# THE GRAPHICAL PLAYER 2011

### Editor
John Burnson

### Projections
Rob McQuown

### Minors Experts
Matt Hagen      Marc Hulet      Melissa Lockard

### Team Experts

| | | |
|---|---|---|
| Bill Baer | Michael Jong | Nick Nelson |
| Matt Bandi | Brian Joseph | Lee Panas |
| Andy Beard | Brian La Shier | Mike Petriello |
| Evan Brunell | Melissa Lockard | David Saltzer |
| Paul Bugala | Jon Lewin | Tom Stephenson |
| Griffin Cooper | Erik Manning | Michael Street |
| Martin Gandy | Joey Matschulat | Lisa Swan |
| David Golebiewski | Brian McGannon | Shawn Weaver |
| Marc Hulet | Rob McQuown | Ricky Zanker |

**ACTA SPORTS**

**www.Rotolympus.com**

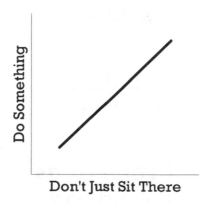

Do Something

Don't Just Sit There

© Copyright 2010 by Whatsoever Things, LLC
Send comments to jburnson@yahoo.com

First Edition: November 2010

Published by ACTA Sports, 4848 N. Clark Street, Skokie, IL 60640, 800-397-2282
info@actasports.com
www.actasports.com
Cover design by Tom A. Wright

Minor-league data courtesy of SABR
www.sabr.org

ISBN 978-0-87946-441-7
Printed in the United States of America

# CONTENTS

Minor-league data on the hitter and pitcher profiles is provided courtesy of SABR. SABR is a not-for-profit membership association open to anyone with an interest in baseball research, statistics, or history. To join SABR, or to buy a gift subscription, visit http://www.sabr.org/.

# DRAFT PACK

These pages compile the projections from the rest of the book. On the position pages, players are rated by mixed-league value ($2L), but single-league values ($1L) and points are also given.

The symbols in the player boxes represent top finishes (either top 25 or top 50) from 2008-2010. Within each group, the symbols are listed in order of rank, not in order of year achieved.

# Mixed League

| $2L | Player | Pos | $1L |
|---|---|---|---|
| $49 | Pujols, Albert | 1B | $40 |
| $38 | Braun, Ryan | LF | $34 |
| $37 | Ramirez, Hanley | SS | $34 |
| $35 | Cabrera, Miguel | 1B | $35 |
| $34 | Halladay, Roy | SP | $35 |
| $32 | Wright, David | 3B | $31 |
| $31 | Tulowitzki, Troy | SS | $29 |
| $30 | Gonzalez, Carlos | CF | $30 |
| $30 | Fielder, Prince | 1B | $28 |
| $30 | Votto, Joey | 1B | $29 |
| $30 | Howard, Ryan | 1B | $27 |
| $29 | Holliday, Matt | LF | $28 |
| $28 | Utley, Chase | 2B | $28 |
| $28 | Teixeira, Mark | 1B | $30 |
| $28 | Hernandez, Felix | SP | $31 |
| $27 | Mauer, Joe | C | $25 |
| $27 | Longoria, Evan | 3B | $30 |
| $26 | Crawford, Carl | LF | $31 |
| $26 | Werth, Jayson | RF | $26 |
| $25 | Wainwright, Adam | SP | $28 |
| $25 | Weeks, Rickie | 2B | $25 |
| $24 | Rollins, Jimmy | SS | $28 |
| $24 | Rodriguez, Alex | 3B | $28 |
| $24 | Kemp, Matt | CF | $26 |
| $24 | Posey, Buster | C | $21 |
| $23 | Beltran, Carlos | CF | $25 |
| $22 | Cruz, Nelson | RF | $25 |
| $22 | Hart, Corey | RF | $25 |
| $22 | McCann, Brian | C | $21 |
| $22 | Choo, Shin-Soo | RF | $27 |
| $22 | Lincecum, Tim | SP | $26 |
| $22 | Hamilton, Josh | LF | $27 |
| $22 | Gonzalez, Adrian | 1B | $23 |
| $22 | Uggla, Dan | 2B | $23 |
| $21 | Johnson, Kelly | 2B | $24 |
| $21 | Sabathia, CC | SP | $27 |
| $21 | Zimmerman, Ryan | 3B | $23 |
| $21 | Kinsler, Ian | 2B | $27 |
| $21 | Hunter, Torii | RF | $27 |
| $21 | Reynolds, Mark | 3B | $23 |
| $21 | Rivera, Mariano | RP | $20 |
| $21 | Phillips, Brandon | 2B | $23 |
| $20 | Cano, Robinson | 2B | $25 |
| $20 | Martinez, Victor | C | $21 |
| $20 | Pence, Hunter | RF | $24 |
| $20 | Upton, Justin | RF | $23 |
| $20 | Dunn, Adam | 1B | $22 |
| $20 | Bruce, Jay | RF | $23 |
| $20 | Johnson, Josh | SP | $23 |
| $20 | Morneau, Justin | 1B | $25 |
| $19 | Soriano, Rafael | RP | $19 |
| $19 | Reyes, Jose | SS | $24 |
| $19 | Pedroia, Dustin | 2B | $25 |
| $19 | Lee, Carlos | LF | $22 |
| $18 | Young, Chris | CF | $22 |
| $18 | Carpenter, Chris | SP | $22 |
| $18 | Markakis, Nick | RF | $24 |
| $18 | Morales, Kendry | 1B | $24 |
| $18 | Lee, Cliff | SP | $22 |
| $18 | Victorino, Shane | CF | $23 |
| $18 | Suzuki, Ichiro | RF | $26 |
| $17 | Bell, Heath | RP | $18 |
| $17 | Kershaw, Clayton | SP | $22 |
| $17 | Soria, Joakim | RP | $17 |
| $17 | Bay, Jason | LF | $22 |
| $17 | Papelbon, Jonathan | RP | $18 |
| $16 | Rios, Alex | CF | $24 |
| $16 | LaRoche, Adam | 1B | $20 |
| $16 | Soto, Geovany | C | $17 |
| $16 | Guerrero, Vladimir | DH | $23 |
| $16 | Latos, Mat | SP | $18 |
| $16 | Ramirez, Aramis | 3B | $20 |
| $16 | Wilson, Brian | RP | $17 |
| $15 | Upton, B.J. | CF | $24 |
| $15 | Verlander, Justin | SP | $22 |
| $15 | Lester, Jon | SP | $22 |
| $15 | Abreu, Bobby | DH | $22 |
| $14 | Street, Huston | RP | $16 |
| $14 | Ethier, Andre | RF | $20 |
| $14 | Konerko, Paul | 1B | $21 |
| $14 | Feliz, Neftali | RP | $16 |
| $14 | Hamels, Cole | SP | $19 |
| $14 | Oswalt, Roy | SP | $19 |
| $14 | Lee, Derrek | 1B | $19 |
| $14 | Greinke, Zack | SP | $21 |
| $14 | Pagan, Angel | CF | $21 |
| $13 | Ross, Cody | CF | $19 |
| $13 | Ellsbury, Jacoby | CF | $23 |
| $13 | McCutchen, Andrew | CF | $20 |
| $13 | Montero, Miguel | C | $15 |
| $13 | Pierre, Juan | LF | $23 |
| $13 | Roberts, Brian | 2B | $21 |
| $13 | Beltre, Adrian | 3B | $21 |
| $13 | Sizemore, Grady | CF | $22 |
| $13 | Youkilis, Kevin | 1B | $20 |

| $2L | Player | Pos | $1L |
|---|---|---|---|
| $13 | Kimbrel, Craig | RP | $15 |
| $13 | Weaver, Jered | SP | $21 |
| $13 | Ramirez, Manny | LF | $20 |
| $13 | Sale, Chris | SP | $18 |
| $13 | Bailey, Andrew | RP | $15 |
| $13 | Doumit, Ryan | C | $15 |
| $12 | Napoli, Mike | C | $16 |
| $12 | Prado, Martin | 2B | $18 |
| $12 | Ibanez, Raul | LF | $18 |
| $12 | Marmol, Carlos | RP | $15 |
| $12 | Jeter, Derek | SS | $20 |
| $12 | Ortiz, David | DH | $19 |
| $12 | Jansen, Kenley | RP | $11 |
| $12 | Rasmus, Colby | CF | $18 |
| $12 | Hudson, Tim | SP | $18 |
| $11 | Soriano, Alfonso | LF | $18 |
| $11 | Santana, Carlos | C | $15 |
| $11 | Young, Michael | 3B | $20 |
| $11 | Stewart, Ian | 3B | $18 |
| $11 | Bourn, Michael | CF | $20 |
| $11 | Drew, Stephen | SS | $18 |
| $11 | Granderson, Curtis | CF | $20 |
| $11 | Bautista, Jose | RF | $20 |
| $11 | Cuddyer, Michael | RF | $19 |
| $11 | Hudson, Dan | SP | $16 |
| $11 | Butler, Billy | 1B | $19 |
| $11 | Valverde, Jose | RP | $13 |
| $11 | Torres, Andres | CF | $18 |
| $11 | Quentin, Carlos | RF | $19 |
| $11 | Broxton, Jonathan | RP | $12 |
| $11 | Loney, James | 1B | $17 |
| $11 | Cain, Matt | SP | $17 |
| $11 | Ludwick, Ryan | RF | $17 |
| $10 | Perez, Chris | RP | $13 |
| $10 | Kuo, Hong-Chih | RP | $10 |
| $10 | Span, Denard | CF | $20 |
| $10 | Byrd, Marlon | CF | $17 |
| $10 | Sandoval, Pablo | 3B | $17 |
| $10 | Stanton, Mike | RF | $16 |
| $10 | Jimenez, Ubaldo | SP | $17 |
| $10 | Huff, Aubrey | 1B | $17 |
| $10 | Hanson, Tommy | SP | $16 |
| $10 | Heyward, Jason | RF | $17 |
| $10 | Jenks, Bobby | RP | $13 |
| $9 | Swisher, Nick | RF | $18 |
| $9 | Axford, John | RP | $13 |
| $9 | Franklin, Ryan | RP | $12 |
| $9 | Smith, Seth | LF | $17 |
| $9 | Crisp, Coco | CF | $20 |
| $9 | Nathan, Joe | RP | $10 |
| $9 | Young, Delmon | LF | $17 |
| $9 | Ramirez, Alexei | SS | $18 |
| $9 | Price, David | SP | $17 |
| $9 | Pena, Carlos | 1B | $17 |
| $9 | Anderson, Brett | SP | $16 |
| $9 | Cordero, Francisco | RP | $12 |
| $9 | Haren, Dan | SP | $17 |
| $9 | Storen, Drew | RP | $12 |
| $8 | Capps, Matt | RP | $11 |
| $8 | Kendrick, Howie | 2B | $18 |
| $8 | Willingham, Josh | LF | $16 |
| $8 | Lidge, Brad | RP | $11 |
| $8 | Jones, Adam | CF | $18 |
| $8 | Nunez, Leo | RP | $12 |
| $8 | Uehara, Koji | RP | $10 |
| $8 | Rodriguez, Francisco ( | RP | $10 |
| $8 | Jackson, Austin | CF | $18 |
| $8 | Ogando, Alexi | RP | $9 |
| $8 | Kuroda, Hiroki | SP | $14 |
| $7 | Zobrist, Ben | RF | $18 |
| $7 | McGehee, Casey | 3B | $15 |
| $7 | Alvarez, Pedro | 3B | $15 |
| $7 | Lyon, Brandon | RP | $11 |
| $7 | Ordonez, Magglio | RF | $17 |
| $7 | Wells, Vernon | CF | $17 |
| $7 | Aardsma, David | RP | $11 |
| $7 | Wilson, C.J. | SP | $15 |
| $7 | Coghlan, Chris | 3B | $16 |
| $7 | Marcum, Shaun | SP | $16 |
| $7 | Walker, Neil | 2B | $15 |
| $7 | Garcia, Jaime | SP | $13 |
| $7 | Thornton, Matt | RP | $8 |
| $7 | Molina, Yadier | C | $12 |
| $6 | Hughes, Phil | SP | $16 |
| $6 | Suzuki, Kurt | C | $12 |
| $6 | Billingsley, Chad | SP | $15 |
| $6 | Lind, Adam | DH | $16 |
| $6 | Polanco, Placido | 3B | $15 |
| $6 | Lewis, Colby | SP | $14 |
| $6 | Olivo, Miguel | C | $11 |
| $6 | Sanchez, Gaby | 1B | $14 |
| $6 | Gregg, Kevin | RP | $10 |
| $6 | Scott, Luke | DH | $16 |
| $6 | DeJesus, David | RF | $16 |
| $6 | Wieters, Matt | C | $12 |

| $2L | Player | Pos | $1L |
|---|---|---|---|
| $6 | Andrus, Elvis | SS | $17 |
| $6 | Madson, Ryan | RP | $7 |
| $5 | Downs, Scott | RP | $7 |
| $5 | Maybin, Cameron | CF | $15 |
| $5 | Martin, Russell | C | $11 |
| $5 | Beckham, Gordon | 2B | $15 |
| $5 | Tabata, Jose | LF | $15 |
| $5 | Gardner, Brett | LF | $17 |
| $5 | Gallardo, Yovani | SP | $13 |
| $5 | Ruiz, Carlos | C | $11 |
| $5 | Gregerson, Luke | RP | $6 |
| $5 | Kubel, Jason | RF | $16 |
| $5 | Meek, Evan | RP | $8 |
| $5 | Colvin, Tyler | RF | $13 |
| $5 | Germano, Justin | RP | $5 |
| $5 | Figgins, Chone | 3B | $17 |
| $5 | Romo, Sergio | RP | $6 |
| $5 | Buchholz, Clay | SP | $13 |
| $4 | Gutierrez, Franklin | CF | $16 |
| $4 | O'Day, Darren | RP | $6 |
| $4 | Posada, Jorge | C | $11 |
| $4 | Scherzer, Max | SP | $14 |
| $4 | Putz, J.J. | RP | $7 |
| $4 | Castro, Starlin | SS | $15 |
| $4 | Sanchez, Jonathan | SP | $12 |
| $4 | Adams, Mike | RP | $4 |
| $4 | Rhodes, Arthur | RP | $5 |
| $4 | Braden, Dallas | SP | $12 |
| $4 | Loe, Kameron | RP | $5 |
| $4 | Santana, Johan | SP | $6 |
| $4 | Kouzmanoff, Kevin | 3B | $15 |
| $4 | Bard, Daniel | RP | $7 |
| $4 | Benoit, Joaquin | RP | $6 |
| $4 | Webb, Brandon | SP | $10 |
| $4 | Escobar, Yunel | SS | $14 |
| $4 | Rivera, Juan | LF | $15 |
| $4 | Kennedy, Ian | SP | $12 |
| $3 | Brown, Domonic | RF | $14 |
| $3 | Bumgarner, Madison | SP | $10 |
| $3 | Ackley, Dustin | 2B | $15 |
| $3 | Rolen, Scott | 3B | $13 |
| $3 | Rodriguez, Wandy | SP | $11 |
| $3 | Matsui, Hideki | DH | $14 |
| $3 | Pierzynski, A.J. | C | $10 |
| $3 | Lilly, Ted | SP | $10 |
| $3 | Devine, Joey | RP | $4 |
| $3 | Davis, Rajai | CF | $16 |
| $3 | Gutierrez, Juan | RP | $7 |
| $3 | Damon, Johnny | DH | $14 |
| $2 | Theriot, Ryan | 2B | $14 |
| $2 | Berkman, Lance | 1B | $15 |
| $2 | Snyder, Chris | C | $9 |
| $2 | McLouth, Nate | CF | $13 |
| $2 | Stubbs, Drew | CF | $13 |
| $2 | Baker, John | C | $9 |
| $2 | Myers, Brett | SP | $11 |
| $2 | Barton, Daric | 1B | $13 |
| $2 | Cabrera, Asdrubal | SS | $14 |
| $2 | Nolasco, Ricky | SP | $10 |
| $2 | Breslow, Craig | RP | $6 |
| $2 | Nakajima, Hiroyuki | SS | $13 |
| $2 | Aybar, Erick | SS | $14 |
| $2 | Cahill, Trevor | SP | $12 |
| $2 | Danks, John | SP | $13 |
| $2 | Garland, Jon | SP | $10 |
| $2 | Balfour, Grant | RP | $4 |
| $2 | Thatcher, Joe | RP | $3 |
| $2 | Tejada, Miguel | 3B | $13 |
| $2 | Betancourt, Rafael | RP | $4 |
| $2 | League, Brandon | RP | $6 |
| $2 | Motte, Jason | RP | $4 |
| $2 | Tejeda, Robinson | RP | $7 |
| $2 | Helton, Todd | 1B | $12 |
| $2 | Hanrahan, Joel | RP | $6 |
| $2 | Scutaro, Marco | SS | $13 |
| $1 | Iwakuma, Hisashi | SP | $9 |
| $1 | Happ, J.A. | SP | $8 |
| $1 | Kintzler, Brandon | RP | $3 |
| $1 | Dempster, Ryan | SP | $10 |
| $1 | Furcal, Rafael | SS | $13 |
| $1 | Morrison, Logan | LF | $12 |
| $1 | Lewis, Fred | LF | $14 |
| $1 | LaPorta, Matt | 1B | $13 |
| $1 | Fowler, Dexter | CF | $13 |
| $1 | Liriano, Francisco | SP | $12 |
| $1 | Brantley, Michael | CF | $14 |
| $1 | McClellan, Kyle | RP | $3 |
| $1 | Capuano, Chris | SP | $7 |
| $1 | Davis, Ike | 1B | $11 |
| $1 | Rodney, Fernando | RP | $6 |
| $1 | Garza, Matt | SP | $12 |
| $1 | Takahashi, Hisanori | RP | $4 |
| $1 | Mujica, Edward | RP | $3 |
| $1 | Peralta, Jhonny | SS | $12 |
| $1 | Lopez, Jose | 3B | $13 |

# Mixed League

| $2L | Pos | $1L |
|---|---|---|
| $0 Duensing, Brian | RP | $9 |
| $0 Wuertz, Mike | RP | $3 |
| $0 Hill, Aaron | 2B | $12 |
| $0 Stauffer, Tim | RP | $3 |
| $0 Figueroa, Nelson | RP | $5 |
| $0 Francisco, Frank | RP | $4 |
| $0 Branyan, Russell | 1B | $13 |
| $0 Gonzalez, Alex | SS | $10 |
| $0 Masset, Nick | RP | $4 |
| $0 Vazquez, Javier | SP | $12 |
| $0 Raburn, Ryan | LF | $13 |
| $0 Iannetta, Chris | C | $8 |
| $0 Richard, Clayton | SP | $8 |
| $0 Lueke, Josh | RP | $2 |
| $0 Moylan, Peter | RP | $3 |
| $0 Marshall, Sean | RP | $4 |
| $0 Pineda, Michael | SP | $7 |
| $0 Jurrjens, Jair | SP | $9 |
| $0 Baker, Scott | SP | $11 |
| $0 Hudson, Orlando | 2B | $12 |
| $0 Borbon, Julio | CF | $13 |
| $0 Chamberlain, Joba | RP | $4 |
| $0 Hafner, Travis | DH | $12 |
| $0 Venters, Jonny | RP | $4 |
| $0 Strop, Pedro | RP | $2 |
| $0 Oliver, Darren | RP | $3 |
| -$1 O'Flaherty, Eric | RP | $2 |
| -$1 Santana, Ervin | SP | $11 |
| -$1 Peralta, Joel | RP | $2 |
| -$1 Jaso, John | C | $8 |
| -$1 Padilla, Vicente | SP | $5 |
| -$1 Sanches, Brian | RP | $2 |
| -$1 Gee, Dillon | SP | $3 |
| -$1 Drew, J.D. | RF | $12 |
| -$1 Slowey, Kevin | SP | $8 |
| -$1 Headley, Chase | 3B | $11 |
| -$1 Belisle, Matt | RP | $2 |
| -$1 Camp, Shawn | RP | $4 |
| -$1 Hardy, J.J. | SS | $12 |
| -$1 Podsednik, Scott | LF | $13 |
| -$1 Frasor, Jason | RP | $3 |
| -$1 Molina, Bengie | C | $8 |
| -$1 Morgan, Nyjer | CF | $12 |
| -$1 Pestano, Vinnie | RP | $1 |
| -$1 Pavano, Carl | SP | $10 |
| -$1 James, Chuck | SP | $1 |
| -$1 Fuentes, Brian | RP | $1 |
| -$1 Dessens, Elmer | RP | $1 |
| -$1 Robertson, David | RP | $3 |
| -$1 Burnett, Sean | RP | $2 |
| -$1 Hellickson, Jeremy | SP | $6 |
| -$1 Escobar, Alcides | SS | $11 |
| -$1 Wheeler, Dan | RP | $2 |
| -$1 Gordon, Alex | LF | $12 |
| -$1 Ziegler, Brad | RP | $2 |
| -$1 Freeman, Freddie | 1B | $9 |
| -$1 Sweeney, Ryan | RF | $11 |
| -$1 Wigginton, Ty | 1B | $12 |
| -$2 Desmond, Ian | SS | $11 |
| -$2 Blake, Casey | 3B | $10 |
| -$2 Hawpe, Brad | RF | $11 |
| -$2 Burrell, Pat | LF | $10 |
| -$2 Casilla, Santiago | RP | $2 |
| -$2 Chacin, Jhoulys | SP | $7 |
| -$2 Strasburg, Stephen | SP | $0 |
| -$2 Aceves, Alfredo | RP | $1 |
| -$2 Duchscherer, Justin | SP | $0 |
| -$2 Clippard, Tyler | RP | $2 |
| -$2 Bray, Bill | RP | $0 |
| -$2 Joyce, Matt | RF | $11 |
| -$2 Lucroy, Jonathan | C | $6 |
| -$2 Lopez, Javier | RP | $1 |
| -$2 Young Jr., Eric | 2B | $11 |
| -$2 Ramirez, Ramon | RP | $1 |
| -$2 Guerrier, Matt | RP | $3 |
| -$2 Dotel, Octavio | RP | $0 |
| -$2 Lindstrom, Matt | RP | $1 |
| -$2 Uribe, Juan | SS | $10 |
| -$2 Dickey, R.A. | SP | $6 |
| -$2 Bedard, Erik | SP | $0 |
| -$2 Wood, Kerry | RP | $2 |
| -$2 Arencibia, JP | C | $7 |
| -$2 Murphy, David | LF | $12 |
| -$2 Crain, Jesse | RP | $2 |
| -$2 Miller, Trever | RP | $0 |
| -$2 Carrasco, D.J. | RP | $1 |
| -$2 Neshek, Pat | RP | $1 |
| -$2 Chapman, Aroldis | RP | $3 |
| -$2 Medlen, Kris | RP | -$1 |
| -$2 Hoffman, Trevor | RP | $0 |
| -$2 Bartlett, Jason | SS | $11 |
| -$3 Resop, Chris | RP | $1 |
| -$3 Spilborghs, Ryan | RF | $10 |
| -$3 Snider, Travis | LF | $11 |
| -$3 Feliciano, Pedro | RP | $1 |
| -$3 Rauch, Jon | RP | $0 |
| -$3 Slaten, Doug | RP | $0 |
| -$3 Lopez, Wilton | RP | $1 |
| -$3 Beckett, Josh | SP | $9 |
| -$3 Cameron, Mike | CF | $11 |
| -$3 Blevins, Jerry | RP | $1 |
| -$3 Freese, David | 3B | $9 |
| -$3 Coffey, Todd | RP | $1 |
| -$3 Peavy, Jake | SP | $9 |
| -$3 Bourjos, Peter | CF | $12 |
| -$3 Shoppach, Kelly | C | $6 |
| -$3 Betancourt, Yuniesky | SS | $11 |
| -$3 Rodriguez, Ivan | C | $6 |
| -$3 Lackey, John | SP | $9 |
| -$3 Cueto, Johnny | SP | $6 |
| -$3 Betemit, Wilson | 3B | $11 |
| -$3 Reyes, Dennys | RP | -$1 |
| -$3 Zambrano, Carlos | SP | $6 |
| -$3 Young, Chris | SP | $1 |
| -$3 Lowe, Derek | SP | $7 |
| -$3 Betemit, Wilson | 3B | $11 |
| -$3 Owens, Rudy | SP | -$1 |
| -$3 Farnsworth, Kyle | RP | $0 |
| -$3 Kohn, Michael | RP | $0 |
| -$3 Gonzalez, Mike | RP | $2 |
| -$3 Atchison, Scott | RP | $0 |
| -$3 Mijares, Jose | RP | $1 |
| -$3 Hernandez, Ramon | C | $6 |
| -$3 Reynolds, Matt | RP | -$1 |
| -$3 Sherrill, George | RP | -$1 |
| -$4 Walker, Tyler | RP | -$1 |
| -$4 Contreras, Jose | RP | $0 |
| -$4 Zimmermann, Jordan | SP | $5 |
| -$4 Choate, Randy | RP | $0 |
| -$4 Walden, Jordan | RP | $1 |
| -$4 Troncoso, Ramon | RP | -$1 |
| -$4 Burton, Jared | RP | -$1 |
| -$4 Avila, Alex | C | $6 |
| -$4 Corpas, Manny | RP | -$2 |
| -$4 Pettitte, Andy | SP | $6 |
| -$4 Perez, Rafael | RP | $1 |
| -$4 DeWitt, Blake | 2B | $9 |
| -$4 Hensley, Clay | RP | $1 |
| -$4 Shields, James | SP | $9 |
| -$4 Frieri, Ernesto | RP | $0 |
| -$4 Perry, Ryan | RP | $1 |
| -$4 Gonzalez, Gio | SP | $9 |
| -$4 Janssen, Casey | RP | $1 |
| -$4 Affeldt, Jeremy | RP | $0 |
| -$4 Niemann, Jeff | SP | $6 |
| -$4 Johnson, Chris | 3B | $9 |
| -$4 Arroyo, Bronson | SP | $6 |
| -$4 Bulger, Jason | RP | $0 |
| -$4 Smith, Joe | RP | $0 |
| -$4 Callaspo, Alberto | 3B | $10 |
| -$4 Kelley, Shawn | RP | $0 |
| -$4 Salas, Fernando | RP | -$1 |
| -$4 Sanchez, Freddy | 2B | $9 |
| -$4 LeBlanc, Wade | SP | $5 |
| -$4 Melancon, Mark | RP | -$1 |
| -$4 DeRosa, Mark | LF | $9 |
| -$4 Torrealba, Yorvit | C | $6 |
| -$4 Fukudome, Kosuke | RF | $9 |
| -$4 Ohman, Will | RP | -$2 |
| -$4 Zumaya, Joel | RP | -$1 |
| -$4 Inge, Brandon | 3B | $10 |
| -$4 Beimel, Joe | RP | -$1 |
| -$4 Hawkins, LaTroy | RP | -$1 |
| -$4 Jepsen, Kevin | RP | $0 |
| -$4 Carlson, Jesse | RP | -$1 |
| -$4 Norberto, Jordan | RP | -$1 |
| -$4 Ring, Royce | RP | -$2 |
| -$4 Russell, Adam | RP | -$1 |
| -$4 Lewis, Jensen | RP | -$1 |
| -$4 Okajima, Hideki | RP | $1 |
| -$4 Pelfrey, Mike | SP | $6 |
| -$4 Cramer, Bobby | SP | -$1 |
| -$4 Webb, Ryan | RP | -$1 |
| -$4 Pena, Brayan | C | $6 |
| -$5 Cohoon, Mark | SP | -$2 |
| -$5 Villanueva, Carlos | RP | -$1 |
| -$5 Marte, Damaso | RP | -$2 |
| -$5 Pineiro, Joel | SP | $6 |
| -$5 Guillen, Jose | RF | $9 |
| -$5 Penny, Brad | SP | $1 |
| -$5 Beltre, Omar | SP | -$1 |
| -$5 Allen, Brandon | 1B | $8 |
| -$5 Veras, Jose | RP | -$2 |
| -$5 Green, Sean | RP | -$2 |
| -$5 Braddock, Zach | RP | -$2 |
| -$5 Martin, J.D. | SP | -$2 |
| -$5 Sanchez, Eduardo | RP | -$2 |
| -$5 Misch, Pat | SP | -$2 |
| -$5 Sanchez, Anibal | SP | $3 |
| -$5 Thole, Josh | C | $5 |
| -$5 Conger, Hank | C | $5 |
| -$5 Maloney, Matt | RP | -$1 |
| -$5 Niese, Jonathon | SP | $5 |
| -$5 Moyer, Jamie | SP | $1 |
| -$5 Acosta, Manny | RP | -$2 |
| -$5 Boggs, Mitchell | RP | -$1 |
| -$5 Wells, Randy | SP | $4 |
| -$5 Luebke, Cory | SP | $0 |
| -$5 Floyd, Gavin | SP | $8 |
| -$5 Elbert, Scott | RP | -$2 |
| -$5 Mock, Garrett | SP | -$2 |
| -$5 Runzler, Dan | RP | -$1 |
| -$5 Pennington, Cliff | SS | $10 |
| -$5 Correia, Kevin | SP | $1 |
| -$5 Hill, Rich | RP | -$1 |
| -$5 Pie, Felix | LF | $10 |
| -$5 Thomas, Brad | RP | -$1 |
| -$5 Wood, Travis | SP | $2 |
| -$6 Rogers, Mark | SP | -$2 |
| -$6 Bernadina, Roger | RF | $9 |
| -$6 Mathis, Jeff | C | $5 |
| -$6 Westbrook, Jake | SP | $4 |
| -$6 Carter, Chris (OAK) | LF | $9 |
| -$6 Sipp, Tony | RP | $0 |
| -$6 Keppinger, Jeff | 2B | $8 |
| -$6 Belisario, Ronald | RP | $0 |
| -$6 Garcia, Freddy | SP | $1 |
| -$6 Rodriguez, Sean | 2B | $9 |
| -$6 Baez, Danys | RP | -$2 |
| -$6 Kearns, Austin | LF | $9 |
| -$6 Durbin, Chad | RP | -$1 |
| -$6 Schumaker, Skip | 2B | $8 |
| -$6 Harang, Aaron | SP | $0 |
| -$6 Linebrink, Scott | RP | $0 |
| -$6 Bautista, Denny | RP | -$2 |
| -$6 Fulchino, Jeff | RP | -$2 |
| -$6 Romero, J.C. | RP | -$2 |
| -$6 Mitre, Sergio | RP | -$1 |
| -$6 Hundley, Nick | C | $4 |
| -$6 Jay, Jon | RF | $8 |
| -$6 Ramos, Cesar | RP | -$2 |
| -$6 Nieve, Fernando | RP | -$2 |
| -$6 Cabrera, Melky | LF | $8 |
| -$6 Hill, Shawn | RP | $1 |
| -$6 Badenhop, Burke | RP | -$1 |
| -$6 Rosales, Adam | 2B | $9 |
| -$6 Hanigan, Ryan | C | $4 |
| -$6 Wolf, Randy | SP | $5 |
| -$6 Thames, Marcus | DH | $9 |
| -$6 Walters, P.J. | RP | -$2 |
| -$6 Vargas, Jason | SP | $7 |
| -$6 Romero, Ricky | SP | $8 |
| -$6 Volquez, Edinson | SP | $3 |
| -$6 Sampson, Chris | RP | -$3 |
| -$6 Buehrle, Mark | SP | $7 |
| -$6 Hunter, Tommy | RP | $4 |
| -$6 Logan, Boone | RP | -$1 |
| -$6 Delcarmen, Manny | RP | -$2 |
| -$6 Jeffress, Jeremy | RP | -$3 |
| -$6 Sonnanstine, Andy | RP | -$1 |
| -$6 Cormier, Lance | RP | -$2 |
| -$6 VandenHurk, Rick | RP | -$2 |
| -$6 Wang, Chien-Ming | SP | $0 |
| -$6 Schlichting, Travis | RP | -$2 |
| -$6 Maine, John | SP | -$3 |
| -$6 Meredith, Cla | RP | -$2 |
| -$6 de la Rosa, Jorge | SP | $3 |
| -$6 Bannister, Brian | SP | -$3 |
| -$6 Smith, Chris | SP | -$3 |
| -$6 Castro, Simon | SP | -$3 |
| -$6 Cecil, Brett | SP | $5 |
| -$6 Santos, Sergio | RP | -$1 |
| -$6 Ondrusek, Logan | RP | -$2 |
| -$7 Valdes, Raul | RP | -$3 |
| -$7 Encarnacion, Edwin | 3B | $9 |
| -$7 Byrdak, Tim | RP | -$3 |
| -$7 McDonald, James | SP | $3 |
| -$7 Moreland, Mitch | 1B | $8 |
| -$7 Schlereth, Daniel | RP | -$2 |
| -$7 Cedeno, Ronny | SS | $8 |
| -$7 Blanton, Joe | SP | $4 |
| -$7 Rodriguez, Francisco ( | RP | -$3 |
| -$7 Jones, Chipper | 3B | $8 |
| -$7 Overbay, Lyle | 1B | $8 |
| -$7 Igarashi, Ryota | RP | -$3 |
| -$7 McCutchen, Daniel | RP | -$3 |
| -$7 Herrmann, Frank | RP | -$2 |
| -$7 Bonderman, Jeremy | SP | -$2 |
| -$7 Judy, Josh | RP | -$1 |
| -$7 Parnell, Bobby | RP | -$1 |
| -$7 Ramos, Wilson | C | $4 |
| -$7 Burres, Brian | SP | -$3 |
| -$7 Wright, Jamey | RP | -$2 |
| -$7 Litsch, Jesse | SP | $0 |
| -$7 Ray, Chris | RP | -$2 |

American League
National League

# First Baseman

Top Finishes Among All Hitters From 2008-10

| | Top 25 | | Top 50 |
|---|---|---|---|
| HR | ■ | HR | □ |
| RBI | ▲ | RBI | △ |
| SB | ● | SB | ○ |

## Projected 2011 Leaders

| Home Runs | $2L |
|---|---|
| 44 Pujols, A | $49 |
| 42 Fielder, P | $30 |
| 39 Howard, R | $30 |
| 39 Dunn, A | $20 |
| 35 Cabrera, M | $35 |
| 34 Gonzalez, A | $22 |
| 33 Pena, C | $9 |
| 33 Votto, J | $30 |
| 33 Teixeira, M | $28 |
| 31 Konerko, P | $14 |
| 30 Morneau, J | $20 |
| 30 LaRoche, A | $16 |
| 27 Branyan, R | $0 |
| 26 Morales, K | $18 |
| 25 LaPorta, M | $1 |

| Runs | $2L |
|---|---|
| 116 Pujols, A | $49 |
| 98 Cabrera, M | $35 |
| 98 Fielder, P | $30 |
| 98 Votto, J | $30 |
| 98 Howard, R | $30 |
| 94 Gonzalez, A | $22 |
| 91 Teixeira, M | $28 |
| 85 Dunn, A | $20 |
| 84 LaRoche, A | $16 |
| 81 Barton, D | $2 |
| 81 Lee, D | $14 |
| 79 Youkilis, K | $13 |
| 78 Morneau, J | $20 |
| 78 Morales, K | $18 |
| 78 Huff, A | $10 |

| Runs Batted In | $2L |
|---|---|
| 131 Pujols, A | $49 |
| 130 Howard, R | $30 |
| 126 Cabrera, M | $35 |
| 112 Fielder, P | $30 |
| 111 Teixeira, M | $28 |
| 104 Votto, J | $30 |
| 104 Dunn, A | $20 |
| 102 Morneau, J | $20 |
| 101 Gonzalez, A | $22 |
| 98 Morales, K | $18 |
| 94 Konerko, P | $14 |
| 91 Loney, J | $11 |
| 90 LaRoche, A | $16 |
| 88 Pena, C | $9 |
| 85 Butler, B | $11 |

| Stolen Bases | $2L |
|---|---|
| 15 Pujols, A | $49 |
| 13 Votto, J | $30 |
| 7 Cabrera, M | $35 |
| 7 Barton, D | $2 |
| 7 Loney, J | $11 |
| 6 Sanchez, G | $6 |
| 6 Huff, A | $10 |
| 6 Lee, D | $14 |
| 5 Youkilis, K | $13 |
| 5 Allen, B | -$5 |
| 4 Berkman, L | $2 |
| 4 Belt, B | -$20 |
| 3 Jones, G | -$10 |
| 3 Pearce, S | -$11 |
| 3 Viciedo, D | -$11 |

| Batting Average | $2L |
|---|---|
| .326 Pujols, A | $49 |
| .305 Cabrera, M | $35 |
| .300 Butler, B | $11 |
| .298 Votto, J | $30 |
| .294 Helton, T | $2 |
| .293 Morneau, J | $20 |
| .291 Youkilis, K | $13 |
| .285 Morales, K | $18 |
| .284 Lee, D | $14 |
| .284 Berkman, L | $2 |
| .283 LaRoche, A | $16 |
| .281 Fielder, P | $30 |
| .281 Huff, A | $10 |
| .280 Loney, J | $11 |
| .279 Teixeira, M | $28 |

### $49 Pujols, Albert ■■■ ▲▲▲

| | PA | HR | R | RBI | SB | BA | $1L | $2L | Pts | RAA |
|---|---|---|---|---|---|---|---|---|---|---|
| '10 | 738 | 42 | 115 | 118 | 14 | .312 | $42 | $41 | 630 | +37 |
| Proj | 725 | 44 | 116 | 131 | 15 | .326 | $40 | $49 | 690 | +59 |

### $30 Votto, Joey ■□□ ▲ ○

| | PA | HR | R | RBI | SB | BA | $1L | $2L | Pts | RAA |
|---|---|---|---|---|---|---|---|---|---|---|
| '10 | 656 | 37 | 106 | 113 | 16 | .324 | $41 | $39 | 540 | +44 |
| Proj | 650 | 33 | 98 | 104 | 13 | .298 | $29 | $30 | 480 | +26 |

### $22 Gonzalez, Adrian ■■■ ▲▲△

| | PA | HR | R | RBI | SB | BA | $1L | $2L | Pts | RAA |
|---|---|---|---|---|---|---|---|---|---|---|
| '10 | 728 | 31 | 87 | 101 | 0 | .298 | $28 | $24 | 470 | +14 |
| Proj | 670 | 34 | 94 | 101 | 0 | .278 | $23 | $22 | 460 | +19 |

### $18 Morales, Kendry ■ ▲

| | PA | HR | R | RBI | SB | BA | $1L | $2L | Pts | RAA |
|---|---|---|---|---|---|---|---|---|---|---|
| '10 | 214 | 11 | 29 | 39 | 0 | .290 | $7 | -$5 | 140 | –2 |
| Proj | 650 | 26 | 78 | 98 | 0 | .285 | $24 | $18 | 390 | –3 |

### $14 Lee, Derrek ■ ▲△

| | PA | HR | R | RBI | SB | BA | $1L | $2L | Pts | RAA |
|---|---|---|---|---|---|---|---|---|---|---|
| '10 | 627 | 19 | 80 | 80 | 1 | .260 | $16 | $9 | 330 | –6 |
| Proj | 575 | 23 | 81 | 81 | 6 | .284 | $19 | $14 | 390 | +15 |

### $11 Loney, James △△△

| | PA | HR | R | RBI | SB | BA | $1L | $2L | Pts | RAA |
|---|---|---|---|---|---|---|---|---|---|---|
| '10 | 657 | 10 | 67 | 88 | 10 | .267 | $16 | $8 | 360 | –21 |
| Proj | 650 | 13 | 72 | 91 | 7 | .280 | $17 | $11 | 400 | –8 |

### $6 Sanchez, Gaby △

| | PA | HR | R | RBI | SB | BA | $1L | $2L | Pts | RAA |
|---|---|---|---|---|---|---|---|---|---|---|
| '10 | 645 | 19 | 72 | 85 | 5 | .273 | $19 | $12 | 380 | –6 |
| Proj | 625 | 19 | 69 | 75 | 6 | .257 | $14 | $6 | 340 | –14 |

### $2 Helton, Todd

| | PA | HR | R | RBI | SB | BA | $1L | $2L | Pts | RAA |
|---|---|---|---|---|---|---|---|---|---|---|
| '10 | 476 | 8 | 48 | 37 | 0 | .256 | $5 | -$6 | 210 | –10 |
| Proj | 525 | 11 | 63 | 58 | 0 | .294 | $12 | $2 | 320 | +6 |

### $0 Branyan, Russell ■□

| | PA | HR | R | RBI | SB | BA | $1L | $2L | Pts | RAA |
|---|---|---|---|---|---|---|---|---|---|---|
| '10 | 431 | 25 | 47 | 57 | 1 | .237 | $12 | $0 | 200 | –3 |
| Proj | 450 | 27 | 54 | 63 | 0 | .243 | $13 | $0 | 230 | +4 |

### -$5 Allen, Brandon

| | PA | HR | R | RBI | SB | BA | $1L | $2L | Pts | RAA |
|---|---|---|---|---|---|---|---|---|---|---|
| '10 | 57 | 1 | 5 | 6 | 0 | .267 | -$4 | -$18 | 20 | +0 |
| Proj | 450 | 23 | 54 | 50 | 5 | .237 | $8 | -$5 | 240 | –3 |

### -$8 Ka'aihue, Kila

| | PA | HR | R | RBI | SB | BA | $1L | $2L | Pts | RAA |
|---|---|---|---|---|---|---|---|---|---|---|
| '10 | 208 | 8 | 22 | 25 | 0 | .217 | $1 | -$13 | 100 | –9 |
| Proj | 450 | 18 | 50 | 50 | 0 | .241 | $7 | -$8 | 240 | –5 |

### -$11 Johnson, Dan

| | PA | HR | R | RBI | SB | BA | $1L | $2L | Pts | RAA |
|---|---|---|---|---|---|---|---|---|---|---|
| '10 | 140 | 7 | 15 | 23 | 1 | .198 | $0 | -$14 | 80 | –2 |
| Proj | 350 | 17 | 39 | 58 | 2 | .227 | $5 | -$11 | 210 | –4 |

### -$11 Pearce, Steve

| | PA | HR | R | RBI | SB | BA | $1L | $2L | Pts | RAA |
|---|---|---|---|---|---|---|---|---|---|---|
| '10 | 38 | 0 | 4 | 5 | 0 | .276 | -$4 | -$19 | 20 | 0 |
| Proj | 300 | 12 | 33 | 36 | 3 | .268 | $5 | -$11 | 190 | +4 |

### -$18 Kotchman, Casey

| | PA | HR | R | RBI | SB | BA | $1L | $2L | Pts | RAA |
|---|---|---|---|---|---|---|---|---|---|---|
| '10 | 463 | 9 | 37 | 51 | 0 | .217 | $3 | -$10 | 200 | –33 |
| Proj | 250 | 5 | 23 | 30 | 0 | .264 | $1 | -$18 | 140 | –10 |

### -$20 Belt, Brandon

| | PA | HR | R | RBI | SB | BA | $1L | $2L | Pts | RAA |
|---|---|---|---|---|---|---|---|---|---|---|
| '10 | --- | -- | --- | --- | -- | ---- | --- | --- | --- | --- |
| Proj | 150 | 4 | 19 | 20 | 4 | .270 | $0 | -$20 | 90 | +1 |

### -$22 Gload, Ross

| | PA | HR | R | RBI | SB | BA | $1L | $2L | Pts | RAA |
|---|---|---|---|---|---|---|---|---|---|---|
| '10 | 141 | 6 | 16 | 22 | 1 | .281 | $1 | -$12 | 100 | –1 |
| Proj | 150 | 3 | 17 | 18 | 2 | .270 | -$1 | -$22 | 90 | –3 |

### -$23 Brown, Jordan

| | PA | HR | R | RBI | SB | BA | $1L | $2L | Pts | RAA |
|---|---|---|---|---|---|---|---|---|---|---|
| '10 | 92 | 0 | 9 | 2 | 0 | .230 | -$4 | -$20 | 30 | –7 |
| Proj | 150 | 3 | 15 | 15 | 0 | .261 | -$2 | -$23 | 70 | –5 |

### -$25 Snyder, Brandon

| | PA | HR | R | RBI | SB | BA | $1L | $2L | Pts | RAA |
|---|---|---|---|---|---|---|---|---|---|---|
| '10 | 20 | 0 | 1 | 3 | 0 | .300 | -$4 | -$20 | 10 | –1 |
| Proj | 100 | 3 | 10 | 12 | 0 | .246 | -$3 | -$25 | 40 | –3 |

### -$26 Davis, Chris

| | PA | HR | R | RBI | SB | BA | $1L | $2L | Pts | RAA |
|---|---|---|---|---|---|---|---|---|---|---|
| '10 | 139 | 1 | 7 | 4 | 3 | .192 | -$4 | -$21 | 30 | –10 |
| Proj | 50 | 3 | 6 | 7 | 1 | .243 | -$4 | -$26 | 20 | –1 |

### $35 Cabrera, Miguel ■■■ ▲▲▲

| | PA | HR | R | RBI | SB | BA | $1L | $2L | Pts | RAA |
|---|---|---|---|---|---|---|---|---|---|---|
| '10 | 680 | 38 | 111 | 126 | 3 | .328 | $41 | $39 | 580 | +40 |
| Proj | 700 | 35 | 98 | 126 | 7 | .305 | $35 | $35 | 520 | +23 |

### $30 Howard, Ryan ■■■ ▲▲▲

| | PA | HR | R | RBI | SB | BA | $1L | $2L | Pts | RAA |
|---|---|---|---|---|---|---|---|---|---|---|
| '10 | 631 | 31 | 87 | 108 | 1 | .276 | $26 | $22 | 380 | +2 |
| Proj | 650 | 39 | 98 | 130 | 0 | .268 | $27 | $30 | 440 | +15 |

### $20 Dunn, Adam ■■■ ▲▲▲

| | PA | HR | R | RBI | SB | BA | $1L | $2L | Pts | RAA |
|---|---|---|---|---|---|---|---|---|---|---|
| '10 | 658 | 38 | 85 | 103 | 0 | .260 | $24 | $20 | 360 | +9 |
| Proj | 650 | 39 | 85 | 104 | 0 | .260 | $22 | $20 | 400 | +19 |

### $16 LaRoche, Adam □□□ ▲

| | PA | HR | R | RBI | SB | BA | $1L | $2L | Pts | RAA |
|---|---|---|---|---|---|---|---|---|---|---|
| '10 | 619 | 25 | 75 | 100 | 0 | .261 | $19 | $13 | 310 | –8 |
| Proj | 600 | 30 | 84 | 90 | 0 | .283 | $20 | $16 | 380 | +15 |

### $13 Youkilis, Kevin □□ ▲△

| | PA | HR | R | RBI | SB | BA | $1L | $2L | Pts | RAA |
|---|---|---|---|---|---|---|---|---|---|---|
| '10 | 438 | 19 | 77 | 62 | 4 | .307 | $21 | $12 | 340 | +18 |
| Proj | 525 | 21 | 79 | 79 | 5 | .291 | $20 | $13 | 370 | +15 |

### $10 Huff, Aubrey ■□ ▲△

| | PA | HR | R | RBI | SB | BA | $1L | $2L | Pts | RAA |
|---|---|---|---|---|---|---|---|---|---|---|
| '10 | 673 | 26 | 100 | 86 | 7 | .290 | $27 | $22 | 480 | +15 |
| Proj | 600 | 18 | 78 | 84 | 6 | .281 | $17 | $10 | 400 | +4 |

### $2 Berkman, Lance □□ ▲ ○

| | PA | HR | R | RBI | SB | BA | $1L | $2L | Pts | RAA |
|---|---|---|---|---|---|---|---|---|---|---|
| '10 | 488 | 14 | 48 | 58 | 3 | .248 | $10 | -$1 | 270 | –2 |
| Proj | 400 | 16 | 56 | 60 | 4 | .284 | $14 | $2 | 280 | +10 |

### $1 LaPorta, Matt

| | PA | HR | R | RBI | SB | BA | $1L | $2L | Pts | RAA |
|---|---|---|---|---|---|---|---|---|---|---|
| '10 | 426 | 12 | 41 | 41 | 0 | .221 | $4 | -$10 | 180 | –20 |
| Proj | 625 | 25 | 69 | 69 | 0 | .244 | $13 | $1 | 320 | –10 |

### -$1 Freeman, Freddie

| | PA | HR | R | RBI | SB | BA | $1L | $2L | Pts | RAA |
|---|---|---|---|---|---|---|---|---|---|---|
| '10 | 24 | 1 | 3 | 1 | 0 | .167 | -$5 | -$20 | 0 | –3 |
| Proj | 600 | 18 | 60 | 72 | 0 | .246 | $9 | -$1 | 310 | –20 |

### -$7 Moreland, Mitch

| | PA | HR | R | RBI | SB | BA | $1L | $2L | Pts | RAA |
|---|---|---|---|---|---|---|---|---|---|---|
| '10 | 178 | 9 | 20 | 25 | 3 | .255 | $4 | -$10 | 110 | +0 |
| Proj | 450 | 18 | 45 | 54 | 0 | .242 | $8 | -$7 | 230 | –13 |

### -$10 Jones, Garrett △

| | PA | HR | R | RBI | SB | BA | $1L | $2L | Pts | RAA |
|---|---|---|---|---|---|---|---|---|---|---|
| '10 | 656 | 21 | 64 | 86 | 7 | .247 | $15 | $7 | 340 | –21 |
| Proj | 300 | 12 | 36 | 39 | 3 | .268 | $6 | -$10 | 180 | –0 |

### -$11 Wallace, Brett

| | PA | HR | R | RBI | SB | BA | $1L | $2L | Pts | RAA |
|---|---|---|---|---|---|---|---|---|---|---|
| '10 | 162 | 2 | 14 | 13 | 0 | .222 | -$3 | -$18 | 30 | –15 |
| Proj | 475 | 14 | 48 | 43 | 0 | .237 | $4 | -$11 | 180 | –26 |

### -$11 Glaus, Troy □ △

| | PA | HR | R | RBI | SB | BA | $1L | $2L | Pts | RAA |
|---|---|---|---|---|---|---|---|---|---|---|
| '10 | 485 | 16 | 52 | 71 | 0 | .240 | $9 | $0 | 250 | –10 |
| Proj | 300 | 12 | 36 | 45 | 0 | .256 | $5 | -$11 | 170 | –1 |

### -$18 Garko, Ryan △

| | PA | HR | R | RBI | SB | BA | $1L | $2L | Pts | RAA |
|---|---|---|---|---|---|---|---|---|---|---|
| '10 | 39 | 0 | 0 | 3 | 0 | .091 | -$5 | -$22 | 0 | –8 |
| Proj | 200 | 8 | 20 | 26 | 0 | .264 | $1 | -$18 | 110 | –4 |

### -$20 Giambi, Jason ■ △

| | PA | HR | R | RBI | SB | BA | $1L | $2L | Pts | RAA |
|---|---|---|---|---|---|---|---|---|---|---|
| '10 | 227 | 6 | 17 | 35 | 2 | .244 | $2 | -$11 | 110 | –5 |
| Proj | 175 | 7 | 19 | 26 | 0 | .238 | $0 | -$20 | 100 | –1 |

### -$22 Sweeney, Mike

| | PA | HR | R | RBI | SB | BA | $1L | $2L | Pts | RAA |
|---|---|---|---|---|---|---|---|---|---|---|
| '10 | 168 | 8 | 21 | 26 | 3 | .252 | $2 | -$10 | 110 | –3 |
| Proj | 150 | 5 | 14 | 20 | 0 | .267 | -$1 | -$22 | 80 | –4 |

### -$24 Gamel, Mat

| | PA | HR | R | RBI | SB | BA | $1L | $2L | Pts | RAA |
|---|---|---|---|---|---|---|---|---|---|---|
| '10 | 17 | 0 | 1 | 1 | 0 | .200 | -$5 | -$21 | 0 | –2 |
| Proj | 125 | 5 | 14 | 15 | 1 | .235 | -$2 | -$24 | 60 | –1 |

### -$26 Alonso, Yonder

| | PA | HR | R | RBI | SB | BA | $1L | $2L | Pts | RAA |
|---|---|---|---|---|---|---|---|---|---|---|
| '10 | 29 | 0 | 2 | 3 | 0 | .207 | -$5 | -$20 | 0 | –3 |
| Proj | 100 | 4 | 8 | 13 | 0 | .224 | -$3 | -$26 | 50 | –2 |

### -$27 Clement, Jeff

| | PA | HR | R | RBI | SB | BA | $1L | $2L | Pts | RAA |
|---|---|---|---|---|---|---|---|---|---|---|
| '10 | 157 | 7 | 11 | 12 | 0 | .201 | $0 | -$9 | 40 | –14 |
| Proj | 50 | 2 | 6 | 6 | 0 | .261 | -$4 | -$27 | 30 | –1 |

### $30 Fielder, Prince ■■■ ▲▲

| | PA | HR | R | RBI | SB | BA | $1L | $2L | Pts | RAA |
|---|---|---|---|---|---|---|---|---|---|---|
| '10 | 731 | 32 | 94 | 83 | 1 | .261 | $22 | $17 | 430 | +5 |
| Proj | 700 | 42 | 98 | 112 | 0 | .281 | $28 | $30 | 490 | +23 |

### $28 Teixeira, Mark ■■■ ▲▲▲

| | PA | HR | R | RBI | SB | BA | $1L | $2L | Pts | RAA |
|---|---|---|---|---|---|---|---|---|---|---|
| '10 | 718 | 33 | 113 | 108 | 0 | .256 | $28 | $23 | 480 | +2 |
| Proj | 650 | 33 | 91 | 111 | 0 | .279 | $30 | $28 | 470 | +20 |

### $20 Morneau, Justin □ ▲▲

| | PA | HR | R | RBI | SB | BA | $1L | $2L | Pts | RAA |
|---|---|---|---|---|---|---|---|---|---|---|
| '10 | 355 | 18 | 53 | 56 | 0 | .345 | $18 | $9 | 280 | +28 |
| Proj | 600 | 30 | 78 | 102 | 0 | .293 | $25 | $20 | 450 | +23 |

### $14 Konerko, Paul ■□ ▲△

| | PA | HR | R | RBI | SB | BA | $1L | $2L | Pts | RAA |
|---|---|---|---|---|---|---|---|---|---|---|
| '10 | 638 | 39 | 89 | 111 | 0 | .312 | $34 | $30 | 480 | +31 |
| Proj | 625 | 31 | 75 | 94 | 0 | .271 | $21 | $14 | 410 | +10 |

### $11 Butler, Billy △

| | PA | HR | R | RBI | SB | BA | $1L | $2L | Pts | RAA |
|---|---|---|---|---|---|---|---|---|---|---|
| '10 | 686 | 15 | 77 | 78 | 0 | .318 | $23 | $16 | 420 | +11 |
| Proj | 650 | 20 | 72 | 85 | 0 | .300 | $19 | $11 | 400 | +7 |

### $9 Pena, Carlos ■■□ ▲▲△

| | PA | HR | R | RBI | SB | BA | $1L | $2L | Pts | RAA |
|---|---|---|---|---|---|---|---|---|---|---|
| '10 | 586 | 28 | 64 | 84 | 5 | .196 | $13 | $3 | 280 | –17 |
| Proj | 550 | 33 | 72 | 88 | 0 | .231 | $17 | $9 | 310 | +4 |

### $2 Barton, Daric

| | PA | HR | R | RBI | SB | BA | $1L | $2L | Pts | RAA |
|---|---|---|---|---|---|---|---|---|---|---|
| '10 | 688 | 10 | 79 | 57 | 7 | .273 | $16 | $6 | 380 | –0 |
| Proj | 675 | 14 | 81 | 68 | 7 | .262 | $13 | $2 | 390 | –3 |

### $1 Davis, Ike

| | PA | HR | R | RBI | SB | BA | $1L | $2L | Pts | RAA |
|---|---|---|---|---|---|---|---|---|---|---|
| '10 | 607 | 19 | 73 | 71 | 3 | .264 | $16 | $8 | 310 | –3 |
| Proj | 625 | 25 | 69 | 75 | 0 | .246 | $11 | $1 | 310 | –11 |

### -$1 Wigginton, Ty

| | PA | HR | R | RBI | SB | BA | $1L | $2L | Pts | RAA |
|---|---|---|---|---|---|---|---|---|---|---|
| '10 | 652 | 22 | 63 | 76 | 0 | .248 | $14 | $4 | 310 | –24 |
| Proj | 500 | 20 | 50 | 60 | 0 | .272 | $12 | -$1 | 270 | –5 |

### -$7 Overbay, Lyle

| | PA | HR | R | RBI | SB | BA | $1L | $2L | Pts | RAA |
|---|---|---|---|---|---|---|---|---|---|---|
| '10 | 615 | 20 | 75 | 67 | 1 | .243 | $14 | $5 | 310 | –12 |
| Proj | 500 | 15 | 55 | 55 | 0 | .249 | $8 | -$7 | 260 | –5 |

### -$11 Nady, Xavier □ △

| | PA | HR | R | RBI | SB | BA | $1L | $2L | Pts | RAA |
|---|---|---|---|---|---|---|---|---|---|---|
| '10 | 347 | 6 | 33 | 33 | 0 | .256 | $2 | -$10 | 110 | –22 |
| Proj | 300 | 12 | 36 | 42 | 0 | .274 | $5 | -$11 | 160 | –5 |

### -$11 Smoak, Justin

| | PA | HR | R | RBI | SB | BA | $1L | $2L | Pts | RAA |
|---|---|---|---|---|---|---|---|---|---|---|
| '10 | 401 | 13 | 40 | 48 | 1 | .218 | $5 | -$7 | 170 | –17 |
| Proj | 450 | 14 | 45 | 50 | 0 | .231 | $5 | -$11 | 200 | –14 |

### -$11 Viciedo, Dayan

| | PA | HR | R | RBI | SB | BA | $1L | $2L | Pts | RAA |
|---|---|---|---|---|---|---|---|---|---|---|
| '10 | 106 | 5 | 17 | 13 | 1 | .308 | $2 | -$13 | 60 | +1 |
| Proj | 300 | 12 | 36 | 36 | 3 | .256 | $5 | -$11 | 150 | –9 |

### -$19 Hoffpauir, Micah

| | PA | HR | R | RBI | SB | BA | $1L | $2L | Pts | RAA |
|---|---|---|---|---|---|---|---|---|---|---|
| '10 | 57 | 0 | 5 | 5 | 0 | .173 | -$5 | -$21 | 10 | –6 |
| Proj | 150 | 6 | 20 | 23 | 0 | .272 | $1 | -$19 | 90 | –1 |

### -$20 Cantu, Jorge □ ▲△

| | PA | HR | R | RBI | SB | BA | $1L | $2L | Pts | RAA |
|---|---|---|---|---|---|---|---|---|---|---|
| '10 | 516 | 11 | 50 | 56 | 0 | .256 | $9 | -$3 | 220 | –24 |
| Proj | 150 | 5 | 18 | 21 | 0 | .276 | $0 | -$20 | 90 | –2 |

### -$22 Trumbo, Mark

| | PA | HR | R | RBI | SB | BA | $1L | $2L | Pts | RAA |
|---|---|---|---|---|---|---|---|---|---|---|
| '10 | 16 | 0 | 2 | 2 | 0 | .067 | -$5 | -$21 | 0 | –3 |
| Proj | 200 | 8 | 16 | 22 | 2 | .214 | -$2 | -$22 | 80 | –13 |

### -$24 Ishikawa, Travis

| | PA | HR | R | RBI | SB | BA | $1L | $2L | Pts | RAA |
|---|---|---|---|---|---|---|---|---|---|---|
| '10 | 175 | 3 | 18 | 22 | 0 | .266 | $0 | -$14 | 90 | –6 |
| Proj | 100 | 3 | 12 | 12 | 1 | .249 | -$2 | -$24 | 50 | –2 |

### -$26 Hosmer, Eric

| | PA | HR | R | RBI | SB | BA | $1L | $2L | Pts | RAA |
|---|---|---|---|---|---|---|---|---|---|---|
| '10 | --- | -- | --- | --- | -- | ---- | --- | --- | --- | --- |
| Proj | 150 | 3 | 11 | 17 | 0 | .221 | -$4 | -$26 | 50 | –9 |

### -$27 Rizzo, Anthony

| | PA | HR | R | RBI | SB | BA | $1L | $2L | Pts | RAA |
|---|---|---|---|---|---|---|---|---|---|---|
| '10 | --- | -- | --- | --- | -- | ---- | --- | --- | --- | --- |
| Proj | 50 | 2 | 5 | 6 | 0 | .251 | -$5 | -$27 | 20 | –2 |

American League
National League

# Third Basemen

| Top Finishes Among All Hitters From 2008-10 | Top 25 | | Top 50 |
|---|---|---|---|
| | ■ | HR | □ |
| | ▲ | RBI | △ |
| | ● | SB | ○ |

## Projected 2011 Leaders

| Home Runs | | $2L |
|---|---|---|
| 39 | Reynolds, M | $21 |
| 35 | Longoria, E | $27 |
| 33 | Rodriguez, A | $24 |
| 30 | Alvarez, P | $7 |
| 29 | Stewart, I | $11 |
| 28 | Ramirez, A | $16 |
| 27 | Wright, D | $32 |
| 26 | Zimmerman, R | $21 |
| 24 | Beltre, A | $13 |
| 24 | Kouzmanoff, K | $4 |
| 20 | McGehee, C | $7 |
| 19 | Sandoval, P | $10 |
| 19 | Lopez, J | $1 |
| 18 | Betemit, W | -$3 |
| 18 | Inge, B | -$4 |

| Runs | | $2L |
|---|---|---|
| 101 | Wright, D | $32 |
| 98 | Longoria, E | $27 |
| 98 | Zimmerman, R | $21 |
| 98 | Reynolds, M | $21 |
| 88 | Coghlan, C | $7 |
| 85 | Young, M | $11 |
| 85 | Polanco, P | $6 |
| 83 | Rodriguez, A | $24 |
| 81 | Stewart, I | $11 |
| 78 | Beltre, A | $13 |
| 78 | Figgins, C | $5 |
| 77 | Ramirez, A | $16 |
| 75 | Sandoval, P | $10 |
| 72 | McGehee, C | $7 |
| 70 | Rolen, S | $3 |

| Runs Batted In | | $2L |
|---|---|---|
| 112 | Longoria, E | $27 |
| 105 | Rodriguez, A | $24 |
| 101 | Wright, D | $32 |
| 99 | Ramirez, A | $16 |
| 98 | Reynolds, M | $21 |
| 96 | Alvarez, P | $7 |
| 91 | Zimmerman, R | $21 |
| 91 | McGehee, C | $7 |
| 84 | Kouzmanoff, K | $4 |
| 81 | Sandoval, P | $10 |
| 81 | Stewart, I | $11 |
| 78 | Beltre, A | $13 |
| 78 | Young, M | $11 |
| 75 | Lopez, J | $1 |
| 72 | Inge, B | -$4 |

| Stolen Bases | | $2L |
|---|---|---|
| 39 | Figgins, C | $5 |
| 20 | Wright, D | $32 |
| 19 | Coghlan, C | $7 |
| 13 | Reynolds, M | $21 |
| 12 | Headley, C | -$1 |
| 12 | Nix, J | -$10 |
| 11 | Rodriguez, A | $24 |
| 11 | Punto, N | -$18 |
| 10 | Morel, B | -$14 |
| 7 | Longoria, E | $27 |
| 7 | Zimmerman, R | $21 |
| 7 | Young, M | $11 |
| 7 | Polanco, P | $6 |
| 6 | Sandoval, P | $10 |
| 6 | Lopez, J | $1 |

| Batting Average | | $2L |
|---|---|---|
| .296 | Wright, D | $32 |
| .291 | Zimmerman, R | $21 |
| .290 | Polanco, P | $6 |
| .290 | Jones, C | -$7 |
| .287 | Beltre, A | $13 |
| .287 | Young, M | $11 |
| .286 | Callaspo, A | -$4 |
| .285 | Ramirez, A | $16 |
| .283 | Sandoval, P | $10 |
| .282 | Rolen, S | $3 |
| .281 | Tejada, M | $2 |
| .279 | Longoria, E | $27 |
| .279 | Izturis, M | -$17 |
| .276 | Rodriguez, A | $24 |
| .270 | Betemit, W | -$3 |

### $32 Wright, David ■■ ▲▲ ●○○

| | PA | HR | R | RBI | SB | BA | $1L | $2L | Pts | RAA |
|---|---|---|---|---|---|---|---|---|---|---|
| '10 | 679 | 29 | 87 | 103 | 19 | .283 | $31 | $26 | 420 | +21 |
| Proj | 675 | 27 | 101 | 101 | 20 | .296 | $31 | $32 | 490 | +36 |

### $21 Zimmerman, Ryan ■□ ▲△

| | PA | HR | R | RBI | SB | BA | $1L | $2L | Pts | RAA |
|---|---|---|---|---|---|---|---|---|---|---|
| '10 | 609 | 25 | 85 | 85 | 4 | .307 | $26 | $20 | 420 | +32 |
| Proj | 650 | 26 | 98 | 91 | 7 | .291 | $23 | $21 | 440 | +23 |

### $13 Beltre, Adrian ■□ ▲

| | PA | HR | R | RBI | SB | BA | $1L | $2L | Pts | RAA |
|---|---|---|---|---|---|---|---|---|---|---|
| '10 | 651 | 28 | 84 | 102 | 2 | .321 | $31 | $26 | 470 | +33 |
| Proj | 600 | 24 | 78 | 78 | 6 | .287 | $21 | $13 | 380 | +14 |

### $10 Sandoval, Pablo □ △

| | PA | HR | R | RBI | SB | BA | $1L | $2L | Pts | RAA |
|---|---|---|---|---|---|---|---|---|---|---|
| '10 | 628 | 13 | 61 | 63 | 3 | .268 | $12 | $3 | 320 | –5 |
| Proj | 625 | 19 | 75 | 81 | 6 | .283 | $17 | $10 | 400 | +12 |

### $7 Coghlan, Chris

| | PA | HR | R | RBI | SB | BA | $1L | $2L | Pts | RAA |
|---|---|---|---|---|---|---|---|---|---|---|
| '10 | 401 | 5 | 60 | 28 | 10 | .268 | $8 | -$3 | 190 | –4 |
| Proj | 625 | 13 | 88 | 56 | 19 | .268 | $16 | $7 | 380 | +8 |

### $4 Kouzmanoff, Kevin △

| | PA | HR | R | RBI | SB | BA | $1L | $2L | Pts | RAA |
|---|---|---|---|---|---|---|---|---|---|---|
| '10 | 588 | 16 | 59 | 71 | 2 | .247 | $12 | $1 | 280 | –18 |
| Proj | 600 | 24 | 66 | 84 | 0 | .259 | $15 | $4 | 330 | +2 |

### $1 Lopez, Jose □ △△

| | PA | HR | R | RBI | SB | BA | $1L | $2L | Pts | RAA |
|---|---|---|---|---|---|---|---|---|---|---|
| '10 | 623 | 10 | 49 | 58 | 3 | .239 | $7 | -$6 | 270 | –31 |
| Proj | 625 | 19 | 63 | 75 | 6 | .266 | $13 | $1 | 350 | –8 |

### -$3 Freese, David

| | PA | HR | R | RBI | SB | BA | $1L | $2L | Pts | RAA |
|---|---|---|---|---|---|---|---|---|---|---|
| '10 | 270 | 4 | 28 | 36 | 1 | .296 | $5 | -$7 | 120 | +0 |
| Proj | 500 | 15 | 55 | 65 | 0 | .259 | $9 | -$3 | 240 | –0 |

### -$4 Callaspo, Alberto

| | PA | HR | R | RBI | SB | BA | $1L | $2L | Pts | RAA |
|---|---|---|---|---|---|---|---|---|---|---|
| '10 | 604 | 10 | 61 | 56 | 5 | .265 | $12 | $1 | 320 | –15 |
| Proj | 550 | 6 | 55 | 50 | 6 | .286 | $10 | -$4 | 310 | –2 |

### -$7 Jones, Chipper

| | PA | HR | R | RBI | SB | BA | $1L | $2L | Pts | RAA |
|---|---|---|---|---|---|---|---|---|---|---|
| '10 | 387 | 10 | 47 | 46 | 5 | .265 | $9 | -$2 | 250 | +12 |
| Proj | 300 | 12 | 45 | 42 | 3 | .290 | $8 | -$7 | 230 | +18 |

### -$11 Teahen, Mark

| | PA | HR | R | RBI | SB | BA | $1L | $2L | Pts | RAA |
|---|---|---|---|---|---|---|---|---|---|---|
| '10 | 262 | 4 | 31 | 25 | 3 | .258 | $3 | -$11 | 110 | –4 |
| Proj | 350 | 7 | 39 | 35 | 4 | .256 | $6 | -$11 | 160 | –4 |

### -$13 Bell, Josh

| | PA | HR | R | RBI | SB | BA | $1L | $2L | Pts | RAA |
|---|---|---|---|---|---|---|---|---|---|---|
| '10 | 161 | 3 | 15 | 12 | 0 | .214 | -$3 | -$18 | 20 | –13 |
| Proj | 450 | 18 | 45 | 45 | 0 | .227 | $5 | -$13 | 160 | –14 |

### -$17 Fields, Josh

| | PA | HR | R | RBI | SB | BA | $1L | $2L | Pts | RAA |
|---|---|---|---|---|---|---|---|---|---|---|
| '10 | 50 | 3 | 5 | 6 | 0 | .306 | -$2 | -$18 | 30 | +1 |
| Proj | 250 | 8 | 28 | 30 | 3 | .245 | $2 | -$17 | 110 | –0 |

### -$20 Helms, Wes

| | PA | HR | R | RBI | SB | BA | $1L | $2L | Pts | RAA |
|---|---|---|---|---|---|---|---|---|---|---|
| '10 | 288 | 4 | 25 | 39 | 0 | .220 | $0 | -$13 | 100 | –13 |
| Proj | 250 | 5 | 23 | 33 | 0 | .250 | $0 | -$20 | 110 | –5 |

### -$21 Fox, Jake

| | PA | HR | R | RBI | SB | BA | $1L | $2L | Pts | RAA |
|---|---|---|---|---|---|---|---|---|---|---|
| '10 | 211 | 7 | 21 | 22 | 0 | .217 | $0 | -$15 | 80 | –10 |
| Proj | 175 | 9 | 18 | 25 | 2 | .238 | $0 | -$21 | 90 | –1 |

### -$21 Francisco, Juan

| | PA | HR | R | RBI | SB | BA | $1L | $2L | Pts | RAA |
|---|---|---|---|---|---|---|---|---|---|---|
| '10 | 59 | 1 | 3 | 7 | 0 | .273 | -$4 | -$19 | 10 | –1 |
| Proj | 150 | 9 | 17 | 21 | 2 | .230 | -$1 | -$21 | 80 | +0 |

### -$25 Cairo, Miguel

| | PA | HR | R | RBI | SB | BA | $1L | $2L | Pts | RAA |
|---|---|---|---|---|---|---|---|---|---|---|
| '10 | 226 | 4 | 30 | 28 | 4 | .290 | $5 | -$8 | 140 | +1 |
| Proj | 100 | 1 | 12 | 10 | 2 | .263 | -$2 | -$25 | 50 | –2 |

### -$26 Pena, Ramiro

| | PA | HR | R | RBI | SB | BA | $1L | $2L | Pts | RAA |
|---|---|---|---|---|---|---|---|---|---|---|
| '10 | 167 | 0 | 18 | 18 | 7 | .227 | $0 | -$15 | 70 | –14 |
| Proj | 150 | 2 | 15 | 12 | 5 | .229 | -$3 | -$26 | 60 | –6 |

### -$27 Hicks, Brandon

| | PA | HR | R | RBI | SB | BA | $1L | $2L | Pts | RAA |
|---|---|---|---|---|---|---|---|---|---|---|
| '10 | 6 | 0 | 7 | 0 | 0 | .000 | -$5 | -$20 | 10 | –1 |
| Proj | 75 | 3 | 9 | 7 | 2 | .201 | -$4 | -$27 | 40 | –0 |

### $27 Longoria, Evan ■□ ▲▲

| | PA | HR | R | RBI | SB | BA | $1L | $2L | Pts | RAA |
|---|---|---|---|---|---|---|---|---|---|---|
| '10 | 673 | 22 | 96 | 104 | 15 | .294 | $31 | $26 | 460 | +26 |
| Proj | 700 | 35 | 98 | 112 | 7 | .279 | $30 | $27 | 470 | +31 |

### $21 Reynolds, Mark ■■□ ▲△△ ○

| | PA | HR | R | RBI | SB | BA | $1L | $2L | Pts | RAA |
|---|---|---|---|---|---|---|---|---|---|---|
| '10 | 603 | 32 | 79 | 85 | 7 | .198 | $14 | $8 | 260 | –5 |
| Proj | 650 | 39 | 98 | 98 | 13 | .244 | $23 | $21 | 390 | +28 |

### $11 Young, Michael △

| | PA | HR | R | RBI | SB | BA | $1L | $2L | Pts | RAA |
|---|---|---|---|---|---|---|---|---|---|---|
| '10 | 722 | 21 | 99 | 91 | 4 | .284 | $25 | $19 | 420 | +6 |
| Proj | 650 | 13 | 85 | 78 | 7 | .287 | $20 | $11 | 360 | +2 |

### $7 McGehee, Casey □ ▲

| | PA | HR | R | RBI | SB | BA | $1L | $2L | Pts | RAA |
|---|---|---|---|---|---|---|---|---|---|---|
| '10 | 675 | 23 | 70 | 104 | 1 | .285 | $23 | $16 | 410 | +12 |
| Proj | 650 | 20 | 72 | 91 | 0 | .265 | $15 | $7 | 350 | +1 |

### $6 Polanco, Placido

| | PA | HR | R | RBI | SB | BA | $1L | $2L | Pts | RAA |
|---|---|---|---|---|---|---|---|---|---|---|
| '10 | 603 | 6 | 76 | 52 | 5 | .298 | $16 | $7 | 340 | –4 |
| Proj | 650 | 7 | 85 | 65 | 7 | .290 | $15 | $6 | 400 | –1 |

### $3 Rolen, Scott

| | PA | HR | R | RBI | SB | BA | $1L | $2L | Pts | RAA |
|---|---|---|---|---|---|---|---|---|---|---|
| '10 | 540 | 20 | 66 | 83 | 1 | .285 | $18 | $11 | 350 | +15 |
| Proj | 500 | 15 | 70 | 65 | 5 | .282 | $13 | $3 | 340 | +18 |

### -$1 Headley, Chase ○

| | PA | HR | R | RBI | SB | BA | $1L | $2L | Pts | RAA |
|---|---|---|---|---|---|---|---|---|---|---|
| '10 | 677 | 11 | 77 | 58 | 17 | .264 | $16 | $7 | 310 | –7 |
| Proj | 620 | 12 | 68 | 62 | 12 | .251 | $11 | -$1 | 300 | +2 |

### -$3 Betemit, Wilson

| | PA | HR | R | RBI | SB | BA | $1L | $2L | Pts | RAA |
|---|---|---|---|---|---|---|---|---|---|---|
| '10 | 317 | 13 | 36 | 43 | 0 | .297 | $10 | -$2 | 180 | +16 |
| Proj | 450 | 18 | 50 | 63 | 0 | .270 | $11 | -$3 | 230 | +14 |

### -$4 Inge, Brandon □

| | PA | HR | R | RBI | SB | BA | $1L | $2L | Pts | RAA |
|---|---|---|---|---|---|---|---|---|---|---|
| '10 | 584 | 13 | 47 | 70 | 4 | .247 | $13 | $7 | 250 | –9 |
| Proj | 600 | 18 | 54 | 72 | 6 | .233 | $10 | -$4 | 250 | –9 |

### -$10 Moustakas, Mike

| | PA | HR | R | RBI | SB | BA | $1L | $2L | Pts | RAA |
|---|---|---|---|---|---|---|---|---|---|---|
| '10 | --- | -- | --- | --- | -- | ---- | --- | --- | --- | --- |
| Proj | 400 | 17 | 47 | 60 | 3 | .262 | $7 | -$10 | 240 | +1 |

### -$12 Valencia, Danny

| | PA | HR | R | RBI | SB | BA | $1L | $2L | Pts | RAA |
|---|---|---|---|---|---|---|---|---|---|---|
| '10 | 322 | 7 | 30 | 40 | 2 | .311 | $9 | -$4 | 180 | +8 |
| Proj | 400 | 12 | 40 | 44 | 0 | .254 | $5 | -$12 | 190 | –3 |

### -$14 Morel, Brent

| | PA | HR | R | RBI | SB | BA | $1L | $2L | Pts | RAA |
|---|---|---|---|---|---|---|---|---|---|---|
| '10 | 70 | 3 | 9 | 7 | 2 | .231 | -$2 | -$17 | 30 | –1 |
| Proj | 250 | 10 | 28 | 30 | 10 | .221 | $4 | -$14 | 140 | –5 |

### -$18 Punto, Nick ○

| | PA | HR | R | RBI | SB | BA | $1L | $2L | Pts | RAA |
|---|---|---|---|---|---|---|---|---|---|---|
| '10 | 290 | 1 | 24 | 20 | 6 | .238 | $0 | -$14 | 110 | –12 |
| Proj | 350 | 0 | 35 | 25 | 11 | .245 | $2 | -$18 | 160 | –7 |

### -$20 Nelson, Chris

| | PA | HR | R | RBI | SB | BA | $1L | $2L | Pts | RAA |
|---|---|---|---|---|---|---|---|---|---|---|
| '10 | 27 | 0 | 7 | 0 | 1 | .280 | -$4 | -$19 | 10 | –1 |
| Proj | 200 | 6 | 24 | 22 | 6 | .227 | $0 | -$20 | 110 | –2 |

### -$21 Feliz, Pedro

| | PA | HR | R | RBI | SB | BA | $1L | $2L | Pts | RAA |
|---|---|---|---|---|---|---|---|---|---|---|
| '10 | 430 | 5 | 36 | 40 | 1 | .218 | -$1 | -$14 | 170 | –34 |
| Proj | 200 | 6 | 20 | 24 | 0 | .257 | $0 | -$21 | 110 | –3 |

### -$23 Murphy, Donnie

| | PA | HR | R | RBI | SB | BA | $1L | $2L | Pts | RAA |
|---|---|---|---|---|---|---|---|---|---|---|
| '10 | 47 | 3 | 9 | 16 | 0 | .318 | -$1 | -$15 | 40 | +4 |
| Proj | 100 | 4 | 14 | 14 | 1 | .255 | -$2 | -$23 | 60 | +2 |

### -$25 LaRoche, Andy

| | PA | HR | R | RBI | SB | BA | $1L | $2L | Pts | RAA |
|---|---|---|---|---|---|---|---|---|---|---|
| '10 | 271 | 4 | 26 | 16 | 1 | .206 | -$3 | -$17 | 90 | –18 |
| Proj | 100 | 3 | 11 | 10 | 1 | .261 | -$3 | -$25 | 50 | +1 |

### -$27 Darnell, James

| | PA | HR | R | RBI | SB | BA | $1L | $2L | Pts | RAA |
|---|---|---|---|---|---|---|---|---|---|---|
| '10 | --- | -- | --- | --- | -- | ---- | --- | --- | --- | --- |
| Proj | 100 | 4 | 9 | 11 | 1 | .208 | -$4 | -$27 | 50 | –1 |

### -$27 Mitchell, Russell

| | PA | HR | R | RBI | SB | BA | $1L | $2L | Pts | RAA |
|---|---|---|---|---|---|---|---|---|---|---|
| '10 | --- | -- | --- | --- | -- | ---- | --- | --- | --- | --- |
| Proj | 100 | 4 | 9 | 10 | 0 | .203 | -$4 | -$27 | 40 | –5 |

### $24 Rodriguez, Alex ■■□ ▲▲▲ ○

| | PA | HR | R | RBI | SB | BA | $1L | $2L | Pts | RAA |
|---|---|---|---|---|---|---|---|---|---|---|
| '10 | 596 | 30 | 74 | 125 | 4 | .270 | $27 | $21 | 430 | +17 |
| Proj | 550 | 33 | 83 | 105 | 11 | .276 | $28 | $24 | 420 | +29 |

### $16 Ramirez, Aramis □□ ▲

| | PA | HR | R | RBI | SB | BA | $1L | $2L | Pts | RAA |
|---|---|---|---|---|---|---|---|---|---|---|
| '10 | 510 | 25 | 61 | 83 | 0 | .241 | $14 | $6 | 300 | –4 |
| Proj | 550 | 28 | 77 | 99 | 0 | .285 | $20 | $16 | 410 | +25 |

### $11 Stewart, Ian □

| | PA | HR | R | RBI | SB | BA | $1L | $2L | Pts | RAA |
|---|---|---|---|---|---|---|---|---|---|---|
| '10 | 449 | 18 | 54 | 61 | 5 | .256 | $13 | $3 | 230 | +1 |
| Proj | 575 | 29 | 81 | 81 | 6 | .263 | $18 | $11 | 360 | +25 |

### $7 Alvarez, Pedro

| | PA | HR | R | RBI | SB | BA | $1L | $2L | Pts | RAA |
|---|---|---|---|---|---|---|---|---|---|---|
| '10 | 387 | 16 | 42 | 64 | 0 | .256 | $9 | -$1 | 180 | +6 |
| Proj | 600 | 30 | 66 | 96 | 0 | .249 | $15 | $7 | 310 | +14 |

### $5 Figgins, Chone ●●●

| | PA | HR | R | RBI | SB | BA | $1L | $2L | Pts | RAA |
|---|---|---|---|---|---|---|---|---|---|---|
| '10 | 702 | 1 | 62 | 35 | 42 | .259 | $16 | $3 | 310 | –19 |
| Proj | 650 | 0 | 78 | 46 | 39 | .266 | $17 | $5 | 360 | –1 |

### $2 Tejada, Miguel

| | PA | HR | R | RBI | SB | BA | $1L | $2L | Pts | RAA |
|---|---|---|---|---|---|---|---|---|---|---|
| '10 | 684 | 15 | 71 | 71 | 2 | .269 | $14 | $6 | 350 | –17 |
| Proj | 550 | 11 | 66 | 66 | 6 | .281 | $13 | $2 | 320 | –5 |

### -$2 Blake, Casey

| | PA | HR | R | RBI | SB | BA | $1L | $2L | Pts | RAA |
|---|---|---|---|---|---|---|---|---|---|---|
| '10 | 574 | 17 | 56 | 64 | 0 | .248 | $9 | $0 | 230 | –9 |
| Proj | 500 | 15 | 60 | 65 | 5 | .260 | $10 | -$2 | 260 | +2 |

### -$4 Johnson, Chris

| | PA | HR | R | RBI | SB | BA | $1L | $2L | Pts | RAA |
|---|---|---|---|---|---|---|---|---|---|---|
| '10 | 364 | 11 | 40 | 52 | 3 | .308 | $12 | $2 | 190 | +8 |
| Proj | 550 | 17 | 55 | 66 | 0 | .256 | $9 | -$4 | 250 | –3 |

### -$7 Encarnacion, Edwin □

| | PA | HR | R | RBI | SB | BA | $1L | $2L | Pts | RAA |
|---|---|---|---|---|---|---|---|---|---|---|
| '10 | 368 | 21 | 47 | 51 | 1 | .244 | $11 | -$1 | 230 | +3 |
| Proj | 400 | 16 | 48 | 52 | 4 | .254 | $9 | -$7 | 230 | +4 |

### -$10 Nix, Jayson

| | PA | HR | R | RBI | SB | BA | $1L | $2L | Pts | RAA |
|---|---|---|---|---|---|---|---|---|---|---|
| '10 | 365 | 14 | 32 | 34 | 1 | .224 | $4 | -$10 | 130 | –15 |
| Proj | 400 | 16 | 44 | 40 | 12 | .239 | $7 | -$10 | 210 | +1 |

### -$12 Baker, Jeff

| | PA | HR | R | RBI | SB | BA | $1L | $2L | Pts | RAA |
|---|---|---|---|---|---|---|---|---|---|---|
| '10 | 224 | 4 | 29 | 21 | 1 | .272 | $2 | -$11 | 100 | –0 |
| Proj | 300 | 9 | 39 | 36 | 3 | .269 | $4 | -$12 | 160 | +5 |

### -$17 Izturis, Maicer

| | PA | HR | R | RBI | SB | BA | $1L | $2L | Pts | RAA |
|---|---|---|---|---|---|---|---|---|---|---|
| '10 | 238 | 3 | 27 | 27 | 7 | .250 | $3 | -$11 | 140 | –5 |
| Proj | 200 | 2 | 28 | 26 | 6 | .279 | $2 | -$17 | 130 | +1 |

### -$19 Mora, Melvin ▲

| | PA | HR | R | RBI | SB | BA | $1L | $2L | Pts | RAA |
|---|---|---|---|---|---|---|---|---|---|---|
| '10 | 356 | 7 | 39 | 45 | 2 | .285 | $8 | -$4 | 200 | +2 |
| Proj | 200 | 4 | 22 | 26 | 2 | .267 | $1 | -$19 | 110 | –4 |

### -$21 Wood, Brandon

| | PA | HR | R | RBI | SB | BA | $1L | $2L | Pts | RAA |
|---|---|---|---|---|---|---|---|---|---|---|
| '10 | 243 | 4 | 20 | 14 | 1 | .146 | -$6 | -$22 | 20 | –34 |
| Proj | 200 | 8 | 22 | 22 | 2 | .231 | $0 | -$21 | 80 | –6 |

### -$21 Conrad, Brooks

| | PA | HR | R | RBI | SB | BA | $1L | $2L | Pts | RAA |
|---|---|---|---|---|---|---|---|---|---|---|
| '10 | 177 | 8 | 31 | 33 | 5 | .250 | $5 | -$7 | 120 | +3 |
| Proj | 150 | 6 | 20 | 18 | 3 | .243 | $0 | -$21 | 80 | +3 |

### -$25 Frazier, Todd

| | PA | HR | R | RBI | SB | BA | $1L | $2L | Pts | RAA |
|---|---|---|---|---|---|---|---|---|---|---|
| '10 | --- | -- | --- | --- | -- | ---- | --- | --- | --- | --- |
| Proj | 100 | 4 | 11 | 11 | 1 | .233 | -$3 | -$25 | 50 | –1 |

### -$25 Marte, Andy

| | PA | HR | R | RBI | SB | BA | $1L | $2L | Pts | RAA |
|---|---|---|---|---|---|---|---|---|---|---|
| '10 | 188 | 5 | 18 | 19 | 0 | .229 | $0 | -$15 | 80 | –5 |
| Proj | 100 | 4 | 10 | 12 | 0 | .254 | -$3 | -$25 | 50 | +1 |

### -$27 Emaus, Brad

| | PA | HR | R | RBI | SB | BA | $1L | $2L | Pts | RAA |
|---|---|---|---|---|---|---|---|---|---|---|
| '10 | --- | -- | --- | --- | -- | ---- | --- | --- | --- | --- |
| Proj | 100 | 3 | 10 | 10 | 2 | .211 | -$4 | -$27 | 50 | –3 |

### -$28 Frandsen, Kevin

| | PA | HR | R | RBI | SB | BA | $1L | $2L | Pts | RAA |
|---|---|---|---|---|---|---|---|---|---|---|
| '10 | 173 | 0 | 24 | 14 | 2 | .250 | $0 | -$15 | 90 | –8 |
| Proj | 50 | 1 | 6 | 5 | 1 | .269 | -$5 | -$28 | 30 | –1 |

American League
National League

# Second Basemen

Top Finishes Among All Hitters From 2008-10

| | Top 25 | Top 50 |
|---|---|---|
| HR | ■ | □ |
| RBI | ▲ | △ |
| SB | ● | ○ |

## Projected 2011 Leaders

| Home Runs | $2L |
|---|---|
| 33 Uggla, D | $22 |
| 30 Weeks, R | $25 |
| 26 Utley, C | $28 |
| 24 Kinsler, I | $21 |
| 22 Hill, A | $0 |
| 20 Johnson, K | $21 |
| 20 Cano, R | $20 |
| 20 Espinosa, D | -$3 |
| 20 Phillips, B | $21 |
| 19 Beckham, G | $5 |
| 18 Walker, N | $7 |
| 17 Rodriguez, S | -$6 |
| 14 Rosales, A | -$6 |
| 13 Pedroia, D | $19 |
| 13 Prado, M | $12 |

| Runs | $2L |
|---|---|
| 120 Weeks, R | $25 |
| 108 Johnson, K | $21 |
| 104 Utley, C | $28 |
| 98 Uggla, D | $22 |
| 98 Pedroia, D | $19 |
| 96 Kinsler, I | $21 |
| 91 Phillips, B | $21 |
| 91 Prado, M | $12 |
| 88 Cano, R | $20 |
| 84 Roberts, B | $13 |
| 78 Theriot, R | $2 |
| 75 Beckham, G | $5 |
| 72 Kendrick, H | $8 |
| 72 Walker, N | $7 |
| 68 Hudson, O | $0 |

| Runs Batted In | $2L |
|---|---|
| 98 Utley, C | $28 |
| 91 Uggla, D | $22 |
| 88 Cano, R | $20 |
| 85 Phillips, B | $21 |
| 78 Walker, N | $7 |
| 75 Weeks, R | $25 |
| 75 Beckham, G | $5 |
| 74 Johnson, K | $21 |
| 72 Kinsler, I | $21 |
| 72 Kendrick, H | $8 |
| 66 Hill, A | $0 |
| 66 DeWitt, B | -$4 |
| 65 Pedroia, D | $19 |
| 65 Prado, M | $12 |
| 60 Espinosa, D | -$3 |

| Stolen Bases | $2L |
|---|---|
| 32 Young Jr., E | -$2 |
| 30 Roberts, B | $13 |
| 26 Phillips, B | $21 |
| 24 Kinsler, I | $21 |
| 24 Theriot, R | $2 |
| 23 Weeks, R | $25 |
| 15 Espinosa, D | -$3 |
| 14 Johnson, K | $21 |
| 13 Utley, C | $28 |
| 13 Pedroia, D | $19 |
| 12 Kendrick, H | $8 |
| 12 Getz, C | -$15 |
| 12 Donald, J | -$9 |
| 11 Sizemore, S | -$14 |
| 9 Rodriguez, S | -$6 |

| Batting Average | $2L |
|---|---|
| .304 Pedroia, D | $19 |
| .297 Cano, R | $20 |
| .297 Prado, M | $12 |
| .294 Infante, O | -$7 |
| .293 Roberts, B | $13 |
| .291 Sanchez, F | -$4 |
| .290 Keppinger, J | -$6 |
| .290 Aviles, M | -$8 |
| .289 Johnson, K | $21 |
| .288 Utley, C | $28 |
| .286 Kinsler, I | $21 |
| .283 Kendrick, H | $8 |
| .282 Hudson, O | $0 |
| .280 Theriot, R | $2 |
| .279 Schumaker, S | -$6 |

### $28 Utley, Chase ■■ ▲△ ○

| | PA | HR | R | RBI | SB | BA | $1L | $2L | Pts | RAA |
|---|---|---|---|---|---|---|---|---|---|---|
| '10 | 514 | 16 | 75 | 65 | 13 | .275 | $19 | $11 | 350 | +12 |
| Proj | 650 | 26 | 104 | 98 | 13 | .288 | $28 | $28 | 480 | +26 |

### $21 Johnson, Kelly □

| | PA | HR | R | RBI | SB | BA | $1L | $2L | Pts | RAA |
|---|---|---|---|---|---|---|---|---|---|---|
| '10 | 672 | 26 | 93 | 71 | 13 | .284 | $26 | $20 | 400 | +30 |
| Proj | 675 | 20 | 108 | 74 | 14 | .289 | $24 | $21 | 430 | +23 |

### $20 Cano, Robinson ■□ ▲

| | PA | HR | R | RBI | SB | BA | $1L | $2L | Pts | RAA |
|---|---|---|---|---|---|---|---|---|---|---|
| '10 | 710 | 29 | 103 | 109 | 3 | .319 | $35 | $32 | 530 | +36 |
| Proj | 675 | 20 | 88 | 88 | 0 | .297 | $25 | $20 | 450 | +21 |

### $12 Prado, Martin

| | PA | HR | R | RBI | SB | BA | $1L | $2L | Pts | RAA |
|---|---|---|---|---|---|---|---|---|---|---|
| '10 | 653 | 15 | 100 | 66 | 5 | .307 | $24 | $18 | 400 | +16 |
| Proj | 650 | 13 | 91 | 65 | 7 | .297 | $18 | $12 | 400 | +14 |

### $5 Beckham, Gordon

| | PA | HR | R | RBI | SB | BA | $1L | $2L | Pts | RAA |
|---|---|---|---|---|---|---|---|---|---|---|
| '10 | 498 | 9 | 58 | 49 | 4 | .252 | $9 | -$3 | 220 | –12 |
| Proj | 625 | 19 | 75 | 75 | 6 | .260 | $15 | $5 | 340 | +1 |

### $0 Hill, Aaron ■□ ▲

| | PA | HR | R | RBI | SB | BA | $1L | $2L | Pts | RAA |
|---|---|---|---|---|---|---|---|---|---|---|
| '10 | 582 | 26 | 70 | 68 | 2 | .205 | $11 | $1 | 300 | –20 |
| Proj | 550 | 22 | 66 | 66 | 6 | .249 | $12 | $0 | 320 | –2 |

### -$3 Espinosa, Danny

| | PA | HR | R | RBI | SB | BA | $1L | $2L | Pts | RAA |
|---|---|---|---|---|---|---|---|---|---|---|
| '10 | 113 | 6 | 16 | 15 | 0 | .214 | -$2 | -$15 | 50 | –2 |
| Proj | 500 | 20 | 60 | 60 | 15 | .216 | $9 | -$3 | 260 | –4 |

### -$6 Keppinger, Jeff

| | PA | HR | R | RBI | SB | BA | $1L | $2L | Pts | RAA |
|---|---|---|---|---|---|---|---|---|---|---|
| '10 | 576 | 6 | 62 | 59 | 4 | .288 | $13 | $3 | 340 | +5 |
| Proj | 475 | 5 | 52 | 48 | 5 | .290 | $8 | -$6 | 290 | +3 |

### -$6 Rosales, Adam

| | PA | HR | R | RBI | SB | BA | $1L | $2L | Pts | RAA |
|---|---|---|---|---|---|---|---|---|---|---|
| '10 | 279 | 7 | 31 | 31 | 2 | .271 | $5 | -$8 | 120 | –2 |
| Proj | 450 | 14 | 54 | 45 | 5 | .257 | $9 | -$6 | 230 | +1 |

### -$8 Aviles, Mike

| | PA | HR | R | RBI | SB | BA | $1L | $2L | Pts | RAA |
|---|---|---|---|---|---|---|---|---|---|---|
| '10 | 448 | 8 | 63 | 32 | 14 | .304 | $15 | $5 | 260 | +4 |
| Proj | 350 | 7 | 46 | 35 | 7 | .290 | $8 | -$8 | 200 | +1 |

### -$10 Lopez, Felipe

| | PA | HR | R | RBI | SB | BA | $1L | $2L | Pts | RAA |
|---|---|---|---|---|---|---|---|---|---|---|
| '10 | 442 | 8 | 52 | 37 | 8 | .233 | $6 | -$6 | 200 | –10 |
| Proj | 400 | 8 | 48 | 36 | 8 | .266 | $6 | -$10 | 220 | +5 |

### -$12 Carroll, Jamey

| | PA | HR | R | RBI | SB | BA | $1L | $2L | Pts | RAA |
|---|---|---|---|---|---|---|---|---|---|---|
| '10 | 417 | 0 | 48 | 23 | 12 | .291 | $8 | -$4 | 200 | +1 |
| Proj | 400 | 0 | 56 | 28 | 8 | .262 | $4 | -$12 | 180 | –8 |

### -$14 Sizemore, Scott

| | PA | HR | R | RBI | SB | BA | $1L | $2L | Pts | RAA |
|---|---|---|---|---|---|---|---|---|---|---|
| '10 | 163 | 3 | 19 | 14 | 0 | .224 | -$1 | -$16 | 60 | –6 |
| Proj | 350 | 11 | 39 | 32 | 11 | .236 | $4 | -$14 | 190 | +4 |

### -$16 Brignac, Reid

| | PA | HR | R | RBI | SB | BA | $1L | $2L | Pts | RAA |
|---|---|---|---|---|---|---|---|---|---|---|
| '10 | 329 | 8 | 39 | 45 | 3 | .256 | $7 | -$5 | 150 | –7 |
| Proj | 300 | 9 | 33 | 33 | 3 | .247 | $3 | -$16 | 140 | –3 |

### -$18 Fontenot, Mike

| | PA | HR | R | RBI | SB | BA | $1L | $2L | Pts | RAA |
|---|---|---|---|---|---|---|---|---|---|---|
| '10 | 261 | 1 | 24 | 25 | 1 | .283 | $2 | -$12 | 110 | –5 |
| Proj | 200 | 4 | 24 | 22 | 2 | .279 | $1 | -$18 | 110 | +4 |

### -$22 Lillibridge, Brent

| | PA | HR | R | RBI | SB | BA | $1L | $2L | Pts | RAA |
|---|---|---|---|---|---|---|---|---|---|---|
| '10 | 101 | 2 | 19 | 16 | 5 | .224 | $0 | -$14 | 50 | –5 |
| Proj | 150 | 3 | 18 | 14 | 8 | .232 | -$1 | -$22 | 70 | –3 |

### -$23 Rhymes, Will

| | PA | HR | R | RBI | SB | BA | $1L | $2L | Pts | RAA |
|---|---|---|---|---|---|---|---|---|---|---|
| '10 | 213 | 1 | 30 | 19 | 0 | .304 | $3 | -$11 | 120 | –0 |
| Proj | 175 | 2 | 18 | 16 | 5 | .242 | -$2 | -$23 | 80 | –7 |

### -$24 Herrera, Jonathan

| | PA | HR | R | RBI | SB | BA | $1L | $2L | Pts | RAA |
|---|---|---|---|---|---|---|---|---|---|---|
| '10 | 258 | 1 | 34 | 21 | 2 | .284 | $2 | -$10 | 120 | –4 |
| Proj | 125 | 1 | 15 | 10 | 4 | .258 | -$2 | -$24 | 60 | –2 |

### -$25 Barney, Darwin

| | PA | HR | R | RBI | SB | BA | $1L | $2L | Pts | RAA |
|---|---|---|---|---|---|---|---|---|---|---|
| '10 | 85 | 0 | 12 | 2 | 0 | .241 | -$4 | -$19 | 30 | –4 |
| Proj | 150 | 2 | 17 | 12 | 2 | .234 | -$3 | -$25 | 70 | –5 |

### $25 Weeks, Rickie ■ ○

| | PA | HR | R | RBI | SB | BA | $1L | $2L | Pts | RAA |
|---|---|---|---|---|---|---|---|---|---|---|
| '10 | 754 | 29 | 112 | 83 | 11 | .269 | $27 | $23 | 410 | +14 |
| Proj | 750 | 30 | 120 | 75 | 23 | .265 | $25 | $25 | 460 | +23 |

### $21 Kinsler, Ian ■ ●●

| | PA | HR | R | RBI | SB | BA | $1L | $2L | Pts | RAA |
|---|---|---|---|---|---|---|---|---|---|---|
| '10 | 462 | 9 | 73 | 45 | 15 | .286 | $17 | $7 | 300 | +10 |
| Proj | 600 | 24 | 96 | 72 | 24 | .286 | $27 | $21 | 470 | +34 |

### $19 Pedroia, Dustin ○○

| | PA | HR | R | RBI | SB | BA | $1L | $2L | Pts | RAA |
|---|---|---|---|---|---|---|---|---|---|---|
| '10 | 352 | 12 | 53 | 41 | 9 | .288 | $13 | $2 | 260 | +14 |
| Proj | 650 | 13 | 98 | 65 | 13 | .304 | $25 | $19 | 460 | +23 |

### $8 Kendrick, Howie

| | PA | HR | R | RBI | SB | BA | $1L | $2L | Pts | RAA |
|---|---|---|---|---|---|---|---|---|---|---|
| '10 | 660 | 10 | 67 | 75 | 14 | .279 | $19 | $10 | 350 | –5 |
| Proj | 600 | 12 | 72 | 72 | 12 | .283 | $18 | $8 | 340 | +3 |

### $3 Ackley, Dustin

| | PA | HR | R | RBI | SB | BA | $1L | $2L | Pts | RAA |
|---|---|---|---|---|---|---|---|---|---|---|
| '10 | -- | -- | -- | -- | -- | --- | --- | --- | --- | --- |
| Proj | 400 | 11 | 54 | 35 | 8 | .251 | $15 | $3 | 230 | +4 |

### $0 Hudson, Orlando

| | PA | HR | R | RBI | SB | BA | $1L | $2L | Pts | RAA |
|---|---|---|---|---|---|---|---|---|---|---|
| '10 | 559 | 6 | 80 | 37 | 10 | .268 | $13 | $2 | 280 | –4 |
| Proj | 525 | 11 | 68 | 47 | 5 | .282 | $12 | $0 | 300 | +11 |

### -$4 DeWitt, Blake

| | PA | HR | R | RBI | SB | BA | $1L | $2L | Pts | RAA |
|---|---|---|---|---|---|---|---|---|---|---|
| '10 | 504 | 5 | 47 | 52 | 3 | .261 | $7 | -$4 | 230 | –7 |
| Proj | 600 | 12 | 60 | 66 | 0 | .255 | $9 | -$4 | 300 | –2 |

### -$6 Rodriguez, Sean

| | PA | HR | R | RBI | SB | BA | $1L | $2L | Pts | RAA |
|---|---|---|---|---|---|---|---|---|---|---|
| '10 | 379 | 9 | 53 | 40 | 13 | .251 | $10 | -$1 | 180 | –8 |
| Proj | 425 | 17 | 51 | 47 | 9 | .239 | $9 | -$6 | 210 | +3 |

### -$7 Infante, Omar

| | PA | HR | R | RBI | SB | BA | $1L | $2L | Pts | RAA |
|---|---|---|---|---|---|---|---|---|---|---|
| '10 | 507 | 8 | 65 | 47 | 7 | .321 | $17 | $8 | 280 | +8 |
| Proj | 375 | 4 | 49 | 41 | 4 | .294 | $8 | -$7 | 210 | +2 |

### -$9 Donald, Jason

| | PA | HR | R | RBI | SB | BA | $1L | $2L | Pts | RAA |
|---|---|---|---|---|---|---|---|---|---|---|
| '10 | 327 | 4 | 39 | 24 | 5 | .253 | $4 | -$10 | 140 | –7 |
| Proj | 575 | 12 | 63 | 52 | 12 | .232 | $7 | -$9 | 250 | –12 |

### -$12 Guzman, Cristian

| | PA | HR | R | RBI | SB | BA | $1L | $2L | Pts | RAA |
|---|---|---|---|---|---|---|---|---|---|---|
| '10 | 399 | 2 | 48 | 26 | 4 | .266 | $5 | -$8 | 160 | –15 |
| Proj | 350 | 4 | 46 | 32 | 4 | .279 | $5 | -$12 | 180 | –8 |

### -$12 Eckstein, David

| | PA | HR | R | RBI | SB | BA | $1L | $2L | Pts | RAA |
|---|---|---|---|---|---|---|---|---|---|---|
| '10 | 492 | 1 | 49 | 29 | 8 | .267 | $5 | -$7 | 230 | –18 |
| Proj | 500 | 5 | 55 | 35 | 5 | .258 | $4 | -$12 | 250 | –15 |

### -$15 Getz, Chris ●

| | PA | HR | R | RBI | SB | BA | $1L | $2L | Pts | RAA |
|---|---|---|---|---|---|---|---|---|---|---|
| '10 | 249 | 0 | 23 | 18 | 15 | .237 | $2 | -$12 | 120 | –11 |
| Proj | 300 | 3 | 33 | 24 | 12 | .263 | $4 | -$15 | 160 | –2 |

### -$16 Barmes, Clint

| | PA | HR | R | RBI | SB | BA | $1L | $2L | Pts | RAA |
|---|---|---|---|---|---|---|---|---|---|---|
| '10 | 442 | 8 | 43 | 50 | 3 | .235 | $4 | -$7 | 200 | –16 |
| Proj | 225 | 7 | 27 | 25 | 5 | .266 | $2 | -$16 | 130 | +3 |

### -$19 Guillen, Carlos

| | PA | HR | R | RBI | SB | BA | $1L | $2L | Pts | RAA |
|---|---|---|---|---|---|---|---|---|---|---|
| '10 | 277 | 6 | 26 | 34 | 1 | .273 | $4 | -$9 | 150 | +1 |
| Proj | 175 | 5 | 21 | 23 | 2 | .274 | $1 | -$19 | 110 | +4 |

### -$22 McDonald, John

| | PA | HR | R | RBI | SB | BA | $1L | $2L | Pts | RAA |
|---|---|---|---|---|---|---|---|---|---|---|
| '10 | 163 | 6 | 27 | 23 | 2 | .250 | $3 | -$11 | 100 | –2 |
| Proj | 200 | 2 | 22 | 20 | 2 | .238 | -$2 | -$22 | 90 | –9 |

### -$24 Valaika, Chris

| | PA | HR | R | RBI | SB | BA | $1L | $2L | Pts | RAA |
|---|---|---|---|---|---|---|---|---|---|---|
| '10 | 40 | 1 | 3 | 2 | 0 | .263 | -$4 | -$19 | 10 | –1 |
| Proj | 150 | 5 | 15 | 15 | 0 | .231 | -$3 | -$24 | 60 | –6 |

### -$24 Tejada, Ruben

| | PA | HR | R | RBI | SB | BA | $1L | $2L | Pts | RAA |
|---|---|---|---|---|---|---|---|---|---|---|
| '10 | 258 | 1 | 28 | 15 | 2 | .213 | -$3 | -$16 | 90 | –18 |
| Proj | 200 | 2 | 20 | 14 | 4 | .228 | -$2 | -$24 | 90 | –8 |

### -$25 Castillo, Luis ○○

| | PA | HR | R | RBI | SB | BA | $1L | $2L | Pts | RAA |
|---|---|---|---|---|---|---|---|---|---|---|
| '10 | 300 | 0 | 28 | 17 | 8 | .235 | $0 | -$14 | 140 | –12 |
| Proj | 100 | 0 | 13 | 7 | 3 | .264 | -$2 | -$25 | 60 | –1 |

### $22 Uggla, Dan ■■■ ▲△△

| | PA | HR | R | RBI | SB | BA | $1L | $2L | Pts | RAA |
|---|---|---|---|---|---|---|---|---|---|---|
| '10 | 676 | 33 | 100 | 105 | 4 | .287 | $30 | $27 | 440 | +34 |
| Proj | 650 | 33 | 98 | 91 | 7 | .271 | $23 | $22 | 420 | +35 |

### $21 Phillips, Brandon △ ●●○

| | PA | HR | R | RBI | SB | BA | $1L | $2L | Pts | RAA |
|---|---|---|---|---|---|---|---|---|---|---|
| '10 | 688 | 18 | 100 | 59 | 16 | .275 | $22 | $16 | 410 | –0 |
| Proj | 650 | 20 | 91 | 85 | 26 | .276 | $24 | $21 | 450 | +12 |

### $13 Roberts, Brian ●●

| | PA | HR | R | RBI | SB | BA | $1L | $2L | Pts | RAA |
|---|---|---|---|---|---|---|---|---|---|---|
| '10 | 262 | 4 | 28 | 15 | 12 | .278 | $5 | -$9 | 140 | +3 |
| Proj | 600 | 12 | 84 | 54 | 30 | .293 | $22 | $13 | 420 | +30 |

### $7 Walker, Neil

| | PA | HR | R | RBI | SB | BA | $1L | $2L | Pts | RAA |
|---|---|---|---|---|---|---|---|---|---|---|
| '10 | 470 | 12 | 57 | 66 | 2 | .296 | $15 | $6 | 270 | +10 |
| Proj | 600 | 18 | 72 | 78 | 6 | .272 | $15 | $7 | 350 | +9 |

### $2 Theriot, Ryan ○○○

| | PA | HR | R | RBI | SB | BA | $1L | $2L | Pts | RAA |
|---|---|---|---|---|---|---|---|---|---|---|
| '10 | 643 | 2 | 72 | 29 | 20 | .270 | $12 | $1 | 280 | –22 |
| Proj | 600 | 6 | 78 | 42 | 24 | .280 | $14 | $2 | 360 | +7 |

### -$2 Young Jr., Eric ○

| | PA | HR | R | RBI | SB | BA | $1L | $2L | Pts | RAA |
|---|---|---|---|---|---|---|---|---|---|---|
| '10 | 189 | 0 | 26 | 8 | 17 | .244 | $2 | -$12 | 100 | –6 |
| Proj | 450 | 5 | 63 | 27 | 32 | .244 | $11 | -$2 | 250 | –8 |

### -$4 Sanchez, Freddy

| | PA | HR | R | RBI | SB | BA | $1L | $2L | Pts | RAA |
|---|---|---|---|---|---|---|---|---|---|---|
| '10 | 480 | 7 | 55 | 47 | 3 | .292 | $11 | $1 | 240 | –1 |
| Proj | 450 | 9 | 59 | 45 | 0 | .291 | $9 | -$4 | 260 | +7 |

### -$6 Schumaker, Skip

| | PA | HR | R | RBI | SB | BA | $1L | $2L | Pts | RAA |
|---|---|---|---|---|---|---|---|---|---|---|
| '10 | 531 | 5 | 66 | 42 | 5 | .265 | $9 | -$2 | 260 | –12 |
| Proj | 475 | 5 | 67 | 38 | 5 | .279 | $8 | -$6 | 260 | –2 |

### -$7 Hall, Bill

| | PA | HR | R | RBI | SB | BA | $1L | $2L | Pts | RAA |
|---|---|---|---|---|---|---|---|---|---|---|
| '10 | 382 | 18 | 44 | 46 | 9 | .247 | $11 | -$1 | 190 | +6 |
| Proj | 400 | 12 | 48 | 48 | 4 | .248 | $8 | -$7 | 180 | –1 |

### -$9 Ellis, Mark

| | PA | HR | R | RBI | SB | BA | $1L | $2L | Pts | RAA |
|---|---|---|---|---|---|---|---|---|---|---|
| '10 | 496 | 5 | 45 | 49 | 7 | .291 | $11 | $0 | 250 | –2 |
| Proj | 400 | 8 | 44 | 44 | 8 | .263 | $7 | -$9 | 220 | –3 |

### -$12 Lowrie, Jed

| | PA | HR | R | RBI | SB | BA | $1L | $2L | Pts | RAA |
|---|---|---|---|---|---|---|---|---|---|---|
| '10 | 197 | 9 | 31 | 24 | 1 | .287 | $5 | -$8 | 150 | +12 |
| Proj | 350 | 7 | 39 | 42 | 0 | .257 | $5 | -$12 | 190 | +7 |

### -$13 Murphy, Dan

| | PA | HR | R | RBI | SB | BA | $1L | $2L | Pts | RAA |
|---|---|---|---|---|---|---|---|---|---|---|
| '10 | -- | -- | -- | -- | -- | --- | --- | --- | --- | --- |
| Proj | 300 | 9 | 33 | 36 | 3 | .260 | $4 | -$13 | 180 | +4 |

### -$15 Kennedy, Adam ○

| | PA | HR | R | RBI | SB | BA | $1L | $2L | Pts | RAA |
|---|---|---|---|---|---|---|---|---|---|---|
| '10 | 390 | 3 | 43 | 31 | 14 | .249 | $6 | -$6 | 200 | –9 |
| Proj | 200 | 2 | 22 | 18 | 6 | .263 | $3 | -$15 | 110 | +1 |

### -$17 Sogard, Eric

| | PA | HR | R | RBI | SB | BA | $1L | $2L | Pts | RAA |
|---|---|---|---|---|---|---|---|---|---|---|
| '10 | 9 | 0 | 0 | 0 | 0 | .429 | -$4 | -$20 | 0 | +1 |
| Proj | 400 | 8 | 40 | 40 | 8 | .220 | $2 | -$17 | 190 | –13 |

### -$21 Lugo, Julio

| | PA | HR | R | RBI | SB | BA | $1L | $2L | Pts | RAA |
|---|---|---|---|---|---|---|---|---|---|---|
| '10 | 264 | 0 | 26 | 20 | 5 | .249 | $1 | -$14 | 80 | –17 |
| Proj | 175 | 2 | 19 | 16 | 7 | .258 | -$1 | -$21 | 90 | +0 |

### -$22 Blanco, Andres

| | PA | HR | R | RBI | SB | BA | $1L | $2L | Pts | RAA |
|---|---|---|---|---|---|---|---|---|---|---|
| '10 | 186 | 0 | 17 | 13 | 0 | .277 | -$1 | -$16 | 70 | –6 |
| Proj | 175 | 2 | 18 | 16 | 2 | .271 | -$1 | -$22 | 90 | –2 |

### -$24 Amarista, Alexi

| | PA | HR | R | RBI | SB | BA | $1L | $2L | Pts | RAA |
|---|---|---|---|---|---|---|---|---|---|---|
| '10 | -- | -- | -- | -- | -- | --- | --- | --- | --- | --- |
| Proj | 100 | 2 | 12 | 8 | 5 | .261 | -$2 | -$24 | 60 | +0 |

### -$24 Casilla, Alexi

| | PA | HR | R | RBI | SB | BA | $1L | $2L | Pts | RAA |
|---|---|---|---|---|---|---|---|---|---|---|
| '10 | 170 | 1 | 26 | 20 | 6 | .276 | $3 | -$11 | 110 | –1 |
| Proj | 100 | 1 | 12 | 8 | 4 | .257 | -$3 | -$24 | 50 | –2 |

### -$25 Tolbert, Matt

| | PA | HR | R | RBI | SB | BA | $1L | $2L | Pts | RAA |
|---|---|---|---|---|---|---|---|---|---|---|
| '10 | 100 | 1 | 8 | 18 | 1 | .230 | -$2 | -$17 | 50 | –4 |
| Proj | 100 | 1 | 11 | 10 | 2 | .253 | -$3 | -$25 | 50 | –2 |

American League
National League

# Shortstops

Top Finishes Among All Hitters From 2008-10

| | Top 25 | | Top 50 |
|---|---|---|---|
| | ■ | HR | □ |
| | ▲ | RBI | △ |
| | ● | SB | ○ |

## Projected 2011 Leaders

| Home Runs | $2L | Runs | $2L | Runs Batted In | $2L | Stolen Bases | $2L | Batting Average | $2L |
|---|---|---|---|---|---|---|---|---|---|
| 27 Tulowitzki, T | $31 | 111 Ramirez, H | $37 | 101 Tulowitzki, T | $31 | 42 Reyes, J | $19 | .308 Ramirez, H | $37 |
| 26 Ramirez, H | $37 | 108 Tulowitzki, T | $31 | 85 Ramirez, H | $37 | 39 Andrus, E | $6 | .298 Tulowitzki, T | $31 |
| 21 Rollins, J | $24 | 105 Rollins, J | $24 | 78 Peralta, J | $1 | 35 Rollins, J | $24 | .287 Reyes, J | $19 |
| 20 Drew, S | $11 | 95 Jeter, D | $12 | 77 Rollins, J | $24 | 33 Ramirez, H | $37 | .285 Drew, S | $11 |
| 19 Gonzalez, A | $0 | 90 Reyes, J | $19 | 75 Gonzalez, A | $0 | 25 Escobar, A | -$1 | .283 Castro, S | $4 |
| 18 Ramirez, A | $9 | 85 Drew, S | $11 | 72 Ramirez, A | $9 | 24 Pennington, C | -$5 | .283 Furcal, R | $1 |
| 18 Peralta, J | $1 | 85 Andrus, E | $6 | 72 Drew, S | $11 | 20 Jeter, D | $12 | .280 Jeter, D | $12 |
| 15 Hardy, J | -$1 | 84 Scutaro, M | $2 | 65 Uribe, J | -$2 | 20 Desmond, I | -$2 | .280 Renteria, E | -$17 |
| 15 Desmond, I | -$2 | 78 Escobar, Y | $4 | 61 Jeter, D | $12 | 20 Bartlett, J | -$2 | .279 Betancourt, Y | -$3 |
| 15 Uribe, J | -$2 | 75 Aybar, E | $2 | 61 Betancourt, Y | -$3 | 20 Castro, S | $4 | .278 Escobar, Y | $4 |
| 14 Jeter, D | $12 | 75 Escobar, A | -$1 | 60 Escobar, Y | $4 | 19 Furcal, R | $1 | .274 Rollins, J | $24 |
| 12 Reyes, J | $19 | 72 Ramirez, A | $9 | 60 Cabrera, A | $2 | 19 Aybar, E | $2 | .273 Cabrera, O | -$9 |
| 12 Escobar, Y | $4 | 72 Cabrera, A | $2 | 60 Hardy, J | -$1 | 15 Ryan, B | -$8 | .273 Abreu, T | -$23 |
| 12 Scutaro, M | $2 | 72 Castro, S | $4 | 59 Castro, S | $4 | 15 Izturis, C | -$13 | .272 Ramirez, A | $9 |
| 11 Betancourt, Y | -$3 | 71 Furcal, R | $1 | 54 Reyes, J | $19 | 14 Tulowitzki, T | $31 | .272 Scutaro, M | $2 |

### $37 Ramirez, Hanley ■ ▲ ●●●

| | PA | HR | R | RBI | SB | BA | $1L | $2L | Pts | RAA |
|---|---|---|---|---|---|---|---|---|---|---|
| '10 | 631 | 21 | 92 | 76 | 32 | .300 | $32 | $26 | 450 | +33 |
| Proj | 650 | 26 | 111 | 85 | 33 | .308 | $34 | $37 | 550 | +62 |

### $19 Reyes, Jose ●●

| | PA | HR | R | RBI | SB | BA | $1L | $2L | Pts | RAA |
|---|---|---|---|---|---|---|---|---|---|---|
| '10 | 607 | 11 | 83 | 54 | 30 | .282 | $23 | $14 | 400 | +9 |
| Proj | 600 | 12 | 90 | 54 | 42 | .287 | $24 | $19 | 460 | +28 |

### $9 Ramirez, Alexei

| | PA | HR | R | RBI | SB | BA | $1L | $2L | Pts | RAA |
|---|---|---|---|---|---|---|---|---|---|---|
| '10 | 628 | 18 | 83 | 70 | 13 | .282 | $23 | $15 | 370 | +7 |
| Proj | 600 | 18 | 72 | 72 | 12 | .272 | $18 | $9 | 350 | +3 |

### $4 Escobar, Yunel

| | PA | HR | R | RBI | SB | BA | $1L | $2L | Pts | RAA |
|---|---|---|---|---|---|---|---|---|---|---|
| '10 | 568 | 4 | 60 | 35 | 6 | .256 | $7 | -$5 | 260 | -6 |
| Proj | 600 | 12 | 78 | 60 | 6 | .278 | $14 | $4 | 350 | +12 |

### $2 Aybar, Erick ○

| | PA | HR | R | RBI | SB | BA | $1L | $2L | Pts | RAA |
|---|---|---|---|---|---|---|---|---|---|---|
| '10 | 590 | 5 | 69 | 29 | 22 | .253 | $11 | -$1 | 260 | -15 |
| Proj | 625 | 6 | 75 | 50 | 19 | .270 | $14 | $2 | 330 | -3 |

### $1 Peralta, Jhonny △

| | PA | HR | R | RBI | SB | BA | $1L | $2L | Pts | RAA |
|---|---|---|---|---|---|---|---|---|---|---|
| '10 | 617 | 15 | 60 | 81 | 1 | .249 | $13 | $3 | 310 | +2 |
| Proj | 600 | 18 | 66 | 78 | 0 | .256 | $12 | $1 | 290 | +6 |

### -$1 Escobar, Alcides

| | PA | HR | R | RBI | SB | BA | $1L | $2L | Pts | RAA |
|---|---|---|---|---|---|---|---|---|---|---|
| '10 | 559 | 4 | 57 | 41 | 10 | .235 | $5 | -$7 | 240 | -20 |
| Proj | 625 | 6 | 75 | 50 | 25 | .245 | $11 | -$1 | 300 | -18 |

### -$2 Bartlett, Jason ●○

| | PA | HR | R | RBI | SB | BA | $1L | $2L | Pts | RAA |
|---|---|---|---|---|---|---|---|---|---|---|
| '10 | 533 | 4 | 71 | 47 | 11 | .254 | $11 | $0 | 260 | -6 |
| Proj | 500 | 5 | 65 | 45 | 20 | .269 | $11 | -$2 | 280 | +4 |

### -$7 Cedeno, Ronny

| | PA | HR | R | RBI | SB | BA | $1L | $2L | Pts | RAA |
|---|---|---|---|---|---|---|---|---|---|---|
| '10 | 506 | 8 | 42 | 38 | 12 | .256 | $7 | -$5 | 200 | -6 |
| Proj | 500 | 10 | 50 | 50 | 10 | .257 | $8 | -$7 | 230 | +0 |

### -$13 Izturis, Cesar ●

| | PA | HR | R | RBI | SB | BA | $1L | $2L | Pts | RAA |
|---|---|---|---|---|---|---|---|---|---|---|
| '10 | 514 | 1 | 42 | 28 | 11 | .230 | $2 | -$12 | 190 | -29 |
| Proj | 500 | 0 | 45 | 30 | 15 | .262 | $4 | -$13 | 240 | -13 |

### -$18 Blum, Geoff

| | PA | HR | R | RBI | SB | BA | $1L | $2L | Pts | RAA |
|---|---|---|---|---|---|---|---|---|---|---|
| '10 | 220 | 2 | 22 | 28 | 0 | .267 | $0 | -$14 | 100 | -1 |
| Proj | 250 | 5 | 25 | 30 | 0 | .266 | $1 | -$18 | 130 | +2 |

### -$19 Janish, Paul

| | PA | HR | R | RBI | SB | BA | $1L | $2L | Pts | RAA |
|---|---|---|---|---|---|---|---|---|---|---|
| '10 | 230 | 5 | 23 | 25 | 1 | .260 | $1 | -$12 | 120 | +0 |
| Proj | 300 | 6 | 33 | 27 | 3 | .246 | $0 | -$19 | 150 | +1 |

### -$22 Manzella, Tommy

| | PA | HR | R | RBI | SB | BA | $1L | $2L | Pts | RAA |
|---|---|---|---|---|---|---|---|---|---|---|
| '10 | 283 | 1 | 17 | 21 | 0 | .225 | -$4 | -$18 | 50 | -19 |
| Proj | 300 | 3 | 24 | 24 | 3 | .232 | -$1 | -$22 | 100 | -10 |

### -$23 Greene, Tyler

| | PA | HR | R | RBI | SB | BA | $1L | $2L | Pts | RAA |
|---|---|---|---|---|---|---|---|---|---|---|
| '10 | 126 | 2 | 14 | 10 | 2 | .221 | -$3 | -$17 | 50 | -4 |
| Proj | 150 | 5 | 18 | 12 | 6 | .225 | -$1 | -$23 | 70 | +1 |

### -$26 Valdez, Wilson

| | PA | HR | R | RBI | SB | BA | $1L | $2L | Pts | RAA |
|---|---|---|---|---|---|---|---|---|---|---|
| '10 | 370 | 4 | 37 | 35 | 7 | .258 | $5 | -$8 | 180 | -6 |
| Proj | 100 | 1 | 12 | 8 | 2 | .254 | -$3 | -$26 | 50 | -0 |

### -$26 Cozart, Zach

| | PA | HR | R | RBI | SB | BA | $1L | $2L | Pts | RAA |
|---|---|---|---|---|---|---|---|---|---|---|
| '10 | --- | --- | --- | --- | --- | --- | --- | --- | --- | --- |
| Proj | 100 | 3 | 10 | 9 | 1 | .215 | -$4 | -$26 | 40 | -2 |

### -$28 Worth, Danny

| | PA | HR | R | RBI | SB | BA | $1L | $2L | Pts | RAA |
|---|---|---|---|---|---|---|---|---|---|---|
| '10 | 115 | 2 | 10 | 8 | 1 | .255 | -$2 | -$17 | 50 | -3 |
| Proj | 100 | 1 | 8 | 7 | 2 | .219 | -$5 | -$28 | 30 | -3 |

### -$28 Tolleson, Steven

| | PA | HR | R | RBI | SB | BA | $1L | $2L | Pts | RAA |
|---|---|---|---|---|---|---|---|---|---|---|
| '10 | 53 | 1 | 5 | 4 | 0 | .286 | -$3 | -$18 | 20 | +1 |
| Proj | 50 | 1 | 5 | 4 | 2 | .228 | -$5 | -$28 | 20 | -1 |

### -$28 Maysonet, Edwin

| | PA | HR | R | RBI | SB | BA | $1L | $2L | Pts | RAA |
|---|---|---|---|---|---|---|---|---|---|---|
| '10 | --- | --- | --- | --- | --- | --- | --- | --- | --- | --- |
| Proj | 50 | 1 | 5 | 4 | 1 | .236 | -$5 | -$28 | 20 | -1 |

### $31 Tulowitzki, Troy ■□ ▲△ ○

| | PA | HR | R | RBI | SB | BA | $1L | $2L | Pts | RAA |
|---|---|---|---|---|---|---|---|---|---|---|
| '10 | 533 | 27 | 89 | 95 | 11 | .315 | $31 | $26 | 440 | +44 |
| Proj | 675 | 27 | 108 | 101 | 14 | .298 | $29 | $31 | 500 | +43 |

### $12 Jeter, Derek ●○

| | PA | HR | R | RBI | SB | BA | $1L | $2L | Pts | RAA |
|---|---|---|---|---|---|---|---|---|---|---|
| '10 | 743 | 10 | 111 | 67 | 18 | .270 | $23 | $15 | 410 | +5 |
| Proj | 675 | 14 | 95 | 61 | 20 | .280 | $20 | $12 | 400 | +17 |

### $6 Andrus, Elvis ●●

| | PA | HR | R | RBI | SB | BA | $1L | $2L | Pts | RAA |
|---|---|---|---|---|---|---|---|---|---|---|
| '10 | 674 | 0 | 88 | 35 | 32 | .265 | $17 | $6 | 320 | -10 |
| Proj | 650 | 7 | 85 | 46 | 39 | .259 | $17 | $6 | 360 | +6 |

### $2 Cabrera, Asdrubal ○

| | PA | HR | R | RBI | SB | BA | $1L | $2L | Pts | RAA |
|---|---|---|---|---|---|---|---|---|---|---|
| '10 | 425 | 3 | 39 | 29 | 6 | .276 | $6 | -$7 | 170 | -7 |
| Proj | 600 | 6 | 72 | 60 | 12 | .271 | $14 | $2 | 310 | +4 |

### $2 Scutaro, Marco

| | PA | HR | R | RBI | SB | BA | $1L | $2L | Pts | RAA |
|---|---|---|---|---|---|---|---|---|---|---|
| '10 | 696 | 11 | 92 | 56 | 5 | .275 | $17 | $8 | 380 | +8 |
| Proj | 600 | 12 | 84 | 54 | 6 | .272 | $13 | $2 | 360 | +19 |

### $0 Gonzalez, Alex □ △

| | PA | HR | R | RBI | SB | BA | $1L | $2L | Pts | RAA |
|---|---|---|---|---|---|---|---|---|---|---|
| '10 | 642 | 23 | 74 | 88 | 1 | .250 | $16 | $9 | 340 | +3 |
| Proj | 625 | 19 | 69 | 75 | 0 | .248 | $10 | $0 | 300 | -3 |

### -$2 Desmond, Ian ○

| | PA | HR | R | RBI | SB | BA | $1L | $2L | Pts | RAA |
|---|---|---|---|---|---|---|---|---|---|---|
| '10 | 577 | 10 | 59 | 65 | 17 | .269 | $15 | $6 | 280 | -3 |
| Proj | 500 | 15 | 50 | 50 | 20 | .250 | $11 | -$2 | 270 | +8 |

### -$3 Betancourt, Yuniesky

| | PA | HR | R | RBI | SB | BA | $1L | $2L | Pts | RAA |
|---|---|---|---|---|---|---|---|---|---|---|
| '10 | 589 | 16 | 60 | 78 | 2 | .259 | $14 | $4 | 320 | -4 |
| Proj | 550 | 11 | 55 | 61 | 6 | .279 | $11 | -$3 | 320 | +6 |

### -$8 Ryan, Brendan

| | PA | HR | R | RBI | SB | BA | $1L | $2L | Pts | RAA |
|---|---|---|---|---|---|---|---|---|---|---|
| '10 | 491 | 2 | 50 | 36 | 11 | .223 | $2 | -$10 | 210 | -23 |
| Proj | 500 | 5 | 60 | 35 | 15 | .250 | $7 | -$8 | 260 | -4 |

### -$14 Hairston, Jerry ○

| | PA | HR | R | RBI | SB | BA | $1L | $2L | Pts | RAA |
|---|---|---|---|---|---|---|---|---|---|---|
| '10 | 478 | 10 | 53 | 50 | 9 | .244 | $8 | -$2 | 240 | -11 |
| Proj | 310 | 6 | 37 | 31 | 6 | .247 | $3 | -$14 | 170 | -0 |

### -$18 Wilson, Jack

| | PA | HR | R | RBI | SB | BA | $1L | $2L | Pts | RAA |
|---|---|---|---|---|---|---|---|---|---|---|
| '10 | 211 | 0 | 17 | 14 | 1 | .249 | -$2 | -$17 | 60 | -10 |
| Proj | 300 | 3 | 27 | 27 | 3 | .268 | $1 | -$18 | 140 | -3 |

### -$20 Sanchez, Angel

| | PA | HR | R | RBI | SB | BA | $1L | $2L | Pts | RAA |
|---|---|---|---|---|---|---|---|---|---|---|
| '10 | 272 | 0 | 30 | 25 | 0 | .277 | $1 | -$12 | 110 | -6 |
| Proj | 300 | 3 | 30 | 27 | 0 | .254 | -$1 | -$20 | 130 | -3 |

### -$22 Counsell, Craig

| | PA | HR | R | RBI | SB | BA | $1L | $2L | Pts | RAA |
|---|---|---|---|---|---|---|---|---|---|---|
| '10 | 230 | 2 | 16 | 21 | 1 | .250 | -$2 | -$15 | 100 | -4 |
| Proj | 200 | 2 | 22 | 16 | 2 | .257 | -$1 | -$22 | 100 | +1 |

### -$24 Hernandez, Anderson

| | PA | HR | R | RBI | SB | BA | $1L | $2L | Pts | RAA |
|---|---|---|---|---|---|---|---|---|---|---|
| '10 | 119 | 0 | 13 | 3 | 3 | .220 | -$4 | -$19 | 40 | -4 |
| Proj | 150 | 2 | 17 | 12 | 3 | .246 | -$2 | -$24 | 70 | -2 |

### -$26 Wilson, Josh

| | PA | HR | R | RBI | SB | BA | $1L | $2L | Pts | RAA |
|---|---|---|---|---|---|---|---|---|---|---|
| '10 | 388 | 2 | 22 | 25 | 5 | .227 | -$1 | -$16 | 100 | -21 |
| Proj | 150 | 2 | 12 | 12 | 3 | .242 | -$4 | -$26 | 60 | -2 |

### -$27 Hernandez, Diory

| | PA | HR | R | RBI | SB | BA | $1L | $2L | Pts | RAA |
|---|---|---|---|---|---|---|---|---|---|---|
| '10 | 10 | 1 | 5 | 1 | 0 | .111 | -$5 | -$19 | 10 | -1 |
| Proj | 75 | 2 | 7 | 8 | 2 | .240 | -$4 | -$27 | 30 | -1 |

### -$28 Rohlinger, Ryan

| | PA | HR | R | RBI | SB | BA | $1L | $2L | Pts | RAA |
|---|---|---|---|---|---|---|---|---|---|---|
| '10 | 18 | 0 | 1 | 1 | 0 | .200 | -$5 | -$21 | 0 | -1 |
| Proj | 50 | 2 | 6 | 6 | 0 | .234 | -$4 | -$28 | 20 | +0 |

### -$28 Nunez, Eduardo

| | PA | HR | R | RBI | SB | BA | $1L | $2L | Pts | RAA |
|---|---|---|---|---|---|---|---|---|---|---|
| '10 | 53 | 1 | 12 | 7 | 5 | .280 | -$1 | -$16 | 50 | +1 |
| Proj | 50 | 1 | 5 | 5 | 2 | .226 | -$5 | -$28 | 20 | -2 |

### -$28 Cruz, Luis

| | PA | HR | R | RBI | SB | BA | $1L | $2L | Pts | RAA |
|---|---|---|---|---|---|---|---|---|---|---|
| '10 | 17 | 0 | 2 | 1 | 0 | .235 | -$5 | -$20 | 10 | -1 |
| Proj | 50 | 1 | 5 | 4 | 1 | .231 | -$5 | -$28 | 20 | -2 |

### $24 Rollins, Jimmy ●●○

| | PA | HR | R | RBI | SB | BA | $1L | $2L | Pts | RAA |
|---|---|---|---|---|---|---|---|---|---|---|
| '10 | 396 | 8 | 48 | 41 | 17 | .243 | $9 | -$2 | 260 | +4 |
| Proj | 700 | 21 | 105 | 77 | 35 | .274 | $26 | $24 | 550 | +33 |

### $11 Drew, Stephen

| | PA | HR | R | RBI | SB | BA | $1L | $2L | Pts | RAA |
|---|---|---|---|---|---|---|---|---|---|---|
| '10 | 635 | 15 | 83 | 61 | 10 | .278 | $18 | $11 | 370 | +23 |
| Proj | 650 | 20 | 85 | 72 | 7 | .285 | $18 | $11 | 420 | +34 |

### $4 Castro, Starlin

| | PA | HR | R | RBI | SB | BA | $1L | $2L | Pts | RAA |
|---|---|---|---|---|---|---|---|---|---|---|
| '10 | 513 | 3 | 53 | 41 | 10 | .300 | $12 | $1 | 250 | +5 |
| Proj | 650 | 7 | 72 | 59 | 20 | .283 | $15 | $4 | 340 | +3 |

### $2 Nakajima, Hiroyuki

| | PA | HR | R | RBI | SB | BA | $1L | $2L | Pts | RAA |
|---|---|---|---|---|---|---|---|---|---|---|
| '10 | --- | --- | --- | --- | --- | --- | --- | --- | --- | --- |
| Proj | 500 | 15 | 60 | 60 | 10 | .272 | $13 | $2 | 290 | +3 |

### $1 Furcal, Rafael ○

| | PA | HR | R | RBI | SB | BA | $1L | $2L | Pts | RAA |
|---|---|---|---|---|---|---|---|---|---|---|
| '10 | 433 | 8 | 66 | 43 | 22 | .300 | $18 | $8 | 300 | +21 |
| Proj | 475 | 10 | 71 | 38 | 19 | .283 | $13 | $1 | 310 | +20 |

### -$1 Hardy, J.J. □

| | PA | HR | R | RBI | SB | BA | $1L | $2L | Pts | RAA |
|---|---|---|---|---|---|---|---|---|---|---|
| '10 | 376 | 6 | 44 | 38 | 1 | .268 | $6 | -$6 | 190 | +2 |
| Proj | 500 | 15 | 60 | 60 | 0 | .269 | $12 | -$1 | 280 | +12 |

### -$2 Uribe, Juan □ △

| | PA | HR | R | RBI | SB | BA | $1L | $2L | Pts | RAA |
|---|---|---|---|---|---|---|---|---|---|---|
| '10 | 581 | 24 | 64 | 85 | 1 | .248 | $15 | $7 | 330 | +6 |
| Proj | 500 | 15 | 55 | 65 | 0 | .257 | $10 | -$2 | 260 | +8 |

### -$5 Pennington, Cliff ●

| | PA | HR | R | RBI | SB | BA | $1L | $2L | Pts | RAA |
|---|---|---|---|---|---|---|---|---|---|---|
| '10 | 576 | 6 | 64 | 46 | 29 | .250 | $15 | $3 | 300 | -1 |
| Proj | 600 | 6 | 66 | 48 | 24 | .237 | $10 | -$5 | 290 | -2 |

### -$9 Cabrera, Orlando ○

| | PA | HR | R | RBI | SB | BA | $1L | $2L | Pts | RAA |
|---|---|---|---|---|---|---|---|---|---|---|
| '10 | 537 | 4 | 64 | 42 | 11 | .263 | $9 | -$1 | 270 | -7 |
| Proj | 400 | 4 | 48 | 36 | 8 | .273 | $6 | -$9 | 220 | -0 |

### -$17 Renteria, Edgar

| | PA | HR | R | RBI | SB | BA | $1L | $2L | Pts | RAA |
|---|---|---|---|---|---|---|---|---|---|---|
| '10 | 270 | 3 | 26 | 22 | 3 | .276 | $2 | -$11 | 120 | +2 |
| Proj | 225 | 5 | 29 | 23 | 5 | .280 | $2 | -$17 | 130 | +6 |

### -$18 Santiago, Ramon

| | PA | HR | R | RBI | SB | BA | $1L | $2L | Pts | RAA |
|---|---|---|---|---|---|---|---|---|---|---|
| '10 | 367 | 3 | 38 | 22 | 2 | .263 | $3 | -$11 | 140 | -7 |
| Proj | 275 | 3 | 30 | 25 | 3 | .259 | $1 | -$18 | 120 | -4 |

### -$21 Cabrera, Everth ●

| | PA | HR | R | RBI | SB | BA | $1L | $2L | Pts | RAA |
|---|---|---|---|---|---|---|---|---|---|---|
| '10 | 244 | 1 | 22 | 22 | 10 | .208 | -$1 | -$15 | 80 | -15 |
| Proj | 190 | 2 | 23 | 15 | 11 | .222 | -$1 | -$21 | 90 | -3 |

### -$23 Abreu, Tony

| | PA | HR | R | RBI | SB | BA | $1L | $2L | Pts | RAA |
|---|---|---|---|---|---|---|---|---|---|---|
| '10 | 201 | 1 | 16 | 13 | 2 | .233 | -$3 | -$17 | 50 | -10 |
| Proj | 150 | 3 | 18 | 14 | 2 | .273 | -$1 | -$23 | 80 | +2 |

### -$25 Andino, Robert

| | PA | HR | R | RBI | SB | BA | $1L | $2L | Pts | RAA |
|---|---|---|---|---|---|---|---|---|---|---|
| '10 | 66 | 2 | 6 | 6 | 1 | .295 | -$2 | -$17 | 30 | +2 |
| Proj | 100 | 2 | 10 | 8 | 3 | .254 | -$3 | -$25 | 40 | -0 |

### -$26 Ciriaco, Pedro

| | PA | HR | R | RBI | SB | BA | $1L | $2L | Pts | RAA |
|---|---|---|---|---|---|---|---|---|---|---|
| '10 | 6 | 0 | 3 | 1 | 0 | .500 | -$4 | -$19 | 10 | +1 |
| Proj | 100 | 1 | 11 | 8 | 5 | .218 | -$3 | -$26 | 40 | -6 |

### -$27 Navarro, Yamaico

| | PA | HR | R | RBI | SB | BA | $1L | $2L | Pts | RAA |
|---|---|---|---|---|---|---|---|---|---|---|
| '10 | 47 | 0 | 4 | 5 | 0 | .143 | -$5 | -$21 | 0 | -7 |
| Proj | 75 | 2 | 8 | 8 | 1 | .221 | -$5 | -$27 | 30 | -2 |

### -$28 Crosby, Bobby

| | PA | HR | R | RBI | SB | BA | $1L | $2L | Pts | RAA |
|---|---|---|---|---|---|---|---|---|---|---|
| '10 | 191 | 1 | 9 | 13 | 0 | .220 | -$5 | -$19 | 50 | -8 |
| Proj | 50 | 1 | 6 | 5 | 1 | .250 | -$4 | -$28 | 20 | +0 |

### -$28 Diaz, Argenis

| | PA | HR | R | RBI | SB | BA | $1L | $2L | Pts | RAA |
|---|---|---|---|---|---|---|---|---|---|---|
| '10 | 37 | 0 | 0 | 2 | 0 | .242 | -$5 | -$21 | 0 | -2 |
| Proj | 100 | 1 | 8 | 8 | 1 | .218 | -$5 | -$28 | 30 | -3 |

### -$29 Navarro, Oswaldo

| | PA | HR | R | RBI | SB | BA | $1L | $2L | Pts | RAA |
|---|---|---|---|---|---|---|---|---|---|---|
| '10 | 25 | 0 | 2 | 0 | 0 | .050 | -$6 | -$21 | 0 | -3 |
| Proj | 50 | 1 | 5 | 4 | 1 | .236 | -$5 | -$29 | 20 | -1 |

American League
National League

# Outfielders

| Top Finishes Among All Hitters From 2008-10 | Top 25 | | Top 50 |
|---|---|---|---|
| | ■ | HR | □ |
| | ▲ | RBI | △ |
| | ● | SB | ○ |

## Projected 2011 Leaders

| Home Runs | $2L |
|---|---|
| 36 Stanton, M | $10 |
| 35 Braun, R | $38 |
| 33 Werth, J | $26 |
| 33 Bruce, J | $20 |
| 31 Lee, C | $19 |
| 30 Cruz, N | $22 |
| 30 Bay, J | $17 |
| 30 Bautista, J | $11 |
| 30 Swisher, N | $9 |
| 29 Hamilton, J | $22 |
| 28 Ramirez, M | $13 |
| 28 Quentin, C | $11 |
| 27 Gonzalez, C | $30 |
| 26 Soriano, A | $11 |
| 26 Holliday, M | $29 |

| Runs | $2L |
|---|---|
| 112 Braun, R | $38 |
| 101 Gonzalez, C | $30 |
| 98 Holliday, M | $29 |
| 98 Crawford, C | $26 |
| 98 Werth, J | $26 |
| 98 Victorino, S | $18 |
| 91 Kemp, M | $24 |
| 91 Hart, C | $22 |
| 91 Upton, J | $20 |
| 91 Bruce, J | $20 |
| 91 Young, C | $18 |
| 91 Upton, B | $15 |
| 91 Young, C | -$3 |
| 91 Markakis, N | $18 |
| 91 Span, D | $10 |

| Runs Batted In | $2L |
|---|---|
| 119 Braun, R | $38 |
| 104 Holliday, M | $29 |
| 100 Lee, C | $19 |
| 98 Hunter, T | $21 |
| 95 Gonzalez, C | $30 |
| 95 Choo, S | $22 |
| 92 Hamilton, J | $22 |
| 91 Werth, J | $26 |
| 91 Kemp, M | $24 |
| 91 Hart, C | $22 |
| 90 Beltran, C | $23 |
| 90 Cruz, N | $22 |
| 90 Bay, J | $17 |
| 90 Ibanez, R | $12 |
| 90 Young, D | $9 |

| Stolen Bases | $2L |
|---|---|
| 52 Pierre, J | $13 |
| 50 Bourn, M | $11 |
| 46 Ellsbury, J | $13 |
| 46 Crawford, C | $26 |
| 41 Davis, R | $3 |
| 40 Gardner, B | $5 |
| 39 Upton, B | $15 |
| 36 Crisp, C | $9 |
| 35 Suzuki, I | $18 |
| 35 Morgan, N | -$1 |
| 33 Victorino, S | $18 |
| 31 Pagan, A | $14 |
| 31 Brantley, M | $1 |
| 31 Bourjos, P | -$3 |
| 30 McCutchen, A | $13 |

| Batting Average | $2L |
|---|---|
| .307 Suzuki, I | $18 |
| .306 Hamilton, J | $22 |
| .304 Holliday, M | $29 |
| .298 Markakis, N | $18 |
| .295 Ordonez, M | $7 |
| .294 Braun, R | $38 |
| .294 Gonzalez, C | $30 |
| .292 DeJesus, D | $6 |
| .290 Byrd, M | $10 |
| .288 Crawford, C | $26 |
| .288 Choo, S | $22 |
| .287 Ethier, A | $14 |
| .286 Jackson, C | -$11 |
| .285 Pence, H | $20 |
| .285 Lee, C | $19 |

### $38 Braun, Ryan ■■□ ▲▲▲ ○

| | PA | HR | R | RBI | SB | BA | $1L | $2L | Pts | RAA |
|---|---|---|---|---|---|---|---|---|---|---|
| '10 | 686 | 25 | 101 | 103 | 14 | .304 | $33 | $29 | 490 | +24 |
| Proj | 700 | 35 | 112 | 119 | 21 | .294 | $34 | $38 | 560 | +34 |

### $26 Crawford, Carl △ ●●●

| | PA | HR | R | RBI | SB | BA | $1L | $2L | Pts | RAA |
|---|---|---|---|---|---|---|---|---|---|---|
| '10 | 666 | 19 | 110 | 90 | 47 | .307 | $41 | $36 | 520 | +18 |
| Proj | 650 | 13 | 98 | 78 | 46 | .288 | $31 | $26 | 470 | +3 |

### $23 Beltran, Carlos □ ▲ ●

| | PA | HR | R | RBI | SB | BA | $1L | $2L | Pts | RAA |
|---|---|---|---|---|---|---|---|---|---|---|
| '10 | 260 | 7 | 21 | 27 | 3 | .255 | $2 | -$11 | 140 | +1 |
| Proj | 600 | 24 | 90 | 90 | 18 | .283 | $25 | $23 | 470 | +38 |

### $22 Choo, Shin-Soo △ ○○

| | PA | HR | R | RBI | SB | BA | $1L | $2L | Pts | RAA |
|---|---|---|---|---|---|---|---|---|---|---|
| '10 | 657 | 22 | 81 | 90 | 22 | .300 | $30 | $24 | 440 | +17 |
| Proj | 675 | 20 | 88 | 95 | 20 | .288 | $27 | $22 | 440 | +17 |

### $20 Pence, Hunter □□□ △ ○

| | PA | HR | R | RBI | SB | BA | $1L | $2L | Pts | RAA |
|---|---|---|---|---|---|---|---|---|---|---|
| '10 | 660 | 25 | 93 | 91 | 18 | .282 | $29 | $23 | 430 | -2 |
| Proj | 650 | 26 | 85 | 85 | 13 | .285 | $24 | $20 | 420 | +7 |

### $19 Lee, Carlos □□□ ▲▲△

| | PA | HR | R | RBI | SB | BA | $1L | $2L | Pts | RAA |
|---|---|---|---|---|---|---|---|---|---|---|
| '10 | 650 | 24 | 67 | 89 | 3 | .246 | $15 | $8 | 390 | -17 |
| Proj | 625 | 31 | 75 | 100 | 6 | .285 | $22 | $19 | 460 | +14 |

### $18 Victorino, Shane ●●●

| | PA | HR | R | RBI | SB | BA | $1L | $2L | Pts | RAA |
|---|---|---|---|---|---|---|---|---|---|---|
| '10 | 653 | 18 | 84 | 69 | 34 | .259 | $24 | $16 | 440 | +2 |
| Proj | 650 | 13 | 98 | 65 | 33 | .277 | $23 | $18 | 470 | +12 |

### $16 Rios, Alex △ ●●○

| | PA | HR | R | RBI | SB | BA | $1L | $2L | Pts | RAA |
|---|---|---|---|---|---|---|---|---|---|---|
| '10 | 621 | 21 | 89 | 88 | 34 | .284 | $32 | $25 | 440 | +7 |
| Proj | 625 | 19 | 81 | 75 | 25 | .274 | $24 | $16 | 410 | +10 |

### $14 Pagan, Angel ●

| | PA | HR | R | RBI | SB | BA | $1L | $2L | Pts | RAA |
|---|---|---|---|---|---|---|---|---|---|---|
| '10 | 638 | 11 | 80 | 69 | 37 | .290 | $27 | $19 | 410 | +7 |
| Proj | 625 | 13 | 81 | 69 | 31 | .282 | $21 | $14 | 410 | +12 |

### $13 McCutchen, Andrew ●○

| | PA | HR | R | RBI | SB | BA | $1L | $2L | Pts | RAA |
|---|---|---|---|---|---|---|---|---|---|---|
| '10 | 654 | 16 | 94 | 56 | 33 | .286 | $27 | $20 | 440 | +19 |
| Proj | 600 | 18 | 84 | 54 | 30 | .280 | $20 | $13 | 420 | +25 |

### $13 Ramirez, Manny ■ ▲

| | PA | HR | R | RBI | SB | BA | $1L | $2L | Pts | RAA |
|---|---|---|---|---|---|---|---|---|---|---|
| '10 | 324 | 9 | 38 | 42 | 1 | .298 | $9 | -$3 | 190 | +10 |
| Proj | 550 | 28 | 77 | 88 | 0 | .284 | $20 | $13 | 380 | +26 |

### $11 Soriano, Alfonso □□ ○

| | PA | HR | R | RBI | SB | BA | $1L | $2L | Pts | RAA |
|---|---|---|---|---|---|---|---|---|---|---|
| '10 | 551 | 24 | 67 | 79 | 5 | .258 | $17 | $9 | 320 | +6 |
| Proj | 525 | 26 | 74 | 68 | 11 | .269 | $18 | $11 | 330 | +10 |

### $11 Bautista, Jose ■ ▲

| | PA | HR | R | RBI | SB | BA | $1L | $2L | Pts | RAA |
|---|---|---|---|---|---|---|---|---|---|---|
| '10 | 685 | 54 | 109 | 124 | 9 | .260 | $38 | $35 | 580 | +38 |
| Proj | 600 | 30 | 78 | 84 | 6 | .253 | $20 | $11 | 400 | +14 |

### $11 Quentin, Carlos ■□ ▲△

| | PA | HR | R | RBI | SB | BA | $1L | $2L | Pts | RAA |
|---|---|---|---|---|---|---|---|---|---|---|
| '10 | 530 | 26 | 73 | 87 | 2 | .243 | $18 | $10 | 350 | -8 |
| Proj | 550 | 28 | 77 | 88 | 6 | .260 | $19 | $11 | 370 | -3 |

### $10 Byrd, Marlon △

| | PA | HR | R | RBI | SB | BA | $1L | $2L | Pts | RAA |
|---|---|---|---|---|---|---|---|---|---|---|
| '10 | 631 | 12 | 84 | 66 | 5 | .293 | $19 | $11 | 340 | +1 |
| Proj | 600 | 18 | 78 | 72 | 6 | .290 | $17 | $10 | 370 | +17 |

### $9 Swisher, Nick ■□□ △

| | PA | HR | R | RBI | SB | BA | $1L | $2L | Pts | RAA |
|---|---|---|---|---|---|---|---|---|---|---|
| '10 | 635 | 29 | 91 | 89 | 1 | .288 | $26 | $20 | 390 | +13 |
| Proj | 600 | 30 | 84 | 78 | 0 | .259 | $18 | $9 | 360 | +14 |

### $9 Young, Delmon ▲

| | PA | HR | R | RBI | SB | BA | $1L | $2L | Pts | RAA |
|---|---|---|---|---|---|---|---|---|---|---|
| '10 | 618 | 21 | 77 | 112 | 5 | .298 | $27 | $21 | 420 | +6 |
| Proj | 600 | 18 | 72 | 90 | 6 | .279 | $18 | $9 | 340 | -9 |

### $8 Jackson, Austin ●

| | PA | HR | R | RBI | SB | BA | $1L | $2L | Pts | RAA |
|---|---|---|---|---|---|---|---|---|---|---|
| '10 | 679 | 4 | 103 | 41 | 27 | .293 | $23 | $14 | 320 | +2 |
| Proj | 675 | 7 | 88 | 54 | 27 | .264 | $18 | $8 | 320 | -4 |

### $7 Wells, Vernon ■ △ ○

| | PA | HR | R | RBI | SB | BA | $1L | $2L | Pts | RAA |
|---|---|---|---|---|---|---|---|---|---|---|
| '10 | 651 | 31 | 79 | 88 | 6 | .273 | $25 | $17 | 440 | +19 |
| Proj | 600 | 18 | 72 | 78 | 12 | .264 | $17 | $7 | 390 | +9 |

### $30 Gonzalez, Carlos ■ ▲ ●

| | PA | HR | R | RBI | SB | BA | $1L | $2L | Pts | RAA |
|---|---|---|---|---|---|---|---|---|---|---|
| '10 | 644 | 34 | 111 | 117 | 26 | .336 | $46 | $44 | 530 | +47 |
| Proj | 675 | 27 | 101 | 95 | 20 | .294 | $30 | $30 | 450 | +23 |

### $26 Werth, Jayson ■□□ △△ ○○

| | PA | HR | R | RBI | SB | BA | $1L | $2L | Pts | RAA |
|---|---|---|---|---|---|---|---|---|---|---|
| '10 | 658 | 27 | 106 | 85 | 13 | .296 | $30 | $26 | 440 | +25 |
| Proj | 650 | 33 | 98 | 91 | 20 | .277 | $26 | $26 | 450 | +26 |

### $22 Cruz, Nelson ■ ○○

| | PA | HR | R | RBI | SB | BA | $1L | $2L | Pts | RAA |
|---|---|---|---|---|---|---|---|---|---|---|
| '10 | 450 | 22 | 60 | 78 | 17 | .318 | $26 | $18 | 360 | +23 |
| Proj | 600 | 30 | 78 | 90 | 18 | .280 | $28 | $22 | 400 | +16 |

### $22 Hamilton, Josh ■■ ▲▲

| | PA | HR | R | RBI | SB | BA | $1L | $2L | Pts | RAA |
|---|---|---|---|---|---|---|---|---|---|---|
| '10 | 576 | 32 | 95 | 100 | 8 | .359 | $39 | $35 | 490 | +51 |
| Proj | 575 | 29 | 81 | 92 | 12 | .306 | $27 | $22 | 430 | +36 |

### $20 Upton, Justin □ ○○

| | PA | HR | R | RBI | SB | BA | $1L | $2L | Pts | RAA |
|---|---|---|---|---|---|---|---|---|---|---|
| '10 | 576 | 17 | 73 | 69 | 18 | .273 | $20 | $12 | 300 | -1 |
| Proj | 650 | 26 | 91 | 85 | 20 | .277 | $23 | $20 | 400 | +14 |

### $18 Young, Chris □ △ ●

| | PA | HR | R | RBI | SB | BA | $1L | $2L | Pts | RAA |
|---|---|---|---|---|---|---|---|---|---|---|
| '10 | 664 | 27 | 94 | 91 | 28 | .257 | $28 | $23 | 430 | +16 |
| Proj | 650 | 26 | 91 | 78 | 20 | .266 | $22 | $18 | 410 | +19 |

### $18 Suzuki, Ichiro ●●●

| | PA | HR | R | RBI | SB | BA | $1L | $2L | Pts | RAA |
|---|---|---|---|---|---|---|---|---|---|---|
| '10 | 745 | 6 | 74 | 43 | 42 | .315 | $28 | $18 | 420 | -6 |
| Proj | 700 | 7 | 84 | 49 | 35 | .307 | $26 | $18 | 430 | -6 |

### $15 Upton, B.J. ●●●

| | PA | HR | R | RBI | SB | BA | $1L | $2L | Pts | RAA |
|---|---|---|---|---|---|---|---|---|---|---|
| '10 | 611 | 18 | 89 | 62 | 42 | .237 | $25 | $16 | 360 | +6 |
| Proj | 650 | 20 | 91 | 72 | 39 | .251 | $24 | $15 | 400 | +18 |

### $13 Ross, Cody △

| | PA | HR | R | RBI | SB | BA | $1L | $2L | Pts | RAA |
|---|---|---|---|---|---|---|---|---|---|---|
| '10 | 573 | 14 | 71 | 65 | 9 | .269 | $16 | $7 | 280 | -3 |
| Proj | 600 | 24 | 78 | 84 | 6 | .276 | $19 | $13 | 370 | +18 |

### $13 Pierre, Juan ●●●

| | PA | HR | R | RBI | SB | BA | $1L | $2L | Pts | RAA |
|---|---|---|---|---|---|---|---|---|---|---|
| '10 | 734 | 1 | 96 | 47 | 68 | .275 | $31 | $21 | 460 | -30 |
| Proj | 650 | 0 | 85 | 46 | 52 | .279 | $23 | $13 | 430 | -18 |

### $12 Ibanez, Raul ■ ▲△

| | PA | HR | R | RBI | SB | BA | $1L | $2L | Pts | RAA |
|---|---|---|---|---|---|---|---|---|---|---|
| '10 | 647 | 16 | 75 | 83 | 4 | .275 | $18 | $10 | 370 | +3 |
| Proj | 600 | 24 | 78 | 90 | 6 | .272 | $18 | $12 | 410 | +19 |

### $11 Bourn, Michael ●●●

| | PA | HR | R | RBI | SB | BA | $1L | $2L | Pts | RAA |
|---|---|---|---|---|---|---|---|---|---|---|
| '10 | 610 | 2 | 84 | 38 | 52 | .265 | $23 | $12 | 350 | -6 |
| Proj | 625 | 6 | 88 | 38 | 50 | .265 | $20 | $11 | 360 | -3 |

### $11 Cuddyer, Michael ■ △

| | PA | HR | R | RBI | SB | BA | $1L | $2L | Pts | RAA |
|---|---|---|---|---|---|---|---|---|---|---|
| '10 | 682 | 14 | 93 | 81 | 7 | .271 | $20 | $13 | 400 | -11 |
| Proj | 650 | 20 | 85 | 85 | 7 | .270 | $19 | $11 | 390 | -3 |

### $11 Ludwick, Ryan ■ ▲△

| | PA | HR | R | RBI | SB | BA | $1L | $2L | Pts | RAA |
|---|---|---|---|---|---|---|---|---|---|---|
| '10 | 553 | 17 | 63 | 69 | 0 | .251 | $11 | $2 | 260 | -15 |
| Proj | 535 | 21 | 75 | 86 | 5 | .273 | $17 | $11 | 320 | -3 |

### $10 Stanton, Mike

| | PA | HR | R | RBI | SB | BA | $1L | $2L | Pts | RAA |
|---|---|---|---|---|---|---|---|---|---|---|
| '10 | 402 | 22 | 45 | 59 | 5 | .259 | $13 | $3 | 200 | +2 |
| Proj | 600 | 36 | 72 | 84 | 6 | .244 | $16 | $10 | 340 | +9 |

### $9 Smith, Seth

| | PA | HR | R | RBI | SB | BA | $1L | $2L | Pts | RAA |
|---|---|---|---|---|---|---|---|---|---|---|
| '10 | 399 | 17 | 55 | 52 | 2 | .246 | $9 | $0 | 250 | -1 |
| Proj | 550 | 22 | 77 | 72 | 6 | .276 | $17 | $9 | 360 | +11 |

### $8 Willingham, Josh

| | PA | HR | R | RBI | SB | BA | $1L | $2L | Pts | RAA |
|---|---|---|---|---|---|---|---|---|---|---|
| '10 | 454 | 16 | 54 | 56 | 8 | .268 | $13 | $4 | 280 | +11 |
| Proj | 550 | 22 | 72 | 72 | 6 | .272 | $16 | $8 | 340 | +13 |

### $7 Zobrist, Ben □ △ ○○

| | PA | HR | R | RBI | SB | BA | $1L | $2L | Pts | RAA |
|---|---|---|---|---|---|---|---|---|---|---|
| '10 | 656 | 10 | 77 | 75 | 24 | .238 | $17 | $8 | 370 | -15 |
| Proj | 600 | 18 | 72 | 72 | 18 | .258 | $18 | $7 | 380 | +3 |

### $6 DeJesus, David

| | PA | HR | R | RBI | SB | BA | $1L | $2L | Pts | RAA |
|---|---|---|---|---|---|---|---|---|---|---|
| '10 | 396 | 5 | 46 | 37 | 3 | .318 | $10 | -$1 | 230 | +3 |
| Proj | 625 | 13 | 75 | 63 | 6 | .292 | $16 | $6 | 380 | +4 |

### $29 Holliday, Matt ■□ ▲▲ ●

| | PA | HR | R | RBI | SB | BA | $1L | $2L | Pts | RAA |
|---|---|---|---|---|---|---|---|---|---|---|
| '10 | 685 | 28 | 95 | 103 | 9 | .312 | $33 | $29 | 500 | +31 |
| Proj | 650 | 26 | 98 | 104 | 13 | .304 | $28 | $29 | 500 | +36 |

### $24 Kemp, Matt ■□ ▲△ ●●○

| | PA | HR | R | RBI | SB | BA | $1L | $2L | Pts | RAA |
|---|---|---|---|---|---|---|---|---|---|---|
| '10 | 672 | 28 | 82 | 89 | 19 | .249 | $23 | $17 | 350 | -4 |
| Proj | 650 | 26 | 91 | 91 | 26 | .272 | $26 | $24 | 420 | +18 |

### $22 Hart, Corey ■ ▲△ ●

| | PA | HR | R | RBI | SB | BA | $1L | $2L | Pts | RAA |
|---|---|---|---|---|---|---|---|---|---|---|
| '10 | 616 | 31 | 91 | 102 | 7 | .283 | $28 | $24 | 400 | +9 |
| Proj | 650 | 26 | 91 | 91 | 20 | .276 | $25 | $22 | 440 | +5 |

### $21 Hunter, Torii □ △△ ○○

| | PA | HR | R | RBI | SB | BA | $1L | $2L | Pts | RAA |
|---|---|---|---|---|---|---|---|---|---|---|
| '10 | 652 | 23 | 76 | 90 | 9 | .281 | $24 | $17 | 390 | -1 |
| Proj | 650 | 26 | 85 | 98 | 20 | .280 | $27 | $21 | 440 | +7 |

### $20 Bruce, Jay □

| | PA | HR | R | RBI | SB | BA | $1L | $2L | Pts | RAA |
|---|---|---|---|---|---|---|---|---|---|---|
| '10 | 578 | 25 | 80 | 70 | 5 | .281 | $21 | $14 | 330 | +7 |
| Proj | 650 | 33 | 91 | 85 | 7 | .268 | $23 | $20 | 400 | +9 |

### $18 Markakis, Nick ▲

| | PA | HR | R | RBI | SB | BA | $1L | $2L | Pts | RAA |
|---|---|---|---|---|---|---|---|---|---|---|
| '10 | 718 | 12 | 79 | 60 | 7 | .297 | $20 | $11 | 400 | +5 |
| Proj | 700 | 21 | 91 | 84 | 7 | .298 | $24 | $18 | 440 | +12 |

### $17 Bay, Jason ■□ ▲▲

| | PA | HR | R | RBI | SB | BA | $1L | $2L | Pts | RAA |
|---|---|---|---|---|---|---|---|---|---|---|
| '10 | 404 | 6 | 48 | 47 | 10 | .259 | $8 | -$3 | 210 | -3 |
| Proj | 600 | 30 | 90 | 90 | 12 | .265 | $21 | $17 | 410 | +23 |

### $14 Ethier, Andre ■□ ▲

| | PA | HR | R | RBI | SB | BA | $1L | $2L | Pts | RAA |
|---|---|---|---|---|---|---|---|---|---|---|
| '10 | 596 | 23 | 71 | 82 | 2 | .292 | $21 | $14 | 370 | +10 |
| Proj | 600 | 24 | 78 | 84 | 6 | .287 | $20 | $14 | 410 | +13 |

### $13 Ellsbury, Jacoby ●●

| | PA | HR | R | RBI | SB | BA | $1L | $2L | Pts | RAA |
|---|---|---|---|---|---|---|---|---|---|---|
| '10 | 84 | 0 | 10 | 5 | 7 | .192 | -$2 | -$18 | 40 | -7 |
| Proj | 575 | 6 | 81 | 46 | 46 | .280 | $23 | $13 | 400 | +8 |

### $13 Sizemore, Grady ■ △ ●

| | PA | HR | R | RBI | SB | BA | $1L | $2L | Pts | RAA |
|---|---|---|---|---|---|---|---|---|---|---|
| '10 | 140 | 0 | 15 | 13 | 4 | .211 | -$2 | -$18 | 40 | -10 |
| Proj | 600 | 24 | 84 | 66 | 24 | .263 | $22 | $13 | 400 | +24 |

### $12 Rasmus, Colby □

| | PA | HR | R | RBI | SB | BA | $1L | $2L | Pts | RAA |
|---|---|---|---|---|---|---|---|---|---|---|
| '10 | 543 | 23 | 85 | 66 | 12 | .276 | $22 | $15 | 310 | +18 |
| Proj | 600 | 24 | 84 | 66 | 12 | .265 | $18 | $12 | 370 | +22 |

### $11 Granderson, Curtis □□ ○

| | PA | HR | R | RBI | SB | BA | $1L | $2L | Pts | RAA |
|---|---|---|---|---|---|---|---|---|---|---|
| '10 | 531 | 24 | 76 | 67 | 12 | .247 | $19 | $10 | 320 | +6 |
| Proj | 600 | 24 | 84 | 66 | 18 | .260 | $20 | $11 | 380 | +15 |

### $11 Torres, Andres ●

| | PA | HR | R | RBI | SB | BA | $1L | $2L | Pts | RAA |
|---|---|---|---|---|---|---|---|---|---|---|
| '10 | 572 | 16 | 84 | 63 | 26 | .268 | $22 | $14 | 360 | +16 |
| Proj | 600 | 18 | 84 | 60 | 24 | .265 | $18 | $11 | 370 | +20 |

### $10 Span, Denard ●○○

| | PA | HR | R | RBI | SB | BA | $1L | $2L | Pts | RAA |
|---|---|---|---|---|---|---|---|---|---|---|
| '10 | 705 | 3 | 85 | 58 | 26 | .264 | $18 | $8 | 400 | -13 |
| Proj | 700 | 7 | 91 | 63 | 28 | .271 | $20 | $10 | 420 | +2 |

### $10 Heyward, Jason

| | PA | HR | R | RBI | SB | BA | $1L | $2L | Pts | RAA |
|---|---|---|---|---|---|---|---|---|---|---|
| '10 | 625 | 18 | 83 | 72 | 11 | .277 | $21 | $13 | 370 | +10 |
| Proj | 600 | 18 | 84 | 66 | 12 | .270 | $17 | $10 | 380 | +8 |

### $9 Crisp, Coco ●○

| | PA | HR | R | RBI | SB | BA | $1L | $2L | Pts | RAA |
|---|---|---|---|---|---|---|---|---|---|---|
| '10 | 328 | 8 | 51 | 38 | 32 | .279 | $17 | $5 | 260 | +9 |
| Proj | 600 | 12 | 78 | 60 | 36 | .261 | $20 | $9 | 400 | +9 |

### $8 Jones, Adam

| | PA | HR | R | RBI | SB | BA | $1L | $2L | Pts | RAA |
|---|---|---|---|---|---|---|---|---|---|---|
| '10 | 622 | 19 | 76 | 69 | 7 | .284 | $21 | $12 | 310 | -4 |
| Proj | 550 | 17 | 72 | 66 | 11 | .279 | $18 | $8 | 300 | -2 |

### $7 Ordonez, Magglio ▲

| | PA | HR | R | RBI | SB | BA | $1L | $2L | Pts | RAA |
|---|---|---|---|---|---|---|---|---|---|---|
| '10 | 365 | 12 | 56 | 59 | 1 | .303 | $14 | $4 | 270 | +10 |
| Proj | 525 | 16 | 63 | 79 | 0 | .295 | $17 | $7 | 340 | +6 |

### $5 Maybin, Cameron

| | PA | HR | R | RBI | SB | BA | $1L | $2L | Pts | RAA |
|---|---|---|---|---|---|---|---|---|---|---|
| '10 | 323 | 8 | 46 | 28 | 9 | .234 | $5 | -$7 | 130 | -11 |
| Proj | 600 | 18 | 84 | 54 | 18 | .247 | $15 | $5 | 310 | +7 |

**$5 Tabata, Jose** ○

| | PA | HR | R | RBI | SB | BA | $1L | $2L | Pts | RAA |
|---|---|---|---|---|---|---|---|---|---|---|
| '10 | 441 | 4 | 61 | 35 | 19 | .299 | $15 | $4 | 260 | –3 |
| Proj | 600 | 12 | 78 | 54 | 24 | .275 | $15 | $5 | 360 | +1 |

**$5 Colvin, Tyler**

| | PA | HR | R | RBI | SB | BA | $1L | $2L | Pts | RAA |
|---|---|---|---|---|---|---|---|---|---|---|
| '10 | 397 | 20 | 60 | 56 | 6 | .254 | $13 | $4 | 240 | –1 |
| Proj | 625 | 25 | 75 | 75 | 13 | .236 | $13 | $5 | 330 | –17 |

**$3 Brown, Domonic**

| | PA | HR | R | RBI | SB | BA | $1L | $2L | Pts | RAA |
|---|---|---|---|---|---|---|---|---|---|---|
| '10 | 71 | 2 | 8 | 13 | 2 | .210 | -$3 | -$17 | 30 | –5 |
| Proj | 450 | 18 | 66 | 66 | 24 | .226 | $14 | $3 | 320 | –16 |

**$2 Stubbs, Drew** ●

| | PA | HR | R | RBI | SB | BA | $1L | $2L | Pts | RAA |
|---|---|---|---|---|---|---|---|---|---|---|
| '10 | 585 | 22 | 91 | 77 | 30 | .255 | $26 | $19 | 340 | +5 |
| Proj | 500 | 15 | 70 | 50 | 25 | .238 | $13 | $2 | 270 | +1 |

**$1 Fowler, Dexter** ●

| | PA | HR | R | RBI | SB | BA | $1L | $2L | Pts | RAA |
|---|---|---|---|---|---|---|---|---|---|---|
| '10 | 505 | 6 | 73 | 36 | 13 | .260 | $11 | $1 | 260 | –1 |
| Proj | 550 | 6 | 77 | 44 | 22 | .257 | $13 | $1 | 300 | +4 |

**$0 Borbon, Julio** ○

| | PA | HR | R | RBI | SB | BA | $1L | $2L | Pts | RAA |
|---|---|---|---|---|---|---|---|---|---|---|
| '10 | 468 | 3 | 60 | 42 | 15 | .276 | $12 | $1 | 230 | –17 |
| Proj | 500 | 5 | 65 | 45 | 25 | .268 | $13 | $0 | 290 | –10 |

**-$1 Morgan, Nyjer** ●●

| | PA | HR | R | RBI | SB | BA | $1L | $2L | Pts | RAA |
|---|---|---|---|---|---|---|---|---|---|---|
| '10 | 578 | 0 | 60 | 24 | 34 | .253 | $11 | -$1 | 250 | –29 |
| Proj | 600 | 0 | 65 | 30 | 35 | .265 | $12 | -$1 | 260 | –15 |

**-$2 Hawpe, Brad** □

| | PA | HR | R | RBI | SB | BA | $1L | $2L | Pts | RAA |
|---|---|---|---|---|---|---|---|---|---|---|
| '10 | 350 | 9 | 31 | 44 | 2 | .245 | $5 | -$8 | 160 | –5 |
| Proj | 400 | 16 | 52 | 60 | 0 | .275 | $11 | -$2 | 240 | +10 |

**-$2 Murphy, David**

| | PA | HR | R | RBI | SB | BA | $1L | $2L | Pts | RAA |
|---|---|---|---|---|---|---|---|---|---|---|
| '10 | 473 | 12 | 54 | 65 | 14 | .291 | $18 | $8 | 310 | +9 |
| Proj | 425 | 13 | 51 | 55 | 9 | .280 | $12 | -$2 | 270 | +11 |

**-$3 Cameron, Mike** □ ○

| | PA | HR | R | RBI | SB | BA | $1L | $2L | Pts | RAA |
|---|---|---|---|---|---|---|---|---|---|---|
| '10 | 180 | 4 | 24 | 15 | 0 | .259 | $1 | -$14 | 70 | –2 |
| Proj | 400 | 16 | 52 | 48 | 8 | .263 | $11 | -$3 | 240 | +15 |

**-$4 DeRosa, Mark**

| | PA | HR | R | RBI | SB | BA | $1L | $2L | Pts | RAA |
|---|---|---|---|---|---|---|---|---|---|---|
| '10 | 104 | 1 | 9 | 10 | 0 | .194 | -$4 | -$19 | 30 | –10 |
| Proj | 400 | 12 | 56 | 52 | 4 | .268 | $9 | -$4 | 240 | +4 |

**-$5 Pie, Felix**

| | PA | HR | R | RBI | SB | BA | $1L | $2L | Pts | RAA |
|---|---|---|---|---|---|---|---|---|---|---|
| '10 | 308 | 5 | 39 | 31 | 5 | .274 | $6 | -$7 | 160 | –8 |
| Proj | 400 | 12 | 52 | 44 | 8 | .271 | $10 | -$5 | 230 | +1 |

**-$6 Kearns, Austin**

| | PA | HR | R | RBI | SB | BA | $1L | $2L | Pts | RAA |
|---|---|---|---|---|---|---|---|---|---|---|
| '10 | 463 | 10 | 55 | 49 | 4 | .263 | $10 | -$1 | 200 | –6 |
| Proj | 500 | 10 | 60 | 55 | 5 | .261 | $9 | -$6 | 240 | –12 |

**-$9 Gomes, Jonny** △

| | PA | HR | R | RBI | SB | BA | $1L | $2L | Pts | RAA |
|---|---|---|---|---|---|---|---|---|---|---|
| '10 | 574 | 18 | 77 | 86 | 5 | .266 | $18 | $11 | 310 | –10 |
| Proj | 300 | 12 | 39 | 42 | 6 | .255 | $6 | -$9 | 170 | +2 |

**-$10 Jennings, Desmond**

| | PA | HR | R | RBI | SB | BA | $1L | $2L | Pts | RAA |
|---|---|---|---|---|---|---|---|---|---|---|
| '10 | 24 | 0 | 5 | 2 | 2 | .190 | -$3 | -$20 | 10 | –2 |
| Proj | 325 | 7 | 39 | 26 | 20 | .244 | $7 | -$10 | 200 | –0 |

**-$11 Jackson, Conor**

| | PA | HR | R | RBI | SB | BA | $1L | $2L | Pts | RAA |
|---|---|---|---|---|---|---|---|---|---|---|
| '10 | 244 | 2 | 25 | 16 | 6 | .236 | $1 | -$14 | 120 | –6 |
| Proj | 300 | 6 | 39 | 36 | 6 | .286 | $6 | -$11 | 210 | +8 |

**-$13 Rowand, Aaron**

| | PA | HR | R | RBI | SB | BA | $1L | $2L | Pts | RAA |
|---|---|---|---|---|---|---|---|---|---|---|
| '10 | 360 | 11 | 42 | 34 | 5 | .230 | $4 | -$8 | 150 | –17 |
| Proj | 300 | 9 | 36 | 36 | 3 | .269 | $4 | -$13 | 160 | +1 |

**-$13 Bowker, John**

| | PA | HR | R | RBI | SB | BA | $1L | $2L | Pts | RAA |
|---|---|---|---|---|---|---|---|---|---|---|
| '10 | 169 | 5 | 16 | 21 | 0 | .219 | -$2 | -$16 | 70 | –9 |
| Proj | 300 | 12 | 33 | 36 | 3 | .254 | $4 | -$13 | 160 | –3 |

**-$14 Reimold, Nolan**

| | PA | HR | R | RBI | SB | BA | $1L | $2L | Pts | RAA |
|---|---|---|---|---|---|---|---|---|---|---|
| '10 | 131 | 3 | 9 | 14 | 0 | .207 | -$3 | -$18 | 50 | –7 |
| Proj | 275 | 11 | 30 | 30 | 3 | .255 | $4 | -$14 | 150 | +0 |

**-$15 McDonald, Darnell**

| | PA | HR | R | RBI | SB | BA | $1L | $2L | Pts | RAA |
|---|---|---|---|---|---|---|---|---|---|---|
| '10 | 364 | 9 | 40 | 34 | 9 | .270 | $9 | -$4 | 170 | +1 |
| Proj | 250 | 5 | 30 | 28 | 8 | .270 | $4 | -$15 | 130 | +1 |

**-$16 Francisco, Ben**

| | PA | HR | R | RBI | SB | BA | $1L | $2L | Pts | RAA |
|---|---|---|---|---|---|---|---|---|---|---|
| '10 | 198 | 6 | 24 | 28 | 8 | .268 | $4 | -$9 | 130 | +1 |
| Proj | 200 | 8 | 26 | 22 | 6 | .267 | $2 | -$16 | 120 | +2 |

**-$18 Parra, Gerardo**

| | PA | HR | R | RBI | SB | BA | $1L | $2L | Pts | RAA |
|---|---|---|---|---|---|---|---|---|---|---|
| '10 | 403 | 3 | 31 | 30 | 1 | .261 | $1 | -$12 | 140 | –17 |
| Proj | 250 | 5 | 28 | 25 | 5 | .263 | $2 | -$18 | 130 | –5 |

**-$18 Craig, Allen**

| | PA | HR | R | RBI | SB | BA | $1L | $2L | Pts | RAA |
|---|---|---|---|---|---|---|---|---|---|---|
| '10 | 125 | 4 | 12 | 18 | 0 | .246 | -$1 | -$16 | 60 | –4 |
| Proj | 225 | 9 | 25 | 29 | 0 | .245 | $1 | -$18 | 110 | –5 |

**-$19 Kalish, Ryan**

| | PA | HR | R | RBI | SB | BA | $1L | $2L | Pts | RAA |
|---|---|---|---|---|---|---|---|---|---|---|
| '10 | 179 | 4 | 26 | 24 | 10 | .252 | $4 | -$10 | 110 | –1 |
| Proj | 200 | 6 | 22 | 22 | 8 | .231 | $1 | -$19 | 110 | –1 |

**$5 Gardner, Brett** ●●

| | PA | HR | R | RBI | SB | BA | $1L | $2L | Pts | RAA |
|---|---|---|---|---|---|---|---|---|---|---|
| '10 | 570 | 5 | 97 | 47 | 47 | .277 | $26 | $17 | 390 | +6 |
| Proj | 500 | 5 | 75 | 40 | 40 | .261 | $17 | $5 | 330 | +3 |

**$4 Gutierrez, Franklin** ○

| | PA | HR | R | RBI | SB | BA | $1L | $2L | Pts | RAA |
|---|---|---|---|---|---|---|---|---|---|---|
| '10 | 634 | 12 | 61 | 64 | 25 | .245 | $16 | $5 | 290 | –14 |
| Proj | 625 | 19 | 75 | 63 | 19 | .253 | $16 | $4 | 310 | –6 |

**$3 Davis, Rajai** ●●●

| | PA | HR | R | RBI | SB | BA | $1L | $2L | Pts | RAA |
|---|---|---|---|---|---|---|---|---|---|---|
| '10 | 561 | 5 | 66 | 52 | 50 | .284 | $25 | $14 | 350 | –3 |
| Proj | 450 | 5 | 54 | 41 | 41 | .271 | $16 | $3 | 290 | +1 |

**$1 Morrison, Logan**

| | PA | HR | R | RBI | SB | BA | $1L | $2L | Pts | RAA |
|---|---|---|---|---|---|---|---|---|---|---|
| '10 | 287 | 2 | 43 | 18 | 0 | .283 | $3 | -$9 | 160 | +6 |
| Proj | 600 | 18 | 72 | 66 | 6 | .258 | $12 | $1 | 360 | +14 |

**$1 Brantley, Michael**

| | PA | HR | R | RBI | SB | BA | $1L | $2L | Pts | RAA |
|---|---|---|---|---|---|---|---|---|---|---|
| '10 | 325 | 3 | 38 | 22 | 10 | .246 | $4 | -$10 | 160 | –12 |
| Proj | 625 | 6 | 69 | 50 | 31 | .251 | $14 | $1 | 360 | –4 |

**-$1 Drew, J.D.**

| | PA | HR | R | RBI | SB | BA | $1L | $2L | Pts | RAA |
|---|---|---|---|---|---|---|---|---|---|---|
| '10 | 549 | 22 | 69 | 68 | 3 | .255 | $16 | $7 | 310 | –2 |
| Proj | 450 | 18 | 63 | 59 | 5 | .266 | $12 | -$1 | 290 | +12 |

**-$1 Gordon, Alex**

| | PA | HR | R | RBI | SB | BA | $1L | $2L | Pts | RAA |
|---|---|---|---|---|---|---|---|---|---|---|
| '10 | 282 | 8 | 34 | 20 | 1 | .215 | $1 | -$13 | 110 | –11 |
| Proj | 525 | 16 | 63 | 53 | 11 | .259 | $12 | -$1 | 270 | +5 |

**-$2 Burrell, Pat** ■

| | PA | HR | R | RBI | SB | BA | $1L | $2L | Pts | RAA |
|---|---|---|---|---|---|---|---|---|---|---|
| '10 | 441 | 20 | 50 | 64 | 0 | .252 | $11 | $2 | 240 | +6 |
| Proj | 400 | 16 | 44 | 60 | 0 | .250 | $10 | -$2 | 210 | +1 |

**-$3 Spilborghs, Ryan**

| | PA | HR | R | RBI | SB | BA | $1L | $2L | Pts | RAA |
|---|---|---|---|---|---|---|---|---|---|---|
| '10 | 388 | 10 | 41 | 39 | 4 | .279 | $8 | -$3 | 190 | –2 |
| Proj | 400 | 12 | 52 | 48 | 8 | .284 | $10 | -$3 | 260 | +11 |

**-$3 Bourjos, Peter**

| | PA | HR | R | RBI | SB | BA | $1L | $2L | Pts | RAA |
|---|---|---|---|---|---|---|---|---|---|---|
| '10 | 193 | 6 | 19 | 15 | 10 | .204 | $1 | -$14 | 90 | –12 |
| Proj | 600 | 12 | 76 | 49 | 31 | .242 | $12 | -$3 | 310 | –16 |

**-$4 Fukudome, Kosuke**

| | PA | HR | R | RBI | SB | BA | $1L | $2L | Pts | RAA |
|---|---|---|---|---|---|---|---|---|---|---|
| '10 | 430 | 13 | 45 | 44 | 7 | .263 | $9 | -$2 | 250 | +2 |
| Proj | 450 | 9 | 59 | 45 | 9 | .272 | $9 | -$4 | 270 | +4 |

**-$6 Bernadina, Roger** ○

| | PA | HR | R | RBI | SB | BA | $1L | $2L | Pts | RAA |
|---|---|---|---|---|---|---|---|---|---|---|
| '10 | 462 | 11 | 52 | 47 | 16 | .246 | $10 | $0 | 230 | –17 |
| Proj | 500 | 10 | 55 | 45 | 25 | .236 | $9 | -$6 | 260 | –12 |

**-$6 Jay, Jon**

| | PA | HR | R | RBI | SB | BA | $1L | $2L | Pts | RAA |
|---|---|---|---|---|---|---|---|---|---|---|
| '10 | 323 | 4 | 47 | 27 | 2 | .300 | $7 | -$5 | 170 | –5 |
| Proj | 500 | 10 | 60 | 45 | 10 | .262 | $8 | -$6 | 260 | –14 |

**-$10 Ankiel, Rick** □

| | PA | HR | R | RBI | SB | BA | $1L | $2L | Pts | RAA |
|---|---|---|---|---|---|---|---|---|---|---|
| '10 | 242 | 6 | 31 | 24 | 3 | .232 | $1 | -$12 | 100 | –3 |
| Proj | 300 | 12 | 39 | 42 | 3 | .266 | $6 | -$10 | 170 | +5 |

**-$11 Jones, Andruw**

| | PA | HR | R | RBI | SB | BA | $1L | $2L | Pts | RAA |
|---|---|---|---|---|---|---|---|---|---|---|
| '10 | 328 | 19 | 41 | 48 | 9 | .230 | $11 | -$1 | 210 | +3 |
| Proj | 300 | 15 | 39 | 42 | 3 | .242 | $6 | -$11 | 180 | +2 |

**-$12 Venable, Will** ●

| | PA | HR | R | RBI | SB | BA | $1L | $2L | Pts | RAA |
|---|---|---|---|---|---|---|---|---|---|---|
| '10 | 453 | 13 | 60 | 51 | 29 | .245 | $16 | $6 | 240 | –11 |
| Proj | 340 | 10 | 41 | 37 | 10 | .235 | $4 | -$12 | 170 | –10 |

**-$13 Milledge, Lastings** ●

| | PA | HR | R | RBI | SB | BA | $1L | $2L | Pts | RAA |
|---|---|---|---|---|---|---|---|---|---|---|
| '10 | 415 | 4 | 38 | 34 | 5 | .277 | $6 | -$7 | 190 | –9 |
| Proj | 350 | 7 | 39 | 35 | 11 | .276 | $5 | -$13 | 200 | +1 |

**-$14 Boesch, Brennan**

| | PA | HR | R | RBI | SB | BA | $1L | $2L | Pts | RAA |
|---|---|---|---|---|---|---|---|---|---|---|
| '10 | 517 | 14 | 49 | 67 | 7 | .256 | $13 | $2 | 260 | –13 |
| Proj | 375 | 11 | 34 | 45 | 4 | .226 | $4 | -$14 | 160 | –19 |

**-$14 Morse, Mike**

| | PA | HR | R | RBI | SB | BA | $1L | $2L | Pts | RAA |
|---|---|---|---|---|---|---|---|---|---|---|
| '10 | 294 | 15 | 36 | 41 | 0 | .289 | $9 | -$2 | 170 | +4 |
| Proj | 250 | 10 | 28 | 33 | 0 | .276 | $3 | -$14 | 140 | +2 |

**-$15 Bradley, Milton**

| | PA | HR | R | RBI | SB | BA | $1L | $2L | Pts | RAA |
|---|---|---|---|---|---|---|---|---|---|---|
| '10 | 280 | 8 | 28 | 29 | 8 | .205 | $3 | -$12 | 110 | –13 |
| Proj | 250 | 8 | 30 | 30 | 3 | .256 | $3 | -$15 | 130 | –1 |

**-$17 Diaz, Matt**

| | PA | HR | R | RBI | SB | BA | $1L | $2L | Pts | RAA |
|---|---|---|---|---|---|---|---|---|---|---|
| '10 | 247 | 7 | 27 | 31 | 3 | .250 | $3 | -$10 | 130 | –6 |
| Proj | 200 | 6 | 24 | 26 | 4 | .269 | $2 | -$17 | 110 | –1 |

**-$18 Hairston, Scott**

| | PA | HR | R | RBI | SB | BA | $1L | $2L | Pts | RAA |
|---|---|---|---|---|---|---|---|---|---|---|
| '10 | 337 | 10 | 34 | 36 | 6 | .210 | $2 | -$10 | 140 | –17 |
| Proj | 230 | 9 | 25 | 28 | 2 | .242 | $1 | -$18 | 130 | –0 |

**-$19 Schierholtz, Nate**

| | PA | HR | R | RBI | SB | BA | $1L | $2L | Pts | RAA |
|---|---|---|---|---|---|---|---|---|---|---|
| '10 | 257 | 3 | 34 | 17 | 4 | .242 | $1 | -$13 | 120 | –15 |
| Proj | 200 | 4 | 24 | 20 | 4 | .274 | $1 | -$19 | 110 | –5 |

**-$20 Maier, Mitch**

| | PA | HR | R | RBI | SB | BA | $1L | $2L | Pts | RAA |
|---|---|---|---|---|---|---|---|---|---|---|
| '10 | 423 | 5 | 41 | 39 | 3 | .263 | $6 | -$7 | 200 | –5 |
| Proj | 250 | 3 | 25 | 23 | 3 | .260 | $0 | -$20 | 110 | –6 |

**$5 Kubel, Jason** □ ▲△

| | PA | HR | R | RBI | SB | BA | $1L | $2L | Pts | RAA |
|---|---|---|---|---|---|---|---|---|---|---|
| '10 | 587 | 21 | 68 | 92 | 0 | .249 | $17 | $8 | 320 | –12 |
| Proj | 525 | 21 | 63 | 84 | 0 | .269 | $16 | $5 | 320 | +1 |

**$4 Rivera, Juan** □ △

| | PA | HR | R | RBI | SB | BA | $1L | $2L | Pts | RAA |
|---|---|---|---|---|---|---|---|---|---|---|
| '10 | 459 | 15 | 53 | 52 | 2 | .252 | $10 | -$1 | 250 | –10 |
| Proj | 525 | 18 | 58 | 74 | 0 | .273 | $15 | $4 | 330 | +3 |

**$2 McLouth, Nate** □ △ ●○

| | PA | HR | R | RBI | SB | BA | $1L | $2L | Pts | RAA |
|---|---|---|---|---|---|---|---|---|---|---|
| '10 | 290 | 6 | 30 | 24 | 7 | .190 | -$1 | -$14 | 120 | –14 |
| Proj | 425 | 17 | 64 | 51 | 17 | .266 | $13 | $2 | 310 | +19 |

**$1 Lewis, Fred** ○○

| | PA | HR | R | RBI | SB | BA | $1L | $2L | Pts | RAA |
|---|---|---|---|---|---|---|---|---|---|---|
| '10 | 481 | 8 | 70 | 36 | 17 | .262 | $13 | $2 | 240 | –8 |
| Proj | 500 | 10 | 75 | 40 | 15 | .269 | $14 | $1 | 280 | +4 |

**$0 Raburn, Ryan**

| | PA | HR | R | RBI | SB | BA | $1L | $2L | Pts | RAA |
|---|---|---|---|---|---|---|---|---|---|---|
| '10 | 410 | 15 | 54 | 62 | 2 | .280 | $14 | $4 | 230 | +2 |
| Proj | 400 | 16 | 56 | 56 | 4 | .271 | $13 | $0 | 240 | +5 |

**-$1 Podsednik, Scott** ●●

| | PA | HR | R | RBI | SB | BA | $1L | $2L | Pts | RAA |
|---|---|---|---|---|---|---|---|---|---|---|
| '10 | 596 | 6 | 63 | 51 | 35 | .297 | $22 | $12 | 330 | –9 |
| Proj | 500 | 5 | 55 | 40 | 25 | .283 | $13 | -$1 | 280 | –3 |

**-$1 Sweeney, Ryan**

| | PA | HR | R | RBI | SB | BA | $1L | $2L | Pts | RAA |
|---|---|---|---|---|---|---|---|---|---|---|
| '10 | 333 | 1 | 41 | 36 | 1 | .294 | $6 | -$7 | 180 | –7 |
| Proj | 600 | 6 | 66 | 60 | 6 | .271 | $11 | -$1 | 310 | –13 |

**-$2 Joyce, Matt**

| | PA | HR | R | RBI | SB | BA | $1L | $2L | Pts | RAA |
|---|---|---|---|---|---|---|---|---|---|---|
| '10 | 263 | 10 | 30 | 40 | 2 | .241 | $5 | -$8 | 160 | +2 |
| Proj | 500 | 20 | 55 | 65 | 5 | .244 | $11 | -$2 | 280 | +2 |

**-$3 Snider, Travis**

| | PA | HR | R | RBI | SB | BA | $1L | $2L | Pts | RAA |
|---|---|---|---|---|---|---|---|---|---|---|
| '10 | 321 | 14 | 36 | 32 | 6 | .255 | $8 | -$5 | 160 | –1 |
| Proj | 500 | 20 | 55 | 65 | 5 | .241 | $11 | -$3 | 220 | –5 |

**-$3 Young, Chris** □ △ ●

| | PA | HR | R | RBI | SB | BA | $1L | $2L | Pts | RAA |
|---|---|---|---|---|---|---|---|---|---|---|
| '10 | 664 | 27 | 94 | 91 | 28 | .257 | $28 | $23 | 430 | +16 |
| Proj | 650 | 26 | 91 | 78 | 20 | .266 | $22 | $18 | 410 | +19 |

**-$5 Guillen, Jose** △

| | PA | HR | R | RBI | SB | BA | $1L | $2L | Pts | RAA |
|---|---|---|---|---|---|---|---|---|---|---|
| '10 | 578 | 19 | 55 | 77 | 1 | .258 | $13 | $4 | 270 | –21 |
| Proj | 350 | 11 | 35 | 49 | 0 | .268 | $9 | -$5 | 180 | –9 |

**-$6 Carter, Chris (OAK)**

| | PA | HR | R | RBI | SB | BA | $1L | $2L | Pts | RAA |
|---|---|---|---|---|---|---|---|---|---|---|
| '10 | 78 | 3 | 8 | 7 | 1 | .186 | $0 | -$14 | 30 | –5 |
| Proj | 500 | 25 | 55 | 65 | 5 | .215 | $9 | -$6 | 240 | –4 |

**-$6 Cabrera, Melky**

| | PA | HR | R | RBI | SB | BA | $1L | $2L | Pts | RAA |
|---|---|---|---|---|---|---|---|---|---|---|
| '10 | 520 | 4 | 50 | 42 | 7 | .255 | $6 | -$6 | 240 | –19 |
| Proj | 500 | 10 | 55 | 50 | 10 | .265 | $8 | -$6 | 310 | +2 |

**-$10 Saunders, Michael**

| | PA | HR | R | RBI | SB | BA | $1L | $2L | Pts | RAA |
|---|---|---|---|---|---|---|---|---|---|---|
| '10 | 327 | 10 | 29 | 33 | 6 | .211 | $3 | -$11 | 130 | –12 |
| Proj | 450 | 14 | 50 | 45 | 14 | .225 | $7 | -$10 | 210 | –8 |

**-$11 Taylor, Michael**

| | PA | HR | R | RBI | SB | BA | $1L | $2L | Pts | RAA |
|---|---|---|---|---|---|---|---|---|---|---|
| '10 | --- | --- | --- | --- | --- | ---- | --- | --- | --- | --- |
| Proj | 350 | 14 | 35 | 42 | 11 | .232 | $7 | -$11 | 200 | –7 |

**-$12 Blanco, Gregor**

| | PA | HR | R | RBI | SB | BA | $1L | $2L | Pts | RAA |
|---|---|---|---|---|---|---|---|---|---|---|
| '10 | 270 | 1 | 31 | 14 | 11 | .283 | $4 | -$10 | 130 | +0 |
| Proj | 400 | 4 | 48 | 28 | 12 | .254 | $5 | -$12 | 200 | +3 |

**-$13 Heisey, Chris**

| | PA | HR | R | RBI | SB | BA | $1L | $2L | Pts | RAA |
|---|---|---|---|---|---|---|---|---|---|---|
| '10 | 227 | 8 | 33 | 21 | 1 | .254 | $2 | -$10 | 100 | –5 |
| Proj | 300 | 12 | 39 | 30 | 9 | .240 | $4 | -$13 | 180 | –1 |

**-$14 Cain, Lorenzo**

| | PA | HR | R | RBI | SB | BA | $1L | $2L | Pts | RAA |
|---|---|---|---|---|---|---|---|---|---|---|
| '10 | 158 | 1 | 17 | 13 | 7 | .306 | $2 | -$13 | 80 | +3 |
| Proj | 425 | 9 | 43 | 38 | 17 | .219 | $4 | -$14 | 200 | –11 |

**-$15 Hinske, Eric**

| | PA | HR | R | RBI | SB | BA | $1L | $2L | Pts | RAA |
|---|---|---|---|---|---|---|---|---|---|---|
| '10 | 325 | 11 | 38 | 51 | 0 | .256 | $7 | -$5 | 180 | +0 |
| Proj | 250 | 10 | 33 | 33 | 3 | .253 | $3 | -$15 | 150 | +7 |

**-$16 Jackson, Brett**

| | PA | HR | R | RBI | SB | BA | $1L | $2L | Pts | RAA |
|---|---|---|---|---|---|---|---|---|---|---|
| '10 | --- | --- | --- | --- | --- | ---- | --- | --- | --- | --- |
| Proj | 150 | 6 | 23 | 17 | 5 | .237 | $2 | -$16 | 80 | +0 |

**-$18 Nix, Layne**

| | PA | HR | R | RBI | SB | BA | $1L | $2L | Pts | RAA |
|---|---|---|---|---|---|---|---|---|---|---|
| '10 | 186 | 4 | 16 | 18 | 0 | .291 | $0 | -$13 | 80 | +1 |
| Proj | 200 | 10 | 24 | 24 | 0 | .260 | $1 | -$18 | 110 | +4 |

**-$18 Patterson, Corey** ○

| | PA | HR | R | RBI | SB | BA | $1L | $2L | Pts | RAA |
|---|---|---|---|---|---|---|---|---|---|---|
| '10 | 343 | 8 | 43 | 32 | 21 | .269 | $12 | -$1 | 180 | –6 |
| Proj | 200 | 4 | 22 | 20 | 10 | .255 | $2 | -$18 | 110 | –4 |

**-$19 Gwynn, Tony** ○

| | PA | HR | R | RBI | SB | BA | $1L | $2L | Pts | RAA |
|---|---|---|---|---|---|---|---|---|---|---|
| '10 | 343 | 3 | 30 | 20 | 17 | .204 | $1 | -$13 | 150 | –16 |
| Proj | 300 | 3 | 33 | 18 | 12 | .232 | $1 | -$19 | 140 | –10 |

**-$20 Francoeur, Jeff**

| | PA | HR | R | RBI | SB | BA | $1L | $2L | Pts | RAA |
|---|---|---|---|---|---|---|---|---|---|---|
| '10 | 511 | 13 | 52 | 65 | 8 | .249 | $12 | $1 | 250 | –26 |
| Proj | 175 | 5 | 21 | 23 | 2 | .263 | $0 | -$20 | 100 | –4 |

**-$20 Blanks, Kyle**

| | PA | HR | R | RBI | SB | BA | $1L | $2L | Pts | RAA |
|---|---|---|---|---|---|---|---|---|---|---|
| '10 | 120 | 3 | 14 | 15 | 1 | .157 | -$4 | -$18 | 30 | –8 |
| Proj | 200 | 8 | 22 | 28 | 2 | .222 | $0 | -$20 | 100 | –2 |

**-$20 Crowe, Trevor** ○

| | PA | HR | R | RBI | SB | BA | $1L | $2L | Pts | RAA |
|---|---|---|---|---|---|---|---|---|---|---|
| '10 | 480 | 2 | 48 | 36 | 20 | .251 | $9 | -$4 | 220 | –22 |
| Proj | 225 | 2 | 25 | 18 | 9 | .243 | $0 | -$20 | 110 | –7 |

**-$21 Gibbons, Jay**

| | PA | HR | R | RBI | SB | BA | $1L | $2L | Pts | RAA |
|---|---|---|---|---|---|---|---|---|---|---|
| '10 | 80 | 5 | 11 | 17 | 0 | .280 | $0 | -$15 | 60 | +1 |
| Proj | 150 | 4 | 16 | 22 | 0 | .276 | $0 | -$21 | 90 | –2 |

**-$21 Harris, Willie**

| | PA | HR | R | RBI | SB | BA | $1L | $2L | Pts | RAA |
|---|---|---|---|---|---|---|---|---|---|---|
| '10 | 262 | 10 | 25 | 32 | 5 | .183 | $0 | -$12 | 120 | –11 |
| Proj | 150 | 3 | 20 | 14 | 5 | .254 | $0 | -$21 | 90 | –1 |

**-$22 Wells, Casper**

| | PA | HR | R | RBI | SB | BA | $1L | $2L | Pts | RAA |
|---|---|---|---|---|---|---|---|---|---|---|
| '10 | 99 | 4 | 14 | 17 | 0 | .323 | $1 | -$13 | 70 | +3 |
| Proj | 150 | 8 | 17 | 17 | 3 | .229 | -$1 | -$22 | 80 | –2 |

**-$23 Dickerson, Chris**

| | PA | HR | R | RBI | SB | BA | $1L | $2L | Pts | RAA |
|---|---|---|---|---|---|---|---|---|---|---|
| '10 | 106 | 0 | 11 | 5 | 4 | .206 | -$4 | -$19 | 20 | –8 |
| Proj | 125 | 4 | 15 | 11 | 5 | .244 | -$1 | -$23 | 60 | +1 |

**-$23 Langerhans, Ryan**

| | PA | HR | R | RBI | SB | BA | $1L | $2L | Pts | RAA |
|---|---|---|---|---|---|---|---|---|---|---|
| '10 | 133 | 3 | 16 | 4 | 4 | .196 | -$2 | -$18 | 30 | –3 |
| Proj | 150 | 5 | 17 | 14 | 3 | .239 | -$2 | -$23 | 70 | +1 |

**-$24 Dyson, Jarrod**

| | PA | HR | R | RBI | SB | BA | $1L | $2L | Pts | RAA |
|---|---|---|---|---|---|---|---|---|---|---|
| '10 | 65 | 1 | 11 | 5 | 9 | .211 | -$1 | -$16 | 50 | –1 |
| Proj | 150 | 2 | 17 | 9 | 12 | .207 | -$2 | -$24 | 70 | –6 |

**-$24 Kelly, Don**

| | PA | HR | R | RBI | SB | BA | $1L | $2L | Pts | RAA |
|---|---|---|---|---|---|---|---|---|---|---|
| '10 | 251 | 9 | 30 | 27 | 3 | .244 | $4 | -$9 | 120 | –12 |
| Proj | 125 | 3 | 14 | 11 | 3 | .258 | -$3 | -$24 | 70 | –2 |

**-$25 Carter, Chris (NYN)**

| | PA | HR | R | RBI | SB | BA | $1L | $2L | Pts | RAA |
|---|---|---|---|---|---|---|---|---|---|---|
| '10 | 180 | 4 | 15 | 24 | 1 | .263 | $0 | -$14 | 100 | –4 |
| Proj | 100 | 4 | 10 | 12 | 0 | .263 | -$2 | -$25 | 60 | +1 |

**-$25 Tuiasosopo, Matt**

| | PA | HR | R | RBI | SB | BA | $1L | $2L | Pts | RAA |
|---|---|---|---|---|---|---|---|---|---|---|
| '10 | 138 | 4 | 12 | 11 | 0 | .173 | -$4 | -$19 | 20 | –12 |
| Proj | 150 | 5 | 15 | 15 | 0 | .227 | -$3 | -$25 | 60 | –4 |

**-$25 Johnson, Reed**

| | PA | HR | R | RBI | SB | BA | $1L | $2L | Pts | RAA |
|---|---|---|---|---|---|---|---|---|---|---|
| '10 | 215 | 2 | 24 | 15 | 2 | .262 | $0 | -$14 | 70 | –12 |
| Proj | 100 | 1 | 12 | 10 | 1 | .265 | -$3 | -$25 | 40 | –4 |

**-$25 Paul, Xavier**

| | PA | HR | R | RBI | SB | BA | $1L | $2L | Pts | RAA |
|---|---|---|---|---|---|---|---|---|---|---|
| '10 | 133 | 0 | 16 | 11 | 3 | .231 | -$3 | -$17 | 50 | –8 |
| Proj | 100 | 2 | 11 | 10 | 3 | .241 | -$3 | -$25 | 50 | –2 |

**-$26 Ryal, Rusty**

| | PA | HR | R | RBI | SB | BA | $1L | $2L | Pts | RAA |
|---|---|---|---|---|---|---|---|---|---|---|
| '10 | 222 | 3 | 19 | 11 | 0 | .261 | -$2 | -$16 | 40 | –13 |
| Proj | 100 | 3 | 11 | 10 | 0 | .245 | -$3 | -$26 | 40 | –3 |

**-$26 Nava, Daniel**

| | PA | HR | R | RBI | SB | BA | $1L | $2L | Pts | RAA |
|---|---|---|---|---|---|---|---|---|---|---|
| '10 | 189 | 1 | 23 | 26 | 1 | .242 | $0 | -$14 | 80 | –7 |
| Proj | 100 | 2 | 11 | 12 | 0 | .230 | -$4 | -$26 | 50 | –2 |

**-$27 Evans, Nick**

| | PA | HR | R | RBI | SB | BA | $1L | $2L | Pts | RAA |
|---|---|---|---|---|---|---|---|---|---|---|
| '10 | 37 | 1 | 5 | 5 | 0 | .306 | -$3 | -$19 | 20 | +0 |
| Proj | 75 | 3 | 8 | 8 | 0 | .234 | -$4 | -$27 | 40 | –1 |

**-$27 Mather, Joe**

| | PA | HR | R | RBI | SB | BA | $1L | $2L | Pts | RAA |
|---|---|---|---|---|---|---|---|---|---|---|
| '10 | 64 | 0 | 7 | 3 | 1 | .217 | -$5 | -$20 | 20 | –5 |
| Proj | 50 | 2 | 6 | 6 | 1 | .243 | -$4 | -$27 | 30 | –0 |

**-$20 Denorfia, Chris**

| | PA | HR | R | RBI | SB | BA | $1L | $2L | Pts | RAA |
|---|---|---|---|---|---|---|---|---|---|---|
| '10 | 320 | 9 | 41 | 36 | 8 | .271 | $8 | -$4 | 190 | +1 |
| Proj | 190 | 4 | 23 | 19 | 4 | .249 | $0 | -$20 | 100 | –2 |

**-$21 Wise, DeWayne**

| | PA | HR | R | RBI | SB | BA | $1L | $2L | Pts | RAA |
|---|---|---|---|---|---|---|---|---|---|---|
| '10 | 118 | 3 | 20 | 14 | 4 | .250 | $1 | -$14 | 60 | –3 |
| Proj | 150 | 5 | 21 | 15 | 6 | .254 | $0 | -$21 | 90 | –0 |

**-$21 Martinez, Fernando**

| | PA | HR | R | RBI | SB | BA | $1L | $2L | Pts | RAA |
|---|---|---|---|---|---|---|---|---|---|---|
| '10 | 22 | 0 | 1 | 2 | 0 | .167 | -$5 | -$21 | 0 | –4 |
| Proj | 200 | 6 | 22 | 20 | 2 | .245 | -$1 | -$21 | 90 | –4 |

**-$22 Bonifacio, Emilio** ○

| | PA | HR | R | RBI | SB | BA | $1L | $2L | Pts | RAA |
|---|---|---|---|---|---|---|---|---|---|---|
| '10 | 201 | 0 | 30 | 10 | 12 | .261 | $2 | -$11 | 100 | –4 |
| Proj | 175 | 2 | 25 | 11 | 9 | .251 | $0 | -$22 | 90 | –4 |

**-$22 Young, Delwyn**

| | PA | HR | R | RBI | SB | BA | $1L | $2L | Pts | RAA |
|---|---|---|---|---|---|---|---|---|---|---|
| '10 | 207 | 7 | 22 | 28 | 1 | .236 | $1 | -$12 | 90 | –8 |
| Proj | 150 | 5 | 18 | 18 | 0 | .265 | -$1 | -$22 | 80 | –0 |

**-$23 Gomez, Carlos** ●○

| | PA | HR | R | RBI | SB | BA | $1L | $2L | Pts | RAA |
|---|---|---|---|---|---|---|---|---|---|---|
| '10 | 319 | 5 | 38 | 24 | 18 | .247 | $6 | -$7 | 140 | –11 |
| Proj | 125 | 1 | 16 | 11 | 8 | .244 | -$1 | -$23 | 60 | –4 |

**-$24 Cunningham, Aaron**

| | PA | HR | R | RBI | SB | BA | $1L | $2L | Pts | RAA |
|---|---|---|---|---|---|---|---|---|---|---|
| '10 | 148 | 1 | 17 | 15 | 1 | .288 | -$1 | -$15 | 60 | –6 |
| Proj | 130 | 4 | 14 | 14 | 3 | .237 | -$2 | -$24 | 60 | –3 |

**-$24 Maxwell, Justin**

| | PA | HR | R | RBI | SB | BA | $1L | $2L | Pts | RAA |
|---|---|---|---|---|---|---|---|---|---|---|
| '10 | 133 | 3 | 16 | 12 | 5 | .144 | -$3 | -$18 | 50 | –7 |
| Proj | 100 | 4 | 13 | 10 | 5 | .212 | -$2 | -$24 | 50 | –2 |

**-$24 Bourgeois, Jason**

| | PA | HR | R | RBI | SB | BA | $1L | $2L | Pts | RAA |
|---|---|---|---|---|---|---|---|---|---|---|
| '10 | 136 | 0 | 16 | 3 | 12 | .220 | -$1 | -$16 | 70 | –8 |
| Proj | 100 | 1 | 12 | 8 | 5 | .263 | -$2 | -$24 | 60 | –2 |

**-$25 Hermida, Jeremy**

| | PA | HR | R | RBI | SB | BA | $1L | $2L | Pts | RAA |
|---|---|---|---|---|---|---|---|---|---|---|
| '10 | 239 | 6 | 19 | 29 | 1 | .216 | $0 | -$15 | 90 | –12 |
| Proj | 100 | 3 | 11 | 12 | 1 | .260 | -$3 | -$25 | 50 | –1 |

**-$25 Gerut, Jody**

| | PA | HR | R | RBI | SB | BA | $1L | $2L | Pts | RAA |
|---|---|---|---|---|---|---|---|---|---|---|
| '10 | 74 | 2 | 7 | 8 | 0 | .197 | -$4 | -$19 | 30 | –5 |
| Proj | 75 | 3 | 11 | 9 | 2 | .265 | -$2 | -$25 | 50 | +1 |

**-$25 Thomas, Clete**

| | PA | HR | R | RBI | SB | BA | $1L | $2L | Pts | RAA |
|---|---|---|---|---|---|---|---|---|---|---|
| '10 | --- | -- | --- | --- | -- | ---- | --- | --- | --- | --- |
| Proj | 100 | 2 | 11 | 9 | 4 | .238 | -$3 | -$25 | 50 | –1 |

**-$26 Willits, Reggie**

| | PA | HR | R | RBI | SB | BA | $1L | $2L | Pts | RAA |
|---|---|---|---|---|---|---|---|---|---|---|
| '10 | 182 | 0 | 23 | 8 | 2 | .258 | -$1 | -$16 | 70 | –8 |
| Proj | 100 | 0 | 13 | 7 | 4 | .252 | -$3 | -$26 | 50 | –3 |

**-$26 Roberts, Ryan**

| | PA | HR | R | RBI | SB | BA | $1L | $2L | Pts | RAA |
|---|---|---|---|---|---|---|---|---|---|---|
| '10 | 72 | 2 | 8 | 9 | 0 | .197 | -$4 | -$18 | 30 | –6 |
| Proj | 75 | 2 | 9 | 8 | 2 | .267 | -$3 | -$26 | 50 | +2 |

**-$26 Montanez, Lou**

| | PA | HR | R | RBI | SB | BA | $1L | $2L | Pts | RAA |
|---|---|---|---|---|---|---|---|---|---|---|
| '10 | 58 | 0 | 2 | 3 | 1 | .140 | -$5 | -$22 | 10 | –10 |
| Proj | 75 | 3 | 8 | 8 | 1 | .251 | -$4 | -$26 | 40 | –1 |

**-$27 Stavinoha, Nick**

| | PA | HR | R | RBI | SB | BA | $1L | $2L | Pts | RAA |
|---|---|---|---|---|---|---|---|---|---|---|
| '10 | 126 | 2 | 11 | 9 | 0 | .256 | -$3 | -$18 | 40 | –8 |
| Proj | 75 | 2 | 8 | 8 | 0 | .255 | -$4 | -$27 | 30 | –3 |

**-$27 Nieuwenhuis, Kirk**

| | PA | HR | R | RBI | SB | BA | $1L | $2L | Pts | RAA |
|---|---|---|---|---|---|---|---|---|---|---|
| '10 | --- | -- | --- | --- | -- | ---- | --- | --- | --- | --- |
| Proj | 50 | 2 | 6 | 6 | 2 | .222 | -$4 | -$27 | 30 | +0 |

**-$20 Winn, Randy** ●

| | PA | HR | R | RBI | SB | BA | $1L | $2L | Pts | RAA |
|---|---|---|---|---|---|---|---|---|---|---|
| '10 | 234 | 4 | 23 | 25 | 6 | .239 | $1 | -$12 | 120 | –10 |
| Proj | 175 | 4 | 19 | 18 | 5 | .276 | $0 | -$20 | 100 | –1 |

**-$21 Balentien, Wladimir**

| | PA | HR | R | RBI | SB | BA | $1L | $2L | Pts | RAA |
|---|---|---|---|---|---|---|---|---|---|---|
| '10 | --- | -- | --- | --- | -- | ---- | --- | --- | --- | --- |
| Proj | 150 | 8 | 18 | 18 | 2 | .252 | $0 | -$21 | 90 | +3 |

**-$21 Patterson, Eric**

| | PA | HR | R | RBI | SB | BA | $1L | $2L | Pts | RAA |
|---|---|---|---|---|---|---|---|---|---|---|
| '10 | 204 | 6 | 26 | 16 | 11 | .214 | $3 | -$12 | 90 | –7 |
| Proj | 150 | 3 | 18 | 14 | 8 | .248 | $0 | -$21 | 80 | –4 |

**-$22 Michaels, Jason**

| | PA | HR | R | RBI | SB | BA | $1L | $2L | Pts | RAA |
|---|---|---|---|---|---|---|---|---|---|---|
| '10 | 204 | 8 | 23 | 26 | 0 | .253 | $2 | -$11 | 120 | –2 |
| Proj | 150 | 5 | 18 | 20 | 2 | .258 | -$1 | -$22 | 90 | +0 |

**-$23 Repko, Jason**

| | PA | HR | R | RBI | SB | BA | $1L | $2L | Pts | RAA |
|---|---|---|---|---|---|---|---|---|---|---|
| '10 | 146 | 3 | 19 | 9 | 3 | .228 | -$1 | -$16 | 50 | –8 |
| Proj | 150 | 3 | 17 | 12 | 6 | .243 | -$1 | -$23 | 60 | –6 |

**-$23 Reddick, Josh**

| | PA | HR | R | RBI | SB | BA | $1L | $2L | Pts | RAA |
|---|---|---|---|---|---|---|---|---|---|---|
| '10 | 63 | 1 | 5 | 5 | 1 | .194 | -$4 | -$20 | 20 | –6 |
| Proj | 150 | 6 | 15 | 17 | 2 | .231 | -$2 | -$23 | 70 | –6 |

**-$24 Duncan, Shelley**

| | PA | HR | R | RBI | SB | BA | $1L | $2L | Pts | RAA |
|---|---|---|---|---|---|---|---|---|---|---|
| '10 | 261 | 11 | 29 | 36 | 1 | .231 | $4 | -$9 | 110 | –4 |
| Proj | 100 | 5 | 12 | 14 | 0 | .248 | -$2 | -$24 | 60 | +1 |

**-$24 Church, Ryan**

| | PA | HR | R | RBI | SB | BA | $1L | $2L | Pts | RAA |
|---|---|---|---|---|---|---|---|---|---|---|
| '10 | 239 | 5 | 25 | 25 | 1 | .201 | -$2 | -$15 | 80 | –16 |
| Proj | 100 | 3 | 13 | 12 | 1 | .267 | -$2 | -$24 | 60 | +1 |

**-$25 Kapler, Gabe**

| | PA | HR | R | RBI | SB | BA | $1L | $2L | Pts | RAA |
|---|---|---|---|---|---|---|---|---|---|---|
| '10 | 140 | 2 | 19 | 14 | 1 | .210 | -$2 | -$17 | 60 | –12 |
| Proj | 100 | 3 | 12 | 13 | 1 | .252 | -$3 | -$25 | 60 | –1 |

**-$25 Gillespie, Cole**

| | PA | HR | R | RBI | SB | BA | $1L | $2L | Pts | RAA |
|---|---|---|---|---|---|---|---|---|---|---|
| '10 | 114 | 2 | 11 | 12 | 1 | .231 | -$3 | -$17 | 40 | –6 |
| Proj | 100 | 3 | 12 | 10 | 2 | .244 | -$2 | -$25 | 50 | –0 |

**-$25 Carroll, Brett**

| | PA | HR | R | RBI | SB | BA | $1L | $2L | Pts | RAA |
|---|---|---|---|---|---|---|---|---|---|---|
| '10 | 93 | 2 | 13 | 7 | 2 | .197 | -$3 | -$18 | 20 | –9 |
| Proj | 100 | 3 | 13 | 11 | 1 | .239 | -$3 | -$25 | 50 | –4 |

**-$25 Gross, Gabe**

| | PA | HR | R | RBI | SB | BA | $1L | $2L | Pts | RAA |
|---|---|---|---|---|---|---|---|---|---|---|
| '10 | 246 | 1 | 27 | 25 | 5 | .239 | $1 | -$13 | 110 | –16 |
| Proj | 100 | 2 | 11 | 11 | 2 | .249 | -$3 | -$25 | 50 | –1 |

**-$26 Bogusevic, Brian**

| | PA | HR | R | RBI | SB | BA | $1L | $2L | Pts | RAA |
|---|---|---|---|---|---|---|---|---|---|---|
| '10 | 32 | 0 | 5 | 3 | 1 | .179 | -$5 | -$20 | 10 | –3 |
| Proj | 100 | 2 | 10 | 9 | 3 | .248 | -$3 | -$26 | 40 | –2 |

**-$26 Gentry, Craig**

| | PA | HR | R | RBI | SB | BA | $1L | $2L | Pts | RAA |
|---|---|---|---|---|---|---|---|---|---|---|
| '10 | 35 | 0 | 4 | 3 | 1 | .212 | -$4 | -$20 | 10 | –4 |
| Proj | 100 | 2 | 11 | 7 | 5 | .221 | -$4 | -$26 | 50 | –3 |

**-$26 Inglett, Joe**

| | PA | HR | R | RBI | SB | BA | $1L | $2L | Pts | RAA |
|---|---|---|---|---|---|---|---|---|---|---|
| '10 | 160 | 1 | 15 | 8 | 1 | .254 | -$3 | -$17 | 60 | –5 |
| Proj | 75 | 1 | 8 | 7 | 2 | .278 | -$3 | -$26 | 40 | –2 |

**-$27 Velez, Eugenio** ○

| | PA | HR | R | RBI | SB | BA | $1L | $2L | Pts | RAA |
|---|---|---|---|---|---|---|---|---|---|---|
| '10 | 66 | 2 | 7 | 8 | 0 | .164 | -$4 | -$19 | 30 | –6 |
| Proj | 50 | 1 | 6 | 5 | 3 | .258 | -$4 | -$27 | 30 | –1 |

**-$28 Durango, Luis**

| | PA | HR | R | RBI | SB | BA | $1L | $2L | Pts | RAA |
|---|---|---|---|---|---|---|---|---|---|---|
| '10 | 53 | 0 | 8 | 4 | 5 | .250 | -$3 | -$17 | 30 | –2 |
| Proj | 80 | 1 | 9 | 6 | 4 | .206 | -$4 | -$28 | 40 | –2 |

## Designated Hitters

**$16 Guerrero, Vladimir** ■□ ▲△

| | PA | HR | R | RBI | SB | BA | $1L | $2L | Pts | RAA |
|---|---|---|---|---|---|---|---|---|---|---|
| '10 | 648 | 29 | 83 | 115 | 4 | .300 | $31 | $25 | 470 | +1 |
| Proj | 550 | 28 | 72 | 88 | 6 | .298 | $23 | $16 | 410 | +15 |

**$15 Abreu, Bobby** ▲▲ ●○○

| | PA | HR | R | RBI | SB | BA | $1L | $2L | Pts | RAA |
|---|---|---|---|---|---|---|---|---|---|---|
| '10 | 670 | 20 | 88 | 78 | 24 | .255 | $24 | $16 | 410 | –0 |
| Proj | 600 | 18 | 84 | 84 | 24 | .270 | $22 | $15 | 430 | +14 |

**$12 Ortiz, David** ■□ ▲△△

| | PA | HR | R | RBI | SB | BA | $1L | $2L | Pts | RAA |
|---|---|---|---|---|---|---|---|---|---|---|
| '10 | 620 | 32 | 86 | 102 | 0 | .270 | $26 | $20 | 400 | +15 |
| Proj | 525 | 26 | 74 | 89 | 0 | .272 | $19 | $12 | 370 | +19 |

**$6 Lind, Adam** ■□ ▲

| | PA | HR | R | RBI | SB | BA | $1L | $2L | Pts | RAA |
|---|---|---|---|---|---|---|---|---|---|---|
| '10 | 616 | 23 | 57 | 72 | 0 | .237 | $12 | $1 | 260 | –23 |
| Proj | 600 | 24 | 66 | 84 | 0 | .258 | $16 | $6 | 340 | –1 |

**$6 Scott, Luke** □□

| | PA | HR | R | RBI | SB | BA | $1L | $2L | Pts | RAA |
|---|---|---|---|---|---|---|---|---|---|---|
| '10 | 521 | 27 | 70 | 72 | 2 | .284 | $21 | $13 | 350 | +15 |
| Proj | 500 | 25 | 60 | 70 | 0 | .278 | $16 | $6 | 320 | +17 |

**$3 Matsui, Hideki** □ △△

| | PA | HR | R | RBI | SB | BA | $1L | $2L | Pts | RAA |
|---|---|---|---|---|---|---|---|---|---|---|
| '10 | 564 | 21 | 55 | 84 | 0 | .274 | $17 | $8 | 330 | +2 |
| Proj | 500 | 20 | 55 | 75 | 0 | .273 | $14 | $3 | 300 | –1 |

**$3 Damon, Johnny** ●

| | PA | HR | R | RBI | SB | BA | $1L | $2L | Pts | RAA |
|---|---|---|---|---|---|---|---|---|---|---|
| '10 | 615 | 8 | 81 | 51 | 11 | .271 | $15 | $5 | 350 | –5 |
| Proj | 475 | 10 | 71 | 48 | 14 | .273 | $14 | $3 | 310 | –0 |

**$0 Hafner, Travis**

| | PA | HR | R | RBI | SB | BA | $1L | $2L | Pts | RAA |
|---|---|---|---|---|---|---|---|---|---|---|
| '10 | 472 | 13 | 46 | 50 | 2 | .278 | $11 | $0 | 230 | –3 |
| Proj | 525 | 16 | 58 | 68 | 0 | .263 | $12 | $0 | 280 | –2 |

**-$6 Thames, Marcus** □

| | PA | HR | R | RBI | SB | BA | $1L | $2L | Pts | RAA |
|---|---|---|---|---|---|---|---|---|---|---|
| '10 | 237 | 12 | 22 | 33 | 0 | .288 | $6 | -$7 | 120 | +2 |
| Proj | 350 | 21 | 42 | 53 | 0 | .254 | $9 | -$6 | 180 | –1 |

**-$8 Cust, Jack** ■□

| | PA | HR | R | RBI | SB | BA | $1L | $2L | Pts | RAA |
|---|---|---|---|---|---|---|---|---|---|---|
| '10 | 425 | 13 | 50 | 52 | 2 | .272 | $11 | $0 | 200 | +6 |
| Proj | 400 | 16 | 48 | 52 | 0 | .232 | $7 | -$8 | 170 | –0 |

**-$11 Thome, Jim** ■□ △

| | PA | HR | R | RBI | SB | BA | $1L | $2L | Pts | RAA |
|---|---|---|---|---|---|---|---|---|---|---|
| '10 | 344 | 25 | 48 | 59 | 0 | .283 | $16 | $6 | 260 | +24 |
| Proj | 275 | 14 | 36 | 44 | 0 | .238 | $5 | -$11 | 150 | +2 |

**-$22 Kotsay, Mark**

| | PA | HR | R | RBI | SB | BA | $1L | $2L | Pts | RAA |
|---|---|---|---|---|---|---|---|---|---|---|
| '10 | 362 | 8 | 30 | 31 | 1 | .239 | $2 | -$12 | 180 | –16 |
| Proj | 200 | 4 | 18 | 20 | 2 | .255 | -$2 | -$22 | 110 | –5 |

**-$24 Johnson, Nick**

| | PA | HR | R | RBI | SB | BA | $1L | $2L | Pts | RAA |
|---|---|---|---|---|---|---|---|---|---|---|
| '10 | 98 | 2 | 12 | 8 | 0 | .167 | -$3 | -$19 | 40 | –3 |
| Proj | 100 | 3 | 12 | 12 | 1 | .273 | -$3 | -$24 | 60 | +2 |

**-$24 Miranda, Juan**

| | PA | HR | R | RBI | SB | BA | $1L | $2L | Pts | RAA |
|---|---|---|---|---|---|---|---|---|---|---|
| '10 | 71 | 3 | 7 | 10 | 0 | .219 | -$2 | -$18 | 40 | –2 |
| Proj | 100 | 4 | 10 | 13 | 0 | .249 | -$3 | -$24 | 50 | –0 |

**-$25 Aybar, Willy**

| | PA | HR | R | RBI | SB | BA | $1L | $2L | Pts | RAA |
|---|---|---|---|---|---|---|---|---|---|---|
| '10 | 310 | 6 | 22 | 43 | 0 | .230 | $2 | -$12 | 130 | –16 |
| Proj | 100 | 3 | 9 | 12 | 0 | .253 | -$3 | -$25 | 50 | –1 |

**-$27 Baldelli, Rocco**

| | PA | HR | R | RBI | SB | BA | $1L | $2L | Pts | RAA |
|---|---|---|---|---|---|---|---|---|---|---|
| '10 | 25 | 1 | 3 | 5 | 1 | .208 | -$3 | -$19 | 20 | –2 |
| Proj | 50 | 2 | 6 | 7 | 1 | .241 | -$4 | -$27 | 20 | –1 |

**-$27 Chavez, Eric**

| | PA | HR | R | RBI | SB | BA | $1L | $2L | Pts | RAA |
|---|---|---|---|---|---|---|---|---|---|---|
| '10 | 123 | 1 | 10 | 10 | 0 | .234 | -$3 | -$18 | 30 | –8 |
| Proj | 50 | 2 | 5 | 6 | 1 | .243 | -$5 | -$27 | 20 | –1 |

**-$28 Morales, Jose**

| | PA | HR | R | RBI | SB | BA | $1L | $2L | Pts | RAA |
|---|---|---|---|---|---|---|---|---|---|---|
| '10 | 44 | 0 | 4 | 7 | 0 | .194 | -$1 | -$11 | 10 | –3 |
| Proj | 50 | 1 | 5 | 5 | 0 | .264 | -$5 | -$28 | 20 | –2 |

American League
National League

# Catchers

Top Finishes Among All Hitters From 2008-10

| Top 25 | | Top 50 |
|---|---|---|
| ■ | HR | □ |
| ▲ | RBI | △ |
| ● | SB | ○ |

## Projected 2011 Leaders

| Home Runs | $2L | Runs | $2L | Runs Batted In | $2L | Stolen Bases | $2L | Batting Average | $2L |
|---|---|---|---|---|---|---|---|---|---|
| 24 Posey, B | $24 | 84 Mauer, J | $27 | 88 McCann, B | $22 | 8 Martin, R | $5 | .315 Mauer, J | $27 |
| 24 Santana, C | $11 | 78 Posey, B | $24 | 84 Mauer, J | $27 | 6 Mauer, J | $27 | .296 Martinez, V | $20 |
| 23 Napoli, M | $12 | 66 McCann, B | $22 | 84 Posey, B | $24 | 6 Santana, C | $11 | .288 Posey, B | $24 |
| 22 McCann, B | $22 | 66 Martinez, V | $20 | 83 Martinez, V | $20 | 6 McCann, B | $22 | .287 McCann, B | $22 |
| 20 Soto, G | $16 | 66 Santana, C | $11 | 78 Santana, C | $11 | 6 Molina, Y | $7 | .283 Soto, G | $16 |
| 20 Montero, M | $13 | 65 Montero, M | $13 | 75 Soto, G | $16 | 6 Suzuki, K | $6 | .281 Pena, B | -$4 |
| 19 Olivo, M | $6 | 60 Soto, G | $16 | 66 Suzuki, K | $6 | 5 Thole, J | -$5 | .280 Ruiz, C | $5 |
| 17 Martinez, V | $20 | 59 Napoli, M | $12 | 65 Montero, M | $13 | 5 Doumit, R | $13 | .279 Montero, M | $13 |
| 16 Snyder, C | $2 | 55 Suzuki, K | $6 | 63 Napoli, M | $12 | 5 Napoli, M | $12 | .279 Molina, Y | $7 |
| 16 Arencibia, J | -$2 | 54 Doumit, R | $13 | 61 Molina, Y | $7 | 5 Ruiz, C | $5 | .277 Doumit, R | $13 |
| 15 Wieters, M | $6 | 52 Martin, R | $5 | 60 Wieters, M | $6 | 5 Lucroy, J | -$2 | .273 Molina, B | -$1 |
| 14 Doumit, R | $13 | 52 Baker, J | $2 | 59 Doumit, R | $13 | 4 Mathis, J | -$6 | .272 Martin, R | $5 |
| 14 Lucroy, J | -$2 | 50 Pierzynski, A | $3 | 56 Snyder, C | $2 | 4 Olivo, M | $6 | .270 Hernandez, R | -$3 |
| 13 Posada, J | $4 | 50 Jaso, J | -$1 | 54 Ruiz, C | $5 | 4 Rodriguez, I | -$3 | .270 Hanigan, R | -$6 |
| 13 Shoppach, K | -$3 | 45 Olivo, M | $6 | 53 Olivo, M | $6 | 3 Torrealba, Y | -$4 | .268 Paulino, R | -$8 |

| Player | | PA | HR | R | RBI | SB | BA | $1L | $2L | Pts | RAA |
|---|---|---|---|---|---|---|---|---|---|---|---|
| $27 Mauer, Joe □ △ | '10 | 598 | 9 | 88 | 75 | 1 | .327 | $25 | $24 | 410 | +26 |
| | Proj | 600 | 12 | 84 | 84 | 6 | .315 | $25 | $27 | 420 | +22 |
| $20 Martinez, Victor ▲ | '10 | 543 | 20 | 64 | 79 | 1 | .302 | $24 | $21 | 380 | +21 |
| | Proj | 550 | 17 | 66 | 83 | 0 | .296 | $21 | $20 | 360 | +16 |
| $13 Doumit, Ryan | '10 | 460 | 13 | 42 | 45 | 1 | .251 | $9 | $3 | 210 | –3 |
| | Proj | 450 | 14 | 54 | 59 | 5 | .277 | $15 | $13 | 260 | +8 |
| $7 Molina, Yadier | '10 | 527 | 6 | 34 | 62 | 8 | .262 | $11 | $5 | 260 | –13 |
| | Proj | 550 | 6 | 44 | 61 | 6 | .279 | $12 | $7 | 290 | –5 |
| $6 Wieters, Matt | '10 | 509 | 11 | 37 | 55 | 0 | .249 | $9 | $2 | 210 | –8 |
| | Proj | 500 | 15 | 45 | 60 | 0 | .262 | $12 | $6 | 240 | +3 |
| $4 Posada, Jorge | '10 | 454 | 18 | 49 | 57 | 3 | .248 | $14 | $8 | 240 | +10 |
| | Proj | 325 | 13 | 36 | 46 | 0 | .265 | $11 | $4 | 180 | +10 |
| $2 Baker, John | '10 | 89 | 0 | 7 | 6 | 0 | .218 | -$2 | -$11 | 30 | –5 |
| | Proj | 400 | 8 | 52 | 48 | 0 | .266 | $9 | $2 | 200 | +2 |
| -$1 Molina, Bengie △ | '10 | 420 | 5 | 27 | 36 | 0 | .249 | $5 | -$4 | 180 | –19 |
| | Proj | 325 | 10 | 29 | 46 | 0 | .273 | $8 | -$1 | 190 | –1 |
| -$3 Shoppach, Kelly | '10 | 187 | 5 | 17 | 17 | 0 | .196 | $1 | -$9 | 40 | –8 |
| | Proj | 325 | 13 | 39 | 42 | 0 | .223 | $6 | -$3 | 110 | –6 |
| -$4 Avila, Alex | '10 | 333 | 7 | 28 | 31 | 2 | .228 | $4 | -$4 | 130 | –8 |
| | Proj | 400 | 12 | 36 | 44 | 0 | .233 | $6 | -$4 | 180 | –0 |
| -$5 Thole, Josh | '10 | 228 | 3 | 17 | 17 | 1 | .277 | $3 | -$6 | 110 | +1 |
| | Proj | 475 | 5 | 38 | 43 | 5 | .243 | $5 | -$5 | 210 | –13 |
| -$6 Hundley, Nick | '10 | 307 | 8 | 33 | 43 | 0 | .249 | $7 | $0 | 140 | –5 |
| | Proj | 300 | 9 | 30 | 36 | 0 | .232 | $4 | -$6 | 130 | –5 |
| -$8 Paulino, Ronny | '10 | 348 | 4 | 31 | 37 | 1 | .259 | $5 | -$2 | 160 | –7 |
| | Proj | 225 | 5 | 23 | 25 | 0 | .268 | $3 | -$8 | 110 | +0 |
| -$8 Barajas, Rod | '10 | 345 | 17 | 39 | 47 | 0 | .240 | $9 | $4 | 180 | –8 |
| | Proj | 200 | 8 | 20 | 26 | 0 | .247 | $3 | -$8 | 100 | –2 |
| -$9 Castro, Jason | '10 | 219 | 2 | 26 | 8 | 0 | .205 | -$1 | -$10 | 70 | –11 |
| | Proj | 400 | 8 | 40 | 32 | 0 | .220 | $2 | -$9 | 150 | –14 |
| -$10 Moore, Adam | '10 | 219 | 4 | 12 | 15 | 0 | .195 | -$4 | -$20 | 30 | –19 |
| | Proj | 300 | 9 | 24 | 30 | 0 | .222 | $2 | -$10 | 110 | –13 |
| -$12 Hester, John | '10 | 107 | 2 | 9 | 7 | 1 | .211 | -$1 | -$11 | 30 | –3 |
| | Proj | 150 | 5 | 17 | 17 | 2 | .243 | $1 | -$12 | 70 | –0 |
| -$12 Montero, Jesus | '10 | --- | -- | --- | --- | -- | ---- | --- | --- | --- | --- |
| | Proj | 200 | 10 | 22 | 28 | 0 | .263 | $1 | -$12 | 120 | +2 |
| -$14 Kottaras, George | '10 | 251 | 9 | 24 | 26 | 2 | .203 | $2 | -$5 | 130 | –3 |
| | Proj | 125 | 5 | 14 | 14 | 0 | .231 | $0 | -$14 | 70 | +3 |

| Player | | PA | HR | R | RBI | SB | BA | $1L | $2L | Pts | RAA |
|---|---|---|---|---|---|---|---|---|---|---|---|
| $24 Posey, Buster | '10 | 448 | 18 | 58 | 67 | 0 | .305 | $17 | $9 | 300 | +16 |
| | Proj | 600 | 24 | 78 | 84 | 0 | .288 | $21 | $24 | 380 | +17 |
| $16 Soto, Geovany | '10 | 391 | 17 | 47 | 53 | 0 | .280 | $14 | $10 | 240 | +22 |
| | Proj | 500 | 20 | 60 | 75 | 0 | .283 | $17 | $16 | 310 | +24 |
| $12 Napoli, Mike □ | '10 | 512 | 26 | 60 | 68 | 4 | .238 | $18 | $13 | 250 | +1 |
| | Proj | 450 | 23 | 59 | 63 | 5 | .252 | $16 | $12 | 240 | +10 |
| $6 Suzuki, Kurt △ | '10 | 547 | 13 | 55 | 71 | 3 | .242 | $13 | $8 | 300 | –19 |
| | Proj | 550 | 11 | 55 | 66 | 6 | .256 | $12 | $6 | 300 | –5 |
| $5 Martin, Russell ○ | '10 | 394 | 5 | 45 | 26 | 6 | .248 | $6 | $0 | 180 | –7 |
| | Proj | 400 | 8 | 52 | 44 | 8 | .272 | $11 | $5 | 240 | +5 |
| $3 Pierzynski, A.J. | '10 | 505 | 9 | 43 | 56 | 3 | .270 | $12 | $6 | 260 | –14 |
| | Proj | 500 | 10 | 50 | 50 | 0 | .267 | $10 | $3 | 250 | –11 |
| $0 Iannetta, Chris | '10 | 225 | 9 | 20 | 27 | 1 | .197 | $2 | -$6 | 100 | –4 |
| | Proj | 300 | 12 | 36 | 42 | 0 | .261 | $8 | $0 | 180 | +11 |
| -$2 Lucroy, Jonathan | '10 | 298 | 4 | 24 | 26 | 4 | .253 | $4 | -$4 | 120 | –10 |
| | Proj | 450 | 14 | 41 | 45 | 5 | .233 | $6 | -$2 | 220 | –4 |
| -$3 Rodriguez, Ivan | '10 | 423 | 4 | 32 | 49 | 2 | .266 | $7 | $1 | 170 | –15 |
| | Proj | 350 | 7 | 35 | 35 | 4 | .261 | $6 | -$3 | 160 | –6 |
| -$4 Torrealba, Yorvit | '10 | 365 | 7 | 31 | 37 | 7 | .271 | $9 | $2 | 170 | –2 |
| | Proj | 320 | 6 | 29 | 38 | 3 | .266 | $6 | -$4 | 150 | –1 |
| -$5 Conger, Hank | '10 | 34 | 0 | 2 | 5 | 0 | .172 | -$2 | -$12 | 10 | –2 |
| | Proj | 300 | 9 | 27 | 42 | 3 | .239 | $5 | -$5 | 160 | –2 |
| -$6 Hanigan, Ryan | '10 | 247 | 5 | 25 | 40 | 0 | .300 | $8 | $1 | 160 | +8 |
| | Proj | 300 | 6 | 30 | 30 | 0 | .270 | $4 | -$6 | 160 | +5 |
| -$8 Flores, Jesus | '10 | --- | -- | --- | --- | -- | ---- | --- | --- | --- | --- |
| | Proj | 200 | 6 | 20 | 32 | 0 | .248 | $3 | -$8 | 100 | –1 |
| -$8 Saltalamacchia, Jarrod | '10 | 30 | 0 | 2 | 2 | 0 | .167 | -$2 | -$12 | 10 | –1 |
| | Proj | 250 | 8 | 28 | 28 | 0 | .235 | $3 | -$8 | 100 | –1 |
| -$9 Cervelli, Francisco | '10 | 318 | 0 | 27 | 38 | 1 | .271 | $5 | -$2 | 150 | –7 |
| | Proj | 250 | 3 | 23 | 25 | 0 | .246 | $2 | -$9 | 110 | –6 |
| -$11 Ross, David | '10 | 145 | 2 | 15 | 28 | 0 | .289 | $3 | -$4 | 90 | +6 |
| | Proj | 150 | 5 | 15 | 20 | 0 | .250 | $1 | -$11 | 70 | +2 |
| -$12 Navarro, Dioner | '10 | 142 | 1 | 11 | 7 | 0 | .194 | -$2 | -$12 | 40 | –11 |
| | Proj | 200 | 4 | 18 | 18 | 2 | .250 | $1 | -$12 | 100 | –3 |
| -$13 Schneider, Brian | '10 | 149 | 4 | 17 | 15 | 0 | .240 | $1 | -$7 | 70 | –1 |
| | Proj | 150 | 3 | 14 | 17 | 0 | .258 | $1 | -$13 | 80 | –1 |
| -$14 Towles, J.R. | '10 | 51 | 1 | 3 | 8 | 0 | .191 | -$2 | -$11 | 20 | –4 |
| | Proj | 100 | 3 | 11 | 11 | 2 | .244 | $0 | -$14 | 50 | +0 |

| Player | | PA | HR | R | RBI | SB | BA | $1L | $2L | Pts | RAA |
|---|---|---|---|---|---|---|---|---|---|---|---|
| $22 McCann, Brian △ | '10 | 576 | 21 | 63 | 77 | 5 | .269 | $20 | $17 | 340 | +15 |
| | Proj | 550 | 22 | 66 | 88 | 6 | .287 | $21 | $22 | 390 | +28 |
| $13 Montero, Miguel | '10 | 334 | 9 | 36 | 43 | 0 | .266 | $8 | $2 | 170 | +2 |
| | Proj | 500 | 20 | 65 | 65 | 0 | .279 | $15 | $13 | 300 | +16 |
| $11 Santana, Carlos | '10 | 194 | 6 | 23 | 22 | 3 | .260 | $5 | -$3 | 130 | +10 |
| | Proj | 600 | 24 | 66 | 78 | 6 | .231 | $15 | $11 | 350 | +15 |
| $6 Olivo, Miguel | '10 | 432 | 14 | 55 | 58 | 7 | .269 | $16 | $12 | 210 | +0 |
| | Proj | 375 | 19 | 45 | 53 | 4 | .259 | $11 | $6 | 190 | +5 |
| $5 Ruiz, Carlos | '10 | 446 | 8 | 43 | 53 | 0 | .302 | $13 | $8 | 260 | +14 |
| | Proj | 450 | 9 | 45 | 54 | 5 | .280 | $11 | $5 | 270 | +8 |
| $2 Snyder, Chris | '10 | 386 | 15 | 34 | 48 | 0 | .207 | $5 | $0 | 160 | –7 |
| | Proj | 400 | 16 | 44 | 56 | 0 | .247 | $9 | $2 | 220 | +11 |
| -$1 Jaso, John | '10 | 405 | 5 | 57 | 44 | 4 | .263 | $11 | $5 | 260 | +6 |
| | Proj | 450 | 9 | 50 | 45 | 0 | .246 | $8 | -$1 | 240 | +2 |
| -$2 Arencibia, JP | '10 | 37 | 2 | 3 | 4 | 0 | .143 | -$1 | -$12 | 10 | –3 |
| | Proj | 400 | 16 | 36 | 52 | 0 | .217 | $7 | -$2 | 160 | –15 |
| -$3 Hernandez, Ramon | '10 | 353 | 7 | 30 | 48 | 0 | .297 | $10 | $4 | 190 | +6 |
| | Proj | 300 | 9 | 27 | 39 | 0 | .270 | $6 | -$3 | 170 | +5 |
| -$4 Pena, Brayan | '10 | 174 | 1 | 11 | 19 | 2 | .253 | $2 | -$8 | 70 | –5 |
| | Proj | 300 | 6 | 27 | 33 | 3 | .281 | $6 | -$4 | 160 | +1 |
| -$6 Mathis, Jeff | '10 | 218 | 3 | 19 | 18 | 3 | .195 | $0 | -$9 | 50 | –20 |
| | Proj | 400 | 8 | 40 | 44 | 4 | .221 | $5 | -$6 | 130 | –18 |
| -$7 Ramos, Wilson | '10 | 82 | 1 | 5 | 5 | 0 | .278 | -$1 | -$10 | 30 | –1 |
| | Proj | 300 | 9 | 27 | 36 | 0 | .238 | $4 | -$7 | 120 | –9 |
| -$8 Buck, John | '10 | 438 | 20 | 53 | 66 | 0 | .281 | $18 | $14 | 220 | +6 |
| | Proj | 200 | 8 | 20 | 28 | 0 | .246 | $3 | -$8 | 100 | +1 |
| -$9 Castro, Ramon | '10 | 128 | 8 | 18 | 21 | 1 | .278 | $5 | -$3 | 80 | +3 |
| | Proj | 150 | 8 | 17 | 24 | 0 | .254 | $3 | -$9 | 80 | +2 |
| -$9 Varitek, Jason | '10 | 125 | 7 | 18 | 16 | 0 | .232 | $3 | -$6 | 60 | +0 |
| | Proj | 250 | 8 | 23 | 28 | 0 | .231 | $2 | -$9 | 100 | –1 |
| -$11 May, Lucas | '10 | 39 | 0 | 3 | 6 | 0 | .189 | -$1 | -$12 | 10 | –5 |
| | Proj | 250 | 10 | 23 | 28 | 3 | .202 | $1 | -$11 | 90 | –9 |
| -$12 Laird, Gerald | '10 | 299 | 5 | 22 | 25 | 3 | .207 | $2 | -$8 | 100 | –20 |
| | Proj | 200 | 4 | 20 | 18 | 2 | .239 | $1 | -$12 | 90 | –3 |
| -$13 Quintero, Humberto | '10 | 278 | 4 | 13 | 20 | 0 | .234 | $0 | -$9 | 70 | –17 |
| | Proj | 200 | 4 | 14 | 16 | 0 | .245 | $0 | -$13 | 60 | –8 |
| -$14 Zaun, Gregg | '10 | 117 | 2 | 11 | 14 | 0 | .265 | $1 | -$8 | 60 | –0 |
| | Proj | 125 | 3 | 13 | 14 | 0 | .246 | $0 | -$14 | 60 | +0 |

American League
National League

# Starting Pitcher

Top Finishes Among All Pitchers From 2008-10

| | Top 25 | | Top 50 |
|---|---|---|---|
| | ■ | W | □ |
| | ▲ | Sv | △ |
| | ● | K | ○ |

## Projected 2011 Leaders

| Innings | $2L | Wins | $2L | Strikeouts | $2L | ERA | $2L | WHIP | $2L |
|---|---|---|---|---|---|---|---|---|---|
| 250 Hernandez, F | $28 | 20 Sabathia, C | $21 | 232 Lincecum, T | $22 | 2.96 Halladay, R | $34 | 1.06 Halladay, R | $34 |
| 240 Halladay, R | $34 | 20 Halladay, R | $34 | 225 Sale, C | $13 | 3.00 Hernandez, F | $28 | 1.13 Lee, C | $18 |
| 240 Wainwright, A | $25 | 19 Wainwright, A | $25 | 221 Hernandez, F | $28 | 3.09 Johnson, J | $20 | 1.15 Latos, M | $16 |
| 240 Sabathia, C | $21 | 18 Lester, J | $15 | 215 Morrow, B | -$8 | 3.15 Wainwright, A | $25 | 1.16 Oswalt, R | $14 |
| 220 Lincecum, T | $22 | 17 Hughes, P | $6 | 214 Kershaw, C | $17 | 3.19 Lincecum, T | $22 | 1.17 Hamels, C | $14 |
| 220 Lee, C | $18 | 17 Lincecum, T | $22 | 208 Lester, J | $15 | 3.22 Carpenter, C | $18 | 1.17 Hernandez, F | $28 |
| 220 Kershaw, C | $17 | 17 Jimenez, U | $10 | 204 Gallardo, Y | $5 | 3.29 Kershaw, C | $17 | 1.17 Carpenter, C | $18 |
| 220 Verlander, J | $15 | 16 Hernandez, F | $28 | 203 Verlander, J | $15 | 3.31 Latos, M | $16 | 1.17 Wainwright, A | $25 |
| 220 Lester, J | $15 | 16 Verlander, J | $15 | 198 Sabathia, C | $21 | 3.38 Sale, C | $13 | 1.17 Santana, J | $4 |
| 220 Greinke, Z | $14 | 15 Price, D | $9 | 198 Sanchez, J | $4 | 3.39 Garcia, J | $7 | 1.18 Sabathia, C | $21 |
| 220 Weaver, J | $13 | 15 Kershaw, C | $17 | 196 Wainwright, A | $25 | 3.40 Duchscherer, J | -$2 | 1.19 Johnson, J | $20 |
| 220 Cain, M | $11 | 15 Gallardo, Y | $5 | 195 Kennedy, I | $4 | 3.40 Hudson, T | $12 | 1.21 Strasburg, S | -$2 |
| 220 Jimenez, U | $10 | 15 Carpenter, C | $18 | 193 Scherzer, M | $4 | 3.45 Sabathia, C | $21 | 1.21 Duchscherer, J | -$2 |
| 220 Billingsley, C | $6 | 14 Billingsley, C | $6 | 193 Weaver, J | $13 | 3.51 Santana, J | $4 | 1.21 Verlander, J | $15 |
| 220 Kennedy, I | $4 | 14 Cahill, T | $2 | 192 Greinke, Z | $14 | 3.52 Lee, C | $18 | 1.21 Weaver, J | $13 |

### $34 Halladay, Roy ■■■ ●●●

| | IP | W | Sv | K | ERA | WHIP | $1L | $2L | Pts | RAA |
|---|---|---|---|---|---|---|---|---|---|---|
| '10 | 251 | 21 | 0 | 219 | 2.44 | 1.04 | $36 | $39 | 480 | +50 |
| Proj | 240 | 20 | 0 | 189 | 2.96 | 1.06 | $35 | $34 | 420 | +33 |

### $22 Lincecum, Tim ■■■ ●●●

| | IP | W | Sv | K | ERA | WHIP | $1L | $2L | Pts | RAA |
|---|---|---|---|---|---|---|---|---|---|---|
| '10 | 212 | 16 | 0 | 231 | 3.43 | 1.27 | $17 | $9 | 390 | +21 |
| Proj | 220 | 17 | 0 | 232 | 3.19 | 1.22 | $26 | $22 | 410 | +26 |

### $18 Carpenter, Chris ■■ ○○

| | IP | W | Sv | K | ERA | WHIP | $1L | $2L | Pts | RAA |
|---|---|---|---|---|---|---|---|---|---|---|
| '10 | 235 | 16 | 0 | 179 | 3.22 | 1.18 | $20 | $15 | 350 | +17 |
| Proj | 200 | 15 | 0 | 146 | 3.22 | 1.17 | $22 | $18 | 300 | +18 |

### $16 Latos, Mat ■ ●

| | IP | W | Sv | K | ERA | WHIP | $1L | $2L | Pts | RAA |
|---|---|---|---|---|---|---|---|---|---|---|
| '10 | 185 | 14 | 0 | 189 | 2.92 | 1.08 | $22 | $19 | 350 | +28 |
| Proj | 160 | 11 | 0 | 160 | 3.31 | 1.15 | $18 | $16 | 280 | +16 |

### $14 Hamels, Cole ■□ ●●○

| | IP | W | Sv | K | ERA | WHIP | $1L | $2L | Pts | RAA |
|---|---|---|---|---|---|---|---|---|---|---|
| '10 | 209 | 12 | 0 | 211 | 3.06 | 1.18 | $19 | $15 | 350 | +29 |
| Proj | 200 | 13 | 0 | 175 | 3.67 | 1.17 | $19 | $14 | 310 | +11 |

### $13 Weaver, Jered ■□ ●●○

| | IP | W | Sv | K | ERA | WHIP | $1L | $2L | Pts | RAA |
|---|---|---|---|---|---|---|---|---|---|---|
| '10 | 224 | 13 | 0 | 233 | 3.01 | 1.07 | $27 | $23 | 390 | +28 |
| Proj | 220 | 14 | 0 | 193 | 3.73 | 1.21 | $21 | $13 | 330 | +9 |

### $11 Hudson, Dan

| | IP | W | Sv | K | ERA | WHIP | $1L | $2L | Pts | RAA |
|---|---|---|---|---|---|---|---|---|---|---|
| '10 | 95 | 8 | 0 | 84 | 2.45 | 1.00 | $11 | $9 | 190 | +21 |
| Proj | 180 | 13 | 0 | 171 | 3.55 | 1.25 | $16 | $11 | 290 | +14 |

### $10 Hanson, Tommy □ ○

| | IP | W | Sv | K | ERA | WHIP | $1L | $2L | Pts | RAA |
|---|---|---|---|---|---|---|---|---|---|---|
| '10 | 203 | 10 | 0 | 173 | 3.33 | 1.17 | $15 | $9 | 280 | +14 |
| Proj | 200 | 12 | 0 | 185 | 3.66 | 1.25 | $16 | $10 | 300 | +8 |

### $9 Haren, Dan ■■□ ●●●

| | IP | W | Sv | K | ERA | WHIP | $1L | $2L | Pts | RAA |
|---|---|---|---|---|---|---|---|---|---|---|
| '10 | 235 | 12 | 0 | 216 | 3.91 | 1.27 | $15 | $0 | 320 | +6 |
| Proj | 200 | 12 | 0 | 173 | 3.92 | 1.21 | $17 | $9 | 290 | +5 |

### $7 Marcum, Shaun □ ○

| | IP | W | Sv | K | ERA | WHIP | $1L | $2L | Pts | RAA |
|---|---|---|---|---|---|---|---|---|---|---|
| '10 | 195 | 13 | 0 | 165 | 3.64 | 1.15 | $17 | $8 | 300 | +12 |
| Proj | 200 | 13 | 0 | 164 | 4.02 | 1.22 | $16 | $7 | 280 | +3 |

### $6 Billingsley, Chad ■□□ ●●○

| | IP | W | Sv | K | ERA | WHIP | $1L | $2L | Pts | RAA |
|---|---|---|---|---|---|---|---|---|---|---|
| '10 | 192 | 12 | 0 | 171 | 3.57 | 1.28 | $11 | $2 | 280 | +13 |
| Proj | 220 | 14 | 0 | 189 | 3.84 | 1.31 | $15 | $6 | 320 | +7 |

### $5 Buchholz, Clay ■

| | IP | W | Sv | K | ERA | WHIP | $1L | $2L | Pts | RAA |
|---|---|---|---|---|---|---|---|---|---|---|
| '10 | 174 | 17 | 0 | 120 | 2.33 | 1.20 | $22 | $18 | 310 | +31 |
| Proj | 180 | 14 | 0 | 142 | 3.68 | 1.36 | $13 | $5 | 270 | +6 |

### $4 Braden, Dallas

| | IP | W | Sv | K | ERA | WHIP | $1L | $2L | Pts | RAA |
|---|---|---|---|---|---|---|---|---|---|---|
| '10 | 193 | 11 | 0 | 113 | 3.50 | 1.16 | $15 | $5 | 230 | +12 |
| Proj | 175 | 10 | 0 | 105 | 3.89 | 1.24 | $12 | $4 | 200 | +4 |

### $4 Kennedy, Ian ○

| | IP | W | Sv | K | ERA | WHIP | $1L | $2L | Pts | RAA |
|---|---|---|---|---|---|---|---|---|---|---|
| '10 | 194 | 9 | 0 | 168 | 3.80 | 1.20 | $10 | $2 | 250 | +9 |
| Proj | 220 | 11 | 0 | 195 | 4.01 | 1.30 | $12 | $4 | 290 | +4 |

### $3 Lilly, Ted ■□ ●○○

| | IP | W | Sv | K | ERA | WHIP | $1L | $2L | Pts | RAA |
|---|---|---|---|---|---|---|---|---|---|---|
| '10 | 194 | 10 | 0 | 166 | 3.62 | 1.08 | $15 | $9 | 280 | +13 |
| Proj | 180 | 10 | 0 | 144 | 4.22 | 1.22 | $10 | $3 | 230 | –2 |

### $2 Cahill, Trevor ■

| | IP | W | Sv | K | ERA | WHIP | $1L | $2L | Pts | RAA |
|---|---|---|---|---|---|---|---|---|---|---|
| '10 | 197 | 18 | 0 | 118 | 2.97 | 1.11 | $22 | $17 | 320 | +24 |
| Proj | 200 | 14 | 0 | 119 | 4.04 | 1.30 | $12 | $2 | 240 | +0 |

### $1 Iwakuma, Hisashi

| | IP | W | Sv | K | ERA | WHIP | $1L | $2L | Pts | RAA |
|---|---|---|---|---|---|---|---|---|---|---|
| '10 | --- | -- | -- | --- | ---- | ---- | --- | --- | --- | --- |
| Proj | 180 | 13 | 0 | 107 | 4.04 | 1.30 | $9 | $1 | 220 | +0 |

### $1 Liriano, Francisco ■ ●

| | IP | W | Sv | K | ERA | WHIP | $1L | $2L | Pts | RAA |
|---|---|---|---|---|---|---|---|---|---|---|
| '10 | 192 | 14 | 0 | 201 | 3.62 | 1.26 | $16 | $5 | 330 | +18 |
| Proj | 200 | 13 | 0 | 190 | 4.19 | 1.34 | $12 | $1 | 300 | +1 |

### $0 Vazquez, Javier ■□ ●●

| | IP | W | Sv | K | ERA | WHIP | $1L | $2L | Pts | RAA |
|---|---|---|---|---|---|---|---|---|---|---|
| '10 | 157 | 10 | 0 | 121 | 5.32 | 1.40 | -$1 | -$21 | 180 | –18 |
| Proj | 200 | 14 | 0 | 172 | 4.52 | 1.27 | $12 | $0 | 280 | –8 |

### $28 Hernandez, Felix ■□ ●●●

| | IP | W | Sv | K | ERA | WHIP | $1L | $2L | Pts | RAA |
|---|---|---|---|---|---|---|---|---|---|---|
| '10 | 250 | 13 | 0 | 232 | 2.27 | 1.06 | $36 | $36 | 420 | +43 |
| Proj | 250 | 16 | 0 | 221 | 3.00 | 1.17 | $31 | $28 | 400 | +29 |

### $21 Sabathia, CC ■■■ ●●●

| | IP | W | Sv | K | ERA | WHIP | $1L | $2L | Pts | RAA |
|---|---|---|---|---|---|---|---|---|---|---|
| '10 | 238 | 21 | 0 | 197 | 3.18 | 1.19 | $26 | $18 | 420 | +25 |
| Proj | 240 | 20 | 0 | 198 | 3.45 | 1.18 | $27 | $21 | 400 | +19 |

### $18 Lee, Cliff ■■□ ●●●

| | IP | W | Sv | K | ERA | WHIP | $1L | $2L | Pts | RAA |
|---|---|---|---|---|---|---|---|---|---|---|
| '10 | 212 | 12 | 0 | 185 | 3.18 | 1.00 | $25 | $21 | 340 | +21 |
| Proj | 220 | 14 | 0 | 164 | 3.52 | 1.13 | $23 | $18 | 310 | +14 |

### $15 Verlander, Justin ■■ ●●○

| | IP | W | Sv | K | ERA | WHIP | $1L | $2L | Pts | RAA |
|---|---|---|---|---|---|---|---|---|---|---|
| '10 | 224 | 18 | 0 | 219 | 3.37 | 1.16 | $24 | $16 | 410 | +22 |
| Proj | 220 | 16 | 0 | 203 | 3.64 | 1.21 | $22 | $15 | 360 | +13 |

### $14 Oswalt, Roy ■□ ●○

| | IP | W | Sv | K | ERA | WHIP | $1L | $2L | Pts | RAA |
|---|---|---|---|---|---|---|---|---|---|---|
| '10 | 212 | 13 | 0 | 193 | 2.76 | 1.03 | $26 | $26 | 360 | +34 |
| Proj | 200 | 12 | 0 | 153 | 3.56 | 1.16 | $18 | $14 | 270 | +13 |

### $13 Sale, Chris △

| | IP | W | Sv | K | ERA | WHIP | $1L | $2L | Pts | RAA |
|---|---|---|---|---|---|---|---|---|---|---|
| '10 | 23 | 2 | 4 | 32 | 1.93 | 1.07 | $2 | -$4 | 80 | +7 |
| Proj | 160 | 10 | 87 | 225 | 3.38 | 1.28 | $18 | $13 | 320 | +13 |

### $11 Cain, Matt ■□ ●○○

| | IP | W | Sv | K | ERA | WHIP | $1L | $2L | Pts | RAA |
|---|---|---|---|---|---|---|---|---|---|---|
| '10 | 223 | 13 | 0 | 177 | 3.14 | 1.08 | $22 | $18 | 330 | +26 |
| Proj | 220 | 13 | 0 | 170 | 3.69 | 1.23 | $17 | $11 | 300 | +11 |

### $9 Price, David ■ ●

| | IP | W | Sv | K | ERA | WHIP | $1L | $2L | Pts | RAA |
|---|---|---|---|---|---|---|---|---|---|---|
| '10 | 209 | 19 | 0 | 188 | 2.72 | 1.19 | $26 | $21 | 400 | +32 |
| Proj | 200 | 15 | 0 | 177 | 3.63 | 1.32 | $17 | $9 | 320 | +10 |

### $8 Kuroda, Hiroki ○

| | IP | W | Sv | K | ERA | WHIP | $1L | $2L | Pts | RAA |
|---|---|---|---|---|---|---|---|---|---|---|
| '10 | 196 | 11 | 0 | 159 | 3.39 | 1.16 | $15 | $9 | 280 | +10 |
| Proj | 200 | 12 | 0 | 142 | 3.87 | 1.21 | $14 | $8 | 250 | +2 |

### $7 Garcia, Jaime □

| | IP | W | Sv | K | ERA | WHIP | $1L | $2L | Pts | RAA |
|---|---|---|---|---|---|---|---|---|---|---|
| '10 | 163 | 13 | 0 | 132 | 2.70 | 1.32 | $13 | $8 | 270 | +17 |
| Proj | 180 | 13 | 0 | 153 | 3.39 | 1.37 | $13 | $7 | 270 | +8 |

### $6 Lewis, Colby □ ●

| | IP | W | Sv | K | ERA | WHIP | $1L | $2L | Pts | RAA |
|---|---|---|---|---|---|---|---|---|---|---|
| '10 | 201 | 12 | 0 | 196 | 3.72 | 1.19 | $17 | $6 | 310 | +9 |
| Proj | 180 | 11 | 0 | 171 | 3.99 | 1.25 | $14 | $6 | 270 | +2 |

### $4 Scherzer, Max □ ●●

| | IP | W | Sv | K | ERA | WHIP | $1L | $2L | Pts | RAA |
|---|---|---|---|---|---|---|---|---|---|---|
| '10 | 196 | 12 | 0 | 184 | 3.50 | 1.25 | $16 | $5 | 300 | +13 |
| Proj | 200 | 12 | 0 | 193 | 3.97 | 1.31 | $14 | $4 | 290 | +2 |

### $4 Santana, Johan ■□ ●○

| | IP | W | Sv | K | ERA | WHIP | $1L | $2L | Pts | RAA |
|---|---|---|---|---|---|---|---|---|---|---|
| '10 | 199 | 11 | 0 | 144 | 2.98 | 1.18 | $17 | $12 | 270 | +31 |
| Proj | 80 | 5 | 0 | 64 | 3.51 | 1.17 | $6 | $4 | 120 | +6 |

### $3 Bumgarner, Madison

| | IP | W | Sv | K | ERA | WHIP | $1L | $2L | Pts | RAA |
|---|---|---|---|---|---|---|---|---|---|---|
| '10 | 111 | 7 | 0 | 86 | 3.00 | 1.31 | $5 | -$1 | 160 | +15 |
| Proj | 160 | 10 | 0 | 133 | 3.57 | 1.36 | $10 | $3 | 220 | +10 |

### $2 Myers, Brett ■ ○○

| | IP | W | Sv | K | ERA | WHIP | $1L | $2L | Pts | RAA |
|---|---|---|---|---|---|---|---|---|---|---|
| '10 | 224 | 14 | 0 | 180 | 3.14 | 1.24 | $17 | $11 | 330 | +22 |
| Proj | 220 | 12 | 0 | 175 | 4.05 | 1.30 | $11 | $2 | 270 | –1 |

### $2 Danks, John ■□□ ○○○

| | IP | W | Sv | K | ERA | WHIP | $1L | $2L | Pts | RAA |
|---|---|---|---|---|---|---|---|---|---|---|
| '10 | 213 | 15 | 0 | 162 | 3.72 | 1.22 | $16 | $5 | 310 | +12 |
| Proj | 200 | 13 | 0 | 150 | 4.15 | 1.29 | $13 | $2 | 260 | –0 |

### $1 Happ, J.A. □

| | IP | W | Sv | K | ERA | WHIP | $1L | $2L | Pts | RAA |
|---|---|---|---|---|---|---|---|---|---|---|
| '10 | 87 | 6 | 0 | 70 | 3.40 | 1.37 | $1 | -$6 | 120 | +6 |
| Proj | 160 | 10 | 0 | 126 | 4.00 | 1.32 | $8 | $1 | 210 | +2 |

### $1 Capuano, Chris

| | IP | W | Sv | K | ERA | WHIP | $1L | $2L | Pts | RAA |
|---|---|---|---|---|---|---|---|---|---|---|
| '10 | 66 | 4 | 0 | 54 | 3.95 | 1.30 | -$1 | -$8 | 90 | +4 |
| Proj | 140 | 9 | 0 | 107 | 4.21 | 1.25 | $7 | $1 | 180 | +0 |

### $0 Richard, Clayton ■ ○

| | IP | W | Sv | K | ERA | WHIP | $1L | $2L | Pts | RAA |
|---|---|---|---|---|---|---|---|---|---|---|
| '10 | 202 | 14 | 0 | 153 | 3.75 | 1.41 | $6 | -$6 | 270 | +10 |
| Proj | 180 | 11 | 0 | 134 | 3.95 | 1.36 | $8 | $0 | 230 | +4 |

### $25 Wainwright, Adam ■■ ●●

| | IP | W | Sv | K | ERA | WHIP | $1L | $2L | Pts | RAA |
|---|---|---|---|---|---|---|---|---|---|---|
| '10 | 230 | 20 | 0 | 213 | 2.42 | 1.05 | $34 | $35 | 460 | +46 |
| Proj | 240 | 19 | 0 | 196 | 3.15 | 1.17 | $28 | $25 | 400 | +27 |

### $20 Johnson, Josh ■ ●●

| | IP | W | Sv | K | ERA | WHIP | $1L | $2L | Pts | RAA |
|---|---|---|---|---|---|---|---|---|---|---|
| '10 | 184 | 11 | 0 | 186 | 2.30 | 1.11 | $23 | $23 | 330 | +40 |
| Proj | 200 | 13 | 0 | 179 | 3.09 | 1.19 | $23 | $20 | 330 | +24 |

### $17 Kershaw, Clayton □ ●●

| | IP | W | Sv | K | ERA | WHIP | $1L | $2L | Pts | RAA |
|---|---|---|---|---|---|---|---|---|---|---|
| '10 | 204 | 13 | 0 | 212 | 2.91 | 1.18 | $21 | $17 | 360 | +28 |
| Proj | 220 | 15 | 0 | 214 | 3.30 | 1.26 | $22 | $17 | 370 | +21 |

### $15 Lester, Jon ■■■ ●●○

| | IP | W | Sv | K | ERA | WHIP | $1L | $2L | Pts | RAA |
|---|---|---|---|---|---|---|---|---|---|---|
| '10 | 208 | 19 | 0 | 225 | 3.25 | 1.20 | $23 | $16 | 420 | +22 |
| Proj | 220 | 18 | 0 | 208 | 3.55 | 1.27 | $22 | $15 | 380 | +15 |

### $14 Greinke, Zack ■□ ●●●

| | IP | W | Sv | K | ERA | WHIP | $1L | $2L | Pts | RAA |
|---|---|---|---|---|---|---|---|---|---|---|
| '10 | 220 | 10 | 0 | 181 | 4.17 | 1.25 | $11 | -$4 | 260 | –5 |
| Proj | 220 | 13 | 0 | 192 | 3.60 | 1.21 | $21 | $14 | 320 | +12 |

### $12 Hudson, Tim ■

| | IP | W | Sv | K | ERA | WHIP | $1L | $2L | Pts | RAA |
|---|---|---|---|---|---|---|---|---|---|---|
| '10 | 229 | 17 | 0 | 139 | 2.83 | 1.15 | $23 | $19 | 330 | +39 |
| Proj | 200 | 14 | 0 | 117 | 3.40 | 1.23 | $17 | $12 | 250 | +18 |

### $10 Jimenez, Ubaldo ■■□ ●●●

| | IP | W | Sv | K | ERA | WHIP | $1L | $2L | Pts | RAA |
|---|---|---|---|---|---|---|---|---|---|---|
| '10 | 222 | 19 | 0 | 214 | 2.88 | 1.15 | $26 | $23 | 430 | +36 |
| Proj | 220 | 17 | 0 | 192 | 3.64 | 1.31 | $17 | $10 | 350 | +14 |

### $9 Anderson, Brett □ ○

| | IP | W | Sv | K | ERA | WHIP | $1L | $2L | Pts | RAA |
|---|---|---|---|---|---|---|---|---|---|---|
| '10 | 112 | 7 | 0 | 75 | 2.80 | 1.19 | $9 | $3 | 160 | +14 |
| Proj | 190 | 12 | 0 | 146 | 3.75 | 1.22 | $16 | $9 | 260 | +7 |

### $7 Wilson, C.J. ■ ▲△ ○

| | IP | W | Sv | K | ERA | WHIP | $1L | $2L | Pts | RAA |
|---|---|---|---|---|---|---|---|---|---|---|
| '10 | 204 | 15 | 0 | 170 | 3.35 | 1.25 | $18 | $8 | 320 | +18 |
| Proj | 180 | 13 | 0 | 157 | 3.60 | 1.32 | $15 | $7 | 270 | +10 |

### $6 Hughes, Phil ■ △

| | IP | W | Sv | K | ERA | WHIP | $1L | $2L | Pts | RAA |
|---|---|---|---|---|---|---|---|---|---|---|
| '10 | 176 | 18 | 0 | 146 | 4.19 | 1.25 | $12 | $0 | 310 | +4 |
| Proj | 200 | 17 | 0 | 176 | 4.10 | 1.28 | $16 | $6 | 330 | +4 |

### $5 Gallardo, Yovani ■□ ●●

| | IP | W | Sv | K | ERA | WHIP | $1L | $2L | Pts | RAA |
|---|---|---|---|---|---|---|---|---|---|---|
| '10 | 185 | 14 | 0 | 200 | 3.84 | 1.37 | $9 | -$2 | 320 | +2 |
| Proj | 200 | 15 | 0 | 204 | 3.92 | 1.35 | $13 | $5 | 330 | +3 |

### $4 Sanchez, Jonathan □ ●●○

| | IP | W | Sv | K | ERA | WHIP | $1L | $2L | Pts | RAA |
|---|---|---|---|---|---|---|---|---|---|---|
| '10 | 193 | 13 | 0 | 205 | 3.07 | 1.23 | $17 | $12 | 340 | +21 |
| Proj | 200 | 12 | 0 | 198 | 3.89 | 1.34 | $12 | $4 | 290 | +4 |

### $4 Webb, Brandon ■ ●

| | IP | W | Sv | K | ERA | WHIP | $1L | $2L | Pts | RAA |
|---|---|---|---|---|---|---|---|---|---|---|
| '10 | --- | -- | -- | --- | ---- | ---- | --- | --- | --- | --- |
| Proj | 160 | 11 | 0 | 113 | 3.86 | 1.28 | $10 | $4 | 210 | +5 |

### $3 Rodriguez, Wandy ■ ●○

| | IP | W | Sv | K | ERA | WHIP | $1L | $2L | Pts | RAA |
|---|---|---|---|---|---|---|---|---|---|---|
| '10 | 195 | 11 | 0 | 178 | 3.60 | 1.29 | $10 | $1 | 280 | +1 |
| Proj | 200 | 11 | 0 | 167 | 3.99 | 1.29 | $11 | $3 | 260 | –1 |

### $2 Nolasco, Ricky ■■□ ●●

| | IP | W | Sv | K | ERA | WHIP | $1L | $2L | Pts | RAA |
|---|---|---|---|---|---|---|---|---|---|---|
| '10 | 158 | 14 | 0 | 147 | 4.51 | 1.28 | $5 | -$6 | 260 | –4 |
| Proj | 180 | 13 | 0 | 158 | 4.43 | 1.25 | $10 | $2 | 270 | –6 |

### $2 Garland, Jon ■■□

| | IP | W | Sv | K | ERA | WHIP | $1L | $2L | Pts | RAA |
|---|---|---|---|---|---|---|---|---|---|---|
| '10 | 200 | 14 | 0 | 136 | 3.47 | 1.32 | $10 | $1 | 270 | +13 |
| Proj | 200 | 12 | 0 | 107 | 3.99 | 1.27 | $10 | $2 | 210 | +2 |

### $1 Dempster, Ryan ■■□ ●●●

| | IP | W | Sv | K | ERA | WHIP | $1L | $2L | Pts | RAA |
|---|---|---|---|---|---|---|---|---|---|---|
| '10 | 215 | 15 | 0 | 208 | 3.85 | 1.32 | $11 | $0 | 340 | –4 |
| Proj | 200 | 13 | 0 | 170 | 4.10 | 1.34 | $10 | $1 | 280 | –4 |

### $1 Garza, Matt ■ ●○

| | IP | W | Sv | K | ERA | WHIP | $1L | $2L | Pts | RAA |
|---|---|---|---|---|---|---|---|---|---|---|
| '10 | 205 | 15 | 1 | 150 | 3.91 | 1.25 | $14 | $1 | 290 | +7 |
| Proj | 200 | 14 | 0 | 155 | 4.17 | 1.32 | $12 | $1 | 270 | –1 |

### $0 Pineda, Michael

| | IP | W | Sv | K | ERA | WHIP | $1L | $2L | Pts | RAA |
|---|---|---|---|---|---|---|---|---|---|---|
| '10 | --- | -- | -- | --- | ---- | ---- | --- | --- | --- | --- |
| Proj | 120 | 7 | 8 | 97 | 3.98 | 1.33 | $7 | $0 | 160 | +1 |

**$0 Jurrjens, Jair** ■□ ○○

| | IP | W | Sv | K | ERA | WHIP | $1L | $2L | Pts | RAA |
|---|---|---|---|---|---|---|---|---|---|---|
| '10 | 116 | 7 | 0 | 86 | 4.64 | 1.39 | -$2 | -$14 | 130 | –6 |
| Proj | 200 | 13 | 0 | 141 | 4.08 | 1.34 | $9 | $0 | 250 | +1 |

**-$1 Padilla, Vicente** ■□

| | IP | W | Sv | K | ERA | WHIP | $1L | $2L | Pts | RAA |
|---|---|---|---|---|---|---|---|---|---|---|
| '10 | 95 | 6 | 0 | 84 | 4.07 | 1.08 | $4 | -$3 | 140 | +1 |
| Proj | 120 | 8 | 0 | 86 | 4.33 | 1.25 | $5 | -$1 | 150 | –3 |

**-$1 Pavano, Carl** ■■ ○

| | IP | W | Sv | K | ERA | WHIP | $1L | $2L | Pts | RAA |
|---|---|---|---|---|---|---|---|---|---|---|
| '10 | 221 | 17 | 0 | 117 | 3.75 | 1.19 | $16 | $4 | 280 | +14 |
| Proj | 200 | 13 | 0 | 114 | 4.44 | 1.25 | $10 | -$1 | 220 | –6 |

**-$2 Chacin, Jhoulys**

| | IP | W | Sv | K | ERA | WHIP | $1L | $2L | Pts | RAA |
|---|---|---|---|---|---|---|---|---|---|---|
| '10 | 137 | 9 | 0 | 138 | 3.28 | 1.27 | $9 | $2 | 230 | +4 |
| Proj | 180 | 11 | 0 | 177 | 4.06 | 1.42 | $7 | -$2 | 260 | –6 |

**-$2 Dickey, R.A.**

| | IP | W | Sv | K | ERA | WHIP | $1L | $2L | Pts | RAA |
|---|---|---|---|---|---|---|---|---|---|---|
| '10 | 174 | 11 | 0 | 104 | 2.84 | 1.19 | $14 | $10 | 230 | +24 |
| Proj | 180 | 10 | 0 | 105 | 4.05 | 1.34 | $6 | -$2 | 180 | –0 |

**-$3 Peavy, Jake** ●

| | IP | W | Sv | K | ERA | WHIP | $1L | $2L | Pts | RAA |
|---|---|---|---|---|---|---|---|---|---|---|
| '10 | 107 | 7 | 0 | 93 | 4.63 | 1.23 | $3 | -$8 | 150 | –2 |
| Proj | 40 | 3 | 0 | 34 | 4.40 | 1.28 | $0 | -$3 | 50 | –1 |

**-$3 Zambrano, Carlos** ■ ○

| | IP | W | Sv | K | ERA | WHIP | $1L | $2L | Pts | RAA |
|---|---|---|---|---|---|---|---|---|---|---|
| '10 | 130 | 11 | 0 | 117 | 3.33 | 1.45 | $5 | -$4 | 210 | +9 |
| Proj | 180 | 12 | 0 | 141 | 4.03 | 1.43 | $6 | -$3 | 230 | +1 |

**-$3 Owens, Rudy**

| | IP | W | Sv | K | ERA | WHIP | $1L | $2L | Pts | RAA |
|---|---|---|---|---|---|---|---|---|---|---|
| '10 | -- | -- | -- | -- | -- | -- | -- | -- | -- | -- |
| Proj | 40 | 2 | 1 | 28 | 4.39 | 1.29 | -$1 | -$3 | 50 | –2 |

**-$4 Shields, James** ■□□ ●○○

| | IP | W | Sv | K | ERA | WHIP | $1L | $2L | Pts | RAA |
|---|---|---|---|---|---|---|---|---|---|---|
| '10 | 203 | 13 | 0 | 187 | 5.18 | 1.46 | $0 | -$23 | 250 | –28 |
| Proj | 200 | 13 | 0 | 155 | 4.63 | 1.30 | $9 | -$4 | 250 | –13 |

**-$4 Arroyo, Bronson** ■■■ ○

| | IP | W | Sv | K | ERA | WHIP | $1L | $2L | Pts | RAA |
|---|---|---|---|---|---|---|---|---|---|---|
| '10 | 216 | 17 | 0 | 121 | 3.88 | 1.15 | $14 | $6 | 290 | +11 |
| Proj | 200 | 12 | 0 | 117 | 4.56 | 1.27 | $6 | -$4 | 210 | –9 |

**-$4 Cramer, Bobby**

| | IP | W | Sv | K | ERA | WHIP | $1L | $2L | Pts | RAA |
|---|---|---|---|---|---|---|---|---|---|---|
| '10 | 24 | 2 | 0 | 13 | 3.04 | 1.10 | -$1 | -$7 | 40 | +4 |
| Proj | 40 | 3 | 0 | 35 | 4.33 | 1.48 | -$1 | -$4 | 50 | –1 |

**-$5 Penny, Brad** □

| | IP | W | Sv | K | ERA | WHIP | $1L | $2L | Pts | RAA |
|---|---|---|---|---|---|---|---|---|---|---|
| '10 | 56 | 3 | 0 | 35 | 3.23 | 1.29 | -$1 | -$7 | 60 | +2 |
| Proj | 100 | 6 | 0 | 58 | 4.36 | 1.35 | $1 | -$5 | 100 | –4 |

**-$5 Misch, Pat**

| | IP | W | Sv | K | ERA | WHIP | $1L | $2L | Pts | RAA |
|---|---|---|---|---|---|---|---|---|---|---|
| '10 | 38 | 0 | 0 | 23 | 3.82 | 1.25 | -$4 | -$10 | 20 | –1 |
| Proj | 40 | 2 | 0 | 25 | 4.72 | 1.33 | -$2 | -$5 | 30 | –3 |

**-$5 Moyer, Jamie** ■□

| | IP | W | Sv | K | ERA | WHIP | $1L | $2L | Pts | RAA |
|---|---|---|---|---|---|---|---|---|---|---|
| '10 | 112 | 9 | 0 | 63 | 4.84 | 1.10 | $2 | -$7 | 140 | –9 |
| Proj | 100 | 6 | 0 | 53 | 4.89 | 1.25 | $1 | -$5 | 100 | –9 |

**-$5 Floyd, Gavin** ■□ ○○○

| | IP | W | Sv | K | ERA | WHIP | $1L | $2L | Pts | RAA |
|---|---|---|---|---|---|---|---|---|---|---|
| '10 | 187 | 10 | 0 | 151 | 4.08 | 1.37 | $7 | -$9 | 220 | +0 |
| Proj | 200 | 11 | 0 | 150 | 4.47 | 1.35 | $8 | -$5 | 230 | –9 |

**-$5 Wood, Travis**

| | IP | W | Sv | K | ERA | WHIP | $1L | $2L | Pts | RAA |
|---|---|---|---|---|---|---|---|---|---|---|
| '10 | 103 | 5 | 0 | 86 | 3.51 | 1.08 | $6 | $0 | 140 | +6 |
| Proj | 120 | 6 | 0 | 108 | 4.43 | 1.40 | $2 | -$5 | 140 | –6 |

**-$6 Garcia, Freddy** □

| | IP | W | Sv | K | ERA | WHIP | $1L | $2L | Pts | RAA |
|---|---|---|---|---|---|---|---|---|---|---|
| '10 | 157 | 12 | 0 | 89 | 4.64 | 1.38 | $3 | -$14 | 180 | –8 |
| Proj | 80 | 5 | 0 | 47 | 4.74 | 1.35 | $1 | -$6 | 80 | –5 |

**-$6 Vargas, Jason**

| | IP | W | Sv | K | ERA | WHIP | $1L | $2L | Pts | RAA |
|---|---|---|---|---|---|---|---|---|---|---|
| '10 | 193 | 9 | 0 | 116 | 3.78 | 1.25 | $10 | -$3 | 200 | +9 |
| Proj | 200 | 9 | 0 | 126 | 4.46 | 1.32 | $7 | -$6 | 190 | –8 |

**-$6 Buehrle, Mark** ■□□ ○

| | IP | W | Sv | K | ERA | WHIP | $1L | $2L | Pts | RAA |
|---|---|---|---|---|---|---|---|---|---|---|
| '10 | 210 | 13 | 0 | 99 | 4.28 | 1.40 | $4 | -$15 | 190 | –1 |
| Proj | 200 | 12 | 0 | 95 | 4.47 | 1.32 | $7 | -$6 | 180 | –8 |

**-$6 Maine, John**

| | IP | W | Sv | K | ERA | WHIP | $1L | $2L | Pts | RAA |
|---|---|---|---|---|---|---|---|---|---|---|
| '10 | 40 | 1 | 0 | 39 | 6.13 | 1.82 | -$9 | -$19 | 30 | –9 |
| Proj | 40 | 2 | 0 | 32 | 4.96 | 1.48 | -$3 | -$6 | 40 | –4 |

**-$6 Castro, Simon**

| | IP | W | Sv | K | ERA | WHIP | $1L | $2L | Pts | RAA |
|---|---|---|---|---|---|---|---|---|---|---|
| '10 | -- | -- | -- | -- | -- | -- | -- | -- | -- | -- |
| Proj | 40 | 2 | 4 | 27 | 4.77 | 1.49 | -$3 | -$6 | 30 | –4 |

**-$7 Blanton, Joe** □ ○

| | IP | W | Sv | K | ERA | WHIP | $1L | $2L | Pts | RAA |
|---|---|---|---|---|---|---|---|---|---|---|
| '10 | 176 | 9 | 0 | 134 | 4.82 | 1.42 | -$3 | -$19 | 180 | –17 |
| Proj | 180 | 10 | 0 | 118 | 4.66 | 1.32 | $4 | -$7 | 190 | –13 |

**-$7 Litsch, Jesse** □

| | IP | W | Sv | K | ERA | WHIP | $1L | $2L | Pts | RAA |
|---|---|---|---|---|---|---|---|---|---|---|
| '10 | 47 | 1 | 0 | 16 | 5.79 | 1.46 | -$5 | -$17 | 10 | –7 |
| Proj | 80 | 4 | 0 | 42 | 4.93 | 1.33 | $0 | -$7 | 60 | –7 |

**-$7 Coleman, Casey**

| | IP | W | Sv | K | ERA | WHIP | $1L | $2L | Pts | RAA |
|---|---|---|---|---|---|---|---|---|---|---|
| '10 | 57 | 4 | 0 | 27 | 4.11 | 1.42 | -$3 | -$11 | 60 | +1 |
| Proj | 40 | 2 | 0 | 26 | 4.94 | 1.59 | -$3 | -$7 | 30 | –4 |

**$0 Baker, Scott** ■□ ○○○

| | IP | W | Sv | K | ERA | WHIP | $1L | $2L | Pts | RAA |
|---|---|---|---|---|---|---|---|---|---|---|
| '10 | 170 | 12 | 0 | 148 | 4.49 | 1.34 | $6 | -$10 | 240 | –3 |
| Proj | 200 | 13 | 0 | 155 | 4.41 | 1.28 | $11 | $0 | 260 | –5 |

**-$1 Gee, Dillon**

| | IP | W | Sv | K | ERA | WHIP | $1L | $2L | Pts | RAA |
|---|---|---|---|---|---|---|---|---|---|---|
| '10 | 33 | 2 | 0 | 17 | 2.18 | 1.21 | -$1 | -$6 | 40 | +6 |
| Proj | 80 | 5 | 0 | 66 | 3.73 | 1.35 | $3 | -$1 | 110 | +3 |

**-$1 James, Chuck**

| | IP | W | Sv | K | ERA | WHIP | $1L | $2L | Pts | RAA |
|---|---|---|---|---|---|---|---|---|---|---|
| '10 | -- | -- | -- | -- | -- | -- | -- | -- | -- | -- |
| Proj | 40 | 4 | 6 | 33 | 4.05 | 1.27 | $1 | -$1 | 70 | –0 |

**-$2 Strasburg, Stephen**

| | IP | W | Sv | K | ERA | WHIP | $1L | $2L | Pts | RAA |
|---|---|---|---|---|---|---|---|---|---|---|
| '10 | 68 | 5 | 0 | 92 | 2.91 | 1.07 | $5 | $2 | 150 | +9 |
| Proj | 20 | 1 | 0 | 23 | 3.71 | 1.21 | $0 | -$2 | 40 | +1 |

**-$2 Bedard, Erik**

| | IP | W | Sv | K | ERA | WHIP | $1L | $2L | Pts | RAA |
|---|---|---|---|---|---|---|---|---|---|---|
| '10 | -- | -- | -- | -- | -- | -- | -- | -- | -- | -- |
| Proj | 20 | 1 | 0 | 19 | 3.68 | 1.27 | $0 | -$2 | 30 | +1 |

**-$3 Lackey, John** ■□□ ○○

| | IP | W | Sv | K | ERA | WHIP | $1L | $2L | Pts | RAA |
|---|---|---|---|---|---|---|---|---|---|---|
| '10 | 215 | 14 | 0 | 156 | 4.40 | 1.42 | $6 | -$14 | 250 | –8 |
| Proj | 200 | 13 | 0 | 143 | 4.32 | 1.35 | $9 | -$3 | 240 | –5 |

**-$3 Young, Chris**

| | IP | W | Sv | K | ERA | WHIP | $1L | $2L | Pts | RAA |
|---|---|---|---|---|---|---|---|---|---|---|
| '10 | 20 | 2 | 0 | 15 | 0.90 | 1.05 | -$1 | -$5 | 40 | +8 |
| Proj | 80 | 4 | 0 | 60 | 4.26 | 1.34 | $1 | -$3 | 90 | –1 |

**-$4 Zimmermann, Jordan**

| | IP | W | Sv | K | ERA | WHIP | $1L | $2L | Pts | RAA |
|---|---|---|---|---|---|---|---|---|---|---|
| '10 | 31 | 1 | 0 | 27 | 4.94 | 1.32 | -$5 | -$12 | 30 | –5 |
| Proj | 160 | 8 | 0 | 156 | 4.45 | 1.35 | $5 | -$4 | 210 | –8 |

**-$4 Gonzalez, Gio** ■ ○

| | IP | W | Sv | K | ERA | WHIP | $1L | $2L | Pts | RAA |
|---|---|---|---|---|---|---|---|---|---|---|
| '10 | 201 | 15 | 0 | 171 | 3.23 | 1.31 | $17 | $6 | 320 | +24 |
| Proj | 190 | 12 | 0 | 181 | 4.20 | 1.44 | $9 | -$4 | 260 | –1 |

**-$4 LeBlanc, Wade**

| | IP | W | Sv | K | ERA | WHIP | $1L | $2L | Pts | RAA |
|---|---|---|---|---|---|---|---|---|---|---|
| '10 | 146 | 8 | 0 | 110 | 4.25 | 1.42 | -$1 | -$13 | 160 | +3 |
| Proj | 180 | 10 | 0 | 148 | 4.36 | 1.36 | $5 | -$4 | 210 | –2 |

**-$5 Cohoon, Mark**

| | IP | W | Sv | K | ERA | WHIP | $1L | $2L | Pts | RAA |
|---|---|---|---|---|---|---|---|---|---|---|
| '10 | -- | -- | -- | -- | -- | -- | -- | -- | -- | -- |
| Proj | 40 | 2 | 3 | 24 | 4.35 | 1.41 | -$2 | -$5 | 40 | –2 |

**-$5 Beltre, Omar**

| | IP | W | Sv | K | ERA | WHIP | $1L | $2L | Pts | RAA |
|---|---|---|---|---|---|---|---|---|---|---|
| '10 | 7 | 0 | 0 | 9 | 9.00 | 2.29 | -$5 | -$14 | 0 | –4 |
| Proj | 40 | 4 | 2 | 29 | 4.15 | 1.58 | -$1 | -$5 | 60 | –1 |

**-$5 Sanchez, Anibal** □ ○

| | IP | W | Sv | K | ERA | WHIP | $1L | $2L | Pts | RAA |
|---|---|---|---|---|---|---|---|---|---|---|
| '10 | 195 | 13 | 0 | 157 | 3.55 | 1.34 | $9 | -$1 | 270 | +7 |
| Proj | 140 | 8 | 0 | 110 | 4.15 | 1.44 | $3 | -$5 | 170 | –3 |

**-$5 Wells, Randy** □

| | IP | W | Sv | K | ERA | WHIP | $1L | $2L | Pts | RAA |
|---|---|---|---|---|---|---|---|---|---|---|
| '10 | 194 | 8 | 0 | 144 | 4.26 | 1.40 | $0 | -$14 | 190 | –1 |
| Proj | 180 | 9 | 0 | 127 | 4.30 | 1.37 | $4 | -$5 | 190 | –3 |

**-$5 Mock, Garrett**

| | IP | W | Sv | K | ERA | WHIP | $1L | $2L | Pts | RAA |
|---|---|---|---|---|---|---|---|---|---|---|
| '10 | 3 | 0 | 0 | 3 | 5.40 | 2.70 | -$6 | -$12 | 0 | –0 |
| Proj | 40 | 2 | 0 | 33 | 4.64 | 1.45 | -$2 | -$5 | 40 | –3 |

**-$6 Rogers, Mark**

| | IP | W | Sv | K | ERA | WHIP | $1L | $2L | Pts | RAA |
|---|---|---|---|---|---|---|---|---|---|---|
| '10 | 10 | 0 | 0 | 11 | 1.80 | 0.50 | -$3 | -$7 | 20 | +3 |
| Proj | 40 | 2 | 0 | 46 | 4.53 | 1.56 | -$2 | -$6 | 50 | –2 |

**-$6 Harang, Aaron** ○○

| | IP | W | Sv | K | ERA | WHIP | $1L | $2L | Pts | RAA |
|---|---|---|---|---|---|---|---|---|---|---|
| '10 | 112 | 6 | 0 | 82 | 5.32 | 1.59 | -$8 | -$23 | 100 | –16 |
| Proj | 100 | 5 | 0 | 74 | 4.76 | 1.33 | $0 | -$6 | 110 | –8 |

**-$6 Romero, Ricky** ■□ ○○

| | IP | W | Sv | K | ERA | WHIP | $1L | $2L | Pts | RAA |
|---|---|---|---|---|---|---|---|---|---|---|
| '10 | 210 | 14 | 0 | 174 | 3.73 | 1.29 | $14 | $1 | 300 | +6 |
| Proj | 200 | 12 | 0 | 157 | 4.32 | 1.42 | $8 | -$6 | 240 | –7 |

**-$6 Hunter, Tommy** □

| | IP | W | Sv | K | ERA | WHIP | $1L | $2L | Pts | RAA |
|---|---|---|---|---|---|---|---|---|---|---|
| '10 | 128 | 13 | 0 | 68 | 3.73 | 1.24 | $8 | -$1 | 190 | +8 |
| Proj | 140 | 10 | 0 | 83 | 4.55 | 1.38 | $4 | -$6 | 160 | –6 |

**-$6 de la Rosa, Jorge** ■ ●

| | IP | W | Sv | K | ERA | WHIP | $1L | $2L | Pts | RAA |
|---|---|---|---|---|---|---|---|---|---|---|
| '10 | 122 | 8 | 0 | 113 | 4.22 | 1.32 | $2 | -$7 | 180 | –2 |
| Proj | 160 | 10 | 0 | 140 | 4.59 | 1.39 | $3 | -$6 | 200 | –10 |

**-$6 Cecil, Brett** ■

| | IP | W | Sv | K | ERA | WHIP | $1L | $2L | Pts | RAA |
|---|---|---|---|---|---|---|---|---|---|---|
| '10 | 173 | 15 | 0 | 117 | 4.22 | 1.33 | $8 | -$7 | 240 | –2 |
| Proj | 160 | 11 | 0 | 116 | 4.58 | 1.39 | $5 | -$6 | 200 | –9 |

**-$7 Bonderman, Jeremy**

| | IP | W | Sv | K | ERA | WHIP | $1L | $2L | Pts | RAA |
|---|---|---|---|---|---|---|---|---|---|---|
| '10 | 171 | 8 | 0 | 112 | 5.53 | 1.44 | -$5 | -$28 | 130 | –29 |
| Proj | 40 | 2 | 0 | 27 | 5.31 | 1.43 | -$2 | -$7 | 30 | –6 |

**-$7 Haeger, Charlie**

| | IP | W | Sv | K | ERA | WHIP | $1L | $2L | Pts | RAA |
|---|---|---|---|---|---|---|---|---|---|---|
| '10 | 30 | 0 | 0 | 30 | 8.40 | 2.07 | -$12 | -$23 | 0 | –17 |
| Proj | 40 | 2 | 0 | 33 | 5.16 | 1.53 | -$3 | -$7 | 40 | –5 |

**-$8 Kendrick, Kyle**

| | IP | W | Sv | K | ERA | WHIP | $1L | $2L | Pts | RAA |
|---|---|---|---|---|---|---|---|---|---|---|
| '10 | 181 | 11 | 0 | 84 | 4.73 | 1.37 | -$2 | -$18 | 160 | –14 |
| Proj | 80 | 5 | 0 | 38 | 4.85 | 1.39 | -$2 | -$8 | 70 | –7 |

**-$1 Santana, Ervin** ■■ ●○

| | IP | W | Sv | K | ERA | WHIP | $1L | $2L | Pts | RAA |
|---|---|---|---|---|---|---|---|---|---|---|
| '10 | 223 | 17 | 0 | 169 | 3.92 | 1.32 | $13 | -$2 | 320 | +6 |
| Proj | 200 | 14 | 0 | 154 | 4.34 | 1.31 | $11 | -$1 | 260 | –6 |

**-$1 Slowey, Kevin** □□

| | IP | W | Sv | K | ERA | WHIP | $1L | $2L | Pts | RAA |
|---|---|---|---|---|---|---|---|---|---|---|
| '10 | 156 | 13 | 0 | 116 | 4.45 | 1.29 | $7 | -$7 | 220 | –3 |
| Proj | 140 | 10 | 0 | 104 | 4.51 | 1.25 | $8 | -$1 | 190 | –6 |

**-$1 Hellickson, Jeremy**

| | IP | W | Sv | K | ERA | WHIP | $1L | $2L | Pts | RAA |
|---|---|---|---|---|---|---|---|---|---|---|
| '10 | 36 | 4 | 0 | 33 | 3.47 | 1.10 | $1 | -$5 | 80 | +4 |
| Proj | 120 | 9 | 0 | 129 | 4.39 | 1.35 | $6 | -$1 | 200 | –3 |

**-$2 Duchscherer, Justin**

| | IP | W | Sv | K | ERA | WHIP | $1L | $2L | Pts | RAA |
|---|---|---|---|---|---|---|---|---|---|---|
| '10 | 28 | 2 | 0 | 18 | 2.89 | 1.36 | -$1 | -$8 | 40 | +3 |
| Proj | 20 | 1 | 0 | 13 | 3.40 | 1.21 | $0 | -$2 | 30 | +1 |

**-$3 Beckett, Josh** ■□ ●●

| | IP | W | Sv | K | ERA | WHIP | $1L | $2L | Pts | RAA |
|---|---|---|---|---|---|---|---|---|---|---|
| '10 | 128 | 6 | 0 | 116 | 5.78 | 1.54 | -$6 | -$26 | 120 | –26 |
| Proj | 180 | 11 | 0 | 157 | 4.55 | 1.31 | $9 | -$3 | 240 | –10 |

**-$3 Cueto, Johnny** □□ ○

| | IP | W | Sv | K | ERA | WHIP | $1L | $2L | Pts | RAA |
|---|---|---|---|---|---|---|---|---|---|---|
| '10 | 186 | 12 | 0 | 138 | 3.64 | 1.28 | $9 | $0 | 250 | +13 |
| Proj | 180 | 10 | 0 | 138 | 4.36 | 1.33 | $6 | -$3 | 210 | –5 |

**-$3 Lowe, Derek** ■■■ ○

| | IP | W | Sv | K | ERA | WHIP | $1L | $2L | Pts | RAA |
|---|---|---|---|---|---|---|---|---|---|---|
| '10 | 194 | 16 | 0 | 136 | 4.00 | 1.37 | $6 | -$6 | 270 | +8 |
| Proj | 200 | 13 | 0 | 120 | 4.29 | 1.34 | $7 | -$3 | 230 | –3 |

**-$4 Pettitte, Andy** ■■ ○○

| | IP | W | Sv | K | ERA | WHIP | $1L | $2L | Pts | RAA |
|---|---|---|---|---|---|---|---|---|---|---|
| '10 | 129 | 11 | 0 | 101 | 3.28 | 1.27 | $10 | $1 | 210 | +12 |
| Proj | 140 | 10 | 0 | 97 | 4.31 | 1.37 | $6 | -$4 | 170 | –4 |

**-$4 Niemann, Jeff** □□

| | IP | W | Sv | K | ERA | WHIP | $1L | $2L | Pts | RAA |
|---|---|---|---|---|---|---|---|---|---|---|
| '10 | 174 | 12 | 0 | 131 | 4.39 | 1.26 | $8 | -$7 | 230 | +0 |
| Proj | 150 | 9 | 0 | 109 | 4.44 | 1.34 | $6 | -$4 | 180 | –4 |

**-$4 Pelfrey, Mike** ■□

| | IP | W | Sv | K | ERA | WHIP | $1L | $2L | Pts | RAA |
|---|---|---|---|---|---|---|---|---|---|---|
| '10 | 204 | 15 | 1 | 113 | 3.66 | 1.38 | $7 | -$4 | 250 | +13 |
| Proj | 200 | 13 | 0 | 108 | 4.21 | 1.37 | $6 | -$4 | 210 | –2 |

**-$5 Pineiro, Joel** ■

| | IP | W | Sv | K | ERA | WHIP | $1L | $2L | Pts | RAA |
|---|---|---|---|---|---|---|---|---|---|---|
| '10 | 152 | 10 | 0 | 92 | 3.84 | 1.24 | $8 | -$3 | 180 | +9 |
| Proj | 160 | 10 | 0 | 80 | 4.55 | 1.28 | $6 | -$5 | 160 | –7 |

**-$5 Martin, J.D.**

| | IP | W | Sv | K | ERA | WHIP | $1L | $2L | Pts | RAA |
|---|---|---|---|---|---|---|---|---|---|---|
| '10 | 48 | 1 | 0 | 31 | 4.13 | 1.40 | -$4 | -$12 | 30 | –6 |
| Proj | 40 | 2 | 0 | 27 | 4.58 | 1.37 | -$2 | -$5 | 40 | –4 |

**-$5 Niese, Jonathon** ○

| | IP | W | Sv | K | ERA | WHIP | $1L | $2L | Pts | RAA |
|---|---|---|---|---|---|---|---|---|---|---|
| '10 | 174 | 9 | 0 | 148 | 4.20 | 1.46 | $0 | -$14 | 200 | –11 |
| Proj | 180 | 10 | 0 | 159 | 4.24 | 1.42 | $5 | -$5 | 230 | –8 |

**-$5 Luebke, Cory**

| | IP | W | Sv | K | ERA | WHIP | $1L | $2L | Pts | RAA |
|---|---|---|---|---|---|---|---|---|---|---|
| '10 | 18 | 1 | 0 | 18 | 4.08 | 1.30 | -$4 | -$10 | 30 | +1 |
| Proj | 80 | 4 | 0 | 82 | 4.41 | 1.46 | $0 | -$5 | 110 | –2 |

**-$5 Correia, Kevin** □ ○

| | IP | W | Sv | K | ERA | WHIP | $1L | $2L | Pts | RAA |
|---|---|---|---|---|---|---|---|---|---|---|
| '10 | 145 | 10 | 0 | 115 | 5.40 | 1.49 | -$6 | -$23 | 160 | –17 |
| Proj | 100 | 6 | 0 | 69 | 4.64 | 1.34 | $1 | -$5 | 110 | –5 |

**-$6 Westbrook, Jake**

| | IP | W | Sv | K | ERA | WHIP | $1L | $2L | Pts | RAA |
|---|---|---|---|---|---|---|---|---|---|---|
| '10 | 203 | 10 | 0 | 128 | 4.22 | 1.34 | $3 | -$11 | 200 | +1 |
| Proj | 180 | 9 | 0 | 108 | 4.33 | 1.35 | $4 | -$6 | 170 | –3 |

**-$6 Wolf, Randy** □□□ ○○

| | IP | W | Sv | K | ERA | WHIP | $1L | $2L | Pts | RAA |
|---|---|---|---|---|---|---|---|---|---|---|
| '10 | 216 | 13 | 0 | 142 | 4.17 | 1.39 | $3 | -$12 | 240 | –1 |
| Proj | 200 | 12 | 0 | 134 | 4.47 | 1.36 | $5 | -$6 | 220 | –8 |

**-$6 Volquez, Edinson** ■ ●

| | IP | W | Sv | K | ERA | WHIP | $1L | $2L | Pts | RAA |
|---|---|---|---|---|---|---|---|---|---|---|
| '10 | 63 | 4 | 0 | 67 | 4.31 | 1.50 | -$3 | -$12 | 90 | +1 |
| Proj | 160 | 9 | 0 | 155 | 4.35 | 1.46 | $3 | -$6 | 210 | –3 |

**-$6 Wang, Chien-Ming**

| | IP | W | Sv | K | ERA | WHIP | $1L | $2L | Pts | RAA |
|---|---|---|---|---|---|---|---|---|---|---|
| '10 | -- | -- | -- | -- | -- | -- | -- | -- | -- | -- |
| Proj | 100 | 6 | 0 | 47 | 4.49 | 1.37 | $0 | -$6 | 90 | –5 |

**-$6 Bannister, Brian**

| | IP | W | Sv | K | ERA | WHIP | $1L | $2L | Pts | RAA |
|---|---|---|---|---|---|---|---|---|---|---|
| '10 | 128 | 7 | 0 | 77 | 6.34 | 1.63 | -$10 | -$35 | 80 | –29 |
| Proj | 20 | 1 | 0 | 11 | 5.74 | 1.55 | -$3 | -$6 | 10 | –4 |

**-$7 McDonald, James**

| | IP | W | Sv | K | ERA | WHIP | $1L | $2L | Pts | RAA |
|---|---|---|---|---|---|---|---|---|---|---|
| '10 | 72 | 4 | 0 | 68 | 4.02 | 1.38 | -$2 | -$9 | 100 | +3 |
| Proj | 160 | 7 | 0 | 160 | 4.35 | 1.44 | $3 | -$7 | 200 | –3 |

**-$7 Burres, Brian**

| | IP | W | Sv | K | ERA | WHIP | $1L | $2L | Pts | RAA |
|---|---|---|---|---|---|---|---|---|---|---|
| '10 | 79 | 4 | 0 | 45 | 4.99 | 1.53 | -$7 | -$18 | 60 | –9 |
| Proj | 40 | 2 | 0 | 26 | 5.03 | 1.51 | -$3 | -$7 | 30 | –5 |

**-$7 Coke, Phil**

| | IP | W | Sv | K | ERA | WHIP | $1L | $2L | Pts | RAA |
|---|---|---|---|---|---|---|---|---|---|---|
| '10 | 65 | 7 | 2 | 53 | 3.76 | 1.44 | $2 | -$7 | 120 | +3 |
| Proj | 160 | 10 | 7 | 141 | 4.52 | 1.47 | $5 | -$7 | 220 | –8 |

**-$8 Moseley, Dustin**

| | IP | W | Sv | K | ERA | WHIP | $1L | $2L | Pts | RAA |
|---|---|---|---|---|---|---|---|---|---|---|
| '10 | 65 | 4 | 0 | 33 | 4.96 | 1.42 | -$3 | -$15 | 60 | –4 |
| Proj | 60 | 3 | 0 | 34 | 5.10 | 1.42 | -$2 | -$8 | 50 | –6 |

### -$8 Morris, Bryan
| | IP | W | Sv | K | ERA | WHIP | $1L | $2L | Pts | RAA |
|---|---|---|---|---|---|---|---|---|---|---|
| '10 | — | — | — | — | — | — | — | — | — | — |
| Proj | 40 | 2 | 3 | 27 | 5.15 | 1.55 | -$4 | -$8 | 30 | –5 |

### -$8 Tomlin, Josh
| | IP | W | Sv | K | ERA | WHIP | $1L | $2L | Pts | RAA |
|---|---|---|---|---|---|---|---|---|---|---|
| '10 | 73 | 6 | 0 | 43 | 4.56 | 1.25 | $1 | -$9 | 90 | –2 |
| Proj | 60 | 4 | 0 | 52 | 5.23 | 1.47 | -$1 | -$8 | 70 | –8 |

### -$9 Matsuzaka, Daisuke ■ ○
| | IP | W | Sv | K | ERA | WHIP | $1L | $2L | Pts | RAA |
|---|---|---|---|---|---|---|---|---|---|---|
| '10 | 154 | 9 | 0 | 133 | 4.69 | 1.37 | $3 | -$14 | 190 | –8 |
| Proj | 160 | 10 | 0 | 138 | 4.63 | 1.44 | $4 | -$9 | 200 | –8 |

### -$9 Stammen, Craig
| | IP | W | Sv | K | ERA | WHIP | $1L | $2L | Pts | RAA |
|---|---|---|---|---|---|---|---|---|---|---|
| '10 | 128 | 4 | 0 | 85 | 5.13 | 1.50 | -$8 | -$23 | 80 | –15 |
| Proj | 60 | 2 | 0 | 39 | 5.14 | 1.47 | -$4 | -$9 | 40 | –7 |

### -$9 Leake, Mike
| | IP | W | Sv | K | ERA | WHIP | $1L | $2L | Pts | RAA |
|---|---|---|---|---|---|---|---|---|---|---|
| '10 | 138 | 8 | 0 | 91 | 4.23 | 1.50 | -$3 | -$15 | 140 | –9 |
| Proj | 160 | 9 | 0 | 105 | 4.37 | 1.46 | $1 | -$9 | 160 | –11 |

### -$10 Blackburn, Nick □
| | IP | W | Sv | K | ERA | WHIP | $1L | $2L | Pts | RAA |
|---|---|---|---|---|---|---|---|---|---|---|
| '10 | 161 | 10 | 0 | 68 | 5.42 | 1.45 | -$5 | -$27 | 120 | –22 |
| Proj | 100 | 6 | 0 | 43 | 5.03 | 1.39 | -$1 | -$10 | 80 | –10 |

### -$10 Hammel, Jason
| | IP | W | Sv | K | ERA | WHIP | $1L | $2L | Pts | RAA |
|---|---|---|---|---|---|---|---|---|---|---|
| '10 | 178 | 10 | 0 | 141 | 4.81 | 1.40 | -$2 | -$17 | 200 | –9 |
| Proj | 180 | 10 | 0 | 130 | 4.80 | 1.38 | $1 | -$10 | 190 | –13 |

### -$10 Lyles, Jordan
| | IP | W | Sv | K | ERA | WHIP | $1L | $2L | Pts | RAA |
|---|---|---|---|---|---|---|---|---|---|---|
| '10 | — | — | — | — | — | — | — | — | — | — |
| Proj | 100 | 5 | 7 | 71 | 4.69 | 1.52 | -$3 | -$10 | 90 | –8 |

### -$10 Cook, Aaron ■□
| | IP | W | Sv | K | ERA | WHIP | $1L | $2L | Pts | RAA |
|---|---|---|---|---|---|---|---|---|---|---|
| '10 | 128 | 6 | 0 | 62 | 5.08 | 1.56 | -$9 | -$25 | 80 | –14 |
| Proj | 120 | 7 | 0 | 51 | 4.78 | 1.41 | -$2 | -$10 | 90 | –10 |

### -$11 Guthrie, Jeremy
| | IP | W | Sv | K | ERA | WHIP | $1L | $2L | Pts | RAA |
|---|---|---|---|---|---|---|---|---|---|---|
| '10 | 209 | 11 | 0 | 119 | 3.83 | 1.16 | $14 | $2 | 230 | +10 |
| Proj | 200 | 10 | 0 | 110 | 4.76 | 1.34 | $4 | -$11 | 170 | –14 |

### -$11 Lynn, Lance
| | IP | W | Sv | K | ERA | WHIP | $1L | $2L | Pts | RAA |
|---|---|---|---|---|---|---|---|---|---|---|
| '10 | — | — | — | — | — | — | — | — | — | — |
| Proj | 60 | 3 | 2 | 43 | 5.52 | 1.58 | -$5 | -$11 | 50 | –11 |

### -$11 Zito, Barry ○○
| | IP | W | Sv | K | ERA | WHIP | $1L | $2L | Pts | RAA |
|---|---|---|---|---|---|---|---|---|---|---|
| '10 | 199 | 9 | 0 | 150 | 4.15 | 1.34 | $3 | -$10 | 210 | +1 |
| Proj | 200 | 10 | 0 | 138 | 4.59 | 1.42 | $1 | -$11 | 190 | –10 |

### -$12 Jackson, Edwin ■□ ●○
| | IP | W | Sv | K | ERA | WHIP | $1L | $2L | Pts | RAA |
|---|---|---|---|---|---|---|---|---|---|---|
| '10 | 209 | 10 | 0 | 181 | 4.47 | 1.39 | $5 | -$15 | 240 | –8 |
| Proj | 200 | 10 | 0 | 145 | 4.69 | 1.42 | $4 | -$12 | 200 | –13 |

### -$12 Suppan, Jeff
| | IP | W | Sv | K | ERA | WHIP | $1L | $2L | Pts | RAA |
|---|---|---|---|---|---|---|---|---|---|---|
| '10 | 101 | 3 | 0 | 51 | 5.06 | 1.65 | -$10 | -$25 | 40 | –11 |
| Proj | 60 | 3 | 0 | 28 | 5.58 | 1.55 | -$6 | -$12 | 30 | –11 |

### -$12 Bush, David
| | IP | W | Sv | K | ERA | WHIP | $1L | $2L | Pts | RAA |
|---|---|---|---|---|---|---|---|---|---|---|
| '10 | 174 | 8 | 0 | 107 | 4.54 | 1.51 | -$5 | -$22 | 140 | –22 |
| Proj | 180 | 9 | 0 | 112 | 4.92 | 1.37 | $0 | -$12 | 160 | –23 |

### -$13 Bailey, Homer
| | IP | W | Sv | K | ERA | WHIP | $1L | $2L | Pts | RAA |
|---|---|---|---|---|---|---|---|---|---|---|
| '10 | 109 | 4 | 0 | 100 | 4.46 | 1.37 | -$2 | -$12 | 120 | –1 |
| Proj | 180 | 8 | 0 | 145 | 4.85 | 1.42 | -$1 | -$13 | 180 | –14 |

### -$13 Chatwood, Tyler
| | IP | W | Sv | K | ERA | WHIP | $1L | $2L | Pts | RAA |
|---|---|---|---|---|---|---|---|---|---|---|
| '10 | — | — | — | — | — | — | — | — | — | — |
| Proj | 40 | 2 | 4 | 19 | 6.02 | 1.89 | -$6 | -$13 | 20 | –10 |

### -$13 Harrell, Lucas
| | IP | W | Sv | K | ERA | WHIP | $1L | $2L | Pts | RAA |
|---|---|---|---|---|---|---|---|---|---|---|
| '10 | 24 | 1 | 0 | 15 | 4.88 | 2.13 | -$6 | -$16 | 10 | –6 |
| Proj | 40 | 2 | 2 | 19 | 6.25 | 1.84 | -$6 | -$13 | 10 | –11 |

### -$13 Silva, Carlos
| | IP | W | Sv | K | ERA | WHIP | $1L | $2L | Pts | RAA |
|---|---|---|---|---|---|---|---|---|---|---|
| '10 | 113 | 10 | 0 | 80 | 4.22 | 1.27 | $2 | -$6 | 170 | +1 |
| Proj | 160 | 10 | 0 | 76 | 5.24 | 1.35 | -$2 | -$13 | 130 | –21 |

### -$14 French, Luke
| | IP | W | Sv | K | ERA | WHIP | $1L | $2L | Pts | RAA |
|---|---|---|---|---|---|---|---|---|---|---|
| '10 | 88 | 5 | 0 | 37 | 4.83 | 1.33 | -$1 | -$14 | 70 | –4 |
| Proj | 100 | 5 | 0 | 62 | 5.23 | 1.52 | -$3 | -$14 | 80 | –12 |

### -$14 Masterson, Justin
| | IP | W | Sv | K | ERA | WHIP | $1L | $2L | Pts | RAA |
|---|---|---|---|---|---|---|---|---|---|---|
| '10 | 180 | 6 | 0 | 140 | 4.70 | 1.50 | -$2 | -$23 | 150 | –18 |
| Proj | 180 | 8 | 0 | 148 | 4.63 | 1.51 | $1 | -$14 | 180 | –14 |

### -$14 Porcello, Rick ■
| | IP | W | Sv | K | ERA | WHIP | $1L | $2L | Pts | RAA |
|---|---|---|---|---|---|---|---|---|---|---|
| '10 | 163 | 10 | 0 | 84 | 4.92 | 1.39 | $0 | -$19 | 140 | –16 |
| Proj | 200 | 11 | 0 | 100 | 4.92 | 1.39 | $2 | -$14 | 170 | –19 |

### -$15 Rogers, Esmil
| | IP | W | Sv | K | ERA | WHIP | $1L | $2L | Pts | RAA |
|---|---|---|---|---|---|---|---|---|---|---|
| '10 | 72 | 2 | 0 | 66 | 6.13 | 1.67 | -$11 | -$24 | 50 | –23 |
| Proj | 80 | 4 | 0 | 75 | 5.64 | 1.66 | -$7 | -$15 | 70 | –16 |

### -$16 Paulino, Felipe
| | IP | W | Sv | K | ERA | WHIP | $1L | $2L | Pts | RAA |
|---|---|---|---|---|---|---|---|---|---|---|
| '10 | 92 | 1 | 0 | 83 | 5.11 | 1.54 | -$8 | -$20 | 60 | –18 |
| Proj | 100 | 3 | 0 | 87 | 5.46 | 1.55 | -$6 | -$16 | 80 | –19 |

### -$8 Davis, Wade □
| | IP | W | Sv | K | ERA | WHIP | $1L | $2L | Pts | RAA |
|---|---|---|---|---|---|---|---|---|---|---|
| '10 | 168 | 12 | 0 | 113 | 4.07 | 1.35 | $7 | -$8 | 210 | +6 |
| Proj | 170 | 11 | 0 | 141 | 4.44 | 1.46 | $5 | -$8 | 220 | –4 |

### -$8 Mortensen, Clayton
| | IP | W | Sv | K | ERA | WHIP | $1L | $2L | Pts | RAA |
|---|---|---|---|---|---|---|---|---|---|---|
| '10 | 6 | 0 | 0 | 7 | 4.50 | 1.33 | -$4 | -$11 | 10 | –1 |
| Proj | 40 | 2 | 0 | 30 | 5.58 | 1.54 | -$3 | -$8 | 30 | –7 |

### -$9 Tazawa, Junichi
| | IP | W | Sv | K | ERA | WHIP | $1L | $2L | Pts | RAA |
|---|---|---|---|---|---|---|---|---|---|---|
| '10 | — | — | — | — | — | — | — | — | — | — |
| Proj | 40 | 1 | 0 | 33 | 5.38 | 1.60 | -$3 | -$9 | 30 | –6 |

### -$9 Harden, Rich ●○
| | IP | W | Sv | K | ERA | WHIP | $1L | $2L | Pts | RAA |
|---|---|---|---|---|---|---|---|---|---|---|
| '10 | 92 | 5 | 0 | 75 | 5.58 | 1.66 | -$6 | -$24 | 80 | –16 |
| Proj | 100 | 6 | 0 | 99 | 4.87 | 1.50 | $0 | -$9 | 130 | –9 |

### -$9 Matusz, Brian
| | IP | W | Sv | K | ERA | WHIP | $1L | $2L | Pts | RAA |
|---|---|---|---|---|---|---|---|---|---|---|
| '10 | 176 | 10 | 0 | 143 | 4.30 | 1.34 | $6 | -$10 | 220 | –1 |
| Proj | 180 | 10 | 0 | 156 | 4.54 | 1.44 | $5 | -$9 | 210 | –8 |

### -$10 Ohlendorf, Ross □
| | IP | W | Sv | K | ERA | WHIP | $1L | $2L | Pts | RAA |
|---|---|---|---|---|---|---|---|---|---|---|
| '10 | 108 | 1 | 0 | 79 | 4.07 | 1.38 | -$3 | -$13 | 70 | –1 |
| Proj | 160 | 6 | 0 | 110 | 4.64 | 1.38 | $0 | -$10 | 130 | –11 |

### -$10 Atilano, Luis
| | IP | W | Sv | K | ERA | WHIP | $1L | $2L | Pts | RAA |
|---|---|---|---|---|---|---|---|---|---|---|
| '10 | 86 | 6 | 0 | 40 | 5.15 | 1.49 | -$6 | -$18 | 70 | –14 |
| Proj | 60 | 3 | 0 | 36 | 5.36 | 1.53 | -$4 | -$10 | 50 | –10 |

### -$10 Fister, Doug
| | IP | W | Sv | K | ERA | WHIP | $1L | $2L | Pts | RAA |
|---|---|---|---|---|---|---|---|---|---|---|
| '10 | 171 | 6 | 0 | 93 | 4.11 | 1.28 | $5 | -$10 | 140 | –1 |
| Proj | 190 | 8 | 0 | 120 | 4.64 | 1.37 | $4 | -$10 | 160 | –12 |

### -$10 Burnett, A.J. ■□ ●●
| | IP | W | Sv | K | ERA | WHIP | $1L | $2L | Pts | RAA |
|---|---|---|---|---|---|---|---|---|---|---|
| '10 | 187 | 10 | 0 | 145 | 5.26 | 1.51 | -$3 | -$28 | 180 | –26 |
| Proj | 190 | 11 | 0 | 155 | 4.74 | 1.45 | $4 | -$10 | 220 | –13 |

### -$11 Gorzelanny, Tom
| | IP | W | Sv | K | ERA | WHIP | $1L | $2L | Pts | RAA |
|---|---|---|---|---|---|---|---|---|---|---|
| '10 | 136 | 7 | 1 | 119 | 4.09 | 1.50 | -$1 | -$13 | 170 | –3 |
| Proj | 140 | 7 | 0 | 111 | 4.67 | 1.48 | -$1 | -$11 | 150 | –11 |

### -$11 Willis, Dontrelle
| | IP | W | Sv | K | ERA | WHIP | $1L | $2L | Pts | RAA |
|---|---|---|---|---|---|---|---|---|---|---|
| '10 | 66 | 2 | 0 | 47 | 5.62 | 1.95 | -$12 | -$26 | 30 | –9 |
| Proj | 40 | 2 | 0 | 26 | 5.74 | 1.76 | -$6 | -$11 | 20 | –7 |

### -$11 Kazmir, Scott □ ●
| | IP | W | Sv | K | ERA | WHIP | $1L | $2L | Pts | RAA |
|---|---|---|---|---|---|---|---|---|---|---|
| '10 | 150 | 9 | 0 | 93 | 5.94 | 1.58 | -$8 | -$33 | 120 | –29 |
| Proj | 140 | 9 | 0 | 112 | 4.98 | 1.46 | $1 | -$11 | 160 | –13 |

### -$12 Maholm, Paul ○
| | IP | W | Sv | K | ERA | WHIP | $1L | $2L | Pts | RAA |
|---|---|---|---|---|---|---|---|---|---|---|
| '10 | 185 | 9 | 0 | 102 | 5.10 | 1.56 | -$10 | -$31 | 130 | –28 |
| Proj | 160 | 8 | 0 | 89 | 4.72 | 1.42 | -$1 | -$12 | 130 | –14 |

### -$12 Norris, Bud ○
| | IP | W | Sv | K | ERA | WHIP | $1L | $2L | Pts | RAA |
|---|---|---|---|---|---|---|---|---|---|---|
| '10 | 154 | 9 | 0 | 158 | 4.92 | 1.48 | -$3 | -$19 | 200 | –18 |
| Proj | 160 | 8 | 0 | 163 | 4.80 | 1.51 | -$1 | -$12 | 200 | –15 |

### -$12 Marquis, Jason ■
| | IP | W | Sv | K | ERA | WHIP | $1L | $2L | Pts | RAA |
|---|---|---|---|---|---|---|---|---|---|---|
| '10 | 59 | 2 | 0 | 31 | 6.60 | 1.70 | -$12 | -$24 | 20 | –18 |
| Proj | 140 | 7 | 0 | 71 | 4.83 | 1.43 | -$2 | -$12 | 110 | –12 |

### -$13 Nova, Ivan
| | IP | W | Sv | K | ERA | WHIP | $1L | $2L | Pts | RAA |
|---|---|---|---|---|---|---|---|---|---|---|
| '10 | 42 | 1 | 0 | 26 | 4.50 | 1.45 | -$3 | -$13 | 30 | –1 |
| Proj | 60 | 3 | 0 | 45 | 5.53 | 1.68 | -$5 | -$13 | 40 | –10 |

### -$13 Oliver, Andy
| | IP | W | Sv | K | ERA | WHIP | $1L | $2L | Pts | RAA |
|---|---|---|---|---|---|---|---|---|---|---|
| '10 | 22 | 0 | 0 | 18 | 7.36 | 1.77 | -$6 | -$17 | 0 | –11 |
| Proj | 60 | 3 | 6 | 39 | 5.64 | 1.66 | -$5 | -$13 | 40 | –12 |

### -$13 Britton, Zach
| | IP | W | Sv | K | ERA | WHIP | $1L | $2L | Pts | RAA |
|---|---|---|---|---|---|---|---|---|---|---|
| '10 | — | — | — | — | — | — | — | — | — | — |
| Proj | 100 | 5 | 8 | 59 | 4.83 | 1.59 | -$3 | -$13 | 80 | –10 |

### -$14 Lohse, Kyle ■
| | IP | W | Sv | K | ERA | WHIP | $1L | $2L | Pts | RAA |
|---|---|---|---|---|---|---|---|---|---|---|
| '10 | 92 | 4 | 0 | 54 | 6.55 | 1.78 | -$15 | -$33 | 40 | –30 |
| Proj | 120 | 7 | 0 | 68 | 5.20 | 1.45 | -$4 | -$14 | 100 | –17 |

### -$14 Stewart, Zach
| | IP | W | Sv | K | ERA | WHIP | $1L | $2L | Pts | RAA |
|---|---|---|---|---|---|---|---|---|---|---|
| '10 | — | — | — | — | — | — | — | — | — | — |
| Proj | 40 | 1 | 2 | 23 | 6.44 | 1.82 | -$6 | -$14 | 10 | –12 |

### -$14 Holland, Derek
| | IP | W | Sv | K | ERA | WHIP | $1L | $2L | Pts | RAA |
|---|---|---|---|---|---|---|---|---|---|---|
| '10 | 57 | 3 | 0 | 54 | 4.08 | 1.38 | $0 | -$10 | 80 | –2 |
| Proj | 140 | 7 | 0 | 120 | 5.19 | 1.47 | -$1 | -$14 | 150 | –20 |

### -$15 McAllister, Zach
| | IP | W | Sv | K | ERA | WHIP | $1L | $2L | Pts | RAA |
|---|---|---|---|---|---|---|---|---|---|---|
| '10 | — | — | — | — | — | — | — | — | — | — |
| Proj | 40 | 2 | 4 | 19 | 7.23 | 1.76 | -$7 | -$15 | 10 | –16 |

### -$15 Duke, Zach □
| | IP | W | Sv | K | ERA | WHIP | $1L | $2L | Pts | RAA |
|---|---|---|---|---|---|---|---|---|---|---|
| '10 | 159 | 8 | 0 | 96 | 5.72 | 1.65 | -$15 | -$36 | 100 | –37 |
| Proj | 160 | 8 | 0 | 79 | 5.01 | 1.43 | -$4 | -$15 | 120 | –19 |

### -$16 Bergesen, Brad
| | IP | W | Sv | K | ERA | WHIP | $1L | $2L | Pts | RAA |
|---|---|---|---|---|---|---|---|---|---|---|
| '10 | 170 | 8 | 0 | 81 | 4.98 | 1.44 | -$3 | -$24 | 120 | –20 |
| Proj | 160 | 8 | 0 | 87 | 4.90 | 1.48 | -$1 | -$16 | 130 | –16 |

### -$8 Morrow, Brandon △△ ○
| | IP | W | Sv | K | ERA | WHIP | $1L | $2L | Pts | RAA |
|---|---|---|---|---|---|---|---|---|---|---|
| '10 | 146 | 10 | 0 | 178 | 4.49 | 1.38 | $6 | -$9 | 250 | –4 |
| Proj | 200 | 13 | 0 | 215 | 4.60 | 1.45 | $7 | -$8 | 290 | –10 |

### -$9 Jackson, Jay
| | IP | W | Sv | K | ERA | WHIP | $1L | $2L | Pts | RAA |
|---|---|---|---|---|---|---|---|---|---|---|
| '10 | — | — | — | — | — | — | — | — | — | — |
| Proj | 40 | 2 | 2 | 24 | 5.70 | 1.48 | -$4 | -$9 | 30 | –8 |

### -$9 Huff, David □
| | IP | W | Sv | K | ERA | WHIP | $1L | $2L | Pts | RAA |
|---|---|---|---|---|---|---|---|---|---|---|
| '10 | 80 | 2 | 0 | 37 | 6.21 | 1.69 | -$10 | -$28 | 10 | –22 |
| Proj | 40 | 2 | 0 | 24 | 5.53 | 1.55 | -$3 | -$9 | 20 | –7 |

### -$9 Narveson, Chris □
| | IP | W | Sv | K | ERA | WHIP | $1L | $2L | Pts | RAA |
|---|---|---|---|---|---|---|---|---|---|---|
| '10 | 168 | 12 | 0 | 137 | 4.99 | 1.38 | -$1 | -$16 | 220 | –13 |
| Proj | 180 | 12 | 0 | 152 | 4.87 | 1.39 | $2 | -$9 | 230 | –14 |

### -$10 Ely, John
| | IP | W | Sv | K | ERA | WHIP | $1L | $2L | Pts | RAA |
|---|---|---|---|---|---|---|---|---|---|---|
| '10 | 100 | 4 | 0 | 76 | 5.49 | 1.45 | -$7 | -$20 | 80 | –14 |
| Proj | 80 | 4 | 0 | 75 | 5.12 | 1.50 | -$3 | -$10 | 90 | –9 |

### -$10 Sanabia, Alex
| | IP | W | Sv | K | ERA | WHIP | $1L | $2L | Pts | RAA |
|---|---|---|---|---|---|---|---|---|---|---|
| '10 | 72 | 5 | 0 | 47 | 3.73 | 1.24 | $0 | -$6 | 90 | +4 |
| Proj | 100 | 6 | 0 | 74 | 4.83 | 1.50 | -$2 | -$10 | 100 | –8 |

### -$10 Beachy, Brandon
| | IP | W | Sv | K | ERA | WHIP | $1L | $2L | Pts | RAA |
|---|---|---|---|---|---|---|---|---|---|---|
| '10 | 15 | 0 | 0 | 15 | 3.00 | 1.53 | -$5 | -$11 | 10 | –2 |
| Proj | 100 | 4 | 0 | 99 | 4.41 | 1.61 | -$3 | -$10 | 110 | –11 |

### -$10 Karstens, Jeff
| | IP | W | Sv | K | ERA | WHIP | $1L | $2L | Pts | RAA |
|---|---|---|---|---|---|---|---|---|---|---|
| '10 | 123 | 3 | 0 | 72 | 4.92 | 1.41 | -$6 | -$20 | 70 | –11 |
| Proj | 80 | 3 | 0 | 45 | 5.09 | 1.44 | -$4 | -$10 | 50 | –9 |

### -$10 Detwiler, Ross
| | IP | W | Sv | K | ERA | WHIP | $1L | $2L | Pts | RAA |
|---|---|---|---|---|---|---|---|---|---|---|
| '10 | 30 | 1 | 0 | 17 | 4.25 | 1.62 | -$6 | -$13 | 20 | –7 |
| Proj | 100 | 5 | 0 | 76 | 4.55 | 1.57 | -$3 | -$10 | 100 | –9 |

### -$11 Gomez, Jeanmar
| | IP | W | Sv | K | ERA | WHIP | $1L | $2L | Pts | RAA |
|---|---|---|---|---|---|---|---|---|---|---|
| '10 | 58 | 4 | 0 | 34 | 4.68 | 1.65 | -$4 | -$16 | 50 | –8 |
| Proj | 60 | 3 | 0 | 49 | 5.24 | 1.66 | -$3 | -$11 | 60 | –9 |

### -$11 Drabek, Kyle
| | IP | W | Sv | K | ERA | WHIP | $1L | $2L | Pts | RAA |
|---|---|---|---|---|---|---|---|---|---|---|
| '10 | 17 | 0 | 0 | 12 | 4.76 | 1.35 | -$4 | -$12 | 10 | –1 |
| Proj | 100 | 4 | 0 | 74 | 5.08 | 1.58 | -$2 | -$11 | 80 | –9 |

### -$12 Kawakami, Kenshin
| | IP | W | Sv | K | ERA | WHIP | $1L | $2L | Pts | RAA |
|---|---|---|---|---|---|---|---|---|---|---|
| '10 | 87 | 1 | 0 | 59 | 5.15 | 1.49 | -$8 | -$20 | 40 | –14 |
| Proj | 100 | 4 | 0 | 63 | 4.96 | 1.46 | -$4 | -$12 | 70 | –12 |

### -$12 Mazzaro, Vin
| | IP | W | Sv | K | ERA | WHIP | $1L | $2L | Pts | RAA |
|---|---|---|---|---|---|---|---|---|---|---|
| '10 | 122 | 6 | 0 | 79 | 4.27 | 1.45 | $0 | -$14 | 110 | –10 |
| Proj | 160 | 8 | 0 | 111 | 4.59 | 1.48 | $2 | -$12 | 160 | –13 |

### -$12 Francis, Jeff
| | IP | W | Sv | K | ERA | WHIP | $1L | $2L | Pts | RAA |
|---|---|---|---|---|---|---|---|---|---|---|
| '10 | 104 | 4 | 0 | 67 | 5.00 | 1.36 | -$5 | -$17 | 80 | –10 |
| Proj | 140 | 7 | 0 | 87 | 4.94 | 1.42 | -$2 | -$12 | 120 | –13 |

### -$12 Talbot, Mitch
| | IP | W | Sv | K | ERA | WHIP | $1L | $2L | Pts | RAA |
|---|---|---|---|---|---|---|---|---|---|---|
| '10 | 159 | 10 | 0 | 88 | 4.41 | 1.49 | $0 | -$18 | 150 | –9 |
| Proj | 160 | 9 | 0 | 106 | 4.62 | 1.50 | $1 | -$12 | 160 | –12 |

### -$13 Rowland-Smith, Ryan
| | IP | W | Sv | K | ERA | WHIP | $1L | $2L | Pts | RAA |
|---|---|---|---|---|---|---|---|---|---|---|
| '10 | 109 | 1 | 0 | 49 | 6.75 | 1.69 | -$14 | -$39 | -10 | –40 |
| Proj | 80 | 3 | 0 | 45 | 5.35 | 1.52 | -$4 | -$13 | 50 | –13 |

### -$13 Volstad, Chris □
| | IP | W | Sv | K | ERA | WHIP | $1L | $2L | Pts | RAA |
|---|---|---|---|---|---|---|---|---|---|---|
| '10 | 175 | 12 | 0 | 102 | 4.58 | 1.41 | -$1 | -$16 | 180 | –8 |
| Proj | 160 | 10 | 0 | 101 | 4.89 | 1.45 | -$2 | -$13 | 150 | –14 |

### -$13 Carmona, Fausto □
| | IP | W | Sv | K | ERA | WHIP | $1L | $2L | Pts | RAA |
|---|---|---|---|---|---|---|---|---|---|---|
| '10 | 210 | 13 | 0 | 124 | 3.77 | 1.31 | $11 | -$3 | 240 | +6 |
| Proj | 200 | 11 | 0 | 116 | 4.60 | 1.45 | $3 | -$13 | 180 | –13 |

### -$14 Lannan, John
| | IP | W | Sv | K | ERA | WHIP | $1L | $2L | Pts | RAA |
|---|---|---|---|---|---|---|---|---|---|---|
| '10 | 143 | 8 | 0 | 71 | 4.65 | 1.56 | -$7 | -$22 | 110 | –11 |
| Proj | 160 | 8 | 0 | 80 | 4.73 | 1.46 | -$2 | -$14 | 120 | –13 |

### -$14 Olsen, Scott
| | IP | W | Sv | K | ERA | WHIP | $1L | $2L | Pts | RAA |
|---|---|---|---|---|---|---|---|---|---|---|
| '10 | 81 | 4 | 0 | 53 | 5.56 | 1.48 | -$7 | -$19 | 60 | –14 |
| Proj | 120 | 5 | 0 | 75 | 5.34 | 1.43 | -$4 | -$14 | 90 | –18 |

### -$14 Morton, Charlie
| | IP | W | Sv | K | ERA | WHIP | $1L | $2L | Pts | RAA |
|---|---|---|---|---|---|---|---|---|---|---|
| '10 | 80 | 2 | 0 | 59 | 7.57 | 1.73 | -$16 | -$34 | 20 | –40 |
| Proj | 100 | 5 | 0 | 72 | 5.35 | 1.53 | -$5 | -$14 | 80 | –17 |

### -$15 Chen, Bruce □
| | IP | W | Sv | K | ERA | WHIP | $1L | $2L | Pts | RAA |
|---|---|---|---|---|---|---|---|---|---|---|
| '10 | 140 | 12 | 1 | 98 | 4.17 | 1.38 | $5 | -$8 | 200 | +1 |
| Proj | 200 | 11 | 0 | 115 | 5.06 | 1.48 | $0 | -$15 | 170 | –17 |

### -$15 Lincoln, Brad
| | IP | W | Sv | K | ERA | WHIP | $1L | $2L | Pts | RAA |
|---|---|---|---|---|---|---|---|---|---|---|
| '10 | 53 | 1 | 0 | 25 | 6.66 | 1.54 | -$10 | -$22 | 10 | –16 |
| Proj | 100 | 4 | 0 | 77 | 5.63 | 1.51 | -$6 | -$15 | 80 | –18 |

### -$16 Saunders, Joe ■■
| | IP | W | Sv | K | ERA | WHIP | $1L | $2L | Pts | RAA |
|---|---|---|---|---|---|---|---|---|---|---|
| '10 | 203 | 9 | 0 | 114 | 4.47 | 1.46 | -$4 | -$21 | 160 | –20 |
| Proj | 200 | 11 | 0 | 106 | 4.85 | 1.44 | -$2 | -$16 | 160 | –22 |

American League
National League

# Relief Pitcher

Top Finishes Among All Pitchers From 2008-10

| | Top 25 | Top 50 |
|---|---|---|
| W | ■ | □ |
| Sv | ▲ | △ |
| K | ● | ○ |

## Projected 2011 Leaders

| Innings | $2L | Saves | $2L | Strikeouts | $2L | ERA | $2L | WHIP | $2L |
|---|---|---|---|---|---|---|---|---|---|
| 160 Duensing, B | $0 | 42 Soriano, R | $19 | 108 Marmol, C | $12 | 1.56 Jansen, K | $12 | 0.84 Germano, J | $5 |
| 120 Mejia, J | -$14 | 41 Nunez, L | $8 | 102 Mejia, J | -$14 | 2.16 Germano, J | $5 | 0.96 Rivera, M | $21 |
| 120 Wakefield, T | -$15 | 41 Aardsma, D | $7 | 98 Duensing, B | $0 | 2.20 Soria, J | $17 | 1.04 Soriano, R | $19 |
| 100 Figueroa, N | $0 | 40 Cordero, F | $9 | 95 Chapman, A | -$2 | 2.35 Rivera, M | $21 | 1.05 Kuo, H | $10 |
| 100 Chapman, A | -$2 | 37 Bailey, A | $13 | 94 Cashner, A | -$16 | 2.50 Kuo, H | $10 | 1.07 Gregerson, L | $5 |
| 100 Cashner, A | -$16 | 36 Soria, J | $17 | 91 Kimbrel, C | $13 | 2.51 Ogando, A | $8 | 1.08 Mujica, E | $1 |
| 80 Marmol, C | $12 | 35 Marmol, C | $12 | 88 Bard, D | $4 | 2.57 Adams, M | $4 | 1.10 Adams, M | $4 |
| 80 Cordero, F | $9 | 35 Papelbon, J | $17 | 88 Hanrahan, J | $2 | 2.67 Bell, H | $17 | 1.10 Benoit, J | $4 |
| 80 Storen, D | $9 | 35 Wilson, B | $16 | 85 Jansen, K | $12 | 2.72 Nathan, J | $9 | 1.11 Soria, J | $17 |
| 80 Nunez, L | $8 | 35 Rivera, M | $21 | 82 Rzepczynski, M | -$10 | 2.78 Loe, K | $4 | 1.11 Thornton, M | $7 |
| 80 Lyon, B | $7 | 33 Lidge, B | $8 | 79 Storen, D | $9 | 2.83 Kimbrel, C | $13 | 1.12 Street, H | $14 |
| 80 Meek, E | $5 | 33 Jenks, B | $10 | 79 Figueroa, N | $0 | 2.87 Devine, J | $3 | 1.12 Nathan, J | $9 |
| 80 Bard, D | $4 | 32 Street, H | $14 | 77 Bailey, A | $13 | 2.89 Soriano, R | $19 | 1.12 Thatcher, J | $2 |
| 80 League, B | $2 | 30 Capps, M | $8 | 72 Robertson, D | -$1 | 2.89 Thatcher, J | $2 | 1.14 Kintzler, B | $1 |
| 80 Hanrahan, J | $2 | 29 Broxton, J | $11 | 72 Axford, J | $9 | 2.92 Wilson, B | $16 | 1.14 Uehara, K | $8 |

#### $21 Rivera, Mariano ▲▲▲

| | IP | W | Sv | K | ERA | WHIP | $1L | $2L | Pts | RAA |
|---|---|---|---|---|---|---|---|---|---|---|
| '10 | 60 | 3 | 33 | 45 | 1.80 | 0.83 | $16 | $14 | 260 | +13 |
| Proj | 60 | 4 | 35 | 54 | 2.35 | 0.96 | $20 | $21 | 300 | +10 |

#### $17 Soria, Joakim ▲▲▲

| | IP | W | Sv | K | ERA | WHIP | $1L | $2L | Pts | RAA |
|---|---|---|---|---|---|---|---|---|---|---|
| '10 | 66 | 1 | 43 | 71 | 1.78 | 1.05 | $18 | $15 | 310 | +17 |
| Proj | 60 | 2 | 36 | 65 | 2.20 | 1.11 | $17 | $17 | 260 | +11 |

#### $14 Street, Huston ▲▲△

| | IP | W | Sv | K | ERA | WHIP | $1L | $2L | Pts | RAA |
|---|---|---|---|---|---|---|---|---|---|---|
| '10 | 47 | 4 | 20 | 45 | 3.61 | 1.06 | $6 | $1 | 190 | +0 |
| Proj | 60 | 4 | 32 | 59 | 3.59 | 1.12 | $16 | $14 | 290 | +1 |

#### $13 Bailey, Andrew ▲▲

| | IP | W | Sv | K | ERA | WHIP | $1L | $2L | Pts | RAA |
|---|---|---|---|---|---|---|---|---|---|---|
| '10 | 49 | 1 | 25 | 42 | 1.47 | 0.96 | $11 | $8 | 190 | +14 |
| Proj | 75 | 3 | 37 | 77 | 3.16 | 1.29 | $15 | $13 | 270 | +6 |

#### $11 Valverde, Jose ▲▲▲

| | IP | W | Sv | K | ERA | WHIP | $1L | $2L | Pts | RAA |
|---|---|---|---|---|---|---|---|---|---|---|
| '10 | 63 | 2 | 26 | 63 | 3.00 | 1.16 | $10 | $4 | 220 | +4 |
| Proj | 60 | 2 | 28 | 59 | 3.69 | 1.27 | $13 | $11 | 260 | –0 |

#### $10 Kuo, Hong-Chih △

| | IP | W | Sv | K | ERA | WHIP | $1L | $2L | Pts | RAA |
|---|---|---|---|---|---|---|---|---|---|---|
| '10 | 60 | 3 | 12 | 73 | 1.20 | 0.78 | $12 | $12 | 190 | +19 |
| Proj | 60 | 4 | 4 | 66 | 2.50 | 1.05 | $10 | $10 | 160 | +9 |

#### $9 Franklin, Ryan ▲▲△

| | IP | W | Sv | K | ERA | WHIP | $1L | $2L | Pts | RAA |
|---|---|---|---|---|---|---|---|---|---|---|
| '10 | 65 | 6 | 27 | 42 | 3.46 | 1.03 | $10 | $6 | 240 | +4 |
| Proj | 60 | 3 | 28 | 36 | 3.94 | 1.25 | $12 | $9 | 240 | –1 |

#### $9 Storen, Drew △

| | IP | W | Sv | K | ERA | WHIP | $1L | $2L | Pts | RAA |
|---|---|---|---|---|---|---|---|---|---|---|
| '10 | 55 | 4 | 5 | 52 | 3.58 | 1.27 | $1 | -$5 | 120 | +1 |
| Proj | 80 | 5 | 6 | 79 | 3.78 | 1.32 | $12 | $9 | 250 | –1 |

#### $8 Nunez, Leo ▲▲

| | IP | W | Sv | K | ERA | WHIP | $1L | $2L | Pts | RAA |
|---|---|---|---|---|---|---|---|---|---|---|
| '10 | 65 | 4 | 30 | 71 | 3.46 | 1.28 | $9 | $4 | 260 | +2 |
| Proj | 80 | 4 | 41 | 70 | 4.30 | 1.35 | $12 | $8 | 280 | –5 |

#### $8 Ogando, Alexi

| | IP | W | Sv | K | ERA | WHIP | $1L | $2L | Pts | RAA |
|---|---|---|---|---|---|---|---|---|---|---|
| '10 | 42 | 4 | 0 | 39 | 1.30 | 1.13 | $4 | $0 | 90 | +13 |
| Proj | 60 | 5 | 0 | 55 | 2.51 | 1.18 | $9 | $8 | 140 | +9 |

#### $7 Thornton, Matt △△

| | IP | W | Sv | K | ERA | WHIP | $1L | $2L | Pts | RAA |
|---|---|---|---|---|---|---|---|---|---|---|
| '10 | 61 | 5 | 8 | 81 | 2.67 | 1.01 | $9 | $5 | 180 | +9 |
| Proj | 60 | 4 | 5 | 68 | 2.99 | 1.11 | $8 | $7 | 140 | +6 |

#### $5 Downs, Scott △△

| | IP | W | Sv | K | ERA | WHIP | $1L | $2L | Pts | RAA |
|---|---|---|---|---|---|---|---|---|---|---|
| '10 | 61 | 5 | 0 | 48 | 2.64 | 0.99 | $6 | $1 | 110 | +9 |
| Proj | 60 | 4 | 2 | 48 | 3.18 | 1.19 | $7 | $5 | 130 | +4 |

#### $5 Germano, Justin

| | IP | W | Sv | K | ERA | WHIP | $1L | $2L | Pts | RAA |
|---|---|---|---|---|---|---|---|---|---|---|
| '10 | 35 | 0 | 0 | 29 | 3.31 | 0.99 | $0 | -$7 | 30 | +1 |
| Proj | 40 | 0 | 0 | 32 | 2.16 | 0.84 | $5 | $5 | 50 | +6 |

#### $4 Putz, J.J. △

| | IP | W | Sv | K | ERA | WHIP | $1L | $2L | Pts | RAA |
|---|---|---|---|---|---|---|---|---|---|---|
| '10 | 54 | 7 | 3 | 65 | 2.83 | 1.04 | $7 | $2 | 160 | +6 |
| Proj | 60 | 5 | 4 | 61 | 3.60 | 1.27 | $7 | $4 | 150 | +1 |

#### $4 Loe, Kameron

| | IP | W | Sv | K | ERA | WHIP | $1L | $2L | Pts | RAA |
|---|---|---|---|---|---|---|---|---|---|---|
| '10 | 58 | 3 | 0 | 46 | 2.78 | 1.18 | $1 | -$3 | 80 | +3 |
| Proj | 60 | 3 | 0 | 47 | 2.78 | 1.18 | $5 | $4 | 80 | +3 |

#### $3 Devine, Joey

| | IP | W | Sv | K | ERA | WHIP | $1L | $2L | Pts | RAA |
|---|---|---|---|---|---|---|---|---|---|---|
| '10 | -- | -- | -- | -- | ---- | ---- | --- | --- | --- | --- |
| Proj | 45 | 3 | 0 | 51 | 2.87 | 1.25 | $4 | $3 | 90 | +5 |

#### $2 Balfour, Grant △△

| | IP | W | Sv | K | ERA | WHIP | $1L | $2L | Pts | RAA |
|---|---|---|---|---|---|---|---|---|---|---|
| '10 | 55 | 2 | 0 | 56 | 2.28 | 1.08 | $5 | -$1 | 90 | +9 |
| Proj | 60 | 3 | 3 | 64 | 3.24 | 1.26 | $4 | $2 | 100 | +3 |

#### $2 League, Brandon △

| | IP | W | Sv | K | ERA | WHIP | $1L | $2L | Pts | RAA |
|---|---|---|---|---|---|---|---|---|---|---|
| '10 | 79 | 9 | 6 | 56 | 3.42 | 1.19 | $7 | $0 | 180 | –2 |
| Proj | 80 | 6 | 5 | 62 | 3.89 | 1.28 | $6 | $2 | 140 | –4 |

#### $2 Hanrahan, Joel △△△

| | IP | W | Sv | K | ERA | WHIP | $1L | $2L | Pts | RAA |
|---|---|---|---|---|---|---|---|---|---|---|
| '10 | 70 | 4 | 6 | 100 | 3.62 | 1.21 | $4 | -$2 | 170 | +3 |
| Proj | 80 | 4 | 5 | 88 | 4.34 | 1.41 | $6 | $2 | 200 | –5 |

#### $19 Soriano, Rafael ▲▲

| | IP | W | Sv | K | ERA | WHIP | $1L | $2L | Pts | RAA |
|---|---|---|---|---|---|---|---|---|---|---|
| '10 | 62 | 3 | 45 | 57 | 1.73 | 0.80 | $20 | $20 | 340 | +14 |
| Proj | 60 | 3 | 42 | 61 | 2.89 | 1.05 | $19 | $19 | 320 | +6 |

#### $17 Papelbon, Jonathan ▲▲▲

| | IP | W | Sv | K | ERA | WHIP | $1L | $2L | Pts | RAA |
|---|---|---|---|---|---|---|---|---|---|---|
| '10 | 67 | 5 | 37 | 76 | 3.90 | 1.27 | $12 | $5 | 310 | –4 |
| Proj | 60 | 4 | 35 | 65 | 3.22 | 1.18 | $18 | $17 | 320 | +4 |

#### $14 Feliz, Neftali ▲

| | IP | W | Sv | K | ERA | WHIP | $1L | $2L | Pts | RAA |
|---|---|---|---|---|---|---|---|---|---|---|
| '10 | 69 | 4 | 40 | 71 | 2.73 | 0.88 | $18 | $16 | 330 | +10 |
| Proj | 60 | 4 | 16 | 62 | 3.50 | 1.21 | $16 | $14 | 290 | +2 |

#### $12 Marmol, Carlos ▲△△

| | IP | W | Sv | K | ERA | WHIP | $1L | $2L | Pts | RAA |
|---|---|---|---|---|---|---|---|---|---|---|
| '10 | 78 | 2 | 38 | 138 | 2.55 | 1.18 | $16 | $14 | 360 | +12 |
| Proj | 80 | 3 | 35 | 108 | 3.45 | 1.38 | $15 | $12 | 310 | +3 |

#### $11 Broxton, Jonathan ▲▲△

| | IP | W | Sv | K | ERA | WHIP | $1L | $2L | Pts | RAA |
|---|---|---|---|---|---|---|---|---|---|---|
| '10 | 62 | 5 | 22 | 73 | 4.04 | 1.48 | $4 | -$3 | 220 | –2 |
| Proj | 60 | 4 | 29 | 71 | 3.28 | 1.25 | $12 | $11 | 240 | +3 |

#### $10 Jenks, Bobby ▲▲▲

| | IP | W | Sv | K | ERA | WHIP | $1L | $2L | Pts | RAA |
|---|---|---|---|---|---|---|---|---|---|---|
| '10 | 53 | 1 | 27 | 61 | 4.44 | 1.37 | $5 | -$3 | 200 | –4 |
| Proj | 60 | 2 | 33 | 55 | 4.02 | 1.28 | $13 | $10 | 260 | –2 |

#### $9 Nathan, Joe ▲▲

| | IP | W | Sv | K | ERA | WHIP | $1L | $2L | Pts | RAA |
|---|---|---|---|---|---|---|---|---|---|---|
| '10 | -- | -- | -- | -- | ---- | ---- | --- | --- | --- | --- |
| Proj | 40 | 4 | 0 | 45 | 2.72 | 1.12 | $10 | $9 | 180 | +5 |

#### $8 Capps, Matt ▲▲▲

| | IP | W | Sv | K | ERA | WHIP | $1L | $2L | Pts | RAA |
|---|---|---|---|---|---|---|---|---|---|---|
| '10 | 73 | 5 | 42 | 59 | 2.47 | 1.26 | $16 | $11 | 330 | +6 |
| Proj | 60 | 2 | 30 | 45 | 3.55 | 1.24 | $11 | $8 | 200 | –0 |

#### $8 Uehara, Koji △

| | IP | W | Sv | K | ERA | WHIP | $1L | $2L | Pts | RAA |
|---|---|---|---|---|---|---|---|---|---|---|
| '10 | 44 | 1 | 13 | 55 | 2.86 | 0.95 | $6 | $1 | 140 | +5 |
| Proj | 60 | 2 | 11 | 55 | 3.76 | 1.14 | $10 | $8 | 190 | –0 |

#### $7 Lyon, Brandon ▲△△

| | IP | W | Sv | K | ERA | WHIP | $1L | $2L | Pts | RAA |
|---|---|---|---|---|---|---|---|---|---|---|
| '10 | 78 | 6 | 20 | 54 | 3.12 | 1.27 | $8 | $2 | 220 | +7 |
| Proj | 80 | 5 | 10 | 54 | 3.60 | 1.30 | $11 | $7 | 210 | +2 |

#### $6 Gregg, Kevin ▲▲▲

| | IP | W | Sv | K | ERA | WHIP | $1L | $2L | Pts | RAA |
|---|---|---|---|---|---|---|---|---|---|---|
| '10 | 59 | 2 | 37 | 58 | 3.51 | 1.39 | $10 | $2 | 260 | +3 |
| Proj | 60 | 2 | 14 | 55 | 4.27 | 1.41 | $10 | $6 | 230 | –4 |

#### $5 Gregerson, Luke

| | IP | W | Sv | K | ERA | WHIP | $1L | $2L | Pts | RAA |
|---|---|---|---|---|---|---|---|---|---|---|
| '10 | 78 | 4 | 2 | 89 | 3.22 | 0.83 | $8 | $5 | 160 | +5 |
| Proj | 60 | 3 | 3 | 68 | 3.24 | 1.07 | $6 | $5 | 110 | +4 |

#### $5 Romo, Sergio

| | IP | W | Sv | K | ERA | WHIP | $1L | $2L | Pts | RAA |
|---|---|---|---|---|---|---|---|---|---|---|
| '10 | 62 | 5 | 0 | 70 | 2.18 | 0.97 | $7 | $4 | 140 | +12 |
| Proj | 60 | 4 | 3 | 66 | 3.06 | 1.15 | $6 | $5 | 110 | +5 |

#### $4 Adams, Mike

| | IP | W | Sv | K | ERA | WHIP | $1L | $2L | Pts | RAA |
|---|---|---|---|---|---|---|---|---|---|---|
| '10 | 67 | 4 | 0 | 73 | 1.76 | 1.07 | $7 | $4 | 130 | +16 |
| Proj | 40 | 2 | 2 | 42 | 2.57 | 1.10 | $4 | $4 | 80 | +6 |

#### $4 Bard, Daniel

| | IP | W | Sv | K | ERA | WHIP | $1L | $2L | Pts | RAA |
|---|---|---|---|---|---|---|---|---|---|---|
| '10 | 75 | 1 | 3 | 76 | 1.93 | 1.00 | $9 | $5 | 120 | +16 |
| Proj | 80 | 3 | 6 | 88 | 3.27 | 1.30 | $7 | $4 | 140 | +4 |

#### $3 Gutierrez, Juan △△

| | IP | W | Sv | K | ERA | WHIP | $1L | $2L | Pts | RAA |
|---|---|---|---|---|---|---|---|---|---|---|
| '10 | 57 | 0 | 15 | 47 | 5.08 | 1.38 | -$2 | -$11 | 110 | –8 |
| Proj | 60 | 2 | 6 | 48 | 4.78 | 1.44 | $7 | $3 | 210 | –7 |

#### $2 Thatcher, Joe

| | IP | W | Sv | K | ERA | WHIP | $1L | $2L | Pts | RAA |
|---|---|---|---|---|---|---|---|---|---|---|
| '10 | 35 | 1 | 0 | 45 | 1.29 | 0.86 | $2 | $0 | 70 | +11 |
| Proj | 40 | 2 | 0 | 43 | 2.89 | 1.12 | $3 | $2 | 60 | +4 |

#### $2 Motte, Jason

| | IP | W | Sv | K | ERA | WHIP | $1L | $2L | Pts | RAA |
|---|---|---|---|---|---|---|---|---|---|---|
| '10 | 52 | 4 | 2 | 54 | 2.24 | 1.13 | $4 | $0 | 110 | +11 |
| Proj | 60 | 3 | 4 | 62 | 3.63 | 1.27 | $4 | $2 | 110 | +1 |

#### $1 Kintzler, Brandon

| | IP | W | Sv | K | ERA | WHIP | $1L | $2L | Pts | RAA |
|---|---|---|---|---|---|---|---|---|---|---|
| '10 | 7 | 0 | 0 | 9 | 7.36 | 1.91 | -$7 | -$13 | 0 | –3 |
| Proj | 40 | 3 | 6 | 29 | 3.07 | 1.14 | $3 | $1 | 60 | +3 |

#### $17 Bell, Heath ▲▲

| | IP | W | Sv | K | ERA | WHIP | $1L | $2L | Pts | RAA |
|---|---|---|---|---|---|---|---|---|---|---|
| '10 | 70 | 6 | 47 | 86 | 1.93 | 1.20 | $19 | $18 | 390 | +15 |
| Proj | 60 | 4 | 29 | 62 | 2.67 | 1.15 | $18 | $17 | 300 | +7 |

#### $16 Wilson, Brian ▲▲▲

| | IP | W | Sv | K | ERA | WHIP | $1L | $2L | Pts | RAA |
|---|---|---|---|---|---|---|---|---|---|---|
| '10 | 75 | 3 | 48 | 93 | 1.81 | 1.18 | $19 | $18 | 380 | +18 |
| Proj | 60 | 2 | 35 | 65 | 2.92 | 1.28 | $17 | $16 | 310 | +6 |

#### $13 Kimbrel, Craig

| | IP | W | Sv | K | ERA | WHIP | $1L | $2L | Pts | RAA |
|---|---|---|---|---|---|---|---|---|---|---|
| '10 | 21 | 4 | 1 | 40 | 0.44 | 1.21 | $1 | -$3 | 90 | +7 |
| Proj | 60 | 6 | 1 | 91 | 2.83 | 1.45 | $15 | $13 | 300 | +6 |

#### $12 Jansen, Kenley △

| | IP | W | Sv | K | ERA | WHIP | $1L | $2L | Pts | RAA |
|---|---|---|---|---|---|---|---|---|---|---|
| '10 | 27 | 1 | 4 | 41 | 0.67 | 1.00 | $2 | -$1 | 80 | +10 |
| Proj | 60 | 3 | 6 | 85 | 1.56 | 1.18 | $11 | $12 | 170 | +16 |

#### $10 Perez, Chris ▲△

| | IP | W | Sv | K | ERA | WHIP | $1L | $2L | Pts | RAA |
|---|---|---|---|---|---|---|---|---|---|---|
| '10 | 63 | 2 | 23 | 61 | 1.71 | 1.08 | $12 | $9 | 210 | +13 |
| Proj | 60 | 2 | 12 | 63 | 3.38 | 1.31 | $13 | $10 | 250 | +2 |

#### $9 Axford, John ▲

| | IP | W | Sv | K | ERA | WHIP | $1L | $2L | Pts | RAA |
|---|---|---|---|---|---|---|---|---|---|---|
| '10 | 58 | 8 | 24 | 76 | 2.48 | 1.19 | $12 | $9 | 280 | +9 |
| Proj | 60 | 5 | 11 | 72 | 3.93 | 1.54 | $13 | $9 | 310 | –1 |

#### $9 Cordero, Francisco ▲▲▲

| | IP | W | Sv | K | ERA | WHIP | $1L | $2L | Pts | RAA |
|---|---|---|---|---|---|---|---|---|---|---|
| '10 | 73 | 6 | 40 | 59 | 3.84 | 1.43 | $9 | $3 | 310 | +1 |
| Proj | 80 | 5 | 40 | 70 | 3.77 | 1.40 | $12 | $9 | 270 | +0 |

#### $8 Lidge, Brad ▲▲▲

| | IP | W | Sv | K | ERA | WHIP | $1L | $2L | Pts | RAA |
|---|---|---|---|---|---|---|---|---|---|---|
| '10 | 46 | 1 | 27 | 52 | 2.96 | 1.23 | $6 | $2 | 200 | +5 |
| Proj | 60 | 2 | 33 | 63 | 4.24 | 1.36 | $11 | $8 | 260 | –4 |

#### $8 Rodriguez, Francisco ▲▲▲

| | IP | W | Sv | K | ERA | WHIP | $1L | $2L | Pts | RAA |
|---|---|---|---|---|---|---|---|---|---|---|
| '10 | 57 | 4 | 25 | 67 | 2.20 | 1.15 | $10 | $8 | 240 | +12 |
| Proj | 60 | 3 | 28 | 66 | 3.14 | 1.27 | $10 | $8 | 200 | +5 |

#### $7 Aardsma, David ▲▲

| | IP | W | Sv | K | ERA | WHIP | $1L | $2L | Pts | RAA |
|---|---|---|---|---|---|---|---|---|---|---|
| '10 | 50 | 0 | 31 | 49 | 3.44 | 1.17 | $8 | $2 | 210 | +3 |
| Proj | 70 | 2 | 41 | 70 | 3.80 | 1.37 | $11 | $7 | 240 | +0 |

#### $6 Madson, Ryan △△

| | IP | W | Sv | K | ERA | WHIP | $1L | $2L | Pts | RAA |
|---|---|---|---|---|---|---|---|---|---|---|
| '10 | 53 | 6 | 5 | 64 | 2.55 | 1.04 | $6 | $3 | 160 | +8 |
| Proj | 60 | 4 | 4 | 53 | 3.49 | 1.17 | $7 | $6 | 150 | +2 |

#### $5 Meek, Evan △

| | IP | W | Sv | K | ERA | WHIP | $1L | $2L | Pts | RAA |
|---|---|---|---|---|---|---|---|---|---|---|
| '10 | 80 | 5 | 4 | 70 | 2.14 | 1.05 | $9 | $7 | 160 | +11 |
| Proj | 80 | 4 | 5 | 71 | 3.36 | 1.34 | $8 | $5 | 170 | +2 |

#### $4 O'Day, Darren

| | IP | W | Sv | K | ERA | WHIP | $1L | $2L | Pts | RAA |
|---|---|---|---|---|---|---|---|---|---|---|
| '10 | 62 | 6 | 0 | 45 | 2.03 | 0.89 | $9 | $5 | 130 | +13 |
| Proj | 60 | 5 | 0 | 47 | 2.97 | 1.15 | $6 | $4 | 100 | +6 |

#### $4 Rhodes, Arthur

| | IP | W | Sv | K | ERA | WHIP | $1L | $2L | Pts | RAA |
|---|---|---|---|---|---|---|---|---|---|---|
| '10 | 55 | 4 | 0 | 50 | 2.29 | 1.02 | $4 | $1 | 100 | +11 |
| Proj | 60 | 4 | 3 | 55 | 2.93 | 1.20 | $5 | $4 | 100 | +6 |

#### $4 Benoit, Joaquin

| | IP | W | Sv | K | ERA | WHIP | $1L | $2L | Pts | RAA |
|---|---|---|---|---|---|---|---|---|---|---|
| '10 | 60 | 1 | 1 | 75 | 1.34 | 0.68 | $11 | $9 | 120 | +17 |
| Proj | 60 | 2 | 0 | 54 | 3.38 | 1.10 | $6 | $4 | 90 | +2 |

#### $2 Breslow, Craig △

| | IP | W | Sv | K | ERA | WHIP | $1L | $2L | Pts | RAA |
|---|---|---|---|---|---|---|---|---|---|---|
| '10 | 75 | 4 | 5 | 71 | 3.01 | 1.10 | $7 | $1 | 140 | +8 |
| Proj | 75 | 4 | 1 | 65 | 3.61 | 1.24 | $6 | $2 | 110 | +2 |

#### $2 Betancourt, Rafael △

| | IP | W | Sv | K | ERA | WHIP | $1L | $2L | Pts | RAA |
|---|---|---|---|---|---|---|---|---|---|---|
| '10 | 62 | 5 | 1 | 89 | 3.61 | 0.96 | $5 | $1 | 150 | +3 |
| Proj | 60 | 4 | 3 | 67 | 3.91 | 1.16 | $4 | $2 | 110 | –0 |

#### $2 Tejeda, Robinson

| | IP | W | Sv | K | ERA | WHIP | $1L | $2L | Pts | RAA |
|---|---|---|---|---|---|---|---|---|---|---|
| '10 | 61 | 3 | 0 | 56 | 3.54 | 1.33 | $1 | -$8 | 80 | –1 |
| Proj | 60 | 3 | 0 | 57 | 4.35 | 1.55 | $7 | $2 | 200 | –5 |

#### $1 McClellan, Kyle △

| | IP | W | Sv | K | ERA | WHIP | $1L | $2L | Pts | RAA |
|---|---|---|---|---|---|---|---|---|---|---|
| '10 | 75 | 1 | 2 | 60 | 2.27 | 1.08 | $5 | $2 | 100 | +14 |
| Proj | 70 | 3 | 1 | 53 | 3.35 | 1.26 | $3 | $1 | 80 | +4 |

**$1 Rodney, Fernando** ▲△△

| | IP | W | Sv | K | ERA | WHIP | $1L | $2L | Pts | RAA |
|---|---|---|---|---|---|---|---|---|---|---|
| '10 | 68 | 4 | 14 | 53 | 4.24 | 1.54 | $2 | -$9 | 150 | –2 |
| Proj | 60 | 3 | 7 | 51 | 4.55 | 1.57 | $6 | $1 | 200 | –5 |

**$0 Duensing, Brian**

| | IP | W | Sv | K | ERA | WHIP | $1L | $2L | Pts | RAA |
|---|---|---|---|---|---|---|---|---|---|---|
| '10 | 131 | 10 | 0 | 78 | 2.62 | 1.20 | $13 | $7 | 190 | +17 |
| Proj | 160 | 11 | 0 | 98 | 3.88 | 1.34 | $9 | $0 | 190 | –3 |

**$0 Figueroa, Nelson**

| | IP | W | Sv | K | ERA | WHIP | $1L | $2L | Pts | RAA |
|---|---|---|---|---|---|---|---|---|---|---|
| '10 | 93 | 7 | 1 | 73 | 3.29 | 1.27 | $4 | -$2 | 150 | +4 |
| Proj | 100 | 7 | 0 | 79 | 3.86 | 1.32 | $5 | $0 | 140 | –2 |

**$0 Lueke, Josh**

| | IP | W | Sv | K | ERA | WHIP | $1L | $2L | Pts | RAA |
|---|---|---|---|---|---|---|---|---|---|---|
| '10 | — | — | — | — | — | — | — | — | — | — |
| Proj | 40 | 3 | 9 | 39 | 3.41 | 1.29 | $2 | $0 | 70 | +1 |

**$0 Chamberlain, Joba**

| | IP | W | Sv | K | ERA | WHIP | $1L | $2L | Pts | RAA |
|---|---|---|---|---|---|---|---|---|---|---|
| '10 | 72 | 3 | 3 | 77 | 4.40 | 1.30 | $1 | -$9 | 110 | –5 |
| Proj | 60 | 4 | 1 | 57 | 4.29 | 1.38 | $4 | $0 | 130 | –4 |

**$0 Oliver, Darren**

| | IP | W | Sv | K | ERA | WHIP | $1L | $2L | Pts | RAA |
|---|---|---|---|---|---|---|---|---|---|---|
| '10 | 62 | 1 | 1 | 65 | 2.48 | 1.10 | $5 | -$1 | 90 | +8 |
| Proj | 60 | 3 | 3 | 50 | 3.57 | 1.28 | $3 | $0 | 70 | +1 |

**-$1 Sanches, Brian**

| | IP | W | Sv | K | ERA | WHIP | $1L | $2L | Pts | RAA |
|---|---|---|---|---|---|---|---|---|---|---|
| '10 | 64 | 2 | 0 | 54 | 2.26 | 1.10 | $3 | $0 | 90 | +9 |
| Proj | 60 | 2 | 3 | 52 | 3.56 | 1.29 | $2 | -$1 | 70 | +0 |

**-$1 Frasor, Jason** △△

| | IP | W | Sv | K | ERA | WHIP | $1L | $2L | Pts | RAA |
|---|---|---|---|---|---|---|---|---|---|---|
| '10 | 64 | 3 | 4 | 65 | 3.68 | 1.38 | $2 | -$7 | 110 | –1 |
| Proj | 60 | 3 | 21 | 57 | 3.67 | 1.33 | $3 | -$1 | 80 | –0 |

**-$1 Dessens, Elmer**

| | IP | W | Sv | K | ERA | WHIP | $1L | $2L | Pts | RAA |
|---|---|---|---|---|---|---|---|---|---|---|
| '10 | 47 | 4 | 0 | 16 | 2.30 | 1.21 | $1 | -$4 | 60 | +7 |
| Proj | 40 | 3 | 0 | 20 | 3.43 | 1.28 | $1 | -$1 | 50 | +1 |

**-$1 Wheeler, Dan** △

| | IP | W | Sv | K | ERA | WHIP | $1L | $2L | Pts | RAA |
|---|---|---|---|---|---|---|---|---|---|---|
| '10 | 48 | 2 | 3 | 46 | 3.35 | 1.08 | $3 | -$4 | 90 | +2 |
| Proj | 50 | 2 | 3 | 42 | 4.23 | 1.18 | $2 | -$1 | 60 | –3 |

**-$2 Aceves, Alfredo**

| | IP | W | Sv | K | ERA | WHIP | $1L | $2L | Pts | RAA |
|---|---|---|---|---|---|---|---|---|---|---|
| '10 | 12 | 3 | 1 | 2 | 3.00 | 1.17 | -$1 | -$8 | 40 | +0 |
| Proj | 40 | 3 | 2 | 29 | 3.91 | 1.29 | $1 | -$2 | 60 | –1 |

**-$2 Lopez, Javier**

| | IP | W | Sv | K | ERA | WHIP | $1L | $2L | Pts | RAA |
|---|---|---|---|---|---|---|---|---|---|---|
| '10 | 58 | 4 | 0 | 38 | 2.34 | 1.21 | $2 | -$2 | 90 | +9 |
| Proj | 60 | 3 | 0 | 38 | 3.54 | 1.37 | $1 | -$2 | 60 | +1 |

**-$2 Dotel, Octavio** ▲

| | IP | W | Sv | K | ERA | WHIP | $1L | $2L | Pts | RAA |
|---|---|---|---|---|---|---|---|---|---|---|
| '10 | 64 | 3 | 22 | 75 | 4.08 | 1.31 | $5 | -$2 | 210 | –3 |
| Proj | 40 | 2 | 19 | 49 | 3.96 | 1.33 | $0 | -$2 | 60 | –1 |

**-$2 Crain, Jesse**

| | IP | W | Sv | K | ERA | WHIP | $1L | $2L | Pts | RAA |
|---|---|---|---|---|---|---|---|---|---|---|
| '10 | 68 | 1 | 1 | 62 | 3.04 | 1.18 | $3 | -$4 | 80 | +4 |
| Proj | 60 | 2 | 0 | 49 | 3.81 | 1.34 | $2 | -$2 | 70 | –1 |

**-$2 Neshek, Pat**

| | IP | W | Sv | K | ERA | WHIP | $1L | $2L | Pts | RAA |
|---|---|---|---|---|---|---|---|---|---|---|
| '10 | 9 | 0 | 0 | 9 | 5.00 | 1.67 | -$4 | -$12 | 10 | –1 |
| Proj | 40 | 2 | 0 | 44 | 4.14 | 1.30 | $1 | -$2 | 60 | –2 |

**-$2 Hoffman, Trevor** ▲▲△

| | IP | W | Sv | K | ERA | WHIP | $1L | $2L | Pts | RAA |
|---|---|---|---|---|---|---|---|---|---|---|
| '10 | 47 | 2 | 10 | 30 | 5.89 | 1.44 | -$4 | -$14 | 80 | –10 |
| Proj | 40 | 2 | 19 | 30 | 4.46 | 1.30 | $0 | -$2 | 60 | –3 |

**-$3 Rauch, Jon** ▲△

| | IP | W | Sv | K | ERA | WHIP | $1L | $2L | Pts | RAA |
|---|---|---|---|---|---|---|---|---|---|---|
| '10 | 58 | 3 | 21 | 46 | 3.12 | 1.30 | $7 | $0 | 180 | +6 |
| Proj | 40 | 2 | 6 | 30 | 4.01 | 1.31 | $0 | -$3 | 50 | –1 |

**-$3 Blevins, Jerry**

| | IP | W | Sv | K | ERA | WHIP | $1L | $2L | Pts | RAA |
|---|---|---|---|---|---|---|---|---|---|---|
| '10 | 49 | 2 | 1 | 46 | 3.70 | 1.48 | -$1 | -$10 | 60 | +2 |
| Proj | 50 | 2 | 0 | 48 | 3.98 | 1.37 | $1 | -$3 | 60 | –1 |

**-$3 Farnsworth, Kyle**

| | IP | W | Sv | K | ERA | WHIP | $1L | $2L | Pts | RAA |
|---|---|---|---|---|---|---|---|---|---|---|
| '10 | 65 | 3 | 0 | 65 | 3.34 | 1.14 | $2 | -$4 | 90 | +4 |
| Proj | 60 | 2 | 0 | 57 | 4.25 | 1.35 | $0 | -$3 | 70 | –3 |

**-$3 Atchison, Scott**

| | IP | W | Sv | K | ERA | WHIP | $1L | $2L | Pts | RAA |
|---|---|---|---|---|---|---|---|---|---|---|
| '10 | 60 | 2 | 0 | 41 | 4.50 | 1.28 | -$1 | -$11 | 50 | –10 |
| Proj | 40 | 1 | 0 | 29 | 4.28 | 1.28 | $0 | -$3 | 40 | –5 |

**-$3 Sherrill, George** ▲▲

| | IP | W | Sv | K | ERA | WHIP | $1L | $2L | Pts | RAA |
|---|---|---|---|---|---|---|---|---|---|---|
| '10 | 36 | 2 | 0 | 25 | 6.69 | 1.93 | -$10 | -$21 | 20 | –12 |
| Proj | 40 | 3 | 2 | 36 | 4.08 | 1.44 | -$1 | -$3 | 50 | –1 |

**-$4 Choate, Randy** △

| | IP | W | Sv | K | ERA | WHIP | $1L | $2L | Pts | RAA |
|---|---|---|---|---|---|---|---|---|---|---|
| '10 | 45 | 4 | 0 | 40 | 4.23 | 1.30 | $0 | -$9 | 70 | –3 |
| Proj | 40 | 3 | 0 | 33 | 4.38 | 1.38 | $0 | -$4 | 50 | –3 |

**-$4 Burton, Jared**

| | IP | W | Sv | K | ERA | WHIP | $1L | $2L | Pts | RAA |
|---|---|---|---|---|---|---|---|---|---|---|
| '10 | 3 | 0 | 0 | 1 | 0.00 | 0.00 | -$4 | -$9 | 0 | +2 |
| Proj | 40 | 2 | 2 | 30 | 4.14 | 1.37 | -$1 | -$4 | 40 | –2 |

**-$4 Hensley, Clay** △

| | IP | W | Sv | K | ERA | WHIP | $1L | $2L | Pts | RAA |
|---|---|---|---|---|---|---|---|---|---|---|
| '10 | 75 | 3 | 7 | 77 | 2.16 | 1.11 | $8 | $5 | 160 | +14 |
| Proj | 80 | 4 | 2 | 61 | 4.26 | 1.43 | $1 | -$4 | 110 | –5 |

**$1 Takahashi, Hisanori** △

| | IP | W | Sv | K | ERA | WHIP | $1L | $2L | Pts | RAA |
|---|---|---|---|---|---|---|---|---|---|---|
| '10 | 122 | 10 | 8 | 114 | 3.61 | 1.30 | $8 | $0 | 250 | +4 |
| Proj | 60 | 4 | 2 | 46 | 4.43 | 1.38 | $4 | $1 | 150 | –4 |

**$0 Wuertz, Mike** △△

| | IP | W | Sv | K | ERA | WHIP | $1L | $2L | Pts | RAA |
|---|---|---|---|---|---|---|---|---|---|---|
| '10 | 40 | 2 | 6 | 40 | 4.31 | 1.41 | $0 | -$9 | 80 | –3 |
| Proj | 50 | 3 | 4 | 51 | 3.67 | 1.27 | $3 | $0 | 90 | +0 |

**$0 Francisco, Frank** ▲△

| | IP | W | Sv | K | ERA | WHIP | $1L | $2L | Pts | RAA |
|---|---|---|---|---|---|---|---|---|---|---|
| '10 | 53 | 6 | 2 | 60 | 3.76 | 1.27 | $3 | -$5 | 130 | +1 |
| Proj | 60 | 4 | 26 | 66 | 3.80 | 1.30 | $4 | $0 | 100 | –0 |

**$0 Moylan, Peter**

| | IP | W | Sv | K | ERA | WHIP | $1L | $2L | Pts | RAA |
|---|---|---|---|---|---|---|---|---|---|---|
| '10 | 64 | 6 | 1 | 52 | 2.97 | 1.41 | $1 | -$5 | 110 | +5 |
| Proj | 70 | 5 | 4 | 53 | 3.39 | 1.39 | $3 | $0 | 100 | +2 |

**$0 Venters, Jonny**

| | IP | W | Sv | K | ERA | WHIP | $1L | $2L | Pts | RAA |
|---|---|---|---|---|---|---|---|---|---|---|
| '10 | 83 | 4 | 1 | 93 | 1.95 | 1.20 | $7 | $4 | 150 | +7 |
| Proj | 70 | 3 | 0 | 64 | 3.94 | 1.50 | $4 | $0 | 150 | –4 |

**-$1 O'Flaherty, Eric**

| | IP | W | Sv | K | ERA | WHIP | $1L | $2L | Pts | RAA |
|---|---|---|---|---|---|---|---|---|---|---|
| '10 | 44 | 3 | 0 | 36 | 2.45 | 1.25 | $0 | -$5 | 70 | +6 |
| Proj | 60 | 3 | 0 | 44 | 3.52 | 1.31 | $2 | -$1 | 80 | +1 |

**-$1 Belisle, Matt**

| | IP | W | Sv | K | ERA | WHIP | $1L | $2L | Pts | RAA |
|---|---|---|---|---|---|---|---|---|---|---|
| '10 | 92 | 7 | 1 | 91 | 2.93 | 1.09 | $8 | $4 | 180 | +7 |
| Proj | 60 | 3 | 0 | 46 | 4.20 | 1.26 | $2 | -$1 | 90 | –4 |

**-$1 Pestano, Vinnie**

| | IP | W | Sv | K | ERA | WHIP | $1L | $2L | Pts | RAA |
|---|---|---|---|---|---|---|---|---|---|---|
| '10 | 5 | 0 | 1 | 8 | 3.60 | 1.80 | -$3 | -$11 | 10 | +0 |
| Proj | 40 | 2 | 6 | 39 | 3.44 | 1.33 | $1 | -$1 | 60 | +1 |

**-$1 Robertson, David**

| | IP | W | Sv | K | ERA | WHIP | $1L | $2L | Pts | RAA |
|---|---|---|---|---|---|---|---|---|---|---|
| '10 | 61 | 4 | 1 | 71 | 3.82 | 1.50 | $0 | -$9 | 110 | +2 |
| Proj | 60 | 4 | 0 | 72 | 3.69 | 1.44 | $3 | -$1 | 100 | +1 |

**-$1 Ziegler, Brad** △△

| | IP | W | Sv | K | ERA | WHIP | $1L | $2L | Pts | RAA |
|---|---|---|---|---|---|---|---|---|---|---|
| '10 | 61 | 3 | 0 | 41 | 3.26 | 1.35 | $1 | -$8 | 70 | +3 |
| Proj | 50 | 3 | 2 | 33 | 3.46 | 1.34 | $2 | -$1 | 60 | +2 |

**-$2 Clippard, Tyler**

| | IP | W | Sv | K | ERA | WHIP | $1L | $2L | Pts | RAA |
|---|---|---|---|---|---|---|---|---|---|---|
| '10 | 91 | 11 | 1 | 112 | 3.07 | 1.21 | $9 | $4 | 230 | +8 |
| Proj | 60 | 4 | 1 | 63 | 4.07 | 1.37 | $2 | -$2 | 100 | –2 |

**-$2 Ramirez, Ramon**

| | IP | W | Sv | K | ERA | WHIP | $1L | $2L | Pts | RAA |
|---|---|---|---|---|---|---|---|---|---|---|
| '10 | 69 | 1 | 3 | 46 | 2.99 | 1.14 | $2 | -$3 | 80 | +7 |
| Proj | 60 | 2 | 1 | 44 | 3.66 | 1.35 | $1 | -$2 | 60 | +1 |

**-$2 Lindstrom, Matt** ▲△△

| | IP | W | Sv | K | ERA | WHIP | $1L | $2L | Pts | RAA |
|---|---|---|---|---|---|---|---|---|---|---|
| '10 | 53 | 2 | 23 | 43 | 4.39 | 1.65 | $0 | -$8 | 160 | –2 |
| Proj | 40 | 1 | 19 | 31 | 4.41 | 1.49 | $1 | -$2 | 90 | –3 |

**-$2 Miller, Trever**

| | IP | W | Sv | K | ERA | WHIP | $1L | $2L | Pts | RAA |
|---|---|---|---|---|---|---|---|---|---|---|
| '10 | 36 | 0 | 0 | 22 | 4.00 | 1.28 | -$4 | -$11 | 20 | –1 |
| Proj | 40 | 2 | 3 | 34 | 3.90 | 1.29 | $0 | -$2 | 50 | –1 |

**-$2 Chapman, Aroldis**

| | IP | W | Sv | K | ERA | WHIP | $1L | $2L | Pts | RAA |
|---|---|---|---|---|---|---|---|---|---|---|
| '10 | 13 | 2 | 0 | 19 | 2.03 | 1.05 | -$2 | -$7 | 40 | +2 |
| Proj | 100 | 6 | 0 | 95 | 4.54 | 1.36 | $3 | -$2 | 160 | –10 |

**-$3 Resop, Chris**

| | IP | W | Sv | K | ERA | WHIP | $1L | $2L | Pts | RAA |
|---|---|---|---|---|---|---|---|---|---|---|
| '10 | 21 | 0 | 0 | 26 | 3.86 | 1.33 | -$4 | -$10 | 20 | +0 |
| Proj | 60 | 4 | 7 | 54 | 3.91 | 1.42 | $1 | -$3 | 80 | –2 |

**-$3 Slaten, Doug**

| | IP | W | Sv | K | ERA | WHIP | $1L | $2L | Pts | RAA |
|---|---|---|---|---|---|---|---|---|---|---|
| '10 | 41 | 4 | 0 | 36 | 3.10 | 1.30 | -$1 | -$6 | 80 | +0 |
| Proj | 40 | 2 | 0 | 33 | 3.92 | 1.37 | $0 | -$3 | 50 | –2 |

**-$3 Coffey, Todd**

| | IP | W | Sv | K | ERA | WHIP | $1L | $2L | Pts | RAA |
|---|---|---|---|---|---|---|---|---|---|---|
| '10 | 62 | 2 | 0 | 56 | 4.76 | 1.41 | -$5 | -$14 | 60 | –12 |
| Proj | 60 | 3 | 2 | 46 | 4.22 | 1.30 | $1 | -$3 | 70 | –5 |

**-$3 Kohn, Michael**

| | IP | W | Sv | K | ERA | WHIP | $1L | $2L | Pts | RAA |
|---|---|---|---|---|---|---|---|---|---|---|
| '10 | 21 | 2 | 1 | 20 | 2.11 | 1.55 | -$1 | -$8 | 40 | +5 |
| Proj | 40 | 3 | 1 | 45 | 3.51 | 1.63 | $0 | -$3 | 70 | +1 |

**-$3 Mijares, Jose**

| | IP | W | Sv | K | ERA | WHIP | $1L | $2L | Pts | RAA |
|---|---|---|---|---|---|---|---|---|---|---|
| '10 | 33 | 1 | 0 | 28 | 3.31 | 1.32 | -$1 | -$9 | 40 | +1 |
| Proj | 60 | 3 | 4 | 56 | 3.97 | 1.43 | $1 | -$3 | 80 | –2 |

**-$4 Walker, Tyler**

| | IP | W | Sv | K | ERA | WHIP | $1L | $2L | Pts | RAA |
|---|---|---|---|---|---|---|---|---|---|---|
| '10 | 35 | 1 | 0 | 30 | 3.57 | 1.22 | -$3 | -$8 | 40 | –0 |
| Proj | 40 | 1 | 0 | 33 | 4.23 | 1.32 | -$1 | -$4 | 40 | –3 |

**-$4 Walden, Jordan**

| | IP | W | Sv | K | ERA | WHIP | $1L | $2L | Pts | RAA |
|---|---|---|---|---|---|---|---|---|---|---|
| '10 | 15 | 0 | 1 | 23 | 2.35 | 1.30 | -$2 | -$8 | 30 | +3 |
| Proj | 40 | 2 | 0 | 44 | 5.06 | 1.67 | $1 | -$4 | 110 | –6 |

**-$4 Corpas, Manny** △△

| | IP | W | Sv | K | ERA | WHIP | $1L | $2L | Pts | RAA |
|---|---|---|---|---|---|---|---|---|---|---|
| '10 | 62 | 3 | 10 | 47 | 4.62 | 1.41 | -$2 | -$10 | 110 | –5 |
| Proj | 20 | 1 | 1 | 13 | 4.34 | 1.33 | -$2 | -$4 | 20 | –1 |

**-$4 Frieri, Ernesto**

| | IP | W | Sv | K | ERA | WHIP | $1L | $2L | Pts | RAA |
|---|---|---|---|---|---|---|---|---|---|---|
| '10 | 32 | 1 | 0 | 41 | 1.71 | 1.11 | $0 | -$4 | 60 | +7 |
| Proj | 60 | 3 | 0 | 69 | 4.07 | 1.48 | $0 | -$4 | 90 | –3 |

**$1 Mujica, Edward**

| | IP | W | Sv | K | ERA | WHIP | $1L | $2L | Pts | RAA |
|---|---|---|---|---|---|---|---|---|---|---|
| '10 | 70 | 2 | 0 | 72 | 3.62 | 0.93 | $3 | -$1 | 100 | +2 |
| Proj | 60 | 2 | 0 | 51 | 4.04 | 1.08 | $3 | $1 | 70 | –2 |

**$0 Stauffer, Tim**

| | IP | W | Sv | K | ERA | WHIP | $1L | $2L | Pts | RAA |
|---|---|---|---|---|---|---|---|---|---|---|
| '10 | 83 | 6 | 0 | 61 | 1.85 | 1.08 | $9 | $7 | 140 | +19 |
| Proj | 60 | 3 | 0 | 43 | 3.52 | 1.25 | $3 | $0 | 80 | +2 |

**$0 Masset, Nick**

| | IP | W | Sv | K | ERA | WHIP | $1L | $2L | Pts | RAA |
|---|---|---|---|---|---|---|---|---|---|---|
| '10 | 77 | 4 | 2 | 85 | 3.40 | 1.27 | $2 | -$4 | 130 | +4 |
| Proj | 80 | 4 | 1 | 69 | 3.97 | 1.31 | $4 | $0 | 120 | –2 |

**$0 Marshall, Sean**

| | IP | W | Sv | K | ERA | WHIP | $1L | $2L | Pts | RAA |
|---|---|---|---|---|---|---|---|---|---|---|
| '10 | 75 | 7 | 1 | 90 | 2.65 | 1.11 | $7 | $4 | 180 | +9 |
| Proj | 80 | 5 | 0 | 69 | 4.04 | 1.31 | $4 | $0 | 120 | –3 |

**$0 Strop, Pedro**

| | IP | W | Sv | K | ERA | WHIP | $1L | $2L | Pts | RAA |
|---|---|---|---|---|---|---|---|---|---|---|
| '10 | 11 | 0 | 0 | 11 | 10.13 | 2.63 | -$7 | -$17 | 0 | –7 |
| Proj | 40 | 2 | 4 | 39 | 3.18 | 1.31 | $2 | $0 | 60 | +2 |

**-$1 Peralta, Joel**

| | IP | W | Sv | K | ERA | WHIP | $1L | $2L | Pts | RAA |
|---|---|---|---|---|---|---|---|---|---|---|
| '10 | 49 | 1 | 0 | 49 | 2.02 | 0.80 | $4 | $2 | 80 | +10 |
| Proj | 60 | 2 | 0 | 51 | 4.01 | 1.17 | $2 | -$1 | 70 | –2 |

**-$1 Camp, Shawn**

| | IP | W | Sv | K | ERA | WHIP | $1L | $2L | Pts | RAA |
|---|---|---|---|---|---|---|---|---|---|---|
| '10 | 72 | 4 | 2 | 46 | 2.99 | 1.23 | $4 | -$3 | 100 | +7 |
| Proj | 80 | 4 | 0 | 53 | 3.82 | 1.29 | $4 | -$1 | 90 | –1 |

**-$1 Fuentes, Brian** ▲▲▲

| | IP | W | Sv | K | ERA | WHIP | $1L | $2L | Pts | RAA |
|---|---|---|---|---|---|---|---|---|---|---|
| '10 | 48 | 4 | 24 | 47 | 2.81 | 1.06 | $10 | $5 | 210 | +5 |
| Proj | 40 | 2 | 23 | 37 | 3.60 | 1.29 | $1 | -$1 | 60 | +0 |

**-$1 Burnett, Sean**

| | IP | W | Sv | K | ERA | WHIP | $1L | $2L | Pts | RAA |
|---|---|---|---|---|---|---|---|---|---|---|
| '10 | 63 | 1 | 3 | 62 | 2.14 | 1.14 | $4 | $0 | 100 | +11 |
| Proj | 60 | 2 | 1 | 47 | 3.86 | 1.38 | $2 | -$1 | 90 | –1 |

**-$2 Casilla, Santiago**

| | IP | W | Sv | K | ERA | WHIP | $1L | $2L | Pts | RAA |
|---|---|---|---|---|---|---|---|---|---|---|
| '10 | 55 | 7 | 2 | 56 | 1.95 | 1.19 | $5 | $2 | 150 | +11 |
| Proj | 60 | 5 | 1 | 52 | 3.83 | 1.41 | $2 | -$2 | 90 | –1 |

**-$2 Bray, Bill**

| | IP | W | Sv | K | ERA | WHIP | $1L | $2L | Pts | RAA |
|---|---|---|---|---|---|---|---|---|---|---|
| '10 | 28 | 0 | 0 | 30 | 4.13 | 1.09 | -$3 | -$9 | 30 | –0 |
| Proj | 40 | 2 | 0 | 41 | 4.01 | 1.25 | $0 | -$2 | 50 | –1 |

**-$2 Guerrier, Matt**

| | IP | W | Sv | K | ERA | WHIP | $1L | $2L | Pts | RAA |
|---|---|---|---|---|---|---|---|---|---|---|
| '10 | 71 | 5 | 1 | 42 | 3.17 | 1.10 | $5 | -$2 | 100 | +4 |
| Proj | 80 | 4 | 24 | 49 | 4.08 | 1.27 | $3 | -$2 | 80 | –4 |

**-$2 Wood, Kerry** ▲△△

| | IP | W | Sv | K | ERA | WHIP | $1L | $2L | Pts | RAA |
|---|---|---|---|---|---|---|---|---|---|---|
| '10 | 46 | 3 | 8 | 49 | 3.13 | 1.39 | $3 | -$5 | 120 | +4 |
| Proj | 60 | 3 | 25 | 62 | 3.77 | 1.41 | $2 | -$2 | 80 | –0 |

**-$2 Carrasco, D.J.**

| | IP | W | Sv | K | ERA | WHIP | $1L | $2L | Pts | RAA |
|---|---|---|---|---|---|---|---|---|---|---|
| '10 | 78 | 3 | 0 | 65 | 3.68 | 1.30 | $0 | -$8 | 90 | –4 |
| Proj | 60 | 3 | 0 | 45 | 3.85 | 1.34 | $1 | -$2 | 70 | –2 |

**-$2 Medlen, Kris**

| | IP | W | Sv | K | ERA | WHIP | $1L | $2L | Pts | RAA |
|---|---|---|---|---|---|---|---|---|---|---|
| '10 | 108 | 6 | 0 | 83 | 3.68 | 1.20 | $4 | -$3 | 140 | +0 |
| Proj | 20 | 1 | 0 | 18 | 3.76 | 1.28 | -$1 | -$2 | 30 | –0 |

**-$3 Feliciano, Pedro**

| | IP | W | Sv | K | ERA | WHIP | $1L | $2L | Pts | RAA |
|---|---|---|---|---|---|---|---|---|---|---|
| '10 | 63 | 3 | 0 | 56 | 3.30 | 1.53 | -$2 | -$10 | 80 | +4 |
| Proj | 60 | 3 | 2 | 52 | 3.84 | 1.40 | $1 | -$3 | 70 | –0 |

**-$3 Lopez, Wilton**

| | IP | W | Sv | K | ERA | WHIP | $1L | $2L | Pts | RAA |
|---|---|---|---|---|---|---|---|---|---|---|
| '10 | 67 | 5 | 1 | 50 | 2.96 | 1.06 | $4 | $0 | 110 | +7 |
| Proj | 60 | 3 | 0 | 45 | 4.35 | 1.34 | $1 | -$3 | 80 | –4 |

**-$3 Reyes, Dennys**

| | IP | W | Sv | K | ERA | WHIP | $1L | $2L | Pts | RAA |
|---|---|---|---|---|---|---|---|---|---|---|
| '10 | 38 | 3 | 1 | 25 | 3.55 | 1.45 | -$3 | -$9 | 60 | +2 |
| Proj | 40 | 2 | 0 | 29 | 3.72 | 1.43 | -$1 | -$3 | 50 | +1 |

**-$3 Gonzalez, Mike** △△

| | IP | W | Sv | K | ERA | WHIP | $1L | $2L | Pts | RAA |
|---|---|---|---|---|---|---|---|---|---|---|
| '10 | 25 | 1 | 1 | 31 | 4.01 | 1.30 | -$2 | -$9 | 40 | +0 |
| Proj | 60 | 2 | 27 | 66 | 4.48 | 1.42 | $2 | -$3 | 100 | –5 |

**-$3 Reynolds, Matt**

| | IP | W | Sv | K | ERA | WHIP | $1L | $2L | Pts | RAA |
|---|---|---|---|---|---|---|---|---|---|---|
| '10 | 18 | 1 | 0 | 17 | 2.00 | 0.83 | -$2 | -$6 | 30 | +4 |
| Proj | 40 | 2 | 0 | 42 | 4.27 | 1.41 | -$1 | -$3 | 60 | –2 |

**-$4 Contreras, Jose** △

| | IP | W | Sv | K | ERA | WHIP | $1L | $2L | Pts | RAA |
|---|---|---|---|---|---|---|---|---|---|---|
| '10 | 57 | 6 | 4 | 57 | 3.34 | 1.22 | $3 | -$2 | 140 | +4 |
| Proj | 60 | 4 | 1 | 44 | 4.43 | 1.34 | $0 | -$4 | 70 | –5 |

**-$4 Troncoso, Ramon** △

| | IP | W | Sv | K | ERA | WHIP | $1L | $2L | Pts | RAA |
|---|---|---|---|---|---|---|---|---|---|---|
| '10 | 54 | 2 | 0 | 34 | 4.33 | 1.35 | -$4 | -$12 | 50 | –4 |
| Proj | 40 | 2 | 2 | 27 | 4.09 | 1.38 | -$1 | -$4 | 40 | –2 |

**-$4 Perez, Rafael**

| | IP | W | Sv | K | ERA | WHIP | $1L | $2L | Pts | RAA |
|---|---|---|---|---|---|---|---|---|---|---|
| '10 | 61 | 6 | 0 | 36 | 3.25 | 1.59 | $0 | -$10 | 90 | +4 |
| Proj | 60 | 4 | 0 | 46 | 4.09 | 1.47 | $1 | -$4 | 80 | –2 |

**-$4 Perry, Ryan**

| | IP | W | Sv | K | ERA | WHIP | $1L | $2L | Pts | RAA |
|---|---|---|---|---|---|---|---|---|---|---|
| '10 | 63 | 3 | 2 | 45 | 3.59 | 1.24 | $2 | -$6 | 80 | +2 |
| Proj | 60 | 3 | 1 | 51 | 4.14 | 1.45 | $1 | -$4 | 80 | –2 |

### -$4 Janssen, Casey

| | IP | W | Sv | K | ERA | WHIP | $1L | $2L | Pts | RAA |
|---|---|---|---|---|---|---|---|---|---|---|
| '10 | 69 | 5 | 0 | 63 | 3.67 | 1.38 | $2 | -$8 | 110 | +2 |
| Proj | 60 | 4 | 0 | 44 | 4.26 | 1.40 | $1 | -$4 | 70 | –3 |

### -$4 Smith, Joe

| | IP | W | Sv | K | ERA | WHIP | $1L | $2L | Pts | RAA |
|---|---|---|---|---|---|---|---|---|---|---|
| '10 | 40 | 2 | 0 | 32 | 3.83 | 1.35 | -$1 | -$10 | 50 | 0 |
| Proj | 45 | 2 | 2 | 32 | 4.16 | 1.42 | $0 | -$4 | 40 | –2 |

### -$4 Melancon, Mark

| | IP | W | Sv | K | ERA | WHIP | $1L | $2L | Pts | RAA |
|---|---|---|---|---|---|---|---|---|---|---|
| '10 | 21 | 2 | 0 | 22 | 4.22 | 1.27 | -$4 | -$9 | 40 | –3 |
| Proj | 40 | 2 | 0 | 39 | 4.45 | 1.40 | -$1 | -$4 | 50 | –4 |

### -$4 Beimel, Joe

| | IP | W | Sv | K | ERA | WHIP | $1L | $2L | Pts | RAA |
|---|---|---|---|---|---|---|---|---|---|---|
| '10 | 45 | 1 | 0 | 21 | 3.40 | 1.36 | -$3 | -$10 | 30 | +2 |
| Proj | 40 | 2 | 0 | 21 | 3.95 | 1.43 | -$1 | -$4 | 30 | –1 |

### -$4 Carlson, Jesse

| | IP | W | Sv | K | ERA | WHIP | $1L | $2L | Pts | RAA |
|---|---|---|---|---|---|---|---|---|---|---|
| '10 | 14 | 0 | 1 | 8 | 4.61 | 1.32 | -$3 | -$11 | 10 | –1 |
| Proj | 40 | 1 | 0 | 31 | 4.44 | 1.35 | -$1 | -$4 | 40 | –3 |

### -$4 Russell, Adam

| | IP | W | Sv | K | ERA | WHIP | $1L | $2L | Pts | RAA |
|---|---|---|---|---|---|---|---|---|---|---|
| '10 | 16 | 0 | 0 | 18 | 4.02 | 1.21 | -$4 | -$10 | 20 | –1 |
| Proj | 40 | 2 | 0 | 36 | 4.27 | 1.43 | -$1 | -$4 | 40 | –3 |

### -$4 Webb, Ryan

| | IP | W | Sv | K | ERA | WHIP | $1L | $2L | Pts | RAA |
|---|---|---|---|---|---|---|---|---|---|---|
| '10 | 59 | 3 | 0 | 44 | 2.90 | 1.41 | -$1 | -$7 | 70 | +6 |
| Proj | 60 | 2 | 0 | 49 | 4.10 | 1.43 | -$1 | -$4 | 60 | –3 |

### -$5 Veras, Jose

| | IP | W | Sv | K | ERA | WHIP | $1L | $2L | Pts | RAA |
|---|---|---|---|---|---|---|---|---|---|---|
| '10 | 48 | 3 | 0 | 54 | 3.75 | 1.27 | -$1 | -$7 | 80 | +2 |
| Proj | 40 | 2 | 0 | 39 | 4.56 | 1.43 | -$2 | -$5 | 50 | –3 |

### -$5 Sanchez, Eduardo

| | IP | W | Sv | K | ERA | WHIP | $1L | $2L | Pts | RAA |
|---|---|---|---|---|---|---|---|---|---|---|
| '10 | --- | --- | --- | --- | ---- | ---- | --- | --- | --- | --- |
| Proj | 40 | 1 | 7 | 35 | 4.07 | 1.48 | -$2 | -$5 | 40 | –2 |

### -$5 Boggs, Mitchell

| | IP | W | Sv | K | ERA | WHIP | $1L | $2L | Pts | RAA |
|---|---|---|---|---|---|---|---|---|---|---|
| '10 | 67 | 2 | 0 | 52 | 3.61 | 1.29 | -$1 | -$8 | 70 | +1 |
| Proj | 60 | 3 | 0 | 44 | 4.54 | 1.48 | -$1 | -$5 | 80 | –6 |

### -$5 Hill, Rich

| | IP | W | Sv | K | ERA | WHIP | $1L | $2L | Pts | RAA |
|---|---|---|---|---|---|---|---|---|---|---|
| '10 | 4 | 1 | 0 | 3 | 0.00 | 1.50 | -$3 | -$9 | 10 | +2 |
| Proj | 40 | 2 | 0 | 35 | 4.69 | 1.48 | -$1 | -$5 | 50 | –5 |

### -$6 Belisario, Ronald

| | IP | W | Sv | K | ERA | WHIP | $1L | $2L | Pts | RAA |
|---|---|---|---|---|---|---|---|---|---|---|
| '10 | 55 | 3 | 2 | 38 | 5.04 | 1.28 | -$4 | -$12 | 70 | –6 |
| Proj | 80 | 4 | 1 | 62 | 4.55 | 1.40 | $0 | -$6 | 90 | –6 |

### -$6 Linebrink, Scott

| | IP | W | Sv | K | ERA | WHIP | $1L | $2L | Pts | RAA |
|---|---|---|---|---|---|---|---|---|---|---|
| '10 | 57 | 3 | 0 | 52 | 4.40 | 1.33 | -$1 | -$10 | 70 | –5 |
| Proj | 60 | 2 | 0 | 50 | 4.83 | 1.36 | $0 | -$6 | 60 | –8 |

### -$6 Romero, J.C.

| | IP | W | Sv | K | ERA | WHIP | $1L | $2L | Pts | RAA |
|---|---|---|---|---|---|---|---|---|---|---|
| '10 | 37 | 1 | 3 | 28 | 3.68 | 1.61 | -$4 | -$11 | 50 | –1 |
| Proj | 40 | 2 | 1 | 30 | 4.21 | 1.58 | -$2 | -$6 | 40 | –3 |

### -$6 Nieve, Fernando

| | IP | W | Sv | K | ERA | WHIP | $1L | $2L | Pts | RAA |
|---|---|---|---|---|---|---|---|---|---|---|
| '10 | 42 | 2 | 0 | 38 | 6.00 | 1.40 | -$6 | -$15 | 40 | –9 |
| Proj | 40 | 2 | 0 | 33 | 5.12 | 1.41 | -$2 | -$6 | 40 | –6 |

### -$6 Walters, P.J.

| | IP | W | Sv | K | ERA | WHIP | $1L | $2L | Pts | RAA |
|---|---|---|---|---|---|---|---|---|---|---|
| '10 | 30 | 2 | 0 | 22 | 6.00 | 1.40 | -$6 | -$14 | 30 | –7 |
| Proj | 40 | 2 | 0 | 38 | 5.02 | 1.49 | -$2 | -$6 | 50 | –6 |

### -$6 Delcarmen, Manny

| | IP | W | Sv | K | ERA | WHIP | $1L | $2L | Pts | RAA |
|---|---|---|---|---|---|---|---|---|---|---|
| '10 | 52 | 3 | 0 | 38 | 4.99 | 1.47 | -$5 | -$14 | 50 | –6 |
| Proj | 60 | 3 | 0 | 47 | 4.47 | 1.50 | -$2 | -$6 | 70 | –5 |

### -$6 Cormier, Lance

| | IP | W | Sv | K | ERA | WHIP | $1L | $2L | Pts | RAA |
|---|---|---|---|---|---|---|---|---|---|---|
| '10 | 62 | 4 | 0 | 30 | 3.92 | 1.65 | -$3 | -$14 | 50 | –0 |
| Proj | 40 | 2 | 0 | 20 | 4.43 | 1.52 | -$2 | -$6 | 30 | –3 |

### -$6 Meredith, Cla

| | IP | W | Sv | K | ERA | WHIP | $1L | $2L | Pts | RAA |
|---|---|---|---|---|---|---|---|---|---|---|
| '10 | 15 | 0 | 1 | 7 | 5.40 | 1.47 | -$4 | -$12 | 10 | –2 |
| Proj | 40 | 2 | 0 | 22 | 4.80 | 1.45 | -$2 | -$6 | 30 | –5 |

### -$6 Ondrusek, Logan

| | IP | W | Sv | K | ERA | WHIP | $1L | $2L | Pts | RAA |
|---|---|---|---|---|---|---|---|---|---|---|
| '10 | 59 | 5 | 0 | 39 | 3.68 | 1.18 | $0 | -$6 | 90 | +1 |
| Proj | 60 | 3 | 0 | 48 | 4.62 | 1.49 | -$2 | -$6 | 70 | –6 |

### -$7 Schlereth, Daniel

| | IP | W | Sv | K | ERA | WHIP | $1L | $2L | Pts | RAA |
|---|---|---|---|---|---|---|---|---|---|---|
| '10 | 19 | 2 | 1 | 19 | 2.89 | 1.61 | -$2 | -$9 | 40 | +1 |
| Proj | 40 | 2 | 1 | 46 | 4.33 | 1.72 | -$2 | -$7 | 50 | –3 |

### -$7 McCutchen, Daniel

| | IP | W | Sv | K | ERA | WHIP | $1L | $2L | Pts | RAA |
|---|---|---|---|---|---|---|---|---|---|---|
| '10 | 68 | 2 | 0 | 38 | 6.12 | 1.64 | -$11 | -$24 | 20 | –18 |
| Proj | 40 | 2 | 0 | 30 | 5.16 | 1.47 | -$3 | -$7 | 40 | –7 |

### -$7 Parnell, Bobby

| | IP | W | Sv | K | ERA | WHIP | $1L | $2L | Pts | RAA |
|---|---|---|---|---|---|---|---|---|---|---|
| '10 | 35 | 0 | 0 | 33 | 2.83 | 1.40 | -$3 | -$9 | 30 | +3 |
| Proj | 60 | 2 | 0 | 52 | 4.59 | 1.54 | -$2 | -$7 | 70 | –6 |

### -$7 Albaladejo, Jonathan

| | IP | W | Sv | K | ERA | WHIP | $1L | $2L | Pts | RAA |
|---|---|---|---|---|---|---|---|---|---|---|
| '10 | 11 | 0 | 0 | 8 | 3.97 | 1.50 | -$4 | -$11 | 10 | +0 |
| Proj | 40 | 2 | 0 | 29 | 5.15 | 1.50 | -$2 | -$7 | 40 | –7 |

### -$4 Affeldt, Jeremy △

| | IP | W | Sv | K | ERA | WHIP | $1L | $2L | Pts | RAA |
|---|---|---|---|---|---|---|---|---|---|---|
| '10 | 50 | 4 | 4 | 44 | 4.14 | 1.60 | -$3 | -$11 | 90 | –3 |
| Proj | 60 | 3 | 4 | 49 | 4.06 | 1.45 | $0 | -$4 | 70 | –2 |

### -$4 Kelley, Shawn

| | IP | W | Sv | K | ERA | WHIP | $1L | $2L | Pts | RAA |
|---|---|---|---|---|---|---|---|---|---|---|
| '10 | 25 | 3 | 0 | 26 | 3.96 | 1.52 | -$2 | -$10 | 50 | +0 |
| Proj | 45 | 3 | 0 | 43 | 4.52 | 1.41 | $0 | -$4 | 60 | –4 |

### -$4 Ohman, Will

| | IP | W | Sv | K | ERA | WHIP | $1L | $2L | Pts | RAA |
|---|---|---|---|---|---|---|---|---|---|---|
| '10 | 42 | 0 | 0 | 43 | 3.21 | 1.50 | -$4 | -$10 | 40 | +1 |
| Proj | 20 | 0 | 0 | 18 | 4.12 | 1.48 | -$2 | -$4 | 20 | –1 |

### -$4 Hawkins, LaTroy △

| | IP | W | Sv | K | ERA | WHIP | $1L | $2L | Pts | RAA |
|---|---|---|---|---|---|---|---|---|---|---|
| '10 | 16 | 0 | 0 | 18 | 8.44 | 1.69 | -$8 | -$16 | 10 | –8 |
| Proj | 40 | 2 | 2 | 27 | 4.60 | 1.33 | -$1 | -$4 | 40 | –4 |

### -$4 Norberto, Jordan

| | IP | W | Sv | K | ERA | WHIP | $1L | $2L | Pts | RAA |
|---|---|---|---|---|---|---|---|---|---|---|
| '10 | 20 | 0 | 0 | 15 | 5.85 | 1.90 | -$8 | -$16 | 0 | –4 |
| Proj | 40 | 3 | 6 | 47 | 4.13 | 1.59 | -$1 | -$4 | 60 | –2 |

### -$4 Lewis, Jensen △

| | IP | W | Sv | K | ERA | WHIP | $1L | $2L | Pts | RAA |
|---|---|---|---|---|---|---|---|---|---|---|
| '10 | 36 | 4 | 0 | 29 | 2.97 | 1.29 | $1 | -$6 | 70 | +4 |
| Proj | 40 | 3 | 0 | 36 | 4.48 | 1.45 | -$1 | -$4 | 50 | –3 |

### -$5 Villanueva, Carlos △

| | IP | W | Sv | K | ERA | WHIP | $1L | $2L | Pts | RAA |
|---|---|---|---|---|---|---|---|---|---|---|
| '10 | 53 | 2 | 1 | 67 | 4.61 | 1.33 | -$3 | -$10 | 80 | –3 |
| Proj | 60 | 2 | 0 | 53 | 4.70 | 1.32 | -$1 | -$5 | 70 | –6 |

### -$5 Green, Sean

| | IP | W | Sv | K | ERA | WHIP | $1L | $2L | Pts | RAA |
|---|---|---|---|---|---|---|---|---|---|---|
| '10 | 9 | 0 | 0 | 12 | 3.86 | 1.61 | -$5 | -$11 | 10 | –2 |
| Proj | 40 | 2 | 0 | 29 | 4.25 | 1.46 | -$2 | -$5 | 40 | –3 |

### -$5 Maloney, Matt

| | IP | W | Sv | K | ERA | WHIP | $1L | $2L | Pts | RAA |
|---|---|---|---|---|---|---|---|---|---|---|
| '10 | 21 | 2 | 0 | 13 | 3.05 | 1.21 | -$3 | -$8 | 30 | +2 |
| Proj | 60 | 3 | 0 | 52 | 4.79 | 1.35 | -$1 | -$5 | 70 | –7 |

### -$5 Elbert, Scott

| | IP | W | Sv | K | ERA | WHIP | $1L | $2L | Pts | RAA |
|---|---|---|---|---|---|---|---|---|---|---|
| '10 | 1 | 0 | 0 | 0 | 13.50 | 6.00 | -$6 | -$12 | 0 | –1 |
| Proj | 40 | 2 | 0 | 48 | 4.59 | 1.51 | -$2 | -$5 | 50 | –4 |

### -$5 Thomas, Brad

| | IP | W | Sv | K | ERA | WHIP | $1L | $2L | Pts | RAA |
|---|---|---|---|---|---|---|---|---|---|---|
| '10 | 69 | 6 | 0 | 30 | 3.89 | 1.53 | -$1 | -$12 | 80 | +0 |
| Proj | 40 | 3 | 0 | 21 | 4.29 | 1.55 | -$1 | -$5 | 40 | –2 |

### -$6 Baez, Danys

| | IP | W | Sv | K | ERA | WHIP | $1L | $2L | Pts | RAA |
|---|---|---|---|---|---|---|---|---|---|---|
| '10 | 48 | 3 | 0 | 28 | 5.48 | 1.64 | -$7 | -$17 | 40 | –10 |
| Proj | 40 | 2 | 2 | 22 | 4.77 | 1.42 | -$2 | -$6 | 30 | –5 |

### -$6 Bautista, Denny

| | IP | W | Sv | K | ERA | WHIP | $1L | $2L | Pts | RAA |
|---|---|---|---|---|---|---|---|---|---|---|
| '10 | 34 | 2 | 0 | 44 | 3.74 | 1.54 | -$4 | -$10 | 60 | +1 |
| Proj | 40 | 2 | 0 | 40 | 4.53 | 1.58 | -$2 | -$6 | 50 | –3 |

### -$6 Mitre, Sergio

| | IP | W | Sv | K | ERA | WHIP | $1L | $2L | Pts | RAA |
|---|---|---|---|---|---|---|---|---|---|---|
| '10 | 54 | 0 | 1 | 29 | 3.33 | 1.09 | $1 | -$6 | 40 | +1 |
| Proj | 60 | 2 | 0 | 34 | 4.78 | 1.32 | -$1 | -$6 | 50 | –8 |

### -$6 Hill, Shawn

| | IP | W | Sv | K | ERA | WHIP | $1L | $2L | Pts | RAA |
|---|---|---|---|---|---|---|---|---|---|---|
| '10 | 21 | 1 | 0 | 14 | 2.61 | 1.35 | -$2 | -$9 | 20 | +1 |
| Proj | 80 | 4 | 0 | 45 | 4.43 | 1.40 | $1 | -$6 | 70 | –8 |

### -$6 Sampson, Chris △

| | IP | W | Sv | K | ERA | WHIP | $1L | $2L | Pts | RAA |
|---|---|---|---|---|---|---|---|---|---|---|
| '10 | 30 | 1 | 0 | 16 | 5.93 | 1.68 | -$8 | -$16 | 10 | –8 |
| Proj | 40 | 1 | 0 | 20 | 4.81 | 1.39 | -$3 | -$6 | 20 | –5 |

### -$6 Jeffress, Jeremy

| | IP | W | Sv | K | ERA | WHIP | $1L | $2L | Pts | RAA |
|---|---|---|---|---|---|---|---|---|---|---|
| '10 | 10 | 1 | 0 | 8 | 2.70 | 1.40 | -$4 | -$10 | 20 | +1 |
| Proj | 20 | 1 | 0 | 22 | 5.20 | 1.77 | -$3 | -$6 | 20 | –4 |

### -$6 VandenHurk, Rick

| | IP | W | Sv | K | ERA | WHIP | $1L | $2L | Pts | RAA |
|---|---|---|---|---|---|---|---|---|---|---|
| '10 | 18 | 0 | 0 | 18 | 5.09 | 1.36 | -$4 | -$12 | 10 | –6 |
| Proj | 40 | 2 | 0 | 38 | 5.04 | 1.48 | -$2 | -$6 | 40 | –7 |

### -$6 Smith, Chris

| | IP | W | Sv | K | ERA | WHIP | $1L | $2L | Pts | RAA |
|---|---|---|---|---|---|---|---|---|---|---|
| '10 | 3 | 0 | 0 | 4 | 5.40 | 1.50 | -$5 | -$11 | 0 | –1 |
| Proj | 40 | 1 | 0 | 32 | 5.15 | 1.41 | -$3 | -$6 | 30 | –7 |

### -$7 Valdes, Raul

| | IP | W | Sv | K | ERA | WHIP | $1L | $2L | Pts | RAA |
|---|---|---|---|---|---|---|---|---|---|---|
| '10 | 59 | 3 | 1 | 56 | 4.91 | 1.47 | -$5 | -$14 | 70 | –7 |
| Proj | 40 | 2 | 0 | 29 | 5.02 | 1.49 | -$3 | -$7 | 40 | –6 |

### -$7 Rodriguez, Francisco

| | IP | W | Sv | K | ERA | WHIP | $1L | $2L | Pts | RAA |
|---|---|---|---|---|---|---|---|---|---|---|
| '10 | 47 | 1 | 0 | 36 | 4.37 | 1.52 | -$3 | -$14 | 30 | –2 |
| Proj | 20 | 1 | 0 | 17 | 5.41 | 1.73 | -$3 | -$7 | 20 | –4 |

### -$7 Herrmann, Frank

| | IP | W | Sv | K | ERA | WHIP | $1L | $2L | Pts | RAA |
|---|---|---|---|---|---|---|---|---|---|---|
| '10 | 45 | 0 | 1 | 24 | 4.03 | 1.28 | -$2 | -$11 | 30 | –2 |
| Proj | 40 | 1 | 0 | 28 | 4.89 | 1.51 | -$2 | -$7 | 30 | –6 |

### -$7 Wright, Jamey

| | IP | W | Sv | K | ERA | WHIP | $1L | $2L | Pts | RAA |
|---|---|---|---|---|---|---|---|---|---|---|
| '10 | 58 | 1 | 0 | 28 | 4.17 | 1.37 | -$2 | -$13 | 30 | –7 |
| Proj | 40 | 1 | 0 | 23 | 4.89 | 1.48 | -$2 | -$7 | 20 | –6 |

### -$7 Johnson, Jim △

| | IP | W | Sv | K | ERA | WHIP | $1L | $2L | Pts | RAA |
|---|---|---|---|---|---|---|---|---|---|---|
| '10 | 26 | 1 | 1 | 22 | 3.42 | 1.41 | -$2 | -$10 | 30 | +1 |
| Proj | 60 | 3 | 3 | 41 | 4.61 | 1.53 | -$1 | -$7 | 60 | –6 |

### -$4 Bulger, Jason

| | IP | W | Sv | K | ERA | WHIP | $1L | $2L | Pts | RAA |
|---|---|---|---|---|---|---|---|---|---|---|
| '10 | 24 | 0 | 0 | 25 | 4.88 | 1.67 | -$4 | -$14 | 20 | –3 |
| Proj | 40 | 2 | 0 | 44 | 4.22 | 1.46 | $0 | -$4 | 50 | –2 |

### -$4 Salas, Fernando

| | IP | W | Sv | K | ERA | WHIP | $1L | $2L | Pts | RAA |
|---|---|---|---|---|---|---|---|---|---|---|
| '10 | 31 | 0 | 0 | 29 | 3.52 | 1.40 | -$4 | -$10 | 30 | +1 |
| Proj | 40 | 1 | 0 | 41 | 4.10 | 1.45 | -$1 | -$4 | 50 | –2 |

### -$4 Zumaya, Joel

| | IP | W | Sv | K | ERA | WHIP | $1L | $2L | Pts | RAA |
|---|---|---|---|---|---|---|---|---|---|---|
| '10 | 38 | 2 | 1 | 34 | 2.58 | 1.12 | $2 | -$4 | 60 | +4 |
| Proj | 40 | 2 | 3 | 37 | 4.08 | 1.48 | -$1 | -$4 | 50 | –2 |

### -$4 Jepsen, Kevin

| | IP | W | Sv | K | ERA | WHIP | $1L | $2L | Pts | RAA |
|---|---|---|---|---|---|---|---|---|---|---|
| '10 | 59 | 2 | 0 | 61 | 3.97 | 1.41 | $0 | -$10 | 70 | +1 |
| Proj | 40 | 1 | 0 | 38 | 4.50 | 1.52 | $0 | -$4 | 60 | –3 |

### -$4 Ring, Royce

| | IP | W | Sv | K | ERA | WHIP | $1L | $2L | Pts | RAA |
|---|---|---|---|---|---|---|---|---|---|---|
| '10 | 2 | 0 | 0 | 2 | 15.43 | 2.14 | -$5 | -$13 | 0 | –3 |
| Proj | 20 | 1 | 0 | 17 | 4.49 | 1.44 | -$2 | -$4 | 20 | –2 |

### -$4 Okajima, Hideki

| | IP | W | Sv | K | ERA | WHIP | $1L | $2L | Pts | RAA |
|---|---|---|---|---|---|---|---|---|---|---|
| '10 | 46 | 4 | 0 | 33 | 4.50 | 1.72 | -$3 | -$14 | 60 | –3 |
| Proj | 60 | 4 | 3 | 48 | 4.16 | 1.48 | $1 | -$4 | 80 | –3 |

### -$5 Marte, Damaso △

| | IP | W | Sv | K | ERA | WHIP | $1L | $2L | Pts | RAA |
|---|---|---|---|---|---|---|---|---|---|---|
| '10 | 18 | 0 | 0 | 12 | 4.08 | 1.19 | -$3 | -$10 | 10 | –0 |
| Proj | 20 | 1 | 0 | 18 | 4.83 | 1.43 | -$2 | -$5 | 20 | –2 |

### -$5 Braddock, Zach

| | IP | W | Sv | K | ERA | WHIP | $1L | $2L | Pts | RAA |
|---|---|---|---|---|---|---|---|---|---|---|
| '10 | 34 | 1 | 0 | 41 | 2.94 | 1.43 | -$3 | -$8 | 50 | +4 |
| Proj | 40 | 1 | 0 | 48 | 4.20 | 1.54 | -$2 | -$5 | 50 | –2 |

### -$5 Acosta, Manny

| | IP | W | Sv | K | ERA | WHIP | $1L | $2L | Pts | RAA |
|---|---|---|---|---|---|---|---|---|---|---|
| '10 | 40 | 3 | 1 | 42 | 2.95 | 1.21 | $0 | -$5 | 80 | +5 |
| Proj | 40 | 2 | 0 | 33 | 4.39 | 1.48 | -$2 | -$5 | 40 | –3 |

### -$5 Runzler, Dan

| | IP | W | Sv | K | ERA | WHIP | $1L | $2L | Pts | RAA |
|---|---|---|---|---|---|---|---|---|---|---|
| '10 | 33 | 3 | 0 | 37 | 3.03 | 1.50 | -$2 | -$8 | 60 | +3 |
| Proj | 60 | 4 | 0 | 71 | 4.01 | 1.64 | -$1 | -$5 | 90 | –2 |

### -$6 Sipp, Tony

| | IP | W | Sv | K | ERA | WHIP | $1L | $2L | Pts | RAA |
|---|---|---|---|---|---|---|---|---|---|---|
| '10 | 63 | 2 | 1 | 69 | 4.14 | 1.38 | $0 | -$10 | 80 | –2 |
| Proj | 60 | 2 | 1 | 68 | 4.44 | 1.50 | $0 | -$6 | 80 | –4 |

### -$6 Durbin, Chad

| | IP | W | Sv | K | ERA | WHIP | $1L | $2L | Pts | RAA |
|---|---|---|---|---|---|---|---|---|---|---|
| '10 | 69 | 4 | 0 | 63 | 3.80 | 1.31 | $0 | -$7 | 100 | +2 |
| Proj | 60 | 3 | 0 | 45 | 4.59 | 1.41 | -$1 | -$6 | 60 | –5 |

### -$6 Fulchino, Jeff

| | IP | W | Sv | K | ERA | WHIP | $1L | $2L | Pts | RAA |
|---|---|---|---|---|---|---|---|---|---|---|
| '10 | 47 | 2 | 0 | 46 | 5.51 | 1.58 | -$7 | -$16 | 50 | –9 |
| Proj | 40 | 2 | 1 | 33 | 4.80 | 1.45 | -$2 | -$6 | 40 | –5 |

### -$6 Ramos, Cesar

| | IP | W | Sv | K | ERA | WHIP | $1L | $2L | Pts | RAA |
|---|---|---|---|---|---|---|---|---|---|---|
| '10 | 8 | 0 | 0 | 9 | 11.88 | 2.64 | -$9 | -$17 | 0 | –7 |
| Proj | 40 | 2 | 0 | 29 | 4.81 | 1.46 | -$2 | -$6 | 40 | –5 |

### -$6 Badenhop, Burke

| | IP | W | Sv | K | ERA | WHIP | $1L | $2L | Pts | RAA |
|---|---|---|---|---|---|---|---|---|---|---|
| '10 | 68 | 2 | 1 | 47 | 3.99 | 1.23 | -$1 | -$8 | 70 | –3 |
| Proj | 80 | 3 | 0 | 57 | 4.47 | 1.39 | -$1 | -$6 | 70 | –7 |

### -$6 Logan, Boone

| | IP | W | Sv | K | ERA | WHIP | $1L | $2L | Pts | RAA |
|---|---|---|---|---|---|---|---|---|---|---|
| '10 | 40 | 2 | 0 | 38 | 2.93 | 1.35 | $0 | -$7 | 60 | +5 |
| Proj | 60 | 2 | 0 | 53 | 4.42 | 1.49 | -$1 | -$6 | 60 | –4 |

### -$6 Sonnanstine, Andy □

| | IP | W | Sv | K | ERA | WHIP | $1L | $2L | Pts | RAA |
|---|---|---|---|---|---|---|---|---|---|---|
| '10 | 81 | 3 | 1 | 50 | 4.44 | 1.36 | -$1 | -$13 | 70 | –4 |
| Proj | 50 | 2 | 0 | 31 | 5.09 | 1.34 | -$1 | -$6 | 40 | –8 |

### -$6 Schlichting, Travis

| | IP | W | Sv | K | ERA | WHIP | $1L | $2L | Pts | RAA |
|---|---|---|---|---|---|---|---|---|---|---|
| '10 | 23 | 1 | 0 | 14 | 3.57 | 1.32 | -$4 | -$10 | 20 | +1 |
| Proj | 60 | 3 | 0 | 51 | 4.41 | 1.53 | -$2 | -$6 | 70 | –4 |

### -$6 Santos, Sergio

| | IP | W | Sv | K | ERA | WHIP | $1L | $2L | Pts | RAA |
|---|---|---|---|---|---|---|---|---|---|---|
| '10 | 52 | 2 | 1 | 56 | 2.96 | 1.53 | $0 | -$8 | 80 | +5 |
| Proj | 60 | 2 | 1 | 64 | 3.85 | 1.67 | -$1 | -$6 | 70 | –0 |

### -$7 Byrdak, Tim

| | IP | W | Sv | K | ERA | WHIP | $1L | $2L | Pts | RAA |
|---|---|---|---|---|---|---|---|---|---|---|
| '10 | 39 | 2 | 0 | 29 | 3.49 | 1.55 | -$4 | -$11 | 40 | +2 |
| Proj | 40 | 2 | 0 | 34 | 4.67 | 1.57 | -$3 | -$7 | 40 | –4 |

### -$7 Igarashi, Ryota

| | IP | W | Sv | K | ERA | WHIP | $1L | $2L | Pts | RAA |
|---|---|---|---|---|---|---|---|---|---|---|
| '10 | 30 | 1 | 0 | 25 | 7.12 | 1.55 | -$8 | -$17 | 20 | –10 |
| Proj | 40 | 2 | 0 | 29 | 5.28 | 1.43 | -$3 | -$7 | 30 | –7 |

### -$7 Judy, Josh

| | IP | W | Sv | K | ERA | WHIP | $1L | $2L | Pts | RAA |
|---|---|---|---|---|---|---|---|---|---|---|
| '10 | --- | --- | --- | --- | ---- | ---- | --- | --- | --- | --- |
| Proj | 60 | 1 | 11 | 50 | 4.53 | 1.47 | -$1 | -$7 | 50 | –6 |

### -$7 Ray, Chris

| | IP | W | Sv | K | ERA | WHIP | $1L | $2L | Pts | RAA |
|---|---|---|---|---|---|---|---|---|---|---|
| '10 | 56 | 5 | 2 | 31 | 3.72 | 1.31 | -$1 | -$7 | 90 | +2 |
| Proj | 60 | 4 | 1 | 43 | 4.84 | 1.48 | -$2 | -$7 | 60 | –7 |

### -$7 Monasterios, Carlos

| | IP | W | Sv | K | ERA | WHIP | $1L | $2L | Pts | RAA |
|---|---|---|---|---|---|---|---|---|---|---|
| '10 | 88 | 3 | 0 | 52 | 4.38 | 1.45 | -$5 | -$15 | 60 | –8 |
| Proj | 40 | 2 | 0 | 32 | 4.98 | 1.56 | -$3 | -$7 | 40 | –6 |

# HITTERS

**METHOD:** The team experts built tentative rosters for each MLB team for 2011. Every hitter targeted for 50 PA or more is here. We also included some "players of interest" who might not get much work in 2011 but who could be important later; these hitters are projected for 25 PA.

All told, this section has 560 hitters. These are our best candidates for meaningful playing time in 2011. We know that many fantasy GM's take part in keeper leagues and leagues with deep benches, so this section gives equal treatment to major- and minor-leaguers.

**OUTLOOK:** Beyond the top tier of players, fantasy value becomes more of a matter of opportunity than of skill. For that reason, the commentaries focus on the player's role, his standing in his organization, and his rivals. Key statistical trends and blips are also dealt with. Probable free agents have been assigned a forecast based on their skill, age, and role.

**SIGNAL BARS:** In front of each player's name is a small graph of five columns. The columns represent the player's fantasy value over the past five seasons (2006-2010). You can see whether, and when, a player was productive.

**HEADER:** The fields to the right of the player's name are

**Projected PA | Projected \$1L | Projected Pt**

Beneath a player's name are his positions and games played in MLB in 2010. Positions are listed in descending order from most-played to least-played. (Note that games played at OF can be less than the sum of games played at LF, CF, and RF if a hitter played multiple spots in one game.) Below and to the right are his **Owned** (his ownership percentage as of late August) and his batting hand (LH/RH/BH).

**MINI-BROWSER:** This is a list of players who play the same position and offer similar overall value, though perhaps with different stats. Except for top-rated players, the listed players are directly above the profiled player in projected \$1L. Age is as of April 1, 2011.

**MINORS:** The stats are for 2010. Level "A" includes low-A and high-A (but not rookie).

**VALUES:** We value players by four methods:

\$1L is the player's single-league (AL- or NL-only) auction value, \$2L is his mixed-league (AL/NL) value. Values are calculated for traditional 5x5 leagues: HR, Runs, RBI, SB, and BA.

**Pts** (Points) is the player's value in a points-based league. We use this formula:

| | |
|---|---|
| **Each Base** | 1 point |
| **Run** | 1 point |
| **RBI** | 1 point |
| **Stolen Base** | 2 points |
| **Strikeout** | -1 point |
| **Caught Stealing** | -1 point |

**RAA** (Runs Above Average) is the number of runs created (positive RAA) or squandered (negative RAA) by the hitter versus a hitter with average productivity. More offense-minded positions have tougher benchmarks.

**COMPETITION:** This table pits a player against players who play on the same team (as of press time) and at the player's anticipated primary position in 2011. The player's primary position is generally the position at which he played the most games in 2010, but in some cases the position has been changed to reflect his expected role in 2011.

Players are ranked in descending order of the total number of starts at the position in 2010. The table breaks out games started against right-handed starting pitchers (GSvR) and left-handers (GSvL), as well as games when the player entered for another hitter (Sub). Figures in the table cover a player's entire work for 2010, and not just his work with this team.

**WEEKLY POINTS:** This graph shows weekly points totals from 2008-2010. The white line is a rolling four-week trend.

**TEN-YEAR TRENDS:** This graph shows yearly trends in SLG, OBP, and BA from 2001-10. The darker-colored section shows the usual range for SLG; the lighter-colored section, for OBP and BA. Black points are forecasts for 2011.

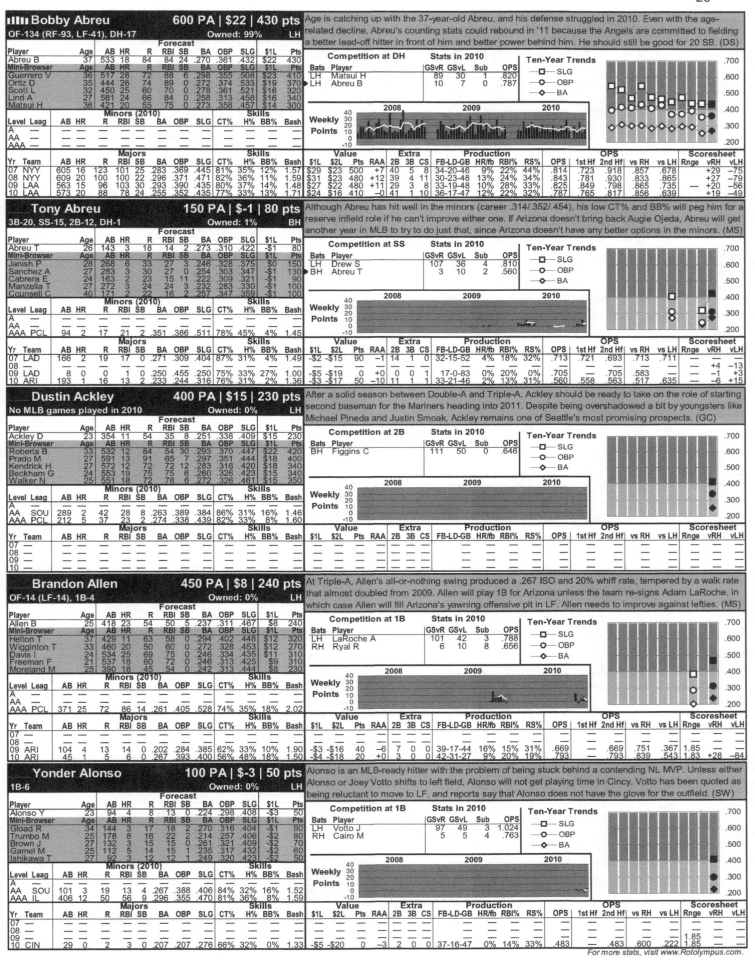

## Bobby Abreu — 600 PA | $22 | 430 pts
OF-134 (RF-93, LF-41), DH-17 · Owned: 99% · LH

Age is catching up with the 37-year-old Abreu, and his defense struggled in 2010. Even with the age-related decline, Abreu's counting stats could rebound in '11 because the Angels are committed to fielding a better lead-off hitter in front of him and better power behind him. He should still be good for 20 SB. (DS)

### Forecast
| Player | Age | AB | HR | R | RBI | SB | BA | OBP | SLG | $1L | Pts |
|---|---|---|---|---|---|---|---|---|---|---|---|
| Abreu B | 37 | 533 | 18 | 84 | 84 | 24 | .270 | .361 | .432 | $22 | 430 |
| Mini-Browser | Age | AB | HR | R | RBI | SB | BA | OBP | SLG | $1L | Pts |
| Guerrero V | 36 | 517 | 28 | 72 | 88 | 6 | .298 | .355 | .508 | $23 | 410 |
| Ortiz D | 35 | 444 | 26 | 74 | 89 | 0 | .272 | .374 | .533 | $19 | 370 |
| Scott L | 32 | 450 | 25 | 60 | 70 | 0 | .278 | .361 | .521 | $16 | 320 |
| Lind A | 27 | 581 | 24 | 66 | 84 | 0 | .273 | .313 | .458 | $16 | 340 |
| Matsui H | 36 | 421 | 20 | 55 | 75 | 0 | .273 | .358 | .457 | $14 | 300 |

### Competition at DH / Stats in 2010
| Bats | Player | GSvR | GSvL | Sub | OPS |
|---|---|---|---|---|---|
| LH | Matsui H | 89 | 30 | 1 | .820 |
| LH | Abreu B | 10 | 7 | 0 | .787 |

Ten-Year Trends: SLG, OBP, BA

### Minors (2010) / Skills
| Level | Leag | AB | HR | R | RBI | SB | BA | OBP | SLG | CT% | H% | BB% | Bash |
|---|---|---|---|---|---|---|---|---|---|---|---|---|---|
| A | — | — | — | — | — | — | — | — | — | — | — | — | — |
| AA | — | — | — | — | — | — | — | — | — | — | — | — | — |
| AAA | — | — | — | — | — | — | — | — | — | — | — | — | — |

### Majors / Skills / Value / Extra / Production / OPS / Scoresheet
| Yr | Team | AB | HR | R | RBI | SB | BA | OBP | SLG | CT% | H% | BB% | Bash | $1L | $2L | Pts | RAA | 2B | 3B | CS | FB-LD-GB | HR/fb | RBI% | RS% | OPS | 1st Hf | 2nd Hf | vs RH | vs LH | Rnge | vRH | vLH |
|---|---|---|---|---|---|---|---|---|---|---|---|---|---|---|---|---|---|---|---|---|---|---|---|---|---|---|---|---|---|---|---|---|
| 07 | NYY | 605 | 16 | 123 | 101 | 25 | .283 | .369 | .445 | 81% | 35% | 12% | 1.57 | $29 | $23 | 500 | +7 | 40 | 5 | 8 | 34-20-46 | 9% | 22% | 44% | .814 | .723 | .918 | .857 | .678 | +29 | -75 |
| 08 | NYY | 609 | 20 | 100 | 100 | 22 | .296 | .371 | .471 | 82% | 36% | 11% | 1.59 | $31 | $23 | 480 | +12 | 39 | 4 | 11 | 30-23-48 | 13% | 24% | 34% | .843 | .781 | .930 | .833 | .865 | +27 | -79 |
| 09 | LAA | 563 | 15 | 96 | 103 | 30 | .293 | .390 | .435 | 80% | 37% | 14% | 1.48 | $27 | $22 | 480 | +11 | 29 | 3 | 8 | 33-19-48 | 10% | 28% | 33% | .825 | .849 | .798 | .865 | .735 | +20 | -56 |
| 10 | LAA | 573 | 20 | 88 | 78 | 24 | .255 | .352 | .435 | 77% | 33% | 13% | 1.71 | $24 | $16 | 410 | -0 | 41 | 1 | 10 | 36-17-47 | 12% | 22% | 32% | .787 | .765 | .817 | .856 | .639 | +19 | +49 |

## Tony Abreu — 150 PA | $-1 | 80 pts
3B-20, SS-15, 2B-12, DH-1 · Owned: 1% · BH

Although Abreu has hit well in the minors (career .314/.352/.454), his low CT% and BB% will peg him for a reserve infield role if he can't improve either one. If Arizona doesn't bring back Augie Ojeda, Abreu will get another year in MLB to try to do just that, since Arizona doesn't have any better options in the minors. (MS)

### Forecast
| Player | Age | AB | HR | R | RBI | SB | BA | OBP | SLG | $1L | Pts |
|---|---|---|---|---|---|---|---|---|---|---|---|
| Abreu T | 26 | 143 | 3 | 18 | 14 | 2 | .273 | .310 | .422 | -$1 | 80 |
| Mini-Browser | Age | AB | HR | R | RBI | SB | BA | OBP | SLG | $1L | Pts |
| Janish P | 28 | 268 | 6 | 33 | 27 | 3 | .246 | .328 | .375 | $0 | 150 |
| Sanchez A | 27 | 283 | 3 | 30 | 27 | 0 | .254 | .303 | .347 | -$1 | 130 |
| Cabrera E | 24 | 163 | 2 | 23 | 15 | 11 | .222 | .309 | .321 | -$1 | 100 |
| Manzella T | 27 | 272 | 3 | 24 | 24 | 3 | .232 | .283 | .330 | -$1 | 100 |
| Counsell C | 40 | 171 | 2 | 22 | 16 | 2 | .257 | .347 | .359 | -$1 | 100 |

### Competition at SS / Stats in 2010
| Bats | Player | GSvR | GSvL | Sub | OPS |
|---|---|---|---|---|---|
| LH | Drew S | 107 | 36 | 4 | .810 |
| BH | Abreu T | 3 | 10 | 2 | .560 |

Ten-Year Trends: SLG, OBP, BA

### Minors (2010) / Skills
| Level | Leag | AB | HR | R | RBI | SB | BA | OBP | SLG | CT% | H% | BB% | Bash |
|---|---|---|---|---|---|---|---|---|---|---|---|---|---|
| A | — | — | — | — | — | — | — | — | — | — | — | — | — |
| AA | — | — | — | — | — | — | — | — | — | — | — | — | — |
| AAA | PCL | 94 | 2 | 17 | 21 | 2 | .351 | .386 | .511 | 78% | 45% | 4% | 1.45 |

### Majors
| Yr | Team | AB | HR | R | RBI | SB | BA | OBP | SLG | CT% | H% | BB% | Bash | $1L | $2L | Pts | RAA | 2B | 3B | CS | FB-LD-GB | HR/fb | RBI% | RS% | OPS | 1st Hf | 2nd Hf | vs RH | vs LH | Rnge | vRH | vLH |
|---|---|---|---|---|---|---|---|---|---|---|---|---|---|---|---|---|---|---|---|---|---|---|---|---|---|---|---|---|---|---|---|---|
| 07 | LAD | 166 | 2 | 19 | 17 | 0 | .271 | .309 | .404 | 87% | 31% | 4% | 1.49 | -$2 | -$15 | 90 | -1 | 14 | 1 | 0 | 32-15-52 | 4% | 18% | 32% | .713 | .721 | .693 | .713 | .711 | | +4 | -13 |
| 08 | — | — | — | — | — | — | — | — | — | — | — | — | — | — | — | — | — | — | — | — | — | — | — | — | — | — | — | — | — | — | — | — |
| 09 | LAD | 8 | 0 | 0 | 1 | 0 | .250 | .455 | .250 | 75% | 33% | 27% | 1.00 | -$5 | -$19 | 0 | +0 | 0 | 0 | 1 | 17-0-83 | 0% | 20% | 0% | .705 | — | .705 | .583 | — | | -1 | +3 |
| 10 | ARI | 193 | 2 | 16 | 13 | 2 | .233 | .244 | .316 | 76% | 31% | 2% | 1.36 | -$3 | -$17 | 50 | -10 | 11 | 1 | 1 | 33-21-46 | 2% | 13% | 31% | .560 | .558 | .563 | .517 | .635 | | -6 | +15 |

## Dustin Ackley — 400 PA | $15 | 230 pts
No MLB games played in 2010 · Owned: 0% · LH

After a solid season between Double-A and Triple-A, Ackley should be ready to take on the role of starting second baseman for the Mariners heading into 2011. Despite being overshadowed a bit by youngsters like Michael Pineda and Justin Smoak, Ackley remains one of Seattle's most promising prospects. (GC)

### Forecast
| Player | Age | AB | HR | R | RBI | SB | BA | OBP | SLG | $1L | Pts |
|---|---|---|---|---|---|---|---|---|---|---|---|
| Ackley D | 23 | 354 | 11 | 54 | 35 | 8 | .251 | .338 | .409 | $15 | 230 |
| Mini-Browser | Age | AB | HR | R | RBI | SB | BA | OBP | SLG | $1L | Pts |
| Roberts B | 33 | 532 | 12 | 84 | 54 | 30 | .293 | .370 | .447 | $22 | 420 |
| Prado M | 27 | 591 | 13 | 91 | 65 | 7 | .297 | .351 | .444 | $18 | 400 |
| Kendrick H | 27 | 572 | 12 | 72 | 72 | 12 | .283 | .318 | .420 | $18 | 340 |
| Beckham G | 24 | 553 | 19 | 75 | 75 | 6 | .260 | .326 | .423 | $15 | 340 |
| Walker N | 25 | 551 | 18 | 72 | 78 | 6 | .272 | .326 | .461 | $15 | 350 |

### Competition at 2B / Stats in 2010
| Bats | Player | GSvR | GSvL | Sub | OPS |
|---|---|---|---|---|---|
| BH | Figgins C | 111 | 50 | 0 | .646 |

Ten-Year Trends: SLG, OBP, BA

### Minors (2010) / Skills
| Level | Leag | AB | HR | R | RBI | SB | BA | OBP | SLG | CT% | H% | BB% | Bash |
|---|---|---|---|---|---|---|---|---|---|---|---|---|---|
| A | — | — | — | — | — | — | — | — | — | — | — | — | — |
| AA | SOU | 289 | 2 | 42 | 28 | 8 | .263 | .389 | .384 | 86% | 31% | 16% | 1.46 |
| AAA | PCL | 212 | 5 | 37 | 23 | 2 | .274 | .338 | .439 | 82% | 33% | 8% | 1.60 |

### Majors
| Yr | Team | AB | HR | R | RBI | SB | BA | OBP | SLG | CT% | H% | BB% | Bash | $1L | $2L | Pts | RAA | 2B | 3B | CS | FB-LD-GB | HR/fb | RBI% | RS% | OPS | 1st Hf | 2nd Hf | vs RH | vs LH | Rnge | vRH | vLH |
|---|---|---|---|---|---|---|---|---|---|---|---|---|---|---|---|---|---|---|---|---|---|---|---|---|---|---|---|---|---|---|---|---|
| 07 | — | — | — | — | — | — | — | — | — | — | — | — | — | — | — | — | — | — | — | — | — | — | — | — | — | — | — | — | — | — | — | — |
| 08 | — | — | — | — | — | — | — | — | — | — | — | — | — | — | — | — | — | — | — | — | — | — | — | — | — | — | — | — | — | — | — | — |
| 09 | — | — | — | — | — | — | — | — | — | — | — | — | — | — | — | — | — | — | — | — | — | — | — | — | — | — | — | — | — | — | — | — |
| 10 | — | — | — | — | — | — | — | — | — | — | — | — | — | — | — | — | — | — | — | — | — | — | — | — | — | — | — | — | — | — | — | — |

## Brandon Allen — 450 PA | $8 | 240 pts
OF-14 (LF-14), 1B-4 · Owned: 0% · LH

At Triple-A, Allen's all-or-nothing swing produced a .267 ISO and 20% whiff rate, tempered by a walk rate that almost doubled from 2009. Allen will play 1B for Arizona unless the team re-signs Adam LaRoche, in which case Allen will fill Arizona's yawning offensive pit in LF. Allen needs to improve against lefties. (MS)

### Forecast
| Player | Age | AB | HR | R | RBI | SB | BA | OBP | SLG | $1L | Pts |
|---|---|---|---|---|---|---|---|---|---|---|---|
| Allen B | 25 | 418 | 23 | 54 | 50 | 5 | .237 | .311 | .467 | $8 | 240 |
| Mini-Browser | Age | AB | HR | R | RBI | SB | BA | OBP | SLG | $1L | Pts |
| Helton T | 37 | 429 | 11 | 63 | 58 | 0 | .294 | .402 | .448 | $12 | 320 |
| Wigginton T | 33 | 460 | 20 | 50 | 60 | 0 | .272 | .328 | .453 | $12 | 270 |
| Davis I | 24 | 534 | 25 | 69 | 75 | 0 | .246 | .334 | .435 | $11 | 310 |
| Freeman F | 21 | 537 | 18 | 60 | 72 | 0 | .246 | .313 | .425 | $9 | 310 |
| Moreland M | 25 | 390 | 18 | 45 | 54 | 0 | .242 | .313 | .444 | $8 | 230 |

### Competition at 1B / Stats in 2010
| Bats | Player | GSvR | GSvL | Sub | OPS |
|---|---|---|---|---|---|
| LH | LaRoche A | 101 | 42 | 3 | .788 |
| RH | Ryal R | 6 | 10 | 8 | .656 |

Ten-Year Trends: SLG, OBP, BA

### Minors (2010) / Skills
| Level | Leag | AB | HR | R | RBI | SB | BA | OBP | SLG | CT% | H% | BB% | Bash |
|---|---|---|---|---|---|---|---|---|---|---|---|---|---|
| A | — | — | — | — | — | — | — | — | — | — | — | — | — |
| AA | — | — | — | — | — | — | — | — | — | — | — | — | — |
| AAA | PCL | 371 | 25 | 72 | 86 | 14 | .261 | .405 | .528 | 74% | 35% | 18% | 2.02 |

### Majors
| Yr | Team | AB | HR | R | RBI | SB | BA | OBP | SLG | CT% | H% | BB% | Bash | $1L | $2L | Pts | RAA | 2B | 3B | CS | FB-LD-GB | HR/fb | RBI% | RS% | OPS | 1st Hf | 2nd Hf | vs RH | vs LH | Rnge | vRH | vLH |
|---|---|---|---|---|---|---|---|---|---|---|---|---|---|---|---|---|---|---|---|---|---|---|---|---|---|---|---|---|---|---|---|---|
| 07 | — | — | — | — | — | — | — | — | — | — | — | — | — | — | — | — | — | — | — | — | — | — | — | — | — | — | — | — | — | — | — | — |
| 08 | — | — | — | — | — | — | — | — | — | — | — | — | — | — | — | — | — | — | — | — | — | — | — | — | — | — | — | — | — | — | — | — |
| 09 | ARI | 104 | 4 | 13 | 14 | 0 | .202 | .284 | .385 | 62% | 33% | 10% | 1.90 | -$3 | -$16 | 40 | -6 | 7 | 0 | 0 | 39-17-44 | 16% | 15% | 31% | .669 | — | .669 | .751 | .367 | 1.85 | | |
| 10 | ARI | 45 | 1 | 5 | 6 | 0 | .267 | .393 | .400 | 56% | 48% | 18% | 1.50 | -$4 | -$18 | 10 | +1 | 1 | 0 | 0 | 42-31-27 | 9% | 20% | 19% | .793 | — | .793 | .839 | .543 | 1.85 | +28 | -84 |

## Yonder Alonso — 100 PA | $-3 | 50 pts
1B-6 · Owned: 0% · LH

Alonso is an MLB-ready hitter with the problem of being stuck behind a contending NL MVP. Unless either Alonso or Joey Votto shifts to left field, Alonso will not get playing time in Cincy. Votto has been quoted as being reluctant to move to LF, and reports say that Alonso does not have the glove for the outfield. (SW)

### Forecast
| Player | Age | AB | HR | R | RBI | SB | BA | OBP | SLG | $1L | Pts |
|---|---|---|---|---|---|---|---|---|---|---|---|
| Alonso Y | 23 | 94 | 4 | 8 | 13 | 0 | .224 | .298 | .408 | -$3 | 50 |
| Mini-Browser | Age | AB | HR | R | RBI | SB | BA | OBP | SLG | $1L | Pts |
| Gload R | 34 | 144 | 3 | 17 | 18 | 2 | .270 | .316 | .404 | -$1 | 90 |
| Trumbo M | 25 | 178 | 8 | 16 | 22 | 2 | .214 | .257 | .406 | -$2 | 80 |
| Brown J | 27 | 132 | 3 | 15 | 15 | 0 | .261 | .321 | .409 | -$2 | 70 |
| Gamel M | 25 | 112 | 5 | 14 | 15 | 1 | .235 | .317 | .432 | -$2 | 60 |
| Ishikawa T | 27 | 92 | 3 | 12 | 12 | 1 | .249 | .320 | .423 | -$2 | 50 |

### Competition at 1B / Stats in 2010
| Bats | Player | GSvR | GSvL | Sub | OPS |
|---|---|---|---|---|---|
| LH | Votto J | 97 | 49 | 3 | 1.024 |
| RH | Cairo M | 5 | 5 | 4 | .763 |

Ten-Year Trends: SLG, OBP, BA

### Minors (2010) / Skills
| Level | Leag | AB | HR | R | RBI | SB | BA | OBP | SLG | CT% | H% | BB% | Bash |
|---|---|---|---|---|---|---|---|---|---|---|---|---|---|
| A | — | — | — | — | — | — | — | — | — | — | — | — | — |
| AA | SOU | 101 | 3 | 19 | 13 | 4 | .267 | .388 | .406 | 84% | 32% | 16% | 1.52 |
| AAA | IL | 406 | 12 | 50 | 56 | 9 | .296 | .355 | .470 | 81% | 36% | 8% | 1.59 |

### Majors
| Yr | Team | AB | HR | R | RBI | SB | BA | OBP | SLG | CT% | H% | BB% | Bash | $1L | $2L | Pts | RAA | 2B | 3B | CS | FB-LD-GB | HR/fb | RBI% | RS% | OPS | 1st Hf | 2nd Hf | vs RH | vs LH | Rnge | vRH | vLH |
|---|---|---|---|---|---|---|---|---|---|---|---|---|---|---|---|---|---|---|---|---|---|---|---|---|---|---|---|---|---|---|---|---|
| 07 | — | — | — | — | — | — | — | — | — | — | — | — | — | — | — | — | — | — | — | — | — | — | — | — | — | — | — | — | — | — | — | — |
| 08 | — | — | — | — | — | — | — | — | — | — | — | — | — | — | — | — | — | — | — | — | — | — | — | — | — | — | — | — | — | — | — | — |
| 09 | — | — | — | — | — | — | — | — | — | — | — | — | — | — | — | — | — | — | — | — | — | — | — | — | — | — | — | — | — | 1.85 | — | — |
| 10 | CIN | 29 | 0 | 2 | 3 | 0 | .207 | .207 | .276 | 66% | 32% | 0% | 1.33 | -$5 | -$20 | 0 | -3 | 2 | 0 | 0 | 37-16-47 | 0% | 14% | 33% | .483 | — | .483 | .600 | .222 | 1.85 | — | — |

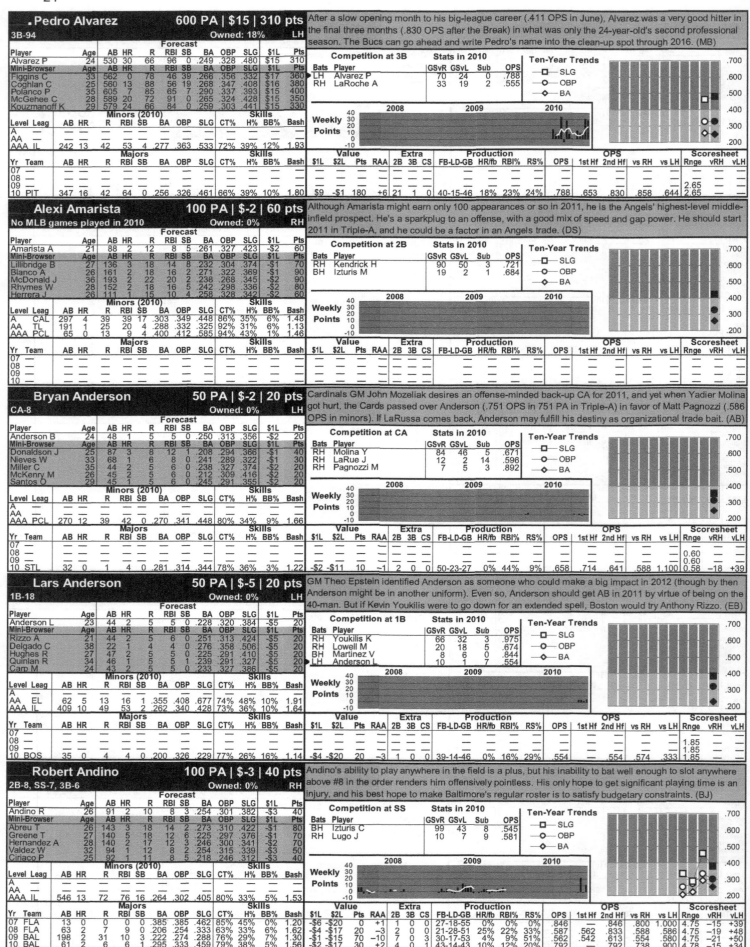

## Pedro Alvarez — 600 PA | $15 | 310 pts
3B-94 — Owned: 18% — LH

### Forecast
| Player | Age | AB | HR | R | RBI | SB | BA | OBP | SLG | $1L | Pts |
|---|---|---|---|---|---|---|---|---|---|---|---|
| Alvarez P | 24 | 530 | 30 | 66 | 96 | 0 | .249 | .328 | .480 | $15 | 310 |
| **Mini-Browser** | Age | AB | HR | R | RBI | SB | BA | OBP | SLG | $1L | Pts |
| Figgins C | 33 | 562 | 0 | 78 | 46 | 39 | .266 | .356 | .332 | $17 | 360 |
| Coghlan C | 25 | 560 | 13 | 88 | 56 | 19 | .268 | .347 | .408 | $15 | 380 |
| Polanco P | 35 | 605 | 7 | 85 | 65 | 7 | .290 | .337 | .393 | $15 | 400 |
| McGehee C | 28 | 589 | 20 | 72 | 91 | 0 | .265 | .324 | .428 | $15 | 350 |
| Kouzmanoff K | 29 | 579 | 24 | 66 | 84 | 0 | .259 | .303 | .441 | $15 | 330 |

### Minors (2010) / Skills
| Level | Leag | AB | HR | R | RBI | SB | BA | OBP | SLG | CT% | H% | BB% | Bash |
|---|---|---|---|---|---|---|---|---|---|---|---|---|---|
| A | — | | | | | | | | | | | | |
| AA | — | | | | | | | | | | | | |
| AAA | IL | 242 | 13 | 42 | 53 | 4 | .277 | .363 | .533 | 72% | 39% | 12% | 1.93 |

### Majors / Skills
| Yr | Team | AB | HR | R | RBI | SB | BA | OBP | SLG | CT% | H% | BB% | Bash |
|---|---|---|---|---|---|---|---|---|---|---|---|---|---|
| 07 | — | | | | | | | | | | | | |
| 08 | — | | | | | | | | | | | | |
| 09 | — | | | | | | | | | | | | |
| 10 | PIT | 347 | 16 | 42 | 64 | 0 | .256 | .326 | .461 | 66% | 39% | 10% | 1.80 |

After a slow opening month to his big-league career (.411 OPS in June), Alvarez was a very good hitter in the final three months (.830 OPS after the Break) in what was only the 24-year-old's second professional season. The Bucs can go ahead and write Pedro's name into the clean-up spot through 2016. (MB)

**Competition at 3B / Stats in 2010**
| Bats | Player | GSvR | GSvL | Sub | OPS |
|---|---|---|---|---|---|
| LH | Alvarez P | 70 | 24 | 16 | .788 |
| RH | LaRoche A | 33 | 19 | 2 | .555 |

Ten-Year Trends: SLG / OBP / BA

| $1L | $2L | Pts | RAA | 2B | 3B | CS | FB-LD-GB | HR/fb | RBI% | RS% | OPS | 1st Hf | 2nd Hf | vs RH | vs LH | Rnge | vRH | vLH |
|---|---|---|---|---|---|---|---|---|---|---|---|---|---|---|---|---|---|---|
| $9 | -$1 | 180 | +6 | 21 | 1 | 0 | 40-15-46 | 18% | 23% | 24% | .788 | .653 | .830 | .858 | .644 | 2.65 | | |

(Rnge 2.65 shown for 09 and 10)

---

## Alexi Amarista — 100 PA | $-2 | 60 pts
No MLB games played in 2010 — Owned: 0% — RH

### Forecast
| Player | Age | AB | HR | R | RBI | SB | BA | OBP | SLG | $1L | Pts |
|---|---|---|---|---|---|---|---|---|---|---|---|
| Amarista A | 21 | 88 | 2 | 12 | 8 | 5 | .261 | .327 | .423 | -$2 | 60 |
| **Mini-Browser** | Age | AB | HR | R | RBI | SB | BA | OBP | SLG | $1L | Pts |
| Lillibridge B | 27 | 136 | 3 | 18 | 14 | 8 | .232 | .304 | .374 | -$1 | 70 |
| Blanco A | 26 | 161 | 2 | 18 | 16 | 2 | .271 | .322 | .369 | -$1 | 90 |
| McDonald J | 36 | 193 | 2 | 22 | 20 | 2 | .238 | .268 | .345 | -$2 | 90 |
| Rhymes W | 28 | 152 | 2 | 18 | 16 | 5 | .242 | .298 | .336 | -$2 | 80 |
| Herrera J | 26 | 111 | 1 | 15 | 10 | 4 | .258 | .328 | .342 | -$2 | 60 |

### Minors (2010) / Skills
| Level | Leag | AB | HR | R | RBI | SB | BA | OBP | SLG | CT% | H% | BB% | Bash |
|---|---|---|---|---|---|---|---|---|---|---|---|---|---|
| A | CAL | 297 | 4 | 39 | 39 | 17 | .303 | .349 | .448 | 86% | 35% | 6% | 1.48 |
| AA | TL | 191 | 1 | 25 | 20 | 4 | .288 | .332 | .325 | 92% | 31% | 6% | 1.13 |
| AAA | PCL | 65 | 0 | 13 | 9 | 4 | .400 | .412 | .585 | 94% | 43% | 1% | 1.46 |

### Majors
| Yr | Team | AB | HR | R | RBI | SB | BA | OBP | SLG | CT% | H% | BB% | Bash |
|---|---|---|---|---|---|---|---|---|---|---|---|---|---|
| 07 | — | | | | | | | | | | | | |
| 08 | — | | | | | | | | | | | | |
| 09 | — | | | | | | | | | | | | |
| 10 | — | | | | | | | | | | | | |

Although Amarista might earn only 100 appearances or so in 2011, he is the Angels' highest-level middle-infield prospect. He's a sparkplug to an offense, with a good mix of speed and gap power. He should start 2011 in Triple-A, and he could be a factor in an Angels trade. (DS)

**Competition at 2B / Stats in 2010**
| Bats | Player | GSvR | GSvL | Sub | OPS |
|---|---|---|---|---|---|
| RH | Kendrick H | 90 | 50 | 3 | .721 |
| BH | Izturis M | 19 | 2 | 1 | .684 |

---

## Bryan Anderson — 50 PA | $-2 | 20 pts
CA-8 — Owned: 0% — LH

### Forecast
| Player | Age | AB | HR | R | RBI | SB | BA | OBP | SLG | $1L | Pts |
|---|---|---|---|---|---|---|---|---|---|---|---|
| Anderson B | 24 | 48 | 1 | 5 | 5 | 0 | .250 | .313 | .356 | -$2 | 20 |
| **Mini-Browser** | Age | AB | HR | R | RBI | SB | BA | OBP | SLG | $1L | Pts |
| Donaldson J | 25 | 87 | 3 | 8 | 12 | 1 | .208 | .294 | .366 | -$1 | 40 |
| Nieves W | 33 | 68 | 1 | 6 | 8 | 0 | .241 | .289 | .322 | -$1 | 30 |
| Miller C | 35 | 44 | 2 | 5 | 6 | 0 | .238 | .327 | .374 | -$2 | 20 |
| McKenry M | 26 | 45 | 2 | 5 | 6 | 0 | .212 | .309 | .416 | -$2 | 20 |
| Santos O | 29 | 45 | 1 | 5 | 5 | 0 | .245 | .291 | .355 | -$2 | 20 |

### Minors (2010) / Skills
| Level | Leag | AB | HR | R | RBI | SB | BA | OBP | SLG | CT% | H% | BB% | Bash |
|---|---|---|---|---|---|---|---|---|---|---|---|---|---|
| A | — | | | | | | | | | | | | |
| AA | — | | | | | | | | | | | | |
| AAA | PCL | 270 | 12 | 39 | 42 | 0 | .270 | .341 | .448 | 80% | 34% | 9% | 1.66 |

### Majors
| Yr | Team | AB | HR | R | RBI | SB | BA | OBP | SLG | CT% | H% | BB% | Bash |
|---|---|---|---|---|---|---|---|---|---|---|---|---|---|
| 07 | — | | | | | | | | | | | | |
| 08 | — | | | | | | | | | | | | |
| 09 | — | | | | | | | | | | | | |
| 10 | STL | 32 | 0 | 1 | 4 | 0 | .281 | .314 | .344 | 78% | 36% | 3% | 1.22 |

Cardinals GM John Mozeliak desires an offense-minded back-up CA for 2011, and yet when Yadier Molina got hurt, the Cards passed over Anderson (.751 OPS in 751 PA in Triple-A) in favor of Matt Pagnozzi (.586 OPS in minors). If LaRussa comes back, Anderson may fulfill his destiny as organizational trade bait. (AB)

**Competition at CA / Stats in 2010**
| Bats | Player | GSvR | GSvL | Sub | OPS |
|---|---|---|---|---|---|
| RH | Molina Y | 84 | 46 | 5 | .671 |
| RH | LaRue J | 12 | 2 | 14 | .596 |
| RH | Pagnozzi M | 7 | 5 | 3 | .892 |

| $1L | $2L | Pts | RAA | 2B | 3B | CS | FB-LD-GB | HR/fb | RBI% | RS% | OPS | 1st Hf | 2nd Hf | vs RH | vs LH | Rnge | vRH | vLH |
|---|---|---|---|---|---|---|---|---|---|---|---|---|---|---|---|---|---|---|
| -$2 | -$11 | 10 | ~1 | 2 | 0 | 0 | 50-23-27 | 0% | 44% | 9% | .658 | .714 | .641 | .588 | 1.100 | 0.58 | -18 | +39 |

(Rnge 0.60 shown for 08 and 09; 0.58 for 10)

---

## Lars Anderson — 50 PA | $-5 | 20 pts
1B-18 — Owned: 0% — LH

### Forecast
| Player | Age | AB | HR | R | RBI | SB | BA | OBP | SLG | $1L | Pts |
|---|---|---|---|---|---|---|---|---|---|---|---|
| Anderson L | 23 | 44 | 2 | 5 | 5 | 0 | .228 | .320 | .384 | -$5 | 20 |
| **Mini-Browser** | Age | AB | HR | R | RBI | SB | BA | OBP | SLG | $1L | Pts |
| Rizzo A | 21 | 44 | 2 | 5 | 6 | 0 | .251 | .313 | .424 | -$5 | 20 |
| Delgado C | 38 | 22 | 1 | 4 | 4 | 0 | .276 | .358 | .506 | -$5 | 20 |
| Hughes R | 27 | 47 | 2 | 5 | 5 | 0 | .225 | .291 | .410 | -$5 | 20 |
| Quinlan R | 34 | 46 | 1 | 5 | 5 | 1 | .239 | .291 | .327 | -$5 | 20 |
| Carp M | 24 | 43 | 2 | 5 | 5 | 0 | .233 | .327 | .386 | -$5 | 20 |

### Minors (2010) / Skills
| Level | Leag | AB | HR | R | RBI | SB | BA | OBP | SLG | CT% | H% | BB% | Bash |
|---|---|---|---|---|---|---|---|---|---|---|---|---|---|
| A | — | | | | | | | | | | | | |
| AA | EL | 62 | 5 | 13 | 16 | 1 | .355 | .408 | .677 | 74% | 48% | 10% | 1.91 |
| AAA | IL | 409 | 10 | 49 | 53 | 2 | .262 | .340 | .428 | 73% | 36% | 10% | 1.64 |

### Majors
| Yr | Team | AB | HR | R | RBI | SB | BA | OBP | SLG | CT% | H% | BB% | Bash |
|---|---|---|---|---|---|---|---|---|---|---|---|---|---|
| 07 | — | | | | | | | | | | | | |
| 08 | — | | | | | | | | | | | | |
| 09 | — | | | | | | | | | | | | |
| 10 | BOS | 35 | 0 | 4 | 4 | 0 | .200 | .326 | .229 | 77% | 26% | 16% | 1.14 |

GM Theo Epstein identified Anderson as someone who could make a big impact in 2012 (though by then Anderson might be in another uniform). Even so, Anderson should get AB in 2011 by virtue of being on the 40-man. But if Kevin Youkilis were to go down for an extended spell, Boston would try Anthony Rizzo. (EB)

**Competition at 1B / Stats in 2010**
| Bats | Player | GSvR | GSvL | Sub | OPS |
|---|---|---|---|---|---|
| RH | Youkilis K | 66 | 32 | 8 | .975 |
| RH | Lowell M | 20 | 18 | 5 | .674 |
| BH | Martinez V | 8 | 6 | 0 | .844 |
| LH | Anderson L | 10 | 1 | 7 | .554 |

| $1L | $2L | Pts | RAA | 2B | 3B | CS | FB-LD-GB | HR/fb | RBI% | RS% | OPS | 1st Hf | 2nd Hf | vs RH | vs LH | Rnge | vRH | vLH |
|---|---|---|---|---|---|---|---|---|---|---|---|---|---|---|---|---|---|---|
| -$4 | -$20 | 20 | -3 | 1 | 0 | 0 | 39-14-46 | 0% | 16% | 29% | .554 | — | .554 | .574 | .333 | 1.85 | | |

(Rnge 1.85 shown for 08, 09, 10)

---

## Robert Andino — 100 PA | $-3 | 40 pts
2B-8, SS-7, 3B-6 — Owned: 0% — RH

### Forecast
| Player | Age | AB | HR | R | RBI | SB | BA | OBP | SLG | $1L | Pts |
|---|---|---|---|---|---|---|---|---|---|---|---|
| Andino R | 26 | 91 | 2 | 10 | 8 | 3 | .254 | .301 | .382 | -$3 | 40 |
| **Mini-Browser** | Age | AB | HR | R | RBI | SB | BA | OBP | SLG | $1L | Pts |
| Abreu T | 26 | 143 | 3 | 18 | 14 | 2 | .273 | .310 | .422 | -$1 | 80 |
| Greene T | 27 | 140 | 5 | 18 | 12 | 6 | .225 | .297 | .376 | -$1 | 70 |
| Hernandez A | 28 | 140 | 2 | 17 | 12 | 2 | .246 | .300 | .341 | -$2 | 70 |
| Valdez W | 32 | 94 | 1 | 12 | 8 | 2 | .254 | .315 | .339 | -$3 | 50 |
| Ciriaco P | 25 | 92 | 2 | 11 | 9 | 8 | .218 | .246 | .312 | -$3 | 40 |

### Minors (2010) / Skills
| Level | Leag | AB | HR | R | RBI | SB | BA | OBP | SLG | CT% | H% | BB% | Bash |
|---|---|---|---|---|---|---|---|---|---|---|---|---|---|
| A | — | | | | | | | | | | | | |
| AA | — | | | | | | | | | | | | |
| AAA | IL | 546 | 13 | 72 | 76 | 16 | .264 | .302 | .405 | 80% | 33% | 5% | 1.53 |

### Majors
| Yr | Team | AB | HR | R | RBI | SB | BA | OBP | SLG | CT% | H% | BB% | Bash |
|---|---|---|---|---|---|---|---|---|---|---|---|---|---|
| 07 | FLA | 13 | 0 | 0 | 0 | 0 | .385 | .385 | .462 | 85% | 45% | 0% | 1.62 |
| 08 | FLA | 63 | 2 | 7 | 9 | 0 | .206 | .254 | .333 | 63% | 33% | 6% | 1.62 |
| 09 | BAL | 198 | 2 | 30 | 13 | 3 | .222 | .274 | .288 | 76% | 29% | 7% | 1.30 |
| 10 | BAL | 61 | 2 | 6 | 6 | 1 | .295 | .333 | .459 | 79% | 38% | 5% | 1.56 |

Andino's ability to play anywhere in the field is a plus, but his inability to bat well enough to slot anywhere above #8 in the order renders him offensively pointless. His only hope to get significant playing time is an injury, and his best hope to make Baltimore's regular roster is to satisfy budgetary constraints. (BJ)

**Competition at SS / Stats in 2010**
| Bats | Player | GSvR | GSvL | Sub | OPS |
|---|---|---|---|---|---|
| BH | Izturis C | 99 | 43 | 8 | .545 |
| RH | Lugo J | 10 | 7 | 9 | .581 |

| Yr | Team | $1L | $2L | Pts | RAA | 2B | 3B | CS | FB-LD-GB | HR/fb | RBI% | RS% | OPS | 1st Hf | 2nd Hf | vs RH | vs LH | Rnge | vRH | vLH |
|---|---|---|---|---|---|---|---|---|---|---|---|---|---|---|---|---|---|---|---|---|
| 07 | FLA | -$6 | -$20 | — | +1 | 0 | 0 | 0 | 27-18-55 | 0% | 0% | 0% | .846 | — | .846 | .800 | 1.000 | 4.75 | -15 | +39 |
| 08 | FLA | -$4 | -$17 | 20 | -3 | 1 | 0 | 0 | 21-28-51 | 25% | 22% | 33% | .587 | .562 | .833 | .588 | .586 | 4.75 | -19 | +48 |
| 09 | BAL | -$1 | -$15 | 70 | -10 | 7 | 4 | 3 | 30-17-53 | 4% | 9% | 51% | .562 | .542 | .613 | .554 | .580 | 4.75 | -21 | +50 |
| 10 | BAL | -$2 | -$17 | 30 | +2 | 1 | 0 | 1 | 43-14-43 | 10% | 12% | 20% | .792 | — | .792 | .738 | .900 | 4.78 | -15 | +34 |

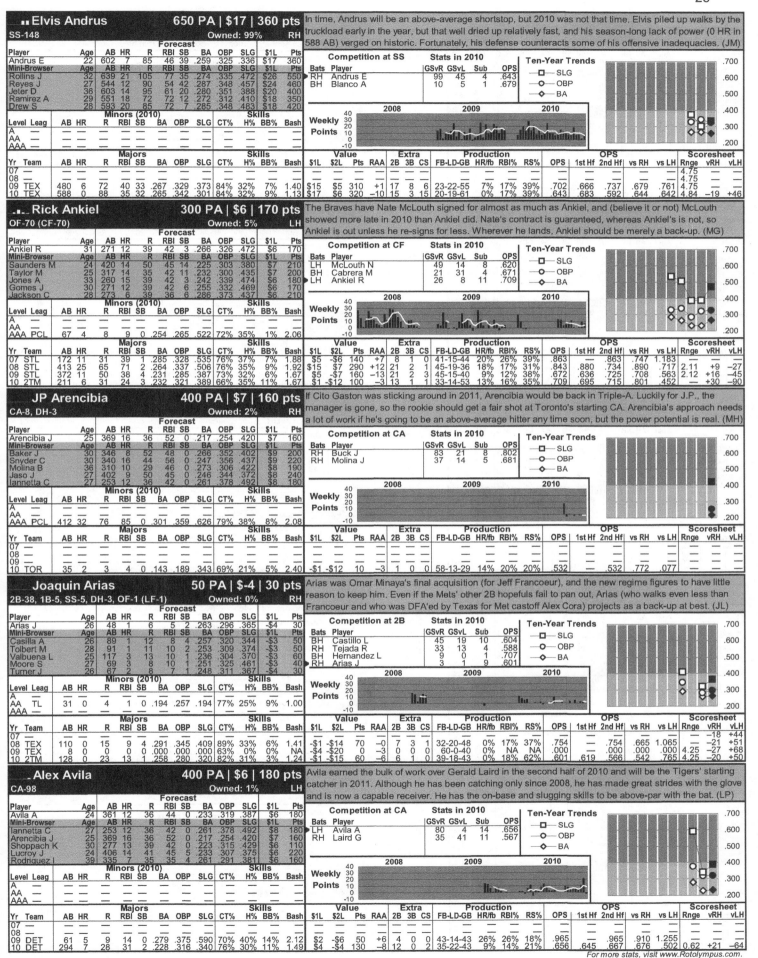

## Elvis Andrus — 650 PA | $17 | 360 pts
SS-148 — Owned: 99% — RH

In time, Andrus will be an above-average shortstop, but 2010 was not that time. Elvis piled up walks by the truckload early in the year, but that well dried up relatively fast, and his season-long lack of power (0 HR in 588 AB) verged on historic. Fortunately, his defense counteracts some of his offensive inadequacies. (JM)

| Player | Age | AB | HR | R | RBI | SB | BA | OBP | SLG | $1L | Pts |
|---|---|---|---|---|---|---|---|---|---|---|---|
| Andrus E | 22 | 602 | 7 | 85 | 46 | 39 | .259 | .325 | .336 | $17 | 360 |
| Rollins J | 32 | 639 | 21 | 105 | 77 | 35 | .274 | .335 | .472 | $26 | 550 |
| Reyes J | 27 | 544 | 12 | 90 | 54 | 42 | .287 | .348 | .457 | $24 | 460 |
| Jeter D | 36 | 603 | 14 | 95 | 61 | 20 | .280 | .351 | .388 | $20 | 400 |
| Ramirez A | 29 | 551 | 18 | 72 | 72 | 12 | .272 | .312 | .410 | $18 | 350 |
| Drew S | 28 | 593 | 20 | 85 | 72 | 7 | .285 | .348 | .483 | $18 | 420 |

| Yr | Team | AB | HR | R | RBI | SB | BA | OBP | SLG | CT% | H% | BB% | Bash |
|---|---|---|---|---|---|---|---|---|---|---|---|---|---|
| 09 | TEX | 480 | 6 | 72 | 40 | 33 | .267 | .329 | .373 | 84% | 32% | 7% | 1.40 |
| 10 | TEX | 588 | 0 | 88 | 35 | 32 | .265 | .342 | .301 | 84% | 32% | 9% | 1.13 |

## Rick Ankiel — 300 PA | $6 | 170 pts
OF-70 (CF-70) — Owned: 5% — LH

The Braves have Nate McLouth signed for almost as much as Ankiel, and (believe it or not) McLouth showed more late in 2010 than Ankiel did. Nate's contract is guaranteed, whereas Ankiel's is not, so Ankiel is out unless he re-signs for less. Wherever he lands, Ankiel should be merely a back-up. (MG)

## JP Arencibia — 400 PA | $7 | 160 pts
CA-8, DH-3 — Owned: 2% — RH

If Cito Gaston was sticking around in 2011, Arencibia would be back in Triple-A. Luckily for J.P., the manager is gone, so the rookie should get a fair shot at Toronto's starting CA. Arencibia's approach needs a lot of work if he's going to be an above-average hitter any time soon, but the power potential is real. (MH)

## Joaquin Arias — 50 PA | $-4 | 30 pts
2B-38, 1B-5, SS-5, DH-3, OF-1 (LF-1) — Owned: 0% — RH

Arias was Omar Minaya's final acquisition (for Jeff Francoeur), and the new regime figures to have little reason to keep him. Even if the Mets' other 2B hopefuls fail to pan out, Arias (who walks even less than Francoeur and who was DFA'ed by Texas for Met castoff Alex Cora) projects as a back-up at best. (JL)

## Alex Avila — 400 PA | $6 | 180 pts
CA-98 — Owned: 1% — LH

Avila earned the bulk of work over Gerald Laird in the second half of 2010 and will be the Tigers' starting catcher in 2011. Although he has been catching only since 2008, he has made great strides with the glove and is now a capable receiver. He has the on-base and slugging skills to be above-par with the bat. (LP)

*For more stats, visit www.Rotolympus.com.*

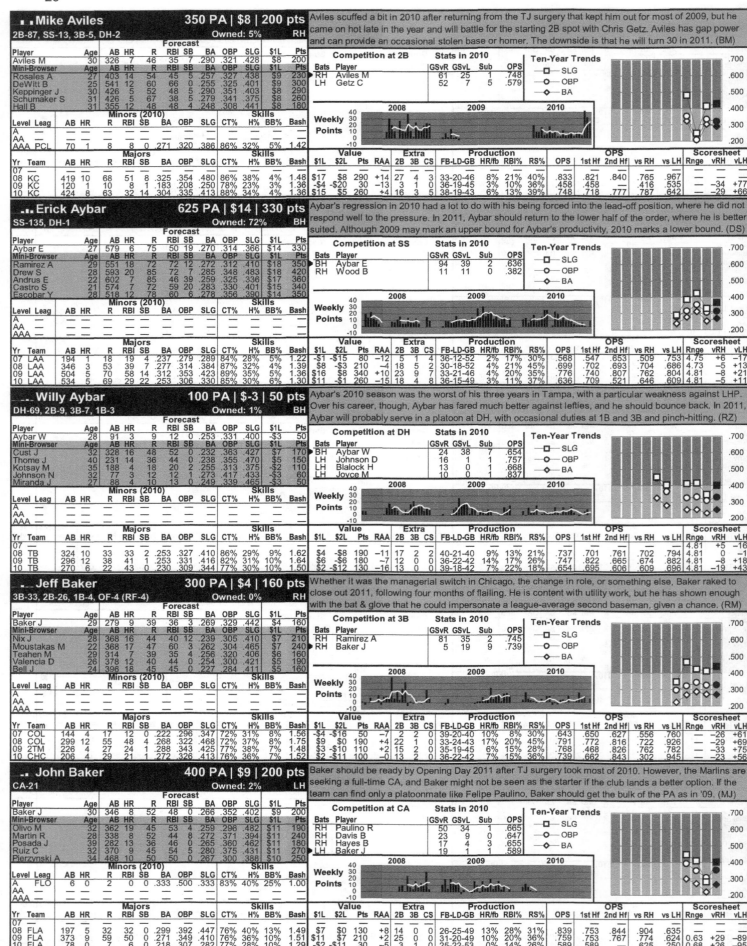

## Mike Aviles — 350 PA | $8 | 200 pts

2B-87, SS-13, 3B-5, DH-2 — Owned: 5% — RH

Aviles scuffed a bit in 2010 after returning from the TJ surgery that kept him out for most of 2009, but he came on hot late in the year and will battle for the starting 2B spot with Chris Getz. Aviles has gap power and can provide an occasional stolen base or homer. The downside is that he will turn 30 in 2011. (BM)

### Forecast

| Player | Age | AB | HR | R | RBI | SB | BA | OBP | SLG | $1L | Pts |
|---|---|---|---|---|---|---|---|---|---|---|---|
| Aviles M | 30 | 326 | 7 | 46 | 35 | 7 | .290 | .321 | .428 | $8 | 200 |

| Mini-Browser | Age | AB | HR | R | RBI | SB | BA | OBP | SLG | $1L | Pts |
|---|---|---|---|---|---|---|---|---|---|---|---|
| Rosales A | 27 | 403 | 14 | 54 | 45 | 5 | .257 | .327 | .438 | $9 | 230 |
| DeWitt B | 25 | 541 | 12 | 60 | 66 | 0 | .255 | .325 | .401 | $9 | 300 |
| Keppinger J | 30 | 426 | 5 | 52 | 48 | 5 | .290 | .351 | .375 | $8 | 290 |
| Schumaker S | 31 | 426 | 5 | 67 | 38 | 5 | .279 | .341 | .375 | $8 | 260 |
| Hall B | 31 | 355 | 12 | 48 | 48 | 4 | .248 | .308 | .441 | $8 | 180 |

### Minors (2010) / Skills

| Level | Leag | AB | HR | R | RBI | SB | BA | OBP | SLG | CT% | H% | BB% | Bash |
|---|---|---|---|---|---|---|---|---|---|---|---|---|---|
| A | — | — | — | — | — | — | — | — | — | — | — | — | — |
| AA | — | — | — | — | — | — | — | — | — | — | — | — | — |
| AAA | PCL | 70 | 1 | 8 | 8 | 0 | .271 | .320 | .386 | 86% | 32% | 5% | 1.42 |

### Majors / Skills / Value / Extra / Production / OPS / Scoresheet

| Yr | Team | AB | HR | R | RBI | SB | BA | OBP | SLG | CT% | H% | BB% | Bash | $1L | $2L | Pts | RAA | 2B | 3B | CS | FB-LD-GB | HR/fb | RBI% | RS% | OPS | 1st Hf | 2nd Hf | vs RH | vs LH | Rnge | vRH | vLH |
|---|---|---|---|---|---|---|---|---|---|---|---|---|---|---|---|---|---|---|---|---|---|---|---|---|---|---|---|---|---|---|---|---|
| 07 | | | | | | | | | | | | | | | | | | | | | | | | | | | | | | | | |
| 08 | KC | 419 | 10 | 68 | 51 | 8 | .325 | .354 | .480 | 86% | 38% | 4% | 1.48 | $17 | $8 | 290 | +14 | 27 | 4 | 3 | 33-20-46 | 8% | 21% | 40% | .833 | .821 | .840 | .765 | .967 | — | −34 | +77 |
| 09 | KC | 120 | 1 | 10 | 8 | 1 | .183 | .208 | .250 | 78% | 23% | 3% | 1.36 | −$4 | −$20 | 30 | −13 | 3 | 1 | 0 | 36-19-45 | 3% | 10% | 36% | .458 | .458 | — | .416 | .535 | — | −5 | +46 |
| 10 | KC | 424 | 8 | 63 | 32 | 14 | .304 | .335 | .413 | 88% | 34% | 4% | 1.36 | $15 | $5 | 260 | +4 | 16 | 3 | 5 | 38-19-43 | 6% | 13% | 39% | .748 | .718 | .777 | .787 | .642 | — | −29 | +66 |

## Erick Aybar — 625 PA | $14 | 330 pts

SS-135, DH-1 — Owned: 72% — BH

Aybar's regression in 2010 had a lot to do with his being forced into the lead-off position, where he did not respond well to the pressure. In 2011, Aybar should return to the lower half of the order, where he is better suited. Although 2009 may mark an upper bound for Aybar's productivity, 2010 marks a lower bound. (DS)

### Forecast

| Player | Age | AB | HR | R | RBI | SB | BA | OBP | SLG | $1L | Pts |
|---|---|---|---|---|---|---|---|---|---|---|---|
| Aybar E | 27 | 579 | 6 | 75 | 50 | 19 | .270 | .314 | .366 | $14 | 330 |

| Mini-Browser | Age | AB | HR | R | RBI | SB | BA | OBP | SLG | $1L | Pts |
|---|---|---|---|---|---|---|---|---|---|---|---|
| Ramirez A | 29 | 551 | 18 | 72 | 72 | 12 | .272 | .312 | .410 | $18 | 350 |
| Drew S | 28 | 593 | 20 | 85 | 72 | 7 | .285 | .348 | .483 | $18 | 420 |
| Andrus E | 22 | 602 | 7 | 85 | 46 | 39 | .259 | .325 | .336 | $17 | 360 |
| Castro S | 21 | 574 | 7 | 72 | 59 | 20 | .283 | .330 | .401 | $15 | 340 |
| Escobar Y | 28 | 518 | 12 | 78 | 60 | 6 | .278 | .356 | .390 | $14 | 350 |

### Minors (2010) / Skills

| Level | Leag | AB | HR | R | RBI | SB | BA | OBP | SLG | CT% | H% | BB% | Bash |
|---|---|---|---|---|---|---|---|---|---|---|---|---|---|
| A | — | — | — | — | — | — | — | — | — | — | — | — | — |
| AA | — | — | — | — | — | — | — | — | — | — | — | — | — |
| AAA | — | — | — | — | — | — | — | — | — | — | — | — | — |

### Majors / Skills / Value / Extra / Production / OPS / Scoresheet

| Yr | Team | AB | HR | R | RBI | SB | BA | OBP | SLG | CT% | H% | BB% | Bash | $1L | $2L | Pts | RAA | 2B | 3B | CS | FB-LD-GB | HR/fb | RBI% | RS% | OPS | 1st Hf | 2nd Hf | vs RH | vs LH | Rnge | vRH | vLH |
|---|---|---|---|---|---|---|---|---|---|---|---|---|---|---|---|---|---|---|---|---|---|---|---|---|---|---|---|---|---|---|---|---|
| 07 | LAA | 194 | 1 | 18 | 19 | 4 | .237 | .279 | .289 | 84% | 28% | 5% | 1.22 | −$1 | −$15 | 80 | −12 | 5 | 1 | 4 | 36-12-52 | 2% | 17% | 30% | .568 | .547 | .653 | .509 | .753 | 4.75 | +6 | −17 |
| 08 | LAA | 346 | 3 | 53 | 39 | 7 | .277 | .314 | .384 | 87% | 32% | 4% | 1.39 | $8 | −$3 | 210 | −4 | 18 | 5 | 2 | 30-18-52 | 4% | 21% | 45% | .699 | .702 | .693 | .704 | .686 | 4.73 | −5 | +13 |
| 09 | LAA | 504 | 5 | 70 | 58 | 14 | .312 | .353 | .423 | 89% | 35% | 5% | 1.36 | $14 | $8 | 340 | +10 | 23 | 9 | 7 | 33-21-46 | 4% | 20% | 35% | .776 | .740 | .807 | .762 | .804 | 4.81 | −8 | +21 |
| 10 | LAA | 534 | 5 | 69 | 29 | 22 | .253 | .306 | .330 | 85% | 30% | 6% | 1.30 | $11 | −$1 | 260 | −15 | 8 | 4 | 16 | 36-15-49 | 3% | 11% | 37% | .636 | .709 | .521 | .646 | .609 | 4.81 | −5 | +11 |

## Willy Aybar — 100 PA | $-3 | 50 pts

DH-69, 2B-9, 3B-7, 1B-3 — Owned: 1% — BH

Aybar's 2010 season was the worst of his three years in Tampa, with a particular weakness against LHP. Over his career, though, Aybar has fared much better against lefties, and he should bounce back. In 2011, Aybar will probably serve in a platoon at DH, with occasional duties at 1B and 3B and pinch-hitting. (RZ)

### Forecast

| Player | Age | AB | HR | R | RBI | SB | BA | OBP | SLG | $1L | Pts |
|---|---|---|---|---|---|---|---|---|---|---|---|
| Aybar W | 28 | 91 | 3 | 9 | 12 | 0 | .253 | .331 | .400 | −$3 | 50 |

| Mini-Browser | Age | AB | HR | R | RBI | SB | BA | OBP | SLG | $1L | Pts |
|---|---|---|---|---|---|---|---|---|---|---|---|
| Cust J | 32 | 328 | 16 | 48 | 52 | 0 | .232 | .363 | .427 | $7 | 170 |
| Thome J | 40 | 231 | 14 | 36 | 44 | 0 | .238 | .355 | .470 | $5 | 150 |
| Kotsay M | 35 | 188 | 4 | 18 | 20 | 2 | .255 | .313 | .375 | −$2 | 110 |
| Johnson N | 32 | 77 | 3 | 12 | 12 | 1 | .273 | .417 | .433 | −$3 | 60 |
| Miranda J | 27 | 88 | 4 | 10 | 13 | 0 | .249 | .339 | .465 | −$4 | 50 |

### Minors (2010) / Skills

| Level | Leag | AB | HR | R | RBI | SB | BA | OBP | SLG | CT% | H% | BB% | Bash |
|---|---|---|---|---|---|---|---|---|---|---|---|---|---|
| A | — | — | — | — | — | — | — | — | — | — | — | — | — |
| AA | — | — | — | — | — | — | — | — | — | — | — | — | — |
| AAA | — | — | — | — | — | — | — | — | — | — | — | — | — |

### Majors / Skills / Value / Extra / Production / OPS / Scoresheet

| Yr | Team | AB | HR | R | RBI | SB | BA | OBP | SLG | CT% | H% | BB% | Bash | $1L | $2L | Pts | RAA | 2B | 3B | CS | FB-LD-GB | HR/fb | RBI% | RS% | OPS | 1st Hf | 2nd Hf | vs RH | vs LH | Rnge | vRH | vLH |
|---|---|---|---|---|---|---|---|---|---|---|---|---|---|---|---|---|---|---|---|---|---|---|---|---|---|---|---|---|---|---|---|---|
| 07 | | | | | | | | | | | | | | | | | | | | | | | | | | | | | | 4.81 | +5 | −16 |
| 08 | TB | 324 | 10 | 33 | 33 | 2 | .253 | .327 | .410 | 86% | 29% | 9% | 1.62 | $4 | −$8 | 190 | −11 | 17 | 2 | 2 | 40-21-40 | 9% | 13% | 21% | .737 | .701 | .761 | .702 | .794 | 4.81 | 0 | −1 |
| 09 | TB | 296 | 12 | 38 | 41 | 1 | .253 | .331 | .416 | 82% | 31% | 10% | 1.64 | $6 | −$6 | 180 | −7 | 12 | 0 | 0 | 36-22-42 | 14% | 17% | 26% | .747 | .822 | .665 | .674 | .882 | 4.81 | −8 | +18 |
| 10 | TB | 270 | 6 | 22 | 43 | 0 | .230 | .309 | .344 | 77% | 30% | 10% | 1.50 | −$2 | −$12 | 130 | −16 | 13 | 0 | 0 | 39-18-42 | 7% | 12% | 22% | .654 | .695 | .606 | .609 | .693 | 4.81 | −19 | +43 |

## Jeff Baker — 300 PA | $4 | 160 pts

3B-33, 2B-26, 1B-4, OF-4 (RF-4) — Owned: 0% — RH

Whether it was the managerial switch in Chicago, the change in role, or something else, Baker raked to close out 2011, following four months of flailing. He is content with utility work, but he has shown enough with the bat & glove that he could impersonate a league-average second baseman, given a chance. (RM)

### Forecast

| Player | Age | AB | HR | R | RBI | SB | BA | OBP | SLG | $1L | Pts |
|---|---|---|---|---|---|---|---|---|---|---|---|
| Baker J | 29 | 279 | 9 | 39 | 36 | 3 | .269 | .329 | .442 | $4 | 160 |

| Mini-Browser | Age | AB | HR | R | RBI | SB | BA | OBP | SLG | $1L | Pts |
|---|---|---|---|---|---|---|---|---|---|---|---|
| Nix J | 28 | 368 | 16 | 44 | 40 | 12 | .239 | .305 | .410 | $7 | 210 |
| Moustakas M | 22 | 368 | 17 | 47 | 60 | 3 | .262 | .304 | .465 | $7 | 240 |
| Teahen M | 29 | 314 | 7 | 39 | 35 | 4 | .256 | .320 | .406 | $6 | 160 |
| Valencia D | 26 | 378 | 12 | 40 | 44 | 0 | .254 | .300 | .421 | $5 | 190 |
| Bell J | 24 | 396 | 18 | 45 | 45 | 0 | .227 | .284 | .411 | $5 | 160 |

### Minors (2010) / Skills

| Level | Leag | AB | HR | R | RBI | SB | BA | OBP | SLG | CT% | H% | BB% | Bash |
|---|---|---|---|---|---|---|---|---|---|---|---|---|---|
| A | — | — | — | — | — | — | — | — | — | — | — | — | — |
| AA | — | — | — | — | — | — | — | — | — | — | — | — | — |
| AAA | — | — | — | — | — | — | — | — | — | — | — | — | — |

### Majors / Skills / Value / Extra / Production / OPS / Scoresheet

| Yr | Team | AB | HR | R | RBI | SB | BA | OBP | SLG | CT% | H% | BB% | Bash | $1L | $2L | Pts | RAA | 2B | 3B | CS | FB-LD-GB | HR/fb | RBI% | RS% | OPS | 1st Hf | 2nd Hf | vs RH | vs LH | Rnge | vRH | vLH |
|---|---|---|---|---|---|---|---|---|---|---|---|---|---|---|---|---|---|---|---|---|---|---|---|---|---|---|---|---|---|---|---|---|
| 07 | COL | 144 | 4 | 17 | 12 | 0 | .222 | .296 | .347 | 72% | 31% | 8% | 1.56 | −$4 | −$16 | 50 | −7 | 2 | 2 | 0 | 39-20-40 | 10% | 8% | 30% | .643 | .650 | .627 | .556 | .760 | — | −26 | +61 |
| 08 | COL | 299 | 12 | 55 | 48 | 4 | .268 | .322 | .468 | 72% | 37% | 8% | 1.75 | $9 | $0 | 190 | +4 | 22 | 1 | 0 | 33-24-43 | 17% | 20% | 45% | .791 | .772 | .816 | .722 | .926 | — | −29 | +69 |
| 09 | 2TM | 226 | 4 | 27 | 24 | 1 | .288 | .343 | .425 | 77% | 38% | 7% | 1.48 | $3 | −$10 | 110 | +2 | 15 | 2 | 0 | 35-19-45 | 6% | 15% | 28% | .768 | .468 | .826 | .762 | .782 | — | −33 | +75 |
| 10 | CHC | 206 | 4 | 29 | 21 | 0 | .272 | .326 | .413 | 76% | 36% | 7% | 1.52 | $2 | −$11 | 100 | −0 | 13 | 2 | 0 | 36-22-42 | 7% | 15% | 36% | .739 | .662 | .843 | .302 | .945 | — | −23 | +69 |

## John Baker — 400 PA | $9 | 200 pts

CA-21 — Owned: 2% — LH

Baker should be ready by Opening Day 2011 after TJ surgery took most of 2010. However, the Marlins are seeking a full-time CA, and Baker might not be seen as the starter if the club lands a better option. If the team can find only a platoonmate like Felipe Paulino, Baker should get the bulk of the PA as in '09. (MJ)

### Forecast

| Player | Age | AB | HR | R | RBI | SB | BA | OBP | SLG | $1L | Pts |
|---|---|---|---|---|---|---|---|---|---|---|---|
| Baker J | 30 | 346 | 8 | 52 | 48 | 0 | .266 | .352 | .402 | $9 | 200 |

| Mini-Browser | Age | AB | HR | R | RBI | SB | BA | OBP | SLG | $1L | Pts |
|---|---|---|---|---|---|---|---|---|---|---|---|
| Olivo M | 32 | 362 | 19 | 45 | 53 | 4 | .259 | .296 | .482 | $11 | 190 |
| Martin R | 28 | 338 | 8 | 52 | 44 | 8 | .272 | .371 | .394 | $11 | 240 |
| Posada J | 39 | 282 | 13 | 36 | 46 | 0 | .265 | .360 | .462 | $11 | 220 |
| Ruiz C | 32 | 370 | 9 | 45 | 54 | 5 | .280 | .375 | .431 | $11 | 270 |
| Pierzynski A | 34 | 468 | 10 | 50 | 50 | 0 | .267 | .300 | .388 | $10 | 250 |

### Minors (2010) / Skills

| Level | Leag | AB | HR | R | RBI | SB | BA | OBP | SLG | CT% | H% | BB% | Bash |
|---|---|---|---|---|---|---|---|---|---|---|---|---|---|
| A | FLO | 6 | 0 | 2 | 0 | 0 | .333 | .500 | .333 | 83% | 40% | 25% | 1.00 |
| AA | — | — | — | — | — | — | — | — | — | — | — | — | — |
| AAA | — | — | — | — | — | — | — | — | — | — | — | — | — |

### Majors / Skills / Value / Extra / Production / OPS / Scoresheet

| Yr | Team | AB | HR | R | RBI | SB | BA | OBP | SLG | CT% | H% | BB% | Bash | $1L | $2L | Pts | RAA | 2B | 3B | CS | FB-LD-GB | HR/fb | RBI% | RS% | OPS | 1st Hf | 2nd Hf | vs RH | vs LH | Rnge | vRH | vLH |
|---|---|---|---|---|---|---|---|---|---|---|---|---|---|---|---|---|---|---|---|---|---|---|---|---|---|---|---|---|---|---|---|---|
| 07 | | | | | | | | | | | | | | | | | | | | | | | | | | | | | | | | |
| 08 | FLA | 197 | 5 | 32 | 32 | 0 | .299 | .392 | .447 | 76% | 40% | 13% | 1.49 | $7 | $0 | 130 | +8 | 14 | 0 | 0 | 26-25-49 | 13% | 28% | 31% | .839 | .753 | .844 | .904 | .635 | — | — | — |
| 09 | FLA | 373 | 9 | 59 | 50 | 0 | .271 | .349 | .410 | 76% | 36% | 10% | 1.51 | $11 | $7 | 210 | +2 | 25 | 0 | 0 | 31-20-49 | 10% | 20% | 36% | .759 | .753 | .767 | .774 | .624 | 0.63 | +29 | −89 |
| 10 | FLA | 78 | 0 | 7 | 6 | 0 | .218 | .307 | .282 | 77% | 28% | 10% | 1.29 | −$2 | −$11 | 30 | — | 3 | 1 | 0 | 25-22-53 | 0% | 14% | 26% | .589 | .589 | — | .625 | .250 | 0.68 | +26 | −95 |

## Rocco Baldelli — 50 PA | $-4 | 20 pts

DH-5, OF-4 (RF-4) — Owned: 0% — RH

Owing to a mitochondrial disorder, which can sit him out for extended stretches, the comeback kid's playing time is hard to predict. Despite that condition, Baldelli can play the outfield, and he is still an excellent weapon against left-handed pitchers. He is a probable replacement for Gabe Kapler. (RZ)

| Player (Forecast) | Age | AB | HR | R | RBI | SB | BA | OBP | SLG | $1L | Pts |
|---|---|---|---|---|---|---|---|---|---|---|---|
| Baldelli R | 29 | 46 | 2 | 6 | 7 | 1 | .241 | .304 | .434 | -$4 | 20 |
| **Mini-Browser** | Age | AB | HR | R | RBI | SB | BA | OBP | SLG | $1L | Pts |
| Thome J | 40 | 231 | 14 | 36 | 44 | 0 | .238 | .355 | .470 | $5 | 150 |
| Kotsay M | 35 | 188 | 4 | 18 | 20 | 2 | .255 | .313 | .375 | -$2 | 110 |
| Johnson N | 32 | 77 | 3 | 12 | 12 | 1 | .273 | .417 | .433 | -$3 | 60 |
| Miranda J | 27 | 88 | 4 | 10 | 13 | 0 | .249 | .339 | .465 | -$3 | 50 |
| Aybar W | 28 | 91 | 3 | 9 | 12 | 0 | .253 | .331 | .400 | -$3 | 50 |

| Level | Leag | AB | HR | R | RBI | SB | BA | OBP | SLG | CT% | H% | BB% | Bash |
|---|---|---|---|---|---|---|---|---|---|---|---|---|---|
| A | FLO | 46 | 0 | 6 | 6 | 0 | .283 | .298 | .370 | 76% | 37% | 2% | 1.31 |
| AA | — | — | — | — | — | — | — | — | — | — | — | — | — |
| AAA | IL | 44 | 2 | 7 | 8 | 0 | .273 | .292 | .477 | 75% | 36% | 2% | 1.75 |

| Yr | Team | AB | HR | R | RBI | SB | BA | OBP | SLG | CT% | H% | BB% | Bash |
|---|---|---|---|---|---|---|---|---|---|---|---|---|---|
| 07 | TB | 137 | 5 | 16 | 12 | 4 | .204 | .268 | .358 | 74% | 27% | 6% | 1.75 |
| 08 | TB | 80 | 4 | 12 | 13 | 0 | .263 | .344 | .475 | 69% | 38% | 8% | 1.81 |
| 09 | BOS | 150 | 7 | 23 | 23 | 1 | .253 | .311 | .433 | 75% | 34% | 7% | 1.71 |
| 10 | TB | 24 | 1 | 3 | 5 | 1 | .208 | .240 | .375 | 79% | 26% | 4% | 1.80 |

**Competition at DH — Stats in 2010**

| Bats | Player | GSvR | GSvL | Sub | OPS |
|---|---|---|---|---|---|
| BH | Aybar W | 24 | 38 | 7 | .654 |
| LH | Johnson D | 16 | 1 | 1 | .757 |
| LH | Blalock H | 13 | 0 | 1 | .668 |
| LH | Joyce M | 10 | 0 | 1 | .837 |

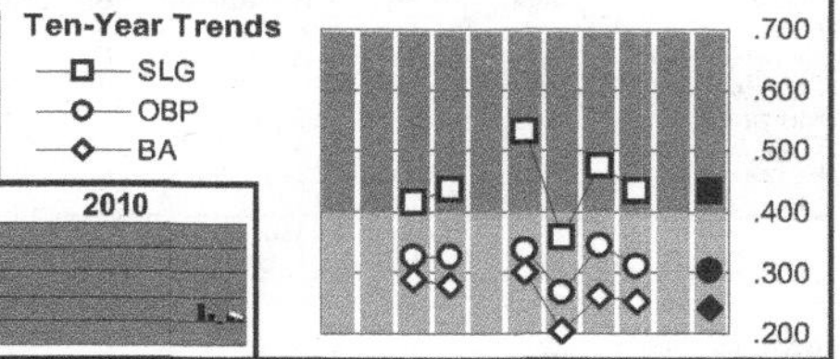


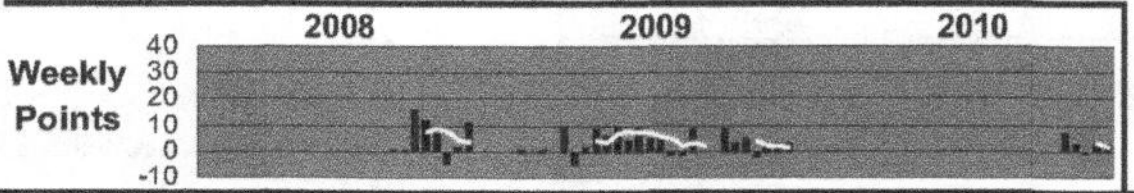


| Yr | $1L | $2L | Pts | RAA | 2B | 3B | CS | FB-LD-GB | HR/fb | RBI% | RS% | OPS | 1st Hf | 2nd Hf | vs RH | vs LH | Rnge | vRH | vLH |
|---|---|---|---|---|---|---|---|---|---|---|---|---|---|---|---|---|---|---|---|
| 07 | -$1 | -$16 | 60 | −11 | 6 | 0 | 1 | 44-18-38 | 11% | 13% | 31% | .626 | .626 | — | .598 | .719 | 0.68 | −11 | +27 |
| 08 | -$1 | -$14 | 40 | −1 | 5 | 0 | 0 | 36-15-49 | 20% | 17% | 30% | .819 | — | .819 | .723 | .882 | 0.68 | −14 | +39 |
| 09 | $2 | -$12 | 90 | −4 | 4 | 1 | 0 | 36-18-46 | 17% | 16% | 36% | .744 | .828 | .631 | .679 | .784 | 0.68 | −27 | +61 |
| 10 | -$3 | -$19 | 20 | −2 | 1 | 0 | 0 | 37-21-42 | 14% | 18% | NA | .615 | — | .615 | .000 | .816 | — | −24 | +45 |

## Wladimir Balentien — 150 PA | $0 | 90 pts

No MLB games played in 2010 — Owned: 0% — RH

Balentien had a strong 2010 in the minors, but when the Reds needed an outfielder, they traded for Willie Bloomquist and made a move to fit him onto the roster, and not Balentien. So Balentien's future is not in Cincinnati, but he could interest another club because he is a decent corner OF with some power. (SW)

| Player (Forecast) | Age | AB | HR | R | RBI | SB | BA | OBP | SLG | $1L | Pts |
|---|---|---|---|---|---|---|---|---|---|---|---|
| Balentien W | 26 | 137 | 8 | 18 | 18 | 2 | .252 | .325 | .484 | $0 | 90 |
| **Mini-Browser** | Age | AB | HR | R | RBI | SB | BA | OBP | SLG | $1L | Pts |
| Crowe T | 27 | 204 | 2 | 25 | 18 | 9 | .243 | .310 | .350 | $0 | 110 |
| Francoeur J | 27 | 166 | 5 | 21 | 23 | 2 | .263 | .310 | .421 | $0 | 100 |
| Denorfia C | 30 | 176 | 4 | 23 | 19 | 4 | .249 | .311 | .382 | $0 | 100 |
| Wise D | 33 | 142 | 5 | 21 | 15 | 6 | .254 | .302 | .446 | $0 | 90 |
| Blanks K | 24 | 180 | 8 | 22 | 28 | 2 | .222 | .322 | .420 | $0 | 100 |

| Level | Leag | AB | HR | R | RBI | SB | BA | OBP | SLG | CT% | H% | BB% | Bash |
|---|---|---|---|---|---|---|---|---|---|---|---|---|---|
| A | — | — | — | — | — | — | — | — | — | — | — | — | — |
| AA | — | — | — | — | — | — | — | — | — | — | — | — | — |
| AAA | IL | 401 | 25 | 71 | 78 | 12 | .282 | .337 | .536 | 79% | 36% | 8% | 1.90 |

| Yr | Team | AB | HR | R | RBI | SB | BA | OBP | SLG | CT% | H% | BB% | Bash |
|---|---|---|---|---|---|---|---|---|---|---|---|---|---|
| 07 | SEA | 3 | 1 | 1 | 4 | 0 | .667 | .500 | 2.000 | 100% | 67% | 0% | 3.00 |
| 08 | SEA | 243 | 7 | 23 | 24 | 0 | .202 | .250 | .342 | 67% | 30% | 6% | 1.69 |
| 09 | 2TM | 265 | 7 | 30 | 24 | 2 | .234 | .305 | .385 | 74% | 32% | 9% | 1.65 |
| 10 | — | — | — | — | — | — | — | — | — | — | — | — | — |

**Competition at LF — Stats in 2010**

| Bats | Player | GSvR | GSvL | Sub | OPS |
|---|---|---|---|---|---|
| RH | Gomes J | 74 | 52 | 3 | .758 |
| LH | Nix L | 29 | 0 | 21 | .805 |
| RH | Heisey C | 4 | 9 | 25 | .757 |

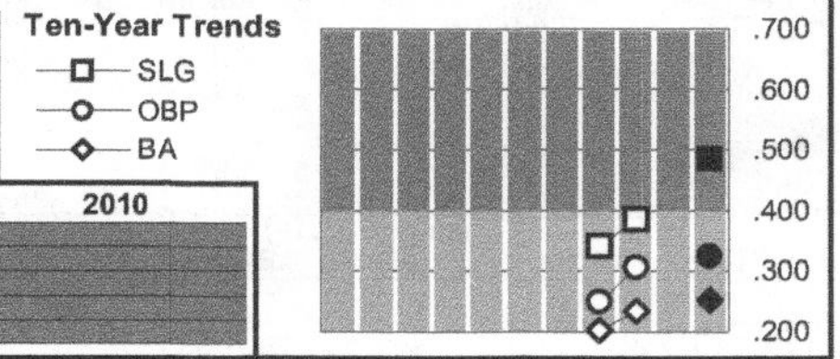


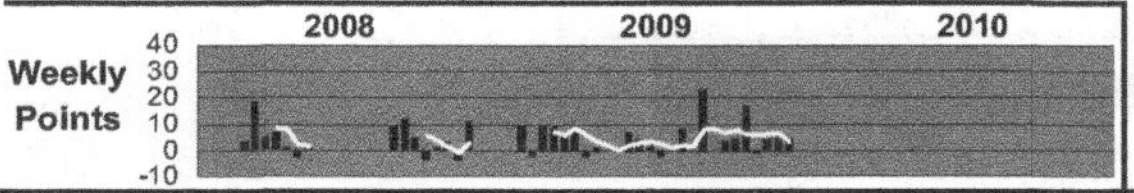


| Yr | $1L | $2L | Pts | RAA | 2B | 3B | CS | FB-LD-GB | HR/fb | RBI% | RS% | OPS | 1st Hf | 2nd Hf | vs RH | vs LH | Rnge | vRH | vLH |
|---|---|---|---|---|---|---|---|---|---|---|---|---|---|---|---|---|---|---|---|
| 07 | -$3 | -$19 | 10 | +2 | 1 | 0 | 0 | 75-25-0 | 33% | 75% | 0% | 2.500 | — | 2.500 | 3.667 | .000 | 2.10 | — | — |
| 08 | -$1 | -$15 | 70 | −17 | 13 | 0 | 1 | 39-14-47 | 11% | 14% | 28% | .592 | .611 | .576 | .578 | .620 | 2.10 | −19 | +47 |
| 09 | -$3 | -$13 | 120 | −7 | 17 | 1 | 1 | 40-15-45 | 9% | 13% | 28% | .690 | .618 | .770 | .758 | .530 | 2.10 | −18 | +42 |
| 10 | — | — | — | — | — | — | — | — | — | — | — | — | — | — | — | — | 2.08 | −4 | +8 |

## Rod Barajas — 200 PA | $3 | 100 pts

CA-96 — Owned: 27% — RH

Talk about first impressions: Barajas got dropped by the Mets and promptly hit 4 HR in his first 8 games as a Dodger. He has always had power, but with a horrendous OBP. That said, Russell Martin is a likely non-tender for LA, so Barajas should be back in his home town and in the mix for significant PT. (MP)

| Player (Forecast) | Age | AB | HR | R | RBI | SB | BA | OBP | SLG | $1L | Pts |
|---|---|---|---|---|---|---|---|---|---|---|---|
| Barajas R | 35 | 186 | 8 | 20 | 26 | 0 | .247 | .292 | .425 | $3 | 100 |
| **Mini-Browser** | Age | AB | HR | R | RBI | SB | BA | OBP | SLG | $1L | Pts |
| Paulino R | 29 | 201 | 5 | 23 | 25 | 0 | .268 | .331 | .400 | $3 | 110 |
| Buck J | 30 | 187 | 8 | 20 | 28 | 0 | .246 | .305 | .450 | $3 | 100 |
| Castro R | 35 | 136 | 8 | 17 | 24 | 0 | .254 | .318 | .474 | $3 | 80 |
| Flores J | 26 | 185 | 6 | 20 | 32 | 0 | .248 | .309 | .411 | $3 | 100 |
| Saltalamacchia J | 25 | 234 | 8 | 28 | 28 | 0 | .235 | .309 | .387 | $3 | 100 |

| Level | Leag | AB | HR | R | RBI | SB | BA | OBP | SLG | CT% | H% | BB% | Bash |
|---|---|---|---|---|---|---|---|---|---|---|---|---|---|
| A | FLO | 17 | 0 | 1 | 2 | 0 | .235 | .235 | .235 | 88% | 27% | 0% | 1.00 |
| AA | — | — | — | — | — | — | — | — | — | — | — | — | — |
| AAA | — | — | — | — | — | — | — | — | — | — | — | — | — |

| Yr | Team | AB | HR | R | RBI | SB | BA | OBP | SLG | CT% | H% | BB% | Bash |
|---|---|---|---|---|---|---|---|---|---|---|---|---|---|
| 07 | PHI | 122 | 4 | 16 | 10 | 0 | .230 | .352 | .393 | 80% | 29% | 14% | 1.71 |
| 08 | TOR | 349 | 11 | 44 | 49 | 0 | .249 | .294 | .410 | 83% | 30% | 5% | 1.64 |
| 09 | TOR | 429 | 19 | 43 | 71 | 1 | .226 | .258 | .403 | 82% | 27% | 4% | 1.78 |
| 10 | 2TM | 313 | 17 | 39 | 47 | 0 | .240 | .284 | .447 | 83% | 29% | 4% | 1.87 |

**Competition at CA — Stats in 2010**

| Bats | Player | GSvR | GSvL | Sub | OPS |
|---|---|---|---|---|---|
| RH | Martin R | 60 | 29 | 4 | .679 |
| RH | Ellis A | 26 | 8 | 9 | .687 |
| RH | Barajas R | 11 | 9 | 3 | .731 |
| RH | Ausmus B | 15 | 4 | 2 | .564 |

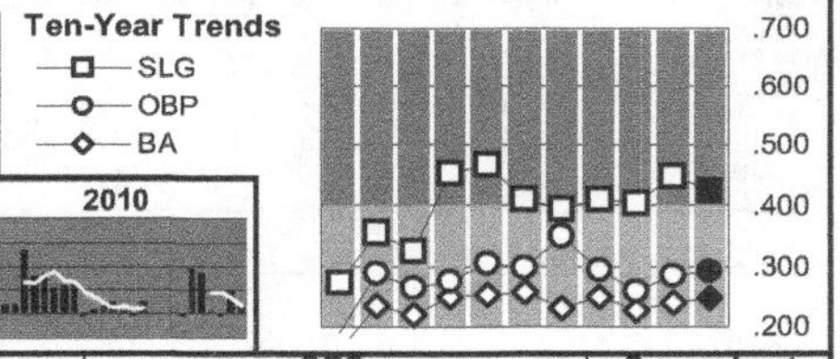


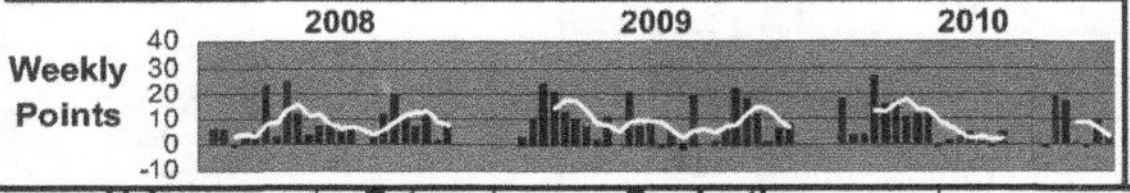


| Yr | $1L | $2L | Pts | RAA | 2B | 3B | CS | FB-LD-GB | HR/fb | RBI% | RS% | OPS | 1st Hf | 2nd Hf | vs RH | vs LH | Rnge | vRH | vLH |
|---|---|---|---|---|---|---|---|---|---|---|---|---|---|---|---|---|---|---|---|
| 07 | -$1 | -$11 | 70 | −1 | 8 | 0 | 1 | 54-15-31 | 8% | 8% | 26% | .745 | .730 | .866 | .685 | .916 | 0.44 | −8 | +25 |
| 08 | $9 | $3 | 190 | −8 | 23 | 0 | 0 | 46-17-37 | 8% | 17% | 33% | .704 | .778 | .616 | .754 | .591 | — | −14 | +38 |
| 09 | $10 | $6 | 230 | −15 | 19 | 0 | 0 | 57-14-29 | 9% | 21% | 24% | .661 | .691 | .623 | .618 | .793 | 0.51 | −9 | +22 |
| 10 | $9 | $4 | 180 | −8 | 14 | 0 | 0 | 66-14-19 | 10% | 19% | 28% | .731 | .707 | .794 | .792 | .552 | — | −12 | +30 |

## Josh Bard — 100 PA | $-1 | 50 pts

CA-39 — Owned: 1% — BH

Although Bard did not exactly have a spectacular season in Seattle in 2010, he was still better at the plate than the Mariners' other catchers, and that distinction could be enough to earn him a back-up role in 2011. (GC)

| Player (Forecast) | Age | AB | HR | R | RBI | SB | BA | OBP | SLG | $1L | Pts |
|---|---|---|---|---|---|---|---|---|---|---|---|
| Bard J | 33 | 90 | 2 | 8 | 10 | 0 | .256 | .330 | .381 | -$1 | 50 |
| **Mini-Browser** | Age | AB | HR | R | RBI | SB | BA | OBP | SLG | $1L | Pts |
| Powell L | 29 | 86 | 4 | 10 | 12 | 0 | .221 | .312 | .384 | -$1 | 40 |
| Hill K | 32 | 95 | 2 | 10 | 10 | 0 | .241 | .304 | .364 | -$1 | 40 |
| Wilson B | 27 | 90 | 2 | 9 | 12 | 0 | .245 | .302 | .380 | -$1 | 40 |
| Castillo W | 23 | 95 | 4 | 9 | 10 | 0 | .221 | .272 | .387 | -$1 | 40 |
| Whiteside E | 31 | 69 | 2 | 8 | 8 | 0 | .239 | .284 | .390 | -$1 | 30 |

| Level | Leag | AB | HR | R | RBI | SB | BA | OBP | SLG | CT% | H% | BB% | Bash |
|---|---|---|---|---|---|---|---|---|---|---|---|---|---|
| A | — | — | — | — | — | — | — | — | — | — | — | — | — |
| AA | — | — | — | — | — | — | — | — | — | — | — | — | — |
| AAA | PCL | 85 | 3 | 7 | 15 | 0 | .235 | .284 | .412 | 79% | 30% | 7% | 1.75 |

| Yr | Team | AB | HR | R | RBI | SB | BA | OBP | SLG | CT% | H% | BB% | Bash |
|---|---|---|---|---|---|---|---|---|---|---|---|---|---|
| 07 | SD | 389 | 5 | 42 | 51 | 0 | .285 | .364 | .404 | 85% | 34% | 11% | 1.41 |
| 08 | SD | 178 | 1 | 11 | 16 | 0 | .202 | .279 | .270 | 86% | 24% | 9% | 1.33 |
| 09 | WAS | 274 | 6 | 20 | 31 | 0 | .230 | .293 | .361 | 82% | 28% | 8% | 1.57 |
| 10 | SEA | 112 | 3 | 9 | 10 | 0 | .214 | .276 | .357 | 76% | 28% | 8% | 1.67 |

**Competition at CA — Stats in 2010**

| Bats | Player | GSvR | GSvL | Sub | OPS |
|---|---|---|---|---|---|
| RH | Moore A | 41 | 17 | 1 | .513 |
| RH | Johnson R | 44 | 13 | 4 | .574 |
| BH | Bard J | 20 | 15 | 4 | .634 |
| RH | Alfonzo E | 5 | 5 | 2 | .537 |

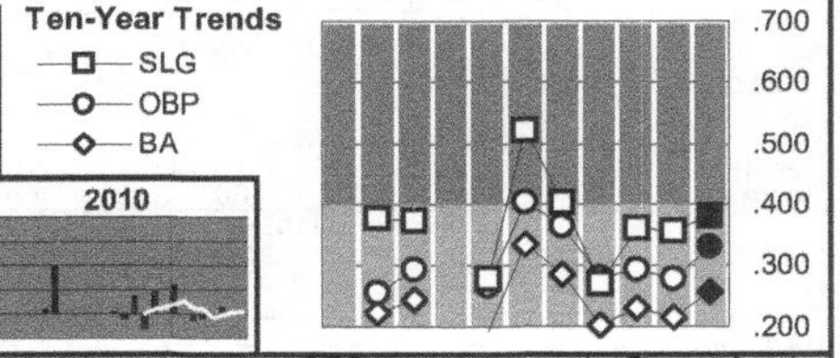


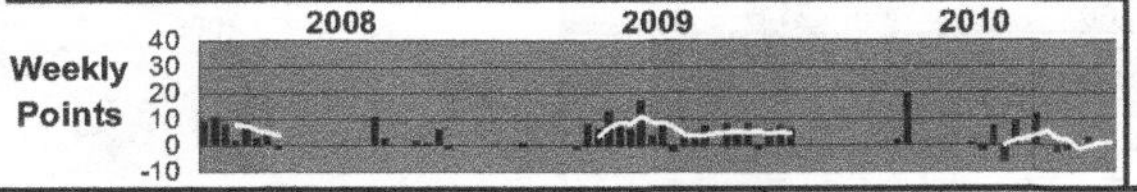


| Yr | $1L | $2L | Pts | RAA | 2B | 3B | CS | FB-LD-GB | HR/fb | RBI% | RS% | OPS | 1st Hf | 2nd Hf | vs RH | vs LH | Rnge | vRH | vLH |
|---|---|---|---|---|---|---|---|---|---|---|---|---|---|---|---|---|---|---|---|
| 07 | $9 | $0 | 240 | +7 | 27 | 2 | 1 | 30-18-52 | 5% | 24% | 24% | .768 | .704 | .834 | .690 | .966 | 0.60 | +7 | −20 |
| 08 | -$2 | -$11 | 70 | −12 | 9 | 0 | 0 | 31-22-47 | 2% | 15% | 19% | .549 | .539 | .575 | .598 | .427 | 0.78 | −11 | +31 |
| 09 | $2 | -$5 | 120 | −9 | 18 | 0 | 1 | 41-19-40 | 6% | 17% | 17% | .655 | .723 | .599 | .653 | .663 | 0.75 | −13 | +33 |
| 10 | $0 | -$10 | 40 | −5 | 7 | 0 | 0 | 46-16-38 | 8% | 13% | 19% | .634 | .631 | .634 | .521 | .797 | 0.78 | −1 | +1 |

## Brian Barden — 50 PA | $-4 | 20 pts

3B-16, SS-7, 2B-2 — Owned: 0% — RH

Barden is one of many players who could potentially handle the utility infield spot for the Marlins. The job offers almost no chance for more than slight playing time (for Barden or anyone) – both Hanley Ramirez and Dan Uggla have played at least 140 games at their positions in each of the past five seasons. (MJ)

| Player (Forecast) | Age | AB | HR | R | RBI | SB | BA | OBP | SLG | $1L | Pts |
|---|---|---|---|---|---|---|---|---|---|---|---|
| Barden B | 29 | 44 | 1 | 6 | 5 | 0 | .249 | .318 | .376 | -$4 | 20 |
| **Mini-Browser** | Age | AB | HR | R | RBI | SB | BA | OBP | SLG | $1L | Pts |
| Pena R | 25 | 144 | 2 | 15 | 12 | 5 | .229 | .285 | .302 | -$3 | 60 |
| Darnell J | 24 | 87 | 4 | 9 | 11 | 1 | .208 | .311 | .393 | -$4 | 50 |
| Hicks B | 25 | 71 | 3 | 9 | 7 | 2 | .201 | .293 | .390 | -$4 | 40 |
| Mitchell R | 26 | 94 | 4 | 9 | 10 | 0 | .203 | .249 | .376 | -$4 | 40 |
| Emaus B | 25 | 90 | 3 | 10 | 10 | 2 | .211 | .282 | .356 | -$4 | 50 |

| Level | Leag | AB | HR | R | RBI | SB | BA | OBP | SLG | CT% | H% | BB% | Bash |
|---|---|---|---|---|---|---|---|---|---|---|---|---|---|
| A | — | — | — | — | — | — | — | — | — | — | — | — | — |
| AA | — | — | — | — | — | — | — | — | — | — | — | — | — |
| AAA | PCL | 184 | 3 | 30 | 23 | 3 | .353 | .407 | .489 | 79% | 45% | 9% | 1.38 |

| Yr | Team | AB | HR | R | RBI | SB | BA | OBP | SLG | CT% | H% | BB% | Bash |
|---|---|---|---|---|---|---|---|---|---|---|---|---|---|
| 07 | 2TM | 35 | 0 | 6 | 0 | 0 | .171 | .216 | .200 | 80% | 21% | 5% | 1.17 |
| 08 | STL | 9 | 0 | 0 | 1 | 0 | .222 | .222 | .222 | 56% | 40% | 0% | 1.00 |
| 09 | STL | 103 | 4 | 13 | 10 | 0 | .233 | .286 | .379 | 80% | 29% | 5% | 1.63 |
| 10 | FLA | 28 | 0 | 2 | 3 | 0 | .179 | .281 | .179 | 57% | 31% | 9% | 1.00 |

**Competition at 3B — Stats in 2010**

| Bats | Player | GSvR | GSvL | Sub | OPS |
|---|---|---|---|---|---|
| RH | Helms W | 29 | 21 | 40 | .646 |
| LH | Tracy C | 22 | 0 | 2 | .628 |
| RH | Barden B | 0 | 0 | 16 | .460 |

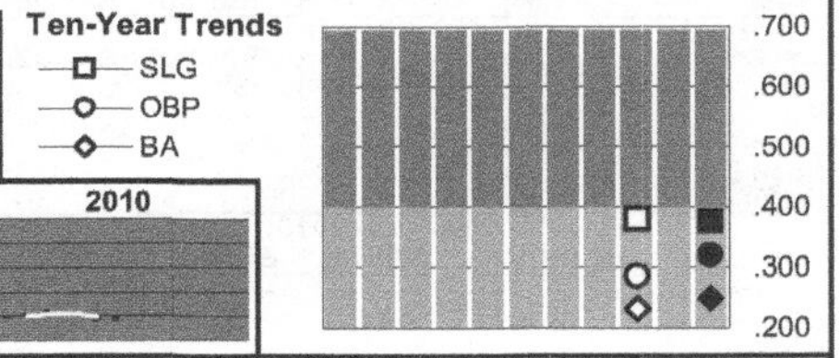


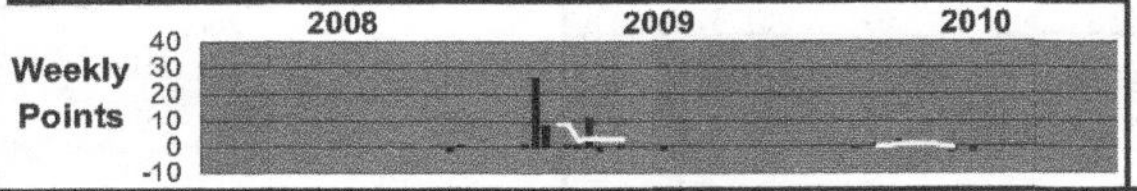


| Yr | $1L | $2L | Pts | RAA | 2B | 3B | CS | FB-LD-GB | HR/fb | RBI% | RS% | OPS | 1st Hf | 2nd Hf | vs RH | vs LH | Rnge | vRH | vLH |
|---|---|---|---|---|---|---|---|---|---|---|---|---|---|---|---|---|---|---|---|
| 07 | -$6 | -$20 | 10 | −4 | 1 | 0 | 0 | 39-11-50 | 0% | 0% | 75% | .416 | .167 | .541 | .399 | .472 | 2.65 | — | — |
| 08 | -$5 | -$19 | 0 | −1 | 0 | 0 | 0 | 20-20-60 | 0% | 14% | 0% | .444 | — | .444 | .500 | .400 | 2.65 | −22 | +54 |
| 09 | -$2 | -$17 | 50 | −5 | 3 | 0 | 0 | 31-19-51 | 16% | 13% | 32% | .664 | .664 | — | .733 | .580 | 2.65 | −21 | +51 |
| 10 | -$5 | -$21 | 0 | −4 | 0 | 0 | 2 | 38-13-50 | 0% | 13% | 22% | .460 | .460 | — | .485 | .400 | 2.67 | −10 | +24 |

*For more stats, visit www.Rotolympus.com.*

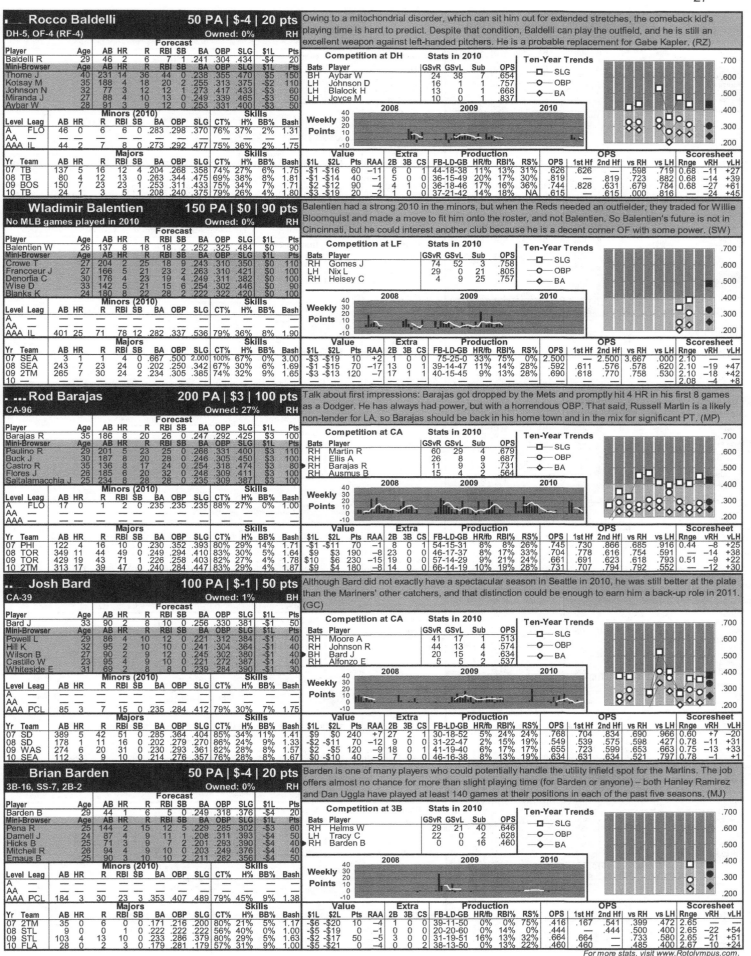

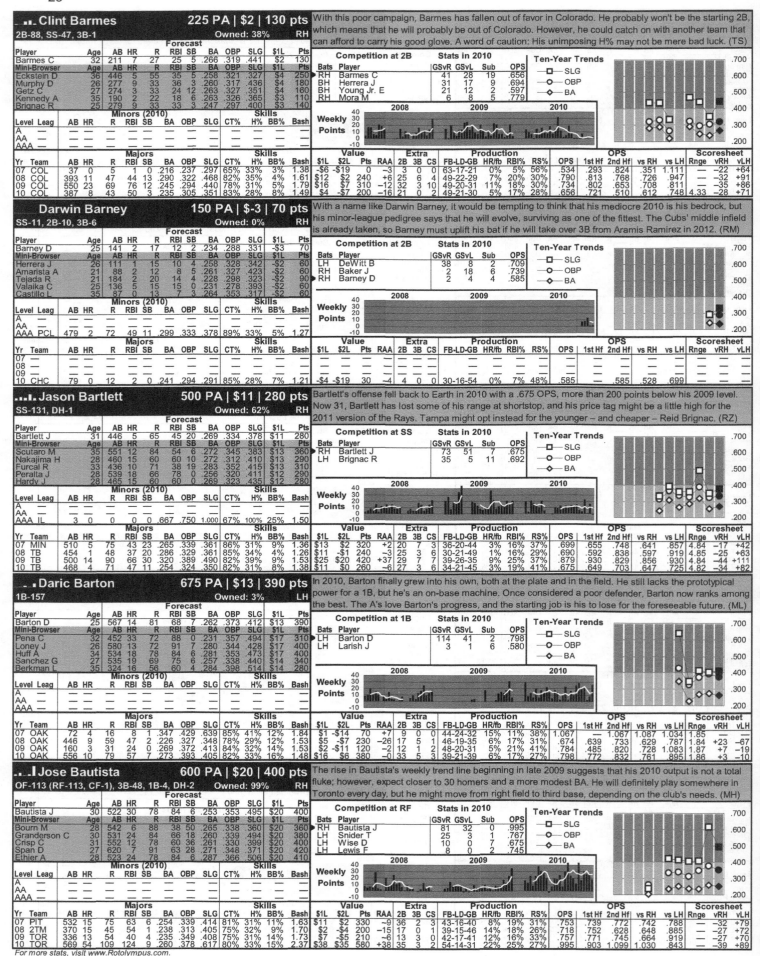

## Clint Barmes — 225 PA | $2 | 130 pts
2B-88, SS-47, 3B-1 — Owned: 38% — RH

With this poor campaign, Barmes has fallen out of favor in Colorado. He probably won't be the starting 2B, which means that he will probably be out of Colorado. However, he could catch on with another team that can afford to carry his good glove. A word of caution: His unimposing H% may not be mere bad luck. (TS)

### Forecast
| Player | Age | AB | HR | R | RBI | SB | BA | OBP | SLG | $1L | Pts |
|---|---|---|---|---|---|---|---|---|---|---|---|
| Barmes C | 32 | 211 | 7 | 27 | 25 | 5 | .266 | .319 | .441 | $2 | 130 |

### Mini-Browser
| Player | Age | AB | HR | R | RBI | SB | BA | OBP | SLG | $1L | Pts |
|---|---|---|---|---|---|---|---|---|---|---|---|
| Eckstein D | 36 | 446 | 5 | 55 | 35 | 5 | .258 | .321 | .327 | $4 | 250 |
| Murphy D | 26 | 277 | 9 | 33 | 36 | 3 | .260 | .317 | .436 | $4 | 180 |
| Getz C | 27 | 274 | 2 | 33 | 24 | 12 | .263 | .327 | .351 | $4 | 160 |
| Kennedy A | 35 | 190 | 2 | 22 | 18 | 6 | .263 | .326 | .365 | $3 | 110 |
| Brignac R | 25 | 279 | 9 | 33 | 33 | 3 | .247 | .297 | .400 | $3 | 140 |

### Minors (2010) / Skills
| Level | Leag | AB | HR | R | RBI | SB | BA | OBP | SLG | CT% | H% | BB% | Bash |
|---|---|---|---|---|---|---|---|---|---|---|---|---|---|
| A | — | | | | | | | | | | | | |
| AA | — | | | | | | | | | | | | |
| AAA | — | | | | | | | | | | | | |

### Competition at 2B / Stats in 2010
| Bats | Player | GSvR | GSvL | Sub | OPS |
|---|---|---|---|---|---|
| RH | Barmes C | 41 | 28 | 19 | .656 |
| BH | Herrera J | 31 | 17 | 9 | .694 |
| BH | Young Jr. E | 21 | 12 | 2 | .597 |
| RH | Mora M | 6 | 8 | 5 | .779 |

### Majors / Skills / Value / Extra / Production / OPS / Scoresheet
| Yr | Team | AB | HR | R | RBI | SB | BA | OBP | SLG | CT% | H% | BB% | Bash | $1L | $2L | Pts | RAA | 2B | 3B | CS | FB-LD-GB | HR/fb | RBI% | RS% | OPS | 1st Hf | 2nd Hf | vs RH | vs LH | Rnge | vRH | vLH |
|---|---|---|---|---|---|---|---|---|---|---|---|---|---|---|---|---|---|---|---|---|---|---|---|---|---|---|---|---|---|---|---|---|
| 07 | COL | 37 | 0 | 5 | 1 | 0 | .216 | .237 | .297 | 65% | 33% | 3% | 1.38 | -$6 | -$19 | 0 | -3 | 0 | 0 | 0 | 63-17-21 | 0% | 5% | 56% | .534 | .293 | .824 | .351 | 1.111 | — | -22 | +64 |
| 08 | COL | 393 | 11 | 47 | 44 | 13 | .290 | .322 | .468 | 82% | 35% | 4% | 1.61 | $12 | $2 | 240 | +6 | 25 | 6 | 4 | 49-22-29 | 7% | 20% | 30% | .790 | .813 | .768 | .726 | .947 | — | -32 | +91 |
| 09 | COL | 550 | 23 | 69 | 76 | 12 | .245 | .294 | .440 | 78% | 31% | 5% | 1.79 | $16 | $7 | 310 | -12 | 32 | 3 | 10 | 49-20-31 | 11% | 18% | 30% | .734 | .802 | .653 | .708 | .811 | 4.33 | -35 | +86 |
| 10 | COL | 387 | 8 | 43 | 50 | 3 | .235 | .305 | .351 | 83% | 28% | 8% | 1.49 | $4 | -$7 | 200 | -16 | 21 | 0 | 2 | 49-21-30 | 9% | 17% | 28% | .656 | .721 | .510 | .612 | .748 | 4.33 | -28 | +71 |

## Darwin Barney — 150 PA | $-3 | 70 pts
SS-11, 2B-10, 3B-6 — Owned: 0% — RH

With a name like Darwin Barney, it would be tempting to think that his mediocre 2010 is his bedrock, but his minor-league pedigree says that he will evolve, surviving as one of the fittest. The Cubs' middle infield is already taken, so Barney must uplift his bat if he will take over 3B from Aramis Ramirez in 2012. (RM)

### Forecast
| Player | Age | AB | HR | R | RBI | SB | BA | OBP | SLG | $1L | Pts |
|---|---|---|---|---|---|---|---|---|---|---|---|
| Barney D | 25 | 141 | 2 | 17 | 12 | 2 | .234 | .288 | .331 | -$3 | 70 |

### Mini-Browser
| Player | Age | AB | HR | R | RBI | SB | BA | OBP | SLG | $1L | Pts |
|---|---|---|---|---|---|---|---|---|---|---|---|
| Herrera J | 26 | 111 | 1 | 15 | 10 | 4 | .258 | .328 | .342 | -$2 | 60 |
| Amarista A | 21 | 88 | 2 | 12 | 8 | 5 | .261 | .327 | .423 | -$2 | 60 |
| Tejada R | 21 | 184 | 2 | 20 | 14 | 4 | .228 | .298 | .323 | -$2 | 90 |
| Valaika C | 25 | 136 | 5 | 15 | 15 | 0 | .231 | .278 | .393 | -$2 | 60 |
| Castillo I | 35 | 87 | 0 | 13 | 7 | 3 | .264 | .333 | .317 | -$2 | 60 |

### Minors (2010) / Skills
| Level | Leag | AB | HR | R | RBI | SB | BA | OBP | SLG | CT% | H% | BB% | Bash |
|---|---|---|---|---|---|---|---|---|---|---|---|---|---|
| A | — | | | | | | | | | | | | |
| AA | — | | | | | | | | | | | | |
| AAA | PCL | 479 | 2 | 72 | 49 | 11 | .299 | .333 | .378 | 89% | 33% | 5% | 1.27 |

### Competition at 2B / Stats in 2010
| Bats | Player | GSvR | GSvL | Sub | OPS |
|---|---|---|---|---|---|
| LH | DeWitt B | 38 | 34 | 5 | .709 |
| RH | Baker J | 2 | 18 | 6 | .739 |
| RH | Barney D | 2 | 4 | 4 | .585 |

### Majors / Skills / Value / Extra / Production / OPS / Scoresheet
| Yr | Team | AB | HR | R | RBI | SB | BA | OBP | SLG | CT% | H% | BB% | Bash | $1L | $2L | Pts | RAA | 2B | 3B | CS | FB-LD-GB | HR/fb | RBI% | RS% | OPS | 1st Hf | 2nd Hf | vs RH | vs LH | Rnge | vRH | vLH |
|---|---|---|---|---|---|---|---|---|---|---|---|---|---|---|---|---|---|---|---|---|---|---|---|---|---|---|---|---|---|---|---|---|
| 07 | — | | | | | | | | | | | | | | | | | | | | | | | | | | | | | | | |
| 08 | — | | | | | | | | | | | | | | | | | | | | | | | | | | | | | | | |
| 09 | — | | | | | | | | | | | | | | | | | | | | | | | | | | | | | | | |
| 10 | CHC | 79 | 0 | 12 | 2 | 0 | .241 | .294 | .291 | 85% | 28% | 7% | 1.21 | -$4 | -$19 | 30 | -4 | 4 | 0 | 0 | 30-16-54 | 0% | 7% | 48% | .585 | — | .585 | .528 | .699 | — | — | — |

## Jason Bartlett — 500 PA | $11 | 280 pts
SS-131, DH-1 — Owned: 62% — RH

Bartlett's offense fell back to Earth in 2010 with a .675 OPS, more than 200 points below his 2009 level. Now 31, Bartlett has lost some of his range at shortstop, and his price tag might be a little high for the 2011 version of the Rays. Tampa might opt instead for the younger – and cheaper – Reid Brignac. (RZ)

### Forecast
| Player | Age | AB | HR | R | RBI | SB | BA | OBP | SLG | $1L | Pts |
|---|---|---|---|---|---|---|---|---|---|---|---|
| Bartlett J | 31 | 446 | 5 | 65 | 45 | 20 | .269 | .334 | .378 | $11 | 280 |

### Mini-Browser
| Player | Age | AB | HR | R | RBI | SB | BA | OBP | SLG | $1L | Pts |
|---|---|---|---|---|---|---|---|---|---|---|---|
| Scutaro M | 35 | 551 | 12 | 84 | 54 | 6 | .272 | .345 | .383 | $13 | 360 |
| Nakajima H | 28 | 460 | 15 | 60 | 60 | 10 | .272 | .312 | .410 | $13 | 290 |
| Furcal R | 33 | 436 | 10 | 71 | 38 | 19 | .283 | .352 | .415 | $13 | 310 |
| Peralta J | 28 | 539 | 18 | 66 | 78 | 0 | .256 | .320 | .411 | $12 | 290 |
| Hardy J | 28 | 465 | 15 | 60 | 60 | 1 | .269 | .323 | .435 | $12 | 280 |

### Minors (2010) / Skills
| Level | Leag | AB | HR | R | RBI | SB | BA | OBP | SLG | CT% | H% | BB% | Bash |
|---|---|---|---|---|---|---|---|---|---|---|---|---|---|
| A | — | | | | | | | | | | | | |
| AA | — | | | | | | | | | | | | |
| AAA | IL | 3 | 0 | 0 | 0 | 0 | .667 | .750 | 1.000 | 67% | 100% | 25% | 1.50 |

### Competition at SS / Stats in 2010
| Bats | Player | GSvR | GSvL | Sub | OPS |
|---|---|---|---|---|---|
| RH | Bartlett J | 73 | 51 | 7 | .675 |
| LH | Brignac R | 35 | 5 | 11 | .692 |

### Majors / Skills / Value / Extra / Production / OPS / Scoresheet
| Yr | Team | AB | HR | R | RBI | SB | BA | OBP | SLG | CT% | H% | BB% | Bash | $1L | $2L | Pts | RAA | 2B | 3B | CS | FB-LD-GB | HR/fb | RBI% | RS% | OPS | 1st Hf | 2nd Hf | vs RH | vs LH | Rnge | vRH | vLH |
|---|---|---|---|---|---|---|---|---|---|---|---|---|---|---|---|---|---|---|---|---|---|---|---|---|---|---|---|---|---|---|---|---|
| 07 | MIN | 510 | 5 | 75 | 43 | 23 | .265 | .339 | .361 | 86% | 31% | 9% | 1.36 | $13 | $2 | 320 | +2 | 20 | 7 | 3 | 36-20-44 | 3% | 16% | 37% | .699 | .655 | .748 | .641 | .857 | 4.84 | -17 | +42 |
| 08 | TB | 454 | 1 | 48 | 37 | 20 | .286 | .329 | .361 | 85% | 34% | 4% | 1.26 | $11 | -$1 | 240 | -3 | 25 | 4 | 6 | 30-21-49 | 1% | 16% | 29% | .690 | .592 | .838 | .597 | .919 | 4.85 | -25 | +63 |
| 09 | TB | 500 | 14 | 90 | 66 | 30 | .320 | .389 | .490 | 82% | 37% | 9% | 1.53 | $25 | $20 | 420 | +37 | 29 | 7 | 7 | 39-26-35 | 9% | 25% | 37% | .879 | .930 | .829 | .856 | .930 | 4.84 | -44 | +111 |
| 10 | TB | 468 | 4 | 71 | 47 | 11 | .254 | .324 | .350 | 82% | 31% | 8% | 1.38 | $11 | $0 | 260 | -6 | 27 | 3 | 6 | 34-21-45 | 3% | 19% | 41% | .675 | .649 | .703 | .647 | .725 | 4.82 | -34 | +72 |

## Daric Barton — 675 PA | $13 | 390 pts
1B-157 — Owned: 3% — LH

In 2010, Barton finally grew into his own, both at the plate and in the field. He still lacks the prototypical power for a 1B, but he's an on-base machine. Once considered a poor defender, Barton now ranks among the best. The A's love Barton's progress, and the starting job is his to lose for the foreseeable future. (ML)

### Forecast
| Player | Age | AB | HR | R | RBI | SB | BA | OBP | SLG | $1L | Pts |
|---|---|---|---|---|---|---|---|---|---|---|---|
| Barton D | 25 | 567 | 14 | 81 | 68 | 7 | .262 | .373 | .412 | $13 | 390 |

### Mini-Browser
| Player | Age | AB | HR | R | RBI | SB | BA | OBP | SLG | $1L | Pts |
|---|---|---|---|---|---|---|---|---|---|---|---|
| Pena C | 32 | 452 | 33 | 72 | 88 | 0 | .231 | .357 | .494 | $17 | 310 |
| Loney J | 26 | 580 | 13 | 72 | 91 | 7 | .280 | .344 | .428 | $17 | 400 |
| Huff A | 34 | 534 | 18 | 78 | 84 | 6 | .281 | .353 | .473 | $17 | 400 |
| Sanchez G | 27 | 535 | 19 | 69 | 75 | 6 | .257 | .338 | .440 | $14 | 340 |
| Berkman L | 35 | 324 | 16 | 56 | 60 | 4 | .284 | .398 | .514 | $14 | 280 |

### Minors (2010) / Skills
| Level | Leag | AB | HR | R | RBI | SB | BA | OBP | SLG | CT% | H% | BB% | Bash |
|---|---|---|---|---|---|---|---|---|---|---|---|---|---|
| A | — | | | | | | | | | | | | |
| AA | — | | | | | | | | | | | | |
| AAA | — | | | | | | | | | | | | |

### Competition at 1B / Stats in 2010
| Bats | Player | GSvR | GSvL | Sub | OPS |
|---|---|---|---|---|---|
| LH | Barton D | 114 | 41 | 2 | .798 |
| LH | Larish J | 3 | 1 | 6 | .580 |

### Majors / Skills / Value / Extra / Production / OPS / Scoresheet
| Yr | Team | AB | HR | R | RBI | SB | BA | OBP | SLG | CT% | H% | BB% | Bash | $1L | $2L | Pts | RAA | 2B | 3B | CS | FB-LD-GB | HR/fb | RBI% | RS% | OPS | 1st Hf | 2nd Hf | vs RH | vs LH | Rnge | vRH | vLH |
|---|---|---|---|---|---|---|---|---|---|---|---|---|---|---|---|---|---|---|---|---|---|---|---|---|---|---|---|---|---|---|---|---|
| 07 | OAK | 72 | 4 | 16 | 8 | 1 | .347 | .429 | .639 | 85% | 41% | 12% | 1.84 | $1 | -$14 | 70 | +7 | 9 | 0 | 0 | 44-24-32 | 15% | 11% | 38% | 1.067 | — | 1.067 | 1.087 | 1.034 | 1.85 | — | — |
| 08 | OAK | 446 | 9 | 59 | 47 | 2 | .226 | .327 | .348 | 78% | 29% | 12% | 1.53 | $5 | -$7 | 230 | -26 | 17 | 5 | 1 | 46-19-35 | 6% | 17% | 31% | .674 | .639 | .733 | .626 | .787 | 1.84 | +23 | -67 |
| 09 | OAK | 160 | 3 | 31 | 24 | 0 | .269 | .372 | .413 | 84% | 31% | 14% | 1.53 | $2 | -$11 | 120 | -2 | 12 | 1 | 2 | 48-20-31 | 5% | 21% | 41% | .784 | .485 | .820 | .728 | 1.083 | 1.87 | +7 | -19 |
| 10 | OAK | 556 | 10 | 79 | 57 | 7 | .273 | .393 | .405 | 82% | 33% | 16% | 1.48 | $16 | $6 | 380 | -0 | 33 | 5 | 3 | 39-21-39 | 6% | 17% | 27% | .798 | .772 | .832 | .761 | .895 | 1.86 | +3 | -10 |

## Jose Bautista — 600 PA | $20 | 400 pts
OF-113 (RF-113, CF-1), 3B-48, 1B-4, DH-2 — Owned: 99% — RH

The rise in Bautista's weekly trend line beginning in late 2009 suggests that his 2010 output is not a total fluke; however, expect closer to 30 homers and a more modest BA. He will definitely play somewhere in Toronto every day, but he might move from right field to third base, depending on the club's needs. (MH)

### Forecast
| Player | Age | AB | HR | R | RBI | SB | BA | OBP | SLG | $1L | Pts |
|---|---|---|---|---|---|---|---|---|---|---|---|
| Bautista J | 30 | 522 | 30 | 78 | 84 | 6 | .253 | .353 | .495 | $20 | 400 |

### Mini-Browser
| Player | Age | AB | HR | R | RBI | SB | BA | OBP | SLG | $1L | Pts |
|---|---|---|---|---|---|---|---|---|---|---|---|
| Bourn M | 28 | 542 | 6 | 88 | 38 | 50 | .265 | .338 | .360 | $20 | 360 |
| Granderson C | 30 | 531 | 24 | 84 | 66 | 18 | .260 | .339 | .494 | $20 | 390 |
| Crisp C | 31 | 552 | 12 | 78 | 60 | 36 | .265 | .330 | .399 | $20 | 400 |
| Span D | 27 | 620 | 7 | 91 | 63 | 28 | .271 | .348 | .371 | $20 | 420 |
| Ethier A | 28 | 523 | 24 | 78 | 84 | 6 | .287 | .366 | .506 | $20 | 410 |

### Minors (2010) / Skills
| Level | Leag | AB | HR | R | RBI | SB | BA | OBP | SLG | CT% | H% | BB% | Bash |
|---|---|---|---|---|---|---|---|---|---|---|---|---|---|
| A | — | | | | | | | | | | | | |
| AA | — | | | | | | | | | | | | |
| AAA | — | | | | | | | | | | | | |

### Competition at RF / Stats in 2010
| Bats | Player | GSvR | GSvL | Sub | OPS |
|---|---|---|---|---|---|
| RH | Bautista J | 81 | 32 | 1 | .995 |
| LH | Snider T | 25 | 3 | 1 | .767 |
| LH | Wise D | 10 | 0 | 7 | .675 |
| LH | Lewis F | 8 | 0 | 2 | .745 |

### Majors / Skills / Value / Extra / Production / OPS / Scoresheet
| Yr | Team | AB | HR | R | RBI | SB | BA | OBP | SLG | CT% | H% | BB% | Bash | $1L | $2L | Pts | RAA | 2B | 3B | CS | FB-LD-GB | HR/fb | RBI% | RS% | OPS | 1st Hf | 2nd Hf | vs RH | vs LH | Rnge | vRH | vLH |
|---|---|---|---|---|---|---|---|---|---|---|---|---|---|---|---|---|---|---|---|---|---|---|---|---|---|---|---|---|---|---|---|---|
| 07 | PIT | 532 | 15 | 75 | 63 | 6 | .254 | .339 | .414 | 81% | 31% | 11% | 1.63 | $2 | $330 | — | -9 | 36 | 2 | 3 | 43-16-40 | 8% | 19% | 31% | .753 | .739 | .772 | .742 | .788 | — | -32 | +79 |
| 08 | 2TM | 370 | 15 | 45 | 54 | 1 | .238 | .313 | .405 | 75% | 32% | 9% | 1.70 | $2 | -$4 | 200 | -15 | 17 | 0 | 1 | 39-15-46 | 14% | 18% | 26% | .718 | .752 | .628 | .648 | .885 | — | -27 | +72 |
| 09 | TOR | 336 | 13 | 54 | 40 | 4 | .235 | .349 | .408 | 75% | 30% | 14% | 1.73 | $7 | -$5 | 210 | -6 | 13 | 3 | 0 | 42-17-41 | 12% | 16% | 33% | .757 | .771 | .745 | .664 | .919 | — | -27 | +70 |
| 10 | TOR | 569 | 54 | 109 | 124 | 9 | .260 | .378 | .617 | 80% | 33% | 15% | 2.37 | $38 | $35 | 580 | +38 | 35 | 3 | 5 | 54-14-31 | 26% | 25% | 27% | .995 | .903 | 1.099 | 1.030 | .843 | — | -39 | +70 |

## Jason Bay — 600 PA | $21 | 410 pts

OF-93 (LF-93) — Owned: 70% — RH

Bay hit only 6 HR in 95 games before missing the final two months of 2010 with a concussion. In Bay's defense, when he batted only .194 in July, he was usually hitting ahead of Jeff Francoeur or the catcher. Consider, too, that David Wright's once-gone power returned in *his* follow-up season at Citi Field. (JL)

| Player | Age | AB | HR | R | RBI | SB | BA | OBP | SLG | $1L | Pts |
|---|---|---|---|---|---|---|---|---|---|---|---|
| Bay J | 32 | 521 | 30 | 90 | 90 | 12 | .265 | .366 | .494 | $21 | 410 |
| **Mini-Browser** | Age | AB | HR | R | RBI | SB | BA | OBP | SLG | $1L | Pts |
| Bruce J | 23 | 582 | 33 | 91 | 85 | 7 | .268 | .338 | .512 | $23 | 400 |
| Young C | 27 | 562 | 26 | 91 | 78 | 20 | .266 | .345 | .496 | $22 | 410 |
| Lee C | 34 | 570 | 31 | 75 | 100 | 6 | .285 | .335 | .493 | $22 | 460 |
| Sizemore G | 28 | 525 | 24 | 84 | 66 | 24 | .263 | .363 | .477 | $22 | 400 |
| Pagan A | 29 | 576 | 13 | 81 | 69 | 31 | .282 | .335 | .437 | $21 | 410 |

| Level | Leag | AB | HR | R | RBI | SB | BA | OBP | SLG | CT% | H% | BB% | Bash |
|---|---|---|---|---|---|---|---|---|---|---|---|---|---|
| A | — | — | — | — | — | — | — | — | — | — | — | — | — |
| AA | — | — | — | — | — | — | — | — | — | — | — | — | — |
| AAA | — | — | — | — | — | — | — | — | — | — | — | — | — |

Competition at LF — Stats in 2010

| Bats | Player | GSvR | GSvL | Sub | OPS |
|---|---|---|---|---|---|
| RH | Bay J | 65 | 27 | 1 | .749 |
| BH | Pagan A | 20 | 6 | 1 | .765 |
| LH | Duda L | 22 | 1 | 1 | .678 |
| LH | Carter C | 14 | 1 | 2 | .706 |

Weekly Points

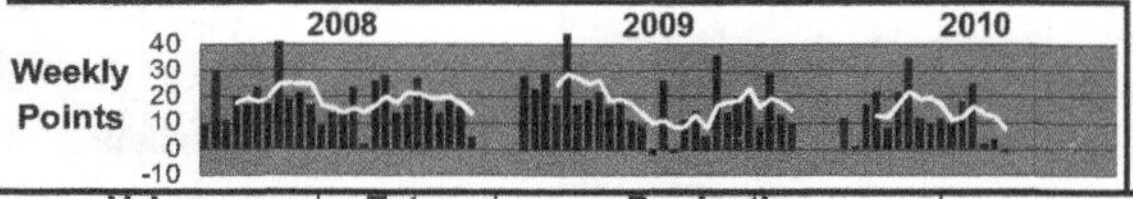
2008
2009
2010
40
30
20
10
0
-10

Ten-Year Trends

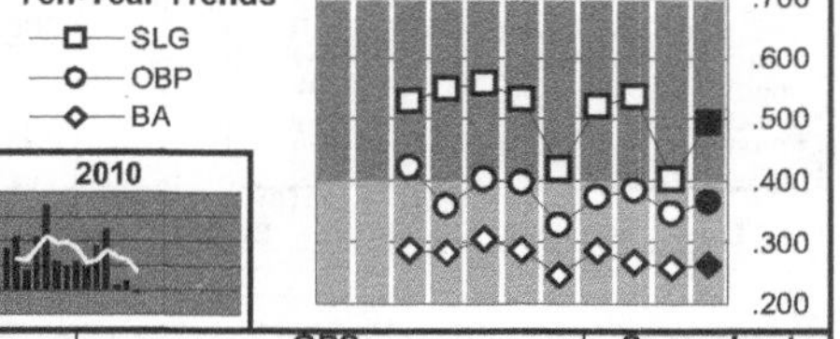
SLG
OBP
BA
.700
.600
.500
.400
.300
.200

| Yr | Team | AB | HR | R | RBI | SB | BA | OBP | SLG | CT% | H% | BB% | Bash | $1L | $2L | Pts | RAA | 2B | 3B | CS | FB-LD-GB | HR/fb | RBI% | RS% | OPS | 1st Hf | 2nd Hf | vs RH | vs LH | Rnge | vRH | vLH |
|---|---|---|---|---|---|---|---|---|---|---|---|---|---|---|---|---|---|---|---|---|---|---|---|---|---|---|---|---|---|---|---|---|
| 07 | PIT | 538 | 21 | 78 | 84 | 4 | .247 | .327 | .418 | 74% | 34% | 10% | 1.69 | $14 | $6 | 310 | –9 | 25 | 2 | 1 | 45-17-38 | 11% | 20% | 32% | .746 | .766 | .714 | .747 | .742 | 2.05 | –22 | +62 |
| 08 | 2TM | 577 | 31 | 111 | 101 | 10 | .286 | .373 | .522 | 76% | 38% | 12% | 1.82 | $25 | $24 | 480 | +28 | 35 | 4 | 0 | 46-17-38 | 15% | 22% | 37% | .895 | .917 | .862 | .907 | .852 | 2.04 | –18 | +48 |
| 09 | BOS | 531 | 36 | 103 | 119 | 13 | .267 | .384 | .537 | 69% | 38% | 15% | 2.01 | $29 | $25 | 460 | +29 | 29 | 3 | 3 | 49-18-33 | 20% | 26% | 32% | .921 | .908 | .939 | .897 | .980 | 2.02 | –6 | +18 |
| 10 | NYM | 348 | 6 | 48 | 47 | 10 | .259 | .347 | .402 | 74% | 35% | 11% | 1.56 | $8 | -$3 | 210 | –3 | 20 | 6 | 0 | 45-19-36 | 5% | 20% | 32% | .749 | .779 | .510 | .748 | .750 | 2.03 | –10 | +26 |

## Gordon Beckham — 625 PA | $15 | 340 pts

2B-126, DH-4 — Owned: 78% — RH

Pitchers adjusted to "The Franchise," and he started the year with stats as barren as a Blockbuster store. But Beckham could adjust, too, and from July 11 until his hand was injured on August 30, he hit a stellar .350/.413/.573. He now looks comfortable at second base and should join the top tier at that position. (RM)

| Player | Age | AB | HR | R | RBI | SB | BA | OBP | SLG | $1L | Pts |
|---|---|---|---|---|---|---|---|---|---|---|---|
| Beckham G | 24 | 553 | 19 | 75 | 75 | 6 | .260 | .326 | .423 | $15 | 340 |
| **Mini-Browser** | Age | AB | HR | R | RBI | SB | BA | OBP | SLG | $1L | Pts |
| Johnson K | 29 | 561 | 20 | 108 | 74 | 14 | .289 | .370 | .501 | $24 | 430 |
| Uggla D | 31 | 576 | 33 | 98 | 91 | 7 | .271 | .366 | .513 | $23 | 420 |
| Roberts B | 33 | 532 | 12 | 84 | 54 | 30 | .293 | .370 | .447 | $22 | 420 |
| Prado M | 27 | 591 | 13 | 91 | 65 | 7 | .297 | .351 | .444 | $18 | 400 |
| Kendrick H | 27 | 572 | 12 | 72 | 72 | 12 | .283 | .318 | .420 | $18 | 340 |

| Level | Leag | AB | HR | R | RBI | SB | BA | OBP | SLG | CT% | H% | BB% | Bash |
|---|---|---|---|---|---|---|---|---|---|---|---|---|---|
| A | — | — | — | — | — | — | — | — | — | — | — | — | — |
| AA | — | — | — | — | — | — | — | — | — | — | — | — | — |
| AAA | — | — | — | — | — | — | — | — | — | — | — | — | — |

Competition at 2B — Stats in 2010

| Bats | Player | GSvR | GSvL | Sub | OPS |
|---|---|---|---|---|---|
| RH | Beckham G | 93 | 32 | 1 | .695 |
| BH | Vizquel O | 17 | 1 | 1 | .673 |
| RH | Lillibridge B | 11 | 7 | 7 | .625 |

Weekly Points

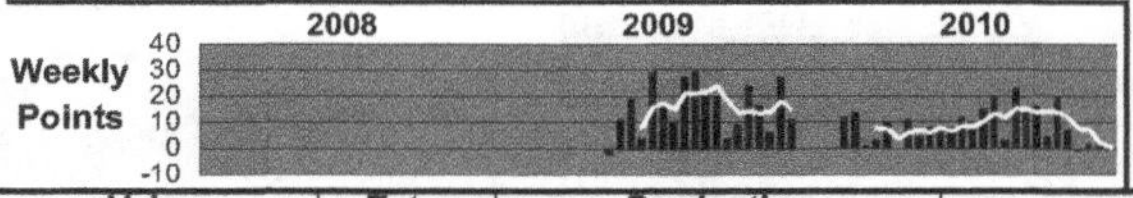
2008
2009
2010
40
30
20
10
0
-10

Ten-Year Trends

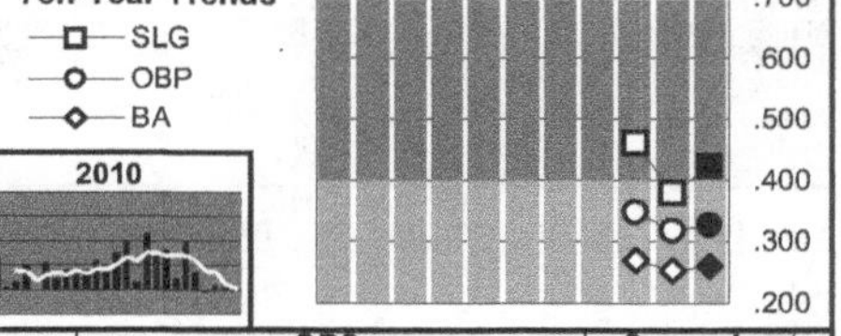
SLG
OBP
BA
.700
.600
.500
.400
.300
.200

| Yr | Team | AB | HR | R | RBI | SB | BA | OBP | SLG | CT% | H% | BB% | Bash | $1L | $2L | Pts | RAA | 2B | 3B | CS | FB-LD-GB | HR/fb | RBI% | RS% | OPS | 1st Hf | 2nd Hf | vs RH | vs LH | Rnge | vRH | vLH |
|---|---|---|---|---|---|---|---|---|---|---|---|---|---|---|---|---|---|---|---|---|---|---|---|---|---|---|---|---|---|---|---|---|
| 07 | — | — | — | — | — | — | — | — | — | — | — | — | — | — | — | — | — | — | — | — | — | — | — | — | — | — | — | — | — | — | — | — |
| 08 | — | — | — | — | — | — | — | — | — | — | — | — | — | — | — | — | — | — | — | — | — | — | — | — | — | — | — | — | — | — | — | — |
| 09 | CHW | 378 | 14 | 58 | 63 | 7 | .270 | .347 | .460 | 83% | 33% | 10% | 1.71 | $12 | $2 | 280 | +8 | 28 | 1 | 4 | 43-17-40 | 10% | 25% | 33% | .808 | .751 | .833 | .774 | .890 | — | — | — |
| 10 | CHW | 444 | 9 | 58 | 49 | 4 | .252 | .317 | .378 | 79% | 32% | 7% | 1.50 | $9 | -$3 | 220 | –12 | 25 | 2 | 6 | 37-17-46 | 7% | 18% | 33% | .695 | .581 | .877 | .705 | .667 | — | –21 | +51 |

## Josh Bell — 450 PA | $5 | 160 pts

3B-50, DH-2 — Owned: 1% — BH

Despite a dip in offense when promoted from Double-A to Triple-A, Bell found himself in the majors by mid-season. He looks to be the everyday 3B in Baltimore, though his combination of infrequent contact and impatience is scary. He has time to pan out, but he needs to make more contact to be relevant. (BJ)

| Player | Age | AB | HR | R | RBI | SB | BA | OBP | SLG | $1L | Pts |
|---|---|---|---|---|---|---|---|---|---|---|---|
| Bell J | 24 | 396 | 18 | 45 | 45 | 0 | .227 | .284 | .411 | $5 | 160 |
| **Mini-Browser** | Age | AB | HR | R | RBI | SB | BA | OBP | SLG | $1L | Pts |
| Jones C | 38 | 248 | 12 | 45 | 42 | 3 | .290 | .401 | .490 | $8 | 230 |
| Nix J | 28 | 368 | 16 | 44 | 40 | 12 | .239 | .305 | .410 | $7 | 210 |
| Moustakas M | 22 | 368 | 17 | 47 | 60 | 3 | .262 | .304 | .465 | $7 | 240 |
| Teahen M | 29 | 314 | 7 | 39 | 35 | 4 | .256 | .320 | .406 | $6 | 160 |
| Valencia D | 26 | 378 | 12 | 40 | 44 | 0 | .254 | .300 | .421 | $5 | 190 |

| Level | Leag | AB | HR | R | RBI | SB | BA | OBP | SLG | CT% | H% | BB% | Bash |
|---|---|---|---|---|---|---|---|---|---|---|---|---|---|
| A | — | — | — | — | — | — | — | — | — | — | — | — | — |
| AA | — | — | — | — | — | — | — | — | — | — | — | — | — |
| AAA | IL | 316 | 13 | 43 | 50 | 2 | .278 | .328 | .481 | 75% | 37% | 7% | 1.73 |

Competition at 3B — Stats in 2010

| Bats | Player | GSvR | GSvL | Sub | OPS |
|---|---|---|---|---|---|
| BH | Bell J | 28 | 12 | 10 | .525 |
| RH | Wigginton T | 16 | 6 | 0 | .727 |

Weekly Points

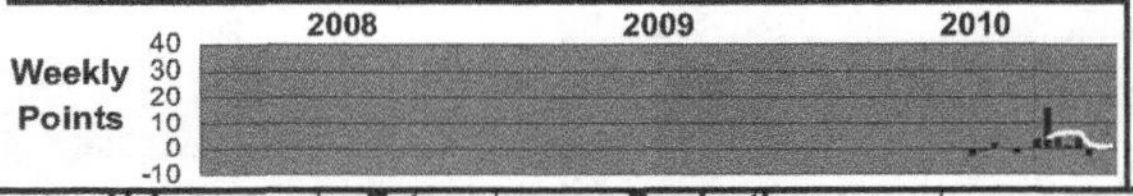
2008
2009
2010
40
30
20
10
0
-10

Ten-Year Trends

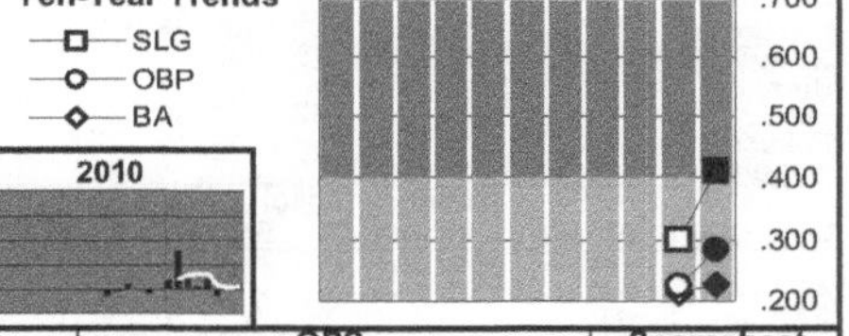
SLG
OBP
BA
.700
.600
.500
.400
.300
.200

| Yr | Team | AB | HR | R | RBI | SB | BA | OBP | SLG | CT% | H% | BB% | Bash | $1L | $2L | Pts | RAA | 2B | 3B | CS | FB-LD-GB | HR/fb | RBI% | RS% | OPS | 1st Hf | 2nd Hf | vs RH | vs LH | Rnge | vRH | vLH |
|---|---|---|---|---|---|---|---|---|---|---|---|---|---|---|---|---|---|---|---|---|---|---|---|---|---|---|---|---|---|---|---|---|
| 07 | — | — | — | — | — | — | — | — | — | — | — | — | — | — | — | — | — | — | — | — | — | — | — | — | — | — | — | — | — | — | — | — |
| 08 | — | — | — | — | — | — | — | — | — | — | — | — | — | — | — | — | — | — | — | — | — | — | — | — | — | — | — | — | — | — | — | — |
| 09 | — | — | — | — | — | — | — | — | — | — | — | — | — | — | — | — | — | — | — | — | — | — | — | — | — | — | — | — | — | — | — | — |
| 10 | BAL | 159 | 3 | 15 | 12 | 0 | .214 | .224 | .302 | 67% | 32% | 1% | 1.41 | -$3 | -$18 | 20 | –13 | 5 | 0 | 1 | 26-17-57 | 11% | 13% | 36% | .525 | .400 | .539 | .474 | .652 | 2.65 | — | — |

## Brandon Belt — 150 PA | $0 | 90 pts

No MLB games played in 2010 — Owned: 0% — LH

Belt emerged in 2010 and become one of San Francisco's top three prospects. He has a build like Darryl Strawberry but lacks the latter's athleticism and power. Belt started 2010 in High-A, and he was not called up when rosters expanded, but he is one of the few credible hitting prospects in the Giants' system. (PB)

| Player | Age | AB | HR | R | RBI | SB | BA | OBP | SLG | $1L | Pts |
|---|---|---|---|---|---|---|---|---|---|---|---|
| Belt B | 22 | 129 | 4 | 19 | 20 | 4 | .270 | .364 | .457 | $0 | 90 |
| **Mini-Browser** | Age | AB | HR | R | RBI | SB | BA | OBP | SLG | $1L | Pts |
| Glaus T | 34 | 246 | 12 | 36 | 45 | 0 | .256 | .365 | .449 | $5 | 170 |
| Wallace B | 24 | 421 | 14 | 48 | 43 | 0 | .237 | .309 | .397 | $4 | 180 |
| Kotchman C | 28 | 218 | 5 | 23 | 30 | 0 | .264 | .331 | .401 | $1 | 140 |
| Garko R | 30 | 182 | 8 | 20 | 26 | 0 | .264 | .339 | .431 | $1 | 110 |
| Hoffpauir M | 31 | 132 | 6 | 20 | 23 | 0 | .272 | .327 | .487 | $1 | 90 |

| Level | Leag | AB | HR | R | RBI | SB | BA | OBP | SLG | CT% | H% | BB% | Bash |
|---|---|---|---|---|---|---|---|---|---|---|---|---|---|
| A | CAL | 269 | 10 | 62 | 62 | 18 | .383 | .492 | .628 | 81% | 47% | 17% | 1.64 |
| AA | EL | 175 | 9 | 26 | 40 | 2 | .337 | .413 | .623 | 81% | 42% | 11% | 1.85 |
| AAA | PCL | 48 | 4 | 11 | 10 | 2 | .229 | .393 | .563 | 69% | 33% | 21% | 2.45 |

Competition at 1B — Stats in 2010

| Bats | Player | GSvR | GSvL | Sub | OPS |
|---|---|---|---|---|---|
| LH | Huff A | 70 | 29 | 1 | .891 |
| RH | Posey B | 19 | 11 | 0 | .862 |
| LH | Ishikawa T | 24 | 1 | 48 | .712 |
| BH | Sandoval P | 8 | 3 | 0 | .732 |

Weekly Points

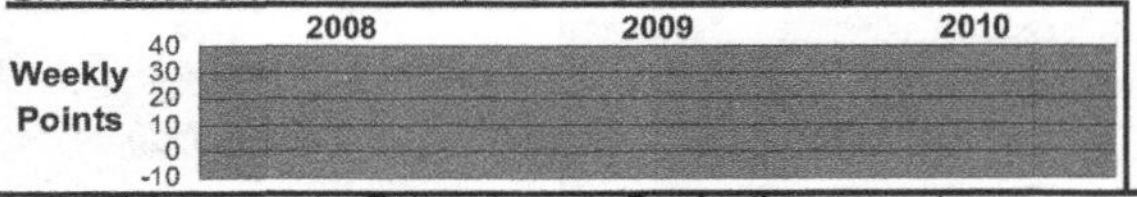
2008
2009
2010
40
30
20
10
0
-10

Ten-Year Trends

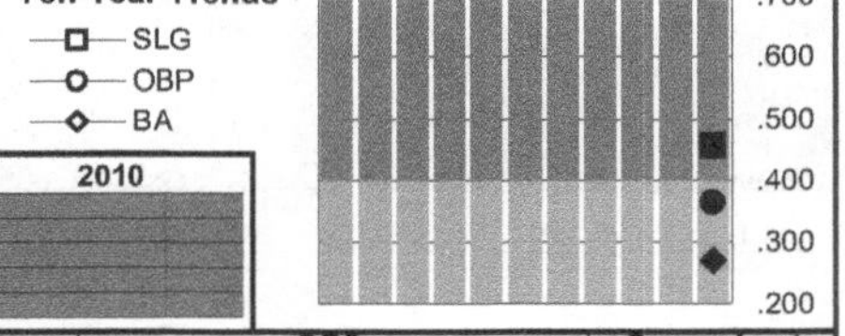
SLG
OBP
BA
.700
.600
.500
.400
.300
.200

| Yr | Team | AB | HR | R | RBI | SB | BA | OBP | SLG | CT% | H% | BB% | Bash | $1L | $2L | Pts | RAA | 2B | 3B | CS | FB-LD-GB | HR/fb | RBI% | RS% | OPS | 1st Hf | 2nd Hf | vs RH | vs LH | Rnge | vRH | vLH |
|---|---|---|---|---|---|---|---|---|---|---|---|---|---|---|---|---|---|---|---|---|---|---|---|---|---|---|---|---|---|---|---|---|
| 07 | — | — | — | — | — | — | — | — | — | — | — | — | — | — | — | — | — | — | — | — | — | — | — | — | — | — | — | — | — | — | — | — |
| 08 | — | — | — | — | — | — | — | — | — | — | — | — | — | — | — | — | — | — | — | — | — | — | — | — | — | — | — | — | — | — | — | — |
| 09 | — | — | — | — | — | — | — | — | — | — | — | — | — | — | — | — | — | — | — | — | — | — | — | — | — | — | — | — | — | — | — | — |
| 10 | — | — | — | — | — | — | — | — | — | — | — | — | — | — | — | — | — | — | — | — | — | — | — | — | — | — | — | — | — | — | — | — |

## Carlos Beltran — 600 PA | $25 | 470 pts

OF-61 (CF-61) — Owned: 65% — BH

Just when Beltran started to regain his form from off-season knee surgery (his September OPS was .967), he was shut down with new knee pain. If he is healthy, Beltran could waive his no-trade clause to play out his contract year elsewhere. If he stays, he could be moved to RF and face more competition for PT. (JL)

| Player | Age | AB | HR | R | RBI | SB | BA | OBP | SLG | $1L | Pts |
|---|---|---|---|---|---|---|---|---|---|---|---|
| Beltran C | 33 | 530 | 24 | 90 | 90 | 18 | .283 | .374 | .512 | $25 | 470 |
| **Mini-Browser** | Age | AB | HR | R | RBI | SB | BA | OBP | SLG | $1L | Pts |
| Hamilton J | 29 | 545 | 29 | 81 | 92 | 12 | .306 | .366 | .534 | $27 | 430 |
| Hunter T | 35 | 580 | 26 | 85 | 98 | 20 | .280 | .344 | .484 | $27 | 440 |
| Werth J | 31 | 563 | 33 | 98 | 91 | 20 | .277 | .379 | .508 | $26 | 450 |
| Kemp M | 26 | 597 | 26 | 91 | 91 | 26 | .272 | .329 | .466 | $26 | 420 |
| Suzuki I | 37 | 638 | 7 | 84 | 49 | 35 | .307 | .353 | .405 | $26 | 430 |

| Level | Leag | AB | HR | R | RBI | SB | BA | OBP | SLG | CT% | H% | BB% | Bash |
|---|---|---|---|---|---|---|---|---|---|---|---|---|---|
| A | FLO | 49 | 0 | 5 | 5 | 0 | .367 | .439 | .469 | 88% | 42% | 12% | 1.28 |
| AA | — | — | — | — | — | — | — | — | — | — | — | — | — |
| AAA | — | — | — | — | — | — | — | — | — | — | — | — | — |

Competition at CF — Stats in 2010

| Bats | Player | GSvR | GSvL | Sub | OPS |
|---|---|---|---|---|---|
| BH | Pagan A | 66 | 25 | 3 | .765 |
| BH | Beltran C | 45 | 13 | 3 | .768 |
| LH | Feliciano J | 8 | 1 | 3 | .563 |
| BH | Matthews Jr. G | 6 | 2 | 2 | .507 |

Weekly Points

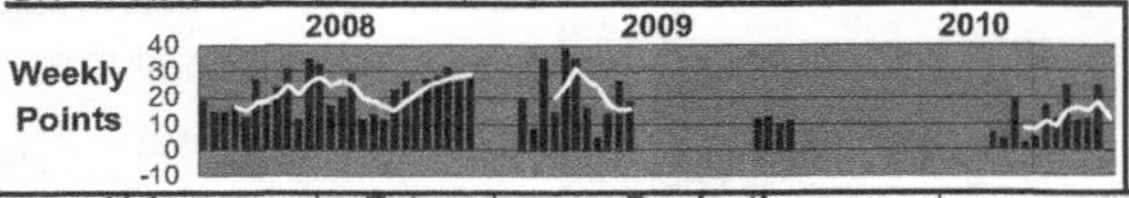
2008
2009
2010
40
30
20
10
0
-10

Ten-Year Trends

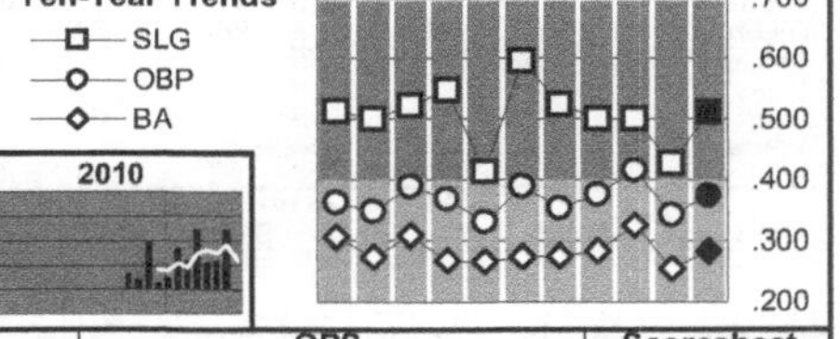
SLG
OBP
BA
.700
.600
.500
.400
.300
.200

| Yr | Team | AB | HR | R | RBI | SB | BA | OBP | SLG | CT% | H% | BB% | Bash | $1L | $2L | Pts | RAA | 2B | 3B | CS | FB-LD-GB | HR/fb | RBI% | RS% | OPS | 1st Hf | 2nd Hf | vs RH | vs LH | Rnge | vRH | vLH |
|---|---|---|---|---|---|---|---|---|---|---|---|---|---|---|---|---|---|---|---|---|---|---|---|---|---|---|---|---|---|---|---|---|
| 07 | NYM | 554 | 33 | 93 | 112 | 23 | .276 | .353 | .525 | 80% | 35% | 11% | 1.90 | $30 | $25 | 500 | +29 | 33 | 3 | 2 | 43-19-38 | 17% | 24% | 31% | .878 | .817 | .967 | .853 | .940 | 2.21 | +10 | –28 |
| 08 | NYM | 606 | 27 | 116 | 112 | 25 | .284 | .376 | .500 | 84% | 34% | 13% | 1.76 | $33 | $28 | 570 | +34 | 40 | 5 | 3 | 33-22-45 | 16% | 23% | 37% | .876 | .839 | .928 | .818 | 1.015 | 2.23 | +9 | –21 |
| 09 | NYM | 308 | 10 | 50 | 48 | 11 | .325 | .415 | .500 | 86% | 38% | 13% | 1.54 | $15 | $3 | 280 | +23 | 22 | 1 | 1 | 35-20-45 | 11% | 22% | 29% | .915 | .952 | .780 | .876 | 1.013 | 2.22 | –21 | +52 |
| 10 | NYM | 220 | 7 | 21 | 27 | 3 | .255 | .341 | .427 | 82% | 31% | 12% | 1.68 | $2 | -$11 | 140 | +1 | 11 | 3 | 1 | 39-19-42 | 10% | 23% | 18% | .768 | — | .768 | .701 | 1.009 | 2.19 | –24 | +59 |

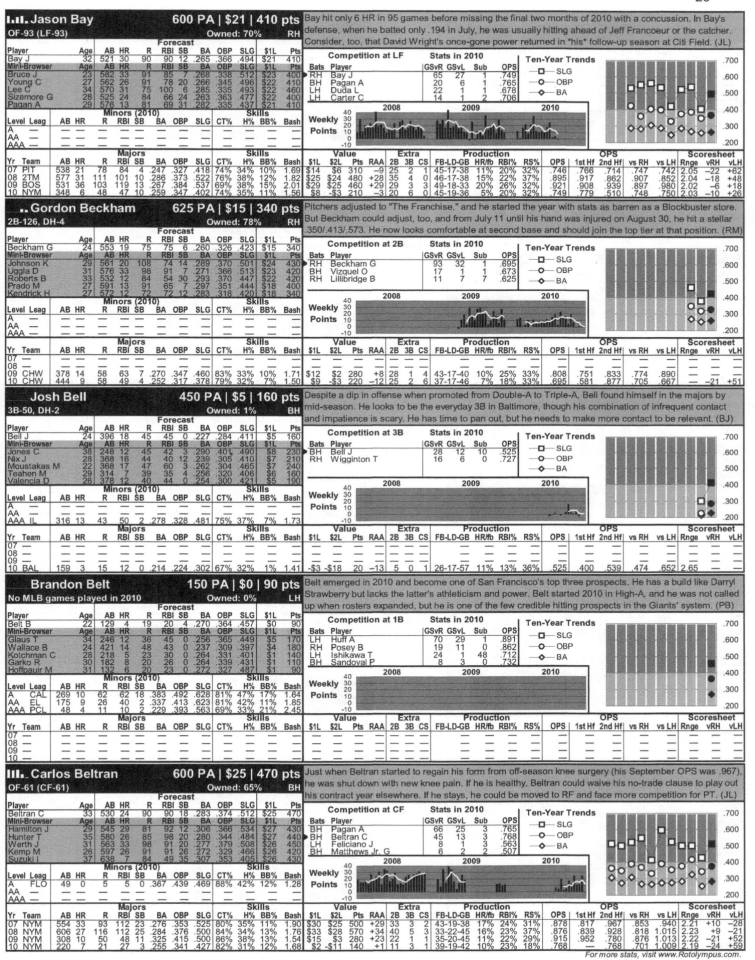

## Adrian Beltre — 600 PA | $21 | 380 pts

3B-154 | Owned: 100% | RH

Beltre had a sublime 2010 campaign, marrying his customary strong Bash with highs in CT% and H%, but the latter are probably not sustainable. However, he clearly answered questions about his offense, and he will get all the playing time that he can handle wherever he lands. Just don't bet on another .320 BA. (EB)

| Player | Age | AB | HR | R | RBI | SB | BA | OBP | SLG | $1L | Pts |
|---|---|---|---|---|---|---|---|---|---|---|---|
| | | Forecast | | | | | | | | | |
| Beltre A | 31 | 544 | 24 | 78 | 78 | 6 | .287 | .334 | .489 | $21 | 380 |
| **Mini-Browser** | Age | AB | HR | R | RBI | SB | BA | OBP | SLG | $1L | Pts |
| Wright D | 28 | 570 | 27 | 101 | 101 | 20 | .296 | .384 | .511 | $31 | 490 |
| Longoria E | 25 | 602 | 35 | 98 | 112 | 7 | .279 | .362 | .516 | $30 | 470 |
| Rodriguez A | 35 | 458 | 33 | 83 | 105 | 11 | .276 | .377 | .537 | $28 | 420 |
| Zimmerman R | 26 | 558 | 26 | 98 | 91 | 7 | .291 | .363 | .507 | $23 | 440 |
| Reynolds M | 27 | 586 | 39 | 98 | 98 | 13 | .244 | .339 | .498 | $23 | 390 |

| Level | Leag | AB | HR | R | RBI | SB | BA | OBP | SLG | CT% | H% | BB% | Bash |
|---|---|---|---|---|---|---|---|---|---|---|---|---|---|
| | | Minors (2010) | | | | | | | | Skills | | | |
| A | — | — | — | — | — | — | — | — | — | — | — | — | — |
| AA | — | — | — | — | — | — | — | — | — | — | — | — | — |
| AAA | — | — | — | — | — | — | — | — | — | — | — | — | — |

**Competition at 3B** — Stats in 2010

| Bats | Player | GSvR | GSvL | Sub | OPS |
|---|---|---|---|---|---|
| RH | Beltre A | 96 | 55 | 3 | .919 |

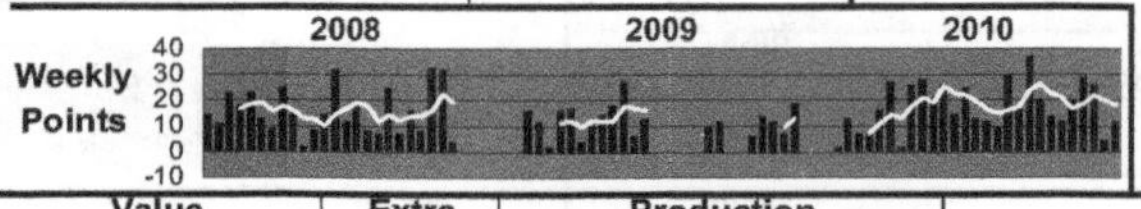

Weekly Points
40
30
20
10
0
-10
2008
2009
2010


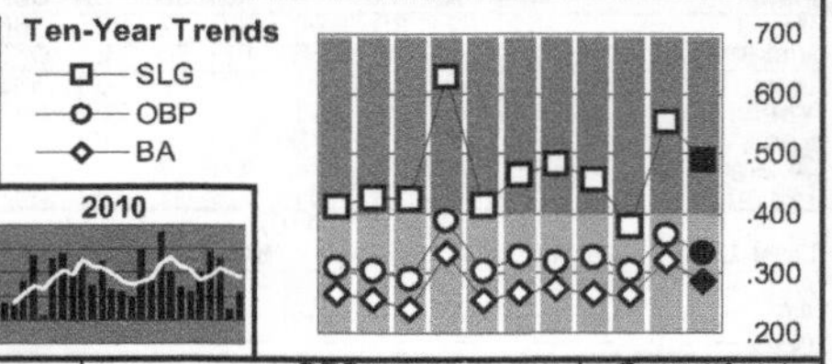

Ten-Year Trends
SLG
OBP
BA
.700
.600
.500
.400
.300
.200


| Yr | Team | AB | HR | R | RBI | SB | BA | OBP | SLG | CT% | H% | BB% | Bash |
|---|---|---|---|---|---|---|---|---|---|---|---|---|---|
| | | Majors | | | | | | | | Skills | | | |
| 07 | SEA | 595 | 26 | 87 | 99 | 14 | .276 | .319 | .482 | 83% | 33% | 6% | 1.75 |
| 08 | SEA | 556 | 25 | 74 | 77 | 8 | .266 | .327 | .457 | 84% | 32% | 8% | 1.72 |
| 09 | SEA | 449 | 8 | 54 | 44 | 13 | .265 | .304 | .379 | 84% | 32% | 4% | 1.43 |
| 10 | BOS | 589 | 28 | 84 | 102 | 2 | .321 | .365 | .553 | 86% | 37% | 6% | 1.72 |

| Yr | $1L | $2L | Pts | RAA | 2B | 3B | CS | FB-LD-GB | HR/fb | RBI% | RS% | OPS | 1st Hf | 2nd Hf | vs RH | vs LH | Rnge | vRH | vLH |
|---|---|---|---|---|---|---|---|---|---|---|---|---|---|---|---|---|---|---|---|
| | Value | | | | Extra | | | Production | | | | OPS | | | | | Scoresheet | | |
| 07 | $24 | $17 | 430 | +13 | 41 | 2 | 2 | 39-17-44 | 13% | 20% | 34% | .802 | .815 | .790 | .780 | .882 | 2.74 | –16 | +47 |
| 08 | $20 | $10 | 380 | +6 | 29 | 1 | 2 | 38-22-40 | 14% | 16% | 28% | .784 | .769 | .808 | .704 | .994 | 2.73 | –16 | +49 |
| 09 | $10 | -$2 | 240 | –11 | 27 | 0 | 2 | 38-16-46 | 6% | 15% | 34% | .683 | .664 | .717 | .616 | .855 | 2.73 | –34 | +89 |
| 10 | $31 | $26 | 470 | +33 | 49 | 2 | 1 | 40-19-40 | 13% | 21% | 27% | .919 | .907 | .933 | .908 | .943 | 2.74 | –40 | +100 |

## Lance Berkman — 400 PA | $14 | 280 pts

1B-93, DH-23 | Owned: 75% | BH

Berkman in 2010 was an unspectacular trade-deadline pick-up who performed as expected. He now hits well only against righties, and he is often hurt. The Yankees are not likely to bring him back – they have more than enough aging stars to slot at DH – but Berkman could be a solid role player elsewhere. (LS)

| Player | Age | AB | HR | R | RBI | SB | BA | OBP | SLG | $1L | Pts |
|---|---|---|---|---|---|---|---|---|---|---|---|
| | | Forecast | | | | | | | | | |
| Berkman L | 35 | 324 | 16 | 56 | 60 | 4 | .284 | .398 | .514 | $14 | 280 |
| **Mini-Browser** | Age | AB | HR | R | RBI | SB | BA | OBP | SLG | $1L | Pts |
| Lee D | 35 | 506 | 23 | 81 | 81 | 6 | .284 | .370 | .488 | $19 | 390 |
| Pena C | 32 | 452 | 33 | 72 | 88 | 0 | .231 | .357 | .494 | $17 | 310 |
| Loney J | 26 | 580 | 13 | 72 | 91 | 7 | .280 | .344 | .428 | $17 | 400 |
| Huff A | 34 | 534 | 18 | 78 | 84 | 6 | .281 | .353 | .473 | $17 | 400 |
| Sanchez G | 27 | 535 | 19 | 69 | 75 | 6 | .257 | .338 | .440 | $14 | 340 |

| Level | Leag | AB | HR | R | RBI | SB | BA | OBP | SLG | CT% | H% | BB% | Bash |
|---|---|---|---|---|---|---|---|---|---|---|---|---|---|
| | | Minors (2010) | | | | | | | | Skills | | | |
| A | — | — | — | — | — | — | — | — | — | — | — | — | — |
| AA | EL | 8 | 0 | 1 | 0 | 0 | .250 | .333 | .250 | 63% | 40% | 11% | 1.00 |
| AAA | PCL | 6 | 1 | 3 | 3 | 0 | .500 | .429 | 1.333 | 67% | 75% | 0% | 2.67 |

**Competition at 1B** — Stats in 2010

| Bats | Player | GSvR | GSvL | Sub | OPS |
|---|---|---|---|---|---|
| BH | Teixeira M | 94 | 54 | 1 | .846 |
| LH | Miranda J | 5 | 0 | 8 | .718 |

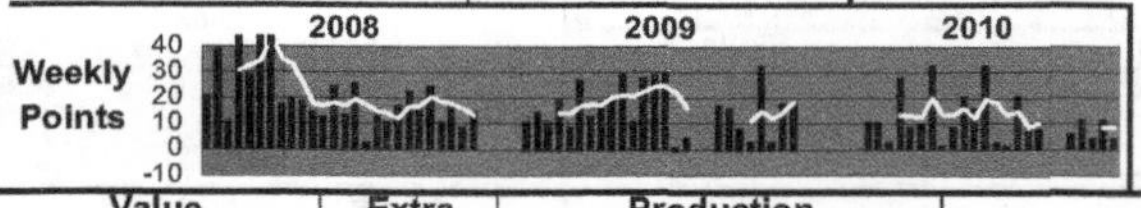

Weekly Points
40
30
20
10
0
-10
2008
2009
2010


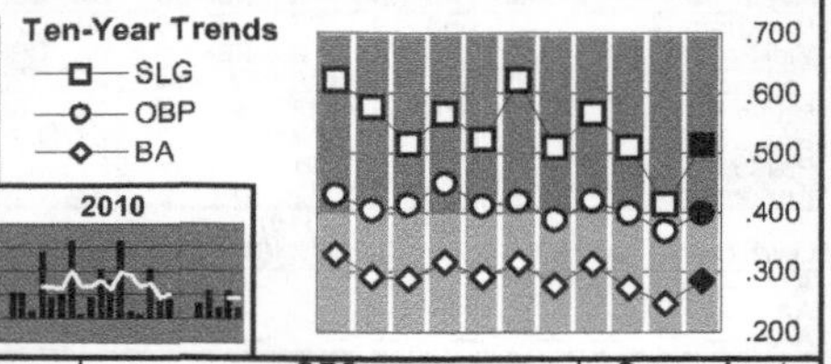

Ten-Year Trends
SLG
OBP
BA
.700
.600
.500
.400
.300
.200


| Yr | Team | AB | HR | R | RBI | SB | BA | OBP | SLG | CT% | H% | BB% | Bash |
|---|---|---|---|---|---|---|---|---|---|---|---|---|---|
| | | Majors | | | | | | | | Skills | | | |
| 07 | HOU | 561 | 34 | 95 | 102 | 7 | .278 | .386 | .510 | 78% | 36% | 14% | 1.83 |
| 08 | HOU | 554 | 29 | 114 | 106 | 18 | .312 | .420 | .567 | 81% | 39% | 14% | 1.82 |
| 09 | HOU | 460 | 25 | 73 | 80 | 7 | .274 | .399 | .509 | 79% | 35% | 17% | 1.86 |
| 10 | 2TM | 404 | 14 | 48 | 58 | 3 | .248 | .368 | .413 | 79% | 31% | 16% | 1.67 |

| Yr | $1L | $2L | Pts | RAA | 2B | 3B | CS | FB-LD-GB | HR/fb | RBI% | RS% | OPS | 1st Hf | 2nd Hf | vs RH | vs LH | Rnge | vRH | vLH |
|---|---|---|---|---|---|---|---|---|---|---|---|---|---|---|---|---|---|---|---|
| | Value | | | | Extra | | | Production | | | | OPS | | | | | Scoresheet | | |
| 07 | $26 | $20 | 460 | +14 | 24 | 2 | 3 | 38-18-44 | 20% | 24% | 27% | .896 | .839 | .962 | .926 | .800 | 1.85 | +31 | –83 |
| 08 | $34 | $30 | 560 | +35 | 46 | 4 | 4 | 39-18-43 | 17% | 26% | 34% | .986 | 1.096 | .821 | 1.057 | .803 | 1.83 | +30 | –84 |
| 09 | $19 | $12 | 400 | +17 | 31 | 1 | 4 | 39-18-43 | 17% | 23% | 24% | .907 | .929 | .869 | .982 | .710 | 1.87 | +22 | –62 |
| 10 | $10 | -$1 | 270 | –2 | 23 | 1 | 2 | 36-16-48 | 12% | 20% | 21% | .781 | .829 | .697 | .847 | .517 | 1.87 | +29 | –76 |

## Roger Bernadina — 500 PA | $9 | 260 pts

OF-130 (RF-78, LF-44, CF-26) | Owned: 1% | LH

Bernadina will open 2011 as the only member of the Nationals' four-man outfield rotation without a clear position. His speed and defense are good enough to secure him 400 AB or so; the rest will depend on his bat. In that department, Bernadina will turn 27 in 2011, and he should improve on his 11 home runs. (PB)

| Player | Age | AB | HR | R | RBI | SB | BA | OBP | SLG | $1L | Pts |
|---|---|---|---|---|---|---|---|---|---|---|---|
| | | Forecast | | | | | | | | | |
| Bernadina R | 26 | 466 | 10 | 55 | 45 | 25 | .236 | .307 | .359 | $9 | 260 |
| **Mini-Browser** | Age | AB | HR | R | RBI | SB | BA | OBP | SLG | $1L | Pts |
| Spilborghs R | 31 | 366 | 12 | 52 | 48 | 8 | .284 | .362 | .455 | $10 | 260 |
| Burrell P | 34 | 320 | 16 | 44 | 60 | 0 | .250 | .361 | .453 | $10 | 210 |
| Pie F | 26 | 384 | 12 | 52 | 44 | 8 | .271 | .320 | .432 | $10 | 230 |
| Fukudome K | 33 | 364 | 9 | 59 | 45 | 9 | .272 | .383 | .436 | $9 | 270 |
| Carter C | 24 | 442 | 25 | 55 | 65 | 5 | .215 | .306 | .437 | $9 | 240 |

| Level | Leag | AB | HR | R | RBI | SB | BA | OBP | SLG | CT% | H% | BB% | Bash |
|---|---|---|---|---|---|---|---|---|---|---|---|---|---|
| | | Minors (2010) | | | | | | | | Skills | | | |
| A | — | — | — | — | — | — | — | — | — | — | — | — | — |
| AA | — | — | — | — | — | — | — | — | — | — | — | — | — |
| AAA | IL | 61 | 2 | 8 | 8 | 7 | .377 | .426 | .541 | 92% | 41% | 9% | 1.43 |

**Competition at RF** — Stats in 2010

| Bats | Player | GSvR | GSvL | Sub | OPS |
|---|---|---|---|---|---|
| RH | Morse M | 38 | 26 | 8 | .870 |
| LH | Bernadina R | 61 | 3 | 14 | .691 |
| LH | Harris W | 26 | 0 | 17 | .653 |
| RH | Maxwell J | 2 | 10 | 17 | .594 |

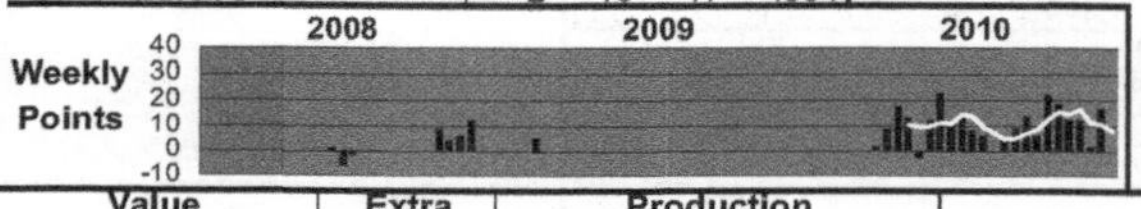

Weekly Points
40
30
20
10
0
-10
2008
2009
2010


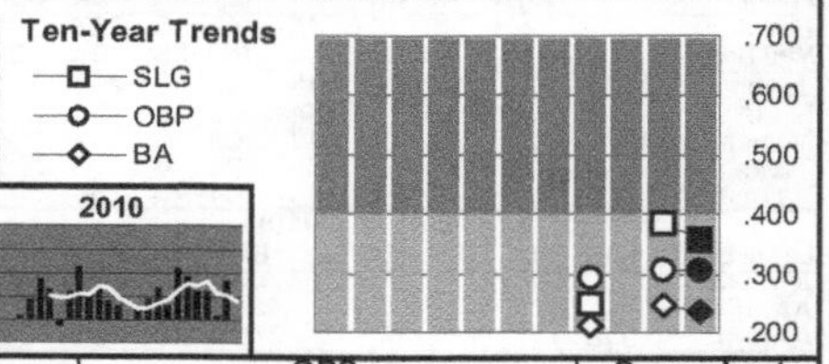

Ten-Year Trends
SLG
OBP
BA
.700
.600
.500
.400
.300
.200


| Yr | Team | AB | HR | R | RBI | SB | BA | OBP | SLG | CT% | H% | BB% | Bash |
|---|---|---|---|---|---|---|---|---|---|---|---|---|---|
| | | Majors | | | | | | | | Skills | | | |
| 07 | — | — | — | — | — | — | — | — | — | — | — | — | — |
| 08 | WAS | 76 | 0 | 10 | 2 | 4 | .211 | .294 | .250 | 72% | 29% | 10% | 1.19 |
| 09 | WAS | 4 | 0 | 1 | 0 | 1 | .250 | .400 | .500 | 75% | 33% | 20% | 2.00 |
| 10 | WAS | 414 | 11 | 52 | 47 | 16 | .246 | .307 | .384 | 78% | 32% | 8% | 1.56 |

| Yr | $1L | $2L | Pts | RAA | 2B | 3B | CS | FB-LD-GB | HR/fb | RBI% | RS% | OPS | 1st Hf | 2nd Hf | vs RH | vs LH | Rnge | vRH | vLH |
|---|---|---|---|---|---|---|---|---|---|---|---|---|---|---|---|---|---|---|---|
| | Value | | | | Extra | | | Production | | | | OPS | | | | | Scoresheet | | |
| 07 | — | — | — | — | — | — | — | — | — | — | — | — | — | — | — | — | — | — | — |
| 08 | -$4 | -$17 | 20 | –7 | 1 | 1 | 3 | 17-15-67 | 0% | 5% | 40% | .544 | .250 | .833 | .536 | .600 | — | — | — |
| 09 | -$4 | -$20 | 0 | +0 | 1 | 0 | 0 | 33-33-33 | 0% | NA | 50% | .900 | .900 | — | .750 | — | 2.12 | +19 | –61 |
| 10 | $10 | $0 | 230 | –17 | 18 | 3 | 2 | 39-13-47 | 9% | 16% | 32% | .691 | .781 | .621 | .681 | .757 | 2.10 | +20 | –60 |

## Yuniesky Betancourt — 550 PA | $11 | 320 pts

SS-151 | Owned: 27% | RH

The Yunigma (as Royals fans have christened him) had a "career year" by old-school standards, but his rates don't wow. He swings at everything (though he doesn't strike out often); he doesn't walk often, either. And yet, he doubled his normal output in HR, aided by a FB trend that has risen three straight years. (BM)

| Player | Age | AB | HR | R | RBI | SB | BA | OBP | SLG | $1L | Pts |
|---|---|---|---|---|---|---|---|---|---|---|---|
| | | Forecast | | | | | | | | | |
| Betancourt Y | 29 | 532 | 11 | 55 | 61 | 6 | .279 | .302 | .413 | $11 | 320 |
| **Mini-Browser** | Age | AB | HR | R | RBI | SB | BA | OBP | SLG | $1L | Pts |
| Peralta J | 28 | 539 | 18 | 66 | 78 | 0 | .256 | .320 | .411 | $12 | 290 |
| Hardy J | 28 | 465 | 15 | 60 | 60 | 0 | .269 | .323 | .435 | $12 | 280 |
| Bartlett J | 31 | 446 | 5 | 65 | 45 | 20 | .269 | .334 | .378 | $11 | 280 |
| Desmond I | 25 | 460 | 15 | 50 | 50 | 20 | .250 | .311 | .403 | $11 | 270 |
| Escobar A | 24 | 561 | 6 | 75 | 50 | 25 | .245 | .290 | .343 | $11 | 300 |

| Level | Leag | AB | HR | R | RBI | SB | BA | OBP | SLG | CT% | H% | BB% | Bash |
|---|---|---|---|---|---|---|---|---|---|---|---|---|---|
| | | Minors (2010) | | | | | | | | Skills | | | |
| A | — | — | — | — | — | — | — | — | — | — | — | — | — |
| AA | — | — | — | — | — | — | — | — | — | — | — | — | — |
| AAA | — | — | — | — | — | — | — | — | — | — | — | — | — |

**Competition at SS** — Stats in 2010

| Bats | Player | GSvR | GSvL | Sub | OPS |
|---|---|---|---|---|---|
| RH | Betancourt Y | 119 | 32 | 0 | .692 |
| RH | Aviles M | 9 | 4 | 0 | .748 |

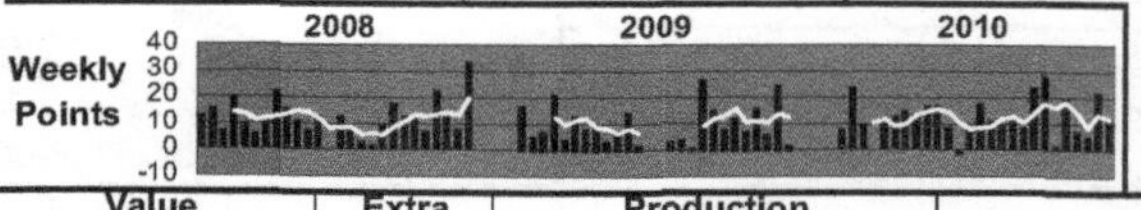

Weekly Points
40
30
20
10
0
-10
2008
2009
2010


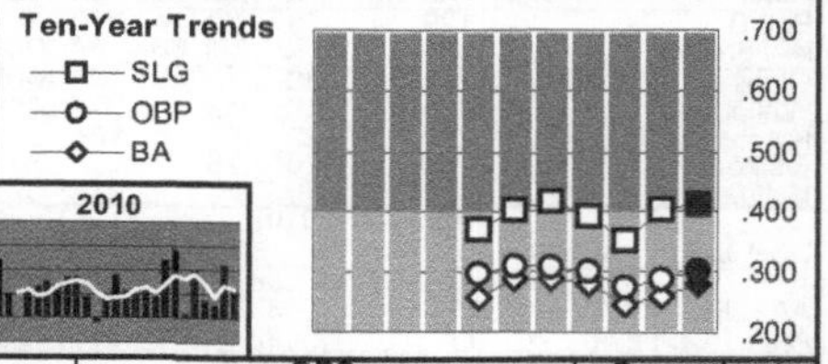

Ten-Year Trends
SLG
OBP
BA
.700
.600
.500
.400
.300
.200


| Yr | Team | AB | HR | R | RBI | SB | BA | OBP | SLG | CT% | H% | BB% | Bash |
|---|---|---|---|---|---|---|---|---|---|---|---|---|---|
| | | Majors | | | | | | | | Skills | | | |
| 07 | SEA | 536 | 9 | 72 | 67 | 5 | .289 | .308 | .418 | 91% | 32% | 3% | 1.45 |
| 08 | SEA | 559 | 7 | 66 | 51 | 4 | .279 | .300 | .392 | 92% | 30% | 3% | 1.40 |
| 09 | 2TM | 470 | 6 | 40 | 49 | 3 | .245 | .274 | .351 | 91% | 27% | 4% | 1.43 |
| 10 | KC | 556 | 16 | 60 | 78 | 2 | .259 | .288 | .405 | 88% | 29% | 4% | 1.56 |

| Yr | $1L | $2L | Pts | RAA | 2B | 3B | CS | FB-LD-GB | HR/fb | RBI% | RS% | OPS | 1st Hf | 2nd Hf | vs RH | vs LH | Rnge | vRH | vLH |
|---|---|---|---|---|---|---|---|---|---|---|---|---|---|---|---|---|---|---|---|
| | Value | | | | Extra | | | Production | | | | OPS | | | | | Scoresheet | | |
| 07 | $14 | $5 | 340 | +4 | 38 | 2 | 4 | 38-19-43 | 5% | 21% | 39% | .725 | .663 | .802 | .673 | .916 | 4.70 | –10 | +28 |
| 08 | $11 | $1 | 320 | –4 | 36 | 3 | 4 | 40-20-40 | 3% | 15% | 35% | .691 | .652 | .746 | .694 | .684 | 4.73 | –19 | +52 |
| 09 | $4 | -$8 | 230 | –17 | 20 | 6 | 3 | 41-17-42 | 3% | 18% | 26% | .625 | .609 | .639 | .573 | .772 | 4.68 | –24 | +62 |
| 10 | $14 | $4 | 320 | –4 | 29 | 2 | 3 | 42-18-40 | 8% | 20% | 29% | .692 | .672 | .716 | .666 | .778 | 4.64 | –20 | +50 |

## Wilson Betemit — 450 PA | $11 | 230 pts

3B-53, DH-14, 1B-5, 2B-2, OF-2 (LF-2) | Owned: 6% | BH

Betemit was a pleasant surprise in 2010, providing some pop after filling in at third for the traded Alberto Callaspo. Betemit's rise to relevancy in KC is suggestive of what Raul Ibanez did in 2001-03. But Betemit's PT may be short-lived, as Mike Moustakas could take at-bats when he is inevitably called up in 2011. (BM)

| Player | Age | AB | HR | R | RBI | SB | BA | OBP | SLG | $1L | Pts |
|---|---|---|---|---|---|---|---|---|---|---|---|
| | | Forecast | | | | | | | | | |
| Betemit W | 29 | 417 | 18 | 50 | 63 | 0 | .270 | .339 | .467 | $11 | 230 |
| **Mini-Browser** | Age | AB | HR | R | RBI | SB | BA | OBP | SLG | $1L | Pts |
| Alvarez P | 24 | 530 | 30 | 66 | 96 | 0 | .249 | .328 | .480 | $15 | 310 |
| Rolen S | 35 | 461 | 15 | 70 | 65 | 5 | .282 | .356 | .466 | $13 | 340 |
| Lopez J | 27 | 587 | 19 | 63 | 75 | 6 | .266 | .294 | .405 | $13 | 350 |
| Tejada M | 36 | 509 | 11 | 66 | 66 | 6 | .281 | .321 | .415 | $13 | 320 |
| Headley C | 26 | 568 | 12 | 68 | 62 | 12 | .251 | .330 | .394 | $11 | 300 |

| Level | Leag | AB | HR | R | RBI | SB | BA | OBP | SLG | CT% | H% | BB% | Bash |
|---|---|---|---|---|---|---|---|---|---|---|---|---|---|
| | | Minors (2010) | | | | | | | | Skills | | | |
| A | — | — | — | — | — | — | — | — | — | — | — | — | — |
| AA | — | — | — | — | — | — | — | — | — | — | — | — | — |
| AAA | PCL | 113 | 2 | 9 | 17 | 1 | .265 | .358 | .407 | 80% | 33% | 13% | 1.53 |

**Competition at 3B** — Stats in 2010

| Bats | Player | GSvR | GSvL | Sub | OPS |
|---|---|---|---|---|---|
| BH | Betemit W | 39 | 12 | 2 | .889 |
| RH | Fields J | 8 | 4 | 0 | .810 |
| LH | Gordon A | 9 | 0 | 1 | .671 |

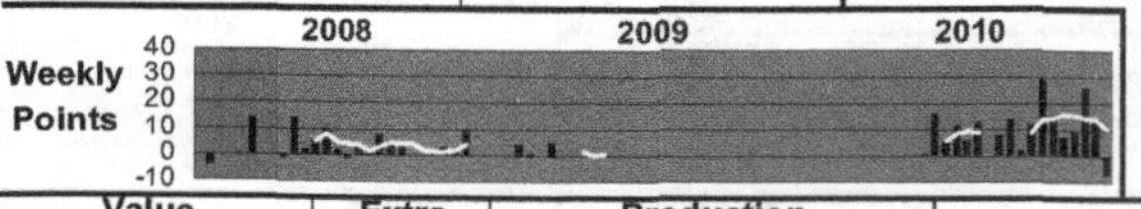

Weekly Points
40
30
20
10
0
-10
2008
2009
2010


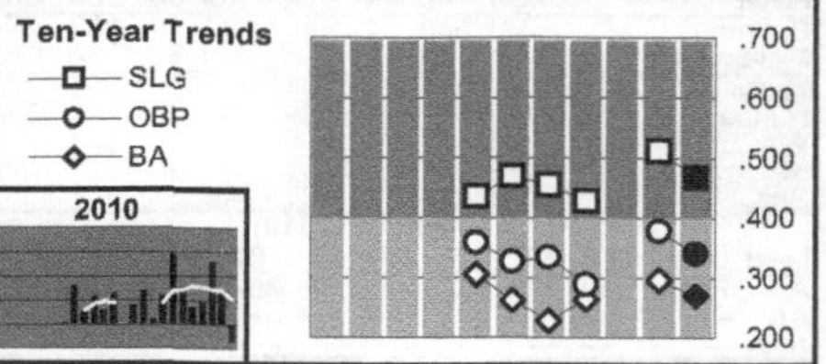

Ten-Year Trends
SLG
OBP
BA
.700
.600
.500
.400
.300
.200


| Yr | Team | AB | HR | R | RBI | SB | BA | OBP | SLG | CT% | H% | BB% | Bash |
|---|---|---|---|---|---|---|---|---|---|---|---|---|---|
| | | Majors | | | | | | | | Skills | | | |
| 07 | 2TM | 240 | 14 | 33 | 50 | 0 | .229 | .333 | .454 | 66% | 35% | 13% | 1.98 |
| 08 | NYY | 189 | 6 | 24 | 25 | 0 | .265 | .289 | .429 | 70% | 38% | 3% | 1.62 |
| 09 | CHW | 45 | 0 | 2 | 3 | 0 | .200 | .280 | .311 | 71% | 28% | 10% | 1.56 |
| 10 | KC | 276 | 13 | 36 | 43 | 0 | .297 | .378 | .511 | 73% | 41% | 11% | 1.72 |

| Yr | $1L | $2L | Pts | RAA | 2B | 3B | CS | FB-LD-GB | HR/fb | RBI% | RS% | OPS | 1st Hf | 2nd Hf | vs RH | vs LH | Rnge | vRH | vLH |
|---|---|---|---|---|---|---|---|---|---|---|---|---|---|---|---|---|---|---|---|
| | Value | | | | Extra | | | Production | | | | OPS | | | | | Scoresheet | | |
| 07 | -$1 | -$7 | 150 | +4 | 12 | 0 | 0 | 40-18-42 | 22% | 27% | 24% | .788 | .802 | .769 | .815 | .670 | 2.68 | +22 | –64 |
| 08 | $2 | -$11 | 80 | –3 | 13 | 0 | 1 | 33-25-43 | 14% | 17% | 35% | .718 | .679 | .769 | .739 | .645 | 2.66 | +18 | –56 |
| 09 | -$4 | -$21 | 10 | –2 | 5 | 0 | 0 | 38-16-47 | 0% | 14% | 14% | .591 | .591 | — | .561 | .650 | 2.66 | +6 | –14 |
| 10 | $10 | -$2 | 180 | +16 | 20 | 0 | 0 | 45-15-40 | 14% | 20% | 22% | .889 | 1.163 | .823 | .873 | .930 | 2.64 | –2 | +5 |

*For more stats, visit www.Rotolympus.com.*

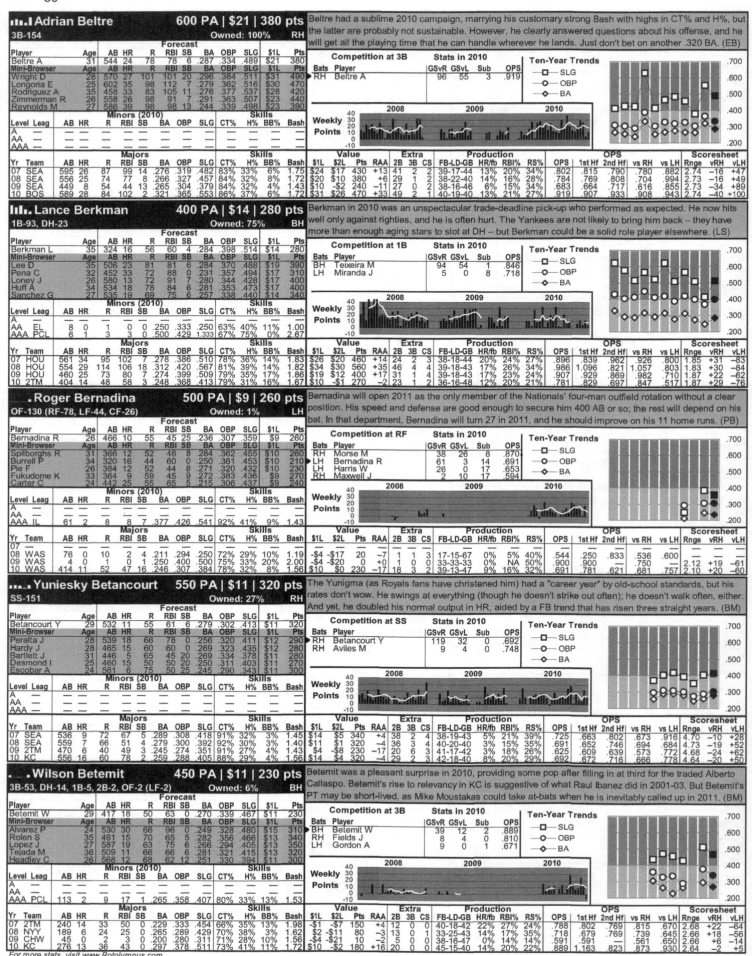

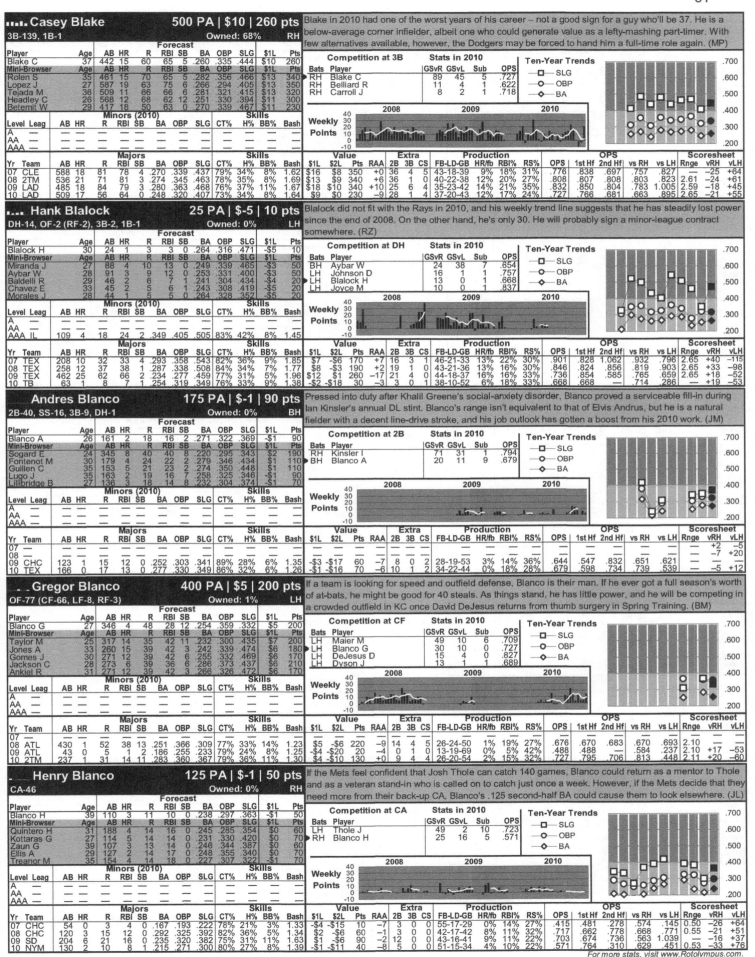

## ....Casey Blake — 500 PA | $10 | 260 pts

**3B-139, 1B-1**  Owned: 68%  RH

Blake in 2010 had one of the worst years of his career – not a good sign for a guy who'll be 37. He is a below-average corner infielder, albeit one who could generate value as a lefty-mashing part-timer. With few alternatives available, however, the Dodgers may be forced to hand him a full-time role again. (MP)

### Forecast

| Player | Age | AB | HR | R | RBI | SB | BA | OBP | SLG | $1L | Pts |
|---|---|---|---|---|---|---|---|---|---|---|---|
| Blake C | 37 | 442 | 15 | 60 | 65 | 5 | .260 | .335 | .444 | $10 | 260 |
| **Mini-Browser** | **Age** | **AB** | **HR** | **R** | **RBI** | **SB** | **BA** | **OBP** | **SLG** | **$1L** | **Pts** |
| Rolen S | 35 | 461 | 15 | 70 | 65 | 5 | .282 | .356 | .466 | $13 | 340 |
| Lopez J | 27 | 587 | 19 | 63 | 75 | 6 | .266 | .294 | .405 | $13 | 350 |
| Tejada M | 36 | 509 | 11 | 66 | 66 | 6 | .281 | .321 | .415 | $13 | 320 |
| Headley C | 26 | 568 | 12 | 68 | 62 | 12 | .251 | .330 | .394 | $11 | 300 |
| Betemit W | 29 | 417 | 18 | 50 | 63 | 0 | .270 | .339 | .467 | $11 | 230 |

**Competition at 3B — Stats in 2010**

| Bats | Player | GSvR | GSvL | Sub | OPS |
|---|---|---|---|---|---|
| RH | Blake C | 89 | 45 | 5 | .727 |
| RH | Belliard R | 11 | 4 | 1 | .622 |
| RH | Carroll J | 8 | 2 | 1 | .718 |

**Ten-Year Trends:** □ SLG  ○ OBP  ◇ BA

**Weekly Points** — 2008 | 2009 | 2010

### Minors (2010) / Skills

| Level | Leag | AB | HR | R | RBI | SB | BA | OBP | SLG | CT% | H% | BB% | Bash |
|---|---|---|---|---|---|---|---|---|---|---|---|---|---|
| A | | — | — | — | — | — | — | — | — | | | | |
| AA | | — | — | — | — | — | — | — | — | | | | |
| AAA | | — | — | — | — | — | — | — | — | | | | |

### Majors / Skills

| Yr | Team | AB | HR | R | RBI | SB | BA | OBP | SLG | CT% | H% | BB% | Bash |
|---|---|---|---|---|---|---|---|---|---|---|---|---|---|
| 07 | CLE | 588 | 18 | 81 | 78 | 4 | .270 | .339 | .437 | 79% | 34% | 8% | 1.62 |
| 08 | 2TM | 536 | 21 | 71 | 81 | 3 | .274 | .345 | .463 | 78% | 35% | 8% | 1.69 |
| 09 | LAD | 485 | 18 | 84 | 79 | 3 | .280 | .363 | .468 | 76% | 37% | 11% | 1.67 |
| 10 | LAD | 509 | 17 | 56 | 64 | 0 | .248 | .320 | .407 | 73% | 34% | 8% | 1.64 |

### Value / Extra / Production / OPS / Scoresheet

| $1L | $2L | Pts | RAA | 2B | 3B | CS | FB-LD-GB | HR/fb | RBI% | RS% | OPS | 1st Hf | 2nd Hf | vs RH | vs LH | Rnge | vRH | vLH |
|---|---|---|---|---|---|---|---|---|---|---|---|---|---|---|---|---|---|---|
| $16 | $8 | 350 | +0 | 36 | 4 | 5 | 43-18-39 | 9% | 18% | 31% | .776 | .838 | .697 | .757 | .827 | — | −25 | +64 |
| $13 | $9 | 340 | +6 | 36 | 1 | 0 | 40-22-38 | 12% | 20% | 27% | .808 | .807 | .808 | .803 | .823 | 2.61 | −24 | +61 |
| $18 | $10 | 340 | +10 | 25 | 6 | 4 | 35-23-42 | 14% | 21% | 35% | .832 | .850 | .804 | .783 | 1.005 | 2.59 | −18 | +45 |
| $9 | $0 | 230 | −9 | 28 | 1 | 4 | 37-20-43 | 12% | 17% | 24% | .727 | .766 | .681 | .663 | .895 | 2.65 | −21 | +55 |

---

## .... Hank Blalock — 25 PA | $-5 | 10 pts

**DH-14, OF-2 (RF-2), 3B-2, 1B-1**  Owned: 0%  LH

Blalock did not fit with the Rays in 2010, and his weekly trend line suggests that he has steadily lost power since the end of 2008. On the other hand, he's only 30. He will probably sign a minor-league contract somewhere. (RZ)

### Forecast

| Player | Age | AB | HR | R | RBI | SB | BA | OBP | SLG | $1L | Pts |
|---|---|---|---|---|---|---|---|---|---|---|---|
| Blalock H | 30 | 24 | 1 | 3 | 3 | 0 | .264 | .316 | .471 | -$5 | 10 |
| **Mini-Browser** | **Age** | **AB** | **HR** | **R** | **RBI** | **SB** | **BA** | **OBP** | **SLG** | **$1L** | **Pts** |
| Miranda J | 27 | 88 | 4 | 10 | 13 | 0 | .249 | .339 | .465 | -$3 | 50 |
| Aybar W | 28 | 91 | 3 | 9 | 12 | 0 | .253 | .331 | .400 | -$3 | 50 |
| Baldelli R | 29 | 46 | 2 | 6 | 7 | 1 | .241 | .304 | .434 | -$4 | 20 |
| Chavez E | 33 | 45 | 2 | 5 | 6 | 1 | .243 | .308 | .419 | -$5 | 20 |
| Morales J | 28 | 44 | 1 | 5 | 6 | 0 | .264 | .328 | .352 | -$5 | 20 |

**Competition at DH — Stats in 2010**

| Bats | Player | GSvR | GSvL | Sub | OPS |
|---|---|---|---|---|---|
| BH | Aybar W | 24 | 38 | 7 | .654 |
| LH | Johnson D | 16 | 1 | 1 | .757 |
| LH | Blalock H | 13 | 0 | 1 | .668 |
| LH | Joyce M | 10 | 0 | 1 | .837 |

**Ten-Year Trends:** □ SLG  ○ OBP  ◇ BA

**Weekly Points** — 2008 | 2009 | 2010

### Minors (2010) / Skills

| Level | Leag | AB | HR | R | RBI | SB | BA | OBP | SLG | CT% | H% | BB% | Bash |
|---|---|---|---|---|---|---|---|---|---|---|---|---|---|
| A | | — | | | | | | | | | | | |
| AA | | — | | | | | | | | | | | |
| AAA | IL | 109 | 4 | 18 | 24 | 2 | .349 | .405 | .505 | 83% | 42% | 8% | 1.45 |

### Majors / Skills

| Yr | Team | AB | HR | R | RBI | SB | BA | OBP | SLG | CT% | H% | BB% | Bash |
|---|---|---|---|---|---|---|---|---|---|---|---|---|---|
| 07 | TEX | 208 | 10 | 32 | 33 | 4 | .293 | .358 | .543 | 82% | 36% | 6% | 1.85 |
| 08 | TEX | 258 | 12 | 37 | 38 | 1 | .287 | .338 | .508 | 84% | 34% | 7% | 1.77 |
| 09 | TEX | 462 | 25 | 62 | 66 | 2 | .234 | .277 | .459 | 77% | 31% | 5% | 1.96 |
| 10 | TB | 63 | 1 | 8 | 7 | 1 | .254 | .319 | .349 | 76% | 33% | 5% | 1.38 |

### Value / Extra / Production / OPS / Scoresheet

| $1L | $2L | Pts | RAA | 2B | 3B | CS | FB-LD-GB | HR/fb | RBI% | RS% | OPS | 1st Hf | 2nd Hf | vs RH | vs LH | Rnge | vRH | vLH |
|---|---|---|---|---|---|---|---|---|---|---|---|---|---|---|---|---|---|---|
| $7 | -$6 | 170 | +7 | 16 | 3 | 1 | 46-21-33 | 13% | 22% | 30% | .901 | .828 | 1.062 | .932 | .796 | 2.65 | +40 | −115 |
| $8 | -$3 | 190 | +2 | 19 | 1 | 0 | 43-21-36 | 13% | 16% | 30% | .846 | .824 | .856 | .819 | .903 | 2.65 | +33 | −98 |
| $12 | $1 | 260 | +17 | 21 | 4 | 0 | 44-18-37 | 16% | 16% | 33% | .736 | .854 | .585 | .765 | .659 | 2.65 | +18 | −52 |
| -$2 | -$18 | 30 | −3 | 3 | 0 | 1 | 38-10-52 | 6% | 18% | 33% | .668 | .668 | — | .714 | .286 | — | +19 | −53 |

---

## Andres Blanco — 175 PA | $-1 | 90 pts

**2B-40, SS-16, 3B-9, DH-1**  Owned: 0%  BH

Pressed into duty after Khalil Greene's social-anxiety disorder, Blanco proved a serviceable fill-in during Ian Kinsler's annual DL stint. Blanco's range isn't equivalent to that of Elvis Andrus, but he is a natural fielder with a decent line-drive stroke, and his job outlook has gotten a boost from his 2010 work. (JM)

### Forecast

| Player | Age | AB | HR | R | RBI | SB | BA | OBP | SLG | $1L | Pts |
|---|---|---|---|---|---|---|---|---|---|---|---|
| Blanco A | 26 | 161 | 2 | 18 | 16 | 2 | .271 | .322 | .369 | -$1 | 90 |
| **Mini-Browser** | **Age** | **AB** | **HR** | **R** | **RBI** | **SB** | **BA** | **OBP** | **SLG** | **$1L** | **Pts** |
| Sogard E | 24 | 345 | 8 | 40 | 40 | 8 | .220 | .295 | .343 | $2 | 190 |
| Fontenot M | 30 | 179 | 4 | 24 | 22 | 2 | .279 | .346 | .434 | $1 | 110 |
| Guillen C | 35 | 153 | 5 | 21 | 23 | 2 | .274 | .350 | .448 | $1 | 110 |
| Lugo J | 35 | 163 | 2 | 19 | 16 | 7 | .258 | .325 | .346 | -$1 | 90 |
| Lillibridge B | 27 | 136 | 3 | 18 | 14 | 8 | .232 | .304 | .374 | -$1 | 70 |

**Competition at 2B — Stats in 2010**

| Bats | Player | GSvR | GSvL | Sub | OPS |
|---|---|---|---|---|---|
| RH | Kinsler I | 71 | 31 | 1 | .794 |
| BH | Blanco A | 20 | 11 | 9 | .679 |

**Ten-Year Trends:** □ SLG  ○ OBP  ◇ BA

**Weekly Points** — 2008 | 2009 | 2010

### Minors (2010) / Skills

| Level | Leag | AB | HR | R | RBI | SB | BA | OBP | SLG | CT% | H% | BB% | Bash |
|---|---|---|---|---|---|---|---|---|---|---|---|---|---|
| A | | — | — | — | — | — | — | — | — | | | | |
| AA | | — | — | — | — | — | — | — | — | | | | |
| AAA | | — | — | — | — | — | — | — | — | | | | |

### Majors / Skills

| Yr | Team | AB | HR | R | RBI | SB | BA | OBP | SLG | CT% | H% | BB% | Bash |
|---|---|---|---|---|---|---|---|---|---|---|---|---|---|
| 07 | — | | | | | | | | | | | | |
| 08 | — | | | | | | | | | | | | |
| 09 | CHC | 123 | 1 | 15 | 12 | 0 | .252 | .303 | .341 | 89% | 28% | 6% | 1.35 |
| 10 | TEX | 166 | 0 | 17 | 13 | 0 | .277 | .330 | .349 | 86% | 32% | 6% | 1.26 |

### Value / Extra / Production / OPS / Scoresheet

| $1L | $2L | Pts | RAA | 2B | 3B | CS | FB-LD-GB | HR/fb | RBI% | RS% | OPS | 1st Hf | 2nd Hf | vs RH | vs LH | Rnge | vRH | vLH |
|---|---|---|---|---|---|---|---|---|---|---|---|---|---|---|---|---|---|---|
| | | | | | | | | | | | | | | | | | +2 | −5 |
| | | | | | | | | | | | | | | | | | −7 | +20 |
| -$3 | -$17 | 60 | −7 | 16 | 8 | 0 | 2 | 28-19-53 | 3% | 14% | 36% | .644 | .547 | .832 | .651 | .621 | — | −5 | +12 |
| -$1 | -$16 | 70 | −6 | 10 | 1 | 2 | 34-22-44 | 0% | 18% | 28% | .679 | .598 | .734 | .739 | .539 | — | −5 | +12 |

---

## _ Gregor Blanco — 400 PA | $5 | 200 pts

**OF-77 (CF-66, LF-8, RF-3)**  Owned: 1%  LH

If a team is looking for speed and outfield defense, Blanco's their man. If he ever got a full season's worth of at-bats, he might be good for 40 steals. As things stand, he has little power, and he will be competing in a crowded outfield in KC once David DeJesus returns from thumb surgery in Spring Training. (BM)

### Forecast

| Player | Age | AB | HR | R | RBI | SB | BA | OBP | SLG | $1L | Pts |
|---|---|---|---|---|---|---|---|---|---|---|---|
| Blanco G | 27 | 346 | 4 | 48 | 28 | 12 | .254 | .359 | .332 | $5 | 200 |
| **Mini-Browser** | **Age** | **AB** | **HR** | **R** | **RBI** | **SB** | **BA** | **OBP** | **SLG** | **$1L** | **Pts** |
| Taylor M | 25 | 317 | 14 | 35 | 42 | 11 | .232 | .300 | .435 | $7 | 200 |
| Jones A | 33 | 260 | 15 | 39 | 42 | 4 | .242 | .339 | .474 | $6 | 180 |
| Gomes J | 30 | 271 | 12 | 39 | 42 | 6 | .255 | .332 | .469 | $6 | 170 |
| Jackson C | 28 | 273 | 6 | 39 | 36 | 6 | .286 | .373 | .437 | $6 | 210 |
| Ankiel R | 31 | 271 | 12 | 39 | 42 | 3 | .266 | .326 | .472 | $6 | 170 |

**Competition at CF — Stats in 2010**

| Bats | Player | GSvR | GSvL | Sub | OPS |
|---|---|---|---|---|---|
| LH | Maier M | 49 | 10 | 6 | .709 |
| LH | Blanco G | 30 | 10 | 0 | .727 |
| LH | DeJesus D | 15 | 4 | 0 | .827 |
| LH | Dyson J | 13 | 1 | 1 | .689 |

**Ten-Year Trends:** □ SLG  ○ OBP  ◇ BA

**Weekly Points** — 2008 | 2009 | 2010

### Minors (2010) / Skills

| Level | Leag | AB | HR | R | RBI | SB | BA | OBP | SLG | CT% | H% | BB% | Bash |
|---|---|---|---|---|---|---|---|---|---|---|---|---|---|
| A | | — | | | | | | | | | | | |
| AA | | — | | | | | | | | | | | |
| AAA | | — | | | | | | | | | | | |

### Majors / Skills

| Yr | Team | AB | HR | R | RBI | SB | BA | OBP | SLG | CT% | H% | BB% | Bash |
|---|---|---|---|---|---|---|---|---|---|---|---|---|---|
| 07 | — | | | | | | | | | | | | |
| 08 | ATL | 430 | 1 | 52 | 38 | 13 | .251 | .366 | .309 | 77% | 33% | 14% | 1.23 |
| 09 | ATL | 43 | 0 | 5 | 1 | 2 | .186 | .255 | .233 | 79% | 24% | 8% | 1.25 |
| 10 | 2TM | 237 | 1 | 31 | 14 | 11 | .283 | .360 | .367 | 79% | 36% | 11% | 1.30 |

### Value / Extra / Production / OPS / Scoresheet

| $1L | $2L | Pts | RAA | 2B | 3B | CS | FB-LD-GB | HR/fb | RBI% | RS% | OPS | 1st Hf | 2nd Hf | vs RH | vs LH | Rnge | vRH | vLH |
|---|---|---|---|---|---|---|---|---|---|---|---|---|---|---|---|---|---|---|
| $5 | -$6 | 220 | −9 | 14 | 4 | 5 | 26-24-50 | 1% | 19% | 27% | .676 | .670 | .683 | .670 | .693 | 2.10 | +17 | −53 |
| -$4 | -$20 | 20 | −4 | 0 | 1 | 0 | 13-19-69 | 0% | 5% | 42% | .488 | .488 | — | .584 | .237 | 2.10 | −6 | −60 |
| -$4 | -$10 | 130 | +0 | 8 | 4 | 4 | 26-20-54 | 2% | 15% | 32% | .727 | .795 | .706 | .813 | .448 | 2.11 | +20 | −60 |

---

## _ Henry Blanco — 125 PA | $-1 | 50 pts

**CA-46**  Owned: 0%  RH

If the Mets feel confident that Josh Thole can catch 140 games, Blanco could return as a mentor to Thole and as a veteran stand-in who is called on to catch just once a week. However, if the Mets decide that they need more from their back-up CA, Blanco's .125 second-half BA could cause them to look elsewhere. (JL)

### Forecast

| Player | Age | AB | HR | R | RBI | SB | BA | OBP | SLG | $1L | Pts |
|---|---|---|---|---|---|---|---|---|---|---|---|
| Blanco H | 39 | 110 | 3 | 11 | 10 | 0 | .238 | .297 | .363 | -$1 | 50 |
| **Mini-Browser** | **Age** | **AB** | **HR** | **R** | **RBI** | **SB** | **BA** | **OBP** | **SLG** | **$1L** | **Pts** |
| Quintero H | 31 | 188 | 4 | 14 | 16 | 0 | .245 | .285 | .354 | $0 | 60 |
| Kottaras G | 27 | 114 | 5 | 14 | 14 | 0 | .231 | .330 | .420 | $0 | 70 |
| Zaun G | 39 | 107 | 3 | 13 | 14 | 0 | .246 | .344 | .387 | $0 | 60 |
| Ellis A | 29 | 127 | 2 | 14 | 17 | 0 | .248 | .355 | .340 | $0 | 70 |
| Treanor M | 35 | 154 | 4 | 14 | 18 | 0 | .227 | .307 | .322 | $0 | 70 |

**Competition at CA — Stats in 2010**

| Bats | Player | GSvR | GSvL | Sub | OPS |
|---|---|---|---|---|---|
| LH | Thole J | 49 | 2 | 10 | .723 |
| RH | Blanco H | 25 | 16 | 5 | .571 |

**Ten-Year Trends:** □ SLG  ○ OBP  ◇ BA

**Weekly Points** — 2008 | 2009 | 2010

### Minors (2010) / Skills

| Level | Leag | AB | HR | R | RBI | SB | BA | OBP | SLG | CT% | H% | BB% | Bash |
|---|---|---|---|---|---|---|---|---|---|---|---|---|---|
| A | | — | | | | | | | | | | | |
| AA | | — | | | | | | | | | | | |
| AAA | | — | | | | | | | | | | | |

### Majors / Skills

| Yr | Team | AB | HR | R | RBI | SB | BA | OBP | SLG | CT% | H% | BB% | Bash |
|---|---|---|---|---|---|---|---|---|---|---|---|---|---|
| 07 | CHC | 54 | 0 | 3 | 4 | 0 | .167 | .193 | .222 | 78% | 21% | 3% | 1.33 |
| 08 | CHC | 120 | 3 | 15 | 12 | 0 | .292 | .325 | .392 | 82% | 36% | 5% | 1.34 |
| 09 | SD | 204 | 6 | 21 | 16 | 0 | .235 | .320 | .382 | 75% | 31% | 11% | 1.63 |
| 10 | NYM | 130 | 2 | 10 | 14 | 0 | .215 | .271 | .300 | 80% | 27% | 8% | 1.39 |

### Value / Extra / Production / OPS / Scoresheet

| $1L | $2L | Pts | RAA | 2B | 3B | CS | FB-LD-GB | HR/fb | RBI% | RS% | OPS | 1st Hf | 2nd Hf | vs RH | vs LH | Rnge | vRH | vLH |
|---|---|---|---|---|---|---|---|---|---|---|---|---|---|---|---|---|---|---|
| -$4 | -$15 | 10 | −7 | 3 | 0 | 0 | 55-17-29 | 0% | 14% | 27% | .415 | .481 | .278 | .574 | .145 | 0.50 | −26 | +64 |
| $2 | -$6 | 60 | −1 | 3 | 0 | 0 | 42-17-42 | 8% | 11% | 32% | .717 | .662 | .778 | .668 | .771 | 0.55 | −21 | +51 |
| -$1 | -$6 | 90 | −2 | 12 | 0 | 0 | 43-16-41 | 9% | 11% | 22% | .703 | .674 | .736 | .563 | 1.039 | — | −16 | +37 |
| -$1 | -$11 | 40 | −8 | 2 | 0 | 0 | 51-15-34 | 7% | 10% | 22% | .571 | .764 | .310 | .629 | .451 | 0.53 | −33 | +76 |

*For more stats, visit www.Rotolympus.com.*

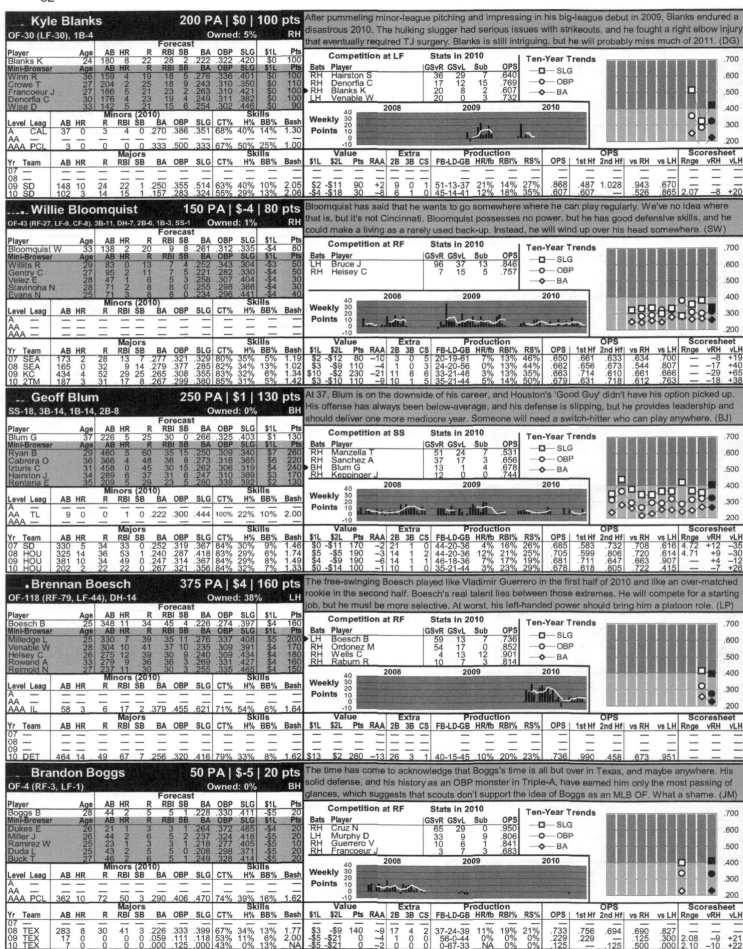

## Kyle Blanks — 200 PA | $0 | 100 pts
OF-30 (LF-30), 1B-4 — Owned: 5% — RH

After pummeling minor-league pitching and impressing in his big-league debut in 2009, Blanks endured a disastrous 2010. The hulking slugger had serious issues with strikeouts, and he fought a right elbow injury that eventually required TJ surgery. Blanks is still intriguing, but he will probably miss much of 2011. (DG)

### Forecast
| Player | Age | AB | HR | R | RBI | SB | BA | OBP | SLG | $1L | Pts |
|---|---|---|---|---|---|---|---|---|---|---|---|
| Blanks K | 24 | 180 | 8 | 22 | 28 | 2 | .222 | .322 | .420 | $0 | 100 |
| Mini-Browser | Age | AB | HR | R | RBI | SB | BA | OBP | SLG | $1L | Pts |
| Winn R | 36 | 159 | 4 | 19 | 18 | 5 | .276 | .336 | .401 | $0 | 100 |
| Crowe T | 27 | 204 | 2 | 25 | 18 | 9 | .243 | .310 | .350 | $0 | 110 |
| Francoeur J | 27 | 166 | 5 | 21 | 23 | 2 | .263 | .310 | .421 | $0 | 100 |
| Denorfia C | 30 | 176 | 4 | 23 | 19 | 4 | .254 | .311 | .382 | $0 | 100 |
| Wise D | 33 | 142 | 5 | 21 | 15 | 6 | .254 | .302 | .446 | $0 | 90 |

### Competition at LF / Stats in 2010
| Bats | Player | GSvR | GSvL | Sub | OPS |
|---|---|---|---|---|---|
| RH | Hairston S | 36 | 29 | 7 | .640 |
| RH | Denorfia C | 17 | 12 | 15 | .769 |
| RH | Blanks K | 20 | 8 | 2 | .607 |
| LH | Venable W | 20 | 0 | 3 | .732 |

### Minors (2010) / Skills
| Level | Leag | AB | HR | R | RBI | SB | BA | OBP | SLG | CT% | H% | BB% | Bash |
|---|---|---|---|---|---|---|---|---|---|---|---|---|---|
| A | CAL | 37 | 0 | 3 | 4 | 0 | .270 | .386 | .351 | 68% | 40% | 14% | 1.30 |
| AA | — | — | | | | | | | | | | | |
| AAA | PCL | 3 | 0 | 0 | 0 | 0 | .333 | .500 | .333 | 67% | 50% | 25% | 1.00 |

### Majors / Skills / Value / Extra / Production / OPS / Scoresheet
| Yr | Team | AB | HR | R | RBI | SB | BA | OBP | SLG | CT% | H% | BB% | Bash | $1L | $2L | Pts | RAA | 2B | 3B | CS | FB-LD-GB | HR/fb | RBI% | RS% | OPS | 1st Hf | 2nd Hf | vs RH | vs LH | Rnge | vRH | vLH |
|---|---|---|---|---|---|---|---|---|---|---|---|---|---|---|---|---|---|---|---|---|---|---|---|---|---|---|---|---|---|---|---|---|
| 07 | — | | | | | | | | | | | | | | | | | | | | | | | | | | | | | | | |
| 08 | — | | | | | | | | | | | | | | | | | | | | | | | | | | | | | | | |
| 09 | SD | 148 | 10 | 24 | 22 | 1 | .250 | .355 | .514 | 63% | 40% | 10% | 2.05 | $2 | -$11 | 90 | +2 | 9 | 0 | 1 | 51-13-37 | 21% | 14% | 27% | .868 | .487 | 1.028 | .943 | .670 | 2.07 | -8 | +20 |
| 10 | SD | 102 | 3 | 14 | 15 | 1 | .157 | .283 | .324 | 55% | 29% | 13% | 2.06 | -$4 | -$18 | 30 | -8 | 4 | 0 | 0 | 45-14-41 | 12% | 18% | 35% | .607 | .607 | — | .526 | .865 | — | | |

## Willie Bloomquist — 150 PA | $-4 | 80 pts
OF-43 (RF-27, LF-9, CF-8), 3B-11, DH-7, 2B-6, 1B-3, SS-1 — Owned: 1% — RH

Bloomquist has said that he wants to go somewhere where he can play regularly. We've no idea where that is, but it's not Cincinnati. Bloomquist possesses no power, but he has good defensive skills, and he could make a living as a rarely used back-up. Instead, he will wind up over his head somewhere. (SW)

### Forecast
| Player | Age | AB | HR | R | RBI | SB | BA | OBP | SLG | $1L | Pts |
|---|---|---|---|---|---|---|---|---|---|---|---|
| Bloomquist W | 33 | 138 | 2 | 20 | 9 | 8 | .261 | .312 | .335 | -$4 | 80 |
| Mini-Browser | Age | AB | HR | R | RBI | SB | BA | OBP | SLG | $1L | Pts |
| Willits R | 29 | 83 | 0 | 13 | 7 | 4 | .252 | .343 | .304 | -$3 | 50 |
| Gentry C | 27 | 95 | 2 | 11 | 7 | 5 | .221 | .282 | .330 | -$4 | 50 |
| Velez E | 28 | 47 | 1 | 6 | 5 | 3 | .258 | .307 | .404 | -$4 | 30 |
| Stavinoha N | 28 | 71 | 2 | 8 | 9 | 0 | .255 | .298 | .388 | -$4 | 30 |
| Evans N | 25 | 71 | 3 | 8 | 9 | 0 | .234 | .296 | .441 | -$4 | 40 |

### Competition at RF / Stats in 2010
| Bats | Player | GSvR | GSvL | Sub | OPS |
|---|---|---|---|---|---|
| LH | Bruce J | 96 | 37 | 13 | .846 |
| RH | Heisey C | 7 | 15 | 5 | .757 |

### Minors (2010) / Skills
| Level | Leag | AB | HR | R | RBI | SB | BA | OBP | SLG | CT% | H% | BB% | Bash |
|---|---|---|---|---|---|---|---|---|---|---|---|---|---|
| A | — | | | | | | | | | | | | |
| AA | — | | | | | | | | | | | | |
| AAA | — | | | | | | | | | | | | |

### Majors / Skills / Value / Extra / Production / OPS / Scoresheet
| Yr | Team | AB | HR | R | RBI | SB | BA | OBP | SLG | CT% | H% | BB% | Bash | $1L | $2L | Pts | RAA | 2B | 3B | CS | FB-LD-GB | HR/fb | RBI% | RS% | OPS | 1st Hf | 2nd Hf | vs RH | vs LH | Rnge | vRH | vLH |
|---|---|---|---|---|---|---|---|---|---|---|---|---|---|---|---|---|---|---|---|---|---|---|---|---|---|---|---|---|---|---|---|---|
| 07 | SEA | 173 | 2 | 28 | 13 | 7 | .277 | .321 | .329 | 80% | 35% | 5% | 1.19 | $2 | -$12 | 80 | -10 | 3 | 0 | 5 | 20-19-61 | 7% | 13% | 46% | .650 | .661 | .633 | .634 | .700 | — | -8 | +19 |
| 08 | SEA | 165 | 0 | 32 | 9 | 14 | .279 | .377 | .285 | 82% | 34% | 13% | 1.02 | $3 | -$9 | 110 | -4 | 1 | 0 | 3 | 24-20-56 | 0% | 13% | 44% | .662 | .656 | .673 | .544 | .807 | — | -17 | +40 |
| 09 | KC | 434 | 4 | 52 | 29 | 25 | .265 | .308 | .355 | 83% | 32% | 6% | 1.34 | $10 | -$2 | 230 | -21 | 11 | 8 | 6 | 33-14-44 | 3% | 13% | 35% | .663 | .714 | .610 | .661 | .666 | — | -29 | +65 |
| 10 | 2TM | 187 | 3 | 31 | 17 | 8 | .267 | .299 | .380 | 85% | 31% | 5% | 1.42 | $3 | -$10 | 110 | -9 | 10 | 1 | 2 | 35-21-44 | 5% | 14% | 50% | .679 | .631 | .718 | .612 | .763 | — | -18 | +38 |

## Geoff Blum — 250 PA | $1 | 130 pts
SS-18, 3B-14, 1B-14, 2B-8 — Owned: 0% — BH

At 37, Blum is on the downside of his career, and Houston's 'Good Guy' didn't have his option picked up. His offense has always been below-average, and his defense is slipping, but he provides leadership and should deliver one more mediocre year. Someone will need a switch-hitter who can play anywhere. (BJ)

### Forecast
| Player | Age | AB | HR | R | RBI | SB | BA | OBP | SLG | $1L | Pts |
|---|---|---|---|---|---|---|---|---|---|---|---|
| Blum G | 37 | 226 | 5 | 25 | 30 | 0 | .266 | .325 | .403 | $1 | 130 |
| Mini-Browser | Age | AB | HR | R | RBI | SB | BA | OBP | SLG | $1L | Pts |
| Ryan B | 29 | 460 | 5 | 60 | 35 | 15 | .250 | .309 | .340 | $7 | 260 |
| Cabrera O | 36 | 366 | 4 | 48 | 36 | 8 | .273 | .316 | .365 | $6 | 220 |
| Izturis C | 31 | 458 | 0 | 45 | 30 | 15 | .262 | .306 | .319 | $4 | 240 |
| Hairston J | 34 | 289 | 6 | 37 | 31 | 6 | .247 | .310 | .369 | $3 | 170 |
| Renteria E | 35 | 209 | 5 | 29 | 23 | 5 | .280 | .339 | .392 | $2 | 130 |

### Competition at SS / Stats in 2010
| Bats | Player | GSvR | GSvL | Sub | OPS |
|---|---|---|---|---|---|
| RH | Manzella T | 51 | 24 | 7 | .531 |
| RH | Sanchez A | 37 | 17 | 3 | .656 |
| BH | Blum G | 13 | 1 | 4 | .678 |
| RH | Keppinger J | 12 | 0 | 0 | .744 |

### Minors (2010) / Skills
| Level | Leag | AB | HR | R | RBI | SB | BA | OBP | SLG | CT% | H% | BB% | Bash |
|---|---|---|---|---|---|---|---|---|---|---|---|---|---|
| A | — | | | | | | | | | | | | |
| AA | TL | 9 | 0 | 0 | 1 | 0 | .222 | .300 | .444 | 100% | 22% | 10% | 2.00 |
| AAA | — | | | | | | | | | | | | |

### Majors / Skills / Value / Extra / Production / OPS / Scoresheet
| Yr | Team | AB | HR | R | RBI | SB | BA | OBP | SLG | CT% | H% | BB% | Bash | $1L | $2L | Pts | RAA | 2B | 3B | CS | FB-LD-GB | HR/fb | RBI% | RS% | OPS | 1st Hf | 2nd Hf | vs RH | vs LH | Rnge | vRH | vLH |
|---|---|---|---|---|---|---|---|---|---|---|---|---|---|---|---|---|---|---|---|---|---|---|---|---|---|---|---|---|---|---|---|---|
| 07 | SD | 330 | 5 | 34 | 33 | 0 | .252 | .319 | .367 | 84% | 30% | 9% | 1.46 | $0 | -$11 | 170 | -2 | 21 | 1 | 0 | 44-20-36 | 4% | 16% | 26% | .685 | .583 | .732 | .708 | .614 | 4.72 | +12 | -35 |
| 08 | HOU | 325 | 14 | 36 | 53 | 1 | .240 | .287 | .418 | 83% | 29% | 6% | 1.74 | $5 | -$5 | 190 | -3 | 14 | 1 | 2 | 44-20-36 | 12% | 21% | 24% | .705 | .599 | .806 | .720 | .614 | 4.71 | +9 | -30 |
| 09 | HOU | 381 | 10 | 34 | 49 | 0 | .247 | .314 | .367 | 84% | 29% | 8% | 1.49 | $4 | -$9 | 190 | -6 | 14 | 0 | 1 | 46-18-36 | 7% | 17% | 19% | .681 | .711 | .647 | .663 | .907 | — | +4 | -12 |
| 10 | HOU | 202 | 2 | 22 | 22 | 0 | .267 | .321 | .356 | 84% | 32% | 7% | 1.33 | $0 | -$14 | 100 | -10 | 11 | 0 | 0 | 35-21-44 | 3% | 23% | 29% | .678 | .618 | .805 | .722 | .415 | — | -7 | +26 |

## Brennan Boesch — 375 PA | $4 | 160 pts
OF-118 (RF-79, LF-44), DH-14 — Owned: 38% — LH

The free-swinging Boesch played like Vladimir Guerrero in the first half of 2010 and like an over-matched rookie in the second half. Boesch's real talent lies between those extremes. He will compete for a starting job, but he must be more selective. At worst, his left-handed power should bring him a platoon role. (LP)

### Forecast
| Player | Age | AB | HR | R | RBI | SB | BA | OBP | SLG | $1L | Pts |
|---|---|---|---|---|---|---|---|---|---|---|---|
| Boesch B | 25 | 348 | 11 | 34 | 45 | 4 | .226 | .274 | .397 | $4 | 160 |
| Mini-Browser | Age | AB | HR | R | RBI | SB | BA | OBP | SLG | $1L | Pts |
| Milledge L | 25 | 330 | 7 | 39 | 35 | 11 | .276 | .337 | .408 | $5 | 200 |
| Venable W | 28 | 304 | 10 | 41 | 37 | 10 | .235 | .309 | .391 | $4 | 170 |
| Heisey C | 26 | 275 | 12 | 39 | 30 | 9 | .240 | .309 | .434 | $4 | 180 |
| Rowand A | 33 | 279 | 9 | 36 | 36 | 3 | .269 | .331 | .427 | $4 | 150 |
| Reimold N | 27 | 237 | 11 | 30 | 30 | 3 | .255 | .335 | .465 | $4 | 150 |

### Competition at RF / Stats in 2010
| Bats | Player | GSvR | GSvL | Sub | OPS |
|---|---|---|---|---|---|
| LH | Boesch B | 59 | 13 | 7 | .736 |
| RH | Ordonez M | 54 | 17 | 0 | .852 |
| RH | Wells C | 4 | 13 | 12 | .901 |
| RH | Raburn R | 10 | 7 | 3 | .814 |

### Minors (2010) / Skills
| Level | Leag | AB | HR | R | RBI | SB | BA | OBP | SLG | CT% | H% | BB% | Bash |
|---|---|---|---|---|---|---|---|---|---|---|---|---|---|
| A | — | | | | | | | | | | | | |
| AA | — | | | | | | | | | | | | |
| AAA | IL | 58 | 3 | 6 | 17 | 2 | .379 | .455 | .621 | 71% | 54% | 6% | 1.64 |

### Majors / Skills / Value / Extra / Production / OPS / Scoresheet
| Yr | Team | AB | HR | R | RBI | SB | BA | OBP | SLG | CT% | H% | BB% | Bash | $1L | $2L | Pts | RAA | 2B | 3B | CS | FB-LD-GB | HR/fb | RBI% | RS% | OPS | 1st Hf | 2nd Hf | vs RH | vs LH | Rnge | vRH | vLH |
|---|---|---|---|---|---|---|---|---|---|---|---|---|---|---|---|---|---|---|---|---|---|---|---|---|---|---|---|---|---|---|---|---|
| 07 | — | | | | | | | | | | | | | | | | | | | | | | | | | | | | | | | |
| 08 | — | | | | | | | | | | | | | | | | | | | | | | | | | | | | | | | |
| 09 | — | | | | | | | | | | | | | | | | | | | | | | | | | | | | | | | |
| 10 | DET | 464 | 14 | 49 | 67 | 4 | .256 | .320 | .416 | 79% | 33% | 8% | 1.62 | $13 | $2 | 260 | -13 | 26 | 3 | 1 | 40-15-45 | 10% | 20% | 23% | .736 | .990 | .458 | .673 | .951 | — | | |

## Brandon Boggs — 50 PA | $-5 | 20 pts
OF-4 (RF-3, LF-1) — Owned: 0% — BH

The time has come to acknowledge that Boggs's time is all but over in Texas, and maybe anywhere. His solid defense, and his history as an OBP monster in Triple-A, have earned him only the most passing of glances, which suggests that scouts don't support the idea of Boggs as an MLB OF. What a shame. (JM)

### Forecast
| Player | Age | AB | HR | R | RBI | SB | BA | OBP | SLG | $1L | Pts |
|---|---|---|---|---|---|---|---|---|---|---|---|
| Boggs B | 28 | 44 | 2 | 5 | 5 | 1 | .228 | .330 | .411 | -$5 | 20 |
| Mini-Browser | Age | AB | HR | R | RBI | SB | BA | OBP | SLG | $1L | Pts |
| Dukes E | 26 | 21 | 1 | 3 | 3 | 1 | .264 | .372 | .465 | -$4 | 20 |
| Miller J | 26 | 44 | 2 | 6 | 5 | 2 | .237 | .324 | .418 | -$5 | 20 |
| Ramirez W | 25 | 23 | 1 | 3 | 3 | 1 | .218 | .277 | .405 | -$5 | 20 |
| Duda L | 25 | 43 | 2 | 5 | 5 | 0 | .208 | .298 | .371 | -$5 | 20 |
| Buck T | 27 | 46 | 2 | 5 | 5 | 2 | .249 | .328 | .414 | -$5 | 20 |

### Competition at RF / Stats in 2010
| Bats | Player | GSvR | GSvL | Sub | OPS |
|---|---|---|---|---|---|
| RH | Cruz N | 65 | 29 | 0 | .950 |
| LH | Murphy D | 33 | 9 | 9 | .806 |
| RH | Guerrero V | 10 | 6 | 1 | .841 |
| RH | Francoeur J | 3 | 7 | 3 | .683 |

### Minors (2010) / Skills
| Level | Leag | AB | HR | R | RBI | SB | BA | OBP | SLG | CT% | H% | BB% | Bash |
|---|---|---|---|---|---|---|---|---|---|---|---|---|---|
| A | — | | | | | | | | | | | | |
| AA | — | | | | | | | | | | | | |
| AAA | PCL | 362 | 10 | 72 | 50 | 3 | .290 | .406 | .470 | 74% | 39% | 16% | 1.62 |

### Majors / Skills / Value / Extra / Production / OPS / Scoresheet
| Yr | Team | AB | HR | R | RBI | SB | BA | OBP | SLG | CT% | H% | BB% | Bash | $1L | $2L | Pts | RAA | 2B | 3B | CS | FB-LD-GB | HR/fb | RBI% | RS% | OPS | 1st Hf | 2nd Hf | vs RH | vs LH | Rnge | vRH | vLH |
|---|---|---|---|---|---|---|---|---|---|---|---|---|---|---|---|---|---|---|---|---|---|---|---|---|---|---|---|---|---|---|---|---|
| 07 | — | | | | | | | | | | | | | | | | | | | | | | | | | | | | | | | |
| 08 | TEX | 283 | 8 | 30 | 41 | 3 | .226 | .333 | .399 | 67% | 34% | 13% | 1.77 | $3 | -$9 | 140 | -9 | 17 | 4 | 2 | 37-24-39 | 11% | 19% | 21% | .733 | .756 | .694 | .690 | .827 | — | | |
| 09 | TEX | 17 | 0 | 3 | 1 | 0 | .059 | .111 | .118 | 53% | 11% | 6% | 2.00 | -$5 | -$21 | 20 | -4 | 1 | 0 | 0 | 56-0-44 | 0% | 0% | 0% | .229 | .229 | — | .125 | .300 | 2.08 | -9 | +21 |
| 10 | TEX | 7 | 0 | 0 | 0 | 0 | .000 | .125 | .000 | 43% | 0% | 13% | NA | -$5 | -$21 | 20 | -3 | 0 | 0 | 0 | 0-67-33 | 0% | 0% | 0% | .125 | .125 | .500 | .000 | .125 | 2.10 | -10 | +24 |

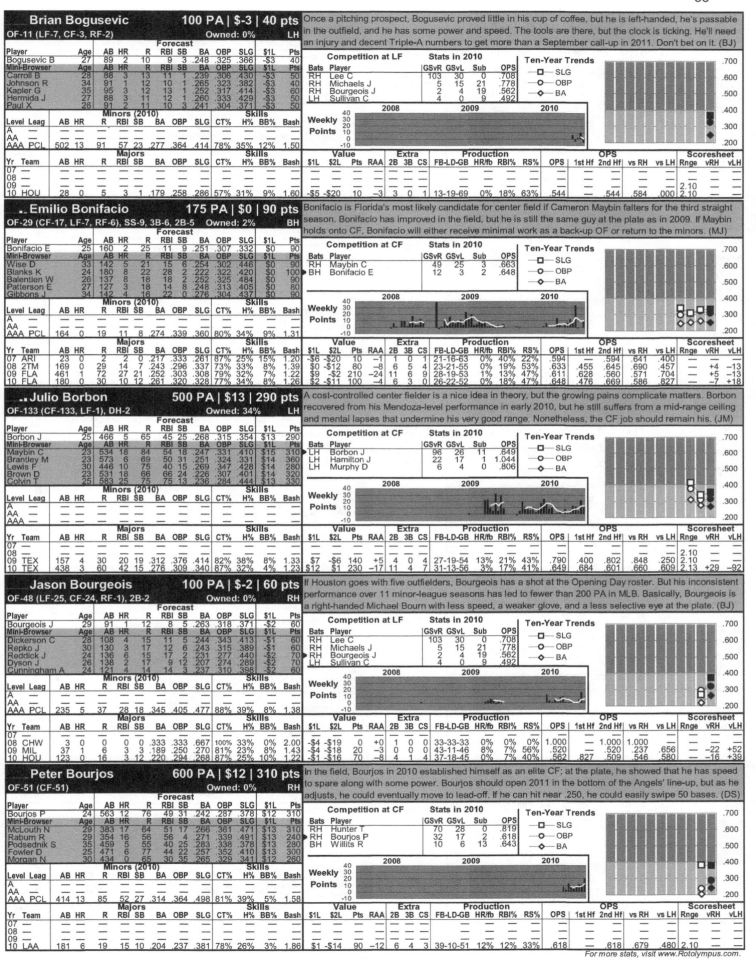

## Brian Bogusevic — 100 PA | $-3 | 40 pts

OF-11 (LF-7, CF-3, RF-2) Owned: 0% LH

| Player | Age | AB | HR | R | RBI | SB | BA | OBP | SLG | $1L | Pts |
|---|---|---|---|---|---|---|---|---|---|---|---|
| Bogusevic B | 27 | 89 | 2 | 10 | 9 | 3 | .248 | .325 | .366 | -$3 | 40 |
| **Mini-Browser** | **Age** | **AB** | **HR** | **R** | **RBI** | **SB** | **BA** | **OBP** | **SLG** | **$1L** | **Pts** |
| Carroll B | 28 | 88 | 3 | 13 | 11 | 1 | .239 | .306 | .430 | -$3 | 50 |
| Johnson R | 34 | 91 | 1 | 12 | 10 | 1 | .265 | .323 | .382 | -$3 | 40 |
| Kapler G | 35 | 95 | 3 | 12 | 13 | 1 | .252 | .317 | .414 | -$3 | 60 |
| Hermida J | 27 | 88 | 3 | 11 | 12 | 1 | .260 | .333 | .429 | -$3 | 50 |
| Paul X | 26 | 91 | 2 | 11 | 10 | 3 | .241 | .304 | .371 | -$3 | 50 |

| Level | Leag | AB | HR | R | RBI | SB | BA | OBP | SLG | CT% | H% | BB% | Bash |
|---|---|---|---|---|---|---|---|---|---|---|---|---|---|
| A | — | — | — | — | — | — | — | — | — | — | — | — | — |
| AA | — | — | — | — | — | — | — | — | — | — | — | — | — |
| AAA | PCL | 502 | 13 | 91 | 57 | 23 | .277 | .364 | .414 | 78% | 35% | 12% | 1.50 |

| Yr | Team | AB | HR | R | RBI | SB | BA | OBP | SLG | CT% | H% | BB% | Bash |
|---|---|---|---|---|---|---|---|---|---|---|---|---|---|
| 07 | — | — | — | — | — | — | — | — | — | — | — | — | — |
| 08 | — | — | — | — | — | — | — | — | — | — | — | — | — |
| 09 | — | — | — | — | — | — | — | — | — | — | — | — | — |
| 10 | HOU | 28 | 0 | 5 | 3 | 1 | .179 | .258 | .286 | 57% | 31% | 9% | 1.60 |

Once a pitching prospect, Bogusevic proved little in his cup of coffee, but he is left-handed, he's passable in the outfield, and he has some power and speed. The tools are there, but the clock is ticking. He'll need an injury and decent Triple-A numbers to get more than a September call-up in 2011. Don't bet on it. (BJ)

**Competition at LF — Stats in 2010**

| Bats | Player | GSvR | GSvL | Sub | OPS |
|---|---|---|---|---|---|
| RH | Lee C | 103 | 30 | 0 | .708 |
| RH | Michaels J | 5 | 15 | 21 | .778 |
| RH | Bourgeois J | 2 | 4 | 19 | .562 |
| LH | Sullivan C | 4 | 0 | 9 | .492 |

**Weekly Points**

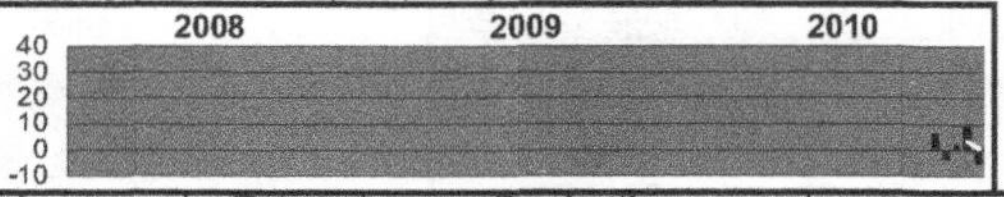


**Ten-Year Trends**

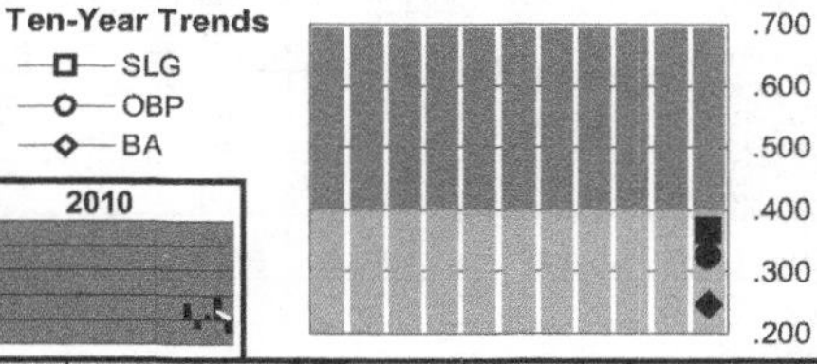


| Yr | $1L | $2L | Pts | RAA | 2B | 3B | CS | FB-LD-GB | HR/fb | RBI% | RS% | OPS | 1st Hf | 2nd Hf | vs RH | vs LH | Rnge | vRH | vLH |
|---|---|---|---|---|---|---|---|---|---|---|---|---|---|---|---|---|---|---|---|
| 07 | — | — | — | — | — | — | — | — | — | — | — | — | — | — | — | — | — | — | — |
| 08 | — | — | — | — | — | — | — | | — | — | — | — | — | — | — | — | — | — | — |
| 09 | — | — | — | — | — | — | — | | — | — | — | — | — | — | — | — | 2.10 | — | — |
| 10 | -$5 | -$20 | 10 | −3 | 3 | 0 | 1 | 13-19-69 | 0% | 18% | 63% | .544 | — | .544 | .584 | .000 | 2.10 | — | — |

## Emilio Bonifacio — 175 PA | $0 | 90 pts

OF-29 (CF-17, LF-7, RF-6), SS-9, 3B-6, 2B-5 Owned: 2% BH

| Player | Age | AB | HR | R | RBI | SB | BA | OBP | SLG | $1L | Pts |
|---|---|---|---|---|---|---|---|---|---|---|---|
| Bonifacio E | 25 | 160 | 2 | 25 | 11 | 9 | .251 | .307 | .332 | $0 | 90 |
| **Mini-Browser** | **Age** | **AB** | **HR** | **R** | **RBI** | **SB** | **BA** | **OBP** | **SLG** | **$1L** | **Pts** |
| Wise D | 33 | 142 | 5 | 21 | 15 | 6 | .254 | .302 | .446 | $0 | 90 |
| Blanks K | 24 | 180 | 8 | 22 | 28 | 2 | .222 | .322 | .420 | $0 | 100 |
| Balentien W | 26 | 137 | 8 | 18 | 18 | 2 | .252 | .325 | .484 | $0 | 90 |
| Patterson E | 27 | 127 | 3 | 18 | 14 | 8 | .248 | .313 | .405 | $0 | 80 |
| Gibbons J | 34 | 142 | 4 | 16 | 22 | 0 | .276 | .304 | .437 | $0 | 90 |

| Level | Leag | AB | HR | R | RBI | SB | BA | OBP | SLG | CT% | H% | BB% | Bash |
|---|---|---|---|---|---|---|---|---|---|---|---|---|---|
| A | — | — | — | — | — | — | — | — | — | — | — | — | — |
| AA | — | — | — | — | — | — | — | — | — | — | — | — | — |
| AAA | PCL | 164 | 0 | 19 | 11 | 8 | .274 | .339 | .360 | 80% | 34% | 9% | 1.31 |

| Yr | Team | AB | HR | R | RBI | SB | BA | OBP | SLG | CT% | H% | BB% | Bash |
|---|---|---|---|---|---|---|---|---|---|---|---|---|---|
| 07 | ARI | 23 | 0 | 2 | 2 | 0 | .217 | .333 | .261 | 87% | 25% | 15% | 1.20 |
| 08 | 2TM | 169 | 0 | 29 | 14 | 7 | .243 | .296 | .337 | 73% | 33% | 8% | 1.39 |
| 09 | FLA | 461 | 1 | 72 | 27 | 21 | .252 | .303 | .308 | 79% | 32% | 7% | 1.22 |
| 10 | FLA | 180 | 0 | 30 | 10 | 12 | .261 | .320 | .328 | 77% | 34% | 8% | 1.26 |

Bonifacio is Florida's most likely candidate for center field if Cameron Maybin falters for the third straight season. Bonifacio has improved in the field, but he is still the same guy at the plate as in 2009. If Maybin holds onto CF, Bonifacio will either receive minimal work as a back-up OF or return to the minors. (MJ)

**Competition at CF — Stats in 2010**

| Bats | Player | GSvR | GSvL | Sub | OPS |
|---|---|---|---|---|---|
| RH | Maybin C | 49 | 25 | 3 | .663 |
| BH | Bonifacio E | 12 | 3 | 2 | .648 |

**Weekly Points**

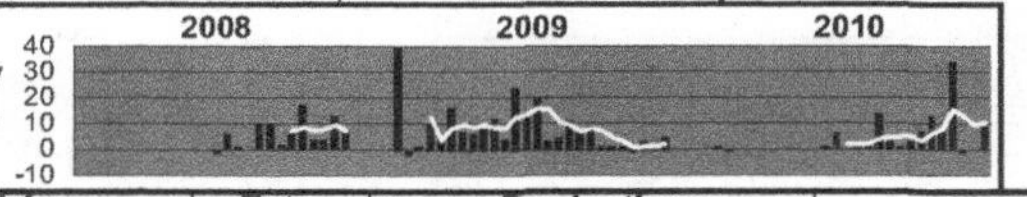


**Ten-Year Trends**

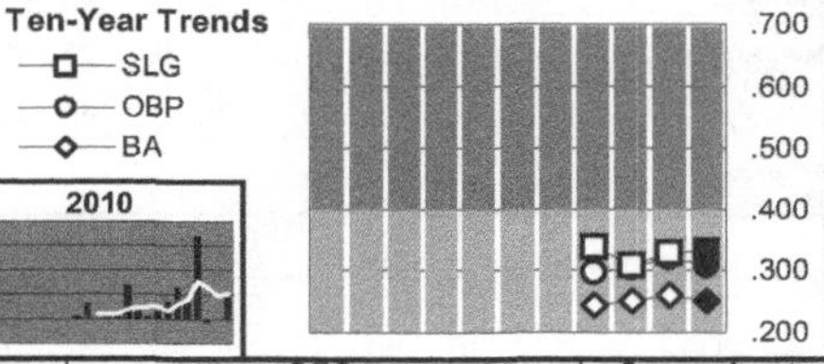


| Yr | $1L | $2L | Pts | RAA | 2B | 3B | CS | FB-LD-GB | HR/fb | RBI% | RS% | OPS | 1st Hf | 2nd Hf | vs RH | vs LH | Rnge | vRH | vLH |
|---|---|---|---|---|---|---|---|---|---|---|---|---|---|---|---|---|---|---|---|
| 07 | -$6 | -$20 | 10 | −1 | 1 | 0 | 1 | 21-16-63 | 0% | 40% | 22% | .594 | — | .594 | .641 | .400 | — | — | — |
| 08 | $0 | -$12 | 80 | −8 | 6 | 5 | 4 | 23-21-55 | 0% | 19% | 53% | .633 | .455 | .645 | .690 | .457 | — | +4 | −13 |
| 09 | $9 | -$2 | 210 | −24 | 11 | 6 | 9 | 28-19-53 | 1% | 13% | 47% | .611 | .628 | .560 | .571 | .704 | — | +5 | −13 |
| 10 | $2 | -$11 | 100 | −4 | 6 | 3 | 0 | 26-22-52 | 0% | 18% | 47% | .648 | .476 | .669 | .586 | .827 | — | −7 | +18 |

## Julio Borbon — 500 PA | $13 | 290 pts

OF-133 (CF-133, LF-1), DH-2 Owned: 34% LH

| Player | Age | AB | HR | R | RBI | SB | BA | OBP | SLG | $1L | Pts |
|---|---|---|---|---|---|---|---|---|---|---|---|
| Borbon J | 25 | 466 | 5 | 65 | 45 | 25 | .268 | .315 | .354 | $13 | 290 |
| **Mini-Browser** | **Age** | **AB** | **HR** | **R** | **RBI** | **SB** | **BA** | **OBP** | **SLG** | **$1L** | **Pts** |
| Maybin C | 23 | 534 | 18 | 84 | 54 | 18 | .247 | .331 | .410 | $15 | 310 |
| Brantley M | 23 | 573 | 6 | 69 | 50 | 31 | .251 | .324 | .331 | $14 | 360 |
| Lewis F | 30 | 446 | 10 | 75 | 40 | 15 | .269 | .347 | .428 | $14 | 280 |
| Brown D | 23 | 531 | 18 | 66 | 66 | 24 | .226 | .307 | .401 | $14 | 320 |
| Colvin T | 25 | 583 | 25 | 75 | 75 | 13 | .236 | .284 | .444 | $13 | 330 |

| Level | Leag | AB | HR | R | RBI | SB | BA | OBP | SLG | CT% | H% | BB% | Bash |
|---|---|---|---|---|---|---|---|---|---|---|---|---|---|
| A | — | — | — | — | — | — | — | — | — | — | — | — | — |
| AA | — | — | — | — | — | — | — | — | — | — | — | — | — |
| AAA | — | — | — | — | — | — | — | — | — | — | — | — | — |

| Yr | Team | AB | HR | R | RBI | SB | BA | OBP | SLG | CT% | H% | BB% | Bash |
|---|---|---|---|---|---|---|---|---|---|---|---|---|---|
| 07 | — | — | — | — | — | — | — | — | — | — | — | — | — |
| 08 | — | — | — | — | — | — | — | — | — | — | — | — | — |
| 09 | TEX | 157 | 4 | 30 | 20 | 19 | .312 | .376 | .414 | 82% | 38% | 8% | 1.33 |
| 10 | TEX | 438 | 3 | 60 | 42 | 15 | .276 | .309 | .340 | 87% | 32% | 4% | 1.23 |

A cost-controlled center fielder is a nice idea in theory, but the growing pains complicate matters. Borbon recovered from his Mendoza-level performance in early 2010, but he still suffers from a mid-range ceiling and mental lapses that undermine his very good range. Nonetheless, the CF job should remain his. (JM)

**Competition at CF — Stats in 2010**

| Bats | Player | GSvR | GSvL | Sub | OPS |
|---|---|---|---|---|---|
| LH | Borbon J | 96 | 26 | 11 | .649 |
| LH | Hamilton J | 22 | 17 | 1 | 1.044 |
| LH | Murphy D | 6 | 4 | 0 | .806 |

**Weekly Points**

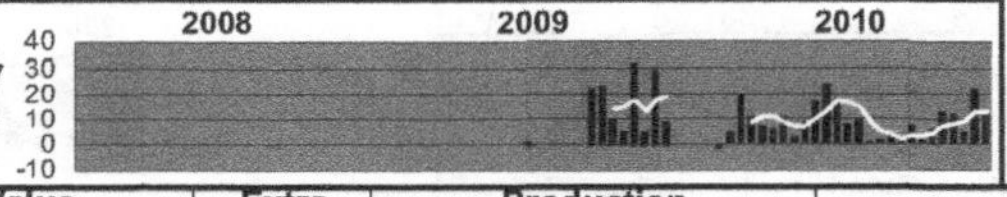


**Ten-Year Trends**

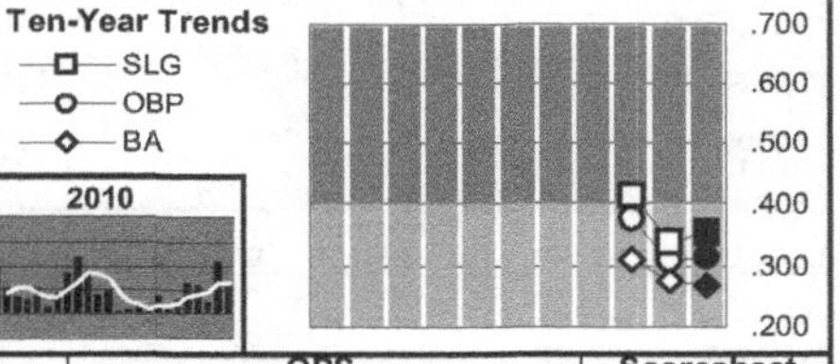


| Yr | $1L | $2L | Pts | RAA | 2B | 3B | CS | FB-LD-GB | HR/fb | RBI% | RS% | OPS | 1st Hf | 2nd Hf | vs RH | vs LH | Rnge | vRH | vLH |
|---|---|---|---|---|---|---|---|---|---|---|---|---|---|---|---|---|---|---|---|
| 07 | — | — | — | — | — | — | — | — | — | — | — | — | — | — | — | — | — | — | — |
| 08 | — | — | — | — | — | — | — | — | — | — | — | — | — | — | — | — | 2.10 | — | — |
| 09 | $7 | -$6 | 140 | +5 | 4 | 0 | 4 | 27-19-54 | 13% | 21% | 43% | .790 | .400 | .802 | .848 | .250 | 2.10 | — | — |
| 10 | $12 | $1 | 230 | −17 | 11 | 4 | 7 | 31-13-56 | 3% | 17% | 41% | .649 | .684 | .601 | .660 | .609 | 2.13 | +29 | −92 |

## Jason Bourgeois — 100 PA | $-2 | 60 pts

OF-48 (LF-25, CF-24, RF-1), 2B-2 Owned: 0% RH

| Player | Age | AB | HR | R | RBI | SB | BA | OBP | SLG | $1L | Pts |
|---|---|---|---|---|---|---|---|---|---|---|---|
| Bourgeois J | 29 | 91 | 1 | 12 | 8 | 5 | .263 | .318 | .371 | -$2 | 60 |
| **Mini-Browser** | **Age** | **AB** | **HR** | **R** | **RBI** | **SB** | **BA** | **OBP** | **SLG** | **$1L** | **Pts** |
| Dickerson C | 28 | 108 | 4 | 15 | 11 | 5 | .244 | .343 | .413 | -$1 | 60 |
| Repko J | 30 | 130 | 3 | 17 | 12 | 6 | .243 | .315 | .389 | -$1 | 60 |
| Reddick J | 24 | 136 | 6 | 15 | 17 | 2 | .231 | .277 | .440 | -$2 | 70 |
| Dyson J | 26 | 138 | 2 | 17 | 9 | 12 | .207 | .274 | .289 | -$2 | 70 |
| Cunningham A | 24 | 121 | 4 | 14 | 14 | 3 | .237 | .310 | .398 | -$2 | 60 |

| Level | Leag | AB | HR | R | RBI | SB | BA | OBP | SLG | CT% | H% | BB% | Bash |
|---|---|---|---|---|---|---|---|---|---|---|---|---|---|
| A | — | — | — | — | — | — | — | — | — | — | — | — | — |
| AA | — | — | — | — | — | — | — | — | — | — | — | — | — |
| AAA | PCL | 235 | 5 | 37 | 28 | 18 | .345 | .405 | .477 | 88% | 39% | 8% | 1.38 |

| Yr | Team | AB | HR | R | RBI | SB | BA | OBP | SLG | CT% | H% | BB% | Bash |
|---|---|---|---|---|---|---|---|---|---|---|---|---|---|
| 07 | — | — | — | — | — | — | — | — | — | — | — | — | — |
| 08 | CHW | 3 | 0 | 0 | 0 | 0 | .333 | .333 | .667 | 100% | 33% | 0% | 2.00 |
| 09 | MIL | 37 | 1 | 6 | 3 | 3 | .189 | .250 | .270 | 81% | 23% | 8% | 1.43 |
| 10 | HOU | 123 | 0 | 16 | 3 | 12 | .220 | .294 | .268 | 87% | 25% | 10% | 1.22 |

If Houston goes with five outfielders, Bourgeois has a shot at the Opening Day roster. But his inconsistent performance over 11 minor-league seasons has led to fewer than 200 PA in MLB. Basically, Bourgeois is a right-handed Michael Bourn with less speed, a weaker glove, and a less selective eye at the plate. (BJ)

**Competition at LF — Stats in 2010**

| Bats | Player | GSvR | GSvL | Sub | OPS |
|---|---|---|---|---|---|
| RH | Lee C | 103 | 30 | 0 | .708 |
| RH | Michaels J | 5 | 15 | 21 | .778 |
| RH | Bourgeois J | 2 | 4 | 19 | .562 |
| LH | Sullivan C | 4 | 0 | 9 | .492 |

**Weekly Points**

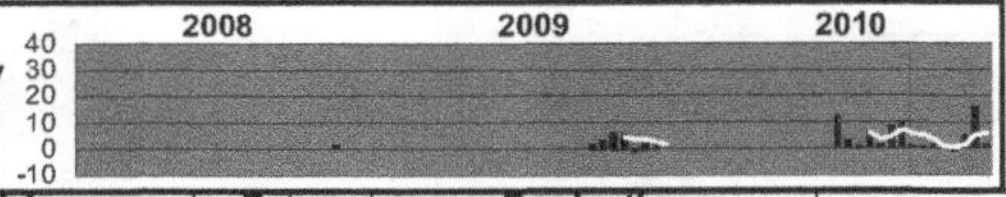


**Ten-Year Trends**

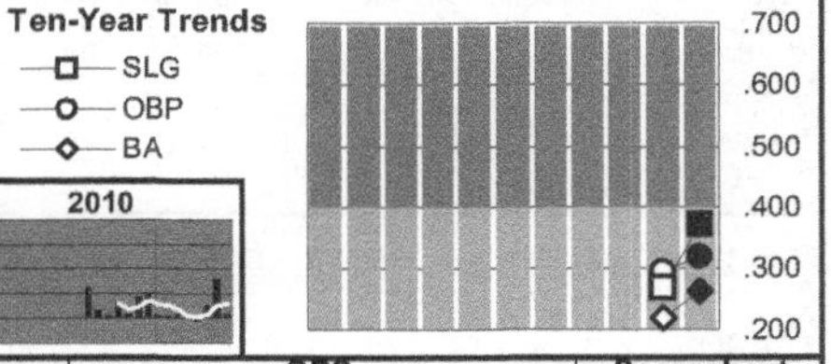


| Yr | $1L | $2L | Pts | RAA | 2B | 3B | CS | FB-LD-GB | HR/fb | RBI% | RS% | OPS | 1st Hf | 2nd Hf | vs RH | vs LH | Rnge | vRH | vLH |
|---|---|---|---|---|---|---|---|---|---|---|---|---|---|---|---|---|---|---|---|
| 07 | — | — | — | — | — | — | — | — | — | — | — | — | — | — | — | — | — | — | — |
| 08 | -$4 | -$19 | 0 | +0 | 1 | 0 | 0 | 33-33-33 | 0% | 0% | 0% | 1.000 | — | 1.000 | 1.000 | — | — | — | — |
| 09 | -$4 | -$18 | 20 | −3 | 0 | 0 | 0 | 43-11-46 | 8% | 7% | 56% | .520 | — | .520 | .237 | .656 | — | −22 | +52 |
| 10 | -$1 | -$16 | 70 | −8 | 4 | 1 | 4 | 37-18-45 | 0% | 7% | 40% | .562 | .827 | .509 | .546 | .580 | — | −16 | +39 |

## Peter Bourjos — 600 PA | $12 | 310 pts

OF-51 (CF-51) Owned: 0% RH

| Player | Age | AB | HR | R | RBI | SB | BA | OBP | SLG | $1L | Pts |
|---|---|---|---|---|---|---|---|---|---|---|---|
| Bourjos P | 24 | 563 | 12 | 76 | 49 | 31 | .242 | .287 | .378 | $12 | 310 |
| **Mini-Browser** | **Age** | **AB** | **HR** | **R** | **RBI** | **SB** | **BA** | **OBP** | **SLG** | **$1L** | **Pts** |
| McLouth N | 29 | 383 | 17 | 64 | 51 | 17 | .266 | .361 | .471 | $13 | 310 |
| Raburn R | 29 | 354 | 16 | 56 | 56 | 4 | .271 | .339 | .491 | $13 | 240 |
| Podsednik S | 35 | 459 | 5 | 55 | 40 | 25 | .283 | .338 | .378 | $13 | 280 |
| Fowler D | 25 | 471 | 6 | 77 | 44 | 22 | .257 | .352 | .410 | $13 | 300 |
| Morgan N | 30 | 434 | 0 | 65 | 30 | 35 | .265 | .329 | .341 | $12 | 260 |

| Level | Leag | AB | HR | R | RBI | SB | BA | OBP | SLG | CT% | H% | BB% | Bash |
|---|---|---|---|---|---|---|---|---|---|---|---|---|---|
| A | — | — | — | — | — | — | — | — | — | — | — | — | — |
| AA | — | — | — | — | — | — | — | — | — | — | — | — | — |
| AAA | PCL | 414 | 13 | 85 | 52 | 27 | .314 | .364 | .498 | 81% | 39% | 5% | 1.58 |

| Yr | Team | AB | HR | R | RBI | SB | BA | OBP | SLG | CT% | H% | BB% | Bash |
|---|---|---|---|---|---|---|---|---|---|---|---|---|---|
| 07 | — | — | — | — | — | — | — | — | — | — | — | — | — |
| 08 | — | — | — | — | — | — | — | — | — | — | — | — | — |
| 09 | — | — | — | — | — | — | — | — | — | — | — | — | — |
| 10 | LAA | 181 | 6 | 19 | 15 | 10 | .204 | .237 | .381 | 78% | 26% | 3% | 1.86 |

In the field, Bourjos in 2010 established himself as an elite CF; at the plate, he showed that he has speed to spare along with some power. Bourjos should open 2011 in the bottom of the Angels' line-up, but as he adjusts, he could eventually move to lead-off. If he can hit near .250, he could easily swipe 50 bases. (DS)

**Competition at CF — Stats in 2010**

| Bats | Player | GSvR | GSvL | Sub | OPS |
|---|---|---|---|---|---|
| RH | Hunter T | 70 | 28 | 0 | .819 |
| RH | Bourjos P | 32 | 17 | 2 | .618 |
| BH | Willits R | 10 | 6 | 13 | .643 |

**Weekly Points**

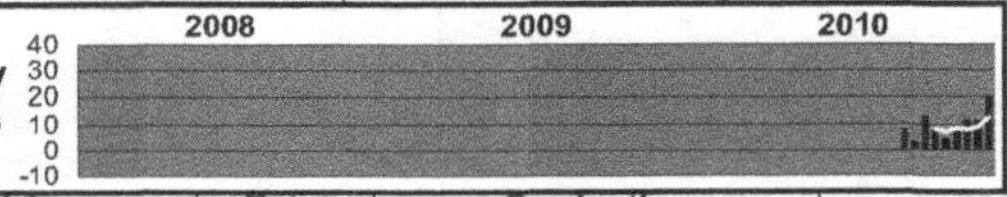


**Ten-Year Trends**

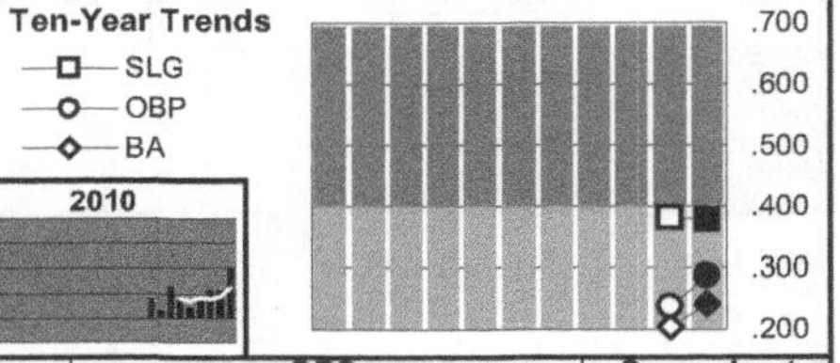


| Yr | $1L | $2L | Pts | RAA | 2B | 3B | CS | FB-LD-GB | HR/fb | RBI% | RS% | OPS | 1st Hf | 2nd Hf | vs RH | vs LH | Rnge | vRH | vLH |
|---|---|---|---|---|---|---|---|---|---|---|---|---|---|---|---|---|---|---|---|
| 07 | — | — | — | — | — | — | — | — | — | — | — | — | — | — | — | — | — | — | — |
| 08 | — | — | — | — | — | — | — | — | — | — | — | — | — | — | — | — | — | — | — |
| 09 | — | — | — | — | — | — | — | — | — | — | — | — | — | — | — | — | — | — | — |
| 10 | $1 | -$14 | 90 | −12 | 6 | 4 | 3 | 39-10-51 | 12% | 12% | 33% | .618 | — | .618 | .679 | .480 | 2.10 | — | — |

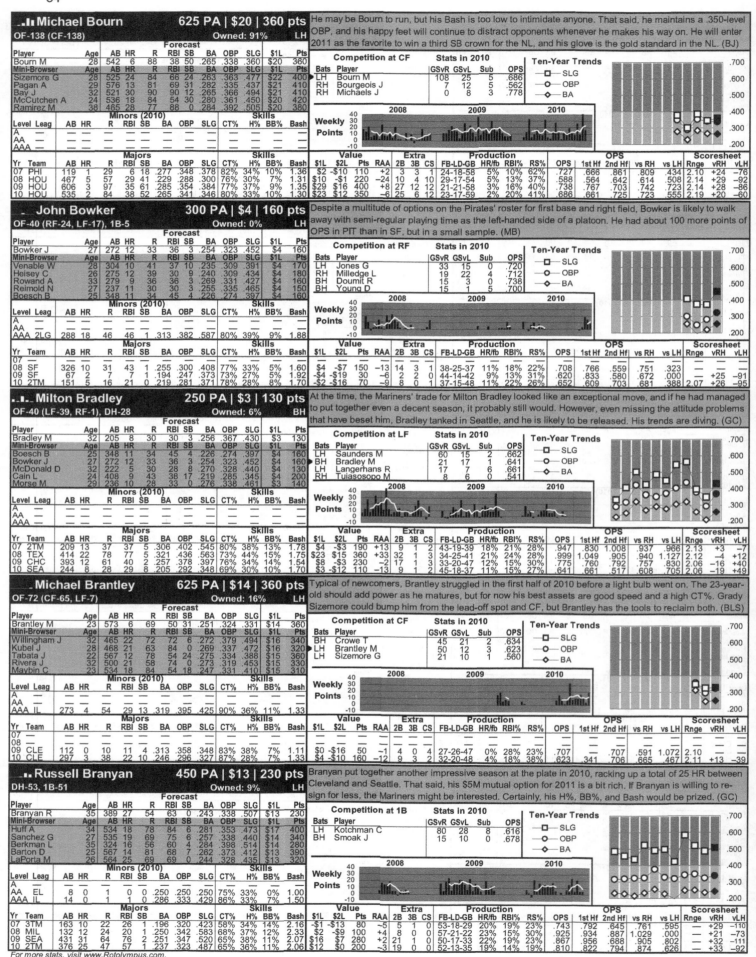

## Michael Bourn — 625 PA | $20 | 360 pts

OF-138 (CF-138) — Owned: 91% — LH

He may be Bourn to run, but his Bash is too low to intimidate anyone. That said, he maintains a .350-level OBP, and his happy feet will continue to distract opponents whenever he makes his way on. He will enter 2011 as the favorite to win a third SB crown for the NL, and his glove is the gold standard in the NL. (BJ)

| Player | Age | AB | HR | R | RBI | SB | BA | OBP | SLG | $1L | Pts |
|---|---|---|---|---|---|---|---|---|---|---|---|
| Bourn M | 28 | 542 | 6 | 88 | 38 | 50 | .265 | .338 | .360 | $20 | 360 |
| **Mini-Browser** | **Age** | **AB** | **HR** | **R** | **RBI** | **SB** | **BA** | **OBP** | **SLG** | **$1L** | **Pts** |
| Sizemore G | 28 | 525 | 24 | 84 | 66 | 24 | .263 | .363 | .477 | $22 | 400 |
| Pagan A | 29 | 576 | 13 | 81 | 69 | 31 | .282 | .335 | .437 | $21 | 410 |
| Bay J | 32 | 521 | 30 | 90 | 90 | 12 | .265 | .366 | .494 | $21 | 410 |
| McCutchen A | 24 | 536 | 18 | 84 | 54 | 30 | .280 | .361 | .450 | $20 | 420 |
| Ramirez M | 38 | 465 | 28 | 77 | 88 | 0 | .284 | .392 | .505 | $20 | 380 |

| Level | Leag | AB | HR | R | RBI | SB | BA | OBP | SLG | CT% | H% | BB% | Bash |
|---|---|---|---|---|---|---|---|---|---|---|---|---|---|
| A | — | — | — | — | — | — | — | — | — | — | — | — | — |
| AA | — | — | — | — | — | — | — | — | — | — | — | — | — |
| AAA | — | — | — | — | — | — | — | — | — | — | — | — | — |

Competition at CF / Stats in 2010

| Bats | Player | GSvR | GSvL | Sub | OPS |
|---|---|---|---|---|---|
| LH | Bourn M | 108 | 25 | 5 | .686 |
| RH | Bourgeois J | 7 | 12 | 5 | .562 |
| RH | Michaels J | 0 | 8 | 3 | .778 |

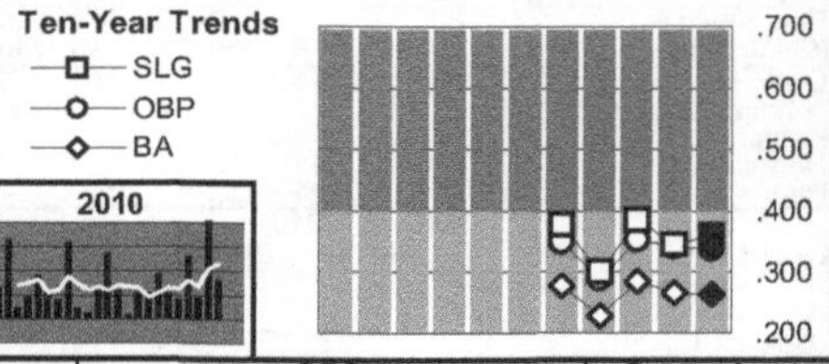


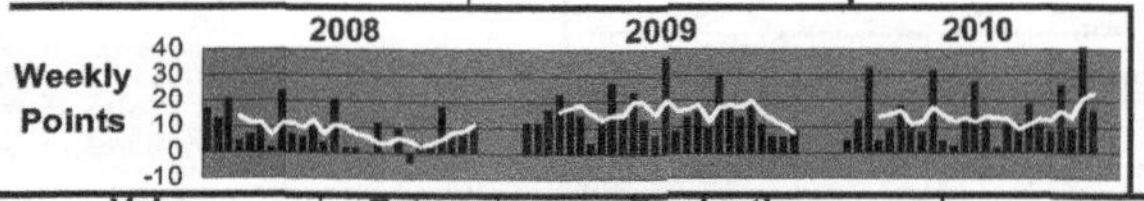


| Yr | Team | AB | HR | R | RBI | SB | BA | OBP | SLG | CT% | H% | BB% | Bash |
|---|---|---|---|---|---|---|---|---|---|---|---|---|---|
| 07 | PHI | 119 | 1 | 29 | 6 | 18 | .277 | .348 | .378 | 82% | 34% | 10% | 1.36 |
| 08 | HOU | 467 | 5 | 57 | 29 | 41 | .229 | .288 | .300 | 76% | 30% | 7% | 1.31 |
| 09 | HOU | 606 | 3 | 97 | 35 | 61 | .285 | .354 | .384 | 77% | 37% | 9% | 1.35 |
| 10 | HOU | 535 | 2 | 84 | 38 | 52 | .265 | .341 | .346 | 80% | 33% | 10% | 1.30 |

| Yr | $1L | $2L | Pts | RAA | 2B | 3B | CS | FB-LD-GB | HR/fb | RBI% | RS% | OPS | 1st Hf | 2nd Hf | vs RH | vs LH | Rnge | vRH | vLH |
|---|---|---|---|---|---|---|---|---|---|---|---|---|---|---|---|---|---|---|---|
| 07 | $2 | -$10 | 110 | +2 | 3 | 3 | 1 | 24-18-58 | 5% | 10% | 62% | .727 | .666 | .861 | .809 | .434 | 2.10 | +24 | –76 |
| 08 | $10 | -$1 | 220 | –24 | 10 | 4 | 10 | 29-17-54 | 5% | 13% | 37% | .588 | .564 | .642 | .614 | .508 | 2.14 | +29 | –92 |
| 09 | $29 | $16 | 400 | +8 | 27 | 12 | 12 | 21-21-58 | 3% | 16% | 40% | .738 | .767 | .703 | .742 | .723 | 2.14 | +28 | –86 |
| 10 | $23 | $12 | 350 | –6 | 25 | 6 | 12 | 23-17-59 | 2% | 20% | 41% | .686 | .661 | .725 | .723 | .555 | 2.19 | +20 | –60 |

## John Bowker — 300 PA | $4 | 160 pts

OF-40 (RF-24, LF-17), 1B-5 — Owned: 0% — LH

Despite a multitude of options on the Pirates' roster for first base and right field, Bowker is likely to walk away with semi-regular playing time as the left-handed side of a platoon. He had about 100 more points of OPS in PIT than in SF, but in a small sample. (MB)

| Player | Age | AB | HR | R | RBI | SB | BA | OBP | SLG | $1L | Pts |
|---|---|---|---|---|---|---|---|---|---|---|---|
| Bowker J | 27 | 272 | 12 | 33 | 36 | 3 | .254 | .323 | .452 | $4 | 160 |
| **Mini-Browser** | **Age** | **AB** | **HR** | **R** | **RBI** | **SB** | **BA** | **OBP** | **SLG** | **$1L** | **Pts** |
| Venable W | 28 | 304 | 10 | 41 | 37 | 10 | .235 | .309 | .391 | $4 | 170 |
| Heisey C | 26 | 275 | 12 | 39 | 30 | 9 | .240 | .309 | .434 | $4 | 180 |
| Rowand A | 33 | 279 | 9 | 36 | 36 | 3 | .269 | .331 | .427 | $4 | 160 |
| Reimold N | 27 | 237 | 11 | 30 | 30 | 3 | .255 | .335 | .465 | $4 | 150 |
| Boesch B | 25 | 348 | 11 | 34 | 45 | 4 | .226 | .274 | .397 | $4 | 160 |

| Level | Leag | AB | HR | R | RBI | SB | BA | OBP | SLG | CT% | H% | BB% | Bash |
|---|---|---|---|---|---|---|---|---|---|---|---|---|---|
| A | — | — | — | — | — | — | — | — | — | — | — | — | — |
| AA | — | — | — | — | — | — | — | — | — | — | — | — | — |
| AAA | 2LG | 288 | 18 | 46 | 46 | 1 | .313 | .382 | .587 | 80% | 39% | 9% | 1.88 |

Competition at RF / Stats in 2010

| Bats | Player | GSvR | GSvL | Sub | OPS |
|---|---|---|---|---|---|
| LH | Jones G | 33 | 15 | 0 | .720 |
| RH | Milledge L | 19 | 22 | 4 | .712 |
| BH | Doumit R | 15 | 3 | 0 | .738 |
| BH | Young D | 15 | 1 | 5 | .700 |

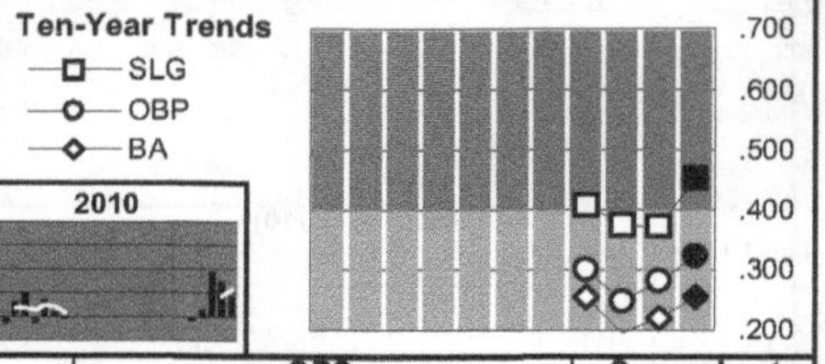


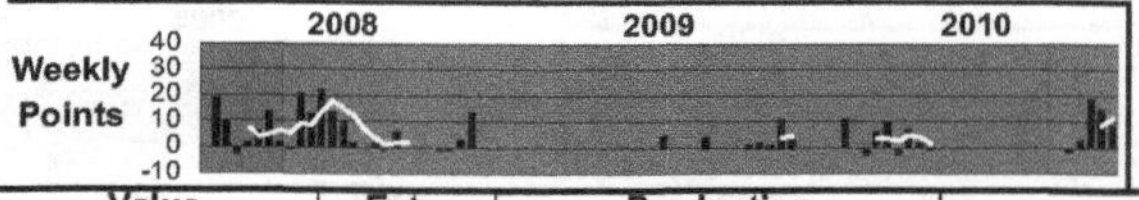


| Yr | Team | AB | HR | R | RBI | SB | BA | OBP | SLG | CT% | H% | BB% | Bash |
|---|---|---|---|---|---|---|---|---|---|---|---|---|---|
| 07 | — | — | — | — | — | — | — | — | — | — | — | — | — |
| 08 | SF | 326 | 10 | 31 | 43 | 1 | .255 | .300 | .408 | 77% | 33% | 5% | 1.60 |
| 09 | SF | 67 | 2 | 7 | 7 | 1 | .194 | .247 | .373 | 73% | 27% | 5% | 1.92 |
| 10 | 2TM | 151 | 5 | 16 | 21 | 0 | .219 | .281 | .371 | 78% | 28% | 8% | 1.70 |

| Yr | $1L | $2L | Pts | RAA | 2B | 3B | CS | FB-LD-GB | HR/fb | RBI% | RS% | OPS | 1st Hf | 2nd Hf | vs RH | vs LH | Rnge | vRH | vLH |
|---|---|---|---|---|---|---|---|---|---|---|---|---|---|---|---|---|---|---|---|
| 07 | — | — | — | — | — | — | — | — | — | — | — | — | — | — | — | — | — | — | — |
| 08 | $4 | -$7 | 150 | –13 | 14 | 3 | 1 | 38-25-37 | 11% | 18% | 22% | .708 | .766 | .559 | .751 | .323 | — | — | — |
| 09 | -$4 | -$19 | 30 | –6 | 2 | 2 | 0 | 44-14-42 | 9% | 13% | 31% | .620 | .833 | .580 | .672 | .000 | — | +25 | –91 |
| 10 | -$2 | -$16 | 70 | –9 | 8 | 0 | 1 | 37-15-48 | 11% | 22% | 26% | .652 | .609 | .703 | .681 | .388 | 2.07 | +26 | –95 |

## Milton Bradley — 250 PA | $3 | 130 pts

OF-40 (LF-39, RF-1), DH-28 — Owned: 6% — BH

At the time, the Mariners' trade for Milton Bradley looked like an exceptional move, and if he had managed to put together even a decent season, it probably still would. However, even missing the attitude problems that have beset him, Bradley tanked in Seattle, and he is likely to be released. His trends are diving. (GC)

| Player | Age | AB | HR | R | RBI | SB | BA | OBP | SLG | $1L | Pts |
|---|---|---|---|---|---|---|---|---|---|---|---|
| Bradley M | 32 | 205 | 8 | 30 | 30 | 3 | .256 | .367 | .430 | $3 | 130 |
| **Mini-Browser** | **Age** | **AB** | **HR** | **R** | **RBI** | **SB** | **BA** | **OBP** | **SLG** | **$1L** | **Pts** |
| Boesch B | 25 | 348 | 11 | 34 | 45 | 4 | .226 | .274 | .397 | $4 | 160 |
| Bowker J | 27 | 272 | 12 | 33 | 36 | 3 | .254 | .323 | .452 | $4 | 160 |
| McDonald D | 32 | 222 | 5 | 30 | 28 | 8 | .270 | .328 | .440 | $4 | 130 |
| Cain L | 24 | 408 | 9 | 43 | 38 | 17 | .219 | .285 | .345 | $4 | 200 |
| Morse M | 29 | 236 | 10 | 28 | 33 | 0 | .276 | .338 | .461 | $3 | 140 |

| Level | Leag | AB | HR | R | RBI | SB | BA | OBP | SLG | CT% | H% | BB% | Bash |
|---|---|---|---|---|---|---|---|---|---|---|---|---|---|
| A | — | — | — | — | — | — | — | — | — | — | — | — | — |
| AA | — | — | — | — | — | — | — | — | — | — | — | — | — |
| AAA | — | — | — | — | — | — | — | — | — | — | — | — | — |

Competition at LF / Stats in 2010

| Bats | Player | GSvR | GSvL | Sub | OPS |
|---|---|---|---|---|---|
| LH | Saunders M | 60 | 15 | 2 | .662 |
| BH | Bradley M | 21 | 17 | 1 | .641 |
| LH | Langerhans R | 17 | 7 | 6 | .661 |
| RH | Tuiasosopo M | 8 | 6 | 0 | .541 |

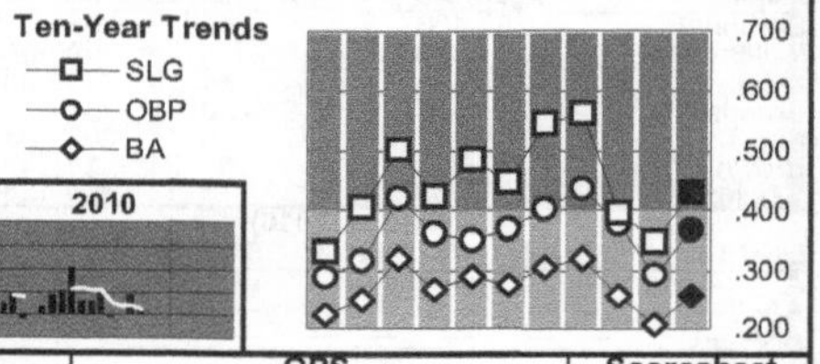


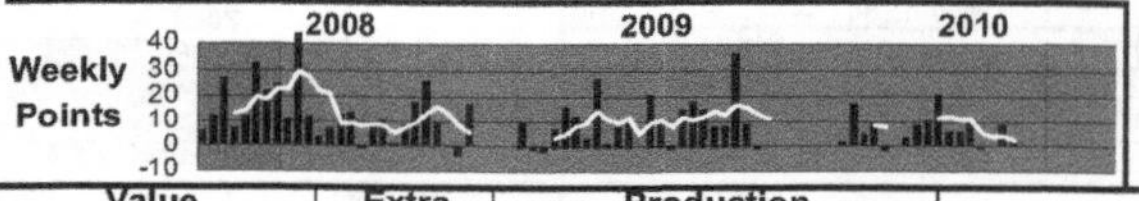


| Yr | Team | AB | HR | R | RBI | SB | BA | OBP | SLG | CT% | H% | BB% | Bash |
|---|---|---|---|---|---|---|---|---|---|---|---|---|---|
| 07 | 2TM | 209 | 13 | 37 | 37 | 5 | .306 | .402 | .545 | 80% | 38% | 13% | 1.78 |
| 08 | TEX | 414 | 22 | 78 | 77 | 5 | .321 | .436 | .563 | 73% | 44% | 15% | 1.75 |
| 09 | CHC | 393 | 12 | 61 | 40 | 2 | .257 | .378 | .397 | 76% | 34% | 14% | 1.54 |
| 10 | SEA | 244 | 8 | 28 | 29 | 8 | .205 | .292 | .348 | 69% | 30% | 10% | 1.70 |

| Yr | $1L | $2L | Pts | RAA | 2B | 3B | CS | FB-LD-GB | HR/fb | RBI% | RS% | OPS | 1st Hf | 2nd Hf | vs RH | vs LH | Rnge | vRH | vLH |
|---|---|---|---|---|---|---|---|---|---|---|---|---|---|---|---|---|---|---|---|
| 07 | $4 | -$3 | 190 | +13 | 9 | 1 | 2 | 43-19-39 | 18% | 21% | 28% | .947 | .830 | 1.008 | .937 | .966 | 2.13 | +3 | –7 |
| 08 | $23 | $15 | 360 | +33 | 32 | 1 | 3 | 34-25-41 | 21% | 24% | 28% | .999 | 1.049 | .905 | .940 | 1.127 | 2.12 | –4 | +12 |
| 09 | $8 | -$3 | 230 | –2 | 17 | 1 | 3 | 33-20-47 | 12% | 15% | 30% | .775 | .760 | .792 | .757 | .830 | 2.06 | –16 | +40 |
| 10 | $3 | -$12 | 110 | –13 | 9 | 1 | 2 | 45-18-37 | 11% | 15% | 27% | .641 | .661 | .517 | .608 | .705 | 2.06 | –19 | +49 |

## Michael Brantley — 625 PA | $14 | 360 pts

OF-72 (CF-65, LF-7) — Owned: 16% — LH

Typical of newcomers, Brantley struggled in the first half of 2010 before a light bulb went on. The 23-year-old should add power as he matures, but for now his best assets are good speed and a high CT%. Grady Sizemore could bump him from the lead-off spot and CF, but Brantley has the tools to reclaim both. (BLS)

| Player | Age | AB | HR | R | RBI | SB | BA | OBP | SLG | $1L | Pts |
|---|---|---|---|---|---|---|---|---|---|---|---|
| Brantley M | 23 | 573 | 6 | 69 | 50 | 31 | .251 | .324 | .331 | $14 | 360 |
| **Mini-Browser** | **Age** | **AB** | **HR** | **R** | **RBI** | **SB** | **BA** | **OBP** | **SLG** | **$1L** | **Pts** |
| Willingham J | 32 | 465 | 22 | 72 | 72 | 6 | .272 | .379 | .494 | $16 | 340 |
| Kubel J | 28 | 468 | 21 | 63 | 84 | 0 | .269 | .337 | .472 | $16 | 320 |
| Tabata J | 22 | 567 | 12 | 78 | 54 | 24 | .275 | .334 | .388 | $15 | 360 |
| Rivera J | 32 | 500 | 21 | 58 | 74 | 0 | .273 | .319 | .453 | $15 | 330 |
| Maybin C | 23 | 534 | 18 | 84 | 54 | 18 | .247 | .331 | .410 | $15 | 310 |

| Level | Leag | AB | HR | R | RBI | SB | BA | OBP | SLG | CT% | H% | BB% | Bash |
|---|---|---|---|---|---|---|---|---|---|---|---|---|---|
| A | — | — | — | — | — | — | — | — | — | — | — | — | — |
| AA | — | — | — | — | — | — | — | — | — | — | — | — | — |
| AAA | IL | 273 | 4 | 54 | 29 | 13 | .319 | .395 | .425 | 90% | 36% | 11% | 1.33 |

Competition at CF / Stats in 2010

| Bats | Player | GSvR | GSvL | Sub | OPS |
|---|---|---|---|---|---|
| BH | Crowe T | 45 | 21 | 2 | .634 |
| LH | Brantley M | 50 | 12 | 3 | .623 |
| LH | Sizemore G | 21 | 10 | 1 | .560 |

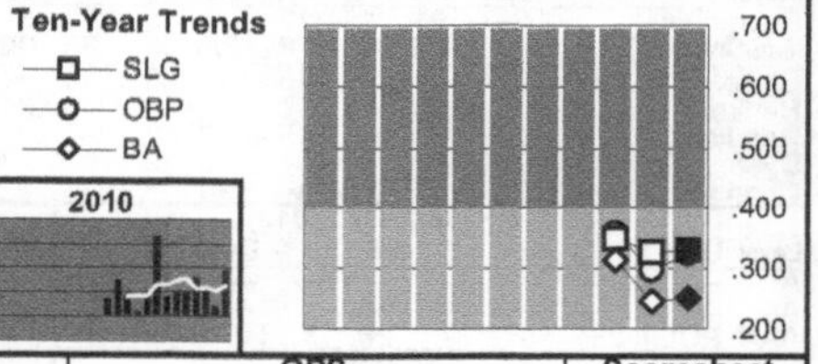

| Yr | Team | AB | HR | R | RBI | SB | BA | OBP | SLG | CT% | H% | BB% | Bash |
|---|---|---|---|---|---|---|---|---|---|---|---|---|---|
| 07 | — | — | — | — | — | — | — | — | — | — | — | — | — |
| 08 | — | — | — | — | — | — | — | — | — | — | — | — | — |
| 09 | CLE | 112 | 0 | 10 | 11 | 4 | .313 | .358 | .348 | 83% | 38% | 7% | 1.11 |
| 10 | CLE | 297 | 3 | 38 | 22 | 10 | .246 | .296 | .327 | 87% | 28% | 7% | 1.33 |

| Yr | $1L | $2L | Pts | RAA | 2B | 3B | CS | FB-LD-GB | HR/fb | RBI% | RS% | OPS | 1st Hf | 2nd Hf | vs RH | vs LH | Rnge | vRH | vLH |
|---|---|---|---|---|---|---|---|---|---|---|---|---|---|---|---|---|---|---|---|
| 07 | — | — | — | — | — | — | — | — | — | — | — | — | — | — | — | — | — | — | — |
| 08 | — | — | — | — | — | — | — | — | — | — | — | — | — | — | — | — | — | — | — |
| 09 | $0 | -$16 | 50 | –1 | 4 | 0 | 4 | 27-26-47 | 0% | 28% | 23% | .707 | — | .707 | .591 | 1.072 | 2.10 | — | — |
| 10 | $4 | -$10 | 160 | –12 | 9 | 3 | 2 | 32-20-48 | 4% | 18% | 38% | .623 | .341 | .706 | .665 | .467 | 2.11 | +13 | –39 |

## Russell Branyan — 450 PA | $13 | 230 pts

DH-53, 1B-51 — Owned: 9% — LH

Branyan put together another impressive season at the plate in 2010, racking up a total of 25 HR between Cleveland and Seattle. That said, his $5M mutual option for 2011 is a bit rich. If Branyan is willing to re-sign for less, the Mariners might be interested. Certainly, his H%, BB%, and Bash would be prized. (GC)

| Player | Age | AB | HR | R | RBI | SB | BA | OBP | SLG | $1L | Pts |
|---|---|---|---|---|---|---|---|---|---|---|---|
| Branyan R | 35 | 389 | 27 | 54 | 63 | 0 | .243 | .338 | .507 | $13 | 230 |
| **Mini-Browser** | **Age** | **AB** | **HR** | **R** | **RBI** | **SB** | **BA** | **OBP** | **SLG** | **$1L** | **Pts** |
| Huff A | 34 | 534 | 18 | 78 | 84 | 6 | .281 | .353 | .473 | $17 | 400 |
| Sanchez G | 27 | 535 | 19 | 69 | 75 | 6 | .257 | .338 | .440 | $14 | 340 |
| Berkman L | 35 | 324 | 16 | 56 | 60 | 4 | .284 | .398 | .514 | $14 | 280 |
| Barton D | 25 | 567 | 14 | 81 | 68 | 7 | .262 | .373 | .412 | $13 | 390 |
| LaPorta M | 26 | 564 | 25 | 69 | 69 | 0 | .244 | .328 | .435 | $13 | 320 |

| Level | Leag | AB | HR | R | RBI | SB | BA | OBP | SLG | CT% | H% | BB% | Bash |
|---|---|---|---|---|---|---|---|---|---|---|---|---|---|
| A | — | — | — | — | — | — | — | — | — | — | — | — | — |
| AA | EL | 8 | 0 | 1 | 0 | 0 | .250 | .250 | .250 | 75% | 33% | 0% | 1.00 |
| AAA | IL | 14 | 0 | 1 | 1 | 0 | .286 | .333 | .429 | 86% | 33% | 7% | 1.50 |

Competition at 1B / Stats in 2010

| Bats | Player | GSvR | GSvL | Sub | OPS |
|---|---|---|---|---|---|
| LH | Kotchman C | 80 | 28 | 8 | .616 |
| BH | Smoak J | 15 | 10 | 0 | .678 |

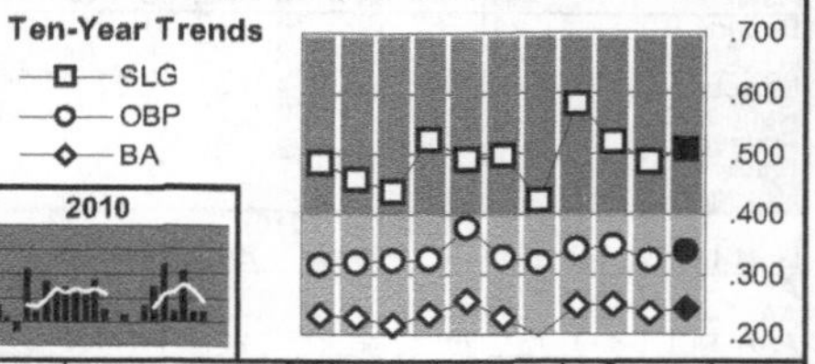


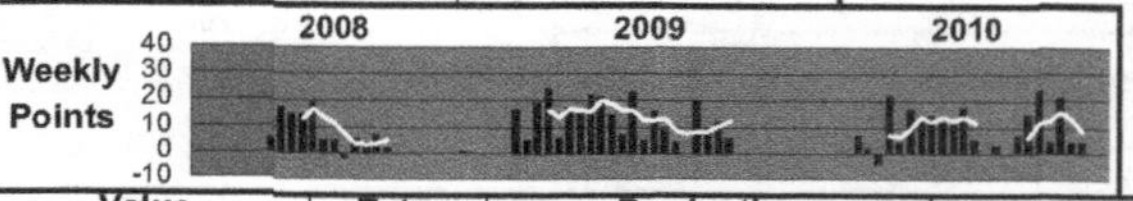


| Yr | Team | AB | HR | R | RBI | SB | BA | OBP | SLG | CT% | H% | BB% | Bash |
|---|---|---|---|---|---|---|---|---|---|---|---|---|---|
| 07 | 3TM | 163 | 10 | 22 | 26 | 1 | .196 | .320 | .423 | 58% | 34% | 14% | 2.16 |
| 08 | MIL | 132 | 12 | 24 | 20 | 1 | .250 | .342 | .583 | 68% | 37% | 12% | 2.33 |
| 09 | SEA | 431 | 31 | 64 | 76 | 2 | .251 | .347 | .520 | 65% | 38% | 11% | 2.07 |
| 10 | 2TM | 376 | 25 | 47 | 57 | 1 | .237 | .323 | .487 | 65% | 36% | 11% | 2.06 |

| Yr | $1L | $2L | Pts | RAA | 2B | 3B | CS | FB-LD-GB | HR/fb | RBI% | RS% | OPS | 1st Hf | 2nd Hf | vs RH | vs LH | Rnge | vRH | vLH |
|---|---|---|---|---|---|---|---|---|---|---|---|---|---|---|---|---|---|---|---|
| 07 | -$1 | -$13 | 80 | –5 | 5 | 1 | 0 | 53-18-29 | 20% | 19% | 23% | .743 | .792 | .645 | .761 | .595 | — | +29 | –110 |
| 08 | $2 | -$9 | 100 | +4 | 8 | 0 | 0 | 57-21-22 | 23% | 15% | 30% | .925 | .934 | .887 | 1.029 | .000 | — | +21 | –73 |
| 09 | $16 | $7 | 280 | +2 | 21 | 1 | 0 | 50-17-33 | 22% | 19% | 23% | .867 | .956 | .688 | .905 | .802 | — | +32 | –111 |
| 10 | $12 | $0 | 200 | –3 | 19 | 0 | 0 | 52-13-35 | 19% | 14% | 19% | .810 | .822 | .794 | .874 | .626 | — | +33 | –92 |

*For more stats, visit www.Rotolympus.com.*

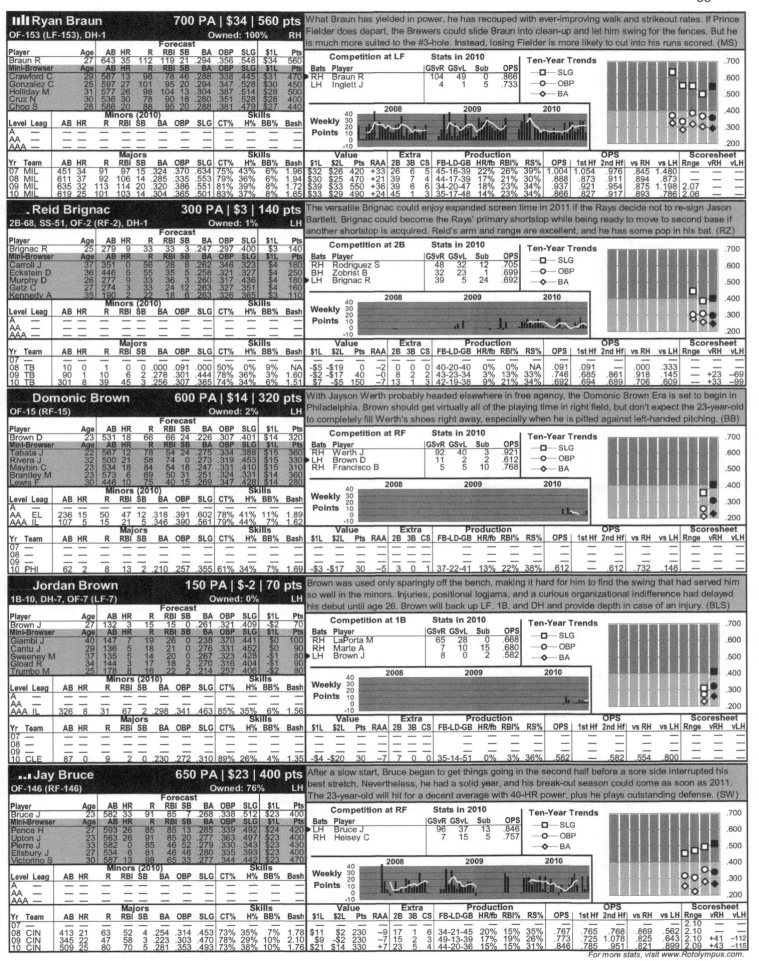

## Ryan Braun — 700 PA | $34 | 560 pts

OF-153 (LF-153), DH-1 — Owned: 100% — RH

What Braun has yielded in power, he has recouped with ever-improving walk and strikeout rates. If Prince Fielder does depart, the Brewers could slide Braun into clean-up and let him swing for the fences. But he is much more suited to the #3-hole. Instead, losing Fielder is more likely to cut into his runs scored. (MS)

| Player | Age | AB | HR | R | RBI | SB | BA | OBP | SLG | $1L | Pts |
|---|---|---|---|---|---|---|---|---|---|---|---|
| Braun R | 27 | 643 | 35 | 112 | 119 | 21 | .294 | .356 | .548 | $34 | 560 |
| **Mini-Browser** | **Age** | **AB** | **HR** | **R** | **RBI** | **SB** | **BA** | **OBP** | **SLG** | **$1L** | **Pts** |
| Crawford C | 29 | 587 | 13 | 98 | 78 | 46 | .288 | .338 | .445 | $31 | 470 |
| Gonzalez C | 25 | 597 | 27 | 101 | 95 | 20 | .294 | .347 | .528 | $30 | 450 |
| Holliday M | 31 | 577 | 26 | 98 | 104 | 13 | .304 | .387 | .514 | $28 | 500 |
| Cruz N | 30 | 536 | 30 | 78 | 90 | 18 | .280 | .351 | .528 | $28 | 400 |
| Choo S | 28 | 586 | 20 | 88 | 95 | 20 | .288 | .381 | .479 | $27 | 440 |

| Level | Leag | AB | HR | R | RBI | SB | BA | OBP | SLG | CT% | H% | BB% | Bash |
|---|---|---|---|---|---|---|---|---|---|---|---|---|---|
| A | — | — | — | — | — | — | — | — | — | — | — | — | — |
| AA | — | — | — | — | — | — | — | — | — | — | — | — | — |
| AAA | — | — | — | — | — | — | — | — | — | — | — | — | — |

Competition at LF — Stats in 2010

| Bats | Player | GSvR | GSvL | Sub | OPS |
|---|---|---|---|---|---|
| RH | Braun R | 104 | 49 | 0 | .866 |
| LH | Inglett J | 4 | 1 | 5 | .733 |

Ten-Year Trends
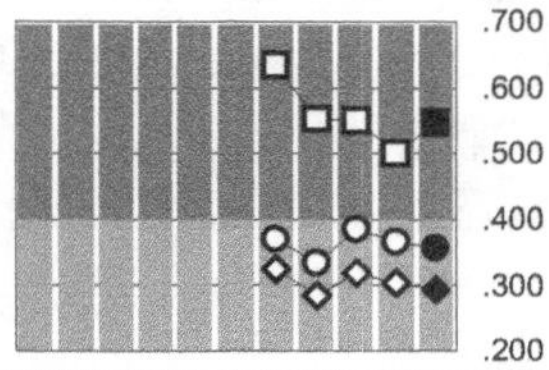

Weekly Points
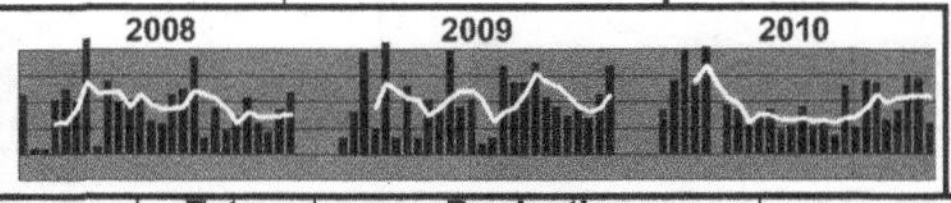

| Yr | Team | AB | HR | R | RBI | SB | BA | OBP | SLG | CT% | H% | BB% | Bash | $1L | $2L | Pts | RAA | 2B | 3B | CS | FB-LD-GB | HR/fb | RBI% | RS% | OPS | 1st Hf | 2nd Hf | vs RH | vs LH | Rnge | vRH | vLH |
|---|---|---|---|---|---|---|---|---|---|---|---|---|---|---|---|---|---|---|---|---|---|---|---|---|---|---|---|---|---|---|---|---|
| 07 | MIL | 451 | 34 | 91 | 97 | 15 | .324 | .370 | .634 | 75% | 43% | 6% | 1.96 | $32 | $26 | 420 | +33 | 26 | 6 | 5 | 45-16-39 | 22% | 26% | 39% | 1.004 | 1.054 | .976 | .845 | 1.480 | — | — | — |
| 08 | MIL | 611 | 37 | 92 | 106 | 14 | .285 | .335 | .553 | 79% | 36% | 6% | 1.94 | $30 | $25 | 470 | +21 | 39 | 7 | 4 | 44-17-39 | 17% | 21% | 30% | .888 | .873 | .911 | .894 | .873 | — | — | — |
| 09 | MIL | 635 | 32 | 113 | 114 | 20 | .320 | .386 | .551 | 81% | 39% | 8% | 1.72 | $39 | $33 | 550 | +36 | 39 | 6 | 6 | 34-20-47 | 18% | 23% | 34% | .937 | .921 | .954 | .875 | 1.198 | 2.07 | — | — |
| 10 | MIL | 619 | 25 | 101 | 103 | 14 | .304 | .365 | .501 | 83% | 37% | 8% | 1.65 | $33 | $29 | 490 | +24 | 45 | 1 | 3 | 35-17-48 | 14% | 23% | 34% | .866 | .827 | .917 | .893 | .786 | 2.06 | — | — |

## Reid Brignac — 300 PA | $3 | 140 pts

2B-68, SS-51, OF-2 (RF-2), DH-1 — Owned: 1% — LH

The versatile Brignac could enjoy expanded screen time in 2011 if the Rays decide not to re-sign Jason Bartlett. Brignac could become the Rays' primary shortstop while being ready to move to second base if another shortstop is acquired. Reid's arm and range are excellent, and he has some pop in his bat. (RZ)

| Player | Age | AB | HR | R | RBI | SB | BA | OBP | SLG | $1L | Pts |
|---|---|---|---|---|---|---|---|---|---|---|---|
| Brignac R | 25 | 279 | 9 | 33 | 33 | 3 | .247 | .297 | .400 | $3 | 140 |
| **Mini-Browser** | **Age** | **AB** | **HR** | **R** | **RBI** | **SB** | **BA** | **OBP** | **SLG** | **$1L** | **Pts** |
| Carroll J | 37 | 351 | 0 | 56 | 28 | 8 | .262 | .346 | .323 | $4 | 180 |
| Eckstein D | 36 | 446 | 5 | 55 | 35 | 5 | .258 | .321 | .327 | $4 | 250 |
| Murphy D | 26 | 277 | 9 | 33 | 36 | 3 | .260 | .317 | .436 | $4 | 180 |
| Getz C | 27 | 274 | 3 | 33 | 24 | 12 | .263 | .327 | .351 | $4 | 160 |
| Kennedy A | 35 | 190 | 2 | 22 | 18 | 6 | .263 | .326 | .365 | $3 | 110 |

| Level | Leag | AB | HR | R | RBI | SB | BA | OBP | SLG | CT% | H% | BB% | Bash |
|---|---|---|---|---|---|---|---|---|---|---|---|---|---|
| A | — | — | — | — | — | — | — | — | — | — | — | — | — |
| AA | — | — | — | — | — | — | — | — | — | — | — | — | — |
| AAA | — | — | — | — | — | — | — | — | — | — | — | — | — |

Competition at 2B — Stats in 2010

| Bats | Player | GSvR | GSvL | Sub | OPS |
|---|---|---|---|---|---|
| RH | Rodriguez S | 48 | 32 | 12 | .705 |
| BH | Zobrist B | 32 | 23 | 1 | .699 |
| LH | Brignac R | 39 | 5 | 24 | .692 |

Ten-Year Trends
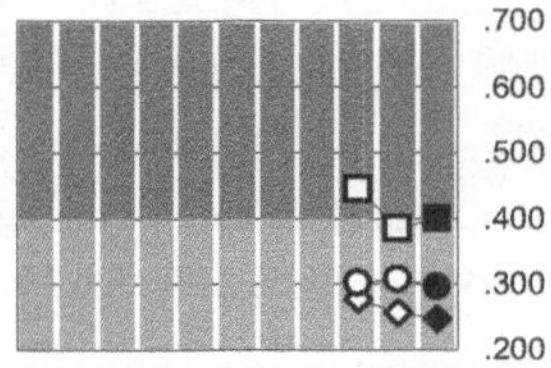

Weekly Points
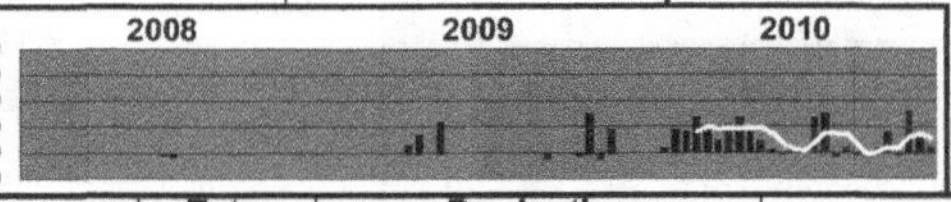

| Yr | Team | AB | HR | R | RBI | SB | BA | OBP | SLG | CT% | H% | BB% | Bash | $1L | $2L | Pts | RAA | 2B | 3B | CS | FB-LD-GB | HR/fb | RBI% | RS% | OPS | 1st Hf | 2nd Hf | vs RH | vs LH | Rnge | vRH | vLH |
|---|---|---|---|---|---|---|---|---|---|---|---|---|---|---|---|---|---|---|---|---|---|---|---|---|---|---|---|---|---|---|---|---|
| 07 | — | — | — | — | — | — | — | — | — | — | — | — | — | — | — | — | — | — | — | — | — | — | — | — | — | — | — | — | — | — | — | — |
| 08 | TB | 10 | 0 | 1 | 0 | 0 | .000 | .091 | .000 | 50% | 0% | 9% | NA | -$5 | -$19 | 0 | −2 | 0 | 0 | 0 | 40-20-40 | 0% | 0% | NA | .091 | .091 | — | .000 | .333 | — | — | — |
| 09 | TB | 90 | 1 | 10 | 6 | 2 | .278 | .301 | .444 | 78% | 36% | 3% | 1.60 | -$2 | -$17 | 40 | −0 | 8 | 2 | 2 | 43-23-34 | 3% | 13% | 33% | .746 | .685 | .861 | .918 | .145 | — | +23 | −69 |
| 10 | TB | 301 | 8 | 39 | 45 | 3 | .256 | .307 | .385 | 74% | 34% | 6% | 1.51 | $7 | -$5 | 150 | −7 | 13 | 1 | 3 | 42-19-38 | 9% | 21% | 34% | .692 | .694 | .689 | .706 | .609 | — | +33 | −99 |

## Domonic Brown — 600 PA | $14 | 320 pts

OF-15 (RF-15) — Owned: 2% — LH

With Jayson Werth probably headed elsewhere in free agency, the Domonic Brown Era is set to begin in Philadelphia. Brown should get virtually all of the playing time in right field, but don't expect the 23-year-old to completely fill Werth's shoes right away, especially when he is pitted against left-handed pitching. (BB)

| Player | Age | AB | HR | R | RBI | SB | BA | OBP | SLG | $1L | Pts |
|---|---|---|---|---|---|---|---|---|---|---|---|
| Brown D | 23 | 531 | 18 | 66 | 66 | 24 | .226 | .307 | .401 | $14 | 320 |
| **Mini-Browser** | **Age** | **AB** | **HR** | **R** | **RBI** | **SB** | **BA** | **OBP** | **SLG** | **$1L** | **Pts** |
| Tabata J | 22 | 567 | 12 | 78 | 54 | 24 | .275 | .334 | .388 | $15 | 360 |
| Rivera J | 32 | 500 | 21 | 58 | 74 | 0 | .273 | .319 | .453 | $15 | 330 |
| Maybin C | 23 | 534 | 18 | 84 | 54 | 18 | .247 | .331 | .410 | $15 | 310 |
| Brantley M | 23 | 573 | 6 | 69 | 50 | 31 | .251 | .324 | .331 | $14 | 360 |
| Lewis F | 30 | 446 | 10 | 75 | 40 | 15 | .269 | .347 | .428 | $14 | 280 |

| Level | Leag | AB | HR | R | RBI | SB | BA | OBP | SLG | CT% | H% | BB% | Bash |
|---|---|---|---|---|---|---|---|---|---|---|---|---|---|
| A | — | — | — | — | — | — | — | — | — | — | — | — | — |
| AA | EL | 236 | 15 | 50 | 47 | 12 | .318 | .391 | .602 | 78% | 41% | 11% | 1.89 |
| AAA | IL | 107 | 5 | 15 | 21 | 5 | .346 | .390 | .561 | 79% | 44% | 7% | 1.62 |

Competition at RF — Stats in 2010

| Bats | Player | GSvR | GSvL | Sub | OPS |
|---|---|---|---|---|---|
| RH | Werth J | 92 | 40 | 3 | .921 |
| LH | Brown D | 11 | 2 | 2 | .612 |
| RH | Francisco B | 5 | 5 | 10 | .768 |

Ten-Year Trends
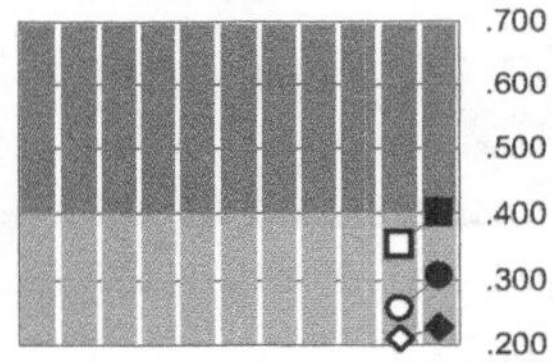

Weekly Points

| Yr | Team | AB | HR | R | RBI | SB | BA | OBP | SLG | CT% | H% | BB% | Bash | $1L | $2L | Pts | RAA | 2B | 3B | CS | FB-LD-GB | HR/fb | RBI% | RS% | OPS | 1st Hf | 2nd Hf | vs RH | vs LH | Rnge | vRH | vLH |
|---|---|---|---|---|---|---|---|---|---|---|---|---|---|---|---|---|---|---|---|---|---|---|---|---|---|---|---|---|---|---|---|---|
| 07 | — | — | — | — | — | — | — | — | — | — | — | — | — | — | — | — | — | — | — | — | — | — | — | — | — | — | — | — | — | — | — | — |
| 08 | — | — | — | — | — | — | — | — | — | — | — | — | — | — | — | — | — | — | — | — | — | — | — | — | — | — | — | — | — | — | — | — |
| 09 | — | — | — | — | — | — | — | — | — | — | — | — | — | — | — | — | — | — | — | — | — | — | — | — | — | — | — | — | — | — | — | — |
| 10 | PHI | 62 | 2 | 8 | 13 | 2 | .210 | .257 | .355 | 61% | 34% | 7% | 1.69 | -$3 | -$17 | 30 | −5 | 3 | 0 | 1 | 37-22-41 | 13% | 22% | 38% | .612 | — | .612 | .732 | .148 | — | — | — |

## Jordan Brown — 150 PA | $-2 | 70 pts

1B-10, DH-7, OF-7 (LF-7) — Owned: 0% — LH

Brown was used only sparingly off the bench, making it hard for him to find the swing that had served him so well in the minors. Injuries, positional logjams, and a curious organizational indifference had delayed his debut until age 26. Brown will back up LF, 1B, and DH and provide depth in case of an injury. (BLS)

| Player | Age | AB | HR | R | RBI | SB | BA | OBP | SLG | $1L | Pts |
|---|---|---|---|---|---|---|---|---|---|---|---|
| Brown J | 27 | 132 | 3 | 15 | 15 | 0 | .261 | .321 | .409 | -$2 | 70 |
| **Mini-Browser** | **Age** | **AB** | **HR** | **R** | **RBI** | **SB** | **BA** | **OBP** | **SLG** | **$1L** | **Pts** |
| Giambi J | 40 | 147 | 7 | 19 | 26 | 0 | .238 | .370 | .441 | $0 | 100 |
| Cantu J | 29 | 136 | 5 | 18 | 21 | 0 | .276 | .331 | .452 | $0 | 90 |
| Sweeney M | 37 | 135 | 5 | 14 | 20 | 0 | .267 | .323 | .428 | -$1 | 80 |
| Gload R | 34 | 144 | 3 | 17 | 18 | 2 | .270 | .316 | .404 | -$1 | 90 |
| Trumbo M | 25 | 178 | 8 | 16 | 22 | 2 | .214 | .257 | .406 | -$2 | 80 |

| Level | Leag | AB | HR | R | RBI | SB | BA | OBP | SLG | CT% | H% | BB% | Bash |
|---|---|---|---|---|---|---|---|---|---|---|---|---|---|
| A | — | — | — | — | — | — | — | — | — | — | — | — | — |
| AA | — | — | — | — | — | — | — | — | — | — | — | — | — |
| AAA | IL | 326 | 8 | 31 | 67 | 2 | .298 | .341 | .463 | 85% | 35% | 6% | 1.56 |

Competition at 1B — Stats in 2010

| Bats | Player | GSvR | GSvL | Sub | OPS |
|---|---|---|---|---|---|
| RH | LaPorta M | 65 | 28 | 0 | .668 |
| RH | Marte A | 7 | 10 | 15 | .680 |
| LH | Brown J | 8 | 0 | 2 | .582 |

Ten-Year Trends
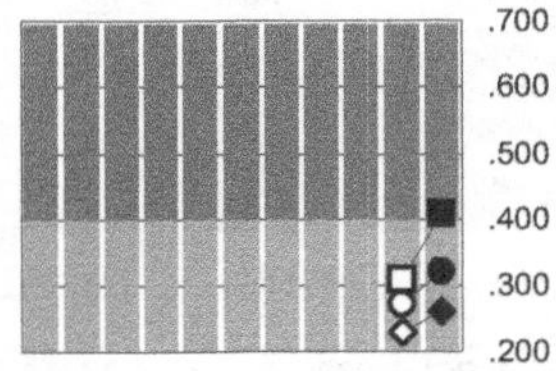

Weekly Points

| Yr | Team | AB | HR | R | RBI | SB | BA | OBP | SLG | CT% | H% | BB% | Bash | $1L | $2L | Pts | RAA | 2B | 3B | CS | FB-LD-GB | HR/fb | RBI% | RS% | OPS | 1st Hf | 2nd Hf | vs RH | vs LH | Rnge | vRH | vLH |
|---|---|---|---|---|---|---|---|---|---|---|---|---|---|---|---|---|---|---|---|---|---|---|---|---|---|---|---|---|---|---|---|---|
| 07 | — | — | — | — | — | — | — | — | — | — | — | — | — | — | — | — | — | — | — | — | — | — | — | — | — | — | — | — | — | — | — | — |
| 08 | — | — | — | — | — | — | — | — | — | — | — | — | — | — | — | — | — | — | — | — | — | — | — | — | — | — | — | — | — | — | — | — |
| 09 | — | — | — | — | — | — | — | — | — | — | — | — | — | — | — | — | — | — | — | — | — | — | — | — | — | — | — | — | — | — | — | — |
| 10 | CLE | 87 | 0 | 9 | 2 | 0 | .230 | .272 | .310 | 89% | 26% | 4% | 1.35 | -$4 | -$20 | 30 | −7 | 7 | 0 | 0 | 35-14-51 | 0% | 3% | 36% | .582 | — | .582 | .554 | .800 | — | — | — |

## Jay Bruce — 650 PA | $23 | 400 pts

OF-146 (RF-146) — Owned: 76% — LH

After a slow start, Bruce began to get things going in the second half before a sore side interrupted his best stretch. Nevertheless, he had a solid year, and his break-out season could come as soon as 2011. The 23-year-old will hit for a decent average with 40-HR power, plus he plays outstanding defense. (SW)

| Player | Age | AB | HR | R | RBI | SB | BA | OBP | SLG | $1L | Pts |
|---|---|---|---|---|---|---|---|---|---|---|---|
| Bruce J | 23 | 582 | 33 | 91 | 85 | 7 | .268 | .338 | .512 | $23 | 400 |
| **Mini-Browser** | **Age** | **AB** | **HR** | **R** | **RBI** | **SB** | **BA** | **OBP** | **SLG** | **$1L** | **Pts** |
| Pence H | 27 | 593 | 26 | 85 | 85 | 13 | .285 | .339 | .492 | $24 | 420 |
| Upton J | 23 | 563 | 26 | 91 | 85 | 20 | .277 | .363 | .497 | $23 | 400 |
| Pierre J | 33 | 582 | 0 | 85 | 46 | 52 | .279 | .330 | .343 | $23 | 430 |
| Ellsbury J | 27 | 534 | 6 | 81 | 46 | 46 | .280 | .335 | .393 | $23 | 400 |
| Victorino S | 30 | 587 | 13 | 98 | 65 | 33 | .277 | .344 | .442 | $23 | 470 |

| Level | Leag | AB | HR | R | RBI | SB | BA | OBP | SLG | CT% | H% | BB% | Bash |
|---|---|---|---|---|---|---|---|---|---|---|---|---|---|
| A | — | — | — | — | — | — | — | — | — | — | — | — | — |
| AA | — | — | — | — | — | — | — | — | — | — | — | — | — |
| AAA | — | — | — | — | — | — | — | — | — | — | — | — | — |

Competition at RF — Stats in 2010

| Bats | Player | GSvR | GSvL | Sub | OPS |
|---|---|---|---|---|---|
| LH | Bruce J | 96 | 37 | 13 | .846 |
| RH | Heisey C | 7 | 15 | 5 | .757 |

Ten-Year Trends
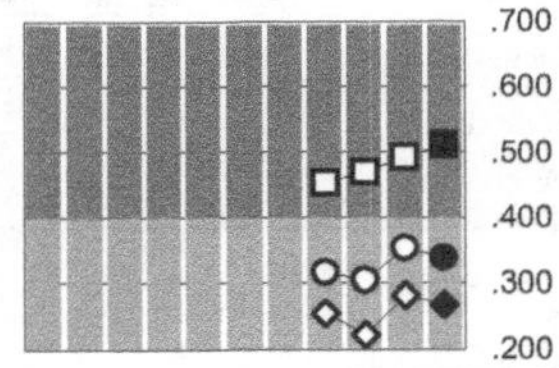

Weekly Points
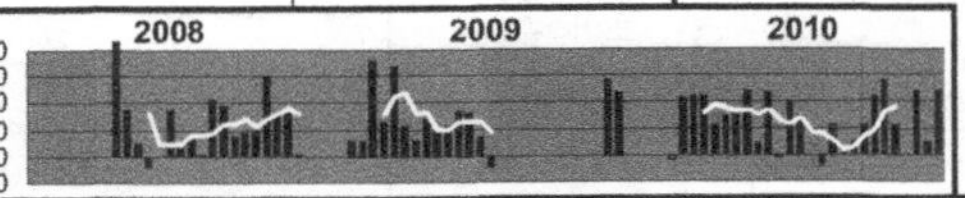

| Yr | Team | AB | HR | R | RBI | SB | BA | OBP | SLG | CT% | H% | BB% | Bash | $1L | $2L | Pts | RAA | 2B | 3B | CS | FB-LD-GB | HR/fb | RBI% | RS% | OPS | 1st Hf | 2nd Hf | vs RH | vs LH | Rnge | vRH | vLH |
|---|---|---|---|---|---|---|---|---|---|---|---|---|---|---|---|---|---|---|---|---|---|---|---|---|---|---|---|---|---|---|---|---|
| 07 | — | — | — | — | — | — | — | — | — | — | — | — | — | — | — | — | — | — | — | — | — | — | — | — | — | — | — | — | — | 2.10 | — | — |
| 08 | CIN | 413 | 21 | 63 | 52 | 4 | .254 | .314 | .453 | 73% | 35% | 7% | 1.78 | $11 | $2 | 230 | −9 | 17 | 1 | 6 | 34-21-45 | 20% | 15% | 35% | .767 | .765 | .768 | .869 | .562 | 2.10 | — | — |
| 09 | CIN | 345 | 22 | 47 | 58 | 3 | .223 | .303 | .470 | 78% | 29% | 10% | 2.10 | $9 | -$2 | 230 | −7 | 15 | 2 | 3 | 49-13-39 | 17% | 19% | 26% | .773 | .725 | 1.078 | .825 | .643 | 2.10 | +41 | −112 |
| 10 | CIN | 509 | 25 | 80 | 70 | 5 | .281 | .353 | .493 | 73% | 38% | 10% | 1.76 | $21 | $14 | 330 | +7 | 23 | 5 | 4 | 44-20-36 | 15% | 15% | 31% | .846 | .785 | .951 | .821 | .899 | 2.09 | +43 | −115 |

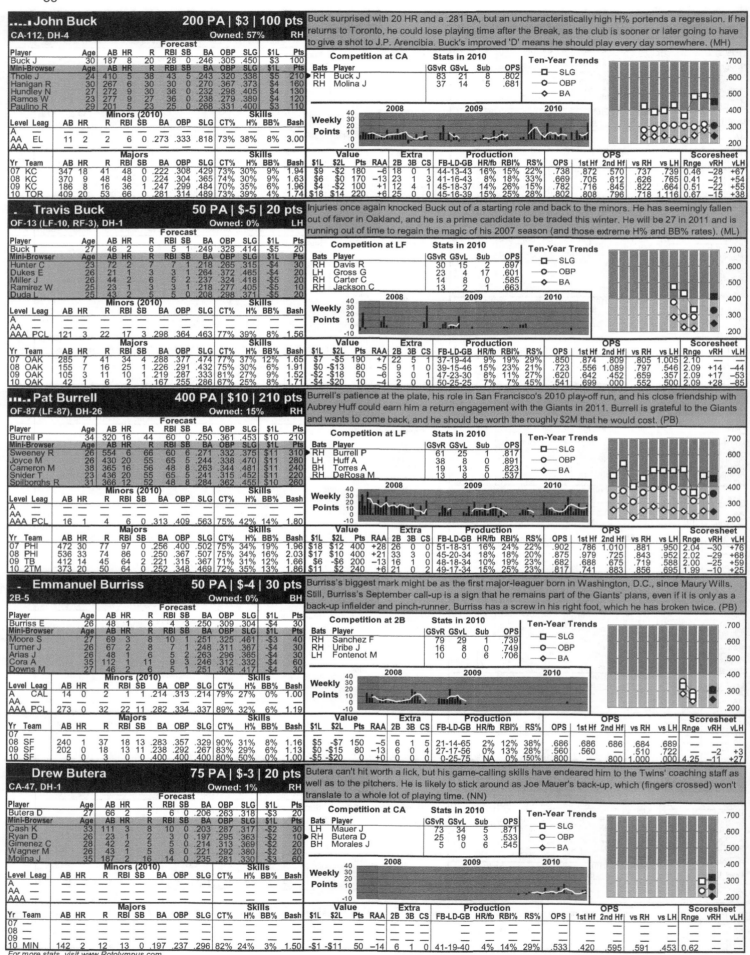

## John Buck — 200 PA | $3 | 100 pts

CA-112, DH-4 — Owned: 57% — RH

Buck surprised with 20 HR and a .281 BA, but an uncharacteristically high H% portends a regression. If he returns to Toronto, he could lose playing time after the Break, as the club is sooner or later going to have to give a shot to J.P. Arencibia. Buck's improved 'D' means he should play every day somewhere. (MH)

**Forecast**

| Player | Age | AB | HR | R | RBI | SB | BA | OBP | SLG | $1L | Pts |
|---|---|---|---|---|---|---|---|---|---|---|---|
| Buck J | 30 | 187 | 8 | 20 | 28 | 0 | .246 | .305 | .450 | $3 | 100 |
| **Mini-Browser** | Age | AB | HR | R | RBI | SB | BA | OBP | SLG | $1L | Pts |
| Thole J | 24 | 410 | 5 | 38 | 43 | 5 | .243 | .320 | .338 | $5 | 210 |
| Hanigan R | 30 | 267 | 6 | 30 | 30 | 0 | .270 | .367 | .373 | $4 | 160 |
| Hundley N | 27 | 272 | 9 | 30 | 36 | 0 | .232 | .298 | .405 | $4 | 130 |
| Ramos W | 23 | 277 | 9 | 27 | 36 | 0 | .238 | .279 | .389 | $4 | 120 |
| Paulino R | 29 | 201 | 5 | 23 | 25 | 0 | .268 | .331 | .400 | $3 | 110 |

**Minors (2010)**

| Level | Leag | AB | HR | R | RBI | SB | BA | OBP | SLG | CT% | H% | BB% | Bash |
|---|---|---|---|---|---|---|---|---|---|---|---|---|---|
| A | — | — | — | — | — | — | — | — | — | — | — | — | — |
| AA | EL | 11 | 2 | 2 | 6 | 0 | .273 | .333 | .818 | 73% | 38% | 8% | 3.00 |
| AAA | — | — | — | — | — | — | — | — | — | — | — | — | — |

**Majors**

| Yr | Team | AB | HR | R | RBI | SB | BA | OBP | SLG | CT% | H% | BB% | Bash | $1L | $2L | Pts | RAA | 2B | 3B | CS | FB-LD-GB | HR/fb | RBI% | RS% | OPS | 1st Hf | 2nd Hf | vs RH | vs LH | Rnge | vRH | vLH |
|---|---|---|---|---|---|---|---|---|---|---|---|---|---|---|---|---|---|---|---|---|---|---|---|---|---|---|---|---|---|---|---|---|
| 07 | KC | 347 | 18 | 41 | 48 | 0 | .222 | .308 | .429 | 73% | 30% | 9% | 1.94 | $9 | -$2 | 180 | −6 | 18 | 0 | 1 | 44-13-43 | 16% | 15% | 22% | .738 | .872 | .570 | .737 | .739 | 0.46 | −28 | +67 |
| 08 | KC | 370 | 9 | 48 | 48 | 0 | .224 | .304 | .365 | 74% | 30% | 9% | 1.63 | $6 | $0 | 170 | −13 | 23 | 1 | 3 | 41-16-43 | 8% | 18% | 33% | .669 | .705 | .612 | .626 | .765 | 0.41 | −21 | +54 |
| 09 | KC | 186 | 8 | 16 | 36 | 1 | .247 | .299 | .484 | 70% | 35% | 6% | 1.96 | $4 | -$2 | 100 | +1 | 12 | 4 | 1 | 45-18-37 | 14% | 26% | 15% | .782 | .716 | .845 | .822 | .664 | 0.51 | −22 | +55 |
| 10 | TOR | 409 | 20 | 53 | 66 | 0 | .281 | .314 | .489 | 73% | 39% | 4% | 1.74 | $18 | $14 | 220 | +6 | 25 | 0 | 0 | 45-16-39 | 15% | 25% | 28% | .802 | .808 | .796 | .718 | 1.116 | 0.67 | −15 | +38 |

**Competition at CA — Stats in 2010**

| Bats | Player | GSvR | GSvL | Sub | OPS |
|---|---|---|---|---|---|
| RH | Buck J | 83 | 21 | 8 | .802 |
| RH | Molina J | 37 | 14 | 5 | .681 |

Ten-Year Trends

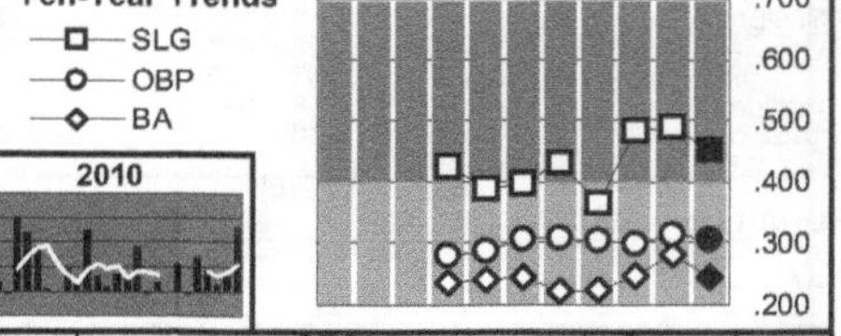
SLG
OBP
BA
.700
.600
.500
.400
.300
.200

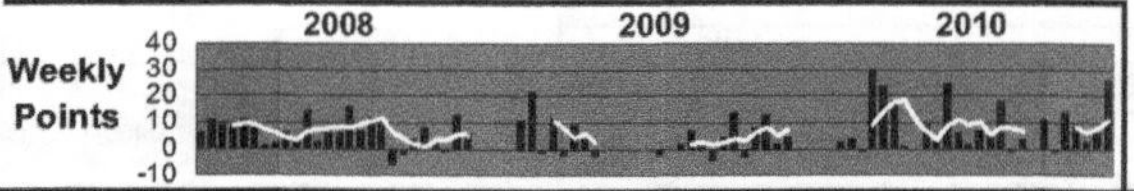
Weekly Points
2008
2009
2010

## Travis Buck — 50 PA | $-5 | 20 pts

OF-13 (LF-10, RF-3), DH-1 — Owned: 0% — LH

Injuries once again knocked Buck out of a starting role and back to the minors. He has seemingly fallen out of favor in Oakland, and he is a prime candidate to be traded this winter. He will be 27 in 2011 and is running out of time to regain the magic of his 2007 season (and those extreme H% and BB% rates). (ML)

**Forecast**

| Player | Age | AB | HR | R | RBI | SB | BA | OBP | SLG | $1L | Pts |
|---|---|---|---|---|---|---|---|---|---|---|---|
| Buck T | 27 | 46 | 2 | 6 | 5 | 1 | .249 | .328 | .414 | -$5 | 20 |
| **Mini-Browser** | Age | AB | HR | R | RBI | SB | BA | OBP | SLG | $1L | Pts |
| Hunter C | 23 | 72 | 2 | 7 | 7 | 1 | .218 | .265 | .315 | -$4 | 30 |
| Dukes E | 26 | 21 | 1 | 3 | 3 | 1 | .264 | .372 | .465 | -$4 | 20 |
| Miller J | 26 | 44 | 2 | 6 | 5 | 2 | .237 | .324 | .418 | -$5 | 20 |
| Ramirez W | 25 | 23 | 1 | 3 | 3 | 1 | .218 | .277 | .405 | -$5 | 10 |
| Duda L | 25 | 43 | 2 | 5 | 5 | 0 | .208 | .298 | .371 | -$5 | 20 |

**Minors (2010)**

| Level | Leag | AB | HR | R | RBI | SB | BA | OBP | SLG | CT% | H% | BB% | Bash |
|---|---|---|---|---|---|---|---|---|---|---|---|---|---|
| A | — | — | — | — | — | — | — | — | — | — | — | — | — |
| AA | — | — | — | — | — | — | — | — | — | — | — | — | — |
| AAA | PCL | 121 | 3 | 22 | 17 | 3 | .298 | .364 | .463 | 77% | 39% | 8% | 1.56 |

**Majors**

| Yr | Team | AB | HR | R | RBI | SB | BA | OBP | SLG | CT% | H% | BB% | Bash | $1L | $2L | Pts | RAA | 2B | 3B | CS | FB-LD-GB | HR/fb | RBI% | RS% | OPS | 1st Hf | 2nd Hf | vs RH | vs LH | Rnge | vRH | vLH |
|---|---|---|---|---|---|---|---|---|---|---|---|---|---|---|---|---|---|---|---|---|---|---|---|---|---|---|---|---|---|---|---|---|
| 07 | OAK | 285 | 7 | 41 | 34 | 4 | .288 | .377 | .474 | 77% | 37% | 12% | 1.65 | $7 | -$5 | 190 | +7 | 22 | 5 | 1 | 37-19-44 | 9% | 19% | 29% | .850 | .874 | .809 | .805 | 1.005 | 2.10 | — | — |
| 08 | OAK | 155 | 7 | 16 | 25 | 1 | .226 | .291 | .432 | 75% | 30% | 6% | 1.91 | $0 | -$13 | 80 | −5 | 9 | 1 | 0 | 39-15-46 | 15% | 23% | 21% | .723 | .556 | 1.089 | .797 | .546 | 2.09 | +14 | −44 |
| 09 | OAK | 105 | 3 | 11 | 10 | 1 | .219 | .287 | .333 | 81% | 27% | 9% | 1.52 | -$2 | -$18 | 50 | −6 | 3 | 0 | 1 | 47-23-30 | 8% | 11% | 27% | .620 | .642 | .452 | .659 | .357 | 2.09 | +17 | −53 |
| 10 | OAK | 42 | 1 | 6 | 2 | 1 | .167 | .255 | .286 | 67% | 25% | 8% | 1.71 | -$4 | -$20 | 10 | −4 | 2 | 0 | 0 | 50-25-25 | 7% | 7% | 45% | .541 | .699 | .000 | .552 | .500 | 2.09 | +28 | −85 |

**Competition at LF — Stats in 2010**

| Bats | Player | GSvR | GSvL | Sub | OPS |
|---|---|---|---|---|---|
| RH | Davis R | 30 | 15 | 2 | .697 |
| LH | Gross G | 23 | 4 | 17 | .601 |
| RH | Carter C | 14 | 8 | 0 | .585 |
| RH | Jackson C | 13 | 2 | 1 | .663 |

Ten-Year Trends

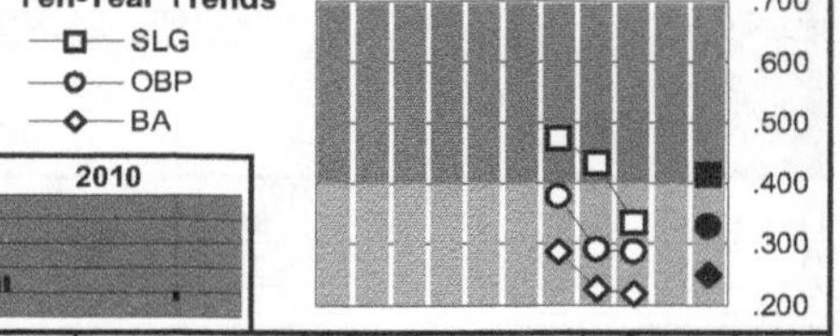
SLG
OBP
BA
.700
.600
.500
.400
.300
.200

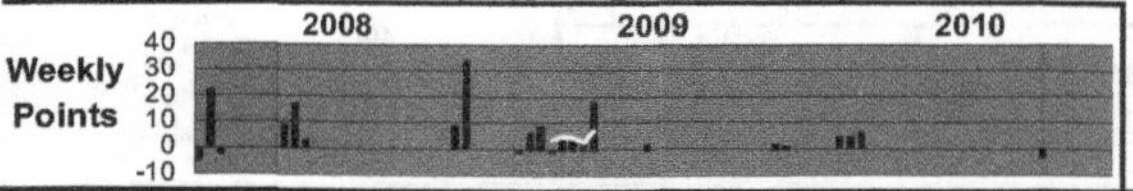
Weekly Points
2008
2009
2010

## Pat Burrell — 400 PA | $10 | 210 pts

OF-87 (LF-87), DH-26 — Owned: 15% — RH

Burrell's patience at the plate, his role in San Francisco's 2010 play-off run, and his close friendship with Aubrey Huff could earn him a return engagement with the Giants in 2011. Burrell is grateful to the Giants and wants to come back, and he should be worth the roughly $2M that he would cost. (PB)

**Forecast**

| Player | Age | AB | HR | R | RBI | SB | BA | OBP | SLG | $1L | Pts |
|---|---|---|---|---|---|---|---|---|---|---|---|
| Burrell P | 34 | 320 | 16 | 44 | 60 | 0 | .250 | .361 | .453 | $10 | 210 |
| **Mini-Browser** | Age | AB | HR | R | RBI | SB | BA | OBP | SLG | $1L | Pts |
| Sweeney R | 26 | 554 | 6 | 66 | 60 | 6 | .271 | .332 | .375 | $11 | 310 |
| Joyce M | 26 | 430 | 20 | 55 | 65 | 5 | .244 | .338 | .470 | $11 | 280 |
| Cameron M | 38 | 365 | 16 | 56 | 48 | 8 | .263 | .344 | .481 | $11 | 240 |
| Snider T | 23 | 436 | 20 | 55 | 65 | 5 | .241 | .315 | .452 | $11 | 220 |
| Spilborghs R | 31 | 366 | 12 | 52 | 48 | 8 | .284 | .362 | .455 | $10 | 260 |

**Minors (2010)**

| Level | Leag | AB | HR | R | RBI | SB | BA | OBP | SLG | CT% | H% | BB% | Bash |
|---|---|---|---|---|---|---|---|---|---|---|---|---|---|
| A | — | — | — | — | — | — | — | — | — | — | — | — | — |
| AA | — | — | — | — | — | — | — | — | — | — | — | — | — |
| AAA | PCL | 16 | 1 | 4 | 6 | 0 | .313 | .409 | .563 | 75% | 42% | 14% | 1.80 |

**Majors**

| Yr | Team | AB | HR | R | RBI | SB | BA | OBP | SLG | CT% | H% | BB% | Bash | $1L | $2L | Pts | RAA | 2B | 3B | CS | FB-LD-GB | HR/fb | RBI% | RS% | OPS | 1st Hf | 2nd Hf | vs RH | vs LH | Rnge | vRH | vLH |
|---|---|---|---|---|---|---|---|---|---|---|---|---|---|---|---|---|---|---|---|---|---|---|---|---|---|---|---|---|---|---|---|---|
| 07 | PHI | 472 | 30 | 77 | 97 | 0 | .256 | .400 | .502 | 75% | 34% | 19% | 1.96 | $18 | $12 | 400 | +28 | 26 | 0 | 0 | 51-18-31 | 16% | 24% | 22% | .902 | .786 | 1.010 | .881 | .950 | 2.04 | −30 | +76 |
| 08 | PHI | 536 | 33 | 74 | 86 | 0 | .250 | .367 | .507 | 75% | 34% | 16% | 2.03 | $17 | $10 | 400 | +21 | 33 | 3 | 0 | 45-20-34 | 18% | 18% | 20% | .875 | .979 | .725 | .843 | .952 | 2.02 | −29 | +68 |
| 09 | TB | 412 | 14 | 45 | 64 | 2 | .221 | .315 | .367 | 71% | 31% | 12% | 1.66 | $6 | -$6 | 200 | −13 | 16 | 1 | 0 | 48-18-34 | 10% | 19% | 23% | .682 | .688 | .675 | .719 | .588 | 2.00 | −25 | +59 |
| 10 | 2TM | 373 | 20 | 50 | 64 | 0 | .252 | .348 | .469 | 72% | 35% | 13% | 1.86 | $11 | $2 | 240 | +6 | 21 | 0 | 2 | 49-17-34 | 15% | 25% | 23% | .817 | .741 | .883 | .856 | .695 | 1.99 | −10 | +25 |

**Competition at LF — Stats in 2010**

| Bats | Player | GSvR | GSvL | Sub | OPS |
|---|---|---|---|---|---|
| RH | Burrell P | 61 | 25 | 1 | .817 |
| LH | Huff A | 38 | 8 | 0 | .891 |
| BH | Torres A | 19 | 13 | 5 | .823 |
| RH | DeRosa M | 13 | 8 | 0 | .537 |

Ten-Year Trends

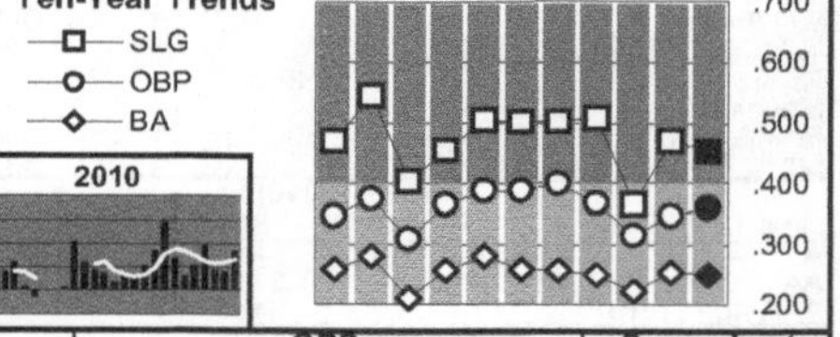
SLG
OBP
BA
.700
.600
.500
.400
.300
.200

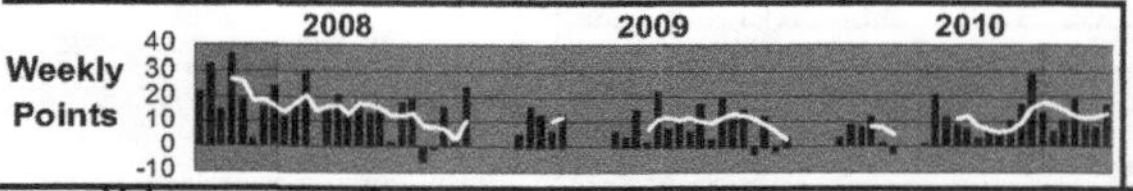
Weekly Points
2008
2009
2010

## Emmanuel Burriss — 50 PA | $-4 | 30 pts

2B-5 — Owned: 0% — BH

Burriss's biggest mark might be as the first major-leaguer born in Washington, D.C., since Maury Wills. Still, Burriss's September call-up is a sign that he remains part of the Giants' plans, even if it is only as a back-up infielder and pinch-runner. Burriss has a screw in his right foot, which he has broken twice. (PB)

**Forecast**

| Player | Age | AB | HR | R | RBI | SB | BA | OBP | SLG | $1L | Pts |
|---|---|---|---|---|---|---|---|---|---|---|---|
| Burriss E | 26 | 48 | 1 | 6 | 4 | 3 | .250 | .309 | .304 | -$4 | 30 |
| **Mini-Browser** | Age | AB | HR | R | RBI | SB | BA | OBP | SLG | $1L | Pts |
| Moore S | 27 | 69 | 3 | 8 | 10 | 1 | .251 | .325 | .461 | -$3 | 40 |
| Turner J | 26 | 67 | 2 | 8 | 7 | 1 | .248 | .311 | .367 | -$4 | 30 |
| Arias J | 26 | 48 | 1 | 6 | 5 | 2 | .263 | .296 | .365 | -$4 | 30 |
| Cora A | 35 | 112 | 1 | 11 | 9 | 3 | .246 | .312 | .332 | -$4 | 60 |
| Downs M | 27 | 46 | 2 | 6 | 5 | 1 | .251 | .306 | .417 | -$4 | 30 |

**Minors (2010)**

| Level | Leag | AB | HR | R | RBI | SB | BA | OBP | SLG | CT% | H% | BB% | Bash |
|---|---|---|---|---|---|---|---|---|---|---|---|---|---|
| A | CAL | 14 | 0 | 2 | 1 | 1 | .214 | .313 | .214 | 79% | 27% | 0% | 1.00 |
| AA | — | — | — | — | — | — | — | — | — | — | — | — | — |
| AAA | PCL | 273 | 0 | 32 | 22 | 11 | .282 | .334 | .337 | 89% | 32% | 6% | 1.19 |

**Majors**

| Yr | Team | AB | HR | R | RBI | SB | BA | OBP | SLG | CT% | H% | BB% | Bash | $1L | $2L | Pts | RAA | 2B | 3B | CS | FB-LD-GB | HR/fb | RBI% | RS% | OPS | 1st Hf | 2nd Hf | vs RH | vs LH | Rnge | vRH | vLH |
|---|---|---|---|---|---|---|---|---|---|---|---|---|---|---|---|---|---|---|---|---|---|---|---|---|---|---|---|---|---|---|---|---|
| 07 | — | — | — | — | — | — | — | — | — | — | — | — | — | — | — | — | — | — | — | — | — | — | — | — | — | — | — | — | — | — | — | — |
| 08 | SF | 240 | 1 | 37 | 18 | 13 | .283 | .357 | .329 | 90% | 31% | 8% | 1.16 | $5 | -$7 | 150 | −5 | 6 | 1 | 5 | 21-14-65 | 2% | 12% | 38% | .686 | .686 | .686 | .684 | .689 | — | — | — |
| 09 | SF | 202 | 0 | 18 | 13 | 11 | .238 | .292 | .267 | 83% | 29% | 6% | 1.13 | $0 | -$15 | 80 | −13 | 6 | 0 | 4 | 27-17-56 | 0% | 13% | 28% | .560 | .560 | — | .510 | .722 | — | −2 | +3 |
| 10 | SF | 5 | 0 | 3 | 0 | 0 | .400 | .400 | .400 | 80% | 50% | 0% | 1.00 | -$5 | -$20 | 0 | +0 | 0 | 0 | 0 | 0-25-75 | NA | 0% | 150% | .800 | — | .800 | 1.000 | .000 | 4.25 | −11 | +27 |

**Competition at 2B — Stats in 2010**

| Bats | Player | GSvR | GSvL | Sub | OPS |
|---|---|---|---|---|---|
| RH | Sanchez F | 79 | 29 | 1 | .739 |
| RH | Uribe J | 16 | 8 | 0 | .749 |
| LH | Fontenot M | 10 | 0 | 6 | .706 |

Ten-Year Trends

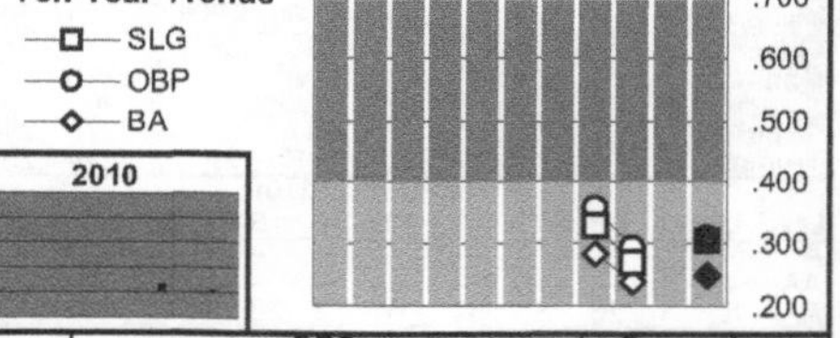
SLG
OBP
BA
.700
.600
.500
.400
.300
.200

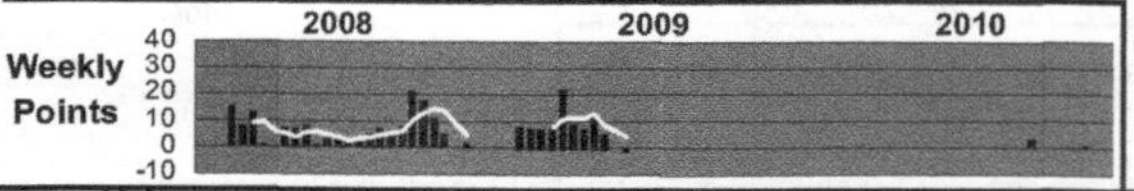
Weekly Points
2008
2009
2010

## Drew Butera — 75 PA | $-3 | 20 pts

CA-47, DH-1 — Owned: 1% — RH

Butera can't hit worth a lick, but his game-calling skills have endeared him to the Twins' coaching staff as well as to the pitchers. He is likely to stick around as Joe Mauer's back-up, which (fingers crossed) won't translate to a whole lot of playing time. (NN)

**Forecast**

| Player | Age | AB | HR | R | RBI | SB | BA | OBP | SLG | $1L | Pts |
|---|---|---|---|---|---|---|---|---|---|---|---|
| Butera D | 27 | 66 | 2 | 5 | 6 | 0 | .206 | .263 | .318 | -$3 | 20 |
| **Mini-Browser** | Age | AB | HR | R | RBI | SB | BA | OBP | SLG | $1L | Pts |
| Cash K | 33 | 111 | 3 | 8 | 10 | 0 | .203 | .287 | .317 | -$2 | 30 |
| Ryan D | 26 | 23 | 1 | 2 | 3 | 0 | .197 | .295 | .363 | -$2 | 10 |
| Gimenez C | 28 | 42 | 2 | 5 | 5 | 0 | .214 | .313 | .369 | -$2 | 20 |
| Wagner M | 26 | 43 | 1 | 5 | 6 | 0 | .221 | .292 | .380 | -$2 | 20 |
| Molina J | 35 | 187 | 2 | 16 | 14 | 0 | .235 | .281 | .330 | -$3 | 60 |

**Minors (2010)**

| Level | Leag | AB | HR | R | RBI | SB | BA | OBP | SLG | CT% | H% | BB% | Bash |
|---|---|---|---|---|---|---|---|---|---|---|---|---|---|
| A | — | — | — | — | — | — | — | — | — | — | — | — | — |
| AA | — | — | — | — | — | — | — | — | — | — | — | — | — |
| AAA | — | — | — | — | — | — | — | — | — | — | — | — | — |

**Majors**

| Yr | Team | AB | HR | R | RBI | SB | BA | OBP | SLG | CT% | H% | BB% | Bash | $1L | $2L | Pts | RAA | 2B | 3B | CS | FB-LD-GB | HR/fb | RBI% | RS% | OPS | 1st Hf | 2nd Hf | vs RH | vs LH | Rnge | vRH | vLH |
|---|---|---|---|---|---|---|---|---|---|---|---|---|---|---|---|---|---|---|---|---|---|---|---|---|---|---|---|---|---|---|---|---|
| 07 | — | — | — | — | — | — | — | — | — | — | — | — | — | — | — | — | — | — | — | — | — | — | — | — | — | — | — | — | — | — | — | — |
| 08 | — | — | — | — | — | — | — | — | — | — | — | — | — | — | — | — | — | — | — | — | — | — | — | — | — | — | — | — | — | — | — | — |
| 09 | — | — | — | — | — | — | — | — | — | — | — | — | — | — | — | — | — | — | — | — | — | — | — | — | — | — | — | — | — | — | — | — |
| 10 | MIN | 142 | 2 | 12 | 13 | 0 | .197 | .237 | .296 | 82% | 24% | 3% | 1.50 | -$1 | -$11 | 50 | −14 | 6 | 1 | 0 | 41-19-40 | 4% | 14% | 29% | .533 | .420 | .595 | .591 | .453 | 0.62 | — | — |

**Competition at CA — Stats in 2010**

| Bats | Player | GSvR | GSvL | Sub | OPS |
|---|---|---|---|---|---|
| LH | Mauer J | 73 | 34 | 5 | .871 |
| RH | Butera D | 25 | 19 | 3 | .533 |
| BH | Morales J | 5 | 0 | 6 | .545 |

Ten-Year Trends

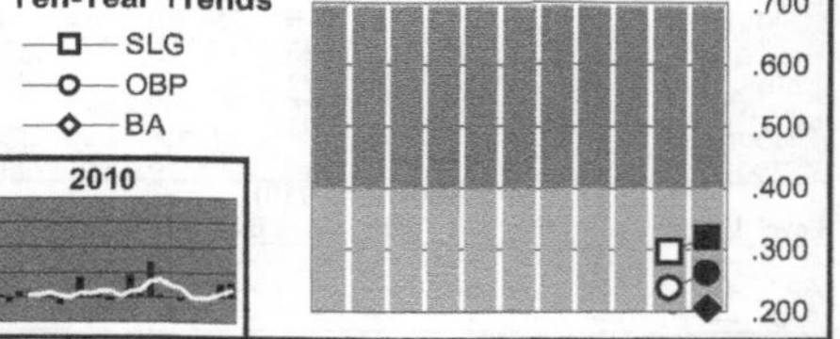
SLG
OBP
BA
.700
.600
.500
.400
.300
.200

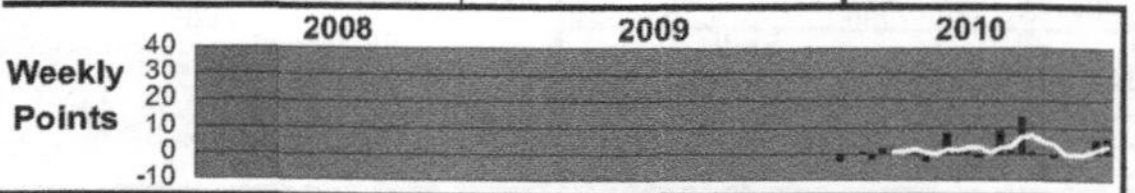
Weekly Points
2008
2009
2010

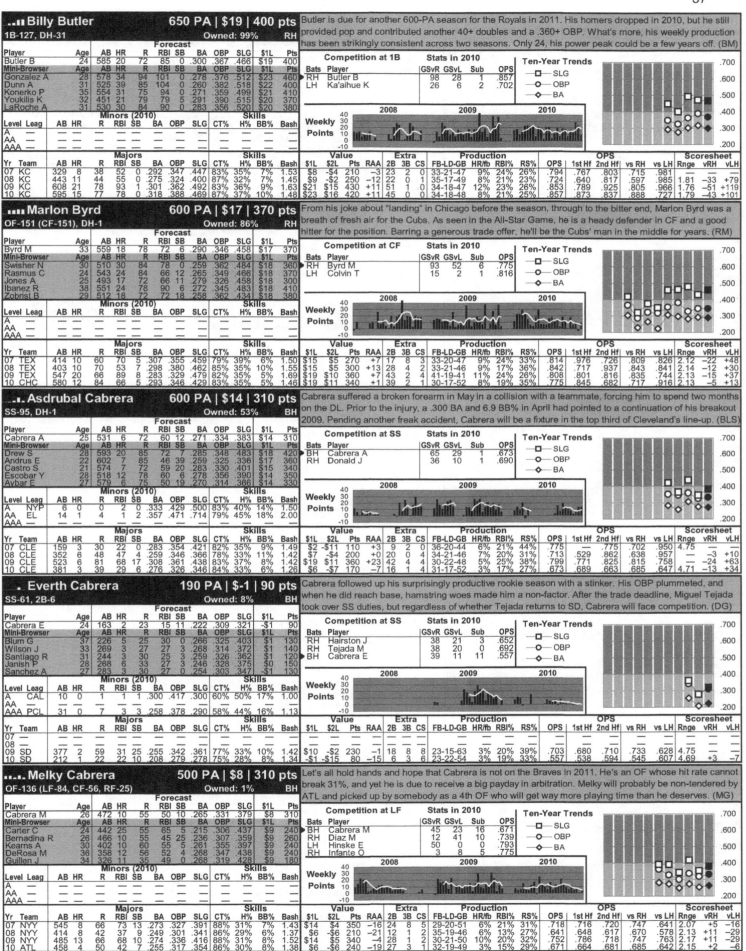

## Billy Butler

**650 PA | $19 | 400 pts**

1B-127, DH-31 | Owned: 99% | RH

Butler is due for another 600-PA season for the Royals in 2011. His homers dropped in 2010, but he still provided pop and contributed another 40+ doubles and a .360+ OBP. What's more, his weekly production has been strikingly consistent across two seasons. Only 24, his power peak could be a few years off. (BM)

| Player | Age | AB | HR | R | RBI | SB | BA | OBP | SLG | $1L | Pts |
|---|---|---|---|---|---|---|---|---|---|---|---|
| | | Forecast | | | | | | | | | |
| Butler B | 24 | 585 | 20 | 72 | 85 | 0 | .300 | .367 | .466 | $19 | 400 |
| **Mini-Browser** | **Age** | **AB** | **HR** | **R** | **RBI** | **SB** | **BA** | **OBP** | **SLG** | **$1L** | **Pts** |
| Gonzalez A | 28 | 578 | 34 | 94 | 101 | 0 | .278 | .376 | .512 | $23 | 460 |
| Dunn A | 31 | 525 | 39 | 85 | 104 | 0 | .260 | .382 | .518 | $22 | 400 |
| Konerko P | 35 | 554 | 31 | 75 | 94 | 0 | .271 | .359 | .499 | $21 | 410 |
| Youkilis K | 32 | 451 | 21 | 79 | 79 | 5 | .291 | .390 | .515 | $20 | 370 |
| LaRoche A | 31 | 530 | 30 | 84 | 90 | 0 | .283 | .356 | .520 | $20 | 380 |

| Level | Leag | AB | HR | R | RBI | SB | BA | OBP | SLG | CT% | H% | BB% | Bash |
|---|---|---|---|---|---|---|---|---|---|---|---|---|---|
| | | Minors (2010) | | | | | | | | Skills | | | |
| A | — | — | — | — | — | — | — | — | — | — | — | — | — |
| AA | — | — | — | — | — | — | — | — | — | — | — | — | — |
| AAA | — | — | — | — | — | — | — | — | — | — | — | — | — |

| Competition at 1B | | Stats in 2010 | | | |
|---|---|---|---|---|---|
| Bats | Player | GSvR | GSvL | Sub | OPS |
| ▶ RH | Butler B | 98 | 28 | 1 | .857 |
| LH | Ka'aihue K | 26 | 6 | 2 | .702 |

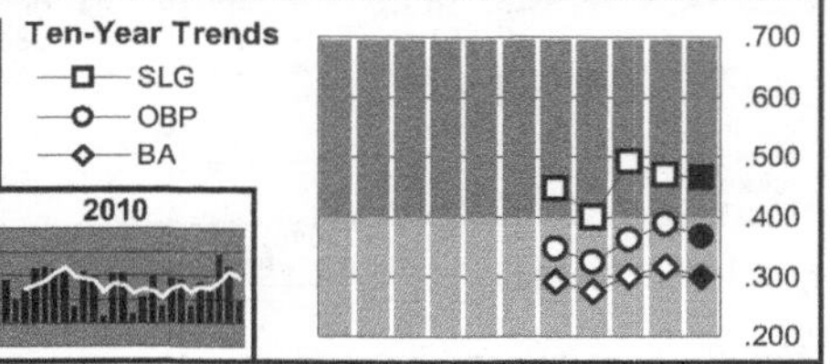


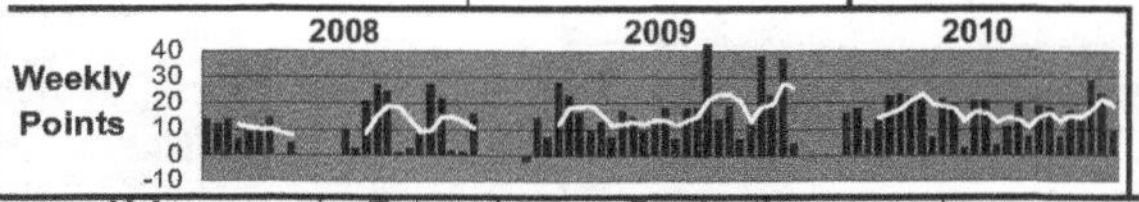


| Yr | Team | AB | HR | R | RBI | SB | BA | OBP | SLG | CT% | H% | BB% | Bash |
|---|---|---|---|---|---|---|---|---|---|---|---|---|---|
| | | Majors | | | | | | | | Skills | | | |
| 07 | KC | 329 | 8 | 38 | 52 | 0 | .292 | .347 | .447 | 83% | 35% | 7% | 1.53 |
| 08 | KC | 443 | 11 | 44 | 55 | 0 | .275 | .324 | .400 | 87% | 32% | 7% | 1.45 |
| 09 | KC | 608 | 21 | 78 | 93 | 1 | .301 | .362 | .492 | 83% | 36% | 9% | 1.63 |
| 10 | KC | 595 | 15 | 77 | 78 | 0 | .318 | .388 | .469 | 87% | 37% | 10% | 1.48 |

| Yr | $1L | $2L | Pts | RAA | 2B | 3B | CS | FB-LD-GB | HR/fb | RBI% | RS% | OPS | 1st Hf | 2nd Hf | vs RH | vs LH | Rnge | vRH | vLH |
|---|---|---|---|---|---|---|---|---|---|---|---|---|---|---|---|---|---|---|---|
| | Value | | | | Extra | | | Production | | | | OPS | | | | | Scoresheet | | |
| 07 | $8 | -$4 | 210 | −3 | 23 | 2 | 0 | 33-21-47 | 9% | 24% | 26% | .794 | .767 | .803 | .715 | .981 | — | — | — |
| 08 | $9 | -$2 | 250 | −12 | 22 | 0 | 1 | 35-17-49 | 8% | 21% | 23% | .724 | .640 | .817 | .597 | .985 | 1.81 | −33 | +79 |
| 09 | $21 | $15 | 430 | +11 | 51 | 1 | 0 | 34-18-47 | 12% | 23% | 26% | .853 | .789 | .925 | .805 | .966 | 1.76 | −51 | +119 |
| 10 | $23 | $16 | 420 | +11 | 45 | 0 | 0 | 34-18-48 | 8% | 21% | 25% | .857 | .873 | .837 | .888 | .727 | 1.79 | −43 | +101 |

## Marlon Byrd

**600 PA | $17 | 370 pts**

OF-151 (CF-151), DH-1 | Owned: 86% | RH

From his joke about "landing" in Chicago before the season, through to the bitter end, Marlon Byrd was a breath of fresh air for the Cubs. As seen in the All-Star Game, he is a heady defender in CF and a good hitter for the position. Barring a generous trade offer, he'll be the Cubs' man in the middle for years. (RM)

| Player | Age | AB | HR | R | RBI | SB | BA | OBP | SLG | $1L | Pts |
|---|---|---|---|---|---|---|---|---|---|---|---|
| | | Forecast | | | | | | | | | |
| Byrd M | 33 | 559 | 18 | 78 | 72 | 6 | .290 | .346 | .458 | $17 | 370 |
| **Mini-Browser** | **Age** | **AB** | **HR** | **R** | **RBI** | **SB** | **BA** | **OBP** | **SLG** | **$1L** | **Pts** |
| Swisher N | 30 | 510 | 30 | 84 | 78 | 0 | .259 | .362 | .484 | $18 | 360 |
| Rasmus C | 24 | 543 | 24 | 84 | 66 | 12 | .265 | .349 | .466 | $18 | 370 |
| Jones A | 25 | 493 | 17 | 72 | 66 | 11 | .279 | .326 | .458 | $18 | 300 |
| Ibanez R | 38 | 551 | 24 | 78 | 90 | 6 | .272 | .345 | .483 | $18 | 410 |
| Zobrist B | 29 | 512 | 18 | 72 | 72 | 18 | .258 | .362 | .434 | $18 | 380 |

| Level | Leag | AB | HR | R | RBI | SB | BA | OBP | SLG | CT% | H% | BB% | Bash |
|---|---|---|---|---|---|---|---|---|---|---|---|---|---|
| | | Minors (2010) | | | | | | | | Skills | | | |
| A | — | — | — | — | — | — | — | — | — | — | — | — | — |
| AA | — | — | — | — | — | — | — | — | — | — | — | — | — |
| AAA | — | — | — | — | — | — | — | — | — | — | — | — | — |

| Competition at CF | | Stats in 2010 | | | |
|---|---|---|---|---|---|
| Bats | Player | GSvR | GSvL | Sub | OPS |
| ▶ RH | Byrd M | 93 | 52 | 6 | .775 |
| LH | Colvin T | 15 | 2 | 1 | .816 |

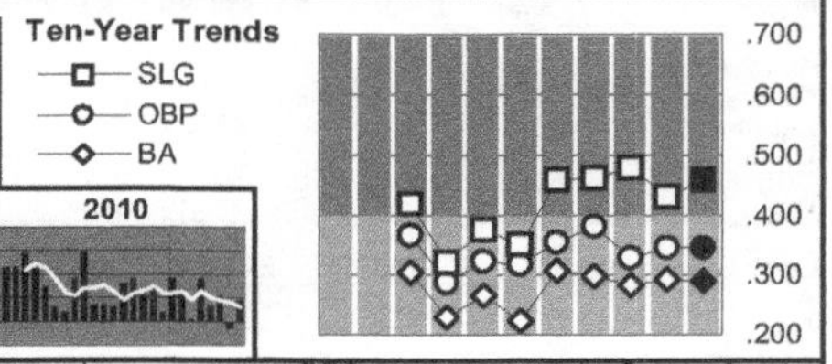


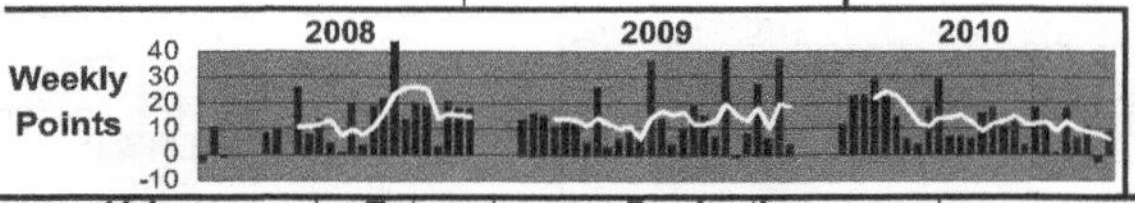


| Yr | Team | AB | HR | R | RBI | SB | BA | OBP | SLG | CT% | H% | BB% | Bash |
|---|---|---|---|---|---|---|---|---|---|---|---|---|---|
| | | Majors | | | | | | | | Skills | | | |
| 07 | TEX | 414 | 10 | 60 | 70 | 5 | .307 | .355 | .459 | 79% | 39% | 6% | 1.50 |
| 08 | TEX | 403 | 10 | 70 | 53 | 7 | .298 | .380 | .462 | 85% | 35% | 10% | 1.55 |
| 09 | TEX | 547 | 20 | 66 | 89 | 8 | .283 | .329 | .479 | 82% | 35% | 5% | 1.69 |
| 10 | CHC | 580 | 12 | 84 | 66 | 5 | .293 | .346 | .429 | 83% | 35% | 5% | 1.46 |

| Yr | $1L | $2L | Pts | RAA | 2B | 3B | CS | FB-LD-GB | HR/fb | RBI% | RS% | OPS | 1st Hf | 2nd Hf | vs RH | vs LH | Rnge | vRH | vLH |
|---|---|---|---|---|---|---|---|---|---|---|---|---|---|---|---|---|---|---|---|
| | Value | | | | Extra | | | Production | | | | OPS | | | | | Scoresheet | | |
| 07 | $15 | $5 | 270 | +7 | 17 | 8 | 3 | 33-20-47 | 9% | 24% | 33% | .814 | .976 | .726 | .809 | .826 | 2.12 | −22 | +48 |
| 08 | $15 | $5 | 300 | +13 | 28 | 4 | 2 | 33-21-46 | 9% | 17% | 36% | .842 | .717 | .937 | .843 | .841 | 2.14 | −12 | +30 |
| 09 | $19 | $10 | 360 | +7 | 43 | 2 | 4 | 41-19-41 | 11% | 24% | 26% | .808 | .801 | .816 | .835 | .744 | 2.13 | −15 | +37 |
| 10 | $19 | $11 | 340 | +1 | 39 | 2 | 1 | 30-17-52 | 8% | 19% | 35% | .775 | .845 | .682 | .717 | .916 | 2.13 | −5 | +13 |

## Asdrubal Cabrera

**600 PA | $14 | 310 pts**

SS-95, DH-1 | Owned: 53% | BH

Cabrera suffered a broken forearm in May in a collision with a teammate, forcing him to spend two months on the DL. Prior to the injury, a .300 BA and 6.9 BB% in April had pointed to a continuation of his breakout 2009. Pending another freak accident, Cabrera will be a fixture in the top third of Cleveland's line-up. (BLS)

| Player | Age | AB | HR | R | RBI | SB | BA | OBP | SLG | $1L | Pts |
|---|---|---|---|---|---|---|---|---|---|---|---|
| | | Forecast | | | | | | | | | |
| Cabrera A | 25 | 531 | 6 | 72 | 60 | 12 | .271 | .334 | .383 | $14 | 310 |
| **Mini-Browser** | **Age** | **AB** | **HR** | **R** | **RBI** | **SB** | **BA** | **OBP** | **SLG** | **$1L** | **Pts** |
| Drew S | 28 | 593 | 20 | 85 | 72 | 7 | .285 | .348 | .483 | $18 | 420 |
| Andrus E | 22 | 602 | 7 | 85 | 46 | 39 | .259 | .325 | .336 | $17 | 360 |
| Castro S | 21 | 574 | 7 | 72 | 59 | 20 | .283 | .330 | .401 | $15 | 340 |
| Escobar Y | 28 | 518 | 12 | 78 | 60 | 6 | .278 | .356 | .390 | $14 | 350 |
| Aybar E | 27 | 579 | 6 | 75 | 50 | 19 | .270 | .314 | .366 | $14 | 330 |

| Level | Leag | AB | HR | R | RBI | SB | BA | OBP | SLG | CT% | H% | BB% | Bash |
|---|---|---|---|---|---|---|---|---|---|---|---|---|---|
| | | Minors (2010) | | | | | | | | Skills | | | |
| A | NYP | 6 | 0 | 0 | 2 | 0 | .333 | .429 | .500 | 83% | 40% | 14% | 1.50 |
| AA | EL | 14 | 1 | 4 | 1 | 2 | .357 | .471 | .714 | 79% | 45% | 18% | 2.00 |
| AAA | — | — | — | — | — | — | — | — | — | — | — | — | — |

| Competition at SS | | Stats in 2010 | | | |
|---|---|---|---|---|---|
| Bats | Player | GSvR | GSvL | Sub | OPS |
| ▶ BH | Cabrera A | 65 | 29 | 1 | .673 |
| RH | Donald J | 36 | 10 | 1 | .690 |

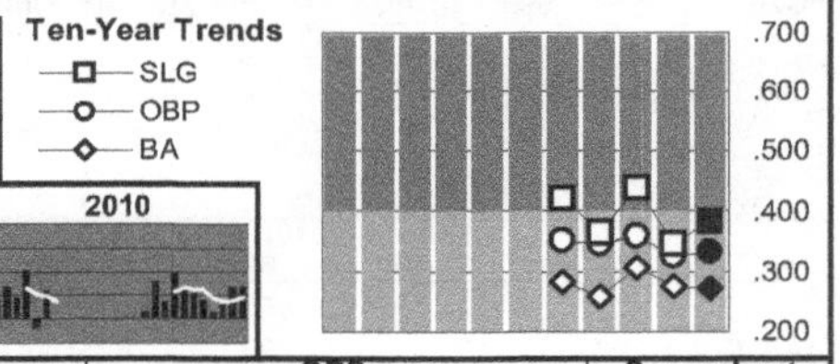


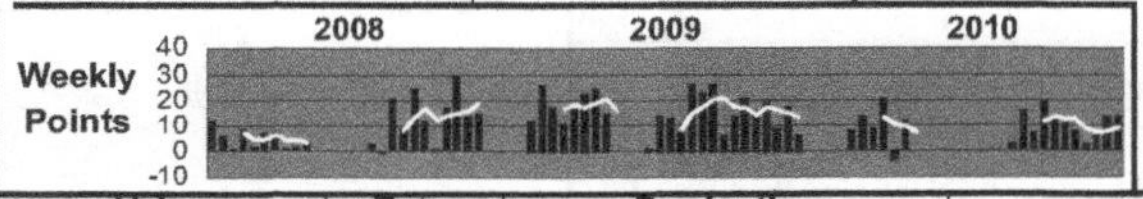


| Yr | Team | AB | HR | R | RBI | SB | BA | OBP | SLG | CT% | H% | BB% | Bash |
|---|---|---|---|---|---|---|---|---|---|---|---|---|---|
| | | Majors | | | | | | | | Skills | | | |
| 07 | CLE | 159 | 3 | 30 | 22 | 0 | .283 | .354 | .421 | 82% | 35% | 9% | 1.49 |
| 08 | CLE | 352 | 6 | 48 | 47 | 4 | .259 | .346 | .366 | 78% | 33% | 11% | 1.42 |
| 09 | CLE | 523 | 6 | 81 | 68 | 17 | .308 | .361 | .438 | 83% | 37% | 8% | 1.42 |
| 10 | CLE | 381 | 3 | 39 | 29 | 6 | .276 | .326 | .346 | 84% | 33% | 6% | 1.26 |

| Yr | $1L | $2L | Pts | RAA | 2B | 3B | CS | FB-LD-GB | HR/fb | RBI% | RS% | OPS | 1st Hf | 2nd Hf | vs RH | vs LH | Rnge | vRH | vLH |
|---|---|---|---|---|---|---|---|---|---|---|---|---|---|---|---|---|---|---|---|
| | Value | | | | Extra | | | Production | | | | OPS | | | | | Scoresheet | | |
| 07 | $2 | -$11 | 110 | +3 | 9 | 2 | 0 | 36-20-44 | 6% | 21% | 44% | .775 | — | .775 | .702 | .950 | 4.75 | — | — |
| 08 | $7 | -$4 | 200 | +0 | 20 | 0 | 4 | 34-21-46 | 7% | 20% | 31% | .713 | .529 | .862 | .638 | .957 | — | −3 | +10 |
| 09 | $19 | $11 | 360 | +23 | 42 | 4 | 4 | 30-22-48 | 5% | 25% | 38% | .799 | .771 | .825 | .815 | .758 | — | −24 | +63 |
| 10 | $6 | -$7 | 170 | −7 | 16 | 1 | 4 | 31-17-52 | 3% | 17% | 27% | .673 | .689 | .663 | .685 | .647 | 4.71 | −13 | +34 |

## Everth Cabrera

**190 PA | $-1 | 90 pts**

SS-61, 2B-6 | Owned: 8% | BH

Cabrera followed up his surprisingly productive rookie season with a stinker. His OBP plummeted, and when he did reach base, hamstring woes made him a non-factor. After the trade deadline, Miguel Tejada took over SS duties, but regardless of whether Tejada returns to SD, Cabrera will face competition. (DG)

| Player | Age | AB | HR | R | RBI | SB | BA | OBP | SLG | $1L | Pts |
|---|---|---|---|---|---|---|---|---|---|---|---|
| | | Forecast | | | | | | | | | |
| Cabrera E | 24 | 163 | 2 | 23 | 15 | 11 | .222 | .309 | .321 | -$1 | 90 |
| **Mini-Browser** | **Age** | **AB** | **HR** | **R** | **RBI** | **SB** | **BA** | **OBP** | **SLG** | **$1L** | **Pts** |
| Blum G | 37 | 226 | 5 | 25 | 30 | 0 | .266 | .325 | .403 | $1 | 130 |
| Wilson J | 33 | 269 | 3 | 27 | 27 | 3 | .268 | .314 | .372 | $1 | 140 |
| Santiago R | 31 | 244 | 3 | 30 | 25 | 3 | .259 | .326 | .362 | $1 | 120 |
| Janish P | 28 | 268 | 6 | 33 | 27 | 3 | .246 | .328 | .375 | $0 | 150 |
| Sanchez A | 27 | 283 | 3 | 30 | 27 | 0 | .254 | .303 | .347 | -$1 | 130 |

| Level | Leag | AB | HR | R | RBI | SB | BA | OBP | SLG | CT% | H% | BB% | Bash |
|---|---|---|---|---|---|---|---|---|---|---|---|---|---|
| | | Minors (2010) | | | | | | | | Skills | | | |
| A | CAL | 10 | 0 | 1 | 1 | 1 | .300 | .417 | .300 | 60% | 50% | 17% | 1.00 |
| AA | — | — | — | — | — | — | — | — | — | — | — | — | — |
| AAA | PCL | 31 | 0 | 7 | 3 | 3 | .258 | .378 | .290 | 58% | 44% | 16% | 1.13 |

| Competition at SS | | Stats in 2010 | | | |
|---|---|---|---|---|---|
| Bats | Player | GSvR | GSvL | Sub | OPS |
| RH | Hairston J | 38 | 21 | 3 | .652 |
| RH | Tejada M | 38 | 20 | 0 | .692 |
| ▶ BH | Cabrera E | 39 | 11 | 11 | .557 |

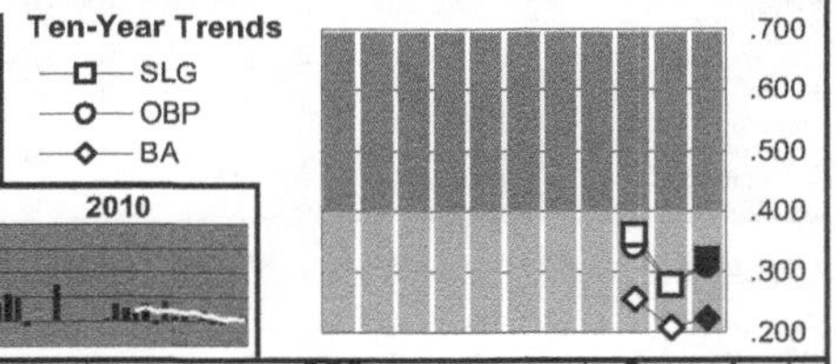


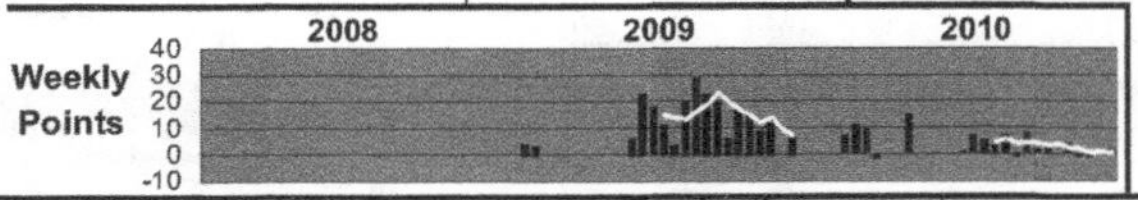


| Yr | Team | AB | HR | R | RBI | SB | BA | OBP | SLG | CT% | H% | BB% | Bash |
|---|---|---|---|---|---|---|---|---|---|---|---|---|---|
| | | Majors | | | | | | | | Skills | | | |
| 07 | — | — | — | — | — | — | — | — | — | — | — | — | — |
| 08 | — | — | — | — | — | — | — | — | — | — | — | — | — |
| 09 | SD | 377 | 2 | 59 | 31 | 25 | .255 | .342 | .361 | 77% | 33% | 10% | 1.42 |
| 10 | SD | 212 | 1 | 22 | 22 | 10 | .208 | .279 | .278 | 75% | 28% | 8% | 1.34 |

| Yr | $1L | $2L | Pts | RAA | 2B | 3B | CS | FB-LD-GB | HR/fb | RBI% | RS% | OPS | 1st Hf | 2nd Hf | vs RH | vs LH | Rnge | vRH | vLH |
|---|---|---|---|---|---|---|---|---|---|---|---|---|---|---|---|---|---|---|---|
| | Value | | | | Extra | | | Production | | | | OPS | | | | | Scoresheet | | |
| 07 | — | — | — | — | — | — | — | — | — | — | — | — | — | — | — | — | — | — | — |
| 08 | — | — | — | — | — | — | — | — | — | — | — | — | — | — | — | — | — | — | — |
| 09 | $10 | -$2 | 230 | −1 | 18 | 8 | 8 | 23-15-63 | 3% | 20% | 39% | .703 | .680 | .710 | .733 | .628 | 4.75 | — | — |
| 10 | -$1 | -$15 | 80 | −15 | 6 | 3 | 6 | 23-22-54 | 3% | 19% | 33% | .557 | .538 | .594 | .545 | .607 | 4.69 | +3 | −7 |

## Melky Cabrera

**500 PA | $8 | 310 pts**

OF-136 (LF-84, CF-56, RF-25) | Owned: 1% | BH

Let's all hold hands and hope that Cabrera is not on the Braves in 2011. He's an OF whose hit rate cannot break 31%, and yet he is due to receive a big payday in arbitration. Melky will probably be non-tendered by ATL and picked up by somebody as a 4th OF who will get way more playing time than he deserves. (MG)

| Player | Age | AB | HR | R | RBI | SB | BA | OBP | SLG | $1L | Pts |
|---|---|---|---|---|---|---|---|---|---|---|---|
| | | Forecast | | | | | | | | | |
| Cabrera M | 26 | 472 | 10 | 55 | 50 | 10 | .265 | .331 | .379 | $8 | 310 |
| **Mini-Browser** | **Age** | **AB** | **HR** | **R** | **RBI** | **SB** | **BA** | **OBP** | **SLG** | **$1L** | **Pts** |
| Carter C | 24 | 442 | 25 | 55 | 65 | 5 | .215 | .306 | .437 | $9 | 240 |
| Bernadina R | 26 | 466 | 10 | 55 | 45 | 25 | .236 | .307 | .359 | $9 | 260 |
| Kearns A | 30 | 402 | 10 | 60 | 55 | 5 | .261 | .355 | .397 | $9 | 240 |
| DeRosa M | 36 | 358 | 12 | 56 | 52 | 4 | .268 | .347 | .438 | $9 | 240 |
| Guillen J | 34 | 326 | 11 | 35 | 49 | 0 | .268 | .319 | .428 | $9 | 180 |

| Level | Leag | AB | HR | R | RBI | SB | BA | OBP | SLG | CT% | H% | BB% | Bash |
|---|---|---|---|---|---|---|---|---|---|---|---|---|---|
| | | Minors (2010) | | | | | | | | Skills | | | |
| A | — | — | — | — | — | — | — | — | — | — | — | — | — |
| AA | — | — | — | — | — | — | — | — | — | — | — | — | — |
| AAA | — | — | — | — | — | — | — | — | — | — | — | — | — |

| Competition at LF | | Stats in 2010 | | | |
|---|---|---|---|---|---|
| Bats | Player | GSvR | GSvL | Sub | OPS |
| ▶ BH | Cabrera M | 45 | 23 | 16 | .671 |
| RH | Diaz M | 12 | 41 | 10 | .739 |
| LH | Hinske E | 50 | 0 | 0 | .793 |
| RH | Infante O | 3 | 8 | 5 | .775 |

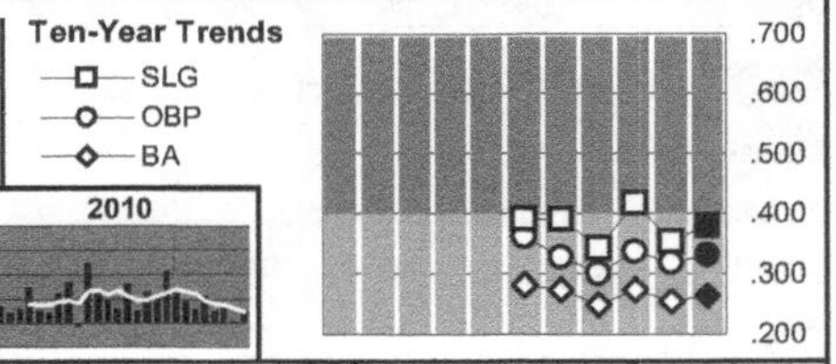


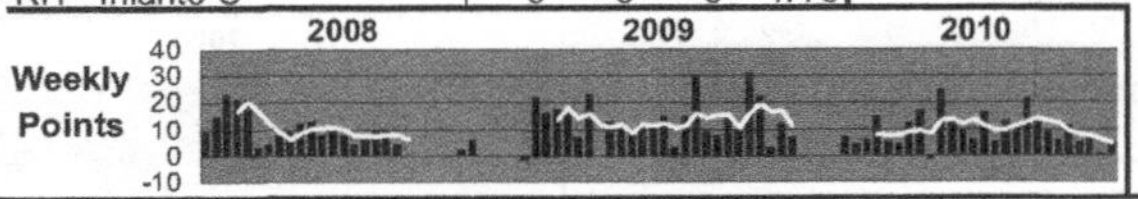


| Yr | Team | AB | HR | R | RBI | SB | BA | OBP | SLG | CT% | H% | BB% | Bash |
|---|---|---|---|---|---|---|---|---|---|---|---|---|---|
| | | Majors | | | | | | | | Skills | | | |
| 07 | NYY | 545 | 8 | 66 | 73 | 13 | .273 | .327 | .391 | 88% | 31% | 7% | 1.43 |
| 08 | NYY | 414 | 8 | 42 | 37 | 9 | .249 | .301 | .341 | 86% | 29% | 6% | 1.37 |
| 09 | NYY | 485 | 13 | 66 | 68 | 10 | .274 | .336 | .416 | 88% | 31% | 8% | 1.52 |
| 10 | ATL | 458 | 4 | 50 | 42 | 7 | .255 | .317 | .354 | 86% | 30% | 8% | 1.38 |

| Yr | $1L | $2L | Pts | RAA | 2B | 3B | CS | FB-LD-GB | HR/fb | RBI% | RS% | OPS | 1st Hf | 2nd Hf | vs RH | vs LH | Rnge | vRH | vLH |
|---|---|---|---|---|---|---|---|---|---|---|---|---|---|---|---|---|---|---|---|
| | Value | | | | Extra | | | Production | | | | OPS | | | | | Scoresheet | | |
| 07 | $14 | $4 | 350 | −16 | 24 | 8 | 5 | 29-20-51 | 6% | 21% | 31% | .718 | .716 | .720 | .747 | .641 | 2.07 | +5 | −16 |
| 08 | $6 | -$6 | 210 | −21 | 12 | 1 | 2 | 35-19-46 | 6% | 13% | 27% | .641 | .648 | .617 | .670 | .578 | 2.13 | +11 | −29 |
| 09 | $14 | $5 | 340 | −4 | 28 | 1 | 2 | 30-21-50 | 10% | 20% | 32% | .752 | .786 | .718 | .747 | .763 | 2.17 | +11 | −29 |
| 10 | $6 | -$6 | 240 | −19 | 27 | 3 | 1 | 32-19-49 | 3% | 15% | 29% | .671 | .664 | .681 | .685 | .642 | 2.15 | +2 | −6 |

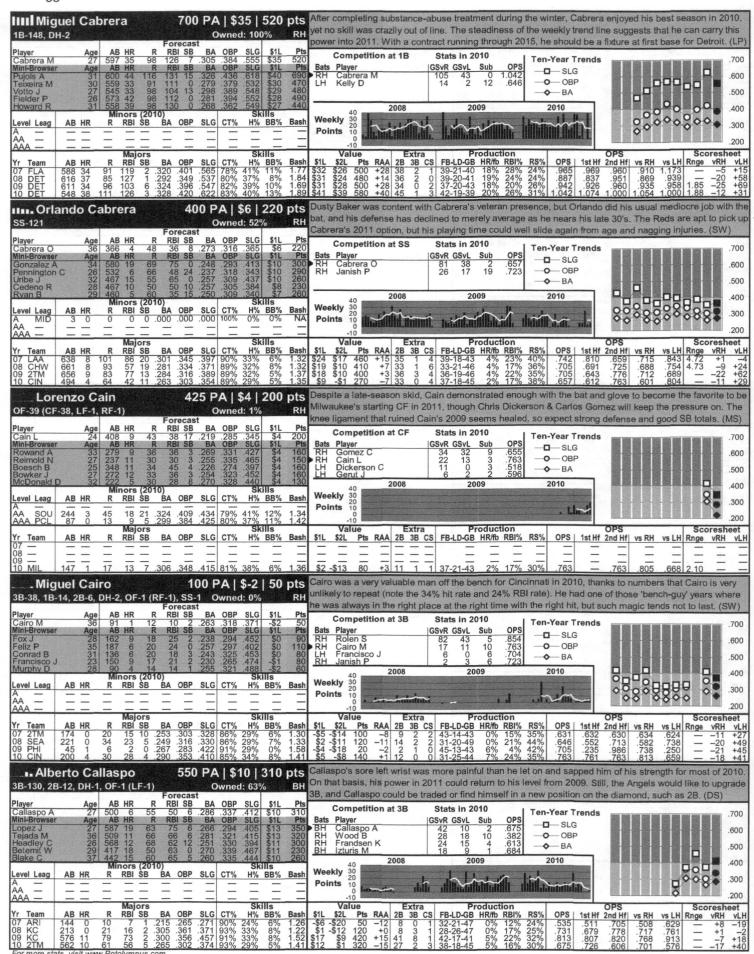

## IIIII Miguel Cabrera — 700 PA | $35 | 520 pts

1B-148, DH-2    Owned: 100%    RH

After completing substance-abuse treatment during the winter, Cabrera enjoyed his best season in 2010, yet no skill was crazily out of line. The steadiness of the weekly trend line suggests that he can carry this power into 2011. With a contract running through 2015, he should be a fixture at first base for Detroit. (LP)

### Forecast

| Player | Age | AB | HR | R | RBI | SB | BA | OBP | SLG | $1L | Pts |
|---|---|---|---|---|---|---|---|---|---|---|---|
| Cabrera M | 27 | 597 | 35 | 98 | 126 | 7 | .305 | .384 | .555 | $35 | 520 |
| Mini-Browser | Age | AB | HR | R | RBI | SB | BA | OBP | SLG | $1L | Pts |
| Pujols A | 31 | 600 | 44 | 116 | 131 | 15 | .326 | .436 | .618 | $40 | 690 |
| Teixeira M | 30 | 559 | 33 | 101 | 111 | 0 | .279 | .379 | .532 | $30 | 470 |
| Votto J | 27 | 545 | 33 | 98 | 104 | 13 | .298 | .389 | .548 | $29 | 480 |
| Fielder P | 26 | 573 | 42 | 98 | 112 | 0 | .281 | .394 | .552 | $28 | 490 |
| Howard R | 31 | 558 | 39 | 98 | 130 | 0 | .268 | .362 | .549 | $27 | 440 |

### Minors (2010) / Skills

| Level | Leag | AB | HR | R | RBI | SB | BA | OBP | SLG | CT% | H% | BB% | Bash |
|---|---|---|---|---|---|---|---|---|---|---|---|---|---|
| A | — | — | — | — | — | — | — | — | — | — | — | — | — |
| AA | — | — | — | — | — | — | — | — | — | — | — | — | — |
| AAA | — | — | — | — | — | — | — | — | — | — | — | — | — |

### Competition at 1B / Stats in 2010

| Bats | Player | GSvR | GSvL | Sub | OPS |
|---|---|---|---|---|---|
| RH | Cabrera M | 105 | 43 | 0 | 1.042 |
| LH | Kelly D | 14 | 2 | 12 | .646 |

### Majors / Skills / Value / Extra / Production / OPS / Scoresheet

| Yr | Team | AB | HR | R | RBI | SB | BA | OBP | SLG | CT% | H% | BB% | Bash | $1L | $2L | Pts | RAA | 2B | 3B | CS | FB-LD-GB | HR/fb | RBI% | RS% | OPS | 1st Hf | 2nd Hf | vs RH | vs LH | Rnge | vRH | vLH |
|---|---|---|---|---|---|---|---|---|---|---|---|---|---|---|---|---|---|---|---|---|---|---|---|---|---|---|---|---|---|---|---|---|
| 07 | FLA | 588 | 34 | 91 | 119 | 2 | .320 | .401 | .565 | 78% | 41% | 11% | 1.77 | $32 | $26 | 500 | +28 | 38 | 2 | 1 | 39-21-40 | 18% | 28% | 24% | .965 | .969 | .960 | .910 | 1.173 | — | -5 | +15 |
| 08 | DET | 616 | 37 | 85 | 127 | 1 | .292 | .349 | .537 | 80% | 37% | 8% | 1.84 | $31 | $24 | 480 | +14 | 36 | 2 | 0 | 39-20-41 | 19% | 24% | 24% | .887 | .837 | .951 | .869 | .939 | — | -20 | +58 |
| 09 | DET | 611 | 34 | 96 | 103 | 6 | .324 | .396 | .547 | 82% | 39% | 10% | 1.69 | $31 | $28 | 500 | +28 | 34 | 0 | 2 | 37-20-43 | 18% | 20% | 26% | .942 | .926 | .960 | .935 | .958 | 1.85 | -25 | +69 |
| 10 | DET | 548 | 38 | 111 | 126 | 3 | .328 | .420 | .622 | 83% | 40% | 13% | 1.89 | $41 | $39 | 580 | +40 | 45 | 1 | 3 | 42-19-39 | 20% | 26% | 31% | 1.042 | 1.074 | 1.002 | 1.000 | 1.088 | 1.88 | -12 | +31 |

## IIII. Orlando Cabrera — 400 PA | $6 | 220 pts

SS-121    Owned: 52%    RH

Dusty Baker was content with Cabrera's veteran presence, but Orlando did his usual mediocre job with the bat, and his defense has declined to merely average as he nears his late 30's. The Reds are apt to pick up Cabrera's 2011 option, but his playing time could well slide again from age and nagging injuries. (SW)

### Forecast

| Player | Age | AB | HR | R | RBI | SB | BA | OBP | SLG | $1L | Pts |
|---|---|---|---|---|---|---|---|---|---|---|---|
| Cabrera O | 36 | 366 | 4 | 48 | 36 | 8 | .273 | .316 | .365 | $6 | 220 |
| Mini-Browser | Age | AB | HR | R | RBI | SB | BA | OBP | SLG | $1L | Pts |
| Gonzalez A | 34 | 580 | 19 | 69 | 75 | 0 | .248 | .293 | .413 | $10 | 300 |
| Pennington C | 26 | 532 | 6 | 66 | 48 | 24 | .237 | .318 | .343 | $10 | 290 |
| Uribe J | 32 | 467 | 15 | 55 | 65 | 0 | .257 | .309 | .437 | $10 | 260 |
| Cedeno R | 28 | 467 | 10 | 50 | 50 | 10 | .257 | .305 | .384 | $8 | 230 |
| Ryan B | 29 | 460 | 5 | 60 | 35 | 15 | .250 | .305 | .340 | $7 | 260 |

### Minors (2010) / Skills

| Level | Leag | AB | HR | R | RBI | SB | BA | OBP | SLG | CT% | H% | BB% | Bash |
|---|---|---|---|---|---|---|---|---|---|---|---|---|---|
| A | MID | 3 | 0 | 0 | 0 | 0 | .000 | .000 | .000 | 100% | 0% | 0% | NA |
| AA | — | — | — | — | — | — | — | — | — | — | — | — | — |
| AAA | — | — | — | — | — | — | — | — | — | — | — | — | — |

### Competition at SS / Stats in 2010

| Bats | Player | GSvR | GSvL | Sub | OPS |
|---|---|---|---|---|---|
| RH | Cabrera O | 81 | 38 | 2 | .657 |
| RH | Janish P | 26 | 17 | 19 | .723 |

### Majors / Skills / Value / Extra / Production / OPS / Scoresheet

| Yr | Team | AB | HR | R | RBI | SB | BA | OBP | SLG | CT% | H% | BB% | Bash | $1L | $2L | Pts | RAA | 2B | 3B | CS | FB-LD-GB | HR/fb | RBI% | RS% | OPS | 1st Hf | 2nd Hf | vs RH | vs LH | Rnge | vRH | vLH |
|---|---|---|---|---|---|---|---|---|---|---|---|---|---|---|---|---|---|---|---|---|---|---|---|---|---|---|---|---|---|---|---|---|
| 07 | LAA | 638 | 8 | 101 | 86 | 20 | .301 | .345 | .397 | 90% | 33% | 6% | 1.32 | $24 | $17 | 460 | +15 | 35 | 1 | 4 | 39-18-43 | 4% | 23% | 40% | .742 | .810 | .659 | .715 | .843 | 4.72 | +1 | -4 |
| 08 | CHW | 661 | 8 | 93 | 57 | 19 | .281 | .334 | .371 | 89% | 32% | 8% | 1.32 | $19 | $10 | 410 | +7 | 33 | 1 | 6 | 33-21-46 | 4% | 17% | 36% | .705 | .691 | .725 | .688 | .754 | 4.73 | -9 | +24 |
| 09 | 2TM | 656 | 9 | 83 | 77 | 13 | .284 | .316 | .389 | 89% | 32% | 5% | 1.37 | $18 | $10 | 400 | +3 | 36 | 3 | 4 | 36-19-46 | 4% | 22% | 35% | .705 | .643 | .776 | .712 | .689 | — | -22 | +40 |
| 10 | CIN | 494 | 4 | 64 | 42 | 11 | .263 | .303 | .354 | 89% | 29% | 5% | 1.35 | $9 | -$1 | 270 | -7 | 33 | 4 | 3 | 37-18-45 | 2% | 17% | 38% | .657 | .612 | .763 | .601 | .804 | — | -11 | +29 |

## Lorenzo Cain — 425 PA | $4 | 200 pts

OF-39 (CF-38, LF-1, RF-1)    Owned: 1%    RH

Despite a late-season skid, Cain demonstrated enough with the bat and glove to become the favorite to be Milwaukee's starting CF in 2011, though Chris Dickerson & Carlos Gomez will keep the pressure on. The knee ligament that ruined Cain's 2009 seems healed, so expect strong defense and good SB totals. (MS)

### Forecast

| Player | Age | AB | HR | R | RBI | SB | BA | OBP | SLG | $1L | Pts |
|---|---|---|---|---|---|---|---|---|---|---|---|
| Cain L | 24 | 408 | 9 | 43 | 38 | 17 | .219 | .285 | .345 | $4 | 200 |
| Mini-Browser | Age | AB | HR | R | RBI | SB | BA | OBP | SLG | $1L | Pts |
| Rowand A | 33 | 279 | 9 | 36 | 36 | 3 | .269 | .331 | .427 | $4 | 160 |
| Reimold N | 27 | 237 | 11 | 30 | 30 | 3 | .255 | .335 | .465 | $4 | 150 |
| Boesch B | 25 | 348 | 11 | 34 | 45 | 4 | .226 | .274 | .397 | $4 | 160 |
| Bowker J | 27 | 272 | 12 | 33 | 36 | 3 | .254 | .323 | .452 | $4 | 160 |
| McDonald D | 32 | 222 | 5 | 30 | 28 | 6 | .270 | .328 | .440 | $4 | 130 |

### Minors (2010) / Skills

| Level | Leag | AB | HR | R | RBI | SB | BA | OBP | SLG | CT% | H% | BB% | Bash |
|---|---|---|---|---|---|---|---|---|---|---|---|---|---|
| A | — | — | — | — | — | — | — | — | — | — | — | — | — |
| AA | SOU | 244 | 3 | 45 | 18 | 21 | .324 | .409 | .434 | 79% | 41% | 12% | 1.34 |
| AAA | PCL | 87 | 0 | 13 | 9 | 5 | .299 | .384 | .425 | 80% | 37% | 11% | 1.42 |

### Competition at CF / Stats in 2010

| Bats | Player | GSvR | GSvL | Sub | OPS |
|---|---|---|---|---|---|
| RH | Gomez C | 34 | 32 | 9 | .655 |
| RH | Cain L | 22 | 13 | 3 | .763 |
| LH | Dickerson C | 11 | 0 | 3 | .518 |
| LH | Gerut J | 6 | 2 | 2 | .596 |

### Majors / Skills / Value / Extra / Production / OPS / Scoresheet

| Yr | Team | AB | HR | R | RBI | SB | BA | OBP | SLG | CT% | H% | BB% | Bash | $1L | $2L | Pts | RAA | 2B | 3B | CS | FB-LD-GB | HR/fb | RBI% | RS% | OPS | 1st Hf | 2nd Hf | vs RH | vs LH | Rnge | vRH | vLH |
|---|---|---|---|---|---|---|---|---|---|---|---|---|---|---|---|---|---|---|---|---|---|---|---|---|---|---|---|---|---|---|---|---|
| 07 | — | — | — | — | — | — | — | — | — | — | — | — | — | — | — | — | — | — | — | — | — | — | — | — | — | — | — | — | — | — | — | — |
| 08 | — | — | — | — | — | — | — | — | — | — | — | — | — | — | — | — | — | — | — | — | — | — | — | — | — | — | — | — | — | — | — | — |
| 09 | — | — | — | — | — | — | — | — | — | — | — | — | — | — | — | — | — | — | — | — | — | — | — | — | — | — | — | — | — | — | — | — |
| 10 | MIL | 147 | 1 | 17 | 13 | 7 | .306 | .348 | .415 | 81% | 38% | 6% | 1.36 | $2 | -$13 | 80 | +3 | 11 | 1 | 1 | 37-21-43 | 2% | 17% | 30% | .763 | | .763 | .805 | .668 | 2.10 | | |

## . Miguel Cairo — 100 PA | $-2 | 50 pts

3B-38, 1B-14, 2B-6, DH-2, OF-1 (RF-1), SS-1    Owned: 0%    RH

Cairo was a very valuable man off the bench for Cincinnati in 2010, thanks to numbers that Cairo is very unlikely to repeat (note the 34% hit rate and 24% RBI rate). He had one of those 'bench-guy' years where he was always in the right place at the right time with the right hit, but such magic tends not to last. (SW)

### Forecast

| Player | Age | AB | HR | R | RBI | SB | BA | OBP | SLG | $1L | Pts |
|---|---|---|---|---|---|---|---|---|---|---|---|
| Cairo M | 36 | 91 | 1 | 12 | 10 | 2 | .263 | .318 | .371 | -$2 | 50 |
| Mini-Browser | Age | AB | HR | R | RBI | SB | BA | OBP | SLG | $1L | Pts |
| Fox J | 28 | 162 | 9 | 18 | 25 | 2 | .238 | .294 | .452 | $0 | 90 |
| Feliz P | 35 | 187 | 6 | 20 | 24 | 0 | .257 | .297 | .402 | $0 | 110 |
| Conrad B | 31 | 136 | 6 | 20 | 18 | 3 | .243 | .325 | .453 | $0 | 80 |
| Francisco J | 23 | 150 | 9 | 17 | 21 | 1 | .230 | .265 | .474 | -$1 | 80 |
| Murphy D | 28 | 90 | 4 | 14 | 14 | 1 | .255 | .321 | .448 | -$2 | 60 |

### Minors (2010) / Skills

| Level | Leag | AB | HR | R | RBI | SB | BA | OBP | SLG | CT% | H% | BB% | Bash |
|---|---|---|---|---|---|---|---|---|---|---|---|---|---|
| A | — | — | — | — | — | — | — | — | — | — | — | — | — |
| AA | — | — | — | — | — | — | — | — | — | — | — | — | — |
| AAA | — | — | — | — | — | — | — | — | — | — | — | — | — |

### Competition at 3B / Stats in 2010

| Bats | Player | GSvR | GSvL | Sub | OPS |
|---|---|---|---|---|---|
| RH | Rolen S | 82 | 43 | 5 | .854 |
| RH | Cairo M | 17 | 11 | 10 | .763 |
| LH | Francisco J | 6 | 0 | 6 | .704 |
| RH | Janish P | 2 | 3 | 6 | .723 |

### Majors / Skills / Value / Extra / Production / OPS / Scoresheet

| Yr | Team | AB | HR | R | RBI | SB | BA | OBP | SLG | CT% | H% | BB% | Bash | $1L | $2L | Pts | RAA | 2B | 3B | CS | FB-LD-GB | HR/fb | RBI% | RS% | OPS | 1st Hf | 2nd Hf | vs RH | vs LH | Rnge | vRH | vLH |
|---|---|---|---|---|---|---|---|---|---|---|---|---|---|---|---|---|---|---|---|---|---|---|---|---|---|---|---|---|---|---|---|---|
| 07 | 2TM | 174 | 0 | 20 | 15 | 10 | .253 | .303 | .328 | 86% | 29% | 6% | 1.30 | -$5 | -$14 | 100 | -8 | 9 | 2 | 2 | 43-14-43 | 0% | 15% | 35% | .631 | .632 | .630 | .634 | .624 | — | -11 | +27 |
| 08 | SEA | 221 | 0 | 34 | 23 | 5 | .249 | .316 | .330 | 86% | 29% | 7% | 1.33 | -$2 | -$11 | 120 | -11 | 14 | 2 | 2 | 31-20-49 | 0% | 21% | 44% | .646 | .552 | .713 | .582 | .738 | — | -20 | +49 |
| 09 | PHI | 45 | 1 | 6 | 2 | 0 | .267 | .283 | .422 | 91% | 29% | 0% | 1.58 | -$4 | -$18 | 20 | -2 | 2 | 0 | 0 | 45-13-43 | 6% | 4% | 42% | .705 | .235 | .986 | .738 | .250 | — | -18 | +41 |
| 10 | CIN | 200 | 4 | 30 | 28 | 4 | .290 | .353 | .410 | 85% | 34% | 8% | 1.41 | $5 | -$8 | 140 | +1 | 12 | 0 | 0 | 31-25-44 | 7% | 24% | 35% | .763 | .761 | .763 | .813 | .659 | — | -18 | +41 |

## . Alberto Callaspo — 550 PA | $10 | 310 pts

3B-130, 2B-12, DH-1, OF-1 (LF-1)    Owned: 63%    BH

Callaspo's sore left wrist was more painful than he let on and sapped him of his strength for most of 2010. On that basis, his power in 2011 could return to his level from 2009. Still, the Angels would like to upgrade 3B, and Callaspo could be traded or find himself in a new position on the diamond, such as 2B. (DS)

### Forecast

| Player | Age | AB | HR | R | RBI | SB | BA | OBP | SLG | $1L | Pts |
|---|---|---|---|---|---|---|---|---|---|---|---|
| Callaspo A | 27 | 500 | 6 | 55 | 50 | 6 | .286 | .337 | .412 | $10 | 310 |
| Mini-Browser | Age | AB | HR | R | RBI | SB | BA | OBP | SLG | $1L | Pts |
| Lopez J | 27 | 587 | 19 | 63 | 75 | 6 | .266 | .294 | .405 | $13 | 350 |
| Tejada M | 36 | 509 | 11 | 66 | 66 | 6 | .281 | .321 | .415 | $13 | 320 |
| Headley C | 26 | 568 | 12 | 68 | 62 | 12 | .251 | .330 | .394 | $11 | 300 |
| Betemit W | 29 | 417 | 18 | 50 | 63 | 0 | .270 | .339 | .467 | $11 | 230 |
| Blake C | 37 | 442 | 15 | 60 | 65 | 5 | .260 | .335 | .444 | $10 | 230 |

### Minors (2010) / Skills

| Level | Leag | AB | HR | R | RBI | SB | BA | OBP | SLG | CT% | H% | BB% | Bash |
|---|---|---|---|---|---|---|---|---|---|---|---|---|---|
| A | — | — | — | — | — | — | — | — | — | — | — | — | — |
| AA | — | — | — | — | — | — | — | — | — | — | — | — | — |
| AAA | — | — | — | — | — | — | — | — | — | — | — | — | — |

### Competition at 3B / Stats in 2010

| Bats | Player | GSvR | GSvL | Sub | OPS |
|---|---|---|---|---|---|
| BH | Callaspo A | 42 | 10 | 2 | .675 |
| RH | Wood B | 28 | 18 | 10 | .382 |
| RH | Frandsen K | 24 | 15 | 4 | .613 |
| BH | Izturis M | 18 | 9 | 1 | .684 |

### Majors / Skills / Value / Extra / Production / OPS / Scoresheet

| Yr | Team | AB | HR | R | RBI | SB | BA | OBP | SLG | CT% | H% | BB% | Bash | $1L | $2L | Pts | RAA | 2B | 3B | CS | FB-LD-GB | HR/fb | RBI% | RS% | OPS | 1st Hf | 2nd Hf | vs RH | vs LH | Rnge | vRH | vLH |
|---|---|---|---|---|---|---|---|---|---|---|---|---|---|---|---|---|---|---|---|---|---|---|---|---|---|---|---|---|---|---|---|---|
| 07 | ARI | 144 | 0 | 10 | 7 | 1 | .215 | .265 | .271 | 90% | 24% | 6% | 1.26 | -$6 | -$20 | 50 | -12 | 8 | 0 | 1 | 32-21-47 | 0% | 12% | 24% | .535 | .511 | .705 | .508 | .629 | — | +8 | -19 |
| 08 | KC | 213 | 0 | 21 | 16 | 2 | .305 | .361 | .371 | 93% | 33% | 8% | 1.22 | $1 | -$12 | 120 | +0 | 8 | 3 | 1 | 28-26-47 | 0% | 17% | 25% | .731 | .679 | .778 | .717 | .761 | — | +1 | -2 |
| 09 | KC | 561 | 11 | 79 | 73 | 2 | .300 | .356 | .457 | 91% | 33% | 8% | 1.52 | $17 | $9 | 420 | +15 | 41 | 8 | 1 | 42-17-41 | 5% | 22% | 32% | .813 | .807 | .820 | .768 | .913 | — | -7 | +18 |
| 10 | 2TM | 562 | 10 | 61 | 56 | 5 | .265 | .302 | .374 | 93% | 29% | 5% | 1.41 | $12 | $1 | 320 | -15 | 27 | 2 | 1 | 38-18-45 | 5% | 16% | 30% | .675 | .726 | .606 | .701 | .576 | — | -17 | +41 |

## Mike Cameron — 400 PA | $11 | 240 pts
OF-46 (CF-46)  Owned: 16%  RH

Cameron is still a welcome member of the Red Sox family, believe it or not. He might be platooned slightly in 2011, but he should be considered a starter until the FA market shakes out. The team is expected to bid heavily for Carl Crawford and Jayson Werth, whose arrivals could push Cameron to a 4th OF role. (EB)

### Forecast
| Player | Age | AB | HR | R | RBI | SB | BA | OBP | SLG | $1L | Pts |
|---|---|---|---|---|---|---|---|---|---|---|---|
| Cameron M | 38 | 365 | 16 | 56 | 48 | 8 | .263 | .344 | .481 | $11 | 240 |

| Mini-Browser | Age | AB | HR | R | RBI | SB | BA | OBP | SLG | $1L | Pts |
|---|---|---|---|---|---|---|---|---|---|---|---|
| Morrison L | 23 | 535 | 18 | 72 | 66 | 6 | .258 | .354 | .438 | $12 | 360 |
| Murphy D | 29 | 395 | 13 | 51 | 55 | 9 | .286 | .341 | .454 | $12 | 270 |
| Hawpe B | 31 | 335 | 16 | 52 | 60 | 0 | .275 | .376 | .501 | $11 | 240 |
| Sweeney R | 26 | 554 | 6 | 66 | 60 | 6 | .271 | .332 | .375 | $11 | 310 |
| Joyce M | 26 | 430 | 20 | 55 | 65 | 5 | .244 | .338 | .470 | $11 | 280 |

### Minors (2010) / Skills
| Level | Leag | AB | HR | R | RBI | SB | BA | OBP | SLG | CT% | H% | BB% | Bash |
|---|---|---|---|---|---|---|---|---|---|---|---|---|---|
| A | — | | | | | | | | | | | | |
| AA | EL | 13 | 2 | 4 | 3 | 0 | .385 | .385 | 1.000 | 69% | 56% | 0% | 2.60 |
| AAA | IL | 14 | 1 | 3 | 3 | 0 | .286 | .421 | .571 | 71% | 40% | 21% | 2.00 |

### Majors / Skills / Value / Extra / Production / OPS / Scoresheet
| Yr | Team | AB | HR | R | RBI | SB | BA | OBP | SLG | CT% | H% | BB% | Bash | $1L | $2L | Pts | RAA | 2B | 3B | CS | FB-LD-GB | HR/fb | RBI% | RS% | OPS | 1st Hf | 2nd Hf | vs RH | vs LH | Rnge | vRH | vLH |
|---|---|---|---|---|---|---|---|---|---|---|---|---|---|---|---|---|---|---|---|---|---|---|---|---|---|---|---|---|---|---|---|---|
| 07 | SD | 571 | 21 | 88 | 78 | 18 | .242 | .328 | .431 | 72% | 34% | 10% | 1.78 | $17 | $9 | 350 | +1 | 33 | 6 | 5 | 44-19-37 | 12% | 20% | 35% | .759 | .771 | .742 | .700 | .914 | 2.19 | -15 | +42 |
| 08 | MIL | 444 | 25 | 69 | 70 | 17 | .243 | .331 | .477 | 68% | 36% | 11% | 1.96 | $17 | $9 | 290 | +9 | 25 | 2 | 5 | 46-22-33 | 18% | 21% | 31% | .809 | .801 | .816 | .761 | .951 | 2.17 | -23 | +61 |
| 09 | MIL | 544 | 24 | 78 | 70 | 7 | .250 | .342 | .452 | 71% | 35% | 12% | 1.81 | $16 | $7 | 320 | +10 | 32 | 3 | 3 | 48-17-35 | 13% | 15% | 28% | .795 | .839 | .743 | .748 | .954 | 2.17 | -35 | +90 |
| 10 | BOS | 162 | 4 | 24 | 15 | 0 | .259 | .328 | .401 | 73% | 36% | 8% | 1.55 | $1 | -$1 | 90 | -2 | 11 | 0 | 1 | 55-16-29 | 6% | 13% | 36% | .729 | .758 | .649 | .588 | 1.128 | 2.19 | -29 | +78 |

### Competition at CF / Stats in 2010
| Bats | Player | GSvR | GSvL | Sub | OPS |
|---|---|---|---|---|---|
| RH | McDonald D | 22 | 30 | 17 | .766 |
| RH | Cameron M | 28 | 15 | 3 | .729 |
| LH | Kalish R | 24 | 9 | 5 | .710 |
| LH | Ellsbury J | 11 | 2 | 0 | .485 |

---

## Robinson Cano — 675 PA | $25 | 450 pts
2B-158, DH-2  Owned: 100%  LH

Cano was the Yankees' best hitter in 2010 – an amazing fact in light of the talent on the team. The lion's share of his improvement in 2010 rested on a doubled BB%. The durable Cano (check the weekly logs – he has missed only 8 games in 4 seasons) should continue to excel as he enters his prime years. (LS)

### Forecast
| Player | Age | AB | HR | R | RBI | SB | BA | OBP | SLG | $1L | Pts |
|---|---|---|---|---|---|---|---|---|---|---|---|
| Cano R | 28 | 636 | 20 | 88 | 88 | 0 | .297 | .341 | .485 | $25 | 450 |

| Mini-Browser | Age | AB | HR | R | RBI | SB | BA | OBP | SLG | $1L | Pts |
|---|---|---|---|---|---|---|---|---|---|---|---|
| Utley C | 32 | 542 | 26 | 104 | 98 | 13 | .288 | .387 | .517 | $28 | 480 |
| Kinsler I | 28 | 545 | 24 | 96 | 72 | 24 | .286 | .361 | .486 | $27 | 470 |
| Weeks R | 28 | 651 | 30 | 120 | 75 | 23 | .265 | .363 | .468 | $25 | 460 |
| Pedroia D | 27 | 577 | 13 | 98 | 65 | 13 | .304 | .372 | .465 | $25 | 460 |
| Phillips B | 29 | 589 | 20 | 91 | 85 | 26 | .276 | .329 | .458 | $24 | 450 |

### Minors (2010) / Skills
| Level | Leag | AB | HR | R | RBI | SB | BA | OBP | SLG | CT% | H% | BB% | Bash |
|---|---|---|---|---|---|---|---|---|---|---|---|---|---|
| A | — | | | | | | | | | | | | |
| AA | — | | | | | | | | | | | | |
| AAA | — | | | | | | | | | | | | |

### Majors / Skills / Value / Extra / Production / OPS / Scoresheet
| Yr | Team | AB | HR | R | RBI | SB | BA | OBP | SLG | CT% | H% | BB% | Bash | $1L | $2L | Pts | RAA | 2B | 3B | CS | FB-LD-GB | HR/fb | RBI% | RS% | OPS | 1st Hf | 2nd Hf | vs RH | vs LH | Rnge | vRH | vLH |
|---|---|---|---|---|---|---|---|---|---|---|---|---|---|---|---|---|---|---|---|---|---|---|---|---|---|---|---|---|---|---|---|---|
| 07 | NYY | 617 | 19 | 93 | 97 | 4 | .306 | .353 | .488 | 86% | 36% | 6% | 1.59 | $24 | $18 | 450 | +18 | 41 | 7 | 5 | 31-17-52 | 12% | 21% | 34% | .841 | .741 | .953 | .831 | .864 | 4.23 | +38 | -112 |
| 08 | NYY | 597 | 14 | 70 | 72 | 2 | .271 | .305 | .410 | 89% | 30% | 4% | 1.51 | $14 | $5 | 350 | -6 | 39 | 5 | 4 | 33-20-47 | 8% | 17% | 31% | .715 | .643 | .815 | .683 | .794 | 4.29 | +25 | -70 |
| 09 | NYY | 637 | 25 | 103 | 85 | 5 | .320 | .352 | .520 | 90% | 36% | 4% | 1.62 | $27 | $23 | 490 | +29 | 48 | 2 | 3 | 33-20-47 | 13% | 15% | 37% | .871 | .831 | .922 | .869 | .876 | 4.25 | +4 | -10 |
| 10 | NYY | 626 | 29 | 103 | 109 | 3 | .319 | .381 | .534 | 88% | 36% | 8% | 1.67 | $35 | $32 | 530 | +36 | 41 | 3 | 2 | 36-19-44 | 14% | 23% | 31% | .914 | .944 | .878 | .944 | .857 | 4.24 | +4 | -10 |

### Competition at 2B / Stats in 2010
| Bats | Player | GSvR | GSvL | Sub | OPS |
|---|---|---|---|---|---|
| LH | Cano R | 102 | 55 | 1 | .914 |

---

## Jorge Cantu — 150 PA | $0 | 90 pts
3B-89, 1B-63, DH-9, 2B-1  Owned: 73%  RH

Cantu has the visage of another interchangeable piece in the dime-a-dozen bin of LHP-mashers, but his spurts of serious power, and his moderate effectiveness vs. RHP, keep him employed and relevant. His days of playing (a terrible) 2B/3B are over, leaving him tied to 1B/DH, where he's suited to platoon. (JM)

### Forecast
| Player | Age | AB | HR | R | RBI | SB | BA | OBP | SLG | $1L | Pts |
|---|---|---|---|---|---|---|---|---|---|---|---|
| Cantu J | 29 | 136 | 5 | 18 | 21 | 0 | .276 | .331 | .452 | $0 | 90 |

| Mini-Browser | Age | AB | HR | R | RBI | SB | BA | OBP | SLG | $1L | Pts |
|---|---|---|---|---|---|---|---|---|---|---|---|
| Kotchman C | 28 | 218 | 5 | 23 | 30 | 0 | .264 | .331 | .401 | $1 | 140 |
| Garko R | 30 | 182 | 8 | 20 | 26 | 0 | .264 | .339 | .431 | $1 | 110 |
| Hoffpauir M | 31 | 132 | 6 | 20 | 23 | 0 | .272 | .327 | .487 | $0 | 90 |
| Belt B | 22 | 129 | 4 | 19 | 20 | 4 | .270 | .364 | .457 | $0 | 90 |
| Giambi J | 40 | 147 | 7 | 19 | 26 | 0 | .238 | .370 | .441 | $0 | 100 |

### Minors (2010) / Skills
| Level | Leag | AB | HR | R | RBI | SB | BA | OBP | SLG | CT% | H% | BB% | Bash |
|---|---|---|---|---|---|---|---|---|---|---|---|---|---|
| A | — | | | | | | | | | | | | |
| AA | — | | | | | | | | | | | | |
| AAA | — | | | | | | | | | | | | |

### Majors / Skills / Value / Extra / Production / OPS / Scoresheet
| Yr | Team | AB | HR | R | RBI | SB | BA | OBP | SLG | CT% | H% | BB% | Bash | $1L | $2L | Pts | RAA | 2B | 3B | CS | FB-LD-GB | HR/fb | RBI% | RS% | OPS | 1st Hf | 2nd Hf | vs RH | vs LH | Rnge | vRH | vLH |
|---|---|---|---|---|---|---|---|---|---|---|---|---|---|---|---|---|---|---|---|---|---|---|---|---|---|---|---|---|---|---|---|---|
| 07 | 2TM | 115 | 1 | 12 | 13 | 0 | .252 | .331 | .357 | 77% | 33% | 9% | 1.41 | -$8 | -$17 | 50 | -6 | 9 | 0 | 0 | 34-22-45 | 3% | 17% | 26% | .687 | .509 | .860 | .765 | .635 | — | -4 | +11 |
| 08 | FLA | 628 | 29 | 92 | 95 | 6 | .277 | .327 | .481 | 82% | 34% | 6% | 1.74 | $23 | $18 | 430 | -7 | 41 | 0 | 2 | 45-21-34 | 12% | 20% | 32% | .808 | .819 | .792 | .789 | .869 | 1.85 | -13 | +29 |
| 09 | FLA | 585 | 16 | 67 | 100 | 3 | .289 | .345 | .443 | 86% | 34% | 7% | 1.53 | $19 | $10 | 400 | -6 | 42 | 0 | 1 | 43-21-36 | 7% | 21% | 25% | .788 | .787 | .789 | .754 | .892 | 1.84 | +15 | +37 |
| 10 | 2TM | 472 | 11 | 50 | 56 | 0 | .256 | .304 | .392 | 80% | 32% | 5% | 1.53 | $9 | -$3 | 220 | -24 | 29 | 1 | 0 | 39-21-40 | 7% | 17% | 27% | .695 | .734 | .606 | .716 | .647 | 1.84 | -20 | +55 |

### Competition at 1B / Stats in 2010
| Bats | Player | GSvR | GSvL | Sub | OPS |
|---|---|---|---|---|---|
| LH | Moreland M | 35 | 3 | 2 | .833 |
| LH | Davis C | 23 | 7 | 11 | .571 |
| RH | Cantu J | 4 | 17 | 2 | .695 |

---

## Mike Carp — 50 PA | $-5 | 20 pts
1B-9, DH-1, OF-1 (LF-1)  Owned: 0%  LH

Carp continues to perform as a 'Quad-A' player – he is a little too good for the minors but not quite skilled enough to warrant a regular job in the majors. His 2011 season will probably be spent much like his 2010 season – in Triple-A. (GC)

### Forecast
| Player | Age | AB | HR | R | RBI | SB | BA | OBP | SLG | $1L | Pts |
|---|---|---|---|---|---|---|---|---|---|---|---|
| Carp M | 24 | 43 | 2 | 5 | 5 | 0 | .233 | .327 | .386 | -$5 | 20 |

| Mini-Browser | Age | AB | HR | R | RBI | SB | BA | OBP | SLG | $1L | Pts |
|---|---|---|---|---|---|---|---|---|---|---|---|
| Davis C | 25 | 45 | 3 | 6 | 7 | 1 | .243 | .301 | .475 | -$4 | 20 |
| Rizzo A | 21 | 44 | 2 | 5 | 6 | 0 | .251 | .313 | .424 | -$5 | 20 |
| Delgado C | 38 | 22 | 1 | 4 | 4 | 0 | .276 | .358 | .506 | -$5 | 20 |
| Hughes R | 27 | 47 | 2 | 5 | 5 | 0 | .225 | .291 | .410 | -$5 | 20 |
| Quinlan R | 34 | 46 | 1 | 5 | 5 | 1 | .239 | .291 | .327 | -$5 | 20 |

### Minors (2010) / Skills
| Level | Leag | AB | HR | R | RBI | SB | BA | OBP | SLG | CT% | H% | BB% | Bash |
|---|---|---|---|---|---|---|---|---|---|---|---|---|---|
| A | — | | | | | | | | | | | | |
| AA | — | | | | | | | | | | | | |
| AAA | PCL | 409 | 29 | 67 | 76 | 1 | .257 | .328 | .516 | 77% | 33% | 9% | 2.01 |

### Majors / Skills / Value / Extra / Production / OPS / Scoresheet
| Yr | Team | AB | HR | R | RBI | SB | BA | OBP | SLG | CT% | H% | BB% | Bash | $1L | $2L | Pts | RAA | 2B | 3B | CS | FB-LD-GB | HR/fb | RBI% | RS% | OPS | 1st Hf | 2nd Hf | vs RH | vs LH | Rnge | vRH | vLH |
|---|---|---|---|---|---|---|---|---|---|---|---|---|---|---|---|---|---|---|---|---|---|---|---|---|---|---|---|---|---|---|---|---|
| 07 | — | | | | | | | | | | | | | | | | | | | | | | | | | | | | | | | |
| 08 | — | | | | | | | | | | | | | | | | | | | | | | | | | | | | | | | |
| 09 | SEA | 54 | 1 | 7 | 5 | 0 | .315 | .415 | .463 | 81% | 39% | 12% | 1.47 | -$2 | -$17 | 40 | +1 | 3 | 1 | 0 | 36-20-44 | 6% | 15% | 23% | .878 | .913 | .863 | .900 | .730 | 1.85 | — | — |
| 10 | SEA | 37 | 0 | 1 | 0 | 0 | .189 | .268 | .243 | 78% | 24% | 10% | 1.29 | -$5 | -$21 | 10 | -4 | 2 | 0 | 0 | 52-17-31 | 0% | 9% | 0% | .512 | .465 | .714 | .496 | .556 | 1.85 | +24 | -73 |

### Competition at 1B / Stats in 2010
| Bats | Player | GSvR | GSvL | Sub | OPS |
|---|---|---|---|---|---|
| LH | Kotchman C | 80 | 28 | 8 | .616 |
| BH | Smoak J | 15 | 10 | 0 | .678 |

---

## Brett Carroll — 100 PA | $-3 | 50 pts
OF-25 (RF-20, LF-7)  Owned: 0%  RH

Carroll was inconsequential for most of 2010, but he should get brief looks during the 2011 season, if only for his defensive prowess. He is a non-factor at the plate and does not have much of a future with Florida, so expect him to split time between the majors and (moreso) minors. (MJ)

### Forecast
| Player | Age | AB | HR | R | RBI | SB | BA | OBP | SLG | $1L | Pts |
|---|---|---|---|---|---|---|---|---|---|---|---|
| Carroll B | 28 | 88 | 3 | 13 | 11 | 1 | .239 | .306 | .430 | -$3 | 50 |

| Mini-Browser | Age | AB | HR | R | RBI | SB | BA | OBP | SLG | $1L | Pts |
|---|---|---|---|---|---|---|---|---|---|---|---|
| Duncan S | 31 | 89 | 5 | 12 | 14 | 0 | .248 | .338 | .470 | -$2 | 60 |
| Carter C | 28 | 91 | 4 | 10 | 12 | 0 | .263 | .328 | .444 | -$2 | 60 |
| Gillespie C | 26 | 86 | 3 | 12 | 10 | 2 | .244 | .334 | .436 | -$2 | 50 |
| Gerut J | 33 | 68 | 3 | 11 | 9 | 2 | .265 | .322 | .467 | -$3 | 50 |
| Kelly D | 31 | 116 | 3 | 14 | 11 | 3 | .258 | .317 | .380 | -$3 | 70 |

### Minors (2010) / Skills
| Level | Leag | AB | HR | R | RBI | SB | BA | OBP | SLG | CT% | H% | BB% | Bash |
|---|---|---|---|---|---|---|---|---|---|---|---|---|---|
| A | FLO | 17 | 0 | 4 | 0 | 2 | .294 | .520 | .353 | 71% | 42% | 12% | 1.20 |
| AA | — | | | | | | | | | | | | |
| AAA | PCL | 244 | 8 | 32 | 30 | 4 | .221 | .299 | .385 | 78% | 28% | 8% | 1.74 |

### Majors / Skills / Value / Extra / Production / OPS / Scoresheet
| Yr | Team | AB | HR | R | RBI | SB | BA | OBP | SLG | CT% | H% | BB% | Bash | $1L | $2L | Pts | RAA | 2B | 3B | CS | FB-LD-GB | HR/fb | RBI% | RS% | OPS | 1st Hf | 2nd Hf | vs RH | vs LH | Rnge | vRH | vLH |
|---|---|---|---|---|---|---|---|---|---|---|---|---|---|---|---|---|---|---|---|---|---|---|---|---|---|---|---|---|---|---|---|---|
| 07 | FLA | 49 | 0 | 10 | 2 | 0 | .184 | .231 | .204 | 69% | 26% | 6% | 1.11 | -$6 | -$19 | 10 | -7 | 1 | 0 | 0 | 36-18-45 | 0% | 8% | 83% | .435 | .450 | .411 | .317 | .549 | — | — | — |
| 08 | FLA | 17 | 0 | 1 | 1 | 0 | .059 | .111 | .176 | 65% | 9% | 6% | 3.00 | -$5 | -$19 | 0 | -4 | 0 | 1 | 0 | 27-27-45 | 0% | 11% | 250% | .288 | .305 | .000 | .597 | .000 | 2.11 | -21 | +49 |
| 09 | FLA | 141 | 3 | 18 | 18 | 0 | .234 | .306 | .383 | 77% | 31% | 7% | 1.64 | -$2 | -$16 | 70 | -9 | 8 | 2 | 0 | 42-19-39 | 7% | 21% | 33% | .689 | .796 | .568 | .589 | .801 | 2.10 | -17 | +39 |
| 10 | FLA | 76 | 2 | 13 | 7 | 2 | .197 | .311 | .329 | 62% | 32% | 6% | 1.67 | -$3 | -$18 | 20 | -9 | 3 | 0 | 1 | 31-19-50 | 13% | 12% | 42% | .640 | .640 | — | .626 | .661 | 2.10 | -18 | +41 |

### Competition at RF / Stats in 2010
| Bats | Player | GSvR | GSvL | Sub | OPS |
|---|---|---|---|---|---|
| RH | Stanton M | 70 | 27 | 1 | .833 |
| RH | Carroll B | 7 | 9 | 4 | .640 |

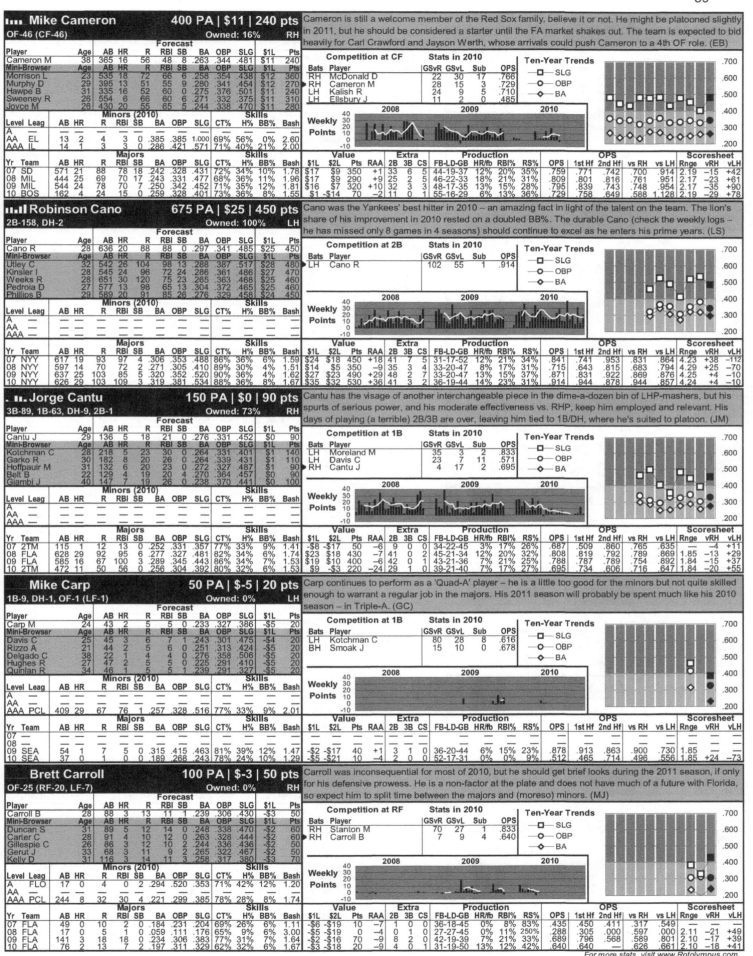

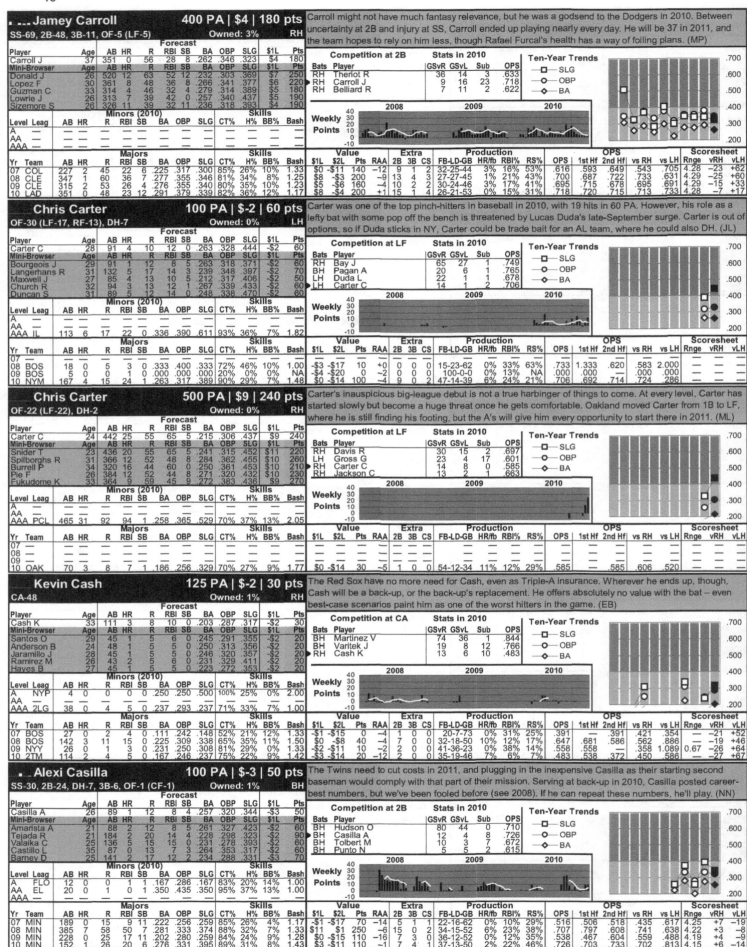

## Jamey Carroll — 400 PA | $4 | 180 pts

SS-69, 2B-48, 3B-11, OF-5 (LF-5)   Owned: 3%   RH

Carroll might not have much fantasy relevance, but he was a godsend to the Dodgers in 2010. Between uncertainty at 2B and injury at SS, Carroll ended up playing nearly every day. He will be 37 in 2011, and the team hopes to rely on him less, though Rafael Furcal's health has a way of foiling plans. (MP)

### Forecast
| Player | Age | AB | HR | R | RBI | SB | BA | OBP | SLG | $1L | Pts |
|---|---|---|---|---|---|---|---|---|---|---|---|
| Carroll J | 37 | 351 | 0 | 56 | 28 | 8 | .262 | .346 | .323 | $4 | 180 |

### Mini-Browser
| Player | Age | AB | HR | R | RBI | SB | BA | OBP | SLG | $1L | Pts |
|---|---|---|---|---|---|---|---|---|---|---|---|
| Donald J | 26 | 520 | 12 | 63 | 52 | 12 | .232 | .303 | .369 | $7 | 250 |
| Lopez F | 30 | 361 | 8 | 48 | 36 | 8 | .266 | .341 | .377 | $6 | 220 |
| Guzman C | 33 | 314 | 4 | 46 | 32 | 4 | .279 | .314 | .389 | $5 | 180 |
| Lowrie J | 26 | 313 | 7 | 39 | 42 | 0 | .257 | .340 | .437 | $5 | 190 |
| Sizemore S | 26 | 326 | 11 | 39 | 32 | 11 | .236 | .318 | .393 | $4 | 190 |

### Minors (2010) / Skills
| Level | Leag | AB | HR | R | RBI | SB | BA | OBP | SLG | CT% | H% | BB% | Bash |
|---|---|---|---|---|---|---|---|---|---|---|---|---|---|
| A | — | — | — | — | — | — | — | — | — | — | — | — | — |
| AA | — | — | — | — | — | — | — | — | — | — | — | — | — |
| AAA | — | — | — | — | — | — | — | — | — | — | — | — | — |

### Majors / Skills
| Yr | Team | AB | HR | R | RBI | SB | BA | OBP | SLG | CT% | H% | BB% | Bash |
|---|---|---|---|---|---|---|---|---|---|---|---|---|---|
| 07 | COL | 227 | 2 | 45 | 22 | 6 | .225 | .317 | .300 | 85% | 26% | 10% | 1.33 |
| 08 | CLE | 347 | 1 | 60 | 36 | 7 | .277 | .355 | .346 | 81% | 34% | 8% | 1.25 |
| 09 | CLE | 315 | 2 | 53 | 26 | 4 | .276 | .355 | .340 | 80% | 35% | 10% | 1.23 |
| 10 | LAD | 351 | 0 | 48 | 23 | 12 | .291 | .379 | .339 | 82% | 36% | 12% | 1.17 |

### Value / Extra / Production / OPS / Scoresheet
| Yr | $1L | $2L | Pts | RAA | 2B | 3B | CS | FB-LD-GB | HR/fb | RBI% | RS% | OPS | 1st Hf | 2nd Hf | vs RH | vs LH | Rnge | vRH | vLH |
|---|---|---|---|---|---|---|---|---|---|---|---|---|---|---|---|---|---|---|---|
| 07 | $0 | -$11 | 140 | -12 | 9 | 1 | 2 | 32-25-44 | 3% | 16% | 53% | .616 | .593 | .649 | .543 | .705 | 4.28 | -23 | +60 |
| 08 | $8 | -$3 | 200 | -9 | 13 | 4 | 3 | 27-27-45 | 1% | 21% | 43% | .700 | .687 | .722 | .733 | .631 | 4.29 | -25 | +60 |
| 09 | $5 | -$6 | 160 | -4 | 10 | 2 | 2 | 30-24-46 | 3% | 17% | 41% | .695 | .715 | .678 | .695 | .691 | 4.29 | -15 | +33 |
| 10 | $8 | -$4 | 200 | +1 | 6 | 2 | 5 | 26-21-53 | 0% | 15% | 31% | .718 | .720 | .715 | .713 | .733 | 4.28 | -7 | +17 |

## Chris Carter — 100 PA | $-2 | 60 pts

OF-30 (LF-17, RF-13), DH-7   Owned: 0%   LH

Carter was one of the top pinch-hitters in baseball in 2010, with 19 hits in 60 PA. However, his role as a lefty bat with some pop off the bench is threatened by Lucas Duda's late-September surge. Carter is out of options, so if Duda sticks in NY, Carter could be trade bait for an AL team, where he could also DH. (JL)

### Forecast
| Player | Age | AB | HR | R | RBI | SB | BA | OBP | SLG | $1L | Pts |
|---|---|---|---|---|---|---|---|---|---|---|---|
| Carter C | 28 | 91 | 4 | 10 | 12 | 0 | .263 | .328 | .444 | -$2 | 60 |

### Mini-Browser
| Player | Age | AB | HR | R | RBI | SB | BA | OBP | SLG | $1L | Pts |
|---|---|---|---|---|---|---|---|---|---|---|---|
| Bourgeois J | 29 | 91 | 1 | 12 | 8 | 5 | .263 | .318 | .371 | -$2 | 60 |
| Langerhans R | 31 | 132 | 5 | 17 | 14 | 1 | .239 | .348 | .397 | -$2 | 70 |
| Maxwell J | 27 | 85 | 4 | 13 | 10 | 5 | .212 | .317 | .406 | -$2 | 50 |
| Church R | 32 | 94 | 3 | 13 | 12 | 1 | .267 | .339 | .433 | -$2 | 60 |
| Duncan S | 31 | 89 | 5 | 12 | 14 | 0 | .248 | .338 | .470 | -$4 | 60 |

### Minors (2010) / Skills
| Level | Leag | AB | HR | R | RBI | SB | BA | OBP | SLG | CT% | H% | BB% | Bash |
|---|---|---|---|---|---|---|---|---|---|---|---|---|---|
| A | — | — | — | — | — | — | — | — | — | — | — | — | — |
| AA | — | — | — | — | — | — | — | — | — | — | — | — | — |
| AAA | IL | 113 | 6 | 17 | 22 | 0 | .336 | .390 | .611 | 93% | 36% | 7% | 1.82 |

### Majors / Skills
| Yr | Team | AB | HR | R | RBI | SB | BA | OBP | SLG | CT% | H% | BB% | Bash |
|---|---|---|---|---|---|---|---|---|---|---|---|---|---|
| 07 | — | — | — | — | — | — | — | — | — | — | — | — | — |
| 08 | BOS | 18 | 0 | 5 | 3 | 0 | .333 | .400 | .333 | 72% | 46% | 10% | 1.00 |
| 09 | BOS | 5 | 0 | 1 | 0 | 0 | .000 | .000 | .000 | 20% | 0% | 0% | NA |
| 10 | NYM | 167 | 4 | 15 | 24 | 1 | .263 | .317 | .389 | 90% | 29% | 7% | 1.48 |

### Value / Extra / Production / OPS / Scoresheet
| Yr | $1L | $2L | Pts | RAA | 2B | 3B | CS | FB-LD-GB | HR/fb | RBI% | RS% | OPS | 1st Hf | 2nd Hf | vs RH | vs LH | Rnge | vRH | vLH |
|---|---|---|---|---|---|---|---|---|---|---|---|---|---|---|---|---|---|---|---|
| 07 | | | | | | | | | | | | | | | | | | | |
| 08 | -$3 | -$17 | 10 | +0 | 0 | 0 | 0 | 15-23-62 | 0% | 33% | 63% | .733 | 1.333 | .620 | .583 | 2.000 | — | — | — |
| 09 | -$4 | -$20 | 0 | -2 | 0 | 0 | 0 | 100-0-0 | 0% | 13% | NA | .000 | .000 | — | .000 | .000 | — | — | — |
| 10 | $0 | -$14 | 100 | -4 | 9 | 0 | 2 | 47-14-39 | 6% | 24% | 21% | .706 | .692 | .714 | .724 | .286 | — | — | — |

## Chris Carter — 500 PA | $9 | 240 pts

OF-22 (LF-22), DH-2   Owned: 0%   RH

Carter's inauspicious big-league debut is not a true harbinger of things to come. At every level, Carter has started slowly but become a huge threat once he gets comfortable. Oakland moved Carter from 1B to LF, where he is still finding his footing, but the A's will give him every opportunity to start there in 2011. (ML)

### Forecast
| Player | Age | AB | HR | R | RBI | SB | BA | OBP | SLG | $1L | Pts |
|---|---|---|---|---|---|---|---|---|---|---|---|
| Carter C | 24 | 442 | 25 | 55 | 65 | 5 | .215 | .306 | .437 | $9 | 240 |

### Mini-Browser
| Player | Age | AB | HR | R | RBI | SB | BA | OBP | SLG | $1L | Pts |
|---|---|---|---|---|---|---|---|---|---|---|---|
| Snider T | 23 | 436 | 20 | 55 | 65 | 5 | .241 | .315 | .452 | $11 | 220 |
| Spilborghs R | 31 | 366 | 12 | 52 | 48 | 8 | .284 | .362 | .455 | $10 | 260 |
| Burrell P | 34 | 320 | 16 | 44 | 60 | 0 | .250 | .361 | .453 | $10 | 210 |
| Pie F | 26 | 384 | 12 | 52 | 44 | 8 | .271 | .320 | .432 | $10 | 230 |
| Fukudome K | 33 | 364 | 9 | 59 | 45 | 9 | .272 | .383 | .436 | $9 | 270 |

### Minors (2010) / Skills
| Level | Leag | AB | HR | R | RBI | SB | BA | OBP | SLG | CT% | H% | BB% | Bash |
|---|---|---|---|---|---|---|---|---|---|---|---|---|---|
| A | — | — | — | — | — | — | — | — | — | — | — | — | — |
| AA | — | — | — | — | — | — | — | — | — | — | — | — | — |
| AAA | PCL | 465 | 31 | 92 | 94 | 1 | .258 | .365 | .529 | 70% | 37% | 13% | 2.05 |

### Majors / Skills
| Yr | Team | AB | HR | R | RBI | SB | BA | OBP | SLG | CT% | H% | BB% | Bash |
|---|---|---|---|---|---|---|---|---|---|---|---|---|---|
| 07 | — | — | — | — | — | — | — | — | — | — | — | — | — |
| 08 | — | — | — | — | — | — | — | — | — | — | — | — | — |
| 09 | — | — | — | — | — | — | — | — | — | — | — | — | — |
| 10 | OAK | 70 | 3 | 8 | 7 | 1 | .186 | .256 | .329 | 70% | 27% | 9% | 1.77 |

### Value / Extra / Production / OPS / Scoresheet
| Yr | $1L | $2L | Pts | RAA | 2B | 3B | CS | FB-LD-GB | HR/fb | RBI% | RS% | OPS | 1st Hf | 2nd Hf | vs RH | vs LH | Rnge | vRH | vLH |
|---|---|---|---|---|---|---|---|---|---|---|---|---|---|---|---|---|---|---|---|
| 07 | | | | | | | | | | | | | | | | | | | |
| 08 | | | | | | | | | | | | | | | | | | | |
| 09 | | | | | | | | | | | | | | | | | | | |
| 10 | $0 | -$14 | 30 | -5 | 1 | 0 | 0 | 54-12-34 | 11% | 12% | 29% | .585 | — | .585 | .606 | .520 | — | — | — |

## Kevin Cash — 125 PA | $-2 | 30 pts

CA-48   Owned: 1%   RH

The Red Sox have no more need for Cash, even as Triple-A insurance. Wherever he ends up, though, Cash will be a back-up, or the back-up's replacement. He offers absolutely no value with the bat — even best-case scenarios paint him as one of the worst hitters in the game. (EB)

### Forecast
| Player | Age | AB | HR | R | RBI | SB | BA | OBP | SLG | $1L | Pts |
|---|---|---|---|---|---|---|---|---|---|---|---|
| Cash K | 33 | 111 | 3 | 8 | 10 | 0 | .203 | .287 | .317 | -$2 | 30 |

### Mini-Browser
| Player | Age | AB | HR | R | RBI | SB | BA | OBP | SLG | $1L | Pts |
|---|---|---|---|---|---|---|---|---|---|---|---|
| Santos O | 29 | 45 | 1 | 5 | 6 | 0 | .245 | .291 | .355 | -$2 | 20 |
| Anderson B | 24 | 48 | 1 | 5 | 5 | 0 | .250 | .313 | .356 | -$2 | 20 |
| Jaramillo J | 28 | 45 | 1 | 5 | 6 | 0 | .246 | .320 | .357 | -$2 | 20 |
| Ramirez M | 26 | 43 | 2 | 5 | 6 | 0 | .231 | .329 | .411 | -$2 | 20 |
| Hayes B | 27 | 45 | 1 | 5 | 5 | 0 | .223 | .272 | .353 | -$2 | 20 |

### Minors (2010) / Skills
| Level | Leag | AB | HR | R | RBI | SB | BA | OBP | SLG | CT% | H% | BB% | Bash |
|---|---|---|---|---|---|---|---|---|---|---|---|---|---|
| A | NYP | 4 | 0 | 0 | 0 | 0 | .250 | .250 | .500 | 100% | 25% | 0% | 2.00 |
| AA | — | — | — | — | — | — | — | — | — | — | — | — | — |
| AAA | 2LG | 38 | 0 | 4 | 5 | 0 | .237 | .293 | .237 | 71% | 33% | 7% | 1.00 |

### Majors / Skills
| Yr | Team | AB | HR | R | RBI | SB | BA | OBP | SLG | CT% | H% | BB% | Bash |
|---|---|---|---|---|---|---|---|---|---|---|---|---|---|
| 07 | BOS | 27 | 0 | 2 | 4 | 0 | .111 | .242 | .148 | 52% | 21% | 12% | 1.33 |
| 08 | BOS | 142 | 3 | 11 | 15 | 0 | .225 | .309 | .338 | 65% | 35% | 11% | 1.50 |
| 09 | NYY | 26 | 0 | 1 | 3 | 0 | .231 | .250 | .308 | 81% | 29% | 0% | 1.33 |
| 10 | 2TM | 114 | 2 | 4 | 11 | 0 | .167 | .246 | .237 | 75% | 22% | 9% | 1.42 |

### Value / Extra / Production / OPS / Scoresheet
| Yr | $1L | $2L | Pts | RAA | 2B | 3B | CS | FB-LD-GB | HR/fb | RBI% | RS% | OPS | 1st Hf | 2nd Hf | vs RH | vs LH | Rnge | vRH | vLH |
|---|---|---|---|---|---|---|---|---|---|---|---|---|---|---|---|---|---|---|---|
| 07 | -$1 | -$15 | 0 | -4 | 1 | 0 | 0 | 20-7-73 | 0% | 31% | 25% | .391 | — | .391 | .421 | .354 | — | -21 | +52 |
| 08 | -$0 | -$8 | 40 | -4 | 7 | 0 | 0 | 32-18-50 | 10% | 12% | 17% | .647 | .681 | .586 | .562 | .886 | — | -19 | +46 |
| 09 | -$2 | -$11 | 0 | -2 | 0 | 0 | 0 | 41-36-23 | 0% | 38% | 14% | .558 | .558 | — | .358 | 1.089 | 0.67 | -26 | +64 |
| 10 | -$3 | -$17 | 20 | -20 | 2 | 0 | 0 | 35-19-46 | 7% | 6% | 7% | .483 | .538 | .372 | .450 | .586 | — | -27 | +64 |

## Alexi Casilla — 100 PA | $-3 | 50 pts

SS-30, 2B-24, DH-7, 3B-6, OF-1 (CF-1)   Owned: 1%   BH

The Twins need to cut costs in 2011, and plugging in the inexpensive Casilla as their starting second baseman would comply with that part of their mission. Serving as back-up in 2010, Casilla posted career-best numbers, but we've been fooled before (see 2008). If he can repeat these numbers, he'll play. (NN)

### Forecast
| Player | Age | AB | HR | R | RBI | SB | BA | OBP | SLG | $1L | Pts |
|---|---|---|---|---|---|---|---|---|---|---|---|
| Casilla A | 26 | 89 | 1 | 12 | 8 | 4 | .257 | .320 | .344 | -$3 | 50 |

### Mini-Browser
| Player | Age | AB | HR | R | RBI | SB | BA | OBP | SLG | $1L | Pts |
|---|---|---|---|---|---|---|---|---|---|---|---|
| Amarista A | 21 | 88 | 2 | 12 | 8 | 5 | .261 | .327 | .423 | -$2 | 60 |
| Tejada R | 21 | 184 | 2 | 20 | 14 | 4 | .228 | .298 | .323 | -$2 | 90 |
| Valaika C | 25 | 136 | 5 | 15 | 13 | 0 | .231 | .278 | .393 | -$2 | 60 |
| Castillo L | 35 | 87 | 0 | 13 | 7 | 3 | .264 | .353 | .317 | -$2 | 60 |
| Barney D | 25 | 141 | 2 | 17 | 12 | 2 | .234 | .288 | .331 | -$3 | 70 |

### Minors (2010) / Skills
| Level | Leag | AB | HR | R | RBI | SB | BA | OBP | SLG | CT% | H% | BB% | Bash |
|---|---|---|---|---|---|---|---|---|---|---|---|---|---|
| A | FLO | 12 | 0 | 1 | 1 | 1 | .167 | .286 | .167 | 83% | 20% | 14% | 1.00 |
| AA | EL | 20 | 0 | 1 | 0 | 1 | .350 | .435 | .350 | 95% | 37% | 13% | 1.00 |
| AAA | — | — | — | — | — | — | — | — | — | — | — | — | — |

### Majors / Skills
| Yr | Team | AB | HR | R | RBI | SB | BA | OBP | SLG | CT% | H% | BB% | Bash |
|---|---|---|---|---|---|---|---|---|---|---|---|---|---|
| 07 | MIN | 189 | 0 | 15 | 9 | 11 | .222 | .256 | .259 | 85% | 26% | 4% | 1.17 |
| 08 | MIN | 385 | 4 | 58 | 50 | 7 | .281 | .333 | .374 | 88% | 32% | 7% | 1.33 |
| 09 | MIN | 228 | 0 | 25 | 17 | 11 | .202 | .280 | .259 | 84% | 24% | 9% | 1.28 |
| 10 | MIN | 152 | 1 | 26 | 20 | 6 | .276 | .331 | .395 | 89% | 31% | 8% | 1.43 |

### Value / Extra / Production / OPS / Scoresheet
| Yr | $1L | $2L | Pts | RAA | 2B | 3B | CS | FB-LD-GB | HR/fb | RBI% | RS% | OPS | 1st Hf | 2nd Hf | vs RH | vs LH | Rnge | vRH | vLH |
|---|---|---|---|---|---|---|---|---|---|---|---|---|---|---|---|---|---|---|---|
| 07 | -$1 | -$17 | 70 | -14 | 5 | 1 | 1 | 22-16-62 | 0% | 10% | 29% | .516 | .506 | .518 | .435 | .617 | 4.25 | +7 | +13 |
| 08 | $11 | -$1 | 250 | -6 | 15 | 2 | 3 | 34-15-52 | 6% | 23% | 38% | .707 | .797 | .608 | .741 | .638 | 4.22 | +3 | -8 |
| 09 | $0 | -$15 | 110 | -16 | 7 | 3 | 7 | 36-12-52 | 0% | 12% | 35% | .538 | .467 | .604 | .559 | .488 | 4.19 | +4 | -9 |
| 10 | $3 | -$11 | 110 | -1 | 7 | 4 | 1 | 37-13-50 | 2% | 23% | 46% | .726 | .703 | .733 | .702 | .813 | 4.25 | +6 | -14 |

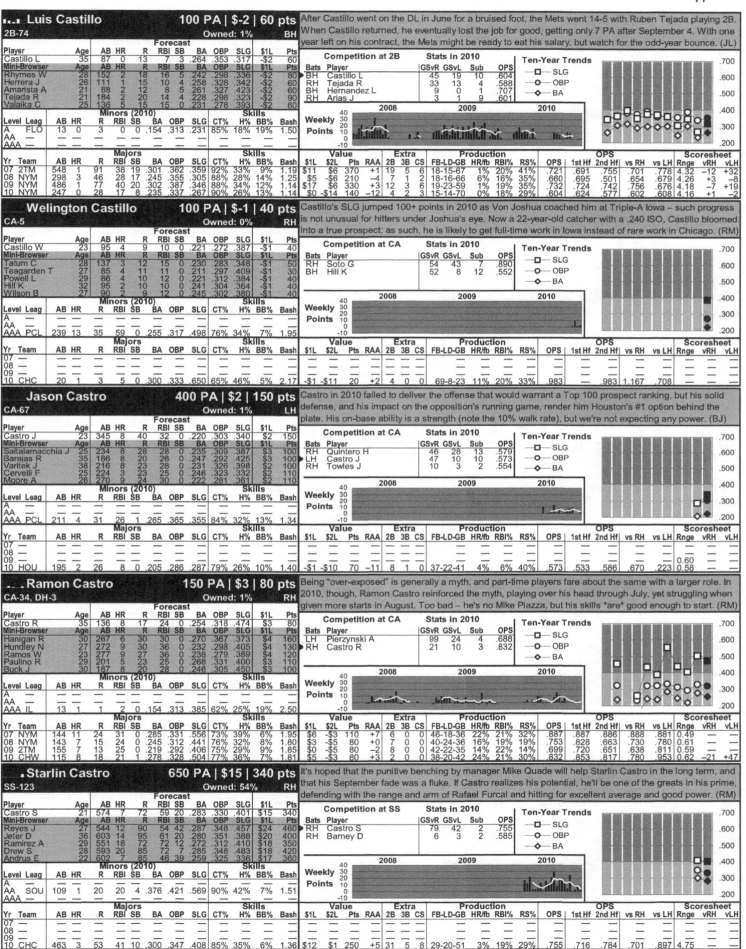

## Luis Castillo — 100 PA | $-2 | 60 pts
**2B-74** — Owned: 1% — BH

After Castillo went on the DL in June for a bruised foot, the Mets went 14-5 with Ruben Tejada playing 2B. When Castillo returned, he eventually lost the job for good, getting only 7 PA after September 4. With one year left on his contract, the Mets might be ready to eat his salary, but watch for the odd-year bounce. (JL)

### Forecast
| Player | Age | AB | HR | R | RBI | SB | BA | OBP | SLG | $1L | Pts |
|---|---|---|---|---|---|---|---|---|---|---|---|
| Castillo L | 35 | 87 | 0 | 13 | 7 | 3 | .264 | .353 | .317 | -$2 | 60 |

| Mini-Browser | Age | AB | HR | R | RBI | SB | BA | OBP | SLG | $1L | Pts |
|---|---|---|---|---|---|---|---|---|---|---|---|
| Rhymes W | 28 | 152 | 2 | 18 | 16 | 5 | .242 | .298 | .336 | -$2 | 80 |
| Herrera J | 26 | 111 | 1 | 15 | 10 | 4 | .258 | .328 | .342 | -$2 | 60 |
| Amarista J | 21 | 88 | 2 | 12 | 8 | 5 | .261 | .327 | .423 | -$2 | 60 |
| Tejada R | 21 | 184 | 2 | 21 | 14 | 4 | .228 | .298 | .323 | -$2 | 90 |
| Valaika C | 25 | 136 | 5 | 15 | 15 | 0 | .231 | .278 | .393 | -$2 | 60 |

### Minors (2010) / Skills
| Level | Leag | AB | HR | R | RBI | SB | BA | OBP | SLG | CT% | H% | BB% | Bash |
|---|---|---|---|---|---|---|---|---|---|---|---|---|---|
| A | FLO | 13 | 0 | 3 | 0 | 0 | .154 | .313 | .231 | 85% | 18% | 19% | 1.50 |
| AA | — | — | — | — | — | — | — | — | — | — | — | — | — |
| AAA | — | — | — | — | — | — | — | — | — | — | — | — | — |

### Competition at 2B / Stats in 2010
| Bats | Player | GSvR | GSvL | Sub | OPS |
|---|---|---|---|---|---|
| BH | Castillo L | 45 | 19 | 10 | .604 |
| RH | Tejada R | 33 | 13 | 4 | .588 |
| BH | Hernandez L | 9 | 0 | 1 | .707 |
| RH | Arias J | 3 | 1 | 9 | .601 |

### Majors / Skills
| Yr | Team | AB | HR | R | RBI | SB | BA | OBP | SLG | CT% | H% | BB% | Bash | $1L | $2L | Pts | RAA | 2B | 3B | CS | FB-LD-GB | HR/fb | RBI% | RS% | OPS | 1st Hf | 2nd Hf | vs RH | vs LH | Rnge | vRH | vLH |
|---|---|---|---|---|---|---|---|---|---|---|---|---|---|---|---|---|---|---|---|---|---|---|---|---|---|---|---|---|---|---|---|---|
| 07 | 2TM | 548 | 1 | 89 | 38 | 19 | .301 | .362 | .359 | 92% | 33% | 9% | 1.19 | $11 | -$6 | 370 | +1 | 19 | 5 | 6 | 18-15-67 | 1% | 20% | 41% | .721 | .691 | .755 | .701 | .778 | 4.32 | -12 | +32 |
| 08 | NYM | 298 | 3 | 46 | 28 | 17 | .245 | .355 | .305 | 88% | 28% | 14% | 1.25 | $5 | -$6 | 210 | -4 | 7 | 1 | 2 | 18-16-66 | 6% | 16% | 35% | .660 | .695 | .501 | .654 | .679 | 4.26 | +3 | -8 |
| 09 | NYM | 486 | 1 | 77 | 40 | 20 | .302 | .387 | .346 | 88% | 34% | 12% | 1.14 | $17 | -$6 | 330 | +3 | 12 | 3 | 6 | 19-23-59 | 1% | 19% | 35% | .732 | .724 | .742 | .756 | .676 | 4.18 | -7 | +19 |
| 10 | NYM | 247 | 0 | 17 | 8 | 3 | .235 | .337 | .267 | 90% | 26% | 13% | 1.14 | $0 | -$14 | 140 | -12 | 4 | 0 | 2 | 15-14-70 | 0% | 18% | 29% | .604 | .624 | .577 | .602 | .608 | 4.16 | +1 | +1 |

---

## Welington Castillo — 100 PA | $-1 | 40 pts
**CA-5** — Owned: 0% — RH

Castillo's SLG jumped 100+ points in 2010 as Von Joshua coached him at Triple-A Iowa – such progress is not unusual for hitters under Joshua's eye. Now a 22-year-old catcher with a .240 ISO, Castillo bloomed into a true prospect; as such, he is likely to get full-time work in Iowa instead of rare work in Chicago. (RM)

### Forecast
| Player | Age | AB | HR | R | RBI | SB | BA | OBP | SLG | $1L | Pts |
|---|---|---|---|---|---|---|---|---|---|---|---|
| Castillo W | 23 | 95 | 4 | 9 | 10 | 0 | .221 | .272 | .387 | -$1 | 40 |

| Mini-Browser | Age | AB | HR | R | RBI | SB | BA | OBP | SLG | $1L | Pts |
|---|---|---|---|---|---|---|---|---|---|---|---|
| Tatum C | 28 | 137 | 3 | 12 | 15 | 0 | .230 | .283 | .348 | -$1 | 50 |
| Teagarden T | 27 | 85 | 4 | 11 | 11 | 0 | .211 | .297 | .409 | -$1 | 30 |
| Powell L | 29 | 86 | 4 | 10 | 12 | 0 | .221 | .312 | .384 | -$1 | 40 |
| Hill K | 32 | 95 | 2 | 10 | 10 | 0 | .241 | .304 | .364 | -$1 | 40 |
| Wilson B | 27 | 90 | 2 | 9 | 12 | 0 | .245 | .302 | .380 | -$1 | 40 |

### Minors (2010) / Skills
| Level | Leag | AB | HR | R | RBI | SB | BA | OBP | SLG | CT% | H% | BB% | Bash |
|---|---|---|---|---|---|---|---|---|---|---|---|---|---|
| A | — | — | — | — | — | — | — | — | — | — | — | — | — |
| AA | — | — | — | — | — | — | — | — | — | — | — | — | — |
| AAA | PCL | 239 | 13 | 35 | 59 | 0 | .255 | .317 | .498 | 76% | 34% | 7% | 1.95 |

### Competition at CA / Stats in 2010
| Bats | Player | GSvR | GSvL | Sub | OPS |
|---|---|---|---|---|---|
| RH | Soto G | 54 | 43 | 7 | .890 |
| BH | Hill K | 52 | 8 | 12 | .552 |

### Majors / Skills
| Yr | Team | AB | HR | R | RBI | SB | BA | OBP | SLG | CT% | H% | BB% | Bash | $1L | $2L | Pts | RAA | 2B | 3B | CS | FB-LD-GB | HR/fb | RBI% | RS% | OPS | 1st Hf | 2nd Hf | vs RH | vs LH | Rnge | vRH | vLH |
|---|---|---|---|---|---|---|---|---|---|---|---|---|---|---|---|---|---|---|---|---|---|---|---|---|---|---|---|---|---|---|---|---|
| 07 | — | — | | | | | | | | | | | | | | | | | | | | | | | | | | | | | | |
| 08 | — | — | | | | | | | | | | | | | | | | | | | | | | | | | | | | | | |
| 09 | — | — | | | | | | | | | | | | | | | | | | | | | | | | | | | | | | |
| 10 | CHC | 20 | 1 | 3 | 5 | 0 | .300 | .333 | .650 | 65% | 46% | 5% | 2.17 | -$1 | -$11 | 20 | +2 | 4 | 0 | 0 | 69-8-23 | 11% | 20% | 33% | .983 | | .983 | 1.167 | .708 | | | |

---

## Jason Castro — 400 PA | $2 | 150 pts
**CA-67** — Owned: 1% — LH

Castro in 2010 failed to deliver the offense that would warrant a Top 100 prospect ranking, but his solid defense, and his impact on the opposition's running game, render him Houston's #1 option behind the plate. His on-base ability is a strength (note the 10% walk rate), but we're not expecting any power. (BJ)

### Forecast
| Player | Age | AB | HR | R | RBI | SB | BA | OBP | SLG | $1L | Pts |
|---|---|---|---|---|---|---|---|---|---|---|---|
| Castro J | 23 | 345 | 8 | 40 | 32 | 0 | .220 | .303 | .340 | $2 | 150 |

| Mini-Browser | Age | AB | HR | R | RBI | SB | BA | OBP | SLG | $1L | Pts |
|---|---|---|---|---|---|---|---|---|---|---|---|
| Saltalamacchia J | 25 | 234 | 8 | 28 | 28 | 0 | .235 | .309 | .387 | $3 | 100 |
| Barajas R | 35 | 186 | 8 | 20 | 26 | 0 | .247 | .292 | .425 | $3 | 100 |
| Varitek J | 38 | 216 | 8 | 23 | 28 | 0 | .231 | .326 | .398 | $2 | 100 |
| Cervelli F | 25 | 224 | 3 | 23 | 25 | 0 | .246 | .323 | .332 | $2 | 110 |
| Moore A | 26 | 270 | 9 | 24 | 30 | 0 | .222 | .281 | .361 | $2 | 110 |

### Minors (2010) / Skills
| Level | Leag | AB | HR | R | RBI | SB | BA | OBP | SLG | CT% | H% | BB% | Bash |
|---|---|---|---|---|---|---|---|---|---|---|---|---|---|
| A | — | — | — | — | — | — | — | — | — | — | — | — | — |
| AA | — | — | — | — | — | — | — | — | — | — | — | — | — |
| AAA | PCL | 211 | 4 | 31 | 26 | 1 | .265 | .365 | .355 | 84% | 32% | 13% | 1.34 |

### Competition at CA / Stats in 2010
| Bats | Player | GSvR | GSvL | Sub | OPS |
|---|---|---|---|---|---|
| RH | Quintero H | 46 | 28 | 13 | .579 |
| LH | Castro J | 47 | 10 | 10 | .573 |
| RH | Towles J | 10 | 3 | 2 | .554 |

### Majors / Skills
| Yr | Team | AB | HR | R | RBI | SB | BA | OBP | SLG | CT% | H% | BB% | Bash | $1L | $2L | Pts | RAA | 2B | 3B | CS | FB-LD-GB | HR/fb | RBI% | RS% | OPS | 1st Hf | 2nd Hf | vs RH | vs LH | Rnge | vRH | vLH |
|---|---|---|---|---|---|---|---|---|---|---|---|---|---|---|---|---|---|---|---|---|---|---|---|---|---|---|---|---|---|---|---|---|
| 07 | — | — | | | | | | | | | | | | | | | | | | | | | | | | | | | | | | |
| 08 | — | — | | | | | | | | | | | | | | | | | | | | | | | | | | | | 0.60 | | |
| 09 | — | — | | | | | | | | | | | | | | | | | | | | | | | | | | | | | | |
| 10 | HOU | 195 | 2 | 26 | 8 | 0 | .205 | .286 | .287 | 79% | 26% | 10% | 1.40 | -$1 | -$10 | 70 | -11 | 8 | 1 | 0 | 37-22-41 | 4% | 6% | 40% | .573 | .533 | .586 | .670 | .223 | 0.58 | | |

---

## Ramon Castro — 150 PA | $3 | 80 pts
**CA-34, DH-3** — Owned: 1% — RH

Being "over-exposed" is generally a myth, and part-time players fare about the same with a larger role. In 2010, though, Ramon Castro reinforced the myth, playing over his head through July, yet struggling when given more starts in August. Too bad – he's no Mike Piazza, but his skills *are* good enough to start. (RM)

### Forecast
| Player | Age | AB | HR | R | RBI | SB | BA | OBP | SLG | $1L | Pts |
|---|---|---|---|---|---|---|---|---|---|---|---|
| Castro R | 35 | 136 | 8 | 17 | 24 | 0 | .254 | .318 | .474 | $3 | 80 |

| Mini-Browser | Age | AB | HR | R | RBI | SB | BA | OBP | SLG | $1L | Pts |
|---|---|---|---|---|---|---|---|---|---|---|---|
| Hanigan R | 30 | 267 | 6 | 30 | 30 | 0 | .270 | .367 | .373 | $4 | 160 |
| Hundley N | 27 | 272 | 9 | 30 | 36 | 0 | .232 | .298 | .405 | $4 | 130 |
| Ramos W | 23 | 277 | 9 | 27 | 36 | 0 | .238 | .279 | .389 | $4 | 120 |
| Paulino R | 29 | 201 | 5 | 23 | 25 | 0 | .268 | .331 | .400 | $3 | 110 |
| Buck J | 30 | 187 | 8 | 20 | 28 | 0 | .246 | .305 | .450 | $3 | 100 |

### Minors (2010) / Skills
| Level | Leag | AB | HR | R | RBI | SB | BA | OBP | SLG | CT% | H% | BB% | Bash |
|---|---|---|---|---|---|---|---|---|---|---|---|---|---|
| A | — | — | — | — | — | — | — | — | — | — | — | — | — |
| AA | — | — | — | — | — | — | — | — | — | — | — | — | — |
| AAA | IL | 13 | 1 | 1 | 2 | 0 | .154 | .313 | .385 | 62% | 25% | 19% | 2.50 |

### Competition at CA / Stats in 2010
| Bats | Player | GSvR | GSvL | Sub | OPS |
|---|---|---|---|---|---|
| LH | Pierzynski A | 99 | 24 | 4 | .688 |
| RH | Castro R | 21 | 10 | 3 | .832 |

### Majors / Skills
| Yr | Team | AB | HR | R | RBI | SB | BA | OBP | SLG | CT% | H% | BB% | Bash | $1L | $2L | Pts | RAA | 2B | 3B | CS | FB-LD-GB | HR/fb | RBI% | RS% | OPS | 1st Hf | 2nd Hf | vs RH | vs LH | Rnge | vRH | vLH |
|---|---|---|---|---|---|---|---|---|---|---|---|---|---|---|---|---|---|---|---|---|---|---|---|---|---|---|---|---|---|---|---|---|
| 07 | NYM | 144 | 11 | 24 | 31 | 0 | .285 | .331 | .556 | 73% | 39% | 6% | 1.95 | $6 | -$3 | 110 | +7 | 6 | 0 | 0 | 46-18-36 | 22% | 21% | 32% | .887 | .887 | .886 | .888 | .881 | 0.49 | — | — |
| 08 | NYM | 143 | 7 | 15 | 24 | 0 | .245 | .312 | .441 | 76% | 32% | 9% | 1.80 | $3 | -$5 | 80 | +0 | 7 | 0 | 0 | 40-24-36 | 16% | 19% | 19% | .753 | .828 | .663 | .730 | .780 | 0.61 | — | — |
| 09 | 2TM | 155 | 7 | 13 | 25 | 0 | .219 | .292 | .406 | 75% | 29% | 9% | 1.85 | $0 | -$5 | 80 | -2 | 8 | 0 | 0 | 42-22-35 | 14% | 22% | 14% | .699 | .720 | .651 | .638 | .811 | 0.59 | — | — |
| 10 | CHW | 115 | 8 | 18 | 21 | 0 | .278 | .328 | .504 | 77% | 36% | 7% | 1.81 | $5 | -$3 | 80 | +3 | 2 | 0 | 0 | 38-20-42 | 24% | 21% | 30% | .832 | .853 | .817 | .780 | .953 | 0.62 | -21 | +47 |

---

## Starlin Castro — 650 PA | $15 | 340 pts
**SS-123** — Owned: 54% — RH

It's hoped that the punitive benching by manager Mike Quade will help Starlin Castro in the long term, and that his September fade was a fluke. If Castro realizes his potential, he'll be one of the greats in his prime, defending with the range and arm of Rafael Furcal and hitting for excellent average and good power. (RM)

### Forecast
| Player | Age | AB | HR | R | RBI | SB | BA | OBP | SLG | $1L | Pts |
|---|---|---|---|---|---|---|---|---|---|---|---|
| Castro S | 21 | 574 | 7 | 72 | 59 | 20 | .283 | .330 | .401 | $15 | 340 |

| Mini-Browser | Age | AB | HR | R | RBI | SB | BA | OBP | SLG | $1L | Pts |
|---|---|---|---|---|---|---|---|---|---|---|---|
| Reyes J | 27 | 544 | 12 | 90 | 54 | 42 | .287 | .348 | .457 | $24 | 460 |
| Jeter D | 36 | 603 | 14 | 95 | 61 | 20 | .280 | .351 | .388 | $20 | 400 |
| Ramirez A | 29 | 551 | 18 | 72 | 72 | 12 | .272 | .312 | .410 | $18 | 350 |
| Drew S | 28 | 593 | 20 | 85 | 72 | 7 | .285 | .348 | .483 | $18 | 420 |
| Andrus E | 22 | 602 | 2 | 85 | 46 | 39 | .259 | .325 | .336 | $17 | 360 |

### Minors (2010) / Skills
| Level | Leag | AB | HR | R | RBI | SB | BA | OBP | SLG | CT% | H% | BB% | Bash |
|---|---|---|---|---|---|---|---|---|---|---|---|---|---|
| A | — | — | — | — | — | — | — | — | — | — | — | — | — |
| AA | SOU | 109 | 1 | 20 | 20 | 4 | .376 | .421 | .569 | 90% | 42% | 7% | 1.51 |
| AAA | — | — | — | — | — | — | — | — | — | — | — | — | — |

### Competition at SS / Stats in 2010
| Bats | Player | GSvR | GSvL | Sub | OPS |
|---|---|---|---|---|---|
| RH | Castro S | 79 | 42 | 2 | .755 |
| RH | Barney D | 6 | 3 | 2 | .585 |

### Majors / Skills
| Yr | Team | AB | HR | R | RBI | SB | BA | OBP | SLG | CT% | H% | BB% | Bash | $1L | $2L | Pts | RAA | 2B | 3B | CS | FB-LD-GB | HR/fb | RBI% | RS% | OPS | 1st Hf | 2nd Hf | vs RH | vs LH | Rnge | vRH | vLH |
|---|---|---|---|---|---|---|---|---|---|---|---|---|---|---|---|---|---|---|---|---|---|---|---|---|---|---|---|---|---|---|---|---|
| 07 | — | — | | | | | | | | | | | | | | | | | | | | | | | | | | | | | | |
| 08 | — | — | | | | | | | | | | | | | | | | | | | | | | | | | | | | | | |
| 09 | — | — | | | | | | | | | | | | | | | | | | | | | | | | | | | | | | |
| 10 | CHC | 463 | 3 | 53 | 41 | 10 | .300 | .347 | .408 | 85% | 35% | 6% | 1.36 | $12 | $1 | 250 | +5 | 31 | 5 | 8 | 29-20-51 | 3% | 19% | 29% | .755 | .716 | .784 | .701 | .897 | 4.75 | — | — |

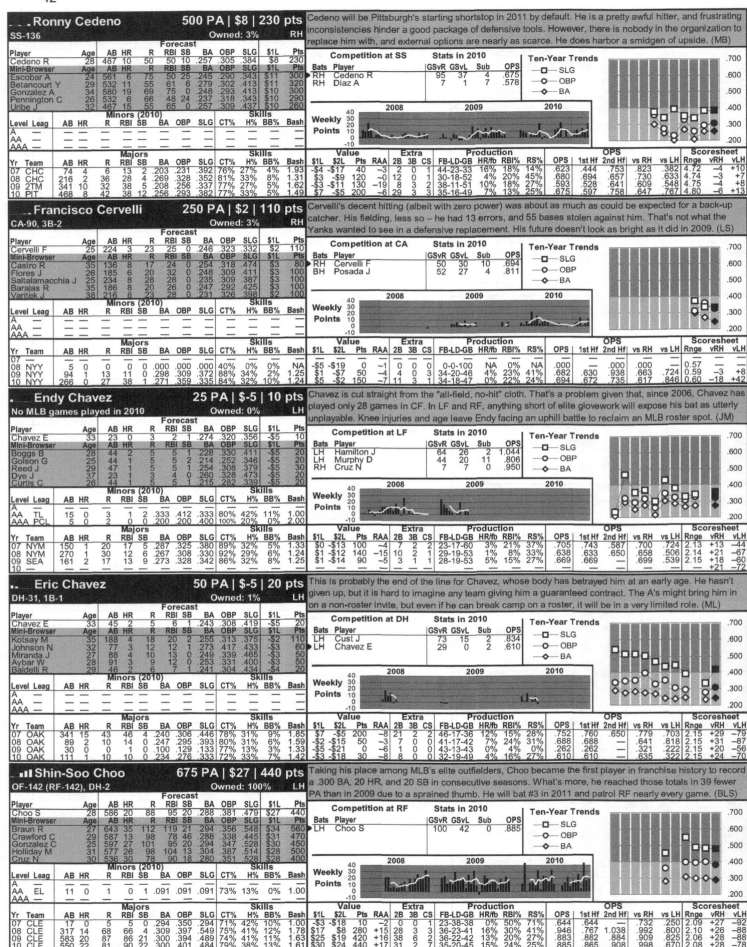

## Ronny Cedeno — 500 PA | $8 | 230 pts

SS-136 — Owned: 3% — RH

Cedeno will be Pittsburgh's starting shortstop in 2011 by default. He is a pretty awful hitter, and frustrating inconsistencies hinder a good package of defensive tools. However, there is nobody in the organization to replace him with, and external options are nearly as scarce. He does harbor a smidgen of upside. (MB)

| Player (Forecast) | Age | AB | HR | R | RBI | SB | BA | OBP | SLG | $1L | Pts |
|---|---|---|---|---|---|---|---|---|---|---|---|
| Cedeno R | 28 | 467 | 10 | 50 | 50 | 10 | .257 | .305 | .384 | $8 | 230 |
| **Mini-Browser** | **Age** | **AB** | **HR** | **R** | **RBI** | **SB** | **BA** | **OBP** | **SLG** | **$1L** | **Pts** |
| Escobar A | 24 | 561 | 6 | 75 | 50 | 25 | .245 | .290 | .343 | $11 | 300 |
| Betancourt Y | 29 | 532 | 11 | 55 | 61 | 6 | .279 | .302 | .413 | $11 | 320 |
| Gonzalez A | 34 | 580 | 19 | 69 | 75 | 0 | .248 | .293 | .413 | $10 | 300 |
| Pennington C | 26 | 532 | 6 | 66 | 48 | 24 | .237 | .318 | .343 | $10 | 290 |
| Uribe J | 32 | 467 | 15 | 55 | 65 | 0 | .257 | .309 | .437 | $10 | 260 |

| Competition at SS | Bats | Player | GSvR | GSvL | Sub | OPS |
|---|---|---|---|---|---|---|
| ▶ | RH | Cedeno R | 95 | 37 | 4 | .675 |
| | RH | Diaz A | 7 | 1 | 7 | .578 |

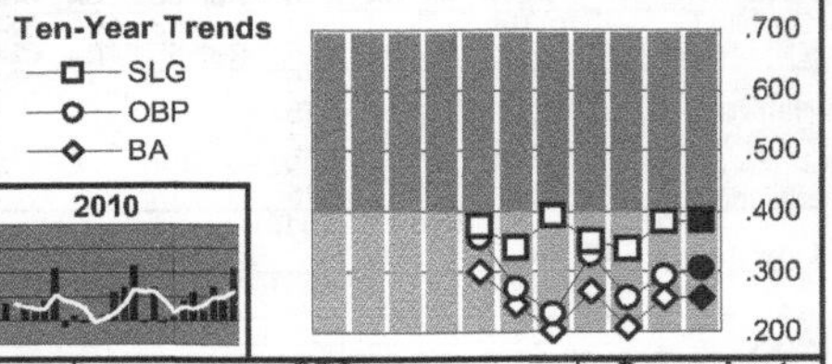


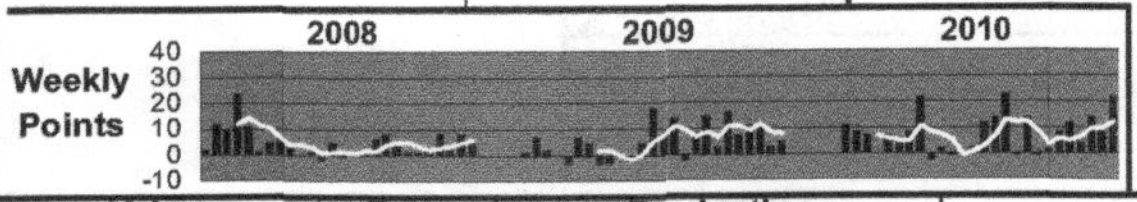


| Minors (2010) Level | Leag | AB | HR | R | RBI | SB | BA | OBP | SLG | CT% | H% | BB% | Bash |
|---|---|---|---|---|---|---|---|---|---|---|---|---|---|
| A | — | — | — | — | — | — | — | — | — | — | — | — | — |
| AA | — | — | — | — | — | — | — | — | — | — | — | — | — |
| AAA | — | — | — | — | — | — | — | — | — | — | — | — | — |

| Majors Yr | Team | AB | HR | R | RBI | SB | BA | OBP | SLG | CT% | H% | BB% | Bash |
|---|---|---|---|---|---|---|---|---|---|---|---|---|---|
| 07 | CHC | 74 | 4 | 6 | 13 | 2 | .203 | .231 | .392 | 76% | 27% | 4% | 1.93 |
| 08 | CHC | 216 | 2 | 36 | 28 | 4 | .269 | .328 | .352 | 81% | 33% | 8% | 1.31 |
| 09 | 2TM | 341 | 10 | 32 | 38 | 5 | .208 | .256 | .337 | 77% | 27% | 5% | 1.62 |
| 10 | PIT | 468 | 8 | 42 | 38 | 12 | .256 | .293 | .382 | 77% | 33% | 5% | 1.49 |

| Yr | Value $1L | $2L | Pts | RAA | Extra 2B | 3B | CS | Production FB-LD-GB | HR/fb | RBI% | RS% | OPS | 1st Hf | 2nd Hf | vs RH | vs LH | Scoresheet Rnge | vRH | vLH |
|---|---|---|---|---|---|---|---|---|---|---|---|---|---|---|---|---|---|---|---|
| 07 | -$4 | -$17 | 40 | −3 | 2 | 0 | 1 | 44-23-33 | 16% | 18% | 14% | .623 | .444 | .753 | .823 | .382 | 4.72 | −4 | +10 |
| 08 | $3 | -$9 | 120 | −0 | 12 | 0 | 1 | 30-18-52 | 4% | 20% | 45% | .680 | .694 | .657 | .730 | .633 | 4.74 | −3 | +7 |
| 09 | -$3 | -$11 | 130 | −19 | 8 | 3 | 2 | 38-11-51 | 10% | 18% | 27% | .593 | .528 | .641 | .609 | .548 | 4.75 | −4 | +8 |
| 10 | $7 | -$5 | 200 | −6 | 29 | 3 | 3 | 35-16-49 | 7% | 13% | 25% | .675 | .597 | .758 | .647 | .767 | 4.80 | −6 | +13 |

## Francisco Cervelli — 250 PA | $2 | 110 pts

CA-90, 3B-2 — Owned: 3% — RH

Cervelli's decent hitting (albeit with zero power) was about as much as could be expected for a back-up catcher. His fielding, less so – he had 13 errors, and 55 bases stolen against him. That's not what the Yanks wanted to see in a defensive replacement. His future doesn't look as bright as it did in 2009. (LS)

| Player (Forecast) | Age | AB | HR | R | RBI | SB | BA | OBP | SLG | $1L | Pts |
|---|---|---|---|---|---|---|---|---|---|---|---|
| Cervelli F | 25 | 224 | 3 | 23 | 25 | 0 | .246 | .323 | .332 | $2 | 110 |
| **Mini-Browser** | **Age** | **AB** | **HR** | **R** | **RBI** | **SB** | **BA** | **OBP** | **SLG** | **$1L** | **Pts** |
| Castro R | 35 | 136 | 8 | 17 | 24 | 0 | .254 | .318 | .474 | $3 | 80 |
| Flores J | 26 | 185 | 6 | 20 | 32 | 0 | .248 | .309 | .411 | $3 | 100 |
| Saltalamacchia J | 25 | 234 | 8 | 28 | 28 | 0 | .235 | .309 | .387 | $3 | 100 |
| Barajas R | 35 | 186 | 8 | 20 | 26 | 0 | .247 | .292 | .425 | $3 | 100 |
| Varitek J | 38 | 216 | 8 | 23 | 28 | 0 | .231 | .326 | .398 | $2 | 100 |

| Competition at CA | Bats | Player | GSvR | GSvL | Sub | OPS |
|---|---|---|---|---|---|---|
| ▶ | RH | Cervelli F | 50 | 30 | 10 | .694 |
| | BH | Posada J | 52 | 27 | 4 | .811 |

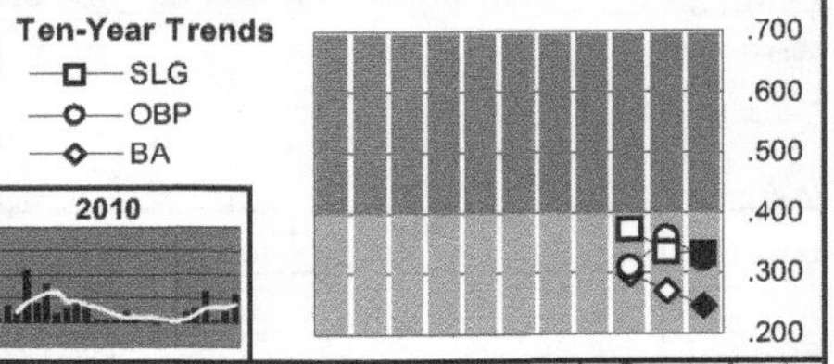


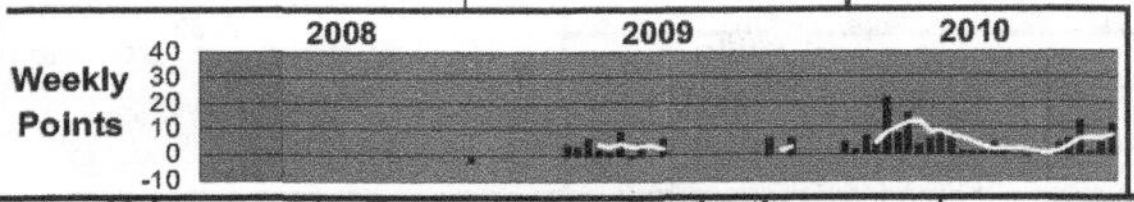


| Minors (2010) Level | Leag | AB | HR | R | RBI | SB | BA | OBP | SLG | CT% | H% | BB% | Bash |
|---|---|---|---|---|---|---|---|---|---|---|---|---|---|
| A | — | — | — | — | — | — | — | — | — | — | — | — | — |
| AA | — | — | — | — | — | — | — | — | — | — | — | — | — |
| AAA | — | — | — | — | — | — | — | — | — | — | — | — | — |

| Majors Yr | Team | AB | HR | R | RBI | SB | BA | OBP | SLG | CT% | H% | BB% | Bash |
|---|---|---|---|---|---|---|---|---|---|---|---|---|---|
| 07 | — | — | — | — | — | — | — | — | — | — | — | — | — |
| 08 | NYY | 5 | 0 | 0 | 0 | 0 | .000 | .000 | .000 | 40% | 0% | 0% | NA |
| 09 | NYY | 94 | 1 | 13 | 11 | 0 | .298 | .309 | .372 | 88% | 34% | 2% | 1.25 |
| 10 | NYY | 266 | 0 | 27 | 38 | 1 | .271 | .359 | .335 | 84% | 32% | 10% | 1.24 |

| Yr | Value $1L | $2L | Pts | RAA | Extra 2B | 3B | CS | Production FB-LD-GB | HR/fb | RBI% | RS% | OPS | 1st Hf | 2nd Hf | vs RH | vs LH | Scoresheet Rnge | vRH | vLH |
|---|---|---|---|---|---|---|---|---|---|---|---|---|---|---|---|---|---|---|---|
| 07 | — | — | — | — | — | — | — | — | — | — | — | — | — | — | — | — | — | — | — |
| 08 | -$5 | -$19 | 0 | −1 | 0 | 0 | 0 | 0-0-100 | NA | 0% | NA | .000 | — | .000 | .000 | — | 0.57 | — | — |
| 09 | $1 | -$7 | 50 | −4 | 4 | 0 | 3 | 34-20-46 | 4% | 23% | 41% | .682 | .630 | .938 | .663 | .724 | 0.59 | −3 | +8 |
| 10 | $5 | -$2 | 150 | −7 | 11 | 3 | 1 | 34-18-47 | 0% | 22% | 24% | .694 | .672 | .735 | .617 | .846 | 0.60 | −18 | +42 |

## Endy Chavez — 25 PA | $-5 | 10 pts

No MLB games played in 2010 — Owned: 0% — LH

Chavez is cut straight from the "all-field, no-hit" cloth. That's a problem given that, since 2006, Chavez has played only 28 games in CF. In LF and RF, anything short of elite glovework will expose his bat as utterly unplayable. Knee injuries and age leave Endy facing an uphill battle to reclaim an MLB roster spot. (JM)

| Player (Forecast) | Age | AB | HR | R | RBI | SB | BA | OBP | SLG | $1L | Pts |
|---|---|---|---|---|---|---|---|---|---|---|---|
| Chavez E | 33 | 23 | 0 | 3 | 2 | 1 | .274 | .320 | .356 | -$5 | 10 |
| **Mini-Browser** | **Age** | **AB** | **HR** | **R** | **RBI** | **SB** | **BA** | **OBP** | **SLG** | **$1L** | **Pts** |
| Boggs B | 28 | 44 | 2 | 5 | 5 | 1 | .228 | .330 | .411 | -$5 | 20 |
| Golson G | 25 | 44 | 1 | 5 | 5 | 2 | .214 | .252 | .346 | -$5 | 20 |
| Reed J | 29 | 47 | 1 | 5 | 5 | 1 | .254 | .308 | .379 | -$5 | 30 |
| Dye J | 37 | 23 | 1 | 3 | 4 | 0 | .260 | .328 | .473 | -$5 | 20 |
| Curtis C | 26 | 44 | 1 | 5 | 5 | 1 | .215 | .282 | .339 | -$5 | 20 |

| Competition at LF | Bats | Player | GSvR | GSvL | Sub | OPS |
|---|---|---|---|---|---|---|
| | LH | Hamilton J | 64 | 26 | 2 | 1.044 |
| | LH | Murphy D | 44 | 20 | 11 | .806 |
| | RH | Cruz N | 7 | 7 | 0 | .950 |

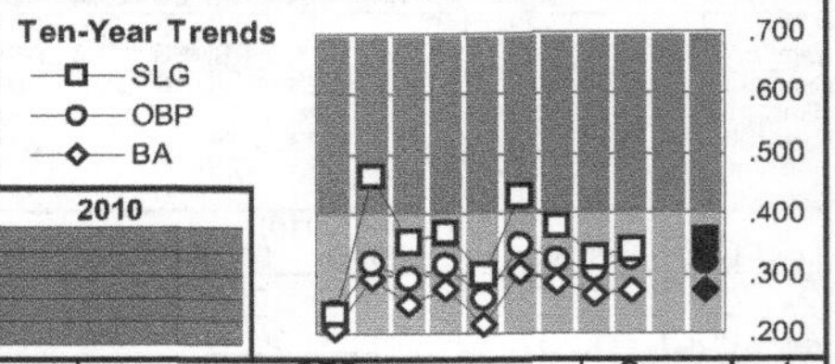


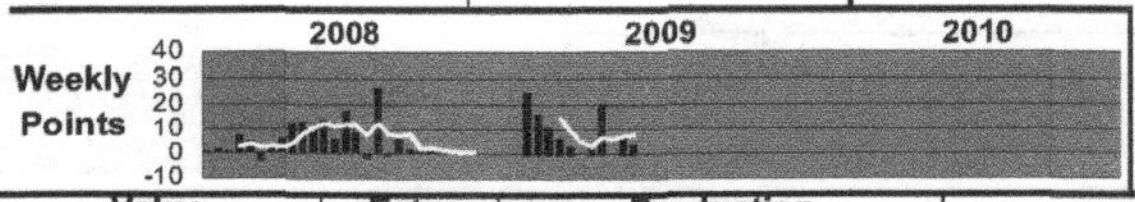


| Minors (2010) Level | Leag | AB | HR | R | RBI | SB | BA | OBP | SLG | CT% | H% | BB% | Bash |
|---|---|---|---|---|---|---|---|---|---|---|---|---|---|
| A | — | — | — | — | — | — | — | — | — | — | — | — | — |
| AA | TL | 15 | 0 | 3 | 1 | 2 | .333 | .412 | .333 | 80% | 42% | 11% | 1.00 |
| AAA | PCL | 5 | 0 | 2 | 0 | 0 | .200 | .200 | .400 | 100% | 20% | 0% | 2.00 |

| Majors Yr | Team | AB | HR | R | RBI | SB | BA | OBP | SLG | CT% | H% | BB% | Bash |
|---|---|---|---|---|---|---|---|---|---|---|---|---|---|
| 07 | NYM | 150 | 1 | 20 | 17 | 5 | .287 | .325 | .380 | 89% | 32% | 5% | 1.33 |
| 08 | NYM | 270 | 1 | 30 | 12 | 6 | .267 | .308 | .330 | 92% | 29% | 6% | 1.24 |
| 09 | SEA | 161 | 2 | 17 | 13 | 9 | .273 | .328 | .342 | 86% | 32% | 8% | 1.25 |
| 10 | — | — | — | — | — | — | — | — | — | — | — | — | — |

| Yr | Value $1L | $2L | Pts | RAA | Extra 2B | 3B | CS | Production FB-LD-GB | HR/fb | RBI% | RS% | OPS | 1st Hf | 2nd Hf | vs RH | vs LH | Scoresheet Rnge | vRH | vLH |
|---|---|---|---|---|---|---|---|---|---|---|---|---|---|---|---|---|---|---|---|
| 07 | $0 | -$13 | 100 | −4 | 7 | 2 | 2 | 23-17-60 | 3% | 21% | 37% | .705 | .743 | .587 | .700 | .724 | 2.13 | +13 | −44 |
| 08 | $1 | -$12 | 140 | −15 | 10 | 2 | 1 | 29-19-53 | 1% | 8% | 33% | .638 | .633 | .650 | .658 | .506 | 2.14 | +21 | −67 |
| 09 | $1 | -$14 | 90 | −5 | 3 | 1 | 1 | 28-19-53 | 5% | 15% | 27% | .669 | .669 | — | .699 | .539 | 2.15 | +18 | −60 |
| 10 | — | — | — | — | — | — | — | — | — | — | — | — | — | — | — | — | — | +21 | −72 |

## Eric Chavez — 50 PA | $-5 | 20 pts

DH-31, 1B-1 — Owned: 1% — LH

This is probably the end of the line for Chavez, whose body has betrayed him at an early age. He hasn't given up, but it is hard to imagine any team giving him a guaranteed contract. The A's might bring him in on a non-roster invite, but even if he can break camp on a roster, it will be in a very limited role. (ML)

| Player (Forecast) | Age | AB | HR | R | RBI | SB | BA | OBP | SLG | $1L | Pts |
|---|---|---|---|---|---|---|---|---|---|---|---|
| Chavez E | 33 | 45 | 2 | 5 | 6 | 1 | .243 | .308 | .419 | -$5 | 20 |
| **Mini-Browser** | **Age** | **AB** | **HR** | **R** | **RBI** | **SB** | **BA** | **OBP** | **SLG** | **$1L** | **Pts** |
| Kotsay M | 35 | 188 | 4 | 18 | 20 | 2 | .255 | .313 | .375 | -$2 | 110 |
| Johnson N | 32 | 77 | 3 | 12 | 12 | 1 | .273 | .417 | .433 | -$3 | 60 |
| Miranda J | 27 | 88 | 4 | 10 | 13 | 0 | .249 | .339 | .465 | -$3 | 50 |
| Aybar W | 28 | 91 | 3 | 9 | 12 | 0 | .253 | .331 | .400 | -$3 | 50 |
| Baldelli R | 29 | 46 | 2 | 6 | 7 | 1 | .241 | .304 | .434 | -$4 | 20 |

| Competition at DH | Bats | Player | GSvR | GSvL | Sub | OPS |
|---|---|---|---|---|---|---|
| | LH | Cust J | 73 | 15 | 2 | .834 |
| ▶ | LH | Chavez E | 29 | 0 | 2 | .610 |

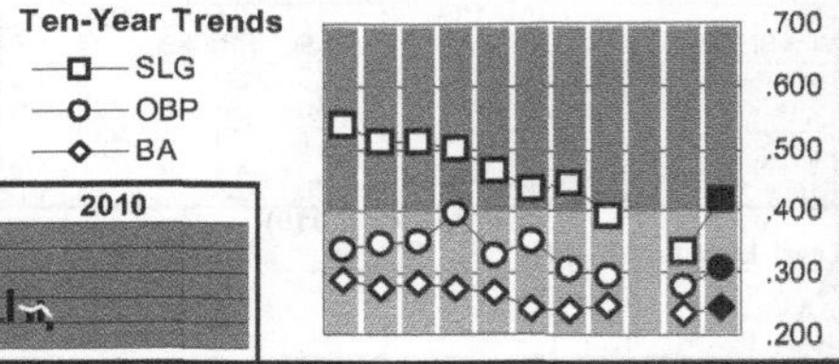


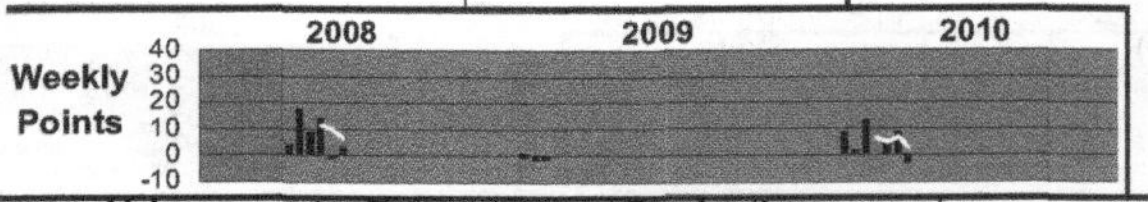


| Minors (2010) Level | Leag | AB | HR | R | RBI | SB | BA | OBP | SLG | CT% | H% | BB% | Bash |
|---|---|---|---|---|---|---|---|---|---|---|---|---|---|
| A | — | — | — | — | — | — | — | — | — | — | — | — | — |
| AA | — | — | — | — | — | — | — | — | — | — | — | — | — |
| AAA | — | — | — | — | — | — | — | — | — | — | — | — | — |

| Majors Yr | Team | AB | HR | R | RBI | SB | BA | OBP | SLG | CT% | H% | BB% | Bash |
|---|---|---|---|---|---|---|---|---|---|---|---|---|---|
| 07 | OAK | 341 | 15 | 43 | 46 | 4 | .240 | .306 | .446 | 78% | 31% | 9% | 1.85 |
| 08 | OAK | 89 | 2 | 10 | 14 | 0 | .247 | .295 | .393 | 80% | 31% | 6% | 1.59 |
| 09 | OAK | 30 | 0 | 0 | 1 | 0 | .100 | .129 | .133 | 77% | 13% | 3% | 1.33 |
| 10 | OAK | 111 | 1 | 10 | 10 | 0 | .234 | .276 | .333 | 72% | 33% | 7% | 1.42 |

| Yr | Value $1L | $2L | Pts | RAA | Extra 2B | 3B | CS | Production FB-LD-GB | HR/fb | RBI% | RS% | OPS | 1st Hf | 2nd Hf | vs RH | vs LH | Scoresheet Rnge | vRH | vLH |
|---|---|---|---|---|---|---|---|---|---|---|---|---|---|---|---|---|---|---|---|
| 07 | $7 | -$5 | 200 | −8 | 21 | 2 | 2 | 46-17-36 | 12% | 15% | 28% | .752 | .760 | .650 | .779 | .703 | 2.15 | +29 | −79 |
| 08 | -$2 | -$15 | 50 | −3 | 7 | 0 | 0 | 41-17-42 | 7% | 24% | 31% | .688 | .688 | — | .641 | .818 | 2.15 | +31 | −87 |
| 09 | -$5 | -$21 | 0 | −6 | 1 | 0 | 0 | 43-13-43 | 0% | 4% | 0% | .262 | .262 | — | .321 | .222 | 2.15 | +20 | −56 |
| 10 | -$3 | -$18 | 30 | −8 | 8 | 0 | 0 | 32-19-49 | 4% | 16% | 27% | .610 | .610 | — | .635 | .322 | 2.15 | +24 | −70 |

## Shin-Soo Choo — 675 PA | $27 | 440 pts

OF-142 (RF-142), DH-2 — Owned: 100% — LH

Taking his place among MLB's elite outfielders, Choo became the first player in franchise history to record a .300 BA, 20 HR, and 20 SB in consecutive seasons. What's more, he reached those totals in 39 fewer PA than in 2009 due to a sprained thumb. He will bat #3 in 2011 and patrol RF nearly every game. (BLS)

| Player (Forecast) | Age | AB | HR | R | RBI | SB | BA | OBP | SLG | $1L | Pts |
|---|---|---|---|---|---|---|---|---|---|---|---|
| Choo S | 28 | 586 | 20 | 88 | 95 | 20 | .288 | .381 | .479 | $27 | 440 |
| **Mini-Browser** | **Age** | **AB** | **HR** | **R** | **RBI** | **SB** | **BA** | **OBP** | **SLG** | **$1L** | **Pts** |
| Braun R | 27 | 643 | 35 | 112 | 119 | 21 | .294 | .356 | .548 | $34 | 560 |
| Crawford C | 29 | 587 | 13 | 98 | 78 | 46 | .288 | .338 | .445 | $31 | 470 |
| Gonzalez C | 25 | 597 | 27 | 101 | 95 | 20 | .294 | .347 | .528 | $30 | 450 |
| Holliday M | 31 | 577 | 26 | 98 | 104 | 13 | .304 | .387 | .514 | $28 | 500 |
| Cruz N | 30 | 536 | 30 | 78 | 90 | 18 | .280 | .351 | .528 | $28 | 400 |

| Competition at RF | Bats | Player | GSvR | GSvL | Sub | OPS |
|---|---|---|---|---|---|---|
| ▶ | LH | Choo S | 100 | 42 | 0 | .885 |

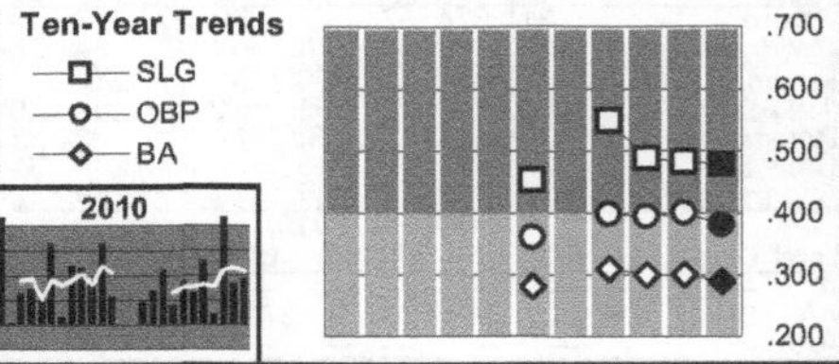


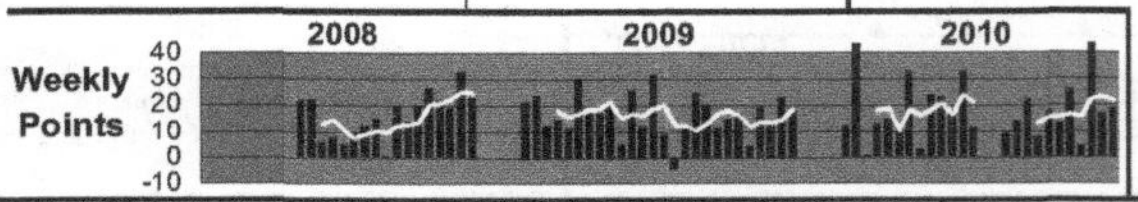


| Minors (2010) Level | Leag | AB | HR | R | RBI | SB | BA | OBP | SLG | CT% | H% | BB% | Bash |
|---|---|---|---|---|---|---|---|---|---|---|---|---|---|
| A | — | — | — | — | — | — | — | — | — | — | — | — | — |
| AA | EL | 11 | 0 | 1 | 0 | 1 | .091 | .091 | .091 | 73% | 13% | 0% | 1.00 |
| AAA | — | — | — | — | — | — | — | — | — | — | — | — | — |

| Majors Yr | Team | AB | HR | R | RBI | SB | BA | OBP | SLG | CT% | H% | BB% | Bash |
|---|---|---|---|---|---|---|---|---|---|---|---|---|---|
| 07 | CLE | 17 | 0 | 5 | 5 | 0 | .294 | .350 | .294 | 71% | 42% | 10% | 1.00 |
| 08 | CLE | 317 | 14 | 68 | 66 | 4 | .309 | .397 | .549 | 75% | 41% | 12% | 1.78 |
| 09 | CLE | 583 | 20 | 87 | 86 | 21 | .300 | .394 | .489 | 74% | 41% | 11% | 1.63 |
| 10 | CLE | 550 | 22 | 81 | 90 | 22 | .300 | .401 | .484 | 79% | 38% | 13% | 1.61 |

| Yr | Value $1L | $2L | Pts | RAA | Extra 2B | 3B | CS | Production FB-LD-GB | HR/fb | RBI% | RS% | OPS | 1st Hf | 2nd Hf | vs RH | vs LH | Scoresheet Rnge | vRH | vLH |
|---|---|---|---|---|---|---|---|---|---|---|---|---|---|---|---|---|---|---|---|
| 07 | -$3 | -$18 | 10 | −2 | 0 | 0 | 1 | 23-38-38 | 0% | 50% | 71% | .644 | .644 | — | .732 | .250 | 2.09 | +27 | −92 |
| 08 | $17 | $8 | 280 | +15 | 28 | 3 | 3 | 36-23-41 | 16% | 30% | 41% | .946 | .767 | 1.038 | .992 | .800 | 2.10 | +26 | −88 |
| 09 | $25 | $19 | 420 | +16 | 38 | 6 | 2 | 36-22-42 | 13% | 20% | 27% | .883 | .882 | .884 | .909 | .825 | 2.06 | +28 | −88 |
| 10 | $30 | $24 | 440 | +17 | 31 | 2 | 7 | 35-20-45 | 15% | 24% | 25% | .885 | .865 | .908 | .998 | .670 | 2.08 | +28 | −78 |

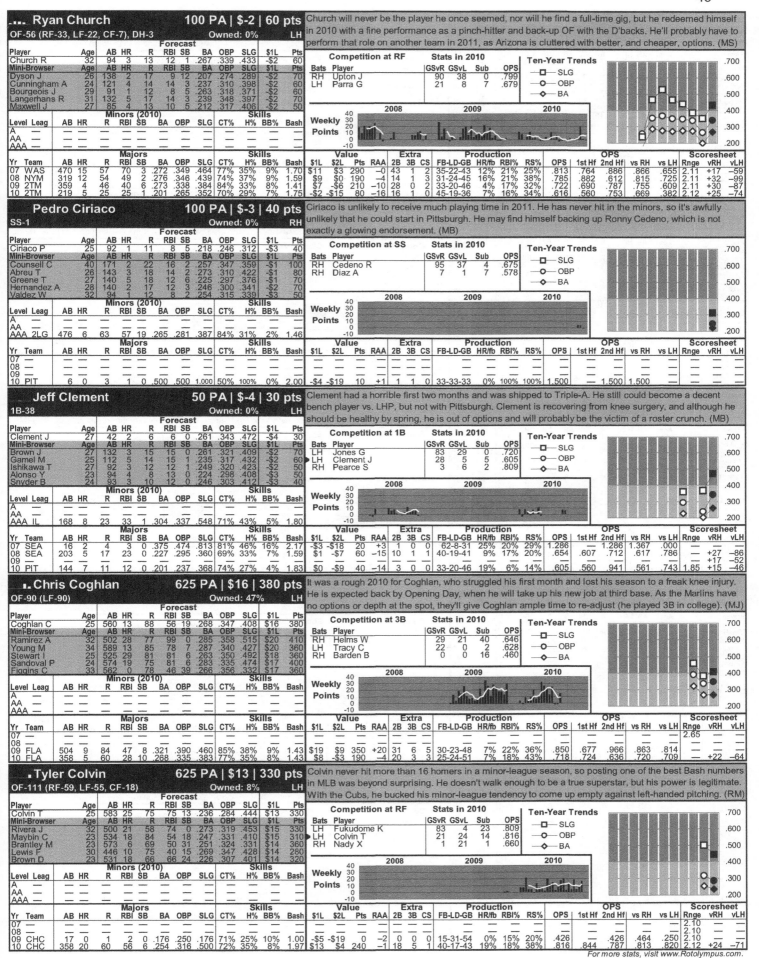

## Ryan Church — 100 PA | $-2 | 60 pts

OF-56 (RF-33, LF-22, CF-7), DH-3 — Owned: 0% — LH

Church will never be the player he once seemed, nor will he find a full-time gig, but he redeemed himself in 2010 with a fine performance as a pinch-hitter and back-up OF with the D'backs. He'll probably have to perform that role on another team in 2011, as Arizona is cluttered with better, and cheaper, options. (MS)

| Player | Age | AB | HR | R | RBI | SB | BA | OBP | SLG | $1L | Pts |
|---|---|---|---|---|---|---|---|---|---|---|---|
| **Forecast** | | | | | | | | | | | |
| Church R | 32 | 94 | 3 | 13 | 12 | 1 | .267 | .339 | .433 | -$2 | 60 |
| **Mini-Browser** | Age | AB | HR | R | RBI | SB | BA | OBP | SLG | $1L | Pts |
| Dyson J | 26 | 138 | 2 | 17 | 9 | 12 | .207 | .274 | .289 | -$2 | 70 |
| Cunningham A | 24 | 121 | 4 | 14 | 14 | 3 | .237 | .310 | .398 | -$2 | 60 |
| Bourgeois J | 29 | 91 | 1 | 12 | 8 | 5 | .263 | .318 | .371 | -$2 | 60 |
| Langerhans R | 31 | 132 | 5 | 17 | 14 | 3 | .239 | .348 | .397 | -$2 | 70 |
| Maxwell J | 27 | 85 | 4 | 13 | 10 | 5 | .212 | .317 | .406 | -$2 | 50 |

| Level | Leag | AB | HR | R | RBI | SB | BA | OBP | SLG | CT% | H% | BB% | Bash |
|---|---|---|---|---|---|---|---|---|---|---|---|---|---|
| **Minors (2010)** | | | | | | | | | | **Skills** | | | |
| A | — | — | — | — | — | — | — | — | — | — | — | — | — |
| AA | — | — | — | — | — | — | — | — | — | — | — | — | — |
| AAA | — | — | — | — | — | — | — | — | — | — | — | — | — |

| Competition at RF | | Stats in 2010 | | | |
|---|---|---|---|---|---|
| Bats | Player | GSvR | GSvL | Sub | OPS |
| RH | Upton J | 90 | 38 | 0 | .799 |
| LH | Parra G | 21 | 8 | 7 | .679 |

Ten-Year Trends

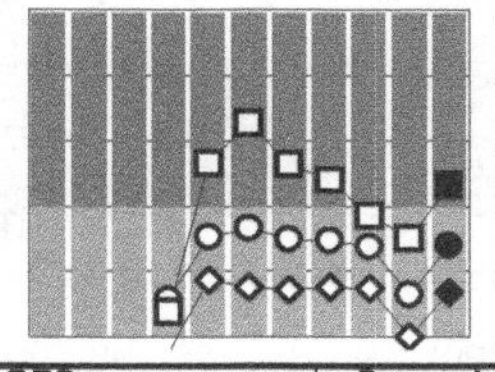

SLG
OBP
BA
.700
.600
.500
.400
.300
.200


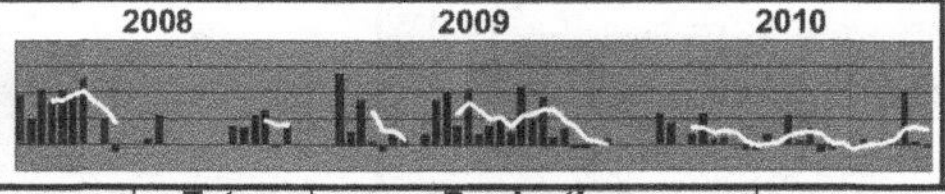

Weekly Points
2008
2009
2010
40
30
20
10
0
-10


| Yr | Team | AB | HR | R | RBI | SB | BA | OBP | SLG | CT% | H% | BB% | Bash | $1L | $2L | Pts | RAA | 2B | 3B | CS | FB-LD-GB | HR/fb | RBI% | RS% | OPS | 1st Hf | 2nd Hf | vs RH | vs LH | Rnge | vRH | vLH |
|---|---|---|---|---|---|---|---|---|---|---|---|---|---|---|---|---|---|---|---|---|---|---|---|---|---|---|---|---|---|---|---|---|
| | | **Majors** | | | | | | | | **Skills** | | | | **Value** | | | | **Extra** | | | **Production** | | | | **OPS** | | | | | **Scoresheet** | | |
| 07 | WAS | 470 | 15 | 57 | 70 | 3 | .272 | .349 | .464 | 77% | 35% | 9% | 1.70 | $11 | $3 | 290 | –0 | 43 | 1 | 2 | 35-22-43 | 12% | 21% | 25% | .813 | .764 | .886 | .866 | .655 | 2.11 | +17 | –59 |
| 08 | NYM | 319 | 12 | 54 | 49 | 2 | .276 | .346 | .439 | 74% | 37% | 9% | 1.59 | $9 | $0 | 190 | –4 | 14 | 1 | 3 | 31-24-45 | 16% | 21% | 38% | .785 | .882 | .612 | .815 | .725 | 2.11 | +32 | –99 |
| 09 | 2TM | 359 | 4 | 46 | 40 | 6 | .273 | .338 | .384 | 84% | 33% | 8% | 1.41 | $7 | -$6 | 210 | –10 | 28 | 0 | 2 | 33-20-46 | 4% | 17% | 32% | .722 | .690 | .787 | .755 | .609 | 2.11 | +30 | –87 |
| 10 | 2TM | 219 | 5 | 25 | 25 | 1 | .201 | .265 | .352 | 70% | 29% | 7% | 1.75 | -$2 | -$15 | 80 | –16 | 16 | 1 | 0 | 45-19-36 | 7% | 16% | 34% | .616 | .560 | .753 | .669 | .382 | 2.12 | +25 | –74 |

## Pedro Ciriaco — 100 PA | $-3 | 40 pts

SS-1 — Owned: 0% — RH

Ciriaco is unlikely to receive much playing time in 2011. He has never hit in the minors, so it's awfully unlikely that he could start in Pittsburgh. He may find himself backing up Ronny Cedeno, which is not exactly a glowing endorsement. (MB)

| Player | Age | AB | HR | R | RBI | SB | BA | OBP | SLG | $1L | Pts |
|---|---|---|---|---|---|---|---|---|---|---|---|
| **Forecast** | | | | | | | | | | | |
| Ciriaco P | 25 | 92 | 1 | 11 | 8 | 5 | .218 | .246 | .312 | -$3 | 40 |
| **Mini-Browser** | Age | AB | HR | R | RBI | SB | BA | OBP | SLG | $1L | Pts |
| Counsell C | 40 | 171 | 2 | 22 | 16 | 2 | .257 | .347 | .359 | -$1 | 100 |
| Abreu T | 26 | 143 | 3 | 18 | 14 | 2 | .273 | .310 | .422 | -$1 | 80 |
| Greene T | 27 | 140 | 5 | 18 | 12 | 6 | .225 | .297 | .376 | -$1 | 70 |
| Hernandez A | 28 | 140 | 2 | 17 | 12 | 3 | .246 | .300 | .341 | -$2 | 70 |
| Valdez W | 32 | 94 | 1 | 12 | 8 | 2 | .254 | .315 | .339 | -$3 | 50 |

| Level | Leag | AB | HR | R | RBI | SB | BA | OBP | SLG | CT% | H% | BB% | Bash |
|---|---|---|---|---|---|---|---|---|---|---|---|---|---|
| **Minors (2010)** | | | | | | | | | | **Skills** | | | |
| A | — | — | — | — | — | — | — | — | — | — | — | — | — |
| AA | — | — | — | — | — | — | — | — | — | — | — | — | — |
| AAA | 2LG | 476 | 6 | 63 | 57 | 19 | .265 | .281 | .387 | 84% | 31% | 2% | 1.46 |

| Competition at SS | | Stats in 2010 | | | |
|---|---|---|---|---|---|
| Bats | Player | GSvR | GSvL | Sub | OPS |
| RH | Cedeno R | 95 | 37 | 4 | .675 |
| RH | Diaz A | 7 | 1 | 7 | .578 |

Ten-Year Trends

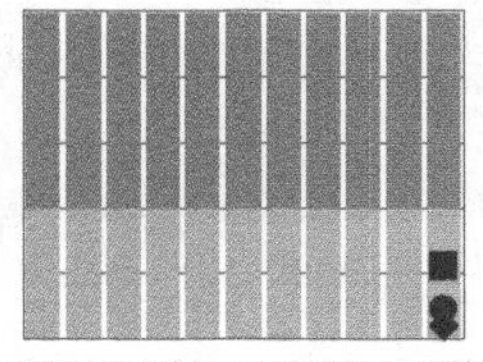

SLG
OBP
BA
.700
.600
.500
.400
.300
.200


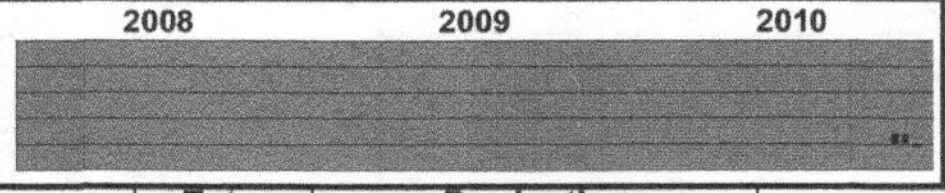

Weekly Points
2008
2009
2010
40
30
20
10
0
-10


| Yr | Team | AB | HR | R | RBI | SB | BA | OBP | SLG | CT% | H% | BB% | Bash | $1L | $2L | Pts | RAA | 2B | 3B | CS | FB-LD-GB | HR/fb | RBI% | RS% | OPS | 1st Hf | 2nd Hf | vs RH | vs LH | Rnge | vRH | vLH |
|---|---|---|---|---|---|---|---|---|---|---|---|---|---|---|---|---|---|---|---|---|---|---|---|---|---|---|---|---|---|---|---|---|
| | | **Majors** | | | | | | | | **Skills** | | | | **Value** | | | | **Extra** | | | **Production** | | | | **OPS** | | | | | **Scoresheet** | | |
| 07 | — | — | — | — | — | — | — | — | — | — | — | — | — | — | — | — | — | — | — | — | — | — | — | — | — | — | — | — | — | — | — | — |
| 08 | — | — | — | — | — | — | — | — | — | — | — | — | — | — | — | — | — | — | — | — | — | — | — | — | — | — | — | — | — | — | — | — |
| 09 | — | — | — | — | — | — | — | — | — | — | — | — | — | — | — | — | — | — | — | — | — | — | — | — | — | — | — | — | — | — | — | — |
| 10 | PIT | 6 | 0 | 3 | 1 | 0 | .500 | .500 | 1.000 | 50% | 100% | 0% | 2.00 | -$4 | -$19 | 10 | +1 | 1 | 1 | 0 | 33-33-33 | 0% | 100% | 100% | 1.500 | — | 1.500 | 1.500 | — | — | — | — |

## Jeff Clement — 50 PA | $-4 | 30 pts

1B-38 — Owned: 0% — LH

Clement had a horrible first two months and was shipped to Triple-A. He still could become a decent bench player vs. LHP, but not with Pittsburgh. Clement is recovering from knee surgery, and although he should be healthy by spring, he is out of options and will probably be the victim of a roster crunch. (MB)

| Player | Age | AB | HR | R | RBI | SB | BA | OBP | SLG | $1L | Pts |
|---|---|---|---|---|---|---|---|---|---|---|---|
| **Forecast** | | | | | | | | | | | |
| Clement J | 27 | 42 | 2 | 6 | 6 | 0 | .261 | .343 | .472 | -$4 | 30 |
| **Mini-Browser** | Age | AB | HR | R | RBI | SB | BA | OBP | SLG | $1L | Pts |
| Brown J | 27 | 132 | 3 | 15 | 15 | 0 | .261 | .321 | .409 | -$2 | 70 |
| Gamel M | 25 | 112 | 5 | 14 | 15 | 1 | .235 | .317 | .432 | -$2 | 60 |
| Ishikawa T | 27 | 92 | 3 | 12 | 12 | 1 | .249 | .320 | .423 | -$2 | 50 |
| Alonso Y | 23 | 94 | 4 | 8 | 13 | 0 | .224 | .298 | .408 | -$3 | 50 |
| Snyder B | 24 | 93 | 3 | 10 | 12 | 0 | .246 | .303 | .412 | -$3 | 40 |

| Level | Leag | AB | HR | R | RBI | SB | BA | OBP | SLG | CT% | H% | BB% | Bash |
|---|---|---|---|---|---|---|---|---|---|---|---|---|---|
| **Minors (2010)** | | | | | | | | | | **Skills** | | | |
| A | — | — | — | — | — | — | — | — | — | — | — | — | — |
| AA | — | — | — | — | — | — | — | — | — | — | — | — | — |
| AAA | IL | 168 | 8 | 23 | 33 | 1 | .304 | .337 | .548 | 71% | 43% | 5% | 1.80 |

| Competition at 1B | | Stats in 2010 | | | |
|---|---|---|---|---|---|
| Bats | Player | GSvR | GSvL | Sub | OPS |
| LH | Jones G | 83 | 29 | 0 | .720 |
| ▸ LH | Clement J | 28 | 5 | 5 | .605 |
| RH | Pearce S | 3 | 6 | 2 | .809 |

Ten-Year Trends

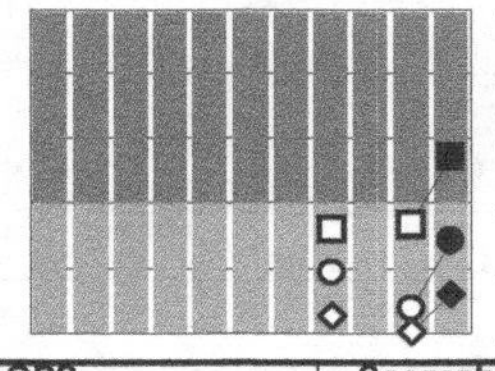

SLG
OBP
BA
.700
.600
.500
.400
.300
.200


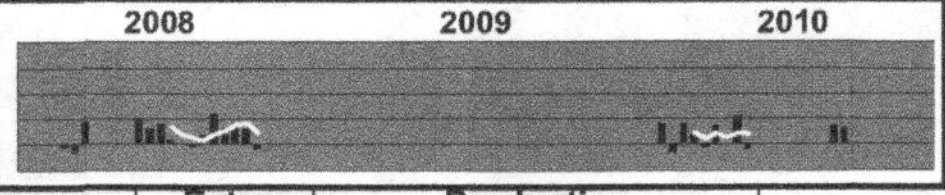

Weekly Points
2008
2009
2010
40
30
20
10
0
-10


| Yr | Team | AB | HR | R | RBI | SB | BA | OBP | SLG | CT% | H% | BB% | Bash | $1L | $2L | Pts | RAA | 2B | 3B | CS | FB-LD-GB | HR/fb | RBI% | RS% | OPS | 1st Hf | 2nd Hf | vs RH | vs LH | Rnge | vRH | vLH |
|---|---|---|---|---|---|---|---|---|---|---|---|---|---|---|---|---|---|---|---|---|---|---|---|---|---|---|---|---|---|---|---|---|
| | | **Majors** | | | | | | | | **Skills** | | | | **Value** | | | | **Extra** | | | **Production** | | | | **OPS** | | | | | **Scoresheet** | | |
| 07 | SEA | 16 | 2 | 4 | 3 | 0 | .375 | .474 | .813 | 81% | 46% | 16% | 2.17 | -$3 | -$18 | 20 | +3 | 1 | 0 | 0 | 62-8-31 | 25% | 20% | 29% | 1.286 | — | 1.286 | 1.367 | .000 | — | — | — |
| 08 | SEA | 203 | 5 | 17 | 23 | 0 | .227 | .295 | .360 | 69% | 33% | 7% | 1.59 | $1 | -$7 | 60 | –15 | 10 | 1 | 1 | 40-19-41 | 9% | 17% | 20% | .654 | .607 | .712 | .617 | .786 | — | +27 | –86 |
| 09 | — | — | — | — | — | — | — | — | — | — | — | — | — | — | — | — | — | — | — | — | — | — | — | — | — | — | — | — | — | — | +17 | –52 |
| 10 | PIT | 144 | 7 | 11 | 12 | 0 | .201 | .237 | .368 | 74% | 27% | 4% | 1.83 | $0 | -$9 | 40 | –14 | 3 | 0 | 0 | 33-20-46 | 19% | 6% | 14% | .605 | .560 | .941 | .561 | .743 | 1.85 | +15 | –46 |

## Chris Coghlan — 625 PA | $16 | 380 pts

OF-90 (LF-90) — Owned: 47% — LH

It was a rough 2010 for Coghlan, who struggled his first month and lost his season to a freak knee injury. He is expected back by Opening Day, when he will take up his new job at third base. As the Marlins have no options or depth at the spot, they'll give Coghlan ample time to re-adjust (he played 3B in college). (MJ)

| Player | Age | AB | HR | R | RBI | SB | BA | OBP | SLG | $1L | Pts |
|---|---|---|---|---|---|---|---|---|---|---|---|
| **Forecast** | | | | | | | | | | | |
| Coghlan C | 25 | 560 | 13 | 88 | 56 | 19 | .268 | .347 | .408 | $16 | 380 |
| **Mini-Browser** | Age | AB | HR | R | RBI | SB | BA | OBP | SLG | $1L | Pts |
| Ramirez A | 32 | 502 | 28 | 77 | 99 | 0 | .285 | .358 | .515 | $20 | 410 |
| Young M | 34 | 589 | 13 | 85 | 78 | 7 | .287 | .340 | .427 | $20 | 360 |
| Stewart I | 25 | 525 | 29 | 81 | 81 | 6 | .263 | .350 | .492 | $18 | 360 |
| Sandoval P | 24 | 574 | 19 | 75 | 81 | 6 | .283 | .335 | .474 | $17 | 400 |
| Figgins C | 33 | 562 | 0 | 78 | 46 | 39 | .266 | .356 | .332 | $17 | 360 |

| Level | Leag | AB | HR | R | RBI | SB | BA | OBP | SLG | CT% | H% | BB% | Bash |
|---|---|---|---|---|---|---|---|---|---|---|---|---|---|
| **Minors (2010)** | | | | | | | | | | **Skills** | | | |
| A | — | — | — | — | — | — | — | — | — | — | — | — | — |
| AA | — | — | — | — | — | — | — | — | — | — | — | — | — |
| AAA | — | — | — | — | — | — | — | — | — | — | — | — | — |

| Competition at 3B | | Stats in 2010 | | | |
|---|---|---|---|---|---|
| Bats | Player | GSvR | GSvL | Sub | OPS |
| RH | Helms W | 29 | 21 | 40 | .646 |
| LH | Tracy C | 22 | 0 | 2 | .628 |
| RH | Barden B | 0 | 0 | 16 | .460 |

Ten-Year Trends

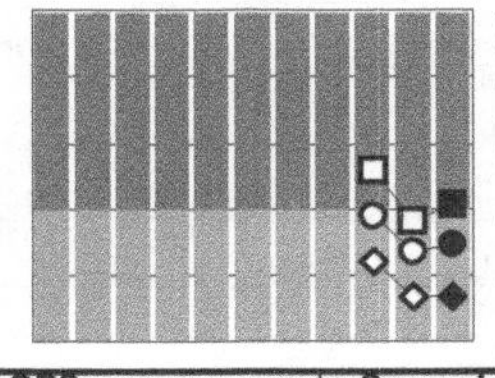

SLG
OBP
BA
.700
.600
.500
.400
.300
.200


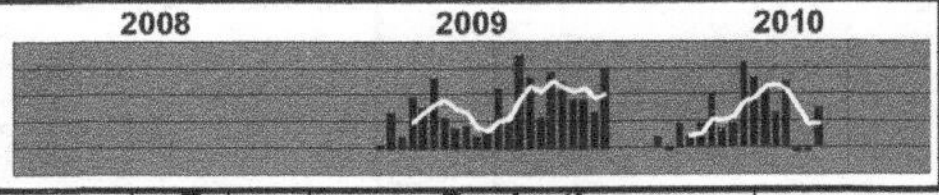

Weekly Points
2008
2009
2010
40
30
20
10
0
-10


| Yr | Team | AB | HR | R | RBI | SB | BA | OBP | SLG | CT% | H% | BB% | Bash | $1L | $2L | Pts | RAA | 2B | 3B | CS | FB-LD-GB | HR/fb | RBI% | RS% | OPS | 1st Hf | 2nd Hf | vs RH | vs LH | Rnge | vRH | vLH |
|---|---|---|---|---|---|---|---|---|---|---|---|---|---|---|---|---|---|---|---|---|---|---|---|---|---|---|---|---|---|---|---|---|
| | | **Majors** | | | | | | | | **Skills** | | | | **Value** | | | | **Extra** | | | **Production** | | | | **OPS** | | | | | **Scoresheet** | | |
| 07 | — | — | — | — | — | — | — | — | — | — | — | — | — | — | — | — | — | — | — | — | — | — | — | — | — | — | — | — | — | 2.65 | — | — |
| 08 | — | — | — | — | — | — | — | — | — | — | — | — | — | — | — | — | — | — | — | — | — | — | — | — | — | — | — | — | — | — | — | — |
| 09 | FLA | 504 | 9 | 84 | 47 | 8 | .321 | .390 | .460 | 85% | 38% | 9% | 1.43 | $19 | $9 | 350 | +20 | 31 | 6 | 5 | 30-23-48 | 7% | 22% | 36% | .850 | .677 | .966 | .863 | .814 | — | — | — |
| 10 | FLA | 358 | 5 | 60 | 28 | 10 | .268 | .335 | .383 | 77% | 35% | 8% | 1.43 | $8 | -$3 | 190 | –4 | 20 | 3 | 3 | 25-24-51 | 7% | 18% | 43% | .718 | .724 | .636 | .720 | .709 | — | +22 | –64 |

## Tyler Colvin — 625 PA | $13 | 330 pts

OF-111 (RF-59, LF-55, CF-18) — Owned: 8% — LH

Colvin never hit more than 16 homers in a minor-league season, so posting one of the best Bash numbers in MLB was beyond surprising. He doesn't walk enough to be a true superstar, but his power is legitimate. With the Cubs, he bucked his minor-league tendency to come up empty against left-handed pitching. (RM)

| Player | Age | AB | HR | R | RBI | SB | BA | OBP | SLG | $1L | Pts |
|---|---|---|---|---|---|---|---|---|---|---|---|
| **Forecast** | | | | | | | | | | | |
| Colvin T | 25 | 583 | 25 | 75 | 75 | 13 | .236 | .284 | .444 | $13 | 330 |
| **Mini-Browser** | Age | AB | HR | R | RBI | SB | BA | OBP | SLG | $1L | Pts |
| Rivera J | 32 | 500 | 21 | 58 | 74 | 0 | .273 | .319 | .453 | $15 | 330 |
| Maybin C | 23 | 534 | 18 | 84 | 54 | 18 | .247 | .331 | .410 | $15 | 310 |
| Brantley M | 23 | 573 | 6 | 69 | 50 | 31 | .251 | .324 | .331 | $14 | 360 |
| Lewis F | 30 | 446 | 10 | 75 | 40 | 15 | .269 | .347 | .428 | $14 | 280 |
| Brown D | 23 | 531 | 18 | 66 | 66 | 24 | .226 | .307 | .401 | $14 | 320 |

| Level | Leag | AB | HR | R | RBI | SB | BA | OBP | SLG | CT% | H% | BB% | Bash |
|---|---|---|---|---|---|---|---|---|---|---|---|---|---|
| **Minors (2010)** | | | | | | | | | | **Skills** | | | |
| A | — | — | — | — | — | — | — | — | — | — | — | — | — |
| AA | — | — | — | — | — | — | — | — | — | — | — | — | — |
| AAA | — | — | — | — | — | — | — | — | — | — | — | — | — |

| Competition at RF | | Stats in 2010 | | | |
|---|---|---|---|---|---|
| Bats | Player | GSvR | GSvL | Sub | OPS |
| LH | Fukudome K | 83 | 4 | 23 | .809 |
| ▸ LH | Colvin T | 21 | 24 | 14 | .816 |
| RH | Nady X | 1 | 21 | 1 | .660 |

Ten-Year Trends

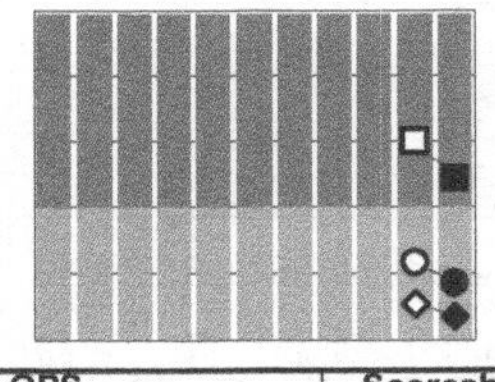

SLG
OBP
BA
.700
.600
.500
.400
.300
.200


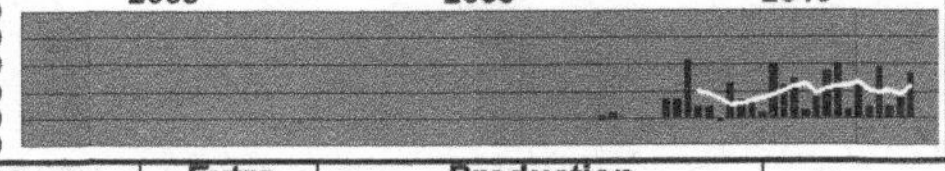

Weekly Points
2008
2009
2010
40
30
20
10
0
-10


| Yr | Team | AB | HR | R | RBI | SB | BA | OBP | SLG | CT% | H% | BB% | Bash | $1L | $2L | Pts | RAA | 2B | 3B | CS | FB-LD-GB | HR/fb | RBI% | RS% | OPS | 1st Hf | 2nd Hf | vs RH | vs LH | Rnge | vRH | vLH |
|---|---|---|---|---|---|---|---|---|---|---|---|---|---|---|---|---|---|---|---|---|---|---|---|---|---|---|---|---|---|---|---|---|
| | | **Majors** | | | | | | | | **Skills** | | | | **Value** | | | | **Extra** | | | **Production** | | | | **OPS** | | | | | **Scoresheet** | | |
| 07 | — | — | — | — | — | — | — | — | — | — | — | — | — | — | — | — | — | — | — | — | — | — | — | — | — | — | — | — | — | 2.10 | — | — |
| 08 | — | — | — | — | — | — | — | — | — | — | — | — | — | — | — | — | — | — | — | — | — | — | — | — | — | — | — | — | — | 2.10 | — | — |
| 09 | CHC | 17 | 0 | 1 | 2 | 0 | .176 | .250 | .176 | 71% | 25% | 10% | 1.00 | -$5 | -$19 | 0 | –2 | 0 | 0 | 0 | 15-31-54 | 0% | 15% | 20% | .426 | — | .426 | .464 | .250 | 2.10 | — | — |
| 10 | CHC | 358 | 20 | 60 | 56 | 6 | .254 | .316 | .500 | 72% | 35% | 8% | 1.97 | $13 | $4 | 240 | –1 | 18 | 5 | 1 | 40-17-43 | 19% | 18% | 38% | .816 | .844 | .787 | .813 | .820 | 2.12 | +24 | –71 |

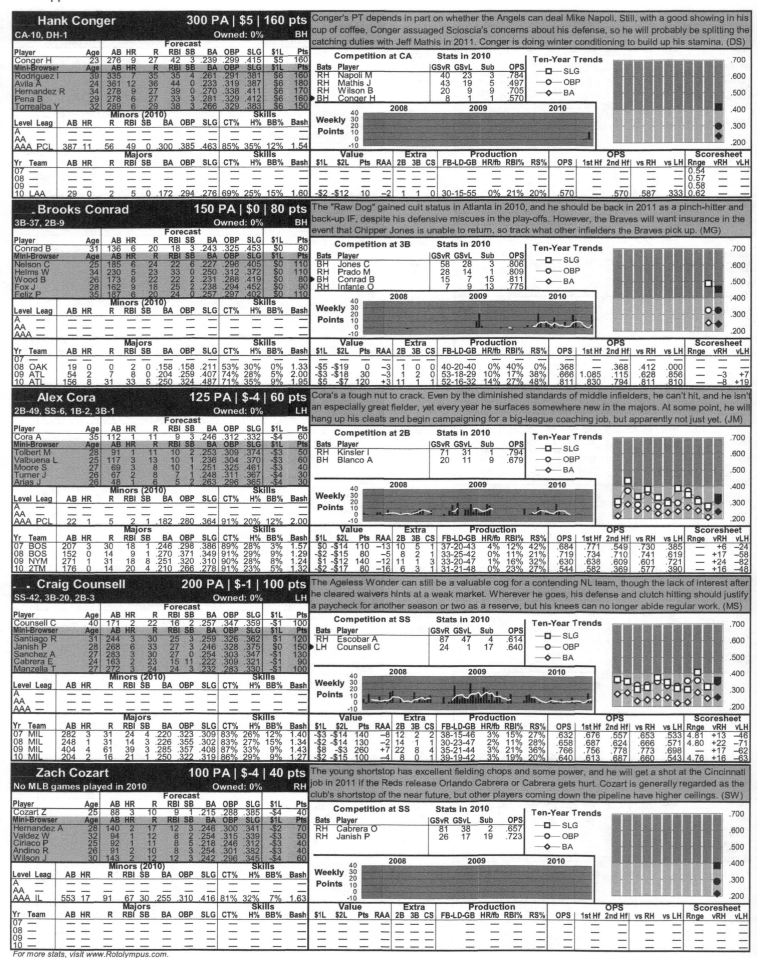

## Hank Conger — 300 PA | $5 | 160 pts
CA-10, DH-1    Owned: 0%    BH

Conger's PT depends in part on whether the Angels can deal Mike Napoli. Still, with a good showing in his cup of coffee, Conger assuaged Scioscia's concerns about his defense, so he will probably be splitting the catching duties with Jeff Mathis in 2011. Conger is doing winter conditioning to build up his stamina. (DS)

### Forecast
| Player | Age | AB | HR | R | RBI | SB | BA | OBP | SLG | $1L | Pts |
|---|---|---|---|---|---|---|---|---|---|---|---|
| Conger H | 23 | 276 | 9 | 27 | 42 | 3 | .239 | .299 | .415 | $5 | 160 |
| Mini-Browser | Age | AB | HR | R | RBI | SB | BA | OBP | SLG | $1L | Pts |
| Rodriguez I | 39 | 335 | 7 | 35 | 35 | 4 | .261 | .291 | .381 | $6 | 160 |
| Avila A | 24 | 361 | 12 | 36 | 44 | 0 | .233 | .319 | .387 | $6 | 180 |
| Hernandez R | 34 | 278 | 9 | 27 | 39 | 0 | .270 | .338 | .411 | $6 | 170 |
| Pena B | 29 | 278 | 6 | 27 | 33 | 3 | .281 | .329 | .412 | $6 | 160 |
| Torrealba Y | 32 | 289 | 6 | 29 | 38 | 1 | .266 | .329 | .383 | $6 | 150 |

### Competition at CA — Stats in 2010
| Bats | Player | GSvR | GSvL | Sub | OPS |
|---|---|---|---|---|---|
| RH | Napoli M | 40 | 23 | 3 | .784 |
| RH | Mathis J | 43 | 19 | 5 | .497 |
| RH | Wilson B | 20 | 9 | 9 | .705 |
| BH | Conger H | 8 | 1 | 1 | .570 |

### Minors (2010) / Skills
| Level | Leag | AB | HR | R | RBI | SB | BA | OBP | SLG | CT% | H% | BB% | Bash |
|---|---|---|---|---|---|---|---|---|---|---|---|---|---|
| A | — | — | — | — | — | — | — | — | — | — | — | — | — |
| AA | — | — | — | — | — | — | — | — | — | — | — | — | — |
| AAA | PCL | 387 | 11 | 56 | 49 | 0 | .300 | .385 | .463 | 85% | 35% | 12% | 1.54 |

### Majors / Skills / Value / Extra / Production / OPS / Scoresheet
| Yr | Team | AB | HR | R | RBI | SB | BA | OBP | SLG | CT% | H% | BB% | Bash | $1L | $2L | Pts | RAA | 2B | 3B | CS | FB-LD-GB | HR/fb | RBI% | RS% | OPS | 1st Hf | 2nd Hf | vs RH | vs LH | Rnge | vRH | vLH |
|---|---|---|---|---|---|---|---|---|---|---|---|---|---|---|---|---|---|---|---|---|---|---|---|---|---|---|---|---|---|---|---|---|
| 07 | — | — | | | | | | | | | | | | | | | | | | | | | | | | | | | | | 0.54 | |
| 08 | — | — | | | | | | | | | | | | | | | | | | | | | | | | | | | | | 0.57 | |
| 09 | — | — | | | | | | | | | | | | | | | | | | | | | | | | | | | | | 0.58 | |
| 10 | LAA | 29 | 0 | 2 | 5 | 0 | .172 | .294 | .276 | 69% | 25% | 15% | 1.60 | -$2 | -$12 | 10 | -2 | 1 | 0 | 30-15-55 | 0% | 21% | 20% | .570 | — | .570 | .587 | .333 | 0.62 | | |

## Brooks Conrad — 150 PA | $0 | 80 pts
3B-37, 2B-9    Owned: 0%    BH

The "Raw Dog" gained cult status in Atlanta in 2010, and he should be back in 2011 as a pinch-hitter and back-up IF, despite his defensive miscues in the play-offs. However, the Braves will want insurance in the event that Chipper Jones is unable to return, so track what other infielders the Braves pick up. (MG)

### Forecast
| Player | Age | AB | HR | R | RBI | SB | BA | OBP | SLG | $1L | Pts |
|---|---|---|---|---|---|---|---|---|---|---|---|
| Conrad B | 31 | 136 | 6 | 20 | 18 | 3 | .243 | .325 | .453 | $0 | 80 |
| Mini-Browser | Age | AB | HR | R | RBI | SB | BA | OBP | SLG | $1L | Pts |
| Nelson C | 25 | 185 | 6 | 24 | 22 | 6 | .227 | .296 | .405 | $0 | 110 |
| Helms W | 34 | 230 | 6 | 23 | 33 | 0 | .250 | .312 | .372 | $0 | 110 |
| Wood B | 26 | 173 | 8 | 22 | 22 | 2 | .231 | .288 | .419 | $0 | 80 |
| Fox J | 28 | 162 | 9 | 18 | 25 | 2 | .238 | .294 | .452 | $0 | 90 |
| Feliz P | 35 | 187 | 6 | 20 | 24 | 0 | .257 | .297 | .402 | $0 | 110 |

### Competition at 3B — Stats in 2010
| Bats | Player | GSvR | GSvL | Sub | OPS |
|---|---|---|---|---|---|
| BH | Jones C | 58 | 28 | 3 | .806 |
| RH | Prado M | 28 | 14 | 1 | .809 |
| BH | Conrad B | 15 | 7 | 15 | .811 |
| RH | Infante O | 7 | 9 | 13 | .775 |

### Minors (2010) / Skills
| Level | Leag | AB | HR | R | RBI | SB | BA | OBP | SLG | CT% | H% | BB% | Bash |
|---|---|---|---|---|---|---|---|---|---|---|---|---|---|
| A | — | — | — | — | — | — | — | — | — | — | — | — | — |
| AA | — | — | — | — | — | — | — | — | — | — | — | — | — |
| AAA | — | — | — | — | — | — | — | — | — | — | — | — | — |

### Majors / Skills / Value / Extra / Production / OPS / Scoresheet
| Yr | Team | AB | HR | R | RBI | SB | BA | OBP | SLG | CT% | H% | BB% | Bash | $1L | $2L | Pts | RAA | 2B | 3B | CS | FB-LD-GB | HR/fb | RBI% | RS% | OPS | 1st Hf | 2nd Hf | vs RH | vs LH | Rnge | vRH | vLH |
|---|---|---|---|---|---|---|---|---|---|---|---|---|---|---|---|---|---|---|---|---|---|---|---|---|---|---|---|---|---|---|---|---|
| 07 | — | — | | | | | | | | | | | | | | | | | | | | | | | | | | | | | | |
| 08 | OAK | 19 | 0 | 0 | 2 | 0 | .158 | .158 | .211 | 53% | 30% | 0% | 1.33 | -$5 | -$19 | 0 | -3 | 1 | 0 | 40-20-40 | 0% | 40% | 0% | .368 | — | .368 | .412 | .000 | — | — | — |
| 09 | ATL | 54 | 2 | 7 | 8 | 0 | .204 | .259 | .407 | 74% | 28% | 5% | 2.00 | -$3 | -$18 | 30 | -3 | 1 | 2 | 53-18-29 | 10% | 17% | 38% | .666 | 1.085 | .115 | .794 | .856 | — | -3 | +7 |
| 10 | ATL | 156 | 8 | 31 | 33 | 5 | .250 | .324 | .487 | 71% | 35% | 9% | 1.95 | $5 | -$7 | 120 | +3 | 11 | 1 | 52-16-32 | 14% | 27% | 48% | .811 | .830 | .794 | .811 | .810 | — | -8 | +19 |

## Alex Cora — 125 PA | $-4 | 60 pts
2B-49, SS-6, 1B-2, 3B-1    Owned: 0%    LH

Cora's a tough nut to crack. Even by the diminished standards of middle infielders, he can't hit, and he isn't an especially great fielder, yet every year he surfaces somewhere new in the majors. At some point, he will hang up his cleats and begin campaigning for a big-league coaching job, but apparently not just yet. (JM)

### Forecast
| Player | Age | AB | HR | R | RBI | SB | BA | OBP | SLG | $1L | Pts |
|---|---|---|---|---|---|---|---|---|---|---|---|
| Cora A | 35 | 112 | 1 | 11 | 9 | 3 | .246 | .312 | .332 | -$4 | 60 |
| Mini-Browser | Age | AB | HR | R | RBI | SB | BA | OBP | SLG | $1L | Pts |
| Tolbert M | 28 | 91 | 1 | 11 | 10 | 2 | .253 | .309 | .374 | -$3 | 50 |
| Valbuena L | 25 | 117 | 3 | 13 | 10 | 1 | .236 | .304 | .370 | -$3 | 60 |
| Moore S | 27 | 69 | 3 | 8 | 10 | 1 | .251 | .325 | .461 | -$3 | 40 |
| Turner J | 26 | 67 | 2 | 8 | 7 | 1 | .248 | .311 | .367 | -$4 | 30 |
| Arias J | 26 | 48 | 1 | 6 | 5 | 2 | .263 | .296 | .365 | -$4 | 30 |

### Competition at 2B — Stats in 2010
| Bats | Player | GSvR | GSvL | Sub | OPS |
|---|---|---|---|---|---|
| RH | Kinsler I | 71 | 31 | 1 | .794 |
| BH | Blanco A | 20 | 11 | 9 | .679 |

### Minors (2010) / Skills
| Level | Leag | AB | HR | R | RBI | SB | BA | OBP | SLG | CT% | H% | BB% | Bash |
|---|---|---|---|---|---|---|---|---|---|---|---|---|---|
| A | — | — | — | — | — | — | — | — | — | — | — | — | — |
| AA | — | — | — | — | — | — | — | — | — | — | — | — | — |
| AAA | PCL | 22 | 1 | 5 | 2 | 1 | .182 | .280 | .364 | 91% | 20% | 12% | 2.00 |

### Majors / Skills / Value / Extra / Production / OPS / Scoresheet
| Yr | Team | AB | HR | R | RBI | SB | BA | OBP | SLG | CT% | H% | BB% | Bash | $1L | $2L | Pts | RAA | 2B | 3B | CS | FB-LD-GB | HR/fb | RBI% | RS% | OPS | 1st Hf | 2nd Hf | vs RH | vs LH | Rnge | vRH | vLH |
|---|---|---|---|---|---|---|---|---|---|---|---|---|---|---|---|---|---|---|---|---|---|---|---|---|---|---|---|---|---|---|---|---|
| 07 | BOS | 207 | 3 | 30 | 18 | 1 | .246 | .298 | .386 | 89% | 28% | 3% | 1.57 | -$9 | -$14 | 110 | -13 | 10 | 5 | 1 | 37-20-43 | 4% | 12% | 42% | .684 | .771 | .549 | .730 | .385 | — | +6 | -24 |
| 08 | BOS | 152 | 0 | 14 | 9 | 1 | .270 | .371 | .349 | 91% | 29% | 9% | 1.29 | -$2 | -$15 | 80 | -5 | 8 | 0 | 1 | 33-25-42 | 0% | 11% | 21% | .719 | .734 | .710 | .741 | .619 | — | +17 | -58 |
| 09 | NYM | 271 | 1 | 31 | 18 | 8 | .251 | .320 | .310 | 90% | 28% | 8% | 1.24 | $1 | -$12 | 140 | -12 | 11 | 1 | 3 | 33-20-47 | 1% | 16% | 32% | .630 | .638 | .609 | .601 | .721 | — | +24 | -82 |
| 10 | 2TM | 176 | 0 | 14 | 20 | 4 | .210 | .266 | .278 | 91% | 23% | 5% | 1.32 | -$2 | -$17 | 80 | -16 | 6 | 3 | 1 | 31-21-48 | 0% | 23% | 27% | .544 | .582 | .369 | .577 | .390 | — | +16 | -48 |

## Craig Counsell — 200 PA | $-1 | 100 pts
SS-42, 3B-20, 2B-3    Owned: 0%    LH

The Ageless Wonder can still be a valuable cog for a contending NL team, though the lack of interest after he cleared waivers hints at a weak market. Wherever he goes, his defense and clutch hitting should justify a paycheck for another season or two as a reserve, but his knees can no longer abide regular work. (MS)

### Forecast
| Player | Age | AB | HR | R | RBI | SB | BA | OBP | SLG | $1L | Pts |
|---|---|---|---|---|---|---|---|---|---|---|---|
| Counsell C | 40 | 171 | 2 | 22 | 16 | 2 | .257 | .347 | .359 | -$1 | 100 |
| Mini-Browser | Age | AB | HR | R | RBI | SB | BA | OBP | SLG | $1L | Pts |
| Santiago R | 31 | 244 | 3 | 30 | 25 | 3 | .259 | .326 | .362 | $1 | 120 |
| Janish P | 28 | 268 | 6 | 33 | 27 | 3 | .246 | .328 | .375 | $0 | 150 |
| Sanchez A | 27 | 283 | 3 | 30 | 27 | 0 | .254 | .303 | .347 | -$1 | 130 |
| Cabrera E | 24 | 163 | 2 | 23 | 15 | 11 | .222 | .309 | .321 | -$1 | 90 |
| Manzella T | 27 | 272 | 3 | 24 | 24 | 3 | .232 | .283 | .330 | -$1 | 100 |

### Competition at SS — Stats in 2010
| Bats | Player | GSvR | GSvL | Sub | OPS |
|---|---|---|---|---|---|
| RH | Escobar A | 87 | 47 | 4 | .614 |
| LH | Counsell C | 24 | 1 | 17 | .640 |

### Minors (2010) / Skills
| Level | Leag | AB | HR | R | RBI | SB | BA | OBP | SLG | CT% | H% | BB% | Bash |
|---|---|---|---|---|---|---|---|---|---|---|---|---|---|
| A | — | — | — | — | — | — | — | — | — | — | — | — | — |
| AA | — | — | — | — | — | — | — | — | — | — | — | — | — |
| AAA | — | — | — | — | — | — | — | — | — | — | — | — | — |

### Majors / Skills / Value / Extra / Production / OPS / Scoresheet
| Yr | Team | AB | HR | R | RBI | SB | BA | OBP | SLG | CT% | H% | BB% | Bash | $1L | $2L | Pts | RAA | 2B | 3B | CS | FB-LD-GB | HR/fb | RBI% | RS% | OPS | 1st Hf | 2nd Hf | vs RH | vs LH | Rnge | vRH | vLH |
|---|---|---|---|---|---|---|---|---|---|---|---|---|---|---|---|---|---|---|---|---|---|---|---|---|---|---|---|---|---|---|---|---|
| 07 | MIL | 282 | 3 | 31 | 24 | 4 | .220 | .323 | .309 | 83% | 26% | 12% | 1.40 | -$3 | -$14 | 140 | -8 | 12 | 2 | 2 | 38-15-46 | 3% | 15% | 27% | .632 | .676 | .557 | .653 | .533 | 4.81 | +13 | -46 |
| 08 | MIL | 248 | 1 | 31 | 14 | 3 | .226 | .355 | .302 | 83% | 27% | 15% | 1.34 | -$2 | -$14 | 130 | -2 | 14 | 1 | 1 | 30-23-47 | 2% | 11% | 28% | .658 | .687 | .624 | .666 | .571 | 4.80 | +22 | -71 |
| 09 | MIL | 404 | 4 | 61 | 39 | 3 | .285 | .357 | .408 | 87% | 33% | 9% | 1.43 | $8 | -$3 | 260 | +7 | 22 | 8 | 4 | 35-21-44 | 3% | 21% | 36% | .766 | .756 | .778 | .773 | .698 | — | +17 | -62 |
| 10 | MIL | 204 | 2 | 16 | 21 | 1 | .250 | .322 | .319 | 86% | 29% | 9% | 1.27 | -$2 | -$15 | 100 | -4 | 8 | 0 | 1 | 39-19-42 | 3% | 19% | 20% | .640 | .613 | .687 | .660 | .543 | 4.76 | +16 | -63 |

## Zach Cozart — 100 PA | $-4 | 40 pts
No MLB games played in 2010    Owned: 0%    RH

The young shortstop has excellent fielding chops and some power, and he will get a shot at the Cincinnati job in 2011 if the Reds release Orlando Cabrera or Cabrera gets hurt. Cozart is generally regarded as the club's shortstop of the near future, but other players coming down the pipeline have higher ceilings. (SW)

### Forecast
| Player | Age | AB | HR | R | RBI | SB | BA | OBP | SLG | $1L | Pts |
|---|---|---|---|---|---|---|---|---|---|---|---|
| Cozart Z | 25 | 88 | 3 | 10 | 9 | 1 | .215 | .288 | .385 | -$4 | 40 |
| Mini-Browser | Age | AB | HR | R | RBI | SB | BA | OBP | SLG | $1L | Pts |
| Hernandez A | 28 | 140 | 2 | 17 | 12 | 3 | .246 | .300 | .341 | -$2 | 70 |
| Valdez W | 32 | 94 | 1 | 12 | 8 | 2 | .254 | .315 | .339 | -$3 | 50 |
| Ciriaco P | 25 | 92 | 3 | 11 | 8 | 5 | .218 | .246 | .312 | -$3 | 40 |
| Andino R | 26 | 91 | 2 | 10 | 8 | 3 | .254 | .301 | .382 | -$3 | 40 |
| Wilson J | 30 | 143 | 2 | 12 | 12 | 3 | .242 | .296 | .345 | -$4 | 40 |

### Competition at SS — Stats in 2010
| Bats | Player | GSvR | GSvL | Sub | OPS |
|---|---|---|---|---|---|
| RH | Cabrera O | 81 | 38 | 2 | .657 |
| RH | Janish P | 26 | 17 | 19 | .723 |

### Minors (2010) / Skills
| Level | Leag | AB | HR | R | RBI | SB | BA | OBP | SLG | CT% | H% | BB% | Bash |
|---|---|---|---|---|---|---|---|---|---|---|---|---|---|
| A | — | — | — | — | — | — | — | — | — | — | — | — | — |
| AA | — | — | — | — | — | — | — | — | — | — | — | — | — |
| AAA | IL | 553 | 17 | 91 | 67 | 30 | .255 | .310 | .416 | 81% | 32% | 7% | 1.63 |

### Majors / Skills / Value / Extra / Production / OPS / Scoresheet
| Yr | Team | AB | HR | R | RBI | SB | BA | OBP | SLG | CT% | H% | BB% | Bash | $1L | $2L | Pts | RAA | 2B | 3B | CS | FB-LD-GB | HR/fb | RBI% | RS% | OPS | 1st Hf | 2nd Hf | vs RH | vs LH | Rnge | vRH | vLH |
|---|---|---|---|---|---|---|---|---|---|---|---|---|---|---|---|---|---|---|---|---|---|---|---|---|---|---|---|---|---|---|---|---|
| 07 | — | — | | | | | | | | | | | | | | | | | | | | | | | | | | | | | | |
| 08 | — | — | | | | | | | | | | | | | | | | | | | | | | | | | | | | | | |
| 09 | — | — | | | | | | | | | | | | | | | | | | | | | | | | | | | | | | |
| 10 | — | — | | | | | | | | | | | | | | | | | | | | | | | | | | | | | | |

## Allen Craig — 225 PA | $1 | 110 pts

OF-34 (RF-30, LF-5), 1B-5, 3B-2, 2B-1 — Owned: 1% — RH

Craig has nothing left to prove in Triple-A (career .928 OPS in two seasons at Memphis). Sporadic playing time in 2010 led to an unimpressive MLB campaign, but barring an unforeseen FA acquisition by St. Louis, Craig should get another shot in 2011 as part of a platoon in right field with Jon Jay. (AB)

### Forecast

| Player | Age | AB | HR | R | RBI | SB | BA | OBP | SLG | $1L | Pts |
|---|---|---|---|---|---|---|---|---|---|---|---|
| Craig A | 26 | 211 | 9 | 25 | 29 | 0 | .245 | .308 | .433 | $1 | 110 |

### Mini-Browser

| Player | Age | AB | HR | R | RBI | SB | BA | OBP | SLG | $1L | Pts |
|---|---|---|---|---|---|---|---|---|---|---|---|
| Diaz M | 33 | 186 | 6 | 24 | 26 | 4 | .269 | .325 | .430 | $2 | 110 |
| Parra G | 23 | 228 | 5 | 28 | 25 | 5 | .263 | .316 | .389 | $1 | 130 |
| Nix L | 30 | 192 | 10 | 24 | 24 | 0 | .260 | .319 | .489 | $1 | 110 |
| Hairston S | 30 | 219 | 9 | 25 | 28 | 2 | .242 | .308 | .433 | $1 | 130 |
| Schierholtz N | 27 | 182 | 4 | 24 | 20 | 4 | .274 | .319 | .445 | $1 | 110 |

### Minors (2010) / Skills

| Level | Leag | AB | HR | R | RBI | SB | BA | OBP | SLG | CT% | H% | BB% | Bash |
|---|---|---|---|---|---|---|---|---|---|---|---|---|---|
| A | — | — | — | — | — | — | — | — | — | — | — | — | — |
| AA | — | — | — | — | — | — | — | — | — | — | — | — | — |
| AAA | PCL | 306 | 14 | 57 | 81 | 1 | .320 | .389 | .549 | 81% | 40% | 10% | 1.71 |

### Competition at RF — Stats in 2010

| Bats | Player | GSvR | GSvL | Sub | OPS |
|---|---|---|---|---|---|
| LH | Jay J | 39 | 5 | 17 | .780 |
| RH | Craig A | 9 | 14 | 7 | .711 |
| BH | Winn R | 12 | 5 | 18 | .663 |
| RH | Stavinoha N | 4 | 12 | 6 | .625 |

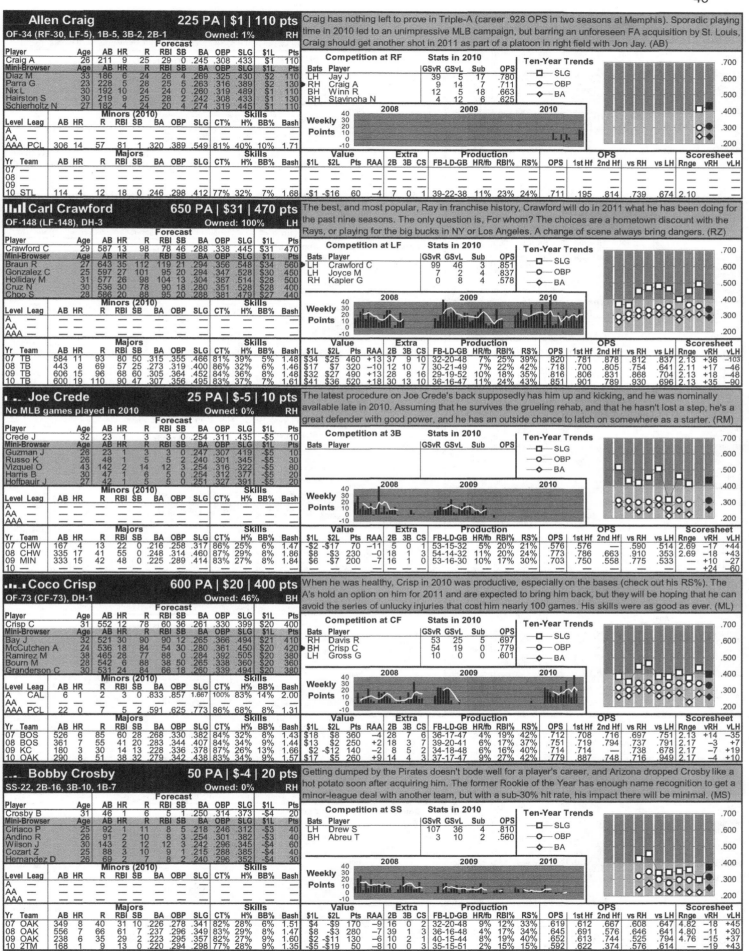

### Majors / Skills / Value / Extra / Production / OPS / Scoresheet

| Yr | Team | AB | HR | R | RBI | SB | BA | OBP | SLG | CT% | H% | BB% | Bash | $1L | $2L | Pts | RAA | 2B | 3B | CS | FB-LD-GB | HR/fb | RBI% | RS% | OPS | 1st Hf | 2nd Hf | vs RH | vs LH | Rnge | vRH | vLH |
|---|---|---|---|---|---|---|---|---|---|---|---|---|---|---|---|---|---|---|---|---|---|---|---|---|---|---|---|---|---|---|---|---|
| 07 | — | — | — | — | — | — | — | — | — | — | — | — | — | — | — | — | — | — | — | — | — | — | — | — | — | — | — | — | — | — | — | — |
| 08 | — | — | — | — | — | — | — | — | — | — | — | — | — | — | — | — | — | — | — | — | — | — | — | — | — | — | — | — | — | — | — | — |
| 09 | — | — | — | — | — | — | — | — | — | — | — | — | — | — | — | — | — | — | — | — | — | — | — | — | — | — | — | — | — | — | — | — |
| 10 | STL | 114 | 4 | 12 | 18 | 0 | .246 | .298 | .412 | 77% | 32% | 7% | 1.68 | -$1 | -$16 | 60 | -4 | 7 | 0 | 1 | 39-22-38 | 11% | 23% | 24% | .711 | .195 | .814 | .739 | .674 | 2.10 | — | — |

---

## Carl Crawford — 650 PA | $31 | 470 pts

OF-148 (LF-148), DH-3 — Owned: 100% — LH

The best, and most popular, Ray in franchise history, Crawford will do in 2011 what he has been doing for the past nine seasons. The only question is, For whom? The choices are a hometown discount with the Rays, or playing for the big bucks in NY or Los Angeles. A change of scene always bring dangers. (RZ)

### Forecast

| Player | Age | AB | HR | R | RBI | SB | BA | OBP | SLG | $1L | Pts |
|---|---|---|---|---|---|---|---|---|---|---|---|
| Crawford C | 29 | 587 | 13 | 98 | 78 | 46 | .288 | .338 | .445 | $31 | 470 |

### Mini-Browser

| Player | Age | AB | HR | R | RBI | SB | BA | OBP | SLG | $1L | Pts |
|---|---|---|---|---|---|---|---|---|---|---|---|
| Braun R | 27 | 643 | 35 | 112 | 119 | 21 | .294 | .356 | .548 | $34 | 560 |
| Gonzalez C | 25 | 597 | 27 | 101 | 95 | 20 | .294 | .347 | .528 | $30 | 450 |
| Holliday M | 31 | 577 | 26 | 98 | 104 | 13 | .304 | .387 | .514 | $28 | 500 |
| Cruz N | 30 | 536 | 30 | 78 | 90 | 18 | .280 | .351 | .528 | $28 | 400 |
| Choo S | 28 | 586 | 20 | 89 | 95 | 20 | .288 | .381 | .479 | $27 | 440 |

### Minors (2010) / Skills

| Level | Leag | AB | HR | R | RBI | SB | BA | OBP | SLG | CT% | H% | BB% | Bash |
|---|---|---|---|---|---|---|---|---|---|---|---|---|---|
| A | — | — | — | — | — | — | — | — | — | — | — | — | — |
| AA | — | — | — | — | — | — | — | — | — | — | — | — | — |
| AAA | — | — | — | — | — | — | — | — | — | — | — | — | — |

### Competition at LF — Stats in 2010

| Bats | Player | GSvR | GSvL | Sub | OPS |
|---|---|---|---|---|---|
| LH | Crawford C | 99 | 46 | 3 | .851 |
| LH | Joyce M | 7 | 2 | 4 | .837 |
| RH | Kapler G | 0 | 8 | 4 | .578 |

### Majors / Skills / Value / Extra / Production / OPS / Scoresheet

| Yr | Team | AB | HR | R | RBI | SB | BA | OBP | SLG | CT% | H% | BB% | Bash | $1L | $2L | Pts | RAA | 2B | 3B | CS | FB-LD-GB | HR/fb | RBI% | RS% | OPS | 1st Hf | 2nd Hf | vs RH | vs LH | Rnge | vRH | vLH |
|---|---|---|---|---|---|---|---|---|---|---|---|---|---|---|---|---|---|---|---|---|---|---|---|---|---|---|---|---|---|---|---|---|
| 07 | TB | 584 | 11 | 93 | 80 | 50 | .315 | .355 | .466 | 81% | 39% | 5% | 1.48 | $34 | $25 | 460 | +13 | 37 | 9 | 10 | 32-20-48 | 7% | 25% | 39% | .820 | .781 | .878 | .812 | .837 | 2.13 | +36 | −103 |
| 08 | TB | 443 | 8 | 69 | 57 | 25 | .273 | .319 | .400 | 86% | 32% | 6% | 1.46 | $17 | $20 | −10 | 12 | 10 | 7 | 30-21-49 | 7% | 22% | 42% | .718 | .700 | .805 | .754 | .641 | 2.11 | +17 | −46 |
| 09 | TB | 606 | 15 | 96 | 68 | 60 | .305 | .364 | .452 | 84% | 36% | 6% | 1.48 | $32 | $27 | 490 | +13 | 28 | 8 | 16 | 29-19-52 | 10% | 18% | 35% | .816 | .806 | .831 | .868 | .704 | 2.13 | +18 | −48 |
| 10 | TB | 600 | 19 | 110 | 90 | 47 | .307 | .356 | .495 | 83% | 37% | 7% | 1.61 | $41 | $36 | 520 | +18 | 30 | 13 | 10 | 36-16-47 | 11% | 24% | 43% | .851 | .901 | .789 | .930 | .696 | 2.13 | +35 | −90 |

---

## Joe Crede — 25 PA | $-5 | 10 pts

No MLB games played in 2010 — Owned: 0% — RH

The latest procedure on Joe Crede's back supposedly has him up and kicking, and he was nominally available late in 2010. Assuming that he survives the grueling rehab, and that he hasn't lost a step, he's a great defender with good power, and he has an outside chance to latch on somewhere as a starter. (RM)

### Forecast

| Player | Age | AB | HR | R | RBI | SB | BA | OBP | SLG | $1L | Pts |
|---|---|---|---|---|---|---|---|---|---|---|---|
| Crede J | 32 | 23 | 1 | 3 | 3 | 0 | .254 | .311 | .435 | -$5 | 10 |

### Mini-Browser

| Player | Age | AB | HR | R | RBI | SB | BA | OBP | SLG | $1L | Pts |
|---|---|---|---|---|---|---|---|---|---|---|---|
| Guzman J | 26 | 23 | 1 | 3 | 3 | 0 | .247 | .307 | .419 | -$5 | 10 |
| Russo K | 26 | 48 | 1 | 5 | 5 | 2 | .240 | .301 | .345 | -$5 | 30 |
| Vizquel O | 43 | 142 | 2 | 14 | 12 | 3 | .254 | .316 | .322 | -$5 | 80 |
| Harris B | 30 | 47 | 1 | 6 | 5 | 0 | .254 | .312 | .377 | -$5 | 20 |
| Hoffpauir J | 27 | 42 | 1 | 5 | 5 | 0 | .251 | .327 | .391 | -$5 | 20 |

### Minors (2010) / Skills

| Level | Leag | AB | HR | R | RBI | SB | BA | OBP | SLG | CT% | H% | BB% | Bash |
|---|---|---|---|---|---|---|---|---|---|---|---|---|---|
| A | — | — | — | — | — | — | — | — | — | — | — | — | — |
| AA | — | — | — | — | — | — | — | — | — | — | — | — | — |
| AAA | — | — | — | — | — | — | — | — | — | — | — | — | — |

### Competition at 3B — Stats in 2010

| Bats | Player | GSvR | GSvL | Sub | OPS |
|---|---|---|---|---|---|

### Majors / Skills / Value / Extra / Production / OPS / Scoresheet

| Yr | Team | AB | HR | R | RBI | SB | BA | OBP | SLG | CT% | H% | BB% | Bash | $1L | $2L | Pts | RAA | 2B | 3B | CS | FB-LD-GB | HR/fb | RBI% | RS% | OPS | 1st Hf | 2nd Hf | vs RH | vs LH | Rnge | vRH | vLH |
|---|---|---|---|---|---|---|---|---|---|---|---|---|---|---|---|---|---|---|---|---|---|---|---|---|---|---|---|---|---|---|---|---|
| 07 | CHW | 167 | 4 | 13 | 22 | 0 | .216 | .258 | .317 | 86% | 25% | 5% | 1.47 | -$2 | -$17 | 70 | −11 | 5 | 0 | 1 | 53-15-32 | 5% | 20% | 21% | .576 | .576 | — | .590 | .514 | 2.69 | −17 | +44 |
| 08 | CHW | 335 | 17 | 41 | 55 | 0 | .248 | .314 | .460 | 87% | 29% | 8% | 1.86 | $8 | -$3 | 230 | −0 | 18 | 1 | 3 | 54-14-32 | 11% | 20% | 24% | .773 | .786 | .663 | .910 | .353 | 2.69 | −18 | +43 |
| 09 | MIN | 333 | 15 | 42 | 48 | 0 | .225 | .289 | .414 | 83% | 27% | 8% | 1.84 | $6 | -$7 | 200 | −7 | 16 | 1 | 0 | 53-16-30 | 10% | 17% | 30% | .703 | .750 | .558 | .775 | .533 | — | +10 | −27 |
| 10 | — | — | — | — | — | — | — | — | — | — | — | — | — | — | — | — | — | — | — | — | — | — | — | — | — | — | — | — | — | +24 | −60 |

---

## Coco Crisp — 600 PA | $20 | 400 pts

OF-73 (CF-73), DH-1 — Owned: 46% — BH

When he was healthy, Crisp in 2010 was productive, especially on the bases (check out his RS%). The A's hold an option on him for 2011 and are expected to bring him back, but they will be hoping that he can avoid the series of unlucky injuries that cost him nearly 100 games. His skills were as good as ever. (ML)

### Forecast

| Player | Age | AB | HR | R | RBI | SB | BA | OBP | SLG | $1L | Pts |
|---|---|---|---|---|---|---|---|---|---|---|---|
| Crisp C | 31 | 552 | 12 | 78 | 60 | 36 | .261 | .330 | .399 | $20 | 400 |

### Mini-Browser

| Player | Age | AB | HR | R | RBI | SB | BA | OBP | SLG | $1L | Pts |
|---|---|---|---|---|---|---|---|---|---|---|---|
| Bay J | 32 | 521 | 30 | 90 | 90 | 12 | .265 | .366 | .494 | $21 | 410 |
| McCutchen A | 24 | 536 | 18 | 84 | 54 | 30 | .280 | .361 | .450 | $20 | 420 |
| Ramirez M | 38 | 465 | 28 | 77 | 88 | 0 | .284 | .392 | .505 | $20 | 380 |
| Bourn M | 28 | 542 | 6 | 87 | 38 | 50 | .265 | .338 | .360 | $20 | 360 |
| Granderson C | 30 | 531 | 24 | 84 | 66 | 18 | .260 | .339 | .494 | $20 | 380 |

### Minors (2010) / Skills

| Level | Leag | AB | HR | R | RBI | SB | BA | OBP | SLG | CT% | H% | BB% | Bash |
|---|---|---|---|---|---|---|---|---|---|---|---|---|---|
| A | CAL | 6 | 1 | 2 | 3 | 0 | .833 | .857 | 1.667 | 100% | 83% | 14% | 2.00 |
| AA | — | — | — | — | — | — | — | — | — | — | — | — | — |
| AAA | PCL | 22 | 0 | 7 | 5 | 2 | .591 | .625 | .773 | 86% | 68% | 8% | 1.31 |

### Competition at CF — Stats in 2010

| Bats | Player | GSvR | GSvL | Sub | OPS |
|---|---|---|---|---|---|
| RH | Davis R | 53 | 25 | 5 | .697 |
| BH | Crisp C | 54 | 19 | 0 | .779 |
| LH | Gross G | 10 | 0 | 0 | .601 |

### Majors / Skills / Value / Extra / Production / OPS / Scoresheet

| Yr | Team | AB | HR | R | RBI | SB | BA | OBP | SLG | CT% | H% | BB% | Bash | $1L | $2L | Pts | RAA | 2B | 3B | CS | FB-LD-GB | HR/fb | RBI% | RS% | OPS | 1st Hf | 2nd Hf | vs RH | vs LH | Rnge | vRH | vLH |
|---|---|---|---|---|---|---|---|---|---|---|---|---|---|---|---|---|---|---|---|---|---|---|---|---|---|---|---|---|---|---|---|---|
| 07 | BOS | 526 | 6 | 85 | 60 | 28 | .268 | .330 | .382 | 84% | 32% | 8% | 1.43 | $18 | $8 | 360 | −4 | 28 | 7 | 6 | 36-17-47 | 4% | 19% | 42% | .712 | .708 | .716 | .697 | .751 | 2.13 | +14 | −35 |
| 08 | BOS | 361 | 7 | 55 | 41 | 20 | .283 | .344 | .407 | 84% | 34% | 9% | 1.44 | $13 | $26 | +2 | 18 | 3 | 7 | 39-20-41 | 6% | 17% | 37% | .751 | .719 | .794 | .737 | .791 | 2.17 | −3 | +7 |
| 09 | KC | 180 | 3 | 30 | 14 | 13 | .228 | .336 | .378 | 87% | 26% | 13% | 1.66 | -$2 | -$12 | 140 | −2 | 5 | 2 | 4 | 34-18-48 | 6% | 16% | 40% | .714 | .714 | — | .738 | .678 | 2.17 | −7 | +19 |
| 10 | OAK | 290 | 8 | 51 | 38 | 32 | .279 | .342 | .438 | 83% | 34% | 9% | 1.57 | $17 | $5 | 260 | +9 | 14 | 4 | 3 | 37-17-47 | 9% | 27% | 42% | .779 | .887 | .748 | .716 | .949 | 2.17 | −4 | +10 |

---

## Bobby Crosby — 50 PA | $-4 | 20 pts

SS-22, 2B-16, 3B-10, 1B-7 — Owned: 0% — RH

Getting dumped by the Pirates doesn't bode well for a player's career, and Arizona dropped Crosby like a hot potato soon after acquiring him. The former Rookie of the Year has enough name recognition to get a minor-league deal with another team, but with a sub-30% hit rate, his impact there will be minimal. (MS)

### Forecast

| Player | Age | AB | HR | R | RBI | SB | BA | OBP | SLG | $1L | Pts |
|---|---|---|---|---|---|---|---|---|---|---|---|
| Crosby B | 31 | 46 | 1 | 6 | 5 | 1 | .250 | .314 | .373 | -$4 | 20 |

### Mini-Browser

| Player | Age | AB | HR | R | RBI | SB | BA | OBP | SLG | $1L | Pts |
|---|---|---|---|---|---|---|---|---|---|---|---|
| Ciriaco P | 25 | 92 | 1 | 11 | 8 | 5 | .218 | .284 | .312 | -$3 | 40 |
| Andino R | 26 | 91 | 2 | 10 | 8 | 3 | .254 | .301 | .382 | -$4 | 40 |
| Wilson J | 30 | 143 | 2 | 12 | 12 | 3 | .242 | .296 | .345 | -$4 | 60 |
| Cozart Z | 25 | 88 | 3 | 10 | 9 | 1 | .215 | .288 | .385 | -$4 | 40 |
| Hernandez D | 26 | 84 | 1 | 8 | 2 | 1 | .240 | .296 | .352 | -$4 | 30 |

### Minors (2010) / Skills

| Level | Leag | AB | HR | R | RBI | SB | BA | OBP | SLG | CT% | H% | BB% | Bash |
|---|---|---|---|---|---|---|---|---|---|---|---|---|---|
| A | — | — | — | — | — | — | — | — | — | — | — | — | — |
| AA | — | — | — | — | — | — | — | — | — | — | — | — | — |
| AAA | — | — | — | — | — | — | — | — | — | — | — | — | — |

### Competition at SS — Stats in 2010

| Bats | Player | GSvR | GSvL | Sub | OPS |
|---|---|---|---|---|---|
| LH | Drew S | 107 | 36 | 4 | .810 |
| BH | Abreu T | 3 | 10 | 2 | .560 |

### Majors / Skills / Value / Extra / Production / OPS / Scoresheet

| Yr | Team | AB | HR | R | RBI | SB | BA | OBP | SLG | CT% | H% | BB% | Bash | $1L | $2L | Pts | RAA | 2B | 3B | CS | FB-LD-GB | HR/fb | RBI% | RS% | OPS | 1st Hf | 2nd Hf | vs RH | vs LH | Rnge | vRH | vLH |
|---|---|---|---|---|---|---|---|---|---|---|---|---|---|---|---|---|---|---|---|---|---|---|---|---|---|---|---|---|---|---|---|---|
| 07 | OAK | 349 | 8 | 40 | 31 | 10 | .226 | .278 | .341 | 82% | 28% | 6% | 1.51 | $4 | -$9 | 170 | −9 | 16 | 0 | 2 | 32-20-48 | 9% | 12% | 33% | .619 | .612 | .667 | .608 | .647 | 4.82 | −18 | +45 |
| 08 | OAK | 556 | 7 | 66 | 61 | 7 | .237 | .296 | .349 | 83% | 29% | 8% | 1.47 | $8 | -$3 | 280 | −7 | 39 | 1 | 2 | 36-16-48 | 4% | 17% | 34% | .645 | .691 | .576 | .646 | .641 | 4.80 | −11 | +30 |
| 09 | OAK | 238 | 6 | 35 | 29 | 2 | .223 | .295 | .357 | 82% | 27% | 9% | 1.60 | -$2 | -$11 | 130 | −6 | 10 | 2 | 1 | 40-15-44 | 8% | 19% | 40% | .652 | .613 | .744 | .525 | .794 | 4.76 | −15 | +37 |
| 10 | 2TM | 168 | 1 | 9 | 13 | 0 | .224 | .298 | .298 | 77% | 28% | 9% | 1.35 | -$5 | -$19 | 50 | −8 | 10 | 0 | 1 | 35-15-51 | 2% | 9% | 15% | .592 | .622 | .374 | .576 | .614 | — | −19 | +43 |

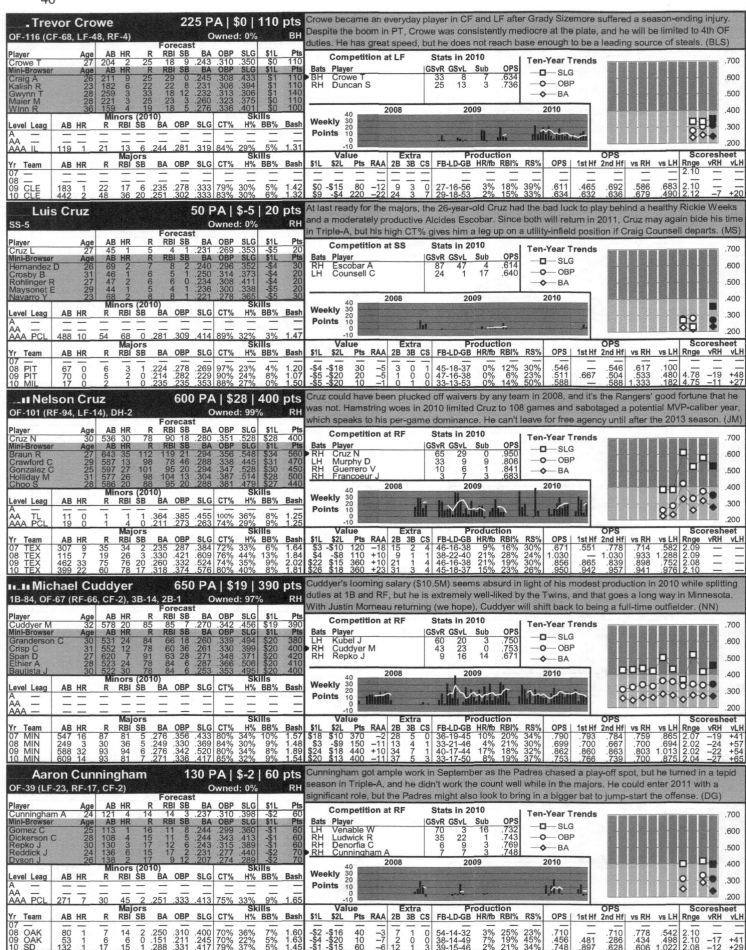

46

## Trevor Crowe — 225 PA | $0 | 110 pts
OF-116 (CF-68, LF-48, RF-4)  Owned: 0%  BH

Crowe became an everyday player in CF and LF after Grady Sizemore suffered a season-ending injury. Despite the boom in PT, Crowe was consistently mediocre at the plate, and he will be limited to 4th OF duties. He has great speed, but he does not reach base enough to be a leading source of steals. (BLS)

### Forecast
| Player | Age | AB | HR | R | RBI | SB | BA | OBP | SLG | $1L | Pts |
|---|---|---|---|---|---|---|---|---|---|---|---|
| Crowe T | 27 | 204 | 2 | 25 | 18 | 9 | .243 | .310 | .350 | $0 | 110 |
| Mini-Browser | Age | AB | HR | R | RBI | SB | BA | OBP | SLG | $1L | Pts |
| Craig A | 26 | 211 | 9 | 25 | 29 | 0 | .245 | .308 | .433 | $1 | 110 |
| Kalish R | 23 | 182 | 6 | 22 | 22 | 8 | .231 | .306 | .394 | $1 | 110 |
| Gwynn T | 28 | 259 | 3 | 33 | 18 | 12 | .232 | .313 | .306 | $1 | 140 |
| Maier M | 28 | 221 | 3 | 25 | 23 | 3 | .260 | .323 | .375 | $0 | 110 |
| Winn R | 36 | 159 | 4 | 19 | 18 | 5 | .276 | .336 | .401 | $0 | 100 |

### Minors (2010) / Skills
| Level | Leag | AB | HR | R | RBI | SB | BA | OBP | SLG | CT% | H% | BB% | Bash |
|---|---|---|---|---|---|---|---|---|---|---|---|---|---|
| A | — |  |  |  |  |  |  |  |  |  |  |  |  |
| AA | — |  |  |  |  |  |  |  |  |  |  |  |  |
| AAA | IL | 119 | 1 | 21 | 13 | 6 | .244 | .281 | .319 | 84% | 29% | 5% | 1.31 |

### Majors / Skills
| Yr | Team | AB | HR | R | RBI | SB | BA | OBP | SLG | CT% | H% | BB% | Bash |
|---|---|---|---|---|---|---|---|---|---|---|---|---|---|
| 07 | — |  |  |  |  |  |  |  |  |  |  |  |  |  |
| 08 | — |  |  |  |  |  |  |  |  |  |  |  |  |  |
| 09 | CLE | 183 | 1 | 22 | 17 | 6 | .235 | .278 | .333 | 79% | 30% | 5% | 1.42 |
| 10 | CLE | 442 | 2 | 48 | 36 | 20 | .251 | .302 | .333 | 83% | 30% | 6% | 1.32 |

**Competition at LF**
| Bats | Player | GSvR | GSvL | Sub | OPS |
|---|---|---|---|---|---|
| BH | Crowe T | 33 | 8 | 7 | .634 |
| RH | Duncan S | 25 | 13 | 3 | .736 |

Ten-Year Trends: □ SLG, ○ OBP, ◇ BA

### Value / Extra / Production / OPS / Scoresheet
| Yr | Team | $1L | $2L | Pts | RAA | 2B | 3B | CS | FB-LD-GB | HR/fb | RBI% | RS% | OPS | 1st Hf | 2nd Hf | vs RH | vs LH | Rnge | vRH | vLH |
|---|---|---|---|---|---|---|---|---|---|---|---|---|---|---|---|---|---|---|---|---|
| 07 | — |  |  |  |  |  |  |  |  |  |  |  |  |  |  |  |  | 2.10 |  |  |
| 08 | — |  |  |  |  |  |  |  |  |  |  |  |  |  |  |  |  |  |  |  |
| 09 | CLE | $0 | -$15 | 80 | -12 | 9 | 3 | 0 | 27-16-56 | 3% | 18% | 39% | .611 | .465 | .692 | .586 | .683 | 2.10 |  |  |
| 10 | CLE | $9 | -$4 | 220 | -22 | 24 | 3 | 7 | 28-18-53 | 2% | 15% | 33% | .634 | .632 | .636 | .679 | .490 | 2.12 | -7 | +20 |

## Luis Cruz — 50 PA | $-5 | 20 pts
SS-5  Owned: 0%  RH

At last ready for the majors, the 26-year-old Cruz had the bad luck to play behind a healthy Rickie Weeks and a moderately productive Alcides Escobar. Since both will return in 2011, Cruz may again bide his time in Triple-A, but his high CT% gives him a leg up on a utility-infield position if Craig Counsell departs. (MS)

### Forecast
| Player | Age | AB | HR | R | RBI | SB | BA | OBP | SLG | $1L | Pts |
|---|---|---|---|---|---|---|---|---|---|---|---|
| Cruz L | 27 | 45 | 1 | 5 | 4 | 1 | .231 | .269 | .353 | -$5 | 20 |
| Mini-Browser | Age | AB | HR | R | RBI | SB | BA | OBP | SLG | $1L | Pts |
| Hernandez D | 26 | 69 | 2 | 7 | 8 | 2 | .240 | .296 | .352 | -$4 | 30 |
| Crosby B | 31 | 46 | 1 | 6 | 5 | 1 | .250 | .314 | .373 | -$4 | 20 |
| Rohlinger R | 27 | 47 | 2 | 6 | 6 | 0 | .234 | .308 | .411 | -$4 | 20 |
| Maysonet E | 29 | 44 | 1 | 5 | 4 | 1 | .236 | .300 | .338 | -$5 | 20 |
| Navarro Y | 23 | 68 | 2 | 8 | 8 | 1 | .221 | .278 | .365 | -$5 | 20 |

### Minors (2010) / Skills
| Level | Leag | AB | HR | R | RBI | SB | BA | OBP | SLG | CT% | H% | BB% | Bash |
|---|---|---|---|---|---|---|---|---|---|---|---|---|---|
| A | — |  |  |  |  |  |  |  |  |  |  |  |  |
| AA | — |  |  |  |  |  |  |  |  |  |  |  |  |
| AAA | PCL | 488 | 10 | 54 | 68 | 10 | .281 | .309 | .414 | 89% | 32% | 3% | 1.47 |

### Majors / Skills
| Yr | Team | AB | HR | R | RBI | SB | BA | OBP | SLG | CT% | H% | BB% | Bash |
|---|---|---|---|---|---|---|---|---|---|---|---|---|---|
| 07 | — |  |  |  |  |  |  |  |  |  |  |  |  |  |
| 08 | PIT | 67 | 0 | 6 | 3 | 1 | .224 | .278 | .269 | 97% | 23% | 4% | 1.20 |
| 09 | PIT | 70 | 0 | 5 | 2 | 0 | .214 | .282 | .229 | 90% | 24% | 8% | 1.07 |
| 10 | MIL | 17 | 0 | 2 | 1 | 0 | .235 | .235 | .353 | 88% | 27% | 0% | 1.50 |

**Competition at SS**
| Bats | Player | GSvR | GSvL | Sub | OPS |
|---|---|---|---|---|---|
| RH | Escobar A | 87 | 47 | 4 | .614 |
| LH | Counsell C | 24 | 1 | 17 | .640 |

Ten-Year Trends: □ SLG, ○ OBP, ◇ BA

### Value / Extra / Production / OPS / Scoresheet
| Yr | Team | $1L | $2L | Pts | RAA | 2B | 3B | CS | FB-LD-GB | HR/fb | RBI% | RS% | OPS | 1st Hf | 2nd Hf | vs RH | vs LH | Rnge | vRH | vLH |
|---|---|---|---|---|---|---|---|---|---|---|---|---|---|---|---|---|---|---|---|---|
| 07 | — |  |  |  |  |  |  |  |  |  |  |  |  |  |  |  |  |  |  |  |
| 08 | PIT | -$4 | -$18 | 30 | -5 | 3 | 0 | 1 | 45-18-37 | 0% | 12% | 30% | .546 |  | .546 | .617 | .100 | 4.78 | -19 | +48 |
| 09 | PIT | -$5 | -$20 | 20 | -5 | 1 | 0 | 0 | 47-16-38 | 0% | 6% | 23% | .511 | .667 | .504 | .533 | .480 | 4.75 | -11 | +27 |
| 10 | MIL | -$5 | -$20 | 10 | -1 | 0 | 1 | 0 | 33-13-53 | 0% | 14% | 50% | .588 |  | .588 | 1.333 | .182 | 4.75 | -11 | +27 |

## Nelson Cruz — 600 PA | $28 | 400 pts
OF-101 (RF-94, LF-14), DH-2  Owned: 99%  RH

Cruz could have been plucked off waivers by any team in 2008, and it's the Rangers' good fortune that he was not. Hamstring woes in 2010 limited Cruz to 108 games and sabotaged a potential MVP-caliber year, which speaks to his per-game dominance. He can't leave for free agency until after the 2013 season. (JM)

### Forecast
| Player | Age | AB | HR | R | RBI | SB | BA | OBP | SLG | $1L | Pts |
|---|---|---|---|---|---|---|---|---|---|---|---|
| Cruz N | 30 | 536 | 30 | 78 | 90 | 18 | .280 | .351 | .528 | $28 | 400 |
| Mini-Browser | Age | AB | HR | R | RBI | SB | BA | OBP | SLG | $1L | Pts |
| Braun R | 27 | 643 | 35 | 112 | 119 | 21 | .294 | .356 | .548 | $34 | 560 |
| Crawford C | 29 | 587 | 13 | 98 | 78 | 46 | .288 | .338 | .445 | $31 | 470 |
| Gonzalez C | 25 | 597 | 27 | 101 | 95 | 20 | .294 | .347 | .528 | $30 | 450 |
| Holliday M | 31 | 577 | 26 | 98 | 104 | 13 | .304 | .387 | .514 | $28 | 500 |
| Choo S | 28 | 586 | 20 | 88 | 95 | 20 | .288 | .381 | .479 | $27 | 440 |

### Minors (2010) / Skills
| Level | Leag | AB | HR | R | RBI | SB | BA | OBP | SLG | CT% | H% | BB% | Bash |
|---|---|---|---|---|---|---|---|---|---|---|---|---|---|
| A | — |  |  |  |  |  |  |  |  |  |  |  |  |
| AA | TL | 11 | 0 | 1 | 1 | 1 | .364 | .385 | .455 | 100% | 36% | 8% | 1.25 |
| AAA | PCL | 19 | 0 | 1 | 4 | 0 | .211 | .273 | .263 | 74% | 29% | 9% | 1.25 |

### Majors / Skills
| Yr | Team | AB | HR | R | RBI | SB | BA | OBP | SLG | CT% | H% | BB% | Bash |
|---|---|---|---|---|---|---|---|---|---|---|---|---|---|
| 07 | TEX | 307 | 9 | 35 | 34 | 2 | .235 | .287 | .384 | 72% | 30% | 6% | 1.64 |
| 08 | TEX | 115 | 7 | 19 | 26 | 3 | .330 | .421 | .609 | 76% | 44% | 13% | 1.84 |
| 09 | TEX | 462 | 33 | 75 | 76 | 20 | .260 | .332 | .524 | 74% | 35% | 9% | 2.02 |
| 10 | TEX | 399 | 22 | 60 | 78 | 17 | .318 | .374 | .576 | 80% | 40% | 8% | 1.81 |

**Competition at RF**
| Bats | Player | GSvR | GSvL | Sub | OPS |
|---|---|---|---|---|---|
| RH | Cruz N | 65 | 29 | 0 | .950 |
| LH | Murphy D | 33 | 9 | 9 | .806 |
| RH | Guerrero V | 10 | 6 | 1 | .841 |
| RH | Francoeur J | 3 | 7 | 3 | .683 |

Ten-Year Trends: □ SLG, ○ OBP, ◇ BA

### Value / Extra / Production / OPS / Scoresheet
| Yr | Team | $1L | $2L | Pts | RAA | 2B | 3B | CS | FB-LD-GB | HR/fb | RBI% | RS% | OPS | 1st Hf | 2nd Hf | vs RH | vs LH | Rnge | vRH | vLH |
|---|---|---|---|---|---|---|---|---|---|---|---|---|---|---|---|---|---|---|---|---|
| 07 | TEX | $3 | -$10 | 120 | -18 | 15 | 2 | 4 | 46-16-38 | 9% | 16% | 30% | .671 | .551 | .736 | .714 | .582 | 2.09 |  |  |
| 08 | TEX | $4 | -$8 | 110 | +10 | 7 | 1 | 1 | 38-22-40 | 21% | 28% | 24% | 1.030 |  | 1.030 | .933 | 1.288 | 2.09 |  |  |
| 09 | TEX | $22 | $15 | 360 | +10 | 21 | 1 | 4 | 46-16-38 | 21% | 19% | 30% | .856 | .865 | .839 | .898 | .752 | 2.08 |  |  |
| 10 | TEX | $26 | $18 | 360 | +23 | 31 | 1 | 4 | 48-18-37 | 15% | 23% | 26% | .950 | .942 | .957 | .941 | .976 | 2.10 |  |  |

## Michael Cuddyer — 650 PA | $19 | 390 pts
1B-84, OF-67 (RF-66, CF-2), 3B-14, 2B-1  Owned: 97%  RH

Cuddyer's looming salary ($10.5M) seems absurd in light of his modest production in 2010 while splitting duties at 1B and RF, but he is extremely well-liked by the Twins, and that goes a long way in Minnesota. With Justin Morneau returning (we hope), Cuddyer will shift back to being a full-time outfielder. (NN)

### Forecast
| Player | Age | AB | HR | R | RBI | SB | BA | OBP | SLG | $1L | Pts |
|---|---|---|---|---|---|---|---|---|---|---|---|
| Cuddyer M | 32 | 578 | 20 | 85 | 85 | 7 | .270 | .342 | .456 | $19 | 390 |
| Mini-Browser | Age | AB | HR | R | RBI | SB | BA | OBP | SLG | $1L | Pts |
| Granderson C | 30 | 531 | 24 | 84 | 66 | 18 | .260 | .339 | .494 | $20 | 380 |
| Crisp C | 31 | 552 | 12 | 78 | 60 | 36 | .261 | .330 | .399 | $20 | 400 |
| Span D | 27 | 620 | 7 | 91 | 63 | 28 | .271 | .348 | .371 | $20 | 420 |
| Ethier A | 28 | 523 | 24 | 78 | 84 | 4 | .287 | .366 | .506 | $20 | 410 |
| Bautista J | 30 | 522 | 30 | 78 | 84 | 6 | .253 | .353 | .495 | $20 | 400 |

### Minors (2010) / Skills
| Level | Leag | AB | HR | R | RBI | SB | BA | OBP | SLG | CT% | H% | BB% | Bash |
|---|---|---|---|---|---|---|---|---|---|---|---|---|---|
| A | — |  |  |  |  |  |  |  |  |  |  |  |  |
| AA | — |  |  |  |  |  |  |  |  |  |  |  |  |
| AAA | — |  |  |  |  |  |  |  |  |  |  |  |  |

### Majors / Skills
| Yr | Team | AB | HR | R | RBI | SB | BA | OBP | SLG | CT% | H% | BB% | Bash |
|---|---|---|---|---|---|---|---|---|---|---|---|---|---|
| 07 | MIN | 547 | 16 | 87 | 81 | 5 | .276 | .356 | .433 | 80% | 34% | 10% | 1.57 |
| 08 | MIN | 249 | 3 | 30 | 36 | 5 | .249 | .330 | .369 | 84% | 30% | 9% | 1.48 |
| 09 | MIN | 588 | 32 | 93 | 94 | 6 | .276 | .342 | .520 | 84% | 30% | 8% | 1.89 |
| 10 | MIN | 609 | 14 | 93 | 81 | 7 | .271 | .336 | .417 | 85% | 32% | 9% | 1.54 |

**Competition at RF**
| Bats | Player | GSvR | GSvL | Sub | OPS |
|---|---|---|---|---|---|
| LH | Kubel J | 60 | 20 | 5 | .750 |
| RH | Cuddyer M | 43 | 23 | 0 | .753 |
| RH | Repko J | 9 | 16 | 14 | .671 |

Ten-Year Trends: □ SLG, ○ OBP, ◇ BA

### Value / Extra / Production / OPS / Scoresheet
| Yr | Team | $1L | $2L | Pts | RAA | 2B | 3B | CS | FB-LD-GB | HR/fb | RBI% | RS% | OPS | 1st Hf | 2nd Hf | vs RH | vs LH | Rnge | vRH | vLH |
|---|---|---|---|---|---|---|---|---|---|---|---|---|---|---|---|---|---|---|---|---|
| 07 | MIN | $18 | $10 | 370 | -2 | 28 | 5 | 0 | 36-19-45 | 10% | 20% | 34% | .790 | .793 | .784 | .759 | .865 | 2.07 | -19 | +41 |
| 08 | MIN | $3 | -$9 | 150 | -11 | 13 | 4 | 1 | 33-21-46 | 4% | 21% | 30% | .699 | .700 | .667 | .700 | .694 | 2.02 | -24 | +57 |
| 09 | MIN | $24 | $18 | 440 | +10 | 34 | 7 | 1 | 40-17-44 | 17% | 18% | 32% | .862 | .860 | .863 | .803 | 1.013 | 2.02 | -22 | +54 |
| 10 | MIN | $20 | $13 | 400 | -11 | 37 | 5 | 3 | 33-17-50 | 8% | 19% | 37% | .753 | .766 | .739 | .700 | .875 | 2.04 | -27 | +65 |

## Aaron Cunningham — 130 PA | $-2 | 60 pts
OF-39 (LF-23, RF-17, CF-2)  Owned: 0%  RH

Cunningham got ample work in September as the Padres chased a play-off spot, but he turned in a tepid season in Triple-A, and he didn't work the count well while in the majors. He could enter 2011 with a significant role, but the Padres might also look to bring in a bigger bat to jump-start the offense. (DG)

### Forecast
| Player | Age | AB | HR | R | RBI | SB | BA | OBP | SLG | $1L | Pts |
|---|---|---|---|---|---|---|---|---|---|---|---|
| Cunningham A | 24 | 121 | 4 | 14 | 14 | 3 | .237 | .310 | .398 | -$2 | 60 |
| Mini-Browser | Age | AB | HR | R | RBI | SB | BA | OBP | SLG | $1L | Pts |
| Gomez C | 25 | 113 | 1 | 16 | 11 | 8 | .244 | .299 | .360 | -$1 | 60 |
| Dickerson C | 28 | 108 | 4 | 15 | 11 | 5 | .244 | .343 | .413 | -$1 | 60 |
| Repko J | 30 | 130 | 4 | 17 | 12 | 6 | .243 | .315 | .389 | -$1 | 60 |
| Reddick J | 24 | 136 | 6 | 15 | 17 | 2 | .231 | .277 | .440 | -$2 | 70 |
| Dyson J | 26 | 138 | 2 | 17 | 9 | 12 | .207 | .274 | .289 | -$2 | 70 |

### Minors (2010) / Skills
| Level | Leag | AB | HR | R | RBI | SB | BA | OBP | SLG | CT% | H% | BB% | Bash |
|---|---|---|---|---|---|---|---|---|---|---|---|---|---|
| A | — |  |  |  |  |  |  |  |  |  |  |  |  |
| AA | — |  |  |  |  |  |  |  |  |  |  |  |  |
| AAA | PCL | 271 | 7 | 30 | 45 | 2 | .251 | .333 | .413 | 75% | 33% | 9% | 1.65 |

### Majors / Skills
| Yr | Team | AB | HR | R | RBI | SB | BA | OBP | SLG | CT% | H% | BB% | Bash |
|---|---|---|---|---|---|---|---|---|---|---|---|---|---|
| 07 | — |  |  |  |  |  |  |  |  |  |  |  |  |  |
| 08 | OAK | 80 | 1 | 7 | 14 | 2 | .250 | .310 | .400 | 70% | 36% | 7% | 1.60 |
| 09 | OAK | 53 | 1 | 6 | 6 | 0 | .151 | .211 | .245 | 70% | 22% | 5% | 1.63 |
| 10 | SD | 132 | 1 | 17 | 15 | 1 | .288 | .331 | .417 | 79% | 37% | 5% | 1.45 |

**Competition at RF**
| Bats | Player | GSvR | GSvL | Sub | OPS |
|---|---|---|---|---|---|
| LH | Venable W | 70 | 3 | 16 | .732 |
| RH | Ludwick R | 35 | 22 | 1 | .743 |
| RH | Denorfia C | 6 | 9 | 3 | .769 |
| RH | Cunningham A | 7 | 7 | 3 | .748 |

Ten-Year Trends: □ SLG, ○ OBP, ◇ BA

### Value / Extra / Production / OPS / Scoresheet
| Yr | Team | $1L | $2L | Pts | RAA | 2B | 3B | CS | FB-LD-GB | HR/fb | RBI% | RS% | OPS | 1st Hf | 2nd Hf | vs RH | vs LH | Rnge | vRH | vLH |
|---|---|---|---|---|---|---|---|---|---|---|---|---|---|---|---|---|---|---|---|---|
| 07 | — |  |  |  |  |  |  |  |  |  |  |  |  |  |  |  |  |  |  |  |
| 08 | OAK | -$2 | -$16 | 40 | -3 | 7 | 1 | 0 | 54-14-32 | 3% | 25% | 23% | .710 |  | .710 | .778 | .542 | 2.10 |  |  |
| 09 | OAK | -$4 | -$20 | 10 | -7 | 2 | 0 | 0 | 38-14-49 | 7% | 19% | 45% | .456 | .481 | .286 | .434 | .498 | 2.10 | -17 | +41 |
| 10 | SD | -$1 | -$15 | 60 | -6 | 12 | 1 | 0 | 39-15-46 | 2% | 21% | 34% | .748 | .897 | .628 | .606 | 1.022 | 2.08 | -12 | +14 |

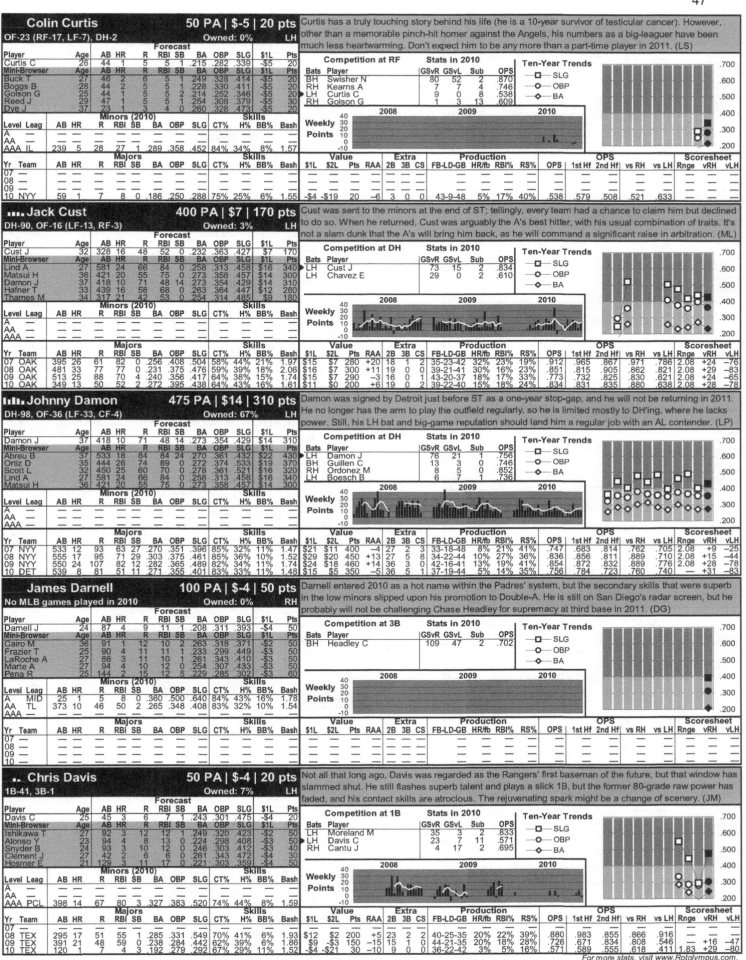

## Colin Curtis — 50 PA | $-5 | 20 pts

OF-23 (RF-17, LF-7), DH-2 — Owned: 0% — LH

Curtis has a truly touching story behind his life (he is a 10-year survivor of testicular cancer). However, other than a memorable pinch-hit homer against the Angels, his numbers as a big-leaguer have been much less heartwarming. Don't expect him to be any more than a part-time player in 2011. (LS)

| Player | Age | AB | HR | R | RBI | SB | BA | OBP | SLG | $1L | Pts |
|---|---|---|---|---|---|---|---|---|---|---|---|
| **Forecast** | | | | | | | | | | | |
| Curtis C | 26 | 44 | 1 | 5 | 5 | 1 | .215 | .282 | .339 | -$5 | 20 |
| **Mini-Browser** | | | | | | | | | | | |
| Buck T | 27 | 46 | 2 | 6 | 5 | 1 | .249 | .328 | .414 | -$5 | 20 |
| Boggs B | 28 | 44 | 2 | 5 | 5 | 1 | .228 | .330 | .411 | -$5 | 20 |
| Golson G | 25 | 44 | 1 | 5 | 5 | 2 | .214 | .252 | .346 | -$5 | 20 |
| Reed J | 29 | 47 | 1 | 5 | 5 | 1 | .254 | .308 | .379 | -$5 | 30 |
| Dye J | 37 | 23 | 1 | 3 | 4 | 0 | .260 | .328 | .473 | -$5 | 20 |

| Level | Leag | AB | HR | R | RBI | SB | BA | OBP | SLG | CT% | H% | BB% | Bash |
|---|---|---|---|---|---|---|---|---|---|---|---|---|---|
| **Minors (2010)** | | | | | | | | | | **Skills** | | | |
| A | — | — | — | — | — | — | — | — | — | — | — | — | — |
| AA | — | — | — | — | — | — | — | — | — | — | — | — | — |
| AAA | IL | 239 | 5 | 28 | 27 | 1 | .289 | .358 | .452 | 84% | 34% | 8% | 1.57 |

| Yr | Team | AB | HR | R | RBI | SB | BA | OBP | SLG | CT% | H% | BB% | Bash |
|---|---|---|---|---|---|---|---|---|---|---|---|---|---|
| **Majors** | | | | | | | | | | **Skills** | | | |
| 07 | — | — | — | — | — | — | — | — | — | — | — | — | — |
| 08 | — | — | — | — | — | — | — | — | — | — | — | — | — |
| 09 | — | — | — | — | — | — | — | — | — | — | — | — | — |
| 10 | NYY | 59 | 1 | 7 | 8 | 0 | .186 | .250 | .288 | 75% | 25% | 6% | 1.55 |

| Yr | $1L | $2L | Pts | RAA | 2B | 3B | CS | FB-LD-GB | HR/fb | RBI% | RS% | OPS | 1st Hf | 2nd Hf | vs RH | vs LH | Rnge | vRH | vLH |
|---|---|---|---|---|---|---|---|---|---|---|---|---|---|---|---|---|---|---|---|
| | **Value** | | | | **Extra** | | | **Production** | | | | **OPS** | | | | | **Scoresheet** | | |
| 07 | — | — | — | — | — | — | — | — | — | — | — | — | — | — | — | — | — | — | — |
| 08 | — | — | — | — | — | — | — | — | — | — | — | — | — | — | — | — | — | — | — |
| 09 | — | — | — | — | — | — | — | — | — | — | — | — | — | — | — | — | — | — | — |
| 10 | -$4 | -$19 | 20 | –6 | 3 | 0 | 0 | 43-9-48 | 5% | 17% | 40% | .538 | .579 | .508 | .521 | .633 | — | — | — |

**Competition at RF — Stats in 2010**

| Bats | Player | GSvR | GSvL | Sub | OPS |
|---|---|---|---|---|---|
| BH | Swisher N | 80 | 52 | 2 | .870 |
| RH | Kearns A | 7 | 7 | 4 | .746 |
| LH | Curtis C | 9 | 0 | 8 | .538 |
| RH | Golson G | 1 | 3 | 13 | .609 |

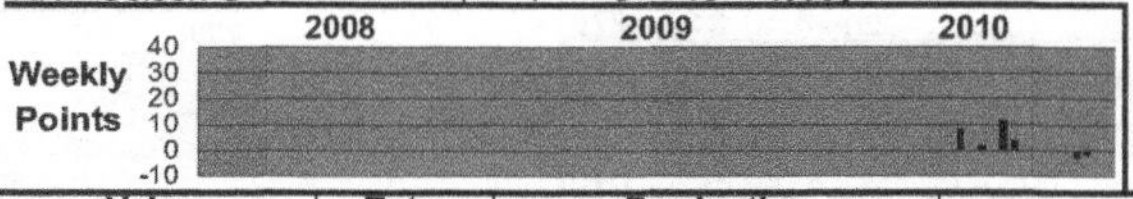


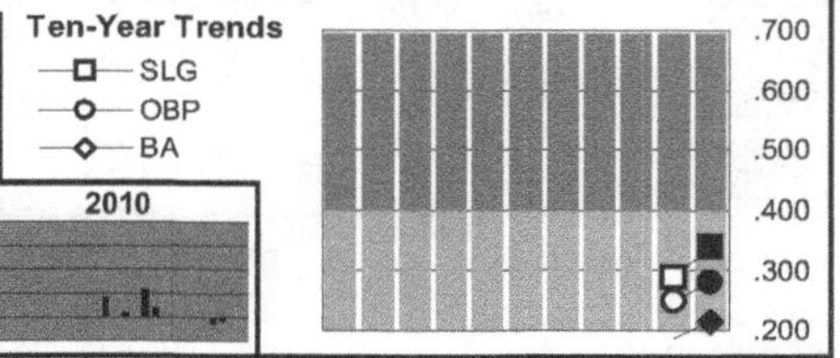


## Jack Cust — 400 PA | $7 | 170 pts

DH-90, OF-16 (LF-13, RF-3) — Owned: 3% — LH

Cust was sent to the minors at the end of ST; tellingly, every team had a chance to claim him but declined to do so. When he returned, Cust was arguably the A's best hitter, with his usual combination of traits. It's not a slam dunk that the A's will bring him back, as he will command a significant raise in arbitration. (ML)

| Player | Age | AB | HR | R | RBI | SB | BA | OBP | SLG | $1L | Pts |
|---|---|---|---|---|---|---|---|---|---|---|---|
| **Forecast** | | | | | | | | | | | |
| Cust J | 32 | 328 | 16 | 48 | 52 | 0 | .232 | .363 | .427 | $7 | 170 |
| **Mini-Browser** | | | | | | | | | | | |
| Lind A | 27 | 581 | 24 | 66 | 84 | 0 | .258 | .313 | .458 | $16 | 340 |
| Matsui H | 36 | 421 | 20 | 55 | 75 | 0 | .273 | .358 | .457 | $14 | 300 |
| Damon J | 37 | 418 | 10 | 71 | 48 | 14 | .273 | .354 | .429 | $14 | 310 |
| Hafner T | 33 | 439 | 16 | 58 | 68 | 0 | .263 | .364 | .447 | $12 | 280 |
| Thames M | 34 | 317 | 21 | 42 | 53 | 0 | .254 | .314 | .485 | $9 | 180 |

| Level | Leag | AB | HR | R | RBI | SB | BA | OBP | SLG | CT% | H% | BB% | Bash |
|---|---|---|---|---|---|---|---|---|---|---|---|---|---|
| **Minors (2010)** | | | | | | | | | | **Skills** | | | |
| A | — | — | — | — | — | — | — | — | — | — | — | — | — |
| AA | — | — | — | — | — | — | — | — | — | — | — | — | — |
| AAA | — | — | — | — | — | — | — | — | — | — | — | — | — |

| Yr | Team | AB | HR | R | RBI | SB | BA | OBP | SLG | CT% | H% | BB% | Bash |
|---|---|---|---|---|---|---|---|---|---|---|---|---|---|
| **Majors** | | | | | | | | | | **Skills** | | | |
| 07 | OAK | 395 | 26 | 61 | 82 | 0 | .256 | .408 | .504 | 58% | 44% | 21% | 1.97 |
| 08 | OAK | 481 | 33 | 77 | 77 | 0 | .231 | .375 | .476 | 59% | 39% | 18% | 2.06 |
| 09 | OAK | 513 | 25 | 88 | 70 | 4 | .240 | .356 | .417 | 64% | 38% | 15% | 1.74 |
| 10 | OAK | 349 | 13 | 50 | 52 | 2 | .272 | .395 | .438 | 64% | 43% | 16% | 1.61 |

| Yr | $1L | $2L | Pts | RAA | 2B | 3B | CS | FB-LD-GB | HR/fb | RBI% | RS% | OPS | 1st Hf | 2nd Hf | vs RH | vs LH | Rnge | vRH | vLH |
|---|---|---|---|---|---|---|---|---|---|---|---|---|---|---|---|---|---|---|---|
| | **Value** | | | | **Extra** | | | **Production** | | | | **OPS** | | | | | **Scoresheet** | | |
| 07 | $15 | $7 | 280 | +20 | 18 | 1 | 2 | 35-23-42 | 32% | 23% | 19% | .912 | .965 | .867 | .971 | .786 | 2.08 | +24 | –76 |
| 08 | $16 | $7 | 300 | +11 | 19 | 0 | 0 | 39-21-41 | 30% | 16% | 23% | .851 | .815 | .905 | .862 | .821 | 2.08 | +29 | –83 |
| 09 | $15 | $7 | 290 | –3 | 16 | 0 | 1 | 43-20-37 | 18% | 17% | 33% | .773 | .732 | .825 | .830 | .621 | 2.08 | +24 | –65 |
| 10 | $11 | $0 | 200 | +6 | 19 | 0 | 2 | 39-22-40 | 15% | 18% | 24% | .834 | .831 | .835 | .880 | .638 | 2.08 | +28 | –78 |

**Competition at DH — Stats in 2010**

| Bats | Player | GSvR | GSvL | Sub | OPS |
|---|---|---|---|---|---|
| LH | Cust J | 73 | 15 | 2 | .834 |
| LH | Chavez E | 29 | 0 | 2 | .610 |

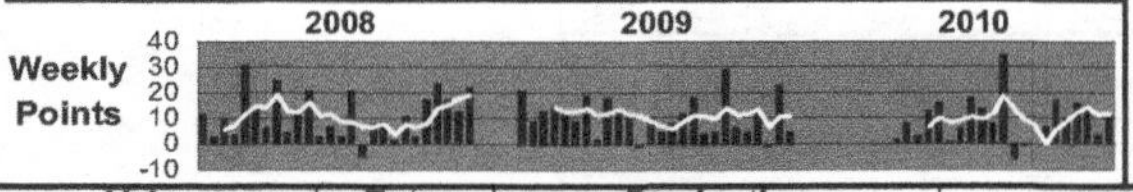


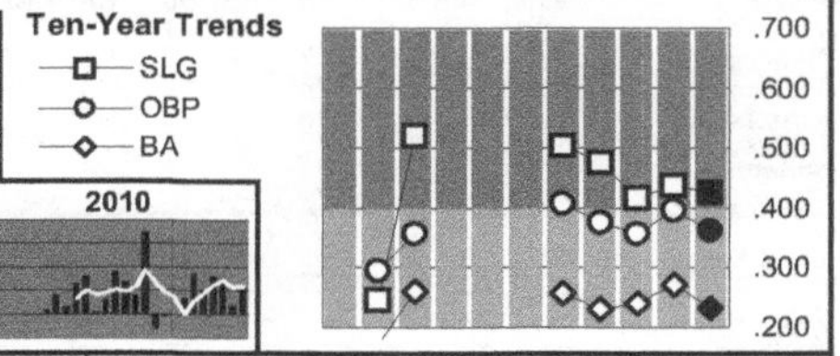


## Johnny Damon — 475 PA | $14 | 310 pts

DH-98, OF-36 (LF-33, CF-4) — Owned: 67% — LH

Damon was signed by Detroit just before ST as a one-year stop-gap, and he will not be returning in 2011. He no longer has the arm to play the outfield regularly, so he is limited mostly to DH'ing, where he lacks power. Still, his LH bat and big-game reputation should land him a regular job with an AL contender. (LP)

| Player | Age | AB | HR | R | RBI | SB | BA | OBP | SLG | $1L | Pts |
|---|---|---|---|---|---|---|---|---|---|---|---|
| **Forecast** | | | | | | | | | | | |
| Damon J | 37 | 418 | 10 | 71 | 48 | 14 | .273 | .354 | .429 | $14 | 310 |
| **Mini-Browser** | | | | | | | | | | | |
| Abreu B | 37 | 533 | 18 | 84 | 84 | 24 | .270 | .361 | .432 | $22 | 430 |
| Ortiz D | 35 | 444 | 26 | 74 | 89 | 0 | .272 | .374 | .533 | $19 | 370 |
| Scott L | 32 | 450 | 25 | 60 | 70 | 0 | .278 | .361 | .521 | $16 | 320 |
| Lind A | 27 | 581 | 24 | 66 | 84 | 0 | .258 | .313 | .458 | $16 | 340 |
| Matsui H | 36 | 421 | 20 | 55 | 75 | 0 | .273 | .358 | .457 | $14 | 300 |

| Level | Leag | AB | HR | R | RBI | SB | BA | OBP | SLG | CT% | H% | BB% | Bash |
|---|---|---|---|---|---|---|---|---|---|---|---|---|---|
| **Minors (2010)** | | | | | | | | | | **Skills** | | | |
| A | — | — | — | — | — | — | — | — | — | — | — | — | — |
| AA | — | — | — | — | — | — | — | — | — | — | — | — | — |
| AAA | — | — | — | — | — | — | — | — | — | — | — | — | — |

| Yr | Team | AB | HR | R | RBI | SB | BA | OBP | SLG | CT% | H% | BB% | Bash |
|---|---|---|---|---|---|---|---|---|---|---|---|---|---|
| **Majors** | | | | | | | | | | **Skills** | | | |
| 07 | NYY | 533 | 12 | 93 | 63 | 27 | .270 | .351 | .396 | 85% | 32% | 11% | 1.47 |
| 08 | NYY | 555 | 17 | 95 | 71 | 29 | .303 | .375 | .461 | 85% | 36% | 10% | 1.52 |
| 09 | NYY | 550 | 24 | 107 | 82 | 12 | .282 | .365 | .489 | 82% | 34% | 11% | 1.74 |
| 10 | DET | 539 | 8 | 81 | 51 | 11 | .271 | .355 | .401 | 83% | 33% | 11% | 1.48 |

| Yr | $1L | $2L | Pts | RAA | 2B | 3B | CS | FB-LD-GB | HR/fb | RBI% | RS% | OPS | 1st Hf | 2nd Hf | vs RH | vs LH | Rnge | vRH | vLH |
|---|---|---|---|---|---|---|---|---|---|---|---|---|---|---|---|---|---|---|---|
| | **Value** | | | | **Extra** | | | **Production** | | | | **OPS** | | | | | **Scoresheet** | | |
| 07 | $21 | $11 | 400 | –4 | 27 | 2 | 3 | 33-18-48 | 8% | 21% | 41% | .747 | .683 | .814 | .762 | .705 | 2.08 | +9 | –25 |
| 08 | $29 | $20 | 450 | +13 | 27 | 5 | 8 | 34-22-44 | 10% | 27% | 36% | .836 | .856 | .811 | .889 | .710 | 2.08 | +15 | –44 |
| 09 | $24 | $18 | 460 | +14 | 36 | 3 | 0 | 42-16-41 | 13% | 19% | 41% | .854 | .872 | .832 | .889 | .776 | 2.08 | +28 | –78 |
| 10 | $15 | $5 | 350 | –5 | 36 | 5 | 1 | 37-19-44 | 5% | 14% | 35% | .756 | .784 | .723 | .760 | .740 | — | +31 | –83 |

**Competition at DH — Stats in 2010**

| Bats | Player | GSvR | GSvL | Sub | OPS |
|---|---|---|---|---|---|
| LH | Damon J | 76 | 21 | 1 | .756 |
| BH | Guillen C | 13 | 3 | 0 | .746 |
| RH | Ordonez M | 8 | 5 | 0 | .852 |
| LH | Boesch B | 6 | 7 | 1 | .736 |

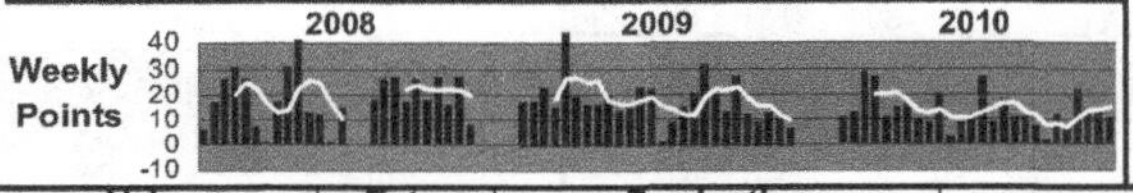


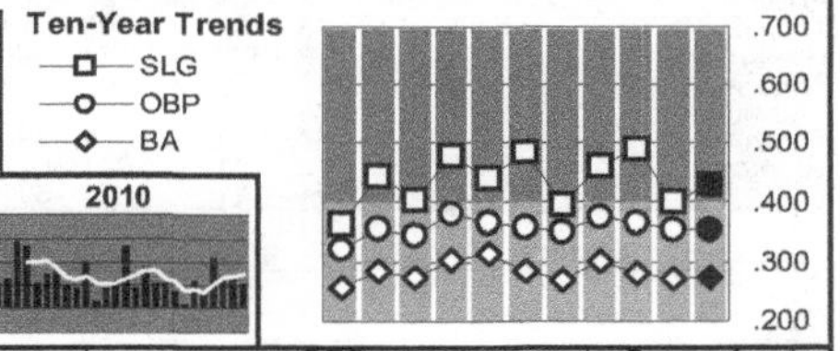


## James Darnell — 100 PA | $-4 | 50 pts

No MLB games played in 2010 — Owned: 0% — RH

Darnell entered 2010 as a hot name within the Padres' system, but the secondary skills that were superb in the low minors slipped upon his promotion to Double-A. He is still on San Diego's radar screen, but he probably will not be challenging Chase Headley for supremacy at third base in 2011. (DG)

| Player | Age | AB | HR | R | RBI | SB | BA | OBP | SLG | $1L | Pts |
|---|---|---|---|---|---|---|---|---|---|---|---|
| **Forecast** | | | | | | | | | | | |
| Darnell J | 24 | 87 | 4 | 9 | 11 | 1 | .208 | .311 | .393 | -$4 | 50 |
| **Mini-Browser** | | | | | | | | | | | |
| Cairo M | 36 | 91 | 1 | 12 | 10 | 2 | .263 | .318 | .371 | -$2 | 50 |
| Frazier T | 25 | 90 | 4 | 11 | 11 | 1 | .233 | .299 | .449 | -$3 | 50 |
| LaRoche A | 27 | 88 | 3 | 11 | 10 | 1 | .261 | .343 | .410 | -$3 | 50 |
| Marte A | 27 | 94 | 4 | 10 | 12 | 0 | .254 | .307 | .433 | -$3 | 50 |
| Pena R | 25 | 144 | 2 | 15 | 12 | 5 | .229 | .285 | .302 | -$3 | 60 |

| Level | Leag | AB | HR | R | RBI | SB | BA | OBP | SLG | CT% | H% | BB% | Bash |
|---|---|---|---|---|---|---|---|---|---|---|---|---|---|
| **Minors (2010)** | | | | | | | | | | **Skills** | | | |
| A | MID | 25 | 1 | 5 | 8 | 0 | .360 | .500 | .640 | 84% | 43% | 16% | 1.78 |
| AA | TL | 373 | 10 | 46 | 50 | 2 | .265 | .348 | .408 | 83% | 32% | 10% | 1.54 |
| AAA | — | — | — | — | — | — | — | — | — | — | — | — | — |

| Yr | Team | AB | HR | R | RBI | SB | BA | OBP | SLG | CT% | H% | BB% | Bash |
|---|---|---|---|---|---|---|---|---|---|---|---|---|---|
| **Majors** | | | | | | | | | | **Skills** | | | |
| 07 | — | — | — | — | — | — | — | — | — | — | — | — | — |
| 08 | — | — | — | — | — | — | — | — | — | — | — | — | — |
| 09 | — | — | — | — | — | — | — | — | — | — | — | — | — |
| 10 | — | — | — | — | — | — | — | — | — | — | — | — | — |

| Yr | $1L | $2L | Pts | RAA | 2B | 3B | CS | FB-LD-GB | HR/fb | RBI% | RS% | OPS | 1st Hf | 2nd Hf | vs RH | vs LH | Rnge | vRH | vLH |
|---|---|---|---|---|---|---|---|---|---|---|---|---|---|---|---|---|---|---|---|
| | **Value** | | | | **Extra** | | | **Production** | | | | **OPS** | | | | | **Scoresheet** | | |
| 07 | — | — | — | — | — | — | — | — | — | — | — | — | — | — | — | — | — | — | — |
| 08 | — | — | — | — | — | — | — | — | — | — | — | — | — | — | — | — | — | — | — |
| 09 | — | — | — | — | — | — | — | — | — | — | — | — | — | — | — | — | — | — | — |
| 10 | — | — | — | — | — | — | — | — | — | — | — | — | — | — | — | — | — | — | — |

**Competition at 3B — Stats in 2010**

| Bats | Player | GSvR | GSvL | Sub | OPS |
|---|---|---|---|---|---|
| BH | Headley C | 109 | 47 | 2 | .702 |

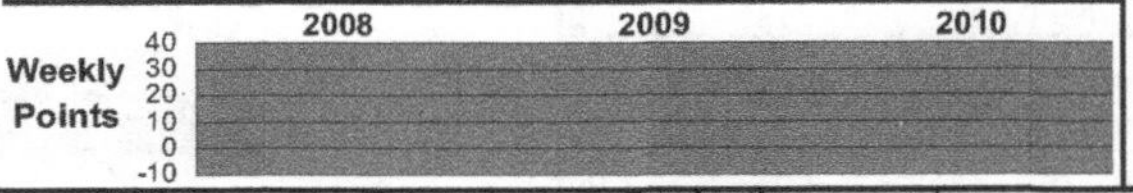


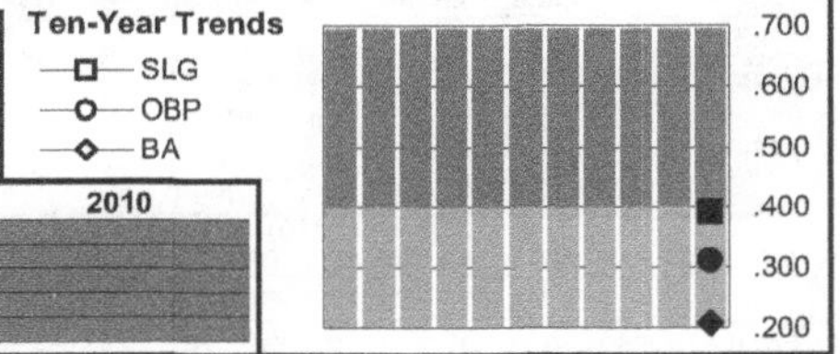


## Chris Davis — 50 PA | $-4 | 20 pts

1B-41, 3B-1 — Owned: 7% — LH

Not all that long ago, Davis was regarded as the Rangers' first baseman of the future, but that window has slammed shut. He still flashes superb talent and plays a slick 1B, but the former 80-grade raw power has faded, and his contact skills are atrocious. The rejuvenating spark might be a change of scenery. (JM)

| Player | Age | AB | HR | R | RBI | SB | BA | OBP | SLG | $1L | Pts |
|---|---|---|---|---|---|---|---|---|---|---|---|
| **Forecast** | | | | | | | | | | | |
| Davis C | 25 | 45 | 3 | 6 | 7 | 1 | .243 | .301 | .475 | -$4 | 20 |
| **Mini-Browser** | | | | | | | | | | | |
| Ishikawa T | 27 | 92 | 3 | 12 | 12 | 1 | .249 | .320 | .423 | -$2 | 50 |
| Alonso Y | 23 | 94 | 4 | 8 | 13 | 0 | .224 | .298 | .408 | -$3 | 50 |
| Snyder B | 24 | 93 | 3 | 10 | 12 | 0 | .246 | .303 | .412 | -$3 | 40 |
| Clement J | 27 | 42 | 2 | 6 | 6 | 0 | .261 | .343 | .472 | -$4 | 30 |
| Hosmer E | 21 | 129 | 3 | 11 | 17 | 0 | .221 | .303 | .359 | -$4 | 50 |

| Level | Leag | AB | HR | R | RBI | SB | BA | OBP | SLG | CT% | H% | BB% | Bash |
|---|---|---|---|---|---|---|---|---|---|---|---|---|---|
| **Minors (2010)** | | | | | | | | | | **Skills** | | | |
| A | — | — | — | — | — | — | — | — | — | — | — | — | — |
| AA | — | — | — | — | — | — | — | — | — | — | — | — | — |
| AAA | PCL | 398 | 14 | 67 | 80 | 3 | .327 | .383 | .520 | 74% | 44% | 8% | 1.59 |

| Yr | Team | AB | HR | R | RBI | SB | BA | OBP | SLG | CT% | H% | BB% | Bash |
|---|---|---|---|---|---|---|---|---|---|---|---|---|---|
| **Majors** | | | | | | | | | | **Skills** | | | |
| 07 | — | — | — | — | — | — | — | — | — | — | — | — | — |
| 08 | TEX | 295 | 17 | 51 | 55 | 1 | .285 | .331 | .549 | 70% | 41% | 6% | 1.93 |
| 09 | TEX | 391 | 21 | 48 | 59 | 0 | .238 | .284 | .442 | 62% | 39% | 6% | 1.86 |
| 10 | TEX | 120 | 1 | 7 | 4 | 3 | .192 | .279 | .292 | 67% | 29% | 11% | 1.52 |

| Yr | $1L | $2L | Pts | RAA | 2B | 3B | CS | FB-LD-GB | HR/fb | RBI% | RS% | OPS | 1st Hf | 2nd Hf | vs RH | vs LH | Rnge | vRH | vLH |
|---|---|---|---|---|---|---|---|---|---|---|---|---|---|---|---|---|---|---|---|
| | **Value** | | | | **Extra** | | | **Production** | | | | **OPS** | | | | | **Scoresheet** | | |
| 07 | — | — | — | — | — | — | — | — | — | — | — | — | — | — | — | — | — | — | — |
| 08 | $12 | $2 | 200 | +5 | 23 | 2 | 2 | 40-25-35 | 20% | 22% | 39% | .880 | .983 | .855 | .866 | .916 | — | — | — |
| 09 | $9 | -$3 | 150 | –15 | 15 | 1 | 0 | 44-21-35 | 20% | 18% | 28% | .726 | .671 | .834 | .808 | .546 | — | +16 | –47 |
| 10 | -$4 | -$21 | 30 | –10 | 9 | 0 | 0 | 36-22-42 | 3% | 5% | 16% | .571 | .589 | .555 | .618 | .411 | 1.83 | +29 | –80 |

**Competition at 1B — Stats in 2010**

| Bats | Player | GSvR | GSvL | Sub | OPS |
|---|---|---|---|---|---|
| LH | Moreland M | 35 | 3 | 2 | .833 |
| LH | Davis C | 23 | 7 | 11 | .571 |
| RH | Cantu J | 4 | 17 | 2 | .695 |

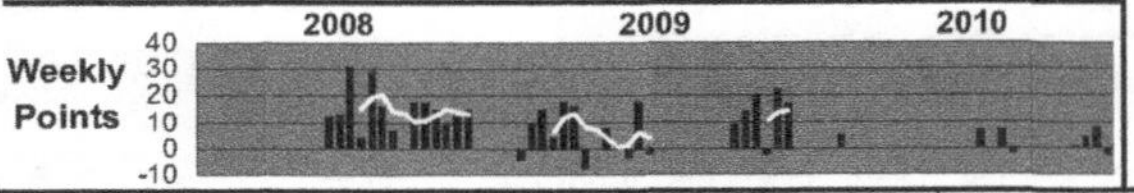


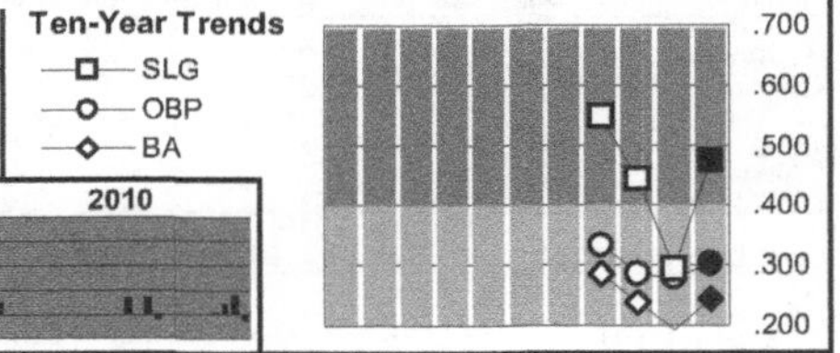

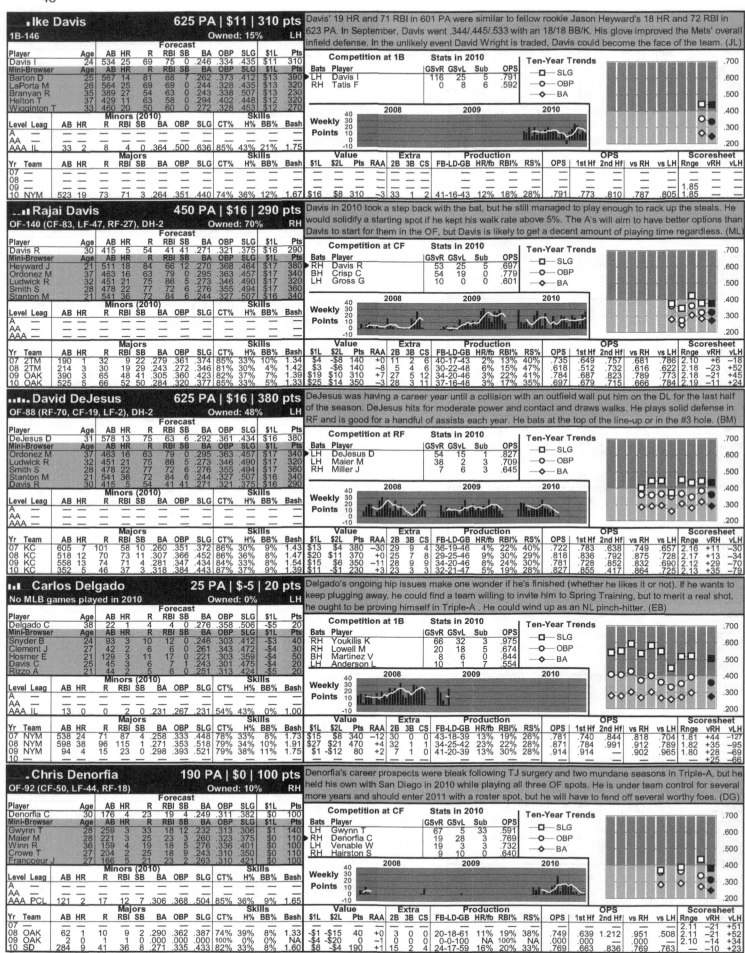

## Ike Davis — 625 PA | $11 | 310 pts
1B-146 — Owned: 15% — LH

Davis' 19 HR and 71 RBI in 601 PA were similar to fellow rookie Jason Heyward's 18 HR and 72 RBI in 623 PA. In September, Davis went .344/.445/.533 with an 18/18 BB/K. His glove improved the Mets' overall infield defense. In the unlikely event David Wright is traded, Davis could become the face of the team. (JL)

### Forecast
| Player | Age | AB | HR | R | RBI | SB | BA | OBP | SLG | $1L | Pts |
|---|---|---|---|---|---|---|---|---|---|---|---|
| Davis I | 24 | 534 | 25 | 69 | 75 | 0 | .246 | .334 | .435 | $11 | 310 |

| Mini-Browser | Age | AB | HR | R | RBI | SB | BA | OBP | SLG | $1L | Pts |
|---|---|---|---|---|---|---|---|---|---|---|---|
| Barton D | 25 | 567 | 14 | 81 | 68 | 7 | .262 | .373 | .412 | $13 | 390 |
| LaPorta M | 26 | 564 | 25 | 69 | 69 | 0 | .244 | .328 | .435 | $13 | 320 |
| Branyan R | 35 | 389 | 27 | 54 | 63 | 0 | .243 | .338 | .507 | $13 | 230 |
| Helton T | 37 | 429 | 11 | 63 | 58 | 0 | .294 | .402 | .448 | $12 | 320 |
| Wigginton T | 33 | 460 | 20 | 50 | 60 | 0 | .272 | .328 | .453 | $12 | 270 |

### Minors (2010) / Skills
| Level | Leag | AB | HR | R | RBI | SB | BA | OBP | SLG | CT% | H% | BB% | Bash |
|---|---|---|---|---|---|---|---|---|---|---|---|---|---|
| A | — | | | | | | | | | | | | |
| AA | — | | | | | | | | | | | | |
| AAA | IL | 33 | 2 | 8 | 4 | 0 | .364 | .500 | .636 | 85% | 43% | 21% | 1.75 |

### Majors / Skills
| Yr | Team | AB | HR | R | RBI | SB | BA | OBP | SLG | CT% | H% | BB% | Bash |
|---|---|---|---|---|---|---|---|---|---|---|---|---|---|
| 07 | — | | | | | | | | | | | | |
| 08 | — | | | | | | | | | | | | |
| 09 | — | | | | | | | | | | | | |
| 10 | NYM | 523 | 19 | 73 | 71 | 3 | .264 | .351 | .440 | 74% | 36% | 12% | 1.67 |

### Competition at 1B / Stats in 2010
| Bats | Player | GSvR | GSvL | Sub | OPS |
|---|---|---|---|---|---|
| LH | Davis I | 116 | 25 | 5 | .791 |
| RH | Tatis F | 0 | 8 | 6 | .592 |

### Value / Extra / Production / OPS / Scoresheet
| | $1L | $2L | Pts | RAA | 2B | 3B | CS | FB-LD-GB | HR/fb | RBI% | RS% | OPS | 1st Hf | 2nd Hf | vs RH | vs LH | Rnge | vRH | vLH |
|---|---|---|---|---|---|---|---|---|---|---|---|---|---|---|---|---|---|---|---|
| 10 | $16 | $8 | 310 | −3 | 33 | 1 | 2 | 41-16-43 | 12% | 18% | 28% | .791 | .773 | .810 | .787 | .805 | 1.85 | | |
| | | | | | | | | | | | | | | | | | 1.85 | | |

---

## Rajai Davis — 450 PA | $16 | 290 pts
OF-140 (CF-83, LF-47, RF-27), DH-2 — Owned: 70% — RH

Davis in 2010 took a step back with the bat, but he still managed to play enough to rack up the steals. He would solidify a starting spot if he kept his walk rate above 5%. The A's will aim to have better options than Davis to start for them in the OF, but Davis is likely to get a decent amount of playing time regardless. (ML)

### Forecast
| Player | Age | AB | HR | R | RBI | SB | BA | OBP | SLG | $1L | Pts |
|---|---|---|---|---|---|---|---|---|---|---|---|
| Davis R | 30 | 415 | 5 | 54 | 41 | 41 | .271 | .321 | .375 | $16 | 290 |

| Mini-Browser | Age | AB | HR | R | RBI | SB | BA | OBP | SLG | $1L | Pts |
|---|---|---|---|---|---|---|---|---|---|---|---|
| Heyward J | 21 | 511 | 18 | 84 | 66 | 12 | .270 | .368 | .464 | $17 | 380 |
| Ordonez M | 37 | 463 | 16 | 63 | 79 | 0 | .295 | .363 | .457 | $17 | 340 |
| Ludwick R | 32 | 451 | 21 | 75 | 86 | 5 | .273 | .346 | .490 | $17 | 320 |
| Smith S | 28 | 478 | 22 | 77 | 72 | 6 | .276 | .355 | .494 | $17 | 360 |
| Stanton M | 21 | 541 | 36 | 72 | 84 | 6 | .244 | .327 | .507 | $16 | 340 |

### Minors (2010) / Skills
| Level | Leag | AB | HR | R | RBI | SB | BA | OBP | SLG | CT% | H% | BB% | Bash |
|---|---|---|---|---|---|---|---|---|---|---|---|---|---|
| A | — | | | | | | | | | | | | |
| AA | — | | | | | | | | | | | | |
| AAA | — | | | | | | | | | | | | |

### Majors / Skills
| Yr | Team | AB | HR | R | RBI | SB | BA | OBP | SLG | CT% | H% | BB% | Bash |
|---|---|---|---|---|---|---|---|---|---|---|---|---|---|
| 07 | 2TM | 190 | 1 | 32 | 9 | 22 | .279 | .361 | .374 | 85% | 33% | 10% | 1.34 |
| 08 | 2TM | 214 | 3 | 30 | 19 | 29 | .243 | .272 | .346 | 81% | 30% | 4% | 1.42 |
| 09 | OAK | 390 | 3 | 65 | 48 | 41 | .305 | .360 | .423 | 82% | 37% | 7% | 1.39 |
| 10 | OAK | 525 | 5 | 66 | 52 | 50 | .284 | .320 | .377 | 85% | 33% | 5% | 1.33 |

### Competition at CF / Stats in 2010
| Bats | Player | GSvR | GSvL | Sub | OPS |
|---|---|---|---|---|---|
| RH | Davis R | 53 | 25 | 5 | .697 |
| BH | Crisp C | 54 | 19 | 0 | .779 |
| LH | Gross G | 10 | 0 | 0 | .601 |

### Value / Extra / Production / OPS / Scoresheet
| Yr | $1L | $2L | Pts | RAA | 2B | 3B | CS | FB-LD-GB | HR/fb | RBI% | RS% | OPS | 1st Hf | 2nd Hf | vs RH | vs LH | Rnge | vRH | vLH |
|---|---|---|---|---|---|---|---|---|---|---|---|---|---|---|---|---|---|---|---|
| 07 | $4 | −$8 | 140 | +0 | 11 | 2 | 6 | 40-17-43 | 2% | 13% | 40% | .735 | .649 | .757 | .681 | .786 | 2.10 | +6 | −18 |
| 08 | $3 | −$6 | 140 | −8 | 5 | 1 | 6 | 30-22-48 | 6% | 15% | 47% | .618 | .512 | .732 | .616 | .622 | 2.18 | −23 | +52 |
| 09 | $19 | $10 | 310 | +7 | 27 | 5 | 12 | 34-20-46 | 3% | 22% | 41% | .784 | .687 | .823 | .789 | .773 | 2.18 | −21 | +45 |
| 10 | $25 | $14 | 350 | −3 | 28 | 3 | 11 | 37-16-48 | 3% | 17% | 35% | .697 | .679 | .715 | .666 | .784 | 2.19 | −11 | +24 |

---

## David DeJesus — 625 PA | $16 | 380 pts
OF-88 (RF-70, CF-19, LF-2), DH-2 — Owned: 48% — LH

DeJesus was having a career year until a collision with an outfield wall put him on the DL for the last half of the season. DeJesus hits for moderate power and contact and draws walks. He plays solid defense in RF and is good for a handful of assists each year. He bats at the top of the line-up or in the #3 hole. (BM)

### Forecast
| Player | Age | AB | HR | R | RBI | SB | BA | OBP | SLG | $1L | Pts |
|---|---|---|---|---|---|---|---|---|---|---|---|
| DeJesus D | 31 | 578 | 13 | 75 | 63 | 6 | .292 | .361 | .434 | $16 | 380 |

| Mini-Browser | Age | AB | HR | R | RBI | SB | BA | OBP | SLG | $1L | Pts |
|---|---|---|---|---|---|---|---|---|---|---|---|
| Ordonez M | 37 | 463 | 16 | 63 | 79 | 0 | .295 | .363 | .457 | $17 | 340 |
| Ludwick R | 32 | 451 | 21 | 75 | 86 | 5 | .273 | .346 | .490 | $17 | 320 |
| Smith S | 28 | 478 | 22 | 77 | 72 | 6 | .276 | .355 | .494 | $17 | 360 |
| Stanton M | 21 | 541 | 36 | 72 | 84 | 6 | .244 | .327 | .507 | $16 | 340 |
| Davis R | 30 | 415 | 5 | 54 | 41 | 41 | .271 | .321 | .375 | $16 | 290 |

### Minors (2010) / Skills
| Level | Leag | AB | HR | R | RBI | SB | BA | OBP | SLG | CT% | H% | BB% | Bash |
|---|---|---|---|---|---|---|---|---|---|---|---|---|---|
| A | — | | | | | | | | | | | | |
| AA | — | | | | | | | | | | | | |
| AAA | — | | | | | | | | | | | | |

### Majors / Skills
| Yr | Team | AB | HR | R | RBI | SB | BA | OBP | SLG | CT% | H% | BB% | Bash |
|---|---|---|---|---|---|---|---|---|---|---|---|---|---|
| 07 | KC | 605 | 7 | 101 | 58 | 10 | .260 | .351 | .372 | 86% | 30% | 9% | 1.43 |
| 08 | KC | 518 | 12 | 70 | 73 | 11 | .307 | .366 | .452 | 86% | 36% | 8% | 1.47 |
| 09 | KC | 558 | 13 | 74 | 71 | 4 | .281 | .347 | .434 | 84% | 33% | 8% | 1.54 |
| 10 | KC | 352 | 5 | 46 | 37 | 3 | .318 | .384 | .443 | 87% | 37% | 9% | 1.39 |

### Competition at RF / Stats in 2010
| Bats | Player | GSvR | GSvL | Sub | OPS |
|---|---|---|---|---|---|
| LH | DeJesus D | 54 | 15 | 1 | .827 |
| LH | Maier M | 38 | 2 | 3 | .709 |
| RH | Miller J | 7 | 6 | 3 | .645 |

### Value / Extra / Production / OPS / Scoresheet
| Yr | $1L | $2L | Pts | RAA | 2B | 3B | CS | FB-LD-GB | HR/fb | RBI% | RS% | OPS | 1st Hf | 2nd Hf | vs RH | vs LH | Rnge | vRH | vLH |
|---|---|---|---|---|---|---|---|---|---|---|---|---|---|---|---|---|---|---|---|
| 07 | $13 | $4 | 380 | −30 | 29 | 9 | 4 | 36-19-46 | 4% | 22% | 40% | .722 | .783 | .638 | .749 | .657 | 2.16 | +11 | −30 |
| 08 | $20 | $11 | 370 | +0 | 25 | 7 | 8 | 29-25-46 | 9% | 30% | 29% | .818 | .836 | .792 | .875 | .728 | 2.17 | +13 | −34 |
| 09 | $15 | $6 | 350 | −11 | 28 | 9 | 9 | 34-20-46 | 8% | 24% | 30% | .781 | .728 | .852 | .832 | .690 | 2.12 | +29 | −70 |
| 10 | $11 | −$1 | 230 | +3 | 23 | 3 | 3 | 32-21-47 | 5% | 19% | 28% | .827 | .855 | .417 | .864 | .725 | 2.13 | +3 | −8 |

---

## Carlos Delgado — 25 PA | $-5 | 20 pts
No MLB games played in 2010 — Owned: 0% — LH

Delgado's ongoing hip issues make one wonder if he's finished (whether he likes it or not). If he wants to keep plugging away, he could find a team willing to invite him to Spring Training, but to merit a real shot, he ought to be proving himself in Triple-A. He could wind up as an NL pinch-hitter. (EB)

### Forecast
| Player | Age | AB | HR | R | RBI | SB | BA | OBP | SLG | $1L | Pts |
|---|---|---|---|---|---|---|---|---|---|---|---|
| Delgado C | 38 | 22 | 1 | 4 | 4 | 0 | .276 | .358 | .506 | −$5 | 20 |

| Mini-Browser | Age | AB | HR | R | RBI | SB | BA | OBP | SLG | $1L | Pts |
|---|---|---|---|---|---|---|---|---|---|---|---|
| Snyder B | 24 | 93 | 3 | 10 | 12 | 0 | .246 | .303 | .412 | −$3 | 40 |
| Clement J | 27 | 42 | 2 | 6 | 6 | 0 | .261 | .343 | .472 | −$4 | 30 |
| Hosmer E | 21 | 129 | 3 | 11 | 17 | 0 | .221 | .303 | .359 | −$4 | 50 |
| Davis C | 25 | 45 | 3 | 4 | 5 | 0 | .243 | .301 | .475 | −$4 | 20 |
| Rizzo A | 21 | 44 | 2 | 5 | 6 | 0 | .251 | .313 | .424 | −$5 | 20 |

### Minors (2010) / Skills
| Level | Leag | AB | HR | R | RBI | SB | BA | OBP | SLG | CT% | H% | BB% | Bash |
|---|---|---|---|---|---|---|---|---|---|---|---|---|---|
| A | — | | | | | | | | | | | | |
| AA | — | | | | | | | | | | | | |
| AAA | IL | 13 | 0 | 0 | 2 | 0 | .231 | .267 | .231 | 54% | 43% | 0% | 1.00 |

### Majors / Skills
| Yr | Team | AB | HR | R | RBI | SB | BA | OBP | SLG | CT% | H% | BB% | Bash |
|---|---|---|---|---|---|---|---|---|---|---|---|---|---|
| 07 | NYM | 538 | 24 | 71 | 87 | 4 | .258 | .333 | .448 | 78% | 33% | 8% | 1.73 |
| 08 | NYM | 598 | 38 | 96 | 115 | 1 | .271 | .353 | .518 | 79% | 34% | 10% | 1.91 |
| 09 | NYM | 94 | 4 | 15 | 23 | 0 | .298 | .393 | .521 | 79% | 38% | 11% | 1.75 |
| 10 | — | | | | | | | | | | | | |

### Competition at 1B / Stats in 2010
| Bats | Player | GSvR | GSvL | Sub | OPS |
|---|---|---|---|---|---|
| RH | Youkilis K | 66 | 32 | 3 | .975 |
| RH | Lowell M | 20 | 18 | 5 | .674 |
| BH | Martinez V | 8 | 6 | 0 | .844 |
| LH | Anderson L | 10 | 1 | 7 | .554 |

### Value / Extra / Production / OPS / Scoresheet
| Yr | $1L | $2L | Pts | RAA | 2B | 3B | CS | FB-LD-GB | HR/fb | RBI% | RS% | OPS | 1st Hf | 2nd Hf | vs RH | vs LH | Rnge | vRH | vLH |
|---|---|---|---|---|---|---|---|---|---|---|---|---|---|---|---|---|---|---|---|
| 07 | $15 | $8 | 340 | −12 | 30 | 0 | 0 | 43-18-39 | 13% | 19% | 26% | .781 | .740 | .844 | .818 | .704 | 1.81 | +44 | −127 |
| 08 | $27 | $21 | 470 | +4 | 32 | 1 | 1 | 34-25-42 | 23% | 22% | 28% | .871 | .784 | .991 | .912 | .789 | 1.82 | +35 | −95 |
| 09 | $1 | −$12 | 80 | +2 | 7 | 1 | 0 | 41-20-39 | 13% | 30% | 28% | .914 | .914 | — | .902 | .965 | 1.80 | +28 | −69 |
| 10 | | | | | | | | | | | | | | | | | | +25 | −66 |

---

## Chris Denorfia — 190 PA | $0 | 100 pts
OF-92 (CF-50, LF-44, RF-18)

Denorfia's career prospects were bleak following TJ surgery and two mundane seasons in Triple-A, but he held his own with San Diego in 2010 while playing all three OF spots. He is under team control for several more years and should enter 2011 with a roster spot, but he will have to fend off several worthy foes. (DG)

Owned: 10% — RH

### Forecast
| Player | Age | AB | HR | R | RBI | SB | BA | OBP | SLG | $1L | Pts |
|---|---|---|---|---|---|---|---|---|---|---|---|
| Denorfia C | 30 | 176 | 4 | 23 | 19 | 4 | .249 | .311 | .382 | $0 | 100 |

| Mini-Browser | Age | AB | HR | R | RBI | SB | BA | OBP | SLG | $1L | Pts |
|---|---|---|---|---|---|---|---|---|---|---|---|
| Gwynn T | 28 | 259 | 3 | 33 | 18 | 12 | .232 | .313 | .306 | $1 | 140 |
| Maier M | 28 | 221 | 3 | 25 | 23 | 3 | .260 | .323 | .375 | $0 | 110 |
| Winn R | 36 | 159 | 4 | 19 | 18 | 5 | .276 | .336 | .401 | $0 | 100 |
| Crowe T | 27 | 204 | 2 | 25 | 18 | 9 | .243 | .310 | .350 | $0 | 110 |
| Francoeur J | 27 | 166 | 5 | 21 | 23 | 2 | .263 | .310 | .421 | $0 | 100 |

### Minors (2010) / Skills
| Level | Leag | AB | HR | R | RBI | SB | BA | OBP | SLG | CT% | H% | BB% | Bash |
|---|---|---|---|---|---|---|---|---|---|---|---|---|---|
| A | — | | | | | | | | | | | | |
| AA | — | | | | | | | | | | | | |
| AAA | PCL | 121 | 2 | 17 | 12 | 7 | .306 | .368 | .504 | 85% | 36% | 9% | 1.65 |

### Competition at CF / Stats in 2010
| Bats | Player | GSvR | GSvL | Sub | OPS |
|---|---|---|---|---|---|
| LH | Gwynn T | 67 | 5 | 33 | .591 |
| RH | Denorfia C | 19 | 28 | 3 | .769 |
| LH | Venable W | 19 | 3 | 3 | .732 |
| RH | Hairston S | 9 | 10 | 0 | .640 |

### Majors / Skills
| Yr | Team | AB | HR | R | RBI | SB | BA | OBP | SLG | CT% | H% | BB% | Bash |
|---|---|---|---|---|---|---|---|---|---|---|---|---|---|
| 07 | | | | | | | | | | | | | |
| 08 | OAK | 62 | 1 | 10 | 9 | 2 | .290 | .362 | .387 | 74% | 39% | 8% | 1.33 |
| 09 | OAK | 4 | 0 | 0 | 0 | 0 | .000 | .000 | .000 | 100% | 0% | 0% | NA |
| 10 | SD | 284 | 9 | 41 | 36 | 8 | .271 | .335 | .433 | 82% | 33% | 8% | 1.60 |

### Value / Extra / Production / OPS / Scoresheet
| Yr | $1L | $2L | Pts | RAA | 2B | 3B | CS | FB-LD-GB | HR/fb | RBI% | RS% | OPS | 1st Hf | 2nd Hf | vs RH | vs LH | Rnge | vRH | vLH |
|---|---|---|---|---|---|---|---|---|---|---|---|---|---|---|---|---|---|---|---|
| 08 | −$1 | −$15 | 40 | +0 | 3 | 0 | 0 | 20-18-61 | 11% | 19% | 38% | .749 | .639 | 1.212 | .951 | .508 | 2.11 | −21 | +51 |
| 09 | −$4 | −$20 | 0 | −1 | 0 | 0 | 0 | 0-0-100 | NA | 100% | 0% | .000 | .000 | — | .000 | — | 2.11 | −21 | +52 |
| 10 | $8 | −$4 | 190 | +2 | 15 | 2 | 4 | 24-17-59 | 11% | 20% | 33% | .769 | .663 | .836 | .769 | .763 | 2.10 | −14 | +34 |
| | | | | | | | | | | | | | | | | | | +23 | |

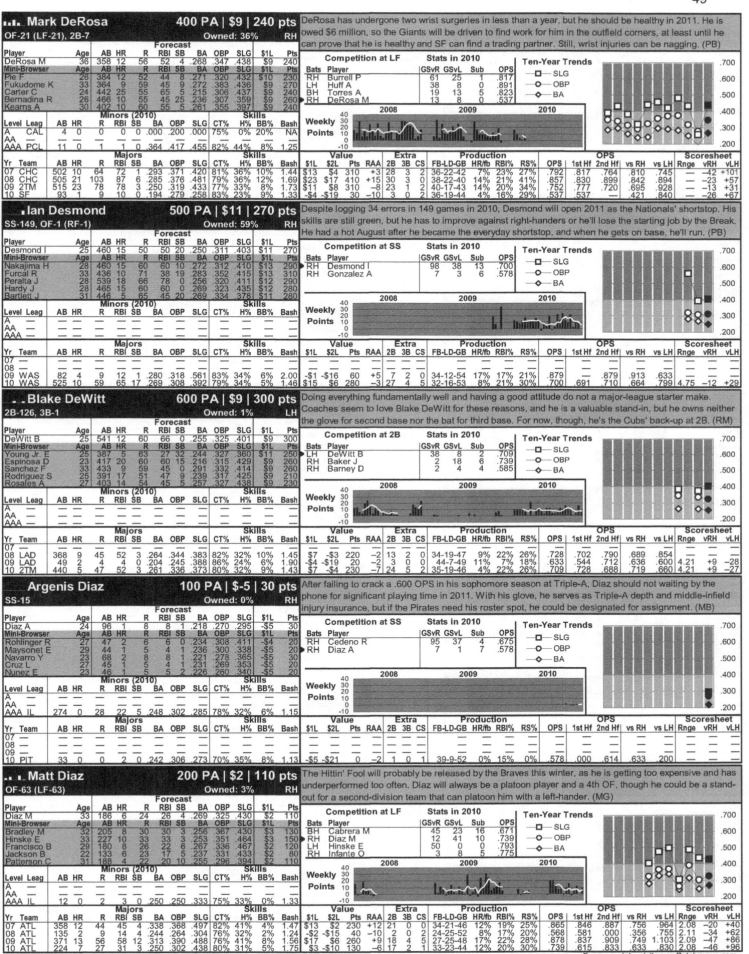

## Mark DeRosa — 400 PA | $9 | 240 pts
OF-21 (LF-21), 2B-7 — Owned: 36% — RH

DeRosa has undergone two wrist surgeries in less than a year, but he should be healthy in 2011. He is owed $6 million, so the Giants will be driven to find work for him in the outfield corners, at least until he can prove that he is healthy and SF can find a trading partner. Still, wrist injuries can be nagging. (PB)

### Forecast
| Player | Age | AB | HR | R | RBI | SB | BA | OBP | SLG | $1L | Pts |
|---|---|---|---|---|---|---|---|---|---|---|---|
| DeRosa M | 36 | 358 | 12 | 56 | 52 | 4 | .268 | .347 | .438 | $9 | 240 |
| Mini-Browser | Age | AB | HR | R | RBI | SB | BA | OBP | SLG | $1L | Pts |
| Pie F | 26 | 384 | 12 | 52 | 44 | 8 | .271 | .320 | .432 | $10 | 230 |
| Fukudome K | 33 | 364 | 9 | 59 | 45 | 9 | .272 | .383 | .436 | $9 | 270 |
| Carter C | 24 | 442 | 25 | 55 | 65 | 5 | .215 | .306 | .437 | $9 | 240 |
| Bernadina R | 26 | 466 | 10 | 55 | 45 | 25 | .236 | .307 | .359 | $9 | 260 |
| Kearns A | 30 | 402 | 10 | 60 | 55 | 5 | .261 | .355 | .397 | $9 | 240 |

### Competition at LF — Stats in 2010
| Bats | Player | GSvR | GSvL | Sub | OPS |
|---|---|---|---|---|---|
| RH | Burrell P | 61 | 25 | 1 | .817 |
| LH | Huff A | 38 | 8 | 0 | .891 |
| BH | Torres A | 19 | 13 | 5 | .823 |
| RH | DeRosa M | 13 | 8 | 0 | .537 |

### Minors (2010)
| Level | Leag | AB | HR | R | RBI | SB | BA | OBP | SLG | CT% | H% | BB% | Bash |
|---|---|---|---|---|---|---|---|---|---|---|---|---|---|
| A | CAL | 4 | 0 | 0 | 0 | 0 | .000 | .200 | .000 | 75% | 0% | 20% | NA |
| AA | — |  |  |  |  |  |  |  |  |  |  |  |  |
| AAA | PCL | 11 | 0 | 1 | 1 | 0 | .364 | .417 | .455 | 82% | 44% | 8% | 1.25 |

### Majors
| Yr | Team | AB | HR | R | RBI | SB | BA | OBP | SLG | CT% | H% | BB% | Bash | $1L | $2L | Pts | RAA | 2B | 3B | CS | FB-LD-GB | HR/fb | RBI% | RS% | OPS | 1st Hf | 2nd Hf | vs RH | vs LH | Rnge | vRH | vLH |
|---|---|---|---|---|---|---|---|---|---|---|---|---|---|---|---|---|---|---|---|---|---|---|---|---|---|---|---|---|---|---|---|---|
| 07 | CHC | 502 | 10 | 64 | 72 | 1 | .293 | .371 | .420 | 81% | 36% | 10% | 1.44 | $13 | $4 | 310 | +3 | 28 | 3 | 2 | 36-22-42 | 7% | 23% | 27% | .792 | .817 | .764 | .810 | .745 | — | -42 | +101 |
| 08 | CHC | 505 | 21 | 103 | 87 | 6 | .285 | .376 | .481 | 79% | 36% | 12% | 1.69 | $23 | $17 | 410 | +15 | 30 | 3 | 0 | 38-22-40 | 14% | 21% | 41% | .857 | .830 | .899 | .842 | .894 | — | -23 | +57 |
| 09 | 2TM | 515 | 23 | 78 | 78 | 3 | .250 | .319 | .433 | 77% | 33% | 8% | 1.73 | $11 | $8 | 310 | -8 | 23 | 1 | 2 | 40-17-43 | 14% | 20% | 34% | .752 | .777 | .720 | .695 | .928 | — | -13 | +31 |
| 10 | SF | 93 | 1 | 9 | 10 | 0 | .194 | .279 | .258 | 83% | 23% | 9% | 1.33 | -$4 | -$19 | 30 | -10 | 3 | 2 | 0 | 36-19-44 | 16% | 29% | 16% | .537 | .537 | — | .421 | .840 | — | -26 | +67 |

## Ian Desmond — 500 PA | $11 | 270 pts
SS-149, OF-1 (RF-1) — Owned: 59% — RH

Despite logging 34 errors in 149 games in 2010, Desmond will open 2011 as the Nationals' shortstop. His skills are still green, but he has to improve against right-handers or he'll lose the starting job by the Break. He had a hot August after he became the everyday shortstop, and when he gets on base, he'll run. (PB)

### Forecast
| Player | Age | AB | HR | R | RBI | SB | BA | OBP | SLG | $1L | Pts |
|---|---|---|---|---|---|---|---|---|---|---|---|
| Desmond I | 25 | 460 | 15 | 50 | 50 | 20 | .250 | .311 | .403 | $11 | 270 |
| Mini-Browser | Age | AB | HR | R | RBI | SB | BA | OBP | SLG | $1L | Pts |
| Nakajima H | 28 | 460 | 15 | 60 | 60 | 10 | .272 | .312 | .410 | $13 | 290 |
| Furcal R | 33 | 436 | 10 | 71 | 38 | 19 | .283 | .352 | .415 | $13 | 310 |
| Peralta J | 28 | 539 | 18 | 66 | 78 | 0 | .256 | .320 | .411 | $12 | 290 |
| Hardy J | 28 | 465 | 15 | 60 | 60 | 0 | .269 | .323 | .435 | $12 | 280 |
| Bartlett J | 31 | 446 | 5 | 65 | 45 | 20 | .269 | .334 | .378 | $11 | 280 |

### Competition at SS — Stats in 2010
| Bats | Player | GSvR | GSvL | Sub | OPS |
|---|---|---|---|---|---|
| RH | Desmond I | 98 | 38 | 13 | .700 |
| RH | Gonzalez A | 7 | 3 | 6 | .578 |

### Minors (2010)
| Level | Leag | AB | HR | R | RBI | SB | BA | OBP | SLG | CT% | H% | BB% | Bash |
|---|---|---|---|---|---|---|---|---|---|---|---|---|---|
| A | — |  |  |  |  |  |  |  |  |  |  |  |  |
| AA | — |  |  |  |  |  |  |  |  |  |  |  |  |
| AAA | — |  |  |  |  |  |  |  |  |  |  |  |  |

### Majors
| Yr | Team | AB | HR | R | RBI | SB | BA | OBP | SLG | CT% | H% | BB% | Bash | $1L | $2L | Pts | RAA | 2B | 3B | CS | FB-LD-GB | HR/fb | RBI% | RS% | OPS | 1st Hf | 2nd Hf | vs RH | vs LH | Rnge | vRH | vLH |
|---|---|---|---|---|---|---|---|---|---|---|---|---|---|---|---|---|---|---|---|---|---|---|---|---|---|---|---|---|---|---|---|---|
| 07 | — |  |  |  |  |  |  |  |  |  |  |  |  |  |  |  |  |  |  |  |  |  |  |  |  |  |  |  |  |  |  |  |
| 08 | — |  |  |  |  |  |  |  |  |  |  |  |  |  |  |  |  |  |  |  |  |  |  |  |  |  |  |  |  |  |  |  |
| 09 | WAS | 82 | 4 | 9 | 12 | 1 | .280 | .318 | .561 | 83% | 34% | 6% | 2.00 | -$1 | -$16 | 60 | +5 | 7 | 2 | 0 | 34-12-54 | 17% | 17% | 21% | .879 | — | .879 | .913 | .633 | — | — |  |
| 10 | WAS | 525 | 10 | 59 | 65 | 17 | .269 | .308 | .392 | 79% | 34% | 5% | 1.46 | $15 | $6 | 280 | -3 | 27 | 4 | 5 | 32-16-53 | 8% | 21% | 30% | .700 | .691 | .710 | .664 | .799 | 4.75 | -12 | +29 |

## Blake DeWitt — 600 PA | $9 | 300 pts
2B-126, 3B-1 — Owned: 1% — LH

Doing everything fundamentally well and having a good attitude do not a major-league starter make. Coaches seem to love Blake DeWitt for these reasons, and he is a valuable stand-in, but he owns neither the glove for second base nor the bat for third base. For now, though, he's the Cubs' back-up at 2B. (RM)

### Forecast
| Player | Age | AB | HR | R | RBI | SB | BA | OBP | SLG | $1L | Pts |
|---|---|---|---|---|---|---|---|---|---|---|---|
| DeWitt B | 25 | 541 | 12 | 60 | 66 | 0 | .255 | .325 | .401 | $9 | 300 |
| Mini-Browser | Age | AB | HR | R | RBI | SB | BA | OBP | SLG | $1L | Pts |
| Young Jr. E | 25 | 387 | 5 | 63 | 27 | 32 | .244 | .327 | .360 | $11 | 250 |
| Espinosa D | 23 | 417 | 20 | 60 | 60 | 15 | .216 | .315 | .429 | $9 | 260 |
| Sanchez F | 33 | 433 | 9 | 59 | 45 | 0 | .291 | .332 | .414 | $9 | 260 |
| Rodriguez S | 25 | 391 | 17 | 51 | 47 | 9 | .239 | .317 | .425 | $9 | 210 |
| Rosales A | 27 | 403 | 14 | 50 | 45 | 5 | .257 | .327 | .438 | $9 | 230 |

### Competition at 2B — Stats in 2010
| Bats | Player | GSvR | GSvL | Sub | OPS |
|---|---|---|---|---|---|
| LH | DeWitt B | 38 | 8 | 2 | .709 |
| RH | Baker J | 2 | 18 | 6 | .739 |
| RH | Barney D | 2 | 4 | 4 | .585 |

### Minors (2010)
| Level | Leag | AB | HR | R | RBI | SB | BA | OBP | SLG | CT% | H% | BB% | Bash |
|---|---|---|---|---|---|---|---|---|---|---|---|---|---|
| A | — |  |  |  |  |  |  |  |  |  |  |  |  |
| AA | — |  |  |  |  |  |  |  |  |  |  |  |  |
| AAA | — |  |  |  |  |  |  |  |  |  |  |  |  |

### Majors
| Yr | Team | AB | HR | R | RBI | SB | BA | OBP | SLG | CT% | H% | BB% | Bash | $1L | $2L | Pts | RAA | 2B | 3B | CS | FB-LD-GB | HR/fb | RBI% | RS% | OPS | 1st Hf | 2nd Hf | vs RH | vs LH | Rnge | vRH | vLH |
|---|---|---|---|---|---|---|---|---|---|---|---|---|---|---|---|---|---|---|---|---|---|---|---|---|---|---|---|---|---|---|---|---|
| 07 | — |  |  |  |  |  |  |  |  |  |  |  |  |  |  |  |  |  |  |  |  |  |  |  |  |  |  |  |  |  |  |  |
| 08 | LAD | 368 | 9 | 45 | 52 | 3 | .264 | .344 | .383 | 82% | 32% | 10% | 1.45 | $7 | -$3 | 220 | -2 | 13 | 2 | 0 | 34-19-47 | 9% | 22% | 26% | .728 | .702 | .790 | .689 | .854 | 4.21 | +9 | -28 |
| 09 | LAD | 49 | 2 | 4 | 4 | 0 | .204 | .245 | .388 | 86% | 24% | 6% | 1.90 | -$4 | -$19 | 20 | -2 | 3 | 0 | 0 | 44-7-49 | 11% | 7% | 18% | .633 | .544 | .712 | .636 | .600 | 4.21 | +9 | -28 |
| 10 | 2TM | 440 | 4 | 47 | 52 | 3 | .264 | .336 | .373 | 80% | 32% | 7% | 1.43 | $7 | -$4 | 230 | -7 | 24 | 5 | 2 | 35-19-46 | 4% | 22% | 26% | .709 | .728 | .688 | .719 | .660 | 4.21 | +9 | -27 |

## Argenis Diaz — 100 PA | $-5 | 30 pts
SS-15 — Owned: 0% — RH

After failing to crack a .600 OPS in his sophomore season at Triple-A, Diaz should not waiting by the phone for significant playing time in 2011. With his glove, he serves as Triple-A depth and middle-infield injury insurance, but if the Pirates need his roster spot, he could be designated for assignment. (MB)

### Forecast
| Player | Age | AB | HR | R | RBI | SB | BA | OBP | SLG | $1L | Pts |
|---|---|---|---|---|---|---|---|---|---|---|---|
| Diaz A | 24 | 96 | 1 | 8 | 8 | 1 | .218 | .270 | .295 | -$5 | 30 |
| Mini-Browser | Age | AB | HR | R | RBI | SB | BA | OBP | SLG | $1L | Pts |
| Rohlinger R | 27 | 47 | 2 | 6 | 6 | 0 | .234 | .308 | .411 | -$4 | 20 |
| Maysonet E | 29 | 44 | 1 | 5 | 4 | 1 | .236 | .300 | .338 | -$5 | 20 |
| Navarro Y | 23 | 68 | 2 | 8 | 8 | 1 | .221 | .278 | .365 | -$5 | 30 |
| Cruz L | 27 | 45 | 1 | 5 | 4 | 1 | .231 | .269 | .353 | -$5 | 20 |
| Nunez E | 23 | 46 | 1 | 5 | 5 | 2 | .226 | .260 | .340 | -$5 | 20 |

### Competition at SS — Stats in 2010
| Bats | Player | GSvR | GSvL | Sub | OPS |
|---|---|---|---|---|---|
| RH | Cedeno R | 95 | 37 | 4 | .675 |
| RH | Diaz A | 7 | 1 | 7 | .578 |

### Minors (2010)
| Level | Leag | AB | HR | R | RBI | SB | BA | OBP | SLG | CT% | H% | BB% | Bash |
|---|---|---|---|---|---|---|---|---|---|---|---|---|---|
| A | — |  |  |  |  |  |  |  |  |  |  |  |  |
| AA | — |  |  |  |  |  |  |  |  |  |  |  |  |
| AAA | IL | 274 | 0 | 28 | 22 | 5 | .248 | .302 | .285 | 78% | 32% | 6% | 1.15 |

### Majors
| Yr | Team | AB | HR | R | RBI | SB | BA | OBP | SLG | CT% | H% | BB% | Bash | $1L | $2L | Pts | RAA | 2B | 3B | CS | FB-LD-GB | HR/fb | RBI% | RS% | OPS | 1st Hf | 2nd Hf | vs RH | vs LH | Rnge | vRH | vLH |
|---|---|---|---|---|---|---|---|---|---|---|---|---|---|---|---|---|---|---|---|---|---|---|---|---|---|---|---|---|---|---|---|---|
| 07 | — |  |  |  |  |  |  |  |  |  |  |  |  |  |  |  |  |  |  |  |  |  |  |  |  |  |  |  |  |  |  |  |
| 08 | — |  |  |  |  |  |  |  |  |  |  |  |  |  |  |  |  |  |  |  |  |  |  |  |  |  |  |  |  |  |  |  |
| 09 | — |  |  |  |  |  |  |  |  |  |  |  |  |  |  |  |  |  |  |  |  |  |  |  |  |  |  |  |  |  |  |  |
| 10 | PIT | 33 | 0 | 2 | 0 | 0 | .242 | .306 | .273 | 70% | 35% | 8% | 1.13 | -$5 | -$21 | 0 | -2 | 1 | 0 | 1 | 39-9-52 | 0% | 15% | 0% | .578 | .000 | .614 | .633 | .200 | — | — |  |

## Matt Diaz — 200 PA | $2 | 110 pts
OF-63 (LF-63) — Owned: 3% — RH

The Hittin' Fool will probably be released by the Braves this winter, as he is getting too expensive and has underperformed his role. Diaz will always be a platoon player and a 4th OF, though he could be a stand-out for a second-division team that can platoon him with a left-hander. (MG)

### Forecast
| Player | Age | AB | HR | R | RBI | SB | BA | OBP | SLG | $1L | Pts |
|---|---|---|---|---|---|---|---|---|---|---|---|
| Diaz M | 33 | 186 | 6 | 24 | 26 | 4 | .269 | .325 | .430 | $2 | 110 |
| Mini-Browser | Age | AB | HR | R | RBI | SB | BA | OBP | SLG | $1L | Pts |
| Bradley M | 32 | 205 | 8 | 30 | 30 | 3 | .256 | .367 | .430 | $3 | 130 |
| Hinske E | 33 | 227 | 10 | 33 | 33 | 3 | .253 | .351 | .464 | $3 | 150 |
| Francisco B | 29 | 180 | 8 | 26 | 22 | 6 | .267 | .336 | .467 | $2 | 120 |
| Jackson B | 22 | 133 | 6 | 23 | 17 | 6 | .237 | .331 | .433 | $2 | 80 |
| Patterson C | 31 | 188 | 4 | 22 | 20 | 10 | .256 | .296 | .394 | $2 | 110 |

### Competition at LF — Stats in 2010
| Bats | Player | GSvR | GSvL | Sub | OPS |
|---|---|---|---|---|---|
| BH | Cabrera M | 45 | 23 | 16 | .671 |
| RH | Diaz M | 12 | 41 | 10 | .739 |
| LH | Hinske E | 50 | 0 | 0 | .793 |
| RH | Infante O | 3 | 8 | 5 | .775 |

### Minors (2010)
| Level | Leag | AB | HR | R | RBI | SB | BA | OBP | SLG | CT% | H% | BB% | Bash |
|---|---|---|---|---|---|---|---|---|---|---|---|---|---|
| A | — |  |  |  |  |  |  |  |  |  |  |  |  |
| AA | — |  |  |  |  |  |  |  |  |  |  |  |  |
| AAA | IL | 4 | 0 | 2 | 3 | 0 | .250 | .250 | .333 | 75% | 33% | 0% | 1.33 |

### Majors
| Yr | Team | AB | HR | R | RBI | SB | BA | OBP | SLG | CT% | H% | BB% | Bash | $1L | $2L | Pts | RAA | 2B | 3B | CS | FB-LD-GB | HR/fb | RBI% | RS% | OPS | 1st Hf | 2nd Hf | vs RH | vs LH | Rnge | vRH | vLH |
|---|---|---|---|---|---|---|---|---|---|---|---|---|---|---|---|---|---|---|---|---|---|---|---|---|---|---|---|---|---|---|---|---|
| 07 | ATL | 358 | 12 | 44 | 45 | 4 | .338 | .368 | .497 | 82% | 41% | 4% | 1.47 | $13 | $2 | 230 | +12 | 21 | 0 | 2 | 34-21-46 | 12% | 19% | 25% | .865 | .846 | .887 | .756 | .964 | 2.08 | -20 | +40 |
| 08 | ATL | 135 | 2 | 9 | 14 | 4 | .244 | .264 | .304 | 76% | 32% | 2% | 1.24 | -$2 | -$15 | 40 | -10 | 2 | 0 | 2 | 24-25-52 | 8% | 17% | 20% | .568 | .581 | .000 | .356 | .755 | 2.11 | -34 | +62 |
| 09 | ATL | 371 | 13 | 56 | 58 | 6 | .313 | .390 | .488 | 76% | 41% | 8% | 1.56 | $17 | $6 | 260 | +9 | 18 | 2 | 3 | 27-25-48 | 17% | 22% | 28% | .878 | .837 | .909 | .749 | 1.103 | 2.09 | -47 | +86 |
| 10 | ATL | 224 | 7 | 27 | 27 | 4 | .250 | .302 | .438 | 80% | 31% | 5% | 1.75 | $3 | -$4 | 130 | -6 | 17 | 2 | 1 | 33-23-44 | 12% | 20% | 30% | .739 | .615 | .833 | .633 | .830 | 2.08 | -46 | +96 |

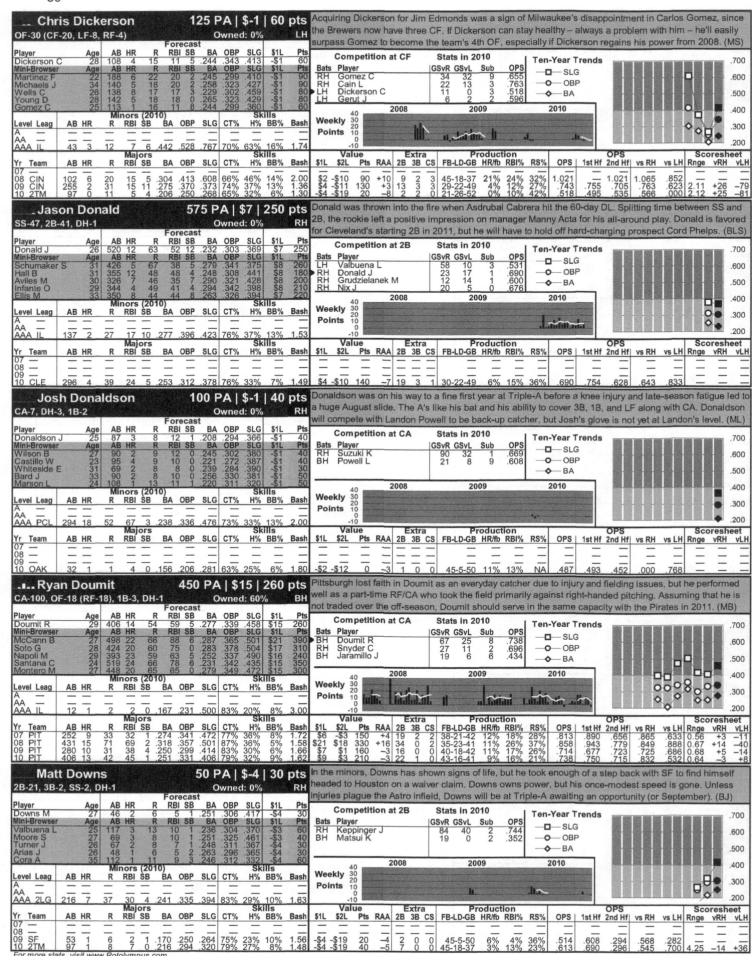

## Chris Dickerson — 125 PA | $-1 | 60 pts
OF-30 (CF-20, LF-8, RF-4) · Owned: 0% · LH

Acquiring Dickerson for Jim Edmonds was a sign of Milwaukee's disappointment in Carlos Gomez, since the Brewers now have three CF. If Dickerson can stay healthy – always a problem with him – he'll easily surpass Gomez to become the team's 4th OF, especially if Dickerson regains his power from 2008. (MS)

### Forecast
| Player | Age | AB | HR | R | RBI | SB | BA | OBP | SLG | $1L | Pts |
|---|---|---|---|---|---|---|---|---|---|---|---|
| Dickerson C | 28 | 108 | 4 | 15 | 11 | 5 | .244 | .343 | .413 | -$1 | 60 |

| Mini-Browser | Age | AB | HR | R | RBI | SB | BA | OBP | SLG | $1L | Pts |
|---|---|---|---|---|---|---|---|---|---|---|---|
| Martinez F | 22 | 188 | 6 | 22 | 20 | 2 | .245 | .299 | .410 | -$1 | 90 |
| Michaels J | 34 | 140 | 5 | 18 | 20 | 2 | .258 | .323 | .427 | -$1 | 90 |
| Wells C | 26 | 138 | 8 | 17 | 17 | 3 | .229 | .302 | .459 | -$1 | 80 |
| Young D | 28 | 142 | 5 | 18 | 18 | 0 | .265 | .323 | .429 | -$1 | 80 |
| Gomez C | 25 | 113 | 3 | 16 | 11 | 6 | .244 | .299 | .360 | -$1 | 60 |

### Minors (2010) / Skills
| Level | Leag | AB | HR | R | RBI | SB | BA | OBP | SLG | CT% | H% | BB% | Bash |
|---|---|---|---|---|---|---|---|---|---|---|---|---|---|
| A | — |  |  |  |  |  |  |  |  |  |  |  |  |
| AA | — |  |  |  |  |  |  |  |  |  |  |  |  |
| AAA | IL | 43 | 3 | 12 | 7 | 6 | .442 | .528 | .767 | 70% | 63% | 16% | 1.74 |

### Majors / Skills / Value / Extra / Production / OPS / Scoresheet
| Yr | Team | AB | HR | R | RBI | SB | BA | OBP | SLG | CT% | H% | BB% | Bash | $1L | $2L | Pts | RAA | 2B | 3B | CS | FB-LD-GB | HR/fb | RBI% | RS% | OPS | 1st Hf | 2nd Hf | vs RH | vs LH | Rnge | vRH | vLH |
|---|---|---|---|---|---|---|---|---|---|---|---|---|---|---|---|---|---|---|---|---|---|---|---|---|---|---|---|---|---|---|---|---|
| 07 | — |  |  |  |  |  |  |  |  |  |  |  |  |  |  |  |  |  |  |  |  |  |  |  |  |  |  |  |  |  |  |  |
| 08 | CIN | 102 | 6 | 20 | 15 | 5 | .304 | .413 | .608 | 66% | 46% | 14% | 2.00 | $2 | -$10 | 90 | +10 | 9 | 2 | 3 | 45-18-37 | 21% | 24% | 32% | 1.021 |  | 1.021 | 1.065 | .852 | 2.11 | +26 | -79 |
| 09 | CIN | 255 | 2 | 31 | 15 | 11 | .275 | .370 | .373 | 74% | 37% | 13% | 1.36 | $4 | -$11 | 130 | +3 | 13 | 3 | 3 | 29-22-49 | 4% | 12% | 27% | .743 | .755 | .705 | .763 | .623 | 2.11 | +25 | -81 |
| 10 | 2TM | 97 | 0 | 11 | 5 | 4 | .206 | .250 | .268 | 65% | 32% | 6% | 1.30 | -$4 | -$13 | 30 | -1 | 4 | 1 | 0 | 21-26-52 | 0% | 11% | 21% | .518 | .495 | .535 | .566 | .000 | 2.12 | +4 | -29 |

## Jason Donald — 575 PA | $7 | 250 pts
SS-47, 2B-41, DH-1 · Owned: 0% · RH

Donald was thrown into the fire when Asdrubal Cabrera hit the 60-day DL. Splitting time between SS and 2B, the rookie left a positive impression on manager Manny Acta for his all-around play. Donald is favored for Cleveland's starting 2B in 2011, but he will have to hold off hard-charging prospect Cord Phelps. (BLS)

### Forecast
| Player | Age | AB | HR | R | RBI | SB | BA | OBP | SLG | $1L | Pts |
|---|---|---|---|---|---|---|---|---|---|---|---|
| Donald J | 26 | 520 | 12 | 63 | 52 | 12 | .232 | .303 | .369 | $7 | 250 |

| Mini-Browser | Age | AB | HR | R | RBI | SB | BA | OBP | SLG | $1L | Pts |
|---|---|---|---|---|---|---|---|---|---|---|---|
| Schumaker S | 31 | 426 | 5 | 67 | 38 | 5 | .279 | .341 | .375 | $8 | 260 |
| Hall B | 31 | 355 | 12 | 48 | 48 | 4 | .248 | .308 | .441 | $8 | 180 |
| Aviles M | 30 | 336 | 7 | 46 | 35 | 7 | .290 | .321 | .428 | $8 | 200 |
| Infante O | 29 | 344 | 4 | 49 | 41 | 4 | .294 | .342 | .398 | $8 | 210 |
| Ellis M | 33 | 350 | 8 | 44 | 44 | 8 | .263 | .326 | .394 | $7 | 220 |

### Minors (2010) / Skills
| Level | Leag | AB | HR | R | RBI | SB | BA | OBP | SLG | CT% | H% | BB% | Bash |
|---|---|---|---|---|---|---|---|---|---|---|---|---|---|
| A | — |  |  |  |  |  |  |  |  |  |  |  |  |
| AA | — |  |  |  |  |  |  |  |  |  |  |  |  |
| AAA | IL | 137 | 2 | 27 | 17 | 10 | .277 | .396 | .423 | 76% | 37% | 13% | 1.53 |

### Majors / Skills / Value / Extra / Production / OPS / Scoresheet
| Yr | Team | AB | HR | R | RBI | SB | BA | OBP | SLG | CT% | H% | BB% | Bash | $1L | $2L | Pts | RAA | 2B | 3B | CS | FB-LD-GB | HR/fb | RBI% | RS% | OPS | 1st Hf | 2nd Hf | vs RH | vs LH | Rnge | vRH | vLH |
|---|---|---|---|---|---|---|---|---|---|---|---|---|---|---|---|---|---|---|---|---|---|---|---|---|---|---|---|---|---|---|---|---|
| 07 | — |  |  |  |  |  |  |  |  |  |  |  |  |  |  |  |  |  |  |  |  |  |  |  |  |  |  |  |  |  |  |  |
| 08 | — |  |  |  |  |  |  |  |  |  |  |  |  |  |  |  |  |  |  |  |  |  |  |  |  |  |  |  |  |  |  |  |
| 09 | — |  |  |  |  |  |  |  |  |  |  |  |  |  |  |  |  |  |  |  |  |  |  |  |  |  |  |  |  |  |  |  |
| 10 | CLE | 296 | 4 | 39 | 24 | 5 | .253 | .312 | .378 | 76% | 33% | 7% | 1.49 | $4 | -$10 | 140 | ~7 | 19 | 3 | 1 | 30-22-49 | 6% | 15% | 36% | .690 | .754 | .628 | .643 | .833 |  |  |  |

## Josh Donaldson — 100 PA | $-1 | 40 pts
CA-7, DH-3, 1B-2 · Owned: 0% · RH

Donaldson was on his way to a fine first year at Triple-A before a knee injury and late-season fatigue led to a huge August slide. The A's like his bat and his ability to cover 3B, 1B, and LF along with CA. Donaldson will compete with Landon Powell to be back-up catcher, but Josh's glove is not yet at Landon's level. (ML)

### Forecast
| Player | Age | AB | HR | R | RBI | SB | BA | OBP | SLG | $1L | Pts |
|---|---|---|---|---|---|---|---|---|---|---|---|
| Donaldson J | 25 | 87 | 3 | 8 | 12 | 1 | .208 | .294 | .366 | -$1 | 40 |

| Mini-Browser | Age | AB | HR | R | RBI | SB | BA | OBP | SLG | $1L | Pts |
|---|---|---|---|---|---|---|---|---|---|---|---|
| Wilson B | 27 | 90 | 2 | 9 | 12 | 0 | .245 | .302 | .380 | -$1 | 40 |
| Castillo W | 23 | 95 | 4 | 9 | 10 | 0 | .221 | .272 | .387 | -$1 | 40 |
| Whiteside E | 31 | 69 | 2 | 8 | 8 | 0 | .239 | .284 | .390 | -$1 | 30 |
| Bard J | 33 | 90 | 2 | 8 | 10 | 0 | .256 | .330 | .381 | -$1 | 50 |
| Marson L | 24 | 108 | 1 | 13 | 11 | 1 | .220 | .311 | .320 | -$1 | 50 |

### Minors (2010) / Skills
| Level | Leag | AB | HR | R | RBI | SB | BA | OBP | SLG | CT% | H% | BB% | Bash |
|---|---|---|---|---|---|---|---|---|---|---|---|---|---|
| A | — |  |  |  |  |  |  |  |  |  |  |  |  |
| AA | — |  |  |  |  |  |  |  |  |  |  |  |  |
| AAA | PCL | 294 | 18 | 52 | 67 | 3 | .238 | .336 | .476 | 73% | 33% | 13% | 2.00 |

### Majors / Skills / Value / Extra / Production / OPS / Scoresheet
| Yr | Team | AB | HR | R | RBI | SB | BA | OBP | SLG | CT% | H% | BB% | Bash | $1L | $2L | Pts | RAA | 2B | 3B | CS | FB-LD-GB | HR/fb | RBI% | RS% | OPS | 1st Hf | 2nd Hf | vs RH | vs LH | Rnge | vRH | vLH |
|---|---|---|---|---|---|---|---|---|---|---|---|---|---|---|---|---|---|---|---|---|---|---|---|---|---|---|---|---|---|---|---|---|
| 07 | — |  |  |  |  |  |  |  |  |  |  |  |  |  |  |  |  |  |  |  |  |  |  |  |  |  |  |  |  |  |  |  |
| 08 | — |  |  |  |  |  |  |  |  |  |  |  |  |  |  |  |  |  |  |  |  |  |  |  |  |  |  |  |  |  |  |  |
| 09 | — |  |  |  |  |  |  |  |  |  |  |  |  |  |  |  |  |  |  |  |  |  |  |  |  |  |  |  |  |  |  |  |
| 10 | OAK | 32 | 1 | 1 | 4 | 0 | .156 | .206 | .281 | 63% | 25% | 6% | 1.80 | -$2 | -$12 | 0 | ~3 | 1 | 0 | 0 | 45-5-50 | 11% | 13% | NA | .487 | .493 | .452 | .000 | .768 |  |  |  |

## Ryan Doumit — 450 PA | $15 | 260 pts
CA-100, OF-18 (RF-18), 1B-3, DH-1 · Owned: 60% · BH

Pittsburgh lost faith in Doumit as an everyday catcher due to injury and fielding issues, but he performed well as a part-time RF/CA who took the field primarily against right-handed pitching. Assuming that he is not traded over the off-season, Doumit should serve in the same capacity with the Pirates in 2011. (MB)

### Forecast
| Player | Age | AB | HR | R | RBI | SB | BA | OBP | SLG | $1L | Pts |
|---|---|---|---|---|---|---|---|---|---|---|---|
| Doumit R | 29 | 406 | 14 | 54 | 59 | 5 | .277 | .339 | .458 | $15 | 260 |

| Mini-Browser | Age | AB | HR | R | RBI | SB | BA | OBP | SLG | $1L | Pts |
|---|---|---|---|---|---|---|---|---|---|---|---|
| McCann B | 27 | 498 | 22 | 66 | 88 | 6 | .287 | .365 | .501 | $21 | 390 |
| Soto G | 28 | 424 | 20 | 60 | 75 | 0 | .283 | .378 | .504 | $17 | 310 |
| Napoli M | 29 | 393 | 23 | 59 | 63 | 5 | .252 | .337 | .490 | $16 | 240 |
| Santana C | 24 | 519 | 24 | 66 | 78 | 6 | .231 | .342 | .435 | $15 | 350 |
| Montero M | 27 | 448 | 20 | 65 | 65 | 0 | .279 | .349 | .472 | $15 | 300 |

### Minors (2010) / Skills
| Level | Leag | AB | HR | R | RBI | SB | BA | OBP | SLG | CT% | H% | BB% | Bash |
|---|---|---|---|---|---|---|---|---|---|---|---|---|---|
| A | — |  |  |  |  |  |  |  |  |  |  |  |  |
| AA | — |  |  |  |  |  |  |  |  |  |  |  |  |
| AAA | IL | 12 | 1 | 2 | 2 | 0 | .167 | .231 | .500 | 83% | 20% | 6% | 3.00 |

### Majors / Skills / Value / Extra / Production / OPS / Scoresheet
| Yr | Team | AB | HR | R | RBI | SB | BA | OBP | SLG | CT% | H% | BB% | Bash | $1L | $2L | Pts | RAA | 2B | 3B | CS | FB-LD-GB | HR/fb | RBI% | RS% | OPS | 1st Hf | 2nd Hf | vs RH | vs LH | Rnge | vRH | vLH |
|---|---|---|---|---|---|---|---|---|---|---|---|---|---|---|---|---|---|---|---|---|---|---|---|---|---|---|---|---|---|---|---|---|
| 07 | PIT | 252 | 9 | 33 | 32 | 1 | .274 | .341 | .472 | 77% | 36% | 8% | 1.72 | $6 | -$3 | 150 | +4 | 19 | 2 | 2 | 38-21-42 | 12% | 18% | 28% | .813 | .890 | .656 | .865 | .633 | 0.56 | +3 | -11 |
| 08 | PIT | 431 | 15 | 71 | 69 | 2 | .318 | .357 | .501 | 87% | 36% | 5% | 1.58 | $21 | $18 | 340 | +16 | 34 | 0 | 2 | 35-23-41 | 11% | 26% | 37% | .858 | .943 | .779 | .849 | .888 | 0.67 | +14 | -40 |
| 09 | PIT | 280 | 10 | 31 | 38 | 4 | .250 | .299 | .414 | 83% | 30% | 6% | 1.66 | $7 | $1 | 160 | -3 | 16 | 0 | 0 | 40-18-42 | 11% | 17% | 26% | .714 | .677 | .723 | .725 | .686 | 0.68 | +5 | -14 |
| 10 | PIT | 406 | 13 | 42 | 45 | 1 | .251 | .331 | .406 | 79% | 32% | 9% | 1.62 | $9 | $3 | 210 | -3 | 22 | 1 | 0 | 43-16-41 | 9% | 16% | 21% | .738 | .750 | .715 | .832 | .532 | 0.64 | -3 | +8 |

## Matt Downs — 50 PA | $-4 | 30 pts
2B-21, 3B-2, SS-2, DH-1 · Owned: 0% · RH

In the minors, Downs has shown signs of life, but he took enough of a step back with SF to find himself headed to Houston on a waiver claim. Downs owns power, but his once-modest speed is gone. Unless injuries plague the Astro infield, Downs will be at Triple-A awaiting an opportunity (or September). (BJ)

### Forecast
| Player | Age | AB | HR | R | RBI | SB | BA | OBP | SLG | $1L | Pts |
|---|---|---|---|---|---|---|---|---|---|---|---|
| Downs M | 27 | 46 | 2 | 6 | 5 | 1 | .251 | .306 | .417 | -$4 | 30 |

| Mini-Browser | Age | AB | HR | R | RBI | SB | BA | OBP | SLG | $1L | Pts |
|---|---|---|---|---|---|---|---|---|---|---|---|
| Valbuena L | 25 | 117 | 3 | 13 | 10 | 1 | .236 | .304 | .370 | -$3 | 60 |
| Moore S | 27 | 69 | 3 | 8 | 10 | 1 | .251 | .325 | .461 | -$4 | 40 |
| Turner J | 26 | 67 | 2 | 8 | 7 | 1 | .248 | .311 | .367 | -$4 | 30 |
| Arias J | 26 | 48 | 1 | 6 | 5 | 2 | .263 | .296 | .365 | -$4 | 30 |
| Cora A | 35 | 112 | 1 | 11 | 9 | 1 | .246 | .312 | .332 | -$4 | 50 |

### Minors (2010) / Skills
| Level | Leag | AB | HR | R | RBI | SB | BA | OBP | SLG | CT% | H% | BB% | Bash |
|---|---|---|---|---|---|---|---|---|---|---|---|---|---|
| A | — |  |  |  |  |  |  |  |  |  |  |  |  |
| AA | — |  |  |  |  |  |  |  |  |  |  |  |  |
| AAA | 2LG | 216 | 7 | 37 | 30 | 4 | .241 | .335 | .394 | 83% | 29% | 10% | 1.63 |

### Majors / Skills / Value / Extra / Production / OPS / Scoresheet
| Yr | Team | AB | HR | R | RBI | SB | BA | OBP | SLG | CT% | H% | BB% | Bash | $1L | $2L | Pts | RAA | 2B | 3B | CS | FB-LD-GB | HR/fb | RBI% | RS% | OPS | 1st Hf | 2nd Hf | vs RH | vs LH | Rnge | vRH | vLH |
|---|---|---|---|---|---|---|---|---|---|---|---|---|---|---|---|---|---|---|---|---|---|---|---|---|---|---|---|---|---|---|---|---|
| 07 | — |  |  |  |  |  |  |  |  |  |  |  |  |  |  |  |  |  |  |  |  |  |  |  |  |  |  |  |  |  |  |  |
| 08 | — |  |  |  |  |  |  |  |  |  |  |  |  |  |  |  |  |  |  |  |  |  |  |  |  |  |  |  |  |  |  |  |
| 09 | SF | 53 | 1 | 6 | 2 | 1 | .170 | .250 | .264 | 75% | 23% | 10% | 1.56 | -$4 | -$19 | 20 | -4 | 2 | 0 | 0 | 45-5-50 | 6% | 4% | 36% | .514 | .608 | .294 | .568 | .282 |  |  |  |
| 10 | 2TM | 97 | 1 | 8 | 7 | 0 | .216 | .294 | .320 | 79% | 27% | 6% | 1.48 | -$4 | -$19 | 40 | -5 | 5 | 0 | 0 | 45-18-37 | 3% | 13% | 23% | .613 | .690 | .296 | .545 | .700 | 4.25 | -14 | +36 |

## J.D. Drew — 450 PA | $12 | 290 pts
OF-133 (RF-133), DH-1 — Owned: 69% — LH

Drew's production on the field in 2010 was lacking, but he made up for it by playing through aches and pains (contrary to his reputation). He remains a top fielder and should bounce back at the plate – his LD rate in 2010 was only 16%, a fact that contributed to his sub-par H%. Should be Boston's #6 hitter. (EB)

### Forecast
| Player | Age | AB | HR | R | RBI | SB | BA | OBP | SLG | $1L | Pts |
|---|---|---|---|---|---|---|---|---|---|---|---|
| Drew J | 35 | 389 | 18 | 63 | 59 | 5 | .266 | .370 | .475 | $12 | 290 |

### Mini-Browser
| Player | Age | AB | HR | R | RBI | SB | BA | OBP | SLG | $1L | Pts |
|---|---|---|---|---|---|---|---|---|---|---|---|
| Podsednik S | 35 | 459 | 5 | 55 | 40 | 25 | .283 | .338 | .378 | $13 | 280 |
| Fowler D | 25 | 471 | 6 | 77 | 44 | 22 | .257 | .352 | .410 | $13 | 300 |
| Morgan N | 30 | 434 | 0 | 65 | 30 | 35 | .265 | .329 | .341 | $12 | 260 |
| Bourjos P | 24 | 563 | 12 | 76 | 49 | 31 | .242 | .287 | .378 | $12 | 310 |
| Gordon A | 27 | 466 | 16 | 63 | 53 | 11 | .259 | .347 | .429 | $12 | 270 |

### Minors (2010) / Skills
| Level | Leag | AB | HR | R | RBI | SB | BA | OBP | SLG | CT% | H% | BB% | Bash |
|---|---|---|---|---|---|---|---|---|---|---|---|---|---|
| A | — | | | | | | | | | | | | |
| AA | — | | | | | | | | | | | | |
| AAA | — | | | | | | | | | | | | |

### Competition at RF — Stats in 2010
| Bats | Player | GSvR | GSvL | Sub | OPS |
|---|---|---|---|---|---|
| LH | Drew J | 90 | 37 | 6 | .793 |
| RH | McDonald D | 6 | 19 | 9 | .766 |
| LH | Reddick J | 7 | 0 | 8 | .529 |

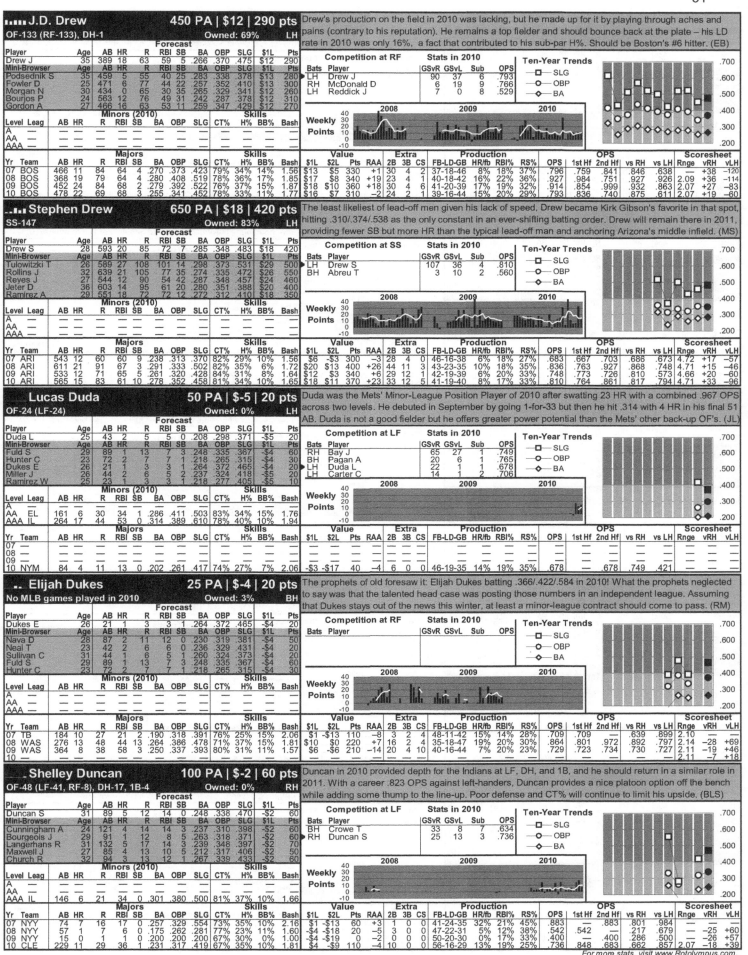

### Majors / Skills / Value / Extra / Production / OPS / Scoresheet
| Yr | Team | AB | HR | R | RBI | SB | BA | OBP | SLG | CT% | H% | BB% | Bash | $1L | $2L | Pts | RAA | 2B | 3B | CS | FB-LD-GB | HR/fb | RBI% | RS% | OPS | 1st Hf | 2nd Hf | vs RH | vs LH | Rnge | vRH | vLH |
|---|---|---|---|---|---|---|---|---|---|---|---|---|---|---|---|---|---|---|---|---|---|---|---|---|---|---|---|---|---|---|---|---|
| 07 | BOS | 466 | 11 | 84 | 64 | 4 | .270 | .373 | .423 | 79% | 34% | 14% | 1.56 | $13 | $13 | 330 | +1 | 30 | 4 | 2 | 37-18-46 | 8% | 18% | 37% | .796 | .759 | .841 | .846 | .638 | | +38 | −120 |
| 08 | BOS | 368 | 19 | 79 | 64 | 4 | .280 | .408 | .519 | 78% | 36% | 17% | 1.85 | $17 | $8 | 340 | +19 | 23 | 4 | 1 | 40-18-42 | 16% | 22% | 36% | .927 | .984 | .751 | .927 | .926 | 2.09 | +36 | −114 |
| 09 | BOS | 452 | 24 | 84 | 68 | 2 | .279 | .392 | .522 | 76% | 37% | 15% | 1.87 | $18 | $10 | 360 | +18 | 30 | 4 | 6 | 41-20-39 | 17% | 19% | 32% | .914 | .854 | .999 | .932 | .863 | 2.07 | +27 | −83 |
| 10 | BOS | 478 | 22 | 69 | 68 | 7 | .255 | .341 | .452 | 78% | 33% | 11% | 1.77 | $16 | $7 | 310 | −2 | 24 | 2 | 1 | 39-16-44 | 15% | 20% | 29% | .793 | .836 | .740 | .875 | .611 | 2.07 | +19 | −60 |

## Stephen Drew — 650 PA | $18 | 420 pts
SS-147 — Owned: 83% — LH

The least likeliest of lead-off men given his lack of speed, Drew became Kirk Gibson's favorite in that spot, hitting .310/.374/.538 as the only constant in an ever-shifting batting order. Drew will remain there in 2011, providing fewer SB but more HR than the typical lead-off man and anchoring Arizona's middle infield. (MS)

### Forecast
| Player | Age | AB | HR | R | RBI | SB | BA | OBP | SLG | $1L | Pts |
|---|---|---|---|---|---|---|---|---|---|---|---|
| Drew S | 28 | 593 | 20 | 85 | 72 | 7 | .285 | .348 | .483 | $18 | 420 |

### Mini-Browser
| Player | Age | AB | HR | R | RBI | SB | BA | OBP | SLG | $1L | Pts |
|---|---|---|---|---|---|---|---|---|---|---|---|
| Tulowitzki T | 26 | 589 | 27 | 108 | 101 | 14 | .298 | .373 | .531 | $29 | 500 |
| Rollins J | 32 | 639 | 21 | 105 | 77 | 35 | .274 | .335 | .472 | $26 | 550 |
| Reyes J | 27 | 544 | 12 | 90 | 54 | 42 | .287 | .344 | .457 | $24 | 460 |
| Jeter D | 36 | 603 | 14 | 95 | 61 | 20 | .280 | .351 | .388 | $20 | 400 |
| Ramirez A | 29 | 551 | 18 | 72 | 72 | 12 | .272 | .312 | .410 | $18 | 350 |

### Minors (2010) / Skills
| Level | Leag | AB | HR | R | RBI | SB | BA | OBP | SLG | CT% | H% | BB% | Bash |
|---|---|---|---|---|---|---|---|---|---|---|---|---|---|
| A | — | | | | | | | | | | | | |
| AA | — | | | | | | | | | | | | |
| AAA | — | | | | | | | | | | | | |

### Competition at SS — Stats in 2010
| Bats | Player | GSvR | GSvL | Sub | OPS |
|---|---|---|---|---|---|
| LH | Drew S | 107 | 36 | 4 | .810 |
| BH | Abreu T | 3 | 10 | 2 | .560 |

### Majors / Skills / Value / Extra / Production / OPS / Scoresheet
| Yr | Team | AB | HR | R | RBI | SB | BA | OBP | SLG | CT% | H% | BB% | Bash | $1L | $2L | Pts | RAA | 2B | 3B | CS | FB-LD-GB | HR/fb | RBI% | RS% | OPS | 1st Hf | 2nd Hf | vs RH | vs LH | Rnge | vRH | vLH |
|---|---|---|---|---|---|---|---|---|---|---|---|---|---|---|---|---|---|---|---|---|---|---|---|---|---|---|---|---|---|---|---|---|
| 07 | ARI | 543 | 12 | 60 | 60 | 9 | .238 | .313 | .370 | 82% | 29% | 10% | 1.56 | $6 | −$3 | 300 | −3 | 28 | 4 | 0 | 46-16-38 | 6% | 18% | 27% | .683 | .667 | .703 | .686 | .673 | 4.72 | +17 | −57 |
| 08 | ARI | 611 | 21 | 91 | 67 | 3 | .291 | .333 | .502 | 82% | 35% | 6% | 1.72 | $20 | $13 | 400 | +26 | 44 | 11 | 3 | 43-23-35 | 10% | 18% | 35% | .836 | .763 | .927 | .868 | .748 | 4.71 | +15 | −46 |
| 09 | ARI | 533 | 12 | 71 | 65 | 5 | .261 | .320 | .428 | 84% | 31% | 6% | 1.64 | $12 | $3 | 340 | +6 | 29 | 12 | 1 | 42-19-39 | 6% | 20% | 33% | .748 | .773 | .726 | .810 | .573 | 4.71 | +20 | −60 |
| 10 | ARI | 565 | 15 | 83 | 61 | 10 | .278 | .352 | .458 | 81% | 34% | 10% | 1.65 | $18 | $11 | 370 | +23 | 33 | 12 | 5 | 41-19-40 | 8% | 17% | 33% | .810 | .764 | .861 | .817 | .794 | 4.71 | +33 | −96 |

## Lucas Duda — 50 PA | $-5 | 20 pts
OF-24 (LF-24) — Owned: 0% — LH

Duda was the Mets' Minor-League Position Player of 2010 after swatting 23 HR with a combined .967 OPS across two levels. He debuted in September by going 1-for-33 but then he hit .314 with 4 HR in his final 51 AB. Duda is not a good fielder but he offers greater power potential than the Mets' other back-up OF's. (JL)

### Forecast
| Player | Age | AB | HR | R | RBI | SB | BA | OBP | SLG | $1L | Pts |
|---|---|---|---|---|---|---|---|---|---|---|---|
| Duda L | 25 | 43 | 2 | 5 | 5 | 0 | .208 | .298 | .371 | −$5 | 20 |

### Mini-Browser
| Player | Age | AB | HR | R | RBI | SB | BA | OBP | SLG | $1L | Pts |
|---|---|---|---|---|---|---|---|---|---|---|---|
| Fuld S | 29 | 89 | 1 | 13 | 7 | 3 | .248 | .335 | .367 | −$4 | 60 |
| Hunter C | 23 | 72 | 2 | 7 | 7 | 1 | .218 | .265 | .315 | −$4 | 30 |
| Dukes E | 26 | 21 | 1 | 3 | 3 | 1 | .264 | .372 | .465 | −$4 | 20 |
| Miller J | 26 | 44 | 2 | 6 | 5 | 2 | .218 | .324 | .418 | −$4 | 20 |
| Ramirez W | 25 | 23 | 1 | 3 | 2 | 1 | .218 | .277 | .405 | −$5 | 10 |

### Minors (2010) / Skills
| Level | Leag | AB | HR | R | RBI | SB | BA | OBP | SLG | CT% | H% | BB% | Bash |
|---|---|---|---|---|---|---|---|---|---|---|---|---|---|
| A | — | | | | | | | | | | | | |
| AA | EL | 161 | 6 | 30 | 34 | 1 | .286 | .411 | .503 | 83% | 34% | 15% | 1.76 |
| AAA | IL | 264 | 17 | 44 | 53 | 0 | .314 | .389 | .610 | 78% | 40% | 10% | 1.94 |

### Competition at LF — Stats in 2010
| Bats | Player | GSvR | GSvL | Sub | OPS |
|---|---|---|---|---|---|
| RH | Bay J | 65 | 27 | 1 | .749 |
| BH | Pagan A | 20 | 6 | 1 | .765 |
| LH | Duda L | 22 | 1 | 1 | .678 |
| LH | Carter C | 14 | 1 | 2 | .706 |

### Majors / Skills / Value / Extra / Production / OPS / Scoresheet
| Yr | Team | AB | HR | R | RBI | SB | BA | OBP | SLG | CT% | H% | BB% | Bash | $1L | $2L | Pts | RAA | 2B | 3B | CS | FB-LD-GB | HR/fb | RBI% | RS% | OPS | 1st Hf | 2nd Hf | vs RH | vs LH | Rnge | vRH | vLH |
|---|---|---|---|---|---|---|---|---|---|---|---|---|---|---|---|---|---|---|---|---|---|---|---|---|---|---|---|---|---|---|---|---|
| 07 | — | | | | | | | | | | | | | | | | | | | | | | | | | | | | | | | |
| 08 | — | | | | | | | | | | | | | | | | | | | | | | | | | | | | | | | |
| 09 | — | | | | | | | | | | | | | | | | | | | | | | | | | | | | | | | |
| 10 | NYM | 84 | 4 | 11 | 13 | 0 | .202 | .261 | .417 | 74% | 27% | 7% | 2.06 | −$3 | −$17 | 40 | −4 | 6 | 0 | 0 | 46-19-35 | 14% | 19% | 35% | .678 | | .678 | .749 | .421 | | | |

## Elijah Dukes — 25 PA | $-4 | 20 pts
No MLB games played in 2010 — Owned: 3% — BH

The prophets of old foresaw it: Elijah Dukes batting .366/.422/.584 in 2010! What the prophets neglected to say was that the talented head case was posting those numbers in an independent league. Assuming that Dukes stays out of the news this winter, at least a minor-league contract should come to pass. (RM)

### Forecast
| Player | Age | AB | HR | R | RBI | SB | BA | OBP | SLG | $1L | Pts |
|---|---|---|---|---|---|---|---|---|---|---|---|
| Dukes E | 26 | 21 | 1 | 3 | 3 | 1 | .264 | .372 | .465 | −$4 | 20 |

### Mini-Browser
| Player | Age | AB | HR | R | RBI | SB | BA | OBP | SLG | $1L | Pts |
|---|---|---|---|---|---|---|---|---|---|---|---|
| Nava D | 28 | 87 | 2 | 11 | 12 | 0 | .230 | .319 | .381 | −$4 | 50 |
| Neal T | 23 | 42 | 2 | 6 | 6 | 0 | .236 | .329 | .431 | −$4 | 20 |
| Sullivan C | 31 | 44 | 1 | 6 | 5 | 1 | .260 | .324 | .373 | −$4 | 20 |
| Fuld S | 29 | 89 | 1 | 13 | 7 | 3 | .248 | .335 | .367 | −$4 | 60 |
| Hunter C | 23 | 72 | 2 | 7 | 7 | 1 | .218 | .265 | .315 | −$4 | 30 |

### Minors (2010) / Skills
| Level | Leag | AB | HR | R | RBI | SB | BA | OBP | SLG | CT% | H% | BB% | Bash |
|---|---|---|---|---|---|---|---|---|---|---|---|---|---|
| A | — | | | | | | | | | | | | |
| AA | — | | | | | | | | | | | | |
| AAA | — | | | | | | | | | | | | |

### Competition at RF — Stats in 2010
| Bats | Player | GSvR | GSvL | Sub | OPS |
|---|---|---|---|---|---|

### Majors / Skills / Value / Extra / Production / OPS / Scoresheet
| Yr | Team | AB | HR | R | RBI | SB | BA | OBP | SLG | CT% | H% | BB% | Bash | $1L | $2L | Pts | RAA | 2B | 3B | CS | FB-LD-GB | HR/fb | RBI% | RS% | OPS | 1st Hf | 2nd Hf | vs RH | vs LH | Rnge | vRH | vLH |
|---|---|---|---|---|---|---|---|---|---|---|---|---|---|---|---|---|---|---|---|---|---|---|---|---|---|---|---|---|---|---|---|---|
| 07 | TB | 184 | 10 | 27 | 21 | 2 | .190 | .318 | .391 | 76% | 25% | 15% | 2.06 | $1 | −$13 | 110 | −8 | 3 | 2 | 4 | 48-11-42 | 15% | 14% | 28% | .709 | .709 | — | .639 | .899 | 2.10 | | |
| 08 | WAS | 276 | 13 | 40 | 44 | 13 | .264 | .386 | .478 | 71% | 37% | 15% | 1.81 | $10 | −$6 | 210 | +7 | 16 | 2 | 4 | 35-18-47 | 19% | 20% | 30% | .864 | .801 | .972 | .892 | .797 | 2.14 | −28 | +69 |
| 09 | WAS | 364 | 8 | 38 | 58 | 9 | .250 | .337 | .393 | 80% | 31% | 11% | 1.57 | $6 | −$6 | 210 | −14 | 24 | 4 | 10 | 40-16-44 | 7% | 20% | 23% | .729 | .723 | .734 | .730 | .727 | 2.11 | −19 | +46 |
| 10 | — | | | | | | | | | | | | | | | | | | | | | | | | | | | | | 2.11 | −7 | +18 |

## Shelley Duncan — 100 PA | $-2 | 60 pts
OF-48 (LF-41, RF-8), DH-17, 1B-4 — Owned: 0% — RH

Duncan in 2010 provided depth for the Indians at LF, DH, and 1B, and he should return in a similar role in 2011. With a career .823 OPS against left-handers, Duncan provides a nice platoon option off the bench while adding some thump to the line-up. Poor defense and CT% will continue to limit his upside. (BLS)

### Forecast
| Player | Age | AB | HR | R | RBI | SB | BA | OBP | SLG | $1L | Pts |
|---|---|---|---|---|---|---|---|---|---|---|---|
| Duncan S | 31 | 89 | 5 | 12 | 14 | 0 | .248 | .338 | .470 | −$2 | 60 |

### Mini-Browser
| Player | Age | AB | HR | R | RBI | SB | BA | OBP | SLG | $1L | Pts |
|---|---|---|---|---|---|---|---|---|---|---|---|
| Cunningham A | 24 | 121 | 4 | 14 | 14 | 3 | .237 | .310 | .398 | −$2 | 60 |
| Bourgeois J | 29 | 91 | 1 | 12 | 8 | 5 | .263 | .318 | .371 | −$2 | 60 |
| Langerhans R | 31 | 132 | 5 | 17 | 14 | 3 | .239 | .348 | .397 | −$2 | 70 |
| Maxwell J | 27 | 85 | 4 | 13 | 10 | 5 | .212 | .317 | .406 | −$2 | 50 |
| Church R | 32 | 94 | 3 | 13 | 12 | 1 | .267 | .339 | .433 | −$2 | 60 |

### Minors (2010) / Skills
| Level | Leag | AB | HR | R | RBI | SB | BA | OBP | SLG | CT% | H% | BB% | Bash |
|---|---|---|---|---|---|---|---|---|---|---|---|---|---|
| A | — | | | | | | | | | | | | |
| AA | — | | | | | | | | | | | | |
| AAA | IL | 146 | 6 | 21 | 34 | 0 | .301 | .380 | .500 | 81% | 37% | 10% | 1.66 |

### Competition at LF — Stats in 2010
| Bats | Player | GSvR | GSvL | Sub | OPS |
|---|---|---|---|---|---|
| BH | Crowe T | 33 | 8 | 7 | .634 |
| RH | Duncan S | 25 | 13 | 3 | .736 |

### Majors / Skills / Value / Extra / Production / OPS / Scoresheet
| Yr | Team | AB | HR | R | RBI | SB | BA | OBP | SLG | CT% | H% | BB% | Bash | $1L | $2L | Pts | RAA | 2B | 3B | CS | FB-LD-GB | HR/fb | RBI% | RS% | OPS | 1st Hf | 2nd Hf | vs RH | vs LH | Rnge | vRH | vLH |
|---|---|---|---|---|---|---|---|---|---|---|---|---|---|---|---|---|---|---|---|---|---|---|---|---|---|---|---|---|---|---|---|---|
| 07 | NYY | 74 | 7 | 16 | 17 | 0 | .257 | .329 | .554 | 73% | 35% | 10% | 2.16 | $1 | −$13 | 60 | +3 | 1 | 0 | 0 | | | | 45% | .883 | | .883 | .801 | .984 | — | | |
| 08 | NYY | 57 | 1 | 7 | 6 | 0 | .175 | .262 | .281 | 77% | 23% | 11% | 1.60 | −$4 | −$18 | 20 | −5 | 3 | 0 | 0 | 47-22-31 | 5% | 12% | 38% | .542 | .542 | | .217 | .679 | — | −25 | +60 |
| 09 | NYY | 15 | 0 | 1 | 0 | 0 | .200 | .200 | .200 | 67% | 30% | 0% | 1.00 | −$4 | −$19 | 0 | −2 | 0 | 0 | 0 | 50-20-30 | 0% | 9% | 33% | .400 | | .400 | .286 | .500 | — | −26 | +57 |
| 10 | CLE | 229 | 11 | 29 | 36 | 0 | .231 | .317 | .419 | 67% | 35% | 10% | 1.81 | $4 | −$9 | 110 | −4 | 10 | 0 | 0 | 56-16-29 | 13% | 19% | 25% | .736 | .848 | .683 | .662 | .857 | 2.07 | −18 | +39 |

*For more stats, visit www.Rotolympus.com.*

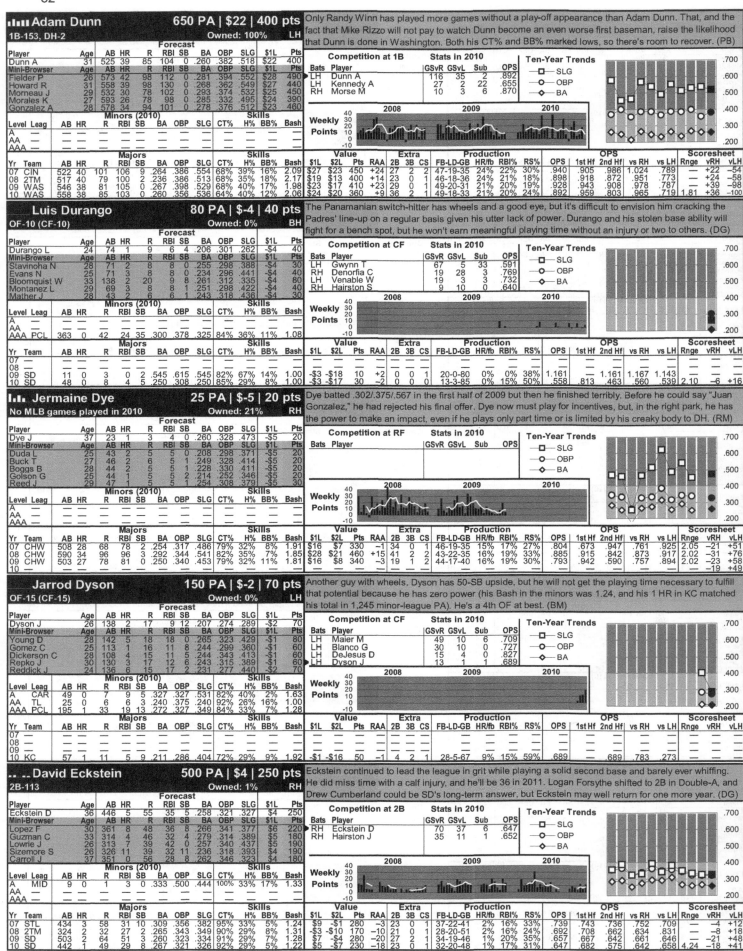

## Adam Dunn — 650 PA | $22 | 400 pts
1B-153, DH-2 — Owned: 100% — LH

Only Randy Winn has played more games without a play-off appearance than Adam Dunn. That, and the fact that Mike Rizzo will not pay to watch Dunn become an even worse first baseman, raise the likelihood that Dunn is done in Washington. Both his CT% and BB% marked lows, so there's room to recover. (PB)

### Forecast
| Player | Age | AB | HR | R | RBI | SB | BA | OBP | SLG | $1L | Pts |
|---|---|---|---|---|---|---|---|---|---|---|---|
| Dunn A | 31 | 525 | 39 | 85 | 104 | 0 | .260 | .382 | .518 | $22 | 400 |

| Mini-Browser | Age | AB | HR | R | RBI | SB | BA | OBP | SLG | $1L | Pts |
|---|---|---|---|---|---|---|---|---|---|---|---|
| Fielder P | 26 | 573 | 42 | 98 | 112 | 0 | .281 | .394 | .552 | $28 | 490 |
| Howard R | 31 | 558 | 39 | 98 | 130 | 0 | .268 | .362 | .549 | $27 | 440 |
| Morneau J | 29 | 532 | 30 | 78 | 102 | 0 | .293 | .374 | .532 | $25 | 450 |
| Morales K | 27 | 593 | 26 | 78 | 98 | 0 | .285 | .332 | .495 | $24 | 390 |
| Gonzalez A | 28 | 578 | 34 | 94 | 101 | 0 | .278 | .376 | .512 | $23 | 460 |

### Minors (2010) / Skills
| Level | Leag | AB | HR | R | RBI | SB | BA | OBP | SLG | CT% | H% | BB% | Bash |
|---|---|---|---|---|---|---|---|---|---|---|---|---|---|
| A | — | — | — | — | — | — | — | — | — | — | — | — | — |
| AA | — | — | — | — | — | — | — | — | — | — | — | — | — |
| AAA | — | — | — | — | — | — | — | — | — | — | — | — | — |

### Majors / Skills / Value / Extra / Production / OPS / Scoresheet
| Yr | Team | AB | HR | R | RBI | SB | BA | OBP | SLG | CT% | H% | BB% | Bash | $1L | $2L | Pts | RAA | 2B | 3B | CS | FB-LD-GB | HR/fb | RBI% | RS% | OPS | 1st Hf | 2nd Hf | vs RH | vs LH | Rnge | vRH | vLH |
|---|---|---|---|---|---|---|---|---|---|---|---|---|---|---|---|---|---|---|---|---|---|---|---|---|---|---|---|---|---|---|---|---|
| 07 | CIN | 522 | 40 | 101 | 106 | 9 | .264 | .386 | .554 | 68% | 39% | 16% | 2.09 | $27 | $23 | 450 | +24 | 27 | 2 | 2 | 47-19-35 | 24% | 22% | 30% | .940 | .905 | .986 | 1.024 | .789 | — | +22 | -54 |
| 08 | 2TM | 517 | 40 | 79 | 100 | 2 | .236 | .386 | .513 | 68% | 35% | 18% | 2.17 | $19 | $13 | 400 | +14 | 23 | 0 | 1 | 46-18-36 | 24% | 21% | 18% | .898 | .918 | .872 | .951 | .773 | — | +24 | -58 |
| 09 | WAS | 546 | 38 | 81 | 105 | 0 | .267 | .398 | .529 | 68% | 40% | 17% | 1.98 | $23 | $17 | 410 | +23 | 29 | 0 | 1 | 49-20-31 | 21% | 20% | 19% | .928 | .943 | .908 | .978 | .787 | — | +39 | -98 |
| 10 | WAS | 558 | 38 | 85 | 103 | 0 | .260 | .356 | .536 | 64% | 40% | 12% | 2.06 | $24 | $20 | 360 | +9 | 36 | 0 | 1 | 49-18-33 | 21% | 20% | 20% | .892 | .965 | .719 | 1.81 | +36 | -100 |

Competition at 1B / Stats in 2010
| Bats | Player | GSvR | GSvL | Sub | OPS |
|---|---|---|---|---|---|
| LH | Dunn A | 116 | 35 | 2 | .892 |
| LH | Kennedy A | 27 | 2 | 22 | .655 |
| RH | Morse M | 10 | 3 | 6 | .870 |

Ten-Year Trends: SLG / OBP / BA

---

## Luis Durango — 80 PA | $-4 | 40 pts
OF-10 (CF-10) — Owned: 0% — BH

The Panamanian switch-hitter has wheels and a good eye, but it's difficult to envision him cracking the Padres' line-up on a regular basis given his utter lack of power. Durango and his stolen base ability will fight for a bench spot, but he won't earn meaningful playing time without an injury or two to others. (DG)

### Forecast
| Player | Age | AB | HR | R | RBI | SB | BA | OBP | SLG | $1L | Pts |
|---|---|---|---|---|---|---|---|---|---|---|---|
| Durango L | 24 | 74 | 1 | 9 | 6 | 4 | .206 | .301 | .262 | -$4 | 40 |

| Mini-Browser | Age | AB | HR | R | RBI | SB | BA | OBP | SLG | $1L | Pts |
|---|---|---|---|---|---|---|---|---|---|---|---|
| Stavinoha N | 28 | 71 | 2 | 8 | 8 | 0 | .255 | .298 | .388 | -$4 | 30 |
| Evans N | 25 | 71 | 3 | 8 | 8 | 0 | .234 | .296 | .441 | -$4 | 30 |
| Bloomquist W | 33 | 138 | 2 | 20 | 9 | 8 | .261 | .312 | .335 | -$4 | 80 |
| Montanez L | 29 | 69 | 3 | 8 | 8 | 1 | .251 | .298 | .422 | -$4 | 40 |
| Mather J | 28 | 43 | 2 | 6 | 6 | 1 | .243 | .318 | .436 | -$4 | 30 |

### Minors (2010) / Skills
| Level | Leag | AB | HR | R | RBI | SB | BA | OBP | SLG | CT% | H% | BB% | Bash |
|---|---|---|---|---|---|---|---|---|---|---|---|---|---|
| A | — | — | — | — | — | — | — | — | — | — | — | — | — |
| AA | — | — | — | — | — | — | — | — | — | — | — | — | — |
| AAA | PCL | 363 | 0 | 42 | 24 | 35 | .300 | .378 | .325 | 84% | 36% | 11% | 1.08 |

### Majors / Skills / Value / Extra / Production / OPS / Scoresheet
| Yr | Team | AB | HR | R | RBI | SB | BA | OBP | SLG | CT% | H% | BB% | Bash | $1L | $2L | Pts | RAA | 2B | 3B | CS | FB-LD-GB | HR/fb | RBI% | RS% | OPS | 1st Hf | 2nd Hf | vs RH | vs LH | Rnge | vRH | vLH |
|---|---|---|---|---|---|---|---|---|---|---|---|---|---|---|---|---|---|---|---|---|---|---|---|---|---|---|---|---|---|---|---|---|
| 07 | — | — | — | — | — | — | — | — | — | — | — | — | — | — | — | — | — | — | — | — | — | — | — | — | — | — | — | — | — | — | — | — |
| 08 | — | — | — | — | — | — | — | — | — | — | — | — | — | — | — | — | — | — | — | — | — | — | — | — | — | — | — | — | — | — | — | — |
| 09 | SD | 11 | 0 | 3 | 0 | 2 | .545 | .615 | .545 | 82% | 67% | 14% | 1.00 | -$3 | -$18 | 10 | +2 | 0 | 0 | 1 | 20-0-80 | 0% | 0% | 38% | 1.161 | — | 1.161 | 1.167 | 1.143 | — | — | — |
| 10 | SD | 48 | 0 | 8 | 4 | 5 | .250 | .308 | .250 | 85% | 29% | 8% | 1.00 | -$3 | -$17 | 30 | -2 | 0 | 0 | 1 | 13-3-85 | 0% | 15% | 50% | .558 | .813 | .463 | .560 | .539 | 2.10 | -6 | +16 |

Competition at CF / Stats in 2010
| Bats | Player | GSvR | GSvL | Sub | OPS |
|---|---|---|---|---|---|
| LH | Gwynn T | 67 | 5 | 33 | .591 |
| RH | Denorfia C | 19 | 28 | 3 | .769 |
| LH | Venable W | 19 | 3 | 3 | .732 |
| RH | Hairston S | 9 | 10 | 0 | .640 |

Ten-Year Trends: SLG / OBP / BA

---

## Jermaine Dye — 25 PA | $-5 | 20 pts
No MLB games played in 2010 — Owned: 21% — RH

Dye batted .302/.375/.567 in the first half of 2009 but then he finished terribly. Before he could say "Juan Gonzalez," he had rejected his final offer. Dye now must play for incentives, but, in the right park, he has the power to make an impact, even if he plays only part time or is limited by his creaky body to DH. (RM)

### Forecast
| Player | Age | AB | HR | R | RBI | SB | BA | OBP | SLG | $1L | Pts |
|---|---|---|---|---|---|---|---|---|---|---|---|
| Dye J | 37 | 23 | 1 | 3 | 4 | 0 | .260 | .328 | .473 | -$5 | 20 |

| Mini-Browser | Age | AB | HR | R | RBI | SB | BA | OBP | SLG | $1L | Pts |
|---|---|---|---|---|---|---|---|---|---|---|---|
| Duda L | 25 | 43 | 2 | 5 | 5 | 0 | .208 | .298 | .371 | -$5 | 20 |
| Buck T | 27 | 46 | 2 | 6 | 5 | 1 | .249 | .328 | .414 | -$5 | 20 |
| Boggs B | 28 | 44 | 2 | 5 | 5 | 1 | .228 | .330 | .411 | -$5 | 20 |
| Golson G | 25 | 44 | 1 | 5 | 2 | 2 | .214 | .252 | .346 | -$5 | 20 |
| Reed J | 29 | 47 | 1 | 5 | 5 | 0 | .254 | .308 | .379 | -$5 | 30 |

### Minors (2010) / Skills
| Level | Leag | AB | HR | R | RBI | SB | BA | OBP | SLG | CT% | H% | BB% | Bash |
|---|---|---|---|---|---|---|---|---|---|---|---|---|---|
| A | — | — | — | — | — | — | — | — | — | — | — | — | — |
| AA | — | — | — | — | — | — | — | — | — | — | — | — | — |
| AAA | — | — | — | — | — | — | — | — | — | — | — | — | — |

### Majors / Skills / Value / Extra / Production / OPS / Scoresheet
| Yr | Team | AB | HR | R | RBI | SB | BA | OBP | SLG | CT% | H% | BB% | Bash | $1L | $2L | Pts | RAA | 2B | 3B | CS | FB-LD-GB | HR/fb | RBI% | RS% | OPS | 1st Hf | 2nd Hf | vs RH | vs LH | Rnge | vRH | vLH |
|---|---|---|---|---|---|---|---|---|---|---|---|---|---|---|---|---|---|---|---|---|---|---|---|---|---|---|---|---|---|---|---|---|
| 07 | CHW | 508 | 28 | 68 | 78 | 2 | .254 | .317 | .486 | 79% | 25% | 8% | 1.91 | $16 | $7 | 330 | -1 | 34 | 0 | 1 | 46-19-35 | 15% | 17% | 27% | .804 | .673 | .947 | .761 | .925 | 2.05 | -21 | +51 |
| 08 | CHW | 590 | 34 | 96 | 96 | 3 | .292 | .344 | .541 | 82% | 35% | 7% | 1.85 | $28 | $21 | 460 | +15 | 41 | 2 | 2 | 43-22-35 | 16% | 19% | 33% | .885 | .915 | .842 | .873 | .917 | 2.02 | -31 | +76 |
| 09 | CHW | 503 | 27 | 78 | 81 | 0 | .250 | .340 | .453 | 79% | 32% | 11% | 1.81 | $16 | $8 | 340 | -3 | 19 | 1 | 2 | 44-17-40 | 16% | 19% | 30% | .793 | .942 | .590 | .757 | .894 | 2.02 | -19 | +58 |
| 10 | — | — | — | — | — | — | — | — | — | — | — | — | — | — | — | — | — | — | — | — | — | — | — | — | — | — | — | — | — | -19 | +49 |

Competition at RF / Stats in 2010
| Bats | Player | GSvR | GSvL | Sub | OPS |
|---|---|---|---|---|---|

Ten-Year Trends: SLG / OBP / BA

---

## Jarrod Dyson — 150 PA | $-2 | 70 pts
OF-15 (CF-15) — Owned: 0% — LH

Another guy with wheels, Dyson has 50-SB upside, but he will not get the playing time necessary to fulfill that potential because he has zero power (his Bash in the minors was 1.24, and his 1 HR in KC matched his total in 1,245 minor-league PA). He's a 4th OF at best. (BM)

### Forecast
| Player | Age | AB | HR | R | RBI | SB | BA | OBP | SLG | $1L | Pts |
|---|---|---|---|---|---|---|---|---|---|---|---|
| Dyson J | 26 | 138 | 2 | 17 | 9 | 12 | .207 | .274 | .289 | -$2 | 70 |

| Mini-Browser | Age | AB | HR | R | RBI | SB | BA | OBP | SLG | $1L | Pts |
|---|---|---|---|---|---|---|---|---|---|---|---|
| Young D | 28 | 142 | 5 | 18 | 18 | 0 | .265 | .323 | .429 | -$1 | 80 |
| Gomez C | 25 | 113 | 1 | 16 | 11 | 8 | .244 | .299 | .360 | -$1 | 60 |
| Dickerson C | 28 | 108 | 4 | 15 | 11 | 5 | .244 | .343 | .413 | -$1 | 60 |
| Repko J | 30 | 130 | 3 | 17 | 12 | 6 | .243 | .315 | .389 | -$1 | 60 |
| Reddick J | 24 | 136 | 6 | 15 | 17 | 2 | .231 | .277 | .440 | -$2 | 70 |

### Minors (2010) / Skills
| Level | Leag | AB | HR | R | RBI | SB | BA | OBP | SLG | CT% | H% | BB% | Bash |
|---|---|---|---|---|---|---|---|---|---|---|---|---|---|
| A | CAR | 49 | 0 | 7 | 9 | 5 | .327 | .327 | .531 | 82% | 40% | 2% | 1.63 |
| AA | TL | 25 | 0 | 6 | 6 | 3 | .240 | .375 | .240 | 92% | 26% | 16% | 1.00 |
| AAA | PCL | 195 | 1 | 33 | 19 | 13 | .272 | .327 | .349 | 84% | 33% | 7% | 1.28 |

### Majors / Skills / Value / Extra / Production / OPS / Scoresheet
| Yr | Team | AB | HR | R | RBI | SB | BA | OBP | SLG | CT% | H% | BB% | Bash | $1L | $2L | Pts | RAA | 2B | 3B | CS | FB-LD-GB | HR/fb | RBI% | RS% | OPS | 1st Hf | 2nd Hf | vs RH | vs LH | Rnge | vRH | vLH |
|---|---|---|---|---|---|---|---|---|---|---|---|---|---|---|---|---|---|---|---|---|---|---|---|---|---|---|---|---|---|---|---|---|
| 07 | — | — | — | — | — | — | — | — | — | — | — | — | — | — | — | — | — | — | — | — | — | — | — | — | — | — | — | — | — | — | — | — |
| 08 | — | — | — | — | — | — | — | — | — | — | — | — | — | — | — | — | — | — | — | — | — | — | — | — | — | — | — | — | — | — | — | — |
| 09 | — | — | — | — | — | — | — | — | — | — | — | — | — | — | — | — | — | — | — | — | — | — | — | — | — | — | — | — | — | — | — | — |
| 10 | KC | 57 | 1 | 11 | 5 | 9 | .211 | .286 | .404 | 72% | 29% | 9% | 1.92 | -$1 | -$16 | 50 | -1 | 4 | 2 | 1 | 28-5-67 | 9% | 15% | 59% | .689 | — | .689 | .783 | .273 | — | — | — |

Competition at CF / Stats in 2010
| Bats | Player | GSvR | GSvL | Sub | OPS |
|---|---|---|---|---|---|
| LH | Maier M | 49 | 10 | 6 | .709 |
| LH | Blanco G | 30 | 10 | 0 | .727 |
| LH | DeJesus D | 15 | 4 | 0 | .827 |
| LH | Dyson J | 13 | 1 | 1 | .689 |

Ten-Year Trends: SLG / OBP / BA

---

## David Eckstein — 500 PA | $4 | 250 pts
2B-113 — Owned: 1% — RH

Eckstein continued to lead the league in grit while playing a solid second base and barely ever whiffing. He did miss time with a calf injury, and he'll be 36 in 2011. Logan Forsythe shifted to 2B in Double-A, and Drew Cumberland could be SD's long-term answer, but Eckstein may well return for one more year. (DG)

### Forecast
| Player | Age | AB | HR | R | RBI | SB | BA | OBP | SLG | $1L | Pts |
|---|---|---|---|---|---|---|---|---|---|---|---|
| Eckstein D | 36 | 446 | 5 | 55 | 35 | 5 | .258 | .321 | .327 | $4 | 250 |

| Mini-Browser | Age | AB | HR | R | RBI | SB | BA | OBP | SLG | $1L | Pts |
|---|---|---|---|---|---|---|---|---|---|---|---|
| Lopez F | 30 | 361 | 8 | 48 | 36 | 8 | .266 | .341 | .377 | $6 | 220 |
| Guzman C | 33 | 314 | 4 | 46 | 32 | 4 | .279 | .314 | .389 | $5 | 180 |
| Lowrie J | 26 | 313 | 7 | 39 | 42 | 0 | .257 | .340 | .437 | $5 | 190 |
| Sizemore S | 26 | 326 | 11 | 39 | 32 | 11 | .236 | .318 | .393 | $4 | 190 |
| Carroll J | 37 | 351 | 4 | 50 | 28 | 8 | .262 | .346 | .323 | $4 | 180 |

### Minors (2010) / Skills
| Level | Leag | AB | HR | R | RBI | SB | BA | OBP | SLG | CT% | H% | BB% | Bash |
|---|---|---|---|---|---|---|---|---|---|---|---|---|---|
| A | MID | 9 | 0 | 1 | 3 | 0 | .333 | .500 | .444 | 100% | 33% | 17% | 1.33 |
| AA | — | — | — | — | — | — | — | — | — | — | — | — | — |
| AAA | — | — | — | — | — | — | — | — | — | — | — | — | — |

### Majors / Skills / Value / Extra / Production / OPS / Scoresheet
| Yr | Team | AB | HR | R | RBI | SB | BA | OBP | SLG | CT% | H% | BB% | Bash | $1L | $2L | Pts | RAA | 2B | 3B | CS | FB-LD-GB | HR/fb | RBI% | RS% | OPS | 1st Hf | 2nd Hf | vs RH | vs LH | Rnge | vRH | vLH |
|---|---|---|---|---|---|---|---|---|---|---|---|---|---|---|---|---|---|---|---|---|---|---|---|---|---|---|---|---|---|---|---|---|
| 07 | STL | 434 | 3 | 58 | 31 | 10 | .309 | .356 | .382 | 95% | 33% | 5% | 1.24 | $9 | $1 | 280 | -3 | 23 | 0 | 1 | 37-22-41 | 2% | 16% | 33% | .739 | .743 | .736 | .752 | .709 | — | -4 | +12 |
| 08 | 2TM | 324 | 2 | 32 | 27 | 2 | .265 | .343 | .349 | 90% | 29% | 8% | 1.31 | -$3 | -$10 | 170 | -10 | 21 | 0 | 1 | 28-20-51 | 2% | 16% | 24% | .692 | .708 | .662 | .634 | .831 | — | -8 | +18 |
| 09 | SD | 503 | 2 | 64 | 51 | 3 | .260 | .323 | .334 | 91% | 29% | 8% | 1.28 | $7 | -$4 | 280 | -20 | 27 | 2 | 1 | 34-19-46 | 1% | 20% | 35% | .657 | .667 | .642 | .661 | .646 | — | -21 | +49 |
| 10 | SD | 442 | 4 | 49 | 29 | 8 | .267 | .321 | .326 | 92% | 29% | 5% | 1.22 | $5 | -$7 | 230 | -18 | 23 | 1 | 0 | 32-20-48 | 1% | 17% | 31% | .647 | .682 | .575 | .642 | .658 | 4.24 | -18 | +41 |

Competition at 2B / Stats in 2010
| Bats | Player | GSvR | GSvL | Sub | OPS |
|---|---|---|---|---|---|
| RH | Eckstein D | 70 | 37 | 6 | .647 |
| RH | Hairston J | 35 | 11 | 1 | .652 |

Ten-Year Trends: SLG / OBP / BA

## A.J. Ellis — 150 PA | $0 | 70 pts
**CA-43** — Owned: 1% — RH

Ellis does not have a home run in professional ball since 2008, and after a less-than-inspiring stint as LA's back-up following Brad Ausmus's injury, his career looked to have stalled headed into his age-30 season. However, he caught fire in September (1.106 OPS in 15 G) and may have played himself into a job. (MP)

| Player | Age | AB | HR | R | RBI | SB | BA | OBP | SLG | $1L | Pts |
|---|---|---|---|---|---|---|---|---|---|---|---|
| Ellis A | 29 | 127 | 2 | 14 | 17 | 0 | .248 | .355 | .340 | $0 | 70 |
| Schneider B | 34 | 128 | 3 | 14 | 17 | 0 | .258 | .343 | .381 | $1 | 80 |
| Towles J | 27 | 90 | 3 | 11 | 11 | 2 | .244 | .331 | .414 | $0 | 50 |
| Quintero H | 31 | 188 | 4 | 14 | 16 | 0 | .245 | .285 | .354 | $0 | 60 |
| Kottaras G | 27 | 114 | 5 | 14 | 14 | 0 | .230 | .320 | .420 | $0 | 60 |
| Zaun G | 39 | 107 | 3 | 13 | 14 | 0 | .246 | .344 | .387 | $0 | 60 |

**Competition at CA — Stats in 2010**

| Bats | Player | GSvR | GSvL | Sub | OPS |
|---|---|---|---|---|---|
| RH | Martin R | 60 | 29 | 4 | .679 |
| RH | Ellis A | 26 | 8 | 9 | .687 |
| RH | Barajas R | 11 | 9 | 3 | .731 |
| RH | Ausmus B | 15 | 4 | 2 | .564 |

## Mark Ellis — 400 PA | $7 | 220 pts
**2B-116, DH-6** — Owned: 0% — RH

Before a ridiculously red-hot September/October, Ellis in 2010 was on his way to a very disappointing year at the plate. Since he turned 30, his Bash has dropped off, as has his speed (note the 6 CS), though he is still an above-average defender. He hits lefties well and could land in a platoon in 2011. (ML)

## Jacoby Ellsbury — 575 PA | $23 | 400 pts
**OF-18 (CF-13, LF-6)** — Owned: 69% — LH

Ellsbury's injuries will not linger in 2011, so the 27-year-old should be back on top of his game, but will it be with Boston? Even his abbreviated 2010 season did not snuff whispers that he may be shipped out. No matter his team, he will lead off, and though his BB% is not high, maybe his age-27 H% will surprise. (EB)

## Brad Emaus — 100 PA | $-4 | 50 pts
**No MLB games played in 2010** — Owned: 0% — RH

Emaus is a dark-horse candidate for Toronto's hot corner in 2011. His bat is better suited for second base, but his defense is a little short at both spots, so he might be relegated to merely a bench role. However, his patience is superb, and he projects to be a Scott Spiezio type. He'll be an injury fill-in in 2011. (MH)

## Edwin Encarnacion — 400 PA | $9 | 230 pts
**3B-95, DH-1** — Owned: 5% — RH

Encarnacion had a late surge that enabled him to reach 20+ homers in only 96 games. He does not hit for average and is a poor defender. Durability is a concern, too, as he has played fewer than 100 games each of the past two years. His return to Toronto is about 50/50; even so, he will be a regular somewhere. (MH)

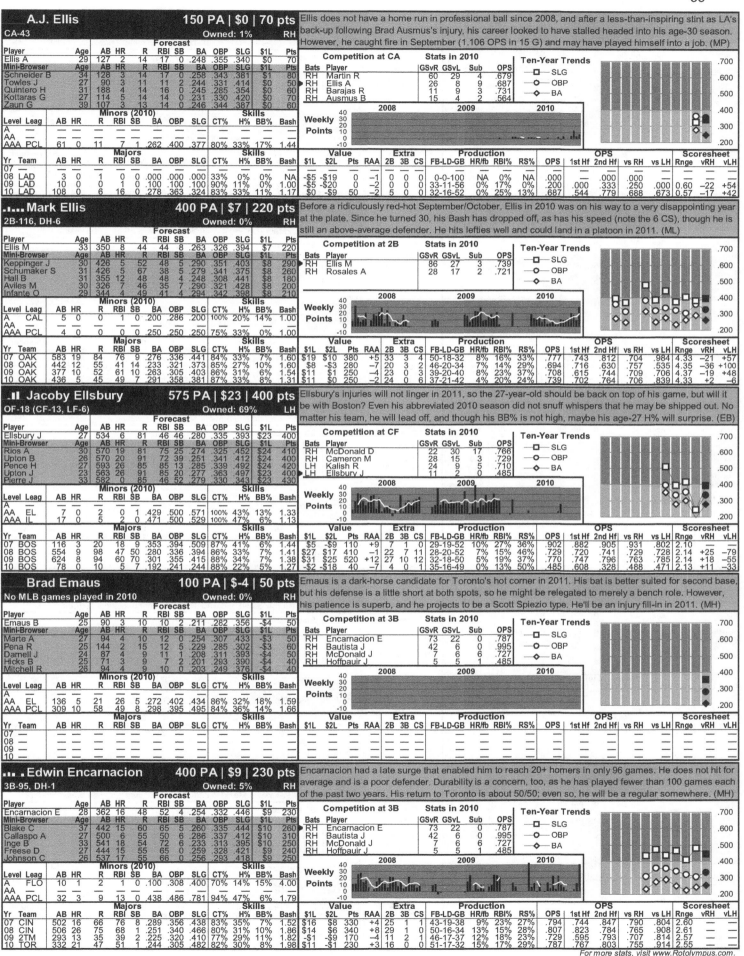

For more stats, visit www.Rotolympus.com.

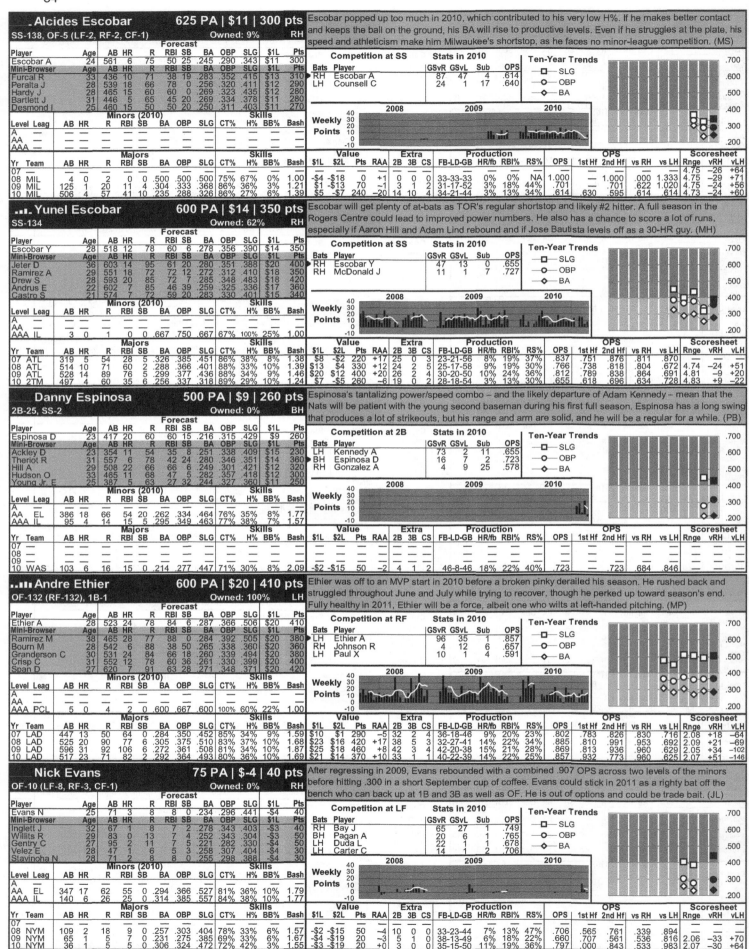

## Alcides Escobar — 625 PA | $11 | 300 pts

SS-138, OF-5 (LF-2, RF-2, CF-1) — Owned: 9% — RH

Escobar popped up too much in 2010, which contributed to his very low H%. If he makes better contact and keeps the ball on the ground, his BA will rise to productive levels. Even if he struggles at the plate, his speed and athleticism make him Milwaukee's shortstop, as he faces no minor-league competition. (MS)

### Forecast

| Player | Age | AB | HR | R | RBI | SB | BA | OBP | SLG | $1L | Pts |
|---|---|---|---|---|---|---|---|---|---|---|---|
| Escobar A | 24 | 561 | 6 | 75 | 50 | 25 | .245 | .290 | .343 | $11 | 300 |
| Mini-Browser | Age | AB | HR | R | RBI | SB | BA | OBP | SLG | $1L | Pts |
| Furcal R | 33 | 436 | 10 | 71 | 38 | 19 | .283 | .352 | .415 | $13 | 310 |
| Peralta J | 28 | 539 | 18 | 66 | 78 | 0 | .256 | .320 | .411 | $12 | 290 |
| Hardy J | 28 | 465 | 15 | 60 | 60 | 0 | .269 | .323 | .435 | $12 | 280 |
| Bartlett J | 31 | 446 | 5 | 65 | 45 | 20 | .269 | .334 | .378 | $11 | 280 |
| Desmond I | 25 | 460 | 15 | 50 | 50 | 20 | .250 | .311 | .403 | $11 | 270 |

### Minors (2010) / Skills

| Level | Leag | AB | HR | R | RBI | SB | BA | OBP | SLG | CT% | H% | BB% | Bash |
|---|---|---|---|---|---|---|---|---|---|---|---|---|---|
| A | — | — | — | — | — | — | — | — | — | — | — | — | — |
| AA | — | — | — | — | — | — | — | — | — | — | — | — | — |
| AAA | — | — | — | — | — | — | — | — | — | — | — | — | — |

### Majors / Skills

| Yr | Team | AB | HR | R | RBI | SB | BA | OBP | SLG | CT% | H% | BB% | Bash |
|---|---|---|---|---|---|---|---|---|---|---|---|---|---|
| 07 | — | — | — | — | — | — | — | — | — | — | — | — | — |
| 08 | MIL | 4 | 0 | 2 | 0 | 0 | .500 | .500 | .500 | 75% | 67% | 0% | 1.00 |
| 09 | MIL | 125 | 1 | 20 | 11 | 4 | .304 | .333 | .368 | 86% | 36% | 3% | 1.21 |
| 10 | MIL | 506 | 4 | 57 | 41 | 10 | .235 | .288 | .326 | 86% | 27% | 6% | 1.39 |

**Competition at SS**

| Bats | Player | GSvR | GSvL | Sub | OPS |
|---|---|---|---|---|---|
| RH | Escobar A | 87 | 47 | 4 | .614 |
| LH | Counsell C | 24 | 1 | 17 | .640 |

**Value / Extra / Production / OPS / Scoresheet**

| Yr | Team | $1L | $2L | Pts | RAA | 2B | 3B | CS | FB-LD-GB | HR/fb | RBI% | RS% | OPS | 1st Hf | 2nd Hf | vs RH | vs LH | Rnge | vRH | vLH |
|---|---|---|---|---|---|---|---|---|---|---|---|---|---|---|---|---|---|---|---|---|
| 07 | | | | | | | | | | | | | | | | | | 4.75 | -26 | +64 |
| 08 | MIL | -$4 | -$18 | 0 | +1 | 0 | 0 | 0 | 33-33-33 | 0% | 0% | NA | 1.000 | — | 1.000 | .000 | 1.333 | 4.75 | -29 | +71 |
| 09 | MIL | $1 | -$13 | 70 | -1 | 3 | 1 | 2 | 31-17-52 | 3% | 18% | 44% | .701 | — | .701 | .622 | 1.020 | 4.75 | -24 | +56 |
| 10 | MIL | $5 | -$7 | 240 | -20 | 14 | 10 | 4 | 34-21-44 | 3% | 13% | 34% | .614 | .630 | .595 | .614 | .614 | 4.73 | -24 | +60 |

## Yunel Escobar — 600 PA | $14 | 350 pts

SS-134 — Owned: 62% — RH

Escobar will get plenty of at-bats as TOR's regular shortstop and likely #2 hitter. A full season in the Rogers Centre could lead to improved power numbers. He also has a chance to score a lot of runs, especially if Aaron Hill and Adam Lind rebound and if Jose Bautista levels off as a 30-HR guy. (MH)

### Forecast

| Player | Age | AB | HR | R | RBI | SB | BA | OBP | SLG | $1L | Pts |
|---|---|---|---|---|---|---|---|---|---|---|---|
| Escobar Y | 28 | 518 | 12 | 78 | 60 | 6 | .278 | .356 | .390 | $14 | 350 |
| Mini-Browser | Age | AB | HR | R | RBI | SB | BA | OBP | SLG | $1L | Pts |
| Jeter D | 36 | 603 | 14 | 95 | 61 | 20 | .289 | .351 | .380 | $20 | 400 |
| Ramirez A | 29 | 551 | 18 | 72 | 72 | 12 | .272 | .312 | .410 | $18 | 350 |
| Drew S | 28 | 593 | 20 | 85 | 72 | 7 | .285 | .348 | .483 | $18 | 420 |
| Andrus E | 22 | 602 | 7 | 85 | 46 | 39 | .259 | .325 | .336 | $17 | 360 |
| Castro S | 21 | 574 | 7 | 72 | 59 | 20 | .283 | .330 | .401 | $15 | 340 |

### Minors (2010) / Skills

| Level | Leag | AB | HR | R | RBI | SB | BA | OBP | SLG | CT% | H% | BB% | Bash |
|---|---|---|---|---|---|---|---|---|---|---|---|---|---|
| A | — | — | — | — | — | — | — | — | — | — | — | — | — |
| AA | — | — | — | — | — | — | — | — | — | — | — | — | — |
| AAA | — | 3 | 0 | 1 | 0 | 0 | .667 | .750 | .667 | 67% | 100% | 25% | 1.00 |

### Majors / Skills

| Yr | Team | AB | HR | R | RBI | SB | BA | OBP | SLG | CT% | H% | BB% | Bash |
|---|---|---|---|---|---|---|---|---|---|---|---|---|---|
| 07 | ATL | 319 | 5 | 54 | 28 | 5 | .326 | .385 | .451 | 86% | 38% | 8% | 1.38 |
| 08 | ATL | 514 | 10 | 71 | 60 | 2 | .288 | .366 | .401 | 88% | 33% | 10% | 1.39 |
| 09 | ATL | 528 | 14 | 89 | 76 | 5 | .299 | .377 | .436 | 88% | 34% | 9% | 1.46 |
| 10 | 2TM | 497 | 4 | 60 | 35 | 6 | .256 | .337 | .318 | 89% | 29% | 10% | 1.24 |

**Competition at SS**

| Bats | Player | GSvR | GSvL | Sub | OPS |
|---|---|---|---|---|---|
| RH | Escobar Y | 47 | 13 | 0 | .655 |
| RH | McDonald J | 11 | 1 | 7 | .727 |

**Value / Extra / Production / OPS / Scoresheet**

| Yr | Team | $1L | $2L | Pts | RAA | 2B | 3B | CS | FB-LD-GB | HR/fb | RBI% | RS% | OPS | 1st Hf | 2nd Hf | vs RH | vs LH | Rnge | vRH | vLH |
|---|---|---|---|---|---|---|---|---|---|---|---|---|---|---|---|---|---|---|---|---|
| 07 | ATL | $8 | -$2 | 220 | +17 | 25 | 0 | 3 | 23-21-56 | 8% | 19% | 37% | .837 | .751 | .876 | .811 | .870 | | | |
| 08 | ATL | $13 | $4 | 330 | +12 | 24 | 2 | 5 | 25-17-58 | 9% | 19% | 30% | .766 | .738 | .818 | .804 | .672 | 4.74 | -24 | +51 |
| 09 | ATL | $20 | $12 | 400 | +20 | 26 | 2 | 4 | 30-20-50 | 10% | 24% | 36% | .812 | .789 | .838 | .864 | .691 | 4.81 | -9 | +20 |
| 10 | 2TM | $7 | -$5 | 260 | -6 | 19 | 0 | 2 | 28-18-54 | 3% | 13% | 30% | .655 | .618 | .696 | .634 | .728 | 4.83 | +9 | -22 |

## Danny Espinosa — 500 PA | $9 | 260 pts

2B-25, SS-2 — Owned: 0% — BH

Espinosa's tantalizing power/speed combo – and the likely departure of Adam Kennedy – mean that the Nats will be patient with the young second baseman during his first full season. Espinosa has a long swing that produces a lot of strikeouts, but his range and arm are solid, and he will be a regular for a while. (PB)

### Forecast

| Player | Age | AB | HR | R | RBI | SB | BA | OBP | SLG | $1L | Pts |
|---|---|---|---|---|---|---|---|---|---|---|---|
| Espinosa D | 23 | 417 | 20 | 60 | 60 | 15 | .216 | .315 | .429 | $9 | 260 |
| Mini-Browser | Age | AB | HR | R | RBI | SB | BA | OBP | SLG | $1L | Pts |
| Ackley D | 23 | 354 | 11 | 54 | 35 | 8 | .251 | .338 | .409 | $15 | 230 |
| Theriot R | 31 | 557 | 6 | 78 | 42 | 24 | .280 | .346 | .351 | $14 | 360 |
| Hill A | 29 | 508 | 22 | 66 | 66 | 6 | .249 | .301 | .421 | $12 | 320 |
| Hudson O | 33 | 465 | 11 | 68 | 47 | 5 | .282 | .357 | .418 | $12 | 300 |
| Young Jr. E | 25 | 387 | 5 | 63 | 27 | 32 | .244 | .327 | .360 | $11 | 250 |

### Minors (2010) / Skills

| Level | Leag | AB | HR | R | RBI | SB | BA | OBP | SLG | CT% | H% | BB% | Bash |
|---|---|---|---|---|---|---|---|---|---|---|---|---|---|
| A | — | — | — | — | — | — | — | — | — | — | — | — | — |
| AA | EL | 386 | 18 | 66 | 54 | 20 | .262 | .334 | .464 | 76% | 35% | 8% | 1.77 |
| AAA | IL | 95 | 4 | 14 | 15 | 5 | .295 | .349 | .463 | 77% | 38% | 7% | 1.57 |

### Majors / Skills

| Yr | Team | AB | HR | R | RBI | SB | BA | OBP | SLG | CT% | H% | BB% | Bash |
|---|---|---|---|---|---|---|---|---|---|---|---|---|---|
| 07 | — | — | — | — | — | — | — | — | — | — | — | — | — |
| 08 | — | — | — | — | — | — | — | — | — | — | — | — | — |
| 09 | — | — | — | — | — | — | — | — | — | — | — | — | — |
| 10 | WAS | 103 | 6 | 16 | 15 | 0 | .214 | .277 | .447 | 71% | 30% | 8% | 2.09 |

**Competition at 2B**

| Bats | Player | GSvR | GSvL | Sub | OPS |
|---|---|---|---|---|---|
| LH | Kennedy A | 73 | 2 | 11 | .655 |
| BH | Espinosa D | 16 | 7 | 2 | .723 |
| RH | Gonzalez A | 4 | 9 | 25 | .578 |

**Value / Extra / Production / OPS / Scoresheet**

| Yr | Team | $1L | $2L | Pts | RAA | 2B | 3B | CS | FB-LD-GB | HR/fb | RBI% | RS% | OPS | 1st Hf | 2nd Hf | vs RH | vs LH | Rnge | vRH | vLH |
|---|---|---|---|---|---|---|---|---|---|---|---|---|---|---|---|---|---|---|---|---|
| 07 | — | | | | | | | | | | | | | | | | | | | |
| 08 | — | | | | | | | | | | | | | | | | | | | |
| 09 | — | | | | | | | | | | | | | | | | | | | |
| 10 | WAS | -$2 | -$15 | 50 | -2 | 4 | 1 | 2 | 46-8-46 | 18% | 22% | 40% | .723 | — | .723 | .684 | .846 | | | |

## Andre Ethier — 600 PA | $20 | 410 pts

OF-132 (RF-132), 1B-1 — Owned: 100% — LH

Ethier was off to an MVP start in 2010 before a broken pinky derailed his season. He rushed back and struggled throughout June and July while trying to recover, though he perked up toward season's end. Fully healthy in 2011, Ethier will be a force, albeit one who wilts at left-handed pitching. (MP)

### Forecast

| Player | Age | AB | HR | R | RBI | SB | BA | OBP | SLG | $1L | Pts |
|---|---|---|---|---|---|---|---|---|---|---|---|
| Ethier A | 28 | 523 | 24 | 78 | 84 | 6 | .287 | .366 | .506 | $20 | 410 |
| Mini-Browser | Age | AB | HR | R | RBI | SB | BA | OBP | SLG | $1L | Pts |
| Ramirez M | 38 | 465 | 28 | 77 | 88 | 0 | .284 | .392 | .505 | $20 | 380 |
| Bourn M | 28 | 542 | 6 | 88 | 38 | 50 | .265 | .338 | .360 | $20 | 360 |
| Granderson C | 30 | 531 | 24 | 84 | 66 | 18 | .256 | .339 | .494 | $20 | 400 |
| Crisp C | 31 | 552 | 12 | 78 | 60 | 36 | .261 | .330 | .399 | $20 | 400 |
| Span D | 27 | 620 | 7 | 91 | 63 | 28 | .271 | .348 | .371 | $20 | 420 |

### Minors (2010) / Skills

| Level | Leag | AB | HR | R | RBI | SB | BA | OBP | SLG | CT% | H% | BB% | Bash |
|---|---|---|---|---|---|---|---|---|---|---|---|---|---|
| A | — | — | — | — | — | — | — | — | — | — | — | — | — |
| AA | — | — | — | — | — | — | — | — | — | — | — | — | — |
| AAA | PCL | 5 | 0 | 4 | 2 | 0 | .600 | .667 | .600 | 100% | 60% | 22% | 1.00 |

### Majors / Skills

| Yr | Team | AB | HR | R | RBI | SB | BA | OBP | SLG | CT% | H% | BB% | Bash |
|---|---|---|---|---|---|---|---|---|---|---|---|---|---|
| 07 | LAD | 447 | 13 | 50 | 64 | 0 | .284 | .350 | .452 | 85% | 34% | 9% | 1.59 |
| 08 | LAD | 525 | 20 | 90 | 77 | 6 | .305 | .375 | .510 | 83% | 37% | 10% | 1.68 |
| 09 | LAD | 596 | 31 | 92 | 106 | 6 | .272 | .361 | .508 | 81% | 34% | 10% | 1.87 |
| 10 | LAD | 517 | 23 | 71 | 82 | 2 | .292 | .364 | .493 | 80% | 36% | 10% | 1.69 |

**Competition at RF**

| Bats | Player | GSvR | GSvL | Sub | OPS |
|---|---|---|---|---|---|
| LH | Ethier A | 96 | 35 | 1 | .857 |
| RH | Johnson R | 4 | 12 | 6 | .657 |
| LH | Paul X | 10 | 1 | 4 | .591 |

**Value / Extra / Production / OPS / Scoresheet**

| Yr | Team | $1L | $2L | Pts | RAA | 2B | 3B | CS | FB-LD-GB | HR/fb | RBI% | RS% | OPS | 1st Hf | 2nd Hf | vs RH | vs LH | Rnge | vRH | vLH |
|---|---|---|---|---|---|---|---|---|---|---|---|---|---|---|---|---|---|---|---|---|
| 07 | LAD | $10 | $1 | 290 | -5 | 32 | 2 | 4 | 36-18-46 | 9% | 20% | 23% | .802 | .783 | .826 | .830 | .716 | 2.08 | +18 | -64 |
| 08 | LAD | $23 | $16 | 420 | +17 | 38 | 5 | 3 | 32-27-41 | 14% | 22% | 34% | .885 | .810 | .991 | .953 | .692 | 2.09 | +21 | -69 |
| 09 | LAD | $25 | $18 | 460 | +8 | 42 | 3 | 1 | 42-20-38 | 15% | 21% | 28% | .869 | .813 | .936 | .960 | .629 | 2.05 | +34 | -102 |
| 10 | LAD | $21 | $14 | 370 | +10 | 33 | 1 | 6 | 40-22-39 | 14% | 22% | 25% | .857 | .932 | .773 | .960 | .625 | 2.07 | +51 | -146 |

## Nick Evans — 75 PA | $-4 | 40 pts

OF-10 (LF-8, RF-3, CF-1) — Owned: 0% — RH

After regressing in 2009, Evans rebounded with a combined .907 OPS across two levels of the minors before hitting .300 in a short September cup of coffee. Evans could stick in 2011 as a righty bat off the bench who can back up at 1B and 3B as well as OF. He is out of options and could be trade bait. (JL)

### Forecast

| Player | Age | AB | HR | R | RBI | SB | BA | OBP | SLG | $1L | Pts |
|---|---|---|---|---|---|---|---|---|---|---|---|
| Evans N | 25 | 71 | 3 | 8 | 8 | 0 | .234 | .296 | .441 | -$4 | 40 |
| Mini-Browser | Age | AB | HR | R | RBI | SB | BA | OBP | SLG | $1L | Pts |
| Inglett J | 32 | 67 | 1 | 8 | 7 | 2 | .278 | .343 | .403 | -$3 | 40 |
| Willits R | 29 | 83 | 0 | 13 | 7 | 4 | .252 | .343 | .304 | -$3 | 50 |
| Gentry C | 27 | 95 | 2 | 11 | 7 | 5 | .221 | .282 | .330 | -$4 | 50 |
| Velez E | 28 | 47 | 1 | 6 | 5 | 3 | .258 | .307 | .404 | -$4 | 30 |
| Stavinoha N | 28 | 71 | 2 | 7 | 8 | 0 | .255 | .298 | .388 | -$4 | 30 |

### Minors (2010) / Skills

| Level | Leag | AB | HR | R | RBI | SB | BA | OBP | SLG | CT% | H% | BB% | Bash |
|---|---|---|---|---|---|---|---|---|---|---|---|---|---|
| A | — | — | — | — | — | — | — | — | — | — | — | — | — |
| AA | EL | 347 | 17 | 62 | 55 | 0 | .294 | .366 | .527 | 81% | 36% | 10% | 1.79 |
| AAA | IL | 140 | 6 | 26 | 25 | 0 | .314 | .385 | .557 | 84% | 38% | 10% | 1.77 |

### Majors / Skills

| Yr | Team | AB | HR | R | RBI | SB | BA | OBP | SLG | CT% | H% | BB% | Bash |
|---|---|---|---|---|---|---|---|---|---|---|---|---|---|
| 07 | — | — | — | — | — | — | — | — | — | — | — | — | — |
| 08 | NYM | 109 | 2 | 18 | 9 | 0 | .257 | .303 | .404 | 78% | 33% | 6% | 1.57 |
| 09 | NYM | 36 | 1 | 5 | 7 | 0 | .231 | .275 | .385 | 69% | 33% | 6% | 1.67 |
| 10 | NYM | 36 | 1 | 5 | 5 | 0 | .306 | .324 | .472 | 72% | 42% | 3% | 1.55 |

**Competition at LF**

| Bats | Player | GSvR | GSvL | Sub | OPS |
|---|---|---|---|---|---|
| RH | Bay J | 65 | 27 | 1 | .749 |
| BH | Pagan A | 20 | 6 | 1 | .765 |
| LH | Duda L | 22 | 1 | 1 | .678 |
| LH | Carter C | 14 | 1 | 2 | .706 |

**Value / Extra / Production / OPS / Scoresheet**

| Yr | Team | $1L | $2L | Pts | RAA | 2B | 3B | CS | FB-LD-GB | HR/fb | RBI% | RS% | OPS | 1st Hf | 2nd Hf | vs RH | vs LH | Rnge | vRH | vLH |
|---|---|---|---|---|---|---|---|---|---|---|---|---|---|---|---|---|---|---|---|---|
| 07 | — | | | | | | | | | | | | | | | | | | | |
| 08 | NYM | -$2 | -$15 | 50 | -4 | 10 | 0 | 0 | 33-23-44 | 7% | 13% | 47% | .706 | .565 | .761 | .339 | .894 | — | — | — |
| 09 | NYM | -$4 | -$19 | 20 | -3 | 5 | 1 | 0 | 38-13-49 | 6% | 18% | 22% | .660 | .707 | .561 | .536 | .816 | 2.06 | -33 | +70 |
| 10 | NYM | -$3 | -$19 | 20 | +0 | 5 | 0 | 0 | 35-15-50 | 11% | 19% | 36% | .797 | .000 | .843 | .533 | .983 | 2.07 | -30 | +64 |

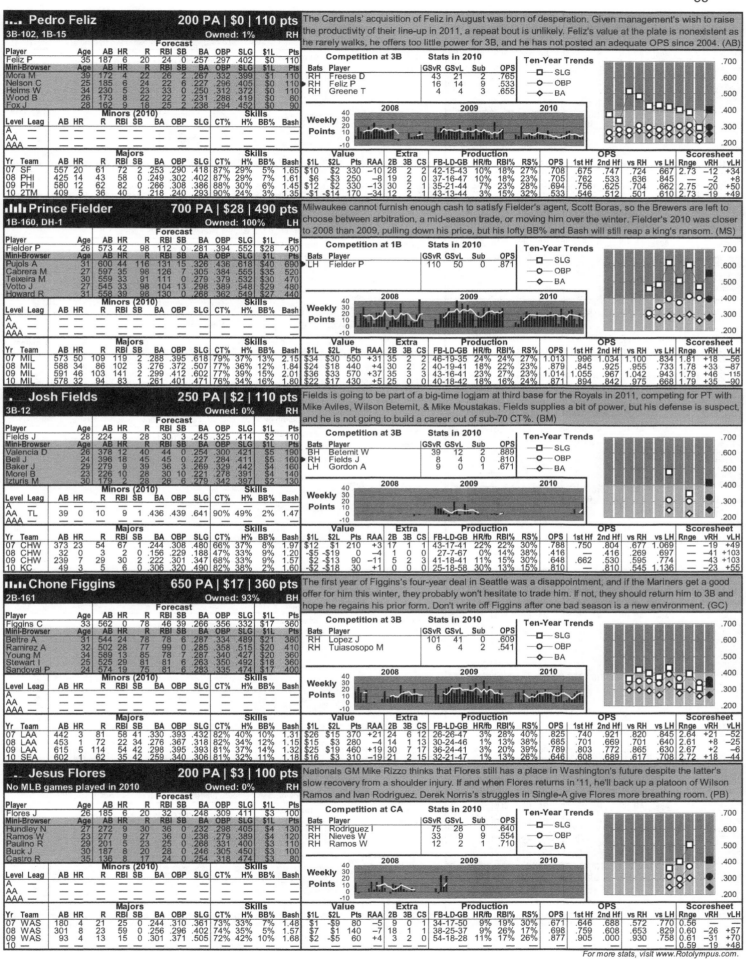

## Pedro Feliz — 200 PA | $0 | 110 pts

3B-102, 1B-15 — Owned: 1% — RH

The Cardinals' acquisition of Feliz in August was born of desperation. Given management's wish to raise the productivity of their line-up in 2011, a repeat bout is unlikely. Feliz's value at the plate is nonexistent as he rarely walks, he offers too little power for 3B, and he has not posted an adequate OPS since 2004. (AB)

| Player | Age | AB | HR | R | RBI | SB | BA | OBP | SLG | $1L | Pts |
|---|---|---|---|---|---|---|---|---|---|---|---|
| **Forecast** | | | | | | | | | | | |
| Feliz P | 35 | 187 | 6 | 20 | 24 | 0 | .257 | .297 | .402 | $0 | 110 |
| **Mini-Browser** | | | | | | | | | | | |
| Mora M | 39 | 172 | 4 | 22 | 26 | 2 | .267 | .332 | .399 | $1 | 110 |
| Nelson C | 25 | 185 | 6 | 24 | 22 | 6 | .227 | .296 | .405 | $0 | 110 |
| Helms W | 34 | 230 | 5 | 23 | 33 | 0 | .250 | .312 | .372 | $0 | 110 |
| Wood B | 26 | 173 | 8 | 22 | 22 | 2 | .231 | .288 | .419 | $0 | 80 |
| Fox J | 28 | 162 | 9 | 18 | 25 | 2 | .238 | .294 | .452 | $0 | 90 |

| Level | Leag | AB | HR | R | RBI | SB | BA | OBP | SLG | CT% | H% | BB% | Bash |
|---|---|---|---|---|---|---|---|---|---|---|---|---|---|
| **Minors (2010)** | | | | | | | | | | | | | |
| A | — | — | — | — | — | — | — | — | — | — | — | — | — |
| AA | — | — | — | — | — | — | — | — | — | — | — | — | — |
| AAA | — | — | — | — | — | — | — | — | — | — | — | — | — |

**Competition at 3B — Stats in 2010**

| Bats | Player | GSvR | GSvL | Sub | OPS |
|---|---|---|---|---|---|
| RH | Freese D | 43 | 21 | 2 | .765 |
| RH | Feliz P | 16 | 14 | 9 | .533 |
| RH | Greene T | 4 | 4 | 3 | .655 |

2008
2009
2010
Weekly Points
40
30
20
10
0
-10

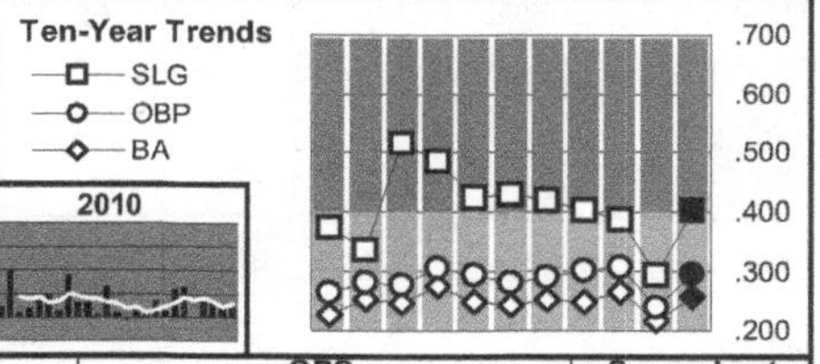
Ten-Year Trends
SLG
OBP
BA
.700
.600
.500
.400
.300
.200

| Yr | Team | AB | HR | R | RBI | SB | BA | OBP | SLG | CT% | H% | BB% | Bash | $1L | $2L | Pts | RAA | 2B | 3B | CS | FB-LD-GB | HR/fb | RBI% | RS% | OPS | 1st Hf | 2nd Hf | vs RH | vs LH | Rnge | vRH | vLH |
|---|---|---|---|---|---|---|---|---|---|---|---|---|---|---|---|---|---|---|---|---|---|---|---|---|---|---|---|---|---|---|---|---|
| | | **Majors** | | | | | | | | **Skills** | | | | **Value** | | | | **Extra** | | | **Production** | | | | **OPS** | | | | | **Scoresheet** | | |
| 07 | SF | 557 | 20 | 61 | 72 | 2 | .253 | .290 | .418 | 87% | 29% | 5% | 1.65 | $10 | $2 | 330 | −10 | 28 | 2 | 2 | 42-15-43 | 10% | 18% | 27% | .708 | .675 | .747 | .724 | .667 | 2.73 | −12 | +34 |
| 08 | PHI | 425 | 14 | 43 | 58 | 0 | .249 | .302 | .402 | 87% | 29% | 7% | 1.61 | $6 | -$3 | 250 | −8 | 19 | 2 | 0 | 37-16-47 | 10% | 18% | 23% | .705 | .762 | .533 | .636 | .845 | — | −2 | +8 |
| 09 | PHI | 580 | 12 | 62 | 82 | 0 | .266 | .308 | .386 | 88% | 30% | 6% | 1.45 | $12 | $2 | 330 | −13 | 30 | 2 | 1 | 35-21-44 | 7% | 23% | 28% | .694 | .756 | .625 | .704 | .662 | 2.75 | −20 | +50 |
| 10 | 2TM | 409 | 5 | 36 | 40 | 1 | .218 | .240 | .293 | 90% | 24% | 3% | 1.35 | -$1 | -$14 | 170 | −34 | 12 | 2 | 1 | 43-13-44 | 3% | 15% | 32% | .533 | .546 | .512 | .501 | .610 | 2.73 | −19 | +49 |

## Prince Fielder — 700 PA | $28 | 490 pts

1B-160, DH-1 — Owned: 100% — LH

Milwaukee cannot furnish enough cash to satisfy Fielder's agent, Scott Boras, so the Brewers are left to choose between arbitration, a mid-season trade, or moving him over the winter. Fielder's 2010 was closer to 2008 than 2009, pulling down his price, but his lofty BB% and Bash will still reap a king's ransom. (MS)

| Player | Age | AB | HR | R | RBI | SB | BA | OBP | SLG | $1L | Pts |
|---|---|---|---|---|---|---|---|---|---|---|---|
| **Forecast** | | | | | | | | | | | |
| Fielder P | 26 | 573 | 42 | 98 | 112 | 0 | .281 | .394 | .552 | $28 | 490 |
| **Mini-Browser** | | | | | | | | | | | |
| Pujols A | 31 | 600 | 44 | 116 | 131 | 15 | .326 | .436 | .618 | $40 | 690 |
| Cabrera M | 27 | 597 | 35 | 98 | 126 | 7 | .305 | .384 | .555 | $35 | 520 |
| Teixeira M | 30 | 559 | 33 | 91 | 111 | 0 | .279 | .379 | .532 | $30 | 470 |
| Votto J | 27 | 545 | 33 | 98 | 104 | 13 | .298 | .389 | .548 | $29 | 480 |
| Howard R | 31 | 558 | 39 | 98 | 130 | 0 | .268 | .362 | .549 | $27 | 440 |

| Level | Leag | AB | HR | R | RBI | SB | BA | OBP | SLG | CT% | H% | BB% | Bash |
|---|---|---|---|---|---|---|---|---|---|---|---|---|---|
| **Minors (2010)** | | | | | | | | | | | | | |
| A | — | — | — | — | — | — | — | — | — | — | — | — | — |
| AA | — | — | — | — | — | — | — | — | — | — | — | — | — |
| AAA | — | — | — | — | — | — | — | — | — | — | — | — | — |

**Competition at 1B — Stats in 2010**

| Bats | Player | GSvR | GSvL | Sub | OPS |
|---|---|---|---|---|---|
| LH | Fielder P | 110 | 50 | 0 | .871 |

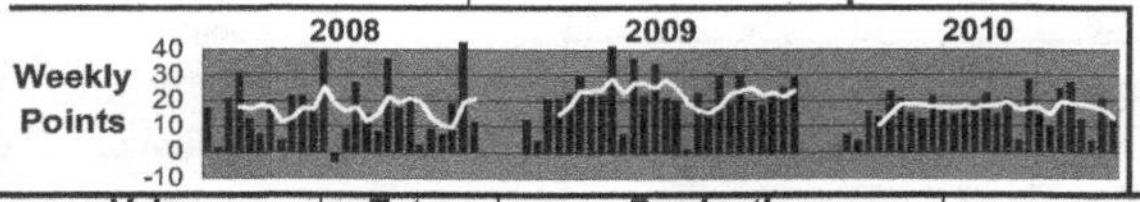
2008
2009
2010
Weekly Points
40
30
20
10
0
-10

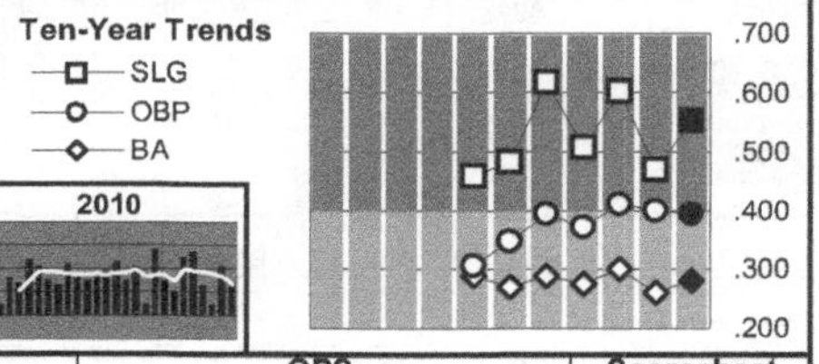
Ten-Year Trends
SLG
OBP
BA
.700
.600
.500
.400
.300
.200

| Yr | Team | AB | HR | R | RBI | SB | BA | OBP | SLG | CT% | H% | BB% | Bash | $1L | $2L | Pts | RAA | 2B | 3B | CS | FB-LD-GB | HR/fb | RBI% | RS% | OPS | 1st Hf | 2nd Hf | vs RH | vs LH | Rnge | vRH | vLH |
|---|---|---|---|---|---|---|---|---|---|---|---|---|---|---|---|---|---|---|---|---|---|---|---|---|---|---|---|---|---|---|---|---|
| | | **Majors** | | | | | | | | **Skills** | | | | **Value** | | | | **Extra** | | | **Production** | | | | **OPS** | | | | | **Scoresheet** | | |
| 07 | MIL | 573 | 50 | 109 | 119 | 2 | .288 | .395 | .618 | 79% | 37% | 13% | 2.15 | $34 | $30 | 550 | +31 | 35 | 2 | 2 | 46-19-35 | 24% | 24% | 27% | 1.013 | .996 | 1.034 | 1.100 | .834 | 1.81 | +18 | −56 |
| 08 | MIL | 588 | 34 | 86 | 102 | 3 | .276 | .372 | .507 | 77% | 36% | 12% | 1.84 | $24 | $18 | 440 | +4 | 30 | 2 | 2 | 40-19-41 | 18% | 22% | 23% | .879 | .845 | .925 | .955 | .733 | 1.78 | +33 | −87 |
| 09 | MIL | 591 | 46 | 103 | 141 | 2 | .299 | .412 | .602 | 77% | 39% | 15% | 2.01 | $36 | $33 | 570 | +37 | 35 | 3 | 3 | 43-16-41 | 23% | 27% | 23% | 1.014 | 1.055 | .967 | 1.042 | .943 | 1.79 | +46 | −115 |
| 10 | MIL | 578 | 32 | 94 | 83 | 1 | .261 | .401 | .471 | 76% | 34% | 16% | 1.80 | $22 | $17 | 430 | +5 | 25 | 0 | 0 | 40-18-42 | 18% | 16% | 24% | .871 | .894 | .842 | .975 | .668 | 1.79 | +35 | −90 |

## Josh Fields — 250 PA | $2 | 110 pts

3B-12 — Owned: 0% — RH

Fields is going to be part of a big-time logjam at third base for the Royals in 2011, competing for PT with Mike Aviles, Wilson Betemit, & Mike Moustakas. Fields supplies a bit of power, but his defense is suspect, and he is not going to build a career out of sub-70 CT%. (BM)

| Player | Age | AB | HR | R | RBI | SB | BA | OBP | SLG | $1L | Pts |
|---|---|---|---|---|---|---|---|---|---|---|---|
| **Forecast** | | | | | | | | | | | |
| Fields J | 28 | 224 | 8 | 28 | 30 | 3 | .245 | .325 | .414 | $2 | 110 |
| **Mini-Browser** | | | | | | | | | | | |
| Valencia D | 26 | 378 | 12 | 40 | 44 | 0 | .254 | .300 | .421 | $5 | 190 |
| Bell J | 24 | 396 | 18 | 45 | 45 | 0 | .227 | .284 | .411 | $5 | 160 |
| Baker J | 29 | 279 | 9 | 39 | 36 | 3 | .269 | .329 | .442 | $4 | 160 |
| Morel B | 23 | 226 | 10 | 28 | 30 | 10 | .221 | .278 | .391 | $4 | 140 |
| Izturis M | 30 | 179 | 2 | 28 | 26 | 6 | .279 | .342 | .397 | $2 | 130 |

| Level | Leag | AB | HR | R | RBI | SB | BA | OBP | SLG | CT% | H% | BB% | Bash |
|---|---|---|---|---|---|---|---|---|---|---|---|---|---|
| **Minors (2010)** | | | | | | | | | | | | | |
| A | — | — | — | — | — | — | — | — | — | — | — | — | — |
| AA | TL | 39 | 0 | 10 | 9 | 1 | .436 | .439 | .641 | 90% | 49% | 2% | 1.47 |
| AAA | — | — | — | — | — | — | — | — | — | — | — | — | — |

**Competition at 3B — Stats in 2010**

| Bats | Player | GSvR | GSvL | Sub | OPS |
|---|---|---|---|---|---|
| BH | Betemit W | 39 | 12 | 2 | .889 |
| RH | Fields J | 8 | 4 | 0 | .810 |
| LH | Gordon A | 9 | 0 | 1 | .671 |

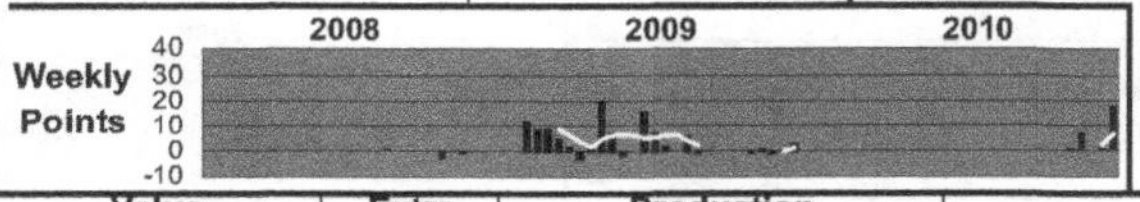
2008
2009
2010
Weekly Points
40
30
20
10
0
-10

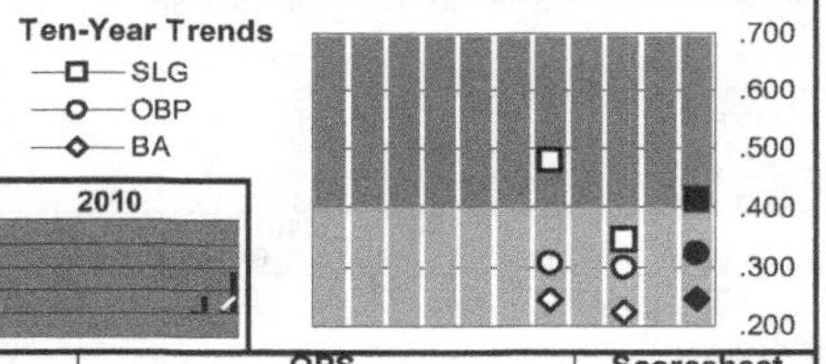
Ten-Year Trends
SLG
OBP
BA
.700
.600
.500
.400
.300
.200

| Yr | Team | AB | HR | R | RBI | SB | BA | OBP | SLG | CT% | H% | BB% | Bash | $1L | $2L | Pts | RAA | 2B | 3B | CS | FB-LD-GB | HR/fb | RBI% | RS% | OPS | 1st Hf | 2nd Hf | vs RH | vs LH | Rnge | vRH | vLH |
|---|---|---|---|---|---|---|---|---|---|---|---|---|---|---|---|---|---|---|---|---|---|---|---|---|---|---|---|---|---|---|---|---|
| | | **Majors** | | | | | | | | **Skills** | | | | **Value** | | | | **Extra** | | | **Production** | | | | **OPS** | | | | | **Scoresheet** | | |
| 07 | CHW | 373 | 23 | 54 | 67 | 1 | .244 | .308 | .480 | 66% | 37% | 8% | 1.97 | $12 | $1 | 210 | +3 | 17 | 1 | 1 | 43-17-41 | 22% | 22% | 30% | .788 | .750 | .804 | .677 | 1.069 | — | −19 | +49 |
| 08 | CHW | 32 | 0 | 3 | 2 | 0 | .156 | .229 | .188 | 47% | 33% | 9% | 1.20 | -$5 | -$19 | 0 | −4 | 1 | 0 | 0 | 27-7-67 | 0% | 14% | 38% | .416 | — | .416 | .269 | .697 | — | −41 | +103 |
| 09 | CHW | 239 | 7 | 29 | 30 | 2 | .222 | .301 | .347 | 68% | 33% | 9% | 1.57 | $2 | -$13 | 90 | −11 | 5 | 2 | 3 | 41-18-41 | 11% | 15% | 30% | .648 | .662 | .530 | .595 | .774 | — | −43 | +103 |
| 10 | KC | 49 | 3 | 5 | 6 | 0 | .306 | .320 | .490 | 82% | 38% | 2% | 1.60 | -$2 | -$18 | 30 | +1 | 0 | 0 | 0 | 25-18-58 | 30% | 13% | 15% | .810 | — | .810 | .545 | 1.136 | — | −23 | +55 |

## Chone Figgins — 650 PA | $17 | 360 pts

2B-161 — Owned: 93% — BH

The first year of Figgins's four-year deal in Seattle was a disappointment, and if the Mariners get a good offer for him this winter, they probably won't hesitate to trade him. If not, they should return him to 3B and hope he regains his prior form. Don't write off Figgins after one bad season is a new environment. (GC)

| Player | Age | AB | HR | R | RBI | SB | BA | OBP | SLG | $1L | Pts |
|---|---|---|---|---|---|---|---|---|---|---|---|
| **Forecast** | | | | | | | | | | | |
| Figgins C | 33 | 562 | 0 | 78 | 46 | 39 | .266 | .356 | .332 | $17 | 360 |
| **Mini-Browser** | | | | | | | | | | | |
| Beltre A | 31 | 544 | 24 | 78 | 78 | 6 | .287 | .334 | .489 | $21 | 380 |
| Ramirez A | 32 | 502 | 28 | 77 | 99 | 0 | .285 | .358 | .515 | $20 | 410 |
| Young M | 34 | 589 | 13 | 85 | 78 | 7 | .287 | .340 | .427 | $20 | 360 |
| Stewart I | 25 | 525 | 29 | 81 | 81 | 6 | .263 | .350 | .492 | $18 | 360 |
| Sandoval P | 24 | 574 | 19 | 75 | 81 | 6 | .283 | .335 | .474 | $17 | 400 |

| Level | Leag | AB | HR | R | RBI | SB | BA | OBP | SLG | CT% | H% | BB% | Bash |
|---|---|---|---|---|---|---|---|---|---|---|---|---|---|
| **Minors (2010)** | | | | | | | | | | | | | |
| A | — | — | — | — | — | — | — | — | — | — | — | — | — |
| AA | — | — | — | — | — | — | — | — | — | — | — | — | — |
| AAA | — | — | — | — | — | — | — | — | — | — | — | — | — |

**Competition at 3B — Stats in 2010**

| Bats | Player | GSvR | GSvL | Sub | OPS |
|---|---|---|---|---|---|
| RH | Lopez J | 101 | 41 | 0 | .609 |
| RH | Tuiasosopo M | 6 | 4 | 2 | .541 |

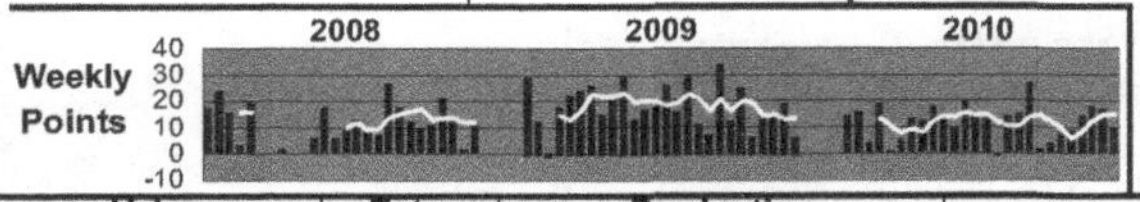
2008
2009
2010
Weekly Points
40
30
20
10
0
-10

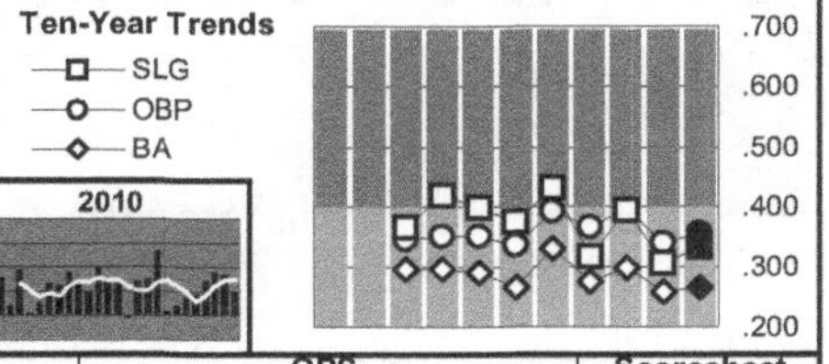
Ten-Year Trends
SLG
OBP
BA
.700
.600
.500
.400
.300
.200

| Yr | Team | AB | HR | R | RBI | SB | BA | OBP | SLG | CT% | H% | BB% | Bash | $1L | $2L | Pts | RAA | 2B | 3B | CS | FB-LD-GB | HR/fb | RBI% | RS% | OPS | 1st Hf | 2nd Hf | vs RH | vs LH | Rnge | vRH | vLH |
|---|---|---|---|---|---|---|---|---|---|---|---|---|---|---|---|---|---|---|---|---|---|---|---|---|---|---|---|---|---|---|---|---|
| | | **Majors** | | | | | | | | **Skills** | | | | **Value** | | | | **Extra** | | | **Production** | | | | **OPS** | | | | | **Scoresheet** | | |
| 07 | LAA | 442 | 3 | 81 | 58 | 41 | .330 | .393 | .432 | 82% | 40% | 10% | 1.31 | $26 | $15 | 370 | +21 | 24 | 6 | 12 | 26-26-47 | 3% | 28% | 40% | .825 | .740 | .921 | .820 | .845 | 2.64 | +21 | −52 |
| 08 | LAA | 453 | 1 | 72 | 22 | 34 | .276 | .367 | .318 | 82% | 34% | 12% | 1.15 | $15 | $3 | 280 | −4 | 14 | 1 | 13 | 30-24-46 | 1% | 13% | 38% | .685 | .701 | .669 | .701 | .640 | 2.61 | +8 | −25 |
| 09 | LAA | 615 | 5 | 114 | 54 | 42 | .298 | .395 | .393 | 81% | 37% | 14% | 1.32 | $25 | $19 | 460 | +19 | 30 | 7 | 17 | 36-24-41 | 3% | 20% | 39% | .789 | .803 | .772 | .865 | .630 | 2.67 | +2 | −6 |
| 10 | SEA | 602 | 1 | 62 | 35 | 42 | .259 | .340 | .306 | 81% | 32% | 11% | 1.18 | $16 | $3 | 310 | −19 | 21 | 2 | 15 | 32-21-47 | 1% | 13% | 26% | .646 | .608 | .689 | .617 | .708 | 2.72 | +18 | −44 |

## Jesus Flores — 200 PA | $3 | 100 pts

No MLB games played in 2010 — Owned: 0% — RH

Nationals GM Mike Rizzo thinks that Flores still has a place in Washington's future despite the latter's slow recovery from a shoulder injury. If and when Flores returns in '11, he'll back up a platoon of Wilson Ramos and Ivan Rodriguez. Derek Norris's struggles in Single-A give Flores more breathing room. (PB)

| Player | Age | AB | HR | R | RBI | SB | BA | OBP | SLG | $1L | Pts |
|---|---|---|---|---|---|---|---|---|---|---|---|
| **Forecast** | | | | | | | | | | | |
| Flores J | 26 | 185 | 6 | 20 | 32 | 0 | .248 | .309 | .411 | $3 | 100 |
| **Mini-Browser** | | | | | | | | | | | |
| Hundley N | 27 | 272 | 9 | 30 | 36 | 0 | .232 | .298 | .405 | $4 | 130 |
| Ramos W | 23 | 277 | 9 | 27 | 36 | 0 | .238 | .279 | .389 | $4 | 120 |
| Paulino R | 29 | 201 | 5 | 23 | 25 | 0 | .268 | .331 | .400 | $3 | 110 |
| Buck J | 30 | 187 | 8 | 20 | 28 | 0 | .246 | .305 | .450 | $3 | 100 |
| Castro R | 35 | 136 | 8 | 17 | 24 | 0 | .254 | .318 | .474 | $3 | 80 |

| Level | Leag | AB | HR | R | RBI | SB | BA | OBP | SLG | CT% | H% | BB% | Bash |
|---|---|---|---|---|---|---|---|---|---|---|---|---|---|
| **Minors (2010)** | | | | | | | | | | | | | |
| A | — | — | — | — | — | — | — | — | — | — | — | — | — |
| AA | — | — | — | — | — | — | — | — | — | — | — | — | — |
| AAA | — | — | — | — | — | — | — | — | — | — | — | — | — |

**Competition at CA — Stats in 2010**

| Bats | Player | GSvR | GSvL | Sub | OPS |
|---|---|---|---|---|---|
| RH | Rodriguez I | 75 | 28 | 0 | .640 |
| RH | Nieves W | 33 | 9 | 9 | .554 |
| RH | Ramos W | 12 | 2 | 1 | .710 |

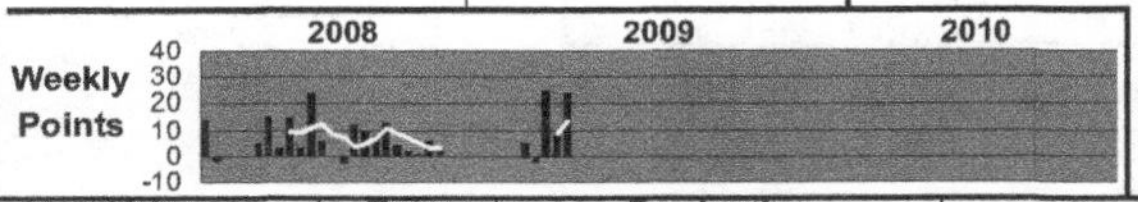
2008
2009
2010
Weekly Points
40
30
20
10
0
-10

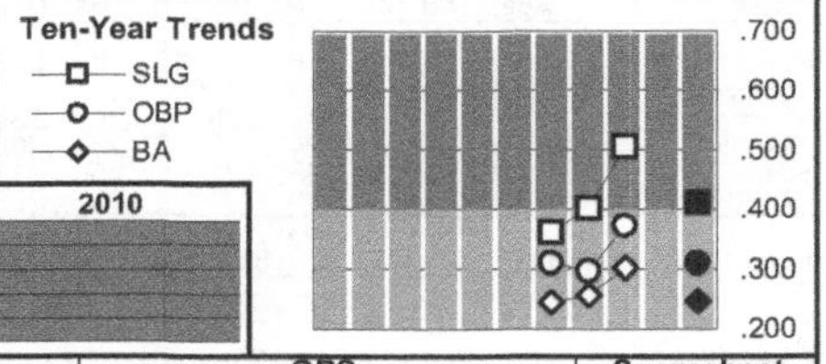
Ten-Year Trends
SLG
OBP
BA
.700
.600
.500
.400
.300
.200

| Yr | Team | AB | HR | R | RBI | SB | BA | OBP | SLG | CT% | H% | BB% | Bash | $1L | $2L | Pts | RAA | 2B | 3B | CS | FB-LD-GB | HR/fb | RBI% | RS% | OPS | 1st Hf | 2nd Hf | vs RH | vs LH | Rnge | vRH | vLH |
|---|---|---|---|---|---|---|---|---|---|---|---|---|---|---|---|---|---|---|---|---|---|---|---|---|---|---|---|---|---|---|---|---|
| | | **Majors** | | | | | | | | **Skills** | | | | **Value** | | | | **Extra** | | | **Production** | | | | **OPS** | | | | | **Scoresheet** | | |
| 07 | WAS | 180 | 4 | 21 | 25 | 0 | .244 | .310 | .361 | 73% | 33% | 7% | 1.48 | $1 | -$9 | 80 | −5 | 9 | 0 | 1 | 34-17-50 | 9% | 19% | 30% | .671 | .646 | .688 | .572 | .770 | 0.56 | — | — |
| 08 | WAS | 301 | 8 | 23 | 59 | 0 | .256 | .296 | .402 | 74% | 35% | 5% | 1.57 | $7 | $1 | 140 | −7 | 18 | 1 | 1 | 38-25-37 | 9% | 26% | 17% | .698 | .759 | .608 | .653 | .829 | 0.60 | −26 | +57 |
| 09 | WAS | 93 | 4 | 13 | 15 | 0 | .301 | .371 | .505 | 72% | 42% | 10% | 1.68 | $2 | -$5 | 60 | +4 | 3 | 2 | 0 | 54-18-28 | 11% | 17% | 26% | .877 | .905 | .000 | .930 | .758 | 0.61 | −31 | +70 |
| 10 | — | — | — | — | — | — | — | — | — | — | — | — | — | — | — | — | — | — | — | — | — | — | — | — | — | — | — | — | — | 0.59 | −19 | +48 |

*For more stats, visit www.Rotolympus.com.*

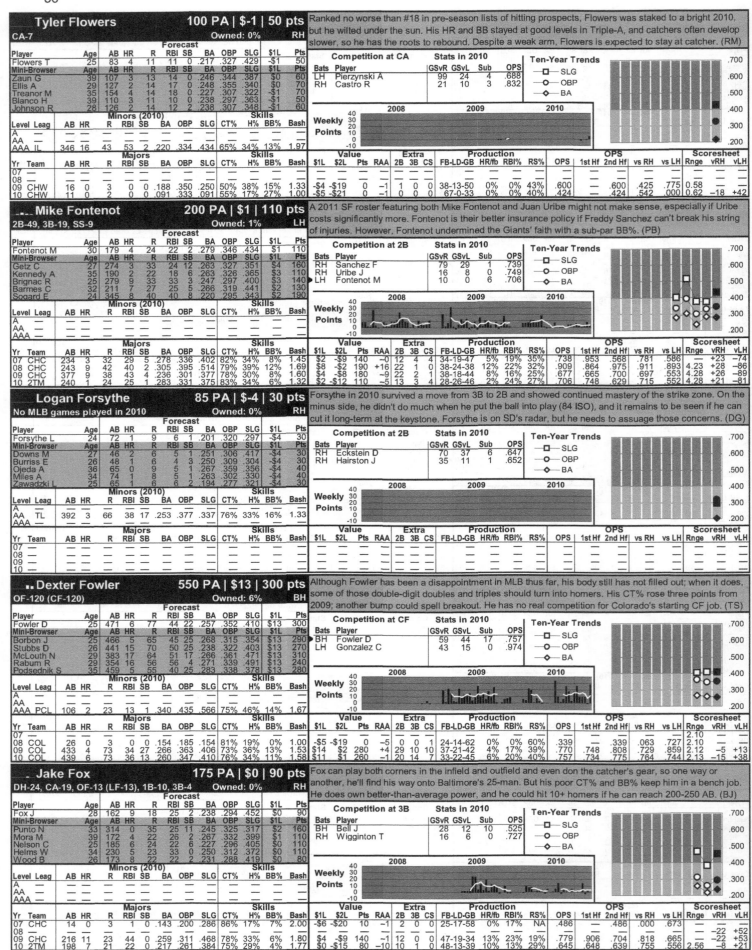

## Tyler Flowers — 100 PA | $-1 | 50 pts

**CA-7** — Owned: 0% — RH

Ranked no worse than #18 in pre-season lists of hitting prospects, Flowers was staked to a bright 2010, but he wilted under the sun. His HR and BB stayed at good levels in Triple-A, and catchers often develop slower, so he has the roots to rebound. Despite a weak arm, Flowers is expected to stay at catcher. (RM)

### Forecast

| Player | Age | AB | HR | R | RBI | SB | BA | OBP | SLG | $1L | Pts |
|---|---|---|---|---|---|---|---|---|---|---|---|
| Flowers T | 25 | 83 | 4 | 11 | 11 | 0 | .217 | .327 | .429 | -$1 | 50 |

| Mini-Browser | Age | AB | HR | R | RBI | SB | BA | OBP | SLG | $1L | Pts |
|---|---|---|---|---|---|---|---|---|---|---|---|
| Zaun G | 39 | 107 | 3 | 13 | 14 | 0 | .246 | .344 | .387 | $0 | 60 |
| Ellis A | 29 | 127 | 2 | 14 | 17 | 0 | .248 | .355 | .340 | $0 | 70 |
| Treanor M | 35 | 154 | 4 | 14 | 18 | 0 | .227 | .307 | .322 | -$1 | 70 |
| Blanco H | 39 | 110 | 3 | 11 | 10 | 0 | .238 | .297 | .363 | -$1 | 50 |
| Johnson R | 28 | 126 | 2 | 14 | 12 | 2 | .238 | .307 | .348 | -$1 | 60 |

### Minors (2010) / Skills

| Level | Leag | AB | HR | R | RBI | SB | BA | OBP | SLG | CT% | H% | BB% | Bash |
|---|---|---|---|---|---|---|---|---|---|---|---|---|---|
| A | — | | | | | | | | | | | | |
| AA | — | | | | | | | | | | | | |
| AAA | IL | 346 | 16 | 43 | 53 | 2 | .220 | .334 | .434 | 65% | 34% | 13% | 1.97 |

### Majors / Skills

| Yr | Team | AB | HR | R | RBI | SB | BA | OBP | SLG | CT% | H% | BB% | Bash |
|---|---|---|---|---|---|---|---|---|---|---|---|---|---|
| 07 | — | | | | | | | | | | | | |
| 08 | — | | | | | | | | | | | | |
| 09 | CHW | 16 | 0 | 3 | 0 | 0 | .188 | .350 | .250 | 50% | 38% | 15% | 1.33 |
| 10 | CHW | 11 | 0 | 2 | 0 | 0 | .091 | .333 | .091 | 55% | 17% | 27% | 1.00 |

### Competition at CA / Stats in 2010

| Bats | Player | GSvR | GSvL | Sub | OPS |
|---|---|---|---|---|---|
| LH | Pierzynski A | 99 | 24 | 4 | .688 |
| RH | Castro R | 21 | 10 | 3 | .832 |

### Value / Extra / Production / OPS / Scoresheet

| Yr | $1L | $2L | Pts | RAA | 2B | 3B | CS | FB-LD-GB | HR/fb | RBI% | RS% | OPS | 1st Hf | 2nd Hf | vs RH | vs LH | Rnge | vRH | vLH |
|---|---|---|---|---|---|---|---|---|---|---|---|---|---|---|---|---|---|---|---|
| 09 | -$4 | -$19 | 0 | -1 | 1 | 0 | 0 | 38-13-50 | 0% | 0% | 43% | .600 | — | .600 | .425 | .775 | 0.58 | | |
| 10 | -$5 | -$21 | 0 | 0 | 0 | 0 | 0 | 67-0-33 | 0% | 0% | 0% | .424 | — | .424 | .542 | .000 | 0.62 | -18 | +42 |

---

## Mike Fontenot — 200 PA | $1 | 110 pts

**2B-49, 3B-19, SS-9** — Owned: 1% — LH

A 2011 SF roster featuring both Mike Fontenot and Juan Uribe might not make sense, especially if Uribe costs significantly more. Fontenot is their better insurance policy if Freddy Sanchez can't break his string of injuries. However, Fontenot undermined the Giants' faith with a sub-par BB%. (PB)

### Forecast

| Player | Age | AB | HR | R | RBI | SB | BA | OBP | SLG | $1L | Pts |
|---|---|---|---|---|---|---|---|---|---|---|---|
| Fontenot M | 30 | 179 | 4 | 24 | 22 | 2 | .279 | .346 | .434 | $1 | 110 |

| Mini-Browser | Age | AB | HR | R | RBI | SB | BA | OBP | SLG | $1L | Pts |
|---|---|---|---|---|---|---|---|---|---|---|---|
| Getz C | 27 | 274 | 3 | 33 | 24 | 12 | .263 | .327 | .351 | $4 | 160 |
| Kennedy A | 35 | 190 | 3 | 22 | 18 | 4 | .263 | .326 | .365 | $3 | 160 |
| Brignac R | 25 | 279 | 9 | 33 | 33 | 3 | .247 | .297 | .400 | $3 | 140 |
| Barmes C | 32 | 211 | 7 | 27 | 25 | 5 | .266 | .319 | .441 | $2 | 130 |
| Sogard E | 24 | 345 | 8 | 40 | 40 | 8 | .220 | .295 | .343 | $2 | 190 |

### Minors (2010) / Skills

| Level | Leag | AB | HR | R | RBI | SB | BA | OBP | SLG | CT% | H% | BB% | Bash |
|---|---|---|---|---|---|---|---|---|---|---|---|---|---|
| A | — | | | | | | | | | | | | |
| AA | — | | | | | | | | | | | | |
| AAA | — | | | | | | | | | | | | |

### Majors / Skills

| Yr | Team | AB | HR | R | RBI | SB | BA | OBP | SLG | CT% | H% | BB% | Bash |
|---|---|---|---|---|---|---|---|---|---|---|---|---|---|
| 07 | CHC | 234 | 3 | 32 | 29 | 5 | .278 | .336 | .402 | 82% | 34% | 8% | 1.45 |
| 08 | CHC | 243 | 9 | 42 | 40 | 2 | .305 | .395 | .514 | 79% | 39% | 12% | 1.69 |
| 09 | CHC | 377 | 9 | 38 | 43 | 4 | .236 | .301 | .377 | 78% | 30% | 8% | 1.60 |
| 10 | 2TM | 240 | 1 | 24 | 25 | 1 | .283 | .331 | .375 | 83% | 34% | 6% | 1.32 |

### Competition at 2B / Stats in 2010

| Bats | Player | GSvR | GSvL | Sub | OPS |
|---|---|---|---|---|---|
| RH | Sanchez F | 79 | 29 | 1 | .739 |
| RH | Uribe J | 16 | 8 | 0 | .749 |
| LH | Fontenot M | 10 | 0 | 6 | .706 |

### Value / Extra / Production / OPS / Scoresheet

| Yr | $1L | $2L | Pts | RAA | 2B | 3B | CS | FB-LD-GB | HR/fb | RBI% | RS% | OPS | 1st Hf | 2nd Hf | vs RH | vs LH | Rnge | vRH | vLH |
|---|---|---|---|---|---|---|---|---|---|---|---|---|---|---|---|---|---|---|---|
| 07 | $2 | -$9 | 140 | -0 | 12 | 4 | 4 | 34-19-47 | 5% | 19% | 35% | .738 | .953 | .568 | .781 | .586 | — | +23 | -74 |
| 08 | $8 | -$2 | 190 | +16 | 22 | 1 | 0 | 38-24-38 | 12% | 22% | 32% | .909 | .864 | .975 | .911 | .893 | 4.23 | +28 | -86 |
| 09 | $4 | -$8 | 180 | -9 | 22 | 2 | 1 | 38-18-44 | 8% | 16% | 25% | .677 | .665 | .700 | .697 | .553 | 4.28 | +26 | -89 |
| 10 | $2 | -$12 | 110 | -5 | 13 | 3 | 4 | 28-26-46 | 2% | 24% | 27% | .706 | .748 | .629 | .715 | .552 | 4.28 | +21 | -81 |

---

## Logan Forsythe — 85 PA | $-4 | 30 pts

**No MLB games played in 2010** — Owned: 0% — RH

Forsythe in 2010 survived a move from 3B to 2B and showed continued mastery of the strike zone. On the minus side, he didn't do much when he put the ball into play (84 ISO), and it remains to be seen if he can cut it long-term at the keystone. Forsythe is on SD's radar, but he needs to assuage those concerns. (DG)

### Forecast

| Player | Age | AB | HR | R | RBI | SB | BA | OBP | SLG | $1L | Pts |
|---|---|---|---|---|---|---|---|---|---|---|---|
| Forsythe L | 24 | 72 | 1 | 9 | 6 | 1 | .201 | .320 | .297 | -$4 | 30 |

| Mini-Browser | Age | AB | HR | R | RBI | SB | BA | OBP | SLG | $1L | Pts |
|---|---|---|---|---|---|---|---|---|---|---|---|
| Downs M | 27 | 46 | 2 | 6 | 5 | 1 | .251 | .306 | .417 | -$4 | 30 |
| Burriss E | 26 | 48 | 1 | 6 | 4 | 3 | .250 | .309 | .304 | -$4 | 30 |
| Ojeda A | 36 | 65 | 0 | 9 | 5 | 1 | .267 | .359 | .356 | -$4 | 40 |
| Miles A | 34 | 74 | 1 | 8 | 5 | 1 | .263 | .302 | .330 | -$4 | 40 |
| Zawadzki L | 25 | 65 | 1 | 6 | 4 | 2 | .194 | .277 | .321 | -$4 | 30 |

### Minors (2010) / Skills

| Level | Leag | AB | HR | R | RBI | SB | BA | OBP | SLG | CT% | H% | BB% | Bash |
|---|---|---|---|---|---|---|---|---|---|---|---|---|---|
| A | — | | | | | | | | | | | | |
| AA | TL | 392 | 3 | 66 | 38 | 17 | .253 | .377 | .337 | 76% | 33% | 16% | 1.33 |
| AAA | — | | | | | | | | | | | | |

### Majors / Skills

| Yr | Team | AB | HR | R | RBI | SB | BA | OBP | SLG | CT% | H% | BB% | Bash |
|---|---|---|---|---|---|---|---|---|---|---|---|---|---|
| 07 | — | | | | | | | | | | | | |
| 08 | — | | | | | | | | | | | | |
| 09 | — | | | | | | | | | | | | |
| 10 | — | | | | | | | | | | | | |

### Competition at 2B / Stats in 2010

| Bats | Player | GSvR | GSvL | Sub | OPS |
|---|---|---|---|---|---|
| RH | Eckstein D | 70 | 37 | 6 | .647 |
| RH | Hairston J | 35 | 11 | 1 | .652 |

---

## Dexter Fowler — 550 PA | $13 | 300 pts

**OF-120 (CF-120)** — Owned: 6% — BH

Although Fowler has been a disappointment in MLB thus far, his body still has not filled out; when it does, some of those double-digit doubles and triples should turn into homers. His CT% rose three points from 2009; another bump could spell breakout. He has no real competition for Colorado's starting CF job. (TS)

### Forecast

| Player | Age | AB | HR | R | RBI | SB | BA | OBP | SLG | $1L | Pts |
|---|---|---|---|---|---|---|---|---|---|---|---|
| Fowler D | 25 | 471 | 6 | 77 | 44 | 22 | .257 | .352 | .410 | $13 | 300 |

| Mini-Browser | Age | AB | HR | R | RBI | SB | BA | OBP | SLG | $1L | Pts |
|---|---|---|---|---|---|---|---|---|---|---|---|
| Borbon J | 25 | 466 | 5 | 65 | 45 | 25 | .268 | .315 | .354 | $13 | 290 |
| Stubbs D | 26 | 441 | 15 | 70 | 50 | 25 | .238 | .322 | .403 | $13 | 270 |
| McLouth N | 29 | 383 | 17 | 64 | 51 | 17 | .266 | .361 | .471 | $13 | 310 |
| Raburn R | 29 | 354 | 16 | 56 | 56 | 4 | .271 | .339 | .491 | $13 | 240 |
| Podsednik S | 35 | 459 | 5 | 55 | 40 | 25 | .283 | .338 | .378 | $13 | 280 |

### Minors (2010) / Skills

| Level | Leag | AB | HR | R | RBI | SB | BA | OBP | SLG | CT% | H% | BB% | Bash |
|---|---|---|---|---|---|---|---|---|---|---|---|---|---|
| A | — | | | | | | | | | | | | |
| AA | — | | | | | | | | | | | | |
| AAA | PCL | 106 | 2 | 23 | 13 | 1 | .340 | .435 | .566 | 75% | 46% | 14% | 1.67 |

### Majors / Skills

| Yr | Team | AB | HR | R | RBI | SB | BA | OBP | SLG | CT% | H% | BB% | Bash |
|---|---|---|---|---|---|---|---|---|---|---|---|---|---|
| 07 | — | | | | | | | | | | | | |
| 08 | COL | 26 | 0 | 3 | 0 | 0 | .154 | .185 | .154 | 81% | 19% | 0% | 1.00 |
| 09 | COL | 433 | 4 | 73 | 34 | 27 | .266 | .363 | .406 | 73% | 36% | 13% | 1.53 |
| 10 | COL | 439 | 6 | 73 | 36 | 13 | .260 | .347 | .410 | 76% | 34% | 11% | 1.58 |

### Competition at CF / Stats in 2010

| Bats | Player | GSvR | GSvL | Sub | OPS |
|---|---|---|---|---|---|
| BH | Fowler D | 59 | 44 | 17 | .757 |
| LH | Gonzalez C | 43 | 15 | 0 | .974 |

### Value / Extra / Production / OPS / Scoresheet

| Yr | $1L | $2L | Pts | RAA | 2B | 3B | CS | FB-LD-GB | HR/fb | RBI% | RS% | OPS | 1st Hf | 2nd Hf | vs RH | vs LH | Rnge | vRH | vLH |
|---|---|---|---|---|---|---|---|---|---|---|---|---|---|---|---|---|---|---|---|
| 08 | -$5 | -$19 | 0 | -5 | 0 | 0 | 1 | 24-14-62 | 0% | 0% | 60% | .339 | — | .339 | .063 | .727 | 2.10 | | |
| 09 | $14 | $2 | 280 | +4 | 29 | 10 | 10 | 37-21-42 | 4% | 17% | 39% | .770 | .748 | .808 | .729 | .859 | 2.12 | -5 | +13 |
| 10 | $11 | $1 | 260 | -1 | 20 | 14 | 7 | 33-22-45 | 6% | 20% | 40% | .757 | .734 | .775 | .764 | .744 | 2.13 | -15 | +34 |

---

## Jake Fox — 175 PA | $0 | 90 pts

**DH-24, CA-19, OF-13 (LF-13), 1B-10, 3B-4** — Owned: 0% — RH

Fox can play both corners in the infield and outfield and even don the catcher's gear, so one way or another, he'll find his way onto Baltimore's 25-man. But his poor CT% and BB% keep him in a bench job. He does own better-than-average power, and he could hit 10+ homers if he can reach 200-250 AB. (BJ)

### Forecast

| Player | Age | AB | HR | R | RBI | SB | BA | OBP | SLG | $1L | Pts |
|---|---|---|---|---|---|---|---|---|---|---|---|
| Fox J | 28 | 162 | 9 | 18 | 25 | 2 | .238 | .294 | .452 | $0 | 90 |

| Mini-Browser | Age | AB | HR | R | RBI | SB | BA | OBP | SLG | $1L | Pts |
|---|---|---|---|---|---|---|---|---|---|---|---|
| Punto N | 33 | 314 | 0 | 35 | 25 | 11 | .245 | .325 | .317 | $2 | 160 |
| Mora M | 39 | 172 | 4 | 22 | 26 | 2 | .267 | .332 | .399 | $1 | 110 |
| Nelson C | 25 | 185 | 6 | 24 | 22 | 6 | .227 | .296 | .405 | $0 | 110 |
| Helms W | 34 | 230 | 5 | 23 | 33 | 0 | .259 | .312 | .372 | $0 | 110 |
| Wood B | 26 | 173 | 8 | 22 | 22 | 2 | .231 | .288 | .419 | $0 | 80 |

### Minors (2010) / Skills

| Level | Leag | AB | HR | R | RBI | SB | BA | OBP | SLG | CT% | H% | BB% | Bash |
|---|---|---|---|---|---|---|---|---|---|---|---|---|---|
| A | — | | | | | | | | | | | | |
| AA | — | | | | | | | | | | | | |
| AAA | — | | | | | | | | | | | | |

### Majors / Skills

| Yr | Team | AB | HR | R | RBI | SB | BA | OBP | SLG | CT% | H% | BB% | Bash |
|---|---|---|---|---|---|---|---|---|---|---|---|---|---|
| 07 | CHC | 14 | 0 | 3 | 1 | 0 | .143 | .200 | .286 | 86% | 17% | 7% | 2.00 |
| 08 | — | | | | | | | | | | | | |
| 09 | CHC | 216 | 11 | 44 | 44 | 0 | .259 | .311 | .468 | 78% | 33% | 6% | 1.80 |
| 10 | 2TM | 198 | 7 | 21 | 22 | 0 | .217 | .261 | .384 | 75% | 29% | 6% | 1.77 |

### Competition at 3B / Stats in 2010

| Bats | Player | GSvR | GSvL | Sub | OPS |
|---|---|---|---|---|---|
| BH | Bell J | 28 | 12 | 10 | .525 |
| RH | Wigginton T | 16 | 6 | 0 | .727 |

### Value / Extra / Production / OPS / Scoresheet

| Yr | $1L | $2L | Pts | RAA | 2B | 3B | CS | FB-LD-GB | HR/fb | RBI% | RS% | OPS | 1st Hf | 2nd Hf | vs RH | vs LH | Rnge | vRH | vLH |
|---|---|---|---|---|---|---|---|---|---|---|---|---|---|---|---|---|---|---|---|
| 07 | -$6 | -$20 | 10 | -1 | 2 | 0 | 0 | 25-17-58 | 0% | 17% | NA | .486 | — | .486 | .000 | .673 | — | | |
| 09 | $4 | -$15 | 140 | -1 | 12 | 0 | 1 | 47-19-34 | 13% | 23% | 19% | .779 | .906 | .704 | .818 | .665 | 2.56 | -22 | +52 |
| 10 | $0 | -$15 | 80 | -10 | 12 | 0 | 1 | 41-19-39 | 5% | 15% | 29% | .645 | .648 | .639 | .755 | .556 | 2.56 | -8 | +21 |

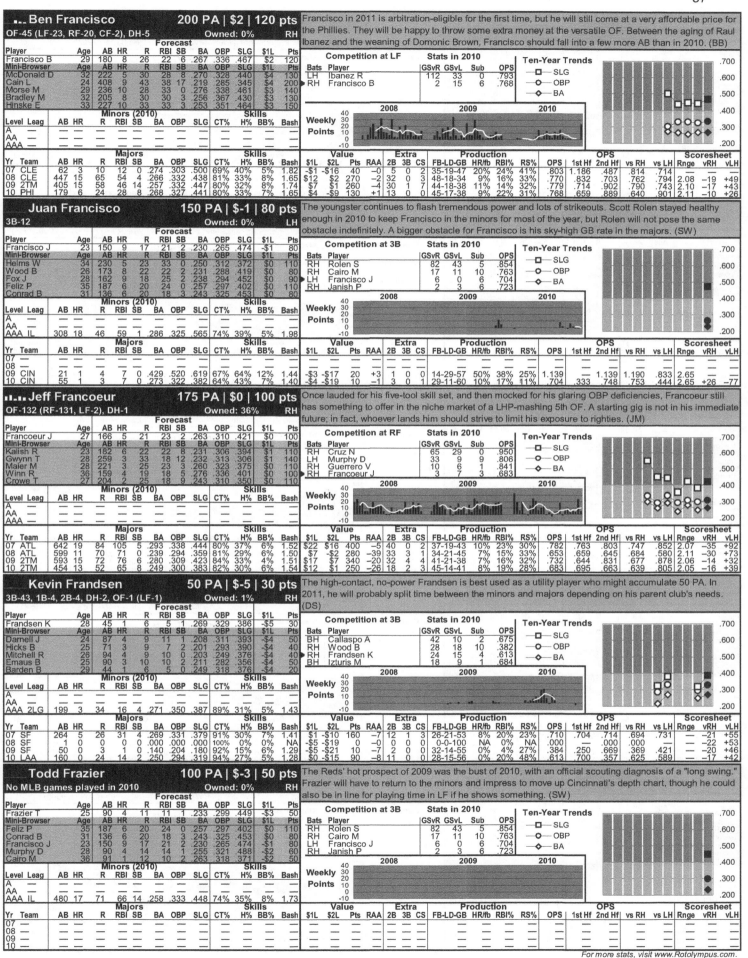

## Ben Francisco — 200 PA | $2 | 120 pts
OF-45 (LF-23, RF-20, CF-2), DH-5 — Owned: 0% — RH

Francisco in 2011 is arbitration-eligible for the first time, but he will still come at a very affordable price for the Phillies. They will be happy to throw some extra money at the versatile OF. Between the aging of Raul Ibanez and the weaning of Domonic Brown, Francisco should fall into a few more AB than in 2010. (BB)

### Forecast
| Player | Age | AB | HR | R | RBI | SB | BA | OBP | SLG | $1L | Pts |
|---|---|---|---|---|---|---|---|---|---|---|---|
| Francisco B | 29 | 180 | 8 | 26 | 22 | 6 | .267 | .336 | .467 | $2 | 120 |

### Mini-Browser
| Player | Age | AB | HR | R | RBI | SB | BA | OBP | SLG | $1L | Pts |
|---|---|---|---|---|---|---|---|---|---|---|---|
| McDonald D | 32 | 222 | 5 | 30 | 28 | 8 | .270 | .328 | .440 | $4 | 130 |
| Cain L | 24 | 408 | 9 | 43 | 38 | 17 | .219 | .285 | .345 | $4 | 200 |
| Morse M | 29 | 236 | 10 | 28 | 33 | 0 | .276 | .338 | .461 | $3 | 140 |
| Bradley M | 32 | 205 | 8 | 30 | 30 | 3 | .256 | .367 | .430 | $3 | 130 |
| Hinske E | 33 | 227 | 10 | 33 | 33 | 3 | .253 | .351 | .464 | $3 | 150 |

### Minors (2010) / Skills
| Level | Leag | AB | HR | R | RBI | SB | BA | OBP | SLG | CT% | H% | BB% | Bash |
|---|---|---|---|---|---|---|---|---|---|---|---|---|---|
| A | — | — | — | — | — | — | — | — | — | — | — | — | — |
| AA | — | — | — | — | — | — | — | — | — | — | — | — | — |
| AAA | — | — | — | — | — | — | — | — | — | — | — | — | — |

### Majors / Skills
| Yr | Team | AB | HR | R | RBI | SB | BA | OBP | SLG | CT% | H% | BB% | Bash |
|---|---|---|---|---|---|---|---|---|---|---|---|---|---|
| 07 | CLE | 62 | 3 | 10 | 12 | 0 | .274 | .303 | .500 | 69% | 40% | 5% | 1.82 |
| 08 | CLE | 447 | 15 | 65 | 54 | 4 | .266 | .332 | .438 | 81% | 33% | 8% | 1.65 |
| 09 | 2TM | 405 | 15 | 58 | 46 | 14 | .257 | .332 | .447 | 80% | 32% | 8% | 1.74 |
| 10 | PHI | 179 | 6 | 24 | 28 | 8 | .268 | .327 | .441 | 80% | 33% | 7% | 1.65 |

### Competition at LF — Stats in 2010
| Bats | Player | GSvR | GSvL | Sub | OPS |
|---|---|---|---|---|---|
| LH | Ibanez R | 112 | 33 | 0 | .793 |
| RH | Francisco B | 2 | 15 | 6 | .768 |

Ten-Year Trends: SLG, OBP, BA

### Value / Extra / Production / OPS / Scoresheet
| Yr | $1L | $2L | Pts | RAA | 2B | 3B | CS | FB-LD-GB | HR/fb | RBI% | RS% | OPS | 1st Hf | 2nd Hf | vs RH | vs LH | Rnge | vRH | vLH |
|---|---|---|---|---|---|---|---|---|---|---|---|---|---|---|---|---|---|---|---|
| 07 | -$1 | -$16 | 40 | -0 | 5 | 0 | 2 | 35-19-47 | 20% | 24% | 41% | .803 | 1.186 | .487 | .814 | .714 | — | — | — |
| 08 | $12 | $2 | 270 | -2 | 32 | 0 | 3 | 48-18-34 | 9% | 16% | 33% | .770 | .832 | .703 | .762 | .794 | 2.08 | -19 | +49 |
| 09 | $7 | $1 | 260 | -4 | 30 | 1 | 7 | 44-18-38 | 11% | 14% | 32% | .779 | .714 | .902 | .790 | .743 | 2.10 | -17 | +43 |
| 10 | $4 | -$9 | 130 | +1 | 13 | 0 | 0 | 45-17-38 | 9% | 22% | 31% | .768 | .659 | .889 | .640 | .901 | 2.11 | -18 | +26 |

---

## Juan Francisco — 150 PA | $-1 | 80 pts
3B-12 — Owned: 0% — LH

The youngster continues to flash tremendous power and lots of strikeouts. Scott Rolen stayed healthy enough in 2010 to keep Francisco in the minors for most of the year, but Rolen will not pose the same obstacle indefinitely. A bigger obstacle for Francisco is his sky-high GB rate in the majors. (SW)

### Forecast
| Player | Age | AB | HR | R | RBI | SB | BA | OBP | SLG | $1L | Pts |
|---|---|---|---|---|---|---|---|---|---|---|---|
| Francisco J | 23 | 150 | 9 | 17 | 21 | 2 | .230 | .265 | .474 | -$1 | 80 |

### Mini-Browser
| Player | Age | AB | HR | R | RBI | SB | BA | OBP | SLG | $1L | Pts |
|---|---|---|---|---|---|---|---|---|---|---|---|
| Helms W | 34 | 230 | 5 | 23 | 33 | 0 | .250 | .312 | .372 | $0 | 110 |
| Wood B | 26 | 173 | 8 | 22 | 22 | 2 | .231 | .288 | .419 | $0 | 80 |
| Fox J | 28 | 162 | 9 | 18 | 25 | 2 | .238 | .294 | .452 | $0 | 90 |
| Feliz P | 35 | 187 | 6 | 20 | 24 | 0 | .257 | .297 | .402 | $0 | 110 |
| Conrad B | 31 | 136 | 6 | 20 | 18 | 3 | .243 | .325 | .453 | $0 | 80 |

### Minors (2010) / Skills
| Level | Leag | AB | HR | R | RBI | SB | BA | OBP | SLG | CT% | H% | BB% | Bash |
|---|---|---|---|---|---|---|---|---|---|---|---|---|---|
| A | — | — | — | — | — | — | — | — | — | — | — | — | — |
| AA | — | — | — | — | — | — | — | — | — | — | — | — | — |
| AAA | IL | 308 | 18 | 46 | 59 | 1 | .286 | .325 | .565 | 74% | 39% | 5% | 1.98 |

### Majors / Skills
| Yr | Team | AB | HR | R | RBI | SB | BA | OBP | SLG | CT% | H% | BB% | Bash |
|---|---|---|---|---|---|---|---|---|---|---|---|---|---|
| 07 | — | — | — | — | — | — | — | — | — | — | — | — | — |
| 08 | — | — | — | — | — | — | — | — | — | — | — | — | — |
| 09 | CIN | 21 | 1 | 4 | 7 | 0 | .429 | .520 | .619 | 67% | 64% | 12% | 1.44 |
| 10 | CIN | 55 | 1 | 3 | 7 | 0 | .273 | .322 | .382 | 64% | 43% | 7% | 1.40 |

### Competition at 3B — Stats in 2010
| Bats | Player | GSvR | GSvL | Sub | OPS |
|---|---|---|---|---|---|
| RH | Rolen S | 82 | 43 | 5 | .854 |
| RH | Cairo M | 17 | 11 | 10 | .763 |
| LH | Francisco J | 6 | 0 | 6 | .704 |
| RH | Janish P | 2 | 3 | 6 | .723 |

Ten-Year Trends: SLG, OBP, BA

### Value / Extra / Production / OPS / Scoresheet
| Yr | $1L | $2L | Pts | RAA | 2B | 3B | CS | FB-LD-GB | HR/fb | RBI% | RS% | OPS | 1st Hf | 2nd Hf | vs RH | vs LH | Rnge | vRH | vLH |
|---|---|---|---|---|---|---|---|---|---|---|---|---|---|---|---|---|---|---|---|
| 07 | — | — | — | — | — | — | — | — | — | — | — | — | — | — | — | — | — | — | — |
| 08 | — | — | — | — | — | — | — | — | — | — | — | — | — | — | — | — | — | — | — |
| 09 | -$3 | -$17 | 20 | +3 | 1 | 0 | 0 | 14-29-57 | 50% | 38% | 25% | 1.139 | — | 1.139 | 1.190 | .833 | 2.65 | — | — |
| 10 | -$4 | -$19 | 10 | -1 | 3 | 0 | 1 | 29-11-60 | 10% | 17% | 11% | .704 | .333 | .748 | .753 | .444 | 2.65 | +26 | -77 |

---

## Jeff Francoeur — 175 PA | $0 | 100 pts
OF-132 (RF-131, LF-2), DH-1 — Owned: 36% — RH

Once lauded for his five-tool skill set, and then mocked for his glaring OBP deficiencies, Francoeur still has something to offer in the niche market of a LHP-mashing 5th OF. A starting gig is not in his immediate future; in fact, whoever lands him should strive to limit his exposure to righties. (JM)

### Forecast
| Player | Age | AB | HR | R | RBI | SB | BA | OBP | SLG | $1L | Pts |
|---|---|---|---|---|---|---|---|---|---|---|---|
| Francoeur J | 27 | 166 | 5 | 21 | 23 | 2 | .263 | .310 | .421 | $0 | 100 |

### Mini-Browser
| Player | Age | AB | HR | R | RBI | SB | BA | OBP | SLG | $1L | Pts |
|---|---|---|---|---|---|---|---|---|---|---|---|
| Kalish R | 23 | 182 | 6 | 22 | 22 | 8 | .231 | .306 | .394 | $1 | 110 |
| Gwynn T | 28 | 259 | 3 | 33 | 18 | 12 | .232 | .313 | .306 | $1 | 140 |
| Maier M | 28 | 221 | 3 | 25 | 23 | 3 | .260 | .323 | .375 | $1 | 110 |
| Winn R | 36 | 159 | 4 | 19 | 18 | 5 | .276 | .336 | .401 | $0 | 100 |
| Crowe T | 27 | 204 | 2 | 25 | 18 | 9 | .243 | .310 | .350 | $0 | 110 |

### Minors (2010) / Skills
| Level | Leag | AB | HR | R | RBI | SB | BA | OBP | SLG | CT% | H% | BB% | Bash |
|---|---|---|---|---|---|---|---|---|---|---|---|---|---|
| A | — | — | — | — | — | — | — | — | — | — | — | — | — |
| AA | — | — | — | — | — | — | — | — | — | — | — | — | — |
| AAA | — | — | — | — | — | — | — | — | — | — | — | — | — |

### Majors / Skills
| Yr | Team | AB | HR | R | RBI | SB | BA | OBP | SLG | CT% | H% | BB% | Bash |
|---|---|---|---|---|---|---|---|---|---|---|---|---|---|
| 07 | ATL | 642 | 19 | 84 | 105 | 5 | .293 | .338 | .444 | 80% | 37% | 6% | 1.52 |
| 08 | ATL | 599 | 11 | 70 | 71 | 0 | .239 | .294 | .359 | 81% | 29% | 6% | 1.50 |
| 09 | 2TM | 593 | 15 | 72 | 76 | 6 | .280 | .309 | .423 | 84% | 33% | 4% | 1.51 |
| 10 | 2TM | 454 | 13 | 52 | 65 | 8 | .249 | .300 | .383 | 82% | 30% | 6% | 1.54 |

### Competition at RF — Stats in 2010
| Bats | Player | GSvR | GSvL | Sub | OPS |
|---|---|---|---|---|---|
| RH | Cruz N | 65 | 29 | 0 | .950 |
| LH | Murphy D | 33 | 9 | 9 | .806 |
| RH | Guerrero V | 10 | 6 | 1 | .841 |
| RH | Francoeur J | 3 | 7 | 3 | .683 |

Ten-Year Trends: SLG, OBP, BA

### Value / Extra / Production / OPS / Scoresheet
| Yr | $1L | $2L | Pts | RAA | 2B | 3B | CS | FB-LD-GB | HR/fb | RBI% | RS% | OPS | 1st Hf | 2nd Hf | vs RH | vs LH | Rnge | vRH | vLH |
|---|---|---|---|---|---|---|---|---|---|---|---|---|---|---|---|---|---|---|---|
| 07 | $22 | $16 | 400 | -5 | 40 | 0 | 2 | 37-19-43 | 10% | 23% | 30% | .782 | .763 | .803 | .747 | .852 | 2.07 | -35 | +92 |
| 08 | $7 | -$2 | 280 | -39 | 33 | 3 | 1 | 34-21-45 | 7% | 15% | 33% | .653 | .659 | .645 | .684 | .580 | 2.11 | -30 | +73 |
| 09 | $17 | $7 | 340 | -20 | 32 | 4 | 4 | 41-21-38 | 7% | 16% | 32% | .732 | .644 | .831 | .677 | .878 | 2.06 | -14 | +32 |
| 10 | $12 | $1 | 250 | -26 | 18 | 2 | 4 | 45-14-41 | 8% | 19% | 28% | .683 | .695 | .663 | .639 | .805 | 2.05 | -16 | +39 |

---

## Kevin Frandsen — 50 PA | $-5 | 30 pts
3B-43, 1B-4, 2B-4, DH-2, OF-1 (LF-1) — Owned: 1% — RH

The high-contact, no-power Frandsen is best used as a utility player who might accumulate 50 PA. In 2011, he will probably split time between the minors and majors depending on his parent club's needs. (DS)

### Forecast
| Player | Age | AB | HR | R | RBI | SB | BA | OBP | SLG | $1L | Pts |
|---|---|---|---|---|---|---|---|---|---|---|---|
| Frandsen K | 28 | 45 | 1 | 6 | 5 | 1 | .269 | .329 | .386 | -$5 | 30 |

### Mini-Browser
| Player | Age | AB | HR | R | RBI | SB | BA | OBP | SLG | $1L | Pts |
|---|---|---|---|---|---|---|---|---|---|---|---|
| Darnell J | 24 | 87 | 4 | 9 | 11 | 1 | .208 | .311 | .393 | -$4 | 50 |
| Hicks B | 25 | 71 | 3 | 9 | 7 | 2 | .201 | .293 | .390 | -$4 | 40 |
| Mitchell R | 26 | 94 | 4 | 9 | 10 | 0 | .203 | .249 | .376 | -$4 | 40 |
| Emaus B | 25 | 90 | 3 | 10 | 10 | 2 | .211 | .282 | .356 | -$4 | 50 |
| Barden B | 29 | 44 | 1 | 6 | 5 | 0 | .249 | .318 | .376 | -$4 | 20 |

### Minors (2010) / Skills
| Level | Leag | AB | HR | R | RBI | SB | BA | OBP | SLG | CT% | H% | BB% | Bash |
|---|---|---|---|---|---|---|---|---|---|---|---|---|---|
| A | — | — | — | — | — | — | — | — | — | — | — | — | — |
| AA | — | — | — | — | — | — | — | — | — | — | — | — | — |
| AAA | 2LG | 199 | 3 | 34 | 16 | 4 | .271 | .350 | .387 | 89% | 31% | 5% | 1.43 |

### Majors / Skills
| Yr | Team | AB | HR | R | RBI | SB | BA | OBP | SLG | CT% | H% | BB% | Bash |
|---|---|---|---|---|---|---|---|---|---|---|---|---|---|
| 07 | SF | 264 | 5 | 26 | 31 | 4 | .269 | .331 | .379 | 91% | 30% | 7% | 1.41 |
| 08 | SF | 1 | 0 | 0 | 0 | 0 | .000 | .000 | .000 | 100% | 0% | 0% | NA |
| 09 | SF | 50 | 0 | 3 | 1 | 0 | .140 | .204 | .180 | 92% | 15% | 6% | 1.29 |
| 10 | LAA | 160 | 0 | 24 | 14 | 2 | .250 | .294 | .319 | 94% | 27% | 6% | 1.28 |

### Competition at 3B — Stats in 2010
| Bats | Player | GSvR | GSvL | Sub | OPS |
|---|---|---|---|---|---|
| BH | Callaspo A | 42 | 10 | 2 | .675 |
| RH | Wood B | 28 | 18 | 10 | .382 |
| RH | Frandsen K | 24 | 15 | 4 | .613 |
| BH | Izturis M | 18 | 9 | 1 | .684 |

Ten-Year Trends: SLG, OBP, BA

### Value / Extra / Production / OPS / Scoresheet
| Yr | $1L | $2L | Pts | RAA | 2B | 3B | CS | FB-LD-GB | HR/fb | RBI% | RS% | OPS | 1st Hf | 2nd Hf | vs RH | vs LH | Rnge | vRH | vLH |
|---|---|---|---|---|---|---|---|---|---|---|---|---|---|---|---|---|---|---|---|
| 07 | $1 | -$10 | 160 | -7 | 12 | 1 | 3 | 26-21-53 | 8% | 20% | 23% | .710 | .704 | .714 | .694 | .731 | — | -21 | +55 |
| 08 | -$5 | -$19 | 0 | -0 | 0 | 0 | 0 | 0-100-0 | NA | 0% | NA | .000 | — | .000 | .000 | — | — | -22 | +43 |
| 09 | -$5 | -$21 | 10 | -7 | 2 | 0 | 0 | 32-14-55 | 0% | 4% | 27% | .384 | .250 | .669 | .369 | .421 | — | -20 | +46 |
| 10 | $0 | -$15 | 90 | -8 | 11 | 0 | 0 | 28-15-56 | 0% | 20% | 48% | .613 | .700 | .357 | .625 | .589 | — | -17 | +42 |

---

## Todd Frazier — 100 PA | $-3 | 50 pts
No MLB games played in 2010 — Owned: 0% — RH

The Reds' hot prospect of 2009 was the bust of 2010, with an official scouting diagnosis of a "long swing." Frazier will have to return to the minors and impress to move up Cincinnati's depth chart, though he could also be in line for playing time in LF if he shows something. (SW)

### Forecast
| Player | Age | AB | HR | R | RBI | SB | BA | OBP | SLG | $1L | Pts |
|---|---|---|---|---|---|---|---|---|---|---|---|
| Frazier T | 25 | 90 | 4 | 11 | 11 | 1 | .233 | .299 | .449 | -$3 | 50 |

### Mini-Browser
| Player | Age | AB | HR | R | RBI | SB | BA | OBP | SLG | $1L | Pts |
|---|---|---|---|---|---|---|---|---|---|---|---|
| Feliz P | 35 | 187 | 6 | 20 | 24 | 0 | .257 | .297 | .402 | $0 | 110 |
| Conrad B | 31 | 136 | 6 | 20 | 18 | 3 | .243 | .325 | .453 | $0 | 80 |
| Francisco J | 23 | 150 | 9 | 17 | 21 | 2 | .230 | .265 | .474 | -$1 | 80 |
| Murphy D | 28 | 90 | 4 | 14 | 14 | 1 | .255 | .321 | .488 | -$2 | 60 |
| Cairo M | 36 | 91 | 1 | 12 | 10 | 2 | .263 | .318 | .371 | -$2 | 50 |

### Minors (2010) / Skills
| Level | Leag | AB | HR | R | RBI | SB | BA | OBP | SLG | CT% | H% | BB% | Bash |
|---|---|---|---|---|---|---|---|---|---|---|---|---|---|
| A | — | — | — | — | — | — | — | — | — | — | — | — | — |
| AA | — | — | — | — | — | — | — | — | — | — | — | — | — |
| AAA | IL | 480 | 17 | 71 | 66 | 14 | .258 | .333 | .448 | 74% | 35% | 8% | 1.73 |

### Majors / Skills
| Yr | Team | AB | HR | R | RBI | SB | BA | OBP | SLG | CT% | H% | BB% | Bash |
|---|---|---|---|---|---|---|---|---|---|---|---|---|---|
| 07 | — | — | — | — | — | — | — | — | — | — | — | — | — |
| 08 | — | — | — | — | — | — | — | — | — | — | — | — | — |
| 09 | — | — | — | — | — | — | — | — | — | — | — | — | — |
| 10 | — | — | — | — | — | — | — | — | — | — | — | — | — |

### Competition at 3B — Stats in 2010
| Bats | Player | GSvR | GSvL | Sub | OPS |
|---|---|---|---|---|---|
| RH | Rolen S | 82 | 43 | 5 | .854 |
| RH | Cairo M | 17 | 11 | 10 | .763 |
| LH | Francisco J | 6 | 0 | 6 | .704 |
| RH | Janish P | 2 | 3 | 6 | .723 |

Ten-Year Trends: SLG, OBP, BA

### Value / Extra / Production / OPS / Scoresheet
| Yr | $1L | $2L | Pts | RAA | 2B | 3B | CS | FB-LD-GB | HR/fb | RBI% | RS% | OPS | 1st Hf | 2nd Hf | vs RH | vs LH | Rnge | vRH | vLH |
|---|---|---|---|---|---|---|---|---|---|---|---|---|---|---|---|---|---|---|---|
| 07 | — | — | — | — | — | — | — | — | — | — | — | — | — | — | — | — | — | — | — |
| 08 | — | — | — | — | — | — | — | — | — | — | — | — | — | — | — | — | — | — | — |
| 09 | — | — | — | — | — | — | — | — | — | — | — | — | — | — | — | — | — | — | — |
| 10 | — | — | — | — | — | — | — | — | — | — | — | — | — | — | — | — | — | — | — |

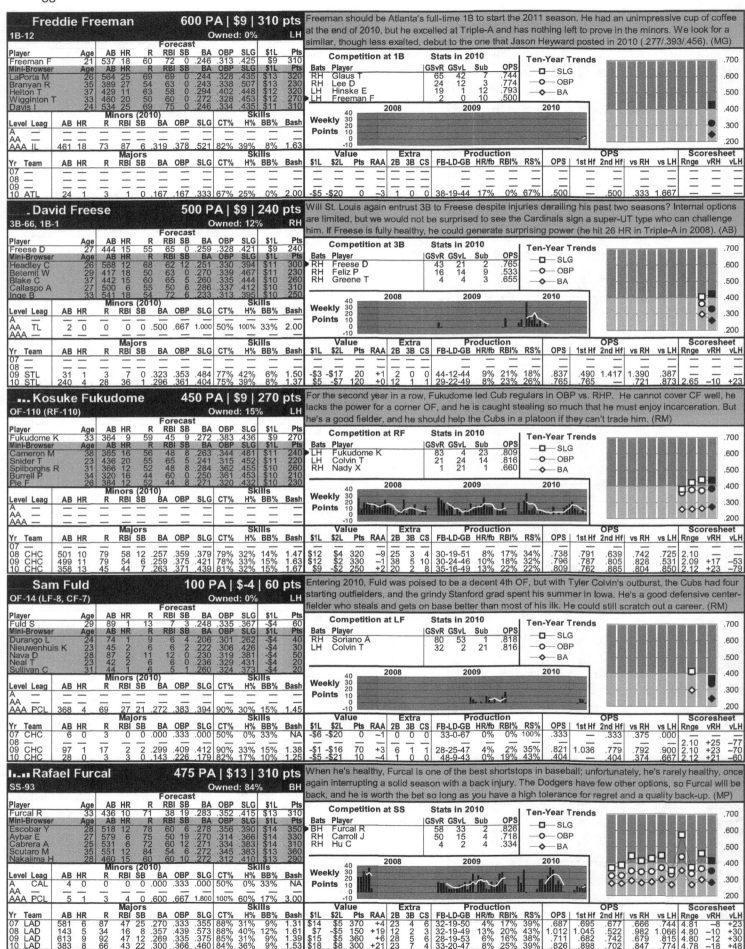

## Freddie Freeman — 600 PA | $9 | 310 pts

1B-12 | Owned: 0% | LH

Freeman should be Atlanta's full-time 1B to start the 2011 season. He had an unimpressive cup of coffee at the end of 2010, but he excelled at Triple-A and has nothing left to prove in the minors. We look for a similar, though less exalted, debut to the one that Jason Heyward posted in 2010 (.277/.393/.456). (MG)

| Player | Age | AB | HR | R | RBI | SB | BA | OBP | SLG | $1L | Pts |
|---|---|---|---|---|---|---|---|---|---|---|---|
| Freeman F | 21 | 537 | 18 | 60 | 72 | 0 | .246 | .313 | .425 | $9 | 310 |
| **Mini-Browser** | **Age** | **AB** | **HR** | **R** | **RBI** | **SB** | **BA** | **OBP** | **SLG** | **$1L** | **Pts** |
| LaPorta M | 26 | 564 | 25 | 69 | 69 | 0 | .244 | .328 | .435 | $13 | 320 |
| Branyan R | 35 | 389 | 27 | 54 | 63 | 0 | .243 | .338 | .507 | $13 | 230 |
| Helton T | 37 | 429 | 11 | 63 | 58 | 0 | .294 | .402 | .448 | $12 | 320 |
| Wigginton T | 33 | 460 | 20 | 50 | 60 | 0 | .272 | .328 | .453 | $12 | 270 |
| Davis I | 24 | 534 | 25 | 69 | 75 | 0 | .246 | .334 | .435 | $11 | 310 |

Minors (2010)

| Level | Leag | AB | HR | R | RBI | SB | BA | OBP | SLG | CT% | H% | BB% | Bash |
|---|---|---|---|---|---|---|---|---|---|---|---|---|---|
| A | — | — | — | — | — | — | — | — | — | — | — | — | — |
| AA | — | — | — | — | — | — | — | — | — | — | — | — | — |
| AAA | IL | 461 | 18 | 73 | 87 | 6 | .319 | .378 | .521 | 82% | 39% | 8% | 1.63 |

Majors

| Yr | Team | AB | HR | R | RBI | SB | BA | OBP | SLG | CT% | H% | BB% | Bash |
|---|---|---|---|---|---|---|---|---|---|---|---|---|---|
| 07 | — | — | — | — | — | — | — | — | — | — | — | — | — |
| 08 | — | — | — | — | — | — | — | — | — | — | — | — | — |
| 09 | — | — | — | — | — | — | — | — | — | — | — | — | — |
| 10 | ATL | 24 | 1 | 3 | 1 | 0 | .167 | .167 | .333 | 67% | 25% | 0% | 2.00 |

| Yr | $1L | $2L | Pts | RAA | 2B | 3B | CS | FB-LD-GB | HR/fb | RBI% | RS% | OPS | 1st Hf | 2nd Hf | vs RH | vs LH | Rnge | vRH | vLH |
|---|---|---|---|---|---|---|---|---|---|---|---|---|---|---|---|---|---|---|---|
| 07 | — | — | — | — | — | — | — | — | — | — | — | — | — | — | — | — | — | — | — |
| 08 | — | — | — | — | — | — | — | — | — | — | — | — | — | — | — | — | — | — | — |
| 09 | — | — | — | — | — | — | — | — | — | — | — | — | — | — | — | — | — | — | — |
| 10 | -$5 | -$20 | 0 | −3 | 1 | 0 | 0 | 38-19-44 | 17% | 0% | 67% | .500 | — | .500 | .333 | 1.667 | — | — | — |

Competition at 1B — Stats in 2010

| Bats | Player | GSvR | GSvL | Sub | OPS |
|---|---|---|---|---|---|
| RH | Glaus T | 65 | 42 | 7 | .744 |
| RH | Lee D | 24 | 12 | 3 | .774 |
| LH | Hinske E | 19 | 1 | 12 | .793 |
| LH | Freeman F | 2 | 0 | 10 | .500 |

Ten-Year Trends

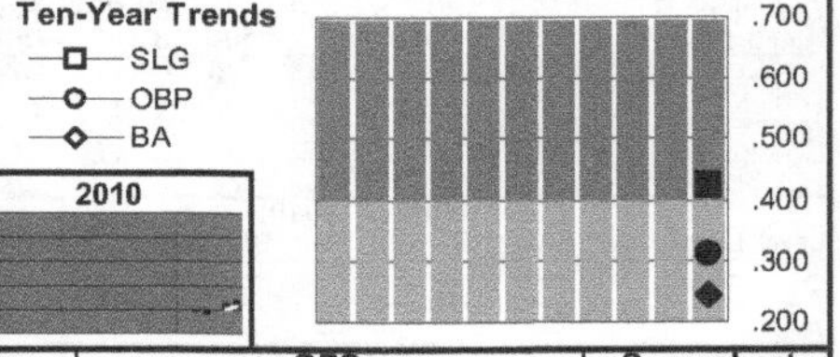
SLG
OBP
BA
.700
.600
.500
.400
.300
.200

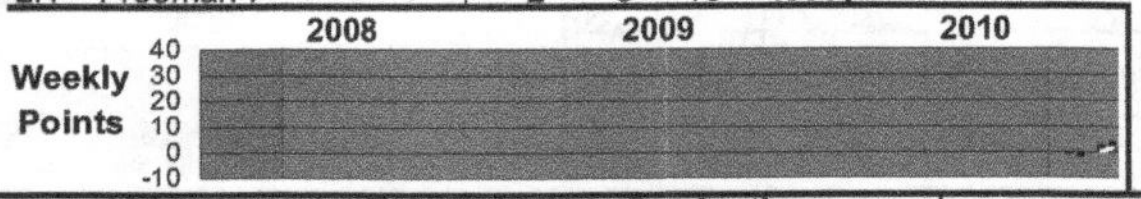
2008
2009
2010
Weekly
Points
40
30
20
10
0
-10

## David Freese — 500 PA | $9 | 240 pts

3B-66, 1B-1 | Owned: 12% | RH

Will St. Louis again entrust 3B to Freese despite injuries derailing his past two seasons? Internal options are limited, but we would not be surprised to see the Cardinals sign a super-UT type who can challenge him. If Freese is fully healthy, he could generate surprising power (he hit 26 HR in Triple-A in 2008). (AB)

| Player | Age | AB | HR | R | RBI | SB | BA | OBP | SLG | $1L | Pts |
|---|---|---|---|---|---|---|---|---|---|---|---|
| Freese D | 27 | 444 | 15 | 55 | 65 | 0 | .259 | .328 | .421 | $9 | 240 |
| **Mini-Browser** | **Age** | **AB** | **HR** | **R** | **RBI** | **SB** | **BA** | **OBP** | **SLG** | **$1L** | **Pts** |
| Headley C | 26 | 568 | 12 | 68 | 62 | 12 | .251 | .330 | .394 | $11 | 300 |
| Betemit W | 29 | 417 | 18 | 50 | 63 | 0 | .270 | .339 | .467 | $11 | 230 |
| Blake C | 37 | 442 | 15 | 60 | 65 | 5 | .260 | .335 | .444 | $10 | 260 |
| Callaspo A | 27 | 500 | 6 | 55 | 50 | 6 | .286 | .337 | .412 | $10 | 310 |
| Inge B | 33 | 541 | 18 | 54 | 72 | 6 | .233 | .313 | .395 | $10 | 250 |

Minors (2010)

| Level | Leag | AB | HR | R | RBI | SB | BA | OBP | SLG | CT% | H% | BB% | Bash |
|---|---|---|---|---|---|---|---|---|---|---|---|---|---|
| A | — | — | — | — | — | — | — | — | — | — | — | — | — |
| AA | TL | 2 | 0 | 0 | 0 | 0 | .500 | .667 | 1.000 | 50% | 100% | 33% | 2.00 |
| AAA | — | — | — | — | — | — | — | — | — | — | — | — | — |

Majors

| Yr | Team | AB | HR | R | RBI | SB | BA | OBP | SLG | CT% | H% | BB% | Bash |
|---|---|---|---|---|---|---|---|---|---|---|---|---|---|
| 07 | — | — | — | — | — | — | — | — | — | — | — | — | — |
| 08 | — | — | — | — | — | — | — | — | — | — | — | — | — |
| 09 | STL | 31 | 1 | 3 | 7 | 0 | .323 | .353 | .484 | 77% | 42% | 6% | 1.50 |
| 10 | STL | 240 | 4 | 28 | 36 | 1 | .296 | .361 | .404 | 75% | 39% | 8% | 1.37 |

| Yr | $1L | $2L | Pts | RAA | 2B | 3B | CS | FB-LD-GB | HR/fb | RBI% | RS% | OPS | 1st Hf | 2nd Hf | vs RH | vs LH | Rnge | vRH | vLH |
|---|---|---|---|---|---|---|---|---|---|---|---|---|---|---|---|---|---|---|---|
| 07 | — | — | — | — | — | — | — | — | — | — | — | — | — | — | — | — | — | — | — |
| 08 | — | — | — | — | — | — | — | — | — | — | — | — | — | — | — | — | — | — | — |
| 09 | -$3 | -$17 | 20 | +1 | 2 | 0 | 0 | 44-12-44 | 9% | 21% | 18% | .837 | .490 | 1.417 | 1.390 | .387 | — | — | — |
| 10 | $5 | -$7 | 120 | +0 | 12 | 1 | 1 | 29-22-49 | 8% | 23% | 26% | .765 | .765 | — | .721 | .873 | 2.65 | −10 | +23 |

Competition at 3B — Stats in 2010

| Bats | Player | GSvR | GSvL | Sub | OPS |
|---|---|---|---|---|---|
| RH | Freese D | 43 | 21 | 2 | .765 |
| RH | Feliz P | 16 | 14 | 9 | .533 |
| RH | Greene T | 4 | 4 | 3 | .655 |

Ten-Year Trends

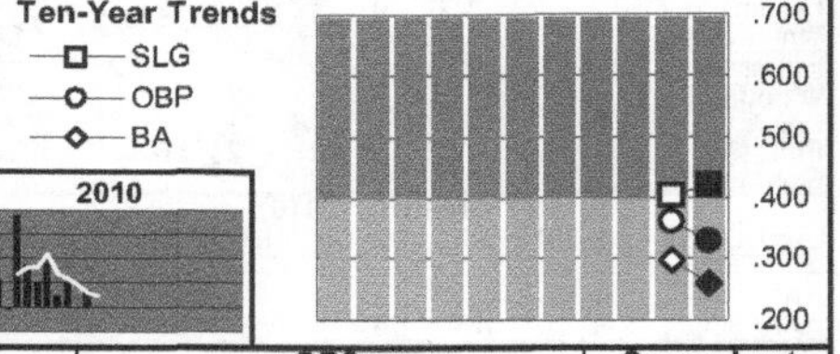
SLG
OBP
BA
.700
.600
.500
.400
.300
.200

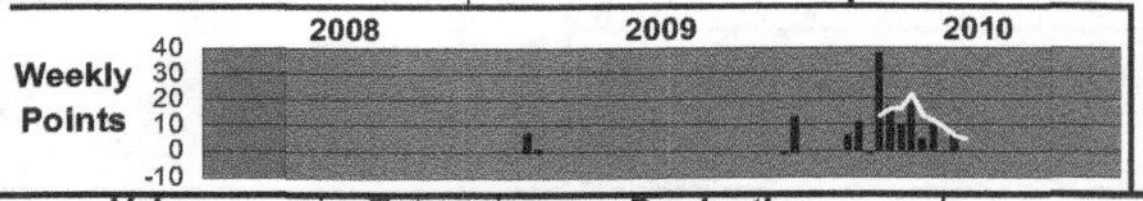
2008
2009
2010
Weekly
Points
40
30
20
10
0
-10

## Kosuke Fukudome — 450 PA | $9 | 270 pts

OF-110 (RF-110) | Owned: 15% | LH

For the second year in a row, Fukudome led Cub regulars in OBP vs. RHP. He cannot cover CF well, he lacks the power for a corner OF, and he is caught stealing so much that he must enjoy incarceration. But he's a good fielder, and he should help the Cubs in a platoon if they can't trade him. (RM)

| Player | Age | AB | HR | R | RBI | SB | BA | OBP | SLG | $1L | Pts |
|---|---|---|---|---|---|---|---|---|---|---|---|
| Fukudome K | 33 | 364 | 9 | 59 | 45 | 9 | .272 | .383 | .436 | $9 | 270 |
| **Mini-Browser** | **Age** | **AB** | **HR** | **R** | **RBI** | **SB** | **BA** | **OBP** | **SLG** | **$1L** | **Pts** |
| Cameron M | 38 | 365 | 16 | 56 | 48 | 8 | .263 | .344 | .481 | $11 | 240 |
| Snider T | 23 | 436 | 20 | 55 | 65 | 5 | .241 | .315 | .452 | $11 | 220 |
| Spilborghs R | 31 | 366 | 12 | 52 | 48 | 8 | .284 | .362 | .455 | $10 | 260 |
| Burrell P | 34 | 320 | 16 | 44 | 60 | 0 | .250 | .361 | .453 | $10 | 210 |
| Pie F | 26 | 384 | 12 | 52 | 44 | 8 | .271 | .320 | .432 | $10 | 230 |

Minors (2010)

| Level | Leag | AB | HR | R | RBI | SB | BA | OBP | SLG | CT% | H% | BB% | Bash |
|---|---|---|---|---|---|---|---|---|---|---|---|---|---|
| A | — | — | — | — | — | — | — | — | — | — | — | — | — |
| AA | — | — | — | — | — | — | — | — | — | — | — | — | — |
| AAA | — | — | — | — | — | — | — | — | — | — | — | — | — |

Majors

| Yr | Team | AB | HR | R | RBI | SB | BA | OBP | SLG | CT% | H% | BB% | Bash |
|---|---|---|---|---|---|---|---|---|---|---|---|---|---|
| 07 | — | — | — | — | — | — | — | — | — | — | — | — | — |
| 08 | CHC | 501 | 10 | 79 | 58 | 12 | .257 | .359 | .379 | 79% | 32% | 14% | 1.47 |
| 09 | CHC | 499 | 11 | 79 | 54 | 6 | .259 | .375 | .421 | 78% | 33% | 15% | 1.63 |
| 10 | CHC | 358 | 13 | 45 | 44 | 7 | .263 | .371 | .439 | 81% | 32% | 15% | 1.67 |

| Yr | $1L | $2L | Pts | RAA | 2B | 3B | CS | FB-LD-GB | HR/fb | RBI% | RS% | OPS | 1st Hf | 2nd Hf | vs RH | vs LH | Rnge | vRH | vLH |
|---|---|---|---|---|---|---|---|---|---|---|---|---|---|---|---|---|---|---|---|
| 07 | — | — | — | — | — | — | — | — | — | — | — | — | — | — | — | — | — | — | — |
| 08 | $12 | $4 | 320 | −9 | 25 | 3 | 4 | 30-19-51 | 8% | 17% | 34% | .738 | .791 | .639 | .742 | .725 | 2.10 | — | — |
| 09 | $12 | $2 | 330 | −1 | 38 | 5 | 10 | 30-24-46 | 10% | 18% | 32% | .796 | .787 | .805 | .828 | .531 | 2.09 | +17 | −53 |
| 10 | $9 | -$2 | 250 | +2 | 20 | 2 | 8 | 35-16-49 | 13% | 22% | 22% | .809 | .762 | .885 | .804 | .850 | 2.12 | +23 | −79 |

Competition at RF — Stats in 2010

| Bats | Player | GSvR | GSvL | Sub | OPS |
|---|---|---|---|---|---|
| LH | Fukudome K | 83 | 4 | 23 | .809 |
| LH | Colvin T | 21 | 24 | 14 | .816 |
| RH | Nady X | 1 | 21 | 1 | .660 |

Ten-Year Trends

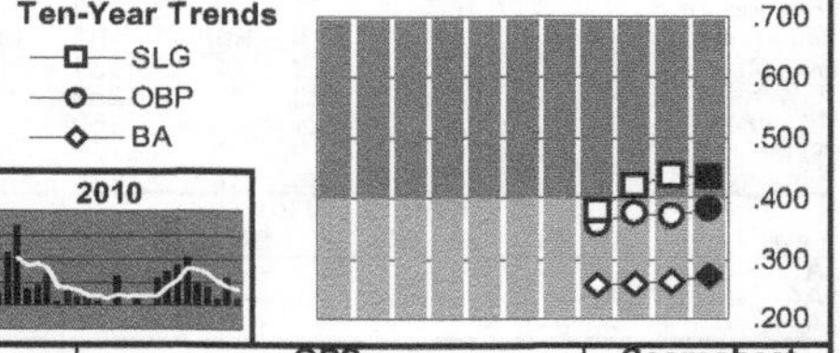
SLG
OBP
BA
.700
.600
.500
.400
.300
.200

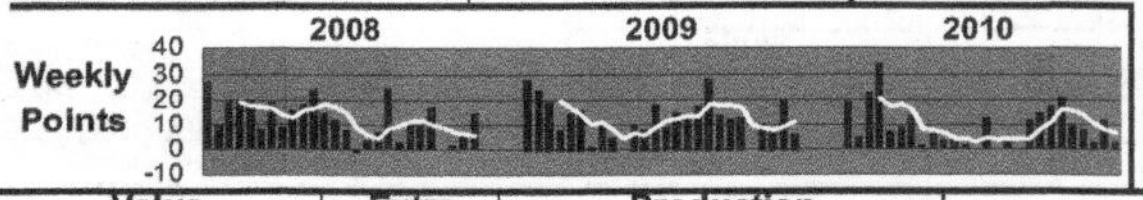
2008
2009
2010
Weekly
Points
40
30
20
10
0
-10

## Sam Fuld — 100 PA | $-4 | 60 pts

OF-14 (LF-8, CF-7) | Owned: 0% | LH

Entering 2010, Fuld was poised to be a decent 4th OF, but with Tyler Colvin's outburst, the Cubs had four starting outfielders, and the grindy Stanford grad spent his summer in Iowa. He's a good defensive center-fielder who steals and gets on base better than most of his ilk. He could still scratch out a career. (RM)

| Player | Age | AB | HR | R | RBI | SB | BA | OBP | SLG | $1L | Pts |
|---|---|---|---|---|---|---|---|---|---|---|---|
| Fuld S | 29 | 89 | 1 | 13 | 7 | 3 | .248 | .335 | .367 | -$4 | 60 |
| **Mini-Browser** | **Age** | **AB** | **HR** | **R** | **RBI** | **SB** | **BA** | **OBP** | **SLG** | **$1L** | **Pts** |
| Durango L | 24 | 74 | 1 | 9 | 6 | 4 | .206 | .301 | .262 | -$4 | 40 |
| Nieuwenhuis K | 23 | 45 | 2 | 6 | 6 | 2 | .222 | .306 | .426 | -$4 | 30 |
| Nava D | 28 | 87 | 2 | 11 | 12 | 0 | .230 | .319 | .381 | -$4 | 50 |
| Neal T | 23 | 42 | 2 | 6 | 6 | 0 | .236 | .329 | .431 | -$4 | 20 |
| Sullivan C | 31 | 44 | 1 | 6 | 5 | 1 | .260 | .324 | .373 | -$4 | 20 |

Minors (2010)

| Level | Leag | AB | HR | R | RBI | SB | BA | OBP | SLG | CT% | H% | BB% | Bash |
|---|---|---|---|---|---|---|---|---|---|---|---|---|---|
| A | — | — | — | — | — | — | — | — | — | — | — | — | — |
| AA | — | — | — | — | — | — | — | — | — | — | — | — | — |
| AAA | PCL | 368 | 4 | 69 | 27 | 21 | .272 | .383 | .394 | 90% | 30% | 15% | 1.45 |

Majors

| Yr | Team | AB | HR | R | RBI | SB | BA | OBP | SLG | CT% | H% | BB% | Bash |
|---|---|---|---|---|---|---|---|---|---|---|---|---|---|
| 07 | CHC | 6 | 0 | 3 | 0 | 0 | .000 | .333 | .000 | 50% | 0% | 33% | NA |
| 08 | — | — | — | — | — | — | — | — | — | — | — | — | — |
| 09 | CHC | 97 | 1 | 17 | 2 | 2 | .299 | .409 | .412 | 90% | 33% | 15% | 1.38 |
| 10 | CHC | 28 | 0 | 3 | 3 | 0 | .143 | .226 | .179 | 82% | 17% | 10% | 1.25 |

| Yr | $1L | $2L | Pts | RAA | 2B | 3B | CS | FB-LD-GB | HR/fb | RBI% | RS% | OPS | 1st Hf | 2nd Hf | vs RH | vs LH | Rnge | vRH | vLH |
|---|---|---|---|---|---|---|---|---|---|---|---|---|---|---|---|---|---|---|---|
| 07 | -$6 | -$20 | 0 | −1 | 0 | 0 | 0 | 33-0-67 | 0% | 0% | 100% | .333 | — | .333 | .375 | .000 | — | — | — |
| 08 | — | — | — | — | — | — | — | — | — | — | — | — | — | — | — | — | 2.10 | +25 | −77 |
| 09 | -$1 | -$16 | 70 | +3 | 6 | 1 | 1 | 28-25-47 | 4% | 2% | 35% | .821 | 1.036 | .779 | .792 | .900 | 2.10 | +23 | −70 |
| 10 | -$5 | -$21 | 10 | −4 | 1 | 0 | 0 | 48-9-43 | 0% | 19% | 43% | .404 | — | .404 | .374 | .667 | 2.12 | +21 | −60 |

Competition at LF — Stats in 2010

| Bats | Player | GSvR | GSvL | Sub | OPS |
|---|---|---|---|---|---|
| RH | Soriano A | 80 | 53 | 1 | .818 |
| LH | Colvin T | 32 | 2 | 21 | .816 |

Ten-Year Trends

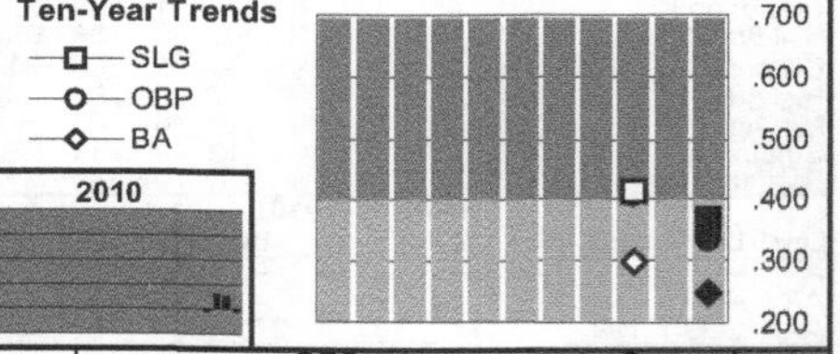
SLG
OBP
BA
.700
.600
.500
.400
.300
.200

2008
2009
2010
Weekly
Points
40
30
20
10
0
-10

## Rafael Furcal — 475 PA | $13 | 310 pts

SS-93 | Owned: 84% | BH

When he's healthy, Furcal is one of the best shortstops in baseball; unfortunately, he's rarely healthy, once again interrupting a solid season with a back injury. The Dodgers have few other options, so Furcal will be back, and he is worth the bet so long as you have a high tolerance for regret and a quality back-up. (MP)

| Player | Age | AB | HR | R | RBI | SB | BA | OBP | SLG | $1L | Pts |
|---|---|---|---|---|---|---|---|---|---|---|---|
| Furcal R | 33 | 436 | 10 | 71 | 38 | 19 | .283 | .352 | .415 | $13 | 310 |
| **Mini-Browser** | **Age** | **AB** | **HR** | **R** | **RBI** | **SB** | **BA** | **OBP** | **SLG** | **$1L** | **Pts** |
| Escobar Y | 28 | 518 | 12 | 78 | 60 | 6 | .278 | .356 | .390 | $14 | 350 |
| Aybar E | 27 | 579 | 6 | 75 | 50 | 19 | .270 | .314 | .366 | $14 | 330 |
| Cabrera A | 25 | 531 | 6 | 72 | 60 | 12 | .271 | .334 | .383 | $14 | 310 |
| Scutaro M | 35 | 551 | 12 | 84 | 54 | 6 | .272 | .345 | .383 | $13 | 360 |
| Nakajima H | 28 | 460 | 15 | 60 | 60 | 10 | .272 | .312 | .410 | $13 | 290 |

Minors (2010)

| Level | Leag | AB | HR | R | RBI | SB | BA | OBP | SLG | CT% | H% | BB% | Bash |
|---|---|---|---|---|---|---|---|---|---|---|---|---|---|
| A | CAL | 4 | 0 | 0 | 0 | 0 | .000 | .333 | .000 | 50% | 0% | 33% | NA |
| AA | — | — | — | — | — | — | — | — | — | — | — | — | — |
| AAA | PCL | 5 | 1 | 3 | 4 | 0 | .600 | .667 | 1.800 | 100% | 60% | 17% | 3.00 |

Majors

| Yr | Team | AB | HR | R | RBI | SB | BA | OBP | SLG | CT% | H% | BB% | Bash |
|---|---|---|---|---|---|---|---|---|---|---|---|---|---|
| 07 | LAD | 581 | 6 | 87 | 47 | 25 | .270 | .333 | .355 | 88% | 31% | 9% | 1.31 |
| 08 | LAD | 143 | 5 | 34 | 16 | 8 | .357 | .439 | .573 | 88% | 40% | 12% | 1.61 |
| 09 | LAD | 613 | 9 | 92 | 47 | 12 | .269 | .335 | .375 | 85% | 31% | 9% | 1.39 |
| 10 | LAD | 383 | 8 | 66 | 43 | 22 | .300 | .366 | .460 | 84% | 36% | 9% | 1.53 |

| Yr | $1L | $2L | Pts | RAA | 2B | 3B | CS | FB-LD-GB | HR/fb | RBI% | RS% | OPS | 1st Hf | 2nd Hf | vs RH | vs LH | Rnge | vRH | vLH |
|---|---|---|---|---|---|---|---|---|---|---|---|---|---|---|---|---|---|---|---|
| 07 | $14 | $5 | 370 | +4 | 23 | 4 | 6 | 32-19-50 | 4% | 17% | 39% | .687 | .695 | .677 | .666 | .744 | 4.81 | −8 | +23 |
| 08 | $7 | -$5 | 150 | +19 | 12 | 2 | 3 | 32-19-49 | 13% | 20% | 43% | 1.012 | 1.045 | .522 | .982 | 1.066 | 4.80 | −10 | +30 |
| 09 | $15 | $5 | 360 | +6 | 28 | 5 | 6 | 28-19-53 | 6% | 16% | 38% | .711 | .682 | .742 | .679 | .815 | 4.80 | −12 | +30 |
| 10 | $18 | $8 | 300 | +21 | 23 | 7 | 4 | 33-20-47 | 8% | 25% | 39% | .826 | .898 | .702 | .847 | .774 | 4.78 | −18 | +48 |

Competition at SS — Stats in 2010

| Bats | Player | GSvR | GSvL | Sub | OPS |
|---|---|---|---|---|---|
| BH | Furcal R | 58 | 33 | 2 | .826 |
| RH | Carroll J | 50 | 15 | 4 | .718 |
| RH | Hu C | 4 | 2 | 4 | .334 |

Ten-Year Trends

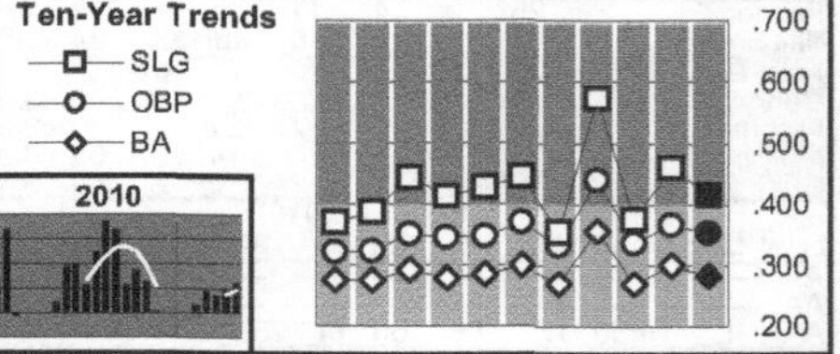
SLG
OBP
BA
.700
.600
.500
.400
.300
.200

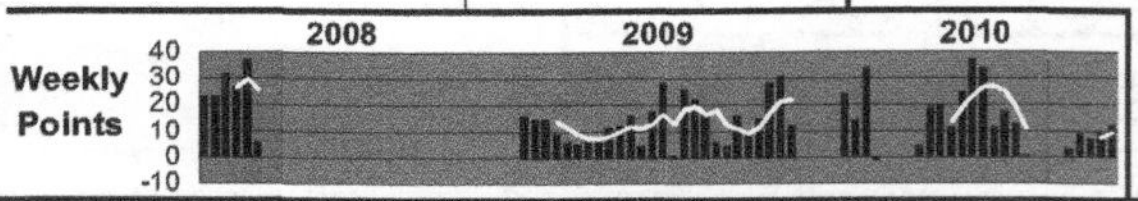
2008
2009
2010
Weekly
Points
40
30
20
10
0
-10

*For more stats, visit www.Rotolympus.com.*

## Mat Gamel

**125 PA | $-2 | 60 pts**

3B-3, OF-1 (LF-1) — Owned: 0% — LH

Gamel's bad luck continued in 2010 when a shoulder injury again delayed his full-season debut. Since first base is the only position open to Gamel, either he or Prince Fielder must go. The Crew will give one more shot to the cheaper Gamel, since they have invested so much in him, but he has to stop striking out. (MS)

**Forecast**

| Player | Age | AB | HR | R | RBI | SB | BA | OBP | SLG | $1L | Pts |
|---|---|---|---|---|---|---|---|---|---|---|---|
| Gamel M | 25 | 112 | 5 | 14 | 15 | 1 | .235 | .317 | .432 | -$2 | 60 |
| **Mini-Browser** | **Age** | **AB** | **HR** | **R** | **RBI** | **SB** | **BA** | **OBP** | **SLG** | **$1L** | **Pts** |
| Cantu J | 29 | 136 | 5 | 18 | 21 | 0 | .276 | .331 | .452 | $0 | 90 |
| Sweeney M | 37 | 135 | 5 | 14 | 20 | 0 | .267 | .323 | .428 | -$1 | 80 |
| Gload R | 34 | 144 | 3 | 17 | 18 | 2 | .270 | .316 | .404 | -$1 | 90 |
| Trumbo M | 25 | 178 | 8 | 16 | 22 | 2 | .214 | .257 | .406 | -$2 | 80 |
| Brown J | 27 | 132 | 3 | 15 | 15 | 0 | .261 | .321 | .409 | -$2 | 70 |

**Minors (2010)** / **Skills**

| Level | Leag | AB | HR | R | RBI | SB | BA | OBP | SLG | CT% | H% | BB% | Bash |
|---|---|---|---|---|---|---|---|---|---|---|---|---|---|
| A | FLO | 20 | 0 | 3 | 2 | 0 | .100 | .308 | .150 | 60% | 17% | 23% | 1.50 |
| AA | SOU | 28 | 1 | 6 | 5 | 0 | .393 | .469 | .571 | 68% | 58% | 13% | 1.45 |
| AAA | PCL | 311 | 13 | 54 | 67 | 3 | .309 | .387 | .511 | 79% | 39% | 11% | 1.66 |

**Competition at 1B** — **Stats in 2010**

| Bats | Player | GSvR | GSvL | Sub | OPS |
|---|---|---|---|---|---|
| LH | Fielder P | 110 | 50 | 0 | .871 |

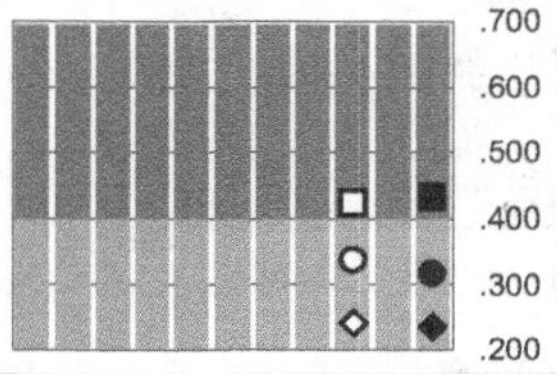


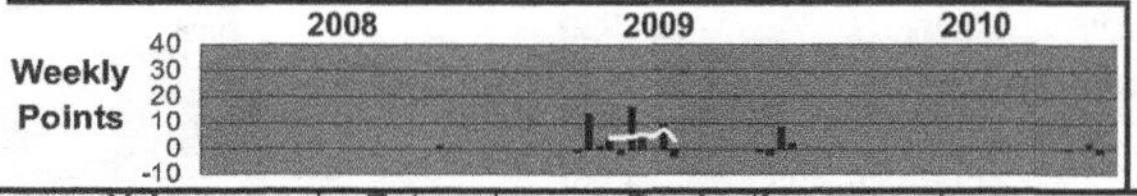


**Majors** / **Skills** / **Value** / **Extra** / **Production** / **OPS** / **Scoresheet**

| Yr | Team | AB | HR | R | RBI | SB | BA | OBP | SLG | CT% | H% | BB% | Bash | $1L | $2L | Pts | RAA | 2B | 3B | CS | FB-LD-GB | HR/fb | RBI% | RS% | OPS | 1st Hf | 2nd Hf | vs RH | vs LH | Rnge | vRH | vLH |
|---|---|---|---|---|---|---|---|---|---|---|---|---|---|---|---|---|---|---|---|---|---|---|---|---|---|---|---|---|---|---|---|---|
| 07 | — | — | — | — | — | — | — | — | — | — | — | — | — | — | — | — | — | — | — | — | — | — | — | — | — | — | — | — | — | — | — | — |
| 08 | MIL | 2 | 0 | 0 | 0 | 0 | .500 | .500 | 1.000 | 50% | 100% | 0% | 2.00 | -$5 | -$19 | 0 | +1 | 1 | 0 | 0 | 0-100-0 | NA | NA | 0% | 1.500 | — | 1.500 | 1.500 | — | — | — | — |
| 09 | MIL | 128 | 5 | 11 | 20 | 1 | .242 | .338 | .422 | 58% | 42% | 12% | 1.74 | -$1 | -$16 | 50 | –3 | 6 | 1 | 0 | 51-27-23 | 13% | 19% | 13% | .760 | .778 | .671 | .739 | .855 | — | +23 | –71 |
| 10 | MIL | 15 | 0 | 1 | 1 | 0 | .200 | .294 | .267 | 47% | 43% | 6% | 1.33 | -$5 | -$21 | 0 | –2 | 1 | 0 | 0 | 29-29-43 | 0% | 17% | 20% | .561 | — | .561 | .497 | 1.000 | — | +19 | –62 |

## Brett Gardner

**500 PA | $17 | 330 pts**

OF-146 (LF-123, CF-45), DH-2 — Owned: 91% — LH

Gardner exceeded all expectations in LF, hitting over .300 in the first half and hitting 5 home runs. He fell off in the second half, but even with a .232 BA, his OBP was .364, and the Yanks scored him at every turn. Unless NY makes a deal for someone like Carl Crawford, Gardner should continue to hone his craft. (LS)

**Forecast**

| Player | Age | AB | HR | R | RBI | SB | BA | OBP | SLG | $1L | Pts |
|---|---|---|---|---|---|---|---|---|---|---|---|
| Gardner B | 27 | 441 | 5 | 75 | 40 | 40 | .261 | .357 | .363 | $17 | 330 |
| **Mini-Browser** | **Age** | **AB** | **HR** | **R** | **RBI** | **SB** | **BA** | **OBP** | **SLG** | **$1L** | **Pts** |
| Jones A | 25 | 493 | 17 | 72 | 66 | 11 | .279 | .326 | .458 | $18 | 300 |
| Ibanez R | 38 | 551 | 24 | 78 | 90 | 6 | .272 | .345 | .483 | $18 | 410 |
| Zobrist B | 29 | 512 | 18 | 72 | 72 | 18 | .258 | .362 | .434 | $18 | 380 |
| Byrd M | 33 | 559 | 18 | 78 | 72 | 6 | .290 | .346 | .458 | $17 | 370 |
| Wells V | 32 | 568 | 18 | 72 | 78 | 12 | .264 | .318 | .452 | $17 | 390 |

**Minors (2010)** / **Skills**

| Level | Leag | AB | HR | R | RBI | SB | BA | OBP | SLG | CT% | H% | BB% | Bash |
|---|---|---|---|---|---|---|---|---|---|---|---|---|---|
| A | — | — | — | — | — | — | — | — | — | — | — | — | — |
| AA | — | — | — | — | — | — | — | — | — | — | — | — | — |
| AAA | — | — | — | — | — | — | — | — | — | — | — | — | — |

**Competition at LF** — **Stats in 2010**

| Bats | Player | GSvR | GSvL | Sub | OPS |
|---|---|---|---|---|---|
| LH | Gardner B | 81 | 30 | 12 | .762 |
| RH | Kearns A | 3 | 17 | 2 | .746 |
| RH | Thames M | 4 | 15 | 6 | .841 |
| RH | Russo K | 4 | 6 | 1 | .470 |

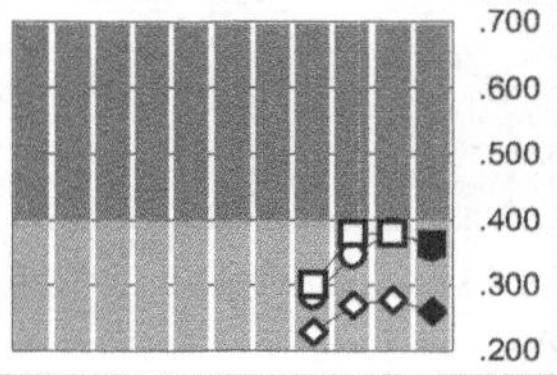


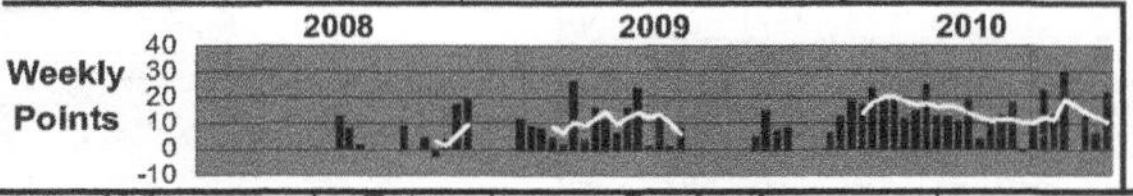


**Majors** / **Skills** / **Value** / **Extra** / **Production** / **OPS** / **Scoresheet**

| Yr | Team | AB | HR | R | RBI | SB | BA | OBP | SLG | CT% | H% | BB% | Bash | $1L | $2L | Pts | RAA | 2B | 3B | CS | FB-LD-GB | HR/fb | RBI% | RS% | OPS | 1st Hf | 2nd Hf | vs RH | vs LH | Rnge | vRH | vLH |
|---|---|---|---|---|---|---|---|---|---|---|---|---|---|---|---|---|---|---|---|---|---|---|---|---|---|---|---|---|---|---|---|---|
| 07 | — | — | — | — | — | — | — | — | — | — | — | — | — | — | — | — | — | — | — | — | — | — | — | — | — | — | — | — | — | — | — | — |
| 08 | NYY | 127 | 0 | 18 | 16 | 13 | .228 | .283 | .299 | 76% | 30% | 6% | 1.31 | $1 | -$12 | 80 | –9 | 5 | 2 | 1 | 35-17-48 | 0% | 25% | 46% | .582 | .429 | .643 | .656 | .250 | — | — | — |
| 09 | NYY | 248 | 3 | 48 | 23 | 26 | .270 | .345 | .379 | 84% | 32% | 9% | 1.40 | $9 | -$3 | 200 | –4 | 6 | 6 | 5 | 33-18-49 | 4% | 19% | 48% | .724 | .757 | .624 | .708 | .781 | 2.12 | +27 | –82 |
| 10 | NYY | 477 | 5 | 97 | 47 | 47 | .277 | .383 | .379 | 79% | 35% | 14% | 1.37 | $26 | $17 | 390 | +6 | 20 | 7 | 9 | 28-19-53 | 5% | 16% | 44% | .762 | .811 | .698 | .778 | .725 | 2.15 | +21 | –64 |

## Ryan Garko

**200 PA | $1 | 110 pts**

1B-6, DH-5 — Owned: 0% — RH

If Garko could do just one other thing besides mashing lefties, he might not have spent 2010 entrenched in Triple-A. Alas, he does not. Garko has proven moderately useful in the past, but teams don't generally lust after bad-fielding, platoon-only first basemen with mediocre power. Expect an NRI. (JM)

**Forecast**

| Player | Age | AB | HR | R | RBI | SB | BA | OBP | SLG | $1L | Pts |
|---|---|---|---|---|---|---|---|---|---|---|---|
| Garko R | 30 | 182 | 8 | 20 | 26 | 0 | .264 | .339 | .431 | $1 | 110 |
| **Mini-Browser** | **Age** | **AB** | **HR** | **R** | **RBI** | **SB** | **BA** | **OBP** | **SLG** | **$1L** | **Pts** |
| Nady X | 32 | 274 | 12 | 36 | 42 | 0 | .274 | .327 | .452 | $5 | 160 |
| Pearce S | 27 | 280 | 12 | 33 | 36 | 3 | .268 | .342 | .483 | $5 | 190 |
| Glaus T | 34 | 246 | 12 | 36 | 45 | 0 | .256 | .365 | .449 | $5 | 170 |
| Wallace B | 24 | 421 | 14 | 48 | 43 | 0 | .237 | .309 | .397 | $4 | 180 |
| Kotchman C | 28 | 218 | 5 | 23 | 30 | 0 | .264 | .331 | .401 | $1 | 140 |

**Minors (2010)** / **Skills**

| Level | Leag | AB | HR | R | RBI | SB | BA | OBP | SLG | CT% | H% | BB% | Bash |
|---|---|---|---|---|---|---|---|---|---|---|---|---|---|
| A | — | — | — | — | — | — | — | — | — | — | — | — | — |
| AA | — | — | — | — | — | — | — | — | — | — | — | — | — |
| AAA | PCL | 340 | 12 | 42 | 48 | 1 | .235 | .326 | .379 | 82% | 29% | 11% | 1.61 |

**Competition at 1B** — **Stats in 2010**

| Bats | Player | GSvR | GSvL | Sub | OPS |
|---|---|---|---|---|---|
| LH | Moreland M | 35 | 3 | 2 | .833 |
| LH | Davis C | 23 | 7 | 11 | .571 |
| RH | Cantu J | 4 | 17 | 2 | .695 |

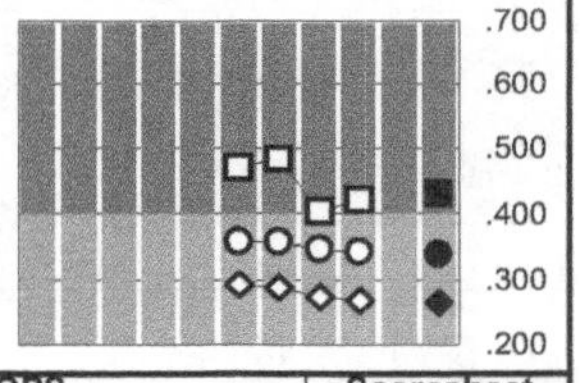


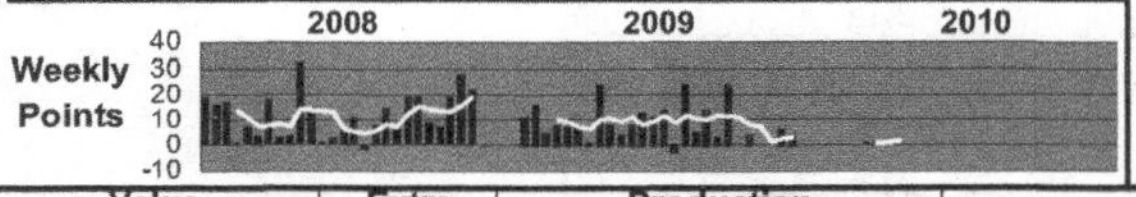


**Majors** / **Skills** / **Value** / **Extra** / **Production** / **OPS** / **Scoresheet**

| Yr | Team | AB | HR | R | RBI | SB | BA | OBP | SLG | CT% | H% | BB% | Bash | $1L | $2L | Pts | RAA | 2B | 3B | CS | FB-LD-GB | HR/fb | RBI% | RS% | OPS | 1st Hf | 2nd Hf | vs RH | vs LH | Rnge | vRH | vLH |
|---|---|---|---|---|---|---|---|---|---|---|---|---|---|---|---|---|---|---|---|---|---|---|---|---|---|---|---|---|---|---|---|---|
| 07 | CLE | 484 | 21 | 62 | 61 | 0 | .289 | .359 | .483 | 81% | 36% | 6% | 1.67 | $15 | $5 | 300 | –5 | 29 | 1 | 1 | 44-19-38 | 12% | 14% | 24% | .842 | .821 | .864 | .812 | .914 | 1.83 | –20 | +52 |
| 08 | CLE | 495 | 14 | 61 | 90 | 0 | .273 | .346 | .404 | 83% | 33% | 8% | 1.48 | $15 | $5 | 310 | –18 | 21 | 1 | 0 | 41-20-39 | 8% | 25% | 26% | .750 | .668 | .868 | .714 | .857 | 1.81 | –26 | +65 |
| 09 | 2TM | 354 | 13 | 39 | 51 | 0 | .268 | .344 | .421 | 86% | 31% | 7% | 1.57 | $3 | -$4 | 220 | –13 | 13 | 1 | 0 | 40-17-43 | 11% | 19% | 21% | .765 | .797 | .720 | .713 | .870 | 1.80 | –28 | +70 |
| 10 | TEX | 33 | 0 | 0 | 3 | 0 | .091 | .167 | .091 | 88% | 10% | 8% | 1.00 | -$5 | -$22 | 0 | –8 | 0 | 0 | 0 | 48-3-48 | 0% | 16% | 0% | .258 | .258 | — | .237 | .269 | — | –28 | +66 |

## Craig Gentry

**100 PA | $-4 | 50 pts**

OF-15 (CF-7, LF-6, RF-4) — Owned: 0% — RH

Gentry is frequently cited as one of the best defensive OF's in the TEX organization, a label that he gained through plus-plus speed and great instincts. However, worries about his bat linger, and at 27, he has shed his youth-induced luster. Maybe he can be a late-blooming poor man's Willy Taveras somewhere. (JM)

**Forecast**

| Player | Age | AB | HR | R | RBI | SB | BA | OBP | SLG | $1L | Pts |
|---|---|---|---|---|---|---|---|---|---|---|---|
| Gentry C | 27 | 95 | 2 | 11 | 7 | 5 | .221 | .282 | .330 | -$4 | 50 |
| **Mini-Browser** | **Age** | **AB** | **HR** | **R** | **RBI** | **SB** | **BA** | **OBP** | **SLG** | **$1L** | **Pts** |
| Ryal R | 28 | 90 | 3 | 11 | 10 | 0 | .245 | .297 | .423 | -$3 | 40 |
| Thomas C | 27 | 88 | 2 | 11 | 9 | 4 | .238 | .320 | .380 | -$3 | 50 |
| Gross G | 31 | 88 | 2 | 11 | 11 | 2 | .249 | .339 | .402 | -$3 | 50 |
| Inglett J | 32 | 67 | 1 | 8 | 7 | 2 | .278 | .343 | .403 | -$3 | 40 |
| Willits R | 29 | 83 | 0 | 13 | 7 | 4 | .252 | .343 | .304 | -$3 | 50 |

**Minors (2010)** / **Skills**

| Level | Leag | AB | HR | R | RBI | SB | BA | OBP | SLG | CT% | H% | BB% | Bash |
|---|---|---|---|---|---|---|---|---|---|---|---|---|---|
| A | — | — | — | — | — | — | — | — | — | — | — | — | — |
| AA | — | — | — | — | — | — | — | — | — | — | — | — | — |
| AAA | PCL | 259 | 4 | 43 | 35 | 12 | .309 | .393 | .413 | 82% | 38% | 10% | 1.34 |

**Competition at CF** — **Stats in 2010**

| Bats | Player | GSvR | GSvL | Sub | OPS |
|---|---|---|---|---|---|
| LH | Borbon J | 96 | 26 | 11 | .649 |
| LH | Hamilton J | 22 | 17 | 1 | 1.044 |
| LH | Murphy D | 6 | 4 | 0 | .806 |

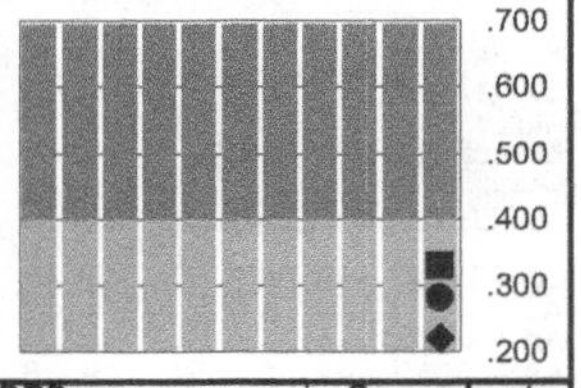


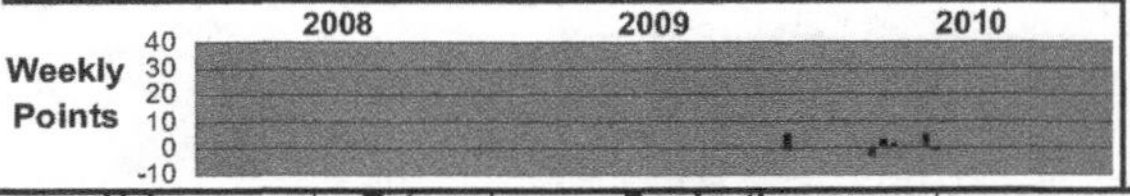


**Majors** / **Skills** / **Value** / **Extra** / **Production** / **OPS** / **Scoresheet**

| Yr | Team | AB | HR | R | RBI | SB | BA | OBP | SLG | CT% | H% | BB% | Bash | $1L | $2L | Pts | RAA | 2B | 3B | CS | FB-LD-GB | HR/fb | RBI% | RS% | OPS | 1st Hf | 2nd Hf | vs RH | vs LH | Rnge | vRH | vLH |
|---|---|---|---|---|---|---|---|---|---|---|---|---|---|---|---|---|---|---|---|---|---|---|---|---|---|---|---|---|---|---|---|---|
| 07 | — | — | — | — | — | — | — | — | — | — | — | — | — | — | — | — | — | — | — | — | — | — | — | — | — | — | — | — | — | — | — | — |
| 08 | — | — | — | — | — | — | — | — | — | — | — | — | — | — | — | — | — | — | — | — | — | — | — | — | — | — | — | — | — | — | — | — |
| 09 | TEX | 17 | 0 | 4 | 1 | 0 | .118 | .211 | .176 | 71% | 17% | 11% | 1.50 | -$4 | -$19 | 0 | –2 | 1 | 0 | 0 | 42-25-33 | 0% | 8% | 100% | .387 | — | .387 | .277 | .750 | — | — | — |
| 10 | TEX | 33 | 0 | 4 | 3 | 1 | .212 | .229 | .212 | 67% | 32% | 3% | 1.00 | -$4 | -$20 | 10 | –4 | 0 | 0 | 0 | 48-9-43 | 0% | 20% | 50% | .441 | .441 | — | .633 | .348 | 2.12 | –18 | +44 |

## Jody Gerut

**75 PA | $-2 | 50 pts**

OF-18 (CF-10, LF-6, RF-4) — Owned: 0% — LH

After the Brewers waived Gerut, the Padres signed him the same day they lost Tony Gwynn Jr., but San Diego never called up Gerut. Gerut's history makes him a signable asset, but his limp performance with Milwaukee means that deal will probably put him in the minors, where he'll await an injury call-up. (MS)

**Forecast**

| Player | Age | AB | HR | R | RBI | SB | BA | OBP | SLG | $1L | Pts |
|---|---|---|---|---|---|---|---|---|---|---|---|
| Gerut J | 33 | 68 | 3 | 11 | 9 | 2 | .265 | .322 | .467 | -$2 | 50 |
| **Mini-Browser** | **Age** | **AB** | **HR** | **R** | **RBI** | **SB** | **BA** | **OBP** | **SLG** | **$1L** | **Pts** |
| Maxwell J | 27 | 85 | 4 | 13 | 10 | 5 | .212 | .317 | .406 | -$2 | 50 |
| Church R | 32 | 94 | 3 | 13 | 12 | 1 | .267 | .339 | .433 | -$2 | 60 |
| Duncan S | 31 | 89 | 5 | 12 | 14 | 0 | .248 | .338 | .470 | -$2 | 60 |
| Carter C | 28 | 91 | 4 | 10 | 12 | 0 | .263 | .328 | .444 | -$2 | 60 |
| Gillespie C | 26 | 86 | 3 | 12 | 10 | 2 | .244 | .336 | .436 | -$2 | 50 |

**Minors (2010)** / **Skills**

| Level | Leag | AB | HR | R | RBI | SB | BA | OBP | SLG | CT% | H% | BB% | Bash |
|---|---|---|---|---|---|---|---|---|---|---|---|---|---|
| A | — | — | — | — | — | — | — | — | — | — | — | — | — |
| AA | — | — | — | — | — | — | — | — | — | — | — | — | — |
| AAA | PCL | 53 | 1 | 7 | 11 | 0 | .302 | .393 | .434 | 91% | 33% | 11% | 1.44 |

**Competition at CF** — **Stats in 2010**

| Bats | Player | GSvR | GSvL | Sub | OPS |
|---|---|---|---|---|---|
| RH | Gomez C | 34 | 32 | 9 | .655 |
| RH | Cain L | 22 | 13 | 3 | .763 |
| LH | Dickerson C | 11 | 0 | 3 | .518 |
| LH | Gerut J | 6 | 2 | 2 | .596 |

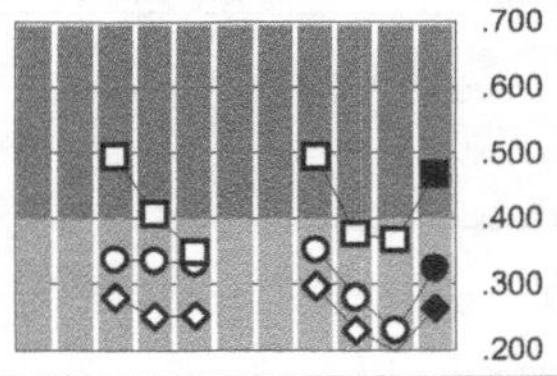


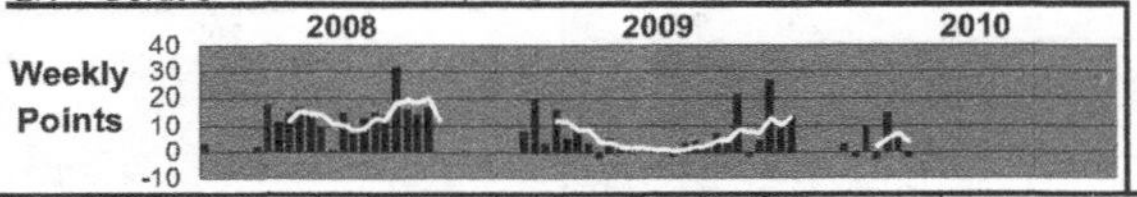


**Majors** / **Skills** / **Value** / **Extra** / **Production** / **OPS** / **Scoresheet**

| Yr | Team | AB | HR | R | RBI | SB | BA | OBP | SLG | CT% | H% | BB% | Bash | $1L | $2L | Pts | RAA | 2B | 3B | CS | FB-LD-GB | HR/fb | RBI% | RS% | OPS | 1st Hf | 2nd Hf | vs RH | vs LH | Rnge | vRH | vLH |
|---|---|---|---|---|---|---|---|---|---|---|---|---|---|---|---|---|---|---|---|---|---|---|---|---|---|---|---|---|---|---|---|---|
| 07 | — | — | — | — | — | — | — | — | — | — | — | — | — | — | — | — | — | — | — | — | — | — | — | — | — | — | — | — | — | 2.05 | +28 | –96 |
| 08 | SD | 328 | 14 | 46 | 43 | 6 | .296 | .351 | .494 | 84% | 35% | 8% | 1.67 | $11 | $1 | 240 | +13 | 15 | 4 | 4 | 36-17-47 | 14% | 22% | 29% | .845 | .750 | .996 | .826 | .923 | — | — | — |
| 09 | 2TM | 274 | 9 | 40 | 35 | 6 | .230 | .279 | .376 | 84% | 27% | 6% | 1.63 | $4 | -$8 | 160 | –10 | 13 | 0 | 2 | 33-20-47 | 12% | 18% | 42% | .654 | .535 | .802 | .660 | .606 | 2.16 | +15 | –49 |
| 10 | MIL | 71 | 2 | 7 | 8 | 0 | .197 | .230 | .366 | 76% | 26% | 4% | 1.86 | -$4 | -$19 | 30 | –5 | 4 | 1 | 1 | 29-10-61 | 13% | 13% | 33% | .596 | .596 | — | .444 | .981 | 2.16 | +12 | –41 |

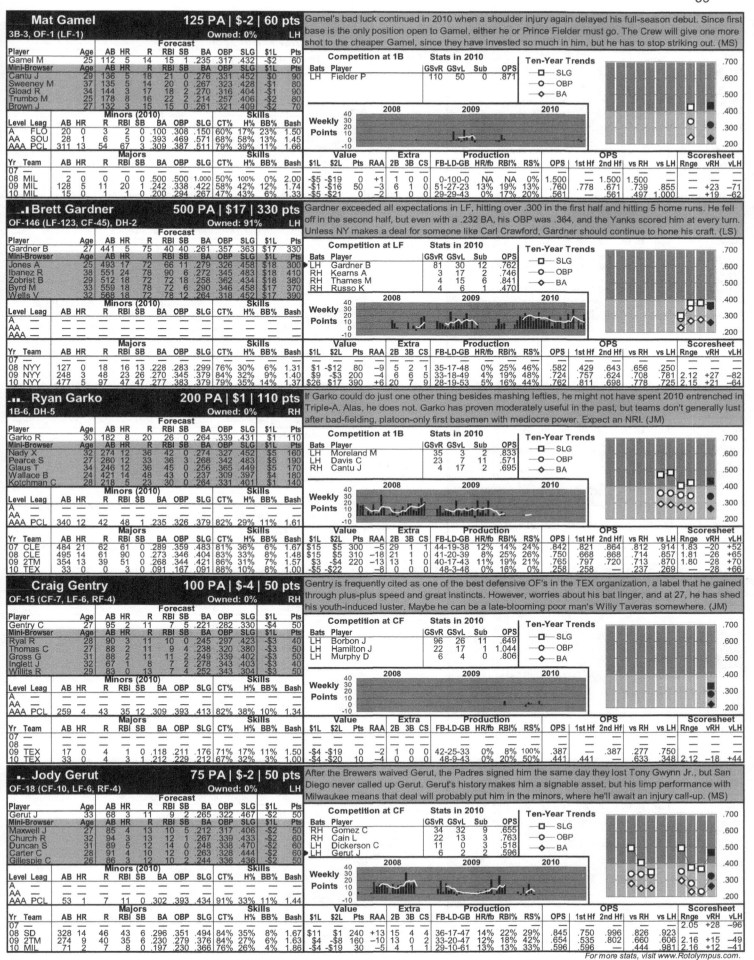

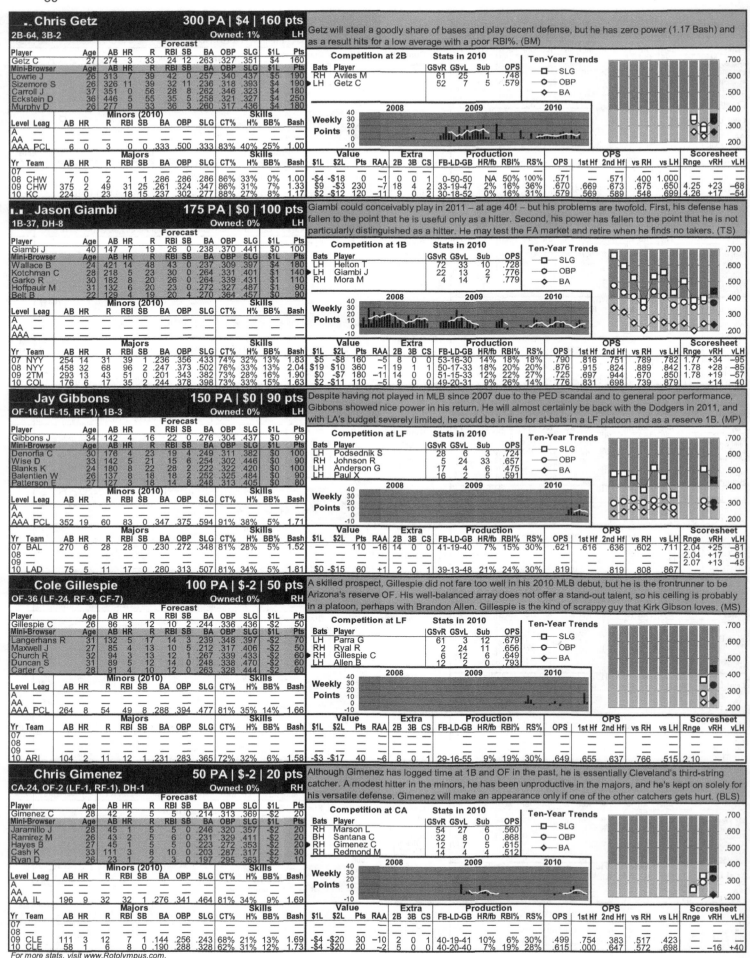

## Chris Getz — 300 PA | $4 | 160 pts

2B-64, 3B-2 — Owned: 1% — LH

Getz will steal a goodly share of bases and play decent defense, but he has zero power (1.17 Bash) and as a result hits for a low average with a poor RBI%. (BM)

| Player | Age | AB | HR | R | RBI | SB | BA | OBP | SLG | $1L | Pts |
|---|---|---|---|---|---|---|---|---|---|---|---|
| **Forecast** | | | | | | | | | | | |
| Getz C | 27 | 274 | 3 | 33 | 24 | 12 | .263 | .327 | .351 | $4 | 160 |
| **Mini-Browser** | | | | | | | | | | | |
| Lowrie J | 26 | 313 | 7 | 39 | 42 | 0 | .257 | .340 | .437 | $5 | 190 |
| Sizemore S | 26 | 326 | 11 | 39 | 32 | 11 | .236 | .318 | .393 | $4 | 190 |
| Carroll J | 37 | 351 | 0 | 56 | 28 | 8 | .262 | .346 | .323 | $4 | 180 |
| Eckstein D | 36 | 446 | 5 | 55 | 35 | 5 | .258 | .321 | .327 | $4 | 250 |
| Murphy D | 26 | 277 | 9 | 33 | 36 | 3 | .260 | .317 | .436 | $4 | 180 |

Competition at 2B — Stats in 2010

| Bats | Player | GSvR | GSvL | Sub | OPS |
|---|---|---|---|---|---|
| RH | Aviles M | 61 | 25 | 1 | .748 |
| LH | Getz C | 52 | 7 | 5 | .579 |

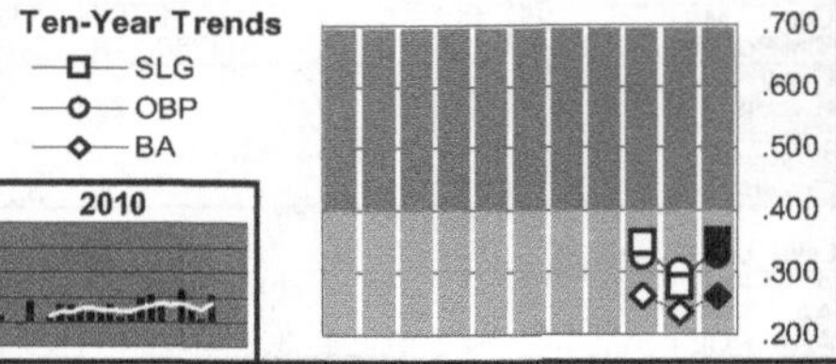


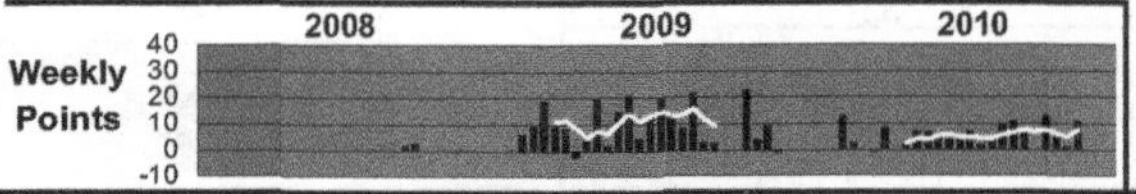


Minors (2010) / Skills

| Level | Leag | AB | HR | R | RBI | SB | BA | OBP | SLG | CT% | H% | BB% | Bash |
|---|---|---|---|---|---|---|---|---|---|---|---|---|---|
| A | — | — | — | — | — | — | — | — | — | — | — | — | — |
| AA | — | — | — | — | — | — | — | — | — | — | — | — | — |
| AAA | PCL | 6 | 0 | 3 | 0 | 0 | .333 | .500 | .333 | 83% | 40% | 25% | 1.00 |

Majors / Skills / Value / Extra / Production / OPS / Scoresheet

| Yr | Team | AB | HR | R | RBI | SB | BA | OBP | SLG | CT% | H% | BB% | Bash | $1L | $2L | Pts | RAA | 2B | 3B | CS | FB-LD-GB | HR/fb | RBI% | RS% | OPS | 1st Hf | 2nd Hf | vs RH | vs LH | Rnge | vRH | vLH |
|---|---|---|---|---|---|---|---|---|---|---|---|---|---|---|---|---|---|---|---|---|---|---|---|---|---|---|---|---|---|---|---|---|
| 07 | — | — | — | — | — | — | — | — | — | — | — | — | — | — | — | — | — | — | — | — | — | — | — | — | — | — | — | — | — | — | — | — |
| 08 | CHW | 7 | 0 | 2 | 1 | 1 | .286 | .286 | .286 | 86% | 33% | 0% | 1.00 | -$4 | -$18 | 0 | –1 | 0 | 0 | 1 | 0-50-50 | NA | 50% | 100% | .571 | — | .571 | .400 | 1.000 | — | — | — |
| 09 | CHW | 375 | 2 | 49 | 31 | 25 | .261 | .324 | .347 | 86% | 31% | 7% | 1.33 | $9 | -$3 | 230 | –7 | 18 | 4 | 2 | 33-19-47 | 2% | 16% | 36% | .670 | .669 | .673 | .675 | .650 | 4.25 | +23 | –68 |
| 10 | KC | 224 | 0 | 23 | 18 | 15 | .237 | .302 | .277 | 88% | 27% | 8% | 1.17 | $2 | -$12 | 120 | –11 | 9 | 0 | 2 | 30-18-52 | 0% | 16% | 31% | .579 | .569 | .589 | .548 | .699 | 4.26 | +17 | –54 |

## Jason Giambi — 175 PA | $0 | 100 pts

1B-37, DH-8 — Owned: 0% — LH

Giambi could conceivably play in 2011 – at age 40! – but his problems are twofold. First, his defense has fallen to the point that he is useful only as a hitter. Second, his power has fallen to the point that he is not particularly distinguished as a hitter. He may test the FA market and retire when he finds no takers. (TS)

| Player | Age | AB | HR | R | RBI | SB | BA | OBP | SLG | $1L | Pts |
|---|---|---|---|---|---|---|---|---|---|---|---|
| **Forecast** | | | | | | | | | | | |
| Giambi J | 40 | 147 | 7 | 19 | 26 | 0 | .238 | .370 | .441 | $0 | 100 |
| **Mini-Browser** | | | | | | | | | | | |
| Wallace B | 24 | 421 | 14 | 48 | 43 | 0 | .237 | .309 | .397 | $4 | 180 |
| Kotchman C | 28 | 218 | 5 | 23 | 30 | 0 | .264 | .331 | .401 | $1 | 140 |
| Garko R | 30 | 182 | 8 | 20 | 26 | 0 | .264 | .339 | .431 | $1 | 110 |
| Hoffpauir M | 31 | 132 | 6 | 20 | 23 | 0 | .272 | .327 | .487 | $1 | 90 |
| Belt B | 22 | 129 | 4 | 19 | 20 | 4 | .270 | .364 | .457 | $0 | 90 |

Competition at 1B — Stats in 2010

| Bats | Player | GSvR | GSvL | Sub | OPS |
|---|---|---|---|---|---|
| LH | Helton T | 72 | 33 | 10 | .728 |
| LH | Giambi J | 22 | 13 | 2 | .776 |
| RH | Mora M | 4 | 14 | 7 | .779 |

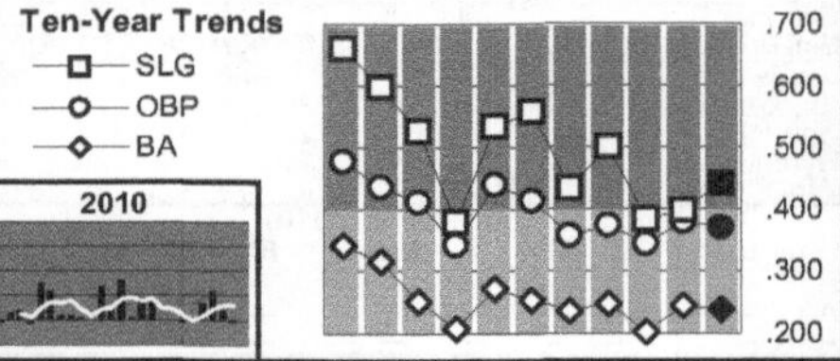


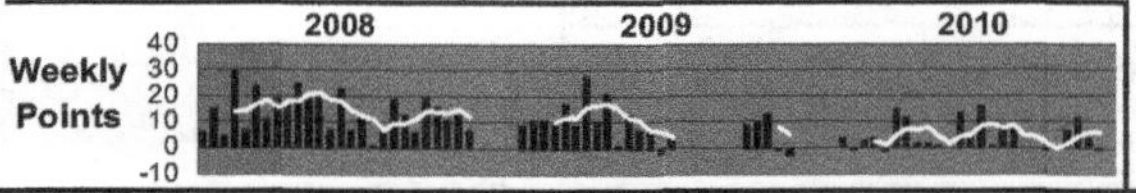


Minors (2010) / Skills

| Level | Leag | AB | HR | R | RBI | SB | BA | OBP | SLG | CT% | H% | BB% | Bash |
|---|---|---|---|---|---|---|---|---|---|---|---|---|---|
| A | — | — | — | — | — | — | — | — | — | — | — | — | — |
| AA | — | — | — | — | — | — | — | — | — | — | — | — | — |
| AAA | — | — | — | — | — | — | — | — | — | — | — | — | — |

Majors / Skills / Value / Extra / Production / OPS / Scoresheet

| Yr | Team | AB | HR | R | RBI | SB | BA | OBP | SLG | CT% | H% | BB% | Bash | $1L | $2L | Pts | RAA | 2B | 3B | CS | FB-LD-GB | HR/fb | RBI% | RS% | OPS | 1st Hf | 2nd Hf | vs RH | vs LH | Rnge | vRH | vLH |
|---|---|---|---|---|---|---|---|---|---|---|---|---|---|---|---|---|---|---|---|---|---|---|---|---|---|---|---|---|---|---|---|---|
| 07 | NYY | 254 | 14 | 31 | 39 | 1 | .236 | .356 | .433 | 74% | 32% | 13% | 1.83 | $5 | -$8 | 160 | –5 | 8 | 0 | 0 | 53-16-30 | 14% | 18% | 18% | .790 | .816 | .751 | .789 | .782 | 1.77 | +34 | –95 |
| 08 | NYY | 458 | 32 | 68 | 96 | 2 | .247 | .373 | .502 | 76% | 33% | 13% | 2.04 | $19 | $10 | 360 | –1 | 19 | 1 | 1 | 50-17-33 | 18% | 20% | 20% | .876 | .915 | .824 | .889 | .842 | 1.78 | +28 | –85 |
| 09 | 2TM | 293 | 13 | 43 | 51 | 0 | .201 | .343 | .382 | 73% | 28% | 16% | 1.90 | $0 | -$7 | 180 | –11 | 14 | 0 | 0 | 51-15-33 | 12% | 22% | 27% | .725 | .697 | .944 | .670 | .850 | 1.78 | +19 | –57 |
| 10 | COL | 176 | 6 | 17 | 35 | 2 | .244 | .378 | .398 | 73% | 33% | 15% | 1.63 | $2 | -$11 | 110 | –5 | 9 | 0 | 0 | 49-20-31 | 9% | 26% | 14% | .776 | .831 | .698 | .739 | .879 | — | +14 | –40 |

## Jay Gibbons — 150 PA | $0 | 90 pts

OF-16 (LF-15, RF-1), 1B-3 — Owned: 0% — LH

Despite having not played in MLB since 2007 due to the PED scandal and to general poor performance, Gibbons showed nice power in his return. He will almost certainly be back with the Dodgers in 2011, and with LA's budget severely limited, he could be in line for at-bats in a LF platoon and as a reserve 1B. (MP)

| Player | Age | AB | HR | R | RBI | SB | BA | OBP | SLG | $1L | Pts |
|---|---|---|---|---|---|---|---|---|---|---|---|
| **Forecast** | | | | | | | | | | | |
| Gibbons J | 34 | 142 | 4 | 16 | 22 | 0 | .276 | .304 | .437 | $0 | 90 |
| **Mini-Browser** | | | | | | | | | | | |
| Denorfia C | 30 | 176 | 4 | 23 | 19 | 4 | .249 | .311 | .382 | $0 | 100 |
| Wise D | 33 | 142 | 5 | 21 | 15 | 6 | .254 | .302 | .446 | $0 | 90 |
| Blanks K | 24 | 180 | 8 | 22 | 28 | 2 | .222 | .322 | .420 | $0 | 100 |
| Balentien W | 26 | 137 | 8 | 18 | 18 | 2 | .252 | .325 | .484 | $0 | 90 |
| Patterson E | 27 | 127 | 3 | 18 | 14 | 8 | .248 | .313 | .405 | $0 | 80 |

Competition at LF — Stats in 2010

| Bats | Player | GSvR | GSvL | Sub | OPS |
|---|---|---|---|---|---|
| LH | Podsednik S | 28 | 6 | 3 | .724 |
| RH | Johnson R | 5 | 24 | 33 | .657 |
| LH | Anderson G | 17 | 4 | 6 | .475 |
| LH | Paul X | 16 | 2 | 5 | .591 |

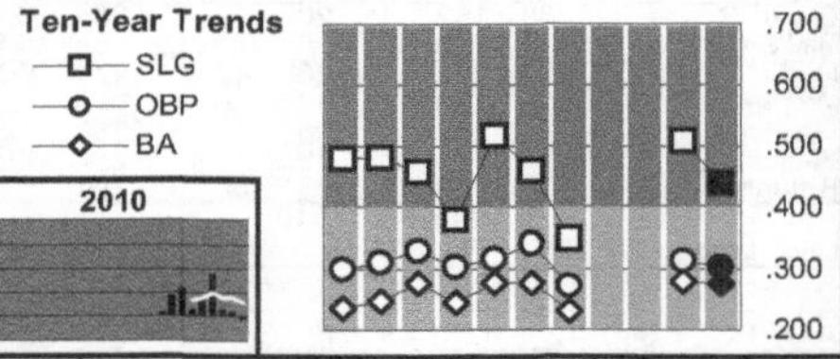


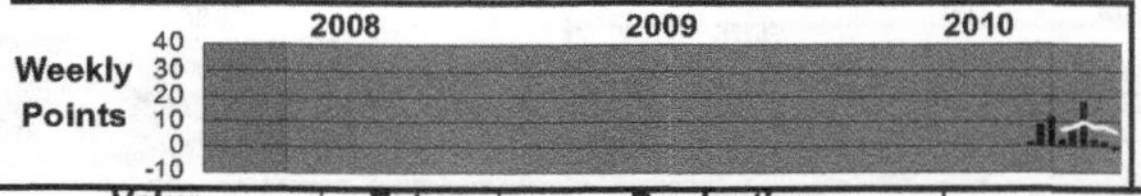


Minors (2010) / Skills

| Level | Leag | AB | HR | R | RBI | SB | BA | OBP | SLG | CT% | H% | BB% | Bash |
|---|---|---|---|---|---|---|---|---|---|---|---|---|---|
| A | — | — | — | — | — | — | — | — | — | — | — | — | — |
| AA | — | — | — | — | — | — | — | — | — | — | — | — | — |
| AAA | PCL | 352 | 19 | 60 | 83 | 0 | .347 | .375 | .594 | 91% | 38% | 5% | 1.71 |

Majors / Skills / Value / Extra / Production / OPS / Scoresheet

| Yr | Team | AB | HR | R | RBI | SB | BA | OBP | SLG | CT% | H% | BB% | Bash | $1L | $2L | Pts | RAA | 2B | 3B | CS | FB-LD-GB | HR/fb | RBI% | RS% | OPS | 1st Hf | 2nd Hf | vs RH | vs LH | Rnge | vRH | vLH |
|---|---|---|---|---|---|---|---|---|---|---|---|---|---|---|---|---|---|---|---|---|---|---|---|---|---|---|---|---|---|---|---|---|
| 07 | BAL | 270 | 6 | 28 | 28 | 0 | .230 | .272 | .348 | 81% | 28% | 5% | 1.52 | — | — | 110 | –16 | 14 | 0 | 0 | 41-19-40 | 7% | 15% | 30% | .621 | .616 | .636 | .602 | .711 | 2.04 | +25 | –81 |
| 08 | — | — | — | — | — | — | — | — | — | — | — | — | — | — | — | — | — | — | — | — | — | — | — | — | — | — | — | — | — | 2.04 | +17 | –61 |
| 09 | — | — | — | — | — | — | — | — | — | — | — | — | — | — | — | — | — | — | — | — | — | — | — | — | — | — | — | — | — | 2.07 | +13 | –45 |
| 10 | LAD | 75 | 5 | 11 | 17 | 0 | .280 | .313 | .507 | 81% | 34% | 5% | 1.81 | $0 | -$15 | 60 | +1 | 2 | 0 | 1 | 39-13-48 | 21% | 24% | 30% | .819 | — | .819 | .808 | .867 | — | — | — |

## Cole Gillespie — 100 PA | $-2 | 50 pts

OF-36 (LF-24, RF-9, CF-7) — Owned: 0% — RH

A skilled prospect, Gillespie did not fare too well in his 2010 MLB debut, but he is the frontrunner to be Arizona's reserve OF. His well-balanced array does not offer a stand-out talent, so his ceiling is probably in a platoon, perhaps with Brandon Allen. Gillespie is the kind of scrappy guy that Kirk Gibson loves. (MS)

| Player | Age | AB | HR | R | RBI | SB | BA | OBP | SLG | $1L | Pts |
|---|---|---|---|---|---|---|---|---|---|---|---|
| **Forecast** | | | | | | | | | | | |
| Gillespie C | 26 | 86 | 3 | 12 | 10 | 2 | .244 | .336 | .436 | -$2 | 50 |
| **Mini-Browser** | | | | | | | | | | | |
| Langerhans R | 31 | 132 | 5 | 17 | 14 | 3 | .239 | .348 | .397 | -$2 | 70 |
| Maxwell J | 27 | 85 | 4 | 13 | 10 | 5 | .212 | .317 | .406 | -$2 | 50 |
| Church R | 32 | 94 | 3 | 13 | 12 | 1 | .267 | .339 | .433 | -$2 | 60 |
| Duncan S | 31 | 89 | 5 | 12 | 14 | 0 | .248 | .338 | .470 | -$2 | 60 |
| Carter C | 28 | 91 | 4 | 10 | 12 | 0 | .263 | .328 | .444 | -$2 | 60 |

Competition at LF — Stats in 2010

| Bats | Player | GSvR | GSvL | Sub | OPS |
|---|---|---|---|---|---|
| LH | Parra G | 61 | 3 | 12 | .679 |
| RH | Ryal R | 2 | 24 | 11 | .656 |
| RH | Gillespie C | 6 | 12 | 6 | .649 |
| LH | Allen B | 12 | 2 | 0 | .793 |

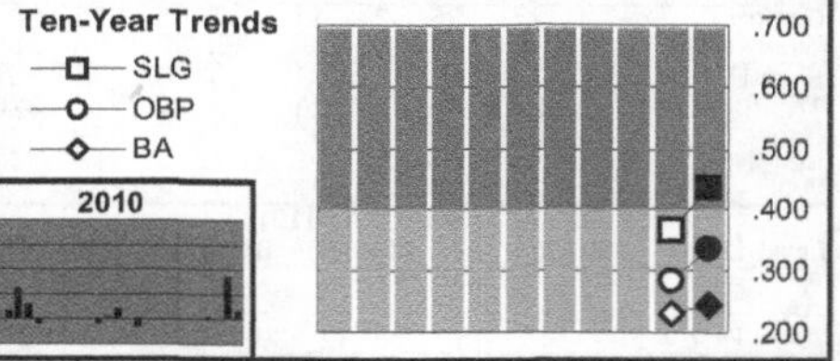


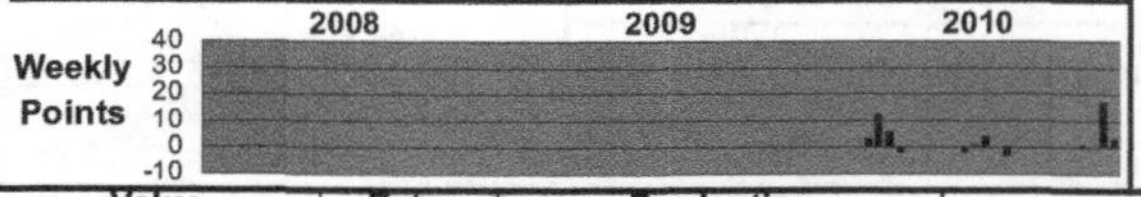


Minors (2010) / Skills

| Level | Leag | AB | HR | R | RBI | SB | BA | OBP | SLG | CT% | H% | BB% | Bash |
|---|---|---|---|---|---|---|---|---|---|---|---|---|---|
| A | — | — | — | — | — | — | — | — | — | — | — | — | — |
| AA | — | — | — | — | — | — | — | — | — | — | — | — | — |
| AAA | PCL | 264 | 8 | 54 | 49 | 8 | .288 | .394 | .477 | 81% | 35% | 14% | 1.66 |

Majors / Skills / Value / Extra / Production / OPS / Scoresheet

| Yr | Team | AB | HR | R | RBI | SB | BA | OBP | SLG | CT% | H% | BB% | Bash | $1L | $2L | Pts | RAA | 2B | 3B | CS | FB-LD-GB | HR/fb | RBI% | RS% | OPS | 1st Hf | 2nd Hf | vs RH | vs LH | Rnge | vRH | vLH |
|---|---|---|---|---|---|---|---|---|---|---|---|---|---|---|---|---|---|---|---|---|---|---|---|---|---|---|---|---|---|---|---|---|
| 07 | — | — | — | — | — | — | — | — | — | — | — | — | — | — | — | — | — | — | — | — | — | — | — | — | — | — | — | — | — | — | — | — |
| 08 | — | — | — | — | — | — | — | — | — | — | — | — | — | — | — | — | — | — | — | — | — | — | — | — | — | — | — | — | — | — | — | — |
| 09 | — | — | — | — | — | — | — | — | — | — | — | — | — | — | — | — | — | — | — | — | — | — | — | — | — | — | — | — | — | — | — | — |
| 10 | ARI | 104 | 2 | 11 | 12 | 1 | .231 | .283 | .365 | 72% | 32% | 6% | 1.58 | -$3 | -$17 | 40 | –6 | 8 | 0 | 1 | 29-16-55 | 9% | 19% | 30% | .649 | .655 | .637 | .766 | .515 | 2.10 | — | — |

## Chris Gimenez — 50 PA | $-2 | 20 pts

CA-24, OF-2 (LF-1, RF-1), DH-1 — Owned: 0% — RH

Although Gimenez has logged time at 1B and OF in the past, he is essentially Cleveland's third-string catcher. A modest hitter in the minors, he has been unproductive in the majors, and he's kept on solely for his versatile defense. Gimenez will make an appearance only if one of the other catchers gets hurt. (BLS)

| Player | Age | AB | HR | R | RBI | SB | BA | OBP | SLG | $1L | Pts |
|---|---|---|---|---|---|---|---|---|---|---|---|
| **Forecast** | | | | | | | | | | | |
| Gimenez C | 28 | 42 | 2 | 5 | 5 | 0 | .214 | .313 | .369 | -$2 | 20 |
| **Mini-Browser** | | | | | | | | | | | |
| Jaramillo J | 28 | 45 | 1 | 5 | 5 | 0 | .246 | .320 | .357 | -$2 | 20 |
| Ramirez M | 26 | 43 | 2 | 5 | 6 | 0 | .231 | .329 | .411 | -$2 | 20 |
| Hayes B | 27 | 45 | 1 | 5 | 5 | 0 | .223 | .272 | .353 | -$2 | 20 |
| Cash K | 33 | 111 | 3 | 8 | 10 | 0 | .203 | .287 | .317 | -$2 | 30 |
| Ryan D | 26 | 23 | 1 | 2 | 3 | 0 | .197 | .295 | .363 | -$2 | 10 |

Competition at CA — Stats in 2010

| Bats | Player | GSvR | GSvL | Sub | OPS |
|---|---|---|---|---|---|
| RH | Marson L | 54 | 27 | 6 | .560 |
| BH | Santana C | 32 | 8 | 0 | .868 |
| RH | Gimenez C | 12 | 7 | 5 | .615 |
| RH | Redmond M | 14 | 4 | 4 | .512 |

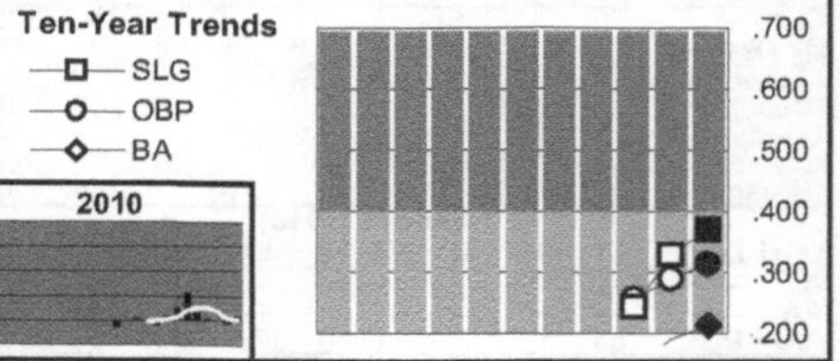


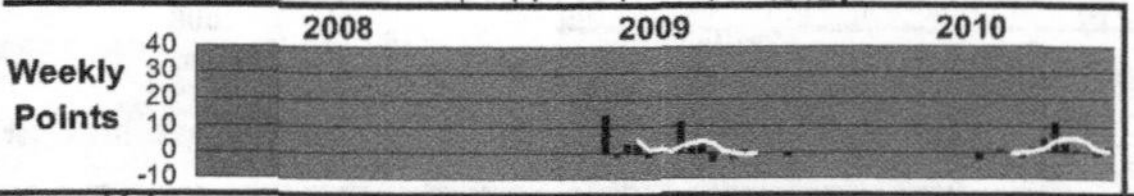


Minors (2010) / Skills

| Level | Leag | AB | HR | R | RBI | SB | BA | OBP | SLG | CT% | H% | BB% | Bash |
|---|---|---|---|---|---|---|---|---|---|---|---|---|---|
| A | — | — | — | — | — | — | — | — | — | — | — | — | — |
| AA | — | — | — | — | — | — | — | — | — | — | — | — | — |
| AAA | IL | 196 | 9 | 32 | 32 | 1 | .276 | .341 | .464 | 81% | 34% | 9% | 1.69 |

Majors / Skills / Value / Extra / Production / OPS / Scoresheet

| Yr | Team | AB | HR | R | RBI | SB | BA | OBP | SLG | CT% | H% | BB% | Bash | $1L | $2L | Pts | RAA | 2B | 3B | CS | FB-LD-GB | HR/fb | RBI% | RS% | OPS | 1st Hf | 2nd Hf | vs RH | vs LH | Rnge | vRH | vLH |
|---|---|---|---|---|---|---|---|---|---|---|---|---|---|---|---|---|---|---|---|---|---|---|---|---|---|---|---|---|---|---|---|---|
| 07 | — | — | — | — | — | — | — | — | — | — | — | — | — | — | — | — | — | — | — | — | — | — | — | — | — | — | — | — | — | — | — | — |
| 08 | — | — | — | — | — | — | — | — | — | — | — | — | — | — | — | — | — | — | — | — | — | — | — | — | — | — | — | — | — | — | — | — |
| 09 | CLE | 111 | 3 | 12 | 7 | 1 | .144 | .256 | .243 | 68% | 21% | 13% | 1.69 | -$4 | -$20 | 30 | –10 | 2 | 0 | 1 | 40-19-41 | 10% | 6% | 30% | .499 | .754 | .383 | .517 | .423 | — | — | — |
| 10 | CLE | 58 | 1 | 6 | 8 | 0 | .190 | .288 | .328 | 62% | 31% | 12% | 1.73 | -$4 | -$20 | 20 | –2 | 5 | 0 | 0 | 40-20-40 | 7% | 19% | 28% | .615 | .000 | .647 | .572 | .698 | — | –16 | +40 |

*For more stats, visit www.Rotolympus.com.*

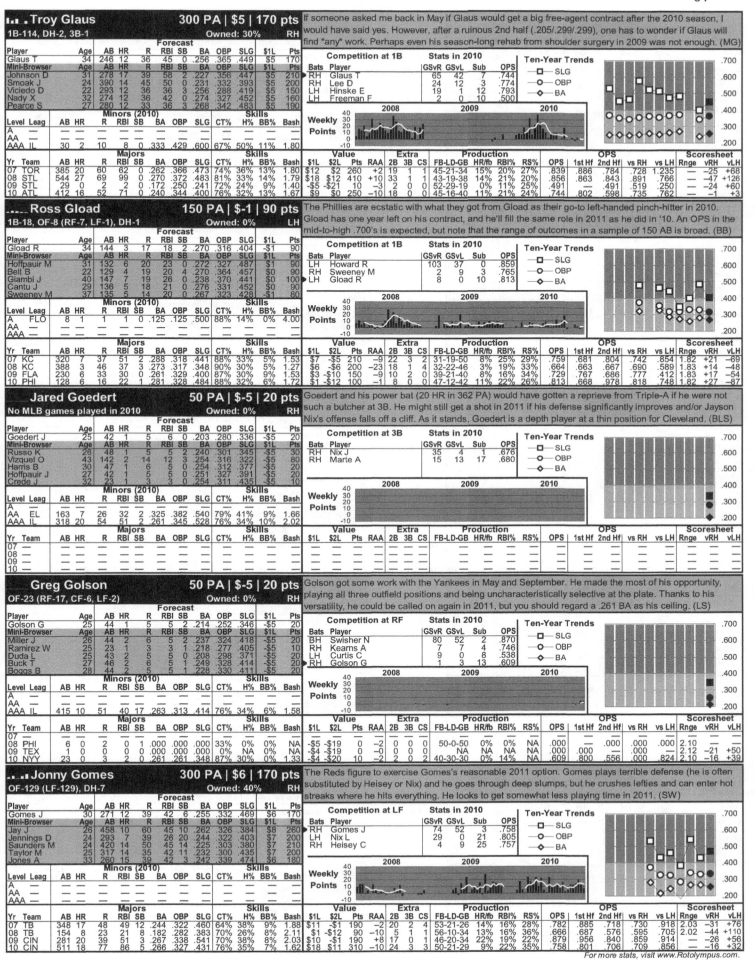

## Troy Glaus — 300 PA | $5 | 170 pts
1B-114, DH-2, 3B-1 — Owned: 30% — RH

If someone asked me back in May if Glaus would get a big free-agent contract after the 2010 season, I would have said yes. However, after a ruinous 2nd half (.205/.299/.299), one has to wonder if Glaus will find *any* work. Perhaps even his season-long rehab from shoulder surgery in 2009 was not enough. (MG)

### Forecast
| Player | Age | AB | HR | R | RBI | SB | BA | OBP | SLG | $1L | Pts |
|---|---|---|---|---|---|---|---|---|---|---|---|
| Glaus T | 34 | 246 | 12 | 36 | 45 | 0 | .256 | .365 | .449 | $5 | 170 |

### Mini-Browser
| Player | Age | AB | HR | R | RBI | SB | BA | OBP | SLG | $1L | Pts |
|---|---|---|---|---|---|---|---|---|---|---|---|
| Johnson D | 31 | 278 | 17 | 39 | 58 | 2 | .227 | .356 | .447 | $5 | 210 |
| Smoak J | 24 | 390 | 14 | 45 | 50 | 0 | .231 | .332 | .393 | $5 | 200 |
| Viciedo D | 22 | 293 | 12 | 36 | 36 | 3 | .256 | .288 | .419 | $5 | 150 |
| Nady X | 32 | 274 | 12 | 36 | 36 | 3 | .274 | .327 | .452 | $5 | 160 |
| Pearce S | 27 | 280 | 12 | 33 | 36 | 3 | .268 | .342 | .453 | $5 | 190 |

### Minors (2010) / Skills
| Level | Leag | AB | HR | R | RBI | SB | BA | OBP | SLG | CT% | H% | BB% | Bash |
|---|---|---|---|---|---|---|---|---|---|---|---|---|---|
| A | — | | | | | | | | | | | | |
| AA | — | | | | | | | | | | | | |
| AAA | IL | 30 | 2 | 10 | 8 | 0 | .333 | .429 | .600 | 67% | 50% | 11% | 1.80 |

### Competition at 1B / Stats in 2010
| Bats | Player | GSvR | GSvL | Sub | OPS |
|---|---|---|---|---|---|
| RH | Glaus T | 65 | 42 | 7 | .744 |
| RH | Lee D | 24 | 12 | 3 | .774 |
| LH | Hinske E | 19 | 1 | 12 | .793 |
| LH | Freeman F | 2 | 0 | 10 | .500 |

Ten-Year Trends: SLG / OBP / BA

### Majors / Skills
| Yr | Team | AB | HR | R | RBI | SB | BA | OBP | SLG | CT% | H% | BB% | Bash | $1L | $2L | Pts | RAA | 2B | 3B | CS | FB-LD-GB | HR/fb | RBI% | RS% | OPS | 1st Hf | 2nd Hf | vs RH | vs LH | Rnge | vRH | vLH |
|---|---|---|---|---|---|---|---|---|---|---|---|---|---|---|---|---|---|---|---|---|---|---|---|---|---|---|---|---|---|---|---|---|
| 07 | TOR | 385 | 20 | 60 | 62 | 0 | .262 | .366 | .473 | 74% | 36% | 13% | 1.80 | $12 | $12 | 260 | +2 | 19 | 1 | 1 | 45-21-34 | 15% | 20% | 27% | .839 | .886 | .784 | .728 | 1.235 | — | -25 | +68 |
| 08 | STL | 544 | 27 | 69 | 99 | 0 | .270 | .372 | .483 | 81% | 33% | 14% | 1.79 | $18 | $12 | 410 | +10 | 33 | 1 | 1 | 43-19-38 | 14% | 21% | 20% | .856 | .863 | .843 | .891 | .766 | — | -47 | +126 |
| 09 | STL | 29 | 0 | 2 | 2 | 0 | .172 | .250 | .241 | 72% | 24% | 9% | 1.40 | -$5 | -$21 | 10 | -3 | 2 | 0 | 0 | 52-29-19 | 0% | 11% | 25% | .491 | | — | .491 | .519 | .250 | — | -1 | +60 |
| 10 | ATL | 412 | 16 | 52 | 71 | 0 | .240 | .344 | .400 | 76% | 32% | 13% | 1.67 | $9 | $0 | 250 | -10 | 18 | 0 | 0 | 45-16-40 | 11% | 21% | 24% | .744 | .802 | .598 | .735 | .762 | — | — | +3 |

## Ross Gload — 150 PA | $-1 | 90 pts
1B-18, OF-8 (RF-7, LF-1), DH-1 — Owned: 0% — LH

The Phillies are ecstatic with what they got from Gload as their go-to left-handed pinch-hitter in 2010. Gload has one year left on his contract, and he'll fill the same role in 2011 as he did in '10. An OPS in the mid-to-high .700's is expected, but note that the range of outcomes in a sample of 150 AB is broad. (BB)

### Forecast
| Player | Age | AB | HR | R | RBI | SB | BA | OBP | SLG | $1L | Pts |
|---|---|---|---|---|---|---|---|---|---|---|---|
| Gload R | 34 | 144 | 3 | 17 | 18 | 2 | .270 | .316 | .404 | -$1 | 90 |

### Mini-Browser
| Player | Age | AB | HR | R | RBI | SB | BA | OBP | SLG | $1L | Pts |
|---|---|---|---|---|---|---|---|---|---|---|---|
| Hoffpauir M | 31 | 132 | 6 | 20 | 23 | 0 | .272 | .327 | .487 | $0 | 90 |
| Belt B | 22 | 129 | 4 | 19 | 20 | 4 | .270 | .364 | .457 | $0 | 90 |
| Giambi J | 40 | 147 | 5 | 19 | 26 | 0 | .238 | .370 | .441 | $0 | 100 |
| Cantu J | 29 | 136 | 5 | 18 | 21 | 0 | .276 | .331 | .452 | $0 | 90 |
| Sweeney M | 37 | 135 | 5 | 14 | 20 | 0 | .267 | .323 | .428 | -$1 | 80 |

### Minors (2010) / Skills
| Level | Leag | AB | HR | R | RBI | SB | BA | OBP | SLG | CT% | H% | BB% | Bash |
|---|---|---|---|---|---|---|---|---|---|---|---|---|---|
| A | FLO | 8 | 1 | 1 | 1 | 0 | .125 | .125 | .500 | 88% | 14% | 0% | 4.00 |
| AA | — | | | | | | | | | | | | |
| AAA | — | | | | | | | | | | | | |

### Competition at 1B / Stats in 2010
| Bats | Player | GSvR | GSvL | Sub | OPS |
|---|---|---|---|---|---|
| LH | Howard R | 103 | 37 | 0 | .859 |
| RH | Sweeney M | 2 | 9 | 3 | .765 |
| LH | Gload R | 8 | 0 | 10 | .813 |

Ten-Year Trends: SLG / OBP / BA

### Majors / Skills
| Yr | Team | AB | HR | R | RBI | SB | BA | OBP | SLG | CT% | H% | BB% | Bash | $1L | $2L | Pts | RAA | 2B | 3B | CS | FB-LD-GB | HR/fb | RBI% | RS% | OPS | 1st Hf | 2nd Hf | vs RH | vs LH | Rnge | vRH | vLH |
|---|---|---|---|---|---|---|---|---|---|---|---|---|---|---|---|---|---|---|---|---|---|---|---|---|---|---|---|---|---|---|---|---|
| 07 | KC | 320 | 7 | 37 | 51 | 2 | .288 | .318 | .441 | 88% | 33% | 5% | 1.53 | $7 | -$5 | 210 | -9 | 22 | 3 | 2 | 31-19-50 | 8% | 25% | 29% | .759 | .681 | .804 | .742 | .854 | 1.82 | +21 | -69 |
| 08 | KC | 388 | 3 | 46 | 37 | 3 | .273 | .317 | .348 | 90% | 30% | 5% | 1.27 | $6 | -$5 | 200 | -23 | 18 | 1 | 4 | 32-22-46 | 3% | 19% | 33% | .664 | .663 | .667 | .690 | .589 | 1.83 | +14 | -48 |
| 09 | FLA | 230 | 6 | 33 | 30 | 0 | .261 | .329 | .400 | 87% | 30% | 9% | 1.53 | $3 | -$10 | 150 | -9 | 10 | 2 | 0 | 39-21-40 | 8% | 16% | 34% | .729 | .767 | .686 | .777 | .412 | 1.83 | +17 | -54 |
| 10 | PHI | 128 | 6 | 16 | 22 | 1 | .281 | .328 | .484 | 88% | 32% | 6% | 1.72 | $1 | -$12 | 100 | -1 | 8 | 0 | 0 | 47-12-42 | 11% | 22% | 26% | .813 | .668 | .978 | .818 | .748 | 1.82 | +27 | -87 |

## Jared Goedert — 50 PA | $-5 | 20 pts
No MLB games played in 2010 — Owned: 0% — RH

Goedert and his power bat (20 HR in 362 PA) would have gotten a reprieve from Triple-A if he were not such a butcher at 3B. He might still get a shot in 2011 if his defense significantly improves and/or Jayson Nix's offense falls off a cliff. As it stands, Goedert is a depth player at a thin position for Cleveland. (BLS)

### Forecast
| Player | Age | AB | HR | R | RBI | SB | BA | OBP | SLG | $1L | Pts |
|---|---|---|---|---|---|---|---|---|---|---|---|
| Goedert J | 25 | 42 | 1 | 5 | 6 | 0 | .203 | .280 | .336 | -$5 | 20 |

### Mini-Browser
| Player | Age | AB | HR | R | RBI | SB | BA | OBP | SLG | $1L | Pts |
|---|---|---|---|---|---|---|---|---|---|---|---|
| Russo K | 26 | 48 | 1 | 5 | 5 | 2 | .240 | .301 | .345 | -$5 | 30 |
| Vizquel O | 43 | 142 | 2 | 14 | 12 | 3 | .254 | .316 | .322 | -$5 | 80 |
| Harris B | 30 | 47 | 1 | 6 | 5 | 0 | .254 | .323 | .377 | -$5 | 20 |
| Hoffpauir J | 27 | 43 | 1 | 5 | 5 | 0 | .251 | .327 | .391 | -$5 | 20 |
| Crede J | 32 | 43 | 1 | 3 | 3 | 0 | .254 | .311 | .435 | -$5 | 10 |

### Minors (2010) / Skills
| Level | Leag | AB | HR | R | RBI | SB | BA | OBP | SLG | CT% | H% | BB% | Bash |
|---|---|---|---|---|---|---|---|---|---|---|---|---|---|
| A | — | | | | | | | | | | | | |
| AA | EL | 163 | 7 | 26 | 32 | 2 | .325 | .382 | .540 | 79% | 41% | 9% | 1.66 |
| AAA | IL | 318 | 20 | 54 | 51 | 2 | .261 | .345 | .528 | 76% | 34% | 10% | 2.02 |

### Competition at 3B / Stats in 2010
| Bats | Player | GSvR | GSvL | Sub | OPS |
|---|---|---|---|---|---|
| RH | Nix J | 35 | 4 | 1 | .676 |
| RH | Marte A | 15 | 13 | 17 | .680 |

Ten-Year Trends: SLG / OBP / BA

### Majors / Skills
| Yr | Team | AB | HR | R | RBI | SB | BA | OBP | SLG | CT% | H% | BB% | Bash | $1L | $2L | Pts | RAA | 2B | 3B | CS | FB-LD-GB | HR/fb | RBI% | RS% | OPS | 1st Hf | 2nd Hf | vs RH | vs LH | Rnge | vRH | vLH |
|---|---|---|---|---|---|---|---|---|---|---|---|---|---|---|---|---|---|---|---|---|---|---|---|---|---|---|---|---|---|---|---|---|
| 07 | — | | | | | | | | | | | | | | | | | | | | | | | | | | | | | | | |
| 08 | — | | | | | | | | | | | | | | | | | | | | | | | | | | | | | | | |
| 09 | — | | | | | | | | | | | | | | | | | | | | | | | | | | | | | | | |
| 10 | — | | | | | | | | | | | | | | | | | | | | | | | | | | | | | | | |

## Greg Golson — 50 PA | $-5 | 20 pts
OF-23 (RF-17, CF-6, LF-2) — Owned: 0% — RH

Golson got some work with the Yankees in May and September. He made the most of his opportunity, playing all three outfield positions and being uncharacteristically selective at the plate. Thanks to his versatility, he could be called on again in 2011, but you should regard a .261 BA as his ceiling. (LS)

### Forecast
| Player | Age | AB | HR | R | RBI | SB | BA | OBP | SLG | $1L | Pts |
|---|---|---|---|---|---|---|---|---|---|---|---|
| Golson G | 25 | 44 | 1 | 5 | 5 | 2 | .214 | .252 | .346 | -$5 | 20 |

### Mini-Browser
| Player | Age | AB | HR | R | RBI | SB | BA | OBP | SLG | $1L | Pts |
|---|---|---|---|---|---|---|---|---|---|---|---|
| Miller J | 26 | 44 | 2 | 6 | 5 | 2 | .237 | .324 | .418 | -$5 | 20 |
| Ramirez W | 25 | 23 | 1 | 3 | 3 | 1 | .218 | .277 | .405 | -$5 | 10 |
| Duda L | 25 | 43 | 2 | 5 | 5 | 0 | .208 | .298 | .371 | -$5 | 20 |
| Buck T | 27 | 46 | 2 | 5 | 5 | 1 | .249 | .328 | .414 | -$5 | 20 |
| Boggs B | 28 | 44 | 2 | 5 | 5 | 1 | .228 | .330 | .411 | -$5 | 20 |

### Minors (2010) / Skills
| Level | Leag | AB | HR | R | RBI | SB | BA | OBP | SLG | CT% | H% | BB% | Bash |
|---|---|---|---|---|---|---|---|---|---|---|---|---|---|
| A | — | | | | | | | | | | | | |
| AA | — | | | | | | | | | | | | |
| AAA | IL | 415 | 10 | 51 | 40 | 17 | .263 | .313 | .414 | 76% | 34% | 6% | 1.58 |

### Competition at RF / Stats in 2010
| Bats | Player | GSvR | GSvL | Sub | OPS |
|---|---|---|---|---|---|
| BH | Swisher N | 80 | 52 | 2 | .870 |
| RH | Kearns A | 7 | 7 | 4 | .746 |
| LH | Curtis C | 9 | 0 | 8 | .538 |
| RH | Golson G | 1 | 3 | 13 | .609 |

Ten-Year Trends: SLG / OBP / BA

### Majors / Skills
| Yr | Team | AB | HR | R | RBI | SB | BA | OBP | SLG | CT% | H% | BB% | Bash | $1L | $2L | Pts | RAA | 2B | 3B | CS | FB-LD-GB | HR/fb | RBI% | RS% | OPS | 1st Hf | 2nd Hf | vs RH | vs LH | Rnge | vRH | vLH |
|---|---|---|---|---|---|---|---|---|---|---|---|---|---|---|---|---|---|---|---|---|---|---|---|---|---|---|---|---|---|---|---|---|
| 07 | — | | | | | | | | | | | | | | | | | | | | | | | | | | | | | | | |
| 08 | PHI | 6 | 0 | 2 | 0 | 1 | .000 | .000 | .000 | 33% | 0% | 0% | NA | -$5 | -$19 | 0 | -2 | 0 | 0 | 0 | 50-0-50 | 0% | 0% | NA | .000 | | — | .000 | .000 | .000 | 2.10 | — | — |
| 09 | TEX | 1 | 0 | 0 | 0 | 0 | .000 | .000 | .000 | 0% | 0% | NA | NA | -$4 | -$19 | 0 | -0 | 0 | 0 | 0 | NA | NA | NA | NA | .000 | .000 | — | .000 | .000 | — | 2.12 | -21 | +50 |
| 10 | NYY | 22 | 0 | 2 | 0 | 2 | .261 | .261 | .348 | 87% | 30% | 0% | 1.33 | -$4 | -$19 | 20 | -2 | 2 | 0 | 0 | 40-30-30 | 0% | 14% | NA | .609 | .000 | .556 | .000 | .824 | 2.10 | -16 | +39 |

## Jonny Gomes — 300 PA | $6 | 170 pts
OF-129 (LF-129), DH-7 — Owned: 40% — RH

The Reds figure to exercise Gomes's reasonable 2011 option. Gomes plays terrible defense (he is often substituted by Heisey or Nix) and he goes through deep slumps, but he crushes lefties and can enter hot streaks where he hits everything. He looks to get somewhat less playing time in 2011. (SW)

### Forecast
| Player | Age | AB | HR | R | RBI | SB | BA | OBP | SLG | $1L | Pts |
|---|---|---|---|---|---|---|---|---|---|---|---|
| Gomes J | 30 | 271 | 12 | 39 | 42 | 6 | .255 | .332 | .469 | $6 | 170 |

### Mini-Browser
| Player | Age | AB | HR | R | RBI | SB | BA | OBP | SLG | $1L | Pts |
|---|---|---|---|---|---|---|---|---|---|---|---|
| Jay J | 26 | 458 | 10 | 60 | 45 | 10 | .262 | .326 | .384 | $8 | 260 |
| Jennings D | 24 | 293 | 7 | 39 | 26 | 20 | .244 | .322 | .403 | $7 | 200 |
| Saunders M | 24 | 420 | 14 | 50 | 45 | 14 | .225 | .303 | .380 | $7 | 210 |
| Taylor M | 25 | 317 | 14 | 35 | 42 | 11 | .232 | .300 | .435 | $7 | 180 |
| Jones A | 33 | 260 | 15 | 39 | 42 | 3 | .242 | .339 | .474 | $6 | 180 |

### Minors (2010) / Skills
| Level | Leag | AB | HR | R | RBI | SB | BA | OBP | SLG | CT% | H% | BB% | Bash |
|---|---|---|---|---|---|---|---|---|---|---|---|---|---|
| A | — | | | | | | | | | | | | |
| AA | — | | | | | | | | | | | | |
| AAA | — | | | | | | | | | | | | |

### Competition at LF / Stats in 2010
| Bats | Player | GSvR | GSvL | Sub | OPS |
|---|---|---|---|---|---|
| RH | Gomes J | 74 | 52 | 3 | .758 |
| LH | Nix L | 29 | 0 | 21 | .805 |
| RH | Heisey C | 4 | 9 | 25 | .757 |

Ten-Year Trends: SLG / OBP / BA

### Majors / Skills
| Yr | Team | AB | HR | R | RBI | SB | BA | OBP | SLG | CT% | H% | BB% | Bash | $1L | $2L | Pts | RAA | 2B | 3B | CS | FB-LD-GB | HR/fb | RBI% | RS% | OPS | 1st Hf | 2nd Hf | vs RH | vs LH | Rnge | vRH | vLH |
|---|---|---|---|---|---|---|---|---|---|---|---|---|---|---|---|---|---|---|---|---|---|---|---|---|---|---|---|---|---|---|---|---|
| 07 | TB | 348 | 17 | 48 | 49 | 12 | .244 | .322 | .460 | 64% | 38% | 9% | 1.88 | $11 | -$5 | 190 | -2 | 20 | 2 | 4 | 53-21-26 | 14% | 16% | 28% | .782 | .885 | .718 | .730 | .918 | 2.03 | -31 | +76 |
| 08 | TB | 154 | 8 | 23 | 21 | 8 | .182 | .282 | .383 | 70% | 26% | 8% | 2.11 | $1 | -$12 | 90 | -10 | 9 | 1 | 0 | 56-10-34 | 13% | 16% | 36% | .666 | .687 | .576 | .595 | .705 | 2.02 | -44 | +110 |
| 09 | CIN | 281 | 20 | 39 | 51 | 3 | .267 | .338 | .541 | 70% | 38% | 8% | 2.03 | $10 | -$1 | 190 | +8 | 17 | 0 | 3 | 46-20-34 | 22% | 19% | 22% | .879 | .956 | .840 | .859 | .914 | — | -26 | +56 |
| 10 | CIN | 511 | 18 | 77 | 86 | 5 | .266 | .327 | .431 | 76% | 35% | 7% | 1.62 | $18 | $11 | 310 | -10 | 24 | 3 | 6 | 50-21-29 | 9% | 20% | 35% | .758 | .801 | .706 | .709 | .856 | — | -16 | +32 |

*For more stats, visit www.Rotolympus.com.*

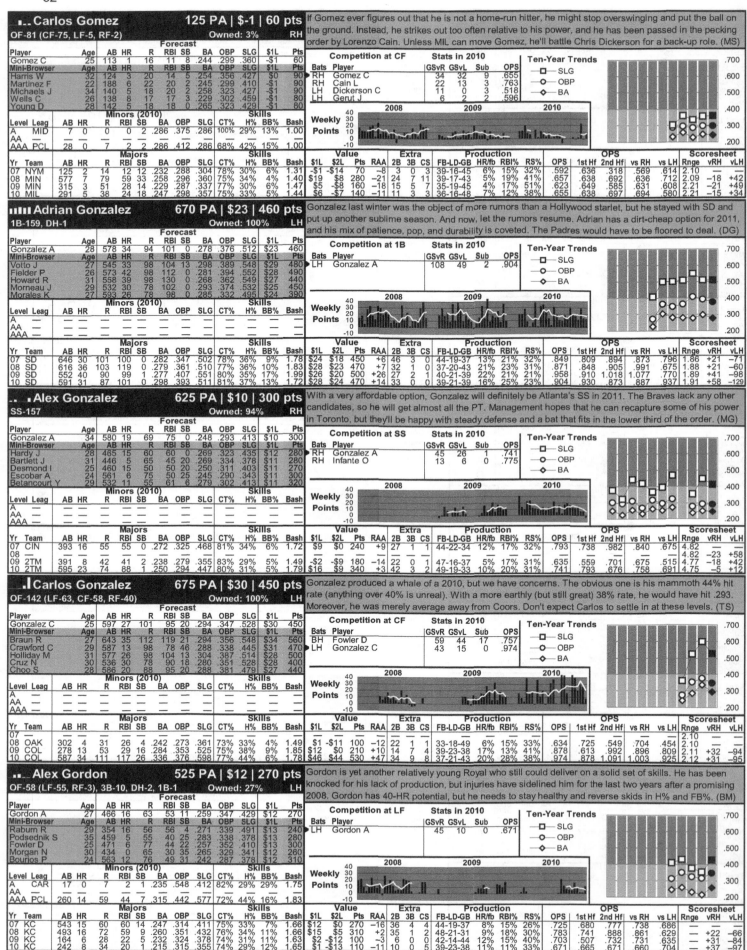

## Carlos Gomez — 125 PA | $-1 | 60 pts

OF-81 (CF-75, LF-5, RF-2) — Owned: 3% — RH

If Gomez ever figures out that he is not a home-run hitter, he might stop overswinging and put the ball on the ground. Instead, he strikes out too often relative to his power, and he has been passed in the pecking order by Lorenzo Cain. Unless MIL can move Gomez, he'll battle Chris Dickerson for a back-up role. (MS)

| Player | Age | AB | HR | R | RBI | SB | BA | OBP | SLG | $1L | Pts |
|---|---|---|---|---|---|---|---|---|---|---|---|
| Gomez C | 25 | 113 | 1 | 16 | 11 | 8 | .244 | .299 | .360 | -$1 | 60 |
| **Mini-Browser** | **Age** | **AB** | **HR** | **R** | **RBI** | **SB** | **BA** | **OBP** | **SLG** | **$1L** | **Pts** |
| Harris W | 32 | 124 | 3 | 20 | 14 | 5 | .254 | .356 | .427 | $0 | 90 |
| Martinez F | 22 | 188 | 6 | 22 | 20 | 2 | .245 | .299 | .410 | -$1 | 90 |
| Michaels J | 34 | 140 | 5 | 18 | 20 | 2 | .258 | .323 | .427 | -$1 | 90 |
| Wells C | 26 | 138 | 8 | 17 | 17 | 3 | .229 | .302 | .459 | -$1 | 80 |
| Young D | 28 | 142 | 5 | 18 | 18 | 0 | .265 | .323 | .429 | -$1 | 80 |

| Level | Leag | AB | HR | R | RBI | SB | BA | OBP | SLG | CT% | H% | BB% | Bash |
|---|---|---|---|---|---|---|---|---|---|---|---|---|---|
| A | MID | 7 | 0 | 0 | 0 | 2 | .286 | .375 | .286 | 100% | 29% | 13% | 1.00 |
| AA | — | — | — | — | — | — | — | — | — | — | — | — | — |
| AAA | PCL | 28 | 0 | 7 | 2 | 2 | .286 | .412 | .286 | 68% | 42% | 15% | 1.00 |

**Competition at CF — Stats in 2010**

| Bats | Player | GSvR | GSvL | Sub | OPS |
|---|---|---|---|---|---|
| RH | Gomez C | 34 | 32 | 9 | .655 |
| RH | Cain L | 22 | 13 | 3 | .763 |
| LH | Dickerson C | 11 | 0 | 3 | .518 |
| LH | Gerut J | 6 | 2 | 2 | .596 |

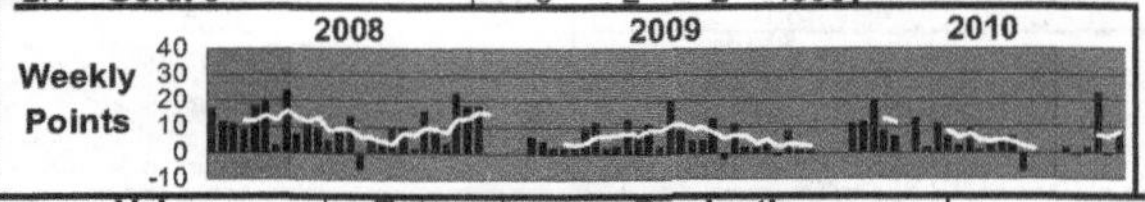
Weekly Points
2008
2009
2010
40
30
20
10
0
-10

Ten-Year Trends
SLG
OBP
BA

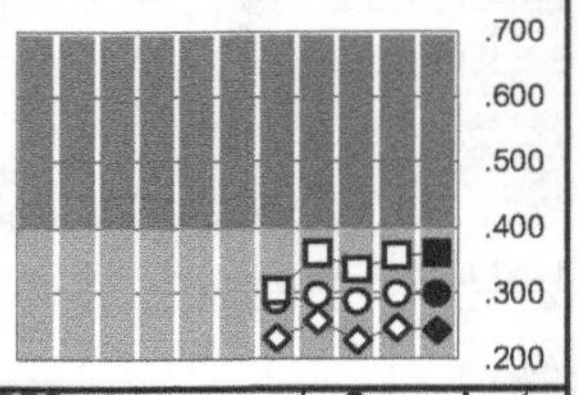
.700
.600
.500
.400
.300
.200

| Yr | Team | AB | HR | R | RBI | SB | BA | OBP | SLG | CT% | H% | BB% | Bash | $1L | $2L | Pts | RAA | 2B | 3B | CS | FB-LD-GB | HR/fb | RBI% | RS% | OPS | 1st Hf | 2nd Hf | vs RH | vs LH | Rnge | vRH | vLH |
|---|---|---|---|---|---|---|---|---|---|---|---|---|---|---|---|---|---|---|---|---|---|---|---|---|---|---|---|---|---|---|---|---|
| 07 | NYM | 125 | 2 | 14 | 12 | 12 | .232 | .288 | .304 | 78% | 30% | 6% | 1.31 | -$1 | -$14 | 70 | −8 | 3 | 0 | 3 | 39-16-45 | 6% | 15% | 32% | .592 | .636 | .318 | .569 | .614 | 2.10 | — | — |
| 08 | MIN | 577 | 7 | 79 | 59 | 33 | .258 | .296 | .360 | 75% | 34% | 4% | 1.40 | $19 | $8 | 280 | −21 | 24 | 7 | 11 | 39-17-43 | 5% | 19% | 41% | .657 | .638 | .692 | .636 | .712 | 2.09 | −18 | +42 |
| 09 | MIN | 315 | 3 | 51 | 28 | 14 | .229 | .287 | .337 | 77% | 30% | 6% | 1.47 | $5 | -$8 | 160 | −18 | 15 | 5 | 7 | 35-19-45 | 4% | 17% | 51% | .623 | .649 | .585 | .631 | .608 | 2.21 | −21 | +49 |
| 10 | MIL | 291 | 5 | 38 | 24 | 18 | .247 | .298 | .357 | 75% | 33% | 5% | 1.44 | $6 | -$7 | 140 | −11 | 11 | 3 | 3 | 36-16-48 | 7% | 12% | 38% | .655 | .638 | .697 | .694 | .580 | 2.21 | −15 | +34 |

## Adrian Gonzalez — 670 PA | $23 | 460 pts

1B-159, DH-1 — Owned: 100% — LH

Gonzalez last winter was the object of more rumors than a Hollywood starlet, but he stayed with SD and put up another sublime season. And now, let the rumors resume. Adrian has a dirt-cheap option for 2011, and his mix of patience, pop, and durability is coveted. The Padres would have to be floored to deal. (DG)

| Player | Age | AB | HR | R | RBI | SB | BA | OBP | SLG | $1L | Pts |
|---|---|---|---|---|---|---|---|---|---|---|---|
| Gonzalez A | 28 | 578 | 34 | 94 | 101 | 0 | .278 | .376 | .512 | $23 | 460 |
| **Mini-Browser** | **Age** | **AB** | **HR** | **R** | **RBI** | **SB** | **BA** | **OBP** | **SLG** | **$1L** | **Pts** |
| Votto J | 27 | 545 | 33 | 98 | 104 | 13 | .298 | .389 | .548 | $29 | 480 |
| Fielder P | 26 | 573 | 42 | 98 | 112 | 0 | .281 | .394 | .552 | $28 | 490 |
| Howard R | 31 | 558 | 39 | 98 | 130 | 0 | .268 | .362 | .549 | $27 | 440 |
| Morneau J | 29 | 532 | 30 | 78 | 102 | 0 | .293 | .374 | .532 | $25 | 450 |
| Morales K | 27 | 593 | 26 | 78 | 98 | 0 | .285 | .332 | .495 | $24 | 390 |

| Level | Leag | AB | HR | R | RBI | SB | BA | OBP | SLG | CT% | H% | BB% | Bash |
|---|---|---|---|---|---|---|---|---|---|---|---|---|---|
| A | — | — | — | — | — | — | — | — | — | — | — | — | — |
| AA | — | — | — | — | — | — | — | — | — | — | — | — | — |
| AAA | — | — | — | — | — | — | — | — | — | — | — | — | — |

**Competition at 1B — Stats in 2010**

| Bats | Player | GSvR | GSvL | Sub | OPS |
|---|---|---|---|---|---|
| LH | Gonzalez A | 108 | 49 | 2 | .904 |

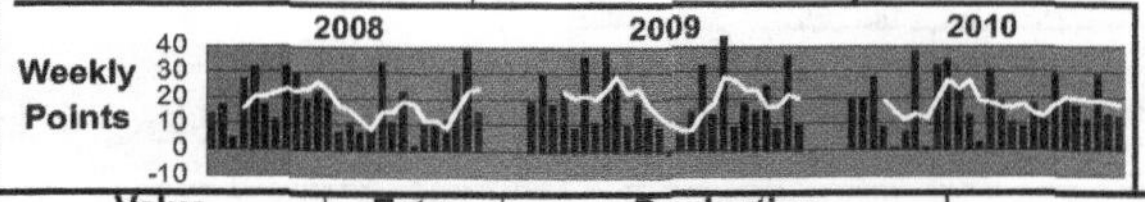
Weekly Points
2008
2009
2010
40
30
20
10
0
-10

Ten-Year Trends
SLG
OBP
BA

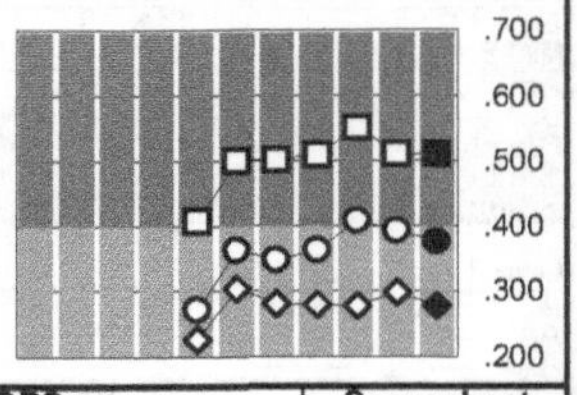
.700
.600
.500
.400
.300
.200

| Yr | Team | AB | HR | R | RBI | SB | BA | OBP | SLG | CT% | H% | BB% | Bash | $1L | $2L | Pts | RAA | 2B | 3B | CS | FB-LD-GB | HR/fb | RBI% | RS% | OPS | 1st Hf | 2nd Hf | vs RH | vs LH | Rnge | vRH | vLH |
|---|---|---|---|---|---|---|---|---|---|---|---|---|---|---|---|---|---|---|---|---|---|---|---|---|---|---|---|---|---|---|---|---|
| 07 | SD | 646 | 30 | 101 | 100 | 0 | .282 | .347 | .502 | 78% | 36% | 9% | 1.78 | $24 | $18 | 450 | +6 | 46 | 3 | 0 | 44-19-37 | 13% | 21% | 32% | .849 | .809 | .894 | .873 | .796 | 1.86 | +21 | −71 |
| 08 | SD | 616 | 36 | 103 | 119 | 0 | .279 | .361 | .510 | 77% | 36% | 10% | 1.83 | $28 | $23 | 470 | +7 | 32 | 1 | 0 | 37-20-43 | 21% | 23% | 31% | .871 | .848 | .905 | .991 | .675 | 1.88 | +21 | −60 |
| 09 | SD | 552 | 40 | 90 | 99 | 1 | .277 | .407 | .551 | 80% | 35% | 17% | 1.99 | $26 | $20 | 500 | +26 | 27 | 2 | 1 | 40-21-39 | 22% | 21% | 21% | .958 | .910 | 1.018 | 1.077 | .770 | 1.89 | +41 | −98 |
| 10 | SD | 591 | 31 | 87 | 101 | 0 | .298 | .393 | .511 | 81% | 37% | 13% | 1.72 | $28 | $24 | 470 | +14 | 33 | 0 | 0 | 39-21-39 | 16% | 25% | 23% | .904 | .930 | .873 | .887 | .937 | 1.91 | +58 | −129 |

## Alex Gonzalez — 625 PA | $10 | 300 pts

SS-157 — Owned: 94% — RH

With a very affordable option, Gonzalez will definitely be Atlanta's SS in 2011. The Braves lack any other candidates, so he will get almost all the PT. Management hopes that he can recapture some of his power in Toronto, but they'll be happy with steady defense and a bat that fits in the lower third of the order. (MG)

| Player | Age | AB | HR | R | RBI | SB | BA | OBP | SLG | $1L | Pts |
|---|---|---|---|---|---|---|---|---|---|---|---|
| Gonzalez A | 34 | 580 | 19 | 69 | 75 | 0 | .248 | .293 | .413 | $10 | 300 |
| **Mini-Browser** | **Age** | **AB** | **HR** | **R** | **RBI** | **SB** | **BA** | **OBP** | **SLG** | **$1L** | **Pts** |
| Hardy J | 28 | 465 | 15 | 60 | 60 | 0 | .269 | .323 | .435 | $12 | 280 |
| Bartlett J | 31 | 446 | 5 | 65 | 45 | 20 | .269 | .334 | .378 | $11 | 280 |
| Desmond I | 25 | 460 | 15 | 50 | 50 | 20 | .250 | .311 | .403 | $11 | 270 |
| Escobar A | 24 | 561 | 6 | 75 | 50 | 25 | .245 | .290 | .343 | $11 | 300 |
| Betancourt Y | 29 | 532 | 11 | 55 | 61 | 6 | .279 | .302 | .413 | $11 | 320 |

| Level | Leag | AB | HR | R | RBI | SB | BA | OBP | SLG | CT% | H% | BB% | Bash |
|---|---|---|---|---|---|---|---|---|---|---|---|---|---|
| A | — | — | — | — | — | — | — | — | — | — | — | — | — |
| AA | — | — | — | — | — | — | — | — | — | — | — | — | — |
| AAA | — | — | — | — | — | — | — | — | — | — | — | — | — |

**Competition at SS — Stats in 2010**

| Bats | Player | GSvR | GSvL | Sub | OPS |
|---|---|---|---|---|---|
| RH | Gonzalez A | 45 | 26 | 1 | .741 |
| RH | Infante O | 13 | 6 | 0 | .775 |

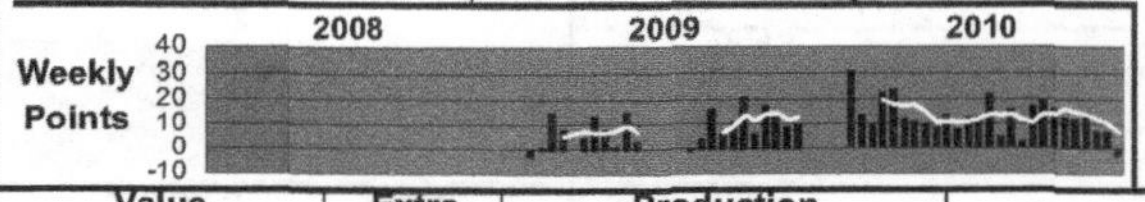
Weekly Points
2008
2009
2010
40
30
20
10
0
-10

Ten-Year Trends
SLG
OBP
BA

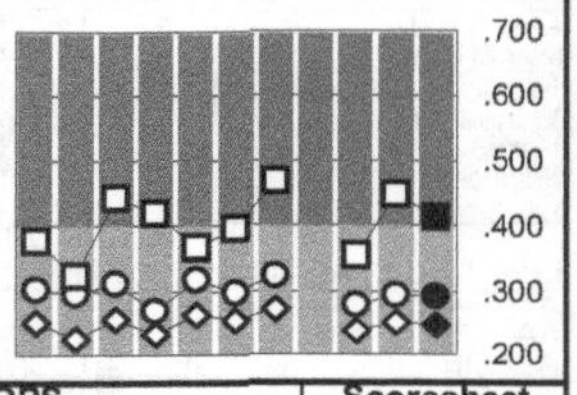
.700
.600
.500
.400
.300
.200

| Yr | Team | AB | HR | R | RBI | SB | BA | OBP | SLG | CT% | H% | BB% | Bash | $1L | $2L | Pts | RAA | 2B | 3B | CS | FB-LD-GB | HR/fb | RBI% | RS% | OPS | 1st Hf | 2nd Hf | vs RH | vs LH | Rnge | vRH | vLH |
|---|---|---|---|---|---|---|---|---|---|---|---|---|---|---|---|---|---|---|---|---|---|---|---|---|---|---|---|---|---|---|---|---|
| 07 | CIN | 393 | 16 | 55 | 55 | 0 | .272 | .325 | .468 | 81% | 34% | 6% | 1.72 | $9 | $0 | 240 | +9 | 27 | 1 | 1 | 44-22-34 | 12% | 17% | 32% | .793 | .738 | .982 | .840 | .675 | 4.82 | — | — |
| 08 | — | — | — | — | — | — | — | — | — | — | — | — | — | — | — | — | — | — | — | — | — | — | — | — | — | — | — | — | — | 4.82 | −23 | +58 |
| 09 | 2TM | 391 | 8 | 42 | 41 | 2 | .238 | .279 | .355 | 83% | 29% | 5% | 1.49 | -$2 | -$9 | 180 | −14 | 22 | 0 | 1 | 47-16-37 | 5% | 17% | 31% | .635 | .559 | .701 | .675 | .515 | 4.77 | −18 | +42 |
| 10 | 2TM | 595 | 23 | 74 | 88 | 1 | .250 | .294 | .447 | 80% | 31% | 5% | 1.79 | $16 | $9 | 340 | +3 | 42 | 3 | 2 | 49-19-33 | 10% | 20% | 31% | .741 | .793 | .676 | .758 | .691 | 4.75 | −5 | +12 |

## Carlos Gonzalez — 675 PA | $30 | 450 pts

OF-142 (LF-63, CF-58, RF-40) — Owned: 100% — LH

Gonzalez produced a whale of a 2010, but we have concerns. The obvious one is his mammoth 44% hit rate (anything over 40% is unreal). With a more earthly (but still great) 38% rate, he would have hit .293. Moreover, he was merely average away from Coors. Don't expect Carlos to settle in at these levels. (TS)

| Player | Age | AB | HR | R | RBI | SB | BA | OBP | SLG | $1L | Pts |
|---|---|---|---|---|---|---|---|---|---|---|---|
| Gonzalez C | 25 | 597 | 27 | 101 | 95 | 20 | .294 | .347 | .528 | $30 | 450 |
| **Mini-Browser** | **Age** | **AB** | **HR** | **R** | **RBI** | **SB** | **BA** | **OBP** | **SLG** | **$1L** | **Pts** |
| Braun R | 27 | 643 | 35 | 112 | 119 | 21 | .294 | .356 | .548 | $34 | 560 |
| Crawford C | 29 | 587 | 13 | 98 | 78 | 46 | .288 | .338 | .445 | $31 | 470 |
| Holliday M | 31 | 577 | 26 | 98 | 104 | 13 | .304 | .387 | .514 | $28 | 500 |
| Cruz N | 30 | 536 | 30 | 78 | 90 | 18 | .280 | .351 | .528 | $28 | 400 |
| Choo S | 28 | 586 | 20 | 88 | 95 | 20 | .288 | .381 | .479 | $27 | 440 |

| Level | Leag | AB | HR | R | RBI | SB | BA | OBP | SLG | CT% | H% | BB% | Bash |
|---|---|---|---|---|---|---|---|---|---|---|---|---|---|
| A | — | — | — | — | — | — | — | — | — | — | — | — | — |
| AA | — | — | — | — | — | — | — | — | — | — | — | — | — |
| AAA | — | — | — | — | — | — | — | — | — | — | — | — | — |

**Competition at CF — Stats in 2010**

| Bats | Player | GSvR | GSvL | Sub | OPS |
|---|---|---|---|---|---|
| BH | Fowler D | 59 | 44 | 17 | .757 |
| LH | Gonzalez C | 43 | 15 | 0 | .974 |

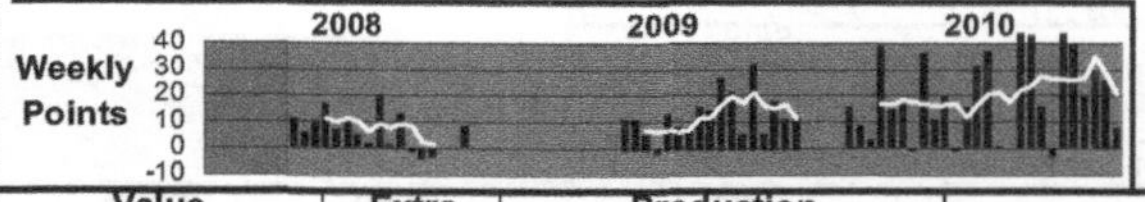
Weekly Points
2008
2009
2010
40
30
20
10
0
-10

Ten-Year Trends
SLG
OBP
BA

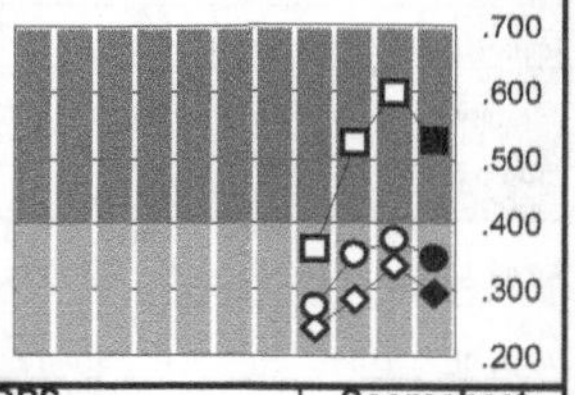
.700
.600
.500
.400
.300
.200

| Yr | Team | AB | HR | R | RBI | SB | BA | OBP | SLG | CT% | H% | BB% | Bash | $1L | $2L | Pts | RAA | 2B | 3B | CS | FB-LD-GB | HR/fb | RBI% | RS% | OPS | 1st Hf | 2nd Hf | vs RH | vs LH | Rnge | vRH | vLH |
|---|---|---|---|---|---|---|---|---|---|---|---|---|---|---|---|---|---|---|---|---|---|---|---|---|---|---|---|---|---|---|---|---|
| 07 | — | — | — | — | — | — | — | — | — | — | — | — | — | — | — | — | — | — | — | — | — | — | — | — | — | — | — | — | — | 2.10 | — | — |
| 08 | OAK | 302 | 4 | 31 | 26 | 4 | .242 | .273 | .361 | 73% | 33% | 4% | 1.49 | $1 | -$11 | 100 | −12 | 22 | 1 | 1 | 33-18-49 | 6% | 15% | 33% | .634 | .725 | .549 | .704 | .454 | 2.10 | — | — |
| 09 | COL | 278 | 13 | 53 | 29 | 16 | .284 | .353 | .525 | 75% | 38% | 9% | 1.85 | $12 | $0 | 210 | +10 | 14 | 7 | 4 | 39-23-38 | 17% | 13% | 41% | .878 | .613 | .992 | .896 | .809 | 2.11 | +32 | −94 |
| 10 | COL | 587 | 34 | 111 | 117 | 26 | .336 | .376 | .598 | 77% | 44% | 6% | 1.78 | $46 | $44 | 530 | +47 | 34 | 9 | 8 | 37-21-43 | 20% | 28% | 38% | .974 | .878 | 1.091 | 1.003 | .925 | 2.12 | +31 | −95 |

## Alex Gordon — 525 PA | $12 | 270 pts

OF-58 (LF-55, RF-3), 3B-10, DH-2, 1B-1 — Owned: 27% — LH

Gordon is yet another relatively young Royal who still could deliver on a solid set of skills. He has been knocked for his lack of production, but injuries have sidelined him for the last two years after a promising 2008. Gordon has 40-HR potential, but he needs to stay healthy and reverse skids in H% and FB%. (BM)

| Player | Age | AB | HR | R | RBI | SB | BA | OBP | SLG | $1L | Pts |
|---|---|---|---|---|---|---|---|---|---|---|---|
| Gordon A | 27 | 466 | 16 | 63 | 53 | 11 | .259 | .347 | .429 | $12 | 270 |
| **Mini-Browser** | **Age** | **AB** | **HR** | **R** | **RBI** | **SB** | **BA** | **OBP** | **SLG** | **$1L** | **Pts** |
| Raburn R | 29 | 354 | 16 | 56 | 56 | 4 | .271 | .339 | .491 | $13 | 240 |
| Podsednik S | 35 | 459 | 5 | 55 | 40 | 25 | .283 | .338 | .378 | $13 | 280 |
| Fowler D | 25 | 471 | 6 | 77 | 44 | 22 | .257 | .352 | .410 | $13 | 300 |
| Morgan N | 30 | 434 | 0 | 65 | 30 | 35 | .265 | .329 | .341 | $12 | 260 |
| Bourjos P | 24 | 563 | 12 | 76 | 49 | 31 | .242 | .287 | .378 | $12 | 310 |

| Level | Leag | AB | HR | R | RBI | SB | BA | OBP | SLG | CT% | H% | BB% | Bash |
|---|---|---|---|---|---|---|---|---|---|---|---|---|---|
| A | CAR | 17 | 0 | 7 | 2 | 1 | .235 | .548 | .412 | 82% | 29% | 29% | 1.75 |
| AA | — | — | — | — | — | — | — | — | — | — | — | — | — |
| AAA | PCL | 260 | 14 | 59 | 44 | 7 | .315 | .442 | .577 | 72% | 44% | 16% | 1.83 |

**Competition at LF — Stats in 2010**

| Bats | Player | GSvR | GSvL | Sub | OPS |
|---|---|---|---|---|---|
| LH | Gordon A | 45 | 10 | 0 | .671 |

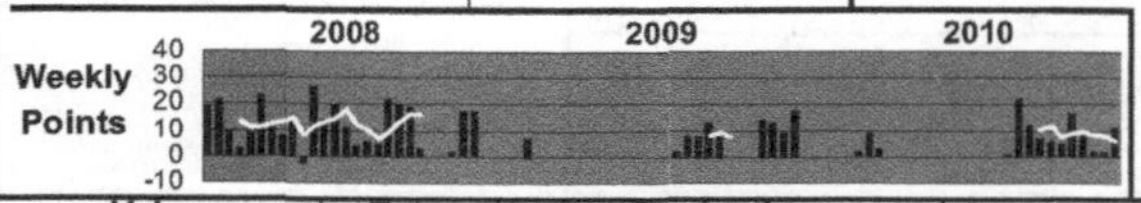
Weekly Points
2008
2009
2010
40
30
20
10
0
-10

Ten-Year Trends
SLG
OBP
BA

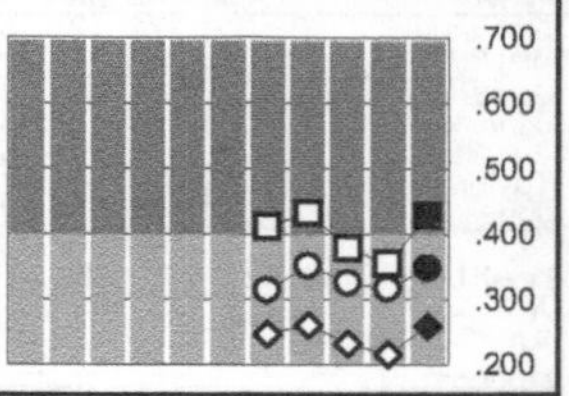
.700
.600
.500
.400
.300
.200

| Yr | Team | AB | HR | R | RBI | SB | BA | OBP | SLG | CT% | H% | BB% | Bash | $1L | $2L | Pts | RAA | 2B | 3B | CS | FB-LD-GB | HR/fb | RBI% | RS% | OPS | 1st Hf | 2nd Hf | vs RH | vs LH | Rnge | vRH | vLH |
|---|---|---|---|---|---|---|---|---|---|---|---|---|---|---|---|---|---|---|---|---|---|---|---|---|---|---|---|---|---|---|---|---|
| 07 | KC | 543 | 15 | 60 | 60 | 14 | .247 | .314 | .411 | 75% | 33% | 7% | 1.66 | $12 | $0 | 270 | −16 | 36 | 4 | 4 | 44-19-37 | 8% | 15% | 26% | .725 | .680 | .777 | .738 | .686 | — | — | — |
| 08 | KC | 493 | 16 | 72 | 59 | 9 | .260 | .351 | .432 | 76% | 34% | 11% | 1.66 | $15 | $5 | 310 | +2 | 35 | 1 | 2 | 48-21-31 | 9% | 18% | 30% | .783 | .741 | .888 | .861 | .629 | — | +22 | −66 |
| 09 | KC | 164 | 6 | 28 | 22 | 5 | .232 | .324 | .378 | 74% | 31% | 11% | 1.63 | $2 | -$12 | 100 | −3 | 6 | 0 | 0 | 42-14-44 | 12% | 15% | 40% | .703 | .507 | .732 | .731 | .635 | — | +31 | −84 |
| 10 | KC | 242 | 8 | 34 | 20 | 1 | .215 | .315 | .355 | 74% | 29% | 12% | 1.65 | $1 | -$13 | 110 | −11 | 10 | 0 | 5 | 39-23-38 | 11% | 11% | 33% | .671 | .665 | .671 | .660 | .704 | — | +37 | −97 |

*For more stats, visit www.Rotolympus.com.*

## Curtis Granderson — 600 PA | $20 | 380 pts

OF-134 (CF-134) — Owned: 96% — LH

Between being on the DL and hitting poorly, Granderson's 2010 season was shaping up to be a dog. However, some work with hitting coach Kevin Long got him back on track, and Granderson hit 14 homers in the last two months of the season. Now we (and Granderson) know what he is capable of in 2011. (LS)

| Player | Age | AB | HR | R | RBI | SB | BA | OBP | SLG | $1L | Pts |
|---|---|---|---|---|---|---|---|---|---|---|---|
| | | Forecast | | | | | | | | | |
| Granderson C | 30 | 531 | 24 | 84 | 66 | 18 | .260 | .339 | .494 | $20 | 380 |
| **Mini-Browser** | **Age** | **AB** | **HR** | **R** | **RBI** | **SB** | **BA** | **OBP** | **SLG** | **$1L** | **Pts** |
| Pagan A | 29 | 576 | 13 | 81 | 69 | 31 | .282 | .335 | .437 | $21 | 410 |
| Bay J | 32 | 521 | 30 | 90 | 90 | 12 | .265 | .366 | .494 | $21 | 410 |
| McCutchen A | 24 | 536 | 18 | 84 | 54 | 30 | .280 | .361 | .450 | $20 | 420 |
| Ramirez M | 38 | 465 | 28 | 77 | 88 | 0 | .284 | .392 | .505 | $20 | 380 |
| Bourn M | 28 | 542 | 6 | 88 | 38 | 50 | .265 | .338 | .360 | $20 | 360 |

| Level | Leag | AB | HR | R | RBI | SB | BA | OBP | SLG | CT% | H% | BB% | Bash |
|---|---|---|---|---|---|---|---|---|---|---|---|---|---|
| | | Minors (2010) | | | | | | | | Skills | | | |
| A | — | — | — | — | — | — | — | — | — | — | — | — | — |
| AA | — | — | — | — | — | — | — | — | — | — | — | — | — |
| AAA | IL | 16 | 0 | 0 | 2 | 0 | .250 | .333 | .250 | 88% | 29% | 11% | 1.00 |

| Competition at CF | | Stats in 2010 | | | |
|---|---|---|---|---|---|
| Bats | Player | GSvR | GSvL | Sub | OPS |
| LH | Granderson C | 87 | 36 | 11 | .792 |
| LH | Gardner B | 22 | 23 | 0 | .762 |

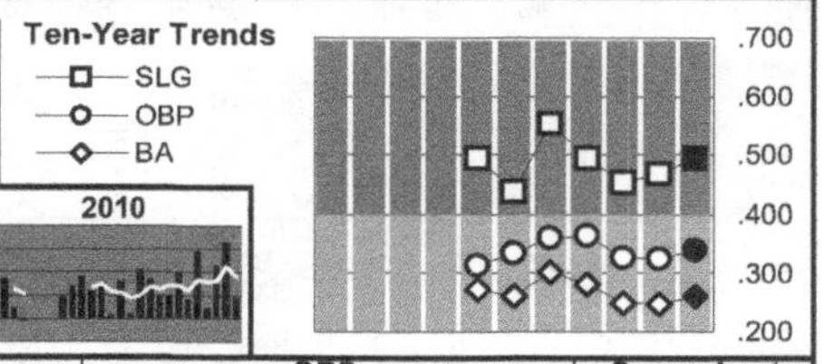


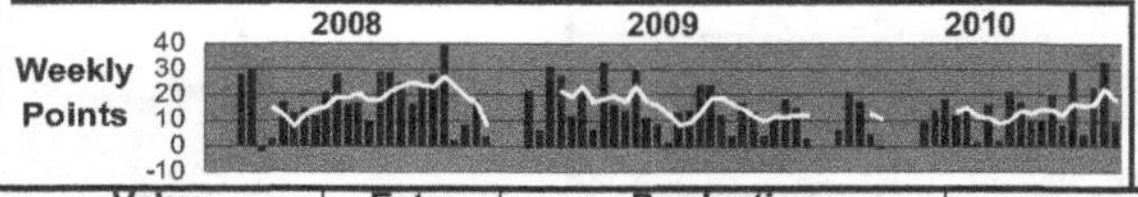


| Yr | Team | AB | HR | R | RBI | SB | BA | OBP | SLG | CT% | H% | BB% | Bash | $1L | $2L | Pts | RAA | 2B | 3B | CS | FB-LD-GB | HR/fb | RBI% | RS% | OPS | 1st Hf | 2nd Hf | vs RH | vs LH | Rnge | vRH | vLH |
|---|---|---|---|---|---|---|---|---|---|---|---|---|---|---|---|---|---|---|---|---|---|---|---|---|---|---|---|---|---|---|---|---|
| | | Majors | | | | | | | | Skills | | | | Value | | | | Extra | | | Production | | | | OPS | | | | | Scoresheet | | |
| 07 | DET | 612 | 23 | 122 | 74 | 26 | .302 | .361 | .552 | 77% | 39% | 8% | 1.83 | $31 | $25 | 500 | +34 | 38 | 23 | 1 | 45-21-34 | 11% | 20% | 45% | .913 | .884 | .948 | 1.014 | .494 | 2.19 | +21 | −70 |
| 08 | DET | 553 | 22 | 112 | 66 | 12 | .280 | .365 | .494 | 80% | 35% | 11% | 1.76 | $24 | $16 | 430 | +23 | 26 | 13 | 4 | 41-19-40 | 12% | 20% | 43% | .858 | .838 | .878 | .900 | .739 | 2.20 | +48 | −160 |
| 09 | DET | 631 | 30 | 91 | 71 | 20 | .249 | .327 | .453 | 78% | 32% | 10% | 1.82 | $21 | $13 | 410 | +7 | 23 | 8 | 6 | 49-21-29 | 13% | 15% | 30% | .780 | .789 | .769 | .897 | .484 | 2.20 | +49 | −158 |
| 10 | NYY | 466 | 24 | 76 | 67 | 12 | .247 | .324 | .468 | 75% | 33% | 10% | 1.90 | $19 | $10 | 320 | +6 | 17 | 7 | 2 | 47-20-33 | 14% | 16% | 36% | .792 | .718 | .861 | .866 | .647 | 2.19 | +50 | −142 |

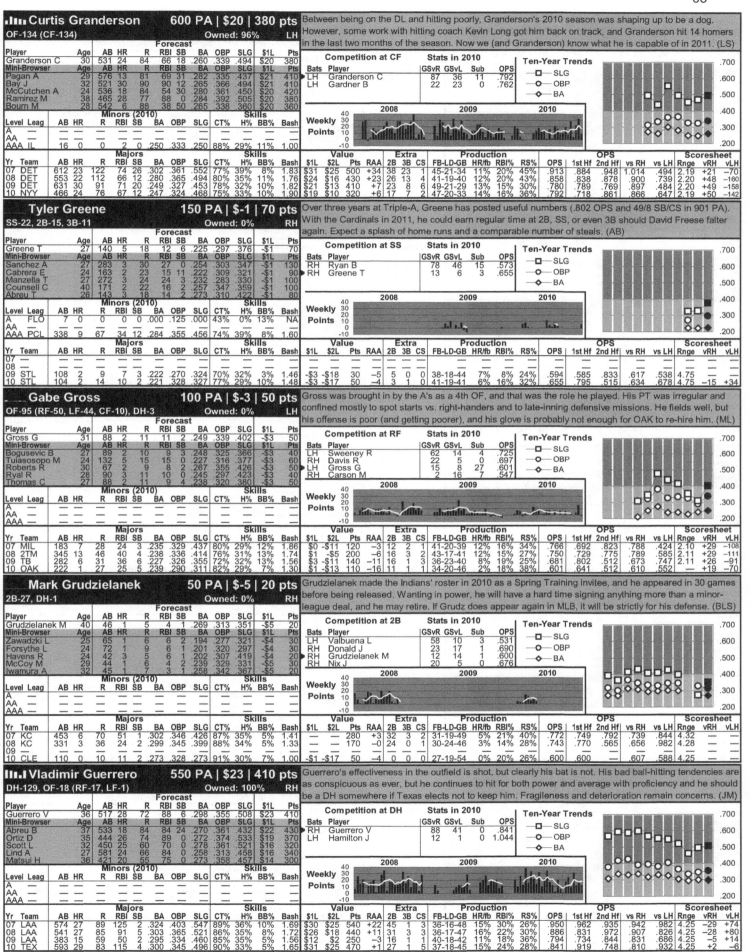

## Tyler Greene — 150 PA | $-1 | 70 pts

SS-22, 2B-15, 3B-11 — Owned: 0% — RH

Over three years at Triple-A, Greene has posted useful numbers (.802 OPS and 49/8 SB/CS in 901 PA). With the Cardinals in 2011, he could earn regular time at 2B, SS, or even 3B should David Freese falter again. Expect a splash of home runs and a comparable number of steals. (AB)

| Player | Age | AB | HR | R | RBI | SB | BA | OBP | SLG | $1L | Pts |
|---|---|---|---|---|---|---|---|---|---|---|---|
| | | Forecast | | | | | | | | | |
| Greene T | 27 | 140 | 5 | 18 | 12 | 6 | .225 | .297 | .376 | -$1 | 70 |
| **Mini-Browser** | **Age** | **AB** | **HR** | **R** | **RBI** | **SB** | **BA** | **OBP** | **SLG** | **$1L** | **Pts** |
| Sanchez A | 27 | 283 | 3 | 30 | 27 | 0 | .254 | .303 | .347 | -$1 | 130 |
| Cabrera E | 24 | 163 | 2 | 23 | 15 | 11 | .222 | .309 | .321 | -$1 | 90 |
| Manzella T | 27 | 272 | 3 | 24 | 24 | 3 | .232 | .283 | .330 | -$1 | 100 |
| Counsell C | 40 | 171 | 2 | 22 | 16 | 2 | .257 | .347 | .359 | -$1 | 100 |
| Abreu T | 26 | 143 | 3 | 18 | 14 | 2 | .273 | .310 | .422 | -$1 | 80 |

| Level | Leag | AB | HR | R | RBI | SB | BA | OBP | SLG | CT% | H% | BB% | Bash |
|---|---|---|---|---|---|---|---|---|---|---|---|---|---|
| | | Minors (2010) | | | | | | | | Skills | | | |
| A | FLO | 7 | 0 | 0 | 0 | 0 | .000 | .125 | .000 | 43% | 0% | 13% | NA |
| AA | — | — | — | — | — | — | — | — | — | — | — | — | — |
| AAA | PCL | 338 | 9 | 67 | 34 | 12 | .284 | .355 | .456 | 74% | 39% | 8% | 1.60 |

| Competition at SS | | Stats in 2010 | | | |
|---|---|---|---|---|---|
| Bats | Player | GSvR | GSvL | Sub | OPS |
| RH | Ryan B | 78 | 46 | 15 | .573 |
| RH | Greene T | 13 | 6 | 3 | .655 |

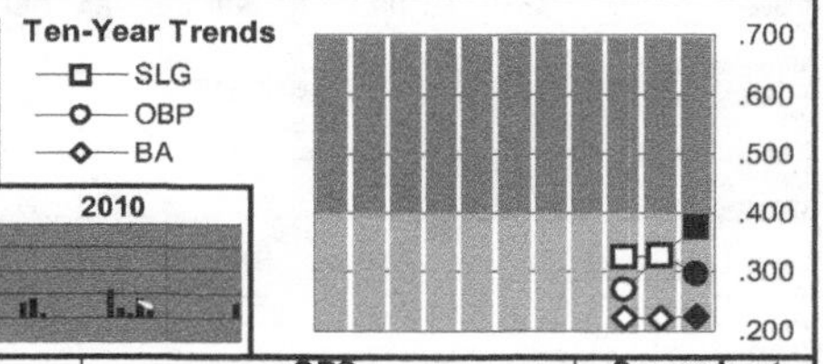


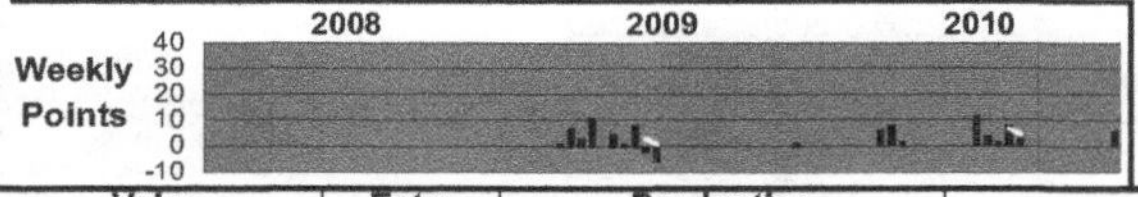


| Yr | Team | AB | HR | R | RBI | SB | BA | OBP | SLG | CT% | H% | BB% | Bash | $1L | $2L | Pts | RAA | 2B | 3B | CS | FB-LD-GB | HR/fb | RBI% | RS% | OPS | 1st Hf | 2nd Hf | vs RH | vs LH | Rnge | vRH | vLH |
|---|---|---|---|---|---|---|---|---|---|---|---|---|---|---|---|---|---|---|---|---|---|---|---|---|---|---|---|---|---|---|---|---|
| | | Majors | | | | | | | | Skills | | | | Value | | | | Extra | | | Production | | | | OPS | | | | | Scoresheet | | |
| 07 | — | — | — | — | — | — | — | — | — | — | — | — | — | — | — | — | — | — | — | — | — | — | — | — | — | — | — | — | — | — | — | — |
| 08 | — | — | — | — | — | — | — | — | — | — | — | — | — | — | — | — | — | — | — | — | — | — | — | — | — | — | — | — | — | — | — | — |
| 09 | STL | 108 | 2 | 9 | 7 | 3 | .222 | .270 | .324 | 70% | 32% | 3% | 1.46 | -$3 | -$18 | 30 | −5 | 5 | 0 | 0 | 38-18-44 | 7% | 8% | 24% | .594 | .585 | .833 | .617 | .538 | 4.75 | — | — |
| 10 | STL | 104 | 2 | 14 | 10 | 2 | .221 | .328 | .327 | 77% | 29% | 10% | 1.48 | -$3 | -$17 | 50 | −4 | 3 | 1 | 0 | 41-19-41 | 6% | 16% | 32% | .655 | .795 | .515 | .634 | .678 | 4.75 | −15 | +34 |

## Gabe Gross — 100 PA | $-3 | 50 pts

OF-95 (RF-50, LF-44, CF-10), DH-3 — Owned: 0% — LH

Gross was brought in by the A's as a 4th OF, and that was the role he played. His PT was irregular and confined mostly to spot starts vs. right-handers and to late-inning defensive missions. He fields well, but his offense is poor (and getting poorer), and his glove is probably not enough for OAK to re-hire him. (ML)

| Player | Age | AB | HR | R | RBI | SB | BA | OBP | SLG | $1L | Pts |
|---|---|---|---|---|---|---|---|---|---|---|---|
| | | Forecast | | | | | | | | | |
| Gross G | 31 | 88 | 2 | 11 | 11 | 2 | .249 | .339 | .402 | -$3 | 50 |
| **Mini-Browser** | **Age** | **AB** | **HR** | **R** | **RBI** | **SB** | **BA** | **OBP** | **SLG** | **$1L** | **Pts** |
| Bogusevic B | 27 | 89 | 2 | 10 | 9 | 3 | .248 | .325 | .366 | -$3 | 40 |
| Tuiasosopo M | 24 | 132 | 5 | 15 | 15 | 0 | .227 | .316 | .377 | -$3 | 60 |
| Roberts R | 30 | 67 | 2 | 9 | 8 | 2 | .267 | .355 | .426 | -$3 | 50 |
| Ryal R | 28 | 90 | 3 | 11 | 10 | 0 | .245 | .297 | .423 | -$3 | 40 |
| Thomas C | 27 | 88 | 2 | 11 | 9 | 4 | .238 | .320 | .380 | -$3 | 50 |

| Level | Leag | AB | HR | R | RBI | SB | BA | OBP | SLG | CT% | H% | BB% | Bash |
|---|---|---|---|---|---|---|---|---|---|---|---|---|---|
| | | Minors (2010) | | | | | | | | Skills | | | |
| A | — | — | — | — | — | — | — | — | — | — | — | — | — |
| AA | — | — | — | — | — | — | — | — | — | — | — | — | — |
| AAA | — | — | — | — | — | — | — | — | — | — | — | — | — |

| Competition at RF | | Stats in 2010 | | | |
|---|---|---|---|---|---|
| Bats | Player | GSvR | GSvL | Sub | OPS |
| LH | Sweeney R | 62 | 14 | 4 | .725 |
| RH | Davis R | 22 | 5 | 0 | .697 |
| LH | Gross G | 15 | 8 | 27 | .601 |
| RH | Carson M | 2 | 16 | 7 | .547 |

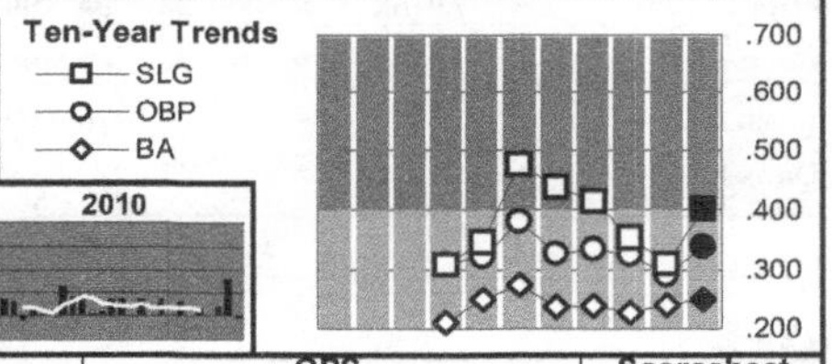


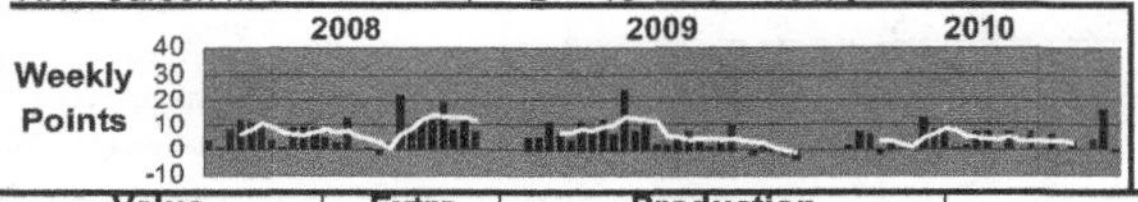


| Yr | Team | AB | HR | R | RBI | SB | BA | OBP | SLG | CT% | H% | BB% | Bash | $1L | $2L | Pts | RAA | 2B | 3B | CS | FB-LD-GB | HR/fb | RBI% | RS% | OPS | 1st Hf | 2nd Hf | vs RH | vs LH | Rnge | vRH | vLH |
|---|---|---|---|---|---|---|---|---|---|---|---|---|---|---|---|---|---|---|---|---|---|---|---|---|---|---|---|---|---|---|---|---|
| | | Majors | | | | | | | | Skills | | | | Value | | | | Extra | | | Production | | | | OPS | | | | | Scoresheet | | |
| 07 | MIL | 183 | 7 | 28 | 24 | 3 | .235 | .329 | .437 | 80% | 29% | 12% | 1.86 | $0 | -$11 | 120 | −3 | 12 | 2 | 1 | 41-20-39 | 12% | 16% | 34% | .766 | .692 | .823 | .788 | .424 | 2.10 | +29 | −108 |
| 08 | 2TM | 345 | 13 | 46 | 40 | 4 | .238 | .336 | .414 | 76% | 31% | 13% | 1.74 | $1 | -$5 | 200 | −6 | 16 | 3 | 2 | 43-17-41 | 12% | 15% | 27% | .750 | .729 | .775 | .789 | .585 | 2.11 | +29 | −111 |
| 09 | TB | 282 | 6 | 31 | 36 | 6 | .227 | .326 | .355 | 72% | 32% | 13% | 1.56 | $3 | -$11 | 140 | −11 | 16 | 1 | 3 | 36-23-40 | 8% | 19% | 25% | .681 | .802 | .512 | .673 | .747 | 2.11 | +26 | −91 |
| 10 | OAK | 222 | 1 | 27 | 25 | 5 | .239 | .290 | .311 | 82% | 29% | 7% | 1.30 | $1 | -$13 | 110 | −16 | 11 | 1 | 1 | 34-20-46 | 2% | 18% | 38% | .601 | .641 | .512 | .610 | .552 | — | +19 | −70 |

## Mark Grudzielanek — 50 PA | $-5 | 20 pts

2B-27, DH-1 — Owned: 0% — RH

Grudzielanek made the Indians' roster in 2010 as a Spring Training invitee, and he appeared in 30 games before being released. Wanting in power, he will have a hard time signing anything more than a minor-league deal, and he may retire. If Grudz does appear again in MLB, it will be strictly for his defense. (BLS)

| Player | Age | AB | HR | R | RBI | SB | BA | OBP | SLG | $1L | Pts |
|---|---|---|---|---|---|---|---|---|---|---|---|
| | | Forecast | | | | | | | | | |
| Grudzielanek M | 40 | 46 | 1 | 5 | 4 | 1 | .269 | .313 | .351 | -$5 | 20 |
| **Mini-Browser** | **Age** | **AB** | **HR** | **R** | **RBI** | **SB** | **BA** | **OBP** | **SLG** | **$1L** | **Pts** |
| Zawadzki L | 25 | 65 | 1 | 6 | 6 | 2 | .194 | .277 | .321 | -$4 | 30 |
| Forsythe L | 24 | 72 | 1 | 9 | 6 | 1 | .201 | .320 | .297 | -$4 | 30 |
| Havens R | 24 | 42 | 3 | 5 | 6 | 1 | .202 | .307 | .419 | -$4 | 20 |
| McCoy M | 29 | 44 | 1 | 6 | 4 | 2 | .239 | .329 | .331 | -$5 | 30 |
| Iwamura A | 32 | 45 | 1 | 7 | 3 | 1 | .258 | .342 | .367 | -$5 | 20 |

| Level | Leag | AB | HR | R | RBI | SB | BA | OBP | SLG | CT% | H% | BB% | Bash |
|---|---|---|---|---|---|---|---|---|---|---|---|---|---|
| | | Minors (2010) | | | | | | | | Skills | | | |
| A | — | — | — | — | — | — | — | — | — | — | — | — | — |
| AA | — | — | — | — | — | — | — | — | — | — | — | — | — |
| AAA | — | — | — | — | — | — | — | — | — | — | — | — | — |

| Competition at 2B | | Stats in 2010 | | | |
|---|---|---|---|---|---|
| Bats | Player | GSvR | GSvL | Sub | OPS |
| LH | Valbuena L | 58 | 10 | 3 | .531 |
| RH | Donald J | 23 | 17 | 1 | .690 |
| RH | Grudzielanek M | 12 | 14 | 1 | .600 |
| RH | Nix J | 20 | 5 | 0 | .676 |

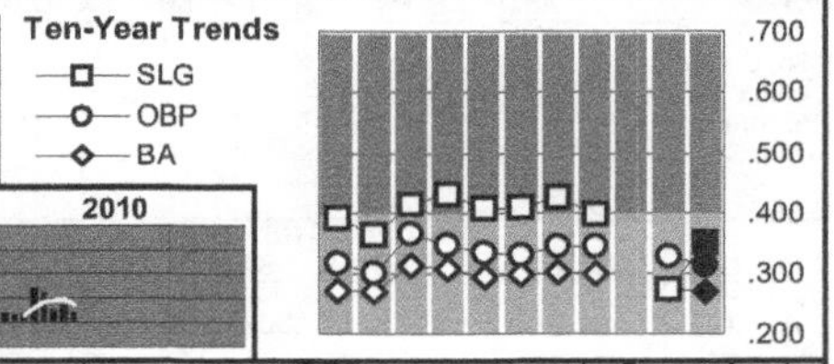


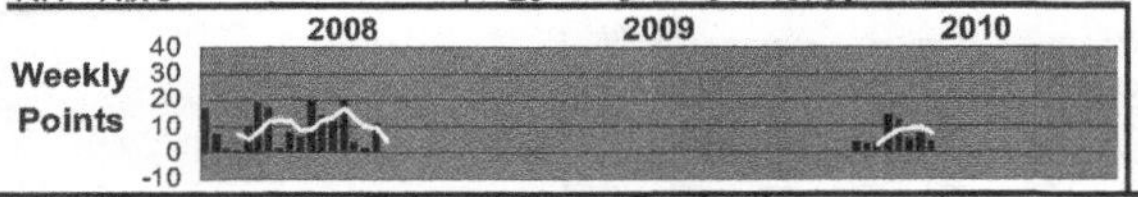


| Yr | Team | AB | HR | R | RBI | SB | BA | OBP | SLG | CT% | H% | BB% | Bash | $1L | $2L | Pts | RAA | 2B | 3B | CS | FB-LD-GB | HR/fb | RBI% | RS% | OPS | 1st Hf | 2nd Hf | vs RH | vs LH | Rnge | vRH | vLH |
|---|---|---|---|---|---|---|---|---|---|---|---|---|---|---|---|---|---|---|---|---|---|---|---|---|---|---|---|---|---|---|---|---|
| | | Majors | | | | | | | | Skills | | | | Value | | | | Extra | | | Production | | | | OPS | | | | | Scoresheet | | |
| 07 | KC | 453 | 6 | 70 | 51 | 1 | .302 | .346 | .426 | 87% | 35% | 5% | 1.41 | — | — | 280 | +3 | 32 | 3 | 2 | 31-19-49 | 5% | 21% | 40% | .772 | .749 | .792 | .739 | .844 | 4.32 | — | — |
| 08 | KC | 331 | 3 | 36 | 24 | 2 | .299 | .345 | .399 | 88% | 34% | 5% | 1.33 | — | — | 170 | −0 | 24 | 0 | 1 | 30-24-46 | 3% | 14% | 28% | .743 | .770 | .565 | .656 | .982 | 4.28 | — | — |
| 09 | — | — | — | — | — | — | — | — | — | — | — | — | — | — | — | — | — | — | — | — | — | — | — | — | — | — | — | — | — | — | — | — |
| 10 | CLE | 110 | 0 | 10 | 11 | 2 | .273 | .328 | .273 | 91% | 30% | 7% | 1.00 | -$1 | -$17 | 50 | −4 | 0 | 0 | 0 | 27-19-54 | 0% | 20% | 26% | .600 | .600 | — | .607 | .588 | 4.25 | — | — |

## Vladimir Guerrero — 550 PA | $23 | 410 pts

DH-129, OF-18 (RF-17, LF-1) — Owned: 100% — RH

Guerrero's effectiveness in the outfield is shot, but clearly his bat is not. His bad ball-hitting tendencies are as conspicuous as ever, but he continues to hit for both power and average with proficiency and he should be a DH somewhere if Texas elects not to keep him. Fragileness and deterioration remain concerns. (JM)

| Player | Age | AB | HR | R | RBI | SB | BA | OBP | SLG | $1L | Pts |
|---|---|---|---|---|---|---|---|---|---|---|---|
| | | Forecast | | | | | | | | | |
| Guerrero V | 36 | 517 | 28 | 72 | 88 | 6 | .298 | .355 | .508 | $23 | 410 |
| **Mini-Browser** | **Age** | **AB** | **HR** | **R** | **RBI** | **SB** | **BA** | **OBP** | **SLG** | **$1L** | **Pts** |
| Abreu B | 37 | 533 | 18 | 84 | 84 | 24 | .270 | .361 | .432 | $22 | 430 |
| Ortiz D | 35 | 444 | 26 | 74 | 89 | 0 | .272 | .374 | .533 | $19 | 370 |
| Scott L | 32 | 450 | 25 | 60 | 70 | 0 | .278 | .361 | .521 | $16 | 320 |
| Lind A | 27 | 581 | 24 | 66 | 84 | 0 | .258 | .313 | .458 | $16 | 340 |
| Matsui H | 36 | 421 | 20 | 55 | 75 | 0 | .273 | .358 | .457 | $14 | 300 |

| Level | Leag | AB | HR | R | RBI | SB | BA | OBP | SLG | CT% | H% | BB% | Bash |
|---|---|---|---|---|---|---|---|---|---|---|---|---|---|
| | | Minors (2010) | | | | | | | | Skills | | | |
| A | — | — | — | — | — | — | — | — | — | — | — | — | — |
| AA | — | — | — | — | — | — | — | — | — | — | — | — | — |
| AAA | — | — | — | — | — | — | — | — | — | — | — | — | — |

| Competition at DH | | Stats in 2010 | | | |
|---|---|---|---|---|---|
| Bats | Player | GSvR | GSvL | Sub | OPS |
| RH | Guerrero V | 88 | 41 | 0 | .841 |
| LH | Hamilton J | 12 | 1 | 0 | 1.044 |

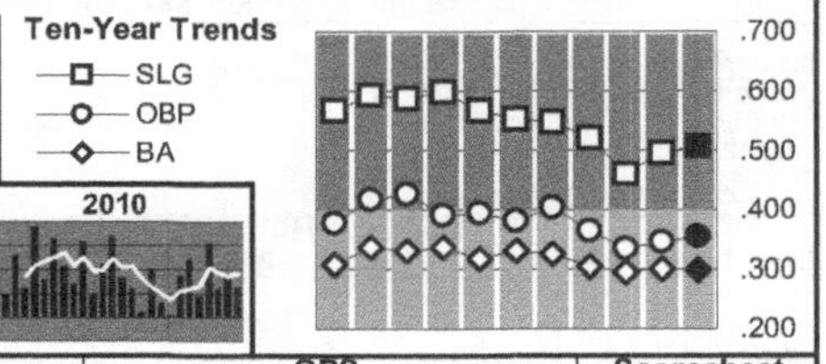


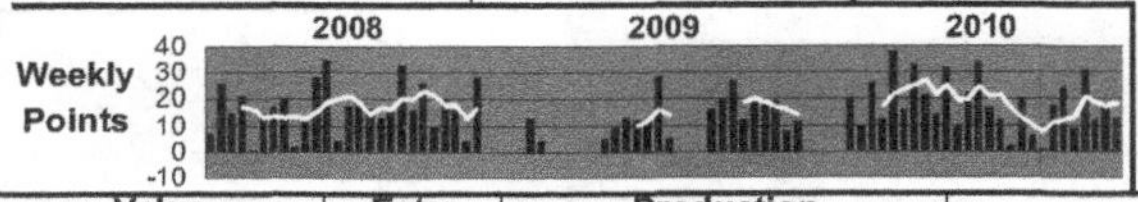


| Yr | Team | AB | HR | R | RBI | SB | BA | OBP | SLG | CT% | H% | BB% | Bash | $1L | $2L | Pts | RAA | 2B | 3B | CS | FB-LD-GB | HR/fb | RBI% | RS% | OPS | 1st Hf | 2nd Hf | vs RH | vs LH | Rnge | vRH | vLH |
|---|---|---|---|---|---|---|---|---|---|---|---|---|---|---|---|---|---|---|---|---|---|---|---|---|---|---|---|---|---|---|---|---|
| | | Majors | | | | | | | | Skills | | | | Value | | | | Extra | | | Production | | | | OPS | | | | | Scoresheet | | |
| 07 | LAA | 574 | 27 | 89 | 125 | 2 | .324 | .403 | .547 | 89% | 36% | 10% | 1.69 | $30 | $25 | 540 | +22 | 45 | 1 | 3 | 36-16-48 | 15% | 30% | 26% | .950 | .962 | .935 | .942 | .982 | 4.25 | −29 | +74 |
| 08 | LAA | 541 | 27 | 85 | 91 | 5 | .303 | .365 | .521 | 86% | 35% | 8% | 1.72 | $26 | $18 | 440 | +11 | 31 | 3 | 3 | 36-17-47 | 16% | 22% | 30% | .886 | .831 | .972 | .907 | .826 | 4.25 | −28 | +80 |
| 09 | LAA | 383 | 15 | 59 | 50 | 2 | .295 | .334 | .460 | 85% | 35% | 5% | 1.56 | $12 | $2 | 250 | −3 | 16 | 1 | 1 | 40-18-42 | 11% | 18% | 36% | .794 | .734 | .844 | .831 | .686 | 4.25 | −5 | +14 |
| 10 | TEX | 593 | 29 | 83 | 115 | 4 | .300 | .345 | .496 | 90% | 33% | 5% | 1.65 | $31 | $25 | 470 | +1 | 27 | 1 | 5 | 37-18-45 | 15% | 24% | 28% | .841 | .919 | .748 | .810 | .932 | 4.25 | +2 | −6 |

## Carlos Guillen — 175 PA | $1 | 110 pts

2B-47, DH-16, OF-4 (LF-4) — Owned: 2% — BH

Guillen's 2010 season ended with knee surgery, and he might not be ready for Opening Day. If the Tigers acquire a veteran left-handed hitter over the winter, they could eat the final year of his contract. Otherwise, once he is ready to go, he will be a utility man splitting time between outfield, second base, and DH. (LP)

| Player | Age | AB | HR | R | RBI | SB | BA | OBP | SLG | $1L | Pts |
|---|---|---|---|---|---|---|---|---|---|---|---|
| Guillen C | 35 | 153 | 5 | 21 | 23 | 2 | .274 | .350 | .448 | $1 | 110 |
| **Mini-Browser** | **Age** | **AB** | **HR** | **R** | **RBI** | **SB** | **BA** | **OBP** | **SLG** | **$1L** | **Pts** |
| Kennedy A | 35 | 190 | 2 | 22 | 18 | 6 | .263 | .326 | .365 | $3 | 110 |
| Brignac R | 25 | 279 | 9 | 33 | 33 | 3 | .247 | .297 | .400 | $3 | 140 |
| Barmes C | 32 | 211 | 7 | 27 | 25 | 5 | .266 | .319 | .441 | $2 | 130 |
| Sogard E | 24 | 345 | 8 | 40 | 40 | 8 | .220 | .295 | .343 | $2 | 190 |
| Fontenot M | 30 | 179 | 4 | 24 | 22 | 2 | .279 | .346 | .434 | $1 | 110 |

Minors (2010)

| Level | Leag | AB | HR | R | RBI | SB | BA | OBP | SLG | CT% | H% | BB% | Bash |
|---|---|---|---|---|---|---|---|---|---|---|---|---|---|
| A | MID | 6 | 0 | 0 | 0 | 0 | .333 | .429 | .333 | 100% | 33% | 14% | 1.00 |
| AA | — | — | — | — | — | — | — | — | — | — | — | — | — |
| AAA | IL | 18 | 1 | 5 | 2 | 0 | .333 | .400 | .667 | 78% | 43% | 10% | 2.00 |

Competition at 2B — Stats in 2010

| Bats | Player | GSvR | GSvL | Sub | OPS |
|---|---|---|---|---|---|
| LH | Rhymes W | 37 | 9 | 7 | .763 |
| BH | Guillen C | 33 | 12 | 2 | .746 |
| RH | Sizemore S | 23 | 13 | 4 | .631 |
| RH | Raburn R | 11 | 5 | 2 | .814 |

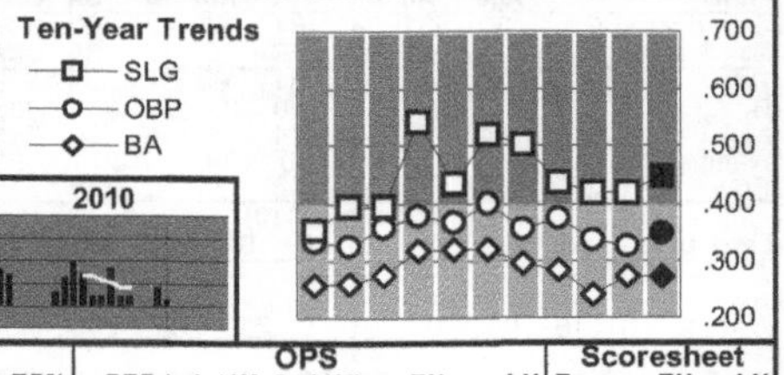

| Yr | Team | AB | HR | R | RBI | SB | BA | OBP | SLG | CT% | H% | BB% | Bash | $1L | $2L | Pts | RAA | 2B | 3B | CS | FB-LD-GB | HR/fb | RBI% | RS% | OPS | 1st Hf | 2nd Hf | vs RH | vs LH | Rnge | vRH | vLH |
|---|---|---|---|---|---|---|---|---|---|---|---|---|---|---|---|---|---|---|---|---|---|---|---|---|---|---|---|---|---|---|---|---|
| 07 | DET | 564 | 21 | 86 | 102 | 13 | .296 | .357 | .502 | 84% | 35% | 9% | 1.69 | $25 | $18 | 450 | +21 | 35 | 9 | 8 | 41-20-39 | 11% | 24% | 32% | .859 | .968 | .747 | .843 | .921 | — | +9 | −24 |
| 08 | DET | 420 | 10 | 68 | 54 | 9 | .286 | .376 | .436 | 84% | 34% | 12% | 1.53 | $14 | $4 | 310 | +15 | 29 | 2 | 3 | 35-20-45 | 8% | 19% | 34% | .811 | .797 | .858 | .810 | .818 | — | +7 | −20 |
| 09 | DET | 277 | 11 | 36 | 41 | 1 | .242 | .339 | .419 | 80% | 30% | 12% | 1.73 | $5 | -$8 | 180 | −0 | 10 | 3 | 3 | 44-20-36 | 11% | 20% | 26% | .757 | .512 | .874 | .757 | .758 | — | −4 | +12 |
| 10 | DET | 253 | 6 | 26 | 34 | 1 | .273 | .327 | .419 | 84% | 33% | 8% | 1.54 | $4 | -$9 | 150 | +1 | 17 | 1 | 2 | 36-14-50 | 8% | 18% | 24% | .746 | .788 | .581 | .786 | .629 | — | −2 | +7 |

## Jose Guillen — 350 PA | $9 | 180 pts

DH-84, OF-60 (RF-60) — Owned: 44% — RH

Guillen's exclusion from the Giants' play-off roster might have been due to a sore neck, but it also speaks to Guillen's declining production over 2010 and to the liability that Guillen has become in the field. Given the logjam in SF's outfield with Mark DeRosa returning, Guillen probably will not return to San Fran. (PB)

| Player | Age | AB | HR | R | RBI | SB | BA | OBP | SLG | $1L | Pts |
|---|---|---|---|---|---|---|---|---|---|---|---|
| Guillen J | 34 | 326 | 11 | 35 | 49 | 0 | .268 | .319 | .428 | $9 | 180 |
| **Mini-Browser** | **Age** | **AB** | **HR** | **R** | **RBI** | **SB** | **BA** | **OBP** | **SLG** | **$1L** | **Pts** |
| Fukudome K | 33 | 364 | 9 | 59 | 45 | 9 | .272 | .383 | .436 | $9 | 270 |
| Carter C | 24 | 442 | 25 | 55 | 65 | 5 | .215 | .306 | .437 | $9 | 240 |
| Bernadina R | 26 | 466 | 10 | 55 | 45 | 25 | .236 | .307 | .359 | $9 | 260 |
| Kearns A | 30 | 402 | 10 | 60 | 55 | 5 | .261 | .355 | .397 | $9 | 240 |
| DeRosa M | 36 | 358 | 12 | 56 | 52 | 4 | .268 | .347 | .438 | $9 | 240 |

Minors (2010)

| Level | Leag | AB | HR | R | RBI | SB | BA | OBP | SLG | CT% | H% | BB% | Bash |
|---|---|---|---|---|---|---|---|---|---|---|---|---|---|
| A | — | — | — | — | — | — | — | — | — | — | — | — | — |
| AA | — | — | — | — | — | — | — | — | — | — | — | — | — |
| AAA | — | — | — | — | — | — | — | — | — | — | — | — | — |

Competition at RF — Stats in 2010

| Bats | Player | GSvR | GSvL | Sub | OPS |
|---|---|---|---|---|---|
| BH | Torres A | 28 | 15 | 0 | .823 |
| LH | Schierholtz N | 31 | 10 | 68 | .676 |
| RH | Guillen J | 28 | 10 | 0 | .730 |
| LH | Huff A | 28 | 6 | 0 | .891 |

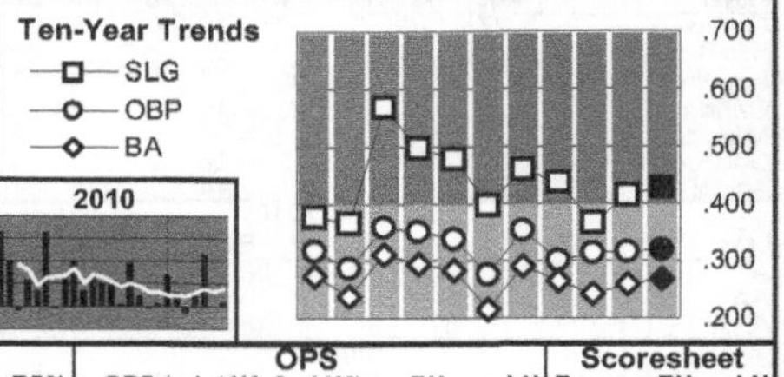


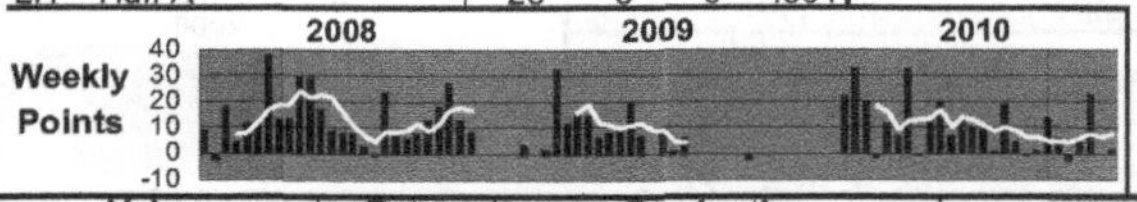


| Yr | Team | AB | HR | R | RBI | SB | BA | OBP | SLG | CT% | H% | BB% | Bash | $1L | $2L | Pts | RAA | 2B | 3B | CS | FB-LD-GB | HR/fb | RBI% | RS% | OPS | 1st Hf | 2nd Hf | vs RH | vs LH | Rnge | vRH | vLH |
|---|---|---|---|---|---|---|---|---|---|---|---|---|---|---|---|---|---|---|---|---|---|---|---|---|---|---|---|---|---|---|---|---|
| 07 | SEA | 593 | 23 | 84 | 99 | 5 | .290 | .353 | .460 | 80% | 36% | 6% | 1.59 | $23 | $16 | 390 | −5 | 28 | 2 | 1 | 36-16-48 | 13% | 21% | 29% | .813 | .795 | .830 | .741 | 1.049 | 2.09 | +1 | −3 |
| 08 | KC | 598 | 20 | 66 | 97 | 2 | .264 | .300 | .438 | 82% | 32% | 4% | 1.66 | $17 | $8 | 340 | −19 | 42 | 1 | 1 | 35-18-47 | 12% | 21% | 27% | .738 | .756 | .709 | .656 | .936 | 2.04 | −35 | +93 |
| 09 | KC | 281 | 9 | 30 | 40 | 1 | .242 | .314 | .367 | 82% | 29% | 7% | 1.51 | $4 | -$10 | 150 | −15 | 8 | 0 | 0 | 40-14-46 | 10% | 21% | 24% | .681 | .691 | .522 | .743 | .554 | 2.03 | −48 | +124 |
| 10 | 2TM | 524 | 19 | 55 | 77 | 1 | .258 | .314 | .416 | 78% | 33% | 6% | 1.61 | $13 | $4 | 270 | −21 | 22 | 2 | 0 | 39-17-45 | 12% | 19% | 22% | .730 | .807 | .606 | .755 | .632 | 2.02 | −25 | +60 |

## Franklin Gutierrez — 625 PA | $16 | 310 pts

OF-146 (CF-146), DH-5 — Owned: 47% — RH

Gutierrez came on like gangbusters in 2010, posting an .861 OPS in April and a .792 OPS in May. In the following four months, though, his OBP never cracked .280. Ultimately, Gutierrez is not strong enough to overcome his poor CT%. But it's clear he can turn up the juice in short stretches that earn more PT. (GC)

| Player | Age | AB | HR | R | RBI | SB | BA | OBP | SLG | $1L | Pts |
|---|---|---|---|---|---|---|---|---|---|---|---|
| Gutierrez F | 28 | 568 | 19 | 75 | 63 | 19 | .253 | .313 | .393 | $16 | 310 |
| **Mini-Browser** | **Age** | **AB** | **HR** | **R** | **RBI** | **SB** | **BA** | **OBP** | **SLG** | **$1L** | **Pts** |
| Ludwick R | 32 | 451 | 21 | 75 | 86 | 5 | .273 | .346 | .490 | $17 | 320 |
| Smith S | 28 | 478 | 22 | 77 | 72 | 6 | .276 | .355 | .494 | $17 | 360 |
| Stanton M | 21 | 541 | 36 | 72 | 84 | 6 | .244 | .327 | .507 | $16 | 340 |
| Davis R | 30 | 415 | 5 | 54 | 41 | 41 | .271 | .321 | .375 | $16 | 290 |
| DeJesus D | 31 | 578 | 13 | 75 | 63 | 6 | .292 | .361 | .434 | $16 | 380 |

Minors (2010)

| Level | Leag | AB | HR | R | RBI | SB | BA | OBP | SLG | CT% | H% | BB% | Bash |
|---|---|---|---|---|---|---|---|---|---|---|---|---|---|
| A | — | — | — | — | — | — | — | — | — | — | — | — | — |
| AA | — | — | — | — | — | — | — | — | — | — | — | — | — |
| AAA | — | — | — | — | — | — | — | — | — | — | — | — | — |

Competition at CF — Stats in 2010

| Bats | Player | GSvR | GSvL | Sub | OPS |
|---|---|---|---|---|---|
| RH | Gutierrez F | 102 | 43 | 1 | .666 |
| LH | Saunders M | 7 | 5 | 2 | .662 |

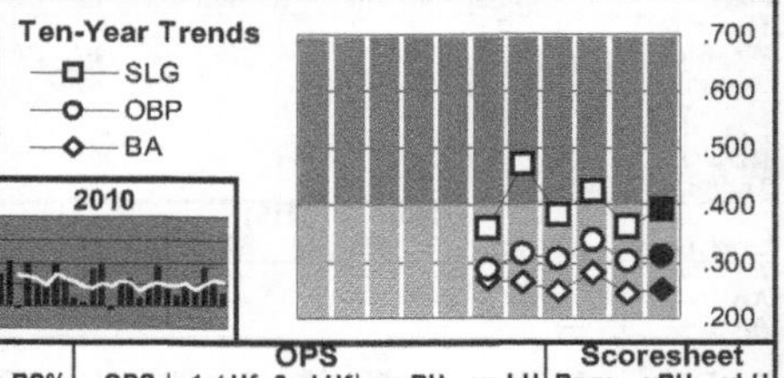


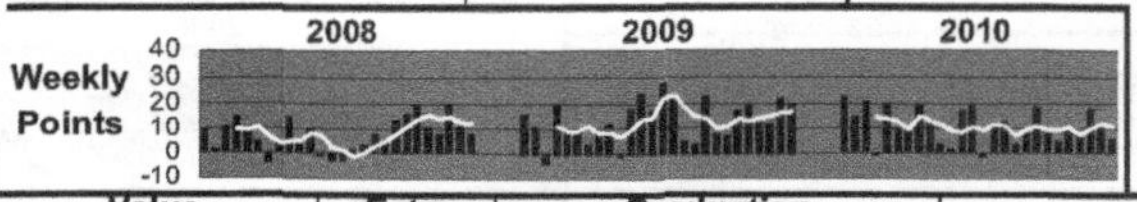


| Yr | Team | AB | HR | R | RBI | SB | BA | OBP | SLG | CT% | H% | BB% | Bash | $1L | $2L | Pts | RAA | 2B | 3B | CS | FB-LD-GB | HR/fb | RBI% | RS% | OPS | 1st Hf | 2nd Hf | vs RH | vs LH | Rnge | vRH | vLH |
|---|---|---|---|---|---|---|---|---|---|---|---|---|---|---|---|---|---|---|---|---|---|---|---|---|---|---|---|---|---|---|---|---|
| 07 | CLE | 271 | 13 | 41 | 36 | 8 | .266 | .318 | .472 | 72% | 37% | 7% | 1.78 | $8 | -$4 | 160 | +2 | 13 | 2 | 3 | 42-15-43 | 16% | 14% | 35% | .790 | .811 | .783 | .722 | .920 | 2.09 | −18 | +44 |
| 08 | CLE | 399 | 8 | 54 | 41 | 9 | .248 | .307 | .383 | 78% | 32% | 6% | 1.55 | $8 | -$4 | 200 | −12 | 26 | 2 | 3 | 41-17-42 | 6% | 15% | 37% | .691 | .579 | .816 | .659 | .755 | 2.10 | −27 | +64 |
| 09 | SEA | 565 | 18 | 85 | 70 | 16 | .283 | .339 | .425 | 78% | 36% | 7% | 1.50 | $20 | $12 | 350 | +3 | 24 | 1 | 5 | 36-19-45 | 11% | 21% | 35% | .764 | .801 | .727 | .681 | .963 | 2.14 | −30 | +68 |
| 10 | SEA | 568 | 12 | 61 | 64 | 25 | .245 | .303 | .363 | 76% | 32% | 8% | 1.48 | $16 | $5 | 290 | −14 | 25 | 3 | 3 | 42-16-42 | 7% | 18% | 28% | .666 | .717 | .601 | .653 | .704 | 2.21 | −35 | +83 |

## Cristian Guzman — 350 PA | $5 | 180 pts

2B-72, SS-23, OF-8 (RF-8), DH-4 — Owned: 38% — BH

LASIK is said to have helped resurrect Guzman's career, but his greatest enemy now is time. Guzman reluctantly joined the Rangers' cause in 2010 and promptly failed to produce (and then got hurt) during Ian Kinsler's DL stay. With his sliding Bash, Guzman is on the fast track to veteran UT IF purgatory. (JM)

| Player | Age | AB | HR | R | RBI | SB | BA | OBP | SLG | $1L | Pts |
|---|---|---|---|---|---|---|---|---|---|---|---|
| Guzman C | 33 | 314 | 4 | 46 | 32 | 4 | .279 | .314 | .389 | $5 | 180 |
| **Mini-Browser** | **Age** | **AB** | **HR** | **R** | **RBI** | **SB** | **BA** | **OBP** | **SLG** | **$1L** | **Pts** |
| Aviles M | 30 | 326 | 7 | 46 | 35 | 7 | .290 | .321 | .428 | $8 | 200 |
| Infante O | 29 | 344 | 4 | 49 | 41 | 4 | .294 | .342 | .398 | $8 | 210 |
| Ellis M | 33 | 350 | 8 | 44 | 44 | 8 | .263 | .326 | .394 | $7 | 220 |
| Donald J | 26 | 520 | 12 | 63 | 52 | 12 | .232 | .303 | .369 | $7 | 250 |
| Lopez F | 30 | 361 | 8 | 48 | 36 | 8 | .266 | .341 | .377 | $6 | 220 |

Minors (2010)

| Level | Leag | AB | HR | R | RBI | SB | BA | OBP | SLG | CT% | H% | BB% | Bash |
|---|---|---|---|---|---|---|---|---|---|---|---|---|---|
| A | — | — | — | — | — | — | — | — | — | — | — | — | — |
| AA | TL | 13 | 0 | 1 | 3 | 1 | .308 | .438 | .308 | 92% | 33% | 19% | 1.00 |
| AAA | — | — | — | — | — | — | — | — | — | — | — | — | — |

Competition at 2B — Stats in 2010

| Bats | Player | GSvR | GSvL | Sub | OPS |
|---|---|---|---|---|---|
| RH | Kinsler I | 71 | 31 | 1 | .794 |
| BH | Blanco A | 20 | 11 | 9 | .679 |

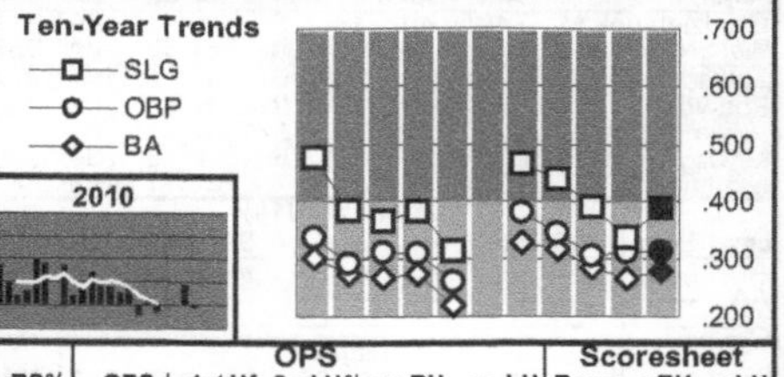


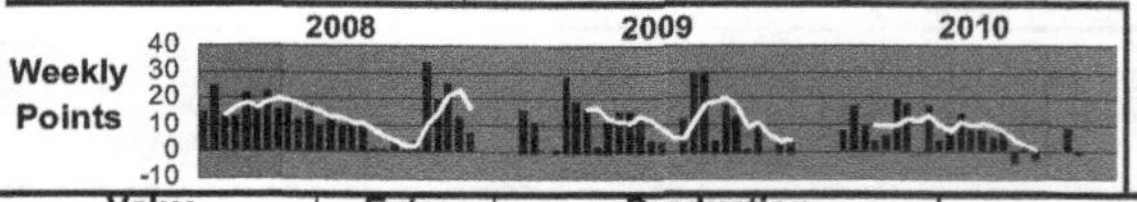


| Yr | Team | AB | HR | R | RBI | SB | BA | OBP | SLG | CT% | H% | BB% | Bash | $1L | $2L | Pts | RAA | 2B | 3B | CS | FB-LD-GB | HR/fb | RBI% | RS% | OPS | 1st Hf | 2nd Hf | vs RH | vs LH | Rnge | vRH | vLH |
|---|---|---|---|---|---|---|---|---|---|---|---|---|---|---|---|---|---|---|---|---|---|---|---|---|---|---|---|---|---|---|---|---|
| 07 | WAS | 174 | 2 | 31 | 14 | 2 | .328 | .380 | .466 | 88% | 37% | 8% | 1.42 | $1 | -$10 | 120 | +7 | 6 | 6 | 0 | 23-17-60 | 6% | 22% | 41% | .846 | .850 | .000 | .856 | .810 | — | +15 | −40 |
| 08 | WAS | 579 | 9 | 77 | 55 | 6 | .316 | .345 | .440 | 90% | 35% | 4% | 1.39 | $18 | $9 | 360 | +8 | 35 | 5 | 5 | 25-23-53 | 7% | 20% | 34% | .786 | .765 | .834 | .731 | .905 | — | +6 | −15 |
| 09 | WAS | 531 | 6 | 74 | 52 | 4 | .284 | .306 | .390 | 86% | 33% | 3% | 1.37 | $12 | $2 | 280 | −11 | 24 | 7 | 5 | 29-17-54 | 5% | 19% | 42% | .696 | .726 | .654 | .679 | .748 | — | −15 | +37 |
| 10 | 2TM | 365 | 2 | 48 | 26 | 4 | .266 | .311 | .337 | 83% | 32% | 5% | 1.27 | $5 | -$8 | 160 | −15 | 12 | 4 | 2 | 29-19-52 | 2% | 16% | 38% | .648 | .712 | .427 | .598 | .752 | — | −20 | +51 |

## Jesus Guzman — 25 PA | $-5 | 10 pts

No MLB games played in 2010 — Owned: 0% — RH

Guzman began his career as a bat-first middle infielder, but he was unable to improve his fielding, and lately he gets work at 3B and LF. He did not surface on the prospect radars of his former organizations, Oakland and Seattle, but he has shown he can handle Pacific Coast League pitching with Fresno. (PB)

| Player | Age | AB | HR | R | RBI | SB | BA | OBP | SLG | $1L | Pts |
|---|---|---|---|---|---|---|---|---|---|---|---|
| Guzman J | 26 | 23 | 1 | 3 | 3 | 0 | .247 | .307 | .419 | -$5 | 10 |
| **Mini-Browser** | **Age** | **AB** | **HR** | **R** | **RBI** | **SB** | **BA** | **OBP** | **SLG** | **$1L** | **Pts** |
| Hicks B | 25 | 71 | 3 | 9 | 7 | 2 | .201 | .293 | .390 | -$4 | 40 |
| Mitchell R | 26 | 94 | 4 | 9 | 10 | 0 | .203 | .249 | .376 | -$4 | 40 |
| Emaus B | 25 | 90 | 3 | 10 | 10 | 2 | .211 | .282 | .356 | -$4 | 50 |
| Barden B | 29 | 44 | 1 | 6 | 5 | 0 | .249 | .318 | .376 | -$4 | 20 |
| Frandsen K | 28 | 45 | 1 | 6 | 5 | 1 | .269 | .329 | .386 | -$5 | 30 |

Minors (2010)

| Level | Leag | AB | HR | R | RBI | SB | BA | OBP | SLG | CT% | H% | BB% | Bash |
|---|---|---|---|---|---|---|---|---|---|---|---|---|---|
| A | — | — | — | — | — | — | — | — | — | — | — | — | — |
| AA | — | — | — | — | — | — | — | — | — | — | — | — | — |
| AAA | PCL | 445 | 18 | 66 | 72 | 6 | .321 | .376 | .510 | 85% | 38% | 8% | 1.59 |

Competition at 3B — Stats in 2010

| Bats | Player | GSvR | GSvL | Sub | OPS |
|---|---|---|---|---|---|
| BH | Sandoval P | 102 | 37 | 4 | .732 |
| RH | Uribe J | 16 | 9 | 1 | .749 |

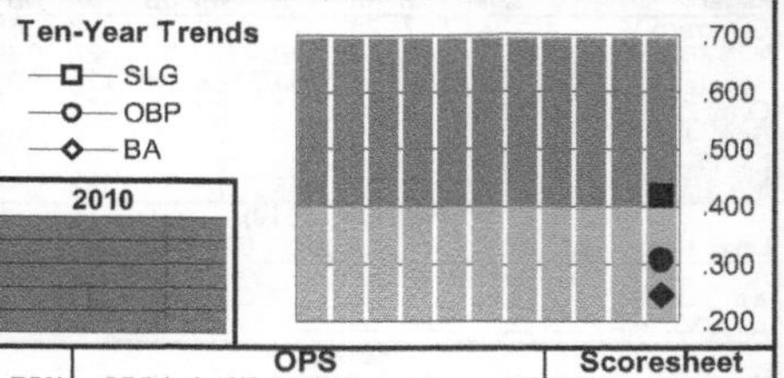


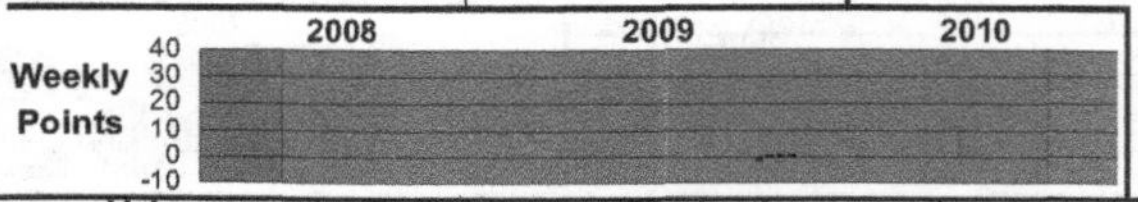


| Yr | Team | AB | HR | R | RBI | SB | BA | OBP | SLG | CT% | H% | BB% | Bash | $1L | $2L | Pts | RAA | 2B | 3B | CS | FB-LD-GB | HR/fb | RBI% | RS% | OPS | 1st Hf | 2nd Hf | vs RH | vs LH | Rnge | vRH | vLH |
|---|---|---|---|---|---|---|---|---|---|---|---|---|---|---|---|---|---|---|---|---|---|---|---|---|---|---|---|---|---|---|---|---|
| 07 | — | — | — | — | — | — | — | — | — | — | — | — | — | — | — | — | — | — | — | — | — | — | — | — | — | — | — | — | — | — | — | — |
| 08 | — | — | — | — | — | — | — | — | — | — | — | — | — | — | — | — | — | — | — | — | — | — | — | — | — | — | — | — | — | — | — | — |
| 09 | SF | 20 | 0 | 0 | 0 | 0 | .250 | .250 | .250 | 85% | 29% | 0% | 1.00 | -$5 | -$20 | 0 | −2 | 0 | 0 | 0 | 6/18/1976 | 0% | 0% | 0% | .500 | .200 | .800 | .571 | .462 | — | — | — |
| 10 | — | — | — | — | — | — | — | — | — | — | — | — | — | — | — | — | — | — | — | — | — | — | — | — | — | — | — | — | — | — | −14 | +34 |

*For more stats, visit www.Rotolympus.com.*

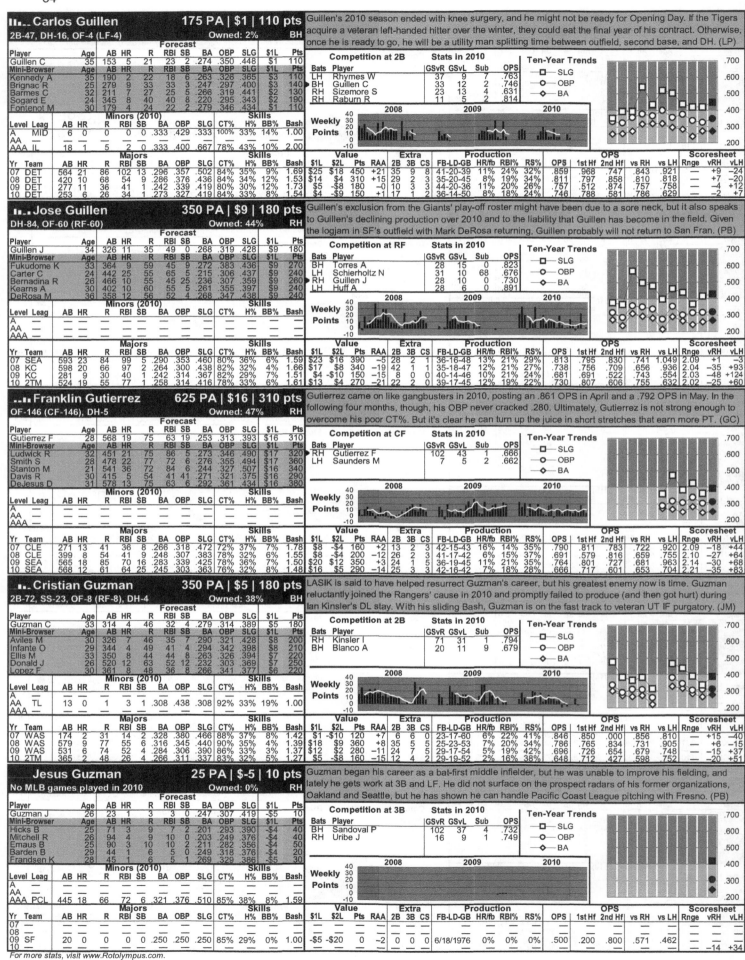

## Tony Gwynn — 300 PA | $1 | 140 pts

OF-105 (CF-105) — Owned: 1% — LH

Gwynn in 2010 suffered some lousy luck on batted balls (a 25% hit rate), and he broke a bone in his right hand, but he had a good BB% and played a crisp CF. It is not clear if the Padres view him as anything but an extra OF, so he'll compete with the likes of Aaron Cunningham, Chris Denorfia, and Will Venable. (DG)

**Forecast**

| Player | Age | AB | HR | R | RBI | SB | BA | OBP | SLG | $1L | Pts |
|---|---|---|---|---|---|---|---|---|---|---|---|
| Gwynn T | 28 | 259 | 3 | 33 | 18 | 12 | .232 | .313 | .306 | $1 | 140 |
| **Mini-Browser** | Age | AB | HR | R | RBI | SB | BA | OBP | SLG | $1L | Pts |
| Nix L | 30 | 192 | 10 | 24 | 24 | 0 | .260 | .319 | .489 | $1 | 110 |
| Hairston S | 30 | 219 | 9 | 25 | 28 | 2 | .242 | .308 | .433 | $1 | 130 |
| Schierholtz N | 27 | 182 | 4 | 24 | 20 | 4 | .274 | .319 | .445 | $1 | 110 |
| Craig A | 26 | 211 | 9 | 25 | 29 | 0 | .245 | .308 | .433 | $1 | 110 |
| Kalish R | 23 | 182 | 6 | 22 | 22 | 8 | .231 | .306 | .394 | $1 | 110 |

**Minors (2010)**

| Level | Leag | AB | HR | R | RBI | SB | BA | OBP | SLG | CT% | H% | BB% | Bash |
|---|---|---|---|---|---|---|---|---|---|---|---|---|---|
| A | — | — | — | — | — | — | — | — | — | — | — | — | — |
| AA | — | — | — | — | — | — | — | — | — | — | — | — | — |
| AAA | — | — | — | — | — | — | — | — | — | — | — | — | — |

**Competition at CF — Stats in 2010**

| Bats | Player | GSvR | GSvL | Sub | OPS |
|---|---|---|---|---|---|
| LH | Gwynn T | 67 | 5 | 33 | .591 |
| RH | Denorfia C | 19 | 28 | 3 | .769 |
| LH | Venable W | 19 | 3 | 3 | .732 |
| RH | Hairston S | 9 | 10 | 0 | .640 |

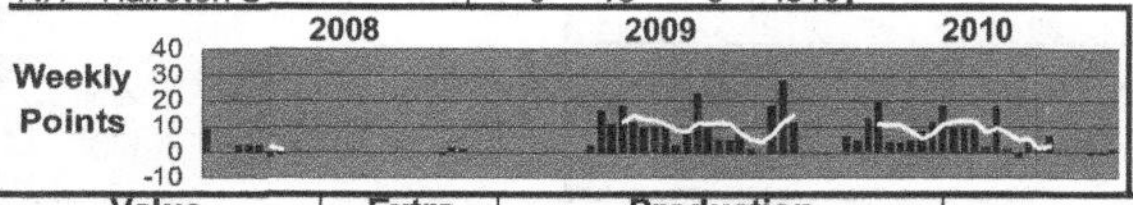
Weekly Points
2008
2009
2010

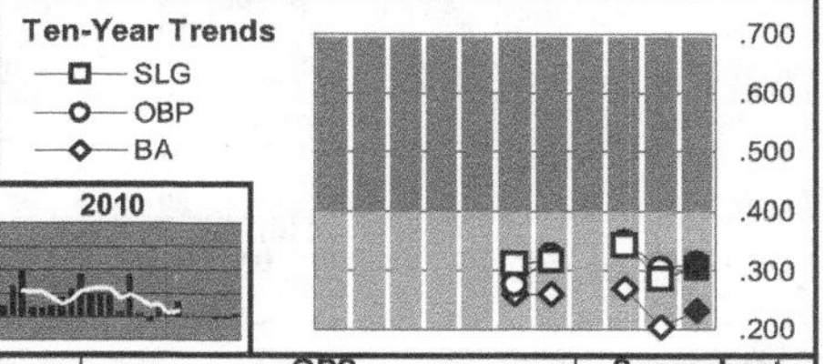
Ten-Year Trends
SLG
OBP
BA

**Majors**

| Yr | Team | AB | HR | R | RBI | SB | BA | OBP | SLG | CT% | H% | BB% | Bash | $1L | $2L | Pts | RAA | 2B | 3B | CS | FB-LD-GB | HR/fb | RBI% | RS% | OPS | 1st Hf | 2nd Hf | vs RH | vs LH | Rnge | vRH | vLH |
|---|---|---|---|---|---|---|---|---|---|---|---|---|---|---|---|---|---|---|---|---|---|---|---|---|---|---|---|---|---|---|---|---|
| 07 | MIL | 123 | 0 | 13 | 10 | 8 | .260 | .326 | .317 | 80% | 32% | 9% | 1.22 | -$2 | -$15 | 60 | −3 | 3 | 2 | 1 | 29-18-53 | 0% | 19% | 30% | .643 | .694 | .500 | .639 | .666 | 2.12 | +21 | −73 |
| 08 | MIL | 42 | 0 | 5 | 1 | 3 | .190 | .271 | .214 | 83% | 23% | 8% | 1.13 | -$4 | -$18 | 20 | −5 | 1 | 0 | 1 | 34-26-40 | 0% | 4% | 38% | .485 | .521 | .286 | .397 | 2.000 | 2.12 | +19 | −65 |
| 09 | SD | 393 | 2 | 59 | 21 | 11 | .270 | .350 | .344 | 83% | 32% | 11% | 1.27 | $7 | -$6 | 210 | −8 | 11 | 6 | 7 | 30-24-46 | 2% | 15% | 37% | .693 | .768 | .639 | .763 | .501 | 2.14 | +13 | −45 |
| 10 | SD | 289 | 3 | 30 | 20 | 17 | .204 | .304 | .287 | 83% | 25% | 12% | 1.41 | $1 | -$13 | 150 | −16 | 9 | 3 | 4 | 35-19-46 | 4% | 13% | 28% | .591 | .630 | .465 | .547 | .872 | 2.17 | +30 | −88 |

## Travis Hafner — 525 PA | $12 | 280 pts

DH-109 — Owned: 3% — LH

Hafner has regained enough strength in his right shoulder to start five games in a row before needing a rest; as a result, he compiled the most PA in a season for him since 2007. The 30-HR power is gone, but Hafner is still a potent hitter when healthy, as evidenced by his .329/.409/.523 line after the Break. (BLS)

**Forecast**

| Player | Age | AB | HR | R | RBI | SB | BA | OBP | SLG | $1L | Pts |
|---|---|---|---|---|---|---|---|---|---|---|---|
| Hafner T | 33 | 439 | 16 | 58 | 68 | 0 | .263 | .364 | .447 | $12 | 280 |
| **Mini-Browser** | Age | AB | HR | R | RBI | SB | BA | OBP | SLG | $1L | Pts |
| Ortiz D | 35 | 444 | 26 | 74 | 89 | 0 | .272 | .374 | .533 | $19 | 370 |
| Scott L | 32 | 450 | 25 | 60 | 70 | 0 | .278 | .361 | .521 | $16 | 320 |
| Lind A | 27 | 581 | 24 | 66 | 84 | 0 | .258 | .313 | .458 | $16 | 340 |
| Matsui H | 36 | 421 | 20 | 55 | 75 | 0 | .273 | .358 | .457 | $14 | 300 |
| Damon J | 37 | 418 | 10 | 71 | 48 | 14 | .273 | .354 | .429 | $14 | 310 |

**Minors (2010)**

| Level | Leag | AB | HR | R | RBI | SB | BA | OBP | SLG | CT% | H% | BB% | Bash |
|---|---|---|---|---|---|---|---|---|---|---|---|---|---|
| A | — | — | — | — | — | — | — | — | — | — | — | — | — |
| AA | — | — | — | — | — | — | — | — | — | — | — | — | — |
| AAA | — | — | — | — | — | — | — | — | — | — | — | — | — |

**Competition at DH — Stats in 2010**

| Bats | Player | GSvR | GSvL | Sub | OPS |
|---|---|---|---|---|---|
| LH | Hafner T | 92 | 16 | 1 | .824 |
| RH | Duncan S | 6 | 9 | 2 | .736 |

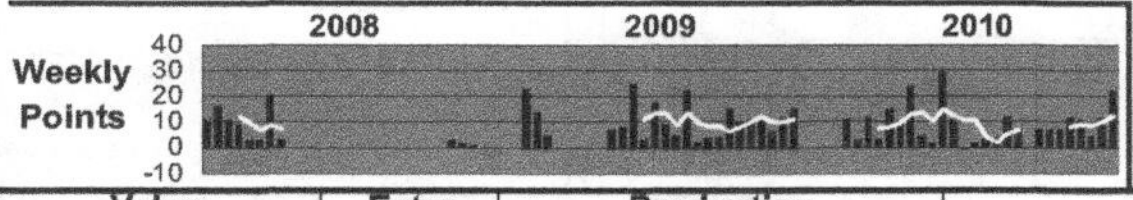
Weekly Points
2008
2009
2010

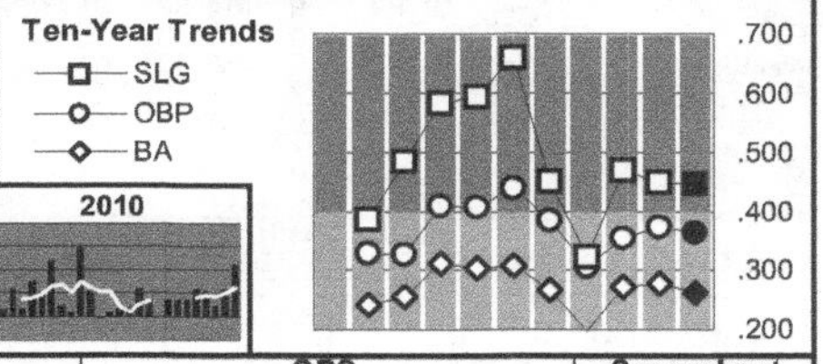
Ten-Year Trends
SLG
OBP
BA

**Majors**

| Yr | Team | AB | HR | R | RBI | SB | BA | OBP | SLG | CT% | H% | BB% | Bash | $1L | $2L | Pts | RAA | 2B | 3B | CS | FB-LD-GB | HR/fb | RBI% | RS% | OPS | 1st Hf | 2nd Hf | vs RH | vs LH | Rnge | vRH | vLH |
|---|---|---|---|---|---|---|---|---|---|---|---|---|---|---|---|---|---|---|---|---|---|---|---|---|---|---|---|---|---|---|---|---|
| 07 | CLE | 545 | 24 | 80 | 100 | 1 | .266 | .385 | .451 | 79% | 34% | 15% | 1.70 | $19 | $11 | 410 | +3 | 25 | 2 | 1 | 35-17-48 | 16% | 23% | 24% | .837 | .849 | .821 | .836 | .837 | — | +15 | −36 |
| 08 | CLE | 198 | 5 | 21 | 24 | 1 | .197 | .305 | .323 | 72% | 27% | 11% | 1.64 | -$1 | -$15 | 80 | −17 | 10 | 0 | 1 | 33-25-42 | 10% | 18% | 24% | .628 | .677 | .437 | .637 | .602 | 2.17 | +6 | −13 |
| 09 | CLE | 338 | 16 | 46 | 49 | 0 | .272 | .355 | .470 | 80% | 34% | 11% | 1.73 | $9 | -$1 | 230 | +1 | 19 | 0 | 0 | 40-21-39 | 15% | 17% | 25% | .826 | .944 | .746 | .866 | .696 | 2.17 | +15 | −37 |
| 10 | CLE | 396 | 13 | 46 | 50 | 2 | .278 | .374 | .449 | 76% | 36% | 11% | 1.62 | $11 | $0 | 230 | −3 | 29 | 0 | 1 | 38-19-43 | 11% | 16% | 21% | .824 | .756 | .932 | .863 | .706 | 2.17 | +26 | −77 |

## Jerry Hairston — 310 PA | $3 | 170 pts

SS-62, 2B-47, OF-12 (RF-8, LF-4), 3B-3 — Owned: 18% — RH

Hairston in 2010 roamed all around the field and contributed value with his glove, though he remained an easy out at the plate and had his season ended early by a fractured tibia and a sore elbow. He would like to return to San Diego, and the Padres seem interested in keeping the free-agent-to-be in a UT role. (DG)

**Forecast**

| Player | Age | AB | HR | R | RBI | SB | BA | OBP | SLG | $1L | Pts |
|---|---|---|---|---|---|---|---|---|---|---|---|
| Hairston J | 34 | 289 | 6 | 37 | 31 | 6 | .247 | .310 | .369 | $3 | 170 |
| **Mini-Browser** | Age | AB | HR | R | RBI | SB | BA | OBP | SLG | $1L | Pts |
| Uribe J | 32 | 467 | 15 | 55 | 65 | 0 | .257 | .309 | .437 | $10 | 260 |
| Cedeno R | 28 | 467 | 10 | 50 | 50 | 10 | .257 | .305 | .384 | $8 | 230 |
| Ryan B | 29 | 460 | 5 | 60 | 35 | 15 | .250 | .309 | .340 | $7 | 260 |
| Cabrera O | 36 | 366 | 4 | 48 | 36 | 8 | .273 | .316 | .365 | $6 | 220 |
| Izturis C | 31 | 458 | 0 | 45 | 30 | 15 | .262 | .306 | .319 | $4 | 240 |

**Minors (2010)**

| Level | Leag | AB | HR | R | RBI | SB | BA | OBP | SLG | CT% | H% | BB% | Bash |
|---|---|---|---|---|---|---|---|---|---|---|---|---|---|
| A | — | — | — | — | — | — | — | — | — | — | — | — | — |
| AA | — | — | — | — | — | — | — | — | — | — | — | — | — |
| AAA | — | — | — | — | — | — | — | — | — | — | — | — | — |

**Competition at SS — Stats in 2010**

| Bats | Player | GSvR | GSvL | Sub | OPS |
|---|---|---|---|---|---|
| RH | Hairston J | 38 | 21 | 3 | .652 |
| RH | Tejada M | 38 | 20 | 0 | .692 |
| BH | Cabrera E | 39 | 11 | 11 | .557 |

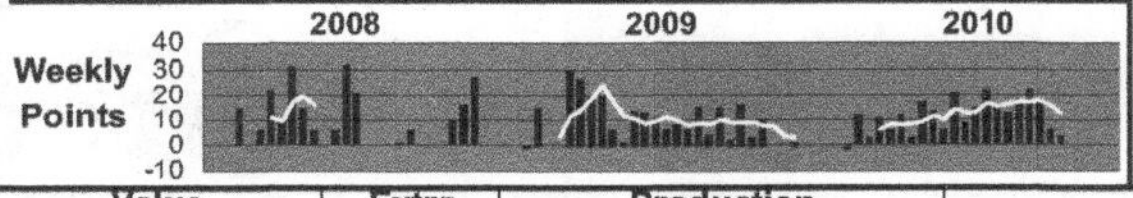
Weekly Points
2008
2009
2010

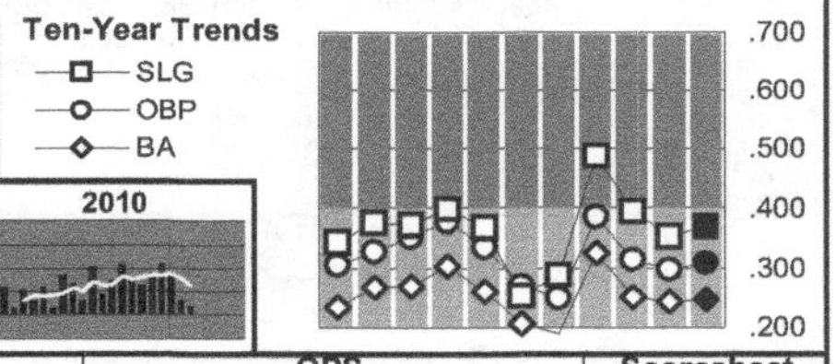
Ten-Year Trends
SLG
OBP
BA

**Majors**

| Yr | Team | AB | HR | R | RBI | SB | BA | OBP | SLG | CT% | H% | BB% | Bash | $1L | $2L | Pts | RAA | 2B | 3B | CS | FB-LD-GB | HR/fb | RBI% | RS% | OPS | 1st Hf | 2nd Hf | vs RH | vs LH | Rnge | vRH | vLH |
|---|---|---|---|---|---|---|---|---|---|---|---|---|---|---|---|---|---|---|---|---|---|---|---|---|---|---|---|---|---|---|---|---|
| 07 | TEX | 159 | 3 | 22 | 16 | 5 | .189 | .249 | .289 | 85% | 22% | 6% | 1.53 | -$1 | -$16 | 80 | −13 | 7 | 0 | 1 | 52-14-35 | 4% | 21% | 46% | .538 | .636 | .324 | .512 | .566 | — | −3 | +5 |
| 08 | CIN | 261 | 6 | 47 | 36 | 15 | .326 | .384 | .487 | 86% | 38% | 8% | 1.49 | $12 | $2 | 220 | +17 | 20 | 2 | 3 | 41-28-32 | 7% | 26% | 39% | .871 | .893 | .815 | .824 | .966 | — | −4 | +9 |
| 09 | 2TM | 383 | 10 | 62 | 39 | 7 | .251 | .315 | .394 | 86% | 29% | 7% | 1.57 | $4 | -$3 | 240 | −2 | 23 | 1 | 4 | 43-23-34 | 7% | 16% | 42% | .710 | .688 | .757 | .694 | .741 | 4.70 | −23 | +49 |
| 10 | SD | 430 | 10 | 53 | 50 | 9 | .244 | .299 | .353 | 87% | 28% | 6% | 1.45 | $8 | -$2 | 240 | −11 | 13 | 2 | 6 | 44-16-40 | 6% | 20% | 33% | .652 | .647 | .663 | .642 | .678 | 4.71 | −21 | +48 |

## Scott Hairston — 230 PA | $1 | 130 pts

OF-85 (LF-72, CF-19, RF-6), DH-1 — Owned: 0% — RH

Slowed in 2010 by hamstring and hip ailments and not showing his typical power, the younger Hairston is a prime non-tender candidate. He's a decent OF option when healthy, but his brittleness might lead SD to cut him loose and instead explore the FA market or give more PT to a guy like Aaron Cunningham. (DG)

**Forecast**

| Player | Age | AB | HR | R | RBI | SB | BA | OBP | SLG | $1L | Pts |
|---|---|---|---|---|---|---|---|---|---|---|---|
| Hairston S | 30 | 219 | 9 | 25 | 28 | 2 | .242 | .308 | .433 | $1 | 130 |
| **Mini-Browser** | Age | AB | HR | R | RBI | SB | BA | OBP | SLG | $1L | Pts |
| Jackson B | 22 | 133 | 6 | 23 | 17 | 5 | .237 | .331 | .433 | $2 | 80 |
| Patterson C | 31 | 188 | 4 | 22 | 20 | 10 | .255 | .296 | .394 | $2 | 110 |
| Diaz M | 33 | 186 | 6 | 24 | 26 | 4 | .269 | .325 | .430 | $2 | 110 |
| Parra G | 23 | 228 | 5 | 28 | 25 | 5 | .263 | .316 | .389 | $2 | 130 |
| Nix L | 30 | 192 | 10 | 24 | 24 | 0 | .260 | .319 | .489 | $1 | 110 |

**Minors (2010)**

| Level | Leag | AB | HR | R | RBI | SB | BA | OBP | SLG | CT% | H% | BB% | Bash |
|---|---|---|---|---|---|---|---|---|---|---|---|---|---|
| A | CAL | 7 | 0 | 1 | 1 | 0 | .571 | .727 | .714 | 86% | 67% | 36% | 1.25 |
| AA | — | — | — | — | — | — | — | — | — | — | — | — | — |
| AAA | — | — | — | — | — | — | — | — | — | — | — | — | — |

**Competition at LF — Stats in 2010**

| Bats | Player | GSvR | GSvL | Sub | OPS |
|---|---|---|---|---|---|
| RH | Hairston S | 36 | 29 | 7 | .640 |
| RH | Denorfia C | 17 | 12 | 15 | .769 |
| RH | Blanks K | 20 | 8 | 2 | .607 |
| LH | Venable W | 20 | 0 | 3 | .732 |

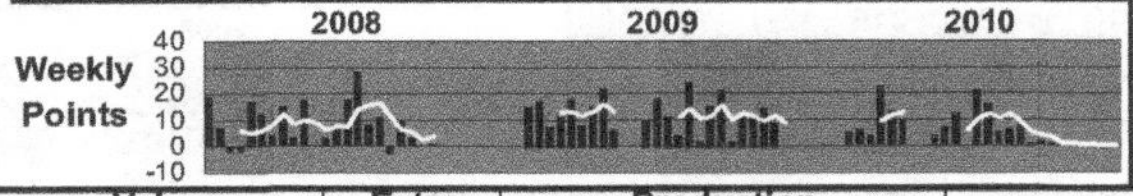
Weekly Points
2008
2009
2010

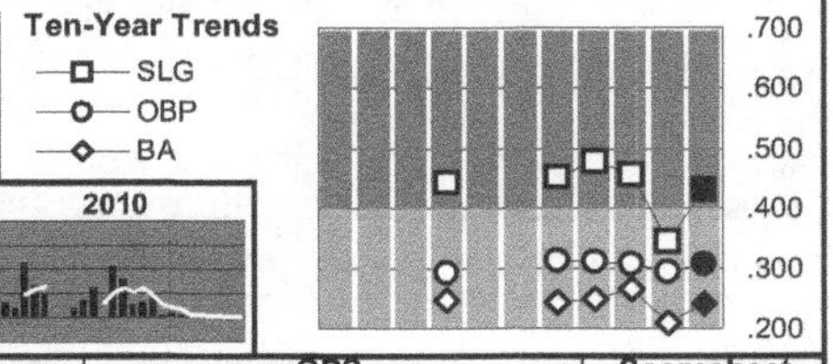
Ten-Year Trends
SLG
OBP
BA

**Majors**

| Yr | Team | AB | HR | R | RBI | SB | BA | OBP | SLG | CT% | H% | BB% | Bash | $1L | $2L | Pts | RAA | 2B | 3B | CS | FB-LD-GB | HR/fb | RBI% | RS% | OPS | 1st Hf | 2nd Hf | vs RH | vs LH | Rnge | vRH | vLH |
|---|---|---|---|---|---|---|---|---|---|---|---|---|---|---|---|---|---|---|---|---|---|---|---|---|---|---|---|---|---|---|---|---|
| 07 | 2TM | 263 | 11 | 37 | 36 | 2 | .243 | .313 | .452 | 79% | 31% | 9% | 1.86 | $3 | -$8 | 170 | −2 | 18 | 2 | 0 | 50-15-34 | 10% | 18% | 33% | .765 | .691 | .867 | .801 | .689 | 2.08 | −20 | +47 |
| 08 | SD | 326 | 17 | 42 | 31 | 3 | .248 | .312 | .479 | 74% | 33% | 8% | 1.93 | $6 | -$5 | 180 | −2 | 18 | 3 | 1 | 48-14-37 | 14% | 11% | 26% | .791 | .811 | .714 | .708 | .896 | 2.09 | −14 | +33 |
| 09 | 2TM | 430 | 17 | 50 | 64 | 11 | .265 | .307 | .456 | 81% | 33% | 5% | 1.72 | $9 | $2 | 270 | −3 | 27 | 2 | 3 | 51-15-34 | 10% | 20% | 26% | .763 | .870 | .649 | .694 | .920 | 2.12 | −24 | +52 |
| 10 | SD | 295 | 10 | 34 | 36 | 6 | .210 | .295 | .346 | 77% | 27% | 9% | 1.65 | $2 | -$10 | 140 | −17 | 10 | 0 | 1 | 51-15-34 | 9% | 16% | 27% | .640 | .714 | .452 | .633 | .655 | 2.13 | −38 | +82 |

## Bill Hall — 400 PA | $8 | 180 pts

OF-65 (LF-55, RF-9, CF-7), 2B-51, SS-6, 3B-5 — Owned: 13% — RH

Hall's strong 2010 season off the bench should get him a long look somewhere as a starter, and he would be right to grab any chance. The Red Sox have enough depth, and not enough work to spread around, for Hall to luck into 380 PA again. Boston also might have enough wisdom not to pay for elevated rates. (EB)

**Forecast**

| Player | Age | AB | HR | R | RBI | SB | BA | OBP | SLG | $1L | Pts |
|---|---|---|---|---|---|---|---|---|---|---|---|
| Hall B | 31 | 355 | 12 | 48 | 48 | 4 | .248 | .308 | .441 | $8 | 180 |
| **Mini-Browser** | Age | AB | HR | R | RBI | SB | BA | OBP | SLG | $1L | Pts |
| Rodriguez S | 25 | 391 | 17 | 51 | 47 | 9 | .239 | .317 | .425 | $9 | 210 |
| Rosales A | 27 | 403 | 14 | 54 | 45 | 5 | .257 | .327 | .438 | $9 | 230 |
| DeWitt B | 25 | 541 | 12 | 60 | 66 | 0 | .255 | .325 | .401 | $9 | 300 |
| Keppinger J | 30 | 426 | 5 | 52 | 48 | 5 | .290 | .351 | .403 | $8 | 290 |
| Schumaker S | 31 | 426 | 5 | 67 | 38 | 5 | .279 | .341 | .375 | $8 | 260 |

**Minors (2010)**

| Level | Leag | AB | HR | R | RBI | SB | BA | OBP | SLG | CT% | H% | BB% | Bash |
|---|---|---|---|---|---|---|---|---|---|---|---|---|---|
| A | — | — | — | — | — | — | — | — | — | — | — | — | — |
| AA | — | — | — | — | — | — | — | — | — | — | — | — | — |
| AAA | — | — | — | — | — | — | — | — | — | — | — | — | — |

**Competition at 2B — Stats in 2010**

| Bats | Player | GSvR | GSvL | Sub | OPS |
|---|---|---|---|---|---|
| RH | Pedroia D | 51 | 24 | 0 | .860 |
| RH | Hall B | 26 | 19 | 6 | .772 |
| BH | Lowrie J | 15 | 11 | 2 | .907 |
| RH | Scutaro M | 6 | 10 | 0 | .721 |

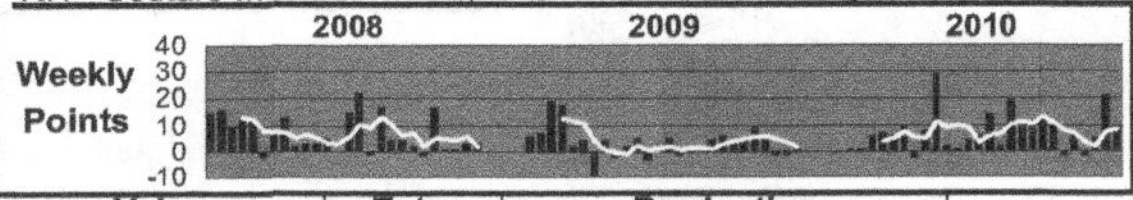
Weekly Points
2008
2009
2010

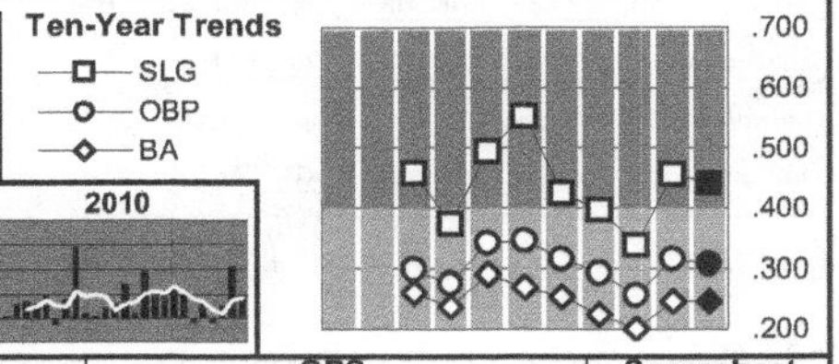
Ten-Year Trends
SLG
OBP
BA

**Majors**

| Yr | Team | AB | HR | R | RBI | SB | BA | OBP | SLG | CT% | H% | BB% | Bash | $1L | $2L | Pts | RAA | 2B | 3B | CS | FB-LD-GB | HR/fb | RBI% | RS% | OPS | 1st Hf | 2nd Hf | vs RH | vs LH | Rnge | vRH | vLH |
|---|---|---|---|---|---|---|---|---|---|---|---|---|---|---|---|---|---|---|---|---|---|---|---|---|---|---|---|---|---|---|---|---|
| 07 | MIL | 452 | 14 | 59 | 63 | 4 | .254 | .315 | .425 | 72% | 35% | 8% | 1.67 | $9 | $0 | 230 | −2 | 35 | 0 | 5 | 41-23-36 | 10% | 20% | 31% | .740 | .784 | .660 | .713 | .795 | — | −30 | +79 |
| 08 | MIL | 404 | 15 | 50 | 55 | 5 | .225 | .293 | .396 | 69% | 33% | 8% | 1.76 | $6 | -$3 | 180 | −11 | 22 | 1 | 6 | 40-21-39 | 13% | 19% | 30% | .689 | .725 | .618 | .557 | .893 | — | −27 | +70 |
| 09 | 2TM | 334 | 8 | 32 | 36 | 2 | .201 | .258 | .338 | 64% | 31% | 7% | 1.69 | -$5 | -$14 | 90 | −18 | 20 | 1 | 2 | 43-18-39 | 9% | 15% | 28% | .596 | .595 | .597 | .589 | .606 | — | −41 | +86 |
| 10 | BOS | 344 | 18 | 44 | 46 | 9 | .247 | .316 | .456 | 70% | 35% | 9% | 1.85 | $11 | -$1 | 190 | +6 | 16 | 1 | 1 | 44-18-38 | 17% | 16% | 25% | .772 | .755 | .787 | .841 | .680 | — | −33 | +68 |

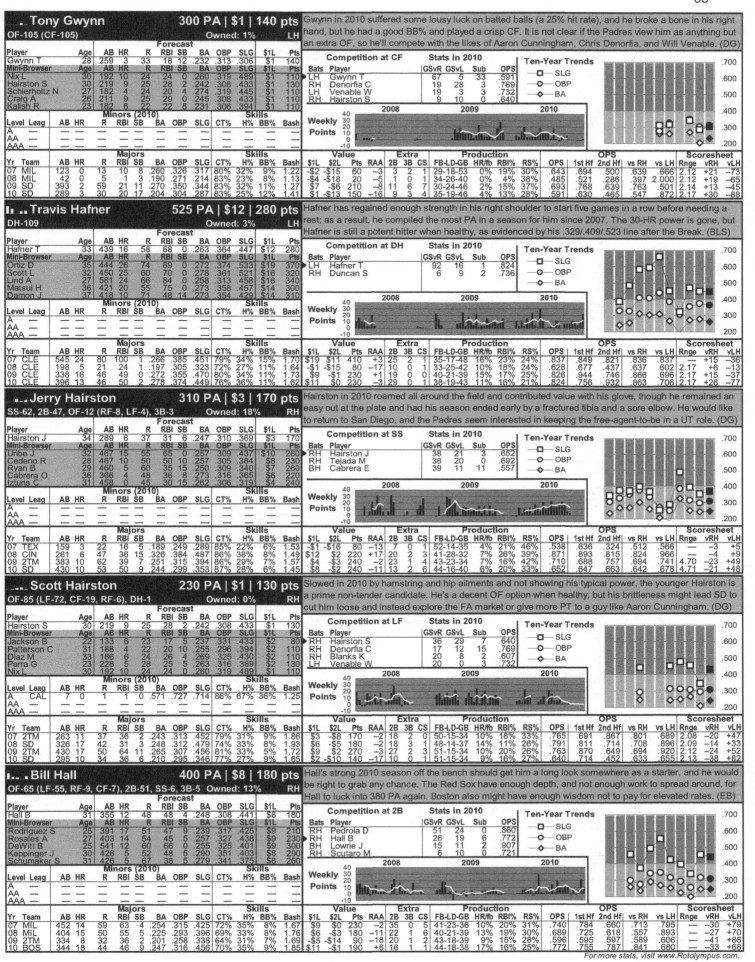

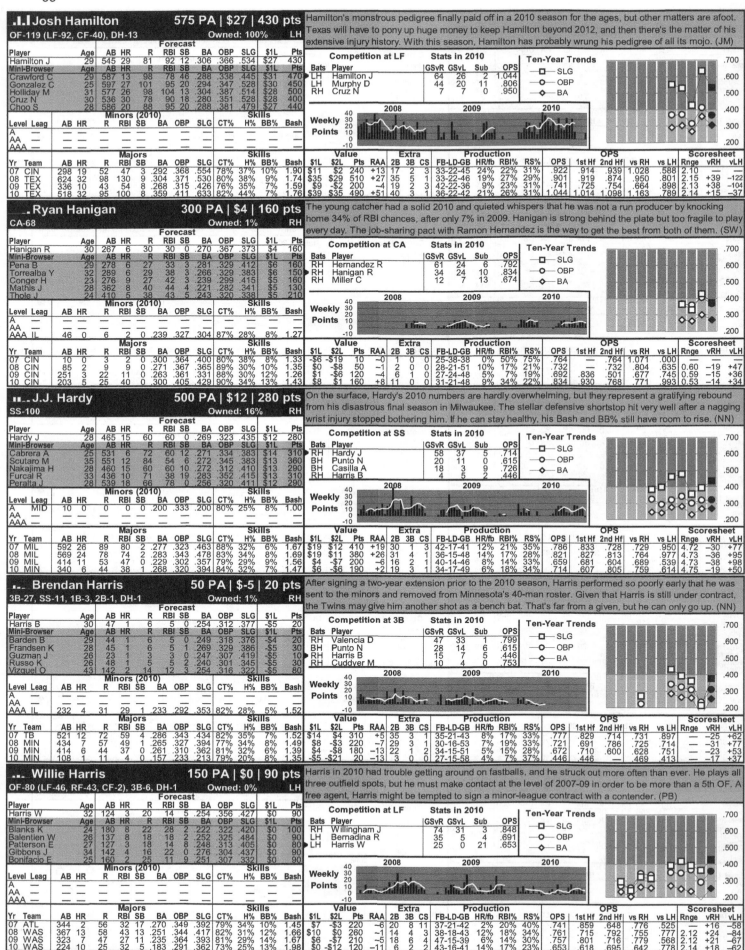

## Josh Hamilton — 575 PA | $27 | 430 pts
OF-119 (LF-92, CF-40), DH-13  Owned: 100%  LH

Hamilton's monstrous pedigree finally paid off in a 2010 season for the ages, but other matters are afoot. Texas will have to pony up huge money to keep Hamilton beyond 2012, and then there's the matter of his extensive injury history. With this season, Hamilton has probably wrung his pedigree of all its mojo. (JM)

### Forecast
| Player | Age | AB | HR | R | RBI | SB | BA | OBP | SLG | $1L | Pts |
|---|---|---|---|---|---|---|---|---|---|---|---|
| Hamilton J | 29 | 545 | 29 | 81 | 92 | 12 | .306 | .366 | .534 | $27 | 430 |

| Mini-Browser | Age | AB | HR | R | RBI | SB | BA | OBP | SLG | $1L | Pts |
|---|---|---|---|---|---|---|---|---|---|---|---|
| Crawford C | 29 | 587 | 13 | 98 | 78 | 46 | .288 | .338 | .445 | $31 | 470 |
| Gonzalez C | 25 | 597 | 27 | 101 | 95 | 20 | .294 | .347 | .528 | $30 | 450 |
| Holliday M | 31 | 577 | 26 | 98 | 104 | 13 | .304 | .387 | .514 | $28 | 400 |
| Cruz N | 30 | 536 | 30 | 79 | 90 | 18 | .280 | .351 | .528 | $28 | 400 |
| Choo S | 28 | 586 | 20 | 88 | 95 | 20 | .288 | .381 | .479 | $27 | 440 |

### Minors (2010) / Skills
| Level | Leag | AB | HR | R | RBI | SB | BA | OBP | SLG | CT% | H% | BB% | Bash |
|---|---|---|---|---|---|---|---|---|---|---|---|---|---|
| A | — | | | | | | | | | | | | |
| AA | — | | | | | | | | | | | | |
| AAA | — | | | | | | | | | | | | |

### Competition at LF | Stats in 2010
| Bats | Player | GSvR | GSvL | Sub | OPS |
|---|---|---|---|---|---|
| LH | Hamilton J | 64 | 26 | 2 | 1.044 |
| LH | Murphy D | 44 | 20 | 11 | .806 |
| RH | Cruz N | 7 | 7 | 0 | .950 |

### Majors / Skills / Value / Extra / Production / OPS / Scoresheet
| Yr | Team | AB | HR | R | RBI | SB | BA | OBP | SLG | CT% | H% | BB% | Bash | $1L | $2L | Pts | RAA | 2B | 3B | CS | FB-LD-GB | HR/fb | RBI% | RS% | OPS | 1st Hf | 2nd Hf | vs RH | vs LH | Rnge | vRH | vLH |
|---|---|---|---|---|---|---|---|---|---|---|---|---|---|---|---|---|---|---|---|---|---|---|---|---|---|---|---|---|---|---|---|---|
| 07 | CIN | 298 | 19 | 52 | 47 | 3 | .292 | .368 | .554 | 78% | 37% | 10% | 1.90 | $11 | $2 | 240 | +13 | 17 | 2 | 3 | 33-22-45 | 24% | 22% | 31% | .922 | .914 | .939 | 1.028 | .588 | 2.10 | — | — |
| 08 | TEX | 624 | 32 | 98 | 130 | 9 | .304 | .371 | .530 | 80% | 38% | 9% | 1.74 | $35 | $29 | 510 | +27 | 35 | 5 | 1 | 33-22-46 | 19% | 27% | 29% | .901 | .919 | .874 | .950 | .801 | 2.15 | +39 | -122 |
| 09 | TEX | 336 | 10 | 43 | 54 | 8 | .268 | .315 | .426 | 76% | 35% | 7% | 1.59 | $9 | -$2 | 200 | -4 | 19 | 2 | 3 | 42-22-36 | 9% | 23% | 31% | .741 | .725 | .754 | .664 | .898 | 2.13 | +38 | -104 |
| 10 | TEX | 518 | 32 | 95 | 100 | 8 | .359 | .411 | .633 | 82% | 44% | 7% | 1.76 | $39 | $35 | 490 | +51 | 40 | 3 | 1 | 36-22-42 | 21% | 26% | 30% | 1.044 | 1.011 | 1.098 | 1.163 | .789 | 2.14 | +15 | -37 |

## Ryan Hanigan — 300 PA | $4 | 160 pts
CA-68  Owned: 1%  RH

The young catcher had a solid 2010 and quieted whispers that he was not a run producer by knocking home 34% of RBI chances, after only 7% in 2009. Hanigan is strong behind the plate but too fragile to play every day. The job-sharing pact with Ramon Hernandez is the way to get the best from both of them. (SW)

### Forecast
| Player | Age | AB | HR | R | RBI | SB | BA | OBP | SLG | $1L | Pts |
|---|---|---|---|---|---|---|---|---|---|---|---|
| Hanigan R | 30 | 267 | 6 | 30 | 30 | 0 | .270 | .367 | .373 | $4 | 160 |

| Mini-Browser | Age | AB | HR | R | RBI | SB | BA | OBP | SLG | $1L | Pts |
|---|---|---|---|---|---|---|---|---|---|---|---|
| Pena B | 29 | 278 | 6 | 27 | 33 | 3 | .281 | .329 | .412 | $6 | 160 |
| Torrealba Y | 32 | 289 | 6 | 29 | 38 | 5 | .266 | .329 | .383 | $6 | 150 |
| Conger H | 23 | 276 | 9 | 27 | 42 | 3 | .239 | .299 | .415 | $5 | 160 |
| Mathis J | 28 | 362 | 8 | 40 | 44 | 4 | .221 | .282 | .341 | $5 | 130 |
| Thole J | 24 | 410 | 5 | 38 | 43 | 5 | .243 | .320 | .338 | $5 | 210 |

### Minors (2010) / Skills
| Level | Leag | AB | HR | R | RBI | SB | BA | OBP | SLG | CT% | H% | BB% | Bash |
|---|---|---|---|---|---|---|---|---|---|---|---|---|---|
| A | — | | | | | | | | | | | | |
| AA | — | | | | | | | | | | | | |
| AAA | IL | 46 | 0 | 6 | 2 | 0 | .239 | .327 | .304 | 87% | 28% | 8% | 1.27 |

### Competition at CA | Stats in 2010
| Bats | Player | GSvR | GSvL | Sub | OPS |
|---|---|---|---|---|---|
| RH | Hernandez R | 61 | 24 | 6 | .792 |
| RH | Hanigan R | 34 | 24 | 10 | .834 |
| RH | Miller C | 12 | 7 | 13 | .674 |

### Majors / Skills / Value / Extra / Production / OPS / Scoresheet
| Yr | Team | AB | HR | R | RBI | SB | BA | OBP | SLG | CT% | H% | BB% | Bash | $1L | $2L | Pts | RAA | 2B | 3B | CS | FB-LD-GB | HR/fb | RBI% | RS% | OPS | 1st Hf | 2nd Hf | vs RH | vs LH | Rnge | vRH | vLH |
|---|---|---|---|---|---|---|---|---|---|---|---|---|---|---|---|---|---|---|---|---|---|---|---|---|---|---|---|---|---|---|---|---|
| 07 | CIN | 10 | 0 | 3 | 2 | 0 | .300 | .364 | .400 | 80% | 38% | 8% | 1.33 | -$6 | -$19 | 10 | -0 | 1 | 0 | 0 | 25-38-38 | 0% | 50% | 75% | .764 | — | .764 | 1.071 | .000 | — | — | — |
| 08 | CIN | 85 | 2 | 9 | 9 | 0 | .271 | .367 | .365 | 89% | 30% | 10% | 1.35 | $0 | -$8 | 50 | -1 | 2 | 0 | 0 | 28-21-51 | 10% | 17% | 21% | .732 | — | .732 | .804 | .635 | 0.60 | -19 | +47 |
| 09 | CIN | 251 | 3 | 22 | 11 | 0 | .263 | .361 | .331 | 88% | 30% | 12% | 1.26 | $1 | -$6 | 120 | -4 | 6 | 1 | 0 | 27-24-48 | 5% | 7% | 19% | .692 | .836 | .501 | .677 | .745 | 0.59 | -15 | +34 |
| 10 | CIN | 203 | 5 | 25 | 40 | 0 | .300 | .405 | .429 | 90% | 34% | 13% | 1.43 | $8 | $1 | 160 | +8 | 11 | 0 | 0 | 31-21-48 | 9% | 34% | 22% | .834 | .930 | .768 | .771 | .993 | 0.53 | -14 | +34 |

## J.J. Hardy — 500 PA | $12 | 280 pts
SS-100  Owned: 16%  RH

On the surface, Hardy's 2010 numbers are hardly overwhelming, but they represent a gratifying rebound from his disastrous final season in Milwaukee. The stellar defensive shortstop hit very well after a nagging wrist injury stopped bothering him. If he can stay healthy, his Bash and BB% still have room to rise. (NN)

### Forecast
| Player | Age | AB | HR | R | RBI | SB | BA | OBP | SLG | $1L | Pts |
|---|---|---|---|---|---|---|---|---|---|---|---|
| Hardy J | 28 | 465 | 15 | 60 | 60 | 0 | .269 | .323 | .435 | $12 | 280 |

| Mini-Browser | Age | AB | HR | R | RBI | SB | BA | OBP | SLG | $1L | Pts |
|---|---|---|---|---|---|---|---|---|---|---|---|
| Cabrera A | 25 | 531 | 6 | 72 | 60 | 12 | .271 | .334 | .383 | $14 | 310 |
| Scutaro M | 35 | 551 | 12 | 84 | 54 | 6 | .272 | .345 | .383 | $13 | 360 |
| Nakajima H | 28 | 460 | 15 | 60 | 60 | 10 | .272 | .312 | .410 | $13 | 290 |
| Furcal J | 33 | 436 | 10 | 71 | 38 | 19 | .283 | .352 | .415 | $13 | 310 |
| Peralta J | 28 | 539 | 18 | 66 | 78 | 0 | .256 | .320 | .411 | $12 | 290 |

### Minors (2010) / Skills
| Level | Leag | AB | HR | R | RBI | SB | BA | OBP | SLG | CT% | H% | BB% | Bash |
|---|---|---|---|---|---|---|---|---|---|---|---|---|---|
| A | MID | 10 | 0 | 0 | 0 | 0 | .200 | .333 | .200 | 80% | 25% | 8% | 1.00 |
| AA | — | | | | | | | | | | | | |
| AAA | — | | | | | | | | | | | | |

### Competition at SS | Stats in 2010
| Bats | Player | GSvR | GSvL | Sub | OPS |
|---|---|---|---|---|---|
| RH | Hardy J | 58 | 37 | 5 | .714 |
| BH | Punto N | 20 | 11 | 0 | .615 |
| BH | Casilla A | 18 | 3 | 9 | .726 |
| RH | Harris B | 4 | 5 | 2 | .446 |

### Majors / Skills / Value / Extra / Production / OPS / Scoresheet
| Yr | Team | AB | HR | R | RBI | SB | BA | OBP | SLG | CT% | H% | BB% | Bash | $1L | $2L | Pts | RAA | 2B | 3B | CS | FB-LD-GB | HR/fb | RBI% | RS% | OPS | 1st Hf | 2nd Hf | vs RH | vs LH | Rnge | vRH | vLH |
|---|---|---|---|---|---|---|---|---|---|---|---|---|---|---|---|---|---|---|---|---|---|---|---|---|---|---|---|---|---|---|---|---|
| 07 | MIL | 592 | 26 | 89 | 80 | 2 | .277 | .323 | .463 | 88% | 32% | 6% | 1.67 | $19 | $12 | 410 | +19 | 30 | 1 | 3 | 42-17-41 | 12% | 21% | 35% | .786 | .833 | .728 | .729 | .950 | 4.72 | -30 | +77 |
| 08 | MIL | 569 | 24 | 78 | 74 | 2 | .283 | .343 | .478 | 83% | 34% | 8% | 1.69 | $19 | $11 | 380 | +26 | 31 | 4 | 1 | 36-15-48 | 14% | 17% | 28% | .821 | .827 | .813 | .764 | .977 | 4.73 | -36 | +95 |
| 09 | MIL | 414 | 11 | 53 | 47 | 0 | .229 | .302 | .357 | 79% | 29% | 9% | 1.56 | $4 | -$7 | 200 | -6 | 16 | 2 | 1 | 40-14-46 | 8% | 14% | 33% | .659 | .681 | .604 | .689 | .539 | 4.73 | -38 | +98 |
| 10 | MIN | 340 | 6 | 44 | 38 | 1 | .268 | .320 | .394 | 84% | 32% | 7% | 1.47 | $6 | -$6 | 190 | +2 | 19 | 3 | 1 | 34-17-49 | 6% | 18% | 34% | .714 | .607 | .805 | .759 | .614 | 4.75 | -19 | +50 |

## Brendan Harris — 50 PA | $-5 | 20 pts
3B-27, SS-11, 1B-3, 2B-1, DH-1  Owned: 1%  RH

After signing a two-year extension prior to the 2010 season, Harris performed so poorly early that he was sent to the minors and removed from Minnesota's 40-man roster. Given that Harris is still under contract, the Twins may give him another shot as a bench bat. That's far from a given, but he can only go up. (NN)

### Forecast
| Player | Age | AB | HR | R | RBI | SB | BA | OBP | SLG | $1L | Pts |
|---|---|---|---|---|---|---|---|---|---|---|---|
| Harris B | 30 | 47 | 1 | 6 | 5 | 0 | .254 | .312 | .377 | -$5 | 20 |

| Mini-Browser | Age | AB | HR | R | RBI | SB | BA | OBP | SLG | $1L | Pts |
|---|---|---|---|---|---|---|---|---|---|---|---|
| Barden B | 29 | 44 | 1 | 6 | 5 | 0 | .249 | .318 | .376 | -$4 | 20 |
| Frandsen K | 28 | 45 | 1 | 6 | 5 | 1 | .269 | .329 | .386 | -$5 | 30 |
| Guzman J | 26 | 23 | 1 | 3 | 3 | 0 | .247 | .307 | .419 | -$5 | 10 |
| Russo K | 26 | 48 | 1 | 5 | 5 | 2 | .240 | .301 | .345 | -$5 | 30 |
| Vizquel O | 43 | 142 | 2 | 14 | 12 | 3 | .254 | .316 | .322 | -$5 | 80 |

### Minors (2010) / Skills
| Level | Leag | AB | HR | R | RBI | SB | BA | OBP | SLG | CT% | H% | BB% | Bash |
|---|---|---|---|---|---|---|---|---|---|---|---|---|---|
| A | — | | | | | | | | | | | | |
| AA | — | | | | | | | | | | | | |
| AAA | IL | 232 | 4 | 31 | 29 | 1 | .233 | .292 | .353 | 82% | 28% | 5% | 1.52 |

### Competition at 3B | Stats in 2010
| Bats | Player | GSvR | GSvL | Sub | OPS |
|---|---|---|---|---|---|
| RH | Valencia D | 47 | 33 | 1 | .799 |
| BH | Punto N | 28 | 14 | 6 | .615 |
| RH | Harris B | 15 | 7 | 5 | .446 |
| RH | Cuddyer M | 10 | 4 | 0 | .753 |

### Majors / Skills / Value / Extra / Production / OPS / Scoresheet
| Yr | Team | AB | HR | R | RBI | SB | BA | OBP | SLG | CT% | H% | BB% | Bash | $1L | $2L | Pts | RAA | 2B | 3B | CS | FB-LD-GB | HR/fb | RBI% | RS% | OPS | 1st Hf | 2nd Hf | vs RH | vs LH | Rnge | vRH | vLH |
|---|---|---|---|---|---|---|---|---|---|---|---|---|---|---|---|---|---|---|---|---|---|---|---|---|---|---|---|---|---|---|---|---|
| 07 | TB | 521 | 12 | 72 | 59 | 4 | .286 | .343 | .434 | 82% | 35% | 7% | 1.52 | $14 | $4 | 310 | +5 | 35 | 3 | 1 | 35-21-43 | 8% | 17% | 33% | .777 | .829 | .714 | .731 | .897 | — | -25 | +62 |
| 08 | MIN | 434 | 7 | 57 | 49 | 1 | .265 | .327 | .394 | 77% | 34% | 8% | 1.49 | $8 | -$3 | 220 | -7 | 29 | 3 | 1 | 30-16-53 | 7% | 19% | 33% | .721 | .691 | .786 | .725 | .714 | — | -31 | +77 |
| 09 | MIN | 414 | 6 | 44 | 37 | 0 | .261 | .310 | .362 | 81% | 32% | 6% | 1.39 | $4 | -$8 | 180 | -13 | 22 | 1 | 2 | 34-15-51 | 5% | 15% | 28% | .672 | .710 | .600 | .628 | .751 | — | -23 | +53 |
| 10 | MIN | 108 | 1 | 11 | 4 | 0 | .157 | .233 | .213 | 79% | 20% | 8% | 1.35 | -$5 | -$21 | 20 | -13 | 10 | 0 | 0 | 27-15-58 | 4% | 7% | 37% | .446 | .446 | — | .469 | .413 | — | -17 | +37 |

## Willie Harris — 150 PA | $0 | 90 pts
OF-80 (LF-46, RF-43, CF-2), 3B-6, DH-1  Owned: 0%  LH

Harris in 2010 had trouble getting around on fastballs, and he struck out more often than ever. He plays all three outfield spots, but he must make contact at the level of 2007-09 in order to be more than a 5th OF. A free agent, Harris might be tempted to sign a minor-league contract with a contender. (PB)

### Forecast
| Player | Age | AB | HR | R | RBI | SB | BA | OBP | SLG | $1L | Pts |
|---|---|---|---|---|---|---|---|---|---|---|---|
| Harris W | 32 | 124 | 3 | 20 | 14 | 5 | .254 | .356 | .427 | $0 | 90 |

| Mini-Browser | Age | AB | HR | R | RBI | SB | BA | OBP | SLG | $1L | Pts |
|---|---|---|---|---|---|---|---|---|---|---|---|
| Blanks K | 24 | 180 | 8 | 22 | 28 | 2 | .222 | .322 | .420 | $0 | 100 |
| Balentien W | 26 | 137 | 8 | 18 | 18 | 2 | .252 | .325 | .484 | $0 | 90 |
| Patterson E | 27 | 127 | 3 | 18 | 14 | 8 | .248 | .313 | .405 | $0 | 80 |
| Gibbons J | 34 | 142 | 4 | 16 | 22 | 0 | .276 | .304 | .437 | $0 | 90 |
| Bonifacio E | 25 | 160 | 2 | 25 | 11 | 9 | .251 | .307 | .332 | $0 | 90 |

### Minors (2010) / Skills
| Level | Leag | AB | HR | R | RBI | SB | BA | OBP | SLG | CT% | H% | BB% | Bash |
|---|---|---|---|---|---|---|---|---|---|---|---|---|---|
| A | — | | | | | | | | | | | | |
| AA | — | | | | | | | | | | | | |
| AAA | — | | | | | | | | | | | | |

### Competition at LF | Stats in 2010
| Bats | Player | GSvR | GSvL | Sub | OPS |
|---|---|---|---|---|---|
| RH | Willingham J | 74 | 31 | 3 | .848 |
| LH | Bernadina R | 35 | 5 | 4 | .691 |
| LH | Harris W | 25 | 0 | 21 | .653 |

### Majors / Skills / Value / Extra / Production / OPS / Scoresheet
| Yr | Team | AB | HR | R | RBI | SB | BA | OBP | SLG | CT% | H% | BB% | Bash | $1L | $2L | Pts | RAA | 2B | 3B | CS | FB-LD-GB | HR/fb | RBI% | RS% | OPS | 1st Hf | 2nd Hf | vs RH | vs LH | Rnge | vRH | vLH |
|---|---|---|---|---|---|---|---|---|---|---|---|---|---|---|---|---|---|---|---|---|---|---|---|---|---|---|---|---|---|---|---|---|
| 07 | ATL | 344 | 2 | 56 | 32 | 17 | .270 | .349 | .392 | 79% | 34% | 10% | 1.45 | $7 | -$3 | 220 | -6 | 20 | 8 | 11 | 37-21-42 | 2% | 20% | 40% | .741 | .859 | .648 | .776 | .525 | — | +16 | -58 |
| 08 | WAS | 367 | 13 | 58 | 43 | 13 | .251 | .344 | .417 | 82% | 31% | 12% | 1.66 | $10 | $0 | 260 | -1 | 14 | 4 | 3 | 38-18-43 | 12% | 18% | 34% | .761 | .715 | .792 | .755 | .777 | 2.12 | +24 | -84 |
| 09 | WAS | 247 | 4 | 47 | 27 | 11 | .235 | .364 | .393 | 81% | 29% | 14% | 1.67 | $6 | -$7 | 210 | -5 | 18 | 6 | 4 | 47-15-39 | 6% | 14% | 30% | .757 | .801 | .716 | .779 | .568 | 2.12 | +21 | -67 |
| 10 | WAS | 224 | 10 | 25 | 32 | 5 | .183 | .291 | .362 | 73% | 25% | 14% | 1.98 | $3 | -$12 | 120 | -11 | 6 | 2 | 1 | 43-16-41 | 14% | 17% | 23% | .653 | .618 | .695 | .642 | .778 | 2.14 | +18 | -61 |

## Corey Hart — 650 PA | $25 | 440 pts

OF-141 (RF-141) — Owned: 99% — RH

Hart's breakout in 2010 was the product of surges in H%, Bash, and (especially) HR/FB. Note, though, that his CT% continued to slip, and that he still can't meet a .350 OBP. If nothing else, the three-year deal that Milwaukee struck with Hart in August means that he will play through any weakening of his numbers. (MS)

| Player | Age | AB | HR | R | RBI | SB | BA | OBP | SLG | $1L | Pts |
|---|---|---|---|---|---|---|---|---|---|---|---|
| | | Forecast | | | | | | | | | |
| Hart C | 29 | 589 | 26 | 91 | 91 | 20 | .276 | .335 | .500 | $25 | 440 |
| **Mini-Browser** | Age | AB | HR | R | RBI | SB | BA | OBP | SLG | $1L | Pts |
| Hunter T | 35 | 580 | 26 | 85 | 98 | 20 | .280 | .344 | .484 | $27 | 440 |
| Werth J | 31 | 563 | 33 | 98 | 91 | 20 | .277 | .379 | .508 | $26 | 450 |
| Kemp M | 26 | 597 | 26 | 91 | 91 | 26 | .272 | .329 | .466 | $26 | 420 |
| Suzuki I | 37 | 638 | 7 | 84 | 49 | 35 | .307 | .353 | .405 | $26 | 430 |
| Beltran C | 33 | 530 | 24 | 90 | 90 | 18 | .283 | .374 | .512 | $25 | 470 |

| Level | Leag | AB | HR | R | RBI | SB | BA | OBP | SLG | CT% | H% | BB% | Bash |
|---|---|---|---|---|---|---|---|---|---|---|---|---|---|
| | | Minors (2010) | | | | | | | | Skills | | | |
| A | — | — | — | — | — | — | — | — | — | — | — | — | — |
| AA | — | — | — | — | — | — | — | — | — | — | — | — | — |
| AAA | — | — | — | — | — | — | — | — | — | — | — | — | — |

| Yr | Team | AB | HR | R | RBI | SB | BA | OBP | SLG | CT% | H% | BB% | Bash |
|---|---|---|---|---|---|---|---|---|---|---|---|---|---|
| | | Majors | | | | | | | | Skills | | | |
| 07 | MIL | 505 | 24 | 86 | 81 | 23 | .295 | .353 | .539 | 80% | 37% | 6% | 1.83 |
| 08 | MIL | 612 | 20 | 76 | 91 | 23 | .268 | .300 | .459 | 82% | 33% | 4% | 1.71 |
| 09 | MIL | 419 | 12 | 64 | 48 | 11 | .260 | .335 | .418 | 78% | 33% | 9% | 1.61 |
| 10 | MIL | 558 | 31 | 91 | 102 | 7 | .283 | .340 | .525 | 75% | 38% | 7% | 1.85 |

| Yr | $1L | $2L | Pts | RAA | 2B | 3B | CS | FB-LD-GB | HR/fb | RBI% | RS% | OPS | 1st Hf | 2nd Hf | vs RH | vs LH | Rnge | vRH | vLH |
|---|---|---|---|---|---|---|---|---|---|---|---|---|---|---|---|---|---|---|---|
| | Value | | | | Extra | | | Production | | | | OPS | | | | | Scoresheet | | |
| 07 | $26 | $19 | 420 | +8 | 33 | 9 | 7 | 46-17-37 | 13% | 26% | 36% | .892 | .876 | .906 | .824 | 1.032 | 2.09 | — | — |
| 08 | $22 | $14 | 400 | –14 | 45 | 6 | 7 | 40-19-40 | 10% | 21% | 32% | .759 | .831 | .659 | .745 | .797 | 2.10 | — | — |
| 09 | $12 | $1 | 250 | –9 | 24 | 3 | 6 | 42-17-41 | 9% | 16% | 36% | .753 | .743 | .780 | .773 | .690 | 2.09 | — | — |
| 10 | $28 | $24 | 400 | +9 | 34 | 4 | 6 | 44-18-38 | 17% | 22% | 34% | .865 | .918 | .802 | .827 | .973 | 2.07 | — | — |

**Competition at RF — Stats in 2010**

| Bats | Player | GSvR | GSvL | Sub | OPS |
|---|---|---|---|---|---|
| RH | Hart C | 91 | 47 | 3 | .865 |
| LH | Inglett J | 8 | 2 | 4 | .733 |

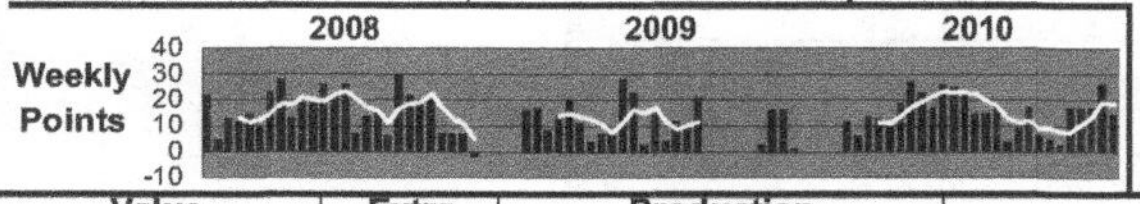


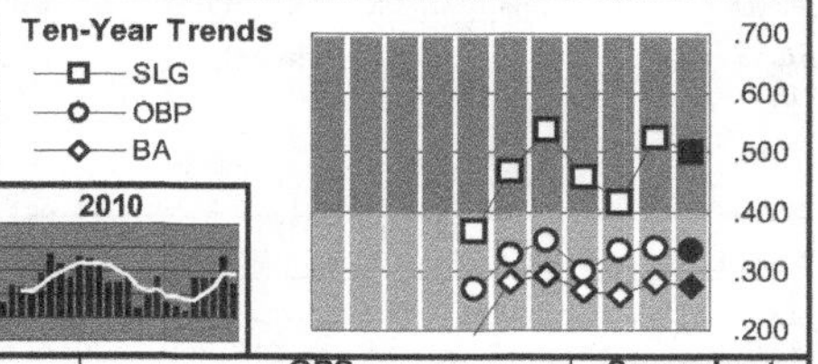


## Reese Havens — 50 PA | $-4 | 20 pts

No MLB games played in 2010 — Owned: 0% — LH

Havens – a good defender with power – could be the Mets' top 2B prospect, if he can only stay healthy. A first-round pick in 2008, Havens was transitioned from SS to 2B in 2010, but oblique injuries derailed his season. He reportedly might need back surgery, which could jeopardize his 2011. (JL)

| Player | Age | AB | HR | R | RBI | SB | BA | OBP | SLG | $1L | Pts |
|---|---|---|---|---|---|---|---|---|---|---|---|
| | | Forecast | | | | | | | | | |
| Havens R | 24 | 42 | 3 | 5 | 6 | 1 | .202 | .307 | .419 | -$4 | 20 |
| **Mini-Browser** | Age | AB | HR | R | RBI | SB | BA | OBP | SLG | $1L | Pts |
| Burriss E | 26 | 48 | 1 | 6 | 4 | 3 | .250 | .309 | .304 | -$4 | 30 |
| Ojeda A | 36 | 65 | 0 | 9 | 5 | 1 | .267 | .359 | .356 | -$4 | 40 |
| Miles A | 34 | 74 | 1 | 8 | 5 | 1 | .263 | .302 | .330 | -$4 | 40 |
| Zawadzki L | 25 | 65 | 1 | 6 | 6 | 2 | .194 | .277 | .321 | -$4 | 30 |
| Forsythe L | 24 | 72 | 1 | 9 | 6 | 1 | .201 | .320 | .297 | -$4 | 30 |

| Level | Leag | AB | HR | R | RBI | SB | BA | OBP | SLG | CT% | H% | BB% | Bash |
|---|---|---|---|---|---|---|---|---|---|---|---|---|---|
| | | Minors (2010) | | | | | | | | Skills | | | |
| A | FLO | 57 | 3 | 9 | 7 | 0 | .281 | .369 | .509 | 68% | 41% | 12% | 1.81 |
| AA | EL | 68 | 6 | 12 | 12 | 0 | .338 | .400 | .662 | 78% | 43% | 8% | 1.96 |
| AAA | — | — | — | — | — | — | — | — | — | — | — | — | — |

| Yr | Team | AB | HR | R | RBI | SB | BA | OBP | SLG | CT% | H% | BB% | Bash |
|---|---|---|---|---|---|---|---|---|---|---|---|---|---|
| | | Majors | | | | | | | | Skills | | | |
| 07 | — | — | — | — | — | — | — | — | — | — | — | — | — |
| 08 | — | — | — | — | — | — | — | — | — | — | — | — | — |
| 09 | — | — | — | — | — | — | — | — | — | — | — | — | — |
| 10 | — | — | — | — | — | — | — | — | — | — | — | — | — |

| Yr | $1L | $2L | Pts | RAA | 2B | 3B | CS | FB-LD-GB | HR/fb | RBI% | RS% | OPS | 1st Hf | 2nd Hf | vs RH | vs LH | Rnge | vRH | vLH |
|---|---|---|---|---|---|---|---|---|---|---|---|---|---|---|---|---|---|---|---|
| | Value | | | | Extra | | | Production | | | | OPS | | | | | Scoresheet | | |
| 07 | — | — | — | — | — | — | — | — | — | — | — | — | — | — | — | — | — | — | — |
| 08 | — | — | — | — | — | — | — | — | — | — | — | — | — | — | — | — | — | — | — |
| 09 | — | — | — | — | — | — | — | — | — | — | — | — | — | — | — | — | — | — | — |
| 10 | — | — | — | — | — | — | — | — | — | — | — | — | — | — | — | — | — | — | — |

**Competition at 2B — Stats in 2010**

| Bats | Player | GSvR | GSvL | Sub | OPS |
|---|---|---|---|---|---|
| BH | Castillo L | 45 | 19 | 10 | .604 |
| RH | Tejada R | 33 | 13 | 4 | .588 |
| BH | Hernandez L | 9 | 0 | 1 | .707 |
| RH | Arias J | 3 | 1 | 9 | .601 |

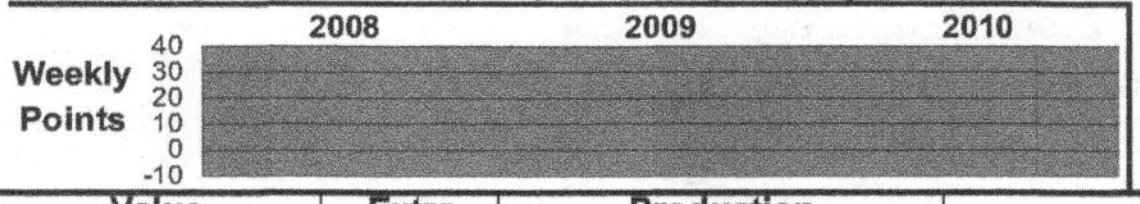


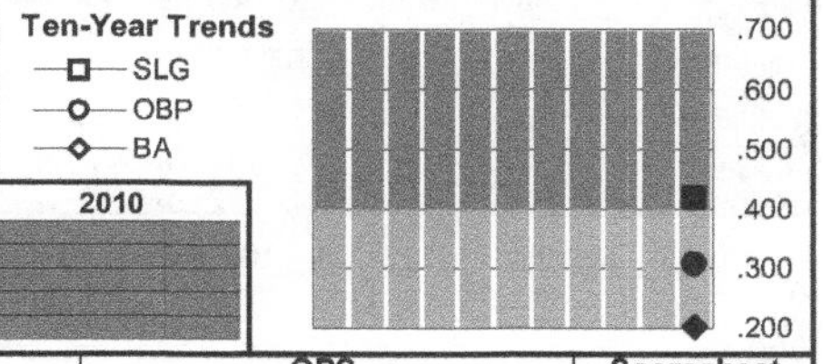


## Brad Hawpe — 400 PA | $11 | 240 pts

OF-66 (RF-66), 1B-9, DH-8 — Owned: 41% — LH

Hawpe struggled all of 2010 with a wipeout of power, but his weekly trends point to a decline that began in June 2009. He was released by Colorado in August and then signed on with Tampa Bay, where he hit only .179/.304/.333 in 39 AB. It can't help Hawpe in '11 to have to adjust to DH'ing and to AL East pitchers. (RZ)

| Player | Age | AB | HR | R | RBI | SB | BA | OBP | SLG | $1L | Pts |
|---|---|---|---|---|---|---|---|---|---|---|---|
| | | Forecast | | | | | | | | | |
| Hawpe B | 31 | 335 | 16 | 52 | 60 | 0 | .275 | .376 | .501 | $11 | 240 |
| **Mini-Browser** | Age | AB | HR | R | RBI | SB | BA | OBP | SLG | $1L | Pts |
| Bourjos P | 24 | 563 | 12 | 76 | 49 | 31 | .242 | .287 | .378 | $12 | 310 |
| Gordon A | 27 | 466 | 16 | 63 | 53 | 11 | .259 | .347 | .429 | $12 | 270 |
| Drew J | 35 | 389 | 18 | 63 | 59 | 5 | .266 | .370 | .475 | $12 | 290 |
| Morrison L | 23 | 535 | 18 | 72 | 66 | 6 | .258 | .354 | .438 | $12 | 360 |
| Murphy D | 29 | 395 | 13 | 51 | 55 | 9 | .280 | .341 | .454 | $12 | 270 |

| Level | Leag | AB | HR | R | RBI | SB | BA | OBP | SLG | CT% | H% | BB% | Bash |
|---|---|---|---|---|---|---|---|---|---|---|---|---|---|
| | | Minors (2010) | | | | | | | | Skills | | | |
| A | 2LG | 10 | 0 | 0 | 1 | 0 | .200 | .385 | .300 | 70% | 29% | 23% | 1.50 |
| AA | — | — | — | — | — | — | — | — | — | — | — | — | — |
| AAA | PCL | 9 | 0 | 2 | 0 | 0 | .222 | .300 | .333 | 67% | 33% | 10% | 1.50 |

| Yr | Team | AB | HR | R | RBI | SB | BA | OBP | SLG | CT% | H% | BB% | Bash |
|---|---|---|---|---|---|---|---|---|---|---|---|---|---|
| | | Majors | | | | | | | | Skills | | | |
| 07 | COL | 516 | 29 | 80 | 116 | 0 | .291 | .387 | .539 | 73% | 40% | 13% | 1.85 |
| 08 | COL | 488 | 25 | 69 | 85 | 2 | .283 | .381 | .498 | 73% | 39% | 13% | 1.76 |
| 09 | COL | 501 | 23 | 82 | 86 | 1 | .285 | .384 | .519 | 71% | 40% | 13% | 1.82 |
| 10 | 2TM | 298 | 9 | 31 | 44 | 2 | .245 | .338 | .419 | 71% | 34% | 12% | 1.71 |

| Yr | $1L | $2L | Pts | RAA | 2B | 3B | CS | FB-LD-GB | HR/fb | RBI% | RS% | OPS | 1st Hf | 2nd Hf | vs RH | vs LH | Rnge | vRH | vLH |
|---|---|---|---|---|---|---|---|---|---|---|---|---|---|---|---|---|---|---|---|
| | Value | | | | Extra | | | Production | | | | OPS | | | | | Scoresheet | | |
| 07 | $24 | $18 | 420 | +22 | 33 | 4 | 2 | 43-21-36 | 18% | 26% | 25% | .926 | .949 | .898 | 1.002 | .679 | 2.02 | +22 | –93 |
| 08 | $19 | $11 | 340 | +15 | 24 | 3 | 2 | 39-23-38 | 18% | 22% | 23% | .879 | .835 | .931 | .897 | .826 | 2.02 | +39 | –136 |
| 09 | $20 | $12 | 360 | +19 | 42 | 3 | 3 | 36-20-43 | 18% | 20% | 29% | .903 | .973 | .813 | .955 | .775 | 2.00 | +34 | –105 |
| 10 | $5 | -$8 | 160 | –5 | 21 | 2 | 1 | 40-20-41 | 10% | 21% | 20% | .758 | .808 | .653 | .730 | .821 | 2.01 | +27 | –78 |

**Competition at RF — Stats in 2010**

| Bats | Player | GSvR | GSvL | Sub | OPS |
|---|---|---|---|---|---|
| BH | Zobrist B | 64 | 34 | 5 | .699 |
| LH | Joyce M | 45 | 1 | 7 | .837 |
| RH | Kapler G | 2 | 29 | 8 | .578 |

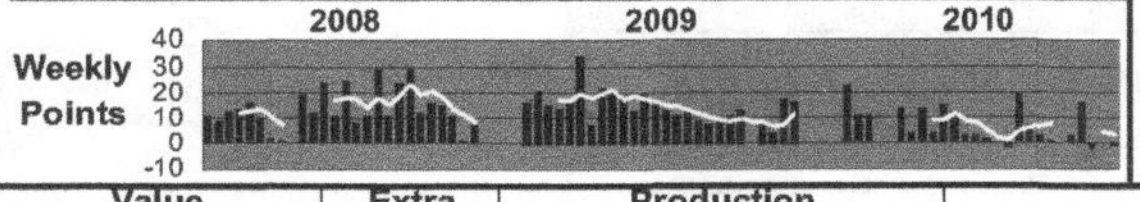


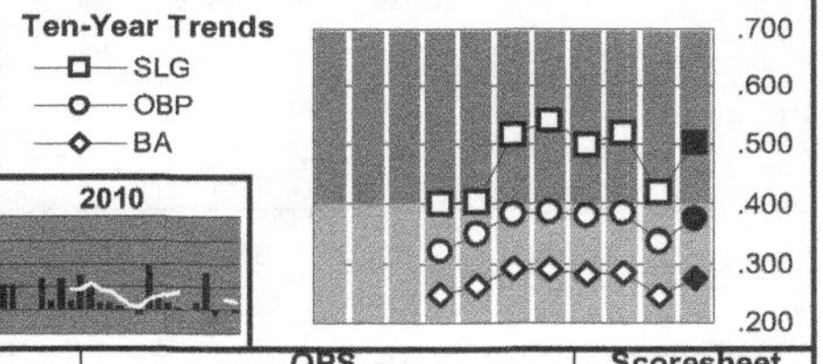


## Brett Hayes — 50 PA | $-2 | 20 pts

CA-24 — Owned: 0% — RH

Hayes will enter 2011 as Florida's emergency third catcher, and he will spend most of the season in the minors. He combines a very low CT% with a very high FB% – a sure recipe for a rotten BA. If the Marlins sign a free-agent catcher over the winter, Hayes will garner few at-bats in MLB. (MJ)

| Player | Age | AB | HR | R | RBI | SB | BA | OBP | SLG | $1L | Pts |
|---|---|---|---|---|---|---|---|---|---|---|---|
| | | Forecast | | | | | | | | | |
| Hayes B | 27 | 45 | 1 | 5 | 5 | 0 | .223 | .272 | .353 | -$2 | 20 |
| **Mini-Browser** | Age | AB | HR | R | RBI | SB | BA | OBP | SLG | $1L | Pts |
| McKenry M | 26 | 45 | 2 | 5 | 6 | 0 | .212 | .309 | .416 | -$2 | 20 |
| Santos O | 29 | 45 | 1 | 5 | 6 | 0 | .245 | .291 | .355 | -$2 | 20 |
| Anderson B | 24 | 48 | 1 | 5 | 5 | 0 | .250 | .313 | .356 | -$2 | 20 |
| Jaramillo J | 28 | 45 | 1 | 5 | 5 | 0 | .246 | .320 | .357 | -$2 | 20 |
| Ramirez M | 26 | 43 | 2 | 5 | 6 | 0 | .231 | .329 | .411 | -$2 | 20 |

| Level | Leag | AB | HR | R | RBI | SB | BA | OBP | SLG | CT% | H% | BB% | Bash |
|---|---|---|---|---|---|---|---|---|---|---|---|---|---|
| | | Minors (2010) | | | | | | | | Skills | | | |
| A | FLO | 23 | 2 | 6 | 7 | 0 | .217 | .333 | .522 | 70% | 31% | 15% | 2.40 |
| AA | — | — | — | — | — | — | — | — | — | — | — | — | — |
| AAA | PCL | 59 | 1 | 7 | 5 | 0 | .220 | .254 | .322 | 85% | 26% | 3% | 1.46 |

| Yr | Team | AB | HR | R | RBI | SB | BA | OBP | SLG | CT% | H% | BB% | Bash |
|---|---|---|---|---|---|---|---|---|---|---|---|---|---|
| | | Majors | | | | | | | | Skills | | | |
| 07 | — | — | — | — | — | — | — | — | — | — | — | — | — |
| 08 | — | — | — | — | — | — | — | — | — | — | — | — | — |
| 09 | FLA | 11 | 1 | 5 | 2 | 0 | .273 | .333 | .636 | 64% | 43% | 0% | 2.33 |
| 10 | FLA | 77 | 2 | 6 | 6 | 0 | .208 | .265 | .390 | 66% | 31% | 7% | 1.88 |

| Yr | $1L | $2L | Pts | RAA | 2B | 3B | CS | FB-LD-GB | HR/fb | RBI% | RS% | OPS | 1st Hf | 2nd Hf | vs RH | vs LH | Rnge | vRH | vLH |
|---|---|---|---|---|---|---|---|---|---|---|---|---|---|---|---|---|---|---|---|
| | Value | | | | Extra | | | Production | | | | OPS | | | | | Scoresheet | | |
| 07 | — | — | — | — | — | — | — | — | — | — | — | — | — | — | — | — | — | — | — |
| 08 | — | — | — | — | — | — | — | — | — | — | — | — | — | — | — | — | — | — | — |
| 09 | -$4 | -$18 | 10 | +0 | 1 | 0 | 0 | 29-29-43 | 50% | 17% | 133% | .970 | .650 | 1.143 | .708 | 1.667 | 0.60 | — | — |
| 10 | -$4 | -$19 | 20 | –3 | 6 | 1 | 0 | 58-10-32 | 7% | 11% | 20% | .655 | .669 | .642 | .692 | .486 | 0.58 | –18 | +46 |

**Competition at CA — Stats in 2010**

| Bats | Player | GSvR | GSvL | Sub | OPS |
|---|---|---|---|---|---|
| RH | Paulino R | 50 | 34 | 1 | .665 |
| RH | Davis B | 23 | 9 | 0 | .647 |
| RH | Hayes B | 17 | 4 | 3 | .655 |
| LH | Baker J | 19 | 1 | 1 | .589 |

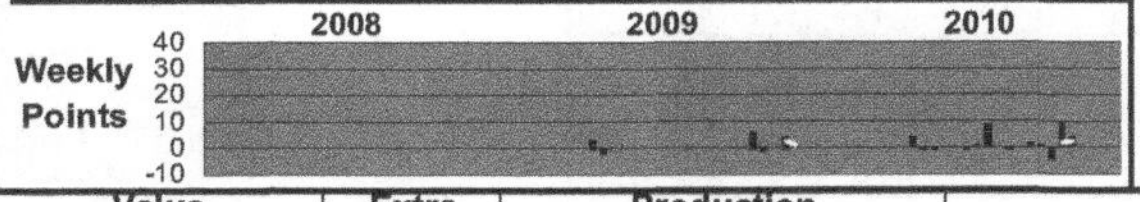


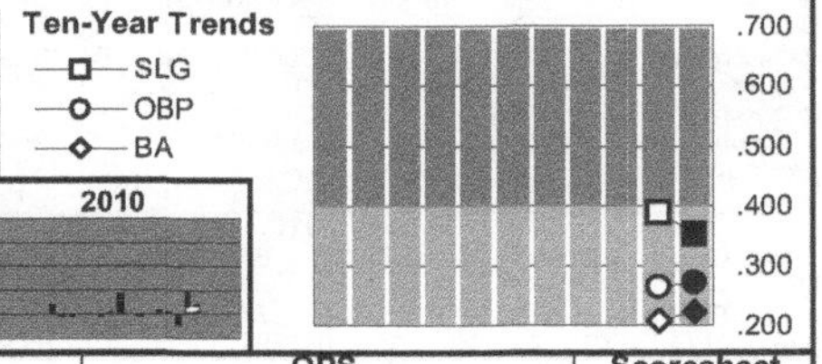


## Chase Headley — 620 PA | $11 | 300 pts

3B-158 — Owned: 82% — BH

Since his full-season debut, Headley has gradually sacrificed power for contact; the only rate that he has affected is his SLG, and in the wrong way. Luckily, he benefits from a lackluster 2010 season by prospect James Darnell, and his job is not in jeopardy. Headley did make a smooth switch back to third base. (DG)

| Player | Age | AB | HR | R | RBI | SB | BA | OBP | SLG | $1L | Pts |
|---|---|---|---|---|---|---|---|---|---|---|---|
| | | Forecast | | | | | | | | | |
| Headley C | 26 | 568 | 12 | 68 | 62 | 12 | .251 | .330 | .394 | $11 | 300 |
| **Mini-Browser** | Age | AB | HR | R | RBI | SB | BA | OBP | SLG | $1L | Pts |
| Kouzmanoff K | 29 | 579 | 24 | 66 | 84 | 0 | .259 | .303 | .441 | $15 | 330 |
| Alvarez P | 24 | 530 | 30 | 66 | 96 | 0 | .249 | .328 | .480 | $15 | 310 |
| Rolen S | 35 | 461 | 15 | 70 | 65 | 5 | .282 | .356 | .466 | $13 | 340 |
| Lopez J | 27 | 587 | 19 | 63 | 75 | 6 | .266 | .294 | .405 | $13 | 350 |
| Tejada M | 36 | 509 | 11 | 66 | 66 | 6 | .281 | .321 | .415 | $13 | 320 |

| Level | Leag | AB | HR | R | RBI | SB | BA | OBP | SLG | CT% | H% | BB% | Bash |
|---|---|---|---|---|---|---|---|---|---|---|---|---|---|
| | | Minors (2010) | | | | | | | | Skills | | | |
| A | — | — | — | — | — | — | — | — | — | — | — | — | — |
| AA | — | — | — | — | — | — | — | — | — | — | — | — | — |
| AAA | — | — | — | — | — | — | — | — | — | — | — | — | — |

| Yr | Team | AB | HR | R | RBI | SB | BA | OBP | SLG | CT% | H% | BB% | Bash |
|---|---|---|---|---|---|---|---|---|---|---|---|---|---|
| | | Majors | | | | | | | | Skills | | | |
| 07 | SD | 18 | 0 | 1 | 0 | 0 | .222 | .333 | .278 | 78% | 29% | 10% | 1.25 |
| 08 | SD | 331 | 9 | 34 | 38 | 4 | .269 | .337 | .420 | 69% | 39% | 8% | 1.56 |
| 09 | SD | 543 | 12 | 62 | 64 | 10 | .262 | .342 | .392 | 76% | 35% | 10% | 1.50 |
| 10 | SD | 610 | 11 | 77 | 58 | 17 | .264 | .327 | .375 | 77% | 34% | 8% | 1.42 |

| Yr | $1L | $2L | Pts | RAA | 2B | 3B | CS | FB-LD-GB | HR/fb | RBI% | RS% | OPS | 1st Hf | 2nd Hf | vs RH | vs LH | Rnge | vRH | vLH |
|---|---|---|---|---|---|---|---|---|---|---|---|---|---|---|---|---|---|---|---|
| | Value | | | | Extra | | | Production | | | | OPS | | | | | Scoresheet | | |
| 07 | -$6 | -$20 | 0 | –1 | 1 | 0 | 0 | 43-21-36 | 0% | 0% | 14% | .611 | .535 | 2.000 | .733 | .333 | — | — | — |
| 08 | $5 | -$6 | 140 | +0 | 19 | 2 | 1 | 37-25-38 | 11% | 18% | 22% | .757 | .829 | .727 | .756 | .757 | 2.65 | +5 | –15 |
| 09 | $13 | $1 | 290 | –0 | 31 | 2 | 2 | 38-17-45 | 8% | 17% | 25% | .734 | .674 | .798 | .765 | .671 | — | –2 | +4 |
| 10 | $16 | $7 | 310 | –7 | 29 | 3 | 5 | 36-18-46 | 6% | 15% | 32% | .702 | .686 | .724 | .753 | .589 | 2.64 | +3 | –9 |

**Competition at 3B — Stats in 2010**

| Bats | Player | GSvR | GSvL | Sub | OPS |
|---|---|---|---|---|---|
| BH | Headley C | 109 | 47 | 2 | .702 |

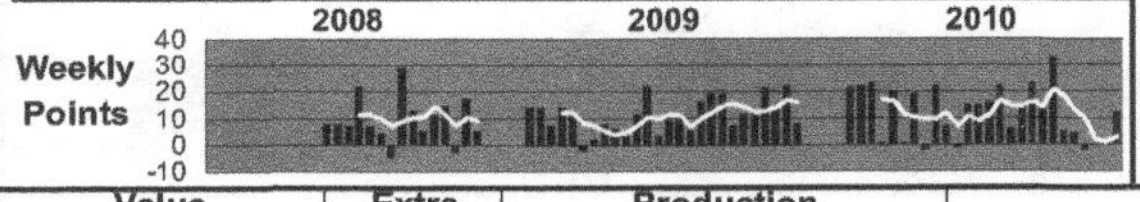


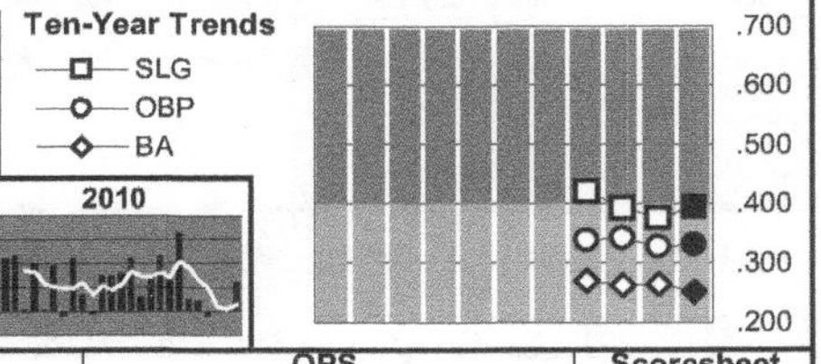

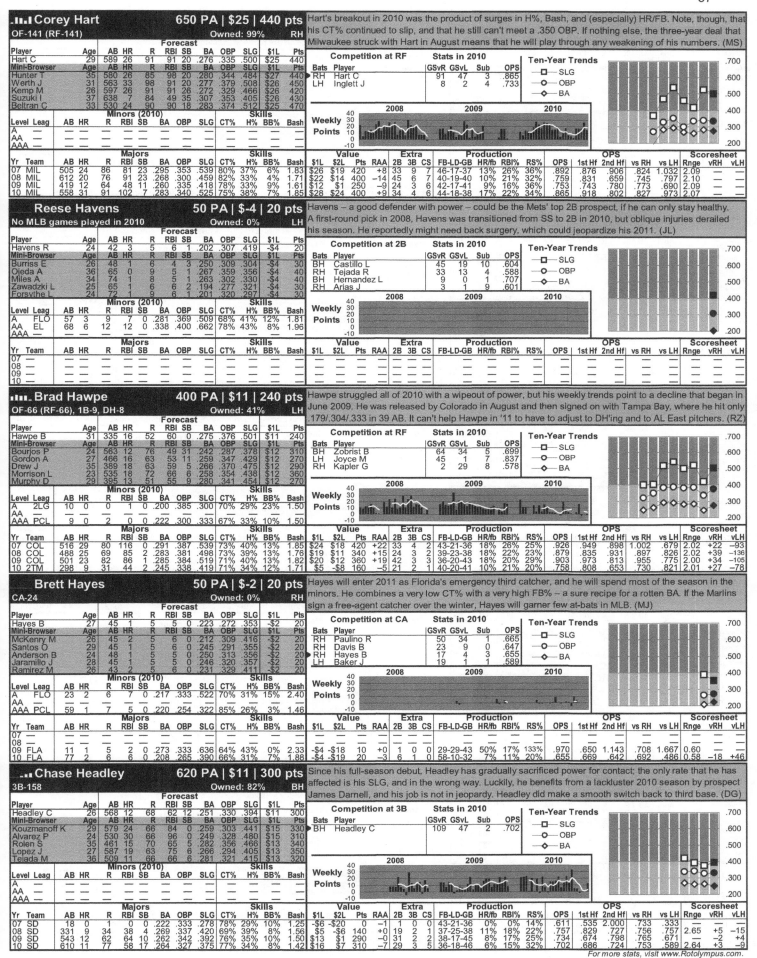

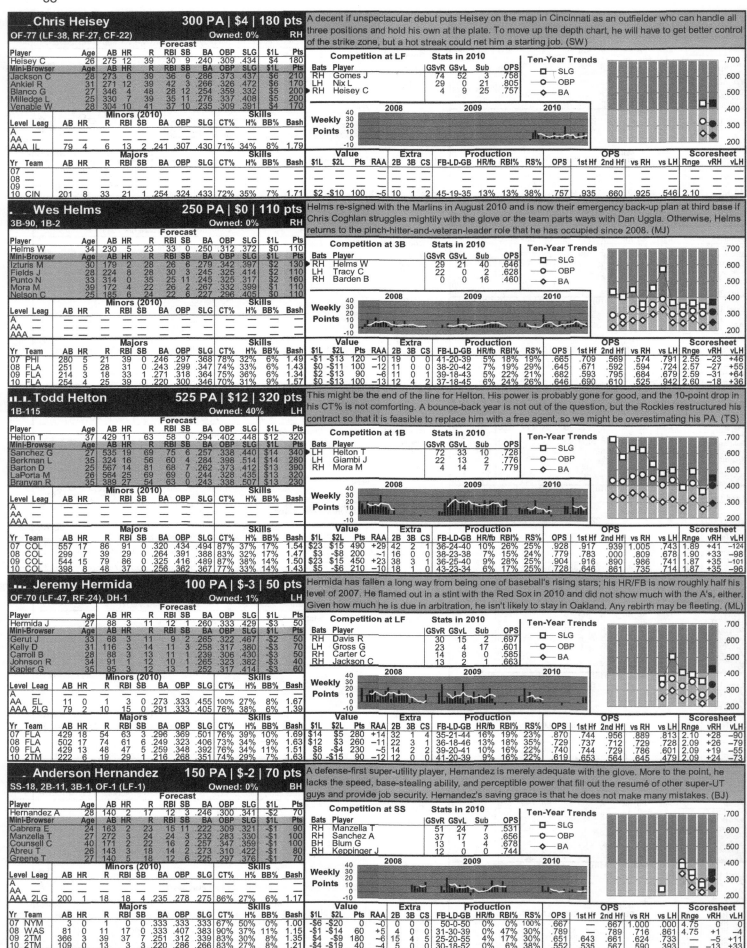

## Chris Heisey — 300 PA | $4 | 180 pts
**OF-77 (LF-38, RF-27, CF-22)** — Owned: 0% — RH

A decent if unspectacular debut puts Heisey on the map in Cincinnati as an outfielder who can handle all three positions and hold his own at the plate. To move up the depth chart, he will have to get better control of the strike zone, but a hot streak could net him a starting job. (SW)

### Forecast
| Player | Age | AB | HR | R | RBI | SB | BA | OBP | SLG | $1L | Pts |
|---|---|---|---|---|---|---|---|---|---|---|---|
| Heisey C | 26 | 275 | 12 | 39 | 30 | 9 | .240 | .309 | .434 | $4 | 180 |
| **Mini-Browser** | **Age** | **AB** | **HR** | **R** | **RBI** | **SB** | **BA** | **OBP** | **SLG** | **$1L** | **Pts** |
| Jackson C | 28 | 273 | 6 | 39 | 36 | 6 | .286 | .373 | .437 | $6 | 210 |
| Ankiel R | 31 | 271 | 12 | 39 | 42 | 3 | .266 | .326 | .472 | $6 | 170 |
| Blanco G | 27 | 346 | 4 | 48 | 28 | 12 | .254 | .359 | .332 | $5 | 200 |
| Milledge L | 25 | 330 | 7 | 39 | 35 | 11 | .276 | .337 | .408 | $5 | 200 |
| Venable W | 28 | 304 | 10 | 41 | 37 | 10 | .235 | .309 | .391 | $4 | 170 |

### Competition at LF / Stats in 2010
| Bats | Player | GSvR | GSvL | Sub | OPS |
|---|---|---|---|---|---|
| RH | Gomes J | 74 | 52 | 3 | .758 |
| LH | Nix L | 29 | 0 | 21 | .805 |
| RH | Heisey C | 4 | 9 | 25 | .757 |

### Minors (2010)
| Level | Leag | AB | HR | R | RBI | SB | BA | OBP | SLG | CT% | H% | BB% | Bash |
|---|---|---|---|---|---|---|---|---|---|---|---|---|---|
| A | — | | | | | | | | | | | | |
| AA | — | | | | | | | | | | | | |
| AAA | IL | 79 | 4 | 6 | 13 | 2 | .241 | .307 | .430 | 71% | 34% | 8% | 1.79 |

### Majors
| Yr | Team | AB | HR | R | RBI | SB | BA | OBP | SLG | CT% | H% | BB% | Bash |
|---|---|---|---|---|---|---|---|---|---|---|---|---|---|
| 07 | — | | | | | | | | | | | | |
| 08 | — | | | | | | | | | | | | |
| 09 | — | | | | | | | | | | | | |
| 10 | CIN | 201 | 8 | 33 | 14 | 1 | .254 | .324 | .433 | 72% | 35% | 7% | 1.71 |

| $1L | $2L | Pts | RAA | 2B | 3B | CS | FB-LD-GB | HR/fb | RBI% | RS% | OPS | 1st Hf | 2nd Hf | vs RH | vs LH | Rnge | vRH | vLH |
|---|---|---|---|---|---|---|---|---|---|---|---|---|---|---|---|---|---|---|
| $2 | -$10 | 100 | -5 | 1 | 0 | 2 | 45-19-35 | 13% | 13% | 38% | .757 | .935 | .660 | .925 | .546 | 2.10 | | |

---

## Wes Helms — 250 PA | $0 | 110 pts
**3B-90, 1B-2** — Owned: 0% — RH

Helms re-signed with the Marlins in August 2010 and is now their emergency back-up plan at third base if Chris Coghlan struggles mightily with the glove or the team parts ways with Dan Uggla. Otherwise, Helms returns to the pinch-hitter-and-veteran-leader role that he has occupied since 2008. (MJ)

### Forecast
| Player | Age | AB | HR | R | RBI | SB | BA | OBP | SLG | $1L | Pts |
|---|---|---|---|---|---|---|---|---|---|---|---|
| Helms W | 34 | 230 | 5 | 23 | 33 | 0 | .250 | .312 | .372 | $0 | 110 |
| **Mini-Browser** | **Age** | **AB** | **HR** | **R** | **RBI** | **SB** | **BA** | **OBP** | **SLG** | **$1L** | **Pts** |
| Izturis M | 30 | 179 | 2 | 28 | 26 | 6 | .279 | .342 | .397 | $2 | 130 |
| Fields J | 28 | 224 | 8 | 28 | 30 | 3 | .245 | .325 | .414 | $2 | 90 |
| Punto N | 33 | 314 | 0 | 35 | 25 | 11 | .245 | .325 | .317 | $2 | 160 |
| Mora M | 39 | 172 | 4 | 22 | 26 | 2 | .267 | .332 | .399 | $1 | 110 |
| Nelson C | 25 | 185 | 6 | 24 | 22 | 6 | .227 | .296 | .405 | $0 | 110 |

### Competition at 3B / Stats in 2010
| Bats | Player | GSvR | GSvL | Sub | OPS |
|---|---|---|---|---|---|
| RH | Helms W | 29 | 21 | 40 | .646 |
| LH | Tracy C | 22 | 0 | 2 | .628 |
| RH | Barden B | 0 | 0 | 16 | .460 |

### Minors (2010)
| Level | Leag | AB | HR | R | RBI | SB | BA | OBP | SLG | CT% | H% | BB% | Bash |
|---|---|---|---|---|---|---|---|---|---|---|---|---|---|
| A | — | | | | | | | | | | | | |
| AA | — | | | | | | | | | | | | |
| AAA | — | | | | | | | | | | | | |

### Majors
| Yr | Team | AB | HR | R | RBI | SB | BA | OBP | SLG | CT% | H% | BB% | Bash |
|---|---|---|---|---|---|---|---|---|---|---|---|---|---|
| 07 | PHI | 280 | 5 | 21 | 39 | 0 | .246 | .297 | .368 | 78% | 32% | 6% | 1.49 |
| 08 | FLA | 251 | 5 | 28 | 31 | 0 | .243 | .299 | .347 | 74% | 33% | 6% | 1.43 |
| 09 | FLA | 214 | 3 | 18 | 33 | 1 | .271 | .318 | .364 | 75% | 36% | 6% | 1.34 |
| 10 | FLA | 254 | 4 | 25 | 39 | 0 | .220 | .300 | .346 | 70% | 31% | 9% | 1.57 |

| Yr | $1L | $2L | Pts | RAA | 2B | 3B | CS | FB-LD-GB | HR/fb | RBI% | RS% | OPS | 1st Hf | 2nd Hf | vs RH | vs LH | Rnge | vRH | vLH |
|---|---|---|---|---|---|---|---|---|---|---|---|---|---|---|---|---|---|---|---|
| 07 | $-1 | -$13 | 120 | -10 | 19 | 0 | 0 | 41-20-39 | 5% | 18% | 19% | .665 | .709 | .569 | .574 | .791 | 2.55 | -23 | +46 |
| 08 | $0 | -$11 | 100 | -12 | 11 | 0 | 0 | 38-20-42 | 7% | 19% | 29% | .645 | .671 | .592 | .594 | .724 | 2.57 | -27 | +55 |
| 09 | $2 | -$13 | 90 | -6 | 11 | 0 | 1 | 39-18-43 | 5% | 22% | 21% | .682 | .593 | .795 | .684 | .679 | 2.59 | -31 | +64 |
| 10 | $0 | -$13 | 100 | -13 | 12 | 4 | 2 | 37-18-45 | 6% | 24% | 26% | .646 | .690 | .610 | .525 | .942 | 2.60 | -18 | +36 |

---

## Todd Helton — 525 PA | $12 | 320 pts
**1B-115** — Owned: 40% — LH

This might be the end of the line for Helton. His power is probably gone for good, and the 10-point drop in his CT% is not comforting. A bounce-back year is not out of the question, but the Rockies restructured his contract so that it is feasible to replace him with a free agent, so we might be overestimating his PA. (TS)

### Forecast
| Player | Age | AB | HR | R | RBI | SB | BA | OBP | SLG | $1L | Pts |
|---|---|---|---|---|---|---|---|---|---|---|---|
| Helton T | 37 | 429 | 11 | 63 | 58 | 0 | .294 | .402 | .448 | $12 | 320 |
| **Mini-Browser** | **Age** | **AB** | **HR** | **R** | **RBI** | **SB** | **BA** | **OBP** | **SLG** | **$1L** | **Pts** |
| Sanchez G | 27 | 535 | 19 | 69 | 75 | 6 | .257 | .338 | .440 | $14 | 340 |
| Berkman L | 35 | 324 | 16 | 56 | 60 | 4 | .284 | .398 | .514 | $14 | 280 |
| Barton D | 25 | 567 | 14 | 81 | 68 | 7 | .262 | .373 | .412 | $13 | 390 |
| LaPorta M | 26 | 564 | 25 | 69 | 69 | 0 | .244 | .328 | .435 | $13 | 320 |
| Branyan R | 35 | 389 | 27 | 54 | 63 | 0 | .243 | .338 | .507 | $13 | 230 |

### Competition at 1B / Stats in 2010
| Bats | Player | GSvR | GSvL | Sub | OPS |
|---|---|---|---|---|---|
| LH | Helton T | 72 | 33 | 10 | .728 |
| LH | Giambi J | 22 | 13 | 2 | .776 |
| RH | Mora M | 4 | 14 | 7 | .779 |

### Minors (2010)
| Level | Leag | AB | HR | R | RBI | SB | BA | OBP | SLG | CT% | H% | BB% | Bash |
|---|---|---|---|---|---|---|---|---|---|---|---|---|---|
| A | — | | | | | | | | | | | | |
| AA | — | | | | | | | | | | | | |
| AAA | — | | | | | | | | | | | | |

### Majors
| Yr | Team | AB | HR | R | RBI | SB | BA | OBP | SLG | CT% | H% | BB% | Bash |
|---|---|---|---|---|---|---|---|---|---|---|---|---|---|
| 07 | COL | 557 | 17 | 86 | 91 | 0 | .320 | .434 | .494 | 83% | 37% | 17% | 1.54 |
| 08 | COL | 299 | 7 | 39 | 29 | 0 | .264 | .391 | .388 | 83% | 32% | 17% | 1.47 |
| 09 | COL | 544 | 15 | 79 | 86 | 0 | .325 | .416 | .489 | 87% | 38% | 14% | 1.50 |
| 10 | COL | 398 | 8 | 48 | 37 | 0 | .256 | .362 | .367 | 77% | 33% | 14% | 1.43 |

| Yr | $1L | $2L | Pts | RAA | 2B | 3B | CS | FB-LD-GB | HR/fb | RBI% | RS% | OPS | 1st Hf | 2nd Hf | vs RH | vs LH | Rnge | vRH | vLH |
|---|---|---|---|---|---|---|---|---|---|---|---|---|---|---|---|---|---|---|---|
| 07 | $23 | $15 | 490 | +29 | 42 | 2 | 1 | 36-24-40 | 10% | 26% | 25% | .928 | .917 | .939 | 1.005 | .743 | 1.89 | +41 | -124 |
| 08 | $3 | -$8 | 200 | ~1 | 16 | 0 | 0 | 38-23-38 | 7% | 15% | 24% | .779 | .783 | .000 | .809 | .678 | 1.90 | +33 | -98 |
| 09 | $23 | $15 | 450 | +23 | 38 | 3 | 1 | 36-25-40 | 9% | 28% | 25% | .904 | .916 | .890 | .986 | .741 | 1.87 | +35 | -101 |
| 10 | $5 | -$6 | 210 | -10 | 18 | 1 | 0 | 43-23-34 | 6% | 17% | 25% | .728 | .646 | .861 | .735 | .714 | 1.87 | +35 | -96 |

---

## Jeremy Hermida — 100 PA | $-3 | 50 pts
**OF-70 (LF-47, RF-24), DH-1** — Owned: 1% — LH

Hermida has fallen a long way from being one of baseball's rising stars; his HR/FB is now roughly half his level of 2007. He flamed out in a stint with the Red Sox in 2010 and did not show much with the A's, either. Given how much he is due in arbitration, he isn't likely to stay in Oakland. Any rebirth may be fleeting. (ML)

### Forecast
| Player | Age | AB | HR | R | RBI | SB | BA | OBP | SLG | $1L | Pts |
|---|---|---|---|---|---|---|---|---|---|---|---|
| Hermida J | 27 | 88 | 3 | 11 | 12 | 1 | .260 | .333 | .429 | -$3 | 50 |
| **Mini-Browser** | **Age** | **AB** | **HR** | **R** | **RBI** | **SB** | **BA** | **OBP** | **SLG** | **$1L** | **Pts** |
| Gerut J | 33 | 68 | 3 | 11 | 9 | 2 | .265 | .322 | .467 | -$2 | 50 |
| Kelly D | 31 | 116 | 3 | 14 | 11 | 3 | .258 | .317 | .380 | -$3 | 70 |
| Carroll B | 28 | 89 | 3 | 13 | 11 | 1 | .239 | .306 | .430 | -$3 | 50 |
| Johnson R | 34 | 91 | 1 | 12 | 10 | 1 | .265 | .323 | .382 | -$3 | 40 |
| Kapler G | 35 | 95 | 3 | 12 | 13 | 1 | .252 | .317 | .414 | -$3 | 60 |

### Competition at LF / Stats in 2010
| Bats | Player | GSvR | GSvL | Sub | OPS |
|---|---|---|---|---|---|
| RH | Davis R | 30 | 15 | 2 | .697 |
| LH | Gross G | 23 | 4 | 17 | .601 |
| RH | Carter C | 14 | 8 | 0 | .585 |
| RH | Jackson C | 13 | 2 | 1 | .663 |

### Minors (2010)
| Level | Leag | AB | HR | R | RBI | SB | BA | OBP | SLG | CT% | H% | BB% | Bash |
|---|---|---|---|---|---|---|---|---|---|---|---|---|---|
| A | — | | | | | | | | | | | | |
| AA | EL | 11 | 0 | 1 | 3 | 0 | .273 | .333 | .455 | 100% | 27% | 8% | 1.67 |
| AAA | 2LG | 79 | 2 | 10 | 15 | 0 | .291 | .333 | .405 | 76% | 38% | 6% | 1.39 |

### Majors
| Yr | Team | AB | HR | R | RBI | SB | BA | OBP | SLG | CT% | H% | BB% | Bash |
|---|---|---|---|---|---|---|---|---|---|---|---|---|---|
| 07 | FLA | 429 | 18 | 54 | 63 | 3 | .296 | .369 | .501 | 76% | 39% | 10% | 1.69 |
| 08 | FLA | 502 | 17 | 74 | 61 | 6 | .249 | .323 | .406 | 73% | 34% | 9% | 1.63 |
| 09 | FLA | 429 | 13 | 48 | 47 | 5 | .259 | .348 | .392 | 76% | 34% | 11% | 1.51 |
| 10 | 2TM | 222 | 6 | 19 | 29 | 1 | .216 | .268 | .351 | 74% | 29% | 7% | 1.63 |

| Yr | $1L | $2L | Pts | RAA | 2B | 3B | CS | FB-LD-GB | HR/fb | RBI% | RS% | OPS | 1st Hf | 2nd Hf | vs RH | vs LH | Rnge | vRH | vLH |
|---|---|---|---|---|---|---|---|---|---|---|---|---|---|---|---|---|---|---|---|
| 07 | $14 | $5 | 280 | +14 | 32 | 1 | 4 | 35-21-44 | 16% | 19% | 23% | .870 | .744 | .956 | .889 | .813 | 2.10 | +28 | -90 |
| 08 | $6 | $3 | 260 | -11 | 22 | 3 | 1 | 36-18-46 | 13% | 18% | 35% | .729 | .737 | .712 | .729 | .728 | 2.09 | +26 | -79 |
| 09 | $8 | -$4 | 230 | -5 | 14 | 2 | 2 | 39-20-41 | 10% | 16% | 22% | .740 | .744 | .729 | .786 | .601 | 2.09 | +19 | -55 |
| 10 | $0 | -$15 | 90 | -12 | 12 | 0 | 0 | 41-20-39 | 9% | 16% | 22% | .619 | .653 | .564 | .645 | .479 | 2.09 | +24 | -73 |

---

## Anderson Hernandez — 150 PA | $-2 | 70 pts
**SS-18, 2B-11, 3B-1, OF-1 (LF-1)** — Owned: 0% — BH

A defense-first super-utility player, Hernandez is merely adequate with the glove. More to the point, he lacks the speed, base-stealing ability, and perceptible power that fill out the resumé of other super-UT guys and provide job security. Hernandez's saving grace is that he does not make many mistakes. (BJ)

### Forecast
| Player | Age | AB | HR | R | RBI | SB | BA | OBP | SLG | $1L | Pts |
|---|---|---|---|---|---|---|---|---|---|---|---|
| Hernandez A | 28 | 140 | 2 | 17 | 12 | 3 | .246 | .300 | .341 | -$2 | 70 |
| **Mini-Browser** | **Age** | **AB** | **HR** | **R** | **RBI** | **SB** | **BA** | **OBP** | **SLG** | **$1L** | **Pts** |
| Cabrera E | 24 | 163 | 2 | 23 | 15 | 11 | .222 | .309 | .321 | -$1 | 90 |
| Manzella T | 27 | 272 | 3 | 24 | 24 | 3 | .232 | .283 | .330 | -$1 | 100 |
| Counsell C | 40 | 171 | 2 | 22 | 16 | 2 | .257 | .347 | .359 | -$1 | 100 |
| Abreu T | 26 | 143 | 3 | 18 | 14 | 2 | .273 | .310 | .422 | -$1 | 80 |
| Greene T | 27 | 140 | 5 | 18 | 12 | 6 | .225 | .297 | .376 | -$1 | 80 |

### Competition at SS / Stats in 2010
| Bats | Player | GSvR | GSvL | Sub | OPS |
|---|---|---|---|---|---|
| RH | Manzella T | 51 | 24 | 7 | .531 |
| RH | Sanchez A | 37 | 17 | 3 | .656 |
| BH | Blum G | 13 | 1 | 4 | .678 |
| RH | Keppinger J | 12 | 0 | 0 | .744 |

### Minors (2010)
| Level | Leag | AB | HR | R | RBI | SB | BA | OBP | SLG | CT% | H% | BB% | Bash |
|---|---|---|---|---|---|---|---|---|---|---|---|---|---|
| A | — | | | | | | | | | | | | |
| AA | — | | | | | | | | | | | | |
| AAA | 2LG | 200 | 1 | 18 | 18 | 4 | .235 | .278 | .275 | 86% | 27% | 6% | 1.17 |

### Majors
| Yr | Team | AB | HR | R | RBI | SB | BA | OBP | SLG | CT% | H% | BB% | Bash |
|---|---|---|---|---|---|---|---|---|---|---|---|---|---|
| 07 | NYM | 3 | 0 | 1 | 0 | 0 | .333 | .333 | .333 | 67% | 50% | 0% | 1.00 |
| 08 | WAS | 81 | 0 | 11 | 17 | 0 | .333 | .407 | .383 | 90% | 37% | 11% | 1.15 |
| 09 | 2TM | 366 | 3 | 39 | 37 | 7 | .251 | .312 | .339 | 83% | 30% | 8% | 1.35 |
| 10 | 2TM | 109 | 2 | 13 | 3 | 3 | .220 | .286 | .266 | 83% | 27% | 6% | 1.21 |

| Yr | $1L | $2L | Pts | RAA | 2B | 3B | CS | FB-LD-GB | HR/fb | RBI% | RS% | OPS | 1st Hf | 2nd Hf | vs RH | vs LH | Rnge | vRH | vLH |
|---|---|---|---|---|---|---|---|---|---|---|---|---|---|---|---|---|---|---|---|
| 07 | $-6 | -$20 | — | | 0 | 0 | 0 | 50-0-50 | 0% | 0% | 100% | .667 | — | .667 | 1.000 | .000 | 4.75 | | |
| 08 | $-1 | -$14 | 60 | +5 | 4 | 0 | 0 | 31-30-39 | 0% | 47% | 30% | .789 | — | .789 | .716 | .861 | 4.75 | +1 | -4 |
| 09 | $4 | -$9 | 180 | -6 | 15 | 4 | 5 | 25-20-55 | 4% | 17% | 30% | .651 | .643 | .661 | .624 | .733 | — | -5 | +11 |
| 10 | $-4 | -$19 | 40 | -7 | 4 | 0 | 6 | 30-18-52 | 6% | 38% | 30% | .552 | .535 | .567 | .590 | .393 | — | -13 | +34 |

*For more stats, visit www.Rotolympus.com.*

## Diory Hernandez — 75 PA | $-4 | 30 pts

SS-4, 2B-1 — Owned: 0% — RH

Diory has not proven that he can hit big-league pitching, and the 26-year-old might find himself fighting for a utility role in 2011. With the question marks about Chipper Jones, the Braves will probably try to acquire some depth in the infield, and Diory could once again be relegated to minor-league emergency fill-in. (MG)

| Player | Age | AB | HR | R | RBI | SB | BA | OBP | SLG | $1L | Pts |
|---|---|---|---|---|---|---|---|---|---|---|---|
| Hernandez D | 26 | 69 | 2 | 7 | 8 | 2 | .240 | .296 | .352 | -$4 | 30 |
| **Mini-Browser** | **Age** | **AB** | **HR** | **R** | **RBI** | **SB** | **BA** | **OBP** | **SLG** | **$1L** | **Pts** |
| Valdez W | 32 | 94 | 1 | 12 | 8 | 2 | .254 | .315 | .339 | -$3 | 50 |
| Ciriaco P | 25 | 92 | 1 | 11 | 8 | 5 | .218 | .246 | .312 | -$3 | 40 |
| Andino R | 26 | 91 | 2 | 10 | 8 | 3 | .254 | .301 | .382 | -$3 | 40 |
| Wilson J | 30 | 143 | 2 | 12 | 12 | 3 | .242 | .296 | .345 | -$4 | 60 |
| Cozart Z | 25 | 88 | 3 | 10 | 9 | 1 | .215 | .288 | .385 | -$4 | 40 |

**Competition at SS — Stats in 2010**

| Bats | Player | GSvR | GSvL | Sub | OPS |
|---|---|---|---|---|---|
| RH | Gonzalez A | 45 | 26 | 1 | .741 |
| RH | Infante O | 13 | 6 | 0 | .775 |

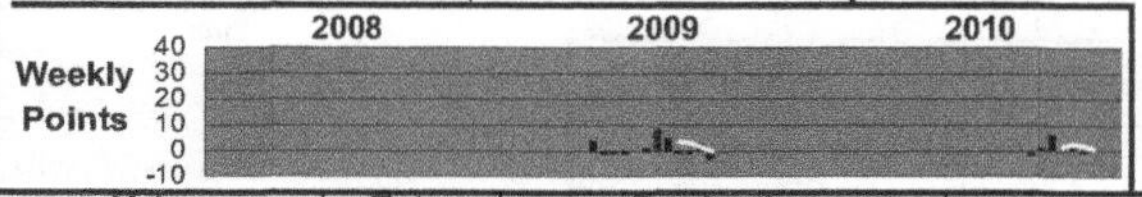
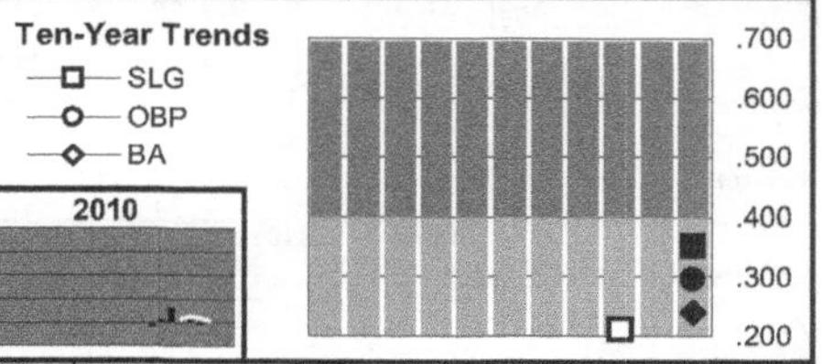

**Minors (2010)**

| Level | Leag | AB | HR | R | RBI | SB | BA | OBP | SLG | CT% | H% | BB% | Bash |
|---|---|---|---|---|---|---|---|---|---|---|---|---|---|
| A | — | — | — | — | — | — | — | — | — | — | — | — | — |
| AA | — | — | — | — | — | — | — | — | — | — | — | — | — |
| AAA | IL | 116 | 0 | 13 | 17 | 3 | .319 | .344 | .414 | 82% | 39% | 3% | 1.30 |

**Majors**

| Yr | Team | AB | HR | R | RBI | SB | BA | OBP | SLG | CT% | H% | BB% | Bash | $1L | $2L | Pts | RAA | 2B | 3B | CS | FB-LD-GB | HR/fb | RBI% | RS% | OPS | 1st Hf | 2nd Hf | vs RH | vs LH | Rnge | vRH | vLH |
|---|---|---|---|---|---|---|---|---|---|---|---|---|---|---|---|---|---|---|---|---|---|---|---|---|---|---|---|---|---|---|---|---|
| 07 | — | — | — | — | — | — | — | — | — | — | — | — | — | — | — | — | — | — | — | — | — | — | — | — | — | — | — | — | — | — | — | — |
| 08 | — | — | — | — | — | — | — | — | — | — | — | — | — | — | — | — | — | — | — | — | — | — | — | — | — | — | — | — | — | — | — | — |
| 09 | ATL | 85 | 1 | 6 | 6 | 0 | .141 | .198 | .212 | 74% | 19% | 6% | 1.50 | -$6 | -$21 | 10 | −11 | 3 | 0 | 1 | 32-14-54 | 5% | 10% | 29% | .410 | .436 | .311 | .477 | .217 | — | — | — |
| 10 | ATL | 9 | 1 | 5 | 1 | 0 | .111 | .111 | .444 | 56% | 20% | 0% | 4.00 | -$5 | -$19 | 10 | −1 | 0 | 0 | 0 | 40-20-40 | 50% | 0% | NA | .556 | — | .556 | .000 | 1.000 | 4.75 | −12 | +30 |

## ▮▮▮▮ Ramon Hernandez — 300 PA | $6 | 170 pts

CA-91, 1B-5 — Owned: 17% — RH

Hernandez in his age-33 season bought himself some time with an atypically high H% and BA. The Reds want to keep him around to work with their young Hispanic pitchers and to share time with Ryan Hanigan. If Ramon is amenable, they'll bring him back; otherwise, another team will bite on the .300-level BA. (SW)

| Player | Age | AB | HR | R | RBI | SB | BA | OBP | SLG | $1L | Pts |
|---|---|---|---|---|---|---|---|---|---|---|---|
| Hernandez R | 34 | 278 | 9 | 27 | 39 | 0 | .270 | .338 | .411 | $6 | 170 |
| **Mini-Browser** | **Age** | **AB** | **HR** | **R** | **RBI** | **SB** | **BA** | **OBP** | **SLG** | **$1L** | **Pts** |
| Arencibia J | 25 | 369 | 16 | 36 | 52 | 0 | .217 | .254 | .420 | $7 | 160 |
| Shoppach K | 30 | 277 | 13 | 39 | 42 | 0 | .223 | .315 | .429 | $6 | 110 |
| Lucroy J | 24 | 406 | 14 | 41 | 45 | 5 | .233 | .307 | .375 | $6 | 220 |
| Rodriguez I | 39 | 335 | 7 | 35 | 35 | 4 | .261 | .291 | .381 | $6 | 160 |
| Avila A | 24 | 361 | 12 | 36 | 44 | 0 | .233 | .319 | .387 | $6 | 180 |

**Competition at CA — Stats in 2010**

| Bats | Player | GSvR | GSvL | Sub | OPS |
|---|---|---|---|---|---|
| ▶ RH | Hernandez R | 61 | 24 | 6 | .792 |
| RH | Hanigan R | 34 | 24 | 10 | .834 |
| RH | Miller C | 12 | 7 | 13 | .674 |

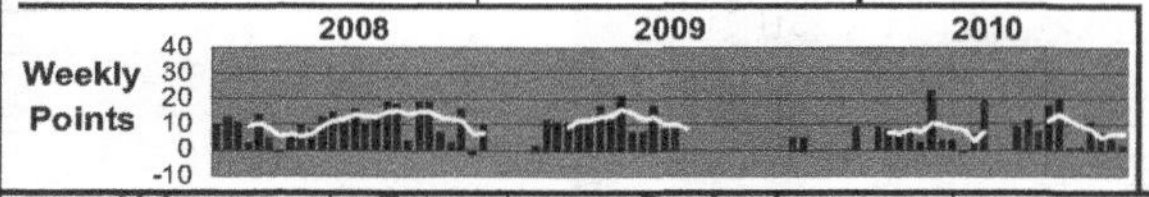
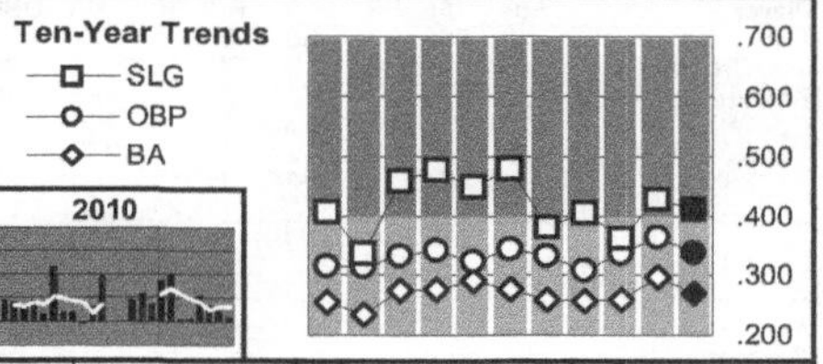

**Minors (2010)**

| Level | Leag | AB | HR | R | RBI | SB | BA | OBP | SLG | CT% | H% | BB% | Bash |
|---|---|---|---|---|---|---|---|---|---|---|---|---|---|
| A | — | — | — | — | — | — | — | — | — | — | — | — | — |
| AA | — | — | — | — | — | — | — | — | — | — | — | — | — |
| AAA | — | — | — | — | — | — | — | — | — | — | — | — | — |

**Majors**

| Yr | Team | AB | HR | R | RBI | SB | BA | OBP | SLG | CT% | H% | BB% | Bash | $1L | $2L | Pts | RAA | 2B | 3B | CS | FB-LD-GB | HR/fb | RBI% | RS% | OPS | 1st Hf | 2nd Hf | vs RH | vs LH | Rnge | vRH | vLH |
|---|---|---|---|---|---|---|---|---|---|---|---|---|---|---|---|---|---|---|---|---|---|---|---|---|---|---|---|---|---|---|---|---|
| 07 | BAL | 364 | 9 | 40 | 62 | 1 | .258 | .333 | .382 | 84% | 31% | 9% | 1.48 | $10 | $0 | 220 | −5 | 18 | 0 | 3 | 35-16-49 | 8% | 25% | 24% | .714 | .696 | .729 | .700 | .754 | 0.51 | −19 | +51 |
| 08 | BAL | 463 | 15 | 49 | 65 | 0 | .257 | .308 | .406 | 87% | 30% | 6% | 1.58 | $12 | $7 | 270 | −7 | 22 | 1 | 0 | 33-20-47 | 11% | 21% | 24% | .714 | .662 | .787 | .726 | .688 | 0.57 | −27 | +71 |
| 09 | CIN | 287 | 5 | 25 | 37 | 1 | .258 | .336 | .362 | 88% | 29% | 10% | 1.41 | $5 | -$2 | 170 | −5 | 13 | 1 | 0 | 32-19-49 | 6% | 23% | 19% | .699 | .693 | .789 | .680 | .748 | 0.68 | −13 | +33 |
| 10 | CIN | 313 | 7 | 30 | 48 | 0 | .297 | .364 | .428 | 84% | 35% | 8% | 1.44 | $10 | $4 | 190 | +6 | 18 | 1 | 0 | 29-20-52 | 9% | 25% | 19% | .792 | .768 | .825 | .786 | .811 | 0.71 | −10 | +25 |

## Jonathan Herrera — 125 PA | $-2 | 60 pts

2B-57, 3B-16, SS-7 — Owned: 1% — BH

Herrera brings a good glove, but he generates almost no offense – and in the hitter-friendly Pacific Coast League! He does achieve a .350 OBP, but his SLG is generally no better. The Rockies will probably keep Herrera around as a UT IF, and he could garner starts during Troy Tulowitzki's annual trip to the DL. (TS)

| Player | Age | AB | HR | R | RBI | SB | BA | OBP | SLG | $1L | Pts |
|---|---|---|---|---|---|---|---|---|---|---|---|
| Herrera J | 26 | 111 | 1 | 15 | 10 | 4 | .258 | .328 | .342 | -$2 | 60 |
| **Mini-Browser** | **Age** | **AB** | **HR** | **R** | **RBI** | **SB** | **BA** | **OBP** | **SLG** | **$1L** | **Pts** |
| Lugo J | 35 | 163 | 2 | 19 | 16 | 7 | .258 | .325 | .346 | -$1 | 90 |
| Lillibridge B | 27 | 136 | 3 | 18 | 14 | 8 | .232 | .304 | .374 | -$1 | 70 |
| Blanco A | 26 | 161 | 2 | 18 | 16 | 2 | .271 | .322 | .369 | -$1 | 90 |
| McDonald J | 36 | 193 | 2 | 22 | 20 | 2 | .238 | .268 | .345 | -$2 | 90 |
| Rhymes W | 28 | 152 | 2 | 18 | 16 | 5 | .242 | .298 | .336 | -$2 | 80 |

**Competition at 2B — Stats in 2010**

| Bats | Player | GSvR | GSvL | Sub | OPS |
|---|---|---|---|---|---|
| RH | Barmes C | 41 | 28 | 19 | .656 |
| ▶ BH | Herrera J | 31 | 17 | 9 | .694 |
| BH | Young Jr. E | 21 | 12 | 2 | .597 |
| RH | Mora M | 6 | 8 | 5 | .779 |

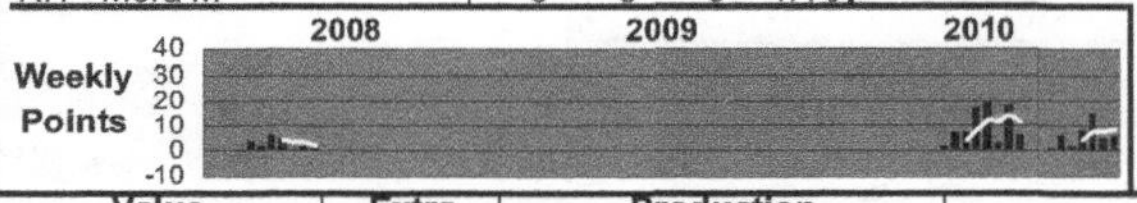
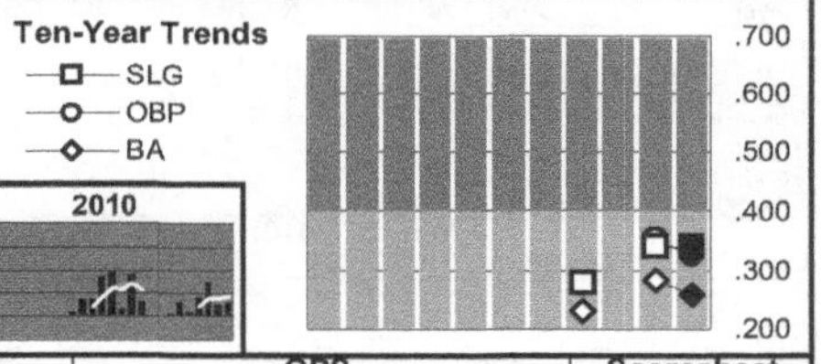

**Minors (2010)**

| Level | Leag | AB | HR | R | RBI | SB | BA | OBP | SLG | CT% | H% | BB% | Bash |
|---|---|---|---|---|---|---|---|---|---|---|---|---|---|
| A | — | — | — | — | — | — | — | — | — | — | — | — | — |
| AA | — | — | — | — | — | — | — | — | — | — | — | — | — |
| AAA | PCL | 222 | 2 | 30 | 17 | 3 | .261 | .340 | .324 | 87% | 30% | 10% | 1.24 |

**Majors**

| Yr | Team | AB | HR | R | RBI | SB | BA | OBP | SLG | CT% | H% | BB% | Bash | $1L | $2L | Pts | RAA | 2B | 3B | CS | FB-LD-GB | HR/fb | RBI% | RS% | OPS | 1st Hf | 2nd Hf | vs RH | vs LH | Rnge | vRH | vLH |
|---|---|---|---|---|---|---|---|---|---|---|---|---|---|---|---|---|---|---|---|---|---|---|---|---|---|---|---|---|---|---|---|---|
| 07 | — | — | — | — | — | — | — | — | — | — | — | — | — | — | — | — | — | — | — | — | — | — | — | — | — | — | — | — | — | — | — | — |
| 08 | COL | 61 | 0 | 5 | 3 | 1 | .230 | .277 | .279 | 84% | 27% | 6% | 1.21 | — | — | 20 | −4 | 1 | 1 | 1 | 21-23-56 | 0% | 12% | 28% | .556 | .556 | — | .579 | .504 | — | — | — |
| 09 | — | — | — | — | — | — | — | — | — | — | — | — | — | — | — | — | — | — | — | — | — | — | — | — | — | — | — | — | — | 4.27 | −1 | +1 |
| 10 | COL | 222 | 1 | 34 | 21 | 2 | .284 | .352 | .342 | 84% | 34% | 10% | 1.21 | $2 | -$10 | 120 | −4 | 6 | 2 | 2 | 32-18-50 | 2% | 21% | 38% | .694 | .701 | .687 | .680 | .722 | — | −3 | +8 |

## John Hester — 150 PA | $1 | 70 pts

CA-33 — Owned: 0% — RH

One reason that Arizona felt comfortable trading Chris Snyder, Hester offers good defense and excellent power potential (career .502 SLG in the minors). In 2011, Hester will back up Miguel Montero, one injury away from a more prominent role. (MS)

| Player | Age | AB | HR | R | RBI | SB | BA | OBP | SLG | $1L | Pts |
|---|---|---|---|---|---|---|---|---|---|---|---|
| Hester J | 27 | 142 | 5 | 17 | 17 | 2 | .243 | .294 | .422 | $1 | 70 |
| **Mini-Browser** | **Age** | **AB** | **HR** | **R** | **RBI** | **SB** | **BA** | **OBP** | **SLG** | **$1L** | **Pts** |
| Varitek J | 38 | 216 | 8 | 23 | 28 | 0 | .231 | .326 | .398 | $2 | 100 |
| Cervelli F | 25 | 224 | 3 | 23 | 25 | 0 | .246 | .323 | .332 | $2 | 110 |
| Moore A | 26 | 270 | 9 | 24 | 30 | 0 | .222 | .281 | .361 | $2 | 110 |
| Castro J | 23 | 345 | 8 | 40 | 32 | 0 | .220 | .303 | .340 | $2 | 150 |
| Ross D | 34 | 126 | 5 | 15 | 20 | 0 | .250 | .350 | .434 | $1 | 70 |

**Competition at CA — Stats in 2010**

| Bats | Player | GSvR | GSvL | Sub | OPS |
|---|---|---|---|---|---|
| LH | Montero M | 57 | 18 | 4 | .770 |
| ▶ RH | Hester J | 11 | 16 | 6 | .640 |

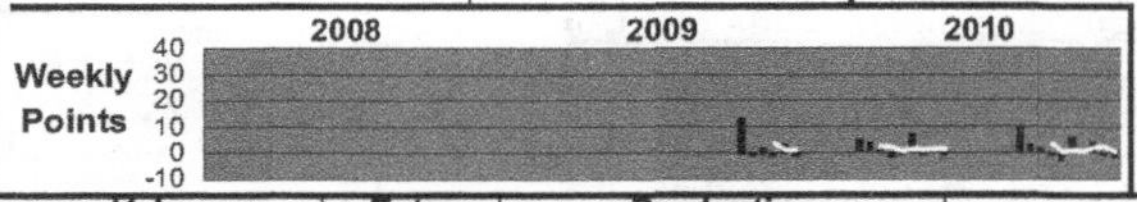
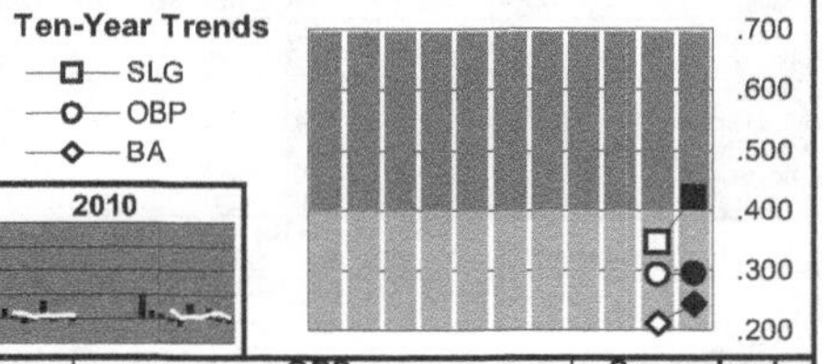

**Minors (2010)**

| Level | Leag | AB | HR | R | RBI | SB | BA | OBP | SLG | CT% | H% | BB% | Bash |
|---|---|---|---|---|---|---|---|---|---|---|---|---|---|
| A | — | — | — | — | — | — | — | — | — | — | — | — | — |
| AA | — | — | — | — | — | — | — | — | — | — | — | — | — |
| AAA | PCL | 138 | 7 | 34 | 29 | 2 | .370 | .440 | .667 | 81% | 46% | 10% | 1.80 |

**Majors**

| Yr | Team | AB | HR | R | RBI | SB | BA | OBP | SLG | CT% | H% | BB% | Bash | $1L | $2L | Pts | RAA | 2B | 3B | CS | FB-LD-GB | HR/fb | RBI% | RS% | OPS | 1st Hf | 2nd Hf | vs RH | vs LH | Rnge | vRH | vLH |
|---|---|---|---|---|---|---|---|---|---|---|---|---|---|---|---|---|---|---|---|---|---|---|---|---|---|---|---|---|---|---|---|---|
| 07 | — | — | — | — | — | — | — | — | — | — | — | — | — | — | — | — | — | — | — | — | — | — | — | — | — | — | — | — | — | — | — | — |
| 08 | — | — | — | — | — | — | — | — | — | — | — | — | — | — | — | — | — | — | — | — | — | — | — | — | — | — | — | — | — | — | — | — |
| 09 | ARI | 28 | 1 | 4 | 4 | 0 | .250 | .300 | .429 | 75% | 33% | 7% | 1.71 | -$4 | -$18 | 20 | 0 | 2 | 0 | 0 | 52-14-33 | 9% | 19% | 38% | .729 | — | .729 | 1.200 | .444 | — | — | — |
| 10 | ARI | 95 | 2 | 9 | 7 | 1 | .211 | .292 | .347 | 66% | 32% | 10% | 1.65 | -$1 | -$11 | 30 | −3 | 7 | 0 | 0 | 46-19-35 | 7% | 10% | 24% | .640 | .500 | .780 | .623 | .661 | 0.59 | −12 | +27 |

## ▮ Jason Heyward — 600 PA | $17 | 380 pts

OF-140 (RF-140) — Owned: 98% — LH

Here is the Braves' everyday RF and emerging cornerstone of their order. Exactly where Heyward bats will depend on whom the Braves acquire to boost the offense and whether Chipper Jones can handle a middle-of-the-order spot. But Heyward should get slotted at #2 or #3. A rise in FB% would be welcome. (MG)

| Player | Age | AB | HR | R | RBI | SB | BA | OBP | SLG | $1L | Pts |
|---|---|---|---|---|---|---|---|---|---|---|---|
| Heyward J | 21 | 511 | 18 | 84 | 66 | 12 | .270 | .368 | .464 | $17 | 380 |
| **Mini-Browser** | **Age** | **AB** | **HR** | **R** | **RBI** | **SB** | **BA** | **OBP** | **SLG** | **$1L** | **Pts** |
| Ibanez R | 38 | 551 | 24 | 78 | 90 | 6 | .272 | .345 | .483 | $18 | 410 |
| Zobrist B | 29 | 512 | 18 | 72 | 72 | 18 | .258 | .362 | .434 | $18 | 380 |
| Byrd M | 33 | 559 | 18 | 78 | 72 | 6 | .290 | .346 | .458 | $17 | 370 |
| Wells V | 32 | 568 | 18 | 72 | 78 | 12 | .264 | .318 | .452 | $17 | 390 |
| Gardner B | 27 | 441 | 5 | 75 | 40 | 40 | .261 | .357 | .363 | $17 | 330 |

**Competition at RF — Stats in 2010**

| Bats | Player | GSvR | GSvL | Sub | OPS |
|---|---|---|---|---|---|
| ▶ LH | Heyward J | 94 | 42 | 4 | .849 |
| BH | Cabrera M | 15 | 9 | 1 | .671 |

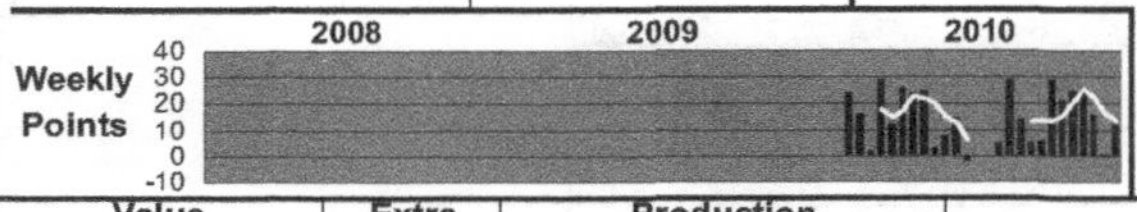
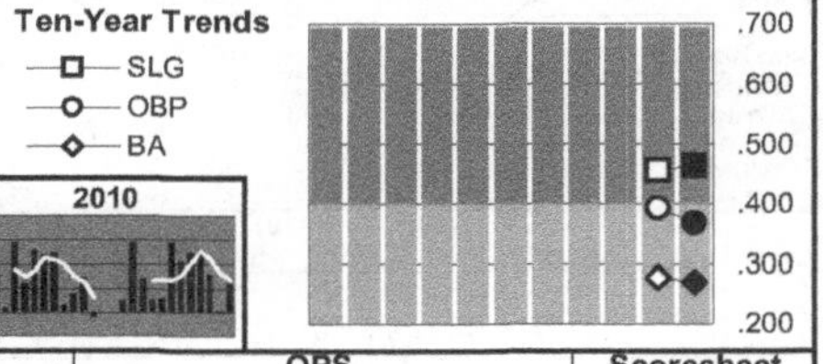

**Minors (2010)**

| Level | Leag | AB | HR | R | RBI | SB | BA | OBP | SLG | CT% | H% | BB% | Bash |
|---|---|---|---|---|---|---|---|---|---|---|---|---|---|
| A | — | — | — | — | — | — | — | — | — | — | — | — | — |
| AA | — | — | — | — | — | — | — | — | — | — | — | — | — |
| AAA | — | — | — | — | — | — | — | — | — | — | — | — | — |

**Majors**

| Yr | Team | AB | HR | R | RBI | SB | BA | OBP | SLG | CT% | H% | BB% | Bash | $1L | $2L | Pts | RAA | 2B | 3B | CS | FB-LD-GB | HR/fb | RBI% | RS% | OPS | 1st Hf | 2nd Hf | vs RH | vs LH | Rnge | vRH | vLH |
|---|---|---|---|---|---|---|---|---|---|---|---|---|---|---|---|---|---|---|---|---|---|---|---|---|---|---|---|---|---|---|---|---|
| 07 | — | — | — | — | — | — | — | — | — | — | — | — | — | — | — | — | — | — | — | — | — | — | — | — | — | — | — | — | — | — | — | — |
| 08 | — | — | — | — | — | — | — | — | — | — | — | — | — | — | — | — | — | — | — | — | — | — | — | — | — | — | — | — | — | 2.10 | — | — |
| 09 | — | — | — | — | — | — | — | — | — | — | — | — | — | — | — | — | — | — | — | — | — | — | — | — | — | — | — | — | — | 2.10 | — | — |
| 10 | ATL | 520 | 18 | 83 | 72 | 11 | .277 | .393 | .456 | 75% | 37% | 15% | 1.65 | $21 | $13 | 370 | +10 | 29 | 5 | 6 | 27-18-55 | 17% | 21% | 29% | .849 | .821 | .875 | .895 | .755 | 2.10 | — | — |

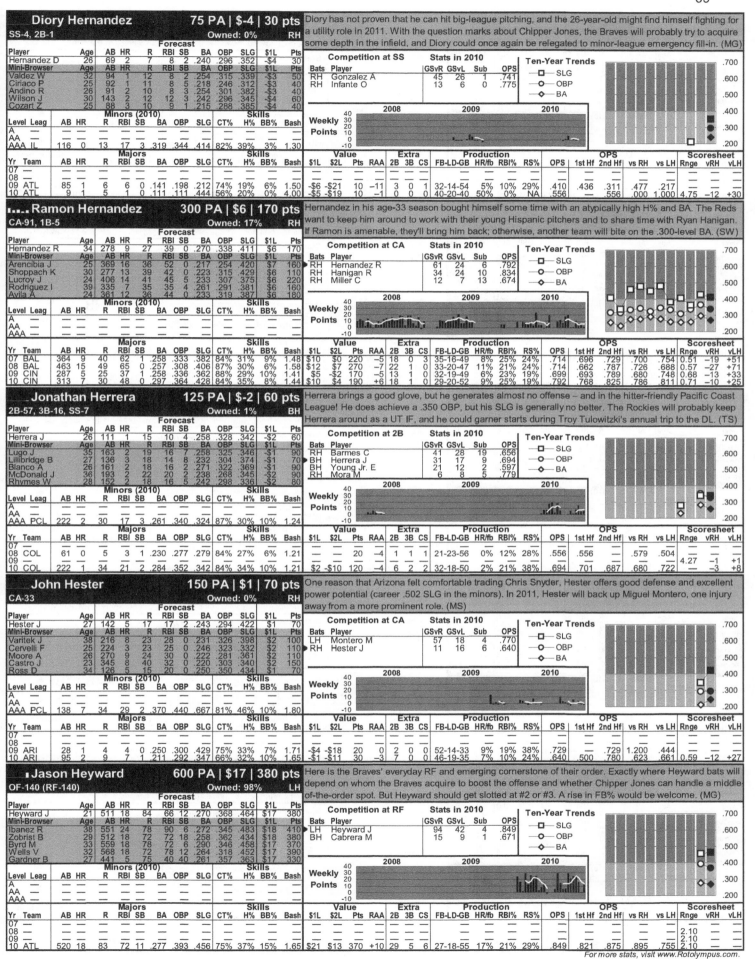

*For more stats, visit www.Rotolympus.com.*

## Brandon Hicks — 75 PA | $-4 | 40 pts

3B-3, SS-2, 2B-1 — Owned: 0% — RH

Like Diory Hernandez, Hicks will probably be minor-league depth for Atlanta in 2011. Hicks has yet to handle big-league pitching — in fact, he has no hits but seven runs scored on pinch-running opportunities — but he could pass Hernandez with a good spring. Even then, Hicks would still toil in the minors. (MG)

### Forecast

| Player | Age | AB | HR | R | RBI | SB | BA | OBP | SLG | $1L | Pts |
|---|---|---|---|---|---|---|---|---|---|---|---|
| Hicks B | 25 | 71 | 3 | 9 | 7 | 2 | .201 | .293 | .390 | -$4 | 40 |

| Mini-Browser | Age | AB | HR | R | RBI | SB | BA | OBP | SLG | $1L | Pts |
|---|---|---|---|---|---|---|---|---|---|---|---|
| Frazier T | 25 | 90 | 4 | 11 | 11 | 1 | .233 | .299 | .449 | -$3 | 50 |
| LaRoche A | 27 | 88 | 3 | 11 | 10 | 1 | .261 | .343 | .410 | -$3 | 50 |
| Marte A | 27 | 94 | 4 | 10 | 12 | 0 | .254 | .307 | .433 | -$3 | 50 |
| Pena R | 25 | 144 | 2 | 15 | 12 | 5 | .229 | .285 | .302 | -$3 | 60 |
| Darnell J | 24 | 87 | 4 | 9 | 11 | 1 | .208 | .311 | .393 | -$4 | 50 |

### Minors (2010) / Skills

| Level | Leag | AB | HR | R | RBI | SB | BA | OBP | SLG | CT% | H% | BB% | Bash |
|---|---|---|---|---|---|---|---|---|---|---|---|---|---|
| A | — | — | | | | | | | | | | | |
| AA | — | — | | | | | | | | | | | |
| AAA | IL | 261 | 7 | 27 | 22 | 10 | .211 | .280 | .333 | 72% | 29% | 7% | 1.58 |

### Majors / Skills

| Yr | Team | AB | HR | R | RBI | SB | BA | OBP | SLG | CT% | H% | BB% | Bash |
|---|---|---|---|---|---|---|---|---|---|---|---|---|---|
| 07 | — | | | | | | | | | | | | |
| 08 | — | | | | | | | | | | | | |
| 09 | — | | | | | | | | | | | | |
| 10 | ATL | 5 | 0 | | 0 | 0 | .000 | .167 | .000 | 60% | 0% | 17% | NA |

**Competition at 3B / Stats in 2010**

| Bats | Player | GSvR | GSvL | Sub | OPS |
|---|---|---|---|---|---|
| BH | Jones C | 58 | 28 | 3 | .806 |
| RH | Prado M | 28 | 14 | 1 | .809 |
| BH | Conrad B | 15 | 7 | 15 | .811 |
| RH | Infante O | 7 | 9 | 13 | .775 |

### Value / Extra / Production / OPS / Scoresheet

| Yr | Team | $1L | $2L | Pts | RAA | 2B | 3B | CS | FB-LD-GB | HR/fb | RBI% | RS% | OPS | 1st Hf | 2nd Hf | vs RH | vs LH | Rnge | vRH | vLH |
|---|---|---|---|---|---|---|---|---|---|---|---|---|---|---|---|---|---|---|---|---|
| 10 | ATL | -$5 | -$20 | 10 | -1 | 0 | 0 | 0 | 33-0-67 | 0% | 0% | NA | .167 | .167 | | .000 | .500 | — | — | — |

---

## .ıl. Aaron Hill — 550 PA | $12 | 320 pts

2B-137, DH-1 — Owned: 91% — RH

Hill was perhaps the biggest disappointment on the 2010 Jays. His offensive numbers slumped horribly as he swung for the fences (see the 13-point jump in FB%). His hit rate is likely to recover, but he will need to level out his swing and look to just hit the ball hard. Despite his struggles, Hill is TOR's everyday 2B. (MH)

### Forecast

| Player | Age | AB | HR | R | RBI | SB | BA | OBP | SLG | $1L | Pts |
|---|---|---|---|---|---|---|---|---|---|---|---|
| Hill A | 29 | 508 | 22 | 66 | 66 | 6 | .249 | .301 | .421 | $12 | 320 |

| Mini-Browser | Age | AB | HR | R | RBI | SB | BA | OBP | SLG | $1L | Pts |
|---|---|---|---|---|---|---|---|---|---|---|---|
| Kendrick H | 27 | 572 | 12 | 72 | 72 | 12 | .283 | .318 | .420 | $18 | 340 |
| Beckham G | 24 | 553 | 19 | 75 | 75 | 6 | .260 | .326 | .423 | $15 | 340 |
| Walker N | 25 | 551 | 18 | 72 | 78 | 6 | .272 | .326 | .461 | $15 | 350 |
| Ackley D | 23 | 354 | 11 | 54 | 35 | 8 | .251 | .338 | .409 | $15 | 230 |
| Theriot R | 31 | 557 | 6 | 78 | 42 | 24 | .280 | .346 | .351 | $14 | 360 |

### Minors (2010) / Skills

| Level | Leag | AB | HR | R | RBI | SB | BA | OBP | SLG | CT% | H% | BB% | Bash |
|---|---|---|---|---|---|---|---|---|---|---|---|---|---|
| A | — | | | | | | | | | | | | |
| AA | — | | | | | | | | | | | | |
| AAA | — | | | | | | | | | | | | |

### Majors / Skills

| Yr | Team | AB | HR | R | RBI | SB | BA | OBP | SLG | CT% | H% | BB% | Bash |
|---|---|---|---|---|---|---|---|---|---|---|---|---|---|
| 07 | TOR | 608 | 17 | 87 | 78 | 4 | .291 | .333 | .459 | 83% | 35% | 6% | 1.58 |
| 08 | TOR | 205 | 2 | 19 | 20 | 4 | .263 | .324 | .361 | 85% | 31% | 7% | 1.37 |
| 09 | TOR | 682 | 36 | 103 | 108 | 6 | .286 | .330 | .499 | 86% | 33% | 6% | 1.74 |
| 10 | TOR | 528 | 26 | 70 | 68 | 2 | .205 | .271 | .394 | 84% | 24% | 7% | 1.93 |

**Competition at 2B / Stats in 2010**

| Bats | Player | GSvR | GSvL | Sub | OPS |
|---|---|---|---|---|---|
| RH | Hill A | 106 | 31 | 6 | .665 |
| RH | McDonald J | 13 | 2 | 8 | .727 |
| RH | McCoy M | 5 | 2 | 7 | .511 |

### Value / Extra / Production / OPS / Scoresheet

| Yr | Team | $1L | $2L | Pts | RAA | 2B | 3B | CS | FB-LD-GB | HR/fb | RBI% | RS% | OPS | 1st Hf | 2nd Hf | vs RH | vs LH | Rnge | vRH | vLH |
|---|---|---|---|---|---|---|---|---|---|---|---|---|---|---|---|---|---|---|---|---|
| 07 | TOR | $19 | $11 | 390 | +13 | 47 | 2 | 3 | 39-21-40 | 9% | 18% | 35% | .792 | .757 | .831 | .753 | .916 | 4.32 | -20 | +49 |
| 08 | TOR | $1 | -$12 | 100 | -5 | 14 | 0 | 2 | 47-17-35 | 2% | 16% | 24% | .685 | .685 | — | .648 | .807 | 4.36 | -22 | +59 |
| 09 | TOR | $29 | $25 | 500 | +21 | 37 | 0 | 2 | 41-20-39 | 15% | 20% | 33% | .829 | .820 | .841 | .806 | .897 | 4.32 | -29 | +76 |
| 10 | TOR | $11 | $1 | 300 | -20 | 22 | 0 | 2 | 54-11-35 | 11% | 15% | 34% | .665 | .631 | .704 | .729 | .451 | 4.31 | -21 | +54 |

---

## Koyie Hill — 100 PA | $-1 | 40 pts

CA-72, 3B-1 — Owned: 0% — BH

Hill in 2010 caught less than 20% of potential base-stealers while posting one of the 10 worst offensive seasons among players with 200+ plate appearances. He is better than these stats, and he could catch on as a back-up, but the decision to play him frequently over Soto was one of Lou Piniella's strangest. (RM)

### Forecast

| Player | Age | AB | HR | R | RBI | SB | BA | OBP | SLG | $1L | Pts |
|---|---|---|---|---|---|---|---|---|---|---|---|
| Hill K | 32 | 95 | 2 | 10 | 10 | 0 | .241 | .304 | .364 | -$1 | 40 |

| Mini-Browser | Age | AB | HR | R | RBI | SB | BA | OBP | SLG | $1L | Pts |
|---|---|---|---|---|---|---|---|---|---|---|---|
| Johnson R | 28 | 126 | 2 | 14 | 12 | 2 | .238 | .307 | .348 | -$1 | 60 |
| Flowers T | 25 | 83 | 4 | 11 | 11 | 0 | .217 | .327 | .429 | -$1 | 50 |
| Tatum C | 28 | 137 | 3 | 12 | 15 | 0 | .230 | .283 | .348 | -$1 | 50 |
| Teagarden T | 27 | 85 | 4 | 11 | 11 | 0 | .211 | .297 | .409 | -$1 | 30 |
| Powell L | 29 | 86 | 4 | 10 | 12 | 0 | .221 | .312 | .384 | -$1 | 40 |

### Minors (2010) / Skills

| Level | Leag | AB | HR | R | RBI | SB | BA | OBP | SLG | CT% | H% | BB% | Bash |
|---|---|---|---|---|---|---|---|---|---|---|---|---|---|
| A | — | | | | | | | | | | | | |
| AA | — | | | | | | | | | | | | |
| AAA | — | | | | | | | | | | | | |

### Majors / Skills

| Yr | Team | AB | HR | R | RBI | SB | BA | OBP | SLG | CT% | H% | BB% | Bash |
|---|---|---|---|---|---|---|---|---|---|---|---|---|---|
| 07 | CHC | 93 | 2 | 7 | 12 | 0 | .161 | .231 | .269 | 81% | 20% | 8% | 1.67 |
| 08 | CHC | 21 | 0 | 0 | 1 | 0 | .095 | .095 | .143 | 43% | 22% | 0% | 1.37 |
| 09 | CHC | 253 | 2 | 26 | 24 | 0 | .237 | .312 | .324 | 69% | 34% | 9% | 1.37 |
| 10 | CHC | 215 | 1 | 18 | 17 | 0 | .214 | .254 | .298 | 72% | 30% | 5% | 1.39 |

**Competition at CA / Stats in 2010**

| Bats | Player | GSvR | GSvL | Sub | OPS |
|---|---|---|---|---|---|
| RH | Soto G | 54 | 43 | 7 | .890 |
| BH | Hill K | 52 | 8 | 12 | .552 |

### Value / Extra / Production / OPS / Scoresheet

| Yr | Team | $1L | $2L | Pts | RAA | 2B | 3B | CS | FB-LD-GB | HR/fb | RBI% | RS% | OPS | 1st Hf | 2nd Hf | vs RH | vs LH | Rnge | vRH | vLH |
|---|---|---|---|---|---|---|---|---|---|---|---|---|---|---|---|---|---|---|---|---|
| 07 | CHC | -$3 | -$14 | 30 | -9 | 4 | 0 | 0 | 40-8-52 | 6% | 15% | 23% | .500 | .447 | .601 | .436 | — | +4 | -11 |
| 08 | CHC | -$3 | -$12 | -10 | -4 | 0 | 0 | 0 | 11/11/1978 | 0% | 8% | 0% | .238 | — | .238 | .167 | .667 | — | +5 | -12 |
| 09 | CHC | $1 | -$5 | 80 | -11 | 14 | 0 | 0 | 28-21-51 | 4% | 15% | 28% | .636 | .615 | .648 | .620 | .714 | 0.58 | -4 | +11 |
| 10 | CHC | -$1 | -$10 | 50 | -16 | 13 | 1 | 0 | 26-22-51 | 3% | 14% | 30% | .552 | .534 | .565 | .523 | .694 | 0.54 | -11 | +31 |

---

## ... Eric Hinske — 250 PA | $3 | 150 pts

OF-50 (LF-50), 1B-32, 3B-1, DH-1 — Owned: 2% — LH

The question is not whether Hinske will find his way back to the post-season in 2011, but for whom. He is a popular player with remarkably stable rates, and Atlanta will probably aim to re-sign him, but if a team offers Hinske a shot at a full-time role (something Atlanta won't do), he will probably jump at that. (MG)

### Forecast

| Player | Age | AB | HR | R | RBI | SB | BA | OBP | SLG | $1L | Pts |
|---|---|---|---|---|---|---|---|---|---|---|---|
| Hinske E | 33 | 227 | 10 | 33 | 33 | 3 | .253 | .351 | .464 | $3 | 150 |

| Mini-Browser | Age | AB | HR | R | RBI | SB | BA | OBP | SLG | $1L | Pts |
|---|---|---|---|---|---|---|---|---|---|---|---|
| Bowker J | 27 | 272 | 12 | 33 | 36 | 3 | .254 | .323 | .452 | $4 | 160 |
| McDonald D | 32 | 222 | 5 | 30 | 28 | 17 | .270 | .328 | .440 | $4 | 130 |
| Cain L | 24 | 408 | 9 | 43 | 38 | 17 | .219 | .285 | .345 | $4 | 200 |
| Morse M | 29 | 236 | 10 | 28 | 33 | 0 | .276 | .338 | .461 | $4 | 140 |
| Bradley M | 32 | 205 | 8 | 30 | 30 | 3 | .256 | .367 | .430 | $3 | 130 |

### Minors (2010) / Skills

| Level | Leag | AB | HR | R | RBI | SB | BA | OBP | SLG | CT% | H% | BB% | Bash |
|---|---|---|---|---|---|---|---|---|---|---|---|---|---|
| A | — | | | | | | | | | | | | |
| AA | — | | | | | | | | | | | | |
| AAA | — | | | | | | | | | | | | |

### Majors / Skills

| Yr | Team | AB | HR | R | RBI | SB | BA | OBP | SLG | CT% | H% | BB% | Bash |
|---|---|---|---|---|---|---|---|---|---|---|---|---|---|
| 07 | BOS | 186 | 6 | 25 | 21 | 3 | .204 | .317 | .398 | 71% | 29% | 13% | 1.95 |
| 08 | TB | 381 | 20 | 59 | 60 | 10 | .247 | .333 | .465 | 77% | 32% | 11% | 1.88 |
| 09 | 2TM | 190 | 8 | 31 | 25 | 1 | .242 | .348 | .432 | 73% | 33% | 12% | 1.77 |
| 10 | ATL | 281 | 11 | 38 | 51 | 0 | .256 | .338 | .456 | 73% | 35% | 10% | 1.78 |

**Competition at LF / Stats in 2010**

| Bats | Player | GSvR | GSvL | Sub | OPS |
|---|---|---|---|---|---|
| BH | Cabrera M | 45 | 23 | 16 | .671 |
| RH | Diaz M | 12 | 41 | 10 | .739 |
| LH | Hinske E | 50 | 0 | 9 | .793 |
| RH | Infante O | 3 | 8 | 5 | .775 |

### Value / Extra / Production / OPS / Scoresheet

| Yr | Team | $1L | $2L | Pts | RAA | 2B | 3B | CS | FB-LD-GB | HR/fb | RBI% | RS% | OPS | 1st Hf | 2nd Hf | vs RH | vs LH | Rnge | vRH | vLH |
|---|---|---|---|---|---|---|---|---|---|---|---|---|---|---|---|---|---|---|---|---|
| 07 | BOS | $0 | -$14 | 100 | -6 | 12 | 3 | 0 | 44-11-45 | 9% | 15% | 30% | .714 | .705 | .723 | .708 | .760 | 2.06 | +34 | -124 |
| 08 | TB | $14 | $3 | 270 | +3 | 21 | 1 | 3 | 41-20-39 | 17% | 18% | 31% | .798 | .873 | .676 | .844 | .488 | — | +26 | -93 |
| 09 | 2TM | -$2 | -$11 | 120 | -1 | 12 | 0 | 0 | 45-18-37 | 13% | 16% | 33% | .780 | .819 | .714 | .778 | .786 | — | +25 | -93 |
| 10 | ATL | $7 | -$5 | 180 | +0 | 21 | 1 | 0 | 47-20-33 | 11% | 22% | 28% | .793 | .817 | .754 | .759 | 1.219 | 2.06 | +26 | -93 |

---

## Jarrett Hoffpauir — 50 PA | $-5 | 20 pts

3B-11, 2B-2 — Owned: 0% — RH

Hoffpauir has proven himself in Triple-A. However, his lack of versatility in the field hurts his worth as a utility player, and his overall game is a little short for an everyday player, even a second baseman. Even so, Hoffpauir could be a useful fill-in if incumbent Aaron Hill gets hurt. (MH)

### Forecast

| Player | Age | AB | HR | R | RBI | SB | BA | OBP | SLG | $1L | Pts |
|---|---|---|---|---|---|---|---|---|---|---|---|
| Hoffpauir J | 27 | 42 | 1 | 5 | 5 | 0 | .251 | .327 | .391 | -$5 | 20 |

| Mini-Browser | Age | AB | HR | R | RBI | SB | BA | OBP | SLG | $1L | Pts |
|---|---|---|---|---|---|---|---|---|---|---|---|
| Frandsen K | 28 | 45 | 1 | 6 | 5 | 1 | .269 | .329 | .386 | -$5 | 30 |
| Guzman J | 26 | 23 | 1 | 3 | 3 | 0 | .247 | .307 | .419 | -$5 | 10 |
| Russo K | 26 | 48 | 1 | 5 | 5 | 2 | .240 | .301 | .345 | -$5 | 30 |
| Vizquel O | 43 | 142 | 2 | 14 | 12 | 3 | .254 | .316 | .322 | -$5 | 80 |
| Harris B | 30 | 47 | 1 | 6 | 6 | 0 | .254 | .312 | .377 | -$5 | 30 |

### Minors (2010) / Skills

| Level | Leag | AB | HR | R | RBI | SB | BA | OBP | SLG | CT% | H% | BB% | Bash |
|---|---|---|---|---|---|---|---|---|---|---|---|---|---|
| A | — | | | | | | | | | | | | |
| AA | — | | | | | | | | | | | | |
| AAA | PCL | 431 | 16 | 73 | 73 | 8 | .295 | .376 | .494 | 92% | 32% | 12% | 1.68 |

### Majors / Skills

| Yr | Team | AB | HR | R | RBI | SB | BA | OBP | SLG | CT% | H% | BB% | Bash |
|---|---|---|---|---|---|---|---|---|---|---|---|---|---|
| 07 | — | | | | | | | | | | | | |
| 08 | — | | | | | | | | | | | | |
| 09 | STL | 12 | 0 | 1 | 2 | 0 | .250 | .438 | .417 | 83% | 30% | 25% | 1.67 |
| 10 | TOR | 34 | 0 | 3 | 0 | 0 | .206 | .250 | .235 | 85% | 24% | 5% | 1.14 |

**Competition at 3B / Stats in 2010**

| Bats | Player | GSvR | GSvL | Sub | OPS |
|---|---|---|---|---|---|
| RH | Encarnacion E | 73 | 22 | 0 | .787 |
| RH | Bautista J | 42 | 6 | 0 | .995 |
| RH | McDonald J | 7 | 6 | 6 | .727 |
| RH | Hoffpauir J | 5 | 5 | 1 | .485 |

### Value / Extra / Production / OPS / Scoresheet

| Yr | Team | $1L | $2L | Pts | RAA | 2B | 3B | CS | FB-LD-GB | HR/fb | RBI% | RS% | OPS | 1st Hf | 2nd Hf | vs RH | vs LH | Rnge | vRH | vLH |
|---|---|---|---|---|---|---|---|---|---|---|---|---|---|---|---|---|---|---|---|---|
| 09 | STL | -$5 | -$19 | 10 | +1 | 2 | 0 | 0 | 50-20-30 | 0% | 25% | 14% | .854 | .854 | | 1.371 | .476 | — | -14 | +34 |
| 10 | TOR | -$5 | -$21 | 10 | -3 | 1 | 0 | 0 | 34-21-45 | 0% | 0% | 11% | .485 | .517 | .333 | .372 | .665 | — | -14 | +34 |

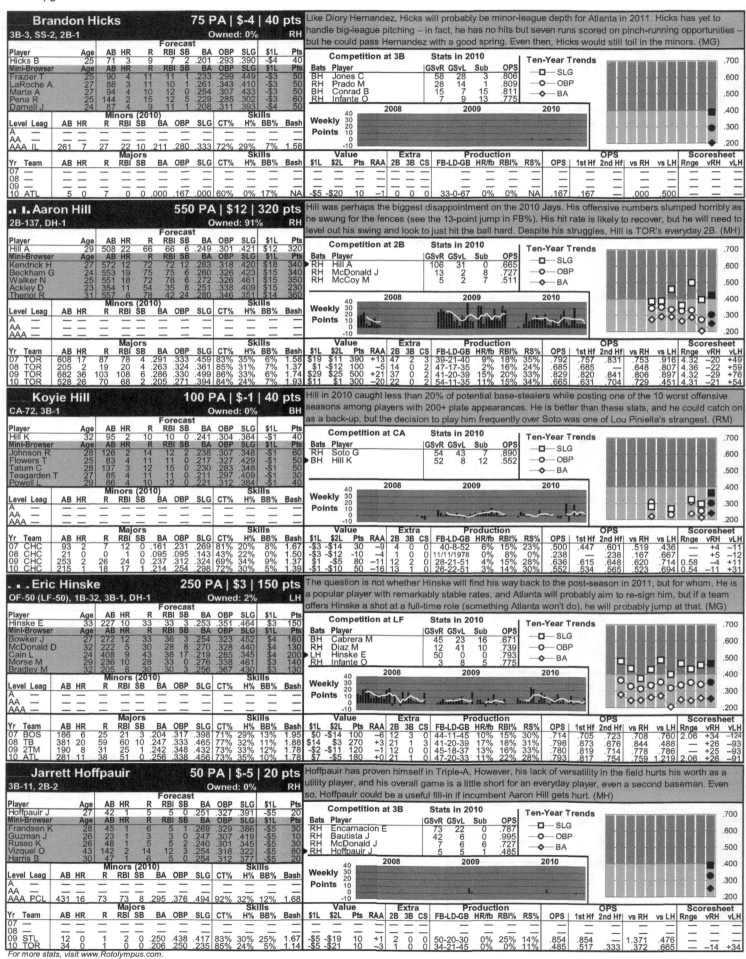

## Micah Hoffpauir — 150 PA | $1 | 90 pts

1B-12, OF-5 (LF-3, RF-2) — Owned: 0% — LH

Hoffpauir is a good enough hitter to occupy a bench role, and in fact he probably wasted his best seasons at Triple-A even though the Cubs have needed lefty bats for years. His defense is functionally limited to 1B, where he is not very good. His September flop removes the slight chance to win the 2011 job. (RM)

**Forecast**

| Player | Age | AB | HR | R | RBI | SB | BA | OBP | SLG | $1L | Pts |
|---|---|---|---|---|---|---|---|---|---|---|---|
| Hoffpauir M | 31 | 132 | 6 | 20 | 23 | 0 | .272 | .327 | .487 | $1 | 90 |
| **Mini-Browser** | Age | AB | HR | R | RBI | SB | BA | OBP | SLG | $1L | Pts |
| Pearce S | 27 | 280 | 12 | 33 | 36 | 3 | .268 | .342 | .483 | $5 | 190 |
| Glaus T | 34 | 246 | 12 | 36 | 45 | 0 | .256 | .365 | .449 | $5 | 170 |
| Wallace B | 24 | 421 | 14 | 48 | 43 | 0 | .237 | .309 | .397 | $4 | 180 |
| Kotchman C | 28 | 218 | 5 | 23 | 30 | 0 | .264 | .331 | .401 | $1 | 140 |
| Garko R | 30 | 182 | 8 | 20 | 26 | 0 | .264 | .339 | .431 | $1 | 110 |

**Minors (2010)**

| Level | Leag | AB | HR | R | RBI | SB | BA | OBP | SLG | CT% | H% | BB% | Bash |
|---|---|---|---|---|---|---|---|---|---|---|---|---|---|
| A | — | — | — | — | — | — | — | — | — | — | — | — | — |
| AA | — | — | — | — | — | — | — | — | — | — | — | — | — |
| AAA | PCL | 427 | 22 | 81 | 95 | 1 | .283 | .368 | .529 | 83% | 34% | 11% | 1.87 |

**Competition at 1B — Stats in 2010**

| Bats | Player | GSvR | GSvL | Sub | OPS |
|---|---|---|---|---|---|
| RH | Nady X | 33 | 17 | 2 | .660 |
| LH | Hoffpauir M | 7 | 1 | 4 | .476 |

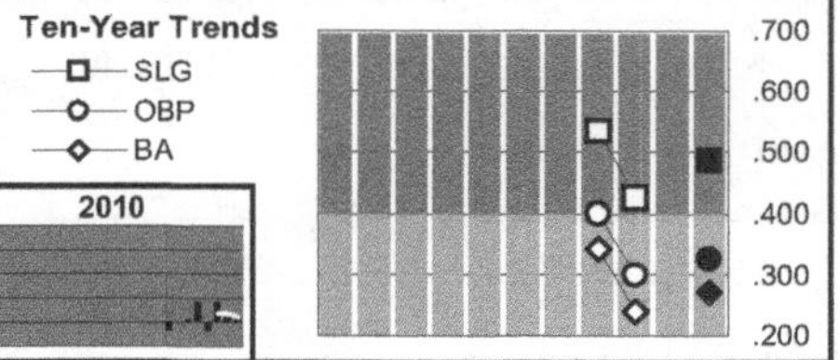


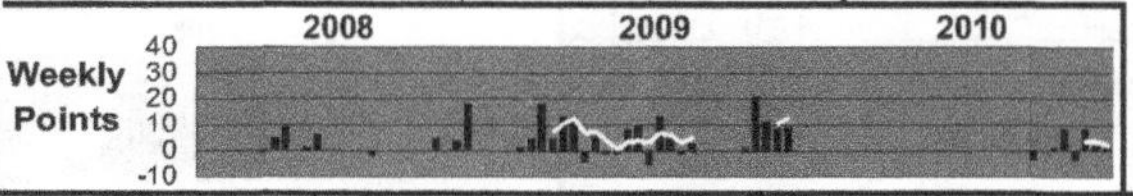


**Majors** (Skills / Value / Extra / Production / OPS / Scoresheet)

| Yr | Team | AB | HR | R | RBI | SB | BA | OBP | SLG | CT% | H% | BB% | Bash | $1L | $2L | Pts | RAA | 2B | 3B | CS | FB-LD-GB | HR/fb | RBI% | RS% | OPS | 1st Hf | 2nd Hf | vs RH | vs LH | Rnge | vRH | vLH |
|---|---|---|---|---|---|---|---|---|---|---|---|---|---|---|---|---|---|---|---|---|---|---|---|---|---|---|---|---|---|---|---|---|
| 07 | — | — | — | — | — | — | — | — | — | — | — | — | — | — | — | — | — | — | — | — | — | — | — | — | — | — | — | — | — | — | — | — |
| 08 | CHC | 73 | 2 | 14 | 8 | 1 | .342 | .400 | .534 | 67% | 51% | 8% | 1.56 | -$1 | -$13 | 40 | +4 | 8 | 0 | 0 | 37-41-22 | 11% | 22% | 40% | .934 | 1.004 | .872 | .953 | .818 | — | — | — |
| 09 | CHC | 234 | 10 | 28 | 35 | 1 | .239 | .300 | .427 | 80% | 30% | 8% | 1.79 | $3 | -$10 | 140 | –8 | 12 | 1 | 0 | 52-21-28 | 10% | 17% | 27% | .727 | .736 | .707 | .749 | .571 | 1.85 | +24 | –74 |
| 10 | CHC | 52 | 0 | 5 | 5 | 0 | .173 | .246 | .231 | 71% | 24% | 9% | 1.33 | -$5 | -$21 | 10 | –6 | 3 | 0 | 0 | 32-16-51 | 0% | 13% | 36% | .476 | — | .476 | .408 | .873 | 1.85 | +23 | –78 |

## Matt Holliday — 650 PA | $28 | 500 pts

OF-155 (LF-155), DH-1 — Owned: 100% — RH

Despite a slow start and having to endure some observers' misguided characterization of him as a poor performer in the clutch, Holliday ended 2010 within 9 points of his career OPS. Even outside Coors Field, he remains an elite hitter, and some metrics suggest that 2010 was his best performance in the field. (AB)

**Forecast**

| Player | Age | AB | HR | R | RBI | SB | BA | OBP | SLG | $1L | Pts |
|---|---|---|---|---|---|---|---|---|---|---|---|
| Holliday M | 31 | 577 | 26 | 98 | 104 | 13 | .304 | .387 | .514 | $28 | 500 |
| **Mini-Browser** | Age | AB | HR | R | RBI | SB | BA | OBP | SLG | $1L | Pts |
| Braun R | 27 | 643 | 35 | 112 | 119 | 21 | .294 | .356 | .548 | $34 | 560 |
| Crawford C | 29 | 587 | 13 | 98 | 78 | 46 | .288 | .338 | .445 | $31 | 470 |
| Gonzalez C | 25 | 597 | 27 | 101 | 95 | 20 | .294 | .347 | .528 | $30 | 450 |
| Cruz N | 30 | 536 | 30 | 78 | 90 | 18 | .280 | .351 | .528 | $28 | 400 |
| Choo S | 28 | 586 | 20 | 88 | 95 | 20 | .288 | .381 | .479 | $27 | 440 |

**Minors (2010)**

| Level | Leag | AB | HR | R | RBI | SB | BA | OBP | SLG | CT% | H% | BB% | Bash |
|---|---|---|---|---|---|---|---|---|---|---|---|---|---|
| A | — | — | — | — | — | — | — | — | — | — | — | — | — |
| AA | — | — | — | — | — | — | — | — | — | — | — | — | — |
| AAA | — | — | — | — | — | — | — | — | — | — | — | — | — |

**Competition at LF — Stats in 2010**

| Bats | Player | GSvR | GSvL | Sub | OPS |
|---|---|---|---|---|---|
| RH | Holliday M | 104 | 51 | 0 | .922 |

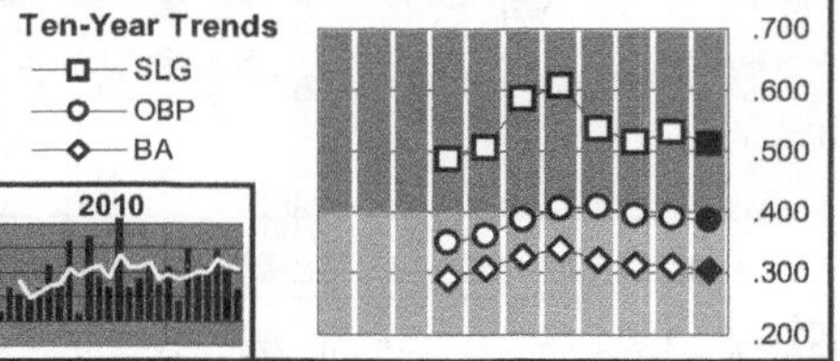


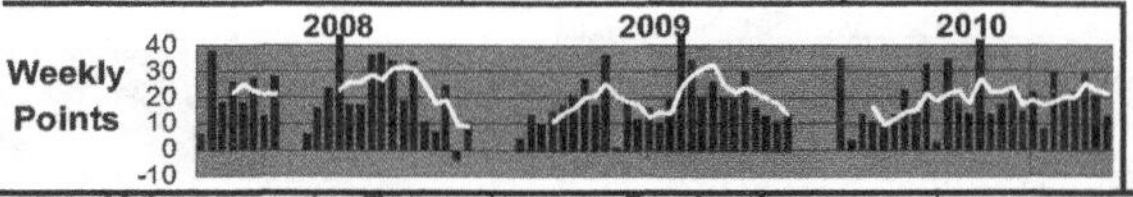


**Majors** (Skills / Value / Extra / Production / OPS / Scoresheet)

| Yr | Team | AB | HR | R | RBI | SB | BA | OBP | SLG | CT% | H% | BB% | Bash | $1L | $2L | Pts | RAA | 2B | 3B | CS | FB-LD-GB | HR/fb | RBI% | RS% | OPS | 1st Hf | 2nd Hf | vs RH | vs LH | Rnge | vRH | vLH |
|---|---|---|---|---|---|---|---|---|---|---|---|---|---|---|---|---|---|---|---|---|---|---|---|---|---|---|---|---|---|---|---|---|
| 07 | COL | 636 | 36 | 120 | 137 | 11 | .340 | .405 | .607 | 80% | 42% | 9% | 1.79 | $43 | $40 | 600 | +53 | 50 | 6 | 4 | 36-20-44 | 19% | 28% | 33% | 1.012 | .964 | 1.073 | 1.028 | .958 | 2.08 | –4 | +12 |
| 08 | COL | 539 | 25 | 107 | 88 | 28 | .321 | .409 | .538 | 81% | 40% | 12% | 1.68 | $34 | $29 | 510 | +41 | 38 | 2 | 2 | 33-22-46 | 17% | 23% | 36% | .947 | .975 | .911 | .963 | .896 | 2.09 | –1 | +4 |
| 09 | 2TM | 581 | 24 | 94 | 109 | 14 | .313 | .394 | .515 | 83% | 38% | 11% | 1.64 | $26 | $24 | 490 | +27 | 39 | 3 | 7 | 39-17-44 | 13% | 26% | 29% | .909 | .792 | 1.047 | .944 | .807 | 2.09 | +1 | –4 |
| 10 | STL | 596 | 28 | 95 | 103 | 9 | .312 | .390 | .532 | 84% | 37% | 10% | 1.70 | $33 | $29 | 500 | +31 | 45 | 1 | 5 | 41-17-42 | 14% | 21% | 29% | .922 | .902 | .944 | .900 | .982 | 2.10 | +5 | –15 |

## Eric Hosmer — 150 PA | $-4 | 50 pts

No MLB games played in 2010 — Owned: 0% — LH

Hosmer could become a fantasy stud in a couple of seasons, but he is likely to spend most of 2011 in Triple-A. He could earn some playing time if Billy Butler or Kila Ka'aihue get injured late in the season. (BM)

**Forecast**

| Player | Age | AB | HR | R | RBI | SB | BA | OBP | SLG | $1L | Pts |
|---|---|---|---|---|---|---|---|---|---|---|---|
| Hosmer E | 21 | 129 | 3 | 11 | 17 | 0 | .221 | .303 | .359 | -$4 | 50 |
| **Mini-Browser** | Age | AB | HR | R | RBI | SB | BA | OBP | SLG | $1L | Pts |
| Gamel M | 25 | 112 | 5 | 14 | 15 | 1 | .235 | .317 | .432 | -$2 | 60 |
| Ishikawa T | 27 | 92 | 3 | 12 | 12 | 1 | .249 | .320 | .423 | -$2 | 50 |
| Alonso Y | 23 | 94 | 4 | 8 | 13 | 0 | .224 | .298 | .408 | -$3 | 50 |
| Snyder B | 24 | 93 | 3 | 10 | 12 | 0 | .246 | .303 | .412 | -$3 | 40 |
| Clement J | 27 | 42 | 2 | 6 | 6 | 0 | .261 | .343 | .472 | -$4 | 30 |

**Minors (2010)**

| Level | Leag | AB | HR | R | RBI | SB | BA | OBP | SLG | CT% | H% | BB% | Bash |
|---|---|---|---|---|---|---|---|---|---|---|---|---|---|
| A | CAR | 325 | 7 | 48 | 51 | 11 | .354 | .429 | .545 | 88% | 40% | 12% | 1.54 |
| AA | TL | 195 | 13 | 39 | 35 | 3 | .313 | .365 | .615 | 86% | 36% | 7% | 1.97 |
| AAA | — | — | — | — | — | — | — | — | — | — | — | — | — |

**Competition at 1B — Stats in 2010**

| Bats | Player | GSvR | GSvL | Sub | OPS |
|---|---|---|---|---|---|
| RH | Butler B | 98 | 28 | 1 | .857 |
| LH | Ka'aihue K | 26 | 6 | 2 | .702 |

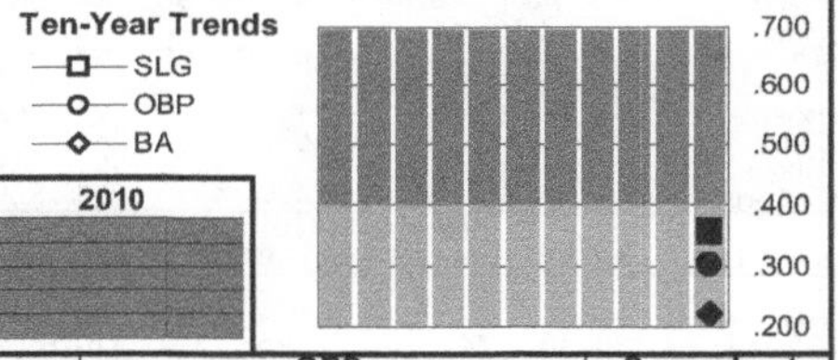


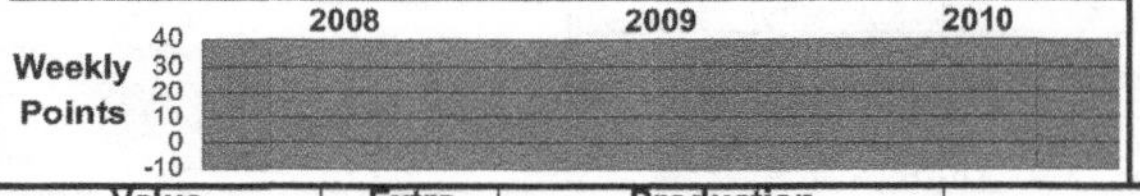


**Majors** (Skills / Value / Extra / Production / OPS / Scoresheet)

| Yr | Team | AB | HR | R | RBI | SB | BA | OBP | SLG | CT% | H% | BB% | Bash | $1L | $2L | Pts | RAA | 2B | 3B | CS | FB-LD-GB | HR/fb | RBI% | RS% | OPS | 1st Hf | 2nd Hf | vs RH | vs LH | Rnge | vRH | vLH |
|---|---|---|---|---|---|---|---|---|---|---|---|---|---|---|---|---|---|---|---|---|---|---|---|---|---|---|---|---|---|---|---|---|
| 07 | — | — | — | — | — | — | — | — | — | — | — | — | — | — | — | — | — | — | — | — | — | — | — | — | — | — | — | — | — | — | — | — |
| 08 | — | — | — | — | — | — | — | — | — | — | — | — | — | — | — | — | — | — | — | — | — | — | — | — | — | — | — | — | — | — | — | — |
| 09 | — | — | — | — | — | — | — | — | — | — | — | — | — | — | — | — | — | — | — | — | — | — | — | — | — | — | — | — | — | — | — | — |
| 10 | — | — | — | — | — | — | — | — | — | — | — | — | — | — | — | — | — | — | — | — | — | — | — | — | — | — | — | — | — | — | — | — |

## Ryan Howard — 650 PA | $27 | 440 pts

1B-140, DH-2 — Owned: 100% — LH

Howard in 2010 signed a five-year, $125M extension that keeps him in Philadelphia through at least 2016. Needless to say, first base is his. His long-term trends suggest that his power has been on the wane for a while, but 2006 and 2010 could be outliers of a steady line. Another 40-HR year is hardly implausible. (BB)

**Forecast**

| Player | Age | AB | HR | R | RBI | SB | BA | OBP | SLG | $1L | Pts |
|---|---|---|---|---|---|---|---|---|---|---|---|
| Howard R | 31 | 558 | 39 | 98 | 130 | 0 | .268 | .362 | .549 | $27 | 440 |
| **Mini-Browser** | Age | AB | HR | R | RBI | SB | BA | OBP | SLG | $1L | Pts |
| Pujols A | 31 | 600 | 44 | 116 | 131 | 15 | .326 | .436 | .618 | $40 | 690 |
| Cabrera M | 27 | 597 | 35 | 98 | 126 | 7 | .305 | .384 | .555 | $35 | 520 |
| Teixeira M | 30 | 559 | 33 | 91 | 111 | 0 | .279 | .379 | .532 | $30 | 470 |
| Votto J | 27 | 545 | 33 | 98 | 104 | 13 | .298 | .389 | .548 | $29 | 480 |
| Fielder P | 26 | 573 | 42 | 98 | 112 | 0 | .281 | .394 | .552 | $28 | 490 |

**Minors (2010)**

| Level | Leag | AB | HR | R | RBI | SB | BA | OBP | SLG | CT% | H% | BB% | Bash |
|---|---|---|---|---|---|---|---|---|---|---|---|---|---|
| A | SAL | 2 | 0 | 0 | 1 | 0 | .500 | .667 | 1.000 | 100% | 50% | 33% | 2.00 |
| AA | — | — | — | — | — | — | — | — | — | — | — | — | — |
| AAA | — | — | — | — | — | — | — | — | — | — | — | — | — |

**Competition at 1B — Stats in 2010**

| Bats | Player | GSvR | GSvL | Sub | OPS |
|---|---|---|---|---|---|
| LH | Howard R | 103 | 37 | 0 | .859 |
| RH | Sweeney M | 2 | 9 | 3 | .765 |
| LH | Gload R | 8 | 0 | 10 | .813 |

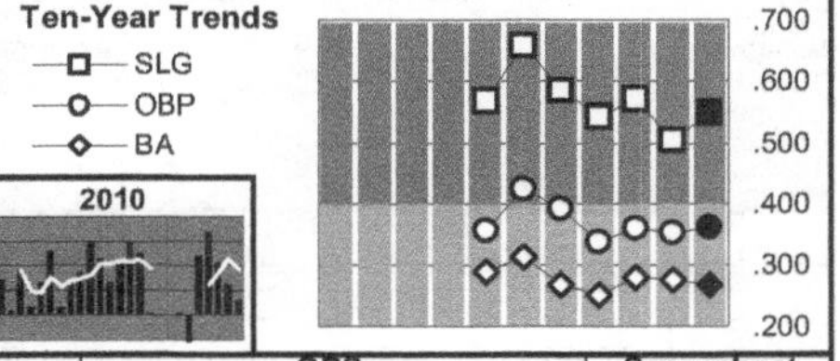


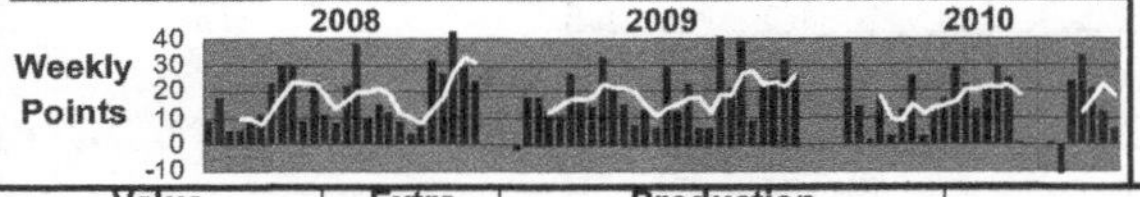


**Majors** (Skills / Value / Extra / Production / OPS / Scoresheet)

| Yr | Team | AB | HR | R | RBI | SB | BA | OBP | SLG | CT% | H% | BB% | Bash | $1L | $2L | Pts | RAA | 2B | 3B | CS | FB-LD-GB | HR/fb | RBI% | RS% | OPS | 1st Hf | 2nd Hf | vs RH | vs LH | Rnge | vRH | vLH |
|---|---|---|---|---|---|---|---|---|---|---|---|---|---|---|---|---|---|---|---|---|---|---|---|---|---|---|---|---|---|---|---|---|
| 07 | PHI | 529 | 47 | 94 | 136 | 1 | .268 | .392 | .584 | 62% | 43% | 16% | 2.18 | $30 | $26 | 450 | +23 | 26 | 0 | 0 | 44-24-31 | 32% | 24% | 23% | .976 | .933 | 1.016 | 1.072 | .826 | 1.82 | +45 | –134 |
| 08 | PHI | 610 | 48 | 105 | 146 | 1 | .251 | .339 | .543 | 67% | 37% | 11% | 2.16 | $30 | $26 | 460 | +7 | 26 | 4 | 1 | 36-22-41 | 32% | 26% | 30% | .881 | .832 | .954 | .966 | .746 | 1.82 | +43 | –103 |
| 09 | PHI | 616 | 45 | 105 | 141 | 8 | .279 | .360 | .571 | 70% | 40% | 11% | 2.05 | $35 | $32 | 500 | +22 | 37 | 4 | 1 | 41-23-36 | 25% | 25% | 29% | .931 | .870 | 1.003 | 1.088 | .653 | 1.82 | +44 | –95 |
| 10 | PHI | 550 | 31 | 87 | 108 | 1 | .276 | .353 | .505 | 71% | 39% | 9% | 1.83 | $26 | $22 | 380 | +2 | 23 | 5 | 1 | 37-23-40 | 21% | 22% | 30% | .859 | .859 | .858 | .876 | .826 | 1.83 | +62 | –137 |

## Orlando Hudson — 525 PA | $12 | 300 pts

2B-124, DH-2 — Owned: 30% — BH

Signed by Minnesota in 2010 to help at second base as well as in the #2 spot in the line-up, Hudson performed as advertised for most of the year, though he slumped horribly in September. It's tough to imagine him back in Minnesota, but he will probably find a starting job somewhere. (NN)

**Forecast**

| Player | Age | AB | HR | R | RBI | SB | BA | OBP | SLG | $1L | Pts |
|---|---|---|---|---|---|---|---|---|---|---|---|
| Hudson O | 33 | 465 | 11 | 68 | 47 | 5 | .282 | .357 | .418 | $12 | 300 |
| **Mini-Browser** | Age | AB | HR | R | RBI | SB | BA | OBP | SLG | $1L | Pts |
| Beckham G | 24 | 553 | 19 | 75 | 75 | 6 | .260 | .326 | .423 | $15 | 340 |
| Walker N | 25 | 551 | 18 | 72 | 78 | 6 | .272 | .326 | .461 | $15 | 350 |
| Ackley D | 23 | 354 | 11 | 54 | 35 | 8 | .251 | .338 | .409 | $15 | 230 |
| Theriot R | 31 | 557 | 6 | 78 | 42 | 24 | .280 | .346 | .351 | $14 | 360 |
| Hill A | 29 | 508 | 22 | 66 | 66 | 6 | .249 | .301 | .421 | $12 | 320 |

**Minors (2010)**

| Level | Leag | AB | HR | R | RBI | SB | BA | OBP | SLG | CT% | H% | BB% | Bash |
|---|---|---|---|---|---|---|---|---|---|---|---|---|---|
| A | — | — | — | — | — | — | — | — | — | — | — | — | — |
| AA | — | — | — | — | — | — | — | — | — | — | — | — | — |
| AAA | — | — | — | — | — | — | — | — | — | — | — | — | — |

**Competition at 2B — Stats in 2010**

| Bats | Player | GSvR | GSvL | Sub | OPS |
|---|---|---|---|---|---|
| BH | Hudson O | 80 | 44 | 0 | .710 |
| BH | Casilla A | 12 | 4 | 8 | .726 |
| BH | Tolbert M | 10 | 3 | 7 | .672 |
| BH | Punto N | 5 | 5 | 2 | .615 |

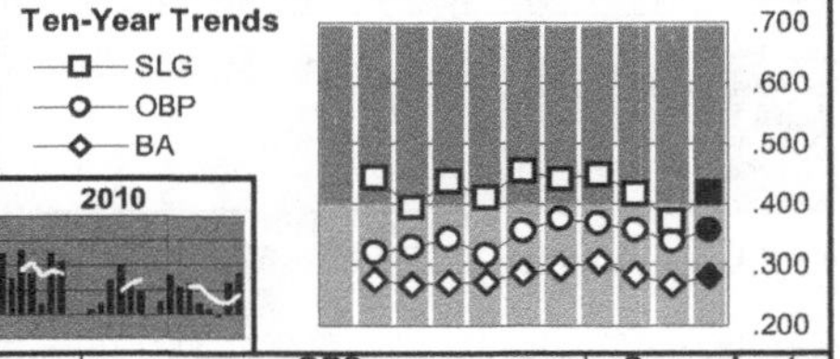


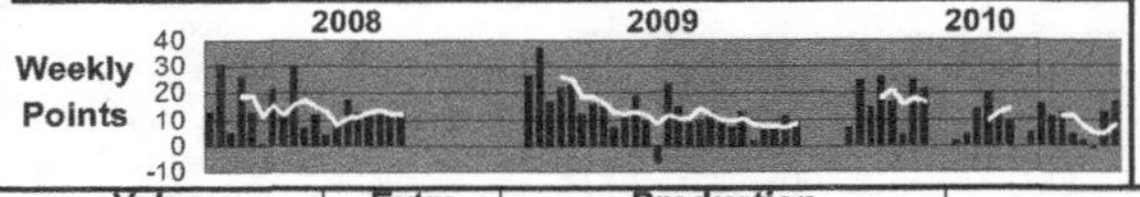


**Majors** (Skills / Value / Extra / Production / OPS / Scoresheet)

| Yr | Team | AB | HR | R | RBI | SB | BA | OBP | SLG | CT% | H% | BB% | Bash | $1L | $2L | Pts | RAA | 2B | 3B | CS | FB-LD-GB | HR/fb | RBI% | RS% | OPS | 1st Hf | 2nd Hf | vs RH | vs LH | Rnge | vRH | vLH |
|---|---|---|---|---|---|---|---|---|---|---|---|---|---|---|---|---|---|---|---|---|---|---|---|---|---|---|---|---|---|---|---|---|
| 07 | ARI | 517 | 10 | 69 | 63 | 10 | .294 | .376 | .441 | 83% | 35% | 12% | 1.50 | $15 | $6 | 360 | +18 | 28 | 9 | 2 | 28-20-52 | 8% | 23% | 28% | .817 | .834 | .788 | .833 | .767 | 4.36 | +4 | –11 |
| 08 | ARI | 407 | 8 | 54 | 41 | 4 | .305 | .367 | .450 | 85% | 36% | 9% | 1.48 | $11 | $1 | 260 | +13 | 29 | 3 | 1 | 29-23-48 | 8% | 18% | 29% | .817 | .816 | .818 | .862 | .720 | 4.36 | –3 | +7 |
| 09 | LAD | 551 | 9 | 74 | 62 | 8 | .283 | .357 | .417 | 82% | 35% | 10% | 1.47 | $16 | $6 | 340 | +7 | 35 | 6 | 1 | 26-19-56 | 8% | 20% | 31% | .774 | .779 | .767 | .747 | .854 | — | +11 | –28 |
| 10 | MIN | 497 | 6 | 80 | 37 | 10 | .268 | .338 | .372 | 82% | 32% | 9% | 1.39 | $13 | $2 | 280 | –4 | 24 | 5 | 3 | 31-21-49 | 5% | 14% | 41% | .710 | .739 | .670 | .711 | .707 | — | –2 | +7 |

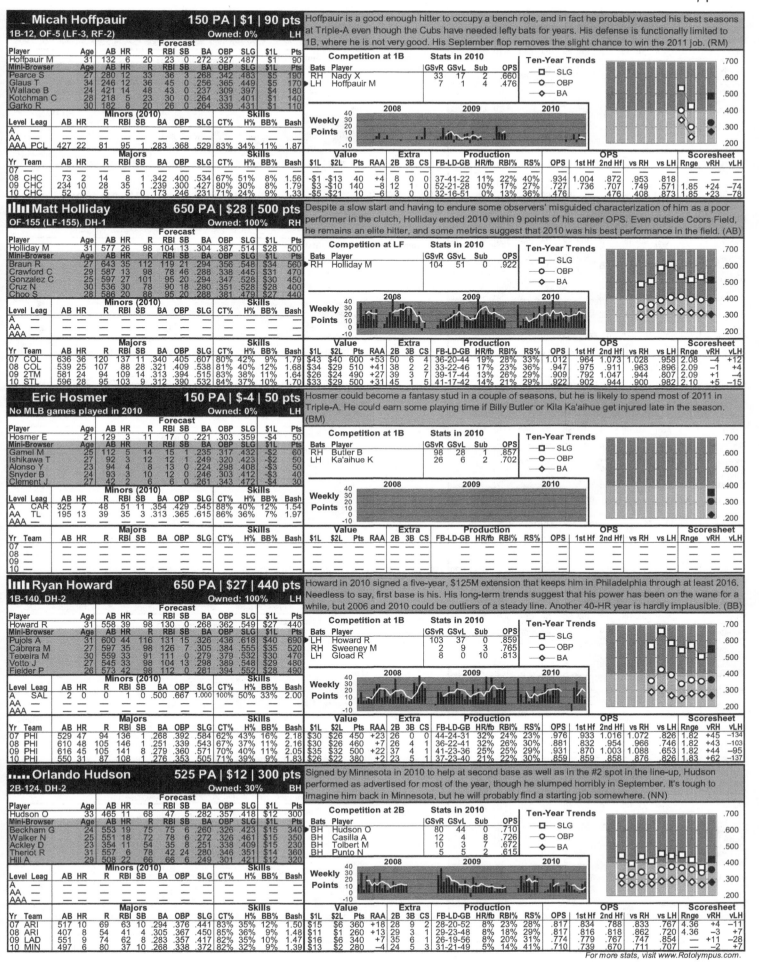

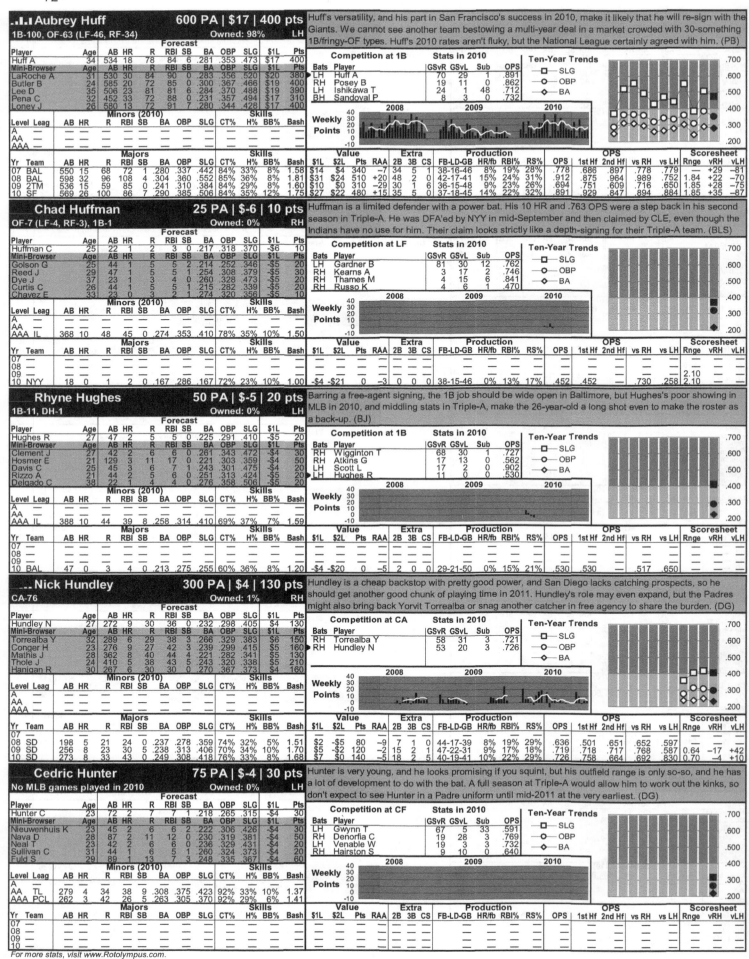

## Aubrey Huff — 600 PA | $17 | 400 pts

1B-100, OF-63 (LF-46, RF-34) — Owned: 98% — LH

Huff's versatility, and his part in San Francisco's success in 2010, make it likely that he will re-sign with the Giants. We cannot see another team bestowing a multi-year deal in a market crowded with 30-something 1B/fringy-OF types. Huff's 2010 rates aren't fluky, but the National League certainly agreed with him. (PB)

| Player | Age | AB | HR | R | RBI | SB | BA | OBP | SLG | $1L | Pts |
|---|---|---|---|---|---|---|---|---|---|---|---|
| **Forecast** | | | | | | | | | | | |
| Huff A | 34 | 534 | 18 | 78 | 84 | 6 | .281 | .353 | .473 | $17 | 400 |
| **Mini-Browser** | | | | | | | | | | | |
| LaRoche A | 31 | 530 | 30 | 84 | 90 | 0 | .283 | .356 | .520 | $20 | 380 |
| Butler B | 24 | 585 | 20 | 72 | 85 | 0 | .300 | .367 | .466 | $19 | 400 |
| Lee D | 35 | 506 | 23 | 81 | 81 | 6 | .284 | .370 | .488 | $19 | 390 |
| Pena C | 32 | 452 | 33 | 72 | 88 | 0 | .231 | .357 | .494 | $17 | 310 |
| Loney J | 26 | 580 | 13 | 72 | 91 | 7 | .280 | .344 | .428 | $17 | 400 |

| Level | Leag | AB | HR | R | RBI | SB | BA | OBP | SLG | CT% | H% | BB% | Bash |
|---|---|---|---|---|---|---|---|---|---|---|---|---|---|
| | | Minors (2010) | | | | | | | | Skills | | | |
| A | — | — | — | — | — | — | — | — | — | — | — | — | — |
| AA | — | — | — | — | — | — | — | — | — | — | — | — | — |
| AAA | — | — | — | — | — | — | — | — | — | — | — | — | — |

Competition at 1B — Stats in 2010

| Bats | Player | GSvR | GSvL | Sub | OPS |
|---|---|---|---|---|---|
| LH | Huff A | 70 | 29 | 1 | .891 |
| RH | Posey B | 19 | 11 | 0 | .862 |
| LH | Ishikawa T | 24 | 1 | 48 | .712 |
| BH | Sandoval P | 8 | 3 | 0 | .732 |

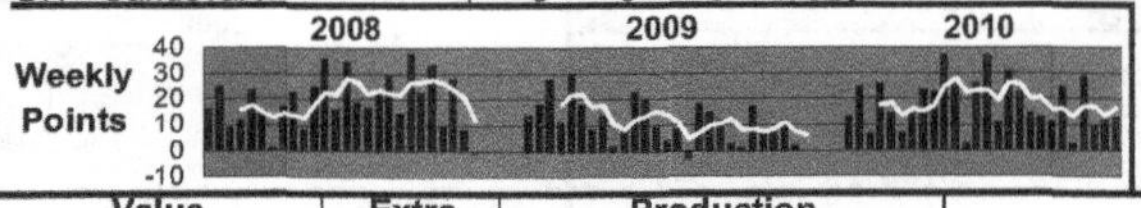


Ten-Year Trends — SLG, OBP, BA

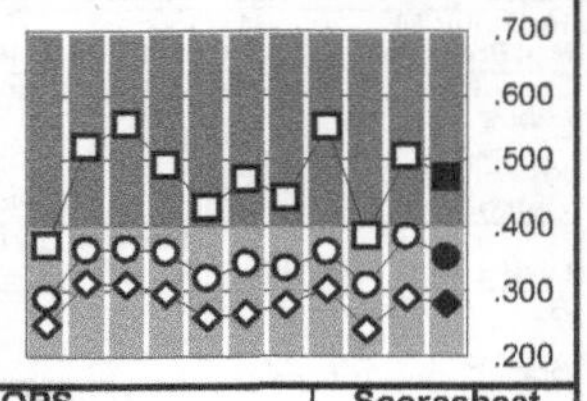


| Yr | Team | AB | HR | R | RBI | SB | BA | OBP | SLG | CT% | H% | BB% | Bash |
|---|---|---|---|---|---|---|---|---|---|---|---|---|---|
| | | Majors | | | | | | | | Skills | | | |
| 07 | BAL | 550 | 15 | 68 | 72 | 1 | .280 | .337 | .442 | 84% | 33% | 8% | 1.58 |
| 08 | BAL | 598 | 32 | 96 | 108 | 4 | .304 | .360 | .552 | 85% | 36% | 8% | 1.81 |
| 09 | 2TM | 536 | 15 | 59 | 85 | 0 | .241 | .310 | .384 | 84% | 29% | 8% | 1.60 |
| 10 | SF | 569 | 26 | 100 | 86 | 7 | .290 | .385 | .506 | 84% | 35% | 12% | 1.75 |

| Yr | $1L | $2L | Pts | RAA | 2B | 3B | CS | FB-LD-GB | HR/fb | RBI% | RS% | OPS | 1st Hf | 2nd Hf | vs RH | vs LH | Rnge | vRH | vLH |
|---|---|---|---|---|---|---|---|---|---|---|---|---|---|---|---|---|---|---|---|
| | Value | | | | Extra | | | Production | | | | OPS | | | | | Scoresheet | | |
| 07 | $14 | $4 | 340 | −7 | 34 | 5 | 1 | 38-16-46 | 8% | 19% | 28% | .778 | .686 | .897 | .778 | .779 | — | +29 | −81 |
| 08 | $31 | $24 | 510 | +20 | 48 | 2 | 0 | 42-17-41 | 15% | 24% | 31% | .912 | .875 | .964 | .989 | .752 | 1.84 | +22 | −70 |
| 09 | $10 | $0 | 310 | −29 | 30 | 1 | 6 | 36-15-48 | 9% | 23% | 26% | .694 | .751 | .609 | .716 | .650 | 1.85 | +28 | −75 |
| 10 | $27 | $22 | 480 | +15 | 35 | 5 | 0 | 37-18-45 | 14% | 22% | 32% | .891 | .929 | .847 | .894 | .884 | 1.85 | +35 | −87 |

## Chad Huffman — 25 PA | $-6 | 10 pts

OF-7 (LF-4, RF-3), 1B-1 — Owned: 0% — RH

Huffman is a limited defender with a power bat. His 10 HR and .763 OPS were a step back in his second season in Triple-A. He was DFA'ed by NYY in mid-September and then claimed by CLE, even though the Indians have no use for him. Their claim looks strictly like a depth-signing for their Triple-A team. (BLS)

| Player | Age | AB | HR | R | RBI | SB | BA | OBP | SLG | $1L | Pts |
|---|---|---|---|---|---|---|---|---|---|---|---|
| **Forecast** | | | | | | | | | | | |
| Huffman C | 25 | 22 | 1 | 2 | 3 | 0 | .217 | .318 | .370 | -$6 | 10 |
| **Mini-Browser** | | | | | | | | | | | |
| Golson G | 25 | 44 | 1 | 5 | 5 | 2 | .214 | .252 | .346 | -$5 | 20 |
| Reed J | 29 | 47 | 1 | 5 | 5 | 1 | .254 | .308 | .379 | -$5 | 30 |
| Dye J | 37 | 23 | 1 | 3 | 4 | 0 | .260 | .328 | .473 | -$5 | 20 |
| Curtis C | 26 | 44 | 1 | 5 | 5 | 1 | .215 | .282 | .339 | -$5 | 20 |
| Chavez E | 33 | 23 | 0 | 3 | 2 | 1 | .274 | .320 | .356 | -$5 | 10 |

| Level | Leag | AB | HR | R | RBI | SB | BA | OBP | SLG | CT% | H% | BB% | Bash |
|---|---|---|---|---|---|---|---|---|---|---|---|---|---|
| | | Minors (2010) | | | | | | | | Skills | | | |
| A | — | — | — | — | — | — | — | — | — | — | — | — | — |
| AA | — | — | — | — | — | — | — | — | — | — | — | — | — |
| AAA | IL | 368 | 10 | 48 | 45 | 0 | .274 | .353 | .410 | 78% | 35% | 10% | 1.50 |

Competition at LF — Stats in 2010

| Bats | Player | GSvR | GSvL | Sub | OPS |
|---|---|---|---|---|---|
| LH | Gardner B | 81 | 30 | 12 | .762 |
| RH | Kearns A | 3 | 17 | 2 | .746 |
| RH | Thames M | 4 | 15 | 6 | .841 |
| RH | Russo K | 4 | 6 | 1 | .470 |

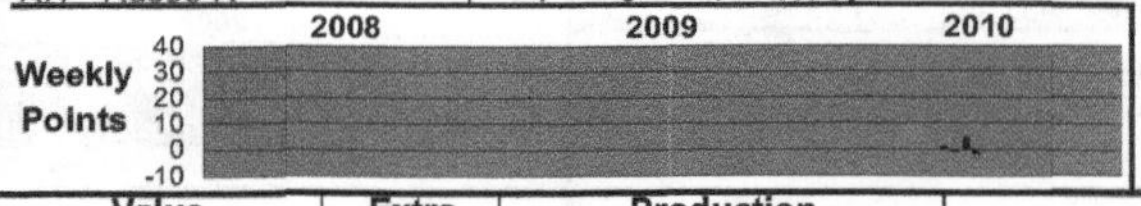


Ten-Year Trends — SLG, OBP, BA

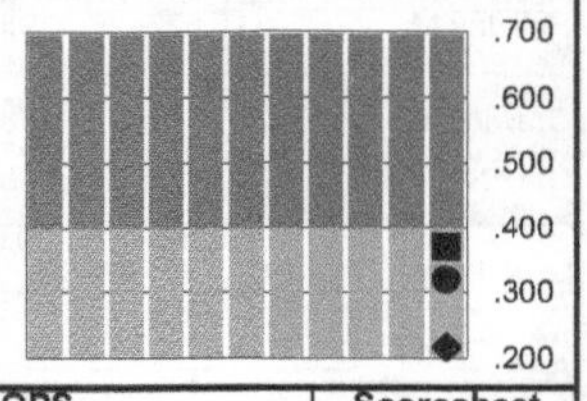


| Yr | Team | AB | HR | R | RBI | SB | BA | OBP | SLG | CT% | H% | BB% | Bash |
|---|---|---|---|---|---|---|---|---|---|---|---|---|---|
| | | Majors | | | | | | | | Skills | | | |
| 07 | — | — | — | — | — | — | — | — | — | — | — | — | — |
| 08 | — | — | — | — | — | — | — | — | — | — | — | — | — |
| 09 | — | — | — | — | — | — | — | — | — | — | — | — | — |
| 10 | NYY | 18 | 0 | 1 | 2 | 0 | .167 | .286 | .167 | 72% | 23% | 10% | 1.00 |

| Yr | $1L | $2L | Pts | RAA | 2B | 3B | CS | FB-LD-GB | HR/fb | RBI% | RS% | OPS | 1st Hf | 2nd Hf | vs RH | vs LH | Rnge | vRH | vLH |
|---|---|---|---|---|---|---|---|---|---|---|---|---|---|---|---|---|---|---|---|
| | Value | | | | Extra | | | Production | | | | OPS | | | | | Scoresheet | | |
| 07 | — | — | — | — | — | — | — | — | — | — | — | — | — | — | — | — | — | — | — |
| 08 | — | — | — | — | — | — | — | — | — | — | — | — | — | — | — | — | — | — | — |
| 09 | — | — | — | — | — | — | — | — | — | — | — | — | — | — | — | — | 2.10 | — | — |
| 10 | -$4 | -$21 | 0 | −3 | 0 | 0 | 0 | 38-15-46 | 0% | 13% | 17% | .452 | .452 | — | .730 | .258 | 2.10 | — | — |

## Rhyne Hughes — 50 PA | $-5 | 20 pts

1B-11, DH-1 — Owned: 0% — LH

Barring a free-agent signing, the 1B job should be wide open in Baltimore, but Hughes's poor showing in MLB in 2010, and middling stats in Triple-A, make the 26-year-old a long shot even to make the roster as a back-up. (BJ)

| Player | Age | AB | HR | R | RBI | SB | BA | OBP | SLG | $1L | Pts |
|---|---|---|---|---|---|---|---|---|---|---|---|
| **Forecast** | | | | | | | | | | | |
| Hughes R | 27 | 47 | 2 | 5 | 5 | 0 | .225 | .291 | .410 | -$5 | 20 |
| **Mini-Browser** | | | | | | | | | | | |
| Clement J | 27 | 42 | 2 | 6 | 6 | 0 | .261 | .343 | .472 | -$4 | 30 |
| Hosmer E | 21 | 129 | 3 | 11 | 17 | 0 | .221 | .303 | .359 | -$4 | 50 |
| Davis C | 25 | 45 | 3 | 6 | 7 | 1 | .243 | .301 | .475 | -$4 | 20 |
| Rizzo A | 21 | 44 | 2 | 5 | 6 | 0 | .251 | .313 | .424 | -$5 | 20 |
| Delgado C | 38 | 22 | 1 | 4 | 4 | 0 | .276 | .358 | .506 | -$5 | 20 |

| Level | Leag | AB | HR | R | RBI | SB | BA | OBP | SLG | CT% | H% | BB% | Bash |
|---|---|---|---|---|---|---|---|---|---|---|---|---|---|
| | | Minors (2010) | | | | | | | | Skills | | | |
| A | — | — | — | — | — | — | — | — | — | — | — | — | — |
| AA | — | — | — | — | — | — | — | — | — | — | — | — | — |
| AAA | IL | 388 | 10 | 44 | 39 | 8 | .258 | .314 | .410 | 69% | 37% | 7% | 1.59 |

Competition at 1B — Stats in 2010

| Bats | Player | GSvR | GSvL | Sub | OPS |
|---|---|---|---|---|---|
| RH | Wigginton T | 68 | 30 | 1 | .727 |
| RH | Atkins G | 17 | 13 | 0 | .562 |
| LH | Scott L | 17 | 2 | 0 | .902 |
| LH | Hughes R | 11 | 0 | 0 | .530 |

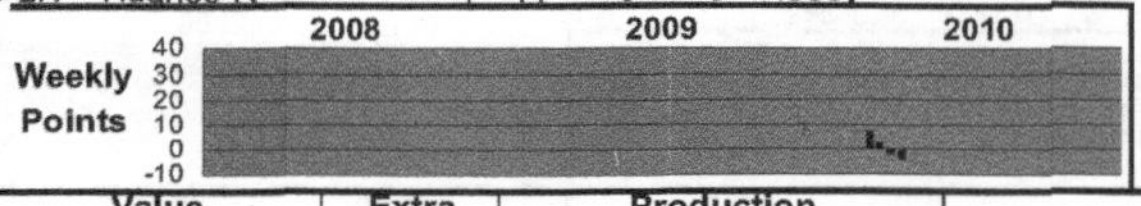


Ten-Year Trends — SLG, OBP, BA

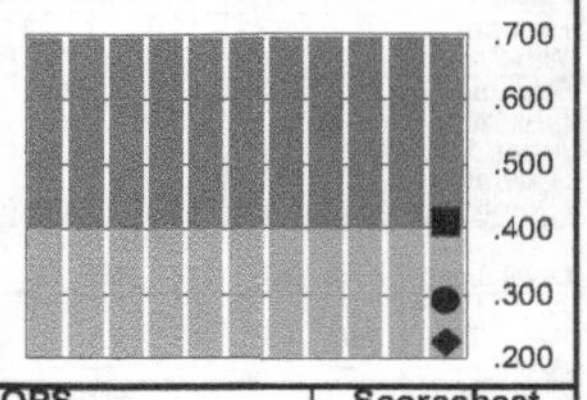


| Yr | Team | AB | HR | R | RBI | SB | BA | OBP | SLG | CT% | H% | BB% | Bash |
|---|---|---|---|---|---|---|---|---|---|---|---|---|---|
| | | Majors | | | | | | | | Skills | | | |
| 07 | — | — | — | — | — | — | — | — | — | — | — | — | — |
| 08 | — | — | — | — | — | — | — | — | — | — | — | — | — |
| 09 | — | — | — | — | — | — | — | — | — | — | — | — | — |
| 10 | BAL | 47 | 0 | 3 | 4 | 0 | .213 | .275 | .255 | 60% | 36% | 8% | 1.20 |

| Yr | $1L | $2L | Pts | RAA | 2B | 3B | CS | FB-LD-GB | HR/fb | RBI% | RS% | OPS | 1st Hf | 2nd Hf | vs RH | vs LH | Rnge | vRH | vLH |
|---|---|---|---|---|---|---|---|---|---|---|---|---|---|---|---|---|---|---|---|
| | Value | | | | Extra | | | Production | | | | OPS | | | | | Scoresheet | | |
| 07 | — | — | — | — | — | — | — | — | — | — | — | — | — | — | — | — | — | — | — |
| 08 | — | — | — | — | — | — | — | — | — | — | — | — | — | — | — | — | — | — | — |
| 09 | — | — | — | — | — | — | — | — | — | — | — | — | — | — | — | — | — | — | — |
| 10 | -$4 | -$20 | 0 | −5 | 2 | 0 | 0 | 29-21-50 | 0% | 15% | 21% | .530 | .530 | — | .517 | .650 | — | — | — |

## Nick Hundley — 300 PA | $4 | 130 pts

CA-76 — Owned: 1% — RH

Hundley is a cheap backstop with pretty good power, and San Diego lacks catching prospects, so he should get another good chunk of playing time in 2011. Hundley's role may even expand, but the Padres might also bring back Yorvit Torrealba or snag another catcher in free agency to share the burden. (DG)

| Player | Age | AB | HR | R | RBI | SB | BA | OBP | SLG | $1L | Pts |
|---|---|---|---|---|---|---|---|---|---|---|---|
| **Forecast** | | | | | | | | | | | |
| Hundley N | 27 | 272 | 9 | 30 | 36 | 0 | .232 | .298 | .405 | $4 | 130 |
| **Mini-Browser** | | | | | | | | | | | |
| Torrealba Y | 32 | 289 | 6 | 29 | 38 | 3 | .266 | .329 | .383 | $6 | 150 |
| Conger H | 23 | 276 | 9 | 27 | 42 | 3 | .239 | .299 | .415 | $5 | 160 |
| Mathis J | 28 | 362 | 8 | 40 | 44 | 4 | .221 | .282 | .341 | $5 | 130 |
| Thole J | 24 | 410 | 5 | 38 | 43 | 5 | .243 | .320 | .338 | $5 | 210 |
| Hanigan R | 30 | 267 | 6 | 30 | 30 | 0 | .270 | .367 | .373 | $4 | 160 |

| Level | Leag | AB | HR | R | RBI | SB | BA | OBP | SLG | CT% | H% | BB% | Bash |
|---|---|---|---|---|---|---|---|---|---|---|---|---|---|
| | | Minors (2010) | | | | | | | | Skills | | | |
| A | — | — | — | — | — | — | — | — | — | — | — | — | — |
| AA | — | — | — | — | — | — | — | — | — | — | — | — | — |
| AAA | — | — | — | — | — | — | — | — | — | — | — | — | — |

Competition at CA — Stats in 2010

| Bats | Player | GSvR | GSvL | Sub | OPS |
|---|---|---|---|---|---|
| RH | Torrealba Y | 58 | 31 | 3 | .721 |
| RH | Hundley N | 53 | 20 | 3 | .726 |

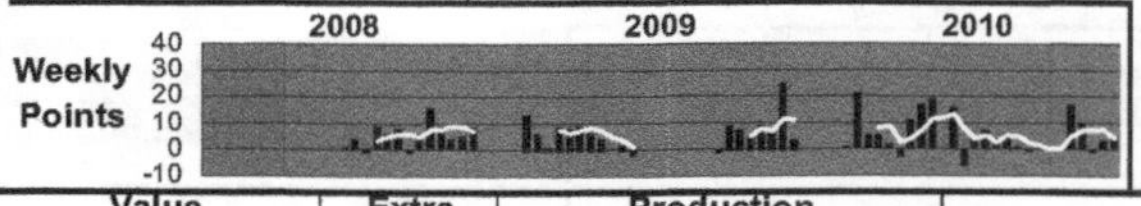


Ten-Year Trends — SLG, OBP, BA

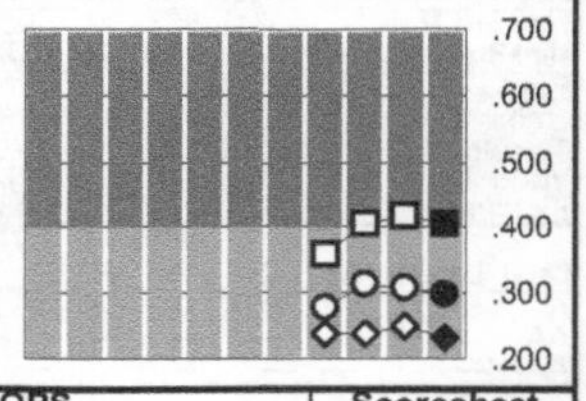


| Yr | Team | AB | HR | R | RBI | SB | BA | OBP | SLG | CT% | H% | BB% | Bash |
|---|---|---|---|---|---|---|---|---|---|---|---|---|---|
| | | Majors | | | | | | | | Skills | | | |
| 07 | — | — | — | — | — | — | — | — | — | — | — | — | — |
| 08 | SD | 198 | 5 | 21 | 24 | 0 | .237 | .278 | .359 | 74% | 32% | 5% | 1.51 |
| 09 | SD | 256 | 8 | 23 | 30 | 5 | .238 | .313 | .406 | 70% | 34% | 10% | 1.70 |
| 10 | SD | 273 | 8 | 33 | 43 | 0 | .249 | .308 | .418 | 76% | 33% | 8% | 1.68 |

| Yr | $1L | $2L | Pts | RAA | 2B | 3B | CS | FB-LD-GB | HR/fb | RBI% | RS% | OPS | 1st Hf | 2nd Hf | vs RH | vs LH | Rnge | vRH | vLH |
|---|---|---|---|---|---|---|---|---|---|---|---|---|---|---|---|---|---|---|---|
| | Value | | | | Extra | | | Production | | | | OPS | | | | | Scoresheet | | |
| 07 | — | — | — | — | — | — | — | — | — | — | — | — | — | — | — | — | — | — | — |
| 08 | $2 | -$5 | 80 | −9 | 7 | 1 | 0 | 44-17-39 | 8% | 19% | 29% | .636 | .501 | .651 | .652 | .597 | — | — | — |
| 09 | $5 | -$2 | 120 | −2 | 15 | 2 | 1 | 47-22-31 | 9% | 17% | 18% | .719 | .718 | .717 | .768 | .587 | 0.64 | −17 | +42 |
| 10 | $7 | $0 | 140 | −5 | 18 | 2 | 5 | 40-19-41 | 10% | 22% | 29% | .726 | .758 | .664 | .692 | .830 | 0.70 | −4 | +10 |

## Cedric Hunter — 75 PA | $-4 | 30 pts

No MLB games played in 2010 — Owned: 0% — LH

Hunter is very young, and he looks promising if you squint, but his outfield range is only so-so, and he has a lot of development to do with the bat. A full season at Triple-A would allow him to work out the kinks, so don't expect to see Hunter in a Padre uniform until mid-2011 at the very earliest. (DG)

| Player | Age | AB | HR | R | RBI | SB | BA | OBP | SLG | $1L | Pts |
|---|---|---|---|---|---|---|---|---|---|---|---|
| **Forecast** | | | | | | | | | | | |
| Hunter C | 23 | 72 | 2 | 7 | 7 | 1 | .218 | .265 | .315 | -$4 | 30 |
| **Mini-Browser** | | | | | | | | | | | |
| Nieuwenhuis K | 23 | 45 | 2 | 6 | 6 | 2 | .222 | .306 | .426 | -$4 | 30 |
| Nava D | 28 | 87 | 2 | 11 | 12 | 0 | .230 | .319 | .381 | -$4 | 50 |
| Neal T | 23 | 42 | 2 | 6 | 6 | 0 | .236 | .329 | .431 | -$4 | 20 |
| Sullivan C | 31 | 44 | 1 | 6 | 5 | 1 | .260 | .324 | .373 | -$4 | 20 |
| Fuld S | 29 | 89 | 1 | 13 | 7 | 3 | .248 | .335 | .367 | -$4 | 60 |

| Level | Leag | AB | HR | R | RBI | SB | BA | OBP | SLG | CT% | H% | BB% | Bash |
|---|---|---|---|---|---|---|---|---|---|---|---|---|---|
| | | Minors (2010) | | | | | | | | Skills | | | |
| A | — | — | — | — | — | — | — | — | — | — | — | — | — |
| AA | TL | 279 | 4 | 34 | 38 | 9 | .308 | .375 | .423 | 92% | 33% | 10% | 1.37 |
| AAA | PCL | 262 | 3 | 42 | 26 | 5 | .263 | .305 | .370 | 92% | 29% | 6% | 1.41 |

Competition at CF — Stats in 2010

| Bats | Player | GSvR | GSvL | Sub | OPS |
|---|---|---|---|---|---|
| LH | Gwynn T | 67 | 5 | 33 | .591 |
| RH | Denorfia C | 19 | 28 | 3 | .769 |
| LH | Venable W | 19 | 3 | 3 | .732 |
| RH | Hairston S | 9 | 10 | 0 | .640 |

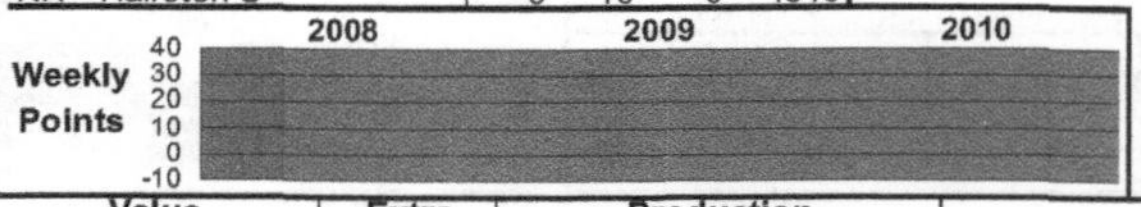


Ten-Year Trends — SLG, OBP, BA

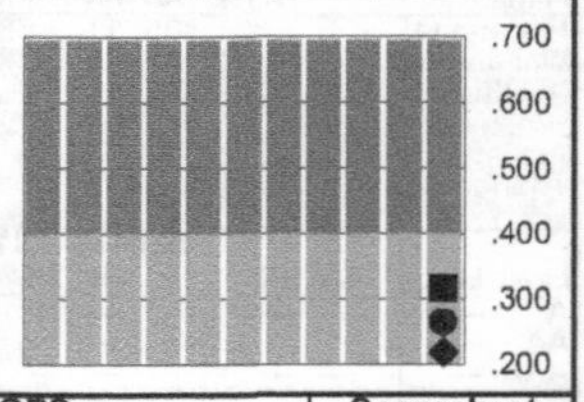


| Yr | Team | AB | HR | R | RBI | SB | BA | OBP | SLG | CT% | H% | BB% | Bash |
|---|---|---|---|---|---|---|---|---|---|---|---|---|---|
| | | Majors | | | | | | | | Skills | | | |
| 07 | — | — | — | — | — | — | — | — | — | — | — | — | — |
| 08 | — | — | — | — | — | — | — | — | — | — | — | — | — |
| 09 | — | — | — | — | — | — | — | — | — | — | — | — | — |
| 10 | — | — | — | — | — | — | — | — | — | — | — | — | — |

| Yr | $1L | $2L | Pts | RAA | 2B | 3B | CS | FB-LD-GB | HR/fb | RBI% | RS% | OPS | 1st Hf | 2nd Hf | vs RH | vs LH | Rnge | vRH | vLH |
|---|---|---|---|---|---|---|---|---|---|---|---|---|---|---|---|---|---|---|---|
| | Value | | | | Extra | | | Production | | | | OPS | | | | | Scoresheet | | |
| 07 | — | — | — | — | — | — | — | — | — | — | — | — | — | — | — | — | — | — | — |
| 08 | — | — | — | — | — | — | — | — | — | — | — | — | — | — | — | — | — | — | — |
| 09 | — | — | — | — | — | — | — | — | — | — | — | — | — | — | — | — | — | — | — |
| 10 | — | — | — | — | — | — | — | — | — | — | — | — | — | — | — | — | — | — | — |

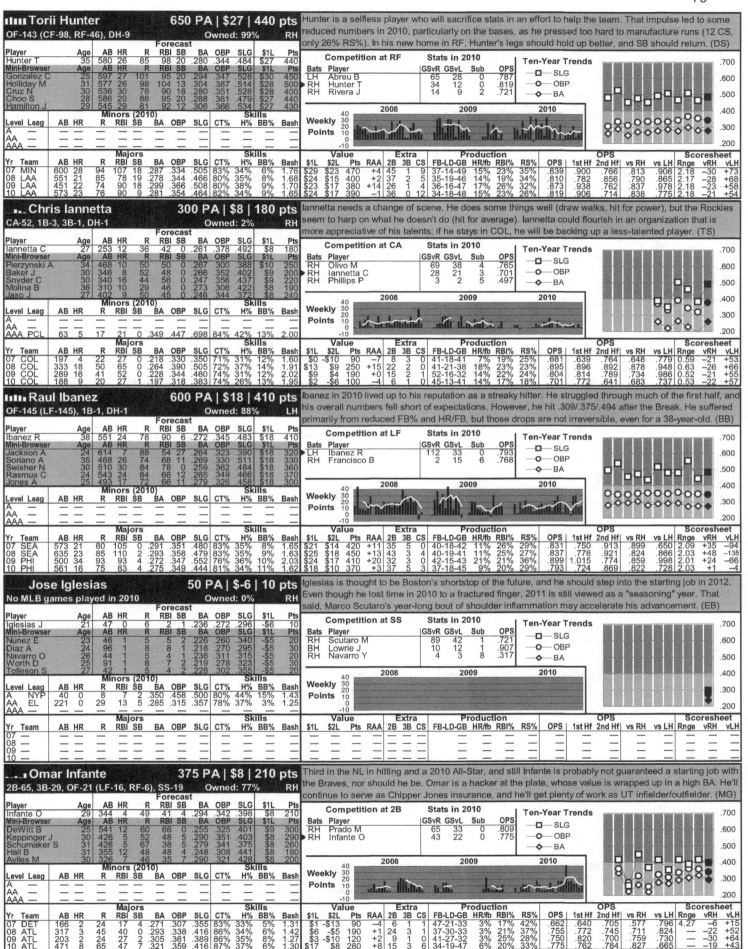

## Torii Hunter — 650 PA | $27 | 440 pts
OF-143 (CF-98, RF-46), DH-9 — Owned: 99% — RH

Hunter is a selfless player who will sacrifice stats in an effort to help the team. That impulse led to some reduced numbers in 2010, particularly on the bases, as he pressed too hard to manufacture runs (12 CS, only 26% RS%). In his new home in RF, Hunter's legs should hold up better, and SB should return. (DS)

### Forecast
| Player | Age | AB | HR | R | RBI | SB | BA | OBP | SLG | $1L | Pts |
|---|---|---|---|---|---|---|---|---|---|---|---|
| Hunter T | 35 | 580 | 26 | 85 | 98 | 20 | .280 | .344 | .484 | $27 | 440 |

### Mini-Browser
| Player | Age | AB | HR | R | RBI | SB | BA | OBP | SLG | $1L | Pts |
|---|---|---|---|---|---|---|---|---|---|---|---|
| Gonzalez C | 25 | 597 | 27 | 101 | 95 | 20 | .294 | .347 | .528 | $30 | 450 |
| Holliday M | 31 | 577 | 26 | 99 | 104 | 13 | .304 | .387 | .514 | $28 | 500 |
| Cruz N | 30 | 536 | 30 | 78 | 90 | 18 | .280 | .351 | .528 | $28 | 400 |
| Choo S | 28 | 586 | 20 | 88 | 95 | 20 | .288 | .381 | .479 | $27 | 440 |
| Hamilton J | 29 | 545 | 29 | 81 | 92 | 12 | .306 | .366 | .534 | $27 | 430 |

### Competition at RF — Stats in 2010
| Bats | Player | GSvR | GSvL | Sub | OPS |
|---|---|---|---|---|---|
| LH | Abreu B | 65 | 28 | 0 | .787 |
| RH | Hunter T | 34 | 12 | 0 | .819 |
| RH | Rivera J | 14 | 9 | 2 | .721 |

### Minors (2010) / Skills
| Level | Leag | AB | HR | R | RBI | SB | BA | OBP | SLG | CT% | H% | BB% | Bash |
|---|---|---|---|---|---|---|---|---|---|---|---|---|---|
| A | — | | | | | | | | | | | | |
| AA | — | | | | | | | | | | | | |
| AAA | — | | | | | | | | | | | | |

### Majors / Skills / Value / Extra / Production / OPS / Scoresheet
| Yr | Team | AB | HR | R | RBI | SB | BA | OBP | SLG | CT% | H% | BB% | Bash | $1L | $2L | Pts | RAA | 2B | 3B | CS | FB-LD-GB | HR/fb | RBI% | RS% | OPS | 1st Hf | 2nd Hf | vs RH | vs LH | Rnge | vRH | vLH |
|---|---|---|---|---|---|---|---|---|---|---|---|---|---|---|---|---|---|---|---|---|---|---|---|---|---|---|---|---|---|---|---|---|
| 07 | MIN | 600 | 28 | 94 | 107 | 18 | .287 | .334 | .505 | 83% | 34% | 6% | 1.76 | $29 | $23 | 470 | +4 | 45 | 1 | 9 | 37-14-49 | 15% | 23% | 35% | .839 | .900 | .766 | .813 | .906 | 2.18 | −30 | +73 |
| 08 | LAA | 551 | 21 | 85 | 78 | 19 | .278 | .344 | .466 | 80% | 35% | 9% | 1.68 | $24 | $15 | 390 | +2 | 37 | 2 | 5 | 35-19-46 | 14% | 19% | 34% | .810 | .782 | .856 | .790 | .865 | 2.17 | −28 | +68 |
| 09 | LAA | 451 | 22 | 74 | 90 | 18 | .299 | .366 | .508 | 80% | 38% | 9% | 1.70 | $23 | $17 | 380 | +14 | 26 | 1 | 4 | 36-16-47 | 17% | 26% | 32% | .873 | .938 | .762 | .837 | .978 | 2.18 | −23 | +58 |
| 10 | LAA | 573 | 23 | 76 | 90 | 9 | .281 | .354 | .464 | 82% | 34% | 9% | 1.65 | $24 | $17 | 390 | −1 | 36 | 4 | 12 | 34-18-48 | 15% | 23% | 26% | .819 | .906 | .714 | .837 | .838 | .775 | −24 | +54 |

## Chris Iannetta — 300 PA | $8 | 180 pts
CA-52, 1B-3, 3B-1, DH-1 — Owned: 2% — RH

Iannetta needs a change of scene. He does some things well (draw walks, hit for power), but the Rockies seem to harp on what he doesn't do (hit for average). Iannetta could flourish in an organization that is more appreciative of his talents; if he stays in COL, he will be backing up a less-talented player. (TS)

### Forecast
| Player | Age | AB | HR | R | RBI | SB | BA | OBP | SLG | $1L | Pts |
|---|---|---|---|---|---|---|---|---|---|---|---|
| Iannetta C | 27 | 253 | 12 | 36 | 42 | 0 | .261 | .378 | .492 | $8 | 180 |

### Mini-Browser
| Player | Age | AB | HR | R | RBI | SB | BA | OBP | SLG | $1L | Pts |
|---|---|---|---|---|---|---|---|---|---|---|---|
| Pierzynski A | 34 | 468 | 10 | 50 | 50 | 0 | .261 | .300 | .388 | $10 | 250 |
| Baker J | 30 | 346 | 8 | 52 | 48 | 0 | .266 | .352 | .402 | $9 | 200 |
| Snyder C | 30 | 340 | 16 | 44 | 56 | 0 | .247 | .336 | .437 | $9 | 220 |
| Molina B | 36 | 310 | 10 | 29 | 46 | 0 | .273 | .306 | .422 | $8 | 190 |
| Jaso J | 27 | 402 | 9 | 50 | 45 | 0 | .246 | .344 | .372 | $8 | 240 |

### Competition at CA — Stats in 2010
| Bats | Player | GSvR | GSvL | Sub | OPS |
|---|---|---|---|---|---|
| RH | Olivo M | 69 | 38 | 4 | .765 |
| RH | Iannetta C | 28 | 21 | 3 | .701 |
| RH | Phillips P | 3 | 2 | 5 | .497 |

### Minors (2010) / Skills
| Level | Leag | AB | HR | R | RBI | SB | BA | OBP | SLG | CT% | H% | BB% | Bash |
|---|---|---|---|---|---|---|---|---|---|---|---|---|---|
| A | — | | | | | | | | | | | | |
| AA | — | | | | | | | | | | | | |
| AAA | PCL | 63 | 5 | 17 | 21 | 0 | .349 | .447 | .698 | 84% | 42% | 13% | 2.00 |

### Majors / Skills / Value / Extra / Production / OPS / Scoresheet
| Yr | Team | AB | HR | R | RBI | SB | BA | OBP | SLG | CT% | H% | BB% | Bash | $1L | $2L | Pts | RAA | 2B | 3B | CS | FB-LD-GB | HR/fb | RBI% | RS% | OPS | 1st Hf | 2nd Hf | vs RH | vs LH | Rnge | vRH | vLH |
|---|---|---|---|---|---|---|---|---|---|---|---|---|---|---|---|---|---|---|---|---|---|---|---|---|---|---|---|---|---|---|---|---|
| 07 | COL | 197 | 4 | 22 | 27 | 0 | .218 | .330 | .350 | 71% | 31% | 12% | 1.60 | $0 | −$10 | 90 | −7 | 8 | 3 | | 41-18-41 | 7% | 19% | 25% | .681 | .639 | .764 | .648 | .779 | 0.59 | −21 | +53 |
| 08 | COL | 333 | 18 | 50 | 65 | 0 | .264 | .390 | .505 | 72% | 37% | 14% | 1.91 | $13 | $4 | 250 | +15 | 22 | 2 | 0 | 41-21-38 | 18% | 23% | 23% | .895 | .896 | .892 | .878 | .948 | 0.63 | −26 | +66 |
| 09 | COL | 289 | 16 | 41 | 52 | 0 | .228 | .344 | .460 | 74% | 31% | 12% | 2.02 | $9 | $4 | 190 | +0 | 15 | 2 | 1 | 52-16-32 | 14% | 22% | 24% | .804 | .814 | .789 | .734 | .986 | 0.52 | −21 | +55 |
| 10 | COL | 188 | 9 | 20 | 27 | 1 | .197 | .318 | .383 | 74% | 26% | 13% | 1.95 | $2 | −$6 | 100 | −4 | 6 | 1 | 0 | 45-13-41 | 14% | 17% | 18% | .701 | .772 | .641 | .683 | .737 | 0.53 | −22 | +57 |

## Raul Ibanez — 600 PA | $18 | 410 pts
OF-145 (LF-145), 1B-1, DH-1 — Owned: 88% — LH

Ibanez in 2010 lived up to his reputation as a streaky hitter. He struggled through much of the first half, and his overall numbers fell short of expectations. However, he hit .309/.375/.494 after the Break. He suffered primarily from reduced FB% and HR/FB, but those drops are not irreversible, even for a 38-year-old. (BB)

### Forecast
| Player | Age | AB | HR | R | RBI | SB | BA | OBP | SLG | $1L | Pts |
|---|---|---|---|---|---|---|---|---|---|---|---|
| Ibanez R | 38 | 551 | 24 | 78 | 90 | 6 | .272 | .345 | .483 | $18 | 410 |

### Mini-Browser
| Player | Age | AB | HR | R | RBI | SB | BA | OBP | SLG | $1L | Pts |
|---|---|---|---|---|---|---|---|---|---|---|---|
| Jackson A | 24 | 614 | 7 | 88 | 54 | 27 | .264 | .323 | .390 | $18 | 320 |
| Soriano A | 35 | 468 | 26 | 74 | 68 | 11 | .269 | .330 | .511 | $18 | 330 |
| Swisher N | 30 | 510 | 30 | 84 | 78 | 0 | .259 | .362 | .484 | $18 | 360 |
| Rasmus C | 24 | 543 | 24 | 84 | 66 | 12 | .265 | .349 | .466 | $18 | 370 |
| Jones A | 25 | 493 | 17 | 72 | 66 | 11 | .279 | .326 | .434 | $18 | 300 |

### Competition at LF — Stats in 2010
| Bats | Player | GSvR | GSvL | Sub | OPS |
|---|---|---|---|---|---|
| LH | Ibanez R | 112 | 33 | 0 | .793 |
| RH | Francisco B | 2 | 15 | 6 | .768 |

### Minors (2010) / Skills
| Level | Leag | AB | HR | R | RBI | SB | BA | OBP | SLG | CT% | H% | BB% | Bash |
|---|---|---|---|---|---|---|---|---|---|---|---|---|---|
| A | — | | | | | | | | | | | | |
| AA | — | | | | | | | | | | | | |
| AAA | — | | | | | | | | | | | | |

### Majors / Skills / Value / Extra / Production / OPS / Scoresheet
| Yr | Team | AB | HR | R | RBI | SB | BA | OBP | SLG | CT% | H% | BB% | Bash | $1L | $2L | Pts | RAA | 2B | 3B | CS | FB-LD-GB | HR/fb | RBI% | RS% | OPS | 1st Hf | 2nd Hf | vs RH | vs LH | Rnge | vRH | vLH |
|---|---|---|---|---|---|---|---|---|---|---|---|---|---|---|---|---|---|---|---|---|---|---|---|---|---|---|---|---|---|---|---|---|
| 07 | SEA | 573 | 21 | 80 | 105 | 0 | .291 | .351 | .480 | 83% | 35% | 8% | 1.65 | $21 | $14 | 420 | +11 | 35 | 5 | 0 | 40-18-42 | 11% | 26% | 29% | .831 | .750 | .913 | .899 | .650 | 2.09 | +35 | −94 |
| 08 | SEA | 635 | 23 | 85 | 110 | 2 | .293 | .358 | .479 | 83% | 35% | 9% | 1.63 | $25 | $18 | 450 | +13 | 43 | 3 | 4 | 40-19-41 | 11% | 25% | 27% | .837 | .776 | .921 | .824 | .866 | 2.03 | +48 | −135 |
| 09 | PHI | 500 | 34 | 93 | 93 | 4 | .272 | .347 | .552 | 76% | 36% | 10% | 2.03 | $24 | $17 | 410 | +20 | 32 | 3 | 0 | 42-15-43 | 21% | 21% | 36% | .899 | 1.015 | .774 | .859 | .998 | 2.01 | +24 | −66 |
| 10 | PHI | 561 | 16 | 75 | 83 | 4 | .275 | .349 | .444 | 81% | 34% | 11% | 1.62 | $18 | $10 | 370 | +3 | 37 | 3 | 1 | 37-18-45 | 9% | 20% | 29% | .793 | .724 | .869 | .822 | .728 | 2.03 | +1 | −4 |

## Jose Iglesias — 50 PA | $-6 | 10 pts
No MLB games played in 2010 — Owned: 0% — RH

Iglesias is thought to be Boston's shortstop of the future, and he should step into the starting job in 2012. Even though he lost time in 2010 to a fractured finger, 2011 is still viewed as a "seasoning" year. That said, Marco Scutaro's year-long bout of shoulder inflammation may accelerate his advancement. (EB)

### Forecast
| Player | Age | AB | HR | R | RBI | SB | BA | OBP | SLG | $1L | Pts |
|---|---|---|---|---|---|---|---|---|---|---|---|
| Iglesias J | 21 | 47 | 0 | 6 | 2 | 1 | .236 | .272 | .296 | −$6 | 10 |

### Mini-Browser
| Player | Age | AB | HR | R | RBI | SB | BA | OBP | SLG | $1L | Pts |
|---|---|---|---|---|---|---|---|---|---|---|---|
| Nunez E | 23 | 46 | 1 | 5 | 5 | 2 | .226 | .260 | .340 | −$5 | 20 |
| Diaz A | 24 | 96 | 1 | 8 | 8 | 1 | .218 | .270 | .295 | −$5 | 30 |
| Navarro O | 26 | 44 | 1 | 5 | 4 | 1 | .236 | .311 | .315 | −$5 | 20 |
| Worth D | 25 | 91 | 3 | 8 | 7 | 2 | .219 | .278 | .323 | −$5 | 30 |
| Tolleson S | 27 | 42 | 1 | 5 | 4 | 2 | .228 | .302 | .355 | −$5 | 20 |

### Competition at SS — Stats in 2010
| Bats | Player | GSvR | GSvL | Sub | OPS |
|---|---|---|---|---|---|
| RH | Scutaro M | 89 | 42 | 1 | .721 |
| BH | Lowrie J | 10 | 12 | 1 | .907 |
| RH | Navarro Y | 4 | 3 | 8 | .317 |

### Minors (2010) / Skills
| Level | Leag | AB | HR | R | RBI | SB | BA | OBP | SLG | CT% | H% | BB% | Bash |
|---|---|---|---|---|---|---|---|---|---|---|---|---|---|
| A | NYP | 40 | 0 | 8 | 7 | 2 | .350 | .458 | .500 | 80% | 44% | 15% | 1.43 |
| AA | EL | 221 | 0 | 29 | 13 | 5 | .285 | .315 | .357 | 78% | 37% | 3% | 1.25 |
| AAA | — | | | | | | | | | | | | |

### Majors / Skills / Value / Extra / Production / OPS / Scoresheet
| Yr | Team | AB | HR | R | RBI | SB | BA | OBP | SLG | CT% | H% | BB% | Bash | $1L | $2L | Pts | RAA | 2B | 3B | CS | FB-LD-GB | HR/fb | RBI% | RS% | OPS | 1st Hf | 2nd Hf | vs RH | vs LH | Rnge | vRH | vLH |
|---|---|---|---|---|---|---|---|---|---|---|---|---|---|---|---|---|---|---|---|---|---|---|---|---|---|---|---|---|---|---|---|---|
| 07 | — | | | | | | | | | | | | | | | | | | | | | | | | | | | | | | | |
| 08 | — | | | | | | | | | | | | | | | | | | | | | | | | | | | | | | | |
| 09 | — | | | | | | | | | | | | | | | | | | | | | | | | | | | | | | | |
| 10 | — | | | | | | | | | | | | | | | | | | | | | | | | | | | | | | | |

## Omar Infante — 375 PA | $8 | 210 pts
2B-65, 3B-29, OF-21 (LF-16, RF-6), SS-19 — Owned: 77% — RH

Third in the NL in hitting and a 2010 All-Star, and still Infante is probably not guaranteed a starting job with the Braves, nor should he be. Omar is a hacker at the plate, whose value is wrapped up in a high BA. He'll continue to serve as Chipper Jones insurance, and he'll get plenty of work as UT infielder/outfielder. (MG)

### Forecast
| Player | Age | AB | HR | R | RBI | SB | BA | OBP | SLG | $1L | Pts |
|---|---|---|---|---|---|---|---|---|---|---|---|
| Infante O | 29 | 344 | 4 | 49 | 41 | 4 | .294 | .342 | .398 | $8 | 210 |

### Mini-Browser
| Player | Age | AB | HR | R | RBI | SB | BA | OBP | SLG | $1L | Pts |
|---|---|---|---|---|---|---|---|---|---|---|---|
| DeWitt B | 25 | 541 | 12 | 60 | 66 | 0 | .255 | .325 | .401 | $9 | 300 |
| Keppinger J | 30 | 426 | 5 | 52 | 48 | 5 | .290 | .351 | .403 | $8 | 290 |
| Schumaker S | 31 | 426 | 5 | 67 | 38 | 5 | .279 | .341 | .375 | $8 | 260 |
| Hall B | 31 | 355 | 12 | 48 | 48 | 4 | .248 | .308 | .441 | $8 | 180 |
| Aviles M | 30 | 326 | 5 | 47 | 46 | 9 | .290 | .321 | .406 | $8 | 200 |

### Competition at 2B — Stats in 2010
| Bats | Player | GSvR | GSvL | Sub | OPS |
|---|---|---|---|---|---|
| RH | Prado M | 65 | 33 | 0 | .809 |
| RH | Infante O | 43 | 22 | 0 | .775 |

### Minors (2010) / Skills
| Level | Leag | AB | HR | R | RBI | SB | BA | OBP | SLG | CT% | H% | BB% | Bash |
|---|---|---|---|---|---|---|---|---|---|---|---|---|---|
| A | — | | | | | | | | | | | | |
| AA | — | | | | | | | | | | | | |
| AAA | — | | | | | | | | | | | | |

### Majors / Skills / Value / Extra / Production / OPS / Scoresheet
| Yr | Team | AB | HR | R | RBI | SB | BA | OBP | SLG | CT% | H% | BB% | Bash | $1L | $2L | Pts | RAA | 2B | 3B | CS | FB-LD-GB | HR/fb | RBI% | RS% | OPS | 1st Hf | 2nd Hf | vs RH | vs LH | Rnge | vRH | vLH |
|---|---|---|---|---|---|---|---|---|---|---|---|---|---|---|---|---|---|---|---|---|---|---|---|---|---|---|---|---|---|---|---|---|
| 07 | DET | 166 | 2 | 24 | 17 | 4 | .271 | .307 | .355 | 83% | 33% | 5% | 1.31 | $1 | −$13 | 90 | −4 | 6 | 1 | 1 | 47-21-33 | 3% | 17% | 42% | .662 | .640 | .705 | .577 | .796 | 4.27 | −6 | +15 |
| 08 | ATL | 317 | 3 | 45 | 40 | 0 | .293 | .338 | .416 | 86% | 34% | 6% | 1.42 | $6 | −$5 | 190 | +1 | 24 | 3 | 1 | 37-30-33 | 3% | 21% | 37% | .755 | .772 | .745 | .711 | .824 | | −22 | +52 |
| 09 | ATL | 203 | 2 | 24 | 27 | 2 | .305 | .364 | .389 | 86% | 35% | 8% | 1.27 | $3 | −$10 | 120 | +2 | 11 | 3 | 0 | 41-27-32 | 3% | 25% | 28% | .750 | .820 | .700 | .759 | .730 | | −30 | +64 |
| 10 | ATL | 471 | 8 | 65 | 47 | 7 | .321 | .359 | .416 | 87% | 37% | 6% | 1.30 | $17 | $8 | 280 | +8 | 15 | 3 | 6 | 34-19-47 | 6% | 20% | 33% | .775 | .762 | .784 | .827 | .665 | | −19 | +43 |

*For more stats, visit www.Rotolympus.com.*

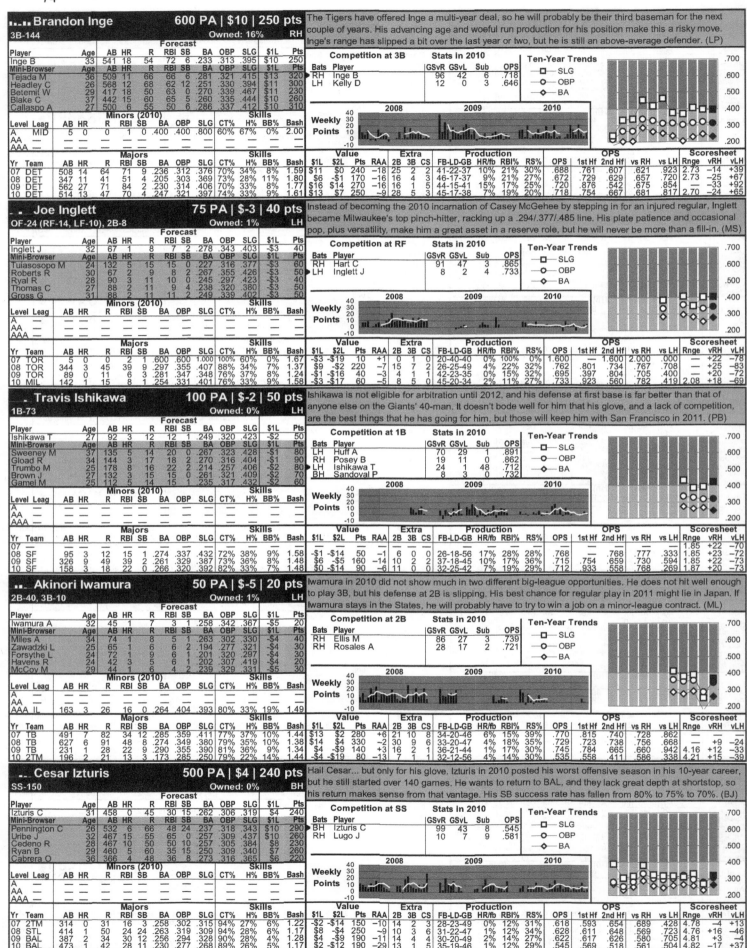

## Brandon Inge — 600 PA | $10 | 250 pts

3B-144 — Owned: 16% — RH

The Tigers have offered Inge a multi-year deal, so he will probably be their third baseman for the next couple of years. His advancing age and woeful run production for his position make this a risky move. Inge's range has slipped a bit over the last year or two, but he is still an above-average defender. (LP)

| Player | Age | AB | HR | R | RBI | SB | BA | OBP | SLG | $1L | Pts |
|---|---|---|---|---|---|---|---|---|---|---|---|
| Inge B | 33 | 541 | 18 | 54 | 72 | 6 | .233 | .313 | .395 | $10 | 250 |
| **Mini-Browser** | **Age** | **AB** | **HR** | **R** | **RBI** | **SB** | **BA** | **OBP** | **SLG** | **$1L** | **Pts** |
| Tejada M | 36 | 509 | 11 | 66 | 66 | 6 | .281 | .321 | .415 | $13 | 320 |
| Headley C | 26 | 568 | 12 | 68 | 62 | 12 | .251 | .330 | .394 | $11 | 300 |
| Betemit W | 29 | 417 | 18 | 50 | 63 | 0 | .270 | .339 | .467 | $11 | 230 |
| Blake C | 37 | 442 | 15 | 60 | 65 | 5 | .260 | .335 | .444 | $10 | 260 |
| Callaspo A | 27 | 500 | 6 | 55 | 50 | 6 | .286 | .337 | .412 | $10 | 310 |

Minors (2010)

| Level | Leag | AB | HR | R | RBI | SB | BA | OBP | SLG | CT% | H% | BB% | Bash |
|---|---|---|---|---|---|---|---|---|---|---|---|---|---|
| A | MID | 5 | 0 | 0 | 1 | 0 | .400 | .400 | .800 | 60% | 67% | 0% | 2.00 |
| AA | — | — | — | — | — | — | — | — | — | — | — | — | — |
| AAA | — | — | — | — | — | — | — | — | — | — | — | — | — |

Competition at 3B — Stats in 2010

| Bats | Player | GSvR | GSvL | Sub | OPS |
|---|---|---|---|---|---|
| RH | Inge B | 96 | 42 | 6 | .718 |
| LH | Kelly D | 12 | 0 | 3 | .646 |

Ten-Year Trends (SLG, OBP, BA)

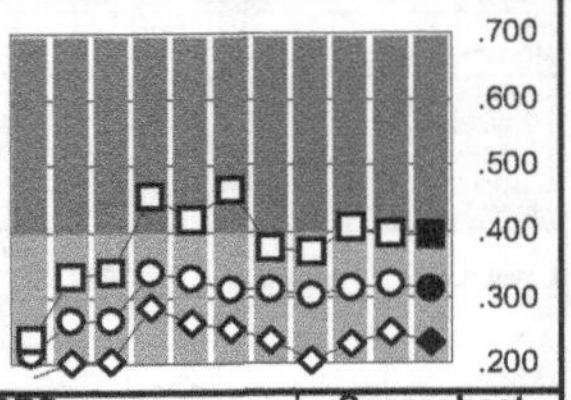

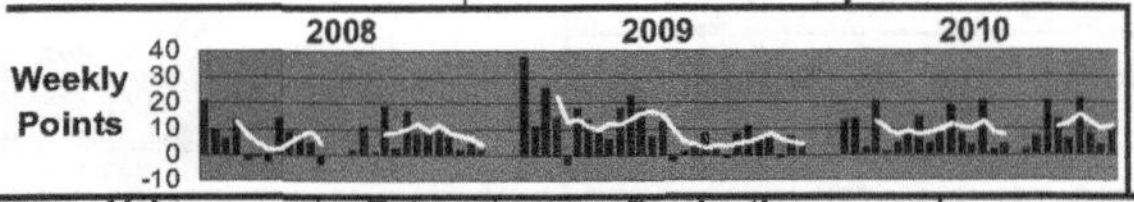

Majors

| Yr | Team | AB | HR | R | RBI | SB | BA | OBP | SLG | CT% | H% | BB% | Bash |
|---|---|---|---|---|---|---|---|---|---|---|---|---|---|
| 07 | DET | 508 | 14 | 64 | 71 | 9 | .236 | .312 | .376 | 70% | 34% | 8% | 1.59 |
| 08 | DET | 347 | 11 | 41 | 51 | 4 | .205 | .303 | .369 | 73% | 28% | 11% | 1.80 |
| 09 | DET | 562 | 27 | 71 | 84 | 2 | .230 | .314 | .406 | 70% | 33% | 8% | 1.77 |
| 10 | DET | 514 | 13 | 47 | 70 | 4 | .247 | .321 | .397 | 74% | 33% | 9% | 1.61 |

| Yr | $1L | $2L | Pts | RAA | 2B | 3B | CS | FB-LD-GB | HR/fb | RBI% | RS% | OPS | 1st Hf | 2nd Hf | vs RH | vs LH | Rnge | vRH | vLH |
|---|---|---|---|---|---|---|---|---|---|---|---|---|---|---|---|---|---|---|---|
| 07 | $11 | $0 | 240 | –18 | 25 | 2 | 2 | 41-22-37 | 10% | 21% | 30% | .688 | .761 | .607 | .621 | .923 | 2.73 | –14 | +39 |
| 08 | $6 | -$1 | 170 | –16 | 16 | 4 | 3 | 46-17-37 | 9% | 21% | 27% | .672 | .729 | .629 | .657 | .720 | 2.73 | –25 | +67 |
| 09 | $16 | $14 | 270 | –16 | 16 | 1 | 5 | 44-15-41 | 15% | 17% | 25% | .720 | .876 | .542 | .675 | .854 | — | –33 | +92 |
| 10 | $13 | $7 | 250 | –9 | 28 | 5 | 3 | 45-17-38 | 7% | 19% | 20% | .718 | .754 | .667 | .681 | .817 | 2.70 | –24 | +65 |

## Joe Inglett — 75 PA | $-3 | 40 pts

OF-24 (RF-14, LF-10), 2B-8 — Owned: 1% — LH

Instead of becoming the 2010 incarnation of Casey McGehee by stepping in for an injured regular, Inglett became Milwaukee's top pinch-hitter, racking up a .294/.377/.485 line. His plate patience and occasional pop, plus versatility, make him a great asset in a reserve role, but he will never be more than a fill-in. (MS)

| Player | Age | AB | HR | R | RBI | SB | BA | OBP | SLG | $1L | Pts |
|---|---|---|---|---|---|---|---|---|---|---|---|
| Inglett J | 32 | 67 | 1 | 8 | 7 | 2 | .278 | .343 | .403 | -$3 | 40 |
| **Mini-Browser** | **Age** | **AB** | **HR** | **R** | **RBI** | **SB** | **BA** | **OBP** | **SLG** | **$1L** | **Pts** |
| Tuiasosopo M | 24 | 132 | 5 | 15 | 15 | 0 | .227 | .316 | .377 | -$3 | 60 |
| Roberts R | 30 | 67 | 2 | 9 | 8 | 2 | .267 | .355 | .426 | -$3 | 50 |
| Ryal R | 28 | 90 | 3 | 11 | 10 | 0 | .245 | .297 | .423 | -$3 | 40 |
| Thomas C | 27 | 88 | 2 | 11 | 9 | 4 | .238 | .320 | .380 | -$3 | 50 |
| Gross G | 31 | 88 | 2 | 11 | 11 | 2 | .249 | .339 | .402 | -$3 | 50 |

Minors (2010)

| Level | Leag | AB | HR | R | RBI | SB | BA | OBP | SLG | CT% | H% | BB% | Bash |
|---|---|---|---|---|---|---|---|---|---|---|---|---|---|
| A | — | — | — | — | — | — | — | — | — | — | — | — | — |
| AA | — | — | — | — | — | — | — | — | — | — | — | — | — |
| AAA | — | — | — | — | — | — | — | — | — | — | — | — | — |

Competition at RF — Stats in 2010

| Bats | Player | GSvR | GSvL | Sub | OPS |
|---|---|---|---|---|---|
| RH | Hart C | 91 | 47 | 3 | .865 |
| LH | Inglett J | 8 | 2 | 4 | .733 |

Ten-Year Trends (SLG, OBP, BA)

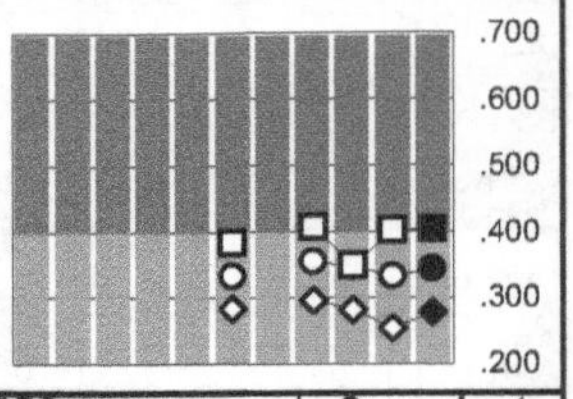

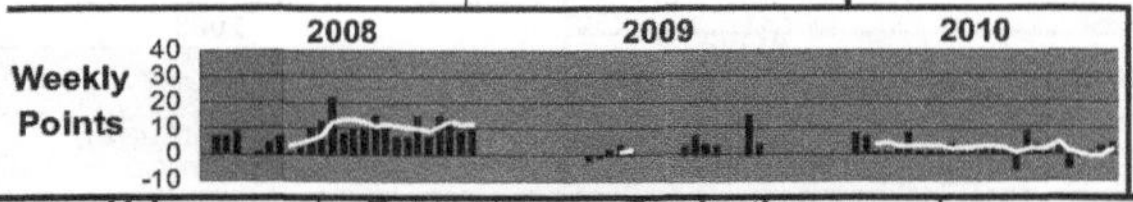

Majors

| Yr | Team | AB | HR | R | RBI | SB | BA | OBP | SLG | CT% | H% | BB% | Bash |
|---|---|---|---|---|---|---|---|---|---|---|---|---|---|
| 07 | TOR | 5 | 0 | 0 | 2 | 1 | .600 | .600 | 1.000 | 100% | 60% | 0% | 1.67 |
| 08 | TOR | 344 | 3 | 45 | 39 | 9 | .297 | .355 | .407 | 88% | 34% | 7% | 1.37 |
| 09 | TOR | 89 | 0 | 11 | 6 | 3 | .281 | .347 | .348 | 76% | 37% | 8% | 1.24 |
| 10 | MIL | 142 | 1 | 15 | 8 | 1 | .254 | .331 | .401 | 76% | 33% | 9% | 1.58 |

| Yr | $1L | $2L | Pts | RAA | 2B | 3B | CS | FB-LD-GB | HR/fb | RBI% | RS% | OPS | 1st Hf | 2nd Hf | vs RH | vs LH | Rnge | vRH | vLH |
|---|---|---|---|---|---|---|---|---|---|---|---|---|---|---|---|---|---|---|---|
| 07 | -$3 | -$19 | 10 | +1 | 0 | 1 | 0 | 20-40-40 | 0% | 100% | 0% | 1.600 | — | 1.600 | 2.000 | .000 | — | +22 | –78 |
| 08 | $9 | -$2 | 220 | –7 | 15 | 7 | 2 | 26-25-49 | 4% | 22% | 32% | .762 | .801 | .734 | .767 | .708 | — | +25 | –83 |
| 09 | -$1 | -$16 | 40 | –3 | 4 | 1 | 1 | 42-23-35 | 0% | 15% | 32% | .695 | .397 | .804 | .705 | .400 | — | +20 | –72 |
| 10 | -$3 | -$17 | 60 | –5 | 8 | 5 | 0 | 45-20-34 | 2% | 11% | 27% | .733 | .923 | .560 | .782 | .419 | 2.08 | +18 | –69 |

## Travis Ishikawa — 100 PA | $-2 | 50 pts

1B-73 — Owned: 0% — LH

Ishikawa is not eligible for arbitration until 2012, and his defense at first base is far better than that of anyone else on the Giants' 40-man. It doesn't bode well for him that his glove, and a lack of competition, are the best things that he has going for him, but those will keep him with San Francisco in 2011. (PB)

| Player | Age | AB | HR | R | RBI | SB | BA | OBP | SLG | $1L | Pts |
|---|---|---|---|---|---|---|---|---|---|---|---|
| Ishikawa T | 27 | 92 | 3 | 12 | 12 | 1 | .249 | .320 | .423 | -$2 | 50 |
| **Mini-Browser** | **Age** | **AB** | **HR** | **R** | **RBI** | **SB** | **BA** | **OBP** | **SLG** | **$1L** | **Pts** |
| Sweeney M | 37 | 135 | 5 | 14 | 20 | 0 | .267 | .323 | .428 | -$1 | 80 |
| Gload R | 34 | 144 | 3 | 17 | 18 | 2 | .270 | .316 | .404 | -$1 | 90 |
| Trumbo M | 25 | 178 | 8 | 16 | 22 | 2 | .214 | .257 | .406 | -$2 | 80 |
| Brown J | 27 | 132 | 3 | 15 | 15 | 0 | .261 | .321 | .409 | -$2 | 70 |
| Gamel M | 25 | 112 | 5 | 14 | 15 | 1 | .235 | .317 | .432 | -$2 | 60 |

Minors (2010)

| Level | Leag | AB | HR | R | RBI | SB | BA | OBP | SLG | CT% | H% | BB% | Bash |
|---|---|---|---|---|---|---|---|---|---|---|---|---|---|
| A | — | — | — | — | — | — | — | — | — | — | — | — | — |
| AA | — | — | — | — | — | — | — | — | — | — | — | — | — |
| AAA | — | — | — | — | — | — | — | — | — | — | — | — | — |

Competition at 1B — Stats in 2010

| Bats | Player | GSvR | GSvL | Sub | OPS |
|---|---|---|---|---|---|
| LH | Huff A | 70 | 29 | 1 | .891 |
| RH | Posey B | 19 | 11 | 0 | .862 |
| LH | Ishikawa T | 24 | 1 | 48 | .712 |
| BH | Sandoval P | 8 | 3 | 0 | .732 |

Ten-Year Trends (SLG, OBP, BA)

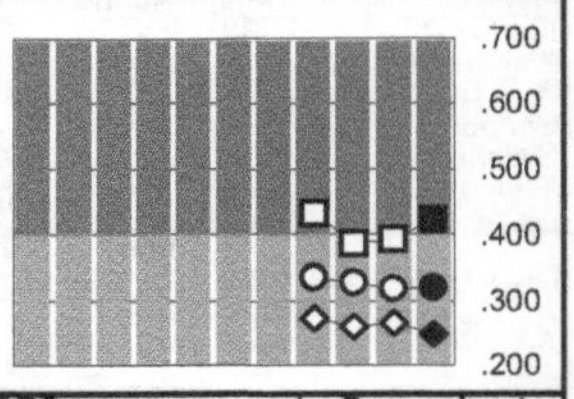

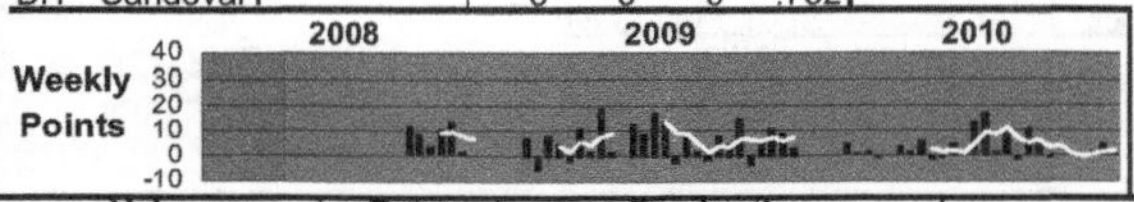

Majors

| Yr | Team | AB | HR | R | RBI | SB | BA | OBP | SLG | CT% | H% | BB% | Bash |
|---|---|---|---|---|---|---|---|---|---|---|---|---|---|
| 07 | — | — | — | — | — | — | — | — | — | — | — | — | — |
| 08 | SF | 95 | 3 | 12 | 15 | 1 | .274 | .337 | .432 | 72% | 38% | 9% | 1.58 |
| 09 | SF | 326 | 9 | 49 | 39 | 2 | .261 | .329 | .387 | 73% | 36% | 8% | 1.48 |
| 10 | SF | 158 | 3 | 18 | 22 | 0 | .266 | .320 | .392 | 82% | 33% | 7% | 1.48 |

| Yr | $1L | $2L | Pts | RAA | 2B | 3B | CS | FB-LD-GB | HR/fb | RBI% | RS% | OPS | 1st Hf | 2nd Hf | vs RH | vs LH | Rnge | vRH | vLH |
|---|---|---|---|---|---|---|---|---|---|---|---|---|---|---|---|---|---|---|---|
| 07 | — | — | — | — | — | — | — | — | — | — | — | — | — | — | — | — | 1.85 | +22 | –70 |
| 08 | -$1 | -$14 | 50 | –1 | 6 | 0 | 0 | 26-18-56 | 17% | 28% | 28% | .768 | — | .768 | .777 | .333 | 1.85 | +23 | –72 |
| 09 | $6 | -$5 | 160 | –14 | 10 | 2 | 2 | 37-18-45 | 10% | 17% | 36% | .715 | .754 | .659 | .730 | .594 | 1.85 | +22 | –73 |
| 10 | $0 | -$14 | 90 | –6 | 11 | 0 | 0 | 32-25-42 | 7% | 19% | 29% | .712 | .933 | .558 | .768 | .269 | 1.87 | +20 | –73 |

## Akinori Iwamura — 50 PA | $-5 | 20 pts

2B-40, 3B-10 — Owned: 1% — LH

Iwamura in 2010 did not show much in two different big-league opportunities. He does not hit well enough to play 3B, but his defense at 2B is slipping. His best chance for regular play in 2011 might lie in Japan. If Iwamura stays in the States, he will probably have to try to win a job on a minor-league contract. (ML)

| Player | Age | AB | HR | R | RBI | SB | BA | OBP | SLG | $1L | Pts |
|---|---|---|---|---|---|---|---|---|---|---|---|
| Iwamura A | 32 | 45 | 1 | 7 | 3 | 1 | .258 | .342 | .367 | -$5 | 20 |
| **Mini-Browser** | **Age** | **AB** | **HR** | **R** | **RBI** | **SB** | **BA** | **OBP** | **SLG** | **$1L** | **Pts** |
| Miles A | 34 | 74 | 1 | 8 | 5 | 1 | .263 | .302 | .330 | -$4 | 40 |
| Zawadzki L | 25 | 65 | 1 | 6 | 6 | 2 | .194 | .277 | .321 | -$4 | 30 |
| Forsythe L | 24 | 72 | 1 | 9 | 6 | 1 | .201 | .320 | .297 | -$4 | 30 |
| Havens R | 24 | 42 | 3 | 5 | 6 | 1 | .202 | .307 | .419 | -$4 | 20 |
| McCoy M | 29 | 44 | 1 | 6 | 4 | 2 | .239 | .329 | .331 | -$5 | 30 |

Minors (2010)

| Level | Leag | AB | HR | R | RBI | SB | BA | OBP | SLG | CT% | H% | BB% | Bash |
|---|---|---|---|---|---|---|---|---|---|---|---|---|---|
| A | — | — | — | — | — | — | — | — | — | — | — | — | — |
| AA | — | — | — | — | — | — | — | — | — | — | — | — | — |
| AAA | IL | 163 | 3 | 26 | 16 | 0 | .264 | .404 | .393 | 80% | 33% | 19% | 1.49 |

Competition at 2B — Stats in 2010

| Bats | Player | GSvR | GSvL | Sub | OPS |
|---|---|---|---|---|---|
| RH | Ellis M | 86 | 27 | 3 | .739 |
| RH | Rosales A | 28 | 17 | 2 | .721 |

Ten-Year Trends (SLG, OBP, BA)

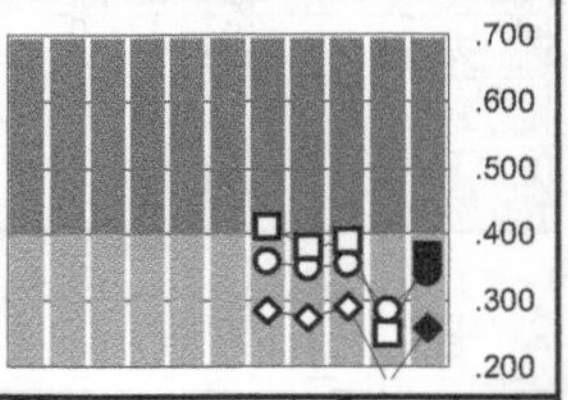

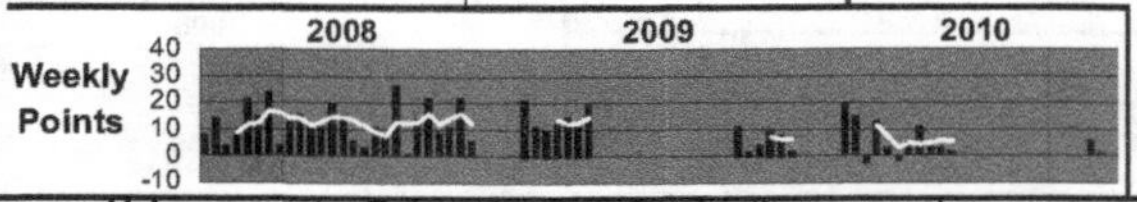

Majors

| Yr | Team | AB | HR | R | RBI | SB | BA | OBP | SLG | CT% | H% | BB% | Bash |
|---|---|---|---|---|---|---|---|---|---|---|---|---|---|
| 07 | TB | 491 | 7 | 82 | 34 | 12 | .285 | .359 | .411 | 77% | 37% | 10% | 1.44 |
| 08 | TB | 627 | 6 | 91 | 48 | 8 | .274 | .349 | .380 | 79% | 35% | 10% | 1.38 |
| 09 | TB | 231 | 1 | 28 | 22 | 9 | .290 | .355 | .390 | 81% | 36% | 9% | 1.34 |
| 10 | 2TM | 196 | 2 | 21 | 13 | 3 | .173 | .285 | .250 | 79% | 22% | 14% | 1.44 |

| Yr | $1L | $2L | Pts | RAA | 2B | 3B | CS | FB-LD-GB | HR/fb | RBI% | RS% | OPS | 1st Hf | 2nd Hf | vs RH | vs LH | Rnge | vRH | vLH |
|---|---|---|---|---|---|---|---|---|---|---|---|---|---|---|---|---|---|---|---|
| 07 | $13 | $2 | 280 | +6 | 21 | 10 | 8 | 34-20-46 | 6% | 15% | 39% | .770 | .815 | .740 | .728 | .862 | — | — | — |
| 08 | $14 | $4 | 330 | –2 | 30 | 9 | 6 | 33-20-47 | 4% | 18% | 35% | .729 | .723 | .738 | .756 | .668 | — | +9 | –24 |
| 09 | $4 | -$9 | 140 | +3 | 16 | 2 | 1 | 36-21-44 | 1% | 17% | 30% | .745 | .784 | .665 | .660 | .942 | 4.16 | +12 | –33 |
| 10 | -$4 | -$19 | 80 | –13 | 7 | 1 | 1 | 32-12-56 | 4% | 14% | 30% | .535 | .558 | .411 | .586 | .338 | 4.21 | +15 | –39 |

## Cesar Izturis — 500 PA | $4 | 240 pts

SS-150 — Owned: 0% — BH

Hail Cesar... but only for his glove. Izturis in 2010 posted his worst offensive season in his 10-year career, but he still started over 140 games. He wants to return to BAL, and they lack great depth at shortstop, so his return makes sense from that vantage. His SB success rate has fallen from 80% to 75% to 70%. (BJ)

| Player | Age | AB | HR | R | RBI | SB | BA | OBP | SLG | $1L | Pts |
|---|---|---|---|---|---|---|---|---|---|---|---|
| Izturis C | 31 | 458 | 0 | 45 | 30 | 15 | .262 | .306 | .319 | $4 | 240 |
| **Mini-Browser** | **Age** | **AB** | **HR** | **R** | **RBI** | **SB** | **BA** | **OBP** | **SLG** | **$1L** | **Pts** |
| Pennington C | 26 | 532 | 6 | 66 | 48 | 24 | .237 | .318 | .343 | $10 | 290 |
| Uribe J | 32 | 467 | 15 | 55 | 65 | 0 | .257 | .309 | .437 | $10 | 260 |
| Cedeno R | 28 | 467 | 10 | 50 | 50 | 10 | .257 | .305 | .384 | $8 | 230 |
| Ryan B | 29 | 460 | 5 | 60 | 35 | 15 | .250 | .309 | .340 | $7 | 260 |
| Cabrera O | 36 | 366 | 4 | 48 | 36 | 8 | .273 | .316 | .365 | $6 | 220 |

Minors (2010)

| Level | Leag | AB | HR | R | RBI | SB | BA | OBP | SLG | CT% | H% | BB% | Bash |
|---|---|---|---|---|---|---|---|---|---|---|---|---|---|
| A | — | — | — | — | — | — | — | — | — | — | — | — | — |
| AA | — | — | — | — | — | — | — | — | — | — | — | — | — |
| AAA | — | — | — | — | — | — | — | — | — | — | — | — | — |

Competition at SS — Stats in 2010

| Bats | Player | GSvR | GSvL | Sub | OPS |
|---|---|---|---|---|---|
| BH | Izturis C | 99 | 43 | 8 | .545 |
| RH | Lugo J | 10 | 7 | 9 | .581 |

Ten-Year Trends (SLG, OBP, BA)

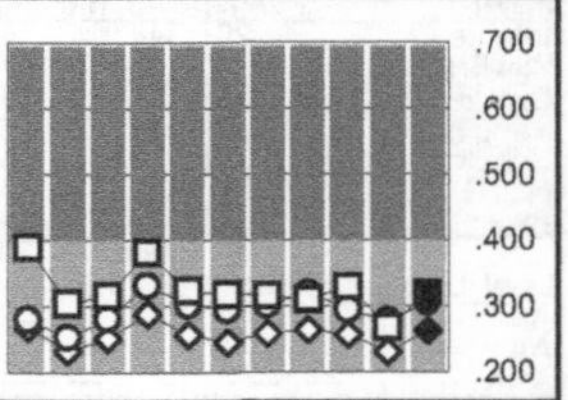

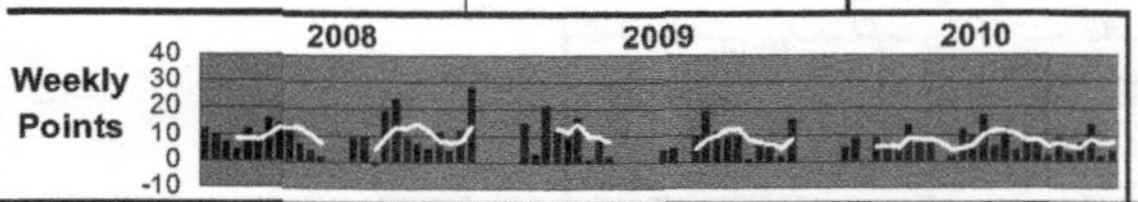

Majors

| Yr | Team | AB | HR | R | RBI | SB | BA | OBP | SLG | CT% | H% | BB% | Bash |
|---|---|---|---|---|---|---|---|---|---|---|---|---|---|
| 07 | 2TM | 314 | 0 | 31 | 16 | 3 | .258 | .302 | .315 | 94% | 27% | 6% | 1.22 |
| 08 | STL | 414 | 1 | 50 | 24 | 24 | .263 | .319 | .309 | 94% | 28% | 6% | 1.17 |
| 09 | BAL | 387 | 2 | 34 | 30 | 12 | .256 | .294 | .328 | 90% | 28% | 4% | 1.28 |
| 10 | BAL | 473 | 1 | 42 | 28 | 11 | .230 | .277 | .268 | 89% | 26% | 5% | 1.17 |

| Yr | $1L | $2L | Pts | RAA | 2B | 3B | CS | FB-LD-GB | HR/fb | RBI% | RS% | OPS | 1st Hf | 2nd Hf | vs RH | vs LH | Rnge | vRH | vLH |
|---|---|---|---|---|---|---|---|---|---|---|---|---|---|---|---|---|---|---|---|
| 07 | -$2 | -$14 | 150 | –10 | 14 | 2 | 3 | 28-23-49 | 0% | 12% | 31% | .618 | .593 | .654 | .689 | .428 | 4.78 | –4 | +13 |
| 08 | $8 | -$4 | 250 | –9 | 10 | 3 | 6 | 31-22-47 | 1% | 12% | 34% | .628 | .611 | .648 | .569 | .723 | 4.76 | +16 | –46 |
| 09 | $4 | -$9 | 190 | –11 | 14 | 4 | 4 | 30-20-49 | 2% | 14% | 27% | .622 | .617 | .626 | .580 | .705 | 4.81 | +3 | –4 |
| 10 | $2 | -$12 | 190 | –29 | 13 | 1 | 5 | 35-19-46 | 1% | 12% | 29% | .545 | .569 | .518 | .561 | .504 | 4.82 | –17 | +37 |

*For more stats, visit www.Rotolympus.com.*

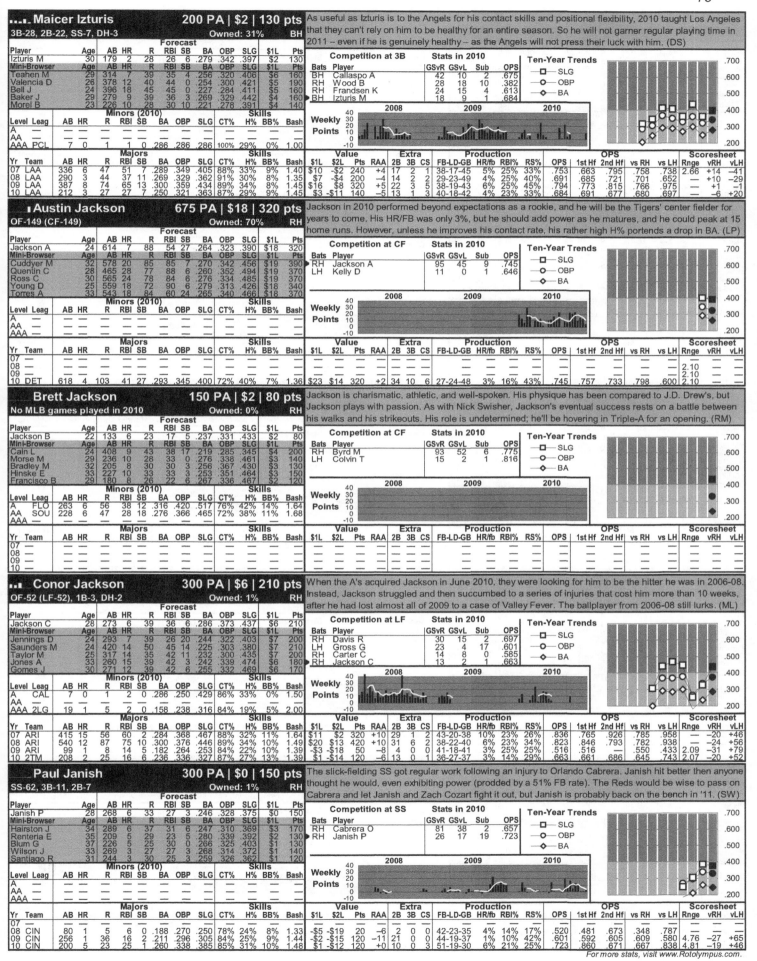

## Maicer Izturis — 200 PA | $2 | 130 pts
3B-28, 2B-22, SS-7, DH-3  Owned: 31%  BH

As useful as Izturis is to the Angels for his contact skills and positional flexibility, 2010 taught Los Angeles that they can't rely on him to be healthy for an entire season. So he will not garner regular playing time in 2011 – even if he is genuinely healthy – as the Angels will not press their luck with him. (DS)

| Player | Age | AB | HR | R | RBI | SB | BA | OBP | SLG | $1L | Pts |
|---|---|---|---|---|---|---|---|---|---|---|---|
| Izturis M | 30 | 179 | 2 | 28 | 26 | 6 | .279 | .342 | .397 | $2 | 130 |
| Teahen M | 29 | 314 | 7 | 39 | 35 | 4 | .256 | .320 | .406 | $6 | 160 |
| Valencia D | 26 | 378 | 12 | 40 | 44 | 0 | .254 | .300 | .425 | $5 | 190 |
| Bell J | 24 | 396 | 18 | 45 | 45 | 0 | .227 | .284 | .411 | $5 | 160 |
| Baker J | 29 | 279 | 9 | 39 | 36 | 3 | .269 | .329 | .442 | $4 | 160 |
| Morel B | 23 | 280 | 10 | 28 | 30 | 10 | .221 | .278 | .391 | $4 | 140 |

Competition at 3B:
BH Callaspo A 42 10 2 .675
RH Wood B 28 18 10 .382
RH Frandsen K 24 15 4 .613
BH Izturis M 18 9 1 .684

Ten-Year Trends: SLG, OBP, BA

Minors (2010) — AAA PCL 7 0 1 1 0 .286 .286 .286 100% 29% 0% 1.00

| Yr | Team | AB | HR | R | RBI | SB | BA | OBP | SLG | CT% | H% | BB% | Bash | $1L | $2L | Pts | RAA |
|---|---|---|---|---|---|---|---|---|---|---|---|---|---|---|---|---|---|
| 07 | LAA | 336 | 6 | 47 | 51 | 7 | .289 | .349 | .405 | 88% | 33% | 9% | 1.40 | $10 | -$2 | 240 | +4 |
| 08 | LAA | 290 | 3 | 44 | 37 | 11 | .269 | .329 | .362 | 91% | 30% | 8% | 1.35 | $7 | -$4 | 200 | -4 |
| 09 | LAA | 387 | 8 | 74 | 65 | 13 | .300 | .359 | .434 | 89% | 34% | 8% | 1.45 | $16 | $8 | 320 | +5 |
| 10 | LAA | 212 | 3 | 27 | 27 | 7 | .250 | .321 | .363 | 87% | 29% | 9% | 1.45 | $3 | -$11 | 140 | -5 |

## Austin Jackson — 675 PA | $18 | 320 pts
OF-149 (CF-149)  Owned: 70%  RH

Jackson in 2010 performed beyond expectations as a rookie, and he will be the Tigers' center fielder for years to come. His HR/FB was only 3%, but he should add power as he matures, and he could peak at 15 home runs. However, unless he improves his contact rate, his rather high H% portends a drop in BA. (LP)

| Player | Age | AB | HR | R | RBI | SB | BA | OBP | SLG | $1L | Pts |
|---|---|---|---|---|---|---|---|---|---|---|---|
| Jackson A | 24 | 614 | 7 | 88 | 54 | 27 | .264 | .323 | .390 | $18 | 320 |
| Cuddyer M | 32 | 578 | 20 | 85 | 85 | 7 | .270 | .342 | .456 | $19 | 390 |
| Quentin C | 28 | 465 | 28 | 77 | 88 | 6 | .260 | .352 | .494 | $19 | 370 |
| Ross D | 30 | 565 | 24 | 78 | 84 | 6 | .276 | .334 | .485 | $19 | 370 |
| Young D | 25 | 559 | 14 | 72 | 90 | 6 | .279 | .313 | .466 | $18 | 340 |
| Torres A | 33 | 543 | 18 | 84 | 60 | 24 | .265 | .340 | .466 | $18 | 370 |

Competition at CF:
RH Jackson A 95 45 9 .745
LH Kelly D 11 0 1 .646

| Yr | Team | AB | HR | R | RBI | SB | BA | OBP | SLG | CT% | H% | BB% | Bash | $1L | $2L | Pts | RAA |
|---|---|---|---|---|---|---|---|---|---|---|---|---|---|---|---|---|---|
| 10 | DET | 618 | 4 | 103 | 41 | 27 | .293 | .345 | .400 | 72% | 40% | 7% | 1.36 | $23 | $14 | 320 | +2 |

## Brett Jackson — 150 PA | $2 | 80 pts
No MLB games played in 2010  Owned: 0%  RH

Jackson is charismatic, athletic, and well-spoken. His physique has been compared to J.D. Drew's, but Jackson plays with passion. As with Nick Swisher, Jackson's eventual success rests on a battle between his walks and his strikeouts. His role is undetermined; he'll be hovering in Triple-A for an opening. (RM)

| Player | Age | AB | HR | R | RBI | SB | BA | OBP | SLG | $1L | Pts |
|---|---|---|---|---|---|---|---|---|---|---|---|
| Jackson B | 22 | 133 | 6 | 23 | 17 | 5 | .237 | .331 | .433 | $2 | 80 |
| Cain L | 24 | 408 | 9 | 43 | 38 | 17 | .219 | .285 | .345 | $4 | 200 |
| Morse M | 29 | 236 | 10 | 28 | 33 | 0 | .276 | .338 | .461 | $3 | 140 |
| Bradley M | 32 | 205 | 8 | 30 | 30 | 3 | .256 | .347 | .430 | $3 | 130 |
| Hinske E | 33 | 227 | 10 | 33 | 33 | 3 | .253 | .351 | .464 | $3 | 150 |
| Francisco B | 29 | 180 | 8 | 26 | 22 | 6 | .267 | .336 | .467 | $2 | 120 |

Competition at CF:
RH Byrd M 93 52 6 .775
LH Colvin T 15 2 1 .816

Minors (2010):
A FLO 263 6 56 38 12 .316 .420 .517 76% 42% 14% 1.64
AA SOU 228 6 47 28 18 .276 .366 .465 72% 38% 11% 1.68

## Conor Jackson — 300 PA | $6 | 210 pts
OF-52 (LF-52), 1B-3, DH-2  Owned: 1%  RH

When the A's acquired Jackson in June 2010, they were looking for him to be the hitter he was in 2006-08. Instead, Jackson struggled and then succumbed to a series of injuries that cost him more than 10 weeks, after he had lost almost all of 2009 to a case of Valley Fever. The ballplayer from 2006-08 still lurks. (ML)

| Player | Age | AB | HR | R | RBI | SB | BA | OBP | SLG | $1L | Pts |
|---|---|---|---|---|---|---|---|---|---|---|---|
| Jackson C | 28 | 273 | 6 | 39 | 36 | 6 | .286 | .373 | .437 | $6 | 210 |
| Jennings D | 24 | 293 | 7 | 39 | 26 | 20 | .244 | .322 | .403 | $7 | 200 |
| Saunders M | 24 | 420 | 14 | 50 | 45 | 14 | .225 | .303 | .380 | $7 | 210 |
| Taylor M | 25 | 317 | 14 | 35 | 42 | 11 | .242 | .300 | .435 | $7 | 200 |
| Jones A | 33 | 260 | 15 | 39 | 42 | 3 | .242 | .339 | .474 | $6 | 180 |
| Gomes J | 30 | 271 | 12 | 39 | 42 | 6 | .255 | .332 | .469 | $6 | 170 |

Competition at LF:
RH Davis R 30 15 2 .697
LH Gross G 23 4 17 .601
RH Carter C 14 8 0 .585
RH Jackson C 13 2 1 .663

Minors (2010):
A CAL 7 0 1 2 0 .286 .250 .429 86% 33% 0% 1.50
AAA 2LG 19 1 5 2 0 .158 .238 .316 84% 19% 5% 2.00

| Yr | Team | AB | HR | R | RBI | SB | BA | OBP | SLG | CT% | H% | BB% | Bash | $1L | $2L | Pts | RAA |
|---|---|---|---|---|---|---|---|---|---|---|---|---|---|---|---|---|---|
| 07 | ARI | 415 | 15 | 56 | 60 | 2 | .284 | .368 | .467 | 88% | 32% | 11% | 1.64 | $11 | -$2 | 320 | +10 |
| 08 | ARI | 540 | 12 | 87 | 75 | 10 | .300 | .376 | .446 | 89% | 34% | 10% | 1.49 | $20 | $13 | 420 | +10 |
| 09 | ARI | 99 | 1 | 9 | 14 | 5 | .182 | .264 | .253 | 84% | 22% | 10% | 1.39 | -$3 | -$18 | 120 | -6 |
| 10 | 2TM | 208 | 2 | 25 | 16 | 6 | .236 | .336 | .327 | 87% | 27% | 14% | 1.39 | $1 | -$12 | 120 | -6 |

## Paul Janish — 300 PA | $0 | 150 pts
SS-62, 3B-11, 2B-7  Owned: 1%  RH

The slick-fielding SS got regular work following an injury to Orlando Cabrera. Janish hit better then anyone thought he would, even exhibiting power (prodded by a 51% FB rate). The Reds would be wise to pass on Cabrera and let Janish and Zach Cozart fight it out, but Janish is probably back on the bench in '11. (SW)

| Player | Age | AB | HR | R | RBI | SB | BA | OBP | SLG | $1L | Pts |
|---|---|---|---|---|---|---|---|---|---|---|---|
| Janish P | 28 | 268 | 6 | 33 | 27 | 3 | .246 | .328 | .375 | $0 | 150 |
| Hairston J | 34 | 289 | 6 | 37 | 31 | 6 | .247 | .310 | .369 | $2 | 170 |
| Renteria E | 35 | 209 | 5 | 29 | 23 | 6 | .280 | .339 | .392 | $2 | 130 |
| Blum G | 37 | 226 | 5 | 25 | 30 | 0 | .266 | .325 | .403 | $1 | 130 |
| Wilson J | 33 | 269 | 3 | 27 | 27 | 3 | .258 | .314 | .372 | $1 | 140 |
| Santiago R | 31 | 244 | 3 | 30 | 25 | 3 | .259 | .326 | .362 | $1 | 120 |

Competition at SS:
RH Cabrera O 81 38 2 .657
RH Janish P 26 17 19 .723

| Yr | Team | AB | HR | R | RBI | SB | BA | OBP | SLG | CT% | H% | BB% | Bash | $1L | $2L | Pts | RAA |
|---|---|---|---|---|---|---|---|---|---|---|---|---|---|---|---|---|---|
| 08 | CIN | 80 | 1 | 5 | 6 | 0 | .188 | .270 | .250 | 78% | 24% | 8% | 1.33 | -$5 | -$19 | 20 | -6 |
| 09 | CIN | 256 | 1 | 36 | 16 | 2 | .211 | .296 | .305 | 84% | 25% | 9% | 1.44 | -$2 | -$15 | 120 | -11 |
| 10 | CIN | 200 | 5 | 23 | 25 | 1 | .260 | .338 | .385 | 85% | 31% | 10% | 1.48 | $1 | -$12 | 120 | +0 |

*For more stats, visit www.Rotolympus.com.*

## Jason Jaramillo — 50 PA | $-2 | 20 pts
CA-31 — Owned: 0% — BH

Jaramillo in 2010 was awful in limited playing time with Pittsburgh, and he wasn't much better in Triple-A. He is basically 40-man roster depth, but he could luck into a back-up role if either Ryan Doumit or Chris Snyder is traded. (MB)

### Forecast

| Player | Age | AB | HR | R | RBI | SB | BA | OBP | SLG | $1L | Pts |
|---|---|---|---|---|---|---|---|---|---|---|---|
| Jaramillo J | 28 | 45 | 1 | 5 | 5 | 0 | .246 | .320 | .357 | -$2 | 20 |

| Mini-Browser | Age | AB | HR | R | RBI | SB | BA | OBP | SLG | $1L | Pts |
|---|---|---|---|---|---|---|---|---|---|---|---|
| Nieves W | 33 | 68 | 1 | 6 | 8 | 0 | .241 | .289 | .322 | -$1 | 30 |
| Miller C | 35 | 44 | 2 | 5 | 6 | 0 | .238 | .327 | .374 | -$2 | 20 |
| McKenry M | 26 | 45 | 2 | 5 | 6 | 0 | .212 | .309 | .416 | -$2 | 20 |
| Santos O | 29 | 45 | 1 | 5 | 6 | 0 | .245 | .291 | .355 | -$2 | 20 |
| Anderson B | 24 | 45 | 1 | 5 | 5 | 0 | .250 | .313 | .356 | -$2 | 20 |

### Minors (2010) / Skills

| Level | Leag | AB | HR | R | RBI | SB | BA | OBP | SLG | CT% | H% | BB% | Bash |
|---|---|---|---|---|---|---|---|---|---|---|---|---|---|
| A | — | | | | | | | | | | | | |
| AA | — | | | | | | | | | | | | |
| AAA | IL | 88 | 1 | 3 | 13 | 0 | .239 | .281 | .307 | 82% | 29% | 5% | 1.29 |

### Majors / Skills

| Yr | Team | AB | HR | R | RBI | SB | BA | OBP | SLG | CT% | H% | BB% | Bash |
|---|---|---|---|---|---|---|---|---|---|---|---|---|---|
| 07 | — | | | | | | | | | | | | |
| 08 | — | | | | | | | | | | | | |
| 09 | PIT | 206 | 3 | 20 | 26 | 1 | .252 | .309 | .364 | 84% | 30% | 8% | 1.44 |
| 10 | PIT | 87 | 1 | 2 | 6 | 0 | .149 | .227 | .207 | 84% | 18% | 8% | 1.38 |

### Value / Extra / Production / OPS / Scoresheet

| Yr | $1L | $2L | Pts | RAA | 2B | 3B | CS | FB-LD-GB | HR/fb | RBI% | RS% | OPS | 1st Hf | 2nd Hf | vs RH | vs LH | Rnge | vRH | vLH |
|---|---|---|---|---|---|---|---|---|---|---|---|---|---|---|---|---|---|---|---|
| 07 | | | | | | | | | | | | | | | | | 0.60 | | |
| 08 | | | | | | | | | | | | | | | | | 0.60 | | |
| 09 | $3 | -$4 | 110 | -4 | 14 | 0 | 1 | 32-20-49 | 5% | 18% | 26% | .673 | .717 | .557 | .701 | .510 | 0.60 | | |
| 10 | -$4 | -$14 | 20 | -11 | 2 | 0 | 0 | 38-12-50 | 4% | 9% | 5% | .434 | .489 | .243 | .332 | .741 | 0.59 | -1 | +4 |

## John Jaso — 450 PA | $8 | 240 pts
CA-96, DH-9, 1B-1 — Owned: 11% — LH

The biggest surprise of 2010 for Tampa Bay, Jaso ascended to the starting catcher's job in his first full season thanks to a stellar OBP. Although his rates are apt to retreat, he is a favorite to win the starting job again in 2011, sharing time with Kelly Shoppach. (RZ)

### Forecast

| Player | Age | AB | HR | R | RBI | SB | BA | OBP | SLG | $1L | Pts |
|---|---|---|---|---|---|---|---|---|---|---|---|
| Jaso J | 27 | 402 | 9 | 50 | 45 | 0 | .246 | .344 | .372 | $8 | 240 |

| Mini-Browser | Age | AB | HR | R | RBI | SB | BA | OBP | SLG | $1L | Pts |
|---|---|---|---|---|---|---|---|---|---|---|---|
| Ruiz C | 32 | 370 | 9 | 45 | 54 | 5 | .280 | .375 | .431 | $11 | 270 |
| Pierzynski A | 34 | 468 | 10 | 50 | 50 | 0 | .267 | .300 | .388 | $10 | 250 |
| Baker J | 30 | 346 | 8 | 52 | 48 | 0 | .266 | .352 | .402 | $9 | 200 |
| Snyder C | 30 | 340 | 16 | 44 | 56 | 0 | .247 | .356 | .437 | $9 | 220 |
| Molina B | 36 | 310 | 10 | 29 | 46 | 0 | .273 | .306 | .422 | $8 | 190 |

### Minors (2010) / Skills

| Level | Leag | AB | HR | R | RBI | SB | BA | OBP | SLG | CT% | H% | BB% | Bash |
|---|---|---|---|---|---|---|---|---|---|---|---|---|---|
| A | — | | | | | | | | | | | | |
| AA | — | | | | | | | | | | | | |
| AAA | IL | 11 | 0 | 1 | 2 | 0 | .364 | .333 | .455 | 82% | 44% | 0% | 1.25 |

### Majors / Skills

| Yr | Team | AB | HR | R | RBI | SB | BA | OBP | SLG | CT% | H% | BB% | Bash |
|---|---|---|---|---|---|---|---|---|---|---|---|---|---|
| 07 | — | | | | | | | | | | | | |
| 08 | TB | 10 | 0 | 2 | 0 | 0 | .200 | .200 | .200 | 80% | 25% | 0% | 1.00 |
| 09 | — | | | | | | | | | | | | |
| 10 | TB | 339 | 5 | 57 | 44 | 4 | .263 | .372 | .378 | 88% | 30% | 15% | 1.44 |

### Value / Extra / Production / OPS / Scoresheet

| Yr | $1L | $2L | Pts | RAA | 2B | 3B | CS | FB-LD-GB | HR/fb | RBI% | RS% | OPS | 1st Hf | 2nd Hf | vs RH | vs LH | Rnge | vRH | vLH |
|---|---|---|---|---|---|---|---|---|---|---|---|---|---|---|---|---|---|---|---|
| 07 | | | | | | | | | | | | | | | | | | | |
| 08 | | | 0 | -1 | 0 | 0 | 0 | 38-25-38 | 0% | 0% | 100% | .400 | | .400 | .250 | 1.000 | 0.57 | | |
| 09 | | | | | | | | | | | | | | | | | 0.58 | +22 | -66 |
| 10 | TB | $11 | $5 | 260 | +6 | 18 | 3 | 0 | 37-17-46 | 5% | 23% | 36% | .750 | .771 | .727 | .772 | .610 | 0.62 | +23 | -67 |

## Jon Jay — 500 PA | $8 | 260 pts
OF-88 (RF-61, CF-27, LF-9) — Owned: 9% — LH

Jay's ridiculous July (.431/.500/.667) convinced the Cardinals that Ryan Ludwick was expendable. Jay's subsequent (and unsurprising) letdown left him with overall numbers that were more reflective of his skills. Between his fielding rep and LaRussa's "feel for the game," Jay should get most starts in RF vs. RH. (AB)

### Forecast

| Player | Age | AB | HR | R | RBI | SB | BA | OBP | SLG | $1L | Pts |
|---|---|---|---|---|---|---|---|---|---|---|---|
| Jay J | 26 | 458 | 10 | 60 | 45 | 10 | .262 | .326 | .384 | $8 | 260 |

| Mini-Browser | Age | AB | HR | R | RBI | SB | BA | OBP | SLG | $1L | Pts |
|---|---|---|---|---|---|---|---|---|---|---|---|
| Bernadina R | 26 | 466 | 10 | 55 | 45 | 25 | .236 | .307 | .359 | $9 | 260 |
| Kearns A | 30 | 402 | 10 | 60 | 55 | 5 | .261 | .355 | .397 | $9 | 240 |
| DeRosa M | 36 | 358 | 12 | 56 | 52 | 4 | .268 | .347 | .438 | $9 | 240 |
| Guillen J | 34 | 326 | 11 | 35 | 49 | 0 | .268 | .319 | .428 | $9 | 180 |
| Cabrera M | 26 | 472 | 10 | 55 | 50 | 10 | .265 | .331 | .379 | $8 | 310 |

### Minors (2010) / Skills

| Level | Leag | AB | HR | R | RBI | SB | BA | OBP | SLG | CT% | H% | BB% | Bash |
|---|---|---|---|---|---|---|---|---|---|---|---|---|---|
| A | — | | | | | | | | | | | | |
| AA | — | | | | | | | | | | | | |
| AAA | PCL | 165 | 4 | 31 | 32 | 13 | .321 | .394 | .491 | 87% | 37% | 9% | 1.53 |

### Majors / Skills

| Yr | Team | AB | HR | R | RBI | SB | BA | OBP | SLG | CT% | H% | BB% | Bash |
|---|---|---|---|---|---|---|---|---|---|---|---|---|---|
| 07 | — | | | | | | | | | | | | |
| 08 | — | | | | | | | | | | | | |
| 09 | — | | | | | | | | | | | | |
| 10 | STL | 287 | 4 | 47 | 27 | 2 | .300 | .359 | .422 | 83% | 36% | 7% | 1.41 |

### Value / Extra / Production / OPS / Scoresheet

| Yr | $1L | $2L | Pts | RAA | 2B | 3B | CS | FB-LD-GB | HR/fb | RBI% | RS% | OPS | 1st Hf | 2nd Hf | vs RH | vs LH | Rnge | vRH | vLH |
|---|---|---|---|---|---|---|---|---|---|---|---|---|---|---|---|---|---|---|---|
| 07 | | | | | | | | | | | | | | | | | 2.10 | | |
| 08 | | | | | | | | | | | | | | | | | | | |
| 09 | | | | | | | | | | | | | | | | | 2.10 | | |
| 10 | STL | $7 | -$5 | 170 | -5 | 19 | 2 | 4 | 32-19-49 | 5% | 19% | 39% | .780 | .989 | .715 | .791 | .741 | 2.10 | | |

## Desmond Jennings — 325 PA | $7 | 200 pts
OF-10 (RF-5, CF-4, LF-2), DH-2 — Owned: 0% — RH

This top prospect will eventually be patrolling the Rays' outfield, but he may take a detour in Triple-A to start the 2011 season. He has yet to be tested in the majors, but he has no apparent weakness, and he should be a future everyday player. (RZ)

### Forecast

| Player | Age | AB | HR | R | RBI | SB | BA | OBP | SLG | $1L | Pts |
|---|---|---|---|---|---|---|---|---|---|---|---|
| Jennings D | 24 | 293 | 7 | 39 | 26 | 20 | .244 | .322 | .403 | $7 | 200 |

| Mini-Browser | Age | AB | HR | R | RBI | SB | BA | OBP | SLG | $1L | Pts |
|---|---|---|---|---|---|---|---|---|---|---|---|
| Kearns A | 30 | 402 | 10 | 60 | 55 | 5 | .261 | .355 | .397 | $9 | 240 |
| DeRosa M | 36 | 358 | 12 | 56 | 52 | 4 | .268 | .347 | .438 | $9 | 240 |
| Guillen J | 34 | 326 | 11 | 35 | 49 | 0 | .268 | .319 | .428 | $9 | 180 |
| Cabrera M | 26 | 472 | 10 | 55 | 50 | 10 | .265 | .331 | .379 | $8 | 310 |
| Jay J | 26 | 458 | 10 | 60 | 45 | 10 | .262 | .326 | .384 | $8 | 260 |

### Minors (2010) / Skills

| Level | Leag | AB | HR | R | RBI | SB | BA | OBP | SLG | CT% | H% | BB% | Bash |
|---|---|---|---|---|---|---|---|---|---|---|---|---|---|
| A | — | | | | | | | | | | | | |
| AA | — | | | | | | | | | | | | |
| AAA | IL | 399 | 3 | 82 | 36 | 37 | .278 | .362 | .393 | 83% | 33% | 10% | 1.41 |

### Majors / Skills

| Yr | Team | AB | HR | R | RBI | SB | BA | OBP | SLG | CT% | H% | BB% | Bash |
|---|---|---|---|---|---|---|---|---|---|---|---|---|---|
| 07 | — | | | | | | | | | | | | |
| 08 | — | | | | | | | | | | | | |
| 09 | — | | | | | | | | | | | | |
| 10 | TB | 21 | 0 | 5 | 2 | 2 | .190 | .292 | .333 | 81% | 24% | 16% | 1.75 |

### Value / Extra / Production / OPS / Scoresheet

| Yr | $1L | $2L | Pts | RAA | 2B | 3B | CS | FB-LD-GB | HR/fb | RBI% | RS% | OPS | 1st Hf | 2nd Hf | vs RH | vs LH | Rnge | vRH | vLH |
|---|---|---|---|---|---|---|---|---|---|---|---|---|---|---|---|---|---|---|---|
| 07 | | | | | | | | | | | | | | | | | | | |
| 08 | | | | | | | | | | | | | | | | | 2.10 | | |
| 09 | | | | | | | | | | | | | | | | | 2.10 | | |
| 10 | TB | -$3 | -$20 | 12 | | | | | 41-12-47 | 0% | 18% | 71% | .625 | | .625 | .350 | .879 | 2.10 | | |

## Derek Jeter — 675 PA | $20 | 400 pts
SS-151, DH-5 — Owned: 100% — RH

The customarily consistent Jeter had an uncharacteristically terrible 2010. He slumped for three months and finished with career-worst numbers in virtually every hitting category. That said, the aberrant nature of this season suggests that we should not yet announce the start of a decline, even for a 36-year-old. (LS)

### Forecast

| Player | Age | AB | HR | R | RBI | SB | BA | OBP | SLG | $1L | Pts |
|---|---|---|---|---|---|---|---|---|---|---|---|
| Jeter D | 36 | 603 | 14 | 95 | 61 | 20 | .280 | .351 | .388 | $20 | 400 |

| Mini-Browser | Age | AB | HR | R | RBI | SB | BA | OBP | SLG | $1L | Pts |
|---|---|---|---|---|---|---|---|---|---|---|---|
| Ramirez H | 27 | 591 | 26 | 111 | 85 | 33 | .308 | .387 | .528 | $34 | 550 |
| Tulowitzki T | 26 | 589 | 27 | 108 | 101 | 14 | .298 | .373 | .531 | $29 | 500 |
| Rollins J | 32 | 639 | 21 | 105 | 77 | 35 | .274 | .335 | .472 | $26 | 550 |
| Reyes J | 27 | 544 | 12 | 90 | 54 | 42 | .287 | .348 | .457 | $24 | 460 |
| Ramirez A | 29 | 551 | 18 | 77 | 72 | 12 | .272 | .312 | .410 | $18 | 350 |

### Minors (2010) / Skills

| Level | Leag | AB | HR | R | RBI | SB | BA | OBP | SLG | CT% | H% | BB% | Bash |
|---|---|---|---|---|---|---|---|---|---|---|---|---|---|
| A | — | | | | | | | | | | | | |
| AA | — | | | | | | | | | | | | |
| AAA | — | | | | | | | | | | | | |

### Majors / Skills

| Yr | Team | AB | HR | R | RBI | SB | BA | OBP | SLG | CT% | H% | BB% | Bash |
|---|---|---|---|---|---|---|---|---|---|---|---|---|---|
| 07 | NYY | 639 | 12 | 102 | 73 | 15 | .322 | .388 | .452 | 84% | 38% | 8% | 1.40 |
| 08 | NYY | 596 | 11 | 88 | 69 | 11 | .300 | .363 | .408 | 86% | 35% | 8% | 1.36 |
| 09 | NYY | 634 | 18 | 107 | 66 | 30 | .334 | .406 | .465 | 89% | 37% | 10% | 1.39 |
| 10 | NYY | 663 | 10 | 111 | 67 | 18 | .270 | .340 | .370 | 84% | 32% | 8% | 1.37 |

### Value / Extra / Production / OPS / Scoresheet

| Yr | Team | $1L | $2L | Pts | RAA | 2B | 3B | CS | FB-LD-GB | HR/fb | RBI% | RS% | OPS | 1st Hf | 2nd Hf | vs RH | vs LH | Rnge | vRH | vLH |
|---|---|---|---|---|---|---|---|---|---|---|---|---|---|---|---|---|---|---|---|---|
| 07 | NYY | $26 | $19 | 400 | +32 | 39 | 4 | 8 | 24-20-56 | 9% | 21% | 34% | .840 | .871 | .803 | .830 | .876 | 4.71 | -24 | +61 |
| 08 | NYY | $21 | $12 | 380 | +16 | 25 | 3 | 8 | 24-18-58 | 9% | 22% | 34% | .771 | .740 | .815 | .750 | .822 | 4.67 | -21 | +59 |
| 09 | NYY | $31 | $23 | 500 | +51 | 27 | 1 | 5 | 23-20-57 | 15% | 18% | 33% | .871 | .857 | .888 | .817 | 1.010 | 4.69 | -17 | +65 |
| 10 | NYY | $23 | $15 | 410 | +45 | 30 | 3 | 5 | 18-16-66 | 10% | 17% | 42% | .710 | .732 | .683 | .632 | .874 | 4.74 | -26 | +65 |

*For more stats, visit www.Rotolympus.com.*

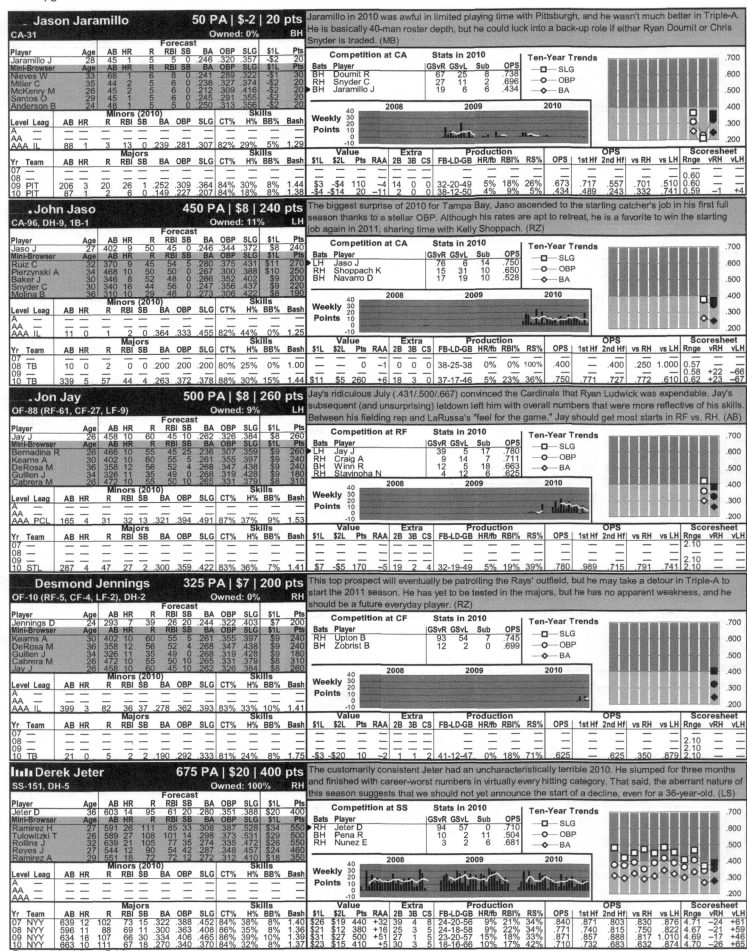

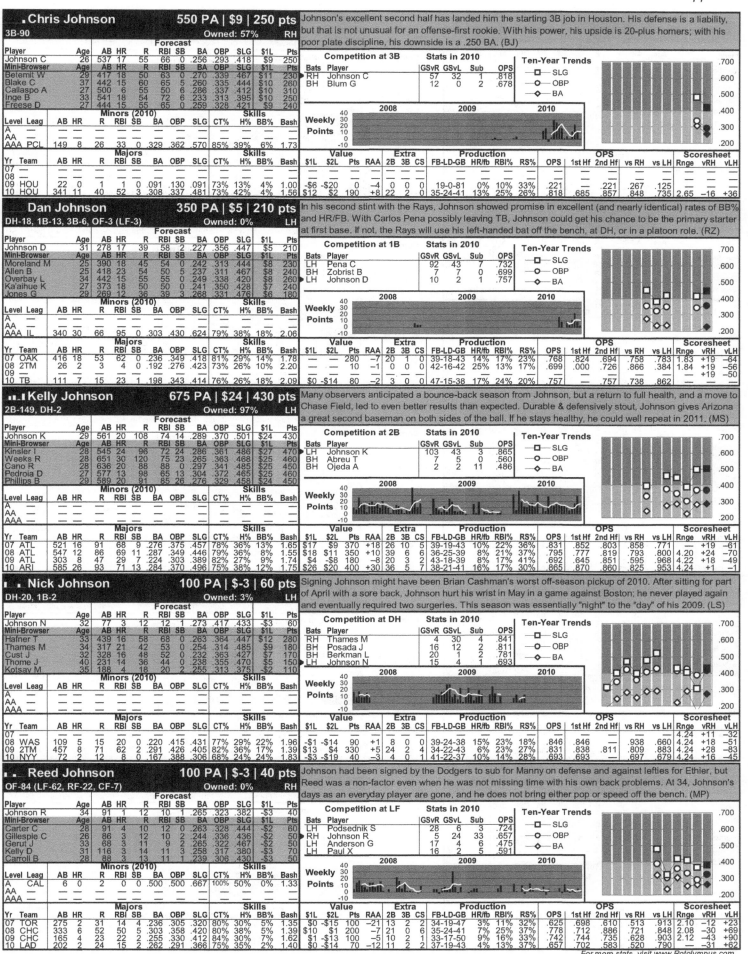

## Chris Johnson — 550 PA | $9 | 250 pts
3B-90 | Owned: 57% | RH

Johnson's excellent second half has landed him the starting 3B job in Houston. His defense is a liability, but that is not unusual for an offense-first rookie. With his power, his upside is 20-plus homers; with his poor plate discipline, his downside is a .250 BA. (BJ)

| Player | Age | AB | HR | R | RBI | SB | BA | OBP | SLG | $1L | Pts |
|---|---|---|---|---|---|---|---|---|---|---|---|
| Johnson C | 26 | 537 | 17 | 55 | 66 | 0 | .256 | .293 | .418 | $9 | 250 |
| Mini-Browser | Age | AB | HR | R | RBI | SB | BA | OBP | SLG | $1L | Pts |
| Betemit W | 29 | 417 | 18 | 50 | 63 | 0 | .270 | .339 | .467 | $11 | 230 |
| Blake C | 37 | 442 | 15 | 60 | 65 | 5 | .260 | .335 | .444 | $10 | 260 |
| Callaspo A | 27 | 500 | 6 | 55 | 50 | 6 | .286 | .337 | .412 | $10 | 310 |
| Inge B | 33 | 541 | 18 | 55 | 72 | 6 | .233 | .313 | .395 | $9 | 250 |
| Freese D | 27 | 444 | 15 | 55 | 65 | 0 | .259 | .328 | .421 | $9 | 240 |

Competition at 3B | Stats in 2010

| Bats | Player | GSvR | GSvL | Sub | OPS |
|---|---|---|---|---|---|
| RH | Johnson C | 57 | 32 | 1 | .818 |
| BH | Blum G | 12 | 0 | 2 | .678 |

| Level | Leag | AB | HR | R | RBI | SB | BA | OBP | SLG | CT% | H% | BB% | Bash |
|---|---|---|---|---|---|---|---|---|---|---|---|---|---|
| A | — | — | — | — | — | — | — | — | — | — | — | — | — |
| AA | — | — | — | — | — | — | — | — | — | — | — | — | — |
| AAA | PCL | 149 | 8 | 26 | 33 | 0 | .329 | .362 | .570 | 85% | 39% | 6% | 1.73 |

| Yr | Team | AB | HR | R | RBI | SB | BA | OBP | SLG | CT% | H% | BB% | Bash | $1L | $2L | Pts | RAA | 2B | 3B | CS | FB-LD-GB | HR/fb | RBI% | RS% | OPS | 1st Hf | 2nd Hf | vs RH | vs LH | Rnge | vRH | vLH |
|---|---|---|---|---|---|---|---|---|---|---|---|---|---|---|---|---|---|---|---|---|---|---|---|---|---|---|---|---|---|---|---|---|
| 07 | | | | | | | | | | | | | | | | | | | | | | | | | | | | | | | | |
| 08 | | | | | | | | | | | | | | | | | | | | | | | | | | | | | | | | |
| 09 | HOU | 22 | 0 | 1 | 1 | 0 | .091 | .130 | .091 | 73% | 13% | 4% | 1.00 | -$6 | -$20 | 0 | -4 | 0 | 0 | 0 | 19-0-81 | 0% | 10% | 33% | .221 | — | .221 | .267 | .125 | — | — | — |
| 10 | HOU | 341 | 11 | 40 | 52 | 3 | .308 | .337 | .481 | 73% | 42% | 4% | 1.56 | $12 | $2 | 190 | +8 | 22 | 2 | 0 | 35-24-41 | 13% | 25% | 26% | .818 | .685 | .857 | .848 | .735 | 2.65 | -16 | +36 |

## Dan Johnson — 350 PA | $5 | 210 pts
DH-18, 1B-13, 3B-6, OF-3 (LF-3) | Owned: 0% | LH

In his second stint with the Rays, Johnson showed promise in excellent (and nearly identical) rates of BB% and HR/FB. With Carlos Pena possibly leaving TB, Johnson could get his chance to be the primary starter at first base. If not, the Rays will use his left-handed bat off the bench, at DH, or in a platoon role. (RZ)

| Player | Age | AB | HR | R | RBI | SB | BA | OBP | SLG | $1L | Pts |
|---|---|---|---|---|---|---|---|---|---|---|---|
| Johnson D | 31 | 278 | 17 | 39 | 58 | 2 | .227 | .356 | .447 | $5 | 210 |
| Mini-Browser | Age | AB | HR | R | RBI | SB | BA | OBP | SLG | $1L | Pts |
| Moreland M | 25 | 390 | 18 | 45 | 54 | 0 | .242 | .313 | .444 | $8 | 230 |
| Allen B | 25 | 418 | 23 | 54 | 50 | 5 | .237 | .311 | .467 | $8 | 240 |
| Overbay L | 34 | 442 | 15 | 55 | 55 | 0 | .249 | .338 | .420 | $8 | 260 |
| Ka'aihue K | 27 | 373 | 18 | 50 | 50 | 0 | .241 | .350 | .428 | $7 | 240 |
| Jones G | 29 | 269 | 12 | 36 | 39 | 2 | .268 | .331 | .476 | $6 | 180 |

Competition at 1B | Stats in 2010

| Bats | Player | GSvR | GSvL | Sub | OPS |
|---|---|---|---|---|---|
| LH | Pena C | 92 | 43 | 7 | .732 |
| BH | Zobrist B | 7 | 7 | 0 | .699 |
| LH | Johnson D | 10 | 2 | 1 | .757 |

| Level | Leag | AB | HR | R | RBI | SB | BA | OBP | SLG | CT% | H% | BB% | Bash |
|---|---|---|---|---|---|---|---|---|---|---|---|---|---|
| A | — | — | — | — | — | — | — | — | — | — | — | — | — |
| AA | — | — | — | — | — | — | — | — | — | — | — | — | — |
| AAA | IL | 340 | 30 | 66 | 95 | 0 | .303 | .430 | .624 | 79% | 38% | 18% | 2.06 |

| Yr | Team | AB | HR | R | RBI | SB | BA | OBP | SLG | CT% | H% | BB% | Bash | $1L | $2L | Pts | RAA | 2B | 3B | CS | FB-LD-GB | HR/fb | RBI% | RS% | OPS | 1st Hf | 2nd Hf | vs RH | vs LH | Rnge | vRH | vLH |
|---|---|---|---|---|---|---|---|---|---|---|---|---|---|---|---|---|---|---|---|---|---|---|---|---|---|---|---|---|---|---|---|---|
| 07 | OAK | 416 | 18 | 53 | 62 | 0 | .236 | .349 | .418 | 81% | 29% | 14% | 1.78 | — | — | 280 | -7 | 20 | 1 | 0 | 39-18-43 | 14% | 17% | 23% | .768 | .824 | .694 | .758 | .783 | 1.83 | +19 | -64 |
| 08 | 2TM | 26 | 2 | 3 | 4 | 0 | .192 | .276 | .423 | 73% | 26% | 10% | 2.20 | — | — | 10 | -1 | 0 | 0 | 0 | 42-16-42 | 25% | 13% | 17% | .699 | .000 | .726 | .866 | .384 | 1.84 | +19 | -56 |
| 09 | | — | — | — | — | — | — | — | — | — | — | — | — | — | — | — | — | — | — | — | — | — | — | — | — | — | — | — | — | — | +19 | -50 |
| 10 | TB | 111 | 7 | 15 | 23 | 1 | .198 | .343 | .414 | 76% | 26% | 18% | 2.09 | $0 | -$14 | 80 | -2 | 3 | 0 | 0 | 47-15-38 | 17% | 24% | 20% | .757 | — | .757 | .738 | .862 | | | |

## Kelly Johnson — 675 PA | $24 | 430 pts
2B-149, DH-2 | Owned: 97% | LH

Many observers anticipated a bounce-back season from Johnson, but a return to full health, and a move to Chase Field, led to even better results than expected. Durable & defensively stout, Johnson gives Arizona a great second baseman on both sides of the ball. If he stays healthy, he could well repeat in 2011. (MS)

| Player | Age | AB | HR | R | RBI | SB | BA | OBP | SLG | $1L | Pts |
|---|---|---|---|---|---|---|---|---|---|---|---|
| Johnson K | 29 | 561 | 20 | 108 | 74 | 14 | .289 | .370 | .501 | $24 | 430 |
| Mini-Browser | Age | AB | HR | R | RBI | SB | BA | OBP | SLG | $1L | Pts |
| Kinsler I | 28 | 545 | 24 | 96 | 72 | 24 | .286 | .361 | .486 | $27 | 470 |
| Weeks R | 28 | 651 | 30 | 120 | 75 | 23 | .265 | .363 | .468 | $25 | 460 |
| Cano R | 28 | 636 | 20 | 88 | 88 | 0 | .297 | .341 | .485 | $25 | 450 |
| Pedroia D | 27 | 577 | 13 | 98 | 65 | 13 | .304 | .372 | .465 | $25 | 460 |
| Phillips B | 29 | 589 | 20 | 91 | 85 | 26 | .276 | .329 | .458 | $24 | 450 |

Competition at 2B | Stats in 2010

| Bats | Player | GSvR | GSvL | Sub | OPS |
|---|---|---|---|---|---|
| LH | Johnson K | 103 | 43 | 3 | .865 |
| BH | Abreu T | 7 | 5 | 0 | .560 |
| BH | Ojeda A | 2 | 2 | 11 | .486 |

| Level | Leag | AB | HR | R | RBI | SB | BA | OBP | SLG | CT% | H% | BB% | Bash |
|---|---|---|---|---|---|---|---|---|---|---|---|---|---|
| A | — | — | — | — | — | — | — | — | — | — | — | — | — |
| AA | — | — | — | — | — | — | — | — | — | — | — | — | — |
| AAA | — | — | — | — | — | — | — | — | — | — | — | — | — |

| Yr | Team | AB | HR | R | RBI | SB | BA | OBP | SLG | CT% | H% | BB% | Bash | $1L | $2L | Pts | RAA | 2B | 3B | CS | FB-LD-GB | HR/fb | RBI% | RS% | OPS | 1st Hf | 2nd Hf | vs RH | vs LH | Rnge | vRH | vLH |
|---|---|---|---|---|---|---|---|---|---|---|---|---|---|---|---|---|---|---|---|---|---|---|---|---|---|---|---|---|---|---|---|---|
| 07 | ATL | 521 | 16 | 91 | 68 | 9 | .276 | .375 | .457 | 78% | 36% | 13% | 1.65 | $17 | $9 | 370 | +18 | 26 | 10 | 5 | 39-19-43 | 10% | 22% | 36% | .831 | .852 | .803 | .858 | .771 | — | +19 | -61 |
| 08 | ATL | 547 | 12 | 86 | 69 | 11 | .287 | .349 | .446 | 79% | 36% | 8% | 1.55 | $18 | $11 | 350 | +10 | 39 | 6 | 6 | 36-25-39 | 7% | 21% | 37% | .795 | .777 | .819 | .793 | .800 | 4.20 | +24 | -70 |
| 09 | ATL | 303 | 8 | 47 | 29 | 7 | .224 | .303 | .389 | 82% | 27% | 9% | 1.74 | $4 | -$8 | 180 | -8 | 20 | 3 | 2 | 43-18-39 | 8% | 17% | 41% | .692 | .645 | .851 | .595 | .968 | 4.22 | +18 | -49 |
| 10 | ARI | 585 | 26 | 93 | 71 | 13 | .284 | .370 | .496 | 75% | 38% | 12% | 1.75 | $26 | $20 | 400 | +30 | 36 | 5 | 7 | 38-21-41 | 16% | 17% | 30% | .865 | .870 | .860 | .825 | .953 | 4.24 | +1 | -1 |

## Nick Johnson — 100 PA | $-3 | 60 pts
DH-20, 1B-2 | Owned: 3% | LH

Signing Johnson might have been Brian Cashman's worst off-season pickup of 2010. After sitting for part of April with a sore back, Johnson hurt his wrist in May in a game against Boston; he never played again and eventually required two surgeries. This season was essentially "night" to the "day" of his 2009. (LS)

| Player | Age | AB | HR | R | RBI | SB | BA | OBP | SLG | $1L | Pts |
|---|---|---|---|---|---|---|---|---|---|---|---|
| Johnson N | 32 | 77 | 3 | 12 | 12 | 1 | .273 | .417 | .433 | -$3 | 60 |
| Mini-Browser | Age | AB | HR | R | RBI | SB | BA | OBP | SLG | $1L | Pts |
| Hafner T | 33 | 439 | 16 | 58 | 68 | 0 | .263 | .364 | .447 | $12 | 280 |
| Thames M | 34 | 317 | 21 | 42 | 53 | 0 | .254 | .314 | .485 | $9 | 180 |
| Cust J | 32 | 328 | 16 | 48 | 52 | 0 | .232 | .363 | .427 | $7 | 170 |
| Thome J | 40 | 231 | 14 | 36 | 44 | 0 | .238 | .355 | .470 | $5 | 150 |
| Kotsay M | 35 | 188 | 4 | 18 | 20 | 2 | .255 | .313 | .375 | -$2 | 110 |

Competition at DH | Stats in 2010

| Bats | Player | GSvR | GSvL | Sub | OPS |
|---|---|---|---|---|---|
| RH | Thames M | 4 | 30 | 4 | .841 |
| BH | Posada J | 16 | 12 | 2 | .811 |
| BH | Berkman L | 20 | 1 | 2 | .781 |
| LH | Johnson N | 15 | 4 | 1 | .693 |

| Level | Leag | AB | HR | R | RBI | SB | BA | OBP | SLG | CT% | H% | BB% | Bash |
|---|---|---|---|---|---|---|---|---|---|---|---|---|---|
| A | — | — | — | — | — | — | — | — | — | — | — | — | — |
| AA | — | — | — | — | — | — | — | — | — | — | — | — | — |
| AAA | — | — | — | — | — | — | — | — | — | — | — | — | — |

| Yr | Team | AB | HR | R | RBI | SB | BA | OBP | SLG | CT% | H% | BB% | Bash | $1L | $2L | Pts | RAA | 2B | 3B | CS | FB-LD-GB | HR/fb | RBI% | RS% | OPS | 1st Hf | 2nd Hf | vs RH | vs LH | Rnge | vRH | vLH |
|---|---|---|---|---|---|---|---|---|---|---|---|---|---|---|---|---|---|---|---|---|---|---|---|---|---|---|---|---|---|---|---|---|
| 07 | | | | | | | | | | | | | | | | | | | | | | | | | | | | | | 4.24 | +11 | -32 |
| 08 | WAS | 109 | 5 | 15 | 20 | 0 | .220 | .415 | .431 | 77% | 29% | 22% | 1.96 | -$1 | -$14 | 90 | +1 | 8 | 0 | 0 | 39-24-38 | 15% | 23% | 18% | .846 | .846 | — | .938 | .660 | 4.24 | +18 | -51 |
| 09 | 2TM | 457 | 8 | 71 | 62 | 2 | .291 | .426 | .405 | 82% | 36% | 17% | 1.39 | $13 | -$4 | 330 | +5 | 24 | 2 | 4 | 34-22-43 | 6% | 23% | 27% | .831 | .838 | .811 | .809 | .883 | 4.24 | +28 | -51 |
| 10 | NYY | 72 | 2 | 12 | 8 | 0 | .167 | .388 | .306 | 68% | 24% | 24% | 1.83 | -$3 | -$19 | 40 | -3 | 1 | 0 | 0 | 41-22-37 | 10% | 14% | 26% | .693 | .693 | — | .697 | .673 | 4.24 | +16 | -50 |

## Reed Johnson — 100 PA | $-3 | 40 pts
OF-84 (LF-62, RF-22, CF-7) | Owned: 0% | RH

Johnson had been signed by the Dodgers to sub for Manny on defense and against lefties for Ethier, but Reed was a non-factor even when he was not missing time with his own back problems. At 34, Johnson's days as an everyday player are gone, and he does not bring either pop or speed off the bench. (MP)

| Player | Age | AB | HR | R | RBI | SB | BA | OBP | SLG | $1L | Pts |
|---|---|---|---|---|---|---|---|---|---|---|---|
| Johnson R | 34 | 91 | 1 | 12 | 10 | 1 | .265 | .323 | .382 | -$3 | 40 |
| Mini-Browser | Age | AB | HR | R | RBI | SB | BA | OBP | SLG | $1L | Pts |
| Carter C | 28 | 91 | 4 | 10 | 12 | 0 | .263 | .328 | .444 | -$2 | 60 |
| Gillespie C | 26 | 86 | 3 | 12 | 10 | 2 | .244 | .336 | .436 | -$2 | 50 |
| Gerut J | 33 | 81 | 3 | 9 | 9 | 2 | .265 | .322 | .467 | -$3 | 50 |
| Kelly D | 31 | 116 | 3 | 14 | 11 | 3 | .258 | .317 | .380 | -$3 | 70 |
| Carroll B | 28 | 88 | 3 | 13 | 11 | 1 | .239 | .306 | .430 | -$3 | 50 |

Competition at LF | Stats in 2010

| Bats | Player | GSvR | GSvL | Sub | OPS |
|---|---|---|---|---|---|
| LH | Podsednik S | 28 | 6 | 3 | .724 |
| RH | Johnson R | 5 | 24 | 33 | .657 |
| LH | Anderson G | 17 | 4 | 6 | .475 |
| LH | Paul X | 16 | 2 | 11 | .591 |

| Level | Leag | AB | HR | R | RBI | SB | BA | OBP | SLG | CT% | H% | BB% | Bash |
|---|---|---|---|---|---|---|---|---|---|---|---|---|---|
| A | CAL | 6 | 0 | 2 | 0 | 0 | .500 | .500 | .667 | 100% | 50% | 0% | 1.33 |
| AA | — | — | — | — | — | — | — | — | — | — | — | — | — |
| AAA | — | — | — | — | — | — | — | — | — | — | — | — | — |

| Yr | Team | AB | HR | R | RBI | SB | BA | OBP | SLG | CT% | H% | BB% | Bash | $1L | $2L | Pts | RAA | 2B | 3B | CS | FB-LD-GB | HR/fb | RBI% | RS% | OPS | 1st Hf | 2nd Hf | vs RH | vs LH | Rnge | vRH | vLH |
|---|---|---|---|---|---|---|---|---|---|---|---|---|---|---|---|---|---|---|---|---|---|---|---|---|---|---|---|---|---|---|---|---|
| 07 | TOR | 275 | 2 | 31 | 14 | 4 | .236 | .305 | .320 | 80% | 30% | 5% | 1.35 | $0 | -$15 | 100 | -21 | 13 | 2 | 2 | 34-19-47 | 3% | 11% | 32% | .625 | .698 | .610 | .513 | .913 | 2.10 | -12 | +23 |
| 08 | CHC | 333 | 6 | 52 | 50 | 5 | .303 | .358 | .420 | 80% | 38% | 5% | 1.39 | $10 | -$1 | 200 | -7 | 21 | 0 | 6 | 35-24-41 | 7% | 25% | 37% | .778 | .712 | .886 | .721 | .848 | 2.08 | -30 | +69 |
| 09 | CHC | 165 | 4 | 23 | 22 | 2 | .255 | .330 | .412 | 84% | 30% | 5% | 1.62 | $1 | -$13 | 100 | -5 | 11 | 2 | 1 | 33-17-50 | 9% | 16% | 33% | .742 | .744 | .735 | .628 | .903 | 2.12 | -43 | +90 |
| 10 | LAD | 202 | 2 | 24 | 15 | 2 | .262 | .291 | .366 | 79% | 35% | 2% | 1.40 | $-14 | -$24 | 70 | -12 | 11 | 2 | 1 | 37-19-43 | 4% | 13% | 37% | .657 | .702 | .583 | .520 | .790 | | -31 | +62 |

For more stats, visit www.Rotolympus.com.

## Rob Johnson — 150 PA | $-1 | 60 pts

CA-61 — Owned: 1% — RH

Forecast

| Player | Age | AB | HR | R | RBI | SB | BA | OBP | SLG | $1L | Pts |
|---|---|---|---|---|---|---|---|---|---|---|---|
| Johnson R | 28 | 126 | 2 | 14 | 12 | 2 | .238 | .307 | .348 | -$1 | 60 |
| **Mini-Browser** | **Age** | **AB** | **HR** | **R** | **RBI** | **SB** | **BA** | **OBP** | **SLG** | **$1L** | **Pts** |
| Kottaras G | 27 | 114 | 5 | 14 | 14 | 0 | .231 | .330 | .420 | $0 | 70 |
| Zaun G | 39 | 107 | 3 | 13 | 14 | 0 | .246 | .344 | .387 | $0 | 60 |
| Ellis A | 29 | 127 | 2 | 14 | 17 | 0 | .248 | .355 | .340 | $0 | 70 |
| Treanor M | 35 | 154 | 4 | 14 | 18 | 0 | .227 | .307 | .322 | -$1 | 70 |
| Blanco H | 39 | 110 | 3 | 11 | 10 | 0 | .238 | .297 | .363 | -$1 | 50 |

Minors (2010)

| Level | Leag | AB | HR | R | RBI | SB | BA | OBP | SLG | CT% | H% | BB% | Bash |
|---|---|---|---|---|---|---|---|---|---|---|---|---|---|
| A | — | — | — | — | — | — | — | — | — | — | — | — | — |
| AA | — | — | — | — | — | — | — | — | — | — | — | — | — |
| AAA | — | — | — | — | — | — | — | — | — | — | — | — | — |

Majors

| Yr | Team | AB | HR | R | RBI | SB | BA | OBP | SLG | CT% | H% | BB% | Bash | $1L | $2L | Pts | RAA | 2B | 3B | CS | FB-LD-GB | HR/fb | RBI% | RS% | OPS | 1st Hf | 2nd Hf | vs RH | vs LH | Rnge | vRH | vLH |
|---|---|---|---|---|---|---|---|---|---|---|---|---|---|---|---|---|---|---|---|---|---|---|---|---|---|---|---|---|---|---|---|---|
| 07 | SEA | 3 | 0 | 1 | 0 | 1 | .333 | .333 | .333 | 100% | 33% | 0% | 1.00 | -$4 | -$20 | 0 | +0 | 0 | 0 | 0 | 100-0-0 | 0% | 0% | 100% | .667 | — | .667 | .667 | — | — | — | — |
| 08 | SEA | 31 | 1 | 2 | 2 | 0 | .129 | .129 | .226 | 81% | 16% | 0% | 1.75 | -$2 | -$11 | 0 | −5 | 0 | 0 | 0 | 42-13-46 | 10% | 8% | 33% | .355 | — | .355 | .300 | .455 | 0.57 | −22 | +53 |
| 09 | SEA | 258 | 2 | 21 | 27 | 1 | .213 | .289 | .326 | 77% | 28% | 9% | 1.53 | $0 | -$7 | 100 | −13 | 19 | 2 | 1 | 33-21-46 | 3% | 17% | 23% | .615 | .598 | .634 | .672 | .493 | 0.61 | −22 | +53 |
| 10 | SEA | 178 | 2 | 24 | 13 | 1 | .191 | .293 | .281 | 74% | 26% | 12% | 1.47 | $0 | -$10 | 70 | −12 | 10 | 0 | 1 | 36-12-52 | 4% | 13% | 37% | .574 | .620 | .311 | .562 | .610 | 0.62 | −5 | +13 |

Johnson in 2010 posted a lowly .574 OPS in his time with Seattle (after a mere .615 OPS in 2009), and the fact that he was not recalled when rosters expanded in September says a lot about his standing with the club. You can't survive in MLB as a low-contact ground-baller. He won't have much of a role in '11. (GC)

Competition at CA — Stats in 2010

| Bats | Player | GSvR | GSvL | Sub | OPS |
|---|---|---|---|---|---|
| RH | Moore A | 41 | 17 | 1 | .513 |
| RH | Johnson R | 44 | 13 | 4 | .574 |
| BH | Bard J | 20 | 15 | 4 | .634 |
| RH | Alfonzo E | 5 | 5 | 2 | .537 |

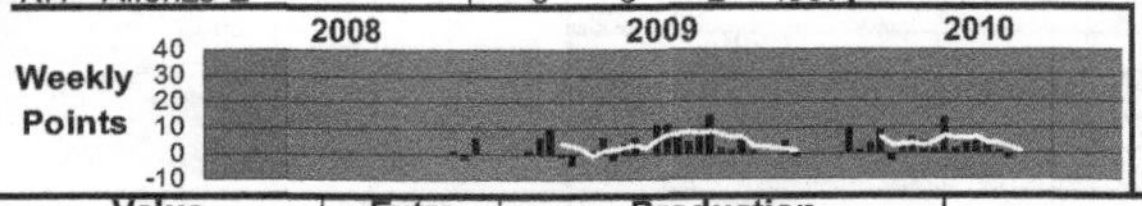


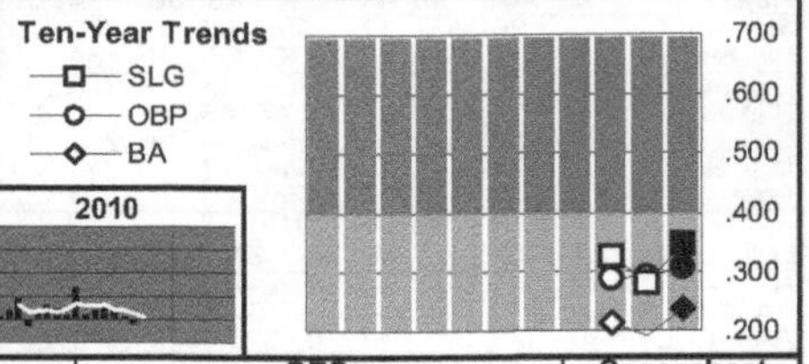


## Adam Jones — 550 PA | $18 | 300 pts

OF-149 (CF-149) — Owned: 94% — RH

Forecast

| Player | Age | AB | HR | R | RBI | SB | BA | OBP | SLG | $1L | Pts |
|---|---|---|---|---|---|---|---|---|---|---|---|
| Jones A | 25 | 493 | 17 | 72 | 66 | 11 | .279 | .326 | .458 | $18 | 300 |
| **Mini-Browser** | **Age** | **AB** | **HR** | **R** | **RBI** | **SB** | **BA** | **OBP** | **SLG** | **$1L** | **Pts** |
| Torres A | 33 | 543 | 18 | 84 | 60 | 24 | .265 | .340 | .466 | $18 | 370 |
| Jackson A | 24 | 614 | 7 | 88 | 54 | 27 | .264 | .323 | .390 | $18 | 320 |
| Soriano A | 35 | 468 | 26 | 74 | 68 | 11 | .269 | .330 | .511 | $18 | 330 |
| Swisher N | 30 | 510 | 30 | 84 | 78 | 0 | .259 | .362 | .484 | $18 | 360 |
| Rasmus C | 24 | 543 | 24 | 84 | 66 | 12 | .265 | .349 | .466 | $18 | 370 |

Minors (2010)

| Level | Leag | AB | HR | R | RBI | SB | BA | OBP | SLG | CT% | H% | BB% | Bash |
|---|---|---|---|---|---|---|---|---|---|---|---|---|---|
| A | — | — | — | — | — | — | — | — | — | — | — | — | — |
| AA | — | — | — | — | — | — | — | — | — | — | — | — | — |
| AAA | — | — | — | — | — | — | — | — | — | — | — | — | — |

Majors

| Yr | Team | AB | HR | R | RBI | SB | BA | OBP | SLG | CT% | H% | BB% | Bash | $1L | $2L | Pts | RAA | 2B | 3B | CS | FB-LD-GB | HR/fb | RBI% | RS% | OPS | 1st Hf | 2nd Hf | vs RH | vs LH | Rnge | vRH | vLH |
|---|---|---|---|---|---|---|---|---|---|---|---|---|---|---|---|---|---|---|---|---|---|---|---|---|---|---|---|---|---|---|---|---|
| 07 | SEA | 65 | 2 | 16 | 4 | 2 | .246 | .300 | .400 | 68% | 36% | 6% | 1.63 | -$1 | -$16 | 30 | −2 | 2 | 1 | 1 | 39-27-34 | 12% | 6% | 74% | .700 | — | .700 | .506 | .941 | 2.14 | −17 | +44 |
| 08 | BAL | 477 | 9 | 61 | 57 | 10 | .270 | .311 | .400 | 77% | 35% | 4% | 1.48 | $13 | $2 | 240 | −10 | 21 | 7 | 3 | 35-18-47 | 7% | 19% | 35% | .711 | .732 | .663 | .728 | .660 | 2.12 | −26 | +63 |
| 09 | BAL | 473 | 19 | 83 | 70 | 10 | .277 | .335 | .457 | 80% | 34% | 7% | 1.65 | $18 | $10 | 330 | +5 | 22 | 3 | 4 | 28-17-55 | 18% | 22% | 41% | .792 | .838 | .695 | .864 | .665 | 2.18 | −17 | +41 |
| 10 | BAL | 581 | 19 | 76 | 69 | 7 | .284 | .325 | .442 | 80% | 36% | 4% | 1.56 | $21 | $12 | 310 | −4 | 25 | 5 | 7 | 37-17-46 | 11% | 17% | 31% | .767 | .757 | .781 | .804 | .666 | 2.18 | +6 | −14 |

The fact that Jones made it through 2010 in relative health brings greater promise to his age-25 campaign. A perennial Gold Glove candidate and solid performer at the plate, Jones is capable of blasting 25 HR, but he needs better judgment on the basepaths. He'll play center field for as long as he can take the field. (BJ)

Competition at CF — Stats in 2010

| Bats | Player | GSvR | GSvL | Sub | OPS |
|---|---|---|---|---|---|
| RH | Jones A | 100 | 48 | 1 | .767 |
| LH | Patterson C | 7 | 1 | 2 | .721 |

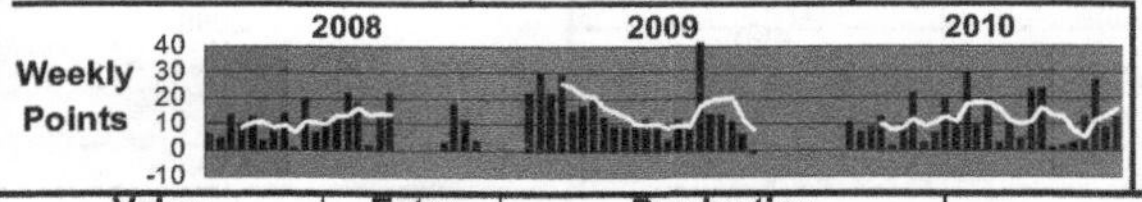


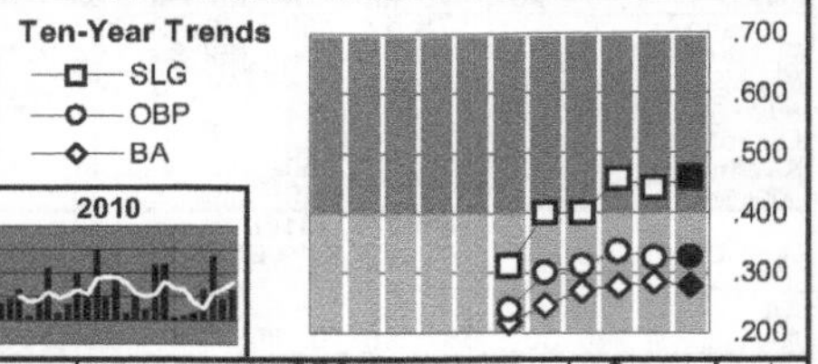


## Andruw Jones — 300 PA | $6 | 180 pts

OF-89 (RF-62, CF-17, LF-12), DH-14 — Owned: 7% — RH

Forecast

| Player | Age | AB | HR | R | RBI | SB | BA | OBP | SLG | $1L | Pts |
|---|---|---|---|---|---|---|---|---|---|---|---|
| Jones A | 33 | 260 | 15 | 39 | 42 | 3 | .242 | .339 | .474 | $6 | 180 |
| **Mini-Browser** | **Age** | **AB** | **HR** | **R** | **RBI** | **SB** | **BA** | **OBP** | **SLG** | **$1L** | **Pts** |
| Cabrera M | 26 | 472 | 10 | 55 | 50 | 10 | .265 | .331 | .379 | $8 | 310 |
| Jay J | 26 | 458 | 10 | 60 | 45 | 10 | .262 | .326 | .384 | $8 | 260 |
| Jennings D | 24 | 293 | 7 | 39 | 26 | 20 | .244 | .322 | .403 | $7 | 200 |
| Saunders M | 24 | 420 | 14 | 50 | 45 | 14 | .225 | .303 | .380 | $7 | 210 |
| Taylor M | 25 | 317 | 14 | 35 | 42 | 11 | .232 | .300 | .435 | $7 | 200 |

Minors (2010)

| Level | Leag | AB | HR | R | RBI | SB | BA | OBP | SLG | CT% | H% | BB% | Bash |
|---|---|---|---|---|---|---|---|---|---|---|---|---|---|
| A | — | — | — | — | — | — | — | — | — | — | — | — | — |
| AA | — | — | — | — | — | — | — | — | — | — | — | — | — |
| AAA | — | — | — | — | — | — | — | — | — | — | — | — | — |

Majors

| Yr | Team | AB | HR | R | RBI | SB | BA | OBP | SLG | CT% | H% | BB% | Bash | $1L | $2L | Pts | RAA | 2B | 3B | CS | FB-LD-GB | HR/fb | RBI% | RS% | OPS | 1st Hf | 2nd Hf | vs RH | vs LH | Rnge | vRH | vLH |
|---|---|---|---|---|---|---|---|---|---|---|---|---|---|---|---|---|---|---|---|---|---|---|---|---|---|---|---|---|---|---|---|---|
| 07 | ATL | 572 | 26 | 83 | 94 | 5 | .222 | .311 | .413 | 76% | 29% | 11% | 1.86 | $13 | $7 | 350 | −21 | 27 | 2 | 2 | 44-17-39 | 13% | 18% | 32% | .724 | .720 | .728 | .694 | .785 | 2.19 | −6 | +15 |
| 08 | LAD | 209 | 3 | 21 | 14 | 0 | .158 | .256 | .249 | 64% | 25% | 11% | 1.58 | -$6 | -$19 | 40 | −23 | 8 | 1 | 1 | 39-13-48 | 6% | 9% | 31% | .505 | .513 | .474 | .436 | .631 | 2.19 | −16 | +42 |
| 09 | TEX | 281 | 17 | 43 | 43 | 5 | .214 | .323 | .459 | 74% | 29% | 13% | 2.15 | $7 | -$6 | 200 | −2 | 18 | 0 | 1 | 50-16-34 | 16% | 16% | 29% | .782 | .869 | .643 | .793 | .762 | — | −26 | +57 |
| 10 | CHW | 278 | 19 | 41 | 48 | 9 | .230 | .341 | .486 | 74% | 31% | 14% | 2.11 | $11 | -$1 | 210 | +3 | 12 | 1 | 2 | 44-11-44 | 21% | 20% | 24% | .827 | .769 | .945 | .781 | .931 | 2.10 | −19 | +40 |

Jones was signed by the White Sox for a fraction of the $13M that Jim Thome got in 2009, and Andruw slugged about as well as the 2009 version of Thome. He also shed enough weight to patrol all 3 OF slots, with good range at the corners. He could start for a desperate team, else he will be a 4th OF w/pop. (RM)

Competition at RF — Stats in 2010

| Bats | Player | GSvR | GSvL | Sub | OPS |
|---|---|---|---|---|---|
| RH | Quentin C | 80 | 23 | 1 | .821 |
| RH | Jones A | 26 | 15 | 21 | .827 |
| LH | Teahen M | 10 | 0 | 0 | .709 |

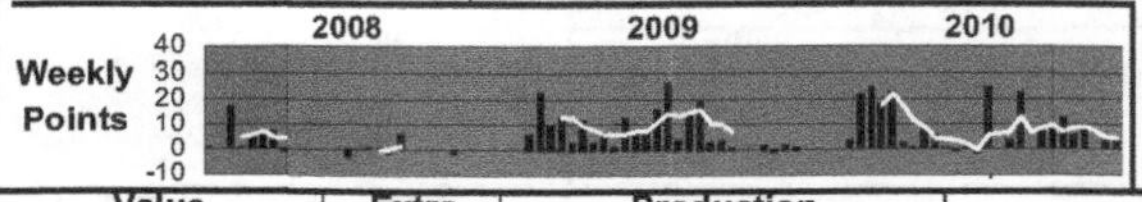


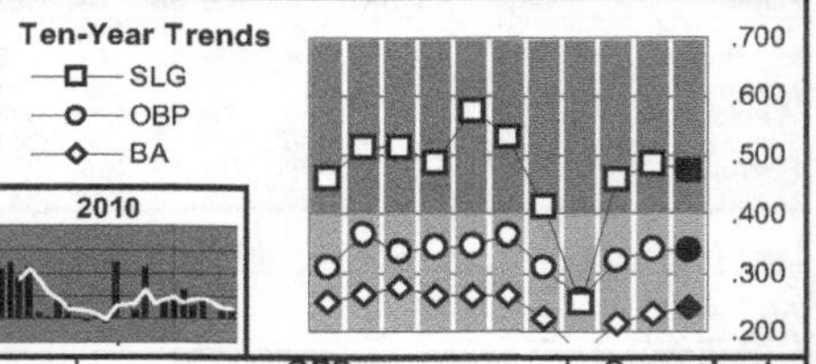


## Chipper Jones — 300 PA | $8 | 230 pts

3B-89, DH-1 — Owned: 47% — BH

Forecast

| Player | Age | AB | HR | R | RBI | SB | BA | OBP | SLG | $1L | Pts |
|---|---|---|---|---|---|---|---|---|---|---|---|
| Jones C | 38 | 248 | 12 | 45 | 42 | 3 | .290 | .401 | .490 | $8 | 230 |
| **Mini-Browser** | **Age** | **AB** | **HR** | **R** | **RBI** | **SB** | **BA** | **OBP** | **SLG** | **$1L** | **Pts** |
| Callaspo A | 27 | 500 | 6 | 55 | 50 | 6 | .286 | .337 | .412 | $10 | 310 |
| Inge B | 33 | 541 | 18 | 54 | 72 | 6 | .233 | .313 | .395 | $10 | 250 |
| Freese D | 27 | 444 | 15 | 55 | 65 | 0 | .259 | .328 | .421 | $9 | 240 |
| Johnson C | 26 | 537 | 17 | 55 | 66 | 0 | .256 | .293 | .418 | $9 | 250 |
| Encarnacion E | 28 | 362 | 16 | 48 | 52 | 4 | .254 | .332 | .446 | $9 | 230 |

Minors (2010)

| Level | Leag | AB | HR | R | RBI | SB | BA | OBP | SLG | CT% | H% | BB% | Bash |
|---|---|---|---|---|---|---|---|---|---|---|---|---|---|
| A | — | — | — | — | — | — | — | — | — | — | — | — | — |
| AA | — | — | — | — | — | — | — | — | — | — | — | — | — |
| AAA | — | — | — | — | — | — | — | — | — | — | — | — | — |

Majors

| Yr | Team | AB | HR | R | RBI | SB | BA | OBP | SLG | CT% | H% | BB% | Bash | $1L | $2L | Pts | RAA | 2B | 3B | CS | FB-LD-GB | HR/fb | RBI% | RS% | OPS | 1st Hf | 2nd Hf | vs RH | vs LH | Rnge | vRH | vLH |
|---|---|---|---|---|---|---|---|---|---|---|---|---|---|---|---|---|---|---|---|---|---|---|---|---|---|---|---|---|---|---|---|---|
| 07 | ATL | 513 | 29 | 108 | 102 | 5 | .337 | .425 | .604 | 85% | 39% | 13% | 1.79 | $32 | $27 | 540 | +58 | 42 | 4 | 1 | 37-19-44 | 18% | 24% | 35% | 1.029 | 1.011 | 1.046 | 1.171 | .803 | 2.58 | +19 | −61 |
| 08 | ATL | 439 | 22 | 82 | 75 | 4 | .364 | .470 | .574 | 86% | 42% | 16% | 1.58 | $27 | $21 | 450 | +56 | 24 | 1 | 0 | 33-24-43 | 17% | 24% | 26% | 1.044 | 1.086 | .955 | 1.047 | 1.040 | 2.63 | +32 | −81 |
| 09 | ATL | 488 | 18 | 80 | 71 | 4 | .264 | .388 | .430 | 82% | 32% | 16% | 1.63 | $16 | $6 | 380 | +16 | 23 | 2 | 1 | 35-20-45 | 13% | 22% | 29% | .818 | .878 | .750 | .772 | .912 | 2.66 | +19 | −47 |
| 10 | ATL | 317 | 10 | 47 | 46 | 5 | .265 | .381 | .426 | 85% | 31% | 16% | 1.61 | $9 | -$2 | 250 | +12 | 21 | 0 | 0 | 44-18-38 | 8% | 21% | 27% | .806 | .770 | .924 | .828 | .766 | 2.63 | −16 | +37 |

All eyes will be on Chipper this spring as he tries to come back from his second ACL injury. His mobility at third base will be the biggest question, and that could limit his effectiveness as an NL'er. Ideally, he would return as a DH, but he will not leave Atlanta. Any struggles in the field could translate to the plate. (MG)

Competition at 3B — Stats in 2010

| Bats | Player | GSvR | GSvL | Sub | OPS |
|---|---|---|---|---|---|
| BH | Jones C | 58 | 28 | 3 | .806 |
| RH | Prado M | 28 | 14 | 1 | .809 |
| BH | Conrad B | 15 | 7 | 15 | .811 |
| RH | Infante O | 7 | 9 | 13 | .775 |

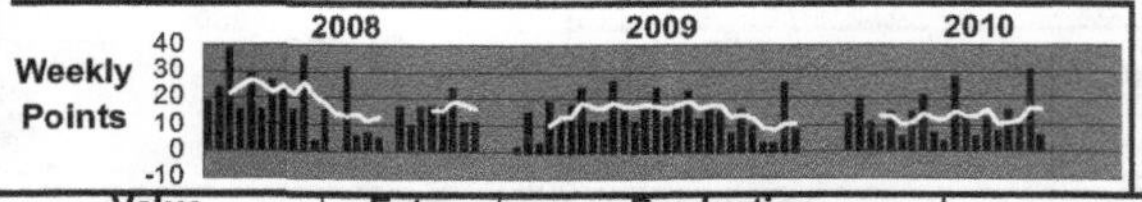


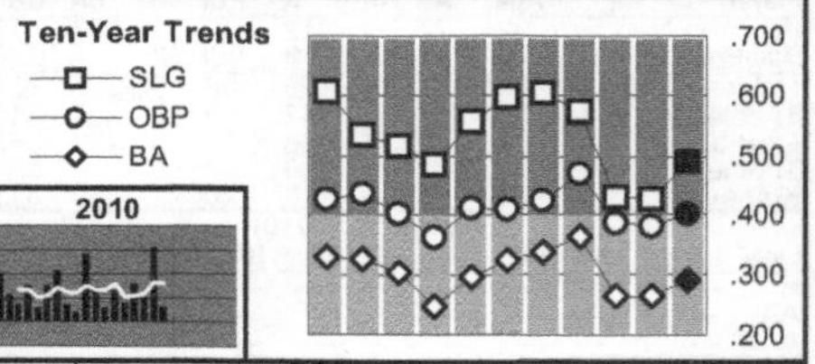


## Garrett Jones — 300 PA | $6 | 180 pts

1B-112, OF-49 (RF-48, LF-1), DH-1 — Owned: 85% — LH

Forecast

| Player | Age | AB | HR | R | RBI | SB | BA | OBP | SLG | $1L | Pts |
|---|---|---|---|---|---|---|---|---|---|---|---|
| Jones G | 29 | 269 | 12 | 36 | 39 | 3 | .268 | .331 | .476 | $6 | 180 |
| **Mini-Browser** | **Age** | **AB** | **HR** | **R** | **RBI** | **SB** | **BA** | **OBP** | **SLG** | **$1L** | **Pts** |
| Freeman F | 21 | 537 | 18 | 60 | 72 | 0 | .246 | .313 | .425 | $9 | 310 |
| Moreland M | 25 | 390 | 18 | 45 | 54 | 0 | .242 | .313 | .444 | $8 | 230 |
| Allen B | 25 | 418 | 23 | 54 | 50 | 5 | .237 | .311 | .467 | $8 | 240 |
| Overbay L | 34 | 442 | 15 | 55 | 55 | 0 | .249 | .338 | .420 | $8 | 260 |
| Ka'aihue K | 27 | 373 | 18 | 50 | 50 | 0 | .241 | .350 | .428 | $7 | 240 |

Minors (2010)

| Level | Leag | AB | HR | R | RBI | SB | BA | OBP | SLG | CT% | H% | BB% | Bash |
|---|---|---|---|---|---|---|---|---|---|---|---|---|---|
| A | — | — | — | — | — | — | — | — | — | — | — | — | — |
| AA | — | — | — | — | — | — | — | — | — | — | — | — | — |
| AAA | — | — | — | — | — | — | — | — | — | — | — | — | — |

Majors

| Yr | Team | AB | HR | R | RBI | SB | BA | OBP | SLG | CT% | H% | BB% | Bash | $1L | $2L | Pts | RAA | 2B | 3B | CS | FB-LD-GB | HR/fb | RBI% | RS% | OPS | 1st Hf | 2nd Hf | vs RH | vs LH | Rnge | vRH | vLH |
|---|---|---|---|---|---|---|---|---|---|---|---|---|---|---|---|---|---|---|---|---|---|---|---|---|---|---|---|---|---|---|---|---|
| 07 | MIN | 77 | 2 | 7 | 5 | 1 | .208 | .262 | .338 | 74% | 28% | 7% | 1.63 | -$3 | -$19 | 20 | −7 | 2 | 1 | 1 | 48-17-34 | 7% | 6% | 25% | .600 | .347 | .629 | .671 | .231 | — | — | — |
| 08 | — | — | — | — | — | — | — | — | — | — | — | — | — | — | — | — | — | — | — | — | — | — | — | — | — | — | — | — | — | 1.85 | +27 | −85 |
| 09 | PIT | 314 | 21 | 45 | 44 | 10 | .293 | .372 | .567 | 76% | 39% | 11% | 1.93 | $14 | $2 | 250 | +14 | 21 | 1 | 2 | 41-18-40 | 21% | 17% | 21% | .938 | 1.131 | .909 | 1.046 | .698 | — | +25 | −78 |
| 10 | PIT | 592 | 21 | 64 | 86 | 7 | .247 | .306 | .414 | 79% | 31% | 8% | 1.68 | $15 | $7 | 340 | −21 | 34 | 1 | 3 | 39-17-44 | 11% | 20% | 24% | .720 | .768 | .659 | .775 | .621 | 1.84 | +36 | −102 |

Stellar stats in 350 PA in his 2009 debut earned Jones a full season in the clean-up slot, and not even a replacement-level performance (and a .621 OPS vs. LHP) could pry him out. In 2011, Pittsburgh plans to use Jones as a platoon piece, a role that should propel him to above-average offensive production. (MB)

Competition at 1B — Stats in 2010

| Bats | Player | GSvR | GSvL | Sub | OPS |
|---|---|---|---|---|---|
| LH | Jones G | 83 | 29 | 0 | .720 |
| LH | Clement J | 28 | 5 | 5 | .605 |
| RH | Pearce S | 3 | 6 | 2 | .809 |

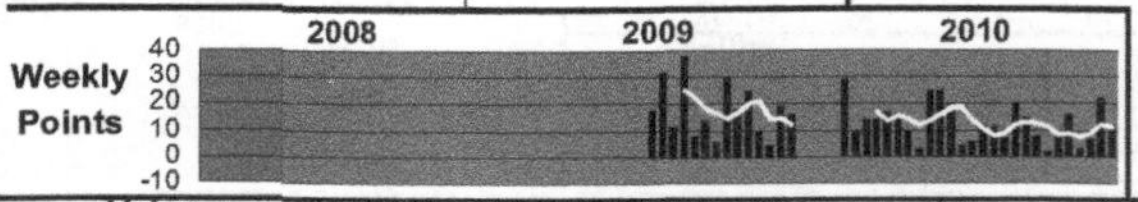


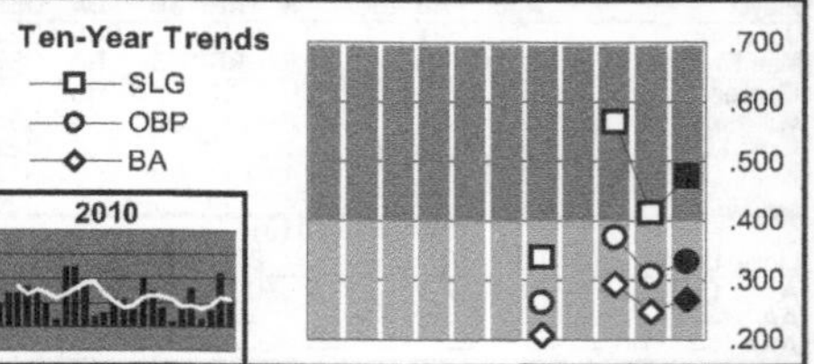

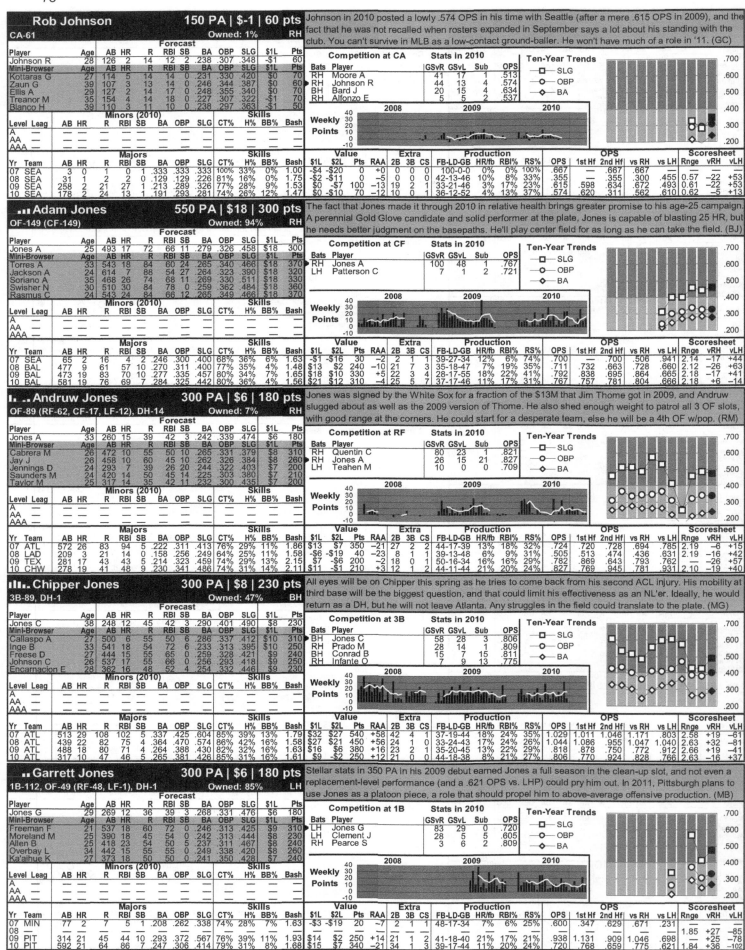

## Matt Joyce — 500 PA | $11 | 280 pts
OF-63 (RF-53, LF-13), DH-11 · Owned: 1% · LH

No more minor leagues for Joyce, he is here to stay. Joe Maddon was reluctant to employ Joyce against left-handed pitchers, but that stance should soften in 2011. Joyce will still be platooned on occasion, and he might play LF more often than he did in 2010 in order to allow other hitters to play RF. (RZ)

### Forecast
| Player | Age | AB | HR | R | RBI | SB | BA | OBP | SLG | $1L | Pts |
|---|---|---|---|---|---|---|---|---|---|---|---|
| Joyce M | 26 | 430 | 20 | 55 | 65 | 5 | .244 | .338 | .470 | $11 | 280 |

### Mini-Browser
| Player | Age | AB | HR | R | RBI | SB | BA | OBP | SLG | $1L | Pts |
|---|---|---|---|---|---|---|---|---|---|---|---|
| Drew J | 35 | 389 | 18 | 63 | 59 | 5 | .266 | .370 | .475 | $12 | 290 |
| Morrison L | 23 | 535 | 18 | 72 | 66 | 6 | .258 | .354 | .438 | $12 | 360 |
| Murphy D | 29 | 395 | 13 | 51 | 55 | 9 | .280 | .341 | .454 | $12 | 270 |
| Hawpe B | 31 | 335 | 16 | 52 | 60 | 0 | .275 | .376 | .501 | $11 | 240 |
| Sweeney R | 26 | 554 | 6 | 66 | 60 | 6 | .271 | .332 | .375 | $11 | 310 |

### Competition at RF — Stats in 2010
| Bats | Player | GSvR | GSvL | Sub | OPS |
|---|---|---|---|---|---|
| BH | Zobrist B | 64 | 34 | 5 | .699 |
| LH | Joyce M | 45 | 1 | 7 | .837 |
| RH | Kapler G | 2 | 29 | 8 | .578 |

### Minors (2010)
| Level | Leag | AB | HR | R | RBI | SB | BA | OBP | SLG | CT% | H% | BB% | Bash |
|---|---|---|---|---|---|---|---|---|---|---|---|---|---|
| A | FLO | 29 | 2 | 6 | 8 | 1 | .379 | .525 | .759 | 72% | 52% | 25% | 2.00 |
| AA | | | | | | | | | | | | | |
| AAA | IL | 92 | 3 | 18 | 12 | 1 | .293 | .435 | .478 | 77% | 38% | 19% | 1.63 |

### Majors
| Yr | Team | AB | HR | R | RBI | SB | BA | OBP | SLG | CT% | H% | BB% | Bash | $1L | $2L | Pts | RAA | 2B | 3B | CS | FB-LD-GB | HR/fb | RBI% | RS% | OPS | 1st Hf | 2nd Hf | vs RH | vs LH | Rnge | vRH | vLH |
|---|---|---|---|---|---|---|---|---|---|---|---|---|---|---|---|---|---|---|---|---|---|---|---|---|---|---|---|---|---|---|---|---|
| 07 | — | | | | | | | | | | | | | | | | | | | | | | | | | | | | | | | |
| 08 | DET | 242 | 12 | 40 | 33 | 0 | .252 | .339 | .492 | 73% | 34% | 11% | 1.95 | $5 | -$6 | 160 | +1 | 16 | 3 | 2 | 47-17-35 | 14% | 16% | 34% | .831 | .969 | .742 | .842 | .711 | — | — | — |
| 09 | TB | 32 | 3 | 3 | 7 | 1 | .188 | .270 | .500 | 78% | 24% | 8% | 2.67 | -$3 | -$19 | 20 | -1 | 1 | 0 | 0 | 50-12-38 | 23% | 21% | 0% | .770 | .770 | — | .773 | .750 | 2.08 | +23 | -78 |
| 09 | TB | 216 | 10 | 40 | 2 | .241 | .360 | .477 | 75% | 32% | 15% | 1.98 | $1 | -$8 | 160 | +2 | 15 | 3 | 2 | 49-18-33 | 13% | 26% | 32% | .690 | .870 | .910 | .263 | 2.08 | +23 | -78 | | | | |

---

## Kila Ka'aihue — 450 PA | $7 | 240 pts
1B-34, DH-15 · Owned: 0% · LH

Kila is the perfect back-up 1B. He struggled in his first month in 2010 but finished on a roll. He already exhibits big-time power (1.82 Bash), and his walk rate will rise to minor-league levels in time (he had 10 BB in his last 15 games). His main obstacle is a reluctance by the Royals' front office to play him. (BM)

### Forecast
| Player | Age | AB | HR | R | RBI | SB | BA | OBP | SLG | $1L | Pts |
|---|---|---|---|---|---|---|---|---|---|---|---|
| Ka'aihue K | 27 | 373 | 18 | 50 | 50 | 0 | .241 | .350 | .428 | $7 | 240 |

### Mini-Browser
| Player | Age | AB | HR | R | RBI | SB | BA | OBP | SLG | $1L | Pts |
|---|---|---|---|---|---|---|---|---|---|---|---|
| Davis I | 24 | 534 | 25 | 69 | 75 | 0 | .246 | .334 | .425 | $11 | 310 |
| Freeman F | 21 | 537 | 18 | 60 | 72 | 0 | .246 | .313 | .425 | $9 | 310 |
| Moreland M | 25 | 390 | 18 | 45 | 54 | 0 | .242 | .313 | .444 | $8 | 230 |
| Allen B | 25 | 418 | 23 | 54 | 50 | 5 | .237 | .311 | .467 | $8 | 240 |
| Overbay L | 34 | 442 | 15 | 55 | 55 | 0 | .249 | .338 | .420 | $8 | 260 |

### Competition at 1B — Stats in 2010
| Bats | Player | GSvR | GSvL | Sub | OPS |
|---|---|---|---|---|---|
| RH | Butler B | 98 | 28 | 1 | .857 |
| LH | Ka'aihue K | 26 | 6 | 2 | .702 |

### Minors (2010)
| Level | Leag | AB | HR | R | RBI | SB | BA | OBP | SLG | CT% | H% | BB% | Bash |
|---|---|---|---|---|---|---|---|---|---|---|---|---|---|
| A | | | | | | | | | | | | | |
| AA | | | | | | | | | | | | | |
| AAA | PCL | 323 | 24 | 67 | 78 | 2 | .319 | .463 | .598 | 79% | 41% | 21% | 1.87 |

### Majors
| Yr | Team | AB | HR | R | RBI | SB | BA | OBP | SLG | CT% | H% | BB% | Bash | $1L | $2L | Pts | RAA | 2B | 3B | CS | FB-LD-GB | HR/fb | RBI% | RS% | OPS | 1st Hf | 2nd Hf | vs RH | vs LH | Rnge | vRH | vLH |
|---|---|---|---|---|---|---|---|---|---|---|---|---|---|---|---|---|---|---|---|---|---|---|---|---|---|---|---|---|---|---|---|---|
| 07 | — | | | | | | | | | | | | | | | | | | | | | | | | | | | | | | | |
| 08 | KC | 21 | 1 | 4 | 1 | 0 | .286 | .375 | .429 | 90% | 32% | 13% | 1.50 | -$3 | -$18 | 20 | +0 | 0 | 0 | 0 | 47-11-42 | 11% | 0% | 38% | .804 | — | .804 | .785 | 1.000 | 1.85 | +23 | -69 |
| 09 | — | | | | | | | | | | | | | | | | | | | | | | | | | | | | | | | |
| 10 | KC | 180 | 8 | 22 | 25 | 0 | .217 | .307 | .394 | 78% | 28% | 12% | 1.82 | $1 | -$13 | 100 | -9 | 6 | 1 | 1 | 49-15-35 | 11% | 15% | 25% | .702 | .500 | .706 | .684 | .754 | 1.85 | +23 | -70 |

---

## Ryan Kalish — 200 PA | $1 | 110 pts
OF-51 (CF-38, LF-12, RF-2) · Owned: 1% · LH

Kalish looks ticketed for a full year in Pawtucket in 2011, but he is widely considered to be the eventual successor to either Cameron, Drew, or Ellsbury in CF (where his bat is already average) or RF. Kalish's game needs refinement, but he seems to have locked up the title of "first call-up in the case of injury." (EB)

### Forecast
| Player | Age | AB | HR | R | RBI | SB | BA | OBP | SLG | $1L | Pts |
|---|---|---|---|---|---|---|---|---|---|---|---|
| Kalish R | 23 | 182 | 6 | 22 | 22 | 8 | .231 | .306 | .394 | $1 | 110 |

### Mini-Browser
| Player | Age | AB | HR | R | RBI | SB | BA | OBP | SLG | $1L | Pts |
|---|---|---|---|---|---|---|---|---|---|---|---|
| Parra G | 23 | 228 | 5 | 28 | 25 | 5 | .263 | .316 | .389 | $2 | 130 |
| Nix L | 30 | 192 | 10 | 24 | 24 | 0 | .260 | .319 | .489 | $1 | 110 |
| Hairston S | 30 | 219 | 9 | 25 | 28 | 2 | .242 | .308 | .433 | $1 | 130 |
| Schierholtz N | 27 | 182 | 4 | 24 | 20 | 4 | .274 | .319 | .445 | $1 | 110 |
| Craig A | 26 | 211 | 9 | 25 | 29 | 1 | .245 | .308 | .431 | $1 | 110 |

### Competition at CF — Stats in 2010
| Bats | Player | GSvR | GSvL | Sub | OPS |
|---|---|---|---|---|---|
| RH | McDonald D | 22 | 30 | 17 | .766 |
| RH | Cameron M | 28 | 15 | 3 | .729 |
| LH | Kalish R | 24 | 9 | 5 | .710 |
| LH | Ellsbury J | 11 | 2 | 0 | .485 |

### Minors (2010)
| Level | Leag | AB | HR | R | RBI | SB | BA | OBP | SLG | CT% | H% | BB% | Bash |
|---|---|---|---|---|---|---|---|---|---|---|---|---|---|
| A | | | | | | | | | | | | | |
| AA | EL | 150 | 8 | 35 | 29 | 13 | .293 | .404 | .527 | 86% | 34% | 15% | 1.80 |
| AAA | IL | 143 | 5 | 22 | 18 | 12 | .294 | .356 | .476 | 78% | 38% | 9% | 1.62 |

### Majors
| Yr | Team | AB | HR | R | RBI | SB | BA | OBP | SLG | CT% | H% | BB% | Bash | $1L | $2L | Pts | RAA | 2B | 3B | CS | FB-LD-GB | HR/fb | RBI% | RS% | OPS | 1st Hf | 2nd Hf | vs RH | vs LH | Rnge | vRH | vLH |
|---|---|---|---|---|---|---|---|---|---|---|---|---|---|---|---|---|---|---|---|---|---|---|---|---|---|---|---|---|---|---|---|---|
| 07 | — | | | | | | | | | | | | | | | | | | | | | | | | | | | | | | | |
| 08 | — | | | | | | | | | | | | | | | | | | | | | | | | | | | | | | | |
| 09 | — | | | | | | | | | | | | | | | | | | | | | | | | | | | | 2.10 | | | |
| 10 | BOS | 163 | 4 | 26 | 24 | 10 | .252 | .305 | .405 | 77% | 33% | 7% | 1.61 | $4 | -$10 | 110 | -1 | 11 | 1 | 1 | 36-18-46 | 9% | 22% | 44% | .710 | — | .710 | .748 | .599 | 2.10 | | |

---

## Gabe Kapler — 100 PA | $-3 | 60 pts
OF-50 (RF-39, LF-12, CF-2), DH-5 · Owned: 0% · RH

Kapler's reputation derives from playing good defense and smashing left-handed pitching. In 2010, though, he could not produce against either righties or lefties. If no team grants him another chance, Kapler could re-retire. Even in 2009, he was merely ordinary at the plate for his position. (RZ)

### Forecast
| Player | Age | AB | HR | R | RBI | SB | BA | OBP | SLG | $1L | Pts |
|---|---|---|---|---|---|---|---|---|---|---|---|
| Kapler G | 35 | 95 | 3 | 12 | 13 | 1 | .252 | .317 | .414 | -$3 | 60 |

### Mini-Browser
| Player | Age | AB | HR | R | RBI | SB | BA | OBP | SLG | $1L | Pts |
|---|---|---|---|---|---|---|---|---|---|---|---|
| Gillespie C | 26 | 86 | 3 | 12 | 10 | 2 | .244 | .336 | .436 | -$2 | 50 |
| Gerut J | 33 | 68 | 3 | 11 | 9 | 2 | .265 | .322 | .467 | -$2 | 50 |
| Kelly D | 31 | 116 | 3 | 14 | 11 | 3 | .258 | .317 | .380 | -$3 | 70 |
| Carroll B | 28 | 88 | 3 | 13 | 11 | 1 | .239 | .306 | .430 | -$3 | 50 |
| Johnson R | 34 | 91 | 1 | 12 | 10 | 1 | .265 | .323 | .382 | -$3 | 50 |

### Competition at RF — Stats in 2010
| Bats | Player | GSvR | GSvL | Sub | OPS |
|---|---|---|---|---|---|
| BH | Zobrist B | 64 | 34 | 5 | .699 |
| LH | Joyce M | 45 | 1 | 7 | .837 |
| RH | Kapler G | 2 | 29 | 8 | .578 |

### Minors (2010)
| Level | Leag | AB | HR | R | RBI | SB | BA | OBP | SLG | CT% | H% | BB% | Bash |
|---|---|---|---|---|---|---|---|---|---|---|---|---|---|
| A | FLO | 13 | 0 | 0 | 1 | 0 | .077 | .143 | .077 | 77% | 10% | 7% | 1.00 |
| AA | | | | | | | | | | | | | |
| AAA | | | | | | | | | | | | | |

### Majors
| Yr | Team | AB | HR | R | RBI | SB | BA | OBP | SLG | CT% | H% | BB% | Bash | $1L | $2L | Pts | RAA | 2B | 3B | CS | FB-LD-GB | HR/fb | RBI% | RS% | OPS | 1st Hf | 2nd Hf | vs RH | vs LH | Rnge | vRH | vLH |
|---|---|---|---|---|---|---|---|---|---|---|---|---|---|---|---|---|---|---|---|---|---|---|---|---|---|---|---|---|---|---|---|---|
| 07 | — | | | | | | | | | | | | | | | | | | | | | | | | | | | | | | -25 | +56 |
| 08 | MIL | 229 | 8 | 36 | 38 | 3 | .301 | .340 | .498 | 83% | 36% | 5% | 1.65 | $7 | -$4 | 170 | +3 | 14 | 1 | 2 | 36-18-46 | 12% | 22% | 37% | .838 | .869 | .780 | .747 | 1.001 | 2.10 | -21 | +47 |
| 09 | TB | 205 | 8 | 26 | 32 | 5 | .239 | .329 | .439 | 81% | 30% | 12% | 1.84 | $3 | -$10 | 150 | -2 | 15 | 1 | 2 | 41-22-36 | 11% | 21% | 26% | .768 | .839 | .681 | .357 | .931 | 2.12 | -31 | +74 |
| 10 | TB | 124 | 3 | 19 | 13 | 1 | .210 | .288 | .290 | 81% | 26% | 8% | 1.38 | -$2 | -$17 | 60 | -12 | 4 | 0 | 1 | 40-19-42 | 5% | 17% | 45% | .578 | .596 | .510 | .640 | .560 | 2.12 | -48 | +90 |

---

## Austin Kearns — 500 PA | $9 | 240 pts
OF-118 (LF-91, RF-32, CF-5), DH-2 · Owned: 6% · RH

Kearns, a trade-deadline pick-up for the Yankees, started out strong in his first month but then slumped, and he eventually lost PT to the team's September call-ups. Kearns is unlikely to be back in pinstripes in 2011, and he is not suited to his natural assignment of facing LHP. (LS)

### Forecast
| Player | Age | AB | HR | R | RBI | SB | BA | OBP | SLG | $1L | Pts |
|---|---|---|---|---|---|---|---|---|---|---|---|
| Kearns A | 30 | 402 | 10 | 60 | 55 | 5 | .261 | .355 | .397 | $9 | 240 |

### Mini-Browser
| Player | Age | AB | HR | R | RBI | SB | BA | OBP | SLG | $1L | Pts |
|---|---|---|---|---|---|---|---|---|---|---|---|
| Burrell P | 34 | 320 | 16 | 44 | 60 | 0 | .250 | .361 | .453 | $10 | 210 |
| Pie F | 26 | 384 | 12 | 52 | 44 | 8 | .271 | .320 | .432 | $10 | 230 |
| Fukudome K | 33 | 364 | 9 | 59 | 45 | 9 | .272 | .383 | .436 | $9 | 270 |
| Carter C | 24 | 442 | 25 | 55 | 65 | 5 | .215 | .306 | .437 | $9 | 240 |
| Bernadina R | 26 | 466 | 10 | 55 | 45 | 25 | .236 | .307 | .359 | $9 | 260 |

### Competition at LF — Stats in 2010
| Bats | Player | GSvR | GSvL | Sub | OPS |
|---|---|---|---|---|---|
| LH | Gardner B | 81 | 30 | 12 | .762 |
| RH | Kearns A | 3 | 17 | 2 | .746 |
| RH | Thames M | 4 | 15 | 6 | .841 |
| RH | Russo K | 4 | 6 | 1 | .470 |

### Minors (2010)
| Level | Leag | AB | HR | R | RBI | SB | BA | OBP | SLG | CT% | H% | BB% | Bash |
|---|---|---|---|---|---|---|---|---|---|---|---|---|---|
| A | | | | | | | | | | | | | |
| AA | | | | | | | | | | | | | |
| AAA | | | | | | | | | | | | | |

### Majors
| Yr | Team | AB | HR | R | RBI | SB | BA | OBP | SLG | CT% | H% | BB% | Bash | $1L | $2L | Pts | RAA | 2B | 3B | CS | FB-LD-GB | HR/fb | RBI% | RS% | OPS | 1st Hf | 2nd Hf | vs RH | vs LH | Rnge | vRH | vLH |
|---|---|---|---|---|---|---|---|---|---|---|---|---|---|---|---|---|---|---|---|---|---|---|---|---|---|---|---|---|---|---|---|---|
| 07 | WAS | 587 | 16 | 84 | 74 | 2 | .266 | .355 | .411 | 82% | 32% | 10% | 1.54 | $14 | $6 | 370 | -5 | 35 | 1 | 2 | 35-20-45 | 10% | 18% | 30% | .765 | .692 | .851 | .728 | .553 | 2.11 | -30 | +76 |
| 08 | WAS | 313 | 7 | 40 | 32 | 2 | .217 | .311 | .316 | 80% | 27% | 10% | 1.46 | $0 | -$11 | 140 | -19 | 10 | 2 | 3 | 32-21-47 | 9% | 14% | 32% | .627 | .614 | .647 | .676 | .496 | 2.12 | -40 | +105 |
| 09 | WAS | 174 | 3 | 20 | 17 | 1 | .195 | .304 | .305 | 71% | 28% | 15% | 1.56 | -$3 | -$17 | 70 | -10 | 6 | 2 | 1 | 37-18-46 | 7% | 13% | 25% | .641 | .644 | .597 | .675 | .553 | 2.11 | -17 | +45 |
| 10 | 2TM | 403 | 10 | 55 | 49 | 4 | .263 | .351 | .395 | 71% | 37% | 10% | 1.50 | $10 | -$1 | 200 | -6 | 21 | 1 | 1 | 33-23-44 | 8% | 15% | 30% | .746 | .766 | .705 | .749 | .540 | 2.09 | -1 | +2 |

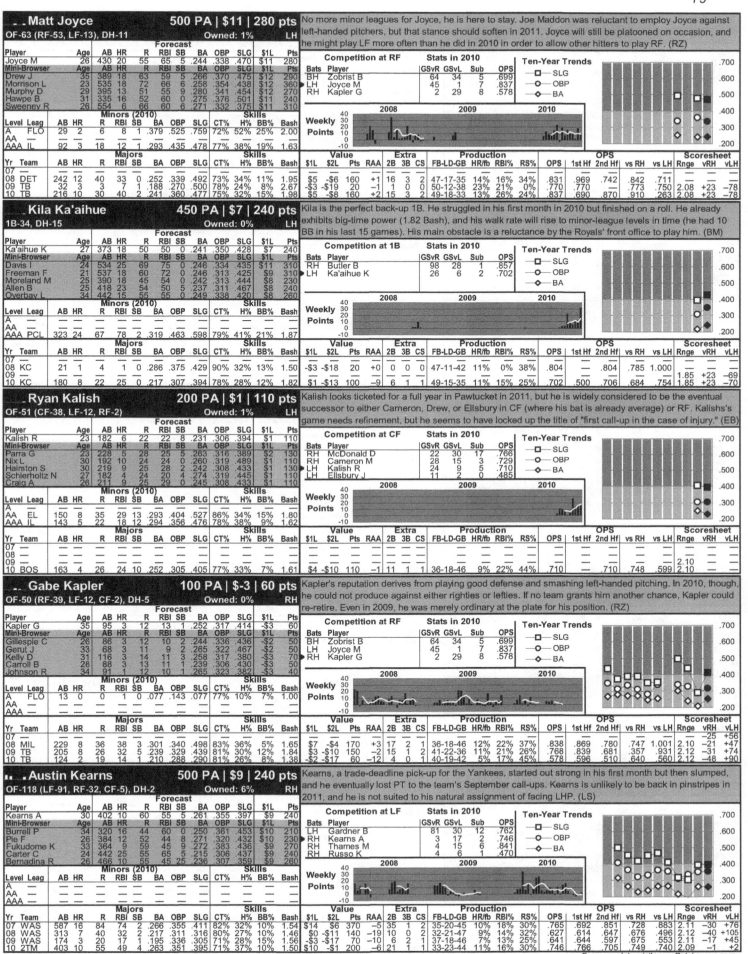

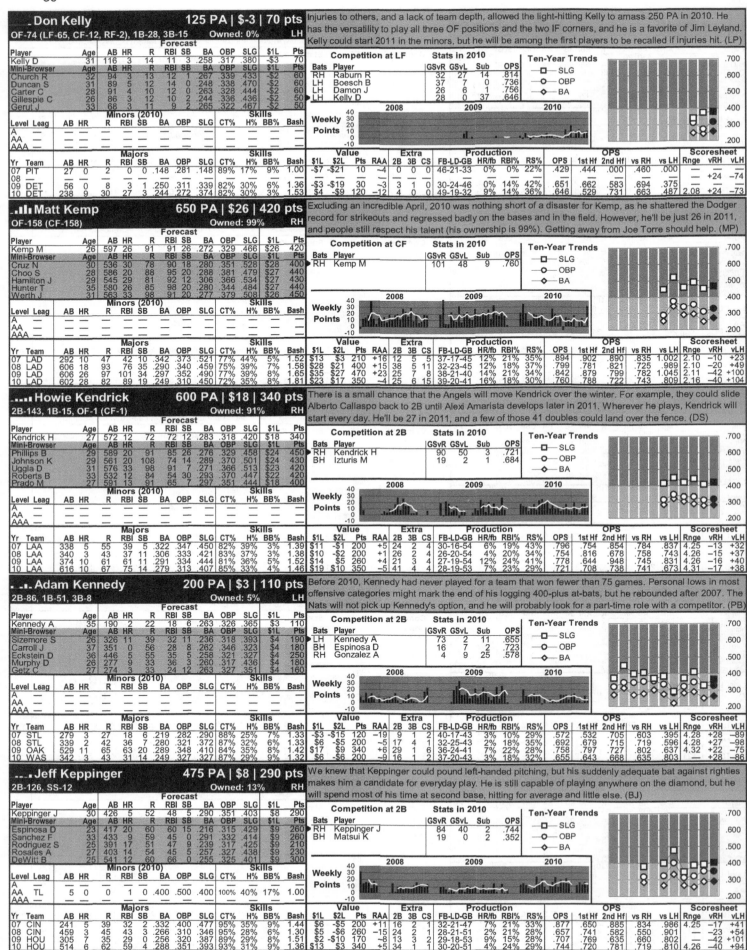

## Don Kelly — 125 PA | $-3 | 70 pts

OF-74 (LF-65, CF-12, RF-2), 1B-28, 3B-15    Owned: 0%    LH

Injuries to others, and a lack of team depth, allowed the light-hitting Kelly to amass 250 PA in 2010. He has the versatility to play all three OF positions and the two IF corners, and he is a favorite of Jim Leyland. Kelly could start 2011 in the minors, but he will be among the first players to be recalled if injuries hit. (LP)

### Forecast
| Player | Age | AB | HR | R | RBI | SB | BA | OBP | SLG | $1L | Pts |
|---|---|---|---|---|---|---|---|---|---|---|---|
| Kelly D | 31 | 116 | 3 | 14 | 11 | 3 | .258 | .317 | .380 | -3 | 70 |

### Mini-Browser
| Player | Age | AB | HR | R | RBI | SB | BA | OBP | SLG | $1L | Pts |
|---|---|---|---|---|---|---|---|---|---|---|---|
| Church R | 32 | 94 | 3 | 13 | 12 | 1 | .267 | .339 | .433 | -2 | 60 |
| Duncan S | 31 | 89 | 5 | 12 | 14 | 0 | .248 | .338 | .470 | -2 | 60 |
| Carter C | 28 | 91 | 4 | 10 | 12 | 0 | .263 | .328 | .444 | -2 | 60 |
| Gillespie C | 26 | 86 | 3 | 12 | 10 | 2 | .244 | .336 | .436 | -2 | 50 |
| Gerut J | 33 | 68 | 3 | 11 | 9 | 2 | .265 | .322 | .467 | -2 | 50 |

### Competition at LF / Stats in 2010
| Bats | Player | GSvR | GSvL | Sub | OPS |
|---|---|---|---|---|---|
| RH | Raburn R | 32 | 27 | 14 | .814 |
| LH | Boesch B | 37 | 7 | 0 | .736 |
| LH | Damon J | 26 | 6 | 1 | .756 |
| LH | Kelly D | 28 | 0 | 37 | .646 |

### Minors (2010) / Skills
| Level | Leag | AB | HR | R | RBI | SB | BA | OBP | SLG | CT% | H% | BB% | Bash |
|---|---|---|---|---|---|---|---|---|---|---|---|---|---|
| A | — | | | | | | | | | | | | |
| AA | — | | | | | | | | | | | | |
| AAA | — | | | | | | | | | | | | |

### Majors / Skills / Value / Extra / Production / OPS / Scoresheet
| Yr | Team | AB | HR | R | RBI | SB | BA | OBP | SLG | CT% | H% | BB% | Bash | $1L | $2L | Pts | RAA | 2B | 3B | CS | FB-LD-GB | HR/fb | RBI% | RS% | OPS | 1st Hf | 2nd Hf | vs RH | vs LH | Rnge | vRH | vLH |
|---|---|---|---|---|---|---|---|---|---|---|---|---|---|---|---|---|---|---|---|---|---|---|---|---|---|---|---|---|---|---|---|---|
| 07 | PIT | 27 | 0 | 2 | 0 | 0 | .148 | .281 | .148 | 89% | 17% | 9% | 1.00 | -7 | -21 | 10 | -4 | 0 | 0 | 0 | 46-21-33 | 0% | 0% | 22% | .429 | .444 | .000 | .460 | .000 | — | +24 | -74 |
| 08 | — | | | | | | | | | | | | | | | | | | | | | | | | | | | | | | | |
| 09 | DET | 56 | 0 | 8 | 3 | 1 | .250 | .311 | .339 | 82% | 30% | 6% | 1.36 | -3 | -19 | 30 | -3 | 3 | 1 | 0 | 30-24-46 | 0% | 14% | 42% | .651 | .662 | .583 | .694 | .375 | — | +24 | -73 |
| 10 | DET | 238 | 9 | 30 | 27 | 3 | .244 | .272 | .374 | 82% | 30% | 3% | 1.53 | 4 | -9 | 120 | -12 | 4 | 0 | 4 | 49-19-32 | 14% | 14% | 36% | .646 | .529 | .731 | .663 | .487 | 2.08 | +24 | -73 |

## Matt Kemp — 650 PA | $26 | 420 pts

OF-158 (CF-158)    Owned: 99%    RH

Excluding an incredible April, 2010 was nothing short of a disaster for Kemp, as he shattered the Dodger record for strikeouts and regressed badly on the bases and in the field. However, he'll be just 26 in 2011, and people still respect his talent (his ownership is 99%). Getting away from Joe Torre should help. (MP)

### Forecast
| Player | Age | AB | HR | R | RBI | SB | BA | OBP | SLG | $1L | Pts |
|---|---|---|---|---|---|---|---|---|---|---|---|
| Kemp M | 26 | 597 | 26 | 91 | 91 | 26 | .272 | .329 | .466 | 26 | 420 |

### Mini-Browser
| Player | Age | AB | HR | R | RBI | SB | BA | OBP | SLG | $1L | Pts |
|---|---|---|---|---|---|---|---|---|---|---|---|
| Cruz N | 30 | 536 | 30 | 78 | 90 | 18 | .280 | .351 | .528 | 28 | 400 |
| Choo S | 28 | 586 | 20 | 88 | 95 | 20 | .288 | .381 | .479 | 27 | 440 |
| Hamilton J | 29 | 545 | 29 | 81 | 92 | 12 | .306 | .366 | .534 | 27 | 430 |
| Hunter T | 35 | 580 | 26 | 85 | 98 | 20 | .280 | .344 | .484 | 27 | 440 |
| Werth J | 31 | 563 | 33 | 98 | 91 | 20 | .277 | .379 | .508 | 26 | 450 |

### Competition at CF / Stats in 2010
| Bats | Player | GSvR | GSvL | Sub | OPS |
|---|---|---|---|---|---|
| RH | Kemp M | 101 | 48 | 9 | .760 |

### Minors (2010) / Skills
| Level | Leag | AB | HR | R | RBI | SB | BA | OBP | SLG | CT% | H% | BB% | Bash |
|---|---|---|---|---|---|---|---|---|---|---|---|---|---|
| A | — | | | | | | | | | | | | |
| AA | — | | | | | | | | | | | | |
| AAA | — | | | | | | | | | | | | |

### Majors / Skills / Value / Extra / Production / OPS / Scoresheet
| Yr | Team | AB | HR | R | RBI | SB | BA | OBP | SLG | CT% | H% | BB% | Bash | $1L | $2L | Pts | RAA | 2B | 3B | CS | FB-LD-GB | HR/fb | RBI% | RS% | OPS | 1st Hf | 2nd Hf | vs RH | vs LH | Rnge | vRH | vLH |
|---|---|---|---|---|---|---|---|---|---|---|---|---|---|---|---|---|---|---|---|---|---|---|---|---|---|---|---|---|---|---|---|---|
| 07 | LAD | 292 | 10 | 47 | 42 | 10 | .342 | .373 | .521 | 77% | 44% | 5% | 1.52 | 13 | 3 | 210 | +16 | 12 | 5 | 5 | 37-17-45 | 12% | 21% | 35% | .894 | .902 | .890 | .835 | 1.002 | 2.10 | -10 | +23 |
| 08 | LAD | 606 | 18 | 93 | 76 | 35 | .290 | .340 | .459 | 75% | 39% | 7% | 1.58 | 28 | 21 | 400 | +15 | 38 | 5 | 11 | 32-23-45 | 12% | 18% | 37% | .799 | .781 | .821 | .725 | .989 | 2.10 | -20 | +49 |
| 09 | LAD | 606 | 26 | 97 | 101 | 34 | .297 | .352 | .490 | 77% | 39% | 8% | 1.65 | 35 | 27 | 470 | +23 | 34 | 7 | 8 | 38-21-40 | 14% | 21% | 34% | .842 | .879 | .799 | .782 | 1.045 | 2.11 | -42 | +100 |
| 10 | LAD | 602 | 28 | 82 | 89 | 19 | .249 | .310 | .450 | 72% | 35% | 8% | 1.81 | 23 | 17 | 350 | -4 | 25 | 6 | 15 | 39-20-41 | 16% | 18% | 30% | .760 | .788 | .722 | .743 | .809 | 2.16 | -40 | +104 |

## Howie Kendrick — 600 PA | $18 | 340 pts

2B-143, 1B-15, OF-1 (CF-1)    Owned: 91%    RH

There is a small chance that the Angels will move Kendrick over the winter. For example, they could slide Alberto Callaspo back to 2B until Alexi Amarista develops later in 2011. Wherever he plays, Kendrick will start every day. He'll be 27 in 2011, and a few of those 41 doubles could land over the fence. (DS)

### Forecast
| Player | Age | AB | HR | R | RBI | SB | BA | OBP | SLG | $1L | Pts |
|---|---|---|---|---|---|---|---|---|---|---|---|
| Kendrick H | 27 | 572 | 12 | 72 | 72 | 12 | .283 | .318 | .420 | 18 | 340 |

### Mini-Browser
| Player | Age | AB | HR | R | RBI | SB | BA | OBP | SLG | $1L | Pts |
|---|---|---|---|---|---|---|---|---|---|---|---|
| Phillips B | 29 | 589 | 20 | 91 | 85 | 26 | .276 | .329 | .458 | 24 | 450 |
| Johnson K | 29 | 561 | 20 | 108 | 74 | 14 | .289 | .370 | .501 | 24 | 430 |
| Uggla D | 31 | 576 | 33 | 98 | 91 | 7 | .271 | .366 | .513 | 23 | 420 |
| Roberts B | 33 | 532 | 12 | 84 | 54 | 30 | .293 | .370 | .447 | 22 | 420 |
| Prado M | 27 | 591 | 13 | 91 | 65 | 7 | .297 | .351 | .444 | 18 | 400 |

### Competition at 2B / Stats in 2010
| Bats | Player | GSvR | GSvL | Sub | OPS |
|---|---|---|---|---|---|
| RH | Kendrick H | 90 | 50 | 3 | .721 |
| BH | Izturis M | 19 | 2 | 1 | .684 |

### Minors (2010) / Skills
| Level | Leag | AB | HR | R | RBI | SB | BA | OBP | SLG | CT% | H% | BB% | Bash |
|---|---|---|---|---|---|---|---|---|---|---|---|---|---|
| A | — | | | | | | | | | | | | |
| AA | — | | | | | | | | | | | | |
| AAA | — | | | | | | | | | | | | |

### Majors / Skills / Value / Extra / Production / OPS / Scoresheet
| Yr | Team | AB | HR | R | RBI | SB | BA | OBP | SLG | CT% | H% | BB% | Bash | $1L | $2L | Pts | RAA | 2B | 3B | CS | FB-LD-GB | HR/fb | RBI% | RS% | OPS | 1st Hf | 2nd Hf | vs RH | vs LH | Rnge | vRH | vLH |
|---|---|---|---|---|---|---|---|---|---|---|---|---|---|---|---|---|---|---|---|---|---|---|---|---|---|---|---|---|---|---|---|---|
| 07 | LAA | 338 | 5 | 55 | 39 | 5 | .322 | .347 | .450 | 82% | 39% | 3% | 1.39 | 11 | -1 | 200 | +5 | 24 | 2 | 4 | 30-16-54 | 6% | 19% | 43% | .796 | .754 | .854 | .784 | .837 | 4.25 | -13 | +32 |
| 08 | LAA | 340 | 3 | 43 | 37 | 11 | .306 | .333 | .421 | 83% | 37% | 3% | 1.38 | 10 | -2 | 200 | +1 | 26 | 2 | 6 | 26-20-54 | 4% | 20% | 34% | .754 | .816 | .678 | .758 | .743 | 4.26 | -15 | +37 |
| 09 | LAA | 374 | 10 | 61 | 61 | 11 | .291 | .334 | .444 | 81% | 36% | 5% | 1.52 | 14 | 5 | 260 | +4 | 21 | 3 | 4 | 27-19-54 | 12% | 24% | 41% | .778 | .644 | .948 | .745 | .831 | 4.26 | -16 | +40 |
| 10 | LAA | 616 | 10 | 67 | 75 | 14 | .279 | .313 | .407 | 85% | 33% | 4% | 1.46 | 19 | 10 | 350 | -5 | 41 | 4 | 4 | 28-19-53 | 7% | 23% | 29% | .721 | .708 | .738 | .738 | .673 | 4.31 | -17 | +38 |

## Adam Kennedy — 200 PA | $3 | 110 pts

2B-86, 1B-51, 3B-8    Owned: 5%    LH

Before 2010, Kennedy had never played for a team that won fewer than 75 games. Personal lows in most offensive categories might mark the end of his logging 400-plus at-bats, but he rebounded after 2007. The Nats will not pick up Kennedy's option, and he will probably look for a part-time role with a competitor. (PB)

### Forecast
| Player | Age | AB | HR | R | RBI | SB | BA | OBP | SLG | $1L | Pts |
|---|---|---|---|---|---|---|---|---|---|---|---|
| Kennedy A | 35 | 190 | 2 | 22 | 18 | 6 | .263 | .326 | .365 | 3 | 110 |

### Mini-Browser
| Player | Age | AB | HR | R | RBI | SB | BA | OBP | SLG | $1L | Pts |
|---|---|---|---|---|---|---|---|---|---|---|---|
| Sizemore S | 26 | 326 | 11 | 39 | 32 | 11 | .236 | .318 | .393 | 4 | 190 |
| Carroll J | 37 | 351 | 0 | 56 | 28 | 8 | .262 | .346 | .323 | 4 | 180 |
| Eckstein D | 36 | 446 | 5 | 55 | 35 | 5 | .258 | .321 | .327 | 4 | 250 |
| Murphy D | 26 | 277 | 9 | 33 | 36 | 3 | .260 | .317 | .436 | 4 | 180 |
| Getz C | 27 | 274 | 3 | 33 | 24 | 12 | .263 | .327 | .351 | 4 | 160 |

### Competition at 2B / Stats in 2010
| Bats | Player | GSvR | GSvL | Sub | OPS |
|---|---|---|---|---|---|
| LH | Kennedy A | 73 | 2 | 11 | .655 |
| BH | Espinosa D | 16 | 7 | 2 | .723 |
| RH | Gonzalez A | 4 | 9 | 25 | .578 |

### Minors (2010) / Skills
| Level | Leag | AB | HR | R | RBI | SB | BA | OBP | SLG | CT% | H% | BB% | Bash |
|---|---|---|---|---|---|---|---|---|---|---|---|---|---|
| A | — | | | | | | | | | | | | |
| AA | — | | | | | | | | | | | | |
| AAA | — | | | | | | | | | | | | |

### Majors / Skills / Value / Extra / Production / OPS / Scoresheet
| Yr | Team | AB | HR | R | RBI | SB | BA | OBP | SLG | CT% | H% | BB% | Bash | $1L | $2L | Pts | RAA | 2B | 3B | CS | FB-LD-GB | HR/fb | RBI% | RS% | OPS | 1st Hf | 2nd Hf | vs RH | vs LH | Rnge | vRH | vLH |
|---|---|---|---|---|---|---|---|---|---|---|---|---|---|---|---|---|---|---|---|---|---|---|---|---|---|---|---|---|---|---|---|---|
| 07 | STL | 279 | 3 | 27 | 18 | 6 | .219 | .282 | .290 | 88% | 25% | 7% | 1.33 | -3 | -15 | 120 | -19 | 9 | 1 | 2 | 40-17-43 | 3% | 10% | 29% | .572 | .532 | .705 | .603 | .395 | 4.28 | +28 | -89 |
| 08 | STL | 339 | 2 | 42 | 36 | 7 | .280 | .321 | .372 | 87% | 32% | 6% | 1.33 | 6 | -5 | 200 | -5 | 17 | 4 | 1 | 32-25-43 | 2% | 18% | 35% | .692 | .679 | .715 | .719 | .596 | 4.28 | +27 | -98 |
| 09 | OAK | 529 | 11 | 65 | 63 | 20 | .289 | .348 | .410 | 84% | 35% | 8% | 1.42 | 17 | 9 | 340 | +6 | 29 | 1 | 6 | 36-24-41 | 7% | 22% | 28% | .758 | .797 | .727 | .802 | .637 | 4.32 | +22 | -75 |
| 10 | WAS | 342 | 3 | 43 | 31 | 14 | .249 | .327 | .327 | 87% | 29% | 9% | 1.32 | 6 | -6 | 200 | -9 | 16 | 1 | 2 | 37-20-43 | 3% | 18% | 32% | .655 | .643 | .668 | .635 | .803 | — | +28 | -86 |

## Jeff Keppinger — 475 PA | $8 | 290 pts

2B-126, SS-12    Owned: 13%    RH

We knew that Keppinger could pound left-handed pitching, but his suddenly adequate bat against righties makes him a candidate for everyday play. He is still capable of playing anywhere on the diamond, but he will spend most of his time at second base, hitting for average and little else. (BJ)

### Forecast
| Player | Age | AB | HR | R | RBI | SB | BA | OBP | SLG | $1L | Pts |
|---|---|---|---|---|---|---|---|---|---|---|---|
| Keppinger J | 30 | 426 | 5 | 52 | 48 | 5 | .290 | .351 | .403 | 8 | 290 |

### Mini-Browser
| Player | Age | AB | HR | R | RBI | SB | BA | OBP | SLG | $1L | Pts |
|---|---|---|---|---|---|---|---|---|---|---|---|
| Espinosa D | 23 | 417 | 20 | 60 | 60 | 15 | .216 | .315 | .429 | 9 | 260 |
| Sanchez F | 33 | 433 | 9 | 59 | 45 | 0 | .291 | .332 | .414 | 9 | 260 |
| Rodriguez S | 25 | 391 | 17 | 51 | 47 | 9 | .239 | .317 | .425 | 9 | 210 |
| Rosales S | 27 | 403 | 14 | 54 | 45 | 5 | .257 | .327 | .438 | 9 | 230 |
| DeWitt B | 25 | 541 | 12 | 60 | 66 | 9 | .255 | .325 | .401 | 9 | 300 |

### Competition at 2B / Stats in 2010
| Bats | Player | GSvR | GSvL | Sub | OPS |
|---|---|---|---|---|---|
| RH | Keppinger J | 84 | 40 | 2 | .744 |
| BH | Matsui K | 19 | 0 | 2 | .352 |

### Minors (2010) / Skills
| Level | Leag | AB | HR | R | RBI | SB | BA | OBP | SLG | CT% | H% | BB% | Bash |
|---|---|---|---|---|---|---|---|---|---|---|---|---|---|
| A | — | | | | | | | | | | | | |
| AA | TL | 5 | 0 | 0 | 1 | 0 | .400 | .500 | .400 | 100% | 40% | 17% | 1.00 |
| AAA | — | | | | | | | | | | | | |

### Majors / Skills / Value / Extra / Production / OPS / Scoresheet
| Yr | Team | AB | HR | R | RBI | SB | BA | OBP | SLG | CT% | H% | BB% | Bash | $1L | $2L | Pts | RAA | 2B | 3B | CS | FB-LD-GB | HR/fb | RBI% | RS% | OPS | 1st Hf | 2nd Hf | vs RH | vs LH | Rnge | vRH | vLH |
|---|---|---|---|---|---|---|---|---|---|---|---|---|---|---|---|---|---|---|---|---|---|---|---|---|---|---|---|---|---|---|---|---|
| 07 | CIN | 241 | 5 | 39 | 32 | 2 | .332 | .400 | .477 | 95% | 35% | 9% | 1.44 | 16 | 2 | 1 | 32-21-47 | 7% | 21% | 33% | .877 | .650 | .885 | .834 | .986 | 4.25 | -17 | +41 |
| 08 | CIN | 459 | 3 | 45 | 43 | 3 | .266 | .310 | .346 | 95% | 28% | 6% | 1.30 | -5 | -6 | 260 | -15 | 24 | 2 | 1 | 28-21-51 | 2% | 19% | 23% | .657 | .741 | .582 | .550 | .901 | — | -23 | +54 |
| 09 | HOU | 305 | 7 | 35 | 29 | 0 | .256 | .320 | .387 | 89% | 29% | 8% | 1.51 | 2 | -10 | 120 | -8 | 13 | 3 | 2 | 29-18-53 | 9% | 15% | 28% | .707 | .769 | .635 | .660 | .802 | — | -42 | +101 |
| 10 | HOU | 514 | 6 | 62 | 59 | 0 | .288 | .351 | .393 | 93% | 31% | 9% | 1.36 | 13 | 3 | 340 | +5 | 34 | 1 | 3 | 30-20-51 | 4% | 24% | 29% | .744 | .720 | .781 | .719 | .810 | 4.26 | -40 | +94 |

## Ian Kinsler — 600 PA | $27 | 470 pts

2B-103 — Owned: 99% — RH

Kinsler has done everything necessary to be a Chase Utley-esque monster: hit for power, hit for average, draw walks, play elite defense, etc. The problem is that Kinsler never seems to do them at the same time, much less stay healthy while doing them. TEX is lucky to have a great 2B but he could be even better. (JM)

| Player | Age | AB | HR | R | RBI | SB | BA | OBP | SLG | $1L | Pts |
|---|---|---|---|---|---|---|---|---|---|---|---|
| Kinsler I | 28 | 545 | 24 | 96 | 72 | 24 | .286 | .361 | .486 | $27 | 470 |
| **Mini-Browser** | **Age** | **AB** | **HR** | **R** | **RBI** | **SB** | **BA** | **OBP** | **SLG** | **$1L** | **Pts** |
| Utley C | 32 | 542 | 26 | 104 | 98 | 13 | .288 | .387 | .517 | $28 | 480 |
| Weeks R | 28 | 651 | 30 | 120 | 75 | 23 | .265 | .363 | .468 | $25 | 460 |
| Cano R | 28 | 636 | 20 | 88 | 88 | 0 | .297 | .341 | .485 | $25 | 450 |
| Pedroia D | 27 | 577 | 13 | 98 | 65 | 13 | .304 | .372 | .465 | $25 | 460 |
| Phillips B | 29 | 589 | 20 | 91 | 85 | 26 | .276 | .329 | .458 | $24 | 450 |

Minors (2010) / Skills

| Level | Leag | AB | HR | R | RBI | SB | BA | OBP | SLG | CT% | H% | BB% | Bash |
|---|---|---|---|---|---|---|---|---|---|---|---|---|---|
| A | — | — | — | — | — | — | — | — | — | — | — | — | — |
| AA | TL | 19 | 0 | 3 | 6 | 2 | .263 | .348 | .368 | 84% | 31% | 9% | 1.40 |
| AAA | — | — | — | — | — | — | — | — | — | — | — | — | — |

Competition at 2B — Stats in 2010

| Bats | Player | GSvR | GSvL | Sub | OPS |
|---|---|---|---|---|---|
| RH | Kinsler I | 71 | 31 | 1 | .794 |
| BH | Blanco A | 20 | 11 | 9 | .679 |

Ten-Year Trends: SLG, OBP, BA

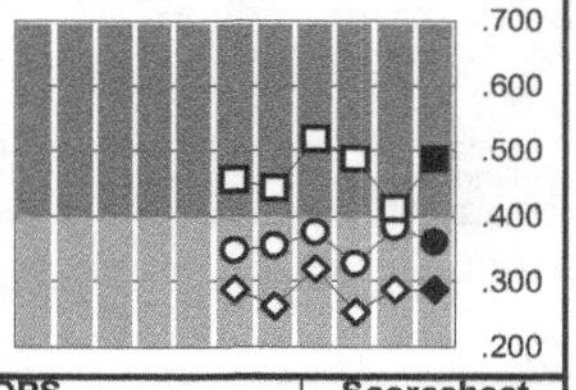


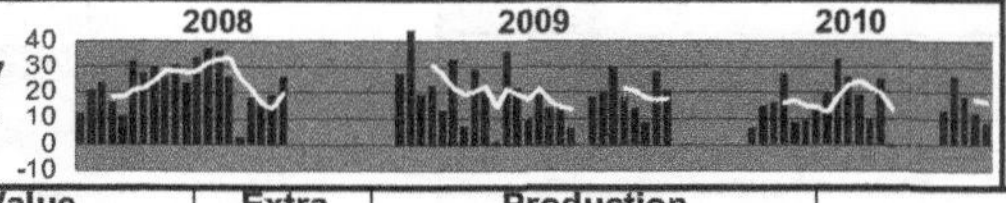


Majors / Skills

| Yr | Team | AB | HR | R | RBI | SB | BA | OBP | SLG | CT% | H% | BB% | Bash |
|---|---|---|---|---|---|---|---|---|---|---|---|---|---|
| 07 | TEX | 483 | 20 | 96 | 61 | 23 | .263 | .355 | .441 | 83% | 32% | 11% | 1.68 |
| 08 | TEX | 518 | 18 | 102 | 71 | 26 | .319 | .375 | .517 | 87% | 37% | 8% | 1.62 |
| 09 | TEX | 566 | 31 | 101 | 86 | 31 | .253 | .327 | .488 | 86% | 29% | 9% | 1.93 |
| 10 | TEX | 391 | 9 | 73 | 45 | 15 | .286 | .382 | .412 | 85% | 34% | 12% | 1.44 |

Value / Extra / Production / OPS / Scoresheet

| Yr | $1L | $2L | Pts | RAA | 2B | 3B | CS | FB-LD-GB | HR/fb | RBI% | RS% | OPS | 1st Hf | 2nd Hf | vs RH | vs LH | Rnge | vRH | vLH |
|---|---|---|---|---|---|---|---|---|---|---|---|---|---|---|---|---|---|---|---|
| 07 | $22 | $12 | 390 | +11 | 22 | 2 | 2 | 46-20-35 | 11% | 17% | 43% | .796 | .787 | .807 | .732 | .999 | 4.26 | −12 | +32 |
| 08 | $30 | $23 | 470 | +32 | 41 | 4 | 2 | 43-24-32 | 9% | 25% | 42% | .892 | .945 | .717 | .915 | .828 | 4.28 | −27 | +69 |
| 09 | $27 | $22 | 500 | +16 | 32 | 4 | 5 | 54-16-30 | 12% | 25% | 40% | .814 | .816 | .811 | .738 | 1.011 | 4.26 | −21 | +55 |
| 10 | $17 | $7 | 300 | +10 | 20 | 1 | 5 | 42-18-40 | 7% | 18% | 39% | .794 | .831 | .734 | .743 | .957 | 4.32 | −21 | +54 |

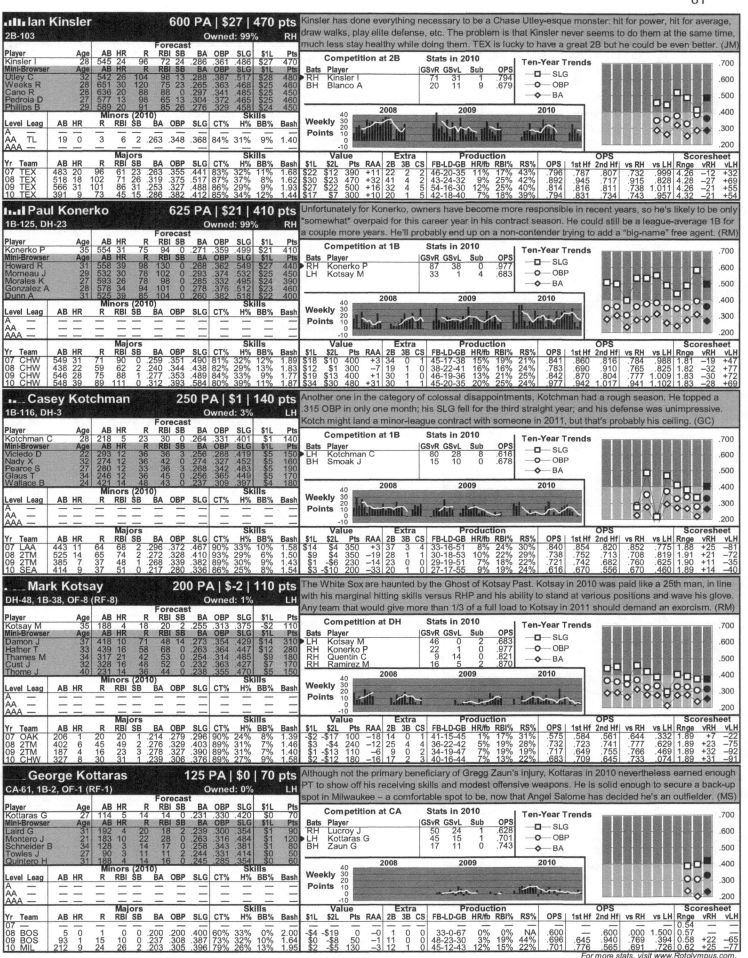

## Paul Konerko — 625 PA | $21 | 410 pts

1B-125, DH-23 — Owned: 99% — RH

Unfortunately for Konerko, owners have become more responsible in recent years, so he's likely to be only *somewhat* overpaid for this career year in his contract season. He could still be a league-average 1B for a couple more years. He'll probably end up on a non-contender trying to add a "big-name" free agent. (RM)

| Player | Age | AB | HR | R | RBI | SB | BA | OBP | SLG | $1L | Pts |
|---|---|---|---|---|---|---|---|---|---|---|---|
| Konerko P | 35 | 554 | 31 | 75 | 94 | 0 | .271 | .359 | .499 | $21 | 410 |
| **Mini-Browser** | **Age** | **AB** | **HR** | **R** | **RBI** | **SB** | **BA** | **OBP** | **SLG** | **$1L** | **Pts** |
| Howard R | 31 | 558 | 39 | 98 | 130 | 0 | .268 | .362 | .549 | $27 | 440 |
| Morneau J | 29 | 532 | 30 | 78 | 102 | 0 | .293 | .374 | .532 | $25 | 450 |
| Morales K | 27 | 593 | 26 | 78 | 98 | 0 | .285 | .332 | .495 | $24 | 390 |
| Gonzalez A | 28 | 578 | 34 | 94 | 101 | 0 | .278 | .376 | .512 | $23 | 460 |
| Dunn A | 31 | 525 | 39 | 85 | 104 | 0 | .260 | .382 | .518 | $22 | 400 |

Minors (2010) / Skills

| Level | Leag | AB | HR | R | RBI | SB | BA | OBP | SLG | CT% | H% | BB% | Bash |
|---|---|---|---|---|---|---|---|---|---|---|---|---|---|
| A | — | — | — | — | — | — | — | — | — | — | — | — | — |
| AA | — | — | — | — | — | — | — | — | — | — | — | — | — |
| AAA | — | — | — | — | — | — | — | — | — | — | — | — | — |

Competition at 1B — Stats in 2010

| Bats | Player | GSvR | GSvL | Sub | OPS |
|---|---|---|---|---|---|
| RH | Konerko P | 87 | 38 | 0 | .977 |
| LH | Kotsay M | 33 | 1 | 4 | .683 |

Ten-Year Trends: SLG, OBP, BA

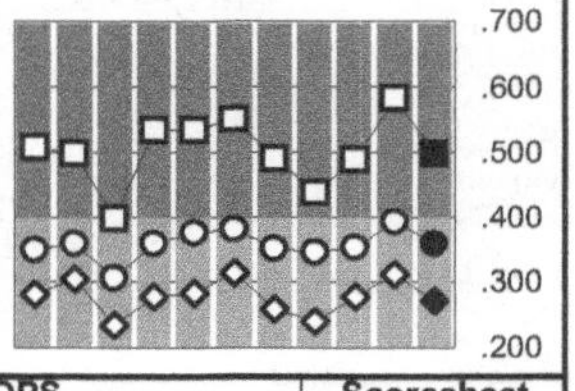


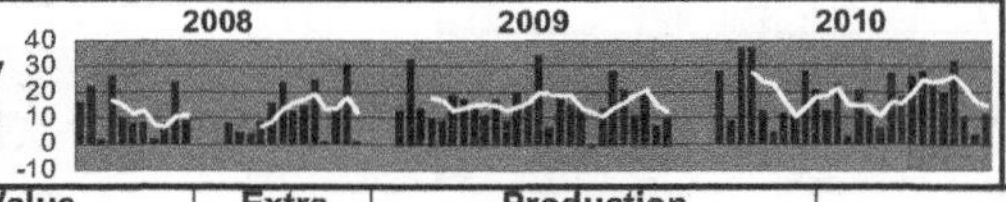


Majors / Skills

| Yr | Team | AB | HR | R | RBI | SB | BA | OBP | SLG | CT% | H% | BB% | Bash |
|---|---|---|---|---|---|---|---|---|---|---|---|---|---|
| 07 | CHW | 549 | 31 | 71 | 90 | 0 | .259 | .351 | .490 | 81% | 32% | 12% | 1.89 |
| 08 | CHW | 438 | 22 | 59 | 62 | 2 | .240 | .344 | .438 | 82% | 29% | 13% | 1.83 |
| 09 | CHW | 546 | 28 | 75 | 88 | 1 | .277 | .353 | .489 | 84% | 33% | 9% | 1.77 |
| 10 | CHW | 548 | 39 | 89 | 111 | 0 | .312 | .393 | .584 | 80% | 39% | 11% | 1.87 |

Value / Extra / Production / OPS / Scoresheet

| Yr | $1L | $2L | Pts | RAA | 2B | 3B | CS | FB-LD-GB | HR/fb | RBI% | RS% | OPS | 1st Hf | 2nd Hf | vs RH | vs LH | Rnge | vRH | vLH |
|---|---|---|---|---|---|---|---|---|---|---|---|---|---|---|---|---|---|---|---|
| 07 | $18 | $10 | 400 | +3 | 34 | 0 | 1 | 45-17-38 | 15% | 19% | 21% | .841 | .860 | .816 | .784 | .988 | 1.81 | −19 | +47 |
| 08 | $12 | $1 | 300 | −7 | 19 | 1 | 0 | 38-22-41 | 16% | 16% | 24% | .783 | .690 | .910 | .765 | .825 | 1.82 | −32 | +77 |
| 09 | $19 | $13 | 400 | +1 | 30 | 1 | 0 | 46-19-36 | 13% | 21% | 25% | .842 | .870 | .804 | .777 | 1.009 | 1.83 | −30 | +72 |
| 10 | $34 | $30 | 480 | +31 | 30 | 1 | 1 | 45-20-35 | 20% | 25% | 24% | .977 | .942 | 1.017 | .941 | 1.102 | 1.83 | −28 | +69 |

## Casey Kotchman — 250 PA | $1 | 140 pts

1B-116, DH-3 — Owned: 3% — LH

Another one in the category of colossal disappointments, Kotchman had a rough season. He topped a .315 OBP in only one month; his SLG fell for the third straight year; and his defense was unimpressive. Kotch might land a minor-league contract with someone in 2011, but that's probably his ceiling. (GC)

| Player | Age | AB | HR | R | RBI | SB | BA | OBP | SLG | $1L | Pts |
|---|---|---|---|---|---|---|---|---|---|---|---|
| Kotchman C | 28 | 218 | 5 | 23 | 30 | 0 | .264 | .331 | .401 | $1 | 140 |
| **Mini-Browser** | **Age** | **AB** | **HR** | **R** | **RBI** | **SB** | **BA** | **OBP** | **SLG** | **$1L** | **Pts** |
| Viciedo D | 22 | 293 | 12 | 36 | 36 | 3 | .256 | .288 | .419 | $5 | 150 |
| Nady X | 32 | 274 | 12 | 36 | 42 | 0 | .274 | .327 | .452 | $5 | 160 |
| Pearce S | 27 | 280 | 12 | 33 | 36 | 3 | .268 | .342 | .483 | $5 | 190 |
| Glaus T | 34 | 246 | 12 | 36 | 45 | 0 | .256 | .365 | .449 | $5 | 170 |
| Wallace B | 24 | 421 | 14 | 48 | 43 | 0 | .237 | .309 | .397 | $4 | 180 |

Minors (2010) / Skills

| Level | Leag | AB | HR | R | RBI | SB | BA | OBP | SLG | CT% | H% | BB% | Bash |
|---|---|---|---|---|---|---|---|---|---|---|---|---|---|
| A | — | — | — | — | — | — | — | — | — | — | — | — | — |
| AA | — | — | — | — | — | — | — | — | — | — | — | — | — |
| AAA | — | — | — | — | — | — | — | — | — | — | — | — | — |

Competition at 1B — Stats in 2010

| Bats | Player | GSvR | GSvL | Sub | OPS |
|---|---|---|---|---|---|
| LH | Kotchman C | 80 | 28 | 8 | .616 |
| BH | Smoak J | 15 | 10 | 0 | .678 |

Ten-Year Trends: SLG, OBP, BA

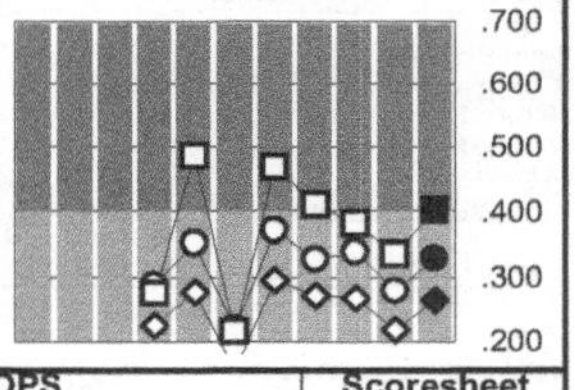


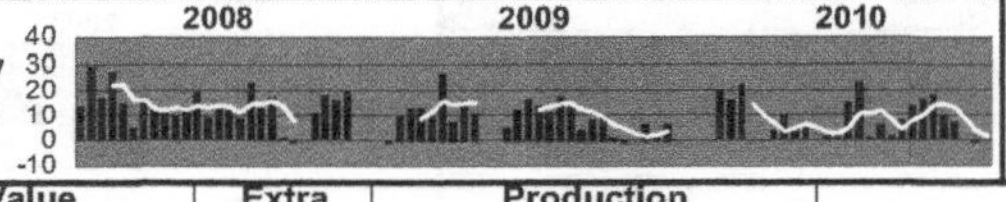


Majors / Skills

| Yr | Team | AB | HR | R | RBI | SB | BA | OBP | SLG | CT% | H% | BB% | Bash |
|---|---|---|---|---|---|---|---|---|---|---|---|---|---|
| 07 | LAA | 443 | 11 | 64 | 68 | 2 | .296 | .372 | .467 | 90% | 33% | 10% | 1.58 |
| 08 | 2TM | 525 | 14 | 65 | 74 | 2 | .272 | .328 | .410 | 93% | 29% | 6% | 1.50 |
| 09 | 2TM | 385 | 7 | 37 | 48 | 1 | .268 | .339 | .382 | 89% | 30% | 9% | 1.43 |
| 10 | SEA | 414 | 9 | 37 | 51 | 0 | .217 | .280 | .336 | 86% | 25% | 8% | 1.54 |

Value / Extra / Production / OPS / Scoresheet

| Yr | $1L | $2L | Pts | RAA | 2B | 3B | CS | FB-LD-GB | HR/fb | RBI% | RS% | OPS | 1st Hf | 2nd Hf | vs RH | vs LH | Rnge | vRH | vLH |
|---|---|---|---|---|---|---|---|---|---|---|---|---|---|---|---|---|---|---|---|
| 07 | $14 | $4 | 350 | +3 | 37 | 3 | 4 | 33-16-51 | 8% | 24% | 30% | .840 | .854 | .820 | .852 | .775 | 1.88 | +25 | −81 |
| 08 | $9 | $4 | 350 | −19 | 28 | 1 | 1 | 30-18-53 | 10% | 22% | 29% | .738 | .752 | .713 | .708 | .819 | 1.91 | +21 | −72 |
| 09 | $1 | -$6 | 230 | −14 | 23 | 0 | 0 | 29-19-51 | 7% | 18% | 22% | .721 | .742 | .682 | .760 | .625 | 1.90 | +11 | −35 |
| 10 | $3 | -$10 | 200 | −33 | 20 | 1 | 0 | 27-17-55 | 9% | 19% | 24% | .616 | .670 | .556 | .670 | .460 | 1.89 | +14 | −40 |

## Mark Kotsay — 200 PA | $-2 | 110 pts

DH-48, 1B-38, OF-8 (RF-8) — Owned: 1% — LH

The White Sox are haunted by the Ghost of Kotsay Past. Kotsay in 2010 was paid like a 25th man, in line with his marginal hitting skills versus RHP and his ability to stand at various positions and wave his glove. Any team that would give more than 1/3 of a full load to Kotsay in 2011 should demand an exorcism. (RM)

| Player | Age | AB | HR | R | RBI | SB | BA | OBP | SLG | $1L | Pts |
|---|---|---|---|---|---|---|---|---|---|---|---|
| Kotsay M | 35 | 188 | 4 | 18 | 20 | 2 | .255 | .313 | .375 | -$2 | 110 |
| **Mini-Browser** | **Age** | **AB** | **HR** | **R** | **RBI** | **SB** | **BA** | **OBP** | **SLG** | **$1L** | **Pts** |
| Damon J | 37 | 418 | 10 | 71 | 48 | 14 | .273 | .354 | .429 | $14 | 310 |
| Hafner T | 33 | 439 | 16 | 58 | 68 | 0 | .263 | .364 | .447 | $12 | 280 |
| Thames M | 34 | 317 | 21 | 42 | 53 | 0 | .254 | .314 | .485 | $9 | 180 |
| Cust J | 32 | 328 | 16 | 48 | 52 | 0 | .232 | .363 | .427 | $7 | 170 |
| Thome J | 40 | 231 | 14 | 36 | 44 | 0 | .238 | .355 | .470 | $5 | 150 |

Minors (2010) / Skills

| Level | Leag | AB | HR | R | RBI | SB | BA | OBP | SLG | CT% | H% | BB% | Bash |
|---|---|---|---|---|---|---|---|---|---|---|---|---|---|
| A | — | — | — | — | — | — | — | — | — | — | — | — | — |
| AA | — | — | — | — | — | — | — | — | — | — | — | — | — |
| AAA | — | — | — | — | — | — | — | — | — | — | — | — | — |

Competition at DH — Stats in 2010

| Bats | Player | GSvR | GSvL | Sub | OPS |
|---|---|---|---|---|---|
| LH | Kotsay M | 46 | 0 | 2 | .683 |
| RH | Konerko P | 22 | 1 | 0 | .977 |
| RH | Quentin C | 9 | 14 | 0 | .821 |
| RH | Ramirez M | 16 | 5 | 2 | .870 |

Ten-Year Trends: SLG, OBP, BA

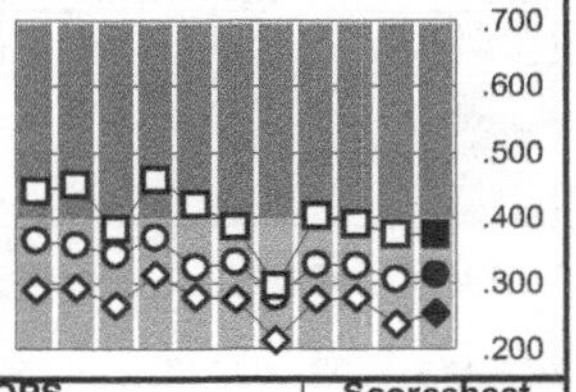


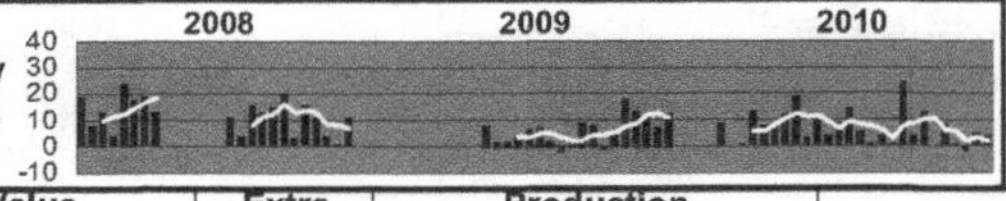


Majors / Skills

| Yr | Team | AB | HR | R | RBI | SB | BA | OBP | SLG | CT% | H% | BB% | Bash |
|---|---|---|---|---|---|---|---|---|---|---|---|---|---|
| 07 | OAK | 206 | 1 | 20 | 20 | 1 | .214 | .279 | .296 | 90% | 24% | 8% | 1.39 |
| 08 | 2TM | 402 | 6 | 45 | 49 | 2 | .276 | .329 | .403 | 89% | 31% | 7% | 1.46 |
| 09 | 2TM | 187 | 4 | 16 | 23 | 3 | .278 | .327 | .390 | 89% | 31% | 7% | 1.40 |
| 10 | CHW | 327 | 8 | 30 | 31 | 1 | .239 | .306 | .376 | 89% | 27% | 9% | 1.58 |

Value / Extra / Production / OPS / Scoresheet

| Yr | $1L | $2L | Pts | RAA | 2B | 3B | CS | FB-LD-GB | HR/fb | RBI% | RS% | OPS | 1st Hf | 2nd Hf | vs RH | vs LH | Rnge | vRH | vLH |
|---|---|---|---|---|---|---|---|---|---|---|---|---|---|---|---|---|---|---|---|
| 07 | -$2 | -$17 | 100 | −18 | 14 | 0 | 1 | 41-15-45 | 1% | 17% | 31% | .575 | .584 | .561 | .644 | .332 | 1.89 | +7 | −22 |
| 08 | $3 | -$4 | 240 | −12 | 25 | 4 | 4 | 36-22-42 | 5% | 19% | 28% | .732 | .723 | .741 | .777 | .629 | 1.89 | +23 | −75 |
| 09 | $1 | -$13 | 110 | −6 | 9 | 0 | 2 | 34-19-47 | 7% | 19% | 19% | .717 | .649 | .755 | .766 | .469 | 1.89 | +32 | −92 |
| 10 | $2 | -$12 | 180 | −16 | 17 | 2 | 3 | 40-16-44 | 7% | 13% | 22% | .683 | .709 | .645 | .733 | .074 | 1.89 | +31 | −91 |

## George Kottaras — 125 PA | $0 | 70 pts

CA-61, 1B-2, OF-1 (RF-1) — Owned: 0% — LH

Although not the primary beneficiary of Gregg Zaun's injury, Kottaras in 2010 nevertheless earned enough PT to show off his receiving skills and modest offensive weapons. He is solid enough to secure a back-up spot in Milwaukee – a comfortable spot to be, now that Angel Salome has decided he's an outfielder. (MS)

| Player | Age | AB | HR | R | RBI | SB | BA | OBP | SLG | $1L | Pts |
|---|---|---|---|---|---|---|---|---|---|---|---|
| Kottaras G | 27 | 114 | 5 | 14 | 14 | 0 | .231 | .330 | .420 | $0 | 70 |
| **Mini-Browser** | **Age** | **AB** | **HR** | **R** | **RBI** | **SB** | **BA** | **OBP** | **SLG** | **$1L** | **Pts** |
| Laird G | 31 | 192 | 4 | 20 | 18 | 2 | .239 | .300 | .354 | $1 | 90 |
| Montero J | 21 | 183 | 10 | 22 | 28 | 0 | .263 | .316 | .484 | $1 | 120 |
| Schneider B | 34 | 128 | 3 | 14 | 17 | 0 | .258 | .343 | .381 | $1 | 80 |
| Towles J | 27 | 90 | 3 | 11 | 11 | 2 | .244 | .331 | .414 | $0 | 50 |
| Quintero H | 31 | 188 | 4 | 14 | 16 | 0 | .245 | .285 | .354 | $0 | 60 |

Minors (2010) / Skills

| Level | Leag | AB | HR | R | RBI | SB | BA | OBP | SLG | CT% | H% | BB% | Bash |
|---|---|---|---|---|---|---|---|---|---|---|---|---|---|
| A | — | — | — | — | — | — | — | — | — | — | — | — | — |
| AA | — | — | — | — | — | — | — | — | — | — | — | — | — |
| AAA | — | — | — | — | — | — | — | — | — | — | — | — | — |

Competition at CA — Stats in 2010

| Bats | Player | GSvR | GSvL | Sub | OPS |
|---|---|---|---|---|---|
| RH | Lucroy J | 50 | 24 | 1 | .628 |
| LH | Kottaras G | 45 | 15 | 1 | .701 |
| BH | Zaun G | 17 | 11 | 0 | .743 |

Ten-Year Trends: SLG, OBP, BA

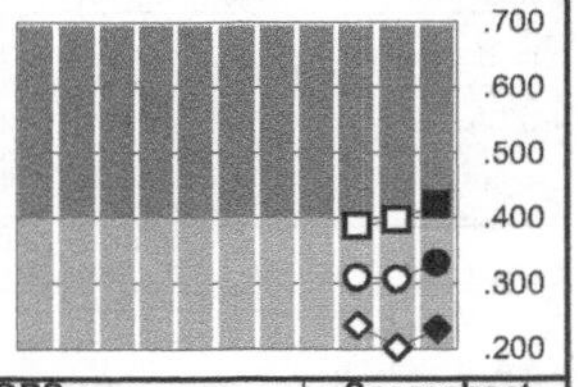


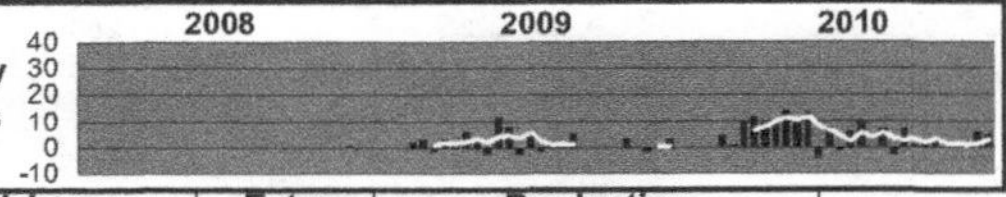


Majors / Skills

| Yr | Team | AB | HR | R | RBI | SB | BA | OBP | SLG | CT% | H% | BB% | Bash |
|---|---|---|---|---|---|---|---|---|---|---|---|---|---|
| 07 | — | — | — | — | — | — | — | — | — | — | — | — | — |
| 08 | BOS | 5 | 0 | 1 | 0 | 0 | .200 | .200 | .400 | 60% | 33% | 0% | 2.00 |
| 09 | BOS | 93 | 1 | 15 | 10 | 0 | .237 | .308 | .387 | 73% | 32% | 10% | 1.64 |
| 10 | MIL | 212 | 9 | 24 | 26 | 2 | .203 | .305 | .396 | 79% | 26% | 13% | 1.95 |

Value / Extra / Production / OPS / Scoresheet

| Yr | $1L | $2L | Pts | RAA | 2B | 3B | CS | FB-LD-GB | HR/fb | RBI% | RS% | OPS | 1st Hf | 2nd Hf | vs RH | vs LH | Rnge | vRH | vLH |
|---|---|---|---|---|---|---|---|---|---|---|---|---|---|---|---|---|---|---|---|
| 07 | — | — | — | — | — | — | — | — | — | — | — | — | — | — | — | — | 0.54 | — | — |
| 08 | -$4 | -$19 | 0 | −0 | 1 | 0 | 0 | 33-0-67 | 0% | 0% | NA | .600 | — | .600 | .000 | 1.500 | 0.57 | — | — |
| 09 | $0 | -$8 | 50 | −1 | 11 | 0 | 0 | 48-23-30 | 3% | 19% | 44% | .696 | .645 | .940 | .769 | .394 | 0.58 | +22 | −65 |
| 10 | $2 | -$5 | 130 | −3 | 12 | 1 | 0 | 45-12-43 | 12% | 15% | 22% | .701 | .776 | .565 | .691 | .726 | 0.62 | +25 | −77 |

*For more stats, visit www.Rotolympus.com.*

## ▪▪▪▪ Kevin Kouzmanoff — 600 PA | $15 | 330 pts

3B-142 — Owned: 19% — RH

Kouzmanoff was signed to be a steady glove at 3B for the A's, who were also hopeful that he would hit for more power out of Petco. But his defense was disappointing, and his SLG actually fell (for the third year in a row). The bright side is that there is little breadth between Kouz's bad seasons and his good ones. (ML)

| Player | Age | AB | HR | R | RBI | SB | BA | OBP | SLG | $1L | Pts |
|---|---|---|---|---|---|---|---|---|---|---|---|
| | | Forecast | | | | | | | | | |
| Kouzmanoff K | 29 | 579 | 24 | 66 | 84 | 0 | .259 | .303 | .441 | $15 | 330 |
| **Mini-Browser** | **Age** | **AB** | **HR** | **R** | **RBI** | **SB** | **BA** | **OBP** | **SLG** | **$1L** | **Pts** |
| Sandoval P | 24 | 574 | 19 | 75 | 81 | 6 | .283 | .335 | .474 | $17 | 400 |
| Figgins C | 33 | 562 | 0 | 78 | 46 | 39 | .266 | .356 | .332 | $17 | 360 |
| Coghlan C | 25 | 560 | 13 | 88 | 56 | 19 | .268 | .347 | .408 | $16 | 380 |
| Polanco P | 35 | 605 | 7 | 85 | 65 | 7 | .290 | .337 | .393 | $15 | 400 |
| McGehee C | 28 | 589 | 20 | 72 | 91 | 0 | .265 | .324 | .428 | $15 | 350 |

| Level | Leag | AB | HR | R | RBI | SB | BA | OBP | SLG | CT% | H% | BB% | Bash |
|---|---|---|---|---|---|---|---|---|---|---|---|---|---|
| | | Minors (2010) | | | | | | | | Skills | | | |
| A | — | — | — | — | — | — | — | — | — | — | — | — | — |
| AA | — | — | — | — | — | — | — | — | — | — | — | — | — |
| AAA | — | — | — | — | — | — | — | — | — | — | — | — | — |

Competition at 3B — Stats in 2010

| Bats | Player | GSvR | GSvL | Sub | OPS |
|---|---|---|---|---|---|
| RH | Kouzmanoff K | 99 | 41 | 2 | .679 |
| LH | Iwamura A | 7 | 2 | 1 | .535 |

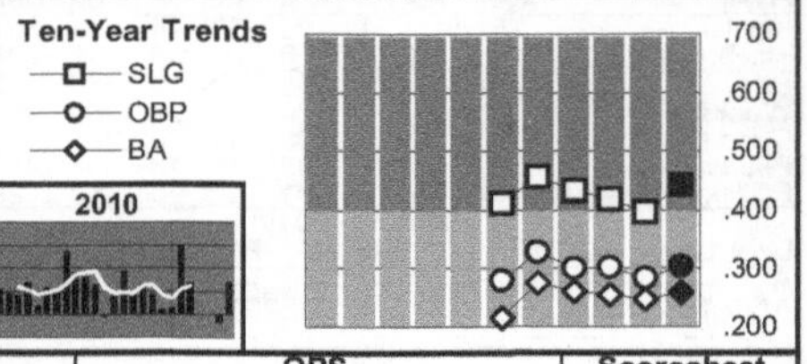
Ten-Year Trends
SLG
OBP
BA
.700
.600
.500
.400
.300
.200

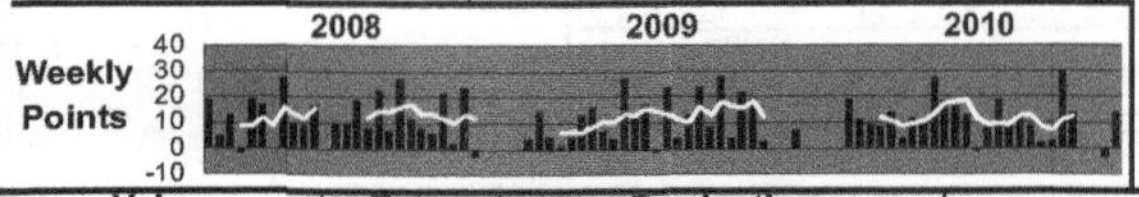
Weekly Points
2008
2009
2010
40
30
20
10
0
-10

| Yr | Team | AB | HR | R | RBI | SB | BA | OBP | SLG | CT% | H% | BB% | Bash |
|---|---|---|---|---|---|---|---|---|---|---|---|---|---|
| | | Majors | | | | | | | | Skills | | | |
| 07 | SD | 484 | 18 | 57 | 74 | 1 | .275 | .329 | .457 | 81% | 34% | 6% | 1.66 |
| 08 | SD | 624 | 23 | 71 | 84 | 0 | .260 | .299 | .433 | 78% | 33% | 3% | 1.67 |
| 09 | SD | 529 | 18 | 50 | 88 | 1 | .255 | .302 | .420 | 80% | 32% | 5% | 1.64 |
| 10 | OAK | 551 | 16 | 59 | 71 | 2 | .247 | .283 | .396 | 83% | 30% | 4% | 1.60 |

| Yr | $1L | $2L | Pts | RAA | 2B | 3B | CS | FB-LD-GB | HR/fb | RBI% | RS% | OPS | 1st Hf | 2nd Hf | vs RH | vs LH | Rnge | vRH | vLH |
|---|---|---|---|---|---|---|---|---|---|---|---|---|---|---|---|---|---|---|---|
| | Value | | | | Extra | | | Production | | | | OPS | | | | | Scoresheet | | |
| 07 | $12 | $4 | 290 | +1 | 30 | 2 | 0 | 41-18-41 | 11% | 22% | 25% | .786 | .673 | .890 | .706 | .972 | 2.65 | –13 | +34 |
| 08 | $14 | $7 | 310 | –14 | 31 | 4 | 0 | 39-22-40 | 12% | 18% | 27% | .732 | .761 | .694 | .762 | .661 | 2.65 | –34 | +84 |
| 09 | $12 | $2 | 280 | –12 | 31 | 1 | 0 | 36-20-44 | 12% | 20% | 21% | .722 | .686 | .778 | .677 | .835 | 2.63 | –21 | +50 |
| 10 | $12 | $1 | 280 | –18 | 32 | 1 | 1 | 40-17-43 | 9% | 16% | 29% | .679 | .688 | .664 | .663 | .724 | 2.67 | –11 | +29 |

## ▪▪▪▪ Jason Kubel — 525 PA | $16 | 320 pts

OF-98 (RF-83, LF-16), DH-42 — Owned: 94% — LH

After a breakout 2009 campaign, Kubel's H% dropped off substantially in 2010, but even in a down year he managed 20 HR and almost 100 RBI. His defensive weakness in the outfield was heavily exposed, but he is expected to return to regular DH duty in 2011, with Michael Cuddyer shifting back to right field. (NN)

| Player | Age | AB | HR | R | RBI | SB | BA | OBP | SLG | $1L | Pts |
|---|---|---|---|---|---|---|---|---|---|---|---|
| | | Forecast | | | | | | | | | |
| Kubel J | 28 | 468 | 21 | 63 | 84 | 0 | .269 | .337 | .472 | $16 | 320 |
| **Mini-Browser** | **Age** | **AB** | **HR** | **R** | **RBI** | **SB** | **BA** | **OBP** | **SLG** | **$1L** | **Pts** |
| Stanton M | 21 | 541 | 36 | 72 | 84 | 6 | .244 | .327 | .507 | $16 | 340 |
| Davis R | 30 | 415 | 5 | 54 | 41 | 41 | .271 | .321 | .375 | $16 | 290 |
| DeJesus D | 31 | 578 | 13 | 75 | 63 | 6 | .292 | .361 | .434 | $16 | 380 |
| Gutierrez F | 28 | 568 | 19 | 75 | 63 | 19 | .253 | .313 | .393 | $16 | 310 |
| Willingham J | 32 | 465 | 22 | 72 | 72 | 6 | .272 | .379 | .494 | $16 | 340 |

| Level | Leag | AB | HR | R | RBI | SB | BA | OBP | SLG | CT% | H% | BB% | Bash |
|---|---|---|---|---|---|---|---|---|---|---|---|---|---|
| | | Minors (2010) | | | | | | | | Skills | | | |
| A | — | — | — | — | — | — | — | — | — | — | — | — | — |
| AA | — | — | — | — | — | — | — | — | — | — | — | — | — |
| AAA | — | — | — | — | — | — | — | — | — | — | — | — | — |

Competition at RF — Stats in 2010

| Bats | Player | GSvR | GSvL | Sub | OPS |
|---|---|---|---|---|---|
| LH | Kubel J | 60 | 20 | 3 | .750 |
| RH | Cuddyer M | 43 | 23 | 0 | .753 |
| RH | Repko J | 9 | 16 | 14 | .671 |

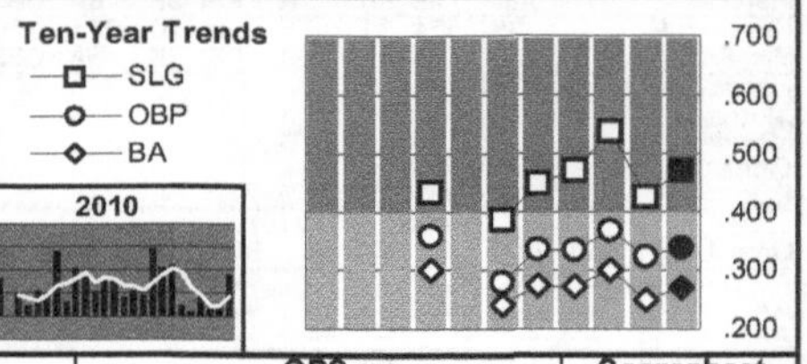
Ten-Year Trends
SLG
OBP
BA
.700
.600
.500
.400
.300
.200

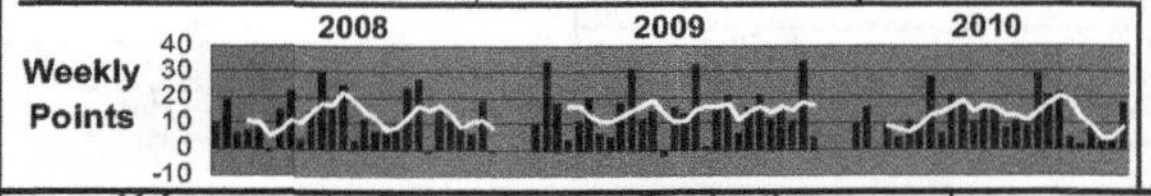
Weekly Points
2008
2009
2010
40
30
20
10
0
-10

| Yr | Team | AB | HR | R | RBI | SB | BA | OBP | SLG | CT% | H% | BB% | Bash |
|---|---|---|---|---|---|---|---|---|---|---|---|---|---|
| | | Majors | | | | | | | | Skills | | | |
| 07 | MIN | 418 | 13 | 49 | 65 | 5 | .273 | .335 | .450 | 81% | 34% | 9% | 1.65 |
| 08 | MIN | 463 | 20 | 74 | 78 | 0 | .272 | .335 | .471 | 80% | 34% | 9% | 1.73 |
| 09 | MIN | 514 | 28 | 73 | 103 | 1 | .300 | .369 | .539 | 79% | 38% | 10% | 1.80 |
| 10 | MIN | 518 | 21 | 68 | 92 | 0 | .249 | .323 | .427 | 78% | 32% | 10% | 1.71 |

| Yr | $1L | $2L | Pts | RAA | 2B | 3B | CS | FB-LD-GB | HR/fb | RBI% | RS% | OPS | 1st Hf | 2nd Hf | vs RH | vs LH | Rnge | vRH | vLH |
|---|---|---|---|---|---|---|---|---|---|---|---|---|---|---|---|---|---|---|---|
| | Value | | | | Extra | | | Production | | | | OPS | | | | | Scoresheet | | |
| 07 | $11 | $1 | 270 | –1 | 31 | 2 | 0 | 35-22-43 | 11% | 24% | 25% | .785 | .706 | .891 | .810 | .667 | 2.06 | +18 | –63 |
| 08 | $17 | $8 | 320 | +0 | 22 | 5 | 1 | 41-20-40 | 13% | 20% | 35% | .805 | .792 | .824 | .833 | .704 | 2.05 | +20 | –73 |
| 09 | $23 | $16 | 400 | +18 | 35 | 2 | 1 | 42-20-39 | 16% | 22% | 24% | .907 | .914 | .900 | 1.014 | .643 | 2.02 | +25 | –84 |
| 10 | $17 | $8 | 320 | –12 | 23 | 3 | 1 | 43-19-38 | 12% | 20% | 28% | .750 | .787 | .706 | .792 | .655 | 2.04 | +42 | –123 |

## ▪▪▪▪ Gerald Laird — 200 PA | $1 | 90 pts

CA-87 — Owned: 1% — RH

A miserable season at the plate caused Laird to lose his starting job to Alex Avila. Laird is a free agent and will not be back with the Tigers. He remains above-average at receiving, and even his bat should generate hits at a rate above 26%. He wants to start, but he might have to settle for a back-up or half-time role. (LP)

| Player | Age | AB | HR | R | RBI | SB | BA | OBP | SLG | $1L | Pts |
|---|---|---|---|---|---|---|---|---|---|---|---|
| | | Forecast | | | | | | | | | |
| Laird G | 31 | 192 | 4 | 20 | 18 | 2 | .239 | .300 | .354 | $1 | 90 |
| **Mini-Browser** | **Age** | **AB** | **HR** | **R** | **RBI** | **SB** | **BA** | **OBP** | **SLG** | **$1L** | **Pts** |
| Castro J | 23 | 345 | 8 | 40 | 32 | 0 | .220 | .303 | .340 | $2 | 150 |
| Ross D | 34 | 126 | 5 | 15 | 20 | 0 | .250 | .350 | .434 | $1 | 70 |
| Hester J | 27 | 142 | 5 | 17 | 17 | 2 | .243 | .294 | .422 | $1 | 70 |
| May L | 26 | 235 | 10 | 23 | 28 | 3 | .202 | .257 | .372 | $1 | 90 |
| Navarro D | 27 | 184 | 4 | 18 | 18 | 2 | .250 | .306 | .362 | $1 | 100 |

| Level | Leag | AB | HR | R | RBI | SB | BA | OBP | SLG | CT% | H% | BB% | Bash |
|---|---|---|---|---|---|---|---|---|---|---|---|---|---|
| | | Minors (2010) | | | | | | | | Skills | | | |
| A | — | — | — | — | — | — | — | — | — | — | — | — | — |
| AA | — | — | — | — | — | — | — | — | — | — | — | — | — |
| AAA | — | — | — | — | — | — | — | — | — | — | — | — | — |

Competition at CA — Stats in 2010

| Bats | Player | GSvR | GSvL | Sub | OPS |
|---|---|---|---|---|---|
| LH | Avila A | 80 | 4 | 14 | .656 |
| RH | Laird G | 35 | 41 | 11 | .567 |

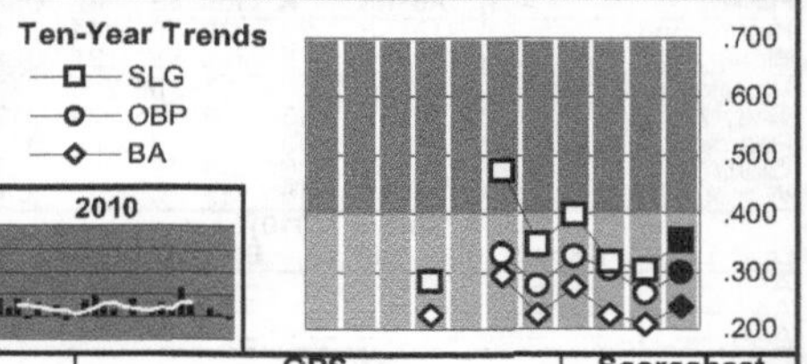
Ten-Year Trends
SLG
OBP
BA
.700
.600
.500
.400
.300
.200

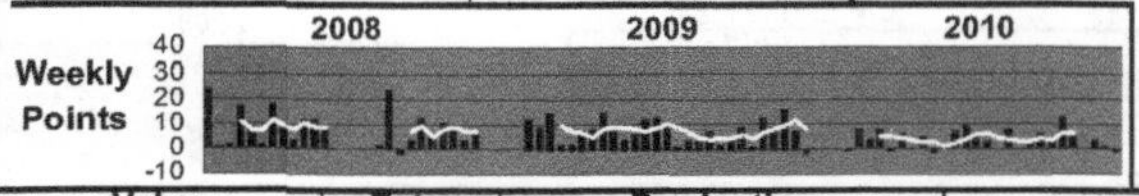
Weekly Points
2008
2009
2010
40
30
20
10
0
-10

| Yr | Team | AB | HR | R | RBI | SB | BA | OBP | SLG | CT% | H% | BB% | Bash |
|---|---|---|---|---|---|---|---|---|---|---|---|---|---|
| | | Majors | | | | | | | | Skills | | | |
| 07 | TEX | 407 | 9 | 48 | 47 | 6 | .224 | .278 | .349 | 75% | 30% | 7% | 1.56 |
| 08 | TEX | 344 | 6 | 54 | 41 | 2 | .276 | .329 | .398 | 82% | 34% | 6% | 1.44 |
| 09 | DET | 413 | 4 | 49 | 33 | 5 | .225 | .306 | .320 | 84% | 27% | 8% | 1.42 |
| 10 | DET | 270 | 5 | 22 | 25 | 3 | .207 | .263 | .304 | 79% | 26% | 6% | 1.46 |

| Yr | $1L | $2L | Pts | RAA | 2B | 3B | CS | FB-LD-GB | HR/fb | RBI% | RS% | OPS | 1st Hf | 2nd Hf | vs RH | vs LH | Rnge | vRH | vLH |
|---|---|---|---|---|---|---|---|---|---|---|---|---|---|---|---|---|---|---|---|
| | Value | | | | Extra | | | Production | | | | OPS | | | | | Scoresheet | | |
| 07 | $8 | -$3 | 170 | –19 | 18 | 3 | 2 | 55-12-33 | 6% | 18% | 34% | .627 | .625 | .628 | .603 | .691 | 0.50 | –31 | +74 |
| 08 | $10 | $4 | 190 | –5 | 24 | 0 | 4 | 41-22-38 | 5% | 18% | 41% | .727 | .797 | .648 | .731 | .719 | 0.50 | –33 | +80 |
| 09 | $4 | -$1 | 200 | –22 | 23 | 2 | 0 | 44-14-41 | 3% | 14% | 32% | .626 | .690 | .546 | .591 | .730 | 0.58 | –20 | +49 |
| 10 | $2 | -$8 | 100 | –20 | 11 | 0 | 1 | 42-15-43 | 6% | 13% | 24% | .567 | .524 | .635 | .611 | .501 | 0.56 | –19 | +48 |

## Ryan Langerhans — 150 PA | $-2 | 70 pts

OF-40 (LF-30, RF-8, CF-2), 1B-6, DH-3 — Owned: 0% — LH

Langerhans in 2010 continued to do what he does best: walk a lot and play good defense at all three outfield spots. The Mariners would be wise to bring him back in the same capacity in 2011. Not that it matters, but Langerhans was ridiculously unlucky on RBI%, scoring only 1 of 42 baserunners. (GC)

| Player | Age | AB | HR | R | RBI | SB | BA | OBP | SLG | $1L | Pts |
|---|---|---|---|---|---|---|---|---|---|---|---|
| | | Forecast | | | | | | | | | |
| Langerhans R | 31 | 132 | 5 | 17 | 14 | 3 | .239 | .348 | .397 | -$2 | 70 |
| **Mini-Browser** | **Age** | **AB** | **HR** | **R** | **RBI** | **SB** | **BA** | **OBP** | **SLG** | **$1L** | **Pts** |
| Repko J | 30 | 130 | 3 | 17 | 12 | 6 | .243 | .315 | .389 | -$1 | 60 |
| Reddick J | 24 | 136 | 6 | 15 | 17 | 2 | .231 | .277 | .440 | -$2 | 70 |
| Dyson J | 26 | 138 | 2 | 17 | 9 | 12 | .207 | .274 | .289 | -$2 | 70 |
| Cunningham A | 24 | 121 | 4 | 14 | 14 | 3 | .237 | .310 | .398 | -$2 | 60 |
| Bourgeois J | 29 | 91 | 1 | 12 | 8 | 5 | .263 | .318 | .371 | -$2 | 60 |

| Level | Leag | AB | HR | R | RBI | SB | BA | OBP | SLG | CT% | H% | BB% | Bash |
|---|---|---|---|---|---|---|---|---|---|---|---|---|---|
| | | Minors (2010) | | | | | | | | Skills | | | |
| A | — | — | — | — | — | — | — | — | — | — | — | — | — |
| AA | — | — | — | — | — | — | — | — | — | — | — | — | — |
| AAA | PCL | 39 | 0 | 8 | 3 | 3 | .282 | .391 | .410 | 72% | 39% | 15% | 1.45 |

Competition at LF — Stats in 2010

| Bats | Player | GSvR | GSvL | Sub | OPS |
|---|---|---|---|---|---|
| LH | Saunders M | 60 | 15 | 2 | .662 |
| BH | Bradley M | 21 | 17 | 1 | .641 |
| LH | Langerhans R | 17 | 7 | 6 | .661 |
| RH | Tuiasosopo M | 8 | 6 | 0 | .541 |

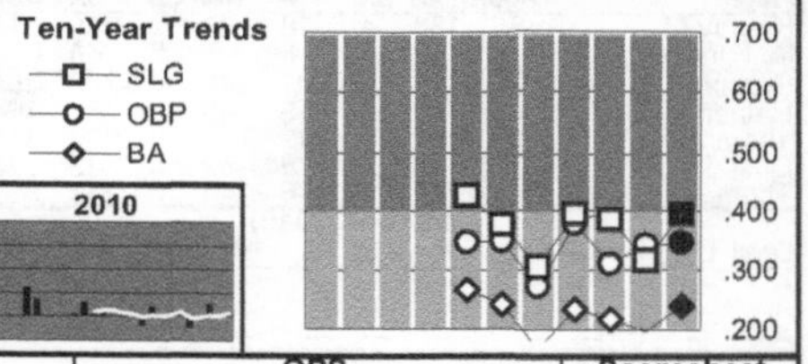
Ten-Year Trends
SLG
OBP
BA
.700
.600
.500
.400
.300
.200

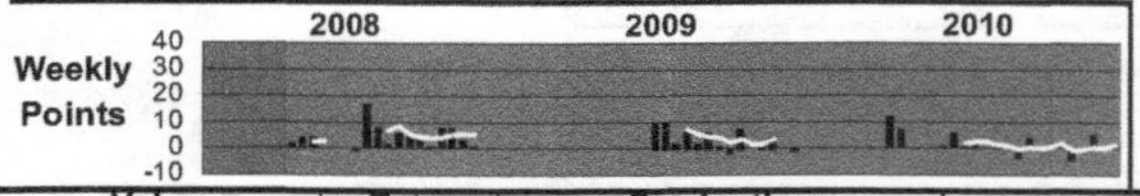
Weekly Points
2008
2009
2010
40
30
20
10
0
-10

| Yr | Team | AB | HR | R | RBI | SB | BA | OBP | SLG | CT% | H% | BB% | Bash |
|---|---|---|---|---|---|---|---|---|---|---|---|---|---|
| | | Majors | | | | | | | | Skills | | | |
| 07 | 3TM | 210 | 6 | 27 | 23 | 3 | .167 | .272 | .305 | 61% | 27% | 12% | 1.83 |
| 08 | WAS | 111 | 3 | 17 | 12 | 2 | .234 | .380 | .396 | 72% | 33% | 18% | 1.69 |
| 09 | SEA | 101 | 3 | 12 | 10 | 0 | .218 | .311 | .386 | 72% | 30% | 11% | 1.77 |
| 10 | SEA | 107 | 3 | 16 | 4 | 4 | .196 | .344 | .318 | 52% | 38% | 18% | 1.62 |

| Yr | $1L | $2L | Pts | RAA | 2B | 3B | CS | FB-LD-GB | HR/fb | RBI% | RS% | OPS | 1st Hf | 2nd Hf | vs RH | vs LH | Rnge | vRH | vLH |
|---|---|---|---|---|---|---|---|---|---|---|---|---|---|---|---|---|---|---|---|
| | Value | | | | Extra | | | Production | | | | OPS | | | | | Scoresheet | | |
| 07 | -$8 | -$16 | 70 | –17 | 7 | 2 | 1 | 43-13-44 | 11% | 17% | 35% | .576 | .563 | .612 | .551 | .711 | 2.11 | +14 | –52 |
| 08 | -$2 | -$14 | 70 | +1 | 5 | 2 | 0 | 31-25-44 | 12% | 14% | 29% | .776 | .485 | .891 | .755 | .858 | — | +10 | –40 |
| 09 | -$2 | -$18 | 50 | –5 | 6 | 1 | 1 | 47-16-37 | 9% | 12% | 26% | .697 | .764 | .659 | .698 | .683 | 2.10 | +11 | –35 |
| 10 | -$2 | -$18 | 30 | –3 | 2 | 1 | 1 | 43-20-38 | 13% | 2% | 31% | .661 | .787 | .572 | .810 | .322 | 2.10 | +20 | –59 |

## ▪▪ Matt LaPorta — 625 PA | $13 | 320 pts

1B-93, DH-8, OF-7 (LF-7) — Owned: 3% — RH

Recovery from off-season hip surgery disrupted LaPorta's mechanics early in 2010, forcing him to play catch-up the rest of the season. Bouncing between 1B and LF for the first two months also did not help. Cleveland has a lot riding on LaPorta's development, and they'll continue to run him out at first base. (BLS)

| Player | Age | AB | HR | R | RBI | SB | BA | OBP | SLG | $1L | Pts |
|---|---|---|---|---|---|---|---|---|---|---|---|
| | | Forecast | | | | | | | | | |
| LaPorta M | 26 | 564 | 25 | 69 | 69 | 0 | .244 | .328 | .435 | $13 | 320 |
| **Mini-Browser** | **Age** | **AB** | **HR** | **R** | **RBI** | **SB** | **BA** | **OBP** | **SLG** | **$1L** | **Pts** |
| Loney J | 26 | 580 | 13 | 72 | 91 | 7 | .280 | .344 | .428 | $17 | 400 |
| Huff A | 34 | 534 | 18 | 78 | 84 | 6 | .281 | .353 | .473 | $17 | 400 |
| Sanchez G | 27 | 535 | 19 | 69 | 75 | 6 | .257 | .338 | .440 | $14 | 340 |
| Berkman L | 35 | 324 | 16 | 56 | 60 | 4 | .284 | .398 | .514 | $14 | 280 |
| Barton D | 25 | 567 | 14 | 81 | 68 | 7 | .262 | .373 | .412 | $13 | 390 |

| Level | Leag | AB | HR | R | RBI | SB | BA | OBP | SLG | CT% | H% | BB% | Bash |
|---|---|---|---|---|---|---|---|---|---|---|---|---|---|
| | | Minors (2010) | | | | | | | | Skills | | | |
| A | — | — | — | — | — | — | — | — | — | — | — | — | — |
| AA | — | — | — | — | — | — | — | — | — | — | — | — | — |
| AAA | IL | 69 | 5 | 7 | 16 | 0 | .362 | .457 | .638 | 86% | 42% | 15% | 1.76 |

Competition at 1B — Stats in 2010

| Bats | Player | GSvR | GSvL | Sub | OPS |
|---|---|---|---|---|---|
| RH | LaPorta M | 65 | 28 | 0 | .668 |
| RH | Marte A | 7 | 10 | 15 | .680 |
| LH | Brown J | 8 | 0 | 2 | .582 |

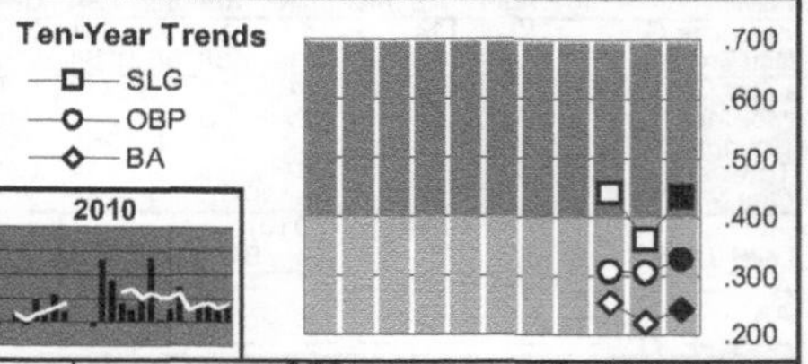
Ten-Year Trends
SLG
OBP
BA
.700
.600
.500
.400
.300
.200

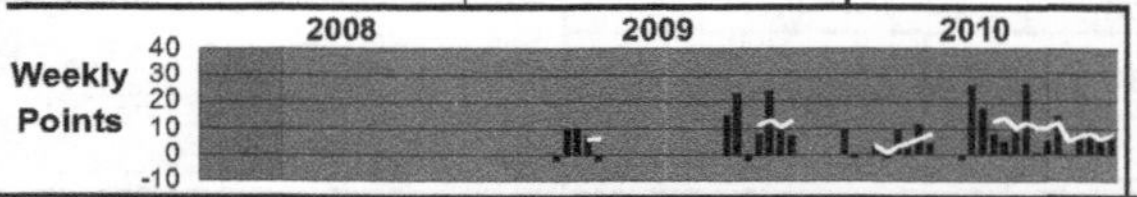
Weekly Points
2008
2009
2010
40
30
20
10
0
-10

| Yr | Team | AB | HR | R | RBI | SB | BA | OBP | SLG | CT% | H% | BB% | Bash |
|---|---|---|---|---|---|---|---|---|---|---|---|---|---|
| | | Majors | | | | | | | | Skills | | | |
| 07 | — | — | — | — | — | — | — | — | — | — | — | — | — |
| 08 | — | — | — | — | — | — | — | — | — | — | — | — | — |
| 09 | CLE | 181 | 7 | 29 | 21 | 2 | .254 | .308 | .442 | 80% | 32% | 6% | 1.74 |
| 10 | CLE | 376 | 12 | 41 | 41 | 0 | .221 | .306 | .362 | 78% | 28% | 11% | 1.64 |

| Yr | $1L | $2L | Pts | RAA | 2B | 3B | CS | FB-LD-GB | HR/fb | RBI% | RS% | OPS | 1st Hf | 2nd Hf | vs RH | vs LH | Rnge | vRH | vLH |
|---|---|---|---|---|---|---|---|---|---|---|---|---|---|---|---|---|---|---|---|
| | Value | | | | Extra | | | Production | | | | OPS | | | | | Scoresheet | | |
| 07 | — | — | — | — | — | — | — | — | — | — | — | — | — | — | — | — | — | — | — |
| 08 | — | — | — | — | — | — | — | — | — | — | — | — | — | — | — | — | — | — | — |
| 09 | $2 | -$11 | 110 | –5 | 13 | 0 | 0 | 42-18-40 | 11% | 15% | 41% | .750 | .571 | .805 | .769 | .680 | — | — | — |
| 10 | $4 | -$10 | 180 | –20 | 15 | 1 | 0 | 45-13-42 | 9% | 15% | 25% | .668 | .717 | .631 | .679 | .635 | — | –12 | +29 |

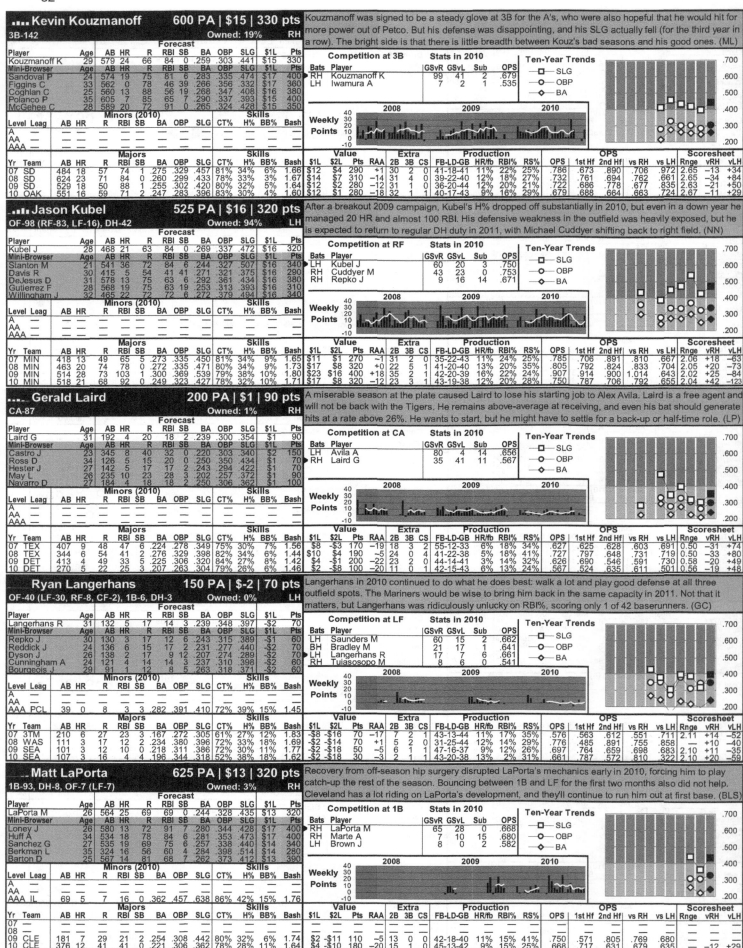

## Adam LaRoche — 600 PA | $20 | 380 pts

1B-146, DH-2 | Owned: 96% | LH

LaRoche in 2010 was the consistent run producer that Arizona has lacked at first base, even though he is not spectacular in the HR department. The D'backs declined his $7.5M option for 2011, but LaRoche will find work with a team that needs a steady, if unspectacular, first baseman. (MS)

| Player | Age | AB | HR | R | RBI | SB | BA | OBP | SLG | $1L | Pts |
|---|---|---|---|---|---|---|---|---|---|---|---|
| **Forecast** | | | | | | | | | | | |
| LaRoche A | 31 | 530 | 30 | 84 | 90 | 0 | .283 | .356 | .520 | $20 | 380 |
| **Mini-Browser** | | | | | | | | | | | |
| Morales K | 27 | 593 | 26 | 78 | 98 | 0 | .285 | .332 | .495 | $24 | 390 |
| Gonzalez A | 28 | 578 | 34 | 94 | 101 | 0 | .278 | .376 | .512 | $23 | 460 |
| Dunn A | 31 | 525 | 39 | 85 | 104 | 0 | .260 | .382 | .518 | $22 | 400 |
| Konerko P | 35 | 554 | 31 | 75 | 94 | 0 | .271 | .359 | .499 | $21 | 410 |
| Youkilis K | 32 | 451 | 21 | 79 | 79 | 5 | .291 | .390 | .515 | $20 | 370 |

| Minors (2010) Level | Leag | AB | HR | R | RBI | SB | BA | OBP | SLG | CT% | H% | BB% | Bash |
|---|---|---|---|---|---|---|---|---|---|---|---|---|---|
| A | — | — | — | — | — | — | — | — | — | — | — | — | — |
| AA | — | — | — | — | — | — | — | — | — | — | — | — | — |
| AAA | — | — | — | — | — | — | — | — | — | — | — | — | — |

| Majors Yr | Team | AB | HR | R | RBI | SB | BA | OBP | SLG | CT% | H% | BB% | Bash |
|---|---|---|---|---|---|---|---|---|---|---|---|---|---|
| 07 | PIT | 563 | 21 | 71 | 88 | 1 | .272 | .345 | .458 | 77% | 35% | 10% | 1.69 |
| 08 | PIT | 492 | 25 | 66 | 85 | 1 | .270 | .341 | .500 | 75% | 36% | 10% | 1.85 |
| 09 | 3TM | 555 | 25 | 78 | 83 | 2 | .277 | .355 | .488 | 74% | 37% | 11% | 1.76 |
| 10 | ARI | 560 | 25 | 75 | 100 | 0 | .261 | .320 | .468 | 69% | 38% | 8% | 1.79 |

| Yr | $1L | $2L | Pts | RAA | 2B | 3B | CS | FB-LD-GB | HR/fb | RBI% | RS% | OPS | 1st Hf | 2nd Hf | vs RH | vs LH | Rnge | vRH | vLH |
|---|---|---|---|---|---|---|---|---|---|---|---|---|---|---|---|---|---|---|---|
| 07 | $16 | $8 | 350 | −2 | 42 | 0 | 1 | 44-21-36 | 11% | 22% | 25% | .803 | .763 | .854 | .802 | .808 | 1.83 | +27 | −105 |
| 08 | $17 | $9 | 330 | +2 | 32 | 3 | 1 | 43-20-37 | 16% | 19% | 25% | .841 | .764 | .975 | .870 | .765 | 1.88 | +22 | −69 |
| 09 | $15 | $12 | 360 | +5 | 38 | 2 | 2 | 43-22-35 | 14% | 20% | 27% | .843 | .784 | .915 | .902 | .706 | 1.86 | +19 | −54 |
| 10 | $19 | $13 | 310 | −8 | 37 | 2 | 1 | 44-18-38 | 15% | 23% | 29% | .788 | .787 | .788 | .802 | .758 | 1.85 | +32 | −88 |

Competition at 1B — Stats in 2010

| Bats | Player | GSvR | GSvL | Sub | OPS |
|---|---|---|---|---|---|
| LH | LaRoche A | 101 | 42 | 3 | .788 |
| RH | Ryal R | 6 | 10 | 8 | .656 |

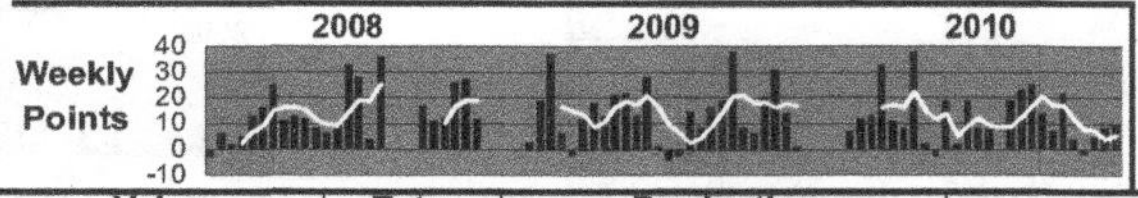


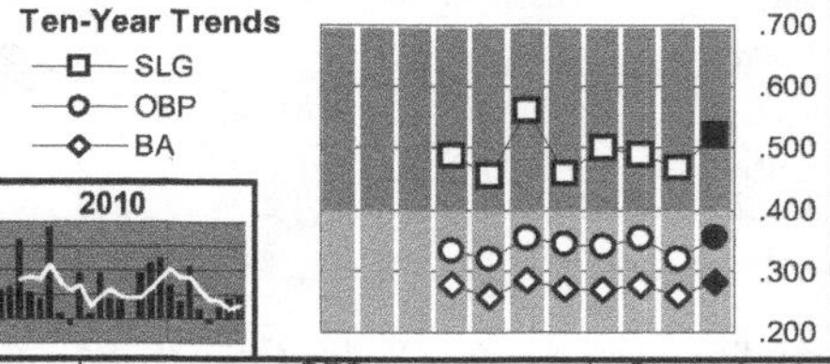


## Andy LaRoche — 100 PA | $-3 | 50 pts

3B-54, 2B-6, 1B-2, DH-1 | Owned: 0% | RH

LaRoche totally flopped in what was likely his final chance with the Pirates in 2010. By season's end, he barely resembled a major-league hitter, possibly as a result of chronic back issues. Even if he's healthy, his H% is too unpredictable (and bad) for him to be counted on. (MB)

| Player | Age | AB | HR | R | RBI | SB | BA | OBP | SLG | $1L | Pts |
|---|---|---|---|---|---|---|---|---|---|---|---|
| **Forecast** | | | | | | | | | | | |
| LaRoche A | 27 | 88 | 3 | 11 | 10 | 1 | .261 | .343 | .410 | -$3 | 50 |
| **Mini-Browser** | | | | | | | | | | | |
| Conrad B | 31 | 136 | 6 | 20 | 18 | 3 | .243 | .325 | .453 | $0 | 80 |
| Francisco J | 23 | 150 | 9 | 17 | 21 | 2 | .230 | .265 | .474 | -$1 | 80 |
| Murphy D | 28 | 90 | 4 | 14 | 14 | 1 | .255 | .321 | .488 | -$2 | 60 |
| Cairo M | 36 | 91 | 1 | 12 | 10 | 2 | .263 | .318 | .371 | -$2 | 50 |
| Frazier T | 25 | 90 | 4 | 11 | 11 | 1 | .233 | .299 | .449 | -$3 | 50 |

| Minors (2010) Level | Leag | AB | HR | R | RBI | SB | BA | OBP | SLG | CT% | H% | BB% | Bash |
|---|---|---|---|---|---|---|---|---|---|---|---|---|---|
| A | — | — | — | — | — | — | — | — | — | — | — | — | — |
| AA | — | — | — | — | — | — | — | — | — | — | — | — | — |
| AAA | — | — | — | — | — | — | — | — | — | — | — | — | — |

| Majors Yr | Team | AB | HR | R | RBI | SB | BA | OBP | SLG | CT% | H% | BB% | Bash |
|---|---|---|---|---|---|---|---|---|---|---|---|---|---|
| 07 | LAD | 93 | 1 | 16 | 10 | 2 | .226 | .365 | .312 | 74% | 30% | 17% | 1.38 |
| 08 | 2TM | 223 | 5 | 17 | 18 | 2 | .166 | .252 | .256 | 83% | 20% | 9% | 1.54 |
| 09 | PIT | 524 | 12 | 64 | 64 | 3 | .258 | .330 | .401 | 84% | 31% | 8% | 1.56 |
| 10 | PIT | 247 | 4 | 26 | 16 | 1 | .206 | .268 | .287 | 83% | 25% | 7% | 1.39 |

| Yr | $1L | $2L | Pts | RAA | 2B | 3B | CS | FB-LD-GB | HR/fb | RBI% | RS% | OPS | 1st Hf | 2nd Hf | vs RH | vs LH | Rnge | vRH | vLH |
|---|---|---|---|---|---|---|---|---|---|---|---|---|---|---|---|---|---|---|---|
| 07 | -$4 | -$17 | 50 | −3 | 5 | 0 | 1 | 40-19-41 | 4% | 17% | 37% | .677 | .700 | .645 | .737 | .510 | 2.65 | — | — |
| 08 | -$6 | -$18 | 80 | −21 | 5 | 0 | 0 | 35-16-49 | 8% | 10% | 21% | .508 | .635 | .476 | .532 | .446 | 2.65 | −16 | +40 |
| 09 | $11 | $0 | 310 | −7 | 29 | 5 | 1 | 34-17-49 | 8% | 19% | 29% | .731 | .737 | .724 | .690 | .855 | 2.69 | −11 | +28 |
| 10 | -$3 | -$17 | 90 | −18 | 8 | 0 | 1 | 33-17-50 | 6% | 12% | 32% | .555 | .601 | .356 | .485 | .683 | 2.70 | −19 | +50 |

Competition at 3B — Stats in 2010

| Bats | Player | GSvR | GSvL | Sub | OPS |
|---|---|---|---|---|---|
| LH | Alvarez P | 70 | 24 | 0 | .788 |
| RH | LaRoche A | 33 | 19 | 2 | .555 |

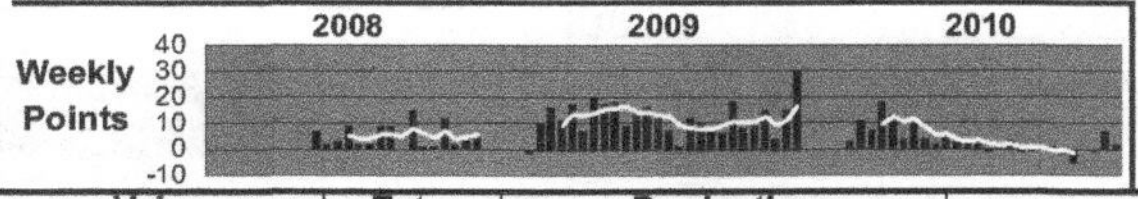


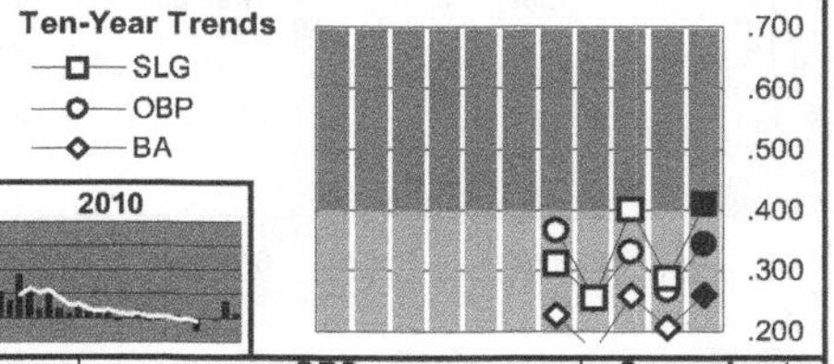


## Carlos Lee — 625 PA | $22 | 460 pts

OF-133 (LF-133), 1B-20, DH-7 | Owned: 97% | RH

Although Lee in 2010 endured his worst offensive season, he swatted 20+ HR for the 11th straight season and even was able to assist at first base. His SLG has nosedived since 2008, but that was a rarefied year for him, and 2010 was the first instance of a truly un-Lee-like hit rate. Blame an unlucky 16% LD%. (BJ)

| Player | Age | AB | HR | R | RBI | SB | BA | OBP | SLG | $1L | Pts |
|---|---|---|---|---|---|---|---|---|---|---|---|
| **Forecast** | | | | | | | | | | | |
| Lee C | 34 | 570 | 31 | 75 | 100 | 6 | .285 | .335 | .493 | $22 | 460 |
| **Mini-Browser** | | | | | | | | | | | |
| Pierre J | 33 | 582 | 0 | 85 | 46 | 52 | .279 | .330 | .343 | $23 | 430 |
| Ellsbury J | 27 | 534 | 6 | 81 | 46 | 46 | .280 | .335 | .393 | $23 | 400 |
| Victorino S | 30 | 587 | 13 | 98 | 65 | 33 | .277 | .344 | .442 | $23 | 470 |
| Bruce J | 23 | 582 | 33 | 91 | 85 | 7 | .268 | .338 | .512 | $23 | 400 |
| Young C | 27 | 562 | 26 | 91 | 78 | 20 | .266 | .345 | .496 | $22 | 410 |

| Minors (2010) Level | Leag | AB | HR | R | RBI | SB | BA | OBP | SLG | CT% | H% | BB% | Bash |
|---|---|---|---|---|---|---|---|---|---|---|---|---|---|
| A | — | — | — | — | — | — | — | — | — | — | — | — | — |
| AA | — | — | — | — | — | — | — | — | — | — | — | — | — |
| AAA | — | — | — | — | — | — | — | — | — | — | — | — | — |

| Majors Yr | Team | AB | HR | R | RBI | SB | BA | OBP | SLG | CT% | H% | BB% | Bash |
|---|---|---|---|---|---|---|---|---|---|---|---|---|---|
| 07 | HOU | 627 | 32 | 93 | 119 | 10 | .303 | .354 | .528 | 90% | 34% | 7% | 1.74 |
| 08 | HOU | 436 | 28 | 61 | 100 | 4 | .314 | .368 | .569 | 89% | 35% | 8% | 1.81 |
| 09 | HOU | 610 | 26 | 65 | 102 | 5 | .300 | .343 | .489 | 92% | 33% | 6% | 1.63 |
| 10 | HOU | 605 | 24 | 67 | 89 | 3 | .246 | .291 | .417 | 90% | 27% | 6% | 1.69 |

| Yr | $1L | $2L | Pts | RAA | 2B | 3B | CS | FB-LD-GB | HR/fb | RBI% | RS% | OPS | 1st Hf | 2nd Hf | vs RH | vs LH | Rnge | vRH | vLH |
|---|---|---|---|---|---|---|---|---|---|---|---|---|---|---|---|---|---|---|---|
| 07 | $31 | $26 | 550 | +22 | 43 | 1 | 5 | 46-16-38 | 12% | 24% | 28% | .882 | .869 | .898 | .859 | .956 | 2.03 | −3 | +9 |
| 08 | $24 | $17 | 400 | +25 | 27 | 0 | 1 | 44-21-35 | 16% | 26% | 22% | .937 | .899 | 1.110 | .930 | .959 | 2.03 | −10 | +27 |
| 09 | $24 | $15 | 460 | +12 | 35 | 1 | 3 | 44-20-36 | 11% | 22% | 19% | .831 | .838 | .824 | .816 | .892 | 2.03 | −16 | +42 |
| 10 | $15 | $8 | 390 | −17 | 29 | 1 | 3 | 46-16-39 | 10% | 19% | 26% | .708 | .682 | .738 | .689 | .771 | 2.03 | −12 | +33 |

Competition at LF — Stats in 2010

| Bats | Player | GSvR | GSvL | Sub | OPS |
|---|---|---|---|---|---|
| RH | Lee C | 103 | 30 | 0 | .708 |
| RH | Michaels J | 5 | 15 | 21 | .778 |
| RH | Bourgeois J | 2 | 4 | 19 | .562 |
| LH | Sullivan C | 4 | 0 | 9 | .492 |

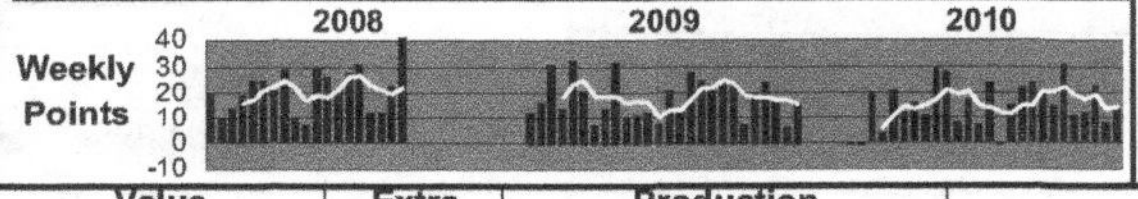


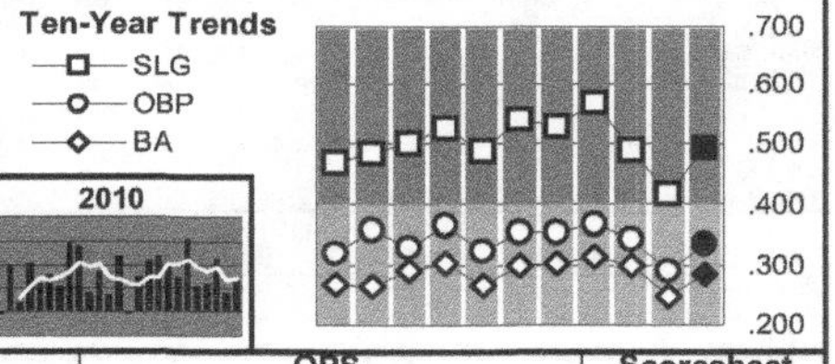


## Derrek Lee — 575 PA | $19 | 390 pts

1B-144, DH-3 | Owned: 91% | RH

Chronic back pain really hurt Lee in 2010 (see his subdued weekly trends), but he still has good power and plays good defense, and with all the changes around the league at first base this winter, some team will wager on a return to double-digit RAA. In Atlanta, Freddie Freeman will finally get the call in 2011. (MG)

| Player | Age | AB | HR | R | RBI | SB | BA | OBP | SLG | $1L | Pts |
|---|---|---|---|---|---|---|---|---|---|---|---|
| **Forecast** | | | | | | | | | | | |
| Lee D | 35 | 506 | 23 | 81 | 81 | 6 | .284 | .370 | .488 | $19 | 390 |
| **Mini-Browser** | | | | | | | | | | | |
| Dunn A | 31 | 525 | 39 | 85 | 104 | 0 | .260 | .382 | .518 | $22 | 400 |
| Konerko P | 35 | 554 | 31 | 75 | 94 | 0 | .271 | .359 | .499 | $21 | 410 |
| Youkilis K | 32 | 451 | 21 | 79 | 79 | 5 | .291 | .390 | .515 | $20 | 370 |
| LaRoche A | 31 | 530 | 30 | 84 | 90 | 0 | .283 | .356 | .520 | $20 | 380 |
| Butler B | 24 | 585 | 20 | 72 | 85 | 0 | .300 | .367 | .466 | $19 | 400 |

| Minors (2010) Level | Leag | AB | HR | R | RBI | SB | BA | OBP | SLG | CT% | H% | BB% | Bash |
|---|---|---|---|---|---|---|---|---|---|---|---|---|---|
| A | — | — | — | — | — | — | — | — | — | — | — | — | — |
| AA | — | — | — | — | — | — | — | — | — | — | — | — | — |
| AAA | — | — | — | — | — | — | — | — | — | — | — | — | — |

| Majors Yr | Team | AB | HR | R | RBI | SB | BA | OBP | SLG | CT% | H% | BB% | Bash |
|---|---|---|---|---|---|---|---|---|---|---|---|---|---|
| 07 | CHC | 567 | 22 | 91 | 82 | 6 | .317 | .400 | .513 | 80% | 40% | 11% | 1.62 |
| 08 | CHC | 623 | 20 | 93 | 90 | 8 | .291 | .361 | .462 | 81% | 36% | 10% | 1.59 |
| 09 | CHC | 532 | 35 | 91 | 111 | 1 | .306 | .393 | .579 | 80% | 39% | 12% | 1.89 |
| 10 | 2TM | 547 | 19 | 80 | 80 | 1 | .260 | .347 | .428 | 76% | 34% | 12% | 1.65 |

| Yr | $1L | $2L | Pts | RAA | 2B | 3B | CS | FB-LD-GB | HR/fb | RBI% | RS% | OPS | 1st Hf | 2nd Hf | vs RH | vs LH | Rnge | vRH | vLH |
|---|---|---|---|---|---|---|---|---|---|---|---|---|---|---|---|---|---|---|---|
| 07 | $25 | $18 | 430 | +19 | 43 | 1 | 5 | 38-21-41 | 13% | 23% | 29% | .913 | .890 | .941 | .885 | 1.015 | 1.90 | −9 | +23 |
| 08 | $24 | $16 | 440 | +7 | 41 | 3 | 2 | 34-21-45 | 12% | 21% | 31% | .823 | .880 | .733 | .785 | .948 | 1.87 | −16 | +45 |
| 09 | $29 | $24 | 480 | +32 | 36 | 2 | 0 | 46-19-35 | 18% | 25% | 27% | .972 | .865 | 1.092 | .986 | .900 | 1.85 | −26 | +71 |
| 10 | $16 | $9 | 330 | −6 | 35 | 0 | 3 | 38-23-40 | 12% | 19% | 31% | .774 | .695 | .888 | .773 | .777 | 1.86 | −10 | +28 |

Competition at 1B — Stats in 2010

| Bats | Player | GSvR | GSvL | Sub | OPS |
|---|---|---|---|---|---|
| RH | Glaus T | 65 | 42 | 7 | .744 |
| RH | Lee D | 24 | 12 | 3 | .774 |
| LH | Hinske E | 19 | 1 | 12 | .793 |
| LH | Freeman F | 2 | 0 | 10 | .500 |

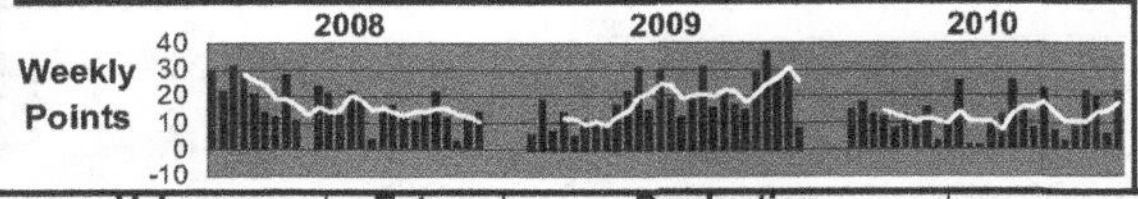


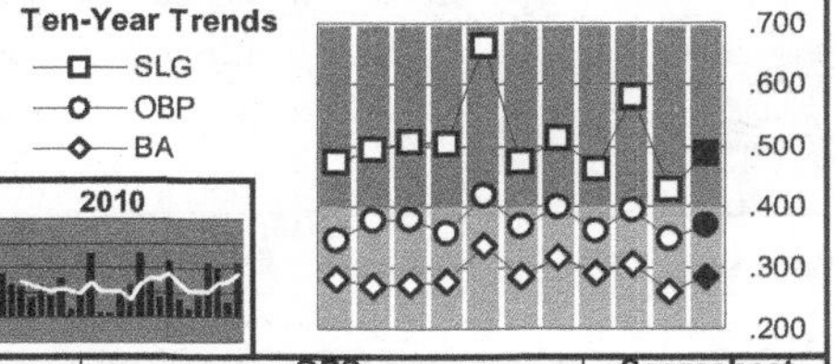


## Fred Lewis — 500 PA | $14 | 280 pts

OF-99 (LF-84, RF-10, CF-7), DH-8 | Owned: 1% | LH

Lewis was a pleasant surprise for Toronto after they acquired him for next to nothing. Unfortunately, his bat is unremarkable for a corner outfielder, and his glove is average at best in spite of his good speed. Toronto might not have at-bats to distribute to warrant holding onto Lewis. (MH)

| Player | Age | AB | HR | R | RBI | SB | BA | OBP | SLG | $1L | Pts |
|---|---|---|---|---|---|---|---|---|---|---|---|
| **Forecast** | | | | | | | | | | | |
| Lewis F | 30 | 446 | 10 | 75 | 40 | 15 | .269 | .347 | .428 | $14 | 280 |
| **Mini-Browser** | | | | | | | | | | | |
| Kubel J | 28 | 468 | 21 | 63 | 84 | 0 | .269 | .337 | .472 | $16 | 320 |
| Tabata J | 22 | 567 | 12 | 78 | 54 | 24 | .275 | .334 | .388 | $15 | 360 |
| Rivera J | 32 | 500 | 21 | 58 | 74 | 0 | .273 | .319 | .453 | $15 | 330 |
| Maybin C | 23 | 534 | 18 | 84 | 54 | 18 | .247 | .331 | .410 | $15 | 310 |
| Brantley M | 23 | 573 | 6 | 69 | 50 | 31 | .251 | .324 | .331 | $14 | 360 |

| Minors (2010) Level | Leag | AB | HR | R | RBI | SB | BA | OBP | SLG | CT% | H% | BB% | Bash |
|---|---|---|---|---|---|---|---|---|---|---|---|---|---|
| A | — | — | — | — | — | — | — | — | — | — | — | — | — |
| AA | — | — | — | — | — | — | — | — | — | — | — | — | — |
| AAA | PCL | 22 | 1 | 6 | 6 | 2 | .409 | .536 | .773 | 91% | 45% | 21% | 1.89 |

| Majors Yr | Team | AB | HR | R | RBI | SB | BA | OBP | SLG | CT% | H% | BB% | Bash |
|---|---|---|---|---|---|---|---|---|---|---|---|---|---|
| 07 | SF | 157 | 3 | 34 | 19 | 5 | .287 | .374 | .408 | 80% | 36% | 11% | 1.42 |
| 08 | SF | 468 | 9 | 81 | 40 | 21 | .282 | .351 | .440 | 74% | 38% | 10% | 1.56 |
| 09 | SF | 295 | 4 | 49 | 20 | 8 | .258 | .348 | .390 | 72% | 36% | 11% | 1.51 |
| 10 | TOR | 428 | 8 | 70 | 36 | 17 | .262 | .332 | .414 | 76% | 35% | 8% | 1.58 |

| Yr | $1L | $2L | Pts | RAA | 2B | 3B | CS | FB-LD-GB | HR/fb | RBI% | RS% | OPS | 1st Hf | 2nd Hf | vs RH | vs LH | Rnge | vRH | vLH |
|---|---|---|---|---|---|---|---|---|---|---|---|---|---|---|---|---|---|---|---|
| 07 | $2 | -$10 | 110 | +1 | 6 | 2 | 1 | 30-15-55 | 8% | 20% | 48% | .782 | .798 | .747 | .807 | .667 | 2.10 | +23 | −73 |
| 08 | $16 | $7 | 290 | +5 | 25 | 11 | 7 | 28-18-54 | 9% | 17% | 41% | .791 | .798 | .776 | .809 | .728 | 2.10 | +24 | −78 |
| 09 | $5 | -$8 | 150 | −5 | 21 | 3 | 4 | 27-21-52 | 7% | 12% | 40% | .738 | .719 | .785 | .795 | .492 | 2.09 | +22 | −73 |
| 10 | $13 | $2 | 240 | −8 | 31 | 5 | 6 | 34-18-47 | 7% | 16% | 41% | .745 | .779 | .683 | .776 | .636 | 2.09 | +28 | −90 |

Competition at LF — Stats in 2010

| Bats | Player | GSvR | GSvL | Sub | OPS |
|---|---|---|---|---|---|
| LH | Lewis F | 67 | 15 | 2 | .745 |
| LH | Snider T | 41 | 8 | 4 | .767 |
| LH | Lind A | 10 | 6 | 0 | .712 |
| LH | Wise D | 7 | 0 | 3 | .675 |

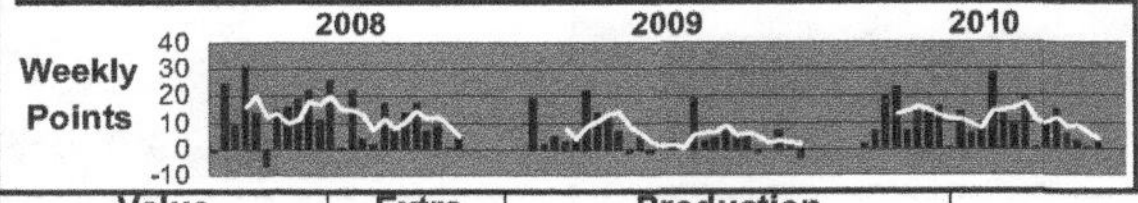


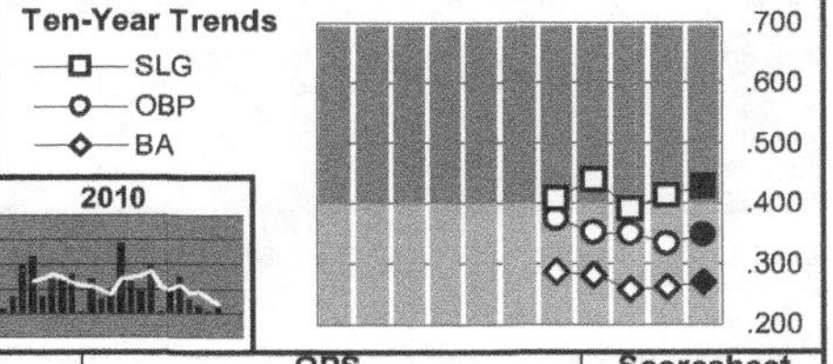


For more stats, visit www.Rotolympus.com.

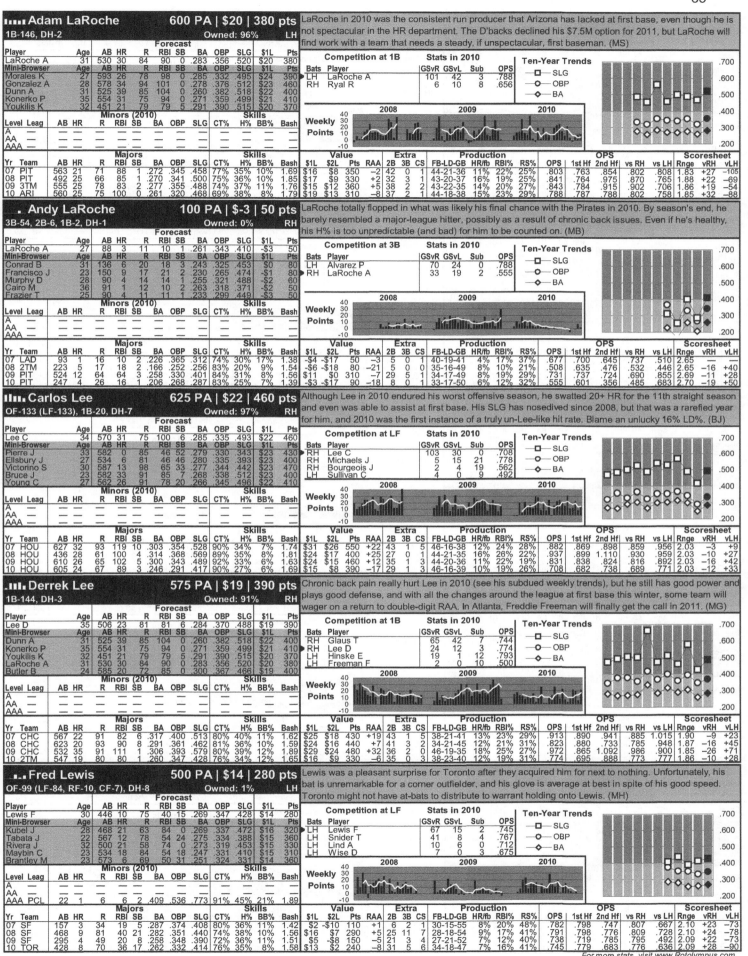

## Brent Lillibridge — 150 PA | $-1 | 70 pts

2B-25, DH-15, OF-8 (CF-6, LF-1, RF-1), SS-4, 3B-3 Owned: 0% RH

At first, 2010 brought renewed hope for former prospect Brent Lillibridge, as he came up in June and hit out of his mind for two months. And then midnight struck. Lillibridge is quick (he was easily Ozzie's choice to pinch-run), and he can handle SS, but the latter trait is superfluous on a team with Omar Vizquel. (RM)

Forecast

| Player | Age | AB | HR | R | RBI | SB | BA | OBP | SLG | $1L | Pts |
|---|---|---|---|---|---|---|---|---|---|---|---|
| Lillibridge B | 27 | 136 | 3 | 18 | 14 | 8 | .232 | .304 | .374 | -$1 | 70 |
| **Mini-Browser** | Age | AB | HR | R | RBI | SB | BA | OBP | SLG | $1L | Pts |
| Barmes C | 32 | 211 | 7 | 27 | 25 | 5 | .266 | .319 | .441 | $2 | 130 |
| Sogard E | 24 | 345 | 8 | 40 | 40 | 8 | .220 | .295 | .343 | $2 | 190 |
| Fontenot M | 30 | 179 | 4 | 24 | 22 | 2 | .279 | .346 | .434 | $1 | 110 |
| Guillen C | 35 | 153 | 5 | 21 | 23 | 2 | .274 | .350 | .448 | $1 | 110 |
| Lugo J | 35 | 163 | 2 | 19 | 16 | 7 | .258 | .325 | .346 | -$1 | 90 |

Minors (2010) / Skills

| Level | Leag | AB | HR | R | RBI | SB | BA | OBP | SLG | CT% | H% | BB% | Bash |
|---|---|---|---|---|---|---|---|---|---|---|---|---|---|
| A | — | — | — | — | — | — | — | — | — | — | — | — | — |
| AA | — | — | — | — | — | — | — | — | — | — | — | — | — |
| AAA | IL | 185 | 4 | 26 | 16 | 19 | .270 | .330 | .378 | 75% | 36% | 8% | 1.40 |

Competition at 2B — Stats in 2010

| Bats | Player | GSvR | GSvL | Sub | OPS |
|---|---|---|---|---|---|
| RH | Beckham G | 93 | 32 | 1 | .695 |
| BH | Vizquel O | 17 | 1 | 1 | .673 |
| RH | Lillibridge B | 11 | 7 | 7 | .625 |

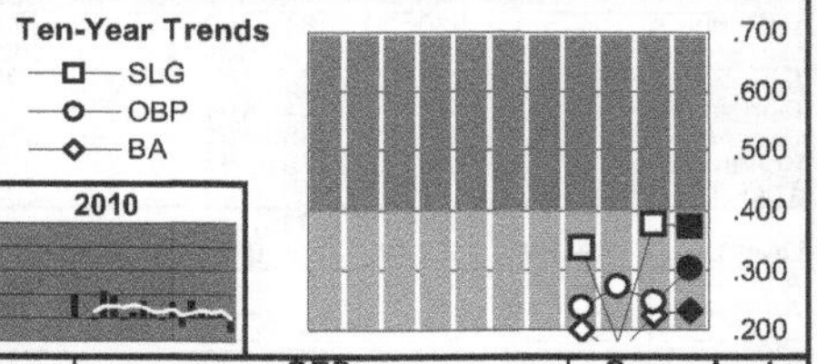


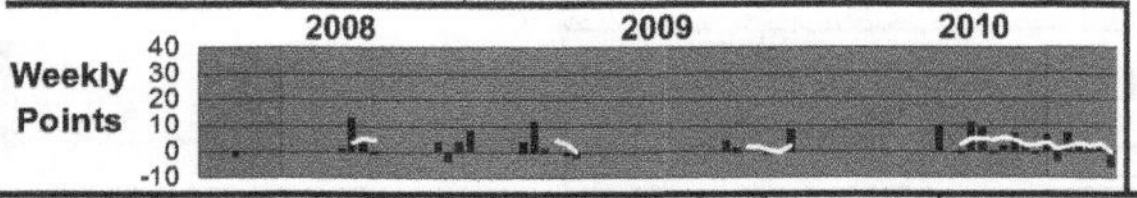


Majors / Skills / Value / Extra / Production / OPS / Scoresheet

| Yr | Team | AB | HR | R | RBI | SB | BA | OBP | SLG | CT% | H% | BB% | Bash | $1L | $2L | Pts | RAA | 2B | 3B | CS | FB-LD-GB | HR/fb | RBI% | RS% | OPS | 1st Hf | 2nd Hf | vs RH | vs LH | Rnge | vRH | vLH |
|---|---|---|---|---|---|---|---|---|---|---|---|---|---|---|---|---|---|---|---|---|---|---|---|---|---|---|---|---|---|---|---|---|
| 07 | — | — | — | — | — | — | — | — | — | — | — | — | — | — | — | — | — | — | — | — | — | — | — | — | — | — | — | — | — | — | — | — |
| 08 | ATL | 80 | 1 | 9 | 8 | 2 | .200 | .238 | .338 | 71% | 28% | 4% | 1.69 | -$4 | -$17 | 30 | −5 | 6 | 1 | 0 | 44-11-45 | 4% | 17% | 42% | .576 | .677 | .484 | .649 | .480 | — | — | — |
| 09 | CHW | 95 | 0 | 9 | 3 | 6 | .158 | .273 | .179 | 73% | 22% | 13% | 1.13 | -$4 | -$19 | 30 | −10 | 2 | 0 | 3 | 34-19-47 | 0% | 5% | 30% | .452 | .451 | .451 | .439 | .481 | — | — | — |
| 10 | CHW | 98 | 2 | 19 | 16 | 5 | .224 | .248 | .378 | 63% | 35% | 3% | 1.68 | $0 | -$14 | 50 | −5 | 5 | 2 | 3 | 39-25-36 | 9% | 25% | 74% | .625 | 1.342 | .416 | .459 | .949 | — | — | — |

## Adam Lind — 600 PA | $16 | 340 pts

DH-122, OF-16 (LF-16), 1B-11 Owned: 81% LH

Coming off a break-out 2010, Lind pressed and turned in a carbon copy of his career-worst 2007 season. Of the last four seasons, the anomaly now appears to be 2009 and its 20% HR/FB. Everything could come together again, as it did in 2009, but it's unlikely. If Lyle Overbay leaves TOR, Lind might move to 1B. (MH)

Forecast

| Player | Age | AB | HR | R | RBI | SB | BA | OBP | SLG | $1L | Pts |
|---|---|---|---|---|---|---|---|---|---|---|---|
| Lind A | 27 | 581 | 24 | 66 | 84 | 0 | .258 | .313 | .458 | $16 | 340 |
| **Mini-Browser** | Age | AB | HR | R | RBI | SB | BA | OBP | SLG | $1L | Pts |
| Guerrero V | 36 | 517 | 28 | 72 | 88 | 6 | .298 | .355 | .508 | $23 | 410 |
| Abreu B | 37 | 533 | 18 | 84 | 84 | 24 | .270 | .361 | .432 | $22 | 430 |
| Ortiz D | 35 | 444 | 26 | 74 | 89 | 0 | .272 | .374 | .533 | $19 | 370 |
| Scott L | 32 | 450 | 25 | 60 | 70 | 0 | .278 | .361 | .521 | $16 | 320 |
| Matsui H | 36 | 421 | 20 | 55 | 75 | 0 | .273 | .358 | .457 | $14 | 300 |

Minors (2010) / Skills

| Level | Leag | AB | HR | R | RBI | SB | BA | OBP | SLG | CT% | H% | BB% | Bash |
|---|---|---|---|---|---|---|---|---|---|---|---|---|---|
| A | — | — | — | — | — | — | — | — | — | — | — | — | — |
| AA | — | — | — | — | — | — | — | — | — | — | — | — | — |
| AAA | — | — | — | — | — | — | — | — | — | — | — | — | — |

Competition at DH — Stats in 2010

| Bats | Player | GSvR | GSvL | Sub | OPS |
|---|---|---|---|---|---|
| LH | Lind A | 103 | 17 | 2 | .712 |

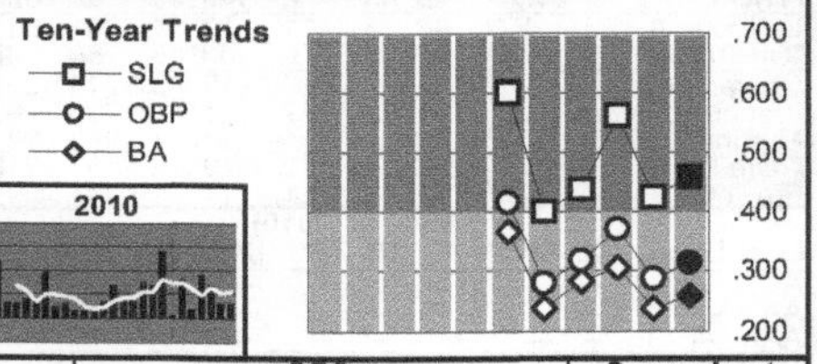


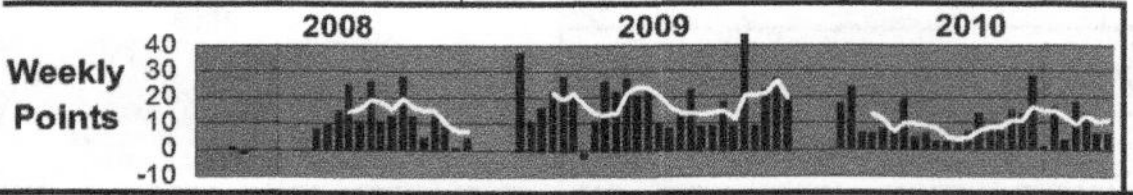


Majors / Skills / Value / Extra / Production / OPS / Scoresheet

| Yr | Team | AB | HR | R | RBI | SB | BA | OBP | SLG | CT% | H% | BB% | Bash | $1L | $2L | Pts | RAA | 2B | 3B | CS | FB-LD-GB | HR/fb | RBI% | RS% | OPS | 1st Hf | 2nd Hf | vs RH | vs LH | Rnge | vRH | vLH |
|---|---|---|---|---|---|---|---|---|---|---|---|---|---|---|---|---|---|---|---|---|---|---|---|---|---|---|---|---|---|---|---|---|
| 07 | TOR | 290 | 11 | 34 | 46 | 1 | .238 | .278 | .400 | 78% | 31% | 5% | 1.68 | $5 | -$8 | 150 | −15 | 14 | 0 | 2 | 37-19-45 | 13% | 24% | 31% | .678 | .657 | .771 | .720 | .542 | — | +22 | −75 |
| 08 | TOR | 326 | 9 | 48 | 40 | 2 | .282 | .316 | .439 | 82% | 34% | 5% | 1.55 | $8 | -$3 | 190 | −8 | 16 | 4 | 0 | 30-19-51 | 11% | 19% | 39% | .755 | .776 | .748 | .781 | .688 | — | +27 | −86 |
| 09 | TOR | 587 | 35 | 93 | 114 | 1 | .305 | .370 | .562 | 81% | 38% | 9% | 1.84 | $29 | $24 | 490 | +25 | 46 | 0 | 1 | 37-20-43 | 20% | 25% | 28% | .932 | .928 | .938 | .992 | .780 | — | +26 | −79 |
| 10 | TOR | 569 | 23 | 57 | 72 | 0 | .237 | .287 | .425 | 75% | 32% | 6% | 1.79 | $12 | $1 | 260 | −23 | 32 | 3 | 0 | 40-19-41 | 13% | 17% | 22% | .712 | .640 | .807 | .829 | .341 | — | +32 | −89 |

## James Loney — 650 PA | $17 | 400 pts

1B-160 Owned: 92% LH

Loney is nothing if not consistent, but consistent sub-par production from a first baseman gains urgency when his salary climbs. Loney is a prime candidate to be dangled by LA this winter in hopes that another team sees his sweet swing as tempting enough to offer starting pitching. (MP)

Forecast

| Player | Age | AB | HR | R | RBI | SB | BA | OBP | SLG | $1L | Pts |
|---|---|---|---|---|---|---|---|---|---|---|---|
| Loney J | 26 | 580 | 13 | 72 | 91 | 7 | .280 | .344 | .428 | $17 | 400 |
| **Mini-Browser** | Age | AB | HR | R | RBI | SB | BA | OBP | SLG | $1L | Pts |
| Youkilis K | 32 | 451 | 21 | 79 | 79 | 5 | .291 | .390 | .515 | $20 | 370 |
| LaRoche A | 31 | 530 | 30 | 84 | 90 | 0 | .283 | .356 | .520 | $20 | 380 |
| Butler B | 24 | 585 | 20 | 72 | 85 | 0 | .300 | .367 | .466 | $19 | 400 |
| Lee D | 35 | 506 | 23 | 81 | 81 | 6 | .284 | .370 | .488 | $19 | 390 |
| Pena C | 32 | 452 | 33 | 72 | 88 | 0 | .231 | .357 | .494 | $17 | 310 |

Minors (2010) / Skills

| Level | Leag | AB | HR | R | RBI | SB | BA | OBP | SLG | CT% | H% | BB% | Bash |
|---|---|---|---|---|---|---|---|---|---|---|---|---|---|
| A | — | — | — | — | — | — | — | — | — | — | — | — | — |
| AA | — | — | — | — | — | — | — | — | — | — | — | — | — |
| AAA | — | — | — | — | — | — | — | — | — | — | — | — | — |

Competition at 1B — Stats in 2010

| Bats | Player | GSvR | GSvL | Sub | OPS |
|---|---|---|---|---|---|
| LH | Loney J | 109 | 40 | 11 | .723 |
| RH | Belliard R | 1 | 7 | 2 | .622 |

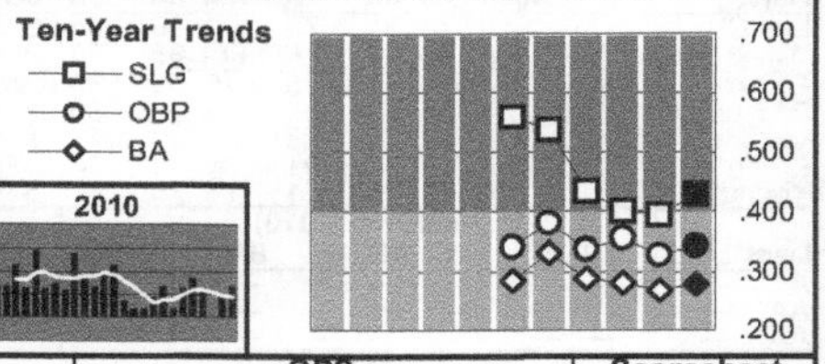


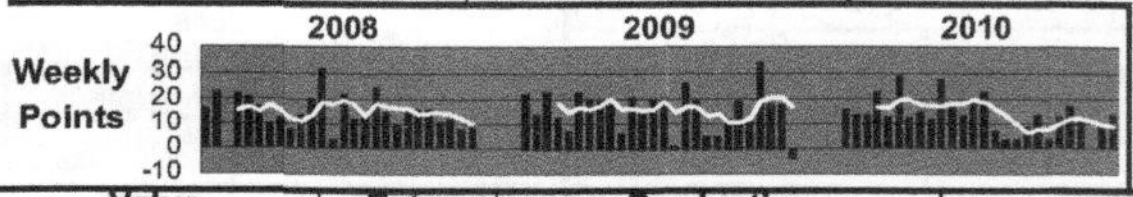


Majors / Skills / Value / Extra / Production / OPS / Scoresheet

| Yr | Team | AB | HR | R | RBI | SB | BA | OBP | SLG | CT% | H% | BB% | Bash | $1L | $2L | Pts | RAA | 2B | 3B | CS | FB-LD-GB | HR/fb | RBI% | RS% | OPS | 1st Hf | 2nd Hf | vs RH | vs LH | Rnge | vRH | vLH |
|---|---|---|---|---|---|---|---|---|---|---|---|---|---|---|---|---|---|---|---|---|---|---|---|---|---|---|---|---|---|---|---|---|
| 07 | LAD | 344 | 15 | 41 | 67 | 0 | .331 | .381 | .538 | 86% | 39% | 7% | 1.62 | $14 | $4 | 270 | +12 | 18 | 4 | 1 | 36-22-42 | 14% | 28% | 20% | .919 | 1.044 | .882 | .939 | .866 | 1.85 | +23 | −76 |
| 08 | LAD | 595 | 13 | 66 | 90 | 7 | .289 | .338 | .434 | 86% | 34% | 7% | 1.50 | $18 | $10 | 380 | −11 | 35 | 6 | 4 | 34-22-44 | 7% | 21% | 26% | .772 | .796 | .737 | .815 | .664 | 1.85 | +23 | −68 |
| 09 | LAD | 576 | 13 | 73 | 90 | 7 | .281 | .357 | .399 | 88% | 32% | 11% | 1.42 | $18 | $10 | 410 | −10 | 25 | 2 | 3 | 35-22-43 | 7% | 23% | 27% | .756 | .752 | .762 | .750 | .779 | 1.84 | +27 | −76 |
| 10 | LAD | 588 | 10 | 67 | 88 | 10 | .267 | .329 | .395 | 84% | 32% | 8% | 1.48 | $16 | $8 | 360 | −21 | 41 | 2 | 5 | 32-25-43 | 6% | 22% | 28% | .723 | .803 | .616 | .785 | .575 | 1.85 | +21 | −62 |

## Evan Longoria — 700 PA | $30 | 470 pts

3B-151 Owned: 100% RH

Longoria is the Rays' franchise player. In 2010, he was caught stealing for the first time, but his success rate is still 75%. In 2011, his HR/FB should revert to the high teens, which in 2010 would have gotten him back to 30 HR. Longoria will try to start every game again and perch in the #3 or #4 spot in the order. (RZ)

Forecast

| Player | Age | AB | HR | R | RBI | SB | BA | OBP | SLG | $1L | Pts |
|---|---|---|---|---|---|---|---|---|---|---|---|
| Longoria E | 25 | 602 | 35 | 98 | 112 | 7 | .279 | .362 | .516 | $30 | 470 |
| **Mini-Browser** | Age | AB | HR | R | RBI | SB | BA | OBP | SLG | $1L | Pts |
| Wright D | 28 | 570 | 27 | 101 | 101 | 20 | .296 | .384 | .511 | $31 | 490 |
| Rodriguez A | 35 | 458 | 33 | 83 | 105 | 11 | .276 | .377 | .537 | $28 | 420 |
| Zimmerman R | 26 | 558 | 26 | 98 | 91 | 7 | .291 | .363 | .507 | $23 | 440 |
| Reynolds M | 27 | 586 | 39 | 98 | 98 | 13 | .244 | .339 | .498 | $23 | 390 |
| Beltre A | 31 | 544 | 24 | 78 | 78 | 6 | .287 | .334 | .489 | $21 | 380 |

Minors (2010) / Skills

| Level | Leag | AB | HR | R | RBI | SB | BA | OBP | SLG | CT% | H% | BB% | Bash |
|---|---|---|---|---|---|---|---|---|---|---|---|---|---|
| A | — | — | — | — | — | — | — | — | — | — | — | — | — |
| AA | — | — | — | — | — | — | — | — | — | — | — | — | — |
| AAA | — | — | — | — | — | — | — | — | — | — | — | — | — |

Competition at 3B — Stats in 2010

| Bats | Player | GSvR | GSvL | Sub | OPS |
|---|---|---|---|---|---|
| RH | Longoria E | 99 | 52 | 0 | .879 |

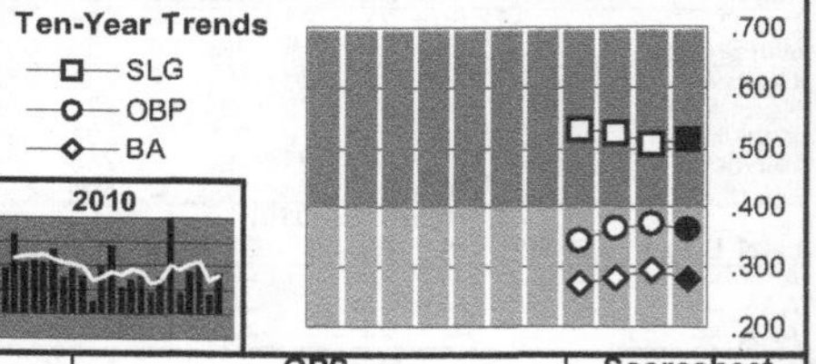


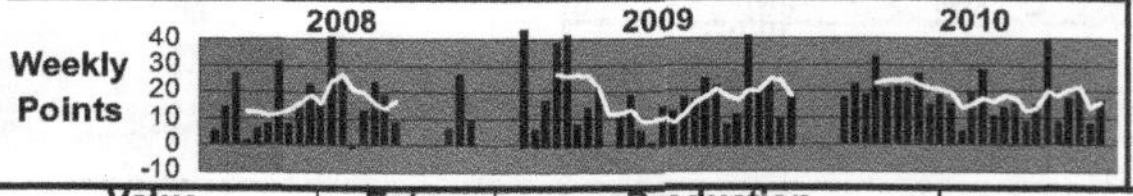


Majors / Skills / Value / Extra / Production / OPS / Scoresheet

| Yr | Team | AB | HR | R | RBI | SB | BA | OBP | SLG | CT% | H% | BB% | Bash | $1L | $2L | Pts | RAA | 2B | 3B | CS | FB-LD-GB | HR/fb | RBI% | RS% | OPS | 1st Hf | 2nd Hf | vs RH | vs LH | Rnge | vRH | vLH |
|---|---|---|---|---|---|---|---|---|---|---|---|---|---|---|---|---|---|---|---|---|---|---|---|---|---|---|---|---|---|---|---|---|
| 07 | — | — | — | — | — | — | — | — | — | — | — | — | — | — | — | — | — | — | — | — | — | — | — | — | — | — | — | — | — | 2.65 | — | — |
| 08 | TB | 448 | 27 | 67 | 85 | 7 | .272 | .343 | .531 | 73% | 37% | 9% | 1.95 | $21 | $12 | 330 | +18 | 31 | 2 | 0 | 42-20-39 | 19% | 20% | 27% | .874 | .861 | .902 | .890 | .830 | 2.65 | — | — |
| 09 | TB | 584 | 33 | 100 | 113 | 9 | .281 | .364 | .526 | 76% | 37% | 11% | 1.87 | $28 | $23 | 470 | +29 | 44 | 0 | 0 | 42-19-39 | 18% | 24% | 32% | .889 | .898 | .880 | .881 | .909 | 2.70 | −12 | +30 |
| 10 | TB | 574 | 22 | 96 | 104 | 15 | .294 | .372 | .507 | 78% | 38% | 11% | 1.72 | $31 | $26 | 460 | +26 | 46 | 5 | 5 | 43-20-37 | 11% | 24% | 33% | .879 | .895 | .857 | .845 | .956 | 2.73 | −10 | +23 |

## Felipe Lopez — 400 PA | $6 | 220 pts

3B-60, 2B-27, SS-25, 1B-2, OF-1 (RF-1) Owned: 38% BH

After the injury to David Freese, Lopez was given regular playing time at 3B. He failed to capitalize on this opportunity and was released after exhibiting pathetic offense, struggling defense, and habitual tardiness. Boston picked him up, but he could enter free agency in 2011. Lopez might need just renewed focus. (AB)

Forecast

| Player | Age | AB | HR | R | RBI | SB | BA | OBP | SLG | $1L | Pts |
|---|---|---|---|---|---|---|---|---|---|---|---|
| Lopez F | 30 | 361 | 8 | 48 | 36 | 8 | .266 | .341 | .377 | $6 | 220 |
| **Mini-Browser** | Age | AB | HR | R | RBI | SB | BA | OBP | SLG | $1L | Pts |
| Hall B | 31 | 355 | 12 | 48 | 48 | 4 | .248 | .308 | .441 | $8 | 180 |
| Aviles M | 30 | 326 | 7 | 46 | 35 | 7 | .290 | .321 | .428 | $8 | 200 |
| Infante O | 29 | 344 | 4 | 49 | 41 | 4 | .294 | .342 | .398 | $8 | 210 |
| Ellis M | 33 | 350 | 8 | 44 | 44 | 8 | .263 | .326 | .394 | $7 | 220 |
| Donald J | 26 | 520 | 12 | 63 | 52 | 12 | .232 | .303 | .369 | $7 | 250 |

Minors (2010) / Skills

| Level | Leag | AB | HR | R | RBI | SB | BA | OBP | SLG | CT% | H% | BB% | Bash |
|---|---|---|---|---|---|---|---|---|---|---|---|---|---|
| A | — | — | — | — | — | — | — | — | — | — | — | — | — |
| AA | — | — | — | — | — | — | — | — | — | — | — | — | — |
| AAA | — | — | — | — | — | — | — | — | — | — | — | — | — |

Competition at 2B — Stats in 2010

| Bats | Player | GSvR | GSvL | Sub | OPS |
|---|---|---|---|---|---|
| LH | Schumaker S | 103 | 15 | 5 | .667 |
| BH | Miles A | 4 | 14 | 32 | .627 |
| RH | Greene T | 2 | 10 | 3 | .655 |

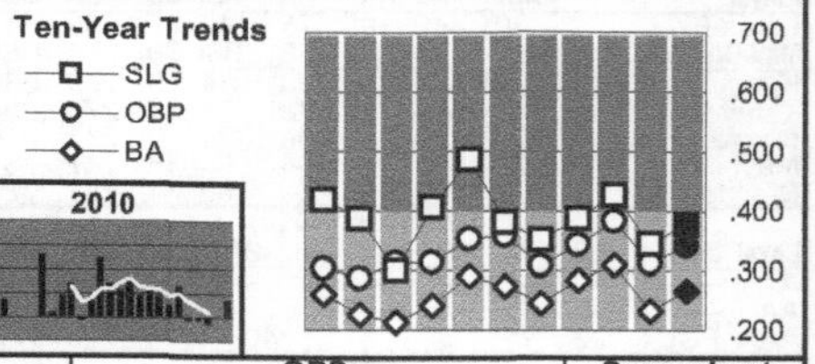


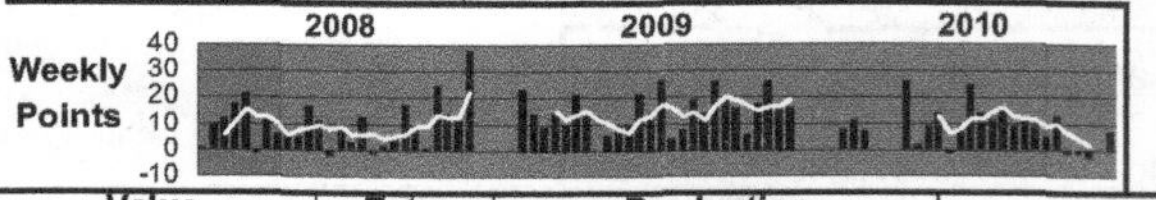


Majors / Skills / Value / Extra / Production / OPS / Scoresheet

| Yr | Team | AB | HR | R | RBI | SB | BA | OBP | SLG | CT% | H% | BB% | Bash | $1L | $2L | Pts | RAA | 2B | 3B | CS | FB-LD-GB | HR/fb | RBI% | RS% | OPS | 1st Hf | 2nd Hf | vs RH | vs LH | Rnge | vRH | vLH |
|---|---|---|---|---|---|---|---|---|---|---|---|---|---|---|---|---|---|---|---|---|---|---|---|---|---|---|---|---|---|---|---|---|
| 07 | WAS | 603 | 9 | 70 | 50 | 24 | .245 | .308 | .352 | 82% | 30% | 8% | 1.43 | $10 | $0 | 320 | −18 | 25 | 6 | 9 | 30-20-50 | 6% | 17% | 31% | .659 | .645 | .677 | .633 | .720 | — | +30 | −80 |
| 08 | 2TM | 481 | 6 | 64 | 46 | 8 | .283 | .343 | .387 | 83% | 34% | 8% | 1.37 | $11 | $1 | 260 | −2 | 28 | 2 | 8 | 31-19-50 | 5% | 18% | 33% | .730 | .619 | .903 | .727 | .736 | — | +7 | −18 |
| 09 | 2TM | 604 | 9 | 88 | 57 | 6 | .310 | .383 | .427 | 83% | 37% | 10% | 1.38 | $20 | $10 | 380 | +21 | 38 | 3 | 6 | 26-22-52 | 7% | 21% | 31% | .810 | .779 | .847 | .802 | .835 | 4.28 | −7 | +17 |
| 10 | 2TM | 391 | 8 | 52 | 37 | 8 | .233 | .311 | .345 | 79% | 29% | 10% | 1.48 | $6 | -$6 | 200 | −10 | 18 | 1 | 2 | 34-18-48 | 8% | 20% | 34% | .656 | .737 | .560 | .626 | .718 | — | −4 | +11 |

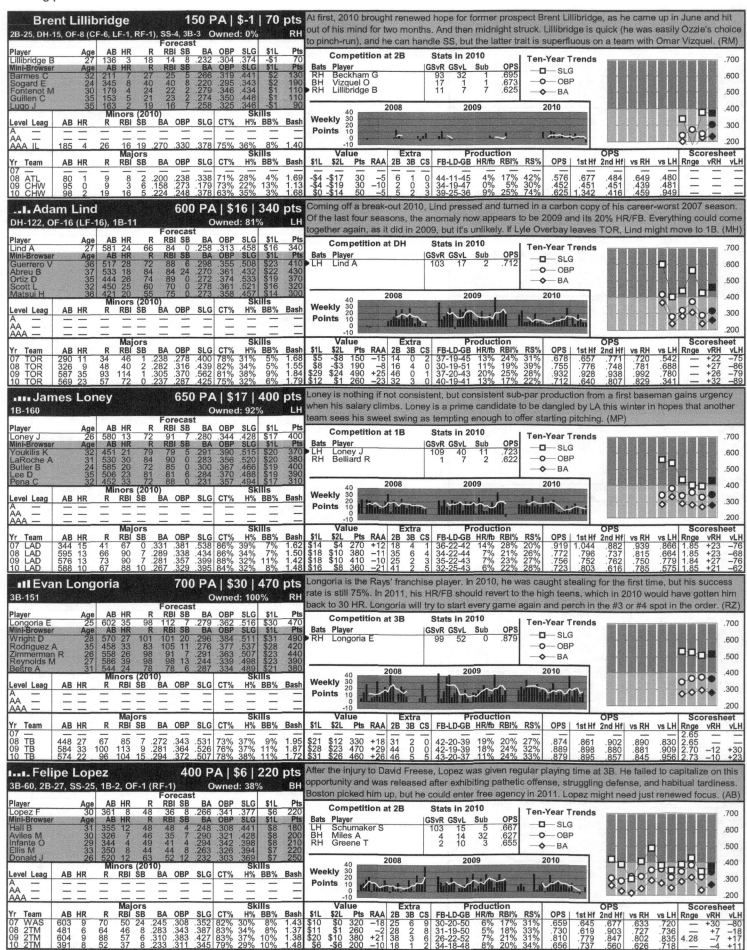

## Jose Lopez — 625 PA | $13 | 350 pts

3B-142, DH-8 — Owned: 58% — RH

Although the move to third base might have propped up Lopez's defense, it did nothing for his offense. After hitting like an average 3B in 2009, Lopez lost 150 points of OPS. There's almost no chance that SEA will pick up his option, but his power potential might draw interest from a team like the White Sox. (GC)

**Forecast**

| Player | Age | AB | HR | R | RBI | SB | BA | OBP | SLG | $1L | Pts |
|---|---|---|---|---|---|---|---|---|---|---|---|
| Lopez J | 27 | 587 | 19 | 63 | 75 | 6 | .266 | .294 | .405 | $13 | 350 |
| **Mini-Browser** | Age | AB | HR | R | RBI | SB | BA | OBP | SLG | $1L | Pts |
| Polanco P | 35 | 605 | 7 | 85 | 65 | 7 | .290 | .337 | .393 | $15 | 400 |
| McGehee C | 28 | 589 | 20 | 72 | 91 | 0 | .265 | .324 | .428 | $15 | 350 |
| Kouzmanoff K | 29 | 579 | 24 | 66 | 84 | 0 | .259 | .303 | .441 | $15 | 330 |
| Alvarez P | 24 | 530 | 30 | 66 | 96 | 0 | .249 | .328 | .480 | $15 | 310 |
| Rolen S | 35 | 461 | 15 | 70 | 65 | 5 | .282 | .356 | .466 | $13 | 340 |

**Minors (2010)** / Skills

| Level | Leag | AB | HR | R | RBI | SB | BA | OBP | SLG | CT% | H% | BB% | Bash |
|---|---|---|---|---|---|---|---|---|---|---|---|---|---|
| A | — | — | — | — | — | — | — | — | — | — | — | — | — |
| AA | — | — | — | — | — | — | — | — | — | — | — | — | — |
| AAA | — | — | — | — | — | — | — | — | — | — | — | — | — |

**Competition at 3B** — Stats in 2010

| Bats | Player | GSvR | GSvL | Sub | OPS |
|---|---|---|---|---|---|
| RH | Lopez J | 101 | 41 | 0 | .609 |
| RH | Tuiasosopo M | 6 | 4 | 2 | .541 |

Ten-Year Trends

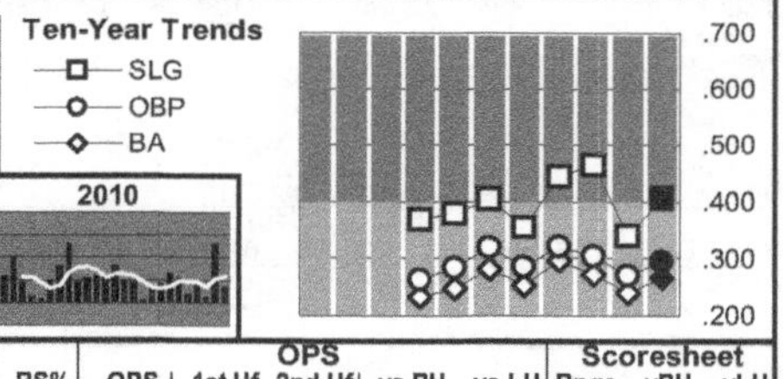

Weekly Points

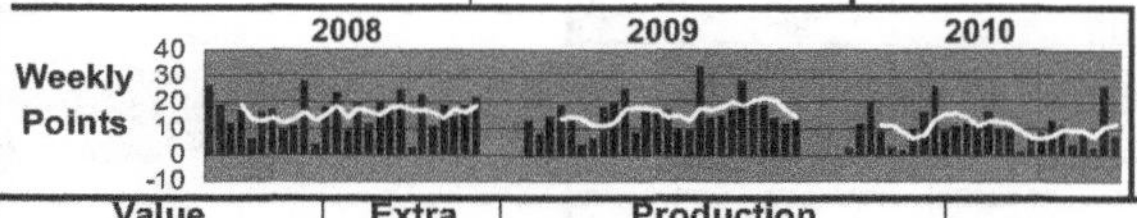

**Majors** / Skills / Value / Extra / Production / OPS / Scoresheet

| Yr | Team | AB | HR | R | RBI | SB | BA | OBP | SLG | CT% | H% | BB% | Bash | $1L | $2L | Pts | RAA | 2B | 3B | CS | FB-LD-GB | HR/fb | RBI% | RS% | OPS | 1st Hf | 2nd Hf | vs RH | vs LH | Rnge | vRH | vLH |
|---|---|---|---|---|---|---|---|---|---|---|---|---|---|---|---|---|---|---|---|---|---|---|---|---|---|---|---|---|---|---|---|---|
| 07 | SEA | 524 | 11 | 58 | 62 | 2 | .252 | .284 | .355 | 88% | 29% | 4% | 1.41 | $8 | -$3 | 260 | −26 | 17 | 2 | 3 | 37-17-46 | 6% | 18% | 32% | .639 | .737 | .519 | .642 | .629 | — | −25 | +64 |
| 08 | SEA | 644 | 17 | 80 | 89 | 6 | .297 | .322 | .443 | 90% | 33% | 4% | 1.49 | $22 | $14 | 420 | +2 | 41 | 1 | 3 | 36-20-44 | 8% | 22% | 31% | .764 | .729 | .814 | .765 | .763 | — | −23 | +62 |
| 09 | SEA | 613 | 25 | 69 | 96 | 3 | .272 | .303 | .463 | 89% | 31% | 4% | 1.70 | $19 | $12 | 410 | −2 | 42 | 0 | 3 | 41-19-41 | 11% | 21% | 26% | .766 | .716 | .820 | .770 | .759 | — | −13 | +33 |
| 10 | SEA | 593 | 10 | 49 | 58 | 3 | .239 | .270 | .339 | 89% | 27% | 4% | 1.42 | $7 | -$6 | 270 | −31 | 29 | 0 | 2 | 38-18-43 | 5% | 15% | 25% | .609 | .610 | .608 | .584 | .681 | — | −7 | +18 |

## Jed Lowrie — 350 PA | $5 | 190 pts

2B-28, SS-23, 1B-7, 3B-1 — Owned: 1% — BH

Lowrie's prior two seasons were essentially a wash, but 2010 changed matters once he returned from mono. His performance opened the door for a gig as shortstop, and he will battle Marco Scutaro in ST. At worst, Lowrie will work steady as the middle-IF back-up, and he could be a fantastic trade chip. (EB)

**Forecast**

| Player | Age | AB | HR | R | RBI | SB | BA | OBP | SLG | $1L | Pts |
|---|---|---|---|---|---|---|---|---|---|---|---|
| Lowrie J | 26 | 313 | 7 | 39 | 42 | 0 | .257 | .340 | .437 | $5 | 190 |
| **Mini-Browser** | Age | AB | HR | R | RBI | SB | BA | OBP | SLG | $1L | Pts |
| Infante O | 29 | 344 | 4 | 49 | 41 | 4 | .294 | .342 | .398 | $8 | 210 |
| Ellis M | 33 | 350 | 8 | 44 | 44 | 8 | .263 | .326 | .394 | $7 | 220 |
| Donald J | 26 | 520 | 12 | 63 | 52 | 12 | .232 | .303 | .369 | $7 | 250 |
| Lopez F | 30 | 361 | 8 | 48 | 36 | 8 | .266 | .341 | .377 | $6 | 220 |
| Guzman C | 33 | 314 | 4 | 46 | 32 | 4 | .279 | .314 | .389 | $5 | 180 |

**Minors (2010)** / Skills

| Level | Leag | AB | HR | R | RBI | SB | BA | OBP | SLG | CT% | H% | BB% | Bash |
|---|---|---|---|---|---|---|---|---|---|---|---|---|---|
| A | NYP | 15 | 0 | 2 | 5 | 0 | .400 | .524 | .467 | 93% | 43% | 24% | 1.17 |
| AA | — | — | — | — | — | — | — | — | — | — | — | — | — |
| AAA | IL | 15 | 1 | 3 | 4 | 1 | .333 | .353 | .733 | 73% | 45% | 6% | 2.20 |

**Competition at 2B** — Stats in 2010

| Bats | Player | GSvR | GSvL | Sub | OPS |
|---|---|---|---|---|---|
| RH | Pedroia D | 51 | 24 | 0 | .860 |
| RH | Hall B | 26 | 19 | 6 | .772 |
| BH | Lowrie J | 15 | 11 | 2 | .907 |
| RH | Scutaro M | 6 | 10 | 0 | .721 |

Ten-Year Trends

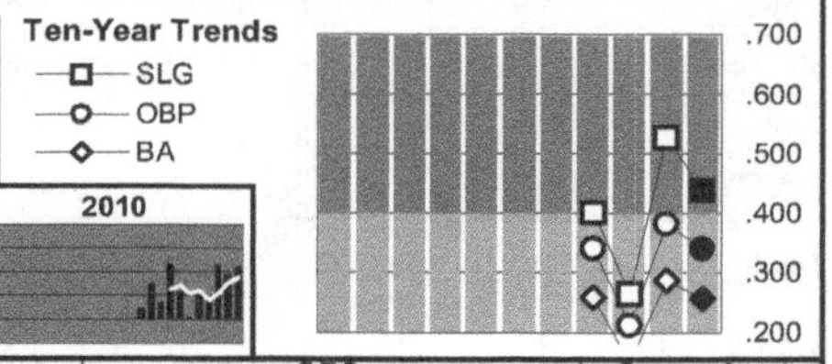

Weekly Points

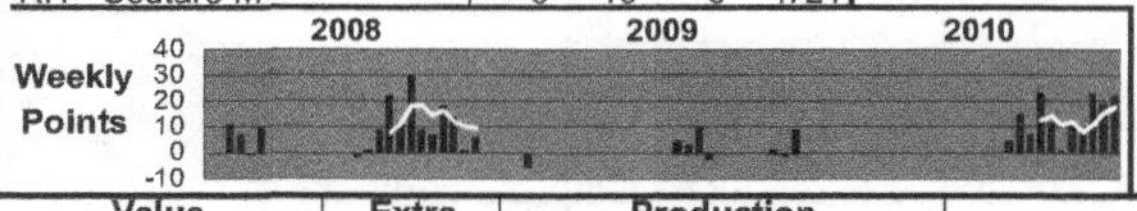

**Majors** / Skills / Value / Extra / Production / OPS / Scoresheet

| Yr | Team | AB | HR | R | RBI | SB | BA | OBP | SLG | CT% | H% | BB% | Bash | $1L | $2L | Pts | RAA | 2B | 3B | CS | FB-LD-GB | HR/fb | RBI% | RS% | OPS | 1st Hf | 2nd Hf | vs RH | vs LH | Rnge | vRH | vLH |
|---|---|---|---|---|---|---|---|---|---|---|---|---|---|---|---|---|---|---|---|---|---|---|---|---|---|---|---|---|---|---|---|---|
| 07 | — | — | — | — | — | — | — | — | — | — | — | — | — | — | — | — | — | — | — | — | — | — | — | — | — | — | — | — | — | — | — | — |
| 08 | BOS | 260 | 2 | 34 | 46 | 1 | .258 | .339 | .400 | 74% | 35% | 11% | 1.55 | $3 | -$8 | 150 | +0 | 25 | 3 | 0 | 43-25-32 | 2% | 25% | 32% | .739 | .733 | .740 | .653 | .934 | — | — | — |
| 09 | BOS | 68 | 2 | 5 | 11 | 0 | .147 | .211 | .265 | 71% | 21% | 8% | 1.80 | -$4 | -$19 | 20 | −7 | 2 | 0 | 0 | 66-10-24 | 6% | 20% | 21% | .475 | .206 | .572 | .391 | .687 | — | −16 | +39 |
| 10 | BOS | 171 | 9 | 31 | 24 | 1 | .287 | .381 | .526 | 85% | 34% | 13% | 1.84 | $5 | -$8 | 150 | +12 | 14 | 0 | 1 | 54-16-29 | 11% | 18% | 33% | .907 | — | .907 | .823 | 1.025 | — | −20 | +51 |

## Jonathan Lucroy — 450 PA | $6 | 220 pts

CA-75 — Owned: 0% — RH

One of Milwaukee's great rookie stories from '10, Lucroy virtually bypassed Double-A on his way to MLB. In the absence of any real organizational pressure at catcher, Lucroy will be the Brewers' starting backstop in 2010 and beyond, a window that will allow the power that he presented in the minors to develop. (MS)

**Forecast**

| Player | Age | AB | HR | R | RBI | SB | BA | OBP | SLG | $1L | Pts |
|---|---|---|---|---|---|---|---|---|---|---|---|
| Lucroy J | 24 | 406 | 14 | 41 | 45 | 5 | .233 | .307 | .375 | $6 | 220 |
| **Mini-Browser** | Age | AB | HR | R | RBI | SB | BA | OBP | SLG | $1L | Pts |
| Molina B | 36 | 310 | 10 | 29 | 46 | 0 | .273 | .306 | .422 | $8 | 190 |
| Jaso J | 27 | 402 | 9 | 50 | 45 | 0 | .246 | .344 | .372 | $8 | 240 |
| Iannetta C | 27 | 253 | 12 | 36 | 42 | 0 | .261 | .378 | .492 | $8 | 180 |
| Arencibia J | 25 | 369 | 16 | 36 | 52 | 0 | .217 | .254 | .420 | $7 | 160 |
| Shoppach K | 30 | 277 | 13 | 39 | 42 | 0 | .223 | .315 | .429 | $6 | 110 |

**Minors (2010)** / Skills

| Level | Leag | AB | HR | R | RBI | SB | BA | OBP | SLG | CT% | H% | BB% | Bash |
|---|---|---|---|---|---|---|---|---|---|---|---|---|---|
| A | — | — | — | — | — | — | — | — | — | — | — | — | — |
| AA | SOU | 42 | 0 | 8 | 5 | 0 | .452 | .500 | .524 | 93% | 49% | 9% | 1.16 |
| AAA | PCL | 80 | 2 | 8 | 11 | 0 | .238 | .265 | .363 | 83% | 29% | 4% | 1.53 |

**Competition at CA** — Stats in 2010

| Bats | Player | GSvR | GSvL | Sub | OPS |
|---|---|---|---|---|---|
| RH | Lucroy J | 50 | 24 | 1 | .628 |
| LH | Kottaras G | 45 | 15 | 1 | .701 |
| BH | Zaun G | 17 | 11 | 0 | .743 |

Ten-Year Trends

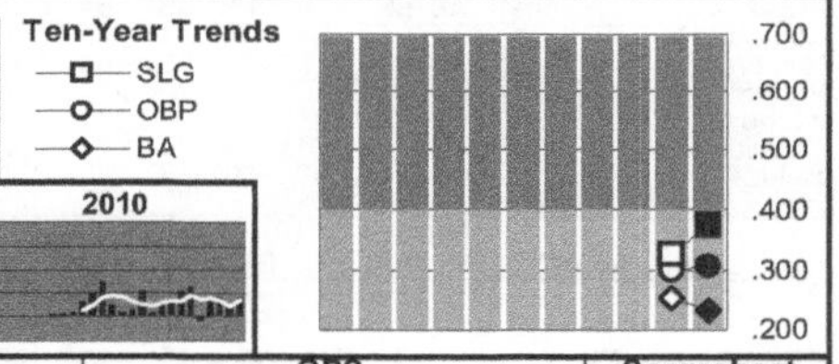

Weekly Points

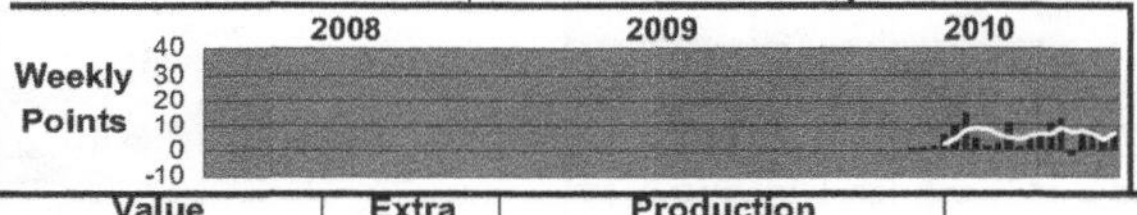

**Majors** / Skills / Value / Extra / Production / OPS / Scoresheet

| Yr | Team | AB | HR | R | RBI | SB | BA | OBP | SLG | CT% | H% | BB% | Bash | $1L | $2L | Pts | RAA | 2B | 3B | CS | FB-LD-GB | HR/fb | RBI% | RS% | OPS | 1st Hf | 2nd Hf | vs RH | vs LH | Rnge | vRH | vLH |
|---|---|---|---|---|---|---|---|---|---|---|---|---|---|---|---|---|---|---|---|---|---|---|---|---|---|---|---|---|---|---|---|---|
| 07 | — | — | — | — | — | — | — | — | — | — | — | — | — | — | — | — | — | — | — | — | — | — | — | — | — | — | — | — | — | — | — | — |
| 08 | — | — | — | — | — | — | — | — | — | — | — | — | — | — | — | — | — | — | — | — | — | — | — | — | — | — | — | — | — | — | — | — |
| 09 | — | — | — | — | — | — | — | — | — | — | — | — | — | — | — | — | — | — | — | — | — | — | — | — | — | — | — | — | — | — | — | — |
| 10 | MIL | 277 | 4 | 24 | 26 | 4 | .253 | .300 | .329 | 84% | 30% | 6% | 1.30 | $4 | -$4 | 120 | −10 | 9 | 0 | 2 | 38-19-44 | 5% | 14% | 24% | .628 | .672 | .608 | .589 | .735 | — | — | — |

## Ryan Ludwick — 535 PA | $17 | 320 pts

OF-126 (RF-126, CF-5, LF-1), DH-1 — Owned: 87% — RH

Ludwick had a slightly disappointing 2010 in which he endured a nagging calf injury and displayed only mid-range pop. Still, he will be worth his arbitration award, and he should be SD's everyday right-fielder. His new park won't help, but Ludwick should fare better in his second go. Just stop gazing at 2008. (DG)

**Forecast**

| Player | Age | AB | HR | R | RBI | SB | BA | OBP | SLG | $1L | Pts |
|---|---|---|---|---|---|---|---|---|---|---|---|
| Ludwick R | 32 | 451 | 21 | 75 | 86 | 5 | .273 | .346 | .490 | $17 | 320 |
| **Mini-Browser** | Age | AB | HR | R | RBI | SB | BA | OBP | SLG | $1L | Pts |
| Byrd M | 33 | 559 | 18 | 78 | 72 | 6 | .290 | .346 | .458 | $17 | 370 |
| Wells V | 32 | 568 | 18 | 72 | 78 | 12 | .264 | .318 | .452 | $17 | 390 |
| Gardner B | 27 | 441 | 5 | 75 | 40 | 40 | .261 | .357 | .363 | $17 | 330 |
| Heyward J | 21 | 511 | 18 | 84 | 66 | 12 | .270 | .368 | .464 | $17 | 380 |
| Ordonez M | 37 | 463 | 16 | 63 | 79 | 0 | .295 | .363 | .457 | $17 | 340 |

**Minors (2010)** / Skills

| Level | Leag | AB | HR | R | RBI | SB | BA | OBP | SLG | CT% | H% | BB% | Bash |
|---|---|---|---|---|---|---|---|---|---|---|---|---|---|
| A | — | — | — | — | — | — | — | — | — | — | — | — | — |
| AA | — | — | — | — | — | — | — | — | — | — | — | — | — |
| AAA | PCL | 9 | 2 | 2 | 5 | 0 | .333 | .273 | 1.111 | 67% | 50% | 0% | 3.33 |

**Competition at RF** — Stats in 2010

| Bats | Player | GSvR | GSvL | Sub | OPS |
|---|---|---|---|---|---|
| LH | Venable W | 70 | 3 | 16 | .732 |
| RH | Ludwick R | 35 | 22 | 1 | .743 |
| RH | Denorfia C | 6 | 9 | 3 | .769 |
| RH | Cunningham A | 7 | 7 | 3 | .748 |

Ten-Year Trends

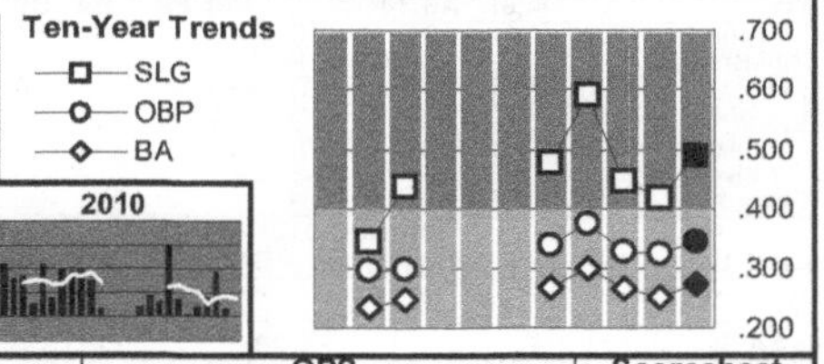

Weekly Points

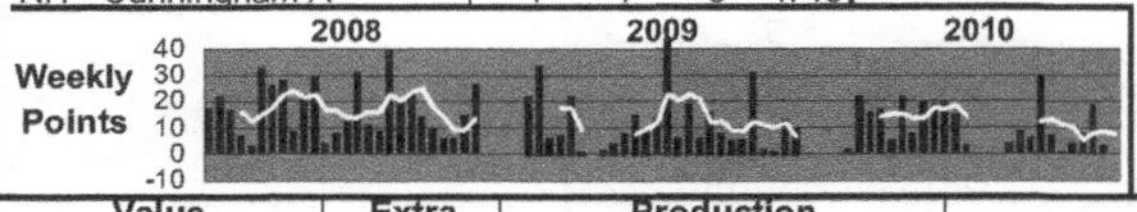

**Majors** / Skills / Value / Extra / Production / OPS / Scoresheet

| Yr | Team | AB | HR | R | RBI | SB | BA | OBP | SLG | CT% | H% | BB% | Bash | $1L | $2L | Pts | RAA | 2B | 3B | CS | FB-LD-GB | HR/fb | RBI% | RS% | OPS | 1st Hf | 2nd Hf | vs RH | vs LH | Rnge | vRH | vLH |
|---|---|---|---|---|---|---|---|---|---|---|---|---|---|---|---|---|---|---|---|---|---|---|---|---|---|---|---|---|---|---|---|---|
| 07 | STL | 303 | 14 | 42 | 52 | 4 | .267 | .339 | .479 | 76% | 35% | 8% | 1.79 | $8 | -$2 | 200 | −2 | 22 | 0 | 4 | 47-16-37 | 13% | 21% | 28% | .818 | .779 | .841 | .909 | .684 | — | — | — |
| 08 | STL | 538 | 37 | 104 | 113 | 4 | .299 | .375 | .591 | 73% | 41% | 10% | 1.98 | $31 | $27 | 460 | +28 | 40 | 3 | 4 | 47-26-27 | 20% | 23% | 35% | .966 | .962 | .971 | .985 | .929 | 2.11 | −4 | +9 |
| 09 | STL | 486 | 22 | 63 | 97 | 4 | .265 | .329 | .447 | 78% | 34% | 8% | 1.68 | $17 | $9 | 320 | −9 | 20 | 1 | 2 | 48-19-33 | 12% | 25% | 26% | .775 | .829 | .720 | .787 | .742 | 2.10 | −1 | +2 |
| 10 | 2TM | 490 | 17 | 63 | 69 | 0 | .251 | .325 | .418 | 75% | 33% | 9% | 1.67 | $11 | $2 | 260 | −15 | 27 | 2 | 4 | 45-23-32 | 10% | 23% | 28% | .743 | .822 | .652 | .800 | .609 | 2.08 | −6 | +14 |

## Julio Lugo — 175 PA | $-1 | 90 pts

2B-60, SS-26, 3B-7, DH-2, OF-1 (LF-1) — Owned: 1% — RH

Far removed from his seasons of playing every day, Lugo in 2010 watched his OPS (and PA) trickle to all-time lows. His worth is waning since there are plenty of franchises who have younger and cheaper utility fielders in their farm system. But "veterans" like Lugo always find a GM with an old yearbook. (BJ)

**Forecast**

| Player | Age | AB | HR | R | RBI | SB | BA | OBP | SLG | $1L | Pts |
|---|---|---|---|---|---|---|---|---|---|---|---|
| Lugo J | 35 | 163 | 2 | 19 | 16 | 7 | .258 | .325 | .346 | -$1 | 90 |
| **Mini-Browser** | Age | AB | HR | R | RBI | SB | BA | OBP | SLG | $1L | Pts |
| Brignac R | 25 | 279 | 9 | 33 | 33 | 3 | .247 | .297 | .400 | $3 | 140 |
| Barmes C | 32 | 211 | 7 | 27 | 25 | 5 | .266 | .319 | .441 | $2 | 130 |
| Sogard E | 24 | 345 | 8 | 40 | 40 | 8 | .220 | .295 | .343 | $2 | 190 |
| Fontenot M | 30 | 179 | 4 | 24 | 22 | 2 | .279 | .346 | .434 | $1 | 110 |
| Guillen C | 35 | 153 | 5 | 21 | 23 | 2 | .274 | .350 | .448 | $1 | 110 |

**Minors (2010)** / Skills

| Level | Leag | AB | HR | R | RBI | SB | BA | OBP | SLG | CT% | H% | BB% | Bash |
|---|---|---|---|---|---|---|---|---|---|---|---|---|---|
| A | — | — | — | — | — | — | — | — | — | — | — | — | — |
| AA | — | — | — | — | — | — | — | — | — | — | — | — | — |
| AAA | — | — | — | — | — | — | — | — | — | — | — | — | — |

**Competition at 2B** — Stats in 2010

| Bats | Player | GSvR | GSvL | Sub | OPS |
|---|---|---|---|---|---|
| BH | Roberts B | 43 | 15 | 1 | .745 |
| RH | Lugo J | 24 | 24 | 12 | .581 |
| RH | Wigginton T | 27 | 12 | 1 | .727 |
| LH | Moore S | 19 | 0 | 3 | .611 |

Ten-Year Trends

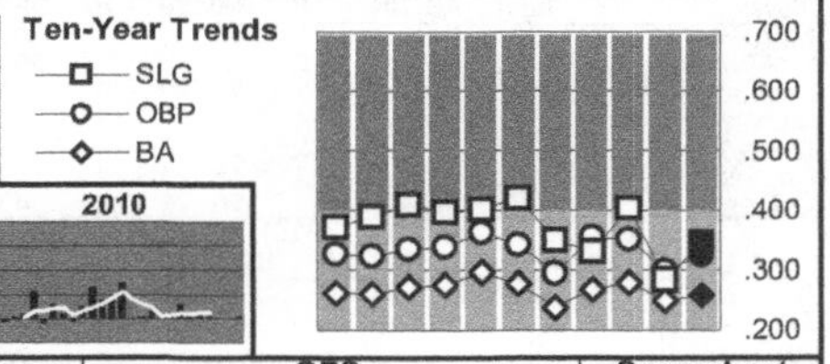

Weekly Points

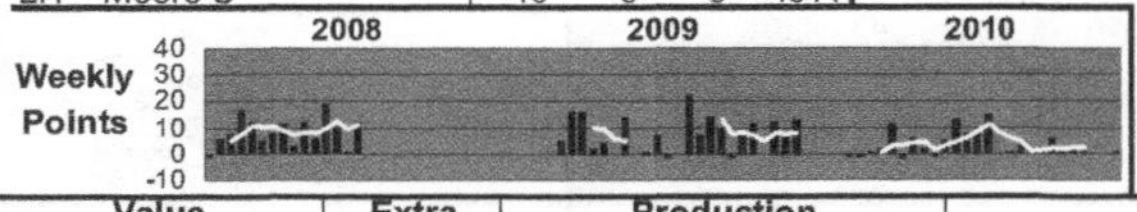

**Majors** / Skills / Value / Extra / Production / OPS / Scoresheet

| Yr | Team | AB | HR | R | RBI | SB | BA | OBP | SLG | CT% | H% | BB% | Bash | $1L | $2L | Pts | RAA | 2B | 3B | CS | FB-LD-GB | HR/fb | RBI% | RS% | OPS | 1st Hf | 2nd Hf | vs RH | vs LH | Rnge | vRH | vLH |
|---|---|---|---|---|---|---|---|---|---|---|---|---|---|---|---|---|---|---|---|---|---|---|---|---|---|---|---|---|---|---|---|---|
| 07 | BOS | 570 | 8 | 71 | 73 | 33 | .237 | .294 | .349 | 86% | 28% | 8% | 1.47 | $16 | $5 | 370 | −15 | 36 | 2 | 6 | 37-17-46 | 5% | 21% | 36% | .643 | .568 | .728 | .640 | .651 | — | −8 | +20 |
| 08 | BOS | 261 | 1 | 27 | 22 | 12 | .268 | .355 | .330 | 80% | 33% | 11% | 1.23 | $4 | -$9 | 140 | −4 | 13 | 0 | 4 | 23-18-60 | 2% | 13% | 24% | .685 | .685 | — | .668 | .749 | — | −10 | +26 |
| 09 | 2TM | 257 | 3 | 40 | 21 | 9 | .280 | .352 | .405 | 82% | 34% | 10% | 1.44 | $1 | -$8 | 170 | +4 | 13 | 5 | 0 | 38-21-40 | 4% | 16% | 37% | .756 | .719 | .784 | .761 | .748 | — | −18 | +45 |
| 10 | BAL | 241 | 0 | 26 | 20 | 5 | .249 | .298 | .282 | 79% | 31% | 6% | 1.13 | $1 | -$14 | 80 | −17 | 4 | 2 | 7 | 31-20-49 | 0% | 16% | 34% | .581 | .615 | .499 | .487 | .716 | — | −16 | +37 |

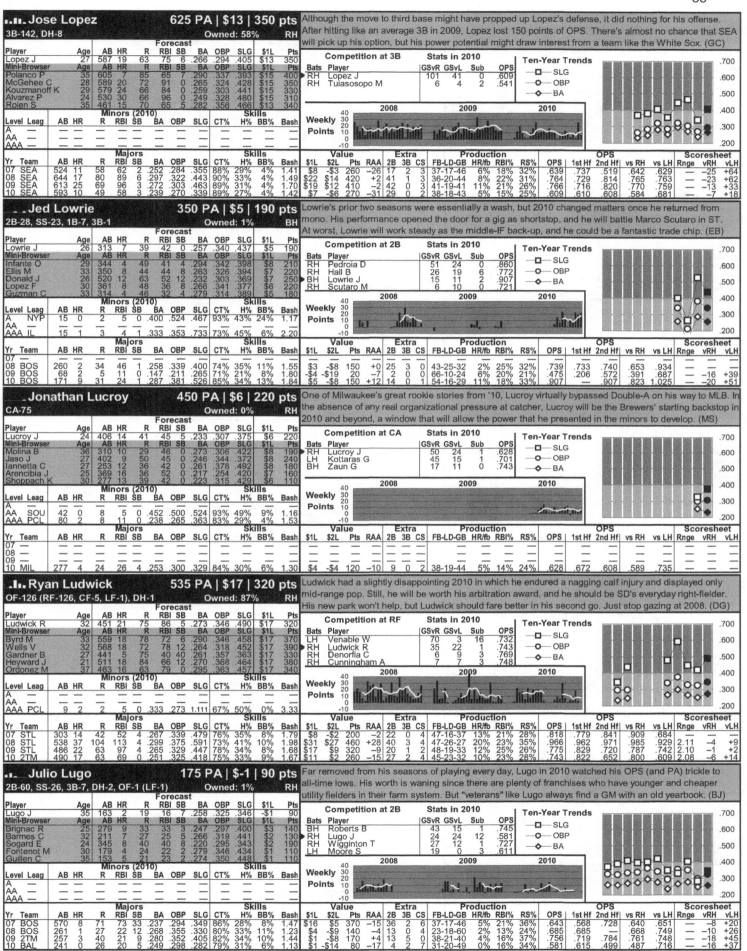

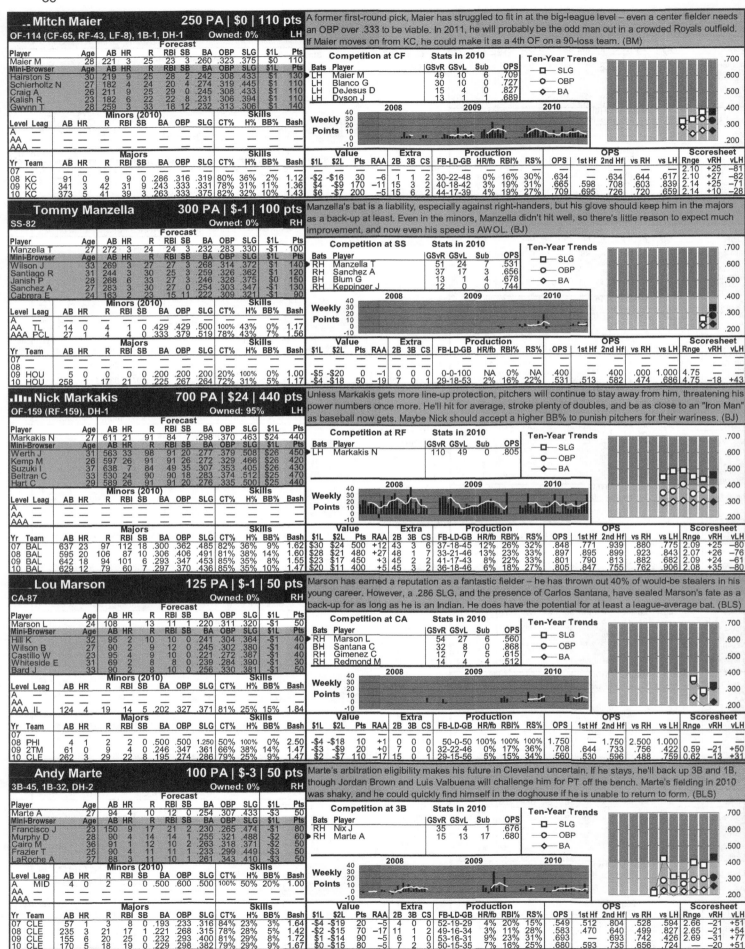

## Mitch Maier — 250 PA | $0 | 110 pts
OF-114 (CF-65, RF-43, LF-8), 1B-1, DH-1  Owned: 0%  LH

A former first-round pick, Maier has struggled to fit in at the big-league level – even a center fielder needs an OBP over .333 to be viable. In 2011, he will probably be the odd man out in a crowded Royals outfield. If Maier moves on from KC, he could make it as a 4th OF on a 90-loss team. (BM)

### Forecast
| Player | Age | AB | HR | R | RBI | SB | BA | OBP | SLG | $1L | Pts |
|---|---|---|---|---|---|---|---|---|---|---|---|
| Maier M | 28 | 221 | 3 | 25 | 23 | 3 | .260 | .323 | .375 | $0 | 110 |

| Mini-Browser | Age | AB | HR | R | RBI | SB | BA | OBP | SLG | $1L | Pts |
|---|---|---|---|---|---|---|---|---|---|---|---|
| Hairston S | 30 | 219 | 9 | 25 | 28 | 2 | .242 | .308 | .433 | $1 | 130 |
| Schierholtz N | 27 | 182 | 4 | 24 | 20 | 4 | .274 | .319 | .445 | $1 | 110 |
| Craig A | 26 | 211 | 9 | 20 | 29 | 0 | .245 | .308 | .433 | $1 | 110 |
| Kalish R | 23 | 182 | 6 | 22 | 22 | 8 | .231 | .306 | .394 | $1 | 110 |
| Gwynn T | 28 | 259 | 3 | 33 | 18 | 12 | .232 | .313 | .306 | $1 | 140 |

### Competition at CF / Stats in 2010
| Bats | Player | GSvR | GSvL | Sub | OPS |
|---|---|---|---|---|---|
| LH | Maier M | 49 | 10 | 6 | .709 |
| LH | Blanco G | 30 | 10 | 0 | .727 |
| LH | DeJesus D | 15 | 4 | 0 | .827 |
| LH | Dyson J | 13 | 1 | 1 | .689 |

### Minors (2010) / Skills
| Level | Leag | AB | HR | R | RBI | SB | BA | OBP | SLG | CT% | H% | BB% | Bash |
|---|---|---|---|---|---|---|---|---|---|---|---|---|---|
| A | — | — | — | — | — | — | — | — | — | — | — | — | — |
| AA | — | — | — | — | — | — | — | — | — | — | — | — | — |
| AAA | — | — | — | — | — | — | — | — | — | — | — | — | — |

### Majors / Skills / Value / Extra / Production / OPS / Scoresheet
| Yr | Team | AB | HR | R | RBI | SB | BA | OBP | SLG | CT% | H% | BB% | Bash | $1L | $2L | Pts | RAA | 2B | 3B | CS | FB-LD-GB | HR/fb | RBI% | RS% | OPS | 1st Hf | 2nd Hf | vs RH | vs LH | Rnge | vRH | vLH |
|---|---|---|---|---|---|---|---|---|---|---|---|---|---|---|---|---|---|---|---|---|---|---|---|---|---|---|---|---|---|---|---|---|
| 07 | — | — | — | — | — | — | — | — | — | — | — | — | — | | | | | | | | | | | | | | | | | 2.10 | +25 | −81 |
| 08 | KC | 91 | 0 | 9 | 9 | 0 | .286 | .316 | .319 | 80% | 36% | 2% | 1.12 | −$2 | −$16 | 30 | −6 | 1 | 1 | 2 | 30-22-48 | 0% | 16% | 30% | .634 | — | .634 | .644 | .617 | 2.10 | +27 | −81 |
| 09 | KC | 341 | 3 | 42 | 31 | 9 | .243 | .333 | .331 | 78% | 31% | 11% | 1.36 | $4 | −$9 | 170 | −11 | 15 | 3 | 2 | 40-18-42 | 3% | 19% | 31% | .665 | .598 | .708 | .603 | .839 | 2.14 | +25 | −71 |
| 10 | KC | 373 | 5 | 41 | 39 | 5 | .263 | .333 | .375 | 82% | 32% | 10% | 1.43 | $6 | −$7 | 200 | −5 | 13 | 5 | 2 | 44-17-39 | 4% | 19% | 27% | .709 | .695 | .726 | .720 | .659 | 2.14 | +10 | −28 |

## Tommy Manzella — 300 PA | $-1 | 100 pts
SS-82  Owned: 0%  RH

Manzella's bat is a liability, especially against right-handers, but his glove should keep him in the majors as a back-up at least. Even in the minors, Manzella didn't hit well, so there's little reason to expect much improvement, and now even his speed is AWOL. (BJ)

### Forecast
| Player | Age | AB | HR | R | RBI | SB | BA | OBP | SLG | $1L | Pts |
|---|---|---|---|---|---|---|---|---|---|---|---|
| Manzella T | 27 | 272 | 3 | 24 | 24 | 3 | .232 | .283 | .330 | −$1 | 100 |

| Mini-Browser | Age | AB | HR | R | RBI | SB | BA | OBP | SLG | $1L | Pts |
|---|---|---|---|---|---|---|---|---|---|---|---|
| Wilson J | 33 | 269 | 3 | 27 | 27 | 3 | .268 | .314 | .372 | $1 | 140 |
| Santiago R | 31 | 244 | 3 | 30 | 25 | 3 | .259 | .326 | .362 | $1 | 120 |
| Janish P | 28 | 268 | 6 | 33 | 27 | 3 | .246 | .328 | .375 | $0 | 150 |
| Sanchez A | 27 | 283 | 3 | 30 | 27 | 0 | .254 | .303 | .347 | $1 | 130 |
| Cabrera E | 24 | 163 | 2 | 23 | 15 | 11 | .222 | .309 | .321 | −$1 | 90 |

### Competition at SS / Stats in 2010
| Bats | Player | GSvR | GSvL | Sub | OPS |
|---|---|---|---|---|---|
| RH | Manzella T | 51 | 24 | 7 | .531 |
| RH | Sanchez A | 37 | 17 | 3 | .656 |
| BH | Blum G | 13 | 1 | 4 | .678 |
| RH | Keppinger J | 12 | 0 | 1 | .744 |

### Minors (2010) / Skills
| Level | Leag | AB | HR | R | RBI | SB | BA | OBP | SLG | CT% | H% | BB% | Bash |
|---|---|---|---|---|---|---|---|---|---|---|---|---|---|
| A | — | — | — | — | — | — | — | — | — | — | — | — | — |
| AA | TL | 14 | 0 | 4 | 1 | 0 | .429 | .429 | .500 | 100% | 43% | 0% | 1.17 |
| AAA | PCL | 27 | 1 | 4 | 4 | 0 | .333 | .379 | .519 | 78% | 43% | 7% | 1.56 |

### Majors / Skills / Value / Extra / Production / OPS / Scoresheet
| Yr | Team | AB | HR | R | RBI | SB | BA | OBP | SLG | CT% | H% | BB% | Bash | $1L | $2L | Pts | RAA | 2B | 3B | CS | FB-LD-GB | HR/fb | RBI% | RS% | OPS | 1st Hf | 2nd Hf | vs RH | vs LH | Rnge | vRH | vLH |
|---|---|---|---|---|---|---|---|---|---|---|---|---|---|---|---|---|---|---|---|---|---|---|---|---|---|---|---|---|---|---|---|---|
| 07 | — | — | — | — | — | — | — | — | — | — | — | — | — | | | | | | | | | | | | | | | | | | | |
| 08 | — | — | — | — | — | — | — | — | — | — | — | — | — | | | | | | | | | | | | | | | | | | | |
| 09 | HOU | 5 | 0 | 0 | 0 | 0 | .200 | .200 | .200 | 20% | 100% | 0% | 1.00 | −$5 | −$20 | 0 | −1 | 0 | 0 | 0 | 0-0-100 | NA | 0% | NA | .400 | — | .400 | .000 | 1.000 | 4.75 | | |
| 10 | HOU | 258 | 1 | 17 | 21 | 0 | .225 | .267 | .264 | 72% | 31% | 5% | 1.17 | −$4 | −$18 | 50 | −19 | 7 | 0 | 1 | 29-18-53 | 2% | 16% | 22% | .531 | .513 | .582 | .474 | .686 | 4.75 | −18 | +43 |

## Nick Markakis — 700 PA | $24 | 440 pts
OF-159 (RF-159), DH-1  Owned: 95%  LH

Unless Markakis gets more line-up protection, pitchers will continue to stay away from him, threatening his power numbers once more. He'll hit for average, stroke plenty of doubles, and be as close to an "Iron Man" as baseball now gets. Maybe Nick should accept a higher BB% to punish pitchers for their wariness. (BJ)

### Forecast
| Player | Age | AB | HR | R | RBI | SB | BA | OBP | SLG | $1L | Pts |
|---|---|---|---|---|---|---|---|---|---|---|---|
| Markakis N | 27 | 611 | 21 | 91 | 84 | 7 | .298 | .370 | .463 | $24 | 440 |

| Mini-Browser | Age | AB | HR | R | RBI | SB | BA | OBP | SLG | $1L | Pts |
|---|---|---|---|---|---|---|---|---|---|---|---|
| Werth J | 31 | 563 | 33 | 98 | 91 | 20 | .277 | .379 | .508 | $26 | 450 |
| Kemp M | 26 | 597 | 26 | 91 | 91 | 26 | .272 | .329 | .466 | $26 | 420 |
| Suzuki I | 37 | 638 | 7 | 84 | 49 | 35 | .307 | .353 | .405 | $26 | 430 |
| Beltran C | 33 | 530 | 24 | 90 | 90 | 18 | .283 | .374 | .512 | $25 | 470 |
| Hart C | 29 | 589 | 26 | 91 | 91 | 20 | .276 | .335 | .500 | $25 | 440 |

### Competition at RF
| Bats | Player | GSvR | GSvL | Sub | OPS |
|---|---|---|---|---|---|
| LH | Markakis N | 110 | 49 | 0 | .805 |

### Minors (2010) / Skills
| Level | Leag | AB | HR | R | RBI | SB | BA | OBP | SLG | CT% | H% | BB% | Bash |
|---|---|---|---|---|---|---|---|---|---|---|---|---|---|
| A | — | — | — | — | — | — | — | — | — | — | — | — | — |
| AA | — | — | — | — | — | — | — | — | — | — | — | — | — |
| AAA | — | — | — | — | — | — | — | — | — | — | — | — | — |

### Majors / Skills / Value / Extra / Production / OPS / Scoresheet
| Yr | Team | AB | HR | R | RBI | SB | BA | OBP | SLG | CT% | H% | BB% | Bash | $1L | $2L | Pts | RAA | 2B | 3B | CS | FB-LD-GB | HR/fb | RBI% | RS% | OPS | 1st Hf | 2nd Hf | vs RH | vs LH | Rnge | vRH | vLH |
|---|---|---|---|---|---|---|---|---|---|---|---|---|---|---|---|---|---|---|---|---|---|---|---|---|---|---|---|---|---|---|---|---|
| 07 | BAL | 637 | 23 | 97 | 112 | 18 | .300 | .362 | .485 | 82% | 36% | 9% | 1.62 | $30 | $24 | 500 | +12 | 43 | 3 | 6 | 37-18-45 | 12% | 26% | 32% | .848 | .771 | .939 | .880 | .775 | 2.09 | +25 | −80 |
| 08 | BAL | 595 | 20 | 106 | 87 | 10 | .306 | .406 | .491 | 81% | 38% | 14% | 1.60 | $28 | $21 | 480 | +27 | 48 | 3 | 7 | 33-21-46 | 13% | 23% | 33% | .897 | .895 | .899 | .923 | .843 | 2.07 | +26 | −76 |
| 09 | BAL | 642 | 18 | 94 | 101 | 6 | .293 | .347 | .453 | 85% | 35% | 8% | 1.55 | $23 | $17 | 450 | +3 | 45 | 2 | 2 | 41-17-43 | 8% | 22% | 33% | .801 | .790 | .813 | .882 | .682 | 2.09 | +24 | −61 |
| 10 | BAL | 629 | 12 | 79 | 60 | 7 | .297 | .370 | .436 | 85% | 35% | 10% | 1.47 | $20 | $11 | 450 | +5 | 45 | 3 | 2 | 36-18-46 | 6% | 18% | 27% | .805 | .847 | .755 | .762 | .906 | 2.08 | +35 | −80 |

## Lou Marson — 125 PA | $-1 | 50 pts
CA-87  Owned: 0%  RH

Marson has earned a reputation as a fantastic fielder – he has thrown out 40% of would-be stealers in his young career. However, a .286 SLG, and the presence of Carlos Santana, have sealed Marson's fate as a back-up for as long as he is an Indian. He does have the potential for at least a league-average bat. (BLS)

### Forecast
| Player | Age | AB | HR | R | RBI | SB | BA | OBP | SLG | $1L | Pts |
|---|---|---|---|---|---|---|---|---|---|---|---|
| Marson L | 24 | 108 | 1 | 13 | 11 | 1 | .220 | .311 | .320 | −$1 | 50 |

| Mini-Browser | Age | AB | HR | R | RBI | SB | BA | OBP | SLG | $1L | Pts |
|---|---|---|---|---|---|---|---|---|---|---|---|
| Hill K | 32 | 95 | 2 | 10 | 10 | 0 | .241 | .304 | .364 | −$1 | 40 |
| Wilson B | 27 | 90 | 2 | 9 | 12 | 0 | .245 | .302 | .380 | −$1 | 40 |
| Castillo W | 23 | 95 | 4 | 9 | 10 | 0 | .221 | .272 | .387 | −$1 | 40 |
| Whiteside E | 31 | 69 | 2 | 8 | 8 | 0 | .239 | .284 | .390 | −$1 | 40 |
| Bard J | 33 | 90 | 2 | 8 | 10 | 0 | .256 | .330 | .381 | −$1 | 50 |

### Competition at CA / Stats in 2010
| Bats | Player | GSvR | GSvL | Sub | OPS |
|---|---|---|---|---|---|
| RH | Marson L | 54 | 27 | 6 | .560 |
| BH | Santana C | 32 | 8 | 0 | .868 |
| RH | Gimenez C | 12 | 7 | 5 | .615 |
| RH | Redmond M | 14 | 4 | 4 | .512 |

### Minors (2010) / Skills
| Level | Leag | AB | HR | R | RBI | SB | BA | OBP | SLG | CT% | H% | BB% | Bash |
|---|---|---|---|---|---|---|---|---|---|---|---|---|---|
| A | — | — | — | — | — | — | — | — | — | — | — | — | — |
| AA | — | — | — | — | — | — | — | — | — | — | — | — | — |
| AAA | IL | 124 | 4 | 19 | 14 | 5 | .202 | .327 | .371 | 81% | 25% | 15% | 1.84 |

### Majors / Skills / Value / Extra / Production / OPS / Scoresheet
| Yr | Team | AB | HR | R | RBI | SB | BA | OBP | SLG | CT% | H% | BB% | Bash | $1L | $2L | Pts | RAA | 2B | 3B | CS | FB-LD-GB | HR/fb | RBI% | RS% | OPS | 1st Hf | 2nd Hf | vs RH | vs LH | Rnge | vRH | vLH |
|---|---|---|---|---|---|---|---|---|---|---|---|---|---|---|---|---|---|---|---|---|---|---|---|---|---|---|---|---|---|---|---|---|
| 07 | — | — | — | — | — | — | — | — | — | — | — | — | — | | | | | | | | | | | | | | | | | | | |
| 08 | PHI | 4 | 1 | 2 | 1 | 0 | .500 | .500 | 1.250 | 50% | 100% | 0% | 2.50 | −$4 | −$18 | 10 | +1 | 0 | 0 | 0 | 50-0-50 | 100% | 100% | 100% | 1.750 | — | 1.750 | 2.500 | 1.000 | 0.59 | −21 | +50 |
| 09 | 2TM | 61 | 0 | 9 | 4 | 0 | .246 | .347 | .361 | 66% | 38% | 14% | 1.47 | −$3 | −$9 | 20 | +0 | 7 | 0 | 0 | 32-22-46 | 0% | 17% | 36% | .708 | .644 | .733 | .756 | .422 | 0.59 | −21 | +50 |
| 10 | CLE | 262 | 3 | 29 | 22 | 8 | .195 | .274 | .286 | 79% | 25% | 9% | 1.47 | $2 | −$7 | 110 | −17 | 15 | 0 | 1 | 29-15-56 | 5% | 15% | 34% | .560 | .530 | .596 | .488 | .759 | 0.62 | −13 | +50 |

## Andy Marte — 100 PA | $-3 | 50 pts
3B-45, 1B-32, DH-2  Owned: 0%  RH

Marte's arbitration eligibility makes his future in Cleveland uncertain. If he stays, he'll back up 3B and 1B, though Jordan Brown and Luis Valbuena will challenge him for PT off the bench. Marte's fielding in 2010 was shaky, and he could quickly find himself in the doghouse if he is unable to return to form. (BLS)

### Forecast
| Player | Age | AB | HR | R | RBI | SB | BA | OBP | SLG | $1L | Pts |
|---|---|---|---|---|---|---|---|---|---|---|---|
| Marte A | 27 | 94 | 4 | 10 | 12 | 0 | .254 | .307 | .433 | −$3 | 50 |

| Mini-Browser | Age | AB | HR | R | RBI | SB | BA | OBP | SLG | $1L | Pts |
|---|---|---|---|---|---|---|---|---|---|---|---|
| Francisco J | 23 | 150 | 9 | 17 | 21 | 2 | .230 | .265 | .474 | −$1 | 80 |
| Murphy D | 28 | 90 | 4 | 14 | 14 | 1 | .255 | .321 | .488 | −$2 | 60 |
| Cairo M | 36 | 91 | 1 | 12 | 10 | 2 | .263 | .318 | .371 | −$2 | 50 |
| Frazier T | 25 | 90 | 4 | 11 | 11 | 1 | .233 | .299 | .449 | −$3 | 50 |
| LaRoche A | 27 | 88 | 3 | 11 | 10 | 1 | .261 | .343 | .410 | −$3 | 50 |

### Competition at 3B / Stats in 2010
| Bats | Player | GSvR | GSvL | Sub | OPS |
|---|---|---|---|---|---|
| RH | Nix J | 35 | 4 | 1 | .676 |
| RH | Marte A | 15 | 13 | 17 | .680 |

### Minors (2010) / Skills
| Level | Leag | AB | HR | R | RBI | SB | BA | OBP | SLG | CT% | H% | BB% | Bash |
|---|---|---|---|---|---|---|---|---|---|---|---|---|---|
| A | MID | 4 | 0 | 2 | 0 | 0 | .500 | .600 | .500 | 100% | 50% | 20% | 1.00 |
| AA | — | — | — | — | — | — | — | — | — | — | — | — | — |
| AAA | — | — | — | — | — | — | — | — | — | — | — | — | — |

### Majors / Skills / Value / Extra / Production / OPS / Scoresheet
| Yr | Team | AB | HR | R | RBI | SB | BA | OBP | SLG | CT% | H% | BB% | Bash | $1L | $2L | Pts | RAA | 2B | 3B | CS | FB-LD-GB | HR/fb | RBI% | RS% | OPS | 1st Hf | 2nd Hf | vs RH | vs LH | Rnge | vRH | vLH |
|---|---|---|---|---|---|---|---|---|---|---|---|---|---|---|---|---|---|---|---|---|---|---|---|---|---|---|---|---|---|---|---|---|
| 07 | CLE | 57 | 1 | 3 | 8 | 0 | .193 | .233 | .316 | 84% | 23% | 3% | 1.64 | −$4 | −$19 | 20 | −5 | 4 | 0 | 0 | 52-19-29 | 4% | 20% | 15% | .549 | .512 | .804 | .528 | .594 | 2.66 | −21 | +51 |
| 08 | CLE | 235 | 3 | 21 | 17 | 1 | .221 | .268 | .315 | 78% | 28% | 5% | 1.42 | −$2 | −$15 | 70 | −17 | 11 | 1 | 2 | 49-16-34 | 3% | 11% | 28% | .583 | .470 | .640 | .499 | .827 | 2.65 | −21 | +54 |
| 09 | CLE | 155 | 6 | 20 | 25 | 0 | .232 | .293 | .400 | 81% | 29% | 8% | 1.72 | $1 | −$14 | 90 | −5 | 6 | 1 | 0 | 53-16-31 | 9% | 23% | 31% | .693 | — | .693 | .742 | .426 | 2.69 | −31 | +77 |
| 10 | CLE | 170 | 5 | 18 | 19 | 0 | .229 | .298 | .382 | 79% | 29% | 9% | 1.67 | $0 | −$15 | 80 | −5 | 7 | 2 | 3 | 50-15-35 | 7% | 16% | 25% | .680 | .593 | .735 | .656 | .724 | | −20 | +54 |

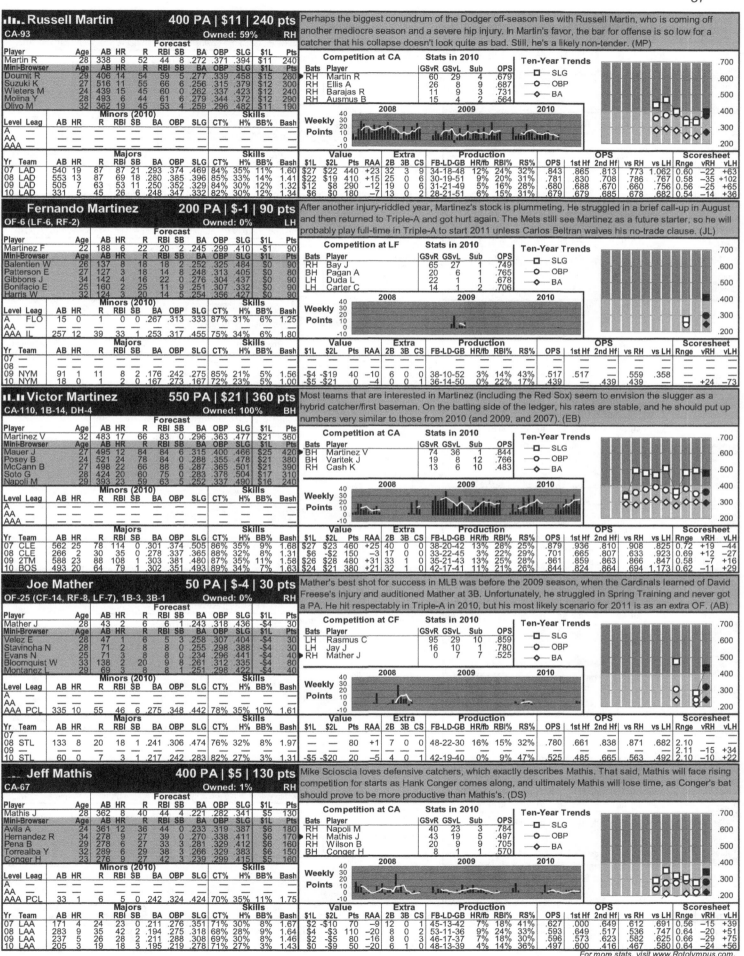

## Russell Martin — 400 PA | $11 | 240 pts
**CA-93** — Owned: 59% — RH

Perhaps the biggest conundrum of the Dodger off-season lies with Russell Martin, who is coming off another mediocre season and a severe hip injury. In Martin's favor, the bar for offense is so low for a catcher that his collapse doesn't look quite as bad. Still, he's a likely non-tender. (MP)

### Forecast
| Player | Age | AB | HR | R | RBI | SB | BA | OBP | SLG | $1L | Pts |
|---|---|---|---|---|---|---|---|---|---|---|---|
| Martin R | 28 | 338 | 8 | 52 | 44 | 8 | .272 | .371 | .394 | $11 | 240 |

### Mini-Browser
| Player | Age | AB | HR | R | RBI | SB | BA | OBP | SLG | $1L | Pts |
|---|---|---|---|---|---|---|---|---|---|---|---|
| Doumit R | 29 | 406 | 14 | 54 | 59 | 5 | .277 | .339 | .458 | $15 | 260 |
| Suzuki K | 27 | 516 | 15 | 55 | 66 | 6 | .256 | .315 | .379 | $12 | 300 |
| Wieters M | 24 | 439 | 15 | 45 | 60 | 0 | .262 | .337 | .423 | $12 | 240 |
| Molina Y | 28 | 493 | 6 | 44 | 61 | 6 | .279 | .344 | .372 | $12 | 290 |
| Olivo M | 32 | 362 | 19 | 45 | 53 | 4 | .259 | .296 | .482 | $11 | 190 |

### Competition at CA — Stats in 2010
| Bats | Player | GSvR | GSvL | Sub | OPS |
|---|---|---|---|---|---|
| RH | Martin R | 60 | 29 | 4 | .679 |
| RH | Ellis A | 26 | 8 | 9 | .687 |
| RH | Barajas R | 11 | 9 | 3 | .731 |
| RH | Ausmus B | 15 | 4 | 2 | .564 |

### Minors (2010) / Skills
| Level | Leag | AB | HR | R | RBI | SB | BA | OBP | SLG | CT% | H% | BB% | Bash |
|---|---|---|---|---|---|---|---|---|---|---|---|---|---|
| A | — | — | — | — | — | — | — | — | — | — | — | — | — |
| AA | — | — | — | — | — | — | — | — | — | — | — | — | — |
| AAA | — | — | — | — | — | — | — | — | — | — | — | — | — |

### Majors / Skills / Value / Extra / Production / OPS / Scoresheet
| Yr | Team | AB | HR | R | RBI | SB | BA | OBP | SLG | CT% | H% | BB% | Bash | $1L | $2L | Pts | RAA | 2B | 3B | CS | FB-LD-GB | HR/fb | RBI% | RS% | OPS | 1st Hf | 2nd Hf | vs RH | vs LH | Rnge | vRH | vLH |
|---|---|---|---|---|---|---|---|---|---|---|---|---|---|---|---|---|---|---|---|---|---|---|---|---|---|---|---|---|---|---|---|---|
| 07 | LAD | 540 | 19 | 87 | 87 | 21 | .293 | .374 | .469 | 84% | 35% | 11% | 1.60 | $27 | $22 | 440 | +23 | 32 | 3 | 9 | 34-18-48 | 12% | 24% | 32% | .843 | .865 | .813 | .773 | 1.062 | 0.60 | −22 | +63 |
| 08 | LAD | 553 | 13 | 87 | 69 | 18 | .280 | .385 | .396 | 85% | 33% | 14% | 1.41 | $22 | $19 | 410 | +15 | 25 | 0 | 6 | 30-19-51 | 9% | 20% | 31% | .781 | .830 | .708 | .780 | .767 | 0.58 | −35 | +102 |
| 09 | LAD | 505 | 7 | 63 | 53 | 11 | .250 | .352 | .329 | 84% | 30% | 12% | 1.32 | $12 | $8 | 290 | −12 | 19 | 0 | 6 | 31-21-49 | 5% | 16% | 28% | .680 | .688 | .670 | .660 | .756 | 0.56 | −25 | +65 |
| 10 | LAD | 331 | 5 | 45 | 26 | 6 | .248 | .347 | .332 | 82% | 30% | 12% | 1.34 | $6 | $0 | 180 | −7 | 13 | 0 | 2 | 28-21-51 | 6% | 15% | 31% | .679 | .679 | .685 | .678 | .682 | 0.54 | −14 | +36 |

---

## Fernando Martinez — 200 PA | $-1 | 90 pts
**OF-6 (LF-6, RF-2)** — Owned: 0% — LH

After another injury-riddled year, Martinez's stock is plummeting. He struggled in a brief call-up in August and then returned to Triple-A and got hurt again. The Mets still see Martinez as a future starter, so he will probably play full-time in Triple-A to start 2011 unless Carlos Beltran waives his no-trade clause. (JL)

### Forecast
| Player | Age | AB | HR | R | RBI | SB | BA | OBP | SLG | $1L | Pts |
|---|---|---|---|---|---|---|---|---|---|---|---|
| Martinez F | 22 | 188 | 6 | 22 | 20 | 2 | .245 | .299 | .410 | -$1 | 90 |

### Mini-Browser
| Player | Age | AB | HR | R | RBI | SB | BA | OBP | SLG | $1L | Pts |
|---|---|---|---|---|---|---|---|---|---|---|---|
| Balentien W | 26 | 137 | 8 | 18 | 18 | 2 | .252 | .325 | .484 | $0 | 90 |
| Patterson E | 27 | 127 | 3 | 18 | 14 | 6 | .248 | .313 | .405 | $0 | 80 |
| Gibbons J | 34 | 142 | 4 | 16 | 22 | 0 | .276 | .304 | .437 | $0 | 90 |
| Bonifacio E | 25 | 160 | 2 | 25 | 11 | 9 | .251 | .307 | .332 | $0 | 90 |
| Harris W | 32 | 124 | 3 | 20 | 14 | 5 | .254 | .356 | .427 | $0 | 90 |

### Competition at LF — Stats in 2010
| Bats | Player | GSvR | GSvL | Sub | OPS |
|---|---|---|---|---|---|
| RH | Bay J | 65 | 27 | 1 | .749 |
| BH | Pagan A | 20 | 6 | 1 | .765 |
| LH | Duda L | 22 | 1 | 1 | .678 |
| LH | Carter C | 14 | 1 | 2 | .706 |

### Minors (2010) / Skills
| Level | Leag | AB | HR | R | RBI | SB | BA | OBP | SLG | CT% | H% | BB% | Bash |
|---|---|---|---|---|---|---|---|---|---|---|---|---|---|
| A | FLO | 15 | 0 | 1 | 0 | 0 | .267 | .313 | .333 | 87% | 31% | 6% | 1.25 |
| AA | — | — | — | — | — | — | — | — | — | — | — | — | — |
| AAA | IL | 257 | 12 | 39 | 31 | 1 | .253 | .317 | .455 | 75% | 34% | 6% | 1.80 |

### Majors / Skills / Value / Extra / Production / OPS / Scoresheet
| Yr | Team | AB | HR | R | RBI | SB | BA | OBP | SLG | CT% | H% | BB% | Bash | $1L | $2L | Pts | RAA | 2B | 3B | CS | FB-LD-GB | HR/fb | RBI% | RS% | OPS | 1st Hf | 2nd Hf | vs RH | vs LH | Rnge | vRH | vLH |
|---|---|---|---|---|---|---|---|---|---|---|---|---|---|---|---|---|---|---|---|---|---|---|---|---|---|---|---|---|---|---|---|---|
| 07 | — | — | — | — | — | — | — | — | — | — | — | — | — | — | — | — | — | — | — | — | — | — | — | — | — | — | — | — | — | — | — | — |
| 08 | — | — | — | — | — | — | — | — | — | — | — | — | — | — | — | — | — | — | — | — | — | — | — | — | — | — | — | — | — | — | — | — |
| 09 | NYM | 91 | 1 | 11 | 8 | 2 | .176 | .242 | .275 | 85% | 21% | 5% | 1.56 | -$4 | -$19 | 40 | −10 | 6 | 0 | 0 | 38-10-52 | 3% | 14% | 43% | .517 | .517 | — | .559 | .358 | — | — | — |
| 10 | NYM | 18 | 0 | 1 | 2 | 0 | .167 | .273 | .167 | 72% | 23% | 5% | 1.00 | -$5 | -$21 | 0 | −4 | 0 | 0 | 1 | 36-14-50 | 0% | 22% | 17% | .439 | — | .439 | .439 | — | — | +24 | −73 |

---

## Victor Martinez — 550 PA | $21 | 360 pts
**CA-110, 1B-14, DH-4** — Owned: 100% — BH

Most teams that are interested in Martinez (including the Red Sox) seem to envision the slugger as a hybrid catcher/first baseman. On the batting side of the ledger, his rates are stable, and he should put up numbers very similar to those from 2010 (and 2009, and 2007). (EB)

### Forecast
| Player | Age | AB | HR | R | RBI | SB | BA | OBP | SLG | $1L | Pts |
|---|---|---|---|---|---|---|---|---|---|---|---|
| Martinez V | 32 | 483 | 17 | 66 | 83 | 0 | .296 | .363 | .477 | $21 | 360 |

### Mini-Browser
| Player | Age | AB | HR | R | RBI | SB | BA | OBP | SLG | $1L | Pts |
|---|---|---|---|---|---|---|---|---|---|---|---|
| Mauer J | 27 | 495 | 12 | 84 | 84 | 6 | .315 | .400 | .466 | $25 | 420 |
| Posey B | 24 | 521 | 24 | 78 | 84 | 0 | .288 | .355 | .478 | $21 | 380 |
| McCann B | 27 | 498 | 22 | 66 | 88 | 5 | .287 | .365 | .501 | $21 | 390 |
| Soto G | 28 | 424 | 20 | 60 | 75 | 0 | .283 | .378 | .504 | $17 | 310 |
| Napoli M | 29 | 393 | 23 | 59 | 63 | 5 | .252 | .337 | .490 | $16 | 240 |

### Competition at CA — Stats in 2010
| Bats | Player | GSvR | GSvL | Sub | OPS |
|---|---|---|---|---|---|
| BH | Martinez V | 74 | 36 | 1 | .844 |
| BH | Varitek J | 19 | 8 | 12 | .766 |
| RH | Cash K | 13 | 6 | 10 | .483 |

### Minors (2010) / Skills
| Level | Leag | AB | HR | R | RBI | SB | BA | OBP | SLG | CT% | H% | BB% | Bash |
|---|---|---|---|---|---|---|---|---|---|---|---|---|---|
| A | — | — | — | — | — | — | — | — | — | — | — | — | — |
| AA | — | — | — | — | — | — | — | — | — | — | — | — | — |
| AAA | — | — | — | — | — | — | — | — | — | — | — | — | — |

### Majors / Skills / Value / Extra / Production / OPS / Scoresheet
| Yr | Team | AB | HR | R | RBI | SB | BA | OBP | SLG | CT% | H% | BB% | Bash | $1L | $2L | Pts | RAA | 2B | 3B | CS | FB-LD-GB | HR/fb | RBI% | RS% | OPS | 1st Hf | 2nd Hf | vs RH | vs LH | Rnge | vRH | vLH |
|---|---|---|---|---|---|---|---|---|---|---|---|---|---|---|---|---|---|---|---|---|---|---|---|---|---|---|---|---|---|---|---|---|
| 07 | CLE | 562 | 25 | 78 | 114 | 0 | .301 | .374 | .505 | 86% | 35% | 9% | 1.68 | $27 | $23 | 460 | +25 | 40 | 0 | 0 | 38-20-42 | 13% | 28% | 25% | .879 | .936 | .810 | .807 | 1.062 | 0.72 | +19 | −44 |
| 08 | CLE | 266 | 2 | 30 | 35 | 0 | .278 | .337 | .365 | 88% | 32% | 8% | 1.31 | $6 | -$2 | 150 | −3 | 17 | 0 | 0 | 33-22-45 | 3% | 22% | 29% | .701 | .665 | .807 | .633 | .923 | 0.69 | +12 | −27 |
| 09 | 2TM | 588 | 23 | 88 | 108 | 1 | .303 | .381 | .480 | 87% | 35% | 11% | 1.58 | $26 | $28 | 480 | +31 | 33 | 1 | 0 | 35-21-43 | 13% | 25% | 28% | .861 | .859 | .863 | .866 | .847 | 0.58 | −7 | +16 |
| 10 | BOS | 493 | 20 | 64 | 79 | 1 | .302 | .351 | .493 | 89% | 34% | 7% | 1.63 | $24 | $21 | 380 | +21 | 32 | 1 | 0 | 42-17-41 | 11% | 21% | 26% | .844 | .824 | .864 | .694 | 1.173 | 0.62 | −11 | +29 |

---

## Joe Mather — 50 PA | $-4 | 30 pts
**OF-25 (CF-14, RF-8, LF-7, 1B-3, 3B-1)** — Owned: 0% — RH

Mather's best shot for success in MLB was before the 2009 season, when the Cardinals learned of David Freese's injury and auditioned Mather at 3B. Unfortunately, he struggled in Spring Training and never got a PA. He hit respectably in Triple-A in 2010, but his most likely scenario for 2011 is as an extra OF. (AB)

### Forecast
| Player | Age | AB | HR | R | RBI | SB | BA | OBP | SLG | $1L | Pts |
|---|---|---|---|---|---|---|---|---|---|---|---|
| Mather J | 28 | 43 | 2 | 6 | 6 | 1 | .243 | .318 | .436 | -$4 | 30 |

### Mini-Browser
| Player | Age | AB | HR | R | RBI | SB | BA | OBP | SLG | $1L | Pts |
|---|---|---|---|---|---|---|---|---|---|---|---|
| Velez E | 28 | 47 | 1 | 6 | 5 | 3 | .258 | .307 | .404 | -$4 | 30 |
| Stavinoha N | 28 | 71 | 2 | 8 | 8 | 0 | .255 | .298 | .388 | -$4 | 30 |
| Evans N | 25 | 71 | 3 | 8 | 10 | 0 | .234 | .296 | .441 | -$4 | 40 |
| Bloomquist W | 33 | 138 | 2 | 20 | 9 | 8 | .261 | .312 | .335 | -$4 | 80 |
| Montanez L | 29 | 69 | 3 | 8 | 8 | 1 | .251 | .298 | .422 | -$4 | 40 |

### Competition at CF — Stats in 2010
| Bats | Player | GSvR | GSvL | Sub | OPS |
|---|---|---|---|---|---|
| LH | Rasmus C | 95 | 29 | 10 | .859 |
| LH | Jay J | 16 | 10 | 1 | .780 |
| RH | Mather J | 0 | 7 | 7 | .525 |

### Minors (2010) / Skills
| Level | Leag | AB | HR | R | RBI | SB | BA | OBP | SLG | CT% | H% | BB% | Bash |
|---|---|---|---|---|---|---|---|---|---|---|---|---|---|
| A | — | — | — | — | — | — | — | — | — | — | — | — | — |
| AA | — | — | — | — | — | — | — | — | — | — | — | — | — |
| AAA | PCL | 335 | 10 | 55 | 46 | 6 | .275 | .348 | .442 | 78% | 35% | 10% | 1.61 |

### Majors / Skills / Value / Extra / Production / OPS / Scoresheet
| Yr | Team | AB | HR | R | RBI | SB | BA | OBP | SLG | CT% | H% | BB% | Bash | $1L | $2L | Pts | RAA | 2B | 3B | CS | FB-LD-GB | HR/fb | RBI% | RS% | OPS | 1st Hf | 2nd Hf | vs RH | vs LH | Rnge | vRH | vLH |
|---|---|---|---|---|---|---|---|---|---|---|---|---|---|---|---|---|---|---|---|---|---|---|---|---|---|---|---|---|---|---|---|---|
| 07 | — | — | — | — | — | — | — | — | — | — | — | — | — | — | — | — | — | — | — | — | — | — | — | — | — | — | — | — | — | — | — | — |
| 08 | STL | 133 | 8 | 20 | 18 | 1 | .241 | .306 | .474 | 76% | 32% | 8% | 1.97 | — | — | 80 | +1 | 7 | 0 | 0 | 48-22-30 | 16% | 15% | 32% | .780 | .661 | .838 | .871 | .682 | 2.10 | — | — |
| 09 | — | — | — | — | — | — | — | — | — | — | — | — | — | — | — | — | — | — | — | — | — | — | — | — | — | — | — | — | — | 2.11 | −15 | +34 |
| 10 | STL | 60 | 0 | 7 | 3 | 1 | .217 | .242 | .283 | 82% | 27% | 3% | 1.31 | -$5 | -$20 | 20 | −5 | 4 | 0 | 1 | 42-19-40 | 0% | 9% | 47% | .525 | .485 | .665 | .563 | .492 | 2.10 | −10 | +22 |

---

## Jeff Mathis — 400 PA | $5 | 130 pts
**CA-67** — Owned: 1% — RH

Mike Scioscia loves defensive catchers, which exactly describes Mathis. That said, Mathis will face rising competition for starts as Hank Conger comes along, and ultimately Mathis will lose time, as Conger's bat should prove to be more productive than Mathis's. (DS)

### Forecast
| Player | Age | AB | HR | R | RBI | SB | BA | OBP | SLG | $1L | Pts |
|---|---|---|---|---|---|---|---|---|---|---|---|
| Mathis J | 28 | 362 | 8 | 40 | 44 | 4 | .221 | .282 | .341 | $5 | 130 |

### Mini-Browser
| Player | Age | AB | HR | R | RBI | SB | BA | OBP | SLG | $1L | Pts |
|---|---|---|---|---|---|---|---|---|---|---|---|
| Avila A | 24 | 361 | 12 | 36 | 44 | 0 | .233 | .319 | .387 | $6 | 180 |
| Hernandez R | 34 | 278 | 5 | 27 | 39 | 0 | .270 | .338 | .411 | $6 | 170 |
| Pena B | 29 | 278 | 6 | 27 | 33 | 3 | .281 | .329 | .412 | $6 | 160 |
| Torrealba Y | 32 | 289 | 6 | 29 | 38 | 3 | .266 | .329 | .383 | $5 | 150 |
| Conger H | 23 | 276 | 9 | 27 | 42 | 5 | .239 | .299 | .415 | $5 | 160 |

### Competition at CA — Stats in 2010
| Bats | Player | GSvR | GSvL | Sub | OPS |
|---|---|---|---|---|---|
| RH | Napoli M | 40 | 23 | 3 | .784 |
| RH | Mathis J | 43 | 19 | 5 | .497 |
| RH | Wilson B | 20 | 9 | 9 | .705 |
| BH | Conger H | 8 | 1 | 1 | .570 |

### Minors (2010) / Skills
| Level | Leag | AB | HR | R | RBI | SB | BA | OBP | SLG | CT% | H% | BB% | Bash |
|---|---|---|---|---|---|---|---|---|---|---|---|---|---|
| A | — | — | — | — | — | — | — | — | — | — | — | — | — |
| AA | — | — | — | — | — | — | — | — | — | — | — | — | — |
| AAA | PCL | 33 | 1 | 6 | 5 | 0 | .242 | .324 | .424 | 70% | 35% | 11% | 1.75 |

### Majors / Skills / Value / Extra / Production / OPS / Scoresheet
| Yr | Team | AB | HR | R | RBI | SB | BA | OBP | SLG | CT% | H% | BB% | Bash | $1L | $2L | Pts | RAA | 2B | 3B | CS | FB-LD-GB | HR/fb | RBI% | RS% | OPS | 1st Hf | 2nd Hf | vs RH | vs LH | Rnge | vRH | vLH |
|---|---|---|---|---|---|---|---|---|---|---|---|---|---|---|---|---|---|---|---|---|---|---|---|---|---|---|---|---|---|---|---|---|
| 07 | LAA | 171 | 4 | 24 | 23 | 0 | .211 | .276 | .351 | 71% | 30% | 8% | 1.67 | $2 | -$10 | 70 | −9 | 12 | 0 | 1 | 45-13-42 | 7% | 18% | 41% | .627 | .000 | .649 | .612 | .691 | 0.56 | −15 | +39 |
| 08 | LAA | 283 | 9 | 35 | 42 | 1 | .194 | .275 | .318 | 68% | 28% | 9% | 1.64 | $4 | -$3 | 110 | −20 | 8 | 0 | 2 | 53-11-36 | 9% | 24% | 33% | .593 | .649 | .517 | .536 | .747 | 0.64 | −20 | +51 |
| 09 | LAA | 237 | 5 | 26 | 28 | 2 | .211 | .288 | .308 | 69% | 30% | 8% | 1.46 | $2 | -$5 | 80 | −16 | 8 | 0 | 3 | 46-17-37 | 7% | 18% | 30% | .596 | .573 | .623 | .680 | .383 | 0.66 | −29 | +75 |
| 10 | LAA | 205 | 3 | 19 | 18 | 3 | .195 | .219 | .278 | 71% | 27% | 3% | 1.43 | $0 | -$9 | 50 | −20 | 6 | 1 | 0 | 48-13-39 | 4% | 14% | 36% | .497 | .600 | .416 | .467 | .580 | 0.64 | −24 | +56 |

## Hideki Matsui — 500 PA | $14 | 300 pts

DH-120, OF-18 (LF-18)    Owned: 52%    LH

With Bobby Abreu already signed and aging into the DH role, Matsui probably will not be back with the Angels. Still, his creaky knees held up well in the second half (.309/.402/.553). His new owner should be content with another season of these rates, since the downside of bad knees is a season like 2008. (DS)

### Forecast

| Player | Age | AB | HR | R | RBI | SB | BA | OBP | SLG | $1L | Pts |
|---|---|---|---|---|---|---|---|---|---|---|---|
| Matsui H | 36 | 421 | 20 | 55 | 75 | 0 | .273 | .358 | .457 | $14 | 300 |
| Mini-Browser | Age | AB | HR | R | RBI | SB | BA | OBP | SLG | $1L | Pts |
| Guerrero V | 36 | 517 | 28 | 72 | 88 | 6 | .298 | .355 | .508 | $23 | 410 |
| Abreu B | 37 | 533 | 18 | 84 | 84 | 24 | .270 | .361 | .432 | $22 | 430 |
| Ortiz D | 35 | 444 | 26 | 74 | 89 | 0 | .272 | .374 | .533 | $19 | 370 |
| Scott L | 32 | 450 | 25 | 60 | 70 | 0 | .278 | .361 | .521 | $16 | 320 |
| Lind A | 27 | 581 | 24 | 66 | 84 | 0 | .258 | .313 | .458 | $16 | 340 |

### Minors (2010) / Skills

| Level | Leag | AB | HR | R | RBI | SB | BA | OBP | SLG | CT% | H% | BB% | Bash |
|---|---|---|---|---|---|---|---|---|---|---|---|---|---|
| A | — | — | — | — | — | — | — | — | — | — | — | — | — |
| AA | — | — | — | — | — | — | — | — | — | — | — | — | — |
| AAA | — | — | — | — | — | — | — | — | — | — | — | — | — |

### Majors / Skills / Value / Extra / Production / OPS / Scoresheet

| Yr | Team | AB | HR | R | RBI | SB | BA | OBP | SLG | CT% | H% | BB% | Bash | $1L | $2L | Pts | RAA | 2B | 3B | CS | FB-LD-GB | HR/fb | RBI% | RS% | OPS | 1st Hf | 2nd Hf | vs RH | vs LH | Rnge | vRH | vLH |
|---|---|---|---|---|---|---|---|---|---|---|---|---|---|---|---|---|---|---|---|---|---|---|---|---|---|---|---|---|---|---|---|---|
| 07 | NYY | 547 | 25 | 100 | 103 | 4 | .285 | .367 | .488 | 87% | 33% | 11% | 1.71 | $24 | $19 | 480 | +10 | 28 | 4 | 2 | 40-17-43 | 13% | 21% | 36% | .855 | .818 | .891 | .872 | .814 | 0.64 | +7 | -19 |
| 08 | NYY | 337 | 9 | 43 | 45 | 0 | .294 | .370 | .424 | 86% | 34% | 10% | 1.44 | $9 | -$3 | 220 | -1 | 17 | 0 | 0 | 34-19-47 | 9% | 20% | 26% | .795 | .862 | .594 | .815 | .751 | 0.64 | +29 | -31 |
| 09 | NYY | 456 | 28 | 62 | 90 | 0 | .274 | .367 | .509 | 84% | 33% | 12% | 1.86 | $18 | $9 | 370 | +11 | 21 | 1 | 1 | 42-20-38 | 17% | 22% | 21% | .876 | .884 | .867 | .835 | .976 | 0.64 | +20 | -54 |
| 10 | LAA | 482 | 21 | 55 | 84 | 0 | .274 | .361 | .459 | 80% | 34% | 12% | 1.67 | $17 | $8 | 330 | +2 | 24 | 1 | 1 | 42-19-39 | 13% | 23% | 19% | .820 | .732 | .955 | .868 | .692 | 0.64 | +8 | -24 |

---

## Joe Mauer — 600 PA | $25 | 420 pts

CA-112, DH-22    Owned: 100%    LH

In his first season after inking a huge extension, Mauer made good with a mostly healthy and productive campaign. It was not realistic to expect a repeat of his 2009 MVP performance (and 20% HR/FB), but the superstar catcher continues to fill out, and some of his doubles should turn back into homers in '11. (NN)

### Forecast

| Player | Age | AB | HR | R | RBI | SB | BA | OBP | SLG | $1L | Pts |
|---|---|---|---|---|---|---|---|---|---|---|---|
| Mauer J | 27 | 495 | 12 | 84 | 84 | 6 | .315 | .400 | .466 | $25 | 420 |
| Mini-Browser | Age | AB | HR | R | RBI | SB | BA | OBP | SLG | $1L | Pts |
| Posey B | 24 | 521 | 24 | 78 | 84 | 0 | .288 | .355 | .478 | $21 | 380 |
| Martinez V | 32 | 483 | 17 | 66 | 83 | 0 | .296 | .363 | .477 | $21 | 360 |
| McCann B | 27 | 498 | 22 | 66 | 88 | 6 | .287 | .365 | .501 | $21 | 390 |
| Soto G | 28 | 424 | 20 | 60 | 75 | 0 | .283 | .378 | .504 | $17 | 310 |
| Napoli M | 29 | 393 | 23 | 59 | 63 | 5 | .252 | .337 | .490 | $16 | 240 |

### Minors (2010) / Skills

| Level | Leag | AB | HR | R | RBI | SB | BA | OBP | SLG | CT% | H% | BB% | Bash |
|---|---|---|---|---|---|---|---|---|---|---|---|---|---|
| A | — | — | — | — | — | — | — | — | — | — | — | — | — |
| AA | — | — | — | — | — | — | — | — | — | — | — | — | — |
| AAA | — | — | — | — | — | — | — | — | — | — | — | — | — |

### Majors / Skills / Value / Extra / Production / OPS / Scoresheet

| Yr | Team | AB | HR | R | RBI | SB | BA | OBP | SLG | CT% | H% | BB% | Bash | $1L | $2L | Pts | RAA | 2B | 3B | CS | FB-LD-GB | HR/fb | RBI% | RS% | OPS | 1st Hf | 2nd Hf | vs RH | vs LH | Rnge | vRH | vLH |
|---|---|---|---|---|---|---|---|---|---|---|---|---|---|---|---|---|---|---|---|---|---|---|---|---|---|---|---|---|---|---|---|---|
| 07 | MIN | 406 | 7 | 62 | 60 | 7 | .293 | .382 | .426 | 87% | 34% | 12% | 1.45 | $16 | $7 | 310 | +12 | 27 | 3 | 1 | 28-18-55 | 7% | 25% | 32% | .808 | .857 | .751 | .877 | .673 | 0.34 | +44 | -117 |
| 08 | MIN | 536 | 9 | 98 | 85 | 1 | .328 | .413 | .451 | 91% | 36% | 13% | 1.38 | $26 | $24 | 460 | +31 | 31 | 4 | 1 | 28-23-49 | 6% | 28% | 35% | .864 | .873 | .853 | .826 | .939 | 0.36 | +36 | -91 |
| 09 | MIN | 523 | 28 | 94 | 96 | 4 | .365 | .444 | .587 | 88% | 42% | 12% | 1.61 | $37 | $37 | 520 | +61 | 30 | 1 | 1 | 30-23-48 | 20% | 28% | 27% | 1.031 | 1.069 | .998 | 1.103 | .910 | 0.37 | +16 | -39 |
| 10 | MIN | 510 | 9 | 88 | 75 | 1 | .327 | .402 | .469 | 90% | 37% | 11% | 1.43 | $25 | $24 | 410 | +26 | 43 | 1 | 1 | 29-24-47 | 7% | 25% | 35% | .871 | .792 | .974 | .978 | .711 | 0.44 | +13 | -32 |

---

## Justin Maxwell — 100 PA | $-2 | 50 pts

OF-51 (RF-29, CF-20, LF-5)    Owned: 0%    RH

Maxwell *looks* like a five-tool player, but unfortunately that's not a fantasy category. Between his seeming tools and his knack for the occasional dramatic home run, Maxwell will earn a shot as the 5th OF, but he'll probably spend 2011 bouncing between Syracuse and Washington once more. (PB)

### Forecast

| Player | Age | AB | HR | R | RBI | SB | BA | OBP | SLG | $1L | Pts |
|---|---|---|---|---|---|---|---|---|---|---|---|
| Maxwell J | 27 | 85 | 4 | 13 | 10 | 5 | .212 | .317 | .406 | -$2 | 50 |
| Mini-Browser | Age | AB | HR | R | RBI | SB | BA | OBP | SLG | $1L | Pts |
| Reddick J | 24 | 136 | 6 | 15 | 17 | 2 | .231 | .277 | .440 | -$2 | 70 |
| Dyson J | 26 | 138 | 2 | 17 | 9 | 12 | .207 | .274 | .289 | -$2 | 70 |
| Cunningham A | 24 | 121 | 4 | 14 | 14 | 3 | .237 | .310 | .398 | -$2 | 60 |
| Bourgeois J | 29 | 91 | 1 | 12 | 8 | 5 | .263 | .318 | .371 | -$2 | 60 |
| Langerhans R | 31 | 132 | 5 | 17 | 14 | 3 | .239 | .348 | .397 | -$2 | 70 |

### Minors (2010) / Skills

| Level | Leag | AB | HR | R | RBI | SB | BA | OBP | SLG | CT% | H% | BB% | Bash |
|---|---|---|---|---|---|---|---|---|---|---|---|---|---|
| A | — | — | — | — | — | — | — | — | — | — | — | — | — |
| AA | — | — | — | — | — | — | — | — | — | — | — | — | — |
| AAA | IL | 230 | 6 | 34 | 21 | 16 | .287 | .390 | .439 | 67% | 43% | 13% | 1.53 |

### Majors / Skills / Value / Extra / Production / OPS / Scoresheet

| Yr | Team | AB | HR | R | RBI | SB | BA | OBP | SLG | CT% | H% | BB% | Bash | $1L | $2L | Pts | RAA | 2B | 3B | CS | FB-LD-GB | HR/fb | RBI% | RS% | OPS | 1st Hf | 2nd Hf | vs RH | vs LH | Rnge | vRH | vLH |
|---|---|---|---|---|---|---|---|---|---|---|---|---|---|---|---|---|---|---|---|---|---|---|---|---|---|---|---|---|---|---|---|---|
| 07 | WAS | 26 | 2 | 5 | 5 | 0 | .269 | .296 | .500 | 69% | 39% | 4% | 1.86 | -$5 | -$18 | 20 | -0 | 0 | 0 | 0 | 44-22-33 | 25% | 17% | 50% | .796 | — | .796 | .282 | 1.125 | | | |
| 08 | | — | — | — | — | — | — | — | — | — | — | — | — | | | | | | | | | | | | | | | | | 2.10 | -27 | +64 |
| 09 | WAS | 89 | 4 | 9 | 6 | 2 | .247 | .343 | .449 | 64% | 39% | 12% | 1.82 | $0 | -$15 | 50 | +0 | 4 | 1 | 1 | 38-14-48 | 19% | 15% | 29% | .793 | .443 | .924 | .897 | .615 | 2.10 | -28 | +65 |
| 10 | WAS | 104 | 3 | 16 | 12 | 5 | .144 | .305 | .288 | 59% | 25% | 19% | 2.00 | -$3 | -$18 | 50 | -7 | 6 | 0 | 1 | 49-16-35 | 10% | 20% | 35% | .594 | .550 | .615 | .407 | .729 | 2.13 | -11 | +25 |

---

## Lucas May — 250 PA | $1 | 90 pts

CA-10, DH-1    Owned: 0%    RH

May might very well be the Royals' Opening Day catcher in 2011, since Jason Kendall is probably out for the season. May flashed decent power in the minors, and his plate discipline improved (12 BB, 19 K) after he came over from the Dodgers in July. But a contact rate of 73% is a strong headwind to success. (BM)

### Forecast

| Player | Age | AB | HR | R | RBI | SB | BA | OBP | SLG | $1L | Pts |
|---|---|---|---|---|---|---|---|---|---|---|---|
| May L | 26 | 235 | 10 | 23 | 28 | 3 | .202 | .257 | .372 | $1 | 90 |
| Mini-Browser | Age | AB | HR | R | RBI | SB | BA | OBP | SLG | $1L | Pts |
| Cervelli F | 25 | 224 | 3 | 23 | 25 | 0 | .246 | .323 | .332 | $2 | 110 |
| Moore A | 26 | 270 | 9 | 30 | 30 | 0 | .222 | .281 | .361 | $2 | 110 |
| Castro J | 23 | 345 | 8 | 40 | 32 | 0 | .220 | .303 | .340 | $2 | 150 |
| Ross D | 34 | 126 | 5 | 15 | 20 | 0 | .250 | .350 | .434 | $1 | 70 |
| Hester J | 27 | 142 | 5 | 17 | 17 | 2 | .243 | .294 | .422 | $1 | 70 |

### Minors (2010) / Skills

| Level | Leag | AB | HR | R | RBI | SB | BA | OBP | SLG | CT% | H% | BB% | Bash |
|---|---|---|---|---|---|---|---|---|---|---|---|---|---|
| A | — | — | — | — | — | — | — | — | — | — | — | — | — |
| AA | SOU | 24 | 0 | 2 | 1 | 0 | .167 | .259 | .208 | 71% | 24% | 7% | 1.25 |
| AAA | 2LG | 351 | 16 | 61 | 58 | 4 | .291 | .355 | .501 | 77% | 38% | 9% | 1.73 |

### Majors / Skills / Value / Extra / Production / OPS / Scoresheet

| Yr | Team | AB | HR | R | RBI | SB | BA | OBP | SLG | CT% | H% | BB% | Bash | $1L | $2L | Pts | RAA | 2B | 3B | CS | FB-LD-GB | HR/fb | RBI% | RS% | OPS | 1st Hf | 2nd Hf | vs RH | vs LH | Rnge | vRH | vLH |
|---|---|---|---|---|---|---|---|---|---|---|---|---|---|---|---|---|---|---|---|---|---|---|---|---|---|---|---|---|---|---|---|---|
| 07 | | — | — | — | — | — | — | — | — | — | — | — | — | | | | | | | | | | | | | | | | | | | |
| 08 | | — | — | — | — | — | — | — | — | — | — | — | — | | | | | | | | | | | | | | | | | 0.60 | | |
| 09 | | — | — | — | — | — | — | — | — | — | — | — | — | | | | | | | | | | | | | | | | | | | |
| 10 | KC | 37 | 0 | 3 | 6 | 0 | .189 | .205 | .216 | 73% | 26% | 0% | 1.14 | -$1 | -$12 | 10 | -5 | 1 | 0 | 1 | 50-11-39 | 0% | 26% | 38% | .421 | — | .421 | .501 | .200 | 0.58 | | |

---

## Cameron Maybin — 600 PA | $15 | 310 pts

OF-77 (CF-77)    Owned: 5%    RH

Maybin in 2011 will be granted Florida's starting CF job for the third season in a row, but management will be even less patient with him than they have been. If Maybin struggles again, the Marlins will pull him from MLB and abandon him in the minors. He will hold his job only if he can nudge up his CT% and BB%. (MJ)

### Forecast

| Player | Age | AB | HR | R | RBI | SB | BA | OBP | SLG | $1L | Pts |
|---|---|---|---|---|---|---|---|---|---|---|---|
| Maybin C | 23 | 534 | 18 | 84 | 54 | 18 | .247 | .331 | .410 | $15 | 310 |
| Mini-Browser | Age | AB | HR | R | RBI | SB | BA | OBP | SLG | $1L | Pts |
| Gutierrez F | 28 | 568 | 19 | 75 | 63 | 19 | .253 | .313 | .393 | $16 | 310 |
| Willingham J | 32 | 465 | 22 | 72 | 72 | 6 | .272 | .379 | .494 | $16 | 340 |
| Kubel J | 28 | 468 | 21 | 63 | 84 | 0 | .269 | .337 | .472 | $16 | 320 |
| Tabata J | 22 | 567 | 12 | 78 | 54 | 24 | .275 | .334 | .388 | $15 | 360 |
| Rivera J | 32 | 500 | 21 | 58 | 74 | 0 | .273 | .319 | .453 | $15 | 330 |

### Minors (2010) / Skills

| Level | Leag | AB | HR | R | RBI | SB | BA | OBP | SLG | CT% | H% | BB% | Bash |
|---|---|---|---|---|---|---|---|---|---|---|---|---|---|
| A | — | — | — | — | — | — | — | — | — | — | — | — | — |
| AA | — | — | — | — | — | — | — | — | — | — | — | — | — |
| AAA | PCL | 130 | 4 | 21 | 23 | 5 | .338 | .407 | .508 | 82% | 42% | 9% | 1.50 |

### Majors / Skills / Value / Extra / Production / OPS / Scoresheet

| Yr | Team | AB | HR | R | RBI | SB | BA | OBP | SLG | CT% | H% | BB% | Bash | $1L | $2L | Pts | RAA | 2B | 3B | CS | FB-LD-GB | HR/fb | RBI% | RS% | OPS | 1st Hf | 2nd Hf | vs RH | vs LH | Rnge | vRH | vLH |
|---|---|---|---|---|---|---|---|---|---|---|---|---|---|---|---|---|---|---|---|---|---|---|---|---|---|---|---|---|---|---|---|---|
| 07 | DET | 49 | 1 | 9 | 4 | 1 | .143 | .208 | .265 | 57% | 25% | 6% | 1.86 | -$3 | -$18 | 20 | -4 | 3 | 0 | 0 | 43-4-54 | 8% | 4% | 70% | .473 | — | .473 | .000 | 2.10 | | | |
| 08 | FLA | 32 | 0 | 9 | 2 | 4 | .500 | .543 | .563 | 75% | 67% | 8% | 1.13 | -$1 | -$14 | 30 | +6 | 2 | 0 | 0 | 21-29-50 | 0% | 25% | 47% | 1.105 | — | 1.105 | 1.160 | .944 | 2.13 | -14 | +37 |
| 09 | FLA | 176 | 4 | 30 | 13 | 1 | .250 | .318 | .409 | 71% | 35% | 9% | 1.64 | $0 | -$14 | 80 | -4 | 12 | 2 | 3 | 28-17-55 | 12% | 9% | 45% | .727 | .589 | .853 | .767 | .646 | 2.15 | -13 | +32 |
| 10 | FLA | 291 | 8 | 46 | 28 | 9 | .234 | .302 | .361 | 68% | 34% | 7% | 1.54 | $0 | -$7 | 130 | -11 | 7 | 3 | 2 | 33-14-53 | 13% | 18% | 43% | .663 | .631 | .717 | .694 | .584 | 2.17 | -9 | +20 |

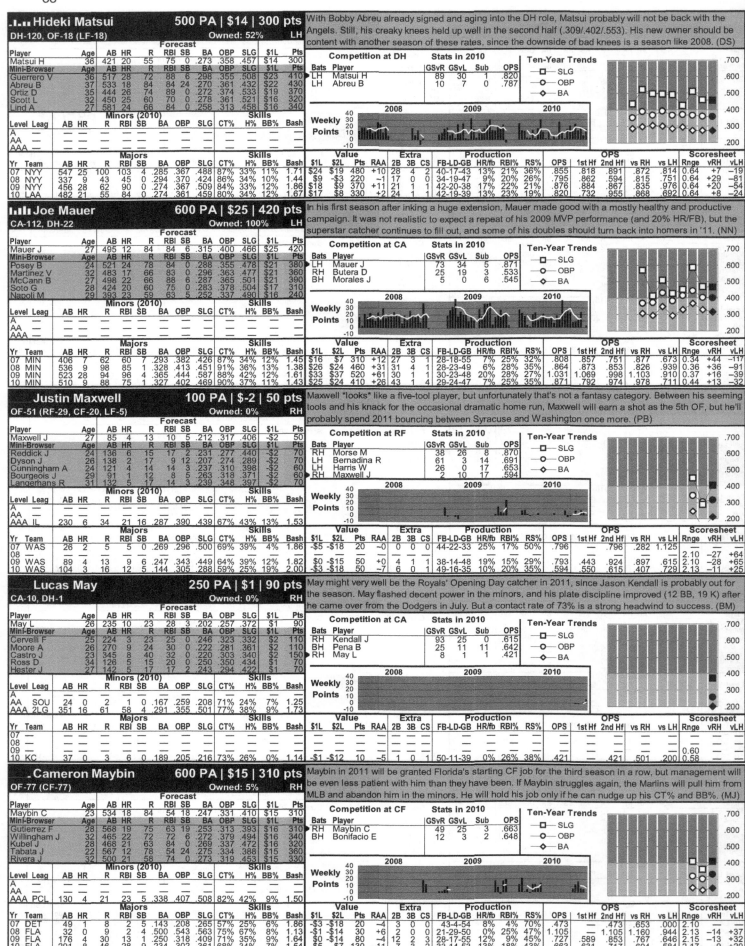

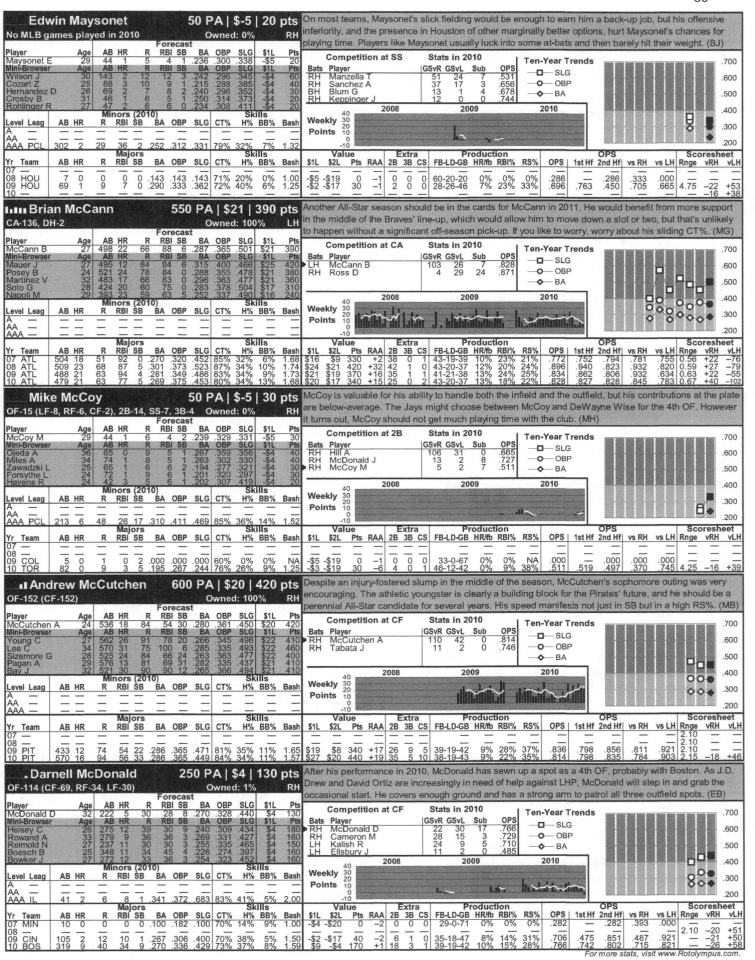

## Edwin Maysonet — 50 PA | $-5 | 20 pts

No MLB games played in 2010 — Owned: 0% — RH

On most teams, Maysonet's slick fielding would be enough to earn him a back-up job, but his offensive inferiority, and the presence in Houston of other marginally better options, hurt Maysonet's chances for playing time. Players like Maysonet usually luck into some at-bats and then barely hit their weight. (BJ)

### Forecast

| Player | Age | AB | HR | R | RBI | SB | BA | OBP | SLG | $1L | Pts |
|---|---|---|---|---|---|---|---|---|---|---|---|
| Maysonet E | 29 | 44 | 1 | 5 | 4 | 1 | .236 | .300 | .338 | -$5 | 20 |

### Mini-Browser

| Player | Age | AB | HR | R | RBI | SB | BA | OBP | SLG | $1L | Pts |
|---|---|---|---|---|---|---|---|---|---|---|---|
| Wilson J | 30 | 143 | 2 | 12 | 12 | 3 | .242 | .296 | .345 | -$4 | 60 |
| Cozart Z | 25 | 88 | 3 | 10 | 9 | 1 | .215 | .288 | .385 | -$4 | 40 |
| Hernandez D | 26 | 69 | 2 | 7 | 8 | 2 | .240 | .296 | .352 | -$4 | 30 |
| Crosby B | 31 | 46 | 1 | 6 | 5 | 1 | .250 | .314 | .373 | -$4 | 20 |
| Rohlinger R | 27 | 47 | 2 | 6 | 6 | 1 | .234 | .308 | .411 | -$4 | 20 |

### Competition at SS — Stats in 2010

| Bats | Player | GSvR | GSvL | Sub | OPS |
|---|---|---|---|---|---|
| RH | Manzella T | 51 | 24 | 7 | .531 |
| RH | Sanchez A | 37 | 17 | 3 | .656 |
| BH | Blum G | 13 | 1 | 4 | .678 |
| RH | Keppinger J | 12 | 0 | 0 | .744 |

### Minors (2010) / Skills

| Level | Leag | AB | HR | R | RBI | SB | BA | OBP | SLG | CT% | H% | BB% | Bash |
|---|---|---|---|---|---|---|---|---|---|---|---|---|---|
| A | — | | | | | | | | | | | | |
| AA | — | | | | | | | | | | | | |
| AAA | PCL | 302 | 2 | 29 | 36 | 2 | .252 | .312 | .331 | 79% | 32% | 7% | 1.32 |

### Majors

| Yr | Team | AB | HR | R | RBI | SB | BA | OBP | SLG | CT% | H% | BB% | Bash | $1L | $2L | Pts | RAA | 2B | 3B | CS | FB-LD-GB | HR/fb | RBI% | RS% | OPS | 1st Hf | 2nd Hf | vs RH | vs LH | Rnge | vRH | vLH |
|---|---|---|---|---|---|---|---|---|---|---|---|---|---|---|---|---|---|---|---|---|---|---|---|---|---|---|---|---|---|---|---|---|
| 07 | — | | | | | | | | | | | | | | | | | | | | | | | | | | | | | | | |
| 08 | HOU | 7 | 0 | 0 | 0 | 0 | .143 | .143 | .143 | 71% | 20% | 0% | 1.00 | -$5 | -$19 | 0 | -1 | 0 | 0 | 0 | 60-20-20 | 0% | 0% | 0% | .286 | — | .286 | .333 | .000 | | -16 | +53 |
| 09 | HOU | 69 | 1 | 9 | 7 | 0 | .290 | .333 | .362 | 72% | 40% | 6% | 1.25 | -$2 | -$17 | 30 | -1 | 2 | 0 | 0 | 28-26-46 | 7% | 23% | 33% | .696 | .763 | .450 | .705 | .665 | 4.75 | -22 | +53 |
| 10 | — | | | | | | | | | | | | | | | | | | | | | | | | | | | | | | -16 | +38 |

## Brian McCann — 550 PA | $21 | 390 pts

CA-136, DH-2 — Owned: 100% — LH

Another All-Star season should be in the cards for McCann in 2011. He would benefit from more support in the middle of the Braves' line-up, which would allow him to move down a slot or two, but that's unlikely to happen without a significant off-season pick-up. If you like to worry, worry about his sliding CT%. (MG)

### Forecast

| Player | Age | AB | HR | R | RBI | SB | BA | OBP | SLG | $1L | Pts |
|---|---|---|---|---|---|---|---|---|---|---|---|
| McCann B | 27 | 498 | 22 | 66 | 88 | 6 | .287 | .365 | .501 | $21 | 390 |

### Mini-Browser

| Player | Age | AB | HR | R | RBI | SB | BA | OBP | SLG | $1L | Pts |
|---|---|---|---|---|---|---|---|---|---|---|---|
| Mauer J | 27 | 495 | 12 | 84 | 84 | 6 | .315 | .400 | .466 | $25 | 420 |
| Posey B | 24 | 521 | 24 | 78 | 84 | 0 | .288 | .355 | .478 | $21 | 380 |
| Martinez V | 32 | 483 | 17 | 66 | 83 | 0 | .296 | .363 | .477 | $21 | 360 |
| Soto G | 28 | 424 | 20 | 60 | 75 | 0 | .283 | .378 | .504 | $17 | 310 |
| Napoli M | 29 | 393 | 23 | 59 | 63 | 5 | .252 | .337 | .490 | $16 | 240 |

### Competition at CA — Stats in 2010

| Bats | Player | GSvR | GSvL | Sub | OPS |
|---|---|---|---|---|---|
| LH | McCann B | 103 | 26 | 7 | .828 |
| RH | Ross D | 4 | 29 | 24 | .871 |

### Minors (2010) / Skills

| Level | Leag | AB | HR | R | RBI | SB | BA | OBP | SLG | CT% | H% | BB% | Bash |
|---|---|---|---|---|---|---|---|---|---|---|---|---|---|
| A | — | | | | | | | | | | | | |
| AA | — | | | | | | | | | | | | |
| AAA | — | | | | | | | | | | | | |

### Majors

| Yr | Team | AB | HR | R | RBI | SB | BA | OBP | SLG | CT% | H% | BB% | Bash | $1L | $2L | Pts | RAA | 2B | 3B | CS | FB-LD-GB | HR/fb | RBI% | RS% | OPS | 1st Hf | 2nd Hf | vs RH | vs LH | Rnge | vRH | vLH |
|---|---|---|---|---|---|---|---|---|---|---|---|---|---|---|---|---|---|---|---|---|---|---|---|---|---|---|---|---|---|---|---|---|
| 07 | ATL | 504 | 18 | 51 | 92 | 0 | .270 | .320 | .452 | 85% | 32% | 6% | 1.68 | $16 | $9 | 330 | +2 | 38 | 0 | 1 | 43-19-39 | 10% | 23% | 21% | .772 | .752 | .794 | .781 | .755 | 0.56 | +22 | -76 |
| 08 | ATL | 509 | 23 | 68 | 87 | 5 | .301 | .373 | .523 | 84% | 34% | 10% | 1.74 | $24 | $21 | 420 | +32 | 42 | 1 | 0 | 43-20-37 | 12% | 20% | 24% | .896 | .940 | .823 | .932 | .820 | 0.59 | +27 | -79 |
| 09 | ATL | 488 | 21 | 63 | 94 | 4 | .281 | .349 | .486 | 83% | 34% | 9% | 1.73 | $21 | $19 | 370 | +16 | 35 | 1 | 1 | 41-21-38 | 13% | 24% | 25% | .834 | .862 | .806 | .932 | .634 | 0.63 | +22 | -55 |
| 10 | ATL | 479 | 21 | 63 | 77 | 5 | .269 | .375 | .453 | 80% | 34% | 13% | 1.68 | $20 | $17 | 340 | +15 | 25 | 0 | 2 | 43-20-37 | 13% | 18% | 22% | .828 | .827 | .828 | .845 | .783 | 0.67 | +40 | -102 |

## Mike McCoy — 50 PA | $-5 | 30 pts

OF-15 (LF-8, RF-6, CF-2), 2B-14, SS-7, 3B-4 — Owned: 0% — RH

McCoy is valuable for his ability to handle both the infield and the outfield, but his contributions at the plate are below-average. The Jays might choose between McCoy and DeWayne Wise for the 4th OF. However it turns out, McCoy should not get much playing time with the club. (MH)

### Forecast

| Player | Age | AB | HR | R | RBI | SB | BA | OBP | SLG | $1L | Pts |
|---|---|---|---|---|---|---|---|---|---|---|---|
| McCoy M | 29 | 44 | 1 | 6 | 4 | 2 | .239 | .329 | .331 | -$5 | 30 |

### Mini-Browser

| Player | Age | AB | HR | R | RBI | SB | BA | OBP | SLG | $1L | Pts |
|---|---|---|---|---|---|---|---|---|---|---|---|
| Ojeda A | 36 | 65 | 0 | 9 | 5 | 1 | .267 | .359 | .356 | -$4 | 40 |
| Miles A | 34 | 74 | 1 | 8 | 5 | 1 | .263 | .302 | .330 | -$4 | 40 |
| Zawadzki L | 25 | 65 | 1 | 6 | 6 | 2 | .194 | .277 | .321 | -$4 | 30 |
| Forsythe L | 24 | 72 | 1 | 9 | 6 | 1 | .201 | .320 | .297 | -$4 | 30 |
| Havens R | 24 | 42 | 3 | 5 | 6 | 1 | .202 | .307 | .419 | -$4 | 20 |

### Competition at 2B — Stats in 2010

| Bats | Player | GSvR | GSvL | Sub | OPS |
|---|---|---|---|---|---|
| RH | Hill A | 106 | 31 | 0 | .665 |
| RH | McDonald J | 13 | 2 | 8 | .727 |
| RH | McCoy M | 5 | 2 | 7 | .511 |

### Minors (2010) / Skills

| Level | Leag | AB | HR | R | RBI | SB | BA | OBP | SLG | CT% | H% | BB% | Bash |
|---|---|---|---|---|---|---|---|---|---|---|---|---|---|
| A | — | | | | | | | | | | | | |
| AA | — | | | | | | | | | | | | |
| AAA | PCL | 213 | 6 | 48 | 26 | 17 | .310 | .411 | .469 | 85% | 36% | 14% | 1.52 |

### Majors

| Yr | Team | AB | HR | R | RBI | SB | BA | OBP | SLG | CT% | H% | BB% | Bash | $1L | $2L | Pts | RAA | 2B | 3B | CS | FB-LD-GB | HR/fb | RBI% | RS% | OPS | 1st Hf | 2nd Hf | vs RH | vs LH | Rnge | vRH | vLH |
|---|---|---|---|---|---|---|---|---|---|---|---|---|---|---|---|---|---|---|---|---|---|---|---|---|---|---|---|---|---|---|---|---|
| 07 | — | | | | | | | | | | | | | | | | | | | | | | | | | | | | | | | |
| 08 | — | | | | | | | | | | | | | | | | | | | | | | | | | | | | | | | |
| 09 | COL | 5 | 0 | 1 | 0 | 2 | .000 | .000 | .000 | 60% | 0% | 0% | NA | -$5 | -$19 | 0 | -1 | 0 | 0 | NA | 33-0-67 | 0% | 0% | NA | .000 | — | .000 | .000 | .000 | 4.25 | -16 | +39 |
| 10 | TOR | 82 | 0 | 9 | 3 | 5 | .195 | .267 | .244 | 76% | 26% | 9% | 1.25 | -$3 | -$19 | 30 | -6 | 4 | 0 | 1 | 46-12-42 | 0% | 9% | 38% | .511 | .519 | .497 | .370 | .745 | 4.25 | -16 | +39 |

## Andrew McCutchen — 600 PA | $20 | 420 pts

OF-152 (CF-152) — Owned: 100% — RH

Despite an injury-fostered slump in the middle of the season, McCutchen's sophomore outing was very encouraging. The athletic youngster is clearly a building block for the Pirates' future, and he should be a perennial All-Star candidate for several years. His speed manifests not just in SB but in a high RS%. (MB)

### Forecast

| Player | Age | AB | HR | R | RBI | SB | BA | OBP | SLG | $1L | Pts |
|---|---|---|---|---|---|---|---|---|---|---|---|
| McCutchen A | 24 | 536 | 18 | 84 | 54 | 30 | .280 | .361 | .450 | $20 | 420 |

### Mini-Browser

| Player | Age | AB | HR | R | RBI | SB | BA | OBP | SLG | $1L | Pts |
|---|---|---|---|---|---|---|---|---|---|---|---|
| Young C | 27 | 562 | 26 | 91 | 78 | 20 | .266 | .345 | .496 | $22 | 410 |
| Lee C | 34 | 570 | 31 | 75 | 100 | 6 | .285 | .335 | .493 | $22 | 460 |
| Sizemore G | 28 | 525 | 24 | 84 | 66 | 24 | .263 | .363 | .477 | $22 | 400 |
| Pagan A | 29 | 576 | 13 | 81 | 69 | 31 | .282 | .335 | .437 | $21 | 410 |
| Bay J | 32 | 521 | 30 | 90 | 90 | 12 | .265 | .366 | .494 | $21 | 410 |

### Competition at CF — Stats in 2010

| Bats | Player | GSvR | GSvL | Sub | OPS |
|---|---|---|---|---|---|
| RH | McCutchen A | 110 | 42 | 0 | .814 |
| RH | Tabata J | 11 | 2 | 0 | .746 |

### Minors (2010) / Skills

| Level | Leag | AB | HR | R | RBI | SB | BA | OBP | SLG | CT% | H% | BB% | Bash |
|---|---|---|---|---|---|---|---|---|---|---|---|---|---|
| A | — | | | | | | | | | | | | |
| AA | — | | | | | | | | | | | | |
| AAA | — | | | | | | | | | | | | |

### Majors

| Yr | Team | AB | HR | R | RBI | SB | BA | OBP | SLG | CT% | H% | BB% | Bash | $1L | $2L | Pts | RAA | 2B | 3B | CS | FB-LD-GB | HR/fb | RBI% | RS% | OPS | 1st Hf | 2nd Hf | vs RH | vs LH | Rnge | vRH | vLH |
|---|---|---|---|---|---|---|---|---|---|---|---|---|---|---|---|---|---|---|---|---|---|---|---|---|---|---|---|---|---|---|---|---|
| 07 | — | | | | | | | | | | | | | | | | | | | | | | | | | | | | | 2.10 | | |
| 08 | — | | | | | | | | | | | | | | | | | | | | | | | | | | | | | 2.10 | | |
| 09 | PIT | 433 | 12 | 74 | 54 | 22 | .286 | .365 | .471 | 81% | 35% | 11% | 1.65 | $19 | $8 | 340 | +17 | 26 | 9 | 5 | 39-19-42 | 9% | 28% | 37% | .836 | .798 | .856 | .811 | .921 | 2.10 | | |
| 10 | PIT | 570 | 16 | 94 | 56 | 33 | .286 | .365 | .449 | 84% | 34% | 11% | 1.57 | $27 | $20 | 440 | +19 | 35 | 5 | 10 | 38-19-43 | 9% | 22% | 35% | .814 | .798 | .835 | .784 | .903 | 2.15 | -18 | +46 |

## Darnell McDonald — 250 PA | $4 | 130 pts

OF-114 (CF-69, RF-34, LF-30) — Owned: 1% — RH

After his performance in 2010, McDonald has sewn up a spot as a 4th OF, probably with Boston. As J.D. Drew and David Ortiz are increasingly in need of help against LHP, McDonald will step in and grab the occasional start. He covers enough ground and has a strong arm to patrol all three outfield spots. (EB)

### Forecast

| Player | Age | AB | HR | R | RBI | SB | BA | OBP | SLG | $1L | Pts |
|---|---|---|---|---|---|---|---|---|---|---|---|
| McDonald D | 32 | 222 | 5 | 30 | 28 | 8 | .270 | .328 | .440 | $4 | 130 |

### Mini-Browser

| Player | Age | AB | HR | R | RBI | SB | BA | OBP | SLG | $1L | Pts |
|---|---|---|---|---|---|---|---|---|---|---|---|
| Heisey C | 26 | 275 | 12 | 39 | 36 | 9 | .240 | .309 | .434 | $4 | 180 |
| Rowand A | 33 | 279 | 9 | 36 | 36 | 3 | .269 | .331 | .427 | $4 | 160 |
| Reimold N | 27 | 237 | 11 | 30 | 45 | 3 | .255 | .335 | .465 | $4 | 150 |
| Boesch B | 25 | 348 | 11 | 34 | 45 | 4 | .256 | .274 | .397 | $4 | 160 |
| Bowker J | 27 | 272 | 12 | 33 | 36 | 3 | .254 | .323 | .452 | $4 | 160 |

### Competition at CF — Stats in 2010

| Bats | Player | GSvR | GSvL | Sub | OPS |
|---|---|---|---|---|---|
| RH | McDonald D | 22 | 30 | 17 | .766 |
| RH | Cameron M | 28 | 15 | 3 | .729 |
| LH | Kalish R | 24 | 9 | 5 | .710 |
| LH | Ellsbury J | 11 | 2 | 0 | .485 |

### Minors (2010) / Skills

| Level | Leag | AB | HR | R | RBI | SB | BA | OBP | SLG | CT% | H% | BB% | Bash |
|---|---|---|---|---|---|---|---|---|---|---|---|---|---|
| A | — | | | | | | | | | | | | |
| AA | — | | | | | | | | | | | | |
| AAA | IL | 41 | 2 | 6 | 8 | 1 | .341 | .372 | .683 | 83% | 41% | 5% | 2.00 |

### Majors

| Yr | Team | AB | HR | R | RBI | SB | BA | OBP | SLG | CT% | H% | BB% | Bash | $1L | $2L | Pts | RAA | 2B | 3B | CS | FB-LD-GB | HR/fb | RBI% | RS% | OPS | 1st Hf | 2nd Hf | vs RH | vs LH | Rnge | vRH | vLH |
|---|---|---|---|---|---|---|---|---|---|---|---|---|---|---|---|---|---|---|---|---|---|---|---|---|---|---|---|---|---|---|---|---|
| 07 | MIN | 10 | 0 | 0 | 0 | 0 | .100 | .182 | .100 | 70% | 14% | 9% | 1.00 | -$4 | -$20 | 0 | -2 | 0 | 0 | 0 | 29-0-71 | 0% | 0% | 0% | .282 | — | .282 | .393 | .000 | | | |
| 08 | — | | | | | | | | | | | | | | | | | | | | | | | | | | | | | 2.10 | -20 | +51 |
| 09 | CIN | 105 | 2 | 12 | 10 | 1 | .267 | .333 | .400 | 70% | 38% | 5% | 1.50 | -$2 | -$17 | 40 | -2 | 6 | 1 | 1 | 35-18-47 | 8% | 14% | 31% | .706 | .475 | .851 | .487 | .921 | | -21 | +50 |
| 10 | BOS | 319 | 9 | 40 | 34 | 9 | .270 | .336 | .429 | 73% | 37% | 5% | 1.59 | $9 | -$4 | 170 | +1 | 18 | 3 | 1 | 39-19-42 | 10% | 15% | 28% | .766 | .742 | .802 | .715 | .821 | | -26 | +58 |

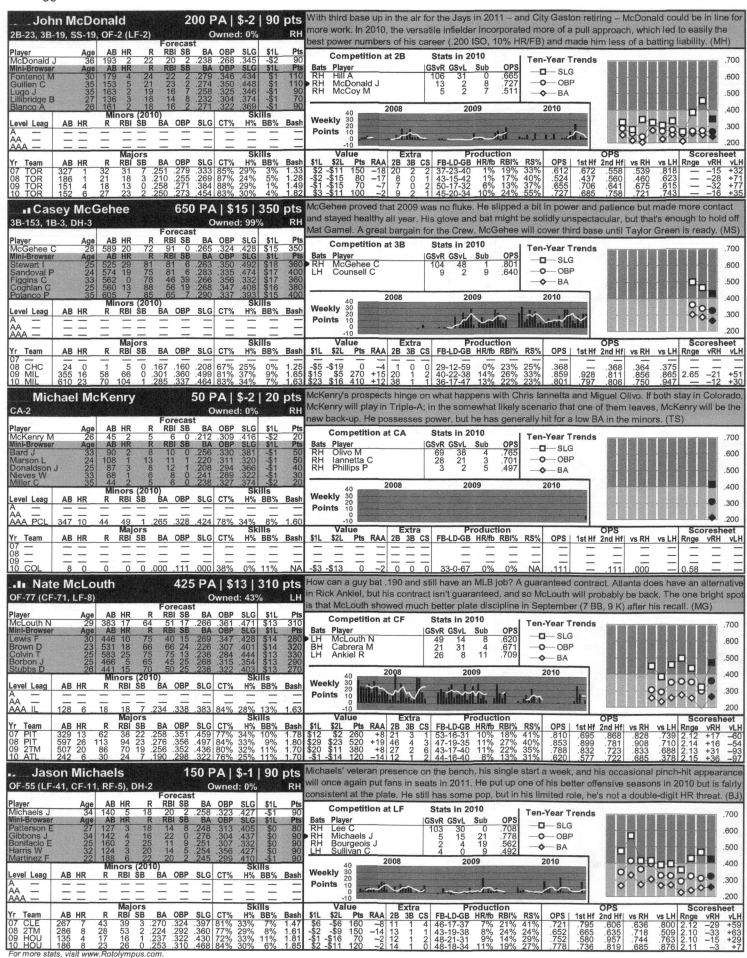

## John McDonald — 200 PA | $-2 | 90 pts

2B-23, 3B-19, SS-19, OF-2 (LF-2) — Owned: 0% — RH

With third base up in the air for the Jays in 2011 – and City Gaston retiring – McDonald could be in line for more work. In 2010, the versatile infielder incorporated more of a pull approach, which led to easily the best power numbers of his career (.200 ISO, 10% HR/FB) and made him less of a batting liability. (MH)

**Forecast**

| Player | Age | AB | HR | R | RBI | SB | BA | OBP | SLG | $1L | Pts |
|---|---|---|---|---|---|---|---|---|---|---|---|
| McDonald J | 36 | 193 | 2 | 22 | 20 | 2 | .238 | .268 | .345 | -$2 | 90 |
| **Mini-Browser** | **Age** | **AB** | **HR** | **R** | **RBI** | **SB** | **BA** | **OBP** | **SLG** | **$1L** | **Pts** |
| Fontenot M | 30 | 179 | 4 | 24 | 22 | 2 | .279 | .346 | .434 | $1 | 110 |
| Guillen C | 35 | 153 | 5 | 21 | 23 | 2 | .274 | .350 | .448 | $1 | 110 |
| Lugo J | 35 | 163 | 2 | 19 | 16 | 7 | .258 | .325 | .346 | -$1 | 90 |
| Lillibridge B | 27 | 136 | 3 | 18 | 14 | 8 | .232 | .304 | .374 | -$1 | 70 |
| Blanco A | 26 | 161 | 2 | 18 | 16 | 2 | .271 | .322 | .369 | -$1 | 90 |

**Minors (2010)**

| Level | Leag | AB | HR | R | RBI | SB | BA | OBP | SLG | CT% | H% | BB% | Bash |
|---|---|---|---|---|---|---|---|---|---|---|---|---|---|
| A | — | — | — | — | — | — | — | — | — | — | — | — | — |
| AA | — | — | — | — | — | — | — | — | — | — | — | — | — |
| AAA | — | — | — | — | — | — | — | — | — | — | — | — | — |

**Competition at 2B — Stats in 2010**

| Bats | Player | GSvR | GSvL | Sub | OPS |
|---|---|---|---|---|---|
| RH | Hill A | 106 | 31 | 0 | .665 |
| RH | McDonald J | 13 | 2 | 8 | .727 |
| RH | McCoy M | 5 | 2 | 7 | .511 |

Ten-Year Trends

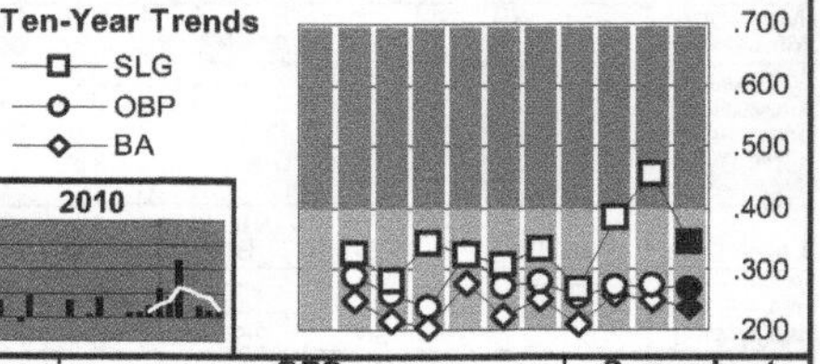


Weekly Points

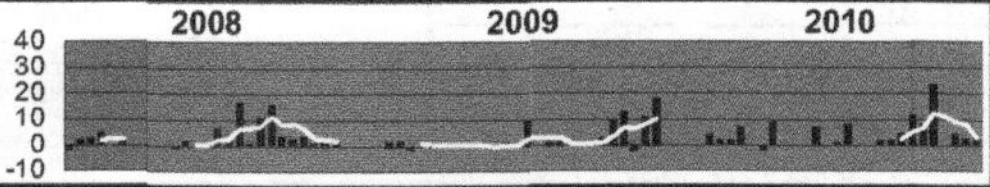


**Majors**

| Yr | Team | AB | HR | R | RBI | SB | BA | OBP | SLG | CT% | H% | BB% | Bash |
|---|---|---|---|---|---|---|---|---|---|---|---|---|---|
| 07 | TOR | 327 | 1 | 32 | 31 | 7 | .251 | .279 | .333 | 85% | 29% | 3% | 1.33 |
| 08 | TOR | 186 | 1 | 21 | 18 | 3 | .210 | .255 | .269 | 87% | 24% | 5% | 1.28 |
| 09 | TOR | 151 | 4 | 18 | 13 | 0 | .258 | .271 | .384 | 88% | 29% | 1% | 1.49 |
| 10 | TOR | 152 | 6 | 27 | 23 | 2 | .250 | .273 | .454 | 83% | 30% | 4% | 1.82 |

| Yr | Value $1L | $2L | Pts | RAA | Extra 2B | 3B | CS | Production FB-LD-GB | HR/fb | RBI% | RS% | OPS | 1st Hf | 2nd Hf | vs RH | vs LH | Scoresheet Rnge | vRH | vLH |
|---|---|---|---|---|---|---|---|---|---|---|---|---|---|---|---|---|---|---|---|
| 07 | $2 | -$11 | 150 | −18 | 20 | 2 | 2 | 37-23-40 | 1% | 19% | 33% | .612 | .672 | .558 | .539 | .818 | — | −15 | +32 |
| 08 | -$2 | -$15 | 80 | −17 | 8 | 0 | 1 | 43-15-42 | 1% | 17% | 40% | .524 | .437 | .560 | .460 | .623 | — | −28 | +71 |
| 09 | -$1 | -$15 | 70 | −7 | 7 | 0 | 2 | 50-17-32 | 6% | 13% | 37% | .655 | .706 | .641 | .675 | .615 | — | −32 | +77 |
| 10 | $3 | -$11 | 100 | −2 | 9 | 2 | 1 | 45-20-34 | 10% | 24% | 55% | .727 | .685 | .758 | .721 | .743 | — | −16 | +35 |

## Casey McGehee — 650 PA | $15 | 350 pts

3B-153, 1B-3, DH-3 — Owned: 99% — RH

McGehee proved that 2009 was no fluke. He slipped a bit in power and patience but made more contact and stayed healthy all year. His glove and bat might be solidly unspectacular, but that's enough to hold off Mat Gamel. A great bargain for the Crew, McGehee will cover third base until Taylor Green is ready. (MS)

**Forecast**

| Player | Age | AB | HR | R | RBI | SB | BA | OBP | SLG | $1L | Pts |
|---|---|---|---|---|---|---|---|---|---|---|---|
| McGehee C | 28 | 589 | 20 | 72 | 91 | 0 | .265 | .324 | .428 | $15 | 350 |
| **Mini-Browser** | **Age** | **AB** | **HR** | **R** | **RBI** | **SB** | **BA** | **OBP** | **SLG** | **$1L** | **Pts** |
| Stewart I | 25 | 525 | 29 | 81 | 81 | 6 | .263 | .350 | .492 | $18 | 360 |
| Sandoval P | 24 | 574 | 19 | 75 | 81 | 6 | .283 | .335 | .474 | $17 | 400 |
| Figgins C | 33 | 562 | 0 | 78 | 46 | 39 | .266 | .356 | .332 | $17 | 360 |
| Coghlan C | 25 | 560 | 13 | 88 | 56 | 19 | .268 | .347 | .408 | $16 | 380 |
| Polanco P | 35 | 605 | 7 | 85 | 65 | 7 | .290 | .337 | .393 | $15 | 400 |

**Minors (2010)**

| Level | Leag | AB | HR | R | RBI | SB | BA | OBP | SLG | CT% | H% | BB% | Bash |
|---|---|---|---|---|---|---|---|---|---|---|---|---|---|
| A | — | — | — | — | — | — | — | — | — | — | — | — | — |
| AA | — | — | — | — | — | — | — | — | — | — | — | — | — |
| AAA | — | — | — | — | — | — | — | — | — | — | — | — | — |

**Competition at 3B — Stats in 2010**

| Bats | Player | GSvR | GSvL | Sub | OPS |
|---|---|---|---|---|---|
| RH | McGehee C | 104 | 48 | 1 | .801 |
| LH | Counsell C | 9 | 2 | 9 | .640 |

Ten-Year Trends

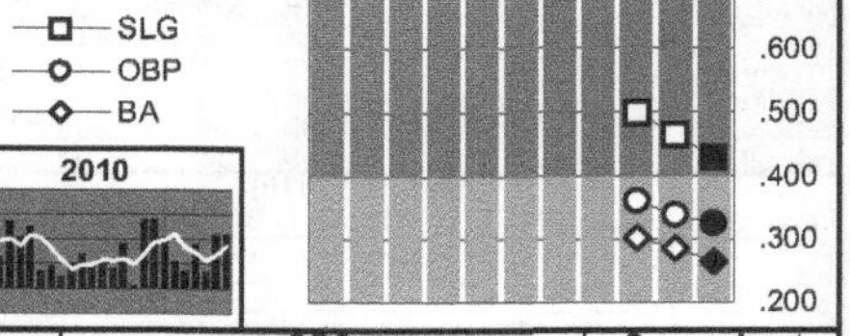


Weekly Points

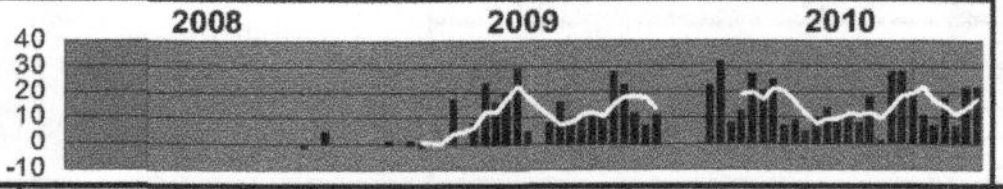


**Majors**

| Yr | Team | AB | HR | R | RBI | SB | BA | OBP | SLG | CT% | H% | BB% | Bash |
|---|---|---|---|---|---|---|---|---|---|---|---|---|---|
| 07 | — | — | — | — | — | — | — | — | — | — | — | — | — |
| 08 | CHC | 24 | 0 | 1 | 5 | 0 | .167 | .160 | .208 | 67% | 25% | 0% | 1.25 |
| 09 | MIL | 355 | 16 | 58 | 66 | 0 | .301 | .360 | .499 | 81% | 37% | 9% | 1.65 |
| 10 | MIL | 610 | 23 | 70 | 104 | 1 | .285 | .337 | .464 | 83% | 34% | 7% | 1.63 |

| Yr | Value $1L | $2L | Pts | RAA | Extra 2B | 3B | CS | Production FB-LD-GB | HR/fb | RBI% | RS% | OPS | 1st Hf | 2nd Hf | vs RH | vs LH | Scoresheet Rnge | vRH | vLH |
|---|---|---|---|---|---|---|---|---|---|---|---|---|---|---|---|---|---|---|---|
| 07 | — | — | — | — | — | — | — | — | — | — | — | — | — | — | — | — | — | — | — |
| 08 | -$5 | -$19 | 0 | −4 | 1 | 0 | 0 | 29-12-59 | 0% | 23% | 25% | .368 | — | .368 | .364 | .375 | — | — | — |
| 09 | $15 | $5 | 270 | +15 | 20 | 1 | 2 | 40-22-38 | 14% | 26% | 33% | .859 | .928 | .811 | .856 | .865 | 2.65 | −21 | +51 |
| 10 | $23 | $16 | 410 | +12 | 38 | 1 | 1 | 36-17-47 | 13% | 22% | 23% | .801 | .797 | .806 | .750 | .947 | — | −12 | +30 |

## Michael McKenry — 50 PA | $-2 | 20 pts

CA-2 — Owned: 0% — RH

McKenry's prospects hinge on what happens with Chris Iannetta and Miguel Olivo. If both stay in Colorado, McKenry will play in Triple-A; in the somewhat likely scenario that one of them leaves, McKenry will be the new back-up. He possesses power, but he has generally hit for a low BA in the minors. (TS)

**Forecast**

| Player | Age | AB | HR | R | RBI | SB | BA | OBP | SLG | $1L | Pts |
|---|---|---|---|---|---|---|---|---|---|---|---|
| McKenry M | 26 | 45 | 2 | 5 | 6 | 0 | .212 | .309 | .416 | -$2 | 20 |
| **Mini-Browser** | **Age** | **AB** | **HR** | **R** | **RBI** | **SB** | **BA** | **OBP** | **SLG** | **$1L** | **Pts** |
| Bard J | 33 | 90 | 2 | 8 | 10 | 0 | .256 | .330 | .381 | -$1 | 50 |
| Marson L | 24 | 108 | 1 | 13 | 11 | 1 | .220 | .311 | .320 | -$1 | 50 |
| Donaldson J | 25 | 87 | 3 | 8 | 12 | 1 | .208 | .294 | .366 | -$1 | 40 |
| Nieves W | 33 | 68 | 1 | 6 | 8 | 0 | .241 | .289 | .322 | -$1 | 30 |
| Miller C | 35 | 44 | 2 | 5 | 6 | 0 | .238 | .327 | .374 | -$2 | 20 |

**Minors (2010)**

| Level | Leag | AB | HR | R | RBI | SB | BA | OBP | SLG | CT% | H% | BB% | Bash |
|---|---|---|---|---|---|---|---|---|---|---|---|---|---|
| A | — | — | — | — | — | — | — | — | — | — | — | — | — |
| AA | — | — | — | — | — | — | — | — | — | — | — | — | — |
| AAA | PCL | 347 | 10 | 44 | 49 | 1 | .265 | .328 | .424 | 78% | 34% | 8% | 1.60 |

**Competition at CA — Stats in 2010**

| Bats | Player | GSvR | GSvL | Sub | OPS |
|---|---|---|---|---|---|
| RH | Olivo M | 69 | 38 | 4 | .765 |
| RH | Iannetta C | 28 | 21 | 3 | .701 |
| RH | Phillips P | 3 | 2 | 5 | .497 |

Ten-Year Trends

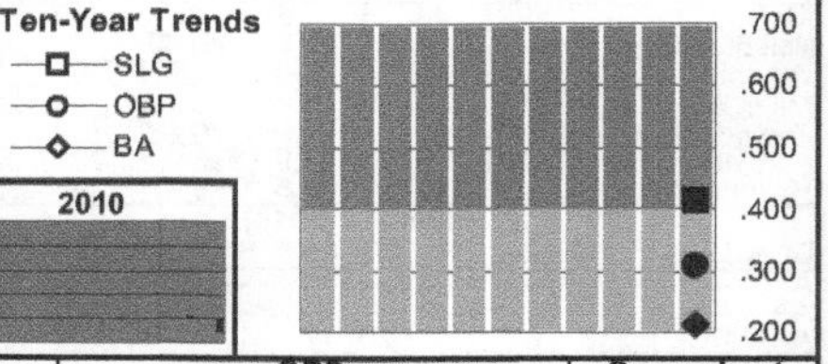


Weekly Points

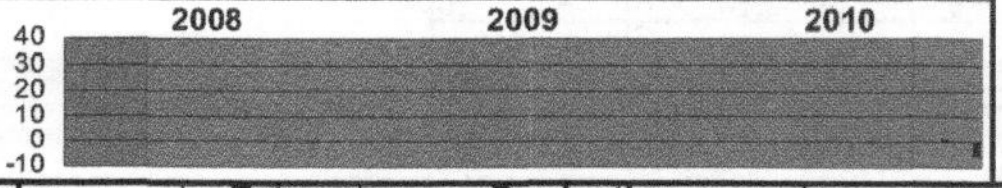


**Majors**

| Yr | Team | AB | HR | R | RBI | SB | BA | OBP | SLG | CT% | H% | BB% | Bash |
|---|---|---|---|---|---|---|---|---|---|---|---|---|---|
| 07 | — | — | — | — | — | — | — | — | — | — | — | — | — |
| 08 | — | — | — | — | — | — | — | — | — | — | — | — | — |
| 09 | — | — | — | — | — | — | — | — | — | — | — | — | — |
| 10 | COL | 8 | 0 | 0 | 0 | 0 | .000 | .111 | .000 | 38% | 0% | 11% | NA |

| Yr | Value $1L | $2L | Pts | RAA | Extra 2B | 3B | CS | Production FB-LD-GB | HR/fb | RBI% | RS% | OPS | 1st Hf | 2nd Hf | vs RH | vs LH | Scoresheet Rnge | vRH | vLH |
|---|---|---|---|---|---|---|---|---|---|---|---|---|---|---|---|---|---|---|---|
| 07 | — | — | — | — | — | — | — | — | — | — | — | — | — | — | — | — | — | — | — |
| 08 | — | — | — | — | — | — | — | — | — | — | — | — | — | — | — | — | — | — | — |
| 09 | — | — | — | — | — | — | — | — | — | — | — | — | — | — | — | — | — | — | — |
| 10 | -$3 | -$13 | 0 | −2 | 0 | 0 | 0 | 33-0-67 | 0% | 0% | NA | .111 | — | .111 | .000 | — | 0.58 | — | — |

## Nate McLouth — 425 PA | $13 | 310 pts

OF-77 (CF-71, LF-8) — Owned: 43% — LH

How can a guy bat .190 and still have an MLB job? A guaranteed contract. Atlanta does have an alternative in Rick Ankiel, but his contract isn't guaranteed, and so McLouth will probably be back. The one bright spot is that McLouth showed much better plate discipline in September (7 BB, 9 K) after his recall. (MG)

**Forecast**

| Player | Age | AB | HR | R | RBI | SB | BA | OBP | SLG | $1L | Pts |
|---|---|---|---|---|---|---|---|---|---|---|---|
| McLouth N | 29 | 383 | 17 | 64 | 51 | 17 | .266 | .361 | .471 | $13 | 310 |
| **Mini-Browser** | **Age** | **AB** | **HR** | **R** | **RBI** | **SB** | **BA** | **OBP** | **SLG** | **$1L** | **Pts** |
| Lewis F | 30 | 446 | 10 | 75 | 40 | 15 | .269 | .347 | .428 | $14 | 280 |
| Brown D | 23 | 531 | 18 | 66 | 66 | 24 | .226 | .307 | .401 | $14 | 320 |
| Colvin T | 25 | 583 | 25 | 75 | 75 | 13 | .236 | .284 | .444 | $13 | 330 |
| Borbon J | 25 | 466 | 5 | 65 | 45 | 25 | .268 | .315 | .354 | $13 | 290 |
| Stubbs D | 26 | 441 | 15 | 70 | 50 | 25 | .238 | .322 | .403 | $13 | 270 |

**Minors (2010)**

| Level | Leag | AB | HR | R | RBI | SB | BA | OBP | SLG | CT% | H% | BB% | Bash |
|---|---|---|---|---|---|---|---|---|---|---|---|---|---|
| A | — | — | — | — | — | — | — | — | — | — | — | — | — |
| AA | — | — | — | — | — | — | — | — | — | — | — | — | — |
| AAA | IL | 128 | 6 | 18 | 18 | 7 | .234 | .338 | .383 | 84% | 28% | 13% | 1.63 |

**Competition at CF — Stats in 2010**

| Bats | Player | GSvR | GSvL | Sub | OPS |
|---|---|---|---|---|---|
| LH | McLouth N | 49 | 14 | 8 | .620 |
| BH | Cabrera M | 21 | 31 | 4 | .671 |
| LH | Ankiel R | 26 | 8 | 11 | .709 |

Ten-Year Trends

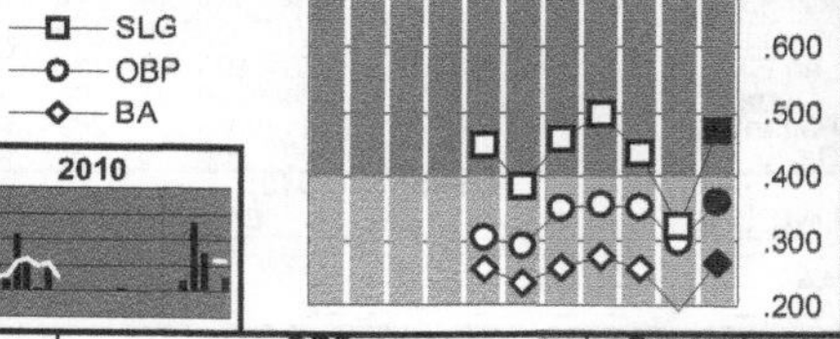


Weekly Points

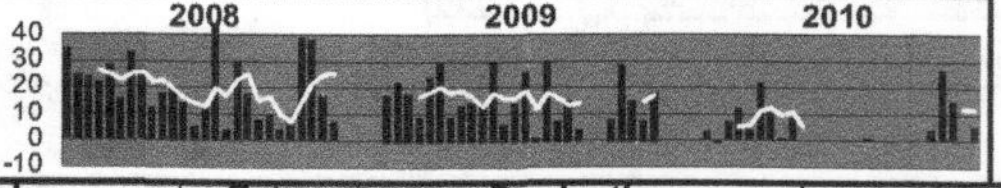


**Majors**

| Yr | Team | AB | HR | R | RBI | SB | BA | OBP | SLG | CT% | H% | BB% | Bash |
|---|---|---|---|---|---|---|---|---|---|---|---|---|---|
| 07 | PIT | 329 | 13 | 62 | 38 | 22 | .258 | .351 | .459 | 77% | 34% | 10% | 1.78 |
| 08 | PIT | 597 | 26 | 113 | 94 | 23 | .276 | .356 | .497 | 84% | 33% | 9% | 1.80 |
| 09 | 2TM | 507 | 20 | 86 | 70 | 19 | .256 | .352 | .436 | 80% | 32% | 11% | 1.70 |
| 10 | ATL | 242 | 6 | 30 | 24 | 7 | .190 | .298 | .322 | 76% | 25% | 11% | 1.70 |

| Yr | Value $1L | $2L | Pts | RAA | Extra 2B | 3B | CS | Production FB-LD-GB | HR/fb | RBI% | RS% | OPS | 1st Hf | 2nd Hf | vs RH | vs LH | Scoresheet Rnge | vRH | vLH |
|---|---|---|---|---|---|---|---|---|---|---|---|---|---|---|---|---|---|---|---|
| 07 | $12 | $2 | 260 | +8 | 21 | 3 | 1 | 53-16-31 | 10% | 18% | 41% | .810 | .695 | .868 | .828 | .739 | 2.12 | +17 | −60 |
| 08 | $29 | $23 | 520 | +19 | 46 | 4 | 3 | 47-19-35 | 11% | 27% | 40% | .853 | .899 | .781 | .908 | .710 | 2.14 | +16 | −54 |
| 09 | $20 | $11 | 380 | +8 | 27 | 2 | 6 | 43-17-40 | 11% | 22% | 35% | .788 | .832 | .723 | .833 | .688 | 2.13 | +31 | −93 |
| 10 | -$1 | -$14 | 120 | −14 | 12 | 1 | 2 | 44-16-40 | 8% | 13% | 31% | .620 | .577 | .722 | .685 | .378 | 2.15 | +36 | −97 |

## Jason Michaels — 150 PA | $-1 | 90 pts

OF-55 (LF-41, CF-11, RF-5), DH-2 — Owned: 0% — RH

Michaels' veteran presence on the bench, his single start a week, and his occasional pinch-hit appearance will once again put fans in seats in 2011. He put up one of his better offensive seasons in 2010 but is fairly consistent at the plate. He still has some pop, but in his limited role, he's not a double-digit HR threat. (BJ)

**Forecast**

| Player | Age | AB | HR | R | RBI | SB | BA | OBP | SLG | $1L | Pts |
|---|---|---|---|---|---|---|---|---|---|---|---|
| Michaels J | 34 | 140 | 5 | 18 | 20 | 2 | .258 | .323 | .427 | -$1 | 90 |
| **Mini-Browser** | **Age** | **AB** | **HR** | **R** | **RBI** | **SB** | **BA** | **OBP** | **SLG** | **$1L** | **Pts** |
| Patterson E | 27 | 127 | 3 | 18 | 14 | 8 | .248 | .313 | .405 | $0 | 80 |
| Gibbons J | 34 | 142 | 4 | 16 | 22 | 0 | .276 | .304 | .437 | $0 | 90 |
| Bonifacio E | 25 | 160 | 2 | 25 | 11 | 9 | .251 | .307 | .332 | $0 | 90 |
| Harris W | 32 | 124 | 3 | 20 | 14 | 5 | .254 | .356 | .427 | $0 | 90 |
| Martinez F | 22 | 188 | 6 | 22 | 20 | 2 | .245 | .299 | .410 | -$1 | 90 |

**Minors (2010)**

| Level | Leag | AB | HR | R | RBI | SB | BA | OBP | SLG | CT% | H% | BB% | Bash |
|---|---|---|---|---|---|---|---|---|---|---|---|---|---|
| A | — | — | — | — | — | — | — | — | — | — | — | — | — |
| AA | — | — | — | — | — | — | — | — | — | — | — | — | — |
| AAA | — | — | — | — | — | — | — | — | — | — | — | — | — |

**Competition at LF — Stats in 2010**

| Bats | Player | GSvR | GSvL | Sub | OPS |
|---|---|---|---|---|---|
| RH | Lee C | 103 | 30 | 0 | .708 |
| RH | Michaels J | 5 | 15 | 21 | .778 |
| RH | Bourgeois J | 2 | 4 | 19 | .562 |
| LH | Sullivan C | 4 | 0 | 9 | .492 |

Ten-Year Trends

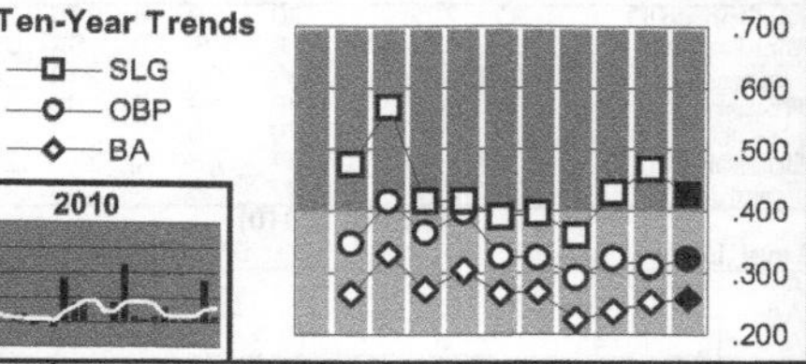


Weekly Points

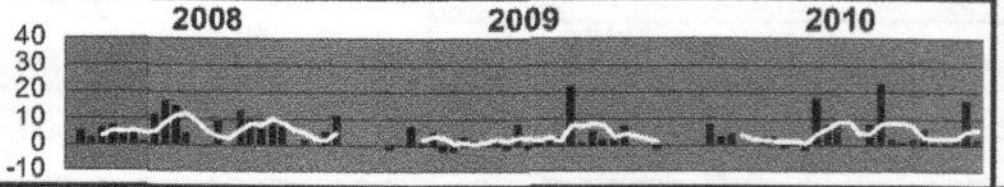


**Majors**

| Yr | Team | AB | HR | R | RBI | SB | BA | OBP | SLG | CT% | H% | BB% | Bash |
|---|---|---|---|---|---|---|---|---|---|---|---|---|---|
| 07 | CLE | 267 | 7 | 43 | 39 | 3 | .270 | .324 | .397 | 81% | 33% | 7% | 1.47 |
| 08 | 2TM | 286 | 8 | 28 | 53 | 2 | .224 | .292 | .360 | 77% | 29% | 8% | 1.61 |
| 09 | HOU | 135 | 4 | 17 | 16 | 1 | .237 | .322 | .430 | 72% | 33% | 11% | 1.81 |
| 10 | HOU | 186 | 8 | 23 | 26 | 0 | .253 | .310 | .468 | 84% | 30% | 6% | 1.85 |

| Yr | Value $1L | $2L | Pts | RAA | Extra 2B | 3B | CS | Production FB-LD-GB | HR/fb | RBI% | RS% | OPS | 1st Hf | 2nd Hf | vs RH | vs LH | Scoresheet Rnge | vRH | vLH |
|---|---|---|---|---|---|---|---|---|---|---|---|---|---|---|---|---|---|---|---|
| 07 | $6 | -$6 | 160 | −8 | 11 | 1 | 4 | 46-17-37 | 7% | 21% | 41% | .721 | .795 | .606 | .636 | .800 | 2.12 | −29 | +59 |
| 08 | -$2 | -$9 | 150 | −14 | 13 | 1 | 1 | 43-19-38 | 8% | 24% | 24% | .652 | .665 | .635 | .718 | .509 | 2.10 | −33 | +63 |
| 09 | -$1 | -$16 | 70 | −2 | 12 | 1 | 2 | 48-21-31 | 9% | 14% | 29% | .752 | .580 | .957 | .744 | .763 | 2.10 | −15 | +29 |
| 10 | $2 | -$11 | 120 | −2 | 14 | 1 | 0 | 48-18-34 | 11% | 19% | 27% | .778 | .736 | .819 | .685 | .876 | 2.11 | −3 | +7 |

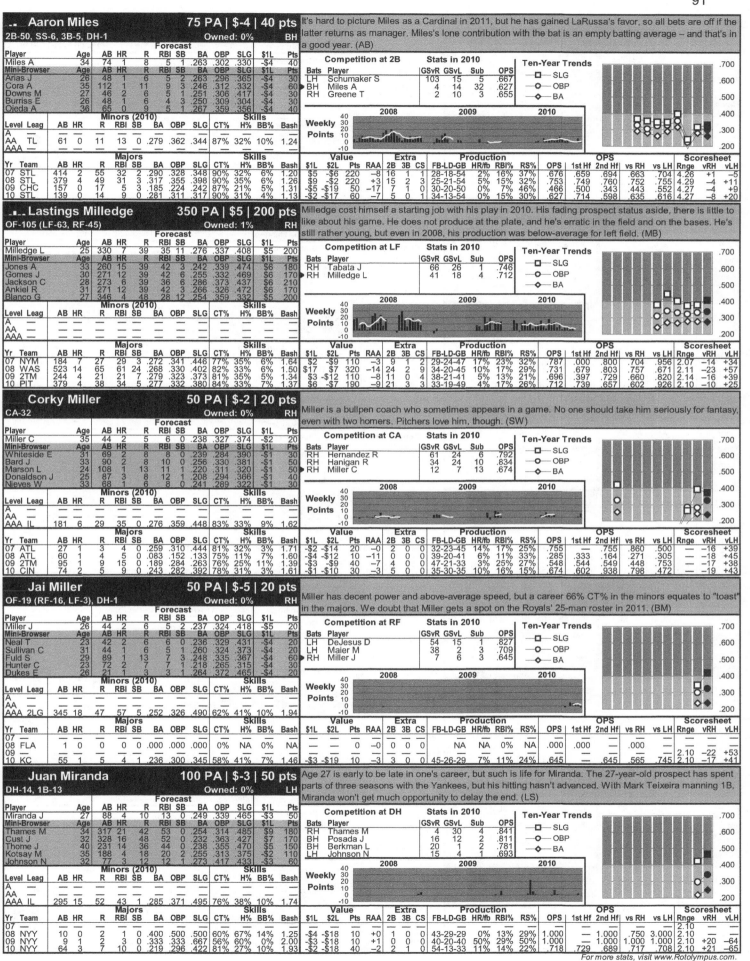

## Aaron Miles — 75 PA | $-4 | 40 pts
2B-50, SS-6, 3B-5, DH-1  Owned: 0%  BH

It's hard to picture Miles as a Cardinal in 2011, but he has gained LaRussa's favor, so all bets are off if the latter returns as manager. Miles's lone contribution with the bat is an empty batting average – and that's in a good year. (AB)

### Forecast
| Player | Age | AB | HR | R | RBI | SB | BA | OBP | SLG | $1L | Pts |
|---|---|---|---|---|---|---|---|---|---|---|---|
| Miles A | 34 | 74 | 1 | 8 | 5 | 1 | .263 | .302 | .330 | -$4 | 40 |
| Mini-Browser | Age | AB | HR | R | RBI | SB | BA | OBP | SLG | $1L | Pts |
| Arias J | 26 | 48 | 1 | 6 | 5 | 2 | .263 | .296 | .365 | -$4 | 30 |
| Cora A | 35 | 112 | 1 | 11 | 9 | 3 | .246 | .312 | .332 | -$4 | 60 |
| Downs M | 27 | 46 | 2 | 6 | 5 | 1 | .251 | .306 | .417 | -$4 | 30 |
| Burriss E | 26 | 48 | 1 | 6 | 4 | 3 | .250 | .309 | .304 | -$4 | 30 |
| Ojeda A | 36 | 65 | 0 | 9 | 5 | 1 | .267 | .359 | .359 | -$4 | 40 |

### Competition at 2B / Stats in 2010
| Bats | Player | GSvR | GSvL | Sub | OPS |
|---|---|---|---|---|---|
| LH | Schumaker S | 103 | 15 | 5 | .667 |
| BH | Miles A | 4 | 14 | 32 | .627 |
| RH | Greene T | 2 | 10 | 3 | .655 |

### Minors (2010) / Skills
| Level | Leag | AB | HR | R | RBI | SB | BA | OBP | SLG | CT% | H% | BB% | Bash |
|---|---|---|---|---|---|---|---|---|---|---|---|---|---|
| A | — | | | | | | | | | | | | |
| AA | TL | 61 | 0 | 11 | 13 | 0 | .279 | .362 | .344 | 87% | 32% | 10% | 1.24 |
| AAA | — | | | | | | | | | | | | |

### Majors
| Yr | Team | AB | HR | R | RBI | SB | BA | OBP | SLG | CT% | H% | BB% | Bash | $1L | $2L | Pts | RAA | 2B | 3B | CS | FB-LD-GB | HR/fb | RBI% | RS% | OPS | 1st Hf | 2nd Hf | vs RH | vs LH | Rnge | vRH | vLH |
|---|---|---|---|---|---|---|---|---|---|---|---|---|---|---|---|---|---|---|---|---|---|---|---|---|---|---|---|---|---|---|---|---|
| 07 | STL | 414 | 2 | 55 | 32 | 2 | .290 | .328 | .348 | 90% | 32% | 6% | 1.20 | -$5 | -$6 | 220 | -8 | 16 | 1 | 1 | 28-18-54 | 2% | 16% | 37% | .676 | .659 | .694 | .663 | .704 | 4.26 | +1 | -5 |
| 08 | STL | 379 | 4 | 49 | 31 | 3 | .317 | .355 | .398 | 90% | 35% | 6% | 1.26 | $9 | -$2 | 220 | +3 | 15 | 2 | 3 | 25-21-54 | 5% | 15% | 32% | .753 | .749 | .760 | .752 | .704 | 4.29 | -4 | +11 |
| 09 | CHC | 157 | 0 | 17 | 5 | 3 | .185 | .224 | .242 | 87% | 21% | 5% | 1.31 | -$5 | -$19 | 50 | -17 | 7 | 1 | 0 | 30-20-50 | 0% | 7% | 46% | .466 | .500 | .343 | .443 | .552 | 4.27 | -4 | +9 |
| 10 | STL | 139 | 0 | 14 | 9 | 0 | .281 | .311 | .317 | 90% | 31% | 4% | 1.13 | -$2 | -$17 | 60 | -7 | 5 | 1 | 0 | 34-13-54 | 0% | 15% | 30% | .627 | .714 | .635 | .616 | .627 | 4.27 | -8 | +20 |

## Lastings Milledge — 350 PA | $5 | 200 pts
OF-105 (LF-63, RF-45)  Owned: 1%  RH

Milledge cost himself a starting job with his play in 2010. His fading prospect status aside, there is little to like about his game. He does not produce at the plate, and he's erratic in the field and on the bases. He's still rather young, but even in 2008, his production was below-average for left field. (MB)

### Forecast
| Player | Age | AB | HR | R | RBI | SB | BA | OBP | SLG | $1L | Pts |
|---|---|---|---|---|---|---|---|---|---|---|---|
| Milledge L | 25 | 330 | 7 | 39 | 35 | 11 | .276 | .337 | .408 | $5 | 200 |
| Mini-Browser | Age | AB | HR | R | RBI | SB | BA | OBP | SLG | $1L | Pts |
| Jones C | 33 | 260 | 15 | 39 | 42 | 3 | .242 | .339 | .474 | $6 | 180 |
| Gomes J | 30 | 271 | 12 | 39 | 42 | 6 | .255 | .332 | .469 | $6 | 170 |
| Jackson C | 28 | 271 | 12 | 39 | 36 | 6 | .266 | .373 | .437 | $6 | 210 |
| Ankiel R | 31 | 271 | 12 | 39 | 42 | 3 | .266 | .326 | .472 | $6 | 170 |
| Blanco G | 27 | 346 | 4 | 48 | 28 | 12 | .254 | .359 | .332 | $5 | 200 |

### Competition at LF / Stats in 2010
| Bats | Player | GSvR | GSvL | Sub | OPS |
|---|---|---|---|---|---|
| RH | Tabata J | 66 | 26 | 1 | .746 |
| RH | Milledge L | 41 | 18 | 4 | .712 |

### Majors
| Yr | Team | AB | HR | R | RBI | SB | BA | OBP | SLG | CT% | H% | BB% | Bash | $1L | $2L | Pts | RAA | 2B | 3B | CS | FB-LD-GB | HR/fb | RBI% | RS% | OPS | 1st Hf | 2nd Hf | vs RH | vs LH | Rnge | vRH | vLH |
|---|---|---|---|---|---|---|---|---|---|---|---|---|---|---|---|---|---|---|---|---|---|---|---|---|---|---|---|---|---|---|---|---|
| 07 | NYM | 184 | 7 | 27 | 29 | 3 | .272 | .341 | .446 | 77% | 35% | 6% | 1.64 | $2 | -$9 | 110 | -3 | 9 | 1 | 2 | 29-24-47 | 17% | 23% | 32% | .787 | .000 | .800 | .704 | .956 | 2.07 | -14 | +34 |
| 08 | WAS | 523 | 14 | 65 | 61 | 24 | .268 | .330 | .402 | 82% | 33% | 6% | 1.50 | $17 | $7 | 320 | -14 | 24 | 2 | 9 | 34-20-45 | 10% | 17% | 29% | .731 | .679 | .803 | .757 | .671 | 2.11 | -23 | +57 |
| 09 | 2TM | 244 | 4 | 21 | 21 | 7 | .279 | .323 | .373 | 81% | 35% | 5% | 1.34 | $5 | -$12 | 110 | -8 | 11 | 0 | 4 | 38-21-41 | 5% | 13% | 21% | .696 | .397 | .729 | .660 | .820 | 2.14 | -16 | +34 |
| 10 | PIT | 379 | 4 | 38 | 34 | 5 | .277 | .332 | .380 | 84% | 33% | 7% | 1.37 | $6 | -$7 | 190 | -9 | 21 | 3 | 3 | 33-19-49 | 4% | 17% | 26% | .712 | .739 | .657 | .602 | .926 | 2.10 | -10 | +25 |

## Corky Miller — 50 PA | $-2 | 20 pts
CA-32  Owned: 0%  RH

Miller is a bullpen coach who sometimes appears in a game. No one should take him seriously for fantasy, even with two homers. Pitchers love him, though. (SW)

### Forecast
| Player | Age | AB | HR | R | RBI | SB | BA | OBP | SLG | $1L | Pts |
|---|---|---|---|---|---|---|---|---|---|---|---|
| Miller C | 35 | 44 | 2 | 5 | 6 | 0 | .238 | .327 | .374 | -$2 | 20 |
| Mini-Browser | Age | AB | HR | R | RBI | SB | BA | OBP | SLG | $1L | Pts |
| Whiteside E | 31 | 69 | 2 | 8 | 8 | 0 | .239 | .284 | .390 | -$1 | 30 |
| Bard J | 33 | 90 | 2 | 8 | 10 | 0 | .256 | .330 | .381 | -$1 | 30 |
| Marson L | 24 | 108 | 1 | 13 | 11 | 1 | .220 | .311 | .320 | -$1 | 50 |
| Donaldson J | 25 | 87 | 3 | 8 | 12 | 1 | .208 | .294 | .366 | -$1 | 40 |
| Nieves W | 33 | 68 | 2 | 6 | 8 | 0 | .241 | .289 | .322 | -$1 | 30 |

### Competition at CA / Stats in 2010
| Bats | Player | GSvR | GSvL | Sub | OPS |
|---|---|---|---|---|---|
| RH | Hernandez R | 61 | 24 | 6 | .792 |
| RH | Hanigan R | 34 | 24 | 10 | .834 |
| RH | Miller C | 12 | 7 | 13 | .674 |

### Minors (2010) / Skills
| Level | Leag | AB | HR | R | RBI | SB | BA | OBP | SLG | CT% | H% | BB% | Bash |
|---|---|---|---|---|---|---|---|---|---|---|---|---|---|
| A | — | | | | | | | | | | | | |
| AA | — | | | | | | | | | | | | |
| AAA | IL | 181 | 6 | 29 | 35 | 0 | .276 | .359 | .448 | 83% | 33% | 9% | 1.62 |

### Majors
| Yr | Team | AB | HR | R | RBI | SB | BA | OBP | SLG | CT% | H% | BB% | Bash | $1L | $2L | Pts | RAA | 2B | 3B | CS | FB-LD-GB | HR/fb | RBI% | RS% | OPS | 1st Hf | 2nd Hf | vs RH | vs LH | Rnge | vRH | vLH |
|---|---|---|---|---|---|---|---|---|---|---|---|---|---|---|---|---|---|---|---|---|---|---|---|---|---|---|---|---|---|---|---|---|
| 07 | ATL | 27 | 1 | 3 | 4 | 0 | .259 | .310 | .444 | 81% | 32% | 3% | 1.71 | -$2 | -$14 | 20 | -0 | 2 | 0 | 0 | 32-23-45 | 14% | 17% | 25% | .755 | — | .755 | .860 | .500 | — | -16 | +39 |
| 08 | ATL | 60 | 1 | 4 | 5 | 0 | .083 | .152 | .133 | 75% | 11% | 7% | 1.60 | -$4 | -$12 | 10 | -11 | 0 | 0 | 0 | 39-20-41 | 6% | 11% | 33% | .285 | .333 | .164 | .271 | .305 | — | -18 | +45 |
| 09 | 2TM | 95 | 1 | 9 | 15 | 0 | .189 | .284 | .263 | 76% | 25% | 11% | 1.39 | -$3 | -$9 | 40 | -7 | 4 | 0 | 0 | 47-21-33 | 3% | 25% | 27% | .548 | .544 | .549 | .448 | .753 | — | -17 | +38 |
| 10 | CIN | 74 | 2 | 5 | 9 | 0 | .243 | .282 | .392 | 78% | 31% | 3% | 1.61 | -$3 | -$10 | 20 | -3 | 5 | 0 | 0 | 35-30-35 | 10% | 16% | 15% | .674 | .602 | .938 | .798 | .472 | — | -19 | +43 |

## Jai Miller — 50 PA | $-5 | 20 pts
OF-19 (RF-16, LF-3), DH-1  Owned: 0%  RH

Miller has decent power and above-average speed, but a career 66% CT% in the minors equates to "toast" in the majors. We doubt that Miller gets a spot on the Royals' 25-man roster in 2011. (BM)

### Forecast
| Player | Age | AB | HR | R | RBI | SB | BA | OBP | SLG | $1L | Pts |
|---|---|---|---|---|---|---|---|---|---|---|---|
| Miller J | 26 | 44 | 2 | 6 | 5 | 2 | .237 | .324 | .418 | -$5 | 20 |
| Mini-Browser | Age | AB | HR | R | RBI | SB | BA | OBP | SLG | $1L | Pts |
| Neal T | 23 | 42 | 2 | 6 | 6 | 0 | .236 | .329 | .431 | -$4 | 20 |
| Sullivan C | 31 | 44 | 1 | 6 | 5 | 1 | .260 | .324 | .373 | -$4 | 20 |
| Fuld S | 29 | 89 | 1 | 13 | 7 | 7 | .248 | .335 | .367 | -$4 | 60 |
| Hunter C | 23 | 72 | 2 | 7 | 7 | 1 | .218 | .265 | .315 | -$4 | 20 |
| Dukes E | 26 | 21 | 1 | 3 | 3 | 1 | .264 | .372 | .465 | -$4 | 20 |

### Competition at RF / Stats in 2010
| Bats | Player | GSvR | GSvL | Sub | OPS |
|---|---|---|---|---|---|
| LH | DeJesus D | 54 | 15 | 1 | .827 |
| LH | Maier M | 38 | 2 | 3 | .709 |
| RH | Miller J | 7 | 6 | 3 | .645 |

### Minors (2010) / Skills
| Level | Leag | AB | HR | R | RBI | SB | BA | OBP | SLG | CT% | H% | BB% | Bash |
|---|---|---|---|---|---|---|---|---|---|---|---|---|---|
| A | — | | | | | | | | | | | | |
| AA | — | | | | | | | | | | | | |
| AAA | 2LG | 345 | 18 | 47 | 57 | 5 | .252 | .326 | .490 | 62% | 41% | 10% | 1.94 |

### Majors
| Yr | Team | AB | HR | R | RBI | SB | BA | OBP | SLG | CT% | H% | BB% | Bash | $1L | $2L | Pts | RAA | 2B | 3B | CS | FB-LD-GB | HR/fb | RBI% | RS% | OPS | 1st Hf | 2nd Hf | vs RH | vs LH | Rnge | vRH | vLH |
|---|---|---|---|---|---|---|---|---|---|---|---|---|---|---|---|---|---|---|---|---|---|---|---|---|---|---|---|---|---|---|---|---|
| 07 | — | | | | | | | | | | | | | | | | | | | | | | | | | | | | | 2.10 | | |
| 08 | FLA | 1 | 0 | 0 | 0 | 0 | .000 | .000 | .000 | 0% | NA | 0% | NA | — | — | 0 | -0 | 0 | 0 | 0 | NA | NA | 0% | NA | .000 | .000 | — | .000 | — | 2.10 | -22 | +53 |
| 09 | — | | | | | | | | | | | | | | | | | | | | | | | | | | | | | 2.10 | | |
| 10 | KC | 55 | 1 | 5 | 4 | 1 | .236 | .300 | .345 | 58% | 41% | 7% | 1.46 | -$3 | -$19 | 20 | -2 | 1 | 0 | 0 | 45-26-29 | 7% | 11% | 24% | .645 | — | .645 | .565 | .745 | 2.10 | -17 | +41 |

## Juan Miranda — 100 PA | $-3 | 50 pts
DH-14, 1B-13  Owned: 0%  LH

Age 27 is early to be late in one's career, but such is life for Miranda. The 27-year-old prospect has spent parts of three seasons with the Yankees, but his hitting hasn't advanced. With Mark Teixeira manning 1B, Miranda won't get much opportunity to delay the end. (LS)

### Forecast
| Player | Age | AB | HR | R | RBI | SB | BA | OBP | SLG | $1L | Pts |
|---|---|---|---|---|---|---|---|---|---|---|---|
| Miranda J | 27 | 88 | 4 | 10 | 13 | 0 | .249 | .339 | .465 | -$3 | 50 |
| Mini-Browser | Age | AB | HR | R | RBI | SB | BA | OBP | SLG | $1L | Pts |
| Thames M | 34 | 317 | 21 | 42 | 53 | 0 | .254 | .314 | .485 | $9 | 180 |
| Cust J | 32 | 328 | 16 | 48 | 52 | 0 | .232 | .363 | .427 | $7 | 170 |
| Thome J | 40 | 231 | 14 | 36 | 44 | 0 | .238 | .355 | .470 | $5 | 150 |
| Kotsay M | 35 | 188 | 4 | 18 | 20 | 2 | .255 | .313 | .375 | -$2 | 110 |
| Johnson N | 32 | 77 | 3 | 12 | 12 | 1 | .273 | .417 | .433 | -$3 | 50 |

### Competition at DH / Stats in 2010
| Bats | Player | GSvR | GSvL | Sub | OPS |
|---|---|---|---|---|---|
| RH | Thames M | 4 | 30 | 4 | .841 |
| BH | Posada J | 16 | 12 | 2 | .811 |
| BH | Berkman L | 20 | 1 | 2 | .781 |
| LH | Johnson N | 15 | 4 | 1 | .693 |

### Minors (2010) / Skills
| Level | Leag | AB | HR | R | RBI | SB | BA | OBP | SLG | CT% | H% | BB% | Bash |
|---|---|---|---|---|---|---|---|---|---|---|---|---|---|
| A | — | | | | | | | | | | | | |
| AA | — | | | | | | | | | | | | |
| AAA | IL | 295 | 15 | 52 | 43 | 1 | .285 | .371 | .495 | 76% | 38% | 10% | 1.74 |

### Majors
| Yr | Team | AB | HR | R | RBI | SB | BA | OBP | SLG | CT% | H% | BB% | Bash | $1L | $2L | Pts | RAA | 2B | 3B | CS | FB-LD-GB | HR/fb | RBI% | RS% | OPS | 1st Hf | 2nd Hf | vs RH | vs LH | Rnge | vRH | vLH |
|---|---|---|---|---|---|---|---|---|---|---|---|---|---|---|---|---|---|---|---|---|---|---|---|---|---|---|---|---|---|---|---|---|
| 07 | — | | | | | | | | | | | | | | | | | | | | | | | | | | | | | 2.10 | | |
| 08 | NYY | 10 | 0 | 2 | 1 | 0 | .400 | .500 | .500 | 60% | 67% | 14% | 1.25 | -$4 | -$18 | 10 | +0 | 1 | 0 | 0 | 43-29-29 | 0% | 13% | 29% | 1.000 | — | 1.000 | .750 | 3.000 | 2.10 | — | — |
| 09 | NYY | 9 | 1 | 2 | 3 | 0 | .333 | .333 | .667 | 56% | 60% | 0% | 2.00 | -$3 | -$18 | 10 | +1 | 0 | 0 | 0 | 40-20-40 | 50% | 29% | 50% | 1.000 | — | 1.000 | .750 | — | 2.10 | +20 | -64 |
| 10 | NYY | 64 | 3 | 7 | 10 | 0 | .219 | .296 | .422 | 81% | 27% | 10% | 1.93 | -$3 | -$18 | 40 | -2 | 2 | 1 | 0 | 54-13-33 | 11% | 14% | 22% | .718 | .729 | .689 | .717 | .708 | 2.10 | +21 | -65 |

## Russell Mitchell — 100 PA | $-4 | 40 pts

No MLB games played in 2010 — Owned: 0% — RH

Mitchell's performance in Triple-A was fueled largely by the offensive haven of his home park, and he contributed little in a September call-up. However, he makes the minimum and offers nice versatility by manning five positions, and that might be enough to earn him a spot on the Dodger bench in 2011. (MP)

### Forecast

| Player | Age | AB | HR | R | RBI | SB | BA | OBP | SLG | $1L | Pts |
|---|---|---|---|---|---|---|---|---|---|---|---|
| Mitchell R | 26 | 94 | 4 | 9 | 10 | 0 | .203 | .249 | .376 | -$4 | 40 |

| Mini-Browser | Age | AB | HR | R | RBI | SB | BA | OBP | SLG | $1L | Pts |
|---|---|---|---|---|---|---|---|---|---|---|---|
| LaRoche A | 27 | 88 | 3 | 11 | 10 | 1 | .261 | .343 | .410 | -$3 | 50 |
| Marte A | 27 | 94 | 4 | 10 | 12 | 0 | .254 | .307 | .433 | -$3 | 50 |
| Pena R | 25 | 144 | 2 | 15 | 12 | 5 | .229 | .285 | .302 | -$3 | 50 |
| Darnell J | 24 | 87 | 4 | 9 | 11 | 1 | .208 | .311 | .393 | -$4 | 50 |
| Hicks B | 25 | 71 | 5 | 9 | 7 | 2 | .201 | .293 | .390 | -$4 | 40 |

### Minors (2010) / Skills

| Level | Leag | AB | HR | R | RBI | SB | BA | OBP | SLG | CT% | H% | BB% | Bash |
|---|---|---|---|---|---|---|---|---|---|---|---|---|---|
| A | — | | | | | | | | | | | | |
| AA | — | | | | | | | | | | | | |
| AAA | PCL | 505 | 23 | 97 | 87 | 1 | .315 | .363 | .535 | 85% | 37% | 7% | 1.70 |

### Majors / Skills / Value / Extra / Production / OPS / Scoresheet

| Yr | Team | AB | HR | R | RBI | SB | BA | OBP | SLG | CT% | H% | BB% | Bash |
|---|---|---|---|---|---|---|---|---|---|---|---|---|---|
| 07 | — | | | | | | | | | | | | |
| 08 | — | | | | | | | | | | | | |
| 09 | — | | | | | | | | | | | | |
| 10 | — | | | | | | | | | | | | |

**Competition at 3B** — Stats in 2010

| Bats | Player | GSvR | GSvL | Sub | OPS |
|---|---|---|---|---|---|
| RH | Blake C | 89 | 45 | 5 | .727 |
| RH | Belliard R | 11 | 4 | 1 | .622 |
| RH | Carroll J | 8 | 2 | 1 | .718 |

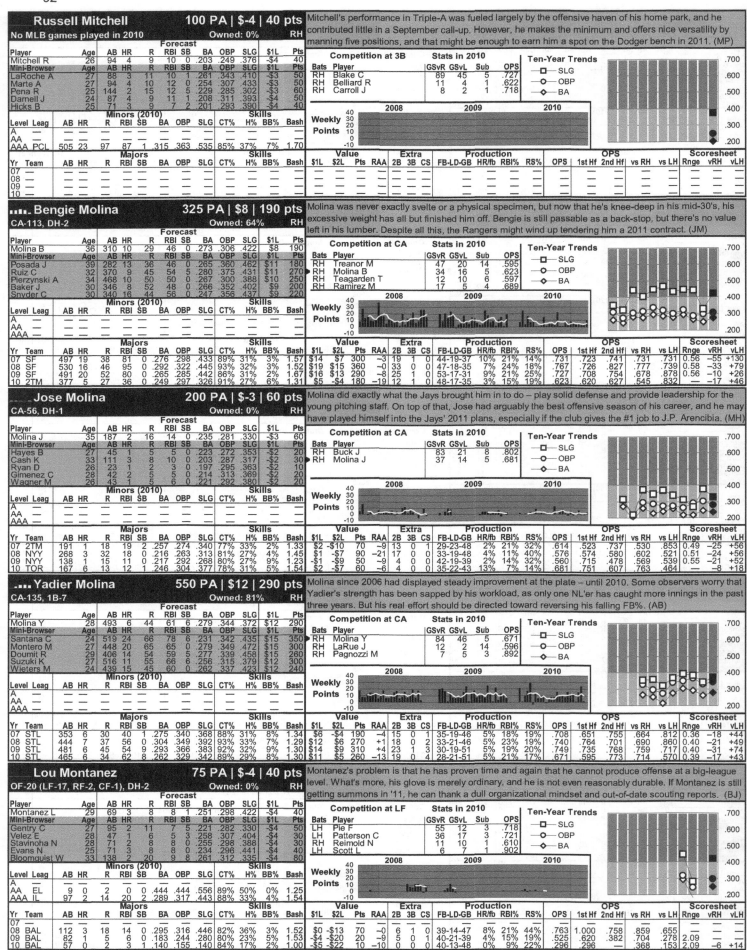

---

## Bengie Molina — 325 PA | $8 | 190 pts

CA-113, DH-2 — Owned: 64% — RH

Molina was never exactly svelte or a physical specimen, but now that he's knee-deep in his mid-30's, his excessive weight has all but finished him off. Bengie is still passable as a back-stop, but there's no value left in his lumber. Despite all this, the Rangers might wind up tendering him a 2011 contract. (JM)

### Forecast

| Player | Age | AB | HR | R | RBI | SB | BA | OBP | SLG | $1L | Pts |
|---|---|---|---|---|---|---|---|---|---|---|---|
| Molina B | 36 | 310 | 10 | 29 | 46 | 0 | .273 | .306 | .422 | $8 | 190 |

| Mini-Browser | Age | AB | HR | R | RBI | SB | BA | OBP | SLG | $1L | Pts |
|---|---|---|---|---|---|---|---|---|---|---|---|
| Posada J | 39 | 282 | 13 | 36 | 46 | 0 | .265 | .360 | .462 | $11 | 180 |
| Ruiz C | 32 | 370 | 9 | 45 | 54 | 1 | .280 | .375 | .431 | $11 | 270 |
| Pierzynski A | 34 | 468 | 10 | 50 | 50 | 0 | .267 | .300 | .388 | $10 | 250 |
| Baker J | 30 | 346 | 8 | 52 | 48 | 1 | .266 | .352 | .402 | $9 | 200 |
| Snyder C | 30 | 340 | 16 | 44 | 56 | 0 | .247 | .356 | .437 | $9 | 220 |

### Minors (2010) / Skills

| Level | Leag | AB | HR | R | RBI | SB | BA | OBP | SLG | CT% | H% | BB% | Bash |
|---|---|---|---|---|---|---|---|---|---|---|---|---|---|
| A | — | | | | | | | | | | | | |
| AA | — | | | | | | | | | | | | |
| AAA | — | | | | | | | | | | | | |

### Majors

| Yr | Team | AB | HR | R | RBI | SB | BA | OBP | SLG | CT% | H% | BB% | Bash | $1L | $2L | Pts | RAA | 2B | 3B | CS | FB-LD-GB | HR/fb | RBI% | RS% | OPS | 1st Hf | 2nd Hf | vs RH | vs LH | Rnge | vRH | vLH |
|---|---|---|---|---|---|---|---|---|---|---|---|---|---|---|---|---|---|---|---|---|---|---|---|---|---|---|---|---|---|---|---|---|
| 07 | SF | 497 | 19 | 38 | 81 | 0 | .276 | .298 | .433 | 89% | 31% | 3% | 1.57 | $14 | $7 | 300 | -3 | 19 | 1 | 0 | 44-19-37 | 10% | 21% | 14% | .731 | .723 | .741 | .731 | .731 | 0.56 | -55 | +130 |
| 08 | SF | 530 | 16 | 46 | 95 | 0 | .292 | .322 | .445 | 93% | 32% | 3% | 1.52 | $19 | $15 | 360 | -0 | 33 | 0 | 0 | 47-18-35 | 7% | 24% | 18% | .767 | .726 | .827 | .777 | .739 | 0.58 | -33 | +79 |
| 09 | SF | 491 | 20 | 52 | 80 | 0 | .265 | .285 | .442 | 86% | 31% | 2% | 1.67 | $16 | $13 | 290 | -8 | 25 | 1 | 0 | 53-17-31 | 9% | 21% | 29% | .727 | .708 | .754 | .678 | .878 | 0.56 | -10 | +26 |
| 10 | 2TM | 377 | 5 | 27 | 36 | 0 | .249 | .297 | .326 | 91% | 27% | 6% | 1.31 | $5 | -$4 | 180 | -19 | 12 | 1 | 0 | 48-17-35 | 3% | 15% | 19% | .623 | .620 | .627 | .545 | .832 | — | -17 | +46 |

**Competition at CA** — Stats in 2010

| Bats | Player | GSvR | GSvL | Sub | OPS |
|---|---|---|---|---|---|
| RH | Treanor M | 47 | 20 | 14 | .595 |
| RH | Molina B | 34 | 16 | 5 | .623 |
| RH | Teagarden T | 12 | 10 | 6 | .597 |
| RH | Ramirez M | 17 | 5 | 4 | .689 |

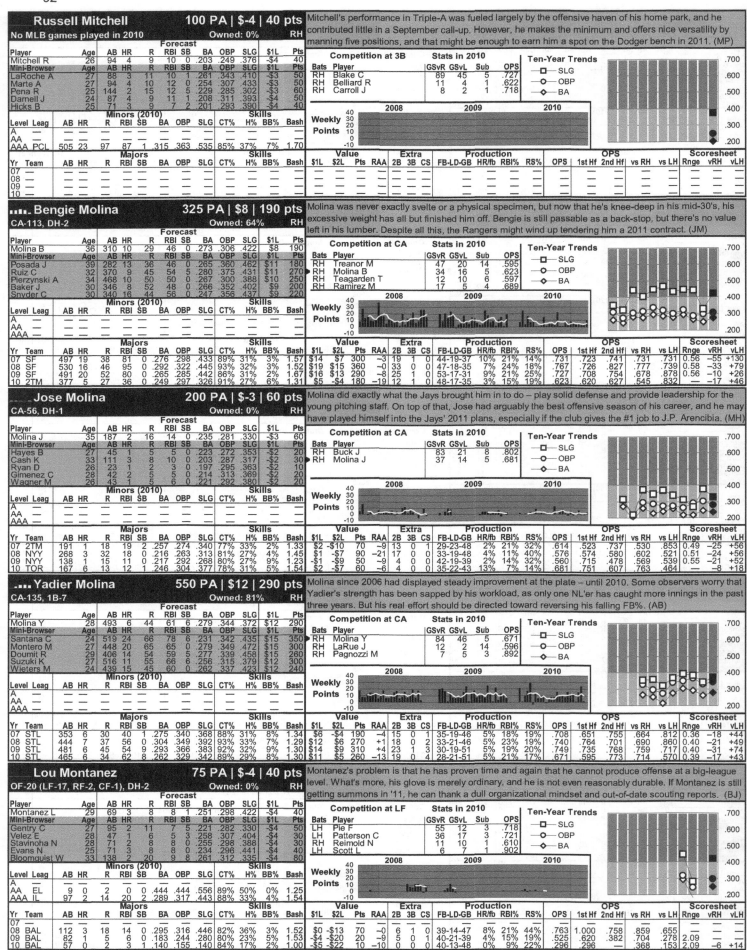

---

## Jose Molina — 200 PA | $-3 | 60 pts

CA-56, DH-1 — Owned: 0% — RH

Molina did exactly what the Jays brought him in to do – play solid defense and provide leadership for the young pitching staff. On top of that, Jose had arguably the best offensive season of his career, and he may have played himself into the Jays' 2011 plans, especially if the club gives the #1 job to J.P. Arencibia. (MH)

### Forecast

| Player | Age | AB | HR | R | RBI | SB | BA | OBP | SLG | $1L | Pts |
|---|---|---|---|---|---|---|---|---|---|---|---|
| Molina J | 35 | 187 | 2 | 16 | 14 | 0 | .235 | .281 | .330 | -$3 | 60 |

| Mini-Browser | Age | AB | HR | R | RBI | SB | BA | OBP | SLG | $1L | Pts |
|---|---|---|---|---|---|---|---|---|---|---|---|
| Hayes B | 27 | 45 | 1 | 5 | 5 | 0 | .223 | .272 | .353 | -$2 | 20 |
| Cash K | 33 | 111 | 3 | 8 | 10 | 0 | .203 | .287 | .317 | -$2 | 30 |
| Ryan D | 26 | 23 | 1 | 2 | 3 | 0 | .197 | .295 | .363 | -$2 | 10 |
| Gimenez C | 28 | 42 | 2 | 5 | 5 | 0 | .214 | .313 | .369 | -$2 | 20 |
| Wagner M | 26 | 43 | 1 | 4 | 6 | 0 | .221 | .292 | .380 | -$2 | 20 |

### Minors (2010) / Skills

| Level | Leag | AB | HR | R | RBI | SB | BA | OBP | SLG | CT% | H% | BB% | Bash |
|---|---|---|---|---|---|---|---|---|---|---|---|---|---|
| A | — | | | | | | | | | | | | |
| AA | — | | | | | | | | | | | | |
| AAA | — | | | | | | | | | | | | |

### Majors

| Yr | Team | AB | HR | R | RBI | SB | BA | OBP | SLG | CT% | H% | BB% | Bash | $1L | $2L | Pts | RAA | 2B | 3B | CS | FB-LD-GB | HR/fb | RBI% | RS% | OPS | 1st Hf | 2nd Hf | vs RH | vs LH | Rnge | vRH | vLH |
|---|---|---|---|---|---|---|---|---|---|---|---|---|---|---|---|---|---|---|---|---|---|---|---|---|---|---|---|---|---|---|---|---|
| 07 | 2TM | 191 | 1 | 18 | 19 | 2 | .257 | .274 | .340 | 77% | 33% | 2% | 1.33 | $2 | -$10 | 70 | -9 | 13 | 0 | 1 | 29-23-48 | 2% | 21% | 32% | .614 | .523 | .737 | .530 | .853 | 0.49 | -25 | +56 |
| 08 | NYY | 268 | 3 | 32 | 18 | 0 | .216 | .263 | .313 | 81% | 27% | 4% | 1.45 | $1 | -$7 | 90 | -21 | 17 | 0 | 0 | 33-19-48 | 4% | 11% | 40% | .576 | .574 | .580 | .602 | .521 | 0.51 | -24 | +56 |
| 09 | NYY | 138 | 1 | 15 | 11 | 0 | .217 | .292 | .268 | 80% | 27% | 9% | 1.23 | -$1 | -$9 | 50 | -9 | 4 | 0 | 0 | 42-19-39 | 2% | 14% | 32% | .560 | .715 | .478 | .569 | .530 | 0.55 | -21 | +52 |
| 10 | TOR | 167 | 6 | 13 | 12 | 1 | .246 | .304 | .377 | 78% | 31% | 5% | 1.54 | $2 | -$7 | 60 | -6 | 4 | 0 | 0 | 35-22-43 | 13% | 7% | 20% | .681 | .751 | .607 | .763 | .464 | — | -8 | +18 |

**Competition at CA** — Stats in 2010

| Bats | Player | GSvR | GSvL | Sub | OPS |
|---|---|---|---|---|---|
| RH | Buck J | 83 | 21 | 8 | .802 |
| RH | Molina J | 37 | 14 | 5 | .681 |

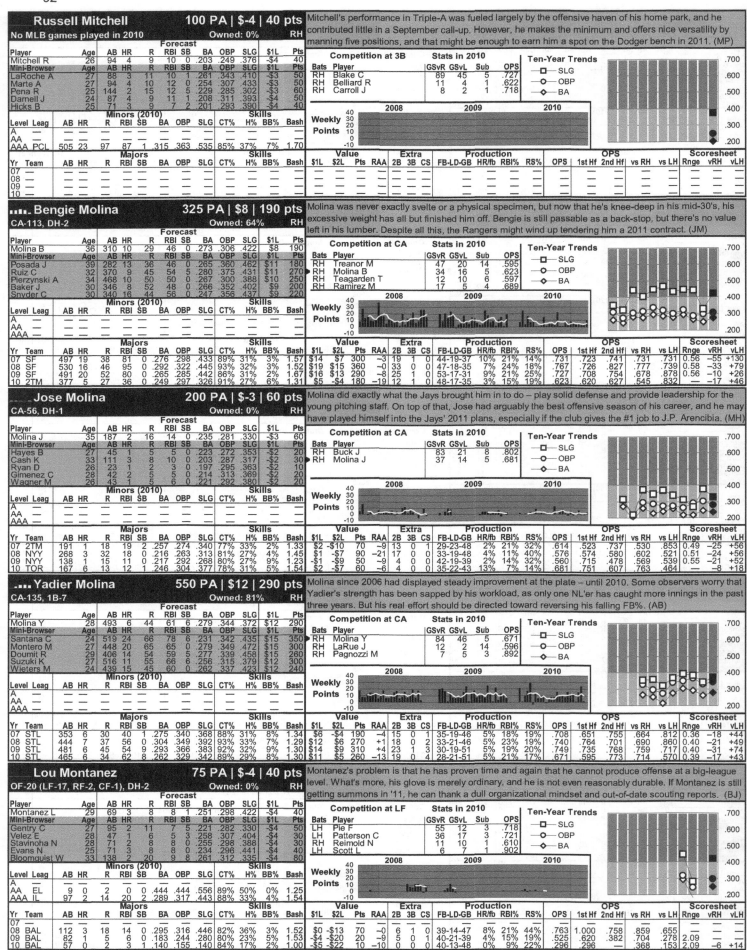

---

## Yadier Molina — 550 PA | $12 | 290 pts

CA-135, 1B-7 — Owned: 81% — RH

Molina since 2006 had displayed steady improvement at the plate – until 2010. Some observers worry that Yadier's strength has been sapped by his workload, as only one NL'er has caught more innings in the past three years. But his real effort should be directed toward reversing his falling FB%. (AB)

### Forecast

| Player | Age | AB | HR | R | RBI | SB | BA | OBP | SLG | $1L | Pts |
|---|---|---|---|---|---|---|---|---|---|---|---|
| Molina Y | 28 | 493 | 6 | 44 | 61 | 6 | .279 | .344 | .372 | $12 | 290 |

| Mini-Browser | Age | AB | HR | R | RBI | SB | BA | OBP | SLG | $1L | Pts |
|---|---|---|---|---|---|---|---|---|---|---|---|
| Santana C | 24 | 519 | 24 | 66 | 78 | 6 | .231 | .342 | .435 | $15 | 350 |
| Montero M | 27 | 448 | 20 | 65 | 65 | 0 | .279 | .349 | .472 | $15 | 300 |
| Doumit R | 29 | 406 | 14 | 54 | 59 | 5 | .277 | .339 | .458 | $15 | 260 |
| Suzuki K | 27 | 516 | 11 | 55 | 66 | 6 | .256 | .315 | .379 | $12 | 300 |
| Wieters M | 24 | 439 | 15 | 45 | 60 | 0 | .262 | .337 | .423 | $12 | 240 |

### Minors (2010) / Skills

| Level | Leag | AB | HR | R | RBI | SB | BA | OBP | SLG | CT% | H% | BB% | Bash |
|---|---|---|---|---|---|---|---|---|---|---|---|---|---|
| A | — | | | | | | | | | | | | |
| AA | — | | | | | | | | | | | | |
| AAA | — | | | | | | | | | | | | |

### Majors

| Yr | Team | AB | HR | R | RBI | SB | BA | OBP | SLG | CT% | H% | BB% | Bash | $1L | $2L | Pts | RAA | 2B | 3B | CS | FB-LD-GB | HR/fb | RBI% | RS% | OPS | 1st Hf | 2nd Hf | vs RH | vs LH | Rnge | vRH | vLH |
|---|---|---|---|---|---|---|---|---|---|---|---|---|---|---|---|---|---|---|---|---|---|---|---|---|---|---|---|---|---|---|---|---|
| 07 | STL | 353 | 6 | 30 | 40 | 1 | .275 | .340 | .368 | 88% | 31% | 8% | 1.34 | $6 | -$4 | 190 | -4 | 15 | 0 | 1 | 35-19-46 | 5% | 18% | 19% | .708 | .651 | .755 | .664 | .812 | 0.36 | -18 | +44 |
| 08 | STL | 444 | 7 | 37 | 56 | 0 | .304 | .349 | .392 | 93% | 32% | 7% | 1.29 | $12 | $6 | 270 | +1 | 18 | 0 | 2 | 33-21-46 | 5% | 23% | 19% | .740 | .764 | .701 | .690 | .860 | 0.40 | -21 | +49 |
| 09 | STL | 481 | 6 | 45 | 54 | 9 | .293 | .366 | .383 | 92% | 32% | 9% | 1.30 | $14 | $9 | 310 | +4 | 23 | 1 | 3 | 30-19-51 | 5% | 19% | 20% | .749 | .735 | .768 | .759 | .717 | 0.40 | -31 | +74 |
| 10 | STL | 465 | 6 | 34 | 62 | 8 | .262 | .329 | .342 | 89% | 29% | 9% | 1.30 | $11 | $5 | 260 | -13 | 19 | 0 | 4 | 28-21-51 | 5% | 21% | 17% | .671 | .595 | .773 | .714 | .570 | 0.39 | -17 | +74 |

**Competition at CA** — Stats in 2010

| Bats | Player | GSvR | GSvL | Sub | OPS |
|---|---|---|---|---|---|
| RH | Molina Y | 84 | 46 | 5 | .671 |
| RH | LaRue J | 12 | 2 | 14 | .596 |
| RH | Pagnozzi M | 7 | 5 | 3 | .892 |

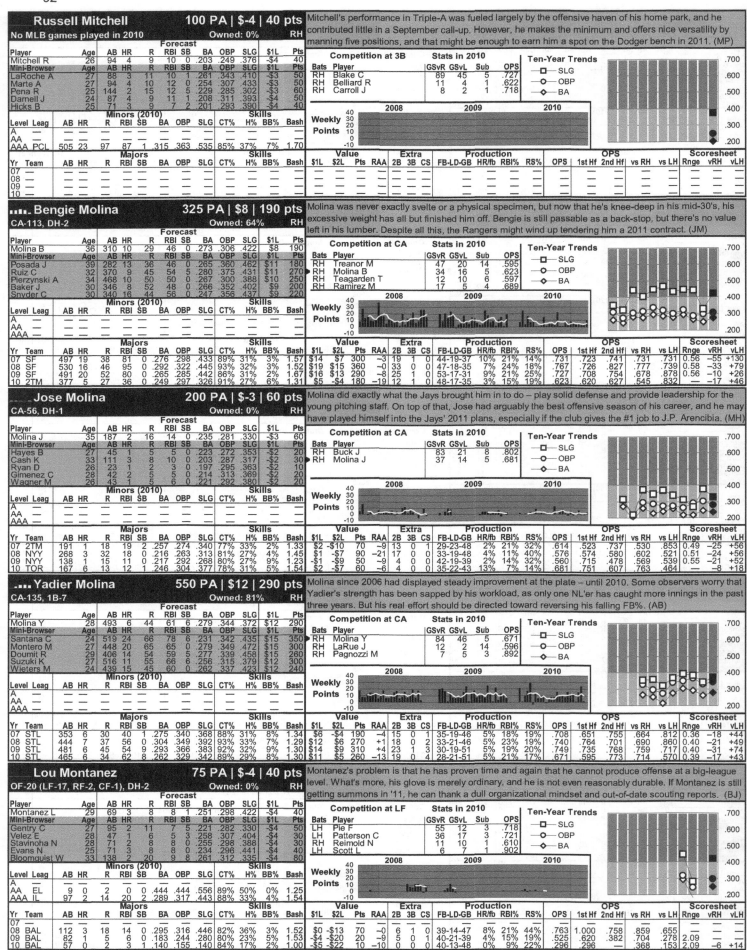

---

## Lou Montanez — 75 PA | $-4 | 40 pts

OF-20 (LF-17, RF-2, CF-1), DH-2 — Owned: 0% — RH

Montanez's problem is that he has proven time and again that he cannot produce offense at a big-league level. What's more, his glove is merely ordinary, and he is not even reasonably durable. If Montanez is still getting summons in '11, he can thank a dull organizational mindset and out-of-date scouting reports. (BJ)

### Forecast

| Player | Age | AB | HR | R | RBI | SB | BA | OBP | SLG | $1L | Pts |
|---|---|---|---|---|---|---|---|---|---|---|---|
| Montanez L | 29 | 69 | 3 | 8 | 8 | 1 | .251 | .298 | .422 | -$4 | 40 |

| Mini-Browser | Age | AB | HR | R | RBI | SB | BA | OBP | SLG | $1L | Pts |
|---|---|---|---|---|---|---|---|---|---|---|---|
| Gentry C | 27 | 95 | 2 | 11 | 7 | 5 | .221 | .282 | .330 | -$4 | 50 |
| Velez E | 28 | 47 | 1 | 6 | 5 | 3 | .258 | .307 | .404 | -$4 | 30 |
| Stavinoha N | 28 | 71 | 2 | 8 | 8 | 0 | .255 | .298 | .388 | -$4 | 30 |
| Evans N | 25 | 71 | 3 | 8 | 8 | 0 | .234 | .296 | .441 | -$4 | 40 |
| Bloomquist W | 33 | 138 | 2 | 20 | 14 | 8 | .261 | .312 | .335 | -$4 | 80 |

### Minors (2010) / Skills

| Level | Leag | AB | HR | R | RBI | SB | BA | OBP | SLG | CT% | H% | BB% | Bash |
|---|---|---|---|---|---|---|---|---|---|---|---|---|---|
| A | — | | | | | | | | | | | | |
| AA | EL | 9 | 0 | 2 | 0 | 0 | .444 | .444 | .556 | 89% | 50% | 0% | 1.25 |
| AAA | IL | 97 | 4 | 14 | 20 | 2 | .289 | .317 | .443 | 88% | 33% | 4% | 1.54 |

### Majors

| Yr | Team | AB | HR | R | RBI | SB | BA | OBP | SLG | CT% | H% | BB% | Bash | $1L | $2L | Pts | RAA | 2B | 3B | CS | FB-LD-GB | HR/fb | RBI% | RS% | OPS | 1st Hf | 2nd Hf | vs RH | vs LH | Rnge | vRH | vLH |
|---|---|---|---|---|---|---|---|---|---|---|---|---|---|---|---|---|---|---|---|---|---|---|---|---|---|---|---|---|---|---|---|---|
| 07 | — | | | | | | | | | | | | | | | | | | | | | | | | | | | | | | | |
| 08 | BAL | 112 | 3 | 18 | 14 | 0 | .295 | .316 | .446 | 82% | 36% | 3% | 1.52 | $0 | -$13 | 70 | -0 | 6 | 1 | 0 | 39-14-47 | 8% | 21% | 44% | .763 | 1.000 | .758 | .859 | .655 | — | — | — |
| 09 | BAL | 82 | 1 | 6 | 6 | 0 | .183 | .244 | .280 | 80% | 22% | 5% | 1.53 | -$4 | -$20 | 20 | -9 | 5 | 0 | 1 | 40-21-39 | 4% | 15% | 19% | .525 | .620 | .382 | .704 | .278 | 2.09 | — | — |
| 10 | BAL | 57 | 0 | 2 | 5 | 0 | .140 | .155 | .140 | 84% | 17% | 2% | 1.00 | -$5 | -$22 | 10 | -10 | 0 | 0 | 0 | 40-13-48 | 0% | 9% | 22% | .296 | .296 | — | .368 | .153 | 2.09 | -6 | +14 |

**Competition at LF** — Stats in 2010

| Bats | Player | GSvR | GSvL | Sub | OPS |
|---|---|---|---|---|---|
| LH | Pie F | 55 | 12 | 3 | .718 |
| LH | Patterson C | 36 | 17 | 3 | .721 |
| RH | Reimold N | 11 | 10 | 1 | .610 |
| LH | Scott L | 6 | 7 | 1 | .902 |

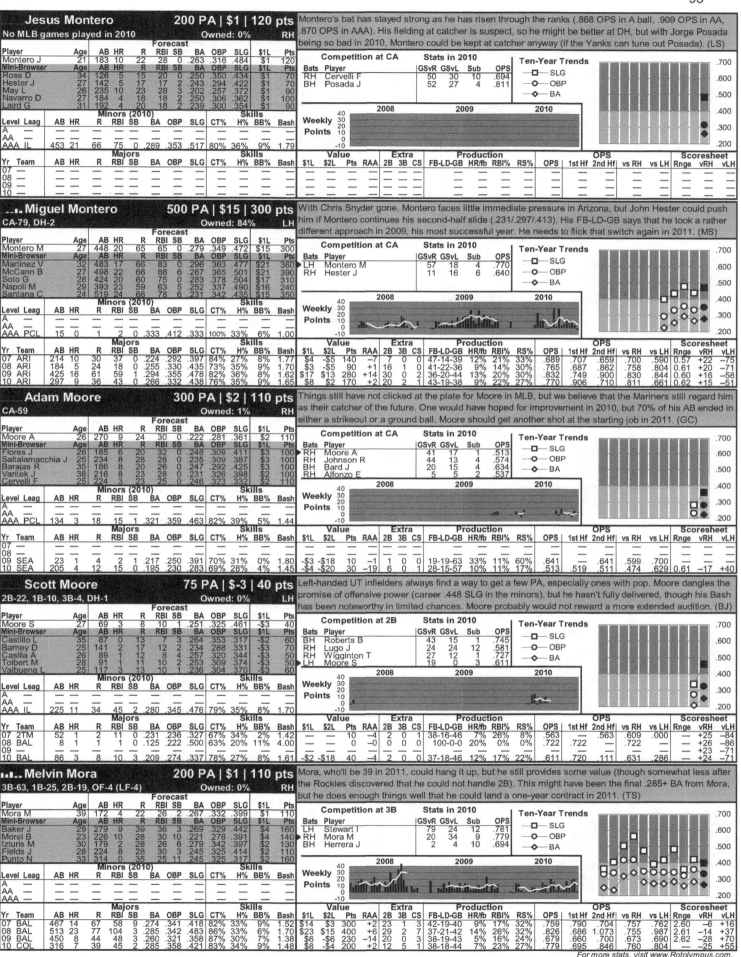

## Jesus Montero

**200 PA | $1 | 120 pts**

No MLB games played in 2010 — Owned: 0% — RH

| Player | Age | AB | HR | R | RBI | SB | BA | OBP | SLG | $1L | Pts |
|---|---|---|---|---|---|---|---|---|---|---|---|
| **Forecast** | | | | | | | | | | | |
| Montero J | 21 | 183 | 10 | 22 | 28 | 0 | .263 | .316 | .484 | $1 | 120 |
| **Mini-Browser** | Age | AB | HR | R | RBI | SB | BA | OBP | SLG | $1L | Pts |
| Ross D | 34 | 126 | 5 | 15 | 20 | 0 | .250 | .350 | .434 | $1 | 70 |
| Hester J | 27 | 142 | 5 | 17 | 17 | 2 | .243 | .294 | .422 | $1 | 70 |
| May L | 26 | 235 | 10 | 23 | 28 | 3 | .202 | .257 | .372 | $1 | 90 |
| Navarro D | 27 | 184 | 4 | 18 | 18 | 2 | .250 | .306 | .362 | $1 | 100 |
| Laird G | 31 | 192 | 4 | 20 | 18 | 2 | .239 | .300 | .354 | $1 | 90 |

| Level | Leag | AB | HR | R | RBI | SB | BA | OBP | SLG | CT% | H% | BB% | Bash |
|---|---|---|---|---|---|---|---|---|---|---|---|---|---|
| **Minors (2010)** | | | | | | | | | | **Skills** | | | |
| A | — | — | — | — | — | — | — | — | — | — | — | — | — |
| AA | — | — | — | — | — | — | — | — | — | — | — | — | — |
| AAA | IL | 453 | 21 | 66 | 75 | 0 | .289 | .353 | .517 | 80% | 36% | 9% | 1.79 |

| Yr | Team | AB | HR | R | RBI | SB | BA | OBP | SLG | CT% | H% | BB% | Bash |
|---|---|---|---|---|---|---|---|---|---|---|---|---|---|
| **Majors** | | | | | | | | | | **Skills** | | | |
| 07 | — | — | — | — | — | — | — | — | — | — | — | — | — |
| 08 | — | — | — | — | — | — | — | — | — | — | — | — | — |
| 09 | — | — | — | — | — | — | — | — | — | — | — | — | — |
| 10 | — | — | — | — | — | — | — | — | — | — | — | — | — |

Montero's bat has stayed strong as he has risen through the ranks (.868 OPS in A ball, .909 OPS in AA, .870 OPS in AAA). His fielding at catcher is suspect, so he might be better at DH, but with Jorge Posada being so bad in 2010, Montero could be kept at catcher anyway (if the Yanks can tune out Posada). (LS)

| Bats | Competition at CA: Player | GSvR | GSvL | Sub | OPS |
|---|---|---|---|---|---|
| | | **Stats in 2010** | | | |
| RH | Cervelli F | 50 | 30 | 10 | .694 |
| BH | Posada J | 52 | 27 | 4 | .811 |

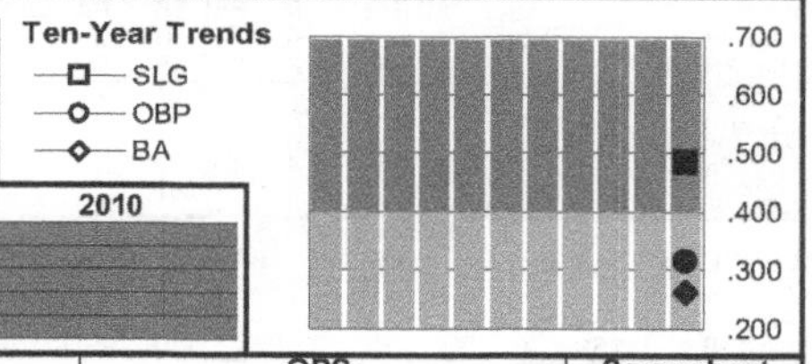


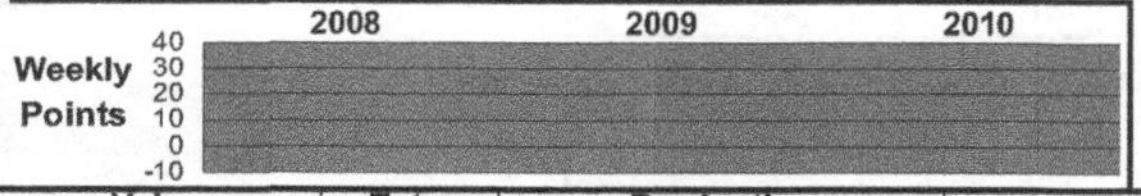


| Yr | $1L | $2L | Pts | RAA | 2B | 3B | CS | FB-LD-GB | HR/fb | RBI% | RS% | OPS | 1st Hf | 2nd Hf | vs RH | vs LH | Rnge | vRH | vLH |
|---|---|---|---|---|---|---|---|---|---|---|---|---|---|---|---|---|---|---|---|
| | **Value** | | | | **Extra** | | | **Production** | | | | **OPS** | | | | | **Scoresheet** | | |
| 07 | — | — | — | — | — | — | — | — | — | — | — | — | — | — | — | — | — | — | — |
| 08 | — | — | — | — | — | — | — | — | — | — | — | — | — | — | — | — | — | — | — |
| 09 | — | — | — | — | — | — | — | — | — | — | — | — | — | — | — | — | — | — | — |
| 10 | — | — | — | — | — | — | — | — | — | — | — | — | — | — | — | — | — | — | — |

## Miguel Montero

**500 PA | $15 | 300 pts**

CA-79, DH-2 — Owned: 84% — LH

| Player | Age | AB | HR | R | RBI | SB | BA | OBP | SLG | $1L | Pts |
|---|---|---|---|---|---|---|---|---|---|---|---|
| **Forecast** | | | | | | | | | | | |
| Montero M | 27 | 448 | 20 | 65 | 65 | 0 | .279 | .349 | .472 | $15 | 300 |
| **Mini-Browser** | Age | AB | HR | R | RBI | SB | BA | OBP | SLG | $1L | Pts |
| Martinez V | 32 | 483 | 17 | 66 | 83 | 0 | .296 | .363 | .477 | $21 | 360 |
| McCann B | 27 | 498 | 22 | 66 | 88 | 6 | .287 | .365 | .501 | $21 | 390 |
| Soto G | 28 | 424 | 20 | 60 | 75 | 0 | .283 | .378 | .504 | $17 | 310 |
| Napoli M | 29 | 393 | 23 | 59 | 63 | 5 | .252 | .337 | .490 | $16 | 240 |
| Santana C | 24 | 519 | 24 | 66 | 78 | 6 | .231 | .342 | .435 | $15 | 350 |

| Level | Leag | AB | HR | R | RBI | SB | BA | OBP | SLG | CT% | H% | BB% | Bash |
|---|---|---|---|---|---|---|---|---|---|---|---|---|---|
| **Minors (2010)** | | | | | | | | | | **Skills** | | | |
| A | — | — | — | — | — | — | — | — | — | — | — | — | — |
| AA | — | — | — | — | — | — | — | — | — | — | — | — | — |
| AAA | PCL | 15 | 0 | 1 | 2 | 0 | .333 | .412 | .333 | 100% | 33% | 6% | 1.00 |

| Yr | Team | AB | HR | R | RBI | SB | BA | OBP | SLG | CT% | H% | BB% | Bash |
|---|---|---|---|---|---|---|---|---|---|---|---|---|---|
| **Majors** | | | | | | | | | | **Skills** | | | |
| 07 | ARI | 214 | 10 | 30 | 37 | 0 | .224 | .292 | .397 | 84% | 27% | 8% | 1.77 |
| 08 | ARI | 184 | 5 | 24 | 18 | 0 | .255 | .330 | .435 | 73% | 35% | 9% | 1.70 |
| 09 | ARI | 425 | 16 | 61 | 59 | 1 | .294 | .355 | .478 | 82% | 36% | 8% | 1.62 |
| 10 | ARI | 297 | 9 | 36 | 43 | 0 | .266 | .332 | .438 | 76% | 35% | 9% | 1.65 |

With Chris Snyder gone, Montero faces little immediate pressure in Arizona, but John Hester could push him if Montero continues his second-half slide (.231/.297/.413). His FB-LD-GB says that he took a rather different approach in 2009, his most successful year. He needs to flick that switch again in 2011. (MS)

| Bats | Competition at CA: Player | GSvR | GSvL | Sub | OPS |
|---|---|---|---|---|---|
| | | **Stats in 2010** | | | |
| LH | Montero M | 57 | 18 | 4 | .770 |
| RH | Hester J | 11 | 16 | 6 | .640 |

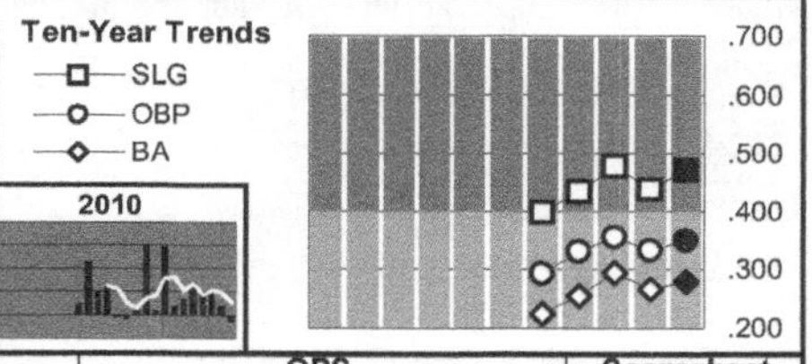


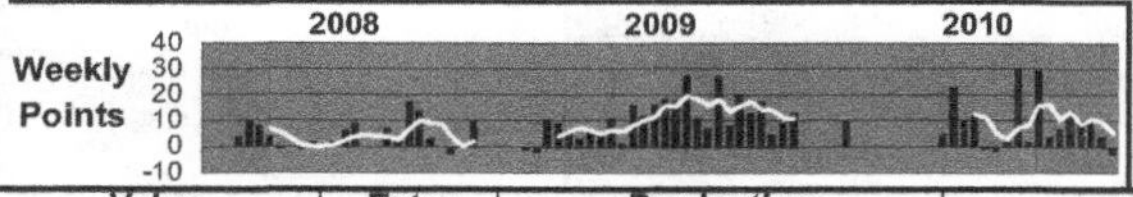


| Yr | $1L | $2L | Pts | RAA | 2B | 3B | CS | FB-LD-GB | HR/fb | RBI% | RS% | OPS | 1st Hf | 2nd Hf | vs RH | vs LH | Rnge | vRH | vLH |
|---|---|---|---|---|---|---|---|---|---|---|---|---|---|---|---|---|---|---|---|
| | **Value** | | | | **Extra** | | | **Production** | | | | **OPS** | | | | | **Scoresheet** | | |
| 07 | $4 | -$5 | 140 | –7 | 7 | 0 | 0 | 47-14-39 | 12% | 21% | 33% | .689 | .707 | .659 | .700 | .590 | 0.57 | +22 | –75 |
| 08 | $3 | -$5 | 90 | +1 | 16 | 1 | 0 | 41-22-36 | 9% | 14% | 30% | .765 | .687 | .862 | .758 | .804 | 0.61 | +20 | –71 |
| 09 | $17 | $13 | 280 | +14 | 30 | 0 | 2 | 36-20-44 | 13% | 20% | 30% | .832 | .749 | .900 | .830 | .844 | 0.60 | +16 | –58 |
| 10 | $8 | $2 | 170 | +2 | 20 | 2 | 1 | 43-19-38 | 9% | 22% | 27% | .770 | .906 | .710 | .811 | .661 | 0.62 | +15 | –51 |

## Adam Moore

**300 PA | $2 | 110 pts**

CA-59 — Owned: 1% — RH

| Player | Age | AB | HR | R | RBI | SB | BA | OBP | SLG | $1L | Pts |
|---|---|---|---|---|---|---|---|---|---|---|---|
| **Forecast** | | | | | | | | | | | |
| Moore A | 26 | 270 | 9 | 24 | 30 | 0 | .222 | .281 | .361 | $2 | 110 |
| **Mini-Browser** | Age | AB | HR | R | RBI | SB | BA | OBP | SLG | $1L | Pts |
| Flores J | 26 | 185 | 6 | 20 | 32 | 0 | .248 | .309 | .411 | $3 | 100 |
| Saltalamacchia J | 25 | 234 | 8 | 28 | 28 | 0 | .235 | .309 | .387 | $3 | 100 |
| Barajas R | 35 | 186 | 8 | 20 | 26 | 0 | .247 | .292 | .425 | $3 | 100 |
| Varitek J | 38 | 216 | 8 | 23 | 28 | 0 | .231 | .326 | .398 | $2 | 100 |
| Cervelli F | 25 | 224 | 3 | 23 | 25 | 0 | .246 | .323 | .332 | $2 | 110 |

| Level | Leag | AB | HR | R | RBI | SB | BA | OBP | SLG | CT% | H% | BB% | Bash |
|---|---|---|---|---|---|---|---|---|---|---|---|---|---|
| **Minors (2010)** | | | | | | | | | | **Skills** | | | |
| A | — | — | — | — | — | — | — | — | — | — | — | — | — |
| AA | — | — | — | — | — | — | — | — | — | — | — | — | — |
| AAA | PCL | 134 | 3 | 18 | 15 | 1 | .321 | .359 | .463 | 82% | 39% | 5% | 1.44 |

| Yr | Team | AB | HR | R | RBI | SB | BA | OBP | SLG | CT% | H% | BB% | Bash |
|---|---|---|---|---|---|---|---|---|---|---|---|---|---|
| **Majors** | | | | | | | | | | **Skills** | | | |
| 07 | — | — | — | — | — | — | — | — | — | — | — | — | — |
| 08 | — | — | — | — | — | — | — | — | — | — | — | — | — |
| 09 | SEA | 23 | 1 | 4 | 2 | 1 | .217 | .250 | .391 | 70% | 31% | 0% | 1.80 |
| 10 | SEA | 205 | 4 | 12 | 15 | 0 | .195 | .230 | .283 | 69% | 28% | 4% | 1.45 |

Things still have not clicked at the plate for Moore in MLB, but we believe that the Mariners still regard him as their catcher of the future. One would have hoped for improvement in 2010, but 70% of his AB ended in either a strikeout or a ground ball. Moore should get another shot at the starting job in 2011. (GC)

| Bats | Competition at CA: Player | GSvR | GSvL | Sub | OPS |
|---|---|---|---|---|---|
| | | **Stats in 2010** | | | |
| RH | Moore A | 41 | 17 | 1 | .513 |
| RH | Johnson R | 44 | 13 | 4 | .574 |
| BH | Bard J | 20 | 15 | 4 | .634 |
| RH | Alfonzo E | 5 | 5 | 2 | .537 |

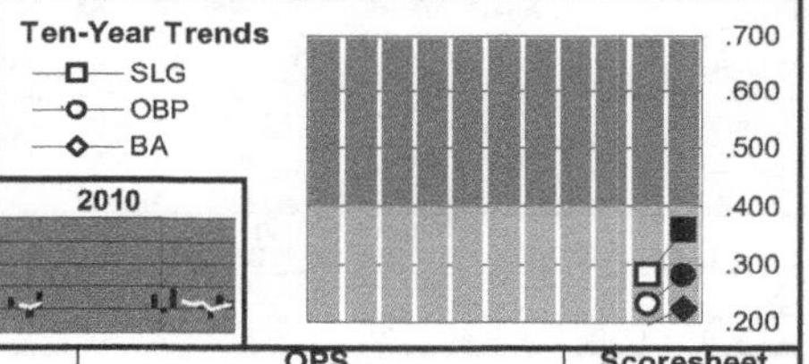


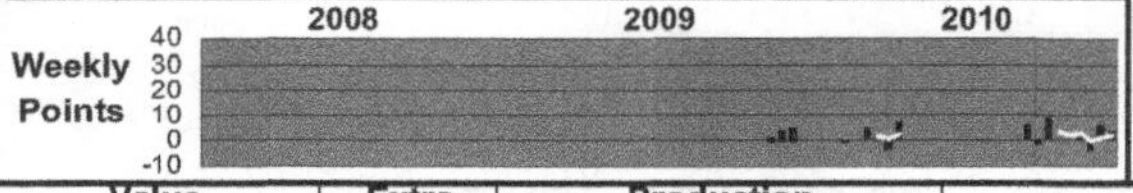


| Yr | $1L | $2L | Pts | RAA | 2B | 3B | CS | FB-LD-GB | HR/fb | RBI% | RS% | OPS | 1st Hf | 2nd Hf | vs RH | vs LH | Rnge | vRH | vLH |
|---|---|---|---|---|---|---|---|---|---|---|---|---|---|---|---|---|---|---|---|
| | **Value** | | | | **Extra** | | | **Production** | | | | **OPS** | | | | | **Scoresheet** | | |
| 07 | — | — | — | — | — | — | — | — | — | — | — | — | — | — | — | — | — | — | — |
| 08 | — | — | — | — | — | — | — | — | — | — | — | — | — | — | — | — | — | — | — |
| 09 | -$3 | -$18 | 10 | –1 | 1 | 0 | 0 | 19-19-63 | 33% | 11% | 60% | .641 | — | .641 | .599 | .700 | — | — | — |
| 10 | -$4 | -$20 | 30 | –19 | 6 | 0 | 1 | 28-15-57 | 10% | 11% | 17% | .513 | .519 | .511 | .474 | .629 | 0.61 | –17 | +40 |

## Scott Moore

**75 PA | $-3 | 40 pts**

2B-22, 1B-10, 3B-4, DH-1 — Owned: 0% — LH

| Player | Age | AB | HR | R | RBI | SB | BA | OBP | SLG | $1L | Pts |
|---|---|---|---|---|---|---|---|---|---|---|---|
| **Forecast** | | | | | | | | | | | |
| Moore S | 27 | 69 | 3 | 8 | 10 | 1 | .251 | .325 | .461 | -$3 | 40 |
| **Mini-Browser** | Age | AB | HR | R | RBI | SB | BA | OBP | SLG | $1L | Pts |
| Castillo L | 35 | 87 | 0 | 13 | 7 | 3 | .264 | .353 | .317 | -$2 | 60 |
| Barney D | 25 | 141 | 2 | 17 | 12 | 2 | .234 | .288 | .331 | -$3 | 70 |
| Casilla A | 26 | 89 | 1 | 12 | 8 | 4 | .257 | .320 | .344 | -$3 | 50 |
| Tolbert M | 28 | 91 | 1 | 11 | 10 | 2 | .253 | .309 | .374 | -$3 | 50 |
| Valbuena L | 25 | 117 | 3 | 13 | 10 | 1 | .236 | .304 | .370 | -$3 | 60 |

| Level | Leag | AB | HR | R | RBI | SB | BA | OBP | SLG | CT% | H% | BB% | Bash |
|---|---|---|---|---|---|---|---|---|---|---|---|---|---|
| **Minors (2010)** | | | | | | | | | | **Skills** | | | |
| A | — | — | — | — | — | — | — | — | — | — | — | — | — |
| AA | — | — | — | — | — | — | — | — | — | — | — | — | — |
| AAA | IL | 225 | 11 | 34 | 45 | 2 | .280 | .345 | .476 | 79% | 35% | 8% | 1.70 |

| Yr | Team | AB | HR | R | RBI | SB | BA | OBP | SLG | CT% | H% | BB% | Bash |
|---|---|---|---|---|---|---|---|---|---|---|---|---|---|
| **Majors** | | | | | | | | | | **Skills** | | | |
| 07 | 2TM | 52 | 1 | 2 | 11 | 0 | .231 | .236 | .327 | 67% | 34% | 2% | 1.42 |
| 08 | BAL | 8 | 1 | 1 | 1 | 0 | .125 | .222 | .500 | 63% | 20% | 11% | 4.00 |
| 09 | — | — | — | — | — | — | — | — | — | — | — | — | — |
| 10 | BAL | 86 | 3 | 8 | 10 | 3 | .209 | .274 | .337 | 78% | 27% | 8% | 1.61 |

Left-handed UT infielders always find a way to get a few PA, especially ones with pop. Moore dangles the promise of offensive power (career .448 SLG in the minors), but he hasn't fully delivered, though his Bash has been noteworthy in limited chances. Moore probably would not reward a more extended audition. (BJ)

| Bats | Competition at 2B: Player | GSvR | GSvL | Sub | OPS |
|---|---|---|---|---|---|
| | | **Stats in 2010** | | | |
| BH | Roberts B | 43 | 15 | 1 | .745 |
| RH | Lugo J | 24 | 24 | 12 | .581 |
| RH | Wigginton T | 27 | 12 | 1 | .727 |
| LH | Moore S | 19 | 0 | 3 | .611 |

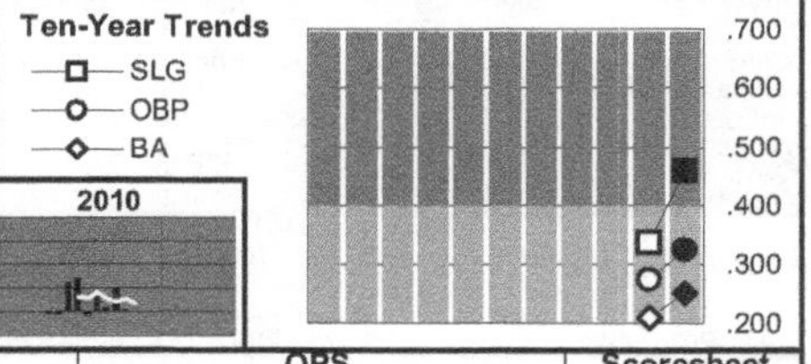


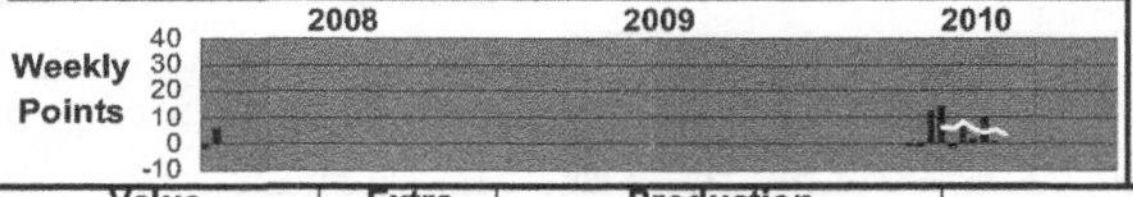


| Yr | $1L | $2L | Pts | RAA | 2B | 3B | CS | FB-LD-GB | HR/fb | RBI% | RS% | OPS | 1st Hf | 2nd Hf | vs RH | vs LH | Rnge | vRH | vLH |
|---|---|---|---|---|---|---|---|---|---|---|---|---|---|---|---|---|---|---|---|
| | **Value** | | | | **Extra** | | | **Production** | | | | **OPS** | | | | | **Scoresheet** | | |
| 07 | — | — | 10 | –4 | 2 | 0 | 1 | 38-16-46 | 7% | 26% | 8% | .563 | — | .563 | .609 | .000 | — | +25 | –84 |
| 08 | — | — | 0 | –0 | 0 | 0 | 0 | 100-0-0 | 20% | 0% | 0% | .722 | .722 | — | .722 | — | — | +26 | –86 |
| 09 | — | — | — | — | — | — | — | — | — | — | — | — | — | — | — | — | — | +23 | –71 |
| 10 | -$2 | -$18 | 40 | –4 | 2 | 0 | 0 | 37-18-46 | 12% | 17% | 22% | .611 | .720 | .111 | .631 | .286 | — | +24 | –71 |

## Melvin Mora

**200 PA | $1 | 110 pts**

3B-63, 1B-25, 2B-19, OF-4 (LF-4) — Owned: 0% — RH

| Player | Age | AB | HR | R | RBI | SB | BA | OBP | SLG | $1L | Pts |
|---|---|---|---|---|---|---|---|---|---|---|---|
| **Forecast** | | | | | | | | | | | |
| Mora M | 39 | 172 | 4 | 22 | 26 | 2 | .267 | .332 | .399 | $1 | 110 |
| **Mini-Browser** | Age | AB | HR | R | RBI | SB | BA | OBP | SLG | $1L | Pts |
| Baker J | 29 | 279 | 9 | 39 | 36 | 3 | .269 | .329 | .442 | $4 | 160 |
| Morel B | 23 | 226 | 10 | 28 | 30 | 10 | .221 | .278 | .391 | $4 | 140 |
| Izturis M | 30 | 179 | 2 | 28 | 26 | 6 | .279 | .342 | .397 | $2 | 130 |
| Fields J | 28 | 224 | 8 | 28 | 30 | 3 | .245 | .325 | .414 | $2 | 110 |
| Punto N | 33 | 314 | 0 | 35 | 25 | 11 | .245 | .325 | .317 | $2 | 160 |

| Level | Leag | AB | HR | R | RBI | SB | BA | OBP | SLG | CT% | H% | BB% | Bash |
|---|---|---|---|---|---|---|---|---|---|---|---|---|---|
| **Minors (2010)** | | | | | | | | | | **Skills** | | | |
| A | — | — | — | — | — | — | — | — | — | — | — | — | — |
| AA | — | — | — | — | — | — | — | — | — | — | — | — | — |
| AAA | — | — | — | — | — | — | — | — | — | — | — | — | — |

| Yr | Team | AB | HR | R | RBI | SB | BA | OBP | SLG | CT% | H% | BB% | Bash |
|---|---|---|---|---|---|---|---|---|---|---|---|---|---|
| **Majors** | | | | | | | | | | **Skills** | | | |
| 07 | BAL | 467 | 14 | 67 | 58 | 9 | .274 | .341 | .418 | 82% | 33% | 9% | 1.52 |
| 08 | BAL | 513 | 23 | 77 | 104 | 3 | .285 | .342 | .483 | 86% | 33% | 6% | 1.70 |
| 09 | BAL | 450 | 8 | 44 | 48 | 3 | .260 | .321 | .358 | 87% | 30% | 7% | 1.38 |
| 10 | COL | 316 | 7 | 39 | 45 | 2 | .285 | .358 | .421 | 83% | 34% | 9% | 1.48 |

Mora, who'll be 39 in 2011, could hang it up, but he still provides some value (though somewhat less after the Rockies discovered that he could not handle 2B). This might have been the final .285+ BA from Mora, but he does enough things well that he could land a one-year contract in 2011. (TS)

| Bats | Competition at 3B: Player | GSvR | GSvL | Sub | OPS |
|---|---|---|---|---|---|
| | | **Stats in 2010** | | | |
| LH | Stewart I | 79 | 24 | 12 | .781 |
| RH | Mora M | 20 | 34 | 9 | .779 |
| BH | Herrera J | 2 | 4 | 10 | .694 |

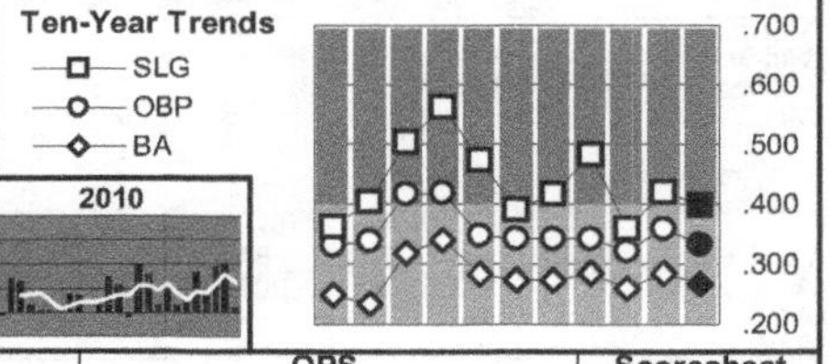


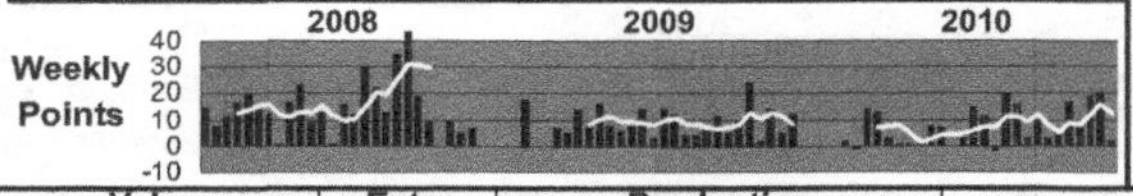


| Yr | $1L | $2L | Pts | RAA | 2B | 3B | CS | FB-LD-GB | HR/fb | RBI% | RS% | OPS | 1st Hf | 2nd Hf | vs RH | vs LH | Rnge | vRH | vLH |
|---|---|---|---|---|---|---|---|---|---|---|---|---|---|---|---|---|---|---|---|
| | **Value** | | | | **Extra** | | | **Production** | | | | **OPS** | | | | | **Scoresheet** | | |
| 07 | $14 | $3 | 300 | +2 | 23 | 1 | 3 | 42-19-40 | 9% | 17% | 32% | .759 | .790 | .704 | .757 | .762 | 2.60 | –6 | +16 |
| 08 | $23 | $15 | 400 | +6 | 29 | 2 | 7 | 37-21-42 | 14% | 26% | 32% | .826 | .686 | 1.073 | .755 | .987 | 2.61 | –14 | +37 |
| 09 | $6 | -$6 | 230 | –14 | 20 | 0 | 3 | 38-19-43 | 5% | 16% | 24% | .679 | .660 | .700 | .673 | .690 | 2.62 | –28 | +70 |
| 10 | $8 | -$4 | 200 | +2 | 12 | 5 | 1 | 38-18-44 | 7% | 23% | 27% | .779 | .695 | .846 | .760 | .804 | — | –25 | +55 |

*For more stats, visit www.Rotolympus.com.*

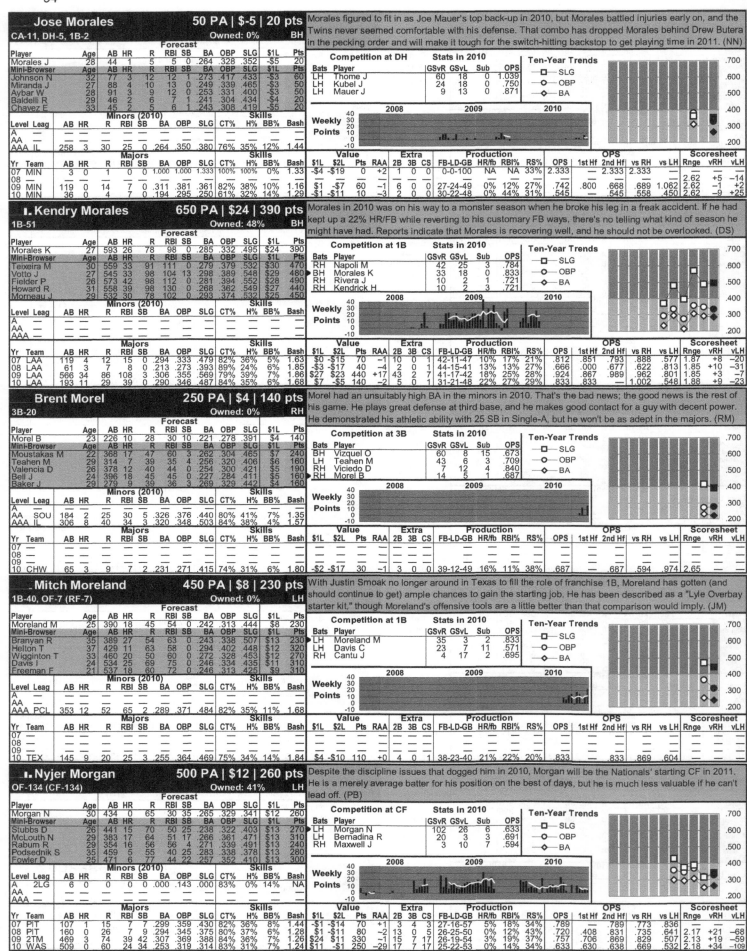

## Jose Morales — 50 PA | $-5 | 20 pts

CA-11, DH-5, 1B-2 | Owned: 0% | BH

Morales figured to fit in as Joe Mauer's top back-up in 2010, but Morales battled injuries early on, and the Twins never seemed comfortable with his defense. That combo has dropped Morales behind Drew Butera in the pecking order and will make it tough for the switch-hitting backstop to get playing time in 2011. (NN)

| Player | Age | AB | HR | R | RBI | SB | BA | OBP | SLG | $1L | Pts |
|---|---|---|---|---|---|---|---|---|---|---|---|
| Morales J | 28 | 44 | 1 | 5 | 5 | 0 | .264 | .328 | .352 | -$5 | 20 |
| **Mini-Browser** | | | | | | | | | | | |
| Johnson N | 32 | 77 | 3 | 12 | 12 | 1 | .273 | .417 | .433 | -$3 | 60 |
| Miranda J | 27 | 88 | 4 | 10 | 13 | 0 | .249 | .339 | .465 | -$3 | 50 |
| Aybar W | 28 | 91 | 3 | 9 | 12 | 0 | .253 | .331 | .400 | -$3 | 50 |
| Baldelli R | 29 | 46 | 2 | 6 | 7 | 1 | .241 | .304 | .434 | -$4 | 20 |
| Chavez E | 33 | 45 | 2 | 5 | 6 | 1 | .243 | .308 | .419 | -$5 | 20 |

| Level | Leag | AB | HR | R | RBI | SB | BA | OBP | SLG | CT% | H% | BB% | Bash |
|---|---|---|---|---|---|---|---|---|---|---|---|---|---|
| A | — | — | — | — | — | — | — | — | — | — | — | — | — |
| AA | — | — | — | — | — | — | — | — | — | — | — | — | — |
| AAA | IL | 258 | 3 | 30 | 25 | 0 | .264 | .350 | .380 | 76% | 35% | 12% | 1.44 |

Competition at DH — Stats in 2010

| Bats | Player | GSvR | GSvL | Sub | OPS |
|---|---|---|---|---|---|
| LH | Thome J | 60 | 18 | 0 | 1.039 |
| LH | Kubel J | 24 | 18 | 0 | .750 |
| LH | Mauer J | 9 | 13 | 0 | .871 |

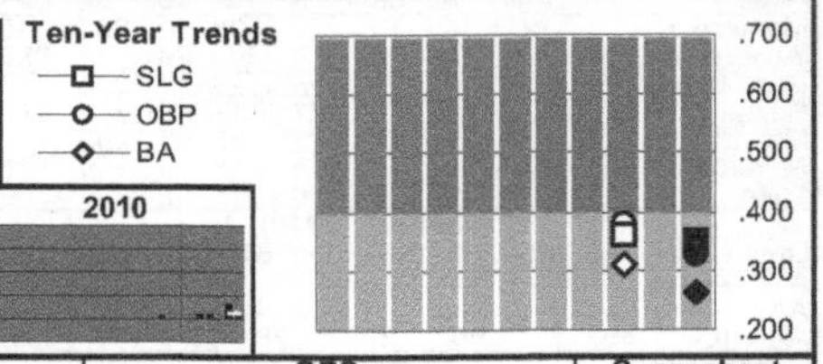


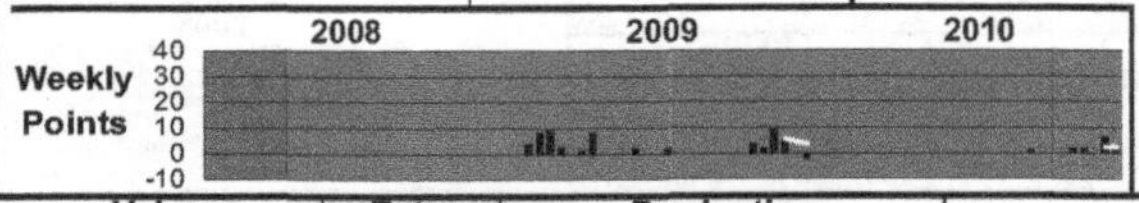


| Yr | Team | AB | HR | R | RBI | SB | BA | OBP | SLG | CT% | H% | BB% | Bash | $1L | $2L | Pts | RAA | 2B | 3B | CS | FB-LD-GB | HR/fb | RBI% | RS% | OPS | 1st Hf | 2nd Hf | vs RH | vs LH | Rnge | vRH | vLH |
|---|---|---|---|---|---|---|---|---|---|---|---|---|---|---|---|---|---|---|---|---|---|---|---|---|---|---|---|---|---|---|---|---|
| 07 | MIN | 3 | 0 | 1 | 0 | 0 | 1.000 | 1.000 | 1.333 | 100% | 100% | 0% | 1.33 | -$4 | -$19 | 0 | +2 | 1 | 0 | 0 | 0-0-100 | NA | NA | 33% | 2.333 | — | 2.333 | 2.333 | — | — | — | — |
| 08 | — | — | — | — | — | — | — | — | — | — | — | — | — | — | — | — | — | — | — | — | — | — | — | — | — | — | — | — | — | 2.62 | +5 | −14 |
| 09 | MIN | 119 | 0 | 14 | 7 | 0 | .311 | .381 | .361 | 82% | 38% | 10% | 1.16 | $1 | -$7 | 60 | −1 | 6 | 0 | 0 | 27-24-49 | 0% | 12% | 27% | .742 | .800 | .668 | .689 | 1.062 | 2.62 | −1 | +2 |
| 10 | MIN | 36 | 0 | 4 | 7 | 0 | .194 | .295 | .250 | 61% | 32% | 14% | 1.29 | -$1 | -$11 | 10 | −3 | 2 | 0 | 0 | 30-22-48 | 0% | 44% | 31% | .545 | — | .545 | .558 | .450 | 2.62 | −9 | +25 |

## Kendry Morales — 650 PA | $24 | 390 pts

1B-51 | Owned: 48% | BH

Morales in 2010 was on his way to a monster season when he broke his leg in a freak accident. If he had kept up a 22% HR/FB while reverting to his customary FB ways, there's no telling what kind of season he might have had. Reports indicate that Morales is recovering well, and he should not be overlooked. (DS)

| Player | Age | AB | HR | R | RBI | SB | BA | OBP | SLG | $1L | Pts |
|---|---|---|---|---|---|---|---|---|---|---|---|
| Morales K | 27 | 593 | 26 | 78 | 98 | 0 | .285 | .332 | .495 | $24 | 390 |
| **Mini-Browser** | | | | | | | | | | | |
| Teixeira M | 30 | 559 | 33 | 91 | 111 | 0 | .279 | .379 | .532 | $30 | 470 |
| Votto J | 27 | 545 | 33 | 98 | 104 | 13 | .298 | .389 | .548 | $29 | 480 |
| Fielder P | 26 | 573 | 42 | 98 | 112 | 0 | .281 | .394 | .552 | $28 | 490 |
| Howard R | 31 | 558 | 39 | 98 | 130 | 0 | .268 | .362 | .549 | $27 | 440 |
| Morneau J | 29 | 532 | 30 | 78 | 102 | 0 | .293 | .374 | .532 | $25 | 450 |

| Level | Leag | AB | HR | R | RBI | SB | BA | OBP | SLG | CT% | H% | BB% | Bash |
|---|---|---|---|---|---|---|---|---|---|---|---|---|---|
| A | — | — | — | — | — | — | — | — | — | — | — | — | — |
| AA | — | — | — | — | — | — | — | — | — | — | — | — | — |
| AAA | — | — | — | — | — | — | — | — | — | — | — | — | — |

Competition at 1B — Stats in 2010

| Bats | Player | GSvR | GSvL | Sub | OPS |
|---|---|---|---|---|---|
| RH | Napoli M | 42 | 25 | 3 | .784 |
| BH | Morales K | 33 | 18 | 0 | .833 |
| RH | Rivera J | 10 | 2 | 1 | .721 |
| RH | Kendrick H | 10 | 2 | 3 | .721 |

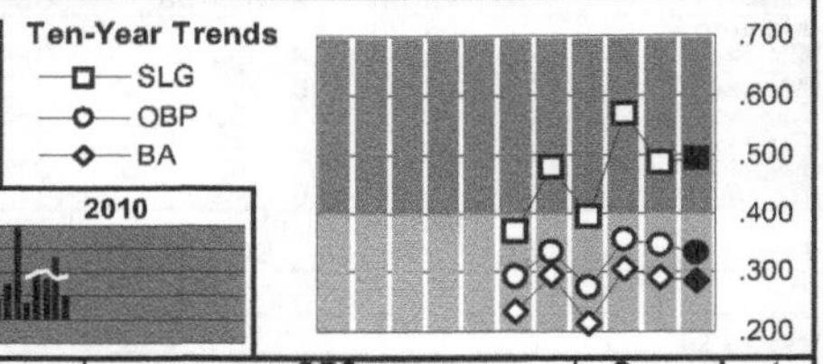


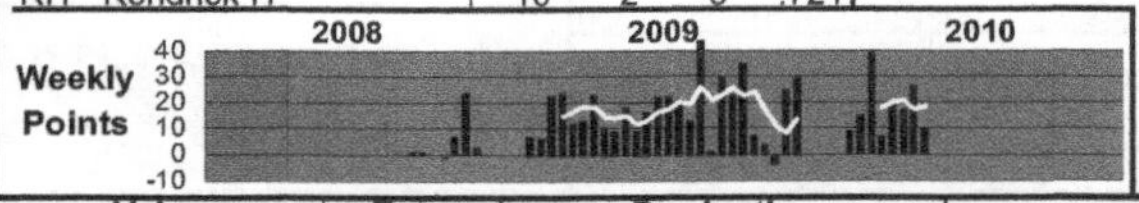


| Yr | Team | AB | HR | R | RBI | SB | BA | OBP | SLG | CT% | H% | BB% | Bash | $1L | $2L | Pts | RAA | 2B | 3B | CS | FB-LD-GB | HR/fb | RBI% | RS% | OPS | 1st Hf | 2nd Hf | vs RH | vs LH | Rnge | vRH | vLH |
|---|---|---|---|---|---|---|---|---|---|---|---|---|---|---|---|---|---|---|---|---|---|---|---|---|---|---|---|---|---|---|---|---|
| 07 | LAA | 119 | 4 | 12 | 15 | 0 | .294 | .333 | .479 | 82% | 36% | 5% | 1.63 | $0 | -$15 | 70 | −1 | 10 | 0 | 1 | 42-11-47 | 10% | 17% | 21% | .812 | .851 | .793 | .888 | .577 | 1.87 | +8 | −20 |
| 08 | LAA | 61 | 3 | 7 | 8 | 0 | .213 | .273 | .393 | 89% | 24% | 6% | 1.85 | -$3 | -$17 | 40 | −4 | 2 | 0 | 1 | 44-15-41 | 13% | 13% | 27% | .666 | .000 | .677 | .622 | .813 | 1.85 | +10 | −31 |
| 09 | LAA | 566 | 34 | 86 | 108 | 3 | .306 | .355 | .569 | 79% | 39% | 7% | 1.86 | $27 | $23 | 440 | +17 | 43 | 2 | 7 | 41-17-42 | 18% | 25% | 28% | .924 | .867 | .989 | .962 | .801 | 1.85 | +3 | −7 |
| 10 | LAA | 193 | 11 | 29 | 39 | 0 | .290 | .346 | .487 | 84% | 35% | 6% | 1.68 | $7 | -$5 | 140 | −2 | 5 | 0 | 1 | 31-21-48 | 22% | 27% | 29% | .833 | .833 | — | 1.002 | .548 | 1.88 | +9 | −23 |

## Brent Morel — 250 PA | $4 | 140 pts

3B-20 | Owned: 0% | RH

Morel had an unsuitably high BA in the minors in 2010. That's the bad news; the good news is the rest of his game. He plays great defense at third base, and he makes good contact for a guy with decent power. He demonstrated his athletic ability with 25 SB in Single-A, but he won't be as adept in the majors. (RM)

| Player | Age | AB | HR | R | RBI | SB | BA | OBP | SLG | $1L | Pts |
|---|---|---|---|---|---|---|---|---|---|---|---|
| Morel B | 23 | 226 | 10 | 28 | 30 | 10 | .221 | .278 | .391 | $4 | 140 |
| **Mini-Browser** | | | | | | | | | | | |
| Moustakas M | 22 | 368 | 17 | 47 | 60 | 3 | .262 | .304 | .465 | $7 | 240 |
| Teahen M | 29 | 314 | 7 | 39 | 35 | 4 | .256 | .320 | .406 | $6 | 160 |
| Valencia D | 26 | 378 | 12 | 40 | 44 | 0 | .254 | .300 | .421 | $5 | 190 |
| Bell J | 24 | 396 | 18 | 45 | 45 | 0 | .227 | .284 | .411 | $5 | 160 |
| Baker J | 29 | 279 | 9 | 39 | 36 | 3 | .269 | .329 | .442 | $4 | 160 |

| Level | Leag | AB | HR | R | RBI | SB | BA | OBP | SLG | CT% | H% | BB% | Bash |
|---|---|---|---|---|---|---|---|---|---|---|---|---|---|
| A | — | — | — | — | — | — | — | — | — | — | — | — | — |
| AA | SOU | 184 | 2 | 25 | 30 | 5 | .326 | .376 | .440 | 80% | 41% | 7% | 1.35 |
| AAA | IL | 306 | 8 | 40 | 34 | 3 | .320 | .348 | .503 | 84% | 38% | 4% | 1.57 |

Competition at 3B — Stats in 2010

| Bats | Player | GSvR | GSvL | Sub | OPS |
|---|---|---|---|---|---|
| BH | Vizquel O | 60 | 8 | 15 | .673 |
| LH | Teahen M | 43 | 6 | 3 | .709 |
| RH | Viciedo D | 7 | 12 | 4 | .840 |
| RH | Morel B | 14 | 5 | 1 | .687 |

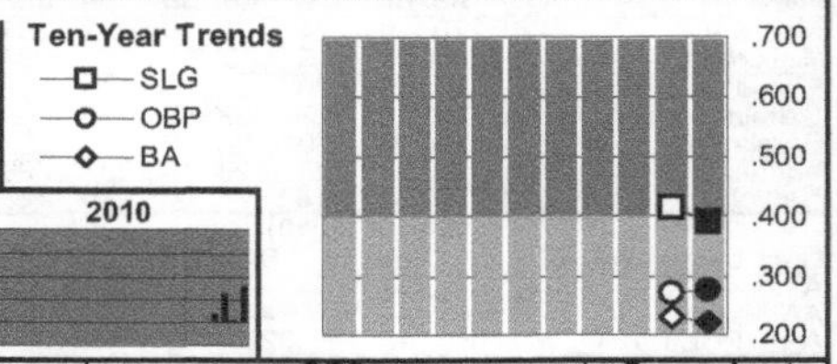


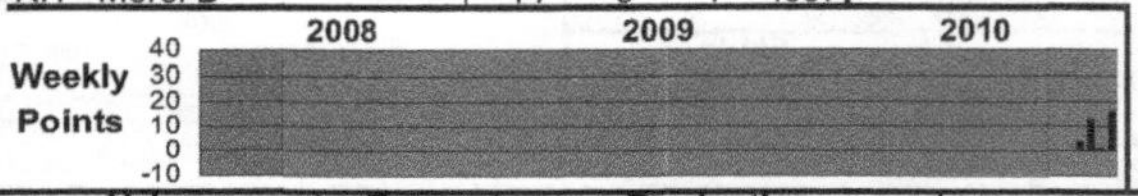


| Yr | Team | AB | HR | R | RBI | SB | BA | OBP | SLG | CT% | H% | BB% | Bash | $1L | $2L | Pts | RAA | 2B | 3B | CS | FB-LD-GB | HR/fb | RBI% | RS% | OPS | 1st Hf | 2nd Hf | vs RH | vs LH | Rnge | vRH | vLH |
|---|---|---|---|---|---|---|---|---|---|---|---|---|---|---|---|---|---|---|---|---|---|---|---|---|---|---|---|---|---|---|---|---|
| 07 | — | — | — | — | — | — | — | — | — | — | — | — | — | — | — | — | — | — | — | — | | — | — | — | — | — | — | — | — | — | — | — |
| 08 | — | — | — | — | — | — | — | — | — | — | — | — | — | — | — | — | — | — | — | — | | — | — | — | — | — | — | — | — | — | — | — |
| 09 | — | — | — | — | — | — | — | — | — | — | — | — | — | — | — | — | — | — | — | — | | — | — | — | — | — | — | — | — | — | — | — |
| 10 | CHW | 65 | 3 | 9 | 7 | 2 | .231 | .271 | .415 | 74% | 31% | 6% | 1.80 | -$2 | -$17 | 30 | −1 | 3 | 0 | 0 | 39-12-49 | 16% | 11% | 38% | .687 | — | .687 | .594 | .974 | 2.65 | — | — |

## Mitch Moreland — 450 PA | $8 | 230 pts

1B-40, OF-7 (RF-7) | Owned: 0% | LH

With Justin Smoak no longer around in Texas to fill the role of franchise 1B, Moreland has gotten (and should continue to get) ample chances to gain the starting job. He has been described as a "Lyle Overbay starter kit," though Moreland's offensive tools are a little better than that comparison would imply. (JM)

| Player | Age | AB | HR | R | RBI | SB | BA | OBP | SLG | $1L | Pts |
|---|---|---|---|---|---|---|---|---|---|---|---|
| Moreland M | 25 | 390 | 18 | 45 | 54 | 0 | .242 | .313 | .444 | $8 | 230 |
| **Mini-Browser** | | | | | | | | | | | |
| Branyan R | 35 | 389 | 27 | 54 | 63 | 0 | .243 | .338 | .507 | $13 | 230 |
| Helton T | 37 | 429 | 11 | 63 | 58 | 0 | .294 | .402 | .448 | $12 | 320 |
| Wigginton T | 33 | 460 | 20 | 50 | 60 | 0 | .272 | .328 | .453 | $12 | 270 |
| Davis I | 24 | 534 | 25 | 69 | 75 | 0 | .246 | .334 | .435 | $11 | 310 |
| Freeman F | 21 | 537 | 18 | 60 | 72 | 0 | .246 | .313 | .425 | $9 | 310 |

| Level | Leag | AB | HR | R | RBI | SB | BA | OBP | SLG | CT% | H% | BB% | Bash |
|---|---|---|---|---|---|---|---|---|---|---|---|---|---|
| A | — | — | — | — | — | — | — | — | — | — | — | — | — |
| AA | — | — | — | — | — | — | — | — | — | — | — | — | — |
| AAA | PCL | 353 | 12 | 52 | 65 | 2 | .289 | .371 | .484 | 82% | 35% | 11% | 1.68 |

Competition at 1B — Stats in 2010

| Bats | Player | GSvR | GSvL | Sub | OPS |
|---|---|---|---|---|---|
| LH | Moreland M | 35 | 3 | 2 | .833 |
| LH | Davis C | 23 | 7 | 11 | .571 |
| RH | Cantu J | 4 | 17 | 2 | .695 |

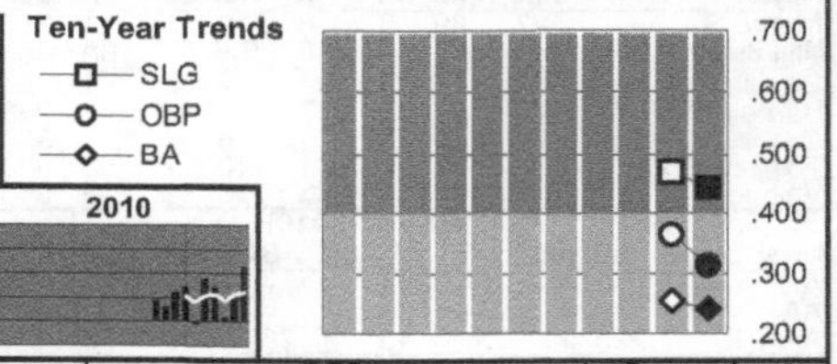


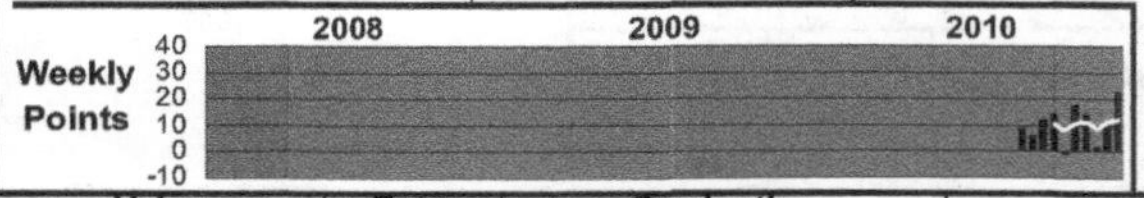


| Yr | Team | AB | HR | R | RBI | SB | BA | OBP | SLG | CT% | H% | BB% | Bash | $1L | $2L | Pts | RAA | 2B | 3B | CS | FB-LD-GB | HR/fb | RBI% | RS% | OPS | 1st Hf | 2nd Hf | vs RH | vs LH | Rnge | vRH | vLH |
|---|---|---|---|---|---|---|---|---|---|---|---|---|---|---|---|---|---|---|---|---|---|---|---|---|---|---|---|---|---|---|---|---|
| 07 | — | — | — | — | — | — | — | — | — | — | — | — | — | — | — | — | — | — | — | — | | — | — | — | — | — | — | — | — | — | — | — |
| 08 | — | — | — | — | — | — | — | — | — | — | — | — | — | — | — | — | — | — | — | — | | — | — | — | — | — | — | — | — | — | — | — |
| 09 | — | — | — | — | — | — | — | — | — | — | — | — | — | — | — | — | — | — | — | — | | — | — | — | — | — | — | — | — | — | — | — |
| 10 | TEX | 145 | 9 | 20 | 25 | 3 | .255 | .364 | .469 | 75% | 34% | 14% | 1.84 | $4 | -$10 | 110 | +0 | 4 | 0 | 1 | 38-23-40 | 21% | 22% | 20% | .833 | — | .833 | .869 | .604 | — | — | — |

## Nyjer Morgan — 500 PA | $12 | 260 pts

OF-134 (CF-134) | Owned: 41% | LH

Despite the discipline issues that dogged him in 2010, Morgan will be the Nationals' starting CF in 2011. He is a merely average batter for his position on the best of days, but he is much less valuable if he can't lead off. (PB)

| Player | Age | AB | HR | R | RBI | SB | BA | OBP | SLG | $1L | Pts |
|---|---|---|---|---|---|---|---|---|---|---|---|
| Morgan N | 30 | 434 | 0 | 65 | 30 | 35 | .265 | .329 | .341 | $12 | 260 |
| **Mini-Browser** | | | | | | | | | | | |
| Stubbs D | 26 | 441 | 15 | 70 | 50 | 25 | .238 | .322 | .403 | $13 | 270 |
| McLouth N | 29 | 383 | 17 | 64 | 51 | 17 | .266 | .361 | .471 | $13 | 310 |
| Raburn R | 29 | 354 | 16 | 56 | 56 | 4 | .271 | .339 | .491 | $13 | 240 |
| Podsednik S | 35 | 459 | 5 | 55 | 40 | 25 | .283 | .338 | .378 | $13 | 280 |
| Fowler D | 25 | 471 | 6 | 77 | 44 | 22 | .257 | .352 | .410 | $13 | 300 |

| Level | Leag | AB | HR | R | RBI | SB | BA | OBP | SLG | CT% | H% | BB% | Bash |
|---|---|---|---|---|---|---|---|---|---|---|---|---|---|
| A | 2LG | 6 | 0 | 0 | 0 | 0 | .000 | .143 | .000 | 83% | 0% | 14% | NA |
| AA | — | — | — | — | — | — | — | — | — | — | — | — | — |
| AAA | — | — | — | — | — | — | — | — | — | — | — | — | — |

Competition at CF — Stats in 2010

| Bats | Player | GSvR | GSvL | Sub | OPS |
|---|---|---|---|---|---|
| LH | Morgan N | 102 | 26 | 6 | .633 |
| LH | Bernadina R | 20 | 3 | 3 | .691 |
| RH | Maxwell J | 3 | 10 | 7 | .594 |

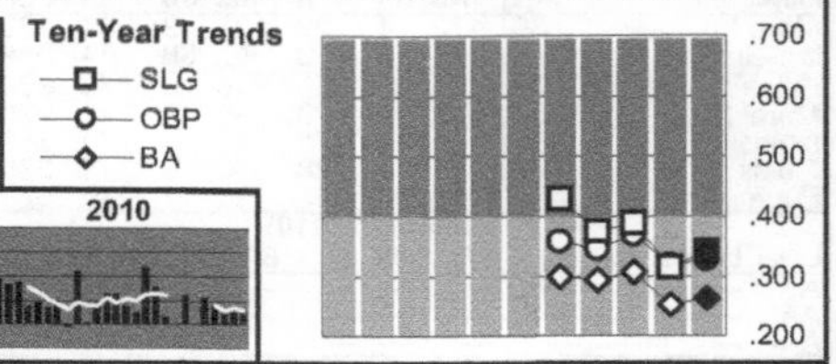


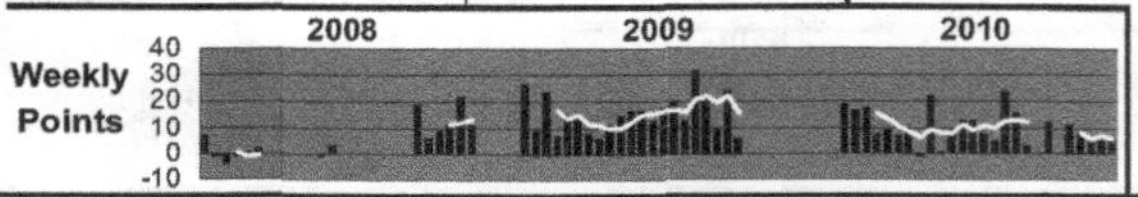


| Yr | Team | AB | HR | R | RBI | SB | BA | OBP | SLG | CT% | H% | BB% | Bash | $1L | $2L | Pts | RAA | 2B | 3B | CS | FB-LD-GB | HR/fb | RBI% | RS% | OPS | 1st Hf | 2nd Hf | vs RH | vs LH | Rnge | vRH | vLH |
|---|---|---|---|---|---|---|---|---|---|---|---|---|---|---|---|---|---|---|---|---|---|---|---|---|---|---|---|---|---|---|---|---|
| 07 | PIT | 107 | 1 | 15 | 7 | 7 | .299 | .359 | .430 | 82% | 36% | 8% | 1.44 | -$1 | -$14 | 70 | +1 | 3 | 4 | 3 | 27-16-57 | 5% | 18% | 34% | .789 | — | .789 | .773 | .836 | — | — | — |
| 08 | PIT | 160 | 0 | 26 | 7 | 9 | .294 | .345 | .375 | 80% | 37% | 6% | 1.28 | $1 | -$11 | 80 | −2 | 13 | 0 | 5 | 26-25-50 | 0% | 12% | 43% | .720 | .408 | .831 | .735 | .641 | 2.17 | +21 | −68 |
| 09 | 2TM | 469 | 3 | 74 | 39 | 42 | .307 | .369 | .388 | 84% | 36% | 7% | 1.26 | $24 | $11 | 330 | −1 | 15 | 7 | 17 | 26-19-54 | 3% | 19% | 37% | .757 | .706 | .869 | .829 | .507 | 2.13 | +19 | −59 |
| 10 | WAS | 509 | 0 | 60 | 24 | 34 | .253 | .319 | .314 | 83% | 31% | 7% | 1.24 | $11 | -$1 | 250 | −29 | 17 | 7 | 17 | 25-22-53 | 0% | 14% | 34% | .633 | .630 | .638 | .669 | .532 | 2.18 | +34 | −109 |

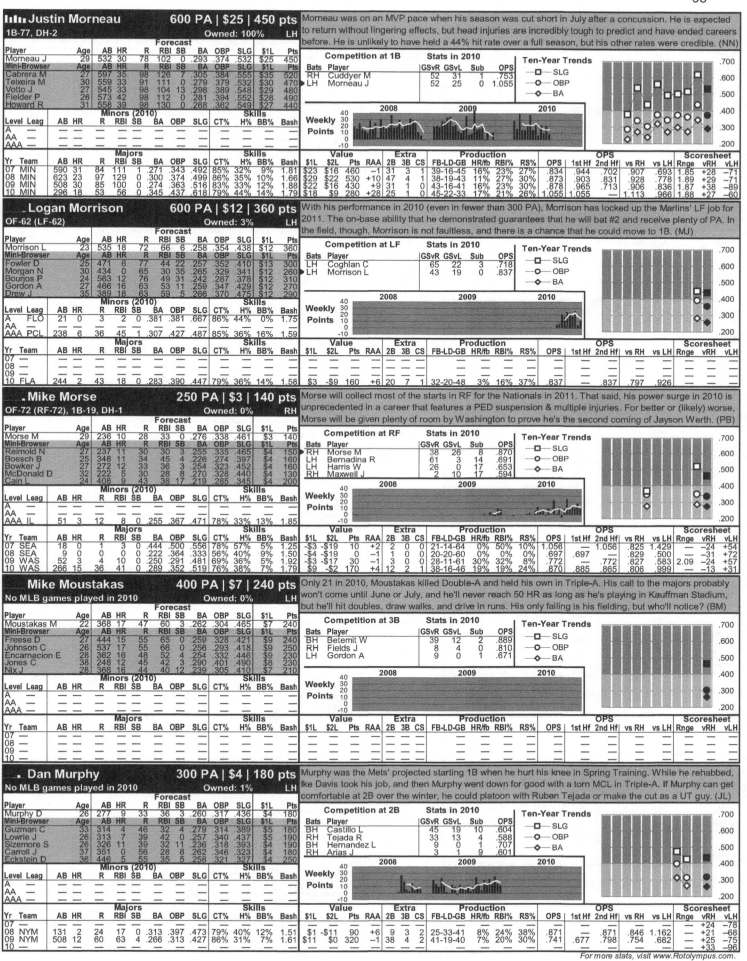

## Justin Morneau — 600 PA | $25 | 450 pts

1B-77, DH-2 — Owned: 100% — LH

| Player | Age | AB | HR | R | RBI | SB | BA | OBP | SLG | $1L | Pts |
|---|---|---|---|---|---|---|---|---|---|---|---|
| Morneau J | 29 | 532 | 30 | 78 | 102 | 0 | .293 | .374 | .532 | $25 | 450 |
| **Mini-Browser** | Age | AB | HR | R | RBI | SB | BA | OBP | SLG | $1L | Pts |
| Cabrera M | 27 | 597 | 35 | 98 | 126 | 7 | .305 | .384 | .555 | $35 | 520 |
| Teixeira M | 30 | 559 | 33 | 91 | 111 | 0 | .279 | .379 | .532 | $30 | 470 |
| Votto J | 27 | 545 | 33 | 98 | 104 | 13 | .298 | .389 | .548 | $29 | 480 |
| Fielder P | 26 | 573 | 42 | 98 | 112 | 0 | .281 | .394 | .552 | $28 | 490 |
| Howard R | 31 | 558 | 39 | 98 | 130 | 0 | .268 | .362 | .549 | $27 | 440 |

Minors (2010)

| Level | Leag | AB | HR | R | RBI | SB | BA | OBP | SLG | CT% | H% | BB% | Bash |
|---|---|---|---|---|---|---|---|---|---|---|---|---|---|
| A | — | — | — | — | — | — | — | — | — | — | — | — | — |
| AA | — | — | — | — | — | — | — | — | — | — | — | — | — |
| AAA | — | — | — | — | — | — | — | — | — | — | — | — | — |

Majors

| Yr | Team | AB | HR | R | RBI | SB | BA | OBP | SLG | CT% | H% | BB% | Bash |
|---|---|---|---|---|---|---|---|---|---|---|---|---|---|
| 07 | MIN | 590 | 31 | 84 | 111 | 1 | .271 | .343 | .492 | 85% | 32% | 9% | 1.81 |
| 08 | MIN | 623 | 23 | 97 | 129 | 0 | .300 | .374 | .499 | 86% | 35% | 10% | 1.66 |
| 09 | MIN | 508 | 30 | 85 | 100 | 0 | .274 | .363 | .516 | 83% | 33% | 12% | 1.88 |
| 10 | MIN | 296 | 18 | 53 | 56 | 0 | .345 | .437 | .618 | 79% | 44% | 14% | 1.79 |

| Yr | Value $1L | $2L | Pts | RAA | Extra 2B | 3B | CS | Production FB-LD-GB | HR/fb | RBI% | RS% | OPS | 1st Hf | 2nd Hf | vs RH | vs LH | Scoresheet Rnge | vRH | vLH |
|---|---|---|---|---|---|---|---|---|---|---|---|---|---|---|---|---|---|---|---|
| 07 | $23 | $16 | 460 | −1 | 31 | 3 | 1 | 39-16-45 | 16% | 23% | 27% | .834 | .944 | .702 | .907 | .693 | 1.85 | +28 | −71 |
| 08 | $29 | $22 | 530 | +10 | 47 | 4 | 1 | 38-19-43 | 11% | 27% | 30% | .873 | .903 | .831 | .928 | .778 | 1.89 | +29 | −71 |
| 09 | $22 | $16 | 430 | +9 | 31 | 1 | 0 | 43-16-41 | 16% | 23% | 30% | .878 | .965 | .713 | .906 | .836 | 1.87 | +38 | −89 |
| 10 | $18 | $9 | 280 | +28 | 25 | 1 | 0 | 45-22-33 | 17% | 21% | 26% | 1.055 | 1.055 | — | 1.113 | .966 | 1.88 | +27 | −60 |

Morneau was on an MVP pace when his season was cut short in July after a concussion. He is expected to return without lingering effects, but head injuries are incredibly tough to predict and have ended careers before. He is unlikely to have held a 44% hit rate over a full season, but his other rates were credible. (NN)

Competition at 1B — Stats in 2010

| Bats | Player | GSvR | GSvL | Sub | OPS |
|---|---|---|---|---|---|
| RH | Cuddyer M | 52 | 31 | 1 | .753 |
| LH | Morneau J | 52 | 25 | 0 | 1.055 |

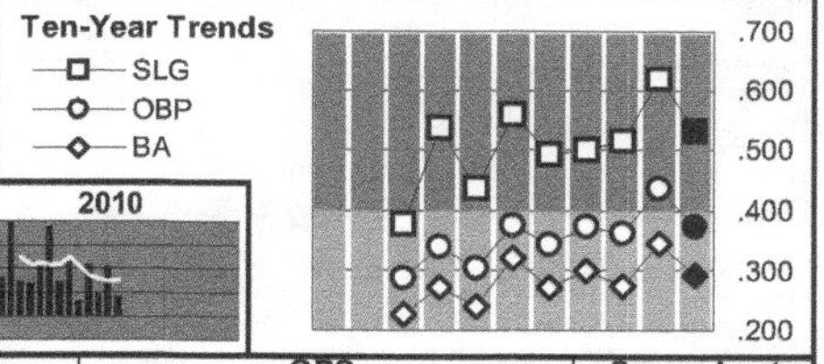

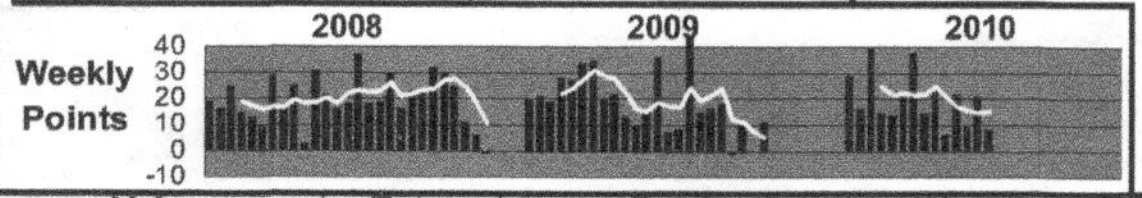

## Logan Morrison — 600 PA | $12 | 360 pts

OF-62 (LF-62) — Owned: 3% — LH

| Player | Age | AB | HR | R | RBI | SB | BA | OBP | SLG | $1L | Pts |
|---|---|---|---|---|---|---|---|---|---|---|---|
| Morrison L | 23 | 535 | 18 | 72 | 66 | 6 | .258 | .354 | .438 | $12 | 360 |
| **Mini-Browser** | Age | AB | HR | R | RBI | SB | BA | OBP | SLG | $1L | Pts |
| Fowler D | 25 | 471 | 6 | 77 | 44 | 22 | .257 | .352 | .410 | $13 | 300 |
| Morgan N | 30 | 434 | 0 | 65 | 30 | 35 | .265 | .329 | .341 | $12 | 260 |
| Bourjos P | 24 | 563 | 12 | 76 | 49 | 31 | .242 | .287 | .378 | $12 | 310 |
| Gordon A | 27 | 466 | 16 | 63 | 53 | 11 | .259 | .347 | .429 | $12 | 270 |
| Drew J | 35 | 389 | 18 | 63 | 59 | 5 | .266 | .370 | .475 | $12 | 290 |

Minors (2010)

| Level | Leag | AB | HR | R | RBI | SB | BA | OBP | SLG | CT% | H% | BB% | Bash |
|---|---|---|---|---|---|---|---|---|---|---|---|---|---|
| A | FLO | 21 | 0 | 3 | 2 | 0 | .381 | .381 | .667 | 86% | 44% | 0% | 1.75 |
| AA | — | — | — | — | — | — | — | — | — | — | — | — | — |
| AAA | PCL | 238 | 6 | 36 | 45 | 1 | .307 | .427 | .487 | 85% | 36% | 16% | 1.59 |

Majors

| Yr | Team | AB | HR | R | RBI | SB | BA | OBP | SLG | CT% | H% | BB% | Bash |
|---|---|---|---|---|---|---|---|---|---|---|---|---|---|
| 07 | — | — | — | — | — | — | — | — | — | — | — | — | — |
| 08 | — | — | — | — | — | — | — | — | — | — | — | — | — |
| 09 | — | — | — | — | — | — | — | — | — | — | — | — | — |
| 10 | FLA | 244 | 2 | 43 | 18 | 0 | .283 | .390 | .447 | 79% | 36% | 14% | 1.58 |

| Yr | Value $1L | $2L | Pts | RAA | Extra 2B | 3B | CS | Production FB-LD-GB | HR/fb | RBI% | RS% | OPS | 1st Hf | 2nd Hf | vs RH | vs LH | Scoresheet Rnge | vRH | vLH |
|---|---|---|---|---|---|---|---|---|---|---|---|---|---|---|---|---|---|---|---|
| 07 | — | — | — | — | — | — | — | — | — | — | — | — | — | — | — | — | — | — | — |
| 08 | — | — | — | — | — | — | — | — | — | — | — | — | — | — | — | — | — | — | — |
| 09 | — | — | — | — | — | — | — | — | — | — | — | — | — | — | — | — | — | — | — |
| 10 | $3 | -$9 | 160 | +6 | 20 | 7 | 1 | 32-20-48 | 3% | 16% | 37% | .837 | — | .837 | .797 | .926 | — | — | — |

With his performance in 2010 (even in fewer than 300 PA), Morrison has locked up the Marlins' LF job for 2011. The on-base ability that he demonstrated guarantees that he will bat #2 and receive plenty of PA. In the field, though, Morrison is not faultless, and there is a chance that he could move to 1B. (MJ)

Competition at LF — Stats in 2010

| Bats | Player | GSvR | GSvL | Sub | OPS |
|---|---|---|---|---|---|
| LH | Coghlan C | 65 | 22 | 3 | .718 |
| LH | Morrison L | 43 | 19 | 0 | .837 |

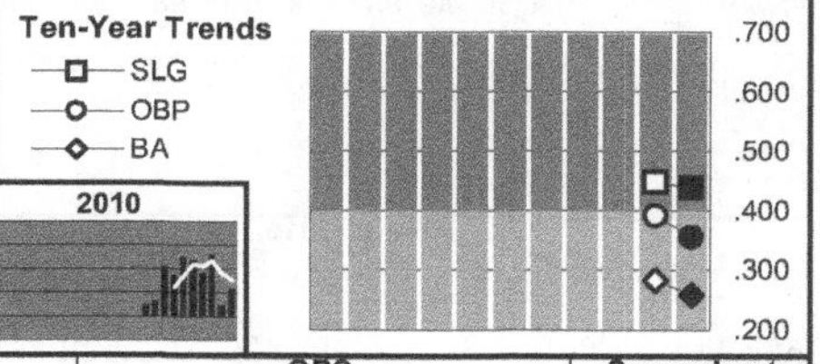

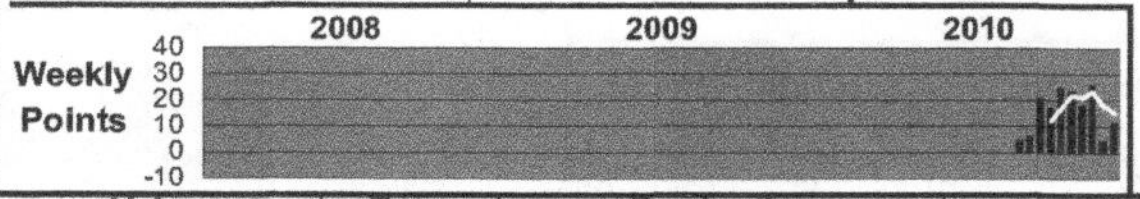

## Mike Morse — 250 PA | $3 | 140 pts

OF-72 (RF-72), 1B-19, DH-1 — Owned: 0% — RH

| Player | Age | AB | HR | R | RBI | SB | BA | OBP | SLG | $1L | Pts |
|---|---|---|---|---|---|---|---|---|---|---|---|
| Morse M | 29 | 236 | 10 | 28 | 33 | 0 | .276 | .338 | .461 | $3 | 140 |
| **Mini-Browser** | Age | AB | HR | R | RBI | SB | BA | OBP | SLG | $1L | Pts |
| Reimold N | 27 | 237 | 11 | 30 | 30 | 3 | .255 | .335 | .465 | $4 | 150 |
| Boesch B | 25 | 348 | 11 | 34 | 45 | 4 | .226 | .274 | .397 | $4 | 160 |
| Bowker J | 27 | 272 | 12 | 33 | 36 | 3 | .254 | .323 | .452 | $4 | 160 |
| McDonald D | 32 | 222 | 5 | 30 | 28 | 8 | .270 | .328 | .440 | $4 | 130 |
| Cain L | 24 | 408 | 9 | 43 | 38 | 17 | .219 | .285 | .345 | $4 | 200 |

Minors (2010)

| Level | Leag | AB | HR | R | RBI | SB | BA | OBP | SLG | CT% | H% | BB% | Bash |
|---|---|---|---|---|---|---|---|---|---|---|---|---|---|
| A | — | — | — | — | — | — | — | — | — | — | — | — | — |
| AA | — | — | — | — | — | — | — | — | — | — | — | — | — |
| AAA | IL | 51 | 3 | 12 | 8 | 0 | .255 | .367 | .471 | 78% | 33% | 13% | 1.85 |

Majors

| Yr | Team | AB | HR | R | RBI | SB | BA | OBP | SLG | CT% | H% | BB% | Bash |
|---|---|---|---|---|---|---|---|---|---|---|---|---|---|
| 07 | SEA | 18 | 0 | 1 | 3 | 0 | .444 | .500 | .556 | 78% | 57% | 5% | 1.25 |
| 08 | SEA | 9 | 0 | 0 | 0 | 0 | .222 | .364 | .333 | 56% | 40% | 9% | 1.50 |
| 09 | WAS | 52 | 3 | 4 | 10 | 0 | .250 | .291 | .481 | 69% | 36% | 5% | 1.92 |
| 10 | WAS | 266 | 15 | 36 | 41 | 0 | .289 | .352 | .519 | 76% | 38% | 7% | 1.79 |

| Yr | Value $1L | $2L | Pts | RAA | Extra 2B | 3B | CS | Production FB-LD-GB | HR/fb | RBI% | RS% | OPS | 1st Hf | 2nd Hf | vs RH | vs LH | Scoresheet Rnge | vRH | vLH |
|---|---|---|---|---|---|---|---|---|---|---|---|---|---|---|---|---|---|---|---|
| 07 | -$3 | -$19 | 10 | +2 | 2 | 0 | 0 | 21-14-64 | 0% | 50% | 10% | 1.056 | — | 1.056 | .825 | 1.429 | — | −24 | +54 |
| 08 | -$4 | -$19 | 0 | −1 | 1 | 0 | 0 | 20-20-60 | 0% | 0% | 0% | .697 | .697 | — | .829 | .500 | — | −31 | +72 |
| 09 | -$3 | -$17 | 30 | −1 | 3 | 0 | 0 | 28-11-61 | 30% | 32% | 8% | .772 | — | .772 | .827 | .583 | 2.09 | −24 | +57 |
| 10 | $9 | -$2 | 170 | +4 | 12 | 2 | 1 | 38-16-46 | 19% | 19% | 24% | .870 | .885 | .865 | .806 | .999 | — | −13 | +31 |

Morse will collect most of the starts in RF for the Nationals in 2011. That said, his power surge in 2010 is unprecedented in a career that features a PED suspension & multiple injuries. For better or (likely) worse, Morse will be given plenty of room by Washington to prove he's the second coming of Jayson Werth. (PB)

Competition at RF — Stats in 2010

| Bats | Player | GSvR | GSvL | Sub | OPS |
|---|---|---|---|---|---|
| RH | Morse M | 38 | 26 | 8 | .870 |
| LH | Bernadina R | 61 | 3 | 14 | .691 |
| LH | Harris W | 26 | 0 | 17 | .653 |
| RH | Maxwell J | 2 | 10 | 17 | .594 |

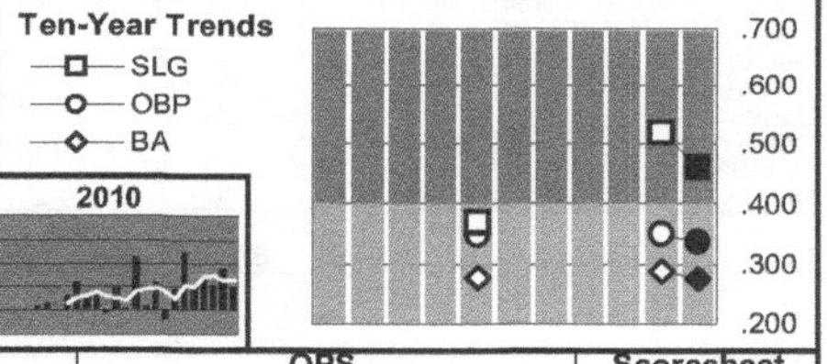

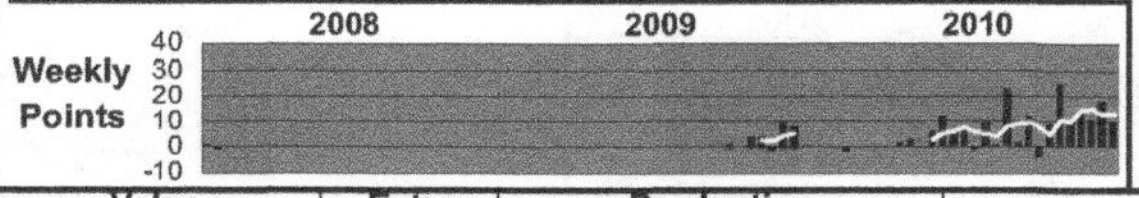

## Mike Moustakas — 400 PA | $7 | 240 pts

No MLB games played in 2010 — Owned: 0% — LH

| Player | Age | AB | HR | R | RBI | SB | BA | OBP | SLG | $1L | Pts |
|---|---|---|---|---|---|---|---|---|---|---|---|
| Moustakas M | 22 | 368 | 17 | 47 | 60 | 3 | .262 | .304 | .465 | $7 | 240 |
| **Mini-Browser** | Age | AB | HR | R | RBI | SB | BA | OBP | SLG | $1L | Pts |
| Freese D | 27 | 444 | 15 | 55 | 65 | 0 | .259 | .328 | .421 | $9 | 240 |
| Johnson C | 26 | 537 | 17 | 55 | 66 | 0 | .256 | .293 | .418 | $9 | 250 |
| Encarnacion E | 28 | 362 | 16 | 48 | 52 | 4 | .254 | .332 | .446 | $9 | 230 |
| Jones C | 38 | 248 | 12 | 45 | 42 | 3 | .290 | .401 | .490 | $8 | 230 |
| Nix J | 28 | 368 | 16 | 44 | 40 | 12 | .239 | .305 | .410 | $7 | 210 |

Minors (2010)

| Level | Leag | AB | HR | R | RBI | SB | BA | OBP | SLG | CT% | H% | BB% | Bash |
|---|---|---|---|---|---|---|---|---|---|---|---|---|---|
| A | — | — | — | — | — | — | — | — | — | — | — | — | — |
| AA | — | — | — | — | — | — | — | — | — | — | — | — | — |
| AAA | — | — | — | — | — | — | — | — | — | — | — | — | — |

Majors

| Yr | Team | AB | HR | R | RBI | SB | BA | OBP | SLG | CT% | H% | BB% | Bash |
|---|---|---|---|---|---|---|---|---|---|---|---|---|---|
| 07 | — | — | — | — | — | — | — | — | — | — | — | — | — |
| 08 | — | — | — | — | — | — | — | — | — | — | — | — | — |
| 09 | — | — | — | — | — | — | — | — | — | — | — | — | — |
| 10 | — | — | — | — | — | — | — | — | — | — | — | — | — |

| Yr | Value $1L | $2L | Pts | RAA | Extra 2B | 3B | CS | Production FB-LD-GB | HR/fb | RBI% | RS% | OPS | 1st Hf | 2nd Hf | vs RH | vs LH | Scoresheet Rnge | vRH | vLH |
|---|---|---|---|---|---|---|---|---|---|---|---|---|---|---|---|---|---|---|---|
| 07 | — | — | — | — | — | — | — | — | — | — | — | — | — | — | — | — | — | — | — |
| 08 | — | — | — | — | — | — | — | — | — | — | — | — | — | — | — | — | — | — | — |
| 09 | — | — | — | — | — | — | — | — | — | — | — | — | — | — | — | — | — | — | — |
| 10 | — | — | — | — | — | — | — | — | — | — | — | — | — | — | — | — | — | — | — |

Only 21 in 2010, Moustakas killed Double-A and held his own in Triple-A. His call to the majors probably won't come until June or July, and he'll never reach 50 HR as long as he's playing in Kauffman Stadium, but he'll hit doubles, draw walks, and drive in runs. His only failing is his fielding, but who'll notice? (BM)

Competition at 3B — Stats in 2010

| Bats | Player | GSvR | GSvL | Sub | OPS |
|---|---|---|---|---|---|
| BH | Betemit W | 39 | 12 | 2 | .889 |
| RH | Fields J | 8 | 4 | 0 | .810 |
| LH | Gordon A | 9 | 0 | 1 | .671 |

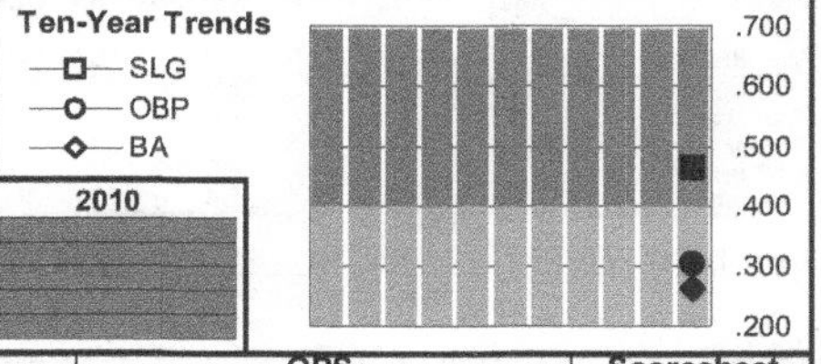

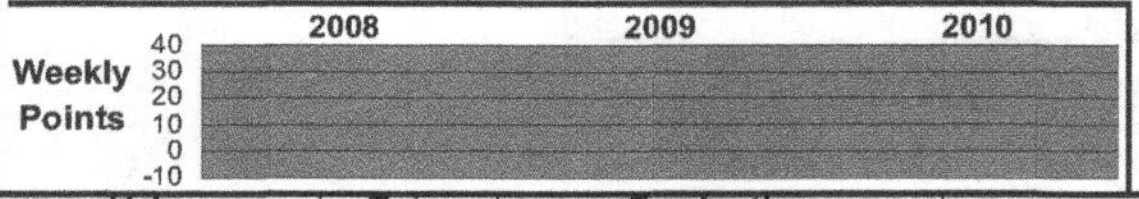

## Dan Murphy — 300 PA | $4 | 180 pts

No MLB games played in 2010 — Owned: 1% — LH

| Player | Age | AB | HR | R | RBI | SB | BA | OBP | SLG | $1L | Pts |
|---|---|---|---|---|---|---|---|---|---|---|---|
| Murphy D | 26 | 277 | 9 | 33 | 36 | 3 | .260 | .317 | .436 | $4 | 180 |
| **Mini-Browser** | Age | AB | HR | R | RBI | SB | BA | OBP | SLG | $1L | Pts |
| Guzman C | 33 | 314 | 4 | 46 | 32 | 4 | .279 | .314 | .389 | $5 | 180 |
| Lowrie J | 26 | 313 | 7 | 39 | 42 | 0 | .257 | .340 | .437 | $5 | 190 |
| Sizemore S | 26 | 326 | 11 | 39 | 32 | 11 | .236 | .318 | .393 | $4 | 190 |
| Carroll J | 37 | 351 | 0 | 56 | 28 | 8 | .262 | .346 | .323 | $4 | 180 |
| Eckstein D | 36 | 446 | 5 | 55 | 35 | 5 | .258 | .321 | .327 | $4 | 250 |

Minors (2010)

| Level | Leag | AB | HR | R | RBI | SB | BA | OBP | SLG | CT% | H% | BB% | Bash |
|---|---|---|---|---|---|---|---|---|---|---|---|---|---|
| A | — | — | — | — | — | — | — | — | — | — | — | — | — |
| AA | — | — | — | — | — | — | — | — | — | — | — | — | — |
| AAA | — | — | — | — | — | — | — | — | — | — | — | — | — |

Majors

| Yr | Team | AB | HR | R | RBI | SB | BA | OBP | SLG | CT% | H% | BB% | Bash |
|---|---|---|---|---|---|---|---|---|---|---|---|---|---|
| 07 | — | — | — | — | — | — | — | — | — | — | — | — | — |
| 08 | NYM | 131 | 2 | 24 | 17 | 0 | .313 | .397 | .473 | 79% | 40% | 12% | 1.51 |
| 09 | NYM | 508 | 12 | 60 | 63 | 4 | .266 | .313 | .427 | 86% | 31% | 7% | 1.61 |
| 10 | — | — | — | — | — | — | — | — | — | — | — | — | — |

| Yr | Value $1L | $2L | Pts | RAA | Extra 2B | 3B | CS | Production FB-LD-GB | HR/fb | RBI% | RS% | OPS | 1st Hf | 2nd Hf | vs RH | vs LH | Scoresheet Rnge | vRH | vLH |
|---|---|---|---|---|---|---|---|---|---|---|---|---|---|---|---|---|---|---|---|
| 07 | — | — | — | — | — | — | — | — | — | — | — | — | — | — | — | — | — | +24 | −78 |
| 08 | $1 | -$11 | 90 | +6 | 9 | 3 | 2 | 25-33-41 | 8% | 24% | 38% | .871 | — | .871 | .846 | 1.162 | — | +21 | −68 |
| 09 | $11 | $0 | 320 | −1 | 38 | 4 | 2 | 41-19-40 | 7% | 20% | 30% | .741 | .677 | .798 | .754 | .682 | — | +25 | −75 |
| 10 | — | — | — | — | — | — | — | — | — | — | — | — | — | — | — | — | — | +33 | −96 |

Murphy was the Mets' projected starting 1B when he hurt his knee in Spring Training. While he rehabbed, Ike Davis took his job, and then Murphy went down for good with a torn MCL in Triple-A. If Murphy can get comfortable at 2B over the winter, he could platoon with Ruben Tejada or make the cut as a UT guy. (JL)

Competition at 2B — Stats in 2010

| Bats | Player | GSvR | GSvL | Sub | OPS |
|---|---|---|---|---|---|
| BH | Castillo L | 45 | 19 | 10 | .604 |
| RH | Tejada R | 33 | 13 | 4 | .588 |
| BH | Hernandez L | 9 | 0 | 1 | .707 |
| RH | Arias J | 3 | 1 | 9 | .601 |

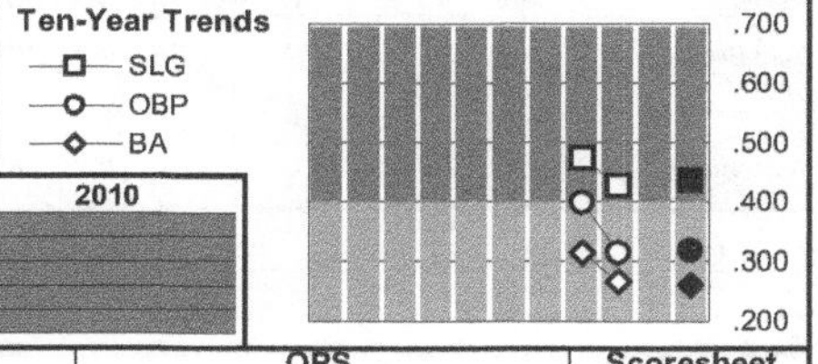

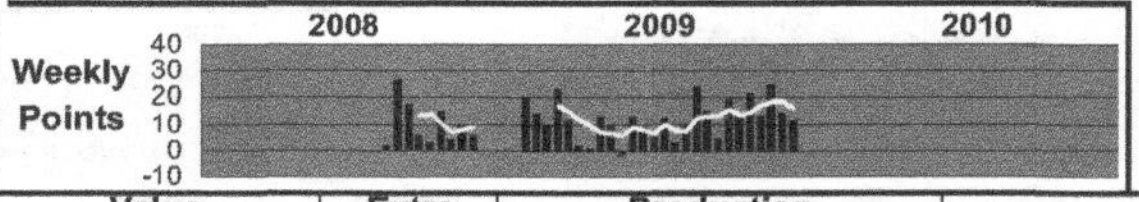

*For more stats, visit www.Rotolympus.com.*

## David Murphy — 425 PA | $12 | 270 pts

OF-125 (LF-75, RF-51, CF-10), DH-1 — Owned: 16% — LH

The Rangers' pillar of consistency flirted with bigger titles in 2010, posting a .290+ BA over a full season for the first time and ratcheting up his game during Josh Hamilton's prolonged absence. It is not illogical to view Murphy as a very good 4th OF and yet pencil him in for 400-450 PA; Texas wants to play him. (JM)

**Forecast**

| Player | Age | AB | HR | R | RBI | SB | BA | OBP | SLG | $1L | Pts |
|---|---|---|---|---|---|---|---|---|---|---|---|
| Murphy D | 29 | 395 | 13 | 51 | 55 | 9 | .280 | .341 | .454 | $12 | 270 |
| Mini-Browser | Age | AB | HR | R | RBI | SB | BA | OBP | SLG | $1L | Pts |
| Morgan N | 30 | 434 | 0 | 65 | 30 | 35 | .265 | .329 | .341 | $12 | 260 |
| Bourjos P | 24 | 563 | 12 | 76 | 49 | 31 | .242 | .287 | .378 | $12 | 310 |
| Gordon A | 27 | 466 | 16 | 63 | 53 | 11 | .259 | .347 | .429 | $12 | 270 |
| Drew J | 35 | 389 | 18 | 63 | 59 | 5 | .266 | .370 | .475 | $12 | 290 |
| Morrison L | 23 | 535 | 18 | 72 | 66 | 6 | .258 | .354 | .438 | $12 | 360 |

**Competition at LF — Stats in 2010**

| Bats | Player | GSvR | GSvL | Sub | OPS |
|---|---|---|---|---|---|
| LH | Hamilton J | 64 | 26 | 2 | 1.044 |
| ▶ LH | Murphy D | 44 | 20 | 11 | .806 |
| RH | Cruz N | 7 | 7 | 0 | .950 |

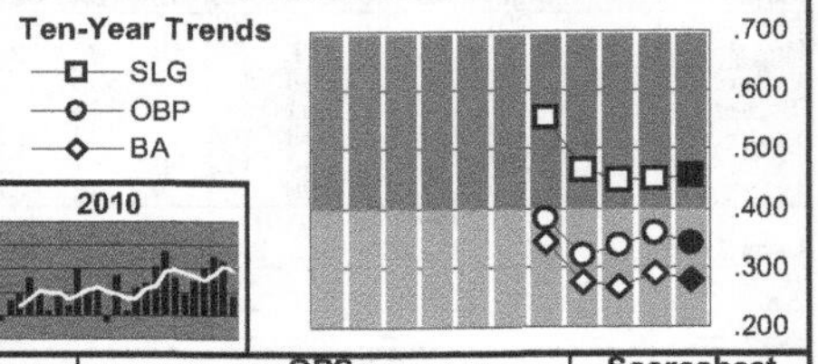


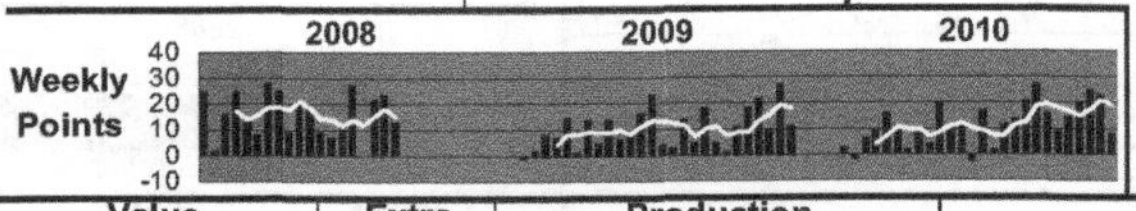


**Minors (2010)**

| Level | Leag | AB | HR | R | RBI | SB | BA | OBP | SLG | CT% | H% | BB% | Bash |
|---|---|---|---|---|---|---|---|---|---|---|---|---|---|
| A | — | — | — | — | — | — | — | — | — | — | — | — | — |
| AA | — | — | — | — | — | — | — | — | — | — | — | — | — |
| AAA | — | — | — | — | — | — | — | — | — | — | — | — | — |

| Majors | | | | | | | | | | Skills | | | | Value | | | | Extra | | | Production | | | | OPS | | | | | Scoresheet | | |
|---|---|---|---|---|---|---|---|---|---|---|---|---|---|---|---|---|---|---|---|---|---|---|---|---|---|---|---|---|---|---|---|---|
| Yr | Team | AB | HR | R | RBI | SB | BA | OBP | SLG | CT% | H% | BB% | Bash | $1L | $2L | Pts | RAA | 2B | 3B | CS | FB-LD-GB | HR/fb | RBI% | RS% | OPS | 1st Hf | 2nd Hf | vs RH | vs LH | Rnge | vRH | vLH |
| 07 | 2TM | 105 | 2 | 17 | 14 | 0 | .343 | .384 | .552 | 81% | 42% | 6% | 1.61 | $1 | -$13 | 80 | +7 | 12 | 2 | 0 | 32-26-42 | 7% | 27% | 37% | .936 | 2.000 | .916 | .901 | 1.071 | 2.10 | +24 | −78 |
| 08 | TEX | 415 | 15 | 64 | 74 | 7 | .275 | .321 | .465 | 83% | 33% | 7% | 1.69 | $16 | $6 | 300 | +1 | 28 | 3 | 2 | 40-18-42 | 11% | 21% | 38% | .786 | .783 | .803 | .835 | .669 | 2.10 | +21 | −68 |
| 09 | TEX | 432 | 17 | 61 | 57 | 9 | .269 | .338 | .447 | 75% | 36% | 10% | 1.66 | $13 | $3 | 270 | +1 | 24 | 1 | 4 | 43-19-38 | 12% | 19% | 30% | .785 | .804 | .769 | .833 | .627 | 2.10 | +25 | −75 |
| 10 | TEX | 419 | 12 | 54 | 65 | 14 | .291 | .358 | .449 | 83% | 35% | 10% | 1.54 | $18 | $8 | 310 | +9 | 26 | 2 | 2 | 36-19-44 | 9% | 25% | 27% | .806 | .712 | .897 | .847 | .696 | 2.08 | +33 | −96 |

## Donnie Murphy — 100 PA | $-2 | 60 pts

3B-4, SS-4, 2B-1 — Owned: 0% — RH

Murphy's PT upside in Florida is limited. He (like Brian Barden) is representative of the players that the Marlins might deploy as a utility infielder or as an emergency option at third base. Murphy is recovering from a season-ending wrist injury, for which he underwent surgery in September. (MJ)

**Forecast**

| Player | Age | AB | HR | R | RBI | SB | BA | OBP | SLG | $1L | Pts |
|---|---|---|---|---|---|---|---|---|---|---|---|
| Murphy D | 28 | 90 | 4 | 14 | 14 | 1 | .255 | .321 | .488 | -$2 | 60 |
| Mini-Browser | Age | AB | HR | R | RBI | SB | BA | OBP | SLG | $1L | Pts |
| Wood B | 26 | 173 | 8 | 22 | 22 | 2 | .231 | .288 | .419 | $0 | 80 |
| Fox J | 28 | 162 | 9 | 18 | 25 | 2 | .238 | .294 | .452 | $0 | 90 |
| Feliz P | 35 | 187 | 6 | 20 | 24 | 0 | .257 | .297 | .402 | $0 | 110 |
| Conrad B | 31 | 136 | 6 | 20 | 18 | 3 | .243 | .325 | .453 | $0 | 80 |
| Francisco J | 23 | 150 | 9 | 17 | 21 | 2 | .230 | .265 | .474 | -$1 | 80 |

**Competition at 3B — Stats in 2010**

| Bats | Player | GSvR | GSvL | Sub | OPS |
|---|---|---|---|---|---|
| RH | Helms W | 29 | 21 | 40 | .646 |
| LH | Tracy C | 22 | 0 | 2 | .628 |
| RH | Barden B | 0 | 0 | 16 | .460 |

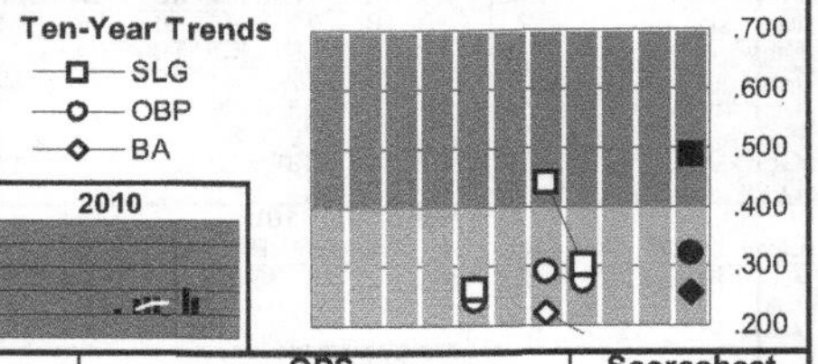


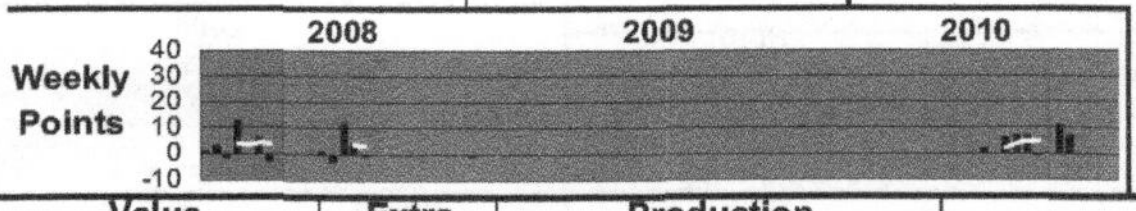


**Minors (2010)**

| Level | Leag | AB | HR | R | RBI | SB | BA | OBP | SLG | CT% | H% | BB% | Bash |
|---|---|---|---|---|---|---|---|---|---|---|---|---|---|
| A | — | — | — | — | — | — | — | — | — | — | — | — | — |
| AA | — | — | — | — | — | — | — | — | — | — | — | — | — |
| AAA | PCL | 206 | 12 | 31 | 35 | 0 | .277 | .335 | .519 | 80% | 35% | 7% | 1.88 |

| Majors | | | | | | | | | | Skills | | | | Value | | | | Extra | | | Production | | | | OPS | | | | | Scoresheet | | |
|---|---|---|---|---|---|---|---|---|---|---|---|---|---|---|---|---|---|---|---|---|---|---|---|---|---|---|---|---|---|---|---|---|
| Yr | Team | AB | HR | R | RBI | SB | BA | OBP | SLG | CT% | H% | BB% | Bash | $1L | $2L | Pts | RAA | 2B | 3B | CS | FB-LD-GB | HR/fb | RBI% | RS% | OPS | 1st Hf | 2nd Hf | vs RH | vs LH | Rnge | vRH | vLH |
| 07 | OAK | 118 | 6 | 21 | 21 | 1 | .220 | .290 | .441 | 70% | 31% | 8% | 2.00 | — | — | 70 | −2 | 8 | 0 | 0 | 46-19-35 | 16% | 19% | 47% | .731 | .000 | .768 | .595 | .968 | — | −14 | +32 |
| 08 | OAK | 103 | 3 | 10 | 13 | 2 | .184 | .274 | .301 | 63% | 29% | 9% | 1.63 | — | — | 30 | −7 | 3 | 0 | 1 | 39-23-38 | 12% | 16% | 24% | .574 | .580 | .522 | .612 | .528 | — | −29 | +70 |
| 09 | — | — | — | — | — | — | — | — | — | — | — | — | — | — | — | — | — | — | — | — | — | — | — | — | — | — | — | — | — | — | −24 | +55 |
| 10 | FLA | 44 | 3 | 9 | 16 | 0 | .318 | .348 | .705 | 57% | 56% | 4% | 2.21 | -$1 | -$15 | 40 | +4 | 6 | 1 | 0 | 36-32-32 | 33% | 39% | 46% | 1.052 | 1.500 | 1.031 | .844 | 1.571 | — | −12 | +26 |

## Xavier Nady — 300 PA | $5 | 160 pts

1B-52, OF-28 (RF-23, LF-6), DH-2 — Owned: 2% — RH

There's talk of Nady being invited back to the Cubs, but he would be a slight (and pricey) upgrade over the freely available names. In his early years, Nady was a decent defensive outfielder, and his ordinary offense was not an issue. Post arm injury, he's a poor-fielding first baseman, and he no longer helps a team. (RM)

**Forecast**

| Player | Age | AB | HR | R | RBI | SB | BA | OBP | SLG | $1L | Pts |
|---|---|---|---|---|---|---|---|---|---|---|---|
| Nady X | 32 | 274 | 12 | 36 | 42 | 0 | .274 | .327 | .452 | $5 | 160 |
| Mini-Browser | Age | AB | HR | R | RBI | SB | BA | OBP | SLG | $1L | Pts |
| Ka'aihue K | 27 | 373 | 18 | 50 | 50 | 0 | .241 | .350 | .428 | $7 | 240 |
| Jones G | 29 | 269 | 12 | 36 | 39 | 3 | .268 | .331 | .476 | $6 | 180 |
| Johnson D | 31 | 278 | 17 | 39 | 58 | 2 | .227 | .356 | .447 | $5 | 210 |
| Smoak J | 24 | 390 | 14 | 45 | 50 | 0 | .231 | .332 | .393 | $5 | 200 |
| Viciedo D | 22 | 293 | 12 | 36 | 36 | 3 | .256 | .288 | .419 | $5 | 150 |

**Competition at 1B — Stats in 2010**

| Bats | Player | GSvR | GSvL | Sub | OPS |
|---|---|---|---|---|---|
| ▶ RH | Nady X | 33 | 17 | 2 | .660 |
| LH | Hoffpauir M | 7 | 1 | 4 | .476 |

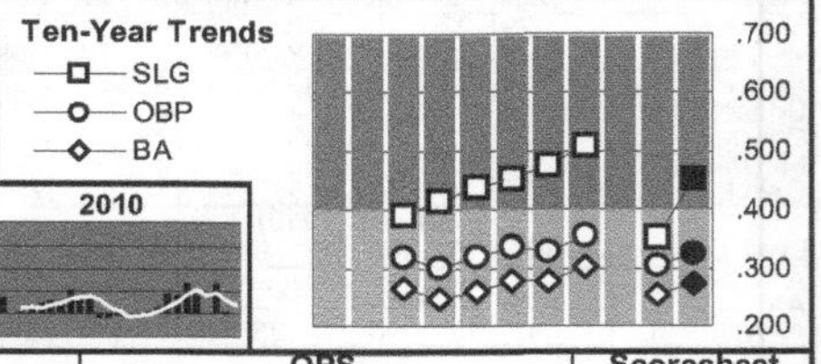


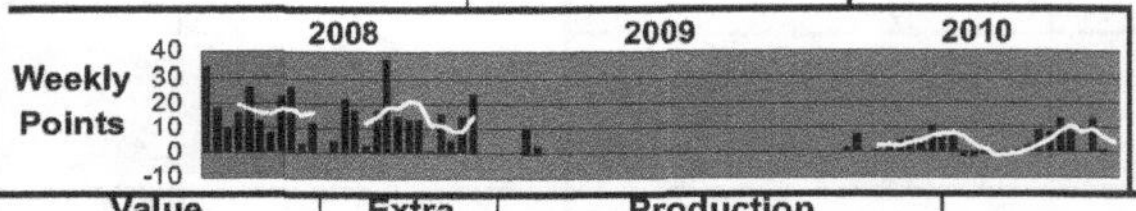


**Minors (2010)**

| Level | Leag | AB | HR | R | RBI | SB | BA | OBP | SLG | CT% | H% | BB% | Bash |
|---|---|---|---|---|---|---|---|---|---|---|---|---|---|
| A | — | — | — | — | — | — | — | — | — | — | — | — | — |
| AA | — | — | — | — | — | — | — | — | — | — | — | — | — |
| AAA | — | — | — | — | — | — | — | — | — | — | — | — | — |

| Majors | | | | | | | | | | Skills | | | | Value | | | | Extra | | | Production | | | | OPS | | | | | Scoresheet | | |
|---|---|---|---|---|---|---|---|---|---|---|---|---|---|---|---|---|---|---|---|---|---|---|---|---|---|---|---|---|---|---|---|---|
| Yr | Team | AB | HR | R | RBI | SB | BA | OBP | SLG | CT% | H% | BB% | Bash | $1L | $2L | Pts | RAA | 2B | 3B | CS | FB-LD-GB | HR/fb | RBI% | RS% | OPS | 1st Hf | 2nd Hf | vs RH | vs LH | Rnge | vRH | vLH |
| 07 | PIT | 431 | 20 | 55 | 72 | 3 | .278 | .330 | .476 | 77% | 36% | 5% | 1.71 | $14 | $5 | 260 | −8 | 23 | 1 | 1 | 40-21-39 | 15% | 23% | 26% | .805 | .848 | .728 | .802 | .819 | 1.87 | −32 | +77 |
| 08 | 2TM | 555 | 25 | 76 | 97 | 2 | .305 | .357 | .510 | 81% | 37% | 6% | 1.67 | $20 | $17 | 400 | +8 | 37 | 1 | 1 | 34-25-41 | 16% | 23% | 27% | .867 | .901 | .825 | .886 | .805 | — | −25 | +68 |
| 09 | NYY | 28 | 0 | 4 | 2 | 0 | .286 | .310 | .429 | 79% | 36% | 3% | 1.50 | -$4 | -$20 | 10 | −1 | 4 | 0 | 0 | 32-27-41 | 0% | 15% | 44% | .739 | .739 | — | .713 | .833 | — | −7 | +17 |
| 10 | CHC | 317 | 6 | 33 | 33 | 0 | .256 | .306 | .353 | 73% | 35% | 5% | 1.38 | -$2 | -$10 | 110 | −22 | 13 | 0 | 0 | 33-20-47 | 8% | 15% | 27% | .660 | .643 | .673 | .667 | .649 | — | −4 | +10 |

## Hiroyuki Nakajima — 500 PA | $13 | 290 pts

No MLB games played in 2010 — Owned: 0% — RH

In his career in Japan, Nakajima has been a gap hitter with good patience (8 BB%) and an 80% CT%. His .482 SLG comes as much from speed (192 doubles and 181 triples) as from power (331 HR). Baltimore, Boston, and Seattle – all teams with Japanese players – are rumored buyers. He can play 2B or SS. (MS)

**Forecast**

| Player | Age | AB | HR | R | RBI | SB | BA | OBP | SLG | $1L | Pts |
|---|---|---|---|---|---|---|---|---|---|---|---|
| Nakajima H | 28 | 460 | 15 | 60 | 60 | 10 | .272 | .312 | .410 | $13 | 290 |
| Mini-Browser | Age | AB | HR | R | RBI | SB | BA | OBP | SLG | $1L | Pts |
| Castro S | 21 | 574 | 7 | 72 | 59 | 20 | .283 | .330 | .401 | $15 | 340 |
| Escobar Y | 28 | 518 | 12 | 78 | 60 | 6 | .278 | .356 | .390 | $14 | 350 |
| Aybar E | 27 | 579 | 6 | 75 | 50 | 19 | .270 | .314 | .366 | $14 | 330 |
| Cabrera A | 25 | 531 | 6 | 72 | 60 | 12 | .271 | .334 | .383 | $14 | 310 |
| Scutaro M | 35 | 551 | 12 | 84 | 54 | 6 | .272 | .345 | .383 | $13 | 360 |

**Competition at SS — Stats in 2010**

| Bats | Player | GSvR | GSvL | Sub | OPS |
|---|---|---|---|---|---|

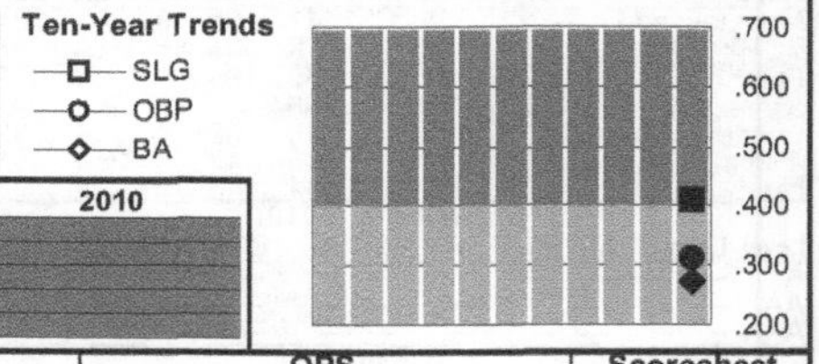


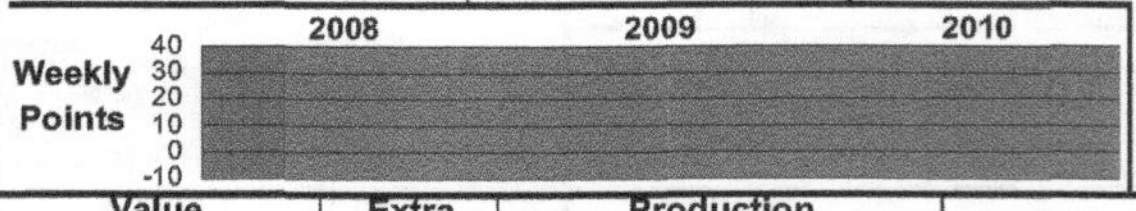


**Minors (2010)**

| Level | Leag | AB | HR | R | RBI | SB | BA | OBP | SLG | CT% | H% | BB% | Bash |
|---|---|---|---|---|---|---|---|---|---|---|---|---|---|
| A | — | — | — | — | — | — | — | — | — | — | — | — | — |
| AA | — | — | — | — | — | — | — | — | — | — | — | — | — |
| AAA | — | — | — | — | — | — | — | — | — | — | — | — | — |

| Majors | | | | | | | | | | Skills | | | | Value | | | | Extra | | | Production | | | | OPS | | | | | Scoresheet | | |
|---|---|---|---|---|---|---|---|---|---|---|---|---|---|---|---|---|---|---|---|---|---|---|---|---|---|---|---|---|---|---|---|---|
| Yr | Team | AB | HR | R | RBI | SB | BA | OBP | SLG | CT% | H% | BB% | Bash | $1L | $2L | Pts | RAA | 2B | 3B | CS | FB-LD-GB | HR/fb | RBI% | RS% | OPS | 1st Hf | 2nd Hf | vs RH | vs LH | Rnge | vRH | vLH |
| 07 | — | — | — | — | — | — | — | — | — | — | — | — | — | — | — | — | — | — | — | — | — | — | — | — | — | — | — | — | — | — | — | — |
| 08 | — | — | — | — | — | — | — | — | — | — | — | — | — | — | — | — | — | — | — | — | — | — | — | — | — | — | — | — | — | — | — | — |
| 09 | — | — | — | — | — | — | — | — | — | — | — | — | — | — | — | — | — | — | — | — | — | — | — | — | — | — | — | — | — | — | — | — |
| 10 | — | — | — | — | — | — | — | — | — | — | — | — | — | — | — | — | — | — | — | — | — | — | — | — | — | — | — | — | — | — | — | — |

## Mike Napoli — 450 PA | $16 | 240 pts

1B-70, CA-66, DH-2 — Owned: 99% — RH

Napoli might be the Angels' biggest trading piece. Although LA does not see him as a catcher, other clubs may accept his defensive shortcomings to play his bat. If Napoli stays in LA, his workload will slip, as he'll share duties with Jeff Mathis and eventually Hank Conger. But a more-rested Napoli might hit better. (DS)

**Forecast**

| Player | Age | AB | HR | R | RBI | SB | BA | OBP | SLG | $1L | Pts |
|---|---|---|---|---|---|---|---|---|---|---|---|
| Napoli M | 29 | 393 | 23 | 59 | 63 | 5 | .252 | .337 | .490 | $16 | 240 |
| Mini-Browser | Age | AB | HR | R | RBI | SB | BA | OBP | SLG | $1L | Pts |
| Mauer J | 27 | 495 | 12 | 84 | 84 | 6 | .315 | .400 | .466 | $25 | 420 |
| Posey B | 24 | 521 | 24 | 78 | 84 | 0 | .288 | .355 | .478 | $21 | 380 |
| Martinez V | 32 | 483 | 17 | 66 | 83 | 0 | .296 | .363 | .477 | $21 | 360 |
| McCann B | 27 | 498 | 22 | 66 | 88 | 6 | .287 | .365 | .501 | $21 | 390 |
| Soto G | 28 | 424 | 20 | 60 | 75 | 0 | .283 | .378 | .504 | $17 | 310 |

**Competition at CA — Stats in 2010**

| Bats | Player | GSvR | GSvL | Sub | OPS |
|---|---|---|---|---|---|
| ▶ RH | Napoli M | 40 | 23 | 3 | .784 |
| RH | Mathis J | 43 | 19 | 5 | .497 |
| RH | Wilson B | 20 | 9 | 9 | .705 |
| BH | Conger H | 8 | 1 | 1 | .570 |

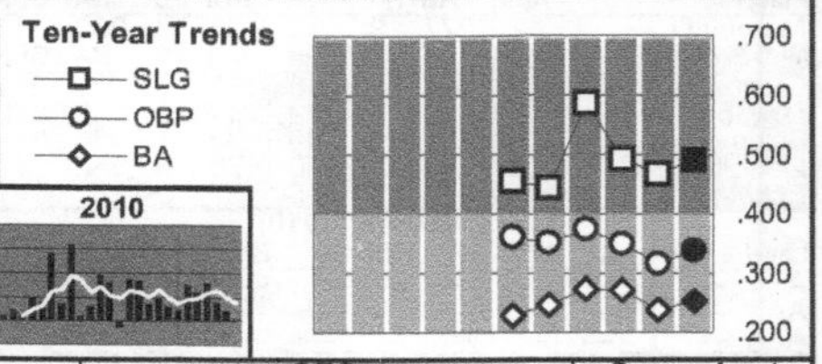


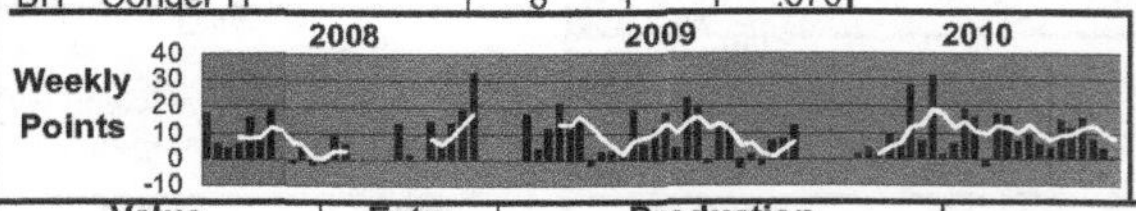


**Minors (2010)**

| Level | Leag | AB | HR | R | RBI | SB | BA | OBP | SLG | CT% | H% | BB% | Bash |
|---|---|---|---|---|---|---|---|---|---|---|---|---|---|
| A | — | — | — | — | — | — | — | — | — | — | — | — | — |
| AA | — | — | — | — | — | — | — | — | — | — | — | — | — |
| AAA | — | — | — | — | — | — | — | — | — | — | — | — | — |

| Majors | | | | | | | | | | Skills | | | | Value | | | | Extra | | | Production | | | | OPS | | | | | Scoresheet | | |
|---|---|---|---|---|---|---|---|---|---|---|---|---|---|---|---|---|---|---|---|---|---|---|---|---|---|---|---|---|---|---|---|---|
| Yr | Team | AB | HR | R | RBI | SB | BA | OBP | SLG | CT% | H% | BB% | Bash | $1L | $2L | Pts | RAA | 2B | 3B | CS | FB-LD-GB | HR/fb | RBI% | RS% | OPS | 1st Hf | 2nd Hf | vs RH | vs LH | Rnge | vRH | vLH |
| 07 | LAA | 219 | 10 | 40 | 34 | 5 | .247 | .351 | .443 | 71% | 35% | 12% | 1.80 | $9 | -$2 | 150 | +3 | 11 | 1 | 2 | 46-19-36 | 14% | 18% | 37% | .794 | .786 | .825 | .783 | .828 | 0.52 | −12 | +29 |
| 08 | LAA | 227 | 20 | 39 | 49 | 7 | .273 | .374 | .586 | 69% | 39% | 13% | 2.15 | $15 | $9 | 200 | +15 | 9 | 1 | 3 | 52-17-31 | 24% | 25% | 23% | .960 | .780 | 1.257 | .954 | .978 | 0.59 | −14 | +36 |
| 09 | LAA | 382 | 20 | 60 | 56 | 3 | .272 | .350 | .492 | 73% | 37% | 9% | 1.81 | $15 | $12 | 240 | +12 | 22 | 1 | 3 | 43-19-38 | 17% | 17% | 31% | .842 | .899 | .773 | .782 | 1.023 | 0.69 | −17 | +43 |
| 10 | LAA | 453 | 26 | 60 | 68 | 4 | .238 | .316 | .468 | 70% | 34% | 8% | 1.96 | $18 | $13 | 250 | +1 | 24 | 1 | 2 | 42-20-38 | 19% | 16% | 25% | .784 | .786 | .780 | .700 | .966 | 0.74 | −22 | +56 |

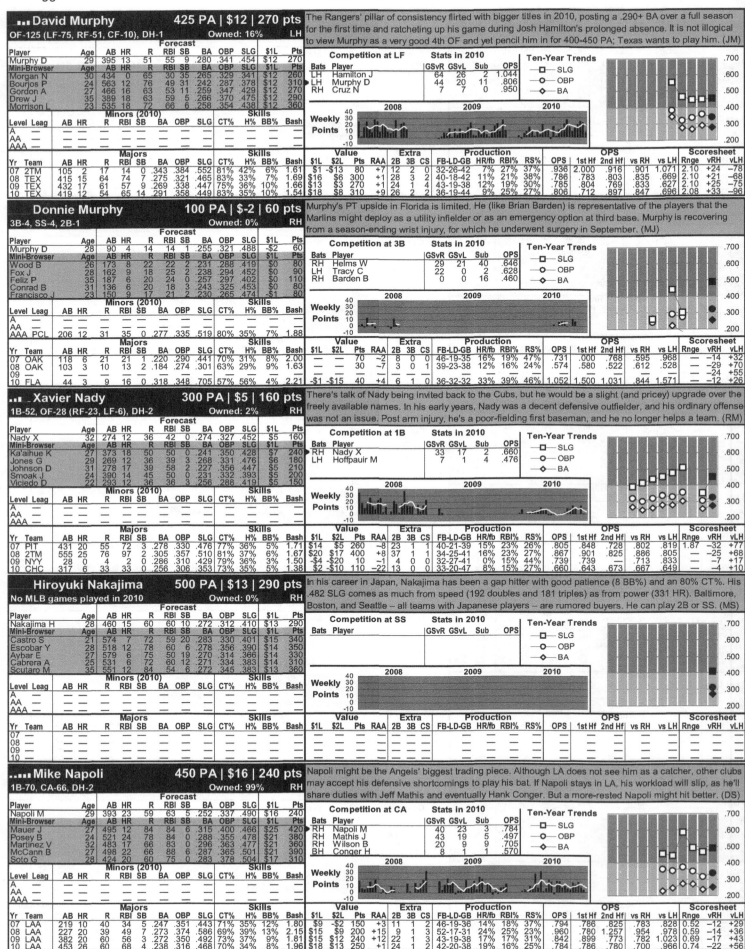

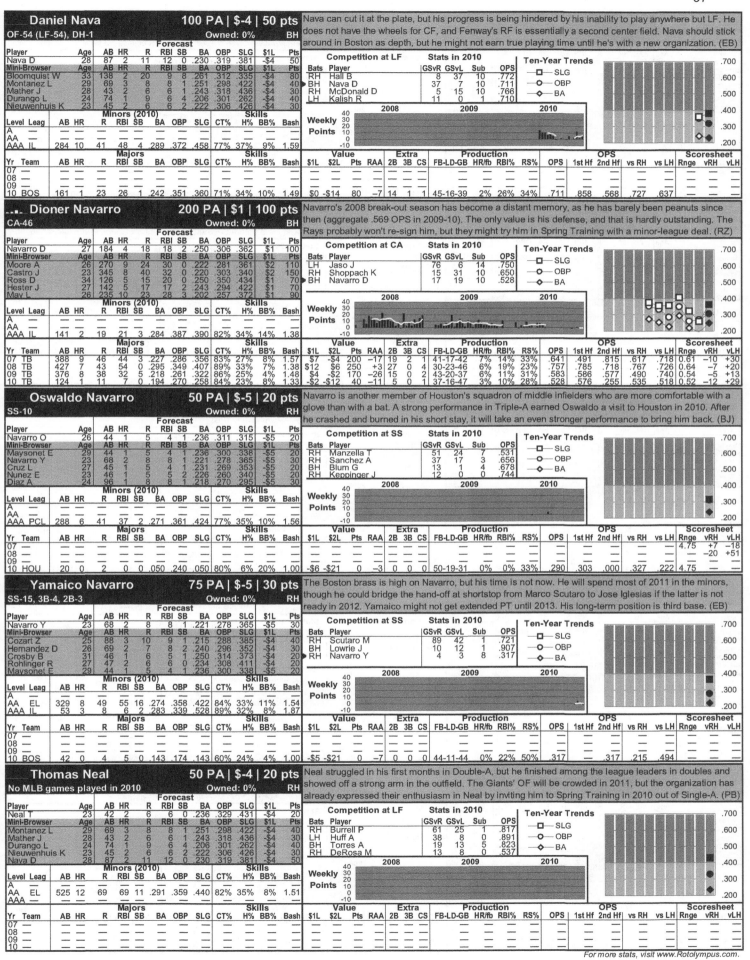

## Daniel Nava — 100 PA | $-4 | 50 pts

OF-54 (LF-54), DH-1    Owned: 0%    BH

Nava can cut it at the plate, but his progress is being hindered by his inability to play anywhere but LF. He does not have the wheels for CF, and Fenway's RF is essentially a second center field. Nava should stick around in Boston as depth, but he might not earn true playing time until he's with a new organization. (EB)

### Forecast
| Player | Age | AB | HR | R | RBI | SB | BA | OBP | SLG | $1L | Pts |
|---|---|---|---|---|---|---|---|---|---|---|---|
| Nava D | 28 | 87 | 2 | 11 | 12 | 0 | .230 | .319 | .381 | -$4 | 50 |

### Mini-Browser
| Player | Age | AB | HR | R | RBI | SB | BA | OBP | SLG | $1L | Pts |
|---|---|---|---|---|---|---|---|---|---|---|---|
| Bloomquist W | 33 | 138 | 2 | 20 | 9 | 8 | .261 | .312 | .335 | -$4 | 80 |
| Montanez L | 29 | 69 | 3 | 8 | 8 | 1 | .251 | .298 | .422 | -$4 | 40 |
| Mather J | 28 | 43 | 2 | 6 | 6 | 1 | .243 | .318 | .436 | -$4 | 30 |
| Durango L | 24 | 74 | 1 | 9 | 6 | 4 | .206 | .301 | .262 | -$4 | 40 |
| Nieuwenhuis K | 23 | 45 | 2 | 6 | 6 | 2 | .222 | .306 | .426 | -$4 | 30 |

### Competition at LF — Stats in 2010
| Bats | Player | GSvR | GSvL | Sub | OPS |
|---|---|---|---|---|---|
| RH | Hall B | 8 | 37 | 10 | .772 |
| BH | Nava D | 37 | 7 | 10 | .711 |
| RH | McDonald D | 5 | 15 | 10 | .766 |
| LH | Kalish R | 11 | 0 | 1 | .710 |

### Minors (2010)
| Level | Leag | AB | HR | R | RBI | SB | BA | OBP | SLG | CT% | H% | BB% | Bash |
|---|---|---|---|---|---|---|---|---|---|---|---|---|---|
| A | — | | | | | | | | | | | | |
| AA | — | | | | | | | | | | | | |
| AAA | IL | 284 | 10 | 41 | 48 | 4 | .289 | .372 | .458 | 77% | 37% | 9% | 1.59 |

### Majors
| Yr | Team | AB | HR | R | RBI | SB | BA | OBP | SLG | CT% | H% | BB% | Bash | $1L | $2L | Pts | RAA | 2B | 3B | CS | FB-LD-GB | HR/fb | RBI% | RS% | OPS | 1st Hf | 2nd Hf | vs RH | vs LH | Rnge | vRH | vLH |
|---|---|---|---|---|---|---|---|---|---|---|---|---|---|---|---|---|---|---|---|---|---|---|---|---|---|---|---|---|---|---|---|---|
| 07 | — | | | | | | | | | | | | | | | | | | | | | | | | | | | | | | | |
| 08 | — | | | | | | | | | | | | | | | | | | | | | | | | | | | | | | | |
| 09 | — | | | | | | | | | | | | | | | | | | | | | | | | | | | | | | | |
| 10 | BOS | 161 | 1 | 23 | 26 | 1 | .242 | .351 | .360 | 71% | 34% | 10% | 1.49 | $0 | -$14 | 80 | -7 | 14 | 1 | 1 | 45-16-39 | 2% | 26% | 34% | .711 | .858 | .568 | .727 | .637 | | | |

---

## Dioner Navarro — 200 PA | $1 | 100 pts

CA-46    Owned: 0%    BH

Navarro's 2008 break-out season has become a distant memory, as he has barely been peanuts since then (aggregate .569 OPS in 2009-10). The only value is his defense, and that is hardly outstanding. The Rays probably won't re-sign him, but they might try him in Spring Training with a minor-league deal. (RZ)

### Forecast
| Player | Age | AB | HR | R | RBI | SB | BA | OBP | SLG | $1L | Pts |
|---|---|---|---|---|---|---|---|---|---|---|---|
| Navarro D | 27 | 184 | 4 | 18 | 18 | 2 | .250 | .306 | .362 | $1 | 100 |

### Mini-Browser
| Player | Age | AB | HR | R | RBI | SB | BA | OBP | SLG | $1L | Pts |
|---|---|---|---|---|---|---|---|---|---|---|---|
| Moore A | 26 | 270 | 9 | 24 | 30 | 0 | .222 | .281 | .361 | $2 | 110 |
| Castro J | 23 | 345 | 4 | 40 | 32 | 0 | .220 | .303 | .340 | $2 | 150 |
| Ross D | 34 | 126 | 5 | 15 | 20 | 0 | .250 | .350 | .434 | $1 | 70 |
| Hester J | 27 | 142 | 5 | 17 | 17 | 2 | .243 | .294 | .422 | $1 | 70 |
| May L | 26 | 235 | 10 | 23 | 28 | 1 | .202 | .257 | .372 | $1 | 90 |

### Competition at CA — Stats in 2010
| Bats | Player | GSvR | GSvL | Sub | OPS |
|---|---|---|---|---|---|
| LH | Jaso J | 76 | 6 | 14 | .750 |
| RH | Shoppach K | 15 | 31 | 10 | .650 |
| BH | Navarro D | 17 | 19 | 10 | .528 |

### Minors (2010)
| Level | Leag | AB | HR | R | RBI | SB | BA | OBP | SLG | CT% | H% | BB% | Bash |
|---|---|---|---|---|---|---|---|---|---|---|---|---|---|
| A | — | | | | | | | | | | | | |
| AA | — | | | | | | | | | | | | |
| AAA | IL | 141 | 2 | 19 | 21 | 3 | .284 | .387 | .390 | 82% | 34% | 14% | 1.38 |

### Majors
| Yr | Team | AB | HR | R | RBI | SB | BA | OBP | SLG | CT% | H% | BB% | Bash | $1L | $2L | Pts | RAA | 2B | 3B | CS | FB-LD-GB | HR/fb | RBI% | RS% | OPS | 1st Hf | 2nd Hf | vs RH | vs LH | Rnge | vRH | vLH |
|---|---|---|---|---|---|---|---|---|---|---|---|---|---|---|---|---|---|---|---|---|---|---|---|---|---|---|---|---|---|---|---|---|
| 07 | TB | 388 | 9 | 46 | 44 | 3 | .227 | .286 | .356 | 83% | 27% | 8% | 1.57 | $7 | -$4 | 200 | -17 | 19 | 2 | 1 | 41-17-42 | 7% | 14% | 33% | .641 | .491 | .815 | .617 | .718 | 0.61 | -10 | +30 |
| 08 | TB | 427 | 7 | 43 | 54 | 0 | .295 | .349 | .407 | 89% | 33% | 7% | 1.38 | $12 | $6 | 250 | +3 | 27 | 0 | 4 | 30-23-46 | 6% | 19% | 23% | .757 | .785 | .718 | .767 | .726 | 0.54 | -7 | +20 |
| 09 | TB | 376 | 8 | 38 | 32 | 5 | .218 | .261 | .322 | 86% | 25% | 4% | 1.48 | $4 | -$2 | 170 | -26 | 15 | 0 | 2 | 43-20-37 | 6% | 11% | 31% | .583 | .586 | .577 | .490 | .740 | 0.54 | -5 | +13 |
| 10 | TB | 124 | 1 | 11 | 7 | 0 | .194 | .270 | .258 | 84% | 23% | 8% | 1.33 | -$2 | -$12 | 40 | -11 | 5 | 0 | 1 | 37-16-47 | 3% | 10% | 28% | .528 | .576 | .255 | .535 | .518 | 0.52 | -12 | +29 |

---

## Oswaldo Navarro — 50 PA | $-5 | 20 pts

SS-10    Owned: 0%    RH

Navarro is another member of Houston's squadron of middle infielders who are more comfortable with a glove than with a bat. A strong performance in Triple-A earned Oswaldo a visit to Houston in 2010. After he crashed and burned in his short stay, it will take an even stronger performance to bring him back. (BJ)

### Forecast
| Player | Age | AB | HR | R | RBI | SB | BA | OBP | SLG | $1L | Pts |
|---|---|---|---|---|---|---|---|---|---|---|---|
| Navarro O | 26 | 44 | 1 | 5 | 4 | 1 | .236 | .311 | .315 | -$5 | 20 |

### Mini-Browser
| Player | Age | AB | HR | R | RBI | SB | BA | OBP | SLG | $1L | Pts |
|---|---|---|---|---|---|---|---|---|---|---|---|
| Maysonet E | 29 | 44 | 1 | 5 | 4 | 1 | .236 | .300 | .338 | -$5 | 20 |
| Navarro Y | 23 | 68 | 2 | 8 | 8 | 1 | .221 | .278 | .365 | -$5 | 30 |
| Cruz L | 27 | 45 | 1 | 5 | 4 | 1 | .231 | .269 | .353 | -$5 | 20 |
| Nunez E | 23 | 46 | 1 | 5 | 5 | 2 | .226 | .260 | .340 | -$5 | 20 |
| Diaz A | 24 | 96 | 1 | 8 | 8 | 1 | .218 | .270 | .295 | -$5 | 30 |

### Competition at SS — Stats in 2010
| Bats | Player | GSvR | GSvL | Sub | OPS |
|---|---|---|---|---|---|
| RH | Manzella T | 51 | 24 | 7 | .531 |
| RH | Sanchez A | 37 | 17 | 3 | .656 |
| BH | Blum G | 13 | 1 | 4 | .678 |
| RH | Keppinger J | 12 | 0 | 0 | .744 |

### Minors (2010)
| Level | Leag | AB | HR | R | RBI | SB | BA | OBP | SLG | CT% | H% | BB% | Bash |
|---|---|---|---|---|---|---|---|---|---|---|---|---|---|
| A | — | | | | | | | | | | | | |
| AA | — | | | | | | | | | | | | |
| AAA | PCL | 288 | 6 | 41 | 37 | 2 | .271 | .361 | .424 | 77% | 35% | 10% | 1.56 |

### Majors
| Yr | Team | AB | HR | R | RBI | SB | BA | OBP | SLG | CT% | H% | BB% | Bash | $1L | $2L | Pts | RAA | 2B | 3B | CS | FB-LD-GB | HR/fb | RBI% | RS% | OPS | 1st Hf | 2nd Hf | vs RH | vs LH | Rnge | vRH | vLH |
|---|---|---|---|---|---|---|---|---|---|---|---|---|---|---|---|---|---|---|---|---|---|---|---|---|---|---|---|---|---|---|---|---|
| 07 | — | | | | | | | | | | | | | | | | | | | | | | | | | | | | | 4.75 | +7 | -18 |
| 08 | — | | | | | | | | | | | | | | | | | | | | | | | | | | | | | | -20 | +51 |
| 09 | — | | | | | | | | | | | | | | | | | | | | | | | | | | | | | | | |
| 10 | HOU | 20 | 0 | 2 | 0 | 0 | .050 | .240 | .050 | 80% | 6% | 20% | 1.00 | -$6 | -$21 | 0 | -3 | 0 | 0 | 0 | 50-19-31 | 0% | 0% | 33% | .290 | .303 | .000 | .327 | .222 | 4.75 | | |

---

## Yamaico Navarro — 75 PA | $-5 | 30 pts

SS-15, 3B-4, 2B-3    Owned: 0%    RH

The Boston brass is high on Navarro, but his time is not now. He will spend most of 2011 in the minors, though he could bridge the hand-off at shortstop from Marco Scutaro to Jose Iglesias if the latter is not ready in 2012. Yamaico might not get extended PT until 2013. His long-term position is third base. (EB)

### Forecast
| Player | Age | AB | HR | R | RBI | SB | BA | OBP | SLG | $1L | Pts |
|---|---|---|---|---|---|---|---|---|---|---|---|
| Navarro Y | 23 | 68 | 2 | 8 | 8 | 1 | .221 | .278 | .365 | -$5 | 30 |

### Mini-Browser
| Player | Age | AB | HR | R | RBI | SB | BA | OBP | SLG | $1L | Pts |
|---|---|---|---|---|---|---|---|---|---|---|---|
| Cozart Z | 25 | 88 | 3 | 10 | 9 | 1 | .215 | .288 | .385 | -$4 | 40 |
| Hernandez D | 26 | 69 | 2 | 7 | 8 | 2 | .240 | .296 | .352 | -$4 | 30 |
| Crosby B | 31 | 46 | 1 | 6 | 5 | 1 | .250 | .314 | .373 | -$4 | 20 |
| Rohlinger R | 27 | 47 | 2 | 6 | 6 | 0 | .234 | .308 | .411 | -$4 | 20 |
| Maysonet E | 29 | 44 | 1 | 5 | 4 | 1 | .236 | .300 | .338 | -$4 | 20 |

### Competition at SS — Stats in 2010
| Bats | Player | GSvR | GSvL | Sub | OPS |
|---|---|---|---|---|---|
| RH | Scutaro M | 89 | 42 | 1 | .721 |
| BH | Lowrie J | 10 | 12 | 1 | .907 |
| RH | Navarro Y | 4 | 3 | 8 | .317 |

### Minors (2010)
| Level | Leag | AB | HR | R | RBI | SB | BA | OBP | SLG | CT% | H% | BB% | Bash |
|---|---|---|---|---|---|---|---|---|---|---|---|---|---|
| A | — | | | | | | | | | | | | |
| AA | EL | 329 | 8 | 49 | 55 | 16 | .274 | .358 | .422 | 84% | 33% | 11% | 1.54 |
| AAA | IL | 53 | 3 | 8 | 6 | 2 | .283 | .339 | .528 | 89% | 32% | 8% | 1.87 |

### Majors
| Yr | Team | AB | HR | R | RBI | SB | BA | OBP | SLG | CT% | H% | BB% | Bash | $1L | $2L | Pts | RAA | 2B | 3B | CS | FB-LD-GB | HR/fb | RBI% | RS% | OPS | 1st Hf | 2nd Hf | vs RH | vs LH | Rnge | vRH | vLH |
|---|---|---|---|---|---|---|---|---|---|---|---|---|---|---|---|---|---|---|---|---|---|---|---|---|---|---|---|---|---|---|---|---|
| 07 | — | | | | | | | | | | | | | | | | | | | | | | | | | | | | | | | |
| 08 | — | | | | | | | | | | | | | | | | | | | | | | | | | | | | | | | |
| 09 | — | | | | | | | | | | | | | | | | | | | | | | | | | | | | | | | |
| 10 | BOS | 42 | 0 | 4 | 5 | 0 | .143 | .174 | .143 | 60% | 24% | 4% | 1.00 | -$5 | -$21 | 0 | -7 | 0 | 0 | 0 | 44-11-44 | 0% | 22% | 50% | .317 | | .317 | .215 | .494 | | | |

---

## Thomas Neal — 50 PA | $-4 | 20 pts

No MLB games played in 2010    Owned: 0%    RH

Neal struggled in his first months in Double-A, but he finished among the league leaders in doubles and showed off a strong arm in the outfield. The Giants' OF will be crowded in 2011, but the organization has already expressed their enthusiasm in Neal by inviting him to Spring Training in 2010 out of Single-A. (PB)

### Forecast
| Player | Age | AB | HR | R | RBI | SB | BA | OBP | SLG | $1L | Pts |
|---|---|---|---|---|---|---|---|---|---|---|---|
| Neal T | 23 | 42 | 2 | 6 | 6 | 0 | .236 | .329 | .431 | -$4 | 20 |

### Mini-Browser
| Player | Age | AB | HR | R | RBI | SB | BA | OBP | SLG | $1L | Pts |
|---|---|---|---|---|---|---|---|---|---|---|---|
| Montanez L | 29 | 69 | 3 | 8 | 8 | 1 | .251 | .298 | .422 | -$4 | 40 |
| Mather J | 28 | 43 | 2 | 6 | 6 | 1 | .243 | .318 | .436 | -$4 | 30 |
| Durango L | 24 | 74 | 1 | 9 | 6 | 4 | .206 | .301 | .262 | -$4 | 40 |
| Nieuwenhuis K | 23 | 45 | 2 | 6 | 6 | 2 | .222 | .306 | .426 | -$4 | 30 |
| Nava D | 28 | 87 | 2 | 11 | 12 | 0 | .230 | .319 | .381 | -$4 | 50 |

### Competition at LF — Stats in 2010
| Bats | Player | GSvR | GSvL | Sub | OPS |
|---|---|---|---|---|---|
| RH | Burrell P | 61 | 25 | 1 | .817 |
| LH | Huff A | 38 | 8 | 0 | .891 |
| BH | Torres A | 19 | 13 | 5 | .823 |
| RH | DeRosa M | 13 | 8 | 0 | .537 |

### Minors (2010)
| Level | Leag | AB | HR | R | RBI | SB | BA | OBP | SLG | CT% | H% | BB% | Bash |
|---|---|---|---|---|---|---|---|---|---|---|---|---|---|
| A | — | | | | | | | | | | | | |
| AA | EL | 525 | 12 | 69 | 69 | 11 | .291 | .359 | .440 | 82% | 35% | 8% | 1.51 |
| AAA | — | | | | | | | | | | | | |

### Majors
| Yr | Team | AB | HR | R | RBI | SB | BA | OBP | SLG | CT% | H% | BB% | Bash |
|---|---|---|---|---|---|---|---|---|---|---|---|---|---|
| 07 | — | | | | | | | | | | | | |
| 08 | — | | | | | | | | | | | | |
| 09 | — | | | | | | | | | | | | |
| 10 | — | | | | | | | | | | | | |

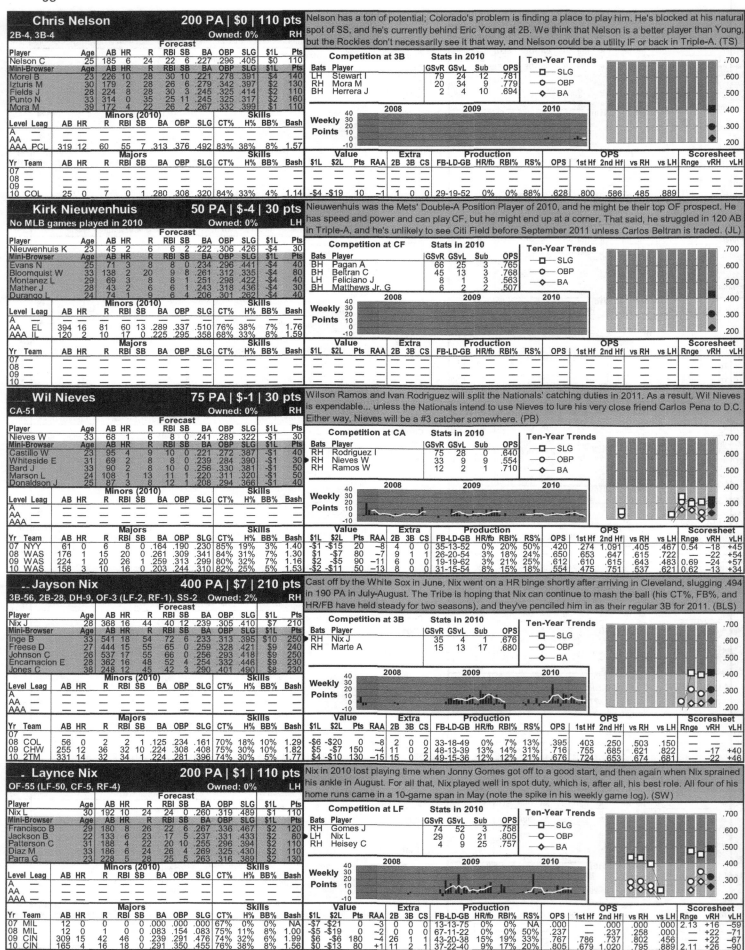

98

## Chris Nelson — 200 PA | $0 | 110 pts
2B-4, 3B-4    Owned: 0%    RH

Nelson has a ton of potential; Colorado's problem is finding a place to play him. He's blocked at his natural spot of SS, and he's currently behind Eric Young at 2B. We think that Nelson is a better player than Young, but the Rockies don't necessarily see it that way, and Nelson could be a utility IF or back in Triple-A. (TS)

### Forecast
| Player | Age | AB | HR | R | RBI | SB | BA | OBP | SLG | $1L | Pts |
|---|---|---|---|---|---|---|---|---|---|---|---|
| Nelson C | 25 | 185 | 6 | 24 | 22 | 6 | .227 | .296 | .405 | $0 | 110 |

### Mini-Browser
| Player | Age | AB | HR | R | RBI | SB | BA | OBP | SLG | $1L | Pts |
|---|---|---|---|---|---|---|---|---|---|---|---|
| Morel B | 23 | 226 | 10 | 28 | 30 | 10 | .221 | .278 | .391 | $4 | 140 |
| Izturis M | 30 | 179 | 2 | 28 | 26 | 6 | .279 | .342 | .397 | $2 | 130 |
| Fields J | 28 | 224 | 8 | 28 | 30 | 3 | .245 | .325 | .414 | $2 | 120 |
| Punto N | 33 | 314 | 0 | 35 | 25 | 11 | .245 | .325 | .317 | $2 | 160 |
| Mora M | 39 | 172 | 4 | 22 | 26 | 2 | .267 | .332 | .399 | $1 | 110 |

### Competition at 3B / Stats in 2010
| Bats | Player | GSvR | GSvL | Sub | OPS |
|---|---|---|---|---|---|
| LH | Stewart I | 79 | 24 | 12 | .781 |
| RH | Mora M | 20 | 34 | 9 | .779 |
| BH | Herrera J | 2 | 4 | 10 | .694 |

### Minors (2010) / Skills
| Level | Leag | AB | HR | R | RBI | SB | BA | OBP | SLG | CT% | H% | BB% | Bash |
|---|---|---|---|---|---|---|---|---|---|---|---|---|---|
| A | — | | | | | | | | | | | | |
| AA | — | | | | | | | | | | | | |
| AAA | PCL | 319 | 12 | 60 | 55 | 7 | .313 | .376 | .492 | 83% | 38% | 8% | 1.57 |

### Majors / Skills / Value / Extra / Production / OPS / Scoresheet
| Yr | Team | AB | HR | R | RBI | SB | BA | OBP | SLG | CT% | H% | BB% | Bash | $1L | $2L | Pts | RAA | 2B | 3B | CS | FB-LD-GB | HR/fb | RBI% | RS% | OPS | 1st Hf | 2nd Hf | vs RH | vs LH | Rnge | vRH | vLH |
|---|---|---|---|---|---|---|---|---|---|---|---|---|---|---|---|---|---|---|---|---|---|---|---|---|---|---|---|---|---|---|---|---|
| 07 | — | | | | | | | | | | | | | | | | | | | | | | | | | | | | | | | |
| 08 | — | | | | | | | | | | | | | | | | | | | | | | | | | | | | | | | |
| 09 | — | | | | | | | | | | | | | | | | | | | | | | | | | | | | | | | |
| 10 | COL | 25 | 0 | 7 | 0 | 1 | .280 | .308 | .320 | 84% | 33% | 4% | 1.14 | -$4 | -$19 | 10 | -1 | 1 | 0 | 0 | 29-19-52 | 0% | 0% | 88% | .628 | .800 | .586 | .485 | .889 | | | |

## Kirk Nieuwenhuis — 50 PA | $-4 | 30 pts
No MLB games played in 2010    Owned: 0%    LH

Nieuwenhuis was the Mets' Double-A Position Player of 2010, and he might be their top OF prospect. He has speed and power and can play CF, but he might end up at a corner. That said, he struggled in 120 AB in Triple-A, and he's unlikely to see Citi Field before September 2011 unless Carlos Beltran is traded. (JL)

### Forecast
| Player | Age | AB | HR | R | RBI | SB | BA | OBP | SLG | $1L | Pts |
|---|---|---|---|---|---|---|---|---|---|---|---|
| Nieuwenhuis K | 23 | 45 | 2 | 6 | 6 | 2 | .222 | .306 | .426 | -$4 | 30 |

### Mini-Browser
| Player | Age | AB | HR | R | RBI | SB | BA | OBP | SLG | $1L | Pts |
|---|---|---|---|---|---|---|---|---|---|---|---|
| Evans N | 25 | 71 | 3 | 8 | 8 | 0 | .234 | .296 | .441 | -$4 | 40 |
| Bloomquist W | 33 | 138 | 2 | 20 | 9 | 8 | .261 | .312 | .335 | -$4 | 40 |
| Montanez L | 29 | 69 | 3 | 8 | 8 | 1 | .251 | .298 | .422 | -$4 | 40 |
| Mather J | 28 | 43 | 2 | 6 | 6 | 1 | .243 | .318 | .436 | -$4 | 40 |
| Durango L | 24 | 74 | 1 | 9 | 6 | 4 | .206 | .301 | .262 | -$4 | 40 |

### Competition at CF / Stats in 2010
| Bats | Player | GSvR | GSvL | Sub | OPS |
|---|---|---|---|---|---|
| BH | Pagan A | 66 | 25 | 3 | .765 |
| BH | Beltran C | 45 | 13 | 3 | .768 |
| LH | Feliciano J | 8 | 1 | 3 | .563 |
| BH | Matthews Jr. G | 6 | 2 | 2 | .507 |

### Minors (2010) / Skills
| Level | Leag | AB | HR | R | RBI | SB | BA | OBP | SLG | CT% | H% | BB% | Bash |
|---|---|---|---|---|---|---|---|---|---|---|---|---|---|
| A | — | | | | | | | | | | | | |
| AA | EL | 394 | 16 | 81 | 60 | 13 | .289 | .337 | .510 | 76% | 38% | 7% | 1.76 |
| AAA | IL | 120 | 2 | 10 | 17 | 0 | .225 | .295 | .358 | 68% | 33% | 8% | 1.59 |

### Majors
| Yr | Team | AB | HR | R | RBI | SB | BA | OBP | SLG | CT% | H% | BB% | Bash |
|---|---|---|---|---|---|---|---|---|---|---|---|---|---|
| 07 | — | | | | | | | | | | | | |
| 08 | — | | | | | | | | | | | | |
| 09 | — | | | | | | | | | | | | |
| 10 | — | | | | | | | | | | | | |

## Wil Nieves — 75 PA | $-1 | 30 pts
CA-51    Owned: 0%    RH

Wilson Ramos and Ivan Rodriguez will split the Nationals' catching duties in 2011. As a result, Wil Nieves is expendable... unless the Nationals intend to use Nieves to lure his very close friend Carlos Pena to D.C. Either way, Nieves will be a #3 catcher somewhere. (PB)

### Forecast
| Player | Age | AB | HR | R | RBI | SB | BA | OBP | SLG | $1L | Pts |
|---|---|---|---|---|---|---|---|---|---|---|---|
| Nieves W | 33 | 68 | 1 | 6 | 8 | 0 | .241 | .289 | .322 | -$1 | 30 |

### Mini-Browser
| Player | Age | AB | HR | R | RBI | SB | BA | OBP | SLG | $1L | Pts |
|---|---|---|---|---|---|---|---|---|---|---|---|
| Castillo W | 23 | 95 | 4 | 9 | 10 | 0 | .221 | .272 | .387 | -$1 | 40 |
| Whiteside E | 31 | 69 | 2 | 8 | 8 | 0 | .239 | .284 | .390 | -$1 | 30 |
| Bard J | 33 | 90 | 2 | 8 | 10 | 0 | .256 | .330 | .381 | -$1 | 50 |
| Marson L | 24 | 108 | 1 | 13 | 11 | 1 | .220 | .311 | .320 | -$1 | 50 |
| Donaldson J | 25 | 87 | 3 | 8 | 12 | 1 | .208 | .294 | .366 | -$1 | 40 |

### Competition at CA / Stats in 2010
| Bats | Player | GSvR | GSvL | Sub | OPS |
|---|---|---|---|---|---|
| RH | Rodriguez I | 75 | 28 | 0 | .640 |
| RH | Nieves W | 33 | 9 | 9 | .554 |
| RH | Ramos W | 12 | 2 | 1 | .710 |

### Minors (2010) / Skills
| Level | Leag | AB | HR | R | RBI | SB | BA | OBP | SLG | CT% | H% | BB% | Bash |
|---|---|---|---|---|---|---|---|---|---|---|---|---|---|
| A | — | | | | | | | | | | | | |
| AA | — | | | | | | | | | | | | |
| AAA | — | | | | | | | | | | | | |

### Majors / Skills / Value / Extra / Production / OPS / Scoresheet
| Yr | Team | AB | HR | R | RBI | SB | BA | OBP | SLG | CT% | H% | BB% | Bash | $1L | $2L | Pts | RAA | 2B | 3B | CS | FB-LD-GB | HR/fb | RBI% | RS% | OPS | 1st Hf | 2nd Hf | vs RH | vs LH | Rnge | vRH | vLH |
|---|---|---|---|---|---|---|---|---|---|---|---|---|---|---|---|---|---|---|---|---|---|---|---|---|---|---|---|---|---|---|---|---|
| 07 | NYY | 61 | 0 | 6 | 8 | 0 | .164 | .190 | .230 | 85% | 19% | 3% | 1.40 | $1 | -$15 | 20 | -8 | 4 | 0 | 0 | 35-13-52 | 0% | 20% | 50% | .420 | .274 | 1.091 | .405 | .467 | 0.54 | -18 | +45 |
| 08 | WAS | 176 | 1 | 15 | 20 | 0 | .261 | .309 | .341 | 84% | 31% | 7% | 1.30 | $1 | -$7 | 80 | -7 | 9 | 1 | 1 | 26-20-54 | 3% | 18% | 24% | .650 | .653 | .647 | .615 | .722 | | -22 | +54 |
| 09 | WAS | 224 | 1 | 20 | 26 | 1 | .259 | .313 | .299 | 80% | 32% | 7% | 1.16 | $2 | -$5 | 90 | -11 | 8 | 0 | 0 | 19-19-62 | 3% | 21% | 25% | .612 | .610 | .615 | .643 | .483 | 0.69 | -24 | +57 |
| 10 | WAS | 158 | 3 | 10 | 16 | 0 | .203 | .244 | .310 | 82% | 25% | 5% | 1.53 | $2 | -$11 | 50 | -13 | 8 | 0 | 0 | 31-15-54 | 8% | 15% | 18% | .554 | .475 | .751 | .537 | .621 | 0.62 | +13 | +34 |

## Jayson Nix — 400 PA | $7 | 210 pts
3B-56, 2B-28, DH-9, OF-3 (LF-2, RF-1), SS-2    Owned: 2%    RH

Cast off by the White Sox in June, Nix went on a HR binge shortly after arriving in Cleveland, slugging .494 in 190 PA in July-August. The Tribe is hoping that Nix can continue to mash the ball (his CT%, FB%, and HR/FB have held steady for two seasons), and they've penciled him in as their regular 3B for 2011. (BLS)

### Forecast
| Player | Age | AB | HR | R | RBI | SB | BA | OBP | SLG | $1L | Pts |
|---|---|---|---|---|---|---|---|---|---|---|---|
| Nix J | 28 | 368 | 16 | 44 | 40 | 12 | .239 | .305 | .410 | $7 | 210 |

### Mini-Browser
| Player | Age | AB | HR | R | RBI | SB | BA | OBP | SLG | $1L | Pts |
|---|---|---|---|---|---|---|---|---|---|---|---|
| Inge B | 33 | 541 | 18 | 54 | 72 | 6 | .233 | .313 | .395 | $10 | 250 |
| Freese D | 27 | 444 | 15 | 55 | 65 | 0 | .259 | .328 | .421 | $9 | 240 |
| Johnson C | 26 | 537 | 17 | 55 | 66 | 0 | .256 | .293 | .418 | $9 | 250 |
| Encarnacion E | 28 | 362 | 16 | 48 | 52 | 4 | .254 | .332 | .446 | $9 | 230 |
| Jones C | 38 | 248 | 12 | 45 | 42 | 3 | .290 | .401 | .460 | $8 | 230 |

### Competition at 3B / Stats in 2010
| Bats | Player | GSvR | GSvL | Sub | OPS |
|---|---|---|---|---|---|
| RH | Nix J | 35 | 4 | 1 | .676 |
| RH | Marte A | 15 | 13 | 17 | .680 |

### Minors (2010)
| Level | Leag | AB | HR | R | RBI | SB | BA | OBP | SLG | CT% | H% | BB% | Bash |
|---|---|---|---|---|---|---|---|---|---|---|---|---|---|
| A | — | | | | | | | | | | | | |
| AA | — | | | | | | | | | | | | |
| AAA | — | | | | | | | | | | | | |

### Majors / Skills / Value / Extra / Production / OPS / Scoresheet
| Yr | Team | AB | HR | R | RBI | SB | BA | OBP | SLG | CT% | H% | BB% | Bash | $1L | $2L | Pts | RAA | 2B | 3B | CS | FB-LD-GB | HR/fb | RBI% | RS% | OPS | 1st Hf | 2nd Hf | vs RH | vs LH | Rnge | vRH | vLH |
|---|---|---|---|---|---|---|---|---|---|---|---|---|---|---|---|---|---|---|---|---|---|---|---|---|---|---|---|---|---|---|---|---|
| 07 | — | | | | | | | | | | | | | | | | | | | | | | | | | | | | | | | |
| 08 | COL | 56 | 0 | 2 | 2 | 1 | .125 | .234 | .161 | 70% | 18% | 10% | 1.29 | -$6 | -$20 | 0 | -8 | 2 | 0 | 0 | 33-18-49 | 0% | 7% | 13% | .395 | .403 | .250 | .503 | .150 | | | |
| 09 | CHW | 255 | 12 | 36 | 32 | 10 | .224 | .308 | .408 | 75% | 30% | 10% | 1.82 | $5 | -$7 | 150 | -4 | 11 | 0 | 2 | 48-13-39 | 13% | 14% | 31% | .716 | .755 | .685 | .621 | .822 | | -17 | +40 |
| 10 | 2TM | 331 | 14 | 32 | 34 | 1 | .224 | .281 | .396 | 74% | 30% | 5% | 1.77 | $4 | -$10 | 130 | -15 | 15 | 0 | 2 | 49-15-36 | 12% | 12% | 21% | .676 | .724 | .653 | .674 | .681 | | -22 | +46 |

## Laynce Nix — 200 PA | $1 | 110 pts
OF-55 (LF-50, CF-5, RF-4)    Owned: 0%    LH

Nix in 2010 lost playing time when Jonny Gomes got off to a good start, and then again when Nix sprained his ankle in August. For all that, Nix played well in spot duty, which is, after all, his best role. All four of his home runs came in a 10-game span in May (note the spike in his weekly game log). (SW)

### Forecast
| Player | Age | AB | HR | R | RBI | SB | BA | OBP | SLG | $1L | Pts |
|---|---|---|---|---|---|---|---|---|---|---|---|
| Nix L | 30 | 192 | 10 | 24 | 24 | 0 | .260 | .319 | .489 | $1 | 110 |

### Mini-Browser
| Player | Age | AB | HR | R | RBI | SB | BA | OBP | SLG | $1L | Pts |
|---|---|---|---|---|---|---|---|---|---|---|---|
| Francisco B | 29 | 180 | 8 | 26 | 22 | 6 | .267 | .336 | .467 | $2 | 120 |
| Jackson B | 22 | 133 | 6 | 23 | 17 | 5 | .237 | .331 | .433 | $2 | 110 |
| Patterson C | 31 | 188 | 4 | 22 | 20 | 10 | .255 | .296 | .394 | $2 | 110 |
| Diaz M | 33 | 186 | 6 | 24 | 26 | 4 | .269 | .325 | .430 | $2 | 120 |
| Parra G | 23 | 228 | 5 | 28 | 25 | 5 | .263 | .316 | .389 | $2 | 130 |

### Competition at LF / Stats in 2010
| Bats | Player | GSvR | GSvL | Sub | OPS |
|---|---|---|---|---|---|
| RH | Gomes J | 74 | 52 | 3 | .758 |
| LH | Nix L | 29 | 0 | 21 | .805 |
| RH | Heisey C | 4 | 9 | 25 | .757 |

### Minors (2010)
| Level | Leag | AB | HR | R | RBI | SB | BA | OBP | SLG | CT% | H% | BB% | Bash |
|---|---|---|---|---|---|---|---|---|---|---|---|---|---|
| A | — | | | | | | | | | | | | |
| AA | — | | | | | | | | | | | | |
| AAA | — | | | | | | | | | | | | |

### Majors / Skills / Value / Extra / Production / OPS / Scoresheet
| Yr | Team | AB | HR | R | RBI | SB | BA | OBP | SLG | CT% | H% | BB% | Bash | $1L | $2L | Pts | RAA | 2B | 3B | CS | FB-LD-GB | HR/fb | RBI% | RS% | OPS | 1st Hf | 2nd Hf | vs RH | vs LH | Rnge | vRH | vLH |
|---|---|---|---|---|---|---|---|---|---|---|---|---|---|---|---|---|---|---|---|---|---|---|---|---|---|---|---|---|---|---|---|---|
| 07 | MIL | 12 | 0 | 0 | 0 | 0 | .000 | .000 | .000 | 67% | 0% | 0% | NA | -$7 | -$21 | 0 | -3 | 0 | 0 | 0 | 13-13-75 | 0% | 0% | NA | .000 | — | .000 | .000 | .000 | 2.13 | +16 | -59 |
| 08 | MIL | 12 | 0 | 1 | 0 | 0 | .083 | .154 | .083 | 75% | 11% | 8% | 1.00 | -$5 | -$19 | 0 | -2 | 0 | 0 | 0 | 67-11-22 | 0% | 0% | 50% | .237 | — | .237 | .258 | .000 | | +22 | -71 |
| 09 | CIN | 309 | 15 | 42 | 46 | 0 | .239 | .291 | .476 | 74% | 32% | 6% | 1.99 | $6 | -$6 | 180 | -4 | 26 | 1 | 1 | 43-20-38 | 15% | 19% | 33% | .767 | .786 | .737 | .802 | .456 | | +22 | -67 |
| 10 | CIN | 165 | 4 | 16 | 18 | 0 | .291 | .350 | .455 | 76% | 38% | 5% | 1.56 | $3 | -$13 | 80 | +1 | 11 | 2 | 1 | 37-22-40 | 9% | 17% | 20% | .805 | .679 | 1.020 | .795 | .889 | 2.11 | +26 | -90 |

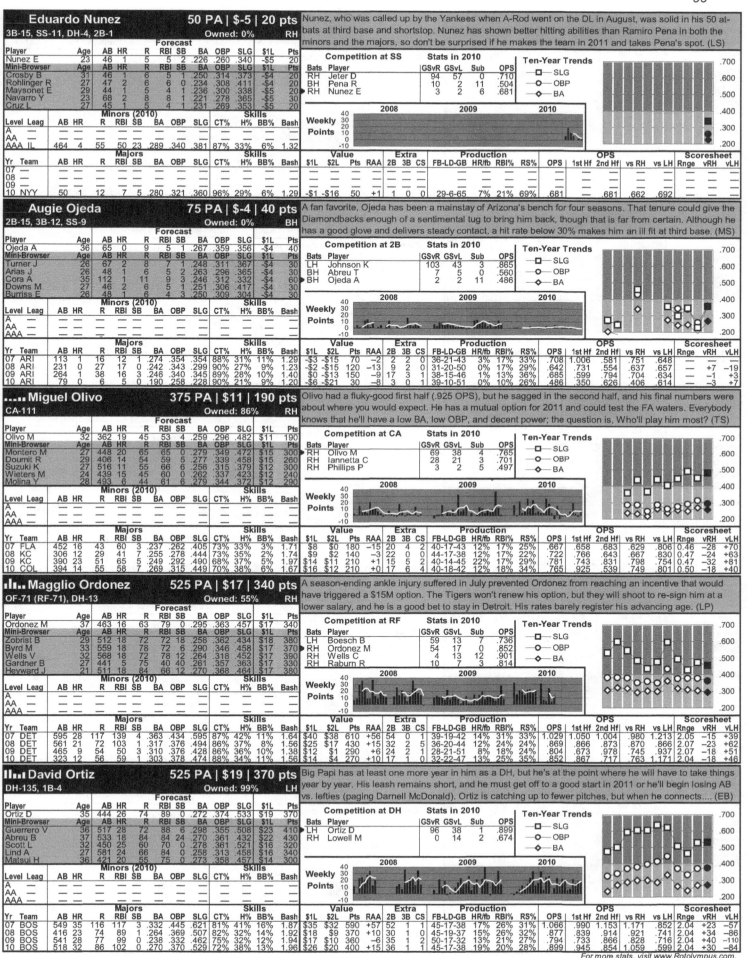

## Eduardo Nunez — 50 PA | $-5 | 20 pts

3B-15, SS-11, DH-4, 2B-1 — Owned: 0% — RH

Nunez, who was called up by the Yankees when A-Rod went on the DL in August, was solid in his 50 at-bats at third base and shortstop. Nunez has shown better hitting abilities than Ramiro Pena in both the minors and the majors, so don't be surprised if he makes the team in 2011 and takes Pena's spot. (LS)

### Forecast

| Player | Age | AB | HR | R | RBI | SB | BA | OBP | SLG | $1L | Pts |
|---|---|---|---|---|---|---|---|---|---|---|---|
| Nunez E | 23 | 46 | 1 | 5 | 5 | 2 | .226 | .260 | .340 | -$5 | 20 |
| **Mini-Browser** | **Age** | **AB** | **HR** | **R** | **RBI** | **SB** | **BA** | **OBP** | **SLG** | **$1L** | **Pts** |
| Crosby B | 31 | 46 | 1 | 6 | 5 | 1 | .250 | .314 | .373 | -$4 | 20 |
| Rohlinger R | 27 | 47 | 2 | 6 | 6 | 0 | .234 | .308 | .411 | -$4 | 20 |
| Maysonet E | 29 | 44 | 1 | 5 | 4 | 1 | .236 | .300 | .338 | -$5 | 20 |
| Navarro Y | 23 | 68 | 2 | 8 | 8 | 1 | .221 | .278 | .365 | -$5 | 30 |
| Cruz L | 27 | 55 | 2 | 5 | 4 | 1 | .231 | .269 | .353 | -$5 | 20 |

### Minors (2010)

| Level | Leag | AB | HR | R | RBI | SB | BA | OBP | SLG | CT% | H% | BB% | Bash |
|---|---|---|---|---|---|---|---|---|---|---|---|---|---|
| A | — | — | — | — | — | — | — | — | — | — | — | — | — |
| AA | — | — | — | — | — | — | — | — | — | — | — | — | — |
| AAA | IL | 464 | 4 | 55 | 50 | 23 | .289 | .340 | .381 | 87% | 33% | 6% | 1.32 |

### Majors / Skills

| Yr | Team | AB | HR | R | RBI | SB | BA | OBP | SLG | CT% | H% | BB% | Bash |
|---|---|---|---|---|---|---|---|---|---|---|---|---|---|
| 07 | — | — | — | — | — | — | — | — | — | — | — | — | — |
| 08 | — | — | — | — | — | — | — | — | — | — | — | — | — |
| 09 | — | — | — | — | — | — | — | — | — | — | — | — | — |
| 10 | NYY | 50 | 1 | 12 | 7 | 5 | .280 | .321 | .360 | 96% | 29% | 6% | 1.29 |

**Competition at SS — Stats in 2010**

| Bats | Player | GSvR | GSvL | Sub | OPS |
|---|---|---|---|---|---|
| RH | Jeter D | 94 | 57 | 0 | .710 |
| BH | Pena R | 10 | 2 | 11 | .504 |
| ► RH | Nunez E | 3 | 2 | 6 | .681 |

**Ten-Year Trends:** SLG, OBP, BA

**Value / Extra / Production / OPS / Scoresheet**

| $1L | $2L | Pts | RAA | 2B | 3B | CS | FB-LD-GB | HR/fb | RBI% | RS% | OPS | 1st Hf | 2nd Hf | vs RH | vs LH | Rnge | vRH | vLH |
|---|---|---|---|---|---|---|---|---|---|---|---|---|---|---|---|---|---|---|
| -$1 | -$16 | 50 | +1 | 1 | 0 | 0 | 29-6-65 | 7% | 21% | 69% | .681 | — | .681 | .662 | .692 | — | — | — |

---

## Augie Ojeda — 75 PA | $-4 | 40 pts

2B-15, 3B-12, SS-9 — Owned: 0% — BH

A fan favorite, Ojeda has been a mainstay of Arizona's bench for four seasons. That tenure could give the Diamondbacks enough of a sentimental tug to bring him back, though that is far from certain. Although he has a good glove and delivers steady contact, a hit rate below 30% makes him an ill fit at third base. (MS)

### Forecast

| Player | Age | AB | HR | R | RBI | SB | BA | OBP | SLG | $1L | Pts |
|---|---|---|---|---|---|---|---|---|---|---|---|
| Ojeda A | 36 | 65 | 0 | 9 | 5 | 1 | .267 | .359 | .356 | -$4 | 40 |
| **Mini-Browser** | **Age** | **AB** | **HR** | **R** | **RBI** | **SB** | **BA** | **OBP** | **SLG** | **$1L** | **Pts** |
| Turner J | 26 | 67 | 2 | 8 | 7 | 1 | .248 | .311 | .367 | -$4 | 30 |
| Arias J | 26 | 48 | 1 | 6 | 5 | 2 | .263 | .296 | .365 | -$4 | 30 |
| Cora A | 35 | 112 | 1 | 11 | 9 | 3 | .246 | .312 | .332 | -$4 | 60 |
| Downs M | 27 | 46 | 2 | 6 | 5 | 1 | .251 | .306 | .417 | -$4 | 30 |
| Burriss E | 26 | 48 | 1 | 6 | 4 | 3 | .250 | .309 | .304 | -$4 | 30 |

### Minors (2010)

| Level | Leag | AB | HR | R | RBI | SB | BA | OBP | SLG | CT% | H% | BB% | Bash |
|---|---|---|---|---|---|---|---|---|---|---|---|---|---|
| A | — | — | — | — | — | — | — | — | — | — | — | — | — |
| AA | — | — | — | — | — | — | — | — | — | — | — | — | — |
| AAA | — | — | — | — | — | — | — | — | — | — | — | — | — |

### Majors / Skills

| Yr | Team | AB | HR | R | RBI | SB | BA | OBP | SLG | CT% | H% | BB% | Bash |
|---|---|---|---|---|---|---|---|---|---|---|---|---|---|
| 07 | ARI | 113 | 1 | 16 | 12 | 1 | .274 | .354 | .354 | 88% | 31% | 11% | 1.29 |
| 08 | ARI | 231 | 0 | 27 | 17 | 0 | .242 | .343 | .299 | 90% | 27% | 9% | 1.23 |
| 09 | ARI | 264 | 1 | 38 | 16 | 3 | .246 | .340 | .345 | 89% | 28% | 10% | 1.40 |
| 10 | ARI | 79 | 0 | 6 | 5 | 0 | .190 | .258 | .228 | 90% | 21% | 9% | 1.20 |

**Competition at 2B — Stats in 2010**

| Bats | Player | GSvR | GSvL | Sub | OPS |
|---|---|---|---|---|---|
| LH | Johnson K | 103 | 43 | 0 | .865 |
| BH | Abreu T | 7 | 5 | 0 | .560 |
| ► BH | Ojeda A | 2 | 2 | 11 | .486 |

**Value / Extra / Production / OPS / Scoresheet**

| Yr | Team | $1L | $2L | Pts | RAA | 2B | 3B | CS | FB-LD-GB | HR/fb | RBI% | RS% | OPS | 1st Hf | 2nd Hf | vs RH | vs LH | Rnge | vRH | vLH |
|---|---|---|---|---|---|---|---|---|---|---|---|---|---|---|---|---|---|---|---|---|
| 07 | ARI | -$3 | -$15 | 70 | -2 | 2 | 2 | 0 | 36-21-43 | 3% | 17% | 33% | .708 | 1.006 | .581 | .751 | .648 | — | +7 | -19 |
| 08 | ARI | -$2 | -$15 | 120 | -13 | 9 | 2 | 0 | 31-20-50 | 0% | 17% | 29% | .642 | .731 | .554 | .637 | .657 | — | -1 | +3 |
| 09 | ARI | $0 | -$13 | 150 | -9 | 17 | 3 | 1 | 38-15-46 | 1% | 13% | 36% | .685 | .599 | .794 | .704 | .634 | — | -3 | +7 |
| 10 | ARI | -$6 | -$21 | 30 | -8 | 3 | 0 | 1 | 39-10-51 | 0% | 10% | 26% | .486 | .350 | .626 | .406 | .614 | — | -3 | +7 |

---

## Miguel Olivo — 375 PA | $11 | 190 pts

CA-111 — Owned: 86% — RH

Olivo had a fluky-good first half (.925 OPS), but he sagged in the second half, and his final numbers were about where you would expect. He has a mutual option for 2011 and could test the FA waters. Everybody knows that he'll have a low BA, low OBP, and decent power; the question is, Who'll play him most? (TS)

### Forecast

| Player | Age | AB | HR | R | RBI | SB | BA | OBP | SLG | $1L | Pts |
|---|---|---|---|---|---|---|---|---|---|---|---|
| Olivo M | 32 | 362 | 19 | 45 | 53 | 4 | .259 | .296 | .482 | $11 | 190 |
| **Mini-Browser** | **Age** | **AB** | **HR** | **R** | **RBI** | **SB** | **BA** | **OBP** | **SLG** | **$1L** | **Pts** |
| Montero M | 27 | 448 | 20 | 65 | 65 | 0 | .279 | .349 | .472 | $15 | 300 |
| Doumit R | 29 | 406 | 14 | 54 | 59 | 5 | .277 | .339 | .458 | $15 | 260 |
| Suzuki K | 27 | 516 | 11 | 55 | 66 | 6 | .256 | .315 | .379 | $12 | 300 |
| Wieters M | 24 | 439 | 15 | 45 | 60 | 0 | .262 | .337 | .423 | $12 | 240 |
| Molina Y | 28 | 493 | 6 | 44 | 61 | 6 | .279 | .344 | .372 | $12 | 290 |

### Minors (2010)

| Level | Leag | AB | HR | R | RBI | SB | BA | OBP | SLG | CT% | H% | BB% | Bash |
|---|---|---|---|---|---|---|---|---|---|---|---|---|---|
| A | — | — | — | — | — | — | — | — | — | — | — | — | — |
| AA | — | — | — | — | — | — | — | — | — | — | — | — | — |
| AAA | — | — | — | — | — | — | — | — | — | — | — | — | — |

### Majors / Skills

| Yr | Team | AB | HR | R | RBI | SB | BA | OBP | SLG | CT% | H% | BB% | Bash |
|---|---|---|---|---|---|---|---|---|---|---|---|---|---|
| 07 | FLA | 452 | 16 | 43 | 60 | 3 | .237 | .262 | .405 | 73% | 33% | 3% | 1.71 |
| 08 | KC | 306 | 12 | 29 | 41 | 7 | .255 | .278 | .444 | 73% | 35% | 2% | 1.74 |
| 09 | KC | 390 | 23 | 51 | 65 | 5 | .249 | .292 | .490 | 68% | 37% | 5% | 1.97 |
| 10 | COL | 394 | 14 | 55 | 58 | 7 | .269 | .315 | .449 | 70% | 38% | 6% | 1.67 |

**Competition at CA — Stats in 2010**

| Bats | Player | GSvR | GSvL | Sub | OPS |
|---|---|---|---|---|---|
| RH | Olivo M | 69 | 38 | 4 | .765 |
| RH | Iannetta C | 28 | 21 | 3 | .701 |
| RH | Phillips P | 3 | 2 | 5 | .497 |

**Value / Extra / Production / OPS / Scoresheet**

| Yr | Team | $1L | $2L | Pts | RAA | 2B | 3B | CS | FB-LD-GB | HR/fb | RBI% | RS% | OPS | 1st Hf | 2nd Hf | vs RH | vs LH | Rnge | vRH | vLH |
|---|---|---|---|---|---|---|---|---|---|---|---|---|---|---|---|---|---|---|---|---|
| 07 | FLA | $8 | $0 | 180 | -15 | 20 | 4 | 3 | 40-17-43 | 12% | 17% | 25% | .667 | .658 | .683 | .629 | .806 | 0.46 | -28 | +70 |
| 08 | KC | $9 | $2 | 140 | -3 | 22 | 0 | 0 | 44-17-38 | 12% | 17% | 22% | .722 | .766 | .643 | .667 | .830 | 0.47 | -24 | +63 |
| 09 | KC | $14 | $11 | 210 | +1 | 15 | 5 | 2 | 40-14-45 | 22% | 17% | 29% | .781 | .743 | .831 | .798 | .754 | 0.47 | -32 | +81 |
| 10 | COL | $16 | $12 | 210 | +0 | 17 | 6 | 4 | 40-18-42 | 12% | 18% | 34% | .765 | .925 | .539 | .749 | .801 | 0.50 | -18 | +40 |

---

## Magglio Ordonez — 525 PA | $17 | 340 pts

OF-71 (RF-71), DH-13 — Owned: 55% — RH

A season-ending ankle injury suffered in July prevented Ordonez from reaching an incentive that would have triggered a $15M option. The Tigers won't renew his option, but they will shoot to re-sign him at a lower salary, and he is a good bet to stay in Detroit. His rates barely register his advancing age. (LP)

### Forecast

| Player | Age | AB | HR | R | RBI | SB | BA | OBP | SLG | $1L | Pts |
|---|---|---|---|---|---|---|---|---|---|---|---|
| Ordonez M | 37 | 463 | 16 | 63 | 79 | 0 | .295 | .363 | .457 | $17 | 340 |
| **Mini-Browser** | **Age** | **AB** | **HR** | **R** | **RBI** | **SB** | **BA** | **OBP** | **SLG** | **$1L** | **Pts** |
| Zobrist B | 29 | 512 | 18 | 72 | 72 | 18 | .258 | .362 | .434 | $18 | 380 |
| Byrd M | 33 | 559 | 18 | 72 | 72 | 6 | .290 | .346 | .458 | $17 | 370 |
| Wells V | 32 | 568 | 18 | 72 | 78 | 12 | .264 | .318 | .452 | $17 | 390 |
| Gardner B | 27 | 441 | 5 | 75 | 40 | 46 | .261 | .357 | .363 | $17 | 330 |
| Heyward J | 21 | 511 | 18 | 84 | 66 | 12 | .270 | .368 | .464 | $17 | 380 |

### Minors (2010)

| Level | Leag | AB | HR | R | RBI | SB | BA | OBP | SLG | CT% | H% | BB% | Bash |
|---|---|---|---|---|---|---|---|---|---|---|---|---|---|
| A | — | — | — | — | — | — | — | — | — | — | — | — | — |
| AA | — | — | — | — | — | — | — | — | — | — | — | — | — |
| AAA | — | — | — | — | — | — | — | — | — | — | — | — | — |

### Majors / Skills

| Yr | Team | AB | HR | R | RBI | SB | BA | OBP | SLG | CT% | H% | BB% | Bash |
|---|---|---|---|---|---|---|---|---|---|---|---|---|---|
| 07 | DET | 595 | 28 | 117 | 139 | 4 | .363 | .434 | .595 | 87% | 42% | 11% | 1.64 |
| 08 | DET | 561 | 21 | 72 | 103 | 1 | .317 | .376 | .494 | 86% | 37% | 8% | 1.56 |
| 09 | DET | 465 | 9 | 54 | 50 | 3 | .310 | .376 | .428 | 86% | 36% | 10% | 1.38 |
| 10 | DET | 323 | 12 | 56 | 59 | 1 | .303 | .378 | .474 | 88% | 34% | 11% | 1.56 |

**Competition at RF — Stats in 2010**

| Bats | Player | GSvR | GSvL | Sub | OPS |
|---|---|---|---|---|---|
| LH | Boesch B | 59 | 13 | 7 | .736 |
| RH | Ordonez M | 54 | 17 | 0 | .852 |
| RH | Wells C | 4 | 13 | 12 | .901 |
| RH | Raburn R | 10 | 7 | 3 | .814 |

**Value / Extra / Production / OPS / Scoresheet**

| Yr | Team | $1L | $2L | Pts | RAA | 2B | 3B | CS | FB-LD-GB | HR/fb | RBI% | RS% | OPS | 1st Hf | 2nd Hf | vs RH | vs LH | Rnge | vRH | vLH |
|---|---|---|---|---|---|---|---|---|---|---|---|---|---|---|---|---|---|---|---|---|
| 07 | DET | $40 | $38 | 610 | +56 | 54 | 0 | 1 | 39-19-42 | 14% | 31% | 33% | 1.029 | 1.050 | 1.004 | .980 | 1.213 | 2.05 | -15 | +39 |
| 08 | DET | $25 | $17 | 430 | +15 | 32 | 2 | 5 | 36-20-44 | 12% | 24% | 24% | .869 | .866 | .873 | .870 | .866 | 2.07 | -23 | +62 |
| 09 | DET | $12 | $1 | 290 | +6 | 24 | 2 | 1 | 28-21-51 | 8% | 18% | 24% | .804 | .673 | .978 | .745 | .937 | 2.07 | -18 | +51 |
| 10 | DET | $14 | $4 | 270 | +10 | 17 | 1 | 0 | 32-22-47 | 15% | 25% | 35% | .852 | .867 | .717 | .763 | 1.171 | 2.04 | -18 | +46 |

---

## David Ortiz — 525 PA | $19 | 370 pts

DH-135, 1B-4 — Owned: 99% — LH

Big Papi has at least one more year in him as a DH, but he's at the point where he will have to take things year by year. His leash remains short, and he must get off to a good start in 2011 or he'll begin losing AB vs. lefties (paging Darnell McDonald). Ortiz is catching up to fewer pitches, but when he connects.... (EB)

### Forecast

| Player | Age | AB | HR | R | RBI | SB | BA | OBP | SLG | $1L | Pts |
|---|---|---|---|---|---|---|---|---|---|---|---|
| Ortiz D | 35 | 444 | 26 | 74 | 89 | 0 | .272 | .374 | .533 | $19 | 370 |
| **Mini-Browser** | **Age** | **AB** | **HR** | **R** | **RBI** | **SB** | **BA** | **OBP** | **SLG** | **$1L** | **Pts** |
| Guerrero V | 36 | 517 | 28 | 72 | 88 | 6 | .298 | .355 | .508 | $23 | 410 |
| Abreu B | 37 | 533 | 19 | 84 | 84 | 24 | .270 | .361 | .432 | $22 | 430 |
| Scott L | 32 | 450 | 25 | 60 | 70 | 0 | .278 | .361 | .521 | $16 | 320 |
| Lind A | 27 | 581 | 24 | 66 | 84 | 0 | .258 | .313 | .458 | $16 | 340 |
| Matsui H | 36 | 421 | 20 | 55 | 75 | 0 | .273 | .358 | .457 | $14 | 300 |

### Minors (2010)

| Level | Leag | AB | HR | R | RBI | SB | BA | OBP | SLG | CT% | H% | BB% | Bash |
|---|---|---|---|---|---|---|---|---|---|---|---|---|---|
| A | — | — | — | — | — | — | — | — | — | — | — | — | — |
| AA | — | — | — | — | — | — | — | — | — | — | — | — | — |
| AAA | — | — | — | — | — | — | — | — | — | — | — | — | — |

### Majors / Skills

| Yr | Team | AB | HR | R | RBI | SB | BA | OBP | SLG | CT% | H% | BB% | Bash |
|---|---|---|---|---|---|---|---|---|---|---|---|---|---|
| 07 | BOS | 549 | 35 | 116 | 117 | 3 | .332 | .445 | .621 | 81% | 41% | 16% | 1.87 |
| 08 | BOS | 416 | 23 | 74 | 89 | 1 | .264 | .369 | .507 | 82% | 32% | 14% | 1.92 |
| 09 | BOS | 541 | 28 | 77 | 99 | 0 | .238 | .332 | .462 | 75% | 32% | 12% | 1.94 |
| 10 | BOS | 518 | 32 | 86 | 102 | 0 | .270 | .370 | .529 | 72% | 38% | 13% | 1.96 |

**Competition at DH — Stats in 2010**

| Bats | Player | GSvR | GSvL | Sub | OPS |
|---|---|---|---|---|---|
| LH | Ortiz D | 96 | 38 | 1 | .899 |
| RH | Lowell M | 0 | 14 | 2 | .674 |

**Value / Extra / Production / OPS / Scoresheet**

| Yr | Team | $1L | $2L | Pts | RAA | 2B | 3B | CS | FB-LD-GB | HR/fb | RBI% | RS% | OPS | 1st Hf | 2nd Hf | vs RH | vs LH | Rnge | vRH | vLH |
|---|---|---|---|---|---|---|---|---|---|---|---|---|---|---|---|---|---|---|---|---|
| 07 | BOS | $35 | $32 | 590 | +57 | 52 | 1 | 0 | 45-17-38 | 17% | 26% | 31% | 1.066 | .990 | 1.153 | 1.171 | .852 | 2.04 | +23 | -57 |
| 08 | BOS | $18 | $9 | 370 | +10 | 30 | 1 | 0 | 45-19-37 | 15% | 26% | 32% | .877 | .839 | .914 | .921 | .741 | 2.04 | +34 | -86 |
| 09 | BOS | $17 | $10 | 360 | -6 | 35 | 1 | 0 | 50-17-32 | 13% | 21% | 27% | .794 | .733 | .866 | .828 | .716 | 2.04 | +40 | -110 |
| 10 | BOS | $26 | $20 | 400 | +15 | 36 | 1 | 0 | 45-17-38 | 19% | 26% | 35% | .899 | .945 | .854 | 1.059 | .599 | 2.04 | +30 | -84 |

*For more stats, visit www.Rotolympus.com.*

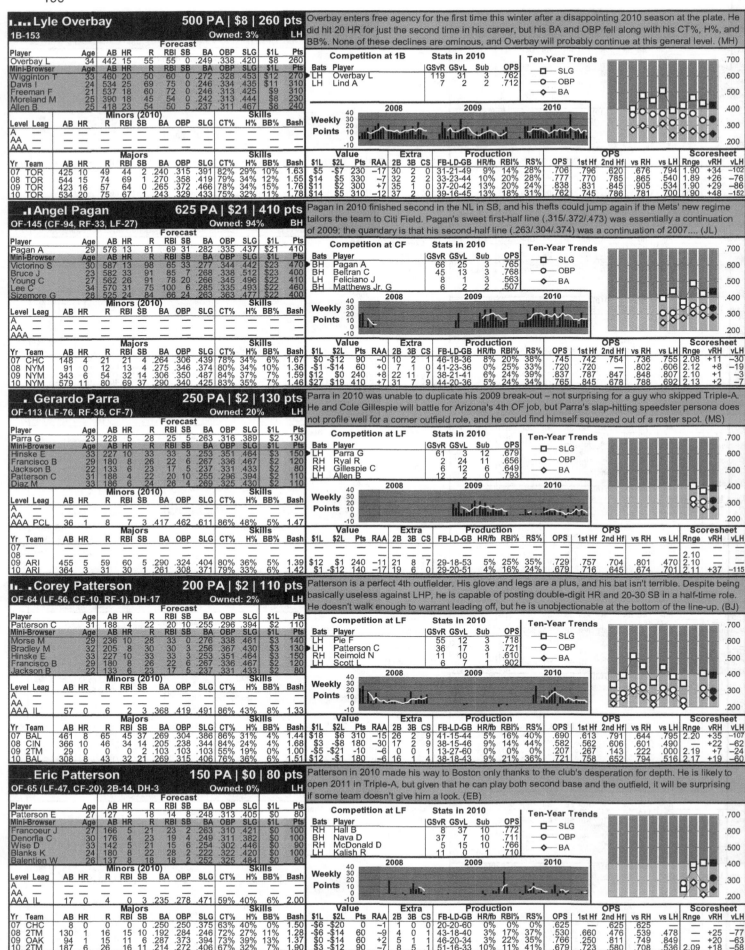

## Lyle Overbay — 500 PA | $8 | 260 pts
1B-153 • Owned: 3% • LH

Overbay enters free agency for the first time this winter after a disappointing 2010 season at the plate. He did hit 20 HR for just the second time in his career, but his BA and OBP fell along with his CT%, H%, and BB%. None of these declines are ominous, and Overbay will probably continue at this general level. (MH)

### Forecast
| Player | Age | AB | HR | R | RBI | SB | BA | OBP | SLG | $1L | Pts |
|---|---|---|---|---|---|---|---|---|---|---|---|
| Overbay L | 34 | 442 | 15 | 55 | 55 | 0 | .249 | .338 | .420 | $8 | 260 |
| Mini-Browser | Age | AB | HR | R | RBI | SB | BA | OBP | SLG | $1L | Pts |
| Wigginton T | 33 | 460 | 20 | 50 | 60 | 0 | .272 | .328 | .453 | $12 | 270 |
| Davis I | 24 | 534 | 25 | 69 | 75 | 0 | .246 | .334 | .445 | $11 | 310 |
| Freeman F | 21 | 537 | 18 | 60 | 72 | 0 | .246 | .313 | .425 | $9 | 310 |
| Moreland M | 25 | 390 | 18 | 45 | 54 | 0 | .242 | .313 | .444 | $8 | 230 |
| Allen B | 25 | 418 | 23 | 54 | 50 | 5 | .237 | .311 | .467 | $8 | 240 |

Minors (2010)
| Level Leag | AB | HR | R | RBI | SB | BA | OBP | SLG | CT% | H% | BB% | Bash |
|---|---|---|---|---|---|---|---|---|---|---|---|---|
| A | — | | | | | | | | | | | |
| AA | — | | | | | | | | | | | |
| AAA | — | | | | | | | | | | | |

### Majors
| Yr Team | AB | HR | R | RBI | SB | BA | OBP | SLG | CT% | H% | BB% | Bash | $1L | $2L | Pts | RAA | 2B | 3B | CS | FB-LD-GB | HR/fb | RBI% | RS% | OPS | 1st Hf | 2nd Hf | vs RH | vs LH | Rnge | vRH | vLH |
|---|---|---|---|---|---|---|---|---|---|---|---|---|---|---|---|---|---|---|---|---|---|---|---|---|---|---|---|---|---|---|---|
| 07 TOR | 425 | 10 | 49 | 44 | 2 | .240 | .315 | .391 | 82% | 29% | 10% | 1.63 | $5 | -$7 | 230 | -17 | 30 | 2 | 0 | 31-21-49 | 9% | 14% | 28% | .706 | .796 | .620 | .676 | .794 | 1.90 | +34 | -102 |
| 08 TOR | 544 | 15 | 74 | 69 | 1 | .270 | .358 | .419 | 79% | 34% | 12% | 1.55 | $14 | $5 | 330 | -7 | 32 | 2 | 3 | 33-23-44 | 10% | 20% | 28% | .777 | .770 | .785 | .865 | .540 | 1.89 | +26 | -76 |
| 09 TOR | 423 | 16 | 57 | 64 | 0 | .265 | .372 | .466 | 78% | 34% | 15% | 1.76 | $11 | $2 | 300 | +7 | 35 | 1 | 0 | 37-20-42 | 13% | 20% | 24% | .838 | .831 | .845 | .905 | .534 | 1.90 | +29 | -86 |
| 10 TOR | 534 | 20 | 75 | 67 | 1 | .243 | .329 | .433 | 75% | 32% | 11% | 1.78 | $8 | -$5 | 300 | -12 | 37 | 2 | 0 | 39-16-45 | 13% | 18% | 31% | .762 | .745 | .786 | .781 | .700 | 1.90 | +48 | -152 |

Competition at 1B / Stats in 2010
| Bats | Player | GSvR | GSvL | Sub | OPS |
|---|---|---|---|---|---|
| LH | Overbay L | 119 | 31 | 3 | .762 |
| LH | Lind A | 7 | 2 | 2 | .712 |

Ten-Year Trends: SLG, OBP, BA

---

## Angel Pagan — 625 PA | $21 | 410 pts
OF-145 (CF-94, RF-33, LF-27) • Owned: 94% • BH

Pagan in 2010 finished second in the NL in SB, and his thefts could jump again if the Mets' new regime tailors the team to Citi Field. Pagan's sweet first-half line (.315/.372/.473) was essentially a continuation of 2009; the quandary is that his second-half line (.263/.304/.374) was a continuation of 2007.... (JL)

### Forecast
| Player | Age | AB | HR | R | RBI | SB | BA | OBP | SLG | $1L | Pts |
|---|---|---|---|---|---|---|---|---|---|---|---|
| Pagan A | 29 | 576 | 13 | 81 | 69 | 31 | .282 | .335 | .437 | $21 | 410 |
| Mini-Browser | Age | AB | HR | R | RBI | SB | BA | OBP | SLG | $1L | Pts |
| Victorino S | 30 | 587 | 13 | 98 | 65 | 33 | .277 | .344 | .442 | $23 | 470 |
| Bruce J | 23 | 582 | 33 | 91 | 85 | 7 | .268 | .338 | .512 | $23 | 400 |
| Young C | 27 | 562 | 26 | 91 | 78 | 20 | .266 | .345 | .496 | $22 | 410 |
| Lee C | 34 | 570 | 31 | 75 | 100 | 6 | .285 | .335 | .493 | $22 | 460 |
| Sizemore G | 28 | 525 | 24 | 84 | 66 | 24 | .263 | .363 | .477 | $22 | 400 |

Minors (2010)
| Level Leag | AB | HR | R | RBI | SB | BA | OBP | SLG | CT% | H% | BB% | Bash |
|---|---|---|---|---|---|---|---|---|---|---|---|---|
| A | — | | | | | | | | | | | |
| AA | — | | | | | | | | | | | |
| AAA | — | | | | | | | | | | | |

### Majors
| Yr Team | AB | HR | R | RBI | SB | BA | OBP | SLG | CT% | H% | BB% | Bash | $1L | $2L | Pts | RAA | 2B | 3B | CS | FB-LD-GB | HR/fb | RBI% | RS% | OPS | 1st Hf | 2nd Hf | vs RH | vs LH | Rnge | vRH | vLH |
|---|---|---|---|---|---|---|---|---|---|---|---|---|---|---|---|---|---|---|---|---|---|---|---|---|---|---|---|---|---|---|---|
| 07 CHC | 148 | 4 | 21 | 21 | 4 | .264 | .306 | .439 | 78% | 34% | 6% | 1.67 | $0 | -$12 | 90 | -0 | 10 | 2 | 1 | 46-18-36 | 8% | 20% | 38% | .745 | .742 | .754 | .736 | .755 | 2.08 | +11 | -30 |
| 08 NYM | 91 | 0 | 12 | 13 | 4 | .275 | .346 | .374 | 80% | 34% | 10% | 1.36 | -$1 | -$14 | 60 | +0 | 7 | 1 | 0 | 41-23-36 | 0% | 25% | 33% | .720 | .720 | — | .802 | .606 | 2.12 | +8 | -19 |
| 09 NYM | 343 | 6 | 54 | 32 | 14 | .306 | .350 | .487 | 84% | 37% | 7% | 1.59 | $12 | $2 | 240 | +8 | 22 | 11 | 7 | 38-21-41 | 6% | 24% | 39% | .837 | .787 | .847 | .848 | .807 | 2.10 | +1 | -3 |
| 10 NYM | 579 | 11 | 80 | 69 | 37 | .290 | .340 | .425 | 83% | 35% | 7% | 1.46 | $27 | $19 | 410 | +7 | 31 | 7 | 9 | 44-20-36 | 5% | 24% | 34% | .765 | .845 | .678 | .788 | .692 | 2.13 | +2 | -7 |

Competition at CF / Stats in 2010
| Bats | Player | GSvR | GSvL | Sub | OPS |
|---|---|---|---|---|---|
| BH | Pagan A | 66 | 25 | 3 | .765 |
| BH | Beltran C | 45 | 13 | 3 | .768 |
| LH | Feliciano J | 8 | 1 | 3 | .563 |
| BH | Matthews Jr. G | 6 | 2 | 2 | .507 |

Ten-Year Trends: SLG, OBP, BA

---

## Gerardo Parra — 250 PA | $2 | 130 pts
OF-113 (LF-76, RF-36, CF-7) • Owned: 20% • LH

Parra in 2010 was unable to duplicate his 2009 break-out – not surprising for a guy who skipped Triple-A. He and Cole Gillespie will battle for Arizona's 4th OF job, but Parra's slap-hitting speedster persona does not profile well for a corner outfield role, and he could find himself squeezed out of a roster spot. (MS)

### Forecast
| Player | Age | AB | HR | R | RBI | SB | BA | OBP | SLG | $1L | Pts |
|---|---|---|---|---|---|---|---|---|---|---|---|
| Parra G | 23 | 228 | 5 | 28 | 25 | 5 | .263 | .316 | .389 | $2 | 130 |
| Mini-Browser | Age | AB | HR | R | RBI | SB | BA | OBP | SLG | $1L | Pts |
| Hinske E | 33 | 227 | 10 | 33 | 33 | 3 | .253 | .351 | .464 | $3 | 150 |
| Francisco B | 29 | 180 | 8 | 26 | 22 | 6 | .267 | .336 | .467 | $2 | 120 |
| Jackson B | 22 | 133 | 6 | 23 | 17 | 5 | .237 | .331 | .433 | $2 | 80 |
| Patterson C | 31 | 188 | 4 | 22 | 20 | 10 | .255 | .296 | .394 | $2 | 110 |
| Diaz M | 33 | 186 | 4 | 24 | 26 | 4 | .269 | .325 | .430 | $2 | 110 |

Minors (2010)
| Level Leag | AB | HR | R | RBI | SB | BA | OBP | SLG | CT% | H% | BB% | Bash |
|---|---|---|---|---|---|---|---|---|---|---|---|---|
| A | — | | | | | | | | | | | |
| AA | — | | | | | | | | | | | |
| AAA PCL | 36 | 1 | 8 | 7 | 3 | .417 | .462 | .611 | 86% | 48% | 5% | 1.47 |

### Majors
| Yr Team | AB | HR | R | RBI | SB | BA | OBP | SLG | CT% | H% | BB% | Bash | $1L | $2L | Pts | RAA | 2B | 3B | CS | FB-LD-GB | HR/fb | RBI% | RS% | OPS | 1st Hf | 2nd Hf | vs RH | vs LH | Rnge | vRH | vLH |
|---|---|---|---|---|---|---|---|---|---|---|---|---|---|---|---|---|---|---|---|---|---|---|---|---|---|---|---|---|---|---|---|
| 07 | | | | | | | | | | | | | | | | | | | | | | | | | | | | | | | |
| 08 | | | | | | | | | | | | | | | | | | | | | | | | | | | | | | | |
| 09 ARI | 455 | 5 | 59 | 60 | 5 | .290 | .324 | .404 | 80% | 36% | 5% | 1.39 | $12 | $1 | 240 | -11 | 21 | 8 | 7 | 29-18-53 | 5% | 25% | 35% | .729 | .757 | .704 | .801 | .470 | 2.10 | — | — |
| 10 ARI | 364 | 3 | 31 | 30 | 1 | .261 | .308 | .371 | 79% | 33% | 6% | 1.42 | $1 | -$12 | 140 | -17 | 19 | 6 | 0 | 29-20-51 | 4% | 16% | 24% | .679 | .716 | .645 | .674 | .701 | 2.11 | +37 | -115 |

Competition at LF / Stats in 2010
| Bats | Player | GSvR | GSvL | Sub | OPS |
|---|---|---|---|---|---|
| LH | Parra G | 61 | 3 | 12 | .679 |
| RH | Ryal R | 2 | 24 | 11 | .656 |
| RH | Gillespie C | 6 | 12 | 6 | .649 |
| LH | Allen B | 12 | 2 | 0 | .793 |

Ten-Year Trends: SLG, OBP, BA

---

## Corey Patterson — 200 PA | $2 | 110 pts
OF-64 (LF-56, CF-10, RF-1), DH-17 • Owned: 2% • LH

Patterson is a perfect 4th outfielder. His glove and legs are a plus, and his bat isn't terrible. Despite being basically useless against LHP, he is capable of posting double-digit HR and 20-30 SB in a half-time role. He doesn't walk enough to warrant leading off, but he is unobjectionable at the bottom of the line-up. (BJ)

### Forecast
| Player | Age | AB | HR | R | RBI | SB | BA | OBP | SLG | $1L | Pts |
|---|---|---|---|---|---|---|---|---|---|---|---|
| Patterson C | 31 | 188 | 4 | 22 | 20 | 10 | .255 | .296 | .394 | $2 | 110 |
| Mini-Browser | Age | AB | HR | R | RBI | SB | BA | OBP | SLG | $1L | Pts |
| Morse M | 29 | 236 | 10 | 28 | 33 | 0 | .276 | .338 | .461 | $3 | 140 |
| Bradley M | 32 | 205 | 8 | 30 | 30 | 3 | .256 | .367 | .430 | $3 | 130 |
| Hinske E | 33 | 227 | 10 | 33 | 33 | 3 | .253 | .351 | .464 | $3 | 150 |
| Francisco B | 29 | 180 | 8 | 26 | 22 | 6 | .267 | .336 | .467 | $2 | 120 |
| Jackson B | 22 | 133 | 6 | 23 | 17 | 5 | .237 | .331 | .433 | $2 | 80 |

Minors (2010)
| Level Leag | AB | HR | R | RBI | SB | BA | OBP | SLG | CT% | H% | BB% | Bash |
|---|---|---|---|---|---|---|---|---|---|---|---|---|
| A | — | | | | | | | | | | | |
| AA | — | | | | | | | | | | | |
| AAA IL | 57 | 0 | 6 | 2 | 3 | .368 | .419 | .491 | 86% | 43% | 8% | 1.33 |

### Majors
| Yr Team | AB | HR | R | RBI | SB | BA | OBP | SLG | CT% | H% | BB% | Bash | $1L | $2L | Pts | RAA | 2B | 3B | CS | FB-LD-GB | HR/fb | RBI% | RS% | OPS | 1st Hf | 2nd Hf | vs RH | vs LH | Rnge | vRH | vLH |
|---|---|---|---|---|---|---|---|---|---|---|---|---|---|---|---|---|---|---|---|---|---|---|---|---|---|---|---|---|---|---|---|
| 07 BAL | 461 | 8 | 65 | 45 | 37 | .269 | .304 | .386 | 86% | 31% | 4% | 1.44 | $18 | $6 | 310 | -15 | 26 | 2 | 9 | 41-15-44 | 5% | 16% | 40% | .690 | .613 | .791 | .644 | .795 | 2.20 | +35 | -107 |
| 08 CIN | 366 | 10 | 46 | 34 | 14 | .205 | .238 | .344 | 84% | 24% | 4% | 1.68 | $3 | -$8 | 180 | -30 | 17 | 2 | 9 | 38-16-46 | 9% | 14% | 44% | .582 | .562 | .606 | .601 | .490 | — | +22 | -67 |
| 09 2TM | 29 | 0 | 2 | 0 | 2 | .103 | .103 | .103 | 55% | 19% | 0% | 1.00 | -$5 | -$21 | -10 | -6 | 0 | 0 | 1 | 13-27-60 | 0% | 0% | 0% | .207 | .267 | .143 | .222 | .000 | 2.19 | +7 | -24 |
| 10 BAL | 308 | 8 | 43 | 32 | 21 | .269 | .315 | .406 | 76% | 36% | 6% | 1.51 | $12 | -$1 | 180 | -6 | 14 | 1 | 4 | 38-18-43 | 9% | 21% | 36% | .721 | .758 | .652 | .794 | .516 | 2.17 | +19 | -60 |

Competition at LF / Stats in 2010
| Bats | Player | GSvR | GSvL | Sub | OPS |
|---|---|---|---|---|---|
| LH | Pie F | 55 | 12 | 3 | .718 |
| LH | Patterson C | 36 | 17 | 3 | .721 |
| RH | Reimold N | 11 | 10 | 1 | .610 |
| LH | Scott L | 6 | 7 | 1 | .902 |

Ten-Year Trends: SLG, OBP, BA

---

## Eric Patterson — 150 PA | $0 | 80 pts
OF-65 (LF-47, CF-20), 2B-14, DH-3 • Owned: 0% • LH

Patterson in 2010 made his way to Boston only thanks to the club's desperation for depth. He is likely to open 2011 in Triple-A, but given that he can play both second base and the outfield, it will be surprising if some team doesn't give him a look. (EB)

### Forecast
| Player | Age | AB | HR | R | RBI | SB | BA | OBP | SLG | $1L | Pts |
|---|---|---|---|---|---|---|---|---|---|---|---|
| Patterson E | 27 | 127 | 3 | 18 | 14 | 8 | .248 | .313 | .405 | $0 | 80 |
| Mini-Browser | Age | AB | HR | R | RBI | SB | BA | OBP | SLG | $1L | Pts |
| Francoeur J | 27 | 166 | 5 | 21 | 23 | 2 | .263 | .310 | .421 | $0 | 100 |
| Denorfia C | 30 | 176 | 4 | 23 | 19 | 4 | .249 | .311 | .382 | $0 | 100 |
| Wise D | 33 | 142 | 5 | 21 | 15 | 6 | .254 | .302 | .446 | $0 | 90 |
| Blanks K | 24 | 180 | 8 | 22 | 28 | 2 | .252 | .322 | .420 | $0 | 100 |
| Balentien W | 26 | 137 | 8 | 18 | 18 | 2 | .252 | .325 | .484 | $0 | 90 |

Minors (2010)
| Level Leag | AB | HR | R | RBI | SB | BA | OBP | SLG | CT% | H% | BB% | Bash |
|---|---|---|---|---|---|---|---|---|---|---|---|---|
| A | — | | | | | | | | | | | |
| AA | — | | | | | | | | | | | |
| AAA IL | 17 | 0 | 4 | 0 | 3 | .235 | .278 | .471 | 59% | 40% | 6% | 2.00 |

### Majors
| Yr Team | AB | HR | R | RBI | SB | BA | OBP | SLG | CT% | H% | BB% | Bash | $1L | $2L | Pts | RAA | 2B | 3B | CS | FB-LD-GB | HR/fb | RBI% | RS% | OPS | 1st Hf | 2nd Hf | vs RH | vs LH | Rnge | vRH | vLH |
|---|---|---|---|---|---|---|---|---|---|---|---|---|---|---|---|---|---|---|---|---|---|---|---|---|---|---|---|---|---|---|---|
| 07 CHC | 8 | 0 | 0 | 0 | 0 | .250 | .250 | .375 | 63% | 40% | 0% | 1.50 | -$6 | -$20 | 0 | -1 | 1 | 0 | 0 | 20-20-60 | 0% | 0% | 0% | .625 | — | .625 | .625 | — | — | — | — |
| 08 2TM | 130 | 1 | 16 | 15 | 10 | .192 | .284 | .246 | 72% | 27% | 11% | 1.28 | -$6 | -$14 | 60 | -9 | 4 | 0 | 1 | 43-18-40 | 3% | 17% | 37% | .530 | .660 | .476 | .539 | .478 | — | +25 | -77 |
| 09 OAK | 94 | 1 | 11 | 6 | 7 | .287 | .373 | .394 | 73% | 39% | 13% | 1.37 | $0 | -$14 | 60 | +2 | 5 | 1 | 1 | 46-20-34 | 3% | 22% | 35% | .766 | .250 | .811 | .749 | .849 | — | +20 | -63 |
| 10 2TM | 187 | 4 | 26 | 16 | 11 | .214 | .272 | .406 | 67% | 32% | 7% | 1.90 | $3 | -$12 | 90 | -7 | 8 | 1 | 1 | 51-16-33 | 9% | 11% | 41% | .679 | .723 | .580 | .708 | .536 | 2.09 | +18 | -58 |

Competition at LF / Stats in 2010
| Bats | Player | GSvR | GSvL | Sub | OPS |
|---|---|---|---|---|---|
| RH | Hall B | 8 | 37 | 10 | .772 |
| BH | Nava D | 37 | 7 | 10 | .711 |
| RH | McDonald D | 5 | 15 | 10 | .766 |
| LH | Kalish R | 11 | 0 | 1 | .710 |

Ten-Year Trends: SLG, OBP, BA

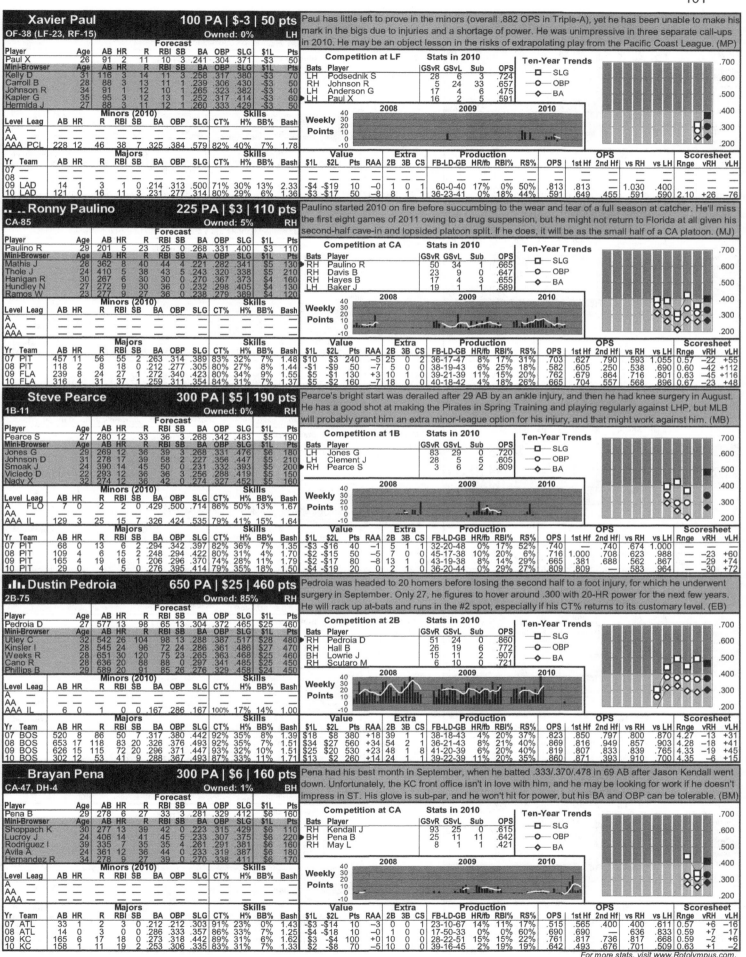

## Xavier Paul — 100 PA | $-3 | 50 pts

OF-38 (LF-23, RF-15) Owned: 0% LH

| Player | Age | AB | HR | R | RBI | SB | BA | OBP | SLG | $1L | Pts |
|---|---|---|---|---|---|---|---|---|---|---|---|
| Paul X | 26 | 91 | 2 | 11 | 10 | 3 | .241 | .304 | .371 | -$3 | 50 |
| **Mini-Browser** | **Age** | **AB** | **HR** | **R** | **RBI** | **SB** | **BA** | **OBP** | **SLG** | **$1L** | **Pts** |
| Kelly D | 31 | 116 | 3 | 14 | 11 | 3 | .258 | .317 | .380 | -$3 | 70 |
| Carroll B | 28 | 88 | 3 | 13 | 11 | 1 | .239 | .306 | .430 | -$3 | 50 |
| Johnson R | 34 | 91 | 1 | 12 | 10 | 1 | .265 | .323 | .382 | -$3 | 40 |
| Kapler G | 35 | 95 | 3 | 12 | 13 | 1 | .252 | .317 | .414 | -$3 | 60 |
| Hermida J | 27 | 88 | 3 | 11 | 12 | 1 | .260 | .333 | .429 | -$3 | 50 |

| Level | Leag | AB | HR | R | RBI | SB | BA | OBP | SLG | CT% | H% | BB% | Bash |
|---|---|---|---|---|---|---|---|---|---|---|---|---|---|
| A | — | — | — | — | — | — | — | — | — | — | — | — | — |
| AA | — | — | — | — | — | — | — | — | — | — | — | — | — |
| AAA | PCL | 228 | 12 | 46 | 38 | 7 | .325 | .384 | .579 | 82% | 40% | 7% | 1.78 |

| Yr | Team | AB | HR | R | RBI | SB | BA | OBP | SLG | CT% | H% | BB% | Bash | $1L | $2L | Pts | RAA | 2B | 3B | CS | FB-LD-GB | HR/fb | RBI% | RS% | OPS | 1st Hf | 2nd Hf | vs RH | vs LH | Rnge | vRH | vLH |
|---|---|---|---|---|---|---|---|---|---|---|---|---|---|---|---|---|---|---|---|---|---|---|---|---|---|---|---|---|---|---|---|---|
| 07 | — | — | — | — | — | — | — | — | — | — | — | — | — | — | — | — | — | — | — | — | — | — | — | — | — | — | — | — | — | — | — | — |
| 08 | — | — | — | — | — | — | — | — | — | — | — | — | — | — | — | — | — | — | — | — | — | — | — | — | — | — | — | — | — | — | — | — |
| 09 | LAD | 14 | 1 | 3 | 1 | 0 | .214 | .313 | .500 | 71% | 30% | 13% | 2.33 | -$4 | -$19 | 10 | –0 | 1 | 0 | 1 | 60-0-40 | 17% | 0% | 50% | .813 | .813 | — | 1.030 | .400 | — | — | — |
| 10 | LAD | 121 | 0 | 16 | 11 | 3 | .231 | .277 | .314 | 80% | 29% | 6% | 1.36 | -$3 | -$17 | 50 | –8 | 8 | 1 | 1 | 36-23-41 | 0% | 18% | 44% | .591 | .649 | .455 | .591 | .590 | 2.10 | +26 | –76 |

Paul has little left to prove in the minors (overall .882 OPS in Triple-A), yet he has been unable to make his mark in the bigs due to injuries and a shortage of power. He was unimpressive in three separate call-ups in 2010. He may be an object lesson in the risks of extrapolating play from the Pacific Coast League. (MP)

| Bats | Player (Competition at LF) | GSvR | GSvL | Sub | OPS |
|---|---|---|---|---|---|
| LH | Podsednik S | 28 | 6 | 3 | .724 |
| RH | Johnson R | 5 | 24 | 33 | .657 |
| LH | Anderson G | 17 | 4 | 6 | .475 |
| LH | Paul X | 16 | 2 | 5 | .591 |

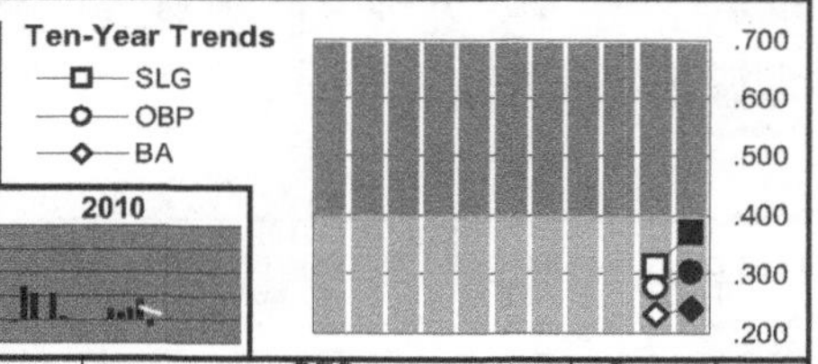


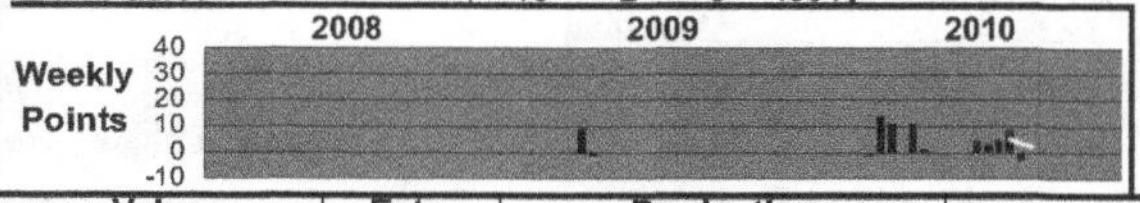


## Ronny Paulino — 225 PA | $3 | 110 pts

CA-85 Owned: 5% RH

| Player | Age | AB | HR | R | RBI | SB | BA | OBP | SLG | $1L | Pts |
|---|---|---|---|---|---|---|---|---|---|---|---|
| Paulino R | 29 | 201 | 5 | 23 | 25 | 0 | .268 | .331 | .400 | $3 | 110 |
| **Mini-Browser** | **Age** | **AB** | **HR** | **R** | **RBI** | **SB** | **BA** | **OBP** | **SLG** | **$1L** | **Pts** |
| Mathis J | 28 | 362 | 8 | 40 | 44 | 4 | .221 | .282 | .341 | $5 | 130 |
| Thole J | 24 | 410 | 5 | 38 | 43 | 5 | .243 | .320 | .338 | $5 | 210 |
| Hanigan R | 30 | 267 | 6 | 30 | 30 | 0 | .270 | .367 | .373 | $4 | 160 |
| Hundley N | 27 | 272 | 9 | 30 | 36 | 0 | .232 | .298 | .405 | $4 | 130 |
| Ramos W | 23 | 277 | 9 | 27 | 36 | 0 | .238 | .279 | .389 | $4 | 120 |

| Level | Leag | AB | HR | R | RBI | SB | BA | OBP | SLG | CT% | H% | BB% | Bash |
|---|---|---|---|---|---|---|---|---|---|---|---|---|---|
| A | — | — | — | — | — | — | — | — | — | — | — | — | — |
| AA | — | — | — | — | — | — | — | — | — | — | — | — | — |
| AAA | — | — | — | — | — | — | — | — | — | — | — | — | — |

| Yr | Team | AB | HR | R | RBI | SB | BA | OBP | SLG | CT% | H% | BB% | Bash | $1L | $2L | Pts | RAA | 2B | 3B | CS | FB-LD-GB | HR/fb | RBI% | RS% | OPS | 1st Hf | 2nd Hf | vs RH | vs LH | Rnge | vRH | vLH |
|---|---|---|---|---|---|---|---|---|---|---|---|---|---|---|---|---|---|---|---|---|---|---|---|---|---|---|---|---|---|---|---|---|
| 07 | PIT | 457 | 11 | 56 | 55 | 2 | .263 | .314 | .389 | 83% | 32% | 7% | 1.48 | $10 | $3 | 240 | –5 | 25 | 0 | 2 | 36-17-47 | 8% | 17% | 31% | .703 | .627 | .790 | .593 | 1.055 | 0.57 | –22 | +55 |
| 08 | PIT | 118 | 2 | 8 | 18 | 0 | .212 | .277 | .305 | 80% | 27% | 8% | 1.44 | -$1 | -$9 | 50 | –7 | 5 | 0 | 0 | 38-19-43 | 6% | 25% | 18% | .582 | .605 | .250 | .538 | .690 | 0.60 | –42 | +112 |
| 09 | FLA | 239 | 8 | 24 | 27 | 1 | .272 | .340 | .423 | 80% | 34% | 9% | 1.55 | $5 | -$1 | 130 | +3 | 10 | 1 | 0 | 39-21-39 | 11% | 15% | 20% | .762 | .679 | .864 | .716 | .801 | 0.63 | –45 | +116 |
| 10 | FLA | 316 | 4 | 31 | 37 | 1 | .259 | .311 | .354 | 84% | 31% | 7% | 1.37 | $5 | -$2 | 160 | –7 | 18 | 0 | 0 | 40-18-42 | 4% | 18% | 26% | .665 | .704 | .557 | .568 | .896 | 0.67 | –23 | +48 |

Paulino started 2010 on fire before succumbing to the wear and tear of a full season at catcher. He'll miss the first eight games of 2011 owing to a drug suspension, but he might not return to Florida at all given his second-half cave-in and lopsided platoon split. If he does, it will be as the small half of a CA platoon. (MJ)

| Bats | Player (Competition at CA) | GSvR | GSvL | Sub | OPS |
|---|---|---|---|---|---|
| RH | Paulino R | 50 | 34 | 1 | .665 |
| RH | Davis B | 23 | 9 | 0 | .647 |
| RH | Hayes B | 17 | 4 | 3 | .655 |
| LH | Baker J | 19 | 1 | 1 | .589 |

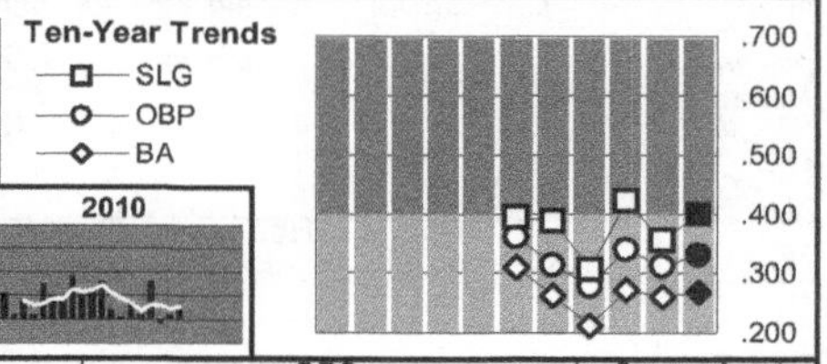


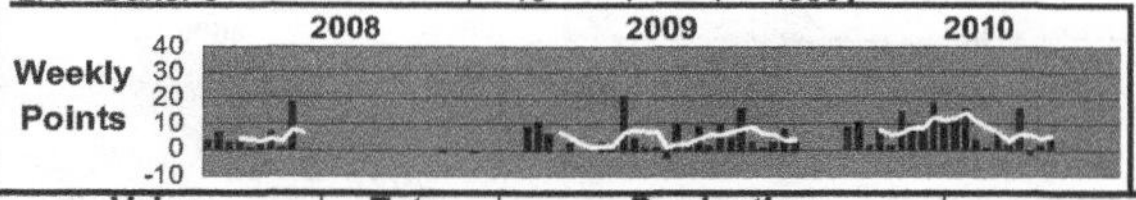


## Steve Pearce — 300 PA | $5 | 190 pts

1B-11 Owned: 0% RH

| Player | Age | AB | HR | R | RBI | SB | BA | OBP | SLG | $1L | Pts |
|---|---|---|---|---|---|---|---|---|---|---|---|
| Pearce S | 27 | 280 | 12 | 33 | 36 | 3 | .268 | .342 | .483 | $5 | 190 |
| **Mini-Browser** | **Age** | **AB** | **HR** | **R** | **RBI** | **SB** | **BA** | **OBP** | **SLG** | **$1L** | **Pts** |
| Jones G | 29 | 269 | 12 | 36 | 39 | 3 | .268 | .331 | .476 | $6 | 180 |
| Johnson D | 31 | 278 | 17 | 39 | 58 | 2 | .227 | .356 | .447 | $5 | 210 |
| Smoak J | 24 | 390 | 14 | 45 | 50 | 0 | .231 | .332 | .393 | $5 | 200 |
| Viciedo D | 22 | 293 | 12 | 36 | 36 | 3 | .256 | .288 | .419 | $5 | 150 |
| Nady X | 32 | 274 | 12 | 36 | 42 | 0 | .274 | .327 | .452 | $5 | 160 |

| Level | Leag | AB | HR | R | RBI | SB | BA | OBP | SLG | CT% | H% | BB% | Bash |
|---|---|---|---|---|---|---|---|---|---|---|---|---|---|
| A | FLO | 7 | 0 | 2 | 2 | 0 | .429 | .500 | .714 | 86% | 50% | 13% | 1.67 |
| AA | — | — | — | — | — | — | — | — | — | — | — | — | — |
| AAA | IL | 129 | 3 | 25 | 15 | 7 | .326 | .424 | .535 | 79% | 41% | 15% | 1.64 |

| Yr | Team | AB | HR | R | RBI | SB | BA | OBP | SLG | CT% | H% | BB% | Bash | $1L | $2L | Pts | RAA | 2B | 3B | CS | FB-LD-GB | HR/fb | RBI% | RS% | OPS | 1st Hf | 2nd Hf | vs RH | vs LH | Rnge | vRH | vLH |
|---|---|---|---|---|---|---|---|---|---|---|---|---|---|---|---|---|---|---|---|---|---|---|---|---|---|---|---|---|---|---|---|---|
| 07 | PIT | 68 | 0 | 13 | 6 | 2 | .294 | .342 | .397 | 82% | 36% | 7% | 1.35 | -$3 | -$16 | 40 | –1 | 5 | 1 | 1 | 32-20-48 | 0% | 17% | 52% | .740 | — | .740 | .674 | 1.000 | — | — | — |
| 08 | PIT | 109 | 4 | 6 | 15 | 2 | .248 | .294 | .422 | 80% | 31% | 4% | 1.70 | -$2 | -$15 | 50 | –5 | 7 | 0 | 0 | 45-17-38 | 10% | 20% | 6% | .716 | 1.000 | .708 | .623 | .988 | — | –23 | +60 |
| 09 | PIT | 165 | 4 | 19 | 16 | 1 | .206 | .296 | .370 | 74% | 28% | 11% | 1.79 | -$2 | -$17 | 80 | –8 | 13 | 1 | 0 | 43-19-38 | 8% | 14% | 29% | .665 | .381 | .688 | .562 | .867 | — | –29 | +74 |
| 10 | PIT | 29 | 0 | 4 | 5 | 0 | .276 | .395 | .414 | 79% | 35% | 18% | 1.50 | -$4 | -$19 | 20 | 0 | 2 | 1 | 0 | 36-20-44 | 0% | 29% | 27% | .809 | .809 | — | .583 | .964 | — | –30 | +72 |

Pearce's bright start was derailed after 29 AB by an ankle injury, and then he had knee surgery in August. He has a good shot at making the Pirates in Spring Training and playing regularly against LHP, but MLB will probably grant him an extra minor-league option for his injury, and that might work against him. (MB)

| Bats | Player (Competition at 1B) | GSvR | GSvL | Sub | OPS |
|---|---|---|---|---|---|
| LH | Jones G | 83 | 29 | 0 | .720 |
| LH | Clement J | 28 | 5 | 5 | .605 |
| RH | Pearce S | 3 | 6 | 2 | .809 |

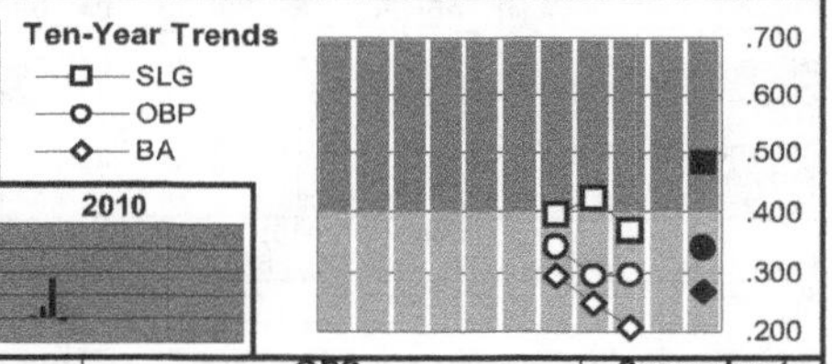


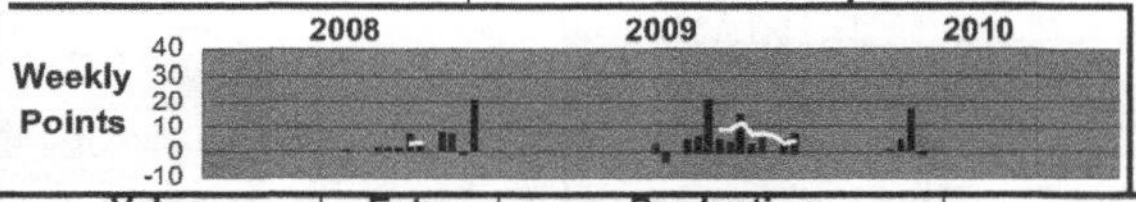


## Dustin Pedroia — 650 PA | $25 | 460 pts

2B-75 Owned: 85% RH

| Player | Age | AB | HR | R | RBI | SB | BA | OBP | SLG | $1L | Pts |
|---|---|---|---|---|---|---|---|---|---|---|---|
| Pedroia D | 27 | 577 | 13 | 98 | 65 | 13 | .304 | .372 | .465 | $25 | 460 |
| **Mini-Browser** | **Age** | **AB** | **HR** | **R** | **RBI** | **SB** | **BA** | **OBP** | **SLG** | **$1L** | **Pts** |
| Utley C | 32 | 542 | 26 | 104 | 98 | 13 | .288 | .387 | .517 | $28 | 480 |
| Kinsler I | 28 | 545 | 24 | 96 | 72 | 24 | .286 | .361 | .486 | $27 | 470 |
| Weeks R | 28 | 651 | 30 | 120 | 75 | 23 | .265 | .363 | .468 | $25 | 460 |
| Cano R | 28 | 636 | 20 | 88 | 88 | 0 | .297 | .341 | .485 | $25 | 450 |
| Phillips B | 29 | 589 | 20 | 91 | 85 | 26 | .276 | .329 | .458 | $24 | 450 |

| Level | Leag | AB | HR | R | RBI | SB | BA | OBP | SLG | CT% | H% | BB% | Bash |
|---|---|---|---|---|---|---|---|---|---|---|---|---|---|
| A | — | — | — | — | — | — | — | — | — | — | — | — | — |
| AA | — | — | — | — | — | — | — | — | — | — | — | — | — |
| AAA | IL | 6 | 0 | 1 | 0 | 0 | .167 | .286 | .167 | 100% | 17% | 14% | 1.00 |

| Yr | Team | AB | HR | R | RBI | SB | BA | OBP | SLG | CT% | H% | BB% | Bash | $1L | $2L | Pts | RAA | 2B | 3B | CS | FB-LD-GB | HR/fb | RBI% | RS% | OPS | 1st Hf | 2nd Hf | vs RH | vs LH | Rnge | vRH | vLH |
|---|---|---|---|---|---|---|---|---|---|---|---|---|---|---|---|---|---|---|---|---|---|---|---|---|---|---|---|---|---|---|---|---|
| 07 | BOS | 520 | 8 | 86 | 50 | 7 | .317 | .380 | .442 | 92% | 35% | 8% | 1.39 | $18 | $8 | 380 | +18 | 39 | 1 | 1 | 38-18-43 | 4% | 20% | 37% | .823 | .850 | .797 | .800 | .870 | 4.27 | –13 | +31 |
| 08 | BOS | 653 | 17 | 118 | 83 | 20 | .326 | .376 | .493 | 92% | 35% | 7% | 1.51 | $34 | $27 | 560 | +34 | 54 | 2 | 1 | 36-21-43 | 8% | 21% | 40% | .869 | .816 | .949 | .857 | .903 | 4.28 | –18 | +41 |
| 09 | BOS | 626 | 15 | 115 | 72 | 20 | .296 | .371 | .447 | 93% | 32% | 10% | 1.51 | $25 | $20 | 530 | +23 | 48 | 1 | 8 | 41-20-39 | 6% | 20% | 40% | .819 | .807 | .833 | .839 | .765 | 4.33 | –19 | +45 |
| 10 | BOS | 302 | 12 | 53 | 41 | 9 | .288 | .367 | .493 | 87% | 33% | 11% | 1.71 | $13 | $2 | 260 | +14 | 24 | 1 | 1 | 39-22-39 | 11% | 20% | 35% | .860 | .871 | .393 | .910 | .700 | 4.35 | –6 | +15 |

Pedroia was headed to 20 homers before losing the second half to a foot injury, for which he underwent surgery in September. Only 27, he figures to hover around .300 with 20-HR power for the next few years. He will rack up at-bats and runs in the #2 spot, especially if his CT% returns to its customary level. (EB)

| Bats | Player (Competition at 2B) | GSvR | GSvL | Sub | OPS |
|---|---|---|---|---|---|
| RH | Pedroia D | 51 | 24 | 0 | .860 |
| RH | Hall B | 26 | 19 | 6 | .772 |
| BH | Lowrie J | 15 | 11 | 2 | .907 |
| RH | Scutaro M | 6 | 10 | 0 | .721 |

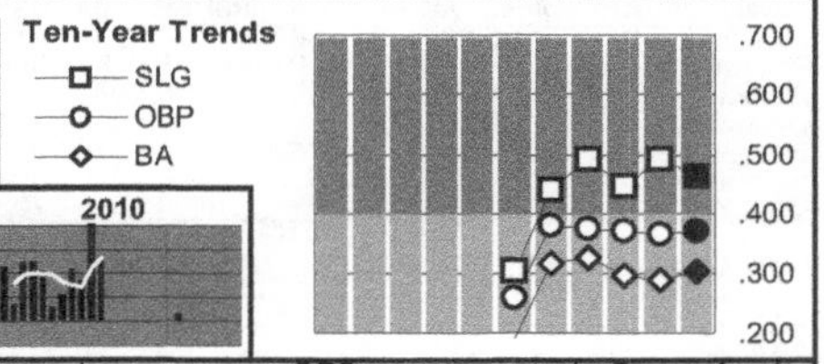


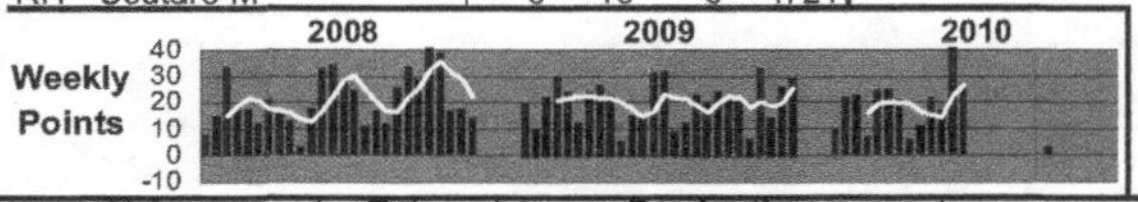


## Brayan Pena — 300 PA | $6 | 160 pts

CA-47, DH-4 Owned: 1% BH

| Player | Age | AB | HR | R | RBI | SB | BA | OBP | SLG | $1L | Pts |
|---|---|---|---|---|---|---|---|---|---|---|---|
| Pena B | 29 | 278 | 6 | 27 | 33 | 3 | .281 | .329 | .412 | $6 | 160 |
| **Mini-Browser** | **Age** | **AB** | **HR** | **R** | **RBI** | **SB** | **BA** | **OBP** | **SLG** | **$1L** | **Pts** |
| Shoppach K | 30 | 277 | 13 | 39 | 42 | 0 | .223 | .315 | .429 | $6 | 110 |
| Lucroy J | 24 | 406 | 14 | 41 | 45 | 5 | .233 | .307 | .375 | $6 | 220 |
| Rodriguez I | 39 | 335 | 7 | 35 | 35 | 4 | .261 | .291 | .381 | $6 | 160 |
| Avila A | 24 | 361 | 12 | 36 | 44 | 0 | .233 | .319 | .387 | $6 | 180 |
| Hernandez R | 34 | 278 | 9 | 27 | 39 | 0 | .270 | .338 | .411 | $6 | 170 |

| Level | Leag | AB | HR | R | RBI | SB | BA | OBP | SLG | CT% | H% | BB% | Bash |
|---|---|---|---|---|---|---|---|---|---|---|---|---|---|
| A | — | — | — | — | — | — | — | — | — | — | — | — | — |
| AA | — | — | — | — | — | — | — | — | — | — | — | — | — |
| AAA | — | — | — | — | — | — | — | — | — | — | — | — | — |

| Yr | Team | AB | HR | R | RBI | SB | BA | OBP | SLG | CT% | H% | BB% | Bash | $1L | $2L | Pts | RAA | 2B | 3B | CS | FB-LD-GB | HR/fb | RBI% | RS% | OPS | 1st Hf | 2nd Hf | vs RH | vs LH | Rnge | vRH | vLH |
|---|---|---|---|---|---|---|---|---|---|---|---|---|---|---|---|---|---|---|---|---|---|---|---|---|---|---|---|---|---|---|---|---|
| 07 | ATL | 33 | 1 | 2 | 3 | 0 | .212 | .212 | .303 | 91% | 23% | 0% | 1.43 | -$3 | -$14 | 10 | –3 | 0 | 0 | 1 | 23-10-67 | 14% | 11% | 17% | .515 | .565 | .400 | .400 | .611 | 0.57 | +6 | –16 |
| 08 | ATL | 14 | 0 | 3 | 0 | 0 | .286 | .333 | .357 | 86% | 33% | 7% | 1.25 | -$4 | -$18 | 10 | –0 | 1 | 0 | 0 | 17-50-33 | 0% | 0% | 60% | .690 | .690 | — | .636 | .833 | 0.59 | +7 | –17 |
| 09 | KC | 165 | 6 | 17 | 18 | 0 | .273 | .318 | .442 | 89% | 31% | 6% | 1.62 | $3 | -$4 | 100 | +0 | 10 | 0 | 0 | 28-22-51 | 15% | 15% | 22% | .761 | .817 | .736 | .817 | .668 | 0.59 | –2 | +6 |
| 10 | KC | 158 | 1 | 11 | 19 | 2 | .253 | .306 | .335 | 83% | 31% | 7% | 1.33 | $2 | -$8 | 70 | –5 | 10 | 0 | 0 | 39-16-45 | 2% | 19% | 19% | .642 | .493 | .676 | .701 | .509 | 0.63 | +1 | –2 |

Pena had his best month in September, when he batted .333/.370/.478 in 69 AB after Jason Kendall went down. Unfortunately, the KC front office isn't in love with him, and he may be looking for work if he doesn't impress in ST. His glove is sub-par, and he won't hit for power, but his BA and OBP can be tolerable. (BM)

| Bats | Player (Competition at CA) | GSvR | GSvL | Sub | OPS |
|---|---|---|---|---|---|
| RH | Kendall J | 93 | 25 | 0 | .615 |
| BH | Pena B | 25 | 11 | 11 | .642 |
| RH | May L | 8 | 1 | 1 | .421 |

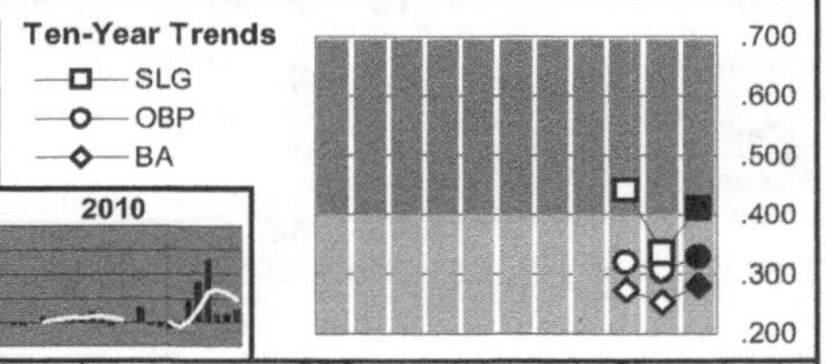


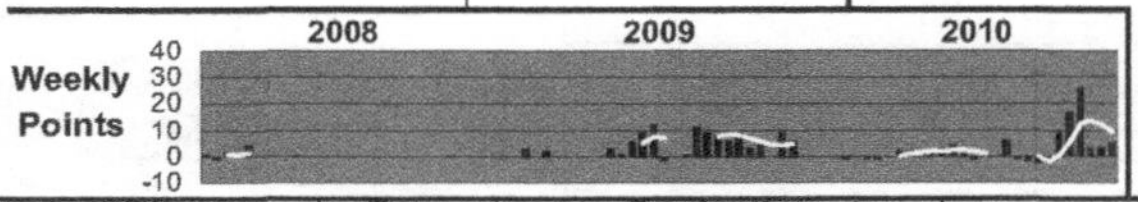

## Carlos Pena — 550 PA | $17 | 310 pts

1B-142, DH-2 — Owned: 94% — LH

Ever since his stellar 2007 campaign, Pena has been up and down. Given his unpredictability, the cost of re-signing him might be too much for the Rays. But given his upside, he would be a worthwhile gamble for a team with weak options at first base. His FB% is very likely to rise in 2011. (RZ)

| Player | Age | AB | HR | R | RBI | SB | BA | OBP | SLG | $1L | Pts |
|---|---|---|---|---|---|---|---|---|---|---|---|
| **Forecast** | | | | | | | | | | | |
| Pena C | 32 | 452 | 33 | 72 | 88 | 0 | .231 | .357 | .494 | $17 | 310 |
| **Mini-Browser** | | | | | | | | | | | |
| Konerko P | 35 | 554 | 31 | 75 | 94 | 0 | .271 | .359 | .499 | $21 | 410 |
| Youkilis K | 32 | 451 | 21 | 79 | 79 | 5 | .291 | .390 | .515 | $20 | 370 |
| LaRoche A | 31 | 530 | 30 | 84 | 90 | 0 | .283 | .356 | .520 | $20 | 380 |
| Butler B | 24 | 585 | 20 | 72 | 85 | 0 | .300 | .367 | .466 | $19 | 400 |
| Lee D | 35 | 506 | 23 | 81 | 81 | 6 | .284 | .370 | .488 | $19 | 390 |

| Level | Leag | AB | HR | R | RBI | SB | BA | OBP | SLG | CT% | H% | BB% | Bash |
|---|---|---|---|---|---|---|---|---|---|---|---|---|---|
| | | Minors (2010) | | | | | | | | Skills | | | |
| A | FLO | 3 | 0 | 1 | 1 | 0 | .667 | .667 | .667 | 100% | 67% | 0% | 1.00 |
| AA | — | — | — | — | — | — | — | — | — | — | — | — | — |
| AAA | — | — | — | — | — | — | — | — | — | — | — | — | — |

| Yr | Team | AB | HR | R | RBI | SB | BA | OBP | SLG | CT% | H% | BB% | Bash |
|---|---|---|---|---|---|---|---|---|---|---|---|---|---|
| | | Majors | | | | | | | | Skills | | | |
| 07 | TB | 490 | 46 | 99 | 121 | 1 | .282 | .411 | .627 | 71% | 40% | 17% | 2.22 |
| 08 | TB | 490 | 31 | 76 | 102 | 1 | .247 | .377 | .494 | 66% | 37% | 16% | 2.00 |
| 09 | TB | 471 | 39 | 91 | 100 | 3 | .227 | .356 | .537 | 65% | 35% | 15% | 2.36 |
| 10 | TB | 484 | 28 | 64 | 84 | 5 | .196 | .325 | .407 | 67% | 29% | 15% | 2.07 |

**Competition at 1B** — Stats in 2010

| Bats | Player | GSvR | GSvL | Sub | OPS |
|---|---|---|---|---|---|
| LH | Pena C | 92 | 43 | 7 | .732 |
| BH | Zobrist B | 7 | 7 | 0 | .699 |
| LH | Johnson D | 10 | 2 | 1 | .757 |

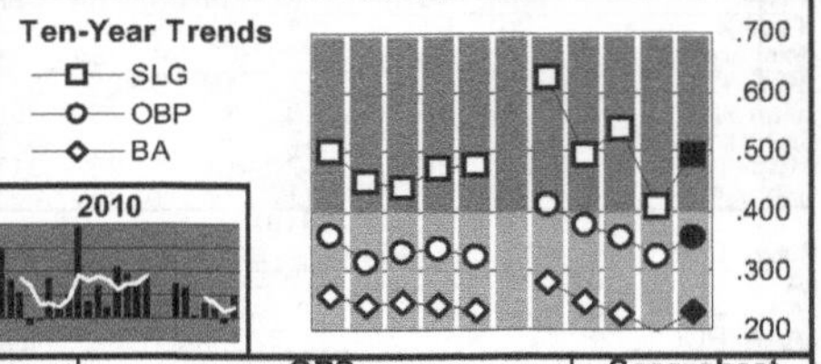


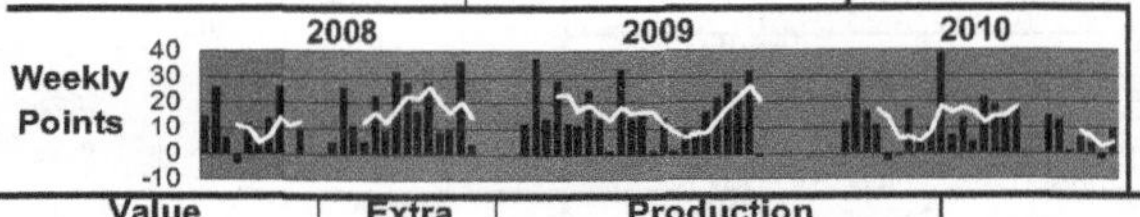


| Yr | $1L | $2L | Pts | RAA | 2B | 3B | CS | FB-LD-GB | HR/fb | RBI% | RS% | OPS | 1st Hf | 2nd Hf | vs RH | vs LH | Rnge | vRH | vLH |
|---|---|---|---|---|---|---|---|---|---|---|---|---|---|---|---|---|---|---|---|
| | Value | | | | Extra | | | Production | | | | OPS | | | | | Scoresheet | | |
| 07 | $31 | $26 | 490 | +36 | 29 | 1 | 0 | 45-18-37 | 29% | 26% | 26% | 1.037 | 1.004 | 1.066 | 1.068 | .953 | — | +29 | –97 |
| 08 | $20 | $12 | 350 | +5 | 24 | 2 | 1 | 50-18-32 | 19% | 22% | 23% | .871 | .778 | .978 | .994 | .654 | 1.83 | +27 | –79 |
| 09 | $21 | $16 | 370 | +6 | 25 | 2 | 3 | 54-17-29 | 24% | 22% | 32% | .893 | .891 | .897 | .936 | .814 | 1.88 | +43 | –115 |
| 10 | $13 | $3 | 280 | –17 | 18 | 0 | 1 | 41-14-45 | 21% | 19% | 22% | .732 | .737 | .724 | .759 | .675 | 1.86 | +45 | –108 |

## Ramiro Pena — 150 PA | $-3 | 60 pts

3B-48, SS-23, 2B-8, DH-2, OF-2 (RF-2) — Owned: 0% — BH

Pena has gotten plenty of chances to shine as a back-up at SS, 3B, and 2B, and although he has been fine with the glove, he is a disappointment with the bat. Being fast is pointless when you hit a lot of fly balls and you rarely walk. In 2011, Pena could lose his spot as the Yankees' UT IF to Eduardo Nunez. (LS)

| Player | Age | AB | HR | R | RBI | SB | BA | OBP | SLG | $1L | Pts |
|---|---|---|---|---|---|---|---|---|---|---|---|
| **Forecast** | | | | | | | | | | | |
| Pena R | 25 | 144 | 2 | 15 | 12 | 5 | .229 | .285 | .302 | -$3 | 60 |
| **Mini-Browser** | | | | | | | | | | | |
| Murphy D | 28 | 90 | 4 | 14 | 14 | 1 | .255 | .321 | .488 | -$2 | 60 |
| Cairo M | 36 | 91 | 1 | 12 | 10 | 2 | .263 | .318 | .371 | -$2 | 50 |
| Frazier T | 25 | 90 | 4 | 11 | 11 | 1 | .233 | .299 | .449 | -$3 | 50 |
| LaRoche A | 27 | 88 | 3 | 11 | 10 | 1 | .261 | .343 | .410 | -$3 | 50 |
| Marte A | 27 | 94 | 4 | 10 | 12 | 0 | .254 | .307 | .433 | -$3 | 50 |

| Level | Leag | AB | HR | R | RBI | SB | BA | OBP | SLG | CT% | H% | BB% | Bash |
|---|---|---|---|---|---|---|---|---|---|---|---|---|---|
| | | Minors (2010) | | | | | | | | Skills | | | |
| A | — | — | — | — | — | — | — | — | — | — | — | — | — |
| AA | — | — | — | — | — | — | — | — | — | — | — | — | — |
| AAA | — | — | — | — | — | — | — | — | — | — | — | — | — |

| Yr | Team | AB | HR | R | RBI | SB | BA | OBP | SLG | CT% | H% | BB% | Bash |
|---|---|---|---|---|---|---|---|---|---|---|---|---|---|
| | | Majors | | | | | | | | Skills | | | |
| 07 | — | — | — | — | — | — | — | — | — | — | — | — | — |
| 08 | — | — | — | — | — | — | — | — | — | — | — | — | — |
| 09 | NYY | 115 | 1 | 17 | 10 | 4 | .287 | .317 | .383 | 83% | 35% | 4% | 1.33 |
| 10 | NYY | 154 | 0 | 18 | 18 | 7 | .227 | .258 | .247 | 82% | 28% | 4% | 1.09 |

**Competition at 3B** — Stats in 2010

| Bats | Player | GSvR | GSvL | Sub | OPS |
|---|---|---|---|---|---|
| RH | Rodriguez A | 79 | 44 | 1 | .847 |
| BH | Pena R | 25 | 3 | 20 | .504 |
| RH | Nunez E | 1 | 9 | 5 | .681 |
| RH | Russo K | 1 | 2 | 13 | .470 |

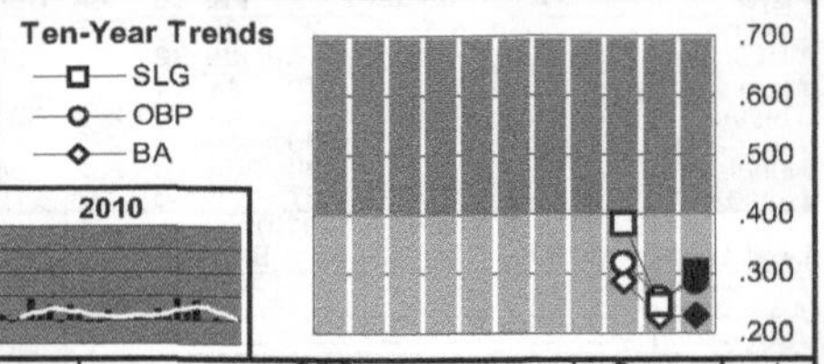


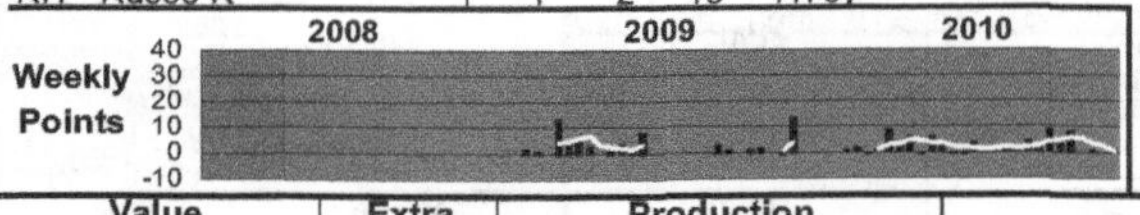


| Yr | $1L | $2L | Pts | RAA | 2B | 3B | CS | FB-LD-GB | HR/fb | RBI% | RS% | OPS | 1st Hf | 2nd Hf | vs RH | vs LH | Rnge | vRH | vLH |
|---|---|---|---|---|---|---|---|---|---|---|---|---|---|---|---|---|---|---|---|
| | Value | | | | Extra | | | Production | | | | OPS | | | | | Scoresheet | | |
| 07 | — | — | — | — | — | — | — | — | — | — | — | — | — | — | — | — | — | — | — |
| 08 | — | — | — | — | — | — | — | — | — | — | — | — | — | — | — | — | — | — | — |
| 09 | $0 | -$15 | 60 | –1 | 6 | 1 | 1 | 39-24-37 | 3% | 17% | 43% | .699 | .657 | .828 | .817 | .274 | — | — | — |
| 10 | $0 | -$15 | 70 | –14 | 1 | 1 | 1 | 40-19-41 | 0% | 17% | 43% | .504 | .446 | .572 | .545 | .343 | — | +5 | –13 |

## Hunter Pence — 650 PA | $24 | 420 pts

OF-156 (RF-156) — Owned: 100% — RH

With Lance Berkman and Roy Oswalt gone, Pence is the face of the franchise in HOU. In 2010, he no longer batted #6 but split his time between #3 and #5. He had unusual success at stealing bases (and scoring runs) in 2010, but his SB rate is still only 67%, and it's too soon to say he's a 20-20 threat. (BJ)

| Player | Age | AB | HR | R | RBI | SB | BA | OBP | SLG | $1L | Pts |
|---|---|---|---|---|---|---|---|---|---|---|---|
| **Forecast** | | | | | | | | | | | |
| Pence H | 27 | 593 | 26 | 85 | 85 | 13 | .285 | .339 | .492 | $24 | 420 |
| **Mini-Browser** | | | | | | | | | | | |
| Beltran C | 33 | 530 | 24 | 90 | 90 | 18 | .283 | .374 | .512 | $25 | 470 |
| Hart C | 29 | 589 | 26 | 91 | 91 | 20 | .276 | .335 | .500 | $25 | 440 |
| Markakis N | 27 | 611 | 21 | 91 | 84 | 7 | .298 | .370 | .463 | $24 | 440 |
| Rios A | 30 | 570 | 19 | 81 | 75 | 25 | .274 | .325 | .452 | $24 | 410 |
| Upton B | 26 | 570 | 20 | 91 | 72 | 39 | .251 | .341 | .412 | $24 | 400 |

| Level | Leag | AB | HR | R | RBI | SB | BA | OBP | SLG | CT% | H% | BB% | Bash |
|---|---|---|---|---|---|---|---|---|---|---|---|---|---|
| | | Minors (2010) | | | | | | | | Skills | | | |
| A | — | — | — | — | — | — | — | — | — | — | — | — | — |
| AA | — | — | — | — | — | — | — | — | — | — | — | — | — |
| AAA | — | — | — | — | — | — | — | — | — | — | — | — | — |

| Yr | Team | AB | HR | R | RBI | SB | BA | OBP | SLG | CT% | H% | BB% | Bash |
|---|---|---|---|---|---|---|---|---|---|---|---|---|---|
| | | Majors | | | | | | | | Skills | | | |
| 07 | HOU | 456 | 17 | 57 | 69 | 11 | .322 | .360 | .539 | 79% | 41% | 5% | 1.67 |
| 08 | HOU | 595 | 25 | 78 | 83 | 11 | .269 | .318 | .466 | 79% | 34% | 6% | 1.73 |
| 09 | HOU | 585 | 25 | 76 | 72 | 14 | .282 | .346 | .472 | 81% | 35% | 9% | 1.67 |
| 10 | HOU | 614 | 25 | 93 | 91 | 18 | .282 | .325 | .461 | 83% | 34% | 6% | 1.64 |

**Competition at RF** — Stats in 2010

| Bats | Player | GSvR | GSvL | Sub | OPS |
|---|---|---|---|---|---|
| RH | Pence H | 111 | 44 | 1 | .786 |

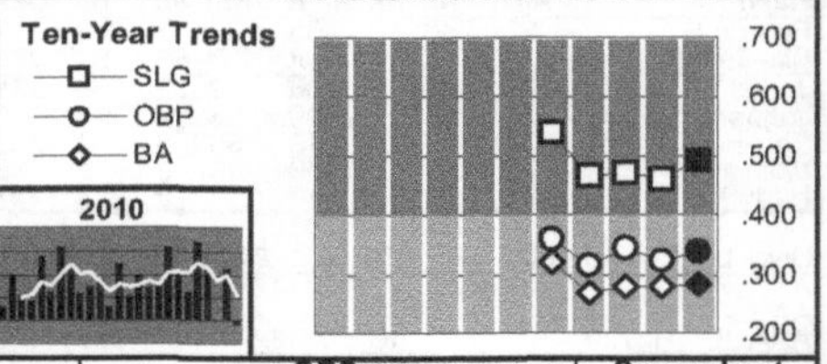


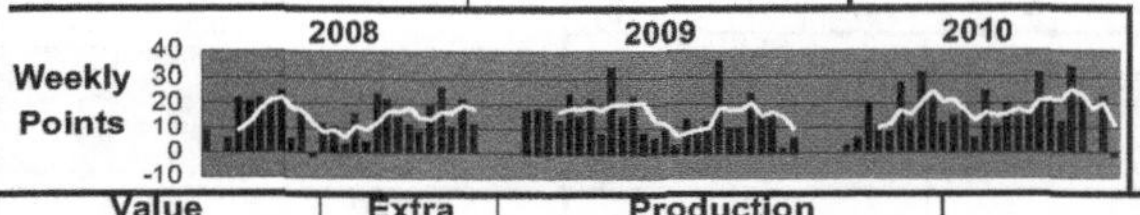


| Yr | $1L | $2L | Pts | RAA | 2B | 3B | CS | FB-LD-GB | HR/fb | RBI% | RS% | OPS | 1st Hf | 2nd Hf | vs RH | vs LH | Rnge | vRH | vLH |
|---|---|---|---|---|---|---|---|---|---|---|---|---|---|---|---|---|---|---|---|
| | Value | | | | Extra | | | Production | | | | OPS | | | | | Scoresheet | | |
| 07 | $19 | $10 | 320 | +16 | 30 | 9 | 5 | 32-19-49 | 15% | 24% | 25% | .899 | .956 | .813 | .872 | .993 | 2.10 | — | — |
| 08 | $20 | $12 | 370 | –8 | 34 | 4 | 10 | 34-14-52 | 15% | 19% | 30% | .783 | .732 | .859 | .804 | .722 | 2.11 | –20 | +54 |
| 09 | $22 | $13 | 390 | +4 | 26 | 5 | 11 | 33-15-53 | 16% | 16% | 26% | .818 | .839 | .792 | .798 | .895 | 2.10 | –10 | +27 |
| 10 | $29 | $23 | 430 | –2 | 29 | 3 | 9 | 32-15-53 | 15% | 21% | 36% | .786 | .743 | .834 | .776 | .820 | 2.11 | –7 | +20 |

## Cliff Pennington — 600 PA | $10 | 290 pts

SS-156 — Owned: 6% — BH

In his first full season in MLB, Pennington established himself as an everyday SS. Although he had a high error count, the A's believe that his defense was a big part of the success of their pitching staff. He was an efficient base-stealer (29/5 SB/CS). If he can raise his BB% to the low teens, he could steal 40 bags. (ML)

| Player | Age | AB | HR | R | RBI | SB | BA | OBP | SLG | $1L | Pts |
|---|---|---|---|---|---|---|---|---|---|---|---|
| **Forecast** | | | | | | | | | | | |
| Pennington C | 26 | 532 | 6 | 66 | 48 | 24 | .237 | .318 | .343 | $10 | 290 |
| **Mini-Browser** | | | | | | | | | | | |
| Bartlett J | 31 | 446 | 5 | 65 | 45 | 20 | .269 | .334 | .378 | $11 | 280 |
| Desmond I | 25 | 460 | 15 | 50 | 50 | 20 | .250 | .311 | .403 | $11 | 270 |
| Escobar A | 24 | 561 | 6 | 75 | 50 | 25 | .245 | .290 | .343 | $11 | 300 |
| Betancourt Y | 29 | 532 | 11 | 55 | 61 | 6 | .279 | .302 | .413 | $11 | 320 |
| Gonzalez A | 34 | 580 | 19 | 69 | 75 | 0 | .248 | .293 | .413 | $10 | 300 |

| Level | Leag | AB | HR | R | RBI | SB | BA | OBP | SLG | CT% | H% | BB% | Bash |
|---|---|---|---|---|---|---|---|---|---|---|---|---|---|
| | | Minors (2010) | | | | | | | | Skills | | | |
| A | — | — | — | — | — | — | — | — | — | — | — | — | — |
| AA | — | — | — | — | — | — | — | — | — | — | — | — | — |
| AAA | — | — | — | — | — | — | — | — | — | — | — | — | — |

| Yr | Team | AB | HR | R | RBI | SB | BA | OBP | SLG | CT% | H% | BB% | Bash |
|---|---|---|---|---|---|---|---|---|---|---|---|---|---|
| | | Majors | | | | | | | | Skills | | | |
| 07 | — | — | — | — | — | — | — | — | — | — | — | — | — |
| 08 | OAK | 99 | 0 | 14 | 9 | 4 | .242 | .339 | .293 | 82% | 30% | 11% | 1.21 |
| 09 | OAK | 208 | 4 | 27 | 21 | 7 | .279 | .342 | .418 | 78% | 36% | 8% | 1.50 |
| 10 | OAK | 508 | 6 | 64 | 46 | 29 | .250 | .319 | .368 | 81% | 31% | 9% | 1.47 |

**Competition at SS** — Stats in 2010

| Bats | Player | GSvR | GSvL | Sub | OPS |
|---|---|---|---|---|---|
| BH | Pennington C | 113 | 34 | 9 | .687 |
| RH | Rosales A | 5 | 8 | 1 | .721 |
| RH | Tolleson S | 0 | 5 | 6 | .748 |

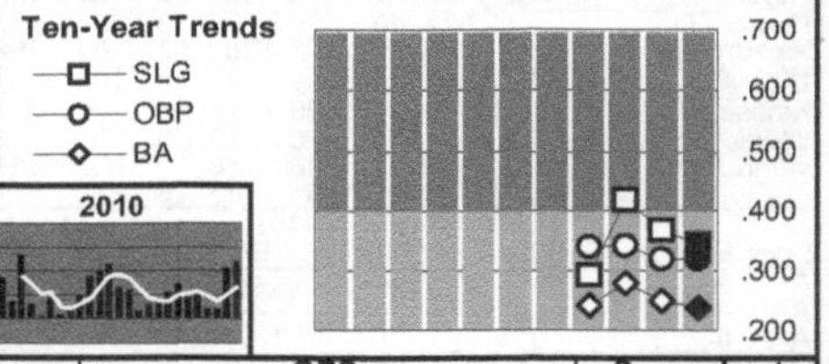


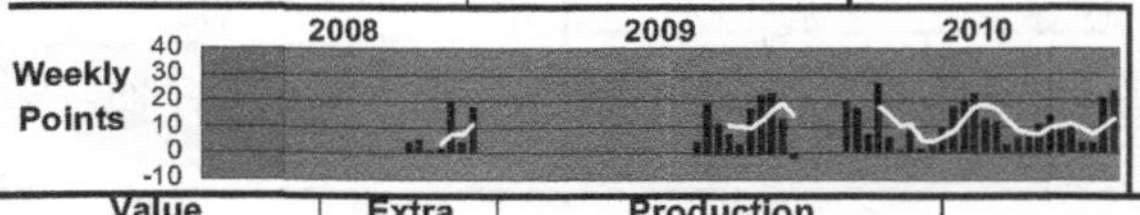


| Yr | $1L | $2L | Pts | RAA | 2B | 3B | CS | FB-LD-GB | HR/fb | RBI% | RS% | OPS | 1st Hf | 2nd Hf | vs RH | vs LH | Rnge | vRH | vLH |
|---|---|---|---|---|---|---|---|---|---|---|---|---|---|---|---|---|---|---|---|
| | Value | | | | Extra | | | Production | | | | OPS | | | | | Scoresheet | | |
| 07 | — | — | — | — | — | — | — | — | — | — | — | — | — | — | — | — | 4.75 | — | — |
| 08 | -$2 | -$15 | 50 | –2 | 5 | 0 | 1 | 46-19-36 | 0% | 18% | 36% | .632 | — | .632 | .609 | .667 | — | — | — |
| 09 | $3 | -$10 | 120 | +4 | 11 | 3 | 5 | 39-18-42 | 6% | 14% | 31% | .760 | — | .760 | .841 | .532 | 4.75 | –2 | +5 |
| 10 | $15 | $3 | 300 | –1 | 26 | 8 | 5 | 43-21-36 | 3% | 17% | 33% | .687 | .726 | .637 | .697 | .655 | 4.71 | +7 | –16 |

## Jhonny Peralta — 600 PA | $12 | 290 pts

3B-100, SS-46, DH-4, 1B-2 — Owned: 50% — RH

Peralta was acquired by the Tigers before the trade deadline, and he played well enough that Detroit will probably keep him for a year. He can play third base, but he will probably be the starting SS until Danny Worth or a young shortstop from outside the organization is ready. If his FB falls, so might his HR. (LP)

| Player | Age | AB | HR | R | RBI | SB | BA | OBP | SLG | $1L | Pts |
|---|---|---|---|---|---|---|---|---|---|---|---|
| **Forecast** | | | | | | | | | | | |
| Peralta J | 28 | 539 | 18 | 66 | 78 | 0 | .256 | .320 | .411 | $12 | 290 |
| **Mini-Browser** | | | | | | | | | | | |
| Aybar E | 27 | 579 | 6 | 75 | 50 | 19 | .270 | .314 | .366 | $14 | 330 |
| Cabrera A | 25 | 531 | 6 | 72 | 60 | 12 | .271 | .334 | .383 | $14 | 310 |
| Scutaro M | 35 | 551 | 12 | 84 | 54 | 6 | .272 | .345 | .383 | $13 | 360 |
| Nakajima H | 28 | 460 | 15 | 60 | 60 | 10 | .272 | .312 | .410 | $13 | 290 |
| Furcal R | 33 | 436 | 10 | 71 | 38 | 19 | .283 | .352 | .415 | $13 | 310 |

| Level | Leag | AB | HR | R | RBI | SB | BA | OBP | SLG | CT% | H% | BB% | Bash |
|---|---|---|---|---|---|---|---|---|---|---|---|---|---|
| | | Minors (2010) | | | | | | | | Skills | | | |
| A | — | — | — | — | — | — | — | — | — | — | — | — | — |
| AA | — | — | — | — | — | — | — | — | — | — | — | — | — |
| AAA | — | — | — | — | — | — | — | — | — | — | — | — | — |

| Yr | Team | AB | HR | R | RBI | SB | BA | OBP | SLG | CT% | H% | BB% | Bash |
|---|---|---|---|---|---|---|---|---|---|---|---|---|---|
| | | Majors | | | | | | | | Skills | | | |
| 07 | CLE | 574 | 21 | 87 | 72 | 4 | .270 | .341 | .430 | 75% | 36% | 9% | 1.59 |
| 08 | CLE | 605 | 23 | 104 | 89 | 3 | .276 | .331 | .473 | 79% | 35% | 7% | 1.71 |
| 09 | CLE | 582 | 11 | 57 | 83 | 0 | .254 | .316 | .375 | 77% | 33% | 8% | 1.47 |
| 10 | 2TM | 551 | 15 | 60 | 81 | 1 | .249 | .311 | .392 | 81% | 31% | 9% | 1.58 |

**Competition at SS** — Stats in 2010

| Bats | Player | GSvR | GSvL | Sub | OPS |
|---|---|---|---|---|---|
| BH | Santiago R | 59 | 8 | 18 | .662 |
| RH | Peralta J | 32 | 13 | 1 | .703 |
| RH | Everett A | 16 | 12 | 3 | .468 |
| RH | Worth D | 10 | 14 | 0 | .653 |

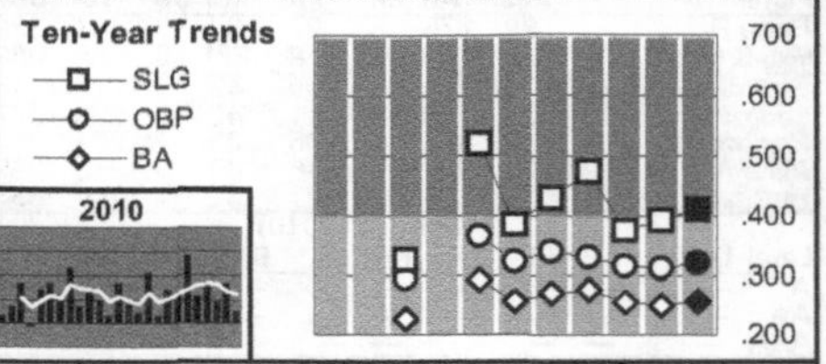


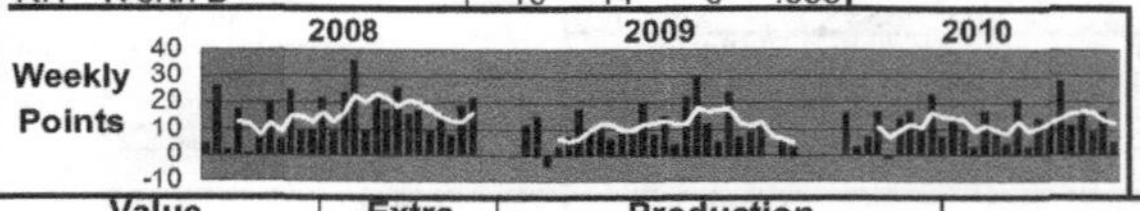


| Yr | $1L | $2L | Pts | RAA | 2B | 3B | CS | FB-LD-GB | HR/fb | RBI% | RS% | OPS | 1st Hf | 2nd Hf | vs RH | vs LH | Rnge | vRH | vLH |
|---|---|---|---|---|---|---|---|---|---|---|---|---|---|---|---|---|---|---|---|
| | Value | | | | Extra | | | Production | | | | OPS | | | | | Scoresheet | | |
| 07 | $17 | $9 | 320 | +16 | 27 | 1 | 4 | 35-19-47 | 14% | 17% | 33% | .771 | .812 | .718 | .754 | .820 | 4.79 | –21 | +52 |
| 08 | $23 | $16 | 410 | +22 | 42 | 4 | 1 | 36-20-44 | 13% | 19% | 41% | .804 | .787 | .824 | .817 | .761 | 4.75 | –16 | +40 |
| 09 | $10 | $0 | 270 | –1 | 35 | 1 | 2 | 31-19-50 | 8% | 20% | 24% | .690 | .710 | .669 | .701 | .661 | 4.70 | –12 | +30 |
| 10 | $13 | $3 | 310 | +2 | 30 | 2 | 0 | 43-22-34 | 8% | 20% | 26% | .703 | .709 | .694 | .677 | .771 | 4.69 | –3 | +8 |

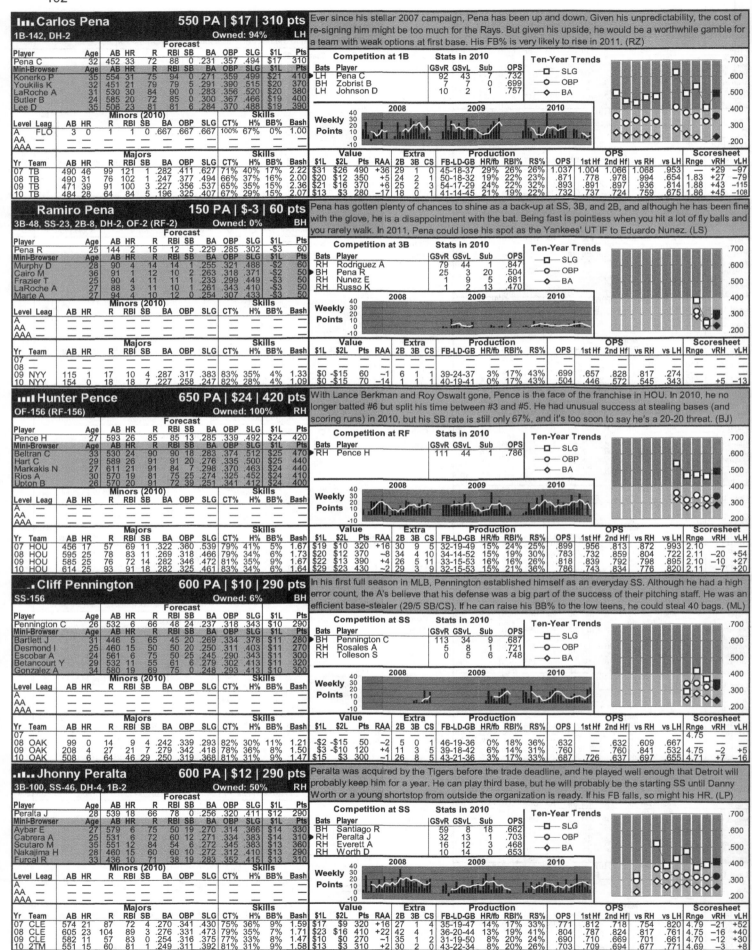

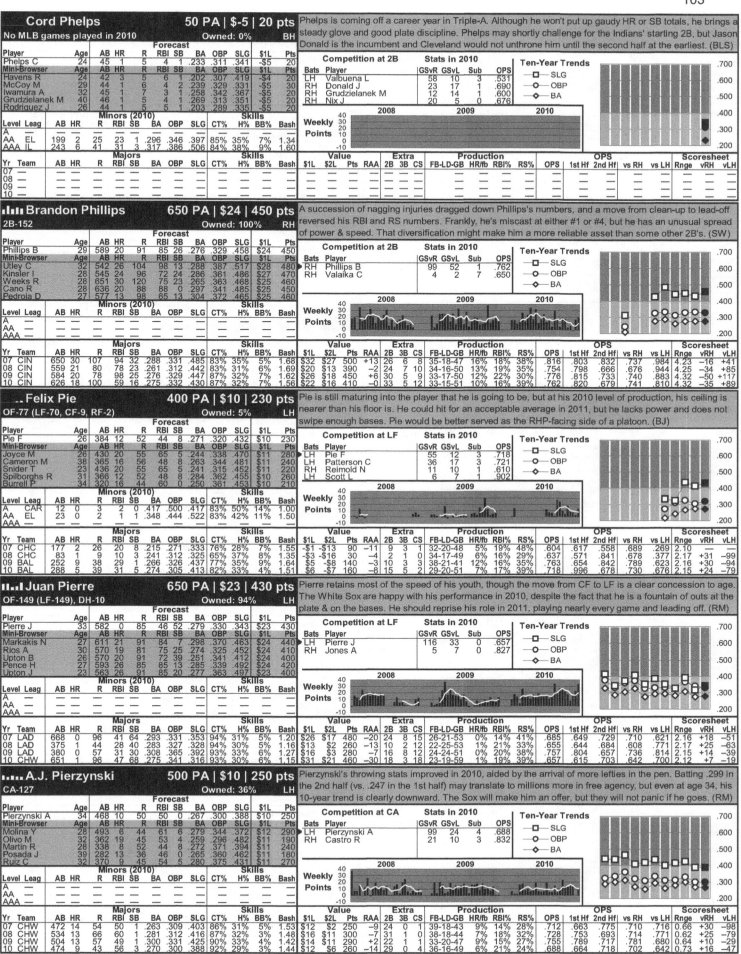

## Cord Phelps — 50 PA | $-5 | 20 pts

No MLB games played in 2010 — Owned: 0% — BH

Phelps is coming off a career year in Triple-A. Although he won't put up gaudy HR or SB totals, he brings a steady glove and good plate discipline. Phelps may shortly challenge for the Indians' starting 2B, but Jason Donald is the incumbent and Cleveland would not unthrone him until the second half at the earliest. (BLS)

| Player | Age | AB | HR | R | RBI | SB | BA | OBP | SLG | $1L | Pts |
|---|---|---|---|---|---|---|---|---|---|---|---|
| Phelps C | 24 | 45 | 1 | 5 | 4 | 1 | .233 | .311 | .341 | -$5 | 20 |
| **Mini-Browser** | **Age** | **AB** | **HR** | **R** | **RBI** | **SB** | **BA** | **OBP** | **SLG** | **$1L** | **Pts** |
| Havens R | 24 | 42 | 3 | 5 | 6 | 1 | .202 | .307 | .419 | -$4 | 20 |
| McCoy M | 29 | 44 | 1 | 6 | 4 | 2 | .239 | .329 | .331 | -$5 | 30 |
| Iwamura A | 32 | 45 | 1 | 7 | 3 | 1 | .258 | .342 | .367 | -$5 | 20 |
| Grudzielanek M | 40 | 46 | 1 | 5 | 4 | 1 | .269 | .313 | .351 | -$5 | 20 |
| Rodriguez J | 26 | 44 | 1 | 5 | 5 | 1 | .203 | .289 | .335 | -$5 | 20 |

Minors (2010) / Skills

| Level | Leag | AB | HR | R | RBI | SB | BA | OBP | SLG | CT% | H% | BB% | Bash |
|---|---|---|---|---|---|---|---|---|---|---|---|---|---|
| A | — | — | — | — | — | — | — | — | — | — | — | — | — |
| AA | EL | 199 | 2 | 25 | 23 | 1 | .296 | .346 | .397 | 85% | 35% | 7% | 1.34 |
| AAA | IL | 243 | 6 | 41 | 31 | 3 | .317 | .386 | .506 | 84% | 38% | 9% | 1.60 |

Majors / Skills

| Yr | Team | AB | HR | R | RBI | SB | BA | OBP | SLG | CT% | H% | BB% | Bash |
|---|---|---|---|---|---|---|---|---|---|---|---|---|---|
| 07 | — | — | — | — | — | — | — | — | — | — | — | — | — |
| 08 | — | — | — | — | — | — | — | — | — | — | — | — | — |
| 09 | — | — | — | — | — | — | — | — | — | — | — | — | — |
| 10 | — | — | — | — | — | — | — | — | — | — | — | — | — |

Competition at 2B — Stats in 2010

| Bats | Player | GSvR | GSvL | Sub | OPS |
|---|---|---|---|---|---|
| LH | Valbuena L | 58 | 10 | 3 | .531 |
| RH | Donald J | 23 | 17 | 1 | .690 |
| RH | Grudzielanek M | 12 | 14 | 1 | .600 |
| RH | Nix J | 20 | 5 | 0 | .676 |

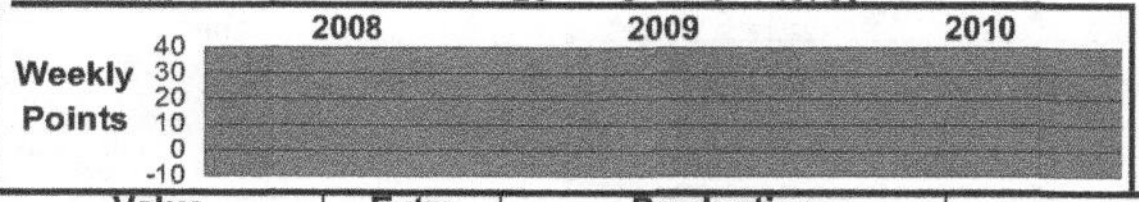


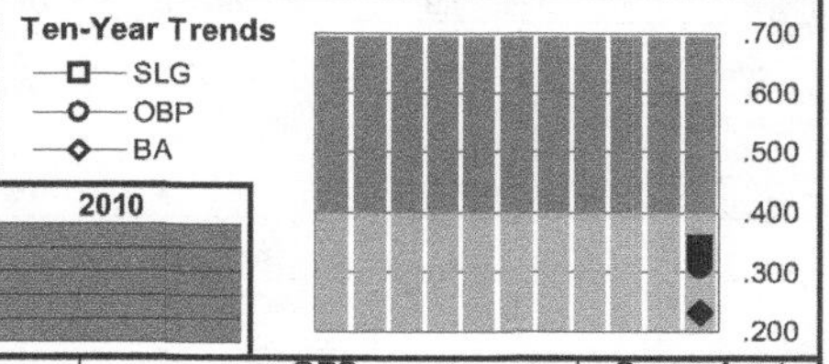


| Yr | $1L | $2L | Pts | RAA | 2B | 3B | CS | FB-LD-GB | HR/fb | RBI% | RS% | OPS | 1st Hf | 2nd Hf | vs RH | vs LH | Rnge | vRH | vLH |
|---|---|---|---|---|---|---|---|---|---|---|---|---|---|---|---|---|---|---|---|
| 07 | — | — | — | — | — | — | — | — | — | — | — | — | — | — | — | — | — | — | — |
| 08 | — | — | — | — | — | — | — | — | — | — | — | — | — | — | — | — | — | — | — |
| 09 | — | — | — | — | — | — | — | — | — | — | — | — | — | — | — | — | — | — | — |
| 10 | — | — | — | — | — | — | — | — | — | — | — | — | — | — | — | — | — | — | — |

## Brandon Phillips — 650 PA | $24 | 450 pts

2B-152 — Owned: 100% — RH

A succession of nagging injuries dragged down Phillips's numbers, and a move from clean-up to lead-off reversed his RBI and RS numbers. Frankly, he's miscast at either #1 or #4, but he has an unusual spread of power & speed. That diversification might make him a more reliable asset than some other 2B's. (SW)

| Player | Age | AB | HR | R | RBI | SB | BA | OBP | SLG | $1L | Pts |
|---|---|---|---|---|---|---|---|---|---|---|---|
| Phillips B | 29 | 589 | 20 | 91 | 85 | 26 | .276 | .329 | .458 | $24 | 450 |
| **Mini-Browser** | **Age** | **AB** | **HR** | **R** | **RBI** | **SB** | **BA** | **OBP** | **SLG** | **$1L** | **Pts** |
| Utley C | 32 | 542 | 26 | 104 | 98 | 13 | .288 | .387 | .517 | $28 | 480 |
| Kinsler I | 28 | 545 | 24 | 96 | 72 | 24 | .286 | .361 | .486 | $27 | 470 |
| Weeks R | 28 | 651 | 30 | 120 | 75 | 23 | .265 | .363 | .468 | $25 | 460 |
| Cano R | 28 | 636 | 20 | 88 | 88 | 0 | .297 | .341 | .485 | $25 | 450 |
| Pedroia D | 27 | 577 | 13 | 98 | 65 | 13 | .304 | .372 | .465 | $25 | 460 |

Minors (2010) / Skills

| Level | Leag | AB | HR | R | RBI | SB | BA | OBP | SLG | CT% | H% | BB% | Bash |
|---|---|---|---|---|---|---|---|---|---|---|---|---|---|
| A | — | — | — | — | — | — | — | — | — | — | — | — | — |
| AA | — | — | — | — | — | — | — | — | — | — | — | — | — |
| AAA | — | — | — | — | — | — | — | — | — | — | — | — | — |

Majors / Skills

| Yr | Team | AB | HR | R | RBI | SB | BA | OBP | SLG | CT% | H% | BB% | Bash |
|---|---|---|---|---|---|---|---|---|---|---|---|---|---|
| 07 | CIN | 650 | 30 | 107 | 94 | 32 | .288 | .331 | .485 | 83% | 35% | 5% | 1.68 |
| 08 | CIN | 559 | 21 | 80 | 78 | 23 | .261 | .312 | .442 | 83% | 31% | 6% | 1.69 |
| 09 | CIN | 584 | 20 | 78 | 98 | 25 | .276 | .329 | .447 | 87% | 32% | 7% | 1.62 |
| 10 | CIN | 626 | 18 | 100 | 59 | 16 | .275 | .332 | .430 | 87% | 32% | 7% | 1.56 |

Competition at 2B — Stats in 2010

| Bats | Player | GSvR | GSvL | Sub | OPS |
|---|---|---|---|---|---|
| RH | Phillips B | 99 | 52 | 1 | .762 |
| RH | Valaika C | 4 | 2 | 7 | .650 |

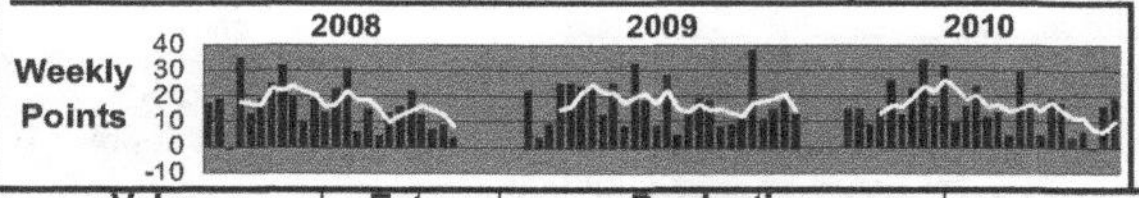


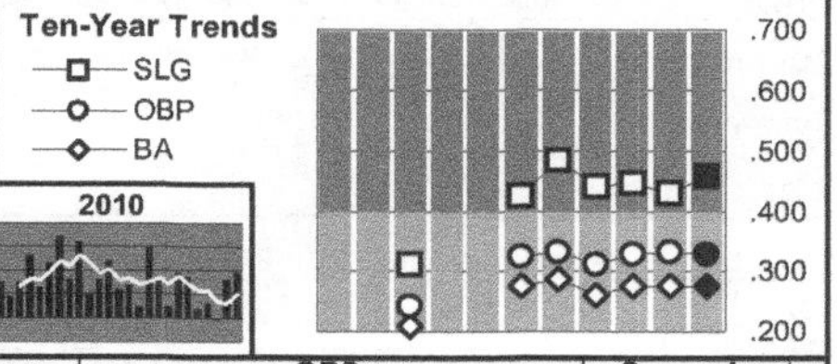


| Yr | $1L | $2L | Pts | RAA | 2B | 3B | CS | FB-LD-GB | HR/fb | RBI% | RS% | OPS | 1st Hf | 2nd Hf | vs RH | vs LH | Rnge | vRH | vLH |
|---|---|---|---|---|---|---|---|---|---|---|---|---|---|---|---|---|---|---|---|
| 07 | $32 | $27 | 500 | +13 | 26 | 6 | 8 | 35-18-47 | 16% | 18% | 38% | .816 | .803 | .832 | .737 | .984 | 4.23 | –16 | +41 |
| 08 | $20 | $13 | 390 | –2 | 24 | 7 | 10 | 34-16-50 | 13% | 19% | 35% | .754 | .798 | .666 | .676 | .944 | 4.25 | –34 | +85 |
| 09 | $26 | $18 | 450 | +6 | 30 | 5 | 9 | 33-17-50 | 12% | 22% | 30% | .776 | .815 | .733 | .740 | .883 | 4.32 | –50 | +117 |
| 10 | $22 | $16 | 410 | –0 | 33 | 5 | 12 | 33-15-51 | 10% | 16% | 39% | .762 | .820 | .679 | .741 | .810 | 4.32 | –35 | +89 |

## Felix Pie — 400 PA | $10 | 230 pts

OF-77 (LF-70, CF-9, RF-2) — Owned: 5% — LH

Pie is still maturing into the player that he is going to be, but at his 2010 level of production, his ceiling is nearer than his floor is. He could hit for an acceptable average in 2011, but he lacks power and does not swipe enough bases. Pie would be better served as the RHP-facing side of a platoon. (BJ)

| Player | Age | AB | HR | R | RBI | SB | BA | OBP | SLG | $1L | Pts |
|---|---|---|---|---|---|---|---|---|---|---|---|
| Pie F | 26 | 384 | 12 | 52 | 44 | 8 | .271 | .320 | .432 | $10 | 230 |
| **Mini-Browser** | **Age** | **AB** | **HR** | **R** | **RBI** | **SB** | **BA** | **OBP** | **SLG** | **$1L** | **Pts** |
| Joyce M | 26 | 430 | 20 | 55 | 65 | 5 | .244 | .338 | .470 | $11 | 280 |
| Cameron M | 38 | 365 | 16 | 56 | 48 | 8 | .263 | .344 | .481 | $11 | 240 |
| Snider T | 23 | 436 | 20 | 55 | 65 | 5 | .241 | .315 | .452 | $11 | 220 |
| Spilborghs R | 31 | 366 | 12 | 52 | 48 | 8 | .284 | .362 | .455 | $10 | 260 |
| Burrell P | 34 | 320 | 16 | 44 | 60 | 0 | .250 | .361 | .453 | $10 | 210 |

Minors (2010) / Skills

| Level | Leag | AB | HR | R | RBI | SB | BA | OBP | SLG | CT% | H% | BB% | Bash |
|---|---|---|---|---|---|---|---|---|---|---|---|---|---|
| A | CAR | 12 | 0 | 3 | 2 | 0 | .417 | .500 | .417 | 83% | 50% | 14% | 1.00 |
| AA | EL | 23 | 0 | 2 | 1 | 1 | .348 | .444 | .522 | 83% | 42% | 11% | 1.50 |
| AAA | — | — | — | — | — | — | — | — | — | — | — | — | — |

Majors / Skills

| Yr | Team | AB | HR | R | RBI | SB | BA | OBP | SLG | CT% | H% | BB% | Bash |
|---|---|---|---|---|---|---|---|---|---|---|---|---|---|
| 07 | CHC | 177 | 2 | 26 | 20 | 8 | .215 | .271 | .333 | 76% | 28% | 7% | 1.55 |
| 08 | CHC | 83 | 1 | 9 | 10 | 3 | .241 | .312 | .325 | 65% | 37% | 8% | 1.35 |
| 09 | BAL | 252 | 9 | 38 | 29 | 1 | .266 | .326 | .437 | 77% | 35% | 9% | 1.64 |
| 10 | BAL | 288 | 5 | 39 | 31 | 5 | .274 | .305 | .413 | 82% | 33% | 4% | 1.51 |

Competition at LF — Stats in 2010

| Bats | Player | GSvR | GSvL | Sub | OPS |
|---|---|---|---|---|---|
| LH | Pie F | 55 | 12 | 3 | .718 |
| LH | Patterson C | 36 | 17 | 3 | .721 |
| RH | Reimold N | 11 | 10 | 1 | .610 |
| LH | Scott L | 6 | 7 | 1 | .902 |

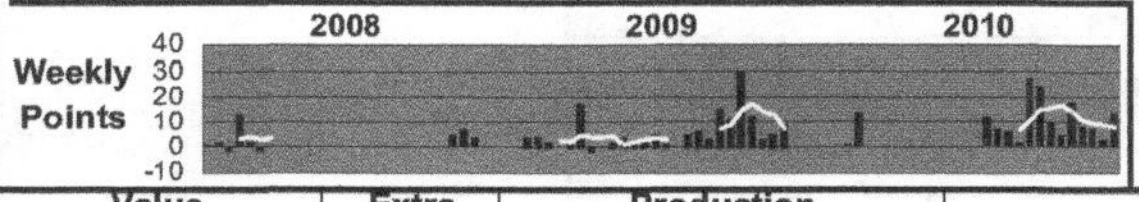


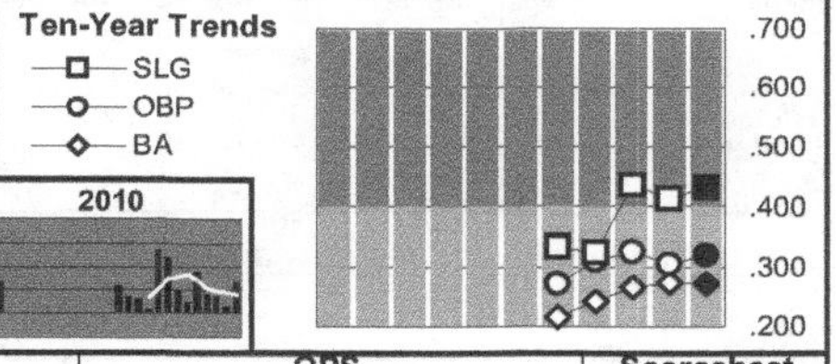


| Yr | $1L | $2L | Pts | RAA | 2B | 3B | CS | FB-LD-GB | HR/fb | RBI% | RS% | OPS | 1st Hf | 2nd Hf | vs RH | vs LH | Rnge | vRH | vLH |
|---|---|---|---|---|---|---|---|---|---|---|---|---|---|---|---|---|---|---|---|
| 07 | -$1 | -$13 | 90 | –11 | 9 | 3 | 1 | 32-20-48 | 5% | 19% | 48% | .604 | .617 | .558 | .689 | .269 | 2.10 | — | — |
| 08 | -$3 | -$16 | 30 | –4 | 2 | 1 | 0 | 34-17-49 | 6% | 16% | 29% | .637 | .571 | .841 | .678 | .377 | 2.17 | +31 | –99 |
| 09 | $5 | -$8 | 140 | –3 | 10 | 3 | 3 | 38-21-41 | 12% | 16% | 35% | .763 | .654 | .842 | .789 | .623 | 2.16 | +30 | –94 |
| 10 | $6 | -$7 | 160 | –8 | 15 | 5 | 2 | 29-20-51 | 7% | 17% | 39% | .718 | .996 | .678 | .730 | .676 | 2.15 | +24 | –79 |

## Juan Pierre — 650 PA | $23 | 430 pts

OF-149 (LF-149), DH-10 — Owned: 94% — LH

Pierre retains most of the speed of his youth, though the move from CF to LF is a clear concession to age. The White Sox are happy with his performance in 2010, despite the fact that he is a fountain of outs at the plate & on the bases. He should reprise his role in 2011, playing nearly every game and leading off. (RM)

| Player | Age | AB | HR | R | RBI | SB | BA | OBP | SLG | $1L | Pts |
|---|---|---|---|---|---|---|---|---|---|---|---|
| Pierre J | 33 | 582 | 0 | 85 | 46 | 52 | .279 | .330 | .343 | $23 | 430 |
| **Mini-Browser** | **Age** | **AB** | **HR** | **R** | **RBI** | **SB** | **BA** | **OBP** | **SLG** | **$1L** | **Pts** |
| Markakis N | 27 | 611 | 21 | 91 | 84 | 7 | .298 | .370 | .463 | $24 | 440 |
| Rios A | 30 | 570 | 19 | 81 | 75 | 25 | .274 | .325 | .452 | $24 | 410 |
| Upton B | 26 | 570 | 20 | 91 | 72 | 39 | .251 | .341 | .412 | $24 | 400 |
| Pence H | 27 | 593 | 26 | 85 | 85 | 13 | .285 | .339 | .492 | $24 | 420 |
| Upton J | 23 | 563 | 26 | 91 | 85 | 20 | .277 | .363 | .497 | $23 | 400 |

Minors (2010) / Skills

| Level | Leag | AB | HR | R | RBI | SB | BA | OBP | SLG | CT% | H% | BB% | Bash |
|---|---|---|---|---|---|---|---|---|---|---|---|---|---|
| A | — | — | — | — | — | — | — | — | — | — | — | — | — |
| AA | — | — | — | — | — | — | — | — | — | — | — | — | — |
| AAA | — | — | — | — | — | — | — | — | — | — | — | — | — |

Majors / Skills

| Yr | Team | AB | HR | R | RBI | SB | BA | OBP | SLG | CT% | H% | BB% | Bash |
|---|---|---|---|---|---|---|---|---|---|---|---|---|---|
| 07 | LAD | 668 | 0 | 96 | 41 | 64 | .293 | .331 | .353 | 94% | 31% | 5% | 1.20 |
| 08 | LAD | 375 | 1 | 44 | 28 | 40 | .283 | .327 | .328 | 94% | 30% | 5% | 1.16 |
| 09 | LAD | 380 | 0 | 57 | 31 | 30 | .308 | .365 | .392 | 93% | 33% | 6% | 1.27 |
| 10 | CHW | 651 | 1 | 96 | 47 | 68 | .275 | .341 | .316 | 93% | 30% | 6% | 1.15 |

Competition at LF — Stats in 2010

| Bats | Player | GSvR | GSvL | Sub | OPS |
|---|---|---|---|---|---|
| LH | Pierre J | 116 | 33 | 0 | .657 |
| RH | Jones A | 5 | 7 | 0 | .827 |

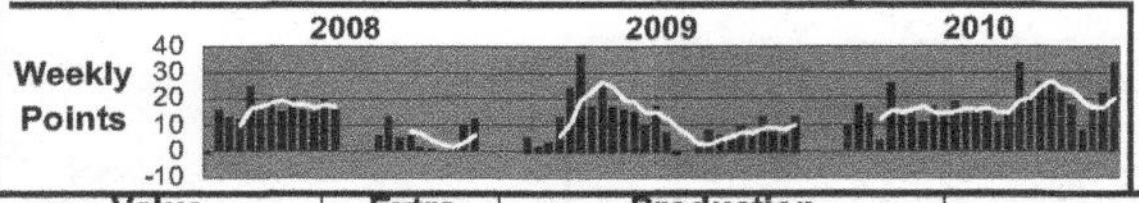


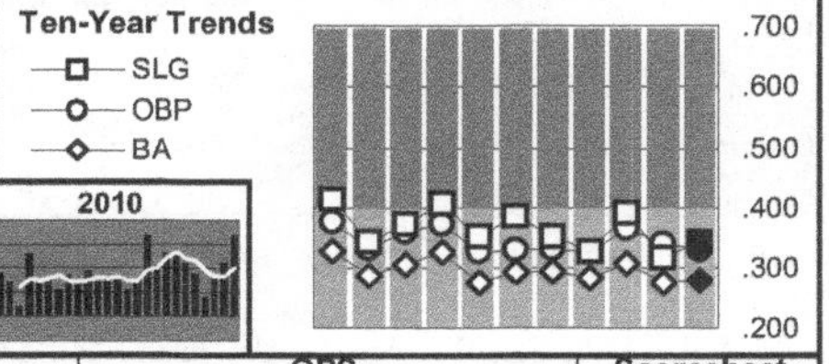


| Yr | $1L | $2L | Pts | RAA | 2B | 3B | CS | FB-LD-GB | HR/fb | RBI% | RS% | OPS | 1st Hf | 2nd Hf | vs RH | vs LH | Rnge | vRH | vLH |
|---|---|---|---|---|---|---|---|---|---|---|---|---|---|---|---|---|---|---|---|
| 07 | $26 | $17 | 480 | –20 | 24 | 8 | 15 | 26-21-53 | 0% | 14% | 41% | .685 | .649 | .729 | .710 | .621 | 2.16 | +18 | –51 |
| 08 | $13 | $2 | 260 | –13 | 10 | 2 | 12 | 22-25-53 | 1% | 21% | 33% | .655 | .644 | .684 | .608 | .771 | 2.17 | +25 | –63 |
| 09 | $16 | $3 | 280 | –7 | 16 | 8 | 12 | 24-24-51 | 0% | 20% | 38% | .757 | .804 | .657 | .736 | .814 | 2.15 | +14 | –39 |
| 10 | $31 | $21 | 460 | –30 | 18 | 3 | 18 | 23-19-59 | 1% | 19% | 39% | .657 | .615 | .703 | .642 | .700 | 2.12 | +7 | –19 |

## A.J. Pierzynski — 500 PA | $10 | 250 pts

CA-127 — Owned: 36% — LH

Pierzynski's throwing stats improved in 2010, aided by the arrival of more lefties in the pen. Batting .299 in the 2nd half (vs. .247 in the 1st half) may translate to millions more in free agency, but even at age 34, his 10-year trend is clearly downward. The Sox will make him an offer, but they will not panic if he goes. (RM)

| Player | Age | AB | HR | R | RBI | SB | BA | OBP | SLG | $1L | Pts |
|---|---|---|---|---|---|---|---|---|---|---|---|
| Pierzynski A | 34 | 468 | 10 | 50 | 50 | 0 | .267 | .300 | .388 | $10 | 250 |
| **Mini-Browser** | **Age** | **AB** | **HR** | **R** | **RBI** | **SB** | **BA** | **OBP** | **SLG** | **$1L** | **Pts** |
| Molina Y | 28 | 493 | 6 | 44 | 61 | 6 | .279 | .344 | .372 | $12 | 290 |
| Olivo M | 32 | 362 | 19 | 45 | 53 | 4 | .259 | .296 | .482 | $11 | 190 |
| Martin R | 28 | 338 | 8 | 52 | 44 | 8 | .272 | .371 | .394 | $11 | 240 |
| Posada J | 39 | 282 | 13 | 36 | 46 | 0 | .265 | .360 | .462 | $11 | 180 |
| Ruiz C | 32 | 370 | 9 | 45 | 54 | 5 | .280 | .375 | .431 | $11 | 270 |

Minors (2010) / Skills

| Level | Leag | AB | HR | R | RBI | SB | BA | OBP | SLG | CT% | H% | BB% | Bash |
|---|---|---|---|---|---|---|---|---|---|---|---|---|---|
| A | — | — | — | — | — | — | — | — | — | — | — | — | — |
| AA | — | — | — | — | — | — | — | — | — | — | — | — | — |
| AAA | — | — | — | — | — | — | — | — | — | — | — | — | — |

Majors / Skills

| Yr | Team | AB | HR | R | RBI | SB | BA | OBP | SLG | CT% | H% | BB% | Bash |
|---|---|---|---|---|---|---|---|---|---|---|---|---|---|
| 07 | CHW | 472 | 14 | 54 | 50 | 1 | .263 | .309 | .403 | 86% | 31% | 5% | 1.53 |
| 08 | CHW | 534 | 13 | 66 | 60 | 1 | .281 | .312 | .416 | 87% | 32% | 3% | 1.48 |
| 09 | CHW | 504 | 13 | 57 | 49 | 1 | .300 | .331 | .425 | 90% | 33% | 4% | 1.42 |
| 10 | CHW | 474 | 9 | 43 | 56 | 3 | .270 | .300 | .388 | 92% | 29% | 3% | 1.44 |

Competition at CA — Stats in 2010

| Bats | Player | GSvR | GSvL | Sub | OPS |
|---|---|---|---|---|---|
| LH | Pierzynski A | 99 | 24 | 4 | .688 |
| RH | Castro R | 21 | 10 | 3 | .832 |

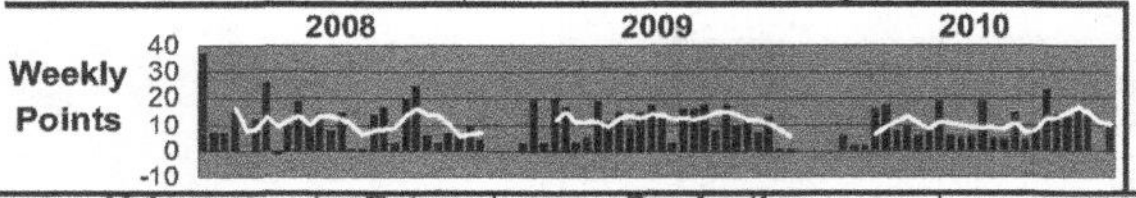


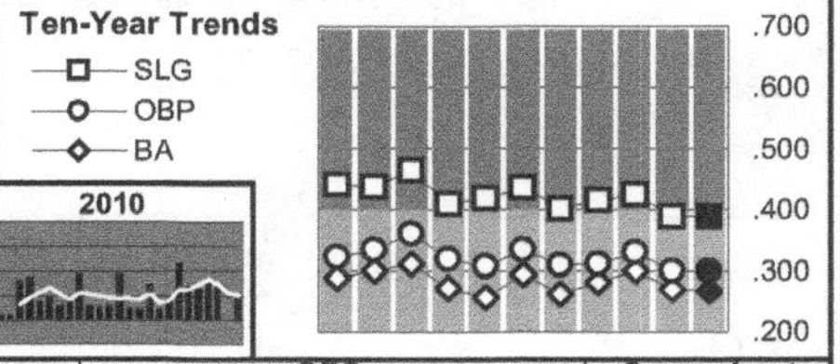


| Yr | $1L | $2L | Pts | RAA | 2B | 3B | CS | FB-LD-GB | HR/fb | RBI% | RS% | OPS | 1st Hf | 2nd Hf | vs RH | vs LH | Rnge | vRH | vLH |
|---|---|---|---|---|---|---|---|---|---|---|---|---|---|---|---|---|---|---|---|
| 07 | $12 | $2 | 250 | –9 | 24 | 0 | 1 | 39-18-43 | 9% | 14% | 28% | .712 | .663 | .775 | .710 | .716 | 0.66 | +30 | –98 |
| 08 | $16 | $11 | 300 | –7 | 31 | 1 | 0 | 38-18-44 | 7% | 18% | 32% | .728 | .753 | .693 | .714 | .771 | 0.62 | +25 | –79 |
| 09 | $14 | $11 | 290 | +2 | 22 | 1 | 1 | 33-20-47 | 9% | 15% | 27% | .755 | .789 | .717 | .781 | .680 | 0.64 | +10 | –29 |
| 10 | $12 | $6 | 260 | –14 | 29 | 0 | 4 | 36-16-49 | 6% | 21% | 24% | .688 | .664 | .718 | .702 | .642 | 0.73 | +16 | –47 |

*For more stats, visit www.Rotolympus.com.*

## Scott Podsednik — 500 PA | $13 | 280 pts

OF-130 (LF-129, CF-6), DH-2 — Owned: 94% — LH

Podsednik was enjoying a decent year in KC, but he faltered badly after being dealt to LA (.313 OBP) before missing most of September with a foot injury. He is nothing without his speed, and he is unlikely to be back with the Dodgers in 2011. He will grab a bench spot somewhere and contribute steals. (MP)

| Player | Age | AB | HR | R | RBI | SB | BA | OBP | SLG | $1L | Pts |
|---|---|---|---|---|---|---|---|---|---|---|---|
| Podsednik S | 35 | 459 | 5 | 55 | 40 | 25 | .283 | .338 | .378 | $13 | 280 |
| **Mini-Browser** | **Age** | **AB** | **HR** | **R** | **RBI** | **SB** | **BA** | **OBP** | **SLG** | **$1L** | **Pts** |
| Colvin T | 25 | 583 | 25 | 75 | 75 | 13 | .236 | .284 | .444 | $13 | 330 |
| Borbon J | 25 | 466 | 5 | 65 | 45 | 25 | .268 | .315 | .354 | $13 | 290 |
| Stubbs D | 26 | 441 | 15 | 70 | 50 | 25 | .238 | .322 | .403 | $13 | 270 |
| McLouth N | 29 | 383 | 17 | 64 | 51 | 17 | .266 | .361 | .471 | $13 | 310 |
| Raburn R | 29 | 354 | 16 | 56 | 56 | 4 | .271 | .339 | .491 | $13 | 240 |

Competition at LF — Stats in 2010

| Bats | Player | GSvR | GSvL | Sub | OPS |
|---|---|---|---|---|---|
| LH | Podsednik S | 28 | 6 | 3 | .724 |
| RH | Johnson R | 5 | 24 | 33 | .657 |
| LH | Anderson G | 17 | 4 | 6 | .475 |
| LH | Paul X | 16 | 2 | 5 | .591 |

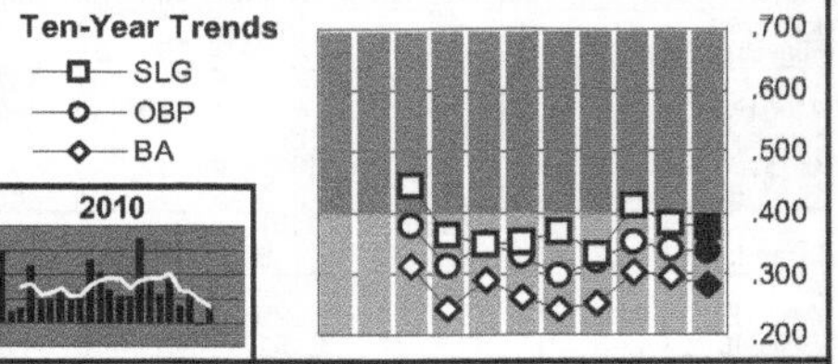


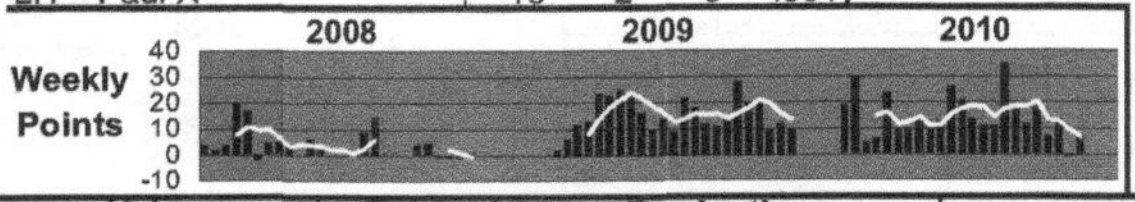


Minors (2010)

| Level | Leag | AB | HR | R | RBI | SB | BA | OBP | SLG | CT% | H% | BB% | Bash |
|---|---|---|---|---|---|---|---|---|---|---|---|---|---|
| A | — | — | — | — | — | — | — | — | — | — | — | — | — |
| AA | — | — | — | — | — | — | — | — | — | — | — | — | — |
| AAA | — | — | — | — | — | — | — | — | — | — | — | — | — |

Majors

| Yr | Team | AB | HR | R | RBI | SB | BA | OBP | SLG | CT% | H% | BB% | Bash |
|---|---|---|---|---|---|---|---|---|---|---|---|---|---|
| 07 | CHW | 214 | 2 | 30 | 11 | 12 | .243 | .299 | .369 | 83% | 29% | 6% | 1.52 |
| 08 | COL | 162 | 1 | 22 | 15 | 12 | .253 | .322 | .333 | 83% | 31% | 9% | 1.32 |
| 09 | CHW | 537 | 7 | 75 | 48 | 30 | .304 | .353 | .412 | 86% | 35% | 7% | 1.36 |
| 10 | 2TM | 539 | 6 | 63 | 51 | 35 | .297 | .342 | .382 | 85% | 35% | 7% | 1.29 |

| Yr | $1L | $2L | Pts | RAA | 2B | 3B | CS | FB-LD-GB | HR/fb | RBI% | RS% | OPS | 1st Hf | 2nd Hf | vs RH | vs LH | Rnge | vRH | vLH |
|---|---|---|---|---|---|---|---|---|---|---|---|---|---|---|---|---|---|---|---|
| 07 | $2 | -$12 | 120 | −11 | 13 | 4 | 5 | 28-19-53 | 4% | 8% | 42% | .668 | .758 | .625 | .622 | .774 | 2.12 | +21 | −66 |
| 08 | $1 | -$11 | 100 | −6 | 8 | 1 | 4 | 24-24-51 | 3% | 22% | 37% | .656 | .579 | .869 | .694 | .333 | — | +25 | −72 |
| 09 | $19 | $10 | 360 | −1 | 25 | 6 | 13 | 30-18-53 | 5% | 20% | 34% | .764 | .739 | .789 | .780 | .723 | 2.13 | +17 | −52 |
| 10 | $22 | $12 | 330 | −9 | 14 | 7 | 15 | 31-19-50 | 4% | 21% | 29% | .724 | .716 | .737 | .754 | .639 | 2.15 | +22 | −65 |

## Placido Polanco — 650 PA | $15 | 400 pts

3B-123, 2B-12 — Owned: 97% — RH

Polanco in 2011 will continue to man the hot corner for the Phillies. Polanco coped all 2010 with floating bone chips in his elbow following a HBP. If his off-season surgery is successful, he should hit .300 again with scant walks and occasional pop. (BB)

| Player | Age | AB | HR | R | RBI | SB | BA | OBP | SLG | $1L | Pts |
|---|---|---|---|---|---|---|---|---|---|---|---|
| Polanco P | 35 | 605 | 7 | 85 | 65 | 7 | .290 | .337 | .393 | $15 | 400 |
| **Mini-Browser** | **Age** | **AB** | **HR** | **R** | **RBI** | **SB** | **BA** | **OBP** | **SLG** | **$1L** | **Pts** |
| Young M | 34 | 589 | 13 | 85 | 78 | 7 | .287 | .340 | .427 | $20 | 360 |
| Stewart I | 25 | 525 | 29 | 81 | 81 | 6 | .263 | .350 | .492 | $18 | 360 |
| Sandoval P | 24 | 574 | 19 | 75 | 81 | 6 | .283 | .335 | .474 | $17 | 400 |
| Figgins C | 33 | 562 | 0 | 78 | 46 | 39 | .266 | .356 | .332 | $17 | 360 |
| Coghlan C | 25 | 560 | 13 | 88 | 56 | 19 | .268 | .347 | .408 | $16 | 380 |

Competition at 3B — Stats in 2010

| Bats | Player | GSvR | GSvL | Sub | OPS |
|---|---|---|---|---|---|
| RH | Polanco P | 82 | 41 | 0 | .726 |
| LH | Dobbs G | 27 | 1 | 8 | .583 |

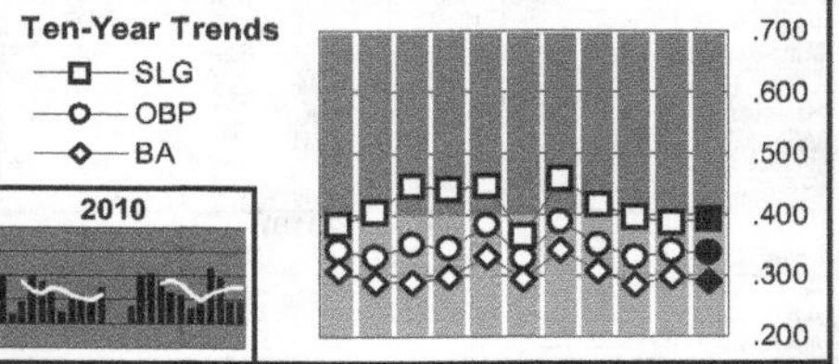


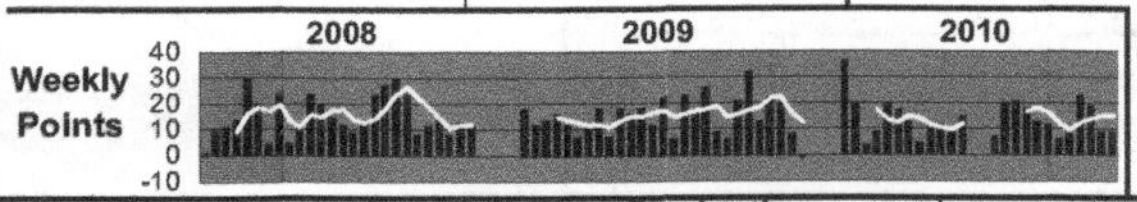


Minors (2010)

| Level | Leag | AB | HR | R | RBI | SB | BA | OBP | SLG | CT% | H% | BB% | Bash |
|---|---|---|---|---|---|---|---|---|---|---|---|---|---|
| A | FLO | 4 | 0 | 1 | 0 | 0 | .250 | .250 | .250 | 100% | 25% | 0% | 1.00 |
| AA | — | — | — | — | — | — | — | — | — | — | — | — | — |
| AAA | — | — | — | — | — | — | — | — | — | — | — | — | — |

Majors

| Yr | Team | AB | HR | R | RBI | SB | BA | OBP | SLG | CT% | H% | BB% | Bash |
|---|---|---|---|---|---|---|---|---|---|---|---|---|---|
| 07 | DET | 587 | 9 | 105 | 67 | 7 | .341 | .388 | .458 | 95% | 36% | 6% | 1.35 |
| 08 | DET | 580 | 8 | 90 | 58 | 7 | .307 | .350 | .417 | 93% | 33% | 6% | 1.36 |
| 09 | DET | 618 | 10 | 82 | 72 | 7 | .285 | .331 | .396 | 93% | 31% | 5% | 1.39 |
| 10 | PHI | 554 | 6 | 76 | 52 | 5 | .298 | .339 | .386 | 92% | 33% | 5% | 1.30 |

| Yr | $1L | $2L | Pts | RAA | 2B | 3B | CS | FB-LD-GB | HR/fb | RBI% | RS% | OPS | 1st Hf | 2nd Hf | vs RH | vs LH | Rnge | vRH | vLH |
|---|---|---|---|---|---|---|---|---|---|---|---|---|---|---|---|---|---|---|---|
| 07 | $25 | $17 | 460 | +20 | 36 | 3 | 3 | 31-24-45 | 5% | 24% | 40% | .846 | .815 | .887 | .857 | .813 | — | −18 | +43 |
| 08 | $19 | $10 | 400 | +4 | 34 | 3 | 1 | 35-19-47 | 4% | 18% | 39% | .768 | .743 | .801 | .741 | .836 | — | −9 | +24 |
| 09 | $16 | $9 | 400 | −9 | 31 | 4 | 2 | 37-20-43 | 5% | 23% | 34% | .727 | .698 | .758 | .723 | .738 | — | −14 | +36 |
| 10 | $16 | $7 | 340 | −4 | 27 | 2 | 0 | 35-20-45 | 3% | 20% | 35% | .726 | .782 | .676 | .749 | .668 | — | −17 | +41 |

## Jorge Posada — 325 PA | $11 | 180 pts

CA-83, DH-30, 1B-1 — Owned: 94% — BH

Posada in 2010 dropped off a little as a hitter (he was hurt several times) and a lot as a catcher (his CS% was just 15%, a career low and even worse than in 2008). 2011 could be Posada's final year in NY, and he might spend much of it at DH. His Bash is still good, and he could bounce back (well, up) at the plate. (LS)

| Player | Age | AB | HR | R | RBI | SB | BA | OBP | SLG | $1L | Pts |
|---|---|---|---|---|---|---|---|---|---|---|---|
| Posada J | 39 | 282 | 13 | 36 | 46 | 0 | .265 | .360 | .462 | $11 | 180 |
| **Mini-Browser** | **Age** | **AB** | **HR** | **R** | **RBI** | **SB** | **BA** | **OBP** | **SLG** | **$1L** | **Pts** |
| Suzuki K | 27 | 516 | 11 | 55 | 66 | 6 | .256 | .315 | .379 | $12 | 300 |
| Wieters M | 24 | 439 | 15 | 45 | 60 | 0 | .262 | .337 | .423 | $12 | 240 |
| Molina Y | 28 | 493 | 6 | 44 | 61 | 6 | .279 | .344 | .372 | $12 | 290 |
| Olivo M | 32 | 362 | 19 | 45 | 53 | 4 | .259 | .296 | .482 | $11 | 190 |
| Martin R | 28 | 338 | 8 | 52 | 44 | 8 | .272 | .371 | .394 | $11 | 240 |

Competition at CA — Stats in 2010

| Bats | Player | GSvR | GSvL | Sub | OPS |
|---|---|---|---|---|---|
| RH | Cervelli F | 50 | 30 | 10 | .694 |
| BH | Posada J | 52 | 27 | 4 | .811 |

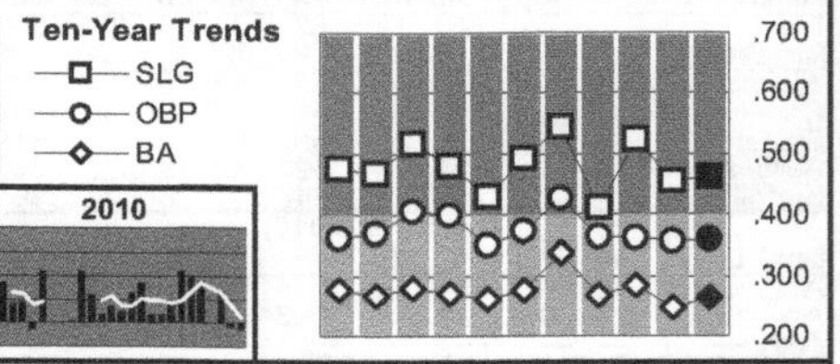

Minors (2010)

| Level | Leag | AB | HR | R | RBI | SB | BA | OBP | SLG | CT% | H% | BB% | Bash |
|---|---|---|---|---|---|---|---|---|---|---|---|---|---|
| A | — | — | — | — | — | — | — | — | — | — | — | — | — |
| AA | — | — | — | — | — | — | — | — | — | — | — | — | — |
| AAA | — | — | — | — | — | — | — | — | — | — | — | — | — |

Majors

| Yr | Team | AB | HR | R | RBI | SB | BA | OBP | SLG | CT% | H% | BB% | Bash |
|---|---|---|---|---|---|---|---|---|---|---|---|---|---|
| 07 | NYY | 506 | 20 | 91 | 90 | 2 | .338 | .426 | .543 | 81% | 42% | 12% | 1.61 |
| 08 | NYY | 168 | 3 | 18 | 22 | 0 | .268 | .364 | .411 | 77% | 35% | 12% | 1.53 |
| 09 | NYY | 383 | 22 | 55 | 81 | 1 | .285 | .363 | .522 | 74% | 39% | 11% | 1.83 |
| 10 | NYY | 383 | 18 | 49 | 57 | 3 | .248 | .357 | .454 | 74% | 33% | 13% | 1.83 |

| Yr | $1L | $2L | Pts | RAA | 2B | 3B | CS | FB-LD-GB | HR/fb | RBI% | RS% | OPS | 1st Hf | 2nd Hf | vs RH | vs LH | Rnge | vRH | vLH |
|---|---|---|---|---|---|---|---|---|---|---|---|---|---|---|---|---|---|---|---|
| 07 | $29 | $24 | 440 | +48 | 42 | 1 | 0 | 37-22-40 | 13% | 21% | 31% | .970 | .901 | 1.061 | .981 | .942 | 0.64 | +11 | −29 |
| 08 | $3 | -$5 | 100 | +2 | 13 | 1 | 0 | 40-21-40 | 6% | 18% | 22% | .775 | .780 | .611 | .793 | .733 | 0.68 | +15 | −38 |
| 09 | $18 | $16 | 280 | +21 | 25 | 0 | 0 | 43-21-36 | 18% | 25% | 24% | .885 | .877 | .894 | .909 | .836 | 0.78 | +1 | −3 |
| 10 | $14 | $8 | 240 | +10 | 23 | 1 | 1 | 38-19-43 | 16% | 17% | 22% | .811 | .838 | .783 | .799 | .833 | 0.84 | +2 | −3 |

## Buster Posey — 600 PA | $21 | 380 pts

CA-76, 1B-30 — Owned: 99% — RH

As a 23-year-old, Posey was the best player on a fantastic Giants team. The college shortstop's ability to play a very competent first base kept his bat in a line-up that sorely needs it. The expected high carry-over of SF's pitching staff means that Posey will have a little more time to concentrate on hitting in 2011. (PB)

| Player | Age | AB | HR | R | RBI | SB | BA | OBP | SLG | $1L | Pts |
|---|---|---|---|---|---|---|---|---|---|---|---|
| Posey B | 24 | 521 | 24 | 78 | 84 | 0 | .288 | .355 | .478 | $21 | 380 |
| **Mini-Browser** | **Age** | **AB** | **HR** | **R** | **RBI** | **SB** | **BA** | **OBP** | **SLG** | **$1L** | **Pts** |
| Mauer J | 27 | 495 | 12 | 84 | 84 | 6 | .315 | .400 | .466 | $25 | 420 |
| Martinez V | 32 | 483 | 17 | 66 | 83 | 0 | .296 | .363 | .477 | $21 | 360 |
| McCann B | 27 | 498 | 22 | 66 | 88 | 6 | .287 | .365 | .501 | $21 | 390 |
| Soto G | 28 | 424 | 20 | 60 | 75 | 0 | .283 | .378 | .504 | $17 | 310 |
| Napoli M | 29 | 393 | 23 | 59 | 63 | 5 | .252 | .337 | .490 | $16 | 240 |

Competition at CA — Stats in 2010

| Bats | Player | GSvR | GSvL | Sub | OPS |
|---|---|---|---|---|---|
| RH | Posey B | 58 | 18 | 0 | .862 |
| RH | Whiteside E | 24 | 8 | 23 | .696 |

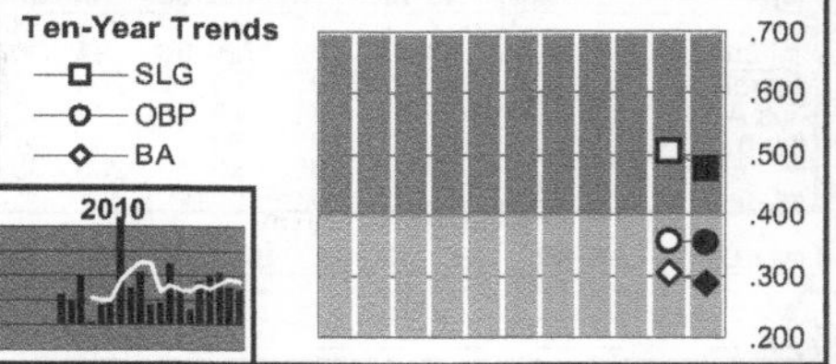


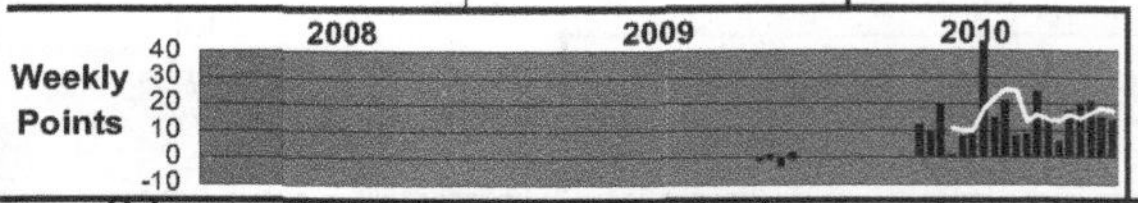


Minors (2010)

| Level | Leag | AB | HR | R | RBI | SB | BA | OBP | SLG | CT% | H% | BB% | Bash |
|---|---|---|---|---|---|---|---|---|---|---|---|---|---|
| A | — | — | — | — | — | — | — | — | — | — | — | — | — |
| AA | — | — | — | — | — | — | — | — | — | — | — | — | — |
| AAA | PCL | 172 | 6 | 31 | 32 | 1 | .349 | .442 | .552 | 83% | 42% | 13% | 1.58 |

Majors

| Yr | Team | AB | HR | R | RBI | SB | BA | OBP | SLG | CT% | H% | BB% | Bash |
|---|---|---|---|---|---|---|---|---|---|---|---|---|---|
| 07 | — | — | — | — | — | — | — | — | — | — | — | — | — |
| 08 | — | — | — | — | — | — | — | — | — | — | — | — | — |
| 09 | SF | 17 | 0 | 1 | 0 | 0 | .118 | .118 | .118 | 76% | 15% | 0% | 1.00 |
| 10 | SF | 406 | 18 | 58 | 67 | 0 | .305 | .357 | .505 | 86% | 35% | 7% | 1.65 |

| Yr | $1L | $2L | Pts | RAA | 2B | 3B | CS | FB-LD-GB | HR/fb | RBI% | RS% | OPS | 1st Hf | 2nd Hf | vs RH | vs LH | Rnge | vRH | vLH |
|---|---|---|---|---|---|---|---|---|---|---|---|---|---|---|---|---|---|---|---|
| 07 | — | — | — | — | — | — | — | — | — | — | — | — | — | — | — | — | — | — | — |
| 08 | — | — | — | — | — | — | — | — | — | — | — | — | — | — | — | — | — | — | — |
| 09 | -$5 | -$20 | 0 | −3 | 0 | 0 | 0 | 31-8-62 | 0% | 0% | 50% | .235 | — | .235 | .333 | .000 | 0.60 | — | — |
| 10 | $17 | $9 | 300 | +16 | 23 | 2 | 2 | 33-18-49 | 15% | 22% | 29% | .862 | .959 | .812 | .832 | .955 | 0.57 | −16 | +37 |

## Landon Powell — 100 PA | $-1 | 40 pts

CA-38, DH-2, 1B-1 — Owned: 1% — BH

Powell is in a tough spot. The A's love his defense, and he has decent power, but Kurt Suzuki plays nearly every day, and Powell can't handle another spot. Powell will enter Spring Training as the favorite for back-up CA, but he will have to fend off the more versatile Josh Donaldson. (ML)

| Player | Age | AB | HR | R | RBI | SB | BA | OBP | SLG | $1L | Pts |
|---|---|---|---|---|---|---|---|---|---|---|---|
| Powell L | 29 | 86 | 4 | 10 | 12 | 0 | .221 | .312 | .384 | -$1 | 40 |
| **Mini-Browser** | **Age** | **AB** | **HR** | **R** | **RBI** | **SB** | **BA** | **OBP** | **SLG** | **$1L** | **Pts** |
| Blanco H | 39 | 110 | 3 | 11 | 10 | 0 | .238 | .297 | .363 | -$1 | 50 |
| Johnson R | 28 | 126 | 2 | 14 | 12 | 2 | .238 | .307 | .348 | -$1 | 60 |
| Flowers T | 25 | 83 | 4 | 11 | 11 | 0 | .217 | .327 | .429 | -$1 | 50 |
| Tatum C | 28 | 137 | 3 | 12 | 15 | 0 | .230 | .283 | .348 | -$1 | 50 |
| Teagarden T | 27 | 85 | 4 | 11 | 11 | 0 | .211 | .297 | .409 | -$1 | 30 |

Competition at CA — Stats in 2010

| Bats | Player | GSvR | GSvL | Sub | OPS |
|---|---|---|---|---|---|
| RH | Suzuki K | 90 | 32 | 1 | .669 |
| BH | Powell L | 21 | 8 | 9 | .608 |

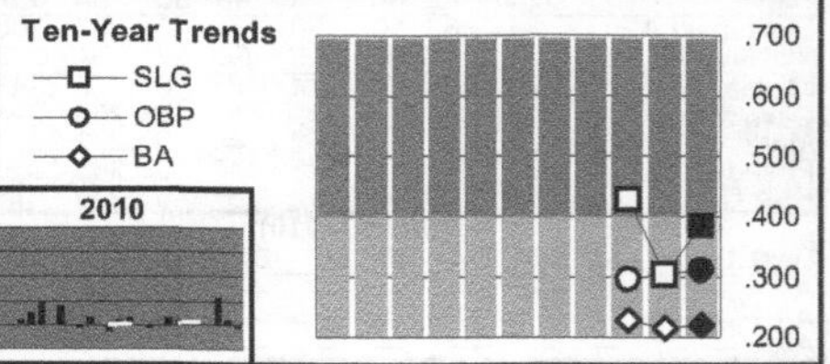


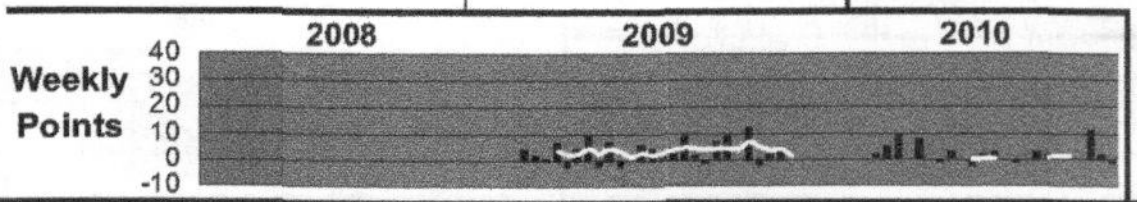


Minors (2010)

| Level | Leag | AB | HR | R | RBI | SB | BA | OBP | SLG | CT% | H% | BB% | Bash |
|---|---|---|---|---|---|---|---|---|---|---|---|---|---|
| A | — | — | — | — | — | — | — | — | — | — | — | — | — |
| AA | — | — | — | — | — | — | — | — | — | — | — | — | — |
| AAA | PCL | 45 | 1 | 6 | 2 | 0 | .200 | .345 | .311 | 80% | 25% | 18% | 1.56 |

Majors

| Yr | Team | AB | HR | R | RBI | SB | BA | OBP | SLG | CT% | H% | BB% | Bash |
|---|---|---|---|---|---|---|---|---|---|---|---|---|---|
| 07 | — | — | — | — | — | — | — | — | — | — | — | — | — |
| 08 | — | — | — | — | — | — | — | — | — | — | — | — | — |
| 09 | OAK | 140 | 7 | 19 | 30 | 0 | .229 | .297 | .429 | 74% | 31% | 9% | 1.88 |
| 10 | OAK | 112 | 2 | 13 | 11 | 1 | .214 | .305 | .304 | 74% | 29% | 12% | 1.42 |

| Yr | $1L | $2L | Pts | RAA | 2B | 3B | CS | FB-LD-GB | HR/fb | RBI% | RS% | OPS | 1st Hf | 2nd Hf | vs RH | vs LH | Rnge | vRH | vLH |
|---|---|---|---|---|---|---|---|---|---|---|---|---|---|---|---|---|---|---|---|
| 07 | — | — | — | — | — | — | — | — | — | — | — | — | — | — | — | — | — | — | — |
| 08 | — | — | — | — | — | — | — | — | — | — | — | — | — | — | — | — | 0.57 | — | — |
| 09 | $3 | -$3 | 90 | −0 | 7 | 0 | 0 | 44-18-38 | 15% | 26% | 31% | .725 | .671 | .781 | .829 | .458 | 0.58 | — | — |
| 10 | $0 | -$9 | 50 | −4 | 4 | 0 | 0 | 46-17-37 | 5% | 16% | 30% | .608 | .682 | .509 | .602 | .624 | 0.58 | +5 | −14 |

*For more stats, visit www.Rotolympus.com.*

## Martin Prado — 650 PA | $18 | 400 pts
2B-98, 3B-43, 1B-5 — Owned: 100% — RH

A finger injury slowed – and then a hip injury ended – Marte-e-e-en's great season. But Prado proved that he can be a valuable second baseman, even an All-Star. After batting in the top third of the Braves' order, he will probably move back to the lead-off spot, where he put up his best numbers (.322/.362/.521). (MG)

### Forecast
| Player | Age | AB | HR | R | RBI | SB | BA | OBP | SLG | $1L | Pts |
|---|---|---|---|---|---|---|---|---|---|---|---|
| Prado M | 27 | 591 | 13 | 91 | 65 | 7 | .297 | .351 | .444 | $18 | 400 |
| Mini-Browser | Age | AB | HR | R | RBI | SB | BA | OBP | SLG | $1L | Pts |
| Pedroia D | 27 | 577 | 13 | 98 | 65 | 13 | .304 | .372 | .465 | $25 | 460 |
| Phillips B | 29 | 589 | 20 | 91 | 85 | 26 | .276 | .329 | .458 | $24 | 450 |
| Johnson K | 29 | 561 | 20 | 108 | 74 | 14 | .289 | .370 | .501 | $24 | 430 |
| Uggla B | 31 | 576 | 33 | 91 | 91 | 7 | .271 | .366 | .513 | $23 | 420 |
| Roberts B | 33 | 532 | 12 | 84 | 54 | 30 | .293 | .370 | .447 | $22 | 420 |

### Minors (2010)
| Level | Leag | AB | HR | R | RBI | SB | BA | OBP | SLG | CT% | H% | BB% | Bash |
|---|---|---|---|---|---|---|---|---|---|---|---|---|---|
| A | — | — | — | — | — | — | — | — | — | — | — | — | — |
| AA | — | — | — | — | — | — | — | — | — | — | — | — | — |
| AAA | IL | 4 | 0 | 0 | 0 | 0 | .250 | .250 | .250 | 100% | 25% | 0% | 1.00 |

### Competition at 2B — Stats in 2010
| Bats | Player | GSvR | GSvL | Sub | OPS |
|---|---|---|---|---|---|
| RH | Prado M | 65 | 33 | 0 | .809 |
| RH | Infante O | 43 | 22 | 0 | .775 |

Ten-Year Trends: SLG, OBP, BA — Weekly Points 2008 / 2009 / 2010

### Majors
| Yr | Team | AB | HR | R | RBI | SB | BA | OBP | SLG | CT% | H% | BB% | Bash | $1L | $2L | Pts | RAA | 2B | 3B | CS | FB-LD-GB | HR/fb | RBI% | RS% | OPS | 1st Hf | 2nd Hf | vs RH | vs LH | Rnge | vRH | vLH |
|---|---|---|---|---|---|---|---|---|---|---|---|---|---|---|---|---|---|---|---|---|---|---|---|---|---|---|---|---|---|---|---|---|
| 07 | ATL | 59 | 0 | 5 | 2 | 0 | .288 | .323 | .339 | 90% | 32% | 5% | 1.18 | -$5 | -$19 | 20 | -1 | 3 | 0 | 0 | 38-19-43 | 0% | 9% | 25% | .662 | .412 | .890 | .954 | .494 | 4.25 | -21 | +49 |
| 08 | ATL | 228 | 2 | 36 | 33 | 3 | .320 | .377 | .461 | 87% | 37% | 8% | 1.44 | $6 | -$5 | 170 | +9 | 18 | 4 | 1 | 35-23-42 | 3% | 26% | 37% | .838 | .755 | .866 | .844 | .829 | 4.25 | -16 | +34 |
| 09 | ATL | 450 | 11 | 64 | 49 | 1 | .307 | .358 | .464 | 87% | 35% | 7% | 1.51 | $14 | $4 | 300 | +12 | 38 | 0 | 3 | 37-20-44 | 8% | 17% | 32% | .822 | .889 | .774 | .774 | .923 | 4.23 | -14 | +28 |
| 10 | ATL | 599 | 15 | 100 | 66 | 5 | .307 | .350 | .459 | 86% | 36% | 6% | 1.49 | $24 | $18 | 400 | +16 | 40 | 3 | 1 | 31-21-48 | 9% | 20% | 40% | .809 | .851 | .741 | .834 | .747 | 4.22 | -24 | +52 |

## Albert Pujols — 725 PA | $40 | 690 pts
1B-157 — Owned: 100% — RH

Even in a typical (for him) season, Pujols is in the discussion for NL MVP. The Cards have stated their intention of signing Pujols to an extension that will "make him a Cardinal for life," but he has offered no guarantees. Expect Mauer-ish rumors all winter. (AB)

### Forecast
| Player | Age | AB | HR | R | RBI | SB | BA | OBP | SLG | $1L | Pts |
|---|---|---|---|---|---|---|---|---|---|---|---|
| Pujols A | 31 | 600 | 44 | 116 | 131 | 15 | .326 | .436 | .618 | $40 | 690 |
| Mini-Browser | Age | AB | HR | R | RBI | SB | BA | OBP | SLG | $1L | Pts |
| Cabrera M | 27 | 597 | 35 | 98 | 126 | 7 | .305 | .384 | .555 | $35 | 520 |
| Teixeira M | 30 | 559 | 33 | 91 | 111 | 0 | .279 | .379 | .532 | $30 | 470 |
| Votto J | 27 | 545 | 33 | 98 | 104 | 13 | .298 | .389 | .548 | $29 | 480 |
| Fielder P | 26 | 573 | 42 | 98 | 112 | 0 | .281 | .394 | .552 | $28 | 490 |
| Howard R | 31 | 558 | 39 | 98 | 130 | 0 | .268 | .362 | .549 | $27 | 440 |

### Minors (2010)
| Level | Leag | AB | HR | R | RBI | SB | BA | OBP | SLG | CT% | H% | BB% | Bash |
|---|---|---|---|---|---|---|---|---|---|---|---|---|---|
| A | — | — | — | — | — | — | — | — | — | — | — | — | — |
| AA | — | — | — | — | — | — | — | — | — | — | — | — | — |
| AAA | — | — | — | — | — | — | — | — | — | — | — | — | — |

### Competition at 1B — Stats in 2010
| Bats | Player | GSvR | GSvL | Sub | OPS |
|---|---|---|---|---|---|
| RH | Pujols A | 103 | 54 | 0 | 1.011 |

Ten-Year Trends: SLG, OBP, BA — Weekly Points 2008 / 2009 / 2010

### Majors
| Yr | Team | AB | HR | R | RBI | SB | BA | OBP | SLG | CT% | H% | BB% | Bash | $1L | $2L | Pts | RAA | 2B | 3B | CS | FB-LD-GB | HR/fb | RBI% | RS% | OPS | 1st Hf | 2nd Hf | vs RH | vs LH | Rnge | vRH | vLH |
|---|---|---|---|---|---|---|---|---|---|---|---|---|---|---|---|---|---|---|---|---|---|---|---|---|---|---|---|---|---|---|---|---|
| 07 | STL | 565 | 32 | 99 | 103 | 2 | .327 | .429 | .568 | 90% | 36% | 14% | 1.74 | $31 | $26 | 560 | +34 | 38 | 1 | 6 | 39-19-42 | 16% | 24% | 26% | .997 | .927 | 1.081 | .942 | 1.140 | 1.91 | +2 | -6 |
| 08 | STL | 524 | 37 | 100 | 116 | 7 | .357 | .462 | .653 | 90% | 40% | 15% | 1.83 | $39 | $34 | 620 | +55 | 44 | 0 | 3 | 37-22-40 | 21% | 28% | 24% | 1.114 | 1.074 | 1.162 | 1.063 | 1.233 | 1.92 | -19 | +47 |
| 09 | STL | 568 | 47 | 124 | 135 | 16 | .327 | .443 | .658 | 89% | 37% | 16% | 2.01 | $46 | $43 | 710 | +52 | 45 | 1 | 4 | 46-16-39 | 20% | 29% | 29% | 1.101 | 1.179 | 1.009 | 1.080 | 1.076 | 1.92 | -35 | +88 |
| 10 | STL | 587 | 42 | 115 | 118 | 14 | .312 | .414 | .596 | 87% | 36% | 14% | 1.91 | $42 | $41 | 630 | +37 | 39 | 1 | 4 | 44-17-38 | 18% | 24% | 29% | 1.011 | .992 | 1.033 | .983 | 1.076 | 1.90 | -25 | +60 |

## Nick Punto — 350 PA | $2 | 160 pts
3B-48, SS-31, 2B-12, DH-1 — Owned: 2% — BH

Despite being treated (and paid) by the Twins as a starting-caliber player, Punto is a utility guy through and through. He's a good one at that, but not worth his $5M option for 2011 after an injury-riddled 2010. That said, he is very well liked by the Twins and could return to the team on a cheaper deal. (NN)

### Forecast
| Player | Age | AB | HR | R | RBI | SB | BA | OBP | SLG | $1L | Pts |
|---|---|---|---|---|---|---|---|---|---|---|---|
| Punto N | 33 | 314 | 0 | 35 | 25 | 11 | .245 | .325 | .317 | $2 | 160 |
| Mini-Browser | Age | AB | HR | R | RBI | SB | BA | OBP | SLG | $1L | Pts |
| Bell J | 24 | 396 | 18 | 45 | 45 | 0 | .227 | .284 | .411 | $5 | 160 |
| Baker J | 29 | 279 | 9 | 39 | 36 | 3 | .269 | .329 | .442 | $4 | 160 |
| Morel B | 23 | 226 | 10 | 28 | 30 | 10 | .221 | .278 | .391 | $4 | 140 |
| Izturis M | 30 | 179 | 2 | 28 | 26 | 6 | .279 | .342 | .397 | $2 | 130 |
| Fields J | 28 | 224 | 8 | 28 | 30 | 3 | .245 | .325 | .414 | $2 | 110 |

### Minors (2010)
| Level | Leag | AB | HR | R | RBI | SB | BA | OBP | SLG | CT% | H% | BB% | Bash |
|---|---|---|---|---|---|---|---|---|---|---|---|---|---|
| A | — | — | — | — | — | — | — | — | — | — | — | — | — |
| AA | — | — | — | — | — | — | — | — | — | — | — | — | — |
| AAA | — | — | — | — | — | — | — | — | — | — | — | — | — |

### Competition at 3B — Stats in 2010
| Bats | Player | GSvR | GSvL | Sub | OPS |
|---|---|---|---|---|---|
| RH | Valencia D | 47 | 33 | 1 | .799 |
| BH | Punto N | 28 | 14 | 6 | .615 |
| RH | Harris B | 15 | 7 | 5 | .446 |
| RH | Cuddyer M | 10 | 4 | 0 | .753 |

Ten-Year Trends: SLG, OBP, BA — Weekly Points 2008 / 2009 / 2010

### Majors
| Yr | Team | AB | HR | R | RBI | SB | BA | OBP | SLG | CT% | H% | BB% | Bash | $1L | $2L | Pts | RAA | 2B | 3B | CS | FB-LD-GB | HR/fb | RBI% | RS% | OPS | 1st Hf | 2nd Hf | vs RH | vs LH | Rnge | vRH | vLH |
|---|---|---|---|---|---|---|---|---|---|---|---|---|---|---|---|---|---|---|---|---|---|---|---|---|---|---|---|---|---|---|---|---|
| 07 | MIN | 472 | 1 | 53 | 25 | 16 | .210 | .291 | .271 | 81% | 26% | 10% | 1.29 | $1 | -$13 | 200 | -31 | 18 | 4 | 6 | 35-15-51 | 1% | 10% | 34% | .562 | .585 | .527 | .599 | .483 | — | 0 | +1 |
| 08 | MIN | 338 | 2 | 43 | 28 | 15 | .284 | .344 | .382 | 83% | 34% | 8% | 1.34 | $8 | -$4 | 200 | -1 | 19 | 4 | 6 | 35-21-45 | 2% | 15% | 33% | .726 | .853 | .670 | .739 | .701 | — | +6 | -13 |
| 09 | MIN | 359 | 1 | 56 | 38 | 16 | .228 | .337 | .284 | 81% | 28% | 14% | 1.24 | $0 | -$6 | 200 | -14 | 15 | 1 | 3 | 33-19-48 | 1% | 20% | 38% | .621 | .543 | .700 | .613 | .642 | — | +10 | -24 |
| 10 | MIN | 252 | 1 | 24 | 20 | 6 | .238 | .313 | .302 | 80% | 30% | 10% | 1.27 | $0 | -$14 | 110 | -12 | 11 | 1 | 2 | 33-15-52 | 2% | 15% | 26% | .615 | .625 | .576 | .618 | .608 | — | -2 | +5 |

## Carlos Quentin — 550 PA | $19 | 370 pts
OF-104 (RF-104), DH-23 — Owned: 93% — RH

The frequent aches, undersized BA, and overblown expectations cost Quentin in "fan respect," but he hit well with RISP, which accounts for the jump in RBI% despite a flat SLG. Although fielding metrics frown, his defensive range is almost average. His 2.0-level Bash is cool but inflated by playing at the Cell. (RM)

### Forecast
| Player | Age | AB | HR | R | RBI | SB | BA | OBP | SLG | $1L | Pts |
|---|---|---|---|---|---|---|---|---|---|---|---|
| Quentin C | 28 | 465 | 28 | 77 | 88 | 6 | .260 | .352 | .494 | $19 | 370 |
| Mini-Browser | Age | AB | HR | R | RBI | SB | BA | OBP | SLG | $1L | Pts |
| Crisp C | 31 | 552 | 12 | 78 | 60 | 36 | .261 | .330 | .399 | $20 | 400 |
| Span D | 27 | 620 | 9 | 91 | 63 | 28 | .271 | .348 | .371 | $20 | 420 |
| Ethier A | 28 | 523 | 24 | 78 | 84 | 6 | .287 | .366 | .506 | $20 | 410 |
| Bautista J | 30 | 522 | 30 | 78 | 84 | 6 | .253 | .353 | .495 | $20 | 400 |
| Cuddyer M | 32 | 578 | 20 | 85 | 85 | 7 | .270 | .342 | .456 | $19 | 390 |

### Minors (2010)
| Level | Leag | AB | HR | R | RBI | SB | BA | OBP | SLG | CT% | H% | BB% | Bash |
|---|---|---|---|---|---|---|---|---|---|---|---|---|---|
| A | — | — | — | — | — | — | — | — | — | — | — | — | — |
| AA | — | — | — | — | — | — | — | — | — | — | — | — | — |
| AAA | — | — | — | — | — | — | — | — | — | — | — | — | — |

### Competition at RF — Stats in 2010
| Bats | Player | GSvR | GSvL | Sub | OPS |
|---|---|---|---|---|---|
| RH | Quentin C | 80 | 23 | 1 | .821 |
| RH | Jones A | 26 | 15 | 21 | .827 |
| LH | Teahen M | 10 | 0 | 0 | .709 |

Ten-Year Trends: SLG, OBP, BA — Weekly Points 2008 / 2009 / 2010

### Majors
| Yr | Team | AB | HR | R | RBI | SB | BA | OBP | SLG | CT% | H% | BB% | Bash | $1L | $2L | Pts | RAA | 2B | 3B | CS | FB-LD-GB | HR/fb | RBI% | RS% | OPS | 1st Hf | 2nd Hf | vs RH | vs LH | Rnge | vRH | vLH |
|---|---|---|---|---|---|---|---|---|---|---|---|---|---|---|---|---|---|---|---|---|---|---|---|---|---|---|---|---|---|---|---|---|
| 07 | ARI | 229 | 5 | 29 | 31 | 2 | .214 | .298 | .349 | 76% | 28% | 7% | 1.63 | -$1 | -$13 | 110 | -20 | 16 | 0 | 2 | 41-16-43 | 7% | 23% | 33% | .647 | .649 | .635 | .670 | .589 | 2.07 | -9 | +23 |
| 08 | CHW | 480 | 36 | 96 | 100 | 7 | .288 | .394 | .571 | 83% | 35% | 12% | 1.99 | $29 | $22 | 470 | +22 | 26 | 1 | 3 | 43-15-41 | 21% | 27% | 32% | .965 | .900 | 1.117 | .975 | .937 | 2.07 | -7 | +18 |
| 09 | CHW | 351 | 21 | 47 | 56 | 0 | .236 | .323 | .456 | 85% | 28% | 8% | 1.93 | $10 | -$2 | 250 | -11 | 14 | 0 | 0 | 47-16-37 | 15% | 18% | 24% | .779 | .783 | .777 | .802 | .716 | 2.05 | -10 | +24 |
| 10 | CHW | 453 | 26 | 73 | 87 | 2 | .243 | .342 | .479 | 82% | 30% | 9% | 1.97 | $18 | $10 | 370 | -8 | 25 | 2 | 2 | 49-14-37 | 14% | 23% | 31% | .821 | .867 | .757 | .838 | .764 | 2.03 | -4 | +12 |

## Robb Quinlan — 50 PA | $-5 | 20 pts
1B-13, OF-4 (RF-3, LF-1), DH-2, 3B-1 — Owned: 0% — RH

After 12 years with the Angels' organization, Quinlan was released in September 2010. He can still offer value with his glove, but for a corner infielder, he has been underwhelming with his bat since 2006. (DS)

### Forecast
| Player | Age | AB | HR | R | RBI | SB | BA | OBP | SLG | $1L | Pts |
|---|---|---|---|---|---|---|---|---|---|---|---|
| Quinlan R | 34 | 46 | 1 | 5 | 5 | 1 | .239 | .291 | .327 | -$5 | 20 |
| Mini-Browser | Age | AB | HR | R | RBI | SB | BA | OBP | SLG | $1L | Pts |
| Hosmer E | 21 | 129 | 3 | 11 | 17 | 0 | .221 | .303 | .359 | -$4 | 50 |
| Davis C | 25 | 45 | 6 | 7 | 14 | 0 | .243 | .301 | .475 | -$4 | 20 |
| Rizzo A | 21 | 44 | 2 | 5 | 6 | 0 | .251 | .313 | .424 | -$5 | 20 |
| Delgado C | 38 | 22 | 1 | 4 | 4 | 0 | .276 | .358 | .506 | -$5 | 20 |
| Hughes R | 27 | 47 | 2 | 5 | 9 | 0 | .225 | .291 | .410 | -$5 | 20 |

### Minors (2010)
| Level | Leag | AB | HR | R | RBI | SB | BA | OBP | SLG | CT% | H% | BB% | Bash |
|---|---|---|---|---|---|---|---|---|---|---|---|---|---|
| A | — | — | — | — | — | — | — | — | — | — | — | — | — |
| AA | — | — | — | — | — | — | — | — | — | — | — | — | — |
| AAA | PCL | 128 | 0 | 13 | 8 | 1 | .258 | .336 | .305 | 82% | 31% | 10% | 1.18 |

### Competition at 1B — Stats in 2010
| Bats | Player | GSvR | GSvL | Sub | OPS |
|---|---|---|---|---|---|
| RH | Napoli M | 42 | 25 | 3 | .784 |
| BH | Morales K | 33 | 18 | 0 | .833 |
| RH | Rivera J | 10 | 2 | 1 | .721 |
| RH | Kendrick H | 10 | 2 | 3 | .721 |

Ten-Year Trends: SLG, OBP, BA — Weekly Points 2008 / 2009 / 2010

### Majors
| Yr | Team | AB | HR | R | RBI | SB | BA | OBP | SLG | CT% | H% | BB% | Bash | $1L | $2L | Pts | RAA | 2B | 3B | CS | FB-LD-GB | HR/fb | RBI% | RS% | OPS | 1st Hf | 2nd Hf | vs RH | vs LH | Rnge | vRH | vLH |
|---|---|---|---|---|---|---|---|---|---|---|---|---|---|---|---|---|---|---|---|---|---|---|---|---|---|---|---|---|---|---|---|---|
| 07 | LAA | 178 | 3 | 21 | 21 | 3 | .247 | .304 | .348 | 85% | 29% | 7% | 1.41 | $0 | -$14 | 100 | -11 | 9 | 0 | 2 | 38-14-48 | 5% | 18% | 32% | .652 | .760 | .514 | .576 | .691 | 1.84 | -39 | +71 |
| 08 | LAA | 164 | 1 | 15 | 11 | 4 | .262 | .326 | .311 | 83% | 32% | 8% | 1.19 | -$1 | -$14 | 70 | -11 | 1 | 2 | 2 | 34-18-48 | 2% | 12% | 24% | .637 | .616 | .666 | .625 | .650 | 1.85 | -29 | +50 |
| 09 | LAA | 115 | 2 | 13 | 14 | 1 | .243 | .275 | .339 | 74% | 33% | 4% | 1.39 | -$1 | -$17 | 40 | -8 | 5 | 0 | 1 | 27-18-55 | 9% | 19% | 35% | .614 | .546 | .702 | .548 | .651 | 1.84 | -18 | +33 |
| 10 | LAA | 33 | 0 | 4 | 2 | 2 | .121 | .182 | .182 | 82% | 15% | 6% | 1.50 | -$4 | -$20 | 10 | -5 | 2 | 0 | 0 | 37-11-52 | 0% | 13% | 67% | .353 | .353 | — | .186 | .641 | — | -12 | +24 |

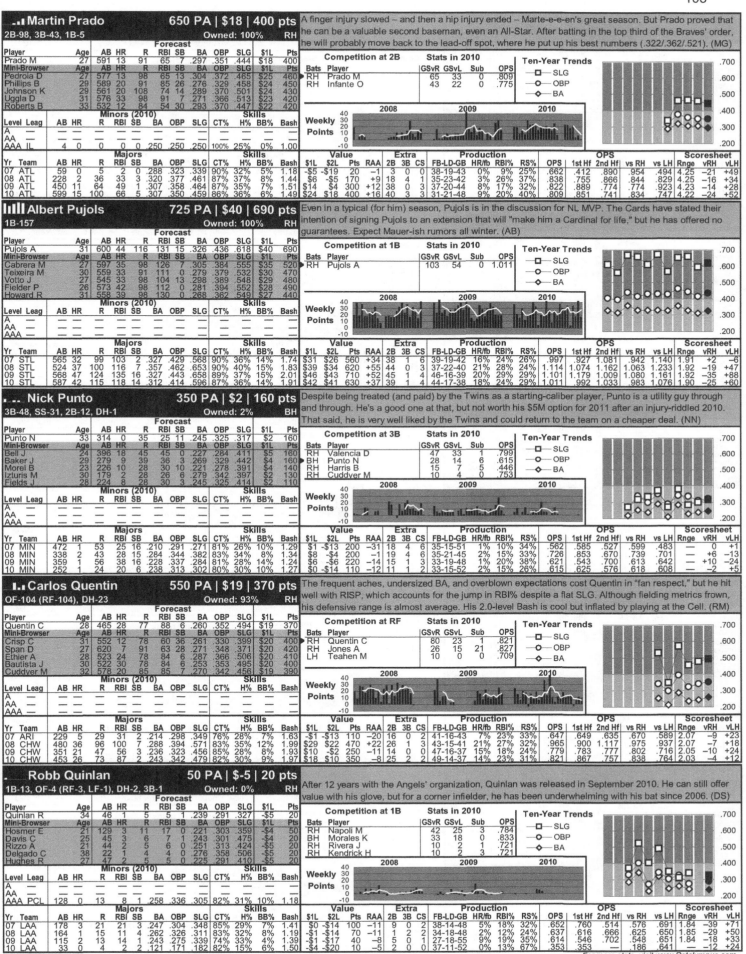

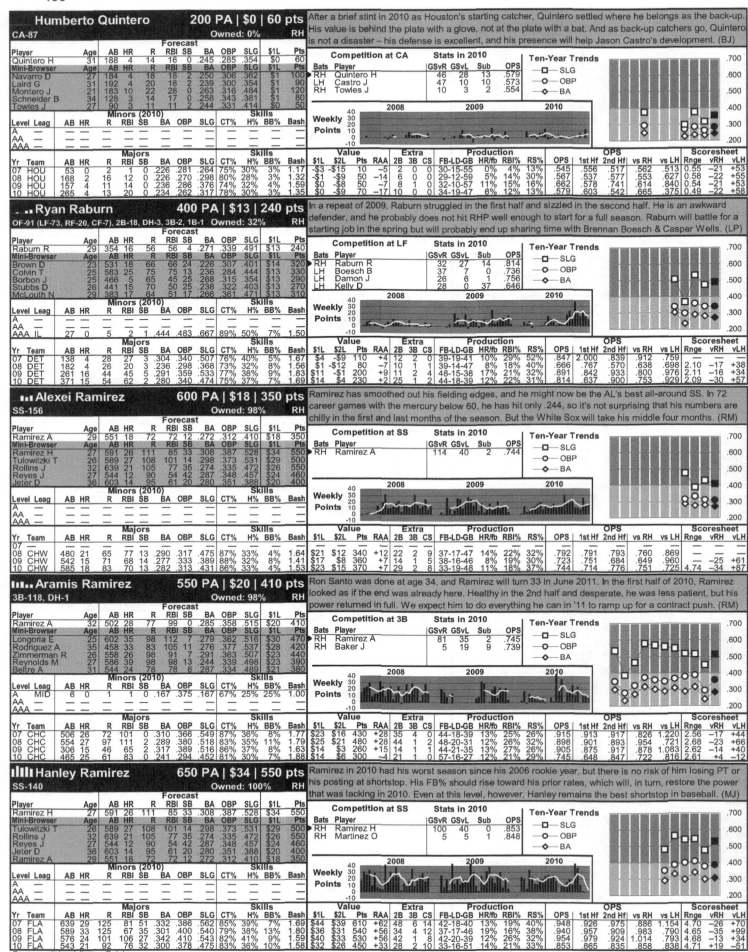

## Humberto Quintero — 200 PA | $0 | 60 pts

CA-87 — Owned: 0% — RH

| Player | Age | AB | HR | R | RBI | SB | BA | OBP | SLG | $1L | Pts |
|---|---|---|---|---|---|---|---|---|---|---|---|
| Quintero H | 31 | 188 | 4 | 14 | 16 | 0 | .245 | .285 | .354 | $0 | 60 |
| **Mini-Browser** | **Age** | **AB** | **HR** | **R** | **RBI** | **SB** | **BA** | **OBP** | **SLG** | **$1L** | **Pts** |
| Navarro D | 27 | 184 | 4 | 18 | 18 | 2 | .250 | .306 | .362 | $1 | 100 |
| Laird G | 31 | 192 | 4 | 20 | 18 | 2 | .239 | .300 | .354 | $1 | 90 |
| Montero J | 21 | 183 | 10 | 22 | 28 | 0 | .263 | .316 | .484 | $1 | 120 |
| Schneider B | 34 | 128 | 3 | 14 | 17 | 0 | .258 | .343 | .381 | $1 | 80 |
| Towles J | 27 | 90 | 3 | 11 | 11 | 2 | .244 | .331 | .414 | $0 | 50 |

Minors (2010)

| Level | Leag | AB | HR | R | RBI | SB | BA | OBP | SLG | CT% | H% | BB% | Bash |
|---|---|---|---|---|---|---|---|---|---|---|---|---|---|
| A | — | — | — | — | — | — | — | — | — | — | — | — | — |
| AA | — | — | — | — | — | — | — | — | — | — | — | — | — |
| AAA | — | — | — | — | — | — | — | — | — | — | — | — | — |

Majors

| Yr | Team | AB | HR | R | RBI | SB | BA | OBP | SLG | CT% | H% | BB% | Bash |
|---|---|---|---|---|---|---|---|---|---|---|---|---|---|
| 07 | HOU | 53 | 0 | 2 | 1 | 0 | .226 | .281 | .264 | 75% | 30% | 3% | 1.17 |
| 08 | HOU | 168 | 2 | 16 | 12 | 0 | .226 | .270 | .298 | 80% | 28% | 3% | 1.32 |
| 09 | HOU | 157 | 4 | 11 | 14 | 0 | .236 | .286 | .376 | 74% | 32% | 4% | 1.59 |
| 10 | HOU | 265 | 4 | 13 | 20 | 0 | .234 | .262 | .317 | 78% | 30% | 3% | 1.35 |

After a brief stint in 2010 as Houston's starting catcher, Quintero settled where he belongs as the back-up. His value is behind the plate with a glove, not at the plate with a bat. And as back-up catchers go, Quintero is not a disaster – his defense is excellent, and his presence will help Jason Castro's development. (BJ)

Competition at CA — Stats in 2010

| Bats | Player | GSvR | GSvL | Sub | OPS |
|---|---|---|---|---|---|
| RH | Quintero H | 46 | 28 | 13 | .579 |
| LH | Castro J | 47 | 10 | 10 | .573 |
| RH | Towles J | 10 | 3 | 2 | .554 |

Ten-Year Trends: SLG, OBP, BA

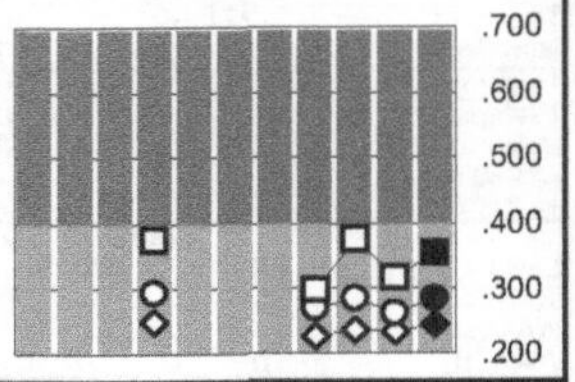


Weekly Points

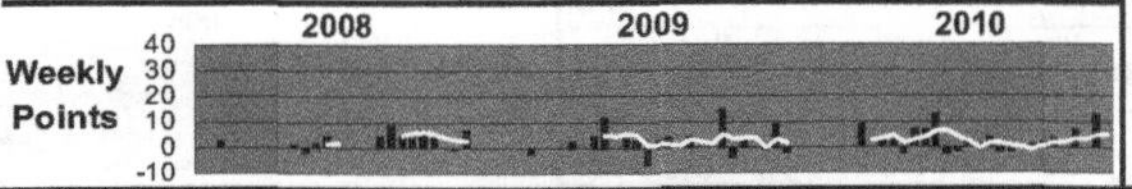


| Yr | $1L | $2L | Pts | RAA | 2B | 3B | CS | FB-LD-GB | HR/fb | RBI% | RS% | OPS | 1st Hf | 2nd Hf | vs RH | vs LH | Rnge | vRH | vLH |
|---|---|---|---|---|---|---|---|---|---|---|---|---|---|---|---|---|---|---|---|
| 07 | -$3 | -$15 | 10 | –5 | 2 | 0 | 0 | 30-15-55 | 0% | 4% | 13% | .545 | .556 | .517 | .562 | .513 | 0.55 | –21 | +53 |
| 08 | -$1 | -$9 | 50 | –14 | 6 | 0 | 0 | 29-12-59 | 5% | 14% | 30% | .567 | .537 | .577 | .553 | .627 | 0.58 | –22 | +55 |
| 09 | $0 | -$8 | 50 | –7 | 8 | 1 | 0 | 32-10-57 | 11% | 15% | 16% | .662 | .578 | .741 | .614 | .840 | 0.54 | –21 | +53 |
| 10 | $0 | -$9 | 70 | –17 | 10 | 0 | 0 | 34-19-47 | 6% | 12% | 13% | .579 | .603 | .542 | .665 | .375 | 0.49 | –22 | +58 |

## Ryan Raburn — 400 PA | $13 | 240 pts

OF-91 (LF-73, RF-20, CF-7), 2B-18, DH-3, 3B-2, 1B-1 — Owned: 32% — RH

| Player | Age | AB | HR | R | RBI | SB | BA | OBP | SLG | $1L | Pts |
|---|---|---|---|---|---|---|---|---|---|---|---|
| Raburn R | 29 | 354 | 16 | 56 | 56 | 4 | .271 | .339 | .491 | $13 | 240 |
| **Mini-Browser** | **Age** | **AB** | **HR** | **R** | **RBI** | **SB** | **BA** | **OBP** | **SLG** | **$1L** | **Pts** |
| Brown D | 23 | 531 | 18 | 66 | 66 | 24 | .226 | .307 | .401 | $14 | 320 |
| Colvin T | 25 | 583 | 25 | 75 | 75 | 13 | .236 | .284 | .444 | $13 | 330 |
| Borbon J | 25 | 466 | 5 | 65 | 45 | 25 | .268 | .315 | .354 | $13 | 290 |
| Stubbs D | 26 | 441 | 15 | 70 | 50 | 25 | .238 | .322 | .403 | $13 | 270 |
| McLouth N | 29 | 383 | 17 | 64 | 51 | 17 | .266 | .361 | .471 | $13 | 310 |

Minors (2010)

| Level | Leag | AB | HR | R | RBI | SB | BA | OBP | SLG | CT% | H% | BB% | Bash |
|---|---|---|---|---|---|---|---|---|---|---|---|---|---|
| A | — | — | — | — | — | — | — | — | — | — | — | — | — |
| AA | — | — | — | — | — | — | — | — | — | — | — | — | — |
| AAA | IL | 27 | 0 | 5 | 2 | 1 | .444 | .483 | .667 | 89% | 50% | 7% | 1.50 |

Majors

| Yr | Team | AB | HR | R | RBI | SB | BA | OBP | SLG | CT% | H% | BB% | Bash |
|---|---|---|---|---|---|---|---|---|---|---|---|---|---|
| 07 | DET | 138 | 4 | 28 | 27 | 3 | .304 | .340 | .507 | 76% | 40% | 5% | 1.67 |
| 08 | DET | 182 | 4 | 26 | 20 | 3 | .236 | .298 | .368 | 73% | 32% | 8% | 1.56 |
| 09 | DET | 261 | 16 | 44 | 45 | 5 | .291 | .359 | .533 | 77% | 38% | 9% | 1.83 |
| 10 | DET | 371 | 15 | 54 | 62 | 2 | .280 | .340 | .474 | 75% | 37% | 7% | 1.69 |

In a repeat of 2009, Raburn struggled in the first half and sizzled in the second half. He is an awkward defender, and he probably does not hit RHP well enough to start for a full season. Raburn will battle for a starting job in the spring but will probably end up sharing time with Brennan Boesch & Casper Wells. (LP)

Competition at LF — Stats in 2010

| Bats | Player | GSvR | GSvL | Sub | OPS |
|---|---|---|---|---|---|
| RH | Raburn R | 32 | 27 | 14 | .814 |
| LH | Boesch B | 37 | 7 | 0 | .736 |
| LH | Damon J | 26 | 6 | 1 | .756 |
| LH | Kelly D | 28 | 0 | 37 | .646 |

Ten-Year Trends: SLG, OBP, BA

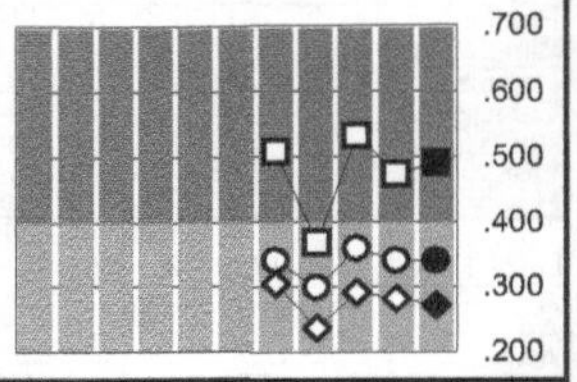


Weekly Points

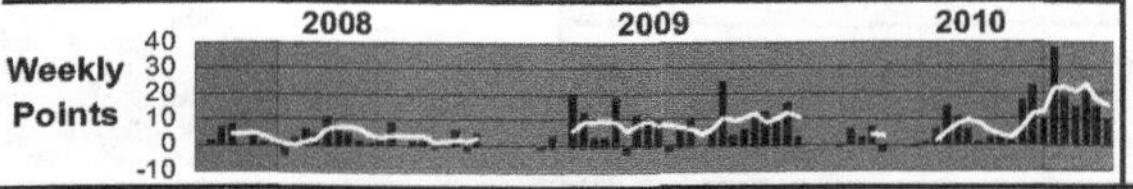


| Yr | $1L | $2L | Pts | RAA | 2B | 3B | CS | FB-LD-GB | HR/fb | RBI% | RS% | OPS | 1st Hf | 2nd Hf | vs RH | vs LH | Rnge | vRH | vLH |
|---|---|---|---|---|---|---|---|---|---|---|---|---|---|---|---|---|---|---|---|
| 07 | $4 | -$9 | 110 | +4 | 12 | 2 | 0 | 39-19-41 | 10% | 29% | 52% | .847 | 2.000 | .839 | .912 | .759 | — | — | — |
| 08 | $1 | -$12 | 80 | –7 | 10 | 1 | 1 | 39-14-47 | 8% | 18% | 40% | .666 | .767 | .570 | .638 | .698 | 2.10 | –17 | +38 |
| 09 | $11 | -$1 | 200 | +9 | 11 | 2 | 4 | 48-15-38 | 17% | 21% | 32% | .891 | .842 | .933 | .800 | .976 | 2.11 | –16 | +34 |
| 10 | $14 | $4 | 230 | +2 | 25 | 1 | 2 | 44-18-39 | 12% | 22% | 31% | .814 | .637 | .900 | .753 | .929 | 2.09 | –30 | +57 |

## Alexei Ramirez — 600 PA | $18 | 350 pts

SS-156 — Owned: 98% — RH

| Player | Age | AB | HR | R | RBI | SB | BA | OBP | SLG | $1L | Pts |
|---|---|---|---|---|---|---|---|---|---|---|---|
| Ramirez A | 29 | 551 | 18 | 72 | 72 | 12 | .272 | .312 | .410 | $18 | 350 |
| **Mini-Browser** | **Age** | **AB** | **HR** | **R** | **RBI** | **SB** | **BA** | **OBP** | **SLG** | **$1L** | **Pts** |
| Ramirez H | 27 | 591 | 26 | 111 | 85 | 33 | .308 | .387 | .528 | $34 | 550 |
| Tulowitzki T | 26 | 589 | 27 | 108 | 101 | 14 | .298 | .373 | .531 | $29 | 500 |
| Rollins J | 32 | 639 | 21 | 105 | 77 | 35 | .274 | .335 | .472 | $26 | 550 |
| Reyes J | 27 | 544 | 12 | 90 | 54 | 42 | .287 | .348 | .457 | $24 | 460 |
| Jeter D | 36 | 603 | 14 | 95 | 61 | 20 | .280 | .351 | .388 | $20 | 400 |

Minors (2010)

| Level | Leag | AB | HR | R | RBI | SB | BA | OBP | SLG | CT% | H% | BB% | Bash |
|---|---|---|---|---|---|---|---|---|---|---|---|---|---|
| A | — | — | — | — | — | — | — | — | — | — | — | — | — |
| AA | — | — | — | — | — | — | — | — | — | — | — | — | — |
| AAA | — | — | — | — | — | — | — | — | — | — | — | — | — |

Majors

| Yr | Team | AB | HR | R | RBI | SB | BA | OBP | SLG | CT% | H% | BB% | Bash |
|---|---|---|---|---|---|---|---|---|---|---|---|---|---|
| 07 | — | — | — | — | — | — | — | — | — | — | — | — | — |
| 08 | CHW | 480 | 21 | 65 | 77 | 13 | .290 | .317 | .475 | 87% | 33% | 4% | 1.64 |
| 09 | CHW | 542 | 15 | 71 | 68 | 14 | .277 | .333 | .389 | 88% | 32% | 8% | 1.41 |
| 10 | CHW | 585 | 18 | 83 | 70 | 13 | .282 | .313 | .431 | 86% | 33% | 4% | 1.53 |

Ramirez has smoothed out his fielding edges, and he might now be the AL's best all-around SS. In 72 career games with the mercury below 60, he has hit only .244, so it's not surprising that his numbers are chilly in the first and last months of the season. But the White Sox will take his middle four months. (RM)

Competition at SS — Stats in 2010

| Bats | Player | GSvR | GSvL | Sub | OPS |
|---|---|---|---|---|---|
| RH | Ramirez A | 114 | 40 | 2 | .744 |

Ten-Year Trends: SLG, OBP, BA

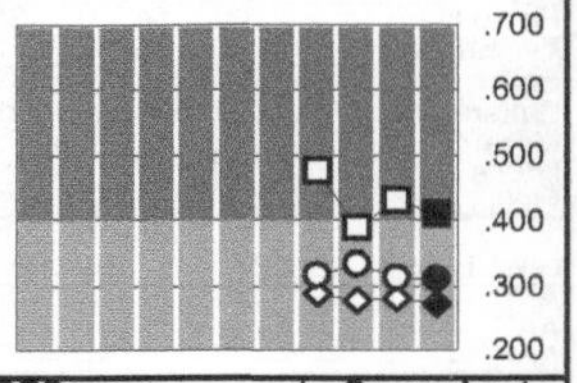


Weekly Points

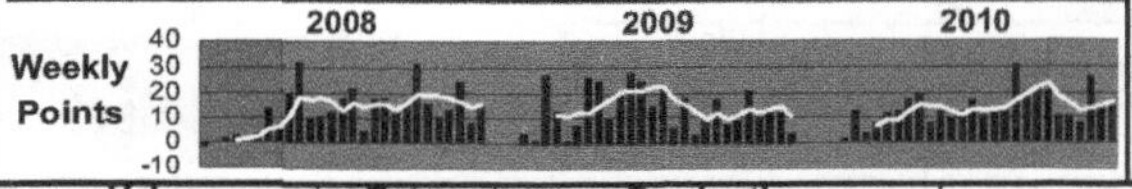


| Yr | $1L | $2L | Pts | RAA | 2B | 3B | CS | FB-LD-GB | HR/fb | RBI% | RS% | OPS | 1st Hf | 2nd Hf | vs RH | vs LH | Rnge | vRH | vLH |
|---|---|---|---|---|---|---|---|---|---|---|---|---|---|---|---|---|---|---|---|
| 07 | — | — | — | — | — | — | — | — | — | — | — | — | — | — | — | — | — | — | — |
| 08 | $21 | $12 | 340 | +12 | 22 | 2 | 9 | 37-17-47 | 14% | 22% | 32% | .792 | .791 | .793 | .760 | .869 | — | — | — |
| 09 | $17 | $8 | 360 | +7 | 14 | 1 | 5 | 38-16-46 | 8% | 19% | 30% | .723 | .751 | .684 | .649 | .960 | — | –25 | +61 |
| 10 | $23 | $15 | 370 | +7 | 29 | 2 | 8 | 33-19-48 | 11% | 18% | 37% | .744 | .714 | .776 | .751 | .725 | 4.74 | –34 | +87 |

## Aramis Ramirez — 550 PA | $20 | 410 pts

3B-118, DH-1 — Owned: 98% — RH

| Player | Age | AB | HR | R | RBI | SB | BA | OBP | SLG | $1L | Pts |
|---|---|---|---|---|---|---|---|---|---|---|---|
| Ramirez A | 32 | 502 | 28 | 77 | 99 | 0 | .285 | .358 | .515 | $20 | 410 |
| **Mini-Browser** | **Age** | **AB** | **HR** | **R** | **RBI** | **SB** | **BA** | **OBP** | **SLG** | **$1L** | **Pts** |
| Longoria E | 25 | 602 | 35 | 98 | 112 | 7 | .279 | .362 | .516 | $30 | 470 |
| Rodriguez A | 35 | 458 | 33 | 83 | 105 | 11 | .276 | .377 | .537 | $28 | 420 |
| Zimmerman R | 26 | 558 | 26 | 98 | 91 | 7 | .291 | .363 | .507 | $23 | 440 |
| Reynolds M | 27 | 586 | 39 | 98 | 98 | 13 | .244 | .339 | .498 | $23 | 390 |
| Beltre A | 31 | 544 | 24 | 78 | 78 | 6 | .287 | .334 | .489 | $21 | 380 |

Minors (2010)

| Level | Leag | AB | HR | R | RBI | SB | BA | OBP | SLG | CT% | H% | BB% | Bash |
|---|---|---|---|---|---|---|---|---|---|---|---|---|---|
| A | MID | 6 | 0 | 1 | 1 | 0 | .167 | .375 | .167 | 67% | 25% | 25% | 1.00 |
| AA | — | — | — | — | — | — | — | — | — | — | — | — | — |
| AAA | — | — | — | — | — | — | — | — | — | — | — | — | — |

Majors

| Yr | Team | AB | HR | R | RBI | SB | BA | OBP | SLG | CT% | H% | BB% | Bash |
|---|---|---|---|---|---|---|---|---|---|---|---|---|---|
| 07 | CHC | 506 | 26 | 72 | 101 | 0 | .310 | .366 | .549 | 87% | 36% | 8% | 1.77 |
| 08 | CHC | 554 | 27 | 97 | 111 | 2 | .289 | .380 | .518 | 83% | 35% | 11% | 1.79 |
| 09 | CHC | 306 | 15 | 46 | 65 | 2 | .317 | .389 | .516 | 86% | 37% | 8% | 1.63 |
| 10 | CHC | 465 | 25 | 61 | 83 | 0 | .241 | .294 | .452 | 81% | 30% | 7% | 1.88 |

Ron Santo was done at age 34, and Ramirez will turn 33 in June 2011. In the first half of 2010, Ramirez looked as if the end was already here. Healthy in the 2nd half and desperate, he was less patient, but his power returned in full. We expect him to do everything he can in '11 to ramp up for a contract push. (RM)

Competition at 3B — Stats in 2010

| Bats | Player | GSvR | GSvL | Sub | OPS |
|---|---|---|---|---|---|
| RH | Ramirez A | 81 | 35 | 2 | .745 |
| RH | Baker J | 5 | 19 | 9 | .739 |

Ten-Year Trends: SLG, OBP, BA

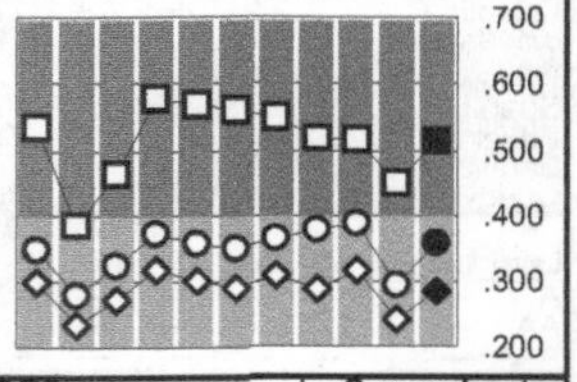


Weekly Points

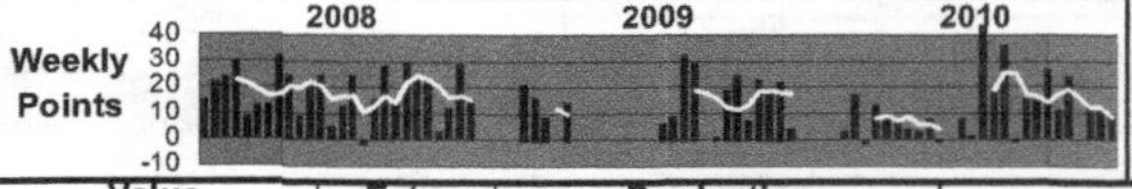


| Yr | $1L | $2L | Pts | RAA | 2B | 3B | CS | FB-LD-GB | HR/fb | RBI% | RS% | OPS | 1st Hf | 2nd Hf | vs RH | vs LH | Rnge | vRH | vLH |
|---|---|---|---|---|---|---|---|---|---|---|---|---|---|---|---|---|---|---|---|
| 07 | $23 | $16 | 430 | +28 | 35 | 4 | 0 | 44-18-39 | 13% | 25% | 26% | .915 | .913 | .917 | .826 | 1.220 | 2.56 | –17 | +44 |
| 08 | $25 | $21 | 480 | +28 | 44 | 1 | 2 | 48-20-31 | 12% | 26% | 32% | .898 | .901 | .893 | .954 | .721 | 2.68 | –23 | +66 |
| 09 | $14 | $3 | 260 | +15 | 14 | 1 | 1 | 44-21-35 | 13% | 27% | 26% | .905 | .875 | .917 | .878 | 1.083 | 2.62 | –14 | +40 |
| 10 | $14 | $6 | 300 | –4 | 21 | 1 | 0 | 57-16-27 | 12% | 21% | 29% | .745 | .648 | .847 | .722 | .816 | 2.61 | +4 | –12 |

## Hanley Ramirez — 650 PA | $34 | 550 pts

SS-140 — Owned: 100% — RH

| Player | Age | AB | HR | R | RBI | SB | BA | OBP | SLG | $1L | Pts |
|---|---|---|---|---|---|---|---|---|---|---|---|
| Ramirez H | 27 | 591 | 26 | 111 | 85 | 33 | .308 | .387 | .528 | $34 | 550 |
| **Mini-Browser** | **Age** | **AB** | **HR** | **R** | **RBI** | **SB** | **BA** | **OBP** | **SLG** | **$1L** | **Pts** |
| Tulowitzki T | 26 | 589 | 27 | 108 | 101 | 14 | .298 | .373 | .531 | $29 | 500 |
| Rollins J | 32 | 639 | 21 | 105 | 77 | 35 | .274 | .335 | .472 | $26 | 550 |
| Reyes J | 27 | 544 | 12 | 90 | 54 | 42 | .287 | .348 | .457 | $24 | 460 |
| Jeter D | 36 | 603 | 14 | 95 | 61 | 20 | .280 | .351 | .388 | $20 | 400 |
| Ramirez A | 29 | 551 | 18 | 72 | 72 | 12 | .272 | .312 | .410 | $18 | 350 |

Minors (2010)

| Level | Leag | AB | HR | R | RBI | SB | BA | OBP | SLG | CT% | H% | BB% | Bash |
|---|---|---|---|---|---|---|---|---|---|---|---|---|---|
| A | — | — | — | — | — | — | — | — | — | — | — | — | — |
| AA | — | — | — | — | — | — | — | — | — | — | — | — | — |
| AAA | — | — | — | — | — | — | — | — | — | — | — | — | — |

Majors

| Yr | Team | AB | HR | R | RBI | SB | BA | OBP | SLG | CT% | H% | BB% | Bash |
|---|---|---|---|---|---|---|---|---|---|---|---|---|---|
| 07 | FLA | 639 | 29 | 125 | 81 | 51 | .332 | .386 | .562 | 85% | 39% | 7% | 1.69 |
| 08 | FLA | 589 | 33 | 125 | 67 | 35 | .301 | .400 | .540 | 79% | 38% | 13% | 1.80 |
| 09 | FLA | 576 | 24 | 101 | 106 | 27 | .342 | .410 | .543 | 82% | 41% | 9% | 1.59 |
| 10 | FLA | 543 | 21 | 92 | 76 | 32 | .300 | .378 | .475 | 83% | 36% | 10% | 1.58 |

Ramirez in 2010 had his worst season since his 2006 rookie year, but there is no risk of him losing PT or his posting at shortstop. His FB% should rise toward his prior rates, which will, in turn, restore the power that was lacking in 2010. Even at this level, however, Hanley remains the best shortstop in baseball. (MJ)

Competition at SS — Stats in 2010

| Bats | Player | GSvR | GSvL | Sub | OPS |
|---|---|---|---|---|---|
| RH | Ramirez H | 100 | 40 | 0 | .853 |
| RH | Martinez O | 5 | 5 | 1 | .848 |

Ten-Year Trends: SLG, OBP, BA

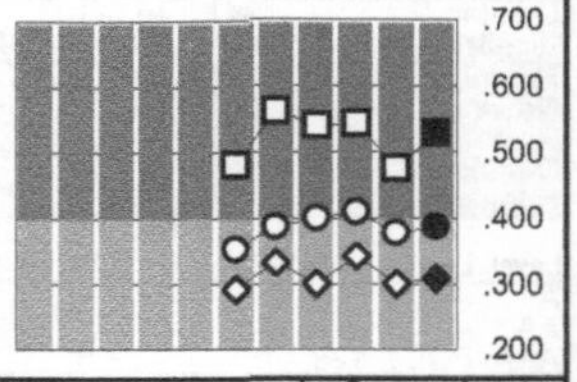


Weekly Points

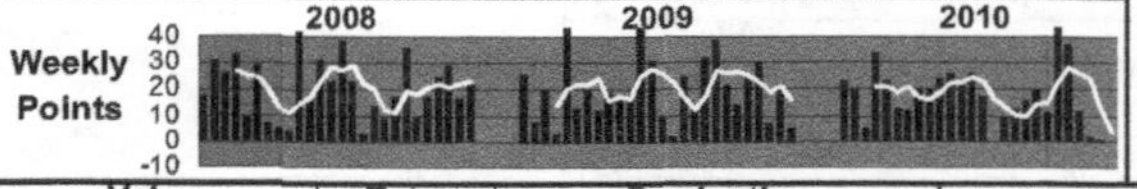


| Yr | $1L | $2L | Pts | RAA | 2B | 3B | CS | FB-LD-GB | HR/fb | RBI% | RS% | OPS | 1st Hf | 2nd Hf | vs RH | vs LH | Rnge | vRH | vLH |
|---|---|---|---|---|---|---|---|---|---|---|---|---|---|---|---|---|---|---|---|
| 07 | $44 | $39 | 610 | +62 | 48 | 6 | 14 | 42-18-40 | 13% | 19% | 40% | .948 | .926 | .975 | .886 | 1.154 | 4.70 | –26 | +70 |
| 08 | $36 | $31 | 540 | +56 | 34 | 4 | 12 | 37-17-46 | 19% | 16% | 38% | .940 | .957 | .909 | .983 | .790 | 4.65 | –35 | +99 |
| 09 | $40 | $33 | 530 | +56 | 42 | 1 | 8 | 42-20-39 | 12% | 26% | 32% | .954 | .979 | .924 | 1.014 | .793 | 4.68 | –13 | +34 |
| 10 | $32 | $26 | 450 | +33 | 28 | 2 | 10 | 33-16-51 | 14% | 21% | 33% | .853 | .865 | .835 | .858 | .838 | 4.71 | +19 | –51 |

*For more stats, visit www.Rotolympus.com.*

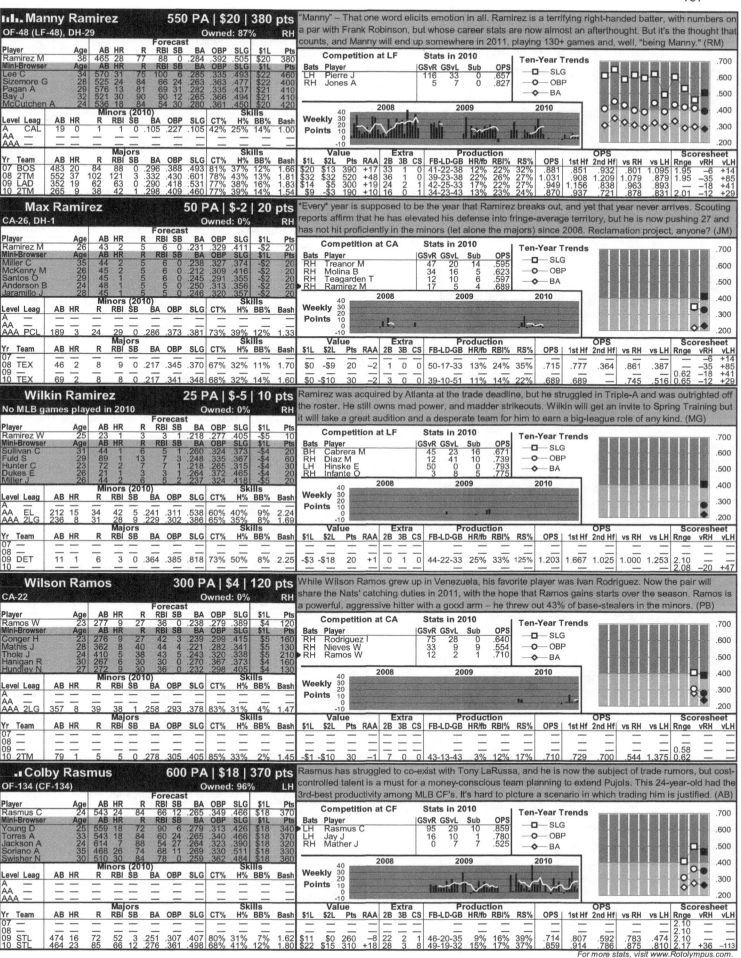

## Manny Ramirez — 550 PA | $20 | 380 pts
OF-48 (LF-48), DH-29 — Owned: 87% — RH

"Manny" – That one word elicits emotion in all. Ramirez is a terrifying right-handed batter, with numbers on a par with Frank Robinson, but whose career stats are now almost an afterthought. But it's the thought that counts, and Manny will end up somewhere in 2011, playing 130+ games and, well, "being Manny." (RM)

### Forecast
| Player | Age | AB | HR | R | RBI | SB | BA | OBP | SLG | $1L | Pts |
|---|---|---|---|---|---|---|---|---|---|---|---|
| Ramirez M | 38 | 465 | 28 | 77 | 88 | 0 | .284 | .392 | .505 | $20 | 380 |
| Mini-Browser | Age | AB | HR | R | RBI | SB | BA | OBP | SLG | $1L | Pts |
| Lee C | 34 | 570 | 31 | 75 | 100 | 6 | .285 | .335 | .493 | $22 | 460 |
| Sizemore G | 28 | 525 | 24 | 84 | 66 | 24 | .263 | .363 | .477 | $22 | 400 |
| Pagan A | 29 | 576 | 13 | 81 | 69 | 31 | .282 | .335 | .437 | $21 | 410 |
| Bay J | 32 | 521 | 30 | 90 | 90 | 12 | .265 | .364 | .494 | $21 | 410 |
| McCutchen A | 24 | 536 | 18 | 84 | 54 | 30 | .280 | .361 | .450 | $20 | 420 |

### Minors (2010)
| Level | Leag | AB | HR | R | RBI | SB | BA | OBP | SLG | CT% | H% | BB% | Bash |
|---|---|---|---|---|---|---|---|---|---|---|---|---|---|
| A | CAL | 19 | 0 | 1 | 1 | 0 | .105 | .227 | .105 | 42% | 25% | 14% | 1.00 |
| AA | — | | | | | | | | | | | | |
| AAA | — | | | | | | | | | | | | |

### Majors / Skills
| Yr | Team | AB | HR | R | RBI | SB | BA | OBP | SLG | CT% | H% | BB% | Bash |
|---|---|---|---|---|---|---|---|---|---|---|---|---|---|
| 07 | BOS | 483 | 20 | 84 | 88 | 0 | .296 | .388 | .493 | 81% | 37% | 12% | 1.66 |
| 08 | 2TM | 552 | 37 | 102 | 121 | 3 | .332 | .430 | .601 | 78% | 43% | 13% | 1.81 |
| 09 | LAD | 352 | 19 | 62 | 63 | 0 | .290 | .418 | .531 | 77% | 38% | 16% | 1.83 |
| 10 | 2TM | 265 | 9 | 38 | 42 | 1 | .298 | .409 | .460 | 77% | 39% | 14% | 1.54 |

### Competition at LF — Stats in 2010
| Bats | Player | GSvR | GSvL | Sub | OPS |
|---|---|---|---|---|---|
| LH | Pierre J | 116 | 33 | 0 | .657 |
| RH | Jones A | 5 | 7 | 0 | .827 |

Ten-Year Trends: SLG, OBP, BA

### Value / Extra / Production / OPS / Scoresheet
| Yr | $1L | $2L | Pts | RAA | 2B | 3B | CS | FB-LD-GB | HR/fb | RBI% | RS% | OPS | 1st Hf | 2nd Hf | vs RH | vs LH | Rnge | vRH | vLH |
|---|---|---|---|---|---|---|---|---|---|---|---|---|---|---|---|---|---|---|---|
| 07 | $20 | $13 | 390 | +17 | 33 | 1 | 0 | 41-22-38 | 12% | 22% | 32% | .881 | .851 | .932 | .801 | 1.095 | 1.95 | -6 | +14 |
| 08 | $32 | $32 | 520 | +48 | 36 | 1 | 0 | 39-23-38 | 22% | 26% | 27% | 1.031 | .908 | 1.209 | 1.079 | .879 | 1.95 | -35 | +85 |
| 09 | $14 | $5 | 300 | +19 | 24 | 2 | 1 | 42-25-33 | 17% | 22% | 27% | .949 | 1.156 | .838 | .963 | .893 | — | -18 | +41 |
| 10 | $9 | -$3 | 190 | +10 | 16 | 1 | 0 | 34-23-43 | 13% | 23% | 24% | .870 | .937 | .721 | .878 | .831 | 2.01 | -12 | +29 |

## Max Ramirez — 50 PA | $-2 | 20 pts
CA-26, DH-1 — Owned: 0% — RH

"Every" year is supposed to be the year that Ramirez breaks out, and yet that year never arrives. Scouting reports affirm that he has elevated his defense into fringe-average territory, but he is now pushing 27 and has not hit proficiently in the minors (let alone the majors) since 2008. Reclamation project, anyone? (JM)

### Forecast
| Player | Age | AB | HR | R | RBI | SB | BA | OBP | SLG | $1L | Pts |
|---|---|---|---|---|---|---|---|---|---|---|---|
| Ramirez M | 26 | 43 | 2 | 5 | 6 | 0 | .231 | .329 | .411 | -$2 | 20 |
| Mini-Browser | Age | AB | HR | R | RBI | SB | BA | OBP | SLG | $1L | Pts |
| Miller C | 35 | 44 | 2 | 5 | 6 | 0 | .238 | .327 | .374 | -$2 | 20 |
| McKenry M | 26 | 45 | 2 | 5 | 6 | 0 | .212 | .309 | .416 | -$2 | 20 |
| Santos O | 29 | 45 | 1 | 5 | 6 | 0 | .245 | .291 | .355 | -$2 | 20 |
| Anderson B | 24 | 48 | 1 | 5 | 5 | 0 | .250 | .313 | .356 | -$2 | 20 |
| Jaramillo J | 28 | 45 | 1 | 5 | 5 | 0 | .246 | .320 | .357 | -$2 | 20 |

### Minors (2010)
| Level | Leag | AB | HR | R | RBI | SB | BA | OBP | SLG | CT% | H% | BB% | Bash |
|---|---|---|---|---|---|---|---|---|---|---|---|---|---|
| A | — | | | | | | | | | | | | |
| AA | — | | | | | | | | | | | | |
| AAA | PCL | 189 | 3 | 24 | 29 | 0 | .286 | .373 | .381 | 73% | 39% | 12% | 1.33 |

### Majors / Skills
| Yr | Team | AB | HR | R | RBI | SB | BA | OBP | SLG | CT% | H% | BB% | Bash |
|---|---|---|---|---|---|---|---|---|---|---|---|---|---|
| 07 | — | | | | | | | | | | | | |
| 08 | TEX | 46 | 2 | 8 | 8 | 0 | .217 | .345 | .370 | 67% | 32% | 11% | 1.70 |
| 09 | — | | | | | | | | | | | | |
| 10 | TEX | 69 | 2 | 8 | 8 | 0 | .217 | .341 | .348 | 68% | 32% | 14% | 1.60 |

### Competition at CA — Stats in 2010
| Bats | Player | GSvR | GSvL | Sub | OPS |
|---|---|---|---|---|---|
| RH | Treanor M | 47 | 20 | 14 | .595 |
| RH | Molina B | 34 | 16 | 5 | .623 |
| RH | Teagarden T | 12 | 10 | 6 | .597 |
| RH | Ramirez M | 17 | 5 | 4 | .689 |

### Value / Extra / Production / OPS / Scoresheet
| Yr | $1L | $2L | Pts | RAA | 2B | 3B | CS | FB-LD-GB | HR/fb | RBI% | RS% | OPS | 1st Hf | 2nd Hf | vs RH | vs LH | Rnge | vRH | vLH |
|---|---|---|---|---|---|---|---|---|---|---|---|---|---|---|---|---|---|---|---|
| 07 | — | | | | | | | | | | | | | | | | | -6 | +14 |
| 08 | $0 | -$9 | 20 | -2 | 1 | 0 | 0 | 50-17-33 | 13% | 24% | 35% | .715 | .777 | .364 | .861 | .387 | | -35 | +85 |
| 09 | | | | | | | | | | | | | | | | | 0.62 | -18 | +41 |
| 10 | $0 | -$10 | 30 | -2 | 1 | 0 | 0 | 39-10-51 | 11% | 14% | 22% | .689 | .689 | — | .745 | .516 | 0.65 | -12 | +29 |

## Wilkin Ramirez — 25 PA | $-5 | 10 pts
No MLB games played in 2010 — Owned: 0% — RH

Ramirez was acquired by Atlanta at the trade deadline, but he struggled in Triple-A and was outrighted off the roster. He still owns mad power, and madder strikeouts. Wilkin will get an invite to Spring Training but it will take a great audition and a desperate team for him to earn a big-league role of any kind. (MG)

### Forecast
| Player | Age | AB | HR | R | RBI | SB | BA | OBP | SLG | $1L | Pts |
|---|---|---|---|---|---|---|---|---|---|---|---|
| Ramirez W | 25 | 23 | 1 | 3 | 3 | 1 | .218 | .277 | .405 | -$5 | 10 |
| Mini-Browser | Age | AB | HR | R | RBI | SB | BA | OBP | SLG | $1L | Pts |
| Sullivan C | 31 | 44 | 1 | 6 | 5 | 1 | .260 | .324 | .373 | -$4 | 20 |
| Fuld S | 29 | 89 | 1 | 13 | 7 | 3 | .248 | .335 | .367 | -$4 | 60 |
| Hunter C | 23 | 72 | 2 | 7 | 7 | 1 | .218 | .265 | .315 | -$4 | 30 |
| Dukes E | 26 | 21 | 1 | 3 | 3 | 1 | .264 | .372 | .465 | -$4 | 20 |
| Miller J | 26 | 44 | 2 | 6 | 5 | 2 | .237 | .320 | .418 | -$5 | 20 |

### Minors (2010)
| Level | Leag | AB | HR | R | RBI | SB | BA | OBP | SLG | CT% | H% | BB% | Bash |
|---|---|---|---|---|---|---|---|---|---|---|---|---|---|
| A | — | | | | | | | | | | | | |
| AA | EL | 212 | 15 | 34 | 42 | 5 | .241 | .311 | .538 | 60% | 40% | 9% | 2.24 |
| AAA | 2LG | 236 | 8 | 31 | 28 | 9 | .229 | .302 | .386 | 65% | 35% | 8% | 1.69 |

### Majors / Skills
| Yr | Team | AB | HR | R | RBI | SB | BA | OBP | SLG | CT% | H% | BB% | Bash |
|---|---|---|---|---|---|---|---|---|---|---|---|---|---|
| 07 | — | | | | | | | | | | | | |
| 08 | — | | | | | | | | | | | | |
| 09 | DET | 11 | 1 | 6 | 3 | 0 | .364 | .385 | .818 | 73% | 50% | 8% | 2.25 |
| 10 | — | | | | | | | | | | | | |

### Competition at LF — Stats in 2010
| Bats | Player | GSvR | GSvL | Sub | OPS |
|---|---|---|---|---|---|
| BH | Cabrera M | 45 | 23 | 16 | .671 |
| RH | Diaz M | 12 | 41 | 10 | .739 |
| LH | Hinske E | 50 | 0 | 0 | .793 |
| RH | Infante O | 3 | 8 | 5 | .775 |

### Value / Extra / Production / OPS / Scoresheet
| Yr | $1L | $2L | Pts | RAA | 2B | 3B | CS | FB-LD-GB | HR/fb | RBI% | RS% | OPS | 1st Hf | 2nd Hf | vs RH | vs LH | Rnge | vRH | vLH |
|---|---|---|---|---|---|---|---|---|---|---|---|---|---|---|---|---|---|---|---|
| 07 | — | | | | | | | | | | | | | | | | | | |
| 08 | — | | | | | | | | | | | | | | | | | | |
| 09 | -$3 | -$18 | 20 | +1 | 0 | 1 | 0 | 44-22-33 | 25% | 33% | 125% | 1.203 | 1.667 | 1.025 | 1.000 | 1.253 | 2.10 | | |
| 10 | | | | | | | | | | | | | | | | | 2.08 | -20 | +47 |

## Wilson Ramos — 300 PA | $4 | 120 pts
CA-22 — Owned: 0% — RH

While Wilson Ramos grew up in Venezuela, his favorite player was Ivan Rodriguez. Now the pair will share the Nats' catching duties in 2011, with the hope that Ramos gains starts over the season. Ramos is a powerful, aggressive hitter with a good arm – he threw out 43% of base-stealers in the minors. (PB)

### Forecast
| Player | Age | AB | HR | R | RBI | SB | BA | OBP | SLG | $1L | Pts |
|---|---|---|---|---|---|---|---|---|---|---|---|
| Ramos W | 23 | 277 | 9 | 27 | 36 | 0 | .238 | .279 | .389 | $4 | 120 |
| Mini-Browser | Age | AB | HR | R | RBI | SB | BA | OBP | SLG | $1L | Pts |
| Conger H | 23 | 276 | 9 | 27 | 42 | 3 | .239 | .299 | .415 | $5 | 160 |
| Mathis J | 28 | 362 | 8 | 40 | 44 | 4 | .221 | .282 | .341 | $5 | 130 |
| Thole J | 24 | 410 | 8 | 38 | 43 | 5 | .243 | .320 | .338 | $5 | 210 |
| Hanigan R | 30 | 267 | 6 | 30 | 30 | 0 | .270 | .367 | .373 | $4 | 160 |
| Hundley N | 27 | 272 | 9 | 30 | 36 | 0 | .232 | .298 | .405 | $4 | 130 |

### Minors (2010)
| Level | Leag | AB | HR | R | RBI | SB | BA | OBP | SLG | CT% | H% | BB% | Bash |
|---|---|---|---|---|---|---|---|---|---|---|---|---|---|
| A | — | | | | | | | | | | | | |
| AA | — | | | | | | | | | | | | |
| AAA | 2LG | 357 | 8 | 39 | 38 | 1 | .258 | .293 | .378 | 83% | 31% | 4% | 1.47 |

### Majors / Skills
| Yr | Team | AB | HR | R | RBI | SB | BA | OBP | SLG | CT% | H% | BB% | Bash |
|---|---|---|---|---|---|---|---|---|---|---|---|---|---|
| 07 | — | | | | | | | | | | | | |
| 08 | — | | | | | | | | | | | | |
| 09 | — | | | | | | | | | | | | |
| 10 | 2TM | 79 | 1 | 8 | 8 | 0 | .278 | .305 | .405 | 85% | 33% | 2% | 1.45 |

### Competition at CA — Stats in 2010
| Bats | Player | GSvR | GSvL | Sub | OPS |
|---|---|---|---|---|---|
| RH | Rodriguez I | 75 | 28 | 0 | .640 |
| RH | Nieves W | 33 | 9 | 9 | .554 |
| RH | Ramos W | 12 | 2 | 1 | .710 |

### Value / Extra / Production / OPS / Scoresheet
| Yr | $1L | $2L | Pts | RAA | 2B | 3B | CS | FB-LD-GB | HR/fb | RBI% | RS% | OPS | 1st Hf | 2nd Hf | vs RH | vs LH | Rnge | vRH | vLH |
|---|---|---|---|---|---|---|---|---|---|---|---|---|---|---|---|---|---|---|---|
| 07 | — | | | | | | | | | | | | | | | | | | |
| 08 | — | | | | | | | | | | | | | | | | | | |
| 09 | | | | | | | | | | | | | | | | | 0.58 | | |
| 10 | 2TM | -$1 | -$18 | 20 | | | | 43-13-43 | 3% | 12% | 17% | .710 | .729 | .700 | .544 | 1.375 | 0.62 | | |

## Colby Rasmus — 600 PA | $18 | 370 pts
OF-134 (CF-134) — Owned: 96% — LH

Rasmus has struggled to co-exist with Tony LaRussa, and he is now the subject of trade rumors, but cost-controlled talent is a must for a money-conscious team planning to extend Pujols. This 24-year-old had the 3rd-best productivity among MLB CF's. It's hard to picture a scenario in which trading him is justified. (AB)

### Forecast
| Player | Age | AB | HR | R | RBI | SB | BA | OBP | SLG | $1L | Pts |
|---|---|---|---|---|---|---|---|---|---|---|---|
| Rasmus C | 24 | 543 | 24 | 84 | 66 | 12 | .265 | .349 | .466 | $18 | 370 |
| Mini-Browser | Age | AB | HR | R | RBI | SB | BA | OBP | SLG | $1L | Pts |
| Young D | 25 | 559 | 18 | 72 | 90 | 6 | .279 | .313 | .426 | $18 | 340 |
| Torres A | 33 | 543 | 18 | 84 | 60 | 24 | .265 | .340 | .466 | $18 | 370 |
| Jackson A | 24 | 614 | 7 | 88 | 54 | 27 | .264 | .323 | .390 | $18 | 320 |
| Soriano A | 35 | 468 | 26 | 74 | 68 | 11 | .269 | .330 | .511 | $18 | 330 |
| Swisher N | 30 | 510 | 30 | 84 | 78 | 0 | .259 | .362 | .484 | $18 | 360 |

### Minors (2010)
| Level | Leag | AB | HR | R | RBI | SB | BA | OBP | SLG | CT% | H% | BB% | Bash |
|---|---|---|---|---|---|---|---|---|---|---|---|---|---|
| A | — | | | | | | | | | | | | |
| AA | — | | | | | | | | | | | | |
| AAA | — | | | | | | | | | | | | |

### Majors / Skills
| Yr | Team | AB | HR | R | RBI | SB | BA | OBP | SLG | CT% | H% | BB% | Bash |
|---|---|---|---|---|---|---|---|---|---|---|---|---|---|
| 07 | — | | | | | | | | | | | | |
| 08 | — | | | | | | | | | | | | |
| 09 | STL | 474 | 16 | 72 | 52 | 3 | .251 | .307 | .407 | 80% | 31% | 7% | 1.62 |
| 10 | STL | 464 | 23 | 85 | 66 | 12 | .276 | .361 | .498 | 68% | 41% | 12% | 1.80 |

### Competition at CF — Stats in 2010
| Bats | Player | GSvR | GSvL | Sub | OPS |
|---|---|---|---|---|---|
| LH | Rasmus C | 95 | 29 | 10 | .859 |
| LH | Jay J | 16 | 10 | 7 | .780 |
| RH | Mather J | 0 | 7 | 7 | .525 |

### Value / Extra / Production / OPS / Scoresheet
| Yr | $1L | $2L | Pts | RAA | 2B | 3B | CS | FB-LD-GB | HR/fb | RBI% | RS% | OPS | 1st Hf | 2nd Hf | vs RH | vs LH | Rnge | vRH | vLH |
|---|---|---|---|---|---|---|---|---|---|---|---|---|---|---|---|---|---|---|---|
| 07 | — | | | | | | | | | | | | | | | | 2.10 | | |
| 08 | — | | | | | | | | | | | | | | | | 2.10 | | |
| 09 | STL | $11 | $0 | 260 | -8 | 22 | 2 | 1 | 46-20-35 | 9% | 16% | 39% | .714 | .807 | .592 | .783 | .474 | 2.10 | |
| 10 | STL | $22 | $15 | 310 | +18 | 28 | 3 | 8 | 49-19-32 | 15% | 17% | 37% | .859 | .914 | .786 | .875 | .810 | 2.17 | +36 | -113 |

## Josh Reddick — 150 PA | $-2 | 70 pts
OF-25 (RF-15, CF-6, LF-6), DH-1  Owned: 0%  LH

Despite going on an absolute tear in Triple-A in the second half (.351/.372/.627), Reddick is quickly being squeezed out in Boston. If he stays in the organization, he'll fight for table scraps as a back-up OF. Given his flashy offense, Reddick would be best served by playing full-time for a second-tier club. (EB)

**Forecast**

| Player | Age | AB | HR | R | RBI | SB | BA | OBP | SLG | $1L | Pts |
|---|---|---|---|---|---|---|---|---|---|---|---|
| Reddick J | 24 | 136 | 6 | 15 | 17 | 2 | .231 | .277 | .440 | -$2 | 70 |
| Mini-Browser | Age | AB | HR | R | RBI | SB | BA | OBP | SLG | $1L | Pts |
| Wells C | 26 | 138 | 8 | 17 | 17 | 3 | .229 | .302 | .459 | -$1 | 80 |
| Young D | 28 | 142 | 5 | 18 | 18 | 0 | .265 | .323 | .429 | -$1 | 80 |
| Gomez C | 25 | 113 | 1 | 16 | 11 | 8 | .244 | .299 | .360 | -$1 | 60 |
| Dickerson C | 28 | 108 | 4 | 15 | 11 | 5 | .244 | .343 | .413 | -$1 | 60 |
| Repko J | 30 | 130 | 3 | 17 | 12 | 6 | .243 | .315 | .389 | -$1 | 60 |

**Minors (2010) / Skills**

| Level | Leag | AB | HR | R | RBI | SB | BA | OBP | SLG | CT% | H% | BB% | Bash |
|---|---|---|---|---|---|---|---|---|---|---|---|---|---|
| A | — | | | | | | | | | | | | |
| AA | — | | | | | | | | | | | | |
| AAA | IL | 451 | 18 | 59 | 65 | 4 | .266 | .301 | .466 | 84% | 32% | 5% | 1.75 |

**Majors / Skills**

| Yr | Team | AB | HR | R | RBI | SB | BA | OBP | SLG | CT% | H% | BB% | Bash |
|---|---|---|---|---|---|---|---|---|---|---|---|---|---|
| 07 | — | | | | | | | | | | | | |
| 08 | — | | | | | | | | | | | | |
| 09 | BOS | 59 | 2 | 5 | 4 | 0 | .169 | .210 | .339 | 71% | 24% | 3% | 2.00 |
| 10 | BOS | 62 | 1 | 5 | 5 | 1 | .194 | .206 | .323 | 76% | 26% | 2% | 1.67 |

**Competition at RF / Stats in 2010**

| Bats | Player | GSvR | GSvL | Sub | OPS |
|---|---|---|---|---|---|
| LH | Drew J | 90 | 37 | 6 | .793 |
| RH | McDonald D | 6 | 19 | 9 | .766 |
| LH | Reddick J | 7 | 0 | 8 | .529 |

**Value / Extra / Production / OPS / Scoresheet**

| $1L | $2L | Pts | RAA | 2B | 3B | CS | FB-LD-GB | HR/fb | RBI% | RS% | OPS | 1st Hf | 2nd Hf | vs RH | vs LH | Rnge | vRH | vLH |
|---|---|---|---|---|---|---|---|---|---|---|---|---|---|---|---|---|---|---|
| -$4 | -$20 | 10 | −6 | 4 | 0 | 0 | 52-17-31 | 9% | 8% | 27% | .549 | | .549 | .530 | .733 | 2.10 | | |
| -$3 | -$20 | 50 | −8 | 5 | 0 | 0 | 43-13-45 | 5% | 10% | 33% | .522 | .568 | .488 | 1.000 | 2.09 | +20 | −61 |

---

## Jeremy Reed — 50 PA | $-5 | 30 pts
OF-9 (LF-6, RF-3), 1B-2  Owned: 0%  LH

Reed in 2010 had a very good spring, but he lost the numbers game and got shipped to Triple-A, where he hit pretty well. Called up to Toronto as an injury replacement, he exhibited good defense but struggled with the bat, and he ended the year back in Triple-A with the White Sox. He'd be a fine 5th OF in the NL. (MH)

**Forecast**

| Player | Age | AB | HR | R | RBI | SB | BA | OBP | SLG | $1L | Pts |
|---|---|---|---|---|---|---|---|---|---|---|---|
| Reed J | 29 | 47 | 1 | 5 | 5 | 1 | .254 | .308 | .379 | -$5 | 30 |
| Mini-Browser | Age | AB | HR | R | RBI | SB | BA | OBP | SLG | $1L | Pts |
| Ramirez W | 25 | 23 | 1 | 3 | 3 | 1 | .218 | .277 | .405 | -$5 | 10 |
| Duda L | 25 | 43 | 2 | 5 | 5 | 0 | .208 | .298 | .371 | -$5 | 20 |
| Buck T | 27 | 46 | 2 | 6 | 5 | 1 | .249 | .328 | .414 | -$5 | 20 |
| Boggs B | 28 | 44 | 2 | 5 | 5 | 1 | .228 | .330 | .411 | -$5 | 20 |
| Golson G | 25 | 44 | 1 | 5 | 2 | 2 | .214 | .242 | .457 | -$5 | 20 |

**Minors (2010) / Skills**

| Level | Leag | AB | HR | R | RBI | SB | BA | OBP | SLG | CT% | H% | BB% | Bash |
|---|---|---|---|---|---|---|---|---|---|---|---|---|---|
| A | — | | | | | | | | | | | | |
| AA | — | | | | | | | | | | | | |
| AAA | 2LG | 323 | 8 | 49 | 36 | 3 | .279 | .342 | .412 | 85% | 33% | 9% | 1.48 |

**Majors / Skills**

| Yr | Team | AB | HR | R | RBI | SB | BA | OBP | SLG | CT% | H% | BB% | Bash |
|---|---|---|---|---|---|---|---|---|---|---|---|---|---|
| 07 | SEA | 17 | 0 | 2 | 0 | 0 | .176 | .176 | .294 | 82% | 21% | 0% | 1.67 |
| 08 | SEA | 286 | 2 | 30 | 31 | 2 | .269 | .314 | .360 | 87% | 31% | 6% | 1.34 |
| 09 | NYM | 161 | 0 | 9 | 9 | 0 | .242 | .301 | .304 | 78% | 31% | 8% | 1.26 |
| 10 | TOR | 21 | 0 | 1 | 3 | 1 | .143 | .217 | .286 | 62% | 23% | 9% | 2.00 |

**Competition at LF / Stats in 2010**

| Bats | Player | GSvR | GSvL | Sub | OPS |
|---|---|---|---|---|---|
| LH | Lewis F | 67 | 15 | 2 | .745 |
| LH | Snider T | 41 | 8 | 4 | .767 |
| LH | Lind A | 10 | 6 | 0 | .712 |
| LH | Wise D | 7 | 0 | 3 | .675 |

**Value / Extra / Production / OPS / Scoresheet**

| $1L | $2L | Pts | RAA | 2B | 3B | CS | FB-LD-GB | HR/fb | RBI% | RS% | OPS | 1st Hf | 2nd Hf | vs RH | vs LH | Rnge | vRH | vLH |
|---|---|---|---|---|---|---|---|---|---|---|---|---|---|---|---|---|---|---|
| -$4 | -$20 | 0 | −2 | 0 | 0 | 0 | 57-7-36 | 0% | 0% | 67% | .471 | | .471 | .471 | | 2.19 | +31 | −109 |
| -$3 | -$10 | 140 | −12 | 18 | 1 | 3 | 28-20-52 | 3% | 20% | 29% | .674 | .674 | .674 | .717 | .231 | 2.13 | +28 | −97 |
| -$4 | -$19 | 40 | −11 | 6 | 2 | 3 | 24-19-57 | 0% | 11% | 17% | .605 | .686 | .508 | .589 | .855 | 2.13 | +23 | −83 |
| -$4 | -$20 | 10 | −2 | 0 | 0 | 0 | 38-23-38 | 20% | 17% | 0% | .503 | .503 | | .490 | .500 | 2.13 | +18 | −68 |

---

## Nolan Reimold — 275 PA | $4 | 150 pts
OF-23 (LF-22, RF-2), DH-12  Owned: 33%  RH

Reimold spent most of 2010 learning first base at Triple-A, and he should get a shot at Baltimore's 1B job now that he's healthy (well, as healthy as he gets). As for his hitting, he has kept a rein on his strikeouts, and with any passable H%, he could reach a .350 OBP. He is still capable of backing up in left field. (BJ)

**Forecast**

| Player | Age | AB | HR | R | RBI | SB | BA | OBP | SLG | $1L | Pts |
|---|---|---|---|---|---|---|---|---|---|---|---|
| Reimold N | 27 | 237 | 11 | 30 | 30 | 3 | .255 | .335 | .465 | $4 | 150 |
| Mini-Browser | Age | AB | HR | R | RBI | SB | BA | OBP | SLG | $1L | Pts |
| Blanco G | 27 | 346 | 4 | 48 | 28 | 12 | .254 | .359 | .332 | $5 | 200 |
| Milledge L | 25 | 330 | 7 | 39 | 35 | 11 | .276 | .337 | .408 | $5 | 200 |
| Venable W | 28 | 304 | 10 | 41 | 37 | 10 | .235 | .309 | .391 | $4 | 170 |
| Heisey C | 26 | 275 | 12 | 39 | 30 | 9 | .240 | .309 | .434 | $4 | 180 |
| Rowand A | 33 | 279 | 9 | 36 | 36 | 3 | .269 | .331 | .427 | $4 | 160 |

**Minors (2010) / Skills**

| Level | Leag | AB | HR | R | RBI | SB | BA | OBP | SLG | CT% | H% | BB% | Bash |
|---|---|---|---|---|---|---|---|---|---|---|---|---|---|
| A | — | | | | | | | | | | | | |
| AA | — | | | | | | | | | | | | |
| AAA | IL | 337 | 10 | 52 | 37 | 9 | .249 | .364 | .374 | 82% | 30% | 13% | 1.50 |

**Majors / Skills**

| Yr | Team | AB | HR | R | RBI | SB | BA | OBP | SLG | CT% | H% | BB% | Bash |
|---|---|---|---|---|---|---|---|---|---|---|---|---|---|
| 07 | — | | | | | | | | | | | | |
| 08 | — | | | | | | | | | | | | |
| 09 | BAL | 358 | 15 | 49 | 45 | 8 | .279 | .365 | .466 | 78% | 36% | 11% | 1.67 |
| 10 | BAL | 116 | 3 | 9 | 14 | 0 | .207 | .282 | .328 | 78% | 27% | 9% | 1.58 |

**Competition at LF / Stats in 2010**

| Bats | Player | GSvR | GSvL | Sub | OPS |
|---|---|---|---|---|---|
| LH | Pie F | 55 | 12 | 3 | .718 |
| LH | Patterson C | 36 | 17 | 3 | .721 |
| RH | Reimold N | 11 | 10 | 1 | .610 |
| LH | Scott L | 6 | 7 | 1 | .902 |

**Value / Extra / Production / OPS / Scoresheet**

| $1L | $2L | Pts | RAA | 2B | 3B | CS | FB-LD-GB | HR/fb | RBI% | RS% | OPS | 1st Hf | 2nd Hf | vs RH | vs LH | Rnge | vRH | vLH |
|---|---|---|---|---|---|---|---|---|---|---|---|---|---|---|---|---|---|---|
| | | | | | | | | | | | | | | | | 2.10 | | |
| | | | | | | | | | | | | | | | | 2.10 | | |
| $11 | $0 | 240 | +9 | 18 | 2 | 2 | 37-14-48 | 14% | 17% | 25% | .831 | .776 | .880 | .841 | .815 | 2.10 | | |
| -$3 | -$18 | 50 | −7 | 5 | 0 | 0 | 39-12-49 | 8% | 14% | 18% | .610 | .639 | .532 | .519 | .735 | 2.08 | −14 | +31 |

---

## Edgar Renteria — 225 PA | $2 | 130 pts
SS-68  Owned: 6%  RH

Renteria has hinted at retirement, as injuries to his groin, hamstring, and biceps battered him in 2010. The Giants will not pick up his $10.5M option, but the 34-year-old could try out at shortstop for the Tigers, or he could make a victory lap with the Marlins. (PB)

**Forecast**

| Player | Age | AB | HR | R | RBI | SB | BA | OBP | SLG | $1L | Pts |
|---|---|---|---|---|---|---|---|---|---|---|---|
| Renteria E | 35 | 209 | 5 | 29 | 23 | 5 | .280 | .339 | .392 | $2 | 130 |
| Mini-Browser | Age | AB | HR | R | RBI | SB | BA | OBP | SLG | $1L | Pts |
| Cedeno R | 28 | 467 | 10 | 50 | 50 | 10 | .257 | .305 | .384 | $8 | 230 |
| Ryan B | 29 | 460 | 5 | 60 | 35 | 15 | .250 | .309 | .340 | $7 | 260 |
| Cabrera O | 36 | 366 | 4 | 48 | 38 | 6 | .273 | .316 | .365 | $6 | 220 |
| Izturis C | 31 | 458 | 0 | 45 | 30 | 15 | .262 | .306 | .319 | $4 | 240 |
| Hairston J | 34 | 289 | 6 | 37 | 31 | 6 | .247 | .310 | .369 | $3 | 170 |

**Minors (2010) / Skills**

| Level | Leag | AB | HR | R | RBI | SB | BA | OBP | SLG | CT% | H% | BB% | Bash |
|---|---|---|---|---|---|---|---|---|---|---|---|---|---|
| A | — | | | | | | | | | | | | |
| AA | — | | | | | | | | | | | | |
| AAA | — | | | | | | | | | | | | |

**Majors / Skills**

| Yr | Team | AB | HR | R | RBI | SB | BA | OBP | SLG | CT% | H% | BB% | Bash |
|---|---|---|---|---|---|---|---|---|---|---|---|---|---|
| 07 | ATL | 494 | 12 | 87 | 57 | 11 | .332 | .390 | .470 | 84% | 39% | 8% | 1.41 |
| 08 | DET | 503 | 10 | 69 | 55 | 6 | .270 | .317 | .382 | 87% | 31% | 7% | 1.41 |
| 09 | SF | 460 | 5 | 50 | 48 | 7 | .250 | .307 | .328 | 85% | 29% | 8% | 1.31 |
| 10 | SF | 243 | 3 | 26 | 22 | 3 | .276 | .332 | .374 | 82% | 34% | 8% | 1.36 |

**Competition at SS / Stats in 2010**

| Bats | Player | GSvR | GSvL | Sub | OPS |
|---|---|---|---|---|---|
| RH | Uribe J | 78 | 23 | 2 | .749 |
| RH | Renteria E | 40 | 22 | 6 | .707 |

**Value / Extra / Production / OPS / Scoresheet**

| $1L | $2L | Pts | RAA | 2B | 3B | CS | FB-LD-GB | HR/fb | RBI% | RS% | OPS | 1st Hf | 2nd Hf | vs RH | vs LH | Rnge | vRH | vLH |
|---|---|---|---|---|---|---|---|---|---|---|---|---|---|---|---|---|---|---|
| $21 | $13 | 360 | +37 | 30 | 1 | 2 | 31-23-46 | 9% | 19% | 38% | .860 | .864 | .850 | .827 | .918 | 4.71 | −35 | +90 |
| $12 | $2 | 300 | +2 | 22 | 2 | 3 | 32-22-46 | 7% | 18% | 36% | .699 | .627 | .812 | .598 | 1.004 | 4.71 | −30 | +77 |
| $6 | -$6 | 230 | −10 | 19 | 2 | 4 | 31-21-48 | 4% | 20% | 30% | .635 | .643 | .622 | .637 | .629 | 4.68 | −44 | +104 |
| $2 | -$11 | 120 | +2 | 11 | 2 | 0 | 37-16-48 | 4% | 15% | 27% | .707 | .711 | .701 | .671 | .794 | 4.71 | −33 | +85 |

---

## Jason Repko — 150 PA | $-1 | 60 pts
OF-48 (RF-39, CF-6, LF-6), DH-3  Owned: 0%  RH

Repko will probably never hit enough to be a major asset, but his outstanding defense in all three OF spots provided a lot of value to a Twins team that sported one of the league's most range-challenged alignments in 2010. It would not be a surprise to see Repko back in a 4th OF role in Minnesota. (NN)

**Forecast**

| Player | Age | AB | HR | R | RBI | SB | BA | OBP | SLG | $1L | Pts |
|---|---|---|---|---|---|---|---|---|---|---|---|
| Repko J | 30 | 130 | 3 | 17 | 12 | 6 | .243 | .315 | .389 | -$1 | 60 |
| Mini-Browser | Age | AB | HR | R | RBI | SB | BA | OBP | SLG | $1L | Pts |
| Michaels J | 34 | 140 | 5 | 18 | 20 | 2 | .258 | .323 | .427 | -$1 | 90 |
| Wells C | 26 | 138 | 8 | 17 | 17 | 3 | .229 | .302 | .459 | -$1 | 80 |
| Young D | 28 | 142 | 5 | 18 | 18 | 0 | .265 | .323 | .429 | -$1 | 80 |
| Gomez C | 25 | 113 | 1 | 16 | 11 | 8 | .244 | .299 | .360 | -$1 | 60 |
| Dickerson C | 28 | 108 | 4 | 15 | 11 | 5 | .244 | .343 | .413 | -$1 | 60 |

**Minors (2010) / Skills**

| Level | Leag | AB | HR | R | RBI | SB | BA | OBP | SLG | CT% | H% | BB% | Bash |
|---|---|---|---|---|---|---|---|---|---|---|---|---|---|
| A | — | | | | | | | | | | | | |
| AA | — | | | | | | | | | | | | |
| AAA | IL | 228 | 6 | 38 | 28 | 10 | .281 | .368 | .412 | 79% | 36% | 11% | 1.47 |

**Majors / Skills**

| Yr | Team | AB | HR | R | RBI | SB | BA | OBP | SLG | CT% | H% | BB% | Bash |
|---|---|---|---|---|---|---|---|---|---|---|---|---|---|
| 07 | — | | | | | | | | | | | | |
| 08 | LAD | 18 | 0 | 0 | 1 | 0 | .167 | .250 | .222 | 50% | 33% | 10% | 1.33 |
| 09 | LAD | 1 | 0 | 1 | 1 | 0 | .000 | .143 | .000 | 60% | 0% | 0% | NA |
| 10 | MIN | 127 | 3 | 19 | 9 | 3 | .228 | .324 | .346 | 70% | 33% | 9% | 1.52 |

**Competition at RF / Stats in 2010**

| Bats | Player | GSvR | GSvL | Sub | OPS |
|---|---|---|---|---|---|
| LH | Kubel J | 60 | 20 | 3 | .750 |
| RH | Cuddyer M | 43 | 23 | 0 | .753 |
| RH | Repko J | 9 | 16 | 14 | .671 |

**Value / Extra / Production / OPS / Scoresheet**

| $1L | $2L | Pts | RAA | 2B | 3B | CS | FB-LD-GB | HR/fb | RBI% | RS% | OPS | 1st Hf | 2nd Hf | vs RH | vs LH | Rnge | vRH | vLH |
|---|---|---|---|---|---|---|---|---|---|---|---|---|---|---|---|---|---|---|
| | | | | | | | | | | | | | | | | 2.13 | −18 | +41 |
| -$5 | -$19 | 0 | −2 | 1 | 0 | 0 | 44-11-44 | 0% | 0% | 0% | .472 | .000 | .748 | .277 | 1.000 | 2.10 | −26 | +62 |
| -$5 | -$20 | 0 | −1 | 0 | 0 | 0 | 25-0-75 | 0% | 14% | 100% | .143 | | .143 | .167 | .000 | 2.09 | −24 | +59 |
| -$1 | -$16 | 50 | −8 | 6 | 0 | 2 | 47-15-38 | 8% | 8% | 36% | .671 | .667 | .671 | .767 | .523 | 2.10 | −19 | +47 |

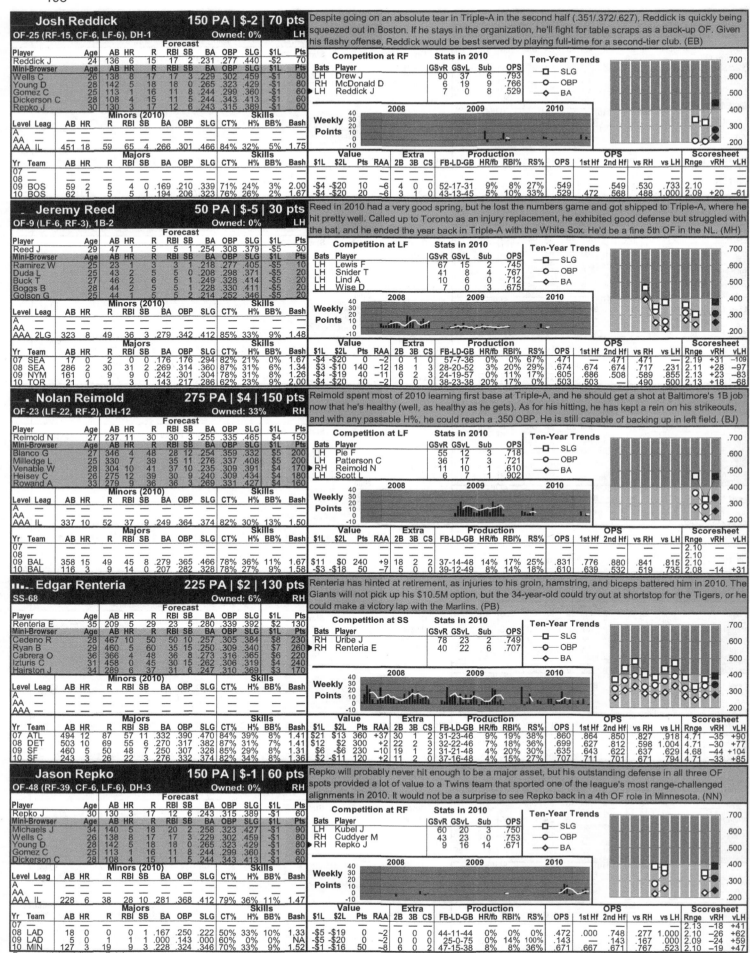

## Jose Reyes — 600 PA | $24 | 460 pts

SS-133 — Owned: 100% — BH

| Player | Age | AB | HR | R | RBI | SB | BA | OBP | SLG | $1L | Pts |
|---|---|---|---|---|---|---|---|---|---|---|---|
| **Forecast** | | | | | | | | | | | |
| Reyes J | 27 | 544 | 12 | 90 | 54 | 42 | .287 | .348 | .457 | $24 | 460 |
| **Mini-Browser** | | | | | | | | | | | |
| Ramirez H | 27 | 591 | 26 | 111 | 85 | 33 | .308 | .387 | .528 | $34 | 550 |
| Tulowitzki T | 26 | 589 | 27 | 108 | 101 | 14 | .298 | .373 | .531 | $29 | 500 |
| Rollins J | 32 | 639 | 21 | 105 | 77 | 35 | .274 | .335 | .472 | $26 | 550 |
| Jeter D | 36 | 603 | 14 | 95 | 61 | 20 | .280 | .351 | .388 | $20 | 400 |
| Ramirez A | 29 | 551 | 18 | 72 | 72 | 12 | .272 | .312 | .410 | $18 | 350 |

| Minors (2010) Level | Leag | AB | HR | R | RBI | SB | BA | OBP | SLG | CT% | H% | BB% | Bash |
|---|---|---|---|---|---|---|---|---|---|---|---|---|---|
| A | FLO | 4 | 0 | 0 | 1 | 0 | .000 | .000 | .000 | 100% | 0% | 0% | NA |
| AA | — | — | — | — | — | — | — | — | — | — | — | — | — |
| AAA | — | — | — | — | — | — | — | — | — | — | — | — | — |

| Majors Yr | Team | AB | HR | R | RBI | SB | BA | OBP | SLG | CT% | H% | BB% | Bash |
|---|---|---|---|---|---|---|---|---|---|---|---|---|---|
| 07 | NYM | 681 | 12 | 119 | 57 | 78 | .280 | .354 | .421 | 89% | 32% | 10% | 1.50 |
| 08 | NYM | 688 | 16 | 113 | 68 | 56 | .297 | .358 | .475 | 88% | 34% | 9% | 1.60 |
| 09 | NYM | 147 | 2 | 18 | 15 | 11 | .279 | .355 | .395 | 87% | 32% | 11% | 1.41 |
| 10 | NYM | 563 | 11 | 83 | 54 | 30 | .282 | .321 | .428 | 89% | 32% | 5% | 1.52 |

Once Reyes recovered from 2009's hamstring woes and a new thyroid issue, he regained his All-Star form (.314 BA, 5 HR, 8 SB in June). But then he hurt his oblique and missed time twice. Batting #3 also baffled him. He could be traded if the Mets' new regime shakes things up, but his foundation remains strong. (JL)

**Competition at SS — Stats in 2010**

| Bats | Player | GSvR | GSvL | Sub | OPS |
|---|---|---|---|---|---|
| BH | Reyes J | 98 | 34 | 1 | .749 |
| RH | Tejada R | 20 | 5 | 3 | .588 |

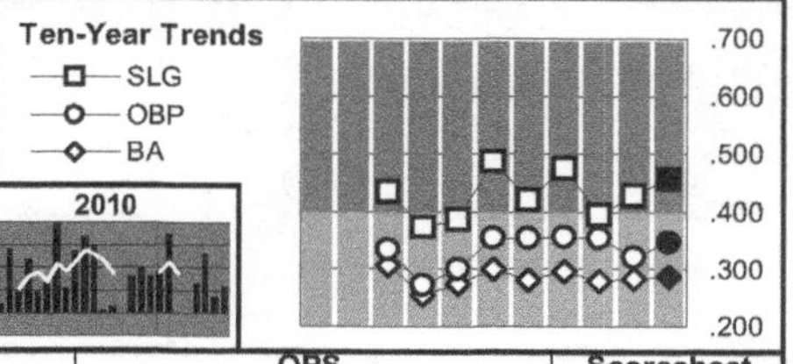


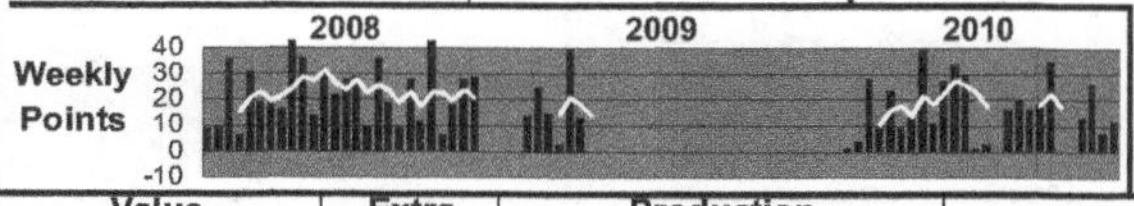


| Yr | $1L | $2L | Pts | RAA | 2B | 3B | CS | FB-LD-GB | HR/fb | RBI% | RS% | OPS | 1st Hf | 2nd Hf | vs RH | vs LH | Rnge | vRH | vLH |
|---|---|---|---|---|---|---|---|---|---|---|---|---|---|---|---|---|---|---|---|
| 07 | $35 | $28 | 600 | +27 | 36 | 12 | 21 | 40-18-42 | 5% | 16% | 42% | .775 | .825 | .719 | .768 | .795 | 4.72 | — | — |
| 08 | $35 | $28 | 590 | +36 | 37 | 19 | 15 | 33-23-44 | 8% | 21% | 38% | .833 | .854 | .804 | .840 | .816 | 4.83 | — | — |
| 09 | $2 | -$12 | 110 | +5 | 7 | 2 | 2 | 40-19-41 | 4% | 19% | 28% | .750 | .750 | — | .662 | 1.086 | 4.77 | — | — |
| 10 | $23 | $14 | 400 | +9 | 29 | 10 | 10 | 40-18-43 | 6% | 20% | 40% | .749 | .731 | .773 | .750 | .744 | 4.74 | — | — |

(Value: $1L–RAA; Extra: 2B–CS; Production: FB-LD-GB–RS%; OPS: OPS–vs LH; Scoresheet: Rnge–vLH)

## Mark Reynolds — 650 PA | $23 | 390 pts

3B-142, 1B-5 — Owned: 98% — RH

| Player | Age | AB | HR | R | RBI | SB | BA | OBP | SLG | $1L | Pts |
|---|---|---|---|---|---|---|---|---|---|---|---|
| **Forecast** | | | | | | | | | | | |
| Reynolds M | 27 | 586 | 39 | 98 | 98 | 13 | .244 | .339 | .498 | $23 | 390 |
| **Mini-Browser** | | | | | | | | | | | |
| Wright D | 28 | 570 | 27 | 101 | 101 | 20 | .296 | .384 | .511 | $31 | 490 |
| Longoria E | 25 | 602 | 35 | 98 | 112 | 7 | .279 | .362 | .516 | $30 | 470 |
| Rodriguez A | 35 | 458 | 33 | 83 | 105 | 11 | .276 | .377 | .537 | $28 | 420 |
| Zimmerman R | 26 | 558 | 26 | 98 | 91 | 7 | .291 | .363 | .507 | $23 | 440 |
| Beltre A | 31 | 544 | 24 | 78 | 78 | 6 | .287 | .334 | .489 | $21 | 380 |

| Minors (2010) Level | Leag | AB | HR | R | RBI | SB | BA | OBP | SLG | CT% | H% | BB% | Bash |
|---|---|---|---|---|---|---|---|---|---|---|---|---|---|
| A | — | — | — | — | — | — | — | — | — | — | — | — | — |
| AA | — | — | — | — | — | — | — | — | — | — | — | — | — |
| AAA | — | — | — | — | — | — | — | — | — | — | — | — | — |

| Majors Yr | Team | AB | HR | R | RBI | SB | BA | OBP | SLG | CT% | H% | BB% | Bash |
|---|---|---|---|---|---|---|---|---|---|---|---|---|---|
| 07 | ARI | 366 | 17 | 62 | 62 | 0 | .279 | .349 | .495 | 65% | 43% | 9% | 1.77 |
| 08 | ARI | 539 | 28 | 87 | 97 | 11 | .239 | .320 | .458 | 62% | 39% | 10% | 1.91 |
| 09 | ARI | 578 | 44 | 98 | 102 | 24 | .260 | .349 | .543 | 61% | 42% | 11% | 2.09 |
| 10 | ARI | 499 | 32 | 79 | 85 | 7 | .198 | .320 | .433 | 58% | 34% | 14% | 2.18 |

Defensive improvement was Reynolds's only step forward in 2010, but he will hold down Arizona's hot corner until 2012 at least, since he'd be tough to trade after a down year. Adjustments to his swing could not contain his strikeouts, but he can still make the ball fly out of Chase when he makes contact. (MS)

**Competition at 3B — Stats in 2010**

| Bats | Player | GSvR | GSvL | Sub | OPS |
|---|---|---|---|---|---|
| RH | Reynolds M | 96 | 45 | 1 | .753 |
| BH | Abreu T | 11 | 5 | 4 | .560 |
| BH | Ojeda A | 1 | 0 | 11 | .486 |

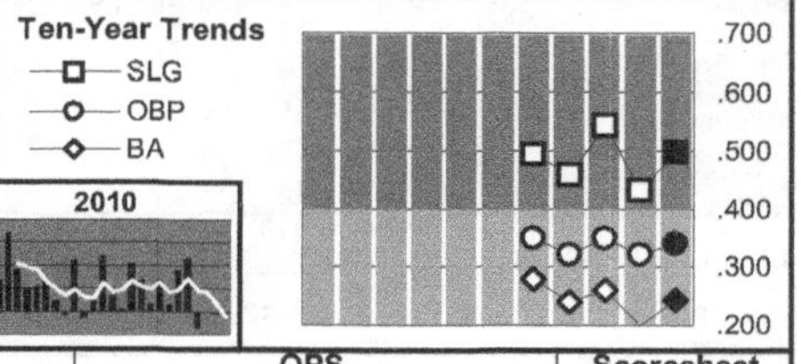


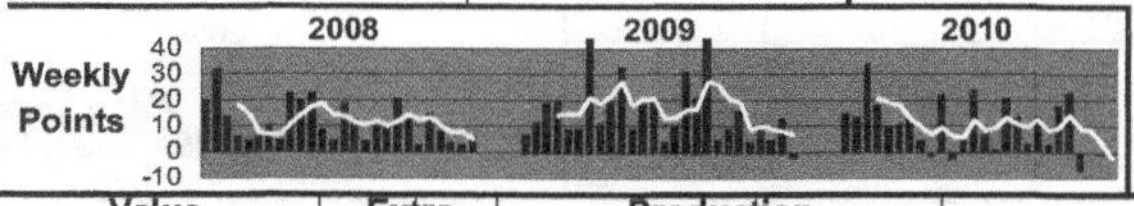


| Yr | $1L | $2L | Pts | RAA | 2B | 3B | CS | FB-LD-GB | HR/fb | RBI% | RS% | OPS | 1st Hf | 2nd Hf | vs RH | vs LH | Rnge | vRH | vLH |
|---|---|---|---|---|---|---|---|---|---|---|---|---|---|---|---|---|---|---|---|
| 07 | $12 | $3 | 210 | +9 | 20 | 4 | 1 | 44-20-36 | 16% | 20% | 35% | .843 | .854 | .836 | .853 | .819 | — | — | — |
| 08 | $19 | $13 | 310 | +6 | 28 | 3 | 2 | 45-19-36 | 18% | 21% | 35% | .779 | .828 | .711 | .706 | .982 | 2.67 | –15 | +38 |
| 09 | $32 | $25 | 410 | +30 | 30 | 1 | 9 | 47-17-35 | 26% | 18% | 29% | .892 | .888 | .898 | .889 | .894 | 2.59 | –30 | +74 |
| 10 | $14 | $8 | 260 | –5 | 17 | 2 | 4 | 55-13-32 | 20% | 19% | 30% | .753 | .800 | .686 | .694 | .913 | 2.60 | –22 | +61 |

## Will Rhymes — 175 PA | $-2 | 80 pts

2B-53 — Owned: 0% — LH

| Player | Age | AB | HR | R | RBI | SB | BA | OBP | SLG | $1L | Pts |
|---|---|---|---|---|---|---|---|---|---|---|---|
| **Forecast** | | | | | | | | | | | |
| Rhymes W | 28 | 152 | 2 | 18 | 16 | 5 | .242 | .298 | .336 | -$2 | 80 |
| **Mini-Browser** | | | | | | | | | | | |
| Guillen C | 35 | 153 | 5 | 21 | 23 | 2 | .274 | .350 | .448 | $1 | 110 |
| Lugo J | 35 | 163 | 2 | 19 | 16 | 7 | .258 | .325 | .346 | -$1 | 90 |
| Lillibridge B | 27 | 136 | 3 | 18 | 14 | 8 | .232 | .304 | .374 | -$1 | 70 |
| Blanco A | 26 | 161 | 2 | 18 | 16 | 2 | .271 | .322 | .369 | -$1 | 90 |
| McDonald J | 36 | 193 | 2 | 22 | 20 | 2 | .238 | .268 | .345 | -$2 | 90 |

| Minors (2010) Level | Leag | AB | HR | R | RBI | SB | BA | OBP | SLG | CT% | H% | BB% | Bash |
|---|---|---|---|---|---|---|---|---|---|---|---|---|---|
| A | — | — | — | — | — | — | — | — | — | — | — | — | — |
| AA | — | — | — | — | — | — | — | — | — | — | — | — | — |
| AAA | IL | 364 | 2 | 59 | 35 | 22 | .305 | .370 | .415 | 90% | 34% | 9% | 1.36 |

| Majors Yr | Team | AB | HR | R | RBI | SB | BA | OBP | SLG | CT% | H% | BB% | Bash |
|---|---|---|---|---|---|---|---|---|---|---|---|---|---|
| 07 | — | — | — | — | — | — | — | — | — | — | — | — | — |
| 08 | — | — | — | — | — | — | — | — | — | — | — | — | — |
| 09 | — | — | — | — | — | — | — | — | — | — | — | — | — |
| 10 | DET | 191 | 1 | 30 | 19 | 0 | .304 | .350 | .414 | 92% | 33% | 7% | 1.36 |

Rhymes's solid performance and hustle down the stretch made him a fan favorite, but the 28-year-old's future is unclear. In 2011, he will get a chance to seize the 2B job, but he is more likely to settle into a UT role. He makes great contact and has good speed, but he has little power and merely average range. (LP)

**Competition at 2B — Stats in 2010**

| Bats | Player | GSvR | GSvL | Sub | OPS |
|---|---|---|---|---|---|
| LH | Rhymes W | 37 | 9 | 7 | .763 |
| BH | Guillen C | 33 | 12 | 2 | .746 |
| RH | Sizemore S | 23 | 13 | 4 | .631 |
| RH | Raburn R | 11 | 5 | 2 | .814 |

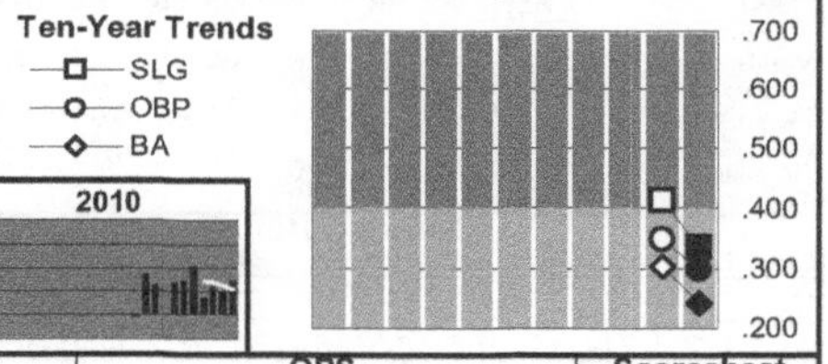


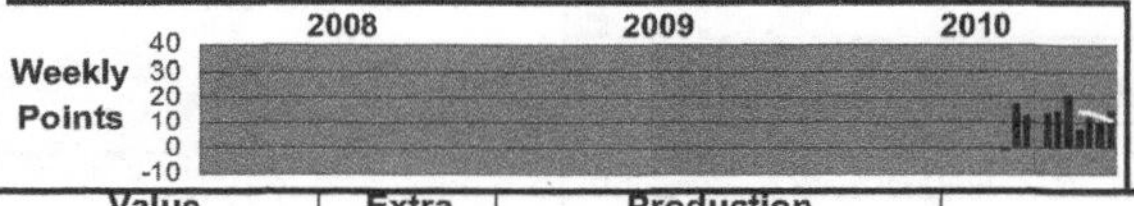


| Yr | $1L | $2L | Pts | RAA | 2B | 3B | CS | FB-LD-GB | HR/fb | RBI% | RS% | OPS | 1st Hf | 2nd Hf | vs RH | vs LH | Rnge | vRH | vLH |
|---|---|---|---|---|---|---|---|---|---|---|---|---|---|---|---|---|---|---|---|
| 07 | — | — | — | — | — | — | — | — | — | — | — | — | — | — | — | — | — | — | — |
| 08 | — | — | — | — | — | — | — | — | — | — | — | — | — | — | — | — | — | — | — |
| 09 | — | — | — | — | — | — | — | — | — | — | — | — | — | — | — | — | — | — | — |
| 10 | $3 | -$11 | 120 | –0 | 12 | 3 | 3 | 33-23-44 | 2% | 18% | 41% | .763 | — | .763 | .741 | .855 | — | — | — |

## Alex Rios — 625 PA | $24 | 410 pts

OF-144 (CF-143, LF-1), DH-2 — Owned: 99% — RH

| Player | Age | AB | HR | R | RBI | SB | BA | OBP | SLG | $1L | Pts |
|---|---|---|---|---|---|---|---|---|---|---|---|
| **Forecast** | | | | | | | | | | | |
| Rios A | 30 | 570 | 19 | 81 | 75 | 25 | .274 | .325 | .452 | $24 | 410 |
| **Mini-Browser** | | | | | | | | | | | |
| Kemp M | 26 | 597 | 26 | 91 | 91 | 26 | .272 | .329 | .466 | $26 | 420 |
| Suzuki I | 37 | 638 | 7 | 84 | 49 | 35 | .307 | .353 | .405 | $26 | 430 |
| Beltran C | 33 | 530 | 24 | 90 | 90 | 18 | .283 | .374 | .512 | $25 | 470 |
| Hart C | 29 | 589 | 26 | 91 | 91 | 20 | .276 | .335 | .500 | $25 | 440 |
| Markakis N | 27 | 611 | 21 | 91 | 84 | 7 | .298 | .370 | .463 | $24 | 440 |

| Minors (2010) Level | Leag | AB | HR | R | RBI | SB | BA | OBP | SLG | CT% | H% | BB% | Bash |
|---|---|---|---|---|---|---|---|---|---|---|---|---|---|
| A | — | — | — | — | — | — | — | — | — | — | — | — | — |
| AA | — | — | — | — | — | — | — | — | — | — | — | — | — |
| AAA | — | — | — | — | — | — | — | — | — | — | — | — | — |

| Majors Yr | Team | AB | HR | R | RBI | SB | BA | OBP | SLG | CT% | H% | BB% | Bash |
|---|---|---|---|---|---|---|---|---|---|---|---|---|---|
| 07 | TOR | 643 | 24 | 114 | 85 | 17 | .297 | .354 | .498 | 84% | 35% | 8% | 1.68 |
| 08 | TOR | 635 | 15 | 91 | 79 | 32 | .291 | .337 | .461 | 82% | 35% | 6% | 1.58 |
| 09 | 2TM | 582 | 17 | 63 | 71 | 24 | .247 | .296 | .395 | 82% | 30% | 6% | 1.60 |
| 10 | CHW | 567 | 21 | 89 | 88 | 34 | .284 | .334 | .457 | 84% | 34% | 6% | 1.61 |

Repeating a disturbing pattern, Rios slumped late in 2010 after having dispelled fears about his huge contract in the first half. If he keeps repeating his career stats and playing stand-out defense, all parties will be happy with the long-term pact. Rios is more likely than most to deliver such consistency. (RM)

**Competition at CF — Stats in 2010**

| Bats | Player | GSvR | GSvL | Sub | OPS |
|---|---|---|---|---|---|
| RH | Rios A | 104 | 37 | 2 | .791 |
| RH | Jones A | 10 | 4 | 3 | .827 |

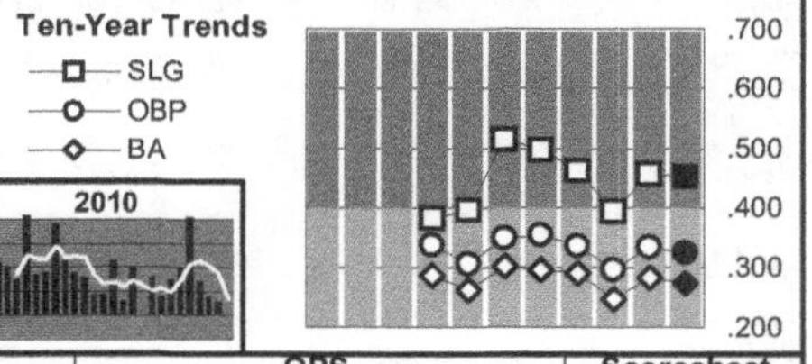


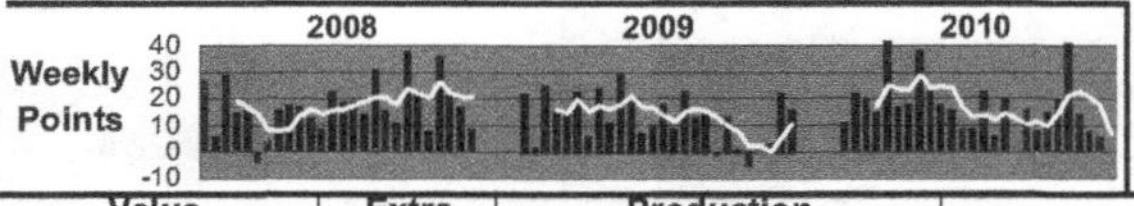


| Yr | $1L | $2L | Pts | RAA | 2B | 3B | CS | FB-LD-GB | HR/fb | RBI% | RS% | OPS | 1st Hf | 2nd Hf | vs RH | vs LH | Rnge | vRH | vLH |
|---|---|---|---|---|---|---|---|---|---|---|---|---|---|---|---|---|---|---|---|
| 07 | $29 | $23 | 500 | +25 | 43 | 7 | 4 | 44-20-36 | 10% | 20% | 39% | .852 | .870 | .831 | .802 | 1.022 | — | –7 | +16 |
| 08 | $28 | $19 | 450 | +15 | 47 | 8 | 8 | 38-21-41 | 7% | 19% | 35% | .798 | .737 | .879 | .818 | .735 | 2.11 | –26 | +69 |
| 09 | $16 | $6 | 340 | –12 | 31 | 2 | 5 | 41-16-43 | 9% | 16% | 27% | .691 | .732 | .623 | .679 | .723 | 2.11 | –18 | +48 |
| 10 | $32 | $25 | 440 | +7 | 29 | 3 | 14 | 38-17-45 | 12% | 22% | 37% | .791 | .878 | .684 | .814 | .717 | 2.13 | –6 | +17 |

## Juan Rivera — 525 PA | $15 | 330 pts

OF-105 (LF-83, RF-25, CF-1), 1B-13, DH-3 — Owned: 37% — RH

| Player | Age | AB | HR | R | RBI | SB | BA | OBP | SLG | $1L | Pts |
|---|---|---|---|---|---|---|---|---|---|---|---|
| **Forecast** | | | | | | | | | | | |
| Rivera J | 32 | 500 | 21 | 58 | 74 | 0 | .273 | .319 | .453 | $15 | 330 |
| **Mini-Browser** | | | | | | | | | | | |
| DeJesus D | 31 | 578 | 13 | 75 | 63 | 6 | .292 | .361 | .434 | $16 | 380 |
| Gutierrez F | 28 | 568 | 19 | 75 | 63 | 19 | .253 | .313 | .393 | $16 | 310 |
| Willingham J | 32 | 465 | 22 | 72 | 72 | 6 | .272 | .379 | .494 | $16 | 340 |
| Kubel J | 28 | 468 | 21 | 63 | 84 | 0 | .269 | .337 | .472 | $16 | 320 |
| Tabata J | 22 | 567 | 12 | 78 | 54 | 24 | .275 | .334 | .388 | $15 | 360 |

| Minors (2010) Level | Leag | AB | HR | R | RBI | SB | BA | OBP | SLG | CT% | H% | BB% | Bash |
|---|---|---|---|---|---|---|---|---|---|---|---|---|---|
| A | — | — | — | — | — | — | — | — | — | — | — | — | — |
| AA | — | — | — | — | — | — | — | — | — | — | — | — | — |
| AAA | — | — | — | — | — | — | — | — | — | — | — | — | — |

| Majors Yr | Team | AB | HR | R | RBI | SB | BA | OBP | SLG | CT% | H% | BB% | Bash |
|---|---|---|---|---|---|---|---|---|---|---|---|---|---|
| 07 | LAA | 43 | 2 | 3 | 8 | 0 | .279 | .295 | .442 | 91% | 31% | 2% | 1.58 |
| 08 | LAA | 256 | 12 | 31 | 45 | 1 | .246 | .282 | .438 | 87% | 28% | 6% | 1.78 |
| 09 | LAA | 529 | 25 | 72 | 88 | 0 | .287 | .332 | .478 | 89% | 32% | 6% | 1.66 |
| 10 | LAA | 416 | 15 | 53 | 52 | 2 | .252 | .312 | .409 | 86% | 29% | 7% | 1.62 |

Rivera has a lot to work on this winter. The Angels are finally willing to trade him because his defense fell off as precipitously as his offense did. If the Angels cannot deal Rivera, he will have a vastly reduced role, but the odds are good that he will transfer. His bat is worthwhile only when his rates peak in concert. (DS)

**Competition at LF — Stats in 2010**

| Bats | Player | GSvR | GSvL | Sub | OPS |
|---|---|---|---|---|---|
| RH | Rivera J | 44 | 36 | 3 | .721 |
| LH | Abreu B | 35 | 6 | 0 | .787 |
| BH | Willits R | 11 | 8 | 25 | .643 |
| LH | Matsui H | 16 | 1 | 1 | .820 |

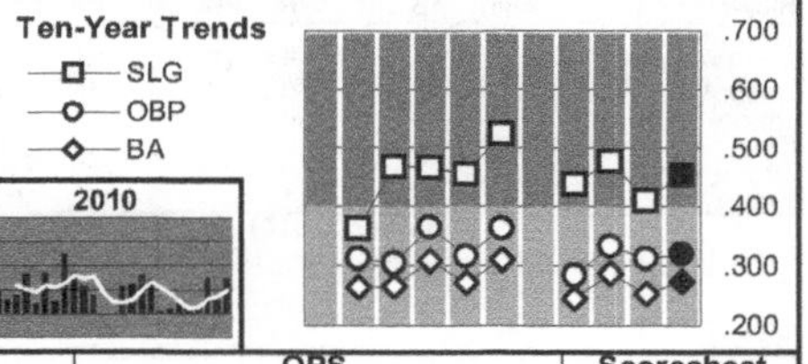


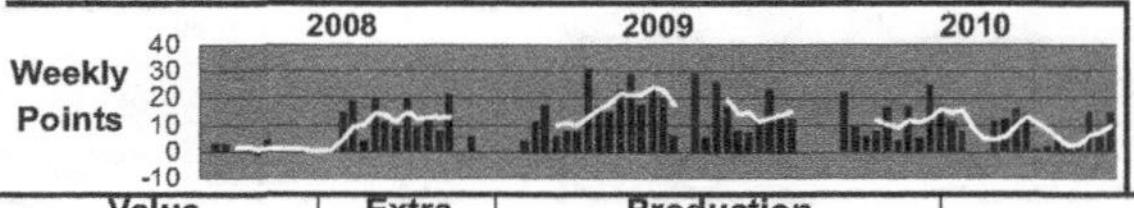


| Yr | $1L | $2L | Pts | RAA | 2B | 3B | CS | FB-LD-GB | HR/fb | RBI% | RS% | OPS | 1st Hf | 2nd Hf | vs RH | vs LH | Rnge | vRH | vLH |
|---|---|---|---|---|---|---|---|---|---|---|---|---|---|---|---|---|---|---|---|
| 07 | -$2 | -$18 | 30 | –1 | 1 | 0 | 0 | 41-15-44 | 13% | 25% | 9% | .737 | — | .737 | .690 | .759 | — | –12 | +29 |
| 08 | $5 | -$6 | 170 | –6 | 13 | 0 | 1 | 48-14-37 | 11% | 22% | 28% | .720 | .667 | .746 | .714 | .730 | 2.08 | –25 | +60 |
| 09 | $19 | $11 | 390 | +7 | 24 | 1 | 1 | 38-18-44 | 14% | 22% | 28% | .810 | .879 | .727 | .730 | 1.030 | 2.07 | –19 | +43 |
| 10 | $10 | -$1 | 250 | –10 | 20 | 0 | 2 | 39-16-46 | 11% | 18% | 30% | .721 | .708 | .741 | .707 | .746 | 2.10 | –31 | +75 |

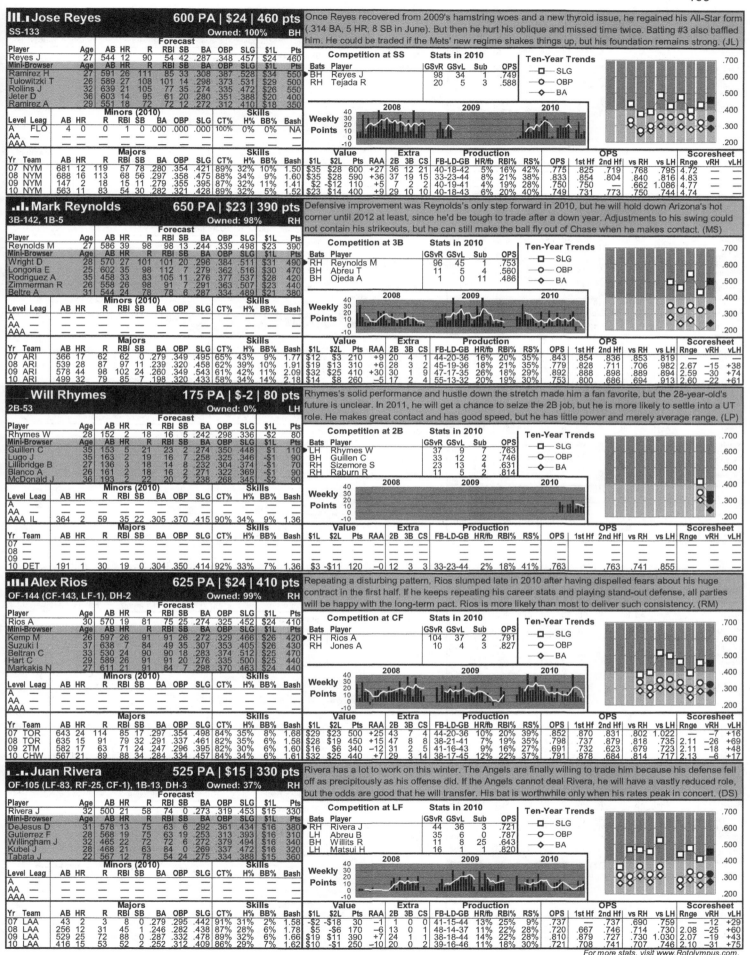

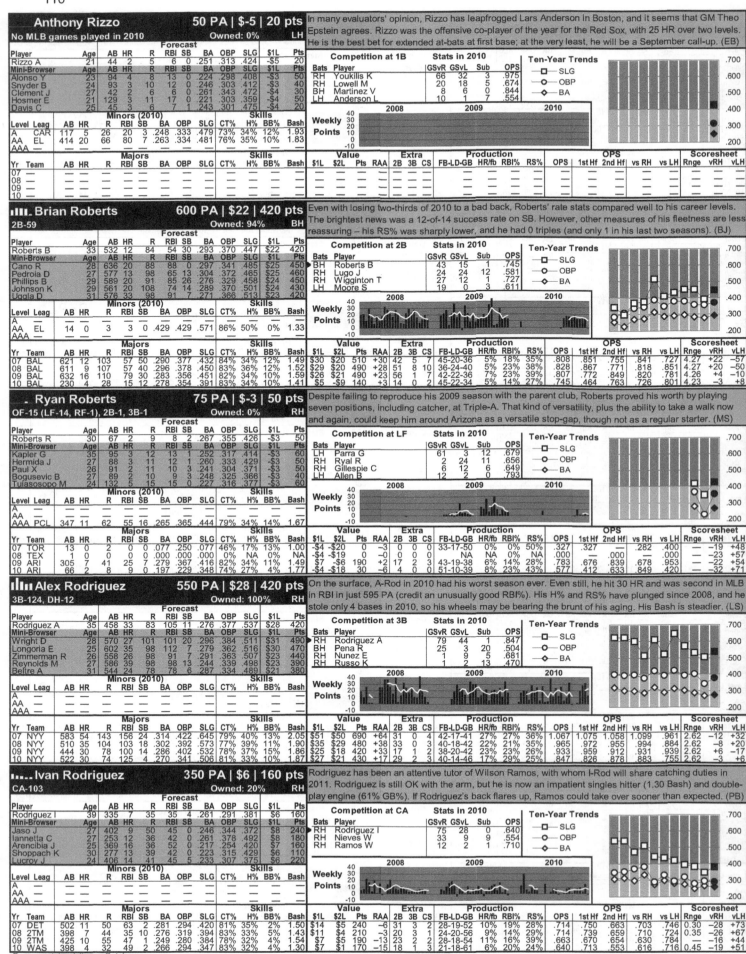

## Anthony Rizzo — 50 PA | $-5 | 20 pts

No MLB games played in 2010 — Owned: 0% — LH

In many evaluators' opinion, Rizzo has leapfrogged Lars Anderson in Boston, and it seems that GM Theo Epstein agrees. Rizzo was the offensive co-player of the year for the Red Sox, with 25 HR over two levels. He is the best bet for extended at-bats at first base; at the very least, he will be a September call-up. (EB)

### Forecast
| Player | Age | AB | HR | R | RBI | SB | BA | OBP | SLG | $1L | Pts |
|---|---|---|---|---|---|---|---|---|---|---|---|
| Rizzo A | 21 | 44 | 2 | 5 | 6 | 0 | .251 | .313 | .424 | -$5 | 20 |
| Mini-Browser | Age | AB | HR | R | RBI | SB | BA | OBP | SLG | $1L | Pts |
| Alonso Y | 23 | 94 | 4 | 8 | 13 | 0 | .224 | .298 | .408 | -$3 | 50 |
| Snyder B | 24 | 93 | 3 | 10 | 12 | 0 | .246 | .303 | .412 | -$3 | 40 |
| Clement J | 27 | 42 | 2 | 6 | 6 | 0 | .261 | .343 | .472 | -$4 | 30 |
| Hosmer E | 21 | 129 | 3 | 11 | 17 | 0 | .221 | .303 | .359 | -$4 | 50 |
| Davis C | 25 | 45 | 3 | 6 | 11 | 0 | .243 | .301 | .475 | -$4 | 20 |

### Minors (2010) / Skills
| Level | Leag | AB | HR | R | RBI | SB | BA | OBP | SLG | CT% | H% | BB% | Bash |
|---|---|---|---|---|---|---|---|---|---|---|---|---|---|
| A | CAR | 117 | 5 | 26 | 20 | 3 | .248 | .333 | .479 | 73% | 34% | 12% | 1.93 |
| AA | EL | 414 | 20 | 66 | 80 | 7 | .263 | .334 | .481 | 76% | 35% | 10% | 1.83 |
| AAA | — | | | | | | | | | | | | |

### Majors / Skills
| Yr | Team | AB | HR | R | RBI | SB | BA | OBP | SLG | CT% | H% | BB% | Bash |
|---|---|---|---|---|---|---|---|---|---|---|---|---|---|
| 07 | — | | | | | | | | | | | | |
| 08 | — | | | | | | | | | | | | |
| 09 | — | | | | | | | | | | | | |
| 10 | — | | | | | | | | | | | | |

Competition at 1B / Stats in 2010
| Bats | Player | GSvR | GSvL | Sub | OPS |
|---|---|---|---|---|---|
| RH | Youkilis K | 66 | 32 | 3 | .975 |
| RH | Lowell M | 20 | 18 | 5 | .674 |
| BH | Martinez V | 8 | 6 | 0 | .844 |
| LH | Anderson L | 10 | 1 | 7 | .554 |

---

## Brian Roberts — 600 PA | $22 | 420 pts

2B-59 — Owned: 94% — BH

Even with losing two-thirds of 2010 to a bad back, Roberts' rate stats compared well to his career levels. The brightest news was a 12-of-14 success rate on SB. However, other measures of his fleetness are less reassuring – his RS% was sharply lower, and he had 0 triples (and only 1 in his last two seasons). (BJ)

### Forecast
| Player | Age | AB | HR | R | RBI | SB | BA | OBP | SLG | $1L | Pts |
|---|---|---|---|---|---|---|---|---|---|---|---|
| Roberts B | 33 | 532 | 12 | 84 | 54 | 30 | .293 | .370 | .447 | $22 | 420 |
| Mini-Browser | Age | AB | HR | R | RBI | SB | BA | OBP | SLG | $1L | Pts |
| Cano R | 28 | 636 | 20 | 88 | 88 | 0 | .297 | .341 | .485 | $25 | 450 |
| Pedroia D | 27 | 577 | 13 | 98 | 65 | 13 | .304 | .372 | .465 | $25 | 460 |
| Phillips B | 29 | 589 | 20 | 91 | 85 | 26 | .276 | .329 | .458 | $24 | 450 |
| Johnson K | 29 | 561 | 20 | 108 | 74 | 14 | .289 | .370 | .501 | $24 | 430 |
| Uggla D | 31 | 576 | 33 | 98 | 91 | 7 | .271 | .366 | .513 | $23 | 420 |

### Minors (2010) / Skills
| Level | Leag | AB | HR | R | RBI | SB | BA | OBP | SLG | CT% | H% | BB% | Bash |
|---|---|---|---|---|---|---|---|---|---|---|---|---|---|
| A | — | | | | | | | | | | | | |
| AA | EL | 14 | 0 | 3 | 3 | 0 | .429 | .429 | .571 | 86% | 50% | 0% | 1.33 |
| AAA | — | | | | | | | | | | | | |

### Majors / Skills
| Yr | Team | AB | HR | R | RBI | SB | BA | OBP | SLG | CT% | H% | BB% | Bash |
|---|---|---|---|---|---|---|---|---|---|---|---|---|---|
| 07 | BAL | 621 | 12 | 103 | 57 | 50 | .290 | .377 | .432 | 84% | 34% | 12% | 1.49 |
| 08 | BAL | 611 | 9 | 107 | 57 | 40 | .296 | .378 | .450 | 83% | 36% | 12% | 1.52 |
| 09 | BAL | 632 | 16 | 110 | 79 | 30 | .283 | .356 | .451 | 82% | 34% | 10% | 1.59 |
| 10 | BAL | 230 | 4 | 28 | 15 | 12 | .278 | .354 | .391 | 83% | 34% | 10% | 1.41 |

Competition at 2B / Stats in 2010
| Bats | Player | GSvR | GSvL | Sub | OPS |
|---|---|---|---|---|---|
| BH | Roberts B | 43 | 15 | 1 | .745 |
| RH | Lugo J | 24 | 24 | 12 | .581 |
| RH | Wigginton T | 27 | 12 | 1 | .727 |
| LH | Moore S | 19 | 0 | 3 | .611 |

### Value / Extra / Production / OPS / Scoresheet
| Yr | Team | $1L | $2L | Pts | RAA | 2B | 3B | CS | FB-LD-GB | HR/fb | RBI% | RS% | OPS | 1st Hf | 2nd Hf | vs RH | vs LH | Rnge | vRH | vLH |
|---|---|---|---|---|---|---|---|---|---|---|---|---|---|---|---|---|---|---|---|---|
| 07 | BAL | $30 | $20 | 510 | +30 | 42 | 5 | 7 | 45-20-36 | 5% | 18% | 35% | .808 | .851 | .755 | .841 | .727 | 4.27 | +22 | -57 |
| 08 | BAL | $29 | $20 | 490 | +28 | 51 | 8 | 10 | 36-24-40 | 5% | 23% | 38% | .828 | .867 | .771 | .818 | .851 | 4.27 | +20 | -50 |
| 09 | BAL | $26 | $21 | 490 | +23 | 56 | 1 | 7 | 42-22-36 | 7% | 23% | 39% | .807 | .772 | .849 | .820 | .781 | 4.26 | +4 | -10 |
| 10 | BAL | $5 | -$9 | 140 | +3 | 14 | 0 | 2 | 45-22-34 | 5% | 14% | 27% | .745 | .464 | .763 | .726 | .801 | 4.23 | -3 | +8 |

---

## Ryan Roberts — 75 PA | $-3 | 50 pts

OF-15 (LF-14, RF-1), 2B-1, 3B-1 — Owned: 0% — RH

Despite failing to reproduce his 2009 season with the parent club, Roberts proved his worth by playing seven positions, including catcher, at Triple-A. That kind of versatility, plus the ability to take a walk now and again, could keep him around Arizona as a versatile stop-gap, though not as a regular starter. (MS)

### Forecast
| Player | Age | AB | HR | R | RBI | SB | BA | OBP | SLG | $1L | Pts |
|---|---|---|---|---|---|---|---|---|---|---|---|
| Roberts R | 30 | 67 | 2 | 9 | 8 | 2 | .267 | .355 | .426 | -$3 | 50 |
| Mini-Browser | Age | AB | HR | R | RBI | SB | BA | OBP | SLG | $1L | Pts |
| Kapler G | 35 | 95 | 3 | 12 | 13 | 1 | .252 | .317 | .414 | -$3 | 60 |
| Hermida J | 27 | 88 | 3 | 11 | 12 | 1 | .260 | .333 | .429 | -$3 | 50 |
| Paul X | 26 | 91 | 2 | 11 | 10 | 3 | .241 | .304 | .371 | -$3 | 50 |
| Bogusevic B | 27 | 89 | 2 | 10 | 9 | 3 | .248 | .325 | .366 | -$3 | 40 |
| Tuiasosopo M | 24 | 132 | 5 | 15 | 15 | 0 | .227 | .316 | .377 | -$3 | 60 |

### Minors (2010) / Skills
| Level | Leag | AB | HR | R | RBI | SB | BA | OBP | SLG | CT% | H% | BB% | Bash |
|---|---|---|---|---|---|---|---|---|---|---|---|---|---|
| A | — | | | | | | | | | | | | |
| AA | — | | | | | | | | | | | | |
| AAA | PCL | 347 | 11 | 62 | 55 | 16 | .265 | .365 | .444 | 79% | 34% | 14% | 1.67 |

### Majors / Skills
| Yr | Team | AB | HR | R | RBI | SB | BA | OBP | SLG | CT% | H% | BB% | Bash |
|---|---|---|---|---|---|---|---|---|---|---|---|---|---|
| 07 | TOR | 13 | 0 | 2 | 0 | 0 | .077 | .250 | .077 | 46% | 17% | 13% | 1.00 |
| 08 | TEX | 1 | 0 | 0 | 0 | 0 | .000 | .000 | .000 | 0% | NA | 0% | NA |
| 09 | ARI | 305 | 7 | 41 | 25 | 7 | .279 | .367 | .416 | 82% | 34% | 11% | 1.49 |
| 10 | ARI | 66 | 2 | 8 | 9 | 0 | .197 | .229 | .348 | 74% | 27% | 4% | 1.77 |

Competition at LF / Stats in 2010
| Bats | Player | GSvR | GSvL | Sub | OPS |
|---|---|---|---|---|---|
| LH | Parra G | 61 | 3 | 12 | .679 |
| RH | Ryal R | 2 | 24 | 11 | .656 |
| RH | Gillespie C | 6 | 12 | 6 | .649 |
| LH | Allen B | 12 | 2 | 0 | .793 |

### Value / Extra / Production / OPS / Scoresheet
| Yr | Team | $1L | $2L | Pts | RAA | 2B | 3B | CS | FB-LD-GB | HR/fb | RBI% | RS% | OPS | 1st Hf | 2nd Hf | vs RH | vs LH | Rnge | vRH | vLH |
|---|---|---|---|---|---|---|---|---|---|---|---|---|---|---|---|---|---|---|---|---|
| 07 | | -$4 | -$20 | 0 | -3 | 0 | 0 | 0 | 33-17-50 | 0% | 0% | 50% | .327 | .327 | — | .282 | .400 | — | -19 | +48 |
| 08 | | -$4 | -$19 | 0 | -0 | 0 | 0 | 0 | NA | NA | 0% | NA | .000 | — | .000 | — | .000 | — | -23 | +57 |
| 09 | | $7 | -$6 | 190 | +2 | 17 | 2 | 3 | 43-19-38 | 6% | 14% | 28% | .783 | .676 | .839 | .678 | .953 | — | -22 | +54 |
| 10 | | -$4 | -$18 | 30 | -6 | 4 | 0 | 2 | 51-10-39 | 8% | 23% | 43% | .577 | .412 | .633 | .849 | .420 | — | -32 | +71 |

---

## Alex Rodriguez — 550 PA | $28 | 420 pts

3B-124, DH-12 — Owned: 100% — RH

On the surface, A-Rod in 2010 had his worst season ever. Even still, he hit 30 HR and was second in MLB in RBI in just 595 PA (credit an unusually good RBI%). His H% and RS% have plunged since 2008, and he stole only 4 bases in 2010, so his wheels may be bearing the brunt of his aging. His Bash is steadier. (LS)

### Forecast
| Player | Age | AB | HR | R | RBI | SB | BA | OBP | SLG | $1L | Pts |
|---|---|---|---|---|---|---|---|---|---|---|---|
| Rodriguez A | 35 | 458 | 33 | 83 | 105 | 11 | .276 | .377 | .537 | $28 | 420 |
| Mini-Browser | Age | AB | HR | R | RBI | SB | BA | OBP | SLG | $1L | Pts |
| Wright D | 28 | 570 | 27 | 101 | 101 | 20 | .296 | .384 | .511 | $31 | 490 |
| Longoria E | 25 | 602 | 35 | 98 | 112 | 7 | .279 | .362 | .516 | $30 | 470 |
| Zimmerman R | 26 | 558 | 26 | 93 | 91 | 7 | .291 | .363 | .507 | $23 | 440 |
| Reynolds M | 27 | 586 | 39 | 98 | 98 | 13 | .244 | .339 | .498 | $23 | 390 |
| Beltre A | 31 | 544 | 24 | 78 | 78 | 6 | .287 | .334 | .489 | $21 | 380 |

### Minors (2010) / Skills
| Level | Leag | AB | HR | R | RBI | SB | BA | OBP | SLG | CT% | H% | BB% | Bash |
|---|---|---|---|---|---|---|---|---|---|---|---|---|---|
| A | — | | | | | | | | | | | | |
| AA | — | | | | | | | | | | | | |
| AAA | — | | | | | | | | | | | | |

### Majors / Skills
| Yr | Team | AB | HR | R | RBI | SB | BA | OBP | SLG | CT% | H% | BB% | Bash |
|---|---|---|---|---|---|---|---|---|---|---|---|---|---|
| 07 | NYY | 583 | 54 | 143 | 156 | 24 | .314 | .422 | .645 | 79% | 40% | 13% | 2.05 |
| 08 | NYY | 510 | 35 | 104 | 103 | 18 | .302 | .392 | .573 | 77% | 39% | 11% | 1.90 |
| 09 | NYY | 444 | 30 | 78 | 100 | 14 | .286 | .402 | .532 | 78% | 37% | 15% | 1.86 |
| 10 | NYY | 522 | 30 | 74 | 125 | 4 | .270 | .341 | .506 | 81% | 33% | 10% | 1.87 |

Competition at 3B / Stats in 2010
| Bats | Player | GSvR | GSvL | Sub | OPS |
|---|---|---|---|---|---|
| RH | Rodriguez A | 79 | 44 | 1 | .847 |
| BH | Pena R | 25 | 3 | 20 | .504 |
| RH | Nunez E | 1 | 9 | 5 | .681 |
| RH | Russo K | 1 | 2 | 13 | .470 |

### Value / Extra / Production / OPS / Scoresheet
| Yr | Team | $1L | $2L | Pts | RAA | 2B | 3B | CS | FB-LD-GB | HR/fb | RBI% | RS% | OPS | 1st Hf | 2nd Hf | vs RH | vs LH | Rnge | vRH | vLH |
|---|---|---|---|---|---|---|---|---|---|---|---|---|---|---|---|---|---|---|---|---|
| 07 | NYY | $51 | $50 | 690 | +64 | 31 | 0 | 4 | 42-17-41 | 27% | 27% | 36% | 1.067 | 1.075 | 1.058 | 1.099 | .961 | 2.62 | -12 | +32 |
| 08 | NYY | $35 | $29 | 480 | +38 | 33 | 0 | 3 | 40-18-42 | 22% | 21% | 35% | .965 | .972 | .955 | .994 | .884 | 2.62 | -8 | +20 |
| 09 | NYY | $25 | $18 | 420 | +33 | 17 | 1 | 2 | 38-20-42 | 23% | 23% | 35% | .933 | .959 | .912 | .931 | .939 | 2.62 | +6 | -17 |
| 10 | NYY | $27 | $21 | 430 | +17 | 29 | 2 | 4 | 40-14-46 | 17% | 29% | 25% | .847 | .826 | .878 | .883 | .755 | 2.62 | -3 | +2 |

---

## Ivan Rodriguez — 350 PA | $6 | 160 pts

CA-103 — Owned: 20% — RH

Rodriguez has been an attentive tutor of Wilson Ramos, with whom I-Rod will share catching duties in 2011. Rodriguez is still OK with the arm, but he is now an impatient singles hitter (1.30 Bash) and double-play engine (61% GB%). If Rodriguez's back flares up, Ramos could take over sooner than expected. (PB)

### Forecast
| Player | Age | AB | HR | R | RBI | SB | BA | OBP | SLG | $1L | Pts |
|---|---|---|---|---|---|---|---|---|---|---|---|
| Rodriguez I | 39 | 335 | 7 | 35 | 35 | 4 | .261 | .291 | .381 | $6 | 160 |
| Mini-Browser | Age | AB | HR | R | RBI | SB | BA | OBP | SLG | $1L | Pts |
| Jaso J | 27 | 402 | 9 | 50 | 45 | 0 | .246 | .344 | .372 | $8 | 240 |
| Iannetta C | 27 | 253 | 12 | 36 | 42 | 0 | .261 | .378 | .492 | $8 | 180 |
| Arencibia J | 25 | 369 | 16 | 36 | 52 | 0 | .217 | .254 | .420 | $7 | 160 |
| Shoppach K | 30 | 277 | 13 | 39 | 42 | 0 | .223 | .315 | .429 | $6 | 110 |
| Lucroy J | 24 | 406 | 14 | 41 | 45 | 5 | .233 | .307 | .375 | $6 | 220 |

### Minors (2010) / Skills
| Level | Leag | AB | HR | R | RBI | SB | BA | OBP | SLG | CT% | H% | BB% | Bash |
|---|---|---|---|---|---|---|---|---|---|---|---|---|---|
| A | — | | | | | | | | | | | | |
| AA | — | | | | | | | | | | | | |
| AAA | — | | | | | | | | | | | | |

### Majors / Skills
| Yr | Team | AB | HR | R | RBI | SB | BA | OBP | SLG | CT% | H% | BB% | Bash |
|---|---|---|---|---|---|---|---|---|---|---|---|---|---|
| 07 | DET | 502 | 11 | 50 | 63 | 2 | .281 | .294 | .420 | 81% | 35% | 2% | 1.50 |
| 08 | 2TM | 398 | 7 | 44 | 35 | 10 | .276 | .319 | .394 | 83% | 33% | 5% | 1.43 |
| 09 | 2TM | 425 | 10 | 45 | 47 | 1 | .249 | .280 | .384 | 78% | 32% | 4% | 1.54 |
| 10 | WAS | 398 | 4 | 32 | 49 | 2 | .266 | .294 | .347 | 82% | 32% | 4% | 1.30 |

Competition at CA / Stats in 2010
| Bats | Player | GSvR | GSvL | Sub | OPS |
|---|---|---|---|---|---|
| RH | Rodriguez I | 75 | 28 | 0 | .640 |
| RH | Nieves W | 33 | 9 | 9 | .554 |
| RH | Ramos W | 12 | 2 | 1 | .710 |

### Value / Extra / Production / OPS / Scoresheet
| Yr | Team | $1L | $2L | Pts | RAA | 2B | 3B | CS | FB-LD-GB | HR/fb | RBI% | RS% | OPS | 1st Hf | 2nd Hf | vs RH | vs LH | Rnge | vRH | vLH |
|---|---|---|---|---|---|---|---|---|---|---|---|---|---|---|---|---|---|---|---|---|
| 07 | | $14 | $5 | 240 | -6 | 31 | 3 | 2 | 24-19-52 | 10% | 12% | 29% | .714 | .750 | .663 | .703 | .746 | 0.30 | -28 | +73 |
| 08 | | $11 | $4 | 210 | -3 | 20 | 3 | 2 | 24-20-56 | 9% | 14% | 29% | .714 | .739 | .659 | .710 | .720 | 0.35 | -26 | +67 |
| 09 | | $7 | $5 | 190 | -13 | 23 | 2 | 2 | 28-18-54 | 11% | 16% | 39% | .663 | .670 | .654 | .630 | .784 | — | -16 | +44 |
| 10 | | $7 | $5 | 170 | -15 | 18 | 1 | 3 | 21-18-61 | 6% | 20% | 24% | .640 | .713 | .553 | .616 | .716 | 0.45 | -19 | +51 |

## Josh Rodriguez — 50 PA | $-5 | 20 pts

No MLB games played in 2010    Owned: 0%    RH

Rodriguez is a leading candidate for Cleveland's UT IF gig. Roster logistics kept him in the minors for all of 2010, but his versatile defense and a solid .293/.372/.486 performance in Triple-A have put him on the team's radar. He is a plus defender up the middle and has logged time at SS, 2B, 3B, and OF. (BLS)

### Forecast

| Player | Age | AB | HR | R | RBI | SB | BA | OBP | SLG | $1L | Pts |
|---|---|---|---|---|---|---|---|---|---|---|---|
| Rodriguez J | 26 | 44 | 1 | 5 | 5 | 1 | .203 | .289 | .335 | -$5 | 20 |

| Mini-Browser | Age | AB | HR | R | RBI | SB | BA | OBP | SLG | $1L | Pts |
|---|---|---|---|---|---|---|---|---|---|---|---|
| Forsythe L | 24 | 72 | 1 | 9 | 6 | 1 | .201 | .320 | .297 | -$4 | 30 |
| Havens R | 24 | 42 | 3 | 5 | 6 | 1 | .202 | .307 | .419 | -$4 | 20 |
| McCoy M | 29 | 44 | 3 | 6 | 4 | 2 | .239 | .329 | .331 | -$5 | 30 |
| Iwamura A | 32 | 45 | 1 | 7 | 3 | 1 | .258 | .342 | .367 | -$5 | 20 |
| Grudzielanek M | 40 | 46 | 1 | 5 | 4 | 1 | .269 | .313 | .351 | -$5 | 20 |

### Minors (2010) / Skills

| Level | Leag | AB | HR | R | RBI | SB | BA | OBP | SLG | CT% | H% | BB% | Bash |
|---|---|---|---|---|---|---|---|---|---|---|---|---|---|
| A | — | — | — | — | — | — | — | — | — | — | — | — | — |
| AA | EL | 63 | 1 | 11 | 11 | 0 | .317 | .405 | .476 | 84% | 38% | 14% | 1.50 |
| AAA | IL | 317 | 12 | 49 | 46 | 6 | .293 | .372 | .486 | 76% | 38% | 11% | 1.66 |

### Competition at 2B / Stats in 2010

| Bats | Player | GSvR | GSvL | Sub | OPS |
|---|---|---|---|---|---|
| LH | Valbuena L | 58 | 10 | 3 | .531 |
| RH | Donald J | 23 | 17 | 1 | .690 |
| RH | Grudzielanek M | 12 | 14 | 1 | .600 |
| RH | Nix J | 20 | 5 | 0 | .676 |

### Majors / Value / Extra / Production / OPS / Scoresheet

| Yr | Team | AB | HR | R | RBI | SB | BA | OBP | SLG | CT% | H% | BB% | Bash | $1L | $2L | Pts | RAA | 2B | 3B | CS | FB-LD-GB | HR/fb | RBI% | RS% | OPS | 1st Hf | 2nd Hf | vs RH | vs LH | Rnge | vRH | vLH |
|---|---|---|---|---|---|---|---|---|---|---|---|---|---|---|---|---|---|---|---|---|---|---|---|---|---|---|---|---|---|---|---|---|
| 07 | — | | | | | | | | | | | | | | | | | | | | | | | | | | | | | | | |
| 08 | — | | | | | | | | | | | | | | | | | | | | | | | | | | | | | | | |
| 09 | — | | | | | | | | | | | | | | | | | | | | | | | | | | | | | | | |
| 10 | — | | | | | | | | | | | | | | | | | | | | | | | | | | | | | | | |

---

## . Sean Rodriguez — 425 PA | $9 | 210 pts

2B-92, OF-21 (CF-9, RF-8, LF-5), 3B-7, SS-5, DH-3, 1B-3    Owned: 7%    RH

Rodriguez is the next Ben Zobrist, as he played every position except pitcher and catcher in 2010. In 2011, Rodriguez should split most of his time between second base and right field. He even stands a chance of seizing second base outright if he can squeeze a few more walks out of his plate appearances. (RZ)

### Forecast

| Player | Age | AB | HR | R | RBI | SB | BA | OBP | SLG | $1L | Pts |
|---|---|---|---|---|---|---|---|---|---|---|---|
| Rodriguez S | 25 | 391 | 17 | 51 | 47 | 9 | .239 | .317 | .425 | $9 | 210 |

| Mini-Browser | Age | AB | HR | R | RBI | SB | BA | OBP | SLG | $1L | Pts |
|---|---|---|---|---|---|---|---|---|---|---|---|
| Hill A | 29 | 508 | 22 | 66 | 66 | 6 | .249 | .301 | .421 | $12 | 320 |
| Hudson O | 33 | 465 | 11 | 68 | 47 | 3 | .282 | .357 | .418 | $12 | 300 |
| Young Jr. E | 25 | 387 | 5 | 63 | 27 | 32 | .244 | .327 | .360 | $11 | 250 |
| Espinosa D | 23 | 417 | 20 | 60 | 60 | 15 | .216 | .315 | .429 | $9 | 260 |
| Sanchez F | 33 | 433 | 9 | 59 | 45 | 0 | .291 | .332 | .414 | $9 | 260 |

### Minors (2010) / Skills

| Level | Leag | AB | HR | R | RBI | SB | BA | OBP | SLG | CT% | H% | BB% | Bash |
|---|---|---|---|---|---|---|---|---|---|---|---|---|---|
| A | — | — | — | — | — | — | — | — | — | — | — | — | — |
| AA | — | — | — | — | — | — | — | — | — | — | — | — | — |
| AAA | — | — | — | — | — | — | — | — | — | — | — | — | — |

### Competition at 2B / Stats in 2010

| Bats | Player | GSvR | GSvL | Sub | OPS |
|---|---|---|---|---|---|
| RH | Rodriguez S | 48 | 32 | 12 | .705 |
| BH | Zobrist B | 32 | 23 | 1 | .699 |
| LH | Brignac R | 39 | 5 | 24 | .692 |

### Majors / Value / Extra / Production / OPS / Scoresheet

| Yr | Team | AB | HR | R | RBI | SB | BA | OBP | SLG | CT% | H% | BB% | Bash | $1L | $2L | Pts | RAA | 2B | 3B | CS | FB-LD-GB | HR/fb | RBI% | RS% | OPS | 1st Hf | 2nd Hf | vs RH | vs LH | Rnge | vRH | vLH |
|---|---|---|---|---|---|---|---|---|---|---|---|---|---|---|---|---|---|---|---|---|---|---|---|---|---|---|---|---|---|---|---|---|
| 07 | — | | | | | | | | | | | | | | | | | | | | | | | | | | | | | | | |
| 08 | LAA | 167 | 3 | 18 | 10 | 3 | .204 | .276 | .317 | 67% | 30% | 7% | 1.56 | -$3 | -$18 | 40 | -11 | 8 | 1 | 1 | 47-12-41 | 6% | 10% | 31% | .593 | .520 | .640 | .639 | .467 | | | |
| 09 | LAA | 25 | 2 | 4 | 4 | 0 | .200 | .276 | .440 | 72% | 28% | 10% | 2.20 | -$3 | -$18 | 20 | -0 | 0 | 1 | 0 | 37-0-63 | 29% | 13% | 33% | .716 | .505 | 1.150 | .786 | .630 | 4.23 | -14 | +35 |
| 10 | TB | 343 | 9 | 53 | 40 | 13 | .251 | .308 | .397 | 72% | 35% | 6% | 1.58 | $10 | -$1 | 180 | -8 | 19 | 2 | 3 | 39-19-42 | 10% | 17% | 42% | .705 | .726 | .666 | .642 | .817 | 4.25 | -8 | +20 |

---

## Ryan Rohlinger — 50 PA | $-4 | 20 pts

SS-4, 3B-3    Owned: 0%    RH

Despite raking in the Pacific League, Rohlinger has looked overmatched at the plate during his cups of coffee with the Giants in three successive seasons. However, any team that employs as many aging and injury-prone infielders as the Giants do can use a versatile short-term replacement like Rohlinger. (PB)

### Forecast

| Player | Age | AB | HR | R | RBI | SB | BA | OBP | SLG | $1L | Pts |
|---|---|---|---|---|---|---|---|---|---|---|---|
| Rohlinger R | 27 | 47 | 2 | 6 | 6 | 0 | .234 | .308 | .411 | -$4 | 20 |

| Mini-Browser | Age | AB | HR | R | RBI | SB | BA | OBP | SLG | $1L | Pts |
|---|---|---|---|---|---|---|---|---|---|---|---|
| Andino R | 26 | 91 | 2 | 10 | 8 | 3 | .254 | .301 | .382 | -$3 | 40 |
| Wilson J | 30 | 143 | 2 | 12 | 12 | 3 | .242 | .296 | .345 | -$4 | 60 |
| Cozart Z | 25 | 88 | 3 | 10 | 9 | 1 | .215 | .288 | .385 | -$4 | 40 |
| Hernandez D | 26 | 69 | 2 | 7 | 8 | 2 | .240 | .296 | .352 | -$4 | 30 |
| Crosby B | 31 | 46 | 1 | 6 | 5 | 1 | .250 | .314 | .353 | -$4 | 20 |

### Minors (2010) / Skills

| Level | Leag | AB | HR | R | RBI | SB | BA | OBP | SLG | CT% | H% | BB% | Bash |
|---|---|---|---|---|---|---|---|---|---|---|---|---|---|
| A | — | — | — | — | — | — | — | — | — | — | — | — | — |
| AA | — | — | — | — | — | — | — | — | — | — | — | — | — |
| AAA | PCL | 283 | 8 | 46 | 48 | 3 | .311 | .392 | .477 | 79% | 39% | 9% | 1.53 |

### Competition at SS / Stats in 2010

| Bats | Player | GSvR | GSvL | Sub | OPS |
|---|---|---|---|---|---|
| RH | Uribe J | 78 | 23 | 2 | .749 |
| RH | Renteria E | 40 | 22 | 6 | .707 |

### Majors / Value / Extra / Production / OPS / Scoresheet

| Yr | Team | AB | HR | R | RBI | SB | BA | OBP | SLG | CT% | H% | BB% | Bash | $1L | $2L | Pts | RAA | 2B | 3B | CS | FB-LD-GB | HR/fb | RBI% | RS% | OPS | 1st Hf | 2nd Hf | vs RH | vs LH | Rnge | vRH | vLH |
|---|---|---|---|---|---|---|---|---|---|---|---|---|---|---|---|---|---|---|---|---|---|---|---|---|---|---|---|---|---|---|---|---|
| 07 | — | | | | | | | | | | | | | | | | | | | | | | | | | | | | | | | |
| 08 | SF | 32 | 0 | 2 | 2 | 0 | .094 | .121 | .188 | 75% | 13% | 3% | 2.00 | -$6 | -$19 | 0 | -6 | 1 | 1 | 1 | 38-8-54 | 0% | 9% | 50% | .309 | — | .309 | .205 | .625 | — | -25 | +59 |
| 09 | SF | 19 | 0 | 4 | 0 | 0 | .158 | .200 | .211 | 68% | 23% | 5% | 1.33 | -$5 | -$19 | 0 | -2 | 1 | 0 | 0 | 31-23-46 | 0% | 36% | 0% | .411 | — | .411 | .636 | .111 | — | -16 | +38 |
| 10 | SF | 15 | 0 | 1 | 1 | 0 | .200 | .294 | .200 | 67% | 30% | 11% | 1.00 | -$5 | -$21 | 0 | -1 | 0 | 0 | 0 | 30-30-40 | 0% | 13% | 20% | .494 | .527 | .000 | .222 | .833 | — | | |

---

## ı.... Scott Rolen — 500 PA | $13 | 340 pts

3B-130    Owned: 96%    RH

The veteran played better, and more often, in 2010 than anyone had a right to expect, but he is unlikely to be as durable at age 35. That will be bad news for the Reds (and for Reds hitters), as Rolen's power was a key to their winning. Still, he has been discounted for three straight years. Clearly, he has the will. (SW)

### Forecast

| Player | Age | AB | HR | R | RBI | SB | BA | OBP | SLG | $1L | Pts |
|---|---|---|---|---|---|---|---|---|---|---|---|
| Rolen S | 35 | 461 | 15 | 70 | 65 | 5 | .282 | .356 | .466 | $13 | 340 |

| Mini-Browser | Age | AB | HR | R | RBI | SB | BA | OBP | SLG | $1L | Pts |
|---|---|---|---|---|---|---|---|---|---|---|---|
| Coghlan C | 25 | 560 | 13 | 88 | 56 | 19 | .268 | .347 | .408 | $16 | 380 |
| Polanco P | 35 | 605 | 7 | 85 | 65 | 7 | .290 | .337 | .393 | $15 | 400 |
| McGehee C | 28 | 589 | 20 | 72 | 91 | 0 | .265 | .324 | .428 | $15 | 350 |
| Kouzmanoff K | 29 | 579 | 24 | 66 | 84 | 0 | .259 | .303 | .441 | $15 | 330 |
| Alvarez P | 24 | 530 | 30 | 66 | 96 | 0 | .249 | .328 | .480 | $15 | 310 |

### Minors (2010) / Skills

| Level | Leag | AB | HR | R | RBI | SB | BA | OBP | SLG | CT% | H% | BB% | Bash |
|---|---|---|---|---|---|---|---|---|---|---|---|---|---|
| A | — | — | — | — | — | — | — | — | — | — | — | — | — |
| AA | — | — | — | — | — | — | — | — | — | — | — | — | — |
| AAA | — | — | — | — | — | — | — | — | — | — | — | — | — |

### Competition at 3B / Stats in 2010

| Bats | Player | GSvR | GSvL | Sub | OPS |
|---|---|---|---|---|---|
| RH | Rolen S | 82 | 43 | 5 | .854 |
| RH | Cairo M | 17 | 11 | 10 | .763 |
| LH | Francisco J | 6 | 0 | 6 | .704 |
| RH | Janish P | 2 | 3 | 6 | .723 |

### Majors / Value / Extra / Production / OPS / Scoresheet

| Yr | Team | AB | HR | R | RBI | SB | BA | OBP | SLG | CT% | H% | BB% | Bash | $1L | $2L | Pts | RAA | 2B | 3B | CS | FB-LD-GB | HR/fb | RBI% | RS% | OPS | 1st Hf | 2nd Hf | vs RH | vs LH | Rnge | vRH | vLH |
|---|---|---|---|---|---|---|---|---|---|---|---|---|---|---|---|---|---|---|---|---|---|---|---|---|---|---|---|---|---|---|---|---|
| 07 | STL | 392 | 8 | 55 | 58 | 5 | .265 | .331 | .398 | 86% | 31% | 8% | 1.50 | $8 | -$2 | 260 | -4 | 24 | 2 | 3 | 43-20-38 | 5% | 21% | 34% | .729 | .725 | .734 | .770 | .616 | 2.74 | -5 | +14 |
| 08 | TOR | 408 | 11 | 50 | 50 | 5 | .262 | .349 | .431 | 83% | 32% | 10% | 1.64 | $10 | $0 | 270 | +3 | 30 | 3 | 0 | 44-21-36 | 7% | 19% | 31% | .780 | .790 | .765 | .787 | .760 | 2.72 | +2 | -5 |
| 09 | 2TM | 475 | 11 | 76 | 67 | 0 | .305 | .368 | .455 | 87% | 35% | 8% | 1.49 | $12 | $8 | 350 | +13 | 36 | 1 | 4 | 41-23-37 | 6% | 22% | 35% | .823 | .847 | .785 | .749 | 1.051 | 2.72 | -3 | +9 |
| 10 | CIN | 471 | 20 | 66 | 83 | 1 | .285 | .358 | .497 | 83% | 34% | 9% | 1.75 | $18 | $11 | 350 | +15 | 34 | 2 | 2 | 44-19-37 | 12% | 21% | 27% | .854 | .909 | .772 | .860 | .840 | 2.72 | -24 | +61 |

---

## ılıı. Jimmy Rollins — 700 PA | $26 | 550 pts

SS-88    Owned: 100%    BH

By RAA, Rollins in 2010 skirted true mediocrity for his position, at least offensively. He even got lucky on RBI (25% RBI%), despite sub-par H% and Bash. He partly compensated by raising his walk rate to 10%. Rollins's performance in 2011 comes down to health (and not just his health in the spring, either). (BB)

### Forecast

| Player | Age | AB | HR | R | RBI | SB | BA | OBP | SLG | $1L | Pts |
|---|---|---|---|---|---|---|---|---|---|---|---|
| Rollins J | 32 | 639 | 21 | 105 | 77 | 35 | .274 | .335 | .472 | $26 | 550 |

| Mini-Browser | Age | AB | HR | R | RBI | SB | BA | OBP | SLG | $1L | Pts |
|---|---|---|---|---|---|---|---|---|---|---|---|
| Ramirez H | 27 | 591 | 26 | 111 | 85 | 33 | .308 | .387 | .528 | $34 | 550 |
| Tulowitzki T | 26 | 589 | 27 | 108 | 101 | 14 | .298 | .373 | .531 | $29 | 500 |
| Reyes J | 27 | 544 | 12 | 90 | 54 | 42 | .287 | .348 | .457 | $24 | 460 |
| Jeter D | 36 | 603 | 14 | 95 | 61 | 20 | .280 | .351 | .388 | $20 | 400 |
| Ramirez A | 29 | 551 | 18 | 72 | 72 | 12 | .272 | .312 | .415 | $18 | 350 |

### Minors (2010) / Skills

| Level | Leag | AB | HR | R | RBI | SB | BA | OBP | SLG | CT% | H% | BB% | Bash |
|---|---|---|---|---|---|---|---|---|---|---|---|---|---|
| A | FLO | 14 | 0 | 2 | 2 | 0 | .143 | .176 | .143 | 93% | 15% | 6% | 1.00 |
| AA | — | — | — | — | — | — | — | — | — | — | — | — | — |
| AAA | — | — | — | — | — | — | — | — | — | — | — | — | — |

### Competition at SS / Stats in 2010

| Bats | Player | GSvR | GSvL | Sub | OPS |
|---|---|---|---|---|---|
| BH | Rollins J | 57 | 29 | 2 | .694 |
| RH | Valdez W | 37 | 14 | 8 | .667 |

### Majors / Value / Extra / Production / OPS / Scoresheet

| Yr | Team | AB | HR | R | RBI | SB | BA | OBP | SLG | CT% | H% | BB% | Bash | $1L | $2L | Pts | RAA | 2B | 3B | CS | FB-LD-GB | HR/fb | RBI% | RS% | OPS | 1st Hf | 2nd Hf | vs RH | vs LH | Rnge | vRH | vLH |
|---|---|---|---|---|---|---|---|---|---|---|---|---|---|---|---|---|---|---|---|---|---|---|---|---|---|---|---|---|---|---|---|---|
| 07 | PHI | 716 | 30 | 139 | 94 | 41 | .296 | .344 | .531 | 88% | 34% | 6% | 1.79 | $39 | $35 | 550 | +44 | 38 | 20 | 6 | 44-20-36 | 11% | 22% | 46% | .875 | .847 | .908 | .857 | .917 | 4.72 | +5 | -16 |
| 08 | PHI | 556 | 11 | 76 | 59 | 47 | .277 | .349 | .437 | 90% | 31% | 9% | 1.58 | $24 | $15 | 470 | +25 | 38 | 9 | 3 | 31-24-45 | 7% | 24% | 32% | .786 | .778 | .794 | .790 | .776 | 4.74 | -5 | +14 |
| 09 | PHI | 672 | 21 | 100 | 77 | 31 | .250 | .296 | .423 | 90% | 26% | 6% | 1.69 | $24 | $16 | 490 | +6 | 43 | 5 | 8 | 41-19-40 | 8% | 20% | 41% | .719 | .642 | .801 | .728 | .692 | 4.83 | +1 | +11 |
| 10 | PHI | 350 | 8 | 48 | 41 | 17 | .243 | .320 | .374 | 91% | 27% | 10% | 1.54 | $9 | -$2 | 260 | +1 | 16 | 3 | 1 | 37-17-46 | 7% | 25% | 34% | .694 | .793 | .642 | .657 | .773 | 4.81 | +1 | -3 |

*For more stats, visit www.Rotolympus.com.*

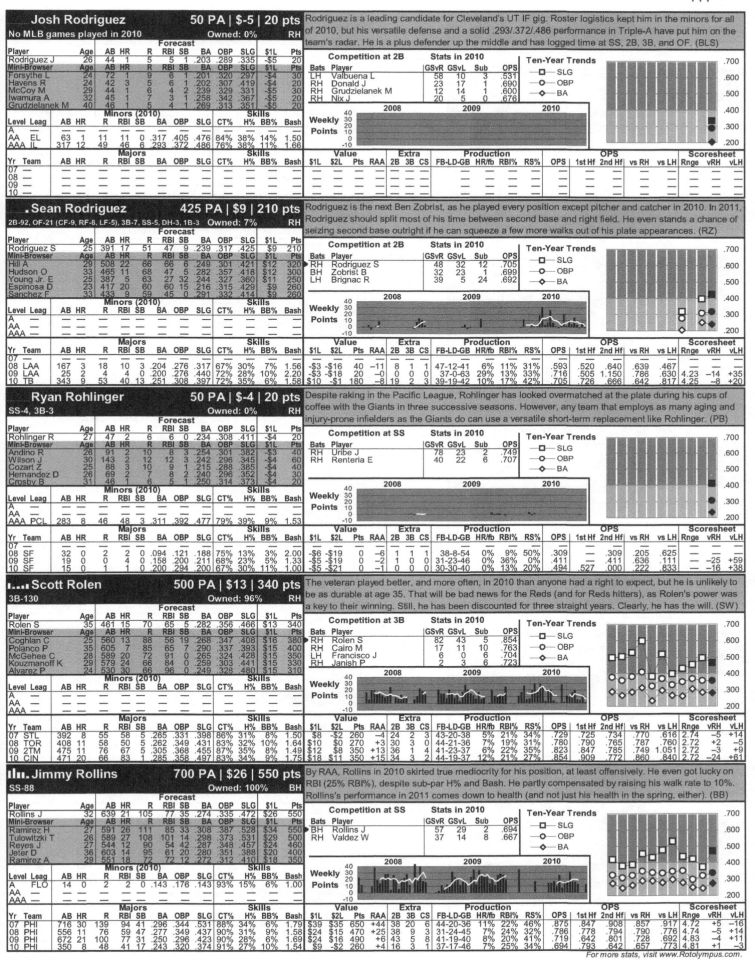

## Adam Rosales

**450 PA | $9 | 230 pts**

2B-47, SS-14, 1B-7, 3B-5, OF-5 (LF-5), DH-4 Owned: 0% RH

Despite being a sub, Rosales was playing nearly every day before an ankle injury ended his season. He displayed some pop and versatility and will probably play a super-sub role once again in 2011. He could compete for the 2B job if Mark Ellis doesn't return, but the A's like what Rosales offers off the bench. (ML)

| | | Forecast | | | | | | | | | |
|---|---|---|---|---|---|---|---|---|---|---|---|
| Player | Age | AB | HR | R | RBI | SB | BA | OBP | SLG | $1L | Pts |
| Rosales A | 27 | 403 | 14 | 54 | 45 | 5 | .257 | .327 | .438 | $9 | 230 |
| Mini-Browser | Age | AB | HR | R | RBI | SB | BA | OBP | SLG | $1L | Pts |
| Hudson O | 33 | 465 | 11 | 68 | 47 | 5 | .282 | .357 | .418 | $12 | 300 |
| Young Jr. E | 25 | 387 | 5 | 63 | 27 | 32 | .244 | .327 | .360 | $11 | 250 |
| Espinosa D | 23 | 417 | 20 | 60 | 60 | 15 | .216 | .315 | .429 | $9 | 260 |
| Sanchez F | 33 | 433 | 9 | 59 | 45 | 0 | .291 | .332 | .414 | $9 | 260 |
| Rodriguez S | 25 | 391 | 17 | 51 | 47 | 9 | .239 | .317 | .425 | $9 | 210 |

| | | Minors (2010) | | | | | | | | Skills | | | |
|---|---|---|---|---|---|---|---|---|---|---|---|---|---|
| Level | Leag | AB | HR | R | RBI | SB | BA | OBP | SLG | CT% | H% | BB% | Bash |
| A | — | — | — | — | — | — | — | — | — | — | — | — | — |
| AA | — | — | — | — | — | — | — | — | — | — | — | — | — |
| AAA | — | — | — | — | — | — | — | — | — | — | — | — | — |

| | | Majors | | | | | | | | Skills | | | |
|---|---|---|---|---|---|---|---|---|---|---|---|---|---|
| Yr | Team | AB | HR | R | RBI | SB | BA | OBP | SLG | CT% | H% | BB% | Bash |
| 07 | — | — | — | — | — | — | — | — | — | — | — | — | — |
| 08 | CIN | 29 | 0 | 0 | 2 | 1 | .207 | .233 | .241 | 86% | 24% | 3% | 1.17 |
| 09 | CIN | 230 | 4 | 23 | 19 | 1 | .213 | .303 | .317 | 80% | 27% | 10% | 1.49 |
| 10 | OAK | 255 | 7 | 31 | 31 | 2 | .271 | .321 | .400 | 75% | 36% | 7% | 1.48 |

**Competition at 2B — Stats in 2010**

| Bats | Player | GSvR | GSvL | Sub | OPS |
|---|---|---|---|---|---|
| RH | Ellis M | 86 | 27 | 3 | .739 |
| ▶ RH | Rosales A | 28 | 17 | 2 | .721 |

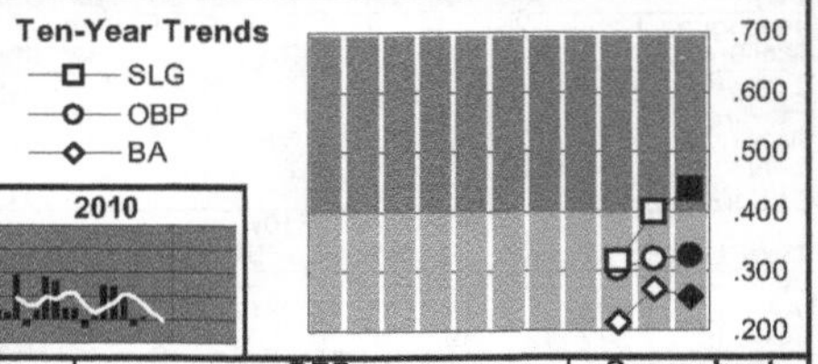


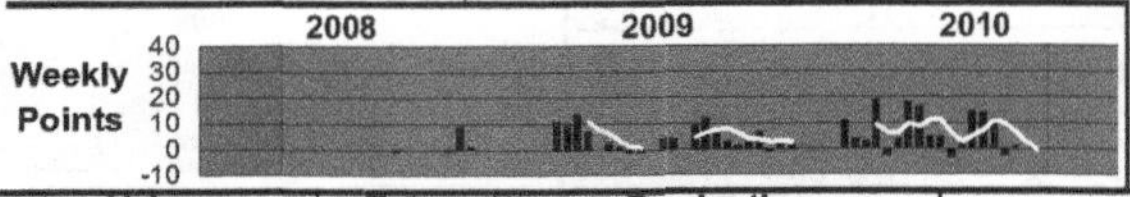


| Value | | | | Extra | | | Production | | | | OPS | | | | | Scoresheet | | |
|---|---|---|---|---|---|---|---|---|---|---|---|---|---|---|---|---|---|---|
| $1L | $2L | Pts | RAA | 2B | 3B | CS | FB-LD-GB | HR/fb | RBI% | RS% | OPS | 1st Hf | 2nd Hf | vs RH | vs LH | Rnge | vRH | vLH |
| — | — | — | — | — | — | — | — | — | — | — | — | — | — | — | — | — | — | — |
| -$5 | -$19 | 10 | −2 | 1 | 0 | 0 | 44-20-36 | 0% | 25% | 0% | .475 | — | .475 | .433 | .545 | — | — | — |
| -$2 | -$17 | 100 | −13 | 10 | 1 | 2 | 40-16-45 | 5% | 12% | 25% | .620 | .571 | .685 | .598 | .693 | — | −22 | +51 |
| $5 | -$8 | 120 | −2 | 8 | 2 | 2 | 34-28-38 | 11% | 17% | 29% | .721 | .744 | .591 | .681 | .794 | — | −19 | +48 |

## Cody Ross

**600 PA | $19 | 370 pts**

OF-151 (CF-89, RF-54, LF-24) Owned: 57% RH

Ross is basically a cheaper, younger version of Aaron Rowand. Once in SF, Ross even showed the power (notably 2 HR off Roy Halladay in the NLCS) that had gone missing in his first five months in Florida. That outburst should make it easier for the Giants to bring Ross back. He can play all three OF positions. (PB)

| | | Forecast | | | | | | | | | |
|---|---|---|---|---|---|---|---|---|---|---|---|
| Player | Age | AB | HR | R | RBI | SB | BA | OBP | SLG | $1L | Pts |
| Ross C | 30 | 565 | 24 | 78 | 84 | 6 | .276 | .334 | .485 | $19 | 370 |
| Mini-Browser | Age | AB | HR | R | RBI | SB | BA | OBP | SLG | $1L | Pts |
| Span D | 27 | 620 | 7 | 91 | 63 | 28 | .271 | .348 | .371 | $20 | 420 |
| Ethier A | 28 | 523 | 24 | 78 | 84 | 6 | .287 | .366 | .506 | $20 | 410 |
| Bautista J | 30 | 522 | 30 | 78 | 84 | 6 | .253 | .353 | .495 | $20 | 400 |
| Cuddyer M | 32 | 578 | 20 | 85 | 85 | 7 | .270 | .342 | .456 | $19 | 390 |
| Quentin C | 28 | 465 | 28 | 77 | 88 | 6 | .260 | .352 | .494 | $19 | 370 |

| | | Minors (2010) | | | | | | | | Skills | | | |
|---|---|---|---|---|---|---|---|---|---|---|---|---|---|
| Level | Leag | AB | HR | R | RBI | SB | BA | OBP | SLG | CT% | H% | BB% | Bash |
| A | — | — | — | — | — | — | — | — | — | — | — | — | — |
| AA | — | — | — | — | — | — | — | — | — | — | — | — | — |
| AAA | — | — | — | — | — | — | — | — | — | — | — | — | — |

| | | Majors | | | | | | | | Skills | | | |
|---|---|---|---|---|---|---|---|---|---|---|---|---|---|
| Yr | Team | AB | HR | R | RBI | SB | BA | OBP | SLG | CT% | H% | BB% | Bash |
| 07 | FLA | 173 | 12 | 35 | 39 | 2 | .335 | .411 | .653 | 78% | 43% | 10% | 1.95 |
| 08 | FLA | 461 | 22 | 59 | 73 | 6 | .260 | .316 | .488 | 75% | 35% | 6% | 1.88 |
| 09 | FLA | 559 | 24 | 73 | 90 | 5 | .270 | .321 | .469 | 78% | 35% | 6% | 1.74 |
| 10 | 2TM | 525 | 14 | 71 | 65 | 9 | .269 | .322 | .413 | 77% | 35% | 6% | 1.54 |

**Competition at CF — Stats in 2010**

| Bats | Player | GSvR | GSvL | Sub | OPS |
|---|---|---|---|---|---|
| BH | Torres A | 63 | 17 | 4 | .823 |
| RH | Rowand A | 51 | 25 | 9 | .659 |
| ▶ RH | Ross C | 6 | 4 | 2 | .735 |

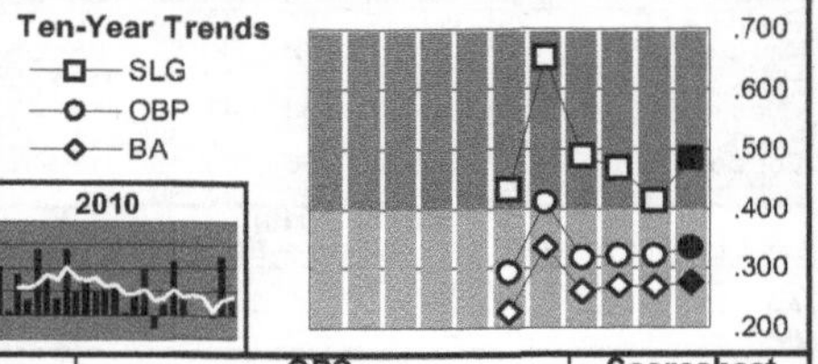


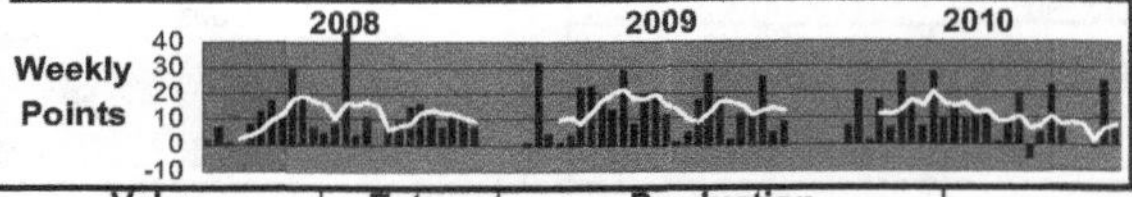


| Value | | | | Extra | | | Production | | | | OPS | | | | | Scoresheet | | |
|---|---|---|---|---|---|---|---|---|---|---|---|---|---|---|---|---|---|---|
| $1L | $2L | Pts | RAA | 2B | 3B | CS | FB-LD-GB | HR/fb | RBI% | RS% | OPS | 1st Hf | 2nd Hf | vs RH | vs LH | Rnge | vRH | vLH |
| $8 | -$3 | 170 | +20 | 19 | 0 | 0 | 38-21-41 | 23% | 31% | 33% | 1.064 | 1.025 | 1.082 | .974 | 1.212 | 2.10 | −34 | +76 |
| $14 | $6 | 280 | +5 | 29 | 5 | 1 | 43-21-36 | 15% | 20% | 27% | .804 | .828 | .777 | .756 | .911 | 2.10 | −41 | +92 |
| $19 | $11 | 340 | +5 | 37 | 1 | 2 | 48-19-33 | 11% | 19% | 29% | .790 | .836 | .733 | .736 | .959 | 2.17 | −36 | +83 |
| $16 | $7 | 280 | −3 | 28 | 3 | 2 | 34-21-46 | 10% | 18% | 34% | .735 | .748 | .714 | .687 | .883 | 2.14 | −32 | +80 |

## David Ross

**150 PA | $1 | 70 pts**

CA-57 Owned: 0% RH

The Braves' slow-and-steady back-up catcher, Ross did not match his power from 2009, but his job is to stand in for Brian McCann about once a week (especially versus LHP), and he performed as well as a back-up can be expected to. Ross is no frills, but he is valuable even in his limited playing time. (MG)

| | | Forecast | | | | | | | | | |
|---|---|---|---|---|---|---|---|---|---|---|---|
| Player | Age | AB | HR | R | RBI | SB | BA | OBP | SLG | $1L | Pts |
| Ross D | 34 | 126 | 5 | 15 | 20 | 0 | .250 | .350 | .434 | $1 | 70 |
| Mini-Browser | Age | AB | HR | R | RBI | SB | BA | OBP | SLG | $1L | Pts |
| Barajas R | 35 | 186 | 8 | 20 | 26 | 0 | .247 | .292 | .425 | $3 | 100 |
| Varitek J | 38 | 216 | 8 | 23 | 28 | 0 | .231 | .326 | .398 | $2 | 100 |
| Cervelli F | 25 | 224 | 3 | 23 | 25 | 0 | .246 | .323 | .332 | $2 | 110 |
| Moore A | 26 | 270 | 9 | 24 | 30 | 0 | .222 | .281 | .361 | $2 | 110 |
| Castro J | 23 | 345 | 8 | 40 | 32 | 0 | .220 | .303 | .340 | $2 | 150 |

| | | Minors (2010) | | | | | | | | Skills | | | |
|---|---|---|---|---|---|---|---|---|---|---|---|---|---|
| Level | Leag | AB | HR | R | RBI | SB | BA | OBP | SLG | CT% | H% | BB% | Bash |
| A | — | — | — | — | — | — | — | — | — | — | — | — | — |
| AA | — | — | — | — | — | — | — | — | — | — | — | — | — |
| AAA | — | — | — | — | — | — | — | — | — | — | — | — | — |

| | | Majors | | | | | | | | Skills | | | |
|---|---|---|---|---|---|---|---|---|---|---|---|---|---|
| Yr | Team | AB | HR | R | RBI | SB | BA | OBP | SLG | CT% | H% | BB% | Bash |
| 07 | CIN | 311 | 17 | 32 | 39 | 0 | .203 | .271 | .399 | 70% | 29% | 9% | 1.97 |
| 08 | 2TM | 142 | 3 | 18 | 13 | 0 | .225 | .369 | .352 | 73% | 31% | 17% | 1.56 |
| 09 | ATL | 128 | 7 | 18 | 20 | 0 | .273 | .380 | .508 | 70% | 39% | 14% | 1.86 |
| 10 | ATL | 121 | 2 | 15 | 28 | 0 | .289 | .392 | .479 | 77% | 38% | 14% | 1.66 |

**Competition at CA — Stats in 2010**

| Bats | Player | GSvR | GSvL | Sub | OPS |
|---|---|---|---|---|---|
| LH | McCann B | 103 | 26 | 7 | .828 |
| ▶ RH | Ross D | 4 | 29 | 24 | .871 |

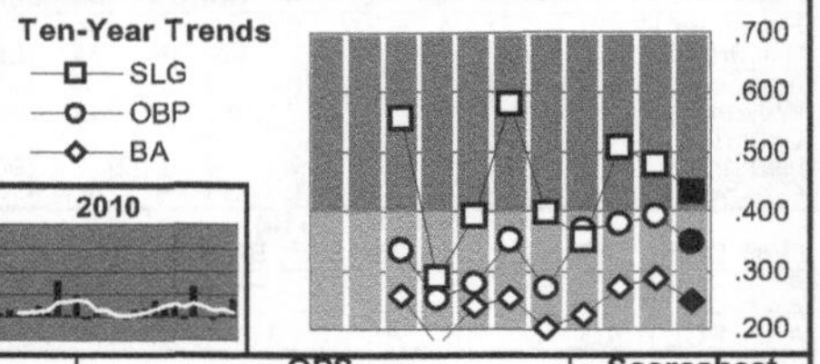


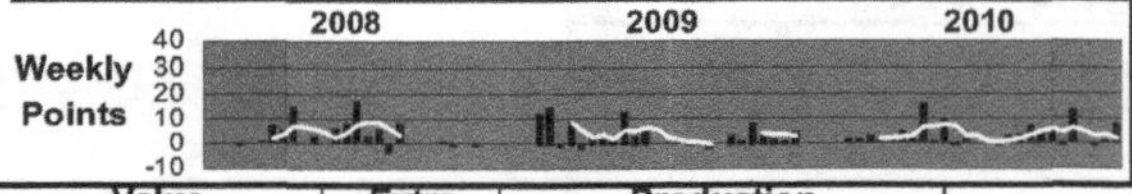


| Value | | | | Extra | | | Production | | | | OPS | | | | | Scoresheet | | |
|---|---|---|---|---|---|---|---|---|---|---|---|---|---|---|---|---|---|---|
| $1L | $2L | Pts | RAA | 2B | 3B | CS | FB-LD-GB | HR/fb | RBI% | RS% | OPS | 1st Hf | 2nd Hf | vs RH | vs LH | Rnge | vRH | vLH |
| $4 | -$5 | 130 | −11 | 10 | 0 | 0 | 48-19-34 | 17% | 12% | 20% | .670 | .658 | .693 | .615 | .761 | 0.41 | −31 | +77 |
| -$2 | -$8 | 70 | −2 | 9 | 0 | 1 | 37-25-38 | 8% | 13% | 24% | .721 | .806 | .499 | .793 | .632 | 0.42 | −40 | +92 |
| $4 | -$3 | 80 | +8 | 9 | 0 | 0 | 49-22-30 | 16% | 17% | 22% | .888 | .908 | .839 | .997 | .648 | 0.50 | −21 | +44 |
| $3 | -$4 | 90 | +6 | 13 | 2 | 1 | 41-21-38 | 5% | 28% | 24% | .871 | .748 | 1.029 | .834 | .886 | 0.57 | −1 | +2 |

## Aaron Rowand

**300 PA | $4 | 160 pts**

OF-85 (CF-85) Owned: 5% RH

Rowand is basically an expensive, older version of Cody Ross. Of course, Rowand is a gamer with a sterling reputation, so he will get more at-bats than he should. He has faded in the second half for the last three seasons (OPS's of .665, .629, and .599), and he ceased getting full-time play in 2010 after May. (PB)

| | | Forecast | | | | | | | | | |
|---|---|---|---|---|---|---|---|---|---|---|---|
| Player | Age | AB | HR | R | RBI | SB | BA | OBP | SLG | $1L | Pts |
| Rowand A | 33 | 279 | 9 | 36 | 36 | 3 | .269 | .331 | .427 | $4 | 160 |
| Mini-Browser | Age | AB | HR | R | RBI | SB | BA | OBP | SLG | $1L | Pts |
| Ankiel R | 31 | 271 | 12 | 39 | 42 | 3 | .266 | .326 | .472 | $6 | 170 |
| Blanco G | 27 | 346 | 4 | 48 | 28 | 12 | .254 | .359 | .332 | $5 | 200 |
| Milledge L | 25 | 330 | 7 | 39 | 35 | 11 | .276 | .337 | .408 | $5 | 200 |
| Venable W | 28 | 304 | 10 | 41 | 37 | 10 | .235 | .309 | .391 | $4 | 170 |
| Heisey C | 26 | 275 | 12 | 39 | 30 | 9 | .240 | .309 | .434 | $4 | 180 |

| | | Minors (2010) | | | | | | | | Skills | | | |
|---|---|---|---|---|---|---|---|---|---|---|---|---|---|
| Level | Leag | AB | HR | R | RBI | SB | BA | OBP | SLG | CT% | H% | BB% | Bash |
| A | — | — | — | — | — | — | — | — | — | — | — | — | — |
| AA | — | — | — | — | — | — | — | — | — | — | — | — | — |
| AAA | — | — | — | — | — | — | — | — | — | — | — | — | — |

| | | Majors | | | | | | | | Skills | | | |
|---|---|---|---|---|---|---|---|---|---|---|---|---|---|
| Yr | Team | AB | HR | R | RBI | SB | BA | OBP | SLG | CT% | H% | BB% | Bash |
| 07 | PHI | 612 | 27 | 105 | 89 | 6 | .309 | .374 | .515 | 81% | 38% | 7% | 1.67 |
| 08 | SF | 549 | 13 | 57 | 70 | 2 | .271 | .339 | .410 | 77% | 35% | 7% | 1.51 |
| 09 | SF | 499 | 15 | 61 | 64 | 4 | .261 | .319 | .419 | 75% | 35% | 5% | 1.61 |
| 10 | SF | 331 | 11 | 42 | 34 | 5 | .230 | .281 | .378 | 78% | 30% | 4% | 1.64 |

**Competition at CF — Stats in 2010**

| Bats | Player | GSvR | GSvL | Sub | OPS |
|---|---|---|---|---|---|
| BH | Torres A | 63 | 17 | 4 | .823 |
| ▶ RH | Rowand A | 51 | 25 | 9 | .659 |
| RH | Ross C | 6 | 4 | 2 | .735 |

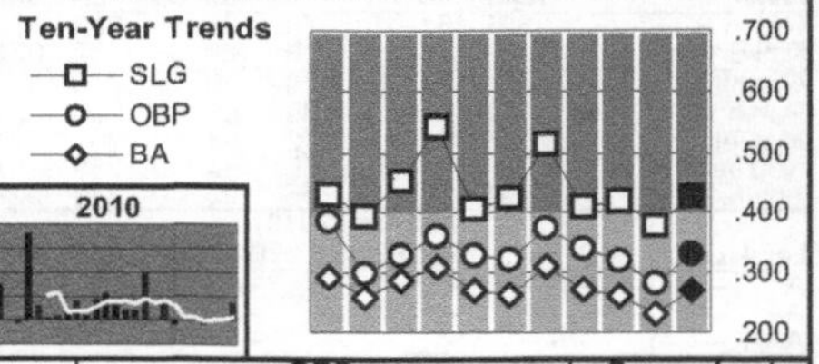


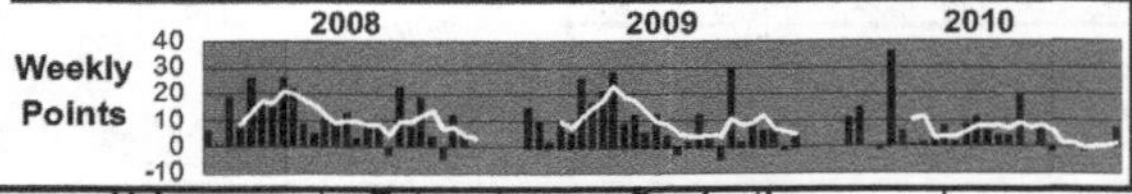


| Value | | | | Extra | | | Production | | | | OPS | | | | | Scoresheet | | |
|---|---|---|---|---|---|---|---|---|---|---|---|---|---|---|---|---|---|---|
| $1L | $2L | Pts | RAA | 2B | 3B | CS | FB-LD-GB | HR/fb | RBI% | RS% | OPS | 1st Hf | 2nd Hf | vs RH | vs LH | Rnge | vRH | vLH |
| $28 | $22 | 450 | +25 | 45 | 0 | 3 | 38-20-43 | 15% | 17% | 34% | .889 | .863 | .915 | .876 | .918 | 2.16 | −21 | +55 |
| $11 | $2 | 270 | −6 | 37 | 0 | 4 | 32-19-49 | 10% | 20% | 23% | .749 | .804 | .665 | .702 | .877 | 2.18 | −18 | +46 |
| $12 | $1 | 250 | −8 | 30 | 2 | 1 | 39-16-45 | 10% | 21% | 29% | .738 | .806 | .629 | .770 | .636 | 2.18 | −26 | +66 |
| $4 | -$8 | 150 | −17 | 12 | 2 | 3 | 37-15-48 | 12% | 19% | 35% | .659 | .681 | .599 | .649 | .682 | 2.17 | −14 | +37 |

## Carlos Ruiz

**450 PA | $11 | 270 pts**

CA-118 Owned: 57% RH

Ruiz in 2010 had a career year; credit a very high (for him) hit rate of 35%. But although the BA may have been fluky, the 12% walk rate and .400 OBP were not – as a #8 hitter in the NL, Ruiz knows exactly what he is doing, and he is content to collect those non-intentional intentional walks. (BB)

| | | Forecast | | | | | | | | | |
|---|---|---|---|---|---|---|---|---|---|---|---|
| Player | Age | AB | HR | R | RBI | SB | BA | OBP | SLG | $1L | Pts |
| Ruiz C | 32 | 370 | 9 | 45 | 54 | 5 | .280 | .375 | .431 | $11 | 270 |
| Mini-Browser | Age | AB | HR | R | RBI | SB | BA | OBP | SLG | $1L | Pts |
| Wieters M | 24 | 439 | 15 | 45 | 60 | 0 | .262 | .337 | .423 | $12 | 240 |
| Molina Y | 28 | 493 | 6 | 44 | 61 | 6 | .279 | .344 | .372 | $12 | 290 |
| Olivo M | 32 | 362 | 19 | 45 | 53 | 4 | .259 | .296 | .482 | $11 | 190 |
| Martin R | 28 | 338 | 8 | 52 | 44 | 8 | .272 | .371 | .394 | $11 | 240 |
| Posada J | 39 | 282 | 13 | 36 | 46 | 0 | .265 | .360 | .462 | $11 | 180 |

| | | Minors (2010) | | | | | | | | Skills | | | |
|---|---|---|---|---|---|---|---|---|---|---|---|---|---|
| Level | Leag | AB | HR | R | RBI | SB | BA | OBP | SLG | CT% | H% | BB% | Bash |
| A | SAL | 8 | 0 | 1 | 1 | 0 | .500 | .500 | .750 | 75% | 67% | 0% | 1.50 |
| AA | — | — | — | — | — | — | — | — | — | — | — | — | — |
| AAA | IL | 2 | 0 | 0 | 0 | 0 | .000 | .333 | .000 | 50% | 0% | 33% | NA |

| | | Majors | | | | | | | | Skills | | | |
|---|---|---|---|---|---|---|---|---|---|---|---|---|---|
| Yr | Team | AB | HR | R | RBI | SB | BA | OBP | SLG | CT% | H% | BB% | Bash |
| 07 | PHI | 374 | 6 | 42 | 54 | 6 | .259 | .340 | .396 | 87% | 30% | 10% | 1.53 |
| 08 | PHI | 320 | 4 | 47 | 31 | 1 | .219 | .320 | .300 | 88% | 25% | 12% | 1.37 |
| 09 | PHI | 322 | 9 | 32 | 43 | 3 | .255 | .355 | .425 | 88% | 29% | 12% | 1.67 |
| 10 | PHI | 371 | 8 | 43 | 53 | 0 | .302 | .400 | .447 | 85% | 35% | 12% | 1.48 |

**Competition at CA — Stats in 2010**

| Bats | Player | GSvR | GSvL | Sub | OPS |
|---|---|---|---|---|---|
| ▶ RH | Ruiz C | 68 | 41 | 9 | .847 |
| LH | Schneider B | 36 | 2 | 8 | .729 |
| RH | Sardinha D | 7 | 2 | 3 | .712 |

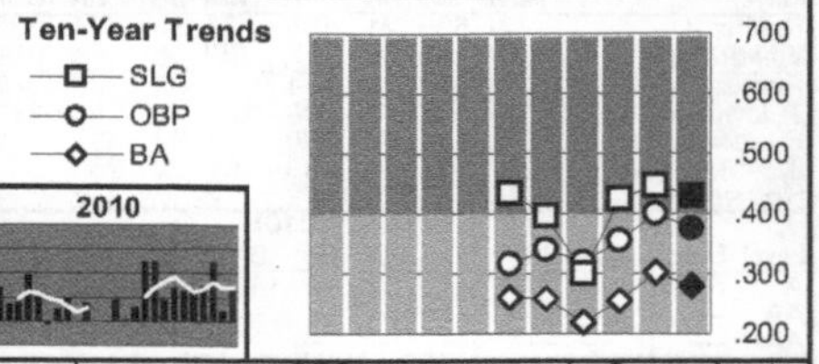


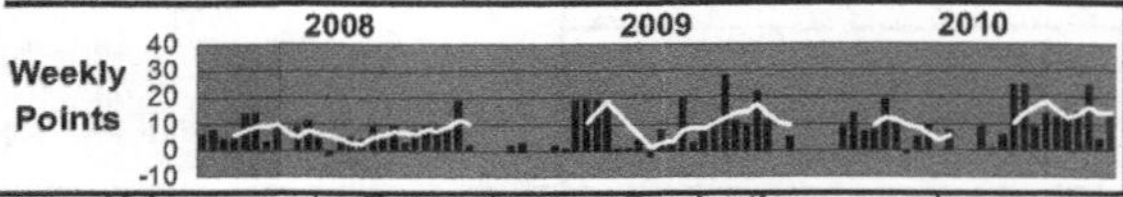


| Value | | | | Extra | | | Production | | | | OPS | | | | | Scoresheet | | |
|---|---|---|---|---|---|---|---|---|---|---|---|---|---|---|---|---|---|---|
| $1L | $2L | Pts | RAA | 2B | 3B | CS | FB-LD-GB | HR/fb | RBI% | RS% | OPS | 1st Hf | 2nd Hf | vs RH | vs LH | Rnge | vRH | vLH |
| $8 | $0 | 250 | −3 | 29 | 2 | 1 | 36-18-46 | 5% | 20% | 26% | .735 | .730 | .741 | .786 | .576 | 0.56 | −20 | +50 |
| $3 | -$3 | 180 | −16 | 14 | 0 | 2 | 29-17-54 | 5% | 16% | 38% | .620 | .573 | .691 | .604 | .679 | 0.58 | −7 | +20 |
| $7 | $2 | 220 | +3 | 26 | 1 | 2 | 39-19-42 | 8% | 22% | 19% | .780 | .703 | .862 | .741 | .894 | 0.62 | −10 | +26 |
| $13 | $8 | 260 | +14 | 28 | 1 | 1 | 35-20-45 | 7% | 21% | 21% | .847 | .794 | .886 | .808 | .940 | 0.60 | −22 | +60 |

*For more stats, visit www.Rotolympus.com.*

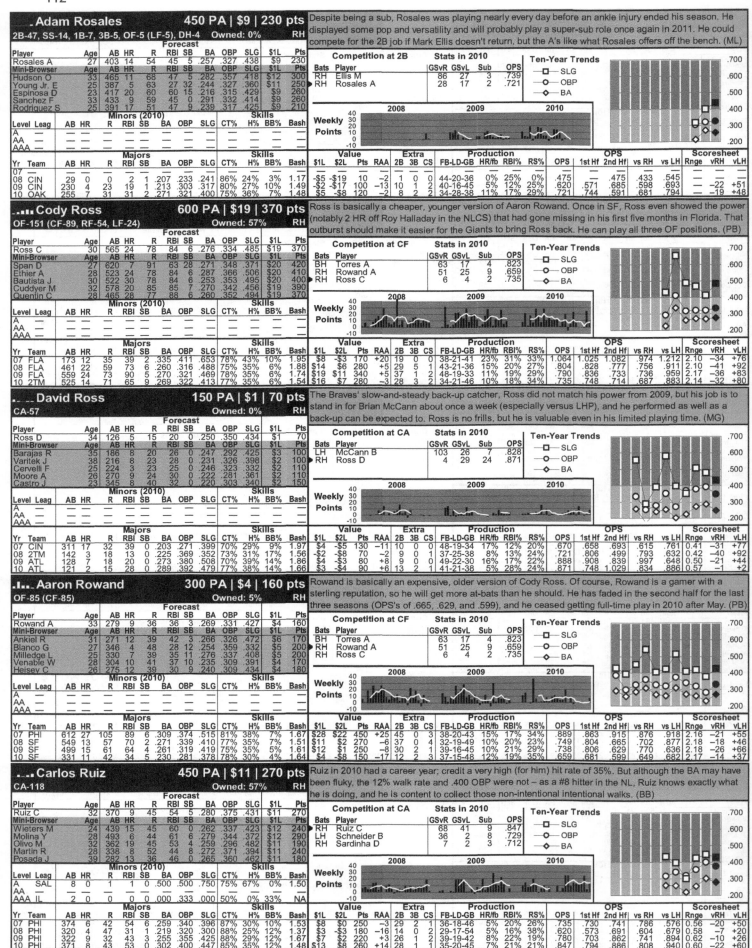

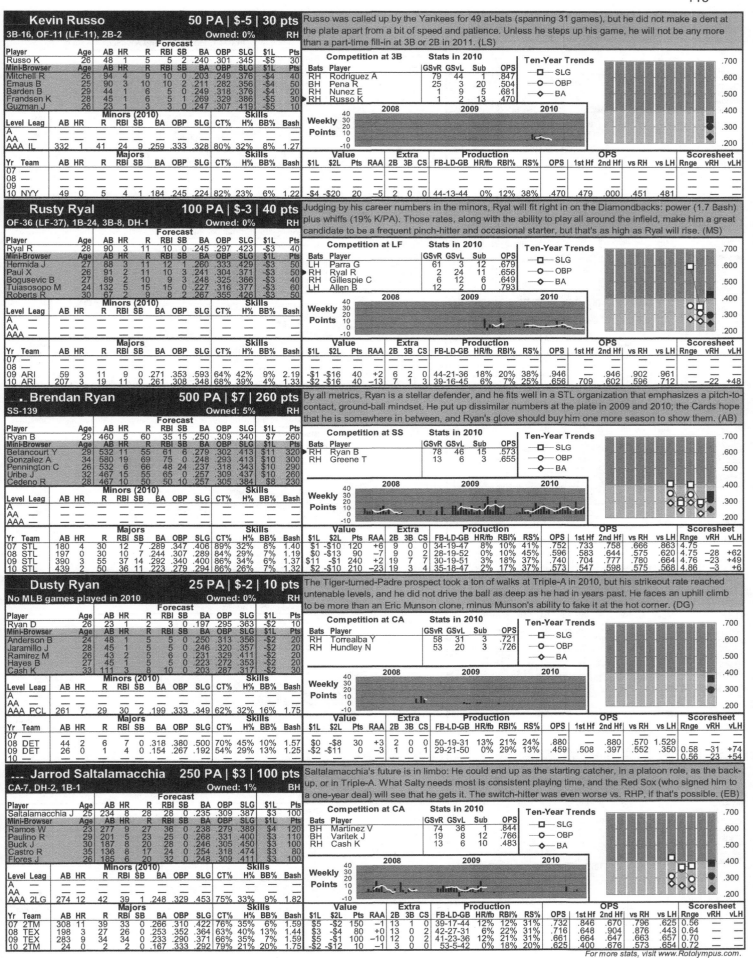

## Kevin Russo — 50 PA | $-5 | 30 pts

3B-16, OF-11 (LF-11), 2B-2 — Owned: 0% — RH

Russo was called up by the Yankees for 49 at-bats (spanning 31 games), but he did not make a dent at the plate apart from a bit of speed and patience. Unless he steps up his game, he will not be any more than a part-time fill-in at 3B or 2B in 2011. (LS)

| Player | Age | AB | HR | R | RBI | SB | BA | OBP | SLG | $1L | Pts |
|---|---|---|---|---|---|---|---|---|---|---|---|
| **Forecast** | | | | | | | | | | | |
| Russo K | 26 | 48 | 1 | 5 | 5 | 2 | .240 | .301 | .345 | -$5 | 30 |
| **Mini-Browser** | Age | AB | HR | R | RBI | SB | BA | OBP | SLG | $1L | Pts |
| Mitchell R | 26 | 94 | 4 | 9 | 10 | 0 | .203 | .249 | .376 | -$4 | 40 |
| Emaus B | 25 | 90 | 3 | 10 | 10 | 2 | .211 | .282 | .356 | -$4 | 50 |
| Barden B | 29 | 44 | 1 | 6 | 5 | 0 | .249 | .318 | .376 | -$4 | 20 |
| Frandsen K | 28 | 45 | 1 | 6 | 5 | 1 | .269 | .329 | .386 | -$5 | 30 |
| Guzman J | 26 | 23 | 1 | 3 | 3 | 0 | .247 | .307 | .419 | -$5 | 10 |

| Level | Leag | AB | HR | R | RBI | SB | BA | OBP | SLG | CT% | H% | BB% | Bash |
|---|---|---|---|---|---|---|---|---|---|---|---|---|---|
| **Minors (2010)** | | | | | | | | | | **Skills** | | | |
| A | — | — | — | — | — | — | — | — | — | — | — | — | — |
| AA | — | — | — | — | — | — | — | — | — | — | — | — | — |
| AAA | IL | 332 | 1 | 41 | 24 | 9 | .259 | .333 | .328 | 80% | 32% | 8% | 1.27 |

| Yr | Team | AB | HR | R | RBI | SB | BA | OBP | SLG | CT% | H% | BB% | Bash |
|---|---|---|---|---|---|---|---|---|---|---|---|---|---|
| **Majors** | | | | | | | | | | **Skills** | | | |
| 07 | — | — | — | — | — | — | — | — | — | — | — | — | — |
| 08 | — | — | — | — | — | — | — | — | — | — | — | — | — |
| 09 | — | — | — | — | — | — | — | — | — | — | — | — | — |
| 10 | NYY | 49 | 0 | 5 | 4 | 1 | .184 | .245 | .224 | 82% | 23% | 6% | 1.22 |

| Yr | $1L | $2L | Pts | RAA | 2B | 3B | CS | FB-LD-GB | HR/fb | RBI% | RS% | OPS | 1st Hf | 2nd Hf | vs RH | vs LH | Rnge | vRH | vLH |
|---|---|---|---|---|---|---|---|---|---|---|---|---|---|---|---|---|---|---|---|
| | **Value** | | | | **Extra** | | | **Production** | | | | **OPS** | | | | | **Scoresheet** | | |
| 07 | — | — | — | — | — | — | — | — | — | — | — | — | — | — | — | — | — | — | — |
| 08 | — | — | — | — | — | — | — | — | — | — | — | — | — | — | — | — | — | — | — |
| 09 | — | — | — | — | — | — | — | — | — | — | — | — | — | — | — | — | — | — | — |
| 10 | -$4 | -$20 | 20 | –5 | 2 | 0 | 0 | 44-13-44 | 0% | 12% | 38% | .470 | .479 | .000 | .451 | .481 | — | — | — |

**Competition at 3B — Stats in 2010**

| Bats | Player | GSvR | GSvL | Sub | OPS |
|---|---|---|---|---|---|
| RH | Rodriguez A | 79 | 44 | 1 | .847 |
| BH | Pena R | 25 | 3 | 20 | .504 |
| RH | Nunez E | 1 | 9 | 5 | .681 |
| RH | Russo K | 1 | 2 | 13 | .470 |

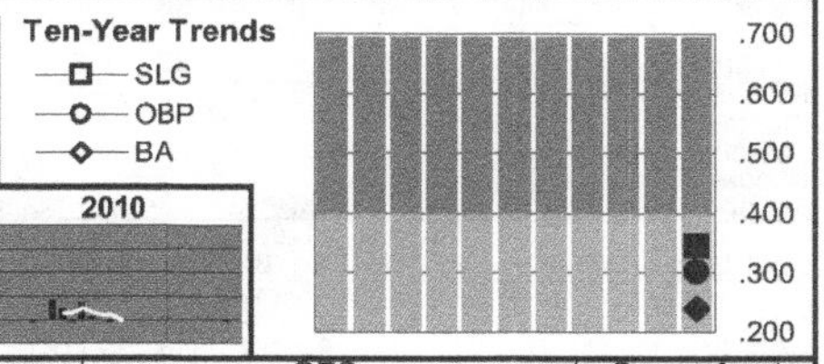


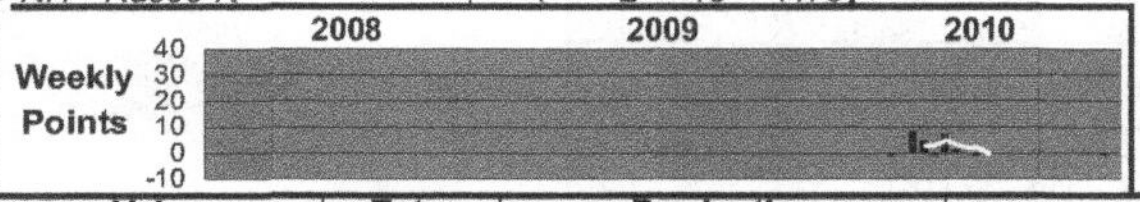


## Rusty Ryal — 100 PA | $-3 | 40 pts

OF-36 (LF-37), 1B-24, 3B-8, DH-1 — Owned: 0% — RH

Judging by his career numbers in the minors, Ryal will fit right in on the Diamondbacks: power (1.7 Bash) plus whiffs (19% K/PA). Those rates, along with the ability to play all around the infield, make him a great candidate to be a frequent pinch-hitter and occasional starter, but that's as high as Ryal will rise. (MS)

| Player | Age | AB | HR | R | RBI | SB | BA | OBP | SLG | $1L | Pts |
|---|---|---|---|---|---|---|---|---|---|---|---|
| **Forecast** | | | | | | | | | | | |
| Ryal R | 28 | 90 | 3 | 11 | 10 | 0 | .245 | .297 | .423 | -$3 | 40 |
| **Mini-Browser** | Age | AB | HR | R | RBI | SB | BA | OBP | SLG | $1L | Pts |
| Hermida J | 27 | 88 | 3 | 11 | 12 | 1 | .260 | .333 | .429 | -$3 | 50 |
| Paul X | 26 | 91 | 2 | 11 | 10 | 3 | .241 | .304 | .371 | -$3 | 50 |
| Bogusevic B | 27 | 89 | 2 | 10 | 9 | 3 | .248 | .325 | .366 | -$3 | 40 |
| Tuiasosopo M | 24 | 132 | 5 | 15 | 15 | 0 | .227 | .316 | .377 | -$3 | 60 |
| Roberts R | 30 | 67 | 2 | 9 | 8 | 2 | .267 | .355 | .426 | -$3 | 50 |

| Level | Leag | AB | HR | R | RBI | SB | BA | OBP | SLG | CT% | H% | BB% | Bash |
|---|---|---|---|---|---|---|---|---|---|---|---|---|---|
| **Minors (2010)** | | | | | | | | | | **Skills** | | | |
| A | — | — | — | — | — | — | — | — | — | — | — | — | — |
| AA | — | — | — | — | — | — | — | — | — | — | — | — | — |
| AAA | — | — | — | — | — | — | — | — | — | — | — | — | — |

| Yr | Team | AB | HR | R | RBI | SB | BA | OBP | SLG | CT% | H% | BB% | Bash |
|---|---|---|---|---|---|---|---|---|---|---|---|---|---|
| **Majors** | | | | | | | | | | **Skills** | | | |
| 07 | — | — | — | — | — | — | — | — | — | — | — | — | — |
| 08 | — | — | — | — | — | — | — | — | — | — | — | — | — |
| 09 | ARI | 59 | 3 | 11 | 9 | 0 | .271 | .353 | .593 | 64% | 42% | 9% | 2.19 |
| 10 | ARI | 207 | 3 | 19 | 11 | 0 | .261 | .308 | .348 | 68% | 39% | 4% | 1.33 |

| Yr | $1L | $2L | Pts | RAA | 2B | 3B | CS | FB-LD-GB | HR/fb | RBI% | RS% | OPS | 1st Hf | 2nd Hf | vs RH | vs LH | Rnge | vRH | vLH |
|---|---|---|---|---|---|---|---|---|---|---|---|---|---|---|---|---|---|---|---|
| | **Value** | | | | **Extra** | | | **Production** | | | | **OPS** | | | | | **Scoresheet** | | |
| 07 | — | — | — | — | — | — | — | — | — | — | — | — | — | — | — | — | — | — | — |
| 08 | — | — | — | — | — | — | — | — | — | — | — | — | — | — | — | — | — | — | — |
| 09 | -$1 | -$16 | 40 | +2 | 6 | 2 | 0 | 44-21-36 | 18% | 20% | 38% | .946 | — | .946 | .902 | .961 | — | — | — |
| 10 | -$2 | -$16 | 40 | –13 | 7 | 1 | 3 | 39-16-45 | 6% | 7% | 25% | .656 | .709 | .602 | .596 | .712 | — | –22 | +48 |

**Competition at LF — Stats in 2010**

| Bats | Player | GSvR | GSvL | Sub | OPS |
|---|---|---|---|---|---|
| LH | Parra G | 61 | 3 | 12 | .679 |
| RH | Ryal R | 2 | 24 | 11 | .656 |
| RH | Gillespie C | 6 | 12 | 6 | .649 |
| LH | Allen B | 12 | 2 | 0 | .793 |

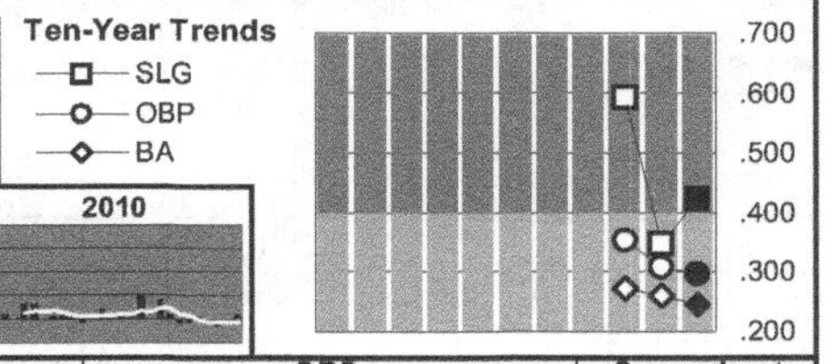


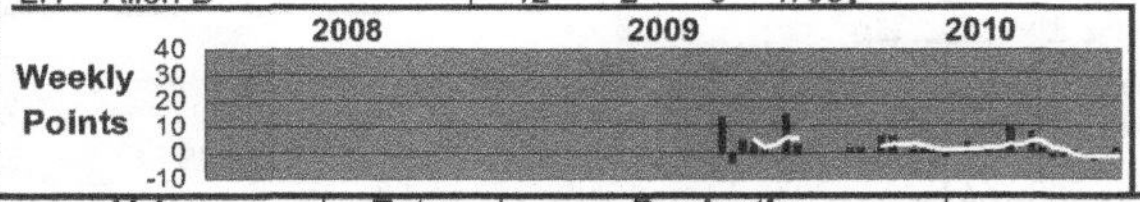


## Brendan Ryan — 500 PA | $7 | 260 pts

SS-139 — Owned: 5% — RH

By all metrics, Ryan is a stellar defender, and he fits well in a STL organization that emphasizes a pitch-to-contact, ground-ball mindset. He put up dissimilar numbers at the plate in 2009 and 2010; the Cards hope that he is somewhere in between, and Ryan's glove should buy him one more season to show them. (AB)

| Player | Age | AB | HR | R | RBI | SB | BA | OBP | SLG | $1L | Pts |
|---|---|---|---|---|---|---|---|---|---|---|---|
| **Forecast** | | | | | | | | | | | |
| Ryan B | 29 | 460 | 5 | 60 | 35 | 15 | .250 | .309 | .340 | $7 | 260 |
| **Mini-Browser** | Age | AB | HR | R | RBI | SB | BA | OBP | SLG | $1L | Pts |
| Betancourt Y | 29 | 532 | 11 | 55 | 61 | 6 | .279 | .302 | .413 | $11 | 320 |
| Gonzalez A | 34 | 580 | 19 | 69 | 75 | 0 | .248 | .293 | .413 | $10 | 300 |
| Pennington C | 26 | 532 | 6 | 66 | 48 | 24 | .237 | .318 | .343 | $10 | 290 |
| Uribe J | 32 | 467 | 15 | 55 | 65 | 0 | .257 | .309 | .437 | $10 | 260 |
| Cedeno R | 28 | 467 | 10 | 50 | 50 | 10 | .257 | .305 | .384 | $8 | 230 |

| Level | Leag | AB | HR | R | RBI | SB | BA | OBP | SLG | CT% | H% | BB% | Bash |
|---|---|---|---|---|---|---|---|---|---|---|---|---|---|
| **Minors (2010)** | | | | | | | | | | **Skills** | | | |
| A | — | — | — | — | — | — | — | — | — | — | — | — | — |
| AA | — | — | — | — | — | — | — | — | — | — | — | — | — |
| AAA | — | — | — | — | — | — | — | — | — | — | — | — | — |

| Yr | Team | AB | HR | R | RBI | SB | BA | OBP | SLG | CT% | H% | BB% | Bash |
|---|---|---|---|---|---|---|---|---|---|---|---|---|---|
| **Majors** | | | | | | | | | | **Skills** | | | |
| 07 | STL | 180 | 4 | 30 | 12 | 7 | .289 | .347 | .406 | 89% | 32% | 8% | 1.40 |
| 08 | STL | 197 | 0 | 30 | 10 | 7 | .244 | .307 | .289 | 84% | 29% | 7% | 1.19 |
| 09 | STL | 390 | 3 | 55 | 37 | 14 | .292 | .340 | .400 | 86% | 34% | 6% | 1.37 |
| 10 | STL | 439 | 2 | 50 | 36 | 11 | .223 | .279 | .294 | 86% | 26% | 7% | 1.32 |

| Yr | $1L | $2L | Pts | RAA | 2B | 3B | CS | FB-LD-GB | HR/fb | RBI% | RS% | OPS | 1st Hf | 2nd Hf | vs RH | vs LH | Rnge | vRH | vLH |
|---|---|---|---|---|---|---|---|---|---|---|---|---|---|---|---|---|---|---|---|
| | **Value** | | | | **Extra** | | | **Production** | | | | **OPS** | | | | | **Scoresheet** | | |
| 07 | $1 | -$10 | 120 | +6 | 9 | 0 | 0 | 34-19-47 | 8% | 10% | 41% | .752 | .733 | .758 | .666 | .863 | 4.75 | — | — |
| 08 | $0 | -$13 | 90 | –7 | 9 | 0 | 2 | 28-19-52 | 0% | 10% | 45% | .596 | .583 | .644 | .575 | .620 | 4.75 | –28 | +62 |
| 09 | $11 | -$1 | 240 | +2 | 19 | 7 | 7 | 30-19-51 | 3% | 18% | 37% | .740 | .704 | .777 | .780 | .664 | 4.76 | –23 | +49 |
| 10 | $2 | -$10 | 210 | –23 | 19 | 3 | 4 | 35-18-47 | 2% | 17% | 37% | .573 | .547 | .598 | .575 | .568 | 4.86 | –3 | +6 |

**Competition at SS — Stats in 2010**

| Bats | Player | GSvR | GSvL | Sub | OPS |
|---|---|---|---|---|---|
| RH | Ryan B | 78 | 46 | 15 | .573 |
| RH | Greene T | 13 | 6 | 3 | .655 |

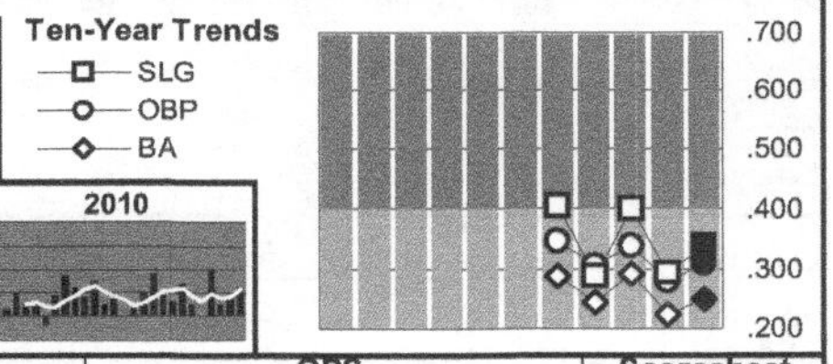


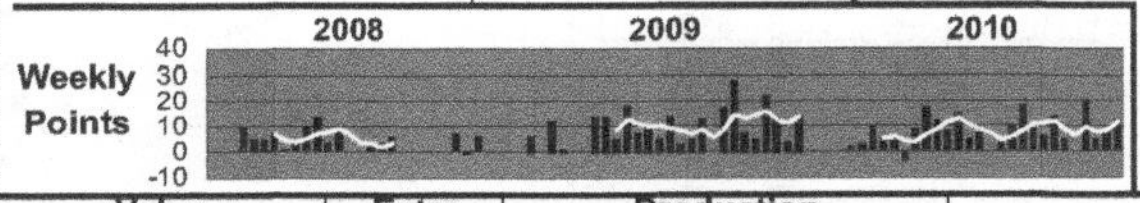


## Dusty Ryan — 25 PA | $-2 | 10 pts

No MLB games played in 2010 — Owned: 0% — RH

The Tiger-turned-Padre prospect took a ton of walks at Triple-A in 2010, but his strikeout rate reached untenable levels, and he did not drive the ball as deep as he had in years past. He faces an uphill climb to be more than an Eric Munson clone, minus Munson's ability to fake it at the hot corner. (DG)

| Player | Age | AB | HR | R | RBI | SB | BA | OBP | SLG | $1L | Pts |
|---|---|---|---|---|---|---|---|---|---|---|---|
| **Forecast** | | | | | | | | | | | |
| Ryan D | 26 | 23 | 1 | 2 | 3 | 0 | .197 | .295 | .363 | -$2 | 10 |
| **Mini-Browser** | Age | AB | HR | R | RBI | SB | BA | OBP | SLG | $1L | Pts |
| Anderson B | 24 | 48 | 1 | 5 | 5 | 0 | .250 | .313 | .356 | -$2 | 20 |
| Jaramillo J | 28 | 45 | 1 | 5 | 5 | 0 | .246 | .320 | .357 | -$2 | 20 |
| Ramirez M | 26 | 43 | 2 | 5 | 6 | 0 | .231 | .329 | .411 | -$2 | 20 |
| Hayes B | 27 | 45 | 1 | 5 | 5 | 0 | .223 | .272 | .353 | -$2 | 20 |
| Cash K | 33 | 111 | 3 | 8 | 10 | 0 | .203 | .287 | .317 | -$2 | 30 |

| Level | Leag | AB | HR | R | RBI | SB | BA | OBP | SLG | CT% | H% | BB% | Bash |
|---|---|---|---|---|---|---|---|---|---|---|---|---|---|
| **Minors (2010)** | | | | | | | | | | **Skills** | | | |
| A | — | — | — | — | — | — | — | — | — | — | — | — | — |
| AA | — | — | — | — | — | — | — | — | — | — | — | — | — |
| AAA | PCL | 261 | 7 | 29 | 30 | 2 | .199 | .333 | .349 | 62% | 32% | 16% | 1.75 |

| Yr | Team | AB | HR | R | RBI | SB | BA | OBP | SLG | CT% | H% | BB% | Bash |
|---|---|---|---|---|---|---|---|---|---|---|---|---|---|
| **Majors** | | | | | | | | | | **Skills** | | | |
| 07 | — | — | — | — | — | — | — | — | — | — | — | — | — |
| 08 | DET | 44 | 2 | 6 | 7 | 0 | .318 | .380 | .500 | 70% | 45% | 10% | 1.57 |
| 09 | DET | 26 | 0 | 1 | 4 | 0 | .154 | .267 | .192 | 54% | 29% | 13% | 1.25 |
| 10 | — | — | — | — | — | — | — | — | — | — | — | — | — |

| Yr | $1L | $2L | Pts | RAA | 2B | 3B | CS | FB-LD-GB | HR/fb | RBI% | RS% | OPS | 1st Hf | 2nd Hf | vs RH | vs LH | Rnge | vRH | vLH |
|---|---|---|---|---|---|---|---|---|---|---|---|---|---|---|---|---|---|---|---|
| | **Value** | | | | **Extra** | | | **Production** | | | | **OPS** | | | | | **Scoresheet** | | |
| 07 | — | — | — | — | — | — | — | — | — | — | — | — | — | — | — | — | — | — | — |
| 08 | $0 | -$8 | 30 | +3 | 2 | 0 | 0 | 50-19-31 | 13% | 21% | 24% | .880 | — | .880 | .570 | 1.529 | — | — | — |
| 09 | -$2 | -$11 | 0 | –3 | 1 | 0 | 1 | 29-21-50 | 0% | 29% | 13% | .459 | .508 | .397 | .552 | .350 | 0.58 | –31 | +74 |
| 10 | — | — | — | — | — | — | — | — | — | — | — | — | — | — | — | — | 0.56 | –23 | +54 |

**Competition at CA — Stats in 2010**

| Bats | Player | GSvR | GSvL | Sub | OPS |
|---|---|---|---|---|---|
| RH | Torrealba Y | 58 | 31 | 3 | .721 |
| RH | Hundley N | 53 | 20 | 3 | .726 |

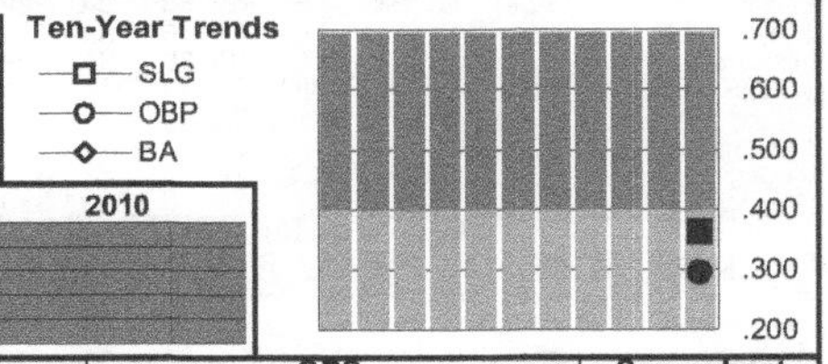


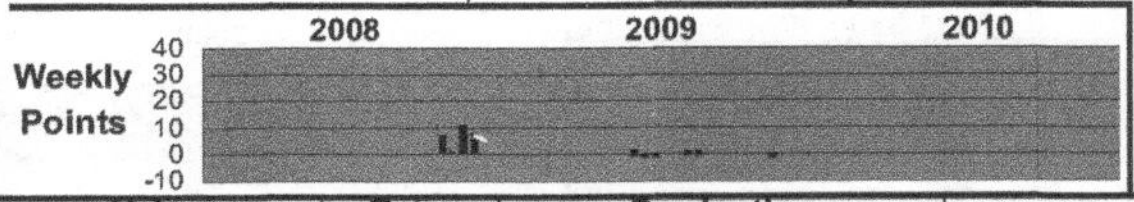


## Jarrod Saltalamacchia — 250 PA | $3 | 100 pts

CA-7, DH-2, 1B-1 — Owned: 1% — BH

Saltalamacchia's future is in limbo: He could end up as the starting catcher, in a platoon role, as the back-up, or in Triple-A. What Salty needs most is consistent playing time, and the Red Sox (who signed him to a one-year deal) will see that he gets it. The switch-hitter was even worse vs. RHP, if that's possible. (EB)

| Player | Age | AB | HR | R | RBI | SB | BA | OBP | SLG | $1L | Pts |
|---|---|---|---|---|---|---|---|---|---|---|---|
| **Forecast** | | | | | | | | | | | |
| Saltalamacchia J | 25 | 234 | 8 | 28 | 28 | 0 | .235 | .309 | .387 | $3 | 100 |
| **Mini-Browser** | Age | AB | HR | R | RBI | SB | BA | OBP | SLG | $1L | Pts |
| Ramos W | 23 | 277 | 9 | 27 | 36 | 0 | .238 | .279 | .389 | $4 | 120 |
| Paulino R | 29 | 201 | 5 | 23 | 25 | 0 | .268 | .331 | .400 | $3 | 110 |
| Buck J | 30 | 187 | 8 | 20 | 28 | 0 | .246 | .305 | .450 | $3 | 100 |
| Castro R | 35 | 136 | 8 | 17 | 24 | 0 | .254 | .318 | .474 | $3 | 80 |
| Flores J | 26 | 185 | 6 | 20 | 32 | 0 | .248 | .309 | .411 | $3 | 100 |

| Level | Leag | AB | HR | R | RBI | SB | BA | OBP | SLG | CT% | H% | BB% | Bash |
|---|---|---|---|---|---|---|---|---|---|---|---|---|---|
| **Minors (2010)** | | | | | | | | | | **Skills** | | | |
| A | — | — | — | — | — | — | — | — | — | — | — | — | — |
| AA | — | — | — | — | — | — | — | — | — | — | — | — | — |
| AAA | 2LG | 274 | 12 | 42 | 39 | 1 | .248 | .329 | .453 | 75% | 33% | 9% | 1.82 |

| Yr | Team | AB | HR | R | RBI | SB | BA | OBP | SLG | CT% | H% | BB% | Bash |
|---|---|---|---|---|---|---|---|---|---|---|---|---|---|
| **Majors** | | | | | | | | | | **Skills** | | | |
| 07 | 2TM | 308 | 11 | 39 | 33 | 0 | .266 | .310 | .422 | 76% | 35% | 6% | 1.59 |
| 08 | TEX | 198 | 3 | 27 | 26 | 0 | .253 | .352 | .364 | 63% | 40% | 13% | 1.44 |
| 09 | TEX | 283 | 9 | 34 | 34 | 0 | .233 | .290 | .371 | 66% | 35% | 7% | 1.59 |
| 10 | 2TM | 24 | 0 | 2 | 2 | 0 | .167 | .333 | .292 | 79% | 21% | 20% | 1.75 |

| Yr | $1L | $2L | Pts | RAA | 2B | 3B | CS | FB-LD-GB | HR/fb | RBI% | RS% | OPS | 1st Hf | 2nd Hf | vs RH | vs LH | Rnge | vRH | vLH |
|---|---|---|---|---|---|---|---|---|---|---|---|---|---|---|---|---|---|---|---|
| | **Value** | | | | **Extra** | | | **Production** | | | | **OPS** | | | | | **Scoresheet** | | |
| 07 | $5 | -$2 | 150 | –1 | 13 | 1 | 0 | 39-17-44 | 12% | 12% | 31% | .732 | .846 | .670 | .796 | .625 | 0.56 | — | — |
| 08 | $3 | -$4 | 80 | +0 | 13 | 0 | 2 | 42-27-31 | 6% | 22% | 31% | .716 | .648 | .904 | .876 | .443 | 0.64 | — | — |
| 09 | $5 | -$1 | 100 | –10 | 12 | 0 | 2 | 41-23-36 | 12% | 21% | 31% | .661 | .664 | .647 | .663 | .657 | 0.70 | — | — |
| 10 | -$2 | -$12 | 10 | –1 | 3 | 0 | 0 | 53-5-42 | 0% | 18% | 20% | .625 | .400 | .676 | .573 | .654 | 0.72 | — | — |

**Competition at CA — Stats in 2010**

| Bats | Player | GSvR | GSvL | Sub | OPS |
|---|---|---|---|---|---|
| BH | Martinez V | 74 | 36 | 1 | .844 |
| BH | Varitek J | 19 | 8 | 12 | .766 |
| RH | Cash K | 13 | 6 | 10 | .483 |

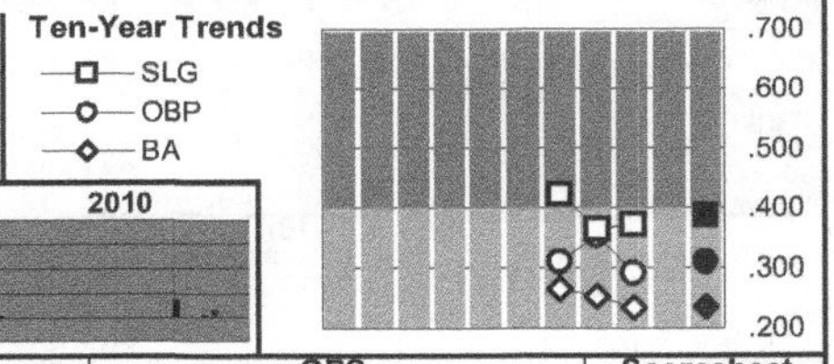


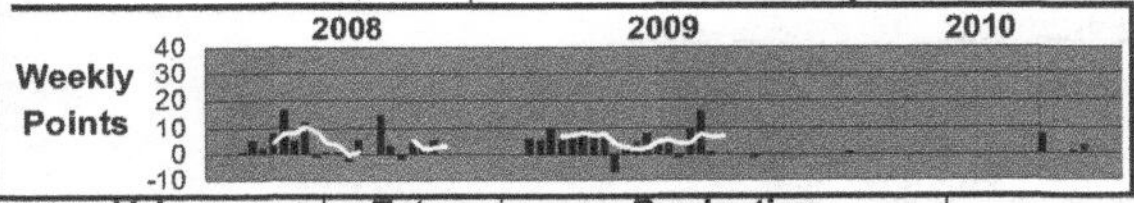


For more stats, visit www.Rotolympus.com.

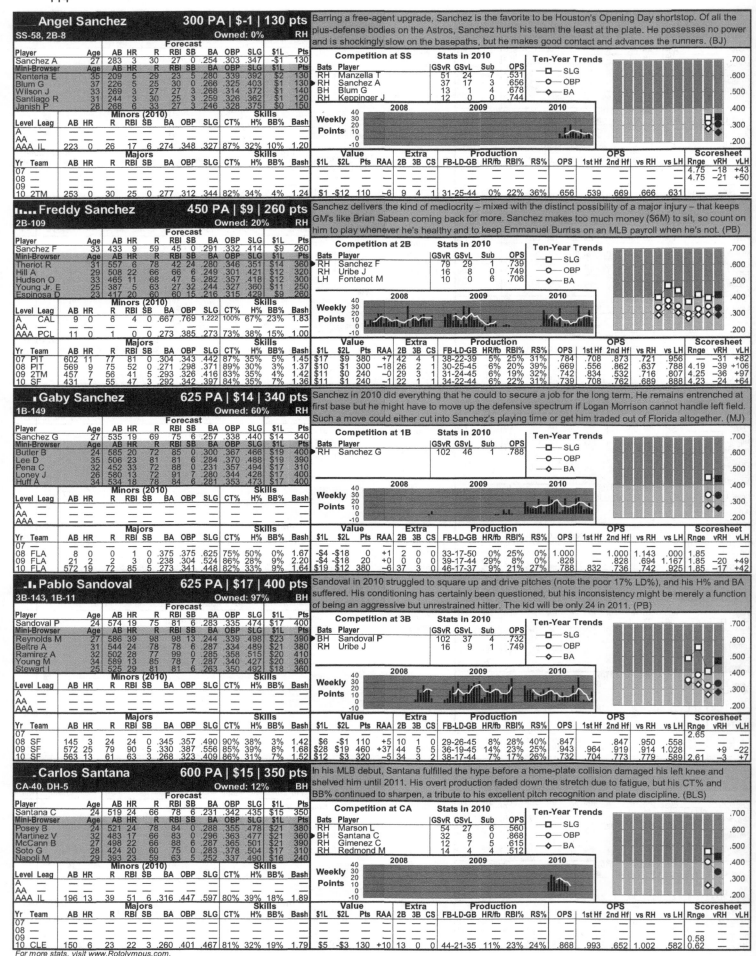

## Angel Sanchez — 300 PA | $-1 | 130 pts

SS-58, 2B-8 — Owned: 0% — RH

Barring a free-agent upgrade, Sanchez is the favorite to be Houston's Opening Day shortstop. Of all the plus-defense bodies on the Astros, Sanchez hurts his team the least at the plate. He possesses no power and is shockingly slow on the basepaths, but he makes good contact and advances the runners. (BJ)

### Forecast

| Player | Age | AB | HR | R | RBI | SB | BA | OBP | SLG | $1L | Pts |
|---|---|---|---|---|---|---|---|---|---|---|---|
| Sanchez A | 27 | 283 | 3 | 30 | 27 | 0 | .254 | .303 | .347 | -$1 | 130 |
| Mini-Browser | Age | AB | HR | R | RBI | SB | BA | OBP | SLG | $1L | Pts |
| Renteria E | 35 | 209 | 5 | 29 | 23 | 5 | .280 | .339 | .392 | $2 | 130 |
| Blum G | 37 | 226 | 5 | 25 | 30 | 0 | .266 | .325 | .403 | $1 | 130 |
| Wilson J | 33 | 269 | 3 | 27 | 27 | 3 | .268 | .314 | .372 | $1 | 140 |
| Santiago R | 31 | 244 | 3 | 30 | 25 | 3 | .259 | .326 | .362 | $1 | 120 |
| Janish P | 28 | 268 | 6 | 33 | 27 | 3 | .246 | .328 | .375 | $0 | 150 |

### Minors (2010) / Skills

| Level | Leag | AB | HR | R | RBI | SB | BA | OBP | SLG | CT% | H% | BB% | Bash |
|---|---|---|---|---|---|---|---|---|---|---|---|---|---|
| A | — | — | — | — | — | — | — | — | — | — | — | — | — |
| AA | — | — | — | — | — | — | — | — | — | — | — | — | — |
| AAA | IL | 223 | 0 | 26 | 17 | 6 | .274 | .348 | .327 | 87% | 32% | 10% | 1.20 |

### Majors / Skills

| Yr | Team | AB | HR | R | RBI | SB | BA | OBP | SLG | CT% | H% | BB% | Bash |
|---|---|---|---|---|---|---|---|---|---|---|---|---|---|
| 07 | — | — | — | — | — | — | — | — | — | — | — | — | — |
| 08 | — | — | — | — | — | — | — | — | — | — | — | — | — |
| 09 | — | — | — | — | — | — | — | — | — | — | — | — | — |
| 10 | 2TM | 253 | 0 | 30 | 25 | 0 | .277 | .312 | .344 | 82% | 34% | 4% | 1.24 |

### Competition at SS / Stats in 2010

| Bats | Player | GSvR | GSvL | Sub | OPS |
|---|---|---|---|---|---|
| RH | Manzella T | 51 | 24 | 7 | .531 |
| RH | Sanchez A | 37 | 17 | 3 | .656 |
| BH | Blum G | 13 | 1 | 4 | .678 |
| RH | Keppinger J | 12 | 0 | 0 | .744 |

### Value / Extra / Production / OPS / Scoresheet

| | $1L | $2L | Pts | RAA | 2B | 3B | CS | FB-LD-GB | HR/fb | RBI% | RS% | OPS | 1st Hf | 2nd Hf | vs RH | vs LH | Rnge | vRH | vLH |
|---|---|---|---|---|---|---|---|---|---|---|---|---|---|---|---|---|---|---|---|
| | | | | | | | | | | | | | | | | | 4.75 | -18 | +43 |
| | | | | | | | | | | | | | | | | | 4.75 | -21 | +50 |
| | $1 | -$12 | 110 | -6 | 9 | 4 | 1 | 31-25-44 | 0% | 22% | 36% | .656 | .539 | .669 | .666 | .631 | | | |

## Freddy Sanchez — 450 PA | $9 | 260 pts

2B-109 — Owned: 20% — RH

Sanchez delivers the kind of mediocrity – mixed with the distinct possibility of a major injury – that keeps GM's like Brian Sabean coming back for more. Sanchez makes too much money ($6M) to sit, so count on him to play whenever he's healthy and to keep Emmanuel Burriss on an MLB payroll when he's not. (PB)

### Forecast

| Player | Age | AB | HR | R | RBI | SB | BA | OBP | SLG | $1L | Pts |
|---|---|---|---|---|---|---|---|---|---|---|---|
| Sanchez F | 33 | 433 | 9 | 59 | 45 | 0 | .291 | .332 | .414 | $9 | 260 |
| Mini-Browser | Age | AB | HR | R | RBI | SB | BA | OBP | SLG | $1L | Pts |
| Theriot R | 31 | 557 | 6 | 78 | 42 | 24 | .280 | .346 | .351 | $14 | 360 |
| Hill A | 29 | 508 | 22 | 66 | 66 | 6 | .249 | .301 | .421 | $12 | 320 |
| Hudson O | 33 | 465 | 11 | 68 | 47 | 5 | .282 | .357 | .418 | $12 | 300 |
| Young Jr. E | 25 | 387 | 5 | 63 | 27 | 32 | .244 | .327 | .360 | $11 | 250 |
| Espinosa D | 23 | 417 | 20 | 60 | 60 | 15 | .216 | .315 | .429 | $9 | 260 |

### Minors (2010) / Skills

| Level | Leag | AB | HR | R | RBI | SB | BA | OBP | SLG | CT% | H% | BB% | Bash |
|---|---|---|---|---|---|---|---|---|---|---|---|---|---|
| A | CAL | 9 | 0 | 6 | 4 | 0 | .667 | .769 | 1.222 | 100% | 67% | 23% | 1.83 |
| AA | — | — | — | — | — | — | — | — | — | — | — | — | — |
| AAA | PCL | 11 | 0 | 1 | 0 | 0 | .273 | .385 | .273 | 73% | 38% | 15% | 1.00 |

### Majors / Skills

| Yr | Team | AB | HR | R | RBI | SB | BA | OBP | SLG | CT% | H% | BB% | Bash |
|---|---|---|---|---|---|---|---|---|---|---|---|---|---|
| 07 | PIT | 602 | 11 | 77 | 81 | 0 | .304 | .343 | .442 | 87% | 35% | 5% | 1.45 |
| 08 | PIT | 569 | 9 | 75 | 52 | 0 | .271 | .298 | .371 | 89% | 30% | 3% | 1.37 |
| 09 | 2TM | 457 | 7 | 56 | 41 | 5 | .293 | .326 | .416 | 83% | 35% | 4% | 1.42 |
| 10 | SF | 431 | 7 | 55 | 47 | 3 | .292 | .342 | .397 | 84% | 35% | 7% | 1.36 |

### Value / Extra / Production / OPS / Scoresheet

| | $1L | $2L | Pts | RAA | 2B | 3B | CS | FB-LD-GB | HR/fb | RBI% | RS% | OPS | 1st Hf | 2nd Hf | vs RH | vs LH | Rnge | vRH | vLH |
|---|---|---|---|---|---|---|---|---|---|---|---|---|---|---|---|---|---|---|---|
| | $17 | $9 | 380 | +7 | 42 | 4 | 1 | 38-22-39 | 5% | 25% | 31% | .784 | .708 | .873 | .721 | .956 | — | -31 | +82 |
| | $10 | $1 | 300 | -18 | 26 | 2 | 1 | 30-25-45 | 6% | 20% | 39% | .669 | .556 | .862 | .637 | .788 | 4.19 | -39 | +106 |
| | $5 | $1 | 240 | -0 | 29 | 3 | 1 | 31-24-45 | 6% | 19% | 32% | .742 | .834 | .532 | .716 | .807 | 4.25 | -36 | +97 |
| | $11 | $1 | 240 | -1 | 22 | 1 | 1 | 34-22-44 | 6% | 22% | 31% | .739 | .708 | .762 | .689 | .888 | 4.23 | -24 | +64 |

## Gaby Sanchez — 625 PA | $14 | 340 pts

1B-149 — Owned: 60% — RH

Sanchez in 2010 did everything that he could to secure a job for the long term. He remains entrenched at first base but he might have to move up the defensive spectrum if Logan Morrison cannot handle left field. Such a move could either cut into Sanchez's playing time or get him traded out of Florida altogether. (MJ)

### Forecast

| Player | Age | AB | HR | R | RBI | SB | BA | OBP | SLG | $1L | Pts |
|---|---|---|---|---|---|---|---|---|---|---|---|
| Sanchez G | 27 | 535 | 19 | 69 | 75 | 6 | .257 | .338 | .440 | $14 | 340 |
| Mini-Browser | Age | AB | HR | R | RBI | SB | BA | OBP | SLG | $1L | Pts |
| Butler B | 24 | 585 | 20 | 72 | 85 | 0 | .300 | .367 | .466 | $19 | 400 |
| Lee D | 35 | 506 | 23 | 81 | 81 | 6 | .284 | .370 | .488 | $19 | 390 |
| Pena C | 32 | 452 | 33 | 72 | 88 | 0 | .231 | .357 | .494 | $17 | 310 |
| Loney J | 26 | 580 | 13 | 72 | 91 | 7 | .280 | .344 | .428 | $17 | 400 |
| Huff A | 34 | 534 | 18 | 78 | 84 | 6 | .281 | .353 | .473 | $17 | 400 |

### Minors (2010) / Skills

| Level | Leag | AB | HR | R | RBI | SB | BA | OBP | SLG | CT% | H% | BB% | Bash |
|---|---|---|---|---|---|---|---|---|---|---|---|---|---|
| A | — | — | — | — | — | — | — | — | — | — | — | — | — |
| AA | — | — | — | — | — | — | — | — | — | — | — | — | — |
| AAA | — | — | — | — | — | — | — | — | — | — | — | — | — |

### Majors / Skills

| Yr | Team | AB | HR | R | RBI | SB | BA | OBP | SLG | CT% | H% | BB% | Bash |
|---|---|---|---|---|---|---|---|---|---|---|---|---|---|
| 07 | — | — | — | — | — | — | — | — | — | — | — | — | — |
| 08 | FLA | 8 | 0 | 0 | 1 | 0 | .375 | .375 | .625 | 75% | 50% | 0% | 1.67 |
| 09 | FLA | 21 | 2 | 3 | 0 | 0 | .238 | .304 | .524 | 86% | 28% | 9% | 2.20 |
| 10 | FLA | 572 | 19 | 72 | 85 | 5 | .273 | .341 | .448 | 82% | 33% | 9% | 1.64 |

### Competition at 1B / Stats in 2010

| Bats | Player | GSvR | GSvL | Sub | OPS |
|---|---|---|---|---|---|
| RH | Sanchez G | 102 | 46 | 1 | .788 |

### Value / Extra / Production / OPS / Scoresheet

| | $1L | $2L | Pts | RAA | 2B | 3B | CS | FB-LD-GB | HR/fb | RBI% | RS% | OPS | 1st Hf | 2nd Hf | vs RH | vs LH | Rnge | vRH | vLH |
|---|---|---|---|---|---|---|---|---|---|---|---|---|---|---|---|---|---|---|---|
| | -$4 | -$18 | 0 | +1 | 2 | 0 | 0 | 33-17-50 | 0% | 25% | 0% | 1.000 | — | 1.000 | 1.143 | .000 | 1.85 | — | — |
| | -$4 | -$18 | 20 | +0 | 0 | 0 | 0 | 39-17-44 | 29% | 24% | 0% | .828 | — | .828 | .694 | 1.167 | 1.85 | -20 | +49 |
| | $19 | $12 | 380 | -6 | 37 | 3 | 0 | 46-17-37 | 9% | 21% | 27% | .788 | .832 | .736 | .742 | .925 | 1.85 | -17 | +42 |

## Pablo Sandoval — 625 PA | $17 | 400 pts

3B-143, 1B-11 — Owned: 97% — BH

Sandoval in 2010 struggled to square up and drive pitches (note the poor 17% LD%), and his H% and BA suffered. His conditioning has certainly been questioned, but his inconsistency might be merely a function of being an aggressive but unrestrained hitter. The kid will be only 24 in 2011. (PB)

### Forecast

| Player | Age | AB | HR | R | RBI | SB | BA | OBP | SLG | $1L | Pts |
|---|---|---|---|---|---|---|---|---|---|---|---|
| Sandoval P | 24 | 574 | 19 | 75 | 81 | 6 | .283 | .335 | .474 | $17 | 400 |
| Mini-Browser | Age | AB | HR | R | RBI | SB | BA | OBP | SLG | $1L | Pts |
| Reynolds M | 27 | 586 | 39 | 98 | 98 | 13 | .244 | .339 | .498 | $23 | 390 |
| Beltre A | 31 | 544 | 24 | 78 | 78 | 6 | .287 | .334 | .489 | $21 | 380 |
| Ramirez A | 32 | 502 | 28 | 77 | 99 | 0 | .285 | .358 | .515 | $20 | 410 |
| Young M | 34 | 589 | 13 | 85 | 78 | 7 | .287 | .340 | .427 | $20 | 360 |
| Stewart I | 25 | 525 | 29 | 81 | 81 | 6 | .263 | .350 | .492 | $18 | 360 |

### Minors (2010) / Skills

| Level | Leag | AB | HR | R | RBI | SB | BA | OBP | SLG | CT% | H% | BB% | Bash |
|---|---|---|---|---|---|---|---|---|---|---|---|---|---|
| A | — | — | — | — | — | — | — | — | — | — | — | — | — |
| AA | — | — | — | — | — | — | — | — | — | — | — | — | — |
| AAA | — | — | — | — | — | — | — | — | — | — | — | — | — |

### Majors / Skills

| Yr | Team | AB | HR | R | RBI | SB | BA | OBP | SLG | CT% | H% | BB% | Bash |
|---|---|---|---|---|---|---|---|---|---|---|---|---|---|
| 07 | — | — | — | — | — | — | — | — | — | — | — | — | — |
| 08 | SF | 145 | 3 | 24 | 24 | 0 | .345 | .357 | .490 | 90% | 38% | 3% | 1.42 |
| 09 | SF | 572 | 25 | 79 | 90 | 5 | .330 | .387 | .556 | 85% | 39% | 8% | 1.68 |
| 10 | SF | 563 | 13 | 61 | 63 | 3 | .268 | .323 | .409 | 86% | 31% | 7% | 1.52 |

### Competition at 3B / Stats in 2010

| Bats | Player | GSvR | GSvL | Sub | OPS |
|---|---|---|---|---|---|
| BH | Sandoval P | 102 | 37 | 4 | .732 |
| RH | Uribe J | 16 | 9 | 1 | .749 |

### Value / Extra / Production / OPS / Scoresheet

| | $1L | $2L | Pts | RAA | 2B | 3B | CS | FB-LD-GB | HR/fb | RBI% | RS% | OPS | 1st Hf | 2nd Hf | vs RH | vs LH | Rnge | vRH | vLH |
|---|---|---|---|---|---|---|---|---|---|---|---|---|---|---|---|---|---|---|---|
| | | | | | | | | | | | | | | | | | 2.65 | — | — |
| | $6 | -$1 | 110 | +5 | 10 | 1 | 0 | 29-26-45 | 8% | 28% | 40% | .847 | — | .847 | .950 | .558 | — | — | — |
| | $28 | $19 | 460 | +37 | 44 | 5 | 5 | 36-19-45 | 14% | 23% | 25% | .943 | .964 | .919 | .914 | 1.028 | — | +9 | -22 |
| | $12 | $3 | 320 | -5 | 34 | 3 | 2 | 38-17-44 | 7% | 17% | 26% | .732 | .704 | .773 | .779 | .589 | 2.61 | -3 | +7 |

## Carlos Santana — 600 PA | $15 | 350 pts

CA-40, DH-5 — Owned: 12% — BH

In his MLB debut, Santana fulfilled the hype before a home-plate collision damaged his left knee and shelved him until 2011. His overt production faded down the stretch due to fatigue, but his CT% and BB% continued to sharpen, a tribute to his excellent pitch recognition and plate discipline. (BLS)

### Forecast

| Player | Age | AB | HR | R | RBI | SB | BA | OBP | SLG | $1L | Pts |
|---|---|---|---|---|---|---|---|---|---|---|---|
| Santana C | 24 | 519 | 24 | 66 | 78 | 6 | .231 | .342 | .435 | $15 | 350 |
| Mini-Browser | Age | AB | HR | R | RBI | SB | BA | OBP | SLG | $1L | Pts |
| Posey B | 24 | 521 | 24 | 78 | 84 | 0 | .288 | .355 | .478 | $21 | 380 |
| Martinez V | 32 | 483 | 17 | 66 | 83 | 0 | .296 | .363 | .477 | $21 | 360 |
| McCann B | 27 | 498 | 22 | 66 | 88 | 2 | .287 | .365 | .501 | $21 | 390 |
| Soto G | 28 | 424 | 20 | 60 | 75 | 0 | .283 | .378 | .504 | $17 | 310 |
| Napoli M | 29 | 393 | 23 | 59 | 63 | 6 | .252 | .337 | .490 | $16 | 240 |

### Minors (2010) / Skills

| Level | Leag | AB | HR | R | RBI | SB | BA | OBP | SLG | CT% | H% | BB% | Bash |
|---|---|---|---|---|---|---|---|---|---|---|---|---|---|
| A | — | — | — | — | — | — | — | — | — | — | — | — | — |
| AA | — | — | — | — | — | — | — | — | — | — | — | — | — |
| AAA | IL | 196 | 13 | 39 | 51 | 6 | .316 | .447 | .597 | 80% | 39% | 18% | 1.89 |

### Majors / Skills

| Yr | Team | AB | HR | R | RBI | SB | BA | OBP | SLG | CT% | H% | BB% | Bash |
|---|---|---|---|---|---|---|---|---|---|---|---|---|---|
| 07 | — | — | — | — | — | — | — | — | — | — | — | — | — |
| 08 | — | — | — | — | — | — | — | — | — | — | — | — | — |
| 09 | — | — | — | — | — | — | — | — | — | — | — | — | — |
| 10 | CLE | 150 | 6 | 23 | 22 | 3 | .260 | .401 | .467 | 81% | 32% | 19% | 1.79 |

### Competition at CA / Stats in 2010

| Bats | Player | GSvR | GSvL | Sub | OPS |
|---|---|---|---|---|---|
| RH | Marson L | 54 | 27 | 6 | .560 |
| BH | Santana C | 32 | 8 | 0 | .868 |
| RH | Gimenez C | 12 | 7 | 5 | .615 |
| RH | Redmond M | 14 | 4 | 4 | .512 |

### Value / Extra / Production / OPS / Scoresheet

| | $1L | $2L | Pts | RAA | 2B | 3B | CS | FB-LD-GB | HR/fb | RBI% | RS% | OPS | 1st Hf | 2nd Hf | vs RH | vs LH | Rnge | vRH | vLH |
|---|---|---|---|---|---|---|---|---|---|---|---|---|---|---|---|---|---|---|---|
| | | | | | | | | | | | | | | | | | 0.58 | — | — |
| | $5 | -$3 | 130 | +10 | 13 | 0 | 0 | 44-21-35 | 11% | 23% | 24% | .868 | .993 | .652 | 1.002 | .582 | 0.62 | — | — |

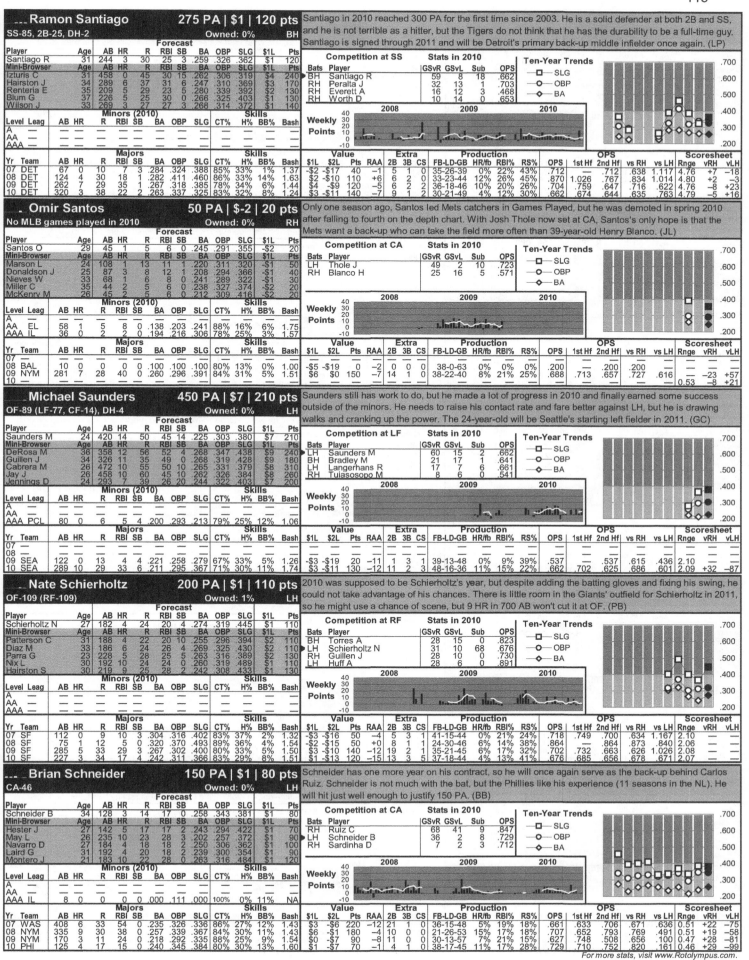

## Ramon Santiago — 275 PA | $1 | 120 pts

SS-85, 2B-25, DH-2 — Owned: 0% — BH

| Player | Age | AB | HR | R | RBI | SB | BA | OBP | SLG | $1L | Pts |
|---|---|---|---|---|---|---|---|---|---|---|---|
| | | Forecast | | | | | | | | | |
| Santiago R | 31 | 244 | 3 | 30 | 25 | 3 | .259 | .326 | .362 | $1 | 120 |
| Mini-Browser | Age | AB | HR | R | RBI | SB | BA | OBP | SLG | $1L | Pts |
| Izturis C | 31 | 458 | 0 | 45 | 30 | 15 | .262 | .306 | .319 | $4 | 240 |
| Hairston J | 34 | 289 | 6 | 37 | 31 | 6 | .247 | .310 | .369 | $3 | 170 |
| Renteria E | 35 | 209 | 5 | 29 | 23 | 5 | .280 | .339 | .392 | $2 | 130 |
| Blum G | 37 | 226 | 5 | 25 | 30 | 0 | .266 | .325 | .403 | $1 | 130 |
| Wilson J | 33 | 269 | 3 | 27 | 27 | 3 | .268 | .314 | .372 | $1 | 140 |

| Level | Leag | AB | HR | R | RBI | SB | BA | OBP | SLG | CT% | H% | BB% | Bash |
|---|---|---|---|---|---|---|---|---|---|---|---|---|---|
| | | Minors (2010) | | | | | | | | Skills | | | |
| A | — | — | — | — | — | — | — | — | — | — | — | — | — |
| AA | — | — | — | — | — | — | — | — | — | — | — | — | — |
| AAA | — | — | — | — | — | — | — | — | — | — | — | — | — |

| Yr | Team | AB | HR | R | RBI | SB | BA | OBP | SLG | CT% | H% | BB% | Bash |
|---|---|---|---|---|---|---|---|---|---|---|---|---|---|
| | | Majors | | | | | | | | Skills | | | |
| 07 | DET | 67 | 0 | 10 | 7 | 3 | .284 | .324 | .388 | 85% | 33% | 1% | 1.37 |
| 08 | DET | 124 | 4 | 30 | 18 | 1 | .282 | .411 | .460 | 86% | 33% | 14% | 1.63 |
| 09 | DET | 262 | 7 | 29 | 35 | 1 | .267 | .318 | .385 | 78% | 34% | 6% | 1.44 |
| 10 | DET | 320 | 3 | 38 | 22 | 2 | .263 | .337 | .325 | 83% | 32% | 8% | 1.24 |

Santiago in 2010 reached 300 PA for the first time since 2003. He is a solid defender at both 2B and SS, and he is not terrible as a hitter, but the Tigers do not think that he has the durability to be a full-time guy. Santiago is signed through 2011 and will be Detroit's primary back-up middle infielder once again. (LP)

**Competition at SS — Stats in 2010**

| Bats | Player | GSvR | GSvL | Sub | OPS |
|---|---|---|---|---|---|
| BH | Santiago R | 59 | 8 | 18 | .662 |
| RH | Peralta J | 32 | 13 | 1 | .703 |
| RH | Everett A | 16 | 12 | 3 | .468 |
| RH | Worth D | 10 | 14 | 0 | .653 |

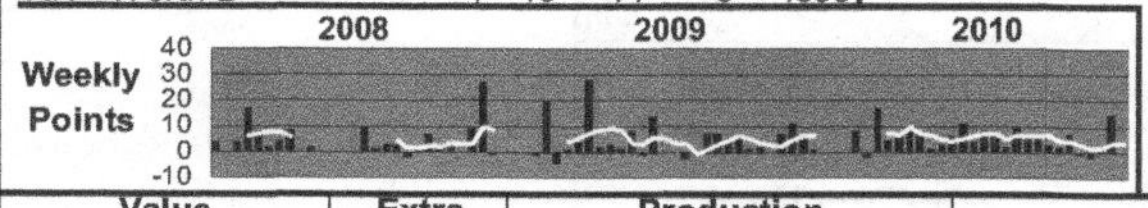


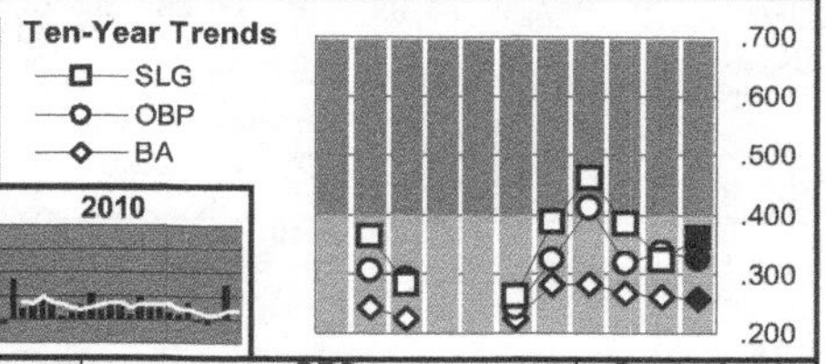


| Yr | $1L | $2L | Pts | RAA | 2B | 3B | CS | FB-LD-GB | HR/fb | RBI% | RS% | OPS | 1st Hf | 2nd Hf | vs RH | vs LH | Rnge | vRH | vLH |
|---|---|---|---|---|---|---|---|---|---|---|---|---|---|---|---|---|---|---|---|
| | Value | | | | Extra | | | Production | | | | OPS | | | | | Scoresheet | | |
| 07 | -$2 | -$17 | 40 | −1 | 5 | 1 | 0 | 35-26-39 | 0% | 22% | 43% | .712 | — | .712 | .638 | 1.117 | 4.76 | +7 | −18 |
| 08 | $2 | -$10 | 110 | +6 | 6 | 2 | 0 | 33-23-44 | 12% | 26% | 45% | .870 | 1.026 | .767 | .834 | 1.014 | 4.80 | +2 | −3 |
| 09 | $4 | -$9 | 120 | −5 | 6 | 2 | 2 | 36-18-46 | 10% | 20% | 26% | .704 | .759 | .647 | .716 | .622 | 4.76 | −8 | +23 |
| 10 | $3 | -$11 | 140 | −7 | 9 | 1 | 2 | 30-21-49 | 4% | 12% | 30% | .662 | .674 | .644 | .635 | .763 | 4.79 | −5 | +16 |

## Omir Santos — 50 PA | $-2 | 20 pts

No MLB games played in 2010 — Owned: 0% — RH

| Player | Age | AB | HR | R | RBI | SB | BA | OBP | SLG | $1L | Pts |
|---|---|---|---|---|---|---|---|---|---|---|---|
| | | Forecast | | | | | | | | | |
| Santos O | 29 | 45 | 1 | 5 | 6 | 0 | .245 | .291 | .355 | -$2 | 20 |
| Mini-Browser | Age | AB | HR | R | RBI | SB | BA | OBP | SLG | $1L | Pts |
| Marson L | 24 | 108 | 1 | 13 | 11 | 1 | .220 | .311 | .320 | -$1 | 50 |
| Donaldson J | 25 | 87 | 3 | 8 | 12 | 1 | .208 | .294 | .366 | -$1 | 40 |
| Nieves W | 33 | 68 | 1 | 6 | 8 | 0 | .241 | .289 | .322 | -$1 | 30 |
| Miller C | 35 | 44 | 2 | 5 | 6 | 0 | .238 | .327 | .374 | -$2 | 20 |
| McKenry M | 26 | 45 | 2 | 5 | 6 | 0 | .212 | .309 | .416 | -$2 | 20 |

| Level | Leag | AB | HR | R | RBI | SB | BA | OBP | SLG | CT% | H% | BB% | Bash |
|---|---|---|---|---|---|---|---|---|---|---|---|---|---|
| | | Minors (2010) | | | | | | | | Skills | | | |
| A | — | — | — | — | — | — | — | — | — | — | — | — | — |
| AA | EL | 58 | 1 | 5 | 8 | 0 | .138 | .203 | .241 | 88% | 16% | 6% | 1.75 |
| AAA | IL | 36 | 0 | 2 | 2 | 0 | .194 | .216 | .306 | 78% | 25% | 3% | 1.57 |

| Yr | Team | AB | HR | R | RBI | SB | BA | OBP | SLG | CT% | H% | BB% | Bash |
|---|---|---|---|---|---|---|---|---|---|---|---|---|---|
| | | Majors | | | | | | | | Skills | | | |
| 07 | — | — | — | — | — | — | — | — | — | — | — | — | — |
| 08 | BAL | 10 | 0 | 0 | 0 | 0 | .100 | .100 | .100 | 80% | 13% | 0% | 1.00 |
| 09 | NYM | 281 | 7 | 28 | 40 | 0 | .260 | .296 | .391 | 84% | 31% | 5% | 1.51 |
| 10 | — | — | — | — | — | — | — | — | — | — | — | — | — |

Only one season ago, Santos led Mets catchers in Games Played, but he was demoted in spring 2010 after falling to fourth on the depth chart. With Josh Thole now set at CA, Santos's only hope is that the Mets want a back-up who can take the field more often than 39-year-old Henry Blanco. (JL)

**Competition at CA — Stats in 2010**

| Bats | Player | GSvR | GSvL | Sub | OPS |
|---|---|---|---|---|---|
| LH | Thole J | 49 | 2 | 10 | .723 |
| RH | Blanco H | 25 | 16 | 5 | .571 |

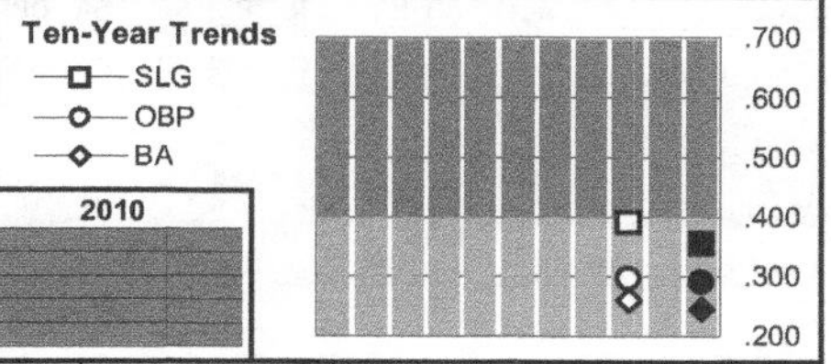


| Yr | $1L | $2L | Pts | RAA | 2B | 3B | CS | FB-LD-GB | HR/fb | RBI% | RS% | OPS | 1st Hf | 2nd Hf | vs RH | vs LH | Rnge | vRH | vLH |
|---|---|---|---|---|---|---|---|---|---|---|---|---|---|---|---|---|---|---|---|
| | Value | | | | Extra | | | Production | | | | OPS | | | | | Scoresheet | | |
| 07 | — | — | — | — | — | — | — | — | — | — | — | — | — | — | — | — | — | — | — |
| 08 | -$5 | -$19 | 0 | −2 | 0 | 0 | 0 | 38-0-63 | 0% | 0% | 0% | .200 | — | .200 | .200 | — | — | — | — |
| 09 | $6 | $0 | 150 | −7 | 14 | 1 | 0 | 38-22-40 | 8% | 21% | 25% | .688 | .713 | .657 | .727 | .616 | — | −23 | +57 |
| 10 | — | — | — | — | — | — | — | — | — | — | — | — | — | — | — | — | 0.53 | −8 | +21 |

## Michael Saunders — 450 PA | $7 | 210 pts

OF-89 (LF-77, CF-14), DH-4 — Owned: 0% — LH

| Player | Age | AB | HR | R | RBI | SB | BA | OBP | SLG | $1L | Pts |
|---|---|---|---|---|---|---|---|---|---|---|---|
| | | Forecast | | | | | | | | | |
| Saunders M | 24 | 420 | 14 | 50 | 45 | 14 | .225 | .303 | .380 | $7 | 210 |
| Mini-Browser | Age | AB | HR | R | RBI | SB | BA | OBP | SLG | $1L | Pts |
| DeRosa M | 36 | 358 | 12 | 56 | 52 | 4 | .268 | .347 | .438 | $9 | 240 |
| Guillen J | 34 | 326 | 11 | 35 | 49 | 0 | .268 | .319 | .428 | $9 | 180 |
| Cabrera M | 26 | 472 | 10 | 55 | 50 | 10 | .265 | .331 | .379 | $8 | 310 |
| Jay J | 26 | 458 | 10 | 60 | 45 | 10 | .262 | .326 | .384 | $8 | 260 |
| Jennings D | 24 | 293 | 7 | 39 | 26 | 20 | .244 | .322 | .403 | $7 | 200 |

| Level | Leag | AB | HR | R | RBI | SB | BA | OBP | SLG | CT% | H% | BB% | Bash |
|---|---|---|---|---|---|---|---|---|---|---|---|---|---|
| | | Minors (2010) | | | | | | | | Skills | | | |
| A | — | — | — | — | — | — | — | — | — | — | — | — | — |
| AA | — | — | — | — | — | — | — | — | — | — | — | — | — |
| AAA | PCL | 80 | 0 | 6 | 5 | 4 | .200 | .293 | .213 | 79% | 25% | 12% | 1.06 |

| Yr | Team | AB | HR | R | RBI | SB | BA | OBP | SLG | CT% | H% | BB% | Bash |
|---|---|---|---|---|---|---|---|---|---|---|---|---|---|
| | | Majors | | | | | | | | Skills | | | |
| 07 | — | — | — | — | — | — | — | — | — | — | — | — | — |
| 08 | — | — | — | — | — | — | — | — | — | — | — | — | — |
| 09 | SEA | 122 | 0 | 13 | 4 | 4 | .221 | .258 | .279 | 67% | 33% | 5% | 1.26 |
| 10 | SEA | 289 | 10 | 29 | 33 | 6 | .211 | .295 | .367 | 71% | 30% | 11% | 1.74 |

Saunders still has work to do, but he made a lot of progress in 2010 and finally earned some success outside of the minors. He needs to raise his contact rate and fare better against LH, but he is drawing walks and cranking up the power. The 24-year-old will be Seattle's starting left fielder in 2011. (GC)

**Competition at LF — Stats in 2010**

| Bats | Player | GSvR | GSvL | Sub | OPS |
|---|---|---|---|---|---|
| LH | Saunders M | 60 | 15 | 2 | .662 |
| BH | Bradley M | 21 | 17 | 1 | .641 |
| LH | Langerhans R | 17 | 7 | 6 | .661 |
| RH | Tuiasosopo M | 8 | 6 | 0 | .541 |

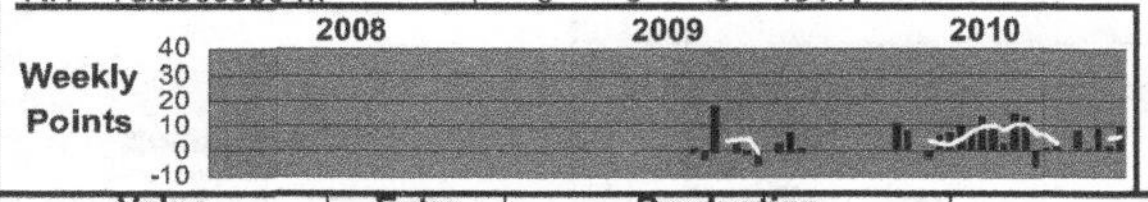


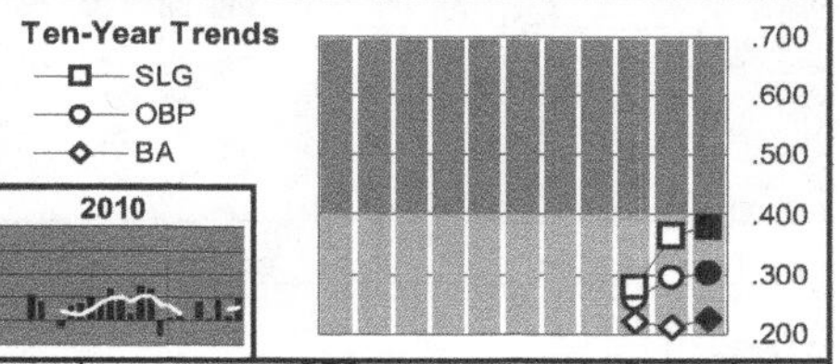


| Yr | $1L | $2L | Pts | RAA | 2B | 3B | CS | FB-LD-GB | HR/fb | RBI% | RS% | OPS | 1st Hf | 2nd Hf | vs RH | vs LH | Rnge | vRH | vLH |
|---|---|---|---|---|---|---|---|---|---|---|---|---|---|---|---|---|---|---|---|
| | Value | | | | Extra | | | Production | | | | OPS | | | | | Scoresheet | | |
| 07 | — | — | — | — | — | — | — | — | — | — | — | — | — | — | — | — | — | — | — |
| 08 | — | — | — | — | — | — | — | — | — | — | — | — | — | — | — | — | — | — | — |
| 09 | -$3 | -$19 | 20 | −11 | 1 | 3 | 1 | 39-13-48 | 0% | 9% | 39% | .537 | — | .537 | .615 | .436 | 2.10 | — | — |
| 10 | $3 | -$11 | 130 | −12 | 11 | 2 | 3 | 48-16-36 | 11% | 15% | 22% | .662 | .702 | .625 | .686 | .601 | 2.09 | +32 | −87 |

## Nate Schierholtz — 200 PA | $1 | 110 pts

OF-109 (RF-109) — Owned: 1% — LH

| Player | Age | AB | HR | R | RBI | SB | BA | OBP | SLG | $1L | Pts |
|---|---|---|---|---|---|---|---|---|---|---|---|
| | | Forecast | | | | | | | | | |
| Schierholtz N | 27 | 182 | 4 | 24 | 20 | 4 | .274 | .319 | .445 | $1 | 110 |
| Mini-Browser | Age | AB | HR | R | RBI | SB | BA | OBP | SLG | $1L | Pts |
| Patterson C | 31 | 188 | 4 | 22 | 20 | 10 | .255 | .296 | .394 | $2 | 110 |
| Diaz M | 33 | 186 | 6 | 24 | 26 | 4 | .269 | .325 | .430 | $2 | 110 |
| Parra G | 23 | 228 | 5 | 28 | 25 | 5 | .263 | .316 | .389 | $2 | 130 |
| Nix L | 30 | 192 | 10 | 24 | 24 | 0 | .260 | .319 | .489 | $1 | 110 |
| Hairston S | 30 | 219 | 9 | 25 | 28 | 2 | .242 | .308 | .433 | $1 | 130 |

| Level | Leag | AB | HR | R | RBI | SB | BA | OBP | SLG | CT% | H% | BB% | Bash |
|---|---|---|---|---|---|---|---|---|---|---|---|---|---|
| | | Minors (2010) | | | | | | | | Skills | | | |
| A | — | — | — | — | — | — | — | — | — | — | — | — | — |
| AA | — | — | — | — | — | — | — | — | — | — | — | — | — |
| AAA | — | — | — | — | — | — | — | — | — | — | — | — | — |

| Yr | Team | AB | HR | R | RBI | SB | BA | OBP | SLG | CT% | H% | BB% | Bash |
|---|---|---|---|---|---|---|---|---|---|---|---|---|---|
| | | Majors | | | | | | | | Skills | | | |
| 07 | SF | 112 | 0 | 9 | 10 | 3 | .304 | .316 | .402 | 83% | 37% | 2% | 1.32 |
| 08 | SF | 75 | 1 | 12 | 5 | 0 | .320 | .370 | .493 | 89% | 36% | 4% | 1.54 |
| 09 | SF | 285 | 5 | 33 | 29 | 3 | .267 | .302 | .400 | 80% | 33% | 5% | 1.50 |
| 10 | SF | 227 | 3 | 34 | 17 | 4 | .242 | .311 | .366 | 83% | 29% | 8% | 1.51 |

2010 was supposed to be Schierholtz's year, but despite adding the batting gloves and fixing his swing, he could not take advantage of his chances. There is little room in the Giants' outfield for Schierholtz in 2011, so he might use a chance of scene, but 9 HR in 700 AB won't cut it at OF. (PB)

**Competition at RF — Stats in 2010**

| Bats | Player | GSvR | GSvL | Sub | OPS |
|---|---|---|---|---|---|
| BH | Torres A | 28 | 15 | 0 | .823 |
| LH | Schierholtz N | 31 | 10 | 68 | .676 |
| RH | Guillen J | 28 | 10 | 0 | .730 |
| LH | Huff A | 28 | 6 | 0 | .891 |

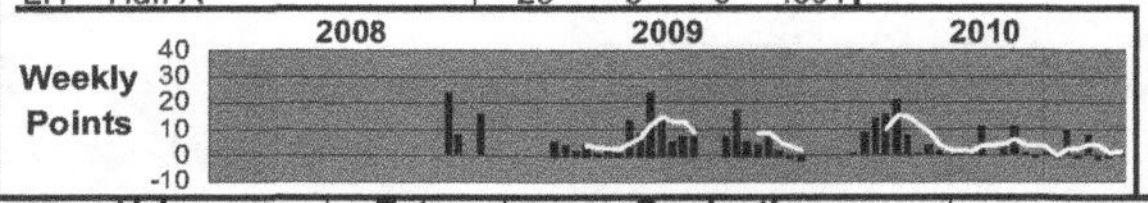


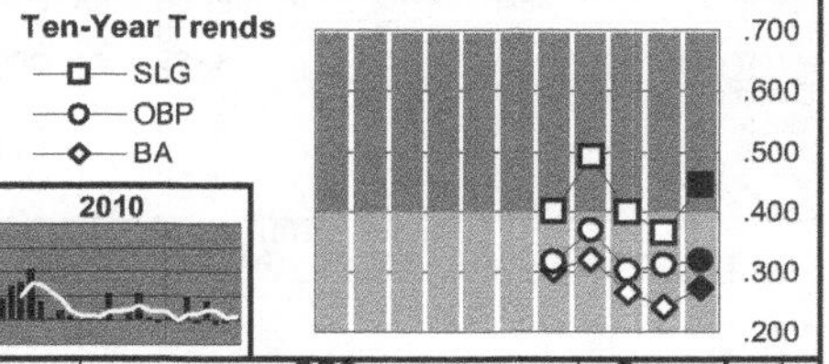


| Yr | $1L | $2L | Pts | RAA | 2B | 3B | CS | FB-LD-GB | HR/fb | RBI% | RS% | OPS | 1st Hf | 2nd Hf | vs RH | vs LH | Rnge | vRH | vLH |
|---|---|---|---|---|---|---|---|---|---|---|---|---|---|---|---|---|---|---|---|
| | Value | | | | Extra | | | Production | | | | OPS | | | | | Scoresheet | | |
| 07 | -$3 | -$16 | 50 | −4 | 5 | 3 | 1 | 41-15-44 | 0% | 21% | 24% | .718 | .749 | .700 | .634 | 1.167 | 2.10 | — | — |
| 08 | -$2 | -$15 | 50 | +0 | 8 | 1 | 1 | 24-30-46 | 6% | 14% | 38% | .864 | — | .864 | .873 | .840 | 2.06 | — | — |
| 09 | $3 | -$10 | 140 | −12 | 19 | 2 | 1 | 35-21-45 | 6% | 17% | 32% | .702 | .732 | .663 | .626 | 1.026 | 2.08 | — | — |
| 10 | $1 | -$13 | 120 | −15 | 13 | 3 | 5 | 37-18-44 | 4% | 13% | 41% | .676 | .685 | .656 | .678 | .671 | 2.07 | — | — |

## Brian Schneider — 150 PA | $1 | 80 pts

CA-46 — Owned: 0% — LH

| Player | Age | AB | HR | R | RBI | SB | BA | OBP | SLG | $1L | Pts |
|---|---|---|---|---|---|---|---|---|---|---|---|
| | | Forecast | | | | | | | | | |
| Schneider B | 34 | 128 | 3 | 14 | 17 | 0 | .258 | .343 | .381 | $1 | 80 |
| Mini-Browser | Age | AB | HR | R | RBI | SB | BA | OBP | SLG | $1L | Pts |
| Hester J | 27 | 142 | 5 | 17 | 17 | 2 | .243 | .294 | .422 | $1 | 70 |
| May L | 26 | 235 | 10 | 23 | 28 | 3 | .202 | .257 | .372 | $1 | 90 |
| Navarro D | 27 | 184 | 4 | 18 | 18 | 2 | .250 | .306 | .362 | $1 | 100 |
| Laird G | 31 | 192 | 4 | 20 | 18 | 2 | .239 | .300 | .354 | $1 | 90 |
| Montero J | 21 | 183 | 10 | 22 | 28 | 0 | .263 | .316 | .484 | $1 | 120 |

| Level | Leag | AB | HR | R | RBI | SB | BA | OBP | SLG | CT% | H% | BB% | Bash |
|---|---|---|---|---|---|---|---|---|---|---|---|---|---|
| | | Minors (2010) | | | | | | | | Skills | | | |
| A | — | — | — | — | — | — | — | — | — | — | — | — | — |
| AA | — | — | — | — | — | — | — | — | — | — | — | — | — |
| AAA | IL | 8 | 0 | 0 | 0 | 0 | .000 | .111 | .000 | 100% | 0% | 11% | NA |

| Yr | Team | AB | HR | R | RBI | SB | BA | OBP | SLG | CT% | H% | BB% | Bash |
|---|---|---|---|---|---|---|---|---|---|---|---|---|---|
| | | Majors | | | | | | | | Skills | | | |
| 07 | WAS | 408 | 6 | 33 | 54 | 0 | .235 | .326 | .336 | 86% | 27% | 12% | 1.43 |
| 08 | NYM | 335 | 9 | 30 | 38 | 0 | .257 | .339 | .367 | 84% | 30% | 11% | 1.43 |
| 09 | NYM | 170 | 3 | 11 | 24 | 0 | .218 | .292 | .335 | 88% | 25% | 9% | 1.54 |
| 10 | PHI | 125 | 4 | 17 | 15 | 0 | .240 | .345 | .384 | 80% | 30% | 13% | 1.60 |

Schneider has one more year on his contract, so he will once again serve as the back-up behind Carlos Ruiz. Schneider is not much with the bat, but the Phillies like his experience (11 seasons in the NL). He will hit just well enough to justify 150 PA. (BB)

**Competition at CA — Stats in 2010**

| Bats | Player | GSvR | GSvL | Sub | OPS |
|---|---|---|---|---|---|
| RH | Ruiz C | 68 | 41 | 9 | .847 |
| LH | Schneider B | 36 | 2 | 8 | .729 |
| RH | Sardinha D | 7 | 2 | 3 | .712 |

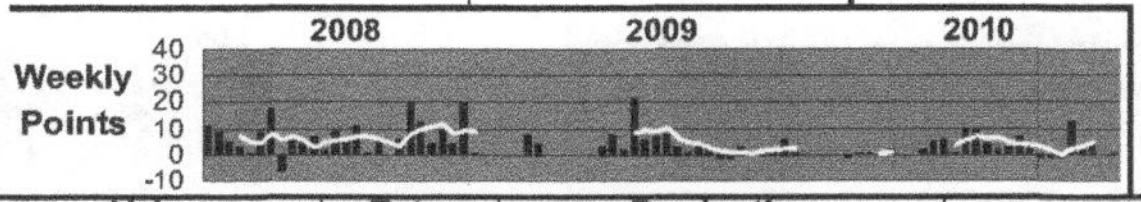


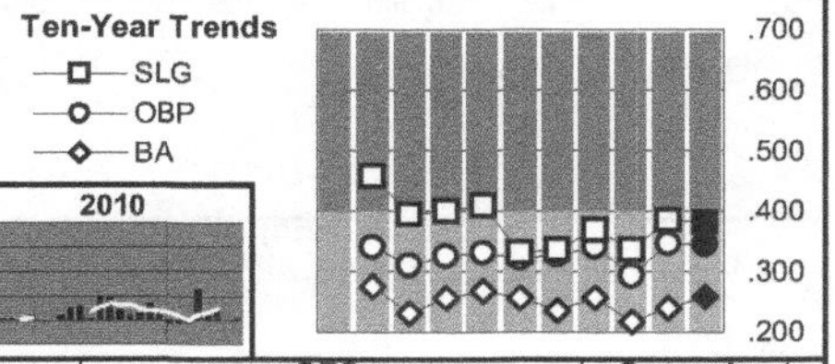


| Yr | $1L | $2L | Pts | RAA | 2B | 3B | CS | FB-LD-GB | HR/fb | RBI% | RS% | OPS | 1st Hf | 2nd Hf | vs RH | vs LH | Rnge | vRH | vLH |
|---|---|---|---|---|---|---|---|---|---|---|---|---|---|---|---|---|---|---|---|
| | Value | | | | Extra | | | Production | | | | OPS | | | | | Scoresheet | | |
| 07 | $3 | -$6 | 220 | −12 | 21 | 1 | 0 | 36-15-48 | 5% | 19% | 18% | .661 | .633 | .706 | .671 | .636 | 0.51 | +22 | −75 |
| 08 | $6 | -$1 | 180 | −4 | 10 | 0 | 0 | 21-26-53 | 15% | 17% | 18% | .707 | .652 | .793 | .769 | .491 | 0.51 | +19 | −58 |
| 09 | $0 | -$7 | 90 | −8 | 11 | 0 | 0 | 30-13-57 | 7% | 21% | 15% | .627 | .748 | .508 | .656 | .100 | 0.47 | +28 | −81 |
| 10 | $1 | -$7 | 70 | −1 | 4 | 1 | 0 | 38-17-45 | 11% | 17% | 28% | .729 | .710 | .752 | .820 | .161 | 0.46 | +29 | −99 |

*For more stats, visit www.Rotolympus.com.*

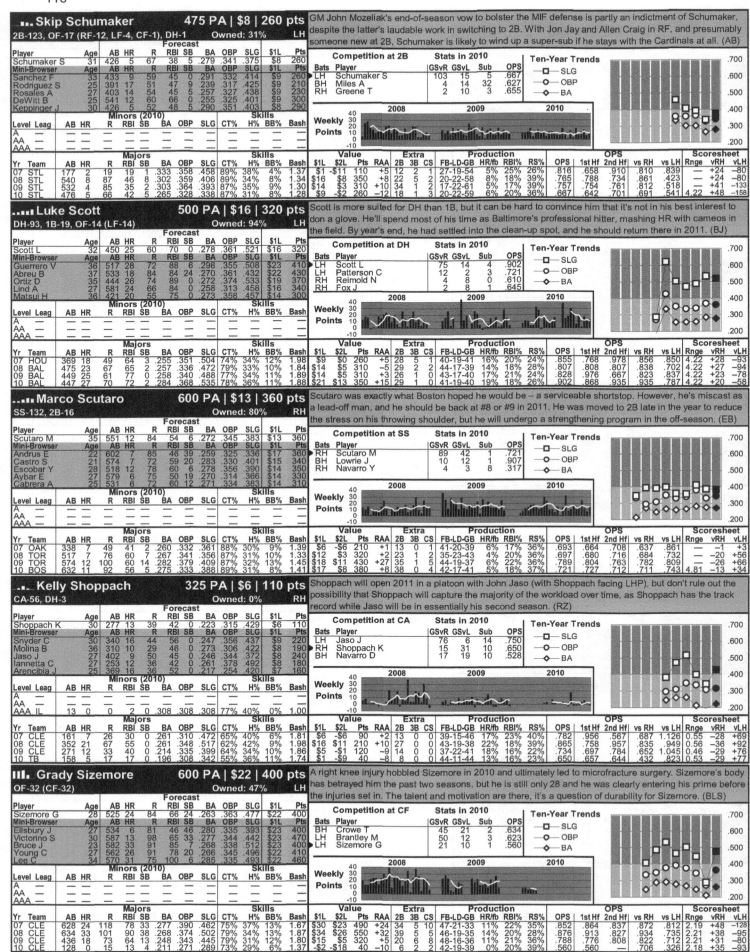

## ... Skip Schumaker — 475 PA | $8 | 260 pts
### 2B-123, OF-17 (RF-12, LF-4, CF-1), DH-1 — Owned: 31% — LH

GM John Mozeliak's end-of-season vow to bolster the MIF defense is partly an indictment of Schumaker, despite the latter's laudable work in switching to 2B. With Jon Jay and Allen Craig in RF, and presumably someone new at 2B, Schumaker is likely to wind up a super-sub if he stays with the Cardinals at all. (AB)

**Forecast**

| Player | Age | AB | HR | R | RBI | SB | BA | OBP | SLG | $1L | Pts |
|---|---|---|---|---|---|---|---|---|---|---|---|
| Schumaker S | 31 | 426 | 5 | 67 | 38 | 5 | .279 | .341 | .375 | $8 | 260 |
| Mini-Browser | Age | AB | HR | R | RBI | SB | BA | OBP | SLG | $1L | Pts |
| Sanchez F | 33 | 433 | 9 | 59 | 45 | 0 | .291 | .332 | .414 | $9 | 260 |
| Rodriguez S | 25 | 391 | 17 | 51 | 47 | 9 | .239 | .317 | .425 | $9 | 210 |
| Rosales A | 27 | 403 | 14 | 54 | 45 | 5 | .257 | .327 | .438 | $9 | 230 |
| DeWitt B | 25 | 541 | 14 | 60 | 66 | 0 | .255 | .325 | .401 | $8 | 300 |
| Keppinger J | 30 | 426 | 5 | 52 | 48 | 5 | .290 | .351 | .403 | $8 | 290 |

**Competition at 2B — Stats in 2010**

| Bats | Player | GSvR | GSvL | Sub | OPS |
|---|---|---|---|---|---|
| LH | Schumaker S | 103 | 15 | 5 | .667 |
| BH | Miles A | 4 | 14 | 32 | .627 |
| RH | Greene T | 2 | 10 | 3 | .655 |

**Ten-Year Trends:** □ SLG ○ OBP ◇ BA

**Minors (2010)** / **Skills**

| Level | Leag | AB | HR | R | RBI | SB | BA | OBP | SLG | CT% | H% | BB% | Bash |
|---|---|---|---|---|---|---|---|---|---|---|---|---|---|
| A | — | — | — | — | — | — | — | — | — | — | — | — | — |
| AA | — | — | — | — | — | — | — | — | — | — | — | — | — |
| AAA | — | — | — | — | — | — | — | — | — | — | — | — | — |

**Majors** / **Skills** / **Value** / **Extra** / **Production** / **OPS** / **Scoresheet**

| Yr | Team | AB | HR | R | RBI | SB | BA | OBP | SLG | CT% | H% | BB% | Bash | $1L | $2L | Pts | RAA | 2B | 3B | CS | FB-LD-GB | HR/fb | RBI% | RS% | OPS | 1st Hf | 2nd Hf | vs RH | vs LH | Rnge | vRH | vLH |
|---|---|---|---|---|---|---|---|---|---|---|---|---|---|---|---|---|---|---|---|---|---|---|---|---|---|---|---|---|---|---|---|---|
| 07 | STL | 177 | 2 | 19 | 19 | 1 | .333 | .358 | .458 | 89% | 38% | 4% | 1.37 | $1 | -$11 | 110 | +5 | 12 | 2 | 1 | 27-19-54 | 5% | 25% | 26% | .816 | .658 | .910 | .810 | .839 | — | +24 | -80 |
| 08 | STL | 540 | 8 | 87 | 46 | 8 | .302 | .359 | .406 | 89% | 34% | 8% | 1.34 | $8 | $8 | 350 | +8 | 22 | 5 | 2 | 20-22-58 | 8% | 18% | 39% | .765 | .788 | .734 | .861 | .423 | — | +24 | -80 |
| 09 | STL | 532 | 4 | 85 | 35 | 2 | .303 | .364 | .393 | 87% | 35% | 9% | 1.30 | $14 | $3 | 310 | +10 | 34 | 1 | 2 | 17-22-61 | 5% | 17% | 39% | .757 | .754 | .761 | .812 | .518 | — | +41 | -133 |
| 10 | STL | 476 | 5 | 66 | 42 | 5 | .265 | .328 | .338 | 87% | 31% | 9% | 1.28 | $8 | -$2 | 260 | -12 | 18 | 1 | 5 | 20-22-59 | 6% | 20% | 36% | .667 | .642 | .701 | .691 | .541 | 4.22 | +48 | -158 |

## ..... Luke Scott — 500 PA | $16 | 320 pts
### DH-93, 1B-19, OF-14 (LF-14) — Owned: 94% — LH

Scott is more suited for DH than 1B, but it can be hard to convince him that it's not in his best interest to don a glove. He'll spend most of his time as Baltimore's professional hitter, mashing HR with cameos in the field. By year's end, he had settled into the clean-up spot, and he should return there in 2011. (BJ)

**Forecast**

| Player | Age | AB | HR | R | RBI | SB | BA | OBP | SLG | $1L | Pts |
|---|---|---|---|---|---|---|---|---|---|---|---|
| Scott L | 32 | 450 | 25 | 60 | 70 | 0 | .278 | .361 | .521 | $16 | 320 |
| Mini-Browser | Age | AB | HR | R | RBI | SB | BA | OBP | SLG | $1L | Pts |
| Guerrero V | 36 | 517 | 28 | 72 | 88 | 6 | .298 | .355 | .508 | $23 | 410 |
| Abreu B | 37 | 533 | 18 | 84 | 84 | 24 | .270 | .361 | .432 | $22 | 430 |
| Ortiz D | 35 | 444 | 26 | 74 | 89 | 0 | .272 | .374 | .533 | $19 | 370 |
| Lind A | 27 | 581 | 24 | 66 | 84 | 0 | .258 | .313 | .458 | $16 | 340 |
| Matsui H | 36 | 421 | 16 | 55 | 75 | 0 | .273 | .358 | .457 | $14 | 300 |

**Competition at DH — Stats in 2010**

| Bats | Player | GSvR | GSvL | Sub | OPS |
|---|---|---|---|---|---|
| LH | Scott L | 75 | 14 | 4 | .902 |
| LH | Patterson C | 12 | 2 | 3 | .721 |
| RH | Reimold N | 4 | 8 | 0 | .610 |
| RH | Fox J | 2 | 8 | 1 | .645 |

**Ten-Year Trends:** □ SLG ○ OBP ◇ BA

**Minors (2010)** / **Skills**

| Level | Leag | AB | HR | R | RBI | SB | BA | OBP | SLG | CT% | H% | BB% | Bash |
|---|---|---|---|---|---|---|---|---|---|---|---|---|---|
| A | — | — | — | — | — | — | — | — | — | — | — | — | — |
| AA | — | — | — | — | — | — | — | — | — | — | — | — | — |
| AAA | — | — | — | — | — | — | — | — | — | — | — | — | — |

**Majors** / **Skills** / **Value** / **Extra** / **Production** / **OPS** / **Scoresheet**

| Yr | Team | AB | HR | R | RBI | SB | BA | OBP | SLG | CT% | H% | BB% | Bash | $1L | $2L | Pts | RAA | 2B | 3B | CS | FB-LD-GB | HR/fb | RBI% | RS% | OPS | 1st Hf | 2nd Hf | vs RH | vs LH | Rnge | vRH | vLH |
|---|---|---|---|---|---|---|---|---|---|---|---|---|---|---|---|---|---|---|---|---|---|---|---|---|---|---|---|---|---|---|---|---|
| 07 | HOU | 369 | 18 | 49 | 64 | 3 | .255 | .351 | .504 | 74% | 34% | 12% | 1.98 | $9 | $0 | 260 | +5 | 28 | 5 | 1 | 40-19-41 | 16% | 20% | 24% | .855 | .768 | .978 | .856 | .850 | 4.22 | +28 | -93 |
| 08 | BAL | 475 | 23 | 67 | 65 | 2 | .257 | .336 | .472 | 79% | 33% | 10% | 1.84 | $14 | $5 | 310 | -5 | 29 | 2 | 1 | 44-17-39 | 14% | 18% | 28% | .807 | .808 | .807 | .838 | .702 | 4.22 | +27 | -94 |
| 09 | BAL | 449 | 25 | 61 | 77 | 0 | .258 | .340 | .488 | 77% | 34% | 11% | 1.89 | $14 | $5 | 310 | +3 | 26 | 1 | 0 | 43-17-40 | 17% | 21% | 24% | .828 | .976 | .667 | .823 | .837 | 4.22 | +23 | -78 |
| 10 | BAL | 447 | 27 | 70 | 72 | 2 | .284 | .368 | .535 | 78% | 36% | 11% | 1.88 | $21 | $13 | 350 | +15 | 29 | 1 | 0 | 41-20-40 | 19% | 18% | 26% | .902 | .868 | .935 | .935 | .787 | 4.22 | +20 | -58 |

## ..... Marco Scutaro — 600 PA | $13 | 360 pts
### SS-132, 2B-16 — Owned: 80% — RH

Scutaro was exactly what Boston hoped he would be – a serviceable shortstop. However, he's miscast as a lead-off man, and he should be back at #8 or #9 in 2011. He was moved to 2B late in the year to reduce the stress on his throwing shoulder, but he will undergo a strengthening program in the off-season. (EB)

**Forecast**

| Player | Age | AB | HR | R | RBI | SB | BA | OBP | SLG | $1L | Pts |
|---|---|---|---|---|---|---|---|---|---|---|---|
| Scutaro M | 35 | 551 | 12 | 84 | 54 | 6 | .272 | .345 | .383 | $13 | 360 |
| Mini-Browser | Age | AB | HR | R | RBI | SB | BA | OBP | SLG | $1L | Pts |
| Andrus E | 22 | 602 | 7 | 85 | 46 | 39 | .259 | .325 | .336 | $17 | 360 |
| Castro S | 21 | 574 | 7 | 72 | 59 | 20 | .283 | .330 | .401 | $15 | 340 |
| Escobar Y | 28 | 518 | 12 | 78 | 60 | 6 | .278 | .356 | .390 | $14 | 350 |
| Aybar E | 27 | 579 | 6 | 75 | 50 | 19 | .270 | .314 | .366 | $14 | 330 |
| Cabrera A | 25 | 531 | 9 | 72 | 60 | 12 | .271 | .334 | .383 | $14 | 310 |

**Competition at SS — Stats in 2010**

| Bats | Player | GSvR | GSvL | Sub | OPS |
|---|---|---|---|---|---|
| RH | Scutaro M | 89 | 42 | 1 | .721 |
| BH | Lowrie J | 10 | 12 | 1 | .907 |
| RH | Navarro Y | 4 | 3 | 8 | .317 |

**Ten-Year Trends:** □ SLG ○ OBP ◇ BA

**Minors (2010)** / **Skills**

| Level | Leag | AB | HR | R | RBI | SB | BA | OBP | SLG | CT% | H% | BB% | Bash |
|---|---|---|---|---|---|---|---|---|---|---|---|---|---|
| A | — | — | — | — | — | — | — | — | — | — | — | — | — |
| AA | — | — | — | — | — | — | — | — | — | — | — | — | — |
| AAA | — | — | — | — | — | — | — | — | — | — | — | — | — |

**Majors** / **Skills** / **Value** / **Extra** / **Production** / **OPS** / **Scoresheet**

| Yr | Team | AB | HR | R | RBI | SB | BA | OBP | SLG | CT% | H% | BB% | Bash | $1L | $2L | Pts | RAA | 2B | 3B | CS | FB-LD-GB | HR/fb | RBI% | RS% | OPS | 1st Hf | 2nd Hf | vs RH | vs LH | Rnge | vRH | vLH |
|---|---|---|---|---|---|---|---|---|---|---|---|---|---|---|---|---|---|---|---|---|---|---|---|---|---|---|---|---|---|---|---|---|
| 07 | OAK | 338 | 7 | 49 | 41 | 2 | .260 | .332 | .361 | 88% | 30% | 9% | 1.39 | $1 | -$6 | 210 | +1 | 13 | 0 | 1 | 41-20-39 | 6% | 17% | 36% | .693 | .664 | .708 | .637 | .861 | — | -1 | +3 |
| 08 | TOR | 517 | 7 | 76 | 60 | 7 | .267 | .341 | .356 | 87% | 31% | 10% | 1.33 | $12 | $3 | 320 | +2 | 23 | 1 | 2 | 35-23-43 | 4% | 20% | 36% | .697 | .680 | .716 | .684 | .732 | — | -20 | +56 |
| 09 | TOR | 574 | 12 | 100 | 60 | 14 | .282 | .379 | .409 | 89% | 32% | 13% | 1.45 | $18 | $11 | 430 | +27 | 35 | 1 | 5 | 44-19-37 | 6% | 22% | 36% | .789 | .804 | .763 | .782 | .809 | — | -26 | +66 |
| 10 | BOS | 632 | 11 | 92 | 56 | 5 | .275 | .333 | .388 | 89% | 31% | 8% | 1.41 | $17 | $8 | 380 | +12 | 38 | 0 | 4 | 42-19-39 | 5% | 18% | 37% | .721 | .727 | .712 | .711 | .743 | 4.81 | -13 | +34 |

## .. Kelly Shoppach — 325 PA | $6 | 110 pts
### CA-56, DH-3 — Owned: 0% — RH

Shoppach will open 2011 in a platoon with John Jaso (with Shoppach facing LHP), but don't rule out the possibility that Shoppach will capture the majority of the workload over time, as Shoppach has the track record while Jaso will be in essentially his second season. (RZ)

**Forecast**

| Player | Age | AB | HR | R | RBI | SB | BA | OBP | SLG | $1L | Pts |
|---|---|---|---|---|---|---|---|---|---|---|---|
| Shoppach K | 30 | 277 | 13 | 39 | 42 | 0 | .223 | .315 | .429 | $6 | 110 |
| Mini-Browser | Age | AB | HR | R | RBI | SB | BA | OBP | SLG | $1L | Pts |
| Snyder C | 30 | 340 | 16 | 44 | 56 | 0 | .247 | .356 | .437 | $9 | 220 |
| Molina B | 36 | 310 | 10 | 29 | 46 | 0 | .273 | .306 | .422 | $8 | 190 |
| Jaso J | 27 | 402 | 9 | 50 | 45 | 0 | .246 | .344 | .372 | $8 | 240 |
| Iannetta C | 27 | 253 | 12 | 36 | 42 | 0 | .261 | .378 | .492 | $8 | 180 |
| Arencibia J | 25 | 369 | 16 | 36 | 52 | 0 | .217 | .254 | .420 | $7 | 160 |

**Competition at CA — Stats in 2010**

| Bats | Player | GSvR | GSvL | Sub | OPS |
|---|---|---|---|---|---|
| LH | Jaso J | 76 | 6 | 14 | .750 |
| RH | Shoppach K | 15 | 31 | 10 | .650 |
| BH | Navarro D | 17 | 19 | 10 | .528 |

**Ten-Year Trends:** □ SLG ○ OBP ◇ BA

**Minors (2010)** / **Skills**

| Level | Leag | AB | HR | R | RBI | SB | BA | OBP | SLG | CT% | H% | BB% | Bash |
|---|---|---|---|---|---|---|---|---|---|---|---|---|---|
| A | — | — | — | — | — | — | — | — | — | — | — | — | — |
| AA | — | — | — | — | — | — | — | — | — | — | — | — | — |
| AAA | IL | 13 | 0 | 0 | 2 | 0 | .308 | .308 | .308 | 77% | 40% | 0% | 1.00 |

**Majors** / **Skills** / **Value** / **Extra** / **Production** / **OPS** / **Scoresheet**

| Yr | Team | AB | HR | R | RBI | SB | BA | OBP | SLG | CT% | H% | BB% | Bash | $1L | $2L | Pts | RAA | 2B | 3B | CS | FB-LD-GB | HR/fb | RBI% | RS% | OPS | 1st Hf | 2nd Hf | vs RH | vs LH | Rnge | vRH | vLH |
|---|---|---|---|---|---|---|---|---|---|---|---|---|---|---|---|---|---|---|---|---|---|---|---|---|---|---|---|---|---|---|---|---|
| 07 | CLE | 161 | 7 | 26 | 30 | 0 | .261 | .310 | .472 | 65% | 40% | 6% | 1.81 | $6 | -$6 | 90 | +2 | 13 | 0 | 0 | 39-15-46 | 17% | 23% | 40% | .782 | .956 | .567 | .687 | 1.126 | 0.55 | -28 | +69 |
| 08 | CLE | 352 | 21 | 67 | 55 | 0 | .261 | .348 | .517 | 62% | 42% | 9% | 1.98 | $16 | $11 | 210 | +10 | 27 | 0 | 0 | 43-19-38 | 22% | 18% | 39% | .865 | .758 | .957 | .835 | .949 | 0.56 | -36 | +92 |
| 09 | CLE | 271 | 12 | 33 | 40 | 0 | .214 | .335 | .399 | 64% | 34% | 10% | 1.86 | $5 | -$1 | 120 | -9 | 14 | 0 | 0 | 37-22-41 | 18% | 16% | 23% | .734 | .697 | .784 | .652 | 1.045 | 0.46 | +24 | +76 |
| 10 | TB | 158 | 5 | 17 | 17 | 0 | .196 | .308 | .342 | 55% | 36% | 11% | 1.74 | $1 | -$9 | 40 | -8 | 8 | 0 | 0 | 44-11-44 | 13% | 16% | 23% | .650 | .657 | .644 | .432 | .823 | 0.53 | -29 | +74 |

## III. Grady Sizemore — 600 PA | $22 | 400 pts
### OF-32 (CF-32) — Owned: 47% — LH

A right knee injury hobbled Sizemore in 2010 and ultimately led to microfracture surgery. Sizemore's body has betrayed him the past two seasons, but he is still only 28 and he was clearly entering his prime before the injuries set in. The talent and motivation are there, it's a question of durability for Sizemore. (BLS)

**Forecast**

| Player | Age | AB | HR | R | RBI | SB | BA | OBP | SLG | $1L | Pts |
|---|---|---|---|---|---|---|---|---|---|---|---|
| Sizemore G | 28 | 525 | 24 | 84 | 66 | 24 | .263 | .363 | .477 | $22 | 400 |
| Mini-Browser | Age | AB | HR | R | RBI | SB | BA | OBP | SLG | $1L | Pts |
| Ellsbury J | 27 | 534 | 6 | 81 | 46 | 46 | .280 | .335 | .393 | $23 | 400 |
| Victorino S | 30 | 587 | 13 | 98 | 65 | 33 | .277 | .344 | .442 | $23 | 470 |
| Bruce J | 23 | 582 | 33 | 91 | 85 | 7 | .268 | .338 | .512 | $23 | 450 |
| Young C | 27 | 562 | 26 | 91 | 78 | 20 | .266 | .345 | .496 | $22 | 410 |
| Lee C | 34 | 570 | 31 | 75 | 100 | 6 | .285 | .335 | .493 | $22 | 460 |

**Competition at CF — Stats in 2010**

| Bats | Player | GSvR | GSvL | Sub | OPS |
|---|---|---|---|---|---|
| BH | Crowe T | 45 | 21 | 2 | .634 |
| LH | Brantley M | 50 | 12 | 3 | .623 |
| LH | Sizemore G | 21 | 10 | 1 | .560 |

**Ten-Year Trends:** □ SLG ○ OBP ◇ BA

**Minors (2010)** / **Skills**

| Level | Leag | AB | HR | R | RBI | SB | BA | OBP | SLG | CT% | H% | BB% | Bash |
|---|---|---|---|---|---|---|---|---|---|---|---|---|---|
| A | — | — | — | — | — | — | — | — | — | — | — | — | — |
| AA | — | — | — | — | — | — | — | — | — | — | — | — | — |
| AAA | — | — | — | — | — | — | — | — | — | — | — | — | — |

**Majors** / **Skills** / **Value** / **Extra** / **Production** / **OPS** / **Scoresheet**

| Yr | Team | AB | HR | R | RBI | SB | BA | OBP | SLG | CT% | H% | BB% | Bash | $1L | $2L | Pts | RAA | 2B | 3B | CS | FB-LD-GB | HR/fb | RBI% | RS% | OPS | 1st Hf | 2nd Hf | vs RH | vs LH | Rnge | vRH | vLH |
|---|---|---|---|---|---|---|---|---|---|---|---|---|---|---|---|---|---|---|---|---|---|---|---|---|---|---|---|---|---|---|---|---|
| 07 | CLE | 628 | 24 | 118 | 78 | 33 | .277 | .390 | .462 | 75% | 37% | 13% | 1.67 | $30 | $23 | 490 | +24 | 34 | 5 | 10 | 47-21-33 | 11% | 22% | 35% | .852 | .864 | .837 | .872 | .812 | 2.19 | +48 | -128 |
| 08 | CLE | 634 | 33 | 101 | 90 | 38 | .268 | .374 | .502 | 79% | 34% | 13% | 1.87 | $34 | $26 | 550 | +32 | 39 | 5 | 5 | 46-19-35 | 14% | 20% | 34% | .876 | .913 | .827 | .934 | .735 | 2.21 | +38 | -95 |
| 09 | CLE | 436 | 18 | 73 | 64 | 13 | .248 | .343 | .445 | 79% | 31% | 11% | 1.80 | $15 | -$5 | 320 | +5 | 20 | 6 | 8 | 48-16-36 | 11% | 21% | 36% | .788 | .776 | .808 | .822 | .712 | 2.21 | +31 | -80 |
| 10 | CLE | 128 | 0 | 15 | 13 | 4 | .211 | .271 | .289 | 73% | 29% | 6% | 1.37 | -$2 | -$18 | 40 | -10 | 4 | 0 | 2 | 42-19-39 | 0% | 16% | 29% | .560 | .560 | — | .706 | .326 | 2.18 | +35 | -74 |

## Scott Sizemore — 350 PA | $4 | 190 pts

2B-40, 3B-6, DH-2 — Owned: 3% — RH

| Player | Age | AB | HR | R | RBI | SB | BA | OBP | SLG | $1L | Pts |
|---|---|---|---|---|---|---|---|---|---|---|---|
| | | Forecast | | | | | | | | | |
| Sizemore S | 26 | 326 | 11 | 39 | 32 | 11 | .236 | .318 | .393 | $4 | 190 |
| **Mini-Browser** | **Age** | **AB** | **HR** | **R** | **RBI** | **SB** | **BA** | **OBP** | **SLG** | **$1L** | **Pts** |
| Ellis M | 33 | 350 | 8 | 44 | 44 | 8 | .263 | .326 | .394 | $7 | 220 |
| Donald J | 26 | 520 | 12 | 63 | 52 | 12 | .232 | .303 | .369 | $7 | 250 |
| Lopez F | 30 | 361 | 8 | 48 | 36 | 8 | .266 | .341 | .377 | $6 | 220 |
| Guzman C | 33 | 314 | 4 | 46 | 32 | 4 | .279 | .314 | .389 | $5 | 180 |
| Lowrie J | 26 | 313 | 7 | 39 | 42 | 0 | .257 | .340 | .437 | $5 | 190 |

Sizemore's sub-par debut was due in part to a lingering ankle injury suffered in the Arizona Fall League. Sizemore is merely adequate in the field, and he won't be handed a roster spot, but with his power (.150 ISO in the minors) and superior patience, he is a good bet to wrestle 2B from Will Rhymes. (LP)

**Competition at 2B — Stats in 2010**

| Bats | Player | GSvR | GSvL | Sub | OPS |
|---|---|---|---|---|---|
| LH | Rhymes W | 37 | 9 | 7 | .763 |
| BH | Guillen C | 33 | 12 | 2 | .746 |
| RH | Sizemore S | 23 | 13 | 4 | .631 |
| RH | Raburn R | 11 | 5 | 2 | .814 |

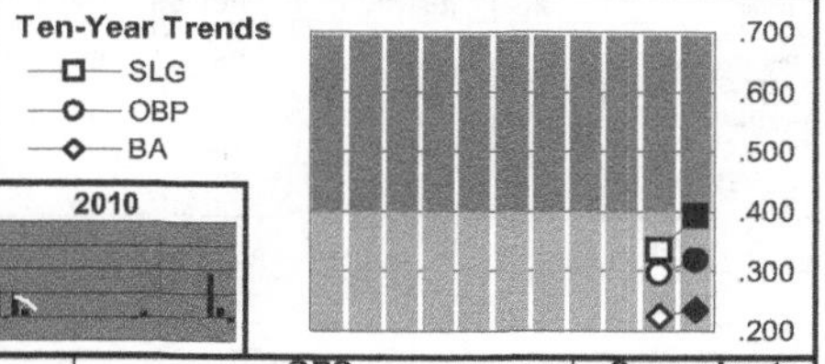

Ten-Year Trends
SLG
OBP
BA
.700
.600
.500
.400
.300
.200


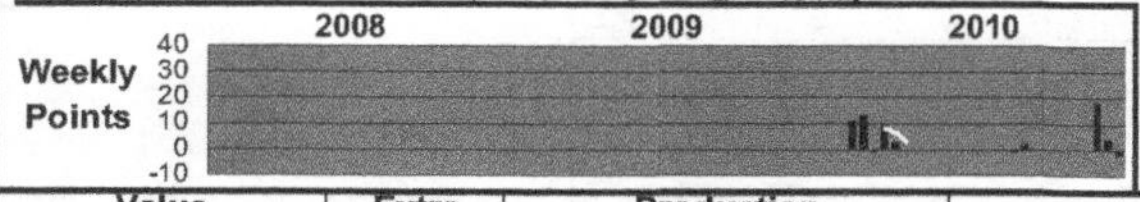

2008
2009
2010
Weekly Points
40
30
20
10
0
-10


| Level | Leag | AB | HR | R | RBI | SB | BA | OBP | SLG | CT% | H% | BB% | Bash |
|---|---|---|---|---|---|---|---|---|---|---|---|---|---|
| | | Minors (2010) | | | | | | | | Skills | | | |
| A | — | — | — | — | — | — | — | — | — | — | — | — | — |
| AA | — | — | — | — | — | — | — | — | — | — | — | — | — |
| AAA | IL | 299 | 9 | 49 | 37 | 2 | .298 | .378 | .472 | 74% | 40% | 9% | 1.58 |

| Yr | Team | AB | HR | R | RBI | SB | BA | OBP | SLG | CT% | H% | BB% | Bash | $1L | $2L | Pts | RAA | 2B | 3B | CS | FB-LD-GB | HR/fb | RBI% | RS% | OPS | 1st Hf | 2nd Hf | vs RH | vs LH | Rnge | vRH | vLH |
|---|---|---|---|---|---|---|---|---|---|---|---|---|---|---|---|---|---|---|---|---|---|---|---|---|---|---|---|---|---|---|---|---|
| | | Majors | | | | | | | | Skills | | | | Value | | | | Extra | | | Production | | | | OPS | | | | | Scoresheet | | |
| 07 | — | — | — | — | — | — | — | — | — | — | — | — | — | — | — | — | — | — | — | — | — | — | — | — | — | — | — | — | — | — | — | — |
| 08 | — | — | — | — | — | — | — | — | — | — | — | — | — | — | — | — | — | — | — | — | — | — | — | — | — | — | — | — | — | — | — | — |
| 09 | — | — | — | — | — | — | — | — | — | — | — | — | — | — | — | — | — | — | — | — | — | — | — | — | — | — | — | — | — | — | — | — |
| 10 | DET | 143 | 3 | 19 | 14 | 0 | .224 | .296 | .336 | 72% | 31% | 9% | 1.50 | -$1 | -$16 | 60 | –6 | 7 | 0 | 0 | 40-22-38 | 7% | 15% | 36% | .631 | .586 | .726 | .610 | .671 | 4.25 | — | — |

## Seth Smith — 550 PA | $17 | 360 pts

OF-101 (LF-71, RF-33) — Owned: 3% — LH

| Player | Age | AB | HR | R | RBI | SB | BA | OBP | SLG | $1L | Pts |
|---|---|---|---|---|---|---|---|---|---|---|---|
| | | Forecast | | | | | | | | | |
| Smith S | 28 | 478 | 22 | 77 | 72 | 6 | .276 | .355 | .494 | $17 | 360 |
| **Mini-Browser** | **Age** | **AB** | **HR** | **R** | **RBI** | **SB** | **BA** | **OBP** | **SLG** | **$1L** | **Pts** |
| Wells V | 32 | 568 | 18 | 72 | 78 | 12 | .264 | .318 | .452 | $17 | 390 |
| Gardner B | 27 | 441 | 5 | 75 | 40 | 40 | .261 | .357 | .363 | $17 | 330 |
| Heyward J | 21 | 511 | 18 | 84 | 66 | 12 | .270 | .368 | .464 | $17 | 380 |
| Ordonez M | 37 | 463 | 16 | 63 | 79 | 0 | .295 | .363 | .457 | $17 | 340 |
| Ludwick R | 32 | 451 | 21 | 75 | 86 | 5 | .273 | .346 | .490 | $17 | 320 |

Smith in 2010 hit for power (1.91 Bash), but his BA fell due to a low H%, owing to an unlikely 16% LD%. That rate – and his BA – should rise, and with Brad Hawpe gone, Smith should get more work. Smith's terrible play against LHP came in a small sample, but he will probably open in a platoon, anyway. (TS)

**Competition at LF — Stats in 2010**

| Bats | Player | GSvR | GSvL | Sub | OPS |
|---|---|---|---|---|---|
| LH | Gonzalez C | 31 | 31 | 1 | .974 |
| LH | Smith S | 57 | 3 | 11 | .783 |
| RH | Spilborghs R | 12 | 21 | 13 | .797 |
| BH | Young Jr. E | 4 | 6 | 0 | .597 |

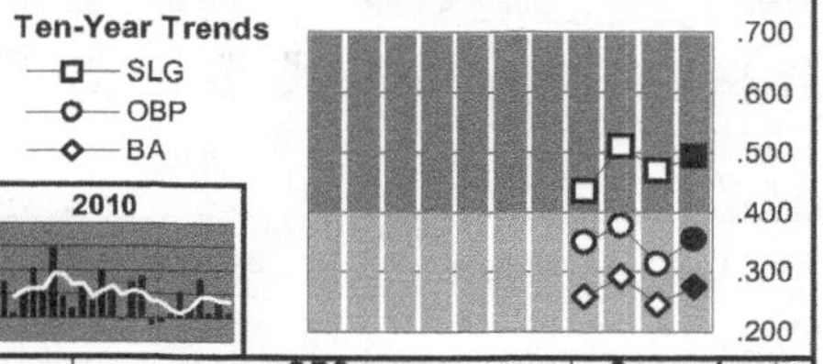

Ten-Year Trends
SLG
OBP
BA
.700
.600
.500
.400
.300
.200


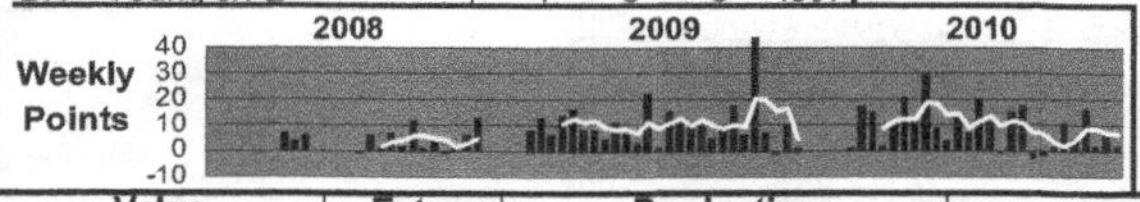

2008
2009
2010
Weekly Points
40
30
20
10
0
-10


| Level | Leag | AB | HR | R | RBI | SB | BA | OBP | SLG | CT% | H% | BB% | Bash |
|---|---|---|---|---|---|---|---|---|---|---|---|---|---|
| | | Minors (2010) | | | | | | | | Skills | | | |
| A | — | — | — | — | — | — | — | — | — | — | — | — | — |
| AA | — | — | — | — | — | — | — | — | — | — | — | — | — |
| AAA | — | — | — | — | — | — | — | — | — | — | — | — | — |

| Yr | Team | AB | HR | R | RBI | SB | BA | OBP | SLG | CT% | H% | BB% | Bash | $1L | $2L | Pts | RAA | 2B | 3B | CS | FB-LD-GB | HR/fb | RBI% | RS% | OPS | 1st Hf | 2nd Hf | vs RH | vs LH | Rnge | vRH | vLH |
|---|---|---|---|---|---|---|---|---|---|---|---|---|---|---|---|---|---|---|---|---|---|---|---|---|---|---|---|---|---|---|---|---|
| | | Majors | | | | | | | | Skills | | | | Value | | | | Extra | | | Production | | | | OPS | | | | | Scoresheet | | |
| 07 | COL | 8 | 0 | 4 | 0 | 0 | .625 | .625 | .875 | 88% | 71% | 0% | 1.40 | -$5 | -$19 | 10 | +2 | 0 | 1 | 0 | 14-57-29 | 0% | 0% | 80% | 1.500 | — | 1.500 | 1.500 | — | — | — | — |
| 08 | COL | 108 | 4 | 13 | 15 | 1 | .259 | .350 | .435 | 79% | 33% | 12% | 1.68 | -$1 | -$14 | 70 | +2 | 7 | 0 | 0 | 34-21-45 | 14% | 22% | 23% | .785 | .662 | .875 | .863 | .083 | 2.10 | +26 | –82 |
| 09 | COL | 335 | 15 | 61 | 55 | 4 | .293 | .378 | .510 | 80% | 37% | 12% | 1.74 | $14 | $3 | 270 | +15 | 20 | 4 | 1 | 42-19-39 | 13% | 25% | 35% | .889 | .919 | .862 | .893 | .868 | 2.10 | +29 | –94 |
| 10 | COL | 358 | 17 | 55 | 52 | 2 | .246 | .314 | .469 | 81% | 30% | 9% | 1.91 | $9 | $0 | 250 | –1 | 19 | 5 | 1 | 48-16-36 | 12% | 20% | 35% | .783 | .894 | .639 | .848 | .393 | 2.09 | +26 | –87 |

## Justin Smoak — 450 PA | $5 | 200 pts

1B-94, DH-5 — Owned: 1% — BH

| Player | Age | AB | HR | R | RBI | SB | BA | OBP | SLG | $1L | Pts |
|---|---|---|---|---|---|---|---|---|---|---|---|
| | | Forecast | | | | | | | | | |
| Smoak J | 24 | 390 | 14 | 45 | 50 | 0 | .231 | .332 | .393 | $5 | 200 |
| **Mini-Browser** | **Age** | **AB** | **HR** | **R** | **RBI** | **SB** | **BA** | **OBP** | **SLG** | **$1L** | **Pts** |
| Allen B | 25 | 418 | 23 | 54 | 50 | 5 | .237 | .311 | .467 | $8 | 240 |
| Overbay L | 34 | 442 | 15 | 55 | 55 | 0 | .249 | .338 | .420 | $8 | 260 |
| Ka'aihue K | 27 | 373 | 18 | 50 | 50 | 0 | .241 | .350 | .428 | $7 | 240 |
| Jones G | 29 | 269 | 12 | 36 | 39 | 3 | .268 | .331 | .476 | $6 | 180 |
| Johnson D | 31 | 278 | 17 | 39 | 58 | 2 | .227 | .356 | .447 | $5 | 210 |

In his first tour with Seattle after being traded from Texas, Smoak looked atrocious (.159/.169/.270 in 65 PA). However, he returned from a stretch in Triple-A as a different person (.340/.421/.580 in 57 PA). He should be given every shot to land the starting first baseman job out of camp in 2011. (GC)

**Competition at 1B — Stats in 2010**

| Bats | Player | GSvR | GSvL | Sub | OPS |
|---|---|---|---|---|---|
| LH | Kotchman C | 80 | 28 | 8 | .616 |
| BH | Smoak J | 15 | 10 | 0 | .678 |

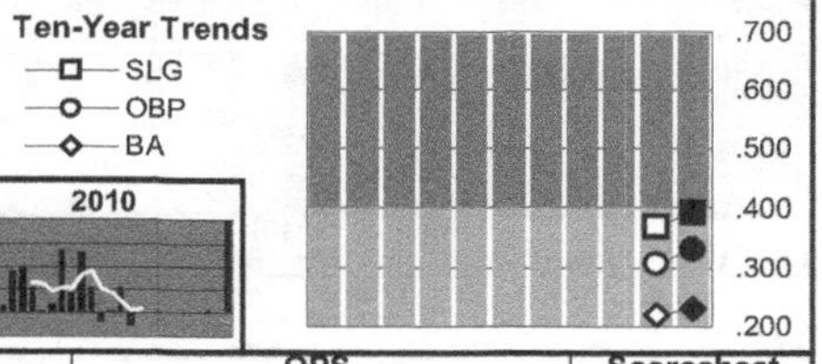

Ten-Year Trends
SLG
OBP
BA
.700
.600
.500
.400
.300
.200


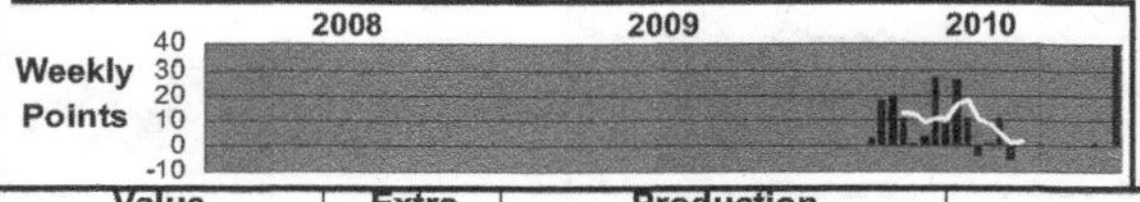

2008
2009
2010
Weekly Points
40
30
20
10
0
-10


| Level | Leag | AB | HR | R | RBI | SB | BA | OBP | SLG | CT% | H% | BB% | Bash |
|---|---|---|---|---|---|---|---|---|---|---|---|---|---|
| | | Minors (2010) | | | | | | | | Skills | | | |
| A | — | — | — | — | — | — | — | — | — | — | — | — | — |
| AA | — | — | — | — | — | — | — | — | — | — | — | — | — |
| AAA | 2LG | 183 | 9 | 33 | 30 | 0 | .279 | .404 | .497 | 78% | 36% | 17% | 1.78 |

| Yr | Team | AB | HR | R | RBI | SB | BA | OBP | SLG | CT% | H% | BB% | Bash | $1L | $2L | Pts | RAA | 2B | 3B | CS | FB-LD-GB | HR/fb | RBI% | RS% | OPS | 1st Hf | 2nd Hf | vs RH | vs LH | Rnge | vRH | vLH |
|---|---|---|---|---|---|---|---|---|---|---|---|---|---|---|---|---|---|---|---|---|---|---|---|---|---|---|---|---|---|---|---|---|
| | | Majors | | | | | | | | Skills | | | | Value | | | | Extra | | | Production | | | | OPS | | | | | Scoresheet | | |
| 07 | — | — | — | — | — | — | — | — | — | — | — | — | — | — | — | — | — | — | — | — | — | — | — | — | — | — | — | — | — | — | — | — |
| 08 | — | — | — | — | — | — | — | — | — | — | — | — | — | — | — | — | — | — | — | — | — | — | — | — | — | — | — | — | — | — | — | — |
| 09 | — | — | — | — | — | — | — | — | — | — | — | — | — | — | — | — | — | — | — | — | — | — | — | — | — | — | — | — | — | 1.85 | — | — |
| 10 | 2TM | 348 | 13 | 40 | 48 | 1 | .218 | .307 | .371 | 74% | 30% | 11% | 1.70 | $5 | -$7 | 170 | –17 | 14 | 0 | 0 | 39-23-38 | 13% | 18% | 25% | .678 | .657 | .727 | .691 | .651 | 1.85 | — | — |

## Travis Snider — 500 PA | $11 | 220 pts

OF-80 (LF-53, RF-29) — Owned: 3% — LH

| Player | Age | AB | HR | R | RBI | SB | BA | OBP | SLG | $1L | Pts |
|---|---|---|---|---|---|---|---|---|---|---|---|
| | | Forecast | | | | | | | | | |
| Snider T | 23 | 436 | 20 | 55 | 65 | 5 | .241 | .315 | .452 | $11 | 220 |
| **Mini-Browser** | **Age** | **AB** | **HR** | **R** | **RBI** | **SB** | **BA** | **OBP** | **SLG** | **$1L** | **Pts** |
| Murphy D | 29 | 395 | 13 | 51 | 55 | 9 | .280 | .341 | .454 | $12 | 270 |
| Hawpe B | 31 | 335 | 16 | 52 | 60 | 0 | .275 | .376 | .501 | $11 | 240 |
| Sweeney R | 26 | 554 | 6 | 66 | 60 | 6 | .271 | .332 | .375 | $11 | 310 |
| Joyce M | 26 | 430 | 20 | 55 | 65 | 5 | .244 | .338 | .470 | $11 | 280 |
| Cameron M | 38 | 365 | 16 | 56 | 48 | 8 | .263 | .344 | .481 | $11 | 240 |

Snider's 2010 season was interrupted by a wrist injury, and when he finally got healthy, he struggled to find work with Toronto. With a new manager on board, Snider should get more PT, but success is not assured. He did swat 6 HR in September, but his contact rate was only 74%, and his ratio of K/BB was 24/2. (MH)

**Competition at LF — Stats in 2010**

| Bats | Player | GSvR | GSvL | Sub | OPS |
|---|---|---|---|---|---|
| LH | Lewis F | 67 | 15 | 2 | .745 |
| LH | Snider T | 41 | 8 | 4 | .767 |
| LH | Lind A | 10 | 6 | 0 | .712 |
| LH | Wise D | 7 | 0 | 3 | .675 |

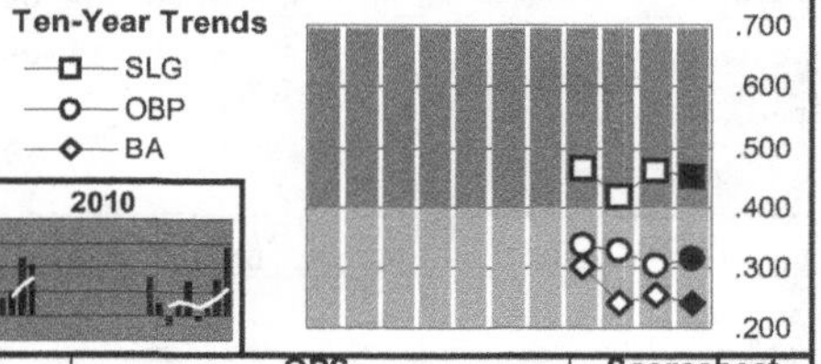

Ten-Year Trends
SLG
OBP
BA
.700
.600
.500
.400
.300
.200


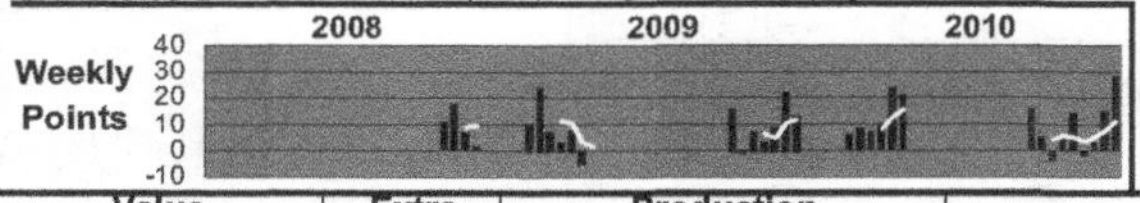

2008
2009
2010
Weekly Points
40
30
20
10
0
-10


| Level | Leag | AB | HR | R | RBI | SB | BA | OBP | SLG | CT% | H% | BB% | Bash |
|---|---|---|---|---|---|---|---|---|---|---|---|---|---|
| | | Minors (2010) | | | | | | | | Skills | | | |
| A | FLO | 4 | 0 | 0 | 0 | 0 | .000 | .000 | .000 | 50% | 0% | 0% | NA |
| AA | EL | 81 | 5 | 14 | 17 | 3 | .296 | .306 | .543 | 74% | 40% | 2% | 1.83 |
| AAA | — | — | — | — | — | — | — | — | — | — | — | — | — |

| Yr | Team | AB | HR | R | RBI | SB | BA | OBP | SLG | CT% | H% | BB% | Bash | $1L | $2L | Pts | RAA | 2B | 3B | CS | FB-LD-GB | HR/fb | RBI% | RS% | OPS | 1st Hf | 2nd Hf | vs RH | vs LH | Rnge | vRH | vLH |
|---|---|---|---|---|---|---|---|---|---|---|---|---|---|---|---|---|---|---|---|---|---|---|---|---|---|---|---|---|---|---|---|---|
| | | Majors | | | | | | | | Skills | | | | Value | | | | Extra | | | Production | | | | OPS | | | | | Scoresheet | | |
| 07 | — | — | — | — | — | — | — | — | — | — | — | — | — | — | — | — | — | — | — | — | — | — | — | — | — | — | — | — | — | 2.10 | — | — |
| 08 | TOR | 73 | 2 | 9 | 13 | 0 | .301 | .338 | .466 | 68% | 44% | 6% | 1.55 | -$1 | -$15 | 40 | +1 | 6 | 0 | 0 | 29-35-37 | 13% | 29% | 28% | .803 | — | .803 | .820 | .732 | 2.10 | — | — |
| 09 | TOR | 241 | 9 | 34 | 29 | 1 | .241 | .328 | .419 | 68% | 36% | 10% | 1.74 | $3 | -$10 | 120 | –4 | 14 | 1 | 1 | 41-15-44 | 14% | 16% | 31% | .748 | .686 | .788 | .775 | .608 | 2.06 | +23 | –71 |
| 10 | TOR | 298 | 14 | 36 | 32 | 6 | .255 | .304 | .463 | 73% | 35% | 7% | 1.82 | $8 | -$5 | 160 | –1 | 20 | 0 | 3 | 35-24-41 | 18% | 15% | 27% | .767 | .806 | .742 | .783 | .702 | 2.08 | +24 | –80 |

## Brandon Snyder — 100 PA | $-3 | 40 pts

1B-10 — Owned: 0% — RH

| Player | Age | AB | HR | R | RBI | SB | BA | OBP | SLG | $1L | Pts |
|---|---|---|---|---|---|---|---|---|---|---|---|
| | | Forecast | | | | | | | | | |
| Snyder B | 24 | 93 | 3 | 10 | 12 | 0 | .246 | .303 | .412 | -$3 | 40 |
| **Mini-Browser** | **Age** | **AB** | **HR** | **R** | **RBI** | **SB** | **BA** | **OBP** | **SLG** | **$1L** | **Pts** |
| Trumbo M | 25 | 178 | 8 | 16 | 22 | 2 | .214 | .257 | .406 | -$2 | 80 |
| Brown J | 27 | 132 | 3 | 15 | 15 | 0 | .261 | .321 | .409 | -$2 | 70 |
| Gamel M | 25 | 112 | 5 | 14 | 15 | 1 | .235 | .317 | .432 | -$2 | 60 |
| Ishikawa T | 27 | 92 | 3 | 12 | 12 | 1 | .249 | .320 | .423 | -$2 | 50 |
| Alonso Y | 23 | 94 | 4 | 8 | 13 | 0 | .224 | .298 | .408 | -$3 | 50 |

Snyder's bat has not been worthless in the minors, but it is better suited for catcher (his drafted position) than for 1B (his new position). That said, Baltimore might be having second thoughts about a player with 165/52 K/BB in two seasons at Triple-A. He played just 10 games in Sept and started only 5 of those. (BJ)

**Competition at 1B — Stats in 2010**

| Bats | Player | GSvR | GSvL | Sub | OPS |
|---|---|---|---|---|---|
| RH | Wigginton T | 68 | 30 | 1 | .727 |
| RH | Atkins G | 17 | 13 | 0 | .562 |
| LH | Scott L | 17 | 2 | 0 | .902 |
| LH | Hughes R | 11 | 0 | 0 | .530 |

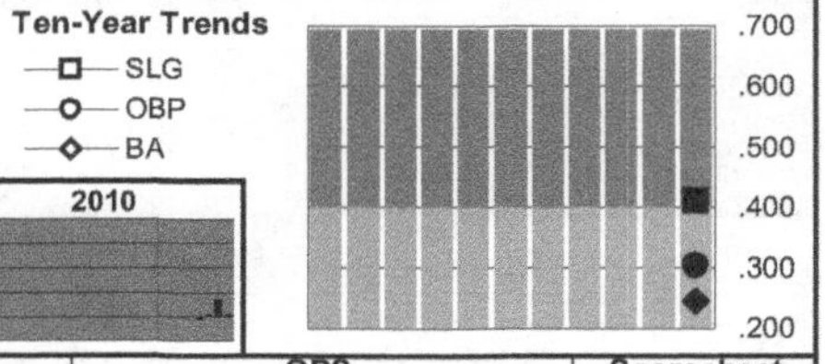

Ten-Year Trends
SLG
OBP
BA
.700
.600
.500
.400
.300
.200


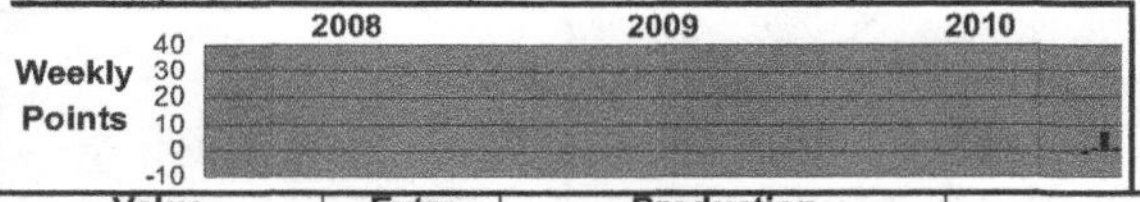

2008
2009
2010
Weekly Points
40
30
20
10
0
-10


| Level | Leag | AB | HR | R | RBI | SB | BA | OBP | SLG | CT% | H% | BB% | Bash |
|---|---|---|---|---|---|---|---|---|---|---|---|---|---|
| | | Minors (2010) | | | | | | | | Skills | | | |
| A | NYP | 13 | 1 | 2 | 4 | 0 | .231 | .231 | .538 | 85% | 27% | 0% | 2.33 |
| AA | — | — | — | — | — | — | — | — | — | — | — | — | — |
| AAA | IL | 339 | 9 | 36 | 43 | 4 | .257 | .324 | .407 | 70% | 37% | 7% | 1.59 |

| Yr | Team | AB | HR | R | RBI | SB | BA | OBP | SLG | CT% | H% | BB% | Bash | $1L | $2L | Pts | RAA | 2B | 3B | CS | FB-LD-GB | HR/fb | RBI% | RS% | OPS | 1st Hf | 2nd Hf | vs RH | vs LH | Rnge | vRH | vLH |
|---|---|---|---|---|---|---|---|---|---|---|---|---|---|---|---|---|---|---|---|---|---|---|---|---|---|---|---|---|---|---|---|---|
| | | Majors | | | | | | | | Skills | | | | Value | | | | Extra | | | Production | | | | OPS | | | | | Scoresheet | | |
| 07 | — | — | — | — | — | — | — | — | — | — | — | — | — | — | — | — | — | — | — | — | — | — | — | — | — | — | — | — | — | — | — | — |
| 08 | — | — | — | — | — | — | — | — | — | — | — | — | — | — | — | — | — | — | — | — | — | — | — | — | — | — | — | — | — | 1.85 | — | — |
| 09 | — | — | — | — | — | — | — | — | — | — | — | — | — | — | — | — | — | — | — | — | — | — | — | — | — | — | — | — | — | — | — | — |
| 10 | BAL | 20 | 0 | 1 | 3 | 0 | .300 | .300 | .400 | 85% | 35% | 0% | 1.33 | -$4 | -$20 | 10 | –1 | 2 | 0 | 1 | 41-12-47 | 0% | 23% | 17% | .700 | — | .700 | .400 | 1.000 | 1.85 | — | — |

*For more stats, visit www.Rotolympus.com.*

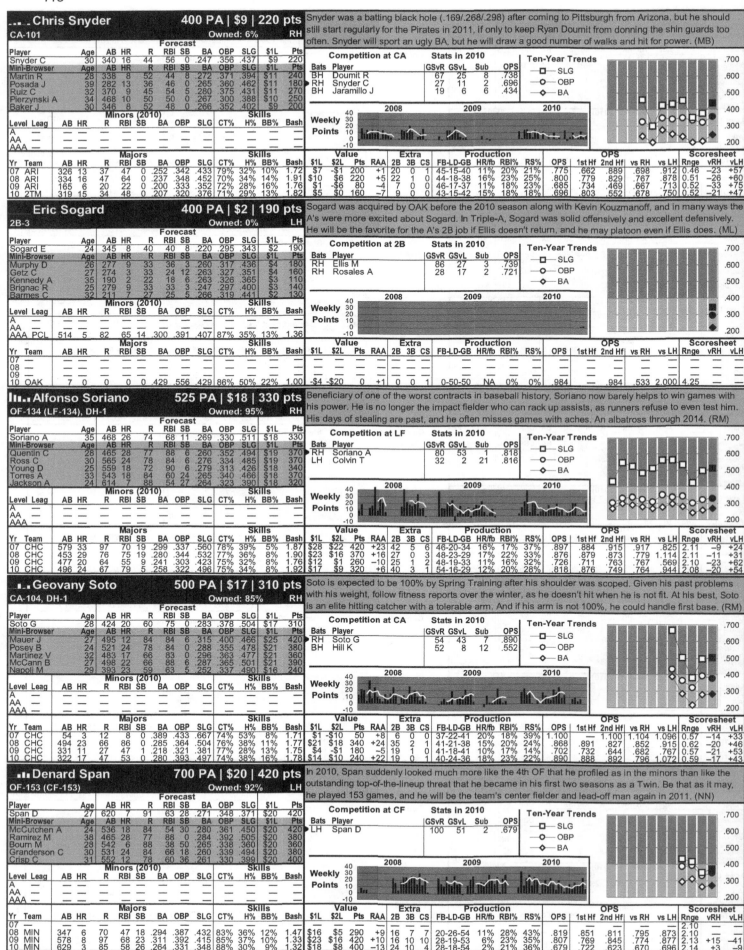

## Chris Snyder — 400 PA | $9 | 220 pts
CA-101 | Owned: 6% | RH

Snyder was a batting black hole (.169/.268/.298) after coming to Pittsburgh from Arizona, but he should still start regularly for the Pirates in 2011, if only to keep Ryan Doumit from donning the shin guards too often. Snyder will sport an ugly BA, but he will draw a good number of walks and hit for power. (MB)

### Forecast
| Player | Age | AB | HR | R | RBI | SB | BA | OBP | SLG | $1L | Pts |
|---|---|---|---|---|---|---|---|---|---|---|---|
| Snyder C | 30 | 340 | 16 | 44 | 56 | 0 | .247 | .356 | .437 | $9 | 220 |
| Mini-Browser | Age | AB | HR | R | RBI | SB | BA | OBP | SLG | $1L | Pts |
| Martin R | 28 | 338 | 8 | 52 | 44 | 8 | .272 | .371 | .394 | $11 | 240 |
| Posada J | 39 | 282 | 13 | 36 | 46 | 0 | .265 | .360 | .462 | $11 | 180 |
| Ruiz C | 32 | 370 | 9 | 45 | 54 | 5 | .280 | .375 | .431 | $11 | 270 |
| Pierzynski A | 34 | 468 | 10 | 50 | 50 | 0 | .267 | .300 | .388 | $10 | 250 |
| Baker J | 30 | 346 | 8 | 52 | 48 | 0 | .266 | .352 | .402 | $9 | 200 |

### Minors (2010) / Skills
| Level | Leag | AB | HR | R | RBI | SB | BA | OBP | SLG | CT% | H% | BB% | Bash |
|---|---|---|---|---|---|---|---|---|---|---|---|---|---|
| A | — | | | | | | | | | | | | |
| AA | — | | | | | | | | | | | | |
| AAA | — | | | | | | | | | | | | |

### Majors / Skills
| Yr | Team | AB | HR | R | RBI | SB | BA | OBP | SLG | CT% | H% | BB% | Bash | $1L | $2L | Pts | RAA | 2B | 3B | CS | FB-LD-GB | HR/fb | RBI% | RS% | OPS | 1st Hf | 2nd Hf | vs RH | vs LH | Rnge | vRH | vLH |
|---|---|---|---|---|---|---|---|---|---|---|---|---|---|---|---|---|---|---|---|---|---|---|---|---|---|---|---|---|---|---|---|---|
| 07 | ARI | 326 | 13 | 37 | 47 | 0 | .252 | .342 | .433 | 79% | 32% | 10% | 1.72 | $7 | -$1 | 200 | +1 | 20 | 0 | 1 | 45-15-40 | 11% | 20% | 21% | .775 | .662 | .889 | .698 | .912 | 0.46 | -23 | +57 |
| 08 | ARI | 334 | 16 | 47 | 64 | 0 | .237 | .348 | .452 | 70% | 34% | 14% | 1.91 | $10 | $6 | 220 | +5 | 22 | 1 | 0 | 44-18-38 | 16% | 23% | 25% | .800 | .779 | .829 | .767 | .878 | 0.51 | -26 | +60 |
| 09 | ARI | 165 | 6 | 20 | 22 | 0 | .200 | .333 | .352 | 72% | 28% | 16% | 1.76 | $1 | -$6 | 80 | -4 | 7 | 0 | 0 | 46-17-37 | 11% | 18% | 23% | .685 | .734 | .469 | .667 | .713 | 0.52 | -33 | +75 |
| 10 | 2TM | 319 | 15 | 34 | 48 | 0 | .207 | .320 | .376 | 71% | 29% | 13% | 1.82 | $5 | -$6 | 160 | -7 | 17 | 1 | 1 | 46-17-36 | 15% | 18% | 18% | .696 | .803 | .552 | .678 | .750 | 0.52 | -21 | +47 |

### Competition at CA / Stats in 2010
| Bats | Player | GSvR | GSvL | Sub | OPS |
|---|---|---|---|---|---|
| BH | Doumit R | 67 | 25 | 8 | .738 |
| RH | Snyder C | 27 | 11 | 2 | .696 |
| BH | Jaramillo J | 19 | 6 | 6 | .434 |

Ten-Year Trends: SLG, OBP, BA

---

## Eric Sogard — 400 PA | $2 | 190 pts
2B-3 | Owned: 0% | LH

Sogard was acquired by OAK before the 2010 season along with Kevin Kouzmanoff, and in many ways the A's were more excited about Sogard. In Triple-A, Sogard was solid offensively and excellent defensively. He will be the favorite for the A's 2B job if Ellis doesn't return, and he may platoon even if Ellis does. (ML)

### Forecast
| Player | Age | AB | HR | R | RBI | SB | BA | OBP | SLG | $1L | Pts |
|---|---|---|---|---|---|---|---|---|---|---|---|
| Sogard E | 24 | 345 | 8 | 40 | 40 | 8 | .220 | .295 | .343 | $2 | 190 |
| Mini-Browser | Age | AB | HR | R | RBI | SB | BA | OBP | SLG | $1L | Pts |
| Murphy D | 26 | 277 | 9 | 33 | 36 | 3 | .260 | .317 | .436 | $4 | 180 |
| Getz C | 27 | 274 | 3 | 33 | 24 | 12 | .263 | .327 | .351 | $4 | 160 |
| Kennedy A | 35 | 190 | 2 | 22 | 18 | 6 | .263 | .326 | .365 | $3 | 110 |
| Brignac R | 25 | 279 | 9 | 33 | 36 | 3 | .247 | .297 | .400 | $3 | 140 |
| Barmes C | 32 | 211 | 7 | 27 | 25 | 5 | .266 | .319 | .441 | $2 | 130 |

### Minors (2010) / Skills
| Level | Leag | AB | HR | R | RBI | SB | BA | OBP | SLG | CT% | H% | BB% | Bash |
|---|---|---|---|---|---|---|---|---|---|---|---|---|---|
| A | — | | | | | | | | | | | | |
| AA | — | | | | | | | | | | | | |
| AAA | PCL | 514 | 5 | 82 | 65 | 14 | .300 | .391 | .407 | 87% | 35% | 13% | 1.36 |

### Majors / Skills
| Yr | Team | AB | HR | R | RBI | SB | BA | OBP | SLG | CT% | H% | BB% | Bash | $1L | $2L | Pts | RAA | 2B | 3B | CS | FB-LD-GB | HR/fb | RBI% | RS% | OPS | 1st Hf | 2nd Hf | vs RH | vs LH | Rnge | vRH | vLH |
|---|---|---|---|---|---|---|---|---|---|---|---|---|---|---|---|---|---|---|---|---|---|---|---|---|---|---|---|---|---|---|---|---|
| 07 | — | | | | | | | | | | | | | | | | | | | | | | | | | | | | | | | |
| 08 | — | | | | | | | | | | | | | | | | | | | | | | | | | | | | | | | |
| 09 | — | | | | | | | | | | | | | | | | | | | | | | | | | | | | | | | |
| 10 | OAK | 7 | 0 | 0 | 0 | 0 | .429 | .556 | .429 | 86% | 50% | 22% | 1.00 | -$4 | -$20 | 0 | +1 | 0 | 0 | 1 | 0-50-50 | NA | 0% | 0% | .984 | — | .984 | .533 | 2.000 | 4.25 | | |

### Competition at 2B / Stats in 2010
| Bats | Player | GSvR | GSvL | Sub | OPS |
|---|---|---|---|---|---|
| RH | Ellis M | 86 | 27 | 3 | .739 |
| RH | Rosales A | 28 | 17 | 2 | .721 |

Ten-Year Trends: SLG, OBP, BA

---

## Alfonso Soriano — 525 PA | $18 | 330 pts
OF-134 (LF-134), DH-1 | Owned: 95% | RH

Beneficiary of one of the worst contracts in baseball history, Soriano now barely helps to win games with his power. He is no longer the impact fielder who can rack up assists, as runners refuse to even test him. His days of stealing are past, and he often misses games with aches. An albatross through 2014. (RM)

### Forecast
| Player | Age | AB | HR | R | RBI | SB | BA | OBP | SLG | $1L | Pts |
|---|---|---|---|---|---|---|---|---|---|---|---|
| Soriano A | 35 | 468 | 26 | 74 | 68 | 11 | .269 | .330 | .511 | $18 | 330 |
| Mini-Browser | Age | AB | HR | R | RBI | SB | BA | OBP | SLG | $1L | Pts |
| Quentin C | 28 | 465 | 28 | 77 | 88 | 6 | .260 | .352 | .494 | $19 | 370 |
| Ross C | 30 | 565 | 24 | 78 | 84 | 6 | .276 | .334 | .485 | $19 | 370 |
| Young D | 25 | 559 | 18 | 72 | 90 | 6 | .279 | .313 | .426 | $19 | 340 |
| Torres A | 33 | 543 | 18 | 84 | 60 | 24 | .265 | .340 | .466 | $18 | 340 |
| Jackson A | 24 | 614 | 7 | 88 | 54 | 27 | .264 | .323 | .390 | $18 | 320 |

### Minors (2010) / Skills
| Level | Leag | AB | HR | R | RBI | SB | BA | OBP | SLG | CT% | H% | BB% | Bash |
|---|---|---|---|---|---|---|---|---|---|---|---|---|---|
| A | — | | | | | | | | | | | | |
| AA | — | | | | | | | | | | | | |
| AAA | — | | | | | | | | | | | | |

### Majors / Skills
| Yr | Team | AB | HR | R | RBI | SB | BA | OBP | SLG | CT% | H% | BB% | Bash | $1L | $2L | Pts | RAA | 2B | 3B | CS | FB-LD-GB | HR/fb | RBI% | RS% | OPS | 1st Hf | 2nd Hf | vs RH | vs LH | Rnge | vRH | vLH |
|---|---|---|---|---|---|---|---|---|---|---|---|---|---|---|---|---|---|---|---|---|---|---|---|---|---|---|---|---|---|---|---|---|
| 07 | CHC | 579 | 33 | 97 | 70 | 19 | .299 | .337 | .560 | 78% | 39% | 5% | 1.87 | $31 | $22 | 420 | +23 | 42 | 5 | 6 | 46-20-34 | 16% | 17% | 37% | .897 | .884 | .915 | .917 | .825 | 2.11 | -9 | +24 |
| 08 | CHC | 453 | 29 | 76 | 75 | 19 | .280 | .344 | .532 | 77% | 36% | 8% | 1.90 | $23 | $16 | 370 | +16 | 27 | 0 | 3 | 48-23-29 | 17% | 22% | 33% | .876 | .879 | .873 | .779 | 1.114 | 2.11 | -11 | +31 |
| 09 | CHC | 477 | 20 | 64 | 55 | 9 | .241 | .303 | .423 | 75% | 32% | 8% | 1.76 | $12 | $5 | 260 | -10 | 25 | 1 | 2 | 48-19-33 | 11% | 16% | 32% | .726 | .711 | .763 | .767 | .569 | 2.10 | -23 | +62 |
| 10 | CHC | 496 | 24 | 67 | 79 | 5 | .258 | .322 | .496 | 75% | 34% | 8% | 1.92 | $17 | $9 | 320 | +6 | 40 | 3 | 1 | 54-16-29 | 12% | 20% | 28% | .818 | .876 | .749 | .764 | .944 | 2.08 | -20 | +54 |

### Competition at LF / Stats in 2010
| Bats | Player | GSvR | GSvL | Sub | OPS |
|---|---|---|---|---|---|
| RH | Soriano A | 80 | 53 | 1 | .818 |
| LH | Colvin T | 32 | 2 | 21 | .816 |

Ten-Year Trends: SLG, OBP, BA

---

## Geovany Soto — 500 PA | $17 | 310 pts
CA-104, DH-1 | Owned: 85% | RH

Soto is expected to be 100% by Spring Training after his shoulder was scoped. Given his past problems with his weight, follow fitness reports over the winter, as he doesn't hit when he is not fit. At his best, Soto is an elite hitting catcher with a tolerable arm. And if his arm is not 100%, he could handle first base. (RM)

### Forecast
| Player | Age | AB | HR | R | RBI | SB | BA | OBP | SLG | $1L | Pts |
|---|---|---|---|---|---|---|---|---|---|---|---|
| Soto G | 28 | 424 | 20 | 60 | 75 | 0 | .283 | .378 | .504 | $17 | 310 |
| Mini-Browser | Age | AB | HR | R | RBI | SB | BA | OBP | SLG | $1L | Pts |
| Mauer J | 27 | 495 | 12 | 84 | 84 | 6 | .315 | .400 | .466 | $25 | 420 |
| Posey B | 24 | 521 | 24 | 78 | 84 | 0 | .288 | .355 | .478 | $21 | 380 |
| Martinez V | 32 | 483 | 17 | 66 | 83 | 0 | .296 | .363 | .477 | $21 | 360 |
| McCann B | 27 | 498 | 22 | 66 | 88 | 2 | .287 | .365 | .501 | $21 | 390 |
| Napoli M | 29 | 393 | 23 | 59 | 63 | 5 | .252 | .337 | .490 | $16 | 240 |

### Minors (2010) / Skills
| Level | Leag | AB | HR | R | RBI | SB | BA | OBP | SLG | CT% | H% | BB% | Bash |
|---|---|---|---|---|---|---|---|---|---|---|---|---|---|
| A | — | | | | | | | | | | | | |
| AA | — | | | | | | | | | | | | |
| AAA | — | | | | | | | | | | | | |

### Majors / Skills
| Yr | Team | AB | HR | R | RBI | SB | BA | OBP | SLG | CT% | H% | BB% | Bash | $1L | $2L | Pts | RAA | 2B | 3B | CS | FB-LD-GB | HR/fb | RBI% | RS% | OPS | 1st Hf | 2nd Hf | vs RH | vs LH | Rnge | vRH | vLH |
|---|---|---|---|---|---|---|---|---|---|---|---|---|---|---|---|---|---|---|---|---|---|---|---|---|---|---|---|---|---|---|---|---|
| 07 | CHC | 54 | 3 | 12 | 8 | 0 | .389 | .433 | .667 | 74% | 53% | 8% | 1.71 | $1 | -$10 | 50 | +8 | 6 | 0 | 0 | 37-22-41 | 20% | 18% | 39% | 1.100 | — | 1.100 | 1.104 | 1.096 | 0.57 | -14 | +33 |
| 08 | CHC | 494 | 23 | 66 | 86 | 0 | .285 | .364 | .504 | 76% | 38% | 11% | 1.77 | $21 | $18 | 340 | +24 | 35 | 2 | 1 | 41-21-38 | 15% | 20% | 24% | .868 | .891 | .827 | .852 | .915 | 0.62 | -20 | +46 |
| 09 | CHC | 331 | 11 | 27 | 47 | 1 | .218 | .321 | .381 | 77% | 28% | 13% | 1.75 | $4 | -$1 | 180 | -5 | 19 | 1 | 0 | 41-18-41 | 10% | 17% | 14% | .702 | .732 | .644 | .682 | .767 | 0.57 | -21 | +53 |
| 10 | CHC | 322 | 17 | 47 | 53 | 0 | .280 | .393 | .497 | 74% | 38% | 16% | 1.78 | $14 | $10 | 240 | +22 | 19 | 0 | 1 | 40-24-36 | 18% | 23% | 22% | .890 | .888 | .892 | .796 | 1.072 | 0.59 | -17 | +41 |

### Competition at CA / Stats in 2010
| Bats | Player | GSvR | GSvL | Sub | OPS |
|---|---|---|---|---|---|
| RH | Soto G | 54 | 43 | 7 | .890 |
| BH | Hill K | 52 | 8 | 12 | .552 |

Ten-Year Trends: SLG, OBP, BA

---

## Denard Span — 700 PA | $20 | 420 pts
OF-153 (CF-153) | Owned: 92% | LH

In 2010, Span suddenly looked much more like the 4th OF that he profiled as in the minors than like the outstanding top-of-the-lineup threat that he became in his first two seasons as a Twin. Be that as it may, he played 153 games, and he will be the team's center fielder and lead-off man again in 2011. (NN)

### Forecast
| Player | Age | AB | HR | R | RBI | SB | BA | OBP | SLG | $1L | Pts |
|---|---|---|---|---|---|---|---|---|---|---|---|
| Span D | 27 | 620 | 7 | 91 | 63 | 28 | .271 | .348 | .371 | $20 | 420 |
| Mini-Browser | Age | AB | HR | R | RBI | SB | BA | OBP | SLG | $1L | Pts |
| McCutchen A | 24 | 536 | 18 | 84 | 54 | 30 | .280 | .361 | .450 | $20 | 420 |
| Ramirez M | 38 | 465 | 28 | 77 | 88 | 0 | .284 | .392 | .505 | $20 | 380 |
| Bourn M | 28 | 542 | 6 | 88 | 38 | 50 | .265 | .338 | .360 | $20 | 360 |
| Granderson C | 30 | 531 | 24 | 84 | 66 | 18 | .260 | .339 | .494 | $20 | 380 |
| Crisp C | 31 | 552 | 12 | 78 | 60 | 36 | .261 | .330 | .399 | $20 | 400 |

### Minors (2010) / Skills
| Level | Leag | AB | HR | R | RBI | SB | BA | OBP | SLG | CT% | H% | BB% | Bash |
|---|---|---|---|---|---|---|---|---|---|---|---|---|---|
| A | — | | | | | | | | | | | | |
| AA | — | | | | | | | | | | | | |
| AAA | — | | | | | | | | | | | | |

### Majors / Skills
| Yr | Team | AB | HR | R | RBI | SB | BA | OBP | SLG | CT% | H% | BB% | Bash | $1L | $2L | Pts | RAA | 2B | 3B | CS | FB-LD-GB | HR/fb | RBI% | RS% | OPS | 1st Hf | 2nd Hf | vs RH | vs LH | Rnge | vRH | vLH |
|---|---|---|---|---|---|---|---|---|---|---|---|---|---|---|---|---|---|---|---|---|---|---|---|---|---|---|---|---|---|---|---|---|
| 07 | — | | | | | | | | | | | | | | | | | | | | | | | | | | | | | 2.10 | | |
| 08 | MIN | 347 | 6 | 70 | 47 | 18 | .294 | .387 | .432 | 83% | 36% | 12% | 1.47 | $16 | $5 | 290 | +9 | 16 | 7 | 7 | 20-26-54 | 11% | 28% | 43% | .819 | .851 | .811 | .795 | .873 | 2.10 | — | — |
| 09 | MIN | 578 | 8 | 97 | 68 | 23 | .311 | .392 | .415 | 85% | 37% | 10% | 1.33 | $23 | $16 | 420 | +10 | 16 | 10 | 10 | 28-19-53 | 6% | 23% | 35% | .807 | .769 | .845 | .774 | .877 | 2.13 | +15 | -41 |
| 10 | MIN | 629 | 3 | 85 | 58 | 26 | .264 | .331 | .348 | 88% | 30% | 9% | 1.32 | $18 | $8 | 400 | -13 | 24 | 10 | 4 | 28-18-54 | 2% | 21% | 36% | .679 | .722 | .623 | .670 | .696 | 2.14 | +3 | -9 |

### Competition at CF / Stats in 2010
| Bats | Player | GSvR | GSvL | Sub | OPS |
|---|---|---|---|---|---|
| LH | Span D | 100 | 51 | 2 | .679 |

Ten-Year Trends: SLG, OBP, BA

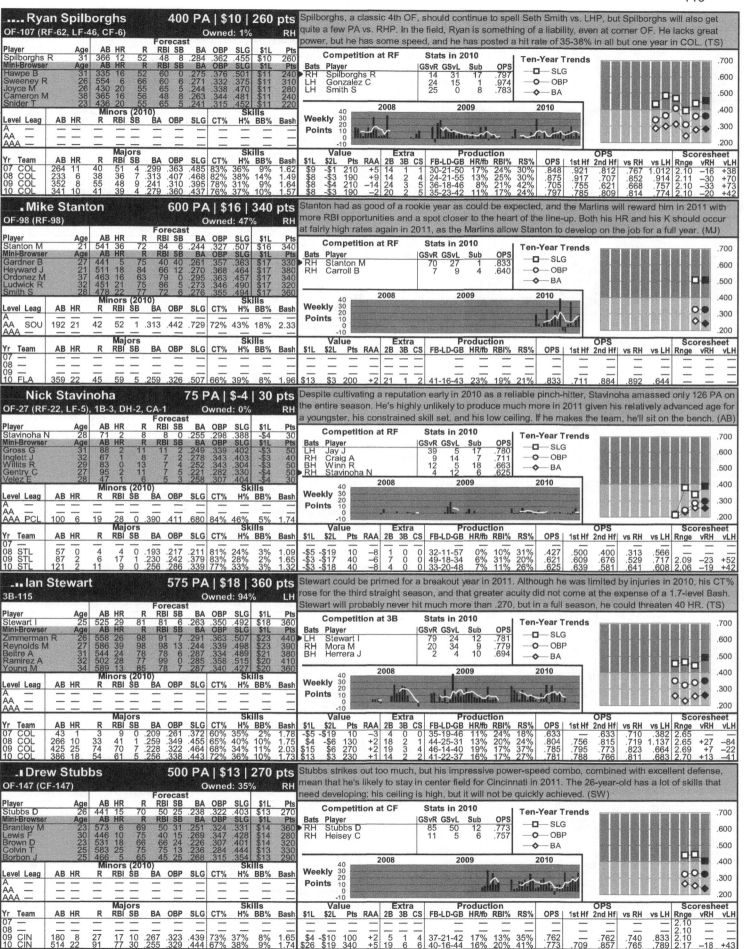

## Ryan Spilborghs — 400 PA | $10 | 260 pts
OF-107 (RF-62, LF-46, CF-6)     Owned: 1%    RH

Spilborghs, a classic 4th OF, should continue to spell Seth Smith vs. LHP, but Spilborghs will also get quite a few PA vs. RHP. In the field, Ryan is something of a liability, even at corner OF. He lacks great power, but he has some speed, and he has posted a hit rate of 35-38% in all but one year in COL. (TS)

### Forecast
| Player | Age | AB | HR | R | RBI | SB | BA | OBP | SLG | $1L | Pts |
|---|---|---|---|---|---|---|---|---|---|---|---|
| Spilborghs R | 31 | 366 | 12 | 52 | 48 | 8 | .284 | .362 | .455 | $10 | 260 |
| Mini-Browser | Age | AB | HR | R | RBI | SB | BA | OBP | SLG | $1L | Pts |
| Hawpe B | 31 | 335 | 16 | 52 | 60 | 0 | .275 | .376 | .501 | $11 | 240 |
| Sweeney R | 26 | 554 | 6 | 66 | 60 | 6 | .271 | .332 | .375 | $11 | 310 |
| Joyce M | 26 | 430 | 20 | 55 | 65 | 5 | .244 | .338 | .470 | $11 | 280 |
| Cameron M | 38 | 365 | 16 | 52 | 48 | 8 | .263 | .344 | .481 | $11 | 240 |
| Snider T | 23 | 436 | 20 | 55 | 65 | 6 | .241 | .315 | .452 | $11 | 220 |

### Minors (2010) / Skills
| Level | Leag | AB | HR | R | RBI | SB | BA | OBP | SLG | CT% | H% | BB% | Bash |
|---|---|---|---|---|---|---|---|---|---|---|---|---|---|
| A | — | — | — | — | — | — | — | — | — | — | — | — | — |
| AA | — | — | — | — | — | — | — | — | — | — | — | — | — |
| AAA | — | — | — | — | — | — | — | — | — | — | — | — | — |

### Competition at RF / Stats in 2010
| Bats | Player | GSvR | GSvL | Sub | OPS |
|---|---|---|---|---|---|
| RH | Spilborghs R | 14 | 31 | 17 | .797 |
| LH | Gonzalez C | 24 | 15 | 1 | .974 |
| LH | Smith S | 25 | 0 | 8 | .783 |

### Majors / Value / Extra / Production / OPS / Scoresheet
| Yr | Team | AB | HR | R | RBI | SB | BA | OBP | SLG | CT% | H% | BB% | Bash | $1L | $2L | Pts | RAA | 2B | 3B | CS | FB-LD-GB | HR/fb | RBI% | RS% | OPS | 1st Hf | 2nd Hf | vs RH | vs LH | Rnge | vRH | vLH |
|---|---|---|---|---|---|---|---|---|---|---|---|---|---|---|---|---|---|---|---|---|---|---|---|---|---|---|---|---|---|---|---|---|
| 07 | COL | 264 | 11 | 40 | 51 | 4 | .299 | .363 | .485 | 83% | 36% | 9% | 1.62 | $9 | -$1 | 210 | +5 | 14 | 1 | 1 | 30-21-50 | 17% | 24% | 30% | .848 | .921 | .812 | .767 | 1.012 | 2.10 | -16 | +38 |
| 08 | COL | 233 | 6 | 38 | 36 | 7 | .313 | .407 | .468 | 82% | 38% | 14% | 1.49 | $8 | -$3 | 190 | +9 | 14 | 2 | 4 | 24-21-55 | 13% | 25% | 30% | .875 | .917 | .707 | .852 | .914 | 2.11 | -30 | +70 |
| 09 | COL | 352 | 10 | 55 | 48 | 9 | .241 | .310 | .395 | 78% | 31% | 9% | 1.64 | $8 | -$4 | 210 | -14 | 24 | 3 | 5 | 36-18-46 | 8% | 21% | 42% | .705 | .755 | .621 | .668 | .757 | 2.10 | -33 | +73 |
| 10 | COL | 341 | 10 | 41 | 39 | 4 | .279 | .360 | .437 | 76% | 37% | 10% | 1.57 | $8 | -$3 | 190 | -2 | 24 | 1 | 6 | 35-23-42 | 11% | 21% | 24% | .797 | .785 | .809 | .814 | .774 | 2.10 | -20 | +44 |

---

## Mike Stanton — 600 PA | $16 | 340 pts
OF-98 (RF-98)     Owned: 47%    RH

Stanton had as good of a rookie year as could be expected, and the Marlins will reward him in 2011 with more RBI opportunities and a spot closer to the heart of the line-up. Both his HR and his K should occur at fairly high rates again in 2011, as the Marlins allow Stanton to develop on the job for a full year. (MJ)

### Forecast
| Player | Age | AB | HR | R | RBI | SB | BA | OBP | SLG | $1L | Pts |
|---|---|---|---|---|---|---|---|---|---|---|---|
| Stanton M | 21 | 541 | 36 | 72 | 84 | 6 | .244 | .327 | .507 | $16 | 340 |
| Mini-Browser | Age | AB | HR | R | RBI | SB | BA | OBP | SLG | $1L | Pts |
| Gardner B | 27 | 441 | 5 | 75 | 40 | 40 | .261 | .357 | .363 | $17 | 330 |
| Heyward J | 21 | 511 | 18 | 84 | 66 | 12 | .270 | .368 | .464 | $17 | 380 |
| Ordonez M | 37 | 463 | 16 | 63 | 79 | 0 | .295 | .363 | .457 | $17 | 340 |
| Ludwick R | 32 | 451 | 21 | 75 | 86 | 5 | .273 | .346 | .490 | $17 | 320 |
| Smith S | 28 | 478 | 22 | 77 | 72 | 6 | .276 | .355 | .494 | $17 | 360 |

### Minors (2010) / Skills
| Level | Leag | AB | HR | R | RBI | SB | BA | OBP | SLG | CT% | H% | BB% | Bash |
|---|---|---|---|---|---|---|---|---|---|---|---|---|---|
| A | — | — | — | — | — | — | — | — | — | — | — | — | — |
| AA | SOU | 192 | 21 | 42 | 52 | 1 | .313 | .442 | .729 | 72% | 43% | 18% | 2.33 |
| AAA | — | — | — | — | — | — | — | — | — | — | — | — | — |

### Competition at RF / Stats in 2010
| Bats | Player | GSvR | GSvL | Sub | OPS |
|---|---|---|---|---|---|
| RH | Stanton M | 70 | 27 | 1 | .833 |
| RH | Carroll B | 7 | 9 | 4 | .640 |

### Majors / Value / Extra / Production / OPS / Scoresheet
| Yr | Team | AB | HR | R | RBI | SB | BA | OBP | SLG | CT% | H% | BB% | Bash | $1L | $2L | Pts | RAA | 2B | 3B | CS | FB-LD-GB | HR/fb | RBI% | RS% | OPS | 1st Hf | 2nd Hf | vs RH | vs LH | Rnge | vRH | vLH |
|---|---|---|---|---|---|---|---|---|---|---|---|---|---|---|---|---|---|---|---|---|---|---|---|---|---|---|---|---|---|---|---|---|
| 07 | — | — | — | — | — | — | — | — | — | — | — | — | — | — | — | — | — | — | — | — | — | — | — | — | — | — | — | — | — | — | — | — |
| 08 | — | — | — | — | — | — | — | — | — | — | — | — | — | — | — | — | — | — | — | — | — | — | — | — | — | — | — | — | — | — | — | — |
| 09 | — | — | — | — | — | — | — | — | — | — | — | — | — | — | — | — | — | — | — | — | — | — | — | — | — | — | — | — | — | — | — | — |
| 10 | FLA | 359 | 22 | 45 | 59 | 5 | .259 | .326 | .507 | 66% | 39% | 8% | 1.96 | $13 | $3 | 200 | +2 | 21 | 1 | 2 | 41-16-43 | 23% | 19% | 21% | .833 | .711 | .884 | .892 | .644 | | | |

---

## Nick Stavinoha — 75 PA | $-4 | 30 pts
OF-27 (RF-22, LF-5), 1B-3, DH-2, CA-1     Owned: 0%    RH

Despite cultivating a reputation early in 2010 as a reliable pinch-hitter, Stavinoha amassed only 126 PA on the entire season. He's highly unlikely to produce much more in 2011 given his relatively advanced age for a youngster, his constrained skill set, and his low ceiling. If he makes the team, he'll sit on the bench. (AB)

### Forecast
| Player | Age | AB | HR | R | RBI | SB | BA | OBP | SLG | $1L | Pts |
|---|---|---|---|---|---|---|---|---|---|---|---|
| Stavinoha N | 28 | 71 | 2 | 8 | 8 | 0 | .255 | .298 | .388 | -$4 | 30 |
| Mini-Browser | Age | AB | HR | R | RBI | SB | BA | OBP | SLG | $1L | Pts |
| Gross G | 31 | 88 | 2 | 11 | 11 | 2 | .249 | .339 | .402 | -$3 | 50 |
| Inglett J | 32 | 67 | 1 | 8 | 7 | 2 | .278 | .343 | .403 | -$3 | 40 |
| Willits R | 29 | 83 | 0 | 13 | 7 | 4 | .252 | .343 | .304 | -$3 | 50 |
| Gentry C | 27 | 95 | 2 | 11 | 7 | 5 | .221 | .282 | .330 | -$4 | 50 |
| Velez E | 28 | 47 | 1 | 6 | 5 | 3 | .258 | .307 | .404 | -$4 | 50 |

### Minors (2010) / Skills
| Level | Leag | AB | HR | R | RBI | SB | BA | OBP | SLG | CT% | H% | BB% | Bash |
|---|---|---|---|---|---|---|---|---|---|---|---|---|---|
| A | — | — | — | — | — | — | — | — | — | — | — | — | — |
| AA | — | — | — | — | — | — | — | — | — | — | — | — | — |
| AAA | PCL | 100 | 6 | 19 | 28 | 0 | .390 | .411 | .680 | 84% | 46% | 5% | 1.74 |

### Competition at RF / Stats in 2010
| Bats | Player | GSvR | GSvL | Sub | OPS |
|---|---|---|---|---|---|
| LH | Jay J | 39 | 5 | 17 | .780 |
| RH | Craig A | 9 | 14 | 7 | .711 |
| BH | Winn R | 12 | 5 | 18 | .663 |
| RH | Stavinoha N | 4 | 12 | 6 | .625 |

### Majors / Value / Extra / Production / OPS / Scoresheet
| Yr | Team | AB | HR | R | RBI | SB | BA | OBP | SLG | CT% | H% | BB% | Bash | $1L | $2L | Pts | RAA | 2B | 3B | CS | FB-LD-GB | HR/fb | RBI% | RS% | OPS | 1st Hf | 2nd Hf | vs RH | vs LH | Rnge | vRH | vLH |
|---|---|---|---|---|---|---|---|---|---|---|---|---|---|---|---|---|---|---|---|---|---|---|---|---|---|---|---|---|---|---|---|---|
| 07 | — | — | — | — | — | — | — | — | — | — | — | — | — | — | — | — | — | — | — | — | — | — | — | — | — | — | — | — | — | — | — | — |
| 08 | STL | 57 | 0 | 4 | 4 | 0 | .193 | .217 | .211 | 81% | 24% | 3% | 1.09 | -$5 | -$19 | 10 | -8 | 1 | 0 | 0 | 32-11-57 | 0% | 10% | 31% | .427 | .500 | .400 | .313 | .566 | — | — | — |
| 09 | STL | 87 | 2 | 6 | 17 | 1 | .230 | .242 | .379 | 83% | 28% | 2% | 1.65 | -$3 | -$17 | 40 | -6 | 7 | 0 | 0 | 49-18-34 | 6% | 31% | 20% | .621 | .609 | .676 | .529 | .779 | 2.09 | -23 | +52 |
| 10 | STL | 121 | 2 | 11 | 9 | 0 | .256 | .286 | .339 | 77% | 33% | 3% | 1.32 | -$3 | -$18 | 40 | -8 | 4 | 0 | 0 | 33-20-48 | 5% | 11% | 26% | .625 | .639 | .581 | .641 | .608 | 2.06 | -19 | +42 |

---

## Ian Stewart — 575 PA | $18 | 360 pts
3B-115     Owned: 94%    LH

Stewart could be primed for a breakout year in 2011. Although he was limited by injuries in 2010, his CT% rose for the third straight season, and that greater acuity did not come at the expense of a 1.7-level Bash. Stewart will probably never hit much more than .270, but in a full season, he could threaten 40 HR. (TS)

### Forecast
| Player | Age | AB | HR | R | RBI | SB | BA | OBP | SLG | $1L | Pts |
|---|---|---|---|---|---|---|---|---|---|---|---|
| Stewart I | 25 | 525 | 29 | 81 | 81 | 6 | .263 | .350 | .492 | $18 | 360 |
| Mini-Browser | Age | AB | HR | R | RBI | SB | BA | OBP | SLG | $1L | Pts |
| Zimmerman R | 26 | 558 | 26 | 98 | 91 | 7 | .291 | .363 | .507 | $23 | 440 |
| Reynolds M | 27 | 586 | 39 | 98 | 98 | 13 | .244 | .339 | .498 | $23 | 390 |
| Beltre A | 31 | 544 | 24 | 78 | 78 | 6 | .287 | .334 | .489 | $21 | 380 |
| Ramirez A | 32 | 502 | 24 | 77 | 99 | 0 | .285 | .358 | .515 | $20 | 410 |
| Young M | 34 | 589 | 13 | 85 | 78 | 7 | .287 | .340 | .427 | $20 | 360 |

### Minors (2010) / Skills
| Level | Leag | AB | HR | R | RBI | SB | BA | OBP | SLG | CT% | H% | BB% | Bash |
|---|---|---|---|---|---|---|---|---|---|---|---|---|---|
| A | — | — | — | — | — | — | — | — | — | — | — | — | — |
| AA | — | — | — | — | — | — | — | — | — | — | — | — | — |
| AAA | — | — | — | — | — | — | — | — | — | — | — | — | — |

### Competition at 3B / Stats in 2010
| Bats | Player | GSvR | GSvL | Sub | OPS |
|---|---|---|---|---|---|
| LH | Stewart I | 79 | 24 | 12 | .781 |
| RH | Mora M | 20 | 34 | 9 | .779 |
| BH | Herrera J | 2 | 4 | 10 | .694 |

### Majors / Value / Extra / Production / OPS / Scoresheet
| Yr | Team | AB | HR | R | RBI | SB | BA | OBP | SLG | CT% | H% | BB% | Bash | $1L | $2L | Pts | RAA | 2B | 3B | CS | FB-LD-GB | HR/fb | RBI% | RS% | OPS | 1st Hf | 2nd Hf | vs RH | vs LH | Rnge | vRH | vLH |
|---|---|---|---|---|---|---|---|---|---|---|---|---|---|---|---|---|---|---|---|---|---|---|---|---|---|---|---|---|---|---|---|---|
| 07 | COL | 43 | 1 | 3 | 9 | 0 | .209 | .261 | .372 | 60% | 35% | 2% | 1.78 | -$5 | -$19 | 10 | -3 | 4 | 0 | 0 | 35-19-46 | 11% | 24% | 18% | .633 | — | .633 | .710 | .382 | 2.65 | — | — |
| 08 | COL | 266 | 10 | 33 | 41 | 1 | .259 | .349 | .455 | 65% | 40% | 10% | 1.75 | $4 | -$6 | 130 | +2 | 18 | 2 | 1 | 44-25-31 | 13% | 20% | 24% | .804 | .756 | .815 | .719 | 1.137 | 2.65 | +27 | -84 |
| 09 | COL | 425 | 25 | 74 | 70 | 7 | .228 | .322 | .464 | 68% | 34% | 11% | 2.03 | $15 | -$6 | 270 | +2 | 19 | 3 | 4 | 46-14-40 | 19% | 17% | 37% | .785 | .795 | .773 | .823 | .664 | 2.69 | +7 | -22 |
| 10 | COL | 386 | 18 | 54 | 61 | 5 | .256 | .338 | .443 | 72% | 36% | 10% | 1.73 | $13 | $3 | 230 | +1 | 22 | 1 | 2 | 41-22-37 | 16% | 17% | 27% | .781 | .788 | .766 | .811 | .683 | 2.70 | +13 | -41 |

---

## Drew Stubbs — 500 PA | $13 | 270 pts
OF-147 (CF-147)     Owned: 35%    RH

Stubbs strikes out too much, but his impressive power-speed combo, combined with excellent defense, mean that he's likely to stay in center field for Cincinnati in 2011. The 26-year-old has a lot of skills that need developing; his ceiling is high, but it will not be quickly achieved. (SW)

### Forecast
| Player | Age | AB | HR | R | RBI | SB | BA | OBP | SLG | $1L | Pts |
|---|---|---|---|---|---|---|---|---|---|---|---|
| Stubbs D | 26 | 441 | 15 | 70 | 50 | 25 | .238 | .322 | .403 | $13 | 270 |
| Mini-Browser | Age | AB | HR | R | RBI | SB | BA | OBP | SLG | $1L | Pts |
| Brantley M | 23 | 573 | 6 | 69 | 50 | 31 | .251 | .324 | .331 | $14 | 360 |
| Lewis F | 30 | 446 | 10 | 75 | 40 | 15 | .269 | .347 | .428 | $14 | 280 |
| Brown D | 23 | 531 | 18 | 66 | 66 | 24 | .226 | .307 | .401 | $14 | 320 |
| Colvin T | 25 | 583 | 25 | 75 | 75 | 13 | .236 | .284 | .444 | $13 | 330 |
| Borbon J | 25 | 466 | 5 | 65 | 45 | 25 | .268 | .315 | .354 | $13 | 290 |

### Minors (2010) / Skills
| Level | Leag | AB | HR | R | RBI | SB | BA | OBP | SLG | CT% | H% | BB% | Bash |
|---|---|---|---|---|---|---|---|---|---|---|---|---|---|
| A | — | — | — | — | — | — | — | — | — | — | — | — | — |
| AA | — | — | — | — | — | — | — | — | — | — | — | — | — |
| AAA | — | — | — | — | — | — | — | — | — | — | — | — | — |

### Competition at CF / Stats in 2010
| Bats | Player | GSvR | GSvL | Sub | OPS |
|---|---|---|---|---|---|
| RH | Stubbs D | 85 | 50 | 12 | .773 |
| RH | Heisey C | 11 | 5 | 6 | .757 |

### Majors / Value / Extra / Production / OPS / Scoresheet
| Yr | Team | AB | HR | R | RBI | SB | BA | OBP | SLG | CT% | H% | BB% | Bash | $1L | $2L | Pts | RAA | 2B | 3B | CS | FB-LD-GB | HR/fb | RBI% | RS% | OPS | 1st Hf | 2nd Hf | vs RH | vs LH | Rnge | vRH | vLH |
|---|---|---|---|---|---|---|---|---|---|---|---|---|---|---|---|---|---|---|---|---|---|---|---|---|---|---|---|---|---|---|---|---|
| 07 | — | — | — | — | — | — | — | — | — | — | — | — | — | — | — | — | — | — | — | — | — | — | — | — | — | — | — | — | 2.10 | — | — |
| 08 | — | — | — | — | — | — | — | — | — | — | — | — | — | — | — | — | — | — | — | — | — | — | — | — | — | — | — | — | 2.10 | — | — |
| 09 | CIN | 180 | 8 | 27 | 17 | 10 | .267 | .323 | .439 | 73% | 37% | 8% | 1.65 | $4 | -$10 | 100 | +2 | 5 | 1 | 4 | 37-21-42 | 17% | 13% | 35% | .762 | — | .762 | .740 | .833 | 2.10 | — | — |
| 10 | CIN | 514 | 22 | 91 | 77 | 30 | .255 | .329 | .444 | 67% | 38% | 9% | 1.74 | $26 | $19 | 340 | +5 | 19 | 6 | 6 | 40-16-44 | 16% | 20% | 41% | .773 | .709 | .857 | .765 | .789 | 2.17 | -18 | +43 |

*For more stats, visit www.Rotolympus.com.*

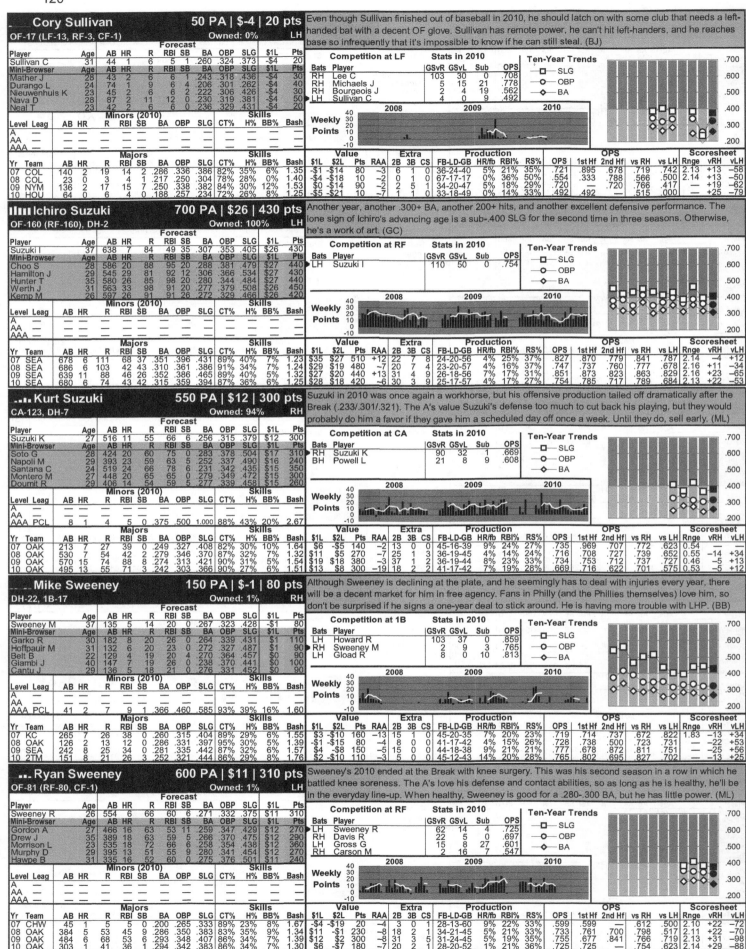

## Cory Sullivan — 50 PA | $-4 | 20 pts

OF-17 (LF-13, RF-3, CF-1) — Owned: 0% — LH

Even though Sullivan finished out of baseball in 2010, he should latch on with some club that needs a left-handed bat with a decent OF glove. Sullivan has remote power, he can't hit left-handers, and he reaches base so infrequently that it's impossible to know if he can still steal. (BJ)

**Forecast**

| Player | Age | AB | HR | R | RBI | SB | BA | OBP | SLG | $1L | Pts |
|---|---|---|---|---|---|---|---|---|---|---|---|
| Sullivan C | 31 | 44 | 1 | 6 | 5 | 1 | .260 | .324 | .373 | -$4 | 20 |
| **Mini-Browser** | Age | AB | HR | R | RBI | SB | BA | OBP | SLG | $1L | Pts |
| Mather J | 28 | 43 | 2 | 6 | 6 | 1 | .243 | .318 | .436 | -$4 | 30 |
| Durango L | 24 | 74 | 1 | 9 | 6 | 4 | .206 | .301 | .262 | -$4 | 40 |
| Nieuwenhuis K | 23 | 45 | 2 | 6 | 6 | 2 | .222 | .306 | .426 | -$4 | 30 |
| Nava D | 28 | 87 | 2 | 11 | 12 | 0 | .230 | .319 | .381 | -$4 | 50 |
| Neal T | 23 | 42 | 2 | 6 | 6 | 0 | .236 | .329 | .431 | -$4 | 20 |

**Minors (2010)** / Skills

| Level | Leag | AB | HR | R | RBI | SB | BA | OBP | SLG | CT% | H% | BB% | Bash |
|---|---|---|---|---|---|---|---|---|---|---|---|---|---|
| A | — | — | — | — | — | — | — | — | — | — | — | — | — |
| AA | — | — | — | — | — | — | — | — | — | — | — | — | — |
| AAA | — | — | — | — | — | — | — | — | — | — | — | — | — |

**Majors** / Skills

| Yr | Team | AB | HR | R | RBI | SB | BA | OBP | SLG | CT% | H% | BB% | Bash |
|---|---|---|---|---|---|---|---|---|---|---|---|---|---|
| 07 | COL | 140 | 2 | 19 | 14 | 2 | .286 | .336 | .386 | 82% | 35% | 6% | 1.35 |
| 08 | COL | 23 | 0 | 3 | 4 | 1 | .217 | .250 | .304 | 78% | 28% | 0% | 1.40 |
| 09 | NYM | 136 | 2 | 17 | 15 | 7 | .250 | .338 | .382 | 84% | 30% | 12% | 1.53 |
| 10 | HOU | 64 | 0 | 6 | 4 | 0 | .188 | .257 | .234 | 72% | 26% | 8% | 1.25 |

| Yr | Value $1L | $2L | Pts | RAA | Extra 2B | 3B | CS | Production FB-LD-GB | HR/fb | RBI% | RS% | OPS | 1st Hf | 2nd Hf | vs RH | vs LH | Scoresheet Rnge | vRH | vLH |
|---|---|---|---|---|---|---|---|---|---|---|---|---|---|---|---|---|---|---|---|
| 07 | -$1 | -$14 | 80 | –3 | 6 | 1 | 0 | 36-24-40 | 5% | 21% | 35% | .721 | .895 | .678 | .719 | .742 | 2.13 | +13 | –58 |
| 08 | -$4 | -$18 | 10 | –2 | 0 | 1 | 0 | 67-17-17 | 0% | 36% | 50% | .554 | .333 | .788 | .566 | .500 | 2.14 | +13 | –50 |
| 09 | $0 | -$14 | 90 | –2 | 2 | 5 | 1 | 34-20-47 | 5% | 18% | 29% | .720 | — | .720 | .766 | .417 | — | +19 | –62 |
| 10 | -$5 | -$21 | 10 | –7 | 1 | 1 | 0 | 33-18-49 | 0% | 14% | 33% | .492 | .492 | — | .515 | .000 | — | +25 | –79 |

**Competition at LF** — Stats in 2010

| Bats | Player | GSvR | GSvL | Sub | OPS |
|---|---|---|---|---|---|
| RH | Lee C | 103 | 30 | 0 | .708 |
| RH | Michaels J | 5 | 15 | 21 | .778 |
| RH | Bourgeois J | 2 | 4 | 19 | .562 |
| ▶LH | Sullivan C | 4 | 0 | 9 | .492 |

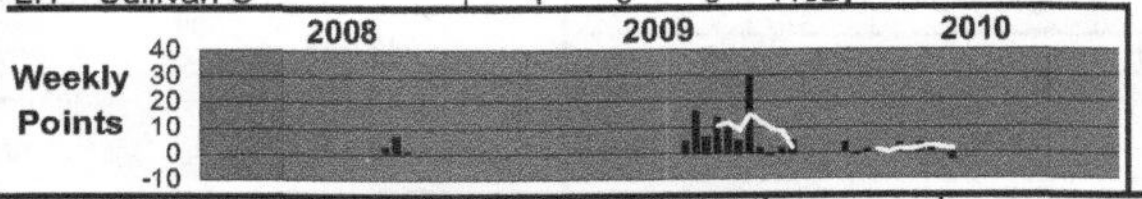


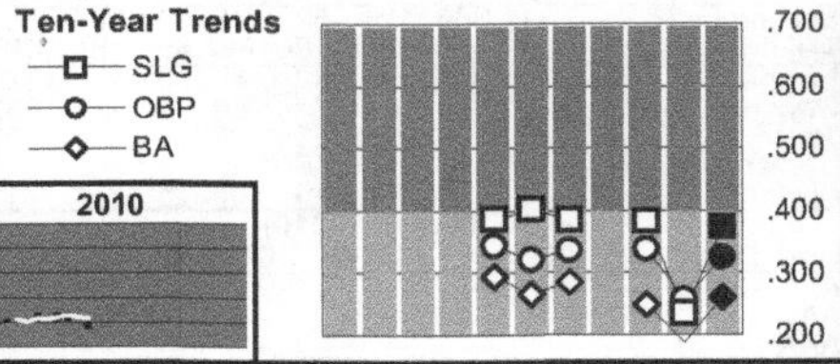


## Ichiro Suzuki — 700 PA | $26 | 430 pts

OF-160 (RF-160), DH-2 — Owned: 100% — LH

Another year, another .300+ BA, another 200+ hits, and another excellent defensive performance. The lone sign of Ichiro's advancing age is a sub-.400 SLG for the second time in three seasons. Otherwise, he's a work of art. (GC)

**Forecast**

| Player | Age | AB | HR | R | RBI | SB | BA | OBP | SLG | $1L | Pts |
|---|---|---|---|---|---|---|---|---|---|---|---|
| Suzuki I | 37 | 638 | 7 | 84 | 49 | 35 | .307 | .353 | .405 | $26 | 430 |
| **Mini-Browser** | Age | AB | HR | R | RBI | SB | BA | OBP | SLG | $1L | Pts |
| Choo S | 28 | 586 | 20 | 88 | 95 | 20 | .288 | .381 | .479 | $27 | 440 |
| Hamilton J | 29 | 545 | 29 | 81 | 92 | 12 | .306 | .366 | .534 | $27 | 430 |
| Hunter T | 35 | 580 | 26 | 85 | 98 | 20 | .280 | .344 | .484 | $27 | 440 |
| Werth J | 31 | 563 | 33 | 98 | 91 | 20 | .277 | .379 | .508 | $26 | 450 |
| Kemp M | 26 | 597 | 26 | 91 | 91 | 26 | .272 | .329 | .466 | $26 | 420 |

**Minors (2010)** / Skills

| Level | Leag | AB | HR | R | RBI | SB | BA | OBP | SLG | CT% | H% | BB% | Bash |
|---|---|---|---|---|---|---|---|---|---|---|---|---|---|
| A | — | — | — | — | — | — | — | — | — | — | — | — | — |
| AA | — | — | — | — | — | — | — | — | — | — | — | — | — |
| AAA | — | — | — | — | — | — | — | — | — | — | — | — | — |

**Majors** / Skills

| Yr | Team | AB | HR | R | RBI | SB | BA | OBP | SLG | CT% | H% | BB% | Bash |
|---|---|---|---|---|---|---|---|---|---|---|---|---|---|
| 07 | SEA | 678 | 6 | 111 | 68 | 37 | .351 | .396 | .431 | 89% | 40% | 7% | 1.23 |
| 08 | SEA | 686 | 6 | 103 | 42 | 43 | .310 | .361 | .386 | 91% | 34% | 7% | 1.24 |
| 09 | SEA | 639 | 11 | 88 | 46 | 26 | .352 | .386 | .465 | 89% | 40% | 5% | 1.32 |
| 10 | SEA | 680 | 6 | 74 | 43 | 42 | .315 | .359 | .394 | 87% | 36% | 6% | 1.25 |

| Yr | Value $1L | $2L | Pts | RAA | Extra 2B | 3B | CS | Production FB-LD-GB | HR/fb | RBI% | RS% | OPS | 1st Hf | 2nd Hf | vs RH | vs LH | Scoresheet Rnge | vRH | vLH |
|---|---|---|---|---|---|---|---|---|---|---|---|---|---|---|---|---|---|---|---|
| 07 | $35 | $27 | 510 | +12 | 22 | 7 | 8 | 24-20-56 | 4% | 25% | 37% | .827 | .870 | .779 | .841 | .787 | 2.14 | –4 | +12 |
| 08 | $29 | $19 | 480 | –7 | 20 | 7 | 4 | 23-20-57 | 4% | 16% | 37% | .747 | .737 | .760 | .777 | .678 | 2.16 | +11 | –34 |
| 09 | $27 | $20 | 440 | +13 | 31 | 4 | 9 | 26-18-56 | 7% | 17% | 31% | .851 | .873 | .823 | .863 | .829 | 2.16 | +23 | –65 |
| 10 | $28 | $18 | 420 | –6 | 30 | 3 | 9 | 25-17-57 | 4% | 17% | 27% | .754 | .785 | .717 | .789 | .684 | 2.13 | +22 | –53 |

**Competition at RF** — Stats in 2010

| Bats | Player | GSvR | GSvL | Sub | OPS |
|---|---|---|---|---|---|
| ▶LH | Suzuki I | 110 | 50 | 0 | .754 |

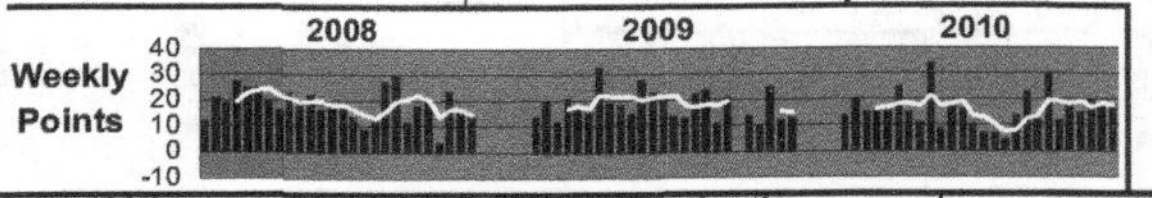


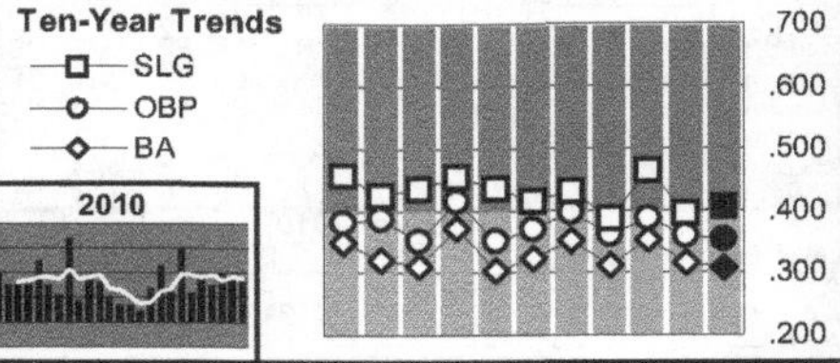


## Kurt Suzuki — 550 PA | $12 | 300 pts

CA-123, DH-7 — Owned: 94% — RH

Suzuki in 2010 was once again a workhorse, but his offensive production tailed off dramatically after the Break (.233/.301/.321). The A's value Suzuki's defense too much to cut back his playing, but they would probably do him a favor if they gave him a scheduled day off once a week. Until they do, sell early. (ML)

**Forecast**

| Player | Age | AB | HR | R | RBI | SB | BA | OBP | SLG | $1L | Pts |
|---|---|---|---|---|---|---|---|---|---|---|---|
| Suzuki K | 27 | 516 | 11 | 55 | 66 | 6 | .256 | .315 | .379 | $12 | 300 |
| **Mini-Browser** | Age | AB | HR | R | RBI | SB | BA | OBP | SLG | $1L | Pts |
| Soto G | 28 | 424 | 20 | 60 | 75 | 0 | .283 | .378 | .504 | $17 | 310 |
| Napoli M | 29 | 393 | 23 | 59 | 63 | 5 | .252 | .337 | .490 | $16 | 240 |
| Santana C | 24 | 519 | 24 | 66 | 78 | 6 | .231 | .342 | .435 | $15 | 350 |
| Montero M | 27 | 448 | 20 | 65 | 65 | 0 | .279 | .349 | .472 | $15 | 300 |
| Doumit R | 29 | 406 | 14 | 54 | 59 | 5 | .277 | .339 | .458 | $15 | 260 |

**Minors (2010)** / Skills

| Level | Leag | AB | HR | R | RBI | SB | BA | OBP | SLG | CT% | H% | BB% | Bash |
|---|---|---|---|---|---|---|---|---|---|---|---|---|---|
| A | — | — | — | — | — | — | — | — | — | — | — | — | — |
| AA | — | — | — | — | — | — | — | — | — | — | — | — | — |
| AAA | PCL | 8 | 1 | 4 | 5 | 0 | .375 | .500 | 1.000 | 88% | 43% | 20% | 2.67 |

**Majors** / Skills

| Yr | Team | AB | HR | R | RBI | SB | BA | OBP | SLG | CT% | H% | BB% | Bash |
|---|---|---|---|---|---|---|---|---|---|---|---|---|---|
| 07 | OAK | 213 | 7 | 27 | 39 | 0 | .249 | .327 | .408 | 82% | 30% | 10% | 1.64 |
| 08 | OAK | 530 | 7 | 54 | 42 | 2 | .279 | .346 | .370 | 87% | 32% | 7% | 1.32 |
| 09 | OAK | 570 | 15 | 74 | 88 | 8 | .274 | .313 | .421 | 90% | 31% | 5% | 1.54 |
| 10 | OAK | 495 | 13 | 55 | 71 | 3 | .242 | .303 | .366 | 90% | 27% | 6% | 1.51 |

| Yr | Value $1L | $2L | Pts | RAA | Extra 2B | 3B | CS | Production FB-LD-GB | HR/fb | RBI% | RS% | OPS | 1st Hf | 2nd Hf | vs RH | vs LH | Scoresheet Rnge | vRH | vLH |
|---|---|---|---|---|---|---|---|---|---|---|---|---|---|---|---|---|---|---|---|
| 07 | $6 | -$5 | 140 | –2 | 13 | 0 | 0 | 45-16-39 | 9% | 24% | 27% | .735 | .969 | .707 | .772 | .623 | 0.54 | — | — |
| 08 | $11 | $5 | 270 | –7 | 25 | 1 | 3 | 36-19-45 | 4% | 14% | 24% | .716 | .708 | .727 | .739 | .652 | 0.55 | –14 | +34 |
| 09 | $19 | $18 | 380 | –3 | 37 | 1 | 2 | 36-19-44 | 8% | 23% | 33% | .734 | .753 | .712 | .737 | .727 | 0.46 | –5 | +13 |
| 10 | $13 | $8 | 300 | –19 | 18 | 2 | 2 | 41-17-42 | 7% | 19% | 28% | .669 | .716 | .622 | .701 | .575 | 0.53 | –5 | +12 |

**Competition at CA** — Stats in 2010

| Bats | Player | GSvR | GSvL | Sub | OPS |
|---|---|---|---|---|---|
| ▶RH | Suzuki K | 90 | 32 | 1 | .669 |
| BH | Powell L | 21 | 8 | 9 | .608 |

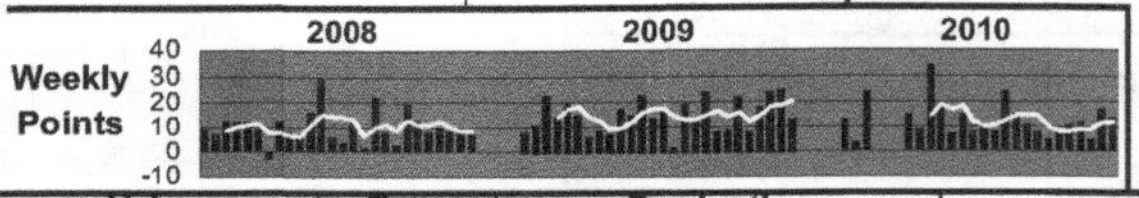


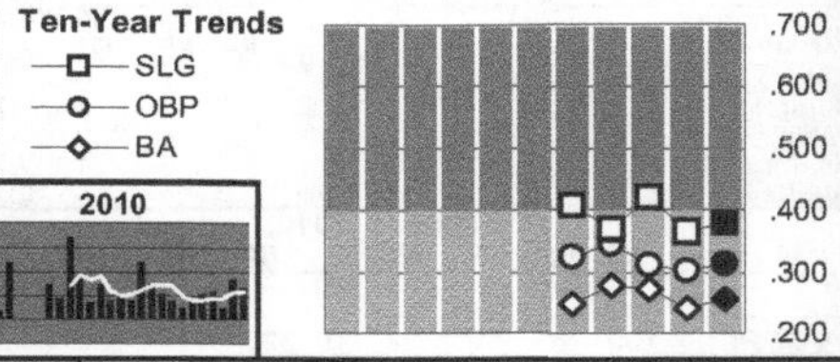


## Mike Sweeney — 150 PA | $-1 | 80 pts

DH-22, 1B-17 — Owned: 1% — RH

Although Sweeney is declining at the plate, and he seemingly has to deal with injuries every year, there will be a decent market for him in free agency. Fans in Philly (and the Phillies themselves) love him, so don't be surprised if he signs a one-year deal to stick around. He is having more trouble with LHP. (BB)

**Forecast**

| Player | Age | AB | HR | R | RBI | SB | BA | OBP | SLG | $1L | Pts |
|---|---|---|---|---|---|---|---|---|---|---|---|
| Sweeney M | 37 | 135 | 5 | 14 | 20 | 0 | .267 | .323 | .428 | -$1 | 80 |
| **Mini-Browser** | Age | AB | HR | R | RBI | SB | BA | OBP | SLG | $1L | Pts |
| Garko R | 30 | 182 | 8 | 20 | 26 | 0 | .264 | .339 | .431 | $1 | 110 |
| Hoffpauir M | 31 | 132 | 6 | 20 | 23 | 0 | .272 | .327 | .487 | $1 | 90 |
| Belt B | 22 | 129 | 4 | 19 | 20 | 4 | .270 | .364 | .457 | $0 | 90 |
| Giambi J | 40 | 147 | 7 | 19 | 26 | 0 | .238 | .370 | .441 | $0 | 100 |
| Cantu J | 29 | 136 | 5 | 18 | 21 | 0 | .276 | .331 | .452 | $0 | 90 |

**Minors (2010)** / Skills

| Level | Leag | AB | HR | R | RBI | SB | BA | OBP | SLG | CT% | H% | BB% | Bash |
|---|---|---|---|---|---|---|---|---|---|---|---|---|---|
| A | — | — | — | — | — | — | — | — | — | — | — | — | — |
| AA | — | — | — | — | — | — | — | — | — | — | — | — | — |
| AAA | PCL | 41 | 2 | 7 | 9 | 1 | .366 | .460 | .585 | 93% | 39% | 16% | 1.60 |

**Majors** / Skills

| Yr | Team | AB | HR | R | RBI | SB | BA | OBP | SLG | CT% | H% | BB% | Bash |
|---|---|---|---|---|---|---|---|---|---|---|---|---|---|
| 07 | KC | 265 | 7 | 26 | 38 | 0 | .260 | .315 | .404 | 89% | 29% | 6% | 1.55 |
| 08 | OAK | 126 | 2 | 13 | 12 | 0 | .286 | .331 | .397 | 95% | 30% | 5% | 1.39 |
| 09 | SEA | 242 | 8 | 25 | 34 | 0 | .281 | .335 | .442 | 87% | 32% | 6% | 1.57 |
| 10 | 2TM | 151 | 8 | 21 | 26 | 3 | .252 | .321 | .444 | 86% | 29% | 8% | 1.76 |

| Yr | Value $1L | $2L | Pts | RAA | Extra 2B | 3B | CS | Production FB-LD-GB | HR/fb | RBI% | RS% | OPS | 1st Hf | 2nd Hf | vs RH | vs LH | Scoresheet Rnge | vRH | vLH |
|---|---|---|---|---|---|---|---|---|---|---|---|---|---|---|---|---|---|---|---|
| 07 | $3 | -$10 | 160 | –13 | 15 | 1 | 0 | 45-20-35 | 7% | 20% | 23% | .719 | .714 | .737 | .672 | .822 | 1.83 | –13 | +34 |
| 08 | -$1 | -$15 | 80 | –4 | 8 | 0 | 0 | 41-17-42 | 4% | 15% | 26% | .728 | .738 | .500 | .723 | .731 | — | –22 | +53 |
| 09 | $4 | -$8 | 150 | –5 | 15 | 0 | 0 | 44-18-38 | 9% | 21% | 21% | .777 | .678 | .872 | .811 | .751 | — | –25 | +56 |
| 10 | $2 | -$10 | 110 | –3 | 5 | 0 | 0 | 45-12-43 | 14% | 20% | 28% | .765 | .802 | .695 | .827 | .702 | — | –13 | +25 |

**Competition at 1B** — Stats in 2010

| Bats | Player | GSvR | GSvL | Sub | OPS |
|---|---|---|---|---|---|
| LH | Howard R | 103 | 37 | 0 | .859 |
| ▶RH | Sweeney M | 2 | 9 | 3 | .765 |
| LH | Gload R | 8 | 0 | 10 | .813 |

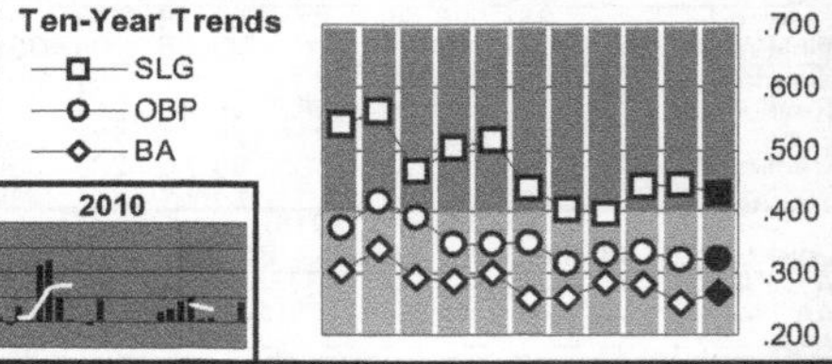


## Ryan Sweeney — 600 PA | $11 | 310 pts

OF-81 (RF-80, CF-1) — Owned: 1% — LH

Sweeney's 2010 ended at the Break with knee surgery. This was his second season in a row in which he battled knee soreness. The A's love his defense and contact abilities, so as long as he is healthy, he'll be in the everyday line-up. When healthy, Sweeney is good for a .280-.300 BA, but he has little power. (ML)

**Forecast**

| Player | Age | AB | HR | R | RBI | SB | BA | OBP | SLG | $1L | Pts |
|---|---|---|---|---|---|---|---|---|---|---|---|
| Sweeney R | 26 | 554 | 6 | 66 | 60 | 6 | .271 | .332 | .375 | $11 | 310 |
| **Mini-Browser** | Age | AB | HR | R | RBI | SB | BA | OBP | SLG | $1L | Pts |
| Gordon A | 27 | 466 | 16 | 63 | 53 | 11 | .259 | .347 | .429 | $12 | 270 |
| Drew J | 35 | 389 | 18 | 63 | 59 | 5 | .266 | .370 | .475 | $12 | 290 |
| Morrison L | 23 | 535 | 18 | 72 | 66 | 6 | .258 | .354 | .438 | $12 | 360 |
| Murphy D | 29 | 395 | 13 | 51 | 55 | 9 | .280 | .341 | .454 | $12 | 280 |
| Hawpe B | 31 | 335 | 16 | 52 | 60 | 0 | .275 | .376 | .501 | $11 | 240 |

**Minors (2010)** / Skills

| Level | Leag | AB | HR | R | RBI | SB | BA | OBP | SLG | CT% | H% | BB% | Bash |
|---|---|---|---|---|---|---|---|---|---|---|---|---|---|
| A | — | — | — | — | — | — | — | — | — | — | — | — | — |
| AA | — | — | — | — | — | — | — | — | — | — | — | — | — |
| AAA | — | — | — | — | — | — | — | — | — | — | — | — | — |

**Majors** / Skills

| Yr | Team | AB | HR | R | RBI | SB | BA | OBP | SLG | CT% | H% | BB% | Bash |
|---|---|---|---|---|---|---|---|---|---|---|---|---|---|
| 07 | CHW | 45 | 1 | 5 | 5 | 0 | .200 | .265 | .333 | 89% | 23% | 8% | 1.67 |
| 08 | OAK | 384 | 5 | 53 | 45 | 9 | .286 | .350 | .383 | 83% | 35% | 9% | 1.34 |
| 09 | OAK | 484 | 6 | 68 | 53 | 6 | .293 | .348 | .407 | 86% | 34% | 7% | 1.39 |
| 10 | OAK | 303 | 1 | 41 | 36 | 1 | .294 | .342 | .383 | 86% | 34% | 7% | 1.30 |

| Yr | Value $1L | $2L | Pts | RAA | Extra 2B | 3B | CS | Production FB-LD-GB | HR/fb | RBI% | RS% | OPS | 1st Hf | 2nd Hf | vs RH | vs LH | Scoresheet Rnge | vRH | vLH |
|---|---|---|---|---|---|---|---|---|---|---|---|---|---|---|---|---|---|---|---|
| 07 | -$4 | -$19 | 20 | –4 | 3 | 0 | 1 | 28-13-60 | 9% | 22% | 33% | .599 | .599 | — | .612 | .500 | 2.10 | +22 | –72 |
| 08 | $11 | -$1 | 230 | –8 | 18 | 2 | 1 | 34-21-45 | 5% | 21% | 33% | .733 | .761 | .700 | .798 | .517 | 2.11 | +22 | –70 |
| 09 | $12 | $2 | 300 | –8 | 31 | 3 | 5 | 31-24-45 | 5% | 19% | 35% | .755 | .677 | .841 | .766 | .719 | 2.13 | +31 | –98 |
| 10 | $6 | -$7 | 180 | –7 | 20 | 2 | 1 | 28-20-52 | 1% | 21% | 36% | .725 | .725 | — | .754 | .623 | 2.14 | +29 | –88 |

**Competition at RF** — Stats in 2010

| Bats | Player | GSvR | GSvL | Sub | OPS |
|---|---|---|---|---|---|
| ▶LH | Sweeney R | 62 | 14 | 4 | .725 |
| RH | Davis R | 22 | 5 | 0 | .697 |
| LH | Gross G | 15 | 8 | 27 | .601 |
| RH | Carson M | 2 | 16 | 7 | .547 |

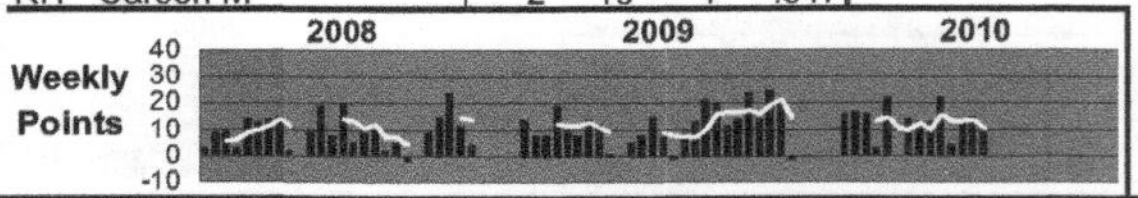


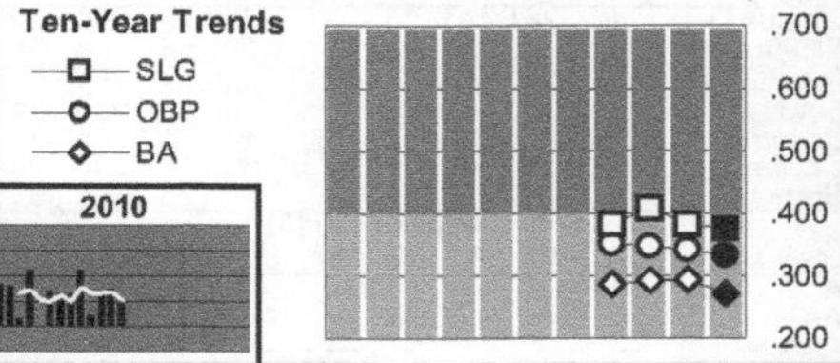

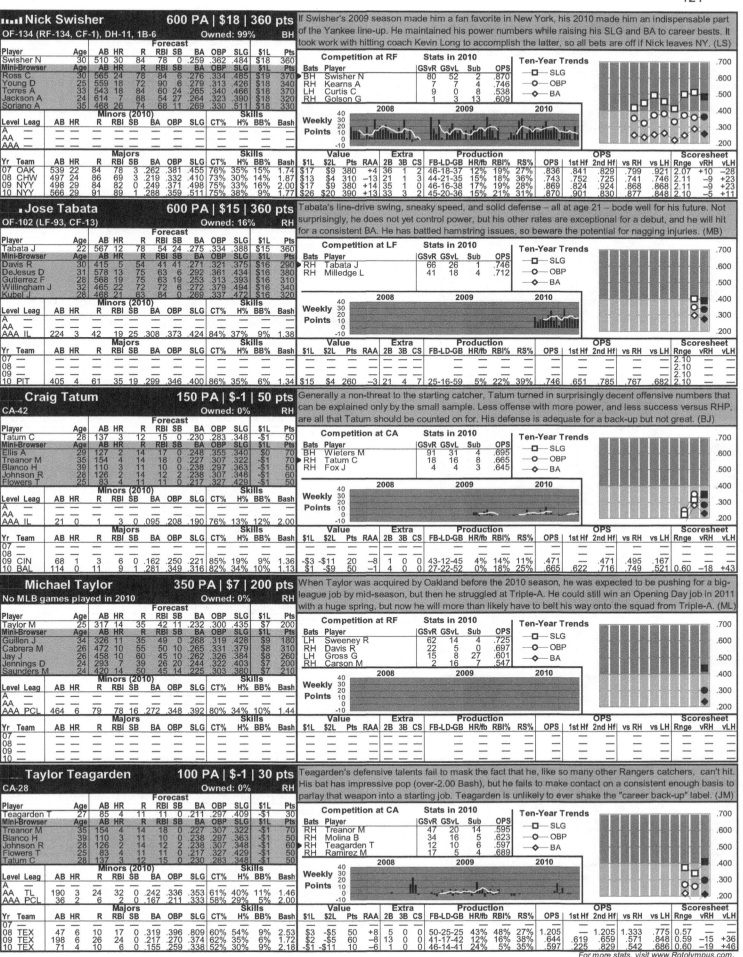

## Nick Swisher — 600 PA | $18 | 360 pts

OF-134 (RF-134, CF-1), DH-11, 1B-6 — Owned: 99% — BH

If Swisher's 2009 season made him a fan favorite in New York, his 2010 made him an indispensable part of the Yankee line-up. He maintained his power numbers while raising his SLG and BA to career bests. It took work with hitting coach Kevin Long to accomplish the latter, so all bets are off if Nick leaves NY. (LS)

### Forecast
| Player | Age | AB | HR | R | RBI | SB | BA | OBP | SLG | $1L | Pts |
|---|---|---|---|---|---|---|---|---|---|---|---|
| Swisher N | 30 | 510 | 30 | 84 | 78 | 0 | .259 | .362 | .484 | $18 | 360 |

### Mini-Browser
| Player | Age | AB | HR | R | RBI | SB | BA | OBP | SLG | $1L | Pts |
|---|---|---|---|---|---|---|---|---|---|---|---|
| Ross C | 30 | 565 | 24 | 78 | 84 | 6 | .276 | .334 | .485 | $19 | 370 |
| Young D | 25 | 559 | 18 | 72 | 90 | 6 | .279 | .313 | .426 | $18 | 340 |
| Torres A | 33 | 543 | 18 | 84 | 60 | 24 | .265 | .340 | .466 | $18 | 370 |
| Jackson A | 24 | 614 | 7 | 88 | 54 | 27 | .264 | .323 | .390 | $18 | 320 |
| Soriano A | 35 | 468 | 26 | 74 | 68 | 11 | .269 | .330 | .511 | $18 | 330 |

### Minors (2010)
| Level | Leag | AB | HR | R | RBI | SB | BA | OBP | SLG | CT% | H% | BB% | Bash |
|---|---|---|---|---|---|---|---|---|---|---|---|---|---|
| A | — | — | — | — | — | — | — | — | — | — | — | — | — |
| AA | — | — | — | — | — | — | — | — | — | — | — | — | — |
| AAA | — | — | — | — | — | — | — | — | — | — | — | — | — |

### Majors
| Yr | Team | AB | HR | R | RBI | SB | BA | OBP | SLG | CT% | H% | BB% | Bash |
|---|---|---|---|---|---|---|---|---|---|---|---|---|---|
| 07 | OAK | 539 | 22 | 84 | 78 | 3 | .262 | .381 | .455 | 76% | 35% | 15% | 1.74 |
| 08 | CHW | 497 | 24 | 86 | 69 | 3 | .219 | .332 | .410 | 73% | 30% | 14% | 1.87 |
| 09 | NYY | 498 | 29 | 84 | 82 | 0 | .249 | .371 | .498 | 75% | 33% | 16% | 2.00 |
| 10 | NYY | 566 | 29 | 91 | 89 | 1 | .288 | .359 | .511 | 75% | 38% | 9% | 1.77 |

### Competition at RF / Stats in 2010
| Bats | Player | GSvR | GSvL | Sub | OPS |
|---|---|---|---|---|---|
| BH | Swisher N | 80 | 52 | 2 | .870 |
| RH | Kearns A | 7 | 7 | 4 | .746 |
| LH | Curtis C | 9 | 0 | 8 | .538 |
| RH | Golson G | 1 | 3 | 13 | .609 |

Ten-Year Trends: □ SLG, ○ OBP, ◇ BA

### Value / Extra / Production / OPS / Scoresheet
| Yr | $1L | $2L | Pts | RAA | 2B | 3B | CS | FB-LD-GB | HR/fb | RBI% | RS% | OPS | 1st Hf | 2nd Hf | vs RH | vs LH | Rnge | vRH | vLH |
|---|---|---|---|---|---|---|---|---|---|---|---|---|---|---|---|---|---|---|---|
| 07 | $17 | $9 | 380 | +4 | 36 | 1 | 2 | 46-18-37 | 12% | 19% | 27% | .836 | .841 | .829 | .799 | .921 | 2.07 | +10 | −28 |
| 08 | $13 | $4 | 310 | −13 | 21 | 1 | 3 | 44-21-35 | 15% | 18% | 36% | .743 | .752 | .725 | .741 | .746 | 2.11 | −9 | +23 |
| 09 | $17 | $8 | 390 | +14 | 35 | 1 | 0 | 46-16-38 | 17% | 19% | 28% | .869 | .824 | .924 | .868 | .868 | 2.11 | −9 | +23 |
| 10 | $26 | $20 | 390 | +13 | 33 | 2 | 1 | 45-20-36 | 15% | 21% | 31% | .870 | .901 | .830 | .877 | .848 | 2.10 | −5 | +11 |

## Jose Tabata — 600 PA | $15 | 360 pts

OF-102 (LF-93, CF-13) — Owned: 16% — RH

Tabata's line-drive swing, sneaky speed, and solid defense – all at age 21 – bode well for his future. Not surprisingly, he does not yet control power, but his other rates are exceptional for a debut, and he will hit for a consistent BA. He has battled hamstring issues, so beware the potential for nagging injuries. (MB)

### Forecast
| Player | Age | AB | HR | R | RBI | SB | BA | OBP | SLG | $1L | Pts |
|---|---|---|---|---|---|---|---|---|---|---|---|
| Tabata J | 22 | 567 | 12 | 78 | 54 | 24 | .275 | .334 | .388 | $15 | 360 |

### Mini-Browser
| Player | Age | AB | HR | R | RBI | SB | BA | OBP | SLG | $1L | Pts |
|---|---|---|---|---|---|---|---|---|---|---|---|
| Davis R | 30 | 415 | 5 | 54 | 41 | 41 | .271 | .321 | .375 | $16 | 290 |
| DeJesus D | 31 | 578 | 13 | 75 | 63 | 6 | .292 | .361 | .434 | $16 | 380 |
| Gutierrez F | 28 | 568 | 19 | 75 | 63 | 19 | .253 | .313 | .393 | $16 | 310 |
| Willingham J | 32 | 465 | 22 | 72 | 72 | 6 | .272 | .379 | .494 | $16 | 340 |
| Kubel J | 28 | 468 | 21 | 63 | 84 | 0 | .269 | .337 | .472 | $16 | 320 |

### Minors (2010)
| Level | Leag | AB | HR | R | RBI | SB | BA | OBP | SLG | CT% | H% | BB% | Bash |
|---|---|---|---|---|---|---|---|---|---|---|---|---|---|
| A | — | — | — | — | — | — | — | — | — | — | — | — | — |
| AA | — | — | — | — | — | — | — | — | — | — | — | — | — |
| AAA | IL | 224 | 3 | 42 | 19 | 25 | .308 | .373 | .424 | 84% | 37% | 9% | 1.38 |

### Majors
| Yr | Team | AB | HR | R | RBI | SB | BA | OBP | SLG | CT% | H% | BB% | Bash |
|---|---|---|---|---|---|---|---|---|---|---|---|---|---|
| 07 | — | — | — | — | — | — | — | — | — | — | — | — | — |
| 08 | — | — | — | — | — | — | — | — | — | — | — | — | — |
| 09 | — | — | — | — | — | — | — | — | — | — | — | — | — |
| 10 | PIT | 405 | 4 | 61 | 35 | 19 | .299 | .346 | .400 | 86% | 35% | 6% | 1.34 |

### Competition at LF / Stats in 2010
| Bats | Player | GSvR | GSvL | Sub | OPS |
|---|---|---|---|---|---|
| RH | Tabata J | 66 | 26 | 1 | .746 |
| RH | Milledge L | 41 | 18 | 4 | .712 |

Ten-Year Trends: □ SLG, ○ OBP, ◇ BA

### Value / Extra / Production / OPS / Scoresheet
| Yr | $1L | $2L | Pts | RAA | 2B | 3B | CS | FB-LD-GB | HR/fb | RBI% | RS% | OPS | 1st Hf | 2nd Hf | vs RH | vs LH | Rnge | vRH | vLH |
|---|---|---|---|---|---|---|---|---|---|---|---|---|---|---|---|---|---|---|---|
| 07 | — | — | — | — | — | — | — | — | — | — | — | — | — | — | — | — | 2.10 | — | — |
| 08 | — | — | — | — | — | — | — | — | — | — | — | — | — | — | — | — | 2.10 | — | — |
| 09 | — | — | — | — | — | — | — | — | — | — | — | — | — | — | — | — | 2.10 | — | — |
| 10 | $15 | $4 | 260 | −3 | 21 | 4 | 7 | 25-16-59 | 5% | 22% | 39% | .746 | .651 | .785 | .767 | .682 | 2.10 | — | — |

## Craig Tatum — 150 PA | $-1 | 50 pts

CA-42 — Owned: 0% — RH

Generally a non-threat to the starting catcher, Tatum turned in surprisingly decent offensive numbers that can be explained only by the small sample. Less offense with more power, and less success versus RHP, are all that Tatum should be counted on for. His defense is adequate for a back-up but not great. (BJ)

### Forecast
| Player | Age | AB | HR | R | RBI | SB | BA | OBP | SLG | $1L | Pts |
|---|---|---|---|---|---|---|---|---|---|---|---|
| Tatum C | 28 | 137 | 3 | 12 | 15 | 0 | .230 | .283 | .348 | -$1 | 50 |

### Mini-Browser
| Player | Age | AB | HR | R | RBI | SB | BA | OBP | SLG | $1L | Pts |
|---|---|---|---|---|---|---|---|---|---|---|---|
| Ellis A | 29 | 127 | 2 | 14 | 17 | 0 | .248 | .355 | .340 | $0 | 70 |
| Treanor M | 35 | 154 | 4 | 14 | 18 | 0 | .227 | .307 | .322 | -$1 | 70 |
| Blanco H | 39 | 110 | 3 | 11 | 10 | 0 | .238 | .297 | .363 | -$1 | 50 |
| Johnson R | 28 | 126 | 2 | 14 | 12 | 2 | .238 | .307 | .348 | -$1 | 60 |
| Flowers T | 25 | 83 | 4 | 11 | 11 | 0 | .217 | .327 | .429 | -$1 | 50 |

### Minors (2010)
| Level | Leag | AB | HR | R | RBI | SB | BA | OBP | SLG | CT% | H% | BB% | Bash |
|---|---|---|---|---|---|---|---|---|---|---|---|---|---|
| A | — | — | — | — | — | — | — | — | — | — | — | — | — |
| AA | — | — | — | — | — | — | — | — | — | — | — | — | — |
| AAA | IL | 21 | 0 | 1 | 3 | 0 | .095 | .208 | .190 | 76% | 13% | 12% | 2.00 |

### Majors
| Yr | Team | AB | HR | R | RBI | SB | BA | OBP | SLG | CT% | H% | BB% | Bash |
|---|---|---|---|---|---|---|---|---|---|---|---|---|---|
| 07 | — | — | — | — | — | — | — | — | — | — | — | — | — |
| 08 | — | — | — | — | — | — | — | — | — | — | — | — | — |
| 09 | CIN | 68 | 1 | 3 | 6 | 0 | .162 | .250 | .221 | 85% | 19% | 9% | 1.36 |
| 10 | BAL | 114 | 0 | 11 | 9 | 1 | .281 | .349 | .316 | 82% | 34% | 10% | 1.13 |

### Competition at CA / Stats in 2010
| Bats | Player | GSvR | GSvL | Sub | OPS |
|---|---|---|---|---|---|
| BH | Wieters M | 91 | 31 | 4 | .695 |
| RH | Tatum C | 18 | 16 | 8 | .665 |
| RH | Fox J | 4 | 4 | 3 | .645 |

Ten-Year Trends: □ SLG, ○ OBP, ◇ BA

### Value / Extra / Production / OPS / Scoresheet
| Yr | $1L | $2L | Pts | RAA | 2B | 3B | CS | FB-LD-GB | HR/fb | RBI% | RS% | OPS | 1st Hf | 2nd Hf | vs RH | vs LH | Rnge | vRH | vLH |
|---|---|---|---|---|---|---|---|---|---|---|---|---|---|---|---|---|---|---|---|
| 07 | — | — | — | — | — | — | — | — | — | — | — | — | — | — | — | — | — | — | — |
| 08 | — | — | — | — | — | — | — | — | — | — | — | — | — | — | — | — | — | — | — |
| 09 | -$3 | -$11 | 20 | −8 | 1 | 0 | 0 | 43-12-45 | 4% | 14% | 11% | .471 | — | .471 | .495 | .167 | — | — | — |
| 10 | $1 | -$9 | 50 | −1 | 4 | 0 | 0 | 27-22-52 | 0% | 18% | 25% | .665 | .622 | .716 | .749 | .521 | 0.60 | −18 | +43 |

## Michael Taylor — 350 PA | $7 | 200 pts

No MLB games played in 2010 — Owned: 0% — RH

When Taylor was acquired by Oakland before the 2010 season, he was expected to be pushing for a big-league job by mid-season, but then he struggled at Triple-A. He could still win an Opening Day job in 2011 with a huge spring, but now he will more than likely have to belt his way onto the squad from Triple-A. (ML)

### Forecast
| Player | Age | AB | HR | R | RBI | SB | BA | OBP | SLG | $1L | Pts |
|---|---|---|---|---|---|---|---|---|---|---|---|
| Taylor M | 25 | 317 | 14 | 35 | 42 | 11 | .232 | .300 | .435 | $7 | 200 |

### Mini-Browser
| Player | Age | AB | HR | R | RBI | SB | BA | OBP | SLG | $1L | Pts |
|---|---|---|---|---|---|---|---|---|---|---|---|
| Guillen J | 34 | 326 | 11 | 35 | 49 | 0 | .268 | .319 | .428 | $9 | 180 |
| Cabrera M | 26 | 472 | 10 | 55 | 50 | 10 | .265 | .331 | .379 | $8 | 310 |
| Jay J | 26 | 458 | 10 | 60 | 45 | 10 | .262 | .326 | .384 | $8 | 260 |
| Jennings D | 24 | 293 | 7 | 39 | 26 | 20 | .244 | .322 | .403 | $7 | 200 |
| Saunders M | 24 | 420 | 14 | 50 | 45 | 14 | .225 | .303 | .380 | $7 | 210 |

### Minors (2010)
| Level | Leag | AB | HR | R | RBI | SB | BA | OBP | SLG | CT% | H% | BB% | Bash |
|---|---|---|---|---|---|---|---|---|---|---|---|---|---|
| A | — | — | — | — | — | — | — | — | — | — | — | — | — |
| AA | — | — | — | — | — | — | — | — | — | — | — | — | — |
| AAA | PCL | 464 | 6 | 79 | 78 | 16 | .272 | .348 | .392 | 80% | 34% | 10% | 1.44 |

### Majors
| Yr | Team | AB | HR | R | RBI | SB | BA | OBP | SLG | CT% | H% | BB% | Bash |
|---|---|---|---|---|---|---|---|---|---|---|---|---|---|
| 07 | — | — | — | — | — | — | — | — | — | — | — | — | — |
| 08 | — | — | — | — | — | — | — | — | — | — | — | — | — |
| 09 | — | — | — | — | — | — | — | — | — | — | — | — | — |
| 10 | — | — | — | — | — | — | — | — | — | — | — | — | — |

### Competition at RF / Stats in 2010
| Bats | Player | GSvR | GSvL | Sub | OPS |
|---|---|---|---|---|---|
| LH | Sweeney R | 62 | 14 | 4 | .725 |
| RH | Davis R | 22 | 5 | 0 | .697 |
| LH | Gross G | 15 | 8 | 27 | .601 |
| RH | Carson M | 2 | 16 | 7 | .547 |

Ten-Year Trends: □ SLG, ○ OBP, ◇ BA

### Value / Extra / Production / OPS / Scoresheet
| Yr | $1L | $2L | Pts | RAA | 2B | 3B | CS | FB-LD-GB | HR/fb | RBI% | RS% | OPS | 1st Hf | 2nd Hf | vs RH | vs LH | Rnge | vRH | vLH |
|---|---|---|---|---|---|---|---|---|---|---|---|---|---|---|---|---|---|---|---|
| 07 | — | — | — | — | — | — | — | — | — | — | — | — | — | — | — | — | — | — | — |
| 08 | — | — | — | — | — | — | — | — | — | — | — | — | — | — | — | — | — | — | — |
| 09 | — | — | — | — | — | — | — | — | — | — | — | — | — | — | — | — | — | — | — |
| 10 | — | — | — | — | — | — | — | — | — | — | — | — | — | — | — | — | — | — | — |

## Taylor Teagarden — 100 PA | $-1 | 30 pts

CA-28 — Owned: 0% — RH

Teagarden's defensive talents fail to mask the fact that he, like so many other Rangers catchers, can't hit. His bat has impressive pop (over-2.00 Bash), but he fails to make contact on a consistent enough basis to parlay that weapon into a starting job. Teagarden is unlikely to ever shake the "career back-up" label. (JM)

### Forecast
| Player | Age | AB | HR | R | RBI | SB | BA | OBP | SLG | $1L | Pts |
|---|---|---|---|---|---|---|---|---|---|---|---|
| Teagarden T | 27 | 85 | 4 | 11 | 11 | 0 | .211 | .297 | .409 | -$1 | 30 |

### Mini-Browser
| Player | Age | AB | HR | R | RBI | SB | BA | OBP | SLG | $1L | Pts |
|---|---|---|---|---|---|---|---|---|---|---|---|
| Treanor M | 35 | 154 | 4 | 14 | 18 | 0 | .227 | .307 | .322 | -$1 | 70 |
| Blanco H | 39 | 110 | 3 | 11 | 10 | 0 | .238 | .297 | .363 | -$1 | 50 |
| Johnson R | 28 | 126 | 2 | 14 | 12 | 2 | .238 | .307 | .348 | -$1 | 60 |
| Flowers T | 25 | 83 | 4 | 11 | 11 | 0 | .217 | .327 | .429 | -$1 | 50 |
| Tatum C | 28 | 137 | 3 | 12 | 15 | 0 | .230 | .283 | .348 | -$1 | 50 |

### Minors (2010)
| Level | Leag | AB | HR | R | RBI | SB | BA | OBP | SLG | CT% | H% | BB% | Bash |
|---|---|---|---|---|---|---|---|---|---|---|---|---|---|
| A | — | — | — | — | — | — | — | — | — | — | — | — | — |
| AA | TL | 190 | 3 | 24 | 32 | 0 | .242 | .336 | .353 | 61% | 40% | 11% | 1.46 |
| AAA | PCL | 36 | 2 | 6 | 2 | 0 | .167 | .211 | .333 | 58% | 29% | 5% | 2.00 |

### Majors
| Yr | Team | AB | HR | R | RBI | SB | BA | OBP | SLG | CT% | H% | BB% | Bash |
|---|---|---|---|---|---|---|---|---|---|---|---|---|---|
| 07 | — | — | — | — | — | — | — | — | — | — | — | — | — |
| 08 | TEX | 47 | 6 | 10 | 17 | 0 | .319 | .396 | .809 | 60% | 54% | 9% | 2.53 |
| 09 | TEX | 198 | 6 | 24 | 26 | 0 | .217 | .270 | .374 | 62% | 35% | 6% | 1.72 |
| 10 | TEX | 71 | 4 | 10 | 6 | 0 | .155 | .259 | .338 | 52% | 38% | 12% | 2.18 |

### Competition at CA / Stats in 2010
| Bats | Player | GSvR | GSvL | Sub | OPS |
|---|---|---|---|---|---|
| RH | Treanor M | 47 | 20 | 14 | .595 |
| RH | Molina B | 34 | 16 | 6 | .623 |
| RH | Teagarden T | 12 | 10 | 6 | .597 |
| RH | Ramirez M | 17 | 5 | 4 | .689 |

Ten-Year Trends: □ SLG, ○ OBP, ◇ BA

### Value / Extra / Production / OPS / Scoresheet
| Yr | $1L | $2L | Pts | RAA | 2B | 3B | CS | FB-LD-GB | HR/fb | RBI% | RS% | OPS | 1st Hf | 2nd Hf | vs RH | vs LH | Rnge | vRH | vLH |
|---|---|---|---|---|---|---|---|---|---|---|---|---|---|---|---|---|---|---|---|
| 07 | — | — | — | — | — | — | — | — | — | — | — | — | — | — | — | — | — | — | — |
| 08 | $3 | -$5 | 50 | +8 | 5 | 0 | 0 | 50-25-25 | 43% | 48% | 27% | 1.205 | — | 1.205 | 1.333 | .775 | 0.57 | — | — |
| 09 | $2 | -$5 | 60 | −8 | 13 | 0 | 0 | 41-17-42 | 12% | 16% | 38% | .644 | .619 | .659 | .571 | .829 | 0.59 | −15 | +36 |
| 10 | -$1 | -$11 | 20 | −6 | 1 | 0 | 0 | 46-14-41 | 24% | 35% | 35% | .597 | .225 | .829 | .542 | .686 | 0.60 | −19 | +46 |

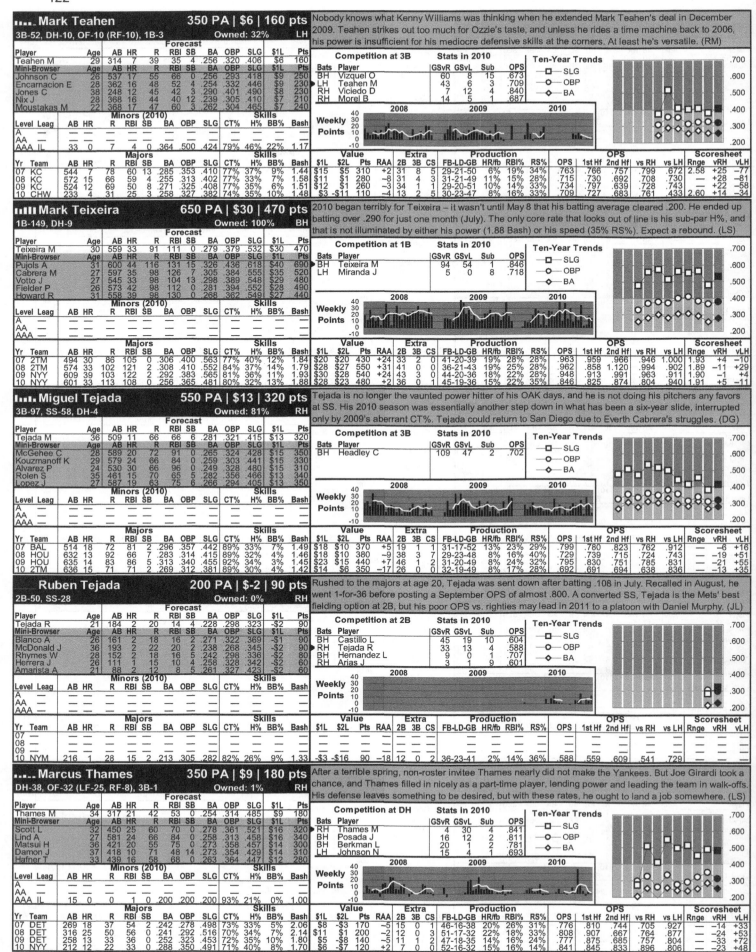

## Mark Teahen — 350 PA | $6 | 160 pts

3B-52, DH-10, OF-10 (RF-10), 1B-3 — Owned: 32% — LH

Nobody knows what Kenny Williams was thinking when he extended Mark Teahen's deal in December 2009. Teahen strikes out too much for Ozzie's taste, and unless he rides a time machine back to 2006, his power is insufficient for his mediocre defensive skills at the corners. At least he's versatile. (RM)

| Player | Age | AB | HR | R | RBI | SB | BA | OBP | SLG | $1L | Pts |
|---|---|---|---|---|---|---|---|---|---|---|---|
| | | Forecast | | | | | | | | | |
| Teahen M | 29 | 314 | 7 | 39 | 35 | 4 | .256 | .320 | .406 | $6 | 160 |
| Mini-Browser | Age | AB | HR | R | RBI | SB | BA | OBP | SLG | $1L | Pts |
| Johnson C | 26 | 537 | 17 | 55 | 66 | 0 | .256 | .293 | .418 | $9 | 250 |
| Encarnacion E | 28 | 362 | 16 | 48 | 52 | 4 | .254 | .332 | .446 | $9 | 230 |
| Jones C | 38 | 248 | 12 | 45 | 42 | 3 | .290 | .401 | .490 | $8 | 230 |
| Nix J | 28 | 368 | 16 | 44 | 40 | 12 | .239 | .305 | .410 | $7 | 210 |
| Moustakas M | 22 | 368 | 17 | 47 | 60 | 3 | .262 | .304 | .465 | $7 | 240 |

**Competition at 3B — Stats in 2010**

| Bats | Player | GSvR | GSvL | Sub | OPS |
|---|---|---|---|---|---|
| BH | Vizquel O | 60 | 8 | 15 | .673 |
| LH | Teahen M | 43 | 6 | 3 | .709 |
| RH | Viciedo D | 7 | 12 | 4 | .840 |
| RH | Morel B | 14 | 5 | 1 | .687 |

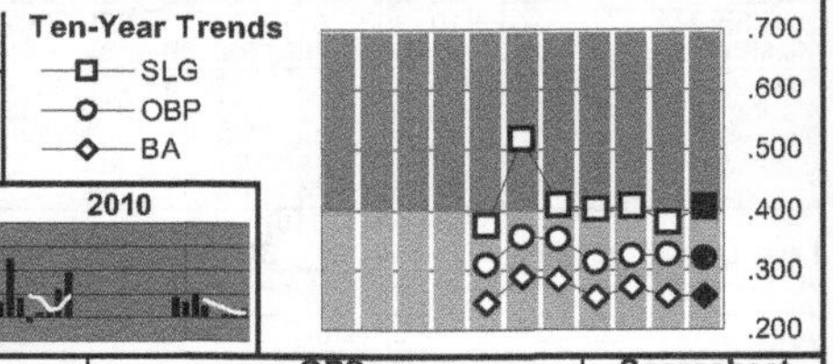


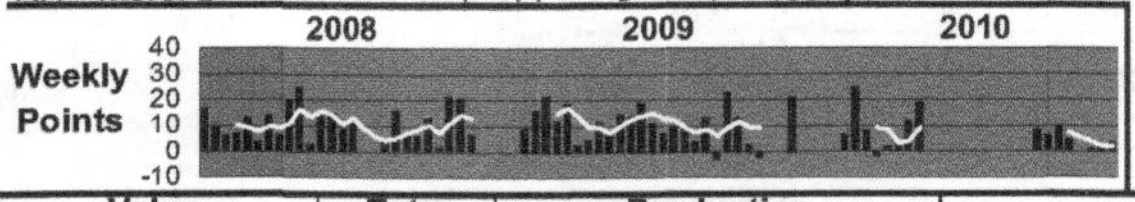


| Level | Leag | AB | HR | R | RBI | SB | BA | OBP | SLG | CT% | H% | BB% | Bash |
|---|---|---|---|---|---|---|---|---|---|---|---|---|---|
| | | Minors (2010) | | | | | | | | Skills | | | |
| A | — | — | — | — | — | — | — | — | — | — | — | — | — |
| AA | — | — | — | — | — | — | — | — | — | — | — | — | — |
| AAA | IL | 33 | 0 | 7 | 4 | 0 | .364 | .500 | .424 | 79% | 46% | 22% | 1.17 |

| Yr | Team | AB | HR | R | RBI | SB | BA | OBP | SLG | CT% | H% | BB% | Bash | $1L | $2L | Pts | RAA | 2B | 3B | CS | FB-LD-GB | HR/fb | RBI% | RS% | OPS | 1st Hf | 2nd Hf | vs RH | vs LH | Rnge | vRH | vLH |
|---|---|---|---|---|---|---|---|---|---|---|---|---|---|---|---|---|---|---|---|---|---|---|---|---|---|---|---|---|---|---|---|---|
| | | Majors | | | | | | | | Skills | | | | Value | | | | Extra | | | Production | | | | OPS | | | | | Scoresheet | | |
| 07 | KC | 544 | 7 | 78 | 60 | 13 | .285 | .353 | .410 | 77% | 37% | 9% | 1.44 | $15 | $5 | 310 | +2 | 31 | 8 | 5 | 29-21-50 | 6% | 19% | 34% | .763 | .766 | .757 | .799 | .672 | 2.58 | +25 | −77 |
| 08 | KC | 572 | 15 | 66 | 59 | 4 | .255 | .313 | .402 | 77% | 33% | 7% | 1.58 | $11 | $1 | 280 | −8 | 31 | 4 | 3 | 31-21-49 | 11% | 15% | 28% | .715 | .730 | .692 | .708 | .730 | — | +28 | −81 |
| 09 | KC | 524 | 12 | 69 | 50 | 8 | .271 | .325 | .408 | 77% | 35% | 6% | 1.51 | $12 | $1 | 260 | −3 | 34 | 1 | 1 | 29-20-51 | 10% | 14% | 33% | .734 | .797 | .639 | .728 | .743 | — | +22 | −58 |
| 10 | CHW | 233 | 4 | 31 | 25 | 3 | .258 | .327 | .382 | 74% | 35% | 10% | 1.48 | $3 | -$11 | 110 | −4 | 13 | 2 | 5 | 30-23-47 | 8% | 16% | 33% | .709 | .727 | .683 | .761 | .433 | 2.60 | +14 | −34 |

## Mark Teixeira — 650 PA | $30 | 470 pts

1B-149, DH-9 — Owned: 100% — BH

2010 began terribly for Teixeira – it wasn't until May 8 that his batting average cleared .200. He ended up batting over .290 for just one month (July). The only core rate that looks out of line is his sub-par H%, and that is not illuminated by either his power (1.88 Bash) or his speed (35% RS%). Expect a rebound. (LS)

| Player | Age | AB | HR | R | RBI | SB | BA | OBP | SLG | $1L | Pts |
|---|---|---|---|---|---|---|---|---|---|---|---|
| | | Forecast | | | | | | | | | |
| Teixeira M | 30 | 559 | 33 | 91 | 111 | 0 | .279 | .379 | .532 | $30 | 470 |
| Mini-Browser | Age | AB | HR | R | RBI | SB | BA | OBP | SLG | $1L | Pts |
| Pujols A | 31 | 600 | 44 | 116 | 131 | 15 | .326 | .436 | .618 | $40 | 690 |
| Cabrera M | 27 | 597 | 35 | 98 | 126 | 7 | .305 | .384 | .555 | $35 | 520 |
| Votto J | 27 | 545 | 33 | 98 | 104 | 13 | .298 | .389 | .548 | $29 | 480 |
| Fielder P | 26 | 573 | 42 | 98 | 112 | 0 | .281 | .394 | .552 | $28 | 490 |
| Howard R | 31 | 558 | 39 | 98 | 130 | 0 | .268 | .362 | .549 | $27 | 440 |

**Competition at 1B — Stats in 2010**

| Bats | Player | GSvR | GSvL | Sub | OPS |
|---|---|---|---|---|---|
| BH | Teixeira M | 94 | 54 | 1 | .846 |
| LH | Miranda J | 5 | 0 | 8 | .718 |

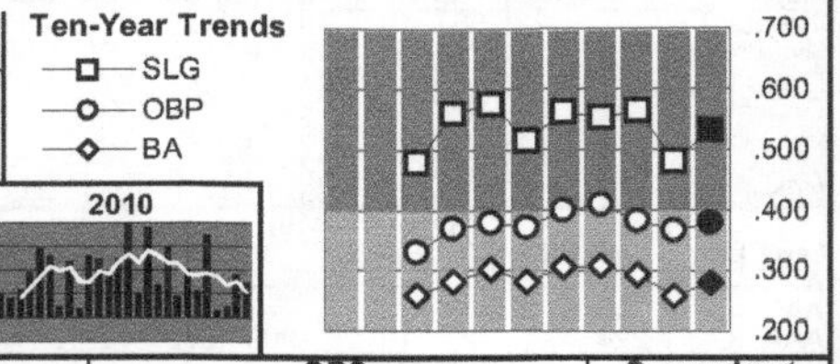


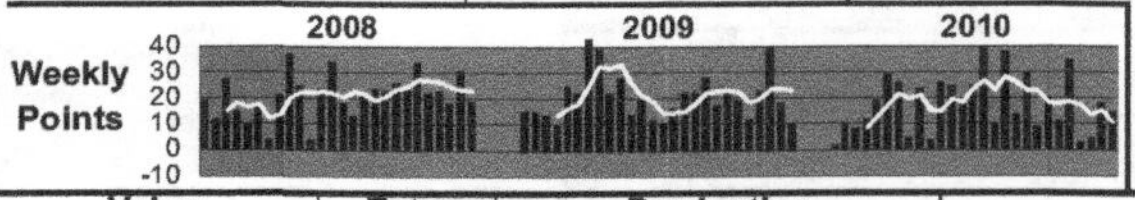


| Level | Leag | AB | HR | R | RBI | SB | BA | OBP | SLG | CT% | H% | BB% | Bash |
|---|---|---|---|---|---|---|---|---|---|---|---|---|---|
| | | Minors (2010) | | | | | | | | Skills | | | |
| A | — | — | — | — | — | — | — | — | — | — | — | — | — |
| AA | — | — | — | — | — | — | — | — | — | — | — | — | — |
| AAA | — | — | — | — | — | — | — | — | — | — | — | — | — |

| Yr | Team | AB | HR | R | RBI | SB | BA | OBP | SLG | CT% | H% | BB% | Bash | $1L | $2L | Pts | RAA | 2B | 3B | CS | FB-LD-GB | HR/fb | RBI% | RS% | OPS | 1st Hf | 2nd Hf | vs RH | vs LH | Rnge | vRH | vLH |
|---|---|---|---|---|---|---|---|---|---|---|---|---|---|---|---|---|---|---|---|---|---|---|---|---|---|---|---|---|---|---|---|---|
| | | Majors | | | | | | | | Skills | | | | Value | | | | Extra | | | Production | | | | OPS | | | | | Scoresheet | | |
| 07 | 2TM | 494 | 30 | 86 | 105 | 0 | .306 | .400 | .563 | 77% | 40% | 12% | 1.84 | $20 | $20 | 430 | +24 | 33 | 2 | 0 | 41-20-39 | 19% | 28% | 28% | .963 | .959 | .966 | .946 | 1.000 | 1.93 | +4 | −10 |
| 08 | 2TM | 574 | 33 | 102 | 121 | 2 | .308 | .410 | .552 | 84% | 37% | 14% | 1.79 | $28 | $27 | 550 | +31 | 41 | 0 | 0 | 36-21-43 | 19% | 25% | 28% | .962 | .858 | 1.120 | .994 | .902 | 1.89 | −11 | +29 |
| 09 | NYY | 609 | 39 | 103 | 122 | 2 | .292 | .383 | .565 | 81% | 36% | 11% | 1.93 | $30 | $28 | 540 | +24 | 43 | 3 | 0 | 44-20-36 | 18% | 22% | 28% | .948 | .913 | .991 | .963 | .911 | 1.90 | −1 | +4 |
| 10 | NYY | 601 | 33 | 113 | 108 | 0 | .256 | .365 | .481 | 80% | 32% | 13% | 1.88 | $28 | $23 | 480 | +2 | 36 | 0 | 1 | 45-19-36 | 15% | 22% | 35% | .846 | .825 | .874 | .804 | .940 | 1.91 | +5 | −11 |

## Miguel Tejada — 550 PA | $13 | 320 pts

3B-97, SS-58, DH-4 — Owned: 81% — RH

Tejada is no longer the vaunted power hitter of his OAK days, and he is not doing his pitchers any favors at SS. His 2010 season was essentially another step down in what has been a six-year slide, interrupted only by 2009's aberrant CT%. Tejada could return to San Diego due to Everth Cabrera's struggles. (DG)

| Player | Age | AB | HR | R | RBI | SB | BA | OBP | SLG | $1L | Pts |
|---|---|---|---|---|---|---|---|---|---|---|---|
| | | Forecast | | | | | | | | | |
| Tejada M | 36 | 509 | 11 | 66 | 66 | 6 | .281 | .321 | .415 | $13 | 320 |
| Mini-Browser | Age | AB | HR | R | RBI | SB | BA | OBP | SLG | $1L | Pts |
| McGehee C | 28 | 589 | 20 | 72 | 91 | 0 | .265 | .324 | .428 | $15 | 350 |
| Kouzmanoff K | 29 | 579 | 24 | 66 | 84 | 0 | .259 | .303 | .441 | $15 | 330 |
| Alvarez P | 24 | 530 | 30 | 66 | 96 | 0 | .249 | .328 | .480 | $15 | 310 |
| Rolen S | 35 | 461 | 15 | 70 | 65 | 5 | .282 | .356 | .466 | $13 | 340 |
| Lopez J | 27 | 587 | 19 | 63 | 75 | 6 | .266 | .294 | .405 | $13 | 350 |

**Competition at 3B — Stats in 2010**

| Bats | Player | GSvR | GSvL | Sub | OPS |
|---|---|---|---|---|---|
| BH | Headley C | 109 | 47 | 2 | .702 |

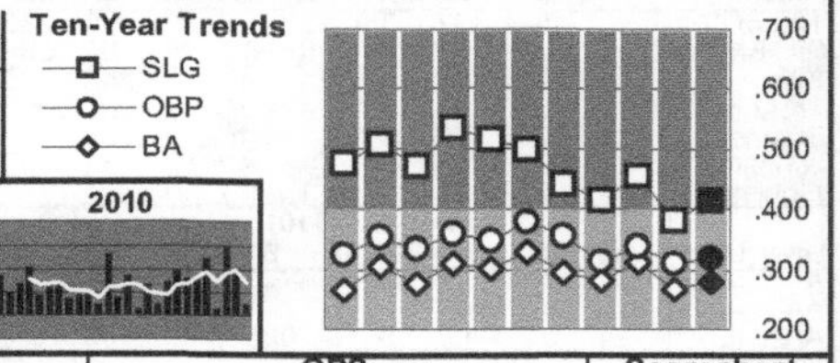


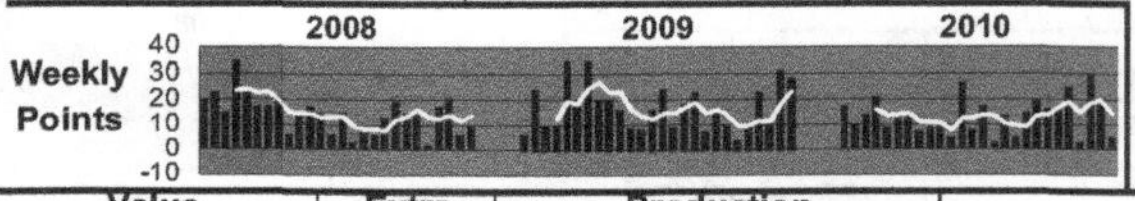


| Level | Leag | AB | HR | R | RBI | SB | BA | OBP | SLG | CT% | H% | BB% | Bash |
|---|---|---|---|---|---|---|---|---|---|---|---|---|---|
| | | Minors (2010) | | | | | | | | Skills | | | |
| A | — | — | — | — | — | — | — | — | — | — | — | — | — |
| AA | — | — | — | — | — | — | — | — | — | — | — | — | — |
| AAA | — | — | — | — | — | — | — | — | — | — | — | — | — |

| Yr | Team | AB | HR | R | RBI | SB | BA | OBP | SLG | CT% | H% | BB% | Bash | $1L | $2L | Pts | RAA | 2B | 3B | CS | FB-LD-GB | HR/fb | RBI% | RS% | OPS | 1st Hf | 2nd Hf | vs RH | vs LH | Rnge | vRH | vLH |
|---|---|---|---|---|---|---|---|---|---|---|---|---|---|---|---|---|---|---|---|---|---|---|---|---|---|---|---|---|---|---|---|---|
| | | Majors | | | | | | | | Skills | | | | Value | | | | Extra | | | Production | | | | OPS | | | | | Scoresheet | | |
| 07 | BAL | 514 | 18 | 72 | 81 | 2 | .296 | .357 | .442 | 89% | 33% | 7% | 1.49 | $18 | $10 | 370 | +5 | 19 | 1 | 1 | 31-17-52 | 13% | 23% | 29% | .799 | .780 | .823 | .762 | .912 | — | −6 | +16 |
| 08 | HOU | 632 | 13 | 92 | 66 | 7 | .283 | .314 | .415 | 89% | 32% | 4% | 1.46 | $18 | $10 | 380 | −9 | 38 | 3 | 7 | 29-23-48 | 8% | 16% | 40% | .729 | .739 | .715 | .724 | .743 | — | −19 | +51 |
| 09 | HOU | 635 | 14 | 83 | 86 | 5 | .313 | .340 | .455 | 92% | 34% | 3% | 1.45 | $23 | $15 | 440 | +7 | 46 | 1 | 2 | 31-20-49 | 8% | 24% | 32% | .795 | .830 | .751 | .785 | .831 | — | −21 | +55 |
| 10 | 2TM | 636 | 15 | 71 | 71 | 2 | .269 | .312 | .381 | 89% | 30% | 4% | 1.42 | $14 | $6 | 350 | −17 | 26 | 0 | 0 | 32-19-49 | 8% | 17% | 28% | .692 | .691 | .694 | .638 | .836 | — | −13 | +35 |

## Ruben Tejada — 200 PA | $-2 | 90 pts

2B-50, SS-28 — Owned: 0% — RH

Rushed to the majors at age 20, Tejada was sent down after batting .108 in July. Recalled in August, he went 1-for-36 before posting a September OPS of almost .800. A converted SS, Tejada is the Mets' best fielding option at 2B, but his poor OPS vs. righties may lead in 2011 to a platoon with Daniel Murphy. (JL)

| Player | Age | AB | HR | R | RBI | SB | BA | OBP | SLG | $1L | Pts |
|---|---|---|---|---|---|---|---|---|---|---|---|
| | | Forecast | | | | | | | | | |
| Tejada R | 21 | 184 | 2 | 20 | 14 | 4 | .228 | .298 | .323 | -$2 | 90 |
| Mini-Browser | Age | AB | HR | R | RBI | SB | BA | OBP | SLG | $1L | Pts |
| Blanco A | 26 | 161 | 2 | 18 | 16 | 2 | .271 | .322 | .369 | -$1 | 90 |
| McDonald J | 36 | 193 | 2 | 22 | 20 | 2 | .238 | .268 | .345 | -$2 | 90 |
| Rhymes W | 28 | 152 | 2 | 18 | 16 | 5 | .242 | .298 | .336 | -$2 | 80 |
| Herrera J | 26 | 111 | 1 | 15 | 10 | 4 | .258 | .328 | .342 | -$2 | 60 |
| Amarista A | 21 | 88 | 2 | 12 | 8 | 5 | .261 | .327 | .423 | -$2 | 60 |

**Competition at 2B — Stats in 2010**

| Bats | Player | GSvR | GSvL | Sub | OPS |
|---|---|---|---|---|---|
| BH | Castillo L | 45 | 19 | 10 | .604 |
| RH | Tejada R | 33 | 13 | 4 | .588 |
| BH | Hernandez L | 9 | 0 | 1 | .707 |
| RH | Arias J | 3 | 1 | 9 | .601 |

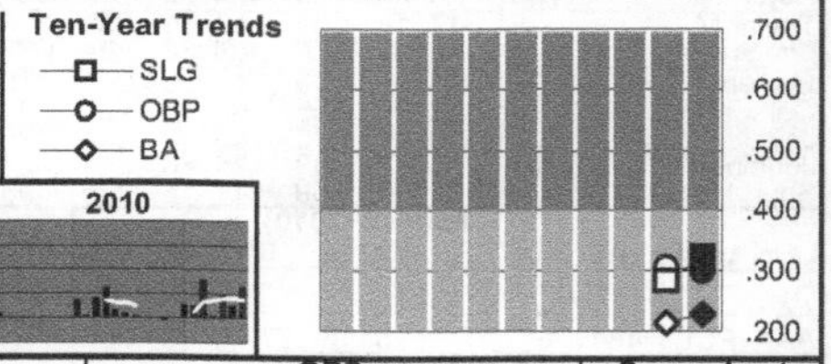


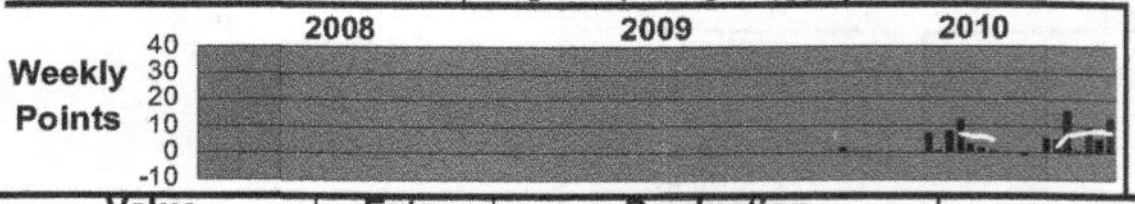


| Level | Leag | AB | HR | R | RBI | SB | BA | OBP | SLG | CT% | H% | BB% | Bash |
|---|---|---|---|---|---|---|---|---|---|---|---|---|---|
| | | Minors (2010) | | | | | | | | Skills | | | |
| A | — | — | — | — | — | — | — | — | — | — | — | — | — |
| AA | — | — | — | — | — | — | — | — | — | — | — | — | — |
| AAA | — | — | — | — | — | — | — | — | — | — | — | — | — |

| Yr | Team | AB | HR | R | RBI | SB | BA | OBP | SLG | CT% | H% | BB% | Bash | $1L | $2L | Pts | RAA | 2B | 3B | CS | FB-LD-GB | HR/fb | RBI% | RS% | OPS | 1st Hf | 2nd Hf | vs RH | vs LH | Rnge | vRH | vLH |
|---|---|---|---|---|---|---|---|---|---|---|---|---|---|---|---|---|---|---|---|---|---|---|---|---|---|---|---|---|---|---|---|---|
| | | Majors | | | | | | | | Skills | | | | Value | | | | Extra | | | Production | | | | OPS | | | | | Scoresheet | | |
| 07 | — | — | — | — | — | — | — | — | — | — | — | — | — | — | — | — | — | — | — | — | — | — | — | — | — | — | — | — | — | — | — | — |
| 08 | — | — | — | — | — | — | — | — | — | — | — | — | — | — | — | — | — | — | — | — | — | — | — | — | — | — | — | — | — | — | — | — |
| 09 | — | — | — | — | — | — | — | — | — | — | — | — | — | — | — | — | — | — | — | — | — | — | — | — | — | — | — | — | — | — | — | — |
| 10 | NYM | 216 | 1 | 28 | 15 | 2 | .213 | .305 | .282 | 82% | 26% | 9% | 1.33 | -$3 | -$16 | 90 | −18 | 12 | 0 | 2 | 36-23-41 | 2% | 14% | 36% | .588 | .559 | .609 | .541 | .729 | — | — | — |

## Marcus Thames — 350 PA | $9 | 180 pts

DH-38, OF-32 (LF-25, RF-8), 3B-1 — Owned: 1% — RH

After a terrible spring, non-roster invitee Thames nearly did not make the Yankees. But Joe Girardi took a chance, and Thames filled in nicely as a part-time player, lending power and leading the team in walk-offs. His defense leaves something to be desired, but with these rates, he ought to land a job somewhere. (LS)

| Player | Age | AB | HR | R | RBI | SB | BA | OBP | SLG | $1L | Pts |
|---|---|---|---|---|---|---|---|---|---|---|---|
| | | Forecast | | | | | | | | | |
| Thames M | 34 | 317 | 21 | 42 | 53 | 0 | .254 | .314 | .485 | $9 | 180 |
| Mini-Browser | Age | AB | HR | R | RBI | SB | BA | OBP | SLG | $1L | Pts |
| Scott L | 32 | 450 | 25 | 60 | 70 | 0 | .278 | .361 | .521 | $16 | 320 |
| Lind A | 27 | 581 | 24 | 66 | 84 | 0 | .258 | .313 | .458 | $16 | 340 |
| Matsui H | 36 | 421 | 20 | 55 | 75 | 0 | .273 | .358 | .457 | $14 | 300 |
| Damon J | 37 | 418 | 10 | 71 | 48 | 14 | .273 | .354 | .429 | $14 | 310 |
| Hafner T | 33 | 439 | 16 | 58 | 68 | 0 | .263 | .364 | .447 | $12 | 280 |

**Competition at DH — Stats in 2010**

| Bats | Player | GSvR | GSvL | Sub | OPS |
|---|---|---|---|---|---|
| RH | Thames M | 4 | 30 | 4 | .841 |
| BH | Posada J | 16 | 12 | 2 | .811 |
| BH | Berkman L | 20 | 1 | 2 | .781 |
| LH | Johnson N | 15 | 4 | 1 | .693 |

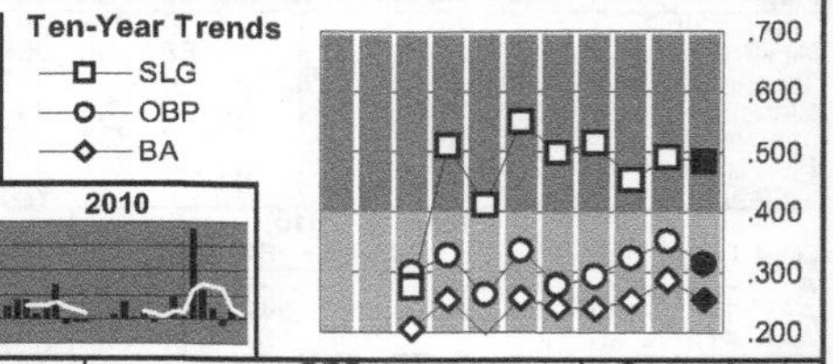


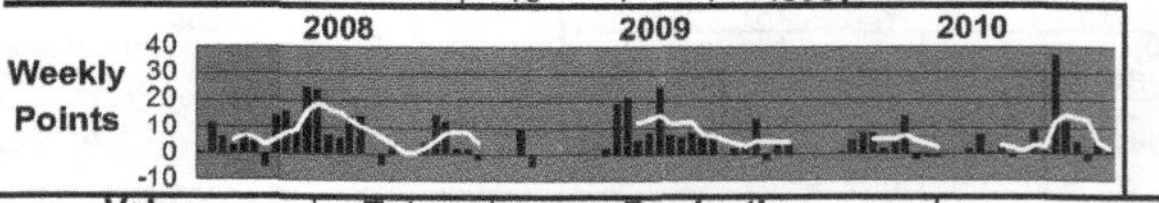


| Level | Leag | AB | HR | R | RBI | SB | BA | OBP | SLG | CT% | H% | BB% | Bash |
|---|---|---|---|---|---|---|---|---|---|---|---|---|---|
| | | Minors (2010) | | | | | | | | Skills | | | |
| A | — | — | — | — | — | — | — | — | — | — | — | — | — |
| AA | — | — | — | — | — | — | — | — | — | — | — | — | — |
| AAA | IL | 15 | 0 | 0 | 1 | 0 | .200 | .200 | .200 | 93% | 21% | 0% | 1.00 |

| Yr | Team | AB | HR | R | RBI | SB | BA | OBP | SLG | CT% | H% | BB% | Bash | $1L | $2L | Pts | RAA | 2B | 3B | CS | FB-LD-GB | HR/fb | RBI% | RS% | OPS | 1st Hf | 2nd Hf | vs RH | vs LH | Rnge | vRH | vLH |
|---|---|---|---|---|---|---|---|---|---|---|---|---|---|---|---|---|---|---|---|---|---|---|---|---|---|---|---|---|---|---|---|---|
| | | Majors | | | | | | | | Skills | | | | Value | | | | Extra | | | Production | | | | OPS | | | | | Scoresheet | | |
| 07 | DET | 269 | 18 | 37 | 54 | 2 | .242 | .278 | .498 | 73% | 33% | 5% | 2.06 | $8 | -$3 | 170 | −5 | 15 | 0 | 1 | 46-16-38 | 20% | 26% | 31% | .776 | .810 | .744 | .705 | .927 | — | −14 | +33 |
| 08 | DET | 316 | 25 | 50 | 56 | 0 | .241 | .292 | .516 | 70% | 34% | 7% | 2.14 | $11 | $1 | 200 | −2 | 12 | 0 | 3 | 51-17-32 | 22% | 18% | 33% | .808 | .907 | .667 | .764 | .877 | — | −24 | +53 |
| 09 | DET | 258 | 13 | 33 | 36 | 0 | .252 | .323 | .453 | 72% | 35% | 10% | 1.80 | $5 | -$8 | 140 | −5 | 11 | 1 | 2 | 47-18-35 | 14% | 16% | 24% | .777 | .875 | .685 | .757 | .804 | — | −33 | +72 |
| 10 | NYY | 212 | 12 | 22 | 33 | 0 | .288 | .350 | .491 | 71% | 40% | 8% | 1.70 | $6 | -$7 | 120 | +2 | 7 | 0 | 0 | 52-16-32 | 15% | 16% | 14% | .841 | .845 | .833 | .896 | .806 | — | −23 | +48 |

*For more stats, visit www.Rotolympus.com.*

## Ryan Theriot — 600 PA | $14 | 360 pts

2B-119, SS-29 — Owned: 81% — RH

Theriot in 2010 was arguably the worst full-time second baseman in baseball. He was allergic to extra-base hits, logging a 1.16 Bash (which explains the 29 RBI in 586 PA). Unfortunately, the Dodgers have few options, and Theriot will probably be their starting 2B again in 2011. His fielding wasn't half-bad.... (MP)

| Player | Age | AB | HR | R | RBI | SB | BA | OBP | SLG | $1L | Pts |
|---|---|---|---|---|---|---|---|---|---|---|---|
| **Forecast** | | | | | | | | | | | |
| Theriot R | 31 | 557 | 6 | 78 | 42 | 24 | .280 | .346 | .351 | $14 | 360 |
| **Mini-Browser** | | | | | | | | | | | |
| Prado M | 27 | 591 | 13 | 91 | 65 | 7 | .297 | .351 | .444 | $18 | 400 |
| Kendrick H | 27 | 572 | 12 | 72 | 72 | 12 | .283 | .318 | .420 | $18 | 340 |
| Beckham G | 24 | 553 | 19 | 75 | 75 | 6 | .260 | .326 | .423 | $15 | 340 |
| Walker N | 25 | 551 | 18 | 72 | 78 | 6 | .272 | .326 | .461 | $15 | 350 |
| Ackley D | 23 | 354 | 11 | 54 | 35 | 8 | .251 | .338 | .409 | $15 | 230 |

| Level | Leag | AB | HR | R | RBI | SB | BA | OBP | SLG | CT% | H% | BB% | Bash |
|---|---|---|---|---|---|---|---|---|---|---|---|---|---|
| **Minors (2010)** | | | | | | | | | | **Skills** | | | |
| A | — | — | — | — | — | — | — | — | — | — | — | — | — |
| AA | — | — | — | — | — | — | — | — | — | — | — | — | — |
| AAA | — | — | — | — | — | — | — | — | — | — | — | — | — |

| Bats | Player | GSvR | GSvL | Sub | OPS |
|---|---|---|---|---|---|
| **Competition at 2B** | | **Stats in 2010** | | | |
| RH | Theriot R | 36 | 14 | 3 | .633 |
| RH | Carroll J | 9 | 16 | 23 | .718 |
| RH | Belliard R | 7 | 11 | 2 | .622 |

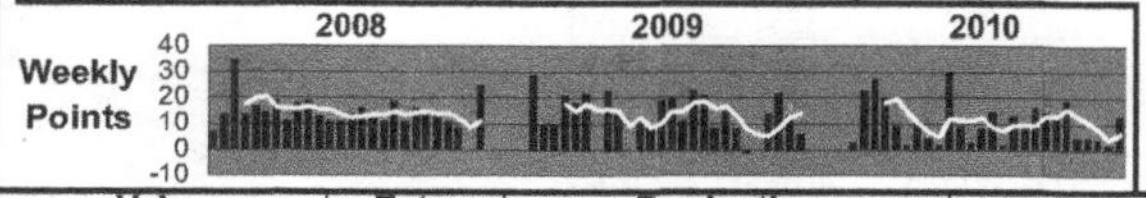


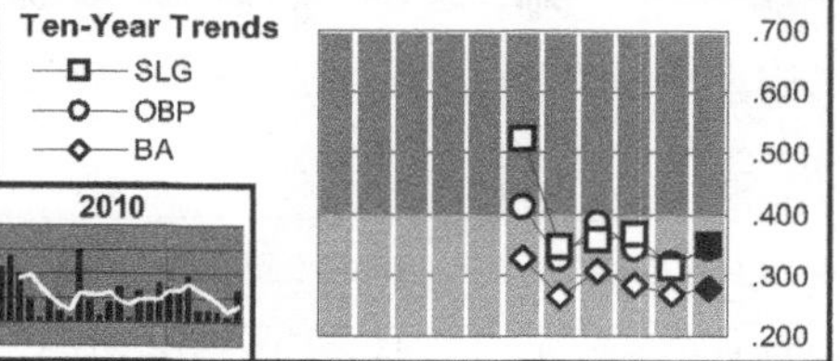


| Yr | Team | AB | HR | R | RBI | SB | BA | OBP | SLG | CT% | H% | BB% | Bash |
|---|---|---|---|---|---|---|---|---|---|---|---|---|---|
| **Majors** | | | | | | | | | | **Skills** | | | |
| 07 | CHC | 537 | 3 | 80 | 45 | 28 | .266 | .326 | .346 | 91% | 29% | 8% | 1.30 |
| 08 | CHC | 580 | 1 | 85 | 38 | 22 | .307 | .387 | .359 | 90% | 34% | 11% | 1.17 |
| 09 | CHC | 602 | 7 | 81 | 54 | 21 | .284 | .343 | .369 | 85% | 34% | 8% | 1.30 |
| 10 | 2TM | 586 | 2 | 72 | 29 | 20 | .270 | .321 | .312 | 87% | 31% | 6% | 1.16 |

| Yr | $1L | $2L | Pts | RAA | 2B | 3B | CS | FB-LD-GB | HR/fb | RBI% | RS% | OPS | 1st Hf | 2nd Hf | vs RH | vs LH | Rnge | vRH | vLH |
|---|---|---|---|---|---|---|---|---|---|---|---|---|---|---|---|---|---|---|---|
| | **Value** | | | | **Extra** | | | **Production** | | | | **OPS** | | | | | **Scoresheet** | | |
| 07 | $13 | $4 | 360 | –6 | 30 | 2 | 4 | 30-21-49 | 2% | 19% | 41% | .672 | .692 | .654 | .634 | .797 | 4.25 | –23 | +53 |
| 08 | $18 | $8 | 380 | +8 | 19 | 4 | 13 | 20-23-57 | 1% | 15% | 33% | .745 | .763 | .719 | .734 | .778 | — | –30 | +77 |
| 09 | $18 | $8 | 350 | –8 | 20 | 5 | 10 | 30-20-50 | 5% | 18% | 33% | .712 | .777 | .634 | .690 | .799 | — | –24 | +65 |
| 10 | $12 | $1 | 280 | –22 | 15 | 2 | 9 | 26-20-54 | 2% | 12% | 35% | .633 | .631 | .636 | .617 | .673 | — | –17 | +49 |

## Josh Thole — 475 PA | $5 | 210 pts

CA-61 — Owned: 1% — LH

Thole is a singles hitter with good rates of CT% and BB% and bad splits versus lefties. His playing time in 2011 depends on the Mets' choice of partner: If 39-year-old Henry Blanco is the back-up, Thole could play 140 games, but if the Mets bring in a younger right-hander with pop, Thole could end up sharing time. (JL)

| Player | Age | AB | HR | R | RBI | SB | BA | OBP | SLG | $1L | Pts |
|---|---|---|---|---|---|---|---|---|---|---|---|
| **Forecast** | | | | | | | | | | | |
| Thole J | 24 | 410 | 5 | 38 | 43 | 5 | .243 | .320 | .338 | $5 | 210 |
| **Mini-Browser** | | | | | | | | | | | |
| Hernandez R | 34 | 278 | 9 | 27 | 39 | 0 | .270 | .338 | .411 | $6 | 170 |
| Pena B | 29 | 278 | 6 | 27 | 33 | 3 | .281 | .329 | .412 | $6 | 160 |
| Torrealba Y | 32 | 289 | 6 | 29 | 38 | 3 | .266 | .329 | .383 | $6 | 150 |
| Conger H | 23 | 276 | 9 | 27 | 42 | 3 | .239 | .299 | .415 | $5 | 160 |
| Mathis J | 28 | 362 | 8 | 40 | 44 | 4 | .221 | .282 | .341 | $5 | 130 |

| Level | Leag | AB | HR | R | RBI | SB | BA | OBP | SLG | CT% | H% | BB% | Bash |
|---|---|---|---|---|---|---|---|---|---|---|---|---|---|
| **Minors (2010)** | | | | | | | | | | **Skills** | | | |
| A | — | — | — | — | — | — | — | — | — | — | — | — | — |
| AA | — | — | — | — | — | — | — | — | — | — | — | — | — |
| AAA | IL | 165 | 2 | 20 | 17 | 0 | .267 | .353 | .430 | 85% | 31% | 12% | 1.61 |

| Bats | Player | GSvR | GSvL | Sub | OPS |
|---|---|---|---|---|---|
| **Competition at CA** | | **Stats in 2010** | | | |
| LH | Thole J | 49 | 2 | 10 | .723 |
| RH | Blanco H | 25 | 16 | 5 | .571 |

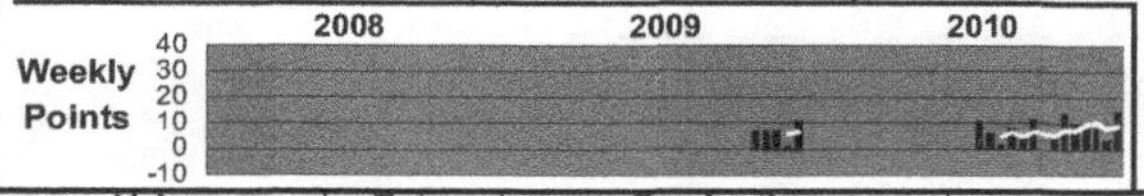


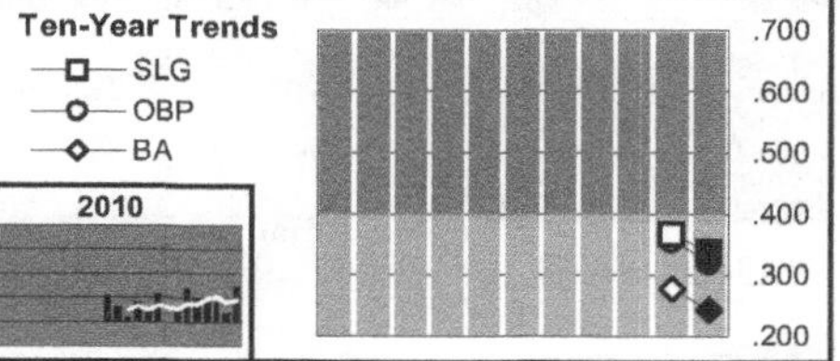


| Yr | Team | AB | HR | R | RBI | SB | BA | OBP | SLG | CT% | H% | BB% | Bash |
|---|---|---|---|---|---|---|---|---|---|---|---|---|---|
| **Majors** | | | | | | | | | | **Skills** | | | |
| 07 | — | — | — | — | — | — | — | — | — | — | — | — | — |
| 08 | — | — | — | — | — | — | — | — | — | — | — | — | — |
| 09 | NYM | 53 | 0 | 2 | 9 | 1 | .321 | .356 | .396 | 91% | 35% | 7% | 1.24 |
| 10 | NYM | 202 | 3 | 17 | 17 | 1 | .277 | .357 | .366 | 88% | 32% | 11% | 1.32 |

| Yr | $1L | $2L | Pts | RAA | 2B | 3B | CS | FB-LD-GB | HR/fb | RBI% | RS% | OPS | 1st Hf | 2nd Hf | vs RH | vs LH | Rnge | vRH | vLH |
|---|---|---|---|---|---|---|---|---|---|---|---|---|---|---|---|---|---|---|---|
| | **Value** | | | | **Extra** | | | **Production** | | | | **OPS** | | | | | **Scoresheet** | | |
| 07 | — | — | — | — | — | — | — | — | — | — | — | — | — | — | — | — | — | — | — |
| 08 | — | — | — | — | — | — | — | — | — | — | — | — | — | — | — | — | — | — | — |
| 09 | $0 | -$9 | 30 | +1 | 2 | 1 | 0 | 20-34-46 | 0% | 33% | 10% | .752 | — | .752 | .783 | .600 | — | — | — |
| 10 | $3 | -$6 | 110 | +1 | 7 | 1 | 0 | 33-23-44 | 5% | 15% | 18% | .723 | 1.188 | .679 | .783 | .343 | 0.56 | +24 | –74 |

## Clete Thomas — 100 PA | $-3 | 50 pts

No MLB games played in 2010 — Owned: 0% — LH

Thomas missed most of 2010 with a knee injury, but he is still in the picture for 2011. He does not make enough contact to be a regular, but his acceptable rates, and ability to play all three OF spots, make him an ideal 4th OF. He will probably open 2011 in Triple-A, but he should be in Detroit by season's end. (LP)

| Player | Age | AB | HR | R | RBI | SB | BA | OBP | SLG | $1L | Pts |
|---|---|---|---|---|---|---|---|---|---|---|---|
| **Forecast** | | | | | | | | | | | |
| Thomas C | 27 | 88 | 2 | 11 | 9 | 4 | .238 | .320 | .380 | -$3 | 50 |
| **Mini-Browser** | | | | | | | | | | | |
| Paul X | 26 | 91 | 2 | 11 | 10 | 3 | .241 | .304 | .371 | -$3 | 50 |
| Bogusevic B | 27 | 89 | 2 | 10 | 9 | 3 | .248 | .325 | .366 | -$3 | 40 |
| Tuiasosopo M | 24 | 132 | 5 | 15 | 15 | 0 | .227 | .316 | .377 | -$3 | 60 |
| Roberts R | 30 | 67 | 2 | 9 | 8 | 2 | .267 | .355 | .426 | -$3 | 50 |
| Ryal R | 28 | 90 | 3 | 11 | 10 | 0 | .245 | .297 | .423 | -$3 | 40 |

| Level | Leag | AB | HR | R | RBI | SB | BA | OBP | SLG | CT% | H% | BB% | Bash |
|---|---|---|---|---|---|---|---|---|---|---|---|---|---|
| **Minors (2010)** | | | | | | | | | | **Skills** | | | |
| A | — | — | — | — | — | — | — | — | — | — | — | — | — |
| AA | — | — | — | — | — | — | — | — | — | — | — | — | — |
| AAA | IL | 71 | 4 | 14 | 13 | 9 | .183 | .318 | .408 | 55% | 33% | 14% | 2.23 |

| Bats | Player | GSvR | GSvL | Sub | OPS |
|---|---|---|---|---|---|
| **Competition at CF** | | **Stats in 2010** | | | |
| RH | Jackson A | 95 | 45 | 9 | .745 |
| LH | Kelly D | 11 | 0 | 1 | .646 |

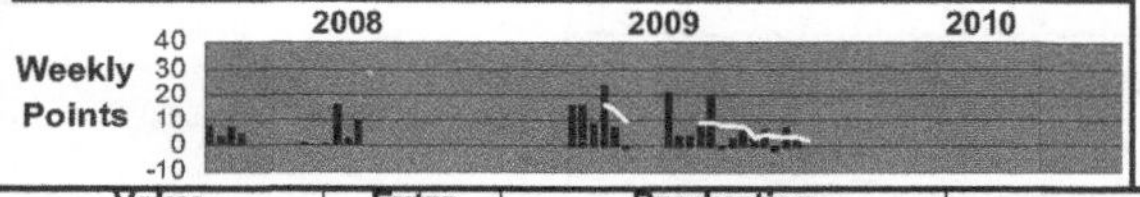


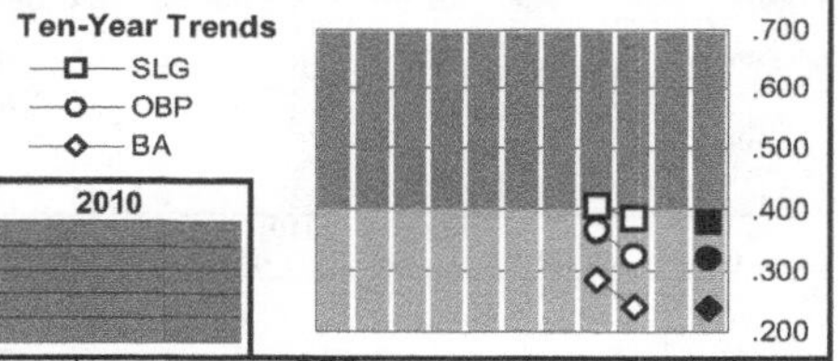


| Yr | Team | AB | HR | R | RBI | SB | BA | OBP | SLG | CT% | H% | BB% | Bash |
|---|---|---|---|---|---|---|---|---|---|---|---|---|---|
| **Majors** | | | | | | | | | | **Skills** | | | |
| 07 | — | — | — | — | — | — | — | — | — | — | — | — | — |
| 08 | DET | 116 | 1 | 7 | 9 | 2 | .284 | .366 | .405 | 78% | 37% | 10% | 1.42 |
| 09 | DET | 275 | 7 | 46 | 39 | 3 | .240 | .324 | .385 | 72% | 33% | 11% | 1.61 |
| 10 | — | — | — | — | — | — | — | — | — | — | — | — | — |

| Yr | $1L | $2L | Pts | RAA | 2B | 3B | CS | FB-LD-GB | HR/fb | RBI% | RS% | OPS | 1st Hf | 2nd Hf | vs RH | vs LH | Rnge | vRH | vLH |
|---|---|---|---|---|---|---|---|---|---|---|---|---|---|---|---|---|---|---|---|
| | **Value** | | | | **Extra** | | | **Production** | | | | **OPS** | | | | | **Scoresheet** | | |
| 07 | — | — | — | — | — | — | — | — | — | — | — | — | — | — | — | — | — | — | — |
| 08 | -$2 | -$15 | 60 | +2 | 9 | 1 | 0 | 41-19-40 | 3% | 16% | 13% | .772 | .772 | — | .746 | .902 | — | — | — |
| 09 | $5 | -$8 | 150 | –2 | 13 | 3 | 0 | 36-16-48 | 10% | 21% | 42% | .709 | .808 | .624 | .721 | .654 | 2.12 | +18 | –59 |
| 10 | — | — | — | — | — | — | — | — | — | — | — | — | — | — | — | — | 2.11 | +18 | –57 |

## Jim Thome — 275 PA | $5 | 150 pts

DH-78 — Owned: 5% — LH

By turning in one of the best seasons of his Hall of Fame career at age 39, Thome in 2010 dashed notions that he was done as a productive player. He would surely like to return to Minnesota, but the aging slugger would probably command a raise, and his Ten-Year Trends show what an oddity 2010 was. (NN)

| Player | Age | AB | HR | R | RBI | SB | BA | OBP | SLG | $1L | Pts |
|---|---|---|---|---|---|---|---|---|---|---|---|
| **Forecast** | | | | | | | | | | | |
| Thome J | 40 | 231 | 14 | 36 | 44 | 0 | .238 | .355 | .470 | $5 | 150 |
| **Mini-Browser** | | | | | | | | | | | |
| Matsui H | 36 | 421 | 20 | 55 | 75 | 0 | .273 | .358 | .457 | $14 | 300 |
| Damon J | 37 | 418 | 10 | 71 | 48 | 14 | .273 | .354 | .429 | $14 | 310 |
| Hafner T | 33 | 439 | 16 | 58 | 68 | 0 | .263 | .364 | .447 | $12 | 280 |
| Thames M | 34 | 317 | 21 | 42 | 53 | 0 | .254 | .314 | .485 | $9 | 180 |
| Cust J | 32 | 328 | 16 | 48 | 52 | 0 | .232 | .363 | .427 | $7 | 170 |

| Level | Leag | AB | HR | R | RBI | SB | BA | OBP | SLG | CT% | H% | BB% | Bash |
|---|---|---|---|---|---|---|---|---|---|---|---|---|---|
| **Minors (2010)** | | | | | | | | | | **Skills** | | | |
| A | — | — | — | — | — | — | — | — | — | — | — | — | — |
| AA | — | — | — | — | — | — | — | — | — | — | — | — | — |
| AAA | — | — | — | — | — | — | — | — | — | — | — | — | — |

| Bats | Player | GSvR | GSvL | Sub | OPS |
|---|---|---|---|---|---|
| **Competition at DH** | | **Stats in 2010** | | | |
| LH | Thome J | 60 | 18 | 0 | 1.039 |
| LH | Kubel J | 24 | 18 | 0 | .750 |
| LH | Mauer J | 9 | 13 | 0 | .871 |

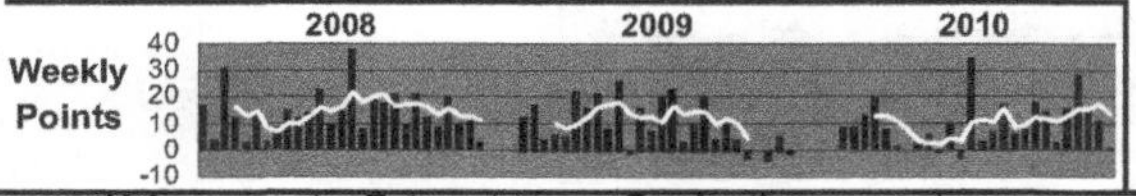


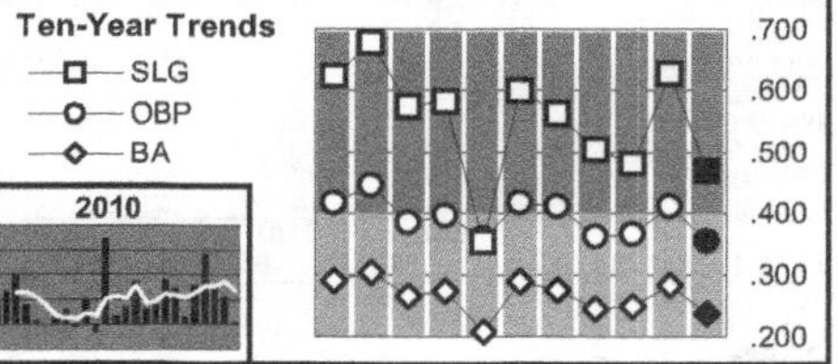


| Yr | Team | AB | HR | R | RBI | SB | BA | OBP | SLG | CT% | H% | BB% | Bash |
|---|---|---|---|---|---|---|---|---|---|---|---|---|---|
| **Majors** | | | | | | | | | | **Skills** | | | |
| 07 | CHW | 432 | 35 | 79 | 96 | 0 | .275 | .410 | .563 | 69% | 40% | 17% | 2.04 |
| 08 | CHW | 503 | 34 | 93 | 90 | 1 | .245 | .362 | .503 | 71% | 35% | 15% | 2.06 |
| 09 | 2TM | 362 | 23 | 55 | 77 | 0 | .249 | .366 | .481 | 66% | 38% | 16% | 1.93 |
| 10 | MIN | 276 | 25 | 48 | 59 | 0 | .283 | .412 | .627 | 70% | 40% | 17% | 2.22 |

| Yr | $1L | $2L | Pts | RAA | 2B | 3B | CS | FB-LD-GB | HR/fb | RBI% | RS% | OPS | 1st Hf | 2nd Hf | vs RH | vs LH | Rnge | vRH | vLH |
|---|---|---|---|---|---|---|---|---|---|---|---|---|---|---|---|---|---|---|---|
| | **Value** | | | | **Extra** | | | **Production** | | | | **OPS** | | | | | **Scoresheet** | | |
| 07 | $22 | $16 | 380 | +26 | 19 | 0 | 1 | 39-18-43 | 30% | 28% | 24% | .973 | .978 | .967 | 1.123 | .663 | 2.11 | +58 | –145 |
| 08 | $21 | $13 | 380 | +10 | 28 | 0 | 0 | 42-18-40 | 23% | 21% | 32% | .865 | .884 | .839 | .868 | .858 | 2.11 | +71 | –175 |
| 09 | $8 | $4 | 250 | +8 | 15 | 0 | 0 | 36-20-44 | 26% | 26% | 24% | .847 | .891 | .773 | .881 | .743 | 2.11 | +39 | –103 |
| 10 | $16 | $6 | 260 | +24 | 16 | 2 | 0 | 38-21-41 | 34% | 21% | 20% | 1.039 | .929 | 1.158 | 1.154 | .769 | — | +21 | –60 |

## Matt Tolbert — 100 PA | $-3 | 50 pts

2B-20, 3B-14, 1B-4, SS-3, DH-2, OF-1 (RF-1) — Owned: 0% — BH

The versatile Tolbert possesses basically every trait that the Twins like in a UT man: He hustles, he fields competently, and he holds his own at the plate. Oh, and he is inexpensive. We can look forward to seeing Tolbert playing in Target Field (albeit in a limited role) for years to come. (NN)

| Player | Age | AB | HR | R | RBI | SB | BA | OBP | SLG | $1L | Pts |
|---|---|---|---|---|---|---|---|---|---|---|---|
| **Forecast** | | | | | | | | | | | |
| Tolbert M | 28 | 91 | 1 | 11 | 10 | 2 | .253 | .309 | .374 | -$3 | 50 |
| **Mini-Browser** | | | | | | | | | | | |
| Tejada R | 21 | 184 | 2 | 20 | 14 | 4 | .228 | .298 | .323 | -$2 | 90 |
| Valaika C | 25 | 136 | 5 | 15 | 15 | 0 | .231 | .278 | .393 | -$2 | 60 |
| Castillo L | 35 | 87 | 0 | 13 | 7 | 3 | .264 | .353 | .317 | -$2 | 60 |
| Barney D | 25 | 141 | 2 | 17 | 12 | 2 | .234 | .288 | .331 | -$3 | 70 |
| Casilla A | 26 | 89 | 1 | 12 | 8 | 4 | .257 | .320 | .344 | -$3 | 50 |

| Level | Leag | AB | HR | R | RBI | SB | BA | OBP | SLG | CT% | H% | BB% | Bash |
|---|---|---|---|---|---|---|---|---|---|---|---|---|---|
| **Minors (2010)** | | | | | | | | | | **Skills** | | | |
| A | — | — | — | — | — | — | — | — | — | — | — | — | — |
| AA | — | — | — | — | — | — | — | — | — | — | — | — | — |
| AAA | IL | 173 | 1 | 19 | 11 | 6 | .283 | .332 | .387 | 83% | 34% | 7% | 1.37 |

| Bats | Player | GSvR | GSvL | Sub | OPS |
|---|---|---|---|---|---|
| **Competition at 2B** | | **Stats in 2010** | | | |
| BH | Hudson O | 80 | 44 | 0 | .710 |
| BH | Casilla A | 12 | 4 | 8 | .726 |
| BH | Tolbert M | 10 | 3 | 7 | .672 |
| BH | Punto N | 5 | 5 | 2 | .615 |

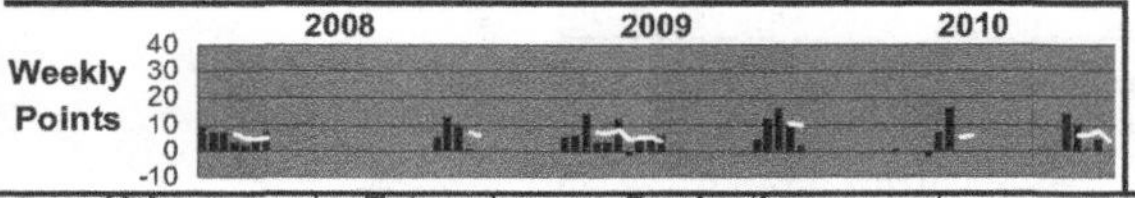


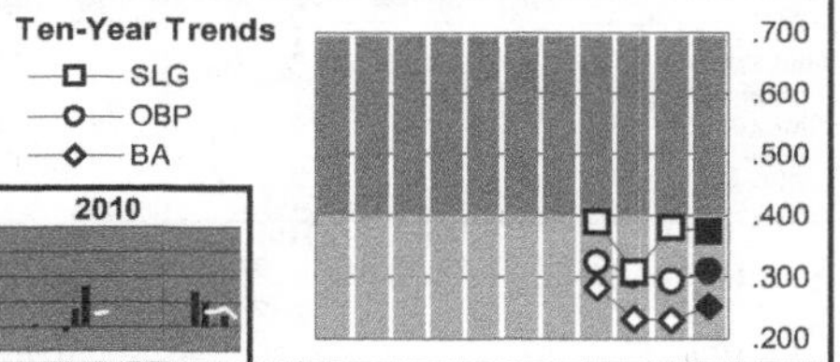


| Yr | Team | AB | HR | R | RBI | SB | BA | OBP | SLG | CT% | H% | BB% | Bash |
|---|---|---|---|---|---|---|---|---|---|---|---|---|---|
| **Majors** | | | | | | | | | | **Skills** | | | |
| 07 | — | — | — | — | — | — | — | — | — | — | — | — | — |
| 08 | MIN | 113 | 0 | 18 | 6 | 7 | .283 | .322 | .389 | 83% | 34% | 6% | 1.38 |
| 09 | MIN | 198 | 2 | 28 | 19 | 6 | .232 | .303 | .308 | 81% | 29% | 9% | 1.33 |
| 10 | MIN | 87 | 1 | 8 | 18 | 1 | .230 | .293 | .379 | 79% | 29% | 9% | 1.65 |

| Yr | $1L | $2L | Pts | RAA | 2B | 3B | CS | FB-LD-GB | HR/fb | RBI% | RS% | OPS | 1st Hf | 2nd Hf | vs RH | vs LH | Rnge | vRH | vLH |
|---|---|---|---|---|---|---|---|---|---|---|---|---|---|---|---|---|---|---|---|
| | **Value** | | | | **Extra** | | | **Production** | | | | **OPS** | | | | | **Scoresheet** | | |
| 07 | — | — | — | — | — | — | — | — | — | — | — | — | — | — | — | — | — | — | — |
| 08 | $0 | -$13 | 70 | –1 | 6 | 3 | 1 | 29-31-41 | 0% | 12% | 46% | .712 | .644 | .897 | .716 | .703 | 4.25 | — | — |
| 09 | $1 | -$13 | 100 | –11 | 7 | 1 | 2 | 34-16-50 | 4% | 17% | 40% | .611 | .497 | .829 | .510 | .890 | — | –1 | +3 |
| 10 | -$2 | -$17 | 50 | –4 | 4 | 3 | 1 | 33-25-42 | 4% | 33% | 25% | .672 | .615 | .737 | .797 | .198 | 4.24 | –17 | +41 |

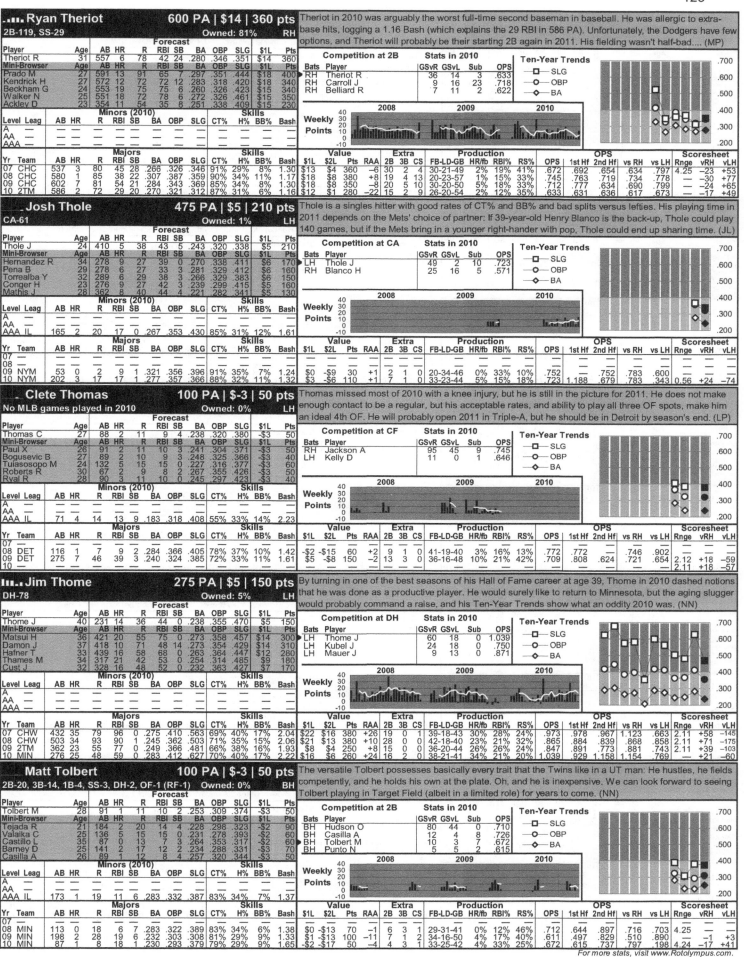

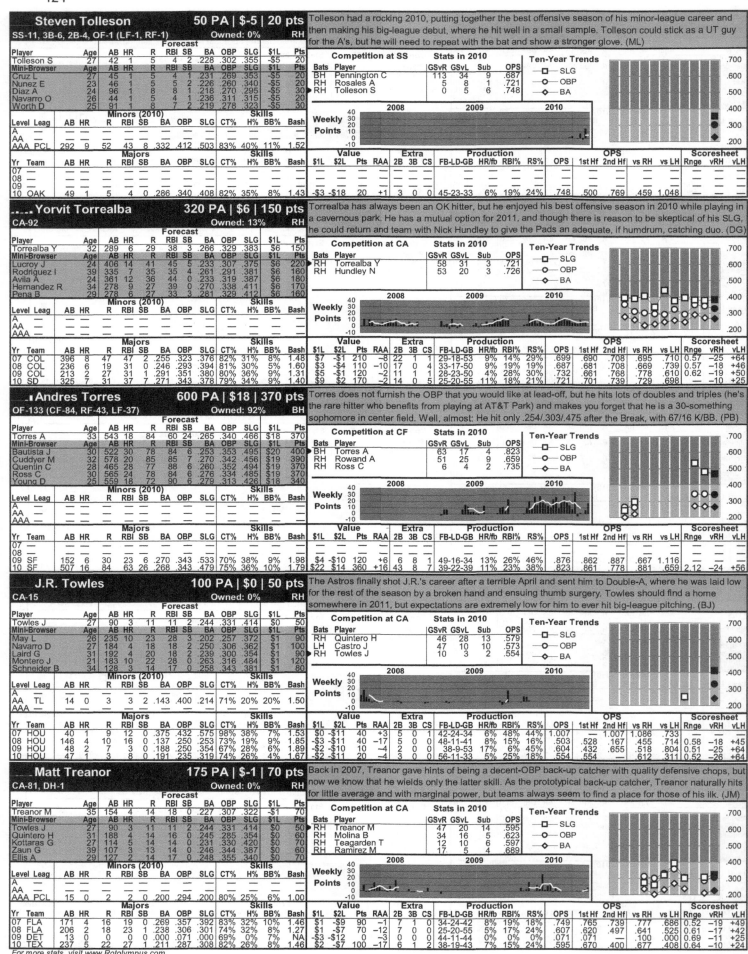

## Steven Tolleson — 50 PA | $-5 | 20 pts
SS-11, 3B-6, 2B-4, OF-1 (LF-1, RF-1) — Owned: 0% — RH

Tolleson had a rocking 2010, putting together the best offensive season of his minor-league career and then making his big-league debut, where he hit well in a small sample. Tolleson could stick as a UT guy for the A's, but he will need to repeat with the bat and show a stronger glove. (ML)

### Forecast
| Player | Age | AB | HR | R | RBI | SB | BA | OBP | SLG | $1L | Pts |
|---|---|---|---|---|---|---|---|---|---|---|---|
| Tolleson S | 27 | 42 | 1 | 5 | 4 | 2 | .228 | .302 | .355 | -$5 | 20 |

| Mini-Browser | Age | AB | HR | R | RBI | SB | BA | OBP | SLG | $1L | Pts |
|---|---|---|---|---|---|---|---|---|---|---|---|
| Cruz L | 27 | 45 | 1 | 5 | 4 | 1 | .231 | .269 | .353 | -$5 | 20 |
| Nunez E | 23 | 46 | 1 | 5 | 5 | 2 | .226 | .260 | .340 | -$5 | 20 |
| Diaz A | 24 | 96 | 2 | 8 | 8 | 1 | .218 | .270 | .295 | -$5 | 30 |
| Navarro O | 26 | 44 | 1 | 5 | 4 | 1 | .236 | .311 | .315 | -$5 | 20 |
| Worth D | 25 | 91 | 1 | 8 | 7 | 2 | .219 | .278 | .323 | -$5 | 30 |

### Minors (2010) / Skills
| Level | Leag | AB | HR | R | RBI | SB | BA | OBP | SLG | CT% | H% | BB% | Bash |
|---|---|---|---|---|---|---|---|---|---|---|---|---|---|
| A | — | | | | | | | | | | | | |
| AA | — | | | | | | | | | | | | |
| AAA | PCL | 292 | 9 | 52 | 43 | 8 | .332 | .412 | .503 | 83% | 40% | 11% | 1.52 |

### Majors / Skills
| Yr | Team | AB | HR | R | RBI | SB | BA | OBP | SLG | CT% | H% | BB% | Bash |
|---|---|---|---|---|---|---|---|---|---|---|---|---|---|
| 07 | — | | | | | | | | | | | | |
| 08 | — | | | | | | | | | | | | |
| 09 | — | | | | | | | | | | | | |
| 10 | OAK | 49 | 1 | 5 | 4 | 0 | .286 | .340 | .408 | 82% | 35% | 8% | 1.43 |

**Competition at SS / Stats in 2010**
| Bats | Player | GSvR | GSvL | Sub | OPS |
|---|---|---|---|---|---|
| BH | Pennington C | 113 | 34 | 9 | .687 |
| RH | Rosales A | 5 | 8 | 1 | .721 |
| RH | Tolleson S | 0 | 5 | 6 | .748 |

### Value / Extra / Production / OPS / Scoresheet
| $1L | $2L | Pts | RAA | 2B | 3B | CS | FB-LD-GB | HR/fb | RBI% | RS% | OPS | 1st Hf | 2nd Hf | vs RH | vs LH | Rnge | vRH | vLH |
|---|---|---|---|---|---|---|---|---|---|---|---|---|---|---|---|---|---|---|
| -$3 | -$18 | 20 | +1 | 3 | 0 | 0 | 45-23-33 | 6% | 19% | 24% | .748 | .500 | .769 | .459 | 1.048 | | | |

---

## Yorvit Torrealba — 320 PA | $6 | 150 pts
CA-92 — Owned: 13% — RH

Torrealba has always been an OK hitter, but he enjoyed his best offensive season in 2010 while playing in a cavernous park. He has a mutual option for 2011, and though there is reason to be skeptical of his SLG, he could return and team with Nick Hundley to give the Pads an adequate, if humdrum, catching duo. (DG)

### Forecast
| Player | Age | AB | HR | R | RBI | SB | BA | OBP | SLG | $1L | Pts |
|---|---|---|---|---|---|---|---|---|---|---|---|
| Torrealba Y | 32 | 289 | 6 | 29 | 38 | 3 | .266 | .329 | .383 | $6 | 150 |

| Mini-Browser | Age | AB | HR | R | RBI | SB | BA | OBP | SLG | $1L | Pts |
|---|---|---|---|---|---|---|---|---|---|---|---|
| Lucroy J | 24 | 406 | 14 | 41 | 45 | 5 | .233 | .307 | .375 | $6 | 220 |
| Rodriguez I | 39 | 335 | 7 | 35 | 35 | 4 | .261 | .291 | .381 | $6 | 160 |
| Avila A | 24 | 361 | 12 | 36 | 44 | 0 | .233 | .319 | .387 | $6 | 180 |
| Hernandez R | 34 | 278 | 9 | 27 | 39 | 0 | .270 | .338 | .411 | $6 | 170 |
| Pena B | 29 | 278 | 6 | 27 | 33 | 1 | .281 | .329 | .409 | $6 | 160 |

### Minors (2010) / Skills
| Level | Leag | AB | HR | R | RBI | SB | BA | OBP | SLG | CT% | H% | BB% | Bash |
|---|---|---|---|---|---|---|---|---|---|---|---|---|---|
| A | — | | | | | | | | | | | | |
| AA | — | | | | | | | | | | | | |
| AAA | — | | | | | | | | | | | | |

### Majors / Skills
| Yr | Team | AB | HR | R | RBI | SB | BA | OBP | SLG | CT% | H% | BB% | Bash |
|---|---|---|---|---|---|---|---|---|---|---|---|---|---|
| 07 | COL | 396 | 8 | 47 | 47 | 2 | .255 | .323 | .376 | 82% | 31% | 8% | 1.48 |
| 08 | COL | 236 | 6 | 19 | 31 | 0 | .246 | .293 | .394 | 81% | 30% | 5% | 1.60 |
| 09 | COL | 213 | 2 | 27 | 31 | 1 | .291 | .351 | .380 | 80% | 36% | 9% | 1.31 |
| 10 | SD | 325 | 7 | 31 | 37 | 7 | .271 | .343 | .378 | 79% | 34% | 9% | 1.40 |

**Competition at CA / Stats in 2010**
| Bats | Player | GSvR | GSvL | Sub | OPS |
|---|---|---|---|---|---|
| RH | Torrealba Y | 58 | 31 | 3 | .721 |
| RH | Hundley N | 53 | 20 | 3 | .726 |

### Value / Extra / Production / OPS / Scoresheet
| Yr | Team | $1L | $2L | Pts | RAA | 2B | 3B | CS | FB-LD-GB | HR/fb | RBI% | RS% | OPS | 1st Hf | 2nd Hf | vs RH | vs LH | Rnge | vRH | vLH |
|---|---|---|---|---|---|---|---|---|---|---|---|---|---|---|---|---|---|---|---|---|
| 07 | COL | $7 | -$1 | 210 | -8 | 22 | 1 | 1 | 29-18-53 | 9% | 14% | 29% | .699 | .690 | .708 | .695 | .710 | 0.57 | -25 | +64 |
| 08 | COL | $3 | -$4 | 110 | -10 | 17 | 0 | 4 | 33-17-50 | 9% | 19% | 19% | .687 | .681 | .708 | .669 | .739 | 0.57 | -18 | +46 |
| 09 | COL | $5 | -$1 | 120 | -2 | 11 | 1 | 1 | 28-20-55 | 4% | 28% | 30% | .732 | .661 | .768 | .778 | .610 | 0.62 | -19 | +50 |
| 10 | SD | $9 | $2 | 170 | -2 | 14 | 0 | 5 | 25-20-55 | 11% | 18% | 21% | .721 | .701 | .739 | .729 | .698 | — | -10 | +25 |

---

## Andres Torres — 600 PA | $18 | 370 pts
OF-133 (CF-84, RF-43, LF-37) — Owned: 92% — BH

Torres does not furnish the OBP that you would like at lead-off, but he hits lots of doubles and triples (he's the rare hitter who benefits from playing at AT&T Park) and makes you forget that he is a 30-something sophomore in center field. Well, almost: He hit only .254/.303/.475 after the Break, with 67/16 K/BB. (PB)

### Forecast
| Player | Age | AB | HR | R | RBI | SB | BA | OBP | SLG | $1L | Pts |
|---|---|---|---|---|---|---|---|---|---|---|---|
| Torres A | 33 | 543 | 18 | 84 | 60 | 24 | .265 | .340 | .466 | $18 | 370 |

| Mini-Browser | Age | AB | HR | R | RBI | SB | BA | OBP | SLG | $1L | Pts |
|---|---|---|---|---|---|---|---|---|---|---|---|
| Bautista J | 30 | 522 | 30 | 78 | 84 | 6 | .253 | .353 | .495 | $20 | 400 |
| Cuddyer M | 32 | 578 | 20 | 85 | 85 | 7 | .270 | .342 | .456 | $19 | 390 |
| Quentin C | 28 | 465 | 28 | 77 | 88 | 4 | .260 | .352 | .494 | $19 | 370 |
| Ross C | 30 | 565 | 24 | 78 | 84 | 6 | .276 | .334 | .485 | $19 | 370 |
| Young D | 25 | 559 | 18 | 72 | 90 | 4 | .279 | .313 | .426 | $18 | 340 |

### Minors (2010) / Skills
| Level | Leag | AB | HR | R | RBI | SB | BA | OBP | SLG | CT% | H% | BB% | Bash |
|---|---|---|---|---|---|---|---|---|---|---|---|---|---|
| A | — | | | | | | | | | | | | |
| AA | — | | | | | | | | | | | | |
| AAA | — | | | | | | | | | | | | |

### Majors / Skills
| Yr | Team | AB | HR | R | RBI | SB | BA | OBP | SLG | CT% | H% | BB% | Bash |
|---|---|---|---|---|---|---|---|---|---|---|---|---|---|
| 07 | — | | | | | | | | | | | | |
| 08 | — | | | | | | | | | | | | |
| 09 | SF | 152 | 6 | 30 | 23 | 6 | .270 | .343 | .533 | 70% | 38% | 9% | 1.98 |
| 10 | SF | 507 | 16 | 84 | 63 | 26 | .268 | .343 | .479 | 75% | 36% | 10% | 1.79 |

**Competition at CF / Stats in 2010**
| Bats | Player | GSvR | GSvL | Sub | OPS |
|---|---|---|---|---|---|
| BH | Torres A | 63 | 17 | 4 | .823 |
| RH | Rowand A | 51 | 25 | 9 | .659 |
| RH | Ross C | 6 | 4 | 2 | .735 |

### Value / Extra / Production / OPS / Scoresheet
| Yr | Team | $1L | $2L | Pts | RAA | 2B | 3B | CS | FB-LD-GB | HR/fb | RBI% | RS% | OPS | 1st Hf | 2nd Hf | vs RH | vs LH | Rnge | vRH | vLH |
|---|---|---|---|---|---|---|---|---|---|---|---|---|---|---|---|---|---|---|---|---|
| 09 | SF | $4 | -$10 | 120 | +6 | 6 | 8 | 1 | 49-16-34 | 13% | 26% | 46% | .876 | .862 | .887 | .667 | 1.116 | — | -10 | +56 |
| 10 | SF | $22 | $14 | 360 | +16 | 43 | 8 | 7 | 39-22-39 | 11% | 23% | 38% | .823 | .861 | .778 | .881 | .659 | 2.12 | -24 | +56 |

---

## J.R. Towles — 100 PA | $0 | 50 pts
CA-15 — Owned: 0% — RH

The Astros finally shot J.R.'s career after a terrible April and sent him to Double-A, where he was laid low for the rest of the season by a broken hand and ensuing thumb surgery. Towles should find a home somewhere in 2011, but expectations are extremely low for him to ever hit big-league pitching. (BJ)

### Forecast
| Player | Age | AB | HR | R | RBI | SB | BA | OBP | SLG | $1L | Pts |
|---|---|---|---|---|---|---|---|---|---|---|---|
| Towles J | 27 | 90 | 3 | 11 | 11 | 2 | .244 | .331 | .414 | $0 | 50 |

| Mini-Browser | Age | AB | HR | R | RBI | SB | BA | OBP | SLG | $1L | Pts |
|---|---|---|---|---|---|---|---|---|---|---|---|
| May L | 26 | 235 | 10 | 23 | 28 | 3 | .202 | .257 | .372 | $1 | 90 |
| Navarro D | 27 | 184 | 4 | 18 | 18 | 2 | .250 | .306 | .362 | $1 | 100 |
| Laird G | 31 | 192 | 4 | 20 | 18 | 2 | .239 | .300 | .354 | $1 | 90 |
| Montero J | 21 | 183 | 10 | 22 | 28 | 0 | .263 | .316 | .484 | $1 | 120 |
| Schneider B | 34 | 128 | 3 | 14 | 17 | 0 | .258 | .343 | .385 | $1 | 80 |

### Minors (2010) / Skills
| Level | Leag | AB | HR | R | RBI | SB | BA | OBP | SLG | CT% | H% | BB% | Bash |
|---|---|---|---|---|---|---|---|---|---|---|---|---|---|
| A | — | | | | | | | | | | | | |
| AA | TL | 14 | 0 | 3 | 3 | 0 | .143 | .400 | .214 | 71% | 20% | 20% | 1.50 |
| AAA | — | | | | | | | | | | | | |

### Majors / Skills
| Yr | Team | AB | HR | R | RBI | SB | BA | OBP | SLG | CT% | H% | BB% | Bash |
|---|---|---|---|---|---|---|---|---|---|---|---|---|---|
| 07 | HOU | 40 | 1 | 9 | 12 | 0 | .375 | .432 | .575 | 98% | 38% | 7% | 1.53 |
| 08 | HOU | 146 | 4 | 10 | 16 | 0 | .137 | .250 | .250 | 73% | 19% | 9% | 1.85 |
| 09 | HOU | 48 | 2 | 7 | 3 | 0 | .188 | .250 | .354 | 67% | 28% | 6% | 1.89 |
| 10 | HOU | 47 | 1 | 3 | 8 | 0 | .191 | .235 | .319 | 74% | 26% | 4% | 1.67 |

**Competition at CA / Stats in 2010**
| Bats | Player | GSvR | GSvL | Sub | OPS |
|---|---|---|---|---|---|
| RH | Quintero H | 46 | 28 | 13 | .579 |
| LH | Castro J | 47 | 10 | 10 | .573 |
| RH | Towles J | 10 | 3 | 2 | .554 |

### Value / Extra / Production / OPS / Scoresheet
| Yr | Team | $1L | $2L | Pts | RAA | 2B | 3B | CS | FB-LD-GB | HR/fb | RBI% | RS% | OPS | 1st Hf | 2nd Hf | vs RH | vs LH | Rnge | vRH | vLH |
|---|---|---|---|---|---|---|---|---|---|---|---|---|---|---|---|---|---|---|---|---|
| 07 | HOU | $0 | -$11 | 40 | +3 | 5 | 0 | 1 | 42-24-34 | 6% | 48% | 44% | 1.007 | — | 1.007 | 1.086 | .733 | 0.58 | -18 | +45 |
| 08 | HOU | -$3 | -$11 | 40 | -17 | 5 | 0 | 0 | 48-11-41 | 8% | 15% | 16% | .503 | .528 | .167 | .455 | .714 | 0.58 | -18 | +45 |
| 09 | HOU | -$2 | -$10 | 10 | -4 | 3 | 0 | 0 | 38-9-53 | 17% | 6% | 45% | .604 | .432 | .655 | .518 | .804 | 0.51 | -25 | +64 |
| 10 | HOU | -$2 | -$11 | 20 | -7 | 3 | 0 | 0 | 56-11-33 | 5% | 25% | 18% | .554 | .554 | — | .612 | .311 | 0.52 | -26 | +64 |

---

## Matt Treanor — 175 PA | $-1 | 70 pts
CA-81, DH-1 — Owned: 0% — RH

Back in 2007, Treanor gave hints of being a decent-OBP back-up catcher with quality defensive chops, but now we know that he wields only the latter skill. As the prototypical back-up catcher, Treanor naturally hits for little average and with marginal power, but teams always seem to find a place for those of his ilk. (JM)

### Forecast
| Player | Age | AB | HR | R | RBI | SB | BA | OBP | SLG | $1L | Pts |
|---|---|---|---|---|---|---|---|---|---|---|---|
| Treanor M | 35 | 154 | 4 | 14 | 18 | 0 | .227 | .307 | .322 | -$1 | 70 |

| Mini-Browser | Age | AB | HR | R | RBI | SB | BA | OBP | SLG | $1L | Pts |
|---|---|---|---|---|---|---|---|---|---|---|---|
| Towles J | 27 | 90 | 3 | 11 | 11 | 2 | .244 | .331 | .414 | $0 | 50 |
| Quintero H | 31 | 188 | 4 | 14 | 16 | 0 | .245 | .285 | .354 | $0 | 60 |
| Kottaras G | 27 | 114 | 5 | 14 | 14 | 0 | .231 | .330 | .420 | $0 | 70 |
| Zaun G | 39 | 107 | 3 | 13 | 14 | 0 | .246 | .344 | .387 | $0 | 60 |
| Ellis A | 29 | 127 | 2 | 14 | 17 | 0 | .248 | .355 | .340 | $0 | 70 |

### Minors (2010) / Skills
| Level | Leag | AB | HR | R | RBI | SB | BA | OBP | SLG | CT% | H% | BB% | Bash |
|---|---|---|---|---|---|---|---|---|---|---|---|---|---|
| A | — | | | | | | | | | | | | |
| AA | — | | | | | | | | | | | | |
| AAA | PCL | 15 | 0 | 2 | 2 | 0 | .200 | .294 | .200 | 80% | 25% | 6% | 1.00 |

### Majors / Skills
| Yr | Team | AB | HR | R | RBI | SB | BA | OBP | SLG | CT% | H% | BB% | Bash |
|---|---|---|---|---|---|---|---|---|---|---|---|---|---|
| 07 | FLA | 171 | 4 | 16 | 19 | 0 | .269 | .357 | .392 | 83% | 32% | 10% | 1.46 |
| 08 | FLA | 206 | 2 | 18 | 23 | 1 | .238 | .306 | .301 | 74% | 32% | 8% | 1.27 |
| 09 | DET | 13 | 0 | 0 | 0 | 0 | .000 | .071 | .000 | 69% | 0% | 7% | NA |
| 10 | TEX | 237 | 5 | 22 | 27 | 0 | .211 | .287 | .308 | 82% | 26% | 8% | 1.46 |

**Competition at CA / Stats in 2010**
| Bats | Player | GSvR | GSvL | Sub | OPS |
|---|---|---|---|---|---|
| RH | Treanor M | 47 | 20 | 14 | .595 |
| RH | Molina B | 34 | 16 | 5 | .623 |
| RH | Teagarden T | 12 | 10 | 6 | .597 |
| RH | Ramirez M | 17 | 5 | 4 | .689 |

### Value / Extra / Production / OPS / Scoresheet
| Yr | Team | $1L | $2L | Pts | RAA | 2B | 3B | CS | FB-LD-GB | HR/fb | RBI% | RS% | OPS | 1st Hf | 2nd Hf | vs RH | vs LH | Rnge | vRH | vLH |
|---|---|---|---|---|---|---|---|---|---|---|---|---|---|---|---|---|---|---|---|---|
| 07 | FLA | $1 | -$9 | 70 | -1 | 7 | 0 | 0 | 34-24-42 | 8% | 19% | 18% | .749 | .765 | .739 | .777 | .686 | 0.52 | -19 | +49 |
| 08 | FLA | $1 | -$7 | 70 | -12 | 7 | 0 | 0 | 25-20-55 | 5% | 17% | 24% | .607 | .620 | .497 | .641 | .525 | 0.61 | -17 | +42 |
| 09 | DET | -$3 | -$12 | -10 | -3 | 0 | 0 | 0 | — | 0% | 0% | 0% | .071 | .071 | — | .100 | .000 | 0.69 | -11 | +25 |
| 10 | TEX | -$2 | -$7 | 100 | -17 | 6 | 1 | 2 | 38-19-43 | 7% | 15% | 24% | .595 | .670 | .400 | .677 | .408 | 0.64 | -26 | +64 |

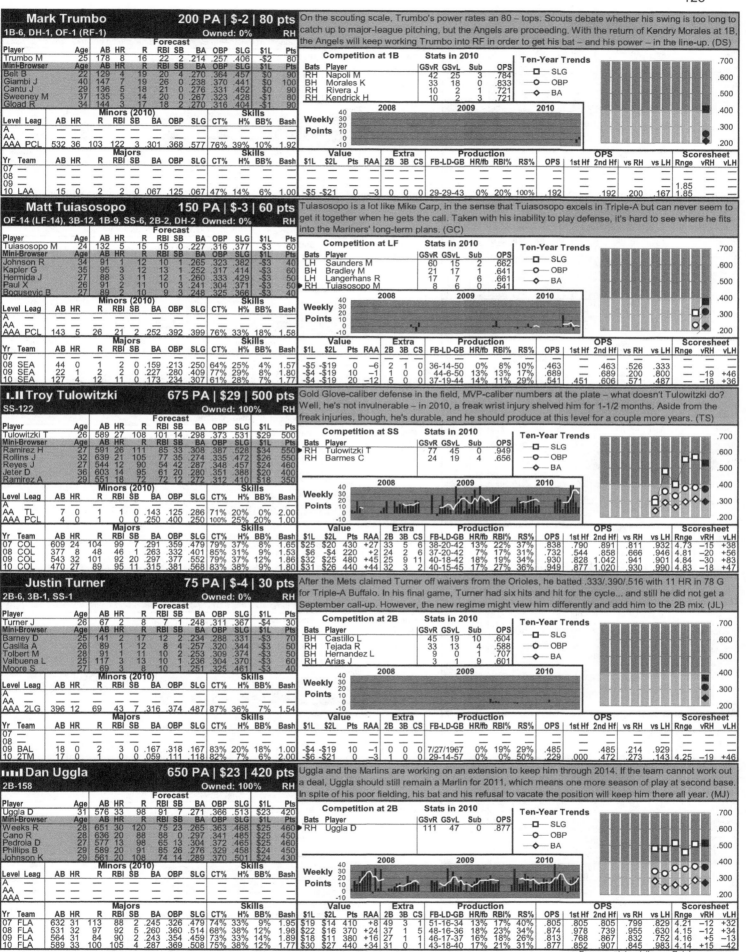

## Mark Trumbo — 200 PA | $-2 | 80 pts
1B-6, DH-1, OF-1 (RF-1)  Owned: 0%  RH

On the scouting scale, Trumbo's power rates an 80 – tops. Scouts debate whether his swing is too long to catch up to major-league pitching, but the Angels are proceeding. With the return of Kendry Morales at 1B, the Angels will keep working Trumbo into RF in order to get his bat – and his power – in the line-up. (DS)

### Forecast
| Player | Age | AB | HR | R | RBI | SB | BA | OBP | SLG | $1L | Pts |
|---|---|---|---|---|---|---|---|---|---|---|---|
| Trumbo M | 25 | 178 | 8 | 16 | 22 | 2 | .214 | .257 | .406 | -$2 | 80 |

### Mini-Browser
| Player | Age | AB | HR | R | RBI | SB | BA | OBP | SLG | $1L | Pts |
|---|---|---|---|---|---|---|---|---|---|---|---|
| Belt B | 22 | 129 | 4 | 19 | 20 | 4 | .250 | .364 | .457 | $0 | 90 |
| Giambi J | 40 | 147 | 7 | 19 | 26 | 0 | .238 | .370 | .441 | $0 | 100 |
| Cantu J | 29 | 136 | 5 | 18 | 21 | 0 | .276 | .331 | .452 | $0 | 90 |
| Sweeney M | 37 | 135 | 5 | 14 | 20 | 0 | .267 | .323 | .428 | -$1 | 80 |
| Gload R | 34 | 144 | 5 | 17 | 18 | 2 | .270 | .316 | .404 | -$1 | 90 |

### Competition at 1B — Stats in 2010
| Bats | Player | GSvR | GSvL | Sub | OPS |
|---|---|---|---|---|---|
| RH | Napoli M | 42 | 25 | 3 | .784 |
| BH | Morales K | 33 | 18 | 0 | .833 |
| RH | Rivera J | 10 | 2 | 1 | .721 |
| RH | Kendrick H | 10 | 2 | 3 | .721 |

Ten-Year Trends: SLG, OBP, BA — 2008 · 2009 · 2010 · Weekly Points

### Minors (2010)
| Level | Leag | AB | HR | R | RBI | SB | BA | OBP | SLG | CT% | H% | BB% | Bash |
|---|---|---|---|---|---|---|---|---|---|---|---|---|---|
| A | — | | | | | | | | | | | | |
| AA | — | | | | | | | | | | | | |
| AAA | PCL | 532 | 36 | 103 | 122 | 3 | .301 | .368 | .577 | 76% | 39% | 10% | 1.92 |

### Majors / Skills / Value / Extra / Production / OPS / Scoresheet
| Yr | Team | AB | HR | R | RBI | SB | BA | OBP | SLG | CT% | H% | BB% | Bash | $1L | $2L | Pts | RAA | 2B | 3B | CS | FB-LD-GB | HR/fb | RBI% | RS% | OPS | 1st Hf | 2nd Hf | vs RH | vs LH | Rnge | vRH | vLH |
|---|---|---|---|---|---|---|---|---|---|---|---|---|---|---|---|---|---|---|---|---|---|---|---|---|---|---|---|---|---|---|---|---|
| 07 | — | | | | | | | | | | | | | | | | | | | | | | | | | | | | | | | |
| 08 | — | | | | | | | | | | | | | | | | | | | | | | | | | | | | | | | |
| 09 | — | | | | | | | | | | | | | | | | | | | | | | | | | | | | | | | |
| 10 | LAA | 15 | 0 | 2 | 2 | 0 | .067 | .125 | .067 | 47% | 14% | 6% | 1.00 | -$5 | -$21 | 0 | -3 | 0 | 0 | 0 | 29-29-43 | 0% | 20% | 100% | .192 | — | .192 | .200 | .167 | 1.85 | 1.85 | — |

## Matt Tuiasosopo — 150 PA | $-3 | 60 pts
OF-14 (LF-14), 3B-12, 1B-9, SS-6, 2B-2, DH-2  Owned: 0%  RH

Tuiasosopo is a lot like Mike Carp, in the sense that Tuiasosopo excels in Triple-A but can never seem to get it together when he gets the call. Taken with his inability to play defense, it's hard to see where he fits into the Mariners' long-term plans. (GC)

### Forecast
| Player | Age | AB | HR | R | RBI | SB | BA | OBP | SLG | $1L | Pts |
|---|---|---|---|---|---|---|---|---|---|---|---|
| Tuiasosopo M | 24 | 132 | 5 | 15 | 15 | 0 | .227 | .316 | .377 | -$3 | 60 |

### Mini-Browser
| Player | Age | AB | HR | R | RBI | SB | BA | OBP | SLG | $1L | Pts |
|---|---|---|---|---|---|---|---|---|---|---|---|
| Johnson R | 34 | 91 | 1 | 12 | 10 | 1 | .265 | .323 | .382 | -$3 | 40 |
| Kapler G | 35 | 95 | 3 | 12 | 13 | 1 | .252 | .317 | .414 | -$3 | 60 |
| Hermida J | 27 | 88 | 3 | 11 | 12 | 1 | .260 | .333 | .429 | -$3 | 50 |
| Paul X | 26 | 91 | 2 | 11 | 10 | 3 | .241 | .304 | .371 | -$3 | 50 |
| Bogusevic B | 27 | 89 | 2 | 10 | 9 | 3 | .248 | .325 | .366 | -$3 | 40 |

### Competition at LF — Stats in 2010
| Bats | Player | GSvR | GSvL | Sub | OPS |
|---|---|---|---|---|---|
| LH | Saunders M | 60 | 15 | 2 | .662 |
| BH | Bradley M | 21 | 17 | 1 | .641 |
| LH | Langerhans R | 17 | 7 | 6 | .661 |
| RH | Tuiasosopo M | 8 | 6 | 0 | .541 |

### Minors (2010)
| Level | Leag | AB | HR | R | RBI | SB | BA | OBP | SLG | CT% | H% | BB% | Bash |
|---|---|---|---|---|---|---|---|---|---|---|---|---|---|
| A | — | | | | | | | | | | | | |
| AA | — | | | | | | | | | | | | |
| AAA | PCL | 143 | 5 | 26 | 21 | 2 | .252 | .392 | .399 | 76% | 33% | 18% | 1.58 |

### Majors
| Yr | Team | AB | HR | R | RBI | SB | BA | OBP | SLG | CT% | H% | BB% | Bash | $1L | $2L | Pts | RAA | 2B | 3B | CS | FB-LD-GB | HR/fb | RBI% | RS% | OPS | 1st Hf | 2nd Hf | vs RH | vs LH | Rnge | vRH | vLH |
|---|---|---|---|---|---|---|---|---|---|---|---|---|---|---|---|---|---|---|---|---|---|---|---|---|---|---|---|---|---|---|---|---|
| 07 | — | | | | | | | | | | | | | | | | | | | | | | | | | | | | | | | |
| 08 | SEA | 44 | 0 | 1 | 2 | 0 | .159 | .213 | .250 | 64% | 25% | 4% | 1.57 | -$5 | -$19 | 0 | -6 | 2 | 1 | 0 | 36-14-50 | 0% | 8% | 10% | .463 | — | .463 | .526 | .333 | — | — | — |
| 09 | SEA | 22 | 3 | 2 | 2 | 0 | .227 | .280 | .409 | 77% | 29% | 8% | 1.42 | -$4 | -$19 | 10 | -1 | 1 | 0 | 0 | 44-6-50 | 13% | 13% | 17% | .689 | — | .689 | .200 | .800 | — | -19 | +46 |
| 10 | SEA | 127 | 4 | 12 | 11 | 0 | .173 | .234 | .307 | 61% | 28% | 8% | 1.77 | -$4 | -$19 | 20 | -12 | 5 | 0 | 0 | 37-19-44 | 14% | 11% | 29% | .541 | .451 | .606 | .571 | .487 | — | -16 | +36 |

## Troy Tulowitzki — 675 PA | $29 | 500 pts
SS-122  Owned: 100%  RH

Gold Glove-caliber defense in the field, MVP-caliber numbers at the plate – what doesn't Tulowitzki do? Well, he's not invulnerable – in 2010, a freak wrist injury shelved him for 1-1/2 months. Aside from the freak injuries, though, he's durable, and he should produce at this level for a couple more years. (TS)

### Forecast
| Player | Age | AB | HR | R | RBI | SB | BA | OBP | SLG | $1L | Pts |
|---|---|---|---|---|---|---|---|---|---|---|---|
| Tulowitzki T | 26 | 589 | 27 | 108 | 101 | 14 | .298 | .373 | .531 | $29 | 500 |

### Mini-Browser
| Player | Age | AB | HR | R | RBI | SB | BA | OBP | SLG | $1L | Pts |
|---|---|---|---|---|---|---|---|---|---|---|---|
| Ramirez H | 27 | 591 | 26 | 111 | 85 | 33 | .308 | .387 | .528 | $34 | 550 |
| Rollins J | 32 | 639 | 21 | 105 | 77 | 35 | .274 | .335 | .472 | $26 | 550 |
| Reyes J | 27 | 544 | 12 | 90 | 54 | 42 | .287 | .348 | .457 | $24 | 460 |
| Jeter D | 36 | 603 | 14 | 95 | 61 | 20 | .280 | .351 | .388 | $20 | 400 |
| Ramirez A | 29 | 551 | 18 | 72 | 72 | 12 | .272 | .312 | .410 | $18 | 350 |

### Competition at SS — Stats in 2010
| Bats | Player | GSvR | GSvL | Sub | OPS |
|---|---|---|---|---|---|
| RH | Tulowitzki T | 77 | 45 | 0 | .949 |
| RH | Barmes C | 24 | 19 | 4 | .656 |

### Minors (2010)
| Level | Leag | AB | HR | R | RBI | SB | BA | OBP | SLG | CT% | H% | BB% | Bash |
|---|---|---|---|---|---|---|---|---|---|---|---|---|---|
| A | — | | | | | | | | | | | | |
| AA | TL | 7 | 0 | 1 | 1 | 0 | 0.143 | .125 | .286 | 71% | 20% | 0% | 2.00 |
| AAA | PCL | 4 | 0 | 1 | 0 | 0 | 0.250 | .400 | .250 | 100% | 25% | 20% | 1.00 |

### Majors
| Yr | Team | AB | HR | R | RBI | SB | BA | OBP | SLG | CT% | H% | BB% | Bash | $1L | $2L | Pts | RAA | 2B | 3B | CS | FB-LD-GB | HR/fb | RBI% | RS% | OPS | 1st Hf | 2nd Hf | vs RH | vs LH | Rnge | vRH | vLH |
|---|---|---|---|---|---|---|---|---|---|---|---|---|---|---|---|---|---|---|---|---|---|---|---|---|---|---|---|---|---|---|---|---|
| 07 | COL | 609 | 24 | 104 | 99 | 7 | .291 | .359 | .479 | 79% | 37% | 8% | 1.65 | $25 | $20 | 430 | +27 | 33 | 5 | 6 | 38-20-42 | 13% | 22% | 37% | .838 | .790 | .891 | .811 | .932 | 4.73 | -15 | +38 |
| 08 | COL | 377 | 8 | 48 | 46 | 1 | .263 | .332 | .401 | 85% | 31% | 9% | 1.53 | $6 | -$4 | 220 | +2 | 24 | 2 | 6 | 37-20-42 | 7% | 17% | 31% | .732 | .544 | .858 | .666 | .946 | 4.81 | -20 | +56 |
| 09 | COL | 543 | 32 | 101 | 92 | 20 | .297 | .377 | .552 | 79% | 37% | 12% | 1.86 | $32 | $25 | 480 | +45 | 25 | 9 | 11 | 40-18-42 | 18% | 19% | 34% | .930 | .828 | 1.042 | .941 | .901 | 4.84 | -30 | +83 |
| 10 | COL | 470 | 27 | 89 | 95 | 11 | .315 | .381 | .568 | 83% | 38% | 9% | 1.81 | $31 | $26 | 440 | +44 | 32 | 3 | 2 | 40-15-45 | 17% | 27% | 36% | .949 | .877 | 1.020 | .930 | .990 | 4.83 | -18 | +47 |

## Justin Turner — 75 PA | $-4 | 30 pts
2B-6, 3B-1, SS-1  Owned: 0%  RH

After the Mets claimed Turner off waivers from the Orioles, he batted .333/.390/.516 with 11 HR in 78 G for Triple-A Buffalo. In his final game, Turner had six hits and hit for the cycle... and still he did not get a September call-up. However, the new regime might view him differently and add him to the 2B mix. (JL)

### Forecast
| Player | Age | AB | HR | R | RBI | SB | BA | OBP | SLG | $1L | Pts |
|---|---|---|---|---|---|---|---|---|---|---|---|
| Turner J | 26 | 67 | 2 | 8 | 7 | 1 | .248 | .311 | .367 | -$4 | 30 |

### Mini-Browser
| Player | Age | AB | HR | R | RBI | SB | BA | OBP | SLG | $1L | Pts |
|---|---|---|---|---|---|---|---|---|---|---|---|
| Barney D | 25 | 141 | 2 | 17 | 12 | 2 | .234 | .288 | .331 | -$3 | 70 |
| Casilla A | 26 | 89 | 1 | 12 | 8 | 4 | .257 | .320 | .344 | -$3 | 50 |
| Tolbert M | 28 | 91 | 1 | 11 | 10 | 2 | .253 | .309 | .374 | -$3 | 50 |
| Valbuena L | 25 | 117 | 3 | 13 | 10 | 1 | .236 | .304 | .370 | -$3 | 60 |
| Moore S | 27 | 69 | 3 | 8 | 10 | 1 | .251 | .325 | .461 | -$3 | 40 |

### Competition at 2B — Stats in 2010
| Bats | Player | GSvR | GSvL | Sub | OPS |
|---|---|---|---|---|---|
| BH | Castillo L | 45 | 19 | 10 | .604 |
| RH | Tejada R | 33 | 13 | 4 | .588 |
| BH | Hernandez L | 9 | 0 | 1 | .707 |
| RH | Arias J | 3 | 1 | 9 | .601 |

### Minors (2010)
| Level | Leag | AB | HR | R | RBI | SB | BA | OBP | SLG | CT% | H% | BB% | Bash |
|---|---|---|---|---|---|---|---|---|---|---|---|---|---|
| A | — | | | | | | | | | | | | |
| AA | — | | | | | | | | | | | | |
| AAA | 2LG | 396 | 12 | 69 | 43 | 7 | .316 | .374 | .487 | 87% | 36% | 7% | 1.54 |

### Majors
| Yr | Team | AB | HR | R | RBI | SB | BA | OBP | SLG | CT% | H% | BB% | Bash | $1L | $2L | Pts | RAA | 2B | 3B | CS | FB-LD-GB | HR/fb | RBI% | RS% | OPS | 1st Hf | 2nd Hf | vs RH | vs LH | Rnge | vRH | vLH |
|---|---|---|---|---|---|---|---|---|---|---|---|---|---|---|---|---|---|---|---|---|---|---|---|---|---|---|---|---|---|---|---|---|
| 07 | — | | | | | | | | | | | | | | | | | | | | | | | | | | | | | | | |
| 08 | — | | | | | | | | | | | | | | | | | | | | | | | | | | | | | | | |
| 09 | BAL | 18 | 0 | 2 | 3 | 0 | .167 | .318 | .167 | 83% | 20% | 18% | 1.00 | -$4 | -$19 | 10 | -1 | 0 | 0 | 0 | 7-27-67 | 0% | 19% | 29% | .485 | — | .485 | .214 | .929 | — | — | — |
| 10 | 2TM | 17 | 0 | 0 | 0 | 0 | .059 | .111 | .118 | 82% | 7% | 6% | 2.00 | -$6 | -$21 | 0 | 0 | 0 | 0 | 0 | 29-14-57 | 0% | 0% | 50% | .229 | .000 | .472 | .273 | .143 | 4.25 | -19 | +44 |

## Dan Uggla — 650 PA | $23 | 420 pts
2B-158  Owned: 100%  RH

Uggla and the Marlins are working on an extension to keep him through 2014. If the team cannot work out a deal, Uggla should still remain a Marlin for 2011, which means one more season of play at second base. In spite of his poor fielding, his bat and his refusal to vacate the position will keep him there all year. (MJ)

### Forecast
| Player | Age | AB | HR | R | RBI | SB | BA | OBP | SLG | $1L | Pts |
|---|---|---|---|---|---|---|---|---|---|---|---|
| Uggla D | 31 | 576 | 33 | 98 | 91 | 7 | .271 | .366 | .513 | $23 | 420 |

### Mini-Browser
| Player | Age | AB | HR | R | RBI | SB | BA | OBP | SLG | $1L | Pts |
|---|---|---|---|---|---|---|---|---|---|---|---|
| Weeks R | 28 | 651 | 30 | 120 | 75 | 23 | .265 | .363 | .468 | $25 | 460 |
| Cano R | 28 | 636 | 20 | 88 | 88 | 0 | .297 | .341 | .485 | $25 | 460 |
| Pedroia D | 27 | 577 | 13 | 98 | 65 | 13 | .304 | .372 | .465 | $25 | 460 |
| Phillips B | 29 | 589 | 20 | 91 | 85 | 26 | .276 | .329 | .458 | $24 | 450 |
| Johnson K | 29 | 561 | 20 | 108 | 74 | 14 | .289 | .370 | .501 | $24 | 430 |

### Competition at 2B — Stats in 2010
| Bats | Player | GSvR | GSvL | Sub | OPS |
|---|---|---|---|---|---|
| RH | Uggla D | 111 | 47 | 0 | .877 |

### Minors (2010)
| Level | Leag | AB | HR | R | RBI | SB | BA | OBP | SLG | CT% | H% | BB% | Bash |
|---|---|---|---|---|---|---|---|---|---|---|---|---|---|
| A | — | | | | | | | | | | | | |
| AA | — | | | | | | | | | | | | |
| AAA | — | | | | | | | | | | | | |

### Majors
| Yr | Team | AB | HR | R | RBI | SB | BA | OBP | SLG | CT% | H% | BB% | Bash | $1L | $2L | Pts | RAA | 2B | 3B | CS | FB-LD-GB | HR/fb | RBI% | RS% | OPS | 1st Hf | 2nd Hf | vs RH | vs LH | Rnge | vRH | vLH |
|---|---|---|---|---|---|---|---|---|---|---|---|---|---|---|---|---|---|---|---|---|---|---|---|---|---|---|---|---|---|---|---|---|
| 07 | FLA | 632 | 31 | 113 | 88 | 2 | .245 | .326 | .479 | 74% | 33% | 9% | 1.95 | $19 | $14 | 410 | +8 | 49 | 3 | 1 | 51-16-34 | 13% | 17% | 40% | .805 | .805 | .805 | .799 | .829 | 4.21 | -12 | +32 |
| 08 | FLA | 531 | 32 | 97 | 92 | 5 | .260 | .360 | .514 | 68% | 38% | 12% | 1.98 | $22 | $16 | 370 | +24 | 37 | 1 | 5 | 48-16-36 | 18% | 23% | 34% | .874 | .978 | .739 | .955 | .630 | 4.15 | -12 | +34 |
| 09 | FLA | 564 | 31 | 84 | 90 | 2 | .243 | .354 | .459 | 73% | 33% | 14% | 1.89 | $18 | $11 | 380 | +16 | 27 | 1 | 3 | 46-17-37 | 16% | 18% | 26% | .813 | .768 | .867 | .832 | .752 | 4.16 | -5 | -13 |
| 10 | FLA | 589 | 33 | 100 | 105 | 4 | .287 | .369 | .508 | 75% | 38% | 12% | 1.77 | $30 | $27 | 440 | +34 | 31 | 0 | 1 | 43-18-40 | 17% | 21% | 31% | .877 | .852 | .907 | .845 | .983 | 4.14 | +15 | -42 |

*For more stats, visit www.Rotolympus.com.*

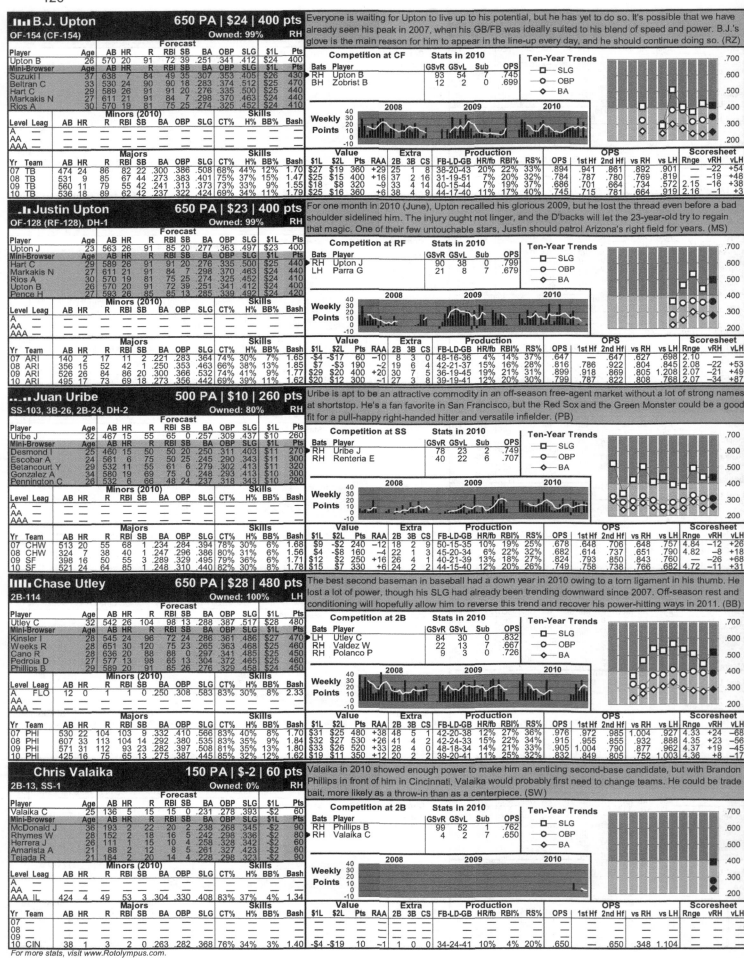

## B.J. Upton — 650 PA | $24 | 400 pts
OF-154 (CF-154) — Owned: 99% — RH

*Everyone is waiting for Upton to live up to his potential, but he has yet to do so. It's possible that we have already seen his peak in 2007, when his GB/FB was ideally suited to his blend of speed and power. B.J.'s glove is the main reason for him to appear in the line-up every day, and he should continue doing so. (RZ)*

### Forecast
| Player | Age | AB | HR | R | RBI | SB | BA | OBP | SLG | $1L | Pts |
|---|---|---|---|---|---|---|---|---|---|---|---|
| Upton B | 26 | 570 | 20 | 91 | 72 | 39 | .251 | .341 | .412 | $24 | 400 |
| Mini-Browser | Age | AB | HR | R | RBI | SB | BA | OBP | SLG | $1L | Pts |
| Suzuki I | 37 | 638 | 7 | 84 | 49 | 35 | .307 | .353 | .405 | $26 | 430 |
| Beltran C | 33 | 530 | 24 | 90 | 90 | 18 | .283 | .374 | .512 | $25 | 470 |
| Hart C | 29 | 589 | 26 | 91 | 91 | 20 | .276 | .335 | .500 | $25 | 440 |
| Markakis N | 27 | 611 | 21 | 91 | 84 | 7 | .298 | .370 | .463 | $24 | 440 |
| Rios A | 30 | 570 | 19 | 81 | 75 | 25 | .274 | .325 | .452 | $24 | 410 |

### Competition at CF / Stats in 2010
| Bats | Player | GSvR | GSvL | Sub | OPS |
|---|---|---|---|---|---|
| RH | Upton B | 93 | 54 | 7 | .745 |
| BH | Zobrist B | 12 | 2 | 0 | .699 |

### Minors (2010) / Skills
| Level | Leag | AB | HR | R | RBI | SB | BA | OBP | SLG | CT% | H% | BB% | Bash |
|---|---|---|---|---|---|---|---|---|---|---|---|---|---|
| A | — | — | — | — | — | — | — | — | — | — | — | — | — |
| AA | — | — | — | — | — | — | — | — | — | — | — | — | — |
| AAA | — | — | — | — | — | — | — | — | — | — | — | — | — |

### Majors / Skills / Value / Extra / Production / OPS / Scoresheet
| Yr | Team | AB | HR | R | RBI | SB | BA | OBP | SLG | CT% | H% | BB% | Bash | $1L | $2L | Pts | RAA | 2B | 3B | CS | FB-LD-GB | HR/fb | RBI% | RS% | OPS | 1st Hf | 2nd Hf | vs RH | vs LH | Rnge | vRH | vLH |
|---|---|---|---|---|---|---|---|---|---|---|---|---|---|---|---|---|---|---|---|---|---|---|---|---|---|---|---|---|---|---|---|---|
| 07 | TB | 474 | 24 | 86 | 82 | 22 | .300 | .386 | .508 | 68% | 44% | 12% | 1.70 | $27 | $19 | 360 | +29 | 25 | 1 | 8 | 38-20-43 | 20% | 22% | 33% | .894 | .941 | .861 | .892 | .901 | — | −22 | +54 |
| 08 | TB | 531 | 9 | 85 | 67 | 44 | .273 | .383 | .401 | 75% | 37% | 15% | 1.47 | $25 | $15 | 400 | +16 | 37 | 2 | 16 | 31-19-51 | 7% | 20% | 32% | .784 | .787 | .780 | .769 | .819 | — | −19 | +48 |
| 09 | TB | 560 | 11 | 79 | 55 | 42 | .241 | .313 | .373 | 73% | 33% | 9% | 1.55 | $18 | $8 | 320 | −9 | 33 | 4 | 14 | 40-15-44 | 7% | 19% | 37% | .686 | .701 | .664 | .734 | .572 | 2.15 | −16 | +38 |
| 10 | TB | 536 | 18 | 89 | 62 | 42 | .237 | .322 | .424 | 69% | 34% | 11% | 1.79 | $25 | $16 | 360 | +6 | 38 | 4 | 16 | 44-17-40 | 10% | 17% | 40% | .745 | .715 | .781 | .745 | .919 | 2.16 | −1 | +3 |

---

## Justin Upton — 650 PA | $23 | 400 pts
OF-128 (RF-128), DH-1 — Owned: 99% — RH

*For one month in 2010 (June), Upton recalled his glorious 2009, but he lost the thread even before a bad shoulder sidelined him. The injury ought not linger, and the D'backs will let the 23-year-old try to regain that magic. One of their few untouchable stars, Justin should patrol Arizona's right field for years. (MS)*

### Forecast
| Player | Age | AB | HR | R | RBI | SB | BA | OBP | SLG | $1L | Pts |
|---|---|---|---|---|---|---|---|---|---|---|---|
| Upton J | 23 | 563 | 26 | 91 | 85 | 20 | .277 | .363 | .497 | $23 | 400 |
| Mini-Browser | Age | AB | HR | R | RBI | SB | BA | OBP | SLG | $1L | Pts |
| Hart C | 29 | 589 | 26 | 91 | 91 | 20 | .276 | .335 | .500 | $25 | 440 |
| Markakis N | 27 | 611 | 21 | 91 | 84 | 7 | .298 | .370 | .463 | $24 | 440 |
| Rios A | 30 | 570 | 19 | 81 | 75 | 25 | .274 | .325 | .452 | $24 | 410 |
| Upton B | 26 | 570 | 20 | 91 | 72 | 39 | .251 | .341 | .412 | $24 | 400 |
| Pence H | 27 | 593 | 26 | 85 | 85 | 13 | .285 | .339 | .492 | $24 | 420 |

### Competition at RF / Stats in 2010
| Bats | Player | GSvR | GSvL | Sub | OPS |
|---|---|---|---|---|---|
| RH | Upton J | 90 | 38 | 0 | .799 |
| LH | Parra G | 21 | 8 | 7 | .679 |

### Minors (2010) / Skills
| Level | Leag | AB | HR | R | RBI | SB | BA | OBP | SLG | CT% | H% | BB% | Bash |
|---|---|---|---|---|---|---|---|---|---|---|---|---|---|
| A | — | — | — | — | — | — | — | — | — | — | — | — | — |
| AA | — | — | — | — | — | — | — | — | — | — | — | — | — |
| AAA | — | — | — | — | — | — | — | — | — | — | — | — | — |

### Majors / Skills / Value / Extra / Production / OPS / Scoresheet
| Yr | Team | AB | HR | R | RBI | SB | BA | OBP | SLG | CT% | H% | BB% | Bash | $1L | $2L | Pts | RAA | 2B | 3B | CS | FB-LD-GB | HR/fb | RBI% | RS% | OPS | 1st Hf | 2nd Hf | vs RH | vs LH | Rnge | vRH | vLH |
|---|---|---|---|---|---|---|---|---|---|---|---|---|---|---|---|---|---|---|---|---|---|---|---|---|---|---|---|---|---|---|---|---|
| 07 | ARI | 140 | 2 | 17 | 11 | 2 | .221 | .283 | .364 | 74% | 30% | 7% | 1.65 | −$4 | −$17 | 60 | −10 | 8 | 3 | 0 | 48-16-36 | 4% | 14% | 37% | .647 | — | .647 | .627 | .698 | 2.10 | — | — |
| 08 | ARI | 356 | 15 | 52 | 42 | 1 | .250 | .353 | .463 | 66% | 38% | 13% | 1.85 | $7 | −$3 | 190 | −2 | 19 | 6 | 4 | 42-21-37 | 15% | 16% | 28% | .816 | .786 | .922 | .804 | .845 | 2.08 | −22 | +53 |
| 09 | ARI | 526 | 26 | 84 | 86 | 20 | .300 | .366 | .532 | 74% | 41% | 9% | 1.77 | $29 | $20 | 400 | +20 | 30 | 7 | 5 | 36-19-45 | 19% | 21% | 31% | .899 | .918 | .869 | .805 | 1.208 | 2.07 | −21 | +49 |
| 10 | ARI | 495 | 17 | 73 | 69 | 18 | .273 | .356 | .442 | 69% | 39% | 11% | 1.62 | $20 | $12 | 300 | −1 | 27 | 3 | 8 | 39-19-41 | 12% | 20% | 30% | .799 | .787 | .822 | .808 | .768 | 2.07 | −34 | +87 |

---

## Juan Uribe — 500 PA | $10 | 260 pts
SS-103, 3B-26, 2B-24, DH-2 — Owned: 80% — RH

*Uribe is apt to be an attractive commodity in an off-season free-agent market without a lot of strong names at shortstop. He's a fan favorite in San Francisco, but the Red Sox and the Green Monster could be a good fit for a pull-happy right-handed hitter and versatile infielder. (PB)*

### Forecast
| Player | Age | AB | HR | R | RBI | SB | BA | OBP | SLG | $1L | Pts |
|---|---|---|---|---|---|---|---|---|---|---|---|
| Uribe J | 32 | 467 | 15 | 55 | 65 | 0 | .257 | .309 | .437 | $10 | 260 |
| Mini-Browser | Age | AB | HR | R | RBI | SB | BA | OBP | SLG | $1L | Pts |
| Desmond I | 25 | 460 | 15 | 50 | 50 | 20 | .250 | .311 | .403 | $11 | 270 |
| Escobar A | 24 | 561 | 6 | 75 | 50 | 25 | .245 | .290 | .343 | $11 | 300 |
| Betancourt Y | 29 | 532 | 11 | 55 | 61 | 6 | .279 | .302 | .413 | $11 | 320 |
| Gonzalez A | 34 | 580 | 19 | 69 | 75 | 0 | .248 | .293 | .413 | $10 | 300 |
| Pennington C | 26 | 532 | 6 | 66 | 48 | 24 | .237 | .318 | .343 | $10 | 290 |

### Competition at SS / Stats in 2010
| Bats | Player | GSvR | GSvL | Sub | OPS |
|---|---|---|---|---|---|
| RH | Uribe J | 78 | 23 | 2 | .749 |
| RH | Renteria E | 40 | 22 | 6 | .707 |

### Minors (2010) / Skills
| Level | Leag | AB | HR | R | RBI | SB | BA | OBP | SLG | CT% | H% | BB% | Bash |
|---|---|---|---|---|---|---|---|---|---|---|---|---|---|
| A | — | — | — | — | — | — | — | — | — | — | — | — | — |
| AA | — | — | — | — | — | — | — | — | — | — | — | — | — |
| AAA | — | — | — | — | — | — | — | — | — | — | — | — | — |

### Majors / Skills / Value / Extra / Production / OPS / Scoresheet
| Yr | Team | AB | HR | R | RBI | SB | BA | OBP | SLG | CT% | H% | BB% | Bash | $1L | $2L | Pts | RAA | 2B | 3B | CS | FB-LD-GB | HR/fb | RBI% | RS% | OPS | 1st Hf | 2nd Hf | vs RH | vs LH | Rnge | vRH | vLH |
|---|---|---|---|---|---|---|---|---|---|---|---|---|---|---|---|---|---|---|---|---|---|---|---|---|---|---|---|---|---|---|---|---|
| 07 | CHW | 513 | 20 | 55 | 68 | 1 | .234 | .284 | .394 | 78% | 30% | 6% | 1.68 | $9 | −$2 | 240 | −12 | 18 | 2 | 9 | 50-15-35 | 10% | 19% | 25% | .678 | .648 | .706 | .648 | .757 | 4.84 | −12 | +26 |
| 08 | CHW | 324 | 7 | 38 | 40 | 1 | .247 | .296 | .386 | 80% | 31% | 6% | 1.56 | $4 | −$8 | 160 | −4 | 22 | 1 | 3 | 45-20-34 | 6% | 22% | 32% | .682 | .614 | .737 | .651 | .790 | 4.82 | −8 | +18 |
| 09 | SF | 398 | 16 | 50 | 55 | 3 | .289 | .329 | .495 | 79% | 30% | 6% | 1.71 | $12 | $2 | 250 | +16 | 26 | 4 | 1 | 40-21-39 | 13% | 18% | 20% | .824 | .793 | .850 | .843 | .760 | — | −26 | +43 |
| 10 | SF | 521 | 24 | 64 | 85 | 1 | .248 | .310 | .440 | 82% | 30% | 6% | 1.78 | $15 | $7 | 330 | +6 | 24 | 2 | 2 | 44-15-40 | 12% | 20% | 26% | .749 | .758 | .738 | .766 | .682 | 4.72 | −11 | +31 |

---

## Chase Utley — 650 PA | $28 | 480 pts
2B-114 — Owned: 100% — LH

*The best second baseman in baseball had a down year in 2010 owing to a torn ligament in his thumb. He lost a lot of power, though his SLG had already been trending downward since 2007. Off-season rest and conditioning will hopefully allow him to reverse this trend and recover his power-hitting ways in 2011. (BB)*

### Forecast
| Player | Age | AB | HR | R | RBI | SB | BA | OBP | SLG | $1L | Pts |
|---|---|---|---|---|---|---|---|---|---|---|---|
| Utley C | 32 | 542 | 26 | 104 | 98 | 13 | .288 | .387 | .517 | $28 | 480 |
| Mini-Browser | Age | AB | HR | R | RBI | SB | BA | OBP | SLG | $1L | Pts |
| Kinsler I | 28 | 545 | 24 | 96 | 72 | 24 | .286 | .361 | .486 | $27 | 470 |
| Weeks R | 28 | 651 | 30 | 120 | 75 | 23 | .265 | .363 | .468 | $25 | 460 |
| Cano R | 28 | 636 | 20 | 88 | 88 | 0 | .297 | .341 | .485 | $25 | 460 |
| Pedroia D | 27 | 577 | 13 | 98 | 65 | 13 | .304 | .372 | .465 | $25 | 460 |
| Phillips B | 29 | 589 | 20 | 91 | 85 | 26 | .276 | .329 | .458 | $24 | 450 |

### Competition at 2B / Stats in 2010
| Bats | Player | GSvR | GSvL | Sub | OPS |
|---|---|---|---|---|---|
| LH | Utley C | 84 | 30 | 0 | .832 |
| RH | Valdez W | 22 | 13 | 7 | .667 |
| RH | Polanco P | 9 | 3 | 0 | .726 |

### Minors (2010) / Skills
| Level | Leag | AB | HR | R | RBI | SB | BA | OBP | SLG | CT% | H% | BB% | Bash |
|---|---|---|---|---|---|---|---|---|---|---|---|---|---|
| A | FLO | 12 | 0 | 1 | 1 | 0 | .250 | .308 | .583 | 83% | 30% | 8% | 2.33 |
| AA | — | — | — | — | — | — | — | — | — | — | — | — | — |
| AAA | — | — | — | — | — | — | — | — | — | — | — | — | — |

### Majors / Skills / Value / Extra / Production / OPS / Scoresheet
| Yr | Team | AB | HR | R | RBI | SB | BA | OBP | SLG | CT% | H% | BB% | Bash | $1L | $2L | Pts | RAA | 2B | 3B | CS | FB-LD-GB | HR/fb | RBI% | RS% | OPS | 1st Hf | 2nd Hf | vs RH | vs LH | Rnge | vRH | vLH |
|---|---|---|---|---|---|---|---|---|---|---|---|---|---|---|---|---|---|---|---|---|---|---|---|---|---|---|---|---|---|---|---|---|
| 07 | PHI | 530 | 22 | 104 | 103 | 9 | .332 | .410 | .566 | 83% | 40% | 8% | 1.70 | $31 | $25 | 480 | +38 | 48 | 5 | 1 | 42-20-38 | 12% | 27% | 36% | .976 | .972 | .985 | 1.004 | .927 | 4.33 | +24 | −68 |
| 08 | PHI | 607 | 33 | 113 | 104 | 14 | .292 | .380 | .535 | 83% | 35% | 9% | 1.84 | $32 | $27 | 530 | +26 | 41 | 4 | 2 | 44-23-33 | 15% | 22% | 34% | .915 | .955 | .855 | .932 | .888 | 4.35 | +23 | −56 |
| 09 | PHI | 571 | 31 | 112 | 93 | 23 | .282 | .397 | .508 | 81% | 35% | 13% | 1.80 | $33 | $26 | 520 | +33 | 28 | 4 | 2 | 48-18-34 | 14% | 21% | 35% | .905 | 1.004 | .790 | .877 | .962 | 4.37 | +19 | −45 |
| 10 | PHI | 425 | 16 | 75 | 65 | 13 | .275 | .387 | .445 | 85% | 32% | 12% | 1.62 | $19 | $11 | 350 | +12 | 20 | 2 | 2 | 39-20-41 | 11% | 20% | 32% | .832 | .849 | .805 | .752 | 1.003 | 4.36 | +8 | −17 |

---

## Chris Valaika — 150 PA | $-2 | 60 pts
2B-13, SS-1 — Owned: 0% — RH

*Valaika in 2010 showed enough power to make him an enticing second-base candidate, but with Brandon Phillips in front of him in Cincinnati, Valaika would probably first need to change teams. He could be trade bait, more likely as a throw-in than as a centerpiece. (SW)*

### Forecast
| Player | Age | AB | HR | R | RBI | SB | BA | OBP | SLG | $1L | Pts |
|---|---|---|---|---|---|---|---|---|---|---|---|
| Valaika C | 25 | 136 | 5 | 15 | 15 | 0 | .231 | .278 | .393 | −$2 | 60 |
| Mini-Browser | Age | AB | HR | R | RBI | SB | BA | OBP | SLG | $1L | Pts |
| McDonald J | 36 | 193 | 2 | 22 | 20 | 2 | .238 | .268 | .345 | −$2 | 90 |
| Rhymes W | 28 | 152 | 2 | 18 | 16 | 5 | .242 | .298 | .336 | −$2 | 80 |
| Herrera J | 26 | 111 | 1 | 15 | 10 | 4 | .258 | .328 | .342 | −$2 | 60 |
| Amarista J | 21 | 88 | 2 | 12 | 8 | 5 | .261 | .327 | .423 | −$2 | 60 |
| Tejada R | 21 | 184 | 2 | 20 | 14 | 4 | .228 | .298 | .323 | −$2 | 90 |

### Competition at 2B / Stats in 2010
| Bats | Player | GSvR | GSvL | Sub | OPS |
|---|---|---|---|---|---|
| RH | Phillips B | 99 | 52 | 1 | .762 |
| RH | Valaika C | 4 | 2 | 7 | .650 |

### Minors (2010) / Skills
| Level | Leag | AB | HR | R | RBI | SB | BA | OBP | SLG | CT% | H% | BB% | Bash |
|---|---|---|---|---|---|---|---|---|---|---|---|---|---|
| A | — | — | — | — | — | — | — | — | — | — | — | — | — |
| AA | — | — | — | — | — | — | — | — | — | — | — | — | — |
| AAA | IL | 424 | 4 | 49 | 53 | 3 | .304 | .330 | .408 | 83% | 37% | 4% | 1.34 |

### Majors / Skills / Value / Extra / Production / OPS / Scoresheet
| Yr | Team | AB | HR | R | RBI | SB | BA | OBP | SLG | CT% | H% | BB% | Bash | $1L | $2L | Pts | RAA | 2B | 3B | CS | FB-LD-GB | HR/fb | RBI% | RS% | OPS | 1st Hf | 2nd Hf | vs RH | vs LH | Rnge | vRH | vLH |
|---|---|---|---|---|---|---|---|---|---|---|---|---|---|---|---|---|---|---|---|---|---|---|---|---|---|---|---|---|---|---|---|---|
| 07 | — | | | | | | | | | | | | | | | | | | | | | | | | | | | | | | | |
| 08 | — | | | | | | | | | | | | | | | | | | | | | | | | | | | | | | | |
| 09 | — | | | | | | | | | | | | | | | | | | | | | | | | | | | | | | | |
| 10 | CIN | 38 | 1 | 3 | 2 | 0 | .263 | .282 | .368 | 76% | 34% | 3% | 1.40 | −$4 | −$19 | 10 | −1 | 1 | 0 | 0 | 34-24-41 | 10% | 4% | 20% | .650 | — | .650 | .348 | 1.104 | — | — | — |

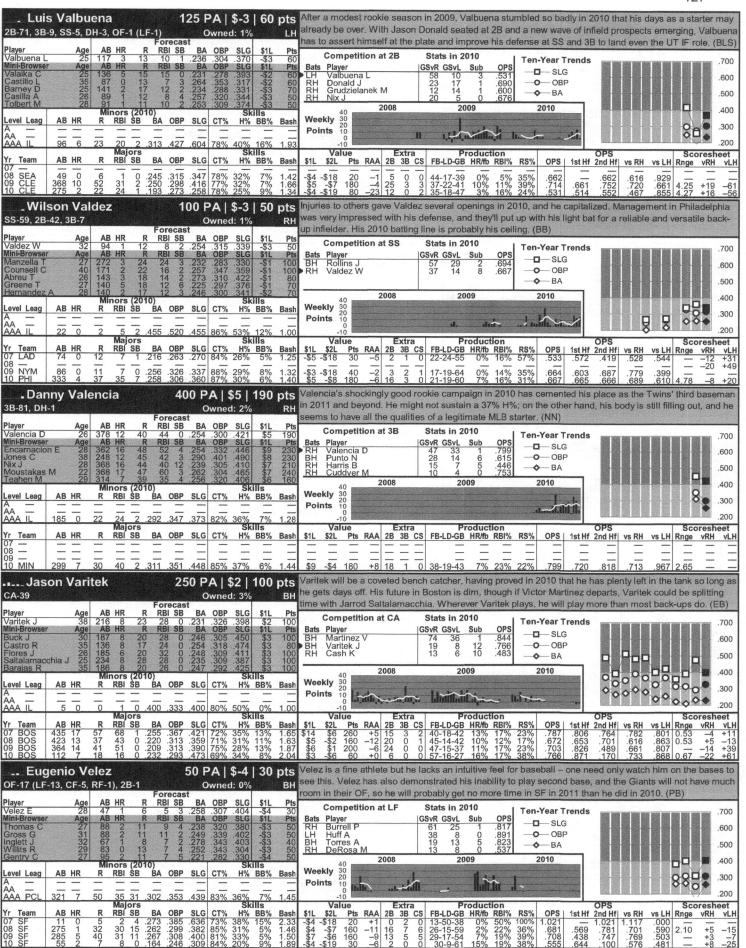

## Luis Valbuena — 125 PA | $-3 | 60 pts

2B-71, 3B-9, SS-5, DH-3, OF-1 (LF-1)  Owned: 1%  LH

After a modest rookie season in 2009, Valbuena stumbled so badly in 2010 that his days as a starter may already be over. With Jason Donald seated at 2B and a new wave of infield prospects emerging, Valbuena has to assert himself at the plate and improve his defense at SS and 3B to land even the UT IF role. (BLS)

### Forecast
| Player | Age | AB | HR | R | RBI | SB | BA | OBP | SLG | $1L | Pts |
|---|---|---|---|---|---|---|---|---|---|---|---|
| Valbuena L | 25 | 117 | 3 | 13 | 10 | 1 | .236 | .304 | .370 | -$3 | 60 |
| Mini-Browser | Age | AB | HR | R | RBI | SB | BA | OBP | SLG | $1L | Pts |
| Valaika C | 25 | 136 | 5 | 15 | 15 | 0 | .231 | .278 | .393 | -$2 | 60 |
| Castillo L | 35 | 87 | 0 | 13 | 7 | 3 | .264 | .353 | .317 | -$2 | 60 |
| Barney D | 25 | 141 | 2 | 17 | 12 | 2 | .234 | .288 | .331 | -$3 | 70 |
| Casilla A | 26 | 89 | 1 | 12 | 8 | 4 | .257 | .320 | .344 | -$3 | 50 |
| Tolbert M | 28 | 91 | 1 | 11 | 10 | 2 | .253 | .309 | .374 | -$3 | 50 |

### Minors (2010)
| Level | Leag | AB | HR | R | RBI | SB | BA | OBP | SLG | CT% | H% | BB% | Bash |
|---|---|---|---|---|---|---|---|---|---|---|---|---|---|
| A | — | | | | | | | | | | | | |
| AA | — | | | | | | | | | | | | |
| AAA | IL | 96 | 6 | 23 | 20 | 2 | .313 | .427 | .604 | 78% | 40% | 16% | 1.93 |

### Majors
| Yr | Team | AB | HR | R | RBI | SB | BA | OBP | SLG | CT% | H% | BB% | Bash | $1L | $2L | Pts | RAA | 2B | 3B | CS | FB-LD-GB | HR/fb | RBI% | RS% | OPS | 1st Hf | 2nd Hf | vs RH | vs LH | Rnge | vRH | vLH |
|---|---|---|---|---|---|---|---|---|---|---|---|---|---|---|---|---|---|---|---|---|---|---|---|---|---|---|---|---|---|---|---|---|
| 07 | — | | | | | | | | | | | | | | | | | | | | | | | | | | | | | | | |
| 08 | SEA | 49 | 0 | 6 | 1 | 0 | .245 | .315 | .347 | 78% | 32% | 7% | 1.42 | -$4 | -$18 | 20 | -1 | 5 | 0 | 0 | 44-17-39 | 0% | 5% | 35% | .662 | — | .662 | .616 | .929 | | | |
| 09 | CLE | 368 | 10 | 52 | 31 | 2 | .250 | .298 | .416 | 77% | 32% | 7% | 1.66 | $5 | -$7 | 180 | -4 | 25 | 3 | 3 | 37-22-41 | 10% | 11% | 39% | .714 | .661 | .752 | .720 | .661 | 4.25 | +19 | -61 |
| 10 | CLE | 275 | 2 | 22 | 24 | 1 | .193 | .273 | .258 | 78% | 25% | 9% | 1.34 | -$4 | -$20 | 60 | -23 | 12 | 0 | 2 | 35-18-47 | 3% | 16% | 24% | .531 | .514 | .552 | .467 | .855 | 4.27 | +16 | -56 |

## Wilson Valdez — 100 PA | $-3 | 50 pts

SS-59, 2B-42, 3B-7  Owned: 1%  RH

Injuries to others gave Valdez several openings in 2010, and he capitalized. Management in Philadelphia was very impressed with his defense, and they'll put up with his light bat for a reliable and versatile back-up infielder. His 2010 batting line is probably his ceiling. (BB)

### Forecast
| Player | Age | AB | HR | R | RBI | SB | BA | OBP | SLG | $1L | Pts |
|---|---|---|---|---|---|---|---|---|---|---|---|
| Valdez W | 32 | 94 | 1 | 12 | 8 | 2 | .254 | .315 | .339 | -$3 | 50 |
| Mini-Browser | Age | AB | HR | R | RBI | SB | BA | OBP | SLG | $1L | Pts |
| Manzella T | 27 | 272 | 3 | 24 | 24 | 3 | .232 | .283 | .330 | -$1 | 100 |
| Counsell C | 40 | 171 | 2 | 22 | 16 | 2 | .257 | .347 | .359 | -$1 | 100 |
| Abreu T | 26 | 143 | 3 | 18 | 14 | 2 | .273 | .310 | .422 | -$1 | 80 |
| Greene T | 27 | 140 | 5 | 18 | 12 | 6 | .225 | .297 | .376 | -$1 | 70 |
| Hernandez A | 28 | 140 | 2 | 17 | 12 | 3 | .246 | .300 | .341 | -$2 | 70 |

### Minors (2010)
| Level | Leag | AB | HR | R | RBI | SB | BA | OBP | SLG | CT% | H% | BB% | Bash |
|---|---|---|---|---|---|---|---|---|---|---|---|---|---|
| A | — | | | | | | | | | | | | |
| AA | — | | | | | | | | | | | | |
| AAA | IL | 22 | 0 | 2 | 5 | 2 | .455 | .520 | .455 | 86% | 53% | 12% | 1.00 |

### Majors
| Yr | Team | AB | HR | R | RBI | SB | BA | OBP | SLG | CT% | H% | BB% | Bash | $1L | $2L | Pts | RAA | 2B | 3B | CS | FB-LD-GB | HR/fb | RBI% | RS% | OPS | 1st Hf | 2nd Hf | vs RH | vs LH | Rnge | vRH | vLH |
|---|---|---|---|---|---|---|---|---|---|---|---|---|---|---|---|---|---|---|---|---|---|---|---|---|---|---|---|---|---|---|---|---|
| 07 | LAD | 74 | 0 | 12 | 7 | 1 | .216 | .263 | .270 | 84% | 26% | 5% | 1.25 | -$5 | -$18 | 30 | -5 | 2 | 1 | 0 | 22-24-55 | 0% | 16% | 57% | .533 | .572 | .419 | .528 | .544 | — | -12 | +31 |
| 08 | — | | | | | | | | | | | | | | | | | | | | | | | | | | | | | | | |
| 09 | NYM | 86 | 0 | 11 | 7 | 0 | .256 | .326 | .337 | 88% | 29% | 8% | 1.32 | -$3 | -$18 | 40 | -2 | 3 | 2 | 1 | 17-19-64 | 0% | 14% | 35% | .664 | .603 | .687 | .779 | .399 | — | -20 | +49 |
| 10 | PHI | 333 | 4 | 37 | 35 | 7 | .258 | .306 | .360 | 87% | 30% | 5% | 1.40 | $5 | -$8 | 180 | -6 | 16 | 3 | 0 | 21-19-60 | 7% | 16% | 31% | .667 | .665 | .666 | .689 | .610 | 4.78 | -8 | +20 |

## Danny Valencia — 400 PA | $5 | 190 pts

3B-81, DH-1  Owned: 2%  RH

Valencia's shockingly good rookie campaign in 2010 has cemented his place as the Twins' third baseman in 2011 and beyond. He might not sustain a 37% H%; on the other hand, his body is still filling out, and he seems to have all the qualities of a legitimate MLB starter. (NN)

### Forecast
| Player | Age | AB | HR | R | RBI | SB | BA | OBP | SLG | $1L | Pts |
|---|---|---|---|---|---|---|---|---|---|---|---|
| Valencia D | 26 | 378 | 12 | 40 | 44 | 0 | .254 | .300 | .421 | $5 | 190 |
| Mini-Browser | Age | AB | HR | R | RBI | SB | BA | OBP | SLG | $1L | Pts |
| Encarnacion E | 28 | 362 | 16 | 48 | 52 | 4 | .254 | .332 | .446 | $9 | 230 |
| Jones C | 38 | 248 | 12 | 45 | 42 | 3 | .290 | .401 | .490 | $8 | 230 |
| Nix J | 28 | 368 | 16 | 44 | 40 | 12 | .239 | .305 | .410 | $7 | 210 |
| Moustakas M | 22 | 368 | 17 | 47 | 60 | 3 | .262 | .304 | .465 | $7 | 240 |
| Teahen M | 29 | 314 | 7 | 39 | 35 | 4 | .256 | .320 | .406 | $6 | 160 |

### Minors (2010)
| Level | Leag | AB | HR | R | RBI | SB | BA | OBP | SLG | CT% | H% | BB% | Bash |
|---|---|---|---|---|---|---|---|---|---|---|---|---|---|
| A | — | | | | | | | | | | | | |
| AA | — | | | | | | | | | | | | |
| AAA | IL | 185 | 0 | 22 | 24 | 2 | .292 | .347 | .373 | 82% | 36% | 7% | 1.28 |

### Majors
| Yr | Team | AB | HR | R | RBI | SB | BA | OBP | SLG | CT% | H% | BB% | Bash | $1L | $2L | Pts | RAA | 2B | 3B | CS | FB-LD-GB | HR/fb | RBI% | RS% | OPS | 1st Hf | 2nd Hf | vs RH | vs LH | Rnge | vRH | vLH |
|---|---|---|---|---|---|---|---|---|---|---|---|---|---|---|---|---|---|---|---|---|---|---|---|---|---|---|---|---|---|---|---|---|
| 07 | — | | | | | | | | | | | | | | | | | | | | | | | | | | | | | | | |
| 08 | — | | | | | | | | | | | | | | | | | | | | | | | | | | | | | | | |
| 09 | — | | | | | | | | | | | | | | | | | | | | | | | | | | | | | | | |
| 10 | MIN | 299 | 7 | 30 | 40 | 2 | .311 | .351 | .448 | 85% | 37% | 6% | 1.44 | $9 | -$4 | 180 | +8 | 18 | 1 | 0 | 38-19-43 | 7% | 23% | 22% | .799 | .720 | .818 | .713 | .967 | 2.65 | — | — |

## Jason Varitek — 250 PA | $2 | 100 pts

CA-39  Owned: 3%  BH

Varitek will be a coveted bench catcher, having proved in 2010 that he has plenty left in the tank so long as he gets days off. His future in Boston is dim, though if Victor Martinez departs, Varitek could be splitting time with Jarrod Saltalamacchia. Wherever Varitek plays, he will play more than most back-ups do. (EB)

### Forecast
| Player | Age | AB | HR | R | RBI | SB | BA | OBP | SLG | $1L | Pts |
|---|---|---|---|---|---|---|---|---|---|---|---|
| Varitek J | 38 | 216 | 8 | 23 | 28 | 0 | .231 | .326 | .398 | $2 | 100 |
| Mini-Browser | Age | AB | HR | R | RBI | SB | BA | OBP | SLG | $1L | Pts |
| Buck J | 30 | 187 | 8 | 20 | 28 | 0 | .246 | .305 | .450 | $3 | 100 |
| Castro R | 35 | 136 | 8 | 17 | 24 | 0 | .254 | .318 | .474 | $3 | 80 |
| Flores J | 26 | 185 | 6 | 20 | 32 | 0 | .248 | .309 | .411 | $3 | 100 |
| Saltalamacchia J | 25 | 234 | 8 | 28 | 28 | 0 | .235 | .309 | .387 | $3 | 100 |
| Barajas R | 35 | 186 | 8 | 20 | 26 | 0 | .247 | .292 | .425 | $3 | 90 |

### Minors (2010)
| Level | Leag | AB | HR | R | RBI | SB | BA | OBP | SLG | CT% | H% | BB% | Bash |
|---|---|---|---|---|---|---|---|---|---|---|---|---|---|
| A | — | | | | | | | | | | | | |
| AA | — | | | | | | | | | | | | |
| AAA | IL | 5 | 0 | 0 | 1 | 0 | .400 | .333 | .400 | 80% | 50% | 0% | 1.00 |

### Majors
| Yr | Team | AB | HR | R | RBI | SB | BA | OBP | SLG | CT% | H% | BB% | Bash | $1L | $2L | Pts | RAA | 2B | 3B | CS | FB-LD-GB | HR/fb | RBI% | RS% | OPS | 1st Hf | 2nd Hf | vs RH | vs LH | Rnge | vRH | vLH |
|---|---|---|---|---|---|---|---|---|---|---|---|---|---|---|---|---|---|---|---|---|---|---|---|---|---|---|---|---|---|---|---|---|
| 07 | BOS | 435 | 17 | 57 | 68 | 1 | .255 | .367 | .421 | 72% | 35% | 13% | 1.65 | $14 | $6 | 260 | +5 | 15 | 3 | 2 | 40-18-42 | 13% | 17% | 23% | .787 | .806 | .764 | .782 | .801 | 0.53 | -4 | +11 |
| 08 | BOS | 423 | 13 | 37 | 43 | 0 | .220 | .313 | .359 | 71% | 31% | 11% | 1.63 | $5 | -$2 | 160 | -12 | 20 | 0 | 1 | 45-14-42 | 10% | 12% | 17% | .672 | .653 | .701 | .616 | .863 | 0.53 | +5 | -13 |
| 09 | BOS | 364 | 14 | 41 | 51 | 0 | .209 | .313 | .390 | 75% | 28% | 11% | 1.87 | $6 | $1 | 200 | -6 | 24 | 0 | 0 | 47-15-37 | 11% | 17% | 23% | .703 | .826 | .489 | .661 | .807 | — | -14 | +39 |
| 10 | BOS | 112 | 7 | 18 | 16 | 0 | .232 | .293 | .473 | 69% | 34% | 8% | 2.04 | $6 | $0 | 60 | +0 | 5 | 0 | 0 | 57-16-27 | 16% | 17% | 38% | .766 | .871 | .170 | .733 | .868 | 0.67 | -22 | +61 |

## Eugenio Velez — 50 PA | $-4 | 30 pts

OF-17 (LF-13, CF-5, RF-1), 2B-1  Owned: 0%  BH

Velez is a fine athlete but he lacks an intuitive feel for baseball – one need only watch him on the bases to see this. Velez has also demonstrated his inability to play second base, and the Giants will not have much room in their OF, so he will probably get no more time in SF in 2011 than he did in 2010. (PB)

### Forecast
| Player | Age | AB | HR | R | RBI | SB | BA | OBP | SLG | $1L | Pts |
|---|---|---|---|---|---|---|---|---|---|---|---|
| Velez E | 28 | 47 | 1 | 6 | 5 | 3 | .258 | .307 | .404 | -$4 | 30 |
| Mini-Browser | Age | AB | HR | R | RBI | SB | BA | OBP | SLG | $1L | Pts |
| Thomas C | 27 | 88 | 2 | 11 | 9 | 4 | .238 | .320 | .380 | -$3 | 50 |
| Gross G | 31 | 88 | 2 | 11 | 11 | 2 | .249 | .339 | .402 | -$3 | 50 |
| Inglett J | 32 | 67 | 1 | 8 | 7 | 2 | .278 | .343 | .403 | -$3 | 40 |
| Willits R | 29 | 83 | 0 | 13 | 7 | 4 | .252 | .343 | .304 | -$3 | 50 |
| Gentry C | 27 | 95 | 2 | 11 | 7 | 5 | .221 | .292 | .330 | -$4 | 50 |

### Minors (2010)
| Level | Leag | AB | HR | R | RBI | SB | BA | OBP | SLG | CT% | H% | BB% | Bash |
|---|---|---|---|---|---|---|---|---|---|---|---|---|---|
| A | — | | | | | | | | | | | | |
| AA | — | | | | | | | | | | | | |
| AAA | PCL | 321 | 7 | 50 | 35 | 31 | .302 | .353 | .439 | 83% | 36% | 7% | 1.45 |

### Majors
| Yr | Team | AB | HR | R | RBI | SB | BA | OBP | SLG | CT% | H% | BB% | Bash | $1L | $2L | Pts | RAA | 2B | 3B | CS | FB-LD-GB | HR/fb | RBI% | RS% | OPS | 1st Hf | 2nd Hf | vs RH | vs LH | Rnge | vRH | vLH |
|---|---|---|---|---|---|---|---|---|---|---|---|---|---|---|---|---|---|---|---|---|---|---|---|---|---|---|---|---|---|---|---|---|
| 07 | SF | 11 | 0 | 5 | 2 | 4 | .273 | .385 | .636 | 73% | 38% | 15% | 2.33 | -$4 | -$18 | 20 | +1 | 0 | 2 | 0 | 13-50-38 | 0% | 50% | 100% | 1.021 | — | 1.021 | 1.117 | .000 | — | — | — |
| 08 | SF | 275 | 1 | 32 | 30 | 15 | .262 | .299 | .382 | 85% | 31% | 5% | 1.46 | -$4 | -$7 | 160 | -11 | 16 | 7 | 6 | 26-18-59 | 2% | 22% | 36% | .681 | .569 | .781 | .701 | .590 | 2.10 | +5 | -15 |
| 09 | SF | 285 | 5 | 40 | 31 | 11 | .267 | .308 | .400 | 81% | 33% | 5% | 1.50 | $7 | -$6 | 160 | -9 | 13 | 5 | 2 | 29-17-54 | 7% | 19% | 39% | .708 | .438 | .747 | .769 | .503 | — | +3 | -7 |
| 10 | SF | 55 | 2 | 7 | 8 | 0 | .164 | .246 | .309 | 84% | 20% | 8% | 1.89 | -$4 | -$19 | 30 | -6 | 2 | 0 | 0 | 30-9-61 | 15% | 19% | 38% | .555 | .644 | .100 | .576 | .481 | — | +8 | -25 |

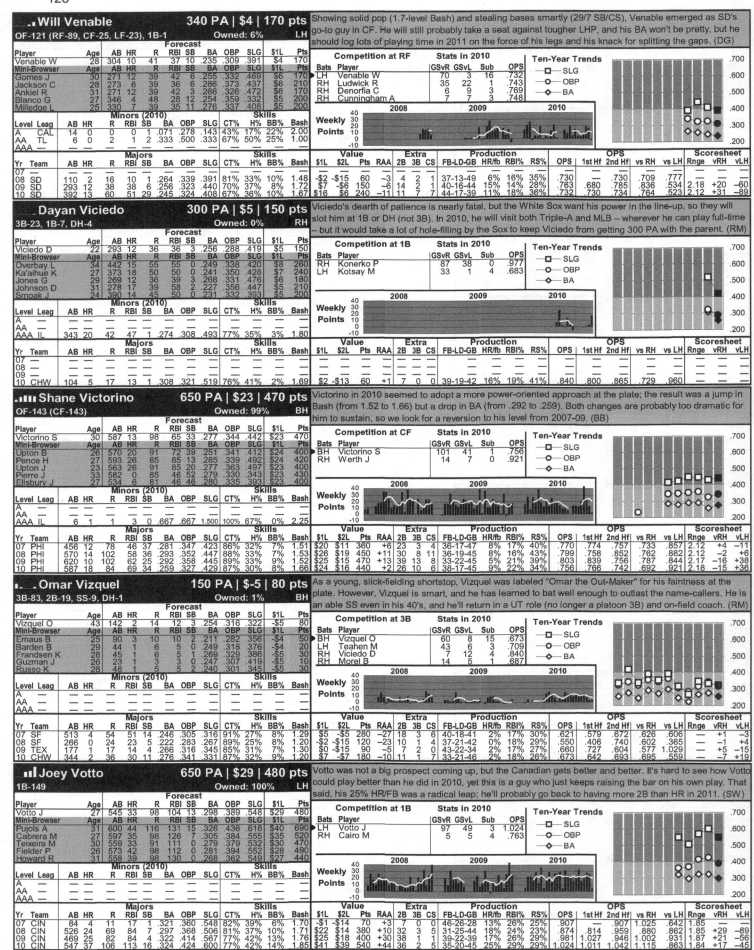

## Will Venable — 340 PA | $4 | 170 pts

OF-121 (RF-89, CF-25, LF-23), 1B-1 — Owned: 6% — LH

Showing solid pop (1.7-level Bash) and stealing bases smartly (29/7 SB/CS), Venable emerged as SD's go-to guy in CF. He will still probably take a seat against tougher LHP, and his BA won't be pretty, but he should log lots of playing time in 2011 on the force of his legs and his knack for splitting the gaps. (DG)

| Player | Age | AB | HR | R | RBI | SB | BA | OBP | SLG | $1L | Pts |
|---|---|---|---|---|---|---|---|---|---|---|---|
| **Forecast** | | | | | | | | | | | |
| Venable W | 28 | 304 | 10 | 41 | 37 | 10 | .235 | .309 | .391 | $4 | 170 |
| **Mini-Browser** | Age | AB | HR | R | RBI | SB | BA | OBP | SLG | $1L | Pts |
| Gomes J | 30 | 271 | 12 | 39 | 42 | 6 | .255 | .332 | .469 | $6 | 170 |
| Jackson C | 28 | 273 | 6 | 39 | 36 | 6 | .286 | .373 | .437 | $6 | 210 |
| Ankiel R | 31 | 271 | 12 | 39 | 42 | 3 | .266 | .326 | .472 | $6 | 170 |
| Blanco G | 27 | 346 | 4 | 48 | 28 | 12 | .254 | .359 | .332 | $5 | 200 |
| Milledge L | 25 | 330 | 7 | 39 | 35 | 11 | .276 | .337 | .408 | $5 | 200 |

**Competition at RF — Stats in 2010**

| Bats | Player | GSvR | GSvL | Sub | OPS |
|---|---|---|---|---|---|
| LH | Venable W | 70 | 3 | 16 | .732 |
| RH | Ludwick R | 35 | 22 | 1 | .743 |
| RH | Denorfia C | 6 | 9 | 3 | .769 |
| RH | Cunningham A | 7 | 7 | 3 | .748 |

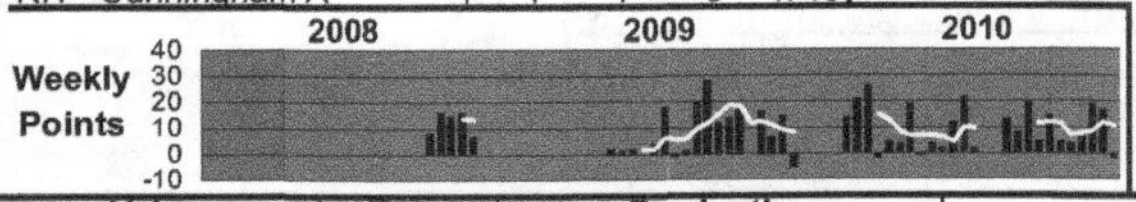


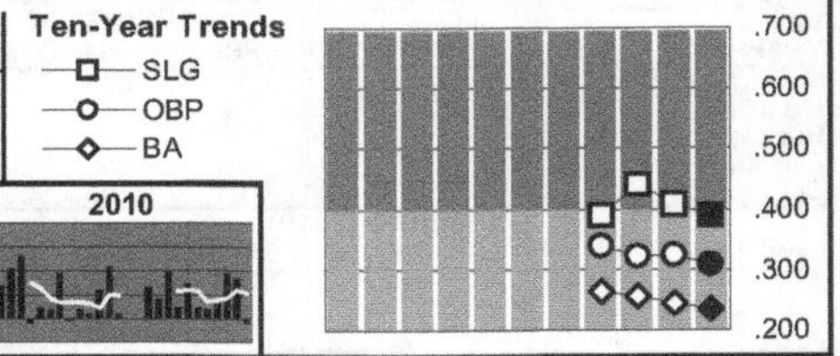


**Minors (2010)**

| Level | Leag | AB | HR | R | RBI | SB | BA | OBP | SLG | CT% | H% | BB% | Bash |
|---|---|---|---|---|---|---|---|---|---|---|---|---|---|
| A | CAL | 14 | 0 | 0 | 0 | 1 | .071 | .278 | .143 | 43% | 17% | 22% | 2.00 |
| AA | TL | 6 | 0 | 2 | 1 | 2 | .333 | .500 | .333 | 67% | 50% | 25% | 1.00 |
| AAA | — | — | — | — | — | — | — | — | — | — | — | — | — |

**Majors**

| Yr | Team | AB | HR | R | RBI | SB | BA | OBP | SLG | CT% | H% | BB% | Bash | $1L | $2L | Pts | RAA | 2B | 3B | CS | FB-LD-GB | HR/fb | RBI% | RS% | OPS | 1st Hf | 2nd Hf | vs RH | vs LH | Rnge | vRH | vLH |
|---|---|---|---|---|---|---|---|---|---|---|---|---|---|---|---|---|---|---|---|---|---|---|---|---|---|---|---|---|---|---|---|---|
| 07 | — | — | — | — | — | — | — | — | — | — | — | — | — | — | — | — | — | — | — | — | — | — | — | — | — | — | — | — | — | — | — | — |
| 08 | SD | 110 | 2 | 16 | 10 | 1 | .264 | .339 | .391 | 81% | 33% | 10% | 1.48 | -$2 | -$15 | 60 | −3 | 4 | 2 | 1 | 37-13-49 | 6% | 16% | 35% | .730 | — | .730 | .709 | .777 | — | — | — |
| 09 | SD | 293 | 12 | 38 | 38 | 6 | .256 | .323 | .440 | 70% | 37% | 8% | 1.72 | $7 | -$6 | 150 | −6 | 14 | 2 | 1 | 40-16-44 | 15% | 14% | 28% | .763 | .680 | .785 | .836 | .534 | 2.18 | +20 | −60 |
| 10 | SD | 392 | 13 | 60 | 51 | 29 | .245 | .324 | .408 | 67% | 36% | 10% | 1.67 | $16 | $6 | 240 | −11 | 11 | 7 | 7 | 44-17-39 | 11% | 18% | 36% | .732 | .730 | .734 | .764 | .523 | 2.12 | +31 | −89 |

## Dayan Viciedo — 300 PA | $5 | 150 pts

3B-23, 1B-7, DH-4 — Owned: 0% — RH

Viciedo's dearth of patience is nearly fatal, but the White Sox want his power in the line-up, so they will slot him at 1B or DH (not 3B). In 2010, he will visit both Triple-A and MLB – wherever he can play full-time – but it would take a lot of hole-filling by the Sox to keep Viciedo from getting 300 PA with the parent. (RM)

| Player | Age | AB | HR | R | RBI | SB | BA | OBP | SLG | $1L | Pts |
|---|---|---|---|---|---|---|---|---|---|---|---|
| **Forecast** | | | | | | | | | | | |
| Viciedo D | 22 | 293 | 12 | 36 | 36 | 3 | .256 | .288 | .419 | $5 | 150 |
| **Mini-Browser** | Age | AB | HR | R | RBI | SB | BA | OBP | SLG | $1L | Pts |
| Overbay L | 34 | 442 | 15 | 55 | 55 | 0 | .249 | .338 | .420 | $8 | 260 |
| Ka'aihue K | 27 | 373 | 18 | 50 | 50 | 0 | .241 | .350 | .428 | $7 | 240 |
| Jones G | 29 | 269 | 12 | 36 | 39 | 3 | .268 | .331 | .476 | $6 | 180 |
| Johnson D | 31 | 278 | 17 | 39 | 58 | 2 | .227 | .356 | .447 | $5 | 210 |
| Smoak J | 24 | 390 | 14 | 45 | 50 | 0 | .231 | .332 | .393 | $5 | 200 |

**Competition at 1B — Stats in 2010**

| Bats | Player | GSvR | GSvL | Sub | OPS |
|---|---|---|---|---|---|
| RH | Konerko P | 87 | 38 | 0 | .977 |
| LH | Kotsay M | 33 | 1 | 4 | .683 |

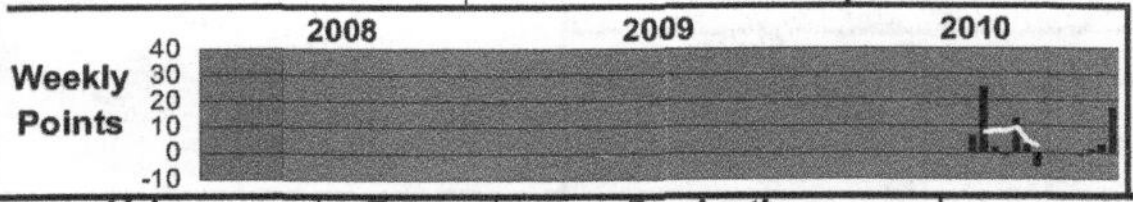


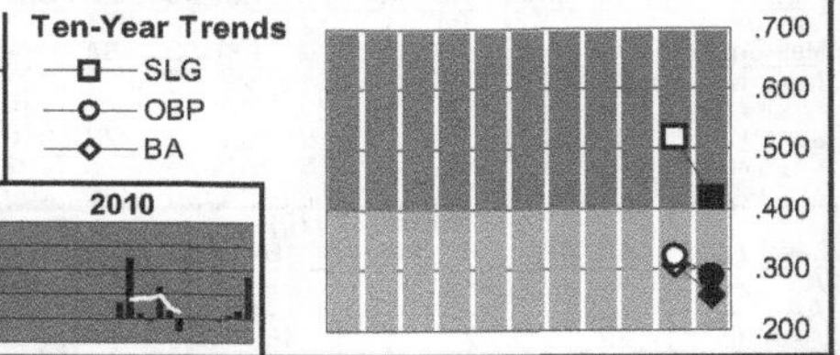


**Minors (2010)**

| Level | Leag | AB | HR | R | RBI | SB | BA | OBP | SLG | CT% | H% | BB% | Bash |
|---|---|---|---|---|---|---|---|---|---|---|---|---|---|
| A | — | — | — | — | — | — | — | — | — | — | — | — | — |
| AA | — | — | — | — | — | — | — | — | — | — | — | — | — |
| AAA | IL | 343 | 20 | 42 | 47 | 1 | .274 | .308 | .493 | 77% | 35% | 3% | 1.80 |

**Majors**

| Yr | Team | AB | HR | R | RBI | SB | BA | OBP | SLG | CT% | H% | BB% | Bash | $1L | $2L | Pts | RAA | 2B | 3B | CS | FB-LD-GB | HR/fb | RBI% | RS% | OPS | 1st Hf | 2nd Hf | vs RH | vs LH | Rnge | vRH | vLH |
|---|---|---|---|---|---|---|---|---|---|---|---|---|---|---|---|---|---|---|---|---|---|---|---|---|---|---|---|---|---|---|---|---|
| 07 | — | — | — | — | — | — | — | — | — | — | — | — | — | — | — | — | — | — | — | — | — | — | — | — | — | — | — | — | — | — | — | — |
| 08 | — | — | — | — | — | — | — | — | — | — | — | — | — | — | — | — | — | — | — | — | — | — | — | — | — | — | — | — | — | — | — | — |
| 09 | — | — | — | — | — | — | — | — | — | — | — | — | — | — | — | — | — | — | — | — | — | — | — | — | — | — | — | — | — | — | — | — |
| 10 | CHW | 104 | 5 | 17 | 13 | 1 | .308 | .321 | .519 | 76% | 41% | 2% | 1.69 | $2 | -$13 | 60 | +1 | 7 | 0 | 0 | 39-19-42 | 16% | 19% | 41% | .840 | .800 | .865 | .729 | .960 | — | — | — |

## Shane Victorino — 650 PA | $23 | 470 pts

OF-143 (CF-143) — Owned: 99% — BH

Victorino in 2010 seemed to adopt a more power-oriented approach at the plate; the result was a jump in Bash (from 1.52 to 1.66) but a drop in BA (from .292 to .259). Both changes are probably too dramatic for him to sustain, so we look for a reversion to his level from 2007-09. (BB)

| Player | Age | AB | HR | R | RBI | SB | BA | OBP | SLG | $1L | Pts |
|---|---|---|---|---|---|---|---|---|---|---|---|
| **Forecast** | | | | | | | | | | | |
| Victorino S | 30 | 587 | 13 | 98 | 65 | 33 | .277 | .344 | .442 | $23 | 470 |
| **Mini-Browser** | Age | AB | HR | R | RBI | SB | BA | OBP | SLG | $1L | Pts |
| Upton B | 26 | 570 | 20 | 91 | 72 | 39 | .251 | .341 | .412 | $24 | 400 |
| Pence H | 27 | 593 | 26 | 85 | 85 | 13 | .285 | .339 | .492 | $24 | 420 |
| Upton J | 23 | 563 | 26 | 91 | 85 | 20 | .277 | .363 | .497 | $23 | 400 |
| Pierre J | 33 | 582 | 0 | 85 | 46 | 52 | .279 | .330 | .343 | $23 | 430 |
| Ellsbury J | 27 | 534 | 6 | 81 | 46 | 46 | .280 | .335 | .393 | $23 | 400 |

**Competition at CF — Stats in 2010**

| Bats | Player | GSvR | GSvL | Sub | OPS |
|---|---|---|---|---|---|
| BH | Victorino S | 101 | 41 | 1 | .756 |
| RH | Werth J | 14 | 7 | 0 | .921 |

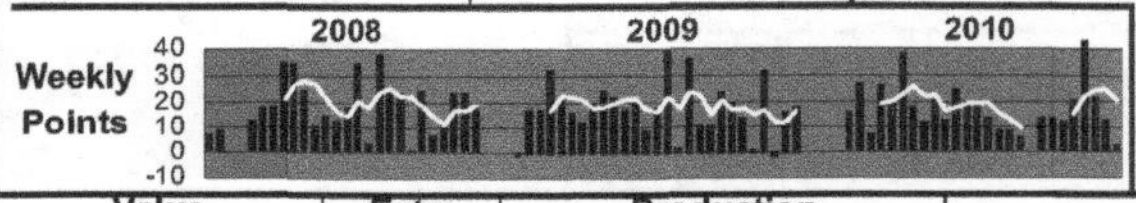


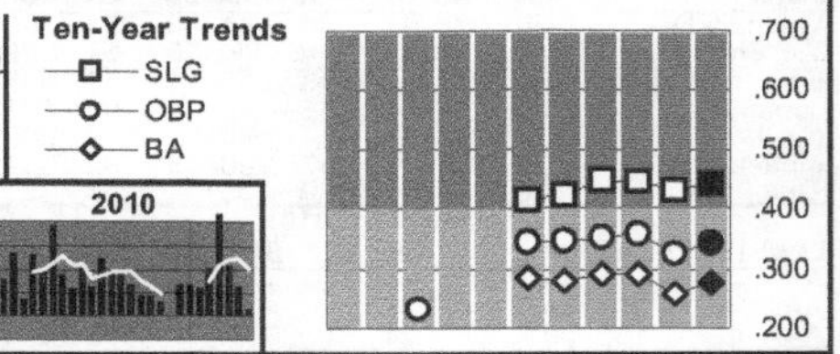


**Minors (2010)**

| Level | Leag | AB | HR | R | RBI | SB | BA | OBP | SLG | CT% | H% | BB% | Bash |
|---|---|---|---|---|---|---|---|---|---|---|---|---|---|
| A | — | — | — | — | — | — | — | — | — | — | — | — | — |
| AA | — | — | — | — | — | — | — | — | — | — | — | — | — |
| AAA | IL | 6 | 1 | 1 | 3 | 0 | .667 | .667 | 1.500 | 100% | 67% | 0% | 2.25 |

**Majors**

| Yr | Team | AB | HR | R | RBI | SB | BA | OBP | SLG | CT% | H% | BB% | Bash | $1L | $2L | Pts | RAA | 2B | 3B | CS | FB-LD-GB | HR/fb | RBI% | RS% | OPS | 1st Hf | 2nd Hf | vs RH | vs LH | Rnge | vRH | vLH |
|---|---|---|---|---|---|---|---|---|---|---|---|---|---|---|---|---|---|---|---|---|---|---|---|---|---|---|---|---|---|---|---|---|
| 07 | PHI | 456 | 12 | 78 | 46 | 37 | .281 | .347 | .423 | 86% | 32% | 7% | 1.51 | $20 | $11 | 360 | +6 | 23 | 3 | 4 | 36-17-47 | 8% | 17% | 40% | .770 | .774 | .757 | .733 | .857 | 2.12 | +4 | −11 |
| 08 | PHI | 570 | 14 | 102 | 58 | 36 | .293 | .352 | .447 | 88% | 33% | 7% | 1.53 | $26 | $19 | 450 | +11 | 30 | 8 | 11 | 36-19-45 | 8% | 16% | 43% | .799 | .758 | .852 | .762 | .882 | 2.12 | −2 | +6 |
| 09 | PHI | 620 | 10 | 102 | 62 | 25 | .292 | .358 | .445 | 89% | 33% | 9% | 1.52 | $25 | $15 | 470 | +13 | 39 | 13 | 8 | 33-22-45 | 5% | 21% | 39% | .803 | .839 | .756 | .787 | .844 | 2.17 | −16 | +38 |
| 10 | PHI | 587 | 18 | 84 | 69 | 34 | .259 | .327 | .429 | 87% | 30% | 8% | 1.66 | $24 | $16 | 440 | +2 | 26 | 10 | 6 | 38-17-45 | 9% | 22% | 34% | .756 | .766 | .742 | .692 | .921 | 2.18 | −15 | +36 |

## Omar Vizquel — 150 PA | $-5 | 80 pts

3B-83, 2B-19, SS-9, DH-1 — Owned: 1% — BH

As a young, slick-fielding shortstop, Vizquel was labeled "Omar the Out-Maker" for his faintness at the plate. However, Vizquel is smart, and he has learned to bat well enough to outlast the name-callers. He is an able SS even in his 40's, and he'll return in a UT role (no longer a platoon 3B) and on-field coach. (RM)

| Player | Age | AB | HR | R | RBI | SB | BA | OBP | SLG | $1L | Pts |
|---|---|---|---|---|---|---|---|---|---|---|---|
| **Forecast** | | | | | | | | | | | |
| Vizquel O | 43 | 142 | 2 | 14 | 12 | 3 | .254 | .316 | .322 | -$5 | 80 |
| **Mini-Browser** | Age | AB | HR | R | RBI | SB | BA | OBP | SLG | $1L | Pts |
| Emaus B | 25 | 90 | 3 | 10 | 10 | 2 | .211 | .282 | .356 | -$4 | 50 |
| Barden B | 29 | 44 | 1 | 6 | 5 | 0 | .249 | .318 | .376 | -$4 | 20 |
| Frandsen K | 28 | 45 | 1 | 6 | 5 | 1 | .269 | .329 | .386 | -$5 | 30 |
| Guzman J | 26 | 23 | 1 | 3 | 3 | 0 | .247 | .307 | .419 | -$5 | 10 |
| Russo K | 26 | 48 | 1 | 5 | 5 | 2 | .240 | .301 | .345 | -$5 | 30 |

**Competition at 3B — Stats in 2010**

| Bats | Player | GSvR | GSvL | Sub | OPS |
|---|---|---|---|---|---|
| BH | Vizquel O | 60 | 8 | 15 | .673 |
| LH | Teahen M | 43 | 6 | 3 | .709 |
| RH | Viciedo D | 7 | 12 | 4 | .840 |
| RH | Morel B | 14 | 5 | 1 | .687 |

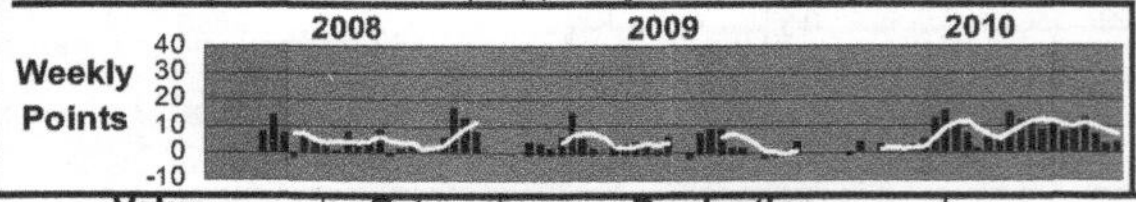


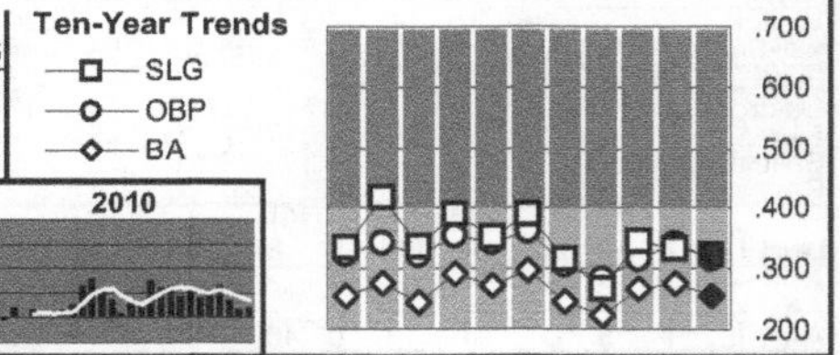


**Minors (2010)**

| Level | Leag | AB | HR | R | RBI | SB | BA | OBP | SLG | CT% | H% | BB% | Bash |
|---|---|---|---|---|---|---|---|---|---|---|---|---|---|
| A | — | — | — | — | — | — | — | — | — | — | — | — | — |
| AA | — | — | — | — | — | — | — | — | — | — | — | — | — |
| AAA | — | — | — | — | — | — | — | — | — | — | — | — | — |

**Majors**

| Yr | Team | AB | HR | R | RBI | SB | BA | OBP | SLG | CT% | H% | BB% | Bash | $1L | $2L | Pts | RAA | 2B | 3B | CS | FB-LD-GB | HR/fb | RBI% | RS% | OPS | 1st Hf | 2nd Hf | vs RH | vs LH | Rnge | vRH | vLH |
|---|---|---|---|---|---|---|---|---|---|---|---|---|---|---|---|---|---|---|---|---|---|---|---|---|---|---|---|---|---|---|---|---|
| 07 | SF | 513 | 4 | 54 | 51 | 14 | .246 | .305 | .316 | 91% | 27% | 8% | 1.29 | $5 | -$5 | 280 | −27 | 18 | 3 | 6 | 40-18-41 | 2% | 17% | 30% | .621 | .579 | .672 | .626 | .606 | — | +1 | −3 |
| 08 | SF | 266 | 0 | 24 | 23 | 5 | .222 | .283 | .267 | 89% | 25% | 8% | 1.20 | -$2 | -$15 | 120 | −23 | 10 | 1 | 4 | 37-21-42 | 0% | 18% | 29% | .550 | .406 | .740 | .602 | .365 | — | −1 | +4 |
| 09 | TEX | 177 | 1 | 17 | 14 | 4 | .266 | .316 | .345 | 85% | 31% | 7% | 1.30 | $0 | -$15 | 90 | −5 | 7 | 2 | 0 | 43-22-34 | 2% | 17% | 27% | .660 | .727 | .604 | .577 | 1.029 | — | +5 | −15 |
| 10 | CHW | 344 | 2 | 36 | 30 | 11 | .276 | .341 | .331 | 87% | 32% | 9% | 1.20 | $7 | -$7 | 180 | −10 | 11 | 1 | 7 | 33-21-46 | 2% | 18% | 26% | .673 | .642 | .693 | .695 | .559 | — | −7 | +19 |

## Joey Votto — 650 PA | $29 | 480 pts

1B-149 — Owned: 100% — LH

Votto was not a big prospect coming up, but the Canadian gets better and better. It's hard to see how Votto could play better than he did in 2010, yet this is a guy who just keeps raising the bar on his own play. That said, his 25% HR/FB was a radical leap; he'll probably go back to having more 2B than HR in 2011. (SW)

| Player | Age | AB | HR | R | RBI | SB | BA | OBP | SLG | $1L | Pts |
|---|---|---|---|---|---|---|---|---|---|---|---|
| **Forecast** | | | | | | | | | | | |
| Votto J | 27 | 545 | 33 | 98 | 104 | 13 | .298 | .389 | .548 | $29 | 480 |
| **Mini-Browser** | Age | AB | HR | R | RBI | SB | BA | OBP | SLG | $1L | Pts |
| Pujols A | 31 | 600 | 44 | 116 | 131 | 15 | .326 | .436 | .618 | $40 | 690 |
| Cabrera M | 27 | 597 | 35 | 98 | 126 | 7 | .305 | .384 | .555 | $35 | 520 |
| Teixeira M | 30 | 559 | 33 | 91 | 111 | 0 | .279 | .379 | .532 | $30 | 470 |
| Fielder P | 26 | 573 | 42 | 98 | 112 | 0 | .281 | .394 | .552 | $28 | 490 |
| Howard R | 31 | 558 | 39 | 98 | 130 | 0 | .268 | .362 | .549 | $27 | 440 |

**Competition at 1B — Stats in 2010**

| Bats | Player | GSvR | GSvL | Sub | OPS |
|---|---|---|---|---|---|
| LH | Votto J | 97 | 49 | 3 | 1.024 |
| RH | Cairo M | 5 | 5 | 4 | .763 |

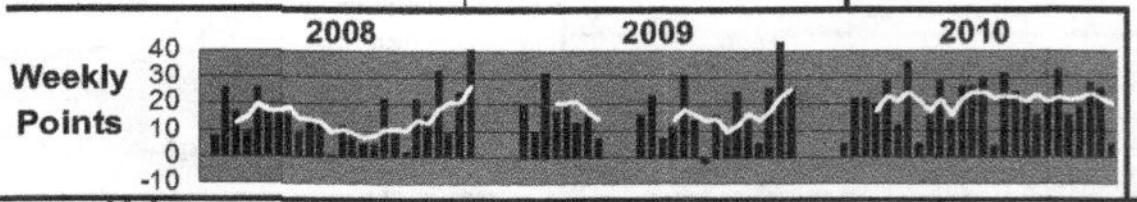


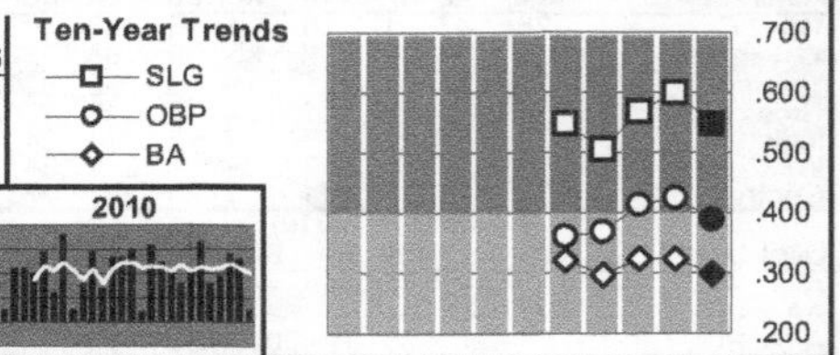


**Minors (2010)**

| Level | Leag | AB | HR | R | RBI | SB | BA | OBP | SLG | CT% | H% | BB% | Bash |
|---|---|---|---|---|---|---|---|---|---|---|---|---|---|
| A | — | — | — | — | — | — | — | — | — | — | — | — | — |
| AA | — | — | — | — | — | — | — | — | — | — | — | — | — |
| AAA | — | — | — | — | — | — | — | — | — | — | — | — | — |

**Majors**

| Yr | Team | AB | HR | R | RBI | SB | BA | OBP | SLG | CT% | H% | BB% | Bash | $1L | $2L | Pts | RAA | 2B | 3B | CS | FB-LD-GB | HR/fb | RBI% | RS% | OPS | 1st Hf | 2nd Hf | vs RH | vs LH | Rnge | vRH | vLH |
|---|---|---|---|---|---|---|---|---|---|---|---|---|---|---|---|---|---|---|---|---|---|---|---|---|---|---|---|---|---|---|---|---|
| 07 | CIN | 84 | 4 | 11 | 17 | 1 | .321 | .360 | .548 | 82% | 39% | 6% | 1.70 | -$1 | -$14 | 70 | +3 | 7 | 0 | 0 | 46-26-28 | 13% | 26% | 25% | .907 | — | .907 | 1.025 | .642 | 1.85 | — | — |
| 08 | CIN | 526 | 24 | 69 | 84 | 7 | .297 | .368 | .506 | 81% | 37% | 10% | 1.71 | $22 | $14 | 380 | +10 | 32 | 3 | 5 | 31-25-44 | 18% | 24% | 23% | .874 | .814 | .959 | .880 | .862 | 1.85 | +29 | −89 |
| 09 | CIN | 469 | 25 | 82 | 84 | 4 | .322 | .414 | .567 | 77% | 42% | 13% | 1.76 | $25 | $18 | 400 | +30 | 38 | 1 | 1 | 39-22-39 | 17% | 26% | 29% | .981 | 1.027 | .946 | 1.002 | .931 | 1.87 | +21 | −56 |
| 10 | CIN | 547 | 37 | 106 | 113 | 16 | .324 | .424 | .600 | 77% | 42% | 14% | 1.85 | $41 | $39 | 540 | +44 | 36 | 2 | 5 | 35-20-45 | 25% | 29% | 29% | 1.024 | 1.011 | 1.042 | 1.115 | .863 | 1.84 | +17 | −45 |

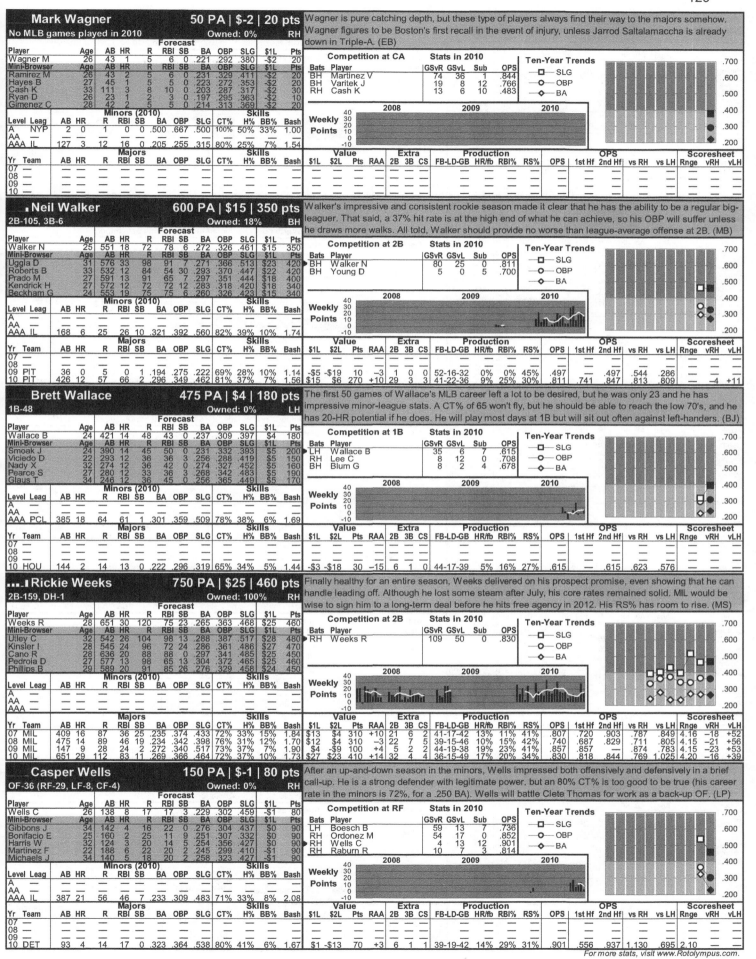

## Mark Wagner — 50 PA | $-2 | 20 pts
No MLB games played in 2010 · Owned: 0% · RH

Wagner is pure catching depth, but these type of players always find their way to the majors somehow. Wagner figures to be Boston's first recall in the event of injury, unless Jarrod Saltalamacchia is already down in Triple-A. (EB)

| Player | Age | AB | HR | R | RBI | SB | BA | OBP | SLG | $1L | Pts |
|---|---|---|---|---|---|---|---|---|---|---|---|
| Wagner M | 26 | 43 | 1 | 5 | 6 | 0 | .221 | .292 | .380 | -$2 | 20 |
| Ramirez M | 26 | 43 | 2 | 5 | 6 | 0 | .231 | .329 | .411 | -$2 | 20 |
| Hayes B | 27 | 45 | 1 | 5 | 2 | 0 | .223 | .272 | .353 | -$2 | 20 |
| Cash K | 33 | 111 | 3 | 8 | 10 | 0 | .203 | .287 | .317 | -$2 | 30 |
| Ryan D | 26 | 23 | 1 | 2 | 5 | 0 | .197 | .295 | .363 | -$2 | 10 |
| Gimenez C | 28 | 42 | 2 | 5 | 5 | 0 | .214 | .313 | .369 | -$2 | 20 |

Minors (2010):
| Level | Leag | AB | HR | R | RBI | SB | BA | OBP | SLG | CT% | H% | BB% | Bash |
|---|---|---|---|---|---|---|---|---|---|---|---|---|---|
| A | NYP | 2 | 0 | 1 | 0 | 0 | .500 | .667 | .500 | 100% | 50% | 33% | 1.00 |
| AAA | IL | 127 | 3 | 12 | 16 | 0 | .205 | .255 | .315 | 80% | 25% | 7% | 1.54 |

Competition at CA (Stats in 2010): BH Martinez V 74/36/1 .844; BH Varitek J 19/8/12 .766; RH Cash K 13/6/10 .483

## Neil Walker — 600 PA | $15 | 350 pts
2B-105, 3B-6 · Owned: 18% · BH

Walker's impressive and consistent rookie season made it clear that he has the ability to be a regular big-leaguer. That said, a 37% hit rate is at the high end of what he can achieve, so his OBP will suffer unless he draws more walks. All told, Walker should provide no worse than league-average offense at 2B. (MB)

| Player | Age | AB | HR | R | RBI | SB | BA | OBP | SLG | $1L | Pts |
|---|---|---|---|---|---|---|---|---|---|---|---|
| Walker N | 25 | 551 | 18 | 72 | 78 | 6 | .272 | .326 | .461 | $15 | 350 |
| Uggla D | 31 | 576 | 33 | 98 | 91 | 7 | .271 | .366 | .513 | $23 | 420 |
| Roberts B | 33 | 532 | 12 | 84 | 54 | 30 | .293 | .370 | .447 | $22 | 420 |
| Prado M | 27 | 591 | 13 | 91 | 65 | 7 | .297 | .351 | .444 | $18 | 400 |
| Kendrick H | 27 | 572 | 12 | 72 | 72 | 12 | .283 | .318 | .420 | $18 | 340 |
| Beckham G | 24 | 553 | 19 | 75 | 75 | 6 | .260 | .326 | .423 | $15 | 340 |

Minors (2010): AAA IL 168 6 25 26 10 .321 .392 .560 82% 39% 10% 1.74

Majors:
| Yr | Team | AB | HR | R | RBI | SB | BA | OBP | SLG | CT% | H% | BB% | Bash | $1L | $2L | Pts | RAA | 2B | 3B | CS | FB-LD-GB | HR/fb | RBI% | RS% | OPS | 1st Hf | 2nd Hf | vs RH | vs LH | Rnge | vRH | vLH |
|---|---|---|---|---|---|---|---|---|---|---|---|---|---|---|---|---|---|---|---|---|---|---|---|---|---|---|---|---|---|---|---|---|
| 09 | PIT | 36 | 0 | 5 | 0 | 1 | .194 | .275 | .222 | 69% | 28% | 10% | 1.14 | -$5 | -$19 | 10 | -3 | 1 | 0 | 0 | 52-16-32 | 0% | 0% | 45% | .497 | — | .497 | .544 | .286 | — | — | — |
| 10 | PIT | 426 | 12 | 57 | 66 | 2 | .296 | .349 | .462 | 81% | 37% | 7% | 1.56 | $15 | $6 | 270 | +10 | 29 | 3 | 3 | 41-22-36 | 9% | 25% | 30% | .811 | .741 | .847 | .813 | .809 | — | -4 | +11 |

Competition at 2B (Stats in 2010): BH Walker N 80/25/0 .811; BH Young D 5/0/5 .700

## Brett Wallace — 475 PA | $4 | 180 pts
1B-48 · Owned: 0% · LH

The first 50 games of Wallace's MLB career left a lot to be desired, but he was only 23 and he has impressive minor-league stats. A CT% of 65 won't fly, but he should be able to reach the low 70's, and he has 20-HR potential if he does. He will play most days at 1B but will sit out often against left-handers. (BJ)

| Player | Age | AB | HR | R | RBI | SB | BA | OBP | SLG | $1L | Pts |
|---|---|---|---|---|---|---|---|---|---|---|---|
| Wallace B | 24 | 421 | 14 | 48 | 43 | 0 | .237 | .309 | .397 | $4 | 180 |
| Smoak J | 24 | 390 | 14 | 45 | 50 | 0 | .231 | .332 | .393 | $5 | 200 |
| Viciedo D | 22 | 293 | 12 | 36 | 36 | 3 | .256 | .288 | .419 | $5 | 150 |
| Nady X | 32 | 274 | 12 | 36 | 42 | 0 | .274 | .327 | .452 | $5 | 160 |
| Pearce S | 27 | 280 | 12 | 33 | 36 | 3 | .268 | .342 | .483 | $5 | 190 |
| Glaus T | 34 | 246 | 12 | 36 | 45 | 0 | .256 | .365 | .449 | $5 | 170 |

Minors (2010): AAA PCL 385 18 64 61 1 .301 .359 .509 78% 38% 6% 1.69

Majors:
| Yr | Team | AB | HR | R | RBI | SB | BA | OBP | SLG | CT% | H% | BB% | Bash | $1L | $2L | Pts | RAA | 2B | 3B | CS | FB-LD-GB | HR/fb | RBI% | RS% | OPS | 1st Hf | 2nd Hf | vs RH | vs LH |
|---|---|---|---|---|---|---|---|---|---|---|---|---|---|---|---|---|---|---|---|---|---|---|---|---|---|---|---|---|---|
| 10 | HOU | 144 | 2 | 14 | 13 | 0 | .222 | .296 | .319 | 65% | 34% | 5% | 1.44 | -$3 | -$18 | 30 | -15 | 6 | 1 | 0 | 44-17-39 | 5% | 16% | 27% | .615 | — | .615 | .623 | .576 |

Competition at 1B (Stats in 2010): LH Wallace B 35/6/7 .615; RH Lee C 8/12/0 .708; BH Blum G 8/2/4 .678

## Rickie Weeks — 750 PA | $25 | 460 pts
2B-159, DH-1 · Owned: 100% · RH

Finally healthy for an entire season, Weeks delivered on his prospect promise, even showing that he can handle leading off. Although he lost some steam after July, his core rates remained solid. MIL would be wise to sign him to a long-term deal before he hits free agency in 2012. His RS% has room to rise. (MS)

| Player | Age | AB | HR | R | RBI | SB | BA | OBP | SLG | $1L | Pts |
|---|---|---|---|---|---|---|---|---|---|---|---|
| Weeks R | 28 | 651 | 30 | 120 | 75 | 23 | .265 | .363 | .468 | $25 | 460 |
| Utley C | 32 | 542 | 26 | 104 | 98 | 13 | .288 | .387 | .517 | $28 | 480 |
| Kinsler I | 28 | 545 | 24 | 96 | 72 | 24 | .286 | .361 | .486 | $27 | 470 |
| Cano R | 28 | 636 | 29 | 100 | 88 | 0 | .297 | .341 | .485 | $25 | 450 |
| Pedroia D | 27 | 577 | 13 | 91 | 65 | 13 | .304 | .372 | .465 | $25 | 460 |
| Phillips B | 29 | 589 | 20 | 91 | 85 | 26 | .276 | .329 | .458 | $24 | 450 |

Majors:
| Yr | Team | AB | HR | R | RBI | SB | BA | OBP | SLG | CT% | H% | BB% | Bash | $1L | $2L | Pts | RAA | 2B | 3B | CS | FB-LD-GB | HR/fb | RBI% | RS% | OPS | 1st Hf | 2nd Hf | vs RH | vs LH | Rnge | vRH | vLH |
|---|---|---|---|---|---|---|---|---|---|---|---|---|---|---|---|---|---|---|---|---|---|---|---|---|---|---|---|---|---|---|---|---|
| 07 | MIL | 409 | 16 | 87 | 36 | 25 | .235 | .374 | .433 | 72% | 33% | 15% | 1.84 | $13 | $4 | 310 | +10 | 21 | 6 | 2 | 41-17-42 | 13% | 11% | 41% | .807 | .720 | .903 | .787 | .849 | 4.16 | -18 | +52 |
| 08 | MIL | 475 | 14 | 89 | 46 | 19 | .234 | .342 | .398 | 76% | 31% | 12% | 1.70 | $12 | $4 | 310 | -3 | 22 | 7 | 5 | 39-15-46 | 10% | 15% | 42% | .740 | .687 | .829 | .711 | .805 | 4.15 | -21 | +56 |
| 09 | MIL | 147 | 9 | 28 | 24 | 2 | .272 | .340 | .517 | 73% | 37% | 7% | 1.90 | $4 | -$9 | 100 | +4 | 5 | 2 | 0 | 44-19-38 | 19% | 23% | 41% | .857 | .857 | — | .874 | .783 | 4.15 | -23 | +53 |
| 10 | MIL | 651 | 29 | 112 | 83 | 11 | .269 | .366 | .464 | 72% | 37% | 10% | 1.73 | $27 | $3 | 410 | +14 | 32 | 4 | 4 | 36-15-49 | 17% | 20% | 34% | .830 | .818 | .844 | .769 | 1.025 | 4.20 | -16 | +39 |

Competition at 2B (Stats in 2010): RH Weeks R 109/50/0 .830

## Casper Wells — 150 PA | $-1 | 80 pts
OF-36 (RF-29, LF-8, CF-4) · Owned: 0% · RH

After an up-and-down season in the minors, Wells impressed both offensively and defensively in a brief call-up. He is a strong defender with legitimate power, but an 80% CT% is too good to be true (his career rate in the minors is 72%, for a .250 BA). Wells will battle Clete Thomas for work as a back-up OF. (LP)

| Player | Age | AB | HR | R | RBI | SB | BA | OBP | SLG | $1L | Pts |
|---|---|---|---|---|---|---|---|---|---|---|---|
| Wells C | 26 | 138 | 8 | 17 | 17 | 3 | .229 | .302 | .459 | -$1 | 80 |
| Gibbons J | 34 | 142 | 4 | 16 | 22 | 0 | .276 | .304 | .437 | $0 | 90 |
| Bonifacio E | 25 | 160 | 2 | 25 | 11 | 6 | .251 | .307 | .332 | $0 | 90 |
| Harris W | 32 | 124 | 3 | 20 | 14 | 5 | .254 | .356 | .427 | $0 | 90 |
| Martinez F | 22 | 188 | 6 | 22 | 20 | 2 | .245 | .299 | .410 | -$1 | 90 |
| Michaels J | 34 | 140 | 5 | 18 | 20 | 2 | .258 | .323 | .427 | -$1 | 80 |

Minors (2010): AAA IL 387 21 56 46 7 .233 .309 .483 71% 33% 8% 2.08

Majors:
| Yr | Team | AB | HR | R | RBI | SB | BA | OBP | SLG | CT% | H% | BB% | Bash | $1L | $2L | Pts | RAA | 2B | 3B | CS | FB-LD-GB | HR/fb | RBI% | RS% | OPS | 1st Hf | 2nd Hf | vs RH | vs LH | Rnge |
|---|---|---|---|---|---|---|---|---|---|---|---|---|---|---|---|---|---|---|---|---|---|---|---|---|---|---|---|---|---|---|
| 10 | DET | 93 | 4 | 14 | 17 | 0 | .323 | .364 | .538 | 80% | 41% | 6% | 1.67 | $1 | -$13 | 70 | +3 | 6 | 1 | 1 | 39-19-42 | 14% | 29% | 31% | .901 | .556 | .937 | 1.130 | .695 | 2.10 |

Competition at RF (Stats in 2010): LH Boesch B 59/13/7 .736; RH Ordonez M 54/17/0 .852; RH Wells C 4/13/12 .901; RH Raburn R 10/7/3 .814

*For more stats, visit www.Rotolympus.com.*

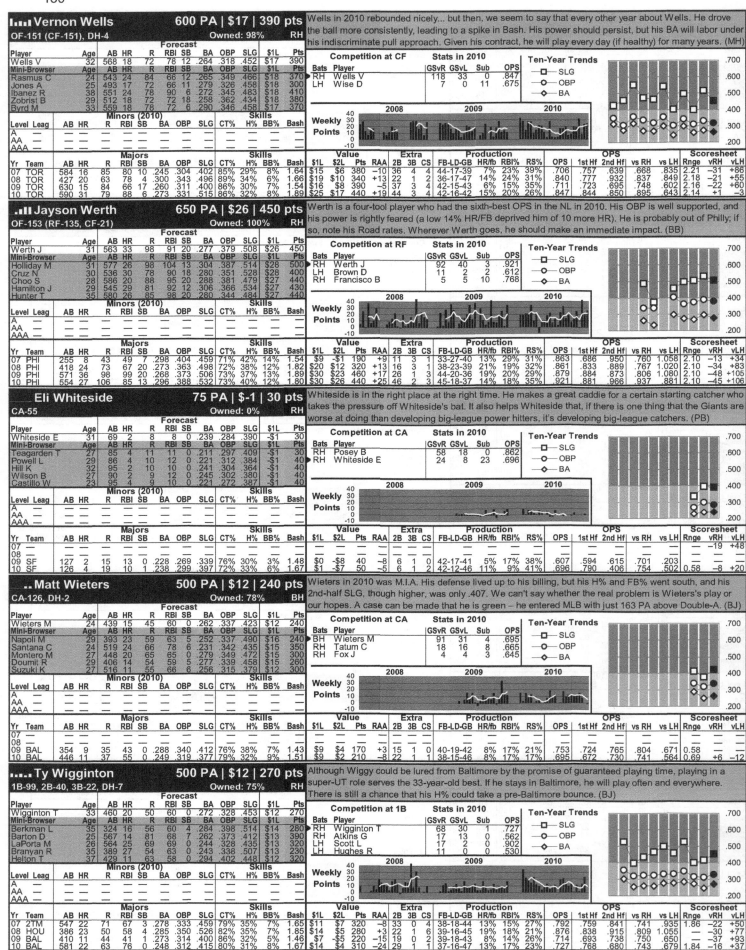

## Vernon Wells — 600 PA | $17 | 390 pts

OF-151 (CF-151), DH-4 — Owned: 98% — RH

Wells in 2010 rebounded nicely... but then, we seem to say that every other year about Wells. He drove the ball more consistently, leading to a spike in Bash. His power should persist, but his BA will labor under his indiscriminate pull approach. Given his contract, he will play every day (if healthy) for many years. (MH)

| Player | Age | AB | HR | R | RBI | SB | BA | OBP | SLG | $1L | Pts |
|---|---|---|---|---|---|---|---|---|---|---|---|
| | | Forecast | | | | | | | | | |
| Wells V | 32 | 568 | 18 | 72 | 78 | 12 | .264 | .318 | .452 | $17 | 390 |
| Mini-Browser | Age | AB | HR | R | RBI | SB | BA | OBP | SLG | $1L | Pts |
| Rasmus C | 24 | 543 | 24 | 84 | 66 | 12 | .265 | .349 | .466 | $18 | 370 |
| Jones A | 25 | 493 | 17 | 72 | 66 | 11 | .279 | .326 | .458 | $18 | 300 |
| Ibanez R | 38 | 551 | 24 | 78 | 90 | 6 | .272 | .345 | .483 | $18 | 410 |
| Zobrist B | 29 | 512 | 18 | 72 | 72 | 18 | .258 | .362 | .434 | $18 | 380 |
| Byrd M | 33 | 559 | 18 | 78 | 72 | 6 | .290 | .346 | .458 | $17 | 370 |

| Level | Leag | AB | HR | R | RBI | SB | BA | OBP | SLG | CT% | H% | BB% | Bash |
|---|---|---|---|---|---|---|---|---|---|---|---|---|---|
| | | Minors (2010) | | | | | | | | Skills | | | |
| A | — | — | — | — | — | — | — | — | — | — | — | — | — |
| AA | — | — | — | — | — | — | — | — | — | — | — | — | — |
| AAA | — | — | — | — | — | — | — | — | — | — | — | — | — |

Competition at CF — Stats in 2010

| Bats | Player | GSvR | GSvL | Sub | OPS |
|---|---|---|---|---|---|
| RH | Wells V | 118 | 33 | 0 | .847 |
| LH | Wise D | 7 | 0 | 11 | .675 |

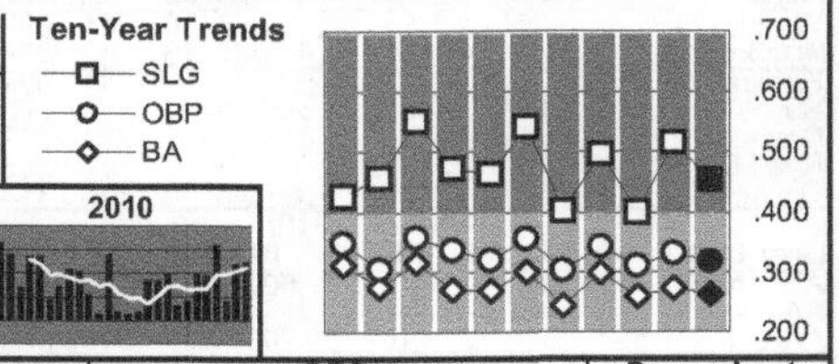


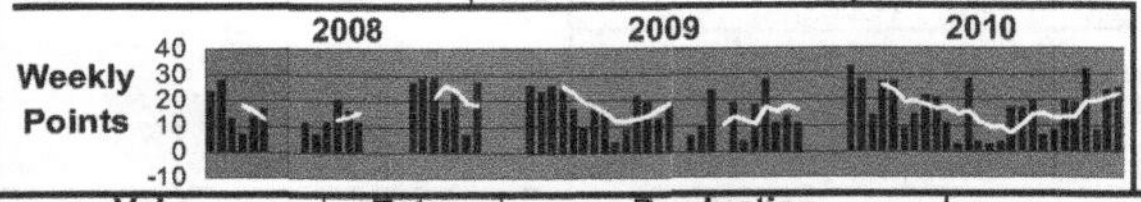


| Yr | Team | AB | HR | R | RBI | SB | BA | OBP | SLG | CT% | H% | BB% | Bash | $1L | $2L | Pts | RAA | 2B | 3B | CS | FB-LD-GB | HR/fb | RBI% | RS% | OPS | 1st Hf | 2nd Hf | vs RH | vs LH | Rnge | vRH | vLH |
|---|---|---|---|---|---|---|---|---|---|---|---|---|---|---|---|---|---|---|---|---|---|---|---|---|---|---|---|---|---|---|---|---|
| | | Majors | | | | | | | | Skills | | | | Value | | | | Extra | | | Production | | | | OPS | | | | | Scoresheet | | |
| 07 | TOR | 584 | 16 | 85 | 80 | 10 | .245 | .304 | .402 | 85% | 29% | 8% | 1.64 | $15 | $6 | 380 | −10 | 36 | 4 | 4 | 44-17-39 | 7% | 23% | 39% | .706 | .757 | .639 | .668 | .835 | 2.21 | −31 | +86 |
| 08 | TOR | 427 | 20 | 63 | 78 | 4 | .300 | .343 | .496 | 89% | 34% | 6% | 1.66 | $19 | $10 | 340 | +13 | 22 | 1 | 2 | 36-17-47 | 14% | 24% | 31% | .840 | .777 | .932 | .837 | .849 | 2.18 | −21 | +55 |
| 09 | TOR | 630 | 15 | 84 | 66 | 17 | .260 | .311 | .400 | 86% | 30% | 7% | 1.54 | $16 | $8 | 390 | −5 | 37 | 3 | 4 | 42-15-43 | 6% | 15% | 35% | .711 | .723 | .695 | .748 | .602 | 2.16 | −22 | +60 |
| 10 | TOR | 590 | 31 | 79 | 88 | 6 | .273 | .331 | .515 | 86% | 32% | 8% | 1.89 | $25 | $17 | 440 | +19 | 44 | 3 | 4 | 42-16-42 | 15% | 20% | 26% | .847 | .844 | .850 | .895 | .643 | 2.14 | +1 | −3 |

## Jayson Werth — 650 PA | $26 | 450 pts

OF-153 (RF-135, CF-21) — Owned: 100% — RH

Werth is a four-tool player who had the sixth-best OPS in the NL in 2010. His OBP is well supported, and his power is rightly feared (a low 14% HR/FB deprived him of 10 more HR). He is probably out of Philly; if so, note his Road rates. Wherever Werth goes, he should make an immediate impact. (BB)

| Player | Age | AB | HR | R | RBI | SB | BA | OBP | SLG | $1L | Pts |
|---|---|---|---|---|---|---|---|---|---|---|---|
| | | Forecast | | | | | | | | | |
| Werth J | 31 | 563 | 33 | 98 | 91 | 20 | .277 | .379 | .508 | $26 | 450 |
| Mini-Browser | Age | AB | HR | R | RBI | SB | BA | OBP | SLG | $1L | Pts |
| Holliday M | 31 | 577 | 26 | 98 | 104 | 13 | .304 | .387 | .514 | $28 | 500 |
| Cruz N | 30 | 536 | 30 | 78 | 90 | 18 | .280 | .351 | .528 | $28 | 400 |
| Choo S | 28 | 586 | 20 | 88 | 95 | 20 | .288 | .381 | .479 | $27 | 440 |
| Hamilton J | 29 | 545 | 29 | 81 | 92 | 12 | .306 | .366 | .534 | $27 | 430 |
| Hunter T | 35 | 580 | 26 | 85 | 98 | 20 | .280 | .344 | .484 | $27 | 440 |

| Level | Leag | AB | HR | R | RBI | SB | BA | OBP | SLG | CT% | H% | BB% | Bash |
|---|---|---|---|---|---|---|---|---|---|---|---|---|---|
| | | Minors (2010) | | | | | | | | Skills | | | |
| A | — | — | — | — | — | — | — | — | — | — | — | — | — |
| AA | — | — | — | — | — | — | — | — | — | — | — | — | — |
| AAA | — | — | — | — | — | — | — | — | — | — | — | — | — |

Competition at RF — Stats in 2010

| Bats | Player | GSvR | GSvL | Sub | OPS |
|---|---|---|---|---|---|
| RH | Werth J | 92 | 40 | 3 | .921 |
| LH | Brown D | 11 | 2 | 2 | .612 |
| RH | Francisco B | 5 | 5 | 10 | .768 |

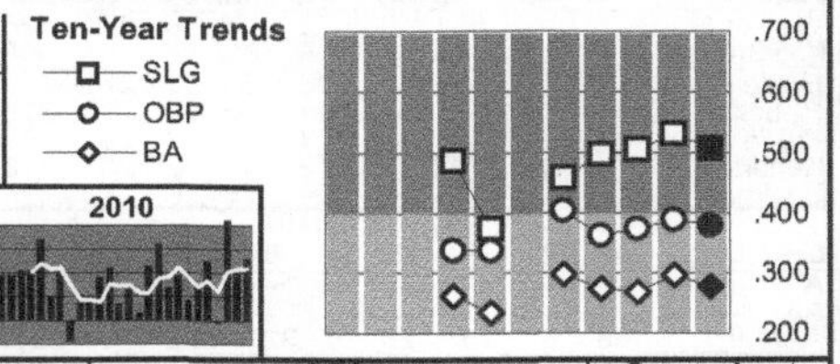


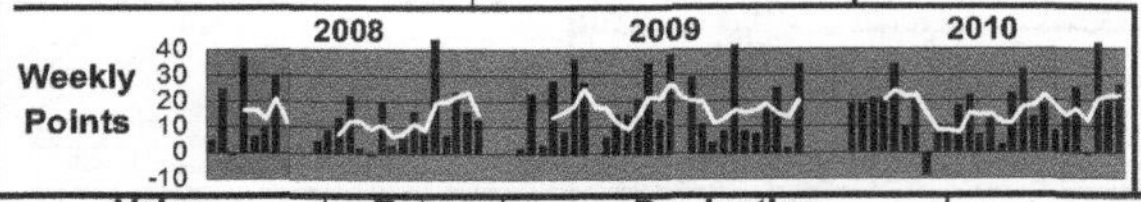


| Yr | Team | AB | HR | R | RBI | SB | BA | OBP | SLG | CT% | H% | BB% | Bash | $1L | $2L | Pts | RAA | 2B | 3B | CS | FB-LD-GB | HR/fb | RBI% | RS% | OPS | 1st Hf | 2nd Hf | vs RH | vs LH | Rnge | vRH | vLH |
|---|---|---|---|---|---|---|---|---|---|---|---|---|---|---|---|---|---|---|---|---|---|---|---|---|---|---|---|---|---|---|---|---|
| | | Majors | | | | | | | | Skills | | | | Value | | | | Extra | | | Production | | | | OPS | | | | | Scoresheet | | |
| 07 | PHI | 255 | 8 | 43 | 49 | 7 | .298 | .404 | .459 | 71% | 42% | 14% | 1.54 | $9 | -$1 | 190 | +9 | 11 | 3 | 1 | 33-27-40 | 13% | 29% | 31% | .863 | .686 | .950 | .760 | 1.058 | 2.10 | −13 | +34 |
| 08 | PHI | 418 | 24 | 73 | 67 | 20 | .273 | .363 | .498 | 72% | 38% | 12% | 1.82 | $20 | $12 | 320 | +13 | 16 | 3 | 1 | 38-23-39 | 21% | 19% | 32% | .861 | .833 | .889 | .767 | 1.020 | 2.10 | −34 | +83 |
| 09 | PHI | 571 | 36 | 98 | 99 | 20 | .268 | .373 | .506 | 73% | 37% | 13% | 1.89 | $30 | $23 | 460 | +17 | 26 | 1 | 3 | 44-20-36 | 19% | 20% | 29% | .879 | .884 | .873 | .806 | 1.080 | 2.10 | −48 | +105 |
| 10 | PHI | 554 | 27 | 106 | 85 | 13 | .296 | .388 | .532 | 73% | 40% | 12% | 1.80 | $30 | $26 | 440 | +25 | 46 | 2 | 3 | 45-18-37 | 14% | 18% | 35% | .921 | .881 | .966 | .937 | .881 | 2.10 | −45 | +106 |

## Eli Whiteside — 75 PA | $-1 | 30 pts

CA-55 — Owned: 0% — RH

Whiteside is in the right place at the right time. He makes a great caddie for a certain starting catcher who takes the pressure off Whiteside's bat. It also helps Whiteside that, if there is one thing that the Giants are worse at doing than developing big-league power hitters, it's developing big-league catchers. (PB)

| Player | Age | AB | HR | R | RBI | SB | BA | OBP | SLG | $1L | Pts |
|---|---|---|---|---|---|---|---|---|---|---|---|
| | | Forecast | | | | | | | | | |
| Whiteside E | 31 | 69 | 2 | 8 | 8 | 0 | .239 | .284 | .390 | -$1 | 30 |
| Mini-Browser | Age | AB | HR | R | RBI | SB | BA | OBP | SLG | $1L | Pts |
| Teagarden T | 27 | 85 | 4 | 11 | 11 | 0 | .211 | .297 | .409 | -$1 | 30 |
| Powell L | 29 | 86 | 4 | 10 | 12 | 0 | .221 | .312 | .384 | -$1 | 40 |
| Hill K | 32 | 95 | 2 | 10 | 10 | 0 | .241 | .304 | .364 | -$1 | 40 |
| Wilson B | 27 | 90 | 2 | 9 | 12 | 0 | .245 | .302 | .380 | -$1 | 40 |
| Castillo W | 23 | 95 | 4 | 9 | 10 | 0 | .221 | .272 | .387 | -$1 | 40 |

| Level | Leag | AB | HR | R | RBI | SB | BA | OBP | SLG | CT% | H% | BB% | Bash |
|---|---|---|---|---|---|---|---|---|---|---|---|---|---|
| | | Minors (2010) | | | | | | | | Skills | | | |
| A | — | — | — | — | — | — | — | — | — | — | — | — | — |
| AA | — | — | — | — | — | — | — | — | — | — | — | — | — |
| AAA | — | — | — | — | — | — | — | — | — | — | — | — | — |

Competition at CA — Stats in 2010

| Bats | Player | GSvR | GSvL | Sub | OPS |
|---|---|---|---|---|---|
| RH | Posey B | 58 | 18 | 0 | .862 |
| RH | Whiteside E | 24 | 8 | 23 | .696 |

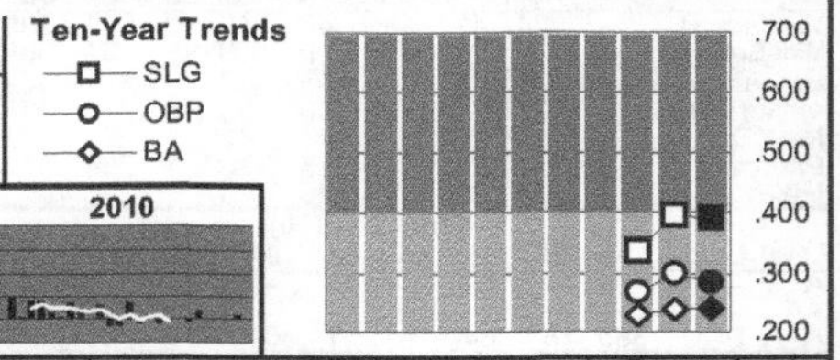


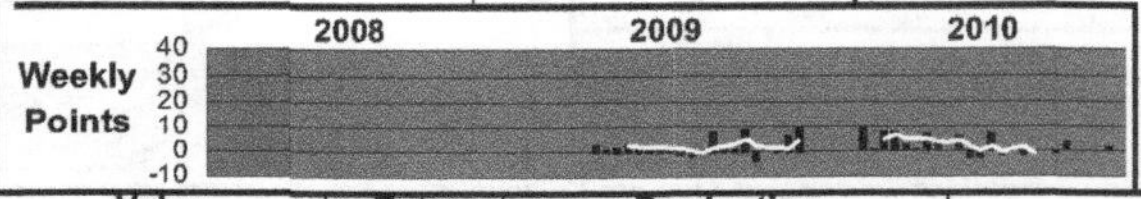


| Yr | Team | AB | HR | R | RBI | SB | BA | OBP | SLG | CT% | H% | BB% | Bash | $1L | $2L | Pts | RAA | 2B | 3B | CS | FB-LD-GB | HR/fb | RBI% | RS% | OPS | 1st Hf | 2nd Hf | vs RH | vs LH | Rnge | vRH | vLH |
|---|---|---|---|---|---|---|---|---|---|---|---|---|---|---|---|---|---|---|---|---|---|---|---|---|---|---|---|---|---|---|---|---|
| | | Majors | | | | | | | | Skills | | | | Value | | | | Extra | | | Production | | | | OPS | | | | | Scoresheet | | |
| 07 | — | — | — | — | — | — | — | — | — | — | — | — | — | — | — | — | — | — | — | — | — | — | — | — | — | — | — | — | — | — | −19 | +48 |
| 08 | — | — | — | — | — | — | — | — | — | — | — | — | — | — | — | — | — | — | — | — | — | — | — | — | — | — | — | — | — | — | — | — |
| 09 | SF | 127 | 2 | 15 | 13 | 0 | .228 | .269 | .339 | 76% | 30% | 3% | 1.48 | $0 | -$8 | 40 | −8 | 6 | 1 | 0 | 42-17-41 | 5% | 17% | 38% | .607 | .594 | .615 | .701 | .203 | — | — | — |
| 10 | SF | 126 | 4 | 19 | 10 | 1 | .238 | .299 | .397 | 72% | 33% | 6% | 1.67 | $1 | -$7 | 50 | −5 | 6 | 1 | 2 | 42-12-46 | 11% | 9% | 41% | .696 | .790 | .406 | .754 | .502 | 0.58 | −8 | +20 |

## Matt Wieters — 500 PA | $12 | 240 pts

CA-126, DH-2 — Owned: 78% — BH

Wieters in 2010 was M.I.A. His defense lived up to his billing, but his H% and FB% went south, and his 2nd-half SLG, though higher, was only .407. We can't say whether the real problem is Wieters's play or our hopes. A case can be made that he is green – he entered MLB with just 163 PA above Double-A. (BJ)

| Player | Age | AB | HR | R | RBI | SB | BA | OBP | SLG | $1L | Pts |
|---|---|---|---|---|---|---|---|---|---|---|---|
| | | Forecast | | | | | | | | | |
| Wieters M | 24 | 439 | 15 | 45 | 60 | 0 | .262 | .337 | .423 | $12 | 240 |
| Mini-Browser | Age | AB | HR | R | RBI | SB | BA | OBP | SLG | $1L | Pts |
| Napoli M | 29 | 393 | 23 | 59 | 63 | 5 | .252 | .337 | .490 | $16 | 240 |
| Santana C | 24 | 519 | 24 | 66 | 78 | 6 | .231 | .342 | .435 | $15 | 350 |
| Montero M | 27 | 448 | 20 | 65 | 65 | 0 | .279 | .349 | .472 | $15 | 300 |
| Doumit R | 29 | 406 | 14 | 54 | 59 | 5 | .277 | .339 | .458 | $15 | 260 |
| Suzuki K | 27 | 516 | 11 | 55 | 66 | 6 | .256 | .315 | .379 | $12 | 300 |

| Level | Leag | AB | HR | R | RBI | SB | BA | OBP | SLG | CT% | H% | BB% | Bash |
|---|---|---|---|---|---|---|---|---|---|---|---|---|---|
| | | Minors (2010) | | | | | | | | Skills | | | |
| A | — | — | — | — | — | — | — | — | — | — | — | — | — |
| AA | — | — | — | — | — | — | — | — | — | — | — | — | — |
| AAA | — | — | — | — | — | — | — | — | — | — | — | — | — |

Competition at CA — Stats in 2010

| Bats | Player | GSvR | GSvL | Sub | OPS |
|---|---|---|---|---|---|
| BH | Wieters M | 91 | 31 | 4 | .695 |
| RH | Tatum C | 18 | 16 | 8 | .665 |
| RH | Fox J | 4 | 4 | 3 | .645 |

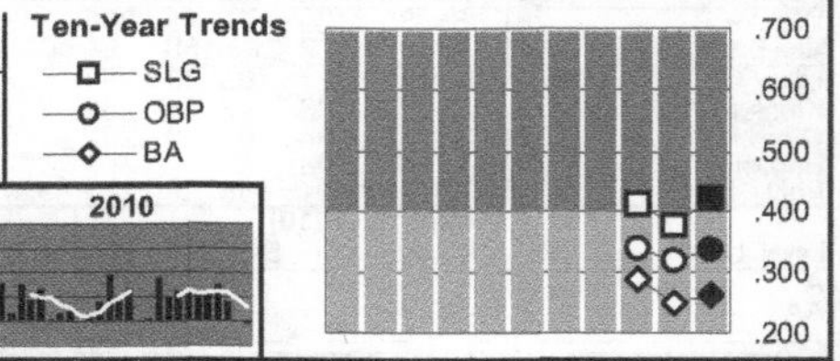

| Yr | Team | AB | HR | R | RBI | SB | BA | OBP | SLG | CT% | H% | BB% | Bash | $1L | $2L | Pts | RAA | 2B | 3B | CS | FB-LD-GB | HR/fb | RBI% | RS% | OPS | 1st Hf | 2nd Hf | vs RH | vs LH | Rnge | vRH | vLH |
|---|---|---|---|---|---|---|---|---|---|---|---|---|---|---|---|---|---|---|---|---|---|---|---|---|---|---|---|---|---|---|---|---|
| | | Majors | | | | | | | | Skills | | | | Value | | | | Extra | | | Production | | | | OPS | | | | | Scoresheet | | |
| 07 | — | — | — | — | — | — | — | — | — | — | — | — | — | — | — | — | — | — | — | — | — | — | — | — | — | — | — | — | — | — | — | — |
| 08 | — | — | — | — | — | — | — | — | — | — | — | — | — | — | — | — | — | — | — | — | — | — | — | — | — | — | — | — | — | — | — | — |
| 09 | BAL | 354 | 9 | 35 | 43 | 0 | .288 | .340 | .412 | 76% | 38% | 7% | 1.43 | $9 | $4 | 170 | +3 | 15 | 1 | 0 | 40-19-42 | 8% | 17% | 21% | .753 | .724 | .765 | .804 | .671 | 0.58 | — | — |
| 10 | BAL | 446 | 11 | 37 | 55 | 0 | .249 | .319 | .377 | 79% | 32% | 9% | 1.51 | $9 | $2 | 210 | −8 | 22 | 1 | 1 | 38-15-46 | 8% | 17% | 17% | .695 | .672 | .730 | .741 | .564 | 0.69 | +6 | −12 |

## Ty Wigginton — 500 PA | $12 | 270 pts

1B-99, 2B-40, 3B-22, DH-7 — Owned: 75% — RH

Although Wiggy could be lured from Baltimore by the promise of guaranteed playing time, playing in a super-UT role serves the 33-year-old best. If he stays in Baltimore, he will play often and everywhere. There is still a chance that his H% could take a pre-Baltimore bounce. (BJ)

| Player | Age | AB | HR | R | RBI | SB | BA | OBP | SLG | $1L | Pts |
|---|---|---|---|---|---|---|---|---|---|---|---|
| | | Forecast | | | | | | | | | |
| Wigginton T | 33 | 460 | 20 | 50 | 60 | 0 | .272 | .328 | .453 | $12 | 270 |
| Mini-Browser | Age | AB | HR | R | RBI | SB | BA | OBP | SLG | $1L | Pts |
| Berkman L | 35 | 324 | 16 | 56 | 60 | 4 | .284 | .398 | .514 | $14 | 280 |
| Barton D | 25 | 567 | 14 | 81 | 68 | 7 | .262 | .373 | .412 | $13 | 390 |
| LaPorta M | 26 | 564 | 25 | 69 | 69 | 0 | .244 | .328 | .435 | $13 | 320 |
| Branyan R | 35 | 389 | 27 | 54 | 63 | 0 | .243 | .338 | .507 | $13 | 230 |
| Helton T | 37 | 429 | 11 | 63 | 58 | 0 | .294 | .402 | .448 | $12 | 320 |

| Level | Leag | AB | HR | R | RBI | SB | BA | OBP | SLG | CT% | H% | BB% | Bash |
|---|---|---|---|---|---|---|---|---|---|---|---|---|---|
| | | Minors (2010) | | | | | | | | Skills | | | |
| A | — | — | — | — | — | — | — | — | — | — | — | — | — |
| AA | — | — | — | — | — | — | — | — | — | — | — | — | — |
| AAA | — | — | — | — | — | — | — | — | — | — | — | — | — |

Competition at 1B — Stats in 2010

| Bats | Player | GSvR | GSvL | Sub | OPS |
|---|---|---|---|---|---|
| RH | Wigginton T | 68 | 30 | 1 | .727 |
| RH | Atkins G | 17 | 13 | 0 | .562 |
| LH | Scott L | 17 | 2 | 0 | .902 |
| LH | Hughes R | 11 | 0 | 0 | .530 |

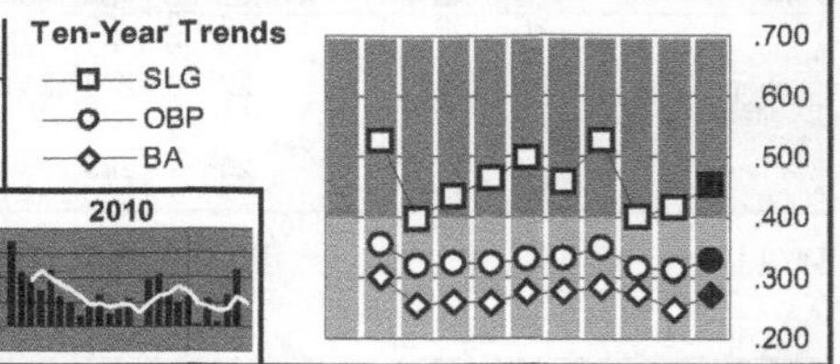

| Yr | Team | AB | HR | R | RBI | SB | BA | OBP | SLG | CT% | H% | BB% | Bash | $1L | $2L | Pts | RAA | 2B | 3B | CS | FB-LD-GB | HR/fb | RBI% | RS% | OPS | 1st Hf | 2nd Hf | vs RH | vs LH | Rnge | vRH | vLH |
|---|---|---|---|---|---|---|---|---|---|---|---|---|---|---|---|---|---|---|---|---|---|---|---|---|---|---|---|---|---|---|---|---|
| | | Majors | | | | | | | | Skills | | | | Value | | | | Extra | | | Production | | | | OPS | | | | | Scoresheet | | |
| 07 | 2TM | 547 | 22 | 71 | 67 | 3 | .278 | .333 | .459 | 79% | 35% | 7% | 1.65 | $11 | $7 | 320 | −8 | 33 | 0 | 4 | 38-18-44 | 13% | 15% | 27% | .792 | .759 | .841 | .741 | .935 | 1.86 | −22 | +50 |
| 08 | HOU | 386 | 23 | 50 | 58 | 4 | .285 | .350 | .526 | 82% | 35% | 7% | 1.85 | $14 | $5 | 280 | +3 | 22 | 1 | 6 | 39-16-45 | 19% | 18% | 21% | .876 | .838 | .915 | .809 | 1.055 | — | −30 | +77 |
| 09 | BAL | 410 | 11 | 44 | 41 | 1 | .273 | .314 | .400 | 86% | 32% | 5% | 1.46 | $7 | -$5 | 220 | −15 | 19 | 0 | 2 | 39-18-43 | 8% | 14% | 26% | .714 | .693 | .738 | .750 | .650 | — | −37 | +93 |
| 10 | BAL | 581 | 22 | 63 | 76 | 0 | .248 | .312 | .415 | 80% | 31% | 8% | 1.67 | $14 | $4 | 310 | −24 | 29 | 1 | 1 | 37-16-47 | 13% | 17% | 23% | .727 | .768 | .680 | .743 | .679 | 1.84 | −16 | +37 |

*For more stats, visit www.Rotolympus.com.*

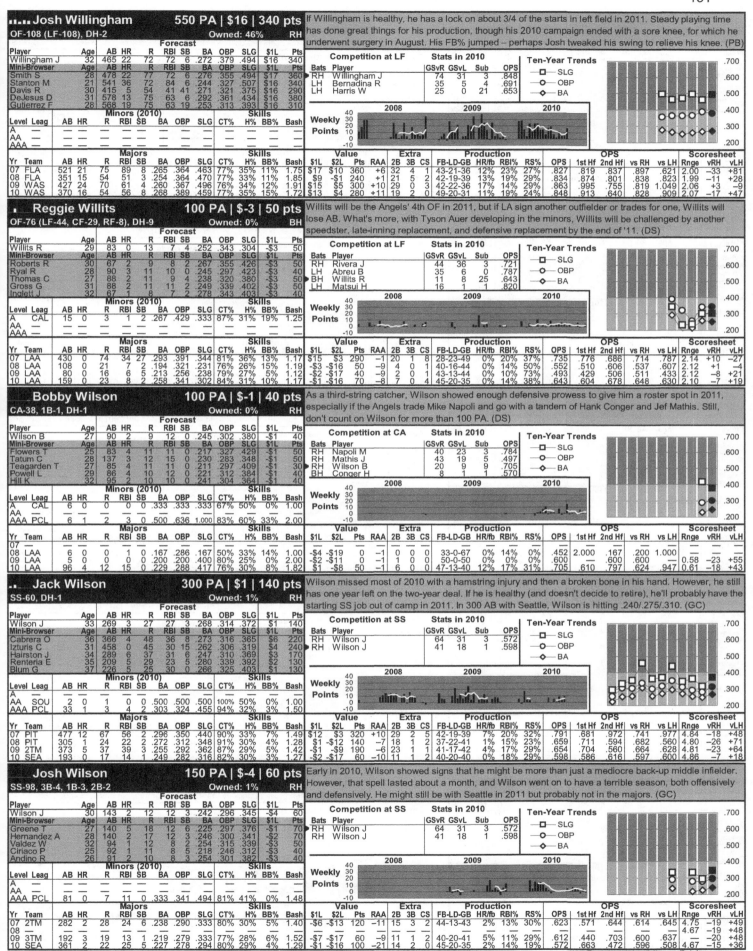

## Josh Willingham — 550 PA | $16 | 340 pts
OF-108 (LF-108), DH-2 — Owned: 46% — RH

If Willingham is healthy, he has a lock on about 3/4 of the starts in left field in 2011. Steady playing time has done great things for his production, though his 2010 campaign ended with a sore knee, for which he underwent surgery in August. His FB% jumped -- perhaps Josh tweaked his swing to relieve his knee. (PB)

| Player | Age | AB | HR | R | RBI | SB | BA | OBP | SLG | $1L | Pts |
|---|---|---|---|---|---|---|---|---|---|---|---|
| Willingham J | 32 | 465 | 22 | 72 | 72 | 6 | .272 | .379 | .494 | $16 | 340 |
| Smith S | 28 | 478 | 22 | 77 | 72 | 6 | .276 | .355 | .494 | $17 | 360 |
| Stanton M | 21 | 541 | 36 | 72 | 84 | 6 | .244 | .327 | .507 | $16 | 340 |
| Davis R | 30 | 415 | 5 | 54 | 41 | 41 | .271 | .321 | .375 | $16 | 290 |
| DeJesus D | 31 | 578 | 13 | 75 | 63 | 6 | .292 | .361 | .434 | $16 | 380 |
| Gutierrez F | 28 | 568 | 19 | 75 | 63 | 19 | .253 | .313 | .393 | $16 | 310 |

Majors:
| Yr | Team | AB | HR | R | RBI | SB | BA | OBP | SLG |
|---|---|---|---|---|---|---|---|---|---|
| 07 | FLA | 521 | 21 | 75 | 89 | 8 | .265 | .364 | .463 |
| 08 | FLA | 351 | 15 | 54 | 51 | 3 | .254 | .364 | .470 |
| 09 | WAS | 427 | 24 | 70 | 61 | 4 | .260 | .367 | .496 |
| 10 | WAS | 370 | 16 | 54 | 56 | 4 | .268 | .389 | .459 |

## Reggie Willits — 100 PA | $-3 | 50 pts
OF-76 (LF-44, CF-29, RF-8), DH-9 — Owned: 0% — BH

Willits will be the Angels' 4th OF in 2011, but if LA sign another outfielder or trades for one, Willits will lose AB. What's more, with Tyson Auer developing in the minors, Willits will be challenged by another speedster, late-inning replacement, and defensive replacement by the end of '11. (DS)

| Player | Age | AB | HR | R | RBI | SB | BA | OBP | SLG | $1L | Pts |
|---|---|---|---|---|---|---|---|---|---|---|---|
| Willits R | 29 | 83 | 0 | 13 | 7 | 4 | .252 | .343 | .304 | $-3 | 50 |

## Bobby Wilson — 100 PA | $-1 | 40 pts
CA-38, 1B-1, DH-1 — Owned: 0% — RH

As a third-string catcher, Wilson showed enough defensive prowess to give him a roster spot in 2011, especially if the Angels trade Mike Napoli and go with a tandem of Hank Conger and Jef Mathis. Still, don't count on Wilson for more than 100 PA. (DS)

| Player | Age | AB | HR | R | RBI | SB | BA | OBP | SLG | $1L | Pts |
|---|---|---|---|---|---|---|---|---|---|---|---|
| Wilson B | 27 | 90 | 2 | 9 | 12 | 0 | .245 | .302 | .380 | $-1 | 40 |

## Jack Wilson — 300 PA | $1 | 140 pts
SS-60, DH-1 — Owned: 1% — RH

Wilson missed most of 2010 with a hamstring injury and then a broken bone in his hand. However, he still has one year left on the two-year deal. If he is healthy (and doesn't decide to retire), he'll probably have the starting SS job out of camp in 2011. In 300 AB with Seattle, Wilson is hitting .240/.275/.310. (GC)

| Player | Age | AB | HR | R | RBI | SB | BA | OBP | SLG | $1L | Pts |
|---|---|---|---|---|---|---|---|---|---|---|---|
| Wilson J | 33 | 269 | 3 | 27 | 27 | 3 | .268 | .314 | .372 | $1 | 140 |

## Josh Wilson — 150 PA | $-4 | 60 pts
SS-98, 3B-4, 1B-3, 2B-2 — Owned: 1% — RH

Early in 2010, Wilson showed signs that he might be more than just a mediocre back-up middle infielder. However, that spell lasted about a month, and Wilson went on to have a terrible season, both offensively and defensively. He might still be with Seattle in 2011 but probably not in the majors. (GC)

| Player | Age | AB | HR | R | RBI | SB | BA | OBP | SLG | $1L | Pts |
|---|---|---|---|---|---|---|---|---|---|---|---|
| Wilson J | 30 | 143 | 2 | 12 | 12 | 3 | .242 | .296 | .345 | $-4 | 60 |

## Randy Winn

**175 PA | $0 | 100 pts**

OF-73 (RF-46, LF-25, CF-9), DH-1 | Owned: 15% | BH

Over 13 big-league seasons, Winn has offered some pop (10+ HR and 30+ doubles from 2002-2008), occasionally efficient speed (seven seasons with greater than 75% SB success rate), near league-average walk rate, and solid defense. Sadly, his skills are eroding. He could find work as a back-up outfielder. (AB)

| Player | Age | AB | HR | R | RBI | SB | BA | OBP | SLG | $1L | Pts |
|---|---|---|---|---|---|---|---|---|---|---|---|
| Winn R | 36 | 159 | 4 | 19 | 18 | 5 | .276 | .336 | .401 | $0 | 100 |
| **Mini-Browser** | **Age** | **AB** | **HR** | **R** | **RBI** | **SB** | **BA** | **OBP** | **SLG** | **$1L** | **Pts** |
| Schierholtz N | 27 | 182 | 4 | 24 | 20 | 4 | .274 | .319 | .445 | $1 | 110 |
| Craig A | 26 | 211 | 9 | 25 | 29 | 0 | .245 | .308 | .433 | $1 | 110 |
| Kalish R | 23 | 182 | 6 | 22 | 22 | 8 | .231 | .306 | .394 | $1 | 110 |
| Gwynn T | 28 | 259 | 3 | 33 | 18 | 12 | .232 | .313 | .306 | $1 | 140 |
| Maier M | 28 | 221 | 3 | 25 | 23 | 3 | .260 | .323 | .375 | $0 | 110 |

| Level | Leag | AB | HR | R | RBI | SB | BA | OBP | SLG | CT% | H% | BB% | Bash |
|---|---|---|---|---|---|---|---|---|---|---|---|---|---|
| A | — | — | — | — | — | — | — | — | — | — | — | — | — |
| AA | — | — | — | — | — | — | — | — | — | — | — | — | — |
| AAA | — | — | — | — | — | — | — | — | — | — | — | — | — |

| Yr | Team | AB | HR | R | RBI | SB | BA | OBP | SLG | CT% | H% | BB% | Bash |
|---|---|---|---|---|---|---|---|---|---|---|---|---|---|
| 07 | SF | 593 | 14 | 73 | 65 | 15 | .300 | .353 | .445 | 86% | 35% | 7% | 1.48 |
| 08 | SF | 598 | 10 | 84 | 64 | 25 | .306 | .363 | .426 | 85% | 36% | 9% | 1.39 |
| 09 | SF | 538 | 2 | 65 | 51 | 16 | .262 | .318 | .353 | 83% | 32% | 8% | 1.35 |
| 10 | 2TM | 205 | 4 | 23 | 25 | 6 | .239 | .307 | .356 | 82% | 29% | 9% | 1.49 |

**Competition at RF — Stats in 2010**

| Bats | Player | GSvR | GSvL | Sub | OPS |
|---|---|---|---|---|---|
| LH | Jay J | 39 | 5 | 17 | .780 |
| RH | Craig A | 9 | 14 | 7 | .711 |
| BH | Winn R | 12 | 5 | 18 | .663 |
| RH | Stavinoha N | 4 | 12 | 6 | .625 |

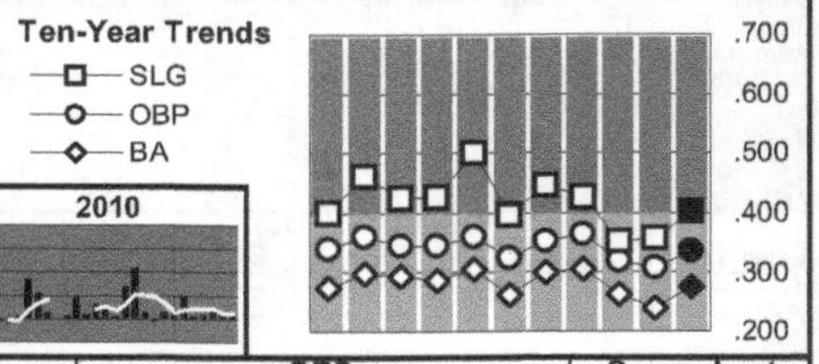
Ten-Year Trends
SLG
OBP
BA
.700
.600
.500
.400
.300
.200

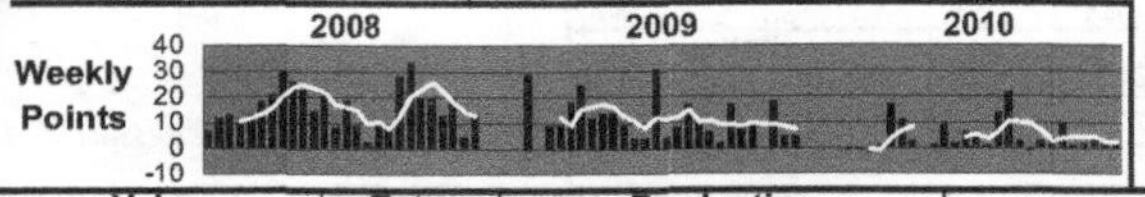
Weekly Points
2008
2009
2010
40
30
20
10
0
-10

| Yr | $1L | $2L | Pts | RAA | 2B | 3B | CS | FB-LD-GB | HR/fb | RBI% | RS% | OPS | 1st Hf | 2nd Hf | vs RH | vs LH | Rnge | vRH | vLH |
|---|---|---|---|---|---|---|---|---|---|---|---|---|---|---|---|---|---|---|---|
| 07 | $19 | $10 | 390 | +0 | 42 | 1 | 3 | 31-19-51 | 9% | 21% | 27% | .798 | .734 | .873 | .736 | .934 | 2.13 | +19 | –55 |
| 08 | $23 | $15 | 420 | +6 | 38 | 2 | 2 | 30-19-51 | 6% | 21% | 32% | .790 | .761 | .826 | .781 | .812 | 2.12 | –7 | +17 |
| 09 | $11 | -$1 | 290 | –22 | 33 | 5 | 2 | 32-22-46 | 1% | 22% | 34% | .671 | .712 | .612 | .751 | .384 | 2.11 | –18 | +44 |
| 10 | $1 | -$12 | 120 | –10 | 8 | 2 | 0 | 31-20-48 | 7% | 16% | 28% | .663 | .608 | .737 | .731 | .440 | — | +13 | –35 |

## DeWayne Wise

**150 PA | $0 | 90 pts**

OF-44 (CF-18, RF-17, LF-10), DH-4 | Owned: 0% | LH

Wise's return to the Jays in 2011 is no sure thing. His solid defense and ability to play all three OF spots make him a valuable 4th outfielder, but his shortcomings at the plate (notably in BB%) reduce his overall worth. He flashes both speed and power, but neither with consistency. (MH)

| Player | Age | AB | HR | R | RBI | SB | BA | OBP | SLG | $1L | Pts |
|---|---|---|---|---|---|---|---|---|---|---|---|
| Wise D | 33 | 142 | 5 | 21 | 15 | 6 | .254 | .302 | .446 | $0 | 90 |
| **Mini-Browser** | **Age** | **AB** | **HR** | **R** | **RBI** | **SB** | **BA** | **OBP** | **SLG** | **$1L** | **Pts** |
| Maier M | 28 | 221 | 3 | 25 | 23 | 3 | .260 | .323 | .375 | $0 | 110 |
| Winn R | 36 | 159 | 4 | 19 | 18 | 5 | .276 | .336 | .401 | $0 | 100 |
| Crowe T | 27 | 204 | 2 | 25 | 18 | 9 | .243 | .310 | .350 | $0 | 110 |
| Francoeur J | 27 | 166 | 5 | 21 | 23 | 2 | .263 | .310 | .421 | $0 | 100 |
| Denorfia C | 30 | 176 | 4 | 23 | 19 | 4 | .249 | .311 | .382 | $0 | 100 |

| Level | Leag | AB | HR | R | RBI | SB | BA | OBP | SLG | CT% | H% | BB% | Bash |
|---|---|---|---|---|---|---|---|---|---|---|---|---|---|
| A | — | — | — | — | — | — | — | — | — | — | — | — | — |
| AA | — | — | — | — | — | — | — | — | — | — | — | — | — |
| AAA | IL | 137 | 4 | 17 | 13 | 2 | .270 | .315 | .511 | 80% | 34% | 5% | 1.89 |

| Yr | Team | AB | HR | R | RBI | SB | BA | OBP | SLG | CT% | H% | BB% | Bash |
|---|---|---|---|---|---|---|---|---|---|---|---|---|---|
| 07 | CIN | 5 | 0 | 1 | 1 | 0 | .200 | .333 | .600 | 80% | 25% | 14% | 3.00 |
| 08 | CHW | 129 | 6 | 20 | 18 | 9 | .248 | .293 | .450 | 75% | 33% | 6% | 1.81 |
| 09 | CHW | 142 | 2 | 17 | 11 | 4 | .225 | .262 | .366 | 81% | 28% | 2% | 1.63 |
| 10 | TOR | 112 | 3 | 20 | 14 | 4 | .250 | .282 | .393 | 74% | 34% | 3% | 1.57 |

**Competition at CF — Stats in 2010**

| Bats | Player | GSvR | GSvL | Sub | OPS |
|---|---|---|---|---|---|
| RH | Wells V | 118 | 33 | 0 | .847 |
| LH | Wise D | 7 | 0 | 11 | .675 |

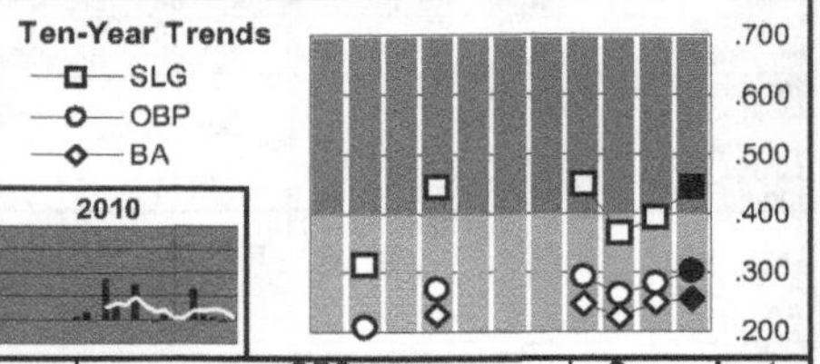
Ten-Year Trends
SLG
OBP
BA
.700
.600
.500
.400
.300
.200

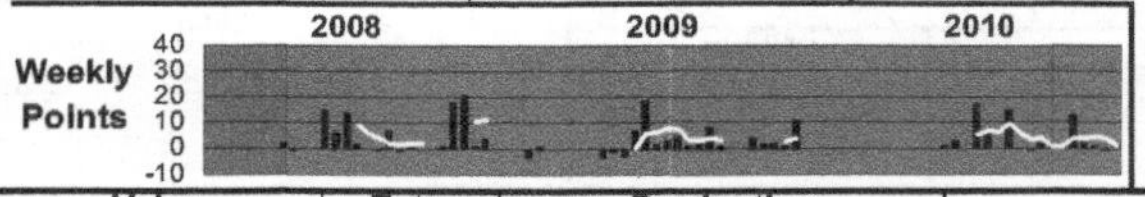
Weekly Points
2008
2009
2010
40
30
20
10
0
-10

| Yr | $1L | $2L | Pts | RAA | 2B | 3B | CS | FB-LD-GB | HR/fb | RBI% | RS% | OPS | 1st Hf | 2nd Hf | vs RH | vs LH | Rnge | vRH | vLH |
|---|---|---|---|---|---|---|---|---|---|---|---|---|---|---|---|---|---|---|---|
| 07 | -$6 | -$20 | 0 | –0 | 0 | 1 | 0 | 25-0-75 | 0% | 50% | 50% | .933 | .933 | — | .933 | — | — | +22 | –75 |
| 08 | $3 | -$10 | 90 | –0 | 4 | 2 | 0 | 42-23-35 | 15% | 19% | 40% | .742 | .972 | .640 | .796 | .286 | — | +24 | –77 |
| 09 | -$1 | -$17 | 60 | –12 | 8 | 3 | 5 | 47-17-36 | 4% | 15% | 41% | .628 | .541 | .763 | .589 | .937 | 2.12 | +26 | –84 |
| 10 | $1 | -$14 | 60 | –3 | 3 | 2 | 0 | 37-22-41 | 10% | 29% | 57% | .675 | .791 | .632 | .679 | .641 | 2.13 | +19 | –64 |

## Brandon Wood

**200 PA | $0 | 80 pts**

3B-56, SS-22, 1B-2, DH-1 | Owned: 1% | RH

If Wood is not traded, he will get a shot to win back the starting 3B job for the Angels, especially if he has a strong showing in the AFL. The Angels have done a lot to work with Wood on sharpening his approach. However, now we're talking about a guy with 13 walks (and a line of .169/.198/.260) in four seasons. (DS)

| Player | Age | AB | HR | R | RBI | SB | BA | OBP | SLG | $1L | Pts |
|---|---|---|---|---|---|---|---|---|---|---|---|
| Wood B | 26 | 173 | 8 | 22 | 22 | 2 | .231 | .288 | .419 | $0 | 80 |
| **Mini-Browser** | **Age** | **AB** | **HR** | **R** | **RBI** | **SB** | **BA** | **OBP** | **SLG** | **$1L** | **Pts** |
| Fields J | 28 | 224 | 8 | 28 | 30 | 3 | .245 | .325 | .414 | $2 | 110 |
| Punto N | 33 | 314 | 0 | 35 | 25 | 11 | .245 | .325 | .317 | $2 | 160 |
| Mora M | 39 | 172 | 4 | 22 | 26 | 2 | .267 | .332 | .399 | $1 | 110 |
| Nelson C | 25 | 185 | 6 | 24 | 22 | 6 | .227 | .296 | .405 | $0 | 110 |
| Helms W | 34 | 230 | 5 | 23 | 33 | 0 | .250 | .312 | .372 | $0 | 110 |

| Level | Leag | AB | HR | R | RBI | SB | BA | OBP | SLG | CT% | H% | BB% | Bash |
|---|---|---|---|---|---|---|---|---|---|---|---|---|---|
| A | — | — | — | — | — | — | — | — | — | — | — | — | — |
| AA | — | — | — | — | — | — | — | — | — | — | — | — | — |
| AAA | PCL | 51 | 1 | 4 | 2 | 0 | .196 | .241 | .255 | 67% | 29% | 6% | 1.30 |

| Yr | Team | AB | HR | R | RBI | SB | BA | OBP | SLG | CT% | H% | BB% | Bash |
|---|---|---|---|---|---|---|---|---|---|---|---|---|---|
| 07 | LAA | 33 | 1 | 2 | 3 | 0 | .152 | .152 | .273 | 64% | 24% | 0% | 1.80 |
| 08 | LAA | 150 | 5 | 12 | 13 | 4 | .200 | .224 | .327 | 71% | 28% | 3% | 1.63 |
| 09 | LAA | 41 | 1 | 5 | 3 | 0 | .195 | .267 | .293 | 54% | 36% | 7% | 1.50 |
| 10 | LAA | 226 | 4 | 20 | 14 | 1 | .146 | .174 | .208 | 69% | 21% | 2% | 1.42 |

**Competition at 3B — Stats in 2010**

| Bats | Player | GSvR | GSvL | Sub | OPS |
|---|---|---|---|---|---|
| BH | Callaspo A | 42 | 10 | 2 | .675 |
| RH | Wood B | 28 | 18 | 10 | .382 |
| RH | Frandsen K | 24 | 15 | 4 | .613 |
| BH | Izturis M | 18 | 9 | 1 | .684 |

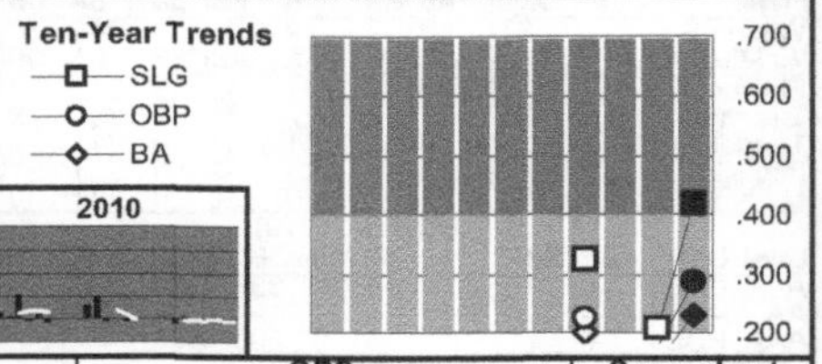
Ten-Year Trends
SLG
OBP
BA
.700
.600
.500
.400
.300
.200

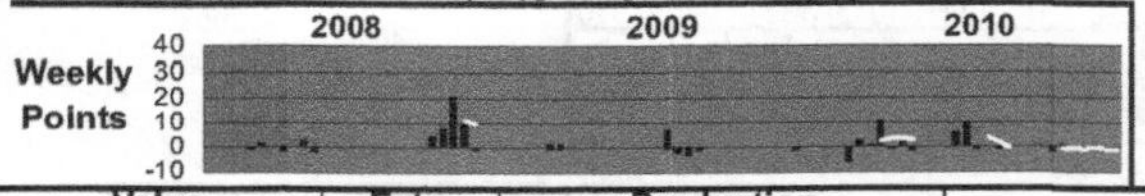
Weekly Points
2008
2009
2010
40
30
20
10
0
-10

| Yr | $1L | $2L | Pts | RAA | 2B | 3B | CS | FB-LD-GB | HR/fb | RBI% | RS% | OPS | 1st Hf | 2nd Hf | vs RH | vs LH | Rnge | vRH | vLH |
|---|---|---|---|---|---|---|---|---|---|---|---|---|---|---|---|---|---|---|---|
| 07 | -$4 | -$20 | 0 | –4 | 1 | 0 | 0 | 38-10-52 | 13% | 10% | 25% | .424 | .182 | .545 | .389 | .467 | — | — | — |
| 08 | -$2 | -$16 | 40 | –11 | 4 | 0 | 0 | 50-14-36 | 9% | 10% | 23% | .551 | .352 | .700 | .621 | .296 | 2.65 | –19 | +49 |
| 09 | -$4 | -$19 | 0 | –4 | 1 | 0 | 0 | 27-27-45 | 17% | 8% | 36% | .559 | .820 | .407 | .508 | .598 | — | –13 | +31 |
| 10 | -$6 | -$22 | 20 | –34 | 2 | 0 | 0 | 52-13-35 | 5% | 9% | 43% | .382 | .418 | .276 | .377 | .392 | — | –8 | +20 |

## Danny Worth

**100 PA | $-5 | 30 pts**

SS-24, 2B-12, 3B-3 | Owned: 0% | RH

Already a capable defender, Worth in 2010 made strides as a hitter before his season was derailed by a heel injury. He cannot be ruled out as an eventual starting shortstop, but his more likely destiny is in UT. Worth will probably start 2011 in Triple-A, but he should get time in the majors later in the year. (LP)

| Player | Age | AB | HR | R | RBI | SB | BA | OBP | SLG | $1L | Pts |
|---|---|---|---|---|---|---|---|---|---|---|---|
| Worth D | 25 | 91 | 1 | 8 | 7 | 2 | .219 | .278 | .323 | -$5 | 30 |
| **Mini-Browser** | **Age** | **AB** | **HR** | **R** | **RBI** | **SB** | **BA** | **OBP** | **SLG** | **$1L** | **Pts** |
| Navarro Y | 23 | 68 | 2 | 8 | 8 | 1 | .221 | .278 | .365 | -$5 | 30 |
| Cruz L | 27 | 45 | 1 | 5 | 4 | 1 | .231 | .269 | .353 | -$5 | 20 |
| Nunez E | 23 | 46 | 1 | 5 | 5 | 2 | .226 | .260 | .340 | -$5 | 20 |
| Diaz A | 24 | 96 | 1 | 8 | 8 | 1 | .218 | .270 | .295 | -$5 | 30 |
| Navarro O | 26 | 44 | 1 | 5 | 4 | 1 | .236 | .311 | .315 | -$5 | 20 |

| Level | Leag | AB | HR | R | RBI | SB | BA | OBP | SLG | CT% | H% | BB% | Bash |
|---|---|---|---|---|---|---|---|---|---|---|---|---|---|
| A | — | — | — | — | — | — | — | — | — | — | — | — | — |
| AA | — | — | — | — | — | — | — | — | — | — | — | — | — |
| AAA | IL | 164 | 2 | 18 | 18 | 12 | .287 | .333 | .354 | 82% | 35% | 6% | 1.23 |

| Yr | Team | AB | HR | R | RBI | SB | BA | OBP | SLG | CT% | H% | BB% | Bash |
|---|---|---|---|---|---|---|---|---|---|---|---|---|---|
| 07 | — | — | — | — | — | — | — | — | — | — | — | — | — |
| 08 | — | — | — | — | — | — | — | — | — | — | — | — | — |
| 09 | — | — | — | — | — | — | — | — | — | — | — | — | — |
| 10 | DET | 106 | 2 | 10 | 8 | 1 | .255 | .295 | .358 | 88% | 29% | 5% | 1.41 |

**Competition at SS — Stats in 2010**

| Bats | Player | GSvR | GSvL | Sub | OPS |
|---|---|---|---|---|---|
| BH | Santiago R | 59 | 8 | 18 | .662 |
| RH | Peralta J | 32 | 13 | 1 | .703 |
| RH | Everett A | 16 | 12 | 3 | .468 |
| RH | Worth D | 10 | 14 | 0 | .653 |

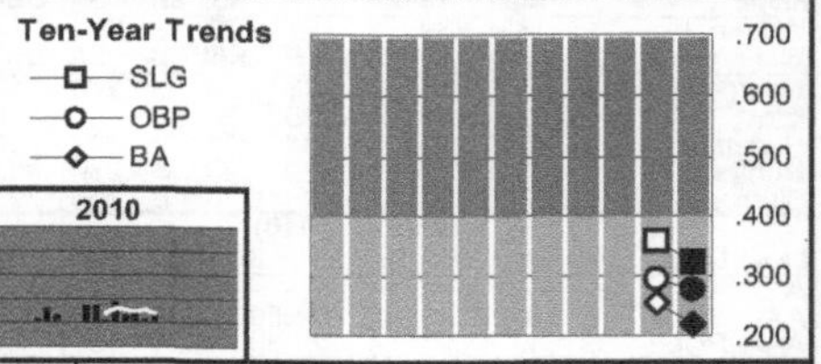
Ten-Year Trends
SLG
OBP
BA
.700
.600
.500
.400
.300
.200

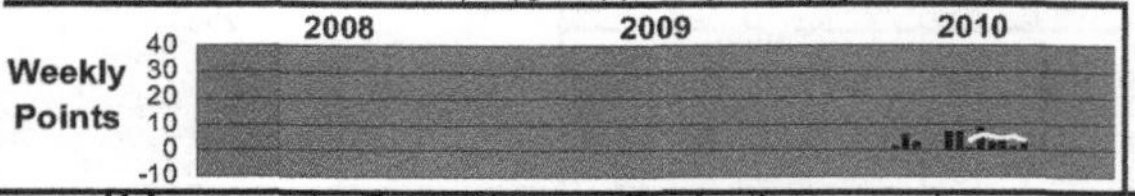
Weekly Points
2008
2009
2010
40
30
20
10
0
-10

| Yr | $1L | $2L | Pts | RAA | 2B | 3B | CS | FB-LD-GB | HR/fb | RBI% | RS% | OPS | 1st Hf | 2nd Hf | vs RH | vs LH | Rnge | vRH | vLH |
|---|---|---|---|---|---|---|---|---|---|---|---|---|---|---|---|---|---|---|---|
| 07 | — | — | — | — | — | — | — | — | — | — | — | — | — | — | — | — | — | — | — |
| 08 | — | — | — | — | — | — | — | — | — | — | — | — | — | — | — | — | — | — | — |
| 09 | — | — | — | — | — | — | — | — | — | — | — | — | — | — | — | — | — | — | — |
| 10 | -$2 | -$17 | 50 | –3 | 5 | 0 | 2 | 32-21-47 | 7% | 13% | 26% | .653 | .672 | .611 | .563 | .766 | — | — | — |

## David Wright

**675 PA | $31 | 490 pts**

3B-155, DH-1 | Owned: 100% | RH

Wright's power reappeared in 2010 – even at Citi Field! – but his BA dipped and his CT% fell again. He hit over .300 for a month only once (June). Wright did not run as much after the Break, but he could re-ignite if the Mets' new regime retools the team. He is unlikely to be traded, but he is no longer untouchable. (JL)

| Player | Age | AB | HR | R | RBI | SB | BA | OBP | SLG | $1L | Pts |
|---|---|---|---|---|---|---|---|---|---|---|---|
| Wright D | 28 | 570 | 27 | 101 | 101 | 20 | .296 | .384 | .511 | $31 | 490 |
| **Mini-Browser** | **Age** | **AB** | **HR** | **R** | **RBI** | **SB** | **BA** | **OBP** | **SLG** | **$1L** | **Pts** |
| Longoria E | 25 | 602 | 35 | 98 | 112 | 7 | .279 | .362 | .516 | $30 | 470 |
| Rodriguez A | 35 | 458 | 33 | 83 | 105 | 11 | .276 | .377 | .537 | $28 | 420 |
| Zimmerman R | 26 | 558 | 26 | 98 | 91 | 7 | .291 | .363 | .507 | $23 | 440 |
| Reynolds M | 27 | 586 | 39 | 98 | 98 | 13 | .244 | .339 | .498 | $23 | 390 |
| Beltre A | 31 | 544 | 24 | 78 | 78 | 6 | .287 | .334 | .489 | $21 | 380 |

| Level | Leag | AB | HR | R | RBI | SB | BA | OBP | SLG | CT% | H% | BB% | Bash |
|---|---|---|---|---|---|---|---|---|---|---|---|---|---|
| A | — | — | — | — | — | — | — | — | — | — | — | — | — |
| AA | — | — | — | — | — | — | — | — | — | — | — | — | — |
| AAA | — | — | — | — | — | — | — | — | — | — | — | — | — |

| Yr | Team | AB | HR | R | RBI | SB | BA | OBP | SLG | CT% | H% | BB% | Bash |
|---|---|---|---|---|---|---|---|---|---|---|---|---|---|
| 07 | NYM | 604 | 30 | 113 | 107 | 34 | .325 | .416 | .546 | 81% | 40% | 13% | 1.68 |
| 08 | NYM | 626 | 33 | 115 | 124 | 15 | .302 | .390 | .534 | 81% | 37% | 13% | 1.77 |
| 09 | NYM | 535 | 10 | 88 | 72 | 27 | .307 | .390 | .447 | 74% | 42% | 12% | 1.46 |
| 10 | NYM | 587 | 29 | 87 | 103 | 19 | .283 | .354 | .503 | 73% | 39% | 10% | 1.78 |

**Competition at 3B — Stats in 2010**

| Bats | Player | GSvR | GSvL | Sub | OPS |
|---|---|---|---|---|---|
| RH | Wright D | 117 | 38 | 0 | .856 |

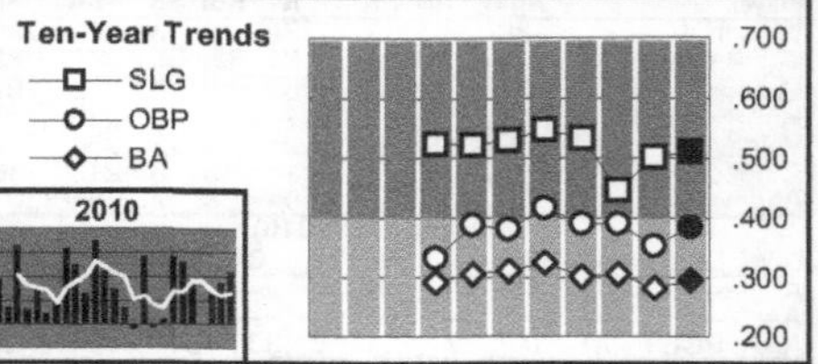
Ten-Year Trends
SLG
OBP
BA
.700
.600
.500
.400
.300
.200

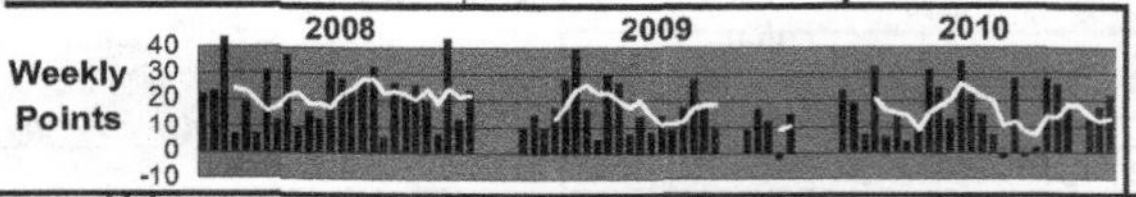
Weekly Points
2008
2009
2010
40
30
20
10
0
-10

| Yr | $1L | $2L | Pts | RAA | 2B | 3B | CS | FB-LD-GB | HR/fb | RBI% | RS% | OPS | 1st Hf | 2nd Hf | vs RH | vs LH | Rnge | vRH | vLH |
|---|---|---|---|---|---|---|---|---|---|---|---|---|---|---|---|---|---|---|---|
| 07 | $40 | $35 | 590 | +57 | 42 | 1 | 5 | 38-23-39 | 16% | 25% | 31% | .963 | .879 | 1.061 | .908 | 1.106 | 2.61 | –11 | +29 |
| 08 | $35 | $32 | 570 | +44 | 42 | 2 | 5 | 38-26-36 | 17% | 24% | 32% | .924 | .878 | .988 | .835 | 1.179 | 2.71 | –21 | +51 |
| 09 | $26 | $16 | 380 | +23 | 39 | 3 | 9 | 36-26-38 | 7% | 20% | 34% | .837 | .872 | .781 | .754 | 1.142 | 2.69 | –45 | +115 |
| 10 | $31 | $26 | 420 | +21 | 36 | 3 | 11 | 43-19-38 | 16% | 23% | 28% | .856 | .924 | .770 | .798 | 1.066 | 2.67 | –48 | +132 |

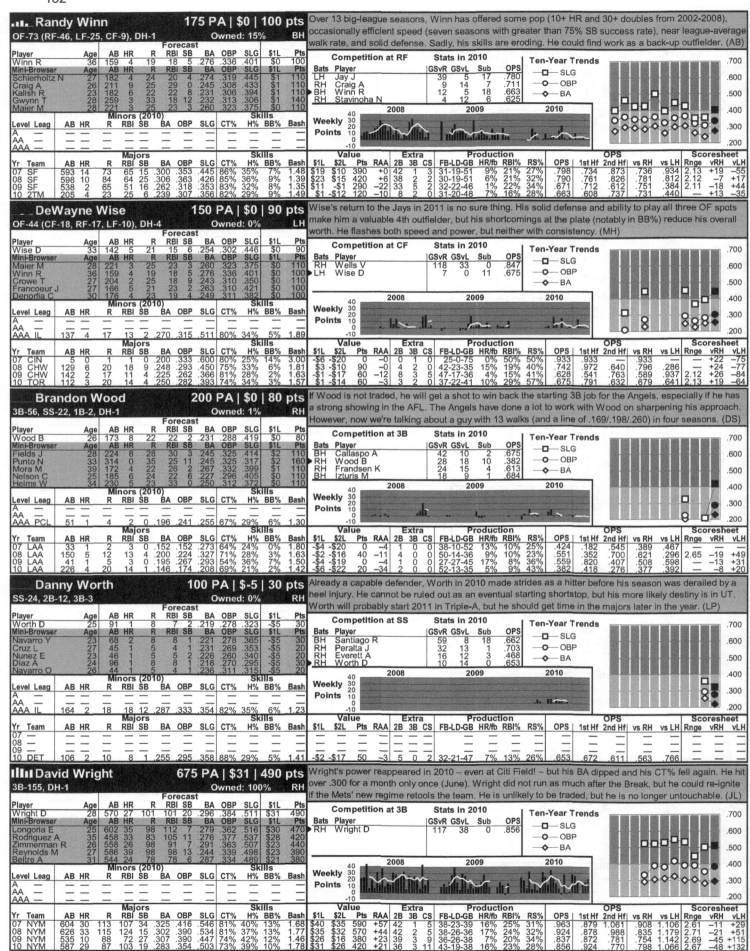

## Kevin Youkilis — 525 PA | $20 | 370 pts
**1B-101, 3B-2**  Owned: 52%  RH

There's no question that Youkilis in 2011 will man either 1B or 3B, the only detail is which one. With Lars Anderson and Anthony Rizzo in the pipeline at 1B, and no fast-advancing third basemen, Youkilis figures to eventually end up at the hot corner. That could happen as early as 2011 if Adrian Beltre moves on. (EB)

### Forecast
| Player | Age | AB | HR | R | RBI | SB | BA | OBP | SLG | $1L | Pts |
|---|---|---|---|---|---|---|---|---|---|---|---|
| Youkilis K | 32 | 451 | 21 | 79 | 79 | 5 | .291 | .390 | .515 | $20 | 370 |

### Mini-Browser
| Player | Age | AB | HR | R | RBI | SB | BA | OBP | SLG | $1L | Pts |
|---|---|---|---|---|---|---|---|---|---|---|---|
| Morneau J | 29 | 532 | 30 | 78 | 102 | 0 | .293 | .374 | .532 | $25 | 450 |
| Morales K | 27 | 593 | 26 | 78 | 98 | 0 | .285 | .332 | .495 | $24 | 390 |
| Gonzalez A | 28 | 578 | 34 | 94 | 101 | 0 | .278 | .376 | .512 | $23 | 460 |
| Dunn A | 31 | 525 | 39 | 85 | 104 | 0 | .260 | .382 | .518 | $22 | 400 |
| Konerko P | 35 | 554 | 31 | 75 | 94 | 0 | .271 | .359 | .499 | $21 | 410 |

### Minors (2010) / Skills
| Level Leag | AB | HR | R | RBI | SB | BA | OBP | SLG | CT% | H% | BB% | Bash |
|---|---|---|---|---|---|---|---|---|---|---|---|---|
| A — | — | — | — | — | — | — | — | — | | | | |
| AA — | — | — | — | — | — | — | — | — | | | | |
| AAA — | — | — | — | — | — | — | — | — | | | | |

### Majors / Skills / Value / Extra / Production / OPS / Scoresheet
| Yr | Team | AB | HR | R | RBI | SB | BA | OBP | SLG | CT% | H% | BB% | Bash | $1L | $2L | Pts | RAA | 2B | 3B | CS | FB-LD-GB | HR/fb | RBI% | RS% | OPS | 1st Hf | 2nd Hf | vs RH | vs LH | Rnge | vRH | vLH |
|---|---|---|---|---|---|---|---|---|---|---|---|---|---|---|---|---|---|---|---|---|---|---|---|---|---|---|---|---|---|---|---|---|
| 07 | BOS | 528 | 16 | 85 | 83 | 4 | .288 | .390 | .453 | 80% | 36% | 12% | 1.57 | $19 | $11 | 380 | +4 | 35 | 2 | 2 | 45-21-34 | 8% | 23% | 30% | .843 | .920 | .747 | .854 | .815 | 1.89 | -13 | +32 |
| 08 | BOS | 538 | 29 | 91 | 115 | 3 | .312 | .390 | .569 | 80% | 39% | 10% | 1.82 | $30 | $24 | 470 | +21 | 43 | 4 | 5 | 44-22-34 | 15% | 27% | 29% | .958 | .933 | .998 | .946 | 1.009 | 1.90 | -8 | +20 |
| 09 | BOS | 491 | 27 | 99 | 94 | 7 | .305 | .413 | .548 | 75% | 41% | 13% | 1.79 | $26 | $21 | 430 | +23 | 36 | 1 | 2 | 44-21-35 | 16% | 24% | 33% | .961 | .985 | .933 | .964 | .953 | 1.89 | -9 | +25 |
| 10 | BOS | 362 | 19 | 77 | 62 | 4 | .307 | .411 | .564 | 81% | 38% | 13% | 1.84 | $21 | $12 | 340 | +18 | 26 | 1 | 4 | 47-16-37 | 14% | 23% | 36% | .975 | .981 | .951 | .863 | 1.311 | 1.89 | -9 | +22 |

### Competition at 1B / Stats in 2010
| Bats | Player | GSvR | GSvL | Sub | OPS |
|---|---|---|---|---|---|
| RH | Youkilis K | 66 | 32 | 3 | .975 |
| RH | Lowell M | 20 | 18 | 5 | .674 |
| BH | Martinez V | 8 | 6 | 0 | .844 |
| LH | Anderson L | 10 | 1 | 7 | .554 |

Ten-Year Trends: □ SLG  ○ OBP  ◇ BA

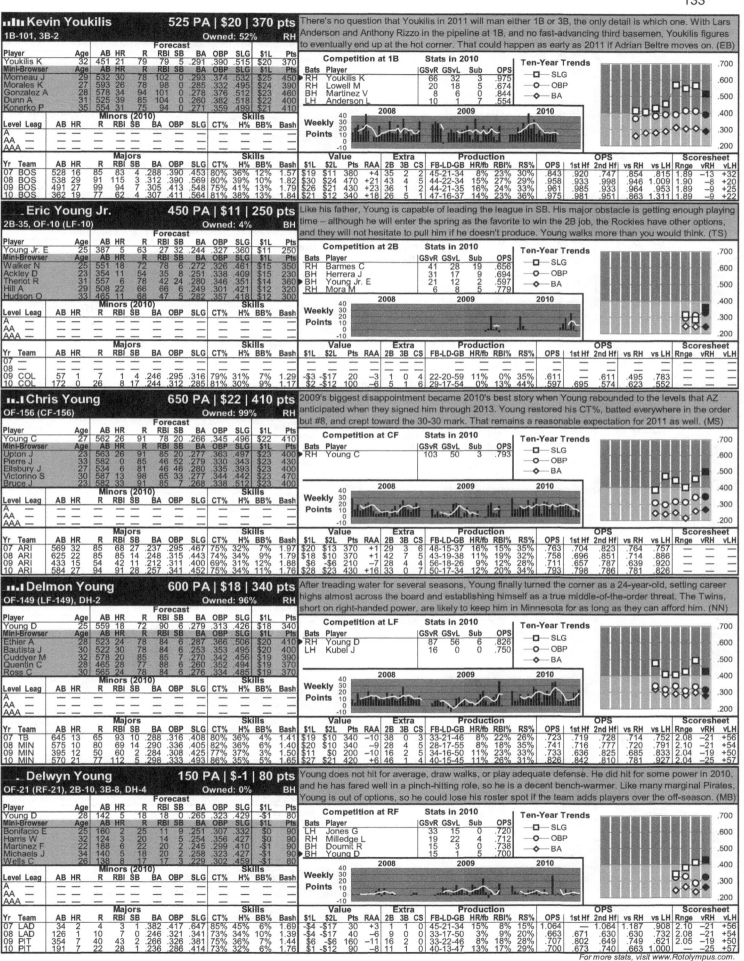

---

## Eric Young Jr. — 450 PA | $11 | 250 pts
**2B-35, OF-10 (LF-10)**  Owned: 4%  BH

Like his father, Young is capable of leading the league in SB. His major obstacle is getting enough playing time – although he will enter the spring as the favorite to win the 2B job, the Rockies have other options, and they will not hesitate to pull him if he doesn't produce. Young walks more than you would think. (TS)

### Forecast
| Player | Age | AB | HR | R | RBI | SB | BA | OBP | SLG | $1L | Pts |
|---|---|---|---|---|---|---|---|---|---|---|---|
| Young Jr. E | 25 | 387 | 5 | 63 | 27 | 32 | .244 | .327 | .360 | $11 | 250 |

### Mini-Browser
| Player | Age | AB | HR | R | RBI | SB | BA | OBP | SLG | $1L | Pts |
|---|---|---|---|---|---|---|---|---|---|---|---|
| Walker N | 25 | 551 | 16 | 72 | 78 | 6 | .272 | .326 | .461 | $15 | 350 |
| Ackley D | 23 | 354 | 11 | 54 | 35 | 8 | .251 | .338 | .409 | $15 | 230 |
| Theriot R | 31 | 557 | 6 | 78 | 42 | 24 | .280 | .346 | .351 | $14 | 360 |
| Hill A | 29 | 508 | 22 | 66 | 66 | 4 | .249 | .301 | .421 | $12 | 320 |
| Hudson O | 33 | 465 | 11 | 68 | 47 | 13 | .282 | .357 | .418 | $12 | 300 |

### Minors (2010) / Skills
| Level Leag | AB | HR | R | RBI | SB | BA | OBP | SLG | CT% | H% | BB% | Bash |
|---|---|---|---|---|---|---|---|---|---|---|---|---|
| A — | — | — | — | — | — | — | — | — | | | | |
| AA — | — | — | — | — | — | — | — | — | | | | |
| AAA — | — | — | — | — | — | — | — | — | | | | |

### Majors / Skills / Value / Extra / Production / OPS / Scoresheet
| Yr | Team | AB | HR | R | RBI | SB | BA | OBP | SLG | CT% | H% | BB% | Bash | $1L | $2L | Pts | RAA | 2B | 3B | CS | FB-LD-GB | HR/fb | RBI% | RS% | OPS | 1st Hf | 2nd Hf | vs RH | vs LH | Rnge | vRH | vLH |
|---|---|---|---|---|---|---|---|---|---|---|---|---|---|---|---|---|---|---|---|---|---|---|---|---|---|---|---|---|---|---|---|---|
| 07 | | | | | | | | | | | | | | | | | | | | | | | | | | | | | | | | |
| 08 | | | | | | | | | | | | | | | | | | | | | | | | | | | | | | | | |
| 09 | COL | 57 | 1 | 7 | 1 | 4 | .246 | .295 | .316 | 79% | 31% | 7% | 1.29 | -$3 | -$17 | 20 | -3 | 1 | 0 | 4 | 22-20-59 | 11% | 0% | 35% | .611 | — | .611 | .495 | .783 | — | — | — |
| 10 | COL | 172 | 0 | 26 | 8 | 17 | .244 | .312 | .285 | 81% | 30% | 9% | 1.17 | $2 | -$12 | 100 | -6 | 5 | 1 | 6 | 29-17-54 | 0% | 13% | 44% | .597 | .695 | .574 | .623 | .552 | — | — | — |

### Competition at 2B / Stats in 2010
| Bats | Player | GSvR | GSvL | Sub | OPS |
|---|---|---|---|---|---|
| RH | Barmes C | 41 | 28 | 19 | .656 |
| BH | Herrera J | 31 | 17 | 9 | .694 |
| BH | Young Jr. E | 21 | 12 | 2 | .597 |
| RH | Mora M | 6 | 8 | 5 | .779 |

---

## Chris Young — 650 PA | $22 | 410 pts
**OF-156 (CF-156)**  Owned: 99%  RH

2009's biggest disappointment became 2010's best story when Young rebounded to the levels that AZ anticipated when they signed him through 2013. Young restored his CT%, batted everywhere in the order but #8, and crept toward the 30-30 mark. That remains a reasonable expectation for 2011 as well. (MS)

### Forecast
| Player | Age | AB | HR | R | RBI | SB | BA | OBP | SLG | $1L | Pts |
|---|---|---|---|---|---|---|---|---|---|---|---|
| Young C | 27 | 562 | 26 | 91 | 78 | 20 | .266 | .345 | .496 | $22 | 410 |

### Mini-Browser
| Player | Age | AB | HR | R | RBI | SB | BA | OBP | SLG | $1L | Pts |
|---|---|---|---|---|---|---|---|---|---|---|---|
| Upton J | 23 | 563 | 26 | 91 | 85 | 20 | .277 | .363 | .497 | $23 | 400 |
| Pierre J | 33 | 582 | 0 | 85 | 46 | 52 | .279 | .330 | .343 | $23 | 430 |
| Ellsbury J | 27 | 534 | 6 | 81 | 46 | 46 | .280 | .335 | .393 | $23 | 400 |
| Victorino S | 30 | 587 | 13 | 98 | 65 | 33 | .277 | .344 | .442 | $23 | 470 |
| Bruce J | 23 | 582 | 33 | 91 | 85 | 7 | .268 | .338 | .512 | $23 | 400 |

### Minors (2010) / Skills
| Level Leag | AB | HR | R | RBI | SB | BA | OBP | SLG | CT% | H% | BB% | Bash |
|---|---|---|---|---|---|---|---|---|---|---|---|---|
| A — | — | — | — | — | — | — | — | — | | | | |
| AA — | — | — | — | — | — | — | — | — | | | | |
| AAA — | — | — | — | — | — | — | — | — | | | | |

### Majors / Skills / Value / Extra / Production / OPS / Scoresheet
| Yr | Team | AB | HR | R | RBI | SB | BA | OBP | SLG | CT% | H% | BB% | Bash | $1L | $2L | Pts | RAA | 2B | 3B | CS | FB-LD-GB | HR/fb | RBI% | RS% | OPS | 1st Hf | 2nd Hf | vs RH | vs LH | Rnge | vRH | vLH |
|---|---|---|---|---|---|---|---|---|---|---|---|---|---|---|---|---|---|---|---|---|---|---|---|---|---|---|---|---|---|---|---|---|
| 07 | ARI | 569 | 32 | 85 | 68 | 27 | .237 | .295 | .467 | 75% | 32% | 7% | 1.97 | $20 | $13 | 370 | +1 | 29 | 3 | 6 | 48-15-37 | 16% | 15% | 35% | .763 | .704 | .823 | .764 | .757 | — | — | — |
| 08 | ARI | 625 | 22 | 85 | 85 | 14 | .248 | .315 | .443 | 74% | 34% | 9% | 1.79 | $18 | $10 | 370 | +1 | 42 | 7 | 5 | 43-19-38 | 11% | 19% | 32% | .758 | .696 | .851 | .714 | .886 | — | — | — |
| 09 | ARI | 433 | 15 | 54 | 42 | 11 | .212 | .311 | .400 | 69% | 31% | 12% | 1.88 | $6 | -$6 | 210 | -7 | 28 | 4 | 4 | 56-18-26 | 9% | 12% | 28% | .711 | .657 | .787 | .639 | .920 | — | — | — |
| 10 | ARI | 584 | 27 | 94 | 91 | 28 | .257 | .341 | .452 | 75% | 34% | 11% | 1.76 | $28 | $23 | 430 | +16 | 33 | 0 | 5 | 50-17-34 | 12% | 20% | 34% | .793 | .798 | .786 | .781 | .826 | — | — | — |

### Competition at CF / Stats in 2010
| Bats | Player | GSvR | GSvL | Sub | OPS |
|---|---|---|---|---|---|
| RH | Young C | 103 | 50 | 3 | .793 |

---

## Delmon Young — 600 PA | $18 | 340 pts
**OF-149 (LF-149), DH-2**  Owned: 96%  RH

After treading water for several seasons, Young finally turned the corner as a 24-year-old, setting career highs almost across the board and establishing himself as a true middle-of-the-order threat. The Twins, short on right-handed power, are likely to keep him in Minnesota for as long as they can afford him. (NN)

### Forecast
| Player | Age | AB | HR | R | RBI | SB | BA | OBP | SLG | $1L | Pts |
|---|---|---|---|---|---|---|---|---|---|---|---|
| Young D | 25 | 559 | 18 | 72 | 90 | 6 | .279 | .313 | .426 | $18 | 340 |

### Mini-Browser
| Player | Age | AB | HR | R | RBI | SB | BA | OBP | SLG | $1L | Pts |
|---|---|---|---|---|---|---|---|---|---|---|---|
| Ethier A | 28 | 523 | 24 | 78 | 84 | 6 | .287 | .366 | .506 | $20 | 410 |
| Bautista J | 30 | 522 | 30 | 78 | 84 | 6 | .253 | .353 | .495 | $20 | 400 |
| Cuddyer M | 32 | 578 | 20 | 85 | 85 | 7 | .270 | .342 | .456 | $19 | 390 |
| Quentin C | 28 | 465 | 28 | 77 | 88 | 4 | .260 | .352 | .494 | $19 | 370 |
| Ross C | 30 | 545 | 24 | 78 | 84 | 6 | .276 | .334 | .485 | $19 | 370 |

### Minors (2010) / Skills
| Level Leag | AB | HR | R | RBI | SB | BA | OBP | SLG | CT% | H% | BB% | Bash |
|---|---|---|---|---|---|---|---|---|---|---|---|---|
| A — | — | — | — | — | — | — | — | — | | | | |
| AA — | — | — | — | — | — | — | — | — | | | | |
| AAA — | — | — | — | — | — | — | — | — | | | | |

### Majors / Skills / Value / Extra / Production / OPS / Scoresheet
| Yr | Team | AB | HR | R | RBI | SB | BA | OBP | SLG | CT% | H% | BB% | Bash | $1L | $2L | Pts | RAA | 2B | 3B | CS | FB-LD-GB | HR/fb | RBI% | RS% | OPS | 1st Hf | 2nd Hf | vs RH | vs LH | Rnge | vRH | vLH |
|---|---|---|---|---|---|---|---|---|---|---|---|---|---|---|---|---|---|---|---|---|---|---|---|---|---|---|---|---|---|---|---|---|
| 07 | TB | 645 | 13 | 65 | 93 | 10 | .288 | .316 | .408 | 80% | 36% | 4% | 1.41 | $19 | $10 | 340 | -10 | 38 | 0 | 3 | 33-21-46 | 8% | 22% | 26% | .723 | .719 | .728 | .714 | .752 | 2.08 | -21 | +56 |
| 08 | MIN | 575 | 10 | 80 | 69 | 14 | .290 | .336 | .405 | 82% | 36% | 6% | 1.40 | $20 | $10 | 340 | -9 | 28 | 4 | 5 | 28-17-55 | 8% | 18% | 30% | .741 | .716 | .777 | .720 | .791 | 2.10 | -21 | +54 |
| 09 | MIN | 395 | 12 | 50 | 60 | 2 | .284 | .308 | .425 | 77% | 37% | 3% | 1.50 | $11 | $0 | 200 | -10 | 16 | 2 | 2 | 34-16-50 | 11% | 23% | 33% | .733 | .636 | .825 | .685 | .833 | 2.04 | -19 | +50 |
| 10 | MIN | 570 | 21 | 77 | 112 | 5 | .298 | .333 | .493 | 86% | 35% | 5% | 1.65 | $27 | $21 | 420 | +6 | 46 | 1 | 4 | 40-15-45 | 11% | 26% | 31% | .826 | .842 | .810 | .781 | .927 | 2.04 | -25 | +57 |

### Competition at LF / Stats in 2010
| Bats | Player | GSvR | GSvL | Sub | OPS |
|---|---|---|---|---|---|
| RH | Young D | 87 | 56 | 6 | .826 |
| LH | Kubel J | 16 | 0 | 0 | .750 |

---

## Delwyn Young — 150 PA | $-1 | 80 pts
**OF-21 (RF-21), 2B-10, 3B-8, DH-4**  Owned: 0%  BH

Young does not hit for average, draw walks, or play adequate defense. He did hit for some power in 2010, and he has fared well in a pinch-hitting role, so he is a decent bench-warmer. Like many marginal Pirates, Young is out of options, so he could lose his roster spot if the team adds players over the off-season. (MB)

### Forecast
| Player | Age | AB | HR | R | RBI | SB | BA | OBP | SLG | $1L | Pts |
|---|---|---|---|---|---|---|---|---|---|---|---|
| Young D | 28 | 142 | 5 | 18 | 18 | 0 | .265 | .323 | .429 | -$1 | 80 |

### Mini-Browser
| Player | Age | AB | HR | R | RBI | SB | BA | OBP | SLG | $1L | Pts |
|---|---|---|---|---|---|---|---|---|---|---|---|
| Bonifacio E | 25 | 160 | 2 | 25 | 11 | 9 | .254 | .307 | .332 | $0 | 90 |
| Harris W | 32 | 124 | 3 | 20 | 14 | 5 | .254 | .356 | .427 | $0 | 90 |
| Martinez F | 22 | 188 | 6 | 22 | 20 | 2 | .245 | .299 | .410 | -$1 | 90 |
| Michaels J | 34 | 143 | 5 | 18 | 20 | 2 | .258 | .323 | .427 | -$1 | 90 |
| Wells C | 26 | 138 | 8 | 17 | 17 | 3 | .229 | .302 | .459 | -$1 | 80 |

### Minors (2010) / Skills
| Level Leag | AB | HR | R | RBI | SB | BA | OBP | SLG | CT% | H% | BB% | Bash |
|---|---|---|---|---|---|---|---|---|---|---|---|---|
| A — | — | — | — | — | — | — | — | — | | | | |
| AA — | — | — | — | — | — | — | — | — | | | | |
| AAA — | — | — | — | — | — | — | — | — | | | | |

### Majors / Skills / Value / Extra / Production / OPS / Scoresheet
| Yr | Team | AB | HR | R | RBI | SB | BA | OBP | SLG | CT% | H% | BB% | Bash | $1L | $2L | Pts | RAA | 2B | 3B | CS | FB-LD-GB | HR/fb | RBI% | RS% | OPS | 1st Hf | 2nd Hf | vs RH | vs LH | Rnge | vRH | vLH |
|---|---|---|---|---|---|---|---|---|---|---|---|---|---|---|---|---|---|---|---|---|---|---|---|---|---|---|---|---|---|---|---|---|
| 07 | LAD | 34 | 2 | 4 | 3 | 1 | .382 | .417 | .647 | 85% | 45% | 6% | 1.69 | -$4 | -$17 | 30 | +3 | 1 | 0 | 1 | 45-21-34 | 15% | 8% | 15% | 1.064 | — | 1.064 | 1.187 | .908 | 2.10 | -21 | +54 |
| 08 | LAD | 126 | 1 | 10 | 7 | 0 | .246 | .321 | .341 | 73% | 34% | 10% | 1.39 | -$4 | -$17 | 40 | -6 | 9 | 0 | 3 | 33-17-50 | 8% | 9% | 20% | .663 | .671 | .630 | .630 | .732 | 2.08 | -21 | +54 |
| 09 | PIT | 354 | 7 | 40 | 43 | 2 | .266 | .326 | .381 | 75% | 36% | 7% | 1.44 | $6 | -$6 | 160 | -11 | 16 | 2 | 0 | 33-22-46 | 8% | 18% | 28% | .707 | .802 | .649 | .749 | .621 | 2.05 | -19 | +50 |
| 10 | PIT | 191 | 7 | 22 | 28 | 1 | .236 | .286 | .414 | 73% | 32% | 6% | 1.76 | $1 | -$12 | 90 | -8 | 11 | 2 | 0 | 40-13-47 | 13% | 17% | 29% | .700 | .673 | .740 | .663 | 1.000 | — | -25 | +57 |

### Competition at RF / Stats in 2010
| Bats | Player | GSvR | GSvL | Sub | OPS |
|---|---|---|---|---|---|
| LH | Jones G | 33 | 15 | 0 | .720 |
| RH | Milledge L | 19 | 22 | 4 | .712 |
| BH | Doumit R | 15 | 3 | 0 | .738 |
| BH | Young D | 15 | 1 | 5 | .700 |

*For more stats, visit www.Rotolympus.com.*

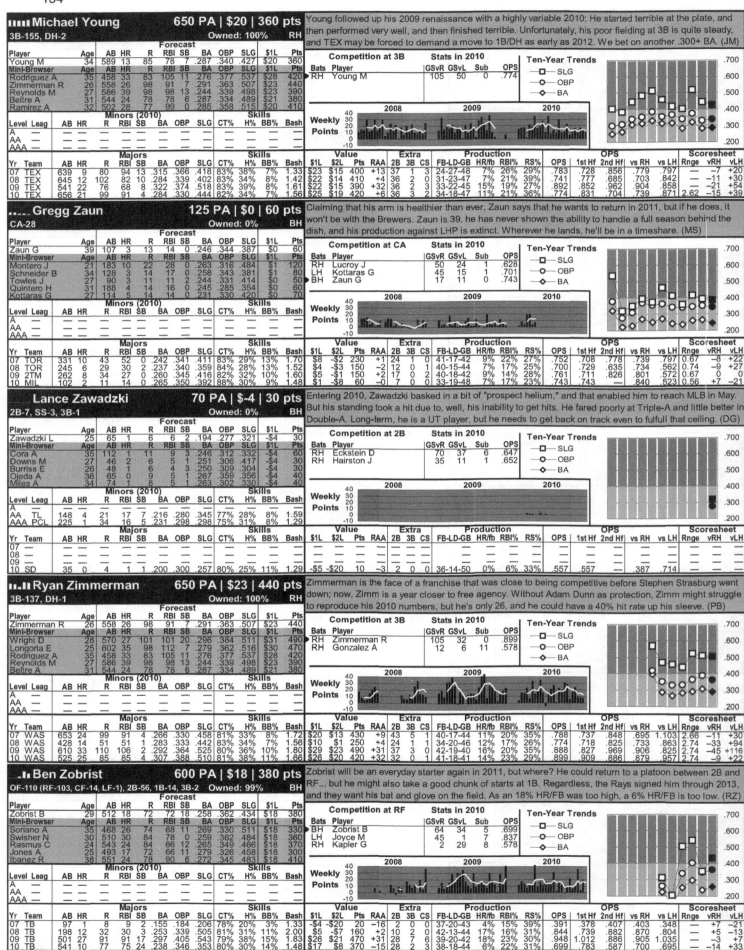

## Michael Young — 650 PA | $20 | 360 pts

3B-155, DH-2 — Owned: 100% — RH

Young followed up his 2009 renaissance with a highly variable 2010: He started terrible at the plate, and then performed very well, and then finished terrible. Unfortunately, his poor fielding at 3B is quite steady, and TEX may be forced to demand a move to 1B/DH as early as 2012. We bet on another .300+ BA. (JM)

| Forecast Player | Age | AB | HR | R | RBI | SB | BA | OBP | SLG | $1L | Pts |
|---|---|---|---|---|---|---|---|---|---|---|---|
| Young M | 34 | 589 | 13 | 85 | 78 | 7 | .287 | .340 | .427 | $20 | 360 |
| **Mini-Browser** | **Age** | **AB** | **HR** | **R** | **RBI** | **SB** | **BA** | **OBP** | **SLG** | **$1L** | **Pts** |
| Rodriguez A | 35 | 458 | 33 | 83 | 105 | 11 | .276 | .377 | .537 | $28 | 420 |
| Zimmerman R | 26 | 558 | 26 | 98 | 91 | 7 | .291 | .363 | .507 | $23 | 440 |
| Reynolds M | 27 | 586 | 39 | 98 | 98 | 13 | .244 | .339 | .498 | $23 | 390 |
| Beltre A | 31 | 544 | 24 | 78 | 78 | 6 | .287 | .334 | .489 | $21 | 380 |
| Ramirez A | 32 | 502 | 28 | 77 | 99 | 0 | .285 | .358 | .515 | $20 | 410 |

| Level | Leag | Minors (2010) AB | HR | R | RBI | SB | BA | OBP | SLG | Skills CT% | H% | BB% | Bash |
|---|---|---|---|---|---|---|---|---|---|---|---|---|---|
| A | — | — | — | — | — | — | — | — | — | — | — | — | — |
| AA | — | — | — | — | — | — | — | — | — | — | — | — | — |
| AAA | — | — | — | — | — | — | — | — | — | — | — | — | — |

| Yr | Team | Majors AB | HR | R | RBI | SB | BA | OBP | SLG | Skills CT% | H% | BB% | Bash |
|---|---|---|---|---|---|---|---|---|---|---|---|---|---|
| 07 | TEX | 639 | 9 | 80 | 94 | 13 | .315 | .366 | .418 | 83% | 38% | 7% | 1.33 |
| 08 | TEX | 645 | 12 | 102 | 82 | 10 | .284 | .339 | .402 | 83% | 34% | 8% | 1.42 |
| 09 | TEX | 541 | 22 | 76 | 68 | 8 | .322 | .374 | .518 | 83% | 39% | 8% | 1.61 |
| 10 | TEX | 656 | 21 | 99 | 91 | 4 | .284 | .330 | .444 | 82% | 34% | 7% | 1.56 |

| Bats | Competition at 3B Player | Stats in 2010 GSvR | GSvL | Sub | OPS |
|---|---|---|---|---|---|
| RH | Young M | 105 | 50 | 0 | .774 |

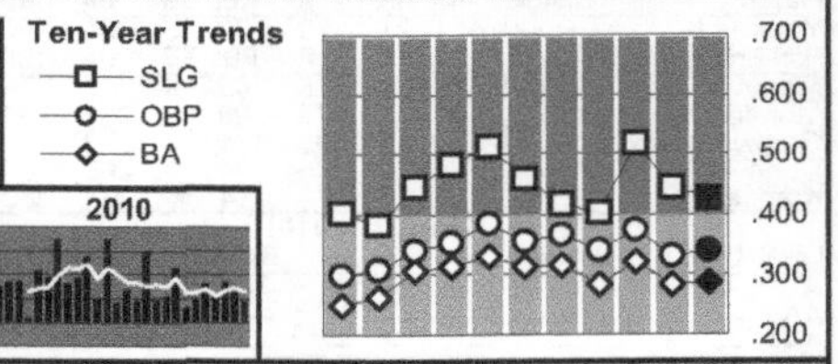


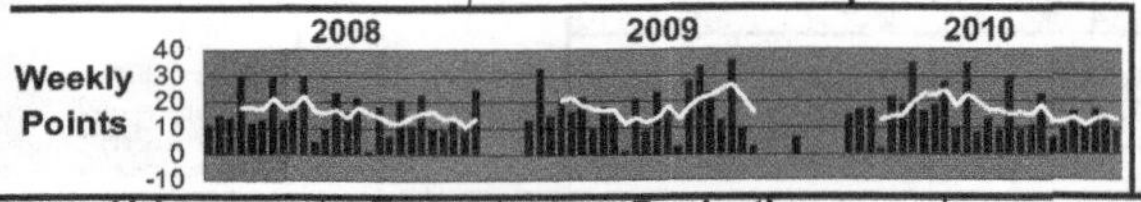


| Yr | Value $1L | $2L | Pts | RAA | Extra 2B | 3B | CS | Production FB-LD-GB | HR/fb | RBI% | RS% | OPS | 1st Hf | 2nd Hf | vs RH | vs LH | Scoresheet Rnge | vRH | vLH |
|---|---|---|---|---|---|---|---|---|---|---|---|---|---|---|---|---|---|---|---|
| 07 | $23 | $15 | 400 | +13 | 37 | 1 | 3 | 24-27-48 | 7% | 26% | 29% | .783 | .728 | .856 | .779 | .797 | — | −7 | +20 |
| 08 | $22 | $14 | 410 | +4 | 36 | 2 | 0 | 31-23-47 | 7% | 21% | 39% | .741 | .777 | .685 | .703 | .842 | — | −11 | +30 |
| 09 | $22 | $15 | 390 | +32 | 36 | 2 | 3 | 33-22-45 | 15% | 19% | 27% | .892 | .852 | .962 | .904 | .858 | — | −21 | +54 |
| 10 | $25 | $19 | 420 | +6 | 36 | 3 | 2 | 34-18-47 | 11% | 21% | 36% | .774 | .831 | .704 | .739 | .871 | 2.62 | −15 | +39 |

## Gregg Zaun — 125 PA | $0 | 60 pts

CA-28 — Owned: 0% — BH

Claiming that his arm is healthier than ever, Zaun says that he wants to return in 2011, but if he does, it won't be with the Brewers. Zaun is 39, he has never shown the ability to handle a full season behind the dish, and his production against LHP is extinct. Wherever he lands, he'll be in a timeshare. (MS)

| Forecast Player | Age | AB | HR | R | RBI | SB | BA | OBP | SLG | $1L | Pts |
|---|---|---|---|---|---|---|---|---|---|---|---|
| Zaun G | 39 | 107 | 3 | 13 | 14 | 0 | .246 | .344 | .387 | $0 | 60 |
| **Mini-Browser** | **Age** | **AB** | **HR** | **R** | **RBI** | **SB** | **BA** | **OBP** | **SLG** | **$1L** | **Pts** |
| Montero J | 21 | 183 | 10 | 22 | 28 | 0 | .263 | .316 | .484 | $1 | 120 |
| Schneider B | 34 | 128 | 3 | 14 | 17 | 0 | .258 | .343 | .381 | $1 | 80 |
| Towles J | 27 | 90 | 3 | 11 | 11 | 2 | .244 | .331 | .414 | $0 | 50 |
| Quintero H | 31 | 188 | 4 | 14 | 16 | 0 | .245 | .285 | .354 | $0 | 60 |
| Kottaras G | 27 | 114 | 5 | 14 | 14 | 0 | .231 | .330 | .420 | $0 | 70 |

| Level | Leag | Minors (2010) AB | HR | R | RBI | SB | BA | OBP | SLG | Skills CT% | H% | BB% | Bash |
|---|---|---|---|---|---|---|---|---|---|---|---|---|---|
| A | — | — | — | — | — | — | — | — | — | — | — | — | — |
| AA | — | — | — | — | — | — | — | — | — | — | — | — | — |
| AAA | — | — | — | — | — | — | — | — | — | — | — | — | — |

| Yr | Team | Majors AB | HR | R | RBI | SB | BA | OBP | SLG | Skills CT% | H% | BB% | Bash |
|---|---|---|---|---|---|---|---|---|---|---|---|---|---|
| 07 | TOR | 331 | 10 | 43 | 52 | 0 | .242 | .341 | .411 | 83% | 29% | 13% | 1.70 |
| 08 | TOR | 245 | 6 | 29 | 30 | 2 | .237 | .340 | .359 | 84% | 28% | 13% | 1.52 |
| 09 | 2TM | 262 | 8 | 34 | 27 | 0 | .260 | .345 | .416 | 82% | 32% | 10% | 1.60 |
| 10 | MIL | 102 | 2 | 11 | 14 | 0 | .265 | .350 | .392 | 88% | 30% | 9% | 1.48 |

| Bats | Competition at CA Player | Stats in 2010 GSvR | GSvL | Sub | OPS |
|---|---|---|---|---|---|
| RH | Lucroy J | 50 | 24 | 1 | .628 |
| LH | Kottaras G | 45 | 15 | 1 | .701 |
| BH | Zaun G | 17 | 11 | 0 | .743 |

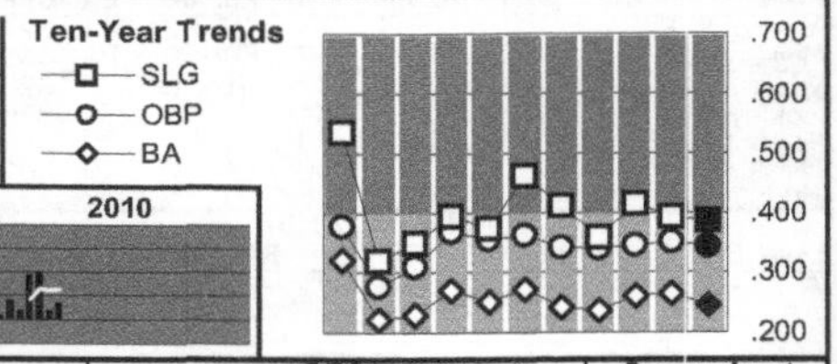


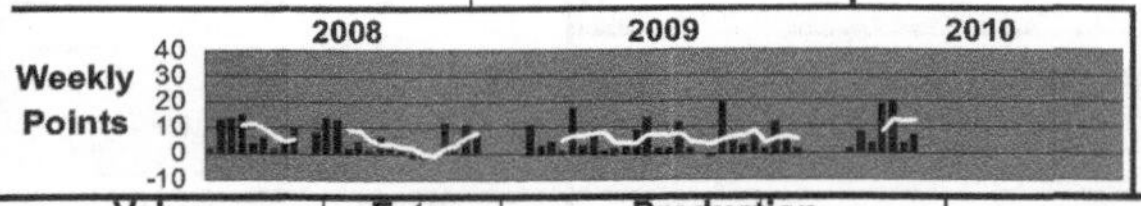


| Yr | Value $1L | $2L | Pts | RAA | Extra 2B | 3B | CS | Production FB-LD-GB | HR/fb | RBI% | RS% | OPS | 1st Hf | 2nd Hf | vs RH | vs LH | Scoresheet Rnge | vRH | vLH |
|---|---|---|---|---|---|---|---|---|---|---|---|---|---|---|---|---|---|---|---|
| 07 | $8 | -$2 | 230 | +1 | 24 | 1 | 0 | 41-17-42 | 9% | 22% | 27% | .752 | .708 | .778 | .739 | .797 | 0.67 | −8 | +22 |
| 08 | $4 | -$3 | 150 | −2 | 12 | 0 | 1 | 40-15-44 | 7% | 17% | 25% | .700 | .729 | .635 | .734 | .562 | 0.74 | −9 | +27 |
| 09 | $5 | -$1 | 150 | +2 | 17 | 0 | 2 | 40-18-42 | 9% | 14% | 28% | .761 | .711 | .826 | .801 | .572 | 0.67 | 0 | 0 |
| 10 | $1 | -$8 | 60 | −0 | 7 | 0 | 0 | 33-19-48 | 7% | 17% | 23% | .743 | .743 | — | .840 | .523 | 0.56 | +7 | −21 |

## Lance Zawadzki — 70 PA | $-4 | 30 pts

2B-7, SS-3, 3B-1 — Owned: 0% — BH

Entering 2010, Zawadzki basked in a bit of "prospect helium," and that enabled him to reach MLB in May. But his standing took a hit due to, well, his inability to get hits. He fared poorly at Triple-A and little better in Double-A. Long-term, he is a UT player, but he needs to get back on track even to fulfull that ceiling. (DG)

| Forecast Player | Age | AB | HR | R | RBI | SB | BA | OBP | SLG | $1L | Pts |
|---|---|---|---|---|---|---|---|---|---|---|---|
| Zawadzki L | 25 | 65 | 1 | 6 | 6 | 2 | .194 | .277 | .321 | -$4 | 30 |
| **Mini-Browser** | **Age** | **AB** | **HR** | **R** | **RBI** | **SB** | **BA** | **OBP** | **SLG** | **$1L** | **Pts** |
| Cora A | 35 | 112 | 1 | 11 | 9 | 3 | .246 | .312 | .332 | -$4 | 60 |
| Downs M | 27 | 46 | 2 | 6 | 5 | 1 | .251 | .306 | .417 | -$4 | 30 |
| Burriss E | 26 | 48 | 1 | 6 | 4 | 3 | .250 | .309 | .304 | -$4 | 30 |
| Ojeda A | 36 | 65 | 0 | 9 | 5 | 1 | .267 | .359 | .356 | -$4 | 40 |
| Miles A | 34 | 74 | 1 | 8 | 5 | 1 | .263 | .302 | .330 | -$4 | 40 |

| Level | Leag | Minors (2010) AB | HR | R | RBI | SB | BA | OBP | SLG | Skills CT% | H% | BB% | Bash |
|---|---|---|---|---|---|---|---|---|---|---|---|---|---|
| A | — | — | — | — | — | — | — | — | — | — | — | — | — |
| AA | TL | 148 | 4 | 21 | 17 | 7 | .216 | .280 | .345 | 77% | 28% | 8% | 1.59 |
| AAA | PCL | 225 | 1 | 34 | 16 | 5 | .231 | .298 | .298 | 75% | 31% | 8% | 1.29 |

| Yr | Team | Majors AB | HR | R | RBI | SB | BA | OBP | SLG | Skills CT% | H% | BB% | Bash |
|---|---|---|---|---|---|---|---|---|---|---|---|---|---|
| 07 | — | — | — | — | — | — | — | — | — | — | — | — | — |
| 08 | — | — | — | — | — | — | — | — | — | — | — | — | — |
| 09 | — | — | — | — | — | — | — | — | — | — | — | — | — |
| 10 | SD | 35 | 0 | 4 | 1 | 1 | .200 | .300 | .257 | 80% | 25% | 11% | 1.29 |

| Bats | Competition at 2B Player | Stats in 2010 GSvR | GSvL | Sub | OPS |
|---|---|---|---|---|---|
| RH | Eckstein D | 70 | 37 | 6 | .647 |
| RH | Hairston J | 35 | 11 | 1 | .652 |

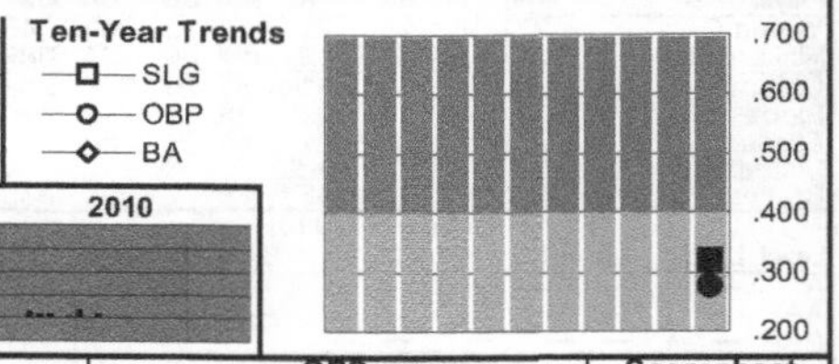


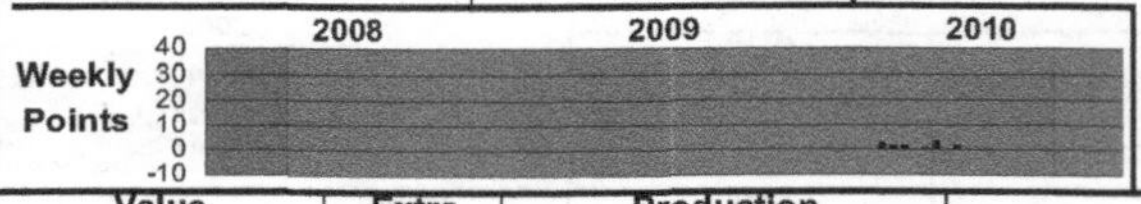


| Yr | Value $1L | $2L | Pts | RAA | Extra 2B | 3B | CS | Production FB-LD-GB | HR/fb | RBI% | RS% | OPS | 1st Hf | 2nd Hf | vs RH | vs LH | Scoresheet Rnge | vRH | vLH |
|---|---|---|---|---|---|---|---|---|---|---|---|---|---|---|---|---|---|---|---|
| 07 | — | — | — | — | — | — | — | — | — | — | — | — | — | — | — | — | — | — | — |
| 08 | — | — | — | — | — | — | — | — | — | — | — | — | — | — | — | — | — | — | — |
| 09 | — | — | — | — | — | — | — | — | — | — | — | — | — | — | — | — | — | — | — |
| 10 | -$5 | -$20 | 10 | −3 | 2 | 0 | 0 | 36-14-50 | 0% | 6% | 33% | .557 | .557 | — | .387 | .714 | — | — | — |

## Ryan Zimmerman — 650 PA | $23 | 440 pts

3B-137, DH-1 — Owned: 100% — RH

Zimmerman is the face of a franchise that was close to being competitive before Stephen Strasburg went down; now, Zimm is a year closer to free agency. Without Adam Dunn as protection, Zimm might struggle to reproduce his 2010 numbers, but he's only 26, and he could have a 40% hit rate up his sleeve. (PB)

| Forecast Player | Age | AB | HR | R | RBI | SB | BA | OBP | SLG | $1L | Pts |
|---|---|---|---|---|---|---|---|---|---|---|---|
| Zimmerman R | 26 | 558 | 26 | 98 | 91 | 7 | .291 | .363 | .507 | $23 | 440 |
| **Mini-Browser** | **Age** | **AB** | **HR** | **R** | **RBI** | **SB** | **BA** | **OBP** | **SLG** | **$1L** | **Pts** |
| Wright D | 28 | 570 | 27 | 101 | 101 | 20 | .296 | .384 | .511 | $31 | 490 |
| Longoria E | 25 | 602 | 35 | 98 | 112 | 7 | .279 | .362 | .516 | $30 | 470 |
| Rodriguez A | 35 | 458 | 33 | 83 | 105 | 11 | .276 | .377 | .537 | $28 | 420 |
| Reynolds M | 27 | 586 | 39 | 98 | 98 | 13 | .244 | .339 | .498 | $23 | 390 |
| Beltre A | 31 | 544 | 24 | 78 | 78 | 6 | .287 | .334 | .489 | $21 | 380 |

| Level | Leag | Minors (2010) AB | HR | R | RBI | SB | BA | OBP | SLG | Skills CT% | H% | BB% | Bash |
|---|---|---|---|---|---|---|---|---|---|---|---|---|---|
| A | — | — | — | — | — | — | — | — | — | — | — | — | — |
| AA | — | — | — | — | — | — | — | — | — | — | — | — | — |
| AAA | — | — | — | — | — | — | — | — | — | — | — | — | — |

| Yr | Team | Majors AB | HR | R | RBI | SB | BA | OBP | SLG | Skills CT% | H% | BB% | Bash |
|---|---|---|---|---|---|---|---|---|---|---|---|---|---|
| 07 | WAS | 653 | 24 | 99 | 91 | 4 | .266 | .330 | .458 | 81% | 33% | 8% | 1.72 |
| 08 | WAS | 428 | 14 | 51 | 51 | 1 | .283 | .333 | .442 | 83% | 34% | 7% | 1.56 |
| 09 | WAS | 610 | 33 | 110 | 106 | 2 | .292 | .364 | .525 | 80% | 36% | 10% | 1.80 |
| 10 | WAS | 525 | 25 | 85 | 85 | 4 | .307 | .388 | .510 | 81% | 38% | 11% | 1.66 |

| Bats | Competition at 3B Player | Stats in 2010 GSvR | GSvL | Sub | OPS |
|---|---|---|---|---|---|
| RH | Zimmerman R | 105 | 32 | 0 | .899 |
| RH | Gonzalez A | 12 | 6 | 11 | .578 |

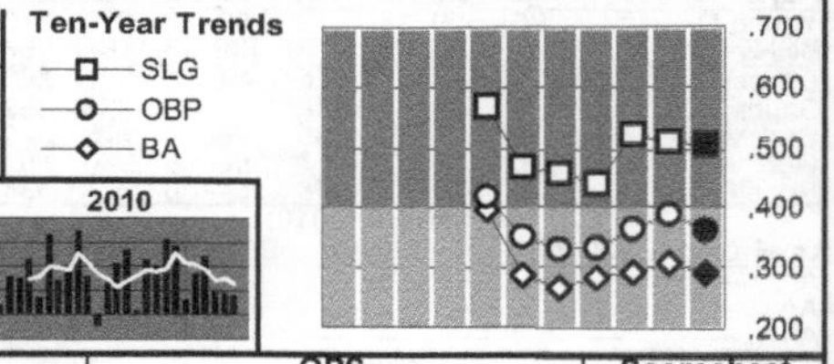


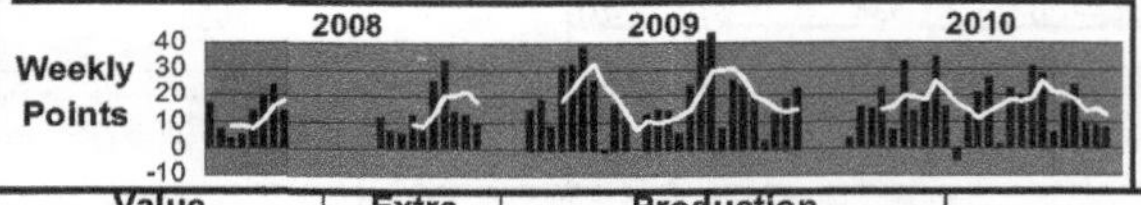


| Yr | Value $1L | $2L | Pts | RAA | Extra 2B | 3B | CS | Production FB-LD-GB | HR/fb | RBI% | RS% | OPS | 1st Hf | 2nd Hf | vs RH | vs LH | Scoresheet Rnge | vRH | vLH |
|---|---|---|---|---|---|---|---|---|---|---|---|---|---|---|---|---|---|---|---|
| 07 | $20 | $13 | 430 | +9 | 43 | 5 | 1 | 40-17-44 | 11% | 20% | 35% | .788 | .737 | .848 | .695 | 1.103 | 2.66 | −11 | +30 |
| 08 | $10 | $1 | 250 | +4 | 24 | 1 | 1 | 34-20-46 | 12% | 17% | 26% | .774 | .718 | .825 | .733 | .863 | 2.74 | −33 | +94 |
| 09 | $29 | $23 | 490 | +31 | 37 | 3 | 0 | 42-19-40 | 16% | 20% | 35% | .888 | .827 | .969 | .906 | .825 | 2.74 | −45 | +116 |
| 10 | $26 | $20 | 420 | +32 | 32 | 0 | 1 | 41-18-41 | 14% | 23% | 29% | .899 | .909 | .886 | .879 | .957 | 2.74 | −9 | +22 |

## Ben Zobrist — 600 PA | $18 | 380 pts

OF-110 (RF-103, CF-14, LF-1), 2B-56, 1B-14, 3B-2 — Owned: 99% — BH

Zobrist will be an everyday starter again in 2011, but where? He could return to a platoon between 2B and RF... but he might also take a good chunk of starts at 1B. Regardless, the Rays signed him through 2013, and they want his bat and glove on the field. As an 18% HR/FB was too high, a 6% HR/FB is too low. (RZ)

| Forecast Player | Age | AB | HR | R | RBI | SB | BA | OBP | SLG | $1L | Pts |
|---|---|---|---|---|---|---|---|---|---|---|---|
| Zobrist B | 29 | 512 | 18 | 72 | 72 | 18 | .258 | .362 | .434 | $18 | 380 |
| **Mini-Browser** | **Age** | **AB** | **HR** | **R** | **RBI** | **SB** | **BA** | **OBP** | **SLG** | **$1L** | **Pts** |
| Soriano A | 35 | 468 | 26 | 74 | 68 | 11 | .269 | .330 | .511 | $18 | 330 |
| Swisher N | 30 | 510 | 30 | 84 | 78 | 0 | .259 | .362 | .484 | $18 | 360 |
| Rasmus C | 24 | 543 | 24 | 84 | 66 | 12 | .265 | .349 | .466 | $18 | 370 |
| Jones A | 25 | 493 | 17 | 72 | 66 | 11 | .279 | .326 | .458 | $18 | 300 |
| Ibanez R | 38 | 551 | 24 | 78 | 90 | 6 | .272 | .345 | .483 | $18 | 410 |

| Level | Leag | Minors (2010) AB | HR | R | RBI | SB | BA | OBP | SLG | Skills CT% | H% | BB% | Bash |
|---|---|---|---|---|---|---|---|---|---|---|---|---|---|
| A | — | — | — | — | — | — | — | — | — | — | — | — | — |
| AA | — | — | — | — | — | — | — | — | — | — | — | — | — |
| AAA | — | — | — | — | — | — | — | — | — | — | — | — | — |

| Yr | Team | Majors AB | HR | R | RBI | SB | BA | OBP | SLG | Skills CT% | H% | BB% | Bash |
|---|---|---|---|---|---|---|---|---|---|---|---|---|---|
| 07 | TB | 97 | 1 | 8 | 9 | 2 | .155 | .184 | .206 | 78% | 20% | 3% | 1.33 |
| 08 | TB | 198 | 12 | 32 | 30 | 3 | .253 | .339 | .505 | 81% | 31% | 11% | 2.00 |
| 09 | TB | 501 | 27 | 91 | 91 | 17 | .297 | .405 | .543 | 79% | 38% | 15% | 1.83 |
| 10 | TB | 541 | 10 | 77 | 75 | 24 | .238 | .346 | .353 | 80% | 30% | 14% | 1.48 |

| Bats | Competition at RF Player | Stats in 2010 GSvR | GSvL | Sub | OPS |
|---|---|---|---|---|---|
| BH | Zobrist B | 64 | 34 | 5 | .699 |
| LH | Joyce M | 45 | 1 | 7 | .837 |
| RH | Kapler G | 2 | 29 | 8 | .578 |

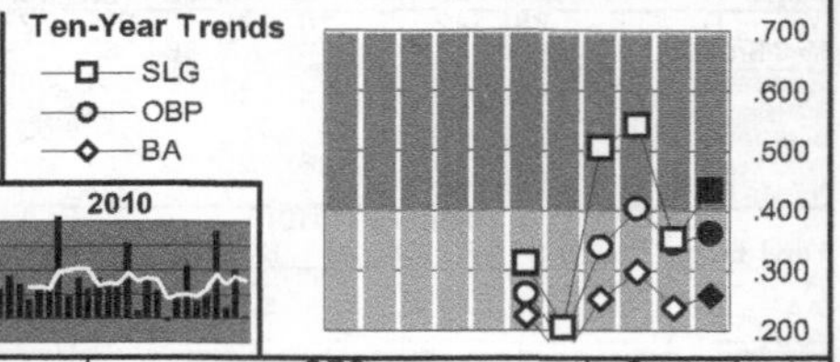


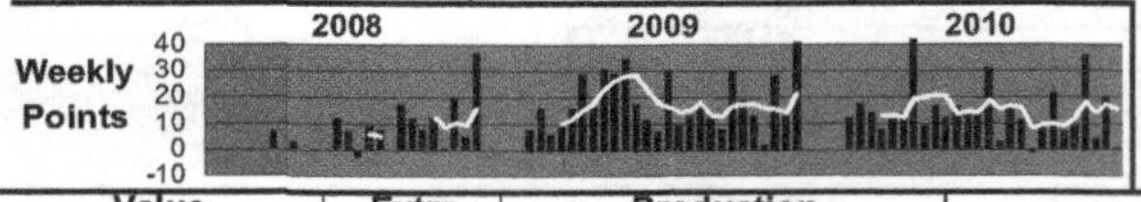


| Yr | Value $1L | $2L | Pts | RAA | Extra 2B | 3B | CS | Production FB-LD-GB | HR/fb | RBI% | RS% | OPS | 1st Hf | 2nd Hf | vs RH | vs LH | Scoresheet Rnge | vRH | vLH |
|---|---|---|---|---|---|---|---|---|---|---|---|---|---|---|---|---|---|---|---|
| 07 | -$4 | -$20 | 20 | −16 | 2 | 0 | 0 | 37-20-43 | 4% | 15% | 39% | .391 | .378 | .407 | .403 | .348 | — | +7 | −21 |
| 08 | $5 | -$7 | 160 | +2 | 10 | 2 | 0 | 42-13-44 | 17% | 16% | 31% | .844 | .739 | .882 | .870 | .804 | — | +5 | −13 |
| 09 | $26 | $21 | 470 | +31 | 28 | 7 | 6 | 39-20-42 | 18% | 23% | 30% | .948 | 1.012 | .886 | .905 | 1.035 | — | −3 | +7 |
| 10 | $17 | $8 | 370 | −15 | 28 | 2 | 3 | 38-18-44 | 6% | 22% | 31% | .699 | .783 | .587 | .700 | .695 | — | −14 | +33 |

*For more stats, visit www.Rotolympus.com.*

# PITCHERS

**METHOD:** The team experts built tentative rosters for each MLB team for 2011. Every pitcher targeted for 40 IP or more is here. We also included some "players of interest" who might not get much work in 2011 but who could be important later; these pitchers are projected for 20 IP.

All told, this section has 495 pitchers. These are our best candidates for meaningful playing time in 2011. We know that many fantasy GM's take part in keeper leagues and leagues with deep benches, so this section gives equal treatment to major- and minor-leaguers.

**OUTLOOK:** Beyond the top tier of players, fantasy value becomes more of a matter of opportunity than of skill. For that reason, the commentaries focus on the player's role, his standing in his organization, and his rivals. Key statistical trends and blips are also dealt with. Probable free agents have been assigned a forecast based on their skill, age, and role.

**SIGNAL BARS:** In front of each player's name is a small graph of five columns. The columns represent the player's fantasy value over the past five seasons (2006-2010). At a glance, you can see whether, and how recently, a player was a productive fantasy asset.

**HEADER:** The fields to the right of the player's name are

**Projected IP | Projected $1L | Projected Pts**

Directly beneath a player's name are his MLB position (SP or RP) and games played in 2010. Positions are listed in descending order from most-played to least-played. Below and to the right are his **Owned** (his ownership percentage in online leagues as of the last weekend in August) and then his pitching hand (LH/RH).

**MINI-BROWSER:** This is a list of players who offer similar overall value, though perhaps with a different breakdown of stats. Unlike with hitters, we bundle both SP's & RP's here. Except for top-rated players, the listed players are directly above the profiled player in projected $1L. Age is as of April 1, 2011.

**MINORS:** The stats are for 2010. Level "A" includes low-A and high-A (but not rookie).

**VALUES:** We value players by four methods:

$1L is the player's single-league (AL- or NL-only) auction value, $2L is his mixed-league (AL/NL) value. Values are calculated for traditional 5x5 leagues: Wins, Saves, K, ERA, WHIP.

**Pts** (Points) is the player's value in a points-based league. We use this formula:

| | |
|---|---|
| **Win** | 10 points |
| **Save** | 5 points |
| **Inning** | 1 point |
| **Strikeout** | 1 point |
| **Hit** | -0.5 point |
| **Walk** | -0.5 point |

**RAA** (Runs Above Average) is the number of runs saved (positive RAA) or surrendered (negative RAA) by the pitcher versus a pitcher with average run allowance. Relievers have a tougher benchmark than do starters.

**COMPETITION:** This table pits a player against players who play on the same team (as of press time) and at the player's anticipated primary position in 2011. The player's primary position is generally the position at which he played the most games in 2010, but in some cases the position has been changed to reflect his expected role in 2011.

Players are ranked in descending order of games played in 2010 (either games started, for SP, or games relieved, for RP). Relievers are pitted against pitchers of the same handedness; starters are not. For starters, the table will shows the top four pitchers on the team in terms of games started. Figures in the table cover a player's entire work for 2010, and not just his work with this team.

**WEEKLY POINTS:** This graph shows weekly points totals from 2008-2010. The white line is a rolling four-week trend.

**TEN-YEAR TRENDS:** This graph shows yearly trends in K/9 and BB/9 from 2001-2010. The darker-colored section shows the usual range for strikeouts; the lighter-colored section, for walks. The black points are forecasts for 2011.

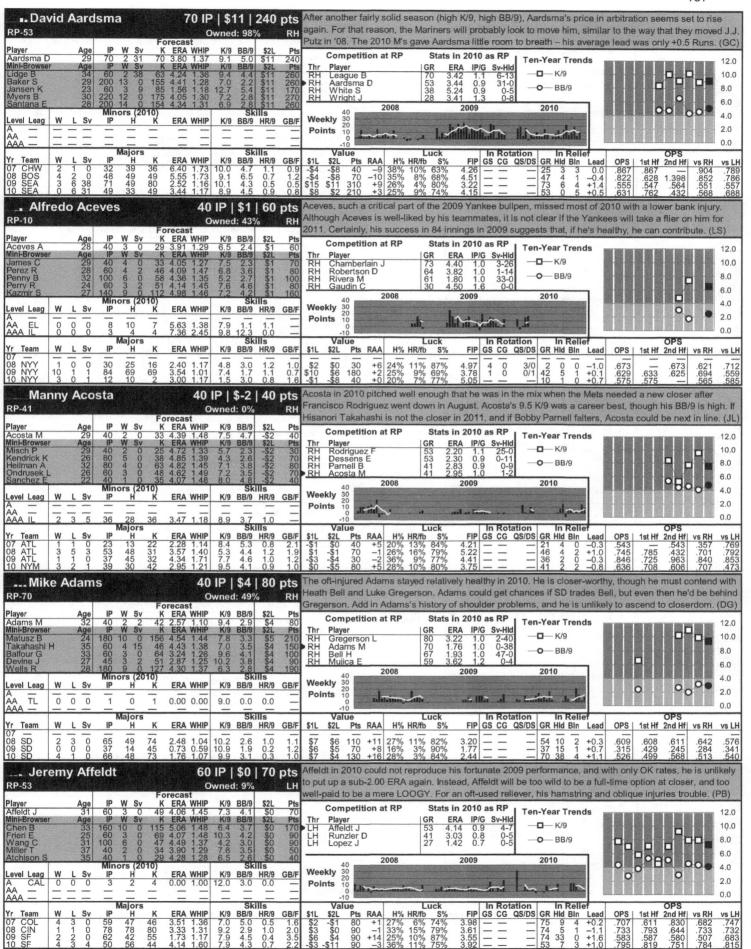

## David Aardsma — 70 IP | $11 | 240 pts

RP-53 Owned: 98% RH

After another fairly solid season (high K/9, high BB/9), Aardsma's price in arbitration seems set to rise again. For that reason, the Mariners will probably look to move him, similar to the way that they moved J.J. Putz in '08. The 2010 M's gave Aardsma little room to breath – his average lead was only +0.5 Runs. (GC)

| Player | Age | IP | W | Sv | K | ERA | WHIP | K/9 | BB/9 | $2L | Pts |
|---|---|---|---|---|---|---|---|---|---|---|---|
| **Forecast** | | | | | | | | | | | |
| Aardsma D | 29 | 70 | 2 | 31 | 70 | 3.80 | 1.37 | 9.1 | 5.0 | $11 | 240 |
| **Mini-Browser** | Age | IP | W | Sv | K | ERA | WHIP | K/9 | BB/9 | $2L | Pts |
| Lidge B | 34 | 60 | 2 | 38 | 63 | 4.24 | 1.36 | 9.4 | 4.4 | $11 | 260 |
| Baker S | 29 | 200 | 13 | 0 | 155 | 4.41 | 1.28 | 7.0 | 2.2 | $11 | 260 |
| Jansen K | 23 | 60 | 3 | 9 | 85 | 1.56 | 1.18 | 12.7 | 5.4 | $11 | 170 |
| Myers B | 30 | 220 | 12 | 0 | 175 | 4.05 | 1.30 | 7.2 | 2.8 | $11 | 270 |
| Santana E | 28 | 200 | 14 | 0 | 154 | 4.34 | 1.31 | 6.9 | 2.8 | $11 | 260 |

Competition at RP — Stats in 2010 as RP

| Thr | Player | GR | ERA | IP/G | Sv-Hld |
|---|---|---|---|---|---|
| RH | League B | 70 | 3.42 | 1.1 | 6-13 |
| RH | Aardsma D | 53 | 3.44 | 0.9 | 31-0 |
| RH | White S | 38 | 5.24 | 0.9 | 0-5 |
| RH | Wright J | 28 | 3.41 | 1.3 | 0-8 |

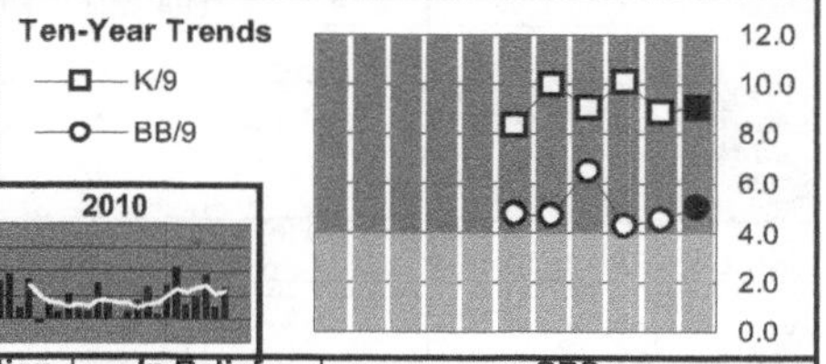
Ten-Year Trends
K/9
BB/9
12.0
10.0
8.0
6.0
4.0
2.0
0.0

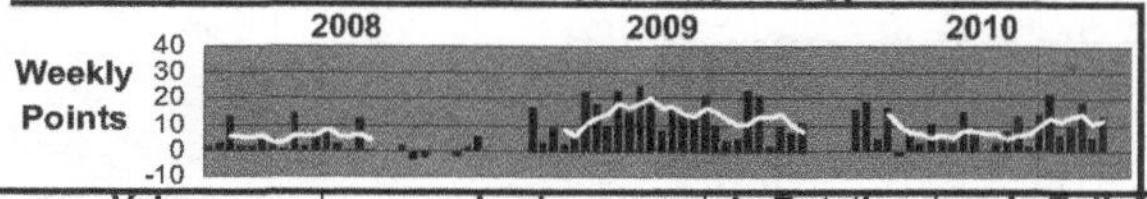
Weekly Points
2008
2009
2010
40
30
20
10
0
-10

Minors (2010)

| Level | Leag | W | L | Sv | IP | H | K | ERA | WHIP | K/9 | BB/9 | HR/9 | GB/F |
|---|---|---|---|---|---|---|---|---|---|---|---|---|---|
| A | — | — | — | — | — | — | — | — | — | — | — | — | — |
| AA | — | — | — | — | — | — | — | — | — | — | — | — | — |
| AAA | — | — | — | — | — | — | — | — | — | — | — | — | — |

Majors

| Yr | Team | W | L | Sv | IP | H | K | ERA | WHIP | K/9 | BB/9 | HR/9 | GB/F | $1L | $2L | Pts | RAA | H% | HR/fb | S% | FIP | GS | CG | QS/DS | GR | Hld | Bln | Lead | OPS | 1st Hf | 2nd Hf | vs RH | vs LH |
|---|---|---|---|---|---|---|---|---|---|---|---|---|---|---|---|---|---|---|---|---|---|---|---|---|---|---|---|---|---|---|---|---|---|
| 07 | CHW | 2 | 1 | 0 | 32 | 39 | 36 | 6.40 | 1.73 | 10.0 | 4.7 | 1.1 | 0.9 | -$4 | -$8 | 40 | –9 | 38% | 10% | 63% | 4.26 | — | — | — | 25 | 3 | 3 | 0.0 | .867 | .867 | — | .904 | .789 |
| 08 | BOS | 4 | 2 | 0 | 48 | 49 | 49 | 5.55 | 1.73 | 9.1 | 6.5 | 0.7 | 1.2 | -$4 | -$8 | 70 | –10 | 35% | 8% | 68% | 4.51 | — | — | — | 47 | 4 | 1 | –0.4 | .822 | .628 | 1.398 | .852 | .786 |
| 09 | SEA | 3 | 6 | 38 | 71 | 49 | 80 | 2.52 | 1.16 | 10.1 | 4.3 | 0.5 | 0.5 | $15 | $11 | 310 | +9 | 26% | 4% | 80% | 3.22 | — | — | — | 73 | 6 | 4 | +1.4 | .555 | .547 | .564 | .551 | .557 |
| 10 | SEA | 0 | 6 | 31 | 49 | 33 | 49 | 3.44 | 1.17 | 8.9 | 4.5 | 0.9 | 0.8 | $8 | $2 | 210 | +3 | 25% | 9% | 74% | 4.15 | — | — | — | 53 | 0 | 5 | +0.5 | .631 | .762 | .432 | .568 | .688 |

## Alfredo Aceves — 40 IP | $1 | 60 pts

RP-10 Owned: 43% RH

Aceves, such a critical part of the 2009 Yankee bullpen, missed most of 2010 with a lower bank injury. Although Aceves is well-liked by his teammates, it is not clear if the Yankees will take a flier on him for 2011. Certainly, his success in 84 innings in 2009 suggests that, if he's healthy, he can contribute. (LS)

| Player | Age | IP | W | Sv | K | ERA | WHIP | K/9 | BB/9 | $2L | Pts |
|---|---|---|---|---|---|---|---|---|---|---|---|
| **Forecast** | | | | | | | | | | | |
| Aceves A | 28 | 40 | 3 | 0 | 29 | 3.91 | 1.29 | 6.5 | 2.4 | $1 | 60 |
| **Mini-Browser** | Age | IP | W | Sv | K | ERA | WHIP | K/9 | BB/9 | $2L | Pts |
| James C | 29 | 40 | 4 | 0 | 33 | 4.05 | 1.27 | 7.5 | 2.3 | $1 | 70 |
| Perez R | 28 | 60 | 4 | 2 | 46 | 4.09 | 1.47 | 6.8 | 3.6 | $1 | 80 |
| Penny B | 32 | 100 | 6 | 0 | 58 | 4.36 | 1.35 | 5.2 | 2.7 | $1 | 100 |
| Perry R | 24 | 60 | 3 | 2 | 51 | 4.14 | 1.45 | 7.6 | 4.6 | $1 | 80 |
| Kazmir S | 27 | 140 | 9 | 0 | 112 | 4.98 | 1.46 | 7.2 | 4.2 | $1 | 160 |

Competition at RP — Stats in 2010 as RP

| Thr | Player | GR | ERA | IP/G | Sv-Hld |
|---|---|---|---|---|---|
| RH | Chamberlain J | 73 | 4.40 | 1.0 | 3-26 |
| RH | Robertson D | 64 | 3.82 | 1.0 | 1-14 |
| RH | Rivera M | 61 | 1.80 | 1.0 | 33-0 |
| RH | Gaudin C | 30 | 4.50 | 1.6 | 0-0 |

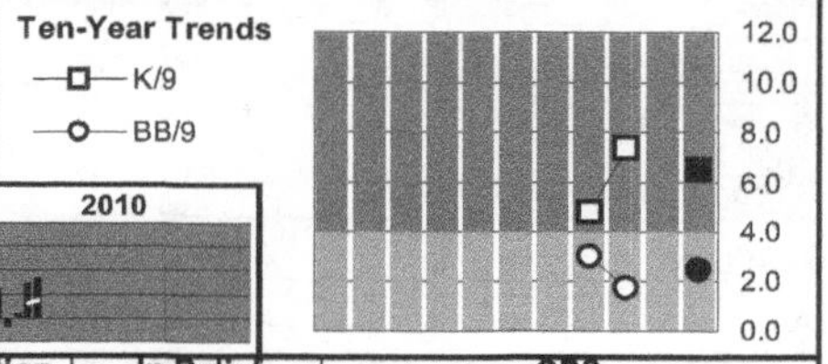
Ten-Year Trends
K/9
BB/9
12.0
10.0
8.0
6.0
4.0
2.0
0.0

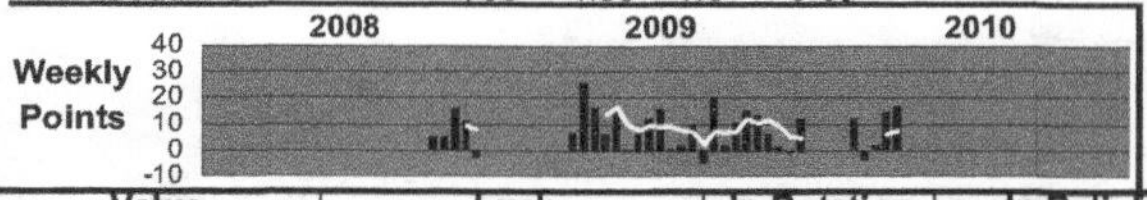
Weekly Points
2008
2009
2010
40
30
20
10
0
-10

Minors (2010)

| Level | Leag | W | L | Sv | IP | H | K | ERA | WHIP | K/9 | BB/9 | HR/9 | GB/F |
|---|---|---|---|---|---|---|---|---|---|---|---|---|---|
| A | — | — | — | — | — | — | — | — | — | — | — | — | — |
| AA | EL | 0 | 0 | 0 | 8 | 10 | 7 | 5.63 | 1.38 | 7.9 | 1.1 | 1.1 | — |
| AAA | IL | 0 | 0 | 0 | 3 | 4 | 4 | 7.36 | 2.45 | 9.8 | 12.3 | 0.0 | — |

Majors

| Yr | Team | W | L | Sv | IP | H | K | ERA | WHIP | K/9 | BB/9 | HR/9 | GB/F | $1L | $2L | Pts | RAA | H% | HR/fb | S% | FIP | GS | CG | QS/DS | GR | Hld | Bln | Lead | OPS | 1st Hf | 2nd Hf | vs RH | vs LH |
|---|---|---|---|---|---|---|---|---|---|---|---|---|---|---|---|---|---|---|---|---|---|---|---|---|---|---|---|---|---|---|---|---|---|
| 07 | — | | | | | | | | | | | | | | | | | | | | | | | | | | | | | | | | |
| 08 | NYY | 1 | 0 | 0 | 30 | 25 | 16 | 2.40 | 1.17 | 4.8 | 3.0 | 1.2 | 1.0 | $2 | $0 | 30 | +6 | 24% | 11% | 87% | 4.97 | 4 | 0 | 3/0 | 2 | 0 | 0 | –1.0 | .673 | — | .673 | .621 | .712 |
| 09 | NYY | 10 | 1 | 1 | 84 | 69 | 69 | 3.54 | 1.01 | 7.4 | 1.7 | 1.1 | 0.7 | $10 | $6 | 180 | +2 | 25% | 9% | 69% | 3.78 | 1 | 0 | 0/1 | 42 | 5 | 1 | +0.1 | .629 | .633 | .625 | .694 | .559 |
| 10 | NYY | 3 | 0 | 1 | 12 | 10 | 2 | 3.00 | 1.17 | 1.5 | 3.0 | 0.8 | 1.6 | -$1 | -$8 | 40 | +0 | 20% | 7% | 77% | 5.05 | — | — | — | 10 | 1 | 0 | +0.7 | .575 | .575 | | .565 | .585 |

## Manny Acosta — 40 IP | $-2 | 40 pts

RP-41 Owned: 0% RH

Acosta in 2010 pitched well enough that he was in the mix when the Mets needed a new closer after Francisco Rodriguez went down in August. Acosta's 9.5 K/9 was a career best, though his BB/9 is high. If Hisanori Takahashi is not the closer in 2011, and if Bobby Parnell falters, Acosta could be next in line. (JL)

| Player | Age | IP | W | Sv | K | ERA | WHIP | K/9 | BB/9 | $2L | Pts |
|---|---|---|---|---|---|---|---|---|---|---|---|
| **Forecast** | | | | | | | | | | | |
| Acosta M | 29 | 40 | 2 | 0 | 33 | 4.39 | 1.48 | 7.5 | 4.7 | -$2 | 40 |
| **Mini-Browser** | Age | IP | W | Sv | K | ERA | WHIP | K/9 | BB/9 | $2L | Pts |
| Misch P | 29 | 40 | 2 | 0 | 25 | 4.72 | 1.33 | 5.7 | 2.3 | -$2 | 30 |
| Kendrick K | 26 | 80 | 5 | 0 | 38 | 4.85 | 1.39 | 4.3 | 2.6 | -$2 | 70 |
| Heilman A | 32 | 80 | 4 | 0 | 63 | 4.82 | 1.45 | 7.1 | 3.8 | -$2 | 80 |
| Ondrusek L | 26 | 60 | 3 | 0 | 48 | 4.62 | 1.49 | 7.2 | 3.5 | -$2 | 70 |
| Sanchez E | 22 | 40 | 1 | 0 | 35 | 4.07 | 1.48 | 8.0 | 4.8 | -$2 | 40 |

Competition at RP — Stats in 2010 as RP

| Thr | Player | GR | ERA | IP/G | Sv-Hld |
|---|---|---|---|---|---|
| RH | Rodriguez F | 53 | 2.20 | 1.1 | 25-0 |
| RH | Dessens E | 53 | 2.30 | 0.9 | 0-11 |
| RH | Parnell B | 41 | 2.83 | 0.9 | 0-9 |
| RH | Acosta M | 41 | 2.95 | 1.0 | 1-2 |

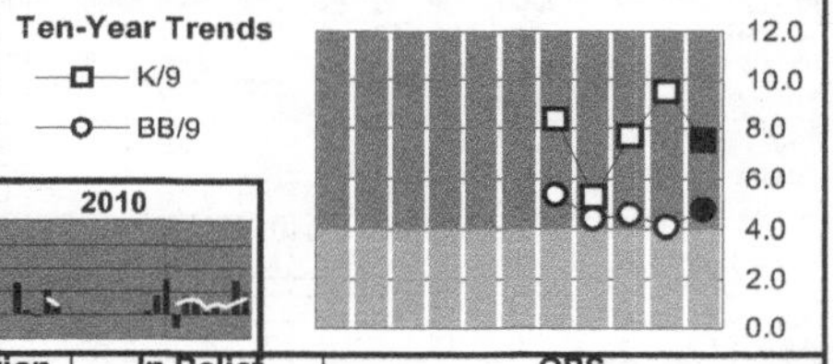
Ten-Year Trends
K/9
BB/9
12.0
10.0
8.0
6.0
4.0
2.0
0.0

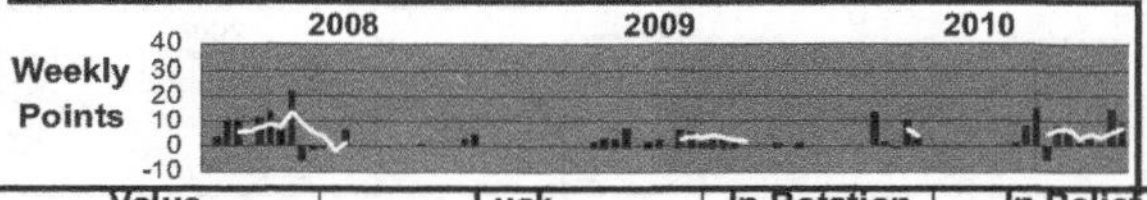
Weekly Points
2008
2009
2010
40
30
20
10
0
-10

Minors (2010)

| Level | Leag | W | L | Sv | IP | H | K | ERA | WHIP | K/9 | BB/9 | HR/9 | GB/F |
|---|---|---|---|---|---|---|---|---|---|---|---|---|---|
| A | — | — | — | — | — | — | — | — | — | — | — | — | — |
| AA | — | — | — | — | — | — | — | — | — | — | — | — | — |
| AAA | IL | 2 | 3 | 5 | 36 | 28 | 36 | 3.47 | 1.18 | 8.9 | 3.7 | 1.0 | — |

Majors

| Yr | Team | W | L | Sv | IP | H | K | ERA | WHIP | K/9 | BB/9 | HR/9 | GB/F | $1L | $2L | Pts | RAA | H% | HR/fb | S% | FIP | GS | CG | QS/DS | GR | Hld | Bln | Lead | OPS | 1st Hf | 2nd Hf | vs RH | vs LH |
|---|---|---|---|---|---|---|---|---|---|---|---|---|---|---|---|---|---|---|---|---|---|---|---|---|---|---|---|---|---|---|---|---|---|
| 07 | ATL | 1 | 1 | 0 | 23 | 13 | 22 | 2.28 | 1.14 | 8.4 | 5.3 | 0.8 | 2.1 | -$1 | $0 | 40 | +5 | 20% | 13% | 84% | 4.21 | — | — | — | 21 | 4 | 0 | –0.3 | .543 | — | .543 | .357 | .769 |
| 08 | ATL | 3 | 5 | 3 | 53 | 48 | 31 | 3.57 | 1.40 | 5.3 | 4.4 | 1.2 | 1.9 | $1 | -$1 | 70 | –1 | 26% | 16% | 79% | 5.22 | — | — | — | 46 | 4 | 2 | +1.0 | .745 | .785 | .432 | .701 | .792 |
| 09 | ATL | 1 | 1 | 0 | 37 | 45 | 32 | 4.34 | 1.71 | 7.7 | 4.6 | 1.0 | 1.2 | -$3 | -$4 | 30 | –2 | 36% | 9% | 77% | 4.41 | — | — | — | 36 | 2 | 0 | –0.3 | .846 | .725 | .963 | .840 | .853 |
| 10 | NYM | 3 | 2 | 1 | 39 | 30 | 42 | 2.95 | 1.21 | 9.5 | 4.1 | 0.9 | 1.0 | $0 | -$5 | 80 | +5 | 28% | 10% | 80% | 3.75 | — | — | — | 41 | 2 | 2 | –0.8 | .636 | .708 | .606 | .707 | .473 |

## Mike Adams — 40 IP | $4 | 80 pts

RP-70 Owned: 49% RH

The oft-injured Adams stayed relatively healthy in 2010. He is closer-worthy, though he must contend with Heath Bell and Luke Gregerson. Adams could get chances if SD trades Bell, but even then he'd be behind Gregerson. Add in Adams's history of shoulder problems, and he is unlikely to ascend to closerdom. (DG)

| Player | Age | IP | W | Sv | K | ERA | WHIP | K/9 | BB/9 | $2L | Pts |
|---|---|---|---|---|---|---|---|---|---|---|---|
| **Forecast** | | | | | | | | | | | |
| Adams M | 32 | 40 | 2 | 2 | 42 | 2.57 | 1.10 | 9.4 | 2.9 | $4 | 80 |
| **Mini-Browser** | Age | IP | W | Sv | K | ERA | WHIP | K/9 | BB/9 | $2L | Pts |
| Matusz B | 24 | 180 | 10 | 0 | 156 | 4.54 | 1.44 | 7.8 | 3.3 | $5 | 210 |
| Takahashi H | 35 | 60 | 4 | 15 | 46 | 4.43 | 1.38 | 7.0 | 3.5 | $4 | 150 |
| Balfour G | 33 | 60 | 3 | 0 | 64 | 3.24 | 1.26 | 9.6 | 4.1 | $4 | 100 |
| Devine J | 27 | 45 | 3 | 2 | 51 | 2.87 | 1.25 | 10.2 | 3.8 | $4 | 90 |
| Wells R | 28 | 180 | 9 | 0 | 127 | 4.30 | 1.37 | 6.3 | 2.8 | $4 | 190 |

Competition at RP — Stats in 2010 as RP

| Thr | Player | GR | ERA | IP/G | Sv-Hld |
|---|---|---|---|---|---|
| RH | Gregerson L | 80 | 3.22 | 1.0 | 2-40 |
| RH | Adams M | 70 | 1.76 | 1.0 | 0-38 |
| RH | Bell H | 67 | 1.93 | 1.0 | 47-0 |
| RH | Mujica E | 59 | 3.62 | 1.2 | 0-4 |

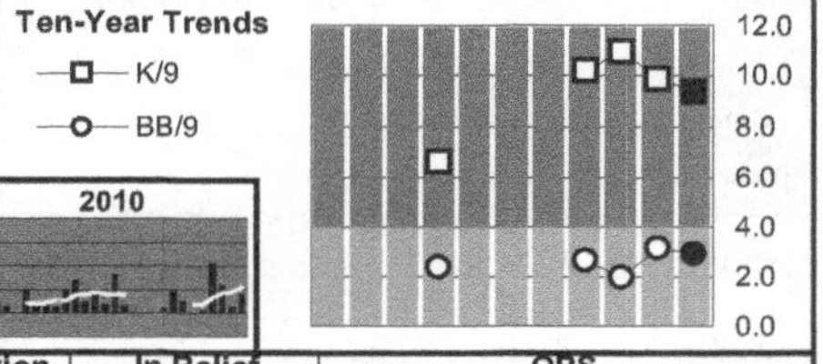
Ten-Year Trends
K/9
BB/9
12.0
10.0
8.0
6.0
4.0
2.0
0.0

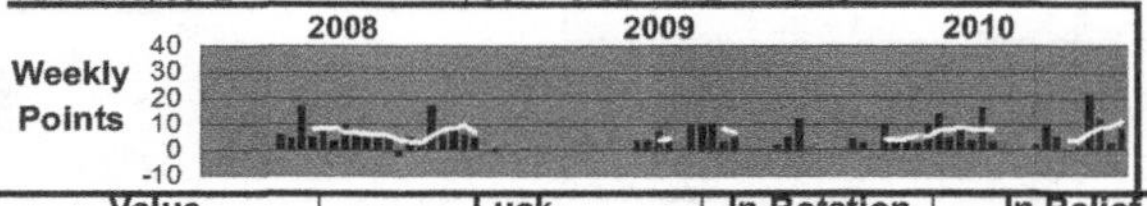
Weekly Points
2008
2009
2010
40
30
20
10
0
-10

Minors (2010)

| Level | Leag | W | L | Sv | IP | H | K | ERA | WHIP | K/9 | BB/9 | HR/9 | GB/F |
|---|---|---|---|---|---|---|---|---|---|---|---|---|---|
| A | — | — | — | — | — | — | — | — | — | — | — | — | — |
| AA | TL | 0 | 0 | 0 | 1 | 0 | 1 | 0.00 | 0.00 | 9.0 | 0.0 | 0.0 | — |
| AAA | — | — | — | — | — | — | — | — | — | — | — | — | — |

Majors

| Yr | Team | W | L | Sv | IP | H | K | ERA | WHIP | K/9 | BB/9 | HR/9 | GB/F | $1L | $2L | Pts | RAA | H% | HR/fb | S% | FIP | GS | CG | QS/DS | GR | Hld | Bln | Lead | OPS | 1st Hf | 2nd Hf | vs RH | vs LH |
|---|---|---|---|---|---|---|---|---|---|---|---|---|---|---|---|---|---|---|---|---|---|---|---|---|---|---|---|---|---|---|---|---|---|
| 07 | — | | | | | | | | | | | | | | | | | | | | | | | | | | | | | | | | |
| 08 | SD | 2 | 3 | 0 | 65 | 49 | 74 | 2.48 | 1.04 | 10.2 | 2.6 | 1.0 | 1.1 | $7 | $6 | 110 | +11 | 27% | 11% | 82% | 3.20 | — | — | — | 54 | 10 | 2 | +0.3 | .609 | .608 | .611 | .642 | .576 |
| 09 | SD | 0 | 0 | 0 | 37 | 14 | 45 | 0.73 | 0.59 | 10.9 | 1.9 | 0.2 | 1.2 | $6 | $5 | 70 | +8 | 16% | 3% | 90% | 1.77 | — | — | — | 37 | 15 | 1 | +0.7 | .315 | .429 | .245 | .284 | .341 |
| 10 | SD | 4 | 1 | 0 | 66 | 48 | 73 | 1.76 | 1.07 | 9.9 | 3.1 | 0.3 | 1.0 | $7 | $4 | 130 | +16 | 28% | 3% | 84% | 2.44 | — | — | — | 70 | 38 | 4 | +1.1 | .526 | .499 | .568 | .513 | .540 |

## Jeremy Affeldt — 60 IP | $0 | 70 pts

RP-53 Owned: 9% LH

Affeldt in 2010 could not reproduce his fortunate 2009 performance, and with only OK rates, he is unlikely to put up a sub-2.00 ERA again. Instead, Affeldt will be too wild to be a full-time option at closer, and too well-paid to be a mere LOOGY. For an oft-used reliever, his hamstring and oblique injuries trouble. (PB)

| Player | Age | IP | W | Sv | K | ERA | WHIP | K/9 | BB/9 | $2L | Pts |
|---|---|---|---|---|---|---|---|---|---|---|---|
| **Forecast** | | | | | | | | | | | |
| Affeldt J | 31 | 60 | 3 | 0 | 49 | 4.06 | 1.45 | 7.3 | 4.1 | $0 | 70 |
| **Mini-Browser** | Age | IP | W | Sv | K | ERA | WHIP | K/9 | BB/9 | $2L | Pts |
| Chen B | 33 | 160 | 10 | 0 | 115 | 5.06 | 1.48 | 6.4 | 3.7 | $0 | 170 |
| Frieri E | 25 | 60 | 3 | 0 | 69 | 4.07 | 1.48 | 10.3 | 4.2 | $0 | 90 |
| Wang C | 31 | 100 | 6 | 0 | 47 | 4.49 | 1.37 | 4.2 | 3.0 | $0 | 90 |
| Miller T | 37 | 40 | 2 | 0 | 34 | 3.90 | 1.29 | 7.6 | 3.5 | $0 | 50 |
| Atchison S | 35 | 40 | 1 | 0 | 29 | 4.28 | 1.28 | 6.5 | 2.6 | $0 | 40 |

Competition at RP — Stats in 2010 as RP

| Thr | Player | GR | ERA | IP/G | Sv-Hld |
|---|---|---|---|---|---|
| LH | Affeldt J | 53 | 4.14 | 0.9 | 4-7 |
| LH | Runzler D | 41 | 3.03 | 0.8 | 0-5 |
| LH | Lopez J | 27 | 1.42 | 0.7 | 0-5 |

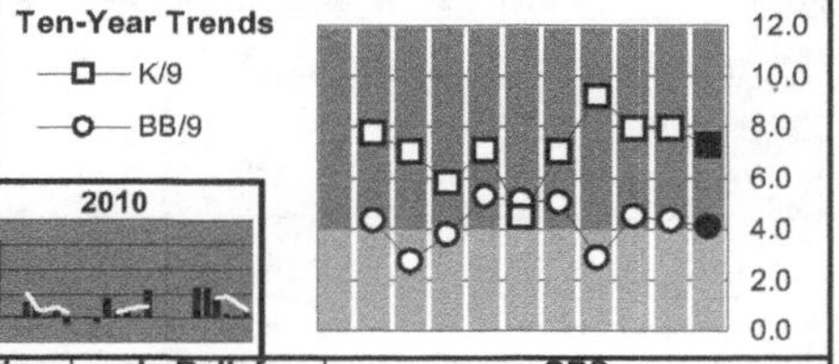
Ten-Year Trends
K/9
BB/9
12.0
10.0
8.0
6.0
4.0
2.0
0.0

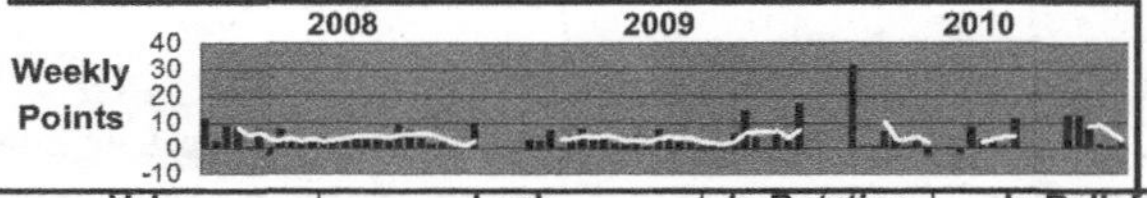
Weekly Points
2008
2009
2010
40
30
20
10
0
-10

Minors (2010)

| Level | Leag | W | L | Sv | IP | H | K | ERA | WHIP | K/9 | BB/9 | HR/9 | GB/F |
|---|---|---|---|---|---|---|---|---|---|---|---|---|---|
| A | CAL | 0 | 0 | 0 | 3 | 2 | 4 | 0.00 | 1.00 | 12.0 | 3.0 | 0.0 | — |
| AA | — | — | — | — | — | — | — | — | — | — | — | — | — |
| AAA | — | — | — | — | — | — | — | — | — | — | — | — | — |

Majors

| Yr | Team | W | L | Sv | IP | H | K | ERA | WHIP | K/9 | BB/9 | HR/9 | GB/F | $1L | $2L | Pts | RAA | H% | HR/fb | S% | FIP | GS | CG | QS/DS | GR | Hld | Bln | Lead | OPS | 1st Hf | 2nd Hf | vs RH | vs LH |
|---|---|---|---|---|---|---|---|---|---|---|---|---|---|---|---|---|---|---|---|---|---|---|---|---|---|---|---|---|---|---|---|---|---|
| 07 | COL | 4 | 3 | 0 | 59 | 47 | 46 | 3.51 | 1.36 | 7.0 | 5.0 | 0.5 | 1.6 | $2 | -$1 | 80 | +1 | 27% | 6% | 74% | 3.98 | — | — | — | 75 | 9 | 4 | +0.2 | .707 | .611 | .830 | .682 | .747 |
| 08 | CIN | 1 | 1 | 0 | 78 | 78 | 80 | 3.33 | 1.31 | 9.2 | 2.9 | 1.0 | 2.0 | $3 | $0 | 90 | –1 | 33% | 15% | 79% | 3.61 | — | — | — | 74 | 5 | 1 | –1.1 | .733 | .793 | .644 | .733 | .732 |
| 09 | SF | 2 | 2 | 0 | 62 | 42 | 55 | 1.73 | 1.17 | 7.9 | 4.5 | 0.4 | 3.5 | $6 | $4 | 90 | +14 | 25% | 10% | 87% | 3.55 | — | — | — | 74 | 33 | 0 | +1.6 | .583 | .587 | .580 | .507 | .683 |
| 10 | SF | 4 | 3 | 4 | 50 | 56 | 44 | 4.14 | 1.60 | 7.9 | 4.3 | 0.7 | 2.2 | -$3 | -$11 | 90 | –3 | 36% | 11% | 75% | 3.92 | — | — | — | 53 | 7 | 3 | +1.0 | .795 | .819 | .751 | .784 | .815 |

*For more stats, visit www.Rotolympus.com.*

## Jonathan Albaladejo — 40 IP | $-2 | 40 pts

RP-10 Owned: 0% RH

Albaladejo nailed down 43 saves for the Yankees' Triple-A affiliate, and he made 10 appearances for New York in mop-up duty (average Lead: -2.2 Runs). His approach in the minors is not translating to MLB – his WHIP has been 1.50 or worse for three straight seasons, and his BB/9 is trending the wrong way. (LS)

| Forecast | | | | | | | | | | | |
|---|---|---|---|---|---|---|---|---|---|---|---|
| Player | Age | IP | W | Sv | K | ERA | WHIP | K/9 | BB/9 | $2L | Pts |
| Albaladejo J | 28 | 40 | 2 | 0 | 29 | 5.15 | 1.50 | 6.6 | 3.9 | -$2 | 40 |
| Mini-Browser | Age | IP | W | Sv | K | ERA | WHIP | K/9 | BB/9 | $2L | Pts |
| Hochevar L | 27 | 160 | 7 | 0 | 109 | 5.29 | 1.46 | 6.2 | 3.2 | -$2 | 130 |
| Saunders J | 29 | 200 | 11 | 0 | 106 | 4.85 | 1.44 | 4.8 | 3.0 | -$2 | 160 |
| Herrmann F | 26 | 40 | 1 | 0 | 28 | 4.89 | 1.51 | 6.3 | 2.6 | -$2 | 30 |
| Ohman W | 33 | 20 | 0 | 0 | 18 | 4.12 | 1.48 | 8.1 | 4.5 | -$2 | 20 |
| Bautista D | 30 | 40 | 2 | 0 | 40 | 4.53 | 1.58 | 9.0 | 5.7 | -$2 | 50 |

| | | Minors (2010) | | | | | | | | Skills | | | |
|---|---|---|---|---|---|---|---|---|---|---|---|---|---|
| Level | Leag | W | L | Sv | IP | H | K | ERA | WHIP | K/9 | BB/9 | HR/9 | GB/F |
| A | — | — | — | — | — | — | — | — | — | — | — | — | — |
| AA | — | — | — | — | — | — | — | — | — | — | — | — | — |
| AAA | IL | 4 | 2 | 43 | 63 | 38 | 82 | 1.42 | 0.88 | 11.7 | 2.6 | 0.4 | — |

| Competition at RP | | Stats in 2010 as RP | | | |
|---|---|---|---|---|---|
| Thr | Player | GR | ERA | IP/G | Sv-Hld |
| RH | Chamberlain J | 73 | 4.40 | 1.0 | 3-26 |
| RH | Robertson D | 64 | 3.82 | 1.0 | 1-14 |
| RH | Rivera M | 61 | 1.80 | 1.0 | 33-0 |
| RH | Gaudin C | 30 | 4.50 | 1.6 | 0-0 |

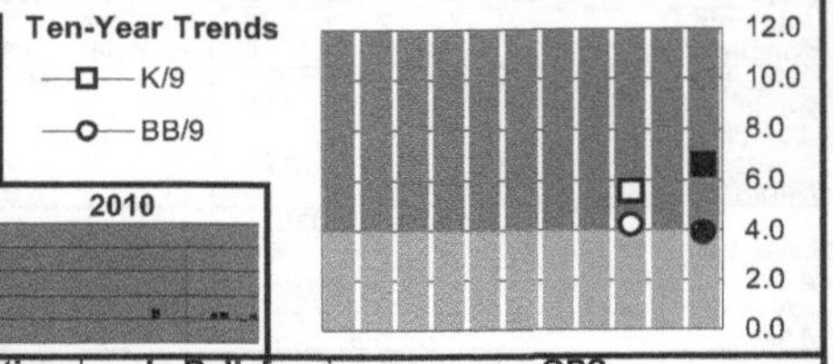


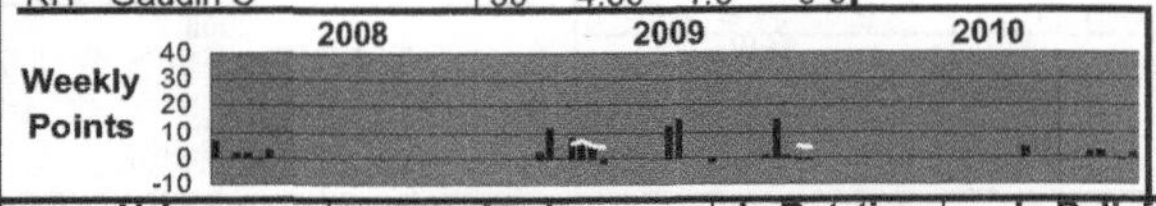


| | | Majors | | | | | | | | Skills | | | | Value | | | | Luck | | | | In Rotation | | | In Relief | | | | OPS | | | | |
|---|---|---|---|---|---|---|---|---|---|---|---|---|---|---|---|---|---|---|---|---|---|---|---|---|---|---|---|---|---|---|---|---|---|
| Yr | Team | W | L | Sv | IP | H | K | ERA | WHIP | K/9 | BB/9 | HR/9 | GB/F | $1L | $2L | Pts | RAA | H% | HR/fb | S% | FIP | GS | CG | QS/DS | GR | Hld | Bln | Lead | OPS | 1st Hf | 2nd Hf | vs RH | vs LH |
| 07 | WAS | 1 | 1 | 0 | 14 | 7 | 12 | 1.88 | 0.63 | 7.5 | 1.3 | 0.6 | 2.2 | $1 | $1 | 30 | +3 | 17% | 10% | 75% | 2.85 | — | — | — | 14 | 2 | 1 | –0.3 | .451 | — | .451 | .299 | .626 |
| 08 | NYY | 0 | 1 | 0 | 13 | 15 | 13 | 3.95 | 1.54 | 8.6 | 4.0 | 0.7 | 1.3 | -$2 | -$3 | 10 | +0 | 38% | 8% | 75% | 3.67 | — | — | — | 7 | 1 | 0 | –2.7 | .839 | .839 | — | .787 | .899 |
| 09 | NYY | 5 | 1 | 0 | 34 | 41 | 21 | 5.24 | 1.66 | 5.5 | 4.2 | 1.6 | 1.8 | -$1 | -$3 | 60 | –8 | 32% | 18% | 73% | 5.75 | — | — | — | 32 | 1 | 1 | –0.2 | .905 | .890 | .938 | 1.020 | .783 |
| 10 | NYY | 0 | 0 | 0 | 11 | 9 | 8 | 3.97 | 1.50 | 6.4 | 6.4 | 0.8 | 1.3 | -$4 | -$11 | 10 | +0 | 26% | 9% | 75% | 5.15 | — | — | — | 10 | 0 | 0 | –2.2 | .713 | — | .713 | .821 | .586 |

## Matt Albers — 40 IP | $-3 | 30 pts

RP-62 Owned: 0% RH

Albers has found his gig as a solid low-pressure-situation middle reliever who is capable of pitching multiple innings or on back-to-back days. His stuff is not good enough for him to contend for a more important bullpen role, and his days as a starter are over, but his curve continues to improve. (BJ)

| Forecast | | | | | | | | | | | |
|---|---|---|---|---|---|---|---|---|---|---|---|
| Player | Age | IP | W | Sv | K | ERA | WHIP | K/9 | BB/9 | $2L | Pts |
| Albers M | 28 | 40 | 2 | 0 | 27 | 5.03 | 1.60 | 6.0 | 4.5 | -$3 | 30 |
| Mini-Browser | Age | IP | W | Sv | K | ERA | WHIP | K/9 | BB/9 | $2L | Pts |
| Castro S | 22 | 40 | 2 | 0 | 27 | 4.77 | 1.49 | 6.1 | 3.9 | -$3 | 30 |
| Britton Z | 23 | 100 | 5 | 0 | 59 | 4.83 | 1.59 | 5.3 | 4.0 | -$3 | 80 |
| Tallet B | 33 | 60 | 3 | 0 | 41 | 5.35 | 1.51 | 6.2 | 4.4 | -$3 | 50 |
| Meche G | 32 | 80 | 3 | 0 | 56 | 5.07 | 1.54 | 6.3 | 4.2 | -$3 | 60 |
| Enright B | 25 | 180 | 10 | 0 | 131 | 4.89 | 1.50 | 6.6 | 2.8 | -$3 | 170 |

| | | Minors (2010) | | | | | | | | Skills | | | |
|---|---|---|---|---|---|---|---|---|---|---|---|---|---|
| Level | Leag | W | L | Sv | IP | H | K | ERA | WHIP | K/9 | BB/9 | HR/9 | GB/F |
| A | — | — | — | — | — | — | — | — | — | — | — | — | — |
| AA | — | — | — | — | — | — | — | — | — | — | — | — | — |
| AAA | — | — | — | — | — | — | — | — | — | — | — | — | — |

| Competition at RP | | Stats in 2010 as RP | | | |
|---|---|---|---|---|---|
| Thr | Player | GR | ERA | IP/G | Sv-Hld |
| RH | Albers M | 62 | 4.52 | 1.2 | 0-7 |
| RH | Simon A | 49 | 4.93 | 1.0 | 17-1 |
| RH | Uehara K | 43 | 2.86 | 1.0 | 13-6 |
| RH | Berken J | 41 | 3.03 | 1.5 | 0-7 |

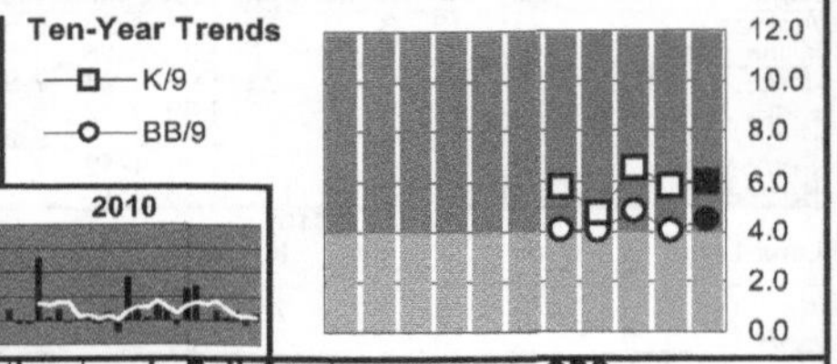

| | | Majors | | | | | | | | Skills | | | | Value | | | | Luck | | | | In Rotation | | | In Relief | | | | OPS | | | | |
|---|---|---|---|---|---|---|---|---|---|---|---|---|---|---|---|---|---|---|---|---|---|---|---|---|---|---|---|---|---|---|---|---|---|
| Yr | Team | W | L | Sv | IP | H | K | ERA | WHIP | K/9 | BB/9 | HR/9 | GB/F | $1L | $2L | Pts | RAA | H% | HR/fb | S% | FIP | GS | CG | QS/DS | GR | Hld | Bln | Lead | OPS | 1st Hf | 2nd Hf | vs RH | vs LH |
| 07 | HOU | 4 | 11 | 0 | 110 | 127 | 71 | 5.86 | 1.60 | 5.8 | 4.1 | 1.5 | 1.4 | -$8 | -$20 | 60 | –27 | 31% | 14% | 66% | 5.39 | 18 | 0 | 8/6 | 13 | 0 | 0 | –0.9 | .859 | .843 | .868 | .858 | .859 |
| 08 | BAL | 3 | 3 | 0 | 49 | 43 | 26 | 3.49 | 1.33 | 4.8 | 4.0 | 0.7 | 1.5 | $1 | -$1 | 50 | +1 | 26% | 8% | 75% | 4.65 | 3 | 0 | 1/1 | 25 | 6 | 2 | +0.0 | .655 | .655 | — | .829 | .468 |
| 09 | BAL | 3 | 6 | 0 | 67 | 80 | 49 | 5.51 | 1.73 | 6.6 | 4.8 | 0.4 | 1.6 | -$3 | -$8 | 50 | –13 | 36% | 4% | 66% | 4.03 | — | — | — | 56 | 10 | 4 | –0.4 | .797 | .728 | .877 | .694 | .929 |
| 10 | BAL | 5 | 3 | 0 | 75 | 78 | 49 | 4.52 | 1.48 | 5.8 | 4.0 | 0.7 | 2.0 | -$2 | -$14 | 80 | –7 | 31% | 9% | 70% | 4.38 | — | — | — | 62 | 7 | 2 | –1.3 | .726 | .749 | .695 | .662 | .819 |

## .. Brett Anderson — 190 IP | $16 | 260 pts

SP-19 Owned: 76% LH

One of the top young lefties in the AL, Anderson in 2010 was outstanding when he was healthy, but he had two stints on the DL with elbow soreness. At season's end, Anderson was pitching without restriction. If he is healthy, and he recovers some of his strikeouts, he should be among the ERA leaders in 2011. (ML)

| Forecast | | | | | | | | | | | |
|---|---|---|---|---|---|---|---|---|---|---|---|
| Player | Age | IP | W | Sv | K | ERA | WHIP | K/9 | BB/9 | $2L | Pts |
| Anderson B | 23 | 190 | 12 | 0 | 146 | 3.75 | 1.22 | 6.9 | 2.2 | $16 | 260 |
| Mini-Browser | Age | IP | W | Sv | K | ERA | WHIP | K/9 | BB/9 | $2L | Pts |
| Cain M | 26 | 220 | 13 | 0 | 170 | 3.69 | 1.23 | 7.0 | 2.9 | $17 | 300 |
| Haren D | 30 | 200 | 12 | 0 | 173 | 3.92 | 1.21 | 7.8 | 1.9 | $17 | 290 |
| Soria J | 26 | 60 | 2 | 32 | 65 | 2.20 | 1.11 | 9.7 | 2.6 | $17 | 260 |
| Hudson T | 35 | 200 | 14 | 0 | 117 | 3.40 | 1.23 | 5.3 | 2.8 | $17 | 250 |
| Hughes P | 24 | 200 | 17 | 0 | 176 | 4.10 | 1.28 | 7.9 | 3.1 | $16 | 330 |

| | | Minors (2010) | | | | | | | | Skills | | | |
|---|---|---|---|---|---|---|---|---|---|---|---|---|---|
| Level | Leag | W | L | Sv | IP | H | K | ERA | WHIP | K/9 | BB/9 | HR/9 | GB/F |
| A | — | — | — | — | — | — | — | — | — | — | — | — | — |
| AA | — | — | — | — | — | — | — | — | — | — | — | — | — |
| AAA | PCL | 1 | 0 | 0 | 13 | 19 | 12 | 4.05 | 1.65 | 8.1 | 2.0 | 0.0 | — |

| Competition at SP | | Stats in 2010 as SP | | | |
|---|---|---|---|---|---|
| Thr | Player | GS | ERA | Supp | W-L |
| LH | Gonzalez G | 33 | 3.23 | 4.3 | 15-9 |
| RH | Cahill T | 30 | 2.97 | 4.6 | 18-8 |
| LH | Braden D | 30 | 3.50 | 3.3 | 11-14 |
| RH | Sheets B | 20 | 4.53 | 4.6 | 4-9 |

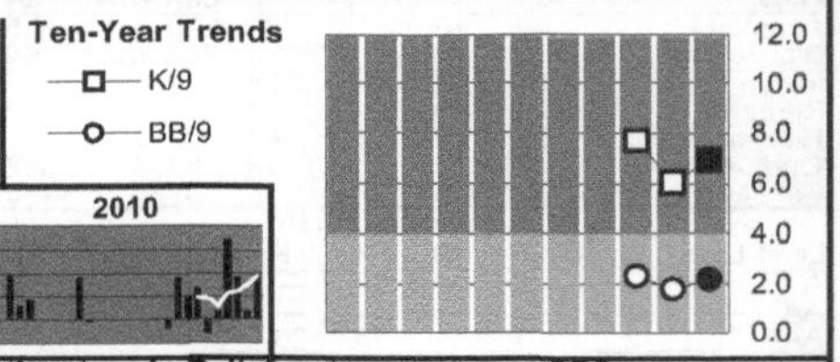


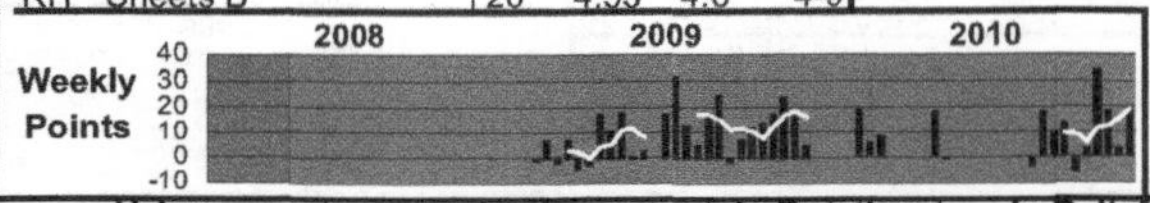


| | | Majors | | | | | | | | Skills | | | | Value | | | | Luck | | | | In Rotation | | | In Relief | | | | OPS | | | | |
|---|---|---|---|---|---|---|---|---|---|---|---|---|---|---|---|---|---|---|---|---|---|---|---|---|---|---|---|---|---|---|---|---|---|
| Yr | Team | W | L | Sv | IP | H | K | ERA | WHIP | K/9 | BB/9 | HR/9 | GB/F | $1L | $2L | Pts | RAA | H% | HR/fb | S% | FIP | GS | CG | QS/DS | GR | Hld | Bln | Lead | OPS | 1st Hf | 2nd Hf | vs RH | vs LH |
| 07 | — | — | — | — | — | — | — | — | — | — | — | — | — | — | — | — | — | — | — | — | — | — | — | — | — | — | — | — | — | — | — | — | — |
| 08 | — | — | — | — | — | — | — | — | — | — | — | — | — | — | — | — | — | — | — | — | — | — | — | — | — | — | — | — | — | — | — | — | — |
| 09 | OAK | 11 | 11 | 0 | 175 | 180 | 150 | 4.06 | 1.28 | 7.7 | 2.3 | 1.0 | 1.5 | $11 | $3 | 240 | –8 | 31% | 11% | 71% | 3.84 | 30 | 1 | 13/5 | — | — | — | — | .711 | .768 | .651 | .683 | .788 |
| 10 | OAK | 7 | 6 | 0 | 112 | 112 | 75 | 2.80 | 1.19 | 6.0 | 1.8 | 0.5 | 1.9 | $9 | $3 | 160 | +14 | 30% | 6% | 77% | 3.25 | 19 | 0 | 13/2 | — | — | — | — | .655 | .560 | .690 | .646 | .685 |

## Jake Arrieta — 140 IP | $-4 | 130 pts

SP-18 Owned: 1% RH

Arrieta displayed poor skills in his MLB debut, but he is only 24, and he matured with each passing month (his September ERA was 2.60, with 6.8 K/9 and 1.0 BB/9). His stuff does not appear to be overly dominant or tricky, and batters get their hits, so we do not foresee an ace. The early review is Jeremy Guthrie II. (BJ)

| Forecast | | | | | | | | | | | |
|---|---|---|---|---|---|---|---|---|---|---|---|
| Player | Age | IP | W | Sv | K | ERA | WHIP | K/9 | BB/9 | $2L | Pts |
| Arrieta J | 25 | 140 | 7 | 0 | 113 | 5.12 | 1.65 | 7.3 | 4.4 | -$4 | 130 |
| Mini-Browser | Age | IP | W | Sv | K | ERA | WHIP | K/9 | BB/9 | $2L | Pts |
| Grabow J | 32 | 40 | 2 | 0 | 29 | 5.17 | 1.58 | 6.4 | 4.6 | -$4 | 30 |
| LeCure S | 26 | 60 | 3 | 0 | 53 | 5.20 | 1.56 | 8.0 | 3.8 | -$4 | 60 |
| Ross T | 23 | 40 | 1 | 0 | 38 | 5.66 | 1.70 | 8.6 | 4.7 | -$4 | 30 |
| Lohse K | 32 | 120 | 7 | 0 | 68 | 5.20 | 1.45 | 5.1 | 2.7 | -$4 | 100 |
| Galarraga A | 29 | 140 | 5 | 0 | 85 | 5.30 | 1.50 | 5.4 | 3.8 | -$4 | 90 |

| | | Minors (2010) | | | | | | | | Skills | | | |
|---|---|---|---|---|---|---|---|---|---|---|---|---|---|
| Level | Leag | W | L | Sv | IP | H | K | ERA | WHIP | K/9 | BB/9 | HR/9 | GB/F |
| A | — | — | — | — | — | — | — | — | — | — | — | — | — |
| AA | — | — | — | — | — | — | — | — | — | — | — | — | — |
| AAA | IL | 6 | 2 | 0 | 73 | 48 | 64 | 1.85 | 1.12 | 7.9 | 4.2 | 0.4 | — |

| Competition at SP | | Stats in 2010 as SP | | | |
|---|---|---|---|---|---|
| Thr | Player | GS | ERA | Supp | W-L |
| RH | Guthrie J | 32 | 3.83 | 3.6 | 11-14 |
| LH | Matusz B | 32 | 4.30 | 3.7 | 10-12 |
| RH | Millwood K | 31 | 5.10 | 3.5 | 4-16 |
| RH | Bergesen B | 28 | 5.02 | 3.9 | 8-12 |

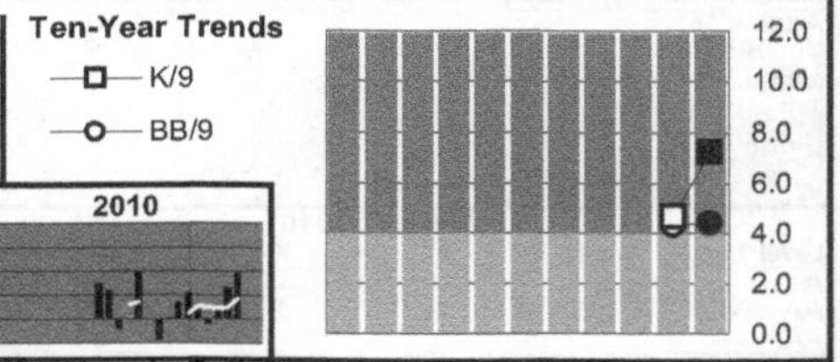

| | | Majors | | | | | | | | Skills | | | | Value | | | | Luck | | | | In Rotation | | | In Relief | | | | OPS | | | | |
|---|---|---|---|---|---|---|---|---|---|---|---|---|---|---|---|---|---|---|---|---|---|---|---|---|---|---|---|---|---|---|---|---|---|
| Yr | Team | W | L | Sv | IP | H | K | ERA | WHIP | K/9 | BB/9 | HR/9 | GB/F | $1L | $2L | Pts | RAA | H% | HR/fb | S% | FIP | GS | CG | QS/DS | GR | Hld | Bln | Lead | OPS | 1st Hf | 2nd Hf | vs RH | vs LH |
| 07 | — | — | — | — | — | — | — | — | — | — | — | — | — | — | — | — | — | — | — | — | — | — | — | — | — | — | — | — | — | — | — | — | — |
| 08 | — | — | — | — | — | — | — | — | — | — | — | — | — | — | — | — | — | — | — | — | — | — | — | — | — | — | — | — | — | — | — | — | — |
| 09 | — | — | — | — | — | — | — | — | — | — | — | — | — | — | — | — | — | — | — | — | — | — | — | — | — | — | — | — | — | — | — | — | — |
| 10 | BAL | 6 | 6 | 0 | 100 | 106 | 52 | 4.66 | 1.53 | 4.7 | 4.3 | 0.8 | 1.1 | -$3 | -$18 | 80 | –8 | 30% | 7% | 70% | 4.86 | 18 | 0 | 10/3 | — | — | — | — | .767 | .753 | .776 | .594 | .898 |

## .. Bronson Arroyo — 200 IP | $6 | 210 pts

SP-33 Owned: 82% RH

The Reds are 99% certain to pick up Arroyo's $11M option, and they will again tap him for the top of their rotation. His sparkling W-L in 2010 owed to a low 24% H%, not to a rebound in K/9. Arroyo is a LAIM-O: a League-Average Innings Muncher. As such, he will be handed the ball so long as he is healthy. (SW)

| Forecast | | | | | | | | | | | |
|---|---|---|---|---|---|---|---|---|---|---|---|
| Player | Age | IP | W | Sv | K | ERA | WHIP | K/9 | BB/9 | $2L | Pts |
| Arroyo B | 34 | 200 | 12 | 0 | 117 | 4.56 | 1.27 | 5.3 | 2.6 | $6 | 210 |
| Mini-Browser | Age | IP | W | Sv | K | ERA | WHIP | K/9 | BB/9 | $2L | Pts |
| Pineda M | 22 | 120 | 7 | 0 | 97 | 3.98 | 1.33 | 7.3 | 3.1 | $7 | 160 |
| Hellickson J | 23 | 120 | 9 | 0 | 129 | 4.39 | 1.35 | 9.7 | 2.6 | $6 | 200 |
| Rodney F | 34 | 60 | 3 | 27 | 51 | 4.55 | 1.57 | 7.6 | 5.2 | $6 | 200 |
| Dickey R | 36 | 180 | 10 | 0 | 105 | 4.05 | 1.34 | 5.2 | 2.9 | $6 | 180 |
| Hanrahan J | 29 | 80 | 4 | 18 | 88 | 4.34 | 1.41 | 9.9 | 4.1 | $6 | 200 |

| | | Minors (2010) | | | | | | | | Skills | | | |
|---|---|---|---|---|---|---|---|---|---|---|---|---|---|
| Level | Leag | W | L | Sv | IP | H | K | ERA | WHIP | K/9 | BB/9 | HR/9 | GB/F |
| A | — | — | — | — | — | — | — | — | — | — | — | — | — |
| AA | — | — | — | — | — | — | — | — | — | — | — | — | — |
| AAA | — | — | — | — | — | — | — | — | — | — | — | — | — |

| Competition at SP | | Stats in 2010 as SP | | | |
|---|---|---|---|---|---|
| Thr | Player | GS | ERA | Supp | W-L |
| RH | Arroyo B | 33 | 3.88 | 4.7 | 17-10 |
| RH | Cueto J | 31 | 3.64 | 4.7 | 12-7 |
| RH | Leake M | 22 | 3.78 | 5.0 | 8-4 |
| RH | Harang A | 20 | 5.22 | 5.1 | 6-7 |

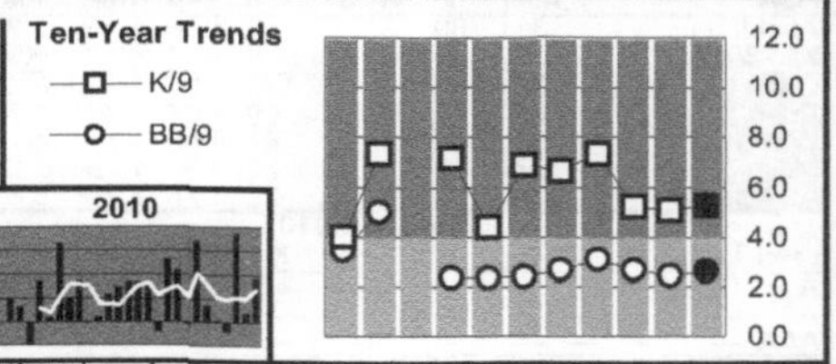


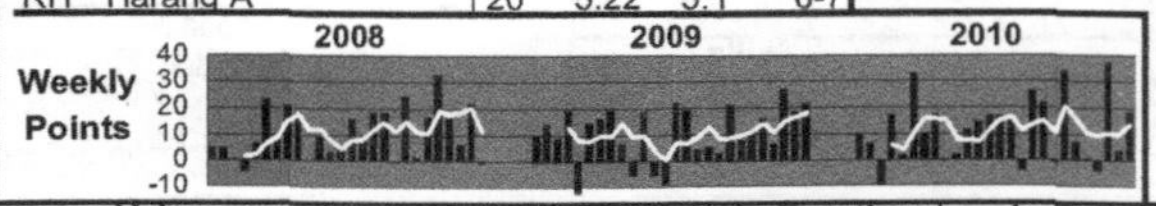


| | | Majors | | | | | | | | Skills | | | | Value | | | | Luck | | | | In Rotation | | | In Relief | | | | OPS | | | | |
|---|---|---|---|---|---|---|---|---|---|---|---|---|---|---|---|---|---|---|---|---|---|---|---|---|---|---|---|---|---|---|---|---|---|
| Yr | Team | W | L | Sv | IP | H | K | ERA | WHIP | K/9 | BB/9 | HR/9 | GB/F | $1L | $2L | Pts | RAA | H% | HR/fb | S% | FIP | GS | CG | QS/DS | GR | Hld | Bln | Lead | OPS | 1st Hf | 2nd Hf | vs RH | vs LH |
| 07 | CIN | 9 | 15 | 0 | 210 | 232 | 156 | 4.23 | 1.40 | 6.7 | 2.7 | 1.2 | 0.8 | $5 | -$9 | 210 | –5 | 32% | 10% | 73% | 4.34 | 34 | 1 | 22/5 | — | — | — | — | .789 | .769 | .811 | .797 | .777 |
| 08 | CIN | 15 | 11 | 0 | 200 | 219 | 163 | 4.77 | 1.44 | 7.3 | 3.1 | 1.3 | 1.2 | $1 | -$10 | 260 | –17 | 32% | 13% | 70% | 4.48 | 34 | 1 | 18/4 | — | — | — | — | .811 | .901 | .701 | .716 | .922 |
| 09 | CIN | 15 | 13 | 0 | 220 | 214 | 127 | 3.84 | 1.27 | 5.2 | 2.7 | 1.3 | 1.2 | $11 | $5 | 260 | +8 | 27% | 12% | 75% | 4.76 | 33 | 3 | 23/6 | — | — | — | — | .737 | .836 | .627 | .687 | .790 |
| 10 | CIN | 17 | 10 | 0 | 215 | 188 | 121 | 3.88 | 1.15 | 5.0 | 2.5 | 1.2 | 1.1 | $14 | $6 | 290 | +11 | 24% | 11% | 71% | 4.65 | 33 | 2 | 21/4 | — | — | — | — | .679 | .677 | .680 | .576 | .786 |

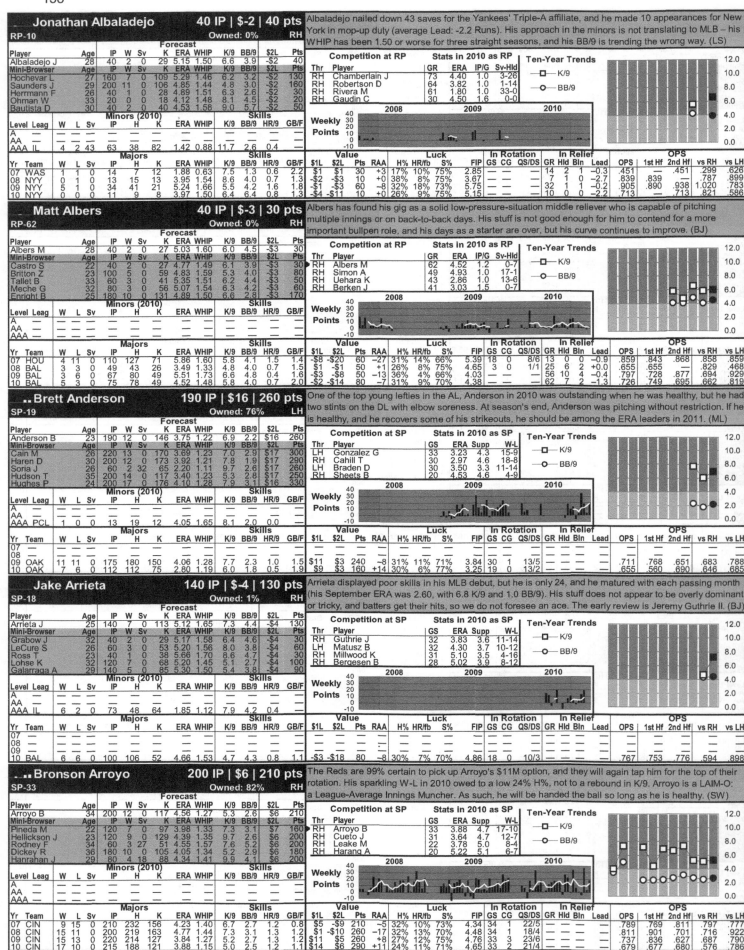

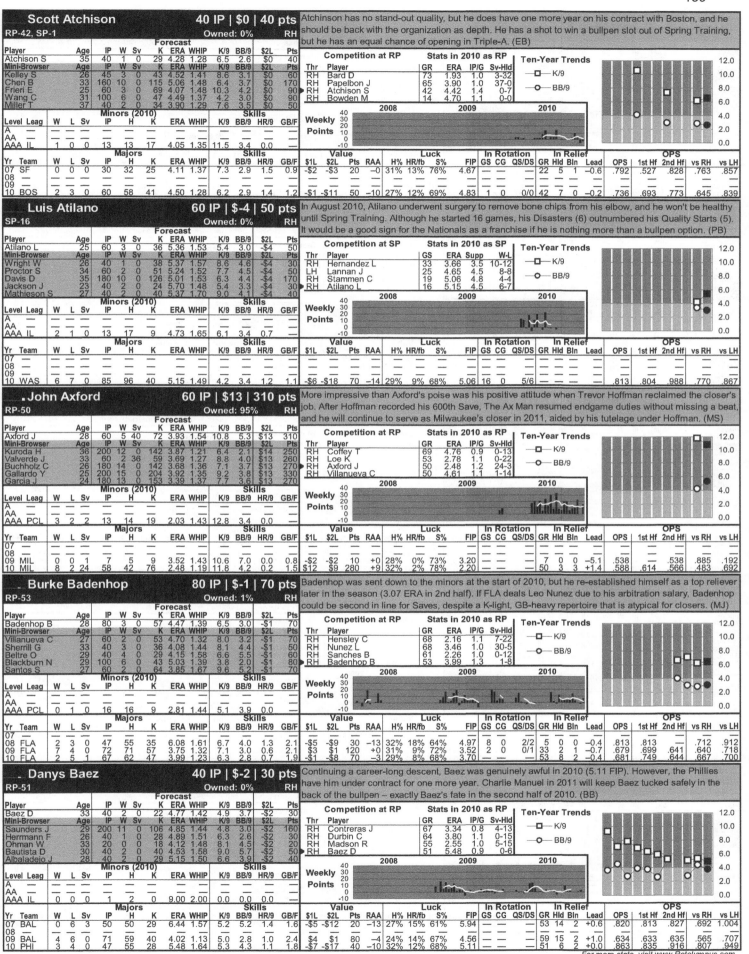

## Scott Atchison — 40 IP | $0 | 40 pts
RP-42, SP-1 — Owned: 0% — RH

Atchinson has no stand-out quality, but he does have one more year on his contract with Boston, and he should be back with the organization as depth. He has a shot to win a bullpen slot out of Spring Training, but he has an equal chance of opening in Triple-A. (EB)

### Forecast
| Player | Age | IP | W | Sv | K | ERA | WHIP | K/9 | BB/9 | $2L | Pts |
|---|---|---|---|---|---|---|---|---|---|---|---|
| Atchison S | 35 | 40 | 1 | 0 | 29 | 4.28 | 1.28 | 6.5 | 2.6 | $0 | 40 |
| Mini-Browser | Age | IP | W | Sv | K | ERA | WHIP | K/9 | BB/9 | $2L | Pts |
| Kelley S | 26 | 45 | 3 | 0 | 43 | 4.52 | 1.41 | 8.6 | 3.1 | $0 | 60 |
| Chen B | 33 | 160 | 10 | 0 | 115 | 5.06 | 1.48 | 6.4 | 3.7 | $0 | 170 |
| Frieri E | 25 | 60 | 3 | 0 | 69 | 4.07 | 1.48 | 10.3 | 4.2 | $0 | 90 |
| Wang C | 31 | 100 | 6 | 0 | 47 | 4.49 | 1.37 | 4.2 | 3.0 | $0 | 90 |
| Miller T | 37 | 40 | 2 | 0 | 34 | 3.90 | 1.29 | 7.6 | 3.5 | $0 | 50 |

### Minors (2010)
| Level | Leag | W | L | Sv | IP | H | K | ERA | WHIP | K/9 | BB/9 | HR/9 | GB/F |
|---|---|---|---|---|---|---|---|---|---|---|---|---|---|
| A | — | | | | | | | | | | | | |
| AA | — | | | | | | | | | | | | |
| AAA | IL | 1 | 0 | 0 | 13 | 13 | 17 | 4.05 | 1.35 | 11.5 | 3.4 | 0.0 | — |

### Majors
| Yr | Team | W | L | Sv | IP | H | K | ERA | WHIP | K/9 | BB/9 | HR/9 | GB/F | $1L | $2L | Pts | RAA | H% | HR/fb | S% | FIP | GS | CG | QS/DS | GR | Hld | Bln | Lead | OPS | 1st Hf | 2nd Hf | vs RH | vs LH |
|---|---|---|---|---|---|---|---|---|---|---|---|---|---|---|---|---|---|---|---|---|---|---|---|---|---|---|---|---|---|---|---|---|---|
| 07 | SF | 0 | 0 | 0 | 30 | 32 | 25 | 4.11 | 1.37 | 7.3 | 2.9 | 1.5 | 0.9 | -$2 | -$3 | 20 | -0 | 31% | 13% | 76% | 4.67 | | | | 22 | 5 | 1 | -0.6 | .792 | .527 | .828 | .763 | .857 |
| 08 | | | | | | | | | | | | | | | | | | | | | | | | | | | | | | | | | |
| 09 | | | | | | | | | | | | | | | | | | | | | | | | | | | | | | | | | |
| 10 | BOS | 2 | 3 | 0 | 60 | 58 | 41 | 4.50 | 1.28 | 6.2 | 2.9 | 1.4 | 1.2 | -$1 | -$11 | 50 | -10 | 27% | 12% | 69% | 4.83 | 1 | 0 | 0/0 | 42 | 7 | 0 | -0.2 | .736 | .693 | .773 | .645 | .839 |

### Competition at RP / Stats in 2010 as RP
| Thr | Player | GR | ERA | IP/G | Sv-Hld |
|---|---|---|---|---|---|
| RH | Bard D | 73 | 1.93 | 1.0 | 3-32 |
| RH | Papelbon J | 65 | 3.90 | 1.0 | 37-0 |
| RH | Atchison S | 42 | 4.42 | 1.4 | 0-7 |
| RH | Bowden M | 14 | 4.70 | 1.1 | 0-0 |

---

## Luis Atilano — 60 IP | $-4 | 50 pts
SP-16 — Owned: 0% — RH

In August 2010, Atilano underwent surgery to remove bone chips from his elbow, and he won't be healthy until Spring Training. Although he started 16 games, his Disasters (6) outnumbered his Quality Starts (5). It would be a good sign for the Nationals as a franchise if he is nothing more than a bullpen option. (PB)

### Forecast
| Player | Age | IP | W | Sv | K | ERA | WHIP | K/9 | BB/9 | $2L | Pts |
|---|---|---|---|---|---|---|---|---|---|---|---|
| Atilano L | 25 | 60 | 3 | 0 | 36 | 5.36 | 1.53 | 5.4 | 3.0 | -$4 | 50 |
| Mini-Browser | Age | IP | W | Sv | K | ERA | WHIP | K/9 | BB/9 | $2L | Pts |
| Wright W | 26 | 40 | 1 | 0 | 38 | 5.37 | 1.57 | 8.6 | 4.6 | -$4 | 30 |
| Proctor S | 34 | 60 | 2 | 0 | 51 | 5.24 | 1.52 | 7.7 | 4.5 | -$4 | 50 |
| Davis D | 35 | 180 | 10 | 0 | 126 | 5.01 | 1.53 | 6.3 | 4.4 | -$4 | 170 |
| Jackson J | 23 | 40 | 2 | 0 | 24 | 5.70 | 1.48 | 5.4 | 3.3 | -$4 | 30 |
| Mathieson S | 27 | 40 | 2 | 0 | 40 | 5.37 | 1.70 | 9.0 | 4.1 | -$4 | 40 |

### Minors (2010)
| Level | Leag | W | L | Sv | IP | H | K | ERA | WHIP | K/9 | BB/9 | HR/9 | GB/F |
|---|---|---|---|---|---|---|---|---|---|---|---|---|---|
| A | — | | | | | | | | | | | | |
| AA | — | | | | | | | | | | | | |
| AAA | IL | 2 | 1 | 0 | 13 | 17 | 9 | 4.73 | 1.65 | 6.1 | 3.4 | 0.7 | — |

### Majors
| Yr | Team | W | L | Sv | IP | H | K | ERA | WHIP | K/9 | BB/9 | HR/9 | GB/F | $1L | $2L | Pts | RAA | H% | HR/fb | S% | FIP | GS | CG | QS/DS | GR | Hld | Bln | Lead | OPS | 1st Hf | 2nd Hf | vs RH | vs LH |
|---|---|---|---|---|---|---|---|---|---|---|---|---|---|---|---|---|---|---|---|---|---|---|---|---|---|---|---|---|---|---|---|---|---|
| 07 | | | | | | | | | | | | | | | | | | | | | | | | | | | | | | | | | |
| 08 | | | | | | | | | | | | | | | | | | | | | | | | | | | | | | | | | |
| 09 | | | | | | | | | | | | | | | | | | | | | | | | | | | | | | | | | |
| 10 | WAS | 6 | 7 | 0 | 85 | 96 | 40 | 5.15 | 1.49 | 4.2 | 3.4 | 1.2 | 1.1 | -$6 | -$18 | 70 | -14 | 29% | 9% | 68% | 5.06 | 16 | 0 | 5/6 | | | | — | .813 | .804 | .988 | .770 | .867 |

### Competition at SP / Stats in 2010 as SP
| Thr | Player | GS | ERA | Supp | W-L |
|---|---|---|---|---|---|
| RH | Hernandez L | 33 | 3.66 | 3.5 | 10-12 |
| LH | Lannan J | 25 | 4.65 | 4.5 | 8-8 |
| RH | Stammen C | 19 | 5.06 | 4.8 | 4-4 |
| RH | Atilano L | 16 | 5.15 | 4.5 | 6-7 |

---

## John Axford — 60 IP | $13 | 310 pts
RP-50 — Owned: 95% — RH

More impressive than Axford's poise was his positive attitude when Trevor Hoffman reclaimed the closer's job. After Hoffman recorded his 600th Save, The Ax Man resumed endgame duties without missing a beat, and he will continue to serve as Milwaukee's closer in 2011, aided by his tutelage under Hoffman. (MS)

### Forecast
| Player | Age | IP | W | Sv | K | ERA | WHIP | K/9 | BB/9 | $2L | Pts |
|---|---|---|---|---|---|---|---|---|---|---|---|
| Axford J | 28 | 60 | 5 | 40 | 72 | 3.93 | 1.54 | 10.8 | 5.3 | $13 | 310 |
| Mini-Browser | Age | IP | W | Sv | K | ERA | WHIP | K/9 | BB/9 | $2L | Pts |
| Kuroda H | 36 | 200 | 12 | 0 | 142 | 3.87 | 1.21 | 6.4 | 2.1 | $14 | 250 |
| Valverde J | 33 | 60 | 2 | 36 | 59 | 3.69 | 1.27 | 8.8 | 4.0 | $13 | 260 |
| Buchholz C | 26 | 180 | 14 | 0 | 142 | 3.68 | 1.36 | 7.1 | 3.7 | $13 | 270 |
| Gallardo Y | 25 | 200 | 15 | 0 | 204 | 3.92 | 1.35 | 9.2 | 3.8 | $13 | 330 |
| Garcia J | 24 | 180 | 13 | 0 | 153 | 3.39 | 1.37 | 7.7 | 3.6 | $13 | 270 |

### Minors (2010)
| Level | Leag | W | L | Sv | IP | H | K | ERA | WHIP | K/9 | BB/9 | HR/9 | GB/F |
|---|---|---|---|---|---|---|---|---|---|---|---|---|---|
| A | — | | | | | | | | | | | | |
| AA | — | | | | | | | | | | | | |
| AAA | PCL | 3 | 2 | 2 | 13 | 14 | 19 | 2.03 | 1.43 | 12.8 | 3.4 | 0.0 | — |

### Majors
| Yr | Team | W | L | Sv | IP | H | K | ERA | WHIP | K/9 | BB/9 | HR/9 | GB/F | $1L | $2L | Pts | RAA | H% | HR/fb | S% | FIP | GS | CG | QS/DS | GR | Hld | Bln | Lead | OPS | 1st Hf | 2nd Hf | vs RH | vs LH |
|---|---|---|---|---|---|---|---|---|---|---|---|---|---|---|---|---|---|---|---|---|---|---|---|---|---|---|---|---|---|---|---|---|---|
| 07 | | | | | | | | | | | | | | | | | | | | | | | | | | | | | | | | | |
| 08 | | | | | | | | | | | | | | | | | | | | | | | | | | | | | | | | | |
| 09 | MIL | 0 | 0 | 1 | 7 | 5 | 9 | 3.52 | 1.43 | 10.6 | 7.0 | 0.0 | 0.8 | -$2 | -$2 | 10 | +0 | 28% | 0% | 73% | 3.20 | | | | 7 | 0 | 0 | -5.1 | .538 | — | .538 | .885 | .192 |
| 10 | MIL | 8 | 2 | 24 | 58 | 42 | 76 | 2.48 | 1.19 | 11.8 | 4.2 | 0.2 | 1.5 | $12 | $9 | 280 | +9 | 32% | 2% | 78% | 2.20 | | | | 50 | 3 | 3 | +1.4 | .588 | .614 | .566 | .483 | .692 |

### Competition at RP / Stats in 2010 as RP
| Thr | Player | GR | ERA | IP/G | Sv-Hld |
|---|---|---|---|---|---|
| RH | Coffey T | 69 | 4.76 | 0.9 | 0-13 |
| RH | Loe K | 53 | 2.78 | 1.1 | 0-22 |
| RH | Axford J | 50 | 2.48 | 1.2 | 24-3 |
| RH | Villanueva C | 50 | 4.61 | 1.1 | 1-14 |

---

## Burke Badenhop — 80 IP | $-1 | 70 pts
RP-53 — Owned: 1% — RH

Badenhop was sent down to the minors at the start of 2010, but he re-established himself as a top reliever later in the season (3.07 ERA in 2nd half). If FLA deals Leo Nunez due to his arbitration salary, Badenhop could be second in line for Saves, despite a K-light, GB-heavy repertoire that is atypical for closers. (MJ)

### Forecast
| Player | Age | IP | W | Sv | K | ERA | WHIP | K/9 | BB/9 | $2L | Pts |
|---|---|---|---|---|---|---|---|---|---|---|---|
| Badenhop B | 28 | 80 | 3 | 0 | 57 | 4.47 | 1.39 | 6.5 | 3.0 | -$1 | 70 |
| Mini-Browser | Age | IP | W | Sv | K | ERA | WHIP | K/9 | BB/9 | $2L | Pts |
| Villanueva C | 27 | 60 | 2 | 0 | 53 | 4.70 | 1.32 | 8.0 | 3.2 | -$1 | 70 |
| Sherrill G | 33 | 40 | 3 | 0 | 36 | 4.08 | 1.44 | 8.1 | 4.4 | -$1 | 50 |
| Beltre O | 29 | 40 | 4 | 0 | 29 | 4.15 | 1.48 | 6.6 | 5.5 | -$1 | 60 |
| Blackburn N | 29 | 100 | 6 | 0 | 43 | 5.03 | 1.39 | 3.8 | 2.0 | -$1 | 80 |
| Santos S | 27 | 60 | 2 | 0 | 64 | 3.85 | 1.67 | 9.6 | 5.2 | -$1 | 70 |

### Minors (2010)
| Level | Leag | W | L | Sv | IP | H | K | ERA | WHIP | K/9 | BB/9 | HR/9 | GB/F |
|---|---|---|---|---|---|---|---|---|---|---|---|---|---|
| A | — | | | | | | | | | | | | |
| AA | — | | | | | | | | | | | | |
| AAA | PCL | 0 | 1 | 0 | 16 | 16 | 9 | 2.81 | 1.44 | 5.1 | 3.9 | 0.0 | — |

### Majors
| Yr | Team | W | L | Sv | IP | H | K | ERA | WHIP | K/9 | BB/9 | HR/9 | GB/F | $1L | $2L | Pts | RAA | H% | HR/fb | S% | FIP | GS | CG | QS/DS | GR | Hld | Bln | Lead | OPS | 1st Hf | 2nd Hf | vs RH | vs LH |
|---|---|---|---|---|---|---|---|---|---|---|---|---|---|---|---|---|---|---|---|---|---|---|---|---|---|---|---|---|---|---|---|---|---|
| 07 | | | | | | | | | | | | | | | | | | | | | | | | | | | | | | | | | |
| 08 | FLA | 2 | 3 | 0 | 47 | 55 | 35 | 6.08 | 1.61 | 6.7 | 4.0 | 1.3 | 2.1 | -$5 | -$9 | 30 | -13 | 32% | 18% | 64% | 4.97 | 8 | 0 | 2/2 | 5 | 0 | 0 | -0.4 | .813 | .813 | — | .712 | .912 |
| 09 | FLA | 7 | 4 | 0 | 72 | 71 | 57 | 3.75 | 1.32 | 7.1 | 3.0 | 0.6 | 2.1 | $3 | $1 | 120 | +0 | 31% | 9% | 72% | 3.52 | 0 | 0 | 0/1 | 33 | 2 | 1 | -0.7 | .679 | .699 | .641 | .640 | .718 |
| 10 | FLA | 2 | 5 | 1 | 67 | 62 | 47 | 3.99 | 1.23 | 6.3 | 2.8 | 0.7 | 1.9 | -$1 | -$8 | 70 | -2 | 29% | 9% | 68% | 3.70 | | | | 53 | 1 | 0 | 0.0 | .681 | .749 | .644 | .667 | .700 |

### Competition at RP / Stats in 2010 as RP
| Thr | Player | GR | ERA | IP/G | Sv-Hld |
|---|---|---|---|---|---|
| RH | Hensley C | 68 | 2.16 | 1.1 | 7-22 |
| RH | Nunez L | 68 | 3.46 | 1.0 | 30-5 |
| RH | Sanches B | 61 | 2.26 | 1.0 | 0-12 |
| RH | Badenhop B | 53 | 3.99 | 1.3 | 1-8 |

---

## Danys Baez — 40 IP | $-2 | 30 pts
RP-51 — Owned: 0% — RH

Continuing a career-long descent, Baez was genuinely awful in 2010 (5.11 FIP). However, the Phillies have him under contract for one more year. Charlie Manuel in 2011 will keep Baez tucked safely in the back of the bullpen – exactly Baez's fate in the second half of 2010. (BB)

### Forecast
| Player | Age | IP | W | Sv | K | ERA | WHIP | K/9 | BB/9 | $2L | Pts |
|---|---|---|---|---|---|---|---|---|---|---|---|
| Baez D | 33 | 40 | 2 | 0 | 22 | 4.77 | 1.42 | 4.9 | 3.7 | -$2 | 30 |
| Mini-Browser | Age | IP | W | Sv | K | ERA | WHIP | K/9 | BB/9 | $2L | Pts |
| Saunders J | 29 | 200 | 11 | 0 | 106 | 4.85 | 1.44 | 4.8 | 3.0 | -$2 | 160 |
| Herrmann F | 26 | 40 | 2 | 0 | 28 | 4.89 | 1.51 | 6.3 | 2.6 | -$2 | 30 |
| Ohman W | 33 | 20 | 0 | 0 | 18 | 4.12 | 1.48 | 8.1 | 4.5 | -$2 | 20 |
| Bautista D | 30 | 40 | 2 | 0 | 40 | 4.53 | 1.58 | 9.0 | 5.7 | -$2 | 40 |
| Albaladejo J | 28 | 40 | 2 | 0 | 29 | 5.15 | 1.50 | 6.6 | 3.9 | -$2 | 40 |

### Minors (2010)
| Level | Leag | W | L | Sv | IP | H | K | ERA | WHIP | K/9 | BB/9 | HR/9 | GB/F |
|---|---|---|---|---|---|---|---|---|---|---|---|---|---|
| A | — | | | | | | | | | | | | |
| AA | — | | | | | | | | | | | | |
| AAA | IL | 0 | 0 | 0 | 1 | 1 | 0 | 9.00 | 2.00 | 0.0 | 0.0 | 0.0 | — |

### Majors
| Yr | Team | W | L | Sv | IP | H | K | ERA | WHIP | K/9 | BB/9 | HR/9 | GB/F | $1L | $2L | Pts | RAA | H% | HR/fb | S% | FIP | GS | CG | QS/DS | GR | Hld | Bln | Lead | OPS | 1st Hf | 2nd Hf | vs RH | vs LH |
|---|---|---|---|---|---|---|---|---|---|---|---|---|---|---|---|---|---|---|---|---|---|---|---|---|---|---|---|---|---|---|---|---|---|
| 07 | BAL | 0 | 6 | 3 | 50 | 50 | 29 | 6.44 | 1.57 | 5.2 | 5.2 | 1.4 | 1.6 | -$5 | -$12 | 20 | -13 | 27% | 15% | 61% | 5.94 | | | | 53 | 14 | 2 | +0.6 | .820 | .813 | .827 | .692 | 1.004 |
| 08 | | | | | | | | | | | | | | | | | | | | | | | | | | | | | | | | | |
| 09 | BAL | 4 | 6 | 0 | 71 | 59 | 40 | 4.02 | 1.13 | 5.0 | 2.8 | 1.0 | 2.4 | $4 | $1 | 80 | -4 | 24% | 14% | 68% | 4.56 | | | | 59 | 15 | 2 | +1.0 | .634 | .633 | .635 | .555 | .707 |
| 10 | PHI | 2 | 5 | 0 | 47 | 55 | 28 | 5.48 | 1.64 | 5.3 | 4.3 | 1.1 | 1.8 | -$7 | -$17 | 30 | -10 | 32% | 12% | 62% | 5.11 | | | | 51 | 6 | 2 | 0.0 | .863 | .835 | .916 | .807 | .949 |

### Competition at RP / Stats in 2010 as RP
| Thr | Player | GR | ERA | IP/G | Sv-Hld |
|---|---|---|---|---|---|
| RH | Contreras J | 67 | 3.34 | 0.9 | 4-13 |
| RH | Durbin C | 64 | 3.80 | 1.1 | 0-15 |
| RH | Madson R | 55 | 2.55 | 1.0 | 5-15 |
| RH | Baez D | 51 | 5.48 | 0.9 | 0-6 |

*For more stats, visit www.Rotolympus.com.*

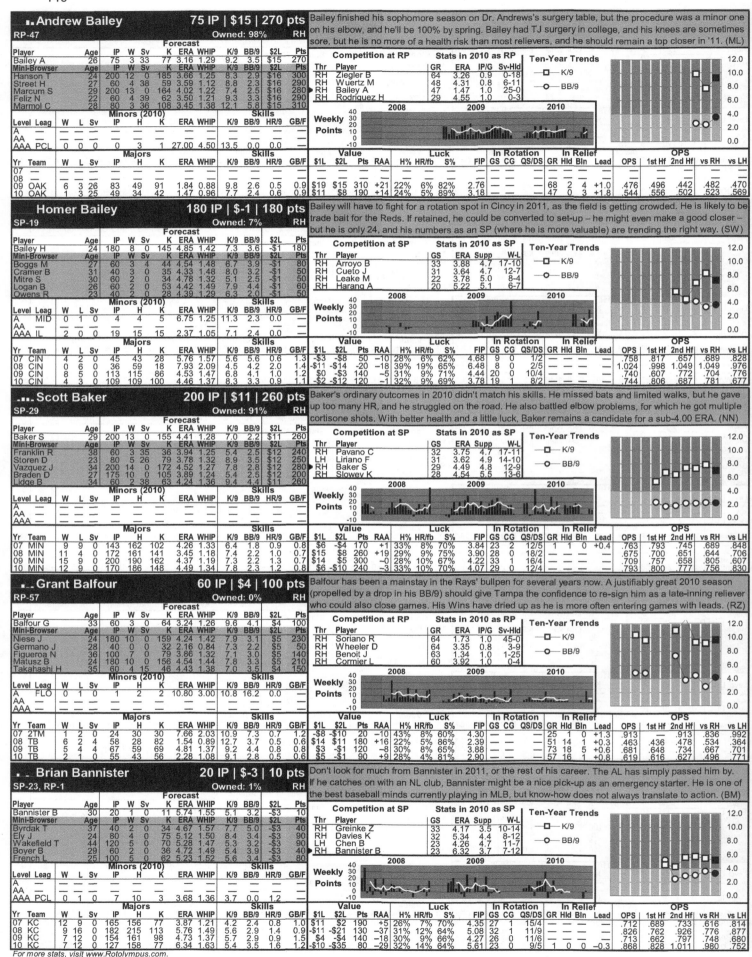

## Andrew Bailey — 75 IP | $15 | 270 pts

RP-47 | Owned: 98% | RH

| Player | Age | IP | W | Sv | K | ERA | WHIP | K/9 | BB/9 | $2L | Pts |
|---|---|---|---|---|---|---|---|---|---|---|---|
| | | Forecast | | | | | | | | | |
| Bailey A | 26 | 75 | 3 | 33 | 77 | 3.16 | 1.29 | 9.2 | 3.5 | $15 | 270 |
| **Mini-Browser** | Age | IP | W | Sv | K | ERA | WHIP | K/9 | BB/9 | $2L | Pts |
| Hanson T | 24 | 200 | 12 | 0 | 185 | 3.66 | 1.25 | 8.3 | 2.9 | $16 | 300 |
| Street H | 27 | 60 | 4 | 38 | 59 | 3.59 | 1.12 | 8.8 | 2.3 | $16 | 290 |
| Marcum S | 29 | 200 | 13 | 0 | 164 | 4.02 | 1.22 | 7.4 | 2.5 | $16 | 280 |
| Feliz N | 22 | 60 | 4 | 39 | 62 | 3.50 | 1.21 | 9.3 | 3.3 | $16 | 290 |
| Marmol C | 28 | 80 | 3 | 36 | 108 | 3.45 | 1.38 | 12.1 | 5.8 | $15 | 310 |

| Level | Leag | W | L | Sv | IP | H | K | ERA | WHIP | K/9 | BB/9 | HR/9 | GB/F |
|---|---|---|---|---|---|---|---|---|---|---|---|---|---|
| | | | | | Minors (2010) | | | | | Skills | | | |
| A | — | — | — | — | — | — | — | — | — | — | — | — | — |
| AA | — | — | — | — | — | — | — | — | — | — | — | — | — |
| AAA | PCL | 0 | 0 | 0 | 0 | 3 | 1 | 27.00 | 4.50 | 13.5 | 0.0 | 0.0 | — |

| Yr | Team | W | L | Sv | IP | H | K | ERA | WHIP | K/9 | BB/9 | HR/9 | GB/F | $1L | $2L | Pts | RAA | H% | HR/fb | S% | FIP | GS | CG | QS/DS | GR | Hld | Bln | Lead | OPS | 1st Hf | 2nd Hf | vs RH | vs LH |
|---|---|---|---|---|---|---|---|---|---|---|---|---|---|---|---|---|---|---|---|---|---|---|---|---|---|---|---|---|---|---|---|---|---|
| | | | | | Majors | | | | | Skills | | | | Value | | | | Luck | | | | In Rotation | | | In Relief | | | | OPS | | | | |
| 07 | — | — | — | — | — | — | — | — | — | — | — | — | — | — | — | — | — | — | — | — | — | — | — | — | — | — | — | — | — | — | — | — | — |
| 08 | — | — | — | — | — | — | — | — | — | — | — | — | — | — | — | — | — | — | — | — | — | — | — | — | — | — | — | — | — | — | — | — | — |
| 09 | OAK | 6 | 3 | 26 | 83 | 49 | 91 | 1.84 | 0.88 | 9.8 | 2.6 | 0.5 | 0.9 | $19 | $15 | 310 | +21 | 22% | 6% | 82% | 2.76 | — | — | — | 68 | 2 | 4 | +1.0 | .476 | .496 | .442 | .482 | .470 |
| 10 | OAK | 1 | 3 | 25 | 49 | 34 | 42 | 1.47 | 0.96 | 7.7 | 2.4 | 0.6 | 0.9 | $11 | $8 | 190 | +14 | 24% | 5% | 89% | 3.18 | — | — | — | 47 | 0 | 3 | +1.8 | .544 | .556 | .502 | .523 | .569 |

Bailey finished his sophomore season on Dr. Andrews's surgery table, but the procedure was a minor one on his elbow, and he'll be 100% by spring. Bailey had TJ surgery in college, and his knees are sometimes sore, but he is no more of a health risk than most relievers, and he should remain a top closer in '11. (ML)

**Competition at RP — Stats in 2010 as RP**

| Thr | Player | GR | ERA | IP/G | Sv-Hld |
|---|---|---|---|---|---|
| RH | Ziegler B | 64 | 3.26 | 0.9 | 0-18 |
| RH | Wuertz M | 48 | 4.31 | 0.8 | 6-11 |
| RH | Bailey A | 47 | 1.47 | 1.0 | 25-0 |
| RH | Rodriguez H | 29 | 4.55 | 1.0 | 0-3 |

**Ten-Year Trends**

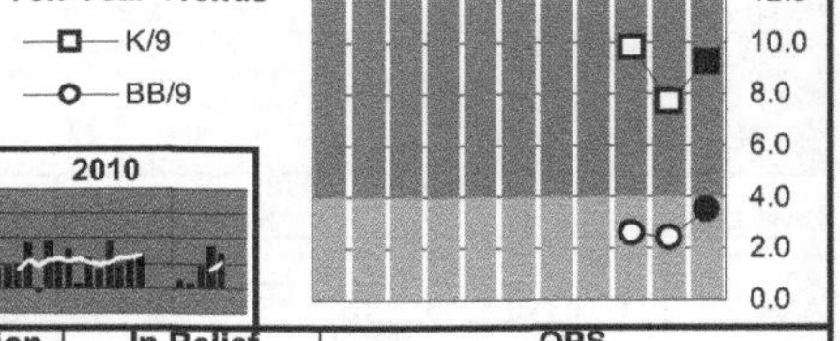

## Homer Bailey — 180 IP | $-1 | 180 pts

SP-19 | Owned: 7% | RH

| Player | Age | IP | W | Sv | K | ERA | WHIP | K/9 | BB/9 | $2L | Pts |
|---|---|---|---|---|---|---|---|---|---|---|---|
| | | Forecast | | | | | | | | | |
| Bailey H | 24 | 180 | 8 | 0 | 145 | 4.85 | 1.42 | 7.3 | 3.6 | -$1 | 180 |
| **Mini-Browser** | Age | IP | W | Sv | K | ERA | WHIP | K/9 | BB/9 | $2L | Pts |
| Boggs M | 27 | 60 | 3 | 4 | 44 | 4.54 | 1.48 | 6.7 | 3.9 | -$1 | 80 |
| Cramer B | 31 | 40 | 3 | 0 | 35 | 4.33 | 1.48 | 8.0 | 3.2 | -$1 | 50 |
| Mitre S | 30 | 60 | 2 | 0 | 34 | 4.78 | 1.32 | 5.1 | 2.5 | -$1 | 50 |
| Logan B | 26 | 60 | 2 | 0 | 53 | 4.42 | 1.49 | 7.9 | 4.4 | -$1 | 60 |
| Owens R | 23 | 40 | 2 | 0 | 28 | 4.39 | 1.29 | 6.3 | 2.0 | -$1 | 50 |

| Level | Leag | W | L | Sv | IP | H | K | ERA | WHIP | K/9 | BB/9 | HR/9 | GB/F |
|---|---|---|---|---|---|---|---|---|---|---|---|---|---|
| | | | | | Minors (2010) | | | | | Skills | | | |
| A | MID | 0 | 1 | 0 | 4 | 4 | 5 | 6.75 | 1.25 | 11.3 | 2.3 | 0.0 | — |
| AA | — | — | — | — | — | — | — | — | — | — | — | — | — |
| AAA | IL | 2 | 0 | 0 | 19 | 15 | 15 | 2.37 | 1.05 | 7.1 | 2.4 | 0.0 | — |

| Yr | Team | W | L | Sv | IP | H | K | ERA | WHIP | K/9 | BB/9 | HR/9 | GB/F | $1L | $2L | Pts | RAA | H% | HR/fb | S% | FIP | GS | CG | QS/DS | GR | Hld | Bln | Lead | OPS | 1st Hf | 2nd Hf | vs RH | vs LH |
|---|---|---|---|---|---|---|---|---|---|---|---|---|---|---|---|---|---|---|---|---|---|---|---|---|---|---|---|---|---|---|---|---|---|
| | | | | | Majors | | | | | Skills | | | | Value | | | | Luck | | | | In Rotation | | | In Relief | | | | OPS | | | | |
| 07 | CIN | 4 | 2 | 0 | 45 | 43 | 28 | 5.76 | 1.57 | 5.6 | 5.6 | 0.6 | 1.3 | -$3 | -$8 | 50 | −10 | 28% | 6% | 62% | 4.68 | 9 | 0 | 1/2 | — | — | — | — | .758 | .817 | .657 | .689 | .828 |
| 08 | CIN | 0 | 6 | 0 | 36 | 59 | 18 | 7.93 | 2.09 | 4.5 | 4.2 | 2.0 | 1.4 | -$11 | -$14 | -20 | −18 | 39% | 19% | 65% | 6.48 | 8 | 0 | 2/5 | — | — | — | — | 1.024 | .998 | 1.049 | 1.049 | .976 |
| 09 | CIN | 8 | 5 | 0 | 113 | 115 | 86 | 4.53 | 1.47 | 6.8 | 4.1 | 1.0 | 1.2 | $0 | -$3 | 140 | −5 | 31% | 9% | 71% | 4.44 | 20 | 0 | 10/4 | — | — | — | — | .740 | .607 | .772 | .704 | .776 |
| 10 | CIN | 4 | 3 | 0 | 109 | 109 | 100 | 4.46 | 1.37 | 8.3 | 3.3 | 0.9 | 1.1 | -$2 | -$12 | 120 | −1 | 32% | 9% | 69% | 3.78 | 19 | 1 | 8/2 | — | — | — | — | .744 | .806 | .687 | .781 | .677 |

Bailey will have to fight for a rotation spot in Cincy in 2011, as the field is getting crowded. He is likely to be trade bait for the Reds. If retained, he could be converted to set-up – he might even make a good closer – but he is only 24, and his numbers as an SP (where he is more valuable) are trending the right way. (SW)

**Competition at SP — Stats in 2010 as SP**

| Thr | Player | GS | ERA | Supp | W-L |
|---|---|---|---|---|---|
| RH | Arroyo B | 33 | 3.88 | 4.7 | 17-10 |
| RH | Cueto J | 31 | 3.64 | 4.7 | 12-7 |
| RH | Leake M | 22 | 3.78 | 5.0 | 8-4 |
| RH | Harang A | 20 | 5.22 | 5.1 | 6-7 |

**Ten-Year Trends**

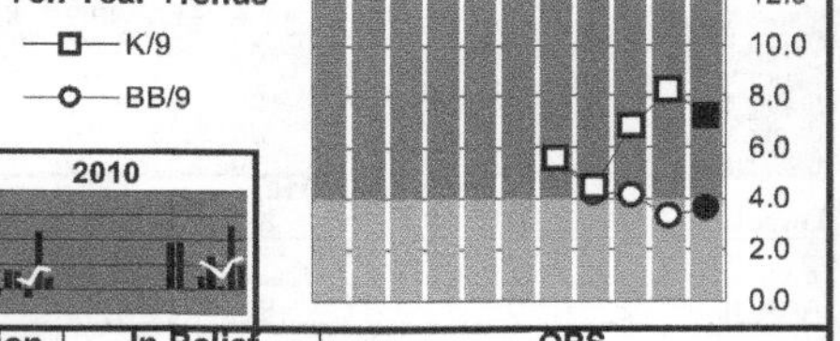


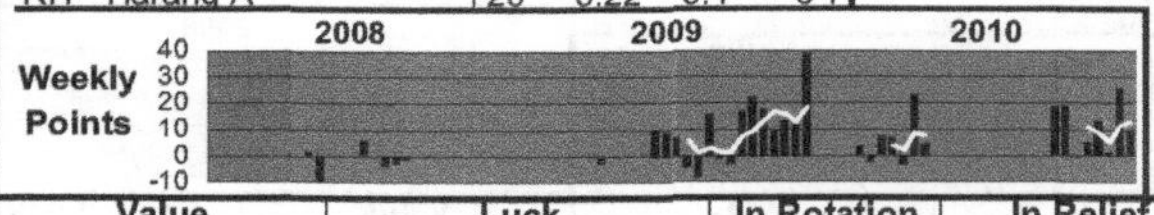


## Scott Baker — 200 IP | $11 | 260 pts

SP-29 | Owned: 91% | RH

| Player | Age | IP | W | Sv | K | ERA | WHIP | K/9 | BB/9 | $2L | Pts |
|---|---|---|---|---|---|---|---|---|---|---|---|
| | | Forecast | | | | | | | | | |
| Baker S | 29 | 200 | 13 | 0 | 155 | 4.41 | 1.28 | 7.0 | 2.2 | $11 | 260 |
| **Mini-Browser** | Age | IP | W | Sv | K | ERA | WHIP | K/9 | BB/9 | $2L | Pts |
| Franklin R | 38 | 60 | 3 | 35 | 36 | 3.94 | 1.25 | 5.4 | 2.5 | $12 | 240 |
| Storen D | 23 | 80 | 5 | 26 | 79 | 3.78 | 1.32 | 8.9 | 3.5 | $12 | 250 |
| Vazquez J | 34 | 200 | 14 | 0 | 172 | 4.52 | 1.27 | 7.8 | 2.8 | $12 | 280 |
| Braden D | 27 | 175 | 10 | 0 | 105 | 3.89 | 1.24 | 5.4 | 2.5 | $12 | 200 |
| Lidge B | 34 | 60 | 2 | 38 | 63 | 4.24 | 1.36 | 9.4 | 4.4 | $11 | 260 |

| Level | Leag | W | L | Sv | IP | H | K | ERA | WHIP | K/9 | BB/9 | HR/9 | GB/F |
|---|---|---|---|---|---|---|---|---|---|---|---|---|---|
| | | | | | Minors (2010) | | | | | Skills | | | |
| A | — | — | — | — | — | — | — | — | — | — | — | — | — |
| AA | — | — | — | — | — | — | — | — | — | — | — | — | — |
| AAA | — | — | — | — | — | — | — | — | — | — | — | — | — |

| Yr | Team | W | L | Sv | IP | H | K | ERA | WHIP | K/9 | BB/9 | HR/9 | GB/F | $1L | $2L | Pts | RAA | H% | HR/fb | S% | FIP | GS | CG | QS/DS | GR | Hld | Bln | Lead | OPS | 1st Hf | 2nd Hf | vs RH | vs LH |
|---|---|---|---|---|---|---|---|---|---|---|---|---|---|---|---|---|---|---|---|---|---|---|---|---|---|---|---|---|---|---|---|---|---|
| | | | | | Majors | | | | | Skills | | | | Value | | | | Luck | | | | In Rotation | | | In Relief | | | | OPS | | | | |
| 07 | MIN | 9 | 9 | 0 | 143 | 162 | 102 | 4.26 | 1.33 | 6.4 | 1.8 | 0.9 | 0.8 | $6 | -$4 | 170 | +1 | 33% | 8% | 70% | 3.84 | 23 | 2 | 12/5 | 1 | 1 | 0 | +0.4 | .763 | .793 | .745 | .689 | .848 |
| 08 | MIN | 11 | 4 | 0 | 172 | 161 | 141 | 3.45 | 1.18 | 7.4 | 2.2 | 1.0 | 0.7 | $15 | $8 | 260 | +19 | 29% | 9% | 75% | 3.90 | 28 | 0 | 18/2 | — | — | — | — | .675 | .700 | .651 | .644 | .706 |
| 09 | MIN | 15 | 9 | 0 | 200 | 190 | 162 | 4.37 | 1.19 | 7.3 | 2.2 | 1.3 | 0.7 | $14 | $5 | 300 | −0 | 28% | 10% | 67% | 4.22 | 33 | 1 | 16/4 | — | — | — | — | .709 | .757 | .658 | .805 | .607 |
| 10 | MIN | 12 | 9 | 0 | 170 | 186 | 148 | 4.49 | 1.34 | 7.8 | 2.3 | 1.2 | 0.8 | $6 | -$10 | 240 | −3 | 33% | 10% | 70% | 4.07 | 29 | 0 | 12/4 | — | — | — | — | .793 | .800 | .777 | .756 | .830 |

Baker's ordinary outcomes in 2010 didn't match his skills. He missed bats and limited walks, but he gave up too many HR, and he struggled on the road. He also battled elbow problems, for which he got multiple cortisone shots. With better health and a little luck, Baker remains a candidate for a sub-4.00 ERA. (NN)

**Competition at SP — Stats in 2010 as SP**

| Thr | Player | GS | ERA | Supp | W-L |
|---|---|---|---|---|---|
| RH | Pavano C | 32 | 3.75 | 4.7 | 17-11 |
| LH | Liriano F | 31 | 3.62 | 4.9 | 14-10 |
| RH | Baker S | 29 | 4.49 | 4.8 | 12-9 |
| RH | Slowey K | 28 | 4.54 | 5.5 | 13-6 |

**Ten-Year Trends**

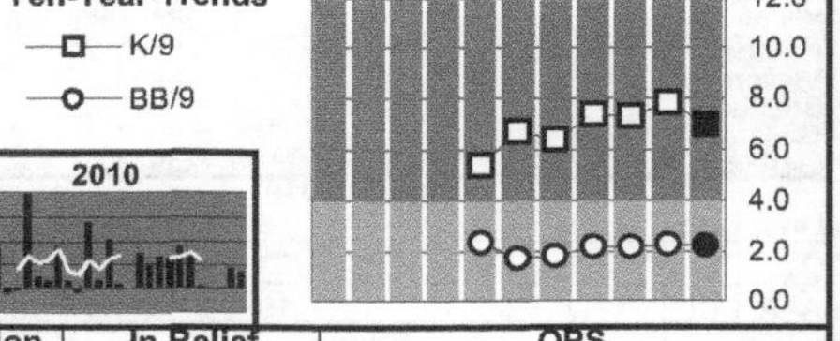


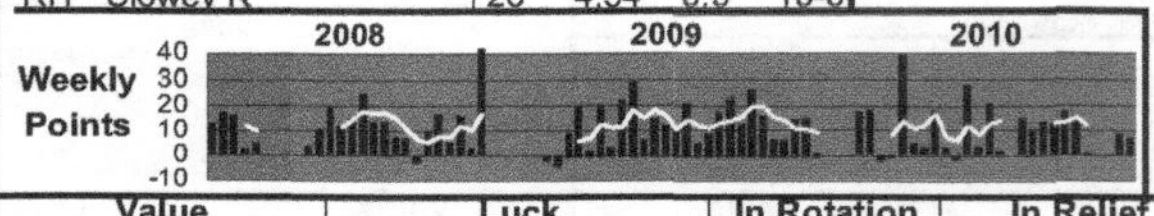


## Grant Balfour — 60 IP | $4 | 100 pts

RP-57 | Owned: 0% | RH

| Player | Age | IP | W | Sv | K | ERA | WHIP | K/9 | BB/9 | $2L | Pts |
|---|---|---|---|---|---|---|---|---|---|---|---|
| | | Forecast | | | | | | | | | |
| Balfour G | 33 | 60 | 3 | 0 | 64 | 3.24 | 1.26 | 9.6 | 4.1 | $4 | 100 |
| **Mini-Browser** | Age | IP | W | Sv | K | ERA | WHIP | K/9 | BB/9 | $2L | Pts |
| Niese J | 24 | 180 | 10 | 0 | 159 | 4.24 | 1.42 | 7.9 | 3.1 | $5 | 230 |
| Germano J | 28 | 40 | 0 | 0 | 32 | 2.16 | 0.84 | 7.3 | 2.2 | $5 | 50 |
| Figueroa N | 36 | 100 | 7 | 0 | 79 | 3.86 | 1.32 | 7.1 | 3.0 | $5 | 140 |
| Matusz B | 24 | 180 | 10 | 0 | 156 | 4.54 | 1.44 | 7.8 | 3.3 | $5 | 210 |
| Takahashi H | 35 | 60 | 4 | 15 | 46 | 4.43 | 1.38 | 7.0 | 3.5 | $4 | 150 |

| Level | Leag | W | L | Sv | IP | H | K | ERA | WHIP | K/9 | BB/9 | HR/9 | GB/F |
|---|---|---|---|---|---|---|---|---|---|---|---|---|---|
| | | | | | Minors (2010) | | | | | Skills | | | |
| A | FLO | 0 | 1 | 0 | 1 | 2 | 2 | 10.80 | 3.00 | 10.8 | 16.2 | 0.0 | — |
| AA | — | — | — | — | — | — | — | — | — | — | — | — | — |
| AAA | — | — | — | — | — | — | — | — | — | — | — | — | — |

| Yr | Team | W | L | Sv | IP | H | K | ERA | WHIP | K/9 | BB/9 | HR/9 | GB/F | $1L | $2L | Pts | RAA | H% | HR/fb | S% | FIP | GS | CG | QS/DS | GR | Hld | Bln | Lead | OPS | 1st Hf | 2nd Hf | vs RH | vs LH |
|---|---|---|---|---|---|---|---|---|---|---|---|---|---|---|---|---|---|---|---|---|---|---|---|---|---|---|---|---|---|---|---|---|---|
| | | | | | Majors | | | | | Skills | | | | Value | | | | Luck | | | | In Rotation | | | In Relief | | | | OPS | | | | |
| 07 | 2TM | 1 | 2 | 0 | 24 | 30 | 30 | 7.66 | 2.03 | 10.9 | 7.3 | 0.7 | 1.2 | -$8 | -$10 | 20 | −10 | 43% | 8% | 60% | 4.30 | — | — | — | 25 | 1 | 0 | +1.3 | .913 | — | .913 | .836 | .992 |
| 08 | TB | 6 | 2 | 4 | 58 | 28 | 82 | 1.54 | 0.89 | 12.7 | 3.7 | 0.5 | 0.6 | $14 | $11 | 180 | +16 | 22% | 5% | 86% | 2.39 | — | — | — | 51 | 14 | 1 | +0.3 | .463 | .436 | .478 | .534 | .364 |
| 09 | TB | 5 | 4 | 4 | 67 | 59 | 69 | 4.81 | 1.37 | 9.2 | 4.4 | 0.8 | 0.8 | $3 | -$1 | 120 | −8 | 30% | 8% | 65% | 3.88 | — | — | — | 73 | 18 | 5 | +0.6 | .681 | .648 | .734 | .667 | .701 |
| 10 | TB | 2 | 1 | 0 | 55 | 43 | 56 | 2.28 | 1.08 | 9.1 | 2.8 | 0.5 | 0.6 | $5 | -$1 | 90 | +9 | 28% | 4% | 81% | 2.90 | — | — | — | 57 | 16 | 1 | +0.8 | .619 | .616 | .627 | .496 | .771 |

Balfour has been a mainstay in the Rays' bullpen for several years now. A justifiably great 2010 season (propelled by a drop in his BB/9) should give Tampa the confidence to re-sign him as a late-inning reliever who could also close games. His Wins have dried up as he is more often entering games with leads. (RZ)

**Competition at RP — Stats in 2010 as RP**

| Thr | Player | GR | ERA | IP/G | Sv-Hld |
|---|---|---|---|---|---|
| RH | Soriano R | 64 | 1.73 | 1.0 | 45-0 |
| RH | Wheeler D | 64 | 3.35 | 0.8 | 3-9 |
| RH | Benoit J | 63 | 1.34 | 1.0 | 1-25 |
| RH | Cormier L | 60 | 3.92 | 1.0 | 0-4 |

**Ten-Year Trends**

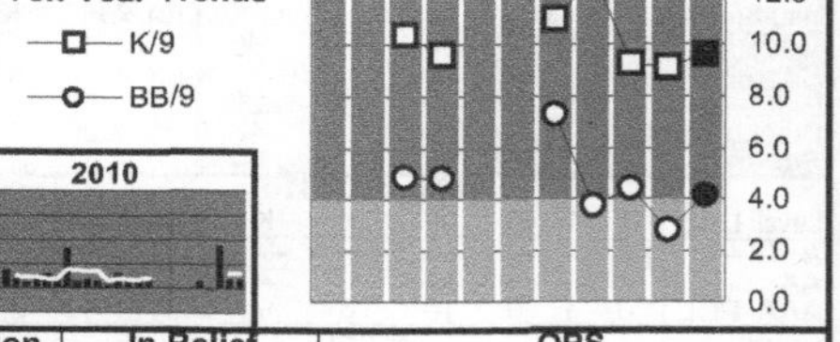


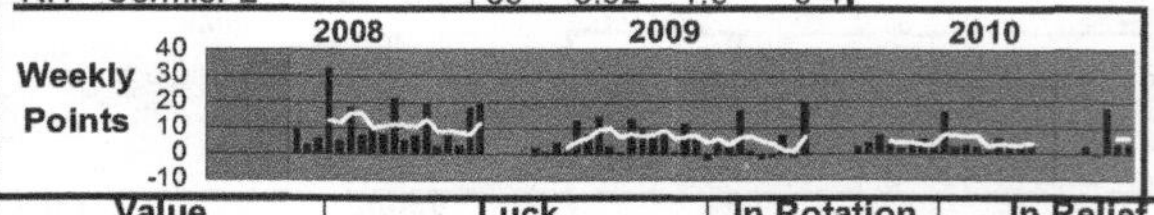


## Brian Bannister — 20 IP | $-3 | 10 pts

SP-23, RP-1 | Owned: 1% | RH

| Player | Age | IP | W | Sv | K | ERA | WHIP | K/9 | BB/9 | $2L | Pts |
|---|---|---|---|---|---|---|---|---|---|---|---|
| | | Forecast | | | | | | | | | |
| Bannister B | 30 | 20 | 1 | 0 | 11 | 5.74 | 1.55 | 5.1 | 3.2 | -$3 | 10 |
| **Mini-Browser** | Age | IP | W | Sv | K | ERA | WHIP | K/9 | BB/9 | $2L | Pts |
| Byrdak T | 37 | 40 | 2 | 0 | 34 | 4.67 | 1.57 | 7.7 | 5.0 | -$3 | 40 |
| Ely J | 24 | 80 | 4 | 0 | 75 | 5.12 | 1.50 | 8.4 | 3.4 | -$3 | 90 |
| Wakefield T | 44 | 120 | 5 | 0 | 70 | 5.28 | 1.47 | 5.3 | 3.2 | -$3 | 90 |
| Boyer B | 29 | 60 | 2 | 0 | 36 | 4.72 | 1.49 | 5.4 | 3.9 | -$3 | 40 |
| French L | 25 | 100 | 5 | 0 | 62 | 5.23 | 1.52 | 5.6 | 3.4 | -$3 | 80 |

| Level | Leag | W | L | Sv | IP | H | K | ERA | WHIP | K/9 | BB/9 | HR/9 | GB/F |
|---|---|---|---|---|---|---|---|---|---|---|---|---|---|
| | | | | | Minors (2010) | | | | | Skills | | | |
| A | — | — | — | — | — | — | — | — | — | — | — | — | — |
| AA | — | — | — | — | — | — | — | — | — | — | — | — | — |
| AAA | PCL | 0 | 1 | 0 | 7 | 10 | 3 | 3.68 | 1.36 | 3.7 | 0.0 | 1.2 | — |

| Yr | Team | W | L | Sv | IP | H | K | ERA | WHIP | K/9 | BB/9 | HR/9 | GB/F | $1L | $2L | Pts | RAA | H% | HR/fb | S% | FIP | GS | CG | QS/DS | GR | Hld | Bln | Lead | OPS | 1st Hf | 2nd Hf | vs RH | vs LH |
|---|---|---|---|---|---|---|---|---|---|---|---|---|---|---|---|---|---|---|---|---|---|---|---|---|---|---|---|---|---|---|---|---|---|
| | | | | | Majors | | | | | Skills | | | | Value | | | | Luck | | | | In Rotation | | | In Relief | | | | OPS | | | | |
| 07 | KC | 12 | 9 | 0 | 165 | 156 | 77 | 3.87 | 1.21 | 4.2 | 2.4 | 0.8 | 1.0 | $11 | $2 | 190 | +5 | 26% | 7% | 70% | 4.35 | 27 | 1 | 15/4 | — | — | — | — | .712 | .689 | .733 | .616 | .814 |
| 08 | KC | 9 | 16 | 0 | 182 | 215 | 113 | 5.76 | 1.49 | 5.6 | 2.9 | 1.4 | 0.9 | -$11 | -$21 | 130 | −37 | 31% | 12% | 64% | 5.08 | 32 | 1 | 11/9 | — | — | — | — | .826 | .762 | .926 | .776 | .877 |
| 09 | KC | 7 | 12 | 0 | 154 | 161 | 98 | 4.73 | 1.37 | 5.7 | 2.9 | 0.9 | 1.5 | $4 | -$4 | 140 | −18 | 30% | 9% | 66% | 4.27 | 26 | 0 | 11/6 | — | — | — | — | .713 | .662 | .797 | .748 | .680 |
| 10 | KC | 7 | 12 | 0 | 127 | 158 | 77 | 6.34 | 1.63 | 5.4 | 3.5 | 1.6 | 1.2 | -$10 | -$35 | 80 | −29 | 32% | 14% | 64% | 5.61 | 23 | 0 | 9/5 | 1 | 0 | 0 | −0.3 | .868 | .828 | 1.011 | .980 | .752 |

Don't look for much from Bannister in 2011, or the rest of his career. The AL has simply passed him by. If he catches on with an NL club, Bannister might be a nice pick-up as an emergency starter. He is one of the best baseball minds currently playing in MLB, but know-how does not always translate to action. (BM)

**Competition at SP — Stats in 2010 as SP**

| Thr | Player | GS | ERA | Supp | W-L |
|---|---|---|---|---|---|
| RH | Greinke Z | 33 | 4.17 | 3.5 | 10-14 |
| RH | Davies K | 32 | 5.34 | 4.4 | 8-12 |
| LH | Chen B | 23 | 4.26 | 4.7 | 11-7 |
| RH | Bannister B | 23 | 6.32 | 3.7 | 7-12 |

**Ten-Year Trends**

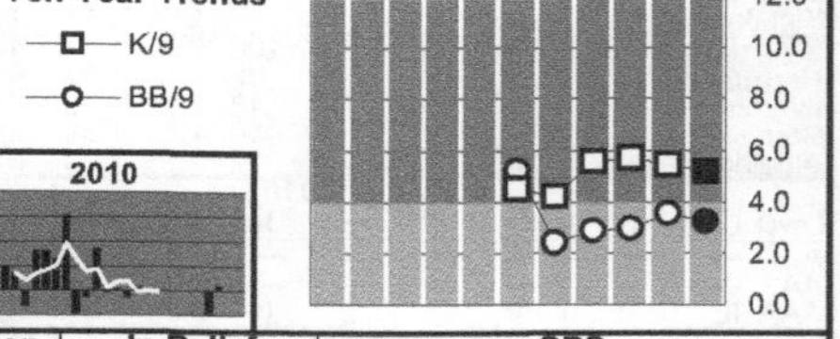


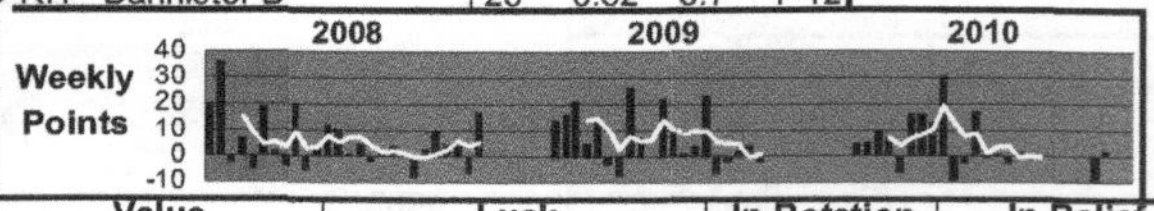

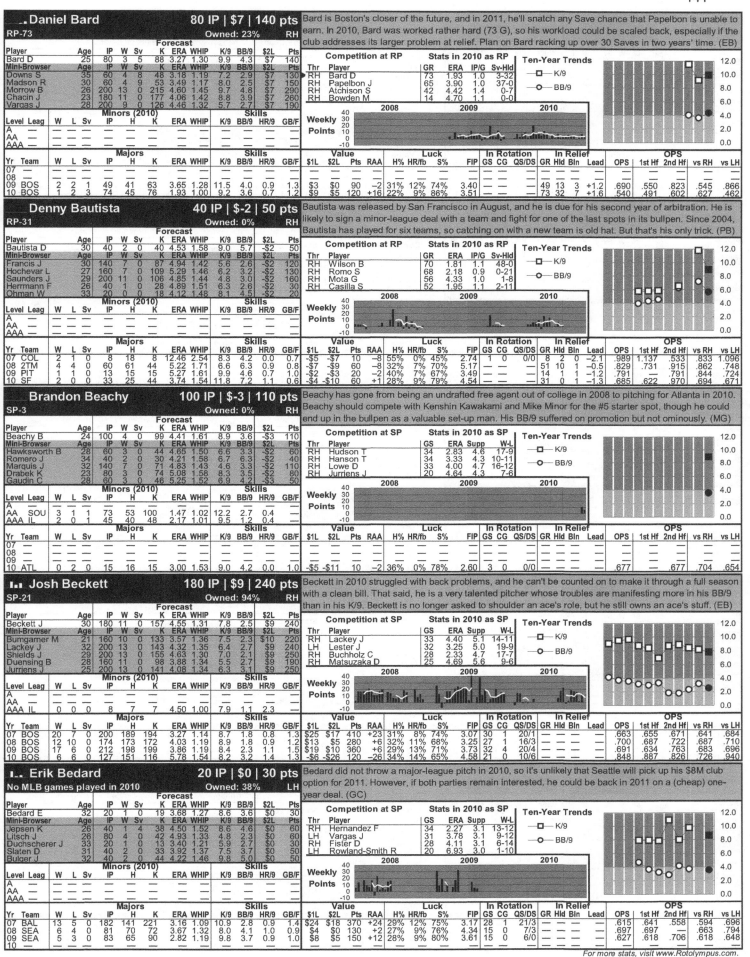

## Daniel Bard — 80 IP | $7 | 140 pts

RP-73    Owned: 23%    RH

Bard is Boston's closer of the future, and in 2011, he'll snatch any Save chance that Papelbon is unable to earn. In 2010, Bard was worked rather hard (73 G), so his workload could be scaled back, especially if the club addresses its larger problem at relief. Plan on Bard racking up over 30 Saves in two years' time. (EB)

### Forecast

| Player | Age | IP | W | Sv | K | ERA | WHIP | K/9 | BB/9 | $2L | Pts |
|---|---|---|---|---|---|---|---|---|---|---|---|
| Bard D | 25 | 80 | 3 | 5 | 88 | 3.27 | 1.30 | 9.9 | 4.3 | $7 | 140 |
| Mini-Browser | Age | IP | W | Sv | K | ERA | WHIP | K/9 | BB/9 | $2L | Pts |
| Downs S | 35 | 60 | 4 | 8 | 48 | 3.18 | 1.19 | 7.2 | 2.9 | $7 | 130 |
| Madson R | 30 | 60 | 4 | 9 | 53 | 3.49 | 1.17 | 8.0 | 2.5 | $7 | 150 |
| Morrow B | 26 | 200 | 13 | 0 | 215 | 4.60 | 1.45 | 9.7 | 4.8 | $7 | 290 |
| Chacin J | 23 | 180 | 11 | 0 | 177 | 4.06 | 1.42 | 8.8 | 3.9 | $7 | 260 |
| Vargas J | 28 | 200 | 9 | 0 | 126 | 4.46 | 1.32 | 5.7 | 2.7 | $7 | 190 |

### Competition at RP — Stats in 2010 as RP

| Thr | Player | GR | ERA | IP/G | Sv-Hld |
|---|---|---|---|---|---|
| RH | Bard D | 73 | 1.93 | 1.0 | 3-32 |
| RH | Papelbon J | 65 | 3.90 | 1.0 | 37-0 |
| RH | Atchison S | 42 | 4.42 | 1.4 | 0-7 |
| RH | Bowden M | 14 | 4.70 | 1.1 | 0-0 |

Ten-Year Trends □ K/9 ○ BB/9

### Minors (2010)

| Level | Leag | W | L | Sv | IP | H | K | ERA | WHIP | K/9 | BB/9 | HR/9 | GB/F |
|---|---|---|---|---|---|---|---|---|---|---|---|---|---|
| A | — | — | — | — | — | — | — | — | — | — | — | — | — |
| AA | — | — | — | — | — | — | — | — | — | — | — | — | — |
| AAA | — | — | — | — | — | — | — | — | — | — | — | — | — |

### Majors

| Yr | Team | W | L | Sv | IP | H | K | ERA | WHIP | K/9 | BB/9 | HR/9 | GB/F | $1L | $2L | Pts | RAA | H% | HR/fb | S% | FIP | GS | CG | QS/DS | GR | Hld | Bln | Lead | OPS | 1st Hf | 2nd Hf | vs RH | vs LH |
|---|---|---|---|---|---|---|---|---|---|---|---|---|---|---|---|---|---|---|---|---|---|---|---|---|---|---|---|---|---|---|---|---|---|
| 07 | — | | | | | | | | | | | | | | | | | | | | | | | | | | | | — | — | — | — | — |
| 08 | — | | | | | | | | | | | | | | | | | | | | | | | | | | | | — | — | — | — | — |
| 09 | BOS | 2 | 2 | 1 | 49 | 41 | 63 | 3.65 | 1.28 | 11.5 | 4.0 | 0.9 | 1.3 | $3 | $0 | 90 | −2 | 31% | 12% | 74% | 3.40 | — | — | — | 49 | 13 | 3 | +1.2 | .690 | .550 | .823 | .545 | .866 |
| 10 | BOS | 1 | 2 | 3 | 74 | 45 | 76 | 1.93 | 1.00 | 9.2 | 3.6 | 0.7 | 1.2 | $9 | $5 | 120 | +16 | 22% | 9% | 86% | 3.51 | — | — | — | 73 | 32 | 7 | +1.6 | .540 | .491 | .602 | .627 | .462 |

## Denny Bautista — 40 IP | $-2 | 50 pts

RP-31    Owned: 0%    RH

Bautista was released by San Francisco in August, and he is due for his second year of arbitration. He is likely to sign a minor-league deal with a team and fight for one of the last spots in its bullpen. Since 2004, Bautista has played for six teams, so catching on with a new team is old hat. But that's his only trick. (PB)

### Forecast

| Player | Age | IP | W | Sv | K | ERA | WHIP | K/9 | BB/9 | $2L | Pts |
|---|---|---|---|---|---|---|---|---|---|---|---|
| Bautista D | 30 | 40 | 2 | 0 | 40 | 4.53 | 1.58 | 9.0 | 5.7 | -$2 | 50 |
| Mini-Browser | Age | IP | W | Sv | K | ERA | WHIP | K/9 | BB/9 | $2L | Pts |
| Francis J | 30 | 140 | 7 | 0 | 87 | 4.94 | 1.42 | 5.6 | 2.6 | -$2 | 120 |
| Hochevar L | 27 | 160 | 7 | 0 | 109 | 5.29 | 1.46 | 6.2 | 3.2 | -$2 | 130 |
| Saunders J | 29 | 200 | 11 | 0 | 106 | 4.85 | 1.44 | 4.8 | 3.0 | -$2 | 160 |
| Herrmann F | 26 | 40 | 1 | 0 | 28 | 4.89 | 1.51 | 6.3 | 2.6 | -$2 | 30 |
| Ohman W | 33 | 20 | 0 | 0 | 18 | 4.12 | 1.48 | 8.1 | 4.5 | -$2 | 20 |

### Competition at RP — Stats in 2010 as RP

| Thr | Player | GR | ERA | IP/G | Sv-Hld |
|---|---|---|---|---|---|
| RH | Wilson B | 70 | 1.81 | 1.1 | 48-0 |
| RH | Romo S | 68 | 2.18 | 0.9 | 0-21 |
| RH | Mota G | 56 | 4.33 | 1.0 | 1-8 |
| RH | Casilla S | 52 | 1.95 | 1.1 | 2-11 |

Ten-Year Trends □ K/9 ○ BB/9

### Minors (2010)

| Level | Leag | W | L | Sv | IP | H | K | ERA | WHIP | K/9 | BB/9 | HR/9 | GB/F |
|---|---|---|---|---|---|---|---|---|---|---|---|---|---|
| A | — | — | — | — | — | — | — | — | — | — | — | — | — |
| AA | — | — | — | — | — | — | — | — | — | — | — | — | — |
| AAA | — | — | — | — | — | — | — | — | — | — | — | — | — |

### Majors

| Yr | Team | W | L | Sv | IP | H | K | ERA | WHIP | K/9 | BB/9 | HR/9 | GB/F | $1L | $2L | Pts | RAA | H% | HR/fb | S% | FIP | GS | CG | QS/DS | GR | Hld | Bln | Lead | OPS | 1st Hf | 2nd Hf | vs RH | vs LH |
|---|---|---|---|---|---|---|---|---|---|---|---|---|---|---|---|---|---|---|---|---|---|---|---|---|---|---|---|---|---|---|---|---|---|
| 07 | COL | 2 | 1 | 0 | 8 | 18 | 8 | 12.46 | 2.54 | 8.3 | 4.2 | 0.0 | 0.7 | -$5 | -$7 | 10 | −8 | 55% | 0% | 45% | 2.74 | 1 | 0 | 0/0 | 8 | 2 | 0 | −2.1 | .989 | 1.137 | .533 | .833 | 1.096 |
| 08 | 2TM | 4 | 4 | 0 | 60 | 61 | 44 | 5.22 | 1.71 | 6.6 | 6.3 | 0.9 | 0.8 | -$7 | -$9 | 60 | −8 | 32% | 7% | 70% | 5.17 | — | — | — | 51 | 10 | 1 | −0.5 | .829 | .731 | .915 | .862 | .748 |
| 09 | PIT | 1 | 1 | 0 | 13 | 15 | 15 | 5.27 | 1.61 | 9.9 | 4.6 | 0.7 | 1.0 | -$2 | -$3 | 20 | −2 | 40% | 7% | 67% | 3.49 | — | — | — | 14 | 1 | 1 | −1.2 | .791 | — | .791 | .844 | .724 |
| 10 | SF | 2 | 0 | 0 | 33 | 25 | 44 | 3.74 | 1.54 | 11.8 | 7.2 | 1.1 | 0.6 | -$4 | -$10 | 60 | +1 | 28% | 9% | 79% | 4.54 | — | — | — | 31 | 0 | 1 | −1.3 | .685 | .622 | .970 | .694 | .671 |

## Brandon Beachy — 100 IP | $-3 | 110 pts

SP-3    Owned: 0%    RH

Beachy has gone from being an undrafted free agent out of college in 2008 to pitching for Atlanta in 2010. Beachy should compete with Kenshin Kawakami and Mike Minor for the #5 starter spot, though he could end up in the bullpen as a valuable set-up man. His BB/9 suffered on promotion but not ominously. (MG)

### Forecast

| Player | Age | IP | W | Sv | K | ERA | WHIP | K/9 | BB/9 | $2L | Pts |
|---|---|---|---|---|---|---|---|---|---|---|---|
| Beachy B | 24 | 100 | 4 | 0 | 99 | 4.41 | 1.61 | 8.9 | 3.6 | -$3 | 110 |
| Mini-Browser | Age | IP | W | Sv | K | ERA | WHIP | K/9 | BB/9 | $2L | Pts |
| Hawksworth B | 28 | 60 | 3 | 0 | 44 | 4.65 | 1.50 | 6.6 | 3.3 | -$2 | 60 |
| Romero J | 34 | 40 | 2 | 0 | 30 | 4.21 | 1.58 | 6.7 | 6.3 | -$2 | 40 |
| Marquis J | 32 | 140 | 7 | 0 | 71 | 4.83 | 1.43 | 4.6 | 3.3 | -$2 | 110 |
| Drabek K | 23 | 80 | 3 | 0 | 74 | 5.08 | 1.58 | 8.3 | 3.5 | -$2 | 80 |
| Gaudin C | 28 | 60 | 3 | 0 | 46 | 5.25 | 1.52 | 6.9 | 4.2 | -$3 | 50 |

### Competition at SP — Stats in 2010 as SP

| Thr | Player | GS | ERA | Supp | W-L |
|---|---|---|---|---|---|
| RH | Hudson T | 34 | 2.83 | 4.6 | 17-9 |
| RH | Hanson T | 34 | 3.33 | 4.3 | 10-11 |
| RH | Lowe D | 33 | 4.00 | 4.7 | 16-12 |
| RH | Jurriens J | 20 | 4.64 | 4.3 | 7-6 |

Ten-Year Trends □ K/9 ○ BB/9

### Minors (2010)

| Level | Leag | W | L | Sv | IP | H | K | ERA | WHIP | K/9 | BB/9 | HR/9 | GB/F |
|---|---|---|---|---|---|---|---|---|---|---|---|---|---|
| A | — | — | — | — | — | — | — | — | — | — | — | — | — |
| AA | SOU | 3 | 1 | 1 | 73 | 53 | 100 | 1.47 | 1.02 | 12.2 | 2.7 | 0.4 | — |
| AAA | IL | 2 | 0 | 1 | 45 | 40 | 48 | 2.17 | 1.01 | 9.5 | 1.2 | 0.4 | — |

### Majors

| Yr | Team | W | L | Sv | IP | H | K | ERA | WHIP | K/9 | BB/9 | HR/9 | GB/F | $1L | $2L | Pts | RAA | H% | HR/fb | S% | FIP | GS | CG | QS/DS | GR | Hld | Bln | Lead | OPS | 1st Hf | 2nd Hf | vs RH | vs LH |
|---|---|---|---|---|---|---|---|---|---|---|---|---|---|---|---|---|---|---|---|---|---|---|---|---|---|---|---|---|---|---|---|---|---|
| 07 | — | | | | | | | | | | | | | | | | | | | | | | | | | | | | — | — | — | — | — |
| 08 | — | | | | | | | | | | | | | | | | | | | | | | | | | | | | — | — | — | — | — |
| 09 | — | | | | | | | | | | | | | | | | | | | | | | | | | | | | — | — | — | — | — |
| 10 | ATL | 0 | 2 | 0 | 15 | 16 | 15 | 3.00 | 1.53 | 9.0 | 4.2 | 0.0 | 1.0 | -$5 | -$11 | 10 | −2 | 36% | 0% | 78% | 2.60 | 3 | 0 | 0/0 | — | — | — | — | .677 | — | .677 | .704 | .654 |

## Josh Beckett — 180 IP | $9 | 240 pts

SP-21    Owned: 94%    RH

Beckett in 2010 struggled with back problems, and he can't be counted on to make it through a full season with a clean bill. That said, he is a very talented pitcher whose troubles are manifesting more in his BB/9 than in his K/9. Beckett is no longer asked to shoulder an ace's role, but he still owns an ace's stuff. (EB)

### Forecast

| Player | Age | IP | W | Sv | K | ERA | WHIP | K/9 | BB/9 | $2L | Pts |
|---|---|---|---|---|---|---|---|---|---|---|---|
| Beckett J | 30 | 180 | 11 | 0 | 157 | 4.55 | 1.31 | 7.8 | 2.5 | $9 | 240 |
| Mini-Browser | Age | IP | W | Sv | K | ERA | WHIP | K/9 | BB/9 | $2L | Pts |
| Bumgarner M | 21 | 160 | 10 | 0 | 133 | 3.57 | 1.36 | 7.5 | 2.3 | $10 | 220 |
| Lackey J | 32 | 200 | 13 | 0 | 143 | 4.32 | 1.35 | 6.4 | 2.7 | $9 | 240 |
| Shields J | 29 | 200 | 13 | 0 | 155 | 4.63 | 1.30 | 7.0 | 2.1 | $9 | 250 |
| Duensing B | 28 | 160 | 11 | 0 | 98 | 3.88 | 1.34 | 5.5 | 2.7 | $9 | 190 |
| Jurriens J | 25 | 200 | 13 | 0 | 141 | 4.08 | 1.34 | 6.3 | 3.1 | $9 | 250 |

### Competition at SP — Stats in 2010 as SP

| Thr | Player | GS | ERA | Supp | W-L |
|---|---|---|---|---|---|
| RH | Lackey J | 33 | 4.40 | 5.1 | 14-11 |
| LH | Lester J | 32 | 3.25 | 5.0 | 19-9 |
| RH | Buchholz C | 28 | 2.33 | 4.7 | 17-7 |
| RH | Matsuzaka D | 25 | 4.69 | 5.6 | 9-6 |

Ten-Year Trends □ K/9 ○ BB/9

### Minors (2010)

| Level | Leag | W | L | Sv | IP | H | K | ERA | WHIP | K/9 | BB/9 | HR/9 | GB/F |
|---|---|---|---|---|---|---|---|---|---|---|---|---|---|
| A | — | — | — | — | — | — | — | — | — | — | — | — | — |
| AA | — | — | — | — | — | — | — | — | — | — | — | — | — |
| AAA | IL | 0 | 0 | 0 | 8 | 7 | 7 | 4.50 | 1.00 | 7.9 | 1.1 | 2.3 | — |

### Majors

| Yr | Team | W | L | Sv | IP | H | K | ERA | WHIP | K/9 | BB/9 | HR/9 | GB/F | $1L | $2L | Pts | RAA | H% | HR/fb | S% | FIP | GS | CG | QS/DS | GR | Hld | Bln | Lead | OPS | 1st Hf | 2nd Hf | vs RH | vs LH |
|---|---|---|---|---|---|---|---|---|---|---|---|---|---|---|---|---|---|---|---|---|---|---|---|---|---|---|---|---|---|---|---|---|---|
| 07 | BOS | 20 | 7 | 0 | 200 | 189 | 194 | 3.27 | 1.14 | 8.7 | 1.8 | 0.8 | 1.3 | $25 | $17 | 410 | +23 | 31% | 8% | 74% | 3.07 | 30 | 1 | 20/1 | — | — | — | — | .663 | .655 | .671 | .641 | .684 |
| 08 | BOS | 12 | 10 | 0 | 174 | 173 | 172 | 4.03 | 1.19 | 8.9 | 1.8 | 0.9 | 1.2 | $13 | $5 | 280 | +6 | 32% | 11% | 68% | 3.25 | 27 | 1 | 16/3 | — | — | — | — | .700 | .687 | .722 | .687 | .710 |
| 09 | BOS | 17 | 6 | 0 | 212 | 198 | 199 | 3.86 | 1.19 | 8.4 | 2.3 | 1.1 | 1.5 | $19 | $10 | 360 | +6 | 29% | 13% | 71% | 3.73 | 32 | 4 | 20/4 | — | — | — | — | .691 | .634 | .763 | .683 | .696 |
| 10 | BOS | 6 | 6 | 0 | 127 | 151 | 116 | 5.78 | 1.54 | 8.2 | 3.2 | 1.4 | 1.3 | -$6 | -$26 | 120 | −26 | 34% | 14% | 65% | 4.58 | 21 | 0 | 10/6 | — | — | — | — | .848 | .887 | .826 | .726 | .940 |

## Erik Bedard — 20 IP | $0 | 30 pts

No MLB games played in 2010    Owned: 38%    LH

Bedard did not throw a major-league pitch in 2010, so it's unlikely that Seattle will pick up his $8M club option for 2011. However, if both parties remain interested, he could be back in 2011 on a (cheap) one-year deal. (GC)

### Forecast

| Player | Age | IP | W | Sv | K | ERA | WHIP | K/9 | BB/9 | $2L | Pts |
|---|---|---|---|---|---|---|---|---|---|---|---|
| Bedard E | 32 | 20 | 1 | 0 | 19 | 3.68 | 1.27 | 8.6 | 3.6 | $0 | 30 |
| Mini-Browser | Age | IP | W | Sv | K | ERA | WHIP | K/9 | BB/9 | $2L | Pts |
| Jepsen K | 26 | 40 | 1 | 4 | 38 | 4.50 | 1.52 | 8.6 | 4.6 | $0 | 60 |
| Litsch J | 26 | 80 | 4 | 0 | 42 | 4.93 | 1.33 | 4.8 | 2.3 | $0 | 60 |
| Duchscherer J | 33 | 20 | 1 | 0 | 13 | 3.40 | 1.21 | 5.9 | 3.7 | $0 | 30 |
| Slaten D | 31 | 40 | 2 | 0 | 33 | 3.92 | 1.37 | 7.5 | 3.7 | $0 | 50 |
| Bulger J | 32 | 40 | 2 | 0 | 44 | 4.22 | 1.46 | 9.8 | 5.0 | $0 | 50 |

### Competition at SP — Stats in 2010 as SP

| Thr | Player | GS | ERA | Supp | W-L |
|---|---|---|---|---|---|
| RH | Hernandez F | 34 | 2.27 | 3.1 | 13-12 |
| LH | Vargas J | 31 | 3.78 | 3.1 | 9-12 |
| RH | Fister D | 28 | 4.11 | 3.1 | 6-14 |
| LH | Rowland-Smith R | 20 | 6.93 | 3.0 | 1-10 |

Ten-Year Trends □ K/9 ○ BB/9

### Minors (2010)

| Level | Leag | W | L | Sv | IP | H | K | ERA | WHIP | K/9 | BB/9 | HR/9 | GB/F |
|---|---|---|---|---|---|---|---|---|---|---|---|---|---|
| A | — | — | — | — | — | — | — | — | — | — | — | — | — |
| AA | — | — | — | — | — | — | — | — | — | — | — | — | — |
| AAA | — | — | — | — | — | — | — | — | — | — | — | — | — |

### Majors

| Yr | Team | W | L | Sv | IP | H | K | ERA | WHIP | K/9 | BB/9 | HR/9 | GB/F | $1L | $2L | Pts | RAA | H% | HR/fb | S% | FIP | GS | CG | QS/DS | GR | Hld | Bln | Lead | OPS | 1st Hf | 2nd Hf | vs RH | vs LH |
|---|---|---|---|---|---|---|---|---|---|---|---|---|---|---|---|---|---|---|---|---|---|---|---|---|---|---|---|---|---|---|---|---|---|
| 07 | BAL | 13 | 5 | 0 | 182 | 141 | 221 | 3.16 | 1.09 | 10.9 | 2.8 | 0.9 | 1.4 | $24 | $18 | 370 | +24 | 29% | 12% | 75% | 3.17 | 28 | 1 | 21/3 | — | — | — | — | .615 | .641 | .558 | .594 | .696 |
| 08 | SEA | 6 | 4 | 0 | 81 | 70 | 72 | 3.67 | 1.32 | 8.0 | 4.1 | 1.0 | 0.9 | $4 | $0 | 130 | +2 | 27% | 9% | 76% | 4.34 | 15 | 0 | 7/3 | — | — | — | — | .697 | .697 | — | .663 | .794 |
| 09 | SEA | 5 | 3 | 0 | 83 | 65 | 90 | 2.82 | 1.19 | 9.8 | 3.7 | 0.9 | 1.0 | $8 | $5 | 150 | +12 | 28% | 9% | 80% | 3.61 | 15 | 0 | 6/0 | — | — | — | — | .627 | .618 | .706 | .618 | .648 |
| 10 | — | | | | | | | | | | | | | | | | | | | | | | | | | | | | — | — | — | — | — |

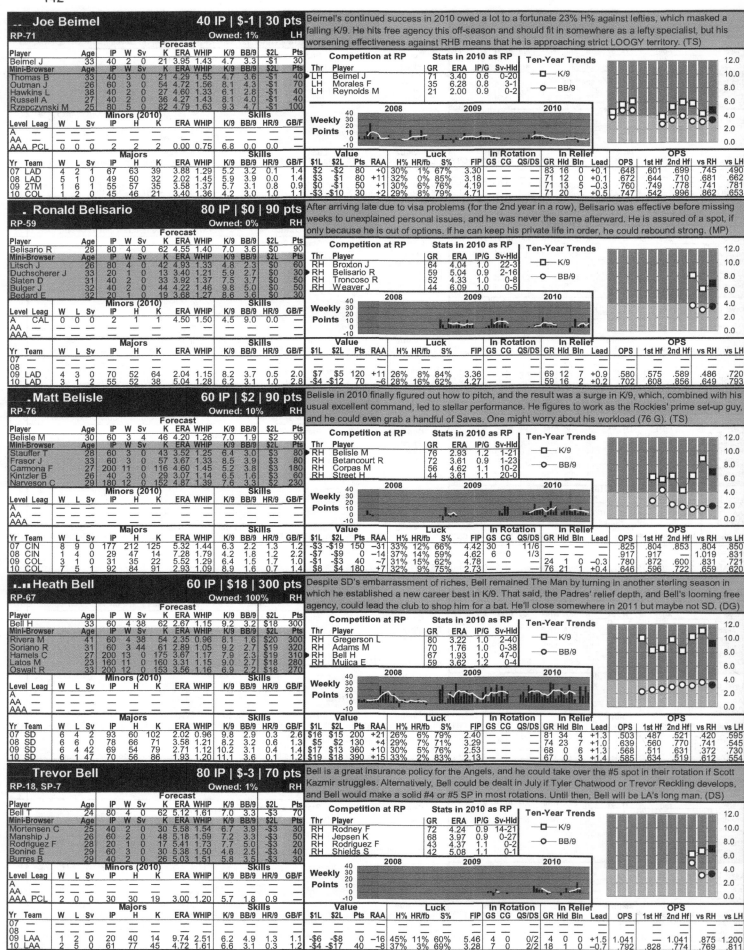

## Joe Beimel — 40 IP | $-1 | 30 pts

RP-71 — Owned: 1% — LH

Beimel's continued success in 2010 owed a lot to a fortunate 23% H% against lefties, which masked a falling K/9. He hits free agency this off-season and should fit in somewhere as a lefty specialist, but his worsening effectiveness against RHB means that he is approaching strict LOOGY territory. (TS)

**Forecast**

| Player | Age | IP | W | Sv | K | ERA | WHIP | K/9 | BB/9 | $2L | Pts |
|---|---|---|---|---|---|---|---|---|---|---|---|
| Beimel J | 33 | 40 | 2 | 0 | 21 | 3.95 | 1.43 | 4.7 | 3.3 | -$1 | 30 |
| **Mini-Browser** | **Age** | **IP** | **W** | **Sv** | **K** | **ERA** | **WHIP** | **K/9** | **BB/9** | **$2L** | **Pts** |
| Thomas B | 33 | 40 | 3 | 0 | 21 | 4.29 | 1.55 | 4.7 | 3.6 | -$1 | 40 |
| Outman J | 26 | 60 | 3 | 0 | 54 | 4.72 | 1.56 | 8.1 | 4.3 | -$1 | 70 |
| Hawkins L | 38 | 40 | 2 | 0 | 27 | 4.60 | 1.33 | 6.1 | 2.8 | -$1 | 40 |
| Russell A | 27 | 40 | 2 | 0 | 36 | 4.27 | 1.43 | 8.1 | 4.0 | -$1 | 40 |
| Rzepczynski M | 25 | 80 | 5 | 0 | 82 | 4.79 | 1.63 | 9.3 | 4.7 | -$1 | 100 |

**Competition at RP — Stats in 2010 as RP**

| Thr | Player | GR | ERA | IP/G | Sv-Hld |
|---|---|---|---|---|---|
| LH | Beimel J | 71 | 3.40 | 0.6 | 0-20 |
| LH | Morales F | 35 | 6.28 | 0.8 | 3-1 |
| LH | Reynolds M | 21 | 2.00 | 0.9 | 0-2 |

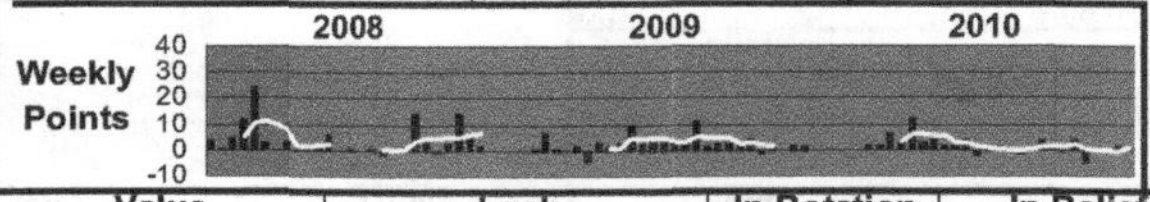

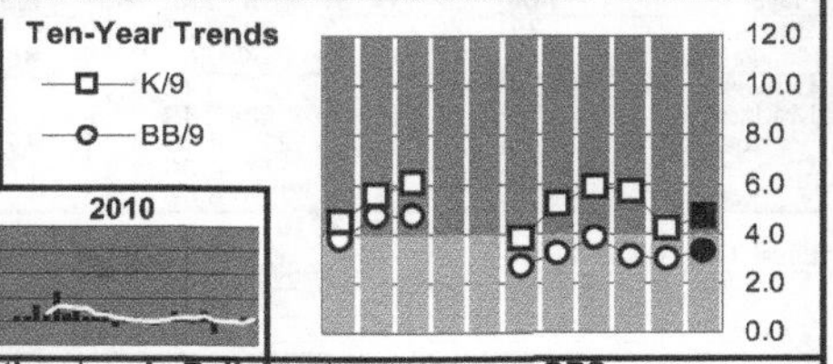

**Minors (2010)**

| Level | Leag | W | L | Sv | IP | H | K | ERA | WHIP | K/9 | BB/9 | HR/9 | GB/F |
|---|---|---|---|---|---|---|---|---|---|---|---|---|---|
| A | — | — | — | — | — | — | — | — | — | — | — | — | — |
| AA | — | — | — | — | — | — | — | — | — | — | — | — | — |
| AAA | PCL | 0 | 0 | 0 | 2 | 2 | 2 | 0.00 | 0.75 | 6.8 | 0.0 | 0.0 | — |

**Majors**

| Yr | Team | W | L | Sv | IP | H | K | ERA | WHIP | K/9 | BB/9 | HR/9 | GB/F | $1L | $2L | Pts | RAA | H% | HR/fb | S% | FIP | GS | CG | QS/DS | GR | Hld | Bln | Lead | OPS | 1st Hf | 2nd Hf | vs RH | vs LH |
|---|---|---|---|---|---|---|---|---|---|---|---|---|---|---|---|---|---|---|---|---|---|---|---|---|---|---|---|---|---|---|---|---|---|
| 07 | LAD | 4 | 2 | 1 | 67 | 63 | 39 | 3.88 | 1.29 | 5.2 | 3.2 | 0.1 | 1.4 | $2 | -$2 | 80 | +0 | 30% | 1% | 67% | 3.30 | — | — | — | 83 | 16 | 0 | +0.1 | .648 | .601 | .699 | .745 | .490 |
| 08 | LAD | 5 | 1 | 0 | 49 | 50 | 32 | 2.02 | 1.45 | 5.9 | 3.9 | 0.0 | 1.4 | $3 | $1 | 80 | +11 | 32% | 0% | 85% | 3.18 | — | — | — | 71 | 12 | 0 | +0.1 | .672 | .644 | .710 | .681 | .662 |
| 09 | 2TM | 1 | 6 | 1 | 55 | 57 | 35 | 3.58 | 1.37 | 5.7 | 3.1 | 0.8 | 0.9 | $0 | -$1 | 50 | +1 | 30% | 6% | 76% | 4.19 | — | — | — | 71 | 13 | 5 | −0.3 | .760 | .749 | .778 | .741 | .781 |
| 10 | COL | 1 | 2 | 0 | 45 | 46 | 21 | 3.40 | 1.36 | 4.2 | 3.0 | 1.0 | 1.1 | -$3 | -$10 | 30 | +2 | 29% | 8% | 79% | 4.71 | — | — | — | 71 | 20 | 1 | +0.5 | .747 | .542 | .996 | .862 | .653 |

## Ronald Belisario — 80 IP | $0 | 90 pts

RP-59 — Owned: 0% — RH

After arriving late due to visa problems (for the 2nd year in a row), Belisario was effective before missing weeks to unexplained personal issues, and he was never the same afterward. He is assured of a spot, if only because he is out of options. If he can keep his private life in order, he could rebound strong. (MP)

**Forecast**

| Player | Age | IP | W | Sv | K | ERA | WHIP | K/9 | BB/9 | $2L | Pts |
|---|---|---|---|---|---|---|---|---|---|---|---|
| Belisario R | 28 | 80 | 4 | 0 | 62 | 4.55 | 1.40 | 7.0 | 3.6 | $0 | 90 |
| **Mini-Browser** | **Age** | **IP** | **W** | **Sv** | **K** | **ERA** | **WHIP** | **K/9** | **BB/9** | **$2L** | **Pts** |
| Litsch J | 26 | 80 | 4 | 0 | 42 | 4.93 | 1.33 | 4.8 | 2.3 | $0 | 60 |
| Duchscherer J | 33 | 20 | 1 | 0 | 13 | 3.40 | 1.21 | 5.9 | 2.7 | $0 | 30 |
| Slaten D | 31 | 40 | 2 | 0 | 33 | 3.92 | 1.37 | 7.5 | 3.7 | $0 | 50 |
| Bulger J | 32 | 40 | 2 | 0 | 44 | 4.22 | 1.46 | 9.8 | 5.0 | $0 | 50 |
| Bedard E | 32 | 20 | 1 | 0 | 19 | 3.68 | 1.27 | 8.6 | 3.6 | $0 | 30 |

**Competition at RP — Stats in 2010 as RP**

| Thr | Player | GR | ERA | IP/G | Sv-Hld |
|---|---|---|---|---|---|
| RH | Broxton J | 64 | 4.04 | 1.0 | 22-3 |
| RH | Belisario R | 59 | 5.04 | 0.9 | 2-16 |
| RH | Troncoso R | 52 | 4.33 | 1.0 | 0-8 |
| RH | Weaver J | 44 | 6.09 | 1.0 | 0-5 |

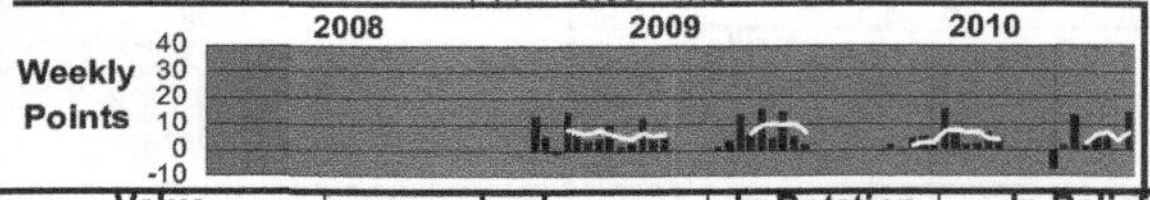

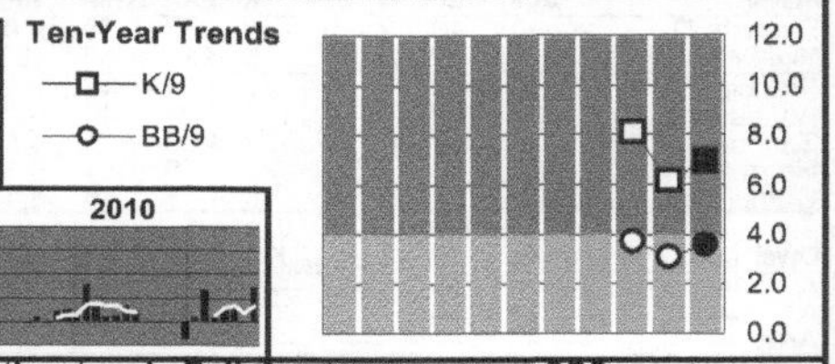

**Minors (2010)**

| Level | Leag | W | L | Sv | IP | H | K | ERA | WHIP | K/9 | BB/9 | HR/9 | GB/F |
|---|---|---|---|---|---|---|---|---|---|---|---|---|---|
| A | CAL | 0 | 0 | 0 | 2 | 1 | 1 | 4.50 | 1.50 | 4.5 | 9.0 | 0.0 | — |
| AA | — | — | — | — | — | — | — | — | — | — | — | — | — |
| AAA | — | — | — | — | — | — | — | — | — | — | — | — | — |

**Majors**

| Yr | Team | W | L | Sv | IP | H | K | ERA | WHIP | K/9 | BB/9 | HR/9 | GB/F | $1L | $2L | Pts | RAA | H% | HR/fb | S% | FIP | GS | CG | QS/DS | GR | Hld | Bln | Lead | OPS | 1st Hf | 2nd Hf | vs RH | vs LH |
|---|---|---|---|---|---|---|---|---|---|---|---|---|---|---|---|---|---|---|---|---|---|---|---|---|---|---|---|---|---|---|---|---|---|
| 07 | — | — | — | — | — | — | — | — | — | — | — | — | — | — | — | — | — | — | — | — | — | — | — | — | — | — | — | — | — | — | — | — | — |
| 08 | — | — | — | — | — | — | — | — | — | — | — | — | — | — | — | — | — | — | — | — | — | — | — | — | — | — | — | — | — | — | — | — | — |
| 09 | LAD | 4 | 3 | 0 | 70 | 52 | 64 | 2.04 | 1.15 | 8.2 | 3.7 | 0.5 | 2.0 | $7 | $5 | 120 | +11 | 26% | 8% | 84% | 3.36 | — | — | — | 69 | 12 | 7 | +0.9 | .580 | .575 | .589 | .486 | .720 |
| 10 | LAD | 3 | 1 | 2 | 55 | 52 | 38 | 5.04 | 1.28 | 6.2 | 3.1 | 1.0 | 2.8 | -$4 | -$12 | 70 | −6 | 28% | 16% | 62% | 4.27 | — | — | — | 59 | 16 | 2 | +0.2 | .702 | .608 | .856 | .649 | .793 |

## Matt Belisle — 60 IP | $2 | 90 pts

RP-76 — Owned: 10% — RH

Belisle in 2010 finally figured out how to pitch, and the result was a surge in K/9, which, combined with his usual excellent command, led to stellar performance. He figures to work as the Rockies' prime set-up guy, and he could even grab a handful of Saves. One might worry about his workload (76 G). (TS)

**Forecast**

| Player | Age | IP | W | Sv | K | ERA | WHIP | K/9 | BB/9 | $2L | Pts |
|---|---|---|---|---|---|---|---|---|---|---|---|
| Belisle M | 30 | 60 | 3 | 4 | 46 | 4.20 | 1.26 | 7.0 | 1.9 | $2 | 90 |
| **Mini-Browser** | **Age** | **IP** | **W** | **Sv** | **K** | **ERA** | **WHIP** | **K/9** | **BB/9** | **$2L** | **Pts** |
| Stauffer T | 28 | 60 | 3 | 0 | 43 | 3.52 | 1.25 | 6.4 | 3.0 | $3 | 80 |
| Frasor J | 33 | 60 | 3 | 0 | 57 | 3.67 | 1.33 | 8.5 | 3.9 | $3 | 80 |
| Carmona F | 27 | 200 | 11 | 0 | 116 | 4.60 | 1.45 | 5.2 | 3.8 | $3 | 180 |
| Kintzler B | 26 | 40 | 3 | 0 | 29 | 3.07 | 1.14 | 6.5 | 1.6 | $3 | 60 |
| Narveson C | 29 | 180 | 12 | 0 | 152 | 4.87 | 1.39 | 7.6 | 3.3 | $2 | 230 |

**Competition at RP — Stats in 2010 as RP**

| Thr | Player | GR | ERA | IP/G | Sv-Hld |
|---|---|---|---|---|---|
| RH | Belisle M | 76 | 2.93 | 1.2 | 1-21 |
| RH | Betancourt R | 72 | 3.61 | 0.9 | 1-23 |
| RH | Corpas M | 56 | 4.62 | 1.1 | 10-2 |
| RH | Street H | 44 | 3.61 | 1.1 | 20-0 |

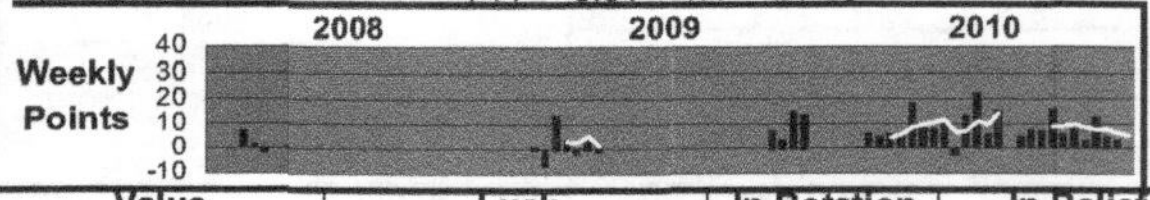

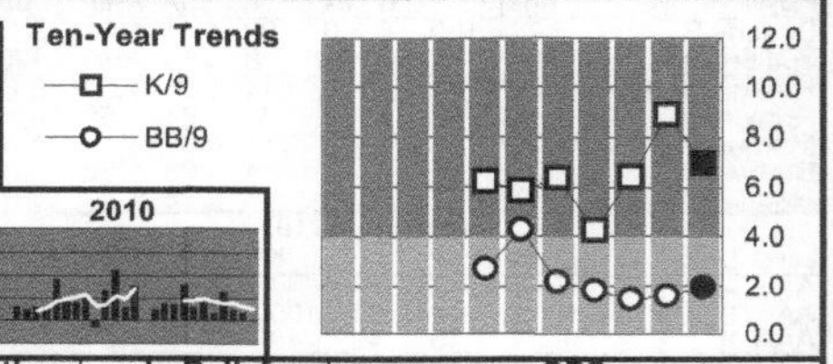

**Minors (2010)**

| Level | Leag | W | L | Sv | IP | H | K | ERA | WHIP | K/9 | BB/9 | HR/9 | GB/F |
|---|---|---|---|---|---|---|---|---|---|---|---|---|---|
| A | — | — | — | — | — | — | — | — | — | — | — | — | — |
| AA | — | — | — | — | — | — | — | — | — | — | — | — | — |
| AAA | — | — | — | — | — | — | — | — | — | — | — | — | — |

**Majors**

| Yr | Team | W | L | Sv | IP | H | K | ERA | WHIP | K/9 | BB/9 | HR/9 | GB/F | $1L | $2L | Pts | RAA | H% | HR/fb | S% | FIP | GS | CG | QS/DS | GR | Hld | Bln | Lead | OPS | 1st Hf | 2nd Hf | vs RH | vs LH |
|---|---|---|---|---|---|---|---|---|---|---|---|---|---|---|---|---|---|---|---|---|---|---|---|---|---|---|---|---|---|---|---|---|---|
| 07 | CIN | 8 | 9 | 0 | 177 | 212 | 125 | 5.32 | 1.44 | 6.3 | 2.2 | 1.3 | 1.2 | -$3 | -$19 | 150 | −31 | 33% | 12% | 66% | 4.42 | 30 | 1 | 11/6 | — | — | — | — | .825 | .804 | .853 | .804 | .850 |
| 08 | CIN | 1 | 4 | 0 | 29 | 47 | 14 | 7.28 | 1.72 | 4.2 | 1.8 | 1.2 | 2.2 | -$7 | -$9 | 0 | −14 | 37% | 14% | 59% | 4.62 | 6 | 0 | 1/3 | — | — | — | — | .917 | .917 | — | 1.019 | .831 |
| 09 | COL | 3 | 1 | 0 | 31 | 35 | 22 | 5.52 | 1.29 | 6.4 | 1.5 | 1.7 | 1.0 | -$1 | -$3 | 40 | −7 | 31% | 15% | 62% | 4.78 | — | — | — | 24 | 1 | 0 | −0.3 | .780 | .872 | .600 | .831 | .721 |
| 10 | COL | 7 | 5 | 1 | 92 | 84 | 91 | 2.93 | 1.09 | 8.9 | 1.6 | 0.7 | 1.4 | $8 | $4 | 180 | +7 | 32% | 9% | 75% | 2.73 | — | — | — | 76 | 21 | 1 | +0.4 | .646 | .596 | .722 | .659 | .620 |

## Heath Bell — 60 IP | $18 | 300 pts

RP-67 — Owned: 100% — RH

Despite SD's embarrassment of riches, Bell remained The Man by turning in another sterling season in which he established a new career best in K/9. That said, the Padres' relief depth, and Bell's looming free agency, could lead the club to shop him for a bat. He'll close somewhere in 2011 but maybe not SD. (DG)

**Forecast**

| Player | Age | IP | W | Sv | K | ERA | WHIP | K/9 | BB/9 | $2L | Pts |
|---|---|---|---|---|---|---|---|---|---|---|---|
| Bell H | 33 | 60 | 4 | 38 | 62 | 2.67 | 1.15 | 9.2 | 3.2 | $18 | 300 |
| **Mini-Browser** | **Age** | **IP** | **W** | **Sv** | **K** | **ERA** | **WHIP** | **K/9** | **BB/9** | **$2L** | **Pts** |
| Rivera M | 41 | 60 | 4 | 38 | 54 | 2.35 | 0.96 | 8.1 | 1.6 | $20 | 300 |
| Soriano R | 31 | 60 | 3 | 44 | 61 | 2.89 | 1.05 | 9.2 | 2.7 | $19 | 320 |
| Hamels C | 27 | 200 | 13 | 0 | 175 | 3.67 | 1.17 | 7.9 | 2.3 | $19 | 310 |
| Latos M | 23 | 160 | 11 | 0 | 160 | 3.31 | 1.15 | 9.0 | 2.7 | $18 | 280 |
| Oswalt R | 33 | 200 | 12 | 0 | 153 | 3.56 | 1.16 | 6.9 | 2.2 | $18 | 270 |

**Competition at RP — Stats in 2010 as RP**

| Thr | Player | GR | ERA | IP/G | Sv-Hld |
|---|---|---|---|---|---|
| RH | Gregerson L | 80 | 3.22 | 1.0 | 2-40 |
| RH | Adams M | 70 | 1.76 | 1.0 | 0-38 |
| RH | Bell H | 67 | 1.93 | 1.0 | 47-0 |
| RH | Mujica E | 59 | 3.62 | 1.2 | 0-4 |

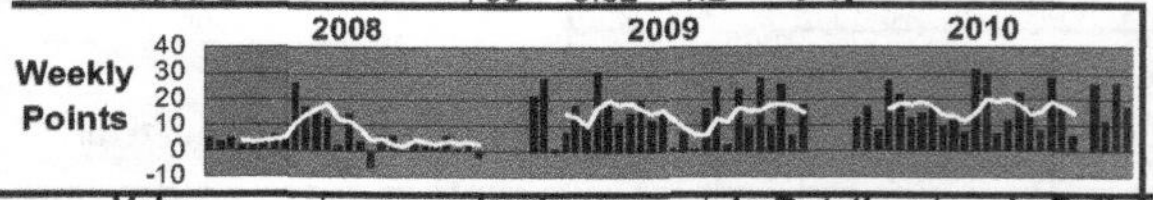

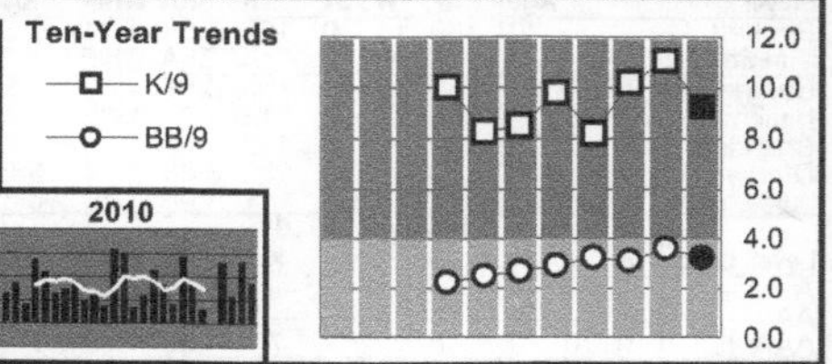

**Minors (2010)**

| Level | Leag | W | L | Sv | IP | H | K | ERA | WHIP | K/9 | BB/9 | HR/9 | GB/F |
|---|---|---|---|---|---|---|---|---|---|---|---|---|---|
| A | — | — | — | — | — | — | — | — | — | — | — | — | — |
| AA | — | — | — | — | — | — | — | — | — | — | — | — | — |
| AAA | — | — | — | — | — | — | — | — | — | — | — | — | — |

**Majors**

| Yr | Team | W | L | Sv | IP | H | K | ERA | WHIP | K/9 | BB/9 | HR/9 | GB/F | $1L | $2L | Pts | RAA | H% | HR/fb | S% | FIP | GS | CG | QS/DS | GR | Hld | Bln | Lead | OPS | 1st Hf | 2nd Hf | vs RH | vs LH |
|---|---|---|---|---|---|---|---|---|---|---|---|---|---|---|---|---|---|---|---|---|---|---|---|---|---|---|---|---|---|---|---|---|---|
| 07 | SD | 6 | 4 | 2 | 93 | 60 | 102 | 2.02 | 0.96 | 9.8 | 2.9 | 0.3 | 2.6 | $16 | $15 | 200 | +21 | 26% | 6% | 79% | 2.40 | — | — | — | 81 | 34 | 4 | +1.3 | .503 | .487 | .521 | .420 | .595 |
| 08 | SD | 6 | 6 | 0 | 78 | 66 | 71 | 3.58 | 1.21 | 8.2 | 3.2 | 0.6 | 1.3 | $5 | $2 | 130 | +4 | 29% | 7% | 71% | 3.29 | — | — | — | 74 | 23 | 7 | +1.0 | .639 | .560 | .770 | .741 | .545 |
| 09 | SD | 6 | 4 | 42 | 69 | 54 | 79 | 2.71 | 1.12 | 10.2 | 3.1 | 0.4 | 1.4 | $17 | $13 | 360 | +10 | 30% | 5% | 76% | 2.53 | — | — | — | 68 | 0 | 6 | +1.3 | .568 | .511 | .631 | .372 | .730 |
| 10 | SD | 6 | 1 | 47 | 70 | 56 | 86 | 1.93 | 1.20 | 11.1 | 3.6 | 0.1 | 1.2 | $19 | $18 | 390 | +15 | 33% | 2% | 83% | 2.13 | — | — | — | 67 | 0 | 3 | +1.4 | .585 | .634 | .519 | .612 | .554 |

## Trevor Bell — 80 IP | $-3 | 70 pts

RP-18, SP-7 — Owned: 1% — RH

Bell is a great insurance policy for the Angels, and he could take over the #5 spot in their rotation if Scott Kazmir struggles. Alternatively, Bell could be dealt in July if Tyler Chatwood or Trevor Reckling develops, and Bell would make a solid #4 or #5 SP in most rotations. Until then, Bell will be LA's long man. (DS)

**Forecast**

| Player | Age | IP | W | Sv | K | ERA | WHIP | K/9 | BB/9 | $2L | Pts |
|---|---|---|---|---|---|---|---|---|---|---|---|
| Bell T | 24 | 80 | 4 | 0 | 62 | 5.12 | 1.61 | 7.0 | 3.3 | -$3 | 70 |
| **Mini-Browser** | **Age** | **IP** | **W** | **Sv** | **K** | **ERA** | **WHIP** | **K/9** | **BB/9** | **$2L** | **Pts** |
| Mortensen C | 25 | 40 | 2 | 0 | 30 | 5.58 | 1.54 | 6.7 | 3.9 | -$3 | 30 |
| Manship J | 26 | 60 | 2 | 0 | 48 | 5.18 | 1.59 | 7.2 | 3.3 | -$3 | 50 |
| Rodriguez F | 28 | 20 | 1 | 0 | 17 | 5.41 | 1.73 | 7.7 | 5.0 | -$3 | 20 |
| Bonine E | 29 | 60 | 3 | 0 | 30 | 5.38 | 1.50 | 4.6 | 2.5 | -$3 | 40 |
| Burres B | 29 | 40 | 2 | 0 | 26 | 5.03 | 1.51 | 5.8 | 3.5 | -$3 | 30 |

**Competition at RP — Stats in 2010 as RP**

| Thr | Player | GR | ERA | IP/G | Sv-Hld |
|---|---|---|---|---|---|
| RH | Rodney F | 72 | 4.24 | 0.9 | 14-21 |
| RH | Jepsen K | 68 | 3.97 | 0.9 | 0-27 |
| RH | Rodriguez F | 43 | 4.37 | 1.1 | 0-2 |
| RH | Shields S | 42 | 5.08 | 1.1 | 0-1 |

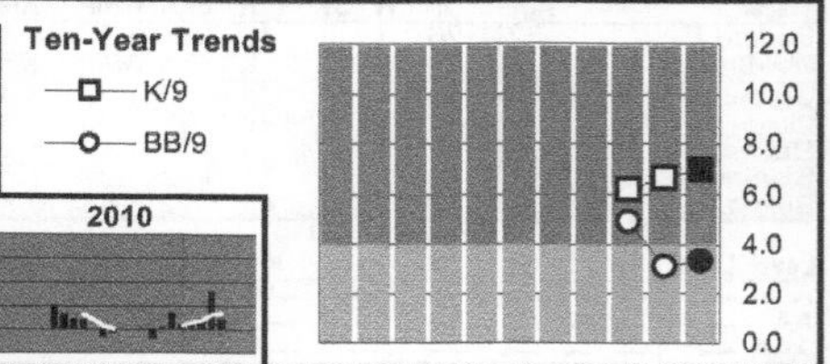

**Minors (2010)**

| Level | Leag | W | L | Sv | IP | H | K | ERA | WHIP | K/9 | BB/9 | HR/9 | GB/F |
|---|---|---|---|---|---|---|---|---|---|---|---|---|---|
| A | — | — | — | — | — | — | — | — | — | — | — | — | — |
| AA | — | — | — | — | — | — | — | — | — | — | — | — | — |
| AAA | PCL | 2 | 0 | 0 | 30 | 30 | 19 | 3.00 | 1.20 | 5.7 | 1.8 | 0.9 | — |

**Majors**

| Yr | Team | W | L | Sv | IP | H | K | ERA | WHIP | K/9 | BB/9 | HR/9 | GB/F | $1L | $2L | Pts | RAA | H% | HR/fb | S% | FIP | GS | CG | QS/DS | GR | Hld | Bln | Lead | OPS | 1st Hf | 2nd Hf | vs RH | vs LH |
|---|---|---|---|---|---|---|---|---|---|---|---|---|---|---|---|---|---|---|---|---|---|---|---|---|---|---|---|---|---|---|---|---|---|
| 07 | — | — | — | — | — | — | — | — | — | — | — | — | — | — | — | — | — | — | — | — | — | — | — | — | — | — | — | — | — | — | — | — | — |
| 08 | — | — | — | — | — | — | — | — | — | — | — | — | — | — | — | — | — | — | — | — | — | — | — | — | — | — | — | — | — | — | — | — | — |
| 09 | LAA | 1 | 2 | 0 | 20 | 40 | 14 | 9.74 | 2.51 | 6.2 | 4.9 | 1.3 | 1.1 | -$6 | -$8 | 0 | −16 | 45% | 11% | 60% | 5.46 | 4 | 0 | 0/2 | 4 | 0 | 0 | +1.5 | 1.041 | — | 1.041 | .875 | 1.200 |
| 10 | LAA | 2 | 5 | 0 | 61 | 77 | 45 | 4.72 | 1.61 | 6.6 | 3.1 | 0.3 | 1.2 | -$4 | -$17 | 40 | −8 | 37% | 3% | 69% | 3.28 | 7 | 0 | 2/2 | 18 | 1 | 0 | −0.7 | .792 | .828 | .774 | .769 | .811 |

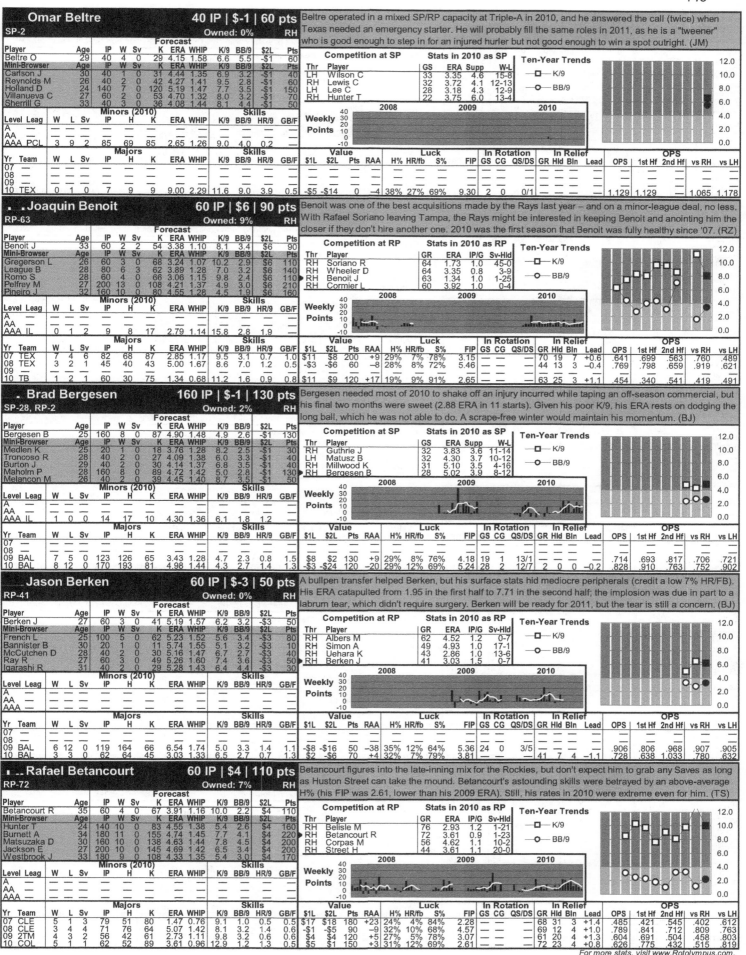

## Omar Beltre — 40 IP | $-1 | 60 pts
**SP-2** — Owned: 0% — RH

Beltre operated in a mixed SP/RP capacity at Triple-A in 2010, and he answered the call (twice) when Texas needed an emergency starter. He will probably fill the same roles in 2011, as he is a "tweener" who is good enough to step in for an injured hurler but not good enough to win a spot outright. (JM)

### Forecast
| Player | Age | IP | W | Sv | K | ERA | WHIP | K/9 | BB/9 | $2L | Pts |
|---|---|---|---|---|---|---|---|---|---|---|---|
| Beltre O | 29 | 40 | 4 | 0 | 29 | 4.15 | 1.58 | 6.6 | 5.5 | -$1 | 60 |
| **Mini-Browser** | **Age** | **IP** | **W** | **Sv** | **K** | **ERA** | **WHIP** | **K/9** | **BB/9** | **$2L** | **Pts** |
| Carlson J | 30 | 40 | 1 | 0 | 31 | 4.44 | 1.35 | 6.9 | 3.2 | -$1 | 40 |
| Reynolds M | 26 | 40 | 2 | 0 | 42 | 4.27 | 1.41 | 9.5 | 2.8 | -$1 | 60 |
| Holland D | 24 | 140 | 7 | 0 | 120 | 5.19 | 1.47 | 7.7 | 3.5 | -$1 | 150 |
| Villanueva C | 27 | 60 | 2 | 0 | 53 | 4.70 | 1.32 | 8.0 | 3.2 | -$1 | 70 |
| Sherrill G | 33 | 40 | 3 | 0 | 36 | 4.08 | 1.44 | 8.1 | 4.4 | -$1 | 50 |

### Minors (2010)
| Level Leag | W | L | Sv | IP | H | K | ERA | WHIP | K/9 | BB/9 | HR/9 | GB/F |
|---|---|---|---|---|---|---|---|---|---|---|---|---|
| A — | | | | | | | | | | | | |
| AA — | | | | | | | | | | | | |
| AAA PCL | 3 | 9 | 2 | 85 | 69 | 85 | 2.65 | 1.26 | 9.0 | 4.0 | 0.2 | — |

### Majors
| Yr Team | W | L | Sv | IP | H | K | ERA | WHIP | K/9 | BB/9 | HR/9 | GB/F |
|---|---|---|---|---|---|---|---|---|---|---|---|---|
| 07 — | | | | | | | | | | | | |
| 08 — | | | | | | | | | | | | |
| 09 — | | | | | | | | | | | | |
| 10 TEX | 0 | 1 | 0 | 7 | 9 | 9 | 9.00 | 2.29 | 11.6 | 9.0 | 3.9 | 0.5 |

### Competition at SP — Stats in 2010 as SP
| Thr | Player | GS | ERA | Supp | W-L |
|---|---|---|---|---|---|
| LH | Wilson C | 33 | 3.35 | 4.6 | 15-8 |
| RH | Lewis C | 32 | 3.72 | 4.1 | 12-13 |
| LH | Lee C | 28 | 3.18 | 4.3 | 12-9 |
| RH | Hunter T | 22 | 3.75 | 6.0 | 13-4 |

### Value / Luck / In Rotation / In Relief / OPS
| $1L | $2L | Pts | RAA | H% | HR/fb | S% | FIP | GS | CG | QS/DS | GR | Hld | Bln | Lead | OPS | 1st Hf | 2nd Hf | vs RH | vs LH |
|---|---|---|---|---|---|---|---|---|---|---|---|---|---|---|---|---|---|---|---|
| -$5 | -$14 | 0 | -4 | 38% | 27% | 69% | 9.30 | 2 | 0 | 0/1 | — | — | — | — | 1.129 | 1.129 | — | 1.065 | 1.178 |

---

## Joaquin Benoit — 60 IP | $6 | 90 pts
**RP-63** — Owned: 9% — RH

Benoit was one of the best acquisitions made by the Rays last year – and on a minor-league deal, no less. With Rafael Soriano leaving Tampa, the Rays might be interested in keeping Benoit and anointing him the closer if they don't hire another one. 2010 was the first season that Benoit was fully healthy since '07. (RZ)

### Forecast
| Player | Age | IP | W | Sv | K | ERA | WHIP | K/9 | BB/9 | $2L | Pts |
|---|---|---|---|---|---|---|---|---|---|---|---|
| Benoit J | 33 | 60 | 2 | 2 | 54 | 3.38 | 1.10 | 8.1 | 3.4 | $6 | 90 |
| **Mini-Browser** | **Age** | **IP** | **W** | **Sv** | **K** | **ERA** | **WHIP** | **K/9** | **BB/9** | **$2L** | **Pts** |
| Gregerson L | 26 | 60 | 3 | 0 | 68 | 3.24 | 1.07 | 10.2 | 2.9 | $6 | 110 |
| League B | 28 | 80 | 6 | 3 | 62 | 3.89 | 1.28 | 7.0 | 3.2 | $6 | 140 |
| Romo S | 28 | 60 | 4 | 0 | 66 | 3.06 | 1.15 | 9.8 | 2.4 | $6 | 110 |
| Pelfrey M | 27 | 200 | 13 | 0 | 108 | 4.21 | 1.37 | 4.9 | 3.0 | $6 | 210 |
| Pineiro J | 32 | 160 | 10 | 0 | 80 | 4.55 | 1.28 | 4.5 | 1.9 | $6 | 160 |

### Minors (2010)
| Level Leag | W | L | Sv | IP | H | K | ERA | WHIP | K/9 | BB/9 | HR/9 | GB/F |
|---|---|---|---|---|---|---|---|---|---|---|---|---|
| A — | | | | | | | | | | | | |
| AA — | | | | | | | | | | | | |
| AAA IL | 0 | 1 | 2 | 9 | 8 | 17 | 2.79 | 1.14 | 15.8 | 2.8 | 1.9 | — |

### Majors
| Yr Team | W | L | Sv | IP | H | K | ERA | WHIP | K/9 | BB/9 | HR/9 | GB/F |
|---|---|---|---|---|---|---|---|---|---|---|---|---|
| 07 TEX | 7 | 4 | 6 | 82 | 68 | 87 | 2.85 | 1.17 | 9.5 | 3.1 | 0.7 | 1.0 |
| 08 TEX | 3 | 2 | 1 | 45 | 40 | 43 | 5.00 | 1.67 | 8.6 | 7.0 | 1.2 | 0.5 |
| 09 — | | | | | | | | | | | | |
| 10 TB | 1 | 2 | 1 | 60 | 30 | 75 | 1.34 | 0.68 | 11.2 | 1.6 | 1.0 | 0.8 |

### Competition at RP — Stats in 2010 as RP
| Thr | Player | GR | ERA | IP/G | Sv-Hld |
|---|---|---|---|---|---|
| RH | Soriano R | 64 | 1.73 | 1.0 | 45-0 |
| RH | Wheeler D | 64 | 3.35 | 0.8 | 3-9 |
| RH | Benoit J | 63 | 1.34 | 1.0 | 1-25 |
| RH | Cormier L | 60 | 3.92 | 1.0 | 0-4 |

### Value / Luck / In Rotation / In Relief / OPS
| $1L | $2L | Pts | RAA | H% | HR/fb | S% | FIP | GS | CG | QS/DS | GR | Hld | Bln | Lead | OPS | 1st Hf | 2nd Hf | vs RH | vs LH |
|---|---|---|---|---|---|---|---|---|---|---|---|---|---|---|---|---|---|---|---|
| $11 | $8 | 200 | +9 | 29% | 7% | 78% | 3.15 | — | — | — | 70 | 19 | 7 | +0.6 | .641 | .699 | .563 | .760 | .489 |
| -$3 | -$6 | 60 | -8 | 28% | 8% | 72% | 5.46 | — | — | — | 44 | 13 | 3 | -0.4 | .769 | .798 | .659 | .919 | .621 |
| $11 | $9 | 120 | +17 | 19% | 9% | 91% | 2.65 | — | — | — | 63 | 25 | 3 | +1.1 | .454 | .340 | .541 | .419 | .491 |

---

## Brad Bergesen — 160 IP | $-1 | 130 pts
**SP-28, RP-2** — Owned: 2% — RH

Bergesen needed most of 2010 to shake off an injury incurred while taping an off-season commercial, but his final two months were sweet (2.88 ERA in 11 starts). Given his poor K/9, his ERA rests on dodging the long ball, which he was not able to do. A scrape-free winter would maintain his momentum. (BJ)

### Forecast
| Player | Age | IP | W | Sv | K | ERA | WHIP | K/9 | BB/9 | $2L | Pts |
|---|---|---|---|---|---|---|---|---|---|---|---|
| Bergesen B | 25 | 160 | 8 | 0 | 87 | 4.90 | 1.48 | 4.9 | 2.6 | -$1 | 130 |
| **Mini-Browser** | **Age** | **IP** | **W** | **Sv** | **K** | **ERA** | **WHIP** | **K/9** | **BB/9** | **$2L** | **Pts** |
| Medlen K | 25 | 20 | 1 | 0 | 18 | 3.76 | 1.28 | 8.2 | 2.5 | -$1 | 30 |
| Troncoso R | 28 | 40 | 2 | 0 | 27 | 4.09 | 1.38 | 6.0 | 3.3 | -$1 | 40 |
| Burton J | 29 | 40 | 2 | 0 | 30 | 4.14 | 1.37 | 6.8 | 3.5 | -$1 | 40 |
| Maholm P | 28 | 160 | 8 | 0 | 89 | 4.72 | 1.42 | 5.0 | 2.8 | -$1 | 130 |
| Melancon M | 26 | 40 | 2 | 0 | 39 | 4.45 | 1.40 | 8.7 | 3.5 | -$1 | 50 |

### Minors (2010)
| Level Leag | W | L | Sv | IP | H | K | ERA | WHIP | K/9 | BB/9 | HR/9 | GB/F |
|---|---|---|---|---|---|---|---|---|---|---|---|---|
| A — | | | | | | | | | | | | |
| AA — | | | | | | | | | | | | |
| AAA IL | 1 | 0 | 0 | 14 | 17 | 10 | 4.30 | 1.36 | 6.1 | 1.8 | 1.2 | — |

### Majors
| Yr Team | W | L | Sv | IP | H | K | ERA | WHIP | K/9 | BB/9 | HR/9 | GB/F |
|---|---|---|---|---|---|---|---|---|---|---|---|---|
| 07 — | | | | | | | | | | | | |
| 08 — | | | | | | | | | | | | |
| 09 BAL | 7 | 5 | 0 | 123 | 126 | 65 | 3.43 | 1.28 | 4.7 | 2.3 | 0.8 | 1.5 |
| 10 BAL | 8 | 12 | 0 | 170 | 193 | 81 | 4.98 | 1.44 | 4.3 | 2.7 | 1.4 | 1.3 |

### Competition at SP — Stats in 2010 as SP
| Thr | Player | GS | ERA | Supp | W-L |
|---|---|---|---|---|---|
| RH | Guthrie J | 32 | 3.83 | 3.6 | 11-14 |
| LH | Matusz B | 32 | 4.30 | 3.7 | 10-12 |
| RH | Millwood K | 31 | 5.10 | 3.5 | 4-16 |
| RH | Bergesen B | 28 | 5.02 | 3.9 | 8-12 |

### Value / Luck / In Rotation / In Relief / OPS
| $1L | $2L | Pts | RAA | H% | HR/fb | S% | FIP | GS | CG | QS/DS | GR | Hld | Bln | Lead | OPS | 1st Hf | 2nd Hf | vs RH | vs LH |
|---|---|---|---|---|---|---|---|---|---|---|---|---|---|---|---|---|---|---|---|
| $8 | $2 | 130 | +9 | 29% | 8% | 76% | 4.18 | 19 | 1 | 13/1 | — | — | — | — | .714 | .693 | .817 | .706 | .721 |
| -$3 | -$24 | 120 | -20 | 29% | 12% | 69% | 5.24 | 28 | 2 | 12/7 | 2 | 0 | 0 | -0.2 | .828 | .910 | .763 | .752 | .902 |

---

## Jason Berken — 60 IP | $-3 | 50 pts
**RP-41** — Owned: 0% — RH

A bullpen transfer helped Berken, but his surface stats hid mediocre peripherals (credit a low 7% HR/FB). His ERA catapulted from 1.95 in the first half to 7.71 in the second half; the implosion was due in part to a labrum tear, which didn't require surgery. Berken will be ready for 2011, but the tear is still a concern. (BJ)

### Forecast
| Player | Age | IP | W | Sv | K | ERA | WHIP | K/9 | BB/9 | $2L | Pts |
|---|---|---|---|---|---|---|---|---|---|---|---|
| Berken J | 27 | 60 | 3 | 0 | 41 | 5.19 | 1.57 | 6.2 | 3.2 | -$3 | 50 |
| **Mini-Browser** | **Age** | **IP** | **W** | **Sv** | **K** | **ERA** | **WHIP** | **K/9** | **BB/9** | **$2L** | **Pts** |
| French L | 25 | 100 | 5 | 0 | 62 | 5.23 | 1.52 | 5.6 | 3.4 | -$3 | 80 |
| Bannister B | 30 | 20 | 1 | 0 | 11 | 5.74 | 1.55 | 5.1 | 3.2 | -$3 | 10 |
| McCutchen D | 28 | 40 | 2 | 0 | 30 | 5.16 | 1.47 | 6.7 | 2.7 | -$3 | 40 |
| Ray R | 27 | 60 | 3 | 0 | 49 | 5.26 | 1.60 | 7.4 | 3.6 | -$3 | 50 |
| Igarashi R | 31 | 40 | 2 | 0 | 29 | 5.28 | 1.43 | 6.4 | 4.4 | -$3 | 30 |

### Minors (2010)
| Level Leag | W | L | Sv | IP | H | K | ERA | WHIP | K/9 | BB/9 | HR/9 | GB/F |
|---|---|---|---|---|---|---|---|---|---|---|---|---|
| A — | | | | | | | | | | | | |
| AA — | | | | | | | | | | | | |
| AAA — | | | | | | | | | | | | |

### Majors
| Yr Team | W | L | Sv | IP | H | K | ERA | WHIP | K/9 | BB/9 | HR/9 | GB/F |
|---|---|---|---|---|---|---|---|---|---|---|---|---|
| 07 — | | | | | | | | | | | | |
| 08 — | | | | | | | | | | | | |
| 09 BAL | 6 | 12 | 0 | 119 | 164 | 66 | 6.54 | 1.74 | 5.0 | 3.3 | 1.4 | 1.1 |
| 10 BAL | 3 | 3 | 0 | 62 | 64 | 45 | 3.03 | 1.33 | 6.5 | 2.7 | 0.7 | 1.3 |

### Competition at RP — Stats in 2010 as RP
| Thr | Player | GR | ERA | IP/G | Sv-Hld |
|---|---|---|---|---|---|
| RH | Albers M | 62 | 4.52 | 1.2 | 0-7 |
| RH | Simon A | 49 | 4.93 | 1.0 | 17-1 |
| RH | Uehara K | 43 | 2.86 | 1.0 | 13-6 |
| RH | Berken J | 41 | 3.03 | 1.5 | 0-7 |

### Value / Luck / In Rotation / In Relief / OPS
| $1L | $2L | Pts | RAA | H% | HR/fb | S% | FIP | GS | CG | QS/DS | GR | Hld | Bln | Lead | OPS | 1st Hf | 2nd Hf | vs RH | vs LH |
|---|---|---|---|---|---|---|---|---|---|---|---|---|---|---|---|---|---|---|---|
| -$8 | -$16 | 50 | -38 | 35% | 12% | 64% | 5.36 | 24 | 0 | 3/5 | — | — | — | — | .906 | .806 | .968 | .907 | .905 |
| -$6 | $0 | 50 | +4 | 32% | 7% | 79% | 4.27 | — | — | — | 41 | 7 | 4 | -1.1 | .728 | .638 | 1.033 | .780 | .632 |

---

## Rafael Betancourt — 60 IP | $4 | 110 pts
**RP-72** — Owned: 7% — RH

Betancourt figures into the late-inning mix for the Rockies, but don't expect him to grab any Saves as long as Huston Street can take the mound. Betancourt's astounding skills were betrayed by an above-average H% (his FIP was 2.61, lower than his 2009 ERA). Still, his rates in 2010 were extreme even for him. (TS)

### Forecast
| Player | Age | IP | W | Sv | K | ERA | WHIP | K/9 | BB/9 | $2L | Pts |
|---|---|---|---|---|---|---|---|---|---|---|---|
| Betancourt R | 35 | 60 | 4 | 0 | 67 | 3.91 | 1.16 | 10.0 | 2.2 | $4 | 110 |
| **Mini-Browser** | **Age** | **IP** | **W** | **Sv** | **K** | **ERA** | **WHIP** | **K/9** | **BB/9** | **$2L** | **Pts** |
| Hunter T | 24 | 140 | 10 | 0 | 83 | 4.55 | 1.38 | 5.4 | 2.6 | $4 | 160 |
| Burnett A | 34 | 180 | 11 | 0 | 155 | 4.74 | 1.45 | 7.7 | 4.1 | $4 | 220 |
| Matsuzaka D | 30 | 160 | 10 | 0 | 138 | 4.63 | 1.44 | 7.8 | 4.5 | $4 | 200 |
| Jackson E | 27 | 200 | 10 | 0 | 145 | 4.69 | 1.42 | 6.5 | 3.4 | $4 | 200 |
| Westbrook J | 33 | 180 | 9 | 0 | 108 | 4.33 | 1.35 | 5.4 | 3.0 | $4 | 170 |

### Minors (2010)
| Level Leag | W | L | Sv | IP | H | K | ERA | WHIP | K/9 | BB/9 | HR/9 | GB/F |
|---|---|---|---|---|---|---|---|---|---|---|---|---|
| A — | | | | | | | | | | | | |
| AA — | | | | | | | | | | | | |
| AAA — | | | | | | | | | | | | |

### Majors
| Yr Team | W | L | Sv | IP | H | K | ERA | WHIP | K/9 | BB/9 | HR/9 | GB/F |
|---|---|---|---|---|---|---|---|---|---|---|---|---|
| 07 CLE | 5 | 1 | 3 | 79 | 51 | 80 | 1.47 | 0.76 | 9.1 | 1.0 | 0.5 | 0.5 |
| 08 CLE | 3 | 4 | 4 | 71 | 76 | 64 | 5.07 | 1.42 | 8.1 | 3.2 | 1.4 | 0.6 |
| 09 2TM | 3 | 4 | 4 | 56 | 42 | 61 | 2.73 | 1.11 | 9.8 | 3.2 | 0.6 | 0.6 |
| 10 COL | 5 | 1 | 1 | 62 | 52 | 89 | 3.61 | 0.96 | 12.9 | 1.2 | 1.3 | 0.5 |

### Competition at RP — Stats in 2010 as RP
| Thr | Player | GR | ERA | IP/G | Sv-Hld |
|---|---|---|---|---|---|
| RH | Belisle M | 76 | 2.93 | 1.2 | 1-21 |
| RH | Betancourt R | 72 | 3.61 | 0.9 | 1-23 |
| RH | Corpas M | 56 | 4.62 | 1.1 | 10-2 |
| RH | Street H | 44 | 3.61 | 1.1 | 20-0 |

### Value / Luck / In Rotation / In Relief / OPS
| $1L | $2L | Pts | RAA | H% | HR/fb | S% | FIP | GS | CG | QS/DS | GR | Hld | Bln | Lead | OPS | 1st Hf | 2nd Hf | vs RH | vs LH |
|---|---|---|---|---|---|---|---|---|---|---|---|---|---|---|---|---|---|---|---|
| $17 | $18 | 150 | +23 | 24% | 4% | 84% | 2.28 | — | — | — | 68 | 31 | 3 | +1.4 | .485 | .421 | .545 | .402 | .612 |
| -$1 | -$5 | 90 | -9 | 32% | 10% | 68% | 4.57 | — | — | — | 69 | 12 | 4 | +1.0 | .789 | .841 | .712 | .809 | .763 |
| $4 | $4 | 120 | +5 | 27% | 5% | 78% | 3.07 | — | — | — | 61 | 20 | 4 | +1.3 | .604 | .691 | .504 | .487 | .803 |
| $5 | $1 | 150 | +3 | 31% | 12% | 69% | 2.61 | — | — | — | 72 | 23 | 4 | +0.8 | .626 | .775 | .432 | .515 | .819 |

## Chad Billingsley — 220 IP | $15 | 320 pts

SP-31 | Owned: 99% | RH

After his rough finish to 2009, Billingsley was one of the biggest question marks heading into 2010, but he ended up being one of the Dodgers' steadiest starters. In his past three seasons, he has 60 Quality Starts to only 9 Disasters. Chad could rocket past 15 Wins – his record in 2010 was hurt by rotten support. (MP)

| Player (Forecast) | Age | IP | W | Sv | K | ERA | WHIP | K/9 | BB/9 | $2L | Pts |
|---|---|---|---|---|---|---|---|---|---|---|---|
| Billingsley C | 26 | 220 | 14 | 0 | 189 | 3.84 | 1.31 | 7.7 | 3.5 | $15 | 320 |
| **Mini-Browser** | **Age** | **IP** | **W** | **Sv** | **K** | **ERA** | **WHIP** | **K/9** | **BB/9** | **$2L** | **Pts** |
| Feliz N | 22 | 60 | 4 | 39 | 62 | 3.50 | 1.21 | 9.3 | 3.3 | $16 | 290 |
| Marmol C | 28 | 80 | 3 | 36 | 108 | 3.45 | 1.38 | 12.1 | 5.8 | $15 | 310 |
| Bailey A | 26 | 75 | 3 | 33 | 77 | 3.16 | 1.29 | 9.2 | 3.5 | $15 | 270 |
| Wilson C | 30 | 180 | 13 | 0 | 157 | 3.60 | 1.32 | 7.9 | 4.3 | $15 | 270 |
| Kimbrel C | 22 | 60 | 6 | 30 | 91 | 2.83 | 1.45 | 13.6 | 6.0 | $15 | 300 |

| Level | Leag | W | L | Sv | IP | H | K | ERA | WHIP | K/9 | BB/9 | HR/9 | GB/F |
|---|---|---|---|---|---|---|---|---|---|---|---|---|---|
| | | | | | Minors (2010) | | | | | Skills | | | |
| A | — | — | — | — | — | — | — | — | — | — | — | — | — |
| AA | — | — | — | — | — | — | — | — | — | — | — | — | — |
| AAA | — | — | — | — | — | — | — | — | — | — | — | — | — |

| Competition at SP: Thr | Player | GS | ERA | Supp | W-L |
|---|---|---|---|---|---|
| LH | Kershaw C | 32 | 2.91 | 3.9 | 13-10 |
| RH | Kuroda H | 31 | 3.39 | 4.3 | 11-13 |
| RH | Billingsley C | 31 | 3.57 | 3.7 | 12-11 |
| LH | Lilly T | 30 | 3.62 | 2.9 | 10-12 |

(Stats in 2010 as SP)

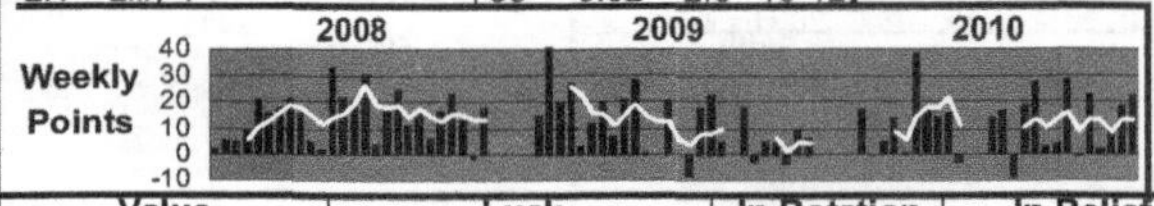
Weekly Points
2008
2009
2010
40
30
20
10
0
-10

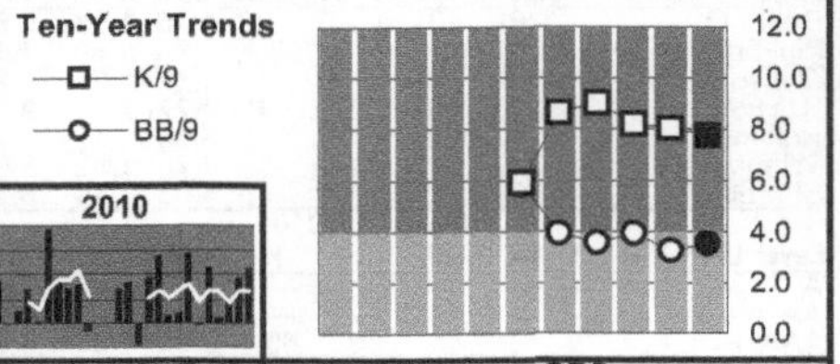
Ten-Year Trends
K/9
BB/9
12.0
10.0
8.0
6.0
4.0
2.0
0.0

| Yr | Team | W | L | Sv | IP | H | K | ERA | WHIP | K/9 | BB/9 | HR/9 | GB/F | $1L | $2L | Pts | RAA | H% | HR/fb | S% | FIP | GS | CG | QS/DS | GR | Hld | Bln | Lead | OPS | 1st Hf | 2nd Hf | vs RH | vs LH |
|---|---|---|---|---|---|---|---|---|---|---|---|---|---|---|---|---|---|---|---|---|---|---|---|---|---|---|---|---|---|---|---|---|---|
| | | Majors | | | | | | | | Skills | | | | Value | | | | Luck | | | | In Rotation | | | In Relief | | | | OPS | | | | |
| 07 | LAD | 12 | 5 | 0 | 147 | 131 | 141 | 3.31 | 1.33 | 8.6 | 3.9 | 0.9 | 1.1 | $12 | $5 | 260 | +17 | 30% | 10% | 78% | 3.91 | 20 | 1 | 9/2 | 23 | 3 | 1 | +0.0 | .701 | .655 | .729 | .660 | .748 |
| 08 | LAD | 16 | 10 | 0 | 200 | 188 | 201 | 3.14 | 1.34 | 9.0 | 3.6 | 0.6 | 1.6 | $17 | $8 | 360 | +23 | 32% | 8% | 78% | 3.30 | 32 | 1 | 20/3 | 3 | 1 | 0 | +0.3 | .687 | .658 | .727 | .614 | .768 |
| 09 | LAD | 12 | 11 | 0 | 196 | 173 | 179 | 4.03 | 1.32 | 8.2 | 3.9 | 0.8 | 1.2 | $9 | $3 | 280 | +3 | 30% | 9% | 71% | 3.82 | 32 | 0 | 22/2 | 1 | 0 | 0 | +0.1 | .703 | .654 | .781 | .693 | .712 |
| 10 | LAD | 12 | 11 | 0 | 191 | 176 | 171 | 3.57 | 1.28 | 8.0 | 3.2 | 0.4 | 1.5 | $11 | $2 | 280 | +13 | 31% | 4% | 71% | 3.04 | 31 | 1 | 18/4 | — | — | — | — | .668 | .741 | .591 | .629 | .703 |

## Nick Blackburn — 100 IP | $-1 | 80 pts

SP-26, RP-2 | Owned: 18% | RH

Blackburn's hittable nature caught up with him in 2010. Over the first four months, he was one of the worst pitchers in MLB, and he was demoted in July. He returned in August and pitched better, if un-Blackburn-like (46 H in 57 IP). That recovery – and his long-term contract – ensures that he will start in 2011. (NN)

| Player (Forecast) | Age | IP | W | Sv | K | ERA | WHIP | K/9 | BB/9 | $2L | Pts |
|---|---|---|---|---|---|---|---|---|---|---|---|
| Blackburn N | 29 | 100 | 6 | 0 | 43 | 5.03 | 1.39 | 3.8 | 2.0 | -$1 | 80 |
| **Mini-Browser** | **Age** | **IP** | **W** | **Sv** | **K** | **ERA** | **WHIP** | **K/9** | **BB/9** | **$2L** | **Pts** |
| Reynolds M | 26 | 40 | 2 | 0 | 42 | 4.27 | 1.41 | 9.5 | 2.8 | -$1 | 60 |
| Holland D | 24 | 140 | 7 | 0 | 120 | 5.19 | 1.47 | 7.7 | 3.5 | -$1 | 150 |
| Villanueva C | 27 | 60 | 2 | 0 | 53 | 4.70 | 1.32 | 8.0 | 3.2 | -$1 | 70 |
| Sherrill G | 33 | 40 | 3 | 0 | 36 | 4.08 | 1.44 | 8.1 | 4.4 | -$1 | 50 |
| Beltre O | 29 | 40 | 4 | 0 | 29 | 4.15 | 1.58 | 6.6 | 5.5 | -$1 | 60 |

| Level | Leag | W | L | Sv | IP | H | K | ERA | WHIP | K/9 | BB/9 | HR/9 | GB/F |
|---|---|---|---|---|---|---|---|---|---|---|---|---|---|
| | | | | | Minors (2010) | | | | | Skills | | | |
| A | — | — | — | — | — | — | — | — | — | — | — | — | — |
| AA | — | — | — | — | — | — | — | — | — | — | — | — | — |
| AAA | IL | 1 | 0 | 0 | 21 | 19 | 13 | 2.49 | 1.15 | 5.4 | 2.5 | 0.8 | — |

| Competition at SP: Thr | Player | GS | ERA | Supp | W-L |
|---|---|---|---|---|---|
| RH | Pavano C | 32 | 3.75 | 4.7 | 17-11 |
| LH | Liriano F | 31 | 3.62 | 4.9 | 14-10 |
| RH | Baker S | 29 | 4.49 | 4.8 | 12-9 |
| RH | Slowey K | 28 | 4.54 | 5.5 | 13-6 |

(Stats in 2010 as SP)

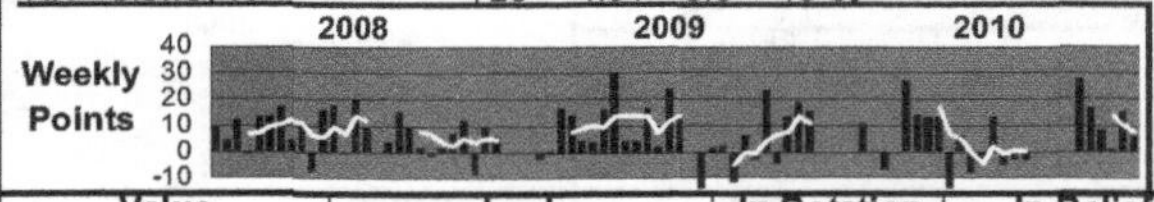
Weekly Points
2008
2009
2010
40
30
20
10
0
-10

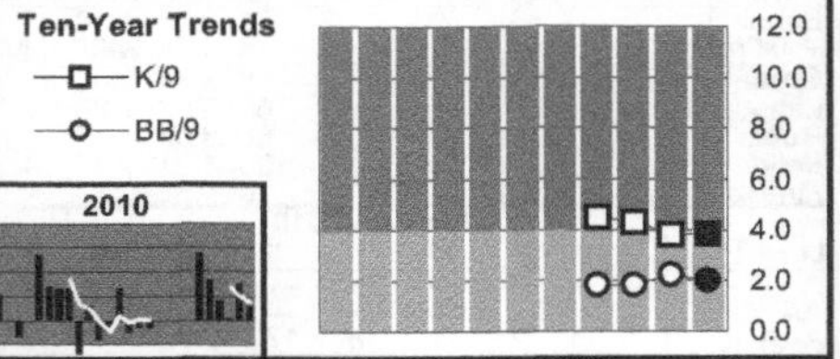
Ten-Year Trends
K/9
BB/9
12.0
10.0
8.0
6.0
4.0
2.0
0.0

| Yr | Team | W | L | Sv | IP | H | K | ERA | WHIP | K/9 | BB/9 | HR/9 | GB/F | $1L | $2L | Pts | RAA | H% | HR/fb | S% | FIP | GS | CG | QS/DS | GR | Hld | Bln | Lead | OPS | 1st Hf | 2nd Hf | vs RH | vs LH |
|---|---|---|---|---|---|---|---|---|---|---|---|---|---|---|---|---|---|---|---|---|---|---|---|---|---|---|---|---|---|---|---|---|---|
| | | Majors | | | | | | | | Skills | | | | Value | | | | Luck | | | | In Rotation | | | In Relief | | | | OPS | | | | |
| 07 | MIN | 0 | 2 | 0 | 11 | 19 | 8 | 7.71 | 1.80 | 6.2 | 1.5 | 1.5 | 0.9 | -$4 | -$6 | 0 | −6 | 41% | 12% | 58% | 4.67 | — | — | — | 6 | 1 | 1 | −0.7 | .908 | — | .908 | .724 | 1.129 |
| 08 | MIN | 11 | 11 | 0 | 193 | 224 | 96 | 4.05 | 1.36 | 4.5 | 1.8 | 1.1 | 1.3 | $4 | -$5 | 180 | −7 | 31% | 10% | 73% | 4.46 | 33 | 0 | 19/7 | — | — | — | — | .771 | .746 | .811 | .765 | .779 |
| 09 | MIN | 11 | 11 | 0 | 205 | 240 | 98 | 4.03 | 1.37 | 4.3 | 1.8 | 1.1 | 1.3 | $9 | -$1 | 180 | −2 | 30% | 9% | 74% | 4.53 | 33 | 3 | 21/6 | — | — | — | — | .768 | .701 | .864 | .706 | .817 |
| 10 | MIN | 10 | 12 | 0 | 161 | 194 | 68 | 5.42 | 1.45 | 3.8 | 2.2 | 1.4 | 1.6 | -$5 | -$27 | 120 | −22 | 31% | 14% | 66% | 5.22 | 26 | 1 | 14/8 | 2 | 0 | 0 | +0.5 | .839 | .943 | .667 | .836 | .843 |

## Joe Blanton — 180 IP | $4 | 190 pts

SP-28, RP-1 | Owned: 18% | RH

Despite a lackluster showing in 2010, Blanton's spot in the Phillies' rotation is secure, as he signed a three year deal on the heels of his uncharacteristically low ERA in 2009. Payback struck in 2010, as both his H% and HR/FB were unkind. His rates in Philly are still decent, and he should be fine as a #4 SP in 2011. (BB)

| Player (Forecast) | Age | IP | W | Sv | K | ERA | WHIP | K/9 | BB/9 | $2L | Pts |
|---|---|---|---|---|---|---|---|---|---|---|---|
| Blanton J | 30 | 180 | 10 | 0 | 118 | 4.66 | 1.32 | 5.9 | 2.4 | $4 | 190 |
| **Mini-Browser** | **Age** | **IP** | **W** | **Sv** | **K** | **ERA** | **WHIP** | **K/9** | **BB/9** | **$2L** | **Pts** |
| Fister D | 27 | 190 | 8 | 0 | 120 | 4.64 | 1.37 | 5.7 | 2.1 | $4 | 160 |
| Masset N | 28 | 80 | 4 | 4 | 69 | 3.97 | 1.31 | 7.8 | 3.4 | $4 | 120 |
| Marshall S | 28 | 80 | 5 | 2 | 69 | 4.04 | 1.31 | 7.7 | 3.1 | $4 | 120 |
| Francisco F | 31 | 60 | 4 | 0 | 66 | 3.80 | 1.30 | 9.9 | 3.6 | $4 | 100 |
| Camp S | 35 | 80 | 4 | 0 | 53 | 3.82 | 1.29 | 5.9 | 2.8 | $4 | 90 |

| Level | Leag | W | L | Sv | IP | H | K | ERA | WHIP | K/9 | BB/9 | HR/9 | GB/F |
|---|---|---|---|---|---|---|---|---|---|---|---|---|---|
| | | | | | Minors (2010) | | | | | Skills | | | |
| A | SAL | 0 | 0 | 0 | 2 | 0 | 2 | 0.00 | 0.00 | 9.0 | 0.0 | 0.0 | — |
| AA | EL | 0 | 1 | 0 | 8 | 9 | 5 | 5.63 | 1.38 | 5.6 | 2.3 | 2.3 | — |
| AAA | — | — | — | — | — | — | — | — | — | — | — | — | — |

| Competition at SP: Thr | Player | GS | ERA | Supp | W-L |
|---|---|---|---|---|---|
| RH | Halladay R | 33 | 2.44 | 4.4 | 21-10 |
| LH | Hamels C | 33 | 3.06 | 3.8 | 12-11 |
| RH | Oswalt R | 32 | 2.73 | 3.0 | 13-13 |
| RH | Kendrick K | 31 | 4.81 | 5.5 | 11-10 |

(Stats in 2010 as SP)

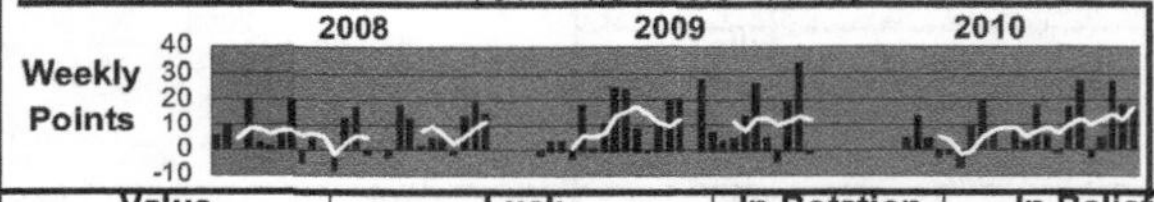
Weekly Points
2008
2009
2010
40
30
20
10
0
-10

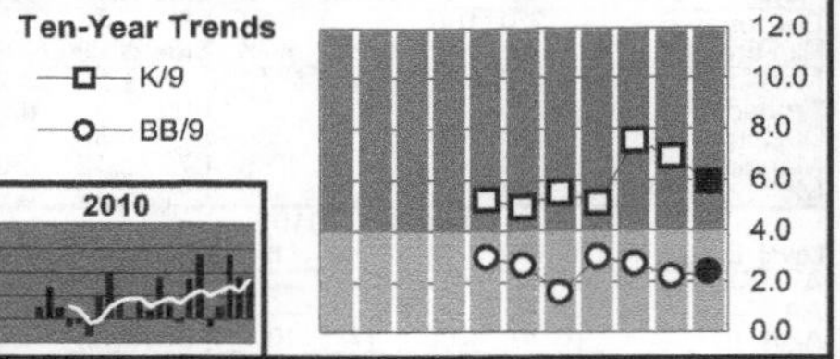
Ten-Year Trends
K/9
BB/9
12.0
10.0
8.0
6.0
4.0
2.0
0.0

| Yr | Team | W | L | Sv | IP | H | K | ERA | WHIP | K/9 | BB/9 | HR/9 | GB/F | $1L | $2L | Pts | RAA | H% | HR/fb | S% | FIP | GS | CG | QS/DS | GR | Hld | Bln | Lead | OPS | 1st Hf | 2nd Hf | vs RH | vs LH |
|---|---|---|---|---|---|---|---|---|---|---|---|---|---|---|---|---|---|---|---|---|---|---|---|---|---|---|---|---|---|---|---|---|---|
| | | Majors | | | | | | | | Skills | | | | Value | | | | Luck | | | | In Rotation | | | In Relief | | | | OPS | | | | |
| 07 | OAK | 14 | 10 | 0 | 230 | 240 | 140 | 3.95 | 1.22 | 5.5 | 1.6 | 0.6 | 1.4 | $15 | $3 | 270 | +7 | 30% | 7% | 68% | 3.51 | 34 | 3 | 20/4 | — | — | — | — | .679 | .625 | .750 | .647 | .714 |
| 08 | 2TM | 9 | 12 | 0 | 197 | 211 | 111 | 4.69 | 1.40 | 5.1 | 3.0 | 1.0 | 1.3 | -$4 | -$11 | 160 | −12 | 29% | 9% | 68% | 4.58 | 33 | 0 | 14/2 | — | — | — | — | .758 | .764 | .747 | .799 | .717 |
| 09 | PHI | 12 | 8 | 0 | 195 | 198 | 163 | 4.05 | 1.32 | 7.5 | 2.7 | 1.4 | 1.0 | $9 | $3 | 260 | +7 | 30% | 13% | 74% | 4.43 | 31 | 0 | 21/3 | — | — | — | — | .759 | .785 | .729 | .792 | .721 |
| 10 | PHI | 9 | 6 | 0 | 175 | 206 | 134 | 4.82 | 1.42 | 6.9 | 2.2 | 1.4 | 1.1 | -$3 | -$19 | 180 | −17 | 33% | 12% | 70% | 4.41 | 28 | 0 | 16/3 | 1 | 0 | 0 | −0.1 | .796 | .859 | .738 | .815 | .774 |

## Jerry Blevins — 50 IP | $1 | 60 pts

RP-63 | Owned: 0% | LH

One bad May (7.71 ERA) hurt Blevins' overall numbers, as he was his customary effective self, especially against left-handed batters. He is the #2 lefty in the A's bullpen behind Craig Breslow and is often asked to pitch to righties as well. If Blevins struggles this spring, he could face a challenge from Josh Outman. (ML)

| Player (Forecast) | Age | IP | W | Sv | K | ERA | WHIP | K/9 | BB/9 | $2L | Pts |
|---|---|---|---|---|---|---|---|---|---|---|---|
| Blevins J | 27 | 50 | 2 | 0 | 48 | 3.98 | 1.37 | 8.7 | 3.1 | $1 | 60 |
| **Mini-Browser** | **Age** | **IP** | **W** | **Sv** | **K** | **ERA** | **WHIP** | **K/9** | **BB/9** | **$2L** | **Pts** |
| Perry R | 24 | 60 | 3 | 2 | 51 | 4.14 | 1.45 | 7.6 | 4.6 | $1 | 80 |
| Kazmir S | 27 | 140 | 9 | 0 | 112 | 4.98 | 1.46 | 7.2 | 4.2 | $1 | 160 |
| Aceves A | 28 | 40 | 3 | 0 | 29 | 3.91 | 1.29 | 6.5 | 2.4 | $1 | 60 |
| Lopez J | 33 | 60 | 3 | 0 | 38 | 3.54 | 1.37 | 5.7 | 3.7 | $1 | 60 |
| Zito B | 32 | 200 | 10 | 0 | 138 | 4.59 | 1.42 | 6.2 | 3.9 | $1 | 190 |

| Level | Leag | W | L | Sv | IP | H | K | ERA | WHIP | K/9 | BB/9 | HR/9 | GB/F |
|---|---|---|---|---|---|---|---|---|---|---|---|---|---|
| | | | | | Minors (2010) | | | | | Skills | | | |
| A | — | — | — | — | — | — | — | — | — | — | — | — | — |
| AA | — | — | — | — | — | — | — | — | — | — | — | — | — |
| AAA | — | — | — | — | — | — | — | — | — | — | — | — | — |

| Competition at RP: Thr | Player | GR | ERA | IP/G | Sv-Hld |
|---|---|---|---|---|---|
| LH | Breslow C | 75 | 3.01 | 1.0 | 5-16 |
| LH | Blevins J | 63 | 3.70 | 0.8 | 1-11 |
| LH | Bowers C | 14 | 4.50 | 1.0 | 0-0 |

(Stats in 2010 as RP)

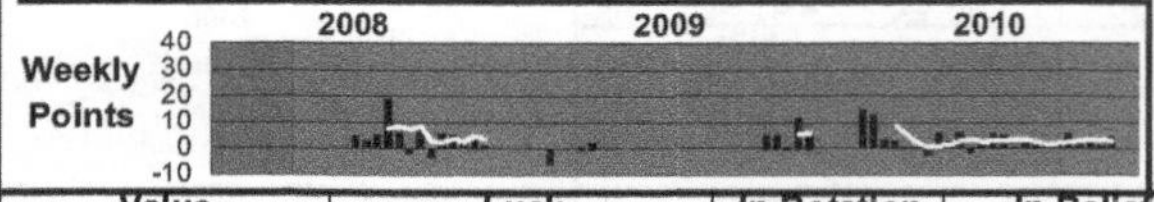
Weekly Points
2008
2009
2010
40
30
20
10
0
-10

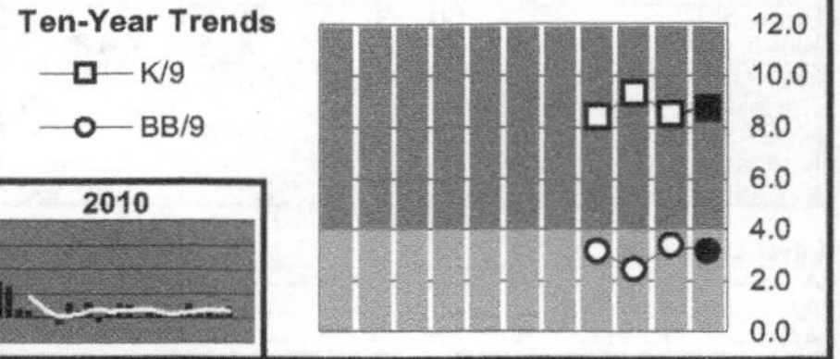
Ten-Year Trends
K/9
BB/9
12.0
10.0
8.0
6.0
4.0
2.0
0.0

| Yr | Team | W | L | Sv | IP | H | K | ERA | WHIP | K/9 | BB/9 | HR/9 | GB/F | $1L | $2L | Pts | RAA | H% | HR/fb | S% | FIP | GS | CG | QS/DS | GR | Hld | Bln | Lead | OPS | 1st Hf | 2nd Hf | vs RH | vs LH |
|---|---|---|---|---|---|---|---|---|---|---|---|---|---|---|---|---|---|---|---|---|---|---|---|---|---|---|---|---|---|---|---|---|---|
| | | Majors | | | | | | | | Skills | | | | Value | | | | Luck | | | | In Rotation | | | In Relief | | | | OPS | | | | |
| 07 | OAK | 0 | 1 | 0 | 4 | 8 | 3 | 9.64 | 2.14 | 5.8 | 3.9 | 1.9 | 0.2 | -$3 | -$5 | 0 | −4 | 37% | 8% | 56% | 6.09 | — | — | — | 6 | 0 | 0 | −0.3 | .965 | — | .965 | 1.080 | .778 |
| 08 | OAK | 1 | 3 | 0 | 37 | 32 | 35 | 3.11 | 1.19 | 8.4 | 3.1 | 0.5 | 1.1 | $2 | $0 | 50 | +3 | 29% | 5% | 74% | 3.17 | — | — | — | 36 | 5 | 1 | −0.9 | .639 | .404 | .663 | .747 | .482 |
| 09 | OAK | 0 | 0 | 0 | 22 | 19 | 23 | 4.84 | 1.12 | 9.3 | 2.4 | 0.8 | 0.6 | -$1 | -$2 | 20 | −2 | 29% | 6% | 57% | 3.21 | — | — | — | 20 | 0 | 0 | +1.8 | .651 | 1.035 | .525 | .617 | .719 |
| 10 | OAK | 2 | 1 | 1 | 48 | 54 | 46 | 3.70 | 1.48 | 8.5 | 3.3 | 1.3 | 1.0 | -$1 | -$10 | 60 | +2 | 33% | 12% | 80% | 4.39 | — | — | — | 63 | 11 | 1 | +0.5 | .758 | .737 | .794 | .892 | .598 |

## Mitchell Boggs — 60 IP | $-1 | 80 pts

RP-61 | Owned: 0% | RH

Boggs' upside metamorphosed in 2010 from back-of-the-rotation starter to high-leverage reliever, as he responded to work in tighter situations with a career-best control. The belief in St. Louis is that the closer's mantle will fall to either Boggs or Jason Motte when Ryan Franklin's contract expires after 2011. (AB)

| Player (Forecast) | Age | IP | W | Sv | K | ERA | WHIP | K/9 | BB/9 | $2L | Pts |
|---|---|---|---|---|---|---|---|---|---|---|---|
| Boggs M | 27 | 60 | 3 | 4 | 44 | 4.54 | 1.48 | 6.7 | 3.9 | -$1 | 80 |
| **Mini-Browser** | **Age** | **IP** | **W** | **Sv** | **K** | **ERA** | **WHIP** | **K/9** | **BB/9** | **$2L** | **Pts** |
| Bush D | 31 | 180 | 9 | 0 | 112 | 4.92 | 1.37 | 5.6 | 2.8 | $0 | 160 |
| Strasburg S | 22 | 20 | 1 | 0 | 23 | 3.71 | 1.21 | 10.4 | 3.2 | $0 | 40 |
| Zumaya J | 26 | 40 | 2 | 0 | 37 | 4.08 | 1.48 | 8.3 | 4.9 | -$1 | 50 |
| Lewis J | 26 | 40 | 3 | 0 | 36 | 4.48 | 1.45 | 8.0 | 4.3 | -$1 | 50 |
| Reyes D | 33 | 40 | 2 | 0 | 29 | 3.72 | 1.43 | 6.4 | 4.5 | -$1 | 50 |

| Level | Leag | W | L | Sv | IP | H | K | ERA | WHIP | K/9 | BB/9 | HR/9 | GB/F |
|---|---|---|---|---|---|---|---|---|---|---|---|---|---|
| | | | | | Minors (2010) | | | | | Skills | | | |
| A | — | — | — | — | — | — | — | — | — | — | — | — | — |
| AA | — | — | — | — | — | — | — | — | — | — | — | — | — |
| AAA | — | — | — | — | — | — | — | — | — | — | — | — | — |

| Competition at RP: Thr | Player | GR | ERA | IP/G | Sv-Hld |
|---|---|---|---|---|---|
| RH | McClellan K | 68 | 2.27 | 1.1 | 2-19 |
| RH | Boggs M | 61 | 3.61 | 1.1 | 0-6 |
| RH | Franklin R | 59 | 3.46 | 1.1 | 27-0 |
| RH | Motte J | 56 | 2.24 | 0.9 | 2-12 |

(Stats in 2010 as RP)

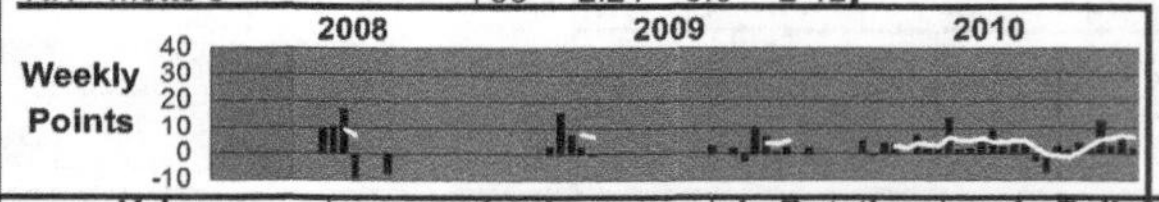
Weekly Points
2008
2009
2010
40
30
20
10
0
-10

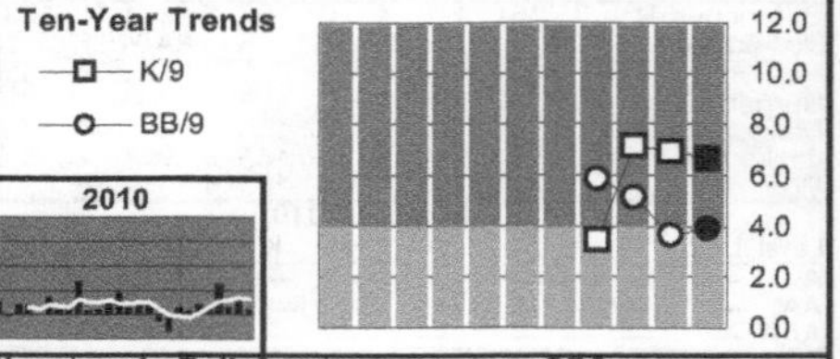
Ten-Year Trends
K/9
BB/9
12.0
10.0
8.0
6.0
4.0
2.0
0.0

| Yr | Team | W | L | Sv | IP | H | K | ERA | WHIP | K/9 | BB/9 | HR/9 | GB/F | $1L | $2L | Pts | RAA | H% | HR/fb | S% | FIP | GS | CG | QS/DS | GR | Hld | Bln | Lead | OPS | 1st Hf | 2nd Hf | vs RH | vs LH |
|---|---|---|---|---|---|---|---|---|---|---|---|---|---|---|---|---|---|---|---|---|---|---|---|---|---|---|---|---|---|---|---|---|---|
| | | Majors | | | | | | | | Skills | | | | Value | | | | Luck | | | | In Rotation | | | In Relief | | | | OPS | | | | |
| 07 | — | — | — | — | — | — | — | — | — | — | — | — | — | — | — | — | — | — | — | — | — | — | — | — | — | — | — | — | — | — | — | — | — |
| 08 | STL | 3 | 2 | 0 | 34 | 42 | 13 | 7.41 | 1.88 | 3.4 | 5.8 | 1.3 | 1.8 | -$7 | -$10 | 20 | −14 | 31% | 14% | 61% | 6.29 | 6 | 0 | 1/2 | 2 | 0 | 0 | −1.0 | .919 | .861 | 1.180 | .736 | 1.060 |
| 09 | STL | 2 | 3 | 0 | 58 | 71 | 46 | 4.19 | 1.79 | 7.1 | 5.1 | 0.5 | 1.8 | -$4 | -$5 | 40 | −2 | 38% | 6% | 76% | 3.99 | 9 | 0 | 2/1 | 7 | 1 | 0 | −0.8 | .856 | .831 | .872 | .667 | 1.096 |
| 10 | STL | 2 | 3 | 0 | 67 | 60 | 52 | 3.61 | 1.29 | 7.0 | 3.6 | 0.7 | 1.7 | -$1 | -$8 | 70 | +1 | 29% | 8% | 73% | 3.82 | — | — | — | 61 | 6 | 0 | +0.3 | .696 | .602 | .824 | .664 | .763 |

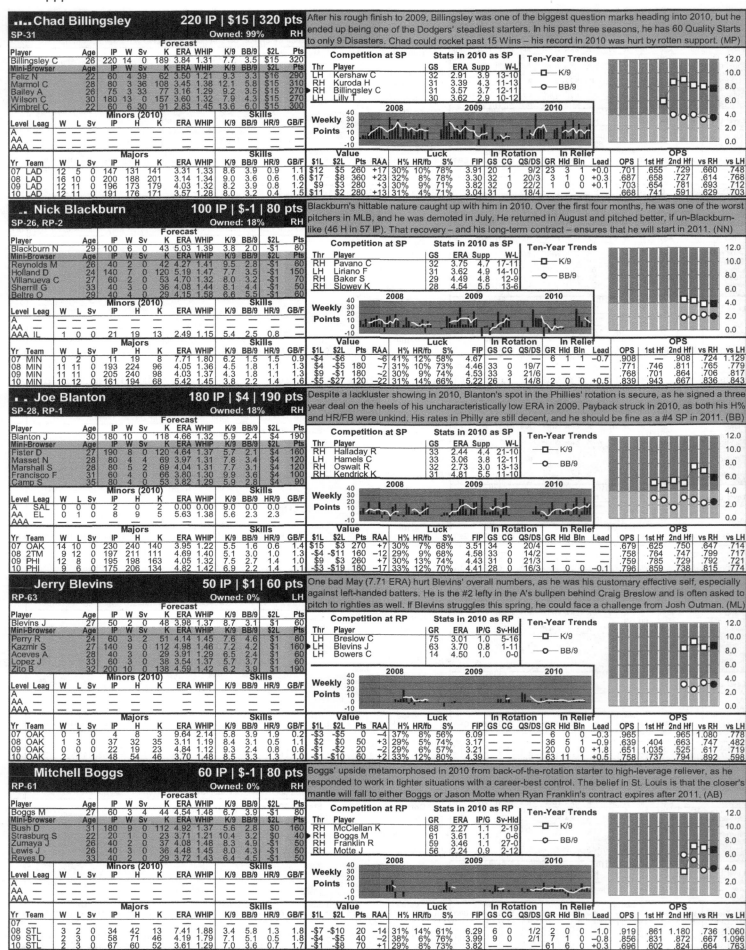

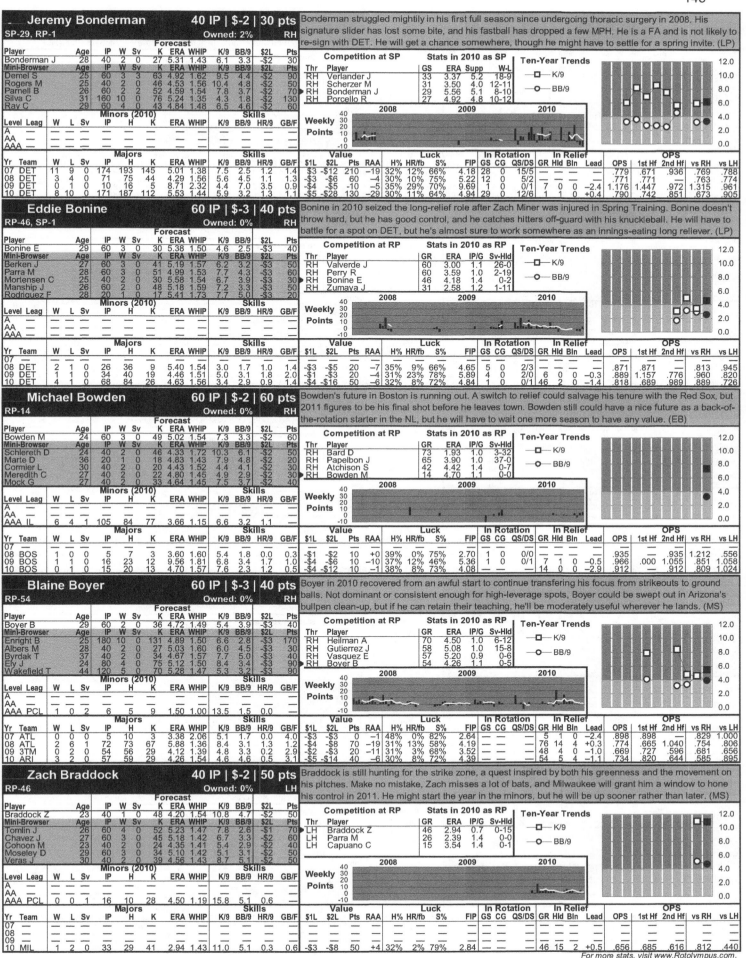

## Jeremy Bonderman — 40 IP | $-2 | 30 pts
**SP-29, RP-1** — Owned: 2% — RH

Bonderman struggled mightily in his first full season since undergoing thoracic surgery in 2008. His signature slider has lost some bite, and his fastball has dropped a few MPH. He is a FA and is not likely to re-sign with DET. He will get a chance somewhere, though he might have to settle for a spring invite. (LP)

| Player | Age | IP | W | Sv | K | ERA | WHIP | K/9 | BB/9 | $2L | Pts |
|---|---|---|---|---|---|---|---|---|---|---|---|
| Bonderman J | 28 | 40 | 2 | 0 | 27 | 5.31 | 1.43 | 6.1 | 3.3 | -$2 | 30 |
| Mini-Browser | Age | IP | W | Sv | K | ERA | WHIP | K/9 | BB/9 | $2L | Pts |
| Demel S | 25 | 60 | 3 | 3 | 63 | 4.92 | 1.62 | 9.5 | 4.4 | -$2 | 90 |
| Rogers M | 25 | 40 | 2 | 0 | 46 | 4.53 | 1.56 | 10.4 | 4.8 | -$2 | 50 |
| Parnell B | 26 | 60 | 2 | 2 | 52 | 4.59 | 1.54 | 7.8 | 3.7 | -$2 | 70 |
| Silva C | 31 | 160 | 10 | 0 | 76 | 5.24 | 1.35 | 4.3 | 1.8 | -$2 | 130 |
| Ray C | 29 | 60 | 4 | 0 | 43 | 4.84 | 1.48 | 6.5 | 4.6 | -$2 | 60 |

**Competition at SP — Stats in 2010 as SP**

| Thr | Player | GS | ERA | Supp | W-L |
|---|---|---|---|---|---|
| RH | Verlander J | 33 | 3.37 | 5.2 | 18-9 |
| RH | Scherzer M | 31 | 3.50 | 4.0 | 12-11 |
| RH | Bonderman J | 29 | 5.56 | 5.1 | 8-10 |
| RH | Porcello R | 27 | 4.92 | 4.8 | 10-12 |

Ten-Year Trends: K/9, BB/9

**Minors (2010)**

| Level | Leag | W | L | Sv | IP | H | K | ERA | WHIP | K/9 | BB/9 | HR/9 | GB/F |
|---|---|---|---|---|---|---|---|---|---|---|---|---|---|
| A | — | | | | | | | | | | | | |
| AA | — | | | | | | | | | | | | |
| AAA | — | | | | | | | | | | | | |

**Majors**

| Yr | Team | W | L | Sv | IP | H | K | ERA | WHIP | K/9 | BB/9 | HR/9 | GB/F | $1L | $2L | Pts | RAA | H% | HR/fb | S% | FIP | GS | CG | QS/DS | GR | Hld | Bln | Lead | OPS | 1st Hf | 2nd Hf | vs RH | vs LH |
|---|---|---|---|---|---|---|---|---|---|---|---|---|---|---|---|---|---|---|---|---|---|---|---|---|---|---|---|---|---|---|---|---|---|
| 07 | DET | 11 | 9 | 0 | 174 | 193 | 145 | 5.01 | 1.38 | 7.5 | 2.5 | 1.2 | 1.4 | -$3 | -$12 | 210 | -19 | 32% | 12% | 66% | 4.18 | 28 | 0 | 15/5 | — | — | — | — | .779 | .671 | .936 | .769 | .788 |
| 08 | DET | 3 | 4 | 0 | 71 | 75 | 44 | 4.29 | 1.56 | 5.6 | 4.5 | 1.1 | 1.3 | -$3 | -$6 | 60 | -4 | 30% | 10% | 75% | 5.22 | 12 | 0 | 5/2 | — | — | — | — | .771 | .771 | — | .763 | .774 |
| 09 | DET | 0 | 1 | 0 | 10 | 16 | 5 | 8.71 | 2.32 | 4.4 | 7.0 | 3.5 | 0.9 | -$4 | -$5 | -10 | -5 | 35% | 29% | 70% | 9.69 | 1 | 0 | 0/1 | 7 | 0 | 0 | -2.4 | 1.176 | 1.447 | .972 | 1.315 | .961 |
| 10 | DET | 8 | 10 | 0 | 171 | 187 | 112 | 5.53 | 1.44 | 5.9 | 3.2 | 1.3 | 1.1 | -$5 | -$28 | 130 | -29 | 30% | 8% | 64% | 4.94 | 29 | 0 | 12/6 | — | — | — | +0.4 | .790 | .742 | .851 | .673 | .905 |

## Eddie Bonine — 60 IP | $-3 | 40 pts
**RP-46, SP-1** — Owned: 0% — RH

Bonine in 2010 seized the long-relief role after Zach Miner was injured in Spring Training. Bonine doesn't throw hard, but he has good control, and he catches hitters off-guard with his knuckleball. He will have to battle for a spot on DET, but he's almost sure to work somewhere as an innings-eating long reliever. (LP)

| Player | Age | IP | W | Sv | K | ERA | WHIP | K/9 | BB/9 | $2L | Pts |
|---|---|---|---|---|---|---|---|---|---|---|---|
| Bonine E | 29 | 60 | 3 | 0 | 30 | 5.38 | 1.50 | 4.6 | 2.5 | -$3 | 40 |
| Mini-Browser | Age | IP | W | Sv | K | ERA | WHIP | K/9 | BB/9 | $2L | Pts |
| Berken J | 27 | 60 | 3 | 0 | 41 | 5.19 | 1.57 | 6.2 | 3.2 | -$3 | 50 |
| Parra M | 28 | 60 | 3 | 0 | 51 | 4.99 | 1.53 | 7.7 | 4.3 | -$3 | 50 |
| Mortensen C | 25 | 40 | 2 | 0 | 30 | 5.58 | 1.54 | 6.7 | 3.9 | -$3 | 30 |
| Manship J | 26 | 60 | 2 | 0 | 48 | 5.18 | 1.59 | 7.2 | 3.3 | -$3 | 50 |
| Rodriguez F | 28 | 20 | 1 | 0 | 17 | 5.41 | 1.73 | 7.7 | 5.0 | -$3 | 20 |

**Competition at RP — Stats in 2010 as RP**

| Thr | Player | GR | ERA | IP/G | Sv-Hld |
|---|---|---|---|---|---|
| RH | Valverde J | 60 | 3.00 | 1.0 | 26-0 |
| RH | Perry R | 60 | 3.59 | 1.0 | 2-19 |
| RH | Bonine E | 46 | 4.18 | 1.4 | 0-2 |
| RH | Zumaya J | 31 | 2.58 | 1.2 | 1-11 |

Ten-Year Trends: K/9, BB/9

**Minors (2010)**

| Level | Leag | W | L | Sv | IP | H | K | ERA | WHIP | K/9 | BB/9 | HR/9 | GB/F |
|---|---|---|---|---|---|---|---|---|---|---|---|---|---|
| A | — | | | | | | | | | | | | |
| AA | — | | | | | | | | | | | | |
| AAA | — | | | | | | | | | | | | |

**Majors**

| Yr | Team | W | L | Sv | IP | H | K | ERA | WHIP | K/9 | BB/9 | HR/9 | GB/F | $1L | $2L | Pts | RAA | H% | HR/fb | S% | FIP | GS | CG | QS/DS | GR | Hld | Bln | Lead | OPS | 1st Hf | 2nd Hf | vs RH | vs LH |
|---|---|---|---|---|---|---|---|---|---|---|---|---|---|---|---|---|---|---|---|---|---|---|---|---|---|---|---|---|---|---|---|---|---|
| 07 | — | | | | | | | | | | | | | | | | | | | | | | | | | | | | | | | | |
| 08 | DET | 2 | 1 | 0 | 26 | 36 | 9 | 5.40 | 1.54 | 3.0 | 1.7 | 1.0 | 1.4 | -$3 | -$5 | 20 | -7 | 35% | 9% | 66% | 4.65 | 5 | 0 | 2/3 | — | — | — | — | .871 | .871 | — | .813 | .945 |
| 09 | DET | 1 | 1 | 0 | 34 | 40 | 19 | 4.46 | 1.51 | 5.0 | 3.1 | 1.8 | 2.0 | -$1 | -$3 | 20 | -4 | 31% | 23% | 78% | 5.89 | 4 | 0 | 0/0 | 6 | 0 | 0 | -0.3 | .889 | 1.157 | .776 | .960 | .820 |
| 10 | DET | 4 | 1 | 0 | 68 | 84 | 26 | 4.63 | 1.56 | 3.4 | 2.9 | 0.9 | 1.4 | -$4 | -$16 | 50 | -6 | 32% | 8% | 72% | 4.84 | 1 | 0 | 0/1 | 46 | 2 | 0 | -1.4 | .818 | .689 | .989 | .889 | .726 |

## Michael Bowden — 60 IP | $-2 | 60 pts
**RP-14** — Owned: 0% — RH

Bowden's future in Boston is running out. A switch to relief could salvage his tenure with the Red Sox, but 2011 figures to be his final shot before he leaves town. Bowden still could have a nice future as a back-of-the-rotation starter in the NL, but he will have to wait one more season to have any value. (EB)

| Player | Age | IP | W | Sv | K | ERA | WHIP | K/9 | BB/9 | $2L | Pts |
|---|---|---|---|---|---|---|---|---|---|---|---|
| Bowden M | 24 | 60 | 3 | 0 | 49 | 5.02 | 1.54 | 7.3 | 3.3 | -$2 | 60 |
| Mini-Browser | Age | IP | W | Sv | K | ERA | WHIP | K/9 | BB/9 | $2L | Pts |
| Schlereth D | 24 | 40 | 2 | 0 | 46 | 4.33 | 1.72 | 10.3 | 6.1 | -$2 | 50 |
| Marte D | 36 | 20 | 1 | 0 | 18 | 4.83 | 1.43 | 7.9 | 4.8 | -$2 | 20 |
| Cormier L | 30 | 40 | 2 | 0 | 20 | 4.43 | 1.52 | 4.4 | 4.1 | -$2 | 20 |
| Meredith C | 27 | 40 | 2 | 0 | 22 | 4.80 | 1.45 | 4.9 | 2.9 | -$2 | 30 |
| Mock G | 27 | 40 | 2 | 0 | 33 | 4.64 | 1.45 | 7.5 | 3.7 | -$2 | 50 |

**Competition at RP — Stats in 2010 as RP**

| Thr | Player | GR | ERA | IP/G | Sv-Hld |
|---|---|---|---|---|---|
| RH | Bard D | 73 | 1.93 | 1.0 | 3-32 |
| RH | Papelbon J | 65 | 3.90 | 1.0 | 37-0 |
| RH | Atchison S | 42 | 4.42 | 1.4 | 0-7 |
| RH | Bowden M | 14 | 4.70 | 1.1 | 0-0 |

Ten-Year Trends: K/9, BB/9

**Minors (2010)**

| Level | Leag | W | L | Sv | IP | H | K | ERA | WHIP | K/9 | BB/9 | HR/9 | GB/F |
|---|---|---|---|---|---|---|---|---|---|---|---|---|---|
| A | — | | | | | | | | | | | | |
| AA | — | | | | | | | | | | | | |
| AAA | IL | 6 | 4 | 1 | 105 | 84 | 77 | 3.66 | 1.15 | 6.6 | 3.2 | 1.1 | — |

**Majors**

| Yr | Team | W | L | Sv | IP | H | K | ERA | WHIP | K/9 | BB/9 | HR/9 | GB/F | $1L | $2L | Pts | RAA | H% | HR/fb | S% | FIP | GS | CG | QS/DS | GR | Hld | Bln | Lead | OPS | 1st Hf | 2nd Hf | vs RH | vs LH |
|---|---|---|---|---|---|---|---|---|---|---|---|---|---|---|---|---|---|---|---|---|---|---|---|---|---|---|---|---|---|---|---|---|---|
| 07 | — | | | | | | | | | | | | | | | | | | | | | | | | | | | | | | | | |
| 08 | BOS | 1 | 0 | 0 | 5 | 7 | 3 | 3.60 | 1.60 | 5.4 | 1.8 | 0.0 | 0.3 | -$1 | -$2 | 10 | +0 | 39% | 0% | 75% | 2.70 | 1 | 0 | 0/0 | — | — | — | — | .935 | — | .935 | 1.212 | .556 |
| 09 | BOS | 0 | 1 | 0 | 16 | 23 | 12 | 9.56 | 1.81 | 6.8 | 3.4 | 1.7 | 1.0 | -$4 | -$6 | 10 | -10 | 37% | 12% | 46% | 5.36 | 1 | 0 | 0/1 | 7 | 1 | 0 | -0.5 | .966 | .000 | 1.055 | .851 | 1.058 |
| 10 | BOS | 0 | 1 | 0 | 15 | 20 | 13 | 4.70 | 1.57 | 7.6 | 2.3 | 1.2 | 0.5 | -$4 | -$12 | 10 | -1 | 38% | 8% | 73% | 4.08 | — | — | — | 14 | 0 | 0 | -2.9 | .912 | — | .912 | .809 | 1.024 |

## Blaine Boyer — 60 IP | $-3 | 40 pts
**RP-54** — Owned: 0% — RH

Boyer in 2010 recovered from an awful start to continue transfering his focus from strikeouts to ground balls. Not dominant or consistent enough for high-leverage spots, Boyer could be swept out in Arizona's bullpen clean-up, but if he can retain their teaching, he'll be moderately useful wherever he lands. (MS)

| Player | Age | IP | W | Sv | K | ERA | WHIP | K/9 | BB/9 | $2L | Pts |
|---|---|---|---|---|---|---|---|---|---|---|---|
| Boyer B | 29 | 60 | 2 | 0 | 36 | 4.72 | 1.49 | 5.4 | 3.9 | -$3 | 40 |
| Mini-Browser | Age | IP | W | Sv | K | ERA | WHIP | K/9 | BB/9 | $2L | Pts |
| Enright B | 25 | 180 | 10 | 0 | 131 | 4.89 | 1.50 | 6.6 | 2.8 | -$3 | 170 |
| Albers M | 28 | 40 | 2 | 0 | 27 | 5.03 | 1.60 | 6.0 | 4.5 | -$3 | 30 |
| Byrdak T | 37 | 40 | 2 | 0 | 34 | 4.67 | 1.57 | 7.7 | 5.0 | -$3 | 40 |
| Ely J | 24 | 80 | 4 | 0 | 75 | 5.12 | 1.50 | 8.4 | 3.4 | -$3 | 90 |
| Wakefield T | 44 | 120 | 5 | 0 | 70 | 5.28 | 1.47 | 5.3 | 3.2 | -$3 | 90 |

**Competition at RP — Stats in 2010 as RP**

| Thr | Player | GR | ERA | IP/G | Sv-Hld |
|---|---|---|---|---|---|
| RH | Heilman A | 70 | 4.50 | 1.0 | 6-12 |
| RH | Gutierrez J | 58 | 5.08 | 1.0 | 15-8 |
| RH | Vasquez E | 57 | 5.20 | 0.9 | 0-6 |
| RH | Boyer B | 54 | 4.26 | 1.1 | 0-5 |

Ten-Year Trends: K/9, BB/9

**Minors (2010)**

| Level | Leag | W | L | Sv | IP | H | K | ERA | WHIP | K/9 | BB/9 | HR/9 | GB/F |
|---|---|---|---|---|---|---|---|---|---|---|---|---|---|
| A | — | | | | | | | | | | | | |
| AA | — | | | | | | | | | | | | |
| AAA | PCL | 1 | 0 | 2 | 6 | 5 | 9 | 1.50 | 1.00 | 13.5 | 1.5 | 0.0 | — |

**Majors**

| Yr | Team | W | L | Sv | IP | H | K | ERA | WHIP | K/9 | BB/9 | HR/9 | GB/F | $1L | $2L | Pts | RAA | H% | HR/fb | S% | FIP | GS | CG | QS/DS | GR | Hld | Bln | Lead | OPS | 1st Hf | 2nd Hf | vs RH | vs LH |
|---|---|---|---|---|---|---|---|---|---|---|---|---|---|---|---|---|---|---|---|---|---|---|---|---|---|---|---|---|---|---|---|---|---|
| 07 | ATL | 0 | 0 | 0 | 5 | 10 | 3 | 3.38 | 2.06 | 5.1 | 1.7 | 0.0 | 4.0 | -$3 | -$3 | 0 | -1 | 48% | 0% | 82% | 2.64 | — | — | — | 5 | 1 | 0 | -2.4 | .898 | .898 | — | .829 | 1.000 |
| 08 | ATL | 2 | 6 | 1 | 72 | 73 | 67 | 5.88 | 1.36 | 8.4 | 3.1 | 1.3 | 1.2 | -$4 | -$8 | 70 | -19 | 31% | 13% | 68% | 4.19 | — | — | — | 76 | 14 | 4 | +0.3 | .774 | .665 | 1.040 | .754 | .806 |
| 09 | 3TM | 3 | 1 | 0 | 54 | 56 | 29 | 4.12 | 1.39 | 4.8 | 3.3 | 0.2 | 2.9 | -$2 | -$3 | 20 | -11 | 31% | 3% | 68% | 3.52 | — | — | — | 48 | 4 | 0 | +1.0 | .669 | .727 | .596 | .681 | .656 |
| 10 | ARI | 3 | 2 | 0 | 57 | 59 | 29 | 4.26 | 1.54 | 4.6 | 4.6 | 0.5 | 3.1 | -$5 | -$14 | 40 | -6 | 30% | 7% | 72% | 4.39 | — | — | — | 54 | 5 | 4 | -1.1 | .734 | .820 | .644 | .585 | .895 |

## Zach Braddock — 40 IP | $-2 | 50 pts
**RP-46** — Owned: 0% — LH

Braddock is still hunting for the strike zone, a quest inspired by both his greenness and the movement on his pitches. Make no mistake, Zach misses a lot of bats, and Milwaukee will grant him a window to hone his control in 2011. He might start the year in the minors, but he will be up sooner rather than later. (MS)

| Player | Age | IP | W | Sv | K | ERA | WHIP | K/9 | BB/9 | $2L | Pts |
|---|---|---|---|---|---|---|---|---|---|---|---|
| Braddock Z | 23 | 40 | 1 | 0 | 48 | 4.20 | 1.54 | 10.8 | 4.7 | -$2 | 50 |
| Mini-Browser | Age | IP | W | Sv | K | ERA | WHIP | K/9 | BB/9 | $2L | Pts |
| Tomlin J | 26 | 60 | 4 | 0 | 52 | 5.23 | 1.47 | 7.8 | 2.6 | -$1 | 70 |
| Chavez J | 27 | 60 | 3 | 0 | 45 | 5.18 | 1.42 | 6.7 | 3.3 | -$2 | 60 |
| Cohoon M | 23 | 40 | 2 | 0 | 24 | 4.35 | 1.41 | 5.4 | 2.9 | -$2 | 40 |
| Moseley D | 29 | 60 | 3 | 0 | 39 | 5.10 | 1.42 | 5.1 | 1.3 | -$2 | 50 |
| Veras J | 30 | 40 | 2 | 0 | 39 | 4.56 | 1.43 | 8.7 | 5.1 | -$2 | 50 |

**Competition at RP — Stats in 2010 as RP**

| Thr | Player | GR | ERA | IP/G | Sv-Hld |
|---|---|---|---|---|---|
| LH | Braddock Z | 46 | 2.94 | 0.9 | 0-15 |
| LH | Parra M | 26 | 2.39 | 1.4 | 0-0 |
| LH | Capuano C | 15 | 3.54 | 1.4 | 0-1 |

Ten-Year Trends: K/9, BB/9

**Minors (2010)**

| Level | Leag | W | L | Sv | IP | H | K | ERA | WHIP | K/9 | BB/9 | HR/9 | GB/F |
|---|---|---|---|---|---|---|---|---|---|---|---|---|---|
| A | — | | | | | | | | | | | | |
| AA | — | | | | | | | | | | | | |
| AAA | PCL | 0 | 0 | 1 | 16 | 10 | 28 | 4.50 | 1.19 | 15.8 | 5.1 | 0.6 | — |

**Majors**

| Yr | Team | W | L | Sv | IP | H | K | ERA | WHIP | K/9 | BB/9 | HR/9 | GB/F | $1L | $2L | Pts | RAA | H% | HR/fb | S% | FIP | GS | CG | QS/DS | GR | Hld | Bln | Lead | OPS | 1st Hf | 2nd Hf | vs RH | vs LH |
|---|---|---|---|---|---|---|---|---|---|---|---|---|---|---|---|---|---|---|---|---|---|---|---|---|---|---|---|---|---|---|---|---|---|
| 07 | — | | | | | | | | | | | | | | | | | | | | | | | | | | | | | | | | |
| 08 | — | | | | | | | | | | | | | | | | | | | | | | | | | | | | | | | | |
| 09 | — | | | | | | | | | | | | | | | | | | | | | | | | | | | | | | | | |
| 10 | MIL | 1 | 2 | 0 | 33 | 29 | 41 | 2.94 | 1.43 | 11.0 | 5.1 | 0.3 | 0.6 | -$3 | -$8 | 50 | +4 | 32% | 2% | 79% | 2.84 | — | — | — | 46 | 15 | 2 | +0.5 | .656 | .685 | .616 | .812 | .440 |

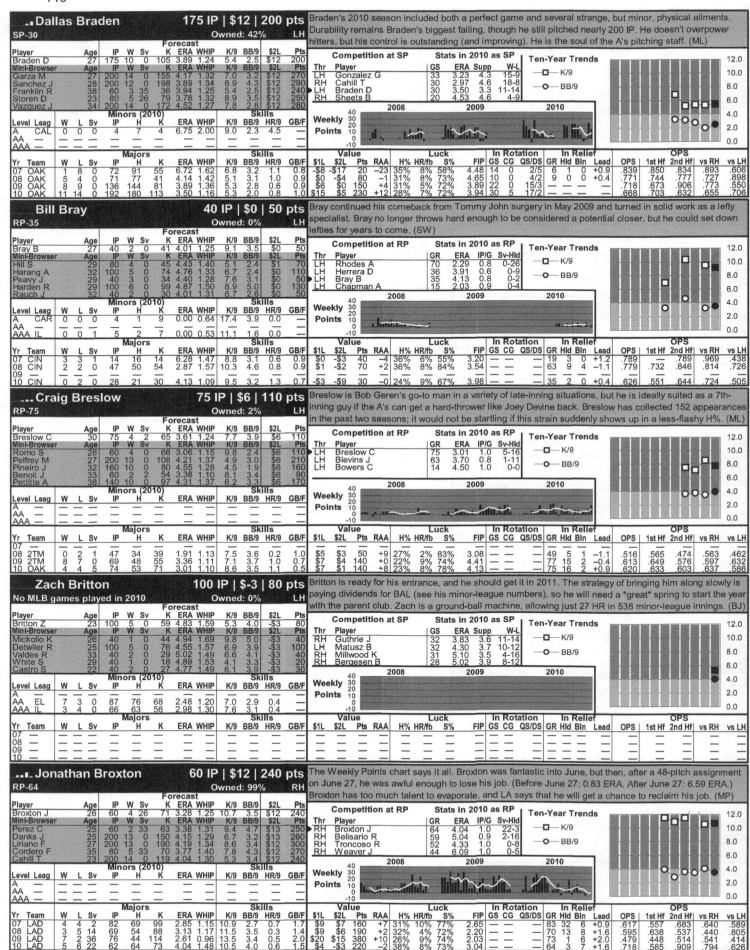

## Dallas Braden — 175 IP | $12 | 200 pts

SP-30 | Owned: 42% | LH

Braden's 2010 season included both a perfect game and several strange, but minor, physical ailments. Durability remains Braden's biggest failing, though he still pitched nearly 200 IP. He doesn't overpower hitters, but his control is outstanding (and improving). He is the soul of the A's pitching staff. (ML)

| Forecast Player | Age | IP | W | Sv | K | ERA | WHIP | K/9 | BB/9 | $2L | Pts |
|---|---|---|---|---|---|---|---|---|---|---|---|
| Braden D | 27 | 175 | 10 | 0 | 105 | 3.89 | 1.24 | 5.4 | 2.5 | $12 | 200 |
| **Mini-Browser** | **Age** | **IP** | **W** | **Sv** | **K** | **ERA** | **WHIP** | **K/9** | **BB/9** | **$2L** | **Pts** |
| Garza M | 27 | 200 | 14 | 0 | 155 | 4.17 | 1.32 | 7.0 | 3.2 | $12 | 270 |
| Sanchez J | 28 | 200 | 12 | 0 | 198 | 3.89 | 1.34 | 8.9 | 4.3 | $12 | 290 |
| Franklin R | 38 | 60 | 3 | 35 | 36 | 3.94 | 1.25 | 5.4 | 2.5 | $12 | 240 |
| Storen D | 23 | 80 | 5 | 26 | 79 | 3.78 | 1.32 | 8.9 | 3.5 | $12 | 250 |
| Vazquez J | 34 | 200 | 14 | 0 | 172 | 4.52 | 1.27 | 7.8 | 2.8 | $12 | 280 |

| Minors (2010) Level | Leag | W | L | Sv | IP | H | K | ERA | WHIP | K/9 | BB/9 | HR/9 | GB/F |
|---|---|---|---|---|---|---|---|---|---|---|---|---|---|
| A | CAL | 0 | 0 | 0 | 4 | 7 | 4 | 6.75 | 2.00 | 9.0 | 2.3 | 4.5 | — |
| AA | — | — | — | — | — | — | — | — | — | — | — | — | — |
| AAA | — | — | — | — | — | — | — | — | — | — | — | — | — |

| Competition at SP Thr | Player | GS | ERA | Supp | W-L |
|---|---|---|---|---|---|
| LH | Gonzalez G | 33 | 3.23 | 4.3 | 15-9 |
| RH | Cahill T | 30 | 2.97 | 4.6 | 18-8 |
| LH | Braden D | 30 | 3.50 | 3.3 | 11-14 |
| RH | Sheets B | 20 | 4.53 | 4.6 | 4-9 |

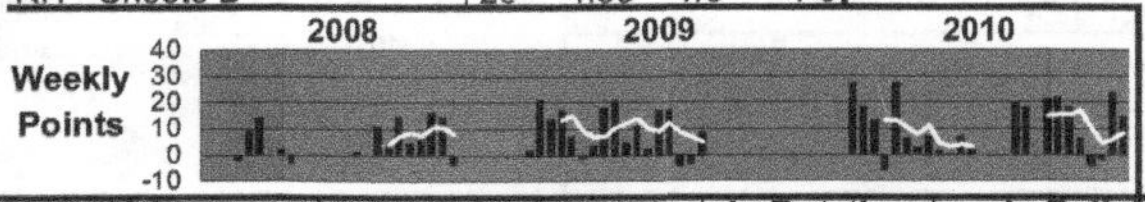


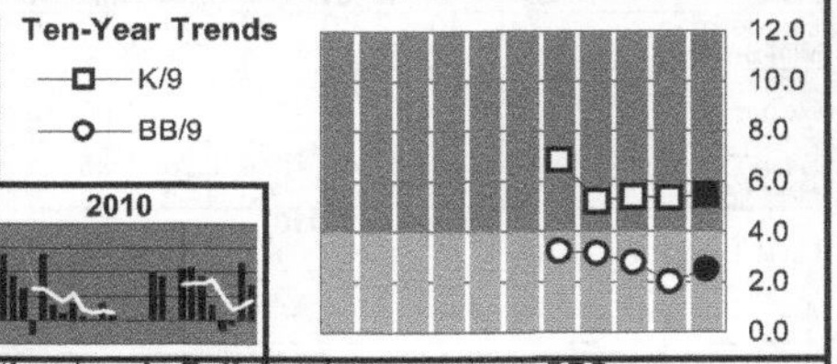


| Yr | Team | W | L | Sv | IP | H | K | ERA | WHIP | K/9 | BB/9 | HR/9 | GB/F | $1L | $2L | Pts | RAA | H% | HR/fb | S% | FIP | GS | CG | QS/DS | GR | Hld | Bln | Lead | OPS | 1st Hf | 2nd Hf | vs RH | vs LH |
|---|---|---|---|---|---|---|---|---|---|---|---|---|---|---|---|---|---|---|---|---|---|---|---|---|---|---|---|---|---|---|---|---|---|
| 07 | OAK | 1 | 8 | 0 | 72 | 91 | 55 | 6.72 | 1.62 | 6.8 | 3.2 | 1.1 | 0.8 | -$8 | -$17 | 20 | -23 | 35% | 8% | 58% | 4.48 | 14 | 0 | 2/5 | 6 | 1 | 0 | +0.9 | .839 | .850 | .834 | .893 | .606 |
| 08 | OAK | 5 | 4 | 0 | 71 | 77 | 41 | 4.14 | 1.42 | 5.1 | 3.1 | 1.0 | 0.9 | $0 | -$4 | 80 | -1 | 31% | 8% | 73% | 4.65 | 10 | 0 | 4/2 | 9 | 0 | 0 | +0.4 | .771 | .744 | .777 | .727 | .898 |
| 09 | OAK | 8 | 9 | 0 | 136 | 144 | 81 | 3.89 | 1.36 | 5.3 | 2.8 | 0.6 | 0.9 | $6 | $0 | 150 | +4 | 31% | 5% | 72% | 3.89 | 22 | 0 | 15/3 | — | — | — | — | .718 | .673 | .906 | .773 | .550 |
| 10 | OAK | 11 | 14 | 0 | 192 | 180 | 113 | 3.50 | 1.16 | 5.3 | 2.0 | 0.8 | 1.0 | $15 | $5 | 230 | +12 | 28% | 7% | 72% | 3.94 | 30 | 5 | 17/2 | — | — | — | — | .668 | .703 | .632 | .655 | .706 |

## Bill Bray — 40 IP | $0 | 50 pts

RP-35 | Owned: 0% | LH

Bray continued his comeback from Tommy John surgery in May 2009 and turned in solid work as a lefty specialist. Bray no longer throws hard enough to be considered a potential closer, but he could set down lefties for years to come. (SW)

| Forecast Player | Age | IP | W | Sv | K | ERA | WHIP | K/9 | BB/9 | $2L | Pts |
|---|---|---|---|---|---|---|---|---|---|---|---|
| Bray B | 27 | 40 | 2 | 0 | 41 | 4.01 | 1.25 | 9.1 | 3.5 | $0 | 50 |
| **Mini-Browser** | **Age** | **IP** | **W** | **Sv** | **K** | **ERA** | **WHIP** | **K/9** | **BB/9** | **$2L** | **Pts** |
| Hill S | 29 | 80 | 4 | 0 | 45 | 4.43 | 1.40 | 5.1 | 2.4 | $1 | 70 |
| Harang A | 32 | 100 | 5 | 0 | 74 | 4.76 | 1.33 | 6.7 | 2.4 | $0 | 110 |
| Peavy J | 29 | 40 | 3 | 0 | 34 | 4.40 | 1.28 | 7.6 | 3.1 | $0 | 50 |
| Harden R | 29 | 100 | 6 | 0 | 99 | 4.87 | 1.50 | 8.9 | 5.0 | $0 | 130 |
| Rauch J | 32 | 40 | 2 | 0 | 30 | 4.01 | 1.31 | 6.7 | 2.6 | $0 | 50 |

| Minors (2010) Level | Leag | W | L | Sv | IP | H | K | ERA | WHIP | K/9 | BB/9 | HR/9 | GB/F |
|---|---|---|---|---|---|---|---|---|---|---|---|---|---|
| A | CAR | 0 | 0 | 0 | 4 | 1 | 9 | 0.00 | 0.64 | 17.4 | 3.9 | 0.0 | — |
| AA | — | — | — | — | — | — | — | — | — | — | — | — | — |
| AAA | IL | 0 | 0 | 1 | 5 | 2 | 7 | 0.00 | 0.53 | 11.1 | 1.6 | 0.0 | — |

| Competition at RP Thr | Player | GR | ERA | IP/G | Sv-Hld |
|---|---|---|---|---|---|
| LH | Rhodes A | 70 | 2.29 | 0.8 | 0-26 |
| LH | Herrera D | 36 | 3.91 | 0.6 | 0-9 |
| LH | Bray B | 35 | 4.13 | 0.8 | 0-2 |
| LH | Chapman A | 15 | 2.03 | 0.9 | 0-4 |

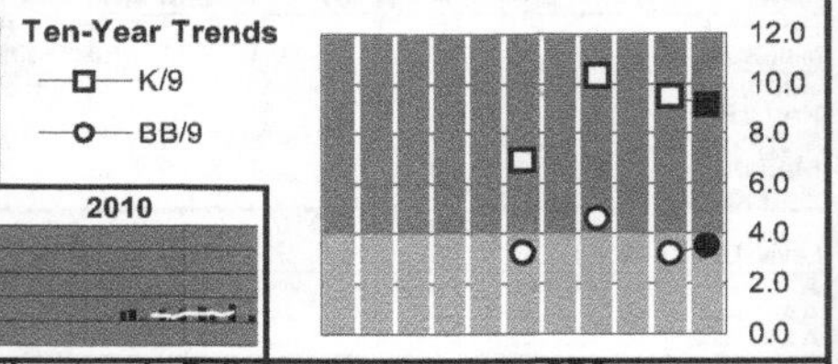


| Yr | Team | W | L | Sv | IP | H | K | ERA | WHIP | K/9 | BB/9 | HR/9 | GB/F | $1L | $2L | Pts | RAA | H% | HR/fb | S% | FIP | GS | CG | QS/DS | GR | Hld | Bln | Lead | OPS | 1st Hf | 2nd Hf | vs RH | vs LH |
|---|---|---|---|---|---|---|---|---|---|---|---|---|---|---|---|---|---|---|---|---|---|---|---|---|---|---|---|---|---|---|---|---|---|
| 07 | CIN | 3 | 3 | 1 | 14 | 16 | 14 | 6.28 | 1.47 | 8.8 | 3.1 | 0.6 | 0.9 | $0 | -$3 | 40 | -4 | 36% | 6% | 55% | 3.20 | — | — | — | 19 | 3 | 0 | +1.2 | .789 | — | .789 | .969 | .438 |
| 08 | CIN | 2 | 2 | 0 | 47 | 50 | 54 | 2.87 | 1.57 | 10.3 | 4.6 | 0.8 | 0.9 | $1 | -$2 | 70 | +2 | 36% | 8% | 84% | 3.54 | — | — | — | 63 | 9 | 4 | -1.1 | .779 | .732 | .846 | .814 | .726 |
| 09 | — | — | — | — | — | — | — | — | — | — | — | — | — | — | — | — | — | — | — | — | — | — | — | — | — | — | — | — | — | — | — | — | — |
| 10 | CIN | 0 | 2 | 0 | 28 | 21 | 30 | 4.13 | 1.09 | 9.5 | 3.2 | 1.3 | 0.7 | -$3 | -$9 | 30 | -0 | 24% | 9% | 67% | 3.98 | — | — | — | 35 | 2 | 0 | +0.4 | .626 | .551 | .644 | .724 | .505 |

## Craig Breslow — 75 IP | $6 | 110 pts

RP-75 | Owned: 2% | LH

Breslow is Bob Geren's go-to man in a variety of late-inning situations, but he is ideally suited as a 7th-inning guy if the A's can get a hard-thrower like Joey Devine back. Breslow has collected 152 appearances in the past two seasons; it would not be startling if this strain suddenly shows up in a less-flashy H%. (ML)

| Forecast Player | Age | IP | W | Sv | K | ERA | WHIP | K/9 | BB/9 | $2L | Pts |
|---|---|---|---|---|---|---|---|---|---|---|---|
| Breslow C | 30 | 75 | 4 | 2 | 65 | 3.61 | 1.24 | 7.7 | 3.9 | $6 | 110 |
| **Mini-Browser** | **Age** | **IP** | **W** | **Sv** | **K** | **ERA** | **WHIP** | **K/9** | **BB/9** | **$2L** | **Pts** |
| Romo S | 28 | 60 | 4 | 0 | 66 | 3.06 | 1.15 | 9.8 | 2.4 | $6 | 110 |
| Pelfrey M | 27 | 200 | 13 | 0 | 108 | 4.21 | 1.37 | 4.9 | 3.0 | $6 | 210 |
| Pineiro J | 32 | 160 | 10 | 0 | 80 | 4.55 | 1.28 | 4.5 | 1.9 | $6 | 160 |
| Benoit J | 33 | 60 | 2 | 2 | 54 | 3.38 | 1.10 | 8.1 | 3.4 | $6 | 90 |
| Pettitte A | 38 | 140 | 10 | 0 | 97 | 4.31 | 1.37 | 6.2 | 3.3 | $6 | 170 |

| Minors (2010) Level | Leag | W | L | Sv | IP | H | K | ERA | WHIP | K/9 | BB/9 | HR/9 | GB/F |
|---|---|---|---|---|---|---|---|---|---|---|---|---|---|
| A | — | — | — | — | — | — | — | — | — | — | — | — | — |
| AA | — | — | — | — | — | — | — | — | — | — | — | — | — |
| AAA | — | — | — | — | — | — | — | — | — | — | — | — | — |

| Competition at RP Thr | Player | GR | ERA | IP/G | Sv-Hld |
|---|---|---|---|---|---|
| LH | Breslow C | 75 | 3.01 | 1.0 | 5-16 |
| LH | Blevins J | 63 | 3.70 | 0.8 | 1-11 |
| LH | Bowers C | 14 | 4.50 | 1.0 | 0-0 |

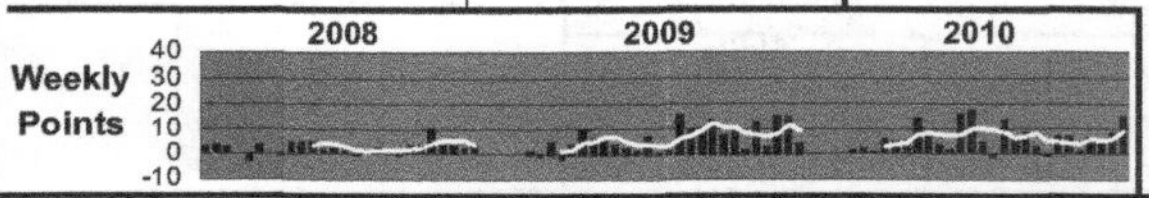


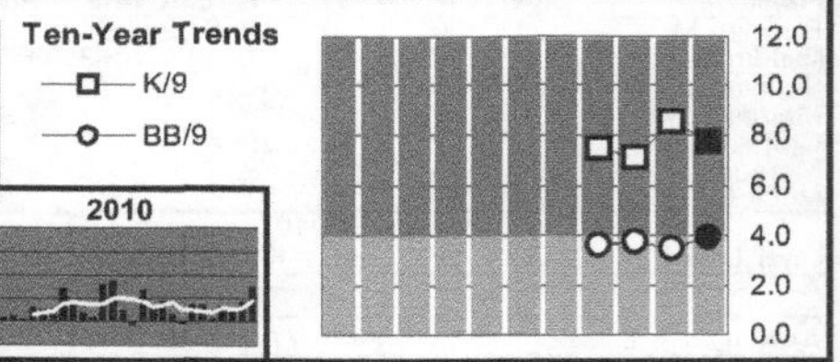


| Yr | Team | W | L | Sv | IP | H | K | ERA | WHIP | K/9 | BB/9 | HR/9 | GB/F | $1L | $2L | Pts | RAA | H% | HR/fb | S% | FIP | GS | CG | QS/DS | GR | Hld | Bln | Lead | OPS | 1st Hf | 2nd Hf | vs RH | vs LH |
|---|---|---|---|---|---|---|---|---|---|---|---|---|---|---|---|---|---|---|---|---|---|---|---|---|---|---|---|---|---|---|---|---|---|
| 07 | — | — | — | — | — | — | — | — | — | — | — | — | — | — | — | — | — | — | — | — | — | — | — | — | — | — | — | — | — | — | — | — | — |
| 08 | 2TM | 0 | 2 | 1 | 47 | 34 | 39 | 1.91 | 1.13 | 7.5 | 3.6 | 0.2 | 1.0 | $5 | $3 | 50 | +9 | 27% | 2% | 83% | 3.08 | — | — | — | 49 | 5 | 1 | -1.1 | .516 | .565 | .474 | .563 | .462 |
| 09 | 2TM | 8 | 7 | 0 | 69 | 48 | 55 | 3.36 | 1.11 | 7.1 | 3.7 | 1.0 | 0.7 | $7 | $4 | 140 | +0 | 22% | 9% | 74% | 4.41 | — | — | — | 77 | 15 | 2 | -0.4 | .613 | .649 | .576 | .597 | .632 |
| 10 | OAK | 4 | 4 | 5 | 74 | 53 | 71 | 3.01 | 1.10 | 8.6 | 3.5 | 1.1 | 0.5 | $7 | $1 | 140 | +8 | 23% | 8% | 78% | 4.13 | — | — | — | 75 | 16 | 2 | +0.9 | .620 | .633 | .603 | .637 | .586 |

## Zach Britton — 100 IP | $-3 | 80 pts

No MLB games played in 2010 | Owned: 0% | LH

Britton is ready for his entrance, and he should get it in 2011. The strategy of bringing him along slowly is paying dividends for BAL (see his minor-league numbers), so he will need a *great* spring to start the year with the parent club. Zach is a ground-ball machine, allowing just 27 HR in 538 minor-league innings. (BJ)

| Forecast Player | Age | IP | W | Sv | K | ERA | WHIP | K/9 | BB/9 | $2L | Pts |
|---|---|---|---|---|---|---|---|---|---|---|---|
| Britton Z | 23 | 100 | 5 | 0 | 59 | 4.83 | 1.59 | 5.3 | 4.0 | -$3 | 80 |
| **Mini-Browser** | **Age** | **IP** | **W** | **Sv** | **K** | **ERA** | **WHIP** | **K/9** | **BB/9** | **$2L** | **Pts** |
| Mickolio K | 26 | 40 | 1 | 0 | 44 | 4.94 | 1.69 | 9.8 | 5.0 | -$3 | 40 |
| Detwiler R | 25 | 100 | 5 | 0 | 76 | 4.55 | 1.57 | 6.9 | 3.9 | -$3 | 100 |
| Valdes R | 33 | 40 | 2 | 0 | 29 | 5.02 | 1.49 | 6.6 | 4.1 | -$3 | 40 |
| White S | 29 | 40 | 1 | 0 | 18 | 4.89 | 1.53 | 4.1 | 3.3 | -$3 | 20 |
| Castro S | 22 | 40 | 2 | 0 | 27 | 4.77 | 1.49 | 6.1 | 3.9 | -$3 | 30 |

| Minors (2010) Level | Leag | W | L | Sv | IP | H | K | ERA | WHIP | K/9 | BB/9 | HR/9 | GB/F |
|---|---|---|---|---|---|---|---|---|---|---|---|---|---|
| A | — | — | — | — | — | — | — | — | — | — | — | — | — |
| AA | EL | 7 | 3 | 0 | 87 | 76 | 68 | 2.48 | 1.20 | 7.0 | 2.9 | 0.4 | — |
| AAA | IL | 3 | 4 | 0 | 66 | 63 | 56 | 2.98 | 1.30 | 7.6 | 3.1 | 0.4 | — |

| Competition at SP Thr | Player | GS | ERA | Supp | W-L |
|---|---|---|---|---|---|
| RH | Guthrie J | 32 | 3.83 | 3.6 | 11-14 |
| LH | Matusz B | 32 | 4.30 | 3.7 | 10-12 |
| RH | Millwood K | 31 | 5.10 | 3.5 | 4-16 |
| RH | Bergesen B | 28 | 5.02 | 3.9 | 8-12 |

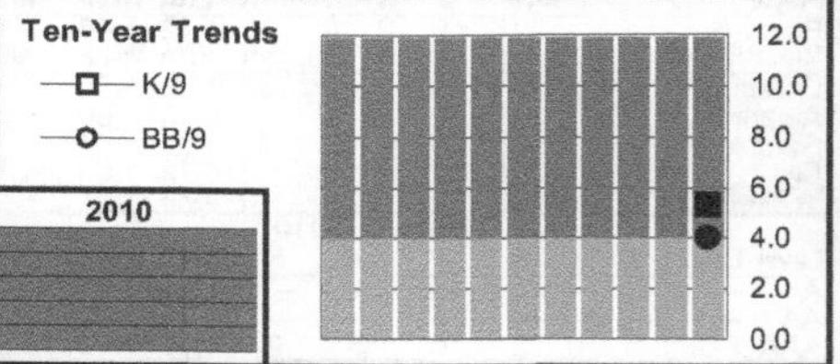


| Yr | Team | W | L | Sv | IP | H | K | ERA | WHIP | K/9 | BB/9 | HR/9 | GB/F | $1L | $2L | Pts | RAA | H% | HR/fb | S% | FIP | GS | CG | QS/DS | GR | Hld | Bln | Lead | OPS | 1st Hf | 2nd Hf | vs RH | vs LH |
|---|---|---|---|---|---|---|---|---|---|---|---|---|---|---|---|---|---|---|---|---|---|---|---|---|---|---|---|---|---|---|---|---|---|
| 07 | — | — | — | — | — | — | — | — | — | — | — | — | — | — | — | — | — | — | — | — | — | — | — | — | — | — | — | — | — | — | — | — | — |
| 08 | — | — | — | — | — | — | — | — | — | — | — | — | — | — | — | — | — | — | — | — | — | — | — | — | — | — | — | — | — | — | — | — | — |
| 09 | — | — | — | — | — | — | — | — | — | — | — | — | — | — | — | — | — | — | — | — | — | — | — | — | — | — | — | — | — | — | — | — | — |
| 10 | — | — | — | — | — | — | — | — | — | — | — | — | — | — | — | — | — | — | — | — | — | — | — | — | — | — | — | — | — | — | — | — | — |

## Jonathan Broxton — 60 IP | $12 | 240 pts

RP-64 | Owned: 99% | RH

The Weekly Points chart says it all. Broxton was fantastic into June, but then, after a 48-pitch assignment on June 27, he was awful enough to lose his job. (Before June 27: 0.83 ERA. After June 27: 6.59 ERA.) Broxton has too much talent to evaporate, and LA says that he will get a chance to reclaim his job. (MP)

| Forecast Player | Age | IP | W | Sv | K | ERA | WHIP | K/9 | BB/9 | $2L | Pts |
|---|---|---|---|---|---|---|---|---|---|---|---|
| Broxton J | 26 | 60 | 4 | 26 | 71 | 3.28 | 1.25 | 10.7 | 3.5 | $12 | 240 |
| **Mini-Browser** | **Age** | **IP** | **W** | **Sv** | **K** | **ERA** | **WHIP** | **K/9** | **BB/9** | **$2L** | **Pts** |
| Perez C | 25 | 60 | 2 | 33 | 63 | 3.38 | 1.31 | 9.4 | 4.7 | $13 | 250 |
| Danks J | 25 | 200 | 13 | 0 | 150 | 4.15 | 1.29 | 6.7 | 3.2 | $13 | 260 |
| Liriano F | 27 | 200 | 13 | 0 | 190 | 4.19 | 1.34 | 8.6 | 3.4 | $12 | 300 |
| Cordero F | 35 | 80 | 5 | 33 | 70 | 3.77 | 1.40 | 7.8 | 4.3 | $12 | 270 |
| Cahill T | 23 | 200 | 14 | 0 | 119 | 4.04 | 1.30 | 5.3 | 3.4 | $12 | 240 |

| Minors (2010) Level | Leag | W | L | Sv | IP | H | K | ERA | WHIP | K/9 | BB/9 | HR/9 | GB/F |
|---|---|---|---|---|---|---|---|---|---|---|---|---|---|
| A | — | — | — | — | — | — | — | — | — | — | — | — | — |
| AA | — | — | — | — | — | — | — | — | — | — | — | — | — |
| AAA | — | — | — | — | — | — | — | — | — | — | — | — | — |

| Competition at RP Thr | Player | GR | ERA | IP/G | Sv-Hld |
|---|---|---|---|---|---|
| RH | Broxton J | 64 | 4.04 | 1.0 | 22-3 |
| RH | Belisario R | 59 | 5.04 | 0.9 | 2-16 |
| RH | Troncoso R | 52 | 4.33 | 1.0 | 0-8 |
| RH | Weaver J | 44 | 6.09 | 1.0 | 0-5 |

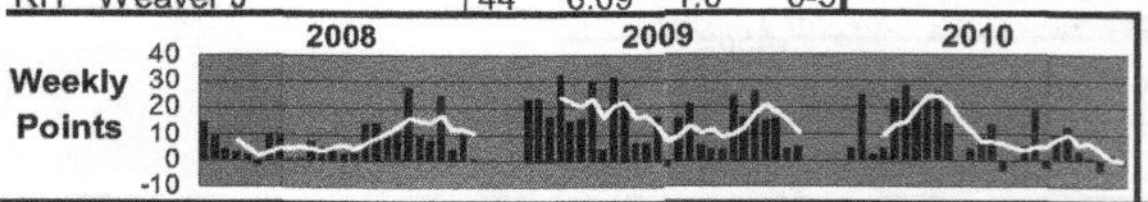


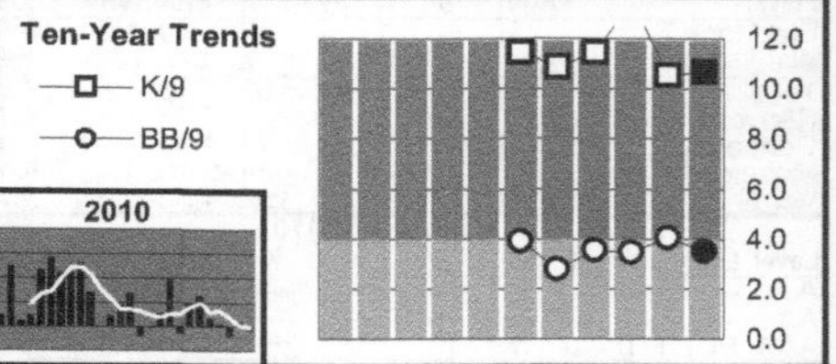


| Yr | Team | W | L | Sv | IP | H | K | ERA | WHIP | K/9 | BB/9 | HR/9 | GB/F | $1L | $2L | Pts | RAA | H% | HR/fb | S% | FIP | GS | CG | QS/DS | GR | Hld | Bln | Lead | OPS | 1st Hf | 2nd Hf | vs RH | vs LH |
|---|---|---|---|---|---|---|---|---|---|---|---|---|---|---|---|---|---|---|---|---|---|---|---|---|---|---|---|---|---|---|---|---|---|
| 07 | LAD | 4 | 4 | 2 | 82 | 69 | 99 | 2.85 | 1.15 | 10.9 | 2.7 | 0.7 | 1.7 | $9 | $7 | 160 | +7 | 31% | 10% | 77% | 2.65 | — | — | — | 83 | 32 | 6 | +0.9 | .617 | .557 | .683 | .640 | .589 |
| 08 | LAD | 3 | 5 | 14 | 69 | 54 | 88 | 3.13 | 1.17 | 11.5 | 3.5 | 0.3 | 1.4 | $9 | $6 | 190 | +2 | 32% | 4% | 72% | 2.20 | — | — | — | 70 | 13 | 8 | +1.6 | .595 | .638 | .537 | .440 | .805 |
| 09 | LAD | 7 | 2 | 36 | 76 | 44 | 114 | 2.61 | 0.96 | 13.5 | 3.4 | 0.5 | 2.0 | $20 | $15 | 380 | +10 | 26% | 9% | 74% | 2.03 | — | — | — | 73 | 1 | 6 | +2.0 | .479 | .448 | .514 | .541 | .414 |
| 10 | LAD | 5 | 6 | 22 | 62 | 64 | 73 | 4.04 | 1.48 | 10.5 | 4.0 | 0.6 | 1.5 | $4 | -$3 | 220 | -2 | 38% | 8% | 73% | 3.04 | — | — | — | 64 | 3 | 7 | +1.6 | .718 | .585 | .909 | .794 | .626 |

*For more stats, visit www.Rotolympus.com.*

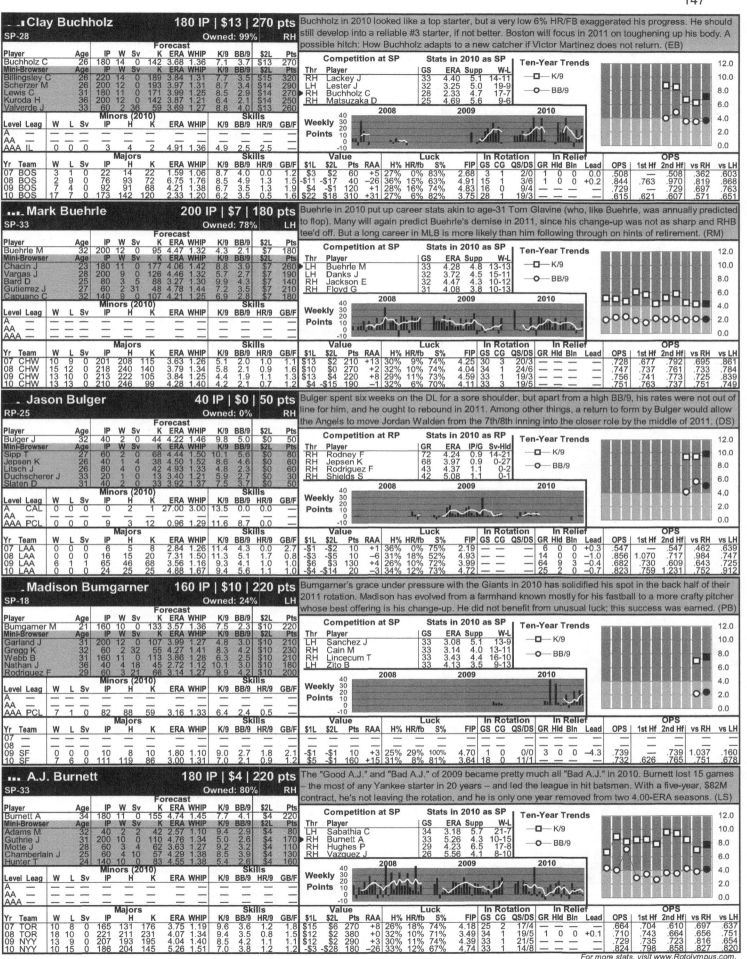

## Clay Buchholz — 180 IP | $13 | 270 pts
**SP-28** — Owned: 99% — RH

Buchholz in 2010 looked like a top starter, but a very low 6% HR/FB exaggerated his progress. He should still develop into a reliable #3 starter, if not better. Boston will focus in 2011 on toughening up his body. A possible hitch: How Buchholz adapts to a new catcher if Victor Martinez does not return. (EB)

### Forecast
| Player | Age | IP | W | Sv | K | ERA | WHIP | K/9 | BB/9 | $2L | Pts |
|---|---|---|---|---|---|---|---|---|---|---|---|
| Buchholz C | 26 | 180 | 14 | 0 | 142 | 3.68 | 1.36 | 7.1 | 3.7 | $13 | 270 |

### Mini-Browser
| Player | Age | IP | W | Sv | K | ERA | WHIP | K/9 | BB/9 | $2L | Pts |
|---|---|---|---|---|---|---|---|---|---|---|---|
| Billingsley C | 26 | 220 | 14 | 0 | 189 | 3.84 | 1.31 | 7.7 | 3.5 | $15 | 320 |
| Scherzer M | 26 | 200 | 12 | 0 | 193 | 3.97 | 1.31 | 8.7 | 3.4 | $14 | 290 |
| Lewis C | 31 | 180 | 11 | 0 | 171 | 3.99 | 1.25 | 8.5 | 2.9 | $14 | 270 |
| Kuroda H | 36 | 200 | 12 | 0 | 142 | 3.87 | 1.21 | 6.4 | 2.1 | $14 | 250 |
| Valverde J | 33 | 60 | 2 | 36 | 59 | 3.69 | 1.27 | 8.8 | 4.0 | $13 | 260 |

### Minors (2010) / Skills
| Level | Leag | W | L | Sv | IP | H | K | ERA | WHIP | K/9 | BB/9 | HR/9 | GB/F |
|---|---|---|---|---|---|---|---|---|---|---|---|---|---|
| A | — | | | | | | | | | | | | |
| AA | — | | | | | | | | | | | | |
| AAA | IL | 0 | 0 | 0 | 3 | 4 | 2 | 4.91 | 1.36 | 4.9 | 2.5 | 2.5 | — |

### Majors / Skills
| Yr | Team | W | L | Sv | IP | H | K | ERA | WHIP | K/9 | BB/9 | HR/9 | GB/F |
|---|---|---|---|---|---|---|---|---|---|---|---|---|---|
| 07 | BOS | 3 | 1 | 0 | 22 | 14 | 22 | 1.59 | 1.06 | 8.7 | 4.0 | 0.0 | 1.2 |
| 08 | BOS | 2 | 9 | 0 | 76 | 93 | 72 | 6.75 | 1.76 | 8.5 | 4.9 | 1.3 | 1.5 |
| 09 | BOS | 7 | 4 | 0 | 92 | 91 | 68 | 4.21 | 1.38 | 6.7 | 3.5 | 1.3 | 1.9 |
| 10 | BOS | 17 | 7 | 0 | 173 | 142 | 120 | 2.33 | 1.20 | 6.2 | 3.5 | 0.5 | 1.6 |

### Competition at SP / Stats in 2010 as SP
| Thr | Player | GS | ERA | Supp | W-L |
|---|---|---|---|---|---|
| RH | Lackey J | 33 | 4.40 | 5.1 | 14-11 |
| LH | Lester J | 32 | 3.25 | 5.0 | 19-9 |
| RH | Buchholz C | 28 | 2.33 | 4.7 | 17-7 |
| RH | Matsuzaka D | 25 | 4.69 | 5.6 | 9-6 |

Weekly Points — 2008 / 2009 / 2010

Ten-Year Trends — K/9 / BB/9

### Value / Luck / In Rotation / In Relief / OPS
| $1L | $2L | Pts | RAA | H% | HR/fb | S% | FIP | GS | CG | QS/DS | GR | Hld | Bln | Lead | OPS | 1st Hf | 2nd Hf | vs RH | vs LH |
|---|---|---|---|---|---|---|---|---|---|---|---|---|---|---|---|---|---|---|---|
| $3 | $2 | 60 | +5 | 27% | 0% | 83% | 2.68 | 3 | 1 | 2/0 | 1 | 0 | 0 | 0.0 | .508 | — | .508 | .362 | .603 |
| -$11 | -$17 | 40 | -26 | 36% | 15% | 63% | 4.91 | 15 | 1 | 3/6 | 1 | 0 | 0 | +0.2 | .844 | .763 | .970 | .819 | .868 |
| $4 | -$1 | 120 | +1 | 28% | 16% | 74% | 4.83 | 16 | 0 | 9/4 | — | — | — | — | .729 | — | .729 | .697 | .763 |
| $22 | $18 | 310 | +31 | 27% | 6% | 82% | 3.75 | 28 | 1 | 19/3 | — | — | — | — | .615 | .621 | .607 | .571 | .651 |

## Mark Buehrle — 200 IP | $7 | 180 pts
**SP-33** — Owned: 78% — LH

Buehrle in 2010 put up career stats akin to age-31 Tom Glavine (who, like Buehrle, was annually predicted to flop). Many will again predict Buehrle's demise in 2011, since his change-up was not as sharp and RHB tee'd off. But a long career in MLB is more likely than him following through on hints of retirement. (RM)

### Forecast
| Player | Age | IP | W | Sv | K | ERA | WHIP | K/9 | BB/9 | $2L | Pts |
|---|---|---|---|---|---|---|---|---|---|---|---|
| Buehrle M | 32 | 200 | 12 | 0 | 95 | 4.47 | 1.32 | 4.3 | 2.1 | $7 | 180 |

### Mini-Browser
| Player | Age | IP | W | Sv | K | ERA | WHIP | K/9 | BB/9 | $2L | Pts |
|---|---|---|---|---|---|---|---|---|---|---|---|
| Chacin J | 23 | 180 | 11 | 0 | 177 | 4.06 | 1.42 | 8.8 | 3.9 | $7 | 260 |
| Vargas J | 28 | 200 | 9 | 0 | 126 | 4.46 | 1.32 | 5.7 | 2.7 | $7 | 190 |
| Bard D | 25 | 80 | 3 | 5 | 88 | 3.27 | 1.30 | 9.9 | 4.3 | $7 | 140 |
| Gutierrez J | 27 | 60 | 2 | 31 | 48 | 4.78 | 1.44 | 7.2 | 3.5 | $7 | 210 |
| Capuano C | 32 | 140 | 9 | 0 | 107 | 4.21 | 1.25 | 6.9 | 2.2 | $7 | 180 |

### Minors (2010) / Skills
| Level | Leag | W | L | Sv | IP | H | K | ERA | WHIP | K/9 | BB/9 | HR/9 | GB/F |
|---|---|---|---|---|---|---|---|---|---|---|---|---|---|
| A | — | | | | | | | | | | | | |
| AA | — | | | | | | | | | | | | |
| AAA | — | | | | | | | | | | | | |

### Majors / Skills
| Yr | Team | W | L | Sv | IP | H | K | ERA | WHIP | K/9 | BB/9 | HR/9 | GB/F |
|---|---|---|---|---|---|---|---|---|---|---|---|---|---|
| 07 | CHW | 10 | 9 | 0 | 201 | 208 | 115 | 3.63 | 1.26 | 5.1 | 2.0 | 1.0 | 1.1 |
| 08 | CHW | 15 | 12 | 0 | 218 | 240 | 140 | 3.79 | 1.34 | 5.8 | 2.1 | 0.9 | 1.6 |
| 09 | CHW | 13 | 10 | 0 | 213 | 222 | 105 | 3.84 | 1.25 | 4.4 | 1.9 | 1.1 | 1.3 |
| 10 | CHW | 13 | 13 | 0 | 210 | 246 | 99 | 4.28 | 1.40 | 4.2 | 2.1 | 0.7 | 1.2 |

### Competition at SP / Stats in 2010 as SP
| Thr | Player | GS | ERA | Supp | W-L |
|---|---|---|---|---|---|
| LH | Buehrle M | 33 | 4.28 | 4.8 | 13-13 |
| LH | Danks J | 32 | 3.72 | 4.5 | 15-11 |
| RH | Jackson E | 32 | 4.47 | 4.3 | 10-12 |
| RH | Floyd G | 31 | 4.08 | 3.8 | 10-13 |

Weekly Points — 2008 / 2009 / 2010

Ten-Year Trends — K/9 / BB/9

### Value / Luck / In Rotation / In Relief / OPS
| $1L | $2L | Pts | RAA | H% | HR/fb | S% | FIP | GS | CG | QS/DS | GR | Hld | Bln | Lead | OPS | 1st Hf | 2nd Hf | vs RH | vs LH |
|---|---|---|---|---|---|---|---|---|---|---|---|---|---|---|---|---|---|---|---|
| $13 | $2 | 210 | +13 | 30% | 9% | 74% | 4.25 | 30 | 3 | 20/3 | — | — | — | — | .728 | .677 | .792 | .695 | .861 |
| $10 | $2 | 270 | +2 | 32% | 10% | 74% | 4.04 | 34 | 1 | 24/6 | — | — | — | — | .747 | .737 | .761 | .733 | .784 |
| $10 | $4 | 220 | +8 | 29% | 11% | 73% | 4.59 | 33 | 1 | 19/3 | — | — | — | — | .756 | .741 | .773 | .725 | .839 |
| $4 | -$15 | 190 | -1 | 32% | 6% | 70% | 4.11 | 33 | 3 | 19/5 | — | — | — | — | .751 | .763 | .737 | .751 | .749 |

## Jason Bulger — 40 IP | $0 | 50 pts
**RP-25** — Owned: 0% — RH

Bulger spent six weeks on the DL for a sore shoulder, but apart from a high BB/9, his rates were not out of line for him, and he ought to rebound in 2011. Among other things, a return to form by Bulger would allow the Angels to move Jordan Walden from the 7th/8th inning into the closer role by the middle of 2011. (DS)

### Forecast
| Player | Age | IP | W | Sv | K | ERA | WHIP | K/9 | BB/9 | $2L | Pts |
|---|---|---|---|---|---|---|---|---|---|---|---|
| Bulger J | 32 | 40 | 2 | 0 | 44 | 4.22 | 1.46 | 9.8 | 5.0 | $0 | 50 |

### Mini-Browser
| Player | Age | IP | W | Sv | K | ERA | WHIP | K/9 | BB/9 | $2L | Pts |
|---|---|---|---|---|---|---|---|---|---|---|---|
| Sipp T | 27 | 60 | 2 | 0 | 68 | 4.44 | 1.50 | 10.1 | 5.6 | $0 | 80 |
| Jepsen K | 26 | 40 | 4 | 4 | 38 | 4.50 | 1.52 | 8.6 | 4.6 | $0 | 60 |
| Litsch J | 26 | 80 | 4 | 0 | 42 | 4.93 | 1.33 | 4.8 | 2.3 | $0 | 60 |
| Duchscherer J | 33 | 20 | 1 | 0 | 13 | 3.40 | 1.21 | 5.9 | 2.7 | $0 | 30 |
| Slaten D | 31 | 40 | 2 | 0 | 33 | 3.92 | 1.37 | 7.5 | 3.7 | $0 | 50 |

### Minors (2010) / Skills
| Level | Leag | W | L | Sv | IP | H | K | ERA | WHIP | K/9 | BB/9 | HR/9 | GB/F |
|---|---|---|---|---|---|---|---|---|---|---|---|---|---|
| A | CAL | 0 | 0 | 0 | 2 | 1 | 27.00 | 3.00 | 13.5 | 0.0 | 0.0 | — | |
| AA | — | | | | | | | | | | | | |
| AAA | PCL | 0 | 0 | 0 | 9 | 3 | 12 | 0.96 | 1.29 | 11.6 | 8.7 | 0.0 | — |

### Majors / Skills
| Yr | Team | W | L | Sv | IP | H | K | ERA | WHIP | K/9 | BB/9 | HR/9 | GB/F |
|---|---|---|---|---|---|---|---|---|---|---|---|---|---|
| 07 | LAA | 0 | 0 | 0 | 6 | 5 | 8 | 2.84 | 1.26 | 11.4 | 4.3 | 0.0 | 2.7 |
| 08 | LAA | 0 | 0 | 0 | 16 | 15 | 20 | 7.31 | 1.50 | 11.3 | 5.1 | 1.7 | 0.8 |
| 09 | LAA | 6 | 1 | 1 | 65 | 46 | 68 | 3.56 | 1.16 | 9.3 | 4.1 | 1.0 | 1.0 |
| 10 | LAA | 0 | 0 | 0 | 24 | 25 | 25 | 4.88 | 1.67 | 9.4 | 5.6 | 1.1 | 1.0 |

### Competition at RP / Stats in 2010 as RP
| Thr | Player | GR | ERA | IP/G | Sv-Hld |
|---|---|---|---|---|---|
| RH | Rodney F | 72 | 4.24 | 0.9 | 14-21 |
| RH | Jepsen K | 68 | 3.97 | 0.9 | 0-27 |
| RH | Rodriguez F | 43 | 4.37 | 1.1 | 0-2 |
| RH | Shields S | 42 | 5.08 | 1.1 | 0-1 |

Weekly Points — 2008 / 2009 / 2010

Ten-Year Trends — K/9 / BB/9

### Value / Luck / In Rotation / In Relief / OPS
| $1L | $2L | Pts | RAA | H% | HR/fb | S% | FIP | GS | CG | QS/DS | GR | Hld | Bln | Lead | OPS | 1st Hf | 2nd Hf | vs RH | vs LH |
|---|---|---|---|---|---|---|---|---|---|---|---|---|---|---|---|---|---|---|---|
| $1 | -$2 | 10 | +1 | 36% | 0% | 75% | 2.19 | — | — | — | 6 | 0 | 0 | +0.3 | .547 | — | .547 | .462 | .639 |
| -$3 | -$5 | 10 | -6 | 31% | 18% | 52% | 4.93 | — | — | — | 14 | 0 | 0 | -1.0 | .856 | 1.070 | .717 | .984 | .747 |
| $6 | $3 | 130 | +4 | 26% | 10% | 72% | 3.99 | — | — | — | 64 | 9 | 3 | -0.4 | .682 | .730 | .609 | .643 | .725 |
| -$4 | -$14 | 20 | -3 | 34% | 12% | 73% | 4.72 | — | — | — | 25 | 2 | 0 | -0.7 | .823 | .759 | 1.231 | .737 | .912 |

## Madison Bumgarner — 160 IP | $10 | 220 pts
**SP-18** — Owned: 24% — LH

Bumgarner's grace under pressure with the Giants in 2010 has solidified his spot in the back half of their 2011 rotation. Madison has evolved from a farmhand known mostly for his fastball to a more crafty pitcher whose best offering is his change-up. He did not benefit from unusual luck; this success was earned. (PB)

### Forecast
| Player | Age | IP | W | Sv | K | ERA | WHIP | K/9 | BB/9 | $2L | Pts |
|---|---|---|---|---|---|---|---|---|---|---|---|
| Bumgarner M | 21 | 160 | 10 | 0 | 133 | 3.57 | 1.36 | 7.5 | 2.3 | $10 | 220 |

### Mini-Browser
| Player | Age | IP | W | Sv | K | ERA | WHIP | K/9 | BB/9 | $2L | Pts |
|---|---|---|---|---|---|---|---|---|---|---|---|
| Garland J | 31 | 200 | 12 | 0 | 107 | 3.99 | 1.27 | 4.8 | 3.0 | $10 | 210 |
| Gregg K | 32 | 60 | 2 | 32 | 55 | 4.27 | 1.41 | 8.3 | 4.2 | $10 | 230 |
| Webb B | 31 | 160 | 10 | 0 | 113 | 3.86 | 1.28 | 6.3 | 2.5 | $10 | 200 |
| Nathan J | 36 | 40 | 4 | 18 | 45 | 2.72 | 1.12 | 10.1 | 3.0 | $10 | 180 |
| Rodriguez F | 29 | 60 | 3 | 21 | 66 | 3.14 | 1.27 | 9.9 | 4.2 | $10 | 200 |

### Minors (2010) / Skills
| Level | Leag | W | L | Sv | IP | H | K | ERA | WHIP | K/9 | BB/9 | HR/9 | GB/F |
|---|---|---|---|---|---|---|---|---|---|---|---|---|---|
| A | — | | | | | | | | | | | | |
| AA | — | | | | | | | | | | | | |
| AAA | PCL | 7 | 1 | 0 | 82 | 88 | 59 | 3.16 | 1.33 | 6.4 | 2.4 | 0.5 | — |

### Majors / Skills
| Yr | Team | W | L | Sv | IP | H | K | ERA | WHIP | K/9 | BB/9 | HR/9 | GB/F |
|---|---|---|---|---|---|---|---|---|---|---|---|---|---|
| 07 | — | | | | | | | | | | | | |
| 08 | — | | | | | | | | | | | | |
| 09 | SF | 0 | 0 | 0 | 10 | 8 | 10 | 1.80 | 1.10 | 9.0 | 2.7 | 1.8 | 2.1 |
| 10 | SF | 7 | 6 | 0 | 111 | 119 | 86 | 3.00 | 1.31 | 7.0 | 2.1 | 0.9 | 1.2 |

### Competition at SP / Stats in 2010 as SP
| Thr | Player | GS | ERA | Supp | W-L |
|---|---|---|---|---|---|
| LH | Sanchez J | 33 | 3.08 | 5.1 | 13-9 |
| RH | Cain M | 33 | 3.14 | 4.0 | 13-11 |
| RH | Lincecum T | 33 | 3.43 | 4.4 | 16-10 |
| LH | Zito B | 33 | 4.13 | 3.5 | 9-13 |

Weekly Points — 2008 / 2009 / 2010

Ten-Year Trends — K/9 / BB/9

### Value / Luck / In Rotation / In Relief / OPS
| $1L | $2L | Pts | RAA | H% | HR/fb | S% | FIP | GS | CG | QS/DS | GR | Hld | Bln | Lead | OPS | 1st Hf | 2nd Hf | vs RH | vs LH |
|---|---|---|---|---|---|---|---|---|---|---|---|---|---|---|---|---|---|---|---|
| -$1 | -$1 | 10 | +3 | 25% | 29% | 100% | 4.70 | 1 | 0 | 0/0 | 3 | 0 | 0 | -4.3 | .739 | — | .739 | 1.037 | .160 |
| $5 | -$1 | 160 | +15 | 31% | 8% | 81% | 3.64 | 18 | 0 | 11/1 | — | — | — | — | .732 | .626 | .765 | .751 | .678 |

## A.J. Burnett — 180 IP | $4 | 220 pts
**SP-33** — Owned: 80% — RH

The "Good A.J." and "Bad A.J." of 2009 became pretty much all "Bad A.J." in 2010. Burnett lost 15 games — the most of any Yankee starter in 20 years — and led the league in hit batsmen. With a five-year, $82M contract, he's not leaving the rotation, and he is only one year removed from two 4.00-ERA seasons. (LS)

### Forecast
| Player | Age | IP | W | Sv | K | ERA | WHIP | K/9 | BB/9 | $2L | Pts |
|---|---|---|---|---|---|---|---|---|---|---|---|
| Burnett A | 34 | 180 | 11 | 0 | 155 | 4.74 | 1.45 | 7.7 | 4.1 | $4 | 220 |

### Mini-Browser
| Player | Age | IP | W | Sv | K | ERA | WHIP | K/9 | BB/9 | $2L | Pts |
|---|---|---|---|---|---|---|---|---|---|---|---|
| Adams M | 32 | 40 | 2 | 2 | 42 | 2.57 | 1.10 | 9.4 | 2.9 | $4 | 80 |
| Guthrie J | 31 | 200 | 10 | 0 | 110 | 4.76 | 1.34 | 5.0 | 2.6 | $4 | 170 |
| Motte J | 28 | 60 | 3 | 4 | 62 | 3.63 | 1.27 | 9.2 | 2.4 | $4 | 110 |
| Chamberlain J | 25 | 60 | 4 | 10 | 57 | 4.29 | 1.38 | 8.5 | 3.9 | $4 | 130 |
| Hunter T | 24 | 140 | 10 | 0 | 83 | 4.55 | 1.38 | 5.4 | 2.6 | $4 | 160 |

### Minors (2010)
| Level | Leag | W | L | Sv | IP | H | K | ERA | WHIP | K/9 | BB/9 | HR/9 | GB/F |
|---|---|---|---|---|---|---|---|---|---|---|---|---|---|
| A | — | | | | | | | | | | | | |
| AA | — | | | | | | | | | | | | |
| AAA | — | | | | | | | | | | | | |

### Majors / Skills
| Yr | Team | W | L | Sv | IP | H | K | ERA | WHIP | K/9 | BB/9 | HR/9 | GB/F |
|---|---|---|---|---|---|---|---|---|---|---|---|---|---|
| 07 | TOR | 10 | 8 | 0 | 165 | 131 | 176 | 3.75 | 1.19 | 9.6 | 3.6 | 1.2 | 1.8 |
| 08 | TOR | 18 | 10 | 0 | 221 | 211 | 231 | 4.07 | 1.34 | 9.4 | 3.5 | 0.8 | 1.5 |
| 09 | NYY | 13 | 9 | 0 | 207 | 193 | 195 | 4.04 | 1.40 | 8.5 | 4.2 | 1.1 | 1.1 |
| 10 | NYY | 10 | 15 | 0 | 186 | 204 | 145 | 5.26 | 1.51 | 7.0 | 3.8 | 1.2 | 1.2 |

### Competition at SP / Stats in 2010 as SP
| Thr | Player | GS | ERA | Supp | W-L |
|---|---|---|---|---|---|
| LH | Sabathia C | 34 | 3.18 | 5.7 | 21-7 |
| RH | Burnett A | 33 | 5.26 | 4.3 | 10-15 |
| RH | Hughes P | 29 | 4.23 | 6.5 | 17-8 |
| RH | Vazquez J | 26 | 5.56 | 4.1 | 8-10 |

Weekly Points — 2008 / 2009 / 2010

Ten-Year Trends — K/9 / BB/9

### Value / Luck / In Rotation / In Relief / OPS
| $1L | $2L | Pts | RAA | H% | HR/fb | S% | FIP | GS | CG | QS/DS | GR | Hld | Bln | Lead | OPS | 1st Hf | 2nd Hf | vs RH | vs LH |
|---|---|---|---|---|---|---|---|---|---|---|---|---|---|---|---|---|---|---|---|
| $9 | $6 | 270 | +8 | 26% | 18% | 74% | 4.18 | 25 | 2 | 17/4 | — | — | — | — | .704 | .704 | .610 | .697 | .637 |
| $12 | $2 | 380 | +0 | 32% | 10% | 71% | 3.49 | 34 | 1 | 19/5 | 1 | 0 | 0 | +0.1 | .710 | .743 | .664 | .656 | .751 |
| $12 | $2 | 290 | +3 | 30% | 11% | 70% | 4.39 | 33 | 1 | 21/5 | — | — | — | — | .729 | .735 | .723 | .816 | .654 |
| -$3 | -$28 | 180 | -26 | 33% | 12% | 67% | 4.74 | 33 | 0 | 14/8 | — | — | — | — | .824 | .798 | .858 | .827 | .820 |

*For more stats, visit www.Rotolympus.com.*

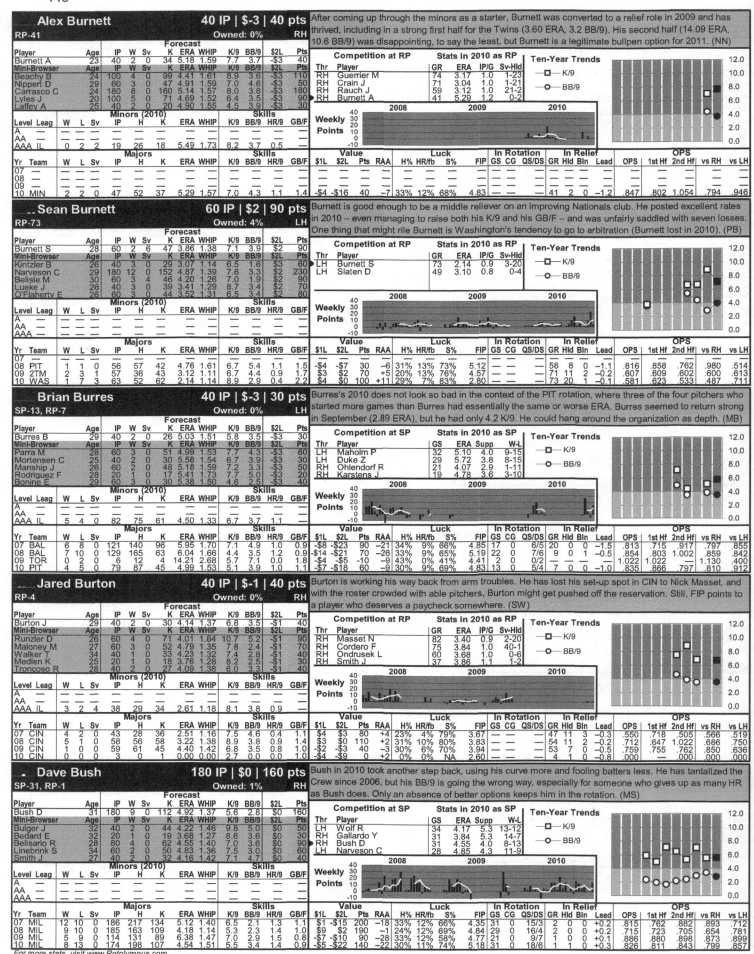

## Alex Burnett — 40 IP | $-3 | 40 pts

RP-41 — Owned: 0% — RH

After coming up through the minors as a starter, Burnett was converted to a relief role in 2009 and has thrived, including in a strong first half for the Twins (3.60 ERA, 3.2 BB/9). His second half (14.09 ERA, 10.6 BB/9) was disappointing, to say the least, but Burnett is a legitimate bullpen option for 2011. (NN)

| Player | Age | IP | W | Sv | K | ERA | WHIP | K/9 | BB/9 | $2L | Pts |
|---|---|---|---|---|---|---|---|---|---|---|---|
| Burnett A | 23 | 40 | 2 | 0 | 34 | 5.18 | 1.59 | 7.7 | 3.7 | -$3 | 40 |
| **Mini-Browser** | **Age** | **IP** | **W** | **Sv** | **K** | **ERA** | **WHIP** | **K/9** | **BB/9** | **$2L** | **Pts** |
| Beachy B | 24 | 100 | 4 | 0 | 99 | 4.41 | 1.61 | 8.9 | 3.6 | -$3 | 110 |
| Nippert D | 29 | 60 | 3 | 0 | 47 | 4.91 | 1.59 | 7.0 | 4.6 | -$3 | 50 |
| Carrasco C | 24 | 180 | 8 | 0 | 160 | 5.14 | 1.57 | 8.0 | 3.8 | -$3 | 180 |
| Lyles J | 20 | 100 | 5 | 0 | 71 | 4.69 | 1.52 | 6.4 | 3.5 | -$3 | 90 |
| Laffey A | 25 | 40 | 2 | 0 | 20 | 4.90 | 1.55 | 4.5 | 3.9 | -$3 | 30 |

| Competition at RP | | Stats in 2010 as RP | | | |
|---|---|---|---|---|---|
| Thr | Player | GR | ERA | IP/G | Sv-Hld |
| RH | Guerrier M | 74 | 3.17 | 1.0 | 1-23 |
| RH | Crain J | 71 | 3.04 | 1.0 | 1-21 |
| RH | Rauch J | 59 | 3.12 | 1.0 | 21-2 |
| RH | Burnett A | 41 | 5.29 | 1.2 | 0-2 |

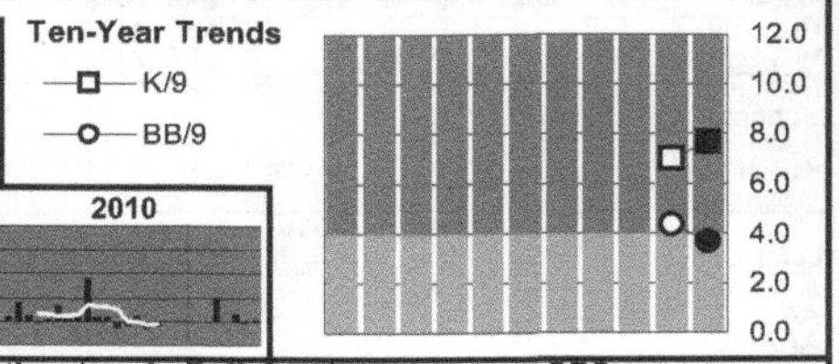
Ten-Year Trends
K/9
BB/9
12.0
10.0
8.0
6.0
4.0
2.0
0.0

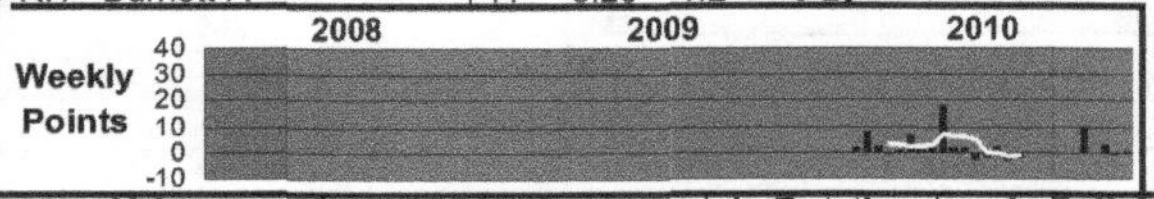
Weekly Points
2008
2009
2010
40
30
20
10
0
-10

| Level | Leag | W | L | Sv | IP | H | K | ERA | WHIP | K/9 | BB/9 | HR/9 | GB/F |
|---|---|---|---|---|---|---|---|---|---|---|---|---|---|
| | | Minors (2010) | | | | | | | | Skills | | | |
| A | — | — | — | — | — | — | — | — | — | — | — | — | — |
| AA | — | — | — | — | — | — | — | — | — | — | — | — | — |
| AAA | IL | 0 | 2 | 2 | 19 | 26 | 18 | 5.49 | 1.73 | 8.2 | 3.7 | 0.5 | — |

| Yr | Team | W | L | Sv | IP | H | K | ERA | WHIP | K/9 | BB/9 | HR/9 | GB/F |
|---|---|---|---|---|---|---|---|---|---|---|---|---|---|
| | | Majors | | | | | | | | Skills | | | |
| 07 | — | — | — | — | — | — | — | — | — | — | — | — | — |
| 08 | — | — | — | — | — | — | — | — | — | — | — | — | — |
| 09 | — | — | — | — | — | — | — | — | — | — | — | — | — |
| 10 | MIN | 2 | 2 | 0 | 47 | 52 | 37 | 5.29 | 1.57 | 7.0 | 4.3 | 1.1 | 1.4 |

| Yr | $1L | $2L | Pts | RAA | H% | HR/fb | S% | FIP | GS | CG | QS/DS | GR | Hld | Bln | Lead | OPS | 1st Hf | 2nd Hf | vs RH | vs LH |
|---|---|---|---|---|---|---|---|---|---|---|---|---|---|---|---|---|---|---|---|---|
| | Value | | | | Luck | | | | In Rotation | | | In Relief | | | | OPS | | | | |
| 07 | — | — | — | — | — | — | — | — | — | — | — | — | — | — | — | — | — | — | — | — |
| 08 | — | — | — | — | — | — | — | — | — | — | — | — | — | — | — | — | — | — | — | — |
| 09 | — | — | — | — | — | — | — | — | — | — | — | — | — | — | — | — | — | — | — | — |
| 10 | -$4 | -$16 | 40 | −7 | 33% | 12% | 68% | 4.83 | — | — | — | 41 | 2 | 0 | −1.2 | .847 | .802 | 1.054 | .794 | .946 |

## Sean Burnett — 60 IP | $2 | 90 pts

RP-73 — Owned: 4% — LH

Burnett is good enough to be a middle reliever on an improving Nationals club. He posted excellent rates in 2010 – even managing to raise both his K/9 and his GB/F – and was unfairly saddled with seven losses. One thing that might rile Burnett is Washington's tendency to go to arbitration (Burnett lost in 2010). (PB)

| Player | Age | IP | W | Sv | K | ERA | WHIP | K/9 | BB/9 | $2L | Pts |
|---|---|---|---|---|---|---|---|---|---|---|---|
| Burnett S | 28 | 60 | 2 | 6 | 47 | 3.86 | 1.38 | 7.1 | 3.9 | $2 | 90 |
| **Mini-Browser** | **Age** | **IP** | **W** | **Sv** | **K** | **ERA** | **WHIP** | **K/9** | **BB/9** | **$2L** | **Pts** |
| Kintzler B | 26 | 40 | 3 | 0 | 29 | 3.07 | 1.14 | 6.5 | 1.6 | $3 | 60 |
| Narveson C | 29 | 180 | 12 | 0 | 152 | 4.87 | 1.39 | 7.6 | 3.3 | $2 | 230 |
| Belisle M | 30 | 60 | 3 | 4 | 46 | 4.20 | 1.26 | 7.0 | 1.9 | $2 | 90 |
| Lueke J | 26 | 40 | 3 | 0 | 39 | 3.41 | 1.29 | 8.7 | 3.4 | $2 | 70 |
| O'Flaherty E | 26 | 60 | 3 | 0 | 44 | 3.52 | 1.31 | 6.5 | 3.4 | $2 | 80 |

| Competition at RP | | Stats in 2010 as RP | | | |
|---|---|---|---|---|---|
| Thr | Player | GR | ERA | IP/G | Sv-Hld |
| LH | Burnett S | 73 | 2.14 | 0.9 | 3-20 |
| LH | Slaten D | 49 | 3.10 | 0.8 | 0-4 |

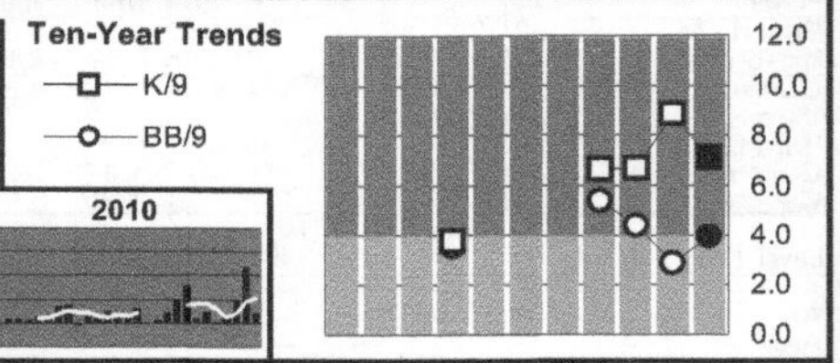
Ten-Year Trends
K/9
BB/9
12.0
10.0
8.0
6.0
4.0
2.0
0.0

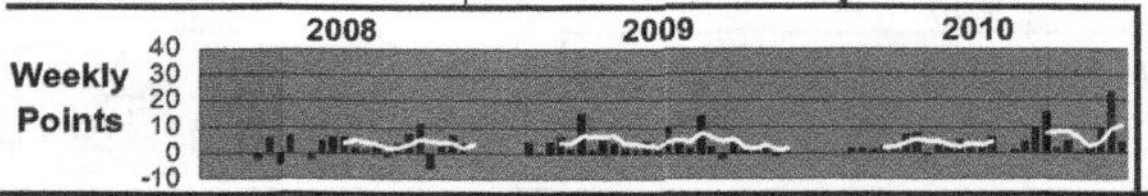
Weekly Points
2008
2009
2010
40
30
20
10
0
-10

| Level | Leag | W | L | Sv | IP | H | K | ERA | WHIP | K/9 | BB/9 | HR/9 | GB/F |
|---|---|---|---|---|---|---|---|---|---|---|---|---|---|
| | | Minors (2010) | | | | | | | | Skills | | | |
| A | — | — | — | — | — | — | — | — | — | — | — | — | — |
| AA | — | — | — | — | — | — | — | — | — | — | — | — | — |
| AAA | — | — | — | — | — | — | — | — | — | — | — | — | — |

| Yr | Team | W | L | Sv | IP | H | K | ERA | WHIP | K/9 | BB/9 | HR/9 | GB/F |
|---|---|---|---|---|---|---|---|---|---|---|---|---|---|
| | | Majors | | | | | | | | Skills | | | |
| 07 | — | — | — | — | — | — | — | — | — | — | — | — | — |
| 08 | PIT | 1 | 1 | 0 | 56 | 57 | 42 | 4.76 | 1.61 | 6.7 | 5.4 | 1.1 | 1.5 |
| 09 | 2TM | 2 | 3 | 1 | 57 | 36 | 43 | 3.12 | 1.11 | 6.7 | 4.4 | 0.9 | 1.7 |
| 10 | WAS | 1 | 7 | 3 | 63 | 52 | 62 | 2.14 | 1.14 | 8.9 | 2.9 | 0.4 | 2.2 |

| Yr | $1L | $2L | Pts | RAA | H% | HR/fb | S% | FIP | GS | CG | QS/DS | GR | Hld | Bln | Lead | OPS | 1st Hf | 2nd Hf | vs RH | vs LH |
|---|---|---|---|---|---|---|---|---|---|---|---|---|---|---|---|---|---|---|---|---|
| | Value | | | | Luck | | | | In Rotation | | | In Relief | | | | OPS | | | | |
| 07 | — | — | — | — | — | — | — | — | — | — | — | — | — | — | — | — | — | — | — | — |
| 08 | -$4 | -$7 | 30 | −6 | 31% | 13% | 73% | 5.12 | — | — | — | 58 | 8 | 0 | −1.1 | .816 | .858 | .762 | .980 | .514 |
| 09 | $3 | $2 | 70 | +5 | 20% | 13% | 76% | 4.57 | — | — | — | 71 | 11 | 2 | −0.2 | .607 | .609 | .602 | .600 | .613 |
| 10 | $4 | $0 | 100 | +11 | 29% | 7% | 83% | 2.80 | — | — | — | 73 | 20 | 1 | −0.1 | .581 | .623 | .533 | .487 | .711 |

## Brian Burres — 40 IP | $-3 | 30 pts

SP-13, RP-7 — Owned: 0% — LH

Burres's 2010 does not look so bad in the context of the PIT rotation, where three of the four pitchers who started more games than Burres had essentially the same or worse ERA. Burres seemed to return strong in September (2.89 ERA), but he had only 4.2 K/9. He could hang around the organization as depth. (MB)

| Player | Age | IP | W | Sv | K | ERA | WHIP | K/9 | BB/9 | $2L | Pts |
|---|---|---|---|---|---|---|---|---|---|---|---|
| Burres B | 29 | 40 | 2 | 0 | 26 | 5.03 | 1.51 | 5.8 | 3.5 | -$3 | 30 |
| **Mini-Browser** | **Age** | **IP** | **W** | **Sv** | **K** | **ERA** | **WHIP** | **K/9** | **BB/9** | **$2L** | **Pts** |
| Parra M | 28 | 60 | 3 | 0 | 51 | 4.99 | 1.53 | 7.7 | 4.3 | -$3 | 60 |
| Mortensen C | 25 | 40 | 2 | 0 | 30 | 5.58 | 1.54 | 6.7 | 3.9 | -$3 | 30 |
| Manship J | 26 | 60 | 2 | 0 | 48 | 5.18 | 1.59 | 7.2 | 3.3 | -$3 | 50 |
| Rodriguez F | 28 | 20 | 1 | 0 | 17 | 5.41 | 1.73 | 7.7 | 5.0 | -$3 | 20 |
| Bonine E | 29 | 60 | 3 | 0 | 30 | 5.38 | 1.50 | 4.6 | 2.5 | -$3 | 40 |

| Competition at SP | | Stats in 2010 as SP | | | |
|---|---|---|---|---|---|
| Thr | Player | GS | ERA | Supp | W-L |
| LH | Maholm P | 32 | 5.10 | 4.0 | 9-15 |
| LH | Duke Z | 29 | 5.72 | 3.8 | 8-15 |
| RH | Ohlendorf R | 21 | 4.07 | 2.9 | 1-11 |
| RH | Karstens J | 19 | 4.78 | 3.6 | 3-10 |

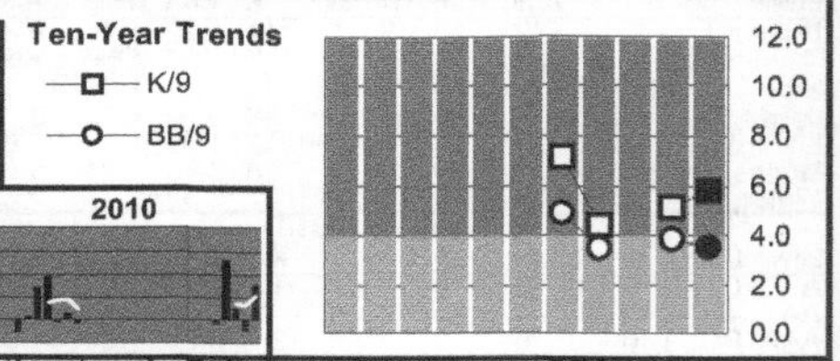
Ten-Year Trends
K/9
BB/9
12.0
10.0
8.0
6.0
4.0
2.0
0.0

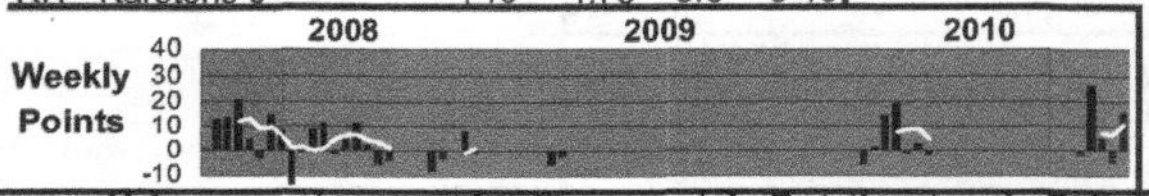
Weekly Points
2008
2009
2010
40
30
20
10
0
-10

| Level | Leag | W | L | Sv | IP | H | K | ERA | WHIP | K/9 | BB/9 | HR/9 | GB/F |
|---|---|---|---|---|---|---|---|---|---|---|---|---|---|
| | | Minors (2010) | | | | | | | | Skills | | | |
| A | — | — | — | — | — | — | — | — | — | — | — | — | — |
| AA | — | — | — | — | — | — | — | — | — | — | — | — | — |
| AAA | IL | 5 | 4 | 0 | 82 | 75 | 61 | 4.50 | 1.33 | 6.7 | 3.7 | 1.1 | — |

| Yr | Team | W | L | Sv | IP | H | K | ERA | WHIP | K/9 | BB/9 | HR/9 | GB/F |
|---|---|---|---|---|---|---|---|---|---|---|---|---|---|
| | | Majors | | | | | | | | Skills | | | |
| 07 | BAL | 6 | 8 | 0 | 121 | 140 | 96 | 5.95 | 1.70 | 7.1 | 4.9 | 1.0 | 0.9 |
| 08 | BAL | 7 | 10 | 0 | 129 | 165 | 63 | 6.04 | 1.66 | 4.4 | 3.5 | 1.2 | 0.9 |
| 09 | TOR | 0 | 2 | 0 | 6 | 12 | 4 | 14.21 | 2.68 | 5.7 | 7.1 | 0.0 | 1.8 |
| 10 | PIT | 4 | 5 | 0 | 79 | 87 | 45 | 4.99 | 1.53 | 5.1 | 3.9 | 1.0 | 1.1 |

| Yr | $1L | $2L | Pts | RAA | H% | HR/fb | S% | FIP | GS | CG | QS/DS | GR | Hld | Bln | Lead | OPS | 1st Hf | 2nd Hf | vs RH | vs LH |
|---|---|---|---|---|---|---|---|---|---|---|---|---|---|---|---|---|---|---|---|---|
| | Value | | | | Luck | | | | In Rotation | | | In Relief | | | | OPS | | | | |
| 07 | -$8 | -$23 | 90 | −21 | 34% | 9% | 66% | 4.85 | 17 | 0 | 6/5 | 20 | 0 | 0 | −1.5 | .813 | .715 | .917 | .797 | .855 |
| 08 | -$14 | -$21 | 70 | −26 | 33% | 9% | 65% | 5.19 | 22 | 0 | 7/6 | 9 | 0 | 1 | −0.5 | .854 | .803 | 1.002 | .859 | .842 |
| 09 | -$4 | -$5 | -10 | −9 | 43% | 0% | 41% | 4.41 | 2 | 0 | 0/2 | — | — | — | — | 1.022 | 1.022 | — | 1.130 | .400 |
| 10 | -$7 | -$18 | 60 | −9 | 30% | 9% | 69% | 4.83 | 13 | 0 | 5/4 | 7 | 0 | 0 | −1.0 | .835 | .866 | .797 | .810 | .912 |

## Jared Burton — 40 IP | $-1 | 40 pts

RP-4 — Owned: 0% — RH

Burton is working his way back from arm troubles. He has lost his set-up spot in CIN to Nick Masset, and with the roster crowded with able pitchers, Burton might get pushed off the reservation. Still, FIP points to a player who deserves a paycheck somewhere. (SW)

| Player | Age | IP | W | Sv | K | ERA | WHIP | K/9 | BB/9 | $2L | Pts |
|---|---|---|---|---|---|---|---|---|---|---|---|
| Burton J | 29 | 40 | 2 | 0 | 30 | 4.14 | 1.37 | 6.8 | 3.5 | -$1 | 40 |
| **Mini-Browser** | **Age** | **IP** | **W** | **Sv** | **K** | **ERA** | **WHIP** | **K/9** | **BB/9** | **$2L** | **Pts** |
| Runzler D | 26 | 60 | 4 | 0 | 71 | 4.01 | 1.64 | 10.7 | 5.2 | -$1 | 90 |
| Maloney M | 27 | 60 | 3 | 0 | 52 | 4.79 | 1.35 | 7.8 | 2.4 | -$1 | 70 |
| Walker T | 34 | 40 | 1 | 0 | 33 | 4.23 | 1.32 | 7.4 | 2.8 | -$1 | 40 |
| Medlen K | 25 | 20 | 1 | 0 | 18 | 3.76 | 1.28 | 8.2 | 2.5 | -$1 | 30 |
| Troncoso R | 28 | 40 | 2 | 0 | 27 | 4.09 | 1.38 | 6.0 | 3.3 | -$1 | 40 |

| Competition at RP | | Stats in 2010 as RP | | | |
|---|---|---|---|---|---|
| Thr | Player | GR | ERA | IP/G | Sv-Hld |
| RH | Masset N | 82 | 3.40 | 0.9 | 2-20 |
| RH | Cordero F | 75 | 3.84 | 1.0 | 40-1 |
| RH | Ondrusek L | 60 | 3.68 | 1.0 | 0-6 |
| RH | Smith J | 37 | 3.86 | 1.1 | 1-2 |

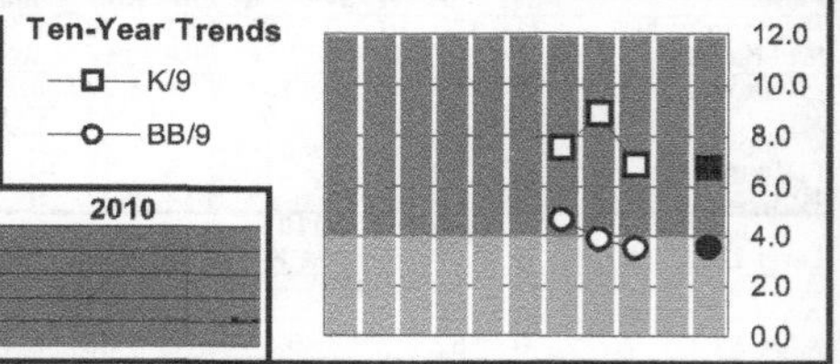
Ten-Year Trends
K/9
BB/9
12.0
10.0
8.0
6.0
4.0
2.0
0.0

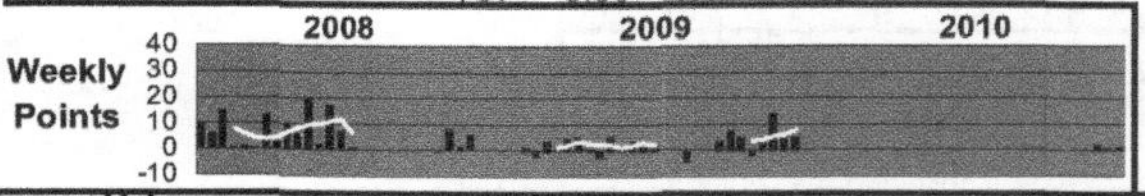
Weekly Points
2008
2009
2010
40
30
20
10
0
-10

| Level | Leag | W | L | Sv | IP | H | K | ERA | WHIP | K/9 | BB/9 | HR/9 | GB/F |
|---|---|---|---|---|---|---|---|---|---|---|---|---|---|
| | | Minors (2010) | | | | | | | | Skills | | | |
| A | — | — | — | — | — | — | — | — | — | — | — | — | — |
| AA | — | — | — | — | — | — | — | — | — | — | — | — | — |
| AAA | IL | 3 | 2 | 4 | 38 | 29 | 34 | 2.61 | 1.18 | 8.1 | 3.8 | 0.9 | — |

| Yr | Team | W | L | Sv | IP | H | K | ERA | WHIP | K/9 | BB/9 | HR/9 | GB/F |
|---|---|---|---|---|---|---|---|---|---|---|---|---|---|
| | | Majors | | | | | | | | Skills | | | |
| 07 | CIN | 4 | 2 | 0 | 43 | 28 | 36 | 2.51 | 1.16 | 7.5 | 4.6 | 0.4 | 1.1 |
| 08 | CIN | 5 | 1 | 0 | 58 | 56 | 58 | 3.22 | 1.38 | 8.9 | 3.8 | 0.9 | 1.4 |
| 09 | CIN | 1 | 0 | 0 | 59 | 61 | 45 | 4.40 | 1.42 | 6.8 | 3.5 | 0.8 | 1.0 |
| 10 | CIN | 0 | 0 | 0 | 3 | 0 | 1 | 0.00 | 0.00 | 2.7 | 0.0 | 0.0 | 1.0 |

| Yr | $1L | $2L | Pts | RAA | H% | HR/fb | S% | FIP | GS | CG | QS/DS | GR | Hld | Bln | Lead | OPS | 1st Hf | 2nd Hf | vs RH | vs LH |
|---|---|---|---|---|---|---|---|---|---|---|---|---|---|---|---|---|---|---|---|---|
| | Value | | | | Luck | | | | In Rotation | | | In Relief | | | | OPS | | | | |
| 07 | $4 | $3 | 80 | +4 | 23% | 4% | 79% | 3.67 | — | — | — | 47 | 11 | 3 | −0.3 | .550 | .718 | .505 | .566 | .519 |
| 08 | $3 | $0 | 110 | +2 | 31% | 10% | 80% | 3.83 | — | — | — | 54 | 11 | 2 | −0.2 | .712 | .647 | 1.022 | .686 | .750 |
| 09 | -$2 | -$3 | 40 | −3 | 30% | 6% | 70% | 3.94 | — | — | — | 53 | 7 | 0 | −0.5 | .759 | .755 | .762 | .850 | .636 |
| 10 | -$4 | -$9 | 0 | +2 | 0% | 0% | NA | 2.60 | — | — | — | 4 | 1 | 0 | −0.8 | .000 | — | .000 | .000 | .000 |

## Dave Bush — 180 IP | $0 | 160 pts

SP-31, RP-1 — Owned: 1% — RH

Bush in 2010 took another step back, using his curve more and fooling batters less. He has tantalized the Crew since 2006, but his BB/9 is going the wrong way, especially for someone who gives up as many HR as Bush does. Only an absence of better options keeps him in the rotation. (MS)

| Player | Age | IP | W | Sv | K | ERA | WHIP | K/9 | BB/9 | $2L | Pts |
|---|---|---|---|---|---|---|---|---|---|---|---|
| Bush D | 31 | 180 | 9 | 0 | 112 | 4.92 | 1.37 | 5.6 | 2.8 | $0 | 160 |
| **Mini-Browser** | **Age** | **IP** | **W** | **Sv** | **K** | **ERA** | **WHIP** | **K/9** | **BB/9** | **$2L** | **Pts** |
| Bulger J | 32 | 40 | 2 | 0 | 44 | 4.22 | 1.46 | 9.8 | 5.0 | $0 | 50 |
| Bedard E | 32 | 20 | 1 | 0 | 19 | 3.68 | 1.27 | 8.6 | 3.6 | $0 | 30 |
| Belisario R | 28 | 80 | 4 | 0 | 62 | 4.55 | 1.40 | 7.0 | 3.6 | $0 | 90 |
| Linebrink S | 34 | 60 | 2 | 0 | 50 | 4.83 | 1.36 | 7.5 | 3.0 | $0 | 60 |
| Smith J | 27 | 40 | 2 | 0 | 32 | 4.16 | 1.42 | 7.1 | 4.7 | $0 | 40 |

| Competition at SP | | Stats in 2010 as SP | | | |
|---|---|---|---|---|---|
| Thr | Player | GS | ERA | Supp | W-L |
| LH | Wolf R | 34 | 4.17 | 5.3 | 13-12 |
| RH | Gallardo Y | 31 | 3.84 | 5.3 | 14-7 |
| RH | Bush D | 31 | 4.55 | 4.0 | 8-13 |
| LH | Narveson C | 28 | 4.85 | 4.3 | 11-9 |

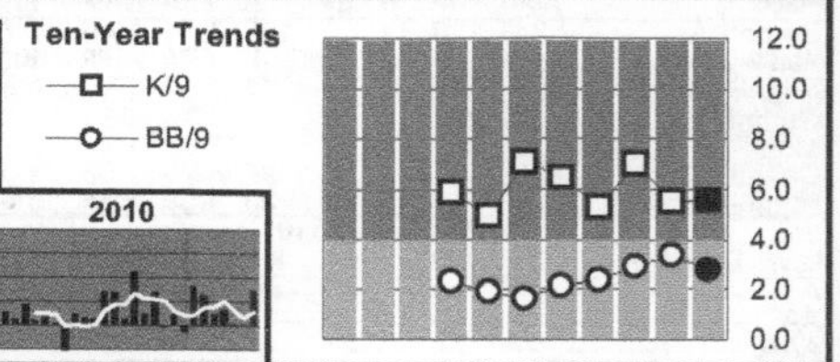
Ten-Year Trends
K/9
BB/9
12.0
10.0
8.0
6.0
4.0
2.0
0.0

Weekly Points
2008
2009
2010
40
30
20
10
0
-10

| Level | Leag | W | L | Sv | IP | H | K | ERA | WHIP | K/9 | BB/9 | HR/9 | GB/F |
|---|---|---|---|---|---|---|---|---|---|---|---|---|---|
| | | Minors (2010) | | | | | | | | Skills | | | |
| A | — | — | — | — | — | — | — | — | — | — | — | — | — |
| AA | — | — | — | — | — | — | — | — | — | — | — | — | — |
| AAA | — | — | — | — | — | — | — | — | — | — | — | — | — |

| Yr | Team | W | L | Sv | IP | H | K | ERA | WHIP | K/9 | BB/9 | HR/9 | GB/F |
|---|---|---|---|---|---|---|---|---|---|---|---|---|---|
| | | Majors | | | | | | | | Skills | | | |
| 07 | MIL | 12 | 10 | 0 | 186 | 217 | 134 | 5.12 | 1.40 | 6.5 | 2.1 | 1.3 | 1.1 |
| 08 | MIL | 9 | 10 | 0 | 185 | 163 | 109 | 4.18 | 1.14 | 5.3 | 2.3 | 1.4 | 1.0 |
| 09 | MIL | 5 | 9 | 0 | 114 | 131 | 89 | 6.38 | 1.47 | 7.0 | 2.9 | 1.5 | 0.8 |
| 10 | MIL | 8 | 13 | 0 | 174 | 198 | 107 | 4.54 | 1.51 | 5.5 | 3.4 | 1.4 | 0.9 |

| Yr | $1L | $2L | Pts | RAA | H% | HR/fb | S% | FIP | GS | CG | QS/DS | GR | Hld | Bln | Lead | OPS | 1st Hf | 2nd Hf | vs RH | vs LH |
|---|---|---|---|---|---|---|---|---|---|---|---|---|---|---|---|---|---|---|---|---|
| | Value | | | | Luck | | | | In Rotation | | | In Relief | | | | OPS | | | | |
| 07 | $1 | -$15 | 200 | −18 | 33% | 12% | 66% | 4.35 | 31 | 0 | 15/3 | 2 | 0 | 0 | +0.2 | .815 | .762 | .882 | .893 | .712 |
| 08 | $9 | $2 | 190 | −1 | 24% | 12% | 69% | 4.84 | 29 | 0 | 16/4 | 2 | 0 | 0 | +0.2 | .715 | .723 | .705 | .654 | .781 |
| 09 | -$7 | -$10 | 90 | −28 | 33% | 12% | 58% | 4.77 | 21 | 0 | 9/7 | 1 | 0 | 0 | +0.1 | .886 | .880 | .898 | .873 | .899 |
| 10 | -$5 | -$22 | 140 | −22 | 30% | 11% | 74% | 5.18 | 31 | 0 | 18/6 | 1 | 1 | 0 | +0.3 | .826 | .811 | .843 | .799 | .857 |

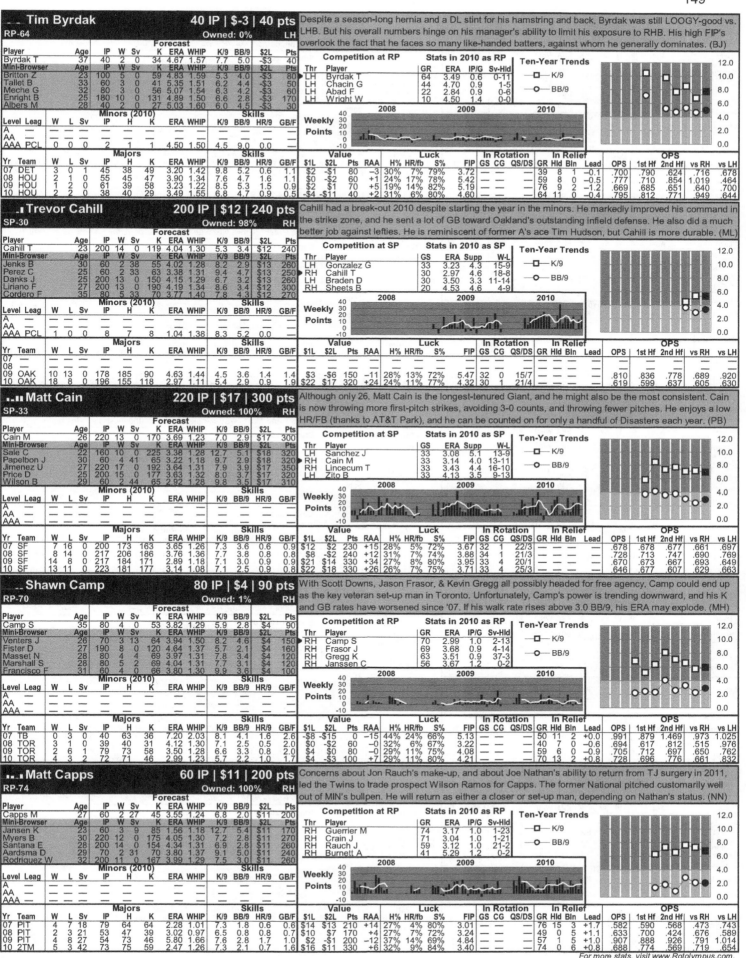

## Tim Byrdak
**40 IP | $-3 | 40 pts**

RP-64 | Owned: 0% | LH

Despite a season-long hernia and a DL stint for his hamstring and back, Byrdak was still LOOGY-good vs. LHB. But his overall numbers hinge on his manager's ability to limit his exposure to RHB. His high FIP's overlook the fact that he faces so many like-handed batters, against whom he generally dominates. (BJ)

Forecast

| Player | Age | IP | W | Sv | K | ERA | WHIP | K/9 | BB/9 | $2L | Pts |
|---|---|---|---|---|---|---|---|---|---|---|---|
| Byrdak T | 37 | 40 | 2 | 0 | 34 | 4.67 | 1.57 | 7.7 | 5.0 | -$3 | 40 |
| **Mini-Browser** | **Age** | **IP** | **W** | **Sv** | **K** | **ERA** | **WHIP** | **K/9** | **BB/9** | **$2L** | **Pts** |
| Britton Z | 23 | 100 | 5 | 0 | 59 | 4.83 | 1.59 | 5.3 | 4.0 | -$3 | 80 |
| Tallet B | 33 | 60 | 3 | 0 | 41 | 5.35 | 1.51 | 6.2 | 4.4 | -$3 | 50 |
| Meche G | 32 | 80 | 3 | 0 | 56 | 5.07 | 1.54 | 6.3 | 4.2 | -$3 | 60 |
| Enright B | 25 | 180 | 10 | 0 | 131 | 4.89 | 1.50 | 6.6 | 2.8 | -$3 | 170 |
| Albers M | 28 | 40 | 2 | 0 | 27 | 5.03 | 1.60 | 6.0 | 4.5 | -$3 | 30 |

Competition at RP — Stats in 2010 as RP

| Thr | Player | GR | ERA | IP/G | Sv-Hld |
|---|---|---|---|---|---|
| LH | Byrdak T | 64 | 3.49 | 0.6 | 0-11 |
| LH | Chacin G | 44 | 4.70 | 0.9 | 1-5 |
| LH | Abad F | 22 | 2.84 | 0.9 | 0-6 |
| LH | Wright W | 10 | 4.50 | 1.4 | 0-0 |

Ten-Year Trends (K/9, BB/9)

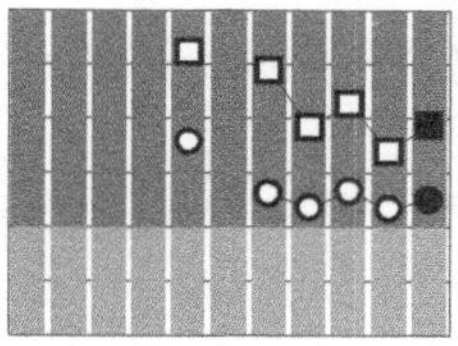


Weekly Points

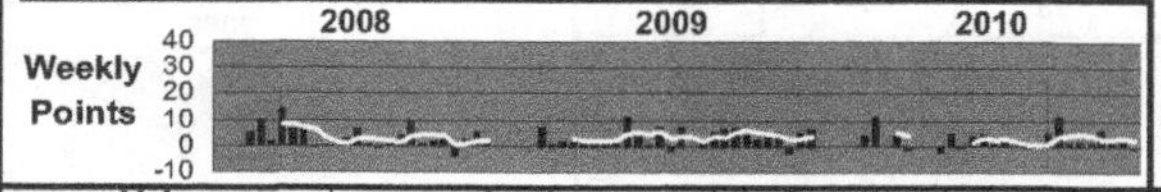


Minors (2010) / Skills

| Level | Leag | W | L | Sv | IP | H | K | ERA | WHIP | K/9 | BB/9 | HR/9 | GB/F |
|---|---|---|---|---|---|---|---|---|---|---|---|---|---|
| A | — | — | — | — | — | — | — | — | — | — | — | — | — |
| AA | — | — | — | — | — | — | — | — | — | — | — | — | — |
| AAA | PCL | 0 | 0 | 0 | 2 | 1 | 1 | 4.50 | 1.50 | 4.5 | 9.0 | 0.0 | — |

Majors / Skills / Value / Luck / In Rotation / In Relief / OPS

| Yr | Team | W | L | Sv | IP | H | K | ERA | WHIP | K/9 | BB/9 | HR/9 | GB/F | $1L | $2L | Pts | RAA | H% | HR/fb | S% | FIP | GS | CG | QS/DS | GR | Hld | Bln | Lead | OPS | 1st Hf | 2nd Hf | vs RH | vs LH |
|---|---|---|---|---|---|---|---|---|---|---|---|---|---|---|---|---|---|---|---|---|---|---|---|---|---|---|---|---|---|---|---|---|---|
| 07 | DET | 3 | 0 | 1 | 45 | 38 | 49 | 3.20 | 1.42 | 9.8 | 5.2 | 0.6 | 1.1 | $2 | -$1 | 80 | –3 | 30% | 7% | 79% | 3.72 | — | — | — | 39 | 8 | 1 | –0.1 | .700 | .790 | .624 | .716 | .678 |
| 08 | HOU | 2 | 1 | 0 | 55 | 45 | 47 | 3.90 | 1.34 | 7.6 | 4.7 | 1.6 | 1.1 | $0 | -$2 | 60 | +1 | 24% | 17% | 78% | 5.42 | — | — | — | 59 | 8 | 0 | –0.5 | .777 | .710 | .854 | 1.019 | .464 |
| 09 | HOU | 1 | 2 | 0 | 61 | 39 | 58 | 3.23 | 1.22 | 8.5 | 5.3 | 1.5 | 0.9 | $2 | $1 | 70 | +5 | 19% | 14% | 82% | 5.19 | — | — | — | 76 | 9 | 2 | –1.2 | .669 | .685 | .651 | .640 | .700 |
| 10 | HOU | 2 | 2 | 0 | 38 | 40 | 29 | 3.49 | 1.55 | 6.8 | 4.7 | 0.9 | 0.5 | -$4 | -$11 | 40 | +2 | 31% | 6% | 80% | 4.60 | — | — | — | 64 | 11 | 0 | –0.4 | .795 | .812 | .771 | .949 | .644 |

## Trevor Cahill
**200 IP | $12 | 240 pts**

SP-30 | Owned: 98% | RH

Cahill had a break-out 2010 despite starting the year in the minors. He markedly improved his command in the strike zone, and he sent a lot of GB toward Oakland's outstanding infield defense. He also did a much better job against lefties. He is reminiscent of former A's ace Tim Hudson, but Cahill is more durable. (ML)

Forecast

| Player | Age | IP | W | Sv | K | ERA | WHIP | K/9 | BB/9 | $2L | Pts |
|---|---|---|---|---|---|---|---|---|---|---|---|
| Cahill T | 23 | 200 | 14 | 0 | 119 | 4.04 | 1.30 | 5.3 | 3.4 | $12 | 240 |
| **Mini-Browser** | **Age** | **IP** | **W** | **Sv** | **K** | **ERA** | **WHIP** | **K/9** | **BB/9** | **$2L** | **Pts** |
| Jenks B | 30 | 60 | 2 | 38 | 55 | 4.02 | 1.28 | 8.2 | 2.9 | $13 | 260 |
| Perez C | 25 | 60 | 2 | 33 | 63 | 3.38 | 1.31 | 9.4 | 4.7 | $13 | 250 |
| Danks J | 25 | 200 | 13 | 0 | 150 | 4.15 | 1.29 | 6.7 | 3.2 | $13 | 260 |
| Liriano F | 27 | 200 | 13 | 0 | 190 | 4.19 | 1.34 | 8.6 | 3.4 | $12 | 300 |
| Cordero F | 35 | 80 | 5 | 33 | 70 | 3.77 | 1.40 | 7.8 | 4.3 | $12 | 270 |

Competition at SP — Stats in 2010 as SP

| Thr | Player | GS | ERA | Supp | W-L |
|---|---|---|---|---|---|
| LH | Gonzalez G | 33 | 3.23 | 4.3 | 15-9 |
| RH | Cahill T | 30 | 2.97 | 4.6 | 18-8 |
| LH | Braden D | 30 | 3.50 | 3.3 | 11-14 |
| RH | Sheets B | 20 | 4.53 | 4.6 | 4-9 |

Ten-Year Trends (K/9, BB/9)

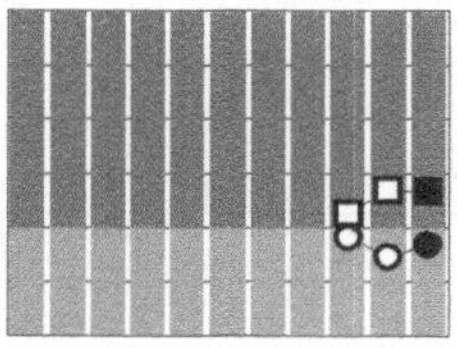


Weekly Points

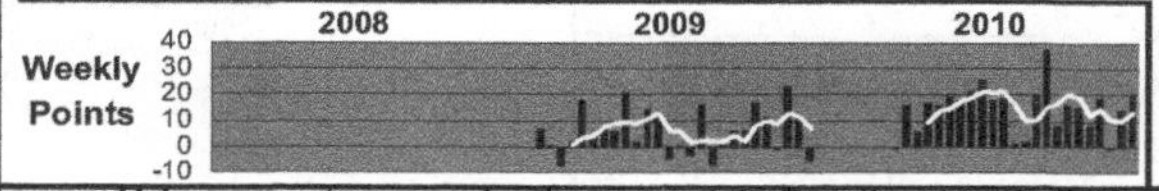


Minors (2010) / Skills

| Level | Leag | W | L | Sv | IP | H | K | ERA | WHIP | K/9 | BB/9 | HR/9 | GB/F |
|---|---|---|---|---|---|---|---|---|---|---|---|---|---|
| A | — | — | — | — | — | — | — | — | — | — | — | — | — |
| AA | — | — | — | — | — | — | — | — | — | — | — | — | — |
| AAA | PCL | 1 | 0 | 0 | 8 | 7 | 8 | 1.04 | 1.38 | 8.3 | 5.2 | 0.0 | — |

Majors / Skills / Value / Luck / In Rotation / In Relief / OPS

| Yr | Team | W | L | Sv | IP | H | K | ERA | WHIP | K/9 | BB/9 | HR/9 | GB/F | $1L | $2L | Pts | RAA | H% | HR/fb | S% | FIP | GS | CG | QS/DS | GR | Hld | Bln | Lead | OPS | 1st Hf | 2nd Hf | vs RH | vs LH |
|---|---|---|---|---|---|---|---|---|---|---|---|---|---|---|---|---|---|---|---|---|---|---|---|---|---|---|---|---|---|---|---|---|---|
| 07 | — | — | — | — | — | — | — | — | — | — | — | — | — | — | — | — | — | — | — | — | — | — | — | — | — | — | — | — | — | — | — | — | — |
| 08 | — | — | — | — | — | — | — | — | — | — | — | — | — | — | — | — | — | — | — | — | — | — | — | — | — | — | — | — | — | — | — | — | — |
| 09 | OAK | 10 | 13 | 0 | 178 | 185 | 90 | 4.63 | 1.44 | 4.5 | 3.6 | 1.4 | 1.4 | $3 | -$6 | 150 | –11 | 28% | 13% | 72% | 5.47 | 32 | 0 | 15/7 | — | — | — | — | .810 | .836 | .778 | .689 | .920 |
| 10 | OAK | 18 | 8 | 0 | 196 | 155 | 118 | 2.97 | 1.11 | 5.4 | 2.9 | 0.9 | 1.9 | $22 | $17 | 320 | +24 | 24% | 11% | 77% | 4.32 | 30 | 1 | 21/4 | — | — | — | — | .619 | .599 | .637 | .605 | .630 |

## Matt Cain
**220 IP | $17 | 300 pts**

SP-33 | Owned: 100% | RH

Although only 26, Matt Cain is the longest-tenured Giant, and he might also be the most consistent. Cain is now throwing more first-pitch strikes, avoiding 3-0 counts, and throwing fewer pitches. He enjoys a low HR/FB (thanks to AT&T Park), and he can be counted on for only a handful of Disasters each year. (PB)

Forecast

| Player | Age | IP | W | Sv | K | ERA | WHIP | K/9 | BB/9 | $2L | Pts |
|---|---|---|---|---|---|---|---|---|---|---|---|
| Cain M | 26 | 220 | 13 | 0 | 170 | 3.69 | 1.23 | 7.0 | 2.9 | $17 | 300 |
| **Mini-Browser** | **Age** | **IP** | **W** | **Sv** | **K** | **ERA** | **WHIP** | **K/9** | **BB/9** | **$2L** | **Pts** |
| Sale C | 22 | 160 | 10 | 0 | 225 | 3.38 | 1.28 | 12.7 | 5.1 | $18 | 320 |
| Papelbon J | 30 | 60 | 4 | 41 | 65 | 3.22 | 1.18 | 9.7 | 2.9 | $18 | 320 |
| Jimenez U | 27 | 220 | 17 | 0 | 192 | 3.64 | 1.31 | 7.9 | 3.9 | $17 | 350 |
| Price D | 25 | 200 | 15 | 0 | 177 | 3.63 | 1.32 | 8.0 | 3.7 | $17 | 320 |
| Wilson B | 29 | 60 | 2 | 44 | 65 | 2.92 | 1.28 | 9.8 | 3.5 | $17 | 310 |

Competition at SP — Stats in 2010 as SP

| Thr | Player | GS | ERA | Supp | W-L |
|---|---|---|---|---|---|
| LH | Sanchez J | 33 | 3.08 | 5.1 | 13-9 |
| RH | Cain M | 33 | 3.14 | 4.0 | 13-11 |
| RH | Lincecum T | 33 | 3.43 | 4.4 | 16-10 |
| LH | Zito B | 33 | 4.13 | 3.5 | 9-13 |

Ten-Year Trends (K/9, BB/9)

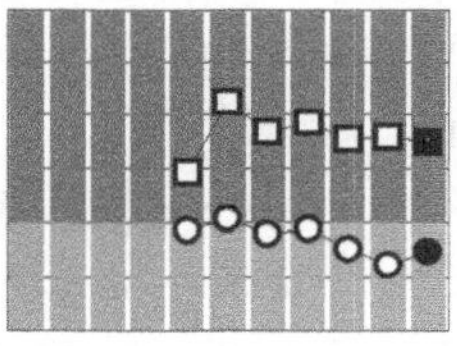


Weekly Points

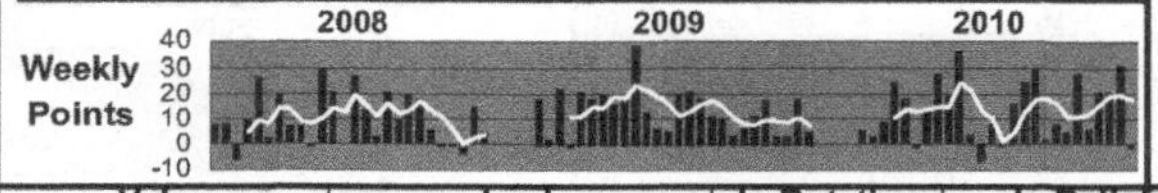


Minors (2010) / Skills

| Level | Leag | W | L | Sv | IP | H | K | ERA | WHIP | K/9 | BB/9 | HR/9 | GB/F |
|---|---|---|---|---|---|---|---|---|---|---|---|---|---|
| A | — | — | — | — | — | — | — | — | — | — | — | — | — |
| AA | — | — | — | — | — | — | — | — | — | — | — | — | — |
| AAA | — | — | — | — | — | — | — | — | — | — | — | — | — |

Majors / Skills / Value / Luck / In Rotation / In Relief / OPS

| Yr | Team | W | L | Sv | IP | H | K | ERA | WHIP | K/9 | BB/9 | HR/9 | GB/F | $1L | $2L | Pts | RAA | H% | HR/fb | S% | FIP | GS | CG | QS/DS | GR | Hld | Bln | Lead | OPS | 1st Hf | 2nd Hf | vs RH | vs LH |
|---|---|---|---|---|---|---|---|---|---|---|---|---|---|---|---|---|---|---|---|---|---|---|---|---|---|---|---|---|---|---|---|---|---|
| 07 | SF | 7 | 16 | 0 | 200 | 173 | 163 | 3.65 | 1.26 | 7.3 | 3.6 | 0.6 | 0.9 | $12 | $2 | 230 | +15 | 28% | 5% | 72% | 3.67 | 32 | 1 | 22/3 | — | — | — | — | .678 | .678 | .677 | .661 | .697 |
| 08 | SF | 8 | 14 | 0 | 217 | 206 | 186 | 3.76 | 1.36 | 7.7 | 3.8 | 0.8 | 0.8 | $8 | -$2 | 240 | +12 | 31% | 7% | 74% | 3.88 | 34 | 1 | 21/3 | — | — | — | — | .728 | .713 | .747 | .690 | .769 |
| 09 | SF | 14 | 8 | 0 | 217 | 184 | 171 | 2.89 | 1.18 | 7.1 | 3.0 | 0.9 | 0.9 | $21 | $14 | 330 | +34 | 27% | 8% | 80% | 3.95 | 33 | 4 | 20/1 | — | — | — | — | .670 | .673 | .667 | .693 | .649 |
| 10 | SF | 13 | 11 | 0 | 223 | 181 | 177 | 3.14 | 1.08 | 7.1 | 2.5 | 0.9 | 0.8 | $22 | $18 | 330 | +26 | 26% | 7% | 75% | 3.71 | 33 | 4 | 25/3 | — | — | — | — | .646 | .677 | .607 | .629 | .663 |

## Shawn Camp
**80 IP | $4 | 90 pts**

RP-70 | Owned: 1% | RH

With Scott Downs, Jason Frasor, & Kevin Gregg all possibly headed for free agency, Camp could end up as the key veteran set-up man in Toronto. Unfortunately, Camp's power is trending downward, and his K and GB rates have worsened since '07. If his walk rate rises above 3.0 BB/9, his ERA may explode. (MH)

Forecast

| Player | Age | IP | W | Sv | K | ERA | WHIP | K/9 | BB/9 | $2L | Pts |
|---|---|---|---|---|---|---|---|---|---|---|---|
| Camp S | 35 | 80 | 4 | 0 | 53 | 3.82 | 1.29 | 5.9 | 2.8 | $4 | 90 |
| **Mini-Browser** | **Age** | **IP** | **W** | **Sv** | **K** | **ERA** | **WHIP** | **K/9** | **BB/9** | **$2L** | **Pts** |
| Venters J | 26 | 70 | 3 | 13 | 64 | 3.94 | 1.50 | 8.2 | 4.6 | $4 | 150 |
| Fister D | 27 | 190 | 8 | 0 | 120 | 4.64 | 1.37 | 5.7 | 2.1 | $4 | 160 |
| Masset N | 28 | 80 | 4 | 4 | 69 | 3.97 | 1.31 | 7.8 | 3.4 | $4 | 120 |
| Marshall S | 28 | 80 | 5 | 2 | 69 | 4.04 | 1.31 | 7.7 | 3.1 | $4 | 120 |
| Francisco F | 31 | 60 | 4 | 0 | 66 | 3.80 | 1.30 | 9.9 | 3.6 | $4 | 100 |

Competition at RP — Stats in 2010 as RP

| Thr | Player | GR | ERA | IP/G | Sv-Hld |
|---|---|---|---|---|---|
| RH | Camp S | 70 | 2.99 | 1.0 | 2-13 |
| RH | Frasor J | 69 | 3.68 | 0.9 | 4-14 |
| RH | Gregg K | 63 | 3.51 | 0.9 | 37-3 |
| RH | Janssen C | 56 | 3.67 | 1.2 | 0-2 |

Ten-Year Trends (K/9, BB/9)

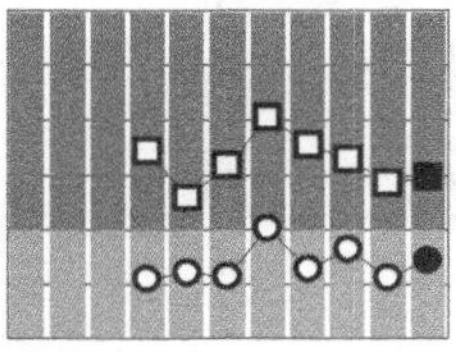


Weekly Points

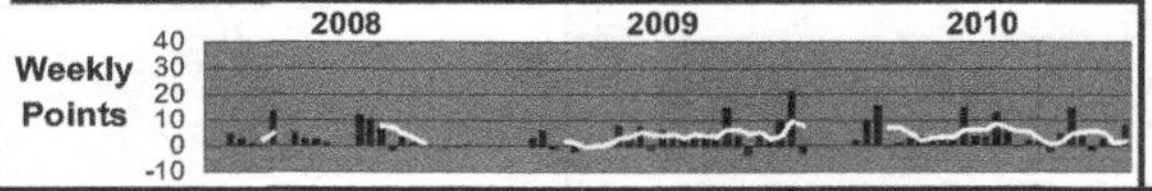


Minors (2010) / Skills

| Level | Leag | W | L | Sv | IP | H | K | ERA | WHIP | K/9 | BB/9 | HR/9 | GB/F |
|---|---|---|---|---|---|---|---|---|---|---|---|---|---|
| A | — | — | — | — | — | — | — | — | — | — | — | — | — |
| AA | — | — | — | — | — | — | — | — | — | — | — | — | — |
| AAA | — | — | — | — | — | — | — | — | — | — | — | — | — |

Majors / Skills / Value / Luck / In Rotation / In Relief / OPS

| Yr | Team | W | L | Sv | IP | H | K | ERA | WHIP | K/9 | BB/9 | HR/9 | GB/F | $1L | $2L | Pts | RAA | H% | HR/fb | S% | FIP | GS | CG | QS/DS | GR | Hld | Bln | Lead | OPS | 1st Hf | 2nd Hf | vs RH | vs LH |
|---|---|---|---|---|---|---|---|---|---|---|---|---|---|---|---|---|---|---|---|---|---|---|---|---|---|---|---|---|---|---|---|---|---|
| 07 | TB | 0 | 3 | 0 | 40 | 63 | 36 | 7.20 | 2.03 | 8.1 | 4.1 | 1.6 | 2.6 | -$8 | -$15 | 0 | –15 | 44% | 24% | 66% | 5.13 | — | — | — | 50 | 11 | 2 | +0.0 | .991 | .879 | 1.469 | .973 | 1.025 |
| 08 | TOR | 3 | 1 | 0 | 39 | 40 | 31 | 4.12 | 1.30 | 7.1 | 2.5 | 0.5 | 2.0 | $0 | -$2 | 60 | –0 | 32% | 6% | 67% | 3.22 | — | — | — | 40 | 7 | 0 | –0.6 | .694 | .617 | .812 | .515 | .976 |
| 09 | TOR | 2 | 6 | 1 | 79 | 73 | 58 | 3.50 | 1.28 | 6.6 | 3.3 | 0.8 | 2.0 | $4 | $0 | 80 | –0 | 29% | 11% | 75% | 4.08 | — | — | — | 59 | 6 | 0 | –0.9 | .705 | .712 | .697 | .650 | .762 |
| 10 | TOR | 4 | 3 | 2 | 72 | 71 | 46 | 2.99 | 1.23 | 5.7 | 2.2 | 1.0 | 1.7 | $4 | -$3 | 100 | +7 | 29% | 11% | 80% | 4.21 | — | — | — | 70 | 13 | 2 | +0.8 | .728 | .696 | .776 | .661 | .832 |

## Matt Capps
**60 IP | $11 | 200 pts**

RP-74 | Owned: 100% | RH

Concerns about Jon Rauch's make-up, and about Joe Nathan's ability to return from TJ surgery in 2011, led the Twins to trade prospect Wilson Ramos for Capps. The former National pitched customarily well out of MIN's bullpen. He will return as either a closer or set-up man, depending on Nathan's status. (NN)

Forecast

| Player | Age | IP | W | Sv | K | ERA | WHIP | K/9 | BB/9 | $2L | Pts |
|---|---|---|---|---|---|---|---|---|---|---|---|
| Capps M | 27 | 60 | 2 | 27 | 45 | 3.55 | 1.24 | 6.8 | 2.0 | $11 | 200 |
| **Mini-Browser** | **Age** | **IP** | **W** | **Sv** | **K** | **ERA** | **WHIP** | **K/9** | **BB/9** | **$2L** | **Pts** |
| Jansen K | 23 | 60 | 3 | 9 | 85 | 1.56 | 1.18 | 12.7 | 5.4 | $11 | 170 |
| Myers B | 30 | 220 | 12 | 0 | 175 | 4.05 | 1.30 | 7.2 | 2.8 | $11 | 270 |
| Santana E | 28 | 200 | 14 | 0 | 154 | 4.34 | 1.31 | 6.9 | 2.8 | $11 | 260 |
| Aardsma D | 29 | 70 | 2 | 31 | 70 | 3.80 | 1.37 | 9.1 | 5.0 | $11 | 240 |
| Rodriguez W | 32 | 200 | 11 | 0 | 167 | 3.99 | 1.29 | 7.5 | 3.0 | $11 | 260 |

Competition at RP — Stats in 2010 as RP

| Thr | Player | GR | ERA | IP/G | Sv-Hld |
|---|---|---|---|---|---|
| RH | Guerrier M | 74 | 3.17 | 1.0 | 1-23 |
| RH | Crain J | 71 | 3.04 | 1.0 | 1-21 |
| RH | Rauch J | 59 | 3.12 | 1.0 | 21-2 |
| RH | Burnett A | 41 | 5.29 | 1.2 | 0-2 |

Ten-Year Trends (K/9, BB/9)

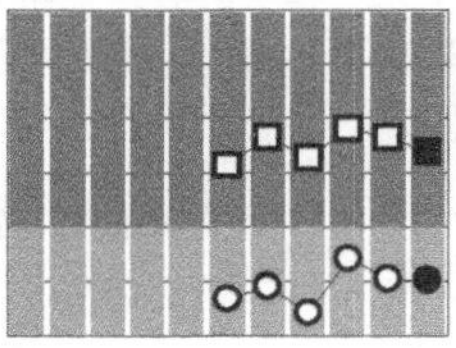


Weekly Points

Minors (2010) / Skills

| Level | Leag | W | L | Sv | IP | H | K | ERA | WHIP | K/9 | BB/9 | HR/9 | GB/F |
|---|---|---|---|---|---|---|---|---|---|---|---|---|---|
| A | — | — | — | — | — | — | — | — | — | — | — | — | — |
| AA | — | — | — | — | — | — | — | — | — | — | — | — | — |
| AAA | — | — | — | — | — | — | — | — | — | — | — | — | — |

Majors / Skills / Value / Luck / In Rotation / In Relief / OPS

| Yr | Team | W | L | Sv | IP | H | K | ERA | WHIP | K/9 | BB/9 | HR/9 | GB/F | $1L | $2L | Pts | RAA | H% | HR/fb | S% | FIP | GS | CG | QS/DS | GR | Hld | Bln | Lead | OPS | 1st Hf | 2nd Hf | vs RH | vs LH |
|---|---|---|---|---|---|---|---|---|---|---|---|---|---|---|---|---|---|---|---|---|---|---|---|---|---|---|---|---|---|---|---|---|---|
| 07 | PIT | 4 | 7 | 18 | 79 | 64 | 64 | 2.28 | 1.01 | 7.3 | 1.8 | 0.6 | 0.6 | $14 | $13 | 210 | +14 | 27% | 4% | 80% | 3.01 | — | — | — | 76 | 15 | 3 | +1.7 | .582 | .590 | .568 | .473 | .743 |
| 08 | PIT | 2 | 3 | 21 | 53 | 47 | 39 | 3.02 | 0.97 | 6.5 | 0.8 | 0.8 | 0.7 | $10 | $7 | 170 | +4 | 27% | 7% | 72% | 3.24 | — | — | — | 49 | 0 | 5 | +1.1 | .633 | .700 | .424 | .676 | .589 |
| 09 | PIT | 4 | 8 | 27 | 54 | 73 | 46 | 5.80 | 1.66 | 7.6 | 2.8 | 1.7 | 1.0 | $2 | -$1 | 200 | –12 | 37% | 14% | 69% | 4.84 | — | — | — | 57 | 1 | 5 | +1.0 | .907 | .888 | .926 | .791 | 1.014 |
| 10 | 2TM | 5 | 3 | 42 | 73 | 75 | 59 | 2.47 | 1.26 | 7.3 | 2.1 | 0.7 | 1.6 | $16 | $11 | 330 | +6 | 32% | 9% | 84% | 3.40 | — | — | — | 74 | 0 | 6 | +0.8 | .688 | .774 | .569 | .719 | .654 |

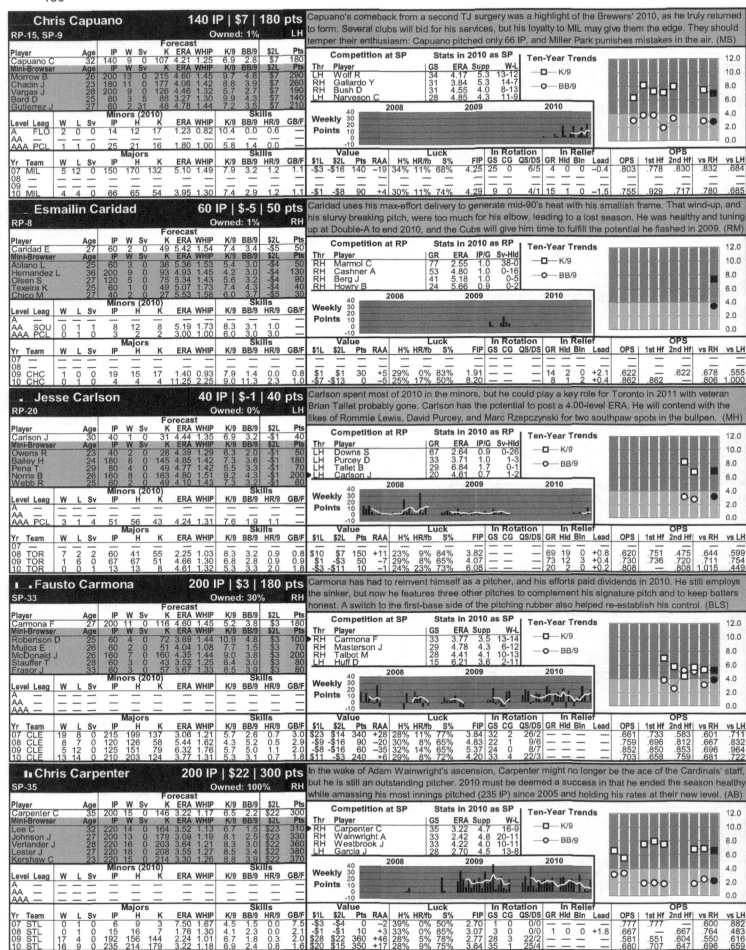

## Chris Capuano — 140 IP | $7 | 180 pts

RP-15, SP-9 — Owned: 1% — LH

Capuano's comeback from a second TJ surgery was a highlight of the Brewers' 2010, as he truly returned to form. Several clubs will bid for his services, but his loyalty to MIL may give them the edge. They should temper their enthusiasm: Capuano pitched only 66 IP, and Miller Park punishes mistakes in the air. (MS)

**Forecast**

| Player | Age | IP | W | Sv | K | ERA | WHIP | K/9 | BB/9 | $2L | Pts |
|---|---|---|---|---|---|---|---|---|---|---|---|
| Capuano C | 32 | 140 | 9 | 0 | 107 | 4.21 | 1.25 | 6.9 | 2.8 | $7 | 180 |
| **Mini-Browser** | **Age** | **IP** | **W** | **Sv** | **K** | **ERA** | **WHIP** | **K/9** | **BB/9** | **$2L** | **Pts** |
| Morrow B | 26 | 200 | 13 | 0 | 215 | 4.60 | 1.45 | 9.7 | 4.8 | $7 | 290 |
| Chacin J | 23 | 180 | 11 | 0 | 177 | 4.06 | 1.42 | 8.8 | 3.9 | $7 | 260 |
| Vargas J | 28 | 200 | 9 | 0 | 126 | 4.46 | 1.32 | 5.7 | 2.7 | $7 | 190 |
| Bard D | 25 | 80 | 3 | 5 | 88 | 3.27 | 1.30 | 9.9 | 4.3 | $7 | 140 |
| Gutierrez J | 27 | 60 | 2 | 31 | 48 | 4.78 | 1.44 | 7.2 | 3.5 | $7 | 210 |

**Minors (2010)** / **Skills**

| Level | Leag | W | L | Sv | IP | H | K | ERA | WHIP | K/9 | BB/9 | HR/9 | GB/F |
|---|---|---|---|---|---|---|---|---|---|---|---|---|---|
| A | FLO | 2 | 0 | 0 | 14 | 12 | 17 | 1.23 | 0.82 | 10.4 | 0.0 | 0.6 | — |
| AA | — | — | — | — | — | — | — | — | — | — | — | — | — |
| AAA | PCL | 1 | 1 | 0 | 25 | 21 | 16 | 1.80 | 1.00 | 5.8 | 1.4 | 0.0 | — |

**Majors** / **Skills**

| Yr | Team | W | L | Sv | IP | H | K | ERA | WHIP | K/9 | BB/9 | HR/9 | GB/F |
|---|---|---|---|---|---|---|---|---|---|---|---|---|---|
| 07 | MIL | 5 | 12 | 0 | 150 | 170 | 132 | 5.10 | 1.49 | 7.9 | 3.2 | 1.2 | 1.1 |
| 08 | — | — | — | — | — | — | — | — | — | — | — | — | — |
| 09 | — | — | — | — | — | — | — | — | — | — | — | — | — |
| 10 | MIL | 4 | 4 | 0 | 66 | 65 | 54 | 3.95 | 1.30 | 7.4 | 2.9 | 1.2 | 1.1 |

| Yr | Value $1L | $2L | Pts | RAA | Luck H% | HR/fb | S% | FIP | In Rotation GS | CG | QS/DS | In Relief GR | Hld | Bln | Lead | OPS | 1st Hf | 2nd Hf | vs RH | vs LH |
|---|---|---|---|---|---|---|---|---|---|---|---|---|---|---|---|---|---|---|---|---|
| 07 | -$3 | -$16 | 140 | −19 | 34% | 11% | 68% | 4.25 | 25 | 0 | 6/5 | 4 | 0 | 0 | −0.4 | .803 | .778 | .830 | .832 | .684 |
| 08 | — | — | — | — | — | — | — | — | — | — | — | — | — | — | — | — | — | — | — | — |
| 09 | — | — | — | — | — | — | — | — | — | — | — | — | — | — | — | — | — | — | — | — |
| 10 | -$1 | -$8 | 90 | +4 | 30% | 11% | 74% | 4.29 | 9 | 0 | 4/1 | 15 | 1 | 0 | −1.5 | .755 | .929 | .717 | .780 | .685 |

**Competition at SP** — Stats in 2010 as SP

| Thr | Player | GS | ERA | Supp | W-L |
|---|---|---|---|---|---|
| LH | Wolf R | 34 | 4.17 | 5.3 | 13-12 |
| RH | Gallardo Y | 31 | 3.84 | 5.3 | 14-7 |
| RH | Bush D | 31 | 4.55 | 4.0 | 8-13 |
| LH | Narveson C | 28 | 4.85 | 4.3 | 11-9 |

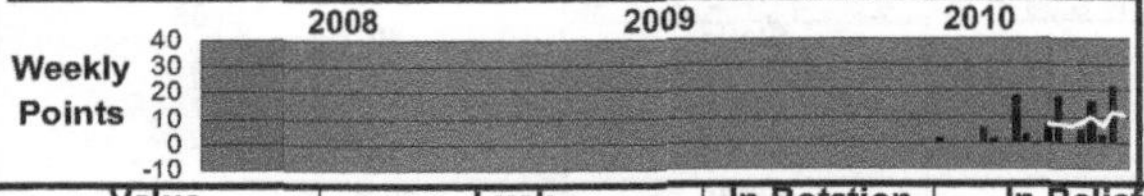


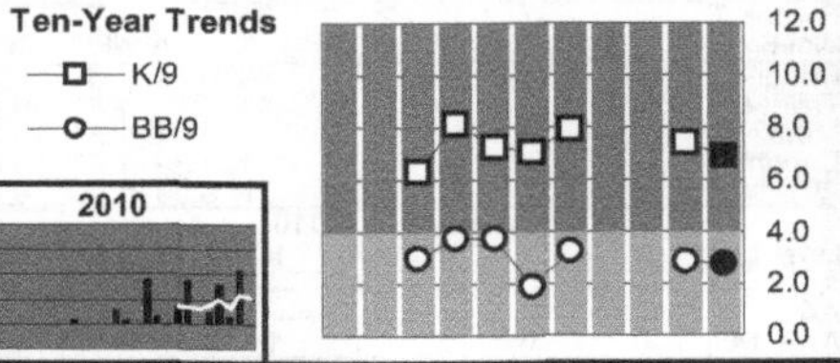


## Esmailin Caridad — 60 IP | $-5 | 50 pts

RP-8 — Owned: 1% — RH

Caridad uses his max-effort delivery to generate mid-90's heat with his smallish frame. That wind-up, and his slurvy breaking pitch, were too much for his elbow, leading to a lost season. He was healthy and tuning up at Double-A to end 2010, and the Cubs will give him time to fulfill the potential he flashed in 2009. (RM)

**Forecast**

| Player | Age | IP | W | Sv | K | ERA | WHIP | K/9 | BB/9 | $2L | Pts |
|---|---|---|---|---|---|---|---|---|---|---|---|
| Caridad E | 27 | 60 | 2 | 0 | 49 | 5.42 | 1.54 | 7.4 | 3.4 | -$5 | 50 |
| **Mini-Browser** | **Age** | **IP** | **W** | **Sv** | **K** | **ERA** | **WHIP** | **K/9** | **BB/9** | **$2L** | **Pts** |
| Atilano L | 25 | 60 | 3 | 0 | 36 | 5.36 | 1.53 | 5.4 | 3.0 | -$4 | 50 |
| Hernandez L | 36 | 200 | 9 | 0 | 93 | 4.93 | 1.45 | 4.2 | 3.0 | -$4 | 130 |
| Olsen S | 27 | 120 | 5 | 0 | 75 | 5.34 | 1.43 | 5.6 | 3.2 | -$4 | 90 |
| Texeira K | 25 | 60 | 1 | 0 | 49 | 5.07 | 1.73 | 7.4 | 4.3 | -$4 | 40 |
| Chico M | 27 | 40 | 2 | 0 | 27 | 5.53 | 1.58 | 6.0 | 3.7 | -$5 | 30 |

**Minors (2010)** / **Skills**

| Level | Leag | W | L | Sv | IP | H | K | ERA | WHIP | K/9 | BB/9 | HR/9 | GB/F |
|---|---|---|---|---|---|---|---|---|---|---|---|---|---|
| A | — | — | — | — | — | — | — | — | — | — | — | — | — |
| AA | SOU | 0 | 1 | 1 | 8 | 12 | 8 | 5.19 | 1.73 | 8.3 | 3.1 | 1.0 | — |
| AAA | PCL | 0 | 1 | 0 | 3 | 2 | 2 | 3.00 | 1.00 | 6.0 | 3.0 | 3.0 | — |

**Majors** / **Skills**

| Yr | Team | W | L | Sv | IP | H | K | ERA | WHIP | K/9 | BB/9 | HR/9 | GB/F |
|---|---|---|---|---|---|---|---|---|---|---|---|---|---|
| 07 | — | — | — | — | — | — | — | — | — | — | — | — | — |
| 08 | — | — | — | — | — | — | — | — | — | — | — | — | — |
| 09 | CHC | 1 | 0 | 0 | 19 | 15 | 17 | 1.40 | 0.93 | 7.9 | 1.4 | 0.0 | 0.8 |
| 10 | CHC | 0 | 1 | 0 | 4 | 4 | 4 | 11.25 | 2.25 | 9.0 | 11.3 | 2.3 | 1.0 |

| Yr | Value $1L | $2L | Pts | RAA | Luck H% | HR/fb | S% | FIP | In Rotation GS | CG | QS/DS | In Relief GR | Hld | Bln | Lead | OPS | 1st Hf | 2nd Hf | vs RH | vs LH |
|---|---|---|---|---|---|---|---|---|---|---|---|---|---|---|---|---|---|---|---|---|
| 07 | — | — | — | — | — | — | — | — | — | — | — | — | — | — | — | — | — | — | — | — |
| 08 | — | — | — | — | — | — | — | — | — | — | — | — | — | — | — | — | — | — | — | — |
| 09 | $1 | $1 | 30 | +5 | 29% | 0% | 83% | 1.91 | — | — | — | 14 | 2 | 0 | +2.1 | .622 | — | .622 | .678 | .555 |
| 10 | -$7 | -$13 | 0 | −5 | 25% | 17% | 50% | 8.20 | — | — | — | 8 | 1 | 2 | +0.4 | .862 | .862 | — | .806 | 1.000 |

**Competition at RP** — Stats in 2010 as RP

| Thr | Player | GR | ERA | IP/G | Sv-Hld |
|---|---|---|---|---|---|
| RH | Marmol C | 77 | 2.55 | 1.0 | 38-0 |
| RH | Cashner A | 53 | 4.80 | 1.0 | 0-16 |
| RH | Berg J | 41 | 5.18 | 1.0 | 0-5 |
| RH | Howry B | 24 | 5.66 | 0.9 | 0-2 |

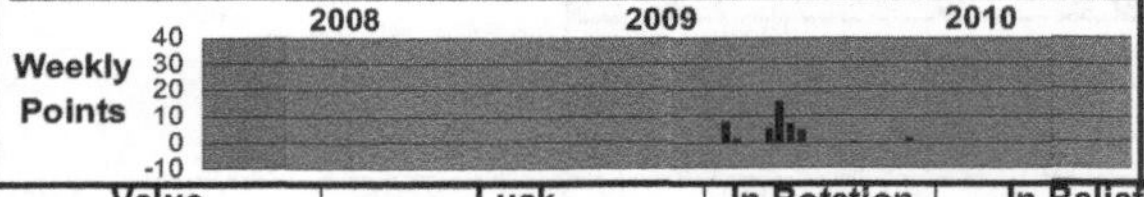


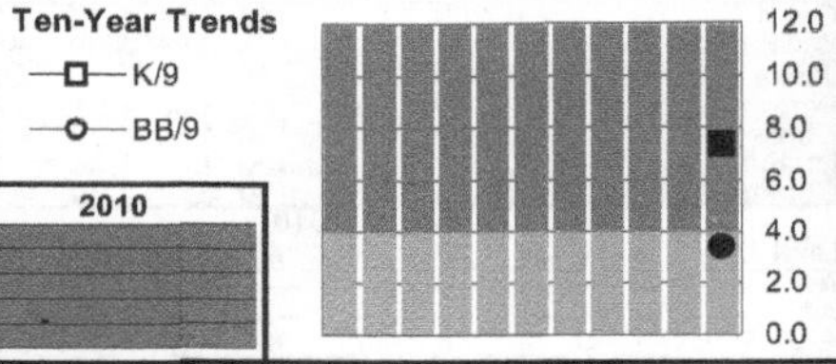


## Jesse Carlson — 40 IP | $-1 | 40 pts

RP-20 — Owned: 0% — LH

Carlson spent most of 2010 in the minors, but he could play a key role for Toronto in 2011 with veteran Brian Tallet probably gone. Carlson has the potential to post a 4.00-level ERA. He will contend with the likes of Rommie Lewis, David Purcey, and Marc Rzepczynski for two southpaw spots in the bullpen. (MH)

**Forecast**

| Player | Age | IP | W | Sv | K | ERA | WHIP | K/9 | BB/9 | $2L | Pts |
|---|---|---|---|---|---|---|---|---|---|---|---|
| Carlson J | 30 | 40 | 1 | 0 | 31 | 4.44 | 1.35 | 6.9 | 3.2 | -$1 | 40 |
| **Mini-Browser** | **Age** | **IP** | **W** | **Sv** | **K** | **ERA** | **WHIP** | **K/9** | **BB/9** | **$2L** | **Pts** |
| Owens R | 23 | 40 | 2 | 0 | 28 | 4.39 | 1.29 | 6.3 | 2.0 | -$1 | 50 |
| Bailey H | 24 | 180 | 8 | 0 | 145 | 4.85 | 1.42 | 7.3 | 3.6 | -$1 | 180 |
| Pena T | 29 | 80 | 4 | 0 | 49 | 4.77 | 1.42 | 5.5 | 3.3 | -$1 | 70 |
| Norris B | 26 | 160 | 8 | 0 | 163 | 4.80 | 1.51 | 9.2 | 4.3 | -$1 | 200 |
| Webb R | 25 | 60 | 2 | 0 | 49 | 4.10 | 1.43 | 7.3 | 3.2 | -$1 | 60 |

**Minors (2010)** / **Skills**

| Level | Leag | W | L | Sv | IP | H | K | ERA | WHIP | K/9 | BB/9 | HR/9 | GB/F |
|---|---|---|---|---|---|---|---|---|---|---|---|---|---|
| A | — | — | — | — | — | — | — | — | — | — | — | — | — |
| AA | — | — | — | — | — | — | — | — | — | — | — | — | — |
| AAA | PCL | 3 | 1 | 4 | 51 | 56 | 43 | 4.24 | 1.31 | 7.6 | 1.9 | 1.1 | — |

**Majors** / **Skills**

| Yr | Team | W | L | Sv | IP | H | K | ERA | WHIP | K/9 | BB/9 | HR/9 | GB/F |
|---|---|---|---|---|---|---|---|---|---|---|---|---|---|
| 07 | — | — | — | — | — | — | — | — | — | — | — | — | — |
| 08 | TOR | 7 | 2 | 2 | 60 | 41 | 55 | 2.25 | 1.03 | 8.3 | 3.2 | 0.9 | 0.8 |
| 09 | TOR | 1 | 6 | 0 | 67 | 67 | 51 | 4.66 | 1.30 | 6.8 | 2.8 | 0.9 | 0.9 |
| 10 | TOR | 0 | 0 | 1 | 13 | 13 | 8 | 4.61 | 1.32 | 5.3 | 3.3 | 2.0 | 1.8 |

| Yr | Value $1L | $2L | Pts | RAA | Luck H% | HR/fb | S% | FIP | In Rotation GS | CG | QS/DS | In Relief GR | Hld | Bln | Lead | OPS | 1st Hf | 2nd Hf | vs RH | vs LH |
|---|---|---|---|---|---|---|---|---|---|---|---|---|---|---|---|---|---|---|---|---|
| 07 | — | — | — | — | — | — | — | — | — | — | — | — | — | — | — | — | — | — | — | — |
| 08 | $10 | $7 | 150 | +11 | 23% | 9% | 84% | 3.82 | — | — | — | 69 | 19 | 0 | +0.8 | .620 | .751 | .475 | .644 | .599 |
| 09 | $1 | -$3 | 50 | −7 | 29% | 8% | 65% | 4.07 | — | — | — | 73 | 12 | 3 | +0.4 | .730 | .736 | .720 | .711 | .754 |
| 10 | -$3 | -$11 | 10 | −1 | 24% | 23% | 73% | 6.08 | — | — | — | 20 | 2 | 0 | +0.2 | .808 | | .808 | 1.015 | .449 |

**Competition at RP** — Stats in 2010 as RP

| Thr | Player | GR | ERA | IP/G | Sv-Hld |
|---|---|---|---|---|---|
| LH | Downs S | 67 | 2.64 | 0.9 | 0-26 |
| LH | Purcey D | 33 | 3.71 | 1.0 | 1-3 |
| LH | Tallet B | 29 | 6.84 | 1.7 | 0-1 |
| LH | Carlson J | 20 | 4.61 | 0.7 | 1-2 |

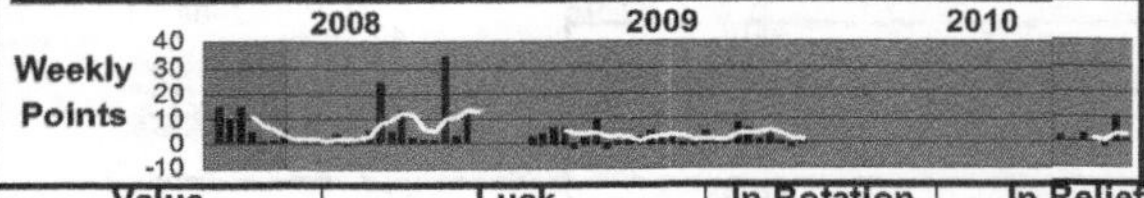


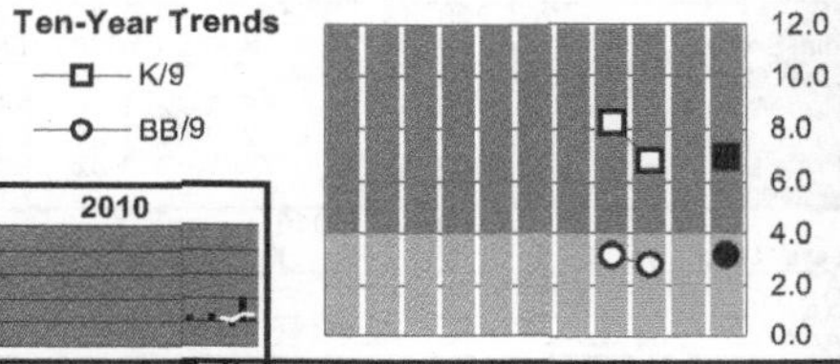


## Fausto Carmona — 200 IP | $3 | 180 pts

SP-33 — Owned: 30% — RH

Carmona has had to reinvent himself as a pitcher, and his efforts paid dividends in 2010. He still employs the sinker, but now he features three other pitches to complement his signature pitch and to keep batters honest. A switch to the first-base side of the pitching rubber also helped re-establish his control. (BLS)

**Forecast**

| Player | Age | IP | W | Sv | K | ERA | WHIP | K/9 | BB/9 | $2L | Pts |
|---|---|---|---|---|---|---|---|---|---|---|---|
| Carmona F | 27 | 200 | 11 | 0 | 116 | 4.60 | 1.45 | 5.2 | 3.8 | $3 | 180 |
| **Mini-Browser** | **Age** | **IP** | **W** | **Sv** | **K** | **ERA** | **WHIP** | **K/9** | **BB/9** | **$2L** | **Pts** |
| Robertson D | 25 | 60 | 4 | 0 | 72 | 3.69 | 1.44 | 10.9 | 4.8 | $3 | 100 |
| Mujica E | 26 | 60 | 2 | 0 | 51 | 4.04 | 1.08 | 7.7 | 1.5 | $3 | 70 |
| McDonald J | 26 | 160 | 7 | 0 | 160 | 4.35 | 1.44 | 9.0 | 3.8 | $3 | 200 |
| Stauffer T | 28 | 60 | 3 | 0 | 43 | 3.52 | 1.25 | 6.4 | 3.0 | $3 | 80 |
| Frasor J | 33 | 60 | 3 | 0 | 57 | 3.67 | 1.33 | 8.5 | 3.9 | $3 | 80 |

**Minors (2010)** / **Skills**

| Level | Leag | W | L | Sv | IP | H | K | ERA | WHIP | K/9 | BB/9 | HR/9 | GB/F |
|---|---|---|---|---|---|---|---|---|---|---|---|---|---|
| A | — | — | — | — | — | — | — | — | — | — | — | — | — |
| AA | — | — | — | — | — | — | — | — | — | — | — | — | — |
| AAA | — | — | — | — | — | — | — | — | — | — | — | — | — |

**Majors** / **Skills**

| Yr | Team | W | L | Sv | IP | H | K | ERA | WHIP | K/9 | BB/9 | HR/9 | GB/F |
|---|---|---|---|---|---|---|---|---|---|---|---|---|---|
| 07 | CLE | 19 | 8 | 0 | 215 | 199 | 137 | 3.06 | 1.21 | 5.7 | 2.6 | 0.7 | 3.0 |
| 08 | CLE | 8 | 7 | 0 | 120 | 126 | 58 | 5.44 | 1.62 | 4.3 | 5.2 | 0.5 | 2.9 |
| 09 | CLE | 5 | 12 | 0 | 125 | 151 | 79 | 6.32 | 1.76 | 5.7 | 5.0 | 1.1 | 2.0 |
| 10 | CLE | 13 | 14 | 0 | 210 | 203 | 124 | 3.77 | 1.31 | 5.3 | 3.1 | 0.7 | 1.8 |

| Yr | Value $1L | $2L | Pts | RAA | Luck H% | HR/fb | S% | FIP | In Rotation GS | CG | QS/DS | In Relief GR | Hld | Bln | Lead | OPS | 1st Hf | 2nd Hf | vs RH | vs LH |
|---|---|---|---|---|---|---|---|---|---|---|---|---|---|---|---|---|---|---|---|---|
| 07 | $23 | $14 | 340 | +28 | 28% | 11% | 77% | 3.84 | 32 | 2 | 26/2 | — | — | — | — | .661 | .733 | .583 | .601 | .711 |
| 08 | -$9 | -$16 | 90 | −20 | 30% | 8% | 65% | 4.83 | 22 | 1 | 9/6 | — | — | — | — | .759 | .696 | .812 | .667 | .832 |
| 09 | -$8 | -$16 | 60 | −35 | 32% | 14% | 65% | 5.37 | 24 | 0 | 8/7 | — | — | — | — | .852 | .850 | .853 | .696 | .964 |
| 10 | $11 | -$3 | 240 | +6 | 29% | 8% | 72% | 4.20 | 33 | 4 | 22/3 | — | — | — | — | .703 | .658 | .759 | .681 | .722 |

**Competition at SP** — Stats in 2010 as SP

| Thr | Player | GS | ERA | Supp | W-L |
|---|---|---|---|---|---|
| RH | Carmona F | 33 | 3.77 | 3.5 | 13-14 |
| RH | Masterson J | 29 | 4.78 | 4.3 | 6-12 |
| RH | Talbot M | 28 | 4.41 | 4.1 | 10-13 |
| LH | Huff D | 15 | 6.21 | 3.6 | 2-11 |

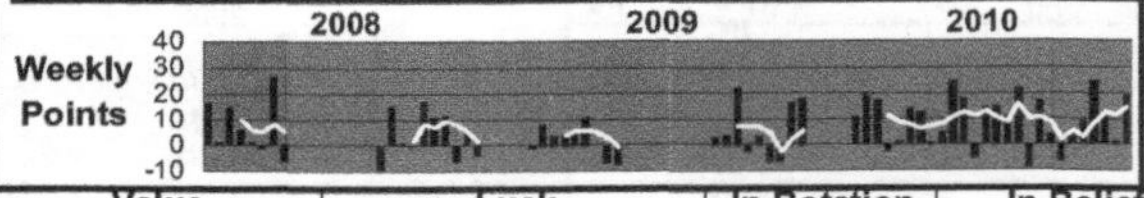


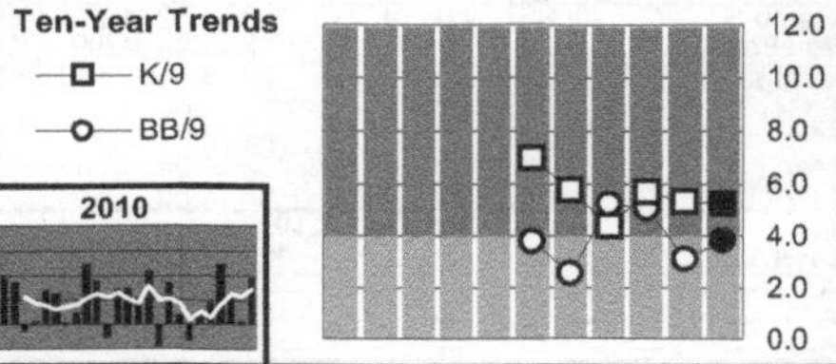


## Chris Carpenter — 200 IP | $22 | 300 pts

SP-35 — Owned: 100% — RH

In the wake of Adam Wainwright's ascension, Carpenter might no longer be the ace of the Cardinals' staff, but he is still an outstanding pitcher. 2010 must be deemed a success in that he ended the season healthy while amassing his most innings pitched (235 IP) since 2005 and holding his rates at their new level. (AB)

**Forecast**

| Player | Age | IP | W | Sv | K | ERA | WHIP | K/9 | BB/9 | $2L | Pts |
|---|---|---|---|---|---|---|---|---|---|---|---|
| Carpenter C | 35 | 200 | 15 | 0 | 146 | 3.22 | 1.17 | 6.5 | 2.2 | $22 | 300 |
| **Mini-Browser** | **Age** | **IP** | **W** | **Sv** | **K** | **ERA** | **WHIP** | **K/9** | **BB/9** | **$2L** | **Pts** |
| Lee C | 32 | 220 | 14 | 0 | 164 | 3.52 | 1.13 | 6.7 | 1.5 | $23 | 310 |
| Johnson J | 27 | 200 | 13 | 0 | 179 | 3.09 | 1.19 | 8.1 | 2.5 | $23 | 330 |
| Verlander J | 28 | 220 | 16 | 0 | 203 | 3.64 | 1.21 | 8.3 | 3.0 | $22 | 360 |
| Lester J | 27 | 220 | 18 | 0 | 208 | 3.55 | 1.27 | 8.5 | 3.4 | $22 | 380 |
| Kershaw C | 23 | 220 | 15 | 0 | 214 | 3.30 | 1.26 | 8.8 | 3.9 | $22 | 370 |

**Minors (2010)** / **Skills**

| Level | Leag | W | L | Sv | IP | H | K | ERA | WHIP | K/9 | BB/9 | HR/9 | GB/F |
|---|---|---|---|---|---|---|---|---|---|---|---|---|---|
| A | — | — | — | — | — | — | — | — | — | — | — | — | — |
| AA | — | — | — | — | — | — | — | — | — | — | — | — | — |
| AAA | — | — | — | — | — | — | — | — | — | — | — | — | — |

**Majors** / **Skills**

| Yr | Team | W | L | Sv | IP | H | K | ERA | WHIP | K/9 | BB/9 | HR/9 | GB/F |
|---|---|---|---|---|---|---|---|---|---|---|---|---|---|
| 07 | STL | 0 | 1 | 0 | 6 | 9 | 3 | 7.50 | 1.67 | 4.5 | 1.5 | 0.0 | 7.5 |
| 08 | STL | 0 | 1 | 0 | 15 | 16 | 7 | 1.76 | 1.30 | 4.1 | 2.3 | 0.0 | 2.1 |
| 09 | STL | 17 | 4 | 0 | 192 | 156 | 144 | 2.24 | 1.01 | 6.7 | 1.8 | 0.3 | 2.0 |
| 10 | STL | 16 | 9 | 0 | 235 | 214 | 179 | 3.22 | 1.18 | 6.9 | 2.4 | 0.8 | 1.6 |

| Yr | Value $1L | $2L | Pts | RAA | Luck H% | HR/fb | S% | FIP | In Rotation GS | CG | QS/DS | In Relief GR | Hld | Bln | Lead | OPS | 1st Hf | 2nd Hf | vs RH | vs LH |
|---|---|---|---|---|---|---|---|---|---|---|---|---|---|---|---|---|---|---|---|---|
| 07 | -$3 | -$4 | 0 | −2 | 39% | 0% | 50% | 2.70 | 1 | 0 | 0/0 | — | — | — | — | .777 | .777 | — | .600 | .882 |
| 08 | -$1 | -$1 | 10 | +3 | 33% | 0% | 85% | 3.07 | 3 | 0 | 0/0 | 1 | 0 | 0 | +1.8 | .667 | — | .667 | .764 | .483 |
| 09 | $28 | $22 | 360 | +46 | 28% | 5% | 78% | 2.77 | 28 | 3 | 22/2 | — | — | — | — | .581 | .551 | .604 | .550 | .616 |
| 10 | $20 | $15 | 350 | +17 | 28% | 9% | 75% | 3.64 | 35 | 1 | 25/4 | — | — | — | — | .680 | .707 | .647 | .696 | .659 |

**Competition at SP** — Stats in 2010 as SP

| Thr | Player | GS | ERA | Supp | W-L |
|---|---|---|---|---|---|
| RH | Carpenter C | 35 | 3.22 | 4.7 | 16-9 |
| RH | Wainwright A | 33 | 2.42 | 4.8 | 20-11 |
| RH | Westbrook J | 33 | 4.22 | 4.0 | 10-11 |
| LH | Garcia J | 28 | 2.70 | 4.5 | 13-8 |

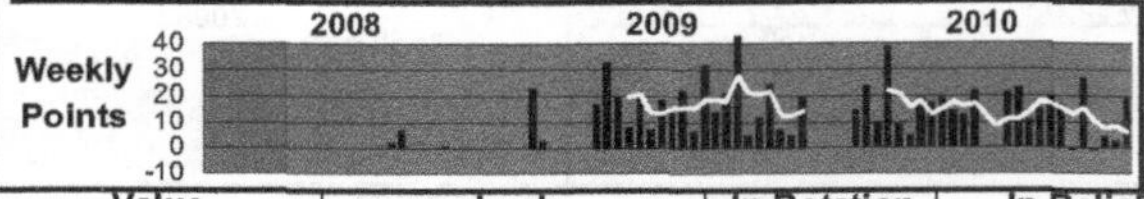


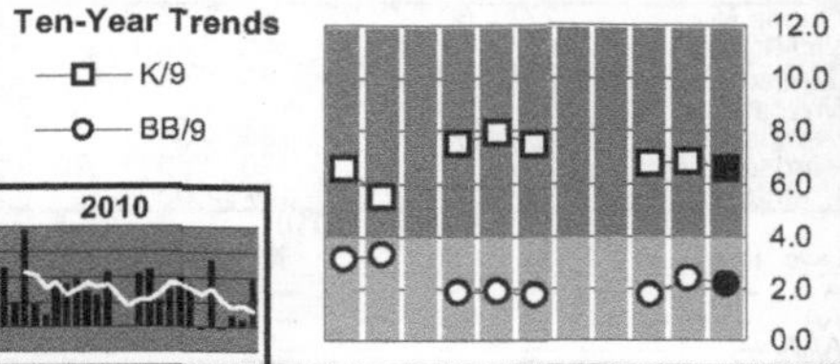


*For more stats, visit www.Rotolympus.com.*

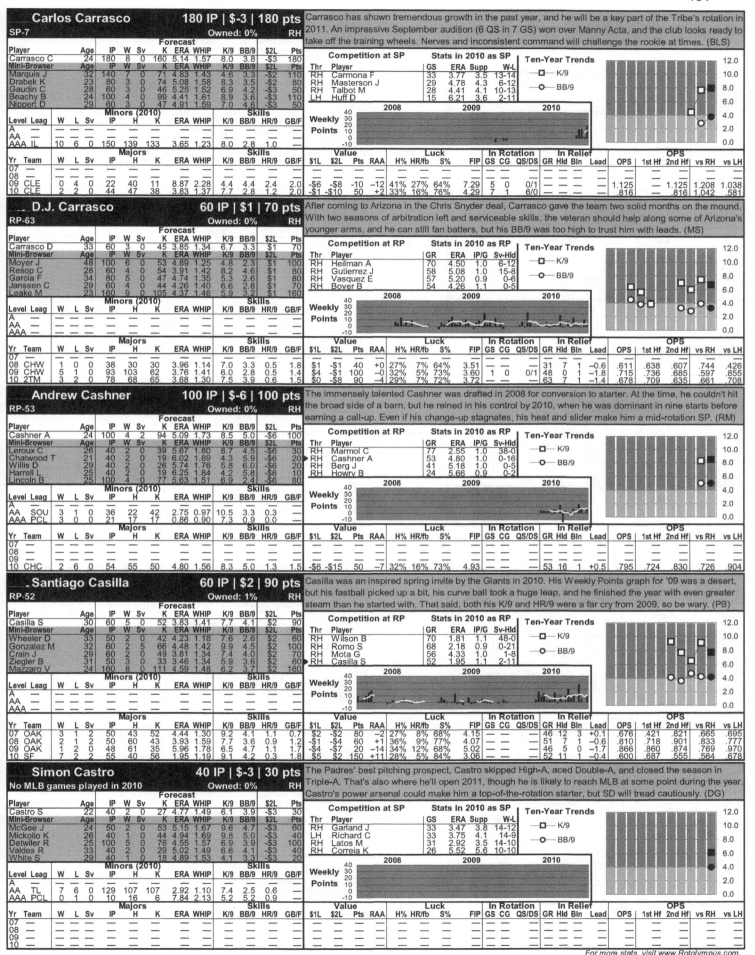

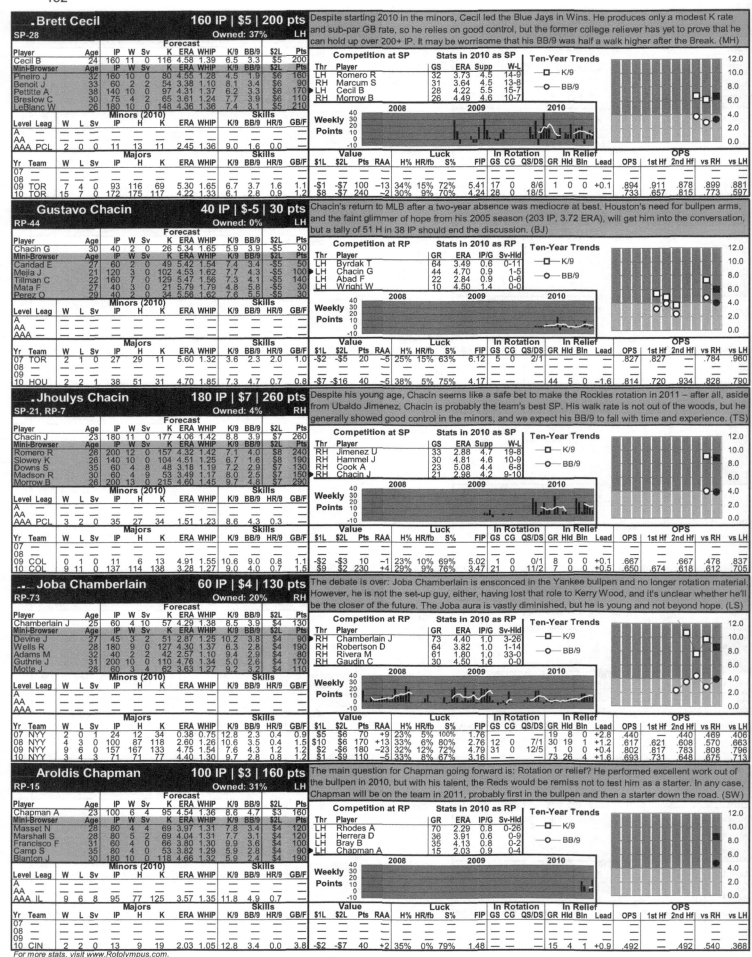

## Brett Cecil — 160 IP | $5 | 200 pts

SP-28 | Owned: 37% | LH

Despite starting 2010 in the minors, Cecil led the Blue Jays in Wins. He produces only a modest K rate and sub-par GB rate, so he relies on good control, but the former college reliever has yet to prove that he can hold up over 200+ IP. It may be worrisome that his BB/9 was half a walk higher after the Break. (MH)

**Forecast**

| Player | Age | IP | W | Sv | K | ERA | WHIP | K/9 | BB/9 | $2L | Pts |
|---|---|---|---|---|---|---|---|---|---|---|---|
| Cecil B | 24 | 160 | 11 | 0 | 116 | 4.58 | 1.39 | 6.5 | 3.3 | $5 | 200 |
| **Mini-Browser** | **Age** | **IP** | **W** | **Sv** | **K** | **ERA** | **WHIP** | **K/9** | **BB/9** | **$2L** | **Pts** |
| Pineiro J | 32 | 160 | 10 | 0 | 80 | 4.55 | 1.28 | 4.5 | 1.9 | $6 | 160 |
| Benoit J | 33 | 60 | 2 | 2 | 54 | 3.38 | 1.10 | 8.1 | 3.4 | $6 | 90 |
| Pettitte A | 38 | 140 | 10 | 0 | 97 | 4.31 | 1.37 | 6.2 | 3.3 | $6 | 170 |
| Breslow C | 30 | 75 | 4 | 2 | 65 | 3.61 | 1.24 | 7.7 | 3.9 | $6 | 110 |
| LeBlanc W | 26 | 180 | 10 | 0 | 148 | 4.36 | 1.36 | 7.4 | 3.1 | $5 | 210 |

**Minors (2010)**

| Level | Leag | W | L | Sv | IP | H | K | ERA | WHIP | K/9 | BB/9 | HR/9 | GB/F |
|---|---|---|---|---|---|---|---|---|---|---|---|---|---|
| A | — | — | — | — | — | — | — | — | — | — | — | — | — |
| AA | — | — | — | — | — | — | — | — | — | — | — | — | — |
| AAA | PCL | 2 | 0 | 0 | 11 | 13 | 11 | 2.45 | 1.36 | 9.0 | 1.6 | 0.0 | — |

**Competition at SP / Stats in 2010 as SP**

| Thr | Player | GS | ERA | Supp | W-L |
|---|---|---|---|---|---|
| LH | Romero R | 32 | 3.73 | 4.5 | 14-9 |
| RH | Marcum S | 31 | 3.64 | 4.5 | 13-8 |
| LH | Cecil B | 28 | 4.22 | 5.5 | 15-7 |
| RH | Morrow B | 26 | 4.49 | 4.6 | 10-7 |

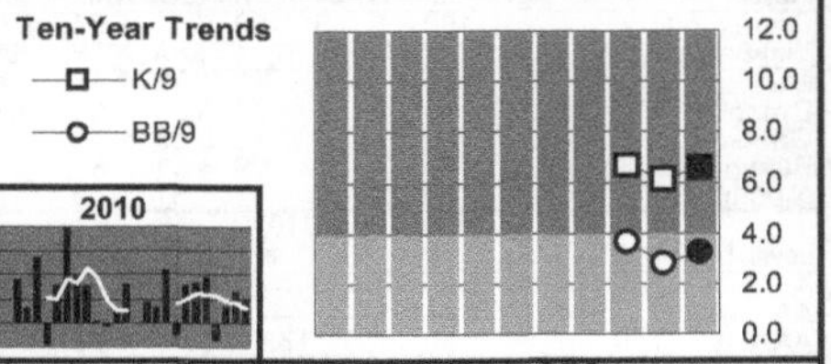


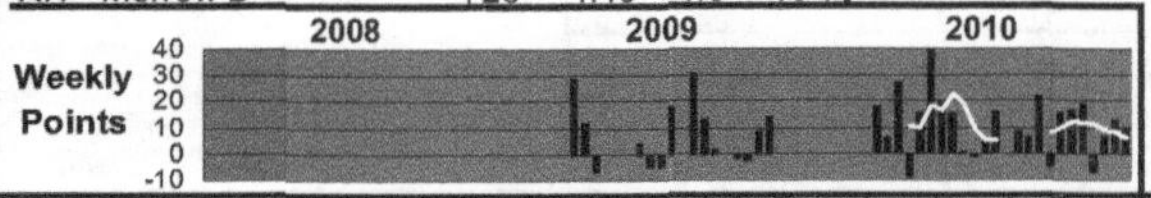


**Majors / Skills / Value / Luck / In Rotation / In Relief / OPS**

| Yr | Team | W | L | Sv | IP | H | K | ERA | WHIP | K/9 | BB/9 | HR/9 | GB/F | $1L | $2L | Pts | RAA | H% | HR/fb | S% | FIP | GS | CG | QS/DS | GR | Hld | Bln | Lead | OPS | 1st Hf | 2nd Hf | vs RH | vs LH |
|---|---|---|---|---|---|---|---|---|---|---|---|---|---|---|---|---|---|---|---|---|---|---|---|---|---|---|---|---|---|---|---|---|---|
| 07 | — | — | — | — | — | — | — | — | — | — | — | — | — | — | — | — | — | — | — | — | — | — | — | — | — | — | — | — | — | — | — | — | — |
| 08 | — | — | — | — | — | — | — | — | — | — | — | — | — | — | — | — | — | — | — | — | — | — | — | — | — | — | — | — | — | — | — | — | — |
| 09 | TOR | 7 | 4 | 0 | 93 | 116 | 69 | 5.30 | 1.65 | 6.7 | 3.7 | 1.6 | 1.1 | -$1 | -$7 | 100 | −13 | 34% | 15% | 72% | 5.41 | 17 | 0 | 8/6 | 1 | 0 | 0 | +0.1 | .894 | .911 | .878 | .899 | .881 |
| 10 | TOR | 15 | 7 | 0 | 172 | 175 | 117 | 4.22 | 1.33 | 6.1 | 2.8 | 0.9 | 1.2 | $8 | -$7 | 240 | −2 | 30% | 9% | 70% | 4.24 | 28 | 0 | 18/5 | — | — | — | — | .733 | .657 | .815 | .773 | .597 |

## Gustavo Chacin — 40 IP | $-5 | 30 pts

RP-44 | Owned: 0% | LH

Chacin's return to MLB after a two-year absence was mediocre at best. Houston's need for bullpen arms, and the faint glimmer of hope from his 2005 season (203 IP, 3.72 ERA), will get him into the conversation, but a tally of 51 H in 38 IP should end the discussion. (BJ)

**Forecast**

| Player | Age | IP | W | Sv | K | ERA | WHIP | K/9 | BB/9 | $2L | Pts |
|---|---|---|---|---|---|---|---|---|---|---|---|
| Chacin G | 30 | 40 | 2 | 0 | 26 | 5.34 | 1.65 | 5.9 | 3.9 | -$5 | 30 |
| **Mini-Browser** | **Age** | **IP** | **W** | **Sv** | **K** | **ERA** | **WHIP** | **K/9** | **BB/9** | **$2L** | **Pts** |
| Caridad E | 27 | 60 | 2 | 0 | 49 | 5.42 | 1.54 | 7.4 | 3.4 | -$5 | 50 |
| Mejia J | 21 | 120 | 3 | 0 | 102 | 4.53 | 1.62 | 7.7 | 4.3 | -$5 | 100 |
| Tillman C | 22 | 160 | 7 | 0 | 129 | 5.47 | 1.56 | 7.3 | 4.1 | -$5 | 140 |
| Mata F | 27 | 40 | 3 | 0 | 21 | 5.79 | 1.79 | 4.8 | 5.8 | -$5 | 30 |
| Perez O | 29 | 40 | 2 | 0 | 34 | 5.56 | 1.62 | 7.6 | 5.5 | -$5 | 30 |

**Minors (2010)**

| Level | Leag | W | L | Sv | IP | H | K | ERA | WHIP | K/9 | BB/9 | HR/9 | GB/F |
|---|---|---|---|---|---|---|---|---|---|---|---|---|---|
| A | — | — | — | — | — | — | — | — | — | — | — | — | — |
| AA | — | — | — | — | — | — | — | — | — | — | — | — | — |
| AAA | — | — | — | — | — | — | — | — | — | — | — | — | — |

**Competition at RP / Stats in 2010 as RP**

| Thr | Player | GR | ERA | IP/G | Sv-Hld |
|---|---|---|---|---|---|
| LH | Byrdak T | 64 | 3.49 | 0.6 | 0-11 |
| LH | Chacin G | 44 | 4.70 | 0.9 | 1-5 |
| LH | Abad F | 22 | 2.84 | 0.9 | 0-6 |
| LH | Wright W | 10 | 4.50 | 1.4 | 0-0 |

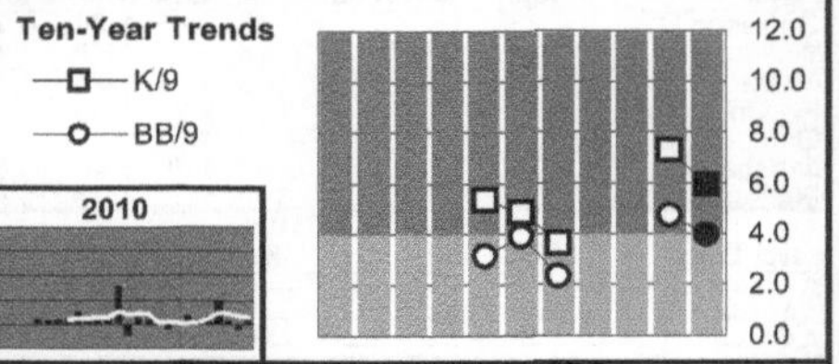


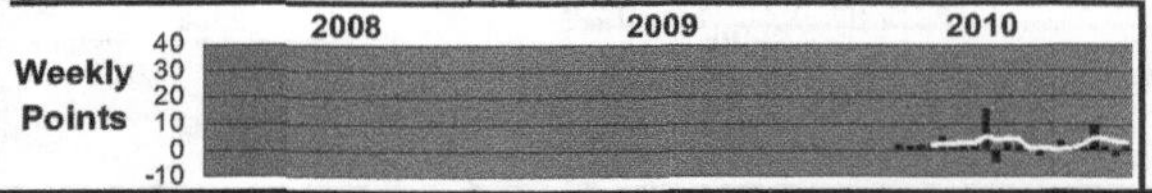


**Majors / Skills / Value / Luck / In Rotation / In Relief / OPS**

| Yr | Team | W | L | Sv | IP | H | K | ERA | WHIP | K/9 | BB/9 | HR/9 | GB/F | $1L | $2L | Pts | RAA | H% | HR/fb | S% | FIP | GS | CG | QS/DS | GR | Hld | Bln | Lead | OPS | 1st Hf | 2nd Hf | vs RH | vs LH |
|---|---|---|---|---|---|---|---|---|---|---|---|---|---|---|---|---|---|---|---|---|---|---|---|---|---|---|---|---|---|---|---|---|---|
| 07 | TOR | 2 | 1 | 0 | 27 | 29 | 11 | 5.60 | 1.32 | 3.6 | 2.3 | 2.0 | 1.0 | -$2 | -$5 | 20 | −5 | 25% | 15% | 63% | 6.12 | 5 | 0 | 2/1 | — | — | — | — | .827 | .827 | — | .784 | .960 |
| 08 | — | — | — | — | — | — | — | — | — | — | — | — | — | — | — | — | — | — | — | — | — | — | — | — | — | — | — | — | — | — | — | — | — |
| 09 | — | — | — | — | — | — | — | — | — | — | — | — | — | — | — | — | — | — | — | — | — | — | — | — | — | — | — | — | — | — | — | — | — |
| 10 | HOU | 2 | 2 | 1 | 38 | 51 | 31 | 4.70 | 1.85 | 7.3 | 4.7 | 0.7 | 0.8 | -$7 | -$16 | 40 | −5 | 38% | 5% | 75% | 4.17 | — | — | — | 44 | 5 | 0 | −1.6 | .814 | .720 | .934 | .828 | .790 |

## Jhoulys Chacin — 180 IP | $7 | 260 pts

SP-21, RP-7 | Owned: 4% | RH

Despite his young age, Chacin seems like a safe bet to make the Rockies rotation in 2011 – after all, aside from Ubaldo Jimenez, Chacin is probably the team's best SP. His walk rate is not out of the woods, but he generally showed good control in the minors, and we expect his BB/9 to fall with time and experience. (TS)

**Forecast**

| Player | Age | IP | W | Sv | K | ERA | WHIP | K/9 | BB/9 | $2L | Pts |
|---|---|---|---|---|---|---|---|---|---|---|---|
| Chacin J | 23 | 180 | 11 | 0 | 177 | 4.06 | 1.42 | 8.8 | 3.9 | $7 | 260 |
| **Mini-Browser** | **Age** | **IP** | **W** | **Sv** | **K** | **ERA** | **WHIP** | **K/9** | **BB/9** | **$2L** | **Pts** |
| Romero R | 26 | 200 | 12 | 0 | 157 | 4.32 | 1.42 | 7.1 | 4.0 | $8 | 240 |
| Slowey K | 26 | 140 | 10 | 0 | 104 | 4.51 | 1.25 | 6.7 | 1.6 | $8 | 190 |
| Downs S | 35 | 60 | 4 | 8 | 48 | 3.18 | 1.19 | 7.2 | 2.9 | $7 | 130 |
| Madson R | 30 | 60 | 4 | 9 | 53 | 3.49 | 1.17 | 8.0 | 2.5 | $7 | 150 |
| Morrow B | 26 | 200 | 13 | 0 | 215 | 4.60 | 1.45 | 9.7 | 4.8 | $7 | 290 |

**Minors (2010)**

| Level | Leag | W | L | Sv | IP | H | K | ERA | WHIP | K/9 | BB/9 | HR/9 | GB/F |
|---|---|---|---|---|---|---|---|---|---|---|---|---|---|
| A | — | — | — | — | — | — | — | — | — | — | — | — | — |
| AA | — | — | — | — | — | — | — | — | — | — | — | — | — |
| AAA | PCL | 3 | 2 | 0 | 35 | 27 | 34 | 1.51 | 1.23 | 8.6 | 4.3 | 0.3 | — |

**Competition at SP / Stats in 2010 as SP**

| Thr | Player | GS | ERA | Supp | W-L |
|---|---|---|---|---|---|
| RH | Jimenez U | 33 | 2.88 | 4.7 | 19-8 |
| RH | Hammel J | 30 | 4.81 | 4.6 | 10-9 |
| RH | Cook A | 23 | 5.08 | 4.4 | 6-8 |
| RH | Chacin J | 21 | 2.98 | 4.2 | 9-10 |

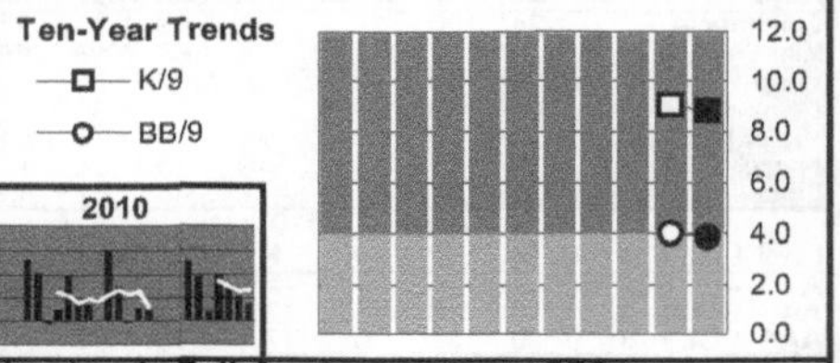


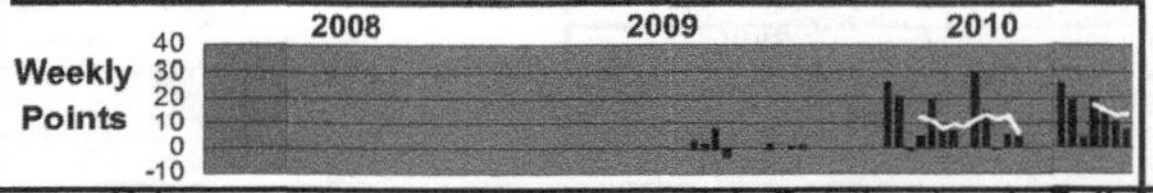


**Majors / Skills / Value / Luck / In Rotation / In Relief / OPS**

| Yr | Team | W | L | Sv | IP | H | K | ERA | WHIP | K/9 | BB/9 | HR/9 | GB/F | $1L | $2L | Pts | RAA | H% | HR/fb | S% | FIP | GS | CG | QS/DS | GR | Hld | Bln | Lead | OPS | 1st Hf | 2nd Hf | vs RH | vs LH |
|---|---|---|---|---|---|---|---|---|---|---|---|---|---|---|---|---|---|---|---|---|---|---|---|---|---|---|---|---|---|---|---|---|---|
| 07 | — | — | — | — | — | — | — | — | — | — | — | — | — | — | — | — | — | — | — | — | — | — | — | — | — | — | — | — | — | — | — | — | — |
| 08 | — | — | — | — | — | — | — | — | — | — | — | — | — | — | — | — | — | — | — | — | — | — | — | — | — | — | — | — | — | — | — | — | — |
| 09 | COL | 0 | 1 | 0 | 11 | 6 | 13 | 4.91 | 1.55 | 10.6 | 9.0 | 0.8 | 1.1 | -$2 | -$3 | 10 | −1 | 23% | 10% | 69% | 5.02 | 1 | 0 | 0/1 | 8 | 0 | 0 | +0.1 | .667 | — | .667 | .478 | .837 |
| 10 | COL | 9 | 11 | 0 | 137 | 114 | 138 | 3.28 | 1.27 | 9.0 | 4.0 | 0.7 | 1.5 | $9 | $2 | 230 | +4 | 29% | 9% | 76% | 3.47 | 21 | 0 | 11/2 | 7 | 0 | 0 | +0.5 | .650 | .674 | .618 | .612 | .705 |

## Joba Chamberlain — 60 IP | $4 | 130 pts

RP-73 | Owned: 20% | RH

The debate is over: Joba Chamberlain is ensconced in the Yankee bullpen and no longer rotation material. However, he is not the set-up guy, either, having lost that role to Kerry Wood, and it's unclear whether he'll be the closer of the future. The Joba aura is vastly diminished, but he is young and not beyond hope. (LS)

**Forecast**

| Player | Age | IP | W | Sv | K | ERA | WHIP | K/9 | BB/9 | $2L | Pts |
|---|---|---|---|---|---|---|---|---|---|---|---|
| Chamberlain J | 25 | 60 | 4 | 10 | 57 | 4.29 | 1.38 | 8.5 | 3.9 | $4 | 130 |
| **Mini-Browser** | **Age** | **IP** | **W** | **Sv** | **K** | **ERA** | **WHIP** | **K/9** | **BB/9** | **$2L** | **Pts** |
| Devine J | 27 | 45 | 3 | 2 | 51 | 2.87 | 1.25 | 10.2 | 3.8 | $4 | 90 |
| Wells R | 28 | 180 | 9 | 0 | 127 | 4.30 | 1.37 | 6.3 | 2.8 | $4 | 190 |
| Adams M | 32 | 40 | 2 | 2 | 42 | 2.57 | 1.10 | 9.4 | 2.9 | $4 | 80 |
| Guthrie J | 31 | 200 | 10 | 0 | 110 | 4.76 | 1.34 | 5.0 | 2.6 | $4 | 170 |
| Motte J | 28 | 60 | 3 | 4 | 62 | 3.63 | 1.27 | 9.2 | 3.2 | $4 | 110 |

**Minors (2010)**

| Level | Leag | W | L | Sv | IP | H | K | ERA | WHIP | K/9 | BB/9 | HR/9 | GB/F |
|---|---|---|---|---|---|---|---|---|---|---|---|---|---|
| A | — | — | — | — | — | — | — | — | — | — | — | — | — |
| AA | — | — | — | — | — | — | — | — | — | — | — | — | — |
| AAA | — | — | — | — | — | — | — | — | — | — | — | — | — |

**Competition at RP / Stats in 2010 as RP**

| Thr | Player | GR | ERA | IP/G | Sv-Hld |
|---|---|---|---|---|---|
| RH | Chamberlain J | 73 | 4.40 | 1.0 | 3-26 |
| RH | Robertson D | 64 | 3.82 | 1.0 | 1-14 |
| RH | Rivera M | 61 | 1.80 | 1.0 | 33-0 |
| RH | Gaudin C | 30 | 4.50 | 1.6 | 0-0 |

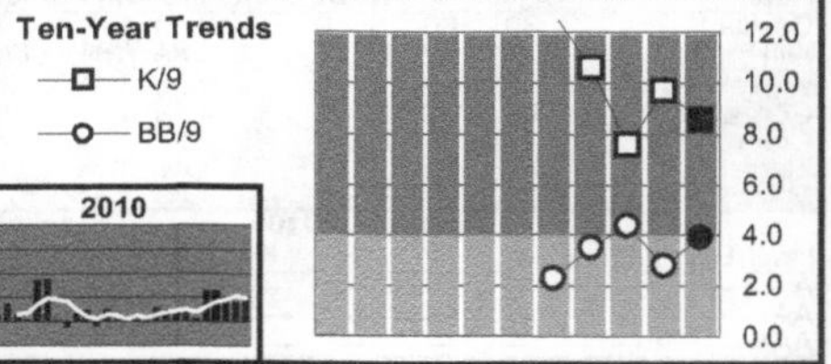


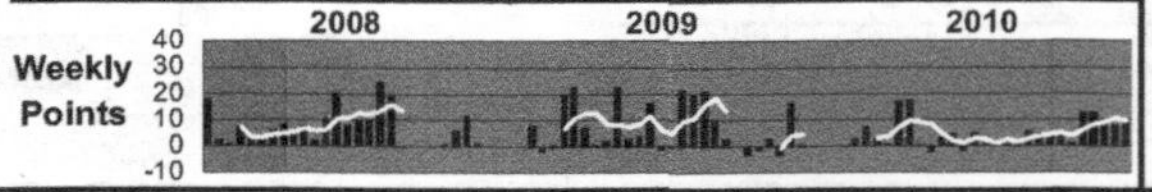


**Majors / Skills / Value / Luck / In Rotation / In Relief / OPS**

| Yr | Team | W | L | Sv | IP | H | K | ERA | WHIP | K/9 | BB/9 | HR/9 | GB/F | $1L | $2L | Pts | RAA | H% | HR/fb | S% | FIP | GS | CG | QS/DS | GR | Hld | Bln | Lead | OPS | 1st Hf | 2nd Hf | vs RH | vs LH |
|---|---|---|---|---|---|---|---|---|---|---|---|---|---|---|---|---|---|---|---|---|---|---|---|---|---|---|---|---|---|---|---|---|---|
| 07 | NYY | 2 | 0 | 1 | 24 | 12 | 34 | 0.38 | 0.75 | 12.8 | 2.3 | 0.4 | 0.9 | $5 | $6 | 70 | +9 | 23% | 5% | 100% | 1.76 | — | — | — | 19 | 8 | 0 | +2.8 | .440 | — | .440 | .469 | .406 |
| 08 | NYY | 4 | 3 | 0 | 100 | 87 | 118 | 2.60 | 1.26 | 10.6 | 3.5 | 0.4 | 1.5 | $10 | $6 | 170 | +13 | 33% | 6% | 80% | 2.76 | 12 | 0 | 7/1 | 30 | 19 | 1 | +1.2 | .617 | .621 | .608 | .570 | .663 |
| 09 | NYY | 9 | 6 | 0 | 157 | 167 | 133 | 4.75 | 1.54 | 7.6 | 4.3 | 1.2 | 1.2 | $2 | -$6 | 180 | −23 | 32% | 12% | 72% | 4.79 | 31 | 0 | 12/5 | 1 | 0 | 0 | +0.4 | .802 | .817 | .783 | .808 | .796 |
| 10 | NYY | 3 | 4 | 3 | 71 | 71 | 77 | 4.40 | 1.30 | 9.7 | 2.8 | 0.8 | 1.2 | $1 | -$9 | 110 | −5 | 33% | 8% | 67% | 3.16 | — | — | — | 73 | 26 | 4 | +1.6 | .693 | .731 | .648 | .675 | .713 |

## Aroldis Chapman — 100 IP | $3 | 160 pts

RP-15 | Owned: 31% | LH

The main question for Chapman going forward is: Rotation or relief? He performed excellent work out of the bullpen in 2010, but with his talent, the Reds would be remiss not to test him as a starter. In any case, Chapman will be on the team in 2011, probably first in the bullpen and then a starter down the road. (SW)

**Forecast**

| Player | Age | IP | W | Sv | K | ERA | WHIP | K/9 | BB/9 | $2L | Pts |
|---|---|---|---|---|---|---|---|---|---|---|---|
| Chapman A | 23 | 100 | 6 | 4 | 95 | 4.54 | 1.36 | 8.6 | 4.7 | $3 | 160 |
| **Mini-Browser** | **Age** | **IP** | **W** | **Sv** | **K** | **ERA** | **WHIP** | **K/9** | **BB/9** | **$2L** | **Pts** |
| Masset N | 28 | 80 | 4 | 4 | 69 | 3.97 | 1.31 | 7.8 | 3.4 | $4 | 120 |
| Marshall S | 28 | 80 | 5 | 2 | 69 | 4.04 | 1.31 | 7.7 | 3.1 | $4 | 120 |
| Francisco F | 31 | 60 | 4 | 0 | 66 | 3.80 | 1.30 | 9.9 | 3.6 | $4 | 100 |
| Camp S | 35 | 80 | 4 | 0 | 53 | 3.82 | 1.29 | 5.9 | 2.8 | $4 | 90 |
| Blanton J | 30 | 180 | 10 | 0 | 118 | 4.66 | 1.32 | 5.9 | 2.4 | $4 | 190 |

**Minors (2010)**

| Level | Leag | W | L | Sv | IP | H | K | ERA | WHIP | K/9 | BB/9 | HR/9 | GB/F |
|---|---|---|---|---|---|---|---|---|---|---|---|---|---|
| A | — | — | — | — | — | — | — | — | — | — | — | — | — |
| AA | — | — | — | — | — | — | — | — | — | — | — | — | — |
| AAA | IL | 9 | 6 | 8 | 95 | 77 | 125 | 3.57 | 1.35 | 11.8 | 4.9 | 0.7 | — |

**Competition at RP / Stats in 2010 as RP**

| Thr | Player | GR | ERA | IP/G | Sv-Hld |
|---|---|---|---|---|---|
| LH | Rhodes A | 70 | 2.29 | 0.8 | 0-26 |
| LH | Herrera D | 36 | 3.91 | 0.6 | 0-9 |
| LH | Bray B | 35 | 4.13 | 0.8 | 0-2 |
| LH | Chapman A | 15 | 2.03 | 0.9 | 0-4 |

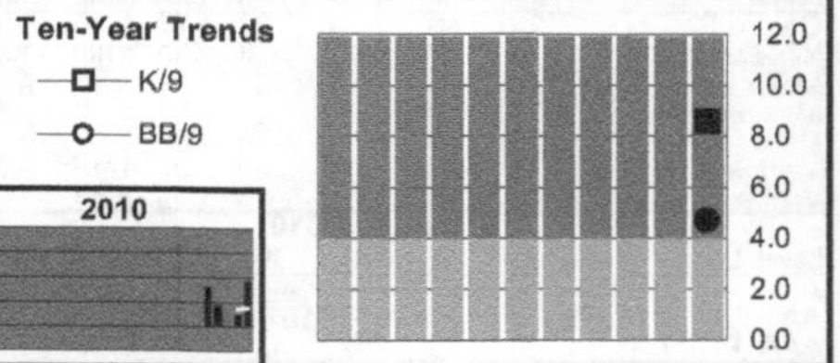

**Majors / Skills / Value / Luck / In Rotation / In Relief / OPS**

| Yr | Team | W | L | Sv | IP | H | K | ERA | WHIP | K/9 | BB/9 | HR/9 | GB/F | $1L | $2L | Pts | RAA | H% | HR/fb | S% | FIP | GS | CG | QS/DS | GR | Hld | Bln | Lead | OPS | 1st Hf | 2nd Hf | vs RH | vs LH |
|---|---|---|---|---|---|---|---|---|---|---|---|---|---|---|---|---|---|---|---|---|---|---|---|---|---|---|---|---|---|---|---|---|---|
| 07 | — | — | — | — | — | — | — | — | — | — | — | — | — | — | — | — | — | — | — | — | — | — | — | — | — | — | — | — | — | — | — | — | — |
| 08 | — | — | — | — | — | — | — | — | — | — | — | — | — | — | — | — | — | — | — | — | — | — | — | — | — | — | — | — | — | — | — | — | — |
| 09 | — | — | — | — | — | — | — | — | — | — | — | — | — | — | — | — | — | — | — | — | — | — | — | — | — | — | — | — | — | — | — | — | — |
| 10 | CIN | 2 | 2 | 0 | 13 | 9 | 19 | 2.03 | 1.05 | 12.8 | 3.4 | 0.0 | 3.8 | -$2 | -$7 | 40 | +2 | 35% | 0% | 79% | 1.48 | — | — | — | 15 | 4 | 1 | +0.9 | .492 | — | .492 | .540 | .368 |

## Tyler Chatwood — 40 IP | $-6 | 20 pts

No MLB games played in 2010 | Owned: 0% | RH

Chatwood is one of the Angels' bright spots in pitching. He dominated Single-A (1.77 ERA in the hitter-friendly Cal League) and saw Triple-A before season's end. With a power arm (92-95 MPH), great curve, and good change-up, Chatwood could be starting for the Angels as soon as the second half of 2011. (DS)

| Player | Age | IP | W | Sv | K | ERA | WHIP | K/9 | BB/9 | $2L | Pts |
|---|---|---|---|---|---|---|---|---|---|---|---|
| Chatwood T | 21 | 40 | 2 | 0 | 19 | 6.02 | 1.89 | 4.3 | 5.9 | -$6 | 20 |
| **Mini-Browser** | **Age** | **IP** | **W** | **Sv** | **K** | **ERA** | **WHIP** | **K/9** | **BB/9** | **$2L** | **Pts** |
| Davies K | 27 | 140 | 6 | 0 | 95 | 5.36 | 1.59 | 6.1 | 4.3 | -$5 | 100 |
| Wood B | 25 | 60 | 2 | 0 | 50 | 5.71 | 1.73 | 7.5 | 4.1 | -$6 | 40 |
| Lopez R | 35 | 180 | 7 | 0 | 104 | 5.25 | 1.43 | 5.2 | 2.4 | -$6 | 120 |
| Suppan J | 36 | 60 | 3 | 0 | 28 | 5.58 | 1.55 | 4.1 | 3.5 | -$6 | 30 |
| Leroux C | 26 | 40 | 2 | 0 | 39 | 5.67 | 1.80 | 8.7 | 4.5 | -$6 | 30 |

Minors (2010)

| Level | Leag | W | L | Sv | IP | H | K | ERA | WHIP | K/9 | BB/9 | HR/9 | GB/F |
|---|---|---|---|---|---|---|---|---|---|---|---|---|---|
| A | CAL | 8 | 3 | 0 | 81 | 71 | 70 | 1.77 | 1.32 | 7.7 | 4.0 | 0.7 | — |
| AA | TL | 4 | 6 | 0 | 68 | 72 | 36 | 3.82 | 1.45 | 4.7 | 3.6 | 0.4 | — |
| AAA | PCL | 1 | 0 | 0 | 5 | 9 | 3 | 6.35 | 1.59 | 4.8 | 0.0 | 1.6 | — |

Majors

| Yr | Team | W | L | Sv | IP | H | K | ERA | WHIP | K/9 | BB/9 | HR/9 | GB/F | $1L | $2L | Pts | RAA | H% | HR/fb | S% | FIP | GS | CG | QS/DS | GR | Hld | Bln | Lead | OPS | 1st Hf | 2nd Hf | vs RH | vs LH |
|---|---|---|---|---|---|---|---|---|---|---|---|---|---|---|---|---|---|---|---|---|---|---|---|---|---|---|---|---|---|---|---|---|---|
| 07 | — | — | — | — | — | — | — | — | — | — | — | — | — | — | — | — | — | — | — | — | — | — | — | — | — | — | — | — | — | — | — | — | — |
| 08 | — | — | — | — | — | — | — | — | — | — | — | — | — | — | — | — | — | — | — | — | — | — | — | — | — | — | — | — | — | — | — | — | — |
| 09 | — | — | — | — | — | — | — | — | — | — | — | — | — | — | — | — | — | — | — | — | — | — | — | — | — | — | — | — | — | — | — | — | — |
| 10 | — | — | — | — | — | — | — | — | — | — | — | — | — | — | — | — | — | — | — | — | — | — | — | — | — | — | — | — | — | — | — | — | — |

Competition at SP / Stats in 2010 as SP

| Thr | Player | GS | ERA | Supp | W-L |
|---|---|---|---|---|---|
| RH | Haren D | 35 | 3.91 | 3.9 | 12-12 |
| RH | Weaver J | 34 | 3.01 | 3.8 | 13-12 |
| RH | Santana E | 33 | 3.92 | 4.9 | 17-10 |
| LH | Kazmir S | 28 | 5.94 | 4.0 | 9-15 |

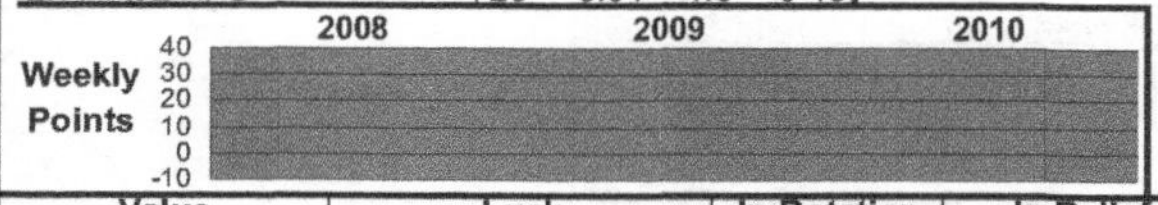
Weekly Points
2008
2009
2010
40
30
20
10
0
-10

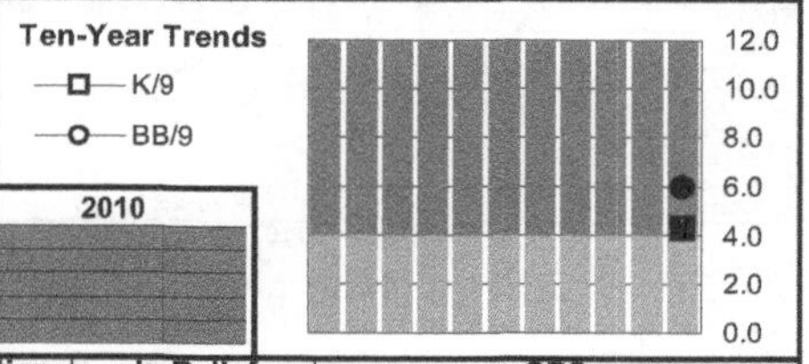
Ten-Year Trends
K/9
BB/9
12.0
10.0
8.0
6.0
4.0
2.0
0.0

## Jesse Chavez — 60 IP | $-2 | 60 pts

RP-51 | Owned: 0% | RH

Chavez was merely a stop-gap for the Royals – in most of his 51 appearances, the outcome wasn't much in doubt. He is generous with home runs and does not exhibit meaningful growth. He might have slightly better luck if he concentrated on LHB. (BM)

| Player | Age | IP | W | Sv | K | ERA | WHIP | K/9 | BB/9 | $2L | Pts |
|---|---|---|---|---|---|---|---|---|---|---|---|
| Chavez J | 27 | 60 | 3 | 0 | 45 | 5.18 | 1.42 | 6.7 | 3.3 | -$2 | 60 |
| **Mini-Browser** | **Age** | **IP** | **W** | **Sv** | **K** | **ERA** | **WHIP** | **K/9** | **BB/9** | **$2L** | **Pts** |
| Russell A | 27 | 40 | 2 | 0 | 36 | 4.27 | 1.43 | 8.1 | 4.0 | -$1 | 40 |
| Rzepczynski M | 25 | 80 | 5 | 0 | 82 | 4.79 | 1.63 | 9.3 | 4.7 | -$1 | 100 |
| Beimel J | 33 | 40 | 2 | 0 | 21 | 3.95 | 1.43 | 4.7 | 3.3 | -$1 | 30 |
| Durbin C | 33 | 60 | 3 | 0 | 45 | 4.59 | 1.41 | 6.8 | 3.9 | -$1 | 60 |
| Tomlin J | 26 | 60 | 4 | 0 | 52 | 5.23 | 1.47 | 7.8 | 2.6 | -$1 | 70 |

Minors (2010)

| Level | Leag | W | L | Sv | IP | H | K | ERA | WHIP | K/9 | BB/9 | HR/9 | GB/F |
|---|---|---|---|---|---|---|---|---|---|---|---|---|---|
| A | — | — | — | — | — | — | — | — | — | — | — | — | — |
| AA | — | — | — | — | — | — | — | — | — | — | — | — | — |
| AAA | — | — | — | — | — | — | — | — | — | — | — | — | — |

Majors

| Yr | Team | W | L | Sv | IP | H | K | ERA | WHIP | K/9 | BB/9 | HR/9 | GB/F | $1L | $2L | Pts | RAA | H% | HR/fb | S% | FIP | GS | CG | QS/DS | GR | Hld | Bln | Lead | OPS | 1st Hf | 2nd Hf | vs RH | vs LH |
|---|---|---|---|---|---|---|---|---|---|---|---|---|---|---|---|---|---|---|---|---|---|---|---|---|---|---|---|---|---|---|---|---|---|
| 07 | — | — | — | — | — | — | — | — | — | — | — | — | — | — | — | — | — | — | — | — | — | — | — | — | — | — | — | — | — | — | — | — | — |
| 08 | PIT | 0 | 1 | 0 | 15 | 20 | 16 | 6.60 | 1.93 | 9.6 | 5.4 | 1.2 | 1.3 | -$4 | -$5 | 10 | –4 | 41% | 13% | 67% | 4.60 | — | — | — | 15 | 0 | 2 | –1.9 | .900 | — | .900 | 1.008 | .727 |
| 09 | PIT | 1 | 4 | 0 | 67 | 69 | 47 | 4.01 | 1.35 | 6.3 | 2.9 | 1.5 | 1.0 | $0 | -$2 | 50 | –3 | 29% | 13% | 76% | 4.91 | — | — | — | 73 | 15 | 4 | +0.4 | .783 | .708 | .864 | .879 | .681 |
| 10 | 2TM | 5 | 5 | 0 | 62 | 69 | 45 | 5.89 | 1.47 | 6.5 | 3.3 | 1.6 | 0.7 | -$4 | -$17 | 70 | –16 | 30% | 11% | 63% | 5.20 | — | — | — | 51 | 6 | 1 | –1.4 | .834 | .756 | .909 | .798 | .884 |

Competition at RP / Stats in 2010 as RP

| Thr | Player | GR | ERA | IP/G | Sv-Hld |
|---|---|---|---|---|---|
| RH | Soria J | 66 | 1.78 | 1.0 | 43-0 |
| RH | Tejeda R | 54 | 3.54 | 1.1 | 0-12 |
| RH | Wood B | 51 | 5.07 | 1.0 | 0-15 |
| RH | Texeira K | 27 | 4.64 | 1.6 | 0-1 |

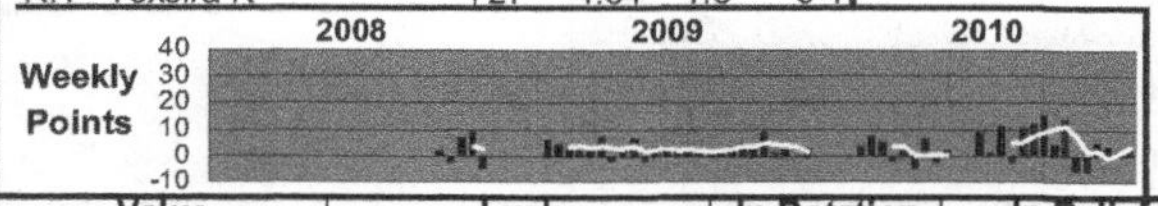
Weekly Points
2008
2009
2010
40
30
20
10
0
-10

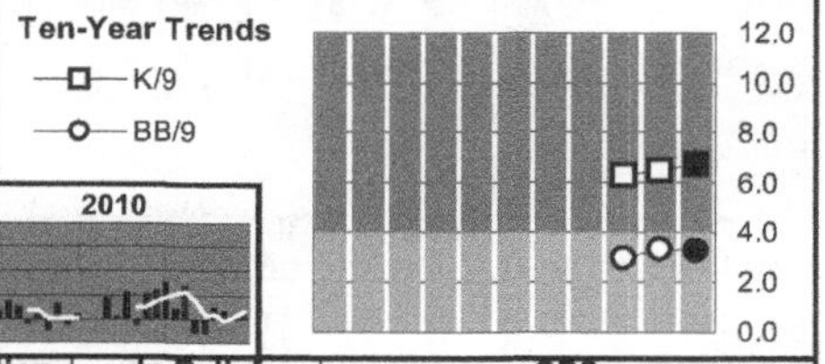
Ten-Year Trends
K/9
BB/9
12.0
10.0
8.0
6.0
4.0
2.0
0.0

## Bruce Chen — 160 IP | $0 | 170 pts

SP-23, RP-10 | Owned: 0% | LH

Chen was a big surprise for the Royals in '10. He led the team with 12 Wins and finished with a 4.17 ERA (versus a career 4.71 ERA entering the season). The source of Chen's riches was a career-low 1.1 HR/9, fed by an 8% HR/FB. But his career rate is 1.6 HR/9. Chen's ERA is a good bet to stray back to 5.00. (BM)

| Player | Age | IP | W | Sv | K | ERA | WHIP | K/9 | BB/9 | $2L | Pts |
|---|---|---|---|---|---|---|---|---|---|---|---|
| Chen B | 33 | 160 | 10 | 0 | 115 | 5.06 | 1.48 | 6.4 | 3.7 | $0 | 170 |
| **Mini-Browser** | **Age** | **IP** | **W** | **Sv** | **K** | **ERA** | **WHIP** | **K/9** | **BB/9** | **$2L** | **Pts** |
| Kohn M | 24 | 40 | 3 | 0 | 45 | 3.51 | 1.63 | 10.1 | 5.8 | $0 | 70 |
| Dotel O | 37 | 40 | 2 | 0 | 49 | 3.96 | 1.33 | 10.9 | 4.4 | $0 | 60 |
| Contreras J | 39 | 60 | 4 | 0 | 44 | 4.43 | 1.34 | 6.5 | 3.1 | $0 | 70 |
| Luebke C | 26 | 80 | 4 | 0 | 82 | 4.41 | 1.46 | 9.2 | 3.1 | $0 | 110 |
| Kelley S | 26 | 45 | 3 | 0 | 43 | 4.52 | 1.41 | 8.6 | 3.1 | $0 | 60 |

Minors (2010)

| Level | Leag | W | L | Sv | IP | H | K | ERA | WHIP | K/9 | BB/9 | HR/9 | GB/F |
|---|---|---|---|---|---|---|---|---|---|---|---|---|---|
| A | — | — | — | — | — | — | — | — | — | — | — | — | — |
| AA | — | — | — | — | — | — | — | — | — | — | — | — | — |
| AAA | PCL | 0 | 1 | 0 | 20 | 13 | 20 | 1.31 | 0.87 | 8.7 | 2.2 | 0.0 | — |

Majors

| Yr | Team | W | L | Sv | IP | H | K | ERA | WHIP | K/9 | BB/9 | HR/9 | GB/F | $1L | $2L | Pts | RAA | H% | HR/fb | S% | FIP | GS | CG | QS/DS | GR | Hld | Bln | Lead | OPS | 1st Hf | 2nd Hf | vs RH | vs LH |
|---|---|---|---|---|---|---|---|---|---|---|---|---|---|---|---|---|---|---|---|---|---|---|---|---|---|---|---|---|---|---|---|---|---|
| 07 | TEX | 0 | 0 | 0 | 10 | 11 | 7 | 7.20 | 1.70 | 6.3 | 5.4 | 2.7 | 0.7 | -$3 | -$5 | 0 | –6 | 27% | 21% | 64% | 7.60 | — | — | — | 5 | 0 | 0 | –1.0 | .970 | .970 | — | .894 | 1.200 |
| 08 | — | — | — | — | — | — | — | — | — | — | — | — | — | — | — | — | — | — | — | — | — | — | — | — | — | — | — | — | — | — | — | — | — |
| 09 | KC | 1 | 6 | 0 | 62 | 74 | 45 | 5.78 | 1.59 | 6.5 | 3.6 | 1.7 | 0.6 | -$3 | -$7 | 30 | –11 | 33% | 12% | 68% | 5.56 | 9 | 0 | 3/2 | 8 | 0 | 0 | –0.1 | .884 | .897 | .878 | .968 | .679 |
| 10 | KC | 12 | 7 | 1 | 140 | 136 | 98 | 4.17 | 1.38 | 6.3 | 3.7 | 1.1 | 0.7 | $5 | -$8 | 200 | +1 | 28% | 8% | 73% | 4.70 | 23 | 1 | 8/2 | 10 | 0 | 0 | –0.5 | .735 | .684 | .763 | .727 | .756 |

Competition at SP / Stats in 2010 as SP

| Thr | Player | GS | ERA | Supp | W-L |
|---|---|---|---|---|---|
| RH | Greinke Z | 33 | 4.17 | 3.5 | 10-14 |
| RH | Davies K | 32 | 5.34 | 4.4 | 8-12 |
| ▶ LH | Chen B | 23 | 4.26 | 4.7 | 11-7 |
| RH | Bannister B | 23 | 6.32 | 3.7 | 7-12 |

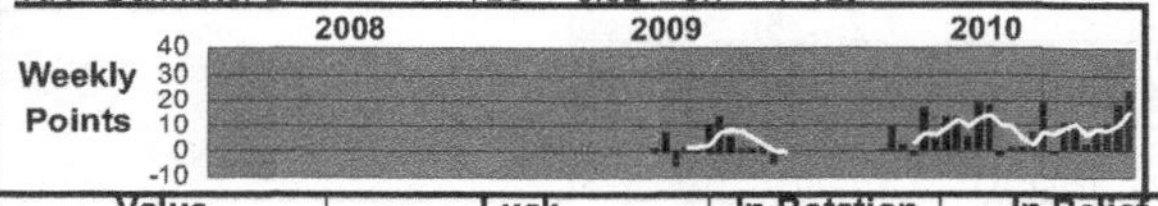
Weekly Points
2008
2009
2010
40
30
20
10
0
-10

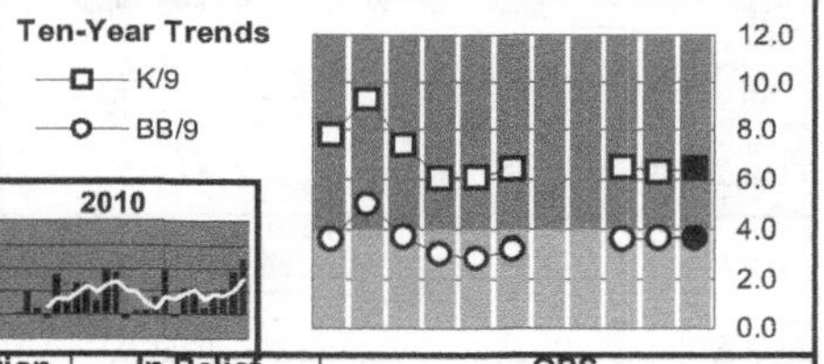
Ten-Year Trends
K/9
BB/9
12.0
10.0
8.0
6.0
4.0
2.0
0.0

## Matt Chico — 40 IP | $-5 | 30 pts

SP-1 | Owned: 0% | LH

Chico's sub-90-MPH fastball and iffy command explain his frequent trips in 2010 between Washington and Syracuse. Chico has an especially hard time after his first trip through the order, so long relief might be his surest path to consistent innings, though he has never played in more than 33 games in one season. (PB)

| Player | Age | IP | W | Sv | K | ERA | WHIP | K/9 | BB/9 | $2L | Pts |
|---|---|---|---|---|---|---|---|---|---|---|---|
| Chico M | 27 | 40 | 2 | 0 | 27 | 5.53 | 1.58 | 6.0 | 3.7 | -$5 | 30 |
| **Mini-Browser** | **Age** | **IP** | **W** | **Sv** | **K** | **ERA** | **WHIP** | **K/9** | **BB/9** | **$2L** | **Pts** |
| Mathieson S | 27 | 40 | 2 | 0 | 40 | 5.37 | 1.70 | 9.0 | 4.1 | -$4 | 40 |
| Atilano L | 25 | 60 | 3 | 0 | 36 | 5.36 | 1.53 | 5.4 | 3.0 | -$4 | 50 |
| Hernandez L | 36 | 200 | 9 | 0 | 93 | 4.93 | 1.45 | 4.2 | 3.0 | -$4 | 130 |
| Olsen S | 27 | 120 | 5 | 0 | 75 | 5.34 | 1.43 | 5.6 | 3.2 | -$4 | 90 |
| Texeira K | 25 | 60 | 1 | 0 | 49 | 5.07 | 1.73 | 7.4 | 4.3 | -$4 | 40 |

Minors (2010)

| Level | Leag | W | L | Sv | IP | H | K | ERA | WHIP | K/9 | BB/9 | HR/9 | GB/F |
|---|---|---|---|---|---|---|---|---|---|---|---|---|---|
| A | — | — | — | — | — | — | — | — | — | — | — | — | — |
| AA | EL | 1 | 2 | 0 | 26 | 26 | 17 | 3.12 | 1.27 | 5.9 | 2.4 | 0.7 | — |
| AAA | IL | 6 | 7 | 0 | 115 | 120 | 69 | 3.73 | 1.33 | 5.4 | 2.6 | 0.9 | — |

Majors

| Yr | Team | W | L | Sv | IP | H | K | ERA | WHIP | K/9 | BB/9 | HR/9 | GB/F | $1L | $2L | Pts | RAA | H% | HR/fb | S% | FIP | GS | CG | QS/DS | GR | Hld | Bln | Lead | OPS | 1st Hf | 2nd Hf | vs RH | vs LH |
|---|---|---|---|---|---|---|---|---|---|---|---|---|---|---|---|---|---|---|---|---|---|---|---|---|---|---|---|---|---|---|---|---|---|
| 07 | WAS | 7 | 9 | 0 | 167 | 183 | 94 | 4.63 | 1.54 | 5.1 | 4.0 | 1.4 | 0.7 | -$3 | -$17 | 120 | –21 | 29% | 10% | 74% | 5.43 | 31 | 0 | 10/5 | — | — | — | — | .824 | .786 | .876 | .833 | .788 |
| 08 | WAS | 0 | 6 | 0 | 48 | 63 | 31 | 6.19 | 1.67 | 5.8 | 3.2 | 1.9 | 1.0 | -$7 | -$10 | 10 | –12 | 34% | 15% | 67% | 5.68 | 8 | 0 | 1/3 | 3 | 0 | 0 | –1.5 | .946 | .946 | — | .920 | 1.009 |
| 09 | — | — | — | — | — | — | — | — | — | — | — | — | — | — | — | — | — | — | — | — | — | — | — | — | — | — | — | — | — | — | — | — | — |
| 10 | WAS | 0 | 0 | 0 | 5 | 6 | 3 | 3.60 | 1.20 | 5.4 | 0.0 | 0.0 | 3.0 | -$5 | -$10 | 0 | +0 | 33% | 0% | 67% | 2.00 | 1 | 0 | 0/0 | — | — | — | — | .699 | .699 | — | .668 | 1.000 |

Competition at RP / Stats in 2010 as RP

| Thr | Player | GR | ERA | IP/G | Sv-Hld |
|---|---|---|---|---|---|
| LH | Burnett S | 73 | 2.14 | 0.9 | 3-20 |
| LH | Slaten D | 49 | 3.10 | 0.8 | 0-4 |

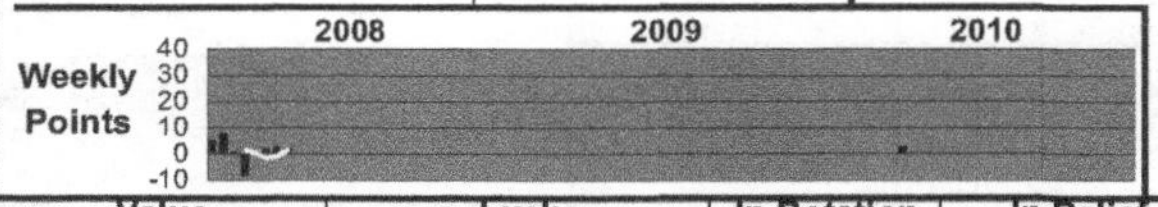
Weekly Points
2008
2009
2010
40
30
20
10
0
-10

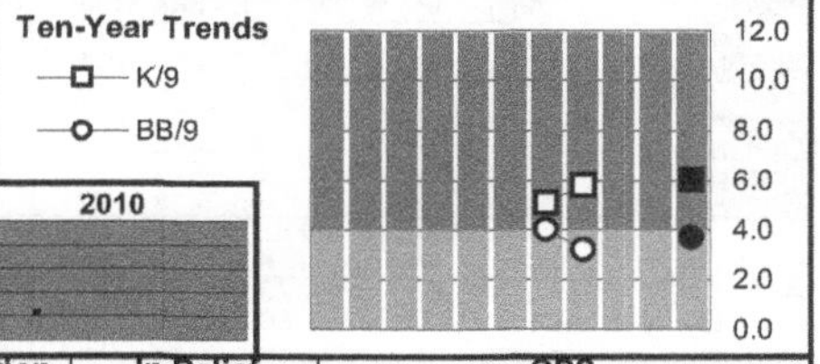
Ten-Year Trends
K/9
BB/9
12.0
10.0
8.0
6.0
4.0
2.0
0.0

## Randy Choate — 40 IP | $0 | 50 pts

RP-85 | Owned: 0% | LH

A cheap lefty specialist, Choate did an excellent job in his second season with the Rays, and he has a .178 batting average against left-handed hitters since 2007 (which he lost to a broken finger). Joe Maddon will again deploy Choate in match-ups, so he'll appear in almost half of the games but garner only 40 IP. (RZ)

| Player | Age | IP | W | Sv | K | ERA | WHIP | K/9 | BB/9 | $2L | Pts |
|---|---|---|---|---|---|---|---|---|---|---|---|
| Choate R | 35 | 40 | 3 | 0 | 33 | 4.38 | 1.38 | 7.4 | 3.5 | $0 | 50 |
| **Mini-Browser** | **Age** | **IP** | **W** | **Sv** | **K** | **ERA** | **WHIP** | **K/9** | **BB/9** | **$2L** | **Pts** |
| Frieri E | 25 | 60 | 3 | 0 | 69 | 4.07 | 1.48 | 10.3 | 4.2 | $0 | 90 |
| Wang C | 31 | 100 | 6 | 0 | 47 | 4.49 | 1.37 | 4.2 | 3.0 | $0 | 90 |
| Miller T | 37 | 40 | 2 | 0 | 34 | 3.90 | 1.29 | 7.6 | 3.5 | $0 | 50 |
| Atchison S | 35 | 40 | 1 | 0 | 29 | 4.28 | 1.28 | 6.5 | 2.6 | $0 | 40 |
| Affeldt J | 31 | 60 | 3 | 0 | 49 | 4.06 | 1.45 | 7.3 | 4.1 | $0 | 70 |

Minors (2010)

| Level | Leag | W | L | Sv | IP | H | K | ERA | WHIP | K/9 | BB/9 | HR/9 | GB/F |
|---|---|---|---|---|---|---|---|---|---|---|---|---|---|
| A | — | — | — | — | — | — | — | — | — | — | — | — | — |
| AA | — | — | — | — | — | — | — | — | — | — | — | — | — |
| AAA | — | — | — | — | — | — | — | — | — | — | — | — | — |

Majors

| Yr | Team | W | L | Sv | IP | H | K | ERA | WHIP | K/9 | BB/9 | HR/9 | GB/F | $1L | $2L | Pts | RAA | H% | HR/fb | S% | FIP | GS | CG | QS/DS | GR | Hld | Bln | Lead | OPS | 1st Hf | 2nd Hf | vs RH | vs LH |
|---|---|---|---|---|---|---|---|---|---|---|---|---|---|---|---|---|---|---|---|---|---|---|---|---|---|---|---|---|---|---|---|---|---|
| 07 | ARI | — | — | — | — | — | — | — | — | — | — | — | — | — | — | — | — | — | — | — | — | — | — | — | — | — | — | — | — | 2.000 | — | — | — |
| 08 | — | — | — | — | — | — | — | — | — | — | — | — | — | — | — | — | — | — | — | — | — | — | — | — | — | — | — | — | — | — | — | — | — |
| 09 | TB | 1 | 0 | 5 | 36 | 28 | 28 | 3.47 | 1.07 | 6.9 | 2.7 | 1.0 | 2.6 | $3 | $1 | 70 | +1 | 25% | 16% | 71% | 4.10 | — | — | — | 61 | 9 | 0 | +0.5 | .588 | .544 | .616 | .880 | .385 |
| 10 | TB | 4 | 3 | 0 | 44 | 41 | 40 | 4.23 | 1.30 | 8.1 | 3.4 | 0.6 | 2.5 | $0 | -$9 | 70 | –3 | 32% | 10% | 67% | 3.52 | — | — | — | 85 | 18 | 2 | +0.3 | .686 | .633 | .739 | 1.162 | .529 |

Competition at RP / Stats in 2010 as RP

| Thr | Player | GR | ERA | IP/G | Sv-Hld |
|---|---|---|---|---|---|
| ▶ LH | Choate R | 85 | 4.23 | 0.5 | 0-18 |

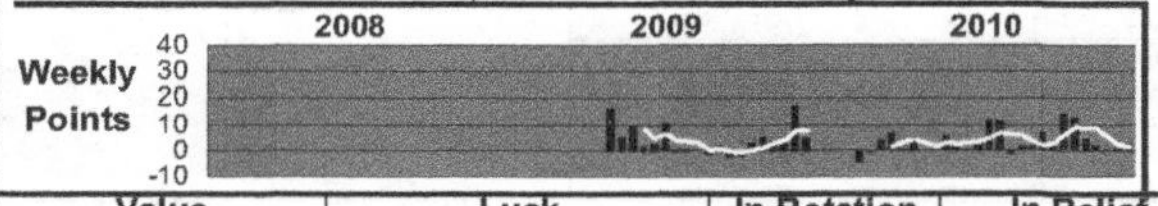
Weekly Points
2008
2009
2010
40
30
20
10
0
-10

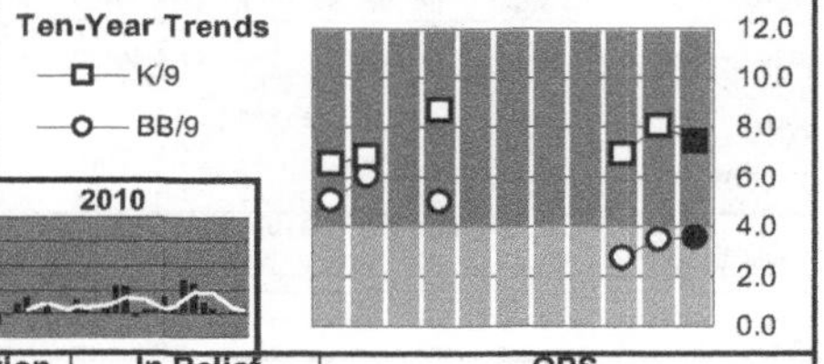
Ten-Year Trends
K/9
BB/9
12.0
10.0
8.0
6.0
4.0
2.0
0.0

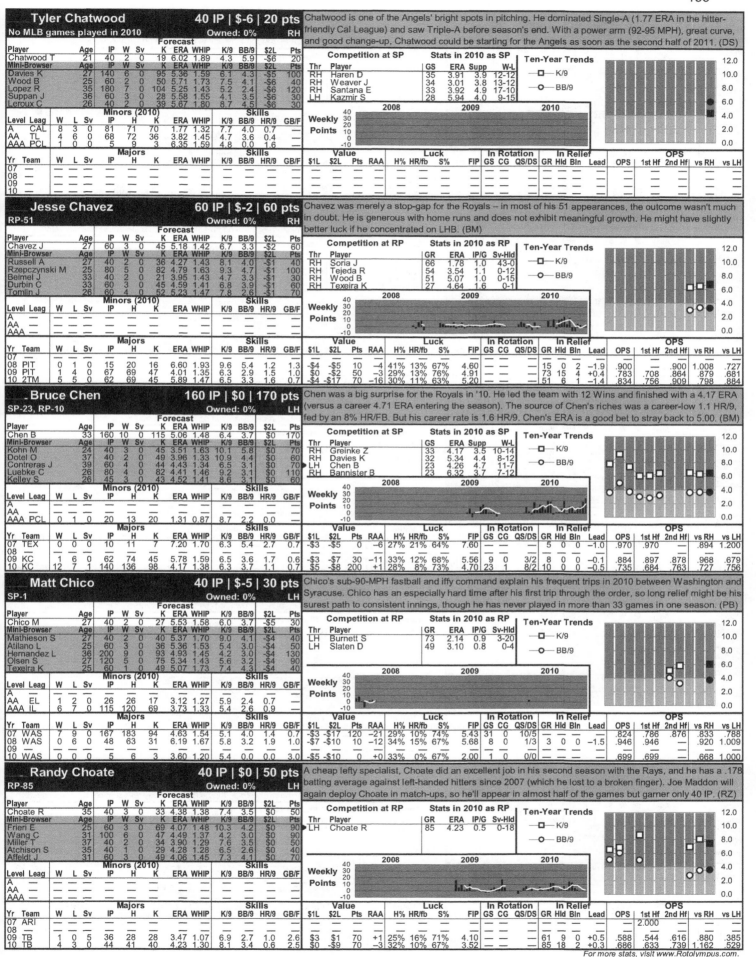

*For more stats, visit www.Rotolympus.com.*

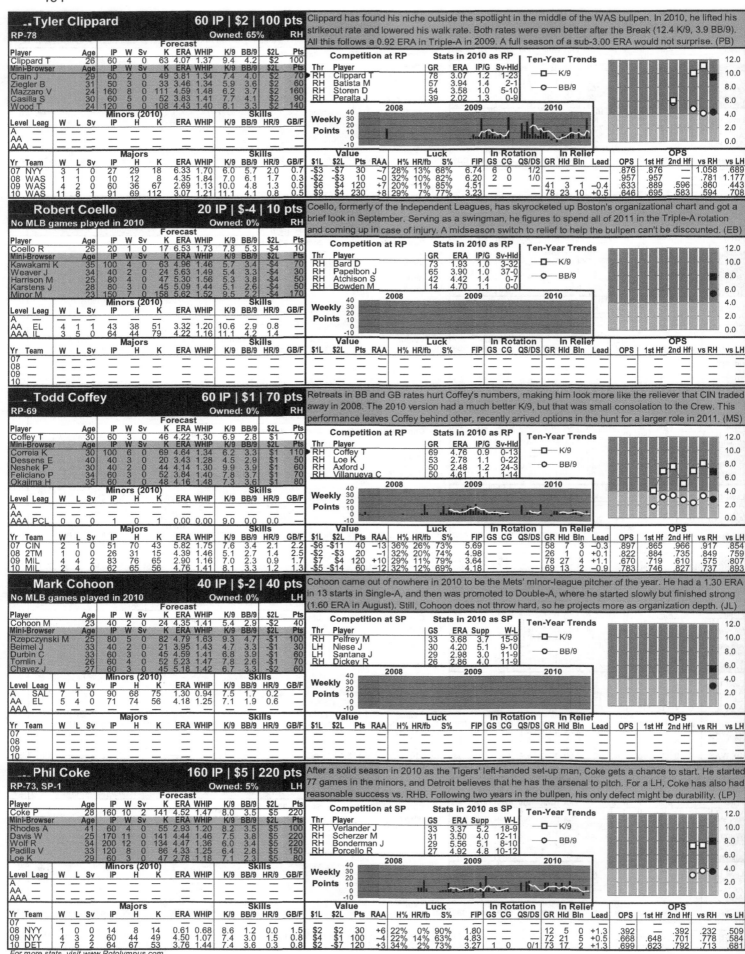

## Tyler Clippard — 60 IP | $2 | 100 pts
RP-78 | Owned: 65% | RH

Clippard has found his niche outside the spotlight in the middle of the WAS bullpen. In 2010, he lifted his strikeout rate and lowered his walk rate. Both rates were even better after the Break (12.4 K/9, 3.9 BB/9). All this follows a 0.92 ERA in Triple-A in 2009. A full season of a sub-3.00 ERA would not surprise. (PB)

### Forecast
| Player | Age | IP | W | Sv | K | ERA | WHIP | K/9 | BB/9 | $2L | Pts |
| --- | --- | --- | --- | --- | --- | --- | --- | --- | --- | --- | --- |
| Clippard T | 26 | 60 | 4 | 0 | 63 | 4.07 | 1.37 | 9.4 | 4.2 | $2 | 100 |
| Mini-Browser | Age | IP | W | Sv | K | ERA | WHIP | K/9 | BB/9 | $2L | Pts |
| Crain J | 29 | 60 | 2 | 0 | 49 | 3.81 | 1.34 | 7.4 | 4.0 | $2 | 70 |
| Ziegler B | 31 | 50 | 3 | 0 | 33 | 3.46 | 1.34 | 5.9 | 3.6 | $2 | 60 |
| Mazzaro V | 24 | 160 | 8 | 0 | 111 | 4.59 | 1.48 | 6.2 | 3.7 | $2 | 160 |
| Casilla S | 30 | 60 | 5 | 0 | 52 | 3.83 | 1.41 | 7.7 | 4.1 | $2 | 90 |
| Wood T | 24 | 120 | 6 | 0 | 108 | 4.43 | 1.40 | 8.1 | 3.3 | $2 | 140 |

### Minors (2010) / Skills
| Level Leag | W | L | Sv | IP | H | K | ERA | WHIP | K/9 | BB/9 | HR/9 | GB/F |
| --- | --- | --- | --- | --- | --- | --- | --- | --- | --- | --- | --- | --- |
| A | — | — | — | — | — | — | — | — | — | — | — | — |
| AA | — | — | — | — | — | — | — | — | — | — | — | — |
| AAA | — | — | — | — | — | — | — | — | — | — | — | — |

### Majors / Skills
| Yr Team | W | L | Sv | IP | H | K | ERA | WHIP | K/9 | BB/9 | HR/9 | GB/F |
| --- | --- | --- | --- | --- | --- | --- | --- | --- | --- | --- | --- | --- |
| 07 NYY | 3 | 1 | 0 | 27 | 29 | 18 | 6.33 | 1.70 | 6.0 | 5.7 | 2.0 | 0.7 |
| 08 WAS | 1 | 1 | 0 | 10 | 12 | 8 | 4.35 | 1.84 | 7.0 | 6.1 | 1.7 | 0.3 |
| 09 WAS | 4 | 2 | 0 | 60 | 36 | 67 | 2.69 | 1.13 | 10.0 | 4.8 | 1.3 | 0.5 |
| 10 WAS | 11 | 8 | 1 | 91 | 69 | 112 | 3.07 | 1.21 | 11.1 | 4.1 | 0.8 | 0.5 |

### Competition at RP / Stats in 2010 as RP
| Thr | Player | GR | ERA | IP/G | Sv-Hld |
| --- | --- | --- | --- | --- | --- |
| RH | Clippard T | 78 | 3.07 | 1.2 | 1-23 |
| RH | Batista M | 57 | 3.94 | 1.4 | 2-1 |
| RH | Storen D | 54 | 3.58 | 1.0 | 5-10 |
| RH | Peralta J | 39 | 2.02 | 1.3 | 0-9 |

### Value / Luck / In Rotation / In Relief / OPS
| Yr | $1L | $2L | Pts | RAA | H% | HR/fb | S% | FIP | GS | CG | QS/DS | GR | Hld | Bln | Lead | OPS | 1st Hf | 2nd Hf | vs RH | vs LH |
| --- | --- | --- | --- | --- | --- | --- | --- | --- | --- | --- | --- | --- | --- | --- | --- | --- | --- | --- | --- | --- |
| 07 | -$3 | -$7 | 30 | ~7 | 28% | 13% | 68% | 6.74 | 6 | 0 | 1/2 | — | — | — | — | .876 | .876 | — | 1.058 | .689 |
| 08 | -$2 | -$3 | 10 | ~0 | 32% | 10% | 82% | 6.20 | 2 | 0 | 1/0 | — | — | — | — | .957 | .957 | — | .781 | 1.177 |
| 09 | $6 | $4 | 120 | +7 | 20% | 11% | 85% | 4.51 | — | — | — | 41 | 3 | 1 | -0.4 | .633 | .889 | .596 | .860 | .443 |
| 10 | $8 | $4 | 230 | +5 | 29% | 7% | 77% | 3.07 | — | — | — | 78 | 23 | 10 | +0.5 | .646 | .695 | .583 | .594 | .708 |

---

## Robert Coello — 20 IP | $-4 | 10 pts
No MLB games played in 2010 | Owned: 0% | RH

Coello, formerly of the Independent Leagues, has skyrocketed up Boston's organizational chart and got a brief look in September. Serving as a swingman, he figures to spend all of 2011 in the Triple-A rotation and coming up in case of injury. A midseason switch to relief to help the bullpen can't be discounted. (EB)

### Forecast
| Player | Age | IP | W | Sv | K | ERA | WHIP | K/9 | BB/9 | $2L | Pts |
| --- | --- | --- | --- | --- | --- | --- | --- | --- | --- | --- | --- |
| Coello R | 26 | 20 | 1 | 0 | 17 | 6.53 | 1.73 | 7.8 | 5.3 | -$4 | 10 |
| Mini-Browser | Age | IP | W | Sv | K | ERA | WHIP | K/9 | BB/9 | $2L | Pts |
| Kawakami K | 35 | 100 | 4 | 0 | 63 | 4.96 | 1.46 | 5.7 | 3.4 | -$4 | 70 |
| Weaver J | 34 | 40 | 4 | 0 | 24 | 5.63 | 1.49 | 5.4 | 3.5 | -$4 | 30 |
| Harrison M | 25 | 80 | 4 | 0 | 47 | 5.30 | 1.56 | 5.3 | 3.8 | -$4 | 50 |
| Karstens J | 28 | 80 | 3 | 0 | 45 | 5.09 | 1.44 | 5.1 | 2.6 | -$4 | 50 |
| Minor M | 23 | 150 | 7 | 0 | 158 | 5.62 | 1.52 | 9.5 | 2.2 | -$4 | 170 |

### Minors (2010) / Skills
| Level Leag | W | L | Sv | IP | H | K | ERA | WHIP | K/9 | BB/9 | HR/9 | GB/F |
| --- | --- | --- | --- | --- | --- | --- | --- | --- | --- | --- | --- | --- |
| A | — | — | — | — | — | — | — | — | — | — | — | — |
| AA EL | 4 | 1 | 1 | 43 | 38 | 51 | 3.32 | 1.20 | 10.6 | 2.9 | 0.8 | — |
| AAA IL | 3 | 5 | 0 | 64 | 44 | 79 | 4.22 | 1.16 | 11.1 | 4.2 | 1.4 | — |

### Majors / Skills
| Yr | W | L | Sv | IP | H | K | ERA | WHIP | K/9 | BB/9 | HR/9 | GB/F |
| --- | --- | --- | --- | --- | --- | --- | --- | --- | --- | --- | --- | --- |
| 07 | — | — | — | — | — | — | — | — | — | — | — | — |
| 08 | — | — | — | — | — | — | — | — | — | — | — | — |
| 09 | — | — | — | — | — | — | — | — | — | — | — | — |
| 10 | — | — | — | — | — | — | — | — | — | — | — | — |

### Competition at RP / Stats in 2010 as RP
| Thr | Player | GR | ERA | IP/G | Sv-Hld |
| --- | --- | --- | --- | --- | --- |
| RH | Bard D | 73 | 1.93 | 1.0 | 3-32 |
| RH | Papelbon J | 65 | 3.90 | 1.0 | 37-0 |
| RH | Atchison S | 42 | 4.42 | 1.4 | 0-7 |
| RH | Bowden M | 14 | 4.70 | 1.1 | 0-0 |

---

## Todd Coffey — 60 IP | $1 | 70 pts
RP-69 | Owned: 0% | RH

Retreats in BB and GB rates hurt Coffey's numbers, making him look more like the reliever that CIN traded away in 2008. The 2010 version had a much better K/9, but that was small consolation to the Crew. This performance leaves Coffey behind other, recently arrived options in the hunt for a larger role in 2011. (MS)

### Forecast
| Player | Age | IP | W | Sv | K | ERA | WHIP | K/9 | BB/9 | $2L | Pts |
| --- | --- | --- | --- | --- | --- | --- | --- | --- | --- | --- | --- |
| Coffey T | 30 | 60 | 3 | 0 | 46 | 4.22 | 1.30 | 6.9 | 2.8 | $1 | 70 |
| Mini-Browser | Age | IP | W | Sv | K | ERA | WHIP | K/9 | BB/9 | $2L | Pts |
| Correia K | 30 | 100 | 6 | 0 | 69 | 4.64 | 1.34 | 6.2 | 3.3 | $1 | 110 |
| Dessens E | 40 | 40 | 3 | 0 | 20 | 3.43 | 1.28 | 4.5 | 2.9 | $1 | 50 |
| Neshek P | 30 | 40 | 2 | 0 | 44 | 4.14 | 1.30 | 9.9 | 3.9 | $1 | 60 |
| Feliciano P | 34 | 60 | 3 | 0 | 52 | 3.84 | 1.40 | 7.8 | 3.7 | $1 | 70 |
| Okajima H | 35 | 60 | 4 | 0 | 48 | 4.16 | 1.48 | 7.3 | 3.6 | $1 | 80 |

### Minors (2010) / Skills
| Level Leag | W | L | Sv | IP | H | K | ERA | WHIP | K/9 | BB/9 | HR/9 | GB/F |
| --- | --- | --- | --- | --- | --- | --- | --- | --- | --- | --- | --- | --- |
| A | — | — | — | — | — | — | — | — | — | — | — | — |
| AA | — | — | — | — | — | — | — | — | — | — | — | — |
| AAA PCL | 0 | 0 | 0 | 1 | 0 | 1 | 0.00 | 0.00 | 9.0 | 0.0 | 0.0 | — |

### Majors / Skills
| Yr Team | W | L | Sv | IP | H | K | ERA | WHIP | K/9 | BB/9 | HR/9 | GB/F |
| --- | --- | --- | --- | --- | --- | --- | --- | --- | --- | --- | --- | --- |
| 07 CIN | 2 | 1 | 0 | 51 | 70 | 43 | 5.82 | 1.75 | 7.6 | 3.4 | 2.1 | 2.2 |
| 08 2TM | 1 | 0 | 0 | 26 | 31 | 15 | 4.39 | 1.46 | 5.1 | 2.7 | 1.4 | 2.5 |
| 09 MIL | 4 | 4 | 2 | 83 | 76 | 65 | 2.90 | 1.16 | 7.0 | 2.3 | 0.9 | 1.7 |
| 10 MIL | 0 | 4 | 0 | 62 | 65 | 56 | 4.76 | 1.41 | 8.1 | 3.3 | 1.2 | 1.3 |

### Competition at RP / Stats in 2010 as RP
| Thr | Player | GR | ERA | IP/G | Sv-Hld |
| --- | --- | --- | --- | --- | --- |
| RH | Coffey T | 69 | 4.76 | 0.9 | 0-13 |
| RH | Loe K | 53 | 2.78 | 1.1 | 0-22 |
| RH | Axford J | 50 | 2.48 | 1.2 | 24-3 |
| RH | Villanueva C | 50 | 4.61 | 1.1 | 1-14 |

### Value / Luck / In Rotation / In Relief / OPS
| Yr | $1L | $2L | Pts | RAA | H% | HR/fb | S% | FIP | GS | CG | QS/DS | GR | Hld | Bln | Lead | OPS | 1st Hf | 2nd Hf | vs RH | vs LH |
| --- | --- | --- | --- | --- | --- | --- | --- | --- | --- | --- | --- | --- | --- | --- | --- | --- | --- | --- | --- | --- |
| 07 | -$6 | -$11 | 40 | -13 | 36% | 26% | 73% | 5.69 | — | — | — | 58 | 7 | 3 | -0.3 | .897 | .865 | .966 | .917 | .854 |
| 08 | -$2 | -$3 | 20 | -1 | 32% | 20% | 74% | 4.98 | — | — | — | 26 | 1 | 0 | +0.1 | .822 | .884 | .735 | .849 | .759 |
| 09 | $7 | $4 | 120 | +10 | 29% | 11% | 79% | 3.64 | — | — | — | 78 | 27 | 4 | +1.1 | .670 | .719 | .610 | .575 | .807 |
| 10 | -$5 | -$14 | 60 | -12 | 34% | 12% | 74% | 4.18 | — | — | — | 69 | 13 | 2 | -0.9 | .783 | .746 | .827 | .737 | .893 |

---

## Mark Cohoon — 40 IP | $-2 | 40 pts
No MLB games played in 2010 | Owned: 0% | LH

Cohoon came out of nowhere in 2010 to be the Mets' minor-league pitcher of the year. He had a 1.30 ERA in 13 starts in Single-A, and then was promoted to Double-A, where he started slowly but finished strong (1.60 ERA in August). Still, Cohoon does not throw hard, so he projects more as organization depth. (JL)

### Forecast
| Player | Age | IP | W | Sv | K | ERA | WHIP | K/9 | BB/9 | $2L | Pts |
| --- | --- | --- | --- | --- | --- | --- | --- | --- | --- | --- | --- |
| Cohoon M | 23 | 40 | 2 | 0 | 24 | 4.35 | 1.41 | 5.4 | 2.9 | -$2 | 40 |
| Mini-Browser | Age | IP | W | Sv | K | ERA | WHIP | K/9 | BB/9 | $2L | Pts |
| Rzepczynski M | 25 | 80 | 5 | 0 | 82 | 4.79 | 1.63 | 9.3 | 4.7 | -$1 | 100 |
| Beimel J | 33 | 40 | 2 | 0 | 21 | 3.95 | 1.43 | 4.7 | 3.3 | -$1 | 30 |
| Durbin C | 33 | 60 | 3 | 0 | 45 | 4.59 | 1.41 | 6.8 | 3.9 | -$1 | 60 |
| Tomlin J | 26 | 60 | 4 | 0 | 52 | 5.23 | 1.47 | 7.8 | 2.6 | -$1 | 60 |
| Chavez J | 27 | 60 | 3 | 0 | 45 | 5.18 | 1.42 | 6.7 | 3.3 | -$2 | 60 |

### Minors (2010) / Skills
| Level Leag | W | L | Sv | IP | H | K | ERA | WHIP | K/9 | BB/9 | HR/9 | GB/F |
| --- | --- | --- | --- | --- | --- | --- | --- | --- | --- | --- | --- | --- |
| A SAL | 7 | 1 | 0 | 90 | 68 | 75 | 1.30 | 0.94 | 7.5 | 1.7 | 0.2 | — |
| AA EL | 5 | 4 | 0 | 71 | 74 | 56 | 4.18 | 1.25 | 7.1 | 1.9 | 0.6 | — |
| AAA | — | — | — | — | — | — | — | — | — | — | — | — |

### Majors / Skills
| Yr | W | L | Sv | IP | H | K | ERA | WHIP | K/9 | BB/9 | HR/9 | GB/F |
| --- | --- | --- | --- | --- | --- | --- | --- | --- | --- | --- | --- | --- |
| 07 | — | — | — | — | — | — | — | — | — | — | — | — |
| 08 | — | — | — | — | — | — | — | — | — | — | — | — |
| 09 | — | — | — | — | — | — | — | — | — | — | — | — |
| 10 | — | — | — | — | — | — | — | — | — | — | — | — |

### Competition at SP / Stats in 2010 as SP
| Thr | Player | GS | ERA | Supp | W-L |
| --- | --- | --- | --- | --- | --- |
| RH | Pelfrey M | 33 | 3.68 | 5.3 | 15-9 |
| LH | Niese J | 30 | 4.20 | 5.1 | 9-10 |
| LH | Santana J | 29 | 2.98 | 3.0 | 11-9 |
| RH | Dickey R | 26 | 2.86 | 4.0 | 11-9 |

---

## Phil Coke — 160 IP | $5 | 220 pts
RP-73, SP-1 | Owned: 5% | LH

After a solid season in 2010 as the Tigers' left-handed set-up man, Coke gets a chance to start. He started 77 games in the minors, and Detroit believes that he has the arsenal to pitch. For a LH, Coke has also had reasonable success vs. RHB. Following two years in the bullpen, his only defect might be durability. (LP)

### Forecast
| Player | Age | IP | W | Sv | K | ERA | WHIP | K/9 | BB/9 | $2L | Pts |
| --- | --- | --- | --- | --- | --- | --- | --- | --- | --- | --- | --- |
| Coke P | 28 | 160 | 10 | 2 | 141 | 4.52 | 1.47 | 8.0 | 3.5 | $5 | 220 |
| Mini-Browser | Age | IP | W | Sv | K | ERA | WHIP | K/9 | BB/9 | $2L | Pts |
| Rhodes A | 41 | 60 | 4 | 0 | 55 | 2.93 | 1.20 | 8.2 | 3.5 | $5 | 100 |
| Davis W | 25 | 170 | 11 | 0 | 141 | 4.44 | 1.46 | 7.5 | 3.8 | $5 | 220 |
| Wolf R | 34 | 200 | 12 | 0 | 134 | 4.47 | 1.36 | 6.0 | 3.4 | $5 | 200 |
| Padilla V | 33 | 120 | 8 | 0 | 86 | 4.33 | 1.25 | 6.4 | 2.8 | $5 | 150 |
| Loe K | 29 | 60 | 3 | 0 | 47 | 2.78 | 1.18 | 7.1 | 2.3 | $5 | 80 |

### Minors (2010) / Skills
| Level Leag | W | L | Sv | IP | H | K | ERA | WHIP | K/9 | BB/9 | HR/9 | GB/F |
| --- | --- | --- | --- | --- | --- | --- | --- | --- | --- | --- | --- | --- |
| A | — | — | — | — | — | — | — | — | — | — | — | — |
| AA | — | — | — | — | — | — | — | — | — | — | — | — |
| AAA | — | — | — | — | — | — | — | — | — | — | — | — |

### Majors / Skills
| Yr Team | W | L | Sv | IP | H | K | ERA | WHIP | K/9 | BB/9 | HR/9 | GB/F |
| --- | --- | --- | --- | --- | --- | --- | --- | --- | --- | --- | --- | --- |
| 07 | — | — | — | — | — | — | — | — | — | — | — | — |
| 08 NYY | 1 | 0 | 0 | 14 | 8 | 14 | 0.61 | 0.68 | 8.6 | 1.2 | 0.0 | 1.5 |
| 09 NYY | 4 | 3 | 1 | 60 | 44 | 49 | 4.50 | 1.07 | 7.4 | 3.0 | 1.5 | 0.8 |
| 10 DET | 7 | 5 | 2 | 64 | 67 | 53 | 3.76 | 1.44 | 7.4 | 3.6 | 0.3 | 0.8 |

### Competition at SP / Stats in 2010 as SP
| Thr | Player | GS | ERA | Supp | W-L |
| --- | --- | --- | --- | --- | --- |
| RH | Verlander J | 33 | 3.37 | 5.2 | 18-9 |
| RH | Scherzer M | 31 | 3.50 | 4.0 | 12-11 |
| RH | Bonderman J | 29 | 5.56 | 5.1 | 8-10 |
| RH | Porcello R | 27 | 4.92 | 4.8 | 10-12 |

### Value / Luck / In Rotation / In Relief / OPS
| Yr | $1L | $2L | Pts | RAA | H% | HR/fb | S% | FIP | GS | CG | QS/DS | GR | Hld | Bln | Lead | OPS | 1st Hf | 2nd Hf | vs RH | vs LH |
| --- | --- | --- | --- | --- | --- | --- | --- | --- | --- | --- | --- | --- | --- | --- | --- | --- | --- | --- | --- | --- |
| 07 | — | — | — | — | — | — | — | — | — | — | — | — | — | — | — | — | — | — | — | — |
| 08 | $2 | $2 | 30 | +6 | 22% | 0% | 90% | 1.80 | — | — | — | 12 | 5 | 0 | +1.3 | .392 | — | .392 | .232 | .509 |
| 09 | $4 | $1 | 100 | -4 | 22% | 14% | 63% | 4.83 | — | — | — | 72 | 21 | 5 | +0.5 | .668 | .648 | .701 | .778 | .584 |
| 10 | -$2 | -$7 | 120 | +3 | 34% | 2% | 73% | 3.27 | 1 | 0 | 0/1 | 73 | 17 | 2 | +1.3 | .699 | .623 | .792 | .713 | .681 |

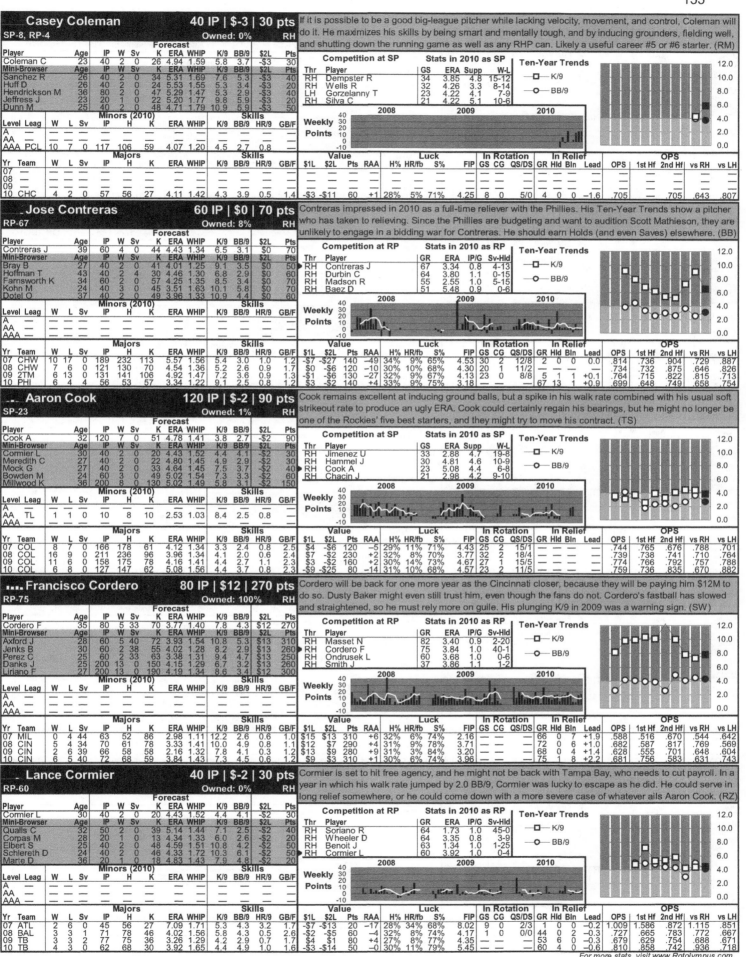

## Casey Coleman — 40 IP | $-3 | 30 pts

SP-8, RP-4 — Owned: 0% — RH

| Player | Age | IP | W | Sv | K | ERA | WHIP | K/9 | BB/9 | $2L | Pts |
|---|---|---|---|---|---|---|---|---|---|---|---|
| Coleman C | 23 | 40 | 2 | 0 | 26 | 4.94 | 1.59 | 5.8 | 3.7 | -$3 | 30 |
| **Mini-Browser** | Age | IP | W | Sv | K | ERA | WHIP | K/9 | BB/9 | $2L | Pts |
| Sanchez R | 26 | 40 | 2 | 0 | 34 | 5.31 | 1.69 | 7.6 | 5.3 | -$3 | 40 |
| Huff D | 26 | 40 | 2 | 0 | 24 | 5.53 | 1.55 | 5.3 | 3.4 | -$3 | 20 |
| Hendrickson M | 36 | 80 | 2 | 0 | 47 | 5.29 | 1.47 | 5.3 | 2.9 | -$3 | 40 |
| Jeffress J | 23 | 20 | 1 | 0 | 22 | 5.20 | 1.77 | 9.8 | 5.9 | -$3 | 20 |
| Dunn M | 25 | 40 | 2 | 0 | 48 | 4.71 | 1.79 | 10.9 | 5.9 | -$3 | 50 |

Minors (2010)

| Level | Leag | W | L | Sv | IP | H | K | ERA | WHIP | K/9 | BB/9 | HR/9 | GB/F |
|---|---|---|---|---|---|---|---|---|---|---|---|---|---|
| A | — | — | — | — | — | — | — | — | — | — | — | — | — |
| AA | — | — | — | — | — | — | — | — | — | — | — | — | — |
| AAA | PCL | 10 | 7 | 0 | 117 | 106 | 59 | 4.07 | 1.20 | 4.5 | 2.7 | 0.8 | — |

Majors

| Yr | Team | W | L | Sv | IP | H | K | ERA | WHIP | K/9 | BB/9 | HR/9 | GB/F |
|---|---|---|---|---|---|---|---|---|---|---|---|---|---|
| 07 | — | — | — | — | — | — | — | — | — | — | — | — | — |
| 08 | — | — | — | — | — | — | — | — | — | — | — | — | — |
| 09 | — | — | — | — | — | — | — | — | — | — | — | — | — |
| 10 | CHC | 4 | 2 | 0 | 57 | 56 | 27 | 4.11 | 1.42 | 4.3 | 3.9 | 0.5 | 1.4 |

| Yr | $1L | $2L | Pts | RAA | H% | HR/fb | S% | FIP | GS | CG | QS/DS | GR | Hld | Bln | Lead | OPS | 1st Hf | 2nd Hf | vs RH | vs LH |
|---|---|---|---|---|---|---|---|---|---|---|---|---|---|---|---|---|---|---|---|---|
| 07 | — | — | — | — | — | — | — | — | — | — | — | — | — | — | — | — | — | — | — | — |
| 08 | — | — | — | — | — | — | — | — | — | — | — | — | — | — | — | — | — | — | — | — |
| 09 | — | — | — | — | — | — | — | — | — | — | — | — | — | — | — | — | — | — | — | — |
| 10 | -$3 | -$11 | 60 | +1 | 28% | 5% | 71% | 4.25 | 8 | 0 | 5/0 | 4 | 0 | 0 | –1.6 | .705 | — | .705 | .643 | .807 |

If it is possible to be a good big-league pitcher while lacking velocity, movement, and control, Coleman will do it. He maximizes his skills by being smart and mentally tough, and by inducing grounders, fielding well, and shutting down the running game as well as any RHP can. Likely a useful career #5 or #6 starter. (RM)

Competition at SP — Stats in 2010 as SP

| Thr | Player | GS | ERA | Supp | W-L |
|---|---|---|---|---|---|
| RH | Dempster R | 34 | 3.85 | 4.8 | 15-12 |
| RH | Wells R | 32 | 4.26 | 3.3 | 8-14 |
| LH | Gorzelanny T | 23 | 4.22 | 4.1 | 7-9 |
| RH | Silva C | 21 | 4.22 | 5.1 | 10-6 |

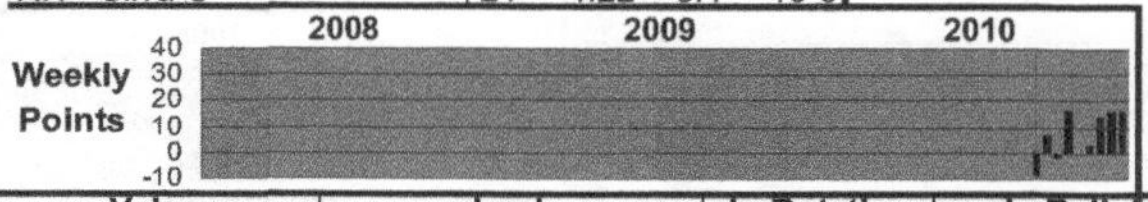


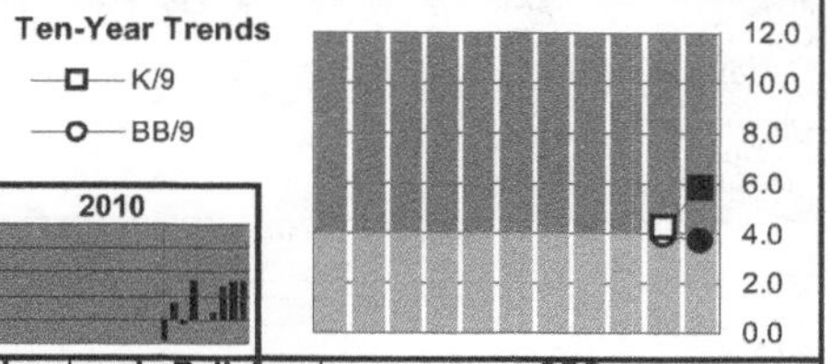


## Jose Contreras — 60 IP | $0 | 70 pts

RP-67 — Owned: 8% — RH

| Player | Age | IP | W | Sv | K | ERA | WHIP | K/9 | BB/9 | $2L | Pts |
|---|---|---|---|---|---|---|---|---|---|---|---|
| Contreras J | 39 | 60 | 4 | 0 | 44 | 4.43 | 1.34 | 6.5 | 3.1 | $0 | 70 |
| **Mini-Browser** | Age | IP | W | Sv | K | ERA | WHIP | K/9 | BB/9 | $2L | Pts |
| Bray B | 27 | 40 | 2 | 0 | 41 | 4.01 | 1.25 | 9.1 | 3.5 | $0 | 50 |
| Hoffman T | 43 | 40 | 2 | 4 | 30 | 4.46 | 1.30 | 6.8 | 2.9 | $0 | 60 |
| Farnsworth K | 34 | 60 | 2 | 0 | 57 | 4.25 | 1.35 | 8.5 | 3.4 | $0 | 70 |
| Kohn M | 24 | 40 | 3 | 0 | 45 | 3.51 | 1.63 | 10.1 | 5.8 | $0 | 70 |
| Dotel O | 37 | 40 | 2 | 0 | 49 | 3.96 | 1.33 | 10.9 | 4.4 | $0 | 60 |

Minors (2010)

| Level | Leag | W | L | Sv | IP | H | K | ERA | WHIP | K/9 | BB/9 | HR/9 | GB/F |
|---|---|---|---|---|---|---|---|---|---|---|---|---|---|
| A | — | — | — | — | — | — | — | — | — | — | — | — | — |
| AA | — | — | — | — | — | — | — | — | — | — | — | — | — |
| AAA | — | — | — | — | — | — | — | — | — | — | — | — | — |

Majors

| Yr | Team | W | L | Sv | IP | H | K | ERA | WHIP | K/9 | BB/9 | HR/9 | GB/F |
|---|---|---|---|---|---|---|---|---|---|---|---|---|---|
| 07 | CHW | 10 | 17 | 0 | 189 | 232 | 113 | 5.57 | 1.56 | 5.4 | 3.0 | 1.0 | 1.2 |
| 08 | CHW | 7 | 6 | 0 | 121 | 130 | 70 | 4.54 | 1.36 | 5.2 | 2.6 | 0.9 | 1.7 |
| 09 | 2TM | 6 | 13 | 0 | 131 | 141 | 106 | 4.92 | 1.47 | 7.2 | 3.6 | 0.9 | 1.3 |
| 10 | PHI | 6 | 4 | 4 | 56 | 53 | 57 | 3.34 | 1.22 | 9.1 | 2.5 | 0.8 | 1.2 |

| Yr | $1L | $2L | Pts | RAA | H% | HR/fb | S% | FIP | GS | CG | QS/DS | GR | Hld | Bln | Lead | OPS | 1st Hf | 2nd Hf | vs RH | vs LH |
|---|---|---|---|---|---|---|---|---|---|---|---|---|---|---|---|---|---|---|---|---|
| 07 | -$7 | -$27 | 140 | –49 | 34% | 9% | 65% | 4.53 | 30 | 2 | 12/8 | 2 | 0 | 0 | 0.0 | .814 | .736 | .904 | .729 | .887 |
| 08 | $0 | -$6 | 120 | –10 | 30% | 10% | 68% | 4.30 | 20 | 1 | 11/2 | — | — | — | — | .734 | .732 | .875 | .646 | .826 |
| 09 | -$1 | -$6 | 130 | –27 | 32% | 9% | 67% | 4.13 | 23 | 0 | 8/8 | 5 | 1 | 1 | +0.1 | .764 | .715 | .822 | .815 | .713 |
| 10 | $3 | -$2 | 140 | +4 | 33% | 9% | 75% | 3.18 | — | — | — | 67 | 13 | 1 | +0.9 | .699 | .648 | .749 | .658 | .754 |

Contreras impressed in 2010 as a full-time reliever with the Phillies. His Ten-Year Trends show a pitcher who has taken to relieving. Since the Phillies are budgeting and want to audition Scott Mathieson, they are unlikely to engage in a bidding war for Contreras. He should earn Holds (and even Saves) elsewhere. (BB)

Competition at RP — Stats in 2010 as RP

| Thr | Player | GR | ERA | IP/G | Sv-Hld |
|---|---|---|---|---|---|
| RH | Contreras J | 67 | 3.34 | 0.8 | 4-13 |
| RH | Durbin C | 64 | 3.80 | 1.1 | 0-15 |
| RH | Madson R | 55 | 2.55 | 1.0 | 5-15 |
| RH | Baez D | 51 | 5.48 | 0.9 | 0-6 |

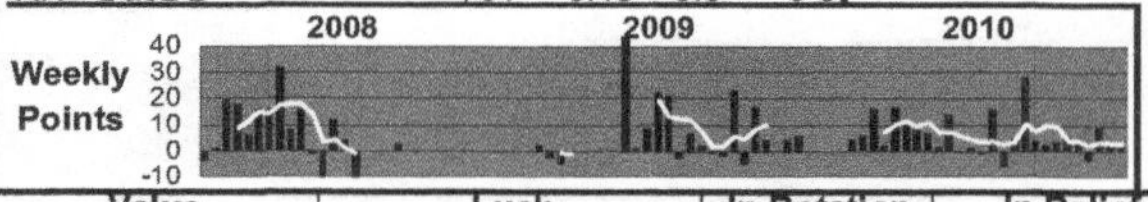


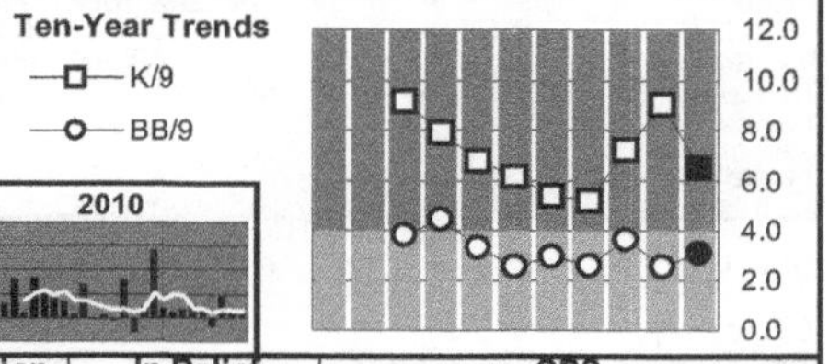


## Aaron Cook — 120 IP | $-2 | 90 pts

SP-23 — Owned: 1% — RH

| Player | Age | IP | W | Sv | K | ERA | WHIP | K/9 | BB/9 | $2L | Pts |
|---|---|---|---|---|---|---|---|---|---|---|---|
| Cook A | 32 | 120 | 7 | 0 | 51 | 4.78 | 1.41 | 3.8 | 2.7 | -$2 | 90 |
| **Mini-Browser** | Age | IP | W | Sv | K | ERA | WHIP | K/9 | BB/9 | $2L | Pts |
| Cormier L | 30 | 40 | 2 | 0 | 20 | 4.43 | 1.52 | 4.4 | 4.1 | -$2 | 30 |
| Meredith C | 27 | 40 | 2 | 0 | 22 | 4.80 | 1.45 | 4.9 | 2.9 | -$2 | 30 |
| Mock G | 27 | 40 | 2 | 0 | 33 | 4.64 | 1.45 | 7.5 | 3.7 | -$2 | 40 |
| Bowden M | 24 | 60 | 3 | 0 | 49 | 5.02 | 1.54 | 7.3 | 3.3 | -$2 | 60 |
| Millwood K | 36 | 200 | 8 | 0 | 130 | 5.02 | 1.49 | 5.8 | 3.1 | -$2 | 150 |

Minors (2010)

| Level | Leag | W | L | Sv | IP | H | K | ERA | WHIP | K/9 | BB/9 | HR/9 | GB/F |
|---|---|---|---|---|---|---|---|---|---|---|---|---|---|
| A | — | — | — | — | — | — | — | — | — | — | — | — | — |
| AA | TL | 1 | 1 | 0 | 10 | 8 | 10 | 2.53 | 1.03 | 8.4 | 2.5 | 0.8 | — |
| AAA | — | — | — | — | — | — | — | — | — | — | — | — | — |

Majors

| Yr | Team | W | L | Sv | IP | H | K | ERA | WHIP | K/9 | BB/9 | HR/9 | GB/F |
|---|---|---|---|---|---|---|---|---|---|---|---|---|---|
| 07 | COL | 8 | 7 | 0 | 166 | 178 | 61 | 4.12 | 1.34 | 3.3 | 2.4 | 0.8 | 2.5 |
| 08 | COL | 16 | 9 | 0 | 211 | 236 | 96 | 3.96 | 1.34 | 4.1 | 2.0 | 0.6 | 2.4 |
| 09 | COL | 11 | 6 | 0 | 158 | 175 | 78 | 4.16 | 1.41 | 4.4 | 2.7 | 1.1 | 2.3 |
| 10 | COL | 6 | 8 | 0 | 127 | 147 | 62 | 5.08 | 1.56 | 4.4 | 3.7 | 0.8 | 2.3 |

| Yr | $1L | $2L | Pts | RAA | H% | HR/fb | S% | FIP | GS | CG | QS/DS | GR | Hld | Bln | Lead | OPS | 1st Hf | 2nd Hf | vs RH | vs LH |
|---|---|---|---|---|---|---|---|---|---|---|---|---|---|---|---|---|---|---|---|---|
| 07 | $4 | -$6 | 120 | –5 | 29% | 11% | 71% | 4.43 | 25 | 2 | 15/1 | — | — | — | — | .744 | .765 | .676 | .788 | .701 |
| 08 | $7 | -$2 | 230 | +2 | 32% | 8% | 70% | 3.77 | 32 | 2 | 18/4 | — | — | — | — | .739 | .738 | .741 | .710 | .764 |
| 09 | $3 | -$2 | 160 | +2 | 30% | 14% | 73% | 4.67 | 27 | 1 | 15/5 | — | — | — | — | .774 | .766 | .792 | .757 | .788 |
| 10 | -$9 | -$25 | 80 | –14 | 31% | 10% | 68% | 4.57 | 23 | 2 | 11/5 | — | — | — | — | .759 | .736 | .835 | .670 | .882 |

Cook remains excellent at inducing ground balls, but a spike in his walk rate combined with his usual soft strikeout rate to produce an ugly ERA. Cook could certainly regain his bearings, but he might no longer be one of the Rockies' five best starters, and they might try to move his contract. (TS)

Competition at SP — Stats in 2010 as SP

| Thr | Player | GS | ERA | Supp | W-L |
|---|---|---|---|---|---|
| RH | Jimenez U | 33 | 2.88 | 4.7 | 19-8 |
| RH | Hammel J | 30 | 4.81 | 4.6 | 10-9 |
| RH | Cook A | 23 | 5.08 | 4.4 | 6-8 |
| RH | Chacin J | 21 | 2.98 | 4.2 | 9-10 |

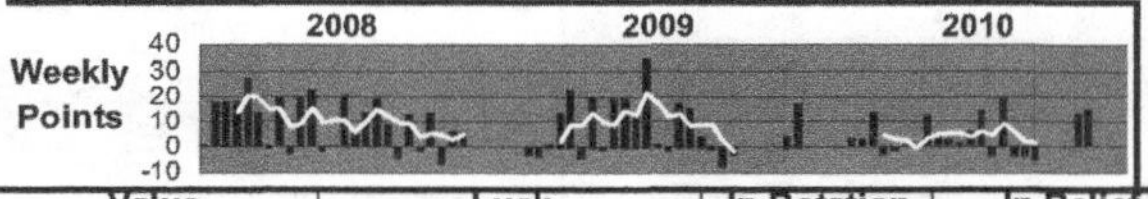


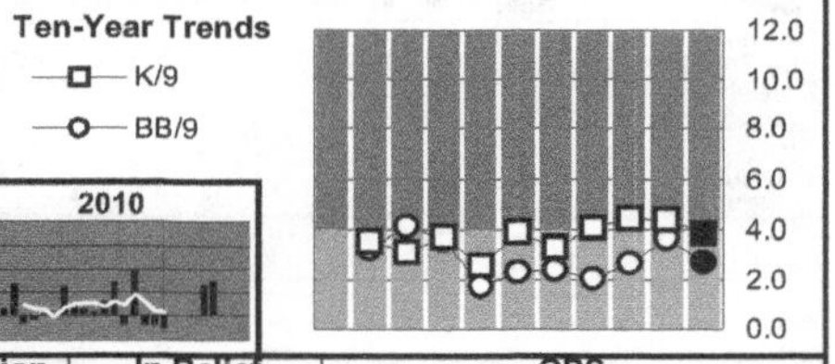


## Francisco Cordero — 80 IP | $12 | 270 pts

RP-75 — Owned: 100% — RH

| Player | Age | IP | W | Sv | K | ERA | WHIP | K/9 | BB/9 | $2L | Pts |
|---|---|---|---|---|---|---|---|---|---|---|---|
| Cordero F | 35 | 80 | 5 | 33 | 70 | 3.77 | 1.40 | 7.8 | 4.3 | $12 | 270 |
| **Mini-Browser** | Age | IP | W | Sv | K | ERA | WHIP | K/9 | BB/9 | $2L | Pts |
| Axford J | 28 | 60 | 5 | 40 | 72 | 3.93 | 1.54 | 10.8 | 5.3 | $13 | 310 |
| Jenks B | 30 | 60 | 2 | 38 | 55 | 4.02 | 1.28 | 8.2 | 2.9 | $13 | 260 |
| Perez C | 25 | 60 | 2 | 33 | 63 | 3.38 | 1.31 | 9.4 | 4.7 | $13 | 250 |
| Danks J | 25 | 200 | 13 | 0 | 150 | 4.15 | 1.29 | 6.7 | 3.2 | $13 | 260 |
| Liriano F | 27 | 200 | 13 | 0 | 190 | 4.19 | 1.34 | 8.6 | 3.4 | $12 | 300 |

Minors (2010)

| Level | Leag | W | L | Sv | IP | H | K | ERA | WHIP | K/9 | BB/9 | HR/9 | GB/F |
|---|---|---|---|---|---|---|---|---|---|---|---|---|---|
| A | — | — | — | — | — | — | — | — | — | — | — | — | — |
| AA | — | — | — | — | — | — | — | — | — | — | — | — | — |
| AAA | — | — | — | — | — | — | — | — | — | — | — | — | — |

Majors

| Yr | Team | W | L | Sv | IP | H | K | ERA | WHIP | K/9 | BB/9 | HR/9 | GB/F |
|---|---|---|---|---|---|---|---|---|---|---|---|---|---|
| 07 | MIL | 0 | 4 | 44 | 63 | 52 | 86 | 2.98 | 1.11 | 12.2 | 2.6 | 0.6 | 1.0 |
| 08 | CIN | 5 | 4 | 34 | 70 | 61 | 78 | 3.33 | 1.41 | 10.0 | 4.9 | 0.8 | 1.1 |
| 09 | CIN | 2 | 6 | 39 | 66 | 58 | 58 | 2.16 | 1.32 | 7.8 | 4.1 | 0.3 | 1.2 |
| 10 | CIN | 6 | 5 | 40 | 72 | 68 | 59 | 3.84 | 1.43 | 7.3 | 4.5 | 0.6 | 1.2 |

| Yr | $1L | $2L | Pts | RAA | H% | HR/fb | S% | FIP | GS | CG | QS/DS | GR | Hld | Bln | Lead | OPS | 1st Hf | 2nd Hf | vs RH | vs LH |
|---|---|---|---|---|---|---|---|---|---|---|---|---|---|---|---|---|---|---|---|---|
| 07 | $15 | $13 | 310 | +6 | 32% | 6% | 74% | 2.16 | — | — | — | 66 | 0 | 7 | +1.9 | .588 | .516 | .670 | .544 | .642 |
| 08 | $12 | $7 | 290 | +4 | 31% | 9% | 78% | 3.71 | — | — | — | 72 | 0 | 6 | +1.0 | .682 | .587 | .817 | .769 | .569 |
| 09 | $13 | $9 | 280 | +9 | 31% | 3% | 84% | 3.20 | — | — | — | 68 | 0 | 4 | +1.4 | .628 | .555 | .701 | .648 | .604 |
| 10 | $9 | $3 | 310 | +1 | 30% | 6% | 74% | 3.96 | — | — | — | 75 | 1 | 8 | +2.2 | .681 | .756 | .583 | .631 | .743 |

Cordero will be back for one more year as the Cincinnati closer, because they will be paying him $12M to do so. Dusty Baker might even still trust him, even though the fans do not. Cordero's fastball has slowed and straightened, so he must rely more on guile. His plunging K/9 in 2009 was a warning sign. (SW)

Competition at RP — Stats in 2010 as RP

| Thr | Player | GR | ERA | IP/G | Sv-Hld |
|---|---|---|---|---|---|
| RH | Masset N | 82 | 3.40 | 0.9 | 2-20 |
| RH | Cordero F | 75 | 3.84 | 1.0 | 40-1 |
| RH | Ondrusek L | 60 | 3.68 | 1.0 | 0-6 |
| RH | Smith J | 37 | 3.86 | 1.1 | 1-2 |

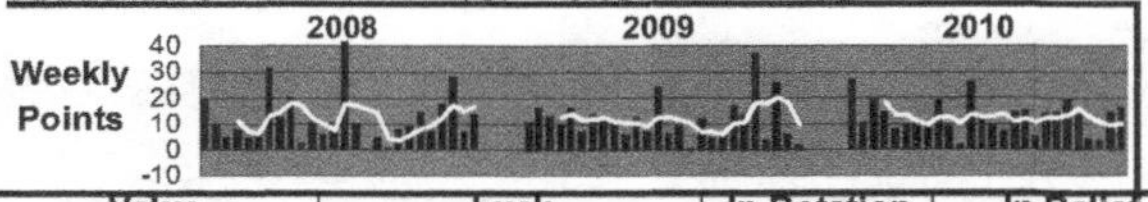


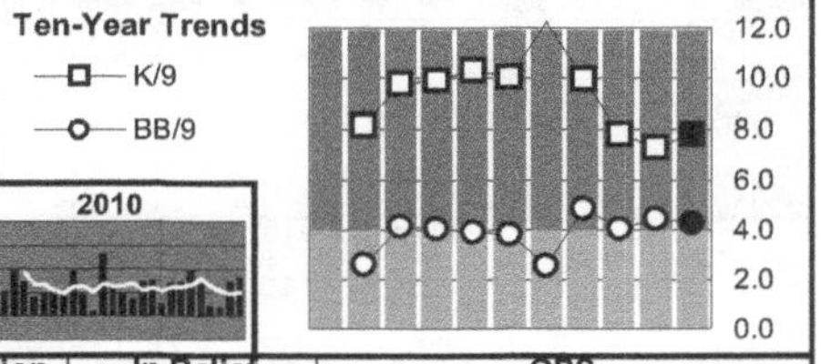


## Lance Cormier — 40 IP | $-2 | 30 pts

RP-60 — Owned: 0% — RH

| Player | Age | IP | W | Sv | K | ERA | WHIP | K/9 | BB/9 | $2L | Pts |
|---|---|---|---|---|---|---|---|---|---|---|---|
| Cormier L | 30 | 40 | 2 | 0 | 20 | 4.43 | 1.52 | 4.4 | 4.1 | -$2 | 30 |
| **Mini-Browser** | Age | IP | W | Sv | K | ERA | WHIP | K/9 | BB/9 | $2L | Pts |
| Qualls C | 32 | 50 | 2 | 0 | 39 | 5.14 | 1.44 | 7.1 | 2.5 | -$2 | 40 |
| Corpas M | 28 | 20 | 1 | 0 | 13 | 4.34 | 1.33 | 6.0 | 2.6 | -$2 | 20 |
| Elbert S | 25 | 40 | 2 | 0 | 48 | 4.59 | 1.51 | 10.8 | 4.2 | -$2 | 50 |
| Schlereth D | 24 | 40 | 2 | 0 | 46 | 4.33 | 1.72 | 10.3 | 6.1 | -$2 | 50 |
| Marte D | 36 | 20 | 1 | 0 | 18 | 4.83 | 1.43 | 7.9 | 4.8 | -$2 | 20 |

Minors (2010)

| Level | Leag | W | L | Sv | IP | H | K | ERA | WHIP | K/9 | BB/9 | HR/9 | GB/F |
|---|---|---|---|---|---|---|---|---|---|---|---|---|---|
| A | — | — | — | — | — | — | — | — | — | — | — | — | — |
| AA | — | — | — | — | — | — | — | — | — | — | — | — | — |
| AAA | — | — | — | — | — | — | — | — | — | — | — | — | — |

Majors

| Yr | Team | W | L | Sv | IP | H | K | ERA | WHIP | K/9 | BB/9 | HR/9 | GB/F |
|---|---|---|---|---|---|---|---|---|---|---|---|---|---|
| 07 | ATL | 2 | 6 | 0 | 45 | 56 | 27 | 7.09 | 1.71 | 5.3 | 4.3 | 3.2 | 1.7 |
| 08 | BAL | 3 | 3 | 1 | 71 | 78 | 46 | 4.02 | 1.56 | 5.8 | 4.3 | 0.5 | 2.6 |
| 09 | TB | 3 | 3 | 2 | 77 | 75 | 36 | 3.26 | 1.29 | 4.2 | 2.9 | 0.7 | 1.7 |
| 10 | TB | 4 | 3 | 0 | 62 | 68 | 30 | 3.92 | 1.65 | 4.4 | 4.9 | 1.0 | 1.6 |

| Yr | $1L | $2L | Pts | RAA | H% | HR/fb | S% | FIP | GS | CG | QS/DS | GR | Hld | Bln | Lead | OPS | 1st Hf | 2nd Hf | vs RH | vs LH |
|---|---|---|---|---|---|---|---|---|---|---|---|---|---|---|---|---|---|---|---|---|
| 07 | -$7 | -$13 | 20 | –17 | 28% | 34% | 68% | 8.02 | 9 | 0 | 2/3 | 1 | 0 | 0 | –0.2 | 1.009 | 1.586 | .872 | 1.115 | .851 |
| 08 | -$2 | -$5 | 60 | –4 | 32% | 8% | 74% | 4.17 | 1 | 0 | 0/0 | 44 | 0 | 2 | –0.3 | .727 | .665 | .783 | .772 | .667 |
| 09 | $4 | $1 | 80 | +4 | 27% | 8% | 77% | 4.35 | — | — | — | 53 | 6 | 0 | –0.3 | .679 | .629 | .754 | .688 | .671 |
| 10 | -$3 | -$14 | 50 | –0 | 30% | 11% | 79% | 5.45 | — | — | — | 60 | 4 | 0 | –0.6 | .810 | .858 | .742 | .936 | .718 |

Cormier is set to hit free agency, and he might not be back with Tampa Bay, who needs to cut payroll. In a year in which his walk rate jumped by 2.0 BB/9, Cormier was lucky to escape as he did. He could serve in long relief somewhere, or he could come down with a more severe case of whatever ails Aaron Cook. (RZ)

Competition at RP — Stats in 2010 as RP

| Thr | Player | GR | ERA | IP/G | Sv-Hld |
|---|---|---|---|---|---|
| RH | Soriano R | 64 | 1.73 | 1.0 | 45-0 |
| RH | Wheeler D | 64 | 3.35 | 0.8 | 3-9 |
| RH | Benoit J | 63 | 1.34 | 1.0 | 1-25 |
| RH | Cormier L | 60 | 3.92 | 1.0 | 0-4 |

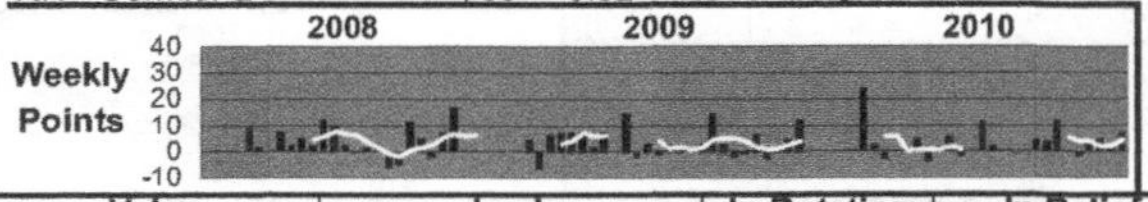


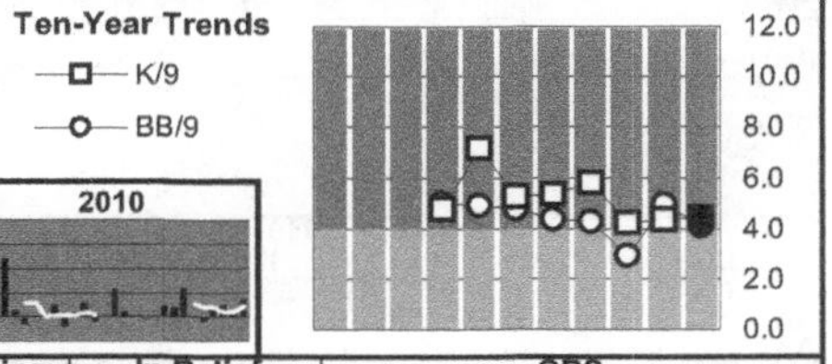

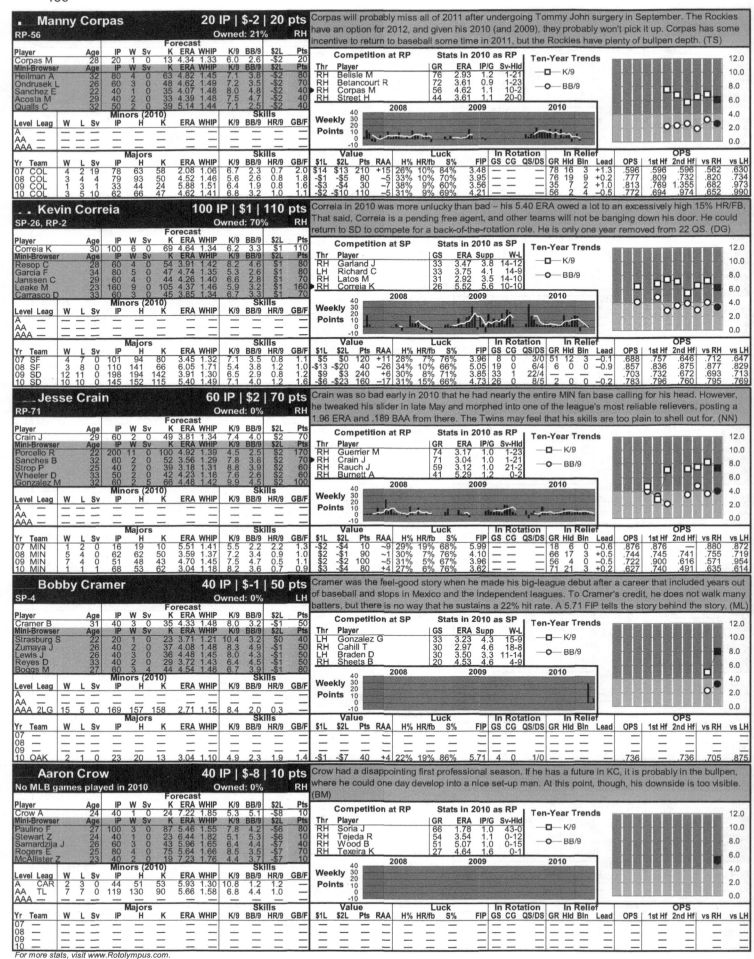

## Manny Corpas — 20 IP | $-2 | 20 pts

RP-56 — Owned: 21% — RH

Corpas will probably miss all of 2011 after undergoing Tommy John surgery in September. The Rockies have an option for 2012, and given his 2010 (and 2009), they probably won't pick it up. Corpas has some incentive to return to baseball some time in 2011, but the Rockies have plenty of bullpen depth. (TS)

| Player | Age | IP | W | Sv | K | ERA | WHIP | K/9 | BB/9 | $2L | Pts |
|---|---|---|---|---|---|---|---|---|---|---|---|
| Corpas M | 28 | 20 | 1 | 0 | 13 | 4.34 | 1.33 | 6.0 | 2.6 | -$2 | 20 |
| **Mini-Browser** | **Age** | **IP** | **W** | **Sv** | **K** | **ERA** | **WHIP** | **K/9** | **BB/9** | **$2L** | **Pts** |
| Heilman A | 32 | 80 | 4 | 0 | 63 | 4.82 | 1.45 | 7.1 | 3.8 | -$2 | 80 |
| Ondrusek L | 26 | 60 | 3 | 0 | 48 | 4.62 | 1.49 | 7.2 | 3.5 | -$2 | 70 |
| Sanchez E | 22 | 40 | 1 | 0 | 35 | 4.07 | 1.48 | 8.0 | 4.8 | -$2 | 40 |
| Acosta M | 29 | 40 | 2 | 0 | 33 | 4.39 | 1.48 | 7.5 | 4.7 | -$2 | 40 |
| Qualls C | 32 | 50 | 2 | 0 | 39 | 5.14 | 1.44 | 7.1 | 2.5 | -$2 | 40 |

Competition at RP / Stats in 2010 as RP

| Thr | Player | GR | ERA | IP/G | Sv-Hld |
|---|---|---|---|---|---|
| RH | Belisle M | 76 | 2.93 | 1.2 | 1-21 |
| RH | Betancourt R | 72 | 3.61 | 0.9 | 1-23 |
| RH | Corpas M | 56 | 4.62 | 1.1 | 10-2 |
| RH | Street H | 44 | 3.61 | 1.1 | 20-0 |

Weekly Points

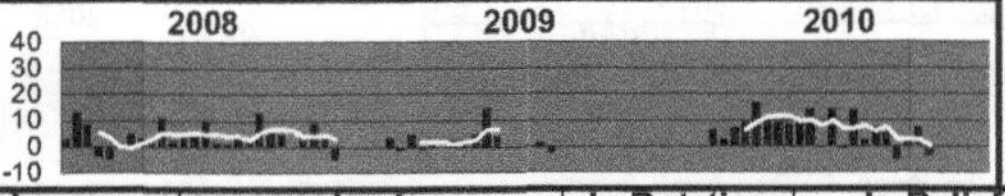


Ten-Year Trends

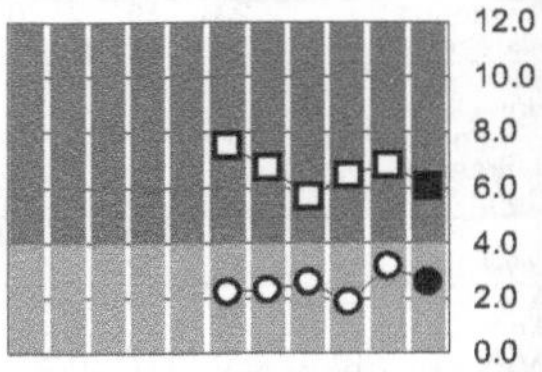


Minors (2010)

| Level | Leag | W | L | Sv | IP | H | K | ERA | WHIP | K/9 | BB/9 | HR/9 | GB/F |
|---|---|---|---|---|---|---|---|---|---|---|---|---|---|
| A | — | — | — | — | — | — | — | — | — | — | — | — | — |
| AA | — | — | — | — | — | — | — | — | — | — | — | — | — |
| AAA | — | — | — | — | — | — | — | — | — | — | — | — | — |

Majors

| Yr | Team | W | L | Sv | IP | H | K | ERA | WHIP | K/9 | BB/9 | HR/9 | GB/F |
|---|---|---|---|---|---|---|---|---|---|---|---|---|---|
| 07 | COL | 4 | 2 | 19 | 78 | 63 | 58 | 2.08 | 1.06 | 6.7 | 2.3 | 0.7 | 2.0 |
| 08 | COL | 3 | 4 | 4 | 79 | 93 | 50 | 4.52 | 1.46 | 5.6 | 2.6 | 0.8 | 1.8 |
| 09 | COL | 1 | 3 | 1 | 33 | 44 | 24 | 5.88 | 1.51 | 6.4 | 1.9 | 0.8 | 1.6 |
| 10 | COL | 3 | 5 | 10 | 62 | 66 | 47 | 4.62 | 1.41 | 6.8 | 3.2 | 1.0 | 1.1 |

| Yr | $1L | $2L | Pts | RAA | H% | HR/fb | S% | FIP | GS | CG | QS/DS | GR | Hld | Bln | Lead | OPS | 1st Hf | 2nd Hf | vs RH | vs LH |
|---|---|---|---|---|---|---|---|---|---|---|---|---|---|---|---|---|---|---|---|---|
| 07 | $14 | $13 | 210 | +15 | 26% | 10% | 84% | 3.48 | — | — | — | 78 | 16 | 3 | +1.3 | .596 | .596 | .596 | .562 | .630 |
| 08 | -$1 | -$5 | 80 | –5 | 33% | 10% | 70% | 3.95 | — | — | — | 76 | 19 | 9 | +0.2 | .777 | .809 | .732 | .820 | .734 |
| 09 | -$3 | -$4 | 30 | –7 | 38% | 9% | 60% | 3.56 | — | — | — | 35 | 7 | 2 | +1.0 | .813 | .769 | 1.355 | .682 | .973 |
| 10 | -$2 | -$10 | 110 | –5 | 31% | 9% | 69% | 4.21 | — | — | — | 56 | 2 | 4 | –0.5 | .772 | .694 | .974 | .652 | .990 |

## Kevin Correia — 100 IP | $1 | 110 pts

SP-26, RP-2 — Owned: 70% — RH

Correia in 2010 was more unlucky than bad – his 5.40 ERA owed a lot to an excessively high 15% HR/FB. That said, Correia is a pending free agent, and other teams will not be banging down his door. He could return to SD to compete for a back-of-the-rotation role. He is only one year removed from 22 QS. (DG)

| Player | Age | IP | W | Sv | K | ERA | WHIP | K/9 | BB/9 | $2L | Pts |
|---|---|---|---|---|---|---|---|---|---|---|---|
| Correia K | 30 | 100 | 6 | 0 | 69 | 4.64 | 1.34 | 6.2 | 3.3 | $1 | 110 |
| **Mini-Browser** | **Age** | **IP** | **W** | **Sv** | **K** | **ERA** | **WHIP** | **K/9** | **BB/9** | **$2L** | **Pts** |
| Resop C | 28 | 60 | 4 | 0 | 54 | 3.91 | 1.42 | 8.2 | 4.6 | $1 | 80 |
| Garcia F | 34 | 80 | 5 | 0 | 47 | 4.74 | 1.35 | 5.3 | 2.6 | $1 | 80 |
| Janssen C | 29 | 60 | 4 | 0 | 44 | 4.26 | 1.40 | 6.6 | 2.8 | $1 | 70 |
| Leake M | 23 | 160 | 9 | 0 | 105 | 4.37 | 1.46 | 5.9 | 3.2 | $1 | 160 |
| Carrasco D | 33 | 60 | 3 | 0 | 45 | 3.85 | 1.34 | 6.7 | 3.3 | $1 | 70 |

Competition at SP / Stats in 2010 as SP

| Thr | Player | GS | ERA | Supp | W-L |
|---|---|---|---|---|---|
| RH | Garland J | 33 | 3.47 | 3.8 | 14-12 |
| LH | Richard C | 33 | 3.75 | 4.1 | 14-9 |
| RH | Latos M | 31 | 2.92 | 3.5 | 14-10 |
| RH | Correia K | 26 | 5.52 | 5.6 | 10-10 |

Weekly Points

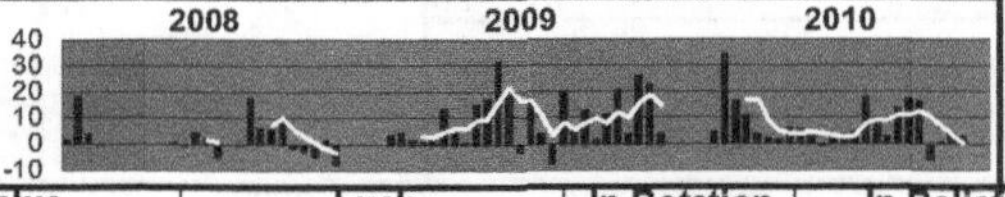


Ten-Year Trends

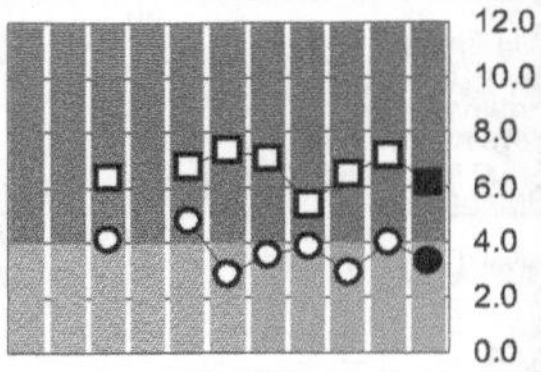


Minors (2010)

| Level | Leag | W | L | Sv | IP | H | K | ERA | WHIP | K/9 | BB/9 | HR/9 | GB/F |
|---|---|---|---|---|---|---|---|---|---|---|---|---|---|
| A | — | — | — | — | — | — | — | — | — | — | — | — | — |
| AA | — | — | — | — | — | — | — | — | — | — | — | — | — |
| AAA | — | — | — | — | — | — | — | — | — | — | — | — | — |

Majors

| Yr | Team | W | L | Sv | IP | H | K | ERA | WHIP | K/9 | BB/9 | HR/9 | GB/F |
|---|---|---|---|---|---|---|---|---|---|---|---|---|---|
| 07 | SF | 4 | 7 | 0 | 101 | 94 | 80 | 3.45 | 1.32 | 7.1 | 3.5 | 0.8 | 1.1 |
| 08 | SF | 3 | 8 | 0 | 110 | 141 | 66 | 6.05 | 1.71 | 5.4 | 3.8 | 1.2 | 1.0 |
| 09 | SD | 12 | 11 | 0 | 198 | 194 | 142 | 3.91 | 1.30 | 6.5 | 2.9 | 0.8 | 1.2 |
| 10 | SD | 10 | 10 | 0 | 145 | 152 | 115 | 5.40 | 1.49 | 7.1 | 4.0 | 1.2 | 1.6 |

| Yr | $1L | $2L | Pts | RAA | H% | HR/fb | S% | FIP | GS | CG | QS/DS | GR | Hld | Bln | Lead | OPS | 1st Hf | 2nd Hf | vs RH | vs LH |
|---|---|---|---|---|---|---|---|---|---|---|---|---|---|---|---|---|---|---|---|---|
| 07 | $5 | $0 | 120 | +11 | 28% | 7% | 76% | 3.96 | 8 | 0 | 3/0 | 51 | 12 | 3 | –0.1 | .688 | .757 | .646 | .712 | .647 |
| 08 | -$13 | -$20 | 40 | –26 | 34% | 10% | 66% | 5.05 | 19 | 0 | 6/4 | 6 | 0 | 0 | –0.9 | .857 | .836 | .875 | .877 | .829 |
| 09 | $9 | $3 | 240 | +6 | 30% | 8% | 71% | 3.85 | 33 | 1 | 22/4 | — | — | — | — | .703 | .732 | .672 | .693 | .713 |
| 10 | -$6 | -$23 | 160 | –17 | 31% | 15% | 66% | 4.73 | 26 | 0 | 8/5 | 2 | 0 | 0 | –0.2 | .783 | .796 | .760 | .795 | .769 |

## Jesse Crain — 60 IP | $2 | 70 pts

RP-71 — Owned: 0% — RH

Crain was so bad early in 2010 that he had nearly the entire MIN fan base calling for his head. However, he tweaked his slider in late May and morphed into one of the league's most reliable relievers, posting a 1.96 ERA and .189 BAA from there. The Twins may feel that his skills are too plain to shell out for. (NN)

| Player | Age | IP | W | Sv | K | ERA | WHIP | K/9 | BB/9 | $2L | Pts |
|---|---|---|---|---|---|---|---|---|---|---|---|
| Crain J | 29 | 60 | 2 | 0 | 49 | 3.81 | 1.34 | 7.4 | 4.0 | $2 | 70 |
| **Mini-Browser** | **Age** | **IP** | **W** | **Sv** | **K** | **ERA** | **WHIP** | **K/9** | **BB/9** | **$2L** | **Pts** |
| Porcello R | 22 | 200 | 11 | 0 | 100 | 4.92 | 1.39 | 4.5 | 2.5 | $2 | 170 |
| Sanches B | 32 | 60 | 2 | 0 | 52 | 3.56 | 1.29 | 7.8 | 3.8 | $2 | 70 |
| Strop P | 25 | 40 | 2 | 0 | 39 | 3.18 | 1.31 | 8.8 | 3.9 | $2 | 60 |
| Wheeler D | 33 | 50 | 2 | 0 | 42 | 4.23 | 1.18 | 7.6 | 2.6 | $2 | 60 |
| Gonzalez M | 32 | 60 | 2 | 5 | 66 | 4.48 | 1.42 | 9.9 | 4.5 | $2 | 100 |

Competition at RP / Stats in 2010 as RP

| Thr | Player | GR | ERA | IP/G | Sv-Hld |
|---|---|---|---|---|---|
| RH | Guerrier M | 74 | 3.17 | 1.0 | 1-23 |
| RH | Crain J | 71 | 3.04 | 1.0 | 1-21 |
| RH | Rauch J | 59 | 3.12 | 1.0 | 21-2 |
| RH | Burnett A | 41 | 5.29 | 1.2 | 0-2 |

Weekly Points

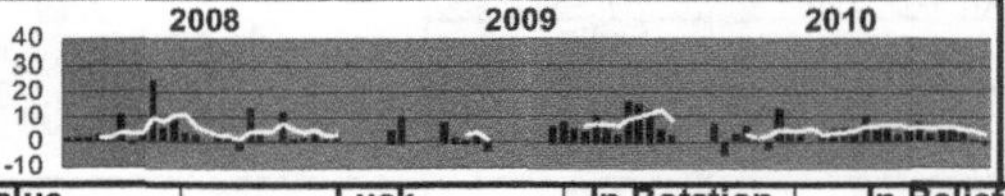


Ten-Year Trends

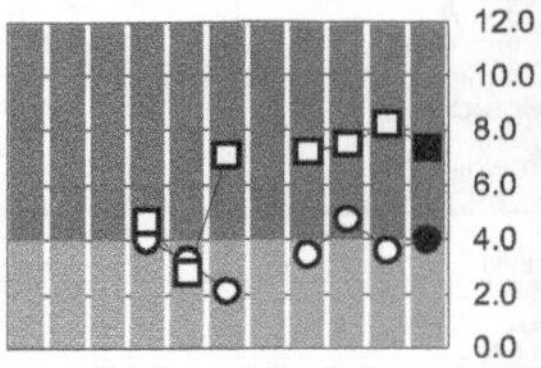


Minors (2010)

| Level | Leag | W | L | Sv | IP | H | K | ERA | WHIP | K/9 | BB/9 | HR/9 | GB/F |
|---|---|---|---|---|---|---|---|---|---|---|---|---|---|
| A | — | — | — | — | — | — | — | — | — | — | — | — | — |
| AA | — | — | — | — | — | — | — | — | — | — | — | — | — |
| AAA | — | — | — | — | — | — | — | — | — | — | — | — | — |

Majors

| Yr | Team | W | L | Sv | IP | H | K | ERA | WHIP | K/9 | BB/9 | HR/9 | GB/F |
|---|---|---|---|---|---|---|---|---|---|---|---|---|---|
| 07 | MIN | 1 | 2 | 0 | 16 | 19 | 10 | 5.51 | 1.41 | 5.5 | 2.2 | 2.2 | 1.3 |
| 08 | MIN | 5 | 4 | 0 | 62 | 62 | 50 | 3.59 | 1.37 | 7.2 | 3.4 | 0.9 | 1.0 |
| 09 | MIN | 7 | 4 | 0 | 51 | 48 | 43 | 4.70 | 1.45 | 7.5 | 4.7 | 0.5 | 1.1 |
| 10 | MIN | 1 | 1 | 1 | 68 | 53 | 62 | 3.04 | 1.18 | 8.2 | 3.6 | 0.7 | 0.9 |

| Yr | $1L | $2L | Pts | RAA | H% | HR/fb | S% | FIP | GS | CG | QS/DS | GR | Hld | Bln | Lead | OPS | 1st Hf | 2nd Hf | vs RH | vs LH |
|---|---|---|---|---|---|---|---|---|---|---|---|---|---|---|---|---|---|---|---|---|
| 07 | -$2 | -$4 | 10 | –9 | 29% | 19% | 68% | 5.99 | — | — | — | 18 | 6 | 0 | –0.6 | .876 | .876 | — | .880 | .872 |
| 08 | $2 | -$1 | 90 | –1 | 30% | 7% | 76% | 4.10 | — | — | — | 66 | 17 | 3 | +0.5 | .744 | .745 | .741 | .755 | .719 |
| 09 | $2 | -$2 | 100 | –5 | 31% | 5% | 67% | 3.96 | — | — | — | 56 | 4 | 0 | –0.5 | .722 | .900 | .616 | .571 | .954 |
| 10 | $3 | -$4 | 80 | +4 | 27% | 6% | 76% | 3.62 | — | — | — | 71 | 21 | 3 | +0.2 | .627 | .740 | .491 | .635 | .614 |

## Bobby Cramer — 40 IP | $-1 | 50 pts

SP-4 — Owned: 0% — LH

Cramer was the feel-good story when he made his big-league debut after a career that included years out of baseball and stops in Mexico and the independent leagues. To Cramer's credit, he does not walk many batters, but there is no way that he sustains a 22% hit rate. A 5.71 FIP tells the story behind the story. (ML)

| Player | Age | IP | W | Sv | K | ERA | WHIP | K/9 | BB/9 | $2L | Pts |
|---|---|---|---|---|---|---|---|---|---|---|---|
| Cramer B | 31 | 40 | 3 | 0 | 35 | 4.33 | 1.48 | 8.0 | 3.2 | -$1 | 50 |
| **Mini-Browser** | **Age** | **IP** | **W** | **Sv** | **K** | **ERA** | **WHIP** | **K/9** | **BB/9** | **$2L** | **Pts** |
| Strasburg S | 22 | 20 | 1 | 0 | 23 | 3.71 | 1.21 | 10.4 | 3.2 | $0 | 40 |
| Zumaya J | 26 | 40 | 2 | 0 | 37 | 4.08 | 1.48 | 8.3 | 4.9 | -$1 | 50 |
| Lewis J | 26 | 40 | 3 | 0 | 36 | 4.48 | 1.45 | 8.0 | 4.3 | -$1 | 50 |
| Reyes D | 33 | 40 | 2 | 0 | 29 | 3.72 | 1.43 | 6.4 | 4.5 | -$1 | 50 |
| Boggs M | 27 | 60 | 3 | 4 | 44 | 4.54 | 1.48 | 6.7 | 3.9 | -$1 | 80 |

Competition at SP / Stats in 2010 as SP

| Thr | Player | GS | ERA | Supp | W-L |
|---|---|---|---|---|---|
| LH | Gonzalez G | 33 | 3.23 | 4.3 | 15-9 |
| RH | Cahill T | 30 | 2.97 | 4.6 | 18-8 |
| LH | Braden D | 30 | 3.50 | 3.3 | 11-14 |
| RH | Sheets B | 20 | 4.53 | 4.6 | 4-9 |

Weekly Points

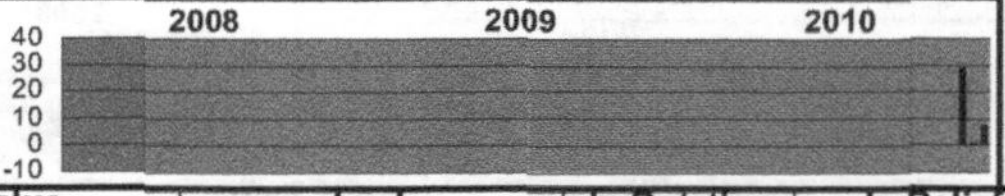


Ten-Year Trends

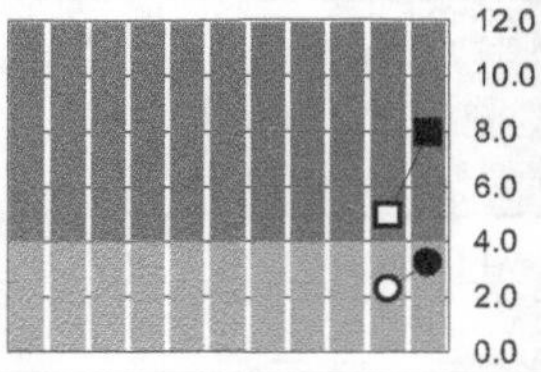


Minors (2010)

| Level | Leag | W | L | Sv | IP | H | K | ERA | WHIP | K/9 | BB/9 | HR/9 | GB/F |
|---|---|---|---|---|---|---|---|---|---|---|---|---|---|
| A | — | — | — | — | — | — | — | — | — | — | — | — | — |
| AA | — | — | — | — | — | — | — | — | — | — | — | — | — |
| AAA | 2LG | 15 | 5 | 0 | 169 | 157 | 158 | 2.71 | 1.15 | 8.4 | 2.0 | 0.3 | — |

Majors

| Yr | Team | W | L | Sv | IP | H | K | ERA | WHIP | K/9 | BB/9 | HR/9 | GB/F |
|---|---|---|---|---|---|---|---|---|---|---|---|---|---|
| 07 | — | — | — | — | — | — | — | — | — | — | — | — | — |
| 08 | — | — | — | — | — | — | — | — | — | — | — | — | — |
| 09 | — | — | — | — | — | — | — | — | — | — | — | — | — |
| 10 | OAK | 2 | 1 | 0 | 23 | 20 | 13 | 3.04 | 1.10 | 4.9 | 2.3 | 1.9 | 1.4 |

| Yr | $1L | $2L | Pts | RAA | H% | HR/fb | S% | FIP | GS | CG | QS/DS | GR | Hld | Bln | Lead | OPS | 1st Hf | 2nd Hf | vs RH | vs LH |
|---|---|---|---|---|---|---|---|---|---|---|---|---|---|---|---|---|---|---|---|---|
| 07 | — | — | — | — | — | — | — | — | — | — | — | — | — | — | — | — | — | — | — | — |
| 08 | — | — | — | — | — | — | — | — | — | — | — | — | — | — | — | — | — | — | — | — |
| 09 | — | — | — | — | — | — | — | — | — | — | — | — | — | — | — | — | — | — | — | — |
| 10 | -$1 | -$7 | 40 | +4 | 22% | 19% | 86% | 5.71 | 4 | 0 | 1/0 | — | — | — | — | .736 | — | .736 | .705 | .875 |

## Aaron Crow — 40 IP | $-8 | 10 pts

No MLB games played in 2010 — Owned: 0% — RH

Crow had a disappointing first professional season. If he has a future in KC, it is probably in the bullpen, where he could one day develop into a nice set-up man. At this point, though, his downside is too visible. (BM)

| Player | Age | IP | W | Sv | K | ERA | WHIP | K/9 | BB/9 | $2L | Pts |
|---|---|---|---|---|---|---|---|---|---|---|---|
| Crow A | 24 | 40 | 1 | 0 | 24 | 7.22 | 1.85 | 5.3 | 5.1 | -$8 | 10 |
| **Mini-Browser** | **Age** | **IP** | **W** | **Sv** | **K** | **ERA** | **WHIP** | **K/9** | **BB/9** | **$2L** | **Pts** |
| Paulino F | 27 | 100 | 3 | 0 | 87 | 5.46 | 1.55 | 7.8 | 4.2 | -$6 | 80 |
| Stewart Z | 24 | 40 | 1 | 0 | 23 | 6.44 | 1.82 | 5.1 | 5.3 | -$6 | 10 |
| Samardzija J | 26 | 60 | 3 | 0 | 43 | 5.96 | 1.65 | 6.4 | 4.4 | -$7 | 40 |
| Rogers E | 25 | 80 | 4 | 0 | 75 | 5.64 | 1.66 | 8.5 | 3.5 | -$7 | 70 |
| McAllister Z | 23 | 40 | 2 | 0 | 19 | 7.23 | 1.76 | 4.4 | 3.7 | -$7 | 10 |

Competition at RP / Stats in 2010 as RP

| Thr | Player | GR | ERA | IP/G | Sv-Hld |
|---|---|---|---|---|---|
| RH | Soria J | 66 | 1.78 | 1.0 | 43-0 |
| RH | Tejeda R | 54 | 3.54 | 1.1 | 0-12 |
| RH | Wood B | 51 | 5.07 | 1.0 | 0-15 |
| RH | Texeira K | 27 | 4.64 | 1.6 | 0-1 |

Weekly Points

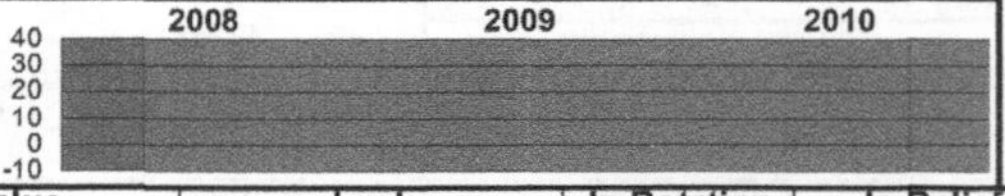


Ten-Year Trends

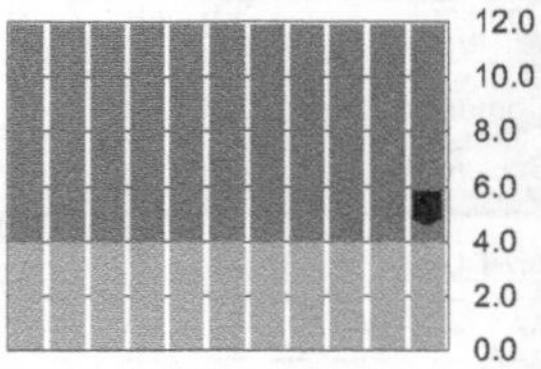


Minors (2010)

| Level | Leag | W | L | Sv | IP | H | K | ERA | WHIP | K/9 | BB/9 | HR/9 | GB/F |
|---|---|---|---|---|---|---|---|---|---|---|---|---|---|
| A | CAR | 2 | 3 | 0 | 44 | 51 | 53 | 5.93 | 1.30 | 10.8 | 1.2 | 1.2 | — |
| AA | TL | 7 | 7 | 0 | 119 | 130 | 90 | 5.66 | 1.58 | 6.8 | 4.4 | 1.0 | — |
| AAA | — | — | — | — | — | — | — | — | — | — | — | — | — |

Majors

| Yr | Team | W | L | Sv | IP | H | K | ERA | WHIP | K/9 | BB/9 | HR/9 | GB/F |
|---|---|---|---|---|---|---|---|---|---|---|---|---|---|
| 07 | — | — | — | — | — | — | — | — | — | — | — | — | — |
| 08 | — | — | — | — | — | — | — | — | — | — | — | — | — |
| 09 | — | — | — | — | — | — | — | — | — | — | — | — | — |
| 10 | — | — | — | — | — | — | — | — | — | — | — | — | — |

| Yr | $1L | $2L | Pts | RAA | H% | HR/fb | S% | FIP | GS | CG | QS/DS | GR | Hld | Bln | Lead | OPS | 1st Hf | 2nd Hf | vs RH | vs LH |
|---|---|---|---|---|---|---|---|---|---|---|---|---|---|---|---|---|---|---|---|---|
| 07 | — | — | — | — | — | — | — | — | — | — | — | — | — | — | — | — | — | — | — | — |
| 08 | — | — | — | — | — | — | — | — | — | — | — | — | — | — | — | — | — | — | — | — |
| 09 | — | — | — | — | — | — | — | — | — | — | — | — | — | — | — | — | — | — | — | — |
| 10 | — | — | — | — | — | — | — | — | — | — | — | — | — | — | — | — | — | — | — | — |

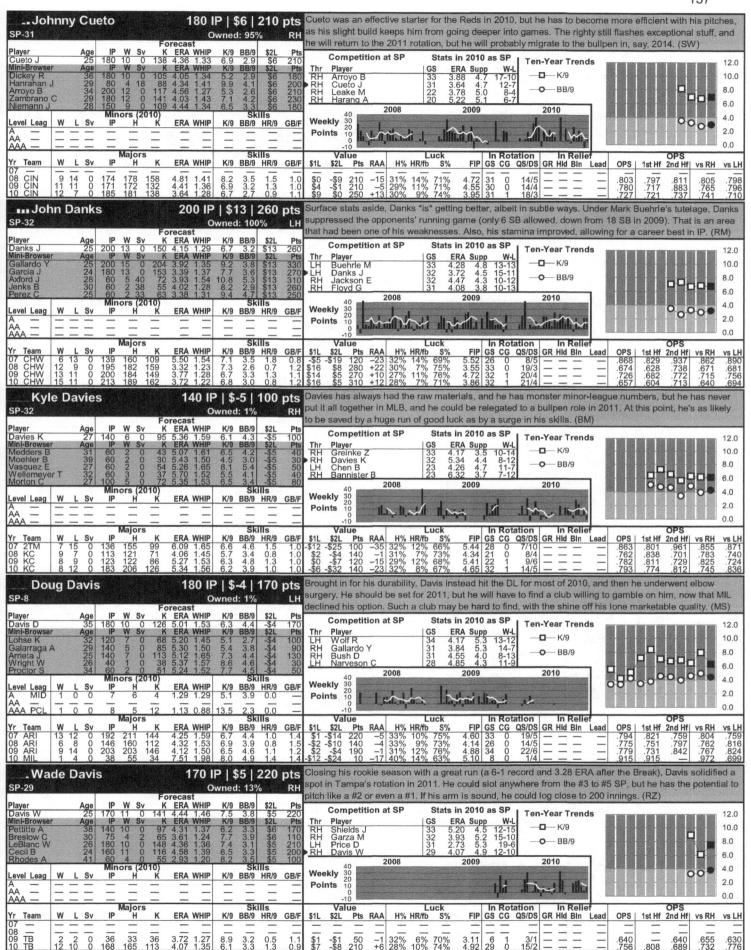

## Johnny Cueto
**180 IP | $6 | 210 pts**

SP-31 | Owned: 95% | RH

Cueto was an effective starter for the Reds in 2010, but he has to become more efficient with his pitches, as his slight build keeps him from going deeper into games. The righty still flashes exceptional stuff, and he will return to the 2011 rotation, but he will probably migrate to the bullpen in, say, 2014. (SW)

| Forecast | | | | | | | | | | | |
|---|---|---|---|---|---|---|---|---|---|---|---|
| Player | Age | IP | W | Sv | K | ERA | WHIP | K/9 | BB/9 | $2L | Pts |
| Cueto J | 25 | 180 | 10 | 0 | 138 | 4.36 | 1.33 | 6.9 | 2.9 | $6 | 210 |
| **Mini-Browser** | Age | IP | W | Sv | K | ERA | WHIP | K/9 | BB/9 | $2L | Pts |
| Dickey R | 36 | 180 | 10 | 0 | 105 | 4.05 | 1.34 | 5.2 | 2.9 | $6 | 180 |
| Hanrahan J | 29 | 80 | 4 | 18 | 88 | 4.34 | 1.41 | 9.9 | 4.1 | $6 | 200 |
| Arroyo B | 34 | 200 | 12 | 0 | 117 | 4.56 | 1.27 | 5.3 | 2.6 | $6 | 210 |
| Zambrano C | 29 | 180 | 12 | 0 | 141 | 4.03 | 1.43 | 7.1 | 4.2 | $6 | 230 |
| Niemann J | 28 | 150 | 9 | 0 | 109 | 4.44 | 1.34 | 6.5 | 3.3 | $6 | 180 |

| Minors (2010) | | | | | | | | | Skills | | | |
|---|---|---|---|---|---|---|---|---|---|---|---|---|
| Level | Leag | W | L | Sv | IP | H | K | ERA | WHIP | K/9 | BB/9 | HR/9 | GB/F |
| A | — | — | — | — | — | — | — | — | — | — | — | — | — |
| AA | — | — | — | — | — | — | — | — | — | — | — | — | — |
| AAA | — | — | — | — | — | — | — | — | — | — | — | — | — |

| Thr | Competition at SP Player | GS | ERA | Supp | W-L |
|---|---|---|---|---|---|
| RH | Arroyo B | 33 | 3.88 | 4.7 | 17-10 |
| RH | ▶ Cueto J | 31 | 3.64 | 4.7 | 12-7 |
| RH | Leake M | 22 | 3.78 | 5.0 | 8-4 |
| RH | Harang A | 20 | 5.22 | 5.1 | 6-7 |

Stats in 2010 as SP

Weekly Points
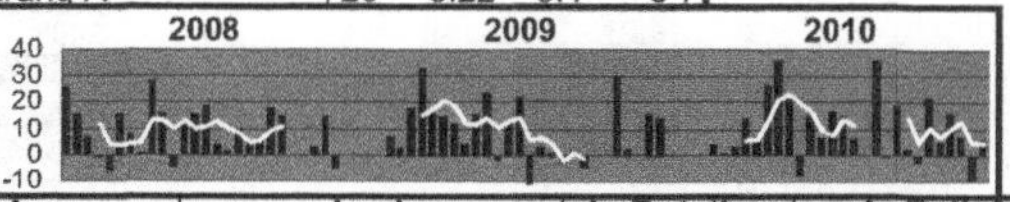
2008
2009
2010
40
30
20
10
0
-10

Ten-Year Trends
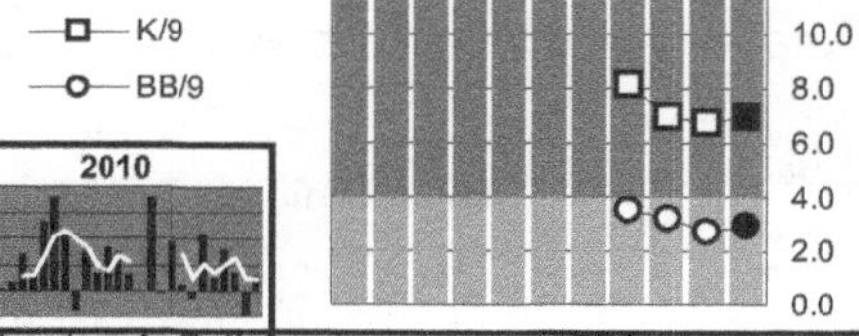
K/9
BB/9
12.0
10.0
8.0
6.0
4.0
2.0
0.0

| Majors | | | | | | | | | | Skills | | | | Value | | | | Luck | | | | In Rotation | | | In Relief | | | | OPS | | | | |
|---|---|---|---|---|---|---|---|---|---|---|---|---|---|---|---|---|---|---|---|---|---|---|---|---|---|---|---|---|---|---|---|---|---|
| Yr | Team | W | L | Sv | IP | H | K | ERA | WHIP | K/9 | BB/9 | HR/9 | GB/F | $1L | $2L | Pts | RAA | H% | HR/fb | S% | FIP | GS | CG | QS/DS | GR | Hld | Bln | Lead | OPS | 1st Hf | 2nd Hf | vs RH | vs LH |
| 07 | — | — | — | — | — | — | — | — | — | — | — | — | — | — | — | — | — | — | — | — | — | — | — | — | — | — | — | — | — | — | — | — | — |
| 08 | CIN | 9 | 14 | 0 | 174 | 178 | 158 | 4.81 | 1.41 | 8.2 | 3.5 | 1.5 | 1.0 | $0 | -$9 | 210 | −15 | 31% | 14% | 71% | 4.72 | 31 | 0 | 14/5 | — | — | — | — | .803 | .797 | .811 | .805 | .798 |
| 09 | CIN | 11 | 11 | 0 | 171 | 172 | 132 | 4.41 | 1.36 | 6.9 | 3.2 | 1.3 | 1.0 | $4 | -$1 | 210 | −5 | 29% | 11% | 71% | 4.55 | 30 | 0 | 14/4 | — | — | — | — | .780 | .717 | .883 | .765 | .796 |
| 10 | CIN | 12 | 7 | 0 | 185 | 181 | 138 | 3.64 | 1.28 | 6.7 | 2.7 | 0.9 | 1.1 | $9 | $0 | 250 | +13 | 30% | 9% | 74% | 3.95 | 31 | 1 | 18/3 | — | — | — | — | .727 | .721 | .737 | .741 | .710 |

## John Danks
**200 IP | $13 | 260 pts**

SP-32 | Owned: 100% | LH

Surface stats aside, Danks *is* getting better, albeit in subtle ways. Under Mark Buehrle's tutelage, Danks suppressed the opponents' running game (only 6 SB allowed, down from 18 SB in 2009). That is an area that had been one of his weaknesses. Also, his stamina improved, allowing for a career best in IP. (RM)

| Forecast | | | | | | | | | | | |
|---|---|---|---|---|---|---|---|---|---|---|---|
| Player | Age | IP | W | Sv | K | ERA | WHIP | K/9 | BB/9 | $2L | Pts |
| Danks J | 25 | 200 | 13 | 0 | 150 | 4.15 | 1.29 | 6.7 | 3.2 | $13 | 260 |
| **Mini-Browser** | Age | IP | W | Sv | K | ERA | WHIP | K/9 | BB/9 | $2L | Pts |
| Gallardo Y | 25 | 200 | 15 | 0 | 204 | 3.92 | 1.35 | 9.2 | 3.8 | $13 | 330 |
| Garcia J | 24 | 180 | 13 | 0 | 153 | 3.39 | 1.37 | 7.7 | 3.6 | $13 | 270 |
| Axford J | 28 | 60 | 5 | 40 | 72 | 3.93 | 1.54 | 10.8 | 5.3 | $13 | 310 |
| Jenks B | 30 | 60 | 2 | 38 | 55 | 4.02 | 1.28 | 8.2 | 2.9 | $13 | 260 |
| Perez C | 25 | 60 | 2 | 33 | 63 | 3.38 | 1.31 | 9.4 | 4.7 | $13 | 250 |

| Minors (2010) | | | | | | | | | Skills | | | |
|---|---|---|---|---|---|---|---|---|---|---|---|---|
| Level | Leag | W | L | Sv | IP | H | K | ERA | WHIP | K/9 | BB/9 | HR/9 | GB/F |
| A | — | — | — | — | — | — | — | — | — | — | — | — | — |
| AA | — | — | — | — | — | — | — | — | — | — | — | — | — |
| AAA | — | — | — | — | — | — | — | — | — | — | — | — | — |

| Thr | Competition at SP Player | GS | ERA | Supp | W-L |
|---|---|---|---|---|---|
| LH | Buehrle M | 33 | 4.28 | 4.8 | 13-13 |
| LH | ▶ Danks J | 32 | 3.72 | 4.5 | 15-11 |
| RH | Jackson E | 32 | 4.47 | 4.3 | 10-12 |
| RH | Floyd G | 31 | 4.08 | 3.8 | 10-13 |

Stats in 2010 as SP

Weekly Points
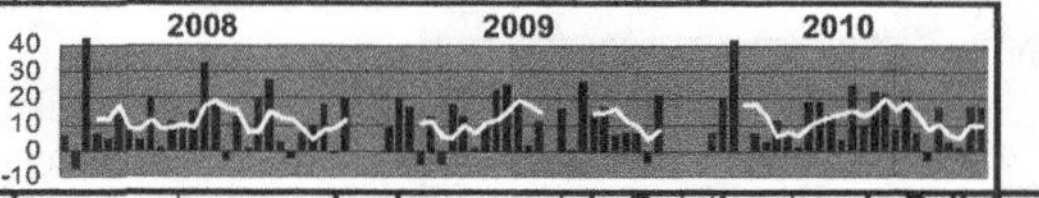
2008
2009
2010
40
30
20
10
0
-10

Ten-Year Trends
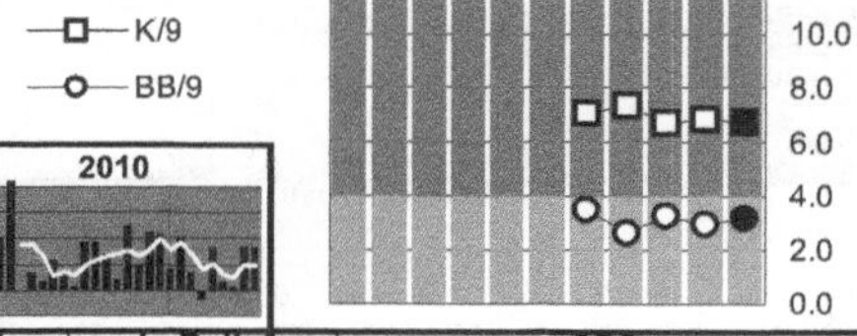
K/9
BB/9
12.0
10.0
8.0
6.0
4.0
2.0
0.0

| Majors | | | | | | | | | | Skills | | | | Value | | | | Luck | | | | In Rotation | | | In Relief | | | | OPS | | | | |
|---|---|---|---|---|---|---|---|---|---|---|---|---|---|---|---|---|---|---|---|---|---|---|---|---|---|---|---|---|---|---|---|---|---|
| Yr | Team | W | L | Sv | IP | H | K | ERA | WHIP | K/9 | BB/9 | HR/9 | GB/F | $1L | $2L | Pts | RAA | H% | HR/fb | S% | FIP | GS | CG | QS/DS | GR | Hld | Bln | Lead | OPS | 1st Hf | 2nd Hf | vs RH | vs LH |
| 07 | CHW | 6 | 13 | 0 | 139 | 160 | 109 | 5.50 | 1.54 | 7.1 | 3.5 | 1.8 | 0.8 | -$5 | -$19 | 120 | −23 | 32% | 14% | 69% | 5.52 | 26 | 0 | 8/5 | — | — | — | — | .868 | .829 | .937 | .862 | .890 |
| 08 | CHW | 12 | 9 | 0 | 195 | 182 | 159 | 3.32 | 1.23 | 7.3 | 2.6 | 0.7 | 1.2 | $16 | $8 | 280 | +22 | 30% | 7% | 75% | 3.55 | 33 | 0 | 19/3 | — | — | — | — | .674 | .628 | .738 | .671 | .681 |
| 09 | CHW | 13 | 11 | 0 | 200 | 184 | 149 | 3.77 | 1.28 | 6.7 | 3.3 | 1.3 | 1.1 | $14 | $5 | 270 | +10 | 27% | 11% | 76% | 4.72 | 32 | 1 | 20/4 | — | — | — | — | .726 | .682 | .772 | .715 | .756 |
| 10 | CHW | 15 | 11 | 0 | 213 | 189 | 162 | 3.72 | 1.22 | 6.8 | 3.0 | 0.8 | 1.2 | $16 | $5 | 310 | +12 | 28% | 7% | 71% | 3.86 | 32 | 1 | 21/4 | — | — | — | — | .657 | .604 | .713 | .640 | .694 |

## Kyle Davies
**140 IP | $-5 | 100 pts**

SP-32 | Owned: 1% | RH

Davies has always had the raw materials, and he has monster minor-league numbers, but he has never put it all together in MLB, and he could be relegated to a bullpen role in 2011. At this point, he's as likely to be saved by a huge run of good luck as by a surge in his skills. (BM)

| Forecast | | | | | | | | | | | |
|---|---|---|---|---|---|---|---|---|---|---|---|
| Player | Age | IP | W | Sv | K | ERA | WHIP | K/9 | BB/9 | $2L | Pts |
| Davies K | 27 | 140 | 6 | 0 | 95 | 5.36 | 1.59 | 6.1 | 4.3 | -$5 | 100 |
| **Mini-Browser** | Age | IP | W | Sv | K | ERA | WHIP | K/9 | BB/9 | $2L | Pts |
| Medders B | 31 | 60 | 2 | 0 | 43 | 5.07 | 1.61 | 6.5 | 4.2 | -$5 | 40 |
| Moehler B | 38 | 60 | 2 | 0 | 30 | 5.43 | 1.50 | 4.5 | 3.0 | -$5 | 30 |
| Vasquez E | 27 | 60 | 2 | 0 | 54 | 5.26 | 1.65 | 8.1 | 5.4 | -$5 | 50 |
| Wellemeyer T | 32 | 60 | 3 | 0 | 37 | 5.70 | 1.52 | 5.5 | 4.1 | -$5 | 40 |
| Morton C | 27 | 100 | 5 | 0 | 72 | 5.35 | 1.53 | 6.5 | 3.4 | -$5 | 80 |

| Minors (2010) | | | | | | | | | Skills | | | |
|---|---|---|---|---|---|---|---|---|---|---|---|---|
| Level | Leag | W | L | Sv | IP | H | K | ERA | WHIP | K/9 | BB/9 | HR/9 | GB/F |
| A | — | — | — | — | — | — | — | — | — | — | — | — | — |
| AA | — | — | — | — | — | — | — | — | — | — | — | — | — |
| AAA | — | — | — | — | — | — | — | — | — | — | — | — | — |

| Thr | Competition at SP Player | GS | ERA | Supp | W-L |
|---|---|---|---|---|---|
| RH | Greinke Z | 33 | 4.17 | 3.5 | 10-14 |
| RH | ▶ Davies K | 32 | 5.34 | 4.4 | 8-12 |
| LH | Chen B | 23 | 4.26 | 4.7 | 11-7 |
| RH | Bannister B | 23 | 6.32 | 3.7 | 7-12 |

Stats in 2010 as SP

Weekly Points
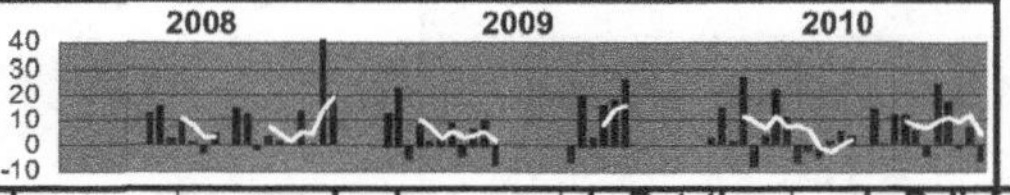
2008
2009
2010
40
30
20
10
0
-10

Ten-Year Trends
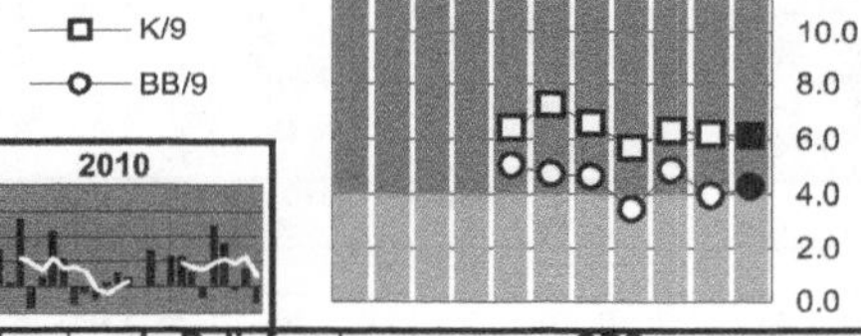
K/9
BB/9
12.0
10.0
8.0
6.0
4.0
2.0
0.0

| Majors | | | | | | | | | | Skills | | | | Value | | | | Luck | | | | In Rotation | | | In Relief | | | | OPS | | | | |
|---|---|---|---|---|---|---|---|---|---|---|---|---|---|---|---|---|---|---|---|---|---|---|---|---|---|---|---|---|---|---|---|---|---|
| Yr | Team | W | L | Sv | IP | H | K | ERA | WHIP | K/9 | BB/9 | HR/9 | GB/F | $1L | $2L | Pts | RAA | H% | HR/fb | S% | FIP | GS | CG | QS/DS | GR | Hld | Bln | Lead | OPS | 1st Hf | 2nd Hf | vs RH | vs LH |
| 07 | 2TM | 7 | 15 | 0 | 136 | 155 | 99 | 6.09 | 1.65 | 6.6 | 4.6 | 1.5 | 1.0 | -$12 | -$25 | 100 | −35 | 32% | 12% | 66% | 5.44 | 28 | 0 | 7/10 | — | — | — | — | .863 | .801 | .961 | .855 | .871 |
| 08 | KC | 9 | 7 | 0 | 113 | 121 | 71 | 4.06 | 1.45 | 5.7 | 3.4 | 0.8 | 1.0 | $2 | -$4 | 140 | −1 | 31% | 7% | 73% | 4.34 | 21 | 0 | 8/4 | — | — | — | — | .762 | .838 | .701 | .783 | .740 |
| 09 | KC | 8 | 9 | 0 | 123 | 122 | 86 | 5.27 | 1.53 | 6.3 | 4.8 | 1.3 | 1.0 | $0 | -$7 | 120 | −15 | 29% | 12% | 68% | 5.41 | 22 | 1 | 9/6 | — | — | — | — | .782 | .811 | .729 | .825 | .724 |
| 10 | KC | 8 | 12 | 0 | 183 | 206 | 126 | 5.34 | 1.56 | 6.2 | 3.9 | 1.0 | 1.0 | -$6 | -$32 | 140 | −23 | 32% | 8% | 67% | 4.65 | 32 | 1 | 14/5 | — | — | — | — | .793 | .774 | .812 | .745 | .836 |

## Doug Davis
**180 IP | $-4 | 170 pts**

SP-8 | Owned: 1% | LH

Brought in for his durability, Davis instead hit the DL for most of 2010, and then he underwent elbow surgery. He should be set for 2011, but he will have to find a club willing to gamble on him, now that MIL declined his option. Such a club may be hard to find, with the shine off his lone marketable quality. (MS)

| Forecast | | | | | | | | | | | |
|---|---|---|---|---|---|---|---|---|---|---|---|
| Player | Age | IP | W | Sv | K | ERA | WHIP | K/9 | BB/9 | $2L | Pts |
| Davis D | 35 | 180 | 10 | 0 | 126 | 5.01 | 1.53 | 6.3 | 4.4 | -$4 | 170 |
| **Mini-Browser** | Age | IP | W | Sv | K | ERA | WHIP | K/9 | BB/9 | $2L | Pts |
| Lohse K | 32 | 120 | 7 | 0 | 68 | 5.20 | 1.45 | 5.1 | 2.7 | -$4 | 100 |
| Galarraga A | 29 | 140 | 5 | 0 | 85 | 5.30 | 1.50 | 5.4 | 3.8 | -$4 | 90 |
| Arrieta J | 25 | 140 | 7 | 0 | 113 | 5.12 | 1.65 | 7.3 | 4.4 | -$4 | 130 |
| Wright W | 26 | 40 | 1 | 0 | 38 | 5.37 | 1.57 | 8.6 | 4.6 | -$4 | 30 |
| Proctor S | 34 | 60 | 2 | 0 | 51 | 5.24 | 1.52 | 7.7 | 4.5 | -$4 | 50 |

| Minors (2010) | | | | | | | | | Skills | | | |
|---|---|---|---|---|---|---|---|---|---|---|---|---|
| Level | Leag | W | L | Sv | IP | H | K | ERA | WHIP | K/9 | BB/9 | HR/9 | GB/F |
| A | MID | 1 | 0 | 0 | 7 | 6 | 4 | 1.29 | 1.29 | 5.1 | 3.9 | 0.0 | — |
| AA | — | — | — | — | — | — | — | — | — | — | — | — | — |
| AAA | PCL | 1 | 0 | 0 | 8 | 5 | 12 | 1.13 | 0.88 | 13.5 | 2.3 | 0.0 | — |

| Thr | Competition at SP Player | GS | ERA | Supp | W-L |
|---|---|---|---|---|---|
| LH | Wolf R | 34 | 4.17 | 5.3 | 13-12 |
| RH | Gallardo Y | 31 | 3.84 | 5.3 | 14-7 |
| RH | Bush D | 31 | 4.55 | 4.0 | 8-13 |
| LH | Narveson C | 28 | 4.85 | 4.3 | 11-9 |

Stats in 2010 as SP

Weekly Points
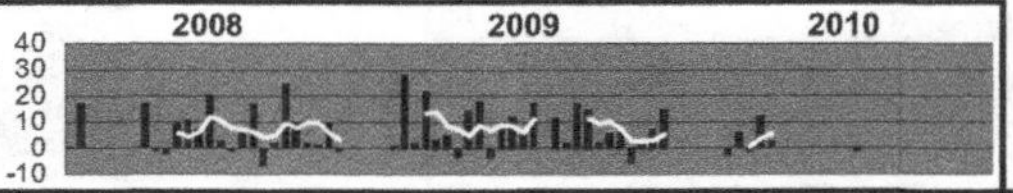
2008
2009
2010
40
30
20
10
0
-10

Ten-Year Trends
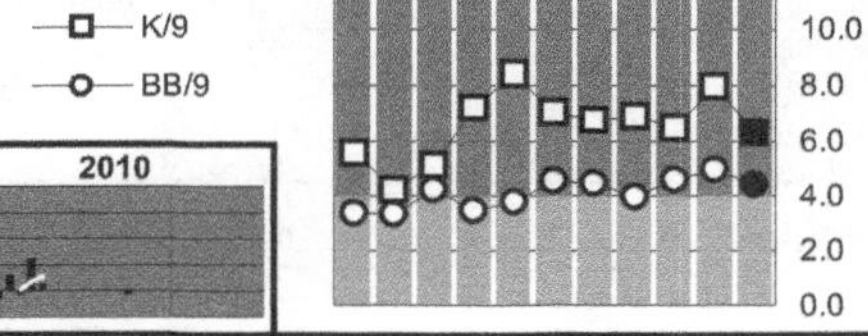
K/9
BB/9
12.0
10.0
8.0
6.0
4.0
2.0
0.0

| Majors | | | | | | | | | | Skills | | | | Value | | | | Luck | | | | In Rotation | | | In Relief | | | | OPS | | | | |
|---|---|---|---|---|---|---|---|---|---|---|---|---|---|---|---|---|---|---|---|---|---|---|---|---|---|---|---|---|---|---|---|---|---|
| Yr | Team | W | L | Sv | IP | H | K | ERA | WHIP | K/9 | BB/9 | HR/9 | GB/F | $1L | $2L | Pts | RAA | H% | HR/fb | S% | FIP | GS | CG | QS/DS | GR | Hld | Bln | Lead | OPS | 1st Hf | 2nd Hf | vs RH | vs LH |
| 07 | ARI | 13 | 12 | 0 | 192 | 211 | 144 | 4.25 | 1.59 | 6.7 | 4.4 | 1.0 | 1.4 | $1 | -$14 | 220 | −5 | 33% | 10% | 75% | 4.60 | 33 | 0 | 19/5 | — | — | — | — | .794 | .821 | .759 | .804 | .759 |
| 08 | ARI | 6 | 8 | 0 | 146 | 160 | 112 | 4.32 | 1.53 | 6.9 | 3.9 | 0.8 | 1.5 | -$2 | -$10 | 140 | −4 | 33% | 9% | 73% | 4.14 | 26 | 0 | 14/5 | — | — | — | — | .775 | .751 | .797 | .762 | .816 |
| 09 | ARI | 9 | 14 | 0 | 203 | 203 | 146 | 4.12 | 1.50 | 6.5 | 4.6 | 1.1 | 1.2 | $2 | -$4 | 190 | −1 | 31% | 12% | 76% | 4.88 | 34 | 0 | 22/6 | — | — | — | — | .779 | .731 | .842 | .767 | .824 |
| 10 | MIL | 1 | 4 | 0 | 38 | 55 | 34 | 7.51 | 1.98 | 8.0 | 4.9 | 1.4 | 1.4 | -$12 | -$24 | 10 | −17 | 40% | 14% | 63% | 5.10 | 8 | 0 | 1/4 | — | — | — | — | .915 | .915 | — | .972 | .699 |

## Wade Davis
**170 IP | $5 | 220 pts**

SP-29 | Owned: 13% | RH

Closing his rookie season with a great run (a 6-1 record and 3.28 ERA after the Break), Davis solidified a spot in Tampa's rotation in 2011. He could slot anywhere from the #3 to #5 SP, but he has the potential to pitch like a #2 or even a #1. If his arm is sound, he could log close to 200 innings. (RZ)

| Forecast | | | | | | | | | | | |
|---|---|---|---|---|---|---|---|---|---|---|---|
| Player | Age | IP | W | Sv | K | ERA | WHIP | K/9 | BB/9 | $2L | Pts |
| Davis W | 25 | 170 | 11 | 0 | 141 | 4.44 | 1.46 | 7.5 | 3.8 | $5 | 220 |
| **Mini-Browser** | Age | IP | W | Sv | K | ERA | WHIP | K/9 | BB/9 | $2L | Pts |
| Pettitte A | 38 | 140 | 10 | 0 | 97 | 4.31 | 1.37 | 6.2 | 3.3 | $6 | 170 |
| Breslow C | 30 | 75 | 4 | 2 | 65 | 3.61 | 1.24 | 7.7 | 3.9 | $6 | 110 |
| LeBlanc W | 26 | 180 | 10 | 0 | 148 | 4.36 | 1.36 | 7.4 | 3.1 | $5 | 210 |
| Cecil B | 24 | 160 | 11 | 0 | 116 | 4.58 | 1.39 | 6.5 | 3.3 | $5 | 200 |
| Rhodes A | 41 | 60 | 4 | 0 | 55 | 2.93 | 1.20 | 8.2 | 3.5 | $5 | 100 |

| Minors (2010) | | | | | | | | | Skills | | | |
|---|---|---|---|---|---|---|---|---|---|---|---|---|
| Level | Leag | W | L | Sv | IP | H | K | ERA | WHIP | K/9 | BB/9 | HR/9 | GB/F |
| A | — | — | — | — | — | — | — | — | — | — | — | — | — |
| AA | — | — | — | — | — | — | — | — | — | — | — | — | — |
| AAA | — | — | — | — | — | — | — | — | — | — | — | — | — |

| Thr | Competition at SP Player | GS | ERA | Supp | W-L |
|---|---|---|---|---|---|
| RH | Shields J | 33 | 5.20 | 4.5 | 12-15 |
| RH | Garza M | 32 | 3.93 | 5.2 | 15-10 |
| LH | Price D | 31 | 2.73 | 5.3 | 19-6 |
| RH | ▶ Davis W | 29 | 4.07 | 4.9 | 12-10 |

Stats in 2010 as SP

Weekly Points
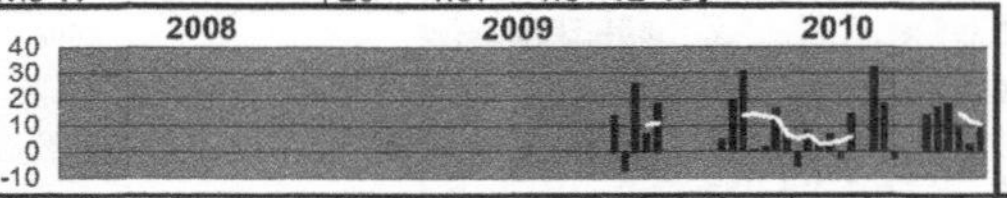
2008
2009
2010
40
30
20
10
0
-10

Ten-Year Trends
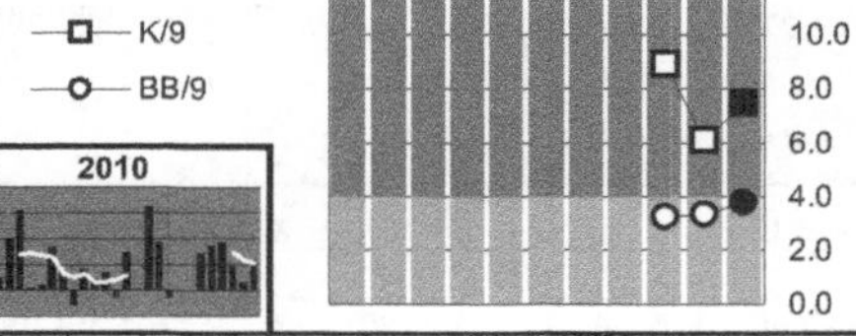
K/9
BB/9
12.0
10.0
8.0
6.0
4.0
2.0
0.0

| Majors | | | | | | | | | | Skills | | | | Value | | | | Luck | | | | In Rotation | | | In Relief | | | | OPS | | | | |
|---|---|---|---|---|---|---|---|---|---|---|---|---|---|---|---|---|---|---|---|---|---|---|---|---|---|---|---|---|---|---|---|---|---|
| Yr | Team | W | L | Sv | IP | H | K | ERA | WHIP | K/9 | BB/9 | HR/9 | GB/F | $1L | $2L | Pts | RAA | H% | HR/fb | S% | FIP | GS | CG | QS/DS | GR | Hld | Bln | Lead | OPS | 1st Hf | 2nd Hf | vs RH | vs LH |
| 07 | — | — | — | — | — | — | — | — | — | — | — | — | — | — | — | — | — | — | — | — | — | — | — | — | — | — | — | — | — | — | — | — | — |
| 08 | — | — | — | — | — | — | — | — | — | — | — | — | — | — | — | — | — | — | — | — | — | — | — | — | — | — | — | — | — | — | — | — | — |
| 09 | TB | 2 | 2 | 0 | 36 | 33 | 36 | 3.72 | 1.27 | 8.9 | 3.2 | 0.5 | 1.1 | $1 | -$1 | 50 | −1 | 32% | 6% | 70% | 3.11 | 6 | 1 | 3/1 | — | — | — | — | .640 | — | .640 | .655 | .630 |
| 10 | TB | 12 | 10 | 0 | 168 | 165 | 113 | 4.07 | 1.35 | 6.1 | 3.3 | 1.3 | 0.9 | $7 | -$8 | 210 | +6 | 28% | 10% | 74% | 4.92 | 29 | 0 | 15/2 | — | — | — | — | .756 | .808 | .689 | .732 | .776 |

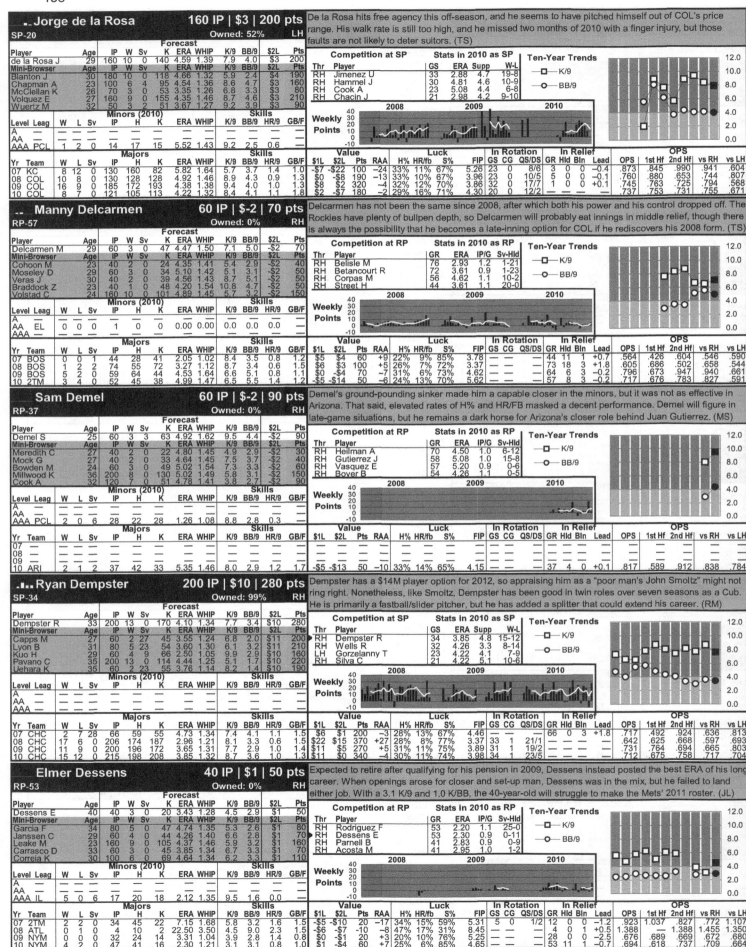

## Jorge de la Rosa — 160 IP | $3 | 200 pts

**SP-20** | Owned: 52% | LH

De la Rosa hits free agency this off-season, and he seems to have pitched himself out of COL's price range. His walk rate is still too high, and he missed two months of 2010 with a finger injury, but those faults are not likely to deter suitors. (TS)

### Forecast

| Player | Age | IP | W | Sv | K | ERA | WHIP | K/9 | BB/9 | $2L | Pts |
|---|---|---|---|---|---|---|---|---|---|---|---|
| de la Rosa J | 29 | 160 | 10 | 0 | 140 | 4.59 | 1.39 | 7.9 | 4.0 | $3 | 200 |
| Mini-Browser | Age | IP | W | Sv | K | ERA | WHIP | K/9 | BB/9 | $2L | Pts |
| Blanton J | 30 | 180 | 10 | 0 | 118 | 4.66 | 1.32 | 5.9 | 2.4 | $4 | 190 |
| Chapman A | 23 | 100 | 6 | 4 | 95 | 4.54 | 1.36 | 8.6 | 4.7 | $3 | 160 |
| McClellan K | 26 | 70 | 3 | 0 | 53 | 3.35 | 1.26 | 6.8 | 3.3 | $3 | 80 |
| Volquez E | 27 | 160 | 9 | 0 | 155 | 4.35 | 1.46 | 8.7 | 4.6 | $3 | 210 |
| Wuertz M | 32 | 50 | 3 | 2 | 51 | 3.67 | 1.27 | 9.2 | 3.9 | $3 | 90 |

### Minors (2010) / Skills

| Level | Leag | W | L | Sv | IP | H | K | ERA | WHIP | K/9 | BB/9 | HR/9 | GB/F |
|---|---|---|---|---|---|---|---|---|---|---|---|---|---|
| A | — | — | — | — | — | — | — | — | — | — | — | — | — |
| AA | — | — | — | — | — | — | — | — | — | — | — | — | — |
| AAA | PCL | 1 | 2 | 0 | 14 | 17 | 15 | 5.52 | 1.43 | 9.2 | 2.5 | 0.6 | — |

### Majors / Skills / Value / Luck / In Rotation / In Relief / OPS

| Yr | Team | W | L | Sv | IP | K | ERA | WHIP | K/9 | BB/9 | HR/9 | GB/F | $1L | $2L | Pts | RAA | H% | HR/fb | S% | FIP | GS | CG | QS/DS | GR | Hld | Bln | Lead | OPS | 1st Hf | 2nd Hf | vs RH | vs LH |
|---|---|---|---|---|---|---|---|---|---|---|---|---|---|---|---|---|---|---|---|---|---|---|---|---|---|---|---|---|---|---|---|---|
| 07 | KC | 8 | 12 | 0 | 130 | 160 | 82 | 5.82 | 1.64 | 5.7 | 3.7 | 1.4 | 1.0 | -$7 | -$22 | 100 | -24 | 33% | 11% | 67% | 5.26 | 23 | 0 | 8/6 | 3 | 0 | | -0.4 | .873 | .845 | .990 | .941 | .604 |
| 08 | COL | 10 | 8 | 0 | 130 | 128 | 128 | 4.92 | 1.46 | 8.9 | 4.3 | 0.9 | 1.3 | $0 | -$8 | 190 | -13 | 33% | 10% | 67% | 3.96 | 23 | 0 | 10/5 | 5 | 0 | 0 | -0.1 | .760 | .880 | .653 | .744 | .807 |
| 09 | COL | 16 | 9 | 0 | 185 | 172 | 193 | 4.38 | 1.38 | 9.4 | 4.0 | 1.1 | 1.3 | $8 | $2 | 320 | -4 | 32% | 12% | 70% | 3.86 | 32 | 0 | 17/7 | 1 | 0 | 0 | +0.1 | .745 | .763 | .725 | .794 | .568 |
| 10 | COL | 8 | 7 | 0 | 121 | 105 | 113 | 4.22 | 1.32 | 8.4 | 4.1 | 1.0 | 1.8 | $2 | -$7 | 180 | -2 | 29% | 16% | 71% | 4.43 | 20 | 0 | 12/2 | | | | | .737 | .753 | .731 | .755 | .671 |

## Manny Delcarmen — 60 IP | $-2 | 70 pts

**RP-57** | Owned: 0% | RH

Delcarmen has not been the same since 2008, after which both his power and his control dropped off. The Rockies have plenty of bullpen depth, so Delcarmen will probably eat innings in middle relief, though there is always the possibility that he becomes a late-inning option for COL if he rediscovers his 2008 form. (TS)

### Forecast

| Player | Age | IP | W | Sv | K | ERA | WHIP | K/9 | BB/9 | $2L | Pts |
|---|---|---|---|---|---|---|---|---|---|---|---|
| Delcarmen M | 29 | 60 | 3 | 0 | 47 | 4.47 | 1.50 | 7.1 | 5.0 | -$2 | 70 |
| Mini-Browser | Age | IP | W | Sv | K | ERA | WHIP | K/9 | BB/9 | $2L | Pts |
| Cohoon M | 23 | 40 | 2 | 0 | 24 | 4.35 | 1.41 | 5.4 | 2.9 | -$2 | 40 |
| Moseley D | 29 | 60 | 3 | 0 | 34 | 5.10 | 1.42 | 5.1 | 3.1 | -$2 | 50 |
| Veras J | 30 | 40 | 2 | 0 | 39 | 4.56 | 1.43 | 8.7 | 5.1 | -$2 | 50 |
| Braddock Z | 23 | 40 | 1 | 0 | 48 | 4.20 | 1.54 | 10.8 | 4.7 | -$2 | 50 |
| Volstad C | 24 | 160 | 10 | 0 | 101 | 4.89 | 1.45 | 5.7 | 3.2 | -$2 | 150 |

### Minors (2010) / Skills

| Level | Leag | W | L | Sv | IP | H | K | ERA | WHIP | K/9 | BB/9 | HR/9 | GB/F |
|---|---|---|---|---|---|---|---|---|---|---|---|---|---|
| A | — | — | — | — | — | — | — | — | — | — | — | — | — |
| AA | EL | 0 | 0 | 0 | 1 | 0 | 0 | 0.00 | 0.00 | 0.0 | 0.0 | 0.0 | — |
| AAA | — | — | — | — | — | — | — | — | — | — | — | — | — |

### Majors / Skills / Value / Luck / In Rotation / In Relief / OPS

| Yr | Team | W | L | Sv | IP | H | K | ERA | WHIP | K/9 | BB/9 | HR/9 | GB/F | $1L | $2L | Pts | RAA | H% | HR/fb | S% | FIP | GS | CG | QS/DS | GR | Hld | Bln | Lead | OPS | 1st Hf | 2nd Hf | vs RH | vs LH |
|---|---|---|---|---|---|---|---|---|---|---|---|---|---|---|---|---|---|---|---|---|---|---|---|---|---|---|---|---|---|---|---|---|---|
| 07 | BOS | 0 | 0 | 1 | 44 | 28 | 41 | 2.05 | 1.02 | 8.4 | 3.5 | 0.8 | 1.2 | $5 | $4 | 60 | +9 | 22% | 9% | 85% | 3.78 | — | — | — | 44 | 11 | 1 | +0.7 | .564 | .426 | .604 | .546 | .590 |
| 08 | BOS | 1 | 2 | 2 | 74 | 55 | 72 | 3.27 | 1.12 | 8.7 | 3.4 | 0.6 | 1.5 | $6 | $3 | 100 | +5 | 26% | 7% | 72% | 3.37 | — | — | — | 73 | 18 | 3 | +1.8 | .605 | .686 | .502 | .658 | .544 |
| 09 | BOS | 5 | 2 | 0 | 59 | 64 | 44 | 4.53 | 1.64 | 6.6 | 5.1 | 0.8 | 1.1 | $0 | -$4 | 50 | -7 | 31% | 6% | 73% | 4.62 | — | — | — | 64 | 6 | 3 | -0.2 | .796 | .673 | .947 | .940 | .661 |
| 10 | 2TM | 3 | 4 | 0 | 52 | 45 | 38 | 4.99 | 1.47 | 6.5 | 5.5 | 1.4 | 1.2 | -$5 | -$14 | 40 | -6 | 24% | 13% | 70% | 5.62 | — | — | — | 57 | 8 | 3 | -0.2 | .717 | .676 | .783 | .827 | .591 |

## Sam Demel — 60 IP | $-2 | 90 pts

**RP-37** | Owned: 0% | RH

Demel's ground-pounding sinker made him a capable closer in the minors, but it was not as effective in Arizona. That said, elevated rates of H% and HR/FB masked a decent performance. Demel will figure in late-game situations, but he remains a dark horse for Arizona's closer role behind Juan Gutierrez. (MS)

### Forecast

| Player | Age | IP | W | Sv | K | ERA | WHIP | K/9 | BB/9 | $2L | Pts |
|---|---|---|---|---|---|---|---|---|---|---|---|
| Demel S | 25 | 60 | 3 | 3 | 63 | 4.92 | 1.62 | 9.5 | 4.4 | -$2 | 90 |
| Mini-Browser | Age | IP | W | Sv | K | ERA | WHIP | K/9 | BB/9 | $2L | Pts |
| Meredith C | 27 | 40 | 2 | 0 | 22 | 4.80 | 1.45 | 4.9 | 2.9 | -$2 | 30 |
| Mock G | 27 | 40 | 2 | 0 | 33 | 4.64 | 1.45 | 7.5 | 3.7 | -$2 | 40 |
| Bowden M | 24 | 60 | 3 | 0 | 49 | 5.02 | 1.54 | 7.3 | 3.3 | -$2 | 60 |
| Millwood K | 36 | 200 | 8 | 0 | 130 | 5.02 | 1.49 | 5.8 | 3.1 | -$2 | 150 |
| Cook A | 32 | 120 | 7 | 0 | 51 | 4.78 | 1.41 | 3.8 | 2.7 | -$2 | 90 |

### Minors (2010) / Skills

| Level | Leag | W | L | Sv | IP | H | K | ERA | WHIP | K/9 | BB/9 | HR/9 | GB/F |
|---|---|---|---|---|---|---|---|---|---|---|---|---|---|
| A | — | — | — | — | — | — | — | — | — | — | — | — | — |
| AA | — | — | — | — | — | — | — | — | — | — | — | — | — |
| AAA | PCL | 2 | 0 | 6 | 28 | 22 | 28 | 1.26 | 1.08 | 8.8 | 2.8 | 0.3 | — |

### Majors / Value / Luck / In Rotation / In Relief / OPS

| Yr | Team | W | L | Sv | IP | K | ERA | WHIP | K/9 | BB/9 | HR/9 | GB/F | $1L | $2L | Pts | RAA | H% | HR/fb | S% | FIP | GS | CG | QS/DS | GR | Hld | Bln | Lead | OPS | 1st Hf | 2nd Hf | vs RH | vs LH |
|---|---|---|---|---|---|---|---|---|---|---|---|---|---|---|---|---|---|---|---|---|---|---|---|---|---|---|---|---|---|---|---|---|
| 07 | — | — | | | | | | | | | | | | | | | | | | | | | | | | | | | | | | |
| 08 | — | — | | | | | | | | | | | | | | | | | | | | | | | | | | | | | | |
| 09 | — | — | | | | | | | | | | | | | | | | | | | | | | | | | | | | | | |
| 10 | ARI | 2 | 1 | 2 | 37 | 42 | 33 | 5.35 | 1.46 | 8.0 | 2.9 | 1.2 | 1.7 | -$5 | -$13 | 50 | -10 | 33% | 14% | 65% | 4.15 | — | — | — | 37 | 4 | 0 | +0.1 | .817 | .589 | .912 | .838 | .784 |

## Ryan Dempster — 200 IP | $10 | 280 pts

**SP-34** | Owned: 99% | RH

Dempster has a $14M player option for 2012, so appraising him as a "poor man's John Smoltz" might not ring right. Nonetheless, like Smoltz, Dempster has been good in twin roles over seven seasons as a Cub. He is primarily a fastball/slider pitcher, but he has added a splitter that could extend his career. (RM)

### Forecast

| Player | Age | IP | W | Sv | K | ERA | WHIP | K/9 | BB/9 | $2L | Pts |
|---|---|---|---|---|---|---|---|---|---|---|---|
| Dempster R | 33 | 200 | 13 | 0 | 170 | 4.10 | 1.34 | 7.7 | 3.4 | $10 | 280 |
| Mini-Browser | Age | IP | W | Sv | K | ERA | WHIP | K/9 | BB/9 | $2L | Pts |
| Capps M | 27 | 60 | 2 | 27 | 45 | 3.55 | 1.24 | 6.8 | 2.0 | $11 | 200 |
| Lyon B | 31 | 80 | 5 | 23 | 54 | 3.60 | 1.30 | 6.1 | 3.2 | $11 | 210 |
| Kuo H | 29 | 60 | 4 | 9 | 66 | 2.50 | 1.05 | 9.9 | 2.9 | $10 | 160 |
| Pavano C | 35 | 200 | 13 | 0 | 114 | 4.44 | 1.25 | 5.1 | 1.7 | $10 | 220 |
| Uehara K | 35 | 60 | 2 | 23 | 55 | 3.76 | 1.14 | 8.2 | 1.4 | $10 | 190 |

### Minors (2010) / Skills

| Level | Leag | W | L | Sv | IP | H | K | ERA | WHIP | K/9 | BB/9 | HR/9 | GB/F |
|---|---|---|---|---|---|---|---|---|---|---|---|---|---|
| A | — | — | — | — | — | — | — | — | — | — | — | — | — |
| AA | — | — | — | — | — | — | — | — | — | — | — | — | — |
| AAA | — | — | — | — | — | — | — | — | — | — | — | — | — |

### Majors / Skills / Value / Luck / In Rotation / In Relief / OPS

| Yr | Team | W | L | Sv | IP | K | ERA | WHIP | K/9 | BB/9 | HR/9 | GB/F | $1L | $2L | Pts | RAA | H% | HR/fb | S% | FIP | GS | CG | QS/DS | GR | Hld | Bln | Lead | OPS | 1st Hf | 2nd Hf | vs RH | vs LH |
|---|---|---|---|---|---|---|---|---|---|---|---|---|---|---|---|---|---|---|---|---|---|---|---|---|---|---|---|---|---|---|---|---|
| 07 | CHC | 2 | 7 | 28 | 66 | 59 | 55 | 4.73 | 1.34 | 7.4 | 4.1 | 1.1 | 1.5 | $6 | $1 | 200 | -3 | 28% | 13% | 67% | 4.46 | — | — | — | 66 | 0 | 3 | +1.8 | .717 | .492 | .924 | .636 | .813 |
| 08 | CHC | 17 | 6 | 0 | 206 | 174 | 187 | 2.96 | 1.21 | 8.1 | 3.3 | 0.6 | 1.5 | $22 | $15 | 370 | +27 | 28% | 8% | 77% | 3.37 | 33 | 1 | 21/1 | — | — | — | — | .642 | .625 | .668 | .597 | .693 |
| 09 | CHC | 11 | 9 | 0 | 200 | 196 | 172 | 3.65 | 1.31 | 7.7 | 2.9 | 1.0 | 1.4 | $11 | $5 | 270 | +5 | 31% | 11% | 75% | 3.89 | 31 | 1 | 19/2 | — | — | — | — | .731 | .764 | .694 | .665 | .803 |
| 10 | CHC | 15 | 12 | 0 | 215 | 198 | 208 | 3.85 | 1.32 | 8.7 | 3.5 | 1.0 | 1.3 | $11 | $5 | 340 | -4 | 30% | 11% | 74% | 3.98 | 34 | 1 | 23/5 | — | — | — | — | .712 | .675 | .758 | .717 | .704 |

## Elmer Dessens — 40 IP | $1 | 50 pts

**RP-53** | Owned: 0% | RH

Expected to retire after qualifying for his pension in 2009, Dessens instead posted the best ERA of his long career. When openings arose for closer and set-up man, Dessens was in the mix, but he failed to land either job. With a 3.1 K/9 and 1.0 K/BB, the 40-year-old will struggle to make the Mets' 2011 roster. (JL)

### Forecast

| Player | Age | IP | W | Sv | K | ERA | WHIP | K/9 | BB/9 | $2L | Pts |
|---|---|---|---|---|---|---|---|---|---|---|---|
| Dessens E | 40 | 40 | 3 | 0 | 20 | 3.43 | 1.28 | 4.5 | 2.9 | $1 | 50 |
| Mini-Browser | Age | IP | W | Sv | K | ERA | WHIP | K/9 | BB/9 | $2L | Pts |
| Garcia F | 34 | 80 | 5 | 0 | 47 | 4.74 | 1.35 | 5.3 | 2.6 | $1 | 80 |
| Janssen C | 29 | 60 | 4 | 0 | 44 | 4.26 | 1.40 | 6.6 | 2.8 | $1 | 70 |
| Leake M | 23 | 160 | 9 | 0 | 105 | 4.37 | 1.46 | 5.9 | 3.2 | $1 | 160 |
| Carrasco D | 33 | 60 | 3 | 0 | 45 | 3.85 | 1.34 | 6.7 | 3.3 | $1 | 70 |
| Correia K | 30 | 100 | 6 | 0 | 69 | 4.64 | 1.34 | 6.2 | 3.1 | $1 | 110 |

### Minors (2010) / Skills

| Level | Leag | W | L | Sv | IP | H | K | ERA | WHIP | K/9 | BB/9 | HR/9 | GB/F |
|---|---|---|---|---|---|---|---|---|---|---|---|---|---|
| A | — | — | — | — | — | — | — | — | — | — | — | — | — |
| AA | — | — | — | — | — | — | — | — | — | — | — | — | — |
| AAA | IL | 5 | 0 | 6 | 17 | 20 | 18 | 2.12 | 1.35 | 9.5 | 1.6 | 0.0 | — |

### Majors / Skills / Value / Luck / In Rotation / In Relief / OPS

| Yr | Team | W | L | Sv | IP | H | K | ERA | WHIP | K/9 | BB/9 | HR/9 | GB/F | $1L | $2L | Pts | RAA | H% | HR/fb | S% | FIP | GS | CG | QS/DS | GR | Hld | Bln | Lead | OPS | 1st Hf | 2nd Hf | vs RH | vs LH |
|---|---|---|---|---|---|---|---|---|---|---|---|---|---|---|---|---|---|---|---|---|---|---|---|---|---|---|---|---|---|---|---|---|
| 07 | 2TM | 2 | 2 | 0 | 34 | 45 | 22 | 7.15 | 1.68 | 5.8 | 3.2 | 1.6 | 1.5 | -$5 | -$10 | 20 | -17 | 34% | 15% | 59% | 5.31 | 5 | 0 | 1/2 | 4 | 0 | 1 | +0.5 | .923 | 1.037 | .772 | 1.107 |
| 08 | ATL | 0 | 1 | 0 | 4 | 10 | 2 | 22.50 | 3.50 | 4.5 | 9.0 | 2.3 | 1.5 | -$6 | -$7 | -10 | -8 | 47% | 17% | 31% | 8.45 | — | — | — | 4 | 0 | 1 | +0.5 | 1.388 | — | 1.388 | 1.455 | 1.350 |
| 09 | NYM | 1 | 0 | 0 | 32 | 24 | 14 | 3.31 | 1.04 | 3.9 | 2.0 | 1.4 | 0.8 | $0 | -$1 | 20 | +3 | 20% | 10% | 76% | 5.25 | — | — | — | 28 | 0 | 0 | -2.5 | .676 | .689 | .669 | .672 | .680 |
| 10 | NYM | 4 | 2 | 0 | 47 | 41 | 16 | 2.30 | 1.21 | 3.1 | 3.1 | 0.8 | 1.6 | $0 | -$4 | 60 | +7 | 25% | 6% | 85% | 4.65 | — | — | — | 53 | 11 | 6 | -0.7 | .694 | .618 | .737 | .709 | .664 |

## Ross Detwiler

**100 IP | $-3 | 100 pts**

SP-5, RP-3 | Owned: 0% | LH

Detwiler stands to gain from the unfortunate end to Stephen Strasburg's 2010 (and 2011) seasons. Ross struggled through a hip injury in 2010 as he tried to dig out from the heap of back-end starters. Strasburg's absence creates daylight for Detwiler, but he needs to find what he keeps forgetting from the minors. (PB)

**Forecast**

| Player | Age | IP | W | Sv | K | ERA | WHIP | K/9 | BB/9 | $2L | Pts |
|---|---|---|---|---|---|---|---|---|---|---|---|
| Detwiler R | 25 | 100 | 5 | 0 | 76 | 4.55 | 1.57 | 6.9 | 3.9 | -$3 | 100 |
| Mini-Browser | Age | IP | W | Sv | K | ERA | WHIP | K/9 | BB/9 | $2L | Pts |
| Sampson C | 32 | 40 | 1 | 0 | 20 | 4.81 | 1.39 | 4.4 | 2.3 | -$3 | 20 |
| Feldman S | 28 | 160 | 9 | 0 | 84 | 5.13 | 1.51 | 4.7 | 3.3 | -$3 | 120 |
| Smith C | 29 | 40 | 1 | 0 | 32 | 5.15 | 1.41 | 7.3 | 3.0 | -$3 | 30 |
| McGee J | 24 | 50 | 2 | 0 | 53 | 5.15 | 1.67 | 9.6 | 4.7 | -$3 | 60 |
| Mickolio K | 26 | 40 | 1 | 0 | 44 | 4.94 | 1.69 | 9.8 | 5.0 | -$3 | 40 |

**Minors (2010)** / **Skills**

| Level | Leag | W | L | Sv | IP | H | K | ERA | WHIP | K/9 | BB/9 | HR/9 | GB/F |
|---|---|---|---|---|---|---|---|---|---|---|---|---|---|
| A | CAR | 0 | 0 | 0 | 6 | 6 | 6 | 1.50 | 1.17 | 9.0 | 1.5 | 1.5 | — |
| AA | EL | 2 | 2 | 0 | 32 | 38 | 31 | 2.48 | 1.38 | 8.5 | 1.9 | 0.3 | — |
| AAA | IL | 1 | 0 | 0 | 5 | 5 | 2 | 1.80 | 1.20 | 3.6 | 1.8 | 0.0 | — |

**Competition at SP** / **Stats in 2010 as SP**

| Thr | Player | GS | ERA | Supp | W-L |
|---|---|---|---|---|---|
| RH | Hernandez L | 33 | 3.66 | 3.5 | 10-12 |
| LH | Lannan J | 25 | 4.65 | 4.5 | 8-8 |
| RH | Stammen C | 19 | 5.06 | 4.8 | 4-4 |
| RH | Atilano L | 16 | 5.15 | 4.5 | 6-7 |

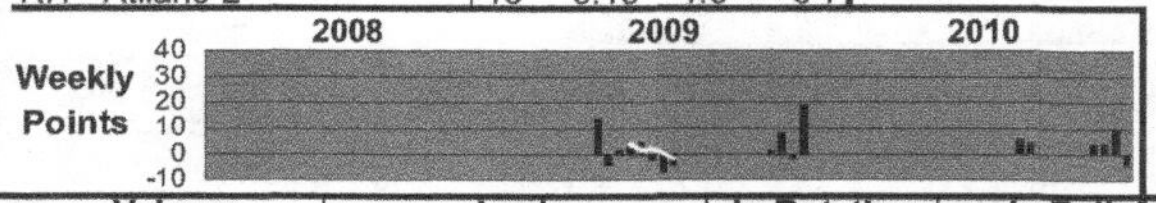


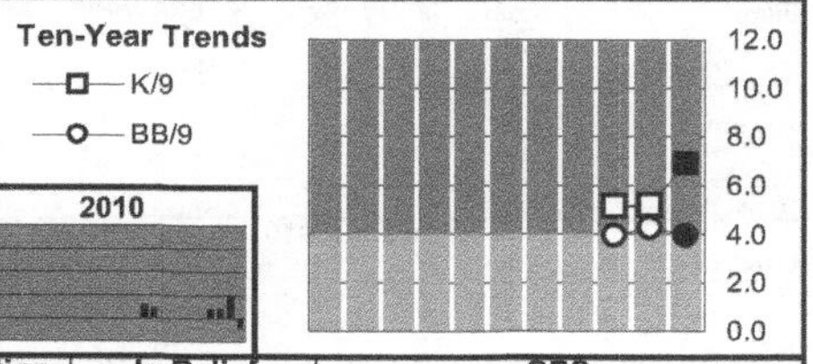


**Majors** / **Skills** / **Value** / **Luck** / **In Rotation** / **In Relief** / **OPS**

| Yr | Team | W | L | Sv | IP | H | K | ERA | WHIP | K/9 | BB/9 | HR/9 | GB/F | $1L | $2L | Pts | RAA | H% | HR/fb | S% | FIP | GS | CG | QS/DS | GR | Hld | Bln | Lead | OPS | 1st Hf | 2nd Hf | vs RH | vs LH |
|---|---|---|---|---|---|---|---|---|---|---|---|---|---|---|---|---|---|---|---|---|---|---|---|---|---|---|---|---|---|---|---|---|---|
| 07 | WAS | 0 | 0 | 0 | 1 | 0 | 1 | 0.00 | 0.00 | 9.0 | 0.0 | 0.0 | 2.0 | -$2 | -$2 | 0 | +0 | 0% | 0% | NA | 1.20 | — | — | — | 1 | 0 | 0 | −6.0 | .000 | — | .000 | .000 | .000 |
| 08 | — | — | — | — | — | — | — | — | — | — | — | — | — | — | — | — | — | — | — | — | — | — | — | — | — | — | — | — | — | — | — | — | — |
| 09 | WAS | 1 | 6 | 0 | 75 | 87 | 43 | 5.00 | 1.59 | 5.1 | 3.9 | 0.4 | 1.3 | -$5 | -$7 | 30 | −6 | 33% | 4% | 67% | 3.89 | 14 | 1 | 4/3 | 1 | 0 | 0 | −0.2 | .767 | .835 | .587 | .783 | .718 |
| 10 | WAS | 1 | 3 | 0 | 29 | 34 | 17 | 4.25 | 1.62 | 5.2 | 4.2 | 1.5 | 1.2 | -$6 | -$13 | 20 | −7 | 31% | 14% | 79% | 5.66 | 5 | 0 | 1/3 | 3 | 0 | 0 | −1.5 | .826 | — | .826 | .780 | 1.024 |

## Joey Devine

**45 IP | $4 | 90 pts**

No MLB games played in 2010 | Owned: 0% | RH

Devine was supposed to return to the A's in 2010 after TJ surgery in 2009, but it never happened, though he was throwing in simulated games at the end of 2010. His health will always be a question, but if he *is* healthy, Devine gives the A's an 8th-inning weapon and a good "Plan B" to Andrew Bailey in the 9th. (ML)

**Forecast**

| Player | Age | IP | W | Sv | K | ERA | WHIP | K/9 | BB/9 | $2L | Pts |
|---|---|---|---|---|---|---|---|---|---|---|---|
| Devine J | 27 | 45 | 3 | 2 | 51 | 2.87 | 1.25 | 10.2 | 3.8 | $4 | 90 |
| Mini-Browser | Age | IP | W | Sv | K | ERA | WHIP | K/9 | BB/9 | $2L | Pts |
| Germano J | 28 | 40 | 0 | 0 | 32 | 2.16 | 0.84 | 7.3 | 2.2 | $5 | 50 |
| Figueroa N | 36 | 100 | 7 | 0 | 79 | 3.86 | 1.32 | 7.1 | 3.0 | $5 | 140 |
| Matusz B | 24 | 180 | 10 | 0 | 156 | 4.54 | 1.44 | 7.8 | 3.3 | $5 | 210 |
| Takahashi H | 35 | 60 | 4 | 15 | 46 | 4.43 | 1.38 | 7.0 | 3.5 | $4 | 150 |
| Balfour G | 33 | 60 | 3 | 0 | 64 | 3.24 | 1.26 | 9.6 | 4.1 | $4 | 100 |

**Minors (2010)** / **Skills**

| Level | Leag | W | L | Sv | IP | H | K | ERA | WHIP | K/9 | BB/9 | HR/9 | GB/F |
|---|---|---|---|---|---|---|---|---|---|---|---|---|---|
| A | — | — | — | — | — | — | — | — | — | — | — | — | — |
| AA | — | — | — | — | — | — | — | — | — | — | — | — | — |
| AAA | — | — | — | — | — | — | — | — | — | — | — | — | — |

**Competition at RP** / **Stats in 2010 as RP**

| Thr | Player | GR | ERA | IP/G | Sv-Hld |
|---|---|---|---|---|---|
| RH | Ziegler B | 64 | 3.26 | 0.9 | 0-18 |
| RH | Wuertz M | 48 | 4.31 | 0.8 | 6-11 |
| RH | Bailey A | 47 | 1.47 | 1.0 | 25-0 |
| RH | Rodriguez H | 29 | 4.55 | 1.0 | 0-3 |

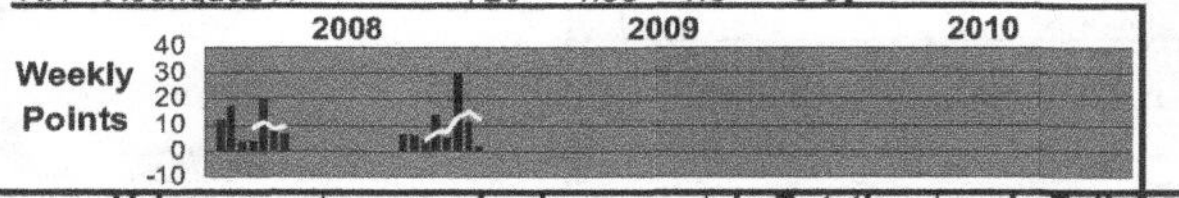


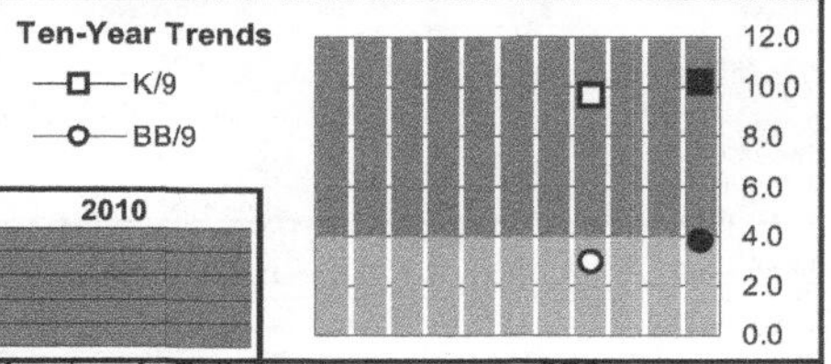


**Majors** / **Skills** / **Value** / **Luck** / **In Rotation** / **In Relief** / **OPS**

| Yr | Team | W | L | Sv | IP | H | K | ERA | WHIP | K/9 | BB/9 | HR/9 | GB/F | $1L | $2L | Pts | RAA | H% | HR/fb | S% | FIP | GS | CG | QS/DS | GR | Hld | Bln | Lead | OPS | 1st Hf | 2nd Hf | vs RH | vs LH |
|---|---|---|---|---|---|---|---|---|---|---|---|---|---|---|---|---|---|---|---|---|---|---|---|---|---|---|---|---|---|---|---|---|---|
| 07 | ATL | 1 | 0 | 0 | 8 | 7 | 7 | 1.08 | 1.80 | 7.6 | 8.6 | 0.0 | 1.6 | -$1 | -$2 | 20 | +3 | 30% | 0% | 93% | 4.40 | — | — | — | 10 | 0 | 0 | −3.0 | .636 | .500 | .671 | .571 | .762 |
| 08 | OAK | 6 | 1 | 1 | 45 | 23 | 49 | 0.59 | 0.83 | 9.7 | 3.0 | 0.0 | 0.9 | $12 | $10 | 140 | +14 | 22% | 0% | 92% | 2.14 | — | — | — | 42 | 11 | 1 | −0.1 | .395 | .496 | .282 | .312 | .515 |
| 09 | — | — | — | — | — | — | — | — | — | — | — | — | — | — | — | — | — | — | — | — | — | — | — | — | — | — | — | — | — | — | — | — | — |
| 10 | — | — | — | — | — | — | — | — | — | — | — | — | — | — | — | — | — | — | — | — | — | — | — | — | — | — | — | — | — | — | — | — | — |

## Thomas Diamond

**60 IP | $-4 | 50 pts**

RP-13, SP-3 | Owned: 0% | RH

Don't be deceived – Diamond is no longer the blazing fastballer that he used to be. However, he has learned how to work with what he has, which is why his strikeout totals appear as strong as ever. His workload more than doubled from 2009, but his arm was rested by relief work in Chicago. (RM)

**Forecast**

| Player | Age | IP | W | Sv | K | ERA | WHIP | K/9 | BB/9 | $2L | Pts |
|---|---|---|---|---|---|---|---|---|---|---|---|
| Diamond T | 27 | 60 | 2 | 0 | 44 | 4.93 | 1.57 | 6.7 | 5.1 | -$4 | 50 |
| Mini-Browser | Age | IP | W | Sv | K | ERA | WHIP | K/9 | BB/9 | $2L | Pts |
| Harrison M | 25 | 80 | 4 | 0 | 47 | 5.30 | 1.56 | 5.3 | 3.8 | -$4 | 50 |
| Karstens J | 28 | 80 | 3 | 0 | 45 | 5.09 | 1.44 | 5.1 | 2.6 | -$4 | 50 |
| Minor M | 23 | 150 | 7 | 0 | 158 | 5.62 | 1.52 | 9.5 | 2.2 | -$4 | 170 |
| Coello R | 26 | 20 | 1 | 0 | 17 | 6.53 | 1.73 | 7.8 | 5.3 | -$4 | 10 |
| Ledezma W | 30 | 40 | 2 | 0 | 36 | 5.28 | 1.59 | 8.1 | 4.3 | -$4 | 40 |

**Minors (2010)** / **Skills**

| Level | Leag | W | L | Sv | IP | H | K | ERA | WHIP | K/9 | BB/9 | HR/9 | GB/F |
|---|---|---|---|---|---|---|---|---|---|---|---|---|---|
| A | — | — | — | — | — | — | — | — | — | — | — | — | — |
| AA | — | — | — | — | — | — | — | — | — | — | — | — | — |
| AAA | PCL | 5 | 4 | 0 | 108 | 86 | 104 | 3.16 | 1.22 | 8.6 | 3.8 | 0.7 | — |

**Competition at RP** / **Stats in 2010 as RP**

| Thr | Player | GR | ERA | IP/G | Sv-Hld |
|---|---|---|---|---|---|
| RH | Marmol C | 77 | 2.55 | 1.0 | 38-0 |
| RH | Cashner A | 53 | 4.80 | 1.0 | 0-16 |
| RH | Berg J | 41 | 5.18 | 1.0 | 0-5 |
| RH | Howry B | 24 | 5.66 | 0.9 | 0-2 |

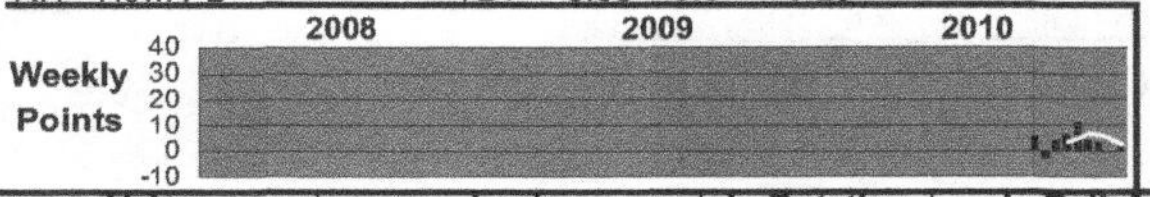


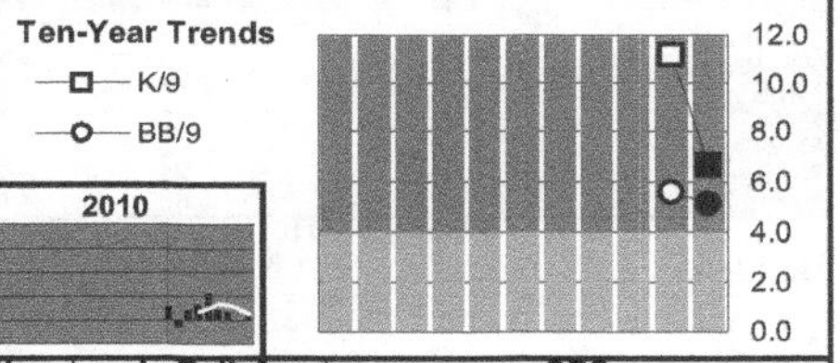


**Majors** / **Skills** / **Value** / **Luck** / **In Rotation** / **In Relief** / **OPS**

| Yr | Team | W | L | Sv | IP | H | K | ERA | WHIP | K/9 | BB/9 | HR/9 | GB/F | $1L | $2L | Pts | RAA | H% | HR/fb | S% | FIP | GS | CG | QS/DS | GR | Hld | Bln | Lead | OPS | 1st Hf | 2nd Hf | vs RH | vs LH |
|---|---|---|---|---|---|---|---|---|---|---|---|---|---|---|---|---|---|---|---|---|---|---|---|---|---|---|---|---|---|---|---|---|---|
| 07 | — | — | — | — | — | — | — | — | — | — | — | — | — | — | — | — | — | — | — | — | — | — | — | — | — | — | — | — | — | — | — | — | — |
| 08 | — | — | — | — | — | — | — | — | — | — | — | — | — | — | — | — | — | — | — | — | — | — | — | — | — | — | — | — | — | — | — | — | — |
| 09 | — | — | — | — | — | — | — | — | — | — | — | — | — | — | — | — | — | — | — | — | — | — | — | — | — | — | — | — | — | — | — | — | — |
| 10 | CHC | 1 | 3 | 0 | 29 | 33 | 36 | 6.83 | 1.76 | 11.2 | 5.6 | 1.6 | 0.6 | -$8 | -$17 | 30 | −10 | 38% | 14% | 63% | 4.82 | 3 | 0 | 1/1 | 13 | 0 | 0 | −0.3 | .875 | — | .875 | .945 | .754 |

## R.A. Dickey

**180 IP | $6 | 180 pts**

SP-26, RP-1 | Owned: 63% | RH

Entering 2010, Dickey had 22 Wins and a 5.43 ERA in seven seasons. And then, at age 35, he finished 7th in the NL with a 2.84 ERA in 174 IP. Dickey was great at home (1.99 ERA) and solid away (3.58 ERA). He is a knuckleballer, so his age is almost irrelevant, but his lack of prior success is very relevant indeed. (JL)

**Forecast**

| Player | Age | IP | W | Sv | K | ERA | WHIP | K/9 | BB/9 | $2L | Pts |
|---|---|---|---|---|---|---|---|---|---|---|---|
| Dickey R | 36 | 180 | 10 | 0 | 105 | 4.05 | 1.34 | 5.2 | 2.9 | $6 | 180 |
| Mini-Browser | Age | IP | W | Sv | K | ERA | WHIP | K/9 | BB/9 | $2L | Pts |
| Lowe D | 37 | 200 | 13 | 0 | 120 | 4.29 | 1.34 | 5.4 | 2.7 | $7 | 230 |
| Tejeda R | 29 | 60 | 3 | 25 | 57 | 4.35 | 1.55 | 8.6 | 5.4 | $7 | 200 |
| Pineda M | 22 | 120 | 7 | 0 | 97 | 3.98 | 1.33 | 7.3 | 3.1 | $7 | 160 |
| Hellickson J | 23 | 120 | 9 | 0 | 129 | 4.39 | 1.35 | 9.7 | 2.6 | $6 | 200 |
| Rodney F | 34 | 60 | 3 | 27 | 51 | 4.55 | 1.57 | 7.6 | 5.2 | $6 | 200 |

**Minors (2010)** / **Skills**

| Level | Leag | W | L | Sv | IP | H | K | ERA | WHIP | K/9 | BB/9 | HR/9 | GB/F |
|---|---|---|---|---|---|---|---|---|---|---|---|---|---|
| A | — | — | — | — | — | — | — | — | — | — | — | — | — |
| AA | — | — | — | — | — | — | — | — | — | — | — | — | — |
| AAA | IL | 4 | 2 | 0 | 60 | 55 | 37 | 2.23 | 1.04 | 5.5 | 1.2 | 0.4 | — |

**Competition at SP** / **Stats in 2010 as SP**

| Thr | Player | GS | ERA | Supp | W-L |
|---|---|---|---|---|---|
| RH | Pelfrey M | 33 | 3.68 | 3.7 | 15-9 |
| LH | Niese J | 30 | 4.20 | 5.1 | 9-10 |
| LH | Santana J | 29 | 2.98 | 3.0 | 11-9 |
| RH | Dickey R | 26 | 2.86 | 4.0 | 11-9 |

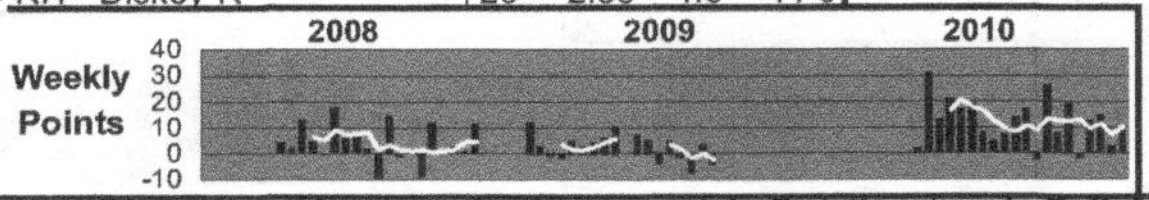


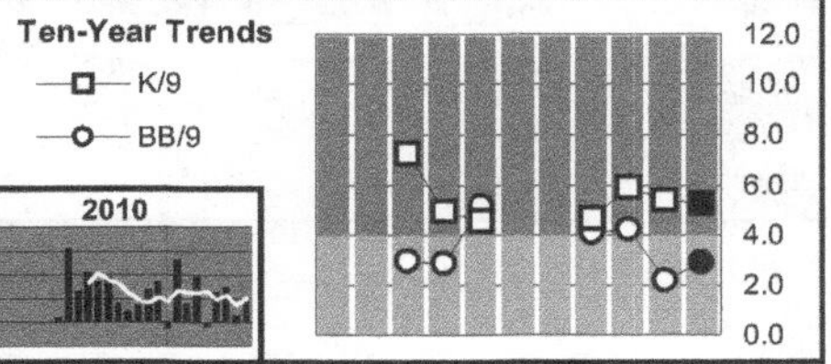


**Majors** / **Skills** / **Value** / **Luck** / **In Rotation** / **In Relief** / **OPS**

| Yr | Team | W | L | Sv | IP | H | K | ERA | WHIP | K/9 | BB/9 | HR/9 | GB/F | $1L | $2L | Pts | RAA | H% | HR/fb | S% | FIP | GS | CG | QS/DS | GR | Hld | Bln | Lead | OPS | 1st Hf | 2nd Hf | vs RH | vs LH |
|---|---|---|---|---|---|---|---|---|---|---|---|---|---|---|---|---|---|---|---|---|---|---|---|---|---|---|---|---|---|---|---|---|---|
| 07 | — | — | — | — | — | — | — | — | — | — | — | — | — | — | — | — | — | — | — | — | — | — | — | — | — | — | — | — | — | — | — | — | — |
| 08 | SEA | 5 | 8 | 0 | 112 | 124 | 58 | 5.21 | 1.56 | 4.6 | 4.1 | 1.2 | 1.3 | -$7 | -$13 | 70 | −10 | 30% | 11% | 69% | 5.37 | 14 | 0 | 6/5 | 18 | 0 | 0 | −2.5 | .805 | .717 | .906 | .801 | .809 |
| 09 | MIN | 1 | 1 | 0 | 64 | 74 | 42 | 4.62 | 1.62 | 5.9 | 4.2 | 1.1 | 1.3 | -$2 | -$5 | 30 | −2 | 32% | 11% | 74% | 5.01 | 1 | 0 | 0/0 | 34 | 1 | 0 | −2.4 | .826 | .756 | 1.165 | .891 | .747 |
| 10 | NYM | 11 | 9 | 0 | 174 | 165 | 104 | 2.84 | 1.19 | 5.4 | 2.2 | 0.7 | 2.0 | $14 | $10 | 230 | +24 | 29% | 8% | 78% | 3.70 | 26 | 2 | 19/2 | 1 | 1 | 0 | +0.5 | .660 | .664 | .657 | .700 | .605 |

## Octavio Dotel

**40 IP | $0 | 60 pts**

RP-68 | Owned: 43% | RH

New Rockie Dotel gave the Dodgers 18.2 mediocre innings in exchange for two good prospects, which made a trade that looked bad at the time seem even worse. Still, Dotel was decent with PIT, and he still records north of 10 K/9. He probably will not close in 2011, but he can be an effective set-up man. (TS)

**Forecast**

| Player | Age | IP | W | Sv | K | ERA | WHIP | K/9 | BB/9 | $2L | Pts |
|---|---|---|---|---|---|---|---|---|---|---|---|
| Dotel O | 37 | 40 | 2 | 0 | 49 | 3.96 | 1.33 | 10.9 | 4.4 | $0 | 60 |
| Mini-Browser | Age | IP | W | Sv | K | ERA | WHIP | K/9 | BB/9 | $2L | Pts |
| Rauch J | 32 | 40 | 2 | 0 | 30 | 4.01 | 1.31 | 6.7 | 2.6 | $0 | 50 |
| Bray B | 27 | 40 | 2 | 0 | 41 | 4.01 | 1.25 | 9.1 | 3.5 | $0 | 50 |
| Hoffman T | 43 | 40 | 2 | 4 | 30 | 4.46 | 1.30 | 6.8 | 2.9 | $0 | 60 |
| Farnsworth K | 34 | 60 | 2 | 0 | 57 | 4.25 | 1.35 | 8.5 | 3.4 | $0 | 70 |
| Kohn M | 24 | 40 | 3 | 0 | 45 | 3.51 | 1.63 | 10.1 | 5.8 | $0 | 70 |

**Minors (2010)** / **Skills**

| Level | Leag | W | L | Sv | IP | H | K | ERA | WHIP | K/9 | BB/9 | HR/9 | GB/F |
|---|---|---|---|---|---|---|---|---|---|---|---|---|---|
| A | — | — | — | — | — | — | — | — | — | — | — | — | — |
| AA | — | — | — | — | — | — | — | — | — | — | — | — | — |
| AAA | — | — | — | — | — | — | — | — | — | — | — | — | — |

**Competition at RP** / **Stats in 2010 as RP**

| Thr | Player | GR | ERA | IP/G | Sv-Hld |
|---|---|---|---|---|---|
| RH | Belisle M | 76 | 2.93 | 1.2 | 1-21 |
| RH | Betancourt R | 72 | 3.61 | 0.9 | 1-23 |
| RH | Corpas M | 56 | 4.62 | 1.1 | 10-2 |
| RH | Street H | 44 | 3.61 | 1.1 | 20-0 |

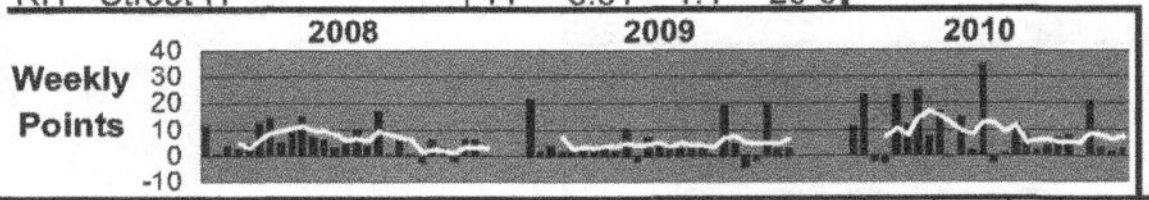


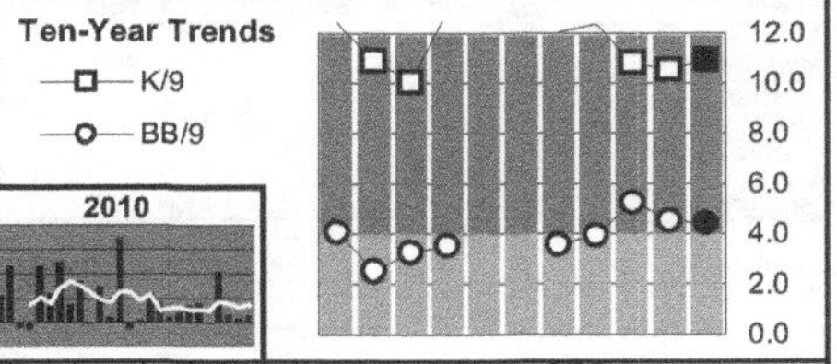


**Majors** / **Skills** / **Value** / **Luck** / **In Rotation** / **In Relief** / **OPS**

| Yr | Team | W | L | Sv | IP | H | K | ERA | WHIP | K/9 | BB/9 | HR/9 | GB/F | $1L | $2L | Pts | RAA | H% | HR/fb | S% | FIP | GS | CG | QS/DS | GR | Hld | Bln | Lead | OPS | 1st Hf | 2nd Hf | vs RH | vs LH |
|---|---|---|---|---|---|---|---|---|---|---|---|---|---|---|---|---|---|---|---|---|---|---|---|---|---|---|---|---|---|---|---|---|---|
| 07 | 2TM | 2 | 1 | 11 | 30 | 29 | 41 | 4.11 | 1.34 | 12.0 | 3.5 | 1.2 | 0.8 | $1 | $0 | 110 | −2 | 33% | 11% | 73% | 3.45 | — | — | — | 33 | 1 | 4 | +1.8 | .748 | .729 | .771 | .740 | .756 |
| 08 | CHW | 4 | 4 | 1 | 67 | 52 | 92 | 3.76 | 1.21 | 12.4 | 3.9 | 1.6 | 0.8 | $5 | $2 | 140 | −4 | 28% | 17% | 77% | 4.18 | — | — | — | 72 | 21 | 4 | +0.7 | .687 | .632 | .782 | .650 | .774 |
| 09 | CHW | 3 | 3 | 0 | 62 | 54 | 75 | 3.32 | 1.44 | 10.8 | 5.2 | 1.0 | 0.6 | $3 | $0 | 100 | +2 | 32% | 9% | 81% | 4.09 | — | — | — | 62 | 16 | 3 | +0.4 | .764 | .747 | .786 | .652 | 1.000 |
| 10 | 3TM | 3 | 4 | 22 | 64 | 52 | 75 | 4.08 | 1.31 | 10.5 | 4.5 | 1.3 | 0.6 | $5 | -$2 | 210 | −3 | 28% | 10% | 73% | 4.23 | — | — | — | 68 | 4 | 6 | +0.1 | .743 | .793 | .682 | .576 | .993 |

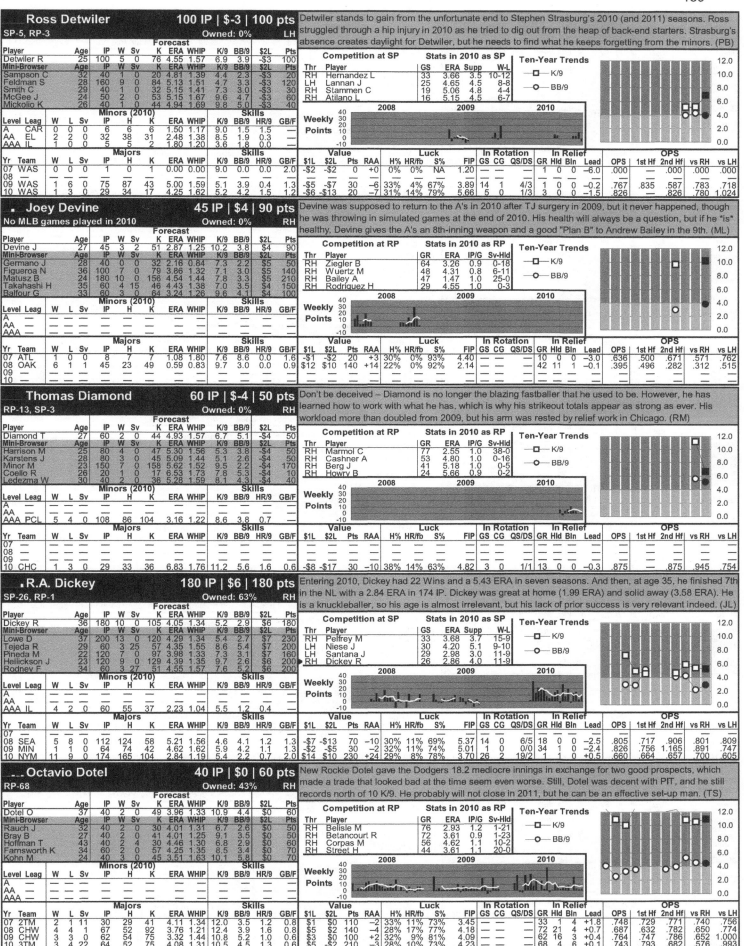

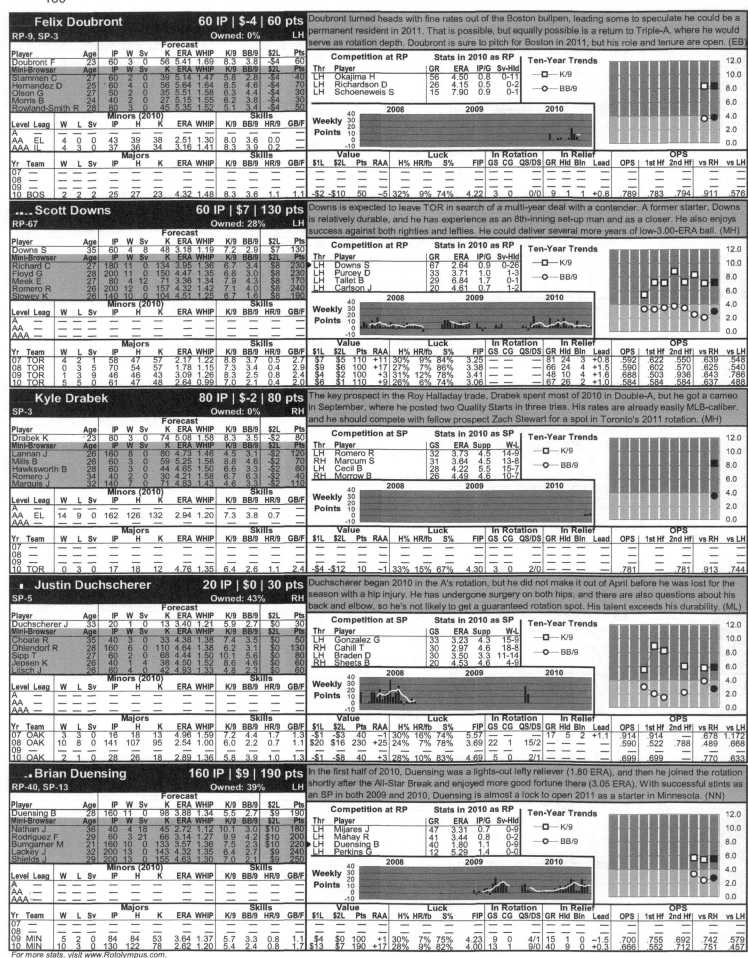

## Felix Doubront — 60 IP | $-4 | 60 pts
RP-9, SP-3 · Owned: 0% · LH

Doubront turned heads with fine rates out of the Boston bullpen, leading some to speculate he could be a permanent resident in 2011. That is possible, but equally possible is a return to Triple-A, where he would serve as rotation depth. Doubront is sure to pitch for Boston in 2011, but his role and tenure are open. (EB)

### Forecast
| Player | Age | IP | W | Sv | K | ERA | WHIP | K/9 | BB/9 | $2L | Pts |
|---|---|---|---|---|---|---|---|---|---|---|---|
| Doubront F | 23 | 60 | 3 | 0 | 56 | 5.41 | 1.69 | 8.3 | 3.8 | -$4 | 60 |

| Mini-Browser | Age | IP | W | Sv | K | ERA | WHIP | K/9 | BB/9 | $2L | Pts |
|---|---|---|---|---|---|---|---|---|---|---|---|
| Stammen C | 27 | 60 | 2 | 0 | 39 | 5.14 | 1.47 | 5.8 | 2.8 | -$4 | 40 |
| Hernandez D | 25 | 60 | 4 | 0 | 56 | 5.64 | 1.64 | 8.5 | 4.6 | -$4 | 70 |
| Olson G | 27 | 50 | 2 | 0 | 35 | 5.51 | 1.58 | 6.3 | 4.4 | -$4 | 30 |
| Morris B | 24 | 40 | 2 | 0 | 27 | 5.15 | 1.55 | 6.2 | 3.8 | -$4 | 30 |
| Rowland-Smith R | 28 | 80 | 5 | 0 | 45 | 5.35 | 1.52 | 5.1 | 3.4 | -$4 | 50 |

### Minors (2010) / Skills
| Level | Leag | W | L | Sv | IP | H | K | ERA | WHIP | K/9 | BB/9 | HR/9 | GB/F |
|---|---|---|---|---|---|---|---|---|---|---|---|---|---|
| A | — | | | | | | | | | | | | |
| AA | EL | 4 | 0 | 0 | 43 | 39 | 38 | 2.51 | 1.30 | 8.0 | 3.6 | 0.0 | |
| AAA | IL | 4 | 3 | 0 | 37 | 36 | 34 | 3.16 | 1.41 | 8.3 | 3.9 | 0.2 | |

### Majors / Skills
| Yr | Team | W | L | Sv | IP | H | K | ERA | WHIP | K/9 | BB/9 | HR/9 | GB/F |
|---|---|---|---|---|---|---|---|---|---|---|---|---|---|
| 07 | — | | | | | | | | | | | | |
| 08 | — | | | | | | | | | | | | |
| 09 | — | | | | | | | | | | | | |
| 10 | BOS | 2 | 2 | 2 | 25 | 27 | 23 | 4.32 | 1.48 | 8.3 | 3.6 | 1.1 | 1.1 |

### Competition at RP / Stats in 2010 as RP
| Thr | Player | GR | ERA | IP/G | Sv-Hld |
|---|---|---|---|---|---|
| LH | Okajima H | 56 | 4.50 | 0.8 | 0-11 |
| LH | Richardson D | 26 | 4.15 | 0.5 | 0-2 |
| LH | Schoeneweis S | 15 | 7.90 | 0.9 | 0-1 |

Ten-Year Trends: K/9, BB/9

### Value / Luck / In Rotation / In Relief / OPS
| $1L | $2L | Pts | RAA | H% | HR/fb | S% | FIP | GS | CG | QS/DS | GR | Hld | Bln | Lead | OPS | 1st Hf | 2nd Hf | vs RH | vs LH |
|---|---|---|---|---|---|---|---|---|---|---|---|---|---|---|---|---|---|---|---|
| -$2 | -$10 | 50 | -5 | 32% | 9% | 74% | 4.22 | 3 | | 0/0 | 9 | 1 | 1 | +0.8 | .789 | .783 | .794 | .911 | .576 |

## Scott Downs — 60 IP | $7 | 130 pts
RP-67 · Owned: 28% · LH

Downs is expected to leave TOR in search of a multi-year deal with a contender. A former starter, Downs is relatively durable, and he has experience as an 8th-inning set-up man and as a closer. He also enjoys success against both righties and lefties. He could deliver several more years of low-3.00-ERA ball. (MH)

### Forecast
| Player | Age | IP | W | Sv | K | ERA | WHIP | K/9 | BB/9 | $2L | Pts |
|---|---|---|---|---|---|---|---|---|---|---|---|
| Downs S | 35 | 60 | 4 | 8 | 48 | 3.18 | 1.19 | 7.2 | 2.9 | $7 | 130 |

| Mini-Browser | Age | IP | W | Sv | K | ERA | WHIP | K/9 | BB/9 | $2L | Pts |
|---|---|---|---|---|---|---|---|---|---|---|---|
| Richard C | 27 | 180 | 11 | 0 | 134 | 3.95 | 1.36 | 6.7 | 3.4 | $8 | 230 |
| Floyd G | 28 | 200 | 11 | 0 | 150 | 4.47 | 1.35 | 6.8 | 3.0 | $8 | 230 |
| Meek E | 27 | 80 | 4 | 12 | 71 | 3.36 | 1.34 | 7.9 | 4.3 | $8 | 170 |
| Romero R | 26 | 200 | 12 | 0 | 157 | 4.32 | 1.42 | 7.1 | 4.0 | $8 | 240 |
| Slowey K | 26 | 140 | 10 | 0 | 104 | 4.51 | 1.25 | 6.7 | 1.6 | $8 | 190 |

### Minors (2010) / Skills
| Level | Leag | W | L | Sv | IP | H | K | ERA | WHIP | K/9 | BB/9 | HR/9 | GB/F |
|---|---|---|---|---|---|---|---|---|---|---|---|---|---|
| A | — | | | | | | | | | | | | |
| AA | — | | | | | | | | | | | | |
| AAA | — | | | | | | | | | | | | |

### Majors / Skills
| Yr | Team | W | L | Sv | IP | H | K | ERA | WHIP | K/9 | BB/9 | HR/9 | GB/F |
|---|---|---|---|---|---|---|---|---|---|---|---|---|---|
| 07 | TOR | 4 | 2 | 1 | 58 | 47 | 57 | 2.17 | 1.22 | 8.8 | 3.7 | 0.5 | 2.7 |
| 08 | TOR | 0 | 3 | 5 | 70 | 54 | 57 | 1.78 | 1.15 | 7.3 | 3.4 | 0.4 | 2.9 |
| 09 | TOR | 1 | 3 | 9 | 46 | 46 | 43 | 3.09 | 1.26 | 8.3 | 2.5 | 0.8 | 2.4 |
| 10 | TOR | 5 | 5 | 0 | 61 | 47 | 48 | 2.64 | 0.99 | 7.0 | 2.1 | 0.4 | 2.4 |

### Competition at RP / Stats in 2010 as RP
| Thr | Player | GR | ERA | IP/G | Sv-Hld |
|---|---|---|---|---|---|
| LH | Downs S | 67 | 2.64 | 0.9 | 0-26 |
| LH | Purcey D | 33 | 3.71 | 1.0 | 1-3 |
| LH | Tallet B | 29 | 6.84 | 1.7 | 0-1 |
| LH | Carlson J | 20 | 4.61 | 0.7 | 1-2 |

Ten-Year Trends: K/9, BB/9

### Value / Luck / In Rotation / In Relief / OPS
| $1L | $2L | Pts | RAA | H% | HR/fb | S% | FIP | GS | CG | QS/DS | GR | Hld | Bln | Lead | OPS | 1st Hf | 2nd Hf | vs RH | vs LH |
|---|---|---|---|---|---|---|---|---|---|---|---|---|---|---|---|---|---|---|---|
| $7 | $5 | 110 | +11 | 30% | 9% | 84% | 3.25 | — | — | — | 81 | 24 | 3 | +0.8 | .592 | .622 | .550 | .639 | .548 |
| $9 | $6 | 100 | +17 | 27% | 7% | 86% | 3.38 | — | — | — | 66 | 24 | 4 | +1.5 | .590 | .602 | .570 | .625 | .540 |
| $4 | $2 | 100 | +3 | 31% | 12% | 78% | 3.41 | — | — | — | 48 | 10 | 4 | +1.6 | .688 | .503 | .936 | .643 | .786 |
| $6 | $1 | 110 | +9 | 26% | 6% | 74% | 3.06 | — | — | — | 67 | 26 | 2 | +1.0 | .584 | .584 | .584 | .637 | .488 |

## Kyle Drabek — 80 IP | $-2 | 80 pts
SP-3 · Owned: 0% · RH

The key prospect in the Roy Halladay trade, Drabek spent most of 2010 in Double-A, but he got a cameo in September, where he posted two Quality Starts in three tries. His rates are already easily MLB-caliber, and he should compete with fellow prospect Zach Stewart for a spot in Toronto's 2011 rotation. (MH)

### Forecast
| Player | Age | IP | W | Sv | K | ERA | WHIP | K/9 | BB/9 | $2L | Pts |
|---|---|---|---|---|---|---|---|---|---|---|---|
| Drabek K | 23 | 80 | 3 | 0 | 74 | 5.08 | 1.58 | 8.3 | 3.5 | -$2 | 80 |

| Mini-Browser | Age | IP | W | Sv | K | ERA | WHIP | K/9 | BB/9 | $2L | Pts |
|---|---|---|---|---|---|---|---|---|---|---|---|
| Lannan J | 26 | 160 | 8 | 0 | 80 | 4.73 | 1.46 | 4.5 | 3.1 | -$2 | 120 |
| Mills B | 26 | 60 | 3 | 0 | 59 | 5.25 | 1.58 | 8.8 | 4.6 | -$2 | 70 |
| Hawksworth B | 28 | 60 | 3 | 0 | 44 | 4.65 | 1.50 | 6.6 | 3.3 | -$2 | 60 |
| Romero J | 34 | 40 | 2 | 0 | 30 | 4.21 | 1.58 | 6.7 | 6.3 | -$2 | 40 |
| Marquis J | 32 | 140 | 7 | 0 | 71 | 4.83 | 1.43 | 4.6 | 3.3 | -$2 | 110 |

### Minors (2010) / Skills
| Level | Leag | W | L | Sv | IP | H | K | ERA | WHIP | K/9 | BB/9 | HR/9 | GB/F |
|---|---|---|---|---|---|---|---|---|---|---|---|---|---|
| A | — | | | | | | | | | | | | |
| AA | EL | 14 | 9 | 0 | 162 | 126 | 132 | 2.94 | 1.20 | 7.3 | 3.8 | 0.7 | |
| AAA | — | | | | | | | | | | | | |

### Majors / Skills
| Yr | Team | W | L | Sv | IP | H | K | ERA | WHIP | K/9 | BB/9 | HR/9 | GB/F |
|---|---|---|---|---|---|---|---|---|---|---|---|---|---|
| 07 | — | | | | | | | | | | | | |
| 08 | — | | | | | | | | | | | | |
| 09 | — | | | | | | | | | | | | |
| 10 | TOR | 0 | 3 | 0 | 17 | 18 | 12 | 4.76 | 1.35 | 6.4 | 2.6 | 1.1 | 2.4 |

### Competition at SP / Stats in 2010 as SP
| Thr | Player | GS | ERA | Supp | W-L |
|---|---|---|---|---|---|
| LH | Romero R | 32 | 3.73 | 4.5 | 14-9 |
| RH | Marcum S | 31 | 3.64 | 4.5 | 13-8 |
| LH | Cecil B | 28 | 4.22 | 5.5 | 15-7 |
| RH | Morrow B | 26 | 4.49 | 4.6 | 10-7 |

Ten-Year Trends: K/9, BB/9

### Value / Luck / In Rotation / In Relief / OPS
| $1L | $2L | Pts | RAA | H% | HR/fb | S% | FIP | GS | CG | QS/DS | GR | Hld | Bln | Lead | OPS | 1st Hf | 2nd Hf | vs RH | vs LH |
|---|---|---|---|---|---|---|---|---|---|---|---|---|---|---|---|---|---|---|---|
| -$4 | -$12 | 10 | -1 | 33% | 15% | 67% | 4.30 | 3 | | 2/0 | | | | | .781 | — | .781 | .913 | .744 |

## Justin Duchscherer — 20 IP | $0 | 30 pts
SP-5 · Owned: 43% · RH

Duchscherer began 2010 in the A's rotation, but he did not make it out of April before he was lost for the season with a hip injury. He has undergone surgery on both hips, and there are also questions about his back and elbow, so he's not likely to get a guaranteed rotation spot. His talent exceeds his durability. (ML)

### Forecast
| Player | Age | IP | W | Sv | K | ERA | WHIP | K/9 | BB/9 | $2L | Pts |
|---|---|---|---|---|---|---|---|---|---|---|---|
| Duchscherer J | 33 | 20 | 1 | 0 | 13 | 3.40 | 1.21 | 5.9 | 2.7 | $0 | 30 |

| Mini-Browser | Age | IP | W | Sv | K | ERA | WHIP | K/9 | BB/9 | $2L | Pts |
|---|---|---|---|---|---|---|---|---|---|---|---|
| Choate R | 35 | 40 | 2 | 0 | 33 | 4.38 | 1.38 | 7.4 | 3.5 | $0 | 50 |
| Ohlendorf R | 28 | 160 | 6 | 0 | 110 | 4.64 | 1.38 | 6.2 | 3.1 | $0 | 130 |
| Sipp T | 27 | 60 | 2 | 0 | 68 | 4.44 | 1.50 | 10.1 | 5.6 | $0 | 80 |
| Jepsen K | 26 | 40 | 1 | 4 | 38 | 4.50 | 1.52 | 8.6 | 4.6 | $0 | 60 |
| Litsch J | 26 | 80 | 4 | 0 | 42 | 4.93 | 1.33 | 4.8 | 2.3 | $0 | 60 |

### Minors (2010) / Skills
| Level | Leag | W | L | Sv | IP | H | K | ERA | WHIP | K/9 | BB/9 | HR/9 | GB/F |
|---|---|---|---|---|---|---|---|---|---|---|---|---|---|
| A | — | | | | | | | | | | | | |
| AA | — | | | | | | | | | | | | |
| AAA | — | | | | | | | | | | | | |

### Majors / Skills
| Yr | Team | W | L | Sv | IP | H | K | ERA | WHIP | K/9 | BB/9 | HR/9 | GB/F |
|---|---|---|---|---|---|---|---|---|---|---|---|---|---|
| 07 | OAK | 3 | 3 | 0 | 16 | 18 | 13 | 4.96 | 1.59 | 7.2 | 4.4 | 1.7 | 1.3 |
| 08 | OAK | 10 | 8 | 0 | 141 | 107 | 95 | 2.54 | 1.00 | 6.0 | 2.2 | 0.7 | 1.1 |
| 09 | — | | | | | | | | | | | | |
| 10 | OAK | 2 | 1 | 0 | 28 | 26 | 18 | 2.89 | 1.36 | 5.8 | 3.9 | 1.0 | 1.3 |

### Competition at SP / Stats in 2010 as SP
| Thr | Player | GS | ERA | Supp | W-L |
|---|---|---|---|---|---|
| LH | Gonzalez G | 33 | 3.23 | 4.5 | 15-9 |
| RH | Cahill T | 30 | 2.97 | 4.6 | 18-8 |
| LH | Braden D | 30 | 3.50 | 3.3 | 11-14 |
| RH | Sheets B | 20 | 4.53 | 4.6 | 4-9 |

Ten-Year Trends: K/9, BB/9

### Value / Luck / In Rotation / In Relief / OPS
| $1L | $2L | Pts | RAA | H% | HR/fb | S% | FIP | GS | CG | QS/DS | GR | Hld | Bln | Lead | OPS | 1st Hf | 2nd Hf | vs RH | vs LH |
|---|---|---|---|---|---|---|---|---|---|---|---|---|---|---|---|---|---|---|---|
| -$1 | -$3 | 40 | -1 | 30% | 16% | 74% | 5.57 | — | | | 17 | 5 | 2 | +1.1 | .914 | .914 | — | .678 | 1.172 |
| $20 | $16 | 230 | +25 | 24% | 7% | 78% | 3.69 | 22 | 1 | 15/2 | | | | | .590 | .522 | .788 | .489 | .668 |
| -$1 | -$8 | 40 | +3 | 28% | 10% | 83% | 4.69 | 5 | | 2/1 | | | | | .699 | .699 | — | .770 | .633 |

## Brian Duensing — 160 IP | $9 | 190 pts
RP-40, SP-13 · Owned: 39% · LH

In the first half of 2010, Duensing was a lights-out lefty reliever (1.80 ERA), and then he joined the rotation shortly after the All-Star Break and enjoyed more good fortune there (3.05 ERA). With successful stints as an SP in both 2009 and 2010, Duensing is almost a lock to open 2011 as a starter in Minnesota. (NN)

### Forecast
| Player | Age | IP | W | Sv | K | ERA | WHIP | K/9 | BB/9 | $2L | Pts |
|---|---|---|---|---|---|---|---|---|---|---|---|
| Duensing B | 28 | 160 | 11 | 0 | 98 | 3.88 | 1.34 | 5.5 | 2.7 | $9 | 190 |

| Mini-Browser | Age | IP | W | Sv | K | ERA | WHIP | K/9 | BB/9 | $2L | Pts |
|---|---|---|---|---|---|---|---|---|---|---|---|
| Nathan J | 36 | 40 | 4 | 18 | 45 | 2.72 | 1.12 | 10.1 | 3.0 | $10 | 180 |
| Rodriguez F | 29 | 60 | 3 | 21 | 66 | 3.14 | 1.27 | 9.9 | 4.2 | $10 | 200 |
| Bumgarner M | 21 | 160 | 9 | 0 | 133 | 3.57 | 1.36 | 7.5 | 2.3 | $10 | 220 |
| Lackey J | 32 | 200 | 13 | 0 | 143 | 4.32 | 1.35 | 6.4 | 2.7 | $9 | 240 |
| Shields J | 29 | 200 | 13 | 0 | 155 | 4.63 | 1.30 | 7.0 | 2.1 | $9 | 250 |

### Minors (2010) / Skills
| Level | Leag | W | L | Sv | IP | H | K | ERA | WHIP | K/9 | BB/9 | HR/9 | GB/F |
|---|---|---|---|---|---|---|---|---|---|---|---|---|---|
| A | — | | | | | | | | | | | | |
| AA | — | | | | | | | | | | | | |
| AAA | — | | | | | | | | | | | | |

### Majors / Skills
| Yr | Team | W | L | Sv | IP | H | K | ERA | WHIP | K/9 | BB/9 | HR/9 | GB/F |
|---|---|---|---|---|---|---|---|---|---|---|---|---|---|
| 07 | — | | | | | | | | | | | | |
| 08 | — | | | | | | | | | | | | |
| 09 | MIN | 5 | 2 | 0 | 84 | 84 | 53 | 3.64 | 1.37 | 5.7 | 3.3 | 0.8 | 1.1 |
| 10 | MIN | 10 | 3 | 0 | 130 | 122 | 78 | 2.62 | 1.20 | 5.4 | 2.4 | 0.8 | 1.7 |

### Competition at RP / Stats in 2010 as RP
| Thr | Player | GR | ERA | IP/G | Sv-Hld |
|---|---|---|---|---|---|
| LH | Mijares J | 47 | 3.31 | 0.7 | 0-9 |
| LH | Mahay R | 41 | 3.44 | 0.8 | 0-2 |
| LH | Duensing B | 40 | 1.80 | 1.1 | 0-9 |
| LH | Perkins G | 12 | 5.29 | 1.4 | 0-0 |

Ten-Year Trends: K/9, BB/9

### Value / Luck / In Rotation / In Relief / OPS
| $1L | $2L | Pts | RAA | H% | HR/fb | S% | FIP | GS | CG | QS/DS | GR | Hld | Bln | Lead | OPS | 1st Hf | 2nd Hf | vs RH | vs LH |
|---|---|---|---|---|---|---|---|---|---|---|---|---|---|---|---|---|---|---|---|
| $4 | $0 | 100 | +1 | 30% | 7% | 75% | 4.23 | 9 | 0 | 4/1 | 15 | 1 | 0 | -1.5 | .700 | .755 | .692 | .742 | .579 |
| $13 | $7 | 190 | +17 | 28% | 9% | 82% | 4.00 | 13 | 1 | 9/0 | 40 | 0 | 0 | +0.3 | .666 | .552 | .712 | .751 | .457 |

## Zach Duke — 160 IP | $-4 | 120 pts
**SP-29** — Owned: 2% — LH

Duke is due a small raise in his final year of arbitration, so given that his 5.72 ERA was the highest of his career, the Pirates are likely to non-tender him. They could try to work out a reduced contract, but we are not counting on seeing Duke again as a Pirate. His plausible "best case" is an ERA in the low 4.00's. (MB)

### Forecast
| Player | Age | IP | W | Sv | K | ERA | WHIP | K/9 | BB/9 | $2L | Pts |
|---|---|---|---|---|---|---|---|---|---|---|---|
| Duke Z | 27 | 160 | 8 | 0 | 79 | 5.01 | 1.43 | 4.5 | 2.4 | -$4 | 120 |
| Mini-Browser | Age | IP | W | Sv | K | ERA | WHIP | K/9 | BB/9 | $2L | Pts |
| Dunn M | 25 | 40 | 2 | 0 | 48 | 4.71 | 1.79 | 10.9 | 5.9 | -$3 | 50 |
| Coleman C | 23 | 40 | 2 | 0 | 26 | 4.94 | 1.59 | 5.8 | 3.7 | -$3 | 30 |
| Gomez J | 23 | 60 | 3 | 0 | 49 | 5.24 | 1.66 | 7.4 | 3.5 | -$3 | 30 |
| Hampton M | 38 | 40 | 2 | 0 | 23 | 5.35 | 1.46 | 5.1 | 3.4 | -$4 | 30 |
| Weinhardt R | 25 | 40 | 2 | 0 | 40 | 5.52 | 1.75 | 9.1 | 3.8 | -$4 | 40 |

### Competition at SP / Stats in 2010 as SP
| Thr | Player | GS | ERA | Supp | W-L |
|---|---|---|---|---|---|
| LH | Maholm P | 32 | 5.10 | 4.0 | 9-15 |
| LH | Duke Z | 29 | 5.72 | 3.8 | 8-15 |
| RH | Ohlendorf R | 21 | 4.07 | 2.9 | 1-11 |
| RH | Karstens J | 19 | 4.78 | 3.6 | 3-10 |

### Minors (2010)
| Level | Leag | W | L | Sv | IP | H | K | ERA | WHIP | K/9 | BB/9 | HR/9 | GB/F |
|---|---|---|---|---|---|---|---|---|---|---|---|---|---|
| A | — | | | | | | | | | | | | — |
| AA | EL | 0 | 0 | 0 | 7 | 5 | 1 | 2.57 | 0.86 | 1.3 | 1.3 | 1.3 | — |
| AAA | — | | | | | | | | | | | | — |

### Majors / Skills
| Yr | Team | W | L | Sv | IP | H | K | ERA | WHIP | K/9 | BB/9 | HR/9 | GB/F | $1L | $2L | Pts | RAA | H% | HR/fb | S% | FIP | GS | CG | QS/DS | GR | Hld | Bln | Lead | OPS | 1st Hf | 2nd Hf | vs RH | vs LH |
|---|---|---|---|---|---|---|---|---|---|---|---|---|---|---|---|---|---|---|---|---|---|---|---|---|---|---|---|---|---|---|---|---|---|
| 07 | PIT | 3 | 8 | 0 | 107 | 161 | 41 | 5.53 | 1.73 | 3.4 | 2.1 | 1.2 | 1.7 | -$10 | -$22 | 20 | -21 | 38% | 12% | 70% | 4.83 | 19 | 0 | 7/5 | 1 | 0 | 0 | +0.3 | .941 | .944 | .917 | .953 | .884 |
| 08 | PIT | 5 | 14 | 0 | 185 | 230 | 87 | 4.82 | 1.50 | 4.2 | 2.3 | 0.9 | 1.6 | -$7 | -$17 | 80 | -20 | 33% | 9% | 69% | 4.36 | 31 | 1 | 14/6 | — | — | — | — | .812 | .821 | .798 | .823 | .749 |
| 09 | PIT | 11 | 16 | 0 | 213 | 231 | 106 | 4.06 | 1.31 | 4.5 | 2.1 | 1.0 | 1.5 | $6 | $0 | 190 | +4 | 31% | 10% | 72% | 4.30 | 32 | 3 | 21/2 | — | — | — | — | .764 | .704 | .845 | .765 | .760 |
| 10 | PIT | 8 | 15 | 0 | 159 | 212 | 96 | 5.72 | 1.65 | 5.4 | 2.9 | 1.4 | 1.5 | -$15 | -$36 | 100 | -37 | 35% | 14% | 68% | 5.00 | 29 | 0 | 12/7 | — | — | — | — | .881 | .909 | .853 | .864 | .947 |

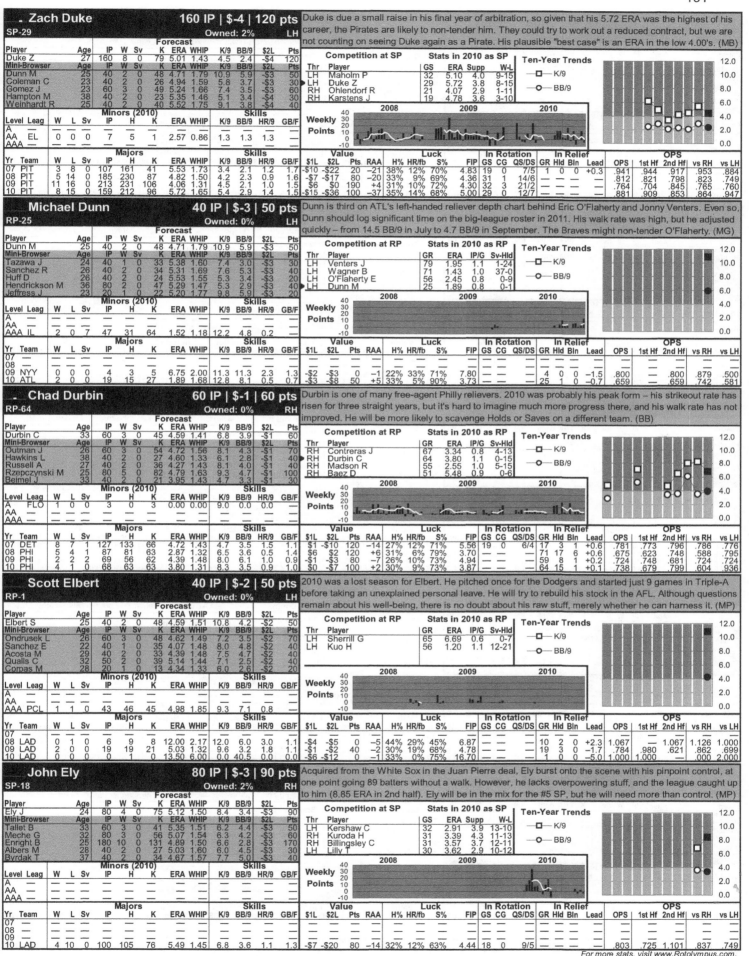

## Michael Dunn — 40 IP | $-3 | 50 pts
**RP-25** — Owned: 0% — LH

Dunn is third on ATL's left-handed reliever depth chart behind Eric O'Flaherty and Jonny Venters. Even so, Dunn should log significant time on the big-league roster in 2011. His walk rate was high, but he adjusted quickly – from 14.5 BB/9 in July to 4.7 BB/9 in September. The Braves might non-tender O'Flaherty. (MG)

### Forecast
| Player | Age | IP | W | Sv | K | ERA | WHIP | K/9 | BB/9 | $2L | Pts |
|---|---|---|---|---|---|---|---|---|---|---|---|
| Dunn M | 25 | 40 | 2 | 0 | 48 | 4.71 | 1.79 | 10.9 | 5.9 | -$3 | 50 |
| Mini-Browser | Age | IP | W | Sv | K | ERA | WHIP | K/9 | BB/9 | $2L | Pts |
| Tazawa J | 24 | 40 | 1 | 0 | 33 | 5.38 | 1.60 | 7.4 | 3.0 | -$3 | 30 |
| Sanchez R | 26 | 40 | 2 | 0 | 34 | 5.31 | 1.69 | 7.6 | 5.3 | -$3 | 40 |
| Huff D | 26 | 40 | 2 | 0 | 24 | 5.53 | 1.55 | 5.3 | 3.4 | -$3 | 40 |
| Hendrickson M | 36 | 80 | 4 | 0 | 47 | 5.29 | 1.47 | 5.3 | 2.9 | -$3 | 40 |
| Jeffress J | 23 | 20 | | | 22 | 5.20 | 1.77 | 9.8 | 5.9 | -$3 | 20 |

### Competition at RP / Stats in 2010 as RP
| Thr | Player | GR | ERA | IP/G | Sv-Hld |
|---|---|---|---|---|---|
| LH | Venters J | 79 | 1.95 | 1.1 | 1-24 |
| LH | Wagner B | 71 | 1.43 | 1.0 | 37-0 |
| LH | O'Flaherty E | 56 | 2.45 | 0.8 | 0-9 |
| LH | Dunn M | 25 | 1.89 | 0.8 | 0-1 |

### Minors (2010)
| Level | Leag | W | L | Sv | IP | H | K | ERA | WHIP | K/9 | BB/9 | HR/9 | GB/F |
|---|---|---|---|---|---|---|---|---|---|---|---|---|---|
| A | — | | | | | | | | | | | | — |
| AA | — | | | | | | | | | | | | — |
| AAA | IL | 2 | 0 | 7 | 47 | 31 | 64 | 1.52 | 1.18 | 12.2 | 4.8 | 0.2 | — |

### Majors / Skills
| Yr | Team | W | L | Sv | IP | H | K | ERA | WHIP | K/9 | BB/9 | HR/9 | GB/F | $1L | $2L | Pts | RAA | H% | HR/fb | S% | FIP | GS | CG | QS/DS | GR | Hld | Bln | Lead | OPS | 1st Hf | 2nd Hf | vs RH | vs LH |
|---|---|---|---|---|---|---|---|---|---|---|---|---|---|---|---|---|---|---|---|---|---|---|---|---|---|---|---|---|---|---|---|---|---|
| 07 | — | | | | | | | | | | | | | | | | | | | | | | | | | | | | | | | | |
| 08 | — | | | | | | | | | | | | | | | | | | | | | | | | | | | | | | | | |
| 09 | NYY | 0 | 0 | 0 | 4 | 3 | 5 | 6.75 | 2.00 | 11.3 | 11.3 | 2.3 | 1.3 | -$2 | -$3 | 0 | -1 | 22% | 33% | 71% | 7.80 | — | — | — | 4 | 0 | 0 | -1.5 | .800 | — | .800 | .879 | .500 |
| 10 | ATL | 2 | 0 | 0 | 19 | 15 | 27 | 1.89 | 1.68 | 12.8 | 8.1 | 0.5 | 0.7 | -$3 | -$8 | 50 | +5 | 33% | 5% | 90% | 3.73 | — | — | — | 25 | 1 | 0 | -0.7 | .659 | — | .659 | .742 | .581 |

## Chad Durbin — 60 IP | $-1 | 60 pts
**RP-64** — Owned: 0% — RH

Durbin is one of many free-agent Philly relievers. 2010 was probably his peak form – his strikeout rate has risen for three straight years, but it's hard to imagine much more progress there, and his walk rate has not improved. He will be more likely to scavenge Holds or Saves on a different team. (BB)

### Forecast
| Player | Age | IP | W | Sv | K | ERA | WHIP | K/9 | BB/9 | $2L | Pts |
|---|---|---|---|---|---|---|---|---|---|---|---|
| Durbin C | 33 | 60 | 3 | 0 | 45 | 4.59 | 1.41 | 6.8 | 3.9 | -$1 | 60 |
| Mini-Browser | Age | IP | W | Sv | K | ERA | WHIP | K/9 | BB/9 | $2L | Pts |
| Outman J | 26 | 60 | 3 | 0 | 54 | 4.72 | 1.56 | 8.1 | 4.3 | -$1 | 70 |
| Hawkins L | 38 | 40 | 2 | 0 | 27 | 4.60 | 1.33 | 6.1 | 2.8 | -$1 | 40 |
| Russell A | 27 | 40 | 2 | 0 | 36 | 4.27 | 1.43 | 8.1 | 4.0 | -$1 | 40 |
| Rzepczynski M | 25 | 80 | 5 | 0 | 82 | 4.79 | 1.63 | 9.3 | 4.7 | -$1 | 100 |
| Beimel J | 33 | 40 | 2 | 0 | 21 | 3.95 | 1.43 | 4.7 | 3.3 | -$1 | 30 |

### Competition at RP / Stats in 2010 as RP
| Thr | Player | GR | ERA | IP/G | Sv-Hld |
|---|---|---|---|---|---|
| RH | Contreras J | 67 | 3.34 | 0.8 | 4-13 |
| RH | Durbin C | 64 | 3.80 | 1.1 | 0-15 |
| RH | Madson R | 55 | 2.55 | 1.0 | 5-15 |
| RH | Baez D | 51 | 5.48 | 0.9 | 0-6 |

### Minors (2010)
| Level | Leag | W | L | Sv | IP | H | K | ERA | WHIP | K/9 | BB/9 | HR/9 | GB/F |
|---|---|---|---|---|---|---|---|---|---|---|---|---|---|
| A | FLO | 1 | 0 | 0 | 3 | 0 | 3 | 0.00 | 0.00 | 9.0 | 0.0 | 0.0 | — |
| AA | — | | | | | | | | | | | | — |
| AAA | — | | | | | | | | | | | | — |

### Majors / Skills
| Yr | Team | W | L | Sv | IP | H | K | ERA | WHIP | K/9 | BB/9 | HR/9 | GB/F | $1L | $2L | Pts | RAA | H% | HR/fb | S% | FIP | GS | CG | QS/DS | GR | Hld | Bln | Lead | OPS | 1st Hf | 2nd Hf | vs RH | vs LH |
|---|---|---|---|---|---|---|---|---|---|---|---|---|---|---|---|---|---|---|---|---|---|---|---|---|---|---|---|---|---|---|---|---|---|
| 07 | DET | 8 | 7 | 1 | 127 | 133 | 66 | 4.72 | 1.43 | 4.7 | 3.5 | 1.5 | 1.1 | $1 | -$10 | 120 | -14 | 27% | 12% | 71% | 5.56 | 19 | 0 | 6/4 | 17 | 3 | 1 | +0.6 | .781 | .773 | .796 | .786 | .776 |
| 08 | PHI | 5 | 4 | 1 | 87 | 81 | 63 | 2.87 | 1.32 | 6.5 | 3.6 | 0.5 | 1.4 | $6 | $2 | 120 | +6 | 31% | 6% | 79% | 3.70 | — | — | — | 71 | 17 | 6 | +0.6 | .675 | .623 | .748 | .588 | .795 |
| 09 | PHI | 2 | 2 | 2 | 69 | 56 | 62 | 4.39 | 1.48 | 8.0 | 6.1 | 1.0 | 0.9 | -$1 | -$3 | 80 | -7 | 26% | 10% | 73% | 4.94 | — | — | — | 59 | 8 | 1 | +0.2 | .724 | .748 | .681 | .724 | .724 |
| 10 | PHI | 4 | 1 | 0 | 68 | 63 | 63 | 3.80 | 1.31 | 8.3 | 3.5 | 0.9 | 1.0 | $0 | -$7 | 100 | +2 | 30% | 9% | 73% | 3.87 | — | — | — | 64 | 15 | 1 | +0.1 | .738 | .679 | .799 | .604 | .936 |

## Scott Elbert — 40 IP | $-2 | 50 pts
**RP-1** — Owned: 0% — LH

2010 was a lost season for Elbert. He pitched once for the Dodgers and started just 9 games in Triple-A before taking an unexplained personal leave. He will try to rebuild his stock in the AFL. Although questions remain about his well-being, there is no doubt about his raw stuff, merely whether he can harness it. (MP)

### Forecast
| Player | Age | IP | W | Sv | K | ERA | WHIP | K/9 | BB/9 | $2L | Pts |
|---|---|---|---|---|---|---|---|---|---|---|---|
| Elbert S | 25 | 40 | 2 | 0 | 48 | 4.59 | 1.51 | 10.8 | 4.2 | -$2 | 50 |
| Mini-Browser | Age | IP | W | Sv | K | ERA | WHIP | K/9 | BB/9 | $2L | Pts |
| Ondrusek L | 26 | 60 | 3 | 0 | 48 | 4.62 | 1.49 | 7.2 | 3.5 | -$2 | 70 |
| Sanchez E | 22 | 40 | 1 | 0 | 35 | 4.07 | 1.48 | 8.0 | 4.8 | -$2 | 40 |
| Acosta M | 29 | 40 | 2 | 0 | 33 | 4.39 | 1.48 | 7.5 | 4.7 | -$2 | 40 |
| Qualls C | 32 | 50 | 2 | 0 | 39 | 5.14 | 1.44 | 7.1 | 2.5 | -$2 | 40 |
| Corpas M | 28 | 20 | 1 | 0 | 13 | 4.34 | 1.33 | 6.0 | 2.6 | -$2 | 20 |

### Competition at RP / Stats in 2010 as RP
| Thr | Player | GR | ERA | IP/G | Sv-Hld |
|---|---|---|---|---|---|
| LH | Sherrill G | 65 | 6.69 | 0.6 | 0-7 |
| LH | Kuo H | 56 | 1.20 | 1.1 | 12-21 |

### Minors (2010)
| Level | Leag | W | L | Sv | IP | H | K | ERA | WHIP | K/9 | BB/9 | HR/9 | GB/F |
|---|---|---|---|---|---|---|---|---|---|---|---|---|---|
| A | — | | | | | | | | | | | | — |
| AA | — | | | | | | | | | | | | — |
| AAA | PCL | 1 | 1 | 0 | 43 | 46 | 45 | 4.98 | 1.85 | 9.3 | 7.1 | 0.8 | — |

### Majors / Skills
| Yr | Team | W | L | Sv | IP | H | K | ERA | WHIP | K/9 | BB/9 | HR/9 | GB/F | $1L | $2L | Pts | RAA | H% | HR/fb | S% | FIP | GS | CG | QS/DS | GR | Hld | Bln | Lead | OPS | 1st Hf | 2nd Hf | vs RH | vs LH |
|---|---|---|---|---|---|---|---|---|---|---|---|---|---|---|---|---|---|---|---|---|---|---|---|---|---|---|---|---|---|---|---|---|---|
| 07 | — | | | | | | | | | | | | | | | | | | | | | | | | | | | | | | | | |
| 08 | LAD | 0 | 1 | 0 | 6 | 9 | 8 | 12.00 | 2.17 | 12.0 | 6.0 | 3.0 | 1.1 | -$4 | -$5 | 20 | -5 | 44% | 29% | 45% | 6.87 | — | — | — | 10 | 2 | 0 | +2.3 | 1.067 | — | 1.067 | 1.126 | 1.000 |
| 09 | LAD | 2 | 0 | 0 | 19 | 19 | 21 | 5.03 | 1.32 | 9.6 | 3.2 | 1.8 | 1.1 | -$1 | -$2 | 40 | -2 | 30% | 19% | 68% | 4.78 | — | — | — | 19 | 3 | 0 | -1.7 | .784 | .980 | .621 | .862 | .699 |
| 10 | LAD | 0 | 0 | 0 | 0 | 1 | 0 | 13.50 | 6.00 | 0.0 | 0.0 | 40.5 | 0.0 | -$4 | -$6 | 12 | -2 | 0% | 0% | 75% | 16.70 | — | — | — | 1 | 0 | 0 | -5.0 | 1.000 | — | 1.000 | .000 | 2.000 |

## John Ely — 80 IP | $-3 | 90 pts
**SP-18** — Owned: 2% — RH

Acquired from the White Sox in the Juan Pierre deal, Ely burst onto the scene with his pinpoint control, at one point going 89 batters without a walk. However, he lacks overpowering stuff, and the league caught up to him (8.85 ERA in 2nd half). Ely will be in the mix for the #5 SP, but he will need more than control. (MP)

### Forecast
| Player | Age | IP | W | Sv | K | ERA | WHIP | K/9 | BB/9 | $2L | Pts |
|---|---|---|---|---|---|---|---|---|---|---|---|
| Ely J | 24 | 80 | 4 | 0 | 75 | 5.12 | 1.50 | 8.4 | 3.4 | -$3 | 90 |
| Mini-Browser | Age | IP | W | Sv | K | ERA | WHIP | K/9 | BB/9 | $2L | Pts |
| Tallet B | 33 | 60 | 3 | 0 | 41 | 5.35 | 1.55 | 6.2 | 4.4 | -$3 | 50 |
| Meche G | 32 | 80 | 3 | 0 | 56 | 5.07 | 1.54 | 6.3 | 4.2 | -$3 | 60 |
| Enright B | 25 | 180 | 10 | 0 | 131 | 4.89 | 1.50 | 6.6 | 2.8 | -$3 | 170 |
| Albers M | 28 | 40 | 2 | 0 | 27 | 5.03 | 1.60 | 6.0 | 4.5 | -$3 | 40 |
| Byrdak T | 37 | 40 | 2 | 0 | 34 | 4.67 | 1.57 | 7.7 | 3.8 | -$3 | 40 |

### Competition at SP / Stats in 2010 as SP
| Thr | Player | GS | ERA | Supp | W-L |
|---|---|---|---|---|---|
| LH | Kershaw C | 32 | 2.91 | 3.9 | 13-10 |
| RH | Kuroda H | 31 | 3.39 | 4.3 | 11-13 |
| RH | Billingsley C | 31 | 3.57 | 3.7 | 12-11 |
| LH | Lilly T | 30 | 3.62 | 2.9 | 10-12 |

### Minors (2010)
| Level | Leag | W | L | Sv | IP | H | K | ERA | WHIP | K/9 | BB/9 | HR/9 | GB/F |
|---|---|---|---|---|---|---|---|---|---|---|---|---|---|
| A | — | | | | | | | | | | | | — |
| AA | — | | | | | | | | | | | | — |
| AAA | — | | | | | | | | | | | | — |

### Majors / Skills
| Yr | Team | W | L | Sv | IP | H | K | ERA | WHIP | K/9 | BB/9 | HR/9 | GB/F | $1L | $2L | Pts | RAA | H% | HR/fb | S% | FIP | GS | CG | QS/DS | GR | Hld | Bln | Lead | OPS | 1st Hf | 2nd Hf | vs RH | vs LH |
|---|---|---|---|---|---|---|---|---|---|---|---|---|---|---|---|---|---|---|---|---|---|---|---|---|---|---|---|---|---|---|---|---|---|
| 07 | — | | | | | | | | | | | | | | | | | | | | | | | | | | | | | | | | |
| 08 | — | | | | | | | | | | | | | | | | | | | | | | | | | | | | | | | | |
| 09 | — | | | | | | | | | | | | | | | | | | | | | | | | | | | | | | | | |
| 10 | LAD | 4 | 10 | 0 | 100 | 105 | 76 | 5.49 | 1.45 | 6.8 | 3.6 | 1.1 | 1.3 | -$7 | -$20 | 80 | -14 | 32% | 12% | 63% | 4.44 | 18 | 0 | 9/5 | — | — | — | — | .803 | .725 | 1.101 | .837 | .749 |

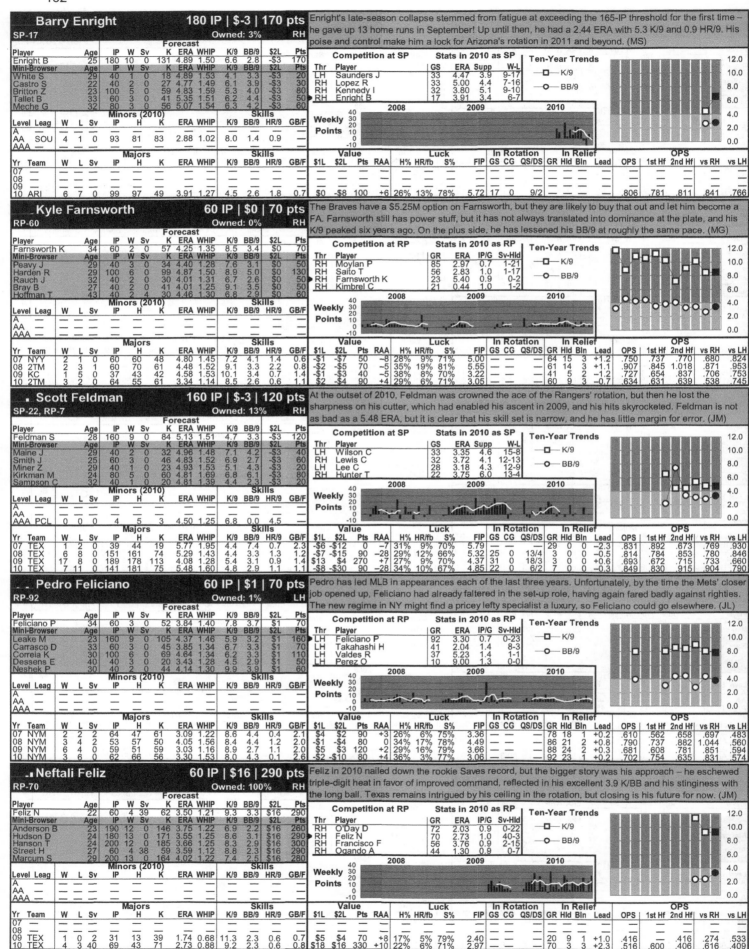

## Barry Enright — 180 IP | $-3 | 170 pts

SP-17 — Owned: 3% — RH

Enright's late-season collapse stemmed from fatigue at exceeding the 165-IP threshold for the first time -- he gave up 13 home runs in September! Up until then, he had a 2.44 ERA with 5.3 K/9 and 0.9 HR/9. His poise and control make him a lock for Arizona's rotation in 2011 and beyond. (MS)

### Forecast

| Player | Age | IP | W | Sv | K | ERA | WHIP | K/9 | BB/9 | $2L | Pts |
|---|---|---|---|---|---|---|---|---|---|---|---|
| Enright B | 25 | 180 | 10 | 0 | 131 | 4.89 | 1.50 | 6.6 | 2.8 | -$3 | 170 |
| Mini-Browser | Age | IP | W | Sv | K | ERA | WHIP | K/9 | BB/9 | $2L | Pts |
| White S | 29 | 40 | 1 | 0 | 18 | 4.89 | 1.53 | 4.1 | 3.3 | -$3 | 20 |
| Castro S | 22 | 40 | 2 | 0 | 27 | 4.77 | 1.49 | 6.1 | 3.9 | -$3 | 30 |
| Britton Z | 23 | 100 | 5 | 0 | 59 | 4.83 | 1.59 | 5.3 | 4.0 | -$3 | 80 |
| Tallet B | 33 | 60 | 3 | 0 | 41 | 5.35 | 1.51 | 6.2 | 4.4 | -$3 | 50 |
| Meche G | 32 | 80 | 3 | 0 | 56 | 5.07 | 1.54 | 6.3 | 4.2 | -$3 | 60 |

### Minors (2010) / Skills

| Level | Leag | W | L | Sv | IP | H | K | ERA | WHIP | K/9 | BB/9 | HR/9 | GB/F |
|---|---|---|---|---|---|---|---|---|---|---|---|---|---|
| A | — | | | | | | | | | | | | |
| AA | SOU | 4 | 1 | 0 | 93 | 81 | 83 | 2.88 | 1.02 | 8.0 | 1.4 | 0.9 | |
| AAA | — | | | | | | | | | | | | |

### Majors / Skills

| Yr | Team | W | L | Sv | IP | H | K | ERA | WHIP | K/9 | BB/9 | HR/9 | GB/F |
|---|---|---|---|---|---|---|---|---|---|---|---|---|---|
| 07 | — | | | | | | | | | | | | |
| 08 | — | | | | | | | | | | | | |
| 09 | — | | | | | | | | | | | | |
| 10 | ARI | 6 | 7 | 0 | 99 | 97 | 49 | 3.91 | 1.27 | 4.5 | 2.6 | 1.8 | 0.7 |

**Competition at SP / Stats in 2010 as SP**

| Thr | Player | GS | ERA | Supp | W-L |
|---|---|---|---|---|---|
| LH | Saunders J | 33 | 4.47 | 3.9 | 9-17 |
| RH | Lopez R | 33 | 5.00 | 4.4 | 7-16 |
| RH | Kennedy I | 32 | 3.80 | 5.1 | 9-10 |
| RH | Enright B | 17 | 3.91 | 3.4 | 6-7 |

Ten-Year Trends: K/9, BB/9

Weekly Points: 2008 / 2009 / 2010

### Value / Luck / In Rotation / In Relief / OPS

| $1L | $2L | Pts | RAA | H% | HR/fb | S% | FIP | GS | CG | QS/DS | GR | Hld | Bln | Lead | OPS | 1st Hf | 2nd Hf | vs RH | vs LH |
|---|---|---|---|---|---|---|---|---|---|---|---|---|---|---|---|---|---|---|---|
| $0 | -$8 | 100 | +6 | 26% | 13% | 78% | 5.72 | 17 | 0 | 9/2 | — | — | — | — | .806 | .781 | .811 | .841 | .766 |

---

## Kyle Farnsworth — 60 IP | $0 | 70 pts

RP-60 — Owned: 0% — RH

The Braves have a $5.25M option on Farnsworth, but they are likely to buy that out and let him become a FA. Farnsworth still has power stuff, but it has not always translated into dominance at the plate, and his K/9 peaked six years ago. On the plus side, he has lessened his BB/9 at roughly the same pace. (MG)

### Forecast

| Player | Age | IP | W | Sv | K | ERA | WHIP | K/9 | BB/9 | $2L | Pts |
|---|---|---|---|---|---|---|---|---|---|---|---|
| Farnsworth K | 34 | 60 | 2 | 0 | 57 | 4.25 | 1.35 | 8.5 | 3.4 | $0 | 70 |
| Mini-Browser | Age | IP | W | Sv | K | ERA | WHIP | K/9 | BB/9 | $2L | Pts |
| Peavy J | 29 | 40 | 2 | 0 | 34 | 4.40 | 1.28 | 7.6 | 3.1 | $0 | 50 |
| Harden R | 29 | 100 | 6 | 0 | 99 | 4.87 | 1.50 | 8.9 | 5.0 | $0 | 130 |
| Rauch J | 32 | 40 | 2 | 0 | 30 | 4.01 | 1.31 | 6.7 | 2.6 | $0 | 50 |
| Bray B | 27 | 40 | 2 | 0 | 41 | 4.01 | 1.25 | 9.1 | 3.5 | $0 | 50 |
| Hoffman T | 43 | 40 | 2 | 4 | 30 | 4.46 | 1.30 | 6.8 | 2.4 | $0 | 60 |

### Minors (2010) / Skills

| Level | Leag | W | L | Sv | IP | H | K | ERA | WHIP | K/9 | BB/9 | HR/9 | GB/F |
|---|---|---|---|---|---|---|---|---|---|---|---|---|---|
| A | — | | | | | | | | | | | | |
| AA | — | | | | | | | | | | | | |
| AAA | — | | | | | | | | | | | | |

### Majors / Skills

| Yr | Team | W | L | Sv | IP | H | K | ERA | WHIP | K/9 | BB/9 | HR/9 | GB/F |
|---|---|---|---|---|---|---|---|---|---|---|---|---|---|
| 07 | NYY | 2 | 1 | 0 | 60 | 60 | 48 | 4.80 | 1.45 | 7.2 | 4.1 | 1.4 | 0.6 |
| 08 | 2TM | 2 | 3 | 1 | 60 | 70 | 61 | 4.48 | 1.52 | 9.1 | 3.3 | 2.2 | 0.8 |
| 09 | KC | 1 | 5 | 0 | 37 | 43 | 42 | 4.58 | 1.53 | 10.1 | 3.4 | 0.7 | 1.4 |
| 10 | 2TM | 3 | 2 | 0 | 64 | 55 | 61 | 3.34 | 1.14 | 8.5 | 2.6 | 0.6 | 1.1 |

**Competition at RP / Stats in 2010 as RP**

| Thr | Player | GR | ERA | IP/G | Sv-Hld |
|---|---|---|---|---|---|
| RH | Moylan P | 85 | 2.97 | 0.7 | 1-21 |
| RH | Saito T | 56 | 2.83 | 1.0 | 1-17 |
| RH | Farnsworth K | 23 | 5.40 | 0.9 | 0-2 |
| RH | Kimbrel C | 21 | 0.44 | 1.0 | 1-2 |

Ten-Year Trends: K/9, BB/9

Weekly Points: 2008 / 2009 / 2010

### Value / Luck / In Rotation / In Relief / OPS

| $1L | $2L | Pts | RAA | H% | HR/fb | S% | FIP | GS | CG | QS/DS | GR | Hld | Bln | Lead | OPS | 1st Hf | 2nd Hf | vs RH | vs LH |
|---|---|---|---|---|---|---|---|---|---|---|---|---|---|---|---|---|---|---|---|
| -$1 | -$7 | 50 | -8 | 28% | 9% | 71% | 5.00 | — | — | — | 64 | 15 | 3 | +1.2 | .750 | .737 | .770 | .680 | .824 |
| -$2 | -$5 | 70 | -5 | 35% | 19% | 81% | 5.55 | — | — | — | 61 | 14 | 3 | +1.1 | .838 | .654 | 1.018 | .871 | .953 |
| -$1 | -$3 | 40 | -5 | 38% | 8% | 70% | 3.22 | — | — | — | 41 | 5 | 2 | -1.2 | .727 | .654 | .837 | .706 | .753 |
| $2 | -$4 | 90 | +4 | 29% | 6% | 71% | 3.05 | — | — | — | 60 | 9 | 3 | -0.7 | .634 | .631 | .639 | .538 | .745 |

---

## Scott Feldman — 160 IP | $-3 | 120 pts

SP-22, RP-7 — Owned: 13% — RH

At the outset of 2010, Feldman was crowned the ace of the Rangers' rotation, but then he lost the sharpness on his cutter, which had enabled his ascent in 2009, and his hits skyrocketed. Feldman is not as bad as a 5.48 ERA, but it is clear that his skill set is narrow, and he has little margin for error. (JM)

### Forecast

| Player | Age | IP | W | Sv | K | ERA | WHIP | K/9 | BB/9 | $2L | Pts |
|---|---|---|---|---|---|---|---|---|---|---|---|
| Feldman S | 28 | 160 | 9 | 0 | 84 | 5.13 | 1.51 | 4.7 | 3.3 | -$3 | 120 |
| Mini-Browser | Age | IP | W | Sv | K | ERA | WHIP | K/9 | BB/9 | $2L | Pts |
| Maine J | 29 | 40 | 2 | 0 | 32 | 4.96 | 1.48 | 7.1 | 4.2 | -$3 | 40 |
| Smith J | 25 | 60 | 3 | 0 | 46 | 4.83 | 1.52 | 6.9 | 2.7 | -$3 | 60 |
| Miner Z | 29 | 40 | 1 | 0 | 23 | 4.93 | 1.53 | 5.1 | 4.3 | -$3 | 40 |
| Kirkman M | 24 | 80 | 5 | 0 | 60 | 4.81 | 1.69 | 6.8 | 6.1 | -$3 | 80 |
| Sampson C | 32 | 40 | 2 | 0 | 20 | 4.81 | 1.39 | 4.4 | 2.7 | -$3 | 50 |

### Minors (2010) / Skills

| Level | Leag | W | L | Sv | IP | H | K | ERA | WHIP | K/9 | BB/9 | HR/9 | GB/F |
|---|---|---|---|---|---|---|---|---|---|---|---|---|---|
| A | — | | | | | | | | | | | | |
| AA | — | | | | | | | | | | | | |
| AAA | PCL | 0 | 0 | 0 | 4 | 5 | 3 | 4.50 | 1.25 | 6.8 | 0.0 | 4.5 | |

### Majors / Skills

| Yr | Team | W | L | Sv | IP | H | K | ERA | WHIP | K/9 | BB/9 | HR/9 | GB/F |
|---|---|---|---|---|---|---|---|---|---|---|---|---|---|
| 07 | TEX | 1 | 2 | 0 | 39 | 44 | 19 | 5.77 | 1.95 | 4.4 | 7.4 | 0.7 | 2.3 |
| 08 | TEX | 6 | 8 | 0 | 151 | 161 | 74 | 5.29 | 1.43 | 4.4 | 3.3 | 1.3 | 1.0 |
| 09 | TEX | 17 | 8 | 0 | 189 | 178 | 113 | 4.08 | 1.28 | 5.4 | 3.1 | 0.9 | 1.4 |
| 10 | TEX | 7 | 11 | 0 | 141 | 181 | 75 | 5.48 | 1.60 | 4.8 | 2.9 | 1.1 | 1.1 |

**Competition at SP / Stats in 2010 as SP**

| Thr | Player | GS | ERA | Supp | W-L |
|---|---|---|---|---|---|
| LH | Wilson C | 33 | 3.35 | 4.6 | 15-8 |
| RH | Lewis C | 32 | 3.72 | 4.1 | 12-13 |
| LH | Lee C | 28 | 3.18 | 4.3 | 12-9 |
| RH | Hunter T | 22 | 3.75 | 6.0 | 13-4 |

Ten-Year Trends: K/9, BB/9

Weekly Points: 2008 / 2009 / 2010

### Value / Luck / In Rotation / In Relief / OPS

| $1L | $2L | Pts | RAA | H% | HR/fb | S% | FIP | GS | CG | QS/DS | GR | Hld | Bln | Lead | OPS | 1st Hf | 2nd Hf | vs RH | vs LH |
|---|---|---|---|---|---|---|---|---|---|---|---|---|---|---|---|---|---|---|---|
| -$6 | -$12 | 0 | -7 | 31% | 9% | 70% | 5.79 | — | — | — | 29 | 0 | 0 | -2.3 | .831 | .892 | .673 | .769 | .930 |
| -$7 | -$15 | 90 | -28 | 29% | 12% | 66% | 5.32 | 25 | 0 | 13/4 | 3 | 0 | 0 | -0.5 | .814 | .784 | .853 | .780 | .846 |
| $13 | $4 | 270 | +7 | 27% | 9% | 70% | 4.37 | 31 | 0 | 18/3 | 3 | 0 | 0 | +0.6 | .693 | .672 | .715 | .733 | .660 |
| -$8 | -$30 | 120 | -28 | 34% | 10% | 67% | 4.85 | 22 | 0 | 6/2 | 2 | 0 | 0 | -0.3 | .849 | .830 | .915 | .904 | .790 |

---

## Pedro Feliciano — 60 IP | $1 | 70 pts

RP-92 — Owned: 1% — LH

Pedro has led MLB in appearances each of the last three years. Unfortunately, by the time the Mets' closer job opened up, Feliciano had already faltered in the set-up role, having again fared badly against righties. The new regime in NY might find a pricey lefty specialist a luxury, so Feliciano could go elsewhere. (JL)

### Forecast

| Player | Age | IP | W | Sv | K | ERA | WHIP | K/9 | BB/9 | $2L | Pts |
|---|---|---|---|---|---|---|---|---|---|---|---|
| Feliciano P | 34 | 60 | 3 | 0 | 52 | 3.84 | 1.40 | 7.8 | 3.7 | $1 | 70 |
| Mini-Browser | Age | IP | W | Sv | K | ERA | WHIP | K/9 | BB/9 | $2L | Pts |
| Leake M | 23 | 160 | 9 | 0 | 105 | 4.37 | 1.46 | 5.9 | 3.3 | $1 | 160 |
| Carrasco D | 33 | 60 | 3 | 0 | 45 | 3.85 | 1.34 | 6.7 | 3.3 | $1 | 70 |
| Correia K | 30 | 100 | 6 | 0 | 69 | 4.64 | 1.34 | 6.2 | 2.9 | $1 | 110 |
| Dessens E | 40 | 40 | 2 | 0 | 20 | 3.43 | 1.28 | 4.5 | 2.9 | $1 | 50 |
| Neshek P | 30 | 40 | 2 | 0 | 44 | 4.14 | 1.30 | 9.9 | 3.5 | $1 | 60 |

### Minors (2010) / Skills

| Level | Leag | W | L | Sv | IP | H | K | ERA | WHIP | K/9 | BB/9 | HR/9 | GB/F |
|---|---|---|---|---|---|---|---|---|---|---|---|---|---|
| A | — | | | | | | | | | | | | |
| AA | — | | | | | | | | | | | | |
| AAA | — | | | | | | | | | | | | |

### Majors / Skills

| Yr | Team | W | L | Sv | IP | H | K | ERA | WHIP | K/9 | BB/9 | HR/9 | GB/F |
|---|---|---|---|---|---|---|---|---|---|---|---|---|---|
| 07 | NYM | 2 | 2 | 2 | 64 | 47 | 61 | 3.09 | 1.22 | 8.6 | 4.4 | 0.4 | 2.1 |
| 08 | NYM | 3 | 4 | 2 | 53 | 57 | 50 | 4.05 | 1.56 | 8.4 | 4.4 | 1.2 | 2.0 |
| 09 | NYM | 6 | 4 | 0 | 59 | 51 | 59 | 3.03 | 1.16 | 8.9 | 2.7 | 1.1 | 2.0 |
| 10 | NYM | 3 | 6 | 0 | 62 | 66 | 56 | 3.30 | 1.53 | 8.0 | 4.3 | 0.1 | 2.6 |

**Competition at RP / Stats in 2010 as RP**

| Thr | Player | GR | ERA | IP/G | Sv-Hld |
|---|---|---|---|---|---|
| LH | Feliciano P | 92 | 3.30 | 0.7 | 0-23 |
| LH | Takahashi H | 41 | 2.04 | 1.4 | 8-3 |
| LH | Valdes R | 37 | 5.23 | 1.4 | 1-1 |
| LH | Perez O | 10 | 9.00 | 1.3 | 0-0 |

Ten-Year Trends: K/9, BB/9

Weekly Points: 2008 / 2009 / 2010

### Value / Luck / In Rotation / In Relief / OPS

| $1L | $2L | Pts | RAA | H% | HR/fb | S% | FIP | GS | CG | QS/DS | GR | Hld | Bln | Lead | OPS | 1st Hf | 2nd Hf | vs RH | vs LH |
|---|---|---|---|---|---|---|---|---|---|---|---|---|---|---|---|---|---|---|---|
| $4 | $2 | 90 | +3 | 26% | 6% | 75% | 3.36 | — | — | — | 78 | 18 | 1 | +0.2 | .610 | .562 | .658 | .697 | .483 |
| -$1 | -$4 | 80 | 0 | 34% | 17% | 78% | 4.49 | — | — | — | 86 | 21 | 2 | +0.8 | .790 | .737 | .882 | 1.044 | .560 |
| $5 | $3 | 120 | +2 | 29% | 16% | 79% | 3.66 | — | — | — | 88 | 24 | 2 | +0.3 | .681 | .608 | .781 | .851 | .594 |
| -$2 | -$10 | 80 | +4 | 36% | 3% | 77% | 3.06 | — | — | — | 92 | 23 | 1 | +0.2 | .702 | .754 | .635 | .831 | .574 |

---

## Neftali Feliz — 60 IP | $16 | 290 pts

RP-70 — Owned: 100% — RH

Feliz in 2010 nailed down the rookie Saves record, but the bigger story was his approach – he eschewed triple-digit heat in favor of improved command, reflected in his excellent 3.9 K/BB and his stinginess with the long ball. Texas remains intrigued by his ceiling in the rotation, but closing is his future for now. (JM)

### Forecast

| Player | Age | IP | W | Sv | K | ERA | WHIP | K/9 | BB/9 | $2L | Pts |
|---|---|---|---|---|---|---|---|---|---|---|---|
| Feliz N | 22 | 60 | 4 | 39 | 62 | 3.50 | 1.21 | 9.3 | 3.3 | $16 | 290 |
| Mini-Browser | Age | IP | W | Sv | K | ERA | WHIP | K/9 | BB/9 | $2L | Pts |
| Anderson B | 23 | 190 | 12 | 0 | 146 | 3.75 | 1.22 | 6.9 | 2.2 | $16 | 260 |
| Hudson D | 24 | 180 | 13 | 0 | 171 | 3.55 | 1.25 | 8.6 | 3.1 | $16 | 290 |
| Hanson T | 24 | 200 | 13 | 0 | 185 | 3.66 | 1.25 | 8.3 | 2.9 | $16 | 300 |
| Street H | 27 | 60 | 4 | 38 | 59 | 3.59 | 1.12 | 8.8 | 2.3 | $16 | 290 |
| Marcum S | 29 | 200 | 13 | 0 | 164 | 4.02 | 1.22 | 7.4 | 2.5 | $16 | 280 |

### Minors (2010) / Skills

| Level | Leag | W | L | Sv | IP | H | K | ERA | WHIP | K/9 | BB/9 | HR/9 | GB/F |
|---|---|---|---|---|---|---|---|---|---|---|---|---|---|
| A | — | | | | | | | | | | | | |
| AA | — | | | | | | | | | | | | |
| AAA | — | | | | | | | | | | | | |

### Majors / Skills

| Yr | Team | W | L | Sv | IP | H | K | ERA | WHIP | K/9 | BB/9 | HR/9 | GB/F |
|---|---|---|---|---|---|---|---|---|---|---|---|---|---|
| 07 | — | | | | | | | | | | | | |
| 08 | — | | | | | | | | | | | | |
| 09 | TEX | 1 | 0 | 2 | 31 | 13 | 39 | 1.74 | 0.68 | 11.3 | 2.3 | 0.6 | 0.7 |
| 10 | TEX | 4 | 3 | 40 | 69 | 43 | 71 | 2.73 | 0.88 | 9.2 | 2.3 | 0.6 | 0.8 |

**Competition at RP / Stats in 2010 as RP**

| Thr | Player | GR | ERA | IP/G | Sv-Hld |
|---|---|---|---|---|---|
| RH | O'Day D | 72 | 2.03 | 0.9 | 0-22 |
| RH | Feliz N | 70 | 2.73 | 1.0 | 40-3 |
| RH | Francisco F | 56 | 3.76 | 0.9 | 2-15 |
| RH | Ogando A | 44 | 1.30 | 0.9 | 0-7 |

Ten-Year Trends: K/9, BB/9

Weekly Points: 2008 / 2009 / 2010

### Value / Luck / In Rotation / In Relief / OPS

| $1L | $2L | Pts | RAA | H% | HR/fb | S% | FIP | GS | CG | QS/DS | GR | Hld | Bln | Lead | OPS | 1st Hf | 2nd Hf | vs RH | vs LH |
|---|---|---|---|---|---|---|---|---|---|---|---|---|---|---|---|---|---|---|---|
| $5 | $4 | 70 | +8 | 17% | 5% | 79% | 2.40 | — | — | — | 20 | 9 | 1 | +1.0 | .416 | | .416 | .274 | .533 |
| $18 | $16 | 330 | +10 | 22% | 6% | 71% | 2.97 | — | — | — | 70 | 3 | 3 | +2.3 | .516 | .600 | .406 | .616 | .409 |

## Nelson Figueroa — 100 IP | $5 | 140 pts

RP-20, SP-11 | Owned: 0% | RH

Fortune shined on Figueroa in 2010, and now he should be upgraded to a contender for a #5 SP on some club. The turnabout is only fair, since Figueroa was miscast as a reliever/spot-starter for too long. His stuff will never dominate, so his upside might be merely league-average, but that's sufficient to prosper. (BJ)

**Forecast**

| Player | Age | IP | W | Sv | K | ERA | WHIP | K/9 | BB/9 | $2L | Pts |
|---|---|---|---|---|---|---|---|---|---|---|---|
| Figueroa N | 36 | 100 | 7 | 0 | 79 | 3.86 | 1.32 | 7.1 | 3.0 | $5 | 140 |
| **Mini-Browser** | Age | IP | W | Sv | K | ERA | WHIP | K/9 | BB/9 | $2L | Pts |
| Loe K | 29 | 60 | 3 | 0 | 47 | 2.78 | 1.18 | 7.1 | 2.3 | $5 | 80 |
| Coke P | 28 | 160 | 10 | 2 | 141 | 4.52 | 1.47 | 8.0 | 3.5 | $5 | 220 |
| Zimmermann J | 24 | 160 | 8 | 0 | 156 | 4.45 | 1.35 | 8.8 | 3.0 | $5 | 210 |
| Niese J | 24 | 180 | 10 | 0 | 159 | 4.24 | 1.42 | 7.9 | 3.1 | $5 | 230 |
| Germano J | 28 | 40 | 0 | 0 | 32 | 2.16 | 0.84 | 7.3 | 2.2 | $5 | 50 |

**Minors (2010)**

| Level | Leag | W | L | Sv | IP | H | K | ERA | WHIP | K/9 | BB/9 | HR/9 | GB/F |
|---|---|---|---|---|---|---|---|---|---|---|---|---|---|
| A | — | — | — | — | — | — | — | — | — | — | — | — | — |
| AA | — | — | — | — | — | — | — | — | — | — | — | — | — |
| AAA | IL | 3 | 0 | 0 | 19 | 10 | 18 | 0.95 | 0.68 | 8.5 | 1.4 | 0.5 | — |

**Majors**

| Yr | Team | W | L | Sv | IP | H | K | ERA | WHIP | K/9 | BB/9 | HR/9 | GB/F |
|---|---|---|---|---|---|---|---|---|---|---|---|---|---|
| 07 | — | — | — | — | — | — | — | — | — | — | — | — | — |
| 08 | NYM | 3 | 3 | 0 | 45 | 48 | 36 | 4.57 | 1.63 | 7.1 | 5.2 | 0.6 | 1.1 |
| 09 | NYM | 3 | 8 | 0 | 70 | 80 | 59 | 4.09 | 1.48 | 7.5 | 3.1 | 1.0 | 1.0 |
| 10 | 2TM | 7 | 4 | 1 | 93 | 84 | 73 | 3.29 | 1.27 | 7.1 | 3.3 | 1.0 | 1.1 |

| Yr | Value $1L | $2L | Pts | RAA | Luck H% | HR/fb | S% | FIP | In Rotation GS | CG | QS/DS | In Relief GR | Hld | Bln | Lead | OPS | 1st Hf | 2nd Hf | vs RH | vs LH |
|---|---|---|---|---|---|---|---|---|---|---|---|---|---|---|---|---|---|---|---|---|
| 07 | — | — | — | — | — | — | — | — | — | — | — | — | — | — | — | — | — | — | — | — |
| 08 | -$3 | -$5 | 50 | −6 | 32% | 5% | 72% | 4.19 | 6 | 0 | 2/1 | 10 | 0 | 1 | −0.7 | .741 | .712 | .902 | .589 | .980 |
| 09 | $0 | -$2 | 80 | −1 | 33% | 9% | 75% | 4.02 | 10 | 1 | 5/2 | 6 | 0 | 0 | −1.4 | .792 | .749 | .796 | .809 | .767 |
| 10 | $4 | -$2 | 150 | +4 | 28% | 9% | 78% | 4.17 | 11 | 0 | 4/1 | 20 | 0 | 0 | −1.1 | .702 | .609 | .735 | .567 | .889 |

**Competition at RP** — Stats in 2010 as RP

| Thr | Player | GR | ERA | IP/G | Sv-Hld |
|---|---|---|---|---|---|
| RH | Lyon B | 79 | 3.12 | 1.0 | 20-19 |
| RH | Lopez W | 68 | 2.96 | 1.0 | 1-14 |
| RH | Lindstrom M | 58 | 4.39 | 0.9 | 23-4 |
| RH | Fulchino J | 50 | 5.51 | 0.9 | 0-5 |

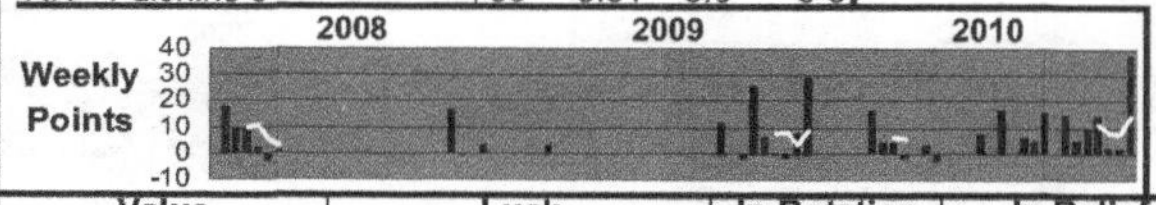


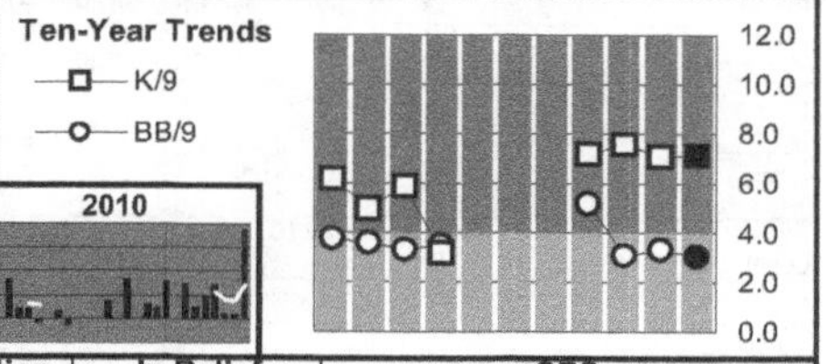


## Doug Fister — 190 IP | $4 | 160 pts

SP-28 | Owned: 20% | RH

Following a largely successful 2010 season, Fister ought to be a lock for the back of Seattle's rotation in 2011. His control is impeccable (his career rate in the minors is 2.1 BB/9), but he does not miss a lot of bats, so fortune and his backing defense play an outsized role in whether he has a good season. (GC)

**Forecast**

| Player | Age | IP | W | Sv | K | ERA | WHIP | K/9 | BB/9 | $2L | Pts |
|---|---|---|---|---|---|---|---|---|---|---|---|
| Fister D | 27 | 190 | 8 | 0 | 120 | 4.64 | 1.37 | 5.7 | 2.1 | $4 | 160 |
| **Mini-Browser** | Age | IP | W | Sv | K | ERA | WHIP | K/9 | BB/9 | $2L | Pts |
| Matsuzaka D | 30 | 160 | 10 | 0 | 138 | 4.63 | 1.44 | 7.8 | 4.5 | $4 | 200 |
| Jackson E | 27 | 200 | 10 | 0 | 145 | 4.69 | 1.42 | 6.5 | 3.4 | $4 | 200 |
| Westbrook J | 33 | 180 | 9 | 0 | 108 | 4.33 | 1.35 | 5.4 | 3.0 | $4 | 170 |
| Betancourt R | 35 | 60 | 4 | 0 | 67 | 3.91 | 1.16 | 10.0 | 2.2 | $4 | 110 |
| Venters J | 26 | 70 | 3 | 13 | 64 | 3.94 | 1.50 | 8.2 | 4.6 | $4 | 150 |

**Minors (2010)**

| Level | Leag | W | L | Sv | IP | H | K | ERA | WHIP | K/9 | BB/9 | HR/9 | GB/F |
|---|---|---|---|---|---|---|---|---|---|---|---|---|---|
| A | — | — | — | — | — | — | — | — | — | — | — | — | — |
| AA | — | — | — | — | — | — | — | — | — | — | — | — | — |
| AAA | PCL | 0 | 0 | 0 | 4 | 4 | 3 | 4.50 | 1.00 | 6.8 | 0.0 | 0.0 | — |

**Majors**

| Yr | Team | W | L | Sv | IP | H | K | ERA | WHIP | K/9 | BB/9 | HR/9 | GB/F |
|---|---|---|---|---|---|---|---|---|---|---|---|---|---|
| 07 | — | — | — | — | — | — | — | — | — | — | — | — | — |
| 08 | — | — | — | — | — | — | — | — | — | — | — | — | — |
| 09 | SEA | 3 | 4 | 0 | 61 | 63 | 36 | 4.13 | 1.28 | 5.3 | 2.2 | 1.6 | 1.1 |
| 10 | SEA | 6 | 14 | 0 | 171 | 187 | 93 | 4.11 | 1.28 | 4.9 | 1.7 | 0.7 | 1.4 |

| Yr | Value $1L | $2L | Pts | RAA | Luck H% | HR/fb | S% | FIP | In Rotation GS | CG | QS/DS | In Relief GR | Hld | Bln | Lead | OPS | 1st Hf | 2nd Hf | vs RH | vs LH |
|---|---|---|---|---|---|---|---|---|---|---|---|---|---|---|---|---|---|---|---|---|
| 07 | — | — | — | — | — | — | — | — | — | — | — | — | — | — | — | — | — | — | — | — |
| 08 | — | — | — | — | — | — | — | — | — | — | — | — | — | — | — | — | — | — | — | — |
| 09 | $2 | -$1 | 60 | +1 | 27% | 14% | 75% | 5.20 | 10 | 0 | 5/2 | 1 | 0 | 0 | −0.2 | .781 | — | .781 | .775 | .786 |
| 10 | $5 | -$10 | 140 | −1 | 31% | 6% | 68% | 3.76 | 28 | 0 | 13/4 | — | — | — | — | .698 | .616 | .770 | .685 | .710 |

**Competition at SP** — Stats in 2010 as SP

| Thr | Player | GS | ERA | Supp | W-L |
|---|---|---|---|---|---|
| RH | Hernandez F | 34 | 2.27 | 3.1 | 13-12 |
| LH | Vargas J | 31 | 3.78 | 3.1 | 9-12 |
| ▸ RH | Fister D | 28 | 4.11 | 3.1 | 6-14 |
| LH | Rowland-Smith R | 20 | 6.93 | 3.0 | 1-10 |

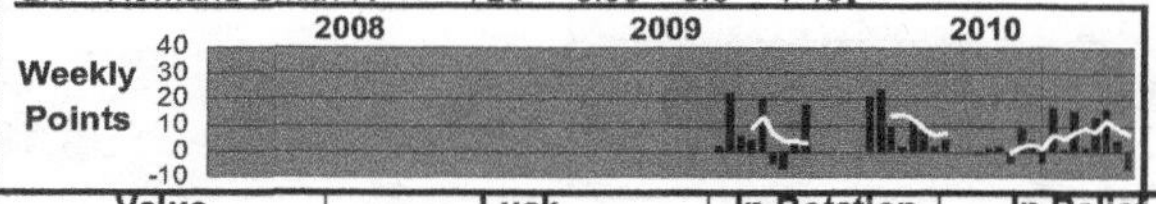


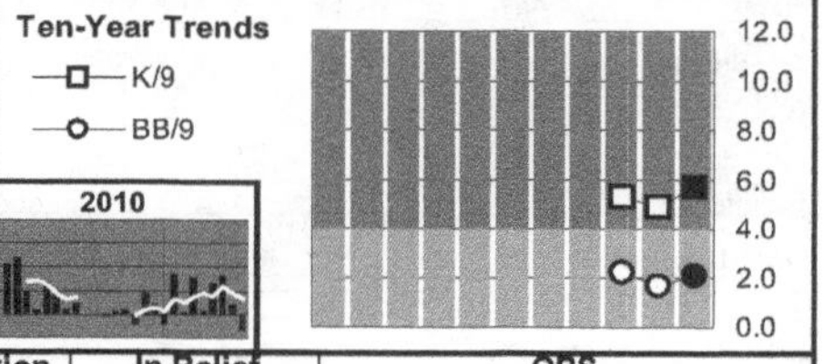


## Gavin Floyd — 200 IP | $8 | 230 pts

SP-31 | Owned: 94% | RH

Before 2009, the White Sox gave Floyd a four-year deal, rare for the organization. Floyd has rewarded the team with two decent seasons that, judging by FIP, should have been better. Floyd does not often throw a Disaster Start, but he need to avoid the high-profile flop against Minnesota (8.06 ERA in four starts). (RM)

**Forecast**

| Player | Age | IP | W | Sv | K | ERA | WHIP | K/9 | BB/9 | $2L | Pts |
|---|---|---|---|---|---|---|---|---|---|---|---|
| Floyd G | 28 | 200 | 11 | 0 | 150 | 4.47 | 1.35 | 6.8 | 3.0 | $8 | 230 |
| **Mini-Browser** | Age | IP | W | Sv | K | ERA | WHIP | K/9 | BB/9 | $2L | Pts |
| Gonzalez G | 25 | 190 | 12 | 0 | 181 | 4.20 | 1.44 | 8.6 | 4.7 | $9 | 260 |
| Ogando A | 27 | 60 | 5 | 4 | 55 | 2.51 | 1.18 | 8.2 | 3.5 | $9 | 140 |
| Happ J | 28 | 160 | 10 | 0 | 126 | 4.00 | 1.32 | 7.1 | 3.6 | $8 | 210 |
| Thornton M | 34 | 60 | 4 | 4 | 68 | 2.99 | 1.11 | 10.2 | 3.0 | $8 | 140 |
| Richard C | 27 | 180 | 11 | 0 | 134 | 3.95 | 1.36 | 6.7 | 3.4 | $8 | 230 |

**Minors (2010)**

| Level | Leag | W | L | Sv | IP | H | K | ERA | WHIP | K/9 | BB/9 | HR/9 | GB/F |
|---|---|---|---|---|---|---|---|---|---|---|---|---|---|
| A | — | — | — | — | — | — | — | — | — | — | — | — | — |
| AA | — | — | — | — | — | — | — | — | — | — | — | — | — |
| AAA | — | — | — | — | — | — | — | — | — | — | — | — | — |

**Majors**

| Yr | Team | W | L | Sv | IP | H | K | ERA | WHIP | K/9 | BB/9 | HR/9 | GB/F |
|---|---|---|---|---|---|---|---|---|---|---|---|---|---|
| 07 | CHW | 1 | 5 | 0 | 70 | 85 | 49 | 5.27 | 1.49 | 6.3 | 2.4 | 2.2 | 1.0 |
| 08 | CHW | 17 | 8 | 0 | 206 | 190 | 145 | 3.84 | 1.26 | 6.3 | 3.1 | 1.3 | 1.0 |
| 09 | CHW | 11 | 11 | 0 | 193 | 178 | 163 | 4.06 | 1.23 | 7.6 | 2.8 | 1.0 | 1.3 |
| 10 | CHW | 10 | 13 | 0 | 187 | 199 | 151 | 4.08 | 1.37 | 7.3 | 2.8 | 0.7 | 1.6 |

| Yr | Value $1L | $2L | Pts | RAA | Luck H% | HR/fb | S% | FIP | In Rotation GS | CG | QS/DS | In Relief GR | Hld | Bln | Lead | OPS | 1st Hf | 2nd Hf | vs RH | vs LH |
|---|---|---|---|---|---|---|---|---|---|---|---|---|---|---|---|---|---|---|---|---|
| 07 | -$3 | -$10 | 40 | −10 | 31% | 18% | 72% | 5.87 | 10 | 0 | 6/3 | 6 | 0 | 0 | −1.6 | .871 | 1.357 | .828 | .828 | .918 |
| 08 | $13 | $4 | 300 | −5 | 26% | 12% | 75% | 4.80 | 33 | 1 | 19/4 | — | — | — | — | .738 | .703 | .777 | .659 | .826 |
| 09 | $13 | $4 | 260 | +2 | 29% | 11% | 69% | 3.94 | 30 | 1 | 19/5 | — | — | — | — | .680 | .675 | .687 | .679 | .680 |
| 10 | $7 | -$9 | 220 | +0 | 33% | 8% | 71% | 3.59 | 31 | 1 | 18/4 | — | — | — | — | .719 | .692 | .757 | .775 | .673 |

**Competition at SP** — Stats in 2010 as SP

| Thr | Player | GS | ERA | Supp | W-L |
|---|---|---|---|---|---|
| LH | Buehrle M | 33 | 4.28 | 4.8 | 13-13 |
| LH | Danks J | 32 | 3.72 | 4.5 | 15-11 |
| RH | Jackson E | 32 | 4.47 | 4.3 | 10-12 |
| ▸ RH | Floyd G | 31 | 4.08 | 3.8 | 10-13 |

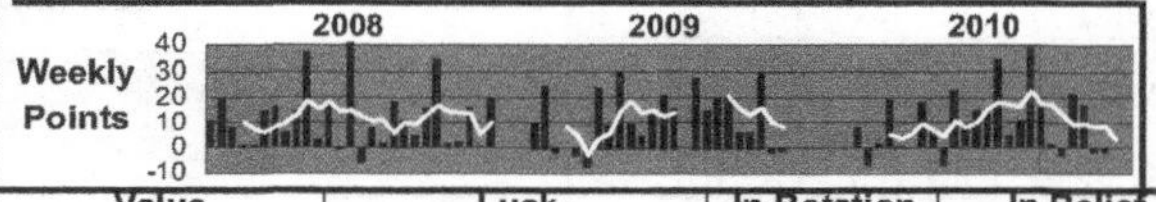


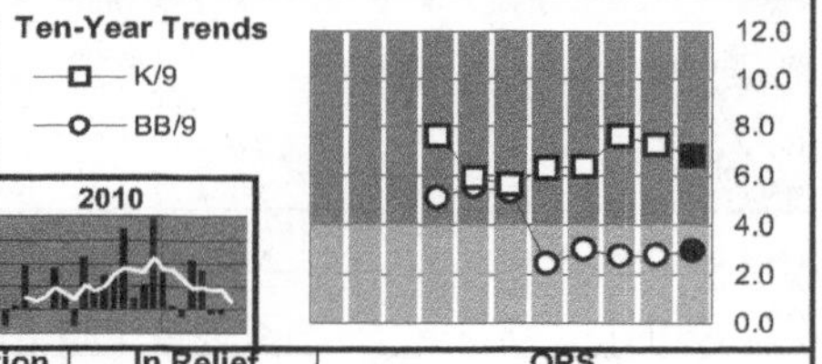


## Jeff Francis — 140 IP | $-2 | 120 pts

SP-19, RP-1 | Owned: 3% | LH

Returning from a shoulder injury, Francis did not resume his 2007 form, but his control was very good, and his FIP was 3.95 (versus 4.05 in 2007). That bodes well for 2011. The Rockies have an option on him; it is not clear if they will pick it up, but they probably will, and Francis will have a rotation spot if healthy. (TS)

**Forecast**

| Player | Age | IP | W | Sv | K | ERA | WHIP | K/9 | BB/9 | $2L | Pts |
|---|---|---|---|---|---|---|---|---|---|---|---|
| Francis J | 30 | 140 | 7 | 0 | 87 | 4.94 | 1.42 | 5.6 | 2.6 | -$2 | 120 |
| **Mini-Browser** | Age | IP | W | Sv | K | ERA | WHIP | K/9 | BB/9 | $2L | Pts |
| Rogers M | 25 | 40 | 2 | 0 | 46 | 4.53 | 1.56 | 10.4 | 4.8 | -$2 | 50 |
| Parnell B | 26 | 60 | 2 | 2 | 52 | 4.59 | 1.54 | 7.8 | 3.7 | -$2 | 70 |
| Silva C | 31 | 160 | 10 | 0 | 76 | 5.24 | 1.35 | 4.3 | 1.8 | -$2 | 130 |
| Ray C | 29 | 60 | 4 | 0 | 43 | 4.84 | 1.48 | 6.5 | 4.6 | -$2 | 60 |
| Bonderman J | 28 | 40 | 2 | 0 | 27 | 5.31 | 1.43 | 6.1 | 3.3 | -$2 | 30 |

**Minors (2010)**

| Level | Leag | W | L | Sv | IP | H | K | ERA | WHIP | K/9 | BB/9 | HR/9 | GB/F |
|---|---|---|---|---|---|---|---|---|---|---|---|---|---|
| A | — | — | — | — | — | — | — | — | — | — | — | — | — |
| AA | TL | 0 | 0 | 0 | 11 | 11 | 5 | 1.54 | 1.11 | 3.9 | 1.5 | 0.8 | — |
| AAA | PCL | 0 | 0 | 0 | 3 | 1 | 3 | 0.00 | 0.67 | 9.0 | 3.0 | 0.0 | — |

**Majors**

| Yr | Team | W | L | Sv | IP | H | K | ERA | WHIP | K/9 | BB/9 | HR/9 | GB/F |
|---|---|---|---|---|---|---|---|---|---|---|---|---|---|
| 07 | COL | 17 | 9 | 0 | 215 | 234 | 165 | 4.22 | 1.38 | 6.9 | 2.6 | 1.0 | 1.2 |
| 08 | COL | 4 | 10 | 0 | 143 | 164 | 94 | 5.01 | 1.48 | 5.9 | 3.1 | 1.3 | 1.2 |
| 09 | — | — | — | — | — | — | — | — | — | — | — | — | — |
| 10 | COL | 4 | 6 | 0 | 104 | 119 | 67 | 5.00 | 1.36 | 5.8 | 2.0 | 0.9 | 1.5 |

| Yr | Value $1L | $2L | Pts | RAA | Luck H% | HR/fb | S% | FIP | In Rotation GS | CG | QS/DS | In Relief GR | Hld | Bln | Lead | OPS | 1st Hf | 2nd Hf | vs RH | vs LH |
|---|---|---|---|---|---|---|---|---|---|---|---|---|---|---|---|---|---|---|---|---|
| 07 | $9 | -$5 | 300 | +3 | 32% | 10% | 72% | 4.05 | 34 | 1 | 19/6 | — | — | — | — | .758 | .746 | .772 | .786 | .663 |
| 08 | -$6 | -$13 | 90 | −13 | 31% | 12% | 69% | 4.81 | 24 | 0 | 12/3 | — | — | — | — | .825 | .846 | .775 | .839 | .772 |
| 09 | — | — | — | — | — | — | — | — | — | — | — | — | — | — | — | — | — | — | — | — |
| 10 | -$5 | -$17 | 80 | −10 | 33% | 10% | 64% | 3.95 | 19 | 0 | 9/3 | 1 | 0 | 0 | −0.2 | .777 | .771 | .784 | .768 | .823 |

**Competition at SP** — Stats in 2010 as SP

| Thr | Player | GS | ERA | Supp | W-L |
|---|---|---|---|---|---|
| RH | Jimenez U | 33 | 2.88 | 4.7 | 19-8 |
| RH | Hammel J | 30 | 4.81 | 4.6 | 10-9 |
| RH | Cook A | 23 | 5.08 | 4.4 | 6-8 |
| RH | Chacin J | 21 | 2.98 | 4.2 | 9-10 |

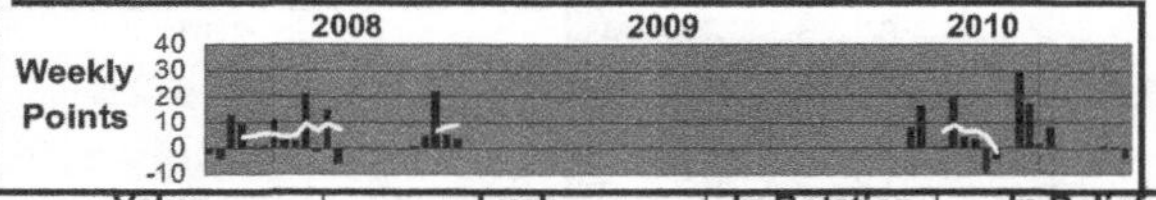


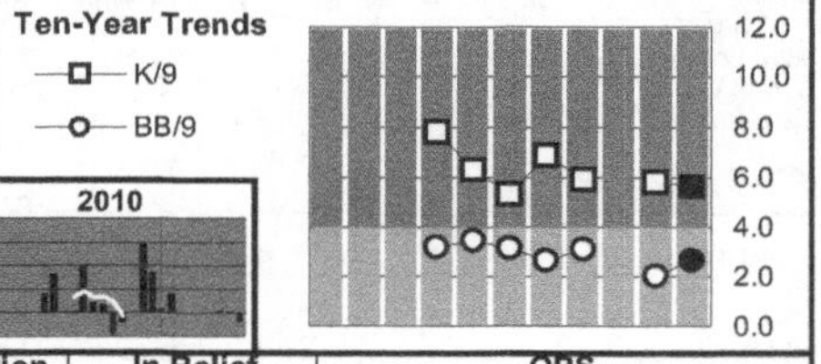


## Frank Francisco — 60 IP | $4 | 100 pts

RP-56 | Owned: 40% | RH

Francisco is in a tricky spot. Despite fashioning a typically excellent campaign, he ceded the closer's role in April and was knocked out of late-season commission by back problems – bad omens for his FA value. He's a virtual lock to close somewhere in 2011, and with a steady 10+ K/9, it'd be a waste if he didn't. (JM)

**Forecast**

| Player | Age | IP | W | Sv | K | ERA | WHIP | K/9 | BB/9 | $2L | Pts |
|---|---|---|---|---|---|---|---|---|---|---|---|
| Francisco F | 31 | 60 | 4 | 0 | 66 | 3.80 | 1.30 | 9.9 | 3.6 | $4 | 100 |
| **Mini-Browser** | Age | IP | W | Sv | K | ERA | WHIP | K/9 | BB/9 | $2L | Pts |
| Betancourt R | 35 | 60 | 4 | 0 | 67 | 3.91 | 1.16 | 10.0 | 2.2 | $4 | 110 |
| Venters J | 26 | 70 | 3 | 13 | 64 | 3.94 | 1.50 | 8.2 | 4.6 | $4 | 150 |
| Fister D | 27 | 190 | 8 | 0 | 120 | 4.64 | 1.37 | 5.7 | 2.1 | $4 | 160 |
| Masset N | 28 | 80 | 4 | 4 | 69 | 3.97 | 1.31 | 7.8 | 3.4 | $4 | 130 |
| Marshall S | 28 | 80 | 5 | 2 | 69 | 4.04 | 1.31 | 7.7 | 3.1 | $4 | 120 |

**Minors (2010)**

| Level | Leag | W | L | Sv | IP | H | K | ERA | WHIP | K/9 | BB/9 | HR/9 | GB/F |
|---|---|---|---|---|---|---|---|---|---|---|---|---|---|
| A | — | — | — | — | — | — | — | — | — | — | — | — | — |
| AA | — | — | — | — | — | — | — | — | — | — | — | — | — |
| AAA | — | — | — | — | — | — | — | — | — | — | — | — | — |

**Majors**

| Yr | Team | W | L | Sv | IP | H | K | ERA | WHIP | K/9 | BB/9 | HR/9 | GB/F |
|---|---|---|---|---|---|---|---|---|---|---|---|---|---|
| 07 | TEX | 1 | 1 | 0 | 59 | 57 | 49 | 4.55 | 1.60 | 7.4 | 5.8 | 0.5 | 0.8 |
| 08 | TEX | 3 | 5 | 5 | 63 | 47 | 83 | 3.13 | 1.15 | 11.8 | 3.7 | 1.0 | 0.7 |
| 09 | TEX | 2 | 3 | 25 | 49 | 40 | 57 | 3.83 | 1.11 | 10.4 | 2.7 | 1.1 | 0.6 |
| 10 | TEX | 6 | 4 | 2 | 52 | 49 | 60 | 3.76 | 1.27 | 10.3 | 3.1 | 0.9 | 1.0 |

| Yr | Value $1L | $2L | Pts | RAA | Luck H% | HR/fb | S% | FIP | In Rotation GS | CG | QS/DS | In Relief GR | Hld | Bln | Lead | OPS | 1st Hf | 2nd Hf | vs RH | vs LH |
|---|---|---|---|---|---|---|---|---|---|---|---|---|---|---|---|---|---|---|---|---|
| 07 | -$2 | -$8 | 40 | −6 | 32% | 4% | 71% | 4.23 | — | — | — | 59 | 21 | 0 | +0.3 | .755 | .662 | .869 | .796 | .701 |
| 08 | $8 | $4 | 140 | +5 | 27% | 9% | 77% | 3.35 | — | — | — | 58 | 12 | 6 | +0.1 | .634 | .712 | .504 | .650 | .617 |
| 09 | $8 | $5 | 200 | +1 | 28% | 9% | 69% | 3.48 | — | — | — | 51 | 4 | 4 | +2.1 | .639 | .588 | .699 | .643 | .637 |
| 10 | $3 | -$5 | 130 | +1 | 33% | 9% | 73% | 3.28 | — | — | — | 56 | 15 | 4 | +1.2 | .681 | .701 | .613 | .765 | .549 |

**Competition at RP** — Stats in 2010 as RP

| Thr | Player | GR | ERA | IP/G | Sv-Hld |
|---|---|---|---|---|---|
| RH | O'Day D | 72 | 2.03 | 0.9 | 0-22 |
| RH | Feliz N | 70 | 2.73 | 1.0 | 40-3 |
| ▸ RH | Francisco F | 56 | 3.76 | 0.9 | 2-15 |
| RH | Ogando A | 44 | 1.30 | 0.9 | 0-7 |

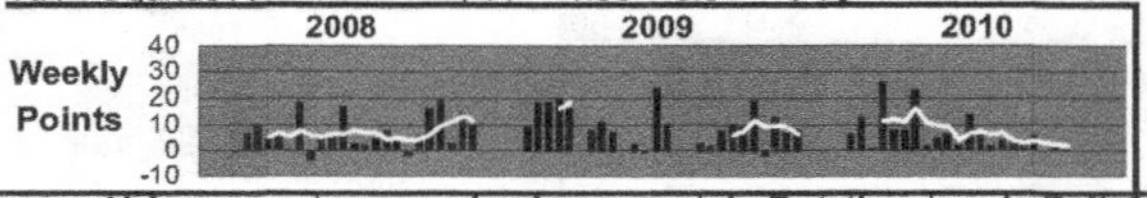


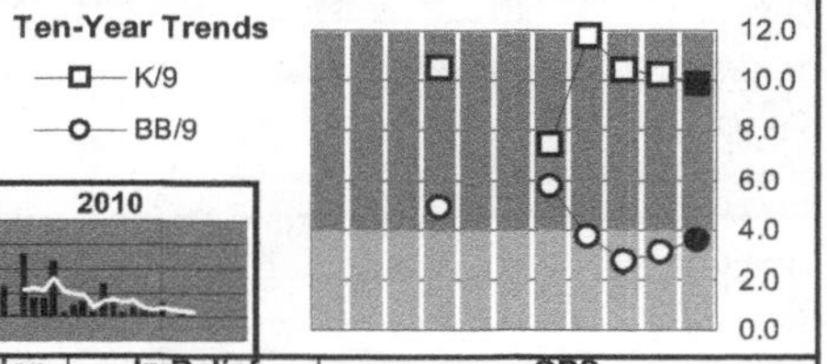


*For more stats, visit www.Rotolympus.com.*

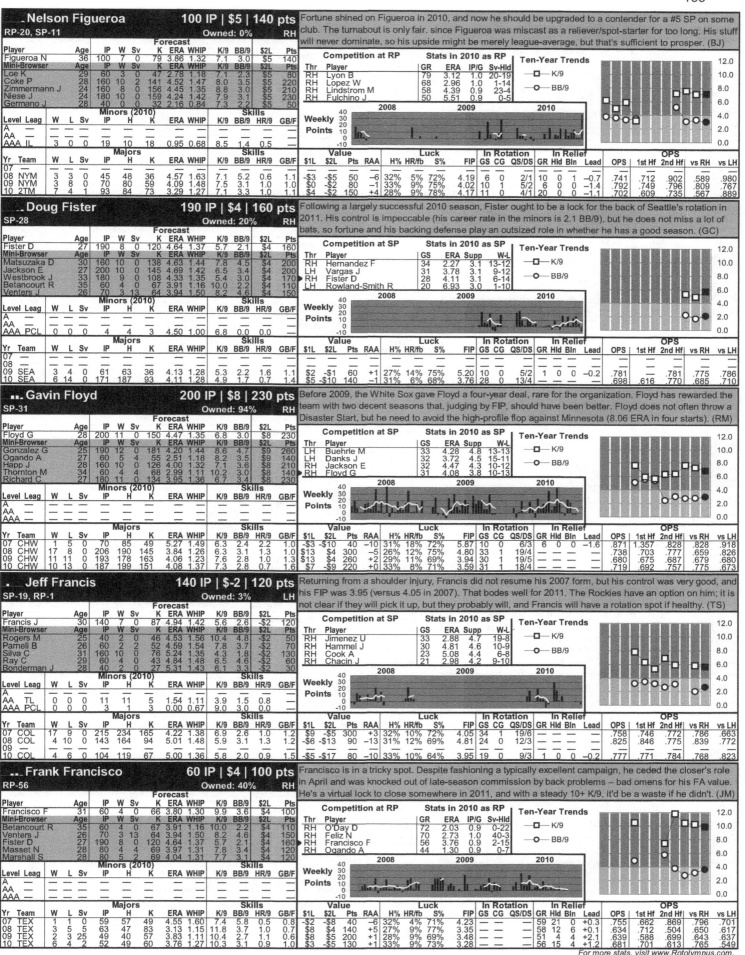

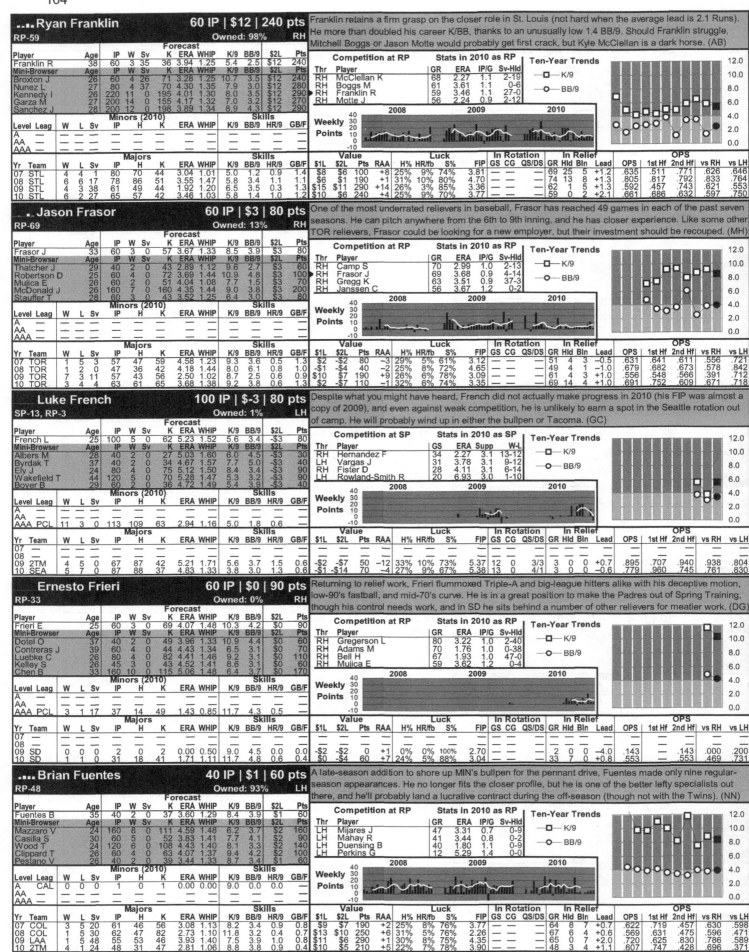

## Ryan Franklin — 60 IP | $12 | 240 pts

RP-59 · Owned: 98% · RH

Franklin retains a firm grasp on the closer role in St. Louis (not hard when the average lead is 2.1 Runs). He more than doubled his career K/BB, thanks to an unusually low 1.4 BB/9. Should Franklin struggle, Mitchell Boggs or Jason Motte would probably get first crack, but Kyle McClellan is a dark horse. (AB)

**Forecast**

| Player | Age | IP | W | Sv | K | ERA | WHIP | K/9 | BB/9 | $2L | Pts |
|---|---|---|---|---|---|---|---|---|---|---|---|
| Franklin R | 38 | 60 | 3 | 35 | 36 | 3.94 | 1.25 | 5.4 | 2.5 | $12 | 240 |
| **Mini-Browser** | **Age** | **IP** | **W** | **Sv** | **K** | **ERA** | **WHIP** | **K/9** | **BB/9** | **$2L** | **Pts** |
| Broxton J | 26 | 60 | 4 | 26 | 71 | 3.28 | 1.25 | 10.7 | 3.5 | $12 | 240 |
| Nunez L | 27 | 80 | 4 | 37 | 70 | 4.30 | 1.35 | 7.9 | 3.0 | $12 | 280 |
| Kennedy I | 26 | 220 | 11 | 0 | 195 | 4.01 | 1.30 | 8.0 | 3.5 | $12 | 290 |
| Garza M | 27 | 200 | 14 | 0 | 155 | 4.17 | 1.32 | 7.0 | 3.2 | $12 | 270 |
| Sanchez J | 28 | 200 | 12 | 0 | 198 | 3.89 | 1.34 | 8.9 | 4.3 | $12 | 290 |

**Minors (2010)**

| Level | Leag | W | L | Sv | IP | H | K | ERA | WHIP | K/9 | BB/9 | HR/9 | GB/F |
|---|---|---|---|---|---|---|---|---|---|---|---|---|---|
| A | — | — | — | — | — | — | — | — | — | — | — | — | — |
| AA | — | — | — | — | — | — | — | — | — | — | — | — | — |
| AAA | — | — | — | — | — | — | — | — | — | — | — | — | — |

**Competition at RP — Stats in 2010 as RP**

| Thr | Player | GR | ERA | IP/G | Sv-Hld |
|---|---|---|---|---|---|
| RH | McClellan K | 68 | 2.27 | 1.1 | 2-19 |
| RH | Boggs M | 61 | 3.61 | 1.1 | 0-6 |
| ▶ RH | Franklin R | 59 | 3.46 | 1.1 | 27-0 |
| RH | Motte J | 56 | 2.24 | 0.9 | 2-12 |

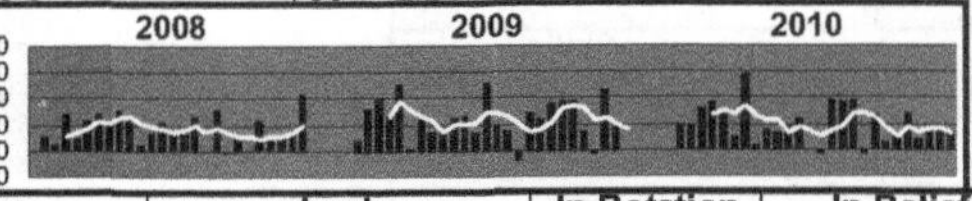


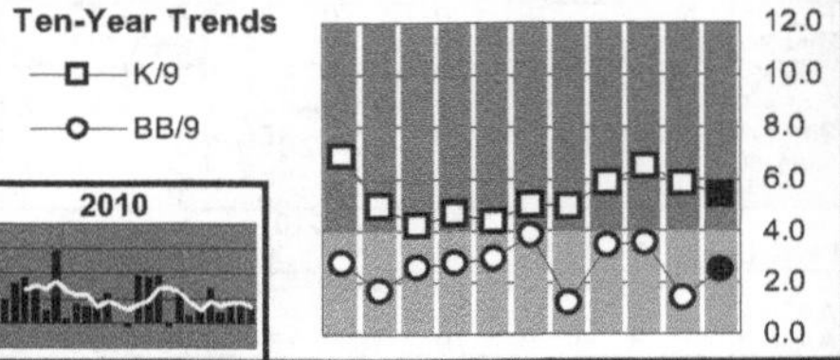


**Majors**

| Yr | Team | W | L | Sv | IP | H | K | ERA | WHIP | K/9 | BB/9 | HR/9 | GB/F | $1L | $2L | Pts | RAA | H% | HR/fb | S% | FIP | GS | CG | QS/DS | GR | Hld | Bln | Lead | OPS | 1st Hf | 2nd Hf | vs RH | vs LH |
|---|---|---|---|---|---|---|---|---|---|---|---|---|---|---|---|---|---|---|---|---|---|---|---|---|---|---|---|---|---|---|---|---|---|
| 07 | STL | 4 | 4 | 1 | 80 | 70 | 44 | 3.04 | 1.01 | 5.0 | 1.2 | 0.9 | 1.4 | $8 | $6 | 100 | +8 | 25% | 9% | 74% | 3.81 | — | — | — | 69 | 25 | 5 | +1.2 | .635 | .511 | .771 | .626 | .646 |
| 08 | STL | 6 | 6 | 17 | 78 | 86 | 51 | 3.55 | 1.47 | 5.8 | 3.4 | 1.1 | 1.1 | $6 | $1 | 190 | +1 | 31% | 10% | 80% | 4.70 | — | — | — | 74 | 13 | 8 | +1.3 | .805 | .817 | .792 | .833 | .764 |
| 09 | STL | 4 | 3 | 38 | 61 | 49 | 44 | 1.92 | 1.20 | 6.5 | 3.5 | 0.3 | 1.3 | $15 | $11 | 290 | +14 | 26% | 3% | 85% | 3.36 | — | — | — | 62 | 1 | 5 | +1.3 | .592 | .457 | .743 | .621 | .553 |
| 10 | STL | 6 | 2 | 27 | 65 | 57 | 42 | 3.46 | 1.03 | 5.8 | 1.4 | 1.0 | 1.2 | $10 | $6 | 240 | +4 | 25% | 9% | 70% | 3.77 | — | — | — | 59 | 0 | 2 | +2.1 | .661 | .686 | .632 | .597 | .750 |

## Jason Frasor — 60 IP | $3 | 80 pts

RP-69 · Owned: 13% · RH

One of the most underrated relievers in baseball, Frasor has reached 49 games in each of the past seven seasons. He can pitch anywhere from the 6th to 9th inning, and he has closer experience. Like some other TOR relievers, Frasor could be looking for a new employer, but their investment should be recouped. (MH)

**Forecast**

| Player | Age | IP | W | Sv | K | ERA | WHIP | K/9 | BB/9 | $2L | Pts |
|---|---|---|---|---|---|---|---|---|---|---|---|
| Frasor J | 33 | 60 | 3 | 0 | 57 | 3.67 | 1.33 | 8.5 | 3.9 | $3 | 80 |
| **Mini-Browser** | **Age** | **IP** | **W** | **Sv** | **K** | **ERA** | **WHIP** | **K/9** | **BB/9** | **$2L** | **Pts** |
| Thatcher J | 29 | 40 | 2 | 0 | 43 | 2.89 | 1.12 | 9.6 | 2.7 | $3 | 60 |
| Robertson D | 25 | 60 | 4 | 0 | 72 | 3.69 | 1.44 | 10.9 | 4.8 | $3 | 100 |
| Mujica E | 26 | 60 | 2 | 0 | 51 | 4.04 | 1.08 | 7.7 | 1.5 | $3 | 70 |
| McDonald J | 26 | 160 | 7 | 0 | 160 | 4.35 | 1.44 | 9.0 | 3.8 | $3 | 200 |
| Stauffer T | 28 | 60 | 3 | 0 | 43 | 3.52 | 1.25 | 6.4 | 3.0 | $3 | 80 |

**Minors (2010)**

| Level | Leag | W | L | Sv | IP | H | K | ERA | WHIP | K/9 | BB/9 | HR/9 | GB/F |
|---|---|---|---|---|---|---|---|---|---|---|---|---|---|
| A | — | — | — | — | — | — | — | — | — | — | — | — | — |
| AA | — | — | — | — | — | — | — | — | — | — | — | — | — |
| AAA | — | — | — | — | — | — | — | — | — | — | — | — | — |

**Competition at RP — Stats in 2010 as RP**

| Thr | Player | GR | ERA | IP/G | Sv-Hld |
|---|---|---|---|---|---|
| RH | Camp S | 70 | 2.99 | 1.0 | 2-13 |
| ▶ RH | Frasor J | 69 | 3.68 | 0.9 | 4-14 |
| RH | Gregg K | 63 | 3.51 | 0.9 | 37-3 |
| RH | Janssen C | 56 | 3.67 | 1.2 | 0-2 |

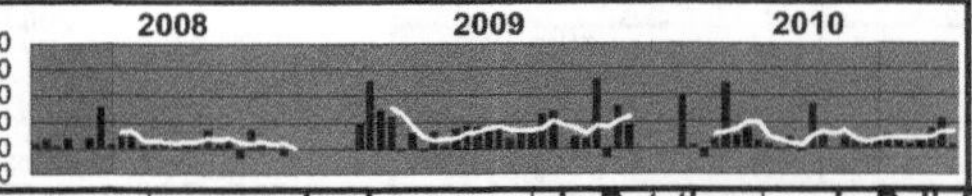


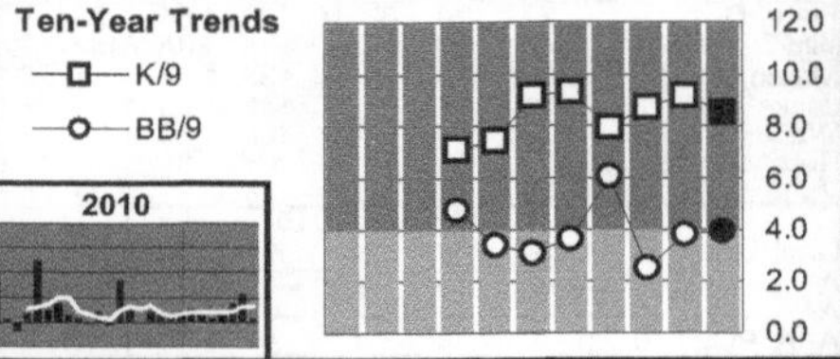


**Majors**

| Yr | Team | W | L | Sv | IP | H | K | ERA | WHIP | K/9 | BB/9 | HR/9 | GB/F | $1L | $2L | Pts | RAA | H% | HR/fb | S% | FIP | GS | CG | QS/DS | GR | Hld | Bln | Lead | OPS | 1st Hf | 2nd Hf | vs RH | vs LH |
|---|---|---|---|---|---|---|---|---|---|---|---|---|---|---|---|---|---|---|---|---|---|---|---|---|---|---|---|---|---|---|---|---|---|
| 07 | TOR | 1 | 5 | 3 | 57 | 47 | 59 | 4.58 | 1.23 | 9.3 | 3.6 | 0.5 | 1.3 | $2 | -$2 | 80 | -3 | 29% | 5% | 61% | 3.12 | — | — | — | 51 | 4 | 3 | -0.5 | .631 | .641 | .611 | .556 | .721 |
| 08 | TOR | 1 | 2 | 0 | 47 | 36 | 42 | 4.18 | 1.44 | 8.0 | 6.1 | 0.8 | 1.0 | -$1 | -$4 | 40 | -2 | 25% | 8% | 72% | 4.65 | — | — | — | 49 | 4 | 1 | -1.0 | .679 | .682 | .673 | .578 | .842 |
| 09 | TOR | 7 | 3 | 11 | 57 | 43 | 56 | 2.50 | 1.02 | 8.7 | 2.5 | 0.6 | 0.9 | $10 | $7 | 190 | +9 | 26% | 6% | 78% | 3.09 | — | — | — | 61 | 4 | 3 | +1.0 | .556 | .548 | .566 | .391 | .712 |
| 10 | TOR | 3 | 4 | 4 | 63 | 61 | 65 | 3.68 | 1.38 | 9.2 | 3.8 | 0.6 | 1.3 | $2 | -$7 | 110 | -1 | 32% | 6% | 74% | 3.35 | — | — | — | 69 | 14 | 4 | +1.0 | .691 | .752 | .609 | .671 | .718 |

## Luke French — 100 IP | $-3 | 80 pts

SP-13, RP-3 · Owned: 1% · LH

Despite what you might have heard, French did not actually make progress in 2010 (his FIP was almost a copy of 2009), and even against weak competition, he is unlikely to earn a spot in the Seattle rotation out of camp. He will probably wind up in either the bullpen or Tacoma. (GC)

**Forecast**

| Player | Age | IP | W | Sv | K | ERA | WHIP | K/9 | BB/9 | $2L | Pts |
|---|---|---|---|---|---|---|---|---|---|---|---|
| French L | 25 | 100 | 5 | 0 | 62 | 5.23 | 1.52 | 5.6 | 3.4 | -$3 | 80 |
| **Mini-Browser** | **Age** | **IP** | **W** | **Sv** | **K** | **ERA** | **WHIP** | **K/9** | **BB/9** | **$2L** | **Pts** |
| Albers M | 28 | 40 | 2 | 0 | 27 | 5.03 | 1.60 | 6.0 | 4.5 | -$3 | 30 |
| Byrdak T | 37 | 40 | 2 | 0 | 34 | 4.67 | 1.57 | 7.7 | 5.0 | -$3 | 40 |
| Ely J | 24 | 80 | 4 | 0 | 75 | 5.12 | 1.50 | 8.4 | 3.4 | -$3 | 90 |
| Wakefield T | 44 | 120 | 5 | 0 | 70 | 5.28 | 1.47 | 5.3 | 3.2 | -$3 | 90 |
| Boyer B | 29 | 60 | 2 | 0 | 36 | 4.72 | 1.49 | 5.4 | 3.9 | -$3 | 40 |

**Minors (2010)**

| Level | Leag | W | L | Sv | IP | H | K | ERA | WHIP | K/9 | BB/9 | HR/9 | GB/F |
|---|---|---|---|---|---|---|---|---|---|---|---|---|---|
| A | — | — | — | — | — | — | — | — | — | — | — | — | — |
| AA | — | — | — | — | — | — | — | — | — | — | — | — | — |
| AAA | PCL | 11 | 3 | 0 | 113 | 109 | 63 | 2.94 | 1.16 | 5.0 | 1.8 | 0.6 | — |

**Competition at SP — Stats in 2010 as SP**

| Thr | Player | GS | ERA | Supp | W-L |
|---|---|---|---|---|---|
| RH | Hernandez F | 34 | 2.27 | 3.1 | 13-12 |
| LH | Vargas J | 31 | 3.78 | 3.1 | 9-12 |
| RH | Fister D | 28 | 4.11 | 3.1 | 6-14 |
| LH | Rowland-Smith R | 20 | 6.93 | 3.0 | 1-10 |

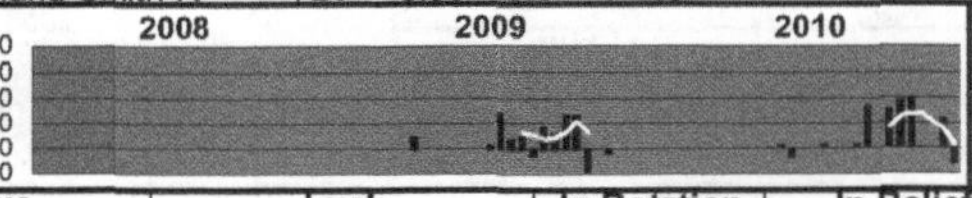


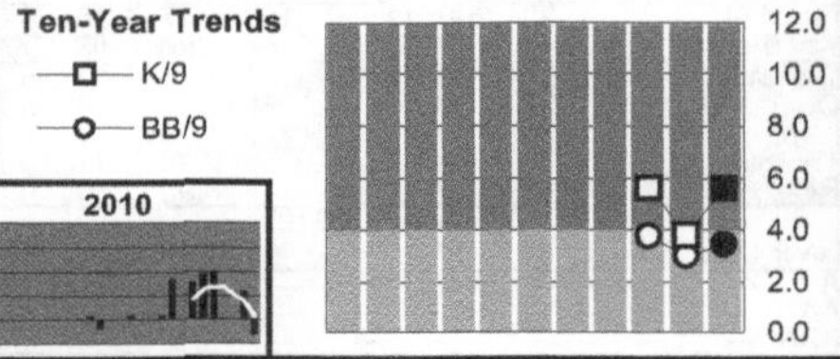


**Majors**

| Yr | Team | W | L | Sv | IP | H | K | ERA | WHIP | K/9 | BB/9 | HR/9 | GB/F | $1L | $2L | Pts | RAA | H% | HR/fb | S% | FIP | GS | CG | QS/DS | GR | Hld | Bln | Lead | OPS | 1st Hf | 2nd Hf | vs RH | vs LH |
|---|---|---|---|---|---|---|---|---|---|---|---|---|---|---|---|---|---|---|---|---|---|---|---|---|---|---|---|---|---|---|---|---|---|
| 07 | — | — | — | — | — | — | — | — | — | — | — | — | — | — | — | — | — | — | — | — | — | — | — | — | — | — | — | — | — | — | — | — | — |
| 08 | — | — | — | — | — | — | — | — | — | — | — | — | — | — | — | — | — | — | — | — | — | — | — | — | — | — | — | — | — | — | — | — | — |
| 09 | 2TM | 4 | 5 | 0 | 67 | 87 | 42 | 5.21 | 1.71 | 5.6 | 3.7 | 1.5 | 0.6 | -$2 | -$7 | 50 | -12 | 33% | 10% | 73% | 5.37 | 12 | 0 | 3/3 | 3 | 0 | 0 | +0.7 | .895 | .707 | .940 | .938 | .804 |
| 10 | SEA | 5 | 7 | 0 | 87 | 88 | 37 | 4.83 | 1.33 | 3.8 | 3.0 | 1.3 | 0.6 | -$1 | -$14 | 70 | -4 | 27% | 9% | 67% | 5.38 | 13 | 0 | 4/1 | 3 | 0 | 0 | -0.6 | .779 | .960 | .745 | .761 | .830 |

## Ernesto Frieri — 60 IP | $0 | 90 pts

RP-33 · Owned: 0% · RH

Returning to relief work, Frieri flummoxed Triple-A and big-league hitters alike with his deceptive motion, low-90's fastball, and mid-70's curve. He is in a great position to make the Padres out of Spring Training, though his control needs work, and in SD he sits behind a number of other relievers for meatier work. (DG)

**Forecast**

| Player | Age | IP | W | Sv | K | ERA | WHIP | K/9 | BB/9 | $2L | Pts |
|---|---|---|---|---|---|---|---|---|---|---|---|
| Frieri E | 25 | 60 | 3 | 0 | 69 | 4.07 | 1.48 | 10.3 | 4.2 | $0 | 90 |
| **Mini-Browser** | **Age** | **IP** | **W** | **Sv** | **K** | **ERA** | **WHIP** | **K/9** | **BB/9** | **$2L** | **Pts** |
| Dotel O | 37 | 40 | 2 | 0 | 49 | 3.96 | 1.33 | 10.9 | 4.4 | $0 | 60 |
| Contreras J | 39 | 60 | 4 | 0 | 44 | 4.43 | 1.34 | 6.5 | 3.1 | $0 | 70 |
| Luebke C | 26 | 80 | 4 | 0 | 82 | 4.41 | 1.46 | 9.2 | 3.1 | $0 | 110 |
| Kelley S | 26 | 45 | 3 | 0 | 43 | 4.52 | 1.41 | 8.6 | 3.1 | $0 | 60 |
| Chen B | 33 | 160 | 10 | 0 | 115 | 5.06 | 1.48 | 6.4 | 3.7 | $0 | 170 |

**Minors (2010)**

| Level | Leag | W | L | Sv | IP | H | K | ERA | WHIP | K/9 | BB/9 | HR/9 | GB/F |
|---|---|---|---|---|---|---|---|---|---|---|---|---|---|
| A | — | — | — | — | — | — | — | — | — | — | — | — | — |
| AA | — | — | — | — | — | — | — | — | — | — | — | — | — |
| AAA | PCL | 3 | 1 | 17 | 37 | 14 | 49 | 1.43 | 0.85 | 11.7 | 4.3 | 0.5 | — |

**Competition at RP — Stats in 2010 as RP**

| Thr | Player | GR | ERA | IP/G | Sv-Hld |
|---|---|---|---|---|---|
| RH | Gregerson L | 80 | 3.22 | 1.0 | 2-40 |
| RH | Adams M | 70 | 1.76 | 1.0 | 0-38 |
| RH | Bell H | 67 | 1.93 | 1.0 | 47-0 |
| RH | Mujica E | 59 | 3.62 | 1.2 | 0-4 |

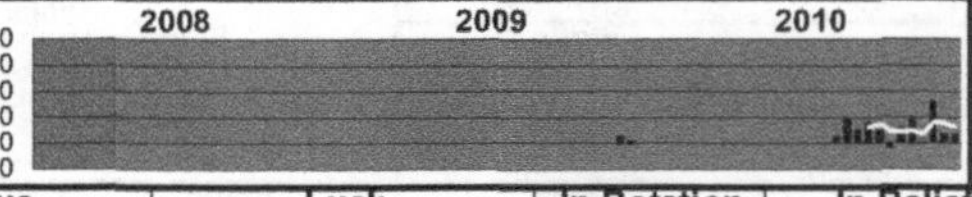


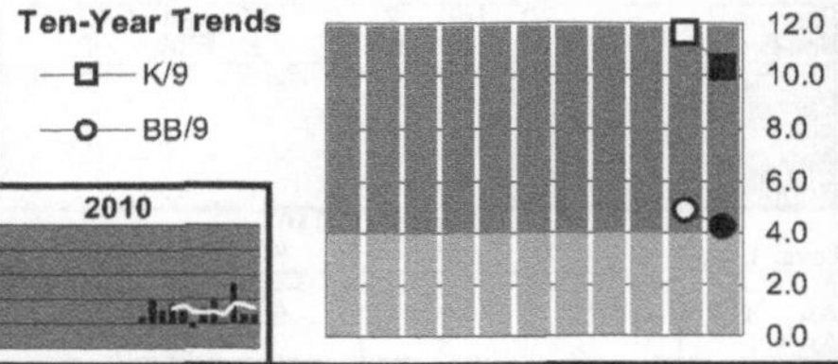


**Majors**

| Yr | Team | W | L | Sv | IP | H | K | ERA | WHIP | K/9 | BB/9 | HR/9 | GB/F | $1L | $2L | Pts | RAA | H% | HR/fb | S% | FIP | GS | CG | QS/DS | GR | Hld | Bln | Lead | OPS | 1st Hf | 2nd Hf | vs RH | vs LH |
|---|---|---|---|---|---|---|---|---|---|---|---|---|---|---|---|---|---|---|---|---|---|---|---|---|---|---|---|---|---|---|---|---|---|
| 07 | — | — | — | — | — | — | — | — | — | — | — | — | — | — | — | — | — | — | — | — | — | — | — | — | — | — | — | — | — | — | — | — | — |
| 08 | — | — | — | — | — | — | — | — | — | — | — | — | — | — | — | — | — | — | — | — | — | — | — | — | — | — | — | — | — | — | — | — | — |
| 09 | SD | 0 | 0 | 0 | 2 | 0 | 2 | 0.00 | 0.50 | 9.0 | 4.5 | 0.0 | 0.0 | -$2 | -$2 | 0 | +1 | 0% | 0% | 100% | 2.70 | — | — | — | 2 | 0 | 0 | -4.0 | .143 | — | .143 | .000 | .200 |
| 10 | SD | 1 | 1 | 0 | 31 | 18 | 41 | 1.71 | 1.11 | 11.7 | 4.8 | 0.6 | 0.4 | $0 | -$4 | 60 | +7 | 24% | 5% | 88% | 3.04 | — | — | — | 33 | 7 | 0 | +0.8 | .553 | — | .553 | .469 | .731 |

## Brian Fuentes — 40 IP | $1 | 60 pts

RP-48 · Owned: 93% · LH

A late-season addition to shore up MIN's bullpen for the pennant drive, Fuentes made only nine regular-season appearances. He no longer fits the closer profile, but he is one of the better lefty specialists out there, and he'll probably land a lucrative contract during the off-season (though not with the Twins). (NN)

**Forecast**

| Player | Age | IP | W | Sv | K | ERA | WHIP | K/9 | BB/9 | $2L | Pts |
|---|---|---|---|---|---|---|---|---|---|---|---|
| Fuentes B | 35 | 40 | 2 | 0 | 37 | 3.60 | 1.29 | 8.4 | 3.9 | $1 | 60 |
| **Mini-Browser** | **Age** | **IP** | **W** | **Sv** | **K** | **ERA** | **WHIP** | **K/9** | **BB/9** | **$2L** | **Pts** |
| Mazzaro V | 24 | 160 | 8 | 0 | 111 | 4.59 | 1.48 | 6.2 | 3.7 | $2 | 160 |
| Casilla S | 30 | 60 | 5 | 0 | 52 | 3.83 | 1.41 | 7.7 | 4.1 | $2 | 90 |
| Wood T | 24 | 120 | 6 | 0 | 108 | 4.43 | 1.40 | 8.1 | 3.3 | $2 | 140 |
| Clippard T | 26 | 60 | 4 | 0 | 63 | 4.07 | 1.37 | 9.4 | 4.2 | $2 | 100 |
| Pestano V | 26 | 40 | 2 | 0 | 39 | 3.44 | 1.33 | 8.7 | 3.4 | $1 | 60 |

**Minors (2010)**

| Level | Leag | W | L | Sv | IP | H | K | ERA | WHIP | K/9 | BB/9 | HR/9 | GB/F |
|---|---|---|---|---|---|---|---|---|---|---|---|---|---|
| A | CAL | 0 | 0 | 0 | 1 | 0 | 1 | 0.00 | 0.00 | 9.0 | 0.0 | 0.0 | — |
| AA | — | — | — | — | — | — | — | — | — | — | — | — | — |
| AAA | — | — | — | — | — | — | — | — | — | — | — | — | — |

**Competition at RP — Stats in 2010 as RP**

| Thr | Player | GR | ERA | IP/G | Sv-Hld |
|---|---|---|---|---|---|
| LH | Mijares J | 47 | 3.31 | 0.7 | 0-9 |
| LH | Mahay R | 41 | 3.44 | 0.8 | 0-2 |
| LH | Duensing B | 40 | 1.80 | 1.1 | 0-9 |
| LH | Perkins G | 12 | 5.29 | 1.4 | 0-0 |

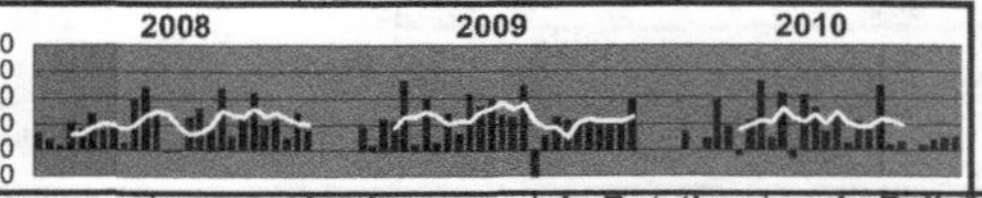


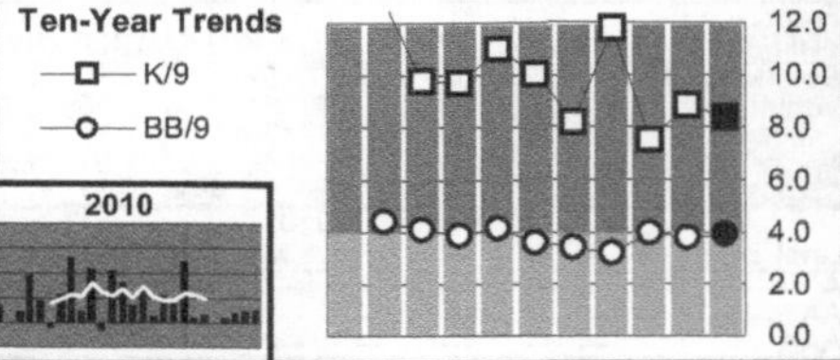


**Majors**

| Yr | Team | W | L | Sv | IP | H | K | ERA | WHIP | K/9 | BB/9 | HR/9 | GB/F | $1L | $2L | Pts | RAA | H% | HR/fb | S% | FIP | GS | CG | QS/DS | GR | Hld | Bln | Lead | OPS | 1st Hf | 2nd Hf | vs RH | vs LH |
|---|---|---|---|---|---|---|---|---|---|---|---|---|---|---|---|---|---|---|---|---|---|---|---|---|---|---|---|---|---|---|---|---|---|
| 07 | COL | 3 | 5 | 20 | 61 | 46 | 56 | 3.08 | 1.13 | 8.2 | 3.4 | 0.9 | 0.8 | $9 | $7 | 190 | +2 | 25% | 8% | 76% | 3.77 | — | — | — | 64 | 8 | 7 | +0.7 | .622 | .719 | .457 | .630 | .598 |
| 08 | COL | 1 | 5 | 30 | 62 | 47 | 82 | 2.73 | 1.10 | 11.8 | 3.2 | 0.4 | 0.7 | $13 | $10 | 250 | +6 | 31% | 5% | 76% | 2.26 | — | — | — | 67 | 6 | 4 | +0.6 | .569 | .631 | .475 | .596 | .471 |
| 09 | LAA | 1 | 5 | 48 | 55 | 53 | 46 | 3.93 | 1.40 | 7.5 | 3.9 | 1.0 | 0.8 | $11 | $6 | 290 | +1 | 30% | 8% | 75% | 4.35 | — | — | — | 65 | 0 | 7 | +2.0 | .720 | .625 | .830 | .786 | .589 |
| 10 | 2TM | 4 | 1 | 24 | 48 | 31 | 47 | 2.81 | 1.06 | 8.8 | 3.8 | 0.9 | 0.4 | $10 | $5 | 210 | +5 | 22% | 7% | 78% | 3.90 | — | — | — | 48 | 3 | 4 | +1.1 | .607 | .747 | .428 | .696 | .371 |

## Jeff Fulchino — 40 IP | $-2 | 40 pts
RP-50  Owned: 0%  RH

Fulchino battled elbow pain in 2010, and he needed surgery in October to put the season behind him. Despite a mid-90's fastball, he is not especially tricky, which makes him hittable even though he gets K's. Fulchino flashes late-inning talent, but he is basically a middle reliever who can go multiple innings. (BJ)

### Forecast
| Player | Age | IP | W | Sv | K | ERA | WHIP | K/9 | BB/9 | $2L | Pts |
|---|---|---|---|---|---|---|---|---|---|---|---|
| Fulchino J | 31 | 40 | 2 | 0 | 33 | 4.80 | 1.45 | 7.4 | 3.6 | -$2 | 40 |

### Mini-Browser
| Player | Age | IP | W | Sv | K | ERA | WHIP | K/9 | BB/9 | $2L | Pts |
|---|---|---|---|---|---|---|---|---|---|---|---|
| Albaladejo J | 28 | 40 | 2 | 0 | 29 | 5.15 | 1.50 | 6.6 | 3.9 | -$2 | 40 |
| Baez D | 33 | 40 | 2 | 0 | 22 | 4.77 | 1.42 | 4.9 | 3.7 | -$2 | 30 |
| Nieve F | 28 | 40 | 2 | 0 | 33 | 5.12 | 1.41 | 7.5 | 3.9 | -$2 | 40 |
| Sanabia A | 22 | 100 | 6 | 0 | 74 | 4.83 | 1.50 | 6.7 | 3.0 | -$2 | 100 |
| Walters P | 26 | 40 | 2 | 0 | 38 | 5.02 | 1.49 | 8.5 | 3.5 | -$2 | 50 |

### Minors (2010) / Skills
| Level | Leag | W | L | Sv | IP | H | K | ERA | WHIP | K/9 | BB/9 | HR/9 | GB/F |
|---|---|---|---|---|---|---|---|---|---|---|---|---|---|
| A | — | — | — | — | — | — | — | — | — | — | — | — | — |
| AA | — | — | — | — | — | — | — | — | — | — | — | — | — |
| AAA | PCL | 0 | 0 | 0 | 4 | 3 | 2 | 0.00 | 1.00 | 4.5 | 2.3 | 0.0 | — |

### Majors / Skills
| Yr | Team | W | L | Sv | IP | H | K | ERA | WHIP | K/9 | BB/9 | HR/9 | GB/F |
|---|---|---|---|---|---|---|---|---|---|---|---|---|---|
| 07 | — | — | — | — | — | — | — | — | — | — | — | — | — |
| 08 | KC | 0 | 1 | 0 | 14 | 21 | 12 | 9.00 | 2.07 | 7.7 | 5.1 | 1.3 | 1.4 |
| 09 | HOU | 6 | 4 | 0 | 82 | 70 | 71 | 3.40 | 1.18 | 7.8 | 3.0 | 0.8 | 1.2 |
| 10 | HOU | 1 | 2 | 0 | 47 | 53 | 46 | 5.51 | 1.58 | 8.7 | 4.2 | 1.3 | 1.1 |

### Competition at RP / Stats in 2010 as RP
| Thr | Player | GR | ERA | IP/G | Sv-Hld |
|---|---|---|---|---|---|
| RH | Lyon B | 79 | 3.12 | 1.0 | 20-19 |
| RH | Lopez W | 68 | 2.96 | 1.0 | 1-14 |
| RH | Lindstrom M | 58 | 4.39 | 0.9 | 23-4 |
| RH | Fulchino J | 50 | 5.51 | 0.9 | 0-5 |

### Value / Luck / In Rotation / In Relief / OPS
| $1L | $2L | Pts | RAA | H% | HR/fb | S% | FIP | GS | CG | QS/DS | GR | Hld | Bln | Lead | OPS | 1st Hf | 2nd Hf | vs RH | vs LH |
|---|---|---|---|---|---|---|---|---|---|---|---|---|---|---|---|---|---|---|---|
| -$6 | -$7 | 0 | -9 | 39% | 12% | 56% | 5.16 | — | — | — | 12 | 0 | 0 | -0.8 | .981 | .938 | 1.011 | .900 | 1.053 |
| $6 | -$3 | 130 | +4 | 29% | 8% | 73% | 3.57 | — | — | — | 61 | 12 | 3 | -0.5 | .680 | .696 | .664 | .652 | .712 |
| -$7 | -$16 | 50 | -9 | 34% | 13% | 68% | 4.57 | — | — | — | 50 | 5 | 1 | -1.7 | .793 | .886 | .632 | .775 | .817 |

## Armando Galarraga — 140 IP | $-4 | 90 pts
SP-24, RP-1  Owned: 3%  RH

Galarraga made headlines in 2010 with his near-perfect game, but he will still have to fight for a job in '11. His control improved, but the mix of low K/9 and GB/F keeps him from being a reliable starter (only 9 QS in 24 GS). With a fair Spring Training, the 29-year-old should retain the #5 spot in Detroit's rotation. (LP)

### Forecast
| Player | Age | IP | W | Sv | K | ERA | WHIP | K/9 | BB/9 | $2L | Pts |
|---|---|---|---|---|---|---|---|---|---|---|---|
| Galarraga A | 29 | 140 | 5 | 0 | 85 | 5.30 | 1.50 | 5.4 | 3.8 | -$4 | 90 |

### Mini-Browser
| Player | Age | IP | W | Sv | K | ERA | WHIP | K/9 | BB/9 | $2L | Pts |
|---|---|---|---|---|---|---|---|---|---|---|---|
| Diamond T | 27 | 60 | 2 | 0 | 44 | 4.93 | 1.57 | 6.7 | 5.1 | -$4 | 50 |
| Grabow J | 32 | 40 | 2 | 0 | 29 | 5.17 | 1.58 | 6.4 | 4.6 | -$4 | 40 |
| LeCure S | 26 | 60 | 3 | 0 | 53 | 5.20 | 1.56 | 8.0 | 3.8 | -$4 | 60 |
| Ross T | 23 | 40 | 1 | 0 | 38 | 5.66 | 1.70 | 8.6 | 4.7 | -$4 | 40 |
| Lohse K | 32 | 120 | 7 | 0 | 68 | 5.20 | 1.45 | 5.1 | 2.7 | -$4 | 100 |

### Minors (2010) / Skills
| Level | Leag | W | L | Sv | IP | H | K | ERA | WHIP | K/9 | BB/9 | HR/9 | GB/F |
|---|---|---|---|---|---|---|---|---|---|---|---|---|---|
| A | — | — | — | — | — | — | — | — | — | — | — | — | — |
| AA | — | — | — | — | — | — | — | — | — | — | — | — | — |
| AAA | IL | 4 | 2 | 0 | 44 | 40 | 40 | 3.65 | 1.22 | 8.1 | 2.8 | 0.8 | — |

### Majors / Skills
| Yr | Team | W | L | Sv | IP | H | K | ERA | WHIP | K/9 | BB/9 | HR/9 | GB/F |
|---|---|---|---|---|---|---|---|---|---|---|---|---|---|
| 07 | TEX | 0 | 0 | 0 | 8 | 8 | 6 | 6.23 | 1.73 | 6.2 | 7.3 | 2.1 | 0.8 |
| 08 | DET | 13 | 7 | 0 | 178 | 152 | 126 | 3.73 | 1.19 | 6.3 | 3.1 | 1.4 | 1.1 |
| 09 | DET | 6 | 10 | 0 | 143 | 158 | 95 | 5.64 | 1.57 | 6.0 | 4.2 | 1.5 | 1.0 |
| 10 | DET | 4 | 9 | 0 | 144 | 143 | 74 | 4.49 | 1.34 | 4.6 | 3.2 | 1.3 | 0.8 |

### Competition at SP / Stats in 2010 as SP
| Thr | Player | GS | ERA | Supp | W-L |
|---|---|---|---|---|---|
| RH | Verlander J | 33 | 3.37 | 5.2 | 18-9 |
| RH | Scherzer M | 31 | 3.50 | 4.0 | 12-11 |
| RH | Bonderman J | 29 | 5.56 | 5.1 | 8-10 |
| RH | Porcello R | 27 | 4.92 | 4.8 | 10-12 |

### Value / Luck / In Rotation / In Relief / OPS
| $1L | $2L | Pts | RAA | H% | HR/fb | S% | FIP | GS | CG | QS/DS | GR | Hld | Bln | Lead | OPS | 1st Hf | 2nd Hf | vs RH | vs LH |
|---|---|---|---|---|---|---|---|---|---|---|---|---|---|---|---|---|---|---|---|
| -$3 | -$4 | 0 | -2 | 24% | 15% | 69% | 7.34 | 1 | 0 | 0/1 | 2 | 0 | 0 | -2.0 | .844 | — | .844 | .683 | .954 |
| $13 | -$6 | 250 | +5 | 24% | 13% | 75% | 4.95 | 28 | 0 | 16/2 | 2 | 0 | 1 | +0.4 | .704 | .657 | .756 | .542 | .834 |
| -$3 | -$12 | 100 | -22 | 30% | 13% | 68% | 5.55 | 25 | 0 | 10/4 | 1 | 0 | 0 | -0.2 | .847 | .863 | .811 | .762 | .924 |
| $0 | -$16 | 90 | -4 | 26% | 9% | 71% | 5.23 | 24 | 2 | 9/4 | 1 | 0 | 0 | +0.3 | .765 | .742 | .780 | .745 | .785 |

## Yovani Gallardo — 200 IP | $13 | 330 pts
SP-31  Owned: 100%  RH

Only a short mid-year DL stint for an oblique strain marred Gallardo's 2010. His Weekly Points graph shows that his second half was rockier than his first, largely because of a 7.75 ERA in August. But he recovered for a 3.77 ERA and three Wins in September. Gallardo's upside is an ERA below 3.00. (MS)

### Forecast
| Player | Age | IP | W | Sv | K | ERA | WHIP | K/9 | BB/9 | $2L | Pts |
|---|---|---|---|---|---|---|---|---|---|---|---|
| Gallardo Y | 25 | 200 | 15 | 0 | 204 | 3.92 | 1.35 | 9.2 | 3.8 | $13 | 330 |

### Mini-Browser
| Player | Age | IP | W | Sv | K | ERA | WHIP | K/9 | BB/9 | $2L | Pts |
|---|---|---|---|---|---|---|---|---|---|---|---|
| Scherzer M | 26 | 200 | 12 | 0 | 193 | 3.97 | 1.31 | 8.7 | 3.4 | $14 | 290 |
| Lewis C | 31 | 180 | 11 | 0 | 171 | 3.99 | 1.33 | 8.5 | 2.9 | $14 | 270 |
| Kuroda H | 36 | 200 | 12 | 0 | 142 | 3.87 | 1.21 | 6.4 | 2.1 | $14 | 250 |
| Valverde J | 33 | 60 | 2 | 36 | 59 | 3.69 | 1.27 | 8.8 | 4.0 | $13 | 260 |
| Buchholz C | 26 | 180 | 14 | 0 | 142 | 3.68 | 1.36 | 7.1 | 3.7 | $13 | 270 |

### Minors (2010) / Skills
| Level | Leag | W | L | Sv | IP | H | K | ERA | WHIP | K/9 | BB/9 | HR/9 | GB/F |
|---|---|---|---|---|---|---|---|---|---|---|---|---|---|
| A | — | — | — | — | — | — | — | — | — | — | — | — | — |
| AA | — | — | — | — | — | — | — | — | — | — | — | — | — |
| AAA | — | — | — | — | — | — | — | — | — | — | — | — | — |

### Majors / Skills
| Yr | Team | W | L | Sv | IP | H | K | ERA | WHIP | K/9 | BB/9 | HR/9 | GB/F |
|---|---|---|---|---|---|---|---|---|---|---|---|---|---|
| 07 | MIL | 9 | 5 | 0 | 110 | 103 | 101 | 3.67 | 1.24 | 8.2 | 3.0 | 1.0 | 1.0 |
| 08 | MIL | 0 | 0 | 0 | 24 | 22 | 20 | 1.88 | 1.25 | 7.5 | 3.0 | 1.1 | 0.8 |
| 09 | MIL | 13 | 12 | 0 | 185 | 150 | 204 | 3.73 | 1.31 | 9.9 | 4.6 | 1.0 | 1.3 |
| 10 | MIL | 14 | 7 | 0 | 185 | 178 | 200 | 3.84 | 1.37 | 9.7 | 3.6 | 0.6 | 1.3 |

### Competition at SP / Stats in 2010 as SP
| Thr | Player | GS | ERA | Supp | W-L |
|---|---|---|---|---|---|
| LH | Wolf R | 34 | 4.17 | 5.3 | 13-12 |
| RH | Gallardo Y | 31 | 3.84 | 5.3 | 14-7 |
| RH | Bush D | 31 | 4.55 | 4.0 | 8-13 |
| LH | Narveson C | 28 | 4.85 | 4.3 | 11-9 |

### Value / Luck / In Rotation / In Relief / OPS
| $1L | $2L | Pts | RAA | H% | HR/fb | S% | FIP | GS | CG | QS/DS | GR | Hld | Bln | Lead | OPS | 1st Hf | 2nd Hf | vs RH | vs LH |
|---|---|---|---|---|---|---|---|---|---|---|---|---|---|---|---|---|---|---|---|
| $8 | $2 | 190 | +6 | 31% | 7% | 72% | 3.32 | 17 | 0 | 12/3 | 3 | 0 | 0 | +0.2 | .676 | .634 | .688 | .665 | .693 |
| $1 | $0 | 20 | +7 | 31% | 10% | 93% | 4.16 | 4 | 0 | 3/0 | — | — | — | — | .723 | .719 | .741 | .619 | .851 |
| $12 | $6 | 320 | +14 | 28% | 12% | 72% | 3.99 | 30 | 1 | 17/4 | — | — | — | — | .701 | .665 | .758 | .752 | .652 |
| $9 | -$2 | 320 | +2 | 33% | 7% | 72% | 3.10 | 31 | 2 | 17/6 | — | — | — | — | .693 | .626 | .789 | .620 | .781 |

## Freddy Garcia — 80 IP | $1 | 80 pts
SP-28  Owned: 10%  RH

Garcia in 2010 piled up twice as many wins as losses, but with his low K/9 and high HR/9, he is back-end-of-the-rotation material. His power dried up in August (4.9 K/9) and especially September (3.8 K/9). Still, as a #5 SP, he was an asset, and he will not vanish from the White Sox until Jake Peavy recovers. (RM)

### Forecast
| Player | Age | IP | W | Sv | K | ERA | WHIP | K/9 | BB/9 | $2L | Pts |
|---|---|---|---|---|---|---|---|---|---|---|---|
| Garcia F | 34 | 80 | 5 | 0 | 47 | 4.74 | 1.35 | 5.3 | 2.6 | $1 | 80 |

### Mini-Browser
| Player | Age | IP | W | Sv | K | ERA | WHIP | K/9 | BB/9 | $2L | Pts |
|---|---|---|---|---|---|---|---|---|---|---|---|
| Blevins J | 27 | 50 | 2 | 0 | 48 | 3.98 | 1.37 | 8.7 | 4.4 | $1 | 60 |
| Ramirez R | 29 | 60 | 3 | 0 | 44 | 3.66 | 1.35 | 6.7 | 4.1 | $1 | 60 |
| Lopez W | 27 | 60 | 3 | 0 | 45 | 4.35 | 1.34 | 6.8 | 1.5 | $1 | 80 |
| Moyer J | 48 | 100 | 6 | 0 | 53 | 4.89 | 1.25 | 4.8 | 2.3 | $1 | 100 |
| Resop C | 28 | 60 | 4 | 0 | 54 | 3.91 | 1.42 | 8.2 | 4.4 | $1 | 80 |

### Minors (2010) / Skills
| Level | Leag | W | L | Sv | IP | H | K | ERA | WHIP | K/9 | BB/9 | HR/9 | GB/F |
|---|---|---|---|---|---|---|---|---|---|---|---|---|---|
| A | — | — | — | — | — | — | — | — | — | — | — | — | — |
| AA | — | — | — | — | — | — | — | — | — | — | — | — | — |
| AAA | — | — | — | — | — | — | — | — | — | — | — | — | — |

### Majors / Skills
| Yr | Team | W | L | Sv | IP | H | K | ERA | WHIP | K/9 | BB/9 | HR/9 | GB/F |
|---|---|---|---|---|---|---|---|---|---|---|---|---|---|
| 07 | PHI | 1 | 5 | 0 | 58 | 74 | 50 | 5.90 | 1.60 | 7.8 | 2.9 | 1.9 | 1.0 |
| 08 | DET | 1 | 1 | 0 | 15 | 11 | 12 | 4.20 | 1.13 | 7.2 | 3.6 | 1.8 | 0.9 |
| 09 | CHW | 3 | 4 | 0 | 56 | 56 | 37 | 4.34 | 1.21 | 5.9 | 1.9 | 0.6 | 1.1 |
| 10 | CHW | 12 | 6 | 0 | 157 | 171 | 89 | 4.64 | 1.38 | 5.1 | 2.6 | 1.3 | 1.1 |

### Competition at SP / Stats in 2010 as SP
| Thr | Player | GS | ERA | Supp | W-L |
|---|---|---|---|---|---|
| LH | Buehrle M | 33 | 4.28 | 4.8 | 13-13 |
| LH | Danks J | 32 | 3.72 | 4.5 | 15-11 |
| RH | Jackson E | 32 | 4.47 | 4.3 | 10-12 |
| RH | Floyd G | 31 | 4.08 | 3.8 | 10-13 |

### Value / Luck / In Rotation / In Relief / OPS
| $1L | $2L | Pts | RAA | H% | HR/fb | S% | FIP | GS | CG | QS/DS | GR | Hld | Bln | Lead | OPS | 1st Hf | 2nd Hf | vs RH | vs LH |
|---|---|---|---|---|---|---|---|---|---|---|---|---|---|---|---|---|---|---|---|
| -$5 | -$12 | 30 | -10 | 36% | 17% | 68% | 5.15 | 11 | 0 | 4/2 | — | — | — | — | .948 | .948 | — | 1.019 | .862 |
| -$1 | -$2 | 20 | -1 | 21% | 16% | 71% | 5.50 | 3 | 0 | 0/0 | — | — | — | — | .702 | — | .702 | .806 | .530 |
| -$2 | -$1 | 60 | +1 | 30% | 5% | 64% | 3.55 | 9 | 0 | 7/2 | — | — | — | — | .690 | — | .690 | .795 | .576 |
| $3 | -$14 | 180 | -8 | 30% | 12% | 70% | 4.93 | 28 | 0 | 18/4 | — | — | — | — | .804 | .785 | .834 | .826 | .784 |

## Jaime Garcia — 180 IP | $13 | 270 pts
SP-28  Owned: 96%  LH

Garcia's rookie campaign turned out better than anyone could have hoped for. We can expect regression in his sophomore season, but even FIP says that the youngster already pitches very well. He should be a solid number #3 SP for the Cards in 2010, so long as he maintains a respectable K/9 and high GB/F. (AB)

### Forecast
| Player | Age | IP | W | Sv | K | ERA | WHIP | K/9 | BB/9 | $2L | Pts |
|---|---|---|---|---|---|---|---|---|---|---|---|
| Garcia J | 24 | 180 | 13 | 0 | 153 | 3.39 | 1.37 | 7.7 | 3.6 | $13 | 270 |

### Mini-Browser
| Player | Age | IP | W | Sv | K | ERA | WHIP | K/9 | BB/9 | $2L | Pts |
|---|---|---|---|---|---|---|---|---|---|---|---|
| Lewis C | 31 | 180 | 11 | 0 | 171 | 3.99 | 1.33 | 8.5 | 2.9 | $14 | 270 |
| Kuroda H | 36 | 200 | 12 | 0 | 142 | 3.87 | 1.21 | 6.4 | 2.1 | $14 | 250 |
| Valverde J | 33 | 60 | 2 | 36 | 59 | 3.69 | 1.27 | 8.8 | 4.0 | $13 | 260 |
| Buchholz C | 26 | 180 | 14 | 0 | 142 | 3.68 | 1.36 | 7.1 | 3.7 | $13 | 270 |
| Gallardo Y | 25 | 200 | 15 | 0 | 204 | 3.92 | 1.35 | 9.2 | 3.8 | $13 | 330 |

### Minors (2010) / Skills
| Level | Leag | W | L | Sv | IP | H | K | ERA | WHIP | K/9 | BB/9 | HR/9 | GB/F |
|---|---|---|---|---|---|---|---|---|---|---|---|---|---|
| A | — | — | — | — | — | — | — | — | — | — | — | — | — |
| AA | — | — | — | — | — | — | — | — | — | — | — | — | — |
| AAA | — | — | — | — | — | — | — | — | — | — | — | — | — |

### Competition at SP / Stats in 2010 as SP
| Thr | Player | GS | ERA | Supp | W-L |
|---|---|---|---|---|---|
| RH | Carpenter C | 35 | 3.22 | 4.7 | 16-9 |
| RH | Wainwright A | 33 | 2.42 | 4.8 | 20-11 |
| RH | Westbrook J | 33 | 4.22 | 4.0 | 10-11 |
| LH | Garcia J | 28 | 2.70 | 4.5 | 13-8 |

### Majors / Skills
| Yr | Team | W | L | Sv | IP | H | K | ERA | WHIP | K/9 | BB/9 | HR/9 | GB/F |
|---|---|---|---|---|---|---|---|---|---|---|---|---|---|
| 07 | — | — | — | — | — | — | — | — | — | — | — | — | — |
| 08 | STL | 1 | 1 | 0 | 16 | 14 | 8 | 5.63 | 1.38 | 4.5 | 4.5 | 2.3 | 3.1 |
| 09 | — | — | — | — | — | — | — | — | — | — | — | — | — |
| 10 | STL | 13 | 8 | 0 | 163 | 151 | 132 | 2.70 | 1.32 | 7.3 | 3.6 | 0.5 | 2.2 |

### Value / Luck / In Rotation / In Relief / OPS
| $1L | $2L | Pts | RAA | H% | HR/fb | S% | FIP | GS | CG | QS/DS | GR | Hld | Bln | Lead | OPS | 1st Hf | 2nd Hf | vs RH | vs LH |
|---|---|---|---|---|---|---|---|---|---|---|---|---|---|---|---|---|---|---|---|
| -$2 | -$3 | 10 | -2 | 21% | 40% | 67% | 6.95 | 1 | 0 | 0/0 | 9 | 3 | 0 | +0.3 | .800 | .393 | .854 | .829 | .713 |
| $13 | $8 | 270 | +17 | 30% | 7% | 81% | 3.48 | 28 | 1 | 19/3 | — | — | — | — | .638 | .600 | .695 | .660 | .550 |

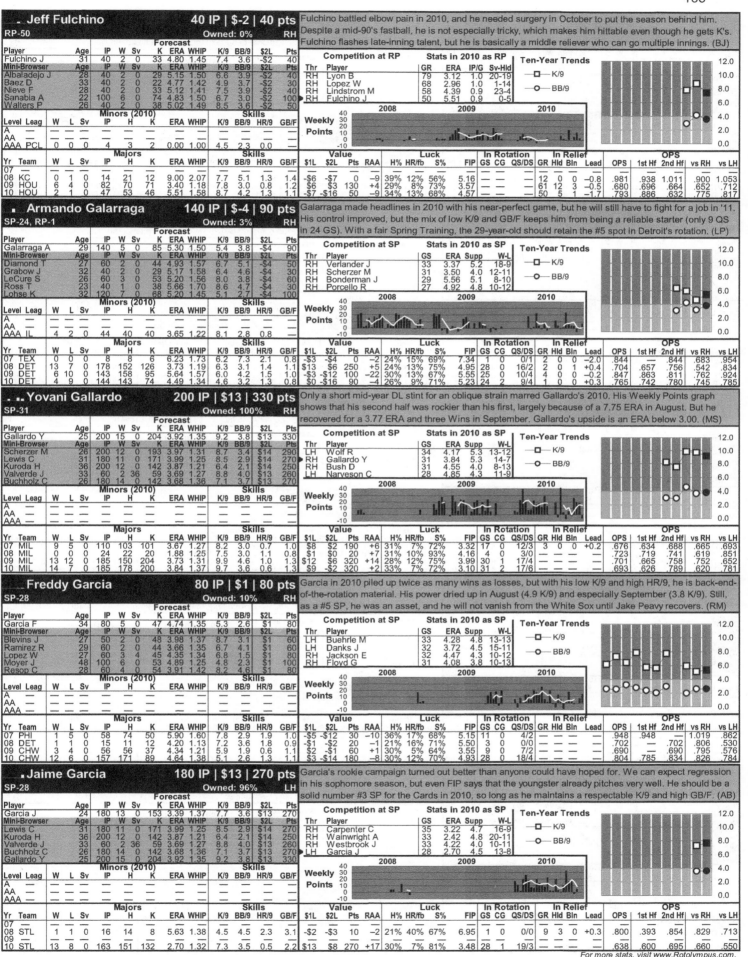

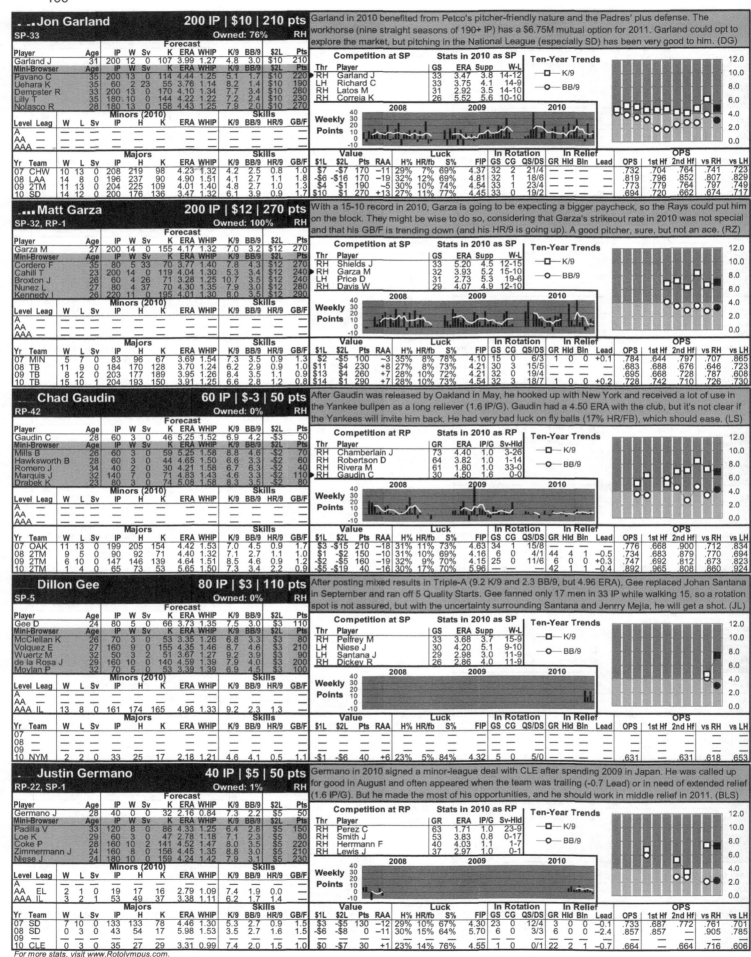

## Jon Garland — 200 IP | $10 | 210 pts

SP-33 | Owned: 76% | RH

Garland in 2010 benefited from Petco's pitcher-friendly nature and the Padres' plus defense. The workhorse (nine straight seasons of 190+ IP) has a $6.75M mutual option for 2011. Garland could opt to explore the market, but pitching in the National League (especially SD) has been very good to him. (DG)

| Player | Age | IP | W | Sv | K | ERA | WHIP | K/9 | BB/9 | $2L | Pts |
|---|---|---|---|---|---|---|---|---|---|---|---|
| Garland J | 31 | 200 | 12 | 0 | 107 | 3.99 | 1.27 | 4.8 | 3.0 | $10 | 210 |
| **Mini-Browser** | **Age** | **IP** | **W** | **Sv** | **K** | **ERA** | **WHIP** | **K/9** | **BB/9** | **$2L** | **Pts** |
| Pavano C | 35 | 200 | 13 | 0 | 114 | 4.44 | 1.25 | 5.1 | 1.7 | $10 | 220 |
| Uehara K | 35 | 60 | 2 | 23 | 55 | 3.76 | 1.14 | 8.2 | 1.4 | $10 | 190 |
| Dempster R | 33 | 200 | 13 | 0 | 170 | 4.10 | 1.34 | 7.7 | 3.4 | $10 | 280 |
| Lilly T | 35 | 180 | 10 | 0 | 144 | 4.22 | 1.22 | 7.2 | 2.4 | $10 | 230 |
| Nolasco R | 28 | 180 | 13 | 0 | 158 | 4.43 | 1.25 | 7.9 | 2.0 | $10 | 270 |

Minors (2010)

| Level | Leag | W | L | Sv | IP | H | K | ERA | WHIP | K/9 | BB/9 | HR/9 | GB/F |
|---|---|---|---|---|---|---|---|---|---|---|---|---|---|
| A | — | — | — | — | — | — | — | — | — | — | — | — | — |
| AA | — | — | — | — | — | — | — | — | — | — | — | — | — |
| AAA | — | — | — | — | — | — | — | — | — | — | — | — | — |

Competition at SP — Stats in 2010 as SP

| Thr | Player | GS | ERA | Supp | W-L |
|---|---|---|---|---|---|
| RH | Garland J | 33 | 3.47 | 3.8 | 14-12 |
| LH | Richard C | 33 | 3.75 | 4.1 | 14-9 |
| RH | Latos M | 31 | 2.92 | 3.5 | 14-10 |
| RH | Correia K | 26 | 5.52 | 5.6 | 10-10 |

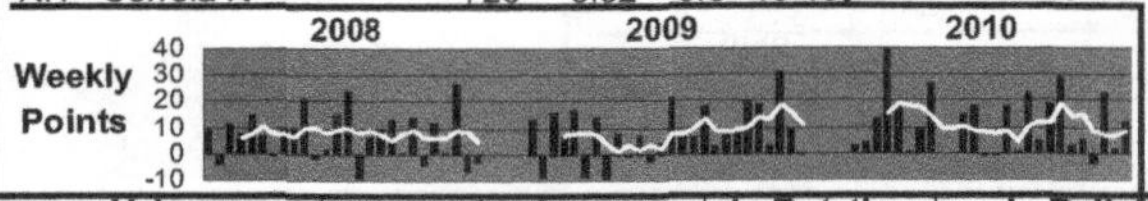


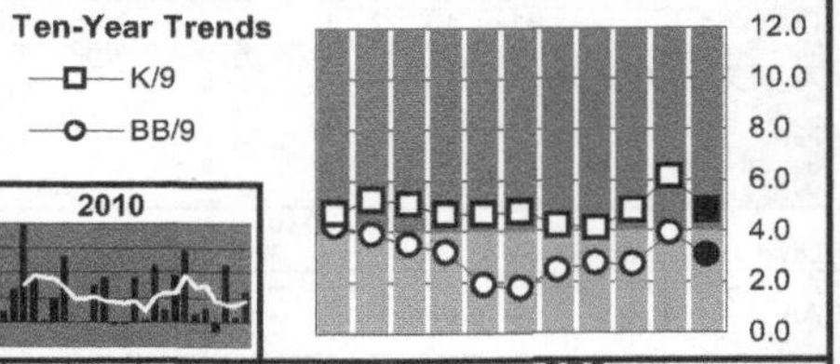


Majors | Skills | Value | Luck | In Rotation | In Relief | OPS

| Yr | Team | W | L | Sv | IP | H | K | ERA | WHIP | K/9 | BB/9 | HR/9 | GB/F | $1L | $2L | Pts | RAA | H% | HR/fb | S% | FIP | GS | CG | QS/DS | GR | Hld | Bln | Lead | OPS | 1st Hf | 2nd Hf | vs RH | vs LH |
|---|---|---|---|---|---|---|---|---|---|---|---|---|---|---|---|---|---|---|---|---|---|---|---|---|---|---|---|---|---|---|---|---|---|
| 07 | CHW | 10 | 13 | 0 | 208 | 219 | 98 | 4.23 | 1.32 | 4.2 | 2.5 | 0.8 | 1.0 | $7 | -$7 | 170 | −11 | 29% | 7% | 69% | 4.37 | 32 | 2 | 21/4 | — | — | — | — | .732 | .704 | .764 | .741 | .723 |
| 08 | LAA | 14 | 8 | 0 | 196 | 237 | 90 | 4.90 | 1.51 | 4.1 | 2.7 | 1.1 | 1.8 | -$6 | -$16 | 170 | −19 | 32% | 12% | 69% | 4.81 | 32 | 1 | 18/6 | — | — | — | — | .819 | .796 | .852 | .807 | .829 |
| 09 | 2TM | 11 | 13 | 0 | 204 | 225 | 109 | 4.01 | 1.40 | 4.8 | 2.7 | 1.0 | 1.3 | $4 | -$1 | 190 | −5 | 30% | 10% | 74% | 4.54 | 33 | 1 | 23/4 | — | — | — | — | .773 | .779 | .764 | .797 | .749 |
| 10 | SD | 14 | 12 | 0 | 200 | 176 | 136 | 3.47 | 1.32 | 6.1 | 3.9 | 0.9 | 1.7 | $10 | $1 | 270 | +13 | 27% | 11% | 77% | 4.45 | 33 | 0 | 19/2 | — | — | — | — | .694 | .720 | .662 | .674 | .717 |

## Matt Garza — 200 IP | $12 | 270 pts

SP-32, RP-1 | Owned: 100% | RH

With a 15-10 record in 2010, Garza is going to be expecting a bigger paycheck, so the Rays could put him on the block. They might be wise to do so, considering that Garza's strikeout rate in 2010 was not special and that his GB/F is trending down (and his HR/9 is going up). A good pitcher, sure, but not an ace. (RZ)

| Player | Age | IP | W | Sv | K | ERA | WHIP | K/9 | BB/9 | $2L | Pts |
|---|---|---|---|---|---|---|---|---|---|---|---|
| Garza M | 27 | 200 | 14 | 0 | 155 | 4.17 | 1.32 | 7.0 | 3.2 | $12 | 270 |
| **Mini-Browser** | **Age** | **IP** | **W** | **Sv** | **K** | **ERA** | **WHIP** | **K/9** | **BB/9** | **$2L** | **Pts** |
| Cordero F | 35 | 80 | 5 | 33 | 70 | 3.77 | 1.40 | 7.8 | 4.3 | $12 | 270 |
| Cahill T | 23 | 200 | 14 | 0 | 119 | 4.04 | 1.30 | 5.3 | 3.4 | $12 | 240 |
| Broxton J | 26 | 60 | 4 | 26 | 71 | 3.28 | 1.25 | 10.7 | 3.5 | $12 | 240 |
| Nunez L | 27 | 80 | 4 | 37 | 70 | 4.30 | 1.35 | 7.9 | 3.0 | $12 | 280 |
| Kennedy I | 26 | 220 | 11 | 0 | 195 | 4.01 | 1.30 | 8.0 | 3.5 | $12 | 290 |

Minors (2010)

| Level | Leag | W | L | Sv | IP | H | K | ERA | WHIP | K/9 | BB/9 | HR/9 | GB/F |
|---|---|---|---|---|---|---|---|---|---|---|---|---|---|
| A | — | — | — | — | — | — | — | — | — | — | — | — | — |
| AA | — | — | — | — | — | — | — | — | — | — | — | — | — |
| AAA | — | — | — | — | — | — | — | — | — | — | — | — | — |

Competition at SP — Stats in 2010 as SP

| Thr | Player | GS | ERA | Supp | W-L |
|---|---|---|---|---|---|
| RH | Shields J | 33 | 5.20 | 4.5 | 12-15 |
| RH | Garza M | 32 | 3.93 | 5.2 | 15-10 |
| LH | Price D | 31 | 2.73 | 5.3 | 19-6 |
| RH | Davis W | 29 | 4.07 | 4.9 | 12-10 |

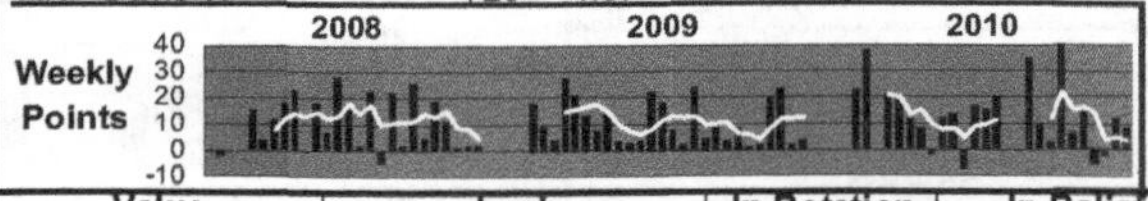


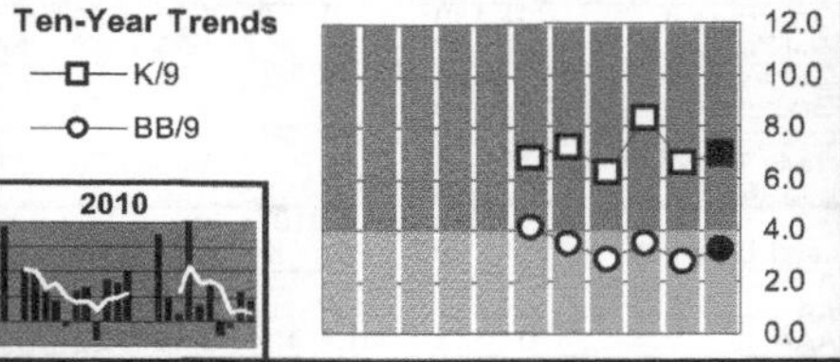


Majors | Skills | Value | Luck | In Rotation | In Relief | OPS

| Yr | Team | W | L | Sv | IP | H | K | ERA | WHIP | K/9 | BB/9 | HR/9 | GB/F | $1L | $2L | Pts | RAA | H% | HR/fb | S% | FIP | GS | CG | QS/DS | GR | Hld | Bln | Lead | OPS | 1st Hf | 2nd Hf | vs RH | vs LH |
|---|---|---|---|---|---|---|---|---|---|---|---|---|---|---|---|---|---|---|---|---|---|---|---|---|---|---|---|---|---|---|---|---|---|
| 07 | MIN | 5 | 7 | 0 | 83 | 96 | 67 | 3.69 | 1.54 | 7.3 | 3.5 | 0.9 | 1.3 | $2 | -$5 | 100 | −3 | 35% | 8% | 78% | 4.10 | 15 | 0 | 6/3 | 1 | 0 | 0 | +0.1 | .784 | .644 | .797 | .707 | .865 |
| 08 | TB | 11 | 9 | 0 | 184 | 170 | 128 | 3.70 | 1.24 | 6.2 | 2.9 | 0.9 | 1.0 | $11 | $4 | 230 | +8 | 27% | 8% | 73% | 4.21 | 30 | 3 | 15/5 | — | — | — | — | .683 | .688 | .676 | .646 | .723 |
| 09 | TB | 8 | 12 | 0 | 203 | 177 | 189 | 3.95 | 1.26 | 8.4 | 3.5 | 1.1 | 0.9 | $13 | $4 | 260 | +7 | 28% | 10% | 72% | 4.21 | 32 | 0 | 19/4 | — | — | — | — | .695 | .668 | .728 | .787 | .608 |
| 10 | TB | 15 | 10 | 1 | 204 | 193 | 150 | 3.91 | 1.25 | 6.6 | 2.8 | 1.2 | 0.8 | $14 | $1 | 290 | +7 | 28% | 10% | 73% | 4.54 | 32 | 3 | 18/7 | 1 | 0 | 0 | +0.2 | .728 | .742 | .710 | .726 | .730 |

## Chad Gaudin — 60 IP | $-3 | 50 pts

RP-42 | Owned: 0% | RH

After Gaudin was released by Oakland in May, he hooked up with New York and received a lot of use in the Yankee bullpen as a long reliever (1.6 IP/G). Gaudin had a 4.50 ERA with the club, but it's not clear if the Yankees will invite him back. He had very bad luck on fly balls (17% HR/FB), which should ease. (LS)

| Player | Age | IP | W | Sv | K | ERA | WHIP | K/9 | BB/9 | $2L | Pts |
|---|---|---|---|---|---|---|---|---|---|---|---|
| Gaudin C | 28 | 60 | 3 | 0 | 46 | 5.25 | 1.52 | 6.9 | 4.2 | -$3 | 50 |
| **Mini-Browser** | **Age** | **IP** | **W** | **Sv** | **K** | **ERA** | **WHIP** | **K/9** | **BB/9** | **$2L** | **Pts** |
| Mills B | 26 | 60 | 3 | 0 | 59 | 5.25 | 1.58 | 8.8 | 4.6 | -$2 | 70 |
| Hawksworth B | 28 | 60 | 3 | 0 | 44 | 4.65 | 1.50 | 6.6 | 3.3 | -$2 | 60 |
| Romero J | 34 | 40 | 2 | 0 | 30 | 4.21 | 1.58 | 6.7 | 6.3 | -$2 | 40 |
| Marquis J | 32 | 140 | 7 | 0 | 71 | 4.83 | 1.43 | 4.6 | 3.3 | -$2 | 110 |
| Drabek K | 23 | 80 | 3 | 0 | 74 | 5.08 | 1.58 | 8.3 | 3.5 | -$2 | 80 |

Minors (2010)

| Level | Leag | W | L | Sv | IP | H | K | ERA | WHIP | K/9 | BB/9 | HR/9 | GB/F |
|---|---|---|---|---|---|---|---|---|---|---|---|---|---|
| A | — | — | — | — | — | — | — | — | — | — | — | — | — |
| AA | — | — | — | — | — | — | — | — | — | — | — | — | — |
| AAA | — | — | — | — | — | — | — | — | — | — | — | — | — |

Competition at RP — Stats in 2010 as RP

| Thr | Player | GR | ERA | IP/G | Sv-Hld |
|---|---|---|---|---|---|
| RH | Chamberlain J | 73 | 4.40 | 1.0 | 3-26 |
| RH | Robertson D | 64 | 3.82 | 1.0 | 1-14 |
| RH | Rivera M | 61 | 1.80 | 1.0 | 33-0 |
| RH | Gaudin C | 30 | 4.50 | 1.6 | 0-0 |

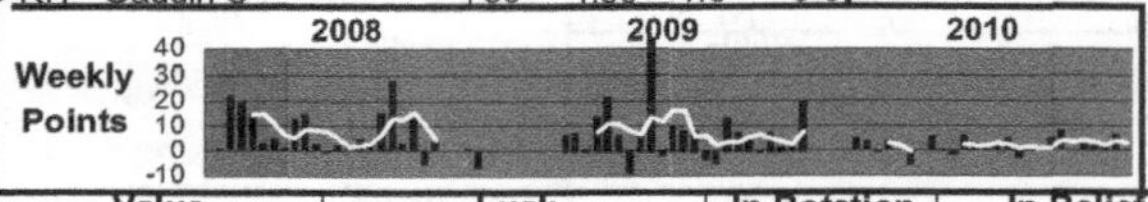


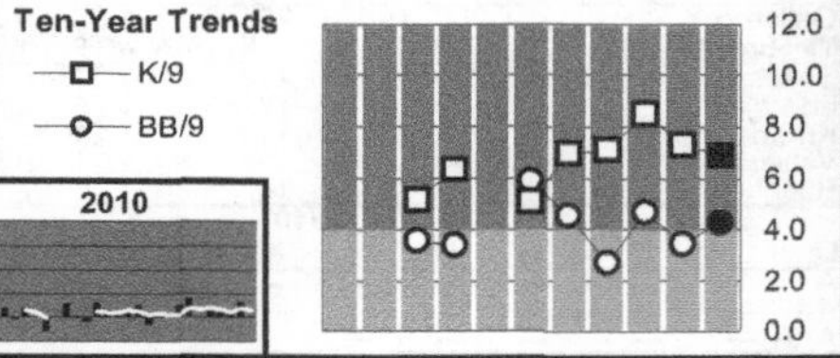


Majors | Skills | Value | Luck | In Rotation | In Relief | OPS

| Yr | Team | W | L | Sv | IP | H | K | ERA | WHIP | K/9 | BB/9 | HR/9 | GB/F | $1L | $2L | Pts | RAA | H% | HR/fb | S% | FIP | GS | CG | QS/DS | GR | Hld | Bln | Lead | OPS | 1st Hf | 2nd Hf | vs RH | vs LH |
|---|---|---|---|---|---|---|---|---|---|---|---|---|---|---|---|---|---|---|---|---|---|---|---|---|---|---|---|---|---|---|---|---|---|
| 07 | OAK | 11 | 13 | 0 | 199 | 205 | 154 | 4.42 | 1.53 | 7.0 | 4.5 | 0.9 | 1.7 | $3 | -$15 | 210 | −18 | 31% | 11% | 73% | 4.63 | 34 | 1 | 15/8 | — | — | — | — | .776 | .668 | .900 | .712 | .834 |
| 08 | 2TM | 9 | 5 | 0 | 90 | 92 | 71 | 4.40 | 1.32 | 7.1 | 2.7 | 1.1 | 1.0 | $1 | -$2 | 150 | −10 | 31% | 10% | 69% | 4.16 | 6 | 0 | 4/1 | 44 | 4 | 1 | −0.5 | .734 | .683 | .879 | .770 | .694 |
| 09 | 2TM | 6 | 10 | 0 | 147 | 146 | 139 | 4.64 | 1.51 | 8.5 | 4.6 | 0.9 | 1.2 | -$2 | -$5 | 160 | −19 | 32% | 9% | 70% | 4.15 | 25 | 0 | 11/6 | 6 | 0 | 0 | +0.3 | .747 | .692 | .812 | .673 | .823 |
| 10 | 2TM | 1 | 4 | 0 | 65 | 73 | 53 | 5.65 | 1.50 | 7.3 | 3.4 | 2.2 | 0.9 | -$5 | -$19 | 40 | −16 | 30% | 17% | 70% | 5.96 | — | — | — | 42 | 1 | 1 | −0.4 | .892 | .965 | .808 | .860 | .924 |

## Dillon Gee — 80 IP | $3 | 110 pts

SP-5 | Owned: 0% | RH

After posting mixed results in Triple-A (9.2 K/9 and 2.3 BB/9, but 4.96 ERA), Gee replaced Johan Santana in September and ran off 5 Quality Starts. Gee fanned only 17 men in 33 IP while walking 15, so a rotation spot is not assured, but with the uncertainty surrounding Santana and Jenrry Mejia, he will get a shot. (JL)

| Player | Age | IP | W | Sv | K | ERA | WHIP | K/9 | BB/9 | $2L | Pts |
|---|---|---|---|---|---|---|---|---|---|---|---|
| Gee D | 24 | 80 | 5 | 0 | 66 | 3.73 | 1.35 | 7.5 | 3.0 | $3 | 110 |
| **Mini-Browser** | **Age** | **IP** | **W** | **Sv** | **K** | **ERA** | **WHIP** | **K/9** | **BB/9** | **$2L** | **Pts** |
| McClellan K | 26 | 70 | 3 | 0 | 53 | 3.35 | 1.26 | 6.8 | 3.3 | $3 | 80 |
| Volquez E | 27 | 160 | 9 | 0 | 155 | 4.35 | 1.46 | 8.7 | 4.6 | $3 | 210 |
| Wuertz M | 32 | 50 | 3 | 2 | 51 | 3.67 | 1.27 | 9.2 | 3.9 | $3 | 90 |
| de la Rosa J | 29 | 160 | 10 | 0 | 140 | 4.59 | 1.39 | 7.9 | 4.0 | $3 | 200 |
| Moylan P | 32 | 70 | 5 | 0 | 53 | 3.39 | 1.39 | 6.9 | 4.5 | $3 | 100 |

Minors (2010)

| Level | Leag | W | L | Sv | IP | H | K | ERA | WHIP | K/9 | BB/9 | HR/9 | GB/F |
|---|---|---|---|---|---|---|---|---|---|---|---|---|---|
| A | — | — | — | — | — | — | — | — | — | — | — | — | — |
| AA | — | — | — | — | — | — | — | — | — | — | — | — | — |
| AAA | IL | 13 | 8 | 0 | 161 | 174 | 165 | 4.96 | 1.33 | 9.2 | 2.3 | 1.3 | — |

Competition at SP — Stats in 2010 as SP

| Thr | Player | GS | ERA | Supp | W-L |
|---|---|---|---|---|---|
| RH | Pelfrey M | 33 | 3.68 | 3.7 | 15-9 |
| LH | Niese J | 30 | 4.20 | 5.1 | 9-10 |
| LH | Santana J | 29 | 2.98 | 3.0 | 11-9 |
| RH | Dickey R | 26 | 2.86 | 4.0 | 11-9 |

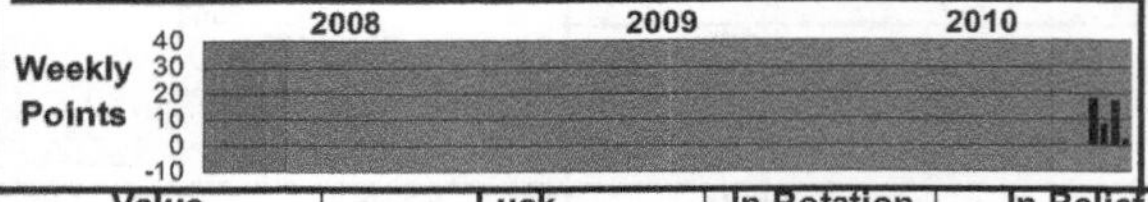


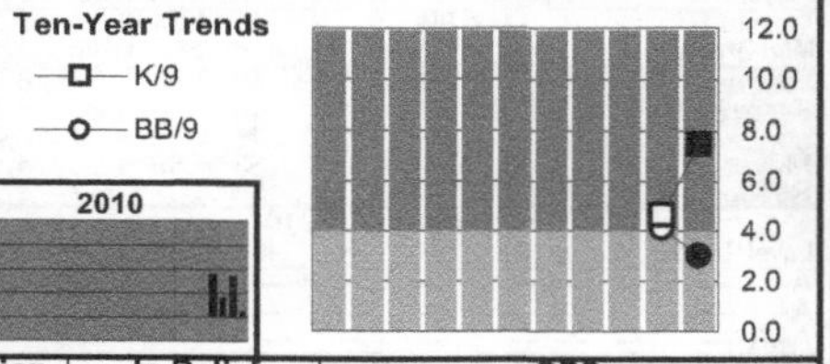


Majors | Skills | Value | Luck | In Rotation | In Relief | OPS

| Yr | Team | W | L | Sv | IP | H | K | ERA | WHIP | K/9 | BB/9 | HR/9 | GB/F | $1L | $2L | Pts | RAA | H% | HR/fb | S% | FIP | GS | CG | QS/DS | GR | Hld | Bln | Lead | OPS | 1st Hf | 2nd Hf | vs RH | vs LH |
|---|---|---|---|---|---|---|---|---|---|---|---|---|---|---|---|---|---|---|---|---|---|---|---|---|---|---|---|---|---|---|---|---|---|
| 07 | — | — | — | — | — | — | — | — | — | — | — | — | — | — | — | — | — | — | — | — | — | — | — | — | — | — | — | — | — | — | — | — | — |
| 08 | — | — | — | — | — | — | — | — | — | — | — | — | — | — | — | — | — | — | — | — | — | — | — | — | — | — | — | — | — | — | — | — | — |
| 09 | — | — | — | — | — | — | — | — | — | — | — | — | — | — | — | — | — | — | — | — | — | — | — | — | — | — | — | — | — | — | — | — | — |
| 10 | NYM | 2 | 2 | 0 | 33 | 25 | 17 | 2.18 | 1.21 | 4.6 | 4.1 | 0.5 | 1.1 | -$1 | -$6 | 40 | +6 | 23% | 5% | 84% | 4.32 | 5 | 0 | 5/0 | — | — | — | — | .631 | — | .631 | .618 | .653 |

## Justin Germano — 40 IP | $5 | 50 pts

RP-22, SP-1 | Owned: 1% | RH

Germano in 2010 signed a minor-league deal with CLE after spending 2009 in Japan. He was called up for good in August and often appeared when the team was trailing (-0.7 Lead) or in need of extended relief (1.6 IP/G). But he made the most of his opportunities, and he should work in middle relief in 2011. (BLS)

| Player | Age | IP | W | Sv | K | ERA | WHIP | K/9 | BB/9 | $2L | Pts |
|---|---|---|---|---|---|---|---|---|---|---|---|
| Germano J | 28 | 40 | 0 | 0 | 32 | 2.16 | 0.84 | 7.3 | 2.2 | $5 | 50 |
| **Mini-Browser** | **Age** | **IP** | **W** | **Sv** | **K** | **ERA** | **WHIP** | **K/9** | **BB/9** | **$2L** | **Pts** |
| Padilla V | 33 | 120 | 8 | 0 | 86 | 4.33 | 1.25 | 6.4 | 2.8 | $5 | 150 |
| Loe K | 29 | 60 | 3 | 0 | 47 | 2.78 | 1.18 | 7.1 | 2.3 | $5 | 80 |
| Coke P | 28 | 160 | 10 | 2 | 141 | 4.52 | 1.47 | 8.0 | 3.5 | $5 | 220 |
| Zimmermann J | 24 | 160 | 8 | 0 | 156 | 4.45 | 1.35 | 8.8 | 3.0 | $5 | 210 |
| Niese J | 24 | 180 | 10 | 0 | 159 | 4.24 | 1.42 | 7.9 | 3.1 | $5 | 230 |

Minors (2010)

| Level | Leag | W | L | Sv | IP | H | K | ERA | WHIP | K/9 | BB/9 | HR/9 | GB/F |
|---|---|---|---|---|---|---|---|---|---|---|---|---|---|
| A | — | — | — | — | — | — | — | — | — | — | — | — | — |
| AA | EL | 2 | 1 | 0 | 19 | 17 | 16 | 2.79 | 1.09 | 7.4 | 1.9 | 0.0 | — |
| AAA | IL | 3 | 2 | 1 | 53 | 49 | 37 | 3.38 | 1.11 | 6.2 | 1.7 | 1.4 | — |

Competition at RP — Stats in 2010 as RP

| Thr | Player | GR | ERA | IP/G | Sv-Hld |
|---|---|---|---|---|---|
| RH | Perez C | 63 | 1.71 | 1.0 | 23-9 |
| RH | Smith J | 53 | 3.83 | 0.8 | 0-17 |
| RH | Herrmann F | 40 | 4.03 | 1.1 | 1-7 |
| RH | Lewis J | 37 | 2.97 | 1.0 | 0-1 |

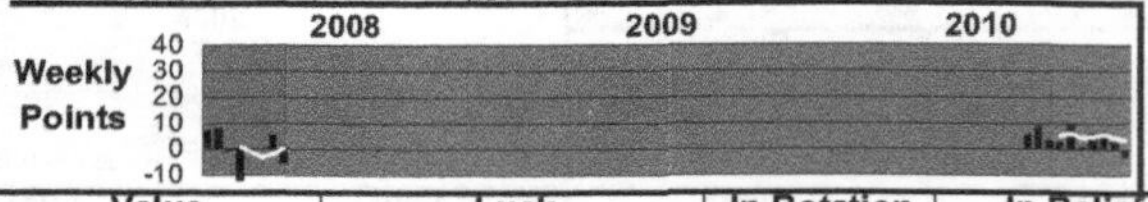


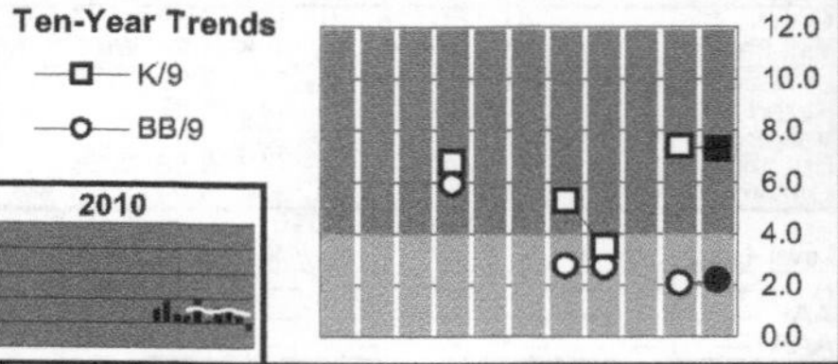


Majors | Skills | Value | Luck | In Rotation | In Relief | OPS

| Yr | Team | W | L | Sv | IP | H | K | ERA | WHIP | K/9 | BB/9 | HR/9 | GB/F | $1L | $2L | Pts | RAA | H% | HR/fb | S% | FIP | GS | CG | QS/DS | GR | Hld | Bln | Lead | OPS | 1st Hf | 2nd Hf | vs RH | vs LH |
|---|---|---|---|---|---|---|---|---|---|---|---|---|---|---|---|---|---|---|---|---|---|---|---|---|---|---|---|---|---|---|---|---|---|
| 07 | SD | 7 | 10 | 0 | 133 | 133 | 78 | 4.46 | 1.30 | 5.3 | 2.7 | 0.9 | 1.5 | $3 | -$5 | 130 | −12 | 29% | 10% | 67% | 4.30 | 23 | 0 | 12/4 | 3 | 0 | 0 | −0.1 | .733 | .687 | .772 | .761 | .701 |
| 08 | SD | 0 | 3 | 0 | 43 | 54 | 17 | 5.98 | 1.53 | 3.5 | 2.7 | 1.6 | 1.5 | -$6 | -$8 | 0 | −11 | 30% | 15% | 64% | 5.70 | 6 | 0 | 3/3 | 6 | 0 | 0 | −2.4 | .857 | .857 | — | .905 | .785 |
| 09 | — | — | — | — | — | — | — | — | — | — | — | — | — | — | — | — | — | — | — | — | — | — | — | — | — | — | — | — | — | — | — | — | — |
| 10 | CLE | 0 | 3 | 0 | 35 | 27 | 29 | 3.31 | 0.99 | 7.4 | 2.0 | 1.5 | 1.0 | $0 | -$7 | 30 | +1 | 23% | 14% | 76% | 4.55 | 1 | 0 | 0/1 | 22 | 2 | 1 | −0.7 | .664 | — | .664 | .716 | .606 |

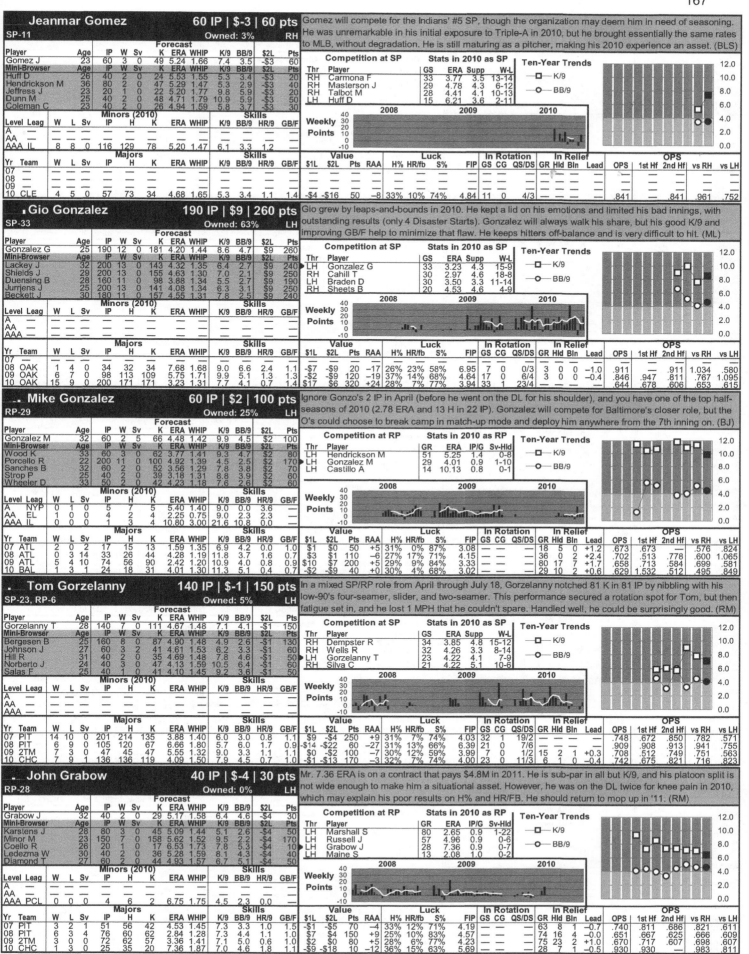

## Jeanmar Gomez — 60 IP | $-3 | 60 pts

SP-11 — Owned: 3% — RH

Gomez will compete for the Indians' #5 SP, though the organization may deem him in need of seasoning. He was unremarkable in his initial exposure to Triple-A in 2010, but he brought essentially the same rates to MLB, without degradation. He is still maturing as a pitcher, making his 2010 experience an asset. (BLS)

**Forecast**

| Player | Age | IP | W | Sv | K | ERA | WHIP | K/9 | BB/9 | $2L | Pts |
|---|---|---|---|---|---|---|---|---|---|---|---|
| Gomez J | 23 | 60 | 3 | 0 | 49 | 5.24 | 1.66 | 7.4 | 3.5 | -$3 | 60 |
| **Mini-Browser** | **Age** | **IP** | **W** | **Sv** | **K** | **ERA** | **WHIP** | **K/9** | **BB/9** | **$2L** | **Pts** |
| Huff D | 26 | 40 | 2 | 0 | 24 | 5.53 | 1.55 | 5.3 | 3.4 | -$3 | 20 |
| Hendrickson M | 36 | 80 | 2 | 0 | 47 | 5.29 | 1.47 | 5.3 | 2.9 | -$3 | 40 |
| Jeffress J | 23 | 20 | 1 | 0 | 22 | 5.20 | 1.77 | 9.8 | 5.9 | -$3 | 20 |
| Dunn M | 25 | 40 | 2 | 0 | 48 | 4.71 | 1.79 | 10.9 | 5.9 | -$3 | 50 |
| Coleman C | 23 | 40 | 2 | 0 | 26 | 4.94 | 1.59 | 5.8 | 3.7 | -$3 | 30 |

**Minors (2010)**

| Level | Leag | W | L | Sv | IP | H | K | ERA | WHIP | K/9 | BB/9 | HR/9 | GB/F |
|---|---|---|---|---|---|---|---|---|---|---|---|---|---|
| A | — | — | — | — | — | — | — | — | — | — | — | — | — |
| AA | — | — | — | — | — | — | — | — | — | — | — | — | — |
| AAA | IL | 8 | 8 | 0 | 116 | 129 | 78 | 5.20 | 1.47 | 6.1 | 3.3 | 1.2 | — |

**Majors**

| Yr | Team | W | L | Sv | IP | H | K | ERA | WHIP | K/9 | BB/9 | HR/9 | GB/F |
|---|---|---|---|---|---|---|---|---|---|---|---|---|---|
| 07 | — | — | — | — | — | — | — | — | — | — | — | — | — |
| 08 | — | — | — | — | — | — | — | — | — | — | — | — | — |
| 09 | — | — | — | — | — | — | — | — | — | — | — | — | — |
| 10 | CLE | 4 | 5 | 0 | 57 | 73 | 34 | 4.68 | 1.65 | 5.3 | 3.4 | 1.1 | 1.4 |

**Competition at SP — Stats in 2010 as SP**

| Thr | Player | GS | ERA | Supp | W-L |
|---|---|---|---|---|---|
| RH | Carmona F | 33 | 3.77 | 3.5 | 13-14 |
| RH | Masterson J | 29 | 4.78 | 4.3 | 6-12 |
| RH | Talbot M | 28 | 4.41 | 4.1 | 10-13 |
| LH | Huff D | 15 | 6.21 | 3.6 | 2-11 |

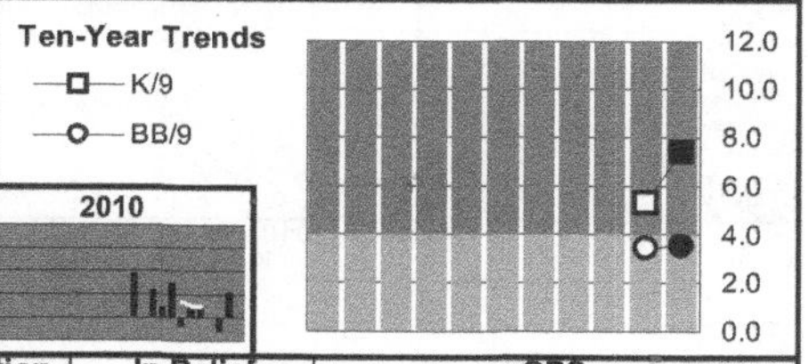


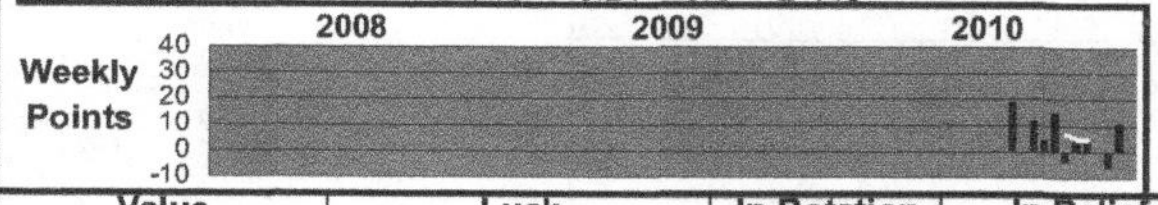


| Yr | $1L | $2L | Pts | RAA | H% | HR/fb | S% | FIP | GS | CG | QS/DS | GR | Hld | Bln | Lead | OPS | 1st Hf | 2nd Hf | vs RH | vs LH |
|---|---|---|---|---|---|---|---|---|---|---|---|---|---|---|---|---|---|---|---|---|
| | **Value** | | | | **Luck** | | | | **In Rotation** | | | **In Relief** | | | | **OPS** | | | | |
| 07 | — | — | — | — | — | — | — | — | — | — | — | — | — | — | — | — | — | — | — | — |
| 08 | — | — | — | — | — | — | — | — | — | — | — | — | — | — | — | — | — | — | — | — |
| 09 | — | — | — | — | — | — | — | — | — | — | — | — | — | — | — | — | — | — | — | — |
| 10 | -$4 | -$16 | 50 | −8 | 33% | 10% | 74% | 4.84 | 11 | 0 | 4/3 | — | — | — | — | .841 | — | .841 | .961 | .752 |

## Gio Gonzalez — 190 IP | $9 | 260 pts

SP-33 — Owned: 63% — LH

Gio grew by leaps-and-bounds in 2010. He kept a lid on his emotions and limited his bad innings, with outstanding results (only 4 Disaster Starts). Gonzalez will always walk his share, but his good K/9 and improving GB/F help to minimize that flaw. He keeps hitters off-balance and is very difficult to hit. (ML)

**Forecast**

| Player | Age | IP | W | Sv | K | ERA | WHIP | K/9 | BB/9 | $2L | Pts |
|---|---|---|---|---|---|---|---|---|---|---|---|
| Gonzalez G | 25 | 190 | 12 | 0 | 181 | 4.20 | 1.44 | 8.6 | 4.7 | $9 | 260 |
| **Mini-Browser** | **Age** | **IP** | **W** | **Sv** | **K** | **ERA** | **WHIP** | **K/9** | **BB/9** | **$2L** | **Pts** |
| Lackey J | 32 | 200 | 13 | 0 | 143 | 4.32 | 1.35 | 6.4 | 2.7 | $9 | 240 |
| Shields J | 29 | 200 | 13 | 0 | 155 | 4.63 | 1.30 | 7.0 | 2.1 | $9 | 250 |
| Duensing B | 28 | 160 | 11 | 0 | 98 | 3.88 | 1.34 | 5.5 | 2.7 | $9 | 190 |
| Jurrjens J | 25 | 200 | 13 | 0 | 141 | 4.08 | 1.34 | 6.3 | 3.1 | $9 | 250 |
| Beckett J | 30 | 180 | 11 | 0 | 157 | 4.55 | 1.31 | 7.8 | 2.5 | $9 | 240 |

**Minors (2010)**

| Level | Leag | W | L | Sv | IP | H | K | ERA | WHIP | K/9 | BB/9 | HR/9 | GB/F |
|---|---|---|---|---|---|---|---|---|---|---|---|---|---|
| A | — | — | — | — | — | — | — | — | — | — | — | — | — |
| AA | — | — | — | — | — | — | — | — | — | — | — | — | — |
| AAA | — | — | — | — | — | — | — | — | — | — | — | — | — |

**Majors**

| Yr | Team | W | L | Sv | IP | H | K | ERA | WHIP | K/9 | BB/9 | HR/9 | GB/F |
|---|---|---|---|---|---|---|---|---|---|---|---|---|---|
| 07 | — | — | — | — | — | — | — | — | — | — | — | — | — |
| 08 | OAK | 1 | 4 | 0 | 34 | 32 | 34 | 7.68 | 1.68 | 9.0 | 6.6 | 2.4 | 1.1 |
| 09 | OAK | 6 | 7 | 0 | 98 | 113 | 109 | 5.75 | 1.71 | 9.9 | 5.1 | 1.3 | 1.3 |
| 10 | OAK | 15 | 9 | 0 | 200 | 171 | 171 | 3.23 | 1.31 | 7.7 | 4.1 | 0.7 | 1.4 |

**Competition at SP — Stats in 2010 as SP**

| Thr | Player | GS | ERA | Supp | W-L |
|---|---|---|---|---|---|
| LH | Gonzalez G | 33 | 3.23 | 4.3 | 15-9 |
| RH | Cahill T | 30 | 2.97 | 4.6 | 18-8 |
| LH | Braden D | 30 | 3.50 | 3.3 | 11-14 |
| RH | Sheets B | 20 | 4.53 | 4.6 | 4-9 |

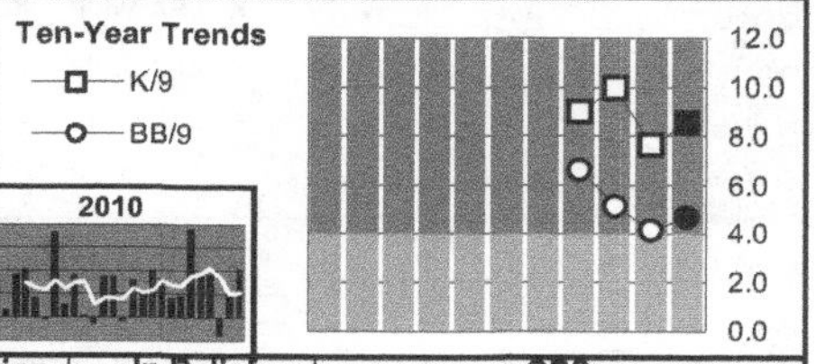


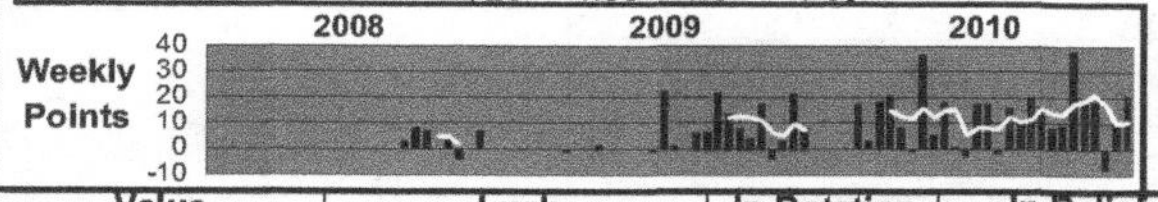


| Yr | $1L | $2L | Pts | RAA | H% | HR/fb | S% | FIP | GS | CG | QS/DS | GR | Hld | Bln | Lead | OPS | 1st Hf | 2nd Hf | vs RH | vs LH |
|---|---|---|---|---|---|---|---|---|---|---|---|---|---|---|---|---|---|---|---|---|
| | **Value** | | | | **Luck** | | | | **In Rotation** | | | **In Relief** | | | | **OPS** | | | | |
| 07 | — | — | — | — | — | — | — | — | — | — | — | — | — | — | — | — | — | — | — | — |
| 08 | -$7 | -$9 | 20 | −17 | 26% | 23% | 58% | 6.95 | 7 | 0 | 0/3 | 3 | 0 | 0 | −1.0 | .911 | — | .911 | 1.034 | .580 |
| 09 | -$2 | -$9 | 120 | −19 | 37% | 14% | 68% | 4.64 | 17 | 0 | 6/4 | 3 | 0 | 0 | −0.4 | .846 | .947 | .811 | .767 | 1.095 |
| 10 | $17 | $6 | 320 | +24 | 28% | 7% | 77% | 3.94 | 33 | 1 | 23/4 | | | | | .644 | .678 | .606 | .653 | .615 |

## Mike Gonzalez — 60 IP | $2 | 100 pts

RP-29 — Owned: 25% — LH

Ignore Gonzo's 2 IP in April (before he went on the DL for his shoulder), and you have one of the top half-seasons of 2010 (2.78 ERA and 13 H in 22 IP). Gonzalez will compete for Baltimore's closer role, but the O's could choose to break camp in match-up mode and deploy him anywhere from the 7th inning on. (BJ)

**Forecast**

| Player | Age | IP | W | Sv | K | ERA | WHIP | K/9 | BB/9 | $2L | Pts |
|---|---|---|---|---|---|---|---|---|---|---|---|
| Gonzalez M | 32 | 60 | 2 | 5 | 66 | 4.48 | 1.42 | 9.9 | 4.5 | $2 | 100 |
| **Mini-Browser** | **Age** | **IP** | **W** | **Sv** | **K** | **ERA** | **WHIP** | **K/9** | **BB/9** | **$2L** | **Pts** |
| Wood K | 33 | 60 | 3 | 0 | 62 | 3.77 | 1.41 | 9.3 | 4.7 | $2 | 80 |
| Porcello R | 22 | 200 | 11 | 0 | 100 | 4.92 | 1.39 | 4.5 | 2.5 | $2 | 170 |
| Sanches B | 32 | 60 | 2 | 0 | 52 | 3.56 | 1.29 | 7.8 | 3.8 | $2 | 70 |
| Strop P | 25 | 40 | 2 | 0 | 39 | 3.18 | 1.31 | 8.8 | 3.9 | $2 | 60 |
| Wheeler D | 33 | 50 | 2 | 0 | 42 | 4.23 | 1.18 | 7.6 | 2.6 | $2 | 60 |

**Minors (2010)**

| Level | Leag | W | L | Sv | IP | H | K | ERA | WHIP | K/9 | BB/9 | HR/9 | GB/F |
|---|---|---|---|---|---|---|---|---|---|---|---|---|---|
| A | NYP | 0 | 1 | 0 | 5 | 7 | 5 | 5.40 | 1.40 | 9.0 | 0.0 | 3.6 | — |
| AA | EL | 1 | 0 | 0 | 4 | 2 | 4 | 2.25 | 0.75 | 9.0 | 2.3 | 2.3 | — |
| AAA | IL | 0 | 0 | 0 | 1 | 3 | 4 | 10.80 | 3.00 | 21.6 | 10.8 | 0.0 | — |

**Majors**

| Yr | Team | W | L | Sv | IP | H | K | ERA | WHIP | K/9 | BB/9 | HR/9 | GB/F |
|---|---|---|---|---|---|---|---|---|---|---|---|---|---|
| 07 | ATL | 2 | 0 | 2 | 17 | 15 | 13 | 1.59 | 1.35 | 6.9 | 4.2 | 0.0 | 1.0 |
| 08 | ATL | 0 | 3 | 14 | 33 | 26 | 44 | 4.28 | 1.19 | 11.8 | 3.7 | 1.6 | 0.7 |
| 09 | ATL | 5 | 4 | 10 | 74 | 56 | 90 | 2.42 | 1.20 | 10.9 | 4.0 | 0.8 | 0.9 |
| 10 | BAL | 1 | 3 | 1 | 24 | 18 | 31 | 4.01 | 1.30 | 11.3 | 5.1 | 0.4 | 0.7 |

**Competition at RP — Stats in 2010 as RP**

| Thr | Player | GR | ERA | IP/G | Sv-Hld |
|---|---|---|---|---|---|
| LH | Hendrickson M | 51 | 5.25 | 1.4 | 0-8 |
| LH | Gonzalez M | 29 | 4.01 | 0.9 | 1-10 |
| LH | Castillo A | 14 | 10.13 | 0.8 | 0-1 |

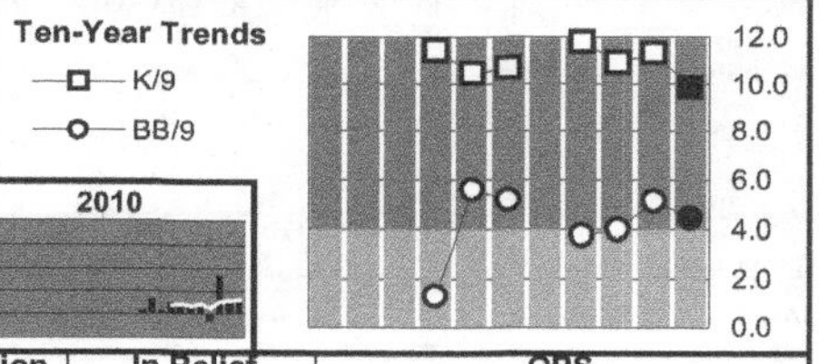


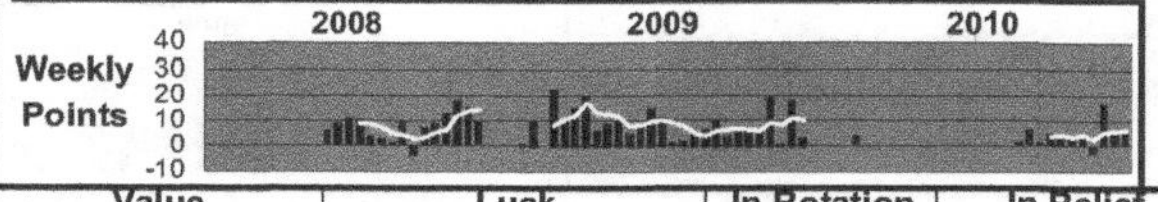


| Yr | $1L | $2L | Pts | RAA | H% | HR/fb | S% | FIP | GS | CG | QS/DS | GR | Hld | Bln | Lead | OPS | 1st Hf | 2nd Hf | vs RH | vs LH |
|---|---|---|---|---|---|---|---|---|---|---|---|---|---|---|---|---|---|---|---|---|
| | **Value** | | | | **Luck** | | | | **In Rotation** | | | **In Relief** | | | | **OPS** | | | | |
| 07 | $1 | $0 | 50 | +5 | 31% | 0% | 87% | 3.08 | — | — | — | 18 | 5 | 0 | +1.2 | .673 | .673 | — | .576 | .824 |
| 08 | $3 | $1 | 110 | −6 | 27% | 17% | 71% | 4.15 | — | — | — | 36 | 0 | 2 | +2.4 | .702 | .513 | .778 | .600 | 1.065 |
| 09 | $10 | $7 | 200 | +5 | 29% | 9% | 84% | 3.33 | — | — | — | 80 | 17 | 7 | +1.7 | .658 | .713 | .584 | .699 | .581 |
| 10 | -$2 | -$9 | 40 | +0 | 30% | 4% | 68% | 3.02 | — | — | — | 29 | 10 | 2 | +0.6 | .629 | 1.532 | .512 | .495 | .849 |

## Tom Gorzelanny — 140 IP | $-1 | 150 pts

SP-23, RP-6 — Owned: 5% — LH

In a mixed SP/RP role from April through July 18, Gorzelanny notched 81 K in 81 IP by nibbling with his low-90's four-seamer, slider, and two-seamer. This performance secured a rotation spot for Tom, but then fatigue set in, and he lost 1 MPH that he couldn't spare. Handled well, he could be surprisingly good. (RM)

**Forecast**

| Player | Age | IP | W | Sv | K | ERA | WHIP | K/9 | BB/9 | $2L | Pts |
|---|---|---|---|---|---|---|---|---|---|---|---|
| Gorzelanny T | 28 | 140 | 7 | 0 | 111 | 4.67 | 1.48 | 7.1 | 4.1 | -$1 | 150 |
| **Mini-Browser** | **Age** | **IP** | **W** | **Sv** | **K** | **ERA** | **WHIP** | **K/9** | **BB/9** | **$2L** | **Pts** |
| Bergesen B | 25 | 160 | 8 | 0 | 87 | 4.90 | 1.48 | 4.9 | 2.6 | -$1 | 130 |
| Johnson J | 27 | 60 | 3 | 2 | 41 | 4.61 | 1.53 | 6.2 | 3.3 | -$1 | 60 |
| Hill R | 31 | 40 | 2 | 0 | 35 | 4.69 | 1.48 | 7.8 | 4.6 | -$1 | 50 |
| Norberto J | 24 | 40 | 3 | 0 | 47 | 4.13 | 1.59 | 10.5 | 6.4 | -$1 | 60 |
| Salas F | 25 | 40 | 1 | 0 | 41 | 4.10 | 1.45 | 9.2 | 3.6 | -$1 | 50 |

**Minors (2010)**

| Level | Leag | W | L | Sv | IP | H | K | ERA | WHIP | K/9 | BB/9 | HR/9 | GB/F |
|---|---|---|---|---|---|---|---|---|---|---|---|---|---|
| A | — | — | — | — | — | — | — | — | — | — | — | — | — |
| AA | — | — | — | — | — | — | — | — | — | — | — | — | — |
| AAA | — | — | — | — | — | — | — | — | — | — | — | — | — |

**Majors**

| Yr | Team | W | L | Sv | IP | H | K | ERA | WHIP | K/9 | BB/9 | HR/9 | GB/F |
|---|---|---|---|---|---|---|---|---|---|---|---|---|---|
| 07 | PIT | 14 | 10 | 0 | 201 | 214 | 135 | 3.88 | 1.40 | 6.0 | 3.0 | 0.8 | 1.1 |
| 08 | PIT | 6 | 9 | 0 | 105 | 120 | 67 | 6.66 | 1.80 | 5.7 | 6.0 | 1.7 | 0.9 |
| 09 | 2TM | 7 | 3 | 0 | 47 | 45 | 47 | 5.55 | 1.32 | 9.0 | 3.3 | 1.1 | 1.1 |
| 10 | CHC | 7 | 9 | 1 | 136 | 136 | 119 | 4.09 | 1.50 | 7.9 | 4.5 | 0.7 | 1.0 |

**Competition at SP — Stats in 2010 as SP**

| Thr | Player | GS | ERA | Supp | W-L |
|---|---|---|---|---|---|
| RH | Dempster R | 34 | 3.85 | 4.8 | 15-12 |
| RH | Wells R | 32 | 4.26 | 3.3 | 8-14 |
| LH | Gorzelanny T | 23 | 4.22 | 4.1 | 7-9 |
| RH | Silva C | 21 | 4.22 | 5.1 | 10-6 |

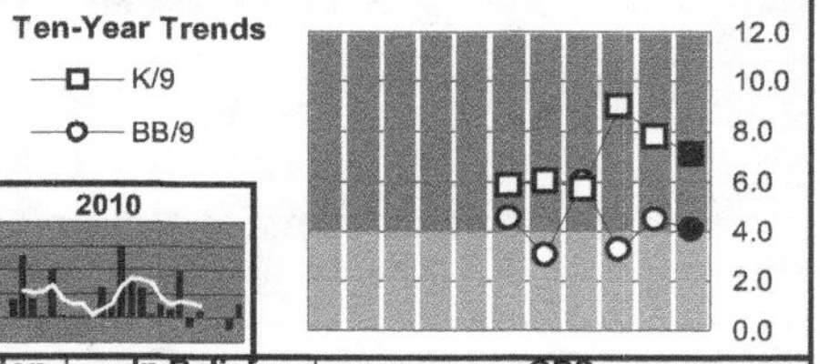


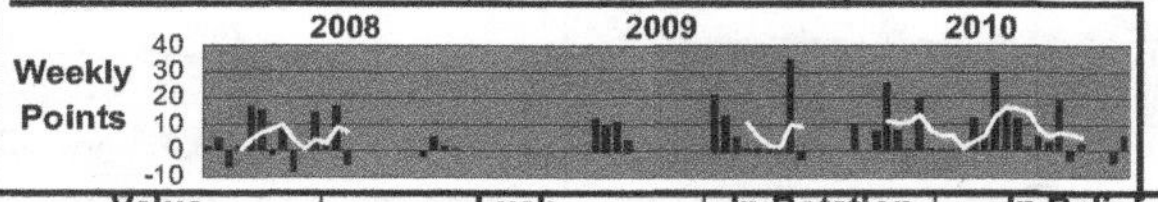


| Yr | $1L | $2L | Pts | RAA | H% | HR/fb | S% | FIP | GS | CG | QS/DS | GR | Hld | Bln | Lead | OPS | 1st Hf | 2nd Hf | vs RH | vs LH |
|---|---|---|---|---|---|---|---|---|---|---|---|---|---|---|---|---|---|---|---|---|
| | **Value** | | | | **Luck** | | | | **In Rotation** | | | **In Relief** | | | | **OPS** | | | | |
| 07 | $9 | -$4 | 250 | +9 | 31% | 7% | 74% | 4.03 | 32 | 1 | 19/2 | — | — | — | — | .748 | .672 | .850 | .782 | .571 |
| 08 | -$14 | -$22 | 60 | −27 | 31% | 13% | 66% | 6.39 | 21 | 0 | 7/6 | — | — | — | — | .909 | .908 | .913 | .941 | .755 |
| 09 | $0 | -$2 | 100 | −7 | 30% | 12% | 59% | 3.99 | 7 | 0 | 1/2 | 15 | 2 | 1 | +0.3 | .708 | .512 | .749 | .751 | .563 |
| 10 | -$1 | -$13 | 170 | −3 | 32% | 7% | 74% | 4.00 | 23 | 0 | 11/3 | 6 | 1 | 0 | −0.4 | .742 | .675 | .821 | .716 | .823 |

## John Grabow — 40 IP | $-4 | 30 pts

RP-28 — Owned: 0% — LH

Mr. 7.36 ERA is on a contract that pays $4.8M in 2011. He is sub-par in all but K/9, and his platoon split is not wide enough to make him a situational asset. However, he was on the DL twice for knee pain in 2010, which may explain his poor results on H% and HR/FB. He should return to mop up in '11. (RM)

**Forecast**

| Player | Age | IP | W | Sv | K | ERA | WHIP | K/9 | BB/9 | $2L | Pts |
|---|---|---|---|---|---|---|---|---|---|---|---|
| Grabow J | 32 | 40 | 2 | 0 | 29 | 5.17 | 1.58 | 6.4 | 4.6 | -$4 | 30 |
| **Mini-Browser** | **Age** | **IP** | **W** | **Sv** | **K** | **ERA** | **WHIP** | **K/9** | **BB/9** | **$2L** | **Pts** |
| Karstens J | 28 | 80 | 3 | 0 | 45 | 5.09 | 1.44 | 5.1 | 2.6 | -$4 | 50 |
| Minor M | 23 | 150 | 7 | 0 | 158 | 5.62 | 1.52 | 9.5 | 2.2 | -$4 | 170 |
| Coello R | 26 | 20 | 1 | 0 | 17 | 6.53 | 1.73 | 7.8 | 5.3 | -$4 | 10 |
| Ledezma W | 30 | 40 | 2 | 0 | 36 | 5.28 | 1.59 | 8.1 | 4.3 | -$4 | 40 |
| Diamond T | 27 | 60 | 2 | 0 | 44 | 4.93 | 1.57 | 6.7 | 5.1 | -$4 | 50 |

**Minors (2010)**

| Level | Leag | W | L | Sv | IP | H | K | ERA | WHIP | K/9 | BB/9 | HR/9 | GB/F |
|---|---|---|---|---|---|---|---|---|---|---|---|---|---|
| A | — | — | — | — | — | — | — | — | — | — | — | — | — |
| AA | — | — | — | — | — | — | — | — | — | — | — | — | — |
| AAA | PCL | 0 | 0 | 0 | 4 | 6 | 2 | 6.75 | 1.75 | 4.5 | 2.3 | 0.0 | — |

**Majors**

| Yr | Team | W | L | Sv | IP | H | K | ERA | WHIP | K/9 | BB/9 | HR/9 | GB/F |
|---|---|---|---|---|---|---|---|---|---|---|---|---|---|
| 07 | PIT | 3 | 2 | 1 | 51 | 56 | 42 | 4.53 | 1.45 | 7.3 | 3.3 | 1.0 | 1.5 |
| 08 | PIT | 6 | 3 | 4 | 76 | 60 | 62 | 2.84 | 1.28 | 7.3 | 4.4 | 1.1 | 1.0 |
| 09 | 2TM | 3 | 0 | 0 | 72 | 62 | 57 | 3.36 | 1.41 | 7.1 | 5.0 | 0.6 | 1.0 |
| 10 | CHC | 1 | 3 | 0 | 25 | 35 | 20 | 7.36 | 1.87 | 7.0 | 4.6 | 1.8 | 1.1 |

**Competition at RP — Stats in 2010 as RP**

| Thr | Player | GR | ERA | IP/G | Sv-Hld |
|---|---|---|---|---|---|
| LH | Marshall S | 80 | 2.65 | 0.9 | 1-22 |
| LH | Russell J | 57 | 4.96 | 0.9 | 0-6 |
| LH | Grabow J | 28 | 7.36 | 0.9 | 0-7 |
| LH | Maine S | 13 | 2.08 | 1.0 | 0-2 |

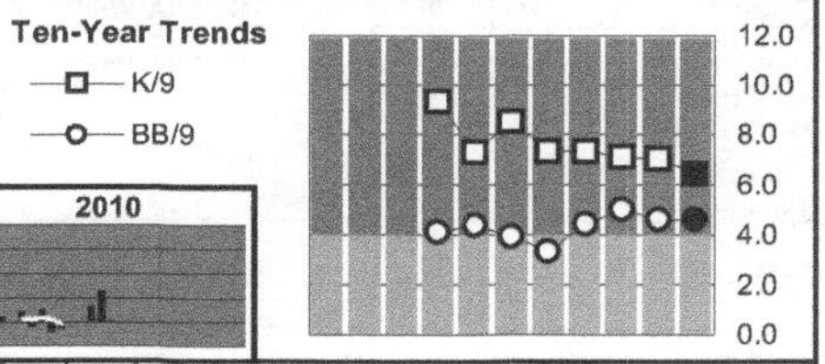


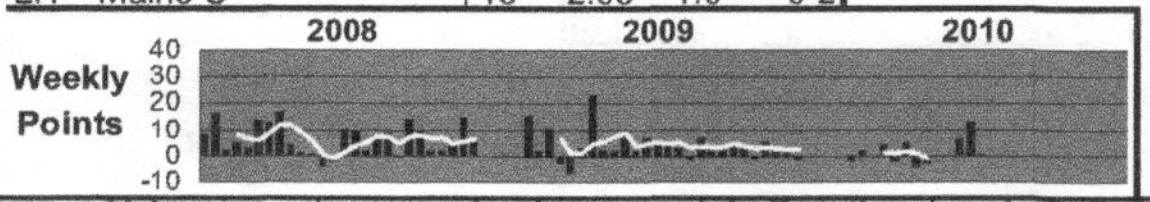


| Yr | $1L | $2L | Pts | RAA | H% | HR/fb | S% | FIP | GS | CG | QS/DS | GR | Hld | Bln | Lead | OPS | 1st Hf | 2nd Hf | vs RH | vs LH |
|---|---|---|---|---|---|---|---|---|---|---|---|---|---|---|---|---|---|---|---|---|
| | **Value** | | | | **Luck** | | | | **In Rotation** | | | **In Relief** | | | | **OPS** | | | | |
| 07 | -$1 | -$5 | 70 | −4 | 33% | 12% | 71% | 4.19 | — | — | — | 63 | 8 | 1 | −0.7 | .740 | .811 | .686 | .821 | .611 |
| 08 | $7 | $4 | 150 | +9 | 25% | 10% | 83% | 4.57 | — | — | — | 74 | 16 | 4 | −0.0 | .651 | .667 | .625 | .666 | .609 |
| 09 | $2 | $0 | 80 | +5 | 28% | 6% | 77% | 4.23 | — | — | — | 75 | 23 | 2 | +1.0 | .670 | .717 | .607 | .698 | .607 |
| 10 | -$9 | -$18 | 10 | −12 | 36% | 15% | 63% | 5.69 | — | — | — | 28 | 7 | 1 | −0.5 | .930 | .930 | — | .983 | .811 |

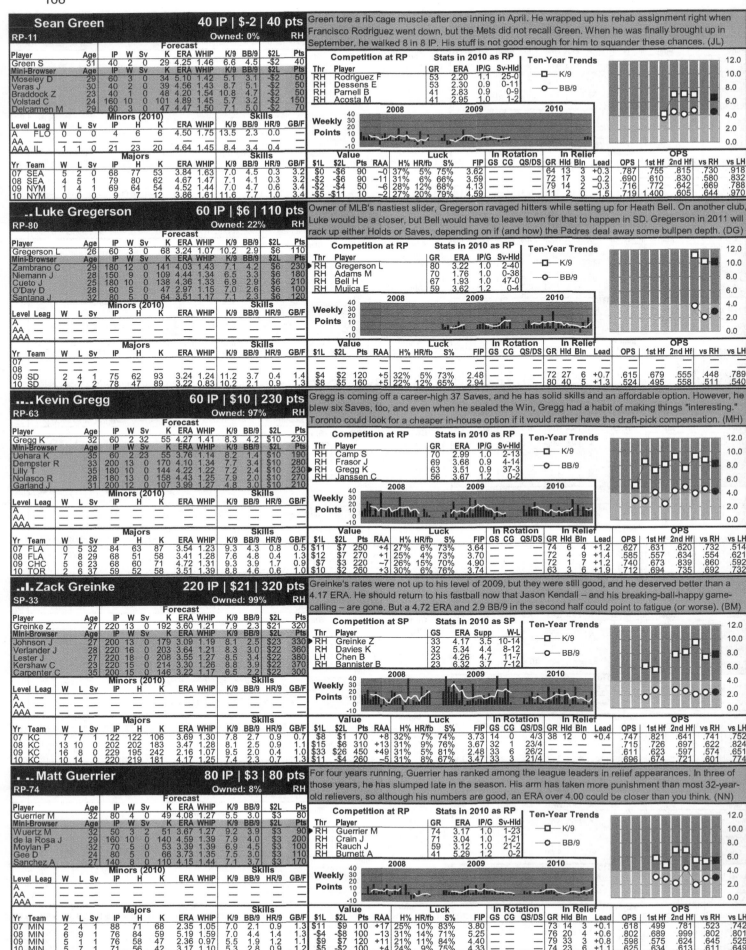

## Sean Green — 40 IP | $-2 | 40 pts

RP-11 — Owned: 0% — RH

Green tore a rib cage muscle after one inning in April. He wrapped up his rehab assignment right when Francisco Rodriguez went down, but the Mets did not recall Green. When he was finally brought up in September, he walked 8 in 8 IP. His stuff is not good enough for him to squander these chances. (JL)

| Player | Age | IP | W | Sv | K | ERA | WHIP | K/9 | BB/9 | $2L | Pts |
|---|---|---|---|---|---|---|---|---|---|---|---|
| Green S | 31 | 40 | 2 | 0 | 29 | 4.25 | 1.46 | 6.6 | 4.5 | -$2 | 40 |
| **Mini-Browser** | **Age** | **IP** | **W** | **Sv** | **K** | **ERA** | **WHIP** | **K/9** | **BB/9** | **$2L** | **Pts** |
| Moseley D | 29 | 60 | 3 | 0 | 34 | 5.10 | 1.42 | 5.1 | 3.1 | -$2 | 50 |
| Veras J | 30 | 40 | 2 | 0 | 39 | 4.56 | 1.43 | 8.7 | 5.1 | -$2 | 50 |
| Braddock Z | 23 | 40 | 1 | 0 | 48 | 4.20 | 1.54 | 10.8 | 4.7 | -$2 | 50 |
| Volstad C | 24 | 160 | 10 | 0 | 101 | 4.89 | 1.45 | 5.7 | 3.2 | -$2 | 150 |
| Delcarmen M | 29 | 60 | 3 | 0 | 47 | 4.47 | 1.50 | 7.1 | 5.0 | -$2 | 70 |

Minors (2010)

| Level | Leag | W | L | Sv | IP | H | K | ERA | WHIP | K/9 | BB/9 | HR/9 | GB/F |
|---|---|---|---|---|---|---|---|---|---|---|---|---|---|
| A | FLO | 0 | 0 | 0 | 4 | 6 | 6 | 4.50 | 1.75 | 13.5 | 2.3 | 0.0 | — |
| AA | — | — | — | — | — | — | — | — | — | — | — | — | — |
| AAA | IL | 1 | 1 | 0 | 21 | 23 | 20 | 4.64 | 1.45 | 8.4 | 3.4 | 0.4 | — |

Competition at RP — Stats in 2010 as RP

| Thr | Player | GR | ERA | IP/G | Sv-Hld |
|---|---|---|---|---|---|
| RH | Rodriguez F | 53 | 2.20 | 1.1 | 25-0 |
| RH | Dessens E | 53 | 2.30 | 0.9 | 0-11 |
| RH | Parnell B | 41 | 2.83 | 0.9 | 0-9 |
| RH | Acosta M | 41 | 2.95 | 1.0 | 1-2 |

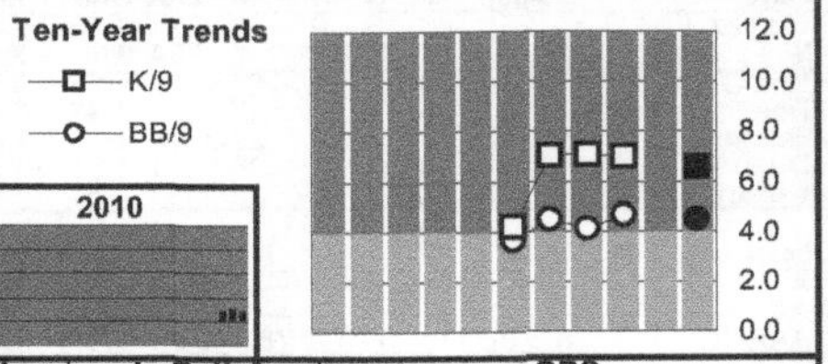


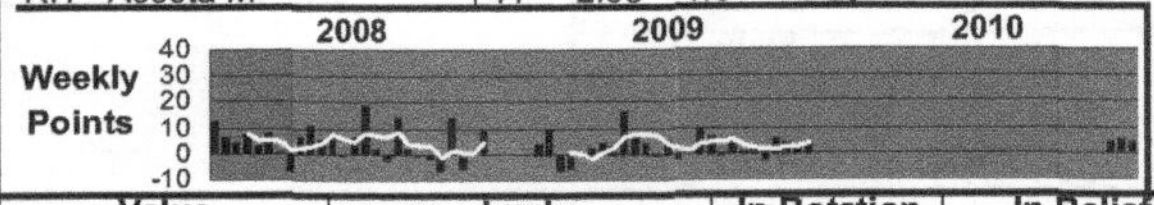


| Yr | Team | W | L | Sv | IP | H | K | ERA | WHIP | K/9 | BB/9 | HR/9 | GB/F | $1L | $2L | Pts | RAA | H% | HR/fb | S% | FIP | GS | CG | QS/DS | GR | Hld | Bln | Lead | OPS | 1st Hf | 2nd Hf | vs RH | vs LH |
|---|---|---|---|---|---|---|---|---|---|---|---|---|---|---|---|---|---|---|---|---|---|---|---|---|---|---|---|---|---|---|---|---|---|
| 07 | SEA | 5 | 2 | 0 | 68 | 77 | 53 | 3.84 | 1.63 | 7.0 | 4.5 | 0.3 | 3.2 | $0 | -$6 | 90 | -0 | 37% | 5% | 75% | 3.62 | — | — | — | 64 | 13 | 3 | +0.3 | .787 | .755 | .815 | .730 | .918 |
| 08 | SEA | 4 | 5 | 1 | 79 | 80 | 62 | 4.67 | 1.47 | 7.1 | 4.1 | 0.3 | 3.2 | -$2 | -$6 | 90 | -11 | 31% | 6% | 66% | 3.59 | — | — | — | 72 | 17 | 3 | -0.2 | .690 | .610 | .830 | .580 | .832 |
| 09 | NYM | 1 | 4 | 1 | 69 | 64 | 54 | 4.52 | 1.44 | 7.0 | 4.7 | 0.6 | 3.4 | -$2 | -$4 | 50 | -6 | 28% | 12% | 68% | 4.13 | — | — | — | 79 | 14 | 2 | -0.3 | .716 | .772 | .642 | .669 | .788 |
| 10 | NYM | 0 | 0 | 0 | 9 | 7 | 12 | 3.86 | 1.61 | 11.6 | 7.7 | 1.0 | 3.4 | -$5 | -$11 | 10 | -2 | 27% | 20% | 79% | 4.59 | — | — | — | 11 | 2 | 0 | -1.5 | .719 | 1.400 | .605 | .644 | .970 |

## Luke Gregerson — 60 IP | $6 | 110 pts

RP-80 — Owned: 22% — RH

Owner of MLB's nastiest slider, Gregerson ravaged hitters while setting up for Heath Bell. On another club, Luke would be a closer, but Bell would have to leave town for that to happen in SD. Gregerson in 2011 will rack up either Holds or Saves, depending on if (and how) the Padres deal away some bullpen depth. (DG)

| Player | Age | IP | W | Sv | K | ERA | WHIP | K/9 | BB/9 | $2L | Pts |
|---|---|---|---|---|---|---|---|---|---|---|---|
| Gregerson L | 26 | 60 | 3 | 0 | 68 | 3.24 | 1.07 | 10.2 | 2.9 | $6 | 110 |
| **Mini-Browser** | **Age** | **IP** | **W** | **Sv** | **K** | **ERA** | **WHIP** | **K/9** | **BB/9** | **$2L** | **Pts** |
| Zambrano C | 29 | 180 | 12 | 0 | 141 | 4.03 | 1.43 | 7.1 | 4.2 | $6 | 230 |
| Niemann J | 28 | 150 | 9 | 0 | 109 | 4.44 | 1.34 | 6.5 | 3.3 | $6 | 180 |
| Cueto J | 25 | 180 | 10 | 0 | 138 | 4.36 | 1.33 | 6.9 | 2.9 | $6 | 210 |
| O'Day D | 28 | 60 | 5 | 0 | 47 | 2.97 | 1.15 | 7.0 | 2.6 | $6 | 100 |
| Santana J | 32 | 80 | 5 | 0 | 64 | 3.51 | 1.17 | 7.1 | 2.3 | $6 | 120 |

Minors (2010)

| Level | Leag | W | L | Sv | IP | H | K | ERA | WHIP | K/9 | BB/9 | HR/9 | GB/F |
|---|---|---|---|---|---|---|---|---|---|---|---|---|---|
| A | — | — | — | — | — | — | — | — | — | — | — | — | — |
| AA | — | — | — | — | — | — | — | — | — | — | — | — | — |
| AAA | — | — | — | — | — | — | — | — | — | — | — | — | — |

Competition at RP — Stats in 2010 as RP

| Thr | Player | GR | ERA | IP/G | Sv-Hld |
|---|---|---|---|---|---|
| ▶ RH | Gregerson L | 80 | 3.22 | 1.0 | 2-40 |
| RH | Adams M | 70 | 1.76 | 1.0 | 0-38 |
| RH | Bell H | 67 | 1.93 | 1.0 | 47-0 |
| RH | Mujica E | 59 | 3.62 | 1.2 | 0-4 |

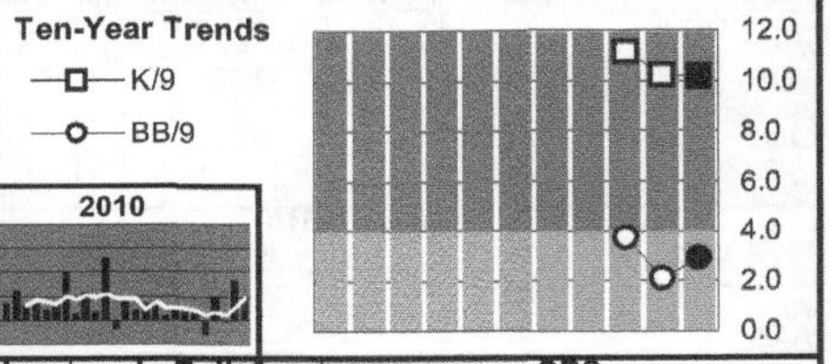


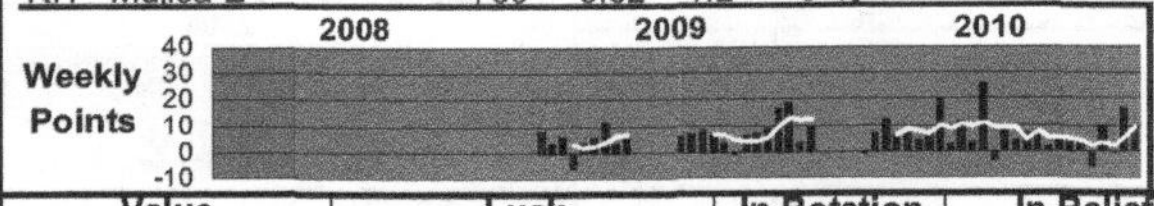


| Yr | Team | W | L | Sv | IP | H | K | ERA | WHIP | K/9 | BB/9 | HR/9 | GB/F | $1L | $2L | Pts | RAA | H% | HR/fb | S% | FIP | GS | CG | QS/DS | GR | Hld | Bln | Lead | OPS | 1st Hf | 2nd Hf | vs RH | vs LH |
|---|---|---|---|---|---|---|---|---|---|---|---|---|---|---|---|---|---|---|---|---|---|---|---|---|---|---|---|---|---|---|---|---|---|
| 07 | — | — | — | — | — | — | — | — | — | — | — | — | — | — | — | — | — | — | — | — | — | — | — | — | — | — | — | — | — | — | — | — | — |
| 08 | — | — | — | — | — | — | — | — | — | — | — | — | — | — | — | — | — | — | — | — | — | — | — | — | — | — | — | — | — | — | — | — | — |
| 09 | SD | 2 | 4 | 1 | 75 | 62 | 93 | 3.24 | 1.24 | 11.2 | 3.7 | 0.4 | 1.4 | $4 | $2 | 120 | +5 | 32% | 5% | 73% | 2.48 | — | — | — | 72 | 27 | 6 | +0.7 | .615 | .679 | .555 | .448 | .789 |
| 10 | SD | 4 | 7 | 2 | 78 | 47 | 89 | 3.22 | 0.83 | 10.2 | 2.1 | 0.9 | 1.3 | $8 | $5 | 160 | +5 | 22% | 12% | 65% | 2.94 | — | — | — | 80 | 40 | 5 | +1.3 | .524 | .495 | .558 | .511 | .540 |

## Kevin Gregg — 60 IP | $10 | 230 pts

RP-63 — Owned: 97% — RH

Gregg is coming off a career-high 37 Saves, and he has solid skills and an affordable option. However, he blew six Saves, too, and even when he sealed the Win, Gregg had a habit of making things "interesting." Toronto could look for a cheaper in-house option if it would rather have the draft-pick compensation. (MH)

| Player | Age | IP | W | Sv | K | ERA | WHIP | K/9 | BB/9 | $2L | Pts |
|---|---|---|---|---|---|---|---|---|---|---|---|
| Gregg K | 32 | 60 | 2 | 32 | 55 | 4.27 | 1.41 | 8.3 | 4.2 | $10 | 230 |
| **Mini-Browser** | **Age** | **IP** | **W** | **Sv** | **K** | **ERA** | **WHIP** | **K/9** | **BB/9** | **$2L** | **Pts** |
| Uehara K | 35 | 60 | 2 | 23 | 55 | 3.76 | 1.14 | 8.2 | 1.4 | $10 | 190 |
| Dempster R | 33 | 200 | 13 | 0 | 170 | 4.10 | 1.34 | 7.7 | 3.4 | $10 | 280 |
| Lilly T | 35 | 180 | 10 | 0 | 144 | 4.22 | 1.22 | 7.2 | 2.4 | $10 | 230 |
| Nolasco R | 28 | 180 | 13 | 0 | 158 | 4.43 | 1.25 | 7.9 | 2.0 | $10 | 270 |
| Garland J | 31 | 200 | 12 | 0 | 107 | 3.99 | 1.27 | 4.8 | 3.0 | $10 | 210 |

Minors (2010)

| Level | Leag | W | L | Sv | IP | H | K | ERA | WHIP | K/9 | BB/9 | HR/9 | GB/F |
|---|---|---|---|---|---|---|---|---|---|---|---|---|---|
| A | — | — | — | — | — | — | — | — | — | — | — | — | — |
| AA | — | — | — | — | — | — | — | — | — | — | — | — | — |
| AAA | — | — | — | — | — | — | — | — | — | — | — | — | — |

Competition at RP — Stats in 2010 as RP

| Thr | Player | GR | ERA | IP/G | Sv-Hld |
|---|---|---|---|---|---|
| RH | Camp S | 70 | 2.99 | 1.0 | 2-13 |
| RH | Frasor J | 69 | 3.68 | 0.9 | 4-14 |
| ▶ RH | Gregg K | 63 | 3.51 | 0.9 | 37-3 |
| RH | Janssen C | 56 | 3.67 | 1.2 | 0-2 |

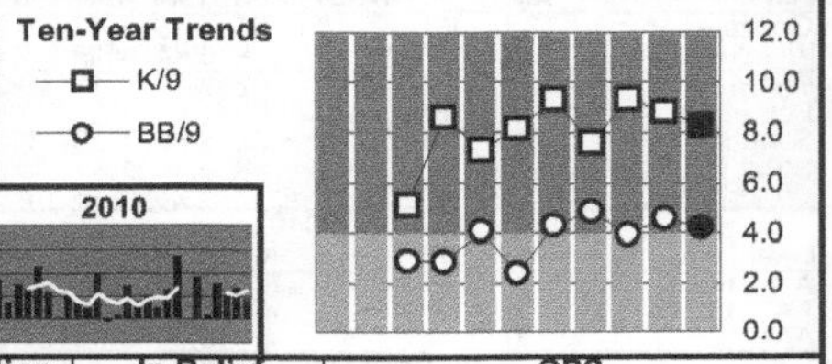


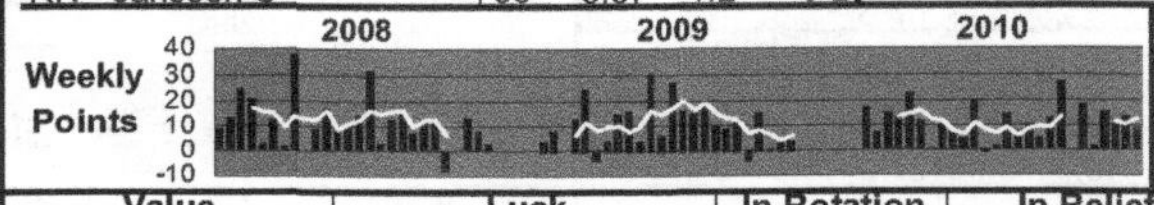


| Yr | Team | W | L | Sv | IP | H | K | ERA | WHIP | K/9 | BB/9 | HR/9 | GB/F | $1L | $2L | Pts | RAA | H% | HR/fb | S% | FIP | GS | CG | QS/DS | GR | Hld | Bln | Lead | OPS | 1st Hf | 2nd Hf | vs RH | vs LH |
|---|---|---|---|---|---|---|---|---|---|---|---|---|---|---|---|---|---|---|---|---|---|---|---|---|---|---|---|---|---|---|---|---|---|
| 07 | FLA | 0 | 5 | 32 | 84 | 63 | 87 | 3.54 | 1.23 | 9.3 | 4.3 | 0.8 | 0.5 | $11 | $7 | 250 | +4 | 27% | 6% | 73% | 3.64 | — | — | — | 74 | 6 | 4 | +1.2 | .627 | .631 | .620 | .732 | .514 |
| 08 | FLA | 7 | 8 | 29 | 68 | 51 | 58 | 3.41 | 1.28 | 7.6 | 4.8 | 0.4 | 1.3 | $12 | $7 | 270 | +1 | 25% | 4% | 73% | 3.70 | — | — | — | 72 | 4 | 9 | +1.4 | .585 | .557 | .634 | .554 | .621 |
| 09 | CHC | 5 | 6 | 23 | 68 | 60 | 71 | 4.72 | 1.31 | 9.3 | 3.9 | 1.7 | 0.9 | $7 | $3 | 220 | -7 | 26% | 15% | 70% | 4.90 | — | — | — | 72 | 1 | 7 | +1.2 | .740 | .673 | .839 | .860 | .592 |
| 10 | TOR | 2 | 6 | 37 | 59 | 52 | 58 | 3.51 | 1.39 | 8.8 | 4.6 | 0.6 | 1.0 | $10 | $2 | 260 | +3 | 30% | 6% | 76% | 3.74 | — | — | — | 63 | 3 | 6 | +1.9 | .712 | .694 | .735 | .692 | .732 |

## Zack Greinke — 220 IP | $21 | 320 pts

SP-33 — Owned: 99% — RH

Greinke's rates were not up to his level of 2009, but they were still good, and he deserved better than a 4.17 ERA. He should return to his fastball now that Jason Kendall – and his breaking-ball-happy game-calling – are gone. But a 4.72 ERA and 2.9 BB/9 in the second half could point to fatigue (or worse). (BM)

| Player | Age | IP | W | Sv | K | ERA | WHIP | K/9 | BB/9 | $2L | Pts |
|---|---|---|---|---|---|---|---|---|---|---|---|
| Greinke Z | 27 | 220 | 13 | 0 | 192 | 3.60 | 1.21 | 7.9 | 2.3 | $21 | 320 |
| **Mini-Browser** | **Age** | **IP** | **W** | **Sv** | **K** | **ERA** | **WHIP** | **K/9** | **BB/9** | **$2L** | **Pts** |
| Johnson J | 27 | 200 | 13 | 0 | 179 | 3.09 | 1.19 | 8.1 | 2.5 | $23 | 330 |
| Verlander J | 28 | 220 | 16 | 0 | 203 | 3.64 | 1.21 | 8.3 | 3.0 | $22 | 360 |
| Lester J | 27 | 220 | 18 | 0 | 208 | 3.55 | 1.27 | 8.5 | 3.4 | $22 | 380 |
| Kershaw C | 23 | 220 | 15 | 0 | 214 | 3.30 | 1.26 | 8.8 | 3.9 | $22 | 370 |
| Carpenter C | 35 | 200 | 15 | 0 | 146 | 3.22 | 1.17 | 6.5 | 2.2 | $22 | 300 |

Minors (2010)

| Level | Leag | W | L | Sv | IP | H | K | ERA | WHIP | K/9 | BB/9 | HR/9 | GB/F |
|---|---|---|---|---|---|---|---|---|---|---|---|---|---|
| A | — | — | — | — | — | — | — | — | — | — | — | — | — |
| AA | — | — | — | — | — | — | — | — | — | — | — | — | — |
| AAA | — | — | — | — | — | — | — | — | — | — | — | — | — |

Competition at SP — Stats in 2010 as SP

| Thr | Player | GS | ERA | Supp | W-L |
|---|---|---|---|---|---|
| ▶ RH | Greinke Z | 33 | 4.17 | 3.5 | 10-14 |
| RH | Davies K | 32 | 5.34 | 4.4 | 8-12 |
| LH | Chen B | 23 | 4.26 | 4.7 | 11-7 |
| RH | Bannister B | 23 | 6.32 | 3.7 | 7-12 |

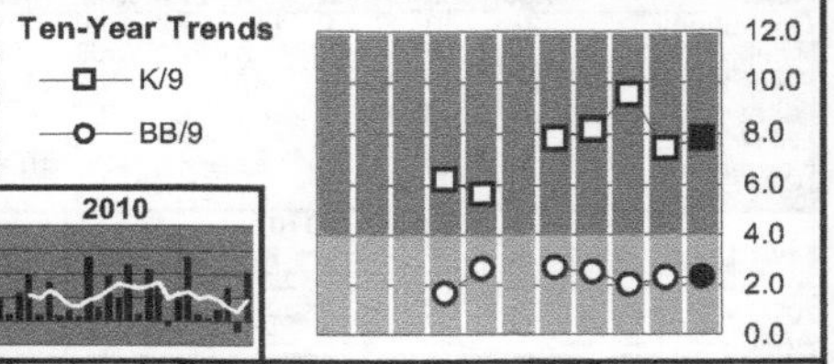


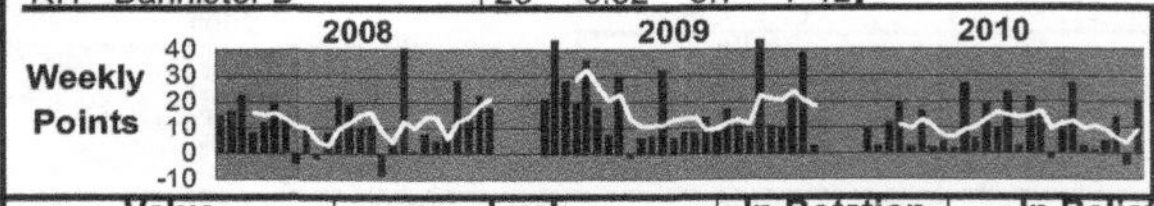


| Yr | Team | W | L | Sv | IP | H | K | ERA | WHIP | K/9 | BB/9 | HR/9 | GB/F | $1L | $2L | Pts | RAA | H% | HR/fb | S% | FIP | GS | CG | QS/DS | GR | Hld | Bln | Lead | OPS | 1st Hf | 2nd Hf | vs RH | vs LH |
|---|---|---|---|---|---|---|---|---|---|---|---|---|---|---|---|---|---|---|---|---|---|---|---|---|---|---|---|---|---|---|---|---|---|
| 07 | KC | 7 | 7 | 1 | 122 | 122 | 106 | 3.69 | 1.30 | 7.8 | 2.7 | 0.9 | 0.7 | $8 | $1 | 170 | +8 | 32% | 7% | 74% | 3.73 | 14 | 0 | 4/3 | 38 | 12 | 0 | +0.4 | .747 | .821 | .641 | .741 | .752 |
| 08 | KC | 13 | 10 | 0 | 202 | 202 | 183 | 3.47 | 1.28 | 8.1 | 2.5 | 0.9 | 1.1 | $15 | $6 | 310 | +13 | 31% | 9% | 76% | 3.67 | 32 | 1 | 23/4 | — | — | — | — | .715 | .726 | .697 | .622 | .824 |
| 09 | KC | 16 | 8 | 0 | 229 | 195 | 242 | 2.16 | 1.07 | 9.5 | 2.0 | 0.4 | 1.0 | $33 | $26 | 450 | +49 | 31% | 5% | 81% | 2.48 | 33 | 6 | 26/2 | — | — | — | — | .611 | .623 | .597 | .574 | .651 |
| 10 | KC | 10 | 14 | 0 | 220 | 219 | 181 | 4.17 | 1.25 | 7.4 | 2.3 | 0.7 | 1.3 | $11 | -$4 | 260 | -5 | 31% | 8% | 67% | 3.47 | 33 | 3 | 21/4 | — | — | — | — | .696 | .674 | .721 | .601 | .774 |

## Matt Guerrier — 80 IP | $3 | 80 pts

RP-74 — Owned: 8% — RH

For four years running, Guerrier has ranked among the league leaders in relief appearances. In three of those years, he has slumped late in the season. His arm has taken more punishment than most 32-year-old relievers, so although his numbers are good, an ERA over 4.00 could be closer than you think. (NN)

| Player | Age | IP | W | Sv | K | ERA | WHIP | K/9 | BB/9 | $2L | Pts |
|---|---|---|---|---|---|---|---|---|---|---|---|
| Guerrier M | 32 | 80 | 4 | 0 | 49 | 4.08 | 1.27 | 5.5 | 3.0 | $3 | 80 |
| **Mini-Browser** | **Age** | **IP** | **W** | **Sv** | **K** | **ERA** | **WHIP** | **K/9** | **BB/9** | **$2L** | **Pts** |
| Wuertz M | 32 | 50 | 3 | 2 | 51 | 3.67 | 1.27 | 9.2 | 3.9 | $3 | 90 |
| de la Rosa J | 29 | 160 | 10 | 0 | 140 | 4.59 | 1.39 | 7.9 | 4.0 | $3 | 200 |
| Moylan P | 32 | 70 | 5 | 0 | 53 | 3.39 | 1.39 | 6.9 | 4.5 | $3 | 100 |
| Gee D | 24 | 80 | 5 | 0 | 66 | 3.73 | 1.35 | 7.5 | 3.0 | $3 | 110 |
| Sanchez A | 27 | 140 | 8 | 0 | 110 | 4.15 | 1.44 | 7.1 | 3.7 | $3 | 170 |

Minors (2010)

| Level | Leag | W | L | Sv | IP | H | K | ERA | WHIP | K/9 | BB/9 | HR/9 | GB/F |
|---|---|---|---|---|---|---|---|---|---|---|---|---|---|
| A | — | — | — | — | — | — | — | — | — | — | — | — | — |
| AA | — | — | — | — | — | — | — | — | — | — | — | — | — |
| AAA | — | — | — | — | — | — | — | — | — | — | — | — | — |

Competition at RP — Stats in 2010 as RP

| Thr | Player | GR | ERA | IP/G | Sv-Hld |
|---|---|---|---|---|---|
| ▶ RH | Guerrier M | 74 | 3.17 | 1.0 | 1-23 |
| RH | Crain J | 71 | 3.04 | 1.0 | 1-21 |
| RH | Rauch J | 59 | 3.12 | 1.0 | 21-2 |
| RH | Burnett A | 41 | 5.29 | 1.2 | 0-2 |

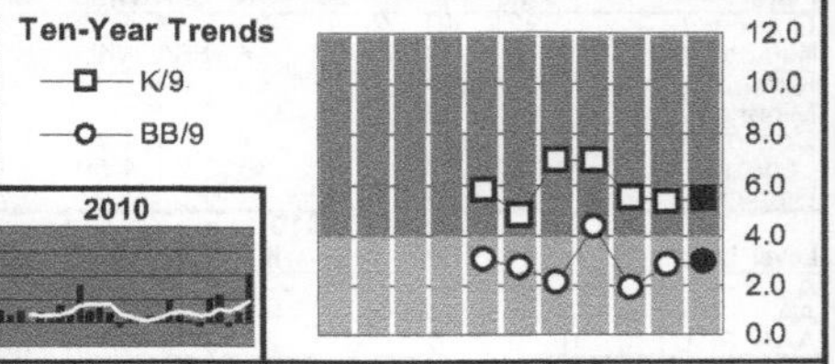


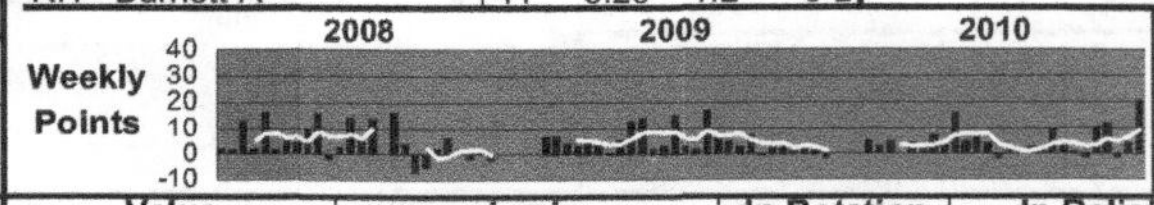


| Yr | Team | W | L | Sv | IP | H | K | ERA | WHIP | K/9 | BB/9 | HR/9 | GB/F | $1L | $2L | Pts | RAA | H% | HR/fb | S% | FIP | GS | CG | QS/DS | GR | Hld | Bln | Lead | OPS | 1st Hf | 2nd Hf | vs RH | vs LH |
|---|---|---|---|---|---|---|---|---|---|---|---|---|---|---|---|---|---|---|---|---|---|---|---|---|---|---|---|---|---|---|---|---|---|
| 07 | MIN | 2 | 4 | 1 | 88 | 71 | 68 | 2.35 | 1.05 | 7.0 | 2.1 | 0.9 | 1.3 | $11 | $9 | 110 | +17 | 25% | 10% | 83% | 3.80 | — | — | — | 73 | 14 | 3 | +0.1 | .618 | .499 | .781 | .523 | .742 |
| 08 | MIN | 6 | 9 | 1 | 76 | 84 | 59 | 5.19 | 1.59 | 7.0 | 4.4 | 1.4 | 1.3 | -$4 | -$8 | 100 | -13 | 31% | 14% | 71% | 5.25 | — | — | — | 76 | 20 | 4 | +0.6 | .802 | .689 | .999 | .802 | .801 |
| 09 | MIN | 5 | 1 | 1 | 76 | 58 | 47 | 2.36 | 0.97 | 5.5 | 1.9 | 1.2 | 1.1 | $9 | $7 | 120 | +11 | 21% | 11% | 84% | 4.40 | — | — | — | 79 | 33 | 3 | +0.8 | .598 | .575 | .624 | .645 | .525 |
| 10 | MIN | 5 | 7 | 1 | 71 | 56 | 42 | 3.17 | 1.10 | 5.3 | 2.8 | 0.9 | 1.2 | $5 | -$2 | 100 | +4 | 24% | 9% | 75% | 4.33 | — | — | — | 74 | 23 | 6 | +1.1 | .625 | .634 | .613 | .611 | .649 |

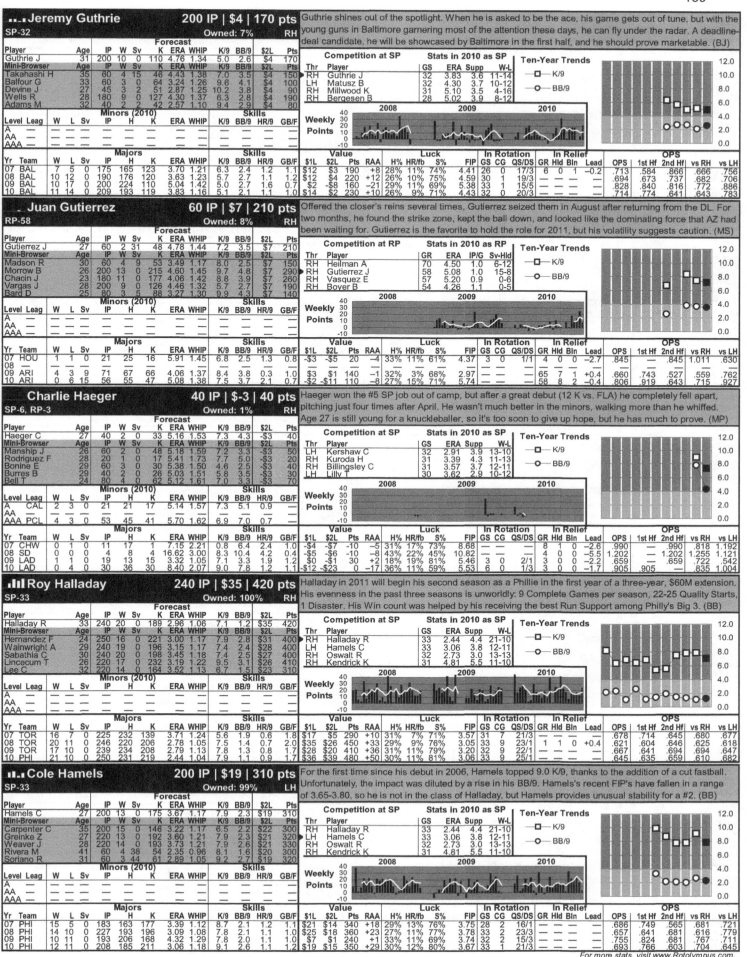

## Jeremy Guthrie — 200 IP | $4 | 170 pts
SP-32 · Owned: 7% · RH

Guthrie shines out of the spotlight. When he is asked to be the ace, his game gets out of tune, but with the young guns in Baltimore garnering most of the attention these days, he can fly under the radar. A deadline-deal candidate, he will be showcased by Baltimore in the first half, and he should prove marketable. (BJ)

### Forecast
| Player | Age | IP | W | Sv | K | ERA | WHIP | K/9 | BB/9 | $2L | Pts |
|---|---|---|---|---|---|---|---|---|---|---|---|
| Guthrie J | 31 | 200 | 10 | 0 | 110 | 4.76 | 1.34 | 5.0 | 2.6 | $4 | 170 |

### Mini-Browser
| Player | Age | IP | W | Sv | K | ERA | WHIP | K/9 | BB/9 | $2L | Pts |
|---|---|---|---|---|---|---|---|---|---|---|---|
| Takahashi H | 35 | 60 | 4 | 15 | 46 | 4.43 | 1.38 | 7.0 | 3.5 | $4 | 150 |
| Balfour G | 33 | 60 | 3 | 0 | 64 | 3.24 | 1.26 | 9.6 | 4.1 | $4 | 100 |
| Devine J | 27 | 45 | 3 | 2 | 51 | 2.87 | 1.25 | 10.2 | 3.8 | $4 | 90 |
| Wells R | 28 | 180 | 9 | 0 | 127 | 4.30 | 1.37 | 6.3 | 2.8 | $4 | 190 |
| Adams M | 32 | 40 | 2 | 2 | 42 | 2.57 | 1.10 | 9.4 | 2.7 | $4 | 80 |

### Minors (2010)
| Level | Leag | W | L | Sv | IP | H | K | ERA | WHIP | K/9 | BB/9 | HR/9 | GB/F |
|---|---|---|---|---|---|---|---|---|---|---|---|---|---|
| A | — | — | — | — | — | — | — | — | — | — | — | — | — |
| AA | — | — | — | — | — | — | — | — | — | — | — | — | — |
| AAA | — | — | — | — | — | — | — | — | — | — | — | — | — |

### Majors / Skills / Value / Luck / In Rotation / In Relief / OPS
| Yr | Team | W | L | Sv | IP | H | K | ERA | WHIP | K/9 | BB/9 | HR/9 | GB/F | $1L | $2L | Pts | RAA | H% | HR/fb | S% | FIP | GS | CG | QS/DS | GR | Hld | Bln | Lead | OPS | 1st Hf | 2nd Hf | vs RH | vs LH |
|---|---|---|---|---|---|---|---|---|---|---|---|---|---|---|---|---|---|---|---|---|---|---|---|---|---|---|---|---|---|---|---|---|---|
| 07 | BAL | 7 | 5 | 0 | 175 | 165 | 123 | 3.70 | 1.21 | 6.3 | 2.4 | 1.2 | 1.1 | $12 | $3 | 190 | +8 | 28% | 11% | 74% | 4.41 | 26 | 0 | 17/3 | 6 | 0 | 1 | -0.2 | .713 | .584 | .866 | .666 | .756 |
| 08 | BAL | 10 | 12 | 0 | 190 | 176 | 120 | 3.63 | 1.23 | 5.7 | 2.7 | 1.1 | 1.2 | $12 | $4 | 220 | +12 | 26% | 10% | 75% | 4.59 | 30 | 1 | 19/3 | — | — | — | — | .694 | .673 | .737 | .682 | .706 |
| 09 | BAL | 10 | 17 | 0 | 200 | 224 | 110 | 5.04 | 1.42 | 5.0 | 2.7 | 1.6 | 0.7 | $2 | -$8 | 160 | -21 | 29% | 11% | 69% | 5.38 | 33 | 1 | 15/5 | — | — | — | — | .828 | .840 | .816 | .772 | .886 |
| 10 | BAL | 11 | 14 | 0 | 209 | 193 | 119 | 3.83 | 1.16 | 5.1 | 2.1 | 1.1 | 1.0 | $14 | $2 | 230 | +10 | 26% | 9% | 71% | 4.43 | 32 | 0 | 20/6 | — | — | — | — | .714 | .774 | .643 | .641 | .783 |

### Competition at SP — Stats in 2010 as SP
| Thr | Player | GS | ERA | Supp | W-L |
|---|---|---|---|---|---|
| RH | Guthrie J | 32 | 3.83 | 3.6 | 11-14 |
| RH | Matusz B | 32 | 4.30 | 3.7 | 10-12 |
| RH | Millwood K | 31 | 5.10 | 3.5 | 4-16 |
| RH | Bergesen B | 28 | 5.02 | 3.9 | 8-12 |

**Ten-Year Trends:** K/9, BB/9

---

## Juan Gutierrez — 60 IP | $7 | 210 pts
RP-58 · Owned: 8% · RH

Offered the closer's reins several times, Gutierrez seized them in August after returning from the DL. For two months, he found the strike zone, kept the ball down, and looked like the dominating force that AZ had been waiting for. Gutierrez is the favorite to hold the role for 2011, but his volatility suggests caution. (MS)

### Forecast
| Player | Age | IP | W | Sv | K | ERA | WHIP | K/9 | BB/9 | $2L | Pts |
|---|---|---|---|---|---|---|---|---|---|---|---|
| Gutierrez J | 27 | 60 | 2 | 31 | 48 | 4.78 | 1.44 | 7.2 | 3.5 | $7 | 210 |

### Mini-Browser
| Player | Age | IP | W | Sv | K | ERA | WHIP | K/9 | BB/9 | $2L | Pts |
|---|---|---|---|---|---|---|---|---|---|---|---|
| Madson R | 30 | 60 | 4 | 9 | 53 | 3.49 | 1.17 | 8.0 | 2.5 | $7 | 150 |
| Morrow B | 26 | 200 | 13 | 0 | 215 | 4.60 | 1.45 | 9.7 | 4.8 | $7 | 290 |
| Chacin J | 23 | 180 | 11 | 0 | 177 | 4.06 | 1.42 | 8.8 | 3.9 | $7 | 260 |
| Vargas J | 28 | 200 | 9 | 0 | 126 | 4.46 | 1.32 | 5.7 | 2.7 | $7 | 190 |
| Bard D | 25 | 80 | 3 | 5 | 88 | 3.27 | 1.30 | 9.9 | 4.3 | $7 | 140 |

### Minors (2010)
| Level | Leag | W | L | Sv | IP | H | K | ERA | WHIP | K/9 | BB/9 | HR/9 | GB/F |
|---|---|---|---|---|---|---|---|---|---|---|---|---|---|
| A | — | — | — | — | — | — | — | — | — | — | — | — | — |
| AA | — | — | — | — | — | — | — | — | — | — | — | — | — |
| AAA | — | — | — | — | — | — | — | — | — | — | — | — | — |

### Majors
| Yr | Team | W | L | Sv | IP | H | K | ERA | WHIP | K/9 | BB/9 | HR/9 | GB/F | $1L | $2L | Pts | RAA | H% | HR/fb | S% | FIP | GS | CG | QS/DS | GR | Hld | Bln | Lead | OPS | 1st Hf | 2nd Hf | vs RH | vs LH |
|---|---|---|---|---|---|---|---|---|---|---|---|---|---|---|---|---|---|---|---|---|---|---|---|---|---|---|---|---|---|---|---|---|---|
| 07 | HOU | 1 | 1 | 0 | 21 | 25 | 16 | 5.91 | 1.45 | 6.8 | 2.5 | 1.3 | 0.8 | -$3 | -$5 | 20 | -4 | 33% | 11% | 61% | 4.37 | 3 | 0 | 1/1 | 4 | 0 | 0 | -2.7 | .845 | — | .845 | 1.011 | .630 |
| 08 | — | — | — | — | — | — | — | — | — | — | — | — | — | — | — | — | — | — | — | — | — | — | — | — | — | — | — | — | — | — | — | — |
| 09 | ARI | 4 | 3 | 9 | 71 | 67 | 66 | 4.06 | 1.37 | 8.4 | 3.8 | 0.3 | 1.0 | $3 | $1 | 140 | -1 | 32% | 3% | 68% | 2.97 | — | — | — | 65 | 7 | 1 | +0.4 | .660 | .743 | .527 | .559 | .762 |
| 10 | ARI | 0 | 6 | 15 | 56 | 55 | 47 | 5.08 | 1.38 | 7.5 | 3.7 | 2.1 | 0.7 | -$2 | -$11 | 110 | -8 | 27% | 15% | 71% | 5.74 | — | — | — | 58 | 8 | 2 | -0.4 | .806 | .919 | .643 | .715 | .927 |

### Competition at RP — Stats in 2010 as RP
| Thr | Player | GR | ERA | IP/G | Sv-Hld |
|---|---|---|---|---|---|
| RH | Heilman A | 70 | 4.50 | 1.0 | 6-12 |
| RH | Gutierrez J | 58 | 5.08 | 1.0 | 15-8 |
| RH | Vasquez E | 57 | 5.20 | 0.9 | 0-6 |
| RH | Boyer B | 54 | 4.26 | 1.1 | 0-5 |

**Ten-Year Trends:** K/9, BB/9

---

## Charlie Haeger — 40 IP | $-3 | 40 pts
SP-6, RP-3 · Owned: 1% · RH

Haeger won the #5 SP job out of camp, but after a great debut (12 K vs. FLA) he completely fell apart, pitching just four times after April. He wasn't much better in the minors, walking more than he whiffed. Age 27 is still young for a knuckleballer, so it's too soon to give up hope, but he has much to prove. (MP)

### Forecast
| Player | Age | IP | W | Sv | K | ERA | WHIP | K/9 | BB/9 | $2L | Pts |
|---|---|---|---|---|---|---|---|---|---|---|---|
| Haeger C | 27 | 40 | 2 | 0 | 33 | 5.16 | 1.53 | 7.3 | 4.3 | -$3 | 40 |

### Mini-Browser
| Player | Age | IP | W | Sv | K | ERA | WHIP | K/9 | BB/9 | $2L | Pts |
|---|---|---|---|---|---|---|---|---|---|---|---|
| Manship J | 26 | 60 | 2 | 0 | 48 | 5.18 | 1.59 | 7.2 | 3.3 | -$3 | 50 |
| Rodriguez F | 28 | 20 | 1 | 0 | 17 | 5.41 | 1.73 | 7.7 | 5.0 | -$3 | 20 |
| Bonine E | 29 | 60 | 3 | 0 | 30 | 5.38 | 1.50 | 4.6 | 2.5 | -$3 | 40 |
| Burres B | 29 | 40 | 2 | 0 | 26 | 5.03 | 1.51 | 5.8 | 3.5 | -$3 | 30 |
| Bell T | 24 | 80 | 4 | 0 | 62 | 5.12 | 1.61 | 7.0 | 3.3 | -$3 | 70 |

### Minors (2010)
| Level | Leag | W | L | Sv | IP | H | K | ERA | WHIP | K/9 | BB/9 | HR/9 | GB/F |
|---|---|---|---|---|---|---|---|---|---|---|---|---|---|
| A | CAL | 2 | 3 | 0 | 21 | 21 | 17 | 5.14 | 1.57 | 7.3 | 5.1 | 0.9 | — |
| AA | — | — | — | — | — | — | — | — | — | — | — | — | — |
| AAA | PCL | 4 | 3 | 0 | 53 | 45 | 41 | 5.70 | 1.62 | 6.9 | 7.0 | 0.7 | — |

### Majors
| Yr | Team | W | L | Sv | IP | H | K | ERA | WHIP | K/9 | BB/9 | HR/9 | GB/F | $1L | $2L | Pts | RAA | H% | HR/fb | S% | FIP | GS | CG | QS/DS | GR | Hld | Bln | Lead | OPS | 1st Hf | 2nd Hf | vs RH | vs LH |
|---|---|---|---|---|---|---|---|---|---|---|---|---|---|---|---|---|---|---|---|---|---|---|---|---|---|---|---|---|---|---|---|---|---|
| 07 | CHW | 0 | 1 | 0 | 11 | 17 | 1 | 7.15 | 2.21 | 0.8 | 6.4 | 2.4 | 1.0 | -$4 | -$7 | -10 | -5 | 31% | 17% | 73% | 8.68 | — | — | 8 | 1 | 0 | -2.6 | .990 | — | .990 | .818 | 1.192 |
| 08 | SD | 0 | 0 | 0 | 4 | 8 | 4 | 16.62 | 3.00 | 8.3 | 10.4 | 4.2 | 0.4 | -$5 | -$6 | -10 | -8 | 43% | 22% | 45% | 10.82 | — | — | 4 | 0 | 0 | -5.5 | 1.202 | — | 1.202 | 1.255 | 1.121 |
| 09 | LAD | 1 | 1 | 0 | 19 | 13 | 15 | 3.32 | 1.15 | 7.1 | 3.3 | 1.9 | 1.2 | $0 | -$1 | 30 | +2 | 18% | 19% | 81% | 5.46 | 3 | 0 | 2/1 | 3 | 0 | 0 | -2.2 | .659 | — | .659 | .722 | .542 |
| 10 | LAD | 0 | 4 | 0 | 30 | 36 | 30 | 8.40 | 2.07 | 9.0 | 7.8 | 1.2 | 1.1 | -$12 | -$23 | -20 | -17 | 36% | 11% | 59% | 5.53 | 6 | 0 | 1/3 | 3 | 0 | 0 | -1.7 | .905 | .905 | — | .835 | 1.004 |

### Competition at SP — Stats in 2010 as SP
| Thr | Player | GS | ERA | Supp | W-L |
|---|---|---|---|---|---|
| LH | Kershaw C | 32 | 2.91 | 3.9 | 13-10 |
| RH | Kuroda H | 31 | 3.39 | 4.3 | 11-13 |
| RH | Billingsley C | 31 | 3.57 | 3.7 | 12-11 |
| LH | Lilly T | 30 | 3.62 | 2.9 | 10-12 |

**Ten-Year Trends:** K/9, BB/9

---

## Roy Halladay — 240 IP | $35 | 420 pts
SP-33 · Owned: 100% · RH

Halladay in 2011 will begin his second season as a Phillie in the first year of a three-year, $60M extension. His evenness in the past three seasons is unworldly: 9 Complete Games per season, 22-25 Quality Starts, 1 Disaster. His Win count was helped by his receiving the best Run Support among Philly's Big 3. (BB)

### Forecast
| Player | Age | IP | W | Sv | K | ERA | WHIP | K/9 | BB/9 | $2L | Pts |
|---|---|---|---|---|---|---|---|---|---|---|---|
| Halladay R | 33 | 240 | 20 | 0 | 189 | 2.96 | 1.06 | 7.1 | 1.2 | $35 | 420 |

### Mini-Browser
| Player | Age | IP | W | Sv | K | ERA | WHIP | K/9 | BB/9 | $2L | Pts |
|---|---|---|---|---|---|---|---|---|---|---|---|
| Hernandez F | 24 | 250 | 16 | 0 | 221 | 3.00 | 1.17 | 7.9 | 2.8 | $31 | 400 |
| Wainwright A | 29 | 240 | 19 | 0 | 196 | 3.15 | 1.17 | 7.4 | 2.4 | $28 | 400 |
| Sabathia C | 30 | 240 | 20 | 0 | 198 | 3.45 | 1.18 | 7.4 | 2.5 | $27 | 400 |
| Lincecum T | 26 | 220 | 17 | 0 | 232 | 3.19 | 1.22 | 9.5 | 3.1 | $26 | 410 |
| Lee C | 32 | 220 | 14 | 0 | 164 | 3.52 | 1.13 | 6.7 | 1.5 | $22 | 310 |

### Minors (2010)
| Level | Leag | W | L | Sv | IP | H | K | ERA | WHIP | K/9 | BB/9 | HR/9 | GB/F |
|---|---|---|---|---|---|---|---|---|---|---|---|---|---|
| A | — | — | — | — | — | — | — | — | — | — | — | — | — |
| AA | — | — | — | — | — | — | — | — | — | — | — | — | — |
| AAA | — | — | — | — | — | — | — | — | — | — | — | — | — |

### Majors
| Yr | Team | W | L | Sv | IP | H | K | ERA | WHIP | K/9 | BB/9 | HR/9 | GB/F | $1L | $2L | Pts | RAA | H% | HR/fb | S% | FIP | GS | CG | QS/DS | GR | Hld | Bln | Lead | OPS | 1st Hf | 2nd Hf | vs RH | vs LH |
|---|---|---|---|---|---|---|---|---|---|---|---|---|---|---|---|---|---|---|---|---|---|---|---|---|---|---|---|---|---|---|---|---|---|
| 07 | TOR | 16 | 7 | 0 | 225 | 232 | 139 | 3.71 | 1.24 | 5.6 | 1.9 | 0.6 | 1.8 | $17 | $5 | 290 | +10 | 31% | 7% | 71% | 3.57 | 31 | 7 | 21/3 | — | — | — | — | .678 | .714 | .645 | .680 | .677 |
| 08 | TOR | 20 | 11 | 0 | 246 | 220 | 206 | 2.78 | 1.05 | 7.5 | 1.4 | 0.7 | 2.0 | $35 | $26 | 450 | +33 | 29% | 9% | 76% | 3.05 | 33 | 9 | 23/1 | 1 | 1 | 0 | +0.4 | .621 | .604 | .646 | .625 | .618 |
| 09 | TOR | 17 | 10 | 0 | 239 | 234 | 208 | 2.79 | 1.13 | 7.8 | 1.3 | 0.8 | 1.7 | $28 | $20 | 410 | +36 | 31% | 10% | 79% | 3.20 | 32 | 9 | 22/1 | — | — | — | — | .667 | .641 | .694 | .694 | .647 |
| 10 | PHI | 21 | 10 | 0 | 250 | 231 | 219 | 2.44 | 1.04 | 7.9 | 1.1 | 0.8 | 1.7 | $36 | $39 | 480 | +50 | 30% | 11% | 81% | 3.01 | 33 | 9 | 25/1 | — | — | — | — | .645 | .636 | .659 | .610 | .682 |

### Competition at SP — Stats in 2010 as SP
| Thr | Player | GS | ERA | Supp | W-L |
|---|---|---|---|---|---|
| RH | Halladay R | 33 | 2.44 | 4.4 | 21-10 |
| LH | Hamels C | 33 | 3.06 | 3.8 | 12-11 |
| RH | Oswalt R | 32 | 2.73 | 3.0 | 13-13 |
| RH | Kendrick K | 31 | 4.81 | 5.5 | 11-10 |

**Ten-Year Trends:** K/9, BB/9

---

## Cole Hamels — 200 IP | $19 | 310 pts
SP-33 · Owned: 99% · LH

For the first time since his debut in 2006, Hamels topped 9.0 K/9, thanks to the addition of a cut fastball. Unfortunately, the impact was diluted by a rise in his BB/9. Hamels's recent FIP's have fallen in a range of 3.65-3.80, so he is not in the class of Halladay, but Hamels provides unusual stability for a #2. (BB)

### Forecast
| Player | Age | IP | W | Sv | K | ERA | WHIP | K/9 | BB/9 | $2L | Pts |
|---|---|---|---|---|---|---|---|---|---|---|---|
| Hamels C | 27 | 200 | 13 | 0 | 175 | 3.67 | 1.17 | 7.9 | 2.3 | $19 | 310 |

### Mini-Browser
| Player | Age | IP | W | Sv | K | ERA | WHIP | K/9 | BB/9 | $2L | Pts |
|---|---|---|---|---|---|---|---|---|---|---|---|
| Carpenter C | 35 | 200 | 15 | 0 | 146 | 3.22 | 1.17 | 6.5 | 2.2 | $22 | 300 |
| Greinke Z | 27 | 220 | 13 | 0 | 192 | 3.60 | 1.21 | 7.9 | 2.3 | $21 | 330 |
| Weaver J | 28 | 220 | 14 | 0 | 193 | 3.73 | 1.21 | 7.9 | 2.6 | $21 | 330 |
| Rivera M | 41 | 60 | 4 | 38 | 54 | 2.35 | 0.96 | 8.1 | 1.6 | $20 | 300 |
| Soriano R | 31 | 60 | 3 | 44 | 61 | 2.89 | 1.05 | 9.2 | 2.7 | $19 | 320 |

### Minors (2010)
| Level | Leag | W | L | Sv | IP | H | K | ERA | WHIP | K/9 | BB/9 | HR/9 | GB/F |
|---|---|---|---|---|---|---|---|---|---|---|---|---|---|
| A | — | — | — | — | — | — | — | — | — | — | — | — | — |
| AA | — | — | — | — | — | — | — | — | — | — | — | — | — |
| AAA | — | — | — | — | — | — | — | — | — | — | — | — | — |

### Majors
| Yr | Team | W | L | Sv | IP | H | K | ERA | WHIP | K/9 | BB/9 | HR/9 | GB/F | $1L | $2L | Pts | RAA | H% | HR/fb | S% | FIP | GS | CG | QS/DS | GR | Hld | Bln | Lead | OPS | 1st Hf | 2nd Hf | vs RH | vs LH |
|---|---|---|---|---|---|---|---|---|---|---|---|---|---|---|---|---|---|---|---|---|---|---|---|---|---|---|---|---|---|---|---|---|---|
| 07 | PHI | 15 | 5 | 0 | 183 | 163 | 177 | 3.39 | 1.12 | 8.7 | 2.1 | 1.2 | 1.1 | $21 | $14 | 340 | +18 | 29% | 13% | 76% | 3.75 | 28 | 2 | 16/1 | — | — | — | — | .686 | .749 | .565 | .681 | .721 |
| 08 | PHI | 14 | 10 | 0 | 227 | 193 | 196 | 3.09 | 1.08 | 7.8 | 2.1 | 1.1 | 1.1 | $25 | $18 | 360 | +23 | 27% | 11% | 77% | 3.78 | 33 | 2 | 23/3 | — | — | — | — | .657 | .641 | .681 | .616 | .779 |
| 09 | PHI | 10 | 11 | 0 | 193 | 206 | 168 | 4.32 | 1.29 | 7.8 | 2.0 | 1.3 | 1.1 | $7 | $1 | 240 | +1 | 33% | 11% | 69% | 3.74 | 32 | 1 | 15/3 | — | — | — | — | .755 | .824 | .681 | .767 | .711 |
| 10 | PHI | 12 | 11 | 0 | 208 | 185 | 211 | 3.06 | 1.18 | 9.1 | 2.6 | 1.1 | 1.2 | $19 | $15 | 350 | +29 | 30% | 12% | 80% | 3.67 | 33 | 1 | 21/3 | — | — | — | — | .693 | .766 | .603 | .704 | .645 |

### Competition at SP — Stats in 2010 as SP
| Thr | Player | GS | ERA | Supp | W-L |
|---|---|---|---|---|---|
| RH | Halladay R | 33 | 2.44 | 4.4 | 21-10 |
| LH | Hamels C | 33 | 3.06 | 3.8 | 12-11 |
| RH | Oswalt R | 32 | 2.73 | 3.0 | 13-13 |
| RH | Kendrick K | 31 | 4.81 | 5.5 | 11-10 |

**Ten-Year Trends:** K/9, BB/9

*For more stats, visit www.Rotolympus.com.*

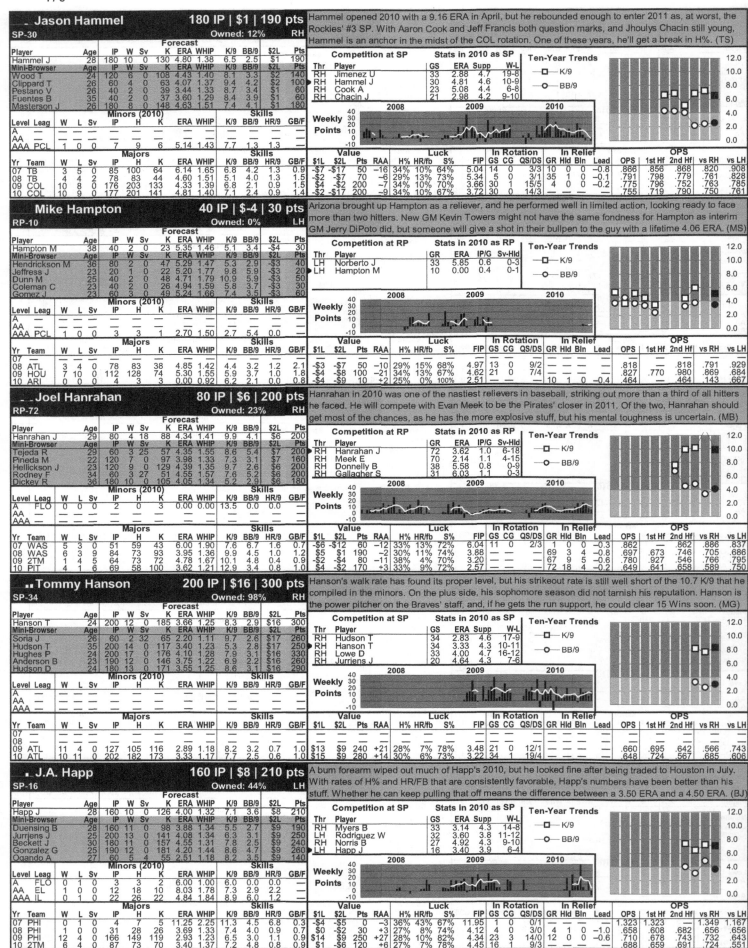

## Jason Hammel — 180 IP | $1 | 190 pts

**SP-30** — Owned: 12% — RH

Hammel opened 2010 with a 9.16 ERA in April, but he rebounded enough to enter 2011 as, at worst, the Rockies' #3 SP. With Aaron Cook and Jeff Francis both question marks, and Jhoulys Chacin still young, Hammel is an anchor in the midst of the COL rotation. One of these years, he'll get a break in H%. (TS)

### Forecast

| Player | Age | IP | W | Sv | K | ERA | WHIP | K/9 | BB/9 | $2L | Pts |
|---|---|---|---|---|---|---|---|---|---|---|---|
| Hammel J | 28 | 180 | 10 | 0 | 130 | 4.80 | 1.38 | 6.5 | 2.5 | $1 | 190 |

| Mini-Browser | Age | IP | W | Sv | K | ERA | WHIP | K/9 | BB/9 | $2L | Pts |
|---|---|---|---|---|---|---|---|---|---|---|---|
| Wood T | 24 | 120 | 6 | 0 | 108 | 4.43 | 1.40 | 8.1 | 3.3 | $2 | 140 |
| Clippard T | 26 | 60 | 4 | 0 | 63 | 4.07 | 1.37 | 9.4 | 4.2 | $2 | 100 |
| Pestano V | 26 | 40 | 2 | 0 | 39 | 3.44 | 1.33 | 8.7 | 3.4 | $1 | 60 |
| Fuentes B | 35 | 40 | 2 | 0 | 37 | 3.60 | 1.29 | 8.4 | 3.9 | $1 | 60 |
| Masterson J | 26 | 180 | 8 | 0 | 148 | 4.63 | 1.51 | 7.4 | 4.1 | $1 | 180 |

### Minors (2010) / Skills

| Level | Leag | W | L | Sv | IP | H | K | ERA | WHIP | K/9 | BB/9 | HR/9 | GB/F |
|---|---|---|---|---|---|---|---|---|---|---|---|---|---|
| A | — | — | — | — | — | — | — | — | — | — | — | — | — |
| AA | — | — | — | — | — | — | — | — | — | — | — | — | — |
| AAA | PCL | 1 | 0 | 0 | 7 | 9 | 6 | 5.14 | 1.43 | 7.7 | 1.3 | 1.3 | — |

### Majors / Skills

| Yr | Team | W | L | Sv | IP | H | K | ERA | WHIP | K/9 | BB/9 | HR/9 | GB/F |
|---|---|---|---|---|---|---|---|---|---|---|---|---|---|
| 07 | TB | 3 | 5 | 0 | 85 | 100 | 64 | 6.14 | 1.65 | 6.8 | 4.2 | 1.3 | 0.9 |
| 08 | TB | 4 | 4 | 2 | 78 | 83 | 44 | 4.60 | 1.51 | 5.1 | 4.0 | 1.3 | 1.5 |
| 09 | COL | 10 | 8 | 0 | 176 | 203 | 133 | 4.33 | 1.39 | 6.8 | 2.1 | 0.9 | 1.5 |
| 10 | COL | 10 | 9 | 0 | 177 | 201 | 141 | 4.81 | 1.40 | 7.1 | 2.4 | 0.9 | 1.4 |

### Competition at SP — Stats in 2010 as SP

| Thr | Player | GS | ERA | Supp | W-L |
|---|---|---|---|---|---|
| RH | Jimenez U | 33 | 2.88 | 4.7 | 19-8 |
| RH | Hammel J | 30 | 4.81 | 4.6 | 10-9 |
| RH | Cook A | 23 | 5.08 | 4.4 | 6-8 |
| RH | Chacin J | 21 | 2.98 | 4.2 | 9-10 |

### Value / Luck / In Rotation / In Relief / OPS

| Yr | $1L | $2L | Pts | RAA | H% | HR/fb | S% | FIP | GS | CG | QS/DS | GR | Hld | Bln | Lead | OPS | 1st Hf | 2nd Hf | vs RH | vs LH |
|---|---|---|---|---|---|---|---|---|---|---|---|---|---|---|---|---|---|---|---|---|
| 07 | -$7 | -$17 | 50 | -16 | 34% | 10% | 64% | 5.04 | 14 | 0 | 3/3 | 10 | | | -0.8 | .866 | .856 | .868 | .820 | .908 |
| 08 | -$2 | -$7 | 70 | -6 | 29% | 13% | 73% | 5.34 | 1 | | 3/1 | 35 | 1 | 0 | -0.1 | .791 | .798 | .779 | .761 | .828 |
| 09 | $4 | -$2 | 200 | -7 | 34% | 10% | 70% | 3.66 | 30 | 1 | 15/5 | 2 | | | -0.2 | .775 | .796 | .752 | .763 | .785 |
| 10 | -$2 | -$17 | 200 | -9 | 34% | 10% | 73% | 3.72 | 30 | 0 | 17/6 | | | | | .755 | .719 | .790 | .750 | .761 |

---

## Mike Hampton — 40 IP | $-4 | 30 pts

**RP-10** — Owned: 0% — LH

Arizona brought up Hampton as a reliever, and he performed well in limited action, looking ready to face more than two hitters. New GM Kevin Towers might not have the same fondness for Hampton as interim GM Jerry DiPoto did, but someone will give a shot in their bullpen to the guy with a lifetime 4.06 ERA. (MS)

### Forecast

| Player | Age | IP | W | Sv | K | ERA | WHIP | K/9 | BB/9 | $2L | Pts |
|---|---|---|---|---|---|---|---|---|---|---|---|
| Hampton M | 38 | 40 | 2 | 0 | 23 | 5.35 | 1.46 | 5.1 | 3.4 | -$4 | 30 |

| Mini-Browser | Age | IP | W | Sv | K | ERA | WHIP | K/9 | BB/9 | $2L | Pts |
|---|---|---|---|---|---|---|---|---|---|---|---|
| Hendrickson M | 36 | 80 | 2 | 0 | 47 | 5.29 | 1.47 | 5.3 | 2.9 | -$3 | 40 |
| Jeffress J | 23 | 20 | 1 | 0 | 22 | 5.20 | 1.77 | 9.8 | 5.9 | -$3 | 20 |
| Dunn M | 25 | 40 | 2 | 0 | 48 | 4.71 | 1.79 | 10.9 | 5.9 | -$3 | 50 |
| Coleman C | 23 | 40 | 2 | 0 | 26 | 4.94 | 1.59 | 5.8 | 3.7 | -$3 | 30 |
| Gomez J | 23 | 60 | 3 | 0 | 49 | 5.24 | 1.66 | 7.4 | 4.3 | -$3 | 60 |

### Minors (2010) / Skills

| Level | Leag | W | L | Sv | IP | H | K | ERA | WHIP | K/9 | BB/9 | HR/9 | GB/F |
|---|---|---|---|---|---|---|---|---|---|---|---|---|---|
| A | — | — | — | — | — | — | — | — | — | — | — | — | — |
| AA | — | — | — | — | — | — | — | — | — | — | — | — | — |
| AAA | PCL | 1 | 0 | 0 | 3 | 3 | 1 | 2.70 | 1.50 | 2.7 | 5.4 | 0.0 | — |

### Majors / Skills

| Yr | Team | W | L | Sv | IP | H | K | ERA | WHIP | K/9 | BB/9 | HR/9 | GB/F |
|---|---|---|---|---|---|---|---|---|---|---|---|---|---|
| 07 | — | — | — | — | — | — | — | — | — | — | — | — | — |
| 08 | ATL | 3 | 4 | 0 | 78 | 83 | 38 | 4.85 | 1.42 | 4.4 | 3.2 | 1.2 | 2.1 |
| 09 | HOU | 7 | 10 | 0 | 112 | 128 | 74 | 5.30 | 1.55 | 5.9 | 3.7 | 1.0 | 1.8 |
| 10 | ARI | 0 | 0 | 0 | 4 | 3 | 3 | 0.00 | 0.92 | 6.2 | 2.1 | 0.0 | 0.8 |

### Competition at RP — Stats in 2010 as RP

| Thr | Player | GR | ERA | IP/G | Sv-Hld |
|---|---|---|---|---|---|
| LH | Norberto J | 33 | 5.85 | 0.6 | 0-3 |
| LH | Hampton M | 10 | 0.00 | 0.4 | 0-1 |

### Value / Luck / In Rotation / In Relief / OPS

| Yr | $1L | $2L | Pts | RAA | H% | HR/fb | S% | FIP | GS | CG | QS/DS | GR | Hld | Bln | Lead | OPS | 1st Hf | 2nd Hf | vs RH | vs LH |
|---|---|---|---|---|---|---|---|---|---|---|---|---|---|---|---|---|---|---|---|---|
| 07 | | | | | | | | | | | | | | | | | | | | |
| 08 | -$3 | -$8 | 50 | -10 | 29% | 15% | 68% | 4.97 | 13 | 0 | 9/2 | | | | | .818 | | .818 | .791 | .929 |
| 09 | -$4 | -$8 | 100 | -21 | 34% | 13% | 67% | 4.62 | 21 | 0 | 7/4 | | | | | .827 | .770 | .980 | .869 | .684 |
| 10 | -$4 | -$9 | 10 | +2 | 25% | 0% | 100% | 2.51 | | | | 10 | 1 | 0 | -0.4 | .464 | | .464 | .143 | .667 |

---

## Joel Hanrahan — 80 IP | $6 | 200 pts

**RP-72** — Owned: 23% — RH

Hanrahan in 2010 was one of the nastiest relievers in baseball, striking out more than a third of all hitters he faced. He will compete with Evan Meek to be the Pirates' closer in 2011. Of the two, Hanrahan should get most of the chances, as he has the more explosive stuff, but his mental toughness is uncertain. (MB)

### Forecast

| Player | Age | IP | W | Sv | K | ERA | WHIP | K/9 | BB/9 | $2L | Pts |
|---|---|---|---|---|---|---|---|---|---|---|---|
| Hanrahan J | 29 | 80 | 4 | 18 | 88 | 4.34 | 1.41 | 9.9 | 4.1 | $6 | 200 |

| Mini-Browser | Age | IP | W | Sv | K | ERA | WHIP | K/9 | BB/9 | $2L | Pts |
|---|---|---|---|---|---|---|---|---|---|---|---|
| Tejeda R | 29 | 60 | 3 | 25 | 57 | 4.35 | 1.55 | 8.6 | 5.4 | $7 | 200 |
| Pineda M | 22 | 120 | 7 | 0 | 97 | 3.98 | 1.33 | 7.3 | 3.1 | $7 | 160 |
| Hellickson J | 23 | 120 | 9 | 0 | 129 | 4.39 | 1.35 | 9.7 | 2.6 | $6 | 200 |
| Rodney F | 34 | 60 | 3 | 27 | 51 | 4.55 | 1.57 | 7.6 | 5.2 | $6 | 200 |
| Dickey R | 36 | 180 | 10 | 0 | 105 | 4.05 | 1.34 | 5.2 | 2.9 | $6 | 180 |

### Minors (2010) / Skills

| Level | Leag | W | L | Sv | IP | H | K | ERA | WHIP | K/9 | BB/9 | HR/9 | GB/F |
|---|---|---|---|---|---|---|---|---|---|---|---|---|---|
| A | FLO | 0 | 0 | 0 | 2 | 0 | 3 | 0.00 | 0.00 | 13.5 | 0.0 | 0.0 | — |
| AA | — | — | — | — | — | — | — | — | — | — | — | — | — |
| AAA | — | — | — | — | — | — | — | — | — | — | — | — | — |

### Majors / Skills

| Yr | Team | W | L | Sv | IP | H | K | ERA | WHIP | K/9 | BB/9 | HR/9 | GB/F |
|---|---|---|---|---|---|---|---|---|---|---|---|---|---|
| 07 | WAS | 5 | 3 | 0 | 51 | 59 | 43 | 6.00 | 1.90 | 7.6 | 6.7 | 1.6 | 0.7 |
| 08 | WAS | 6 | 3 | 9 | 84 | 73 | 93 | 3.95 | 1.36 | 9.9 | 4.5 | 1.0 | 1.2 |
| 09 | 2TM | 1 | 4 | 5 | 64 | 73 | 72 | 4.78 | 1.67 | 10.1 | 4.8 | 0.4 | 0.9 |
| 10 | PIT | 4 | 1 | 6 | 69 | 58 | 100 | 3.62 | 1.21 | 12.9 | 3.4 | 0.8 | 1.0 |

### Competition at RP — Stats in 2010 as RP

| Thr | Player | GR | ERA | IP/G | Sv-Hld |
|---|---|---|---|---|---|
| RH | Hanrahan J | 72 | 3.62 | 1.0 | 6-18 |
| RH | Meek E | 70 | 2.14 | 1.1 | 4-15 |
| RH | Donnelly B | 38 | 5.58 | 0.8 | 0-9 |
| RH | Gallagher S | 31 | 6.03 | 1.1 | 0-3 |

### Value / Luck / In Rotation / In Relief / OPS

| Yr | $1L | $2L | Pts | RAA | H% | HR/fb | S% | FIP | GS | CG | QS/DS | GR | Hld | Bln | Lead | OPS | 1st Hf | 2nd Hf | vs RH | vs LH |
|---|---|---|---|---|---|---|---|---|---|---|---|---|---|---|---|---|---|---|---|---|
| 07 | -$6 | -$12 | 60 | -12 | 33% | 13% | 72% | 6.04 | 11 | 0 | 2/3 | | | | -0.3 | .862 | | .862 | .886 | .837 |
| 08 | $5 | $1 | 190 | -2 | 30% | 11% | 74% | 3.88 | | | | 69 | 3 | 4 | -0.8 | .697 | .673 | .746 | .705 | .686 |
| 09 | -$4 | -$4 | 80 | -11 | 38% | 4% | 70% | 3.20 | | | | 67 | 9 | 5 | -0.6 | .780 | .927 | .746 | .766 | .795 |
| 10 | $4 | -$2 | 170 | +3 | 33% | 9% | 72% | 2.57 | | | | 72 | 18 | 4 | -0.2 | .649 | .641 | .658 | .589 | .750 |

---

## Tommy Hanson — 200 IP | $16 | 300 pts

**SP-34** — Owned: 98% — RH

Hanson's walk rate has found its proper level, but his strikeout rate is still well short of the 10.7 K/9 that he compiled in the minors. On the plus side, his sophomore season did not tarnish his reputation. Hanson is the power pitcher on the Braves' staff, and, if he gets the run support, he could clear 15 Wins soon. (MG)

### Forecast

| Player | Age | IP | W | Sv | K | ERA | WHIP | K/9 | BB/9 | $2L | Pts |
|---|---|---|---|---|---|---|---|---|---|---|---|
| Hanson T | 24 | 200 | 12 | 0 | 185 | 3.66 | 1.25 | 8.3 | 2.9 | $16 | 300 |

| Mini-Browser | Age | IP | W | Sv | K | ERA | WHIP | K/9 | BB/9 | $2L | Pts |
|---|---|---|---|---|---|---|---|---|---|---|---|
| Soria J | 26 | 60 | 2 | 32 | 65 | 2.20 | 1.11 | 9.7 | 2.6 | $17 | 260 |
| Hudson T | 35 | 200 | 14 | 0 | 117 | 3.40 | 1.23 | 5.3 | 2.8 | $17 | 250 |
| Hughes P | 24 | 200 | 17 | 0 | 176 | 4.10 | 1.28 | 7.9 | 3.1 | $16 | 330 |
| Anderson B | 23 | 190 | 12 | 0 | 146 | 3.75 | 1.22 | 6.9 | 2.2 | $16 | 260 |
| Hudson D | 24 | 180 | 13 | 0 | 171 | 3.55 | 1.25 | 8.6 | 3.1 | $16 | 290 |

### Minors (2010) / Skills

| Level | Leag | W | L | Sv | IP | H | K | ERA | WHIP | K/9 | BB/9 | HR/9 | GB/F |
|---|---|---|---|---|---|---|---|---|---|---|---|---|---|
| A | — | — | — | — | — | — | — | — | — | — | — | — | — |
| AA | — | — | — | — | — | — | — | — | — | — | — | — | — |
| AAA | — | — | — | — | — | — | — | — | — | — | — | — | — |

### Majors / Skills

| Yr | Team | W | L | Sv | IP | H | K | ERA | WHIP | K/9 | BB/9 | HR/9 | GB/F |
|---|---|---|---|---|---|---|---|---|---|---|---|---|---|
| 07 | — | — | — | — | — | — | — | — | — | — | — | — | — |
| 08 | — | — | — | — | — | — | — | — | — | — | — | — | — |
| 09 | ATL | 11 | 4 | 0 | 127 | 105 | 116 | 2.89 | 1.18 | 8.2 | 3.2 | 0.7 | 1.0 |
| 10 | ATL | 10 | 11 | 0 | 202 | 182 | 173 | 3.33 | 1.17 | 7.7 | 2.5 | 0.6 | 1.0 |

### Competition at SP — Stats in 2010 as SP

| Thr | Player | GS | ERA | Supp | W-L |
|---|---|---|---|---|---|
| RH | Hudson T | 34 | 2.83 | 4.6 | 17-9 |
| RH | Hanson T | 34 | 3.33 | 4.3 | 10-11 |
| RH | Lowe D | 33 | 4.00 | 4.7 | 16-12 |
| RH | Jurrjens J | 20 | 4.64 | 4.3 | 7-6 |

### Value / Luck / In Rotation / In Relief / OPS

| Yr | $1L | $2L | Pts | RAA | H% | HR/fb | S% | FIP | GS | CG | QS/DS | GR | Hld | Bln | Lead | OPS | 1st Hf | 2nd Hf | vs RH | vs LH |
|---|---|---|---|---|---|---|---|---|---|---|---|---|---|---|---|---|---|---|---|---|
| 07 | | | | | | | | | | | | | | | | | | | | |
| 08 | | | | | | | | | | | | | | | | | | | | |
| 09 | $13 | $9 | 240 | +21 | 28% | 7% | 78% | 3.48 | 21 | 0 | 12/1 | | | | | .660 | .695 | .642 | .566 | .743 |
| 10 | $15 | $9 | 280 | +14 | 30% | 6% | 73% | 3.22 | 34 | 1 | 19/4 | | | | | .648 | .724 | .567 | .685 | .648 |

---

## J.A. Happ — 160 IP | $8 | 210 pts

**SP-16** — Owned: 44% — LH

A bum forearm wiped out much of Happ's 2010, but he looked fine after being traded to Houston in July. With rates of H% and HR/FB that are consistently favorable, Happ's numbers have been better than his stuff. Whether he can keep pulling that off means the difference between a 3.50 ERA and a 4.50 ERA. (BJ)

### Forecast

| Player | Age | IP | W | Sv | K | ERA | WHIP | K/9 | BB/9 | $2L | Pts |
|---|---|---|---|---|---|---|---|---|---|---|---|
| Happ J | 28 | 160 | 10 | 0 | 126 | 4.00 | 1.32 | 7.1 | 3.6 | $8 | 210 |

| Mini-Browser | Age | IP | W | Sv | K | ERA | WHIP | K/9 | BB/9 | $2L | Pts |
|---|---|---|---|---|---|---|---|---|---|---|---|
| Duensing B | 28 | 160 | 11 | 0 | 98 | 3.88 | 1.34 | 5.5 | 2.7 | $9 | 190 |
| Jurrjens J | 25 | 200 | 13 | 0 | 141 | 4.04 | 1.34 | 6.3 | 3.1 | $9 | 250 |
| Beckett J | 30 | 180 | 11 | 0 | 157 | 4.55 | 1.31 | 7.8 | 2.5 | $9 | 240 |
| Gonzalez G | 25 | 190 | 12 | 0 | 181 | 4.20 | 1.44 | 8.6 | 4.7 | $9 | 260 |
| Oganda A | 27 | 60 | 5 | 4 | 55 | 2.51 | 1.18 | 8.2 | 4.0 | $9 | 140 |

### Minors (2010) / Skills

| Level | Leag | W | L | Sv | IP | H | K | ERA | WHIP | K/9 | BB/9 | HR/9 | GB/F |
|---|---|---|---|---|---|---|---|---|---|---|---|---|---|
| A | FLO | 0 | 1 | 0 | 3 | 3 | 2 | 6.00 | 1.00 | 6.0 | 0.0 | 0.0 | — |
| AA | EL | 1 | 0 | 0 | 12 | 18 | 10 | 8.03 | 1.78 | 7.3 | 2.9 | 2.2 | — |
| AAA | IL | 0 | 1 | 0 | 22 | 26 | 22 | 4.84 | 1.84 | 8.9 | 6.0 | 1.2 | — |

### Majors / Skills

| Yr | Team | W | L | Sv | IP | H | K | ERA | WHIP | K/9 | BB/9 | HR/9 | GB/F |
|---|---|---|---|---|---|---|---|---|---|---|---|---|---|
| 07 | PHI | 1 | 0 | 0 | 4 | 7 | 5 | 11.25 | 2.25 | 11.3 | 4.5 | 6.8 | 0.3 |
| 08 | PHI | 1 | 0 | 0 | 31 | 28 | 26 | 3.69 | 1.33 | 7.4 | 4.0 | 0.9 | 0.7 |
| 09 | PHI | 12 | 4 | 0 | 166 | 149 | 119 | 2.93 | 1.23 | 6.5 | 3.0 | 1.1 | 0.6 |
| 10 | 2TM | 6 | 4 | 0 | 87 | 73 | 70 | 3.40 | 1.37 | 7.2 | 4.8 | 0.9 | 0.9 |

### Competition at SP — Stats in 2010 as SP

| Thr | Player | GS | ERA | Supp | W-L |
|---|---|---|---|---|---|
| RH | Myers B | 33 | 3.14 | 4.3 | 14-8 |
| LH | Rodriguez W | 32 | 3.60 | 3.8 | 11-12 |
| RH | Norris B | 27 | 4.92 | 4.3 | 9-10 |
| LH | Happ J | 16 | 3.40 | 3.9 | 6-4 |

### Value / Luck / In Rotation / In Relief / OPS

| Yr | $1L | $2L | Pts | RAA | H% | HR/fb | S% | FIP | GS | CG | QS/DS | GR | Hld | Bln | Lead | OPS | 1st Hf | 2nd Hf | vs RH | vs LH |
|---|---|---|---|---|---|---|---|---|---|---|---|---|---|---|---|---|---|---|---|---|
| 07 | -$4 | -$5 | 0 | -3 | 36% | 43% | 62% | 11.95 | 1 | 0 | 0/1 | | | | | 1.323 | 1.323 | | 1.349 | 1.167 |
| 08 | $0 | -$2 | 30 | +3 | 27% | 8% | 74% | 4.12 | 4 | 0 | 3/0 | 4 | 1 | 0 | -1.0 | .658 | .608 | .682 | .656 | .656 |
| 09 | $14 | $9 | 250 | +27 | 28% | 10% | 82% | 4.34 | 23 | 3 | 14/0 | 12 | 0 | 0 | -0.6 | .710 | .678 | .743 | .732 | .643 |
| 10 | -$6 | -$2 | 170 | +7 | 27% | 7% | 78% | 4.45 | 14 | | 9/3 | | | | | .688 | .659 | .691 | .724 | .551 |

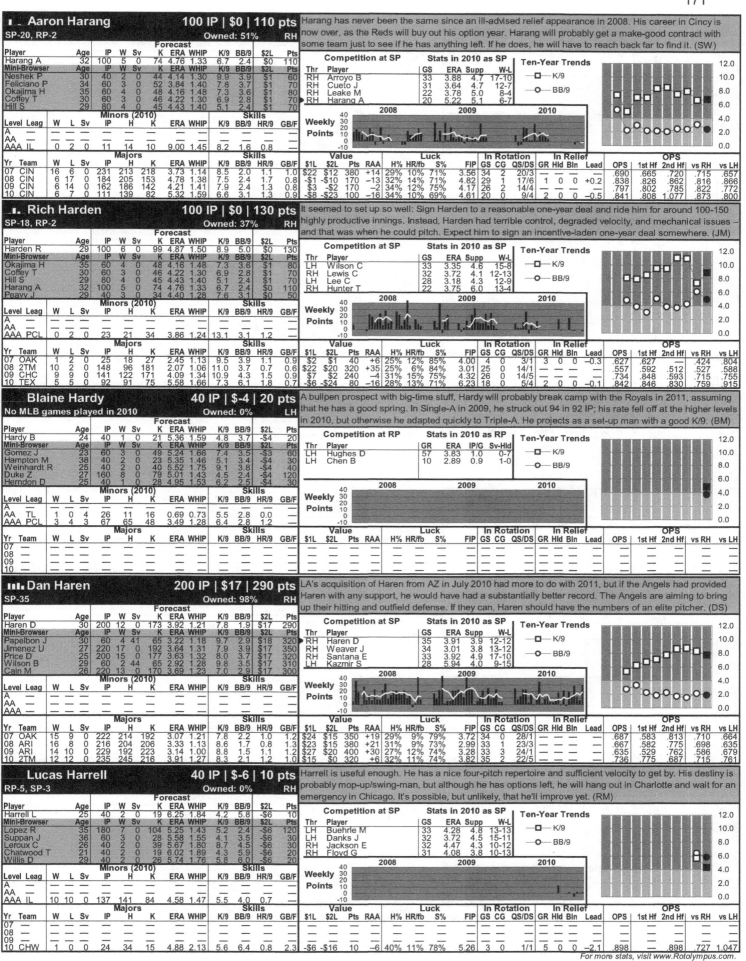

## Aaron Harang — 100 IP | $0 | 110 pts

SP-20, RP-2 — Owned: 51% — RH

Harang has never been the same since an ill-advised relief appearance in 2008. His career in Cincy is now over, as the Reds will buy out his option year. Harang will probably get a make-good contract with some team just to see if he has anything left. If he does, he will have to reach back far to find it. (SW)

| Player | Age | IP | W | Sv | K | ERA | WHIP | K/9 | BB/9 | $2L | Pts |
|---|---|---|---|---|---|---|---|---|---|---|---|
| Harang A | 32 | 100 | 5 | 0 | 74 | 4.76 | 1.33 | 6.7 | 2.4 | $0 | 110 |
| **Mini-Browser** | **Age** | **IP** | **W** | **Sv** | **K** | **ERA** | **WHIP** | **K/9** | **BB/9** | **$2L** | **Pts** |
| Neshek P | 30 | 40 | 2 | 0 | 44 | 4.14 | 1.30 | 9.9 | 3.9 | $1 | 60 |
| Feliciano P | 34 | 60 | 3 | 0 | 52 | 3.84 | 1.40 | 7.8 | 3.7 | $1 | 70 |
| Okajima H | 35 | 60 | 4 | 0 | 48 | 4.16 | 1.48 | 7.3 | 3.6 | $1 | 80 |
| Coffey T | 30 | 60 | 3 | 0 | 46 | 4.22 | 1.30 | 6.9 | 2.8 | $1 | 70 |
| Hill S | 29 | 80 | 4 | 0 | 45 | 4.43 | 1.40 | 5.1 | 2.4 | $1 | 70 |

| Level | Leag | W | L | Sv | IP | H | K | ERA | WHIP | K/9 | BB/9 | HR/9 | GB/F |
|---|---|---|---|---|---|---|---|---|---|---|---|---|---|
| A | — | — | — | — | — | — | — | — | — | — | — | — | — |
| AA | — | — | — | — | — | — | — | — | — | — | — | — | — |
| AAA | IL | 0 | 2 | 0 | 11 | 14 | 10 | 9.00 | 1.45 | 8.2 | 1.6 | 0.8 | — |

| Competition at SP Thr | Player | GS | ERA | Supp | W-L |
|---|---|---|---|---|---|
| RH | Arroyo B | 33 | 3.88 | 4.7 | 17-10 |
| RH | Cueto J | 31 | 3.64 | 4.7 | 12-7 |
| RH | Leake M | 22 | 3.78 | 5.0 | 8-4 |
| RH | Harang A | 20 | 5.22 | 5.1 | 6-7 |

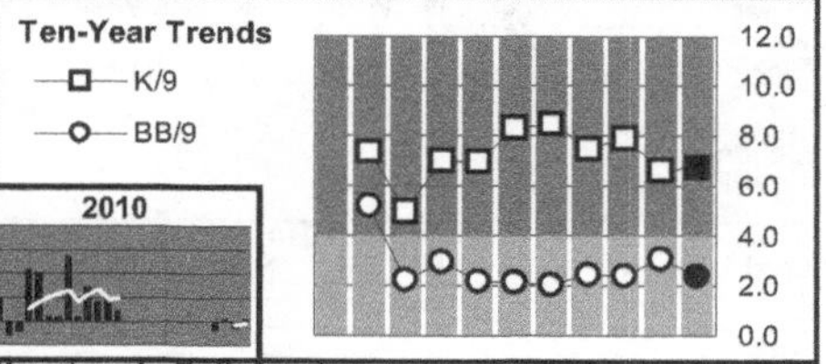


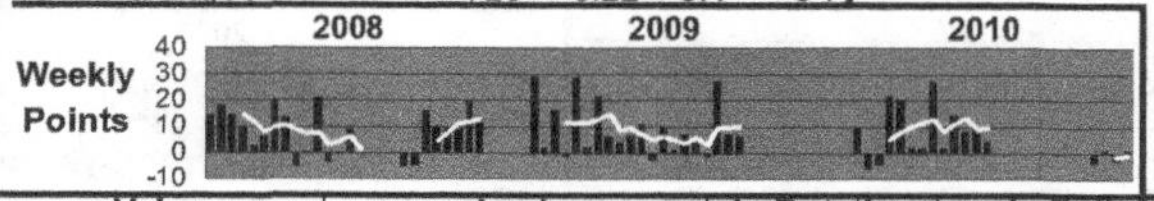


| Yr | Team | W | L | Sv | IP | H | K | ERA | WHIP | K/9 | BB/9 | HR/9 | GB/F |
|---|---|---|---|---|---|---|---|---|---|---|---|---|---|
| 07 | CIN | 16 | 6 | 0 | 231 | 213 | 218 | 3.73 | 1.14 | 8.5 | 2.0 | 1.1 | 1.0 |
| 08 | CIN | 6 | 17 | 0 | 184 | 205 | 153 | 4.78 | 1.38 | 7.5 | 2.4 | 1.7 | 0.8 |
| 09 | CIN | 6 | 14 | 0 | 162 | 186 | 142 | 4.21 | 1.41 | 7.9 | 2.4 | 1.3 | 0.8 |
| 10 | CIN | 6 | 7 | 0 | 111 | 139 | 82 | 5.32 | 1.59 | 6.6 | 3.1 | 1.3 | 0.9 |

| Yr | $1L | $2L | Pts | RAA | H% | HR/fb | S% | FIP | GS | CG | QS/DS | GR | Hld | Bln | Lead | OPS | 1st Hf | 2nd Hf | vs RH | vs LH |
|---|---|---|---|---|---|---|---|---|---|---|---|---|---|---|---|---|---|---|---|---|
| 07 | $22 | $12 | 380 | +14 | 29% | 10% | 71% | 3.56 | 34 | 2 | 20/3 | — | — | — | — | .690 | .665 | .720 | .715 | .657 |
| 08 | -$1 | -$10 | 170 | −13 | 32% | 14% | 71% | 4.82 | 29 | 1 | 17/6 | 1 | 0 | 0 | +0.2 | .838 | .826 | .862 | .816 | .866 |
| 09 | $3 | -$2 | 170 | −2 | 34% | 12% | 75% | 4.17 | 26 | 2 | 14/4 | — | — | — | — | .797 | .802 | .785 | .822 | .772 |
| 10 | -$8 | -$23 | 100 | −16 | 34% | 10% | 69% | 4.61 | 20 | 0 | 9/4 | 2 | 0 | 0 | −0.5 | .841 | .808 | 1.077 | .873 | .800 |

## Rich Harden — 100 IP | $0 | 130 pts

SP-18, RP-2 — Owned: 37% — RH

It seemed to set up so well: Sign Harden to a reasonable one-year deal and ride him for around 100-150 highly productive innings. Instead, Harden had terrible control, degraded velocity, and mechanical issues – and that was when he could pitch. Expect him to sign an incentive-laden one-year deal somewhere. (JM)

| Player | Age | IP | W | Sv | K | ERA | WHIP | K/9 | BB/9 | $2L | Pts |
|---|---|---|---|---|---|---|---|---|---|---|---|
| Harden R | 29 | 100 | 6 | 0 | 99 | 4.87 | 1.50 | 8.9 | 5.0 | $0 | 130 |
| **Mini-Browser** | **Age** | **IP** | **W** | **Sv** | **K** | **ERA** | **WHIP** | **K/9** | **BB/9** | **$2L** | **Pts** |
| Okajima H | 35 | 60 | 4 | 0 | 48 | 4.16 | 1.48 | 7.3 | 3.6 | $1 | 80 |
| Coffey T | 30 | 60 | 3 | 0 | 46 | 4.22 | 1.30 | 6.9 | 2.8 | $1 | 70 |
| Hill S | 29 | 80 | 4 | 0 | 45 | 4.43 | 1.40 | 5.1 | 2.4 | $1 | 70 |
| Harang A | 32 | 100 | 5 | 0 | 74 | 4.76 | 1.33 | 6.7 | 2.4 | $0 | 110 |
| Peavy J | 29 | 40 | 3 | 0 | 34 | 4.40 | 1.28 | 7.6 | 3.1 | $0 | 50 |

| Level | Leag | W | L | Sv | IP | H | K | ERA | WHIP | K/9 | BB/9 | HR/9 | GB/F |
|---|---|---|---|---|---|---|---|---|---|---|---|---|---|
| A | — | — | — | — | — | — | — | — | — | — | — | — | — |
| AA | — | — | — | — | — | — | — | — | — | — | — | — | — |
| AAA | PCL | 0 | 2 | 0 | 23 | 21 | 34 | 3.86 | 1.24 | 13.1 | 3.1 | 1.2 | — |

| Competition at SP Thr | Player | GS | ERA | Supp | W-L |
|---|---|---|---|---|---|
| LH | Wilson C | 33 | 3.35 | 4.6 | 15-8 |
| RH | Lewis C | 32 | 3.72 | 4.1 | 12-13 |
| LH | Lee C | 28 | 3.18 | 4.3 | 12-9 |
| RH | Hunter T | 22 | 3.75 | 6.0 | 13-4 |

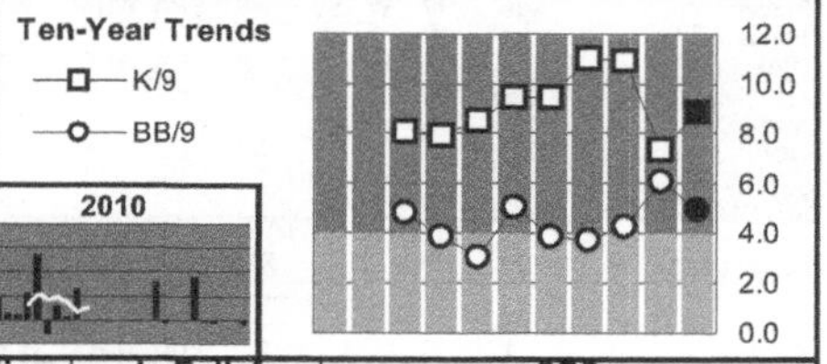


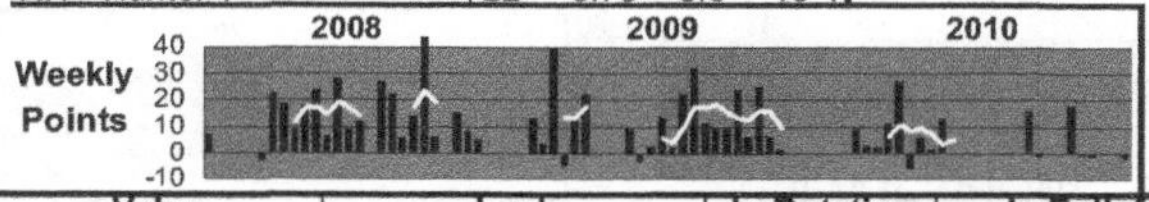


| Yr | Team | W | L | Sv | IP | H | K | ERA | WHIP | K/9 | BB/9 | HR/9 | GB/F |
|---|---|---|---|---|---|---|---|---|---|---|---|---|---|
| 07 | OAK | 1 | 2 | 0 | 25 | 18 | 27 | 2.45 | 1.13 | 9.5 | 3.9 | 1.1 | 0.9 |
| 08 | 2TM | 10 | 2 | 0 | 148 | 96 | 181 | 2.07 | 1.06 | 11.0 | 3.7 | 0.7 | 0.6 |
| 09 | CHC | 9 | 9 | 0 | 141 | 122 | 171 | 4.09 | 1.34 | 10.9 | 4.3 | 1.5 | 0.9 |
| 10 | TEX | 5 | 5 | 0 | 92 | 91 | 75 | 5.58 | 1.66 | 7.3 | 6.1 | 1.8 | 0.7 |

| Yr | $1L | $2L | Pts | RAA | H% | HR/fb | S% | FIP | GS | CG | QS/DS | GR | Hld | Bln | Lead | OPS | 1st Hf | 2nd Hf | vs RH | vs LH |
|---|---|---|---|---|---|---|---|---|---|---|---|---|---|---|---|---|---|---|---|---|
| 07 | $2 | $1 | 40 | +6 | 25% | 12% | 85% | 4.00 | 4 | 0 | 3/1 | 3 | 0 | 0 | −0.3 | .627 | .627 | — | .424 | .804 |
| 08 | $22 | $20 | 320 | +35 | 25% | 6% | 84% | 3.01 | 25 | 0 | 14/1 | — | — | — | — | .557 | .592 | .512 | .527 | .588 |
| 09 | $7 | $2 | 240 | −4 | 31% | 15% | 75% | 4.32 | 26 | 0 | 14/5 | — | — | — | — | .734 | .848 | .593 | .715 | .755 |
| 10 | -$6 | -$24 | 80 | −16 | 28% | 13% | 71% | 6.23 | 18 | 0 | 5/4 | 2 | 0 | 0 | −0.1 | .842 | .846 | .830 | .759 | .915 |

## Blaine Hardy — 40 IP | $-4 | 20 pts

No MLB games played in 2010 — Owned: 0% — LH

A bullpen prospect with big-time stuff, Hardy will probably break camp with the Royals in 2011, assuming that he has a good spring. In Single-A in 2009, he struck out 94 in 92 IP; his rate fell off at the higher levels in 2010, but otherwise he adapted quickly to Triple-A. He projects as a set-up man with a good K/9. (BM)

| Player | Age | IP | W | Sv | K | ERA | WHIP | K/9 | BB/9 | $2L | Pts |
|---|---|---|---|---|---|---|---|---|---|---|---|
| Hardy B | 24 | 40 | 1 | 0 | 21 | 5.36 | 1.59 | 4.8 | 3.7 | -$4 | 20 |
| **Mini-Browser** | **Age** | **IP** | **W** | **Sv** | **K** | **ERA** | **WHIP** | **K/9** | **BB/9** | **$2L** | **Pts** |
| Gomez J | 23 | 60 | 3 | 0 | 49 | 5.24 | 1.66 | 7.4 | 3.5 | -$3 | 60 |
| Hampton M | 38 | 40 | 2 | 0 | 23 | 5.35 | 1.46 | 5.1 | 3.4 | -$4 | 30 |
| Weinhardt R | 25 | 40 | 2 | 0 | 40 | 5.52 | 1.75 | 9.1 | 3.8 | -$4 | 40 |
| Duke Z | 27 | 160 | 8 | 0 | 79 | 5.01 | 1.43 | 4.5 | 2.4 | -$4 | 120 |
| Herndon D | 25 | 40 | 1 | 0 | 28 | 4.95 | 1.53 | 6.2 | 2.5 | -$4 | 30 |

| Level | Leag | W | L | Sv | IP | H | K | ERA | WHIP | K/9 | BB/9 | HR/9 | GB/F |
|---|---|---|---|---|---|---|---|---|---|---|---|---|---|
| A | — | — | — | — | — | — | — | — | — | — | — | — | — |
| AA | TL | 1 | 0 | 4 | 26 | 11 | 16 | 0.69 | 0.73 | 5.5 | 2.8 | 0.0 | — |
| AAA | PCL | 3 | 4 | 3 | 67 | 65 | 48 | 3.49 | 1.28 | 6.4 | 2.8 | 1.2 | — |

| Competition at RP Thr | Player | GR | ERA | IP/G | Sv-Hld |
|---|---|---|---|---|---|
| LH | Hughes D | 57 | 3.83 | 1.0 | 0-7 |
| LH | Chen B | 10 | 2.89 | 0.9 | 1-0 |

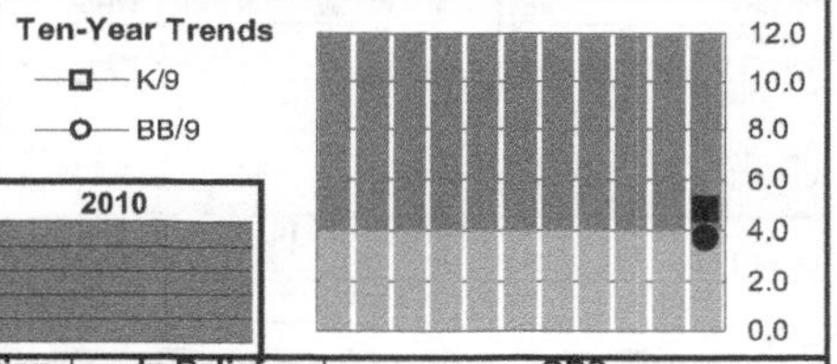


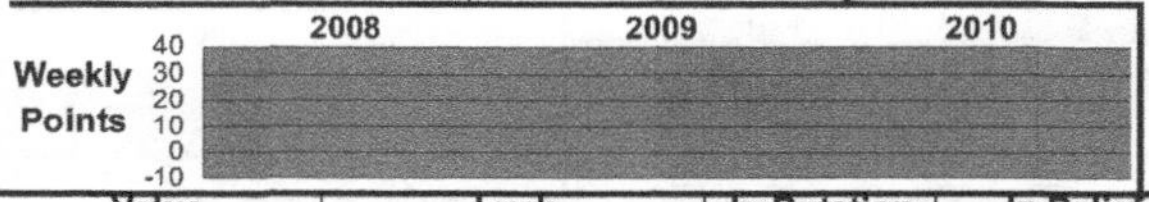


| Yr | Team | W | L | Sv | IP | H | K | ERA | WHIP | K/9 | BB/9 | HR/9 | GB/F |
|---|---|---|---|---|---|---|---|---|---|---|---|---|---|
| 07 | — | — | — | — | — | — | — | — | — | — | — | — | — |
| 08 | — | — | — | — | — | — | — | — | — | — | — | — | — |
| 09 | — | — | — | — | — | — | — | — | — | — | — | — | — |
| 10 | — | — | — | — | — | — | — | — | — | — | — | — | — |

| Yr | $1L | $2L | Pts | RAA | H% | HR/fb | S% | FIP | GS | CG | QS/DS | GR | Hld | Bln | Lead | OPS | 1st Hf | 2nd Hf | vs RH | vs LH |
|---|---|---|---|---|---|---|---|---|---|---|---|---|---|---|---|---|---|---|---|---|
| 07 | — | — | — | — | — | — | — | — | — | — | — | — | — | — | — | — | — | — | — | — |
| 08 | — | — | — | — | — | — | — | — | — | — | — | — | — | — | — | — | — | — | — | — |
| 09 | — | — | — | — | — | — | — | — | — | — | — | — | — | — | — | — | — | — | — | — |
| 10 | — | — | — | — | — | — | — | — | — | — | — | — | — | — | — | — | — | — | — | — |

## Dan Haren — 200 IP | $17 | 290 pts

SP-35 — Owned: 98% — RH

LA's acquisition of Haren from AZ in July 2010 had more to do with 2011, but if the Angels had provided Haren with any support, he would have had a substantially better record. The Angels are aiming to bring up their hitting and outfield defense. If they can, Haren should have the numbers of an elite pitcher. (DS)

| Player | Age | IP | W | Sv | K | ERA | WHIP | K/9 | BB/9 | $2L | Pts |
|---|---|---|---|---|---|---|---|---|---|---|---|
| Haren D | 30 | 200 | 12 | 0 | 173 | 3.92 | 1.21 | 7.8 | 1.9 | $17 | 290 |
| **Mini-Browser** | **Age** | **IP** | **W** | **Sv** | **K** | **ERA** | **WHIP** | **K/9** | **BB/9** | **$2L** | **Pts** |
| Papelbon J | 30 | 60 | 4 | 41 | 65 | 3.22 | 1.18 | 9.7 | 2.9 | $18 | 320 |
| Jimenez U | 27 | 220 | 17 | 0 | 192 | 3.64 | 1.31 | 7.9 | 3.9 | $17 | 350 |
| Price D | 25 | 200 | 15 | 0 | 177 | 3.63 | 1.32 | 8.0 | 3.7 | $17 | 320 |
| Wilson B | 29 | 60 | 2 | 44 | 65 | 2.92 | 1.28 | 9.8 | 3.5 | $17 | 310 |
| Cain M | 26 | 220 | 13 | 0 | 170 | 3.69 | 1.23 | 7.0 | 2.9 | $17 | 300 |

| Level | Leag | W | L | Sv | IP | H | K | ERA | WHIP | K/9 | BB/9 | HR/9 | GB/F |
|---|---|---|---|---|---|---|---|---|---|---|---|---|---|
| A | — | — | — | — | — | — | — | — | — | — | — | — | — |
| AA | — | — | — | — | — | — | — | — | — | — | — | — | — |
| AAA | — | — | — | — | — | — | — | — | — | — | — | — | — |

| Competition at SP Thr | Player | GS | ERA | Supp | W-L |
|---|---|---|---|---|---|
| RH | Haren D | 35 | 3.91 | 3.9 | 12-12 |
| RH | Weaver J | 34 | 3.01 | 3.8 | 13-12 |
| RH | Santana E | 33 | 3.92 | 4.9 | 17-10 |
| LH | Kazmir S | 28 | 5.94 | 4.0 | 9-15 |

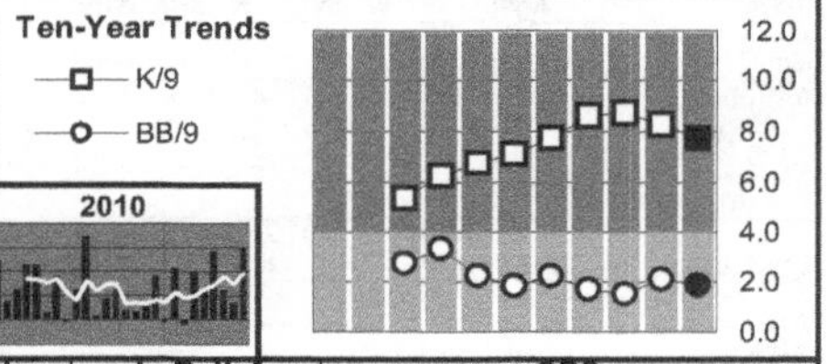


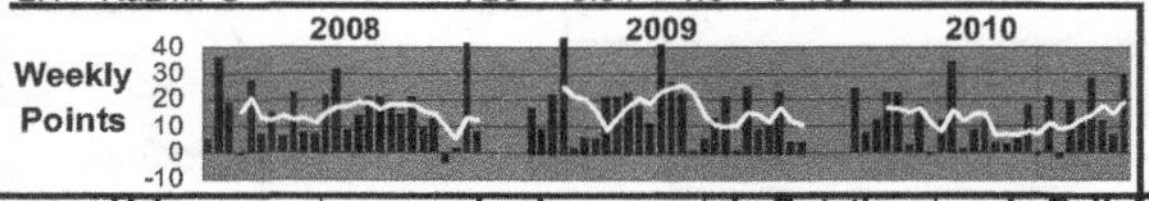


| Yr | Team | W | L | Sv | IP | H | K | ERA | WHIP | K/9 | BB/9 | HR/9 | GB/F |
|---|---|---|---|---|---|---|---|---|---|---|---|---|---|
| 07 | OAK | 15 | 9 | 0 | 222 | 214 | 192 | 3.07 | 1.21 | 7.8 | 2.2 | 1.0 | 1.2 |
| 08 | ARI | 16 | 8 | 0 | 216 | 204 | 206 | 3.33 | 1.13 | 8.6 | 1.7 | 0.8 | 1.3 |
| 09 | ARI | 14 | 10 | 0 | 229 | 192 | 223 | 3.14 | 1.00 | 8.8 | 1.5 | 1.1 | 1.2 |
| 10 | 2TM | 12 | 12 | 0 | 235 | 245 | 216 | 3.91 | 1.27 | 8.3 | 2.1 | 1.2 | 1.0 |

| Yr | $1L | $2L | Pts | RAA | H% | HR/fb | S% | FIP | GS | CG | QS/DS | GR | Hld | Bln | Lead | OPS | 1st Hf | 2nd Hf | vs RH | vs LH |
|---|---|---|---|---|---|---|---|---|---|---|---|---|---|---|---|---|---|---|---|---|
| 07 | $24 | $15 | 350 | +19 | 29% | 9% | 79% | 3.72 | 34 | 0 | 28/1 | — | — | — | — | .687 | .583 | .813 | .710 | .664 |
| 08 | $23 | $15 | 380 | +21 | 31% | 9% | 73% | 2.99 | 33 | 1 | 23/3 | — | — | — | — | .667 | .582 | .775 | .698 | .635 |
| 09 | $27 | $20 | 400 | +30 | 27% | 12% | 74% | 3.28 | 33 | 3 | 24/1 | — | — | — | — | .635 | .529 | .762 | .586 | .679 |
| 10 | $15 | $0 | 320 | +6 | 32% | 11% | 74% | 3.82 | 35 | 2 | 22/5 | — | — | — | — | .736 | .775 | .687 | .715 | .761 |

## Lucas Harrell — 40 IP | $-6 | 10 pts

RP-5, SP-3 — Owned: 0% — RH

Harrell is useful enough. He has a nice four-pitch repertoire and sufficient velocity to get by. His destiny is probably mop-up/swing-man, but although he has options left, he will hang out in Charlotte and wait for an emergency in Chicago. It's possible, but unlikely, that he'll improve yet. (RM)

| Player | Age | IP | W | Sv | K | ERA | WHIP | K/9 | BB/9 | $2L | Pts |
|---|---|---|---|---|---|---|---|---|---|---|---|
| Harrell L | 25 | 40 | 2 | 0 | 19 | 6.25 | 1.84 | 4.2 | 5.8 | -$6 | 10 |
| **Mini-Browser** | **Age** | **IP** | **W** | **Sv** | **K** | **ERA** | **WHIP** | **K/9** | **BB/9** | **$2L** | **Pts** |
| Lopez R | 35 | 180 | 7 | 0 | 104 | 5.25 | 1.43 | 5.2 | 2.4 | -$6 | 120 |
| Suppan J | 36 | 60 | 3 | 0 | 28 | 5.58 | 1.55 | 4.1 | 3.5 | -$6 | 30 |
| Leroux C | 26 | 40 | 2 | 0 | 39 | 5.67 | 1.80 | 8.7 | 4.5 | -$6 | 30 |
| Chatwood T | 21 | 40 | 2 | 0 | 19 | 6.02 | 1.89 | 4.3 | 5.9 | -$6 | 20 |
| Willis D | 29 | 40 | 2 | 0 | 26 | 5.74 | 1.76 | 5.8 | 6.0 | -$6 | 20 |

| Level | Leag | W | L | Sv | IP | H | K | ERA | WHIP | K/9 | BB/9 | HR/9 | GB/F |
|---|---|---|---|---|---|---|---|---|---|---|---|---|---|
| A | — | — | — | — | — | — | — | — | — | — | — | — | — |
| AA | — | — | — | — | — | — | — | — | — | — | — | — | — |
| AAA | IL | 10 | 10 | 0 | 137 | 141 | 84 | 4.58 | 1.47 | 5.5 | 4.0 | 0.7 | — |

| Competition at SP Thr | Player | GS | ERA | Supp | W-L |
|---|---|---|---|---|---|
| LH | Buehrle M | 33 | 4.28 | 4.8 | 13-13 |
| LH | Danks J | 32 | 3.72 | 4.5 | 15-11 |
| RH | Jackson E | 32 | 4.47 | 4.3 | 10-12 |
| RH | Floyd G | 31 | 4.08 | 3.8 | 10-13 |

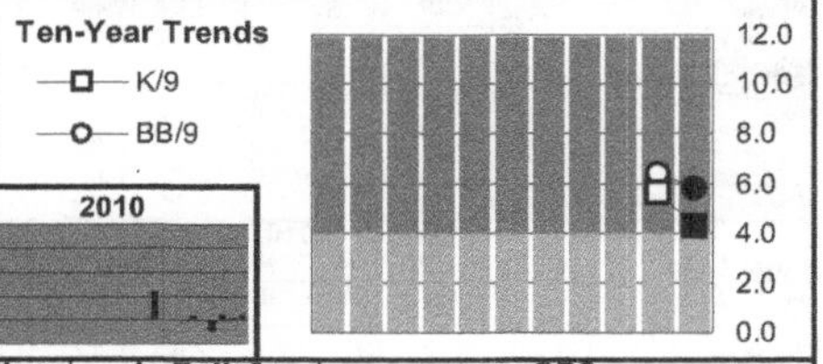


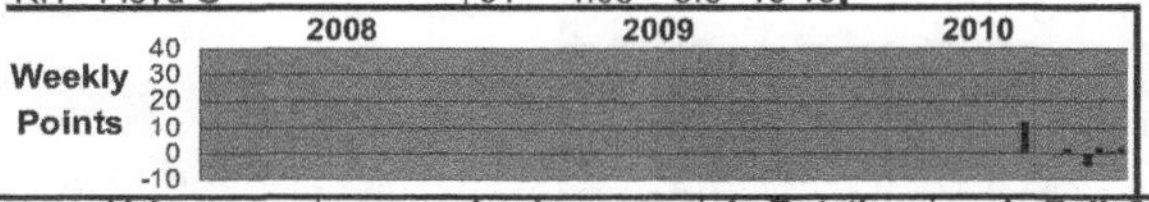


| Yr | Team | W | L | Sv | IP | H | K | ERA | WHIP | K/9 | BB/9 | HR/9 | GB/F |
|---|---|---|---|---|---|---|---|---|---|---|---|---|---|
| 07 | — | — | — | — | — | — | — | — | — | — | — | — | — |
| 08 | — | — | — | — | — | — | — | — | — | — | — | — | — |
| 09 | — | — | — | — | — | — | — | — | — | — | — | — | — |
| 10 | CHW | 1 | 0 | 0 | 24 | 34 | 15 | 4.88 | 2.13 | 5.6 | 6.4 | 0.8 | 2.3 |

| Yr | $1L | $2L | Pts | RAA | H% | HR/fb | S% | FIP | GS | CG | QS/DS | GR | Hld | Bln | Lead | OPS | 1st Hf | 2nd Hf | vs RH | vs LH |
|---|---|---|---|---|---|---|---|---|---|---|---|---|---|---|---|---|---|---|---|---|
| 07 | — | — | — | — | — | — | — | — | — | — | — | — | — | — | — | — | — | — | — | — |
| 08 | — | — | — | — | — | — | — | — | — | — | — | — | — | — | — | — | — | — | — | — |
| 09 | — | — | — | — | — | — | — | — | — | — | — | — | — | — | — | — | — | — | — | — |
| 10 | -$6 | -$16 | 10 | −6 | 40% | 11% | 78% | 5.26 | 3 | 0 | 1/1 | 5 | 0 | 0 | −2.1 | .898 | — | .898 | .727 | 1.047 |

## Matt Harrison 80 IP | $-4 | 50 pts

RP-31, SP-6 Owned: 0% LH

Harrison's still-plus stuff yielded an heightened K/9 in 2010 and aided him in curtailing his susceptibility to RHB, but that breakthrough is less exciting when it's a function of having moved to relief. A trade to the NL could enable Harrison to survive as a #4-5 starter; otherwise, he is a lefty long man and little more. (JM)

Forecast

| Player | Age | IP | W | Sv | K | ERA | WHIP | K/9 | BB/9 | $2L | Pts |
|---|---|---|---|---|---|---|---|---|---|---|---|
| Harrison M | 25 | 80 | 4 | 0 | 47 | 5.30 | 1.56 | 5.3 | 3.8 | -$4 | 50 |
| Mini-Browser | Age | IP | W | Sv | K | ERA | WHIP | K/9 | BB/9 | $2L | Pts |
| Morris B | 24 | 40 | 2 | 0 | 27 | 5.15 | 1.55 | 6.2 | 3.8 | -$4 | 30 |
| Rowland-Smith R | 28 | 80 | 3 | 0 | 45 | 5.35 | 1.52 | 5.1 | 3.4 | -$4 | 50 |
| Doubront F | 23 | 60 | 3 | 0 | 56 | 5.41 | 1.69 | 8.3 | 3.8 | -$4 | 60 |
| Kawakami K | 35 | 100 | 4 | 0 | 63 | 4.96 | 1.46 | 5.7 | 3.4 | -$4 | 70 |
| Weaver J | 34 | 40 | 2 | 0 | 24 | 5.63 | 1.49 | 5.4 | 3.3 | -$4 | 30 |

| | | | | | Minors (2010) | | | | | Skills | | | |
|---|---|---|---|---|---|---|---|---|---|---|---|---|---|
| Level | Leag | W | L | Sv | IP | H | K | ERA | WHIP | K/9 | BB/9 | HR/9 | GB/F |
| A | — | — | — | — | — | — | — | — | — | — | — | — | — |
| AA | — | — | — | — | — | — | — | — | — | — | — | — | — |
| AAA | — | — | — | — | — | — | — | — | — | — | — | — | — |

Competition at RP — Stats in 2010 as RP

| Thr | Player | GR | ERA | IP/G | Sv-Hld |
|---|---|---|---|---|---|
| LH | Oliver D | 64 | 2.48 | 1.0 | 1-14 |
| ▶ LH | Harrison M | 31 | 4.26 | 1.4 | 2-3 |
| LH | Kirkman M | 14 | 1.65 | 1.2 | 0-2 |
| LH | Rapada C | 13 | 4.00 | 0.7 | 0-3 |

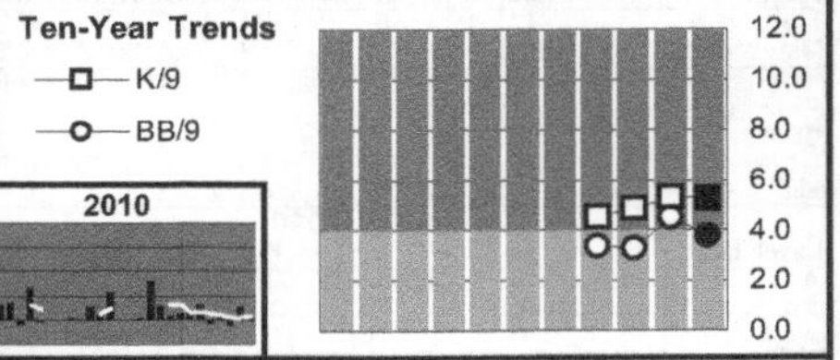


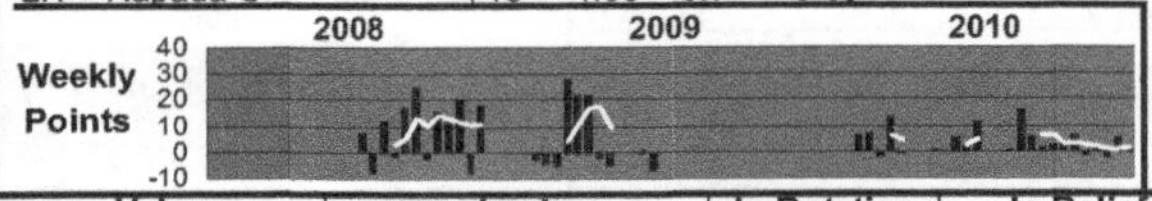


| | | | | | Majors | | | | | Skills | | | | Value | | | | Luck | | | | In Rotation | | | In Relief | | | | OPS | | | | |
|---|---|---|---|---|---|---|---|---|---|---|---|---|---|---|---|---|---|---|---|---|---|---|---|---|---|---|---|---|---|---|---|---|---|
| Yr | Team | W | L | Sv | IP | H | K | ERA | WHIP | K/9 | BB/9 | HR/9 | GB/F | $1L | $2L | Pts | RAA | H% | HR/fb | S% | FIP | GS | CG | QS/DS | GR | Hld | Bln | Lead | OPS | 1st Hf | 2nd Hf | vs RH | vs LH |
| 07 | — | — | — | — | — | — | — | — | — | — | — | — | — | — | — | — | — | — | — | — | — | — | — | — | — | — | — | — | — | — | — | — | — |
| 08 | TEX | 9 | 3 | 0 | 83 | 100 | 42 | 5.49 | 1.57 | 4.5 | 3.3 | 1.3 | 1.1 | -$5 | -$10 | 100 | −19 | 31% | 11% | 67% | 5.27 | 15 | 1 | 6/6 | — | — | — | — | .878 | .896 | .876 | .844 | .971 |
| 09 | TEX | 4 | 5 | 0 | 63 | 81 | 34 | 6.11 | 1.64 | 4.8 | 3.3 | 1.3 | 1.5 | -$3 | -$8 | 40 | −15 | 34% | 13% | 64% | 5.16 | 11 | 2 | 2/4 | — | — | — | — | .876 | .876 | — | .974 | .564 |
| 10 | TEX | 3 | 2 | 2 | 78 | 80 | 46 | 4.71 | 1.52 | 5.3 | 4.5 | 1.1 | 1.4 | -$3 | -$16 | 60 | −10 | 28% | 12% | 72% | 5.28 | 6 | 0 | 3/1 | 31 | 3 | 1 | +0.6 | .755 | .711 | .830 | .770 | .716 |

## LaTroy Hawkins 40 IP | $-1 | 40 pts

RP-18 Owned: 1% RH

Hawk's first year with Milwaukee was a disaster, ending in shoulder surgery. His prognosis is reportedly excellent, though his absence from the bullpen gave auditions for younger and better options. That, plus his advancing age, means that a late-game role in 2011 is far from assured even if he is healthy. (MS)

Forecast

| Player | Age | IP | W | Sv | K | ERA | WHIP | K/9 | BB/9 | $2L | Pts |
|---|---|---|---|---|---|---|---|---|---|---|---|
| Hawkins L | 38 | 40 | 2 | 0 | 27 | 4.60 | 1.33 | 6.1 | 2.8 | -$1 | 40 |
| Mini-Browser | Age | IP | W | Sv | K | ERA | WHIP | K/9 | BB/9 | $2L | Pts |
| Gorzelanny T | 28 | 140 | 7 | 0 | 111 | 4.67 | 1.48 | 7.1 | 4.1 | -$1 | 150 |
| Judy J | 25 | 60 | 1 | 0 | 50 | 4.53 | 1.47 | 7.6 | 3.4 | -$1 | 50 |
| Sonnanstine A | 28 | 50 | 2 | 0 | 31 | 5.09 | 1.34 | 5.5 | 2.4 | -$1 | 40 |
| Thomas B | 33 | 40 | 3 | 0 | 21 | 4.29 | 1.55 | 4.7 | 3.6 | -$1 | 40 |
| Outman J | 26 | 60 | 3 | 0 | 54 | 4.72 | 1.56 | 8.1 | 4.3 | -$1 | 70 |

| | | | | | Minors (2010) | | | | | Skills | | | |
|---|---|---|---|---|---|---|---|---|---|---|---|---|---|
| Level | Leag | W | L | Sv | IP | H | K | ERA | WHIP | K/9 | BB/9 | HR/9 | GB/F |
| A | — | — | — | — | — | — | — | — | — | — | — | — | — |
| AA | — | — | — | — | — | — | — | — | — | — | — | — | — |
| AAA | PCL | 0 | 0 | 1 | 6 | 4 | 1 | 0.00 | 0.63 | 1.4 | 0.0 | 0.0 | — |

Competition at RP — Stats in 2010 as RP

| Thr | Player | GR | ERA | IP/G | Sv-Hld |
|---|---|---|---|---|---|
| RH | Coffey T | 69 | 4.76 | 0.9 | 0-13 |
| RH | Loe K | 53 | 2.78 | 1.1 | 0-22 |
| RH | Axford J | 50 | 2.48 | 1.2 | 24-3 |
| RH | Villanueva C | 50 | 4.61 | 1.1 | 1-14 |

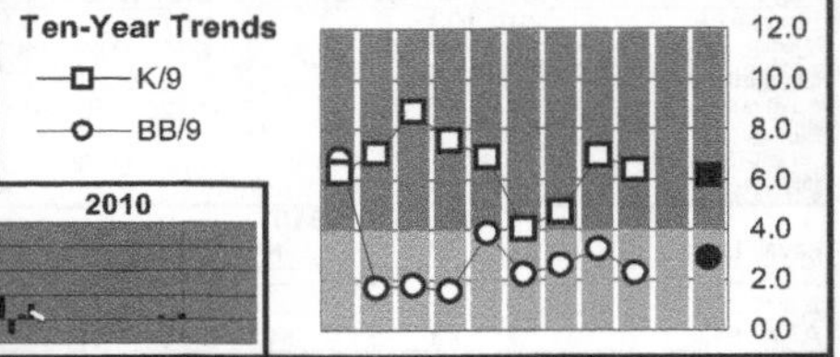


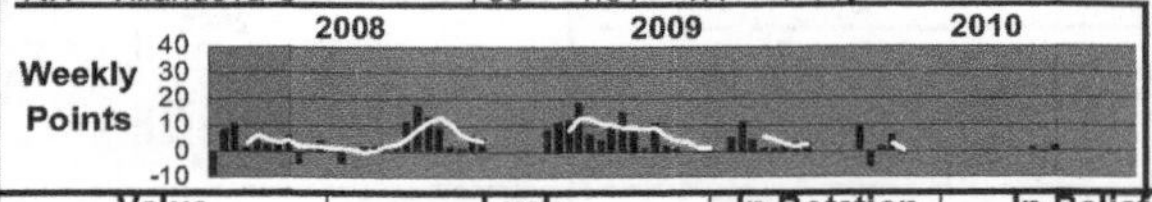


| | | | | | Majors | | | | | Skills | | | | Value | | | | Luck | | | | In Rotation | | | In Relief | | | | OPS | | | | |
|---|---|---|---|---|---|---|---|---|---|---|---|---|---|---|---|---|---|---|---|---|---|---|---|---|---|---|---|---|---|---|---|---|---|
| Yr | Team | W | L | Sv | IP | H | K | ERA | WHIP | K/9 | BB/9 | HR/9 | GB/F | $1L | $2L | Pts | RAA | H% | HR/fb | S% | FIP | GS | CG | QS/DS | GR | Hld | Bln | Lead | OPS | 1st Hf | 2nd Hf | vs RH | vs LH |
| 07 | COL | 2 | 5 | 0 | 55 | 52 | 29 | 3.42 | 1.23 | 4.7 | 2.6 | 1.0 | 3.0 | $2 | -$1 | 50 | +4 | 27% | 16% | 76% | 4.43 | — | — | — | 62 | 18 | 5 | +1.2 | .698 | .780 | .632 | .665 | .735 |
| 08 | 2TM | 3 | 1 | 1 | 62 | 53 | 48 | 3.92 | 1.21 | 7.0 | 3.2 | 0.4 | 1.3 | $0 | $0 | 80 | −1 | 28% | 5% | 67% | 3.40 | — | — | — | 57 | 13 | 1 | +0.1 | .626 | .742 | .440 | .459 | .831 |
| 09 | HOU | 1 | 4 | 11 | 63 | 60 | 45 | 2.13 | 1.20 | 6.4 | 2.3 | 1.0 | 1.5 | $7 | $5 | 120 | +13 | 29% | 12% | 88% | 3.97 | — | — | — | 65 | 19 | 4 | +0.9 | .679 | .665 | .699 | .828 | .529 |
| 10 | MIL | 0 | 3 | 0 | 16 | 21 | 18 | 8.44 | 1.69 | 10.1 | 3.4 | 1.1 | 1.5 | -$8 | -$16 | 10 | −8 | 42% | 13% | 48% | 3.70 | — | — | — | 18 | 6 | 2 | +1.2 | .890 | .809 | 1.084 | .957 | .783 |

## Blake Hawksworth 60 IP | $-2 | 60 pts

RP-37, SP-8 Owned: 3% RH

Hawksworth has taken over the Brad Thompson role in St. Louis by occasionally filling in for the rotation but mostly eating low-leverage innings out of the bullpen. If his unreasonably high H% and HR/FB retreat in 2011, he could furnish an ERA in the mid-4.00's, and that excludes any gains from his rising K/9. (AB)

Forecast

| Player | Age | IP | W | Sv | K | ERA | WHIP | K/9 | BB/9 | $2L | Pts |
|---|---|---|---|---|---|---|---|---|---|---|---|
| Hawksworth B | 28 | 60 | 3 | 0 | 44 | 4.65 | 1.50 | 6.6 | 3.3 | -$2 | 60 |
| Mini-Browser | Age | IP | W | Sv | K | ERA | WHIP | K/9 | BB/9 | $2L | Pts |
| Infante G | 23 | 60 | 3 | 0 | 47 | 4.31 | 1.75 | 7.1 | 7.0 | -$2 | 60 |
| Ramos C | 26 | 40 | 2 | 0 | 29 | 4.81 | 1.46 | 6.5 | 3.4 | -$2 | 40 |
| Wright J | 36 | 40 | 1 | 0 | 23 | 4.89 | 1.48 | 5.2 | 4.4 | -$2 | 20 |
| Lannan J | 26 | 160 | 8 | 0 | 80 | 4.73 | 1.46 | 4.5 | 3.1 | -$2 | 120 |
| Mills B | 26 | 60 | 3 | 0 | 59 | 5.25 | 1.58 | 8.8 | 4.6 | -$2 | 70 |

| | | | | | Minors (2010) | | | | | Skills | | | |
|---|---|---|---|---|---|---|---|---|---|---|---|---|---|
| Level | Leag | W | L | Sv | IP | H | K | ERA | WHIP | K/9 | BB/9 | HR/9 | GB/F |
| A | — | — | — | — | — | — | — | — | — | — | — | — | — |
| AA | — | — | — | — | — | — | — | — | — | — | — | — | — |
| AAA | — | — | — | — | — | — | — | — | — | — | — | — | — |

Competition at RP — Stats in 2010 as RP

| Thr | Player | GR | ERA | IP/G | Sv-Hld |
|---|---|---|---|---|---|
| RH | McClellan K | 68 | 2.27 | 1.1 | 2-19 |
| RH | Boggs M | 61 | 3.61 | 1.1 | 0-6 |
| RH | Franklin R | 59 | 3.46 | 1.1 | 27-0 |
| RH | Motte J | 56 | 2.24 | 0.9 | 2-12 |

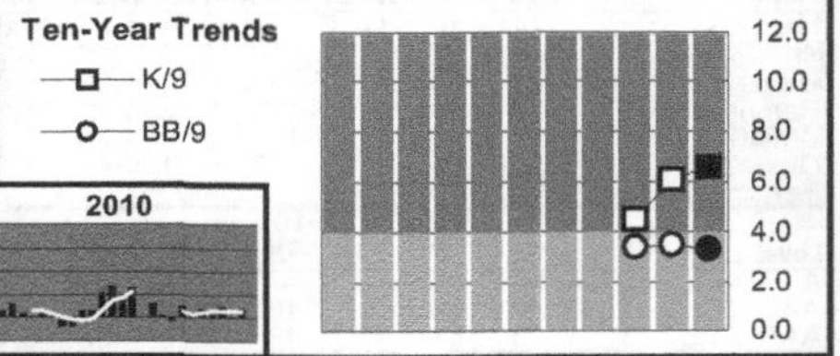


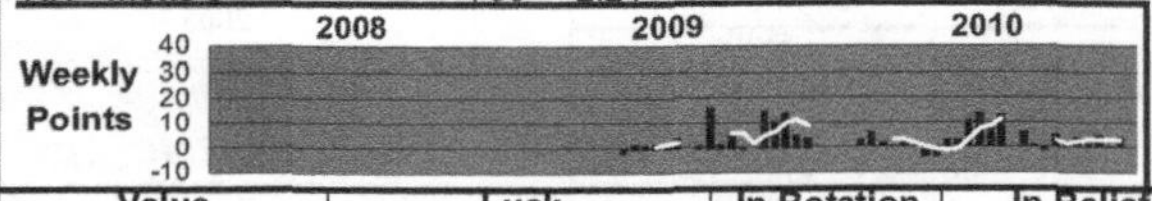


| | | | | | Majors | | | | | Skills | | | | Value | | | | Luck | | | | In Rotation | | | In Relief | | | | OPS | | | | |
|---|---|---|---|---|---|---|---|---|---|---|---|---|---|---|---|---|---|---|---|---|---|---|---|---|---|---|---|---|---|---|---|---|---|
| Yr | Team | W | L | Sv | IP | H | K | ERA | WHIP | K/9 | BB/9 | HR/9 | GB/F | $1L | $2L | Pts | RAA | H% | HR/fb | S% | FIP | GS | CG | QS/DS | GR | Hld | Bln | Lead | OPS | 1st Hf | 2nd Hf | vs RH | vs LH |
| 07 | — | — | — | — | — | — | — | — | — | — | — | — | — | — | — | — | — | — | — | — | — | — | — | — | — | — | — | — | — | — | — | — | — |
| 08 | — | — | — | — | — | — | — | — | — | — | — | — | — | — | — | — | — | — | — | — | — | — | — | — | — | — | — | — | — | — | — | — | — |
| 09 | STL | 4 | 0 | 0 | 40 | 29 | 20 | 2.03 | 1.10 | 4.5 | 3.4 | 0.5 | 1.7 | $4 | $2 | 70 | +8 | 23% | 5% | 83% | 3.98 | — | — | — | 30 | 2 | 0 | −0.8 | .612 | .726 | .555 | .513 | .724 |
| 10 | STL | 4 | 8 | 0 | 90 | 113 | 61 | 4.98 | 1.64 | 6.1 | 3.5 | 1.5 | 1.6 | -$8 | -$21 | 70 | −15 | 34% | 16% | 74% | 5.17 | 8 | 0 | 1/2 | 37 | 4 | 0 | −0.5 | .848 | .839 | .862 | .818 | .886 |

## Aaron Heilman 80 IP | $-2 | 80 pts

RP-70 Owned: 14% RH

Instead of stabilizing Arizona's bullpen, Heilman roiled it, especially when asked to close (8 Blown Saves versus 6 Saves). Diminishing ground-ball and strikeout rates did not help, though the truth is that interest in Heilman has always exceeded his ability to deliver. For his career, he now has 30 Blown Saves. (MS)

Forecast

| Player | Age | IP | W | Sv | K | ERA | WHIP | K/9 | BB/9 | $2L | Pts |
|---|---|---|---|---|---|---|---|---|---|---|---|
| Heilman A | 32 | 80 | 4 | 0 | 63 | 4.82 | 1.45 | 7.1 | 3.8 | -$2 | 80 |
| Mini-Browser | Age | IP | W | Sv | K | ERA | WHIP | K/9 | BB/9 | $2L | Pts |
| Martin J | 28 | 40 | 2 | 0 | 27 | 4.58 | 1.37 | 6.1 | 2.2 | -$2 | 40 |
| Purcey D | 28 | 60 | 3 | 0 | 53 | 4.96 | 1.53 | 7.9 | 4.9 | -$2 | 60 |
| Ring R | 30 | 20 | 1 | 0 | 17 | 4.49 | 1.44 | 7.7 | 4.0 | -$2 | 20 |
| Misch P | 29 | 40 | 2 | 0 | 25 | 4.72 | 1.33 | 5.7 | 2.3 | -$2 | 30 |
| Kendrick K | 26 | 80 | 5 | 0 | 38 | 4.85 | 1.39 | 4.3 | 2.6 | -$2 | 70 |

| | | | | | Minors (2010) | | | | | Skills | | | |
|---|---|---|---|---|---|---|---|---|---|---|---|---|---|
| Level | Leag | W | L | Sv | IP | H | K | ERA | WHIP | K/9 | BB/9 | HR/9 | GB/F |
| A | — | — | — | — | — | — | — | — | — | — | — | — | — |
| AA | — | — | — | — | — | — | — | — | — | — | — | — | — |
| AAA | — | — | — | — | — | — | — | — | — | — | — | — | — |

Competition at RP — Stats in 2010 as RP

| Thr | Player | GR | ERA | IP/G | Sv-Hld |
|---|---|---|---|---|---|
| ▶ RH | Heilman A | 70 | 4.50 | 1.0 | 6-12 |
| RH | Gutierrez J | 58 | 5.08 | 1.0 | 15-8 |
| RH | Vasquez E | 57 | 5.20 | 0.9 | 0-6 |
| RH | Boyer B | 54 | 4.26 | 1.1 | 0-5 |

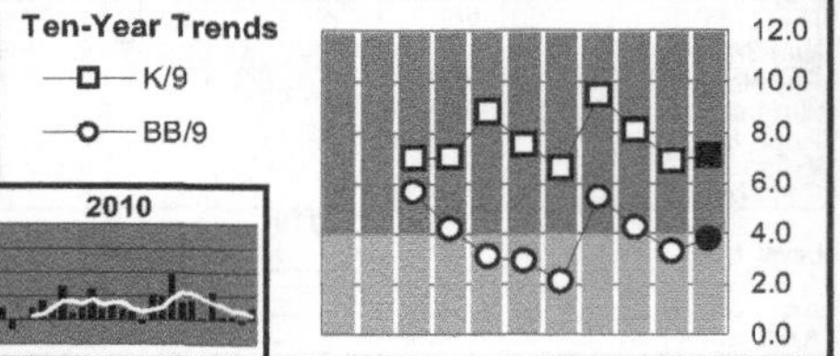


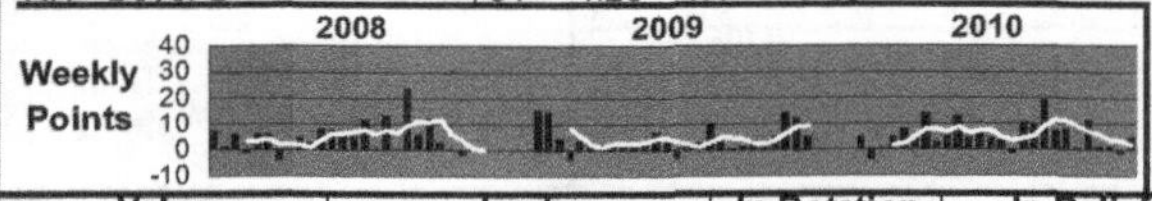


| | | | | | Majors | | | | | Skills | | | | Value | | | | Luck | | | | In Rotation | | | In Relief | | | | OPS | | | | |
|---|---|---|---|---|---|---|---|---|---|---|---|---|---|---|---|---|---|---|---|---|---|---|---|---|---|---|---|---|---|---|---|---|---|
| Yr | Team | W | L | Sv | IP | H | K | ERA | WHIP | K/9 | BB/9 | HR/9 | GB/F | $1L | $2L | Pts | RAA | H% | HR/fb | S% | FIP | GS | CG | QS/DS | GR | Hld | Bln | Lead | OPS | 1st Hf | 2nd Hf | vs RH | vs LH |
| 07 | NYM | 7 | 7 | 1 | 86 | 72 | 63 | 3.03 | 1.07 | 6.6 | 2.1 | 0.8 | 1.3 | $10 | $7 | 150 | +3 | 26% | 9% | 75% | 3.64 | — | — | — | 81 | 22 | 5 | +0.5 | .634 | .705 | .561 | .568 | .738 |
| 08 | NYM | 3 | 8 | 3 | 76 | 75 | 80 | 5.21 | 1.59 | 9.5 | 5.4 | 1.2 | 1.2 | -$4 | -$8 | 100 | −14 | 32% | 13% | 69% | 4.62 | — | — | — | 78 | 15 | 5 | +0.2 | .793 | .723 | .916 | .652 | .991 |
| 09 | CHC | 4 | 4 | 1 | 72 | 68 | 65 | 4.11 | 1.41 | 8.1 | 4.2 | 1.1 | 1.1 | $1 | -$1 | 100 | −1 | 31% | 12% | 74% | 4.43 | — | — | — | 70 | 10 | 6 | +0.6 | .754 | .769 | .727 | .828 | .642 |
| 10 | ARI | 5 | 8 | 6 | 72 | 73 | 55 | 4.50 | 1.38 | 6.9 | 3.3 | 1.1 | 0.8 | -$1 | -$10 | 120 | −5 | 30% | 9% | 70% | 4.38 | — | — | — | 70 | 12 | 8 | +0.6 | .755 | .769 | .736 | .860 | .647 |

## Jeremy Hellickson 120 IP | $6 | 200 pts

RP-6, SP-4 Owned: 11% RH

A top prospect, Hellickson should be a full-time starter in the Rays' rotation some time in 2011. Our lone hesitation is that there may not be a spot for him unless another Ray starter gets hurt or dealt. Certainly, a debut with a 3.93 FIP and 4 Wins says that he is ready. (RZ)

Forecast

| Player | Age | IP | W | Sv | K | ERA | WHIP | K/9 | BB/9 | $2L | Pts |
|---|---|---|---|---|---|---|---|---|---|---|---|
| Hellickson J | 23 | 120 | 9 | 0 | 129 | 4.39 | 1.35 | 9.7 | 2.6 | $6 | 200 |
| Mini-Browser | Age | IP | W | Sv | K | ERA | WHIP | K/9 | BB/9 | $2L | Pts |
| Buehrle M | 32 | 200 | 12 | 0 | 95 | 4.47 | 1.32 | 4.3 | 2.1 | $7 | 180 |
| Putz J | 34 | 60 | 5 | 9 | 61 | 3.60 | 1.27 | 9.1 | 3.8 | $7 | 150 |
| Lowe D | 37 | 200 | 13 | 0 | 120 | 4.29 | 1.34 | 5.4 | 2.7 | $7 | 230 |
| Tejeda R | 29 | 60 | 3 | 25 | 57 | 4.35 | 1.55 | 8.6 | 5.4 | $7 | 200 |
| Pineda M | 22 | 120 | 7 | 0 | 97 | 3.98 | 1.33 | 7.3 | 3.1 | $7 | 160 |

| | | | | | Minors (2010) | | | | | Skills | | | |
|---|---|---|---|---|---|---|---|---|---|---|---|---|---|
| Level | Leag | W | L | Sv | IP | H | K | ERA | WHIP | K/9 | BB/9 | HR/9 | GB/F |
| A | FLO | 0 | 0 | 0 | 1 | 4 | 4 | 21.60 | 3.60 | 21.6 | 10.8 | 0.0 | — |
| AA | — | — | — | — | — | — | — | — | — | — | — | — | — |
| AAA | IL | 12 | 3 | 0 | 117 | 103 | 123 | 2.45 | 1.17 | 9.4 | 2.7 | 0.4 | — |

Competition at SP — Stats in 2010 as SP

| Thr | Player | GS | ERA | Supp | W-L |
|---|---|---|---|---|---|
| RH | Shields J | 33 | 5.20 | 4.5 | 12-15 |
| RH | Garza M | 32 | 3.93 | 5.2 | 15-10 |
| LH | Price D | 31 | 2.73 | 5.3 | 19-6 |
| RH | Davis W | 29 | 4.07 | 4.9 | 12-10 |

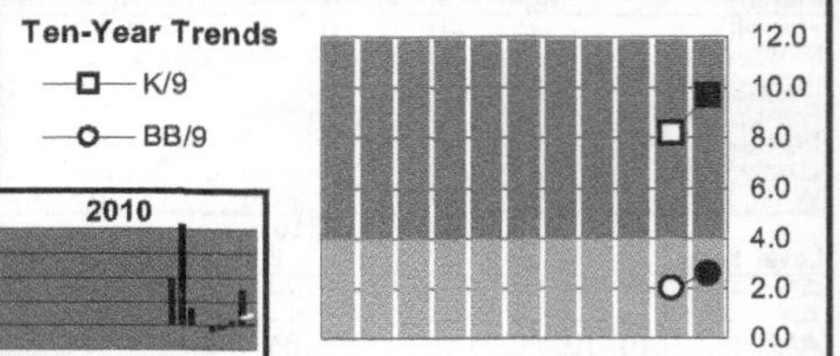

| | | | | | Majors | | | | | Skills | | | | Value | | | | Luck | | | | In Rotation | | | In Relief | | | | OPS | | | | |
|---|---|---|---|---|---|---|---|---|---|---|---|---|---|---|---|---|---|---|---|---|---|---|---|---|---|---|---|---|---|---|---|---|---|
| Yr | Team | W | L | Sv | IP | H | K | ERA | WHIP | K/9 | BB/9 | HR/9 | GB/F | $1L | $2L | Pts | RAA | H% | HR/fb | S% | FIP | GS | CG | QS/DS | GR | Hld | Bln | Lead | OPS | 1st Hf | 2nd Hf | vs RH | vs LH |
| 07 | — | — | — | — | — | — | — | — | — | — | — | — | — | — | — | — | — | — | — | — | — | — | — | — | — | — | — | — | — | — | — | — | — |
| 08 | — | — | — | — | — | — | — | — | — | — | — | — | — | — | — | — | — | — | — | — | — | — | — | — | — | — | — | — | — | — | — | — | — |
| 09 | — | — | — | — | — | — | — | — | — | — | — | — | — | — | — | — | — | — | — | — | — | — | — | — | — | — | — | — | — | — | — | — | — |
| 10 | TB | 4 | 0 | 0 | 36 | 32 | 33 | 3.47 | 1.10 | 8.2 | 2.0 | 1.2 | 0.8 | $1 | -$5 | 80 | +4 | 27% | 10% | 74% | 3.93 | 4 | 0 | 4/0 | 6 | 0 | 1 | +1.2 | .666 | — | .666 | .391 | .906 |

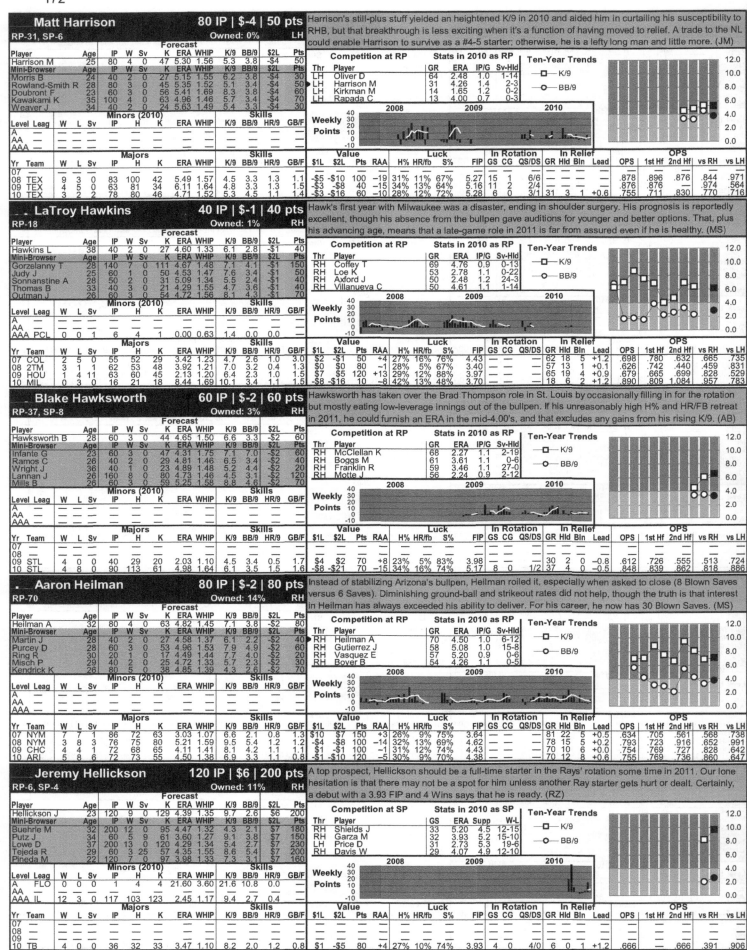

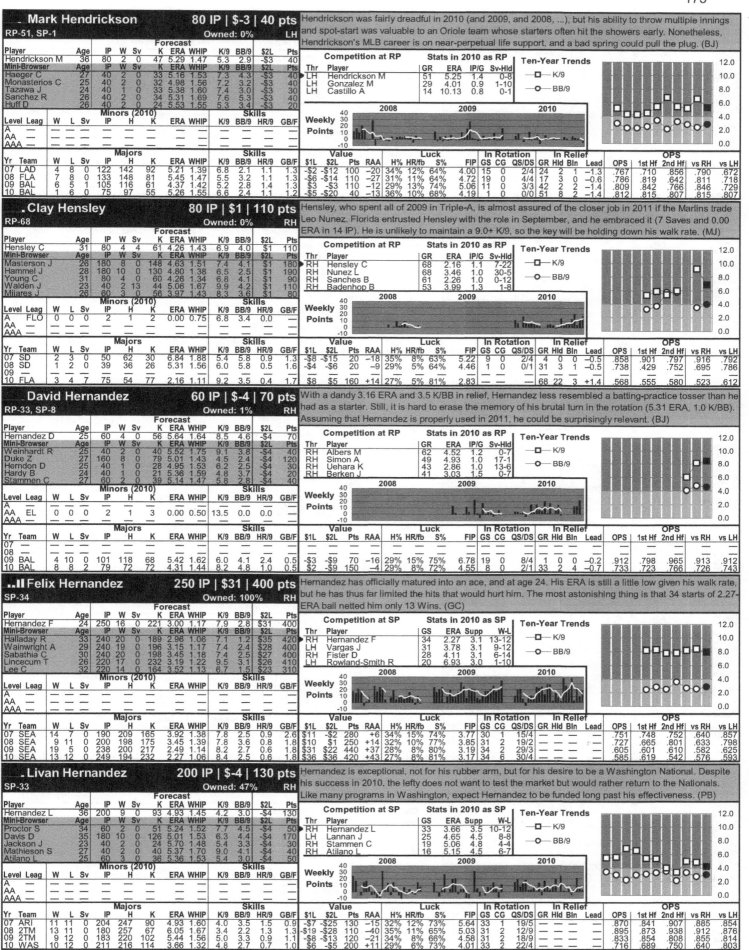

## Mark Hendrickson — 80 IP | $-3 | 40 pts

RP-51, SP-1 — Owned: 0% — LH

Hendrickson was fairly dreadful in 2010 (and 2009, and 2008, ...), but his ability to throw multiple innings and spot-start was valuable to an Oriole team whose starters often hit the showers early. Nonetheless, Hendrickson's MLB career is on near-perpetual life support, and a bad spring could pull the plug. (BJ)

**Forecast**

| Player | Age | IP | W | Sv | K | ERA | WHIP | K/9 | BB/9 | $2L | Pts |
|---|---|---|---|---|---|---|---|---|---|---|---|
| Hendrickson M | 36 | 80 | 2 | 0 | 47 | 5.29 | 1.47 | 5.3 | 2.9 | -$3 | 40 |
| **Mini-Browser** | **Age** | **IP** | **W** | **Sv** | **K** | **ERA** | **WHIP** | **K/9** | **BB/9** | **$2L** | **Pts** |
| Haeger C | 27 | 40 | 2 | 0 | 33 | 5.16 | 1.53 | 7.3 | 4.3 | -$3 | 40 |
| Monasterios C | 25 | 40 | 2 | 0 | 32 | 4.98 | 1.56 | 7.2 | 3.2 | -$3 | 40 |
| Tazawa J | 24 | 40 | 1 | 0 | 33 | 5.38 | 1.60 | 7.4 | 3.0 | -$3 | 30 |
| Sanchez R | 26 | 40 | 2 | 0 | 34 | 5.31 | 1.69 | 7.6 | 5.3 | -$3 | 40 |
| Huff D | 26 | 40 | 2 | 0 | 24 | 5.53 | 1.55 | 5.3 | 3.4 | -$3 | 20 |

**Minors (2010)** / **Skills**

| Level | Leag | W | L | Sv | IP | H | K | ERA | WHIP | K/9 | BB/9 | HR/9 | GB/F |
|---|---|---|---|---|---|---|---|---|---|---|---|---|---|
| A | — | — | — | — | — | — | — | — | — | — | — | — | — |
| AA | — | — | — | — | — | — | — | — | — | — | — | — | — |
| AAA | — | — | — | — | — | — | — | — | — | — | — | — | — |

**Competition at RP** — Stats in 2010 as RP

| Thr | Player | GR | ERA | IP/G | Sv-Hld |
|---|---|---|---|---|---|
| LH | Hendrickson M | 51 | 5.25 | 1.4 | 0-8 |
| LH | Gonzalez M | 29 | 4.01 | 0.9 | 1-10 |
| LH | Castillo A | 14 | 10.13 | 0.8 | 0-1 |

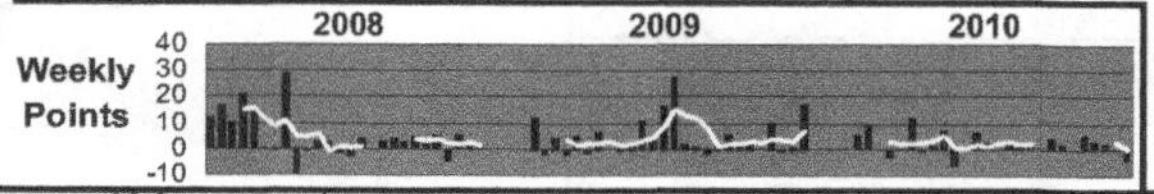
Weekly Points
2008
2009
2010
40
30
20
10
0
-10

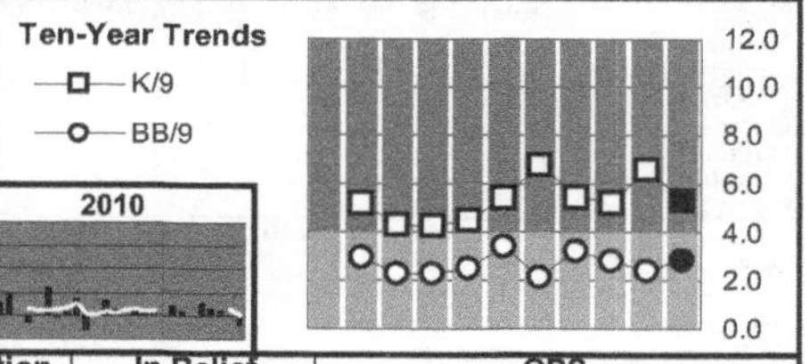
Ten-Year Trends
K/9
BB/9
12.0
10.0
8.0
6.0
4.0
2.0
0.0

**Majors** / **Skills**

| Yr | Team | W | L | Sv | IP | H | K | ERA | WHIP | K/9 | BB/9 | HR/9 | GB/F |
|---|---|---|---|---|---|---|---|---|---|---|---|---|---|
| 07 | LAD | 4 | 8 | 0 | 122 | 142 | 92 | 5.21 | 1.39 | 6.8 | 2.1 | 1.1 | 1.3 |
| 08 | FLA | 7 | 8 | 0 | 133 | 148 | 81 | 5.45 | 1.44 | 5.5 | 3.2 | 1.1 | 1.3 |
| 09 | BAL | 6 | 5 | 1 | 105 | 116 | 61 | 4.37 | 1.42 | 5.2 | 2.8 | 1.4 | 1.3 |
| 10 | BAL | 1 | 6 | 0 | 75 | 97 | 55 | 5.26 | 1.55 | 6.6 | 2.4 | 1.1 | 1.2 |

| Yr | Value $1L | $2L | Pts | RAA | Luck H% | HR/fb | S% | FIP | In Rotation GS | CG | QS/DS | In Relief GR | Hld | Bln | Lead | OPS | 1st Hf | 2nd Hf | vs RH | vs LH |
|---|---|---|---|---|---|---|---|---|---|---|---|---|---|---|---|---|---|---|---|---|
| 07 | -$2 | -$12 | 100 | −20 | 34% | 12% | 64% | 4.00 | 15 | 0 | 2/4 | 24 | 2 | 1 | −1.3 | .767 | .710 | .856 | .790 | .672 |
| 08 | -$6 | -$14 | 110 | −27 | 31% | 11% | 64% | 4.72 | 19 | 0 | 4/4 | 17 | 3 | 0 | −0.6 | .786 | .819 | .642 | .811 | .718 |
| 09 | $3 | -$3 | 110 | −12 | 29% | 13% | 74% | 5.06 | 11 | 0 | 3/3 | 42 | 2 | 2 | −1.4 | .809 | .842 | .766 | .846 | .729 |
| 10 | -$5 | -$20 | 40 | −13 | 36% | 10% | 68% | 4.19 | 1 | 0 | 0/0 | 51 | 8 | 2 | −1.4 | .812 | .815 | .807 | .815 | .807 |

## Clay Hensley — 80 IP | $1 | 110 pts

RP-68 — Owned: 0% — RH

Hensley, who spent all of 2009 in Triple-A, is almost assured of the closer job in 2011 if the Marlins trade Leo Nunez. Florida entrusted Hensley with the role in September, and he embraced it (7 Saves and 0.00 ERA in 14 IP). He is unlikely to maintain a 9.0+ K/9, so the key will be holding down his walk rate. (MJ)

**Forecast**

| Player | Age | IP | W | Sv | K | ERA | WHIP | K/9 | BB/9 | $2L | Pts |
|---|---|---|---|---|---|---|---|---|---|---|---|
| Hensley C | 31 | 80 | 4 | 4 | 61 | 4.26 | 1.43 | 6.9 | 4.0 | $1 | 110 |
| **Mini-Browser** | **Age** | **IP** | **W** | **Sv** | **K** | **ERA** | **WHIP** | **K/9** | **BB/9** | **$2L** | **Pts** |
| Masterson J | 26 | 180 | 8 | 0 | 148 | 4.63 | 1.51 | 7.4 | 4.1 | $1 | 180 |
| Hammel J | 28 | 180 | 10 | 0 | 130 | 4.80 | 1.38 | 6.5 | 2.5 | $1 | 190 |
| Young C | 31 | 80 | 4 | 0 | 60 | 4.26 | 1.34 | 6.8 | 4.1 | $1 | 90 |
| Walden J | 23 | 40 | 2 | 13 | 44 | 5.06 | 1.67 | 9.9 | 4.2 | $1 | 110 |
| Mijares J | 26 | 60 | 3 | 0 | 56 | 3.97 | 1.43 | 8.3 | 3.6 | $1 | 80 |

**Minors (2010)** / **Skills**

| Level | Leag | W | L | Sv | IP | H | K | ERA | WHIP | K/9 | BB/9 | HR/9 | GB/F |
|---|---|---|---|---|---|---|---|---|---|---|---|---|---|
| A | FLO | 0 | 0 | 0 | 2 | 1 | 2 | 0.00 | 0.75 | 6.8 | 3.4 | 0.0 | — |
| AA | — | — | — | — | — | — | — | — | — | — | — | — | — |
| AAA | — | — | — | — | — | — | — | — | — | — | — | — | — |

**Competition at RP** — Stats in 2010 as RP

| Thr | Player | GR | ERA | IP/G | Sv-Hld |
|---|---|---|---|---|---|
| RH | Hensley C | 68 | 2.16 | 1.1 | 7-22 |
| RH | Nunez L | 68 | 3.46 | 1.0 | 30-5 |
| RH | Sanches B | 61 | 2.26 | 1.0 | 0-12 |
| RH | Badenhop B | 53 | 3.99 | 1.3 | 1-8 |

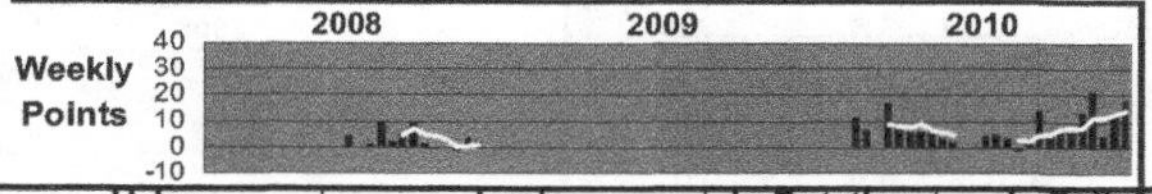
Weekly Points
2008
2009
2010
40
30
20
10
0
-10

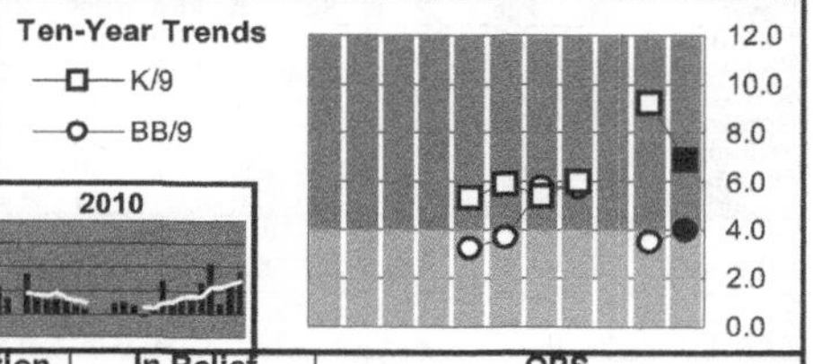
Ten-Year Trends
K/9
BB/9
12.0
10.0
8.0
6.0
4.0
2.0
0.0

**Majors** / **Skills**

| Yr | Team | W | L | Sv | IP | H | K | ERA | WHIP | K/9 | BB/9 | HR/9 | GB/F |
|---|---|---|---|---|---|---|---|---|---|---|---|---|---|
| 07 | SD | 2 | 3 | 0 | 50 | 62 | 30 | 6.84 | 1.88 | 5.4 | 5.8 | 0.9 | 1.3 |
| 08 | SD | 1 | 2 | 0 | 39 | 36 | 26 | 5.31 | 1.56 | 6.0 | 5.8 | 0.5 | 1.6 |
| 09 | — | — | — | — | — | — | — | — | — | — | — | — | — |
| 10 | FLA | 3 | 4 | 7 | 75 | 54 | 77 | 2.16 | 1.11 | 9.2 | 3.5 | 0.4 | 1.7 |

| Yr | Value $1L | $2L | Pts | RAA | Luck H% | HR/fb | S% | FIP | In Rotation GS | CG | QS/DS | In Relief GR | Hld | Bln | Lead | OPS | 1st Hf | 2nd Hf | vs RH | vs LH |
|---|---|---|---|---|---|---|---|---|---|---|---|---|---|---|---|---|---|---|---|---|
| 07 | -$8 | -$15 | 20 | −18 | 35% | 8% | 63% | 5.22 | 9 | 0 | 2/4 | 4 | 0 | 0 | −0.5 | .858 | .901 | .797 | .916 | .792 |
| 08 | -$4 | -$6 | 20 | −9 | 29% | 5% | 64% | 4.46 | 1 | 0 | 0/1 | 31 | 3 | 1 | −0.5 | .738 | .429 | .752 | .695 | .786 |
| 09 | — | — | — | — | — | — | — | — | — | — | — | — | — | — | — | — | — | — | — | — |
| 10 | $8 | $5 | 160 | +14 | 27% | 5% | 81% | 2.83 | — | — | — | 68 | 22 | 3 | +1.4 | .568 | .555 | .580 | .523 | .612 |

## David Hernandez — 60 IP | $-4 | 70 pts

RP-33, SP-8 — Owned: 1% — RH

With a dandy 3.16 ERA and 3.5 K/BB in relief, Hernandez less resembled a batting-practice tosser than he had as a starter. Still, it is hard to erase the memory of his brutal turn in the rotation (5.31 ERA, 1.0 K/BB). Assuming that Hernandez is properly used in 2011, he could be surprisingly relevant. (BJ)

**Forecast**

| Player | Age | IP | W | Sv | K | ERA | WHIP | K/9 | BB/9 | $2L | Pts |
|---|---|---|---|---|---|---|---|---|---|---|---|
| Hernandez D | 25 | 60 | 4 | 0 | 56 | 5.64 | 1.64 | 8.5 | 4.6 | -$4 | 70 |
| **Mini-Browser** | **Age** | **IP** | **W** | **Sv** | **K** | **ERA** | **WHIP** | **K/9** | **BB/9** | **$2L** | **Pts** |
| Weinhardt R | 25 | 40 | 2 | 0 | 40 | 5.52 | 1.75 | 9.1 | 3.8 | -$4 | 40 |
| Duke Z | 27 | 160 | 8 | 0 | 79 | 5.01 | 1.43 | 4.5 | 2.4 | -$4 | 120 |
| Herndon D | 25 | 40 | 1 | 0 | 28 | 4.95 | 1.53 | 6.2 | 2.5 | -$4 | 30 |
| Hardy B | 25 | 40 | 1 | 0 | 21 | 5.36 | 1.59 | 4.8 | 3.7 | -$4 | 20 |
| Stammen C | 27 | 60 | 2 | 0 | 39 | 5.14 | 1.47 | 5.8 | 2.8 | -$4 | 40 |

**Minors (2010)** / **Skills**

| Level | Leag | W | L | Sv | IP | H | K | ERA | WHIP | K/9 | BB/9 | HR/9 | GB/F |
|---|---|---|---|---|---|---|---|---|---|---|---|---|---|
| A | — | — | — | — | — | — | — | — | — | — | — | — | — |
| AA | EL | 0 | 0 | 0 | 2 | 1 | 3 | 0.00 | 0.50 | 13.5 | 0.0 | 0.0 | — |
| AAA | — | — | — | — | — | — | — | — | — | — | — | — | — |

**Competition at RP** — Stats in 2010 as RP

| Thr | Player | GR | ERA | IP/G | Sv-Hld |
|---|---|---|---|---|---|
| RH | Albers M | 62 | 4.52 | 1.2 | 0-7 |
| RH | Simon A | 49 | 4.93 | 1.0 | 17-1 |
| RH | Uehara K | 43 | 2.86 | 1.0 | 13-6 |
| RH | Berken J | 41 | 3.03 | 1.5 | 0-7 |

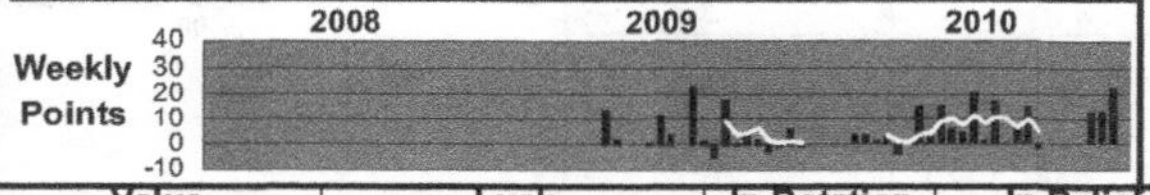
Weekly Points
2008
2009
2010
40
30
20
10
0
-10

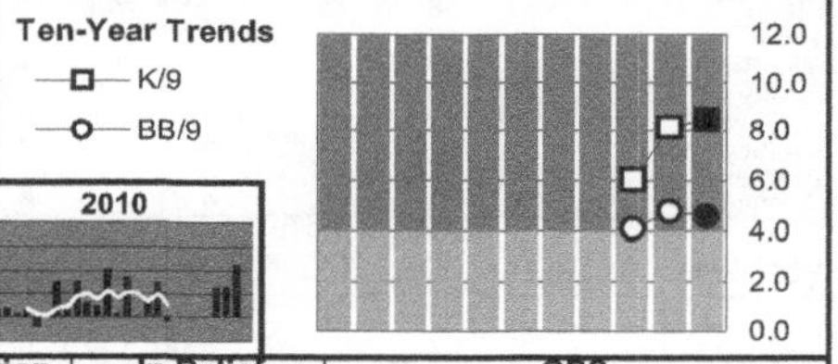
Ten-Year Trends
K/9
BB/9
12.0
10.0
8.0
6.0
4.0
2.0
0.0

**Majors** / **Skills**

| Yr | Team | W | L | Sv | IP | H | K | ERA | WHIP | K/9 | BB/9 | HR/9 | GB/F |
|---|---|---|---|---|---|---|---|---|---|---|---|---|---|
| 07 | — | — | — | — | — | — | — | — | — | — | — | — | — |
| 08 | — | — | — | — | — | — | — | — | — | — | — | — | — |
| 09 | BAL | 4 | 10 | 0 | 101 | 118 | 68 | 5.42 | 1.62 | 6.0 | 4.1 | 2.4 | 0.5 |
| 10 | BAL | 8 | 8 | 2 | 79 | 72 | 72 | 4.31 | 1.44 | 8.2 | 4.8 | 1.0 | 0.5 |

| Yr | Value $1L | $2L | Pts | RAA | Luck H% | HR/fb | S% | FIP | In Rotation GS | CG | QS/DS | In Relief GR | Hld | Bln | Lead | OPS | 1st Hf | 2nd Hf | vs RH | vs LH |
|---|---|---|---|---|---|---|---|---|---|---|---|---|---|---|---|---|---|---|---|---|
| 07 | — | — | — | — | — | — | — | — | — | — | — | — | — | — | — | — | — | — | — | — |
| 08 | — | — | — | — | — | — | — | — | — | — | — | — | — | — | — | — | — | — | — | — |
| 09 | -$3 | -$9 | 70 | −16 | 29% | 15% | 75% | 6.78 | 19 | 0 | 8/4 | 1 | 0 | 0 | −0.2 | .912 | .798 | .965 | .913 | .912 |
| 10 | $2 | -$9 | 150 | −4 | 29% | 8% | 72% | 4.55 | 8 | 0 | 2/1 | 33 | 2 | 4 | −0.7 | .733 | .723 | .766 | .726 | .743 |

## Felix Hernandez — 250 IP | $31 | 400 pts

SP-34 — Owned: 100% — RH

Hernandez has officially matured into an ace, and at age 24. His ERA is still a little low given his walk rate, but he has thus far limited the hits that would hurt him. The most astonishing thing is that 34 starts of 2.27-ERA ball netted him only 13 Wins. (GC)

**Forecast**

| Player | Age | IP | W | Sv | K | ERA | WHIP | K/9 | BB/9 | $2L | Pts |
|---|---|---|---|---|---|---|---|---|---|---|---|
| Hernandez F | 24 | 250 | 16 | 0 | 221 | 3.00 | 1.17 | 7.9 | 2.8 | $31 | 400 |
| **Mini-Browser** | **Age** | **IP** | **W** | **Sv** | **K** | **ERA** | **WHIP** | **K/9** | **BB/9** | **$2L** | **Pts** |
| Halladay R | 33 | 240 | 20 | 0 | 189 | 2.96 | 1.06 | 7.1 | 1.2 | $35 | 420 |
| Wainwright A | 29 | 240 | 19 | 0 | 196 | 3.15 | 1.17 | 7.4 | 2.4 | $28 | 400 |
| Sabathia C | 30 | 240 | 20 | 0 | 198 | 3.45 | 1.18 | 7.4 | 2.5 | $27 | 400 |
| Lincecum T | 26 | 220 | 17 | 0 | 232 | 3.19 | 1.22 | 9.5 | 3.1 | $26 | 410 |
| Lee C | 32 | 220 | 14 | 0 | 164 | 3.52 | 1.13 | 6.7 | 1.5 | $23 | 310 |

**Minors (2010)** / **Skills**

| Level | Leag | W | L | Sv | IP | H | K | ERA | WHIP | K/9 | BB/9 | HR/9 | GB/F |
|---|---|---|---|---|---|---|---|---|---|---|---|---|---|
| A | — | — | — | — | — | — | — | — | — | — | — | — | — |
| AA | — | — | — | — | — | — | — | — | — | — | — | — | — |
| AAA | — | — | — | — | — | — | — | — | — | — | — | — | — |

**Competition at SP** — Stats in 2010 as SP

| Thr | Player | GS | ERA | Supp | W-L |
|---|---|---|---|---|---|
| RH | Hernandez F | 34 | 2.27 | 3.1 | 13-12 |
| LH | Vargas J | 31 | 3.78 | 3.1 | 9-12 |
| RH | Fister D | 28 | 4.11 | 3.1 | 6-14 |
| LH | Rowland-Smith R | 20 | 6.93 | 3.0 | 1-10 |

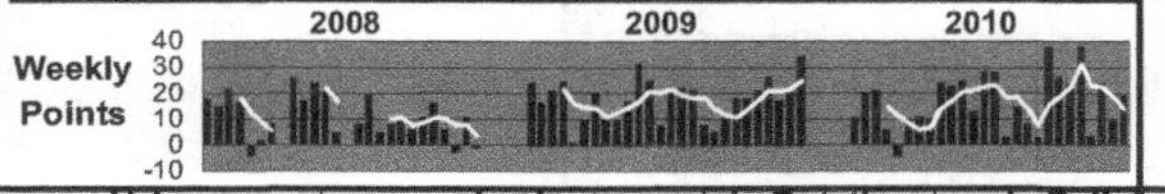
Weekly Points
2008
2009
2010
40
30
20
10
0
-10

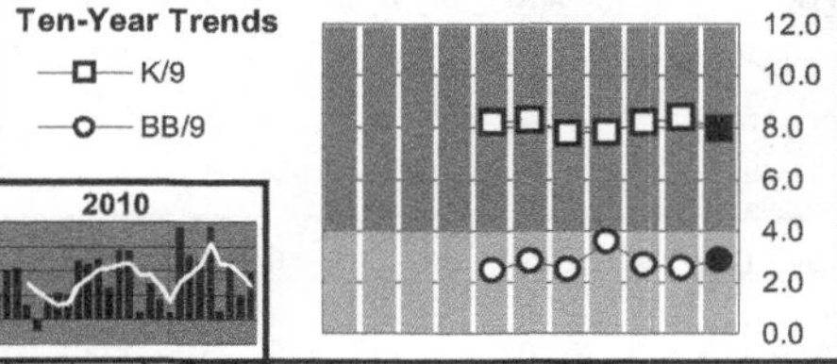
Ten-Year Trends
K/9
BB/9
12.0
10.0
8.0
6.0
4.0
2.0
0.0

**Majors** / **Skills**

| Yr | Team | W | L | Sv | IP | H | K | ERA | WHIP | K/9 | BB/9 | HR/9 | GB/F |
|---|---|---|---|---|---|---|---|---|---|---|---|---|---|
| 07 | SEA | 14 | 7 | 0 | 190 | 209 | 165 | 3.92 | 1.38 | 7.8 | 2.5 | 0.9 | 2.6 |
| 08 | SEA | 9 | 11 | 0 | 200 | 198 | 175 | 3.45 | 1.39 | 7.8 | 3.6 | 0.8 | 1.8 |
| 09 | SEA | 19 | 5 | 0 | 238 | 200 | 217 | 2.49 | 1.14 | 8.2 | 2.7 | 0.6 | 1.8 |
| 10 | SEA | 13 | 12 | 0 | 249 | 194 | 232 | 2.27 | 1.06 | 8.4 | 2.5 | 0.6 | 1.8 |

| Yr | Value $1L | $2L | Pts | RAA | Luck H% | HR/fb | S% | FIP | In Rotation GS | CG | QS/DS | In Relief GR | Hld | Bln | Lead | OPS | 1st Hf | 2nd Hf | vs RH | vs LH |
|---|---|---|---|---|---|---|---|---|---|---|---|---|---|---|---|---|---|---|---|---|
| 07 | $11 | -$2 | 280 | +6 | 34% | 15% | 74% | 3.77 | 30 | 1 | 15/4 | — | — | — | — | .751 | .748 | .752 | .640 | .857 |
| 08 | $10 | $1 | 250 | +14 | 32% | 10% | 77% | 3.85 | 31 | 2 | 19/2 | — | — | — | — | .727 | .665 | .801 | .633 | .798 |
| 09 | $31 | $22 | 440 | +37 | 28% | 8% | 80% | 3.19 | 34 | 2 | 29/3 | — | — | — | — | .605 | .601 | .610 | .582 | .625 |
| 10 | $36 | $36 | 420 | +43 | 27% | 8% | 81% | 3.17 | 34 | 6 | 30/4 | — | — | — | — | .585 | .619 | .542 | .576 | .593 |

## Livan Hernandez — 200 IP | $-4 | 130 pts

SP-33 — Owned: 47% — RH

Hernandez is exceptional, not for his rubber arm, but for his desire to be a Washington National. Despite his success in 2010, the lefty does not want to test the market but would rather return to the Nationals. Like many programs in Washington, expect Hernandez to be funded long past his effectiveness. (PB)

**Forecast**

| Player | Age | IP | W | Sv | K | ERA | WHIP | K/9 | BB/9 | $2L | Pts |
|---|---|---|---|---|---|---|---|---|---|---|---|
| Hernandez L | 36 | 200 | 9 | 0 | 93 | 4.93 | 1.45 | 4.2 | 3.0 | -$4 | 130 |
| **Mini-Browser** | **Age** | **IP** | **W** | **Sv** | **K** | **ERA** | **WHIP** | **K/9** | **BB/9** | **$2L** | **Pts** |
| Proctor S | 34 | 60 | 2 | 0 | 51 | 5.24 | 1.52 | 7.7 | 4.5 | -$4 | 50 |
| Davis D | 35 | 180 | 10 | 0 | 126 | 5.01 | 1.53 | 6.3 | 4.4 | -$4 | 170 |
| Jackson J | 23 | 40 | 2 | 0 | 24 | 5.70 | 1.48 | 5.4 | 3.3 | -$4 | 30 |
| Mathieson S | 27 | 40 | 2 | 0 | 40 | 5.37 | 1.70 | 9.0 | 4.1 | -$4 | 40 |
| Atilano L | 25 | 60 | 3 | 0 | 36 | 5.36 | 1.53 | 5.4 | 3.0 | -$4 | 50 |

**Minors (2010)** / **Skills**

| Level | Leag | W | L | Sv | IP | H | K | ERA | WHIP | K/9 | BB/9 | HR/9 | GB/F |
|---|---|---|---|---|---|---|---|---|---|---|---|---|---|
| A | — | — | — | — | — | — | — | — | — | — | — | — | — |
| AA | — | — | — | — | — | — | — | — | — | — | — | — | — |
| AAA | — | — | — | — | — | — | — | — | — | — | — | — | — |

**Competition at SP** — Stats in 2010 as SP

| Thr | Player | GS | ERA | Supp | W-L |
|---|---|---|---|---|---|
| RH | Hernandez L | 33 | 3.66 | 3.5 | 10-12 |
| LH | Lannan J | 25 | 4.65 | 4.5 | 8-8 |
| RH | Stammen C | 19 | 5.06 | 4.8 | 4-4 |
| RH | Atilano L | 16 | 5.15 | 4.5 | 6-7 |

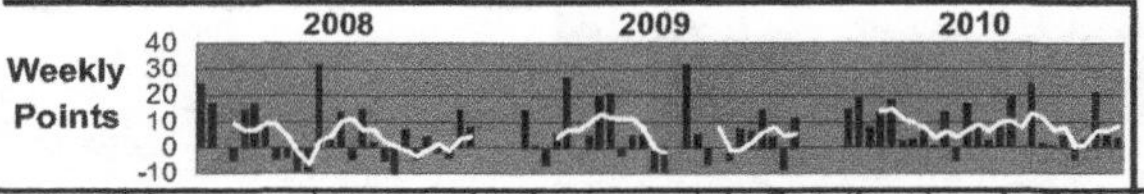
Weekly Points
2008
2009
2010
40
30
20
10
0
-10

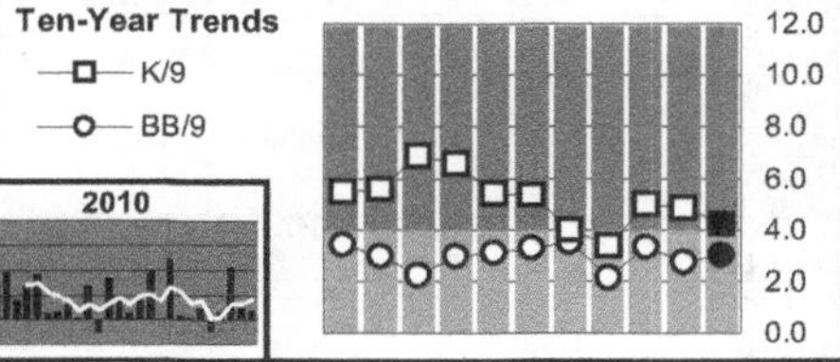
Ten-Year Trends
K/9
BB/9
12.0
10.0
8.0
6.0
4.0
2.0
0.0

**Majors** / **Skills**

| Yr | Team | W | L | Sv | IP | H | K | ERA | WHIP | K/9 | BB/9 | HR/9 | GB/F |
|---|---|---|---|---|---|---|---|---|---|---|---|---|---|
| 07 | ARI | 11 | 11 | 0 | 204 | 247 | 90 | 4.93 | 1.60 | 4.0 | 3.5 | 1.5 | 0.9 |
| 08 | 2TM | 13 | 11 | 0 | 180 | 257 | 67 | 6.05 | 1.67 | 3.4 | 2.2 | 1.3 | 1.3 |
| 09 | 2TM | 9 | 12 | 0 | 183 | 220 | 102 | 5.44 | 1.56 | 5.0 | 3.3 | 0.9 | 1.1 |
| 10 | WAS | 10 | 12 | 0 | 211 | 216 | 114 | 3.66 | 1.32 | 4.8 | 2.7 | 0.7 | 1.0 |

| Yr | Value $1L | $2L | Pts | RAA | Luck H% | HR/fb | S% | FIP | In Rotation GS | CG | QS/DS | In Relief GR | Hld | Bln | Lead | OPS | 1st Hf | 2nd Hf | vs RH | vs LH |
|---|---|---|---|---|---|---|---|---|---|---|---|---|---|---|---|---|---|---|---|---|
| 07 | -$7 | -$25 | 130 | −15 | 32% | 12% | 73% | 5.64 | 33 | 1 | 19/5 | — | — | — | — | .870 | .841 | .907 | .885 | .854 |
| 08 | -$19 | -$28 | 110 | −40 | 35% | 11% | 65% | 5.03 | 31 | 2 | 12/9 | — | — | — | — | .895 | .873 | .938 | .912 | .876 |
| 09 | -$8 | -$13 | 120 | −21 | 34% | 8% | 66% | 4.58 | 31 | 2 | 18/9 | — | — | — | — | .833 | .854 | .808 | .855 | .814 |
| 10 | $6 | -$5 | 200 | +11 | 29% | 6% | 73% | 4.01 | 33 | 2 | 22/4 | — | — | — | — | .716 | .689 | .750 | .640 | .803 |

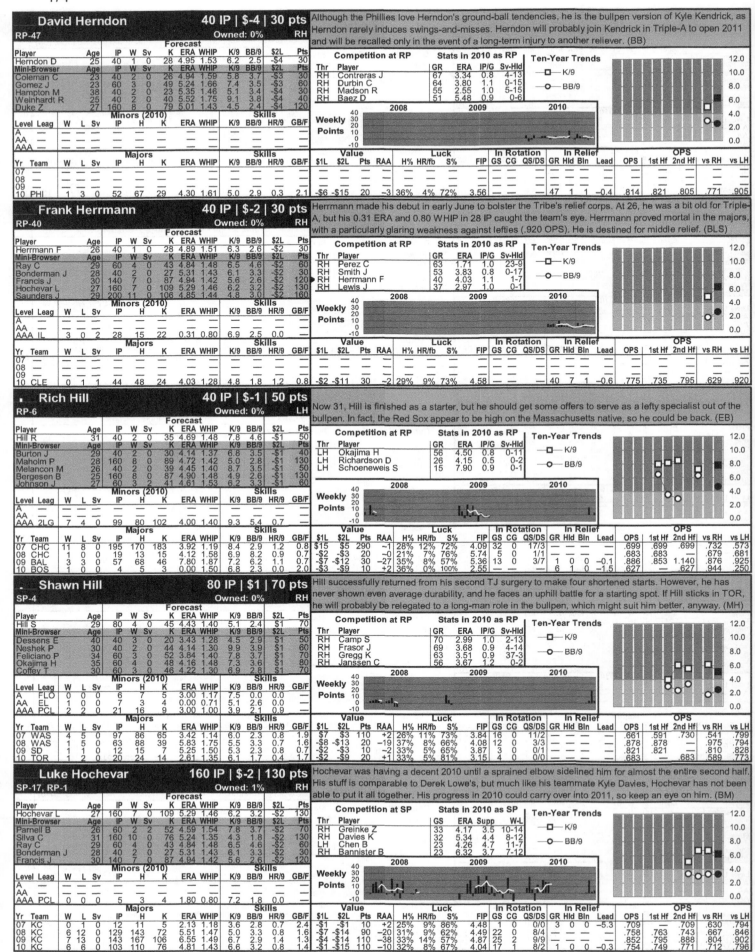

## David Herndon — 40 IP | $-4 | 30 pts

RP-47 — Owned: 0% — RH

Although the Phillies love Herndon's ground-ball tendencies, he is the bullpen version of Kyle Kendrick, as Herndon rarely induces swings-and-misses. Herndon will probably join Kendrick in Triple-A to open 2011 and will be recalled only in the event of a long-term injury to another reliever. (BB)

Forecast

| Player | Age | IP | W | Sv | K | ERA | WHIP | K/9 | BB/9 | $2L | Pts |
|---|---|---|---|---|---|---|---|---|---|---|---|
| Herndon D | 25 | 40 | 1 | 0 | 28 | 4.95 | 1.53 | 6.2 | 2.5 | -$4 | 30 |
| **Mini-Browser** | Age | IP | W | Sv | K | ERA | WHIP | K/9 | BB/9 | $2L | Pts |
| Coleman C | 23 | 40 | 2 | 0 | 26 | 4.94 | 1.59 | 5.8 | 3.7 | -$3 | 30 |
| Gomez J | 23 | 60 | 3 | 0 | 49 | 5.24 | 1.66 | 7.4 | 3.5 | -$3 | 60 |
| Hampton M | 38 | 40 | 2 | 0 | 23 | 5.35 | 1.46 | 5.1 | 3.4 | -$4 | 30 |
| Weinhardt R | 25 | 40 | 2 | 0 | 40 | 5.52 | 1.75 | 9.1 | 3.8 | -$4 | 40 |
| Duke Z | 27 | 160 | 8 | 0 | 79 | 5.01 | 1.43 | 4.5 | 2.4 | -$4 | 120 |

| Competition at RP | | Stats in 2010 as RP | | | |
|---|---|---|---|---|---|
| Thr | Player | GR | ERA | IP/G | Sv-Hld |
| RH | Contreras J | 67 | 3.34 | 0.8 | 4-13 |
| RH | Durbin C | 64 | 3.80 | 1.1 | 0-15 |
| RH | Madson R | 55 | 2.55 | 1.0 | 5-15 |
| RH | Baez D | 51 | 5.48 | 0.9 | 0-6 |

Ten-Year Trends
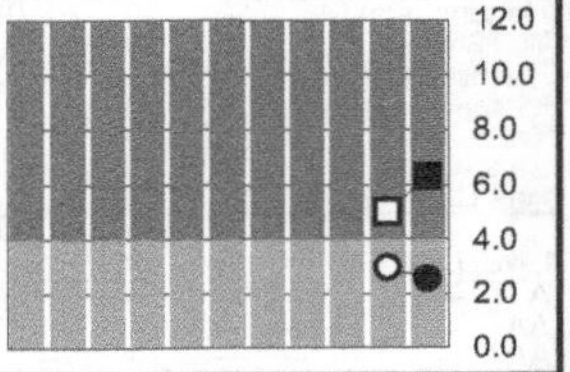


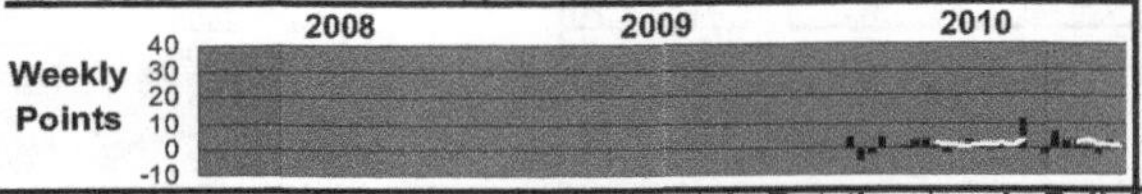


Minors (2010)

| Level | Leag | W | L | Sv | IP | H | K | ERA | WHIP | K/9 | BB/9 | HR/9 | GB/F |
|---|---|---|---|---|---|---|---|---|---|---|---|---|---|
| A | — | — | — | — | — | — | — | — | — | — | — | — | — |
| AA | — | — | — | — | — | — | — | — | — | — | — | — | — |
| AAA | — | — | — | — | — | — | — | — | — | — | — | — | — |

Majors

| Yr | Team | W | L | Sv | IP | H | K | ERA | WHIP | K/9 | BB/9 | HR/9 | GB/F | $1L | $2L | Pts | RAA | H% | HR/fb | S% | FIP | GS | CG | QS/DS | GR | Hld | Bln | Lead | OPS | 1st Hf | 2nd Hf | vs RH | vs LH |
|---|---|---|---|---|---|---|---|---|---|---|---|---|---|---|---|---|---|---|---|---|---|---|---|---|---|---|---|---|---|---|---|---|---|
| 07 | — | — | — | — | — | — | — | — | — | — | — | — | — | — | — | — | — | — | — | — | — | — | — | — | — | — | — | — | — | — | — | — | — |
| 08 | — | — | — | — | — | — | — | — | — | — | — | — | — | — | — | — | — | — | — | — | — | — | — | — | — | — | — | — | — | — | — | — | — |
| 09 | — | — | — | — | — | — | — | — | — | — | — | — | — | — | — | — | — | — | — | — | — | — | — | — | — | — | — | — | — | — | — | — | — |
| 10 | PHI | 1 | 3 | 0 | 52 | 67 | 29 | 4.30 | 1.61 | 5.0 | 2.9 | 0.3 | 2.1 | -$6 | -$15 | 20 | -3 | 36% | 4% | 72% | 3.56 | — | — | — | 47 | 1 | 1 | -0.4 | .814 | .821 | .805 | .771 | .905 |

## Frank Herrmann — 40 IP | $-2 | 30 pts

RP-40 — Owned: 0% — RH

Herrmann made his debut in early June to bolster the Tribe's relief corps. At 26, he was a bit old for Triple-A, but his 0.31 ERA and 0.80 WHIP in 28 IP caught the team's eye. Herrmann proved mortal in the majors, with a particularly glaring weakness against lefties (.920 OPS). He is destined for middle relief. (BLS)

Forecast

| Player | Age | IP | W | Sv | K | ERA | WHIP | K/9 | BB/9 | $2L | Pts |
|---|---|---|---|---|---|---|---|---|---|---|---|
| Herrmann F | 26 | 40 | 1 | 0 | 28 | 4.89 | 1.51 | 6.3 | 2.6 | -$2 | 30 |
| **Mini-Browser** | Age | IP | W | Sv | K | ERA | WHIP | K/9 | BB/9 | $2L | Pts |
| Ray C | 29 | 60 | 4 | 0 | 43 | 4.84 | 1.48 | 6.5 | 4.6 | -$2 | 60 |
| Bonderman J | 28 | 40 | 2 | 0 | 27 | 5.31 | 1.43 | 6.1 | 3.3 | -$2 | 30 |
| Francis J | 30 | 140 | 7 | 0 | 87 | 4.94 | 1.42 | 5.6 | 2.6 | -$2 | 120 |
| Hochevar L | 27 | 160 | 7 | 0 | 109 | 5.29 | 1.46 | 6.2 | 3.2 | -$2 | 130 |
| Saunders J | 29 | 200 | 11 | 0 | 106 | 4.85 | 1.44 | 4.8 | 3.0 | -$2 | 160 |

| Competition at RP | | Stats in 2010 as RP | | | |
|---|---|---|---|---|---|
| Thr | Player | GR | ERA | IP/G | Sv-Hld |
| RH | Perez C | 63 | 1.71 | 1.0 | 23-9 |
| RH | Smith J | 53 | 3.83 | 0.8 | 0-17 |
| RH | Herrmann F | 40 | 4.03 | 1.1 | 1-7 |
| RH | Lewis J | 37 | 2.97 | 1.0 | 0-1 |

Ten-Year Trends
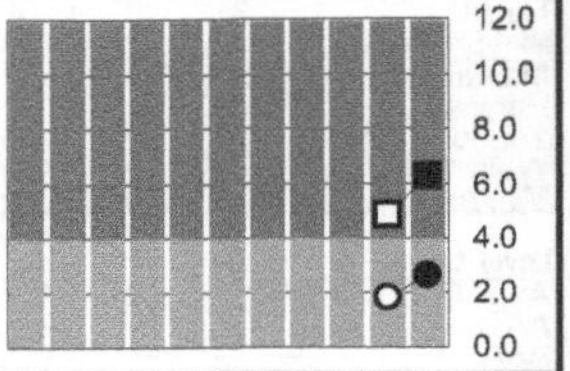


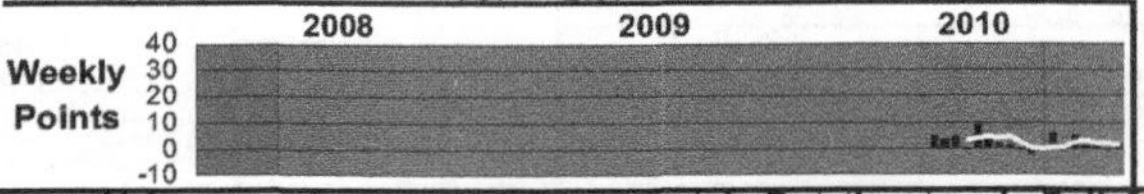


Minors (2010)

| Level | Leag | W | L | Sv | IP | H | K | ERA | WHIP | K/9 | BB/9 | HR/9 | GB/F |
|---|---|---|---|---|---|---|---|---|---|---|---|---|---|
| A | — | — | — | — | — | — | — | — | — | — | — | — | — |
| AA | — | — | — | — | — | — | — | — | — | — | — | — | — |
| AAA | IL | 3 | 0 | 2 | 28 | 15 | 22 | 0.31 | 0.80 | 6.9 | 2.5 | 0.0 | — |

Majors

| Yr | Team | W | L | Sv | IP | H | K | ERA | WHIP | K/9 | BB/9 | HR/9 | GB/F | $1L | $2L | Pts | RAA | H% | HR/fb | S% | FIP | GS | CG | QS/DS | GR | Hld | Bln | Lead | OPS | 1st Hf | 2nd Hf | vs RH | vs LH |
|---|---|---|---|---|---|---|---|---|---|---|---|---|---|---|---|---|---|---|---|---|---|---|---|---|---|---|---|---|---|---|---|---|---|
| 07 | — | — | — | — | — | — | — | — | — | — | — | — | — | — | — | — | — | — | — | — | — | — | — | — | — | — | — | — | — | — | — | — | — |
| 08 | — | — | — | — | — | — | — | — | — | — | — | — | — | — | — | — | — | — | — | — | — | — | — | — | — | — | — | — | — | — | — | — | — |
| 09 | — | — | — | — | — | — | — | — | — | — | — | — | — | — | — | — | — | — | — | — | — | — | — | — | — | — | — | — | — | — | — | — | — |
| 10 | CLE | 0 | 1 | 1 | 44 | 48 | 24 | 4.03 | 1.28 | 4.8 | 1.8 | 1.2 | 0.8 | -$2 | -$11 | 30 | -2 | 29% | 9% | 73% | 4.58 | — | — | — | 40 | 7 | 1 | -0.6 | .775 | .735 | .795 | .629 | .920 |

## Rich Hill — 40 IP | $-1 | 50 pts

RP-6 — Owned: 0% — LH

Now 31, Hill is finished as a starter, but he should get some offers to serve as a lefty specialist out of the bullpen. In fact, the Red Sox appear to be high on the Massachusetts native, so he could be back. (EB)

Forecast

| Player | Age | IP | W | Sv | K | ERA | WHIP | K/9 | BB/9 | $2L | Pts |
|---|---|---|---|---|---|---|---|---|---|---|---|
| Hill R | 31 | 40 | 2 | 0 | 35 | 4.69 | 1.48 | 7.8 | 4.6 | -$1 | 50 |
| **Mini-Browser** | Age | IP | W | Sv | K | ERA | WHIP | K/9 | BB/9 | $2L | Pts |
| Burton J | 29 | 40 | 2 | 0 | 30 | 4.14 | 1.37 | 6.8 | 3.5 | -$1 | 40 |
| Maholm P | 28 | 160 | 8 | 0 | 89 | 4.72 | 1.42 | 5.0 | 2.8 | -$1 | 130 |
| Melancon M | 26 | 40 | 2 | 0 | 39 | 4.45 | 1.40 | 8.7 | 3.5 | -$1 | 50 |
| Bergesen B | 25 | 160 | 8 | 0 | 87 | 4.90 | 1.48 | 4.9 | 2.6 | -$1 | 130 |
| Johnson J | 27 | 60 | 3 | 2 | 41 | 4.61 | 1.53 | 6.2 | 3.3 | -$1 | 60 |

| Competition at RP | | Stats in 2010 as RP | | | |
|---|---|---|---|---|---|
| Thr | Player | GR | ERA | IP/G | Sv-Hld |
| LH | Okajima H | 56 | 4.50 | 0.8 | 0-11 |
| LH | Richardson D | 26 | 4.15 | 0.5 | 0-2 |
| LH | Schoeneweis S | 15 | 7.90 | 0.9 | 0-1 |

Ten-Year Trends
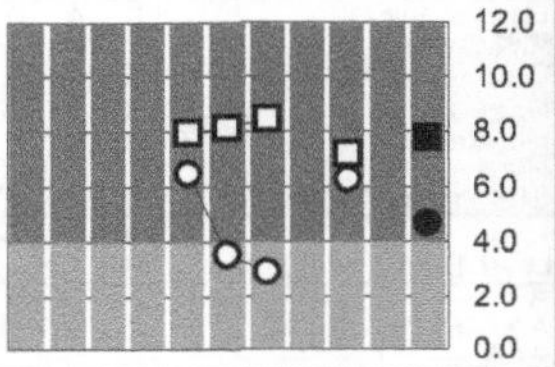


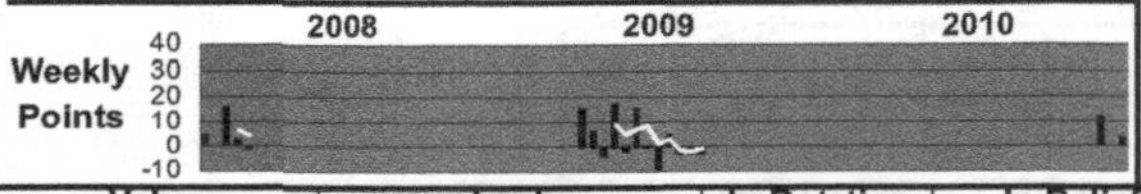


Minors (2010)

| Level | Leag | W | L | Sv | IP | H | K | ERA | WHIP | K/9 | BB/9 | HR/9 | GB/F |
|---|---|---|---|---|---|---|---|---|---|---|---|---|---|
| A | — | — | — | — | — | — | — | — | — | — | — | — | — |
| AA | — | — | — | — | — | — | — | — | — | — | — | — | — |
| AAA | 2LG | 7 | 4 | 0 | 99 | 80 | 102 | 4.00 | 1.40 | 9.3 | 5.4 | 0.7 | — |

Majors

| Yr | Team | W | L | Sv | IP | H | K | ERA | WHIP | K/9 | BB/9 | HR/9 | GB/F | $1L | $2L | Pts | RAA | H% | HR/fb | S% | FIP | GS | CG | QS/DS | GR | Hld | Bln | Lead | OPS | 1st Hf | 2nd Hf | vs RH | vs LH |
|---|---|---|---|---|---|---|---|---|---|---|---|---|---|---|---|---|---|---|---|---|---|---|---|---|---|---|---|---|---|---|---|---|---|
| 07 | CHC | 11 | 8 | 0 | 195 | 170 | 183 | 3.92 | 1.19 | 8.4 | 2.9 | 1.2 | 0.8 | $15 | $5 | 290 | -1 | 28% | 12% | 72% | 4.09 | 32 | 0 | 17/3 | — | — | — | — | .699 | .699 | .699 | .732 | .573 |
| 08 | CHC | 1 | 0 | 0 | 19 | 13 | 15 | 4.12 | 1.58 | 6.9 | 8.2 | 0.9 | 0.7 | -$2 | -$3 | 20 | -0 | 21% | 7% | 76% | 5.74 | 5 | 0 | 1/1 | — | — | — | — | .683 | .683 | — | .679 | .681 |
| 09 | BAL | 3 | 3 | 0 | 57 | 68 | 46 | 7.80 | 1.87 | 7.2 | 6.2 | 1.1 | 0.7 | -$7 | -$12 | 30 | -27 | 35% | 8% | 57% | 5.36 | 13 | 0 | 3/7 | 1 | 0 | 0 | -0.1 | .886 | .853 | 1.140 | .876 | .925 |
| 10 | BOS | 1 | 0 | 0 | 4 | 5 | 3 | 0.00 | 1.50 | 6.8 | 2.3 | 0.0 | 2.0 | -$3 | -$9 | 10 | +2 | 36% | 0% | 100% | 2.55 | — | — | — | 6 | 1 | 0 | -1.5 | .627 | — | .627 | .944 | .250 |

## Shawn Hill — 80 IP | $1 | 70 pts

SP-4 — Owned: 0% — RH

Hill successfully returned from his second TJ surgery to make four shortened starts. However, he has never shown even average durability, and he faces an uphill battle for a starting spot. If Hill sticks in TOR, he will probably be relegated to a long-man role in the bullpen, which might suit him better, anyway. (MH)

Forecast

| Player | Age | IP | W | Sv | K | ERA | WHIP | K/9 | BB/9 | $2L | Pts |
|---|---|---|---|---|---|---|---|---|---|---|---|
| Hill S | 29 | 80 | 4 | 0 | 45 | 4.43 | 1.40 | 5.1 | 2.4 | $1 | 70 |
| **Mini-Browser** | Age | IP | W | Sv | K | ERA | WHIP | K/9 | BB/9 | $2L | Pts |
| Dessens E | 40 | 40 | 3 | 0 | 20 | 3.43 | 1.28 | 4.5 | 2.9 | $1 | 50 |
| Neshek P | 30 | 40 | 2 | 0 | 44 | 4.14 | 1.30 | 9.9 | 3.9 | $1 | 60 |
| Feliciano P | 34 | 60 | 3 | 0 | 52 | 3.84 | 1.40 | 7.8 | 3.7 | $1 | 70 |
| Okajima H | 35 | 60 | 4 | 0 | 48 | 4.16 | 1.48 | 7.3 | 3.6 | $1 | 80 |
| Coffey T | 30 | 60 | 3 | 0 | 46 | 4.22 | 1.30 | 6.9 | 2.8 | $1 | 70 |

| Competition at RP | | Stats in 2010 as RP | | | |
|---|---|---|---|---|---|
| Thr | Player | GR | ERA | IP/G | Sv-Hld |
| RH | Camp S | 70 | 2.99 | 1.0 | 2-13 |
| RH | Frasor J | 69 | 3.68 | 0.9 | 4-14 |
| RH | Gregg K | 63 | 3.51 | 0.9 | 37-3 |
| RH | Janssen C | 56 | 3.67 | 1.2 | 0-2 |

Ten-Year Trends
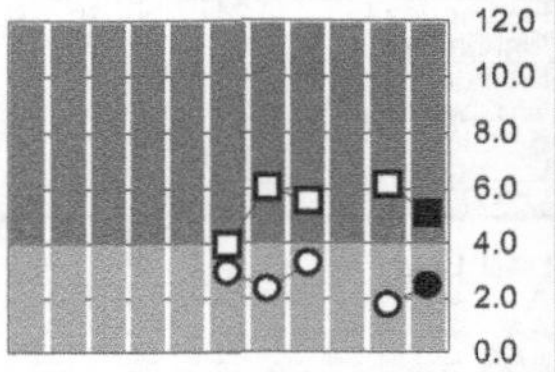


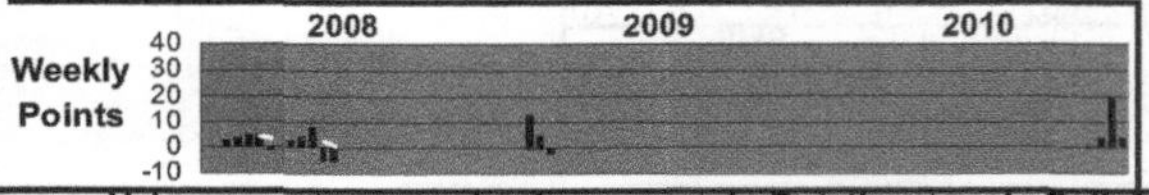


Minors (2010)

| Level | Leag | W | L | Sv | IP | H | K | ERA | WHIP | K/9 | BB/9 | HR/9 | GB/F |
|---|---|---|---|---|---|---|---|---|---|---|---|---|---|
| A | FLO | 0 | 0 | 0 | 6 | 7 | 5 | 3.00 | 1.17 | 7.5 | 0.0 | 0.0 | — |
| AA | EL | 1 | 0 | 0 | 7 | 3 | 4 | 0.00 | 0.71 | 5.1 | 2.6 | 0.0 | — |
| AAA | PCL | 2 | 2 | 0 | 21 | 16 | 9 | 3.00 | 1.00 | 3.9 | 2.1 | 0.9 | — |

Majors

| Yr | Team | W | L | Sv | IP | H | K | ERA | WHIP | K/9 | BB/9 | HR/9 | GB/F | $1L | $2L | Pts | RAA | H% | HR/fb | S% | FIP | GS | CG | QS/DS | GR | Hld | Bln | Lead | OPS | 1st Hf | 2nd Hf | vs RH | vs LH |
|---|---|---|---|---|---|---|---|---|---|---|---|---|---|---|---|---|---|---|---|---|---|---|---|---|---|---|---|---|---|---|---|---|---|
| 07 | WAS | 4 | 5 | 0 | 97 | 86 | 65 | 3.42 | 1.14 | 6.0 | 2.3 | 0.8 | 1.9 | $7 | $3 | 110 | +2 | 26% | 11% | 73% | 3.84 | 16 | 0 | 11/2 | — | — | — | — | .661 | .591 | .730 | .541 | .799 |
| 08 | WAS | 1 | 5 | 0 | 63 | 88 | 39 | 5.83 | 1.75 | 5.5 | 3.3 | 0.7 | 1.6 | -$8 | -$13 | 20 | -19 | 37% | 8% | 66% | 4.08 | 12 | 0 | 3/3 | — | — | — | — | .878 | .878 | — | .975 | .794 |
| 09 | SD | 1 | 1 | 0 | 12 | 15 | 7 | 5.25 | 1.50 | 5.3 | 2.3 | 0.8 | 0.7 | -$2 | -$3 | 10 | -2 | 33% | 5% | 65% | 3.87 | 3 | 0 | 0/1 | — | — | — | — | .821 | .821 | — | .810 | .828 |
| 10 | TOR | 1 | 2 | 0 | 20 | 24 | 14 | 2.61 | 1.35 | 6.1 | 1.7 | 0.4 | 1.7 | -$2 | -$9 | 20 | +1 | 33% | 5% | 81% | 3.15 | 4 | 0 | 0/0 | — | — | — | — | .683 | — | .683 | .589 | .773 |

## Luke Hochevar — 160 IP | $-2 | 130 pts

SP-17, RP-1 — Owned: 1% — RH

Hochevar was having a decent 2010 until a sprained elbow sidelined him for almost the entire second half. His stuff is comparable to Derek Lowe's, but much like his teammate Kyle Davies, Hochevar has not been able to put it all together. His progress in 2010 could carry over into 2011, so keep an eye on him. (BM)

Forecast

| Player | Age | IP | W | Sv | K | ERA | WHIP | K/9 | BB/9 | $2L | Pts |
|---|---|---|---|---|---|---|---|---|---|---|---|
| Hochevar L | 27 | 160 | 7 | 0 | 109 | 5.29 | 1.46 | 6.2 | 3.2 | -$2 | 130 |
| **Mini-Browser** | Age | IP | W | Sv | K | ERA | WHIP | K/9 | BB/9 | $2L | Pts |
| Parnell B | 26 | 60 | 2 | 2 | 52 | 4.59 | 1.54 | 7.8 | 3.7 | -$2 | 70 |
| Silva C | 31 | 160 | 10 | 0 | 76 | 5.24 | 1.35 | 4.3 | 1.8 | -$2 | 130 |
| Ray C | 29 | 60 | 4 | 0 | 43 | 4.84 | 1.48 | 6.5 | 4.6 | -$2 | 60 |
| Bonderman J | 28 | 40 | 2 | 0 | 27 | 5.31 | 1.43 | 6.1 | 3.3 | -$2 | 30 |
| Francis J | 30 | 140 | 7 | 0 | 87 | 4.94 | 1.42 | 5.6 | 2.6 | -$2 | 120 |

| Competition at SP | | Stats in 2010 as SP | | | |
|---|---|---|---|---|---|
| Thr | Player | GS | ERA | Supp | W-L |
| RH | Greinke Z | 33 | 4.17 | 3.5 | 10-14 |
| RH | Davies K | 32 | 5.34 | 4.4 | 8-12 |
| LH | Chen B | 23 | 4.26 | 4.7 | 11-7 |
| RH | Bannister B | 23 | 6.32 | 3.7 | 7-12 |

Ten-Year Trends
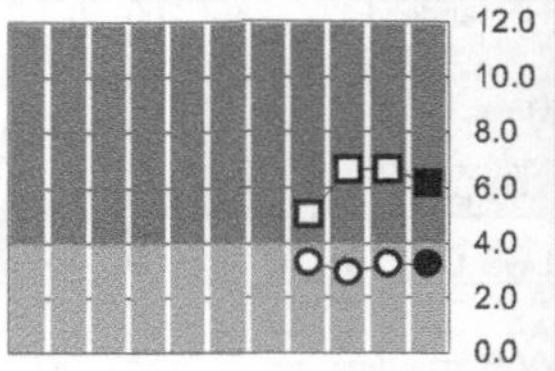


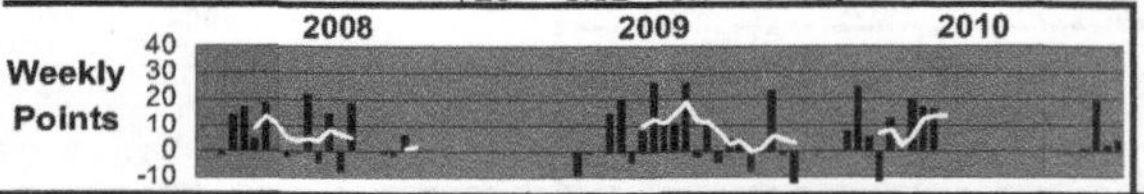


Minors (2010)

| Level | Leag | W | L | Sv | IP | H | K | ERA | WHIP | K/9 | BB/9 | HR/9 | GB/F |
|---|---|---|---|---|---|---|---|---|---|---|---|---|---|
| A | — | — | — | — | — | — | — | — | — | — | — | — | — |
| AA | — | — | — | — | — | — | — | — | — | — | — | — | — |
| AAA | PCL | 0 | 0 | 0 | 5 | 3 | 4 | 1.80 | 0.80 | 7.2 | 1.8 | 0.0 | — |

Majors

| Yr | Team | W | L | Sv | IP | H | K | ERA | WHIP | K/9 | BB/9 | HR/9 | GB/F | $1L | $2L | Pts | RAA | H% | HR/fb | S% | FIP | GS | CG | QS/DS | GR | Hld | Bln | Lead | OPS | 1st Hf | 2nd Hf | vs RH | vs LH |
|---|---|---|---|---|---|---|---|---|---|---|---|---|---|---|---|---|---|---|---|---|---|---|---|---|---|---|---|---|---|---|---|---|---|
| 07 | KC | 0 | 1 | 0 | 12 | 11 | 5 | 2.13 | 1.18 | 3.6 | 2.8 | 0.7 | 2.4 | -$1 | -$1 | 10 | +2 | 25% | 9% | 86% | 4.48 | 1 | 0 | 0/0 | 3 | 0 | 0 | -5.3 | .709 | — | .709 | .630 | .794 |
| 08 | KC | 6 | 12 | 0 | 129 | 143 | 72 | 5.51 | 1.47 | 5.0 | 3.3 | 0.8 | 1.6 | -$7 | -$14 | 90 | -20 | 31% | 9% | 62% | 4.49 | 22 | 0 | 8/4 | — | — | — | — | .758 | .763 | .743 | .667 | .846 |
| 09 | KC | 7 | 13 | 0 | 143 | 167 | 106 | 6.55 | 1.49 | 6.7 | 2.9 | 1.4 | 1.3 | -$4 | -$14 | 110 | -38 | 33% | 14% | 57% | 4.87 | 25 | 2 | 9/9 | — | — | — | — | .852 | .795 | .888 | .804 | .902 |
| 10 | KC | 6 | 6 | 0 | 103 | 110 | 76 | 4.81 | 1.43 | 6.6 | 3.2 | 0.8 | 1.4 | -$1 | -$15 | 110 | -10 | 32% | 8% | 67% | 4.04 | 17 | 1 | 8/2 | 1 | 0 | 0 | -0.3 | .754 | .749 | .771 | .712 | .796 |

## Trevor Hoffman — 40 IP | $0 | 60 pts

RP-50 — Owned: 48% — RH

Hoffman will not return to the Brewers, who declined to make him their primary closer. That role is what it will take to lure Hoffman to another club, since he is not willing to accept the kind of half-year deal that his slow starts merit. A few teams might give him a shot, but retirement is more likely. (MS)

| Player | Age | IP | W | Sv | K | ERA | WHIP | K/9 | BB/9 | $2L | Pts |
|---|---|---|---|---|---|---|---|---|---|---|---|
| **Forecast** | | | | | | | | | | | |
| Hoffman T | 43 | 40 | 2 | 4 | 30 | 4.46 | 1.30 | 6.8 | 2.9 | $0 | 60 |
| **Mini-Browser** | **Age** | **IP** | **W** | **Sv** | **K** | **ERA** | **WHIP** | **K/9** | **BB/9** | **$2L** | **Pts** |
| Harang A | 32 | 100 | 5 | 0 | 74 | 4.76 | 1.33 | 6.7 | 2.4 | $0 | 110 |
| Peavy J | 29 | 40 | 3 | 0 | 34 | 4.40 | 1.28 | 7.6 | 3.1 | $0 | 50 |
| Harden R | 29 | 100 | 6 | 0 | 99 | 4.87 | 1.50 | 8.9 | 5.0 | $0 | 130 |
| Rauch J | 32 | 40 | 2 | 0 | 30 | 4.01 | 1.31 | 6.7 | 2.6 | $0 | 50 |
| Bray B | 27 | 40 | 2 | 0 | 41 | 4.01 | 1.25 | 9.1 | 3.5 | $0 | 50 |

| Level | Leag | W | L | Sv | IP | H | K | ERA | WHIP | K/9 | BB/9 | HR/9 | GB/F |
|---|---|---|---|---|---|---|---|---|---|---|---|---|---|
| | | **Minors (2010)** | | | | | | | | **Skills** | | | |
| A | — | — | — | — | — | — | — | — | — | — | — | — | — |
| AA | — | — | — | — | — | — | — | — | — | — | — | — | — |
| AAA | — | — | — | — | — | — | — | — | — | — | — | — | — |

**Competition at RP** / **Stats in 2010 as RP**

| Thr | Player | GR | ERA | IP/G | Sv-Hld |
|---|---|---|---|---|---|
| RH | Coffey T | 69 | 4.76 | 0.9 | 0-13 |
| RH | Loe K | 53 | 2.78 | 1.1 | 0-22 |
| RH | Axford J | 50 | 2.48 | 1.2 | 24-3 |
| RH | Villanueva C | 50 | 4.61 | 1.1 | 1-14 |

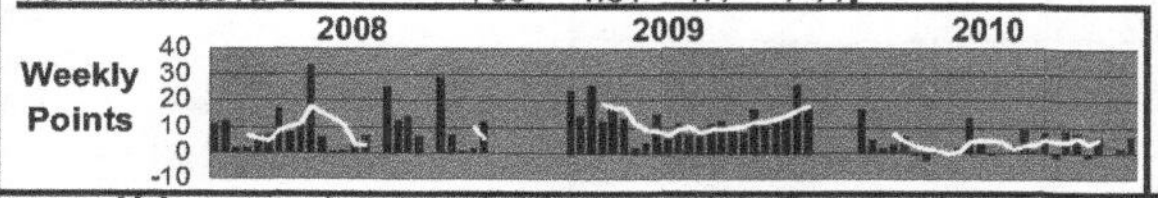


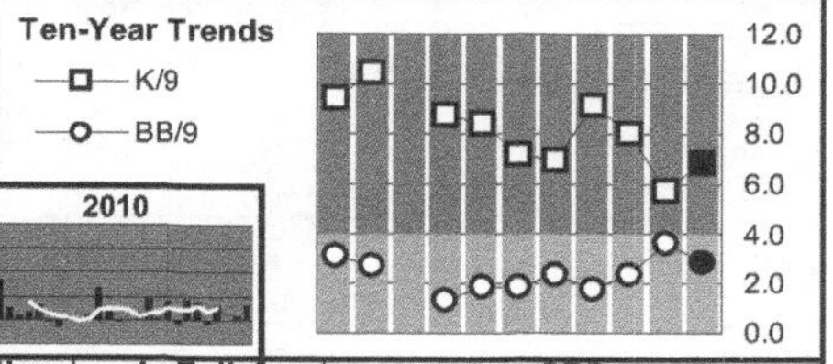


| Yr | Team | W | L | Sv | IP | H | K | ERA | WHIP | K/9 | BB/9 | HR/9 | GB/F |
|---|---|---|---|---|---|---|---|---|---|---|---|---|---|
| | | **Majors** | | | | | | | | **Skills** | | | |
| 07 | SD | 4 | 5 | 42 | 57 | 49 | 44 | 2.98 | 1.12 | 6.9 | 2.4 | 0.3 | 0.6 |
| 08 | SD | 3 | 6 | 30 | 45 | 38 | 46 | 3.77 | 1.04 | 9.1 | 1.8 | 1.6 | 0.8 |
| 09 | MIL | 3 | 2 | 37 | 54 | 35 | 48 | 1.83 | 0.91 | 8.0 | 2.3 | 0.3 | 0.8 |
| 10 | MIL | 2 | 7 | 10 | 47 | 49 | 30 | 5.89 | 1.44 | 5.7 | 3.6 | 1.5 | 0.6 |

| Yr | $1L | $2L | Pts | RAA | H% | HR/fb | S% | FIP | GS | CG | QS/DS |
|---|---|---|---|---|---|---|---|---|---|---|---|
| | **Value** | | | | **Luck** | | | | **In Rotation** | | |
| 07 | $14 | $12 | 300 | +5 | 28% | 2% | 73% | 2.90 | — | — | — |
| 08 | $11 | $7 | 230 | +1 | 26% | 14% | 72% | 4.06 | — | — | — |
| 09 | $16 | $12 | 280 | +13 | 24% | 3% | 81% | 2.68 | — | — | — |
| 10 | -$4 | -$14 | 80 | −10 | 28% | 10% | 62% | 5.33 | — | — | — |

| Yr | GR | Hld | Bln | Lead | OPS | 1st Hf | 2nd Hf | vs RH | vs LH |
|---|---|---|---|---|---|---|---|---|---|
| | **In Relief** | | | | **OPS** | | | | |
| 07 | 61 | 0 | 7 | +1.6 | .634 | .477 | .817 | .492 | .799 |
| 08 | 48 | 0 | 4 | +1.4 | .657 | .768 | .447 | .471 | .862 |
| 09 | 55 | 0 | 4 | +1.7 | .481 | .527 | .436 | .413 | .556 |
| 10 | 50 | 2 | 5 | +0.1 | .832 | 1.019 | .544 | .780 | .892 |

## Derek Holland — 140 IP | $-1 | 150 pts

SP-10, RP-4 — Owned: 0% — LH

Holland in 2010 moved forward developmentally, but knee and shoulder injuries precluded a larger step. He still brandishes legit swing-and-miss stuff, but whispers persist about his mental make-up. Even if he doesn't immediately squeak into the 2011 rotation, his day of reckoning is fast approaching. (JM)

| Player | Age | IP | W | Sv | K | ERA | WHIP | K/9 | BB/9 | $2L | Pts |
|---|---|---|---|---|---|---|---|---|---|---|---|
| **Forecast** | | | | | | | | | | | |
| Holland D | 24 | 140 | 7 | 0 | 120 | 5.19 | 1.47 | 7.7 | 3.5 | -$1 | 150 |
| **Mini-Browser** | **Age** | **IP** | **W** | **Sv** | **K** | **ERA** | **WHIP** | **K/9** | **BB/9** | **$2L** | **Pts** |
| Pena T | 29 | 80 | 4 | 0 | 49 | 4.77 | 1.42 | 5.5 | 3.3 | -$1 | 70 |
| Norris B | 26 | 160 | 8 | 0 | 163 | 4.80 | 1.51 | 9.2 | 4.3 | -$1 | 200 |
| Webb R | 25 | 60 | 2 | 0 | 49 | 4.10 | 1.43 | 7.3 | 3.2 | -$1 | 60 |
| Carlson J | 30 | 40 | 1 | 0 | 31 | 4.44 | 1.35 | 6.9 | 3.2 | -$1 | 40 |
| Reynolds M | 26 | 40 | 2 | 0 | 42 | 4.27 | 1.41 | 9.5 | 2.8 | -$1 | 60 |

| Level | Leag | W | L | Sv | IP | H | K | ERA | WHIP | K/9 | BB/9 | HR/9 | GB/F |
|---|---|---|---|---|---|---|---|---|---|---|---|---|---|
| | | **Minors (2010)** | | | | | | | | **Skills** | | | |
| A | — | — | — | — | — | — | — | — | — | — | — | — | — |
| AA | — | — | — | — | — | — | — | — | — | — | — | — | — |
| AAA | PCL | 6 | 2 | 0 | 62 | 50 | 51 | 1.87 | 1.09 | 7.3 | 2.6 | 0.7 | — |

**Competition at SP** / **Stats in 2010 as SP**

| Thr | Player | GS | ERA | Supp | W-L |
|---|---|---|---|---|---|
| LH | Wilson C | 33 | 3.35 | 4.6 | 15-8 |
| RH | Lewis C | 32 | 3.72 | 4.1 | 12-13 |
| LH | Lee C | 28 | 3.18 | 4.3 | 12-9 |
| RH | Hunter T | 22 | 3.75 | 6.0 | 13-4 |

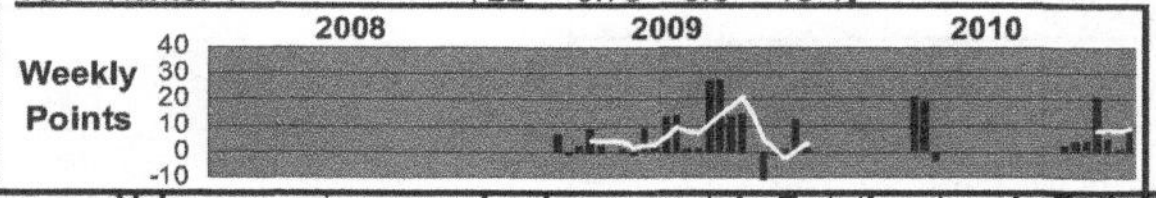


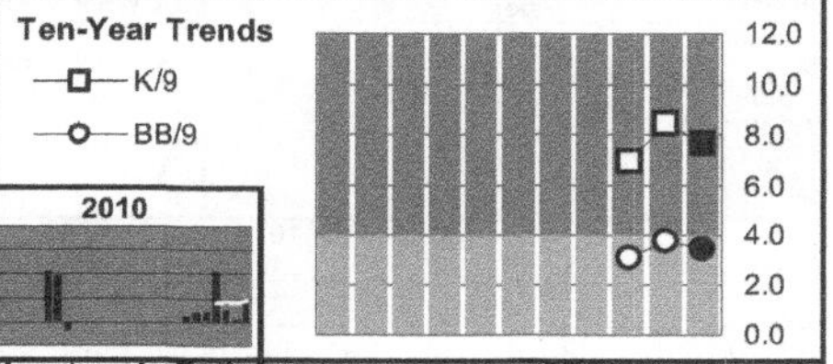


| Yr | Team | W | L | Sv | IP | H | K | ERA | WHIP | K/9 | BB/9 | HR/9 | GB/F |
|---|---|---|---|---|---|---|---|---|---|---|---|---|---|
| | | **Majors** | | | | | | | | **Skills** | | | |
| 07 | — | — | — | — | — | — | — | — | — | — | — | — | — |
| 08 | — | — | — | — | — | — | — | — | — | — | — | — | — |
| 09 | TEX | 8 | 13 | 0 | 138 | 160 | 107 | 6.12 | 1.50 | 7.0 | 3.1 | 1.7 | 1.1 |
| 10 | TEX | 3 | 4 | 0 | 57 | 55 | 54 | 4.08 | 1.38 | 8.5 | 3.8 | 0.9 | 1.0 |

| Yr | $1L | $2L | Pts | RAA | H% | HR/fb | S% | FIP | GS | CG | QS/DS |
|---|---|---|---|---|---|---|---|---|---|---|---|
| | **Value** | | | | **Luck** | | | | **In Rotation** | | |
| 07 | — | — | — | — | — | — | — | — | — | — | — |
| 08 | — | — | — | — | — | — | — | — | — | — | — |
| 09 | -$2 | -$11 | 130 | −30 | 32% | 15% | 62% | 5.22 | 21 | 1 | 4/5 |
| 10 | $0 | -$10 | 80 | −2 | 30% | 8% | 73% | 4.03 | 10 | 0 | 2/3 |

| Yr | GR | Hld | Bln | Lead | OPS | 1st Hf | 2nd Hf | vs RH | vs LH |
|---|---|---|---|---|---|---|---|---|---|
| | **In Relief** | | | | **OPS** | | | | |
| 07 | — | — | — | — | — | — | — | — | — |
| 08 | — | — | — | — | — | — | — | — | — |
| 09 | 12 | 2 | 1 | +0.2 | .856 | .888 | .831 | .870 | .809 |
| 10 | 4 | 1 | 0 | −0.4 | .727 | .782 | .697 | .818 | .362 |

## Daniel Hudson — 180 IP | $16 | 290 pts

SP-14 — Owned: 38% — RH

Low hit and homer rates facilitated Hudson's 1.69 ERA with Arizona, but he also showed excellent control (1.8 BB/9), thereby easing Arizona's loss of Edwin Jackson. In 2011, Hudson would have to pitch his way *out* of the rotation, and he could be part of a triumvirate of young D'back arms for a good long time. (MS)

| Player | Age | IP | W | Sv | K | ERA | WHIP | K/9 | BB/9 | $2L | Pts |
|---|---|---|---|---|---|---|---|---|---|---|---|
| **Forecast** | | | | | | | | | | | |
| Hudson D | 24 | 180 | 13 | 0 | 171 | 3.55 | 1.25 | 8.6 | 3.1 | $16 | 290 |
| **Mini-Browser** | **Age** | **IP** | **W** | **Sv** | **K** | **ERA** | **WHIP** | **K/9** | **BB/9** | **$2L** | **Pts** |
| Haren D | 30 | 200 | 12 | 0 | 173 | 3.92 | 1.21 | 7.8 | 1.9 | $17 | 290 |
| Soria J | 26 | 60 | 2 | 32 | 65 | 2.20 | 1.11 | 9.7 | 2.6 | $17 | 260 |
| Hudson T | 35 | 200 | 14 | 0 | 117 | 3.40 | 1.23 | 5.3 | 2.8 | $17 | 250 |
| Hughes P | 24 | 200 | 17 | 0 | 176 | 4.10 | 1.28 | 7.9 | 3.1 | $16 | 330 |
| Anderson B | 23 | 190 | 12 | 0 | 146 | 3.75 | 1.22 | 6.9 | 2.2 | $16 | 260 |

| Level | Leag | W | L | Sv | IP | H | K | ERA | WHIP | K/9 | BB/9 | HR/9 | GB/F |
|---|---|---|---|---|---|---|---|---|---|---|---|---|---|
| | | **Minors (2010)** | | | | | | | | **Skills** | | | |
| A | — | — | — | — | — | — | — | — | — | — | — | — | — |
| AA | — | — | — | — | — | — | — | — | — | — | — | — | — |
| AAA | IL | 11 | 4 | 0 | 93 | 81 | 108 | 3.47 | 1.20 | 10.4 | 3.0 | 1.3 | — |

**Competition at SP** / **Stats in 2010 as SP**

| Thr | Player | GS | ERA | Supp | W-L |
|---|---|---|---|---|---|
| LH | Saunders J | 33 | 4.47 | 3.9 | 9-17 |
| RH | Lopez R | 33 | 5.00 | 4.4 | 7-16 |
| RH | Kennedy I | 32 | 3.80 | 5.1 | 9-10 |
| RH | Enright B | 17 | 3.91 | 3.4 | 6-7 |

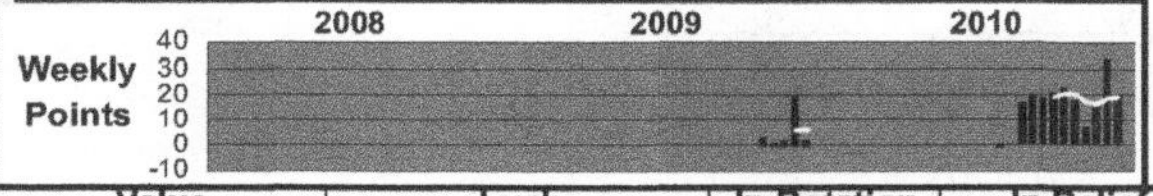


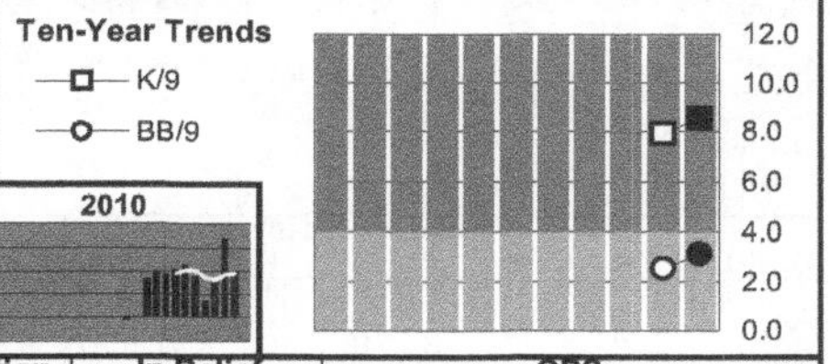


| Yr | Team | W | L | Sv | IP | H | K | ERA | WHIP | K/9 | BB/9 | HR/9 | GB/F |
|---|---|---|---|---|---|---|---|---|---|---|---|---|---|
| | | **Majors** | | | | | | | | **Skills** | | | |
| 07 | — | — | — | — | — | — | — | — | — | — | — | — | — |
| 08 | — | — | — | — | — | — | — | — | — | — | — | — | — |
| 09 | CHW | 1 | 1 | 0 | 18 | 16 | 14 | 3.38 | 1.34 | 6.8 | 4.3 | 1.4 | 0.5 |
| 10 | 2TM | 8 | 2 | 0 | 95 | 68 | 84 | 2.45 | 1.00 | 7.9 | 2.5 | 0.8 | 0.8 |

| Yr | $1L | $2L | Pts | RAA | H% | HR/fb | S% | FIP | GS | CG | QS/DS |
|---|---|---|---|---|---|---|---|---|---|---|---|
| | **Value** | | | | **Luck** | | | | **In Rotation** | | |
| 07 | — | — | — | — | — | — | — | — | — | — | — |
| 08 | — | — | — | — | — | — | — | — | — | — | — |
| 09 | -$1 | -$2 | 20 | +0 | 24% | 9% | 82% | 5.34 | 2 | 0 | 1/0 |
| 10 | $11 | $9 | 190 | +21 | 24% | 7% | 79% | 3.43 | 14 | 0 | 12/1 |

| Yr | GR | Hld | Bln | Lead | OPS | 1st Hf | 2nd Hf | vs RH | vs LH |
|---|---|---|---|---|---|---|---|---|---|
| | **In Relief** | | | | **OPS** | | | | |
| 07 | — | — | — | — | — | — | — | — | — |
| 08 | — | — | — | — | — | — | — | — | — |
| 09 | 4 | 0 | 0 | −1.5 | .711 | — | .711 | .830 | .596 |
| 10 | — | — | — | — | .579 | 1.207 | .548 | .586 | .571 |

## Tim Hudson — 200 IP | $17 | 250 pts

SP-34 — Owned: 100% — RH

Hudson's return from TJ surgery earned him the Comeback Player of the Year in the NL. He re-emerged as the ace of the Braves' staff and was possibly better than before the surgery – he really used his sinker and showed greater pitchability than ever. At 35, though, his arm probably won't be this fresh again. (MG)

| Player | Age | IP | W | Sv | K | ERA | WHIP | K/9 | BB/9 | $2L | Pts |
|---|---|---|---|---|---|---|---|---|---|---|---|
| **Forecast** | | | | | | | | | | | |
| Hudson T | 35 | 200 | 14 | 0 | 117 | 3.40 | 1.23 | 5.3 | 2.8 | $17 | 250 |
| **Mini-Browser** | **Age** | **IP** | **W** | **Sv** | **K** | **ERA** | **WHIP** | **K/9** | **BB/9** | **$2L** | **Pts** |
| Price D | 25 | 200 | 15 | 0 | 177 | 3.63 | 1.32 | 8.0 | 3.7 | $17 | 320 |
| Wilson B | 29 | 60 | 2 | 44 | 65 | 2.92 | 1.28 | 9.8 | 3.5 | $17 | 310 |
| Cain M | 26 | 220 | 13 | 0 | 170 | 3.69 | 1.23 | 7.0 | 2.9 | $17 | 300 |
| Haren D | 30 | 200 | 12 | 0 | 173 | 3.92 | 1.21 | 7.8 | 1.9 | $17 | 290 |
| Soria J | 26 | 60 | 2 | 32 | 65 | 2.20 | 1.11 | 9.7 | 2.6 | $17 | 260 |

| Level | Leag | W | L | Sv | IP | H | K | ERA | WHIP | K/9 | BB/9 | HR/9 | GB/F |
|---|---|---|---|---|---|---|---|---|---|---|---|---|---|
| | | **Minors (2010)** | | | | | | | | **Skills** | | | |
| A | — | — | — | — | — | — | — | — | — | — | — | — | — |
| AA | — | — | — | — | — | — | — | — | — | — | — | — | — |
| AAA | — | — | — | — | — | — | — | — | — | — | — | — | — |

**Competition at SP** / **Stats in 2010 as SP**

| Thr | Player | GS | ERA | Supp | W-L |
|---|---|---|---|---|---|
| RH | Hudson T | 34 | 2.83 | 4.6 | 17-9 |
| RH | Hanson T | 34 | 3.33 | 4.3 | 10-11 |
| RH | Lowe D | 33 | 4.00 | 4.7 | 16-12 |
| RH | Jurrjens J | 20 | 4.64 | 4.3 | 7-6 |

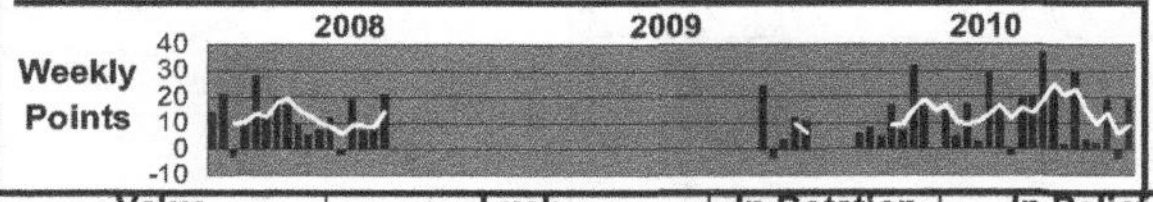


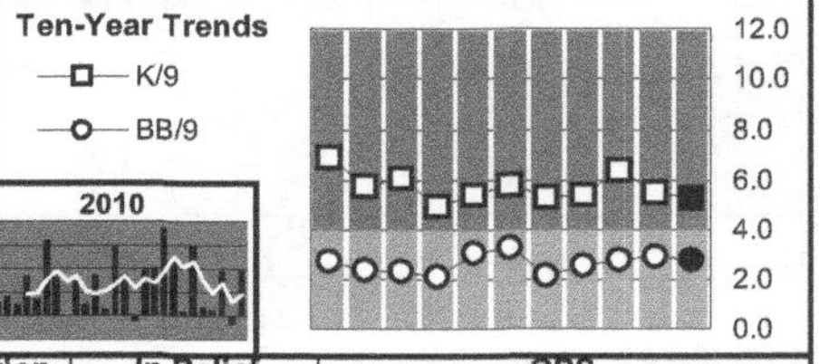


| Yr | Team | W | L | Sv | IP | H | K | ERA | WHIP | K/9 | BB/9 | HR/9 | GB/F |
|---|---|---|---|---|---|---|---|---|---|---|---|---|---|
| | | **Majors** | | | | | | | | **Skills** | | | |
| 07 | ATL | 16 | 10 | 0 | 224 | 221 | 132 | 3.33 | 1.22 | 5.3 | 2.1 | 0.4 | 2.9 |
| 08 | ATL | 11 | 7 | 0 | 142 | 125 | 85 | 3.17 | 1.16 | 5.4 | 2.5 | 0.7 | 2.7 |
| 09 | ATL | 2 | 1 | 0 | 42 | 49 | 30 | 3.61 | 1.46 | 6.4 | 2.8 | 0.9 | 3.1 |
| 10 | ATL | 17 | 9 | 0 | 228 | 189 | 139 | 2.83 | 1.15 | 5.5 | 2.9 | 0.8 | 2.9 |

| Yr | $1L | $2L | Pts | RAA | H% | HR/fb | S% | FIP | GS | CG | QS/DS |
|---|---|---|---|---|---|---|---|---|---|---|---|
| | **Value** | | | | **Luck** | | | | **In Rotation** | | |
| 07 | $19 | $10 | 300 | +24 | 30% | 6% | 72% | 3.31 | 34 | 1 | 25/3 |
| 08 | $13 | $8 | 200 | +17 | 27% | 11% | 75% | 3.85 | 22 | 1 | 16/4 |
| 09 | -$1 | -$2 | 40 | +4 | 34% | 15% | 78% | 3.93 | 7 | 0 | 4/0 |
| 10 | $23 | $19 | 330 | +39 | 25% | 13% | 79% | 4.09 | 34 | 1 | 25/2 |

| Yr | GR | Hld | Bln | Lead | OPS | 1st Hf | 2nd Hf | vs RH | vs LH |
|---|---|---|---|---|---|---|---|---|---|
| | **In Relief** | | | | **OPS** | | | | |
| 07 | — | — | — | — | .660 | .646 | .678 | .647 | .672 |
| 08 | 1 | 0 | 0 | +0.4 | .660 | .661 | .650 | .562 | .749 |
| 09 | — | — | — | — | .768 | — | .768 | .721 | .833 |
| 10 | — | — | — | — | .641 | .610 | .676 | .616 | .667 |

## David Huff — 40 IP | $-3 | 20 pts

SP-15 — Owned: 0% — LH

Huff took a line drive to the head in late May, which could not have helped his season, but his performance had already begun to slip. He has now burned Cleveland twice when handed a rotation spot, and with new faces on the horizon, he may get left behind. Management has been unhappy with Huff's approach. (BLS)

| Player | Age | IP | W | Sv | K | ERA | WHIP | K/9 | BB/9 | $2L | Pts |
|---|---|---|---|---|---|---|---|---|---|---|---|
| **Forecast** | | | | | | | | | | | |
| Huff D | 26 | 40 | 2 | 0 | 24 | 5.53 | 1.55 | 5.3 | 3.4 | -$3 | 20 |
| **Mini-Browser** | **Age** | **IP** | **W** | **Sv** | **K** | **ERA** | **WHIP** | **K/9** | **BB/9** | **$2L** | **Pts** |
| Bell T | 24 | 80 | 4 | 0 | 62 | 5.12 | 1.61 | 7.0 | 3.3 | -$3 | 70 |
| Haeger C | 27 | 40 | 2 | 0 | 33 | 5.16 | 1.53 | 7.3 | 4.3 | -$3 | 40 |
| Monasterios C | 25 | 40 | 2 | 0 | 32 | 4.98 | 1.56 | 7.2 | 3.2 | -$3 | 40 |
| Tazawa J | 24 | 40 | 1 | 0 | 33 | 5.38 | 1.60 | 7.4 | 3.0 | -$3 | 30 |
| Sanchez R | 26 | 40 | 2 | 0 | 34 | 5.31 | 1.69 | 7.6 | 5.3 | -$3 | 40 |

| Level | Leag | W | L | Sv | IP | H | K | ERA | WHIP | K/9 | BB/9 | HR/9 | GB/F |
|---|---|---|---|---|---|---|---|---|---|---|---|---|---|
| | | **Minors (2010)** | | | | | | | | **Skills** | | | |
| A | — | — | — | — | — | — | — | — | — | — | — | — | — |
| AA | — | — | — | — | — | — | — | — | — | — | — | — | — |
| AAA | IL | 8 | 2 | 0 | 74 | 84 | 52 | 4.36 | 1.41 | 6.3 | 2.5 | 1.0 | — |

**Competition at SP** / **Stats in 2010 as SP**

| Thr | Player | GS | ERA | Supp | W-L |
|---|---|---|---|---|---|
| RH | Carmona F | 33 | 3.77 | 3.5 | 13-14 |
| RH | Masterson J | 29 | 4.78 | 4.3 | 6-12 |
| RH | Talbot M | 28 | 4.41 | 4.1 | 10-13 |
| LH | Huff D | 15 | 6.21 | 3.6 | 2-11 |

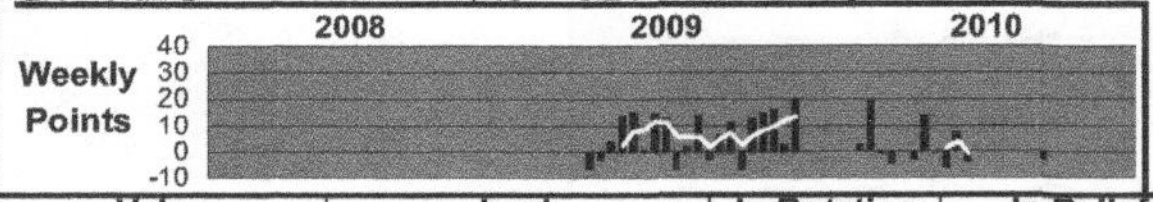


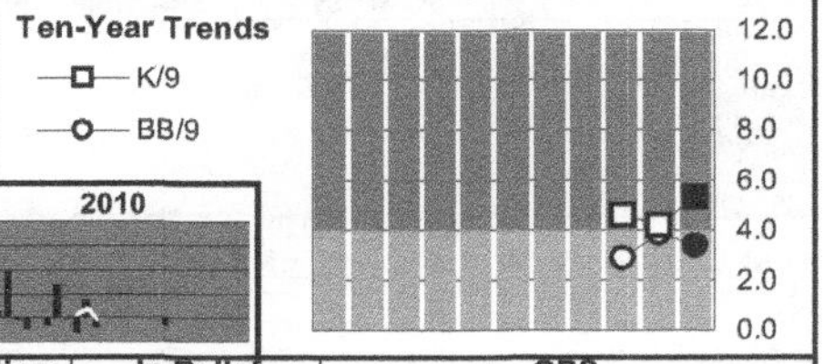


| Yr | Team | W | L | Sv | IP | H | K | ERA | WHIP | K/9 | BB/9 | HR/9 | GB/F |
|---|---|---|---|---|---|---|---|---|---|---|---|---|---|
| | | **Majors** | | | | | | | | **Skills** | | | |
| 07 | — | — | — | — | — | — | — | — | — | — | — | — | — |
| 08 | — | — | — | — | — | — | — | — | — | — | — | — | — |
| 09 | CLE | 11 | 8 | 0 | 128 | 159 | 65 | 5.61 | 1.56 | 4.6 | 2.9 | 1.1 | 0.9 |
| 10 | CLE | 2 | 11 | 0 | 79 | 101 | 37 | 6.21 | 1.69 | 4.2 | 3.8 | 1.6 | 0.8 |

| Yr | $1L | $2L | Pts | RAA | H% | HR/fb | S% | FIP | GS | CG | QS/DS |
|---|---|---|---|---|---|---|---|---|---|---|---|
| | **Value** | | | | **Luck** | | | | **In Rotation** | | |
| 07 | — | — | — | — | — | — | — | — | — | — | — |
| 08 | — | — | — | — | — | — | — | — | — | — | — |
| 09 | -$1 | -$9 | 120 | −19 | 32% | 8% | 65% | 4.87 | 23 | 0 | 8/6 |
| 10 | -$10 | -$28 | 10 | −22 | 31% | 11% | 66% | 5.94 | 15 | 1 | 4/5 |

| Yr | GR | Hld | Bln | Lead | OPS | 1st Hf | 2nd Hf | vs RH | vs LH |
|---|---|---|---|---|---|---|---|---|---|
| | **In Relief** | | | | **OPS** | | | | |
| 07 | — | — | — | — | — | — | — | — | — |
| 08 | — | — | — | — | — | — | — | — | — |
| 09 | — | — | — | — | .834 | .880 | .796 | .806 | .885 |
| 10 | — | — | — | — | .917 | .910 | .965 | .880 | 1.040 |

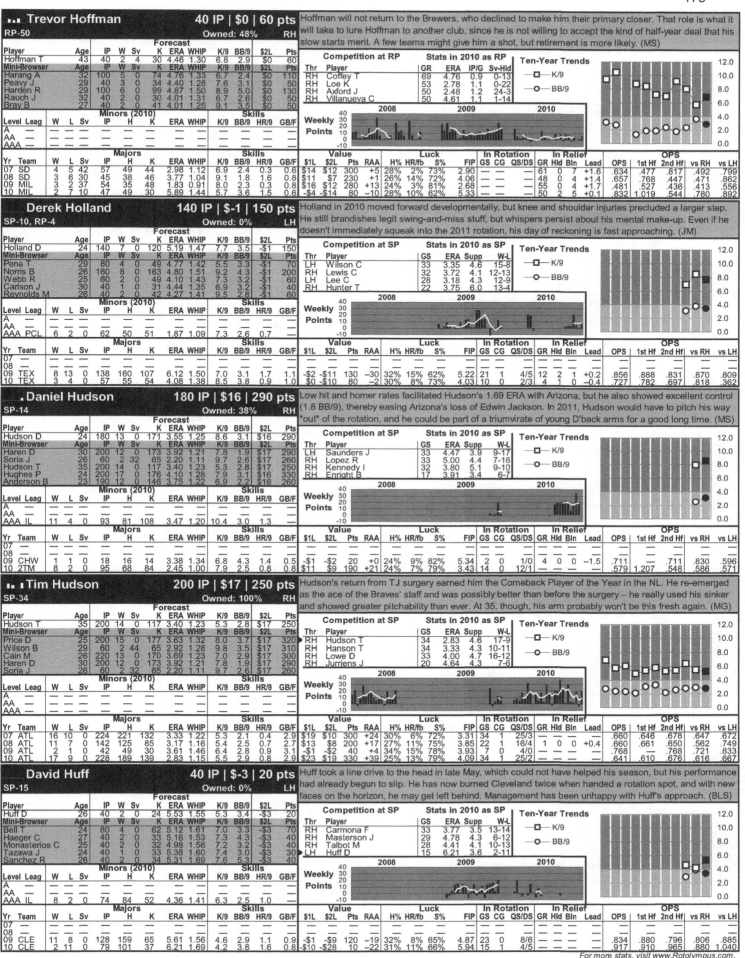

## Phil Hughes — 200 IP | $16 | 330 pts
SP-29, RP-2 — Owned: 99% — RH

Hughes had a breakout 2010, starting as the #5 SP but finishing at #3 with the club's second-most Wins. His hit and HR rates were not unduly favorable, so his success was legit; however, going 176 IP pounded his K/9, and he ran out of gas (he had a 1.9 K/BB in the second half and a 1.5 K/BB in the play-offs). (LS)

### Forecast
| Player | Age | IP | W | Sv | K | ERA | WHIP | K/9 | BB/9 | $2L | Pts |
|---|---|---|---|---|---|---|---|---|---|---|---|
| Hughes P | 24 | 200 | 17 | 0 | 176 | 4.10 | 1.28 | 7.9 | 3.1 | $16 | 330 |

### Mini-Browser
| Player | Age | IP | W | Sv | K | ERA | WHIP | K/9 | BB/9 | $2L | Pts |
|---|---|---|---|---|---|---|---|---|---|---|---|
| Wilson B | 29 | 60 | 2 | 44 | 65 | 2.92 | 1.28 | 9.8 | 3.5 | $17 | 310 |
| Cain M | 26 | 220 | 13 | 0 | 170 | 3.69 | 1.23 | 7.0 | 2.9 | $17 | 300 |
| Haren D | 30 | 200 | 12 | 0 | 173 | 3.92 | 1.21 | 7.8 | 1.9 | $17 | 290 |
| Soria J | 26 | 60 | 2 | 32 | 65 | 2.20 | 1.11 | 9.7 | 2.6 | $17 | 260 |
| Hudson T | 35 | 200 | 14 | 0 | 117 | 3.40 | 1.23 | 5.3 | 2.8 | $17 | 250 |

### Competition at SP — Stats in 2010 as SP
| Thr | Player | GS | ERA | Supp | W-L |
|---|---|---|---|---|---|
| LH | Sabathia C | 34 | 3.18 | 5.7 | 21-7 |
| RH | Burnett A | 33 | 5.26 | 4.3 | 10-15 |
| RH | Hughes P | 29 | 4.23 | 6.5 | 17-8 |
| RH | Vazquez J | 26 | 5.56 | 4.1 | 8-10 |

### Minors (2010)
| Level | Leag | W | L | Sv | IP | H | K | ERA | WHIP | K/9 | BB/9 | HR/9 | GB/F |
|---|---|---|---|---|---|---|---|---|---|---|---|---|---|
| A | — | — | — | — | — | — | — | — | — | — | — | — | — |
| AA | — | — | — | — | — | — | — | — | — | — | — | — | — |
| AAA | — | — | — | — | — | — | — | — | — | — | — | — | — |

### Majors / Skills
| Yr | Team | W | L | Sv | IP | H | K | ERA | WHIP | K/9 | BB/9 | HR/9 | GB/F |
|---|---|---|---|---|---|---|---|---|---|---|---|---|---|
| 07 | NYY | 5 | 3 | 0 | 72 | 64 | 58 | 4.46 | 1.28 | 7.2 | 3.6 | 1.0 | 0.8 |
| 08 | NYY | 0 | 4 | 0 | 34 | 43 | 23 | 6.62 | 1.71 | 6.1 | 4.0 | 0.8 | 0.9 |
| 09 | NYY | 8 | 3 | 3 | 86 | 68 | 96 | 3.03 | 1.12 | 10.0 | 2.9 | 0.8 | 0.8 |
| 10 | NYY | 18 | 8 | 0 | 176 | 162 | 146 | 4.19 | 1.25 | 7.5 | 3.0 | 1.3 | 0.8 |

### Value / Luck / In Rotation / In Relief / OPS
| Yr | $1L | $2L | Pts | RAA | H% | HR/fb | S% | FIP | GS | CG | QS/DS | GR | Hld | Bln | Lead | OPS | 1st Hf | 2nd Hf | vs RH | vs LH |
|---|---|---|---|---|---|---|---|---|---|---|---|---|---|---|---|---|---|---|---|---|
| 07 | $2 | -$3 | 100 | -3 | 27% | 8% | 67% | 4.33 | 13 | 0 | 5/2 | — | — | — | — | .699 | .485 | .732 | .563 | .846 |
| 08 | -$6 | -$9 | 0 | -9 | 35% | 7% | 60% | 4.42 | 8 | 0 | 2/2 | — | — | — | — | .845 | .947 | .611 | .771 | .937 |
| 09 | $11 | $7 | 200 | +11 | 28% | 8% | 76% | 3.25 | 7 | 0 | 2/1 | 44 | 18 | 3 | +0.8 | .635 | .718 | .496 | .546 | .740 |
| 10 | $12 | $5 | 310 | +4 | 28% | 10% | 71% | 4.47 | 29 | 0 | 15/3 | — | — | — | — | .702 | .668 | .747 | .674 | .728 |

## Tommy Hunter — 140 IP | $4 | 160 pts
SP-22, RP-1 — Owned: 40% — RH

Hunter perfectly illustrates the fallacy of following Wins: His 13-4, 3.73 ERA campaign in 2010 belies both his peripherals (5.14 FIP) and his hittability (.281 BAA in the final two months). Hunter is not bad, but he is also no better than a #4 starter on a first-division ballclub. If nothing else, he will keep eating innings. (JM)

### Forecast
| Player | Age | IP | W | Sv | K | ERA | WHIP | K/9 | BB/9 | $2L | Pts |
|---|---|---|---|---|---|---|---|---|---|---|---|
| Hunter T | 24 | 140 | 10 | 0 | 83 | 4.55 | 1.38 | 5.4 | 2.6 | $4 | 160 |

### Mini-Browser
| Player | Age | IP | W | Sv | K | ERA | WHIP | K/9 | BB/9 | $2L | Pts |
|---|---|---|---|---|---|---|---|---|---|---|---|
| Wells R | 28 | 180 | 9 | 0 | 127 | 4.30 | 1.37 | 6.3 | 2.8 | $4 | 190 |
| Adams M | 32 | 40 | 2 | 42 | 42 | 2.57 | 1.10 | 9.4 | 2.9 | $4 | 80 |
| Guthrie J | 31 | 200 | 10 | 0 | 110 | 4.76 | 1.34 | 5.0 | 2.6 | $4 | 170 |
| Motte J | 28 | 60 | 3 | 4 | 62 | 3.63 | 1.27 | 9.2 | 3.2 | $4 | 110 |
| Chamberlain J | 25 | 60 | 4 | 10 | 57 | 4.29 | 1.38 | 8.5 | 3.3 | $4 | 130 |

### Competition at SP — Stats in 2010 as SP
| Thr | Player | GS | ERA | Supp | W-L |
|---|---|---|---|---|---|
| LH | Wilson C | 33 | 3.35 | 4.6 | 15-8 |
| RH | Lewis C | 32 | 3.72 | 4.1 | 12-13 |
| LH | Lee C | 28 | 3.18 | 4.3 | 12-9 |
| RH | Hunter T | 22 | 3.75 | 6.0 | 13-4 |

### Minors (2010)
| Level | Leag | W | L | Sv | IP | H | K | ERA | WHIP | K/9 | BB/9 | HR/9 | GB/F |
|---|---|---|---|---|---|---|---|---|---|---|---|---|---|
| A | — | — | — | — | — | — | — | — | — | — | — | — | — |
| AA | — | — | — | — | — | — | — | — | — | — | — | — | — |
| AAA | PCL | 1 | 2 | 0 | 26 | 28 | 14 | 4.05 | 1.46 | 4.7 | 3.7 | 0.7 | — |

### Majors / Skills
| Yr | Team | W | L | Sv | IP | H | K | ERA | WHIP | K/9 | BB/9 | HR/9 | GB/F |
|---|---|---|---|---|---|---|---|---|---|---|---|---|---|
| 07 | — | — | — | — | — | — | — | — | — | — | — | — | — |
| 08 | TEX | 0 | 0 | 0 | 11 | 23 | 9 | 16.36 | 2.36 | 7.4 | 2.5 | 3.3 | 0.7 |
| 09 | TEX | 9 | 6 | 0 | 112 | 113 | 64 | 4.10 | 1.30 | 5.1 | 2.7 | 1.0 | 0.9 |
| 10 | TEX | 13 | 4 | 0 | 128 | 126 | 68 | 3.73 | 1.24 | 4.8 | 2.3 | 1.5 | 1.0 |

### Value / Luck / In Rotation / In Relief / OPS
| Yr | $1L | $2L | Pts | RAA | H% | HR/fb | S% | FIP | GS | CG | QS/DS | GR | Hld | Bln | Lead | OPS | 1st Hf | 2nd Hf | vs RH | vs LH |
|---|---|---|---|---|---|---|---|---|---|---|---|---|---|---|---|---|---|---|---|---|
| 07 | | | | | | | | | | | | | | | | | | | | |
| 08 | -$8 | -$10 | -10 | -15 | 43% | 18% | 27% | 7.21 | 3 | 0 | 0/3 | — | — | — | — | 1.144 | — | 1.144 | 1.069 | 1.219 |
| 09 | $6 | $0 | 140 | +0 | 28% | 8% | 71% | 4.55 | 19 | 1 | 8/2 | — | — | — | — | .736 | .688 | .748 | .595 | .869 |
| 10 | $8 | -$1 | 190 | +8 | 26% | 12% | 77% | 5.14 | 22 | 1 | 13/3 | 1 | 0 | 0 | +0.7 | .740 | .643 | .788 | .708 | .765 |

## Ryota Igarashi — 40 IP | $-3 | 30 pts
RP-34 — Owned: 0% — RH

After a 1.35 ERA in April, Igarashi briefly took over the set-up role before he strained his hamstring and missed a month. On his return, he was so bad that he was banished to Single-A before rejoining NY, and he ended with a 7.12 ERA. Inferior control was his downfall (he had a career 3.8 BB/9 in Japan). (JL)

### Forecast
| Player | Age | IP | W | Sv | K | ERA | WHIP | K/9 | BB/9 | $2L | Pts |
|---|---|---|---|---|---|---|---|---|---|---|---|
| Igarashi R | 31 | 40 | 2 | 0 | 29 | 5.28 | 1.43 | 6.4 | 4.4 | -$3 | 30 |

### Mini-Browser
| Player | Age | IP | W | Sv | K | ERA | WHIP | K/9 | BB/9 | $2L | Pts |
|---|---|---|---|---|---|---|---|---|---|---|---|
| Boyer B | 29 | 60 | 2 | 0 | 36 | 4.72 | 1.49 | 5.4 | 3.9 | -$3 | 40 |
| French L | 25 | 100 | 5 | 0 | 62 | 5.23 | 1.52 | 5.6 | 3.4 | -$3 | 80 |
| Bannister B | 30 | 20 | 1 | 0 | 11 | 5.74 | 1.55 | 5.1 | 3.2 | -$3 | 10 |
| McCutchen D | 28 | 40 | 2 | 0 | 30 | 5.16 | 1.47 | 6.7 | 2.7 | -$3 | 40 |
| Ray R | 27 | 60 | 3 | 0 | 49 | 5.26 | 1.60 | 7.4 | 3.0 | -$3 | 50 |

### Competition at RP — Stats in 2010 as RP
| Thr | Player | GR | ERA | IP/G | Sv-Hld |
|---|---|---|---|---|---|
| RH | Rodriguez F | 53 | 2.20 | 1.1 | 25-0 |
| RH | Dessens E | 53 | 2.30 | 0.9 | 0-11 |
| RH | Parnell B | 41 | 2.83 | 0.9 | 0-9 |
| RH | Acosta M | 41 | 2.95 | 1.0 | 1-2 |

### Minors (2010)
| Level | Leag | W | L | Sv | IP | H | K | ERA | WHIP | K/9 | BB/9 | HR/9 | GB/F |
|---|---|---|---|---|---|---|---|---|---|---|---|---|---|
| A | FLO | 1 | 0 | 0 | 7 | 10 | 11 | 2.35 | 1.43 | 12.9 | 1.2 | 0.0 | — |
| AA | — | — | — | — | — | — | — | — | — | — | — | — | — |
| AAA | IL | 2 | 1 | 2 | 16 | 18 | 16 | 3.31 | 1.47 | 8.8 | 3.3 | 1.1 | — |

### Majors / Skills
| Yr | Team | W | L | Sv | IP | H | K | ERA | WHIP | K/9 | BB/9 | HR/9 | GB/F |
|---|---|---|---|---|---|---|---|---|---|---|---|---|---|
| 07 | — | — | — | — | — | — | — | — | — | — | — | — | — |
| 08 | — | — | — | — | — | — | — | — | — | — | — | — | — |
| 09 | — | — | — | — | — | — | — | — | — | — | — | — | — |
| 10 | NYM | 1 | 1 | 0 | 30 | 29 | 25 | 7.12 | 1.55 | 7.4 | 5.3 | 1.2 | 0.9 |

### Value / Luck / In Rotation / In Relief / OPS
| Yr | $1L | $2L | Pts | RAA | H% | HR/fb | S% | FIP | GS | CG | QS/DS | GR | Hld | Bln | Lead | OPS | 1st Hf | 2nd Hf | vs RH | vs LH |
|---|---|---|---|---|---|---|---|---|---|---|---|---|---|---|---|---|---|---|---|---|
| 07 | | | | | | | | | | | | | | | | | | | | |
| 08 | | | | | | | | | | | | | | | | | | | | |
| 09 | | | | | | | | | | | | | | | | | | | | |
| 10 | -$8 | -$17 | 20 | -10 | 29% | 10% | 53% | 5.05 | — | — | — | 34 | 2 | 0 | -1.0 | .796 | .817 | .754 | .724 | .915 |

## Gregory Infante — 60 IP | $-2 | 60 pts
RP-5 — Owned: 0% — RH

Another year, another flamethrowing reliever manufactured from thin air by the White Sox. Although not as dramatic as the Sergio Santos miracle, Infante's story is that he was a starter through 2009, and now he touches 98 MPH and has an unhittable curve over which he has no control (yet, mind you). (RM)

### Forecast
| Player | Age | IP | W | Sv | K | ERA | WHIP | K/9 | BB/9 | $2L | Pts |
|---|---|---|---|---|---|---|---|---|---|---|---|
| Infante G | 23 | 60 | 3 | 0 | 47 | 4.31 | 1.75 | 7.1 | 7.0 | -$2 | 60 |

### Mini-Browser
| Player | Age | IP | W | Sv | K | ERA | WHIP | K/9 | BB/9 | $2L | Pts |
|---|---|---|---|---|---|---|---|---|---|---|---|
| Baez D | 33 | 40 | 2 | 0 | 22 | 4.77 | 1.42 | 4.9 | 3.7 | -$2 | 30 |
| Nieve F | 28 | 40 | 2 | 0 | 33 | 5.12 | 1.41 | 7.5 | 3.9 | -$2 | 40 |
| Sanabia A | 22 | 100 | 6 | 0 | 74 | 4.83 | 1.50 | 6.7 | 3.0 | -$2 | 100 |
| Walters P | 26 | 40 | 2 | 0 | 38 | 5.02 | 1.49 | 8.5 | 3.6 | -$2 | 50 |
| Fulchino J | 31 | 40 | 2 | 0 | 33 | 4.80 | 1.45 | 7.4 | 3.6 | -$2 | 40 |

### Competition at RP — Stats in 2010 as RP
| Thr | Player | GR | ERA | IP/G | Sv-Hld |
|---|---|---|---|---|---|
| RH | Putz J | 60 | 2.83 | 0.9 | 3-14 |
| RH | Santos S | 56 | 2.96 | 0.9 | 1-14 |
| RH | Jenks B | 55 | 4.44 | 1.0 | 27-0 |
| RH | Linebrink S | 52 | 4.40 | 1.1 | 0-4 |

### Minors (2010)
| Level | Leag | W | L | Sv | IP | H | K | ERA | WHIP | K/9 | BB/9 | HR/9 | GB/F |
|---|---|---|---|---|---|---|---|---|---|---|---|---|---|
| A | CAR | 1 | 2 | 9 | 33 | 32 | 35 | 3.48 | 1.40 | 9.4 | 4.0 | 0.0 | — |
| AA | SOU | 2 | 2 | 3 | 26 | 23 | 34 | 3.42 | 1.33 | 11.6 | 4.1 | 0.0 | — |
| AAA | — | — | — | — | — | — | — | — | — | — | — | — | — |

### Majors / Skills
| Yr | Team | W | L | Sv | IP | H | K | ERA | WHIP | K/9 | BB/9 | HR/9 | GB/F |
|---|---|---|---|---|---|---|---|---|---|---|---|---|---|
| 07 | — | — | — | — | — | — | — | — | — | — | — | — | — |
| 08 | — | — | — | — | — | — | — | — | — | — | — | — | — |
| 09 | — | — | — | — | — | — | — | — | — | — | — | — | — |
| 10 | CHW | 0 | 0 | 0 | 4 | 2 | 5 | 0.00 | 1.29 | 9.6 | 7.7 | 0.0 | 0.7 |

### Value / Luck / In Rotation / In Relief / OPS
| Yr | $1L | $2L | Pts | RAA | H% | HR/fb | S% | FIP | GS | CG | QS/DS | GR | Hld | Bln | Lead | OPS | 1st Hf | 2nd Hf | vs RH | vs LH |
|---|---|---|---|---|---|---|---|---|---|---|---|---|---|---|---|---|---|---|---|---|
| 07 | | | | | | | | | | | | | | | | | | | | |
| 08 | | | | | | | | | | | | | | | | | | | | |
| 09 | | | | | | | | | | | | | | | | | | | | |
| 10 | -$3 | -$10 | 10 | +2 | 20% | 0% | 100% | 3.73 | — | — | — | 5 | 0 | 0 | -5.0 | .449 | — | .449 | .111 | .786 |

## Hisashi Iwakuma — 180 IP | $9 | pts
No MLB games played in 2010 — Owned: 0% — RH

Japan's second-best pitcher, Iwakuma generates ground balls while registering 6.9 K/9 and 2.0 BB/9. He dominated the 2009 WBC with his slider and splitter. Those pitches, and his ability to keep the ball down, should bring some success in MLB, but elbow and shoulder injuries in 2006-07 are concerns. (MS)

### Forecast
| Player | Age | IP | W | Sv | K | ERA | WHIP | K/9 | BB/9 | $2L | Pts |
|---|---|---|---|---|---|---|---|---|---|---|---|
| Iwakuma H | 29 | 180 | 13 | 0 | 107 | 4.04 | 1.30 | 5.3 | 3.4 | $9 | |

### Mini-Browser
| Player | Age | IP | W | Sv | K | ERA | WHIP | K/9 | BB/9 | $2L | Pts |
|---|---|---|---|---|---|---|---|---|---|---|---|
| Nathan J | 36 | 40 | 4 | 18 | 45 | 2.72 | 1.12 | 10.1 | 3.0 | $10 | 180 |
| Rodriguez F | 29 | 60 | 3 | 21 | 66 | 3.14 | 1.29 | 9.9 | 4.2 | $10 | 200 |
| Bumgarner M | 21 | 160 | 10 | 0 | 133 | 3.57 | 1.36 | 7.5 | 2.3 | $10 | 220 |
| Lackey J | 32 | 180 | 13 | 0 | 143 | 4.32 | 1.35 | 6.4 | 2.7 | $10 | 240 |
| Shields J | 29 | 200 | 13 | 0 | 155 | 4.63 | 1.30 | 7.0 | 2.5 | $9 | 250 |

### Competition at SP — Stats in 2010 as SP
| Thr | Player | GS | ERA | Supp | W-L |
|---|---|---|---|---|---|

### Minors (2010)
| Level | Leag | W | L | Sv | IP | H | K | ERA | WHIP | K/9 | BB/9 | HR/9 | GB/F |
|---|---|---|---|---|---|---|---|---|---|---|---|---|---|
| A | — | — | — | — | — | — | — | — | — | — | — | — | — |
| AA | — | — | — | — | — | — | — | — | — | — | — | — | — |
| AAA | — | — | — | — | — | — | — | — | — | — | — | — | — |

### Majors / Skills
| Yr | Team | W | L | Sv | IP | H | K | ERA | WHIP | K/9 | BB/9 | HR/9 | GB/F |
|---|---|---|---|---|---|---|---|---|---|---|---|---|---|
| 07 | — | — | — | — | — | — | — | — | — | — | — | — | — |
| 08 | — | — | — | — | — | — | — | — | — | — | — | — | — |
| 09 | — | — | — | — | — | — | — | — | — | — | — | — | — |
| 10 | — | — | — | — | — | — | — | — | — | — | — | — | — |

### Value / Luck / In Rotation / In Relief / OPS
| Yr | $1L | $2L | Pts | RAA | H% | HR/fb | S% | FIP | GS | CG | QS/DS | GR | Hld | Bln | Lead | OPS | 1st Hf | 2nd Hf | vs RH | vs LH |
|---|---|---|---|---|---|---|---|---|---|---|---|---|---|---|---|---|---|---|---|---|
| 07 | — | — | — | — | — | — | — | — | — | — | — | — | — | — | — | — | — | — | — | — |
| 08 | — | — | — | — | — | — | — | — | — | — | — | — | — | — | — | — | — | — | — | — |
| 09 | — | — | — | — | — | — | — | — | — | — | — | — | — | — | — | — | — | — | — | — |
| 10 | — | — | — | — | — | — | — | — | — | — | — | — | — | — | — | — | — | — | — | — |

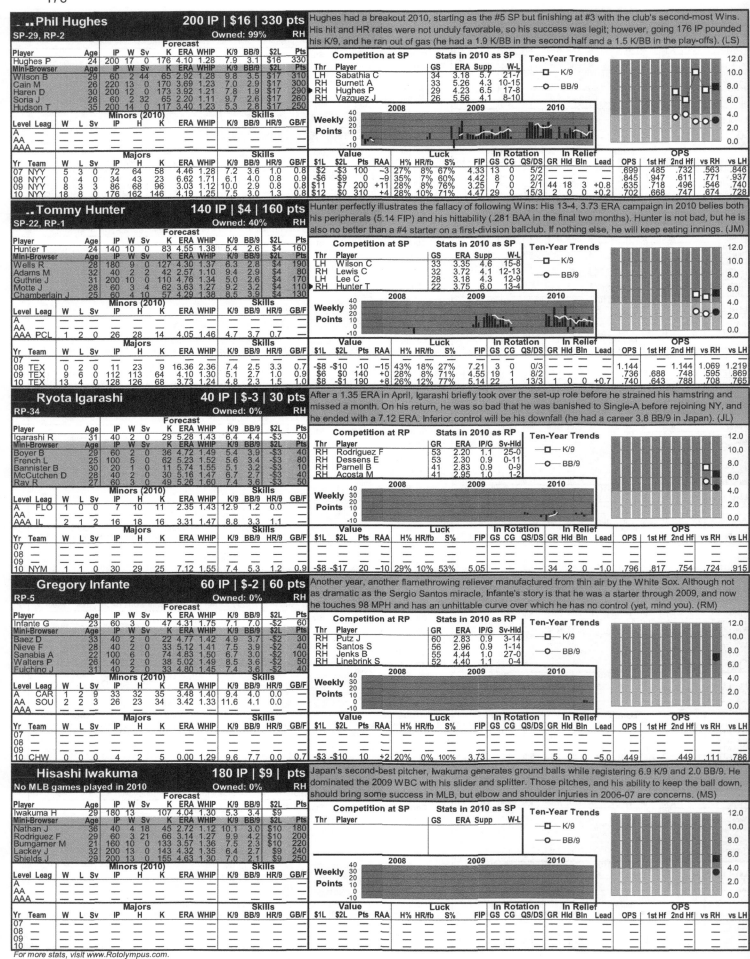

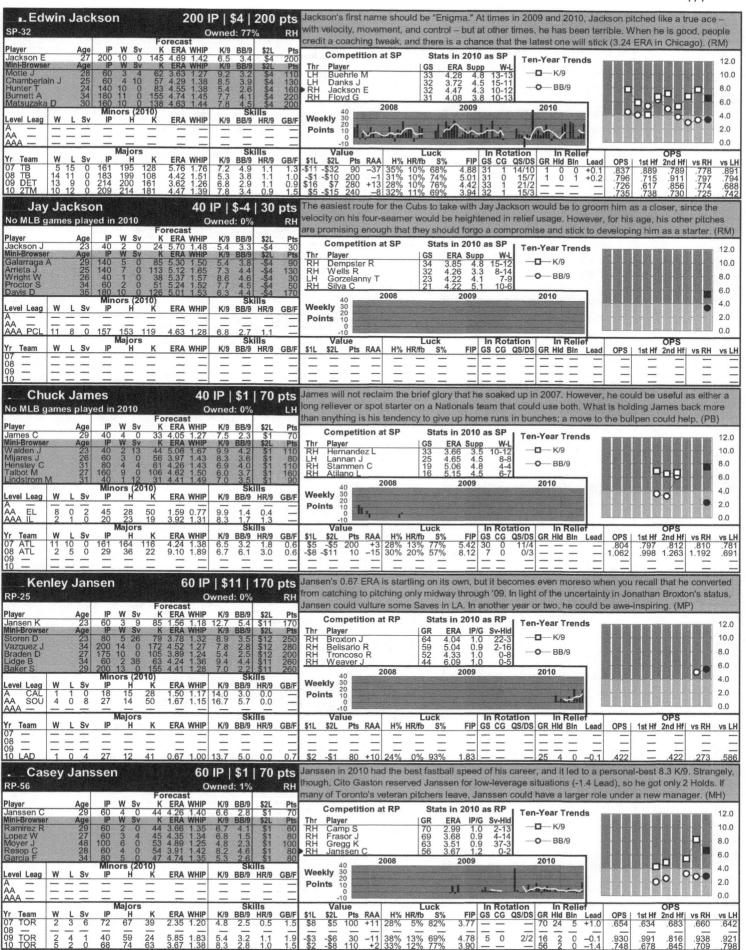

## Edwin Jackson — 200 IP | $4 | 200 pts
**SP-32** — Owned: 77% — RH

Jackson's first name should be "Enigma." At times in 2009 and 2010, Jackson pitched like a true ace – with velocity, movement, and control – but at other times, he has been terrible. When he is good, people credit a coaching tweak, and there is a chance that the latest one will stick (3.24 ERA in Chicago). (RM)

### Forecast
| Player | Age | IP | W | Sv | K | ERA | WHIP | K/9 | BB/9 | $2L | Pts |
|---|---|---|---|---|---|---|---|---|---|---|---|
| Jackson E | 27 | 200 | 10 | 0 | 145 | 4.69 | 1.42 | 6.5 | 3.4 | $4 | 200 |

### Mini-Browser
| Player | Age | IP | W | Sv | K | ERA | WHIP | K/9 | BB/9 | $2L | Pts |
|---|---|---|---|---|---|---|---|---|---|---|---|
| Motte J | 28 | 60 | 3 | 4 | 62 | 3.63 | 1.27 | 9.2 | 3.2 | $4 | 110 |
| Chamberlain J | 25 | 60 | 4 | 10 | 57 | 4.29 | 1.38 | 8.5 | 3.9 | $4 | 130 |
| Hunter T | 24 | 140 | 10 | 0 | 83 | 4.55 | 1.38 | 5.4 | 3.5 | $4 | 160 |
| Burnett A | 34 | 180 | 11 | 0 | 155 | 4.47 | 1.45 | 7.7 | 4.1 | $4 | 220 |
| Matsuzaka D | 30 | 160 | 10 | 0 | 138 | 4.63 | 1.44 | 7.8 | 4.5 | $4 | 200 |

### Competition at SP — Stats in 2010 as SP
| Thr | Player | GS | ERA | Supp | W-L |
|---|---|---|---|---|---|
| LH | Buehrle M | 33 | 4.28 | 4.8 | 13-13 |
| LH | Danks J | 32 | 3.72 | 4.5 | 15-11 |
| RH | Jackson E | 32 | 4.47 | 4.3 | 10-12 |
| RH | Floyd G | 31 | 4.08 | 3.8 | 10-13 |

Ten-Year Trends — K/9, BB/9

### Minors (2010)
| Level | Leag | W | L | Sv | IP | H | K | ERA | WHIP | K/9 | BB/9 | HR/9 | GB/F |
|---|---|---|---|---|---|---|---|---|---|---|---|---|---|
| A | — | — | — | — | — | — | — | — | — | — | — | — | — |
| AA | — | — | — | — | — | — | — | — | — | — | — | — | — |
| AAA | — | — | — | — | — | — | — | — | — | — | — | — | — |

### Majors
| Yr | Team | W | L | Sv | IP | H | K | ERA | WHIP | K/9 | BB/9 | HR/9 | GB/F | $1L | $2L | Pts | RAA | H% | HR/fb | S% | FIP | GS | CG | QS/DS | GR | Hld | Bln | Lead | OPS | 1st Hf | 2nd Hf | vs RH | vs LH |
|---|---|---|---|---|---|---|---|---|---|---|---|---|---|---|---|---|---|---|---|---|---|---|---|---|---|---|---|---|---|---|---|---|---|
| 07 | TB | 5 | 15 | 0 | 161 | 195 | 128 | 5.76 | 1.76 | 7.2 | 4.9 | 1.1 | 1.3 | -$11 | -$32 | 90 | -37 | 35% | 10% | 68% | 4.88 | 31 | 1 | 14/10 | 1 | 0 | 0 | +0.1 | .837 | .889 | .789 | .778 | .891 |
| 08 | TB | 14 | 11 | 0 | 183 | 199 | 108 | 4.42 | 1.51 | 5.3 | 3.8 | 1.1 | 1.1 | -$1 | -$10 | 200 | -1 | 31% | 10% | 74% | 5.01 | 31 | 0 | 15/7 | 1 | 0 | 1 | +0.2 | .796 | .715 | .911 | .797 | .794 |
| 09 | DET | 13 | 9 | 0 | 214 | 200 | 161 | 3.62 | 1.26 | 6.8 | 2.9 | 1.1 | 0.9 | $16 | $7 | 280 | +13 | 28% | 10% | 76% | 4.42 | 33 | 1 | 21/2 | — | — | — | — | .726 | .617 | .856 | .774 | .688 |
| 10 | 2TM | 10 | 12 | 0 | 209 | 214 | 181 | 4.47 | 1.39 | 7.8 | 3.4 | 0.9 | 1.5 | $5 | -$15 | 240 | +2 | 32% | 11% | 69% | 3.94 | 32 | 1 | 15/3 | — | — | — | — | .735 | .738 | .730 | .725 | .742 |

---

## Jay Jackson — 40 IP | $-4 | 30 pts
**No MLB games played in 2010** — Owned: 0% — RH

The easiest route for the Cubs to take with Jay Jackson would be to groom him as a closer, since the velocity on his four-seamer would be heightened in relief usage. However, for his age, his other pitches are promising enough that they should forgo a compromise and stick to developing him as a starter. (RM)

### Forecast
| Player | Age | IP | W | Sv | K | ERA | WHIP | K/9 | BB/9 | $2L | Pts |
|---|---|---|---|---|---|---|---|---|---|---|---|
| Jackson J | 23 | 40 | 2 | 0 | 24 | 5.70 | 1.48 | 5.4 | 3.3 | -$4 | 30 |

### Mini-Browser
| Player | Age | IP | W | Sv | K | ERA | WHIP | K/9 | BB/9 | $2L | Pts |
|---|---|---|---|---|---|---|---|---|---|---|---|
| Galarraga A | 29 | 140 | 5 | 0 | 85 | 5.30 | 1.50 | 5.4 | 3.8 | -$4 | 90 |
| Arrieta J | 25 | 140 | 7 | 0 | 113 | 5.12 | 1.65 | 7.3 | 4.4 | -$4 | 130 |
| Wright W | 26 | 40 | 1 | 0 | 38 | 5.37 | 1.47 | 8.6 | 4.6 | -$4 | 30 |
| Proctor S | 34 | 60 | 2 | 0 | 51 | 5.24 | 1.52 | 7.7 | 4.5 | -$4 | 50 |
| Davis D | 35 | 180 | 10 | 0 | 126 | 5.01 | 1.53 | 6.3 | 4.4 | -$4 | 170 |

### Competition at SP — Stats in 2010 as SP
| Thr | Player | GS | ERA | Supp | W-L |
|---|---|---|---|---|---|
| RH | Dempster R | 34 | 3.85 | 4.8 | 15-12 |
| RH | Wells R | 32 | 4.26 | 3.3 | 8-14 |
| LH | Gorzelanny T | 23 | 4.22 | 4.1 | 7-9 |
| RH | Silva C | 21 | 4.22 | 5.1 | 10-6 |

Ten-Year Trends — K/9, BB/9

### Minors (2010)
| Level | Leag | W | L | Sv | IP | H | K | ERA | WHIP | K/9 | BB/9 | HR/9 | GB/F |
|---|---|---|---|---|---|---|---|---|---|---|---|---|---|
| A | — | — | — | — | — | — | — | — | — | — | — | — | — |
| AA | — | — | — | — | — | — | — | — | — | — | — | — | — |
| AAA | PCL | 11 | 8 | 0 | 157 | 153 | 119 | 4.63 | 1.28 | 6.8 | 2.7 | 1.1 | — |

### Majors
| Yr | Team | W | L | Sv | IP | H | K | ERA | WHIP | K/9 | BB/9 | HR/9 | GB/F |
|---|---|---|---|---|---|---|---|---|---|---|---|---|---|
| 07 | — | — | — | — | — | — | — | — | — | — | — | — | — |
| 08 | — | — | — | — | — | — | — | — | — | — | — | — | — |
| 09 | — | — | — | — | — | — | — | — | — | — | — | — | — |
| 10 | — | — | — | — | — | — | — | — | — | — | — | — | — |

---

## Chuck James — 40 IP | $1 | 70 pts
**No MLB games played in 2010** — Owned: 0% — LH

James will not reclaim the brief glory that he soaked up in 2007. However, he could be useful as either a long reliever or spot starter on a Nationals team that could use both. What is holding James back more than anything is his tendency to give up home runs in bunches; a move to the bullpen could help. (PB)

### Forecast
| Player | Age | IP | W | Sv | K | ERA | WHIP | K/9 | BB/9 | $2L | Pts |
|---|---|---|---|---|---|---|---|---|---|---|---|
| James C | 29 | 40 | 4 | 0 | 33 | 4.05 | 1.27 | 7.5 | 2.3 | $1 | 70 |

### Mini-Browser
| Player | Age | IP | W | Sv | K | ERA | WHIP | K/9 | BB/9 | $2L | Pts |
|---|---|---|---|---|---|---|---|---|---|---|---|
| Walden J | 23 | 40 | 2 | 13 | 44 | 5.06 | 1.67 | 9.9 | 4.2 | $1 | 110 |
| Mijares J | 26 | 60 | 3 | 0 | 56 | 3.97 | 1.43 | 8.3 | 3.6 | $1 | 80 |
| Hensley C | 31 | 80 | 4 | 4 | 61 | 4.26 | 1.43 | 6.9 | 4.0 | $1 | 110 |
| Talbot M | 27 | 160 | 9 | 0 | 106 | 4.62 | 1.50 | 6.0 | 3.7 | $1 | 160 |
| Lindstrom M | 31 | 40 | 1 | 12 | 31 | 4.41 | 1.49 | 7.0 | 3.5 | $1 | 90 |

### Competition at SP — Stats in 2010 as SP
| Thr | Player | GS | ERA | Supp | W-L |
|---|---|---|---|---|---|
| RH | Hernandez L | 33 | 3.66 | 3.5 | 10-12 |
| LH | Lannan J | 25 | 4.65 | 4.5 | 8-8 |
| RH | Stammen C | 19 | 5.06 | 4.8 | 4-4 |
| RH | Atilano L | 16 | 5.15 | 4.5 | 6-7 |

Ten-Year Trends — K/9, BB/9

### Minors (2010)
| Level | Leag | W | L | Sv | IP | H | K | ERA | WHIP | K/9 | BB/9 | HR/9 | GB/F |
|---|---|---|---|---|---|---|---|---|---|---|---|---|---|
| A | — | — | — | — | — | — | — | — | — | — | — | — | — |
| AA | EL | 8 | 0 | 2 | 45 | 28 | 50 | 1.59 | 0.77 | 9.9 | 1.4 | 0.4 | — |
| AAA | IL | 2 | 1 | 0 | 20 | 23 | 19 | 3.92 | 1.31 | 8.3 | 1.7 | 1.3 | — |

### Majors
| Yr | Team | W | L | Sv | IP | H | K | ERA | WHIP | K/9 | BB/9 | HR/9 | GB/F | $1L | $2L | Pts | RAA | H% | HR/fb | S% | FIP | GS | CG | QS/DS | GR | Hld | Bln | Lead | OPS | 1st Hf | 2nd Hf | vs RH | vs LH |
|---|---|---|---|---|---|---|---|---|---|---|---|---|---|---|---|---|---|---|---|---|---|---|---|---|---|---|---|---|---|---|---|---|---|
| 07 | ATL | 11 | 10 | 0 | 161 | 164 | 116 | 4.24 | 1.38 | 6.5 | 3.2 | 1.8 | 0.6 | $5 | -$5 | 90 | +3 | 28% | 13% | 77% | 5.42 | 30 | 0 | 11/4 | — | — | — | — | .804 | .797 | .812 | .810 | .781 |
| 08 | ATL | 2 | 5 | 0 | 29 | 36 | 22 | 9.10 | 1.89 | 6.7 | 6.1 | 3.0 | 0.6 | -$8 | -$11 | 10 | -15 | 30% | 20% | 57% | 8.12 | 7 | 0 | 0/3 | — | — | — | — | 1.062 | .998 | 1.263 | 1.192 | .691 |
| 09 | — | — | — | — | — | — | — | — | — | — | — | — | — | | | | | | | | | | | | | | | | | | | | |
| 10 | — | — | — | — | — | — | — | — | — | — | — | — | — | | | | | | | | | | | | | | | | | | | | |

---

## Kenley Jansen — 60 IP | $11 | 170 pts
**RP-25** — Owned: 0% — RH

Jansen's 0.67 ERA is startling on its own, but it becomes even moreso when you recall that he converted from catching to pitching only midway through '09. In light of the uncertainty in Jonathan Broxton's status, Jansen could vulture some Saves in LA. In another year or two, he could be awe-inspiring. (MP)

### Forecast
| Player | Age | IP | W | Sv | K | ERA | WHIP | K/9 | BB/9 | $2L | Pts |
|---|---|---|---|---|---|---|---|---|---|---|---|
| Jansen K | 23 | 60 | 3 | 9 | 85 | 1.56 | 1.18 | 12.7 | 5.4 | $11 | 170 |

### Mini-Browser
| Player | Age | IP | W | Sv | K | ERA | WHIP | K/9 | BB/9 | $2L | Pts |
|---|---|---|---|---|---|---|---|---|---|---|---|
| Storen D | 23 | 80 | 5 | 26 | 79 | 3.78 | 1.32 | 8.9 | 3.5 | $12 | 250 |
| Vazquez J | 34 | 200 | 14 | 0 | 172 | 4.52 | 1.27 | 7.8 | 2.8 | $12 | 280 |
| Braden D | 27 | 175 | 10 | 0 | 105 | 3.89 | 1.24 | 5.4 | 2.5 | $12 | 200 |
| Lidge B | 34 | 60 | 2 | 38 | 63 | 4.24 | 1.36 | 9.4 | 4.4 | $11 | 260 |
| Baker S | 29 | 200 | 13 | 0 | 155 | 4.41 | 1.28 | 7.0 | 2.2 | $11 | 260 |

### Competition at RP — Stats in 2010 as RP
| Thr | Player | GR | ERA | IP/G | Sv-Hld |
|---|---|---|---|---|---|
| RH | Broxton J | 64 | 4.04 | 1.0 | 22-3 |
| RH | Belisario R | 59 | 5.04 | 0.9 | 2-16 |
| RH | Troncoso R | 52 | 4.33 | 1.0 | 0-8 |
| RH | Weaver J | 44 | 6.09 | 1.0 | 0-5 |

Ten-Year Trends — K/9, BB/9

### Minors (2010)
| Level | Leag | W | L | Sv | IP | H | K | ERA | WHIP | K/9 | BB/9 | HR/9 | GB/F |
|---|---|---|---|---|---|---|---|---|---|---|---|---|---|
| A | CAL | 1 | 1 | 0 | 18 | 15 | 28 | 1.50 | 1.17 | 14.0 | 3.0 | 0.0 | — |
| AA | SOU | 4 | 0 | 8 | 27 | 14 | 50 | 1.67 | 1.15 | 16.7 | 5.7 | 0.0 | — |
| AAA | — | — | — | — | — | — | — | — | — | — | — | — | — |

### Majors
| Yr | Team | W | L | Sv | IP | H | K | ERA | WHIP | K/9 | BB/9 | HR/9 | GB/F | $1L | $2L | Pts | RAA | H% | HR/fb | S% | FIP | GS | CG | QS/DS | GR | Hld | Bln | Lead | OPS | 1st Hf | 2nd Hf | vs RH | vs LH |
|---|---|---|---|---|---|---|---|---|---|---|---|---|---|---|---|---|---|---|---|---|---|---|---|---|---|---|---|---|---|---|---|---|---|
| 07 | — | — | — | — | — | — | — | — | — | — | — | — | — | | | | | | | | | | | | | | | | | | | | |
| 08 | — | — | — | — | — | — | — | — | — | — | — | — | — | | | | | | | | | | | | | | | | | | | | |
| 09 | — | — | — | — | — | — | — | — | — | — | — | — | — | | | | | | | | | | | | | | | | | | | | |
| 10 | LAD | 1 | 0 | 4 | 27 | 12 | 41 | 0.67 | 1.00 | 13.7 | 5.0 | 0.0 | 0.7 | $2 | -$1 | 80 | +10 | 24% | 0% | 93% | 1.83 | — | — | — | 25 | 4 | 0 | -0.1 | .422 | | .422 | .273 | .586 |

---

## Casey Janssen — 60 IP | $1 | 70 pts
**RP-56** — Owned: 1% — RH

Janssen in 2010 had the best fastball speed of his career, and it led to a personal-best 8.3 K/9. Strangely, though, Cito Gaston reserved Janssen for low-leverage situations (-1.4 Lead), so he got only 2 Holds. If many of Toronto's veteran pitchers leave, Janssen could have a larger role under a new manager. (MH)

### Forecast
| Player | Age | IP | W | Sv | K | ERA | WHIP | K/9 | BB/9 | $2L | Pts |
|---|---|---|---|---|---|---|---|---|---|---|---|
| Janssen C | 29 | 60 | 4 | 0 | 44 | 4.26 | 1.40 | 6.6 | 2.8 | $1 | 70 |

### Mini-Browser
| Player | Age | IP | W | Sv | K | ERA | WHIP | K/9 | BB/9 | $2L | Pts |
|---|---|---|---|---|---|---|---|---|---|---|---|
| Ramirez R | 29 | 60 | 2 | 0 | 44 | 3.66 | 1.35 | 6.7 | 4.1 | $1 | 60 |
| Lopez W | 27 | 60 | 3 | 4 | 45 | 4.35 | 1.34 | 6.8 | 1.5 | $1 | 90 |
| Moyer J | 48 | 100 | 6 | 0 | 53 | 4.89 | 1.25 | 4.8 | 2.3 | $1 | 100 |
| Resop C | 28 | 60 | 4 | 0 | 50 | 3.91 | 1.42 | 8.2 | 4.6 | $1 | 80 |
| Garcia F | 34 | 80 | 5 | 0 | 47 | 4.74 | 1.35 | 5.3 | 2.6 | $1 | 80 |

### Competition at RP — Stats in 2010 as RP
| Thr | Player | GR | ERA | IP/G | Sv-Hld |
|---|---|---|---|---|---|
| RH | Camp S | 70 | 2.99 | 1.0 | 2-13 |
| RH | Frasor J | 69 | 3.68 | 0.9 | 4-14 |
| RH | Gregg K | 63 | 3.51 | 0.9 | 37-3 |
| RH | Janssen C | 56 | 3.67 | 1.2 | 0-2 |

Ten-Year Trends — K/9, BB/9

### Minors (2010)
| Level | Leag | W | L | Sv | IP | H | K | ERA | WHIP | K/9 | BB/9 | HR/9 | GB/F |
|---|---|---|---|---|---|---|---|---|---|---|---|---|---|
| A | — | — | — | — | — | — | — | — | — | — | — | — | — |
| AA | — | — | — | — | — | — | — | — | — | — | — | — | — |
| AAA | — | — | — | — | — | — | — | — | — | — | — | — | — |

### Majors
| Yr | Team | W | L | Sv | IP | H | K | ERA | WHIP | K/9 | BB/9 | HR/9 | GB/F | $1L | $2L | Pts | RAA | H% | HR/fb | S% | FIP | GS | CG | QS/DS | GR | Hld | Bln | Lead | OPS | 1st Hf | 2nd Hf | vs RH | vs LH |
|---|---|---|---|---|---|---|---|---|---|---|---|---|---|---|---|---|---|---|---|---|---|---|---|---|---|---|---|---|---|---|---|---|---|
| 07 | TOR | 2 | 3 | 6 | 72 | 67 | 39 | 2.35 | 1.20 | 4.8 | 2.5 | 0.5 | 1.5 | $8 | $5 | 100 | +11 | 28% | 5% | 82% | 3.77 | — | — | — | 70 | 24 | 5 | +1.0 | .654 | .634 | .683 | .660 | .642 |
| 08 | — | — | — | — | — | — | — | — | — | — | — | — | — | | | | | | | | | | | | | | | | | | | | |
| 09 | TOR | 4 | 1 | 0 | 40 | 59 | 24 | 5.85 | 1.83 | 5.4 | 3.2 | 1.1 | 1.9 | -$3 | -$6 | 30 | -11 | 30% | 13% | 69% | 4.78 | 5 | 0 | 0/1 | 16 | 0 | 0 | -0.1 | .930 | .991 | .816 | .938 | .921 |
| 10 | TOR | 5 | 2 | 0 | 68 | 74 | 63 | 3.67 | 1.38 | 8.3 | 2.8 | 1.0 | 1.5 | $2 | -$8 | 110 | +2 | 33% | 12% | 77% | 3.90 | — | — | 2/2 | 56 | 2 | 0 | -1.4 | .748 | .678 | .845 | .709 | .798 |

*For more stats, visit www.Rotolympus.com.*

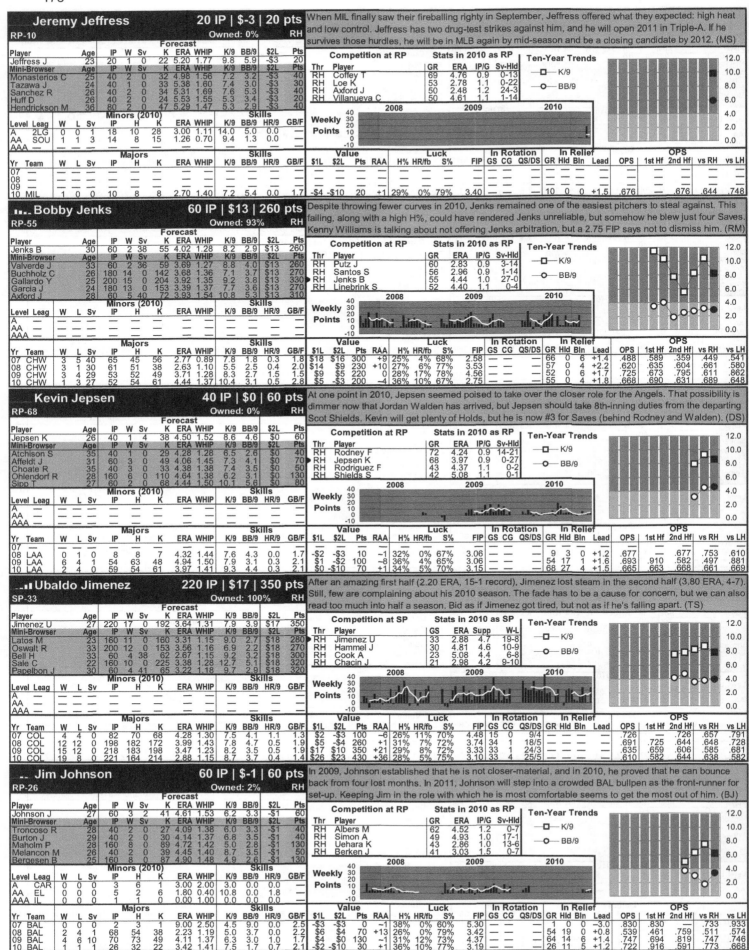

## Jeremy Jeffress — 20 IP | $-3 | 20 pts
RP-10 | Owned: 0% | RH

When MIL finally saw their fireballing righty in September, Jeffress offered what they expected: high heat and low control. Jeffress has two drug-test strikes against him, and he will open 2011 in Triple-A. If he survives those hurdles, he will be in MLB again by mid-season and be a closing candidate by 2012. (MS)

### Forecast
| Player | Age | IP | W | Sv | K | ERA | WHIP | K/9 | BB/9 | $2L | Pts |
|---|---|---|---|---|---|---|---|---|---|---|---|
| Jeffress J | 23 | 20 | 1 | 0 | 22 | 5.20 | 1.77 | 9.8 | 5.9 | -$3 | 20 |
| Mini-Browser | Age | IP | W | Sv | K | ERA | WHIP | K/9 | BB/9 | $2L | Pts |
| Monasterios C | 25 | 40 | 2 | 0 | 32 | 4.98 | 1.56 | 7.2 | 3.2 | -$3 | 40 |
| Tazawa J | 24 | 40 | 1 | 0 | 33 | 5.38 | 1.60 | 7.4 | 3.0 | -$3 | 30 |
| Sanchez R | 26 | 40 | 2 | 0 | 34 | 5.31 | 1.69 | 7.6 | 5.3 | -$3 | 40 |
| Huff D | 26 | 40 | 2 | 0 | 24 | 5.53 | 1.55 | 5.3 | 3.4 | -$3 | 20 |
| Hendrickson M | 36 | 80 | 2 | 0 | 47 | 5.29 | 1.47 | 5.3 | 2.9 | -$3 | 40 |

### Competition at RP / Stats in 2010 as RP
| Thr | Player | GR | ERA | IP/G | Sv-Hld |
|---|---|---|---|---|---|
| RH | Coffey T | 69 | 4.76 | 0.9 | 0-13 |
| RH | Loe K | 53 | 2.78 | 1.1 | 0-22 |
| RH | Axford J | 50 | 2.48 | 1.2 | 24-3 |
| RH | Villanueva C | 50 | 4.61 | 1.1 | 1-14 |

### Minors (2010)
| Level | Leag | W | L | Sv | IP | H | K | ERA | WHIP | K/9 | BB/9 | HR/9 | GB/F |
|---|---|---|---|---|---|---|---|---|---|---|---|---|---|
| A | 2LG | 0 | 0 | 1 | 18 | 10 | 28 | 3.00 | 1.11 | 14.0 | 5.0 | 0.0 | — |
| AA | SOU | 1 | 1 | 3 | 14 | 8 | 15 | 1.26 | 0.70 | 9.4 | 1.3 | 0.0 | — |
| AAA | — | | | | | | | | | | | | |

### Majors / Skills
| Yr | Team | W | L | Sv | IP | H | K | ERA | WHIP | K/9 | BB/9 | HR/9 | GB/F |
|---|---|---|---|---|---|---|---|---|---|---|---|---|---|
| 07 | — | | | | | | | | | | | | |
| 08 | — | | | | | | | | | | | | |
| 09 | — | | | | | | | | | | | | |
| 10 | MIL | 1 | 0 | 0 | 10 | 8 | 8 | 2.70 | 1.40 | 7.2 | 5.4 | 0.0 | 1.7 |

### Value / Luck / In Rotation / In Relief / OPS
| Yr | $1L | $2L | Pts | RAA | H% | HR/fb | S% | FIP | GS | CG | QS/DS | GR | Hld | Bln | Lead | OPS | 1st Hf | 2nd Hf | vs RH | vs LH |
|---|---|---|---|---|---|---|---|---|---|---|---|---|---|---|---|---|---|---|---|---|
| | -$4 | -$10 | 20 | +1 | 29% | 0% | 79% | 3.40 | — | — | — | 10 | 0 | 0 | +1.5 | .676 | — | .676 | .644 | .748 |

## Bobby Jenks — 60 IP | $13 | 260 pts
RP-55 | Owned: 93% | RH

Despite throwing fewer curves in 2010, Jenks remained one of the easiest pitchers to steal against. This failing, along with a high H%, could have rendered Jenks unreliable, but somehow he blew just four Saves. Kenny Williams is talking about not offering Jenks arbitration, but a 2.75 FIP says not to dismiss him. (RM)

### Forecast
| Player | Age | IP | W | Sv | K | ERA | WHIP | K/9 | BB/9 | $2L | Pts |
|---|---|---|---|---|---|---|---|---|---|---|---|
| Jenks B | 30 | 60 | 2 | 38 | 55 | 4.02 | 1.28 | 8.2 | 2.9 | $13 | 260 |
| Mini-Browser | Age | IP | W | Sv | K | ERA | WHIP | K/9 | BB/9 | $2L | Pts |
| Valverde J | 33 | 60 | 2 | 36 | 59 | 3.69 | 1.27 | 8.8 | 4.0 | $13 | 260 |
| Buchholz C | 26 | 180 | 14 | 0 | 142 | 3.68 | 1.36 | 7.1 | 3.7 | $13 | 270 |
| Gallardo Y | 25 | 200 | 15 | 0 | 204 | 3.92 | 1.35 | 9.2 | 3.8 | $13 | 330 |
| Garcia J | 24 | 180 | 13 | 0 | 153 | 3.39 | 1.37 | 7.7 | 3.6 | $13 | 270 |
| Axford J | 28 | 60 | 5 | 40 | 72 | 3.93 | 1.54 | 10.8 | 5.3 | $13 | 310 |

### Competition at RP / Stats in 2010 as RP
| Thr | Player | GR | ERA | IP/G | Sv-Hld |
|---|---|---|---|---|---|
| RH | Putz J | 60 | 2.83 | 0.9 | 3-14 |
| RH | Santos S | 56 | 2.96 | 0.9 | 1-14 |
| RH | Jenks B | 55 | 4.44 | 1.0 | 27-0 |
| RH | Linebrink S | 52 | 4.40 | 1.1 | 0-4 |

### Minors (2010)
| Level | Leag | W | L | Sv | IP | H | K | ERA | WHIP | K/9 | BB/9 | HR/9 | GB/F |
|---|---|---|---|---|---|---|---|---|---|---|---|---|---|
| A | — | | | | | | | | | | | | |
| AA | — | | | | | | | | | | | | |
| AAA | — | | | | | | | | | | | | |

### Majors / Skills
| Yr | Team | W | L | Sv | IP | H | K | ERA | WHIP | K/9 | BB/9 | HR/9 | GB/F |
|---|---|---|---|---|---|---|---|---|---|---|---|---|---|
| 07 | CHW | 3 | 5 | 40 | 65 | 45 | 56 | 2.77 | 0.89 | 7.8 | 1.8 | 0.3 | 1.8 |
| 08 | CHW | 3 | 1 | 30 | 61 | 51 | 38 | 2.63 | 1.10 | 5.5 | 2.5 | 0.4 | 2.0 |
| 09 | CHW | 3 | 4 | 29 | 53 | 52 | 49 | 3.71 | 1.28 | 8.3 | 2.7 | 1.5 | 1.5 |
| 10 | CHW | 1 | 3 | 27 | 52 | 54 | 61 | 4.44 | 1.37 | 10.4 | 3.1 | 0.5 | 2.8 |

### Value / Luck / In Rotation / In Relief / OPS
| Yr | $1L | $2L | Pts | RAA | H% | HR/fb | S% | FIP | GS | CG | QS/DS | GR | Hld | Bln | Lead | OPS | 1st Hf | 2nd Hf | vs RH | vs LH |
|---|---|---|---|---|---|---|---|---|---|---|---|---|---|---|---|---|---|---|---|---|
| 07 | $18 | $16 | 300 | +9 | 25% | 4% | 68% | 2.58 | — | — | — | 66 | 0 | 6 | +1.4 | .488 | .589 | .359 | .449 | .541 |
| 08 | $14 | $9 | 230 | +10 | 27% | 6% | 77% | 3.53 | — | — | — | 57 | 0 | 4 | +2.2 | .620 | .635 | .604 | .661 | .580 |
| 09 | $9 | $5 | 220 | +8 | 28% | 17% | 78% | 4.56 | — | — | — | 52 | 0 | 6 | +1.7 | .725 | .673 | .795 | .611 | .862 |
| 10 | $5 | -$3 | 200 | -4 | 36% | 10% | 67% | 2.75 | — | — | — | 55 | 0 | 4 | +1.8 | .668 | .690 | .631 | .689 | .648 |

## Kevin Jepsen — 40 IP | $0 | 60 pts
RP-68 | Owned: 0% | RH

At one point in 2010, Jepsen seemed poised to take over the closer role for the Angels. That possibility is dimmer now that Jordan Walden has arrived, but Jepsen should take 8th-inning duties from the departing Scot Shields. Kevin will get plenty of Holds, but he is now #3 for Saves (behind Rodney and Walden). (DS)

### Forecast
| Player | Age | IP | W | Sv | K | ERA | WHIP | K/9 | BB/9 | $2L | Pts |
|---|---|---|---|---|---|---|---|---|---|---|---|
| Jepsen K | 26 | 40 | 1 | 4 | 38 | 4.50 | 1.52 | 8.6 | 4.6 | $0 | 60 |
| Mini-Browser | Age | IP | W | Sv | K | ERA | WHIP | K/9 | BB/9 | $2L | Pts |
| Atchison S | 35 | 40 | 1 | 0 | 29 | 4.28 | 1.28 | 6.5 | 2.6 | $0 | 40 |
| Affeldt J | 31 | 60 | 3 | 0 | 49 | 4.06 | 1.45 | 7.3 | 4.1 | $0 | 70 |
| Choate R | 35 | 40 | 3 | 0 | 33 | 4.38 | 1.38 | 7.4 | 3.5 | $0 | 50 |
| Ohlendorf R | 28 | 160 | 6 | 0 | 110 | 4.64 | 1.38 | 6.2 | 3.1 | $0 | 130 |
| Sipp T | 27 | 60 | 2 | 0 | 68 | 4.44 | 1.50 | 10.1 | 5.6 | $0 | 80 |

### Competition at RP / Stats in 2010 as RP
| Thr | Player | GR | ERA | IP/G | Sv-Hld |
|---|---|---|---|---|---|
| RH | Rodney F | 72 | 4.24 | 0.9 | 14-21 |
| RH | Jepsen K | 68 | 3.97 | 0.9 | 0-27 |
| RH | Rodriguez F | 43 | 4.37 | 1.1 | 0-2 |
| RH | Shields S | 42 | 5.08 | 1.1 | 0-1 |

### Minors (2010)
| Level | Leag | W | L | Sv | IP | H | K | ERA | WHIP | K/9 | BB/9 | HR/9 | GB/F |
|---|---|---|---|---|---|---|---|---|---|---|---|---|---|
| A | — | | | | | | | | | | | | |
| AA | — | | | | | | | | | | | | |
| AAA | — | | | | | | | | | | | | |

### Majors / Skills
| Yr | Team | W | L | Sv | IP | H | K | ERA | WHIP | K/9 | BB/9 | HR/9 | GB/F |
|---|---|---|---|---|---|---|---|---|---|---|---|---|---|
| 07 | — | | | | | | | | | | | | |
| 08 | LAA | 0 | 1 | 0 | 8 | 8 | 7 | 4.32 | 1.44 | 7.6 | 4.3 | 0.0 | 1.7 |
| 09 | LAA | 6 | 4 | 1 | 54 | 63 | 48 | 4.94 | 1.50 | 7.9 | 3.1 | 0.3 | 2.1 |
| 10 | LAA | 2 | 4 | 0 | 59 | 54 | 61 | 3.97 | 1.41 | 9.3 | 4.4 | 0.3 | 2.1 |

### Value / Luck / In Rotation / In Relief / OPS
| Yr | $1L | $2L | Pts | RAA | H% | HR/fb | S% | FIP | GS | CG | QS/DS | GR | Hld | Bln | Lead | OPS | 1st Hf | 2nd Hf | vs RH | vs LH |
|---|---|---|---|---|---|---|---|---|---|---|---|---|---|---|---|---|---|---|---|---|
| 07 | | | | | | | | | | | | | | | | | | | | |
| 08 | -$2 | -$3 | 10 | -1 | 32% | 0% | 67% | 3.06 | — | — | — | 9 | 3 | 0 | +1.2 | .677 | — | .677 | .753 | .610 |
| 09 | -$1 | -$3 | 100 | -1 | 34% | 4% | 65% | 3.06 | — | — | — | 54 | 17 | 1 | +1.6 | .693 | .910 | .582 | .497 | .881 |
| 10 | $0 | -$10 | 70 | +1 | 34% | 5% | 70% | 3.15 | — | — | — | 68 | 27 | 4 | +1.5 | .665 | .664 | .668 | .661 | .669 |

## Ubaldo Jimenez — 220 IP | $17 | 350 pts
SP-33 | Owned: 100% | RH

After an amazing first half (2.20 ERA, 15-1 record), Jimenez lost steam in the second half (3.80 ERA, 4-7). Still, few are complaining about his 2010 season. The fade has to be a cause for concern, but we can also read too much into half a season. Bid as if Jimenez got tired, but not as if he's falling apart. (TS)

### Forecast
| Player | Age | IP | W | Sv | K | ERA | WHIP | K/9 | BB/9 | $2L | Pts |
|---|---|---|---|---|---|---|---|---|---|---|---|
| Jimenez U | 27 | 220 | 17 | 0 | 192 | 3.64 | 1.31 | 7.9 | 3.9 | $17 | 350 |
| Mini-Browser | Age | IP | W | Sv | K | ERA | WHIP | K/9 | BB/9 | $2L | Pts |
| Latos M | 23 | 160 | 11 | 0 | 160 | 3.31 | 1.15 | 9.0 | 2.7 | $18 | 280 |
| Oswalt R | 33 | 200 | 12 | 0 | 153 | 3.56 | 1.16 | 6.9 | 2.2 | $18 | 270 |
| Bell H | 33 | 60 | 4 | 38 | 62 | 2.67 | 1.15 | 9.2 | 3.2 | $18 | 300 |
| Sale C | 22 | 160 | 9 | 0 | 225 | 3.38 | 1.28 | 12.7 | 5.1 | $18 | 320 |
| Papelbon J | 30 | 60 | 4 | 41 | 65 | 3.22 | 1.18 | 9.7 | 2.9 | $18 | 320 |

### Competition at SP / Stats in 2010 as SP
| Thr | Player | GS | ERA | Supp | W-L |
|---|---|---|---|---|---|
| RH | Jimenez U | 33 | 2.88 | 4.7 | 19-8 |
| RH | Hammel J | 30 | 4.81 | 4.6 | 10-9 |
| RH | Cook A | 23 | 5.08 | 4.6 | 6-8 |
| RH | Chacin J | 21 | 2.98 | 4.2 | 9-10 |

### Minors (2010)
| Level | Leag | W | L | Sv | IP | H | K | ERA | WHIP | K/9 | BB/9 | HR/9 | GB/F |
|---|---|---|---|---|---|---|---|---|---|---|---|---|---|
| A | — | | | | | | | | | | | | |
| AA | — | | | | | | | | | | | | |
| AAA | — | | | | | | | | | | | | |

### Majors / Skills
| Yr | Team | W | L | Sv | IP | H | K | ERA | WHIP | K/9 | BB/9 | HR/9 | GB/F |
|---|---|---|---|---|---|---|---|---|---|---|---|---|---|
| 07 | COL | 4 | 4 | 0 | 82 | 70 | 68 | 4.28 | 1.30 | 7.5 | 4.1 | 1.1 | 1.3 |
| 08 | COL | 12 | 12 | 0 | 198 | 182 | 172 | 3.99 | 1.43 | 7.8 | 4.7 | 0.5 | 1.9 |
| 09 | COL | 15 | 12 | 0 | 218 | 183 | 198 | 3.47 | 1.23 | 8.2 | 3.5 | 0.5 | 1.9 |
| 10 | COL | 19 | 8 | 0 | 221 | 164 | 214 | 2.88 | 1.15 | 8.7 | 3.0 | 0.4 | 1.4 |

### Value / Luck / In Rotation / In Relief / OPS
| Yr | $1L | $2L | Pts | RAA | H% | HR/fb | S% | FIP | GS | CG | QS/DS | GR | Hld | Bln | Lead | OPS | 1st Hf | 2nd Hf | vs RH | vs LH |
|---|---|---|---|---|---|---|---|---|---|---|---|---|---|---|---|---|---|---|---|---|
| 07 | $2 | -$3 | 100 | -6 | 26% | 11% | 70% | 4.48 | 15 | 0 | 9/4 | — | — | — | .726 | — | .726 | .657 | .791 |
| 08 | $5 | -$4 | 260 | +1 | 31% | 7% | 72% | 3.74 | 34 | 1 | 18/5 | — | — | — | .691 | .725 | .644 | .648 | .728 |
| 09 | $17 | $10 | 350 | +21 | 29% | 8% | 72% | 3.33 | 33 | 3 | 24/3 | — | — | — | .635 | .659 | .606 | .585 | .681 |
| 10 | $26 | $23 | 430 | +36 | 28% | 5% | 75% | 3.10 | 33 | 0 | 25/5 | — | — | — | .610 | .582 | .644 | .638 | .581 |

## Jim Johnson — 60 IP | $-1 | 60 pts
RP-26 | Owned: 2% | RH

In 2009, Johnson established that he is not closer-material, and in 2010, he proved that he can bounce back from four lost months. In 2011, Johnson will step into a crowded BAL bullpen as the front-runner for set-up. Keeping Jim in the role with which he is most comfortable seems to get the most out of him. (BJ)

### Forecast
| Player | Age | IP | W | Sv | K | ERA | WHIP | K/9 | BB/9 | $2L | Pts |
|---|---|---|---|---|---|---|---|---|---|---|---|
| Johnson J | 27 | 60 | 3 | 2 | 41 | 4.61 | 1.53 | 6.2 | 3.3 | -$1 | 60 |
| Mini-Browser | Age | IP | W | Sv | K | ERA | WHIP | K/9 | BB/9 | $2L | Pts |
| Troncoso R | 28 | 40 | 2 | 0 | 27 | 4.09 | 1.38 | 6.0 | 3.3 | -$1 | 40 |
| Burton J | 29 | 40 | 2 | 0 | 30 | 4.14 | 1.37 | 6.8 | 3.5 | -$1 | 40 |
| Maholm P | 28 | 160 | 8 | 0 | 89 | 4.72 | 1.42 | 5.0 | 2.8 | -$1 | 130 |
| Melancon M | 26 | 40 | 2 | 0 | 39 | 4.45 | 1.40 | 8.7 | 3.5 | -$1 | 50 |
| Bergesen B | 25 | 160 | 8 | 0 | 87 | 4.90 | 1.48 | 4.9 | 2.6 | -$1 | 130 |

### Competition at RP / Stats in 2010 as RP
| Thr | Player | GR | ERA | IP/G | Sv-Hld |
|---|---|---|---|---|---|
| RH | Albers M | 62 | 4.52 | 1.2 | 0-7 |
| RH | Simon A | 49 | 4.93 | 1.0 | 17-11 |
| RH | Uehara K | 43 | 2.86 | 1.0 | 13-6 |
| RH | Berken J | 41 | 3.03 | 1.5 | 0-7 |

### Minors (2010)
| Level | Leag | W | L | Sv | IP | H | K | ERA | WHIP | K/9 | BB/9 | HR/9 | GB/F |
|---|---|---|---|---|---|---|---|---|---|---|---|---|---|
| A | CAR | 0 | 0 | 0 | 3 | 6 | 1 | 3.00 | 2.00 | 3.0 | 0.0 | 0.0 | — |
| AA | EL | 0 | 0 | 0 | 4 | 4 | 2 | 1.80 | 0.40 | 10.8 | 0.0 | 1.8 | — |
| AAA | IL | 0 | 0 | 0 | 1 | 0 | 1 | 0.00 | 1.00 | 0.0 | 0.0 | 0.0 | — |

### Majors / Skills
| Yr | Team | W | L | Sv | IP | H | K | ERA | WHIP | K/9 | BB/9 | HR/9 | GB/F |
|---|---|---|---|---|---|---|---|---|---|---|---|---|---|
| 07 | BAL | 1 | 0 | 0 | 3 | 3 | 3 | 9.00 | 2.50 | 4.5 | 9.0 | 0.0 | 2.5 |
| 08 | BAL | 2 | 4 | 1 | 68 | 54 | 38 | 2.23 | 1.19 | 5.0 | 3.7 | 0.0 | 2.2 |
| 09 | BAL | 4 | 6 | 10 | 70 | 73 | 49 | 4.11 | 1.37 | 6.3 | 3.0 | 1.0 | 1.7 |
| 10 | BAL | 1 | 1 | 0 | 26 | 32 | 22 | 3.42 | 1.41 | 7.5 | 0.7 | 0.7 | 2.1 |

### Value / Luck / In Rotation / In Relief / OPS
| Yr | $1L | $2L | Pts | RAA | H% | HR/fb | S% | FIP | GS | CG | QS/DS | GR | Hld | Bln | Lead | OPS | 1st Hf | 2nd Hf | vs RH | vs LH |
|---|---|---|---|---|---|---|---|---|---|---|---|---|---|---|---|---|---|---|---|---|
| 07 | -$3 | -$3 | 0 | -1 | 38% | 0% | 60% | 5.30 | — | — | — | 1 | 0 | 0 | -3.0 | — | — | — | .733 | .933 |
| 08 | $6 | $4 | 70 | +13 | 26% | 2% | 79% | 3.42 | — | — | — | 54 | 19 | 0 | +0.8 | .539 | .461 | .759 | .511 | .574 |
| 09 | -$4 | $0 | 130 | -1 | 31% | 12% | 73% | 4.37 | — | — | — | 64 | 14 | 6 | +1.4 | .747 | .694 | .819 | .747 | .746 |
| 10 | -$2 | -$10 | 30 | -3 | 36% | 10% | 77% | 3.19 | — | — | — | 26 | 11 | 5 | +1.2 | .722 | .916 | .591 | .773 | .646 |

## ▮ Josh Johnson — 200 IP | $23 | 330 pts

SP-28 — Owned: 100% — RH

Johnson was shut down late in 2010 with a nagging back strain and shoulder inflammation, but he is expected to be ready in time to open 2011 for Florida for a second straight year. Through 20 starts, Josh was 13-7 with a 1.61 ERA and 9.4 K/9. Even fighting aches, he improved his overall K/9 and BB/9. (MJ)

| Player | Age | IP | W | Sv | K | ERA | WHIP | K/9 | BB/9 | $2L | Pts |
|---|---|---|---|---|---|---|---|---|---|---|---|
| | | **Forecast** | | | | | | | | | |
| Johnson J | 27 | 200 | 13 | 0 | 179 | 3.09 | 1.19 | 8.1 | 2.5 | $23 | 330 |
| **Mini-Browser** | **Age** | **IP** | **W** | **Sv** | **K** | **ERA** | **WHIP** | **K/9** | **BB/9** | **$2L** | **Pts** |
| Hernandez F | 24 | 250 | 16 | 0 | 221 | 3.00 | 1.17 | 7.9 | 2.8 | $31 | 400 |
| Wainwright A | 29 | 240 | 19 | 0 | 196 | 3.15 | 1.17 | 7.4 | 2.4 | $28 | 400 |
| Sabathia C | 30 | 240 | 20 | 0 | 198 | 3.45 | 1.18 | 7.4 | 2.5 | $27 | 400 |
| Lincecum T | 26 | 220 | 17 | 0 | 232 | 3.19 | 1.22 | 9.5 | 3.1 | $26 | 410 |
| Lee C | 32 | 220 | 14 | 0 | 164 | 3.52 | 1.13 | 6.7 | 1.5 | $23 | 310 |

| Level | Leag | W | L | Sv | IP | H | K | ERA | WHIP | K/9 | BB/9 | HR/9 | GB/F |
|---|---|---|---|---|---|---|---|---|---|---|---|---|---|
| | | **Minors (2010)** | | | | | | | | **Skills** | | | |
| A | — | — | — | — | — | — | — | — | — | — | — | — | — |
| AA | — | — | — | — | — | — | — | — | — | — | — | — | — |
| AAA | — | — | — | — | — | — | — | — | — | — | — | — | — |

| Yr | Team | W | L | Sv | IP | H | K | ERA | WHIP | K/9 | BB/9 | HR/9 | GB/F |
|---|---|---|---|---|---|---|---|---|---|---|---|---|---|
| | | **Majors** | | | | | | | | **Skills** | | | |
| 07 | FLA | 0 | 3 | 0 | 15 | 26 | 14 | 7.47 | 2.43 | 8.0 | 6.9 | 0.6 | 2.0 |
| 08 | FLA | 7 | 1 | 0 | 87 | 91 | 77 | 3.61 | 1.35 | 7.9 | 2.8 | 0.7 | 1.5 |
| 09 | FLA | 15 | 5 | 0 | 209 | 184 | 191 | 3.23 | 1.16 | 8.2 | 2.5 | 0.6 | 1.6 |
| 10 | FLA | 11 | 6 | 0 | 183 | 155 | 186 | 2.30 | 1.11 | 9.1 | 2.4 | 0.3 | 1.4 |

**Competition at SP** — **Stats in 2010 as SP**

| | Thr | Player | GS | ERA | Supp | W-L |
|---|---|---|---|---|---|---|
| | RH | Sanchez A | 32 | 3.55 | 4.8 | 13-12 |
| | RH | Volstad C | 30 | 4.58 | 5.1 | 12-9 |
| ▶ | RH | Johnson J | 28 | 2.30 | 4.3 | 11-6 |
| | RH | Nolasco R | 26 | 4.51 | 4.4 | 14-9 |

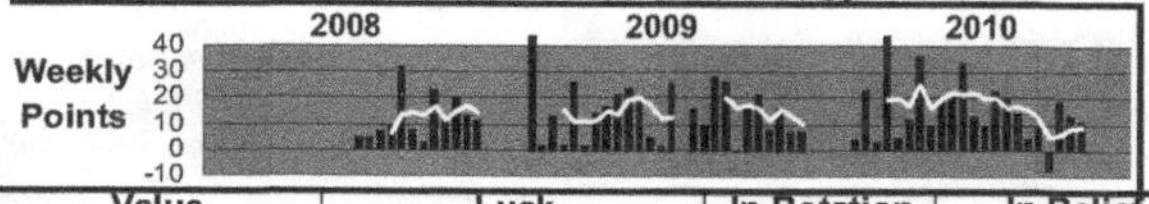
Weekly Points
2008
2009
2010
40
30
20
10
0
-10

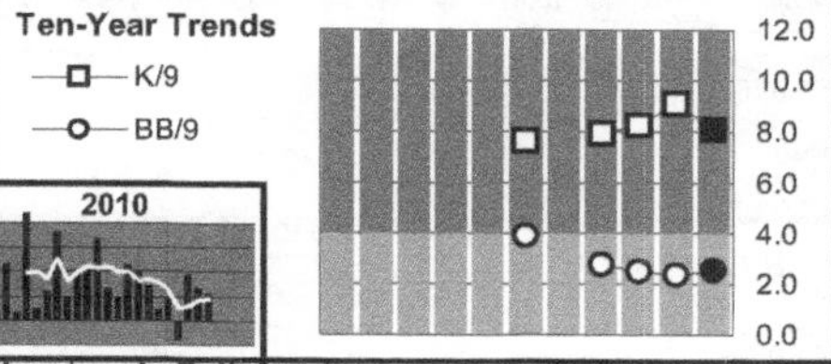
Ten-Year Trends
K/9
BB/9
12.0
10.0
8.0
6.0
4.0
2.0
0.0

| Yr | $1L | $2L | Pts | RAA | H% | HR/fb | S% | FIP | GS | CG | QS/DS | GR | Hld | Bln | Lead | OPS | 1st Hf | 2nd Hf | vs RH | vs LH |
|---|---|---|---|---|---|---|---|---|---|---|---|---|---|---|---|---|---|---|---|---|
| | **Value** | | | | **Luck** | | | | **In Rotation** | | | **In Relief** | | | | **OPS** | | | | |
| 07 | -$6 | -$9 | 0 | −9 | 47% | 8% | 68% | 4.54 | 4 | 0 | 0/2 | — | — | — | — | .982 | .982 | — | .857 | 1.109 |
| 08 | $4 | $0 | 140 | +7 | 34% | 9% | 75% | 3.41 | 14 | 1 | 10/1 | — | — | — | — | .723 | .632 | .729 | .709 | .735 |
| 09 | $20 | $14 | 350 | +26 | 30% | 8% | 73% | 3.08 | 33 | 2 | 23/1 | — | — | — | — | .629 | .595 | .682 | .649 | .611 |
| 10 | $23 | $23 | 330 | +40 | 30% | 4% | 80% | 2.45 | 28 | 1 | 23/1 | — | — | — | — | .607 | .548 | .714 | .602 | .612 |

## Josh Judy — 60 IP | $-1 | 50 pts

No MLB games played in 2010 — Owned: 0% — RH

Judy is a well-regarded relief prospect poised to break into CLE's bullpen in 2011. Only a lack of space on the 40-man postponed his debut. His mid-90's fastball and plus-slider have contributed to a robust career K/9. Judy should break camp with the team and could make a rapid ascent through the RP ranks. (BLS)

| Player | Age | IP | W | Sv | K | ERA | WHIP | K/9 | BB/9 | $2L | Pts |
|---|---|---|---|---|---|---|---|---|---|---|---|
| | | **Forecast** | | | | | | | | | |
| Judy J | 25 | 60 | 1 | 0 | 50 | 4.53 | 1.47 | 7.6 | 3.4 | -$1 | 50 |
| **Mini-Browser** | **Age** | **IP** | **W** | **Sv** | **K** | **ERA** | **WHIP** | **K/9** | **BB/9** | **$2L** | **Pts** |
| Johnson J | 27 | 60 | 3 | 2 | 41 | 4.61 | 1.53 | 6.2 | 3.3 | -$1 | 60 |
| Hill R | 31 | 40 | 2 | 0 | 35 | 4.69 | 1.48 | 7.8 | 4.6 | -$1 | 50 |
| Norberto J | 24 | 40 | 3 | 0 | 47 | 4.13 | 1.59 | 10.5 | 6.4 | -$1 | 60 |
| Salas F | 25 | 40 | 1 | 0 | 41 | 4.10 | 1.45 | 9.2 | 3.6 | -$1 | 50 |
| Gorzelanny T | 28 | 140 | 7 | 0 | 111 | 4.67 | 1.48 | 7.1 | 4.1 | -$1 | 150 |

| Level | Leag | W | L | Sv | IP | H | K | ERA | WHIP | K/9 | BB/9 | HR/9 | GB/F |
|---|---|---|---|---|---|---|---|---|---|---|---|---|---|
| | | **Minors (2010)** | | | | | | | | **Skills** | | | |
| A | — | — | — | — | — | — | — | — | — | — | — | — | — |
| AA | EL | 0 | 0 | 0 | 2 | 6 | 2 | 9.00 | 3.00 | 9.0 | 0.0 | 0.0 | — |
| AAA | IL | 3 | 0 | 2 | 47 | 48 | 55 | 2.68 | 1.32 | 10.5 | 2.7 | 1.0 | — |

| Yr | Team | W | L | Sv | IP | H | K | ERA | WHIP | K/9 | BB/9 | HR/9 | GB/F |
|---|---|---|---|---|---|---|---|---|---|---|---|---|---|
| | | **Majors** | | | | | | | | **Skills** | | | |
| 07 | — | — | — | — | — | — | — | — | — | — | — | — | — |
| 08 | — | — | — | — | — | — | — | — | — | — | — | — | — |
| 09 | — | — | — | — | — | — | — | — | — | — | — | — | — |
| 10 | — | — | — | — | — | — | — | — | — | — | — | — | — |

**Competition at RP** — **Stats in 2010 as RP**

| Thr | Player | GR | ERA | IP/G | Sv-Hld |
|---|---|---|---|---|---|
| RH | Perez C | 63 | 1.71 | 1.0 | 23-9 |
| RH | Smith J | 53 | 3.83 | 0.8 | 0-17 |
| RH | Herrmann F | 40 | 4.03 | 1.1 | 1-7 |
| RH | Lewis J | 37 | 2.97 | 1.0 | 0-1 |

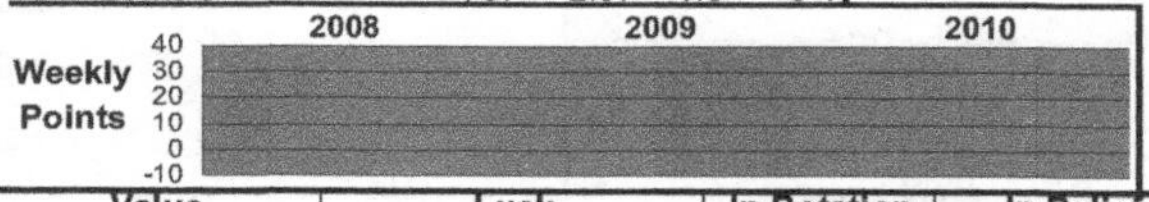
Weekly Points
2008
2009
2010
40
30
20
10
0
-10

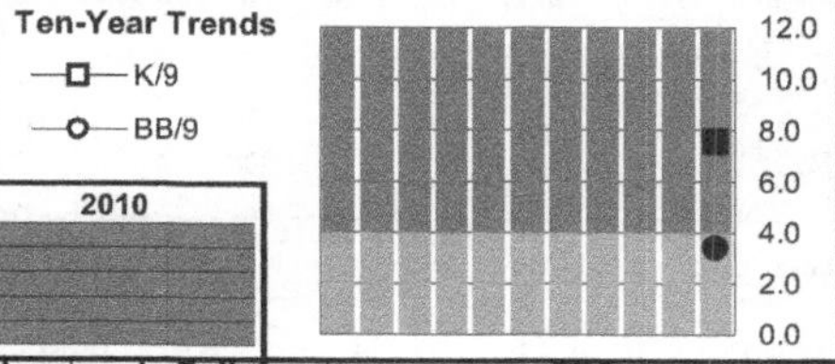
Ten-Year Trends
K/9
BB/9
12.0
10.0
8.0
6.0
4.0
2.0
0.0

| Yr | $1L | $2L | Pts | RAA | H% | HR/fb | S% | FIP | GS | CG | QS/DS | GR | Hld | Bln | Lead | OPS | 1st Hf | 2nd Hf | vs RH | vs LH |
|---|---|---|---|---|---|---|---|---|---|---|---|---|---|---|---|---|---|---|---|---|
| | **Value** | | | | **Luck** | | | | **In Rotation** | | | **In Relief** | | | | **OPS** | | | | |
| 07 | — | — | — | — | — | — | — | — | — | — | — | — | — | — | — | — | — | — | — | — |
| 08 | — | — | — | — | — | — | — | — | — | — | — | — | — | — | — | — | — | — | — | — |
| 09 | — | — | — | — | — | — | — | — | — | — | — | — | — | — | — | — | — | — | — | — |
| 10 | — | — | — | — | — | — | — | — | — | — | — | — | — | — | — | — | — | — | — | — |

## ▮ Jair Jurrjens — 200 IP | $9 | 250 pts

SP-20 — Owned: 86% — RH

Jurrjens in 2010 was coming off 400 innings of 3.10-ERA ball, but injuries limited his assistance at the start and end of the year, and he underwent arthroscopic knee surgery in October. If healthy, Jurrjens could still be one of the best starters on a very deep Atlanta staff. A low HR/9 is key to his success. (MG)

| Player | Age | IP | W | Sv | K | ERA | WHIP | K/9 | BB/9 | $2L | Pts |
|---|---|---|---|---|---|---|---|---|---|---|---|
| | | **Forecast** | | | | | | | | | |
| Jurrjens J | 25 | 200 | 13 | 0 | 141 | 4.08 | 1.34 | 6.3 | 3.1 | $9 | 250 |
| **Mini-Browser** | **Age** | **IP** | **W** | **Sv** | **K** | **ERA** | **WHIP** | **K/9** | **BB/9** | **$2L** | **Pts** |
| Rodriguez F | 29 | 60 | 3 | 21 | 66 | 3.14 | 1.27 | 9.9 | 4.2 | $10 | 200 |
| Bumgarner M | 21 | 160 | 10 | 0 | 133 | 3.57 | 1.36 | 7.5 | 2.3 | $10 | 220 |
| Lackey J | 32 | 200 | 13 | 0 | 143 | 4.32 | 1.35 | 6.4 | 2.7 | $9 | 240 |
| Shields J | 29 | 200 | 13 | 0 | 155 | 4.63 | 1.30 | 7.0 | 2.1 | $9 | 250 |
| Duensing B | 28 | 160 | 11 | 0 | 98 | 3.88 | 1.34 | 5.5 | 2.7 | $9 | 190 |

| Level | Leag | W | L | Sv | IP | H | K | ERA | WHIP | K/9 | BB/9 | HR/9 | GB/F |
|---|---|---|---|---|---|---|---|---|---|---|---|---|---|
| | | **Minors (2010)** | | | | | | | | **Skills** | | | |
| A | — | — | — | — | — | — | — | — | — | — | — | — | — |
| AA | — | — | — | — | — | — | — | — | — | — | — | — | — |
| AAA | IL | 1 | 1 | 0 | 13 | 20 | 9 | 5.54 | 2.00 | 6.2 | 4.2 | 1.4 | — |

| Yr | Team | W | L | Sv | IP | H | K | ERA | WHIP | K/9 | BB/9 | HR/9 | GB/F |
|---|---|---|---|---|---|---|---|---|---|---|---|---|---|
| | | **Majors** | | | | | | | | **Skills** | | | |
| 07 | DET | 3 | 1 | 0 | 30 | 24 | 13 | 4.70 | 1.14 | 3.8 | 3.2 | 1.2 | 0.9 |
| 08 | ATL | 13 | 10 | 0 | 188 | 188 | 139 | 3.68 | 1.37 | 6.6 | 3.3 | 0.5 | 1.9 |
| 09 | ATL | 14 | 10 | 0 | 215 | 186 | 152 | 2.60 | 1.21 | 6.4 | 3.1 | 0.6 | 1.1 |
| 10 | ATL | 7 | 6 | 0 | 116 | 120 | 86 | 4.64 | 1.39 | 6.7 | 3.2 | 1.0 | 1.0 |

**Competition at SP** — **Stats in 2010 as SP**

| | Thr | Player | GS | ERA | Supp | W-L |
|---|---|---|---|---|---|---|
| | RH | Hudson T | 34 | 2.83 | 4.6 | 17-9 |
| | RH | Hanson T | 34 | 3.33 | 4.3 | 10-11 |
| | RH | Lowe D | 33 | 4.00 | 4.7 | 16-12 |
| ▶ | RH | Jurrjens J | 20 | 4.64 | 4.3 | 7-6 |

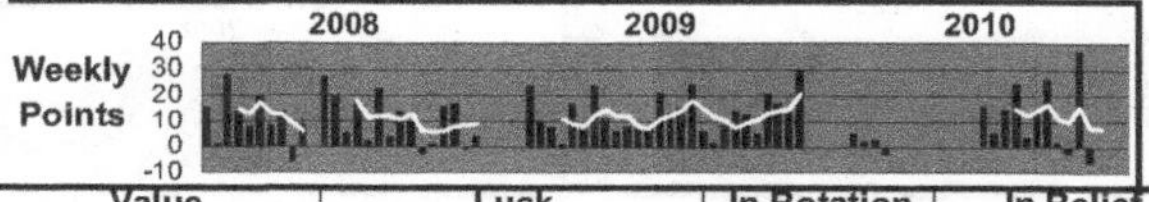
Weekly Points
2008
2009
2010
40
30
20
10
0
-10

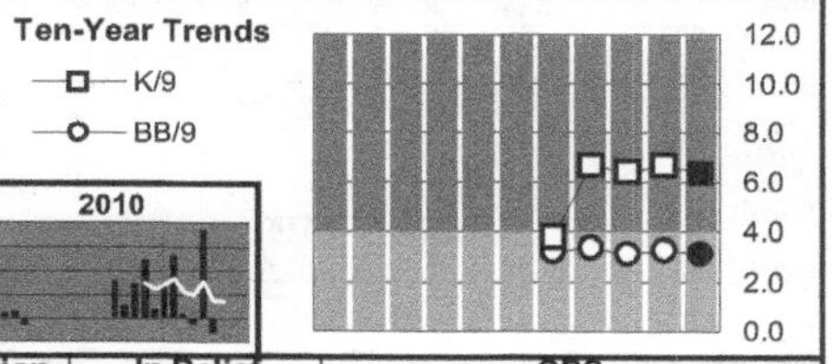
Ten-Year Trends
K/9
BB/9
12.0
10.0
8.0
6.0
4.0
2.0
0.0

| Yr | $1L | $2L | Pts | RAA | H% | HR/fb | S% | FIP | GS | CG | QS/DS | GR | Hld | Bln | Lead | OPS | 1st Hf | 2nd Hf | vs RH | vs LH |
|---|---|---|---|---|---|---|---|---|---|---|---|---|---|---|---|---|---|---|---|---|
| | **Value** | | | | **Luck** | | | | **In Rotation** | | | **In Relief** | | | | **OPS** | | | | |
| 07 | $0 | -$2 | 40 | −1 | 22% | 9% | 61% | 5.22 | 7 | 0 | 1/2 | — | — | — | — | .717 | — | .717 | .509 | .874 |
| 08 | $9 | $0 | 250 | +6 | 31% | 7% | 73% | 3.60 | 31 | 0 | 17/3 | — | — | — | — | .711 | .687 | .744 | .686 | .733 |
| 09 | $21 | $15 | 310 | +35 | 28% | 6% | 81% | 3.74 | 34 | 0 | 25/1 | — | — | — | — | .660 | .686 | .632 | .597 | .729 |
| 10 | -$2 | -$14 | 130 | −6 | 31% | 9% | 68% | 4.26 | 20 | 0 | 10/4 | — | — | — | — | .791 | .739 | .813 | .725 | .873 |

## Jeff Karstens — 80 IP | $-4 | 50 pts

SP-19, RP-7 — Owned: 1% — RH

Although Karstens's final 2010 numbers were unimpressive, he did help solidify an ailing Pirates rotation. This is probably his natural level, so the Pirates are apt to confer his rotation spot on a more talented arm. Karstens will probably hang around as a depth starter, though the Pirates could non-tender him. (MB)

| Player | Age | IP | W | Sv | K | ERA | WHIP | K/9 | BB/9 | $2L | Pts |
|---|---|---|---|---|---|---|---|---|---|---|---|
| | | **Forecast** | | | | | | | | | |
| Karstens J | 28 | 80 | 3 | 0 | 45 | 5.09 | 1.44 | 5.1 | 2.6 | -$4 | 50 |
| **Mini-Browser** | **Age** | **IP** | **W** | **Sv** | **K** | **ERA** | **WHIP** | **K/9** | **BB/9** | **$2L** | **Pts** |
| Rowland-Smith R | 28 | 80 | 3 | 0 | 45 | 5.35 | 1.52 | 5.1 | 3.4 | -$4 | 50 |
| Doubront F | 23 | 60 | 3 | 0 | 56 | 5.41 | 1.69 | 8.3 | 3.8 | -$4 | 60 |
| Kawakami K | 35 | 100 | 4 | 0 | 63 | 4.96 | 1.46 | 5.7 | 3.4 | -$4 | 70 |
| Weaver J | 34 | 40 | 2 | 0 | 24 | 5.63 | 1.49 | 5.4 | 3.3 | -$4 | 30 |
| Harrison M | 25 | 80 | 4 | 0 | 47 | 5.30 | 1.56 | 5.3 | 3.8 | -$4 | 50 |

| Level | Leag | W | L | Sv | IP | H | K | ERA | WHIP | K/9 | BB/9 | HR/9 | GB/F |
|---|---|---|---|---|---|---|---|---|---|---|---|---|---|
| | | **Minors (2010)** | | | | | | | | **Skills** | | | |
| A | — | — | — | — | — | — | — | — | — | — | — | — | — |
| AA | — | — | — | — | — | — | — | — | — | — | — | — | — |
| AAA | IL | 1 | 2 | 0 | 16 | 21 | 12 | 7.31 | 1.44 | 6.8 | 1.1 | 1.7 | — |

| Yr | Team | W | L | Sv | IP | H | K | ERA | WHIP | K/9 | BB/9 | HR/9 | GB/F |
|---|---|---|---|---|---|---|---|---|---|---|---|---|---|
| | | **Majors** | | | | | | | | **Skills** | | | |
| 07 | NYY | 1 | 4 | 0 | 14 | 27 | 5 | 11.05 | 2.45 | 3.1 | 5.5 | 2.5 | 0.5 |
| 08 | PIT | 2 | 6 | 0 | 51 | 56 | 23 | 4.03 | 1.34 | 4.0 | 2.3 | 1.2 | 1.1 |
| 09 | PIT | 4 | 6 | 0 | 108 | 115 | 52 | 5.42 | 1.48 | 4.3 | 3.8 | 1.0 | 0.8 |
| 10 | PIT | 3 | 10 | 0 | 122 | 146 | 72 | 4.92 | 1.41 | 5.3 | 2.0 | 1.5 | 1.1 |

**Competition at SP** — **Stats in 2010 as SP**

| | Thr | Player | GS | ERA | Supp | W-L |
|---|---|---|---|---|---|---|
| | LH | Maholm P | 32 | 5.10 | 4.0 | 9-15 |
| | LH | Duke Z | 29 | 5.72 | 3.8 | 8-15 |
| | RH | Ohlendorf R | 21 | 4.07 | 2.9 | 1-11 |
| ▶ | RH | Karstens J | 19 | 4.78 | 3.6 | 3-10 |

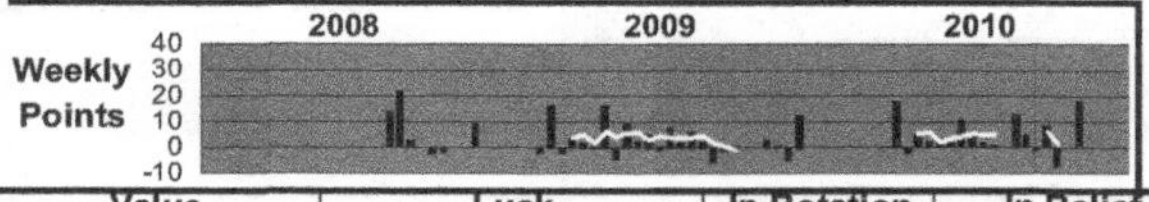
Weekly Points
2008
2009
2010
40
30
20
10
0
-10

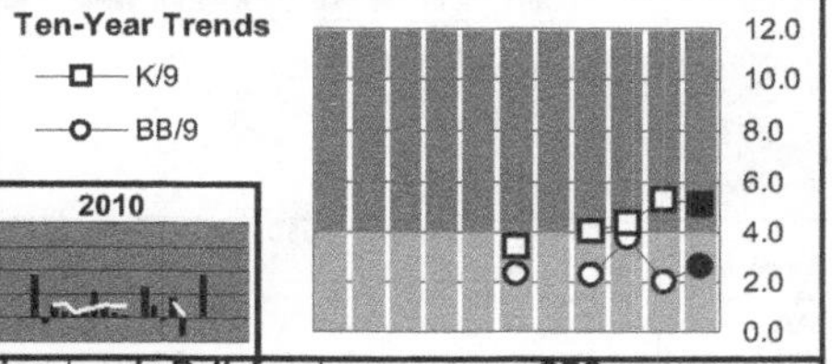
Ten-Year Trends
K/9
BB/9
12.0
10.0
8.0
6.0
4.0
2.0
0.0

| Yr | $1L | $2L | Pts | RAA | H% | HR/fb | S% | FIP | GS | CG | QS/DS | GR | Hld | Bln | Lead | OPS | 1st Hf | 2nd Hf | vs RH | vs LH |
|---|---|---|---|---|---|---|---|---|---|---|---|---|---|---|---|---|---|---|---|---|
| | **Value** | | | | **Luck** | | | | **In Rotation** | | | **In Relief** | | | | **OPS** | | | | |
| 07 | -$7 | -$11 | -10 | −14 | 40% | 13% | 56% | 8.00 | 3 | 0 | 0/2 | 4 | 0 | 0 | −1.7 | 1.167 | 1.216 | 1.145 | 1.010 | 1.335 |
| 08 | -$1 | -$3 | 40 | −7 | 29% | 10% | 74% | 4.84 | 9 | 1 | 5/2 | — | — | — | — | .774 | — | .774 | .812 | .737 |
| 09 | -$5 | -$8 | 60 | −13 | 30% | 7% | 64% | 4.93 | 13 | 0 | 4/1 | 26 | 1 | 0 | −0.3 | .827 | .800 | .886 | .824 | .828 |
| 10 | -$6 | -$20 | 70 | −11 | 31% | 13% | 70% | 4.91 | 19 | 0 | 10/2 | 7 | 0 | 0 | −0.8 | .837 | .888 | .747 | .683 | 1.027 |

## ▮ Kenshin Kawakami — 100 IP | $-4 | 70 pts

SP-16, RP-2 — Owned: 47% — RH

Bobby Cox has lost all confidence in KK. Kawakami has not established that he can post consistent stuff from start to start or go deep into games (only 5.4 IP/G). Atlanta will probably try to move him (maybe back to Japan); if they cannot, they might eat all or part of the remainder of his contract and release him. (MG)

| Player | Age | IP | W | Sv | K | ERA | WHIP | K/9 | BB/9 | $2L | Pts |
|---|---|---|---|---|---|---|---|---|---|---|---|
| | | **Forecast** | | | | | | | | | |
| Kawakami K | 35 | 100 | 4 | 0 | 63 | 4.96 | 1.46 | 5.7 | 3.4 | -$4 | 70 |
| **Mini-Browser** | **Age** | **IP** | **W** | **Sv** | **K** | **ERA** | **WHIP** | **K/9** | **BB/9** | **$2L** | **Pts** |
| Hernandez D | 25 | 60 | 4 | 0 | 56 | 5.64 | 1.64 | 8.5 | 4.6 | -$4 | 70 |
| Olson G | 27 | 50 | 2 | 0 | 35 | 5.51 | 1.58 | 6.3 | 4.4 | -$4 | 30 |
| Morris B | 24 | 40 | 2 | 0 | 27 | 5.15 | 1.55 | 6.2 | 3.8 | -$4 | 30 |
| Rowland-Smith R | 28 | 80 | 3 | 0 | 45 | 5.35 | 1.52 | 5.1 | 3.4 | -$4 | 50 |
| Doubront F | 23 | 60 | 3 | 0 | 56 | 5.41 | 1.69 | 8.3 | 3.8 | -$4 | 60 |

| Level | Leag | W | L | Sv | IP | H | K | ERA | WHIP | K/9 | BB/9 | HR/9 | GB/F |
|---|---|---|---|---|---|---|---|---|---|---|---|---|---|
| | | **Minors (2010)** | | | | | | | | **Skills** | | | |
| A | — | — | — | — | — | — | — | — | — | — | — | — | — |
| AA | — | — | — | — | — | — | — | — | — | — | — | — | — |
| AAA | IL | 0 | 1 | 0 | 21 | 26 | 22 | 4.29 | 1.48 | 9.4 | 2.1 | 2.1 | — |

| Yr | Team | W | L | Sv | IP | H | K | ERA | WHIP | K/9 | BB/9 | HR/9 | GB/F |
|---|---|---|---|---|---|---|---|---|---|---|---|---|---|
| | | **Majors** | | | | | | | | **Skills** | | | |
| 07 | — | — | — | — | — | — | — | — | — | — | — | — | — |
| 08 | — | — | — | — | — | — | — | — | — | — | — | — | — |
| 09 | ATL | 7 | 12 | 1 | 156 | 153 | 105 | 3.86 | 1.34 | 6.0 | 3.3 | 0.9 | 1.1 |
| 10 | ATL | 1 | 10 | 0 | 87 | 98 | 59 | 5.15 | 1.49 | 6.1 | 3.3 | 1.0 | 1.0 |

**Competition at SP** — **Stats in 2010 as SP**

| Thr | Player | GS | ERA | Supp | W-L |
|---|---|---|---|---|---|
| RH | Hudson T | 34 | 2.83 | 4.6 | 17-9 |
| RH | Hanson T | 34 | 3.33 | 4.3 | 10-11 |
| RH | Lowe D | 33 | 4.00 | 4.7 | 16-12 |
| RH | Jurrjens J | 20 | 4.64 | 4.3 | 7-6 |

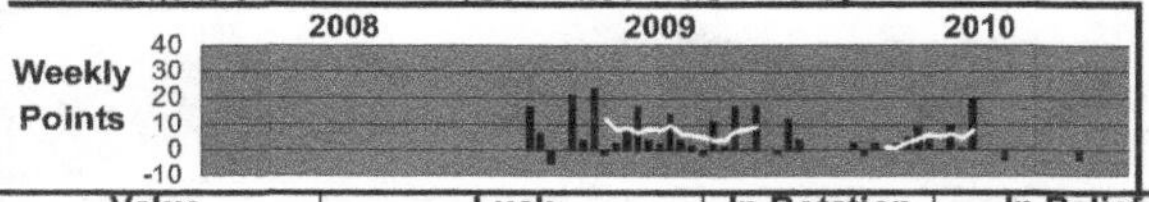
Weekly Points
2008
2009
2010
40
30
20
10
0
-10

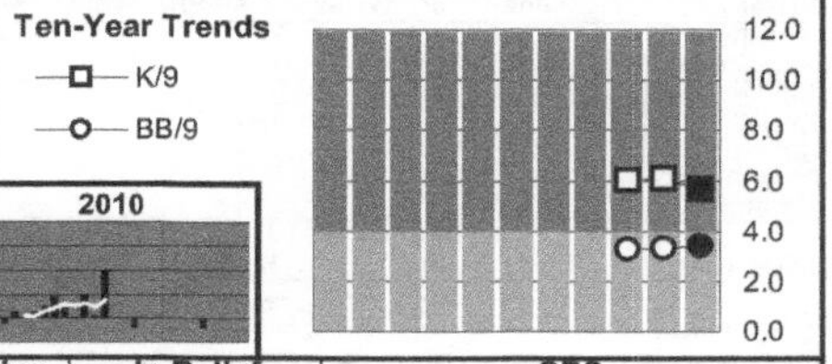
Ten-Year Trends
K/9
BB/9
12.0
10.0
8.0
6.0
4.0
2.0
0.0

| Yr | $1L | $2L | Pts | RAA | H% | HR/fb | S% | FIP | GS | CG | QS/DS | GR | Hld | Bln | Lead | OPS | 1st Hf | 2nd Hf | vs RH | vs LH |
|---|---|---|---|---|---|---|---|---|---|---|---|---|---|---|---|---|---|---|---|---|
| | **Value** | | | | **Luck** | | | | **In Rotation** | | | **In Relief** | | | | **OPS** | | | | |
| 07 | — | — | — | — | — | — | — | — | — | — | — | — | — | — | — | — | — | — | — | — |
| 08 | — | — | — | — | — | — | — | — | — | — | — | — | — | — | — | — | — | — | — | — |
| 09 | $5 | $1 | 160 | +4 | 29% | 8% | 73% | 4.20 | 25 | 0 | 13/3 | 7 | 0 | 0 | +0.3 | .766 | .774 | .755 | .835 | .702 |
| 10 | -$8 | -$20 | 40 | −14 | 32% | 9% | 67% | 4.44 | 16 | 0 | 7/3 | 2 | 0 | 0 | −0.4 | .830 | .784 | 1.434 | .788 | .880 |

*For more stats, visit www.Rotolympus.com.*

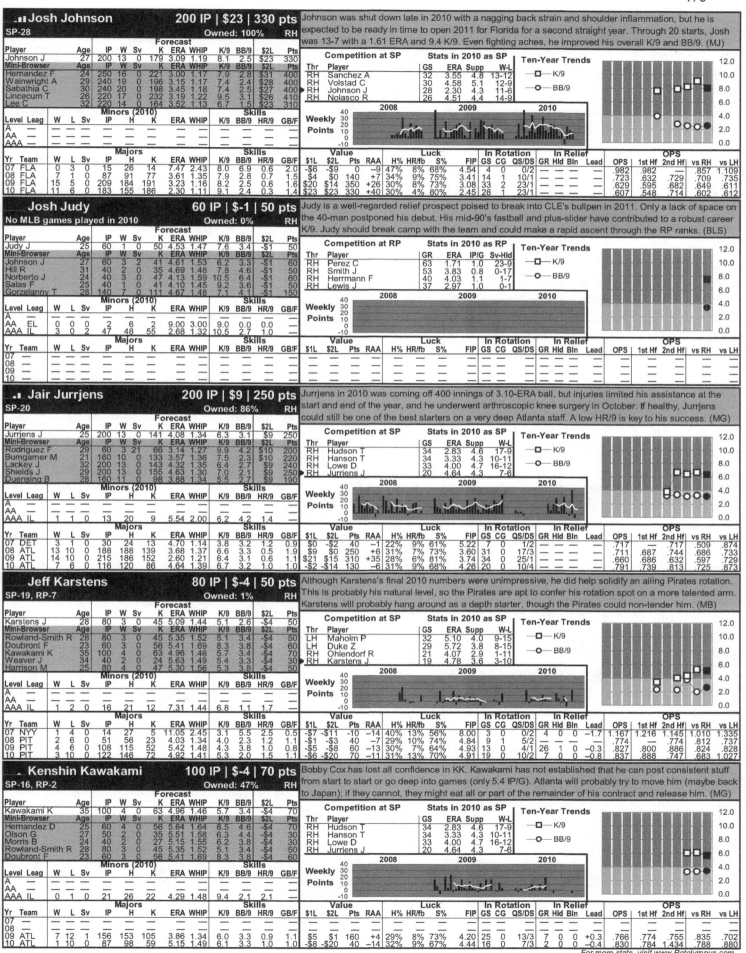

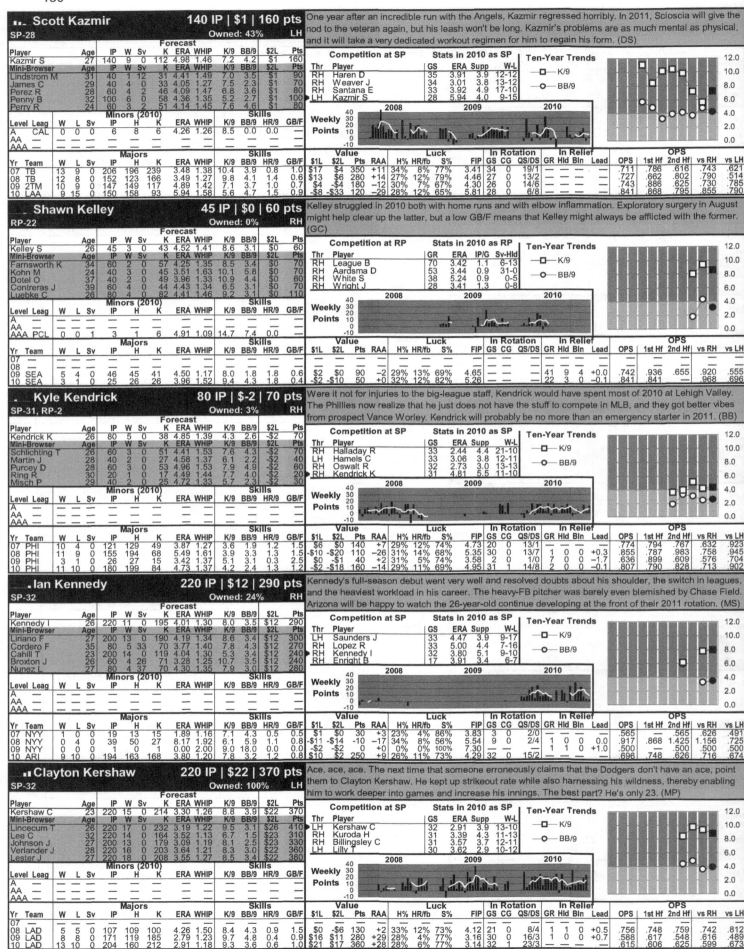

## Scott Kazmir — 140 IP | $1 | 160 pts
**SP-28** — Owned: 43% — LH

One year after an incredible run with the Angels, Kazmir regressed horribly. In 2011, Scioscia will give the nod to the veteran again, but his leash won't be long. Kazmir's problems are as much mental as physical, and it will take a very dedicated workout regimen for him to regain his form. (DS)

### Forecast
| Player | Age | IP | W | Sv | K | ERA | WHIP | K/9 | BB/9 | $2L | Pts |
|---|---|---|---|---|---|---|---|---|---|---|---|
| Kazmir S | 27 | 140 | 9 | 0 | 112 | 4.98 | 1.46 | 7.2 | 4.2 | $1 | 160 |
| **Mini-Browser** | **Age** | **IP** | **W** | **Sv** | **K** | **ERA** | **WHIP** | **K/9** | **BB/9** | **$2L** | **Pts** |
| Lindstrom M | 31 | 40 | 1 | 12 | 31 | 4.41 | 1.49 | 7.0 | 3.5 | $1 | 90 |
| James C | 29 | 40 | 4 | 0 | 33 | 4.05 | 1.27 | 7.5 | 2.3 | $1 | 70 |
| Perez R | 28 | 60 | 4 | 2 | 46 | 4.09 | 1.47 | 6.8 | 3.6 | $1 | 80 |
| Penny B | 32 | 100 | 6 | 0 | 58 | 4.36 | 1.35 | 5.2 | 2.7 | $1 | 100 |
| Perry R | 24 | 60 | 3 | 4 | 51 | 4.14 | 1.45 | 7.6 | 4.3 | $1 | 80 |

### Minors (2010)
| Level | Leag | W | L | Sv | IP | H | K | ERA | WHIP | K/9 | BB/9 | HR/9 | GB/F |
|---|---|---|---|---|---|---|---|---|---|---|---|---|---|
| A | CAL | 0 | 0 | 0 | 6 | 8 | 6 | 4.26 | 1.26 | 8.5 | 0.0 | 0.0 | — |
| AA | — | | | | | | | | | | | | |
| AAA | — | | | | | | | | | | | | |

### Majors
| Yr | Team | W | L | Sv | IP | H | K | ERA | WHIP | K/9 | BB/9 | HR/9 | GB/F | $1L | $2L | Pts | RAA | H% | HR/fb | S% | FIP | GS | CG | QS/DS | GR | Hld | Bln | Lead | OPS | 1st Hf | 2nd Hf | vs RH | vs LH |
|---|---|---|---|---|---|---|---|---|---|---|---|---|---|---|---|---|---|---|---|---|---|---|---|---|---|---|---|---|---|---|---|---|---|
| 07 | TB | 13 | 9 | 0 | 206 | 196 | 239 | 3.48 | 1.38 | 10.4 | 3.9 | 0.8 | 1.0 | $17 | $4 | 350 | +11 | 34% | 8% | 77% | 3.41 | 34 | 0 | 19/1 | — | — | — | — | .711 | .786 | .616 | .743 | .621 |
| 08 | TB | 12 | 8 | 0 | 152 | 123 | 166 | 3.49 | 1.27 | 9.8 | 4.1 | 1.4 | 0.6 | $13 | $6 | 280 | +14 | 27% | 12% | 79% | 4.46 | 27 | 0 | 13/2 | — | — | — | — | .727 | .662 | .802 | .790 | .514 |
| 09 | 2TM | 10 | 9 | 0 | 147 | 149 | 117 | 4.89 | 1.42 | 7.1 | 3.7 | 1.0 | 0.7 | $4 | -$8 | 140 | -12 | 30% | 7% | 67% | 4.30 | 26 | 0 | 14/6 | — | — | — | — | .743 | .886 | .625 | .730 | .785 |
| 10 | LAA | 9 | 15 | 0 | 150 | 158 | 93 | 5.94 | 1.58 | 5.6 | 4.7 | 1.5 | 0.9 | -$8 | -$33 | -20 | -29 | 28% | 12% | 65% | 5.81 | 28 | 0 | 6/8 | — | — | — | — | .841 | .868 | .795 | .855 | .790 |

---

## Shawn Kelley — 45 IP | $0 | 60 pts
**RP-22** — Owned: 0% — RH

Kelley struggled in 2010 both with home runs and with elbow inflammation. Exploratory surgery in August might help clear up the latter, but a low GB/F means that Kelley might always be afflicted with the former. (GC)

### Forecast
| Player | Age | IP | W | Sv | K | ERA | WHIP | K/9 | BB/9 | $2L | Pts |
|---|---|---|---|---|---|---|---|---|---|---|---|
| Kelley S | 26 | 45 | 3 | 0 | 43 | 4.52 | 1.41 | 8.6 | 3.1 | $0 | 60 |
| **Mini-Browser** | **Age** | **IP** | **W** | **Sv** | **K** | **ERA** | **WHIP** | **K/9** | **BB/9** | **$2L** | **Pts** |
| Farnsworth K | 34 | 60 | 2 | 0 | 57 | 4.25 | 1.35 | 8.5 | 3.4 | $0 | 70 |
| Kohn M | 24 | 40 | 2 | 0 | 45 | 3.51 | 1.63 | 10.1 | 5.8 | $0 | 70 |
| Dotel O | 37 | 40 | 2 | 0 | 49 | 3.96 | 1.33 | 10.9 | 4.4 | $0 | 60 |
| Contreras J | 39 | 60 | 4 | 0 | 44 | 4.43 | 1.34 | 6.5 | 3.1 | $0 | 70 |
| Luebke C | 26 | 80 | 4 | 0 | 82 | 4.41 | 1.46 | 9.2 | 3.6 | $0 | 110 |

### Minors (2010)
| Level | Leag | W | L | Sv | IP | H | K | ERA | WHIP | K/9 | BB/9 | HR/9 | GB/F |
|---|---|---|---|---|---|---|---|---|---|---|---|---|---|
| A | — | | | | | | | | | | | | |
| AA | — | | | | | | | | | | | | |
| AAA | PCL | 0 | 0 | 1 | 3 | 1 | 6 | 4.91 | 1.09 | 14.7 | 7.4 | 0.0 | — |

### Majors
| Yr | Team | W | L | Sv | IP | H | K | ERA | WHIP | K/9 | BB/9 | HR/9 | GB/F | $1L | $2L | Pts | RAA | H% | HR/fb | S% | FIP | GS | CG | QS/DS | GR | Hld | Bln | Lead | OPS | 1st Hf | 2nd Hf | vs RH | vs LH |
|---|---|---|---|---|---|---|---|---|---|---|---|---|---|---|---|---|---|---|---|---|---|---|---|---|---|---|---|---|---|---|---|---|---|
| 07 | | | | | | | | | | | | | | | | | | | | | | | | | | | | | | | | | |
| 08 | | | | | | | | | | | | | | | | | | | | | | | | | | | | | | | | | |
| 09 | SEA | 5 | 4 | 0 | 46 | 45 | 41 | 4.50 | 1.17 | 8.0 | 1.8 | 1.8 | 0.6 | $2 | $0 | 90 | -2 | 29% | 13% | 69% | 4.65 | — | — | — | 41 | 9 | 4 | +0.0 | .742 | .936 | .655 | .920 | .555 |
| 10 | SEA | 3 | 1 | 0 | 25 | 26 | 36 | 3.96 | 1.52 | 9.4 | 4.3 | 1.8 | 0.4 | -$2 | -$10 | 50 | 0 | 32% | 12% | 82% | 5.26 | — | — | — | 22 | 3 | 0 | -0.1 | .841 | .841 | — | .968 | .696 |

---

## Kyle Kendrick — 80 IP | $-2 | 70 pts
**SP-31, RP-2** — Owned: 3% — RH

Were it not for injuries to the big-league staff, Kendrick would have spent most of 2010 at Lehigh Valley. The Phillies now realize that he just does not have the stuff to compete in MLB, and they got better vibes from prospect Vance Worley. Kendrick will probably be no more than an emergency starter in 2011. (BB)

### Forecast
| Player | Age | IP | W | Sv | K | ERA | WHIP | K/9 | BB/9 | $2L | Pts |
|---|---|---|---|---|---|---|---|---|---|---|---|
| Kendrick K | 26 | 80 | 5 | 0 | 38 | 4.85 | 1.39 | 4.3 | 2.6 | -$2 | 70 |
| **Mini-Browser** | **Age** | **IP** | **W** | **Sv** | **K** | **ERA** | **WHIP** | **K/9** | **BB/9** | **$2L** | **Pts** |
| Schlichting T | 26 | 60 | 3 | 0 | 51 | 4.41 | 1.53 | 7.6 | 4.3 | -$2 | 70 |
| Martin J | 28 | 40 | 2 | 0 | 27 | 4.58 | 1.37 | 6.1 | 2.2 | -$2 | 40 |
| Purcey D | 28 | 60 | 4 | 0 | 53 | 4.96 | 1.53 | 7.9 | 4.9 | -$2 | 60 |
| Ring R | 30 | 20 | 1 | 0 | 17 | 4.49 | 1.44 | 7.7 | 4.0 | -$2 | 20 |
| Misch P | 29 | 40 | 2 | 0 | 25 | 4.72 | 1.33 | 5.7 | 2.3 | -$2 | 30 |

### Minors (2010)
| Level | Leag | W | L | Sv | IP | H | K | ERA | WHIP | K/9 | BB/9 | HR/9 | GB/F |
|---|---|---|---|---|---|---|---|---|---|---|---|---|---|
| A | — | | | | | | | | | | | | |
| AA | — | | | | | | | | | | | | |
| AAA | — | | | | | | | | | | | | |

### Majors
| Yr | Team | W | L | Sv | IP | H | K | ERA | WHIP | K/9 | BB/9 | HR/9 | GB/F | $1L | $2L | Pts | RAA | H% | HR/fb | S% | FIP | GS | CG | QS/DS | GR | Hld | Bln | Lead | OPS | 1st Hf | 2nd Hf | vs RH | vs LH |
|---|---|---|---|---|---|---|---|---|---|---|---|---|---|---|---|---|---|---|---|---|---|---|---|---|---|---|---|---|---|---|---|---|---|
| 07 | PHI | 10 | 4 | 0 | 121 | 129 | 49 | 3.87 | 1.24 | 3.6 | 1.9 | 1.2 | 1.5 | $6 | $0 | 140 | +7 | 29% | 12% | 74% | 4.73 | 20 | 0 | 13/1 | — | — | — | — | .774 | .794 | .767 | .632 | .923 |
| 08 | PHI | 11 | 9 | 0 | 155 | 194 | 68 | 5.49 | 1.61 | 3.9 | 3.3 | 1.3 | 1.5 | -$10 | -$20 | 110 | -26 | 31% | 14% | 68% | 5.35 | 30 | 0 | 13/7 | 1 | 0 | 0 | +0.3 | .855 | .787 | .983 | .758 | .945 |
| 09 | PHI | 3 | 1 | 0 | 26 | 27 | 15 | 3.42 | 1.37 | 5.1 | 3.1 | 0.3 | 2.5 | $0 | -$1 | 40 | +2 | 31% | 5% | 74% | 3.58 | 2 | 0 | 1/0 | 7 | 0 | 0 | -1.7 | .636 | .899 | .609 | .576 | .704 |
| 10 | PHI | 11 | 10 | 0 | 180 | 199 | 84 | 4.73 | 1.37 | 4.2 | 2.4 | 1.3 | 1.2 | -$2 | -$18 | 160 | -14 | 29% | 11% | 69% | 4.95 | 31 | 1 | 14/8 | — | — | — | -0.1 | .807 | .790 | .828 | .713 | .902 |

---

## Ian Kennedy — 220 IP | $12 | 290 pts
**SP-32** — Owned: 24% — RH

Kennedy's full-season debut went very well and resolved doubts about his shoulder, the switch in leagues, and the heaviest workload in his career. The heavy-FB pitcher was barely even blemished by Chase Field. Arizona will be happy to watch the 26-year-old continue developing at the front of their 2011 rotation. (MS)

### Forecast
| Player | Age | IP | W | Sv | K | ERA | WHIP | K/9 | BB/9 | $2L | Pts |
|---|---|---|---|---|---|---|---|---|---|---|---|
| Kennedy I | 26 | 220 | 11 | 0 | 195 | 4.01 | 1.30 | 8.0 | 3.5 | $12 | 290 |
| **Mini-Browser** | **Age** | **IP** | **W** | **Sv** | **K** | **ERA** | **WHIP** | **K/9** | **BB/9** | **$2L** | **Pts** |
| Liriano F | 27 | 200 | 13 | 0 | 190 | 4.19 | 1.34 | 8.6 | 3.4 | $12 | 300 |
| Cordero F | 35 | 80 | 5 | 33 | 70 | 3.77 | 1.40 | 7.8 | 4.3 | $12 | 270 |
| Cahill T | 23 | 200 | 14 | 0 | 119 | 4.04 | 1.30 | 5.3 | 3.4 | $12 | 240 |
| Broxton J | 26 | 60 | 4 | 26 | 71 | 3.28 | 1.25 | 10.7 | 3.5 | $12 | 240 |
| Nunez L | 27 | 80 | 4 | 37 | 70 | 4.30 | 1.35 | 7.9 | 3.0 | $12 | 280 |

### Minors (2010)
| Level | Leag | W | L | Sv | IP | H | K | ERA | WHIP | K/9 | BB/9 | HR/9 | GB/F |
|---|---|---|---|---|---|---|---|---|---|---|---|---|---|
| A | — | | | | | | | | | | | | |
| AA | — | | | | | | | | | | | | |
| AAA | — | | | | | | | | | | | | |

### Majors
| Yr | Team | W | L | Sv | IP | H | K | ERA | WHIP | K/9 | BB/9 | HR/9 | GB/F | $1L | $2L | Pts | RAA | H% | HR/fb | S% | FIP | GS | CG | QS/DS | GR | Hld | Bln | Lead | OPS | 1st Hf | 2nd Hf | vs RH | vs LH |
|---|---|---|---|---|---|---|---|---|---|---|---|---|---|---|---|---|---|---|---|---|---|---|---|---|---|---|---|---|---|---|---|---|---|
| 07 | NYY | 1 | 0 | 0 | 19 | 13 | 15 | 1.89 | 1.16 | 7.1 | 4.3 | 0.5 | 0.5 | $1 | $0 | 30 | +3 | 23% | 4% | 86% | 3.83 | 3 | 0 | 2/0 | — | — | — | — | .565 | — | .565 | .626 | .491 |
| 08 | NYY | 0 | 4 | 0 | 39 | 50 | 27 | 8.17 | 1.92 | 6.1 | 5.9 | 1.1 | 0.8 | -$15 | -$14 | -10 | -17 | 34% | 8% | 56% | 5.54 | 9 | 0 | 2/4 | 1 | 0 | 0.0 | .917 | .868 | 1.425 | 1.156 | .725 |
| 09 | NYY | 0 | 0 | 0 | 1 | 0 | 1 | 0.00 | 2.00 | 9.0 | 18.0 | 0.0 | 0.0 | -$2 | -$2 | 0 | +0 | 0% | 0% | 100% | 7.30 | — | — | — | 1 | 1 | 0 | +1.0 | .500 | — | .500 | .500 | .500 |
| 10 | ARI | 9 | 10 | 0 | 194 | 163 | 168 | 3.80 | 1.20 | 7.8 | 3.2 | 1.2 | 0.8 | $10 | $22 | 250 | +9 | 26% | 11% | 73% | 4.29 | 32 | 0 | 15/2 | — | — | — | — | .630 | .636 | .626 | .716 | .541 |

---

## Clayton Kershaw — 220 IP | $22 | 370 pts
**SP-32** — Owned: 100% — LH

Ace, ace, ace. The next time that someone erroneously claims that the Dodgers don't have an ace, point them to Clayton Kershaw. He kept up strikeout rate while also harnessing his wildness, thereby enabling him to work deeper into games and increase his innings. The best part? He's only 23. (MP)

### Forecast
| Player | Age | IP | W | Sv | K | ERA | WHIP | K/9 | BB/9 | $2L | Pts |
|---|---|---|---|---|---|---|---|---|---|---|---|
| Kershaw C | 23 | 220 | 15 | 0 | 214 | 3.30 | 1.26 | 8.8 | 3.9 | $22 | 370 |
| **Mini-Browser** | **Age** | **IP** | **W** | **Sv** | **K** | **ERA** | **WHIP** | **K/9** | **BB/9** | **$2L** | **Pts** |
| Lincecum T | 26 | 220 | 17 | 0 | 232 | 3.19 | 1.22 | 9.5 | 3.1 | $22 | 410 |
| Lee C | 32 | 220 | 14 | 0 | 164 | 3.52 | 1.13 | 6.7 | 1.5 | $23 | 310 |
| Johnson J | 27 | 200 | 13 | 0 | 179 | 3.09 | 1.19 | 8.1 | 2.5 | $23 | 330 |
| Verlander J | 28 | 220 | 16 | 0 | 203 | 3.64 | 1.21 | 8.3 | 3.0 | $23 | 360 |
| Lester J | 27 | 220 | 18 | 0 | 208 | 3.55 | 1.27 | 8.5 | 3.4 | $22 | 380 |

### Minors (2010)
| Level | Leag | W | L | Sv | IP | H | K | ERA | WHIP | K/9 | BB/9 | HR/9 | GB/F |
|---|---|---|---|---|---|---|---|---|---|---|---|---|---|
| A | — | | | | | | | | | | | | |
| AA | — | | | | | | | | | | | | |
| AAA | — | | | | | | | | | | | | |

### Majors
| Yr | Team | W | L | Sv | IP | H | K | ERA | WHIP | K/9 | BB/9 | HR/9 | GB/F | $1L | $2L | Pts | RAA | H% | HR/fb | S% | FIP | GS | CG | QS/DS | GR | Hld | Bln | Lead | OPS | 1st Hf | 2nd Hf | vs RH | vs LH |
|---|---|---|---|---|---|---|---|---|---|---|---|---|---|---|---|---|---|---|---|---|---|---|---|---|---|---|---|---|---|---|---|---|---|
| 07 | | | | | | | | | | | | | | | | | | | | | | | | | | | | | | | | | |
| 08 | LAD | 5 | 5 | 0 | 107 | 109 | 100 | 4.26 | 1.50 | 8.4 | 4.3 | 0.9 | 1.5 | $0 | -$6 | 130 | +2 | 33% | 12% | 73% | 4.12 | 21 | 0 | 8/4 | 1 | 0 | 0 | +0.5 | .756 | .748 | .759 | .742 | .812 |
| 09 | LAD | 8 | 8 | 0 | 171 | 119 | 185 | 2.79 | 1.23 | 9.7 | 4.8 | 0.4 | 0.9 | $16 | $11 | 280 | +29 | 28% | 4% | 77% | 3.16 | 30 | 0 | 16/3 | 1 | 0 | 0 | +0.7 | .588 | .617 | .548 | .616 | .489 |
| 10 | LAD | 13 | 10 | 0 | 204 | 160 | 212 | 2.91 | 1.18 | 9.3 | 3.6 | 0.6 | 0.9 | $21 | $17 | 360 | +28 | 28% | 6% | 77% | 3.14 | 32 | 1 | 23/3 | — | — | — | — | .615 | .606 | .625 | .599 | .673 |

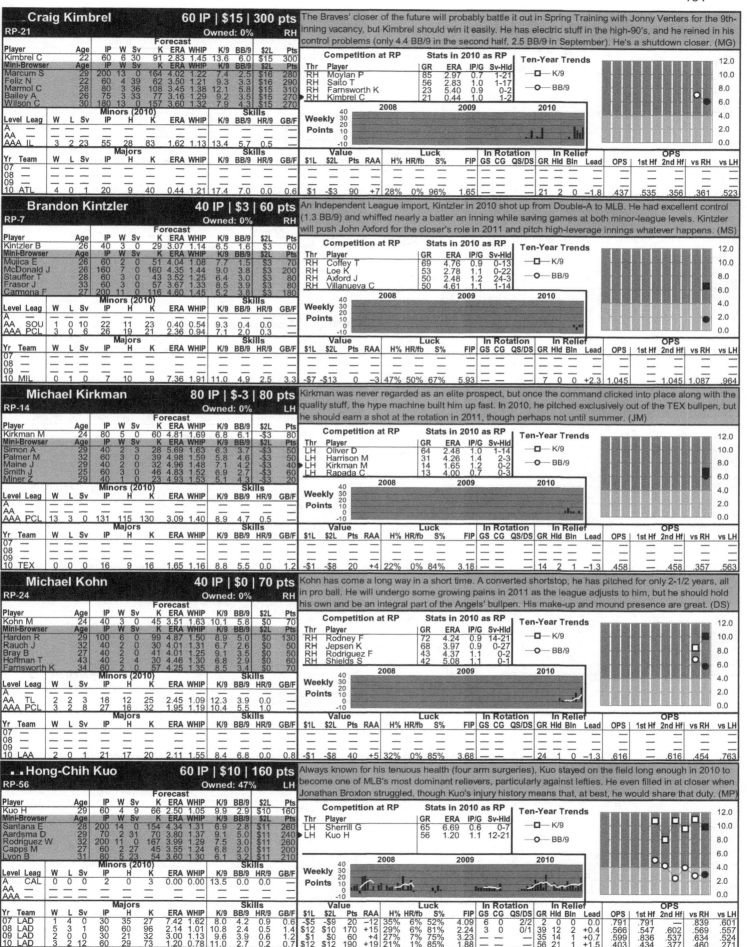

## Craig Kimbrel — 60 IP | $15 | 300 pts
**RP-21** — Owned: 0% — RH

The Braves' closer of the future will probably battle it out in Spring Training with Jonny Venters for the 9th-inning vacancy, but Kimbrel should win it easily. He has electric stuff in the high-90's, and he reined in his control problems (only 4.4 BB/9 in the second half, 2.5 BB/9 in September). He's a shutdown closer. (MG)

### Forecast
| Player | Age | IP | W | Sv | K | ERA | WHIP | K/9 | BB/9 | $2L | Pts |
|---|---|---|---|---|---|---|---|---|---|---|---|
| Kimbrel C | 22 | 60 | 6 | 30 | 91 | 2.83 | 1.45 | 13.6 | 6.0 | $15 | 300 |
| Mini-Browser | Age | IP | W | Sv | K | ERA | WHIP | K/9 | BB/9 | $2L | Pts |
| Marcum S | 29 | 200 | 13 | 0 | 164 | 4.02 | 1.22 | 7.4 | 2.5 | $16 | 280 |
| Feliz N | 22 | 60 | 4 | 39 | 62 | 3.50 | 1.21 | 9.3 | 3.3 | $16 | 290 |
| Marmol C | 28 | 80 | 3 | 36 | 108 | 3.45 | 1.38 | 12.1 | 5.8 | $15 | 310 |
| Bailey A | 26 | 75 | 3 | 33 | 77 | 3.16 | 1.29 | 9.2 | 3.5 | $15 | 270 |
| Wilson C | 30 | 180 | 13 | 0 | 157 | 3.60 | 1.32 | 7.9 | 4.3 | $15 | 270 |

### Minors (2010) / Skills
| Level | Leag | W | L | Sv | IP | H | K | ERA | WHIP | K/9 | BB/9 | HR/9 | GB/F |
|---|---|---|---|---|---|---|---|---|---|---|---|---|---|
| A | — | | | | | | | | | | | | |
| AA | — | | | | | | | | | | | | |
| AAA | IL | 3 | 2 | 23 | 55 | 28 | 83 | 1.62 | 1.13 | 13.4 | 5.7 | 0.5 | — |

### Majors / Skills
| Yr | Team | W | L | Sv | IP | H | K | ERA | WHIP | K/9 | BB/9 | HR/9 | GB/F |
|---|---|---|---|---|---|---|---|---|---|---|---|---|---|
| 07 | — | | | | | | | | | | | | |
| 08 | — | | | | | | | | | | | | |
| 09 | — | | | | | | | | | | | | |
| 10 | ATL | 4 | 0 | 1 | 20 | 9 | 40 | 0.44 | 1.21 | 17.4 | 7.0 | 0.0 | 0.6 |

**Competition at RP / Stats in 2010 as RP**
| Thr | Player | GR | ERA | IP/G | Sv-Hld |
|---|---|---|---|---|---|
| RH | Moylan P | 85 | 2.97 | 0.7 | 1-21 |
| RH | Saito T | 56 | 2.83 | 1.0 | 1-17 |
| RH | Farnsworth K | 23 | 5.40 | 0.9 | 0-2 |
| RH | Kimbrel C | 21 | 0.44 | 1.0 | 1-2 |

Ten-Year Trends: K/9, BB/9

### Value / Luck / In Rotation / In Relief / OPS
| $1L | $2L | Pts | RAA | H% | HR/fb | S% | FIP | GS | CG | QS/DS | GR | Hld | Bln | Lead | OPS | 1st Hf | 2nd Hf | vs RH | vs LH |
|---|---|---|---|---|---|---|---|---|---|---|---|---|---|---|---|---|---|---|---|
| $1 | -$3 | 90 | +7 | 28% | 0% | 96% | 1.65 | — | — | — | 21 | 2 | 0 | -1.8 | .437 | .535 | .356 | .361 | .523 |

## Brandon Kintzler — 40 IP | $3 | 60 pts
**RP-7** — Owned: 0% — RH

An Independent League import, Kintzler in 2010 shot up from Double-A to MLB. He had excellent control (1.3 BB/9) and whiffed nearly a batter an inning while saving games at both minor-league levels. Kintzler will push John Axford for the closer's role in 2011 and pitch high-leverage innings whatever happens. (MS)

### Forecast
| Player | Age | IP | W | Sv | K | ERA | WHIP | K/9 | BB/9 | $2L | Pts |
|---|---|---|---|---|---|---|---|---|---|---|---|
| Kintzler B | 26 | 40 | 3 | 0 | 29 | 3.07 | 1.14 | 6.5 | 1.6 | $3 | 60 |
| Mini-Browser | Age | IP | W | Sv | K | ERA | WHIP | K/9 | BB/9 | $2L | Pts |
| Mujica E | 26 | 60 | 2 | 0 | 51 | 4.04 | 1.08 | 7.7 | 1.5 | $3 | 70 |
| McDonald J | 26 | 160 | 7 | 0 | 160 | 4.35 | 1.44 | 9.0 | 3.8 | $3 | 200 |
| Stauffer T | 28 | 60 | 3 | 0 | 43 | 3.52 | 1.25 | 6.4 | 3.0 | $3 | 80 |
| Frasor J | 33 | 60 | 3 | 0 | 57 | 3.67 | 1.33 | 8.5 | 3.9 | $3 | 80 |
| Carmona F | 27 | 200 | 11 | 0 | 116 | 4.60 | 1.45 | 5.2 | 3.8 | $3 | 180 |

### Minors (2010) / Skills
| Level | Leag | W | L | Sv | IP | H | K | ERA | WHIP | K/9 | BB/9 | HR/9 | GB/F |
|---|---|---|---|---|---|---|---|---|---|---|---|---|---|
| A | — | | | | | | | | | | | | |
| AA | SOU | 1 | 0 | 10 | 22 | 11 | 23 | 0.40 | 0.54 | 9.3 | 0.4 | 0.0 | — |
| AAA | PCL | 3 | 0 | 6 | 26 | 19 | 21 | 2.36 | 0.94 | 7.1 | 2.0 | 0.3 | — |

### Majors / Skills
| Yr | Team | W | L | Sv | IP | H | K | ERA | WHIP | K/9 | BB/9 | HR/9 | GB/F |
|---|---|---|---|---|---|---|---|---|---|---|---|---|---|
| 07 | — | | | | | | | | | | | | |
| 08 | — | | | | | | | | | | | | |
| 09 | — | | | | | | | | | | | | |
| 10 | MIL | 0 | 1 | 0 | 7 | 10 | 9 | 7.36 | 1.91 | 11.0 | 4.9 | 2.5 | 3.3 |

**Competition at RP / Stats in 2010 as RP**
| Thr | Player | GR | ERA | IP/G | Sv-Hld |
|---|---|---|---|---|---|
| RH | Coffey T | 69 | 4.76 | 0.9 | 0-13 |
| RH | Loe K | 53 | 2.78 | 1.1 | 0-22 |
| RH | Axford J | 50 | 2.48 | 1.2 | 24-3 |
| RH | Villanueva C | 50 | 4.61 | 1.1 | 1-14 |

Ten-Year Trends: K/9, BB/9

### Value / Luck / In Rotation / In Relief / OPS
| $1L | $2L | Pts | RAA | H% | HR/fb | S% | FIP | GS | CG | QS/DS | GR | Hld | Bln | Lead | OPS | 1st Hf | 2nd Hf | vs RH | vs LH |
|---|---|---|---|---|---|---|---|---|---|---|---|---|---|---|---|---|---|---|---|
| -$7 | -$13 | 0 | -3 | 47% | 50% | 67% | 5.93 | — | — | — | 7 | 0 | 0 | +2.3 | 1.045 | — | 1.045 | 1.087 | .964 |

## Michael Kirkman — 80 IP | $-3 | 80 pts
**RP-14** — Owned: 0% — LH

Kirkman was never regarded as an elite prospect, but once the command clicked into place along with the quality stuff, the hype machine built him up fast. In 2010, he pitched exclusively out of the TEX bullpen, but he should earn a shot at the rotation in 2011, though perhaps not until summer. (JM)

### Forecast
| Player | Age | IP | W | Sv | K | ERA | WHIP | K/9 | BB/9 | $2L | Pts |
|---|---|---|---|---|---|---|---|---|---|---|---|
| Kirkman M | 24 | 80 | 5 | 0 | 60 | 4.81 | 1.69 | 6.8 | 6.1 | -$3 | 80 |
| Mini-Browser | Age | IP | W | Sv | K | ERA | WHIP | K/9 | BB/9 | $2L | Pts |
| Simon A | 29 | 40 | 2 | 3 | 28 | 5.69 | 1.63 | 6.3 | 3.7 | -$3 | 50 |
| Palmer M | 32 | 60 | 3 | 0 | 39 | 4.98 | 1.59 | 5.8 | 4.6 | -$3 | 50 |
| Maine J | 29 | 40 | 2 | 0 | 32 | 4.96 | 1.48 | 7.1 | 4.2 | -$3 | 40 |
| Smith J | 25 | 60 | 3 | 0 | 46 | 4.83 | 1.52 | 6.9 | 2.7 | -$3 | 60 |
| Miner Z | 29 | 40 | 2 | 0 | 23 | 4.93 | 1.53 | 5.1 | 4.3 | -$3 | 30 |

### Minors (2010) / Skills
| Level | Leag | W | L | Sv | IP | H | K | ERA | WHIP | K/9 | BB/9 | HR/9 | GB/F |
|---|---|---|---|---|---|---|---|---|---|---|---|---|---|
| A | — | | | | | | | | | | | | |
| AA | — | | | | | | | | | | | | |
| AAA | PCL | 13 | 3 | 0 | 131 | 115 | 130 | 3.09 | 1.40 | 8.9 | 4.7 | 0.5 | — |

### Majors / Skills
| Yr | Team | W | L | Sv | IP | H | K | ERA | WHIP | K/9 | BB/9 | HR/9 | GB/F |
|---|---|---|---|---|---|---|---|---|---|---|---|---|---|
| 07 | — | | | | | | | | | | | | |
| 08 | — | | | | | | | | | | | | |
| 09 | — | | | | | | | | | | | | |
| 10 | TEX | 0 | 0 | 0 | 16 | 9 | 16 | 1.65 | 1.16 | 8.8 | 5.5 | 0.0 | 1.2 |

**Competition at RP / Stats in 2010 as RP**
| Thr | Player | GR | ERA | IP/G | Sv-Hld |
|---|---|---|---|---|---|
| LH | Oliver D | 64 | 2.48 | 1.0 | 1-14 |
| LH | Harrison M | 31 | 4.26 | 1.4 | 2-3 |
| LH | Kirkman M | 14 | 1.65 | 1.2 | 0-2 |
| LH | Rapada C | 13 | 4.00 | 0.7 | 0-3 |

Ten-Year Trends: K/9, BB/9

### Value / Luck / In Rotation / In Relief / OPS
| $1L | $2L | Pts | RAA | H% | HR/fb | S% | FIP | GS | CG | QS/DS | GR | Hld | Bln | Lead | OPS | 1st Hf | 2nd Hf | vs RH | vs LH |
|---|---|---|---|---|---|---|---|---|---|---|---|---|---|---|---|---|---|---|---|
| -$1 | -$8 | 20 | +4 | 22% | 0% | 84% | 3.18 | — | — | — | 14 | 2 | 1 | -1.3 | .458 | — | .458 | .357 | .563 |

## Michael Kohn — 40 IP | $0 | 70 pts
**RP-24** — Owned: 0% — RH

Kohn has come a long way in a short time. A converted shortstop, he has pitched for only 2-1/2 years, all in pro ball. He will undergo some growing pains in 2011 as the league adjusts to him, but he should hold his own and be an integral part of the Angels' bullpen. His make-up and mound presence are great. (DS)

### Forecast
| Player | Age | IP | W | Sv | K | ERA | WHIP | K/9 | BB/9 | $2L | Pts |
|---|---|---|---|---|---|---|---|---|---|---|---|
| Kohn M | 24 | 40 | 3 | 0 | 45 | 3.51 | 1.63 | 10.1 | 5.8 | $0 | 70 |
| Mini-Browser | Age | IP | W | Sv | K | ERA | WHIP | K/9 | BB/9 | $2L | Pts |
| Harden R | 29 | 100 | 6 | 0 | 99 | 4.87 | 1.50 | 8.9 | 5.0 | $0 | 130 |
| Rauch J | 32 | 40 | 2 | 0 | 30 | 4.01 | 1.31 | 6.7 | 2.6 | $0 | 50 |
| Bray B | 27 | 40 | 2 | 0 | 41 | 4.01 | 1.25 | 9.1 | 3.5 | $0 | 50 |
| Hoffman T | 43 | 40 | 2 | 4 | 30 | 4.46 | 1.30 | 6.8 | 2.9 | $0 | 60 |
| Farnsworth K | 34 | 60 | 2 | 0 | 57 | 4.25 | 1.35 | 8.5 | 3.4 | $0 | 70 |

### Minors (2010) / Skills
| Level | Leag | W | L | Sv | IP | H | K | ERA | WHIP | K/9 | BB/9 | HR/9 | GB/F |
|---|---|---|---|---|---|---|---|---|---|---|---|---|---|
| A | — | | | | | | | | | | | | |
| AA | TL | 2 | 2 | 3 | 18 | 12 | 25 | 2.45 | 1.09 | 12.3 | 3.9 | 0.0 | — |
| AAA | PCL | 3 | 2 | 8 | 27 | 16 | 32 | 1.95 | 1.19 | 10.4 | 5.5 | 1.0 | — |

### Majors / Skills
| Yr | Team | W | L | Sv | IP | H | K | ERA | WHIP | K/9 | BB/9 | HR/9 | GB/F |
|---|---|---|---|---|---|---|---|---|---|---|---|---|---|
| 07 | — | | | | | | | | | | | | |
| 08 | — | | | | | | | | | | | | |
| 09 | — | | | | | | | | | | | | |
| 10 | LAA | 1 | 1 | 0 | 21 | 17 | 20 | 2.11 | 1.55 | 8.4 | 6.0 | 0.0 | 0.8 |

**Competition at RP / Stats in 2010 as RP**
| Thr | Player | GR | ERA | IP/G | Sv-Hld |
|---|---|---|---|---|---|
| RH | Rodney F | 72 | 4.24 | 0.9 | 14-21 |
| RH | Jepsen K | 68 | 3.97 | 0.9 | 0-27 |
| RH | Rodriguez F | 43 | 4.37 | 1.1 | 0-2 |
| RH | Shields S | 42 | 5.08 | 1.1 | 0-1 |

Ten-Year Trends: K/9, BB/9

### Value / Luck / In Rotation / In Relief / OPS
| $1L | $2L | Pts | RAA | H% | HR/fb | S% | FIP | GS | CG | QS/DS | GR | Hld | Bln | Lead | OPS | 1st Hf | 2nd Hf | vs RH | vs LH |
|---|---|---|---|---|---|---|---|---|---|---|---|---|---|---|---|---|---|---|---|
| -$1 | -$4 | 20 | +5 | 32% | 0% | 85% | 3.68 | — | — | — | 24 | 1 | 0 | -1.3 | .616 | — | .616 | .454 | .763 |

## Hong-Chih Kuo — 60 IP | $10 | 160 pts
**RP-56** — Owned: 47% — LH

Always known for his tenuous health (four arm surgeries), Kuo stayed on the field long enough in 2010 to become one of MLB's most dominant relievers, particularly against lefties. He even filled in at closer when Jonathan Broxton struggled, though Kuo's injury history means that, at best, he would share that duty. (MP)

### Forecast
| Player | Age | IP | W | Sv | K | ERA | WHIP | K/9 | BB/9 | $2L | Pts |
|---|---|---|---|---|---|---|---|---|---|---|---|
| Kuo H | 29 | 60 | 4 | 9 | 66 | 2.50 | 1.05 | 9.9 | 2.9 | $10 | 160 |
| Mini-Browser | Age | IP | W | Sv | K | ERA | WHIP | K/9 | BB/9 | $2L | Pts |
| Santana E | 28 | 200 | 14 | 0 | 154 | 4.34 | 1.31 | 6.9 | 2.8 | $11 | 260 |
| Aardsma D | 29 | 70 | 2 | 31 | 70 | 3.80 | 1.37 | 9.1 | 5.0 | $11 | 240 |
| Rodriguez W | 32 | 200 | 11 | 0 | 167 | 3.99 | 1.29 | 7.5 | 3.0 | $11 | 260 |
| Capps M | 27 | 60 | 2 | 27 | 45 | 3.55 | 1.24 | 6.8 | 2.0 | $11 | 210 |
| Lyon B | 31 | 80 | 5 | 23 | 54 | 3.60 | 1.30 | 6.1 | 3.2 | $11 | 210 |

### Minors (2010) / Skills
| Level | Leag | W | L | Sv | IP | H | K | ERA | WHIP | K/9 | BB/9 | HR/9 | GB/F |
|---|---|---|---|---|---|---|---|---|---|---|---|---|---|
| A | CAL | 0 | 0 | 0 | 2 | 0 | 3 | 0.00 | 0.00 | 13.5 | 0.0 | 0.0 | — |
| AA | — | | | | | | | | | | | | |
| AAA | — | | | | | | | | | | | | |

### Majors / Skills
| Yr | Team | W | L | Sv | IP | H | K | ERA | WHIP | K/9 | BB/9 | HR/9 | GB/F |
|---|---|---|---|---|---|---|---|---|---|---|---|---|---|
| 07 | LAD | 1 | 4 | 0 | 30 | 35 | 27 | 7.42 | 1.62 | 8.0 | 4.2 | 0.9 | 0.6 |
| 08 | LAD | 5 | 3 | 1 | 80 | 60 | 96 | 2.14 | 1.01 | 10.8 | 2.4 | 0.5 | 1.4 |
| 09 | LAD | 0 | 0 | 0 | 30 | 21 | 32 | 3.00 | 1.13 | 9.6 | 3.9 | 0.6 | 1.2 |
| 10 | LAD | 3 | 2 | 12 | 60 | 29 | 73 | 1.20 | 0.78 | 11.0 | 2.7 | 0.2 | 0.7 |

**Competition at RP / Stats in 2010 as RP**
| Thr | Player | GR | ERA | IP/G | Sv-Hld |
|---|---|---|---|---|---|
| LH | Sherrill G | 65 | 6.69 | 0.6 | 0-7 |
| LH | Kuo H | 56 | 1.20 | 1.1 | 12-21 |

Ten-Year Trends: K/9, BB/9

### Value / Luck / In Rotation / In Relief / OPS
| Yr | $1L | $2L | Pts | RAA | H% | HR/fb | S% | FIP | GS | CG | QS/DS | GR | Hld | Bln | Lead | OPS | 1st Hf | 2nd Hf | vs RH | vs LH |
|---|---|---|---|---|---|---|---|---|---|---|---|---|---|---|---|---|---|---|---|---|
| 07 | -$5 | -$9 | 20 | -12 | 35% | 6% | 52% | 4.09 | 6 | 0 | 2/2 | 2 | 0 | 0 | 0.0 | .791 | .791 | — | .839 | .601 |
| 08 | $12 | $10 | 170 | +15 | 29% | 6% | 81% | 2.24 | 3 | 0 | 0/1 | 39 | 12 | 2 | +0.4 | .566 | .547 | .602 | .569 | .557 |
| 09 | $1 | $0 | 60 | +4 | 27% | 7% | 75% | 3.23 | — | — | — | 35 | 14 | 1 | +0.7 | .599 | .836 | .537 | .634 | .524 |
| 10 | $12 | $12 | 190 | +19 | 21% | 6% | 85% | 1.88 | — | — | — | 56 | 21 | 1 | +1.5 | .403 | .434 | .377 | .460 | .271 |

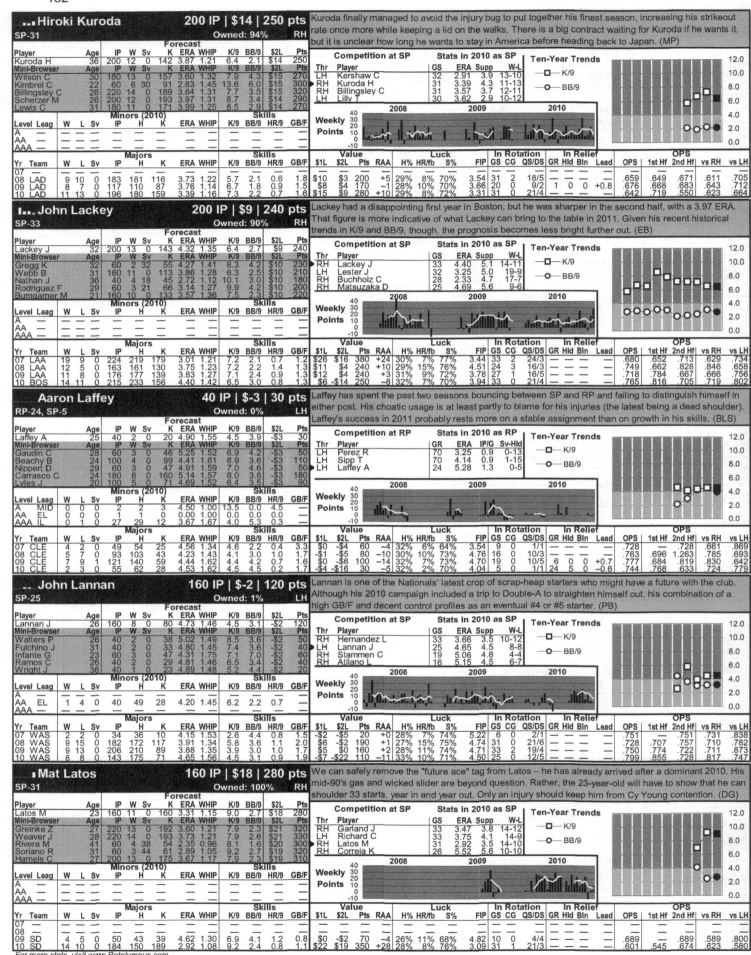

## Hiroki Kuroda — 200 IP | $14 | 250 pts
SP-31 — Owned: 94% — RH

Kuroda finally managed to avoid the injury bug to put together his finest season, increasing his strikeout rate once more while keeping a lid on the walks. There is a big contract waiting for Kuroda if he wants it, but it is unclear how long he wants to stay in America before heading back to Japan. (MP)

### Forecast
| Player | Age | IP | W | Sv | K | ERA | WHIP | K/9 | BB/9 | $2L | Pts |
|---|---|---|---|---|---|---|---|---|---|---|---|
| Kuroda H | 36 | 200 | 12 | 0 | 142 | 3.87 | 1.21 | 6.4 | 2.1 | $14 | 250 |

| Mini-Browser | Age | IP | W | Sv | K | ERA | WHIP | K/9 | BB/9 | $2L | Pts |
|---|---|---|---|---|---|---|---|---|---|---|---|
| Wilson C | 30 | 180 | 13 | 0 | 157 | 3.60 | 1.32 | 7.9 | 4.3 | $15 | 270 |
| Kimbrel C | 22 | 60 | 6 | 30 | 91 | 2.83 | 1.45 | 13.6 | 6.0 | $15 | 300 |
| Billingsley C | 26 | 220 | 14 | 0 | 189 | 3.84 | 1.31 | 7.7 | 3.5 | $15 | 320 |
| Scherzer M | 26 | 200 | 12 | 0 | 193 | 3.97 | 1.31 | 8.7 | 3.4 | $14 | 290 |
| Lewis C | 31 | 180 | 11 | 0 | 171 | 3.99 | 1.25 | 8.5 | 2.9 | $14 | 270 |

### Minors (2010)
| Level | Leag | W | L | Sv | IP | H | K | ERA | WHIP | K/9 | BB/9 | HR/9 | GB/F |
|---|---|---|---|---|---|---|---|---|---|---|---|---|---|
| A | — | — | — | — | — | — | — | — | — | — | — | — | — |
| AA | — | — | — | — | — | — | — | — | — | — | — | — | — |
| AAA | — | — | — | — | — | — | — | — | — | — | — | — | — |

### Majors / Skills / Value / Luck / In Rotation / In Relief / OPS
| Yr | Team | W | L | Sv | IP | H | K | ERA | WHIP | K/9 | BB/9 | HR/9 | GB/F | $1L | $2L | Pts | RAA | H% | HR/fb | S% | FIP | GS | CG | QS/DS | GR | Hld | Bln | Lead | OPS | 1st Hf | 2nd Hf | vs RH | vs LH |
|---|---|---|---|---|---|---|---|---|---|---|---|---|---|---|---|---|---|---|---|---|---|---|---|---|---|---|---|---|---|---|---|---|---|
| 07 | — | | | | | | | | | | | | | | | | | | | | | | | | | | | | | | | | |
| 08 | LAD | 9 | 10 | 0 | 183 | 181 | 116 | 3.73 | 1.22 | 5.7 | 2.1 | 0.6 | 1.8 | $10 | $3 | 200 | +5 | 29% | 8% | 70% | 3.54 | 31 | 2 | 18/5 | — | — | — | — | .659 | .649 | .671 | .611 | .705 |
| 09 | LAD | 8 | 7 | 0 | 117 | 110 | 87 | 3.76 | 1.14 | 6.7 | 1.8 | 0.9 | 1.5 | $8 | $4 | 170 | −1 | 28% | 10% | 70% | 3.66 | 20 | 0 | 9/2 | 1 | 0 | 0 | +0.8 | .676 | .668 | .683 | .643 | .712 |
| 10 | LAD | 11 | 13 | 0 | 196 | 180 | 159 | 3.39 | 1.16 | 7.3 | 2.2 | 0.7 | 1.6 | $15 | $9 | 280 | +10 | 29% | 8% | 72% | 3.31 | 31 | 0 | 21/4 | — | — | — | — | .642 | .677 | .550 | .623 | .664 |

### Competition at SP / Stats in 2010 as SP
| Thr | Player | GS | ERA | Supp | W-L |
|---|---|---|---|---|---|
| LH | Kershaw C | 32 | 2.91 | 3.9 | 13-10 |
| RH | Kuroda H | 31 | 3.39 | 4.3 | 11-13 |
| RH | Billingsley C | 31 | 3.57 | 3.7 | 12-11 |
| LH | Lilly T | 30 | 3.62 | 2.9 | 10-12 |

---

## John Lackey — 200 IP | $9 | 240 pts
SP-33 — Owned: 90% — RH

Lackey had a disappointing first year in Boston, but he was sharper in the second half, with a 3.97 ERA. That figure is more indicative of what Lackey can bring to the table in 2011. Given his recent historical trends in K/9 and BB/9, though, the prognosis becomes less bright further out. (EB)

### Forecast
| Player | Age | IP | W | Sv | K | ERA | WHIP | K/9 | BB/9 | $2L | Pts |
|---|---|---|---|---|---|---|---|---|---|---|---|
| Lackey J | 32 | 200 | 13 | 0 | 143 | 4.32 | 1.35 | 6.4 | 2.7 | $9 | 240 |

| Mini-Browser | Age | IP | W | Sv | K | ERA | WHIP | K/9 | BB/9 | $2L | Pts |
|---|---|---|---|---|---|---|---|---|---|---|---|
| Gregg K | 32 | 60 | 2 | 32 | 55 | 4.27 | 1.41 | 8.3 | 4.2 | $10 | 230 |
| Webb B | 31 | 160 | 11 | 0 | 113 | 3.86 | 1.28 | 6.3 | 2.5 | $10 | 210 |
| Nathan J | 36 | 40 | 4 | 18 | 45 | 2.72 | 1.12 | 10.1 | 3.0 | $10 | 180 |
| Rodriguez F | 29 | 60 | 3 | 21 | 66 | 3.14 | 1.27 | 9.9 | 4.2 | $10 | 200 |
| Bumgarner M | 21 | 160 | 10 | 0 | 133 | 3.57 | 1.36 | 7.5 | 2.3 | $10 | 220 |

### Minors (2010)
| Level | Leag | W | L | Sv | IP | H | K | ERA | WHIP | K/9 | BB/9 | HR/9 | GB/F |
|---|---|---|---|---|---|---|---|---|---|---|---|---|---|
| A | — | — | — | — | — | — | — | — | — | — | — | — | — |
| AA | — | — | — | — | — | — | — | — | — | — | — | — | — |
| AAA | — | — | — | — | — | — | — | — | — | — | — | — | — |

### Majors / Skills / Value / Luck / In Rotation / In Relief / OPS
| Yr | Team | W | L | Sv | IP | H | K | ERA | WHIP | K/9 | BB/9 | HR/9 | GB/F | $1L | $2L | Pts | RAA | H% | HR/fb | S% | FIP | GS | CG | QS/DS | GR | Hld | Bln | Lead | OPS | 1st Hf | 2nd Hf | vs RH | vs LH |
|---|---|---|---|---|---|---|---|---|---|---|---|---|---|---|---|---|---|---|---|---|---|---|---|---|---|---|---|---|---|---|---|---|---|
| 07 | LAA | 19 | 9 | 0 | 224 | 219 | 179 | 3.01 | 1.21 | 7.2 | 2.1 | 0.7 | 1.2 | $26 | $16 | 380 | +24 | 30% | 7% | 77% | 3.44 | 33 | 2 | 24/3 | — | — | — | — | .680 | .652 | .713 | .629 | .734 |
| 08 | LAA | 12 | 5 | 0 | 163 | 161 | 130 | 3.75 | 1.23 | 7.2 | 2.2 | 1.4 | 1.3 | $11 | $4 | 240 | +10 | 29% | 15% | 76% | 4.51 | 24 | 3 | 16/3 | — | — | — | — | .749 | .662 | .828 | .846 | .658 |
| 09 | LAA | 11 | 8 | 0 | 176 | 177 | 139 | 3.83 | 1.27 | 7.1 | 2.4 | 0.9 | 1.3 | $12 | $4 | 240 | +3 | 31% | 9% | 72% | 3.78 | 27 | 1 | 16/5 | — | — | — | — | .718 | .784 | .667 | .666 | .756 |
| 10 | BOS | 14 | 11 | 0 | 215 | 233 | 156 | 4.40 | 1.42 | 6.5 | 3.0 | 0.8 | 1.3 | $6 | −$14 | 250 | −8 | 32% | 7% | 70% | 3.94 | 33 | 0 | 21/4 | — | — | — | — | .765 | .816 | .705 | .719 | .802 |

### Competition at SP / Stats in 2010 as SP
| Thr | Player | GS | ERA | Supp | W-L |
|---|---|---|---|---|---|
| RH | Lackey J | 33 | 4.40 | 5.1 | 14-11 |
| LH | Lester J | 32 | 3.25 | 5.0 | 19-9 |
| RH | Buchholz C | 28 | 2.33 | 4.7 | 17-7 |
| RH | Matsuzaka D | 25 | 4.69 | 5.6 | 9-6 |

---

## Aaron Laffey — 40 IP | $-3 | 30 pts
RP-24, SP-5 — Owned: 0% — LH

Laffey has spent the past two seasons bouncing between SP and RP and failing to distinguish himself in either post. His chaotic usage is at least partly to blame for his injuries (the latest being a dead shoulder). Laffey's success in 2011 probably rests more on a stable assignment than on growth in his skills. (BLS)

### Forecast
| Player | Age | IP | W | Sv | K | ERA | WHIP | K/9 | BB/9 | $2L | Pts |
|---|---|---|---|---|---|---|---|---|---|---|---|
| Laffey A | 25 | 40 | 2 | 0 | 20 | 4.90 | 1.55 | 4.5 | 3.9 | -$3 | 30 |

| Mini-Browser | Age | IP | W | Sv | K | ERA | WHIP | K/9 | BB/9 | $2L | Pts |
|---|---|---|---|---|---|---|---|---|---|---|---|
| Gaudin C | 28 | 60 | 3 | 0 | 46 | 5.25 | 1.52 | 6.9 | 4.2 | -$3 | 50 |
| Beachy B | 24 | 100 | 4 | 0 | 99 | 4.41 | 1.61 | 8.9 | 3.6 | -$3 | 110 |
| Nippert D | 29 | 60 | 3 | 0 | 47 | 4.91 | 1.59 | 7.0 | 4.6 | -$3 | 50 |
| Carrasco C | 24 | 180 | 8 | 0 | 160 | 5.14 | 1.57 | 8.0 | 3.8 | -$3 | 180 |
| Lyles J | 20 | 100 | 5 | 0 | 71 | 4.69 | 1.42 | 6.4 | 3.5 | -$3 | 90 |

### Minors (2010)
| Level | Leag | W | L | Sv | IP | H | K | ERA | WHIP | K/9 | BB/9 | HR/9 | GB/F |
|---|---|---|---|---|---|---|---|---|---|---|---|---|---|
| A | MID | 0 | 0 | 0 | 2 | 2 | 3 | 4.50 | 1.00 | 13.5 | 0.0 | 4.5 | — |
| AA | EL | 0 | 0 | 0 | 1 | 1 | 0 | 0.00 | 0.00 | 0.0 | 0.0 | 0.0 | — |
| AAA | IL | 0 | 1 | 0 | 27 | 29 | 12 | 3.67 | 1.67 | 4.0 | 5.3 | 0.3 | — |

### Majors / Skills / Value / Luck / In Rotation / In Relief / OPS
| Yr | Team | W | L | Sv | IP | H | K | ERA | WHIP | K/9 | BB/9 | HR/9 | GB/F | $1L | $2L | Pts | RAA | H% | HR/fb | S% | FIP | GS | CG | QS/DS | GR | Hld | Bln | Lead | OPS | 1st Hf | 2nd Hf | vs RH | vs LH |
|---|---|---|---|---|---|---|---|---|---|---|---|---|---|---|---|---|---|---|---|---|---|---|---|---|---|---|---|---|---|---|---|---|---|
| 07 | CLE | 4 | 2 | 0 | 49 | 54 | 25 | 4.56 | 1.34 | 4.6 | 2.2 | 0.4 | 3.3 | $0 | -$4 | 60 | −4 | 32% | 6% | 64% | 3.54 | 9 | 0 | 1/1 | — | — | — | — | .728 | — | .728 | .661 | .869 |
| 08 | CLE | 5 | 7 | 0 | 93 | 103 | 43 | 4.23 | 1.43 | 4.1 | 3.0 | 1.0 | 1.7 | -$1 | -$5 | 80 | −10 | 30% | 10% | 73% | 4.76 | 16 | 0 | 10/3 | — | — | — | — | .763 | .696 | 1.263 | .785 | .693 |
| 09 | CLE | 7 | 9 | 1 | 121 | 140 | 59 | 4.44 | 1.62 | 4.4 | 4.2 | 0.7 | 1.6 | $0 | -$6 | 100 | −14 | 32% | 7% | 73% | 4.70 | 19 | 0 | 10/5 | 6 | 0 | 0 | +0.7 | .777 | .684 | .819 | .830 | .642 |
| 10 | CLE | 2 | 3 | 0 | 55 | 62 | 28 | 4.53 | 1.62 | 4.5 | 4.5 | 0.2 | 1.7 | -$4 | -$16 | 30 | −5 | 32% | 2% | 70% | 4.04 | 5 | 0 | 1/1 | 24 | 5 | 0 | −0.6 | .744 | .768 | .633 | .724 | .771 |

### Competition at RP / Stats in 2010 as RP
| Thr | Player | GR | ERA | IP/G | Sv-Hld |
|---|---|---|---|---|---|
| LH | Perez R | 70 | 3.25 | 0.9 | 0-13 |
| LH | Sipp T | 70 | 4.14 | 0.9 | 1-15 |
| LH | Laffey A | 24 | 5.28 | 1.3 | 0-5 |

---

## John Lannan — 160 IP | $-2 | 120 pts
SP-25 — Owned: 1% — LH

Lannan is one of the Nationals' latest crop of scrap-heap starters who might have a future with the club. Although his 2010 campaign included a trip to Double-A to straighten himself out, his combination of a high GB/F and decent control profiles as an eventual #4 or #5 starter. (PB)

### Forecast
| Player | Age | IP | W | Sv | K | ERA | WHIP | K/9 | BB/9 | $2L | Pts |
|---|---|---|---|---|---|---|---|---|---|---|---|
| Lannan J | 26 | 160 | 8 | 0 | 80 | 4.73 | 1.46 | 4.5 | 3.1 | -$2 | 120 |

| Mini-Browser | Age | IP | W | Sv | K | ERA | WHIP | K/9 | BB/9 | $2L | Pts |
|---|---|---|---|---|---|---|---|---|---|---|---|
| Walters P | 26 | 40 | 2 | 0 | 38 | 5.02 | 1.49 | 8.5 | 3.6 | -$2 | 50 |
| Fulchino J | 31 | 40 | 2 | 0 | 33 | 4.80 | 1.45 | 7.4 | 3.6 | -$2 | 40 |
| Infante G | 23 | 60 | 3 | 0 | 47 | 4.31 | 1.75 | 7.1 | 7.0 | -$2 | 60 |
| Ramos C | 26 | 40 | 2 | 0 | 29 | 4.81 | 1.44 | 6.5 | 3.4 | -$2 | 40 |
| Wright J | 36 | 40 | 1 | 0 | 23 | 4.89 | 1.48 | 5.2 | 4.4 | -$2 | 20 |

### Minors (2010)
| Level | Leag | W | L | Sv | IP | H | K | ERA | WHIP | K/9 | BB/9 | HR/9 | GB/F |
|---|---|---|---|---|---|---|---|---|---|---|---|---|---|
| A | — | — | — | — | — | — | — | — | — | — | — | — | — |
| AA | EL | 1 | 4 | 0 | 40 | 49 | 28 | 4.20 | 1.45 | 6.2 | 2.2 | 0.7 | — |
| AAA | — | — | — | — | — | — | — | — | — | — | — | — | — |

### Majors / Skills / Value / Luck / In Rotation / In Relief / OPS
| Yr | Team | W | L | Sv | IP | H | K | ERA | WHIP | K/9 | BB/9 | HR/9 | GB/F | $1L | $2L | Pts | RAA | H% | HR/fb | S% | FIP | GS | CG | QS/DS | GR | Hld | Bln | Lead | OPS | 1st Hf | 2nd Hf | vs RH | vs LH |
|---|---|---|---|---|---|---|---|---|---|---|---|---|---|---|---|---|---|---|---|---|---|---|---|---|---|---|---|---|---|---|---|---|---|
| 07 | WAS | 2 | 2 | 0 | 34 | 36 | 10 | 4.15 | 1.53 | 2.6 | 4.4 | 0.8 | 1.5 | -$2 | -$5 | 20 | +0 | 28% | 7% | 74% | 5.22 | 6 | 0 | 2/1 | — | — | — | — | .751 | — | .751 | .731 | .838 |
| 08 | WAS | 9 | 15 | 0 | 182 | 172 | 117 | 3.91 | 1.34 | 5.8 | 3.6 | 1.1 | 2.0 | $6 | -$2 | 190 | +1 | 27% | 15% | 75% | 4.74 | 31 | 0 | 21/6 | — | — | — | — | .728 | .707 | .767 | .710 | .782 |
| 09 | WAS | 9 | 13 | 0 | 206 | 210 | 89 | 3.88 | 1.35 | 3.9 | 3.0 | 1.0 | 1.7 | $5 | $0 | 160 | +2 | 28% | 11% | 74% | 4.71 | 33 | 2 | 19/4 | — | — | — | — | .750 | .774 | .722 | .711 | .873 |
| 10 | WAS | 8 | 8 | 0 | 143 | 175 | 71 | 4.65 | 1.56 | 4.5 | 3.1 | 0.9 | 1.9 | -$7 | -$22 | 110 | −11 | 33% | 10% | 71% | 4.50 | 25 | 0 | 12/5 | — | — | — | — | .799 | .855 | .728 | .817 | .747 |

### Competition at SP / Stats in 2010 as SP
| Thr | Player | GS | ERA | Supp | W-L |
|---|---|---|---|---|---|
| RH | Hernandez L | 33 | 3.66 | 3.5 | 10-12 |
| LH | Lannan J | 25 | 4.65 | 4.5 | 8-8 |
| RH | Stammen C | 19 | 5.06 | 4.8 | 4-4 |
| RH | Atilano L | 16 | 5.15 | 4.5 | 6-7 |

---

## Mat Latos — 160 IP | $18 | 280 pts
SP-31 — Owned: 100% — RH

We can safely remove the "future ace" tag from Latos – he has already arrived after a dominant 2010. His mid-90's gas and wicked slider are beyond question. Rather, the 23-year-old will have to show that he can shoulder 33 starts, year in and year out. Only an injury should keep him from Cy Young contention. (DG)

### Forecast
| Player | Age | IP | W | Sv | K | ERA | WHIP | K/9 | BB/9 | $2L | Pts |
|---|---|---|---|---|---|---|---|---|---|---|---|
| Latos M | 23 | 160 | 11 | 0 | 160 | 3.31 | 1.15 | 9.0 | 2.7 | $18 | 280 |

| Mini-Browser | Age | IP | W | Sv | K | ERA | WHIP | K/9 | BB/9 | $2L | Pts |
|---|---|---|---|---|---|---|---|---|---|---|---|
| Greinke Z | 27 | 220 | 13 | 0 | 192 | 3.60 | 1.21 | 7.9 | 2.3 | $21 | 320 |
| Weaver J | 28 | 220 | 14 | 0 | 193 | 3.73 | 1.21 | 7.9 | 2.6 | $21 | 330 |
| Rivera M | 41 | 60 | 4 | 38 | 54 | 2.35 | 0.96 | 8.1 | 1.6 | $20 | 300 |
| Soriano R | 31 | 60 | 3 | 44 | 62 | 2.89 | 1.05 | 9.2 | 2.7 | $19 | 320 |
| Hamels C | 27 | 200 | 13 | 0 | 175 | 3.67 | 1.17 | 7.9 | 2.3 | $19 | 310 |

### Minors (2010)
| Level | Leag | W | L | Sv | IP | H | K | ERA | WHIP | K/9 | BB/9 | HR/9 | GB/F |
|---|---|---|---|---|---|---|---|---|---|---|---|---|---|
| A | — | — | — | — | — | — | — | — | — | — | — | — | — |
| AA | — | — | — | — | — | — | — | — | — | — | — | — | — |
| AAA | — | — | — | — | — | — | — | — | — | — | — | — | — |

### Majors / Skills / Value / Luck / In Rotation / In Relief / OPS
| Yr | Team | W | L | Sv | IP | H | K | ERA | WHIP | K/9 | BB/9 | HR/9 | GB/F | $1L | $2L | Pts | RAA | H% | HR/fb | S% | FIP | GS | CG | QS/DS | GR | Hld | Bln | Lead | OPS | 1st Hf | 2nd Hf | vs RH | vs LH |
|---|---|---|---|---|---|---|---|---|---|---|---|---|---|---|---|---|---|---|---|---|---|---|---|---|---|---|---|---|---|---|---|---|---|
| 07 | — | | | | | | | | | | | | | | | | | | | | | | | | | | | | | | | | |
| 08 | — | | | | | | | | | | | | | | | | | | | | | | | | | | | | | | | | |
| 09 | SD | 4 | 5 | 0 | 50 | 43 | 39 | 4.62 | 1.30 | 6.9 | 4.1 | 1.2 | 0.8 | $0 | -$2 | 70 | −4 | 26% | 11% | 68% | 4.82 | 10 | 0 | 4/4 | — | — | — | — | .689 | — | .689 | .589 | .800 |
| 10 | SD | 14 | 10 | 0 | 184 | 150 | 189 | 2.92 | 1.08 | 9.2 | 2.4 | 0.8 | 1.1 | $22 | $19 | 350 | +28 | 28% | 8% | 76% | 3.09 | 31 | 1 | 21/3 | — | — | — | — | .601 | .545 | .674 | .623 | .580 |

### Competition at SP / Stats in 2010 as SP
| Thr | Player | GS | ERA | Supp | W-L |
|---|---|---|---|---|---|
| RH | Garland J | 33 | 3.47 | 3.8 | 14-12 |
| LH | Richard C | 33 | 3.75 | 4.1 | 14-9 |
| RH | Latos M | 31 | 2.92 | 3.5 | 14-10 |
| RH | Correia K | 26 | 5.52 | 5.6 | 10-10 |

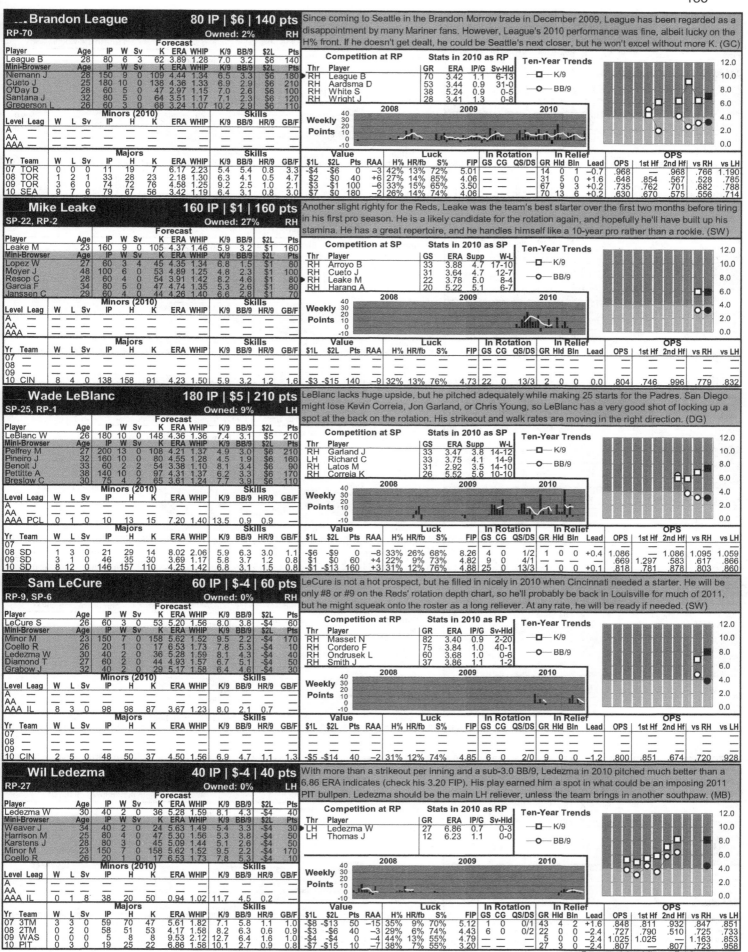

## Brandon League — 80 IP | $6 | 140 pts
RP-70 · Owned: 2% · RH

Since coming to Seattle in the Brandon Morrow trade in December 2009, League has been regarded as a disappointment by many Mariner fans. However, League's 2010 performance was fine, albeit lucky on the H% front. If he doesn't get dealt, he could be Seattle's next closer, but he won't excel without more K. (GC)

### Forecast
| Player | Age | IP | W | Sv | K | ERA | WHIP | K/9 | BB/9 | $2L | Pts |
|---|---|---|---|---|---|---|---|---|---|---|---|
| League B | 28 | 80 | 6 | 3 | 62 | 3.89 | 1.28 | 7.0 | 3.2 | $6 | 140 |

### Mini-Browser
| Player | Age | IP | W | Sv | K | ERA | WHIP | K/9 | BB/9 | $2L | Pts |
|---|---|---|---|---|---|---|---|---|---|---|---|
| Niemann J | 28 | 150 | 9 | 0 | 109 | 4.44 | 1.34 | 6.5 | 3.3 | $6 | 180 |
| Cueto J | 25 | 180 | 10 | 0 | 138 | 4.36 | 1.33 | 6.9 | 2.9 | $6 | 210 |
| O'Day D | 28 | 60 | 5 | 0 | 47 | 2.97 | 1.15 | 7.0 | 2.5 | $6 | 100 |
| Santana J | 32 | 80 | 5 | 0 | 64 | 3.51 | 1.17 | 7.1 | 2.3 | $6 | 120 |
| Gregerson L | 26 | 60 | 3 | 0 | 68 | 3.24 | 1.07 | 10.2 | 2.9 | $6 | 110 |

### Competition at RP — Stats in 2010 as RP
| Thr | Player | GR | ERA | IP/G | Sv-Hld |
|---|---|---|---|---|---|
| RH | League B | 70 | 3.42 | 1.1 | 6-13 |
| RH | Aardsma D | 53 | 3.44 | 0.9 | 31-0 |
| RH | White S | 38 | 5.24 | 0.9 | 0-5 |
| RH | Wright J | 28 | 3.41 | 1.3 | 0-8 |

### Majors
| Yr | Team | W | L | Sv | IP | H | K | ERA | WHIP | K/9 | BB/9 | HR/9 | GB/F |
|---|---|---|---|---|---|---|---|---|---|---|---|---|---|
| 07 | TOR | 0 | 0 | 0 | 11 | 19 | 7 | 6.17 | 2.23 | 5.4 | 5.4 | 0.8 | 3.3 |
| 08 | TOR | 1 | 2 | 1 | 33 | 28 | 23 | 2.18 | 1.30 | 6.3 | 4.1 | 0.5 | 4.7 |
| 09 | TOR | 3 | 6 | 0 | 74 | 72 | 76 | 4.58 | 1.25 | 9.2 | 2.5 | 1.0 | 2.1 |
| 10 | SEA | 9 | 7 | 6 | 79 | 67 | 57 | 3.42 | 1.19 | 6.4 | 3.1 | 0.8 | 3.0 |

| $1L | $2L | Pts | RAA | H% | HR/fb | S% | FIP | GS | CG | QS/DS | GR | Hld | Bln | Lead | OPS | 1st Hf | 2nd Hf | vs RH | vs LH |
|---|---|---|---|---|---|---|---|---|---|---|---|---|---|---|---|---|---|---|---|
| -$4 | -$6 | 0 | -3 | 42% | 13% | 72% | 5.01 | — | — | — | 14 | 0 | 1 | -0.7 | .968 | — | .968 | .766 | 1.190 |
| $2 | $0 | 40 | +6 | 27% | 14% | 85% | 4.06 | — | — | — | 31 | 5 | 0 | +1.6 | .648 | .854 | .567 | .528 | .785 |
| $3 | -$1 | 100 | -6 | 33% | 15% | 65% | 3.50 | — | — | — | 67 | 9 | 3 | +0.2 | .735 | .762 | .701 | .682 | .788 |
| $7 | $0 | 180 | -2 | 26% | 14% | 74% | 4.06 | — | — | — | 70 | 13 | 6 | +0.2 | .630 | .670 | .575 | .556 | .714 |

## Mike Leake — 160 IP | $1 | 160 pts
SP-22, RP-2 · Owned: 27% · RH

Another slight righty for the Reds, Leake was the team's best starter over the first two months before tiring in his first pro season. He is a likely candidate for the rotation again, and hopefully he'll have built up his stamina. He has a great repertoire, and he handles himself like a 10-year pro rather than a rookie. (SW)

### Forecast
| Player | Age | IP | W | Sv | K | ERA | WHIP | K/9 | BB/9 | $2L | Pts |
|---|---|---|---|---|---|---|---|---|---|---|---|
| Leake M | 23 | 160 | 9 | 0 | 105 | 4.37 | 1.46 | 5.9 | 3.2 | $1 | 160 |

### Mini-Browser
| Player | Age | IP | W | Sv | K | ERA | WHIP | K/9 | BB/9 | $2L | Pts |
|---|---|---|---|---|---|---|---|---|---|---|---|
| Lopez W | 27 | 60 | 3 | 4 | 45 | 4.35 | 1.34 | 6.8 | 1.5 | $1 | 80 |
| Moyer J | 48 | 100 | 6 | 0 | 53 | 4.89 | 1.25 | 4.8 | 2.3 | $1 | 100 |
| Resop C | 28 | 60 | 4 | 0 | 54 | 3.91 | 1.42 | 8.2 | 4.6 | $1 | 80 |
| Garcia F | 34 | 80 | 5 | 0 | 47 | 4.74 | 1.35 | 5.3 | 2.6 | $1 | 80 |
| Janssen C | 29 | 60 | 4 | 0 | 44 | 4.26 | 1.40 | 6.6 | 2.8 | $1 | 70 |

### Competition at SP — Stats in 2010 as SP
| Thr | Player | GS | ERA | Supp | W-L |
|---|---|---|---|---|---|
| RH | Arroyo B | 33 | 3.88 | 4.7 | 17-10 |
| RH | Cueto J | 31 | 3.64 | 4.7 | 12-7 |
| RH | Leake M | 22 | 3.78 | 5.0 | 8-4 |
| RH | Harang A | 20 | 5.22 | 5.1 | 6-7 |

### Majors
| Yr | Team | W | L | Sv | IP | H | K | ERA | WHIP | K/9 | BB/9 | HR/9 | GB/F |
|---|---|---|---|---|---|---|---|---|---|---|---|---|---|
| 10 | CIN | 8 | 4 | 0 | 138 | 158 | 91 | 4.23 | 1.50 | 5.9 | 3.2 | 1.0 | 1.6 |

| $1L | $2L | Pts | RAA | H% | HR/fb | S% | FIP | GS | CG | QS/DS | GR | Hld | Bln | Lead | OPS | 1st Hf | 2nd Hf | vs RH | vs LH |
|---|---|---|---|---|---|---|---|---|---|---|---|---|---|---|---|---|---|---|---|
| -$3 | -$15 | 140 | -9 | 32% | 13% | 76% | 4.73 | 22 | 0 | 13/3 | 2 | 0 | 0 | 0.0 | .804 | .746 | .996 | .779 | .832 |

## Wade LeBlanc — 180 IP | $5 | 210 pts
SP-25, RP-1 · Owned: 9% · LH

LeBlanc lacks huge upside, but he pitched adequately while making 25 starts for the Padres. San Diego might lose Kevin Correia, Jon Garland, or Chris Young, so LeBlanc has a very good shot of locking up a spot at the back on the rotation. His strikeout and walk rates are moving in the right direction. (DG)

### Forecast
| Player | Age | IP | W | Sv | K | ERA | WHIP | K/9 | BB/9 | $2L | Pts |
|---|---|---|---|---|---|---|---|---|---|---|---|
| LeBlanc W | 26 | 180 | 10 | 0 | 148 | 4.36 | 1.36 | 7.4 | 3.1 | $5 | 210 |

### Mini-Browser
| Player | Age | IP | W | Sv | K | ERA | WHIP | K/9 | BB/9 | $2L | Pts |
|---|---|---|---|---|---|---|---|---|---|---|---|
| Pelfrey M | 27 | 200 | 13 | 0 | 108 | 4.21 | 1.37 | 4.9 | 3.0 | $6 | 180 |
| Pineiro J | 32 | 160 | 10 | 0 | 80 | 4.55 | 1.28 | 4.5 | 1.9 | $6 | 160 |
| Benoit J | 33 | 60 | 2 | 2 | 54 | 3.38 | 1.10 | 8.1 | 3.4 | $6 | 90 |
| Pettitte A | 38 | 140 | 10 | 0 | 97 | 4.31 | 1.37 | 6.2 | 3.3 | $6 | 170 |
| Breslow C | 30 | 75 | 4 | 2 | 65 | 3.61 | 1.24 | 7.7 | 3.9 | $6 | 110 |

### Competition at SP — Stats in 2010 as SP
| Thr | Player | GS | ERA | Supp | W-L |
|---|---|---|---|---|---|
| RH | Garland J | 33 | 3.47 | 3.8 | 14-12 |
| LH | Richard C | 33 | 3.75 | 4.1 | 14-9 |
| RH | Latos M | 31 | 2.92 | 3.5 | 14-10 |
| RH | Correia K | 26 | 5.52 | 5.6 | 10-10 |

### Minors (2010)
| Level | Leag | W | L | Sv | IP | H | K | ERA | WHIP | K/9 | BB/9 | HR/9 | GB/F |
|---|---|---|---|---|---|---|---|---|---|---|---|---|---|
| AAA | PCL | 0 | 1 | 0 | 10 | 13 | 15 | 7.20 | 1.40 | 13.5 | 0.9 | 0.9 | — |

### Majors
| Yr | Team | W | L | Sv | IP | H | K | ERA | WHIP | K/9 | BB/9 | HR/9 | GB/F |
|---|---|---|---|---|---|---|---|---|---|---|---|---|---|
| 08 | SD | 1 | 3 | 0 | 21 | 29 | 14 | 8.02 | 2.06 | 5.9 | 6.3 | 3.0 | 1.1 |
| 09 | SD | 3 | 1 | 0 | 46 | 35 | 30 | 3.69 | 1.17 | 5.8 | 3.7 | 1.2 | 0.8 |
| 10 | SD | 8 | 12 | 0 | 146 | 157 | 110 | 4.25 | 1.42 | 6.8 | 3.1 | 1.5 | 0.8 |

| $1L | $2L | Pts | RAA | H% | HR/fb | S% | FIP | GS | CG | QS/DS | GR | Hld | Bln | Lead | OPS | 1st Hf | 2nd Hf | vs RH | vs LH |
|---|---|---|---|---|---|---|---|---|---|---|---|---|---|---|---|---|---|---|---|
| -$6 | -$9 | 0 | -8 | 33% | 26% | 68% | 8.26 | 4 | 0 | 1/2 | 1 | 0 | 0 | +0.4 | 1.086 | — | 1.086 | 1.095 | 1.059 |
| $0 | $0 | 60 | +4 | 22% | 9% | 73% | 4.82 | 9 | 0 | 4/1 | 1 | 0 | 0 | — | .669 | 1.297 | .583 | .617 | .866 |
| -$1 | -$13 | 160 | +3 | 31% | 12% | 76% | 4.88 | 25 | 0 | 13/3 | 1 | 0 | 0 | +0.1 | .818 | .781 | .878 | .803 | .860 |

## Sam LeCure — 60 IP | $-4 | 60 pts
RP-9, SP-6 · Owned: 0% · RH

LeCure is not a hot prospect, but he filled in nicely in 2010 when Cincinnati needed a starter. He will be only #8 or #9 on the Reds' rotation depth chart, so he'll probably be back in Louisville for much of 2011, but he might squeak onto the roster as a long reliever. At any rate, he will be ready if needed. (SW)

### Forecast
| Player | Age | IP | W | Sv | K | ERA | WHIP | K/9 | BB/9 | $2L | Pts |
|---|---|---|---|---|---|---|---|---|---|---|---|
| LeCure S | 26 | 60 | 3 | 0 | 53 | 5.20 | 1.56 | 8.0 | 3.8 | -$4 | 60 |

### Mini-Browser
| Player | Age | IP | W | Sv | K | ERA | WHIP | K/9 | BB/9 | $2L | Pts |
|---|---|---|---|---|---|---|---|---|---|---|---|
| Minor M | 23 | 150 | 7 | 0 | 158 | 5.62 | 1.52 | 9.5 | 2.2 | -$4 | 170 |
| Coello R | 26 | 20 | 1 | 0 | 17 | 6.53 | 1.73 | 7.8 | 5.3 | -$4 | 10 |
| Ledezma W | 30 | 40 | 2 | 0 | 36 | 5.28 | 1.59 | 8.1 | 4.3 | -$4 | 40 |
| Diamond T | 27 | 60 | 2 | 0 | 44 | 4.93 | 1.57 | 6.7 | 5.1 | -$4 | 50 |
| Grabow J | 32 | 40 | 2 | 0 | 29 | 5.17 | 1.58 | 6.4 | 4.6 | -$4 | 30 |

### Competition at RP — Stats in 2010 as RP
| Thr | Player | GR | ERA | IP/G | Sv-Hld |
|---|---|---|---|---|---|
| RH | Masset N | 82 | 3.40 | 0.9 | 2-20 |
| RH | Cordero F | 75 | 3.84 | 1.0 | 40-1 |
| RH | Ondrusek L | 60 | 3.68 | 1.0 | 0-6 |
| RH | Smith J | 37 | 3.86 | 1.1 | 1-2 |

### Minors (2010)
| Level | Leag | W | L | Sv | IP | H | K | ERA | WHIP | K/9 | BB/9 | HR/9 | GB/F |
|---|---|---|---|---|---|---|---|---|---|---|---|---|---|
| AAA | IL | 8 | 3 | 0 | 98 | 98 | 87 | 3.67 | 1.23 | 8.0 | 2.1 | 0.7 | — |

### Majors
| Yr | Team | W | L | Sv | IP | H | K | ERA | WHIP | K/9 | BB/9 | HR/9 | GB/F |
|---|---|---|---|---|---|---|---|---|---|---|---|---|---|
| 10 | CIN | 2 | 5 | 0 | 48 | 50 | 37 | 4.50 | 1.56 | 6.9 | 4.7 | 1.1 | 1.3 |

| $1L | $2L | Pts | RAA | H% | HR/fb | S% | FIP | GS | CG | QS/DS | GR | Hld | Bln | Lead | OPS | 1st Hf | 2nd Hf | vs RH | vs LH |
|---|---|---|---|---|---|---|---|---|---|---|---|---|---|---|---|---|---|---|---|
| -$5 | -$14 | 40 | -2 | 31% | 12% | 74% | 4.85 | 6 | 0 | 2/0 | 9 | 0 | 0 | -1.2 | .800 | .851 | .674 | .720 | .928 |

## Wil Ledezma — 40 IP | $-4 | 40 pts
RP-27 · Owned: 0% · LH

With more than a strikeout per inning and a sub-3.0 BB/9, Ledezma in 2010 pitched much better than a 6.86 ERA indicates (check his 3.20 FIP). His play earned him a spot in what could be an imposing 2011 PIT bullpen. Ledezma should be the main LH reliever, unless the team brings in another southpaw. (MB)

### Forecast
| Player | Age | IP | W | Sv | K | ERA | WHIP | K/9 | BB/9 | $2L | Pts |
|---|---|---|---|---|---|---|---|---|---|---|---|
| Ledezma W | 30 | 40 | 2 | 0 | 36 | 5.28 | 1.59 | 8.1 | 4.3 | -$4 | 40 |

### Mini-Browser
| Player | Age | IP | W | Sv | K | ERA | WHIP | K/9 | BB/9 | $2L | Pts |
|---|---|---|---|---|---|---|---|---|---|---|---|
| Weaver J | 34 | 40 | 2 | 0 | 24 | 5.63 | 1.49 | 5.4 | 3.3 | -$4 | 30 |
| Harrison M | 25 | 80 | 4 | 0 | 47 | 5.30 | 1.56 | 5.3 | 3.8 | -$4 | 50 |
| Karstens J | 28 | 80 | 3 | 0 | 45 | 5.09 | 1.44 | 5.1 | 2.6 | -$4 | 50 |
| Minor M | 23 | 150 | 7 | 0 | 158 | 5.62 | 1.52 | 9.5 | 2.2 | -$4 | 170 |
| Coello R | 26 | 20 | 1 | 0 | 17 | 6.53 | 1.73 | 7.8 | 5.3 | -$4 | 10 |

### Competition at RP — Stats in 2010 as RP
| Thr | Player | GR | ERA | IP/G | Sv-Hld |
|---|---|---|---|---|---|
| LH | Ledezma W | 27 | 6.86 | 0.7 | 0-3 |
| LH | Thomas J | 12 | 6.23 | 1.1 | 0-0 |

### Minors (2010)
| Level | Leag | W | L | Sv | IP | H | K | ERA | WHIP | K/9 | BB/9 | HR/9 | GB/F |
|---|---|---|---|---|---|---|---|---|---|---|---|---|---|
| AAA | IL | 2 | 2 | 0 | 38 | 20 | 50 | 0.94 | 1.02 | 11.7 | 4.5 | 0.2 | — |

### Majors
| Yr | Team | W | L | Sv | IP | H | K | ERA | WHIP | K/9 | BB/9 | HR/9 | GB/F |
|---|---|---|---|---|---|---|---|---|---|---|---|---|---|
| 07 | 3TM | 3 | 3 | 0 | 59 | 70 | 47 | 5.61 | 1.82 | 7.1 | 5.8 | 1.1 | 1.0 |
| 08 | 2TM | 0 | 2 | 0 | 58 | 51 | 53 | 4.17 | 1.58 | 8.2 | 6.3 | 0.6 | 0.9 |
| 09 | WAS | 0 | 0 | 0 | 5 | 8 | 8 | 9.53 | 2.12 | 12.7 | 6.4 | 1.6 | 1.0 |
| 10 | PIT | 0 | 3 | 0 | 19 | 25 | 20 | 6.86 | 1.58 | 9.4 | 2.7 | 0.9 | 1.3 |

| $1L | $2L | Pts | RAA | H% | HR/fb | S% | FIP | GS | CG | QS/DS | GR | Hld | Bln | Lead | OPS | 1st Hf | 2nd Hf | vs RH | vs LH |
|---|---|---|---|---|---|---|---|---|---|---|---|---|---|---|---|---|---|---|---|
| -$8 | -$13 | 50 | -15 | 35% | 9% | 70% | 5.12 | 1 | 0 | 0/1 | 43 | 4 | 2 | +1.6 | .848 | .811 | .932 | .847 | .851 |
| -$3 | -$6 | 40 | -3 | 29% | 6% | 74% | 4.43 | 6 | 0 | 0/2 | 22 | 0 | 1 | -2.4 | .727 | .790 | .510 | .725 | .733 |
| -$4 | -$4 | 0 | -4 | 44% | 13% | 55% | 4.79 | — | — | — | 5 | 0 | 0 | -2.4 | 1.025 | 1.025 | — | 1.163 | .853 |
| -$7 | -$14 | 10 | -7 | 38% | 7% | 55% | 3.20 | — | — | — | 27 | 3 | 0 | -2.4 | .807 | — | .807 | .723 | .958 |

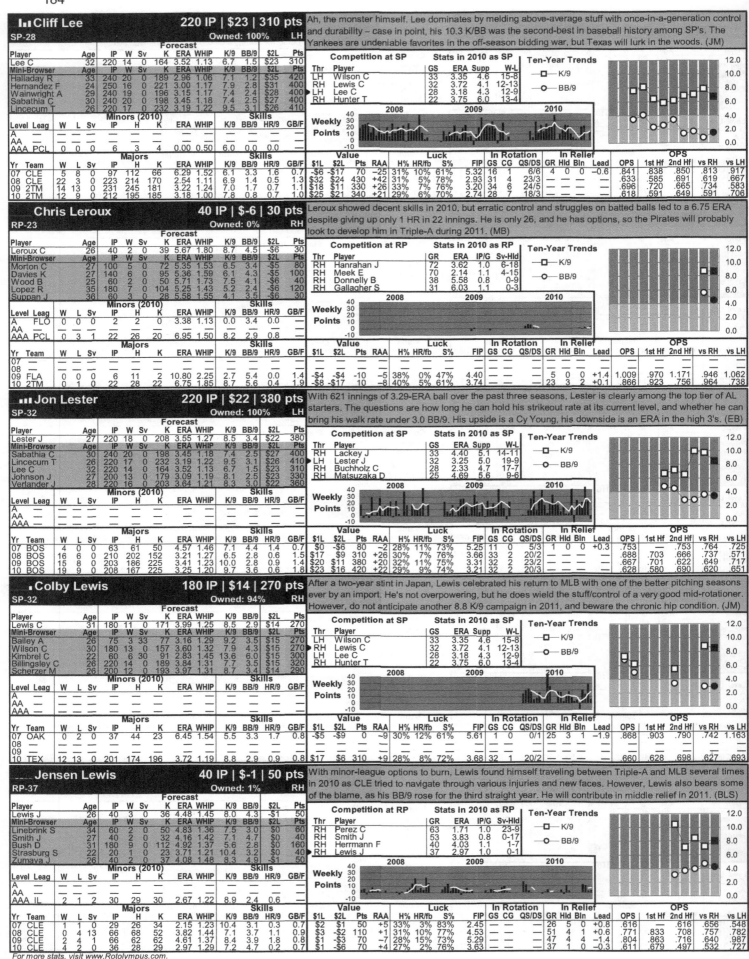

## Cliff Lee

**220 IP | $23 | 310 pts**

SP-28 | Owned: 100% | LH

Forecast

| Player | Age | IP | W | Sv | K | ERA | WHIP | K/9 | BB/9 | $2L | Pts |
|---|---|---|---|---|---|---|---|---|---|---|---|
| Lee C | 32 | 220 | 14 | 0 | 164 | 3.52 | 1.13 | 6.7 | 1.5 | $23 | 310 |
| **Mini-Browser** | **Age** | **IP** | **W** | **Sv** | **K** | **ERA** | **WHIP** | **K/9** | **BB/9** | **$2L** | **Pts** |
| Halladay R | 33 | 240 | 20 | 0 | 189 | 2.96 | 1.06 | 7.1 | 1.2 | $35 | 420 |
| Hernandez F | 24 | 250 | 16 | 0 | 221 | 3.00 | 1.17 | 7.9 | 2.8 | $31 | 400 |
| Wainwright A | 29 | 240 | 19 | 0 | 196 | 3.15 | 1.17 | 7.4 | 2.4 | $28 | 400 |
| Sabathia C | 30 | 240 | 20 | 0 | 198 | 3.45 | 1.18 | 7.4 | 2.5 | $27 | 400 |
| Lincecum T | 26 | 220 | 17 | 0 | 232 | 3.19 | 1.22 | 9.5 | 3.1 | $26 | 410 |

Minors (2010) / Skills

| Level | Leag | W | L | Sv | IP | H | K | ERA | WHIP | K/9 | BB/9 | HR/9 | GB/F |
|---|---|---|---|---|---|---|---|---|---|---|---|---|---|
| A | — | — | — | — | — | — | — | — | — | — | — | — | — |
| AA | — | — | — | — | — | — | — | — | — | — | — | — | — |
| AAA | PCL | 0 | 0 | 0 | 6 | 3 | 4 | 0.00 | 0.50 | 6.0 | 0.0 | 0.0 | — |

Majors / Skills

| Yr | Team | W | L | Sv | IP | H | K | ERA | WHIP | K/9 | BB/9 | HR/9 | GB/F |
|---|---|---|---|---|---|---|---|---|---|---|---|---|---|
| 07 | CLE | 5 | 8 | 0 | 97 | 112 | 66 | 6.29 | 1.52 | 6.1 | 3.3 | 1.6 | 0.7 |
| 08 | CLE | 22 | 3 | 0 | 223 | 214 | 170 | 2.54 | 1.11 | 6.9 | 1.4 | 0.5 | 1.3 |
| 09 | 2TM | 14 | 13 | 0 | 231 | 245 | 181 | 3.22 | 1.24 | 7.0 | 1.7 | 0.7 | 1.1 |
| 10 | 2TM | 12 | 9 | 0 | 212 | 195 | 185 | 3.18 | 1.00 | 7.8 | 0.8 | 0.7 | 1.0 |

Ah, the monster himself. Lee dominates by melding above-average stuff with once-in-a-generation control and durability – case in point, his 10.3 K/BB was the second-best in baseball history among SP's. The Yankees are undeniable favorites in the off-season bidding war, but Texas will lurk in the woods. (JM)

Competition at SP / Stats in 2010 as SP

| Thr | Player | GS | ERA | Supp | W-L |
|---|---|---|---|---|---|
| LH | Wilson C | 33 | 3.35 | 4.6 | 15-8 |
| RH | Lewis C | 32 | 3.72 | 4.1 | 12-13 |
| ▶ LH | Lee C | 28 | 3.18 | 4.3 | 12-9 |
| RH | Hunter T | 22 | 3.75 | 6.0 | 13-4 |

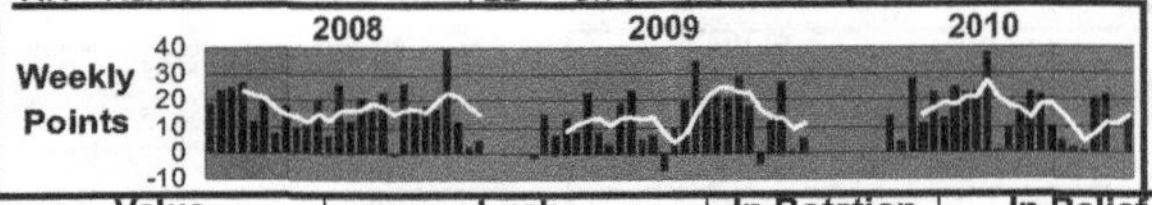


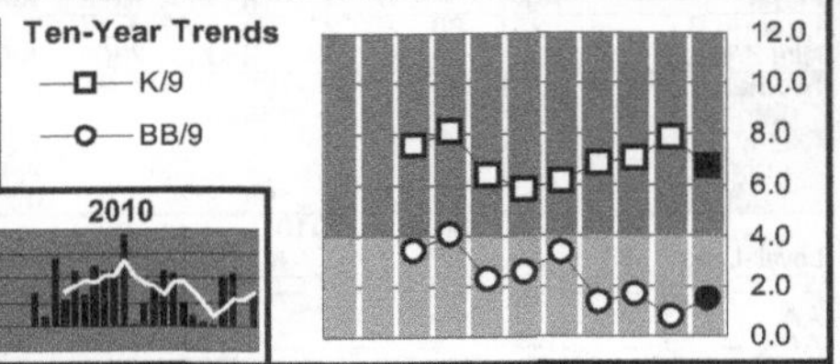


| Yr | $1L | $2L | Pts | RAA | H% | HR/fb | S% | FIP | GS | CG | QS/DS | GR | Hld | Bln | Lead | OPS | 1st Hf | 2nd Hf | vs RH | vs LH |
|---|---|---|---|---|---|---|---|---|---|---|---|---|---|---|---|---|---|---|---|---|
| 07 | -$6 | -$17 | 70 | −25 | 31% | 10% | 61% | 5.32 | 16 | 1 | 6/6 | 4 | 0 | 0 | −0.6 | .841 | .838 | .850 | .813 | .917 |
| 08 | $32 | $24 | 430 | +42 | 31% | 5% | 78% | 2.93 | 31 | 4 | 23/3 | — | — | — | — | .633 | .585 | .691 | .619 | .667 |
| 09 | $18 | $11 | 330 | +26 | 33% | 7% | 76% | 3.20 | 34 | 6 | 24/5 | — | — | — | — | .696 | .720 | .665 | .734 | .583 |
| 10 | $25 | $21 | 340 | +21 | 29% | 6% | 70% | 2.74 | 28 | 7 | 18/3 | — | — | — | — | .618 | .591 | .649 | .591 | .706 |

## Chris Leroux

**40 IP | $-6 | 30 pts**

RP-23 | Owned: 0% | RH

Forecast

| Player | Age | IP | W | Sv | K | ERA | WHIP | K/9 | BB/9 | $2L | Pts |
|---|---|---|---|---|---|---|---|---|---|---|---|
| Leroux C | 26 | 40 | 2 | 0 | 39 | 5.67 | 1.80 | 8.7 | 4.5 | -$6 | 30 |
| **Mini-Browser** | **Age** | **IP** | **W** | **Sv** | **K** | **ERA** | **WHIP** | **K/9** | **BB/9** | **$2L** | **Pts** |
| Morton C | 27 | 100 | 5 | 0 | 72 | 5.35 | 1.53 | 6.5 | 3.4 | -$5 | 80 |
| Davies K | 27 | 140 | 6 | 0 | 95 | 5.36 | 1.59 | 6.1 | 4.3 | -$5 | 100 |
| Wood B | 25 | 60 | 2 | 0 | 50 | 5.71 | 1.73 | 7.5 | 4.1 | -$6 | 40 |
| Lopez R | 35 | 180 | 7 | 0 | 104 | 5.25 | 1.43 | 5.2 | 2.4 | -$6 | 120 |
| Suppan J | 36 | 60 | 3 | 0 | 28 | 5.58 | 1.55 | 4.1 | 3.5 | -$6 | 30 |

Minors (2010) / Skills

| Level | Leag | W | L | Sv | IP | H | K | ERA | WHIP | K/9 | BB/9 | HR/9 | GB/F |
|---|---|---|---|---|---|---|---|---|---|---|---|---|---|
| A | FLO | 0 | 0 | 0 | 2 | 2 | 0 | 3.38 | 1.13 | 0.0 | 3.4 | 0.0 | — |
| AA | — | — | — | — | — | — | — | — | — | — | — | — | — |
| AAA | PCL | 0 | 3 | 1 | 22 | 26 | 20 | 6.95 | 1.50 | 8.2 | 2.9 | 0.8 | — |

Majors / Skills

| Yr | Team | W | L | Sv | IP | H | K | ERA | WHIP | K/9 | BB/9 | HR/9 | GB/F |
|---|---|---|---|---|---|---|---|---|---|---|---|---|---|
| 07 | — | — | — | — | — | — | — | — | — | — | — | — | — |
| 08 | — | — | — | — | — | — | — | — | — | — | — | — | — |
| 09 | FLA | 0 | 0 | 0 | 6 | 11 | 2 | 10.80 | 2.25 | 2.7 | 5.4 | 0.0 | 1.4 |
| 10 | 2TM | 0 | 1 | 0 | 22 | 28 | 22 | 6.75 | 1.85 | 8.7 | 5.6 | 0.4 | 1.9 |

Leroux showed decent skills in 2010, but erratic control and struggles on batted balls led to a 6.75 ERA despite giving up only 1 HR in 22 innings. He is only 26, and he has options, so the Pirates will probably look to develop him in Triple-A during 2011. (MB)

Competition at RP / Stats in 2010 as RP

| Thr | Player | GR | ERA | IP/G | Sv-Hld |
|---|---|---|---|---|---|
| RH | Hanrahan J | 72 | 3.62 | 1.0 | 6-18 |
| RH | Meek E | 70 | 2.14 | 1.1 | 4-15 |
| RH | Donnelly B | 38 | 5.58 | 0.8 | 0-9 |
| RH | Gallagher S | 31 | 6.03 | 1.1 | 0-3 |

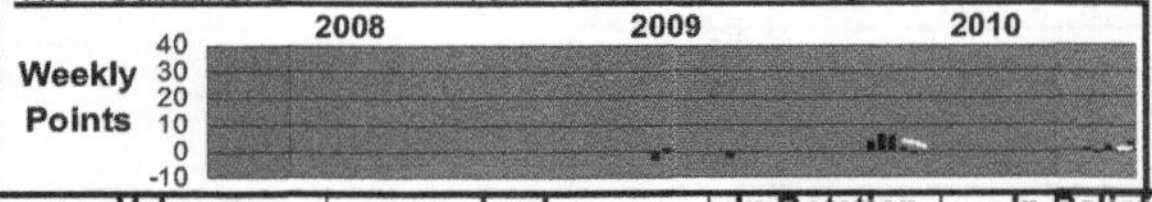


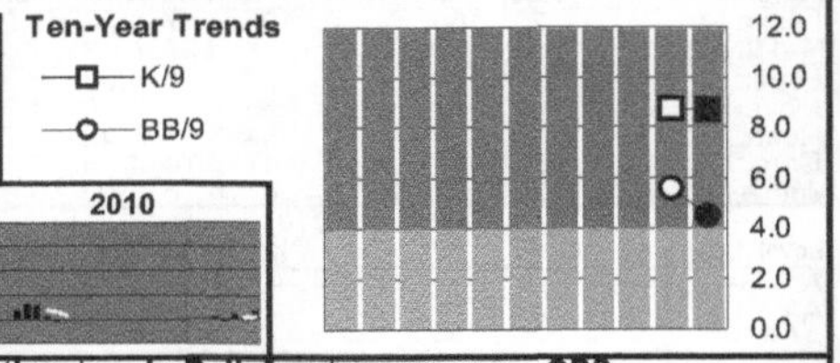


| Yr | $1L | $2L | Pts | RAA | H% | HR/fb | S% | FIP | GS | CG | QS/DS | GR | Hld | Bln | Lead | OPS | 1st Hf | 2nd Hf | vs RH | vs LH |
|---|---|---|---|---|---|---|---|---|---|---|---|---|---|---|---|---|---|---|---|---|
| 07 | — | — | — | — | — | — | — | — | — | — | — | — | — | — | — | — | — | — | — | — |
| 08 | — | — | — | — | — | — | — | — | — | — | — | — | — | — | — | — | — | — | — | — |
| 09 | -$4 | -$4 | -10 | −5 | 38% | 0% | 47% | 4.40 | — | — | — | 5 | 0 | 0 | +1.4 | 1.009 | .970 | 1.171 | .946 | 1.062 |
| 10 | -$8 | -$17 | 10 | −8 | 40% | 5% | 61% | 3.74 | — | — | — | 23 | 3 | 2 | +0.1 | .866 | .923 | .756 | .964 | .738 |

## Jon Lester

**220 IP | $22 | 380 pts**

SP-32 | Owned: 100% | LH

Forecast

| Player | Age | IP | W | Sv | K | ERA | WHIP | K/9 | BB/9 | $2L | Pts |
|---|---|---|---|---|---|---|---|---|---|---|---|
| Lester J | 27 | 220 | 18 | 0 | 208 | 3.55 | 1.27 | 8.5 | 3.4 | $22 | 380 |
| **Mini-Browser** | **Age** | **IP** | **W** | **Sv** | **K** | **ERA** | **WHIP** | **K/9** | **BB/9** | **$2L** | **Pts** |
| Sabathia C | 30 | 240 | 20 | 0 | 198 | 3.45 | 1.18 | 7.4 | 2.5 | $27 | 400 |
| Lincecum T | 26 | 220 | 17 | 0 | 232 | 3.19 | 1.22 | 9.5 | 3.1 | $26 | 410 |
| Lee C | 32 | 220 | 14 | 0 | 164 | 3.52 | 1.13 | 6.7 | 1.5 | $23 | 310 |
| Johnson J | 27 | 200 | 13 | 0 | 179 | 3.09 | 1.19 | 8.1 | 2.5 | $23 | 330 |
| Verlander J | 28 | 220 | 16 | 0 | 203 | 3.64 | 1.21 | 8.3 | 3.0 | $22 | 360 |

Minors (2010) / Skills

| Level | Leag | W | L | Sv | IP | H | K | ERA | WHIP | K/9 | BB/9 | HR/9 | GB/F |
|---|---|---|---|---|---|---|---|---|---|---|---|---|---|
| A | — | — | — | — | — | — | — | — | — | — | — | — | — |
| AA | — | — | — | — | — | — | — | — | — | — | — | — | — |
| AAA | — | — | — | — | — | — | — | — | — | — | — | — | — |

Majors / Skills

| Yr | Team | W | L | Sv | IP | H | K | ERA | WHIP | K/9 | BB/9 | HR/9 | GB/F |
|---|---|---|---|---|---|---|---|---|---|---|---|---|---|
| 07 | BOS | 4 | 0 | 0 | 63 | 61 | 50 | 4.57 | 1.46 | 7.1 | 4.4 | 1.4 | 0.7 |
| 08 | BOS | 16 | 6 | 0 | 210 | 202 | 152 | 3.21 | 1.27 | 6.5 | 2.8 | 0.6 | 1.5 |
| 09 | BOS | 15 | 8 | 0 | 203 | 186 | 225 | 3.41 | 1.23 | 10.0 | 2.8 | 0.9 | 1.4 |
| 10 | BOS | 19 | 9 | 0 | 208 | 167 | 225 | 3.25 | 1.20 | 9.7 | 3.6 | 0.6 | 1.8 |

With 621 innings of 3.29-ERA ball over the past three seasons, Lester is clearly among the top tier of AL starters. The questions are how long he can hold his strikeout rate at its current level, and whether he can bring his walk rate under 3.0 BB/9. His upside is a Cy Young, his downside is an ERA in the high 3's. (EB)

Competition at SP / Stats in 2010 as SP

| Thr | Player | GS | ERA | Supp | W-L |
|---|---|---|---|---|---|
| RH | Lackey J | 33 | 4.40 | 5.1 | 14-11 |
| ▶ LH | Lester J | 32 | 3.25 | 5.0 | 19-9 |
| RH | Buchholz C | 28 | 2.33 | 4.7 | 17-7 |
| RH | Matsuzaka D | 25 | 4.69 | 5.6 | 9-6 |

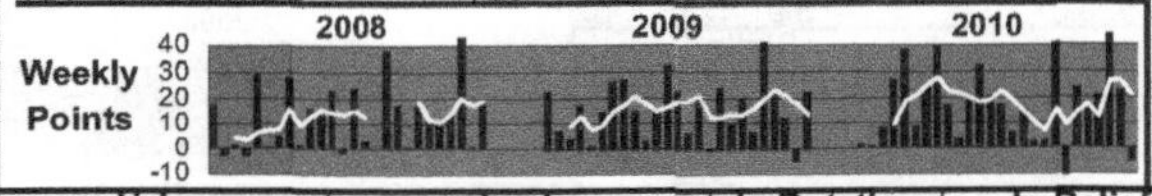


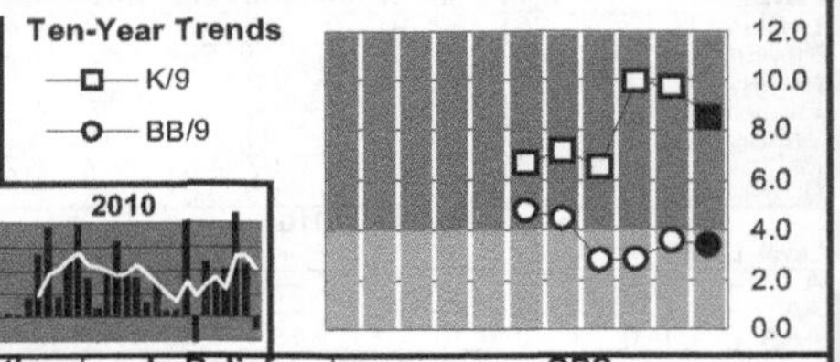


| Yr | $1L | $2L | Pts | RAA | H% | HR/fb | S% | FIP | GS | CG | QS/DS | GR | Hld | Bln | Lead | OPS | 1st Hf | 2nd Hf | vs RH | vs LH |
|---|---|---|---|---|---|---|---|---|---|---|---|---|---|---|---|---|---|---|---|---|
| 07 | $0 | -$6 | 80 | −2 | 28% | 11% | 73% | 5.25 | 11 | 0 | 5/3 | 1 | 0 | 0 | +0.3 | .753 | — | .753 | .764 | .725 |
| 08 | $17 | $9 | 310 | +26 | 30% | 7% | 76% | 3.66 | 33 | 2 | 20/2 | — | — | — | — | .688 | .703 | .666 | .737 | .571 |
| 09 | $20 | $11 | 380 | +20 | 32% | 11% | 75% | 3.31 | 32 | 2 | 23/2 | — | — | — | — | .667 | .701 | .622 | .649 | .717 |
| 10 | $23 | $16 | 420 | +22 | 29% | 9% | 74% | 3.21 | 32 | 2 | 20/3 | — | — | — | — | .628 | .580 | .690 | .620 | .651 |

## Colby Lewis

**180 IP | $14 | 270 pts**

SP-32 | Owned: 94% | RH

Forecast

| Player | Age | IP | W | Sv | K | ERA | WHIP | K/9 | BB/9 | $2L | Pts |
|---|---|---|---|---|---|---|---|---|---|---|---|
| Lewis C | 31 | 180 | 11 | 0 | 171 | 3.99 | 1.25 | 8.5 | 2.9 | $14 | 270 |
| **Mini-Browser** | **Age** | **IP** | **W** | **Sv** | **K** | **ERA** | **WHIP** | **K/9** | **BB/9** | **$2L** | **Pts** |
| Bailey A | 26 | 75 | 3 | 33 | 77 | 3.16 | 1.29 | 9.2 | 3.5 | $15 | 270 |
| Wilson C | 30 | 180 | 13 | 0 | 157 | 3.60 | 1.32 | 7.9 | 4.3 | $15 | 270 |
| Kimbrel C | 22 | 60 | 6 | 30 | 91 | 2.83 | 1.45 | 13.6 | 6.0 | $15 | 300 |
| Billingsley C | 26 | 220 | 14 | 0 | 189 | 3.84 | 1.31 | 7.7 | 3.5 | $15 | 320 |
| Scherzer M | 26 | 200 | 12 | 0 | 193 | 3.97 | 1.31 | 8.7 | 3.4 | $14 | 290 |

Minors (2010) / Skills

| Level | Leag | W | L | Sv | IP | H | K | ERA | WHIP | K/9 | BB/9 | HR/9 | GB/F |
|---|---|---|---|---|---|---|---|---|---|---|---|---|---|
| A | — | — | — | — | — | — | — | — | — | — | — | — | — |
| AA | — | — | — | — | — | — | — | — | — | — | — | — | — |
| AAA | — | — | — | — | — | — | — | — | — | — | — | — | — |

Majors / Skills

| Yr | Team | W | L | Sv | IP | H | K | ERA | WHIP | K/9 | BB/9 | HR/9 | GB/F |
|---|---|---|---|---|---|---|---|---|---|---|---|---|---|
| 07 | OAK | 0 | 2 | 0 | 37 | 44 | 23 | 6.45 | 1.54 | 5.5 | 3.3 | 1.7 | 0.8 |
| 08 | — | — | — | — | — | — | — | — | — | — | — | — | — |
| 09 | — | — | — | — | — | — | — | — | — | — | — | — | — |
| 10 | TEX | 12 | 13 | 0 | 201 | 174 | 196 | 3.72 | 1.19 | 8.8 | 2.9 | 0.9 | 0.8 |

After a two-year stint in Japan, Lewis celebrated his return to MLB with one of the better pitching seasons ever by an import. He's not overpowering, but he does wield the stuff/control of a very good mid-rotationer. However, do not anticipate another 8.8 K/9 campaign in 2011, and beware the chronic hip condition. (JM)

Competition at SP / Stats in 2010 as SP

| Thr | Player | GS | ERA | Supp | W-L |
|---|---|---|---|---|---|
| LH | Wilson C | 33 | 3.35 | 4.6 | 15-8 |
| ▶ RH | Lewis C | 32 | 3.72 | 4.1 | 12-13 |
| LH | Lee C | 28 | 3.18 | 4.3 | 12-9 |
| RH | Hunter T | 22 | 3.75 | 6.0 | 13-4 |

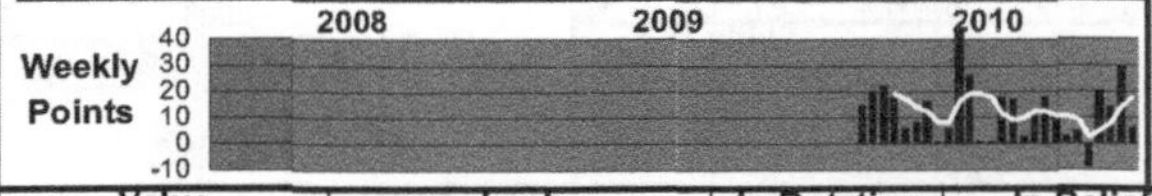


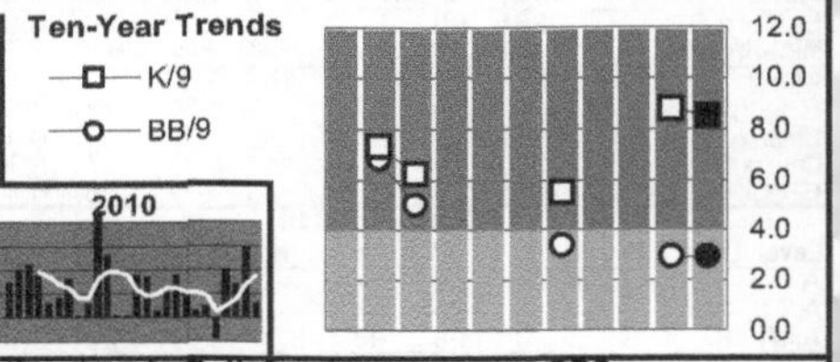


| Yr | $1L | $2L | Pts | RAA | H% | HR/fb | S% | FIP | GS | CG | QS/DS | GR | Hld | Bln | Lead | OPS | 1st Hf | 2nd Hf | vs RH | vs LH |
|---|---|---|---|---|---|---|---|---|---|---|---|---|---|---|---|---|---|---|---|---|
| 07 | -$5 | -$9 | 0 | −9 | 30% | 12% | 61% | 5.61 | 1 | 0 | 0/1 | 25 | 3 | 1 | −1.9 | .868 | .903 | .790 | .742 | 1.163 |
| 08 | — | — | — | — | — | — | — | — | — | — | — | — | — | — | — | — | — | — | — | — |
| 09 | — | — | — | — | — | — | — | — | — | — | — | — | — | — | — | — | — | — | — | — |
| 10 | $17 | $6 | 310 | +9 | 28% | 8% | 72% | 3.68 | 32 | 1 | 20/2 | — | — | — | — | .660 | .628 | .698 | .627 | .693 |

## Jensen Lewis

**40 IP | $-1 | 50 pts**

RP-37 | Owned: 1% | RH

Forecast

| Player | Age | IP | W | Sv | K | ERA | WHIP | K/9 | BB/9 | $2L | Pts |
|---|---|---|---|---|---|---|---|---|---|---|---|
| Lewis J | 26 | 40 | 3 | 0 | 36 | 4.48 | 1.45 | 8.0 | 4.3 | -$1 | 50 |
| **Mini-Browser** | **Age** | **IP** | **W** | **Sv** | **K** | **ERA** | **WHIP** | **K/9** | **BB/9** | **$2L** | **Pts** |
| Linebrink S | 34 | 60 | 2 | 0 | 50 | 4.83 | 1.36 | 7.5 | 3.0 | $0 | 60 |
| Smith J | 27 | 40 | 2 | 0 | 32 | 4.16 | 1.42 | 7.1 | 4.7 | $0 | 40 |
| Bush D | 31 | 180 | 9 | 0 | 112 | 4.92 | 1.37 | 5.6 | 2.8 | $0 | 160 |
| Strasburg S | 22 | 20 | 1 | 0 | 23 | 3.71 | 1.21 | 10.4 | 3.2 | $0 | 40 |
| Zumaya J | 26 | 40 | 2 | 0 | 37 | 4.08 | 1.48 | 8.3 | 4.9 | -$1 | 50 |

Minors (2010) / Skills

| Level | Leag | W | L | Sv | IP | H | K | ERA | WHIP | K/9 | BB/9 | HR/9 | GB/F |
|---|---|---|---|---|---|---|---|---|---|---|---|---|---|
| A | — | — | — | — | — | — | — | — | — | — | — | — | — |
| AA | — | — | — | — | — | — | — | — | — | — | — | — | — |
| AAA | IL | 2 | 1 | 2 | 30 | 29 | 30 | 2.67 | 1.22 | 8.9 | 2.4 | 0.6 | — |

Majors / Skills

| Yr | Team | W | L | Sv | IP | H | K | ERA | WHIP | K/9 | BB/9 | HR/9 | GB/F |
|---|---|---|---|---|---|---|---|---|---|---|---|---|---|
| 07 | CLE | 1 | 1 | 0 | 29 | 26 | 34 | 2.15 | 1.23 | 10.4 | 3.1 | 0.3 | 0.7 |
| 08 | CLE | 0 | 4 | 13 | 66 | 68 | 52 | 3.82 | 1.44 | 7.1 | 3.7 | 1.1 | 0.9 |
| 09 | CLE | 2 | 4 | 1 | 66 | 62 | 62 | 4.61 | 1.37 | 8.4 | 3.9 | 1.8 | 0.8 |
| 10 | CLE | 4 | 2 | 0 | 36 | 28 | 29 | 2.97 | 1.29 | 7.2 | 4.7 | 0.2 | 0.7 |

With minor-league options to burn, Lewis found himself traveling between Triple-A and MLB several times in 2010 as CLE tried to navigate through various injuries and new faces. However, Lewis also bears some of the blame, as his BB/9 rose for the third straight year. He will contribute in middle relief in 2011. (BLS)

Competition at RP / Stats in 2010 as RP

| Thr | Player | GR | ERA | IP/G | Sv-Hld |
|---|---|---|---|---|---|
| RH | Perez C | 63 | 1.71 | 1.0 | 23-9 |
| RH | Smith J | 53 | 3.83 | 0.8 | 0-17 |
| RH | Herrmann F | 40 | 4.03 | 1.1 | 1-7 |
| ▶ RH | Lewis J | 37 | 2.97 | 1.0 | 0-1 |

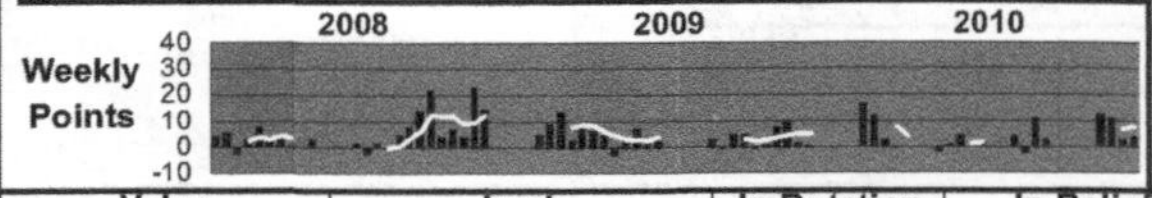


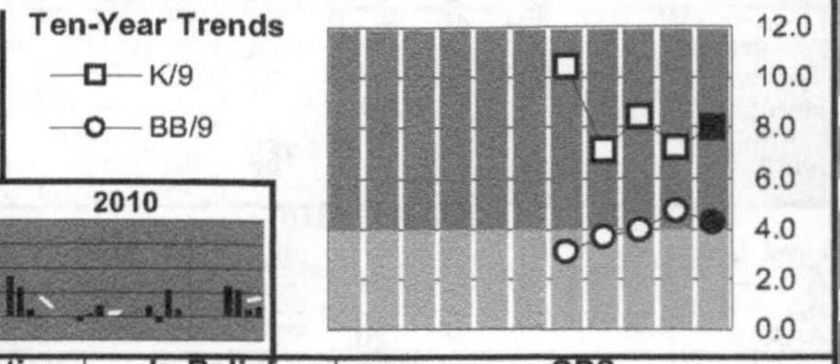


| Yr | $1L | $2L | Pts | RAA | H% | HR/fb | S% | FIP | GS | CG | QS/DS | GR | Hld | Bln | Lead | OPS | 1st Hf | 2nd Hf | vs RH | vs LH |
|---|---|---|---|---|---|---|---|---|---|---|---|---|---|---|---|---|---|---|---|---|
| 07 | $2 | $1 | 50 | +5 | 33% | 3% | 83% | 2.45 | — | — | — | 26 | 5 | 0 | +0.8 | .616 | — | .616 | .656 | .548 |
| 08 | $3 | -$2 | 110 | +1 | 31% | 10% | 77% | 4.53 | — | — | — | 51 | 4 | 1 | +0.6 | .771 | .833 | .708 | .757 | .782 |
| 09 | $1 | -$3 | 70 | −7 | 28% | 15% | 73% | 5.29 | — | — | — | 47 | 4 | 4 | −1.4 | .804 | .863 | .716 | .640 | .987 |
| 10 | $1 | -$6 | 70 | +4 | 27% | 2% | 76% | 3.63 | — | — | — | 37 | 1 | 0 | −0.3 | .611 | .679 | .497 | .532 | .727 |

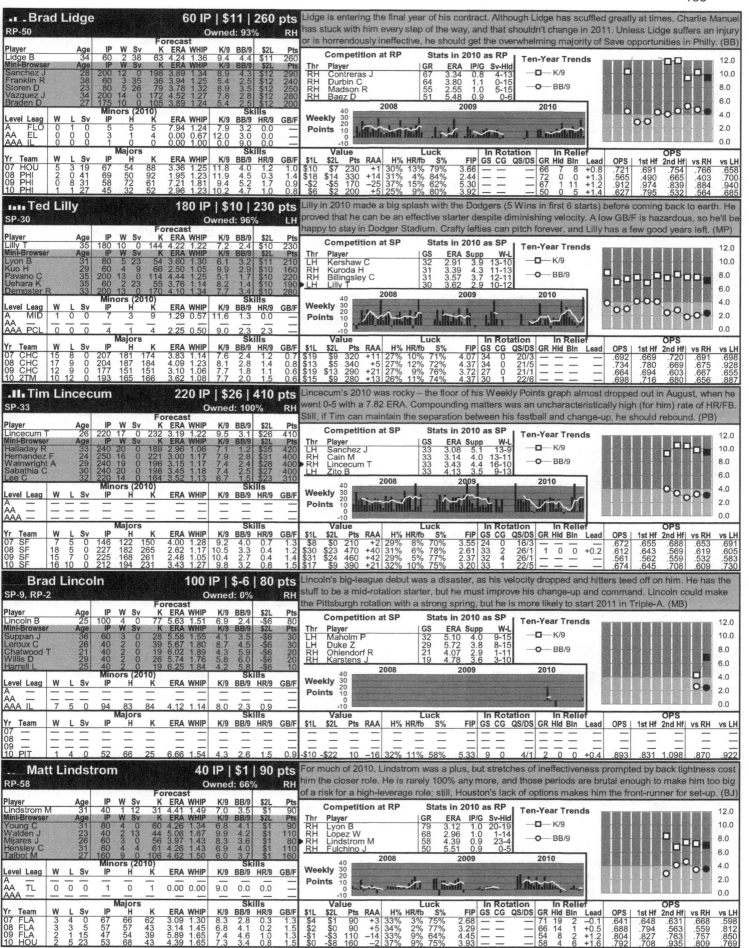

## Brad Lidge — 60 IP | $11 | 260 pts
RP-50    Owned: 93%    RH

Lidge is entering the final year of his contract. Although Lidge has scuffled greatly at times, Charlie Manuel has stuck with him every step of the way, and that shouldn't change in 2011. Unless Lidge suffers an injury or is horrendously ineffective, he should get the overwhelming majority of Save opportunities in Philly. (BB)

### Forecast / Mini-Browser
| Player | Age | IP | W | Sv | K | ERA | WHIP | K/9 | BB/9 | $2L | Pts |
|---|---|---|---|---|---|---|---|---|---|---|---|
| Lidge B | 34 | 60 | 2 | 38 | 63 | 4.24 | 1.36 | 9.4 | 4.3 | $11 | 260 |
| Sanchez J | 28 | 200 | 12 | 0 | 198 | 3.89 | 1.34 | 8.9 | 4.3 | $12 | 290 |
| Franklin R | 38 | 60 | 3 | 35 | 36 | 3.94 | 1.25 | 5.4 | 2.5 | $12 | 240 |
| Storen D | 23 | 80 | 5 | 26 | 79 | 3.78 | 1.32 | 8.9 | 3.5 | $12 | 250 |
| Vazquez J | 34 | 200 | 14 | 0 | 172 | 4.52 | 1.27 | 7.8 | 2.8 | $12 | 280 |
| Braden D | 27 | 175 | 10 | 0 | 105 | 3.89 | 1.24 | 5.4 | 2.5 | $12 | 200 |

### Minors (2010)
| Level Leag | W | L | Sv | IP | H | K | ERA | WHIP | K/9 | BB/9 | HR/9 | GB/F |
|---|---|---|---|---|---|---|---|---|---|---|---|---|
| A FLO | 0 | 1 | 0 | 5 | 5 | 5 | 7.94 | 1.24 | 7.9 | 3.2 | 0.0 | — |
| AA EL | 0 | 0 | 0 | 3 | 1 | 4 | 0.00 | 0.67 | 12.0 | 3.0 | 0.0 | — |
| AAA IL | 0 | 0 | 0 | 1 | 0 | 0 | 0.00 | 1.00 | 0.0 | 9.0 | 0.0 | — |

### Majors
| Yr Team | W | L | Sv | IP | H | K | ERA | WHIP | K/9 | BB/9 | HR/9 | GB/F |
|---|---|---|---|---|---|---|---|---|---|---|---|---|
| 07 HOU | 5 | 3 | 19 | 67 | 54 | 88 | 3.36 | 1.25 | 11.8 | 4.0 | 1.2 | 1.0 |
| 08 PHI | 2 | 0 | 41 | 69 | 50 | 92 | 1.95 | 1.23 | 11.9 | 4.5 | 0.3 | 1.4 |
| 09 PHI | 0 | 8 | 31 | 58 | 72 | 61 | 7.21 | 1.81 | 9.4 | 5.2 | 1.7 | 0.9 |
| 10 PHI | 1 | 1 | 27 | 45 | 32 | 52 | 2.96 | 1.23 | 10.2 | 4.7 | 1.0 | 0.8 |

### Competition at RP / Stats in 2010 as RP
| Thr | Player | GR | ERA | IP/G | Sv-Hld |
|---|---|---|---|---|---|
| RH | Contreras J | 67 | 3.34 | 0.8 | 4-13 |
| RH | Durbin C | 64 | 3.80 | 1.1 | 0-15 |
| RH | Madson R | 55 | 2.55 | 1.0 | 5-15 |
| RH | Baez D | 51 | 5.48 | 0.9 | 0-6 |

### Value / Luck / In Rotation / In Relief / OPS
| Yr | $1L | $2L | Pts | RAA | H% | HR/fb | S% | FIP | GS | CG | QS/DS | GR | Hld | Bln | Lead | OPS | 1st Hf | 2nd Hf | vs RH | vs LH |
|---|---|---|---|---|---|---|---|---|---|---|---|---|---|---|---|---|---|---|---|---|
| 07 | $10 | $7 | 230 | +1 | 30% | 13% | 79% | 3.66 | — | — | — | 66 | 7 | 8 | +0.8 | .721 | .691 | .754 | .766 | .658 |
| 08 | $18 | $14 | 330 | +14 | 31% | 4% | 84% | 2.44 | — | — | — | 72 | 0 | 0 | +1.3 | .565 | .490 | .665 | .403 | .700 |
| 09 | -$2 | -$5 | 170 | -25 | 37% | 15% | 62% | 5.30 | — | — | — | 67 | 1 | 11 | +1.2 | .912 | .974 | .839 | .884 | .940 |
| 10 | $6 | $2 | 200 | +5 | 25% | 9% | 80% | 3.92 | — | — | — | 50 | 0 | 5 | +1.4 | .627 | .795 | .532 | .564 | .685 |

## Ted Lilly — 180 IP | $10 | 230 pts
SP-30    Owned: 96%    LH

Lilly in 2010 made a big splash with the Dodgers (5 Wins in first 6 starts) before coming back to earth. He proved that he can be an effective starter despite diminishing velocity. A low GB/F is hazardous, so he'll be happy to stay in Dodger Stadium. Crafty lefties can pitch forever, and Lilly has a few good years left. (MP)

### Forecast / Mini-Browser
| Player | Age | IP | W | Sv | K | ERA | WHIP | K/9 | BB/9 | $2L | Pts |
|---|---|---|---|---|---|---|---|---|---|---|---|
| Lilly T | 35 | 180 | 10 | 0 | 144 | 4.22 | 1.22 | 7.2 | 2.4 | $10 | 230 |
| Lyon B | 31 | 80 | 5 | 23 | 54 | 3.60 | 1.30 | 6.1 | 3.2 | $11 | 210 |
| Kuo H | 29 | 60 | 4 | 9 | 66 | 2.50 | 1.05 | 9.9 | 2.9 | $10 | 160 |
| Pavano C | 35 | 200 | 13 | 0 | 114 | 4.44 | 1.25 | 5.1 | 1.7 | $10 | 220 |
| Uehara K | 35 | 60 | 2 | 23 | 55 | 3.76 | 1.14 | 8.2 | 1.4 | $10 | 190 |
| Dempster R | 33 | 200 | 13 | 0 | 170 | 4.10 | 1.34 | 7.7 | 3.4 | $10 | 280 |

### Minors (2010)
| Level Leag | W | L | Sv | IP | H | K | ERA | WHIP | K/9 | BB/9 | HR/9 | GB/F |
|---|---|---|---|---|---|---|---|---|---|---|---|---|
| A MID | 1 | 0 | 0 | 7 | 3 | 9 | 1.29 | 0.57 | 11.6 | 1.3 | 0.0 | — |
| AA | — | | | | | | | | | | | |
| AAA PCL | 0 | 0 | 0 | 4 | 1 | 4 | 2.25 | 0.50 | 9.0 | 2.3 | 2.3 | — |

### Majors
| Yr Team | W | L | Sv | IP | H | K | ERA | WHIP | K/9 | BB/9 | HR/9 | GB/F |
|---|---|---|---|---|---|---|---|---|---|---|---|---|
| 07 CHC | 15 | 8 | 0 | 207 | 181 | 174 | 3.83 | 1.14 | 7.6 | 2.4 | 1.2 | 0.7 |
| 08 CHC | 17 | 9 | 0 | 204 | 187 | 184 | 4.09 | 1.23 | 8.1 | 2.8 | 1.4 | 0.8 |
| 09 CHC | 12 | 9 | 0 | 177 | 151 | 151 | 3.10 | 1.06 | 7.7 | 1.8 | 1.1 | 0.6 |
| 10 2TM | 10 | 12 | 0 | 193 | 165 | 166 | 3.62 | 1.08 | 7.7 | 2.0 | 1.6 | 0.6 |

### Competition at SP / Stats in 2010 as SP
| Thr | Player | GS | ERA | Supp | W-L |
|---|---|---|---|---|---|
| LH | Kershaw C | 32 | 2.91 | 3.9 | 13-10 |
| RH | Kuroda H | 31 | 3.39 | 4.3 | 11-13 |
| RH | Billingsley C | 31 | 3.57 | 3.7 | 12-11 |
| LH | Lilly T | 30 | 3.62 | 2.9 | 10-12 |

### Value / Luck / In Rotation / In Relief / OPS
| Yr | $1L | $2L | Pts | RAA | H% | HR/fb | S% | FIP | GS | CG | QS/DS | GR | Hld | Bln | Lead | OPS | 1st Hf | 2nd Hf | vs RH | vs LH |
|---|---|---|---|---|---|---|---|---|---|---|---|---|---|---|---|---|---|---|---|---|
| 07 | $19 | $9 | 320 | +11 | 27% | 10% | 71% | 4.07 | 34 | 0 | 20/3 | — | — | — | — | .692 | .669 | .720 | .691 | .698 |
| 08 | $13 | $5 | 340 | +5 | 27% | 12% | 72% | 4.37 | 34 | 0 | 21/5 | — | — | — | — | .734 | .780 | .669 | .675 | .928 |
| 09 | $19 | $13 | 290 | +21 | 27% | 9% | 76% | 3.72 | 27 | 0 | 21/1 | — | — | — | — | .664 | .694 | .603 | .667 | .655 |
| 10 | $15 | $9 | 280 | +13 | 26% | 11% | 74% | 4.37 | 30 | 1 | 22/6 | — | — | — | — | .698 | .716 | .680 | .656 | .887 |

## Tim Lincecum — 220 IP | $26 | 410 pts
SP-33    Owned: 100%    RH

Lincecum's 2010 was rocky – the floor of his Weekly Points graph almost dropped out in August, when he went 0-5 with a 7.82 ERA. Compounding matters was an uncharacteristically high (for him) rate of HR/FB. Still, if Tim can maintain the separation between his fastball and change-up, he should rebound. (PB)

### Forecast / Mini-Browser
| Player | Age | IP | W | Sv | K | ERA | WHIP | K/9 | BB/9 | $2L | Pts |
|---|---|---|---|---|---|---|---|---|---|---|---|
| Lincecum T | 26 | 220 | 17 | 0 | 232 | 3.19 | 1.22 | 9.5 | 3.1 | $26 | 410 |
| Halladay R | 33 | 240 | 20 | 0 | 189 | 2.96 | 1.06 | 7.1 | 1.2 | $35 | 420 |
| Hernandez F | 24 | 250 | 16 | 0 | 221 | 3.00 | 1.17 | 7.9 | 2.8 | $31 | 400 |
| Wainwright A | 29 | 240 | 19 | 0 | 196 | 3.15 | 1.17 | 7.4 | 2.4 | $28 | 400 |
| Sabathia C | 30 | 240 | 20 | 0 | 198 | 3.45 | 1.18 | 7.4 | 2.5 | $27 | 400 |
| Lee C | 32 | 220 | 14 | 0 | 164 | 3.52 | 1.13 | 6.7 | 1.5 | $23 | 310 |

### Minors (2010)
| Level Leag | W | L | Sv | IP | H | K | ERA | WHIP | K/9 | BB/9 | HR/9 | GB/F |
|---|---|---|---|---|---|---|---|---|---|---|---|---|
| A | — | | | | | | | | | | | |
| AA | — | | | | | | | | | | | |
| AAA | — | | | | | | | | | | | |

### Majors
| Yr Team | W | L | Sv | IP | H | K | ERA | WHIP | K/9 | BB/9 | HR/9 | GB/F |
|---|---|---|---|---|---|---|---|---|---|---|---|---|
| 07 SF | 7 | 5 | 0 | 146 | 122 | 150 | 4.00 | 1.28 | 9.2 | 4.0 | 0.7 | 1.3 |
| 08 SF | 18 | 5 | 0 | 227 | 182 | 265 | 2.62 | 1.17 | 10.5 | 3.3 | 0.4 | 1.2 |
| 09 SF | 15 | 7 | 0 | 225 | 168 | 261 | 2.48 | 1.05 | 10.4 | 2.7 | 0.4 | 1.4 |
| 10 SF | 16 | 10 | 0 | 212 | 194 | 231 | 3.43 | 1.27 | 9.8 | 3.2 | 0.8 | 1.1 |

### Competition at SP / Stats in 2010 as SP
| Thr | Player | GS | ERA | Supp | W-L |
|---|---|---|---|---|---|
| LH | Sanchez J | 33 | 3.08 | 5.1 | 13-9 |
| RH | Cain M | 33 | 3.14 | 4.0 | 13-11 |
| RH | Lincecum T | 33 | 3.43 | 4.4 | 16-10 |
| LH | Zito B | 33 | 4.13 | 3.5 | 9-13 |

### Value / Luck / In Rotation / In Relief / OPS
| Yr | $1L | $2L | Pts | RAA | H% | HR/fb | S% | FIP | GS | CG | QS/DS | GR | Hld | Bln | Lead | OPS | 1st Hf | 2nd Hf | vs RH | vs LH |
|---|---|---|---|---|---|---|---|---|---|---|---|---|---|---|---|---|---|---|---|---|
| 07 | $8 | $0 | 210 | +2 | 29% | 8% | 70% | 3.55 | 24 | 0 | 16/3 | — | — | — | — | .672 | .655 | .688 | .653 | .691 |
| 08 | $30 | $23 | 470 | +40 | 31% | 6% | 78% | 2.61 | 33 | 2 | 26/1 | 1 | 0 | 0 | +0.2 | .612 | .643 | .569 | .619 | .605 |
| 09 | $31 | $24 | 460 | +42 | 29% | 5% | 77% | 2.37 | 32 | 4 | 26/1 | — | — | — | — | .561 | .562 | .559 | .532 | .583 |
| 10 | $17 | $9 | 390 | +21 | 32% | 10% | 75% | 3.20 | 33 | 1 | 22/5 | — | — | — | — | .674 | .645 | .708 | .609 | .730 |

## Brad Lincoln — 100 IP | $-6 | 80 pts
SP-9, RP-2    Owned: 0%    RH

Lincoln's big-league debut was a disaster, as his velocity dropped and hitters teed off on him. He has the stuff to be a mid-rotation starter, but he must improve his change-up and command. Lincoln could make the Pittsburgh rotation with a strong spring, but he is more likely to start 2011 in Triple-A. (MB)

### Forecast / Mini-Browser
| Player | Age | IP | W | Sv | K | ERA | WHIP | K/9 | BB/9 | $2L | Pts |
|---|---|---|---|---|---|---|---|---|---|---|---|
| Lincoln B | 25 | 100 | 4 | 0 | 77 | 5.63 | 1.51 | 6.9 | 2.4 | -$6 | 80 |
| Suppan J | 36 | 60 | 3 | 0 | 28 | 5.58 | 1.55 | 4.1 | 3.5 | -$6 | 30 |
| Leroux C | 26 | 40 | 2 | 0 | 39 | 5.67 | 1.80 | 8.7 | 4.5 | -$6 | 30 |
| Chatwood T | 21 | 40 | 2 | 0 | 19 | 6.02 | 1.89 | 4.3 | 5.9 | -$6 | 20 |
| Willis D | 29 | 40 | 2 | 0 | 26 | 5.74 | 1.76 | 5.8 | 6.0 | -$6 | 20 |
| Harrell L | 25 | 40 | 2 | 0 | 19 | 6.25 | 1.84 | 4.2 | 5.8 | -$6 | 10 |

### Minors (2010)
| Level Leag | W | L | Sv | IP | H | K | ERA | WHIP | K/9 | BB/9 | HR/9 | GB/F |
|---|---|---|---|---|---|---|---|---|---|---|---|---|
| A | — | | | | | | | | | | | |
| AA | — | | | | | | | | | | | |
| AAA IL | 7 | 5 | 0 | 94 | 83 | 84 | 4.12 | 1.14 | 8.0 | 2.3 | 0.9 | — |

### Majors
| Yr Team | W | L | Sv | IP | H | K | ERA | WHIP | K/9 | BB/9 | HR/9 | GB/F |
|---|---|---|---|---|---|---|---|---|---|---|---|---|
| 07 | — | | | | | | | | | | | |
| 08 | — | | | | | | | | | | | |
| 09 | — | | | | | | | | | | | |
| 10 PIT | 1 | 4 | 0 | 52 | 58 | 25 | 6.66 | 1.54 | 4.3 | 1.5 | 1.5 | 0.9 |

### Competition at SP / Stats in 2010 as SP
| Thr | Player | GS | ERA | Supp | W-L |
|---|---|---|---|---|---|
| LH | Maholm P | 32 | 5.10 | 4.0 | 9-15 |
| LH | Duke Z | 29 | 5.72 | 3.8 | 8-15 |
| RH | Ohlendorf R | 21 | 4.07 | 2.9 | 1-11 |
| RH | Karstens J | 19 | 4.78 | 3.6 | 3-10 |

### Value / Luck / In Rotation / In Relief / OPS
| Yr | $1L | $2L | Pts | RAA | H% | HR/fb | S% | FIP | GS | CG | QS/DS | GR | Hld | Bln | Lead | OPS | 1st Hf | 2nd Hf | vs RH | vs LH |
|---|---|---|---|---|---|---|---|---|---|---|---|---|---|---|---|---|---|---|---|---|
| 10 | -$10 | -$20 | 80 | -16 | 32% | 11% | 58% | 5.33 | 9 | 0 | 4/1 | 2 | 0 | 0 | +0.4 | .893 | .831 | 1.098 | .870 | .922 |

## Matt Lindstrom — 40 IP | $1 | 90 pts
RP-58    Owned: 66%    RH

For much of 2010, Lindstrom was a plus, but stretches of ineffectiveness prompted by back tightness cost him the closer role. He is rarely 100% any more, and those periods are brutal enough to make him too big of a risk for a high-leverage role; still, Houston's lack of options makes him the front-runner for set-up. (BJ)

### Forecast / Mini-Browser
| Player | Age | IP | W | Sv | K | ERA | WHIP | K/9 | BB/9 | $2L | Pts |
|---|---|---|---|---|---|---|---|---|---|---|---|
| Lindstrom M | 31 | 40 | 1 | 12 | 31 | 4.41 | 1.49 | 7.0 | 3.5 | $1 | 90 |
| Young C | 31 | 80 | 4 | 0 | 60 | 4.26 | 1.34 | 6.8 | 4.1 | $1 | 90 |
| Walden J | 23 | 40 | 2 | 13 | 44 | 5.06 | 1.67 | 9.9 | 4.2 | $1 | 110 |
| Mijares J | 26 | 60 | 3 | 0 | 56 | 3.97 | 1.43 | 8.3 | 3.6 | $1 | 80 |
| Hensley C | 31 | 80 | 4 | 4 | 61 | 4.26 | 1.43 | 6.9 | 4.0 | $1 | 110 |
| Talbot M | 27 | 160 | 9 | 0 | 106 | 4.62 | 1.50 | 6.0 | 3.7 | $1 | 160 |

### Minors (2010)
| Level Leag | W | L | Sv | IP | H | K | ERA | WHIP | K/9 | BB/9 | HR/9 | GB/F |
|---|---|---|---|---|---|---|---|---|---|---|---|---|
| A | — | | | | | | | | | | | |
| AA TL | 0 | 0 | 0 | 1 | 0 | 1 | 0.00 | 0.00 | 9.0 | 0.0 | 0.0 | — |
| AAA | — | | | | | | | | | | | |

### Majors
| Yr Team | W | L | Sv | IP | H | K | ERA | WHIP | K/9 | BB/9 | HR/9 | GB/F |
|---|---|---|---|---|---|---|---|---|---|---|---|---|
| 07 FLA | 3 | 4 | 0 | 67 | 66 | 62 | 3.09 | 1.30 | 8.3 | 2.8 | 0.3 | 1.3 |
| 08 FLA | 3 | 5 | 5 | 57 | 57 | 43 | 3.14 | 1.45 | 6.8 | 4.1 | 0.2 | 1.5 |
| 09 FLA | 2 | 1 | 15 | 47 | 54 | 39 | 5.89 | 1.65 | 7.4 | 4.6 | 1.0 | 1.3 |
| 10 HOU | 2 | 5 | 23 | 53 | 68 | 43 | 4.39 | 1.46 | 7.3 | 3.4 | 0.8 | 1.5 |

### Competition at RP / Stats in 2010 as RP
| Thr | Player | GR | ERA | IP/G | Sv-Hld |
|---|---|---|---|---|---|
| RH | Lyon B | 79 | 3.12 | 1.0 | 20-19 |
| RH | Lopez W | 68 | 2.96 | 1.0 | 1-14 |
| RH | Lindstrom M | 58 | 4.39 | 0.9 | 23-4 |
| RH | Fulchino J | 50 | 5.51 | 0.9 | 0-5 |

### Value / Luck / In Rotation / In Relief / OPS
| Yr | $1L | $2L | Pts | RAA | H% | HR/fb | S% | FIP | GS | CG | QS/DS | GR | Hld | Bln | Lead | OPS | 1st Hf | 2nd Hf | vs RH | vs LH |
|---|---|---|---|---|---|---|---|---|---|---|---|---|---|---|---|---|---|---|---|---|
| 07 | $4 | $1 | 90 | +3 | 33% | 3% | 75% | 2.68 | — | — | — | 71 | 19 | 2 | -0.1 | .641 | .648 | .631 | .668 | .598 |
| 08 | $2 | $0 | 90 | +5 | 34% | 2% | 77% | 3.29 | — | — | — | 66 | 14 | 1 | +0.5 | .688 | .794 | .563 | .559 | .812 |
| 09 | -$3 | -$6 | 110 | -14 | 33% | 9% | 64% | 4.45 | — | — | — | 54 | 8 | 2 | +1.2 | .804 | .827 | .765 | .757 | .850 |
| 10 | $0 | -$8 | 160 | -2 | 37% | 9% | 75% | 3.93 | — | — | — | 58 | 4 | 6 | +1.6 | .792 | .708 | .935 | .809 | .769 |

## Scott Linebrink — 60 IP | $0 | 60 pts

RP-52 — Owned: 1% — RH

Check out Linebrink's HR/FB in three seasons with the White Sox: 14%, 13%, 13%. Even with solid rates of walks and strikeouts, a 1.5 HR/9 nearly dooms a pitcher to an ERA of 4.50 (or worse). The best way for Linebrink to shed the "bust" label would be to get traded to a park that can better contain his fly balls. (RM)

| Player | Age | IP | W | Sv | K | ERA | WHIP | K/9 | BB/9 | $2L | Pts |
|---|---|---|---|---|---|---|---|---|---|---|---|
| Linebrink S | 34 | 60 | 2 | 0 | 50 | 4.83 | 1.36 | 7.5 | 3.0 | $0 | 60 |
| **Mini-Browser** | **Age** | **IP** | **W** | **Sv** | **K** | **ERA** | **WHIP** | **K/9** | **BB/9** | **$2L** | **Pts** |
| Duchscherer J | 33 | 20 | 1 | 0 | 13 | 3.40 | 1.21 | 5.9 | 2.7 | $0 | 30 |
| Slaten D | 31 | 40 | 2 | 0 | 33 | 3.92 | 1.37 | 7.5 | 3.7 | $0 | 50 |
| Bulger J | 32 | 40 | 2 | 0 | 44 | 4.22 | 1.46 | 9.8 | 5.0 | $0 | 50 |
| Bedard E | 32 | 20 | 1 | 0 | 19 | 3.68 | 1.27 | 8.6 | 3.6 | $0 | 30 |
| Belisario R | 28 | 80 | 4 | 0 | 62 | 4.55 | 1.40 | 7.0 | 3.6 | $0 | 90 |

| Level | Leag | W | L | Sv | IP | H | K | ERA | WHIP | K/9 | BB/9 | HR/9 | GB/F |
|---|---|---|---|---|---|---|---|---|---|---|---|---|---|
| A | — | — | — | — | — | — | — | — | — | — | — | — | — |
| AA | — | — | — | — | — | — | — | — | — | — | — | — | — |
| AAA | — | — | — | — | — | — | — | — | — | — | — | — | — |

Competition at RP — Stats in 2010 as RP

| Thr | Player | GR | ERA | IP/G | Sv-Hld |
|---|---|---|---|---|---|
| RH | Putz J | 60 | 2.83 | 0.9 | 3-14 |
| RH | Santos S | 56 | 2.96 | 0.9 | 1-14 |
| RH | Jenks B | 55 | 4.44 | 1.0 | 27-0 |
| RH | Linebrink S | 52 | 4.40 | 1.1 | 0-4 |

Weekly Points

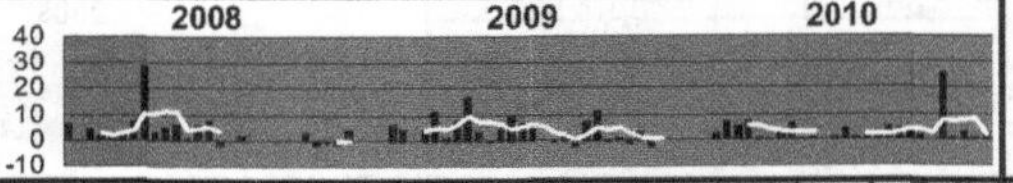


Ten-Year Trends

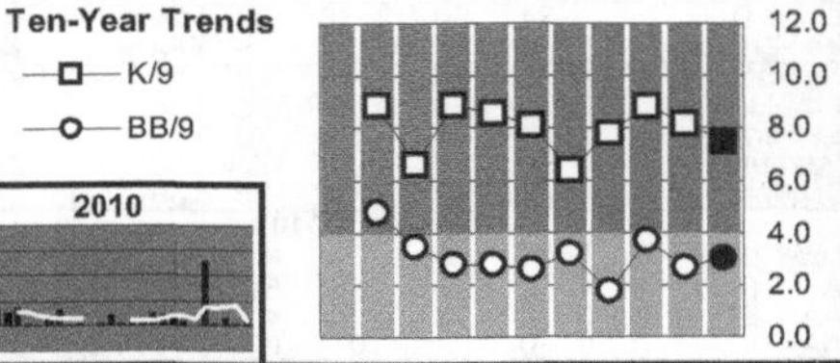


| Yr | Team | W | L | Sv | IP | H | K | ERA | WHIP | K/9 | BB/9 | HR/9 | GB/F |
|---|---|---|---|---|---|---|---|---|---|---|---|---|---|
| 07 | 2TM | 5 | 6 | 1 | 70 | 68 | 50 | 3.71 | 1.32 | 6.4 | 3.2 | 1.5 | 1.1 |
| 08 | CHW | 2 | 2 | 1 | 46 | 41 | 40 | 3.69 | 1.08 | 7.8 | 1.7 | 1.6 | 0.9 |
| 09 | CHW | 3 | 7 | 2 | 56 | 70 | 55 | 4.66 | 1.66 | 8.8 | 3.7 | 1.4 | 1.0 |
| 10 | CHW | 3 | 2 | 0 | 57 | 59 | 52 | 4.40 | 1.33 | 8.2 | 2.7 | 1.7 | 0.6 |

| Yr | $1L | $2L | Pts | RAA | H% | HR/fb | S% | FIP | GS | CG | QS/DS | GR | Hld | Bln | Lead | OPS | 1st Hf | 2nd Hf | vs RH | vs LH |
|---|---|---|---|---|---|---|---|---|---|---|---|---|---|---|---|---|---|---|---|---|
| 07 | $3 | -$1 | 100 | −1 | 27% | 15% | 79% | 5.11 | — | — | — | 71 | 21 | 7 | +1.0 | .742 | .664 | .833 | .773 | .706 |
| 08 | $3 | $1 | 70 | +1 | 26% | 14% | 74% | 4.40 | — | — | — | 50 | 19 | 3 | +2.1 | .677 | .597 | .995 | .717 | .631 |
| 09 | $0 | -$4 | 80 | −9 | 36% | 13% | 76% | 4.66 | — | — | — | 57 | 7 | 2 | +1.3 | .875 | .696 | 1.084 | .871 | .880 |
| 10 | -$1 | -$10 | 70 | −5 | 30% | 13% | 74% | 4.87 | — | — | — | 52 | 4 | 1 | −1.0 | .780 | .807 | .751 | .647 | .901 |

## Francisco Liriano — 200 IP | $12 | 300 pts

SP-31 — Owned: 99% — LH

It was a long road to recovery from Tommy John surgery, but in 2010 Liriano finally resembled the dominant force that torched the league as a rookie back in '06. He is viewed as the team ace, and he will certainly be back for at least 2011. In fact, the Twins would be wise to explore a long-term deal soon. (NN)

| Player | Age | IP | W | Sv | K | ERA | WHIP | K/9 | BB/9 | $2L | Pts |
|---|---|---|---|---|---|---|---|---|---|---|---|
| Liriano F | 27 | 200 | 13 | 0 | 190 | 4.19 | 1.34 | 8.6 | 3.4 | $12 | 300 |
| **Mini-Browser** | **Age** | **IP** | **W** | **Sv** | **K** | **ERA** | **WHIP** | **K/9** | **BB/9** | **$2L** | **Pts** |
| Garcia J | 24 | 180 | 13 | 0 | 153 | 3.39 | 1.37 | 7.7 | 3.6 | $13 | 270 |
| Axford J | 28 | 60 | 5 | 40 | 72 | 3.93 | 1.54 | 10.8 | 5.3 | $13 | 310 |
| Jenks B | 30 | 60 | 2 | 38 | 55 | 4.02 | 1.28 | 8.2 | 2.9 | $13 | 260 |
| Perez C | 25 | 60 | 2 | 33 | 63 | 3.38 | 1.31 | 9.4 | 4.7 | $13 | 250 |
| Danks J | 25 | 200 | 13 | 0 | 150 | 4.15 | 1.29 | 6.7 | 3.2 | $13 | 260 |

| Level | Leag | W | L | Sv | IP | H | K | ERA | WHIP | K/9 | BB/9 | HR/9 | GB/F |
|---|---|---|---|---|---|---|---|---|---|---|---|---|---|
| A | — | — | — | — | — | — | — | — | — | — | — | — | — |
| AA | — | — | — | — | — | — | — | — | — | — | — | — | — |
| AAA | — | — | — | — | — | — | — | — | — | — | — | — | — |

Competition at SP — Stats in 2010 as SP

| Thr | Player | GS | ERA | Supp | W-L |
|---|---|---|---|---|---|
| RH | Pavano C | 32 | 3.75 | 4.7 | 17-11 |
| LH | Liriano F | 31 | 3.62 | 4.9 | 14-10 |
| RH | Baker S | 29 | 4.49 | 4.8 | 12-9 |
| RH | Slowey K | 28 | 4.54 | 5.5 | 13-6 |

Weekly Points

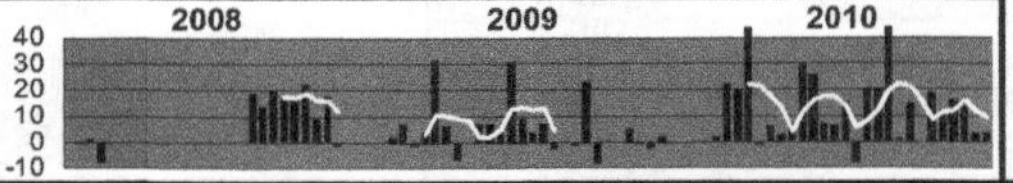


Ten-Year Trends

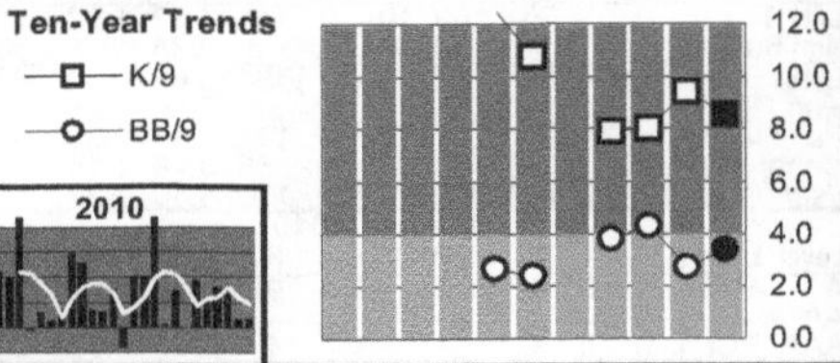


| Yr | Team | W | L | Sv | IP | H | K | ERA | WHIP | K/9 | BB/9 | HR/9 | GB/F |
|---|---|---|---|---|---|---|---|---|---|---|---|---|---|
| 07 | — | — | — | — | — | — | — | — | — | — | — | — | — |
| 08 | MIN | 6 | 4 | 0 | 76 | 74 | 67 | 3.91 | 1.39 | 7.9 | 3.8 | 0.8 | 1.0 |
| 09 | MIN | 5 | 13 | 0 | 136 | 147 | 122 | 5.80 | 1.55 | 8.0 | 4.3 | 1.4 | 1.0 |
| 10 | MIN | 14 | 10 | 0 | 191 | 184 | 201 | 3.62 | 1.26 | 9.4 | 2.7 | 0.4 | 2.0 |

| Yr | $1L | $2L | Pts | RAA | H% | HR/fb | S% | FIP | GS | CG | QS/DS | GR | Hld | Bln | Lead | OPS | 1st Hf | 2nd Hf | vs RH | vs LH |
|---|---|---|---|---|---|---|---|---|---|---|---|---|---|---|---|---|---|---|---|---|
| 07 | — | — | — | — | — | — | — | — | — | — | — | — | — | — | — | — | — | — | — | — |
| 08 | $2 | -$2 | 120 | −3 | 31% | 8% | 74% | 4.00 | 14 | 0 | 7/3 | — | — | — | — | .719 | .924 | .678 | .745 | .637 |
| 09 | -$3 | -$11 | 110 | −26 | 33% | 13% | 65% | 4.94 | 24 | 0 | 10/8 | 5 | 0 | 0 | −0.1 | .830 | .807 | .896 | .899 | .631 |
| 10 | $16 | $5 | 330 | +18 | 34% | 6% | 71% | 2.72 | 31 | 0 | 20/2 | — | — | — | — | .670 | .661 | .681 | .713 | .517 |

## Jesse Litsch — 80 IP | $0 | 60 pts

SP-9 — Owned: 0% — RH

Litsch in 2010 returned from TJ surgery only to injure his hip. He's expected to be healthy for 2011, but his durability is in doubt. He might have lost his starting role in Toronto and could be relegated to the bullpen. As a pitch-to-contact guy with a modest fastball, Litsch might be better off in the NL. (MH)

| Player | Age | IP | W | Sv | K | ERA | WHIP | K/9 | BB/9 | $2L | Pts |
|---|---|---|---|---|---|---|---|---|---|---|---|
| Litsch J | 26 | 80 | 4 | 0 | 42 | 4.93 | 1.33 | 4.8 | 2.3 | $0 | 60 |
| **Mini-Browser** | **Age** | **IP** | **W** | **Sv** | **K** | **ERA** | **WHIP** | **K/9** | **BB/9** | **$2L** | **Pts** |
| Affeldt J | 31 | 60 | 3 | 0 | 49 | 4.06 | 1.45 | 7.3 | 4.1 | $0 | 70 |
| Choate R | 35 | 40 | 3 | 0 | 33 | 4.38 | 1.38 | 7.4 | 3.5 | $0 | 50 |
| Ohlendorf R | 28 | 160 | 6 | 0 | 110 | 4.64 | 1.38 | 6.2 | 3.1 | $0 | 130 |
| Sipp T | 27 | 60 | 2 | 0 | 68 | 4.44 | 1.50 | 10.1 | 5.6 | $0 | 80 |
| Jepsen K | 26 | 40 | 1 | 4 | 38 | 4.50 | 1.52 | 8.6 | 4.6 | $0 | 60 |

| Level | Leag | W | L | Sv | IP | H | K | ERA | WHIP | K/9 | BB/9 | HR/9 | GB/F |
|---|---|---|---|---|---|---|---|---|---|---|---|---|---|
| A | FLO | 1 | 1 | 0 | 15 | 9 | 10 | 1.80 | 0.87 | 6.0 | 2.4 | 0.6 | — |
| AA | — | — | — | — | — | — | — | — | — | — | — | — | — |
| AAA | PCL | 0 | 3 | 0 | 22 | 34 | 13 | 8.18 | 1.68 | 5.3 | 1.2 | 1.6 | — |

Competition at SP — Stats in 2010 as SP

| Thr | Player | GS | ERA | Supp | W-L |
|---|---|---|---|---|---|
| LH | Romero R | 32 | 3.73 | 4.5 | 14-9 |
| RH | Marcum S | 31 | 3.64 | 4.5 | 13-8 |
| LH | Cecil B | 28 | 4.22 | 5.5 | 15-7 |
| RH | Morrow B | 26 | 4.49 | 4.6 | 10-7 |

Weekly Points

Ten-Year Trends

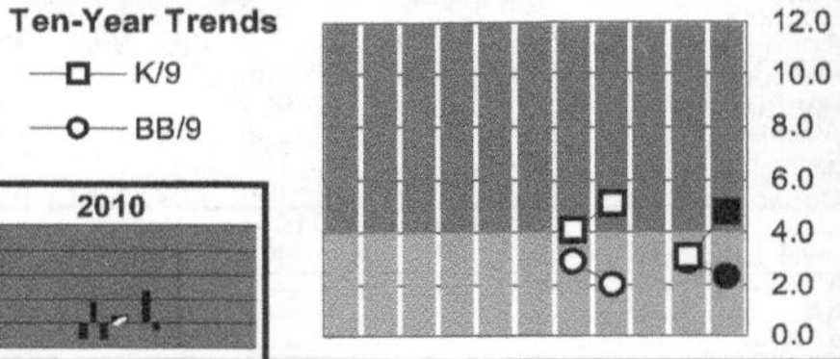


| Yr | Team | W | L | Sv | IP | H | K | ERA | WHIP | K/9 | BB/9 | HR/9 | GB/F |
|---|---|---|---|---|---|---|---|---|---|---|---|---|---|
| 07 | TOR | 7 | 9 | 0 | 111 | 116 | 50 | 3.81 | 1.37 | 4.1 | 2.9 | 1.1 | 1.4 |
| 08 | TOR | 13 | 9 | 0 | 176 | 178 | 99 | 3.58 | 1.23 | 5.1 | 2.0 | 1.0 | 1.5 |
| 09 | TOR | 0 | 1 | 0 | 9 | 14 | 8 | 9.00 | 1.67 | 8.0 | 1.0 | 4.0 | 0.7 |
| 10 | TOR | 1 | 5 | 0 | 46 | 53 | 16 | 5.79 | 1.46 | 3.1 | 2.9 | 1.4 | 1.1 |

| Yr | $1L | $2L | Pts | RAA | H% | HR/fb | S% | FIP | GS | CG | QS/DS | GR | Hld | Bln | Lead | OPS | 1st Hf | 2nd Hf | vs RH | vs LH |
|---|---|---|---|---|---|---|---|---|---|---|---|---|---|---|---|---|---|---|---|---|
| 07 | $4 | -$3 | 110 | −1 | 28% | 11% | 76% | 5.01 | 20 | 0 | 12/3 | — | — | — | — | .761 | .859 | .733 | .646 | .863 |
| 08 | $12 | $5 | 230 | +8 | 28% | 11% | 75% | 4.32 | 28 | 2 | 15/4 | 1 | 0 | 0 | −0.1 | .721 | .775 | .622 | .716 | .725 |
| 09 | -$3 | -$4 | 0 | −5 | 36% | 25% | 55% | 7.63 | 2 | 0 | 0/1 | — | — | — | — | 1.106 | 1.106 | — | 1.559 | .770 |
| 10 | -$5 | -$17 | 10 | −7 | 29% | 10% | 62% | 5.53 | 9 | 0 | 3/2 | — | — | — | — | .822 | .825 | .816 | .805 | .833 |

## Kameron Loe — 60 IP | $5 | 80 pts

RP-53 — Owned: 0% — RH

Loe got his (strikeout) groove back in Japan in 2009, abandoning his slider and change-up for his heater and curve. Shifting to relief might also have enhanced his strikeout rate. The Brewers will use Loe either as a starter or reliever, though his success in the bullpen in 2010 suggests that he will reside there. (MS)

| Player | Age | IP | W | Sv | K | ERA | WHIP | K/9 | BB/9 | $2L | Pts |
|---|---|---|---|---|---|---|---|---|---|---|---|
| Loe K | 29 | 60 | 3 | 0 | 47 | 2.78 | 1.18 | 7.1 | 2.3 | $5 | 80 |
| **Mini-Browser** | **Age** | **IP** | **W** | **Sv** | **K** | **ERA** | **WHIP** | **K/9** | **BB/9** | **$2L** | **Pts** |
| Cecil B | 24 | 160 | 11 | 0 | 116 | 4.58 | 1.39 | 6.5 | 3.3 | $5 | 200 |
| Rhodes A | 41 | 60 | 4 | 0 | 55 | 2.93 | 1.20 | 8.2 | 3.5 | $5 | 100 |
| Davis W | 25 | 170 | 11 | 0 | 141 | 4.44 | 1.46 | 7.5 | 3.8 | $5 | 220 |
| Wolf R | 34 | 200 | 12 | 0 | 134 | 4.47 | 1.36 | 6.0 | 3.4 | $5 | 220 |
| Padilla V | 33 | 120 | 8 | 0 | 86 | 4.33 | 1.25 | 6.4 | 2.8 | $5 | 150 |

| Level | Leag | W | L | Sv | IP | H | K | ERA | WHIP | K/9 | BB/9 | HR/9 | GB/F |
|---|---|---|---|---|---|---|---|---|---|---|---|---|---|
| A | — | — | — | — | — | — | — | — | — | — | — | — | — |
| AA | — | — | — | — | — | — | — | — | — | — | — | — | — |
| AAA | PCL | 4 | 3 | 0 | 62 | 57 | 39 | 3.16 | 1.21 | 5.6 | 2.7 | 0.9 | — |

Competition at RP — Stats in 2010 as RP

| Thr | Player | GR | ERA | IP/G | Sv-Hld |
|---|---|---|---|---|---|
| RH | Coffey T | 69 | 4.76 | 0.9 | 0-13 |
| RH | Loe K | 53 | 2.78 | 1.1 | 0-22 |
| RH | Axford J | 50 | 2.48 | 1.2 | 24-3 |
| RH | Villanueva C | 50 | 4.61 | 1.1 | 1-14 |

Weekly Points

Ten-Year Trends

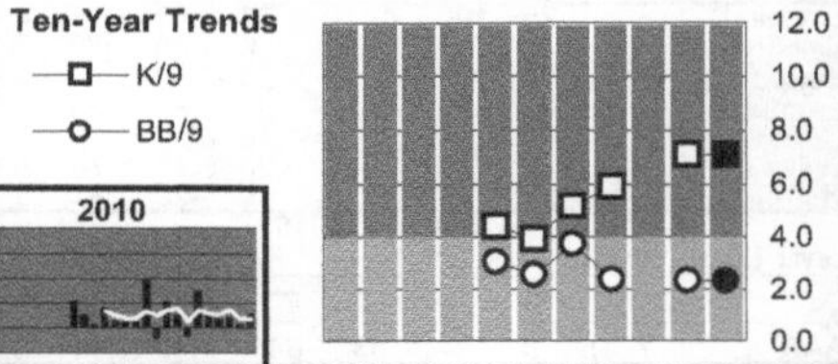


| Yr | Team | W | L | Sv | IP | H | K | ERA | WHIP | K/9 | BB/9 | HR/9 | GB/F |
|---|---|---|---|---|---|---|---|---|---|---|---|---|---|
| 07 | TEX | 6 | 11 | 0 | 136 | 162 | 78 | 5.36 | 1.60 | 5.2 | 3.7 | 0.9 | 2.2 |
| 08 | TEX | 1 | 0 | 0 | 30 | 36 | 20 | 3.23 | 1.43 | 5.9 | 2.3 | 0.9 | 1.5 |
| 09 | — | — | — | — | — | — | — | — | — | — | — | — | — |
| 10 | MIL | 3 | 5 | 0 | 58 | 54 | 46 | 2.78 | 1.18 | 7.1 | 2.3 | 0.9 | 2.4 |

| Yr | $1L | $2L | Pts | RAA | H% | HR/fb | S% | FIP | GS | CG | QS/DS | GR | Hld | Bln | Lead | OPS | 1st Hf | 2nd Hf | vs RH | vs LH |
|---|---|---|---|---|---|---|---|---|---|---|---|---|---|---|---|---|---|---|---|---|
| 07 | -$6 | -$20 | 80 | −35 | 32% | 10% | 67% | 4.63 | 23 | 0 | 9/7 | 5 | 0 | 0 | +0.1 | .810 | .808 | .811 | .725 | .895 |
| 08 | $0 | -$2 | 30 | −4 | 32% | 9% | 80% | 4.05 | — | — | — | 14 | 2 | 1 | −0.2 | .768 | 1.028 | .613 | .505 | 1.095 |
| 09 | — | — | — | — | — | — | — | — | — | — | — | — | — | — | — | — | — | — | — | — |
| 10 | $1 | -$3 | 80 | +3 | 28% | 14% | 81% | 3.73 | — | — | — | 53 | 22 | 2 | +0.3 | .661 | .443 | .778 | .612 | .740 |

## Boone Logan — 60 IP | $-1 | 60 pts

RP-51 — Owned: 1% — LH

Logan was part of the Javier Vazquez-Melky Cabrera swap with Atlanta in December 2009, and he has proven to be the most valuable part of the deal for the Yankees, emerging as the steadiest lefty arm in the bullpen after Damaso Marte went down. Logan's ERA was 3.93 in the first half and 2.08 afterward. (LS)

| Player | Age | IP | W | Sv | K | ERA | WHIP | K/9 | BB/9 | $2L | Pts |
|---|---|---|---|---|---|---|---|---|---|---|---|
| Logan B | 26 | 60 | 2 | 0 | 53 | 4.42 | 1.49 | 7.9 | 4.4 | -$1 | 60 |
| **Mini-Browser** | **Age** | **IP** | **W** | **Sv** | **K** | **ERA** | **WHIP** | **K/9** | **BB/9** | **$2L** | **Pts** |
| Lewis J | 26 | 40 | 3 | 0 | 36 | 4.48 | 1.45 | 8.0 | 4.3 | -$1 | 50 |
| Reyes D | 33 | 40 | 2 | 0 | 29 | 3.72 | 1.43 | 6.4 | 4.5 | -$1 | 50 |
| Boggs M | 27 | 60 | 3 | 4 | 44 | 4.54 | 1.48 | 6.7 | 3.9 | -$1 | 80 |
| Cramer B | 31 | 40 | 3 | 0 | 35 | 4.33 | 1.48 | 8.0 | 3.2 | -$1 | 50 |
| Mitre S | 30 | 60 | 2 | 0 | 34 | 4.78 | 1.32 | 5.1 | 2.5 | -$1 | 50 |

| Level | Leag | W | L | Sv | IP | H | K | ERA | WHIP | K/9 | BB/9 | HR/9 | GB/F |
|---|---|---|---|---|---|---|---|---|---|---|---|---|---|
| A | — | — | — | — | — | — | — | — | — | — | — | — | — |
| AA | — | — | — | — | — | — | — | — | — | — | — | — | — |
| AAA | IL | 0 | 1 | 0 | 21 | 18 | 23 | 2.11 | 1.03 | 9.7 | 1.7 | 0.4 | — |

Competition at RP — Stats in 2010 as RP

| Thr | Player | GR | ERA | IP/G | Sv-Hld |
|---|---|---|---|---|---|
| LH | Logan B | 51 | 2.93 | 0.8 | 0-13 |
| LH | Marte D | 30 | 4.08 | 0.6 | 0-9 |

Weekly Points

Ten-Year Trends

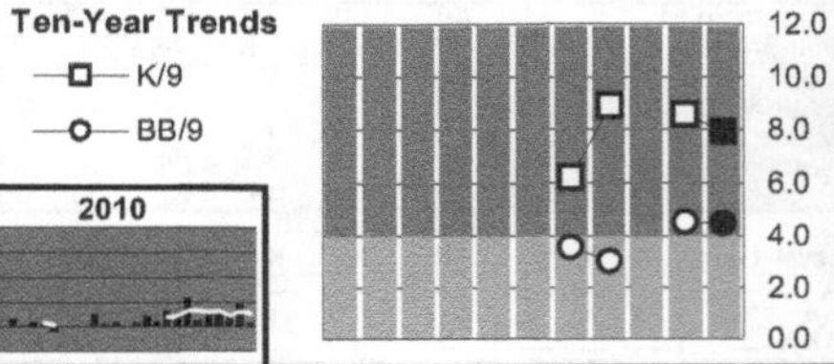


| Yr | Team | W | L | Sv | IP | H | K | ERA | WHIP | K/9 | BB/9 | HR/9 | GB/F |
|---|---|---|---|---|---|---|---|---|---|---|---|---|---|
| 07 | CHW | 2 | 1 | 0 | 50 | 59 | 35 | 4.97 | 1.56 | 6.2 | 3.6 | 1.2 | 1.5 |
| 08 | CHW | 2 | 3 | 0 | 42 | 57 | 42 | 5.95 | 1.68 | 8.9 | 3.0 | 1.5 | 1.3 |
| 09 | ATL | 1 | 1 | 0 | 17 | 21 | 10 | 5.19 | 1.73 | 5.2 | 4.7 | 0.5 | 3.9 |
| 10 | NYY | 2 | 0 | 0 | 40 | 34 | 38 | 2.93 | 1.35 | 8.6 | 4.5 | 0.7 | 1.3 |

| Yr | $1L | $2L | Pts | RAA | H% | HR/fb | S% | FIP | GS | CG | QS/DS | GR | Hld | Bln | Lead | OPS | 1st Hf | 2nd Hf | vs RH | vs LH |
|---|---|---|---|---|---|---|---|---|---|---|---|---|---|---|---|---|---|---|---|---|
| 07 | -$2 | -$8 | 40 | −7 | 33% | 12% | 71% | 4.90 | — | — | — | 68 | 11 | 2 | −0.9 | .802 | .730 | .862 | .968 | .587 |
| 08 | -$5 | -$8 | 40 | −12 | 39% | 15% | 67% | 4.46 | — | — | — | 55 | 3 | 1 | −0.9 | .891 | .693 | 1.369 | .971 | .829 |
| 09 | -$3 | -$3 | 10 | −4 | 33% | 10% | 69% | 4.35 | — | — | — | 20 | 1 | 0 | +0.5 | .767 | .495 | .897 | .932 | .626 |
| 10 | $0 | -$7 | 60 | +5 | 30% | 8% | 80% | 3.88 | — | — | — | 51 | 13 | 0 | +0.4 | .659 | .790 | .537 | .842 | .501 |

*For more stats, visit www.Rotolympus.com.*

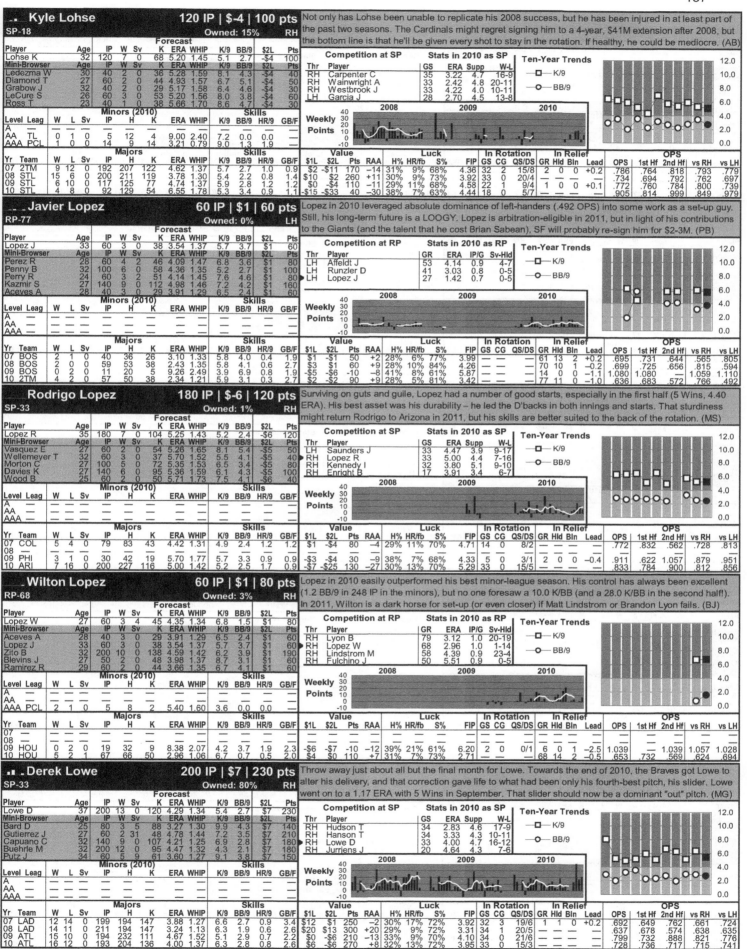

## Kyle Lohse — SP-18 — 120 IP | $-4 | 100 pts — Owned: 15% — RH

Not only has Lohse been unable to replicate his 2008 success, but he has been injured in at least part of the past two seasons. The Cardinals might regret signing him to a 4-year, $41M extension after 2008, but the bottom line is that he'll be given every shot to stay in the rotation. If healthy, he could be mediocre. (AB)

### Forecast

| Player | Age | IP | W | Sv | K | ERA | WHIP | K/9 | BB/9 | $2L | Pts |
|---|---|---|---|---|---|---|---|---|---|---|---|
| Lohse K | 32 | 120 | 7 | 0 | 68 | 5.20 | 1.45 | 5.1 | 2.7 | -$4 | 100 |
| **Mini-Browser** | Age | IP | W | Sv | K | ERA | WHIP | K/9 | BB/9 | $2L | Pts |
| Ledezma W | 30 | 40 | 2 | 0 | 36 | 5.28 | 1.59 | 8.1 | 4.3 | -$4 | 40 |
| Diamond T | 27 | 60 | 2 | 0 | 44 | 4.93 | 1.57 | 6.7 | 5.1 | -$4 | 50 |
| Grabow J | 32 | 40 | 2 | 0 | 29 | 5.17 | 1.58 | 6.4 | 4.6 | -$4 | 30 |
| LeCure S | 26 | 60 | 3 | 0 | 53 | 5.20 | 1.56 | 8.0 | 3.8 | -$4 | 60 |
| Ross T | 23 | 40 | 2 | 0 | 38 | 5.66 | 1.70 | 8.6 | 4.7 | -$4 | 30 |

### Minors (2010) / Skills

| Level | Leag | W | L | Sv | IP | H | K | ERA | WHIP | K/9 | BB/9 | HR/9 | GB/F |
|---|---|---|---|---|---|---|---|---|---|---|---|---|---|
| A | — | | | | | | | | | | | | |
| AA | TL | 0 | 1 | 0 | 5 | 12 | 4 | 9.00 | 2.40 | 7.2 | 0.0 | 0.0 | |
| AAA | PCL | 1 | 0 | 0 | 14 | 9 | 14 | 3.21 | 0.79 | 9.0 | 1.3 | 1.9 | |

### Majors / Skills

| Yr | Team | W | L | Sv | IP | H | K | ERA | WHIP | K/9 | BB/9 | HR/9 | GB/F |
|---|---|---|---|---|---|---|---|---|---|---|---|---|---|
| 07 | 2TM | 9 | 12 | 0 | 192 | 207 | 122 | 4.62 | 1.37 | 5.7 | 2.7 | 1.0 | 0.9 |
| 08 | STL | 15 | 6 | 0 | 200 | 211 | 119 | 3.78 | 1.30 | 5.4 | 2.2 | 0.8 | 1.4 |
| 09 | STL | 6 | 10 | 0 | 117 | 125 | 77 | 4.74 | 1.37 | 5.9 | 2.8 | 1.2 | 1.2 |
| 10 | STL | 4 | 8 | 0 | 92 | 129 | 54 | 6.55 | 1.78 | 5.3 | 3.4 | 0.9 | 1.1 |

### Competition at SP / Stats in 2010 as SP

| Thr | Player | GS | ERA | Supp | W-L |
|---|---|---|---|---|---|
| RH | Carpenter C | 35 | 3.22 | 4.7 | 16-9 |
| RH | Wainwright A | 33 | 2.42 | 4.8 | 20-11 |
| RH | Westbrook J | 33 | 4.22 | 4.0 | 10-11 |
| LH | Garcia J | 28 | 2.70 | 4.5 | 13-8 |

### Value / Luck / In Rotation / In Relief / OPS

| | $1L | $2L | Pts | RAA | H% | HR/fb | S% | FIP | GS | CG | QS/DS | GR | Hld | Bln | Lead | OPS | 1st Hf | 2nd Hf | vs RH | vs LH |
|---|---|---|---|---|---|---|---|---|---|---|---|---|---|---|---|---|---|---|---|---|
| 07 | $2 | -$11 | 170 | -14 | 31% | 9% | 68% | 4.36 | 32 | 2 | 15/8 | 2 | 0 | | +0.2 | .786 | .764 | .818 | .793 | .779 |
| 08 | $10 | $2 | 260 | +11 | 30% | 9% | 73% | 3.92 | 33 | 0 | 20/4 | | | | | .734 | .694 | .792 | .762 | .697 |
| 09 | $0 | -$4 | 110 | -11 | 29% | 11% | 68% | 4.58 | 22 | 1 | 9/4 | 1 | 0 | 0 | +0.1 | .772 | .760 | .784 | .800 | .739 |
| 10 | -$15 | -$33 | 40 | -30 | 38% | 7% | 63% | 4.44 | 18 | 0 | 5/7 | | | | | .905 | .814 | .999 | .849 | .979 |

---

## Javier Lopez — RP-77 — 60 IP | $1 | 60 pts — Owned: 0% — LH

Lopez in 2010 leveraged absolute dominance of left-handers (.492 OPS) into some work as a set-up guy. Still, his long-term future is a LOOGY. Lopez is arbitration-eligible in 2011, but in light of his contributions to the Giants (and the talent that he cost Brian Sabean), SF will probably re-sign him for $2-3M. (PB)

### Forecast

| Player | Age | IP | W | Sv | K | ERA | WHIP | K/9 | BB/9 | $2L | Pts |
|---|---|---|---|---|---|---|---|---|---|---|---|
| Lopez J | 33 | 60 | 3 | 0 | 38 | 3.54 | 1.37 | 5.7 | 3.7 | $1 | 60 |
| **Mini-Browser** | Age | IP | W | Sv | K | ERA | WHIP | K/9 | BB/9 | $2L | Pts |
| Perez R | 28 | 60 | 4 | 2 | 46 | 4.09 | 1.47 | 6.8 | 3.6 | $1 | 80 |
| Penny B | 32 | 100 | 6 | 0 | 58 | 4.36 | 1.35 | 5.2 | 2.7 | $1 | 100 |
| Perry R | 24 | 60 | 3 | 2 | 51 | 4.14 | 1.45 | 7.6 | 4.6 | $1 | 80 |
| Kazmir S | 27 | 140 | 9 | 0 | 112 | 4.98 | 1.46 | 7.2 | 4.2 | $1 | 160 |
| Aceves A | 28 | 40 | 3 | 0 | 29 | 3.91 | 1.29 | 6.5 | 2.4 | $1 | 60 |

### Minors (2010) / Skills

| Level | Leag | W | L | Sv | IP | H | K | ERA | WHIP | K/9 | BB/9 | HR/9 | GB/F |
|---|---|---|---|---|---|---|---|---|---|---|---|---|---|
| A | — | | | | | | | | | | | | |
| AA | — | | | | | | | | | | | | |
| AAA | — | | | | | | | | | | | | |

### Majors / Skills

| Yr | Team | W | L | Sv | IP | H | K | ERA | WHIP | K/9 | BB/9 | HR/9 | GB/F |
|---|---|---|---|---|---|---|---|---|---|---|---|---|---|
| 07 | BOS | 2 | 1 | 0 | 40 | 36 | 26 | 3.10 | 1.33 | 5.8 | 4.0 | 0.4 | 1.9 |
| 08 | BOS | 2 | 0 | 0 | 59 | 53 | 38 | 2.43 | 1.35 | 5.8 | 4.1 | 0.6 | 2.7 |
| 09 | BOS | 0 | 2 | 0 | 11 | 20 | 5 | 9.26 | 2.49 | 3.9 | 6.9 | 0.8 | 1.9 |
| 10 | 2TM | 4 | 2 | 0 | 57 | 50 | 38 | 2.34 | 1.21 | 5.9 | 3.1 | 0.3 | 2.7 |

### Competition at RP / Stats in 2010 as RP

| Thr | Player | GR | ERA | IP/G | Sv-Hld |
|---|---|---|---|---|---|
| LH | Affeldt J | 53 | 4.14 | 0.9 | 4-7 |
| LH | Runzler D | 41 | 3.03 | 0.8 | 0-5 |
| LH | Lopez J | 27 | 1.42 | 0.7 | 0-5 |

### Value / Luck / In Rotation / In Relief / OPS

| | $1L | $2L | Pts | RAA | H% | HR/fb | S% | FIP | GS | CG | QS/DS | GR | Hld | Bln | Lead | OPS | 1st Hf | 2nd Hf | vs RH | vs LH |
|---|---|---|---|---|---|---|---|---|---|---|---|---|---|---|---|---|---|---|---|---|
| 07 | $1 | -$1 | 50 | +2 | 28% | 6% | 77% | 3.99 | | | | 61 | 13 | 2 | +0.2 | .695 | .731 | .644 | .565 | .805 |
| 08 | $3 | $1 | 60 | +9 | 28% | 10% | 84% | 4.26 | | | | 70 | 10 | 1 | -0.2 | .699 | .725 | .656 | .815 | .594 |
| 09 | -$5 | -$6 | -10 | -8 | 41% | 8% | 61% | 5.87 | | | | 14 | 0 | 0 | -1.1 | 1.080 | 1.080 | — | 1.059 | 1.110 |
| 10 | $2 | -$2 | 90 | +9 | 28% | 5% | 81% | 3.42 | | | | 77 | 11 | 0 | -1.0 | .636 | .683 | .572 | .766 | .492 |

---

## Rodrigo Lopez — SP-33 — 180 IP | $-6 | 120 pts — Owned: 1% — RH

Surviving on guts and guile, Lopez had a number of good starts, especially in the first half (5 Wins, 4.40 ERA). His best asset was his durability – he led the D'backs in both innings and starts. That sturdiness might return Rodrigo to Arizona in 2011, but his skills are better suited to the back of the rotation. (MS)

### Forecast

| Player | Age | IP | W | Sv | K | ERA | WHIP | K/9 | BB/9 | $2L | Pts |
|---|---|---|---|---|---|---|---|---|---|---|---|
| Lopez R | 35 | 180 | 7 | 0 | 104 | 5.25 | 1.43 | 5.2 | 2.4 | -$6 | 120 |
| **Mini-Browser** | Age | IP | W | Sv | K | ERA | WHIP | K/9 | BB/9 | $2L | Pts |
| Vasquez E | 27 | 60 | 2 | 0 | 54 | 5.26 | 1.65 | 8.1 | 5.4 | -$5 | 50 |
| Wellemeyer T | 32 | 60 | 3 | 0 | 37 | 5.70 | 1.52 | 5.5 | 4.1 | -$5 | 40 |
| Morton C | 27 | 100 | 5 | 0 | 72 | 5.35 | 1.53 | 6.5 | 3.4 | -$5 | 80 |
| Davies K | 27 | 140 | 6 | 0 | 95 | 5.36 | 1.59 | 6.1 | 4.1 | -$5 | 100 |
| Wood B | 25 | 60 | 2 | 0 | 50 | 5.71 | 1.73 | 7.5 | 4.1 | -$6 | 60 |

### Minors (2010) / Skills

| Level | Leag | W | L | Sv | IP | H | K | ERA | WHIP | K/9 | BB/9 | HR/9 | GB/F |
|---|---|---|---|---|---|---|---|---|---|---|---|---|---|
| A | — | | | | | | | | | | | | |
| AA | — | | | | | | | | | | | | |
| AAA | — | | | | | | | | | | | | |

### Majors / Skills

| Yr | Team | W | L | Sv | IP | H | K | ERA | WHIP | K/9 | BB/9 | HR/9 | GB/F |
|---|---|---|---|---|---|---|---|---|---|---|---|---|---|
| 07 | COL | 5 | 4 | 0 | 79 | 83 | 43 | 4.42 | 1.31 | 4.9 | 2.4 | 1.2 | 1.2 |
| 08 | — | | | | | | | | | | | | |
| 09 | PHI | 3 | 1 | 0 | 30 | 42 | 19 | 5.70 | 1.77 | 5.7 | 3.3 | 0.9 | 0.9 |
| 10 | ARI | 7 | 16 | 0 | 200 | 227 | 116 | 5.00 | 1.42 | 5.2 | 2.5 | 1.7 | 0.9 |

### Competition at SP / Stats in 2010 as SP

| Thr | Player | GS | ERA | Supp | W-L |
|---|---|---|---|---|---|
| LH | Saunders J | 33 | 4.47 | 3.9 | 9-17 |
| RH | Lopez R | 33 | 5.00 | 4.4 | 7-16 |
| RH | Kennedy I | 32 | 3.80 | 5.1 | 9-10 |
| RH | Enright B | 17 | 3.91 | 3.4 | 6-7 |

### Value / Luck / In Rotation / In Relief / OPS

| | $1L | $2L | Pts | RAA | H% | HR/fb | S% | FIP | GS | CG | QS/DS | GR | Hld | Bln | Lead | OPS | 1st Hf | 2nd Hf | vs RH | vs LH |
|---|---|---|---|---|---|---|---|---|---|---|---|---|---|---|---|---|---|---|---|---|
| 07 | $1 | -$4 | 80 | -4 | 29% | 11% | 70% | 4.71 | 14 | 0 | 8/2 | | | | | .772 | .832 | .562 | .728 | .813 |
| 09 | -$3 | -$5 | 30 | -2 | 38% | 7% | 68% | 4.33 | 5 | 0 | 1/2 | 2 | 0 | 0 | -0.4 | .911 | .622 | 1.057 | .879 | .951 |
| 10 | -$7 | -$25 | 130 | -27 | 30% | 13% | 70% | 5.29 | 33 | 0 | 15/5 | | | | | .833 | .784 | .900 | .812 | .856 |

---

## Wilton Lopez — RP-68 — 60 IP | $1 | 80 pts — Owned: 3% — RH

Lopez in 2010 easily outperformed his best minor-league season. His control has always been excellent (1.2 BB/9 in 248 IP in the minors), but no one foresaw a 10.0 K/BB (and a 28.0 K/BB in the second half!). In 2011, Wilton is a dark horse for set-up (or even closer) if Matt Lindstrom or Brandon Lyon fails. (BJ)

### Forecast

| Player | Age | IP | W | Sv | K | ERA | WHIP | K/9 | BB/9 | $2L | Pts |
|---|---|---|---|---|---|---|---|---|---|---|---|
| Lopez W | 27 | 60 | 3 | 4 | 45 | 4.35 | 1.34 | 6.8 | 1.5 | $1 | 80 |
| **Mini-Browser** | Age | IP | W | Sv | K | ERA | WHIP | K/9 | BB/9 | $2L | Pts |
| Aceves A | 28 | 40 | 3 | 0 | 29 | 3.91 | 1.29 | 6.5 | 2.4 | $1 | 60 |
| Lopez J | 33 | 60 | 3 | 0 | 38 | 3.54 | 1.37 | 5.7 | 3.7 | $1 | 60 |
| Zito B | 32 | 200 | 10 | 0 | 138 | 4.59 | 1.42 | 6.2 | 3.9 | $1 | 190 |
| Blevins J | 27 | 50 | 2 | 0 | 48 | 3.98 | 1.37 | 8.7 | 3.1 | $1 | 60 |
| Ramirez R | 29 | 60 | 2 | 0 | 44 | 3.66 | 1.35 | 6.7 | 4.1 | $1 | 60 |

### Minors (2010) / Skills

| Level | Leag | W | L | Sv | IP | H | K | ERA | WHIP | K/9 | BB/9 | HR/9 | GB/F |
|---|---|---|---|---|---|---|---|---|---|---|---|---|---|
| A | — | | | | | | | | | | | | |
| AA | — | | | | | | | | | | | | |
| AAA | PCL | 2 | 1 | 0 | 5 | 8 | 2 | 5.40 | 1.60 | 3.6 | 0.0 | 0.0 | |

### Majors / Skills

| Yr | Team | W | L | Sv | IP | H | K | ERA | WHIP | K/9 | BB/9 | HR/9 | GB/F |
|---|---|---|---|---|---|---|---|---|---|---|---|---|---|
| 07 | — | | | | | | | | | | | | |
| 08 | — | | | | | | | | | | | | |
| 09 | HOU | 0 | 2 | 0 | 19 | 32 | 9 | 8.38 | 2.07 | 4.2 | 3.7 | 1.9 | 2.3 |
| 10 | HOU | 4 | 3 | 0 | 67 | 66 | 50 | 2.96 | 1.06 | 6.7 | 0.7 | 0.5 | 2.0 |

### Competition at RP / Stats in 2010 as RP

| Thr | Player | GR | ERA | IP/G | Sv-Hld |
|---|---|---|---|---|---|
| RH | Lyon B | 79 | 3.12 | 1.0 | 20-19 |
| RH | Lopez W | 68 | 2.96 | 1.0 | 1-14 |
| RH | Lindstrom M | 58 | 4.39 | 0.9 | 23-4 |
| RH | Fulchino J | 50 | 5.51 | 0.9 | 0-5 |

### Value / Luck / In Rotation / In Relief / OPS

| | $1L | $2L | Pts | RAA | H% | HR/fb | S% | FIP | GS | CG | QS/DS | GR | Hld | Bln | Lead | OPS | 1st Hf | 2nd Hf | vs RH | vs LH |
|---|---|---|---|---|---|---|---|---|---|---|---|---|---|---|---|---|---|---|---|---|
| 09 | -$6 | -$7 | -10 | -12 | 39% | 21% | 61% | 6.20 | 2 | 0 | 0/1 | 6 | 0 | 1 | -2.5 | 1.039 | — | 1.039 | 1.057 | 1.028 |
| 10 | $4 | $0 | 110 | +7 | 31% | 7% | 73% | 2.71 | | | | 68 | 14 | 2 | -0.5 | .653 | .732 | .569 | .624 | .694 |

---

## Derek Lowe — SP-33 — 200 IP | $7 | 230 pts — Owned: 80% — RH

Throw away just about all but the final month for Lowe. Towards the end of 2010, the Braves got Lowe to alter his delivery, and that correction gave life to what had been only his fourth-best pitch, his slider. Lowe went on to a 1.17 ERA with 5 Wins in September. That slider should now be a dominant "out" pitch. (MG)

### Forecast

| Player | Age | IP | W | Sv | K | ERA | WHIP | K/9 | BB/9 | $2L | Pts |
|---|---|---|---|---|---|---|---|---|---|---|---|
| Lowe D | 37 | 200 | 13 | 0 | 120 | 4.29 | 1.34 | 5.4 | 2.7 | $7 | 230 |
| **Mini-Browser** | Age | IP | W | Sv | K | ERA | WHIP | K/9 | BB/9 | $2L | Pts |
| Bard D | 25 | 80 | 3 | 5 | 88 | 3.27 | 1.30 | 9.9 | 4.3 | $7 | 140 |
| Gutierrez J | 27 | 60 | 2 | 31 | 48 | 4.78 | 1.44 | 7.2 | 3.5 | $7 | 210 |
| Capuano C | 32 | 140 | 9 | 0 | 107 | 4.21 | 1.25 | 6.9 | 2.8 | $7 | 180 |
| Buehrle M | 32 | 200 | 12 | 0 | 95 | 4.47 | 1.32 | 4.3 | 2.1 | $7 | 180 |
| Putz J | 34 | 60 | 5 | 9 | 61 | 3.60 | 1.27 | 9.1 | 2.8 | $7 | 150 |

### Minors (2010) / Skills

| Level | Leag | W | L | Sv | IP | H | K | ERA | WHIP | K/9 | BB/9 | HR/9 | GB/F |
|---|---|---|---|---|---|---|---|---|---|---|---|---|---|
| A | — | | | | | | | | | | | | |
| AA | — | | | | | | | | | | | | |
| AAA | — | | | | | | | | | | | | |

### Majors / Skills

| Yr | Team | W | L | Sv | IP | H | K | ERA | WHIP | K/9 | BB/9 | HR/9 | GB/F |
|---|---|---|---|---|---|---|---|---|---|---|---|---|---|
| 07 | LAD | 12 | 14 | 0 | 199 | 194 | 147 | 3.88 | 1.27 | 6.6 | 2.7 | 0.6 | 3.4 |
| 08 | LAD | 14 | 11 | 0 | 211 | 194 | 147 | 3.24 | 1.13 | 6.3 | 1.9 | 0.6 | 2.6 |
| 09 | ATL | 15 | 10 | 0 | 194 | 232 | 111 | 4.67 | 1.52 | 5.1 | 2.9 | 0.7 | 2.2 |
| 10 | ATL | 16 | 12 | 0 | 193 | 204 | 136 | 4.00 | 1.37 | 6.3 | 2.8 | 0.8 | 2.6 |

### Competition at SP / Stats in 2010 as SP

| Thr | Player | GS | ERA | Supp | W-L |
|---|---|---|---|---|---|
| RH | Hudson T | 34 | 2.83 | 4.6 | 17-9 |
| RH | Hanson T | 34 | 3.33 | 4.3 | 10-11 |
| RH | Lowe D | 33 | 4.00 | 4.7 | 16-12 |
| RH | Jurrjens J | 20 | 4.64 | 4.3 | 7-6 |

### Value / Luck / In Rotation / In Relief / OPS

| | $1L | $2L | Pts | RAA | H% | HR/fb | S% | FIP | GS | CG | QS/DS | GR | Hld | Bln | Lead | OPS | 1st Hf | 2nd Hf | vs RH | vs LH |
|---|---|---|---|---|---|---|---|---|---|---|---|---|---|---|---|---|---|---|---|---|
| 07 | $12 | $3 | 250 | -2 | 30% | 17% | 72% | 3.92 | 32 | 3 | 19/6 | 1 | 1 | 0 | +0.2 | .692 | .649 | .762 | .661 | .724 |
| 08 | $20 | $13 | 300 | +20 | 29% | 9% | 72% | 3.31 | 34 | 1 | 20/5 | | | | | .637 | .678 | .574 | .638 | .635 |
| 09 | $0 | -$6 | 210 | -13 | 33% | 9% | 70% | 4.10 | 34 | 0 | 21/6 | | | | | .799 | .732 | .888 | .821 | .776 |
| 10 | $6 | -$6 | 270 | +8 | 32% | 13% | 72% | 3.95 | 33 | 0 | 15/3 | | | | | .728 | .736 | .717 | .715 | .741 |

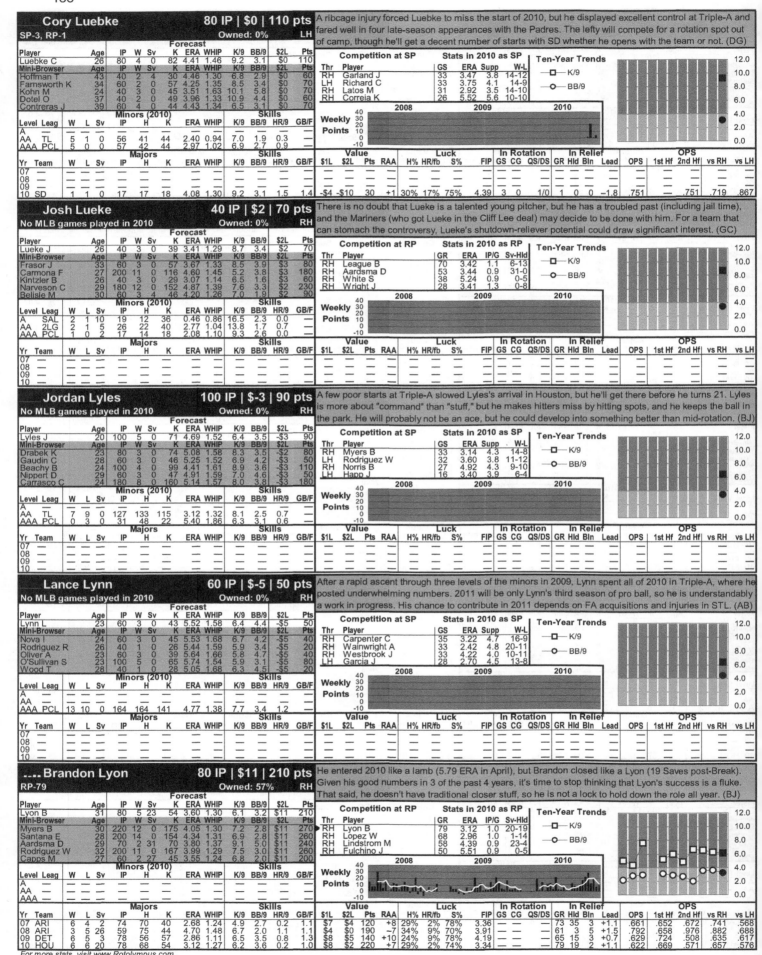

## Cory Luebke — 80 IP | $0 | 110 pts

SP-3, RP-1 — Owned: 0% — LH

| Player | Age | IP | W | Sv | K | ERA | WHIP | K/9 | BB/9 | $2L | Pts |
|---|---|---|---|---|---|---|---|---|---|---|---|
| Luebke C | 26 | 80 | 4 | 0 | 82 | 4.41 | 1.46 | 9.2 | 3.1 | $0 | 110 |
| **Mini-Browser** | **Age** | **IP** | **W** | **Sv** | **K** | **ERA** | **WHIP** | **K/9** | **BB/9** | **$2L** | **Pts** |
| Hoffman T | 43 | 40 | 2 | 4 | 30 | 4.46 | 1.30 | 6.8 | 2.9 | $0 | 60 |
| Farnsworth K | 34 | 60 | 2 | 0 | 57 | 4.25 | 1.35 | 8.5 | 3.4 | $0 | 70 |
| Kohn M | 24 | 40 | 3 | 0 | 45 | 3.51 | 1.63 | 10.1 | 5.8 | $0 | 70 |
| Dotel O | 37 | 40 | 2 | 0 | 49 | 3.96 | 1.33 | 10.9 | 4.4 | $0 | 60 |
| Contreras J | 39 | 60 | 4 | 0 | 44 | 4.43 | 1.34 | 6.5 | 3.1 | $0 | 70 |

| Level | Leag | W | L | Sv | IP | H | K | ERA | WHIP | K/9 | BB/9 | HR/9 | GB/F |
|---|---|---|---|---|---|---|---|---|---|---|---|---|---|
| A | — | — | — | — | — | — | — | — | — | — | — | — | — |
| AA | TL | 5 | 1 | 0 | 56 | 41 | 44 | 2.40 | 0.94 | 7.0 | 1.9 | 0.3 | — |
| AAA | PCL | 5 | 0 | 0 | 57 | 42 | 44 | 2.97 | 1.02 | 6.9 | 2.7 | 0.9 | — |

| Yr | Team | W | L | Sv | IP | H | K | ERA | WHIP | K/9 | BB/9 | HR/9 | GB/F |
|---|---|---|---|---|---|---|---|---|---|---|---|---|---|
| 07 | — | — | — | — | — | — | — | — | — | — | — | — | — |
| 08 | — | — | — | — | — | — | — | — | — | — | — | — | — |
| 09 | — | — | — | — | — | — | — | — | — | — | — | — | — |
| 10 | SD | 1 | 1 | 0 | 17 | 17 | 18 | 4.08 | 1.30 | 9.2 | 3.1 | 1.5 | 1.4 |

A ribcage injury forced Luebke to miss the start of 2010, but he displayed excellent control at Triple-A and fared well in four late-season appearances with the Padres. The lefty will compete for a rotation spot out of camp, though he'll get a decent number of starts with SD whether he opens with the team or not. (DG)

| Thr | Player (Competition at SP) | GS | ERA | Supp | W-L |
|---|---|---|---|---|---|
| RH | Garland J | 33 | 3.47 | 3.8 | 14-12 |
| LH | Richard C | 33 | 3.75 | 4.1 | 14-9 |
| RH | Latos M | 31 | 2.92 | 3.5 | 14-10 |
| RH | Correia K | 26 | 5.52 | 5.6 | 10-10 |

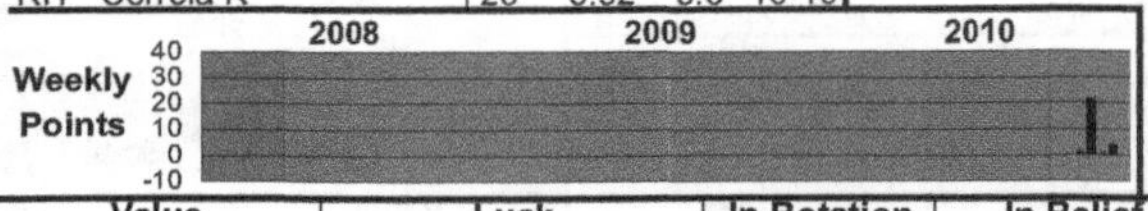


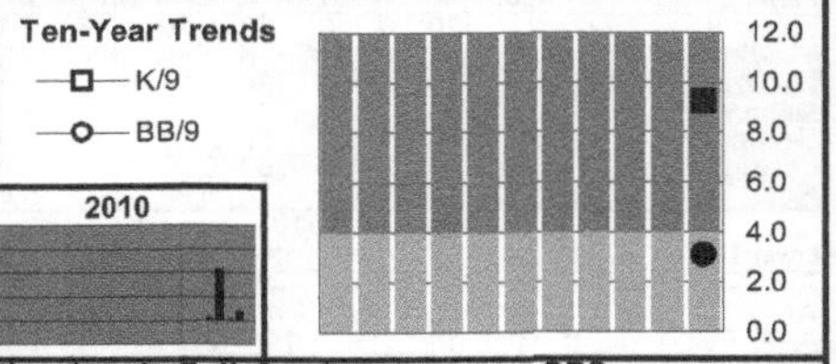


| $1L | $2L | Pts | RAA | H% | HR/fb | S% | FIP | GS | CG | QS/DS | GR | Hld | Bln | Lead | OPS | 1st Hf | 2nd Hf | vs RH | vs LH |
|---|---|---|---|---|---|---|---|---|---|---|---|---|---|---|---|---|---|---|---|
| — | — | — | — | — | — | — | — | — | — | — | — | — | — | — | — | — | — | — | — |
| — | — | — | — | — | — | — | — | — | — | — | — | — | — | — | — | — | — | — | — |
| — | — | — | — | — | — | — | — | — | — | — | — | — | — | — | — | — | — | — | — |
| -$4 | -$10 | 30 | +1 | 30% | 17% | 75% | 4.39 | 3 | 0 | 1/0 | 1 | 0 | 0 | −1.8 | .751 | — | .751 | .719 | .867 |

## Josh Lueke — 40 IP | $2 | 70 pts

No MLB games played in 2010 — Owned: 0% — RH

| Player | Age | IP | W | Sv | K | ERA | WHIP | K/9 | BB/9 | $2L | Pts |
|---|---|---|---|---|---|---|---|---|---|---|---|
| Lueke J | 26 | 40 | 3 | 0 | 39 | 3.41 | 1.29 | 8.7 | 3.4 | $2 | 70 |
| **Mini-Browser** | **Age** | **IP** | **W** | **Sv** | **K** | **ERA** | **WHIP** | **K/9** | **BB/9** | **$2L** | **Pts** |
| Frasor J | 33 | 60 | 3 | 0 | 57 | 3.67 | 1.33 | 8.5 | 3.9 | $3 | 80 |
| Carmona F | 27 | 200 | 11 | 0 | 116 | 4.60 | 1.45 | 5.2 | 3.8 | $3 | 180 |
| Kintzler B | 26 | 40 | 3 | 0 | 29 | 3.07 | 1.14 | 6.5 | 1.6 | $3 | 60 |
| Narveson C | 29 | 180 | 12 | 0 | 152 | 4.87 | 1.39 | 7.6 | 3.3 | $2 | 230 |
| Belisle M | 30 | 60 | 3 | 4 | 46 | 4.20 | 1.26 | 7.0 | 1.9 | $2 | 90 |

| Level | Leag | W | L | Sv | IP | H | K | ERA | WHIP | K/9 | BB/9 | HR/9 | GB/F |
|---|---|---|---|---|---|---|---|---|---|---|---|---|---|
| A | SAL | 2 | 1 | 10 | 19 | 12 | 36 | 0.46 | 0.86 | 16.5 | 2.3 | 0.0 | — |
| AA | 2LG | 2 | 1 | 5 | 26 | 22 | 40 | 2.77 | 1.04 | 13.8 | 1.7 | 0.7 | — |
| AAA | PCL | 1 | 0 | 2 | 17 | 14 | 18 | 2.08 | 1.10 | 9.3 | 2.6 | 0.0 | — |

| Yr | Team | W | L | Sv | IP | H | K | ERA | WHIP | K/9 | BB/9 | HR/9 | GB/F |
|---|---|---|---|---|---|---|---|---|---|---|---|---|---|
| 07 | — | — | — | — | — | — | — | — | — | — | — | — | — |
| 08 | — | — | — | — | — | — | — | — | — | — | — | — | — |
| 09 | — | — | — | — | — | — | — | — | — | — | — | — | — |
| 10 | — | — | — | — | — | — | — | — | — | — | — | — | — |

There is no doubt that Lueke is a talented young pitcher, but he has a troubled past (including jail time), and the Mariners (who got Lueke in the Cliff Lee deal) may decide to be done with him. For a team that can stomach the controversy, Lueke's shutdown-reliever potential could draw significant interest. (GC)

| Thr | Player (Competition at RP) | GR | ERA | IP/G | Sv-Hld |
|---|---|---|---|---|---|
| RH | League B | 70 | 3.42 | 1.1 | 6-13 |
| RH | Aardsma D | 53 | 3.44 | 0.9 | 31-0 |
| RH | White S | 38 | 5.24 | 0.9 | 0-5 |
| RH | Wright J | 28 | 3.41 | 1.3 | 0-8 |

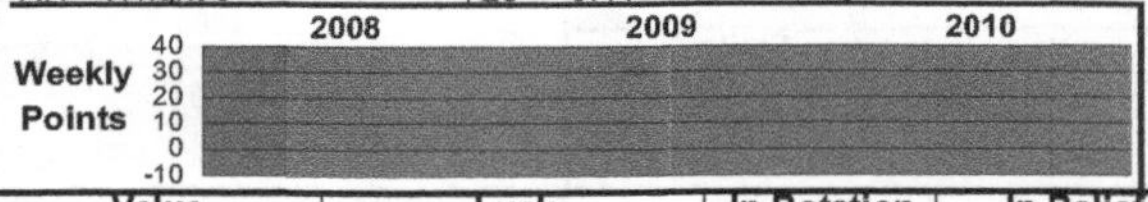


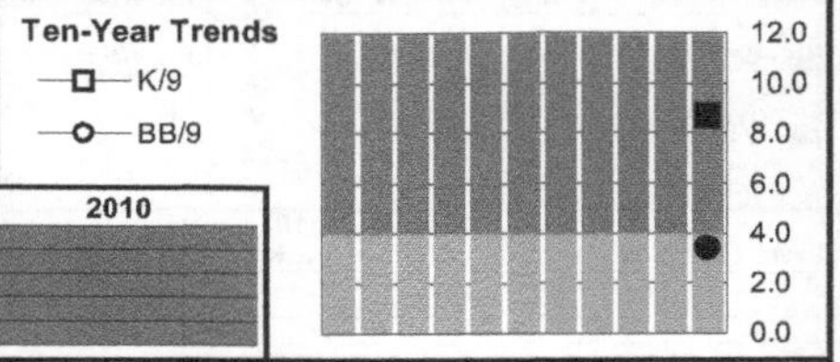


| $1L | $2L | Pts | RAA | H% | HR/fb | S% | FIP | GS | CG | QS/DS | GR | Hld | Bln | Lead | OPS | 1st Hf | 2nd Hf | vs RH | vs LH |
|---|---|---|---|---|---|---|---|---|---|---|---|---|---|---|---|---|---|---|---|
| — | — | — | — | — | — | — | — | — | — | — | — | — | — | — | — | — | — | — | — |
| — | — | — | — | — | — | — | — | — | — | — | — | — | — | — | — | — | — | — | — |
| — | — | — | — | — | — | — | — | — | — | — | — | — | — | — | — | — | — | — | — |
| — | — | — | — | — | — | — | — | — | — | — | — | — | — | — | — | — | — | — | — |

## Jordan Lyles — 100 IP | $-3 | 90 pts

No MLB games played in 2010 — Owned: 0% — RH

| Player | Age | IP | W | Sv | K | ERA | WHIP | K/9 | BB/9 | $2L | Pts |
|---|---|---|---|---|---|---|---|---|---|---|---|
| Lyles J | 20 | 100 | 5 | 0 | 71 | 4.69 | 1.52 | 6.4 | 3.5 | -$3 | 90 |
| **Mini-Browser** | **Age** | **IP** | **W** | **Sv** | **K** | **ERA** | **WHIP** | **K/9** | **BB/9** | **$2L** | **Pts** |
| Drabek K | 23 | 80 | 3 | 0 | 74 | 5.08 | 1.58 | 8.3 | 3.5 | -$2 | 80 |
| Gaudin C | 28 | 60 | 3 | 0 | 46 | 5.25 | 1.52 | 6.9 | 4.2 | -$3 | 50 |
| Beachy B | 24 | 100 | 4 | 0 | 99 | 4.41 | 1.61 | 8.9 | 3.6 | -$3 | 110 |
| Nippert D | 29 | 60 | 3 | 0 | 47 | 4.91 | 1.59 | 7.0 | 4.6 | -$3 | 50 |
| Carrasco C | 24 | 180 | 8 | 0 | 160 | 5.14 | 1.57 | 8.0 | 3.8 | -$3 | 180 |

| Level | Leag | W | L | Sv | IP | H | K | ERA | WHIP | K/9 | BB/9 | HR/9 | GB/F |
|---|---|---|---|---|---|---|---|---|---|---|---|---|---|
| A | — | — | — | — | — | — | — | — | — | — | — | — | — |
| AA | TL | 7 | 9 | 0 | 127 | 133 | 115 | 3.12 | 1.32 | 8.1 | 2.5 | 0.7 | — |
| AAA | PCL | 0 | 3 | 0 | 31 | 48 | 22 | 5.40 | 1.86 | 6.3 | 3.1 | 0.6 | — |

| Yr | Team | W | L | Sv | IP | H | K | ERA | WHIP | K/9 | BB/9 | HR/9 | GB/F |
|---|---|---|---|---|---|---|---|---|---|---|---|---|---|
| 07 | — | — | — | — | — | — | — | — | — | — | — | — | — |
| 08 | — | — | — | — | — | — | — | — | — | — | — | — | — |
| 09 | — | — | — | — | — | — | — | — | — | — | — | — | — |
| 10 | — | — | — | — | — | — | — | — | — | — | — | — | — |

A few poor starts at Triple-A slowed Lyles's arrival in Houston, but he'll get there before he turns 21. Lyles is more about "command" than "stuff," but he makes hitters miss by hitting spots, and he keeps the ball in the park. He will probably not be an ace, but he could develop into something better than mid-rotation. (BJ)

| Thr | Player (Competition at SP) | GS | ERA | Supp | W-L |
|---|---|---|---|---|---|
| RH | Myers B | 33 | 3.14 | 4.3 | 14-8 |
| LH | Rodriguez W | 32 | 3.60 | 3.8 | 11-12 |
| RH | Norris B | 27 | 4.92 | 4.3 | 9-10 |
| LH | Happ J | 16 | 3.40 | 3.9 | 6-4 |

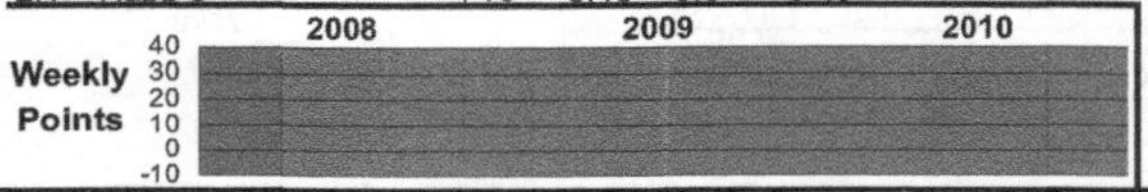


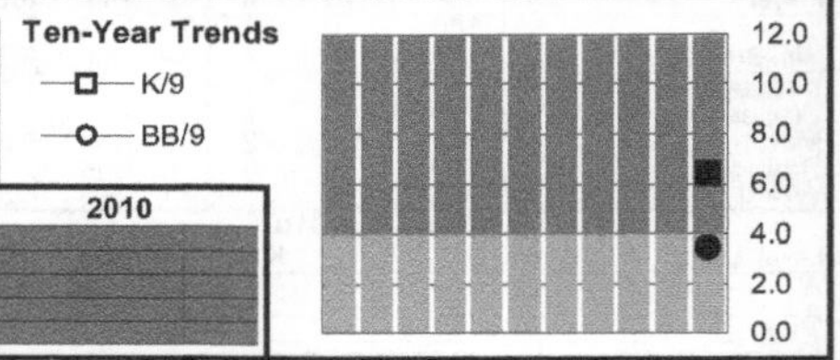


| $1L | $2L | Pts | RAA | H% | HR/fb | S% | FIP | GS | CG | QS/DS | GR | Hld | Bln | Lead | OPS | 1st Hf | 2nd Hf | vs RH | vs LH |
|---|---|---|---|---|---|---|---|---|---|---|---|---|---|---|---|---|---|---|---|
| — | — | — | — | — | — | — | — | — | — | — | — | — | — | — | — | — | — | — | — |
| — | — | — | — | — | — | — | — | — | — | — | — | — | — | — | — | — | — | — | — |
| — | — | — | — | — | — | — | — | — | — | — | — | — | — | — | — | — | — | — | — |
| — | — | — | — | — | — | — | — | — | — | — | — | — | — | — | — | — | — | — | — |

## Lance Lynn — 60 IP | $-5 | 50 pts

No MLB games played in 2010 — Owned: 0% — RH

| Player | Age | IP | W | Sv | K | ERA | WHIP | K/9 | BB/9 | $2L | Pts |
|---|---|---|---|---|---|---|---|---|---|---|---|
| Lynn L | 23 | 60 | 3 | 0 | 43 | 5.52 | 1.58 | 6.4 | 4.4 | -$5 | 50 |
| **Mini-Browser** | **Age** | **IP** | **W** | **Sv** | **K** | **ERA** | **WHIP** | **K/9** | **BB/9** | **$2L** | **Pts** |
| Nova I | 24 | 60 | 3 | 0 | 45 | 5.53 | 1.68 | 6.7 | 4.2 | -$5 | 40 |
| Rodriguez R | 26 | 40 | 1 | 0 | 26 | 5.44 | 1.59 | 5.9 | 3.4 | -$5 | 20 |
| Oliver A | 23 | 60 | 3 | 0 | 39 | 5.64 | 1.66 | 5.8 | 4.7 | -$5 | 40 |
| O'Sullivan S | 23 | 100 | 5 | 0 | 65 | 5.74 | 1.54 | 5.9 | 3.1 | -$5 | 80 |
| Wood T | 28 | 40 | 1 | 0 | 28 | 5.05 | 1.68 | 6.3 | 4.5 | -$5 | 20 |

| Level | Leag | W | L | Sv | IP | H | K | ERA | WHIP | K/9 | BB/9 | HR/9 | GB/F |
|---|---|---|---|---|---|---|---|---|---|---|---|---|---|
| A | — | — | — | — | — | — | — | — | — | — | — | — | — |
| AA | — | — | — | — | — | — | — | — | — | — | — | — | — |
| AAA | PCL | 13 | 10 | 0 | 164 | 164 | 141 | 4.77 | 1.38 | 7.7 | 3.4 | 1.2 | — |

| Yr | Team | W | L | Sv | IP | H | K | ERA | WHIP | K/9 | BB/9 | HR/9 | GB/F |
|---|---|---|---|---|---|---|---|---|---|---|---|---|---|
| 07 | — | — | — | — | — | — | — | — | — | — | — | — | — |
| 08 | — | — | — | — | — | — | — | — | — | — | — | — | — |
| 09 | — | — | — | — | — | — | — | — | — | — | — | — | — |
| 10 | — | — | — | — | — | — | — | — | — | — | — | — | — |

After a rapid ascent through three levels of the minors in 2009, Lynn spent all of 2010 in Triple-A, where he posted underwhelming numbers. 2011 will be only Lynn's third season of pro ball, so he is understandably a work in progress. His chance to contribute in 2011 depends on FA acquisitions and injuries in STL. (AB)

| Thr | Player (Competition at SP) | GS | ERA | Supp | W-L |
|---|---|---|---|---|---|
| RH | Carpenter C | 35 | 3.22 | 4.7 | 16-9 |
| RH | Wainwright A | 33 | 2.42 | 4.8 | 20-11 |
| RH | Westbrook J | 33 | 4.22 | 4.0 | 10-11 |
| LH | Garcia J | 28 | 2.70 | 4.5 | 13-8 |

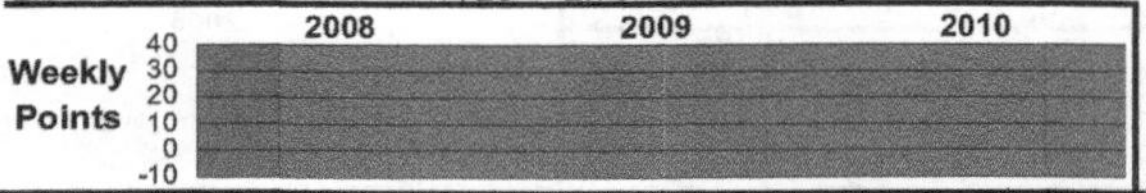


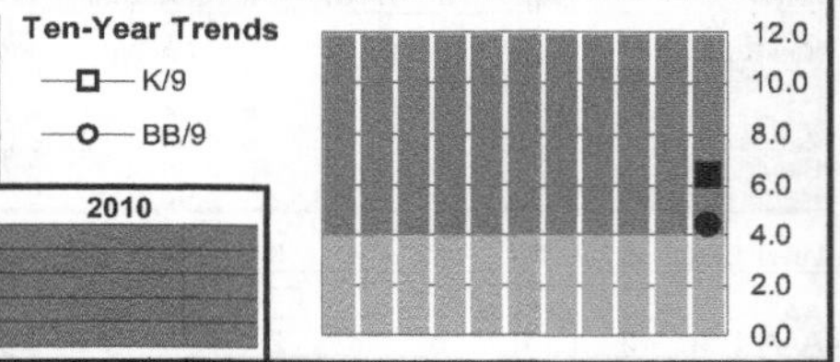


| $1L | $2L | Pts | RAA | H% | HR/fb | S% | FIP | GS | CG | QS/DS | GR | Hld | Bln | Lead | OPS | 1st Hf | 2nd Hf | vs RH | vs LH |
|---|---|---|---|---|---|---|---|---|---|---|---|---|---|---|---|---|---|---|---|
| — | — | — | — | — | — | — | — | — | — | — | — | — | — | — | — | — | — | — | — |
| — | — | — | — | — | — | — | — | — | — | — | — | — | — | — | — | — | — | — | — |
| — | — | — | — | — | — | — | — | — | — | — | — | — | — | — | — | — | — | — | — |
| — | — | — | — | — | — | — | — | — | — | — | — | — | — | — | — | — | — | — | — |

## ..... Brandon Lyon — 80 IP | $11 | 210 pts

RP-79 — Owned: 57% — RH

| Player | Age | IP | W | Sv | K | ERA | WHIP | K/9 | BB/9 | $2L | Pts |
|---|---|---|---|---|---|---|---|---|---|---|---|
| Lyon B | 31 | 80 | 5 | 23 | 54 | 3.60 | 1.30 | 6.1 | 3.2 | $11 | 210 |
| **Mini-Browser** | **Age** | **IP** | **W** | **Sv** | **K** | **ERA** | **WHIP** | **K/9** | **BB/9** | **$2L** | **Pts** |
| Myers B | 30 | 220 | 12 | 0 | 175 | 4.05 | 1.30 | 7.2 | 2.8 | $11 | 270 |
| Santana E | 28 | 200 | 14 | 0 | 154 | 4.34 | 1.31 | 6.9 | 2.8 | $11 | 260 |
| Aardsma D | 29 | 70 | 2 | 31 | 70 | 3.80 | 1.37 | 9.1 | 5.0 | $11 | 240 |
| Rodriguez W | 32 | 200 | 11 | 0 | 167 | 3.99 | 1.29 | 7.5 | 3.0 | $11 | 260 |
| Capps M | 27 | 60 | 2 | 27 | 45 | 3.55 | 1.24 | 6.8 | 2.0 | $11 | 200 |

| Level | Leag | W | L | Sv | IP | H | K | ERA | WHIP | K/9 | BB/9 | HR/9 | GB/F |
|---|---|---|---|---|---|---|---|---|---|---|---|---|---|
| A | — | — | — | — | — | — | — | — | — | — | — | — | — |
| AA | — | — | — | — | — | — | — | — | — | — | — | — | — |
| AAA | — | — | — | — | — | — | — | — | — | — | — | — | — |

| Yr | Team | W | L | Sv | IP | H | K | ERA | WHIP | K/9 | BB/9 | HR/9 | GB/F |
|---|---|---|---|---|---|---|---|---|---|---|---|---|---|
| 07 | ARI | 6 | 4 | 2 | 74 | 70 | 40 | 2.68 | 1.24 | 4.9 | 2.7 | 0.2 | 1.1 |
| 08 | ARI | 3 | 5 | 26 | 59 | 75 | 44 | 4.70 | 1.48 | 6.7 | 2.0 | 1.1 | 1.1 |
| 09 | DET | 6 | 5 | 3 | 78 | 56 | 57 | 2.86 | 1.11 | 6.5 | 3.5 | 0.8 | 1.3 |
| 10 | HOU | 6 | 6 | 20 | 78 | 68 | 54 | 3.12 | 1.27 | 6.2 | 3.6 | 0.2 | 1.0 |

He entered 2010 like a lamb (5.79 ERA in April), but Brandon closed like a Lyon (19 Saves post-Break). Given his good numbers in 3 of the past 4 years, it's time to stop thinking that Lyon's success is a fluke. That said, he doesn't have traditional closer stuff, so he is not a lock to hold down the role all year. (BJ)

| Thr | Player (Competition at RP) | GR | ERA | IP/G | Sv-Hld |
|---|---|---|---|---|---|
| RH | Lyon B | 79 | 3.12 | 1.0 | 20-19 |
| RH | Lopez W | 68 | 2.96 | 1.0 | 1-14 |
| RH | Lindstrom M | 58 | 4.39 | 0.9 | 23-4 |
| RH | Fulchino J | 50 | 5.51 | 0.9 | 0-5 |

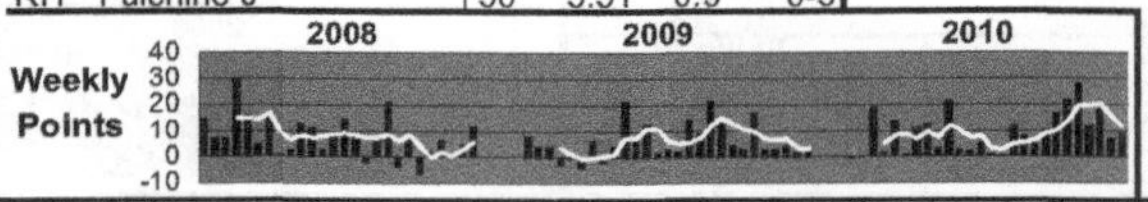


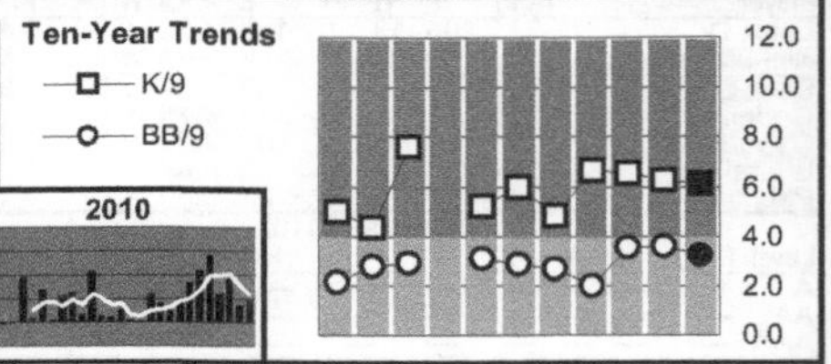


| $1L | $2L | Pts | RAA | H% | HR/fb | S% | FIP | GS | CG | QS/DS | GR | Hld | Bln | Lead | OPS | 1st Hf | 2nd Hf | vs RH | vs LH |
|---|---|---|---|---|---|---|---|---|---|---|---|---|---|---|---|---|---|---|---|
| $7 | $4 | 120 | +8 | 29% | 2% | 78% | 3.36 | — | — | — | 73 | 35 | 3 | +1.1 | .661 | .652 | .672 | .741 | .568 |
| $4 | $0 | 190 | −7 | 34% | 9% | 70% | 3.91 | — | — | — | 61 | 3 | 5 | +1.5 | .792 | .658 | .976 | .882 | .688 |
| $8 | $5 | 140 | +10 | 24% | 9% | 78% | 4.19 | — | — | — | 65 | 15 | 3 | +0.7 | .629 | .724 | .508 | .635 | .617 |
| $8 | $2 | 220 | +7 | 29% | 2% | 74% | 3.34 | — | — | — | 79 | 19 | 2 | +1.1 | .622 | .669 | .571 | .657 | .576 |

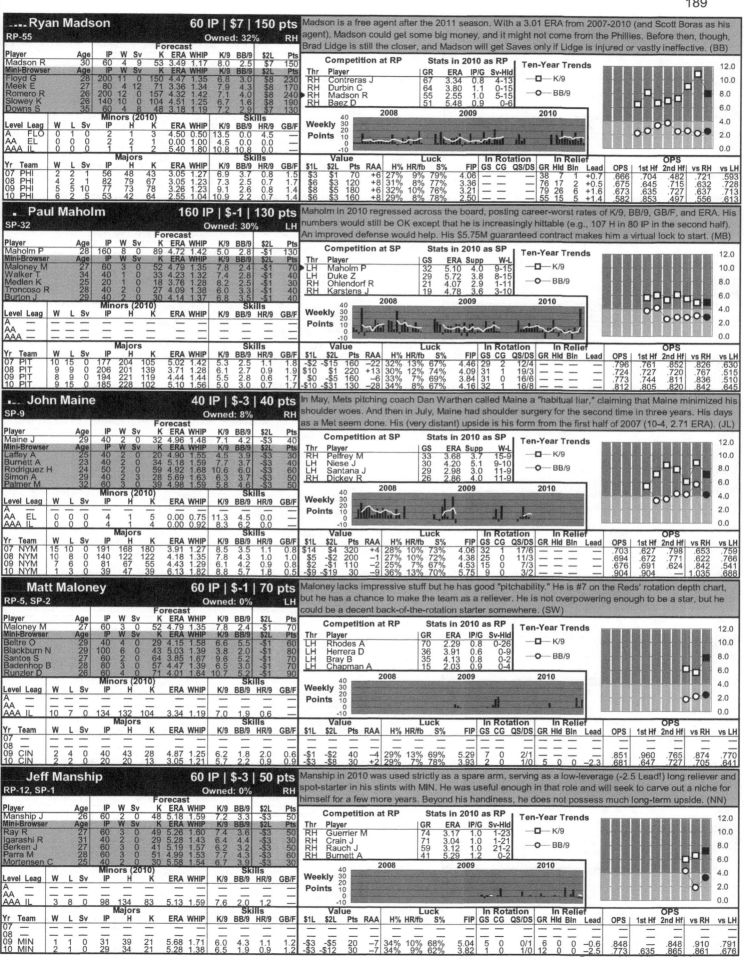

## Ryan Madson — 60 IP | $7 | 150 pts

RP-55 — Owned: 32% — RH

Madson is a free agent after the 2011 season. With a 3.01 ERA from 2007-2010 (and Scott Boras as his agent), Madson could get some big money, and it might not come from the Phillies. Before then, though, Brad Lidge is still the closer, and Madson will get Saves only if Lidge is injured or vastly ineffective. (BB)

| Player | Age | IP | W | Sv | K | ERA | WHIP | K/9 | BB/9 | $2L | Pts |
|---|---|---|---|---|---|---|---|---|---|---|---|
| **Forecast** | | | | | | | | | | | |
| Madson R | 30 | 60 | 4 | 9 | 53 | 3.49 | 1.17 | 8.0 | 2.5 | $7 | 150 |
| **Mini-Browser** | Age | IP | W | Sv | K | ERA | WHIP | K/9 | BB/9 | $2L | Pts |
| Floyd G | 28 | 200 | 11 | 0 | 150 | 4.47 | 1.35 | 6.8 | 3.0 | $8 | 230 |
| Meek E | 27 | 80 | 4 | 12 | 71 | 3.36 | 1.34 | 7.9 | 4.3 | $8 | 170 |
| Romero R | 26 | 200 | 12 | 0 | 157 | 4.32 | 1.42 | 7.1 | 4.0 | $8 | 240 |
| Slowey K | 26 | 140 | 10 | 0 | 104 | 4.51 | 1.25 | 6.7 | 1.6 | $8 | 190 |
| Downs S | 35 | 60 | 4 | 8 | 48 | 3.18 | 1.19 | 7.2 | 2.9 | $7 | 130 |

| Level | Leag | W | L | Sv | IP | H | K | ERA | WHIP | K/9 | BB/9 | HR/9 | GB/F |
|---|---|---|---|---|---|---|---|---|---|---|---|---|---|
| **Minors (2010)** | | | | | | | | | | **Skills** | | | |
| A | FLO | 0 | 1 | 0 | 2 | 1 | 3 | 4.50 | 0.50 | 13.5 | 0.0 | 4.5 | — |
| AA | EL | 0 | 0 | 0 | 2 | 2 | 1 | 0.00 | 1.00 | 4.5 | 0.0 | 0.0 | — |
| AAA | IL | 0 | 0 | 0 | 1 | 1 | 2 | 5.40 | 1.80 | 10.8 | 10.8 | 0.0 | — |

**Competition at RP — Stats in 2010 as RP**

| Thr | Player | GR | ERA | IP/G | Sv-Hld |
|---|---|---|---|---|---|
| RH | Contreras J | 67 | 3.34 | 0.8 | 4-13 |
| RH | Durbin C | 64 | 3.80 | 1.1 | 0-15 |
| ▶ RH | Madson R | 55 | 2.55 | 1.0 | 5-15 |
| RH | Baez D | 51 | 5.48 | 0.9 | 0-6 |

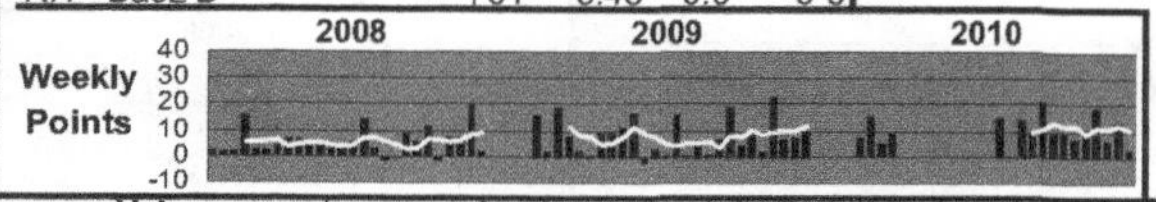


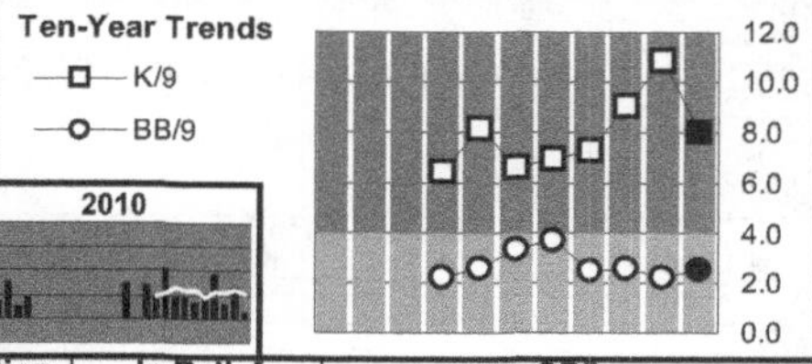


| Yr | Team | W | L | Sv | IP | H | K | ERA | WHIP | K/9 | BB/9 | HR/9 | GB/F | $1L | $2L | Pts | RAA | H% | HR/fb | S% | FIP | GS | CG | QS/DS | GR | Hld | Bln | Lead | OPS | 1st Hf | 2nd Hf | vs RH | vs LH |
|---|---|---|---|---|---|---|---|---|---|---|---|---|---|---|---|---|---|---|---|---|---|---|---|---|---|---|---|---|---|---|---|---|---|
| | | **Majors** | | | | | | | | **Skills** | | | | **Value** | | | | **Luck** | | | | **In Rotation** | | | **In Relief** | | | | **OPS** | | | | |
| 07 | PHI | 2 | 2 | 1 | 56 | 48 | 43 | 3.05 | 1.27 | 6.9 | 3.7 | 0.8 | 1.5 | $3 | $1 | 70 | +6 | 27% | 9% | 79% | 4.06 | — | — | — | 38 | 7 | 1 | +0.7 | .666 | .704 | .482 | .721 | .593 |
| 08 | PHI | 4 | 2 | 1 | 82 | 79 | 67 | 3.05 | 1.23 | 7.3 | 2.5 | 0.7 | 1.7 | $6 | $3 | 120 | +8 | 31% | 8% | 77% | 3.36 | — | — | — | 76 | 17 | 2 | +0.5 | .675 | .645 | .715 | .632 | .728 |
| 09 | PHI | 5 | 5 | 10 | 77 | 73 | 78 | 3.26 | 1.23 | 9.1 | 2.6 | 0.8 | 1.4 | $8 | $5 | 180 | +6 | 32% | 10% | 76% | 3.21 | — | — | — | 79 | 26 | 6 | +1.6 | .673 | .635 | .727 | .637 | .713 |
| 10 | PHI | 6 | 2 | 5 | 53 | 42 | 64 | 2.55 | 1.04 | 10.9 | 2.2 | 0.7 | 1.4 | $6 | $3 | 160 | +8 | 29% | 8% | 78% | 2.50 | — | — | — | 55 | 15 | 5 | +1.4 | .582 | .853 | .497 | .556 | .613 |

## Paul Maholm — 160 IP | $-1 | 130 pts

SP-32 — Owned: 30% — LH

Maholm in 2010 regressed across the board, posting career-worst rates of K/9, BB/9, GB/F, and ERA. His numbers would still be OK except that he is increasingly hittable (e.g., 107 H in 80 IP in the second half). An improved defense would help. His $5.75M guaranteed contract makes him a virtual lock to start. (MB)

| Player | Age | IP | W | Sv | K | ERA | WHIP | K/9 | BB/9 | $2L | Pts |
|---|---|---|---|---|---|---|---|---|---|---|---|
| **Forecast** | | | | | | | | | | | |
| Maholm P | 28 | 160 | 8 | 0 | 89 | 4.72 | 1.42 | 5.0 | 2.8 | -$1 | 130 |
| **Mini-Browser** | Age | IP | W | Sv | K | ERA | WHIP | K/9 | BB/9 | $2L | Pts |
| Maloney M | 27 | 60 | 3 | 0 | 52 | 4.79 | 1.35 | 7.8 | 2.4 | -$1 | 70 |
| Walker T | 34 | 40 | 1 | 0 | 33 | 4.23 | 1.32 | 7.4 | 2.8 | -$1 | 40 |
| Medlen K | 25 | 20 | 1 | 0 | 18 | 3.76 | 1.28 | 8.2 | 2.5 | -$1 | 30 |
| Troncoso R | 28 | 40 | 2 | 0 | 27 | 4.09 | 1.38 | 6.0 | 3.3 | -$1 | 40 |
| Burton J | 29 | 40 | 2 | 0 | 30 | 4.14 | 1.37 | 6.8 | 3.5 | -$1 | 40 |

| Level | Leag | W | L | Sv | IP | H | K | ERA | WHIP | K/9 | BB/9 | HR/9 | GB/F |
|---|---|---|---|---|---|---|---|---|---|---|---|---|---|
| **Minors (2010)** | | | | | | | | | | **Skills** | | | |
| A | — | — | — | — | — | — | — | — | — | — | — | — | — |
| AA | — | — | — | — | — | — | — | — | — | — | — | — | — |
| AAA | — | — | — | — | — | — | — | — | — | — | — | — | — |

**Competition at SP — Stats in 2010 as SP**

| Thr | Player | GS | ERA | Supp | W-L |
|---|---|---|---|---|---|
| ▶ LH | Maholm P | 32 | 5.10 | 4.0 | 9-15 |
| LH | Duke Z | 29 | 5.72 | 3.8 | 8-15 |
| RH | Ohlendorf R | 21 | 4.07 | 2.9 | 1-11 |
| RH | Karstens J | 19 | 4.78 | 3.6 | 3-10 |

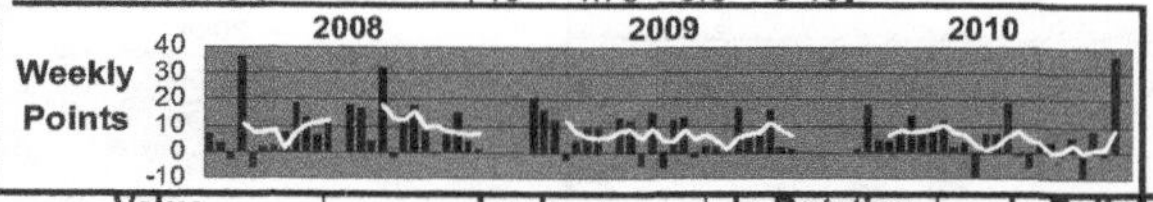


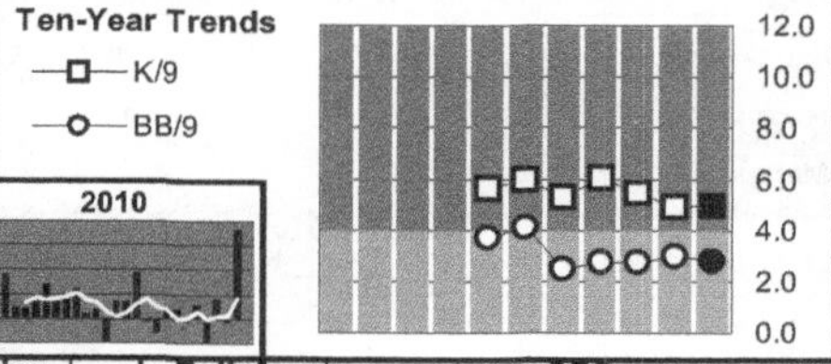


| Yr | Team | W | L | Sv | IP | H | K | ERA | WHIP | K/9 | BB/9 | HR/9 | GB/F | $1L | $2L | Pts | RAA | H% | HR/fb | S% | FIP | GS | CG | QS/DS | GR | Hld | Bln | Lead | OPS | 1st Hf | 2nd Hf | vs RH | vs LH |
|---|---|---|---|---|---|---|---|---|---|---|---|---|---|---|---|---|---|---|---|---|---|---|---|---|---|---|---|---|---|---|---|---|---|
| | | **Majors** | | | | | | | | **Skills** | | | | **Value** | | | | **Luck** | | | | **In Rotation** | | | **In Relief** | | | | **OPS** | | | | |
| 07 | PIT | 10 | 15 | 0 | 177 | 204 | 105 | 5.02 | 1.42 | 5.3 | 2.5 | 1.1 | 1.8 | -$2 | -$15 | 160 | -22 | 32% | 13% | 67% | 4.46 | 29 | 2 | 12/4 | — | — | — | — | .796 | .761 | .852 | .826 | .630 |
| 08 | PIT | 9 | 9 | 0 | 206 | 201 | 139 | 3.71 | 1.28 | 6.1 | 2.7 | 0.9 | 1.9 | $10 | $1 | 220 | +13 | 30% | 12% | 74% | 4.09 | 31 | 1 | 19/3 | — | — | — | — | .724 | .727 | .720 | .767 | .515 |
| 09 | PIT | 8 | 9 | 0 | 194 | 221 | 119 | 4.44 | 1.44 | 5.5 | 2.8 | 0.6 | 1.7 | $0 | -$5 | 160 | -6 | 33% | 7% | 69% | 3.84 | 31 | 0 | 16/6 | — | — | — | — | .773 | .744 | .811 | .836 | .510 |
| 10 | PIT | 9 | 15 | 0 | 185 | 228 | 102 | 5.10 | 1.56 | 5.0 | 3.0 | 0.7 | 1.7 | -$10 | -$31 | 130 | -28 | 34% | 8% | 67% | 4.16 | 32 | 1 | 16/8 | — | — | — | — | .812 | .805 | .820 | .842 | .645 |

## John Maine — 40 IP | $-3 | 40 pts

SP-9 — Owned: 8% — RH

In May, Mets pitching coach Dan Warthen called Maine a "habitual liar," claiming that Maine minimized his shoulder woes. And then in July, Maine had shoulder surgery for the second time in three years. His days as a Met seem done. His (very distant) upside is his form from the first half of 2007 (10-4, 2.71 ERA). (JL)

| Player | Age | IP | W | Sv | K | ERA | WHIP | K/9 | BB/9 | $2L | Pts |
|---|---|---|---|---|---|---|---|---|---|---|---|
| **Forecast** | | | | | | | | | | | |
| Maine J | 29 | 40 | 2 | 0 | 32 | 4.96 | 1.48 | 7.1 | 4.2 | -$3 | 40 |
| **Mini-Browser** | Age | IP | W | Sv | K | ERA | WHIP | K/9 | BB/9 | $2L | Pts |
| Laffey A | 25 | 40 | 2 | 0 | 20 | 4.90 | 1.55 | 4.5 | 3.9 | -$3 | 30 |
| Burnett A | 23 | 40 | 2 | 0 | 34 | 5.18 | 1.59 | 7.7 | 3.7 | -$3 | 40 |
| Rodriguez H | 24 | 50 | 2 | 0 | 59 | 4.92 | 1.68 | 10.6 | 6.0 | -$3 | 60 |
| Simon A | 29 | 40 | 2 | 3 | 28 | 5.69 | 1.63 | 6.3 | 3.7 | -$3 | 50 |
| Palmer M | 32 | 60 | 3 | 0 | 39 | 4.98 | 1.59 | 5.8 | 4.6 | -$3 | 50 |

| Level | Leag | W | L | Sv | IP | H | K | ERA | WHIP | K/9 | BB/9 | HR/9 | GB/F |
|---|---|---|---|---|---|---|---|---|---|---|---|---|---|
| **Minors (2010)** | | | | | | | | | | **Skills** | | | |
| A | — | — | — | — | — | — | — | — | — | — | — | — | — |
| AA | EL | 0 | 0 | 0 | 4 | 1 | 5 | 0.00 | 0.75 | 11.3 | 4.5 | 0.0 | — |
| AAA | IL | 0 | 0 | 0 | 4 | 1 | 4 | 0.00 | 0.92 | 8.3 | 6.2 | 0.0 | — |

**Competition at SP — Stats in 2010 as SP**

| Thr | Player | GS | ERA | Supp | W-L |
|---|---|---|---|---|---|
| RH | Pelfrey M | 33 | 3.68 | 3.7 | 15-9 |
| LH | Niese J | 30 | 4.20 | 5.1 | 9-10 |
| LH | Santana J | 29 | 2.98 | 3.0 | 11-9 |
| RH | Dickey R | 26 | 2.86 | 4.0 | 11-9 |

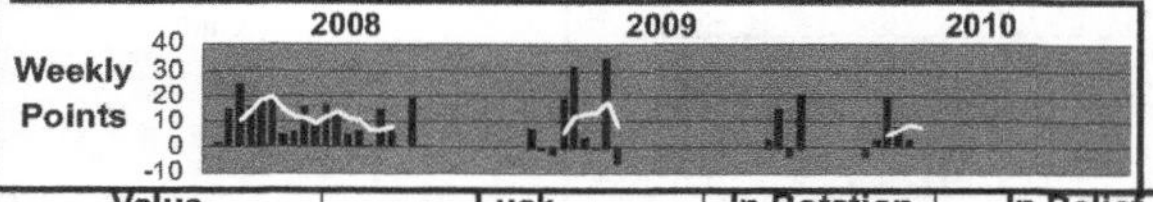


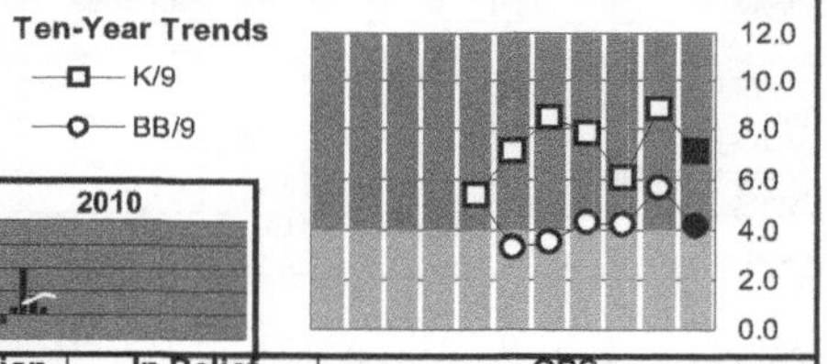


| Yr | Team | W | L | Sv | IP | H | K | ERA | WHIP | K/9 | BB/9 | HR/9 | GB/F | $1L | $2L | Pts | RAA | H% | HR/fb | S% | FIP | GS | CG | QS/DS | GR | Hld | Bln | Lead | OPS | 1st Hf | 2nd Hf | vs RH | vs LH |
|---|---|---|---|---|---|---|---|---|---|---|---|---|---|---|---|---|---|---|---|---|---|---|---|---|---|---|---|---|---|---|---|---|---|
| | | **Majors** | | | | | | | | **Skills** | | | | **Value** | | | | **Luck** | | | | **In Rotation** | | | **In Relief** | | | | **OPS** | | | | |
| 07 | NYM | 15 | 10 | 0 | 191 | 168 | 180 | 3.91 | 1.27 | 8.5 | 3.5 | 1.1 | 0.8 | $14 | $4 | 320 | +4 | 28% | 10% | 73% | 4.06 | 32 | 1 | 17/6 | — | — | — | — | .703 | .627 | .798 | .653 | .759 |
| 08 | NYM | 10 | 8 | 0 | 140 | 122 | 122 | 4.18 | 1.35 | 7.8 | 4.3 | 1.0 | 1.0 | $5 | -$2 | 200 | -1 | 27% | 10% | 72% | 4.38 | 25 | 0 | 11/3 | — | — | — | — | .694 | .672 | .771 | .622 | .766 |
| 09 | NYM | 7 | 6 | 0 | 81 | 67 | 55 | 4.43 | 1.29 | 6.1 | 4.2 | 0.9 | 0.8 | $2 | -$1 | 110 | -2 | 25% | 7% | 67% | 4.53 | 15 | 0 | 7/3 | — | — | — | — | .676 | .691 | .624 | .842 | .541 |
| 10 | NYM | 1 | 3 | 0 | 39 | 47 | 39 | 6.13 | 1.82 | 8.8 | 5.7 | 1.8 | 0.5 | -$9 | -$19 | 30 | -9 | 36% | 13% | 70% | 5.75 | 9 | 0 | 3/2 | — | — | — | — | .904 | .904 | — | 1.035 | .688 |

## Matt Maloney — 60 IP | $-1 | 70 pts

RP-5, SP-2 — Owned: 0% — LH

Maloney lacks impressive stuff but he has good "pitchability." He is #7 on the Reds' rotation depth chart, but he has a chance to make the team as a reliever. He is not overpowering enough to be a star, but he could be a decent back-of-the-rotation starter somewhere. (SW)

| Player | Age | IP | W | Sv | K | ERA | WHIP | K/9 | BB/9 | $2L | Pts |
|---|---|---|---|---|---|---|---|---|---|---|---|
| **Forecast** | | | | | | | | | | | |
| Maloney M | 27 | 60 | 3 | 0 | 52 | 4.79 | 1.35 | 7.8 | 2.4 | -$1 | 70 |
| **Mini-Browser** | Age | IP | W | Sv | K | ERA | WHIP | K/9 | BB/9 | $2L | Pts |
| Beltre O | 29 | 40 | 4 | 0 | 29 | 4.15 | 1.58 | 6.6 | 5.5 | -$1 | 60 |
| Blackburn N | 29 | 100 | 6 | 0 | 43 | 5.03 | 1.39 | 3.8 | 2.0 | -$1 | 80 |
| Santos S | 27 | 60 | 2 | 0 | 64 | 3.85 | 1.67 | 9.6 | 5.2 | -$1 | 70 |
| Badenhop B | 28 | 80 | 3 | 0 | 57 | 4.47 | 1.39 | 6.5 | 3.0 | -$1 | 70 |
| Runzler D | 26 | 60 | 4 | 0 | 71 | 4.01 | 1.64 | 10.7 | 5.2 | -$1 | 90 |

| Level | Leag | W | L | Sv | IP | H | K | ERA | WHIP | K/9 | BB/9 | HR/9 | GB/F |
|---|---|---|---|---|---|---|---|---|---|---|---|---|---|
| **Minors (2010)** | | | | | | | | | | **Skills** | | | |
| A | — | — | — | — | — | — | — | — | — | — | — | — | — |
| AA | — | — | — | — | — | — | — | — | — | — | — | — | — |
| AAA | IL | 10 | 7 | 0 | 134 | 132 | 104 | 3.34 | 1.19 | 7.0 | 1.9 | 0.6 | — |

**Competition at RP — Stats in 2010 as RP**

| Thr | Player | GR | ERA | IP/G | Sv-Hld |
|---|---|---|---|---|---|
| LH | Rhodes A | 70 | 2.29 | 0.8 | 0-26 |
| LH | Herrera D | 36 | 3.91 | 0.6 | 0-9 |
| LH | Bray B | 35 | 4.13 | 0.8 | 0-2 |
| LH | Chapman A | 15 | 2.03 | 0.9 | 0-4 |

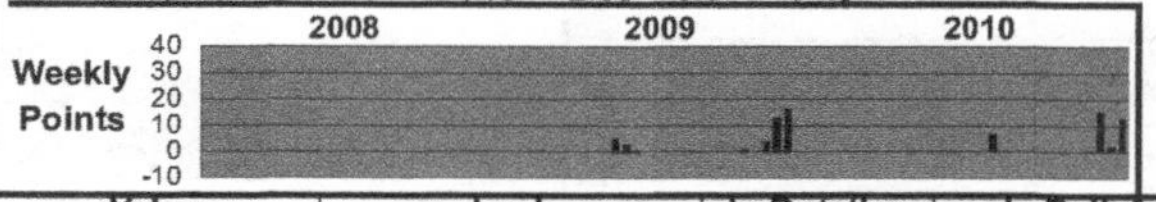


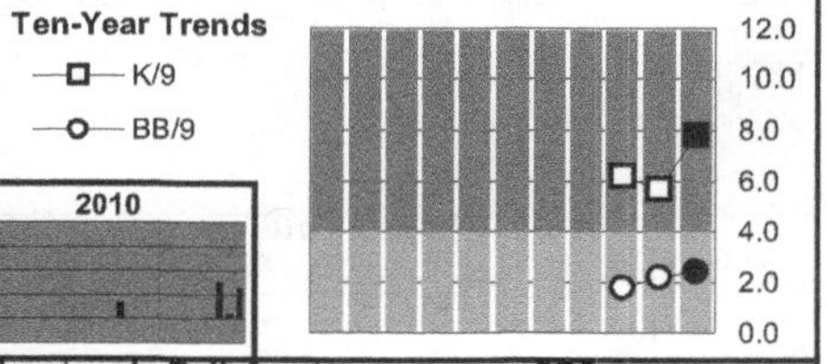


| Yr | Team | W | L | Sv | IP | H | K | ERA | WHIP | K/9 | BB/9 | HR/9 | GB/F | $1L | $2L | Pts | RAA | H% | HR/fb | S% | FIP | GS | CG | QS/DS | GR | Hld | Bln | Lead | OPS | 1st Hf | 2nd Hf | vs RH | vs LH |
|---|---|---|---|---|---|---|---|---|---|---|---|---|---|---|---|---|---|---|---|---|---|---|---|---|---|---|---|---|---|---|---|---|---|
| | | **Majors** | | | | | | | | **Skills** | | | | **Value** | | | | **Luck** | | | | **In Rotation** | | | **In Relief** | | | | **OPS** | | | | |
| 07 | — | — | — | — | — | — | — | — | — | — | — | — | — | — | — | — | — | — | — | — | — | — | — | — | — | — | — | — | — | — | — | — | — |
| 08 | — | — | — | — | — | — | — | — | — | — | — | — | — | — | — | — | — | — | — | — | — | — | — | — | — | — | — | — | — | — | — | — | — |
| 09 | CIN | 2 | 4 | 0 | 40 | 43 | 28 | 4.87 | 1.25 | 6.2 | 1.8 | 2.0 | 0.6 | -$1 | -$2 | 40 | -4 | 29% | 13% | 69% | 5.29 | 7 | 0 | 2/1 | — | — | — | — | .851 | .960 | .765 | .874 | .770 |
| 10 | CIN | 2 | 2 | 0 | 20 | 20 | 13 | 3.05 | 1.21 | 5.7 | 2.2 | 0.9 | 0.9 | -$3 | -$8 | 30 | +2 | 29% | 7% | 78% | 3.93 | 2 | 0 | 1/0 | 5 | 0 | 0 | -2.3 | .681 | .647 | .727 | .705 | .641 |

## Jeff Manship — 60 IP | $-3 | 50 pts

RP-12, SP-1 — Owned: 0% — RH

Manship in 2010 was used strictly as a spare arm, serving as a low-leverage (-2.5 Lead!) long reliever and spot-starter in his stints with MIN. He was useful enough in that role and will seek to carve out a niche for himself for a few more years. Beyond his handiness, he does not possess much long-term upside. (NN)

| Player | Age | IP | W | Sv | K | ERA | WHIP | K/9 | BB/9 | $2L | Pts |
|---|---|---|---|---|---|---|---|---|---|---|---|
| **Forecast** | | | | | | | | | | | |
| Manship J | 26 | 60 | 2 | 0 | 48 | 5.18 | 1.59 | 7.2 | 3.3 | -$3 | 50 |
| **Mini-Browser** | Age | IP | W | Sv | K | ERA | WHIP | K/9 | BB/9 | $2L | Pts |
| Ray R | 27 | 60 | 3 | 0 | 49 | 5.26 | 1.60 | 7.4 | 3.6 | -$3 | 50 |
| Igarashi R | 31 | 40 | 2 | 0 | 29 | 5.28 | 1.43 | 6.4 | 4.4 | -$3 | 30 |
| Berken J | 27 | 60 | 3 | 0 | 41 | 5.19 | 1.57 | 6.2 | 3.2 | -$3 | 50 |
| Parra M | 28 | 60 | 3 | 0 | 51 | 4.99 | 1.53 | 7.7 | 4.3 | -$3 | 60 |
| Mortensen C | 25 | 40 | 2 | 0 | 30 | 5.58 | 1.54 | 6.7 | 3.9 | -$3 | 30 |

| Level | Leag | W | L | Sv | IP | H | K | ERA | WHIP | K/9 | BB/9 | HR/9 | GB/F |
|---|---|---|---|---|---|---|---|---|---|---|---|---|---|
| **Minors (2010)** | | | | | | | | | | **Skills** | | | |
| A | — | — | — | — | — | — | — | — | — | — | — | — | — |
| AA | — | — | — | — | — | — | — | — | — | — | — | — | — |
| AAA | IL | 3 | 8 | 0 | 98 | 134 | 83 | 5.13 | 1.59 | 7.6 | 2.0 | 1.2 | — |

**Competition at RP — Stats in 2010 as RP**

| Thr | Player | GR | ERA | IP/G | Sv-Hld |
|---|---|---|---|---|---|
| RH | Guerrier M | 74 | 3.17 | 1.0 | 1-23 |
| RH | Crain J | 71 | 3.04 | 1.0 | 1-21 |
| RH | Rauch J | 59 | 3.12 | 1.0 | 21-2 |
| RH | Burnett A | 41 | 5.29 | 1.2 | 0-2 |

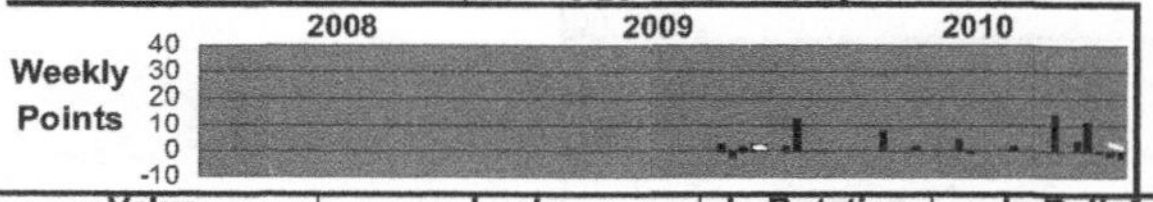


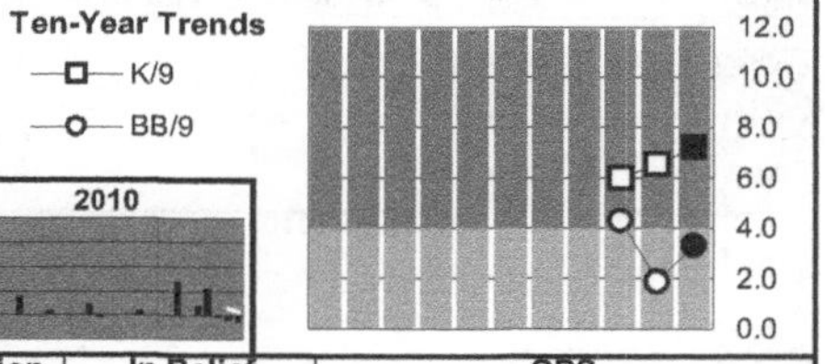


| Yr | Team | W | L | Sv | IP | H | K | ERA | WHIP | K/9 | BB/9 | HR/9 | GB/F | $1L | $2L | Pts | RAA | H% | HR/fb | S% | FIP | GS | CG | QS/DS | GR | Hld | Bln | Lead | OPS | 1st Hf | 2nd Hf | vs RH | vs LH |
|---|---|---|---|---|---|---|---|---|---|---|---|---|---|---|---|---|---|---|---|---|---|---|---|---|---|---|---|---|---|---|---|---|---|
| | | **Majors** | | | | | | | | **Skills** | | | | **Value** | | | | **Luck** | | | | **In Rotation** | | | **In Relief** | | | | **OPS** | | | | |
| 07 | — | — | — | — | — | — | — | — | — | — | — | — | — | — | — | — | — | — | — | — | — | — | — | — | — | — | — | — | — | — | — | — | — |
| 08 | — | — | — | — | — | — | — | — | — | — | — | — | — | — | — | — | — | — | — | — | — | — | — | — | — | — | — | — | — | — | — | — | — |
| 09 | MIN | 1 | 1 | 0 | 31 | 39 | 21 | 5.68 | 1.71 | 6.0 | 4.3 | 1.1 | 1.2 | -$3 | -$5 | 20 | -7 | 34% | 10% | 68% | 5.04 | 5 | 0 | 0/1 | 6 | 0 | 0 | -0.6 | .848 | — | .848 | .910 | .791 |
| 10 | MIN | 2 | 1 | 0 | 29 | 34 | 21 | 5.28 | 1.38 | 6.5 | 1.9 | 0.9 | 1.2 | -$3 | -$12 | 30 | -7 | 34% | 9% | 62% | 3.82 | 1 | 0 | 1/0 | 12 | 0 | 0 | -2.5 | .773 | .635 | .865 | .861 | .676 |

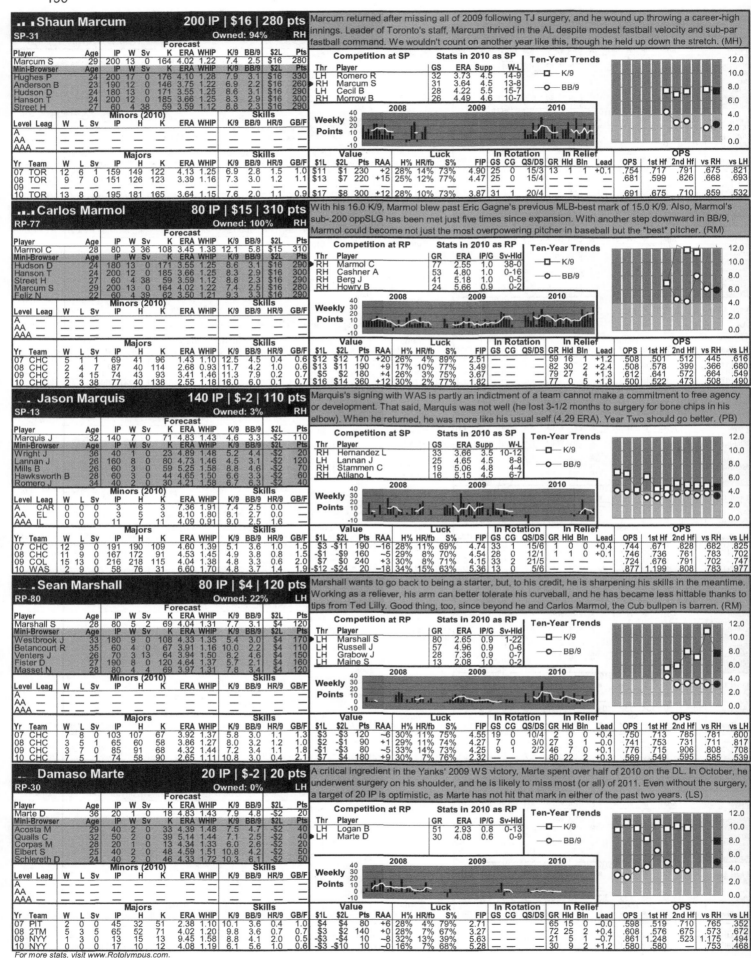

## Shaun Marcum — 200 IP | $16 | 280 pts
SP-31   Owned: 94%   RH

Marcum returned after missing all of 2009 following TJ surgery, and he wound up throwing a career-high innings. Leader of Toronto's staff, Marcum thrived in the AL despite modest fastball velocity and sub-par fastball command. We wouldn't count on another year like this, though he held up down the stretch. (MH)

### Forecast
| Player | Age | IP | W | Sv | K | ERA | WHIP | K/9 | BB/9 | $2L | Pts |
|---|---|---|---|---|---|---|---|---|---|---|---|
| Marcum S | 29 | 200 | 13 | 0 | 164 | 4.02 | 1.22 | 7.4 | 2.5 | $16 | 280 |
| Mini-Browser | Age | IP | W | Sv | K | ERA | WHIP | K/9 | BB/9 | $2L | Pts |
| Hughes P | 24 | 200 | 17 | 0 | 176 | 4.10 | 1.28 | 7.9 | 3.1 | $16 | 330 |
| Anderson B | 23 | 190 | 12 | 0 | 146 | 3.75 | 1.22 | 6.9 | 2.2 | $16 | 260 |
| Hudson D | 24 | 180 | 13 | 0 | 171 | 3.55 | 1.25 | 8.6 | 3.1 | $16 | 290 |
| Hanson T | 24 | 200 | 12 | 0 | 185 | 3.66 | 1.25 | 8.3 | 2.9 | $16 | 300 |
| Street H | 27 | 60 | 4 | 38 | 59 | 3.59 | 1.12 | 8.8 | 2.3 | $16 | 290 |

### Minors (2010) / Skills
| Level | Leag | W | L | Sv | IP | H | K | ERA | WHIP | K/9 | BB/9 | HR/9 | GB/F |
|---|---|---|---|---|---|---|---|---|---|---|---|---|---|
| A | — | — | — | — | — | — | — | — | — | — | — | — | — |
| AA | — | — | — | — | — | — | — | — | — | — | — | — | — |
| AAA | — | — | — | — | — | — | — | — | — | — | — | — | — |

### Majors / Skills / Value / Luck / In Rotation / In Relief / OPS
| Yr | Team | W | L | Sv | IP | H | K | ERA | WHIP | K/9 | BB/9 | HR/9 | GB/F | $1L | $2L | Pts | RAA | H% | HR/fb | S% | FIP | GS | CG | QS/DS | GR | Hld | Bln | Lead | OPS | 1st Hf | 2nd Hf | vs RH | vs LH |
|---|---|---|---|---|---|---|---|---|---|---|---|---|---|---|---|---|---|---|---|---|---|---|---|---|---|---|---|---|---|---|---|---|---|
| 07 | TOR | 12 | 6 | 1 | 159 | 149 | 122 | 4.13 | 1.25 | 6.9 | 2.8 | 1.5 | 1.0 | $11 | $1 | 230 | +2 | 28% | 14% | 73% | 4.90 | 25 | 0 | 15/3 | 13 | 1 | 1 | +0.1 | .754 | .717 | .791 | .675 | .821 |
| 08 | TOR | 9 | 7 | 0 | 151 | 126 | 123 | 3.39 | 1.16 | 7.3 | 3.0 | 1.2 | 1.1 | $13 | $7 | 220 | +15 | 25% | 12% | 77% | 4.47 | 25 | 0 | 15/4 | — | — | — | — | .681 | .599 | .826 | .668 | .693 |
| 09 | | | | | | | | | | | | | | | | | | | | | | | | | | | | | | | | | |
| 10 | TOR | 13 | 8 | 0 | 195 | 181 | 165 | 3.64 | 1.15 | 7.6 | 2.0 | 1.1 | 0.9 | $17 | $8 | 300 | +12 | 28% | 10% | 73% | 3.87 | 31 | 1 | 20/4 | — | — | — | — | .691 | .675 | .710 | .859 | .532 |

### Competition at SP / Stats in 2010 as SP
| Thr | Player | GS | ERA | Supp | W-L |
|---|---|---|---|---|---|
| LH | Romero R | 32 | 3.73 | 4.5 | 14-9 |
| RH | Marcum S | 31 | 3.64 | 4.5 | 13-8 |
| LH | Cecil B | 28 | 4.22 | 5.5 | 15-7 |
| RH | Morrow B | 26 | 4.49 | 4.6 | 10-7 |

---

## Carlos Marmol — 80 IP | $15 | 310 pts
RP-77   Owned: 100%   RH

With his 16.0 K/9, Marmol blew past Eric Gagne's previous MLB-best mark of 15.0 K/9. Also, Marmol's sub-.200 oppSLG has been met just five times since expansion. With another step downward in BB/9, Marmol could become not just the most overpowering pitcher in baseball but the *best* pitcher. (RM)

### Forecast
| Player | Age | IP | W | Sv | K | ERA | WHIP | K/9 | BB/9 | $2L | Pts |
|---|---|---|---|---|---|---|---|---|---|---|---|
| Marmol C | 28 | 80 | 3 | 36 | 108 | 3.45 | 1.38 | 12.1 | 5.8 | $15 | 310 |
| Mini-Browser | Age | IP | W | Sv | K | ERA | WHIP | K/9 | BB/9 | $2L | Pts |
| Hudson D | 24 | 180 | 13 | 0 | 171 | 3.55 | 1.25 | 8.6 | 3.1 | $16 | 290 |
| Hanson T | 24 | 200 | 12 | 0 | 185 | 3.66 | 1.25 | 8.3 | 2.9 | $16 | 300 |
| Street H | 27 | 60 | 4 | 38 | 59 | 3.59 | 1.12 | 8.8 | 2.3 | $16 | 290 |
| Marcum S | 29 | 200 | 13 | 0 | 164 | 4.02 | 1.22 | 7.4 | 2.5 | $16 | 280 |
| Feliz N | 22 | 60 | 4 | 39 | 62 | 3.50 | 1.21 | 9.3 | 3.3 | $16 | 290 |

### Minors (2010) / Skills
| Level | Leag | W | L | Sv | IP | H | K | ERA | WHIP | K/9 | BB/9 | HR/9 | GB/F |
|---|---|---|---|---|---|---|---|---|---|---|---|---|---|
| A | — | — | — | — | — | — | — | — | — | — | — | — | — |
| AA | — | — | — | — | — | — | — | — | — | — | — | — | — |
| AAA | — | — | — | — | — | — | — | — | — | — | — | — | — |

### Majors / Skills / Value / Luck / In Rotation / In Relief / OPS
| Yr | Team | W | L | Sv | IP | H | K | ERA | WHIP | K/9 | BB/9 | HR/9 | GB/F | $1L | $2L | Pts | RAA | H% | HR/fb | S% | FIP | GS | CG | QS/DS | GR | Hld | Bln | Lead | OPS | 1st Hf | 2nd Hf | vs RH | vs LH |
|---|---|---|---|---|---|---|---|---|---|---|---|---|---|---|---|---|---|---|---|---|---|---|---|---|---|---|---|---|---|---|---|---|---|
| 07 | CHC | 5 | 1 | 1 | 69 | 41 | 96 | 1.43 | 1.10 | 12.5 | 4.5 | 0.4 | 0.6 | $12 | $12 | 170 | +20 | 26% | 4% | 89% | 2.51 | — | — | — | 59 | 16 | 1 | +1.2 | .508 | .501 | .512 | .445 | .616 |
| 08 | CHC | 2 | 4 | 7 | 87 | 40 | 114 | 2.68 | 0.93 | 11.7 | 4.2 | 1.0 | 0.6 | $13 | $11 | 190 | +9 | 17% | 10% | 77% | 3.49 | — | — | — | 82 | 30 | 2 | +2.4 | .508 | .578 | .399 | .366 | .680 |
| 09 | CHC | 2 | 4 | 15 | 74 | 43 | 93 | 3.41 | 1.46 | 11.3 | 7.9 | 0.2 | 0.7 | $5 | $2 | 180 | +4 | 26% | 3% | 75% | 3.67 | — | — | — | 79 | 27 | 4 | +1.3 | .612 | .641 | .572 | .664 | .549 |
| 10 | CHC | 2 | 3 | 38 | 77 | 40 | 138 | 2.55 | 1.18 | 16.0 | 6.0 | 0.1 | 0.7 | $16 | $14 | 360 | +12 | 30% | 2% | 77% | 1.82 | — | — | — | 77 | 0 | 5 | +1.8 | .500 | .522 | .473 | .508 | .490 |

### Competition at RP / Stats in 2010 as RP
| Thr | Player | GR | ERA | IP/G | Sv-Hld |
|---|---|---|---|---|---|
| RH | Marmol C | 77 | 2.55 | 1.0 | 38-0 |
| RH | Cashner A | 53 | 4.80 | 1.0 | 0-16 |
| RH | Berg J | 41 | 5.18 | 1.0 | 0-5 |
| RH | Howry B | 24 | 5.66 | 0.9 | 0-2 |

---

## Jason Marquis — 140 IP | $-2 | 110 pts
SP-13   Owned: 3%   RH

Marquis's signing with WAS is partly an indictment of a team cannot make a commitment to free agency or development. That said, Marquis was not well (he lost 3-1/2 months to surgery for bone chips in his elbow). When he returned, he was more like his usual self (4.29 ERA). Year Two should go better. (PB)

### Forecast
| Player | Age | IP | W | Sv | K | ERA | WHIP | K/9 | BB/9 | $2L | Pts |
|---|---|---|---|---|---|---|---|---|---|---|---|
| Marquis J | 32 | 140 | 7 | 0 | 71 | 4.83 | 1.43 | 4.6 | 3.3 | -$2 | 110 |
| Mini-Browser | Age | IP | W | Sv | K | ERA | WHIP | K/9 | BB/9 | $2L | Pts |
| Wright J | 36 | 40 | 1 | 0 | 23 | 4.89 | 1.48 | 5.2 | 4.4 | -$2 | 20 |
| Lannan J | 26 | 160 | 8 | 0 | 80 | 4.73 | 1.46 | 4.5 | 3.1 | -$2 | 120 |
| Mills B | 26 | 60 | 3 | 0 | 59 | 5.25 | 1.58 | 8.8 | 4.6 | -$2 | 70 |
| Hawksworth B | 28 | 60 | 3 | 0 | 44 | 4.65 | 1.50 | 6.6 | 3.3 | -$2 | 60 |
| Romero J | 34 | 40 | 2 | 0 | 30 | 4.21 | 1.58 | 6.7 | 6.3 | -$2 | 40 |

### Minors (2010) / Skills
| Level | Leag | W | L | Sv | IP | H | K | ERA | WHIP | K/9 | BB/9 | HR/9 | GB/F |
|---|---|---|---|---|---|---|---|---|---|---|---|---|---|
| A | CAR | 0 | 0 | 0 | 3 | 6 | 3 | 7.36 | 1.91 | 7.4 | 2.5 | 0.0 | — |
| AA | EL | 0 | 0 | 0 | 3 | 5 | 3 | 8.10 | 1.80 | 8.1 | 2.7 | 0.0 | — |
| AAA | IL | 0 | 0 | 0 | 11 | 7 | 11 | 4.09 | 0.91 | 9.0 | 2.5 | 1.6 | — |

### Majors / Skills / Value / Luck / In Rotation / In Relief / OPS
| Yr | Team | W | L | Sv | IP | H | K | ERA | WHIP | K/9 | BB/9 | HR/9 | GB/F | $1L | $2L | Pts | RAA | H% | HR/fb | S% | FIP | GS | CG | QS/DS | GR | Hld | Bln | Lead | OPS | 1st Hf | 2nd Hf | vs RH | vs LH |
|---|---|---|---|---|---|---|---|---|---|---|---|---|---|---|---|---|---|---|---|---|---|---|---|---|---|---|---|---|---|---|---|---|---|
| 07 | CHC | 12 | 9 | 0 | 191 | 190 | 109 | 4.60 | 1.39 | 5.1 | 3.6 | 1.0 | 1.5 | $3 | -$11 | 190 | -16 | 28% | 11% | 69% | 4.74 | 33 | 1 | 15/6 | 1 | 0 | 0 | +0.4 | .744 | .671 | .828 | .682 | .825 |
| 08 | CHC | 11 | 9 | 0 | 167 | 172 | 91 | 4.53 | 1.45 | 4.9 | 3.8 | 0.8 | 1.5 | -$1 | -$9 | 160 | -5 | 29% | 8% | 70% | 4.54 | 28 | 0 | 12/1 | 1 | 1 | 0 | +0.1 | .746 | .736 | .761 | .783 | .702 |
| 09 | COL | 15 | 13 | 0 | 216 | 218 | 115 | 4.04 | 1.38 | 4.8 | 3.3 | 0.6 | 2.0 | $7 | $0 | 240 | +3 | 30% | 8% | 74% | 4.15 | 33 | 2 | 21/5 | — | — | — | — | .724 | .676 | .791 | .702 | .747 |
| 10 | WAS | 2 | 9 | 0 | 58 | 76 | 31 | 6.60 | 1.70 | 4.8 | 3.7 | 1.4 | 1.9 | -$12 | -$24 | 20 | -18 | 34% | 15% | 63% | 5.36 | 13 | 0 | 5/6 | — | — | — | — | .877 | 1.199 | .508 | .783 | .977 |

### Competition at SP / Stats in 2010 as SP
| Thr | Player | GS | ERA | Supp | W-L |
|---|---|---|---|---|---|
| RH | Hernandez L | 33 | 3.66 | 3.5 | 10-12 |
| LH | Lannan J | 25 | 4.65 | 4.5 | 8-8 |
| RH | Stammen C | 19 | 5.06 | 4.8 | 4-4 |
| RH | Atilano L | 16 | 5.15 | 4.5 | 6-7 |

---

## Sean Marshall — 80 IP | $4 | 120 pts
RP-80   Owned: 22%   LH

Marshall wants to go back to being a starter, but, to his credit, he is sharpening his skills in the meantime. Working as a reliever, his arm can better tolerate his curveball, and he has became less hittable thanks to tips from Ted Lilly. Good thing, too, since beyond he and Carlos Marmol, the Cub bullpen is barren. (RM)

### Forecast
| Player | Age | IP | W | Sv | K | ERA | WHIP | K/9 | BB/9 | $2L | Pts |
|---|---|---|---|---|---|---|---|---|---|---|---|
| Marshall S | 28 | 80 | 5 | 2 | 69 | 4.04 | 1.31 | 7.7 | 3.1 | $4 | 120 |
| Mini-Browser | Age | IP | W | Sv | K | ERA | WHIP | K/9 | BB/9 | $2L | Pts |
| Westbrook J | 33 | 180 | 9 | 0 | 108 | 4.33 | 1.35 | 5.4 | 3.0 | $4 | 170 |
| Betancourt R | 35 | 60 | 4 | 0 | 67 | 3.91 | 1.16 | 10.0 | 2.2 | $4 | 110 |
| Venters J | 26 | 70 | 3 | 13 | 64 | 3.94 | 1.50 | 8.2 | 4.6 | $4 | 150 |
| Fister D | 27 | 190 | 8 | 0 | 120 | 4.64 | 1.37 | 5.7 | 2.1 | $4 | 160 |
| Masset N | 28 | 80 | 4 | 4 | 69 | 3.97 | 1.31 | 7.8 | 3.4 | $4 | 120 |

### Minors (2010) / Skills
| Level | Leag | W | L | Sv | IP | H | K | ERA | WHIP | K/9 | BB/9 | HR/9 | GB/F |
|---|---|---|---|---|---|---|---|---|---|---|---|---|---|
| A | — | — | — | — | — | — | — | — | — | — | — | — | — |
| AA | — | — | — | — | — | — | — | — | — | — | — | — | — |
| AAA | — | — | — | — | — | — | — | — | — | — | — | — | — |

### Majors / Skills / Value / Luck / In Rotation / In Relief / OPS
| Yr | Team | W | L | Sv | IP | H | K | ERA | WHIP | K/9 | BB/9 | HR/9 | GB/F | $1L | $2L | Pts | RAA | H% | HR/fb | S% | FIP | GS | CG | QS/DS | GR | Hld | Bln | Lead | OPS | 1st Hf | 2nd Hf | vs RH | vs LH |
|---|---|---|---|---|---|---|---|---|---|---|---|---|---|---|---|---|---|---|---|---|---|---|---|---|---|---|---|---|---|---|---|---|---|
| 07 | CHC | 7 | 8 | 0 | 103 | 107 | 67 | 3.92 | 1.37 | 5.8 | 3.0 | 1.1 | 1.3 | $3 | -$3 | 120 | -6 | 30% | 11% | 75% | 4.55 | 19 | 0 | 10/4 | 2 | 0 | 1 | +0.4 | .750 | .713 | .785 | .781 | .600 |
| 08 | CHC | 3 | 5 | 1 | 65 | 60 | 58 | 3.86 | 1.27 | 8.0 | 3.2 | 1.2 | 1.0 | $2 | -$1 | 90 | +1 | 29% | 11% | 74% | 4.27 | 7 | 0 | 3/0 | 27 | 3 | 1 | -0.0 | .741 | .753 | .731 | .711 | .817 |
| 09 | CHC | 3 | 7 | 0 | 85 | 91 | 68 | 4.32 | 1.44 | 7.2 | 3.4 | 1.1 | 1.8 | -$1 | -$3 | 90 | -5 | 33% | 14% | 73% | 4.25 | 9 | 1 | 2/2 | 46 | 7 | 0 | +0.1 | .776 | .715 | .906 | .808 | .708 |
| 10 | CHC | 7 | 5 | 1 | 74 | 58 | 90 | 2.65 | 1.11 | 10.8 | 3.0 | 0.4 | 2.1 | $7 | $4 | 180 | +9 | 30% | 7% | 76% | 2.32 | — | — | — | 80 | 22 | 2 | +0.3 | .569 | .549 | .595 | .585 | .551 |

### Competition at RP / Stats in 2010 as RP
| Thr | Player | GR | ERA | IP/G | Sv-Hld |
|---|---|---|---|---|---|
| LH | Marshall S | 80 | 2.65 | 0.9 | 1-22 |
| LH | Russell J | 57 | 4.96 | 0.9 | 0-6 |
| LH | Grabow J | 28 | 7.36 | 0.9 | 0-7 |
| LH | Maine S | 13 | 2.08 | 1.0 | 0-2 |

---

## Damaso Marte — 20 IP | $-2 | 20 pts
RP-30   Owned: 0%   LH

A critical ingredient in the Yanks' 2009 WS victory, Marte spent over half of 2010 on the DL. In October, he underwent surgery on his shoulder, and he is likely to miss most (or all) of 2011. Even without the surgery, a target of 20 IP is optimistic, as Marte has not hit that mark in either of the past two years. (LS)

### Forecast
| Player | Age | IP | W | Sv | K | ERA | WHIP | K/9 | BB/9 | $2L | Pts |
|---|---|---|---|---|---|---|---|---|---|---|---|
| Marte D | 36 | 20 | 1 | 0 | 18 | 4.83 | 1.43 | 7.9 | 4.8 | -$2 | 20 |
| Mini-Browser | Age | IP | W | Sv | K | ERA | WHIP | K/9 | BB/9 | $2L | Pts |
| Acosta M | 29 | 40 | 2 | 0 | 33 | 4.39 | 1.48 | 7.5 | 4.7 | -$2 | 40 |
| Qualls C | 32 | 50 | 2 | 0 | 39 | 5.14 | 1.44 | 7.1 | 2.5 | -$2 | 40 |
| Corpas M | 28 | 20 | 1 | 0 | 13 | 4.34 | 1.33 | 6.0 | 2.6 | -$2 | 10 |
| Elbert S | 25 | 40 | 2 | 0 | 48 | 4.59 | 1.51 | 10.8 | 4.2 | -$2 | 50 |
| Schlereth D | 24 | 40 | 2 | 0 | 46 | 4.33 | 1.72 | 10.3 | 6.1 | -$2 | 50 |

### Minors (2010) / Skills
| Level | Leag | W | L | Sv | IP | H | K | ERA | WHIP | K/9 | BB/9 | HR/9 | GB/F |
|---|---|---|---|---|---|---|---|---|---|---|---|---|---|
| A | — | — | — | — | — | — | — | — | — | — | — | — | — |
| AA | — | — | — | — | — | — | — | — | — | — | — | — | — |
| AAA | — | — | — | — | — | — | — | — | — | — | — | — | — |

### Majors / Skills / Value / Luck / In Rotation / In Relief / OPS
| Yr | Team | W | L | Sv | IP | H | K | ERA | WHIP | K/9 | BB/9 | HR/9 | GB/F | $1L | $2L | Pts | RAA | H% | HR/fb | S% | FIP | GS | CG | QS/DS | GR | Hld | Bln | Lead | OPS | 1st Hf | 2nd Hf | vs RH | vs LH |
|---|---|---|---|---|---|---|---|---|---|---|---|---|---|---|---|---|---|---|---|---|---|---|---|---|---|---|---|---|---|---|---|---|---|
| 07 | PIT | 2 | 0 | 0 | 45 | 32 | 51 | 2.38 | 1.14 | 10.1 | 3.6 | 0.4 | 1.0 | $4 | $4 | 60 | +6 | 28% | 4% | 79% | 2.71 | — | — | — | 65 | 15 | 0 | -0.0 | .598 | .519 | .710 | .765 | .352 |
| 08 | 2TM | 5 | 3 | 5 | 65 | 52 | 71 | 4.02 | 1.20 | 9.8 | 3.6 | 0.7 | 0.7 | $3 | $2 | 140 | +0 | 28% | 7% | 67% | 3.27 | — | — | — | 72 | 25 | 2 | +0.4 | .608 | .576 | .675 | .573 | .672 |
| 09 | NYY | 0 | 0 | 0 | 13 | 15 | 13 | 9.45 | 1.58 | 8.8 | 4.1 | 2.0 | 0.5 | -$3 | -$4 | 10 | -8 | 32% | 13% | 39% | 5.63 | — | — | — | 21 | 5 | 1 | -0.7 | .861 | 1.248 | .523 | 1.175 | .494 |
| 10 | NYY | 0 | 0 | 0 | 17 | 10 | 12 | 4.08 | 1.19 | 6.4 | 5.6 | 1.0 | 0.6 | -$3 | -$10 | 10 | +1 | 16% | 7% | 68% | 5.28 | — | — | — | 30 | 9 | 2 | +1.2 | .580 | .580 | — | .753 | .468 |

### Competition at RP / Stats in 2010 as RP
| Thr | Player | GR | ERA | IP/G | Sv-Hld |
|---|---|---|---|---|---|
| LH | Logan B | 51 | 2.93 | 0.8 | 0-13 |
| LH | Marte D | 30 | 4.08 | 0.6 | 0-9 |

## J.D. Martin

**40 IP | $-2 | 40 pts**

SP-9 — Owned: 0% — RH

Martin is another starting pitcher who will get a longer look in 2011 than he would if Stephen Strasburg were healthy. Nowadays, the former Cleveland top prospect is a soft-tosser who induces a lot of FB (and a lot of easy homers). With a bit more separation between his K/9 and BB/9, Martin could be bearable. (PB)

| Player | Age | IP | W | Sv | K | ERA | WHIP | K/9 | BB/9 | $2L | Pts |
|---|---|---|---|---|---|---|---|---|---|---|---|
| | | Forecast | | | | | | | | | |
| Martin J | 28 | 40 | 2 | 0 | 27 | 4.58 | 1.37 | 6.1 | 2.2 | -$2 | 40 |
| Mini-Browser | Age | IP | W | Sv | K | ERA | WHIP | K/9 | BB/9 | $2L | Pts |
| Volstad C | 24 | 160 | 10 | 0 | 101 | 4.89 | 1.45 | 5.7 | 3.2 | -$2 | 150 |
| Delcarmen M | 29 | 60 | 3 | 0 | 47 | 4.47 | 1.50 | 7.1 | 5.0 | -$2 | 70 |
| Green S | 31 | 40 | 2 | 0 | 29 | 4.25 | 1.46 | 6.6 | 4.5 | -$2 | 40 |
| VandenHurk R | 25 | 40 | 2 | 0 | 38 | 5.04 | 1.48 | 8.5 | 3.9 | -$2 | 40 |
| Schlichting T | 26 | 60 | 3 | 0 | 51 | 4.41 | 1.53 | 7.6 | 4.3 | -$2 | 70 |

| Level | Leag | W | L | Sv | IP | H | K | ERA | WHIP | K/9 | BB/9 | HR/9 | GB/F |
|---|---|---|---|---|---|---|---|---|---|---|---|---|---|
| | | Minors (2010) | | | | | | | | Skills | | | |
| A | — | — | — | — | — | — | — | — | — | — | — | — | — |
| AA | — | — | — | — | — | — | — | — | — | — | — | — | — |
| AAA | IL | 2 | 2 | 0 | 41 | 40 | 25 | 3.51 | 1.17 | 5.5 | 1.8 | 0.7 | — |

| Yr | Team | W | L | Sv | IP | H | K | ERA | WHIP | K/9 | BB/9 | HR/9 | GB/F |
|---|---|---|---|---|---|---|---|---|---|---|---|---|---|
| | | Majors | | | | | | | | Skills | | | |
| 07 | — | — | — | — | — | — | — | — | — | — | — | — | — |
| 08 | — | — | — | — | — | — | — | — | — | — | — | — | — |
| 09 | WAS | 5 | 4 | 0 | 77 | 85 | 37 | 4.44 | 1.42 | 4.3 | 2.8 | 1.6 | 0.8 |
| 10 | WAS | 1 | 5 | 0 | 48 | 56 | 31 | 4.13 | 1.40 | 5.8 | 2.1 | 1.7 | 0.9 |

**Competition at SP** — Stats in 2010 as SP

| Thr | Player | GS | ERA | Supp | W-L |
|---|---|---|---|---|---|
| RH | Hernandez L | 33 | 3.66 | 3.5 | 10-12 |
| LH | Lannan J | 25 | 4.65 | 4.5 | 8-8 |
| RH | Stammen C | 19 | 5.06 | 4.8 | 4-4 |
| RH | Atilano L | 16 | 5.15 | 4.5 | 6-7 |

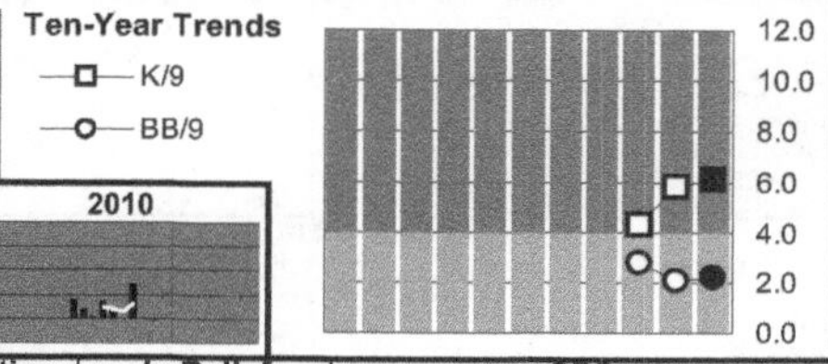


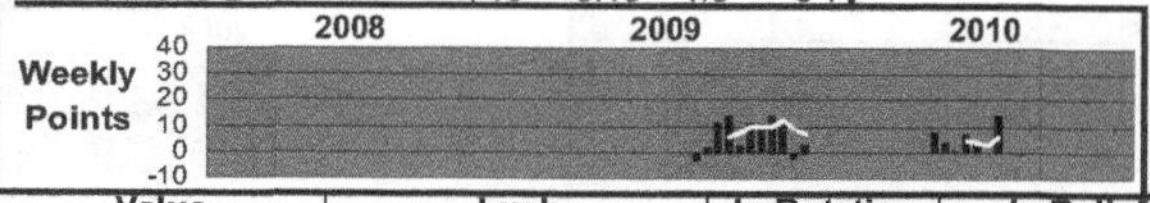


| Yr | $1L | $2L | Pts | RAA | H% | HR/fb | S% | FIP | GS | CG | QS/DS | GR | Hld | Bln | Lead | OPS | 1st Hf | 2nd Hf | vs RH | vs LH |
|---|---|---|---|---|---|---|---|---|---|---|---|---|---|---|---|---|---|---|---|---|
| | Value | | | | Luck | | | | In Rotation | | | In Relief | | | | OPS | | | | |
| 07 | — | — | — | — | — | — | — | — | — | — | — | — | — | — | — | — | — | — | — | — |
| 08 | — | — | — | — | — | — | — | — | — | — | — | — | — | — | — | — | — | — | — | — |
| 09 | -$1 | -$3 | 70 | –2 | 29% | 12% | 75% | 5.54 | 15 | 0 | 5/2 | — | — | — | — | .830 | — | .830 | .814 | .846 |
| 10 | -$4 | -$12 | 30 | –6 | 30% | 13% | 78% | 5.03 | 9 | 0 | 2/1 | — | — | — | — | .820 | .768 | 1.083 | .721 | .934 |

## Nick Masset

**80 IP | $4 | 120 pts**

RP-82 — Owned: 2% — RH

The hard-throwing Masset is the Reds' set-up man and closer-in-waiting. Francisco Cordero still makes a lot of money to record Saves, but if he goes down with an injury, Masset could get the job in the short term. In any case, Masset is the favorite to be the closer in 2012. (SW)

| Player | Age | IP | W | Sv | K | ERA | WHIP | K/9 | BB/9 | $2L | Pts |
|---|---|---|---|---|---|---|---|---|---|---|---|
| | | Forecast | | | | | | | | | |
| Masset N | 28 | 80 | 4 | 4 | 69 | 3.97 | 1.31 | 7.8 | 3.4 | $4 | 120 |
| Mini-Browser | Age | IP | W | Sv | K | ERA | WHIP | K/9 | BB/9 | $2L | Pts |
| Jackson E | 27 | 200 | 10 | 0 | 145 | 4.69 | 1.42 | 6.5 | 3.4 | $4 | 200 |
| Westbrook J | 33 | 180 | 9 | 0 | 108 | 4.33 | 1.35 | 5.4 | 3.0 | $4 | 170 |
| Betancourt R | 35 | 60 | 4 | 0 | 67 | 3.91 | 1.16 | 10.0 | 2.2 | $4 | 110 |
| Venters J | 26 | 70 | 3 | 13 | 64 | 3.94 | 1.50 | 8.2 | 4.6 | $4 | 150 |
| Fister D | 27 | 190 | 8 | 0 | 120 | 4.64 | 1.37 | 5.7 | 2.1 | $4 | 160 |

| Level | Leag | W | L | Sv | IP | H | K | ERA | WHIP | K/9 | BB/9 | HR/9 | GB/F |
|---|---|---|---|---|---|---|---|---|---|---|---|---|---|
| | | Minors (2010) | | | | | | | | Skills | | | |
| A | — | — | — | — | — | — | — | — | — | — | — | — | — |
| AA | — | — | — | — | — | — | — | — | — | — | — | — | — |
| AAA | — | — | — | — | — | — | — | — | — | — | — | — | — |

| Yr | Team | W | L | Sv | IP | H | K | ERA | WHIP | K/9 | BB/9 | HR/9 | GB/F |
|---|---|---|---|---|---|---|---|---|---|---|---|---|---|
| | | Majors | | | | | | | | Skills | | | |
| 07 | CHW | 2 | 3 | 0 | 39 | 52 | 21 | 7.09 | 1.98 | 4.8 | 5.9 | 0.5 | 1.1 |
| 08 | 2TM | 2 | 0 | 1 | 62 | 71 | 43 | 3.92 | 1.56 | 6.2 | 3.8 | 1.0 | 1.9 |
| 09 | CIN | 5 | 1 | 0 | 76 | 54 | 70 | 2.37 | 1.03 | 8.3 | 2.8 | 0.7 | 1.7 |
| 10 | CIN | 4 | 4 | 2 | 76 | 64 | 85 | 3.40 | 1.27 | 10.0 | 3.9 | 0.8 | 1.4 |

**Competition at RP** — Stats in 2010 as RP

| Thr | Player | GR | ERA | IP/G | Sv-Hld |
|---|---|---|---|---|---|
| RH | Masset N | 82 | 3.40 | 0.9 | 2-20 |
| RH | Cordero F | 75 | 3.84 | 1.0 | 40-1 |
| RH | Ondrusek L | 60 | 3.68 | 1.0 | 0-6 |
| RH | Smith J | 37 | 3.86 | 1.1 | 1-2 |

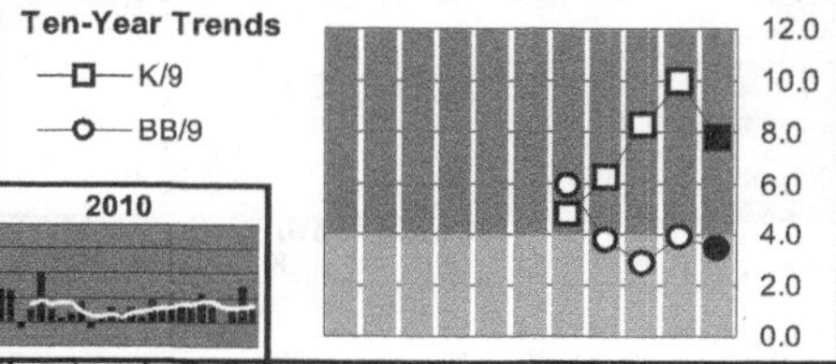


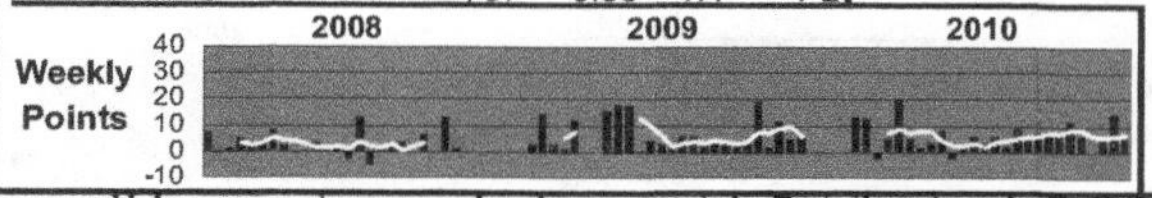


| Yr | $1L | $2L | Pts | RAA | H% | HR/fb | S% | FIP | GS | CG | QS/DS | GR | Hld | Bln | Lead | OPS | 1st Hf | 2nd Hf | vs RH | vs LH |
|---|---|---|---|---|---|---|---|---|---|---|---|---|---|---|---|---|---|---|---|---|
| | Value | | | | Luck | | | | In Rotation | | | In Relief | | | | OPS | | | | |
| 07 | -$7 | -$14 | 10 | –15 | 35% | 4% | 62% | 4.88 | 1 | 0 | 0/0 | 26 | 2 | 1 | –1.0 | .851 | .864 | .542 | .857 | .844 |
| 08 | -$4 | -$5 | 50 | –4 | 34% | 13% | 78% | 4.59 | 1 | 0 | 0/0 | 41 | 2 | 2 | –0.2 | .817 | .766 | .912 | .786 | .874 |
| 09 | $9 | $7 | 140 | +12 | 25% | 10% | 81% | 3.33 | — | — | — | 74 | 20 | 2 | +0.2 | .584 | .458 | .691 | .564 | .618 |
| 10 | $2 | -$4 | 130 | +4 | 30% | 10% | 76% | 3.46 | — | — | — | 82 | 20 | 3 | +0.7 | .643 | .814 | .435 | .660 | .608 |

## Justin Masterson

**180 IP | $1 | 180 pts**

SP-29, RP-5 — Owned: 4% — RH

Masterson has the potential of an outstanding SP, but until he finds a way to tame lefties, he will struggle. Despite an inconsistent 2010 campaign, a late-season surge (1.45 ERA in final 5 starts) secured a spot in the 2011 rotation. Even if he falls short as a starter, a prominent role awaits him in the CLE bullpen. (BLS)

| Player | Age | IP | W | Sv | K | ERA | WHIP | K/9 | BB/9 | $2L | Pts |
|---|---|---|---|---|---|---|---|---|---|---|---|
| | | Forecast | | | | | | | | | |
| Masterson J | 26 | 180 | 8 | 0 | 148 | 4.63 | 1.51 | 7.4 | 4.1 | $1 | 180 |
| Mini-Browser | Age | IP | W | Sv | K | ERA | WHIP | K/9 | BB/9 | $2L | Pts |
| Casilla S | 30 | 60 | 5 | 0 | 52 | 3.83 | 1.41 | 7.7 | 4.1 | $2 | 90 |
| Wood T | 24 | 120 | 6 | 0 | 108 | 4.43 | 1.40 | 8.1 | 3.3 | $2 | 140 |
| Clippard T | 26 | 60 | 4 | 0 | 63 | 4.07 | 1.37 | 9.4 | 4.2 | $2 | 100 |
| Pestano V | 26 | 40 | 2 | 0 | 39 | 3.44 | 1.33 | 8.7 | 3.4 | $1 | 60 |
| Fuentes B | 35 | 40 | 2 | 0 | 37 | 3.60 | 1.29 | 8.4 | 3.9 | $1 | 60 |

| Level | Leag | W | L | Sv | IP | H | K | ERA | WHIP | K/9 | BB/9 | HR/9 | GB/F |
|---|---|---|---|---|---|---|---|---|---|---|---|---|---|
| | | Minors (2010) | | | | | | | | Skills | | | |
| A | — | — | — | — | — | — | — | — | — | — | — | — | — |
| AA | — | — | — | — | — | — | — | — | — | — | — | — | — |
| AAA | — | — | — | — | — | — | — | — | — | — | — | — | — |

| Yr | Team | W | L | Sv | IP | H | K | ERA | WHIP | K/9 | BB/9 | HR/9 | GB/F |
|---|---|---|---|---|---|---|---|---|---|---|---|---|---|
| | | Majors | | | | | | | | Skills | | | |
| 07 | — | — | — | — | — | — | — | — | — | — | — | — | — |
| 08 | BOS | 6 | 5 | 0 | 88 | 68 | 68 | 3.16 | 1.22 | 6.9 | 4.1 | 1.0 | 2.0 |
| 09 | 2TM | 4 | 10 | 0 | 129 | 128 | 119 | 4.52 | 1.45 | 8.3 | 4.2 | 0.8 | 1.7 |
| 10 | CLE | 6 | 13 | 0 | 180 | 197 | 140 | 4.70 | 1.50 | 7.0 | 3.7 | 0.7 | 2.4 |

**Competition at SP** — Stats in 2010 as SP

| Thr | Player | GS | ERA | Supp | W-L |
|---|---|---|---|---|---|
| RH | Carmona F | 33 | 3.77 | 3.5 | 13-14 |
| RH | Masterson J | 29 | 4.78 | 4.3 | 6-12 |
| RH | Talbot M | 28 | 4.41 | 4.1 | 10-13 |
| LH | Huff D | 15 | 6.21 | 3.6 | 2-11 |

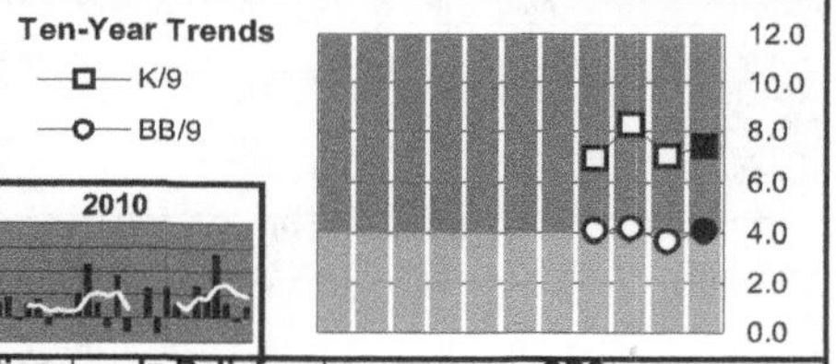


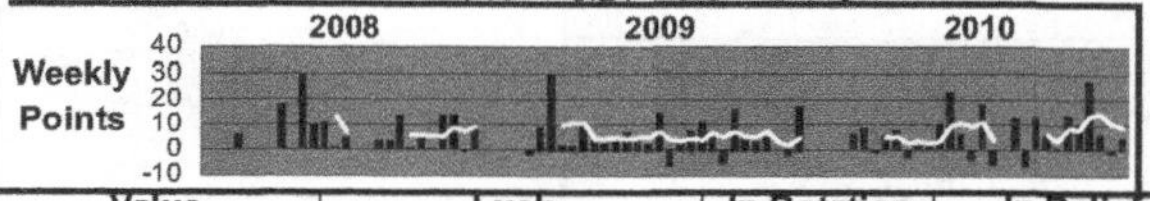


| Yr | $1L | $2L | Pts | RAA | H% | HR/fb | S% | FIP | GS | CG | QS/DS | GR | Hld | Bln | Lead | OPS | 1st Hf | 2nd Hf | vs RH | vs LH |
|---|---|---|---|---|---|---|---|---|---|---|---|---|---|---|---|---|---|---|---|---|
| | Value | | | | Luck | | | | In Rotation | | | In Relief | | | | OPS | | | | |
| 07 | — | — | — | — | — | — | — | — | — | — | — | — | — | — | — | — | — | — | — | — |
| 08 | $7 | $3 | 130 | +13 | 25% | 15% | 79% | 4.59 | 9 | 0 | 5/0 | 27 | 3 | 1 | +0.4 | .674 | .692 | .645 | .572 | .787 |
| 09 | $3 | -$4 | 130 | –9 | 33% | 10% | 70% | 4.01 | 16 | 1 | 6/3 | 26 | 6 | 1 | 0.0 | .740 | .788 | .692 | .591 | .877 |
| 10 | -$2 | -$23 | 150 | –18 | 33% | 10% | 69% | 3.97 | 29 | 1 | 12/8 | 5 | 2 | 0 | +0.4 | .738 | .769 | .691 | .681 | .784 |

## Frank Mata

**40 IP | $-5 | 30 pts**

RP-15 — Owned: 0% — RH

Mata's missteps in MLB were overshadowed by his minor-league success, but he does not have dominant stuff, and his skills do not convert to big upside. That said, with consistent improvement, his workman-like make-up might one day translate to middle relief. (BJ)

| Player | Age | IP | W | Sv | K | ERA | WHIP | K/9 | BB/9 | $2L | Pts |
|---|---|---|---|---|---|---|---|---|---|---|---|
| | | Forecast | | | | | | | | | |
| Mata F | 27 | 40 | 3 | 0 | 21 | 5.79 | 1.79 | 4.8 | 5.8 | -$5 | 30 |
| Mini-Browser | Age | IP | W | Sv | K | ERA | WHIP | K/9 | BB/9 | $2L | Pts |
| Texeira K | 25 | 60 | 1 | 0 | 49 | 5.07 | 1.73 | 7.4 | 4.3 | -$4 | 40 |
| Chico M | 27 | 40 | 2 | 0 | 27 | 5.53 | 1.58 | 6.0 | 3.7 | -$5 | 30 |
| Caridad E | 27 | 60 | 2 | 0 | 49 | 5.42 | 1.54 | 7.4 | 3.4 | -$5 | 50 |
| Mejia J | 21 | 120 | 3 | 0 | 102 | 4.53 | 1.62 | 7.7 | 4.3 | -$5 | 100 |
| Tillman C | 22 | 160 | 7 | 0 | 129 | 5.47 | 1.56 | 7.3 | 4.1 | -$5 | 140 |

| Level | Leag | W | L | Sv | IP | H | K | ERA | WHIP | K/9 | BB/9 | HR/9 | GB/F |
|---|---|---|---|---|---|---|---|---|---|---|---|---|---|
| | | Minors (2010) | | | | | | | | Skills | | | |
| A | — | — | — | — | — | — | — | — | — | — | — | — | — |
| AA | — | — | — | — | — | — | — | — | — | — | — | — | — |
| AAA | IL | 5 | 3 | 8 | 42 | 34 | 30 | 3.16 | 1.27 | 6.3 | 4.2 | 0.4 | — |

| Yr | Team | W | L | Sv | IP | H | K | ERA | WHIP | K/9 | BB/9 | HR/9 | GB/F |
|---|---|---|---|---|---|---|---|---|---|---|---|---|---|
| | | Majors | | | | | | | | Skills | | | |
| 07 | — | — | — | — | — | — | — | — | — | — | — | — | — |
| 08 | — | — | — | — | — | — | — | — | — | — | — | — | — |
| 09 | — | — | — | — | — | — | — | — | — | — | — | — | — |
| 10 | BAL | 0 | 0 | 0 | 17 | 24 | 9 | 7.79 | 1.85 | 4.7 | 4.2 | 1.0 | 2.4 |

**Competition at RP** — Stats in 2010 as RP

| Thr | Player | GR | ERA | IP/G | Sv-Hld |
|---|---|---|---|---|---|
| RH | Albers M | 62 | 4.52 | 1.2 | 0-7 |
| RH | Simon A | 49 | 4.93 | 1.0 | 17-1 |
| RH | Uehara K | 43 | 2.86 | 1.0 | 13-6 |
| RH | Berken J | 41 | 3.03 | 1.5 | 0-7 |

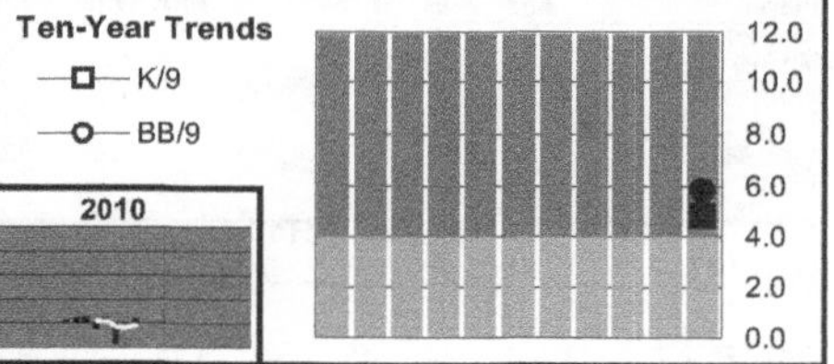


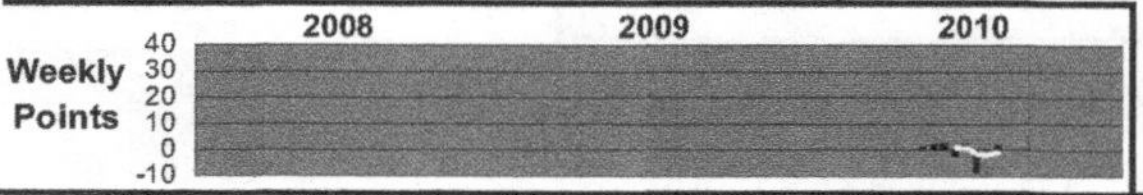


| Yr | $1L | $2L | Pts | RAA | H% | HR/fb | S% | FIP | GS | CG | QS/DS | GR | Hld | Bln | Lead | OPS | 1st Hf | 2nd Hf | vs RH | vs LH |
|---|---|---|---|---|---|---|---|---|---|---|---|---|---|---|---|---|---|---|---|---|
| | Value | | | | Luck | | | | In Rotation | | | In Relief | | | | OPS | | | | |
| 07 | — | — | — | — | — | — | — | — | — | — | — | — | — | — | — | — | — | — | — | — |
| 08 | — | — | — | — | — | — | — | — | — | — | — | — | — | — | — | — | — | — | — | — |
| 09 | — | — | — | — | — | — | — | — | — | — | — | — | — | — | — | — | — | — | — | — |
| 10 | -$6 | -$17 | 0 | –8 | 34% | 13% | 57% | 5.15 | — | — | — | 15 | 1 | 0 | –4.0 | .900 | .941 | .692 | .891 | .913 |

## Scott Mathieson

**40 IP | $-4 | 40 pts**

RP-2 — Owned: 0% — RH

Mathieson's progress in 2011 will tell the Phillies how to handle the impending free agency of Brad Lidge and Ryan Madson. Consequently, Mathieson should receive ample opportunities in the middle innings to show off his stuff. If he impresses, he could be scavenging Holds and even Saves later in the season. (BB)

| Player | Age | IP | W | Sv | K | ERA | WHIP | K/9 | BB/9 | $2L | Pts |
|---|---|---|---|---|---|---|---|---|---|---|---|
| | | Forecast | | | | | | | | | |
| Mathieson S | 27 | 40 | 2 | 0 | 40 | 5.37 | 1.70 | 9.0 | 4.1 | -$4 | 40 |
| Mini-Browser | Age | IP | W | Sv | K | ERA | WHIP | K/9 | BB/9 | $2L | Pts |
| Arrieta J | 25 | 140 | 7 | 0 | 113 | 5.12 | 1.65 | 7.3 | 4.4 | -$4 | 130 |
| Wright W | 26 | 40 | 1 | 0 | 38 | 5.37 | 1.57 | 8.6 | 4.6 | -$4 | 30 |
| Proctor S | 34 | 60 | 2 | 0 | 51 | 5.24 | 1.52 | 7.7 | 4.5 | -$4 | 50 |
| Davis D | 35 | 180 | 10 | 0 | 126 | 5.01 | 1.53 | 6.3 | 4.4 | -$4 | 170 |
| Jackson J | 23 | 40 | 2 | 0 | 24 | 5.70 | 1.48 | 5.4 | 3.3 | -$4 | 30 |

| Level | Leag | W | L | Sv | IP | H | K | ERA | WHIP | K/9 | BB/9 | HR/9 | GB/F |
|---|---|---|---|---|---|---|---|---|---|---|---|---|---|
| | | Minors (2010) | | | | | | | | Skills | | | |
| A | — | — | — | — | — | — | — | — | — | — | — | — | — |
| AA | — | — | — | — | — | — | — | — | — | — | — | — | — |
| AAA | IL | 3 | 6 | 26 | 64 | 49 | 83 | 2.80 | 1.13 | 11.6 | 3.4 | 1.1 | — |

| Yr | Team | W | L | Sv | IP | H | K | ERA | WHIP | K/9 | BB/9 | HR/9 | GB/F |
|---|---|---|---|---|---|---|---|---|---|---|---|---|---|
| | | Majors | | | | | | | | Skills | | | |
| 07 | — | — | — | — | — | — | — | — | — | — | — | — | — |
| 08 | — | — | — | — | — | — | — | — | — | — | — | — | — |
| 09 | — | — | — | — | — | — | — | — | — | — | — | — | — |
| 10 | PHI | 0 | 0 | 0 | 1 | 5 | 1 | 10.80 | 4.20 | 5.4 | 10.8 | 0.0 | 2.5 |

**Competition at RP** — Stats in 2010 as RP

| Thr | Player | GR | ERA | IP/G | Sv-Hld |
|---|---|---|---|---|---|
| RH | Contreras J | 67 | 3.34 | 0.8 | 4-13 |
| RH | Durbin C | 64 | 3.80 | 1.1 | 0-15 |
| RH | Madson R | 55 | 2.55 | 1.0 | 5-15 |
| RH | Baez D | 51 | 5.48 | 0.9 | 0-6 |

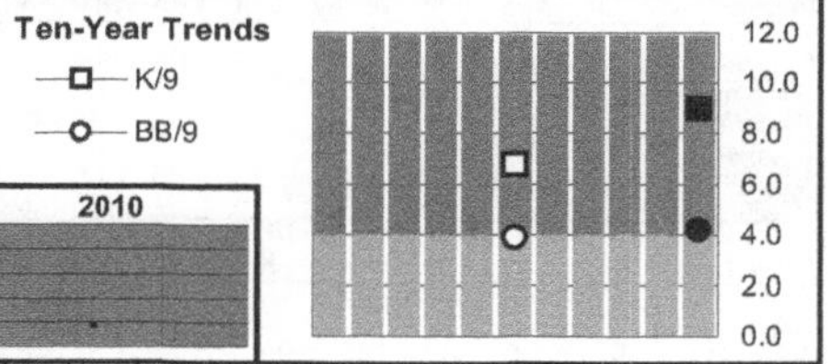


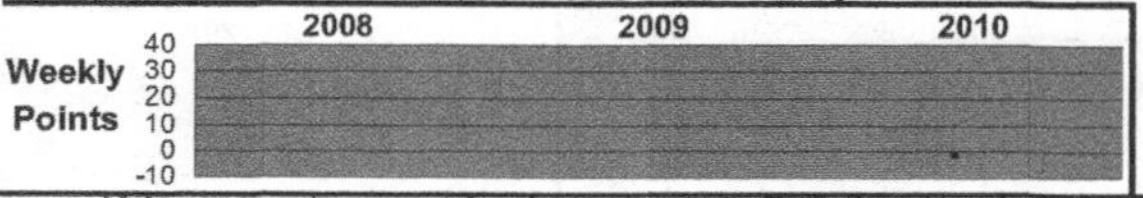


| Yr | $1L | $2L | Pts | RAA | H% | HR/fb | S% | FIP | GS | CG | QS/DS | GR | Hld | Bln | Lead | OPS | 1st Hf | 2nd Hf | vs RH | vs LH |
|---|---|---|---|---|---|---|---|---|---|---|---|---|---|---|---|---|---|---|---|---|
| | Value | | | | Luck | | | | In Rotation | | | In Relief | | | | OPS | | | | |
| 07 | — | — | — | — | — | — | — | — | — | — | — | — | — | — | — | — | — | — | — | — |
| 08 | — | — | — | — | — | — | — | — | — | — | — | — | — | — | — | — | — | — | — | — |
| 09 | — | — | — | — | — | — | — | — | — | — | — | — | — | — | — | — | — | — | — | — |
| 10 | -$6 | -$12 | 0 | –2 | 63% | 0% | 71% | 5.60 | — | — | — | 2 | 0 | 0 | +1.5 | 1.192 | 1.200 | 1.167 | 1.314 | 1.000 |

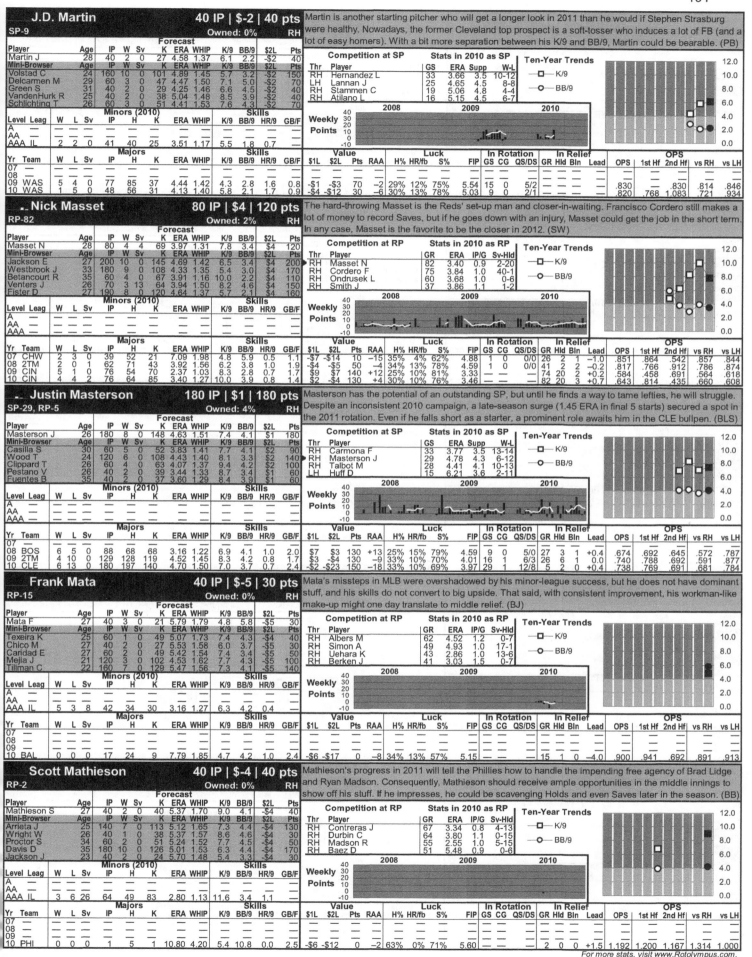

For more stats, visit www.Rotolympus.com.

## Daisuke Matsuzaka — 160 IP | $4 | 200 pts

SP-25 — Owned: 62% — RH

| Player | Age | IP | W | Sv | K | ERA | WHIP | K/9 | BB/9 | $2L | Pts |
|---|---|---|---|---|---|---|---|---|---|---|---|
| **Forecast** | | | | | | | | | | | |
| Matsuzaka D | 30 | 160 | 10 | 0 | 138 | 4.63 | 1.44 | 7.8 | 4.5 | $4 | 200 |
| **Mini-Browser** | Age | IP | W | Sv | K | ERA | WHIP | K/9 | BB/9 | $2L | Pts |
| Guthrie J | 31 | 200 | 10 | 0 | 110 | 4.76 | 1.34 | 5.0 | 2.6 | $4 | 170 |
| Motte J | 28 | 60 | 3 | 4 | 62 | 3.63 | 1.27 | 9.2 | 3.2 | $4 | 110 |
| Chamberlain J | 25 | 60 | 4 | 10 | 57 | 4.29 | 1.38 | 8.5 | 3.9 | $4 | 130 |
| Hunter T | 24 | 140 | 10 | 0 | 83 | 4.55 | 1.38 | 5.4 | 2.6 | $4 | 160 |
| Burnett A | 34 | 180 | 11 | 0 | 155 | 4.74 | 1.45 | 7.7 | 4.1 | $4 | 220 |

Minors (2010) / Skills

| Level | Leag | W | L | Sv | IP | H | K | ERA | WHIP | K/9 | BB/9 | HR/9 | GB/F |
|---|---|---|---|---|---|---|---|---|---|---|---|---|---|
| A | — | — | — | — | — | — | — | — | — | — | — | — | — |
| AA | — | — | — | — | — | — | — | — | — | — | — | — | — |
| AAA | IL | 2 | 0 | 0 | 16 | 11 | 13 | 1.62 | 0.72 | 7.0 | 0.5 | 0.5 | — |

Majors / Skills

| Yr | Team | W | L | Sv | IP | H | K | ERA | WHIP | K/9 | BB/9 | HR/9 | GB/F |
|---|---|---|---|---|---|---|---|---|---|---|---|---|---|
| 07 | BOS | 15 | 12 | 0 | 204 | 191 | 201 | 4.40 | 1.32 | 8.8 | 3.5 | 1.1 | 0.9 |
| 08 | BOS | 18 | 3 | 0 | 167 | 128 | 154 | 2.90 | 1.32 | 8.3 | 5.0 | 0.6 | 0.9 |
| 09 | BOS | 4 | 6 | 0 | 59 | 81 | 54 | 5.76 | 1.87 | 8.2 | 4.6 | 1.5 | 0.8 |
| 10 | BOS | 9 | 6 | 0 | 153 | 137 | 133 | 4.69 | 1.37 | 7.8 | 4.3 | 0.8 | 0.7 |

| Yr | Value $1L | $2L | Pts | RAA | Luck H% | HR/fb | S% | FIP | In Rotation GS | CG | QS/DS | In Relief GR | Hld | Bln | Lead | OPS | 1st Hf | 2nd Hf | vs RH | vs LH |
|---|---|---|---|---|---|---|---|---|---|---|---|---|---|---|---|---|---|---|---|---|
| 07 | $11 | -$3 | 320 | +1 | 30% | 10% | 70% | 4.10 | 32 | 1 | 18/5 | — | — | — | — | .731 | .693 | .782 | .719 | .744 |
| 08 | $17 | $10 | 340 | +25 | 26% | 6% | 80% | 4.08 | 29 | 0 | 14/2 | — | — | — | — | .645 | .640 | .651 | .564 | .718 |
| 09 | -$4 | -$8 | 60 | -9 | 38% | 12% | 72% | 5.19 | 12 | 0 | 3/2 | — | — | — | — | .935 | 1.091 | .674 | .876 | .975 |
| 10 | $3 | -$14 | 190 | -8 | 29% | 7% | 66% | 4.11 | 25 | 0 | 10/3 | — | — | — | — | .706 | .679 | .730 | .626 | .770 |

Matsuzaka is who he is: a frustrating pitcher who nibbles around the plate. That said, his velocity did rise a tick in 2010 after he finally signed on to Boston's shoulder-strengthening program last winter. That little boost might be all it takes to hide Matsuzaka's warts. He should open 2011 as Boston's #5 starter. (EB)

Competition at SP — Stats in 2010 as SP

| Thr | Player | GS | ERA | Supp | W-L |
|---|---|---|---|---|---|
| RH | Lackey J | 33 | 4.40 | 5.1 | 14-11 |
| LH | Lester J | 32 | 3.25 | 5.0 | 19-9 |
| RH | Buchholz C | 28 | 2.33 | 4.7 | 17-7 |
| ▶ RH | Matsuzaka D | 25 | 4.69 | 5.6 | 9-6 |

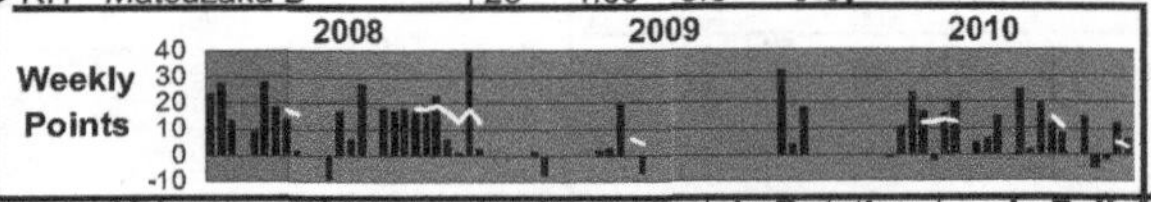


Ten-Year Trends

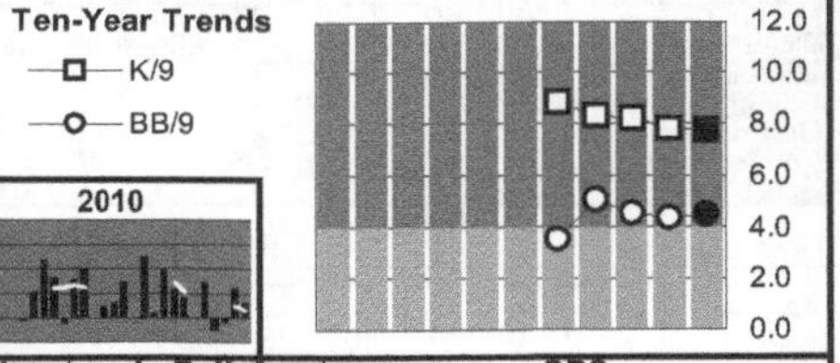


## Brian Matusz — 180 IP | $5 | 210 pts

SP-32 — Owned: 14% — LH

| Player | Age | IP | W | Sv | K | ERA | WHIP | K/9 | BB/9 | $2L | Pts |
|---|---|---|---|---|---|---|---|---|---|---|---|
| **Forecast** | | | | | | | | | | | |
| Matusz B | 24 | 180 | 10 | 0 | 156 | 4.54 | 1.44 | 7.8 | 3.3 | $5 | 210 |
| **Mini-Browser** | Age | IP | W | Sv | K | ERA | WHIP | K/9 | BB/9 | $2L | Pts |
| Coke P | 28 | 160 | 10 | 2 | 141 | 4.52 | 1.47 | 8.0 | 3.5 | $5 | 220 |
| Zimmermann J | 24 | 160 | 8 | 0 | 156 | 4.45 | 1.35 | 8.8 | 3.0 | $5 | 210 |
| Niese J | 24 | 180 | 10 | 0 | 159 | 4.24 | 1.42 | 7.9 | 3.1 | $5 | 230 |
| Germano J | 28 | 40 | 0 | 0 | 32 | 2.16 | 0.84 | 7.3 | 2.2 | $5 | 50 |
| Figueroa N | 36 | 100 | 7 | 0 | 79 | 3.86 | 1.32 | 7.1 | 3.0 | $5 | 140 |

Minors (2010) / Skills

| Level | Leag | W | L | Sv | IP | H | K | ERA | WHIP | K/9 | BB/9 | HR/9 | GB/F |
|---|---|---|---|---|---|---|---|---|---|---|---|---|---|
| A | — | — | — | — | — | — | — | — | — | — | — | — | — |
| AA | — | — | — | — | — | — | — | — | — | — | — | — | — |
| AAA | — | — | — | — | — | — | — | — | — | — | — | — | — |

Majors / Skills

| Yr | Team | W | L | Sv | IP | H | K | ERA | WHIP | K/9 | BB/9 | HR/9 | GB/F |
|---|---|---|---|---|---|---|---|---|---|---|---|---|---|
| 07 | — | — | — | — | — | — | — | — | — | — | — | — | — |
| 08 | — | — | — | — | — | — | — | — | — | — | — | — | — |
| 09 | BAL | 5 | 2 | 0 | 44 | 52 | 38 | 4.63 | 1.48 | 7.7 | 2.8 | 1.2 | 0.7 |
| 10 | BAL | 10 | 12 | 0 | 175 | 173 | 143 | 4.30 | 1.34 | 7.3 | 3.2 | 1.0 | 0.8 |

| Yr | Value $1L | $2L | Pts | RAA | Luck H% | HR/fb | S% | FIP | In Rotation GS | CG | QS/DS | In Relief GR | Hld | Bln | Lead | OPS | 1st Hf | 2nd Hf | vs RH | vs LH |
|---|---|---|---|---|---|---|---|---|---|---|---|---|---|---|---|---|---|---|---|---|
| 07 | — | — | — | — | — | — | — | — | — | — | — | — | — | — | — | — | — | — | — | — |
| 08 | — | — | — | — | — | — | — | — | — | — | — | — | — | — | — | — | — | — | — | — |
| 09 | $1 | -$2 | 80 | -2 | 34% | 9% | 72% | 4.29 | 8 | 0 | 2/1 | — | — | — | — | .823 | — | .823 | .850 | .708 |
| 10 | $6 | -$10 | 220 | -1 | 30% | 8% | 70% | 4.15 | 32 | 0 | 18/7 | — | — | — | — | .718 | .756 | .660 | .755 | .581 |

Matusz has the stuff to be an ace, and he might be nearer to a break-out than you think. His overall numbers in 2010 were OK, but he didn't find his groove until June, and he dominated after August 1 (2.18 ERA, 7-1 record). During that stretch, he faced only one team with a below-average offense. (BJ)

Competition at SP — Stats in 2010 as SP

| Thr | Player | GS | ERA | Supp | W-L |
|---|---|---|---|---|---|
| RH | Guthrie J | 32 | 3.83 | 3.6 | 11-14 |
| ▶ LH | Matusz B | 32 | 4.30 | 3.7 | 10-12 |
| RH | Millwood K | 31 | 5.10 | 3.5 | 4-16 |
| RH | Bergesen B | 28 | 5.02 | 3.9 | 8-12 |

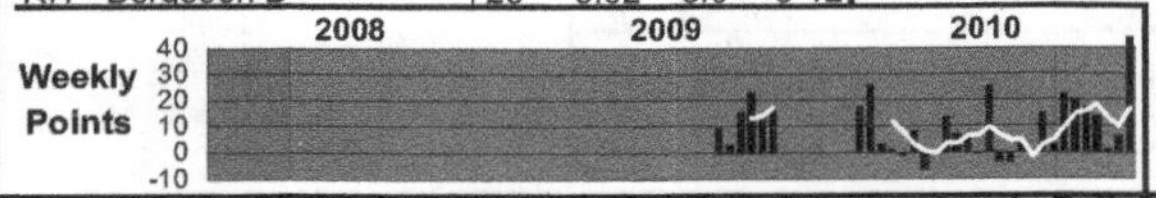


Ten-Year Trends

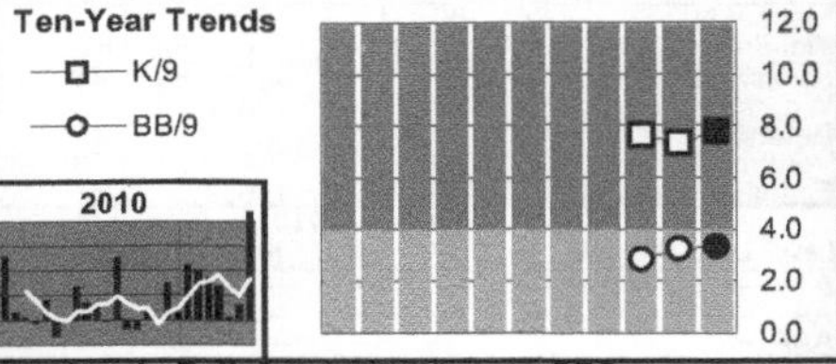


## Yunesky Maya — 120 IP | $-17 | 90 pts

SP-5 — Owned: 0% — RH

| Player | Age | IP | W | Sv | K | ERA | WHIP | K/9 | BB/9 | $2L | Pts |
|---|---|---|---|---|---|---|---|---|---|---|---|
| **Forecast** | | | | | | | | | | | |
| Maya Y | 29 | 120 | 9 | 0 | 83 | 6.23 | 2.00 | 6.2 | 7.6 | -$17 | 90 |
| **Mini-Browser** | Age | IP | W | Sv | K | ERA | WHIP | K/9 | BB/9 | $2L | Pts |
| Rogers E | 25 | 80 | 4 | 0 | 75 | 5.64 | 1.66 | 8.5 | 3.5 | -$7 | 70 |
| McAllister Z | 23 | 40 | 2 | 0 | 19 | 7.23 | 1.76 | 4.4 | 3.7 | -$7 | 10 |
| Crow A | 24 | 40 | 1 | 0 | 24 | 7.22 | 1.85 | 5.3 | 5.1 | -$8 | 10 |
| Reckling T | 21 | 40 | 1 | 0 | 21 | 7.21 | 2.02 | 4.7 | 6.8 | -$9 | 0 |
| West S | 24 | 120 | 6 | 0 | 100 | 5.57 | 1.69 | 7.5 | 4.3 | -$9 | 100 |

Minors (2010) / Skills

| Level | Leag | W | L | Sv | IP | H | K | ERA | WHIP | K/9 | BB/9 | HR/9 | GB/F |
|---|---|---|---|---|---|---|---|---|---|---|---|---|---|
| A | CAR | 0 | 1 | 0 | 4 | 7 | 4 | 13.50 | 2.50 | 9.0 | 6.8 | 2.3 | — |
| AA | — | — | — | — | — | — | — | — | — | — | — | — | — |
| AAA | IL | 1 | 1 | 0 | 10 | 8 | 9 | 0.87 | 1.26 | 7.8 | 4.4 | 0.0 | — |

Majors / Skills

| Yr | Team | W | L | Sv | IP | H | K | ERA | WHIP | K/9 | BB/9 | HR/9 | GB/F |
|---|---|---|---|---|---|---|---|---|---|---|---|---|---|
| 07 | — | — | — | — | — | — | — | — | — | — | — | — | — |
| 08 | — | — | — | — | — | — | — | — | — | — | — | — | — |
| 09 | — | — | — | — | — | — | — | — | — | — | — | — | — |
| 10 | WAS | 0 | 3 | 0 | 26 | 30 | 12 | 5.88 | 1.58 | 4.2 | 3.8 | 1.0 | 0.8 |

| Yr | Value $1L | $2L | Pts | RAA | Luck H% | HR/fb | S% | FIP | In Rotation GS | CG | QS/DS | In Relief GR | Hld | Bln | Lead | OPS | 1st Hf | 2nd Hf | vs RH | vs LH |
|---|---|---|---|---|---|---|---|---|---|---|---|---|---|---|---|---|---|---|---|---|
| 07 | — | — | — | — | — | — | — | — | — | — | — | — | — | — | — | — | — | — | — | — |
| 08 | — | — | — | — | — | — | — | — | — | — | — | — | — | — | — | — | — | — | — | — |
| 09 | — | — | — | — | — | — | — | — | — | — | — | — | — | — | — | — | — | — | — | — |
| 10 | -$8 | -$15 | 0 | -5 | 31% | 8% | 63% | 5.05 | 5 | 0 | 0/0 | — | — | — | — | .831 | — | .831 | .774 | .883 |

Maya has a decent curveball, and he enjoyed easy success in Triple-A, but the strikeouts didn't materialize in MLB, and it is pretty clear that the Nationals overpaid for the Cuban defector. Long-term, he looks bound for the bullpen; however, the Nationals have made an investment, and so... Maya will be an SP in '11. (PB)

Competition at SP — Stats in 2010 as SP

| Thr | Player | GS | ERA | Supp | W-L |
|---|---|---|---|---|---|
| RH | Hernandez L | 33 | 3.66 | 3.5 | 10-12 |
| LH | Lannan J | 25 | 4.65 | 4.5 | 8-8 |
| RH | Stammen C | 19 | 5.06 | 4.8 | 4-4 |
| RH | Atilano L | 16 | 5.15 | 4.5 | 6-7 |

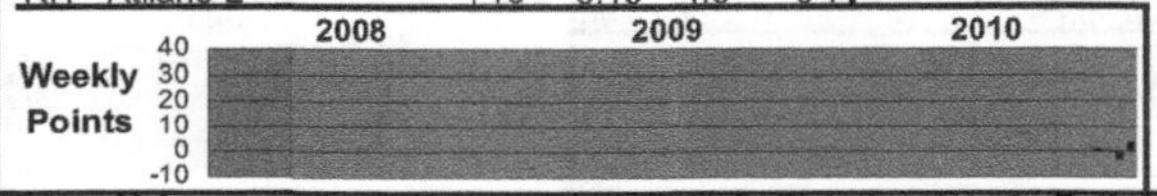


Ten-Year Trends

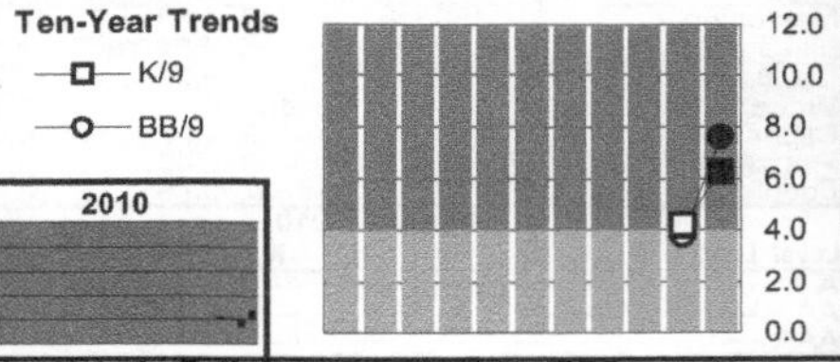


## Vin Mazzaro — 160 IP | $2 | 160 pts

SP-18, RP-6 — Owned: 3% — RH

| Player | Age | IP | W | Sv | K | ERA | WHIP | K/9 | BB/9 | $2L | Pts |
|---|---|---|---|---|---|---|---|---|---|---|---|
| **Forecast** | | | | | | | | | | | |
| Mazzaro V | 24 | 160 | 8 | 0 | 111 | 4.59 | 1.48 | 6.2 | 3.7 | $2 | 160 |
| **Mini-Browser** | Age | IP | W | Sv | K | ERA | WHIP | K/9 | BB/9 | $2L | Pts |
| Strop P | 25 | 40 | 2 | 0 | 39 | 3.18 | 1.31 | 8.8 | 3.9 | $2 | 60 |
| Wheeler D | 33 | 50 | 2 | 0 | 42 | 4.23 | 1.18 | 7.6 | 2.6 | $2 | 60 |
| Gonzalez M | 32 | 60 | 2 | 5 | 66 | 4.48 | 1.42 | 9.9 | 4.5 | $2 | 100 |
| Crain J | 29 | 60 | 2 | 0 | 49 | 3.81 | 1.34 | 7.4 | 4.0 | $2 | 70 |
| Ziegler B | 31 | 50 | 3 | 0 | 33 | 3.46 | 1.34 | 5.9 | 3.6 | $2 | 60 |

Minors (2010) / Skills

| Level | Leag | W | L | Sv | IP | H | K | ERA | WHIP | K/9 | BB/9 | HR/9 | GB/F |
|---|---|---|---|---|---|---|---|---|---|---|---|---|---|
| A | — | — | — | — | — | — | — | — | — | — | — | — | — |
| AA | — | — | — | — | — | — | — | — | — | — | — | — | — |
| AAA | PCL | 3 | 1 | 0 | 37 | 35 | 38 | 3.13 | 1.39 | 9.2 | 4.1 | 0.5 | — |

Majors / Skills

| Yr | Team | W | L | Sv | IP | H | K | ERA | WHIP | K/9 | BB/9 | HR/9 | GB/F |
|---|---|---|---|---|---|---|---|---|---|---|---|---|---|
| 07 | — | — | — | — | — | — | — | — | — | — | — | — | — |
| 08 | — | — | — | — | — | — | — | — | — | — | — | — | — |
| 09 | OAK | 4 | 9 | 0 | 91 | 120 | 59 | 5.32 | 1.74 | 5.8 | 3.8 | 1.2 | 1.0 |
| 10 | OAK | 6 | 8 | 0 | 122 | 127 | 79 | 4.27 | 1.45 | 5.8 | 3.7 | 1.4 | 1.2 |

| Yr | Value $1L | $2L | Pts | RAA | Luck H% | HR/fb | S% | FIP | In Rotation GS | CG | QS/DS | In Relief GR | Hld | Bln | Lead | OPS | 1st Hf | 2nd Hf | vs RH | vs LH |
|---|---|---|---|---|---|---|---|---|---|---|---|---|---|---|---|---|---|---|---|---|
| 07 | — | — | — | — | — | — | — | — | — | — | — | — | — | — | — | — | — | — | — | — |
| 08 | — | — | — | — | — | — | — | — | — | — | — | — | — | — | — | — | — | — | — | — |
| 09 | -$4 | -$9 | 60 | -16 | 35% | 10% | 71% | 5.00 | 17 | 0 | 4/3 | — | — | — | — | .873 | .697 | 1.034 | .836 | .899 |
| 10 | $0 | -$14 | 110 | -10 | 29% | 13% | 75% | 5.25 | 18 | 0 | 12/4 | 6 | 0 | 0 | -0.3 | .765 | .770 | .761 | .733 | .797 |

Although Mazzaro's ERA dropped by a run, his rates barely budged from his rookie season. His raw stuff is better than his numbers, but he still does not hit his locations consistently. The A's want to challenge Mazzaro to shape up, and he will be pushed this spring by Cramer, Mortensen, Outman, and Ross. (ML)

Competition at SP — Stats in 2010 as SP

| Thr | Player | GS | ERA | Supp | W-L |
|---|---|---|---|---|---|
| LH | Gonzalez G | 33 | 3.23 | 4.3 | 15-9 |
| RH | Cahill T | 30 | 2.97 | 4.6 | 18-8 |
| LH | Braden D | 30 | 3.50 | 3.3 | 11-14 |
| RH | Sheets B | 20 | 4.53 | 4.6 | 4-9 |

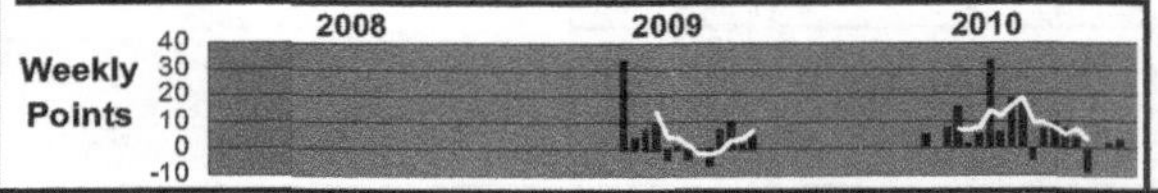


Ten-Year Trends

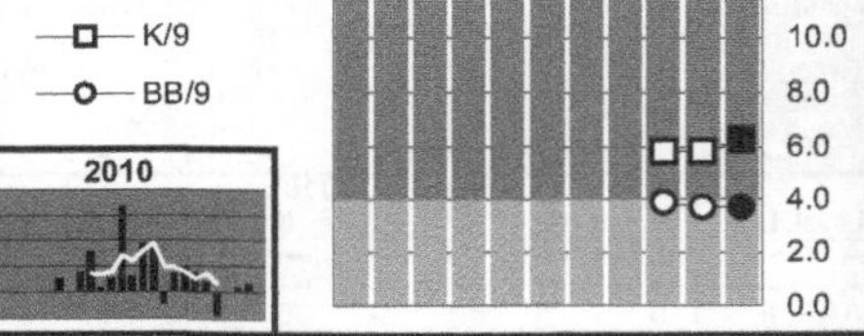


## Zach McAllister — 40 IP | $-7 | 10 pts

No MLB games played in 2010 — Owned: 0% — RH

| Player | Age | IP | W | Sv | K | ERA | WHIP | K/9 | BB/9 | $2L | Pts |
|---|---|---|---|---|---|---|---|---|---|---|---|
| **Forecast** | | | | | | | | | | | |
| McAllister Z | 23 | 40 | 2 | 0 | 19 | 7.23 | 1.76 | 4.4 | 3.7 | -$7 | 10 |
| **Mini-Browser** | Age | IP | W | Sv | K | ERA | WHIP | K/9 | BB/9 | $2L | Pts |
| Richardson D | 27 | 40 | 1 | 0 | 39 | 6.03 | 2.01 | 8.7 | 9.2 | -$6 | 20 |
| Paulino F | 27 | 100 | 3 | 0 | 87 | 5.46 | 1.55 | 7.8 | 4.2 | -$6 | 80 |
| Stewart Z | 24 | 40 | 1 | 0 | 23 | 6.44 | 1.82 | 5.1 | 5.3 | -$6 | 10 |
| Samardzija J | 26 | 60 | 3 | 0 | 43 | 5.96 | 1.65 | 6.4 | 4.4 | -$7 | 40 |
| Rogers E | 25 | 80 | 4 | 0 | 75 | 5.64 | 1.66 | 8.5 | 3.5 | -$7 | 70 |

Minors (2010) / Skills

| Level | Leag | W | L | Sv | IP | H | K | ERA | WHIP | K/9 | BB/9 | HR/9 | GB/F |
|---|---|---|---|---|---|---|---|---|---|---|---|---|---|
| A | — | — | — | — | — | — | — | — | — | — | — | — | — |
| AA | — | — | — | — | — | — | — | — | — | — | — | — | — |
| AAA | 2LG | 9 | 12 | 0 | 149 | 185 | 99 | 5.29 | 1.54 | 6.0 | 2.7 | 1.3 | — |

Majors / Skills

| Yr | Team | W | L | Sv | IP | H | K | ERA | WHIP | K/9 | BB/9 | HR/9 | GB/F |
|---|---|---|---|---|---|---|---|---|---|---|---|---|---|
| 07 | — | — | — | — | — | — | — | — | — | — | — | — | — |
| 08 | — | — | — | — | — | — | — | — | — | — | — | — | — |
| 09 | — | — | — | — | — | — | — | — | — | — | — | — | — |
| 10 | — | — | — | — | — | — | — | — | — | — | — | — | — |

| Yr | Value $1L | $2L | Pts | RAA | Luck H% | HR/fb | S% | FIP | In Rotation GS | CG | QS/DS | In Relief GR | Hld | Bln | Lead | OPS | 1st Hf | 2nd Hf | vs RH | vs LH |
|---|---|---|---|---|---|---|---|---|---|---|---|---|---|---|---|---|---|---|---|---|
| 07 | — | — | — | — | — | — | — | — | — | — | — | — | — | — | — | — | — | — | — | — |
| 08 | — | — | — | — | — | — | — | — | — | — | — | — | — | — | — | — | — | — | — | — |
| 09 | — | — | — | — | — | — | — | — | — | — | — | — | — | — | — | — | — | — | — | — |
| 10 | — | — | — | — | — | — | — | — | — | — | — | — | — | — | — | — | — | — | — | — |

McAllister had lost his luster in the Yankee system before Cleveland acquired him as a PTBNL. He held his own in Triple-A at age 22, after a strong showing in Double-A in 2009. He's a dark horse to win the #5 SP spot, but he could land a role with the Indians after a bit more honing of his skills in the minors. (BLS)

Competition at SP — Stats in 2010 as SP

| Thr | Player | GS | ERA | Supp | W-L |
|---|---|---|---|---|---|
| RH | Carmona F | 33 | 3.77 | 3.5 | 13-14 |
| RH | Masterson J | 29 | 4.78 | 4.3 | 6-12 |
| RH | Talbot M | 28 | 4.41 | 4.1 | 10-13 |
| LH | Huff D | 15 | 6.21 | 3.6 | 2-11 |

Ten-Year Trends

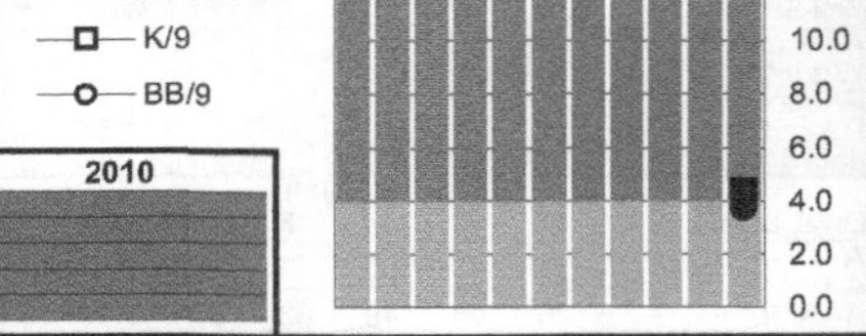

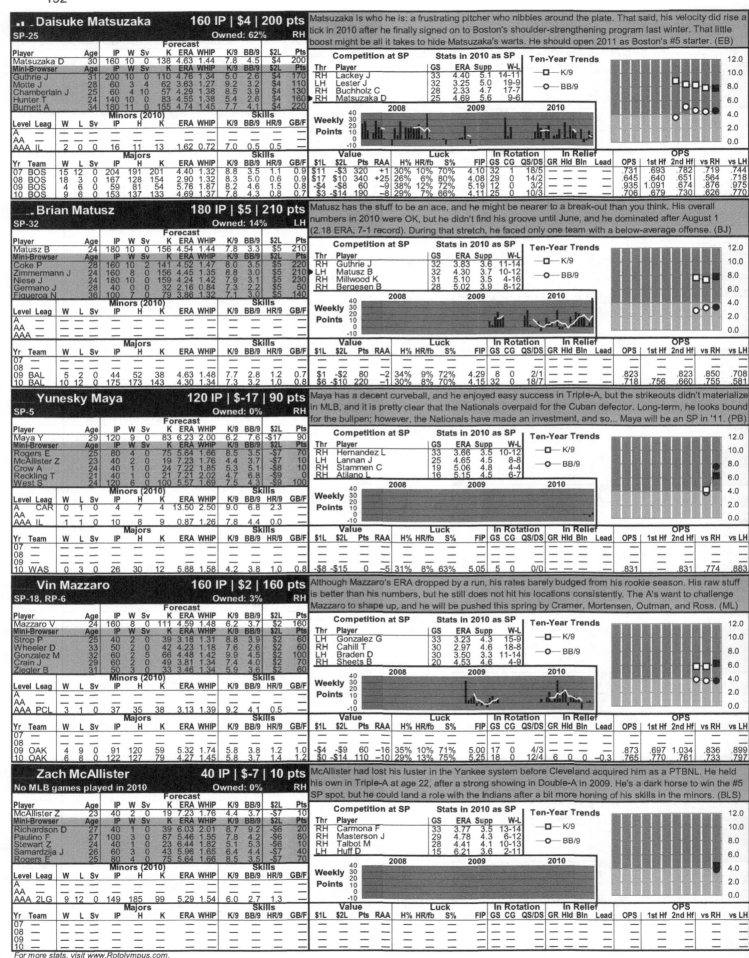

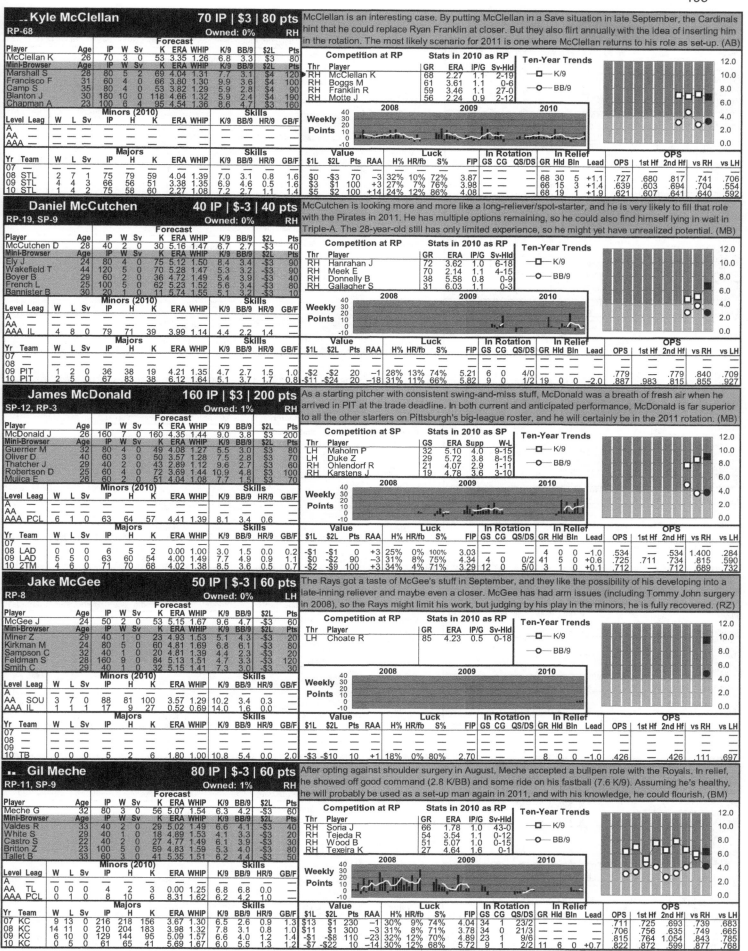

## Kyle McClellan — 70 IP | $3 | 80 pts

RP-68 — Owned: 0% — RH

| Player | Age | IP | W | Sv | K | ERA | WHIP | K/9 | BB/9 | $2L | Pts |
|---|---|---|---|---|---|---|---|---|---|---|---|
| McClellan K | 26 | 70 | 3 | 0 | 53 | 3.35 | 1.26 | 6.8 | 3.3 | $3 | 80 |
| **Mini-Browser** | **Age** | **IP** | **W** | **Sv** | **K** | **ERA** | **WHIP** | **K/9** | **BB/9** | **$2L** | **Pts** |
| Marshall S | 28 | 80 | 5 | 2 | 69 | 4.04 | 1.31 | 7.7 | 3.1 | $4 | 120 |
| Francisco F | 31 | 60 | 4 | 0 | 66 | 3.80 | 1.30 | 9.9 | 3.6 | $4 | 100 |
| Camp S | 35 | 80 | 4 | 0 | 53 | 3.82 | 1.29 | 5.9 | 2.8 | $4 | 90 |
| Blanton J | 30 | 180 | 10 | 0 | 118 | 4.66 | 1.32 | 5.9 | 2.4 | $4 | 190 |
| Chapman A | 23 | 100 | 6 | 4 | 95 | 4.54 | 1.36 | 8.6 | 4.7 | $3 | 160 |

Minors (2010) / Skills

| Level | Leag | W | L | Sv | IP | H | K | ERA | WHIP | K/9 | BB/9 | HR/9 | GB/F |
|---|---|---|---|---|---|---|---|---|---|---|---|---|---|
| A | — | — | — | — | — | — | — | — | — | — | — | — | — |
| AA | — | — | — | — | — | — | — | — | — | — | — | — | — |
| AAA | — | — | — | — | — | — | — | — | — | — | — | — | — |

Majors / Skills

| Yr | Team | W | L | Sv | IP | H | K | ERA | WHIP | K/9 | BB/9 | HR/9 | GB/F |
|---|---|---|---|---|---|---|---|---|---|---|---|---|---|
| 07 | — | — | — | — | — | — | — | — | — | — | — | — | — |
| 08 | STL | 2 | 7 | 1 | 75 | 79 | 59 | 4.04 | 1.39 | 7.0 | 3.1 | 0.8 | 1.6 |
| 09 | STL | 4 | 4 | 3 | 66 | 56 | 51 | 3.38 | 1.35 | 6.9 | 4.6 | 0.5 | 1.6 |
| 10 | STL | 1 | 4 | 2 | 75 | 58 | 60 | 2.27 | 1.08 | 7.2 | 2.7 | 1.1 | 1.4 |

McClellan is an interesting case. By putting McClellan in a Save situation in late September, the Cardinals hint that he could replace Ryan Franklin at closer. But they also flirt annually with the idea of inserting him in the rotation. The most likely scenario for 2011 is one where McClellan returns to his role as set-up. (AB)

Competition at RP / Stats in 2010 as RP

| Thr | Player | GR | ERA | IP/G | Sv-Hld |
|---|---|---|---|---|---|
| RH | McClellan K | 68 | 2.27 | 1.1 | 2-19 |
| RH | Boggs M | 61 | 3.61 | 1.1 | 0-6 |
| RH | Franklin R | 59 | 3.46 | 1.1 | 27-0 |
| RH | Motte J | 56 | 2.24 | 0.9 | 2-12 |

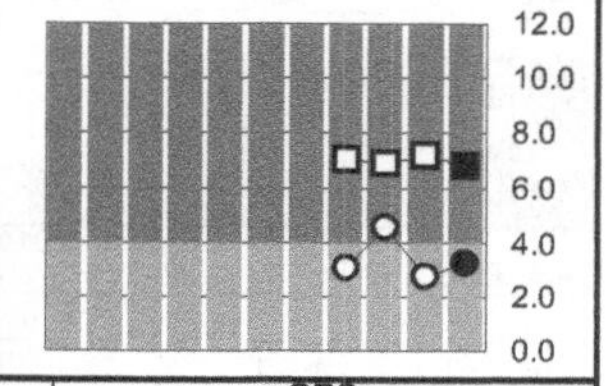


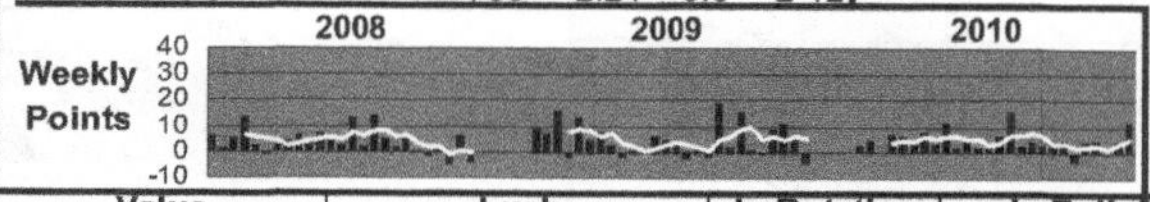


| Yr | $1L | $2L | Pts | RAA | H% | HR/fb | S% | FIP | GS | CG | QS/DS | GR | Hld | Bln | Lead | OPS | 1st Hf | 2nd Hf | vs RH | vs LH |
|---|---|---|---|---|---|---|---|---|---|---|---|---|---|---|---|---|---|---|---|---|
| | Value | | | | Luck | | | | In Rotation | | | In Relief | | | | OPS | | | | |
| 07 | — | — | — | — | — | — | — | — | — | — | — | — | — | — | — | — | — | — | — | — |
| 08 | $0 | -$3 | 70 | −3 | 32% | 10% | 72% | 3.87 | — | — | — | 68 | 30 | 5 | +1.1 | .727 | .680 | .817 | .741 | .706 |
| 09 | $3 | $1 | 100 | +3 | 27% | 7% | 76% | 3.98 | — | — | — | 66 | 15 | 3 | +1.4 | .639 | .603 | .694 | .704 | .554 |
| 10 | $5 | $2 | 100 | +14 | 24% | 12% | 86% | 4.08 | — | — | — | 68 | 19 | 1 | +1.9 | .621 | .607 | .641 | .640 | .592 |

## Daniel McCutchen — 40 IP | $-3 | 40 pts

RP-19, SP-9 — Owned: 0% — RH

| Player | Age | IP | W | Sv | K | ERA | WHIP | K/9 | BB/9 | $2L | Pts |
|---|---|---|---|---|---|---|---|---|---|---|---|
| McCutchen D | 28 | 40 | 2 | 0 | 30 | 5.16 | 1.47 | 6.7 | 2.7 | -$3 | 40 |
| **Mini-Browser** | **Age** | **IP** | **W** | **Sv** | **K** | **ERA** | **WHIP** | **K/9** | **BB/9** | **$2L** | **Pts** |
| Ely J | 24 | 80 | 4 | 0 | 75 | 5.12 | 1.50 | 8.4 | 3.4 | -$3 | 90 |
| Wakefield T | 44 | 120 | 5 | 0 | 70 | 5.28 | 1.47 | 5.3 | 3.2 | -$3 | 90 |
| Boyer B | 29 | 60 | 2 | 0 | 36 | 4.72 | 1.49 | 5.4 | 3.9 | -$3 | 40 |
| French L | 25 | 100 | 5 | 0 | 62 | 5.23 | 1.52 | 5.6 | 3.4 | -$3 | 80 |
| Bannister B | 30 | 20 | 1 | 0 | 11 | 5.74 | 1.55 | 5.1 | 3.2 | -$3 | 10 |

Minors (2010) / Skills

| Level | Leag | W | L | Sv | IP | H | K | ERA | WHIP | K/9 | BB/9 | HR/9 | GB/F |
|---|---|---|---|---|---|---|---|---|---|---|---|---|---|
| A | — | — | — | — | — | — | — | — | — | — | — | — | — |
| AA | — | — | — | — | — | — | — | — | — | — | — | — | — |
| AAA | IL | 4 | 8 | 0 | 79 | 71 | 39 | 3.99 | 1.14 | 4.4 | 2.2 | 1.4 | — |

Majors / Skills

| Yr | Team | W | L | Sv | IP | H | K | ERA | WHIP | K/9 | BB/9 | HR/9 | GB/F |
|---|---|---|---|---|---|---|---|---|---|---|---|---|---|
| 07 | — | — | — | — | — | — | — | — | — | — | — | — | — |
| 08 | — | — | — | — | — | — | — | — | — | — | — | — | — |
| 09 | PIT | 1 | 2 | 0 | 36 | 38 | 19 | 4.21 | 1.35 | 4.7 | 2.7 | 1.5 | 1.0 |
| 10 | PIT | 2 | 5 | 0 | 67 | 83 | 38 | 6.12 | 1.64 | 5.1 | 3.7 | 1.7 | 0.8 |

McCutchen is looking more and more like a long-reliever/spot-starter, and he is very likely to fill that role with the Pirates in 2011. He has multiple options remaining, so he could also find himself lying in wait in Triple-A. The 28-year-old still has only limited experience, so he might yet have unrealized potential. (MB)

Competition at RP / Stats in 2010 as RP

| Thr | Player | GR | ERA | IP/G | Sv-Hld |
|---|---|---|---|---|---|
| RH | Hanrahan J | 72 | 3.62 | 1.0 | 6-18 |
| RH | Meek E | 70 | 2.14 | 1.1 | 4-15 |
| RH | Donnelly B | 38 | 5.58 | 0.8 | 0-9 |
| RH | Gallagher S | 31 | 6.03 | 1.1 | 0-3 |

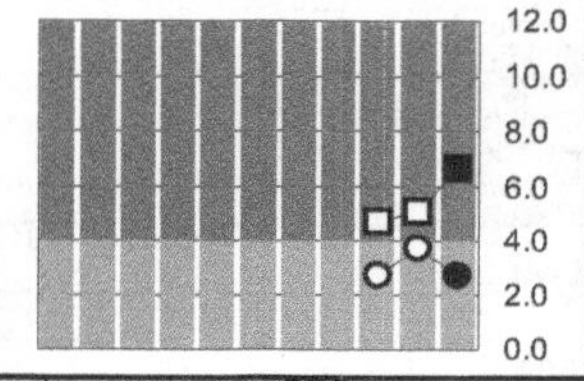


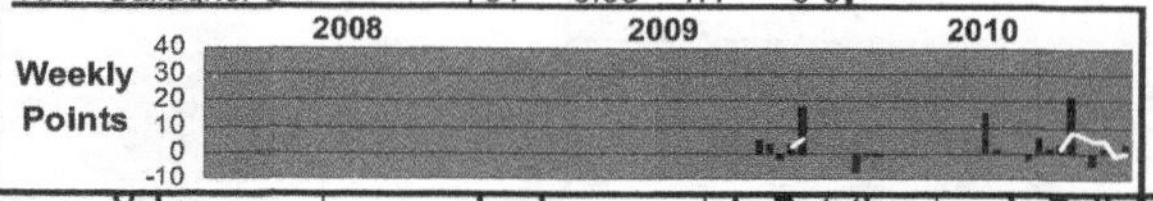


| Yr | $1L | $2L | Pts | RAA | H% | HR/fb | S% | FIP | GS | CG | QS/DS | GR | Hld | Bln | Lead | OPS | 1st Hf | 2nd Hf | vs RH | vs LH |
|---|---|---|---|---|---|---|---|---|---|---|---|---|---|---|---|---|---|---|---|---|
| | Value | | | | Luck | | | | In Rotation | | | In Relief | | | | OPS | | | | |
| 07 | — | — | — | — | — | — | — | — | — | — | — | — | — | — | — | — | — | — | — | — |
| 08 | — | — | — | — | — | — | — | — | — | — | — | — | — | — | — | — | — | — | — | — |
| 09 | -$2 | -$2 | 20 | −1 | 28% | 13% | 74% | 5.21 | 6 | 0 | 4/0 | — | — | — | — | .779 | — | .779 | .840 | .709 |
| 10 | -$11 | -$24 | 20 | −18 | 31% | 11% | 66% | 5.82 | 9 | 0 | 1/2 | 19 | 0 | 0 | −2.0 | .887 | .983 | .815 | .855 | .927 |

## James McDonald — 160 IP | $3 | 200 pts

SP-12, RP-3 — Owned: 1% — RH

| Player | Age | IP | W | Sv | K | ERA | WHIP | K/9 | BB/9 | $2L | Pts |
|---|---|---|---|---|---|---|---|---|---|---|---|
| McDonald J | 26 | 160 | 7 | 0 | 160 | 4.35 | 1.44 | 9.0 | 3.8 | $3 | 200 |
| **Mini-Browser** | **Age** | **IP** | **W** | **Sv** | **K** | **ERA** | **WHIP** | **K/9** | **BB/9** | **$2L** | **Pts** |
| Guerrier M | 32 | 80 | 4 | 0 | 49 | 4.08 | 1.27 | 5.5 | 3.0 | $3 | 80 |
| Oliver D | 40 | 60 | 3 | 0 | 50 | 3.57 | 1.28 | 7.5 | 2.8 | $3 | 70 |
| Thatcher J | 29 | 40 | 2 | 0 | 43 | 2.89 | 1.12 | 9.6 | 2.7 | $3 | 60 |
| Robertson D | 25 | 60 | 4 | 0 | 72 | 3.69 | 1.44 | 10.9 | 4.8 | $3 | 100 |
| Mujica E | 26 | 60 | 2 | 0 | 51 | 4.04 | 1.08 | 7.7 | 1.5 | $3 | 70 |

Minors (2010) / Skills

| Level | Leag | W | L | Sv | IP | H | K | ERA | WHIP | K/9 | BB/9 | HR/9 | GB/F |
|---|---|---|---|---|---|---|---|---|---|---|---|---|---|
| A | — | — | — | — | — | — | — | — | — | — | — | — | — |
| AA | — | — | — | — | — | — | — | — | — | — | — | — | — |
| AAA | PCL | 6 | 1 | 0 | 63 | 64 | 57 | 4.41 | 1.39 | 8.1 | 3.4 | 0.6 | — |

Majors / Skills

| Yr | Team | W | L | Sv | IP | H | K | ERA | WHIP | K/9 | BB/9 | HR/9 | GB/F |
|---|---|---|---|---|---|---|---|---|---|---|---|---|---|
| 07 | — | — | — | — | — | — | — | — | — | — | — | — | — |
| 08 | LAD | 0 | 0 | 0 | 6 | 5 | 2 | 0.00 | 1.00 | 3.0 | 1.5 | 0.0 | 0.2 |
| 09 | LAD | 5 | 5 | 0 | 63 | 60 | 54 | 4.00 | 1.49 | 7.7 | 4.9 | 0.9 | 1.1 |
| 10 | 2TM | 4 | 6 | 0 | 71 | 70 | 68 | 4.02 | 1.38 | 8.5 | 3.6 | 0.5 | 0.7 |

As a starting pitcher with consistent swing-and-miss stuff, McDonald was a breath of fresh air when he arrived in PIT at the trade deadline. In both current and anticipated performance, McDonald is far superior to all the other starters on Pittsburgh's big-league roster, and he will certainly be in the 2011 rotation. (MB)

Competition at SP / Stats in 2010 as SP

| Thr | Player | GS | ERA | Supp | W-L |
|---|---|---|---|---|---|
| LH | Maholm P | 32 | 5.10 | 4.0 | 9-15 |
| LH | Duke Z | 29 | 5.72 | 3.8 | 8-15 |
| RH | Ohlendorf R | 21 | 4.07 | 2.9 | 1-11 |
| RH | Karstens J | 19 | 4.78 | 3.6 | 3-10 |

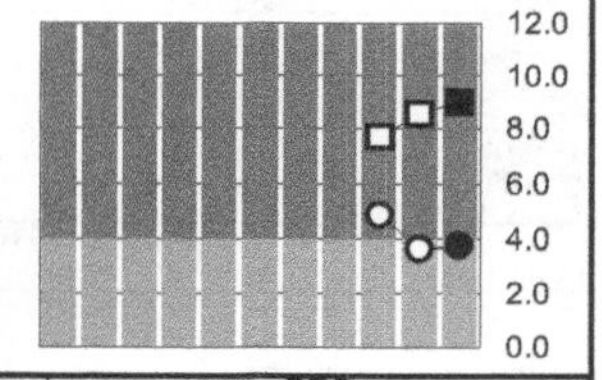


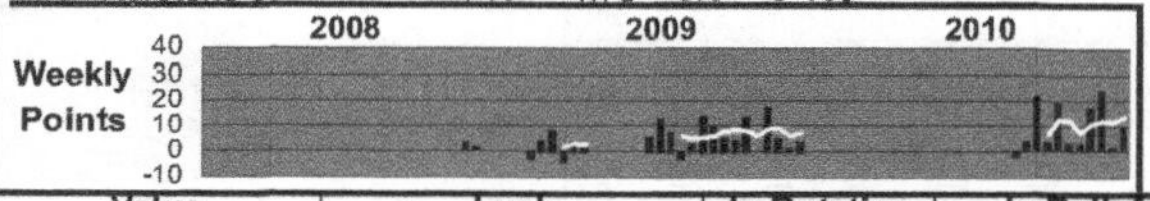


| Yr | $1L | $2L | Pts | RAA | H% | HR/fb | S% | FIP | GS | CG | QS/DS | GR | Hld | Bln | Lead | OPS | 1st Hf | 2nd Hf | vs RH | vs LH |
|---|---|---|---|---|---|---|---|---|---|---|---|---|---|---|---|---|---|---|---|---|
| | Value | | | | Luck | | | | In Rotation | | | In Relief | | | | OPS | | | | |
| 07 | — | — | — | — | — | — | — | — | — | — | — | — | — | — | — | — | — | — | — | — |
| 08 | -$1 | -$1 | 0 | +3 | 25% | 0% | 100% | 3.03 | — | — | — | 4 | 0 | 0 | −1.0 | .534 | — | .534 | 1.400 | .284 |
| 09 | $0 | -$2 | 90 | −3 | 31% | 8% | 75% | 4.34 | 4 | 0 | 0/2 | 41 | 5 | 0 | +0.6 | .725 | .711 | .734 | .815 | .590 |
| 10 | -$2 | -$9 | 100 | +3 | 34% | 4% | 71% | 3.29 | 12 | 0 | 5/0 | 3 | 1 | 0 | +0.1 | .712 | — | .712 | .689 | .732 |

## Jake McGee — 50 IP | $-3 | 60 pts

RP-8 — Owned: 0% — LH

| Player | Age | IP | W | Sv | K | ERA | WHIP | K/9 | BB/9 | $2L | Pts |
|---|---|---|---|---|---|---|---|---|---|---|---|
| McGee J | 24 | 50 | 2 | 0 | 53 | 5.15 | 1.67 | 9.6 | 4.7 | -$3 | 60 |
| **Mini-Browser** | **Age** | **IP** | **W** | **Sv** | **K** | **ERA** | **WHIP** | **K/9** | **BB/9** | **$2L** | **Pts** |
| Miner Z | 29 | 40 | 1 | 0 | 23 | 4.93 | 1.53 | 5.1 | 4.3 | -$3 | 20 |
| Kirkman M | 24 | 80 | 5 | 0 | 60 | 4.81 | 1.69 | 6.8 | 6.1 | -$3 | 80 |
| Sampson C | 32 | 40 | 1 | 0 | 20 | 4.81 | 1.39 | 4.4 | 2.3 | -$3 | 20 |
| Feldman S | 28 | 160 | 9 | 0 | 84 | 5.13 | 1.51 | 4.7 | 3.3 | -$3 | 120 |
| Smith C | 29 | 40 | 1 | 0 | 32 | 5.15 | 1.41 | 7.3 | 3.0 | -$3 | 30 |

Minors (2010) / Skills

| Level | Leag | W | L | Sv | IP | H | K | ERA | WHIP | K/9 | BB/9 | HR/9 | GB/F |
|---|---|---|---|---|---|---|---|---|---|---|---|---|---|
| A | — | — | — | — | — | — | — | — | — | — | — | — | — |
| AA | SOU | 3 | 7 | 0 | 88 | 81 | 100 | 3.57 | 1.29 | 10.2 | 3.4 | 0.3 | — |
| AAA | IL | 1 | 1 | 1 | 17 | 9 | 27 | 0.52 | 0.69 | 14.0 | 1.6 | 0.0 | — |

Majors / Skills

| Yr | Team | W | L | Sv | IP | H | K | ERA | WHIP | K/9 | BB/9 | HR/9 | GB/F |
|---|---|---|---|---|---|---|---|---|---|---|---|---|---|
| 07 | — | — | — | — | — | — | — | — | — | — | — | — | — |
| 08 | — | — | — | — | — | — | — | — | — | — | — | — | — |
| 09 | — | — | — | — | — | — | — | — | — | — | — | — | — |
| 10 | TB | 0 | 0 | 0 | 5 | 2 | 6 | 1.80 | 1.00 | 10.8 | 5.4 | 0.0 | 2.0 |

The Rays got a taste of McGee's stuff in September, and they like the possibility of his developing into a late-inning reliever and maybe even a closer. McGee has had arm issues (including Tommy John surgery in 2008), so the Rays might limit his work, but judging by his play in the minors, he is fully recovered. (RZ)

Competition at RP / Stats in 2010 as RP

| Thr | Player | GR | ERA | IP/G | Sv-Hld |
|---|---|---|---|---|---|
| LH | Choate R | 85 | 4.23 | 0.5 | 0-18 |

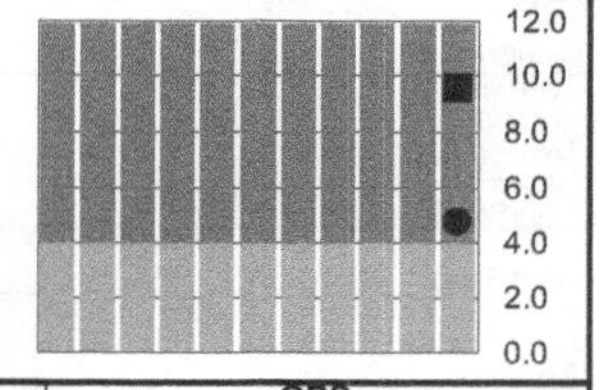


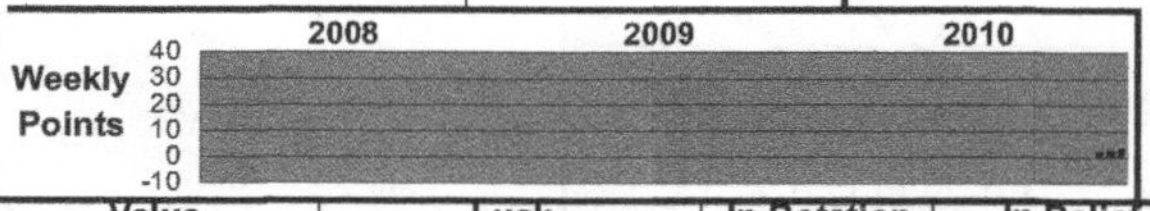


| Yr | $1L | $2L | Pts | RAA | H% | HR/fb | S% | FIP | GS | CG | QS/DS | GR | Hld | Bln | Lead | OPS | 1st Hf | 2nd Hf | vs RH | vs LH |
|---|---|---|---|---|---|---|---|---|---|---|---|---|---|---|---|---|---|---|---|---|
| | Value | | | | Luck | | | | In Rotation | | | In Relief | | | | OPS | | | | |
| 07 | — | — | — | — | — | — | — | — | — | — | — | — | — | — | — | — | — | — | — | — |
| 08 | — | — | — | — | — | — | — | — | — | — | — | — | — | — | — | — | — | — | — | — |
| 09 | — | — | — | — | — | — | — | — | — | — | — | — | — | — | — | — | — | — | — | — |
| 10 | -$3 | -$10 | 10 | +1 | 18% | 0% | 80% | 2.70 | — | — | — | 8 | 0 | 0 | −1.0 | .426 | — | .426 | .111 | .697 |

## Gil Meche — 80 IP | $-3 | 60 pts

RP-11, SP-9 — Owned: 1% — RH

| Player | Age | IP | W | Sv | K | ERA | WHIP | K/9 | BB/9 | $2L | Pts |
|---|---|---|---|---|---|---|---|---|---|---|---|
| Meche G | 32 | 80 | 3 | 0 | 56 | 5.07 | 1.54 | 6.3 | 4.2 | -$3 | 60 |
| **Mini-Browser** | **Age** | **IP** | **W** | **Sv** | **K** | **ERA** | **WHIP** | **K/9** | **BB/9** | **$2L** | **Pts** |
| Valdes R | 33 | 40 | 2 | 0 | 29 | 5.02 | 1.49 | 6.6 | 4.1 | -$3 | 40 |
| White S | 29 | 40 | 1 | 0 | 18 | 4.89 | 1.53 | 4.1 | 3.3 | -$3 | 20 |
| Castro S | 22 | 40 | 2 | 0 | 27 | 4.77 | 1.49 | 6.1 | 3.9 | -$3 | 30 |
| Britton Z | 23 | 100 | 5 | 0 | 59 | 4.83 | 1.59 | 5.3 | 4.0 | -$3 | 80 |
| Tallet B | 33 | 60 | 3 | 0 | 41 | 5.35 | 1.51 | 6.2 | 4.4 | -$3 | 50 |

Minors (2010) / Skills

| Level | Leag | W | L | Sv | IP | H | K | ERA | WHIP | K/9 | BB/9 | HR/9 | GB/F |
|---|---|---|---|---|---|---|---|---|---|---|---|---|---|
| A | — | — | — | — | — | — | — | — | — | — | — | — | — |
| AA | TL | 0 | 0 | 0 | 4 | 2 | 3 | 0.00 | 1.25 | 6.8 | 6.8 | 0.0 | — |
| AAA | PCL | 0 | 1 | 0 | 8 | 10 | 6 | 8.31 | 1.62 | 6.2 | 4.2 | 1.0 | — |

Majors / Skills

| Yr | Team | W | L | Sv | IP | H | K | ERA | WHIP | K/9 | BB/9 | HR/9 | GB/F |
|---|---|---|---|---|---|---|---|---|---|---|---|---|---|
| 07 | KC | 9 | 13 | 0 | 216 | 218 | 156 | 3.67 | 1.30 | 6.5 | 2.6 | 0.9 | 1.3 |
| 08 | KC | 14 | 11 | 0 | 210 | 204 | 183 | 3.98 | 1.32 | 7.8 | 3.1 | 0.8 | 1.0 |
| 09 | KC | 6 | 10 | 0 | 129 | 144 | 95 | 5.09 | 1.57 | 6.6 | 4.0 | 1.2 | 1.4 |
| 10 | KC | 0 | 5 | 0 | 61 | 65 | 41 | 5.69 | 1.67 | 6.0 | 5.5 | 1.3 | 1.2 |

After opting against shoulder surgery in August, Meche accepted a bullpen role with the Royals. In relief, he showed off good command (2.8 K/BB) and some ride on his fastball (7.6 K/9). Assuming he's healthy, he will probably be used as a set-up man again in 2011, and with his knowledge, he could flourish. (BM)

Competition at RP / Stats in 2010 as RP

| Thr | Player | GR | ERA | IP/G | Sv-Hld |
|---|---|---|---|---|---|
| RH | Soria J | 66 | 1.78 | 1.0 | 43-0 |
| RH | Tejeda R | 54 | 3.54 | 1.1 | 0-12 |
| RH | Wood B | 51 | 5.07 | 1.0 | 0-15 |
| RH | Texeira K | 27 | 4.64 | 1.6 | 0-1 |

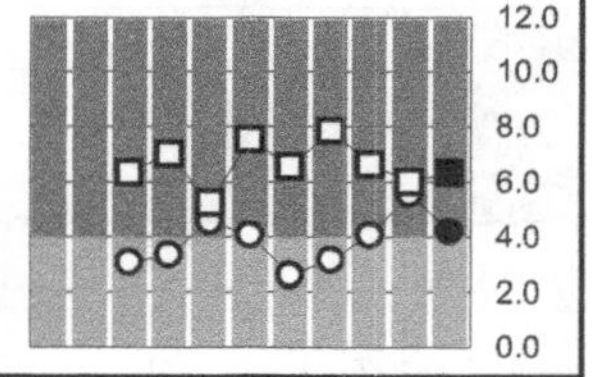


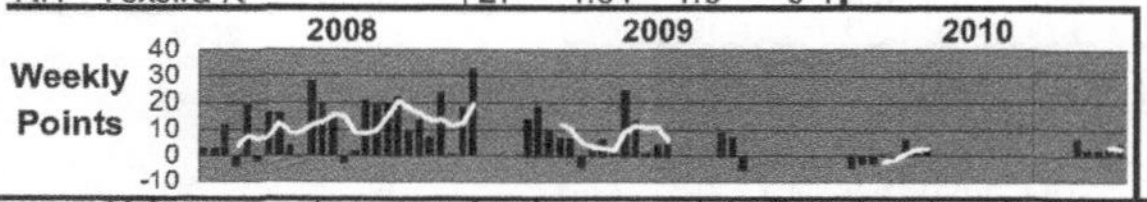


| Yr | $1L | $2L | Pts | RAA | H% | HR/fb | S% | FIP | GS | CG | QS/DS | GR | Hld | Bln | Lead | OPS | 1st Hf | 2nd Hf | vs RH | vs LH |
|---|---|---|---|---|---|---|---|---|---|---|---|---|---|---|---|---|---|---|---|---|
| | Value | | | | Luck | | | | In Rotation | | | In Relief | | | | OPS | | | | |
| 07 | $13 | $1 | 230 | −1 | 30% | 9% | 74% | 4.04 | 34 | 1 | 23/2 | — | — | — | — | .711 | .725 | .693 | .739 | .683 |
| 08 | $11 | $1 | 300 | −3 | 31% | 8% | 71% | 3.78 | 34 | 0 | 21/3 | — | — | — | — | .706 | .756 | .635 | .749 | .665 |
| 09 | -$1 | -$8 | 110 | −23 | 32% | 12% | 70% | 4.89 | 23 | 1 | 9/6 | — | — | — | — | .815 | .764 | 1.054 | .843 | .785 |
| 10 | -$7 | -$22 | 10 | −14 | 30% | 12% | 68% | 5.72 | 9 | 1 | 2/2 | 11 | 6 | 0 | +0.7 | .822 | .872 | .599 | .877 | .768 |

*For more stats, visit www.Rotolympus.com.*

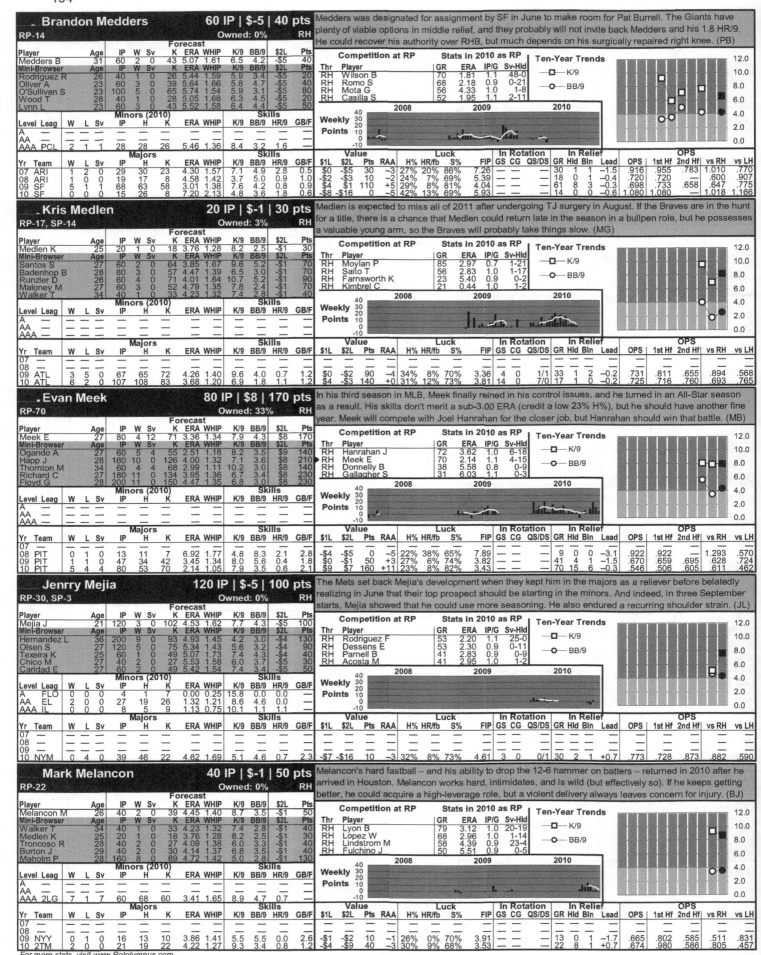

## Brandon Medders — 60 IP | $-5 | 40 pts

RP-14 — Owned: 0% — RH

Medders was designated for assignment by SF in June to make room for Pat Burrell. The Giants have plenty of viable options in middle relief, and they probably will not invite back Medders and his 1.8 HR/9. He could recover his authority over RHB, but much depends on his surgically repaired right knee. (PB)

| Player | Age | IP | W | Sv | K | ERA | WHIP | K/9 | BB/9 | $2L | Pts |
|---|---|---|---|---|---|---|---|---|---|---|---|
| Medders B | 31 | 60 | 2 | 0 | 43 | 5.07 | 1.61 | 6.5 | 4.2 | -$5 | 40 |
| **Mini-Browser** | **Age** | **IP** | **W** | **Sv** | **K** | **ERA** | **WHIP** | **K/9** | **BB/9** | **$2L** | **Pts** |
| Rodriguez R | 26 | 40 | 1 | 0 | 26 | 5.44 | 1.59 | 5.9 | 3.4 | -$5 | 20 |
| Oliver A | 23 | 60 | 3 | 0 | 39 | 5.64 | 1.66 | 5.8 | 4.7 | -$5 | 40 |
| O'Sullivan S | 23 | 100 | 5 | 0 | 65 | 5.74 | 1.54 | 5.9 | 3.1 | -$5 | 80 |
| Wood T | 28 | 40 | 1 | 0 | 28 | 5.05 | 1.68 | 6.3 | 4.5 | -$5 | 20 |
| Lynn L | 23 | 60 | 3 | 0 | 43 | 5.52 | 1.58 | 6.4 | 4.4 | -$5 | 50 |

| Level | Leag | W | L | Sv | IP | H | K | ERA | WHIP | K/9 | BB/9 | HR/9 | GB/F |
|---|---|---|---|---|---|---|---|---|---|---|---|---|---|
| A | — | — | — | — | — | — | — | — | — | — | — | — | — |
| AA | — | — | — | — | — | — | — | — | — | — | — | — | — |
| AAA | PCL | 2 | 1 | 1 | 28 | 28 | 26 | 5.46 | 1.36 | 8.4 | 3.2 | 1.6 | — |

| Yr | Team | W | L | Sv | IP | H | K | ERA | WHIP | K/9 | BB/9 | HR/9 | GB/F | $1L | $2L | Pts | RAA | H% | HR/fb | S% | FIP | GS | CG | QS/DS | GR | Hld | Bln | Lead | OPS | 1st Hf | 2nd Hf | vs RH | vs LH |
|---|---|---|---|---|---|---|---|---|---|---|---|---|---|---|---|---|---|---|---|---|---|---|---|---|---|---|---|---|---|---|---|---|---|
| 07 | ARI | 1 | 2 | 0 | 29 | 30 | 23 | 4.30 | 1.57 | 7.1 | 4.9 | 2.8 | 0.5 | $0 | -$5 | 30 | –3 | 27% | 20% | 86% | 7.26 | — | — | — | 30 | 1 | 1 | –1.5 | .916 | .955 | .783 | 1.010 | .770 |
| 08 | ARI | 1 | 0 | 0 | 19 | 17 | 8 | 4.58 | 1.42 | 3.7 | 5.0 | 0.9 | 1.0 | -$2 | -$3 | 10 | –2 | 24% | 7% | 69% | 5.39 | — | — | — | 18 | 0 | 1 | –0.4 | .720 | .720 | — | .600 | .907 |
| 09 | SF | 5 | 1 | 1 | 68 | 63 | 58 | 3.01 | 1.38 | 7.6 | 4.2 | 0.8 | 0.9 | $4 | $1 | 110 | +5 | 29% | 8% | 81% | 4.04 | — | — | — | 61 | 8 | 3 | –0.3 | .698 | .733 | .658 | .647 | .775 |
| 10 | SF | 0 | 0 | 0 | 15 | 26 | 8 | 7.20 | 2.13 | 4.8 | 3.6 | 1.8 | 0.6 | -$8 | -$16 | 0 | –5 | 42% | 13% | 69% | 5.93 | — | — | — | 14 | 0 | 0 | –0.6 | 1.080 | 1.080 | — | 1.018 | 1.166 |

**Competition at RP — Stats in 2010 as RP**

| Thr | Player | GR | ERA | IP/G | Sv-Hld |
|---|---|---|---|---|---|
| RH | Wilson B | 70 | 1.81 | 1.1 | 48-0 |
| RH | Romo S | 68 | 2.18 | 0.9 | 0-21 |
| RH | Mota G | 56 | 4.33 | 1.0 | 1-8 |
| RH | Casilla S | 52 | 1.95 | 1.1 | 2-11 |

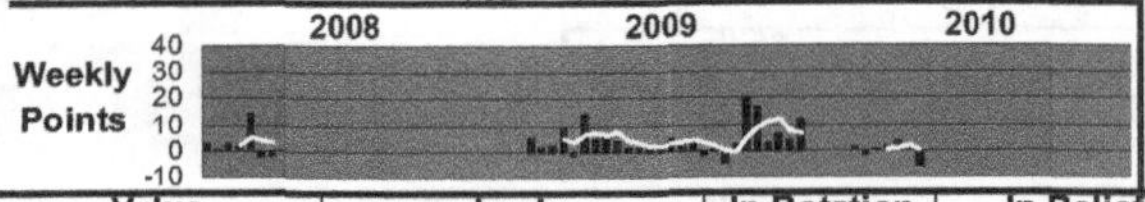


**Ten-Year Trends** — K/9, BB/9

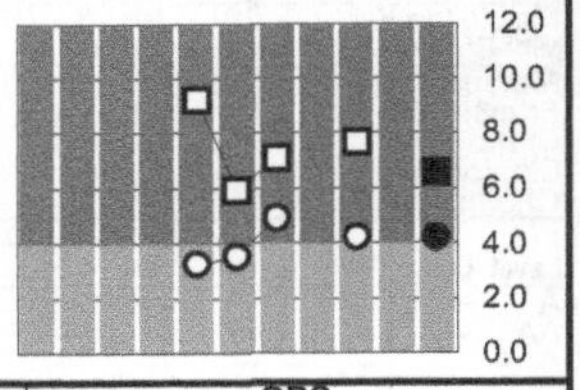


## Kris Medlen — 20 IP | $-1 | 30 pts

RP-17, SP-14 — Owned: 3% — RH

Medlen is expected to miss all of 2011 after undergoing TJ surgery in August. If the Braves are in the hunt for a title, there is a chance that Medlen could return late in the season in a bullpen role, but he possesses a valuable young arm, so the Braves will probably take things slow. (MG)

| Player | Age | IP | W | Sv | K | ERA | WHIP | K/9 | BB/9 | $2L | Pts |
|---|---|---|---|---|---|---|---|---|---|---|---|
| Medlen K | 25 | 20 | 1 | 0 | 18 | 3.76 | 1.28 | 8.2 | 2.5 | -$1 | 30 |
| **Mini-Browser** | **Age** | **IP** | **W** | **Sv** | **K** | **ERA** | **WHIP** | **K/9** | **BB/9** | **$2L** | **Pts** |
| Santos S | 27 | 60 | 2 | 0 | 64 | 3.85 | 1.67 | 9.6 | 5.2 | -$1 | 70 |
| Badenhop B | 28 | 80 | 3 | 0 | 57 | 4.47 | 1.39 | 6.5 | 3.0 | -$1 | 70 |
| Runzler D | 26 | 60 | 4 | 0 | 71 | 4.01 | 1.64 | 10.7 | 5.2 | -$1 | 90 |
| Maloney M | 27 | 60 | 3 | 0 | 52 | 4.79 | 1.35 | 7.8 | 2.4 | -$1 | 70 |
| Walker T | 34 | 40 | 1 | 0 | 33 | 4.23 | 1.32 | 7.4 | 2.8 | -$1 | 40 |

| Level | Leag | W | L | Sv | IP | H | K | ERA | WHIP | K/9 | BB/9 | HR/9 | GB/F |
|---|---|---|---|---|---|---|---|---|---|---|---|---|---|
| A | — | — | — | — | — | — | — | — | — | — | — | — | — |
| AA | — | — | — | — | — | — | — | — | — | — | — | — | — |
| AAA | — | — | — | — | — | — | — | — | — | — | — | — | — |

| Yr | Team | W | L | Sv | IP | H | K | ERA | WHIP | K/9 | BB/9 | HR/9 | GB/F | $1L | $2L | Pts | RAA | H% | HR/fb | S% | FIP | GS | CG | QS/DS | GR | Hld | Bln | Lead | OPS | 1st Hf | 2nd Hf | vs RH | vs LH |
|---|---|---|---|---|---|---|---|---|---|---|---|---|---|---|---|---|---|---|---|---|---|---|---|---|---|---|---|---|---|---|---|---|---|
| 07 | — | — | — | — | — | — | — | — | — | — | — | — | — | — | — | — | — | — | — | — | — | — | — | — | — | — | — | — | — | — | — | — | — |
| 08 | — | — | — | — | — | — | — | — | — | — | — | — | — | — | — | — | — | — | — | — | — | — | — | — | — | — | — | — | — | — | — | — | — |
| 09 | ATL | 3 | 5 | 0 | 67 | 65 | 72 | 4.26 | 1.40 | 9.6 | 4.0 | 0.7 | 1.2 | $0 | -$2 | 90 | –4 | 34% | 8% | 70% | 3.36 | 4 | 0 | 1/1 | 33 | 1 | 2 | –0.2 | .731 | .811 | .655 | .894 | .568 |
| 10 | ATL | 6 | 2 | 0 | 107 | 108 | 83 | 3.68 | 1.20 | 6.9 | 1.8 | 1.1 | 1.2 | $4 | -$3 | 140 | +0 | 31% | 12% | 73% | 3.81 | 14 | 0 | 7/0 | 17 | 1 | 0 | –0.2 | .725 | .716 | .760 | .693 | .765 |

**Competition at RP — Stats in 2010 as RP**

| Thr | Player | GR | ERA | IP/G | Sv-Hld |
|---|---|---|---|---|---|
| RH | Moylan P | 85 | 2.97 | 0.7 | 1-21 |
| RH | Saito T | 56 | 2.83 | 1.0 | 1-17 |
| RH | Farnsworth K | 23 | 5.40 | 0.9 | 0-2 |
| RH | Kimbrel C | 21 | 0.44 | 1.0 | 1-2 |

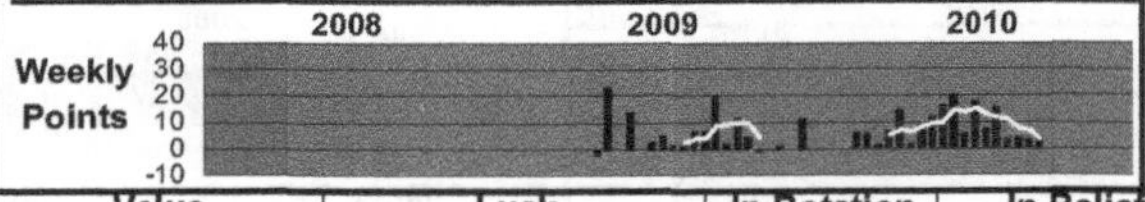


**Ten-Year Trends** — K/9, BB/9

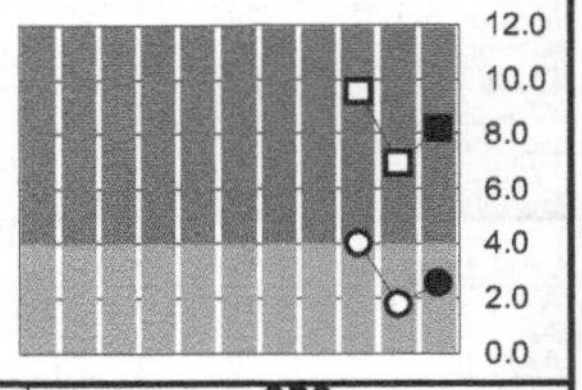


## Evan Meek — 80 IP | $8 | 170 pts

RP-70 — Owned: 33% — RH

In his third season in MLB, Meek finally reined in his control issues, and he turned in an All-Star season as a result. His skills don't merit a sub-3.00 ERA (credit a low 23% H%), but he should have another fine year. Meek will compete with Joel Hanrahan for the closer job, but Hanrahan should win that battle. (MB)

| Player | Age | IP | W | Sv | K | ERA | WHIP | K/9 | BB/9 | $2L | Pts |
|---|---|---|---|---|---|---|---|---|---|---|---|
| Meek E | 27 | 80 | 4 | 12 | 71 | 3.36 | 1.34 | 7.9 | 4.3 | $8 | 170 |
| **Mini-Browser** | **Age** | **IP** | **W** | **Sv** | **K** | **ERA** | **WHIP** | **K/9** | **BB/9** | **$2L** | **Pts** |
| Ogando A | 27 | 60 | 5 | 4 | 55 | 2.51 | 1.18 | 8.2 | 3.5 | $9 | 140 |
| Happ J | 28 | 160 | 10 | 0 | 126 | 4.00 | 1.32 | 7.1 | 3.6 | $8 | 210 |
| Thornton M | 34 | 60 | 4 | 4 | 68 | 2.99 | 1.11 | 10.2 | 3.0 | $8 | 140 |
| Richard C | 27 | 180 | 11 | 0 | 134 | 3.95 | 1.36 | 6.7 | 3.4 | $8 | 230 |
| Floyd G | 28 | 200 | 11 | 0 | 150 | 4.47 | 1.35 | 6.8 | 3.0 | $8 | 230 |

| Level | Leag | W | L | Sv | IP | H | K | ERA | WHIP | K/9 | BB/9 | HR/9 | GB/F |
|---|---|---|---|---|---|---|---|---|---|---|---|---|---|
| A | — | — | — | — | — | — | — | — | — | — | — | — | — |
| AA | — | — | — | — | — | — | — | — | — | — | — | — | — |
| AAA | — | — | — | — | — | — | — | — | — | — | — | — | — |

| Yr | Team | W | L | Sv | IP | H | K | ERA | WHIP | K/9 | BB/9 | HR/9 | GB/F | $1L | $2L | Pts | RAA | H% | HR/fb | S% | FIP | GS | CG | QS/DS | GR | Hld | Bln | Lead | OPS | 1st Hf | 2nd Hf | vs RH | vs LH |
|---|---|---|---|---|---|---|---|---|---|---|---|---|---|---|---|---|---|---|---|---|---|---|---|---|---|---|---|---|---|---|---|---|---|
| 07 | — | — | — | — | — | — | — | — | — | — | — | — | — | — | — | — | — | — | — | — | — | — | — | — | — | — | — | — | — | — | — | — | — |
| 08 | PIT | 0 | 1 | 0 | 13 | 11 | 7 | 6.92 | 1.77 | 4.8 | 8.3 | 2.1 | 2.8 | -$4 | -$5 | 0 | –5 | 22% | 38% | 65% | 7.89 | — | — | — | 9 | 0 | 0 | –3.1 | .922 | .922 | — | 1.293 | .570 |
| 09 | PIT | 1 | 1 | 0 | 47 | 34 | 42 | 3.45 | 1.34 | 8.0 | 5.6 | 0.4 | 1.8 | $0 | -$1 | 50 | +3 | 27% | 6% | 74% | 3.82 | — | — | — | 41 | 4 | 1 | –1.5 | .670 | .659 | .695 | .628 | .724 |
| 10 | PIT | 5 | 4 | 4 | 80 | 53 | 70 | 2.14 | 1.05 | 7.9 | 3.5 | 0.6 | 2.1 | $9 | $7 | 160 | +11 | 23% | 8% | 82% | 3.43 | — | — | — | 70 | 15 | 6 | –0.3 | .546 | .506 | .605 | .611 | .462 |

**Competition at RP — Stats in 2010 as RP**

| Thr | Player | GR | ERA | IP/G | Sv-Hld |
|---|---|---|---|---|---|
| RH | Hanrahan J | 72 | 3.62 | 1.0 | 6-18 |
| RH | Meek E | 70 | 2.14 | 1.1 | 4-15 |
| RH | Donnelly B | 38 | 5.58 | 0.8 | 0-9 |
| RH | Gallagher S | 31 | 6.03 | 1.1 | 0-3 |

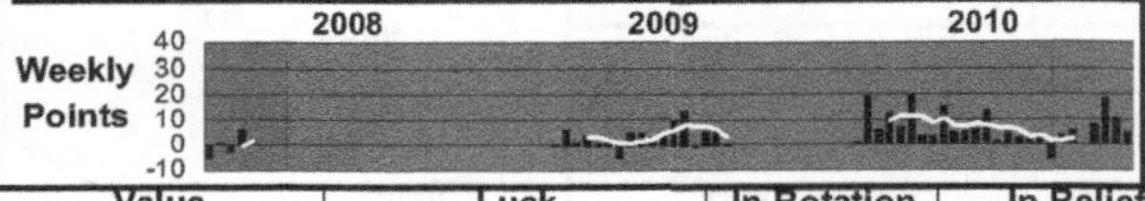


**Ten-Year Trends** — K/9, BB/9

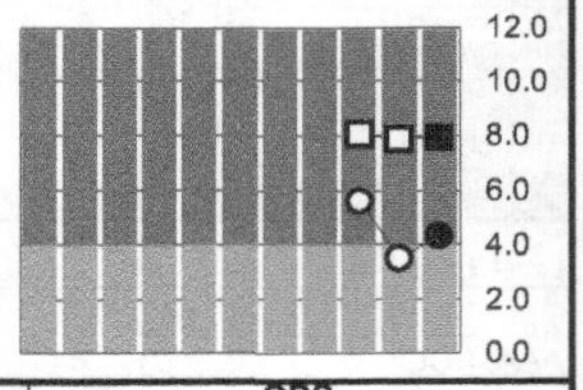


## Jenrry Mejia — 120 IP | $-5 | 100 pts

RP-30, SP-3 — Owned: 0% — RH

The Mets set back Mejia's development when they kept him in the majors as a reliever before belatedly realizing in June that their top prospect should be starting in the minors. And indeed, in three September starts, Mejia showed that he could use more seasoning. He also endured a recurring shoulder strain. (JL)

| Player | Age | IP | W | Sv | K | ERA | WHIP | K/9 | BB/9 | $2L | Pts |
|---|---|---|---|---|---|---|---|---|---|---|---|
| Mejia J | 21 | 120 | 3 | 0 | 102 | 4.53 | 1.62 | 7.7 | 4.3 | -$5 | 100 |
| **Mini-Browser** | **Age** | **IP** | **W** | **Sv** | **K** | **ERA** | **WHIP** | **K/9** | **BB/9** | **$2L** | **Pts** |
| Hernandez L | 36 | 200 | 9 | 0 | 93 | 4.93 | 1.45 | 4.2 | 3.0 | -$4 | 130 |
| Olsen S | 27 | 120 | 5 | 0 | 75 | 5.34 | 1.43 | 5.6 | 3.2 | -$4 | 90 |
| Texeira K | 25 | 60 | 1 | 0 | 49 | 5.07 | 1.73 | 7.4 | 4.3 | -$4 | 40 |
| Chico M | 27 | 40 | 2 | 0 | 27 | 5.53 | 1.58 | 6.0 | 3.7 | -$5 | 30 |
| Caridad E | 27 | 60 | 2 | 0 | 49 | 5.42 | 1.54 | 7.4 | 3.4 | -$5 | 50 |

| Level | Leag | W | L | Sv | IP | H | K | ERA | WHIP | K/9 | BB/9 | HR/9 | GB/F |
|---|---|---|---|---|---|---|---|---|---|---|---|---|---|
| A | FLO | 0 | 0 | 0 | 4 | 1 | 7 | 0.00 | 0.25 | 15.8 | 0.0 | 0.0 | — |
| AA | EL | 2 | 0 | 0 | 27 | 19 | 26 | 1.32 | 1.21 | 8.6 | 4.6 | 0.0 | — |
| AAA | IL | 0 | 0 | 0 | 8 | 5 | 9 | 1.13 | 0.75 | 10.1 | 1.1 | 1.1 | — |

| Yr | Team | W | L | Sv | IP | H | K | ERA | WHIP | K/9 | BB/9 | HR/9 | GB/F | $1L | $2L | Pts | RAA | H% | HR/fb | S% | FIP | GS | CG | QS/DS | GR | Hld | Bln | Lead | OPS | 1st Hf | 2nd Hf | vs RH | vs LH |
|---|---|---|---|---|---|---|---|---|---|---|---|---|---|---|---|---|---|---|---|---|---|---|---|---|---|---|---|---|---|---|---|---|---|
| 07 | — | — | — | — | — | — | — | — | — | — | — | — | — | — | — | — | — | — | — | — | — | — | — | — | — | — | — | — | — | — | — | — | — |
| 08 | — | — | — | — | — | — | — | — | — | — | — | — | — | — | — | — | — | — | — | — | — | — | — | — | — | — | — | — | — | — | — | — | — |
| 09 | — | — | — | — | — | — | — | — | — | — | — | — | — | — | — | — | — | — | — | — | — | — | — | — | — | — | — | — | — | — | — | — | — |
| 10 | NYM | 0 | 4 | 0 | 39 | 46 | 22 | 4.62 | 1.69 | 5.1 | 4.6 | 0.7 | 2.3 | -$7 | -$16 | 10 | –3 | 32% | 8% | 73% | 4.61 | 3 | 0 | 0/1 | 30 | 2 | 1 | +0.7 | .773 | .728 | .873 | .882 | .590 |

**Competition at RP — Stats in 2010 as RP**

| Thr | Player | GR | ERA | IP/G | Sv-Hld |
|---|---|---|---|---|---|
| RH | Rodriguez F | 53 | 2.20 | 1.1 | 25-0 |
| RH | Dessens E | 53 | 2.30 | 0.9 | 0-11 |
| RH | Parnell B | 41 | 2.83 | 0.9 | 0-9 |
| RH | Acosta M | 41 | 2.95 | 1.0 | 1-2 |

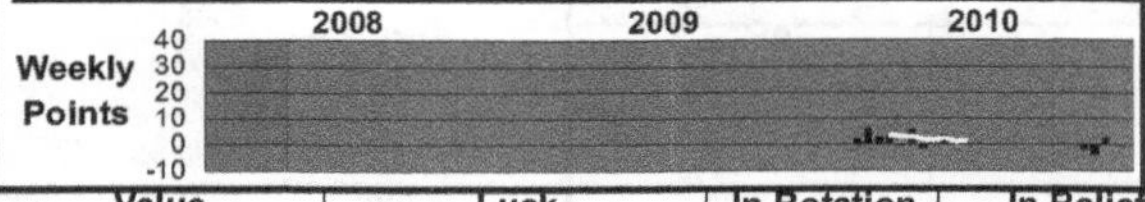


**Ten-Year Trends** — K/9, BB/9

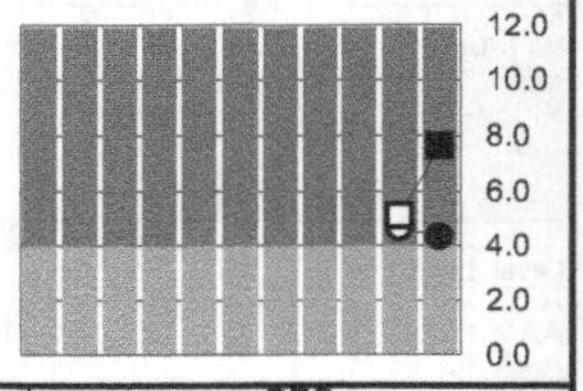


## Mark Melancon — 40 IP | $-1 | 50 pts

RP-22 — Owned: 0% — RH

Melancon's hard fastball – and his ability to drop the 12-6 hammer on batters – returned in 2010 after he arrived in Houston. Melancon works hard, intimidates, and is wild (but effectively so). If he keeps getting better, he could acquire a high-leverage role, but a violent delivery always leaves concern for injury. (BJ)

| Player | Age | IP | W | Sv | K | ERA | WHIP | K/9 | BB/9 | $2L | Pts |
|---|---|---|---|---|---|---|---|---|---|---|---|
| Melancon M | 26 | 40 | 2 | 0 | 39 | 4.45 | 1.40 | 8.7 | 3.5 | -$1 | 50 |
| **Mini-Browser** | **Age** | **IP** | **W** | **Sv** | **K** | **ERA** | **WHIP** | **K/9** | **BB/9** | **$2L** | **Pts** |
| Walker T | 34 | 40 | 1 | 0 | 33 | 4.23 | 1.32 | 7.4 | 2.8 | -$1 | 40 |
| Medlen K | 25 | 20 | 1 | 0 | 18 | 3.76 | 1.28 | 8.2 | 2.5 | -$1 | 30 |
| Troncoso R | 28 | 40 | 2 | 0 | 27 | 4.09 | 1.38 | 6.0 | 3.3 | -$1 | 40 |
| Burton J | 29 | 40 | 2 | 0 | 30 | 4.14 | 1.37 | 6.8 | 3.5 | -$1 | 40 |
| Maholm P | 28 | 160 | 8 | 0 | 89 | 4.72 | 1.42 | 5.0 | 2.8 | -$1 | 130 |

| Level | Leag | W | L | Sv | IP | H | K | ERA | WHIP | K/9 | BB/9 | HR/9 | GB/F |
|---|---|---|---|---|---|---|---|---|---|---|---|---|---|
| A | — | — | — | — | — | — | — | — | — | — | — | — | — |
| AA | — | — | — | — | — | — | — | — | — | — | — | — | — |
| AAA | 2LG | 7 | 1 | 7 | 60 | 68 | 60 | 3.41 | 1.65 | 8.9 | 4.7 | 0.7 | — |

| Yr | Team | W | L | Sv | IP | H | K | ERA | WHIP | K/9 | BB/9 | HR/9 | GB/F | $1L | $2L | Pts | RAA | H% | HR/fb | S% | FIP | GS | CG | QS/DS | GR | Hld | Bln | Lead | OPS | 1st Hf | 2nd Hf | vs RH | vs LH |
|---|---|---|---|---|---|---|---|---|---|---|---|---|---|---|---|---|---|---|---|---|---|---|---|---|---|---|---|---|---|---|---|---|---|
| 07 | — | — | — | — | — | — | — | — | — | — | — | — | — | — | — | — | — | — | — | — | — | — | — | — | — | — | — | — | — | — | — | — | — |
| 08 | — | — | — | — | — | — | — | — | — | — | — | — | — | — | — | — | — | — | — | — | — | — | — | — | — | — | — | — | — | — | — | — | — |
| 09 | NYY | 0 | 1 | 0 | 16 | 13 | 10 | 3.86 | 1.41 | 5.5 | 5.5 | 0.0 | 2.6 | -$1 | -$2 | 10 | –1 | 26% | 0% | 70% | 3.91 | — | — | — | 13 | 0 | 1 | –1.7 | .665 | .802 | .585 | .511 | .831 |
| 10 | 2TM | 2 | 0 | 0 | 21 | 19 | 22 | 4.22 | 1.27 | 9.3 | 3.4 | 0.8 | 1.2 | -$4 | -$9 | 40 | –3 | 30% | 9% | 68% | 3.53 | — | — | — | 22 | 8 | 1 | +0.7 | .674 | .980 | .586 | .805 | .457 |

**Competition at RP — Stats in 2010 as RP**

| Thr | Player | GR | ERA | IP/G | Sv-Hld |
|---|---|---|---|---|---|
| RH | Lyon B | 79 | 3.12 | 1.0 | 20-19 |
| RH | Lopez W | 68 | 2.96 | 1.0 | 1-14 |
| RH | Lindstrom M | 58 | 4.39 | 0.9 | 23-4 |
| RH | Fulchino J | 50 | 5.51 | 0.9 | 0-5 |

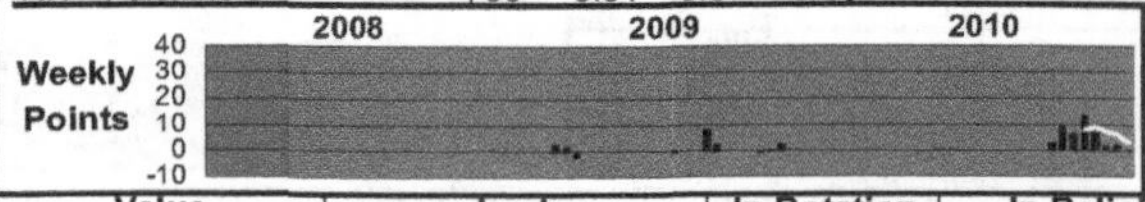


**Ten-Year Trends** — K/9, BB/9

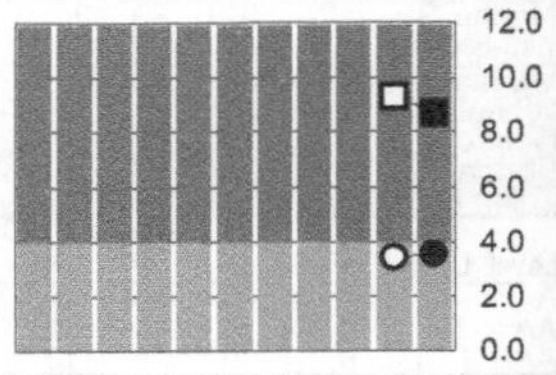

## Cla Meredith — 40 IP | $-2 | 30 pts

RP-21 — Owned: 0% — RH

Moving out of San Diego hasn't helped Meredith, who has been killed by the long ball (7 HR in 43 IP) since relocating to Baltimore. It does not help that both his K/9 and GB/F are ticking down. Meredith's poor rates during his residency in Triple-A indicate that he is well and truly lost, and possibly hurt. (BJ)

| Player | Age | IP | W | Sv | K | ERA | WHIP | K/9 | BB/9 | $2L | Pts |
|---|---|---|---|---|---|---|---|---|---|---|---|
| Meredith C | 27 | 40 | 2 | 0 | 22 | 4.80 | 1.45 | 4.9 | 2.9 | -$2 | 30 |
| **Mini-Browser** | **Age** | **IP** | **W** | **Sv** | **K** | **ERA** | **WHIP** | **K/9** | **BB/9** | **$2L** | **Pts** |
| Corpas M | 28 | 20 | 1 | 0 | 13 | 4.34 | 1.33 | 6.0 | 2.6 | -$2 | 20 |
| Elbert S | 25 | 40 | 2 | 0 | 48 | 4.59 | 1.51 | 10.8 | 4.2 | -$2 | 50 |
| Schlereth D | 24 | 40 | 2 | 0 | 46 | 4.33 | 1.72 | 10.3 | 6.1 | -$2 | 50 |
| Marte D | 36 | 20 | 1 | 0 | 18 | 4.83 | 1.43 | 7.9 | 4.8 | -$2 | 20 |
| Cormier L | 30 | 40 | 2 | 0 | 20 | 4.43 | 1.52 | 4.4 | 4.1 | -$2 | 30 |

Minors (2010) / Skills

| Level | Leag | W | L | Sv | IP | H | K | ERA | WHIP | K/9 | BB/9 | HR/9 | GB/F |
|---|---|---|---|---|---|---|---|---|---|---|---|---|---|
| A | — | — | — | — | — | — | — | — | — | — | — | — | — |
| AA | — | — | — | — | — | — | — | — | — | — | — | — | — |
| AAA | IL | 1 | 2 | 0 | 27 | 32 | 17 | 6.00 | 1.63 | 5.7 | 4.0 | 0.7 | — |

Competition at RP / Stats in 2010 as RP

| Thr | Player | GR | ERA | IP/G | Sv-Hld |
|---|---|---|---|---|---|
| RH | Albers M | 62 | 4.52 | 1.2 | 0-7 |
| RH | Simon A | 49 | 4.93 | 1.0 | 17-1 |
| RH | Uehara K | 43 | 2.86 | 1.0 | 13-6 |
| RH | Berken J | 41 | 3.03 | 1.5 | 0-7 |

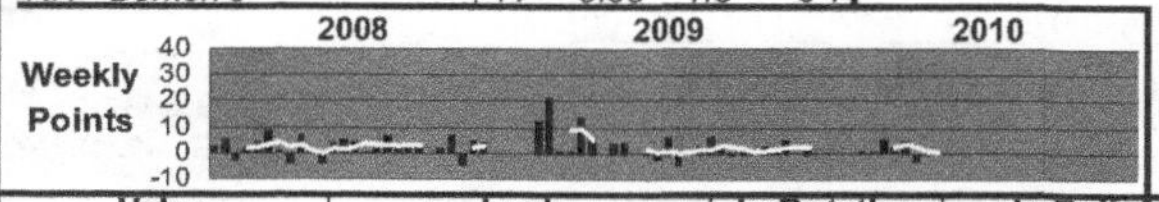


Ten-Year Trends — K/9, BB/9

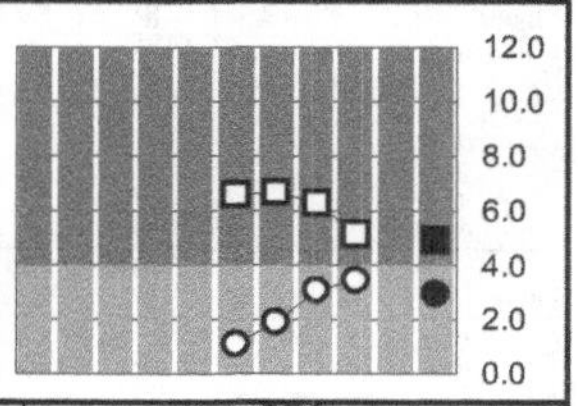


Majors / Skills

| Yr | Team | W | L | Sv | IP | H | K | ERA | WHIP | K/9 | BB/9 | HR/9 | GB/F |
|---|---|---|---|---|---|---|---|---|---|---|---|---|---|
| 07 | SD | 5 | 6 | 0 | 79 | 94 | 59 | 3.50 | 1.39 | 6.7 | 1.9 | 0.7 | 5.3 |
| 08 | SD | 0 | 3 | 0 | 70 | 79 | 49 | 4.09 | 1.46 | 6.3 | 3.1 | 0.8 | 3.9 |
| 09 | 2TM | 4 | 2 | 0 | 65 | 73 | 37 | 3.99 | 1.50 | 5.1 | 3.4 | 0.6 | 3.0 |
| 10 | BAL | 0 | 2 | 1 | 15 | 18 | 7 | 5.40 | 1.47 | 4.2 | 2.4 | 2.4 | 1.5 |

Value / Luck / In Rotation / In Relief / OPS

| Yr | $1L | $2L | Pts | RAA | H% | HR/fb | S% | FIP | GS | CG | QS/DS | GR | Hld | Bln | Lead | OPS | 1st Hf | 2nd Hf | vs RH | vs LH |
|---|---|---|---|---|---|---|---|---|---|---|---|---|---|---|---|---|---|---|---|---|
| 07 | $3 | -$1 | 100 | −2 | 35% | 17% | 76% | 3.34 | — | — | — | 80 | 10 | 5 | +0.6 | .721 | .733 | .708 | .695 | .757 |
| 08 | -$2 | -$5 | 40 | −2 | 34% | 16% | 73% | 3.94 | — | — | — | 73 | 11 | 6 | 0.0 | .736 | .740 | .730 | .677 | .848 |
| 09 | -$2 | -$3 | 60 | −2 | 33% | 9% | 73% | 4.06 | — | — | — | 64 | 4 | 3 | −2.4 | .747 | .761 | .730 | .790 | .691 |
| 10 | -$4 | -$12 | 10 | −2 | 28% | 21% | 72% | 6.63 | — | — | — | 21 | 3 | 1 | −1.5 | .932 | .932 | — | .952 | .881 |

## Kam Mickolio — 40 IP | $-3 | 40 pts

RP-3 — Owned: 0% — RH

Before being derailed by a strained shoulder, Mickolio in 2010 was seen by the Orioles as a future closer. He can be dominating, but he has to be healthy, and now things need to break right in 2011 just for him to make the bullpen. If given a chance, Kam might delight in 2011 as much as he disappointed in 2010. (BJ)

| Player | Age | IP | W | Sv | K | ERA | WHIP | K/9 | BB/9 | $2L | Pts |
|---|---|---|---|---|---|---|---|---|---|---|---|
| Mickolio K | 26 | 40 | 1 | 0 | 44 | 4.94 | 1.69 | 9.8 | 5.0 | -$3 | 40 |
| **Mini-Browser** | **Age** | **IP** | **W** | **Sv** | **K** | **ERA** | **WHIP** | **K/9** | **BB/9** | **$2L** | **Pts** |
| Kirkman M | 24 | 80 | 5 | 0 | 60 | 4.81 | 1.69 | 6.8 | 6.1 | -$3 | 80 |
| Sampson C | 32 | 40 | 1 | 0 | 20 | 4.81 | 1.39 | 4.4 | 2.3 | -$3 | 20 |
| Feldman S | 28 | 160 | 9 | 0 | 84 | 5.13 | 1.51 | 4.7 | 3.3 | -$3 | 120 |
| Smith C | 29 | 40 | 1 | 0 | 32 | 5.15 | 1.41 | 7.3 | 3.0 | -$3 | 30 |
| McGee J | 24 | 50 | 2 | 0 | 53 | 5.15 | 1.67 | 9.6 | 4.7 | -$3 | 60 |

Minors (2010) / Skills

| Level | Leag | W | L | Sv | IP | H | K | ERA | WHIP | K/9 | BB/9 | HR/9 | GB/F |
|---|---|---|---|---|---|---|---|---|---|---|---|---|---|
| A | NYP | 1 | 0 | 0 | 5 | 1 | 7 | 1.80 | 0.40 | 12.6 | 1.8 | 1.8 | — |
| AA | — | — | — | — | — | — | — | — | — | — | — | — | — |
| AAA | IL | 4 | 3 | 0 | 35 | 44 | 48 | 6.37 | 1.73 | 12.2 | 4.3 | 1.0 | — |

Competition at RP / Stats in 2010 as RP

| Thr | Player | GR | ERA | IP/G | Sv-Hld |
|---|---|---|---|---|---|
| RH | Albers M | 62 | 4.52 | 1.2 | 0-7 |
| RH | Simon A | 49 | 4.93 | 1.0 | 17-1 |
| RH | Uehara K | 43 | 2.86 | 1.0 | 13-6 |
| RH | Berken J | 41 | 3.03 | 1.5 | 0-7 |

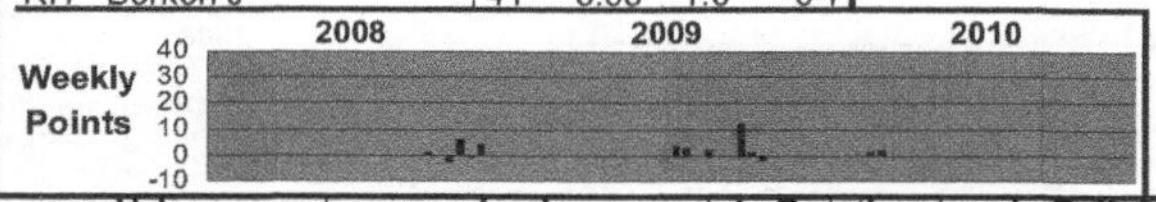


Ten-Year Trends — K/9, BB/9

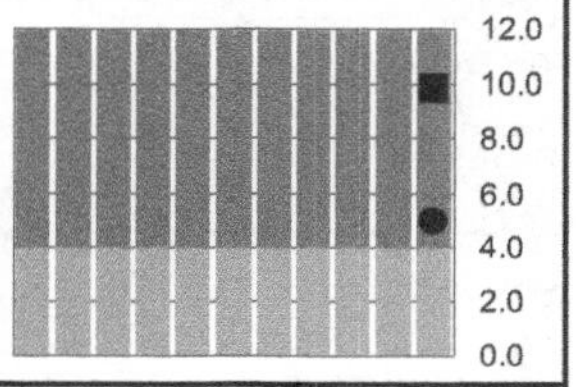


Majors / Skills

| Yr | Team | W | L | Sv | IP | H | K | ERA | WHIP | K/9 | BB/9 | HR/9 | GB/F |
|---|---|---|---|---|---|---|---|---|---|---|---|---|---|
| 07 | — | — | — | — | — | — | — | — | — | — | — | — | — |
| 08 | BAL | 0 | 1 | 0 | 7 | 8 | 8 | 5.87 | 1.57 | 9.4 | 4.7 | 0.0 | 0.8 |
| 09 | BAL | 0 | 2 | 0 | 13 | 11 | 14 | 2.63 | 1.32 | 9.2 | 4.6 | 0.0 | 1.1 |
| 10 | BAL | 0 | 0 | 0 | 3 | 5 | 4 | 7.36 | 2.18 | 9.8 | 7.4 | 2.5 | 0.3 |

Value / Luck / In Rotation / In Relief / OPS

| Yr | $1L | $2L | Pts | RAA | H% | HR/fb | S% | FIP | GS | CG | QS/DS | GR | Hld | Bln | Lead | OPS | 1st Hf | 2nd Hf | vs RH | vs LH |
|---|---|---|---|---|---|---|---|---|---|---|---|---|---|---|---|---|---|---|---|---|
| 07 | — | — | — | — | — | — | — | — | — | — | — | — | — | — | — | — | — | — | — | — |
| 08 | -$2 | -$3 | 0 | −2 | 36% | 0% | 58% | 2.78 | — | — | — | 9 | 0 | 1 | −1.8 | .743 | — | .743 | .921 | .536 |
| 09 | -$1 | -$2 | 10 | +2 | 29% | 0% | 78% | 2.79 | — | — | — | 11 | 2 | 0 | 0.0 | .565 | .000 | .635 | .795 | .301 |
| 10 | -$4 | -$12 | 0 | −1 | 36% | 14% | 71% | 7.12 | — | — | — | 3 | 0 | 0 | −3.7 | 1.046 | 1.046 | — | 1.250 | .833 |

## Jose Mijares — 60 IP | $1 | 80 pts

RP-47 — Owned: 1% — LH

The Twins would not have spent millions of dollars down the stretch for a few weeks of Brian Fuentes if they trusted Mijares as their top lefty reliever. Jose was hurt for much of 2010, and when he could pitch, he was far less effective than before, especially versus LHB. That said, he will probably be back in 2011. (NN)

| Player | Age | IP | W | Sv | K | ERA | WHIP | K/9 | BB/9 | $2L | Pts |
|---|---|---|---|---|---|---|---|---|---|---|---|
| Mijares J | 26 | 60 | 3 | 0 | 56 | 3.97 | 1.43 | 8.3 | 3.6 | $1 | 80 |
| **Mini-Browser** | **Age** | **IP** | **W** | **Sv** | **K** | **ERA** | **WHIP** | **K/9** | **BB/9** | **$2L** | **Pts** |
| Fuentes B | 35 | 40 | 2 | 0 | 37 | 3.60 | 1.29 | 8.4 | 3.9 | $1 | 60 |
| Masterson J | 26 | 180 | 8 | 0 | 148 | 4.63 | 1.51 | 7.4 | 4.1 | $1 | 180 |
| Hammel J | 28 | 180 | 10 | 0 | 130 | 4.80 | 1.38 | 6.5 | 2.5 | $1 | 190 |
| Young C | 31 | 80 | 4 | 0 | 60 | 4.26 | 1.34 | 6.8 | 4.1 | $1 | 90 |
| Walden J | 23 | 40 | 2 | 13 | 44 | 5.06 | 1.67 | 9.9 | 4.2 | $1 | 110 |

Minors (2010) / Skills

| Level | Leag | W | L | Sv | IP | H | K | ERA | WHIP | K/9 | BB/9 | HR/9 | GB/F |
|---|---|---|---|---|---|---|---|---|---|---|---|---|---|
| A | — | — | — | — | — | — | — | — | — | — | — | — | — |
| AA | — | — | — | — | — | — | — | — | — | — | — | — | — |
| AAA | IL | 0 | 0 | 0 | 1 | 6 | 2 | 27.00 | 4.20 | 10.8 | 5.4 | 5.4 | — |

Competition at RP / Stats in 2010 as RP

| Thr | Player | GR | ERA | IP/G | Sv-Hld |
|---|---|---|---|---|---|
| ▶ LH | Mijares J | 47 | 3.31 | 0.7 | 0-9 |
| LH | Mahay R | 41 | 3.44 | 0.8 | 0-2 |
| LH | Duensing B | 40 | 1.80 | 1.1 | 0-9 |
| LH | Perkins G | 12 | 5.29 | 1.4 | 0-0 |

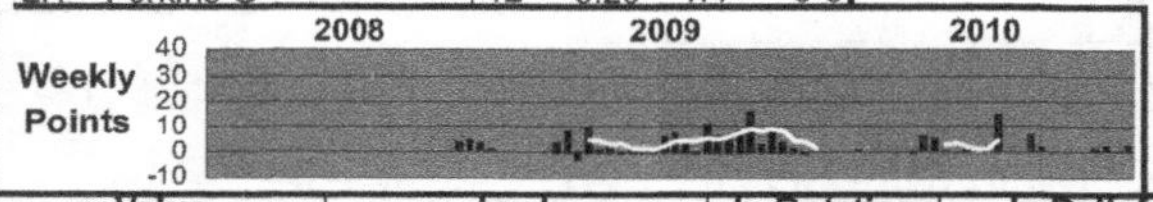


Ten-Year Trends — K/9, BB/9

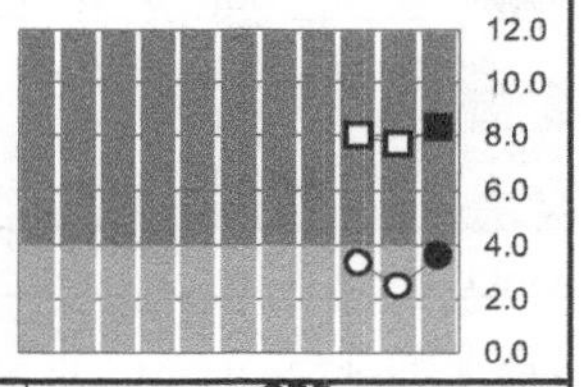


Majors / Skills

| Yr | Team | W | L | Sv | IP | H | K | ERA | WHIP | K/9 | BB/9 | HR/9 | GB/F |
|---|---|---|---|---|---|---|---|---|---|---|---|---|---|
| 07 | — | — | — | — | — | — | — | — | — | — | — | — | — |
| 08 | MIN | 0 | 1 | 0 | 10 | 3 | 5 | 0.87 | 0.29 | 4.4 | 0.0 | 0.0 | 0.8 |
| 09 | MIN | 2 | 2 | 0 | 61 | 50 | 55 | 2.34 | 1.18 | 8.0 | 3.4 | 1.0 | 0.7 |
| 10 | MIN | 1 | 1 | 0 | 32 | 34 | 28 | 3.31 | 1.32 | 7.7 | 2.5 | 1.1 | 0.6 |

Value / Luck / In Rotation / In Relief / OPS

| Yr | $1L | $2L | Pts | RAA | H% | HR/fb | S% | FIP | GS | CG | QS/DS | GR | Hld | Bln | Lead | OPS | 1st Hf | 2nd Hf | vs RH | vs LH |
|---|---|---|---|---|---|---|---|---|---|---|---|---|---|---|---|---|---|---|---|---|
| 07 | — | — | — | — | — | — | — | — | — | — | — | — | — | — | — | — | — | — | — | — |
| 08 | $1 | $1 | 10 | +4 | 11% | 0% | 67% | 2.33 | — | — | — | 10 | 2 | 0 | −0.2 | .206 | — | .206 | .150 | .286 |
| 09 | $5 | $3 | 80 | +11 | 26% | 8% | 86% | 4.11 | — | — | — | 71 | 27 | 1 | +1.0 | .649 | .651 | .646 | .791 | .480 |
| 10 | -$1 | -$9 | 40 | +1 | 32% | 7% | 79% | 4.00 | — | — | — | 47 | 9 | 0 | +0.4 | .768 | .722 | .823 | .761 | .776 |

## Trever Miller — 40 IP | $0 | 50 pts

RP-57 — Owned: 0% — LH

Miller's 2011 option vested in 2010 after he made 45 appearances and ended the year with a sound arm. Miller is the Cards' only returning left-handed specialist (since Dennys Reyes will be a free agent), so he figures to continue being tapped for high-leverage situations against opposing teams' toughest LHB. (AB)

| Player | Age | IP | W | Sv | K | ERA | WHIP | K/9 | BB/9 | $2L | Pts |
|---|---|---|---|---|---|---|---|---|---|---|---|
| Miller T | 37 | 40 | 2 | 0 | 34 | 3.90 | 1.29 | 7.6 | 3.5 | $0 | 50 |
| **Mini-Browser** | **Age** | **IP** | **W** | **Sv** | **K** | **ERA** | **WHIP** | **K/9** | **BB/9** | **$2L** | **Pts** |
| Luebke C | 26 | 80 | 4 | 0 | 82 | 4.41 | 1.46 | 9.2 | 3.1 | $0 | 110 |
| Kelley S | 26 | 45 | 3 | 0 | 43 | 4.52 | 1.41 | 8.6 | 3.1 | $0 | 60 |
| Chen B | 33 | 160 | 10 | 0 | 115 | 5.06 | 1.48 | 6.4 | 3.7 | $0 | 170 |
| Frieri E | 25 | 60 | 3 | 0 | 69 | 4.07 | 1.48 | 10.3 | 4.2 | $0 | 90 |
| Wang C | 31 | 100 | 6 | 0 | 47 | 4.49 | 1.37 | 4.2 | 3.0 | $0 | 90 |

Minors (2010) / Skills

| Level | Leag | W | L | Sv | IP | H | K | ERA | WHIP | K/9 | BB/9 | HR/9 | GB/F |
|---|---|---|---|---|---|---|---|---|---|---|---|---|---|
| A | — | — | — | — | — | — | — | — | — | — | — | — | — |
| AA | — | — | — | — | — | — | — | — | — | — | — | — | — |
| AAA | — | — | — | — | — | — | — | — | — | — | — | — | — |

Competition at RP / Stats in 2010 as RP

| Thr | Player | GR | ERA | IP/G | Sv-Hld |
|---|---|---|---|---|---|
| LH | Reyes D | 59 | 3.55 | 0.6 | 1-6 |
| ▶ LH | Miller T | 57 | 4.00 | 0.6 | 0-11 |

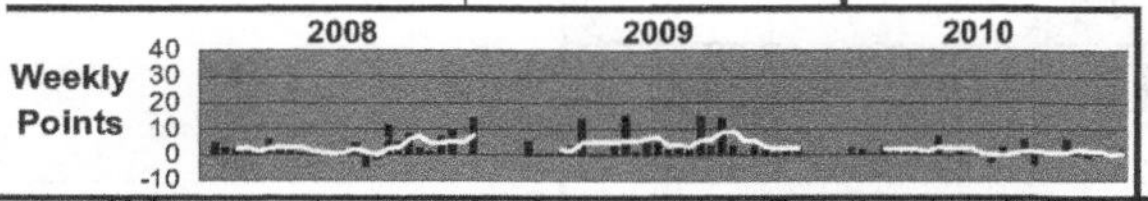


Ten-Year Trends — K/9, BB/9

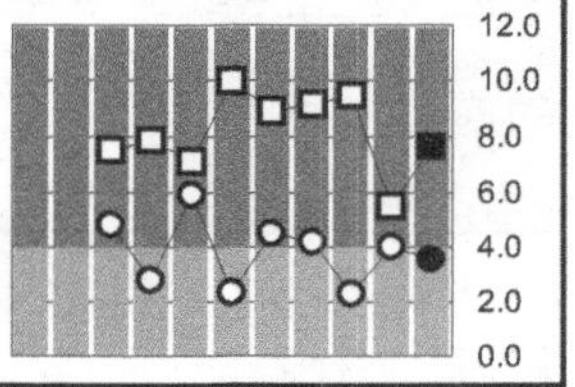


Majors / Skills

| Yr | Team | W | L | Sv | IP | H | K | ERA | WHIP | K/9 | BB/9 | HR/9 | GB/F |
|---|---|---|---|---|---|---|---|---|---|---|---|---|---|
| 07 | HOU | 0 | 0 | 1 | 46 | 45 | 46 | 4.86 | 1.47 | 8.9 | 4.5 | 1.2 | 0.7 |
| 08 | TB | 2 | 0 | 2 | 43 | 39 | 44 | 4.15 | 1.36 | 9.1 | 4.2 | 0.4 | 0.7 |
| 09 | STL | 4 | 1 | 0 | 43 | 31 | 46 | 2.06 | 0.96 | 9.5 | 2.3 | 1.0 | 0.8 |
| 10 | STL | 0 | 1 | 0 | 36 | 30 | 22 | 4.00 | 1.28 | 5.5 | 4.0 | 0.5 | 1.1 |

Value / Luck / In Rotation / In Relief / OPS

| Yr | $1L | $2L | Pts | RAA | H% | HR/fb | S% | FIP | GS | CG | QS/DS | GR | Hld | Bln | Lead | OPS | 1st Hf | 2nd Hf | vs RH | vs LH |
|---|---|---|---|---|---|---|---|---|---|---|---|---|---|---|---|---|---|---|---|---|
| 07 | -$2 | -$6 | 40 | −5 | 30% | 9% | 69% | 4.39 | — | — | — | 76 | 12 | 2 | +0.1 | .777 | .893 | .650 | .902 | .653 |
| 08 | $1 | -$2 | 70 | −2 | 32% | 4% | 68% | 3.25 | — | — | — | 68 | 11 | 1 | +0.5 | .687 | .634 | .748 | .793 | .606 |
| 09 | $5 | $4 | 100 | +9 | 25% | 10% | 86% | 3.34 | — | — | — | 70 | 13 | 1 | +0.3 | .589 | .591 | .585 | .889 | .398 |
| 10 | -$4 | -$11 | 20 | −1 | 27% | 5% | 68% | 4.03 | — | — | — | 57 | 11 | 1 | +1.5 | .640 | .689 | .583 | .759 | .551 |

## Brad Mills — 60 IP | $-2 | 70 pts

RP-4, SP-3 — Owned: 0% — LH

Mills pitched in seven games in MLB, including four appearances out of the bullpen. If he makes the 2011 Blue Jays, it will probably be in relief. In his time in the majors, Mills has been too free with walks. Mix that tendency with below-average velocity and a fly-ball bias, and he is not likely to be an impact pitcher. (MH)

| Player | Age | IP | W | Sv | K | ERA | WHIP | K/9 | BB/9 | $2L | Pts |
|---|---|---|---|---|---|---|---|---|---|---|---|
| Mills B | 26 | 60 | 3 | 0 | 59 | 5.25 | 1.58 | 8.8 | 4.6 | -$2 | 70 |
| **Mini-Browser** | **Age** | **IP** | **W** | **Sv** | **K** | **ERA** | **WHIP** | **K/9** | **BB/9** | **$2L** | **Pts** |
| Fulchino J | 31 | 40 | 2 | 0 | 33 | 4.80 | 1.45 | 7.4 | 3.6 | -$2 | 40 |
| Infante G | 23 | 60 | 3 | 0 | 47 | 4.31 | 1.75 | 7.1 | 7.0 | -$2 | 60 |
| Ramos C | 26 | 40 | 2 | 0 | 29 | 4.81 | 1.46 | 6.5 | 3.4 | -$2 | 40 |
| Wright J | 36 | 40 | 1 | 0 | 23 | 4.89 | 1.48 | 5.2 | 4.4 | -$2 | 20 |
| Lannan J | 26 | 160 | 8 | 0 | 80 | 4.73 | 1.46 | 4.5 | 3.1 | -$2 | 120 |

Minors (2010) / Skills

| Level | Leag | W | L | Sv | IP | H | K | ERA | WHIP | K/9 | BB/9 | HR/9 | GB/F |
|---|---|---|---|---|---|---|---|---|---|---|---|---|---|
| A | — | — | — | — | — | — | — | — | — | — | — | — | — |
| AA | — | — | — | — | — | — | — | — | — | — | — | — | — |
| AAA | PCL | 8 | 6 | 0 | 112 | 118 | 100 | 4.97 | 1.43 | 8.0 | 3.4 | 1.2 | — |

Competition at RP / Stats in 2010 as RP

| Thr | Player | GR | ERA | IP/G | Sv-Hld |
|---|---|---|---|---|---|
| LH | Downs S | 67 | 2.64 | 0.9 | 0-26 |
| LH | Purcey D | 33 | 3.71 | 1.0 | 1-3 |
| LH | Tallet B | 29 | 6.84 | 1.7 | 0-1 |
| LH | Carlson J | 20 | 4.61 | 0.7 | 1-2 |

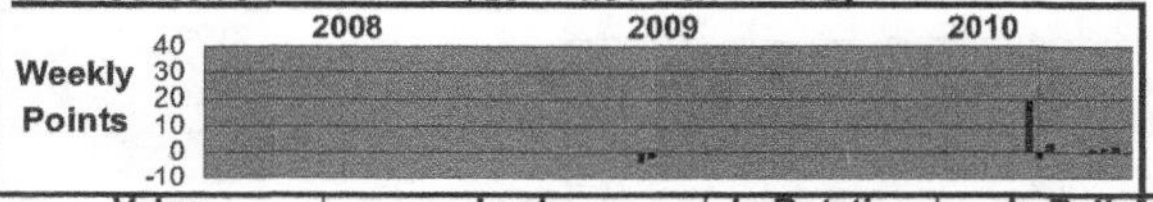


Ten-Year Trends — K/9, BB/9

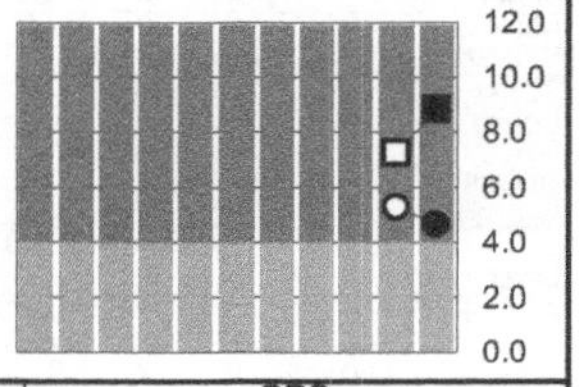


Majors / Skills

| Yr | Team | W | L | Sv | IP | H | K | ERA | WHIP | K/9 | BB/9 | HR/9 | GB/F |
|---|---|---|---|---|---|---|---|---|---|---|---|---|---|
| 07 | — | — | — | — | — | — | — | — | — | — | — | — | — |
| 08 | — | — | — | — | — | — | — | — | — | — | — | — | — |
| 09 | TOR | 0 | 1 | 0 | 7 | 14 | 9 | 14.09 | 2.61 | 10.6 | 7.0 | 4.7 | 0.2 |
| 10 | TOR | 1 | 0 | 0 | 22 | 20 | 18 | 5.64 | 1.48 | 7.3 | 5.2 | 0.8 | 0.8 |

Value / Luck / In Rotation / In Relief / OPS

| Yr | $1L | $2L | Pts | RAA | H% | HR/fb | S% | FIP | GS | CG | QS/DS | GR | Hld | Bln | Lead | OPS | 1st Hf | 2nd Hf | vs RH | vs LH |
|---|---|---|---|---|---|---|---|---|---|---|---|---|---|---|---|---|---|---|---|---|
| 07 | — | — | — | — | — | — | — | — | — | — | — | — | — | — | — | — | — | — | — | — |
| 08 | — | — | — | — | — | — | — | — | — | — | — | — | — | — | — | — | — | — | — | — |
| 09 | -$4 | -$6 | -10 | −9 | 43% | 20% | 50% | 10.08 | 2 | 0 | 0/2 | — | — | — | — | 1.276 | 1.276 | — | 1.395 | .875 |
| 10 | -$4 | -$13 | 20 | −4 | 28% | 6% | 61% | 4.60 | 3 | 0 | 1/1 | 4 | 1 | 0 | −1.7 | .745 | — | .745 | .684 | .836 |

*For more stats, visit www.Rotolympus.com.*

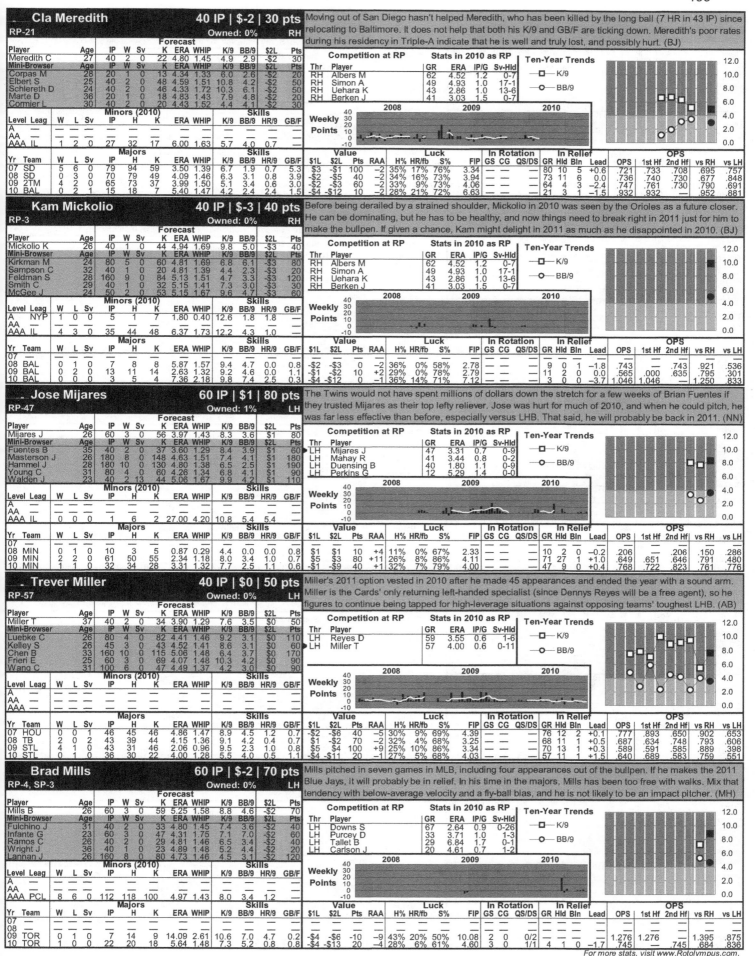

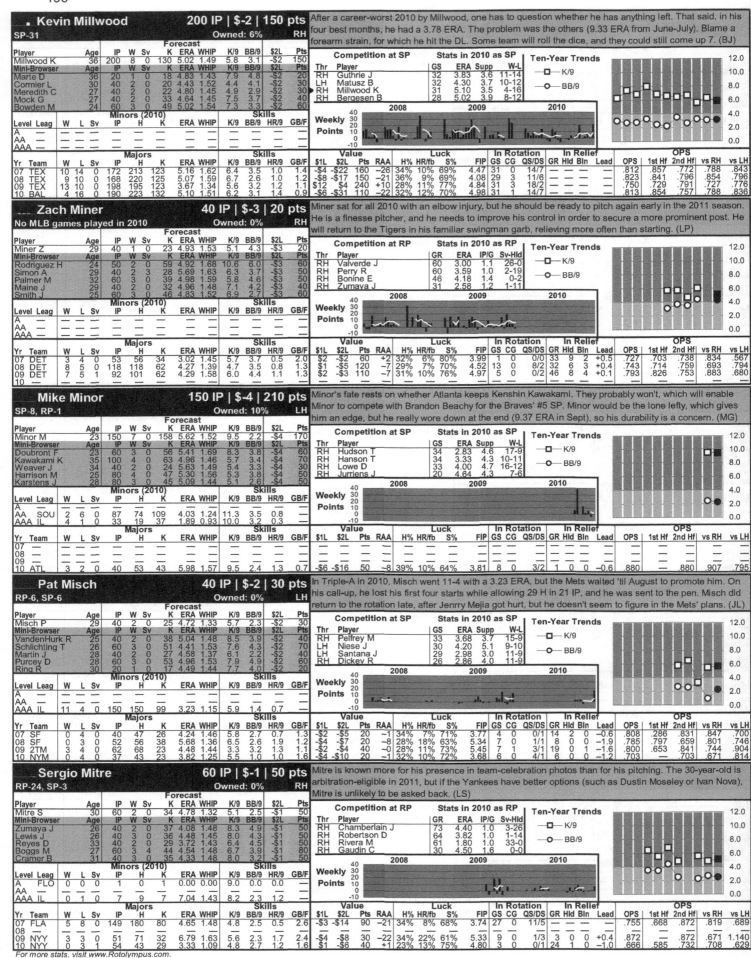

## Kevin Millwood — 200 IP | $-2 | 150 pts

SP-31 — Owned: 6% — RH

| Player | Age | IP | W | Sv | K | ERA | WHIP | K/9 | BB/9 | $2L | Pts |
|---|---|---|---|---|---|---|---|---|---|---|---|
| | | Forecast | | | | | | | | | |
| Millwood K | 36 | 200 | 8 | 0 | 130 | 5.02 | 1.49 | 5.8 | 3.1 | -$2 | 150 |
| Mini-Browser | Age | IP | W | Sv | K | ERA | WHIP | K/9 | BB/9 | $2L | Pts |
| Marte D | 36 | 20 | 1 | 0 | 18 | 4.83 | 1.43 | 7.9 | 4.8 | -$2 | 20 |
| Cormier L | 30 | 40 | 2 | 0 | 20 | 4.43 | 1.52 | 4.4 | 4.1 | -$2 | 30 |
| Meredith C | 27 | 40 | 2 | 0 | 22 | 4.80 | 1.45 | 4.9 | 2.9 | -$2 | 30 |
| Mock G | 27 | 40 | 2 | 0 | 33 | 4.64 | 1.45 | 7.5 | 3.7 | -$2 | 40 |
| Bowden M | 24 | 60 | 3 | 0 | 49 | 5.02 | 1.54 | 7.3 | 3.3 | -$2 | 60 |

| Level | Leag | W | L | Sv | IP | H | K | ERA | WHIP | K/9 | BB/9 | HR/9 | GB/F |
|---|---|---|---|---|---|---|---|---|---|---|---|---|---|
| | | Minors (2010) | | | | | | | | Skills | | | |
| A | — | — | — | — | — | — | — | — | — | — | — | — | — |
| AA | — | — | — | — | — | — | — | — | — | — | — | — | — |
| AAA | — | — | — | — | — | — | — | — | — | — | — | — | — |

| Yr | Team | W | L | Sv | IP | H | K | ERA | WHIP | K/9 | BB/9 | HR/9 | GB/F |
|---|---|---|---|---|---|---|---|---|---|---|---|---|---|
| | | Majors | | | | | | | | Skills | | | |
| 07 | TEX | 10 | 14 | 0 | 172 | 213 | 123 | 5.16 | 1.62 | 6.4 | 3.5 | 1.0 | 1.4 |
| 08 | TEX | 9 | 10 | 0 | 168 | 220 | 125 | 5.07 | 1.59 | 6.7 | 2.6 | 1.0 | 1.2 |
| 09 | TEX | 13 | 10 | 0 | 198 | 195 | 123 | 3.67 | 1.34 | 5.6 | 3.2 | 1.2 | 1.1 |
| 10 | BAL | 4 | 16 | 0 | 190 | 223 | 132 | 5.10 | 1.51 | 6.2 | 3.1 | 1.4 | 0.9 |

After a career-worst 2010 by Millwood, one has to question whether he has anything left. That said, in his four best months, he had a 3.78 ERA. The problem was the others (9.33 ERA from June-July). Blame a forearm strain, for which he hit the DL. Some team will roll the dice, and they could still come up 7. (BJ)

| Thr | Player (Competition at SP) | GS | ERA | Supp | W-L |
|---|---|---|---|---|---|
| | | Stats in 2010 as SP | | | |
| RH | Guthrie J | 32 | 3.83 | 3.6 | 11-14 |
| LH | Matusz B | 32 | 4.30 | 3.7 | 10-12 |
| RH | Millwood K | 31 | 5.10 | 3.5 | 4-16 |
| RH | Bergesen B | 28 | 5.02 | 3.9 | 8-12 |

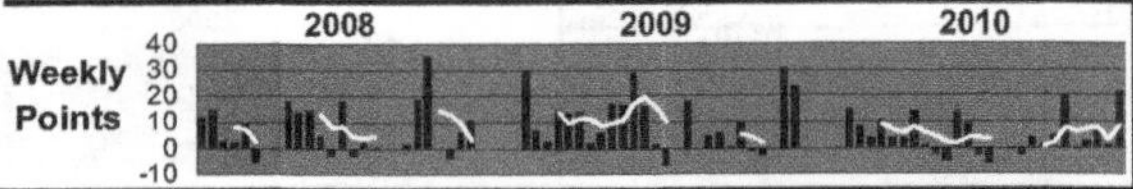


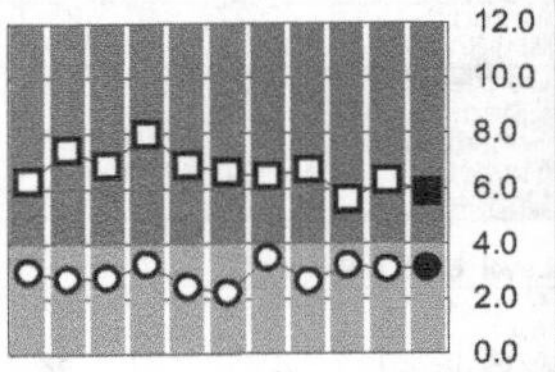


| Yr | $1L | $2L | Pts | RAA | H% | HR/fb | S% | FIP | GS | CG | QS/DS | GR | Hld | Bln | Lead | OPS | 1st Hf | 2nd Hf | vs RH | vs LH |
|---|---|---|---|---|---|---|---|---|---|---|---|---|---|---|---|---|---|---|---|---|
| | Value | | | | Luck | | | | In Rotation | | | In Relief | | | | OPS | | | | |
| 07 | -$4 | -$22 | 160 | –26 | 34% | 10% | 69% | 4.47 | 31 | 0 | 14/7 | — | — | — | — | .812 | .857 | .772 | .788 | .843 |
| 08 | -$8 | -$17 | 150 | –21 | 36% | 9% | 69% | 4.08 | 29 | 3 | 11/6 | — | — | — | — | .823 | .841 | .796 | .854 | .796 |
| 09 | $12 | $4 | 240 | +10 | 28% | 11% | 77% | 4.84 | 31 | 3 | 18/2 | — | — | — | — | .750 | .729 | .791 | .727 | .776 |
| 10 | -$6 | -$31 | 110 | –22 | 32% | 12% | 70% | 4.98 | 31 | 1 | 14/7 | — | — | — | — | .813 | .854 | .757 | .788 | .836 |

## Zach Miner — 40 IP | $-3 | 20 pts

No MLB games played in 2010 — Owned: 0% — RH

| Player | Age | IP | W | Sv | K | ERA | WHIP | K/9 | BB/9 | $2L | Pts |
|---|---|---|---|---|---|---|---|---|---|---|---|
| | | Forecast | | | | | | | | | |
| Miner Z | 29 | 40 | 1 | 0 | 23 | 4.93 | 1.53 | 5.1 | 4.3 | -$3 | 20 |
| Mini-Browser | Age | IP | W | Sv | K | ERA | WHIP | K/9 | BB/9 | $2L | Pts |
| Rodriguez H | 24 | 50 | 2 | 0 | 59 | 4.92 | 1.68 | 10.6 | 6.0 | -$3 | 60 |
| Simon A | 29 | 40 | 2 | 3 | 28 | 5.69 | 1.63 | 6.3 | 3.7 | -$3 | 50 |
| Palmer M | 32 | 60 | 3 | 0 | 39 | 4.98 | 1.59 | 5.8 | 4.6 | -$3 | 50 |
| Maine J | 29 | 40 | 2 | 0 | 32 | 4.96 | 1.48 | 7.1 | 4.2 | -$3 | 40 |
| Smith J | 25 | 60 | 3 | 0 | 46 | 4.83 | 1.52 | 6.9 | 2.7 | -$3 | 60 |

| Level | Leag | W | L | Sv | IP | H | K | ERA | WHIP | K/9 | BB/9 | HR/9 | GB/F |
|---|---|---|---|---|---|---|---|---|---|---|---|---|---|
| | | Minors (2010) | | | | | | | | Skills | | | |
| A | — | — | — | — | — | — | — | — | — | — | — | — | — |
| AA | — | — | — | — | — | — | — | — | — | — | — | — | — |
| AAA | — | — | — | — | — | — | — | — | — | — | — | — | — |

| Yr | Team | W | L | Sv | IP | H | K | ERA | WHIP | K/9 | BB/9 | HR/9 | GB/F |
|---|---|---|---|---|---|---|---|---|---|---|---|---|---|
| | | Majors | | | | | | | | Skills | | | |
| 07 | DET | 3 | 4 | 0 | 53 | 56 | 34 | 3.02 | 1.45 | 5.7 | 3.7 | 0.5 | 2.0 |
| 08 | DET | 8 | 5 | 0 | 118 | 118 | 62 | 4.27 | 1.39 | 4.7 | 3.5 | 0.8 | 1.3 |
| 09 | DET | 7 | 5 | 1 | 92 | 101 | 62 | 4.29 | 1.58 | 6.0 | 4.4 | 1.1 | 1.3 |
| 10 | — | — | — | — | — | — | — | — | — | — | — | — | — |

Miner sat for all 2010 with an elbow injury, but he should be ready to pitch again early in the 2011 season. He is a finesse pitcher, and he needs to improve his control in order to secure a more prominent post. He will return to the Tigers in his familiar swingman garb, relieving more often than starting. (LP)

| Thr | Player (Competition at RP) | GR | ERA | IP/G | Sv-Hld |
|---|---|---|---|---|---|
| | | Stats in 2010 as RP | | | |
| RH | Valverde J | 60 | 3.00 | 1.1 | 26-0 |
| RH | Perry R | 60 | 3.59 | 1.0 | 2-19 |
| RH | Bonine E | 46 | 4.18 | 1.4 | 0-2 |
| RH | Zumaya J | 31 | 2.58 | 1.2 | 1-11 |

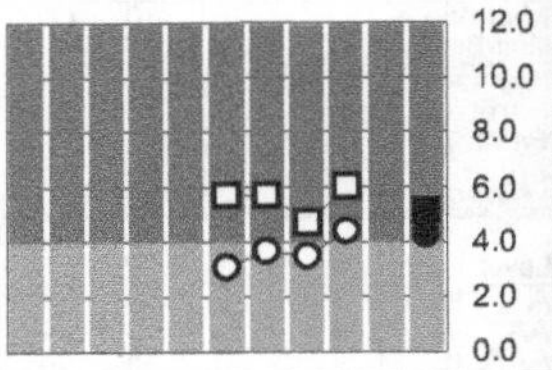


| Yr | $1L | $2L | Pts | RAA | H% | HR/fb | S% | FIP | GS | CG | QS/DS | GR | Hld | Bln | Lead | OPS | 1st Hf | 2nd Hf | vs RH | vs LH |
|---|---|---|---|---|---|---|---|---|---|---|---|---|---|---|---|---|---|---|---|---|
| | Value | | | | Luck | | | | In Rotation | | | In Relief | | | | OPS | | | | |
| 07 | $2 | -$2 | 60 | +2 | 32% | 6% | 80% | 3.99 | 1 | 0 | 0/0 | 33 | 9 | 2 | +0.5 | .727 | .703 | .738 | .834 | .567 |
| 08 | $1 | -$5 | 120 | –7 | 29% | 7% | 70% | 4.52 | 13 | 0 | 8/2 | 32 | 6 | 3 | +0.4 | .743 | .714 | .759 | .693 | .794 |
| 09 | $2 | -$3 | 110 | –7 | 31% | 10% | 76% | 4.97 | 5 | 0 | 0/2 | 46 | 8 | 4 | +0.1 | .793 | .826 | .753 | .883 | .680 |
| 10 | — | — | — | — | — | — | — | — | — | — | — | — | — | — | — | — | — | — | — | — |

## Mike Minor — 150 IP | $-4 | 210 pts

SP-8, RP-1 — Owned: 10% — LH

| Player | Age | IP | W | Sv | K | ERA | WHIP | K/9 | BB/9 | $2L | Pts |
|---|---|---|---|---|---|---|---|---|---|---|---|
| | | Forecast | | | | | | | | | |
| Minor M | 23 | 150 | 7 | 0 | 158 | 5.62 | 1.52 | 9.5 | 2.2 | -$4 | 170 |
| Mini-Browser | Age | IP | W | Sv | K | ERA | WHIP | K/9 | BB/9 | $2L | Pts |
| Doubront F | 23 | 60 | 3 | 0 | 56 | 5.41 | 1.69 | 8.3 | 3.8 | -$4 | 60 |
| Kawakami K | 35 | 100 | 4 | 0 | 63 | 4.96 | 1.46 | 5.7 | 3.4 | -$4 | 70 |
| Weaver J | 34 | 40 | 2 | 0 | 24 | 5.63 | 1.49 | 5.4 | 3.3 | -$4 | 30 |
| Harrison M | 25 | 80 | 4 | 0 | 47 | 5.30 | 1.56 | 5.3 | 3.8 | -$4 | 50 |
| Karstens J | 28 | 80 | 3 | 0 | 45 | 5.09 | 1.44 | 5.1 | 2.6 | -$4 | 50 |

| Level | Leag | W | L | Sv | IP | H | K | ERA | WHIP | K/9 | BB/9 | HR/9 | GB/F |
|---|---|---|---|---|---|---|---|---|---|---|---|---|---|
| | | Minors (2010) | | | | | | | | Skills | | | |
| A | — | — | — | — | — | — | — | — | — | — | — | — | — |
| AA | SOU | 2 | 6 | 0 | 87 | 74 | 109 | 4.03 | 1.24 | 11.3 | 3.5 | 0.8 | — |
| AAA | IL | 4 | 1 | 0 | 33 | 19 | 37 | 1.89 | 0.93 | 10.0 | 3.2 | 0.3 | — |

| Yr | Team | W | L | Sv | IP | H | K | ERA | WHIP | K/9 | BB/9 | HR/9 | GB/F |
|---|---|---|---|---|---|---|---|---|---|---|---|---|---|
| | | Majors | | | | | | | | Skills | | | |
| 07 | — | — | — | — | — | — | — | — | — | — | — | — | — |
| 08 | — | — | — | — | — | — | — | — | — | — | — | — | — |
| 09 | — | — | — | — | — | — | — | — | — | — | — | — | — |
| 10 | ATL | 3 | 2 | 0 | 40 | 53 | 43 | 5.98 | 1.57 | 9.5 | 2.4 | 1.3 | 0.7 |

Minor's fate rests on whether Atlanta keeps Kenshin Kawakami. They probably won't, which will enable Minor to compete with Brandon Beachy for the Braves' #5 SP. Minor would be the lone lefty, which gives him an edge, but he really wore down at the end (9.37 ERA in Sept), so his durability is a concern. (MG)

| Thr | Player (Competition at SP) | GS | ERA | Supp | W-L |
|---|---|---|---|---|---|
| | | Stats in 2010 as SP | | | |
| RH | Hudson T | 34 | 2.83 | 4.6 | 17-9 |
| RH | Hanson T | 34 | 3.33 | 4.3 | 10-11 |
| RH | Lowe D | 33 | 4.00 | 4.7 | 16-12 |
| RH | Jurrjens J | 20 | 4.64 | 4.3 | 7-6 |

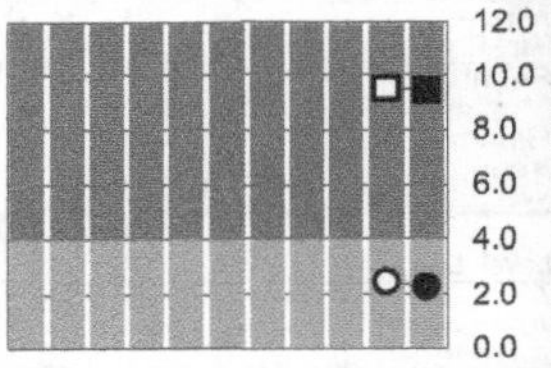


| Yr | $1L | $2L | Pts | RAA | H% | HR/fb | S% | FIP | GS | CG | QS/DS | GR | Hld | Bln | Lead | OPS | 1st Hf | 2nd Hf | vs RH | vs LH |
|---|---|---|---|---|---|---|---|---|---|---|---|---|---|---|---|---|---|---|---|---|
| | Value | | | | Luck | | | | In Rotation | | | In Relief | | | | OPS | | | | |
| 07 | — | — | — | — | — | — | — | — | — | — | — | — | — | — | — | — | — | — | — | — |
| 08 | — | — | — | — | — | — | — | — | — | — | — | — | — | — | — | — | — | — | — | — |
| 09 | — | — | — | — | — | — | — | — | — | — | — | — | — | — | — | — | — | — | — | — |
| 10 | -$6 | -$16 | 50 | –8 | 39% | 10% | 64% | 3.81 | 8 | 0 | 3/2 | 1 | 0 | 0 | –0.6 | .880 | — | .880 | .907 | .795 |

## Pat Misch — 40 IP | $-2 | 30 pts

RP-6, SP-6 — Owned: 0% — LH

| Player | Age | IP | W | Sv | K | ERA | WHIP | K/9 | BB/9 | $2L | Pts |
|---|---|---|---|---|---|---|---|---|---|---|---|
| | | Forecast | | | | | | | | | |
| Misch P | 29 | 40 | 2 | 0 | 25 | 4.72 | 1.33 | 5.7 | 2.3 | -$2 | 30 |
| Mini-Browser | Age | IP | W | Sv | K | ERA | WHIP | K/9 | BB/9 | $2L | Pts |
| VandenHurk R | 25 | 40 | 2 | 0 | 38 | 5.04 | 1.48 | 8.5 | 3.9 | -$2 | 40 |
| Schlichting T | 26 | 60 | 3 | 0 | 51 | 4.41 | 1.53 | 7.6 | 4.3 | -$2 | 70 |
| Martin J | 28 | 40 | 2 | 0 | 27 | 4.58 | 1.37 | 6.1 | 2.2 | -$2 | 40 |
| Purcey D | 28 | 60 | 3 | 0 | 53 | 4.96 | 1.53 | 7.9 | 4.9 | -$2 | 60 |
| Ring R | 30 | 20 | 1 | 0 | 17 | 4.49 | 1.44 | 7.7 | 4.0 | -$2 | 20 |

| Level | Leag | W | L | Sv | IP | H | K | ERA | WHIP | K/9 | BB/9 | HR/9 | GB/F |
|---|---|---|---|---|---|---|---|---|---|---|---|---|---|
| | | Minors (2010) | | | | | | | | Skills | | | |
| A | — | — | — | — | — | — | — | — | — | — | — | — | — |
| AA | — | — | — | — | — | — | — | — | — | — | — | — | — |
| AAA | IL | 11 | 4 | 0 | 150 | 150 | 99 | 3.23 | 1.15 | 5.9 | 1.4 | 0.7 | — |

| Yr | Team | W | L | Sv | IP | H | K | ERA | WHIP | K/9 | BB/9 | HR/9 | GB/F |
|---|---|---|---|---|---|---|---|---|---|---|---|---|---|
| | | Majors | | | | | | | | Skills | | | |
| 07 | SF | 0 | 4 | 0 | 40 | 47 | 26 | 4.24 | 1.46 | 5.8 | 2.7 | 0.7 | 1.3 |
| 08 | SF | 0 | 3 | 0 | 52 | 56 | 38 | 5.68 | 1.36 | 6.5 | 2.6 | 1.9 | 1.2 |
| 09 | 2TM | 3 | 4 | 0 | 62 | 68 | 23 | 4.48 | 1.44 | 3.3 | 3.2 | 1.3 | 1.1 |
| 10 | NYM | 0 | 4 | 0 | 37 | 43 | 23 | 3.82 | 1.25 | 5.5 | 1.0 | 1.0 | 1.6 |

In Triple-A in 2010, Misch went 11-4 with a 3.23 ERA, but the Mets waited 'til August to promote him. On his call-up, he lost his first four starts while allowing 29 H in 21 IP, and he was sent to the pen. Misch did return to the rotation late, after Jenrry Mejia got hurt, but he doesn't seem to figure in the Mets' plans. (JL)

| Thr | Player (Competition at SP) | GS | ERA | Supp | W-L |
|---|---|---|---|---|---|
| | | Stats in 2010 as SP | | | |
| RH | Pelfrey M | 33 | 3.68 | 3.7 | 15-9 |
| LH | Niese J | 30 | 4.20 | 5.1 | 9-10 |
| LH | Santana J | 29 | 2.98 | 3.0 | 11-9 |
| RH | Dickey R | 26 | 2.86 | 4.0 | 11-9 |

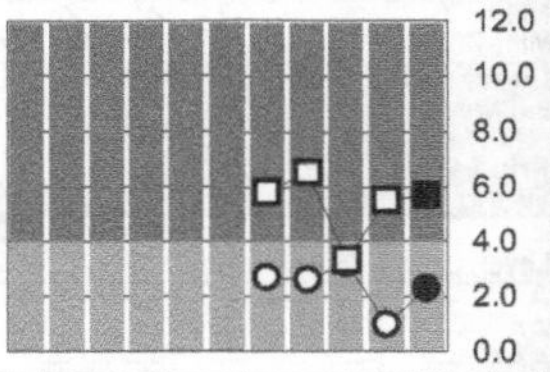


| Yr | $1L | $2L | Pts | RAA | H% | HR/fb | S% | FIP | GS | CG | QS/DS | GR | Hld | Bln | Lead | OPS | 1st Hf | 2nd Hf | vs RH | vs LH |
|---|---|---|---|---|---|---|---|---|---|---|---|---|---|---|---|---|---|---|---|---|
| | Value | | | | Luck | | | | In Rotation | | | In Relief | | | | OPS | | | | |
| 07 | -$2 | -$5 | 20 | –1 | 34% | 7% | 71% | 3.77 | 4 | 0 | 0/1 | 14 | 2 | 0 | –0.6 | .808 | .286 | .831 | .847 | .700 |
| 08 | -$4 | -$7 | 20 | –8 | 28% | 18% | 63% | 5.34 | 7 | 0 | 1/1 | 8 | 0 | 0 | –1.9 | .785 | .797 | .659 | .801 | .746 |
| 09 | -$2 | -$4 | 40 | –0 | 28% | 11% | 73% | 5.45 | 7 | 1 | 3/1 | 19 | 0 | 1 | –1.6 | .800 | .653 | .841 | .744 | .904 |
| 10 | -$4 | -$10 | 20 | –1 | 32% | 10% | 72% | 3.68 | 6 | 0 | 4/1 | 6 | 0 | 0 | –1.2 | .703 | — | .703 | .671 | .814 |

## Sergio Mitre — 60 IP | $-1 | 50 pts

RP-24, SP-3 — Owned: 0% — RH

| Player | Age | IP | W | Sv | K | ERA | WHIP | K/9 | BB/9 | $2L | Pts |
|---|---|---|---|---|---|---|---|---|---|---|---|
| | | Forecast | | | | | | | | | |
| Mitre S | 30 | 60 | 2 | 0 | 34 | 4.78 | 1.32 | 5.1 | 2.5 | -$1 | 50 |
| Mini-Browser | Age | IP | W | Sv | K | ERA | WHIP | K/9 | BB/9 | $2L | Pts |
| Zumaya J | 26 | 40 | 2 | 0 | 37 | 4.08 | 1.48 | 8.3 | 4.9 | -$1 | 50 |
| Lewis J | 26 | 40 | 3 | 0 | 36 | 4.48 | 1.45 | 8.0 | 4.3 | -$1 | 50 |
| Reyes D | 33 | 40 | 2 | 0 | 29 | 3.72 | 1.43 | 6.4 | 4.5 | -$1 | 50 |
| Boggs M | 27 | 60 | 3 | 4 | 44 | 4.54 | 1.48 | 6.7 | 3.9 | -$1 | 80 |
| Cramer B | 31 | 40 | 3 | 0 | 35 | 4.33 | 1.48 | 8.0 | 3.2 | -$1 | 50 |

| Level | Leag | W | L | Sv | IP | H | K | ERA | WHIP | K/9 | BB/9 | HR/9 | GB/F |
|---|---|---|---|---|---|---|---|---|---|---|---|---|---|
| | | Minors (2010) | | | | | | | | Skills | | | |
| A | FLO | 0 | 0 | 0 | 1 | 0 | 1 | 0.00 | 0.00 | 9.0 | 0.0 | 0.0 | — |
| AA | — | — | — | — | — | — | — | — | — | — | — | — | — |
| AAA | IL | 0 | 1 | 0 | 7 | 9 | 7 | 7.04 | 1.43 | 8.2 | 2.3 | 1.2 | — |

| Yr | Team | W | L | Sv | IP | H | K | ERA | WHIP | K/9 | BB/9 | HR/9 | GB/F |
|---|---|---|---|---|---|---|---|---|---|---|---|---|---|
| | | Majors | | | | | | | | Skills | | | |
| 07 | FLA | 5 | 8 | 0 | 149 | 180 | 80 | 4.65 | 1.48 | 4.8 | 2.5 | 0.5 | 2.6 |
| 08 | — | — | — | — | — | — | — | — | — | — | — | — | — |
| 09 | NYY | 3 | 3 | 0 | 51 | 71 | 32 | 6.79 | 1.63 | 5.6 | 2.3 | 1.7 | 2.4 |
| 10 | NYY | 0 | 3 | 1 | 54 | 43 | 29 | 3.33 | 1.09 | 4.8 | 2.7 | 1.2 | 1.6 |

Mitre is known more for his presence in team-celebration photos than for his pitching. The 30-year-old is arbitration-eligible in 2011, but if the Yankees have better options (such as Dustin Moseley or Ivan Nova), Mitre is unlikely to be asked back. (LS)

| Thr | Player (Competition at RP) | GR | ERA | IP/G | Sv-Hld |
|---|---|---|---|---|---|
| | | Stats in 2010 as RP | | | |
| RH | Chamberlain J | 73 | 4.40 | 1.0 | 3-26 |
| RH | Robertson D | 64 | 3.82 | 1.0 | 1-14 |
| RH | Rivera M | 61 | 1.80 | 1.0 | 33-0 |
| RH | Gaudin C | 30 | 4.50 | 1.6 | 0-0 |

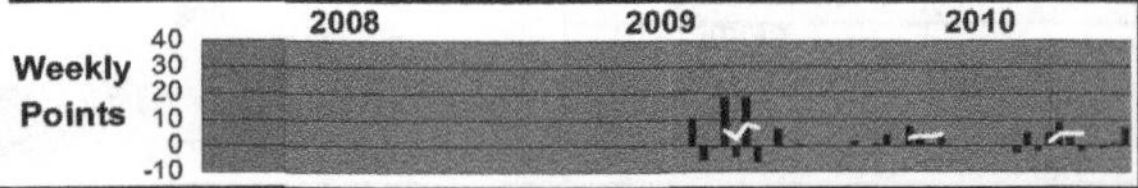


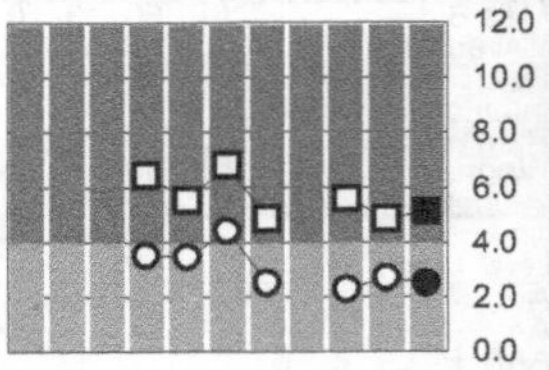


| Yr | $1L | $2L | Pts | RAA | H% | HR/fb | S% | FIP | GS | CG | QS/DS | GR | Hld | Bln | Lead | OPS | 1st Hf | 2nd Hf | vs RH | vs LH |
|---|---|---|---|---|---|---|---|---|---|---|---|---|---|---|---|---|---|---|---|---|
| | Value | | | | Luck | | | | In Rotation | | | In Relief | | | | OPS | | | | |
| 07 | -$3 | -$14 | 90 | –21 | 34% | 8% | 68% | 3.74 | 27 | 0 | 11/5 | — | — | — | — | .755 | .668 | .872 | .819 | .689 |
| 08 | — | — | — | — | — | — | — | — | — | — | — | — | — | — | — | — | — | — | — | — |
| 09 | -$4 | -$8 | 30 | –22 | 34% | 22% | 61% | 5.33 | 9 | 0 | 1/3 | 3 | 0 | 0 | +0.4 | .872 | — | .872 | .671 | 1.140 |
| 10 | $1 | -$6 | 40 | +1 | 23% | 13% | 75% | 4.80 | 3 | 0 | 0/1 | 24 | 1 | 0 | –1.0 | .666 | .585 | .732 | .708 | .629 |

## Garrett Mock

**40 IP | $-2 | 40 pts**

SP-1 — Owned: 0% — RH

Mock was a member of the Nationals' 2010 Opening Day roster, but in April he went down with a neck injury that sidelined him until August. When he is on, Mock can induce ground balls and get strikeouts. Unfortunately, he's more often not on (he has only 4 Quality Starts in 19 tries). (PB)

| Player | Age | IP | W | Sv | K | ERA | WHIP | K/9 | BB/9 | $2L | Pts |
|---|---|---|---|---|---|---|---|---|---|---|---|
| | | Forecast | | | | | | | | | |
| Mock G | 27 | 40 | 2 | 0 | 33 | 4.64 | 1.45 | 7.5 | 3.7 | -$2 | 40 |
| **Mini-Browser** | **Age** | **IP** | **W** | **Sv** | **K** | **ERA** | **WHIP** | **K/9** | **BB/9** | **$2L** | **Pts** |
| Elbert S | 25 | 40 | 2 | 0 | 48 | 4.59 | 1.51 | 10.8 | 4.2 | -$2 | 50 |
| Schlereth D | 24 | 40 | 2 | 0 | 46 | 4.33 | 1.72 | 10.3 | 6.1 | -$2 | 50 |
| Marte D | 36 | 20 | 1 | 0 | 18 | 4.83 | 1.43 | 7.9 | 4.8 | -$2 | 20 |
| Cormier L | 30 | 40 | 2 | 0 | 20 | 4.43 | 1.52 | 4.4 | 4.1 | -$2 | 30 |
| Meredith C | 27 | 40 | 2 | 0 | 22 | 4.80 | 1.45 | 4.9 | 2.9 | -$2 | 30 |

**Competition at SP — Stats in 2010 as SP**

| Thr | Player | GS | ERA | Supp | W-L |
|---|---|---|---|---|---|
| RH | Hernandez L | 33 | 3.66 | 3.5 | 10-12 |
| LH | Lannan J | 25 | 4.65 | 4.5 | 8-8 |
| RH | Stammen C | 19 | 5.06 | 4.8 | 4-4 |
| RH | Atilano L | 16 | 5.15 | 4.5 | 6-7 |

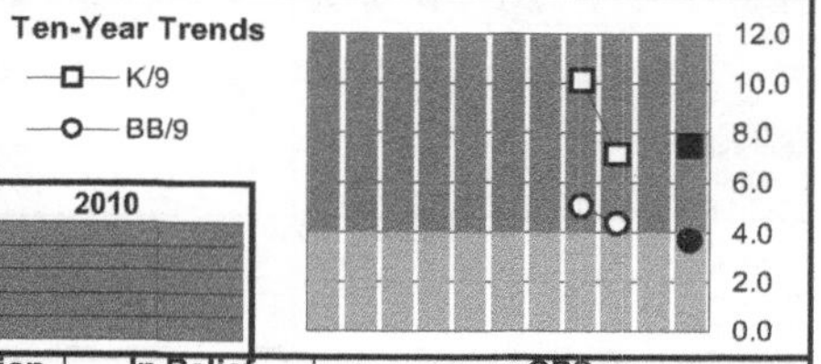
Ten-Year Trends
K/9
BB/9
12.0
10.0
8.0
6.0
4.0
2.0
0.0

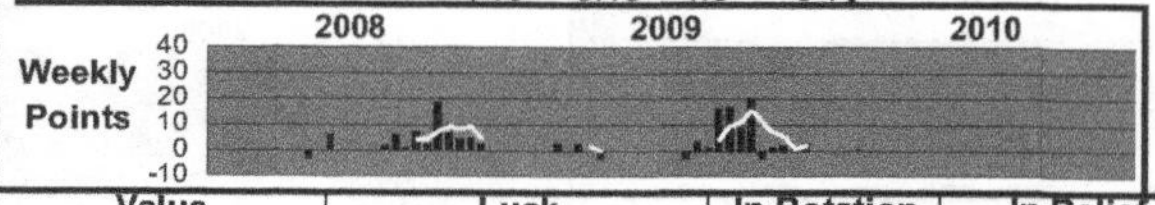
Weekly Points
2008
2009
2010
40
30
20
10
0
-10

| Level | Leag | W | L | Sv | IP | H | K | ERA | WHIP | K/9 | BB/9 | HR/9 | GB/F |
|---|---|---|---|---|---|---|---|---|---|---|---|---|---|
| | | Minors (2010) | | | | | | | | Skills | | | |
| A | 2LG | 0 | 1 | 0 | 11 | 13 | 12 | 3.27 | 1.27 | 9.8 | 0.8 | 0.8 | — |
| AA | EL | 0 | 1 | 0 | 5 | 6 | 0 | 7.20 | 1.60 | 0.0 | 3.6 | 1.8 | — |
| AAA | IL | 1 | 1 | 0 | 11 | 11 | 6 | 4.09 | 1.27 | 4.9 | 2.5 | 0.0 | — |

| Yr | Team | W | L | Sv | IP | H | K | ERA | WHIP | K/9 | BB/9 | HR/9 | GB/F |
|---|---|---|---|---|---|---|---|---|---|---|---|---|---|
| | | Majors | | | | | | | | Skills | | | |
| 07 | — | — | — | — | — | — | — | — | — | — | — | — | — |
| 08 | WAS | 1 | 3 | 0 | 41 | 37 | 46 | 4.17 | 1.46 | 10.1 | 5.0 | 0.9 | 1.2 |
| 09 | WAS | 3 | 10 | 0 | 91 | 114 | 72 | 5.62 | 1.73 | 7.1 | 4.3 | 0.9 | 1.5 |
| 10 | WAS | 0 | 0 | 0 | 3 | 4 | 3 | 5.40 | 2.70 | 8.1 | 13.5 | 5.4 | 0.7 |

| Yr | $1L | $2L | Pts | RAA | H% | HR/fb | S% | FIP | GS | CG | QS/DS | GR | Hld | Bln | Lead | OPS | 1st Hf | 2nd Hf | vs RH | vs LH |
|---|---|---|---|---|---|---|---|---|---|---|---|---|---|---|---|---|---|---|---|---|
| | Value | | | | Luck | | | | In Rotation | | | In Relief | | | | OPS | | | | |
| 07 | — | — | — | — | — | — | — | — | — | — | — | — | — | — | — | — | — | — | — | — |
| 08 | -$1 | -$3 | 50 | +0 | 31% | 10% | 73% | 3.91 | 3 | 0 | 0/0 | 23 | 0 | 0 | –1.8 | .709 | .959 | .622 | .698 | .725 |
| 09 | -$7 | -$10 | 60 | –20 | 36% | 9% | 68% | 4.35 | 15 | 0 | 4/3 | 13 | 4 | 2 | +0.9 | .848 | .769 | .861 | .783 | .909 |
| 10 | -$6 | -$12 | 0 | –0 | 22% | 33% | 100% | 13.70 | 1 | 0 | 0/0 | — | — | — | — | 1.188 | 1.188 | — | 1.500 | .429 |

## Brian Moehler

**60 IP | $-5 | 30 pts**

RP-12, SP-8 — Owned: 0% — RH

Anyone who has seen Moehler pitch should not be surprised that he's from Rockingham, since that's what hitters have recently been doing against him. Moehler hit the DL in July for his groin, and he had surgery in September. At age 39, he might have one more practically terrible year left. (BJ)

| Player | Age | IP | W | Sv | K | ERA | WHIP | K/9 | BB/9 | $2L | Pts |
|---|---|---|---|---|---|---|---|---|---|---|---|
| | | Forecast | | | | | | | | | |
| Moehler B | 39 | 60 | 2 | 0 | 30 | 5.43 | 1.50 | 4.5 | 3.0 | -$5 | 30 |
| **Mini-Browser** | **Age** | **IP** | **W** | **Sv** | **K** | **ERA** | **WHIP** | **K/9** | **BB/9** | **$2L** | **Pts** |
| Oliver A | 23 | 60 | 3 | 0 | 39 | 5.64 | 1.66 | 5.8 | 4.7 | -$5 | 40 |
| O'Sullivan S | 23 | 100 | 5 | 0 | 65 | 5.74 | 1.54 | 5.9 | 3.1 | -$5 | 80 |
| Wood T | 28 | 40 | 1 | 0 | 28 | 5.05 | 1.68 | 6.3 | 4.5 | -$5 | 20 |
| Lynn L | 23 | 60 | 3 | 0 | 43 | 5.52 | 1.58 | 6.4 | 4.4 | -$5 | 50 |
| Medders B | 31 | 60 | 2 | 0 | 43 | 5.07 | 1.61 | 6.5 | 4.2 | -$5 | 40 |

**Competition at RP — Stats in 2010 as RP**

| Thr | Player | GR | ERA | IP/G | Sv-Hld |
|---|---|---|---|---|---|
| RH | Lyon B | 79 | 3.12 | 1.0 | 20-19 |
| RH | Lopez W | 68 | 2.96 | 1.0 | 1-14 |
| RH | Lindstrom M | 58 | 4.39 | 0.9 | 23-4 |
| RH | Fulchino J | 50 | 5.51 | 0.9 | 0-5 |

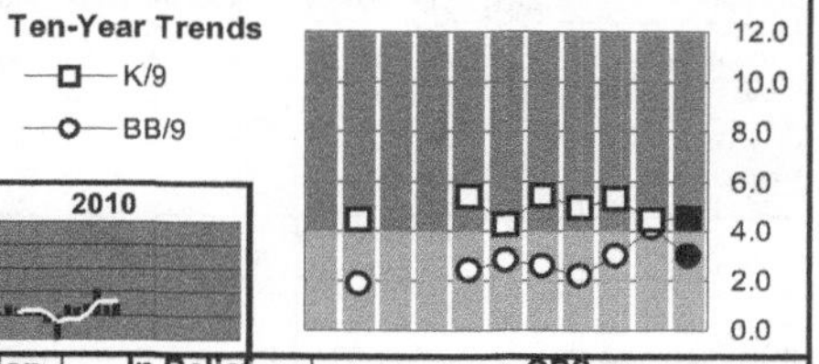
Ten-Year Trends
K/9
BB/9
12.0
10.0
8.0
6.0
4.0
2.0
0.0

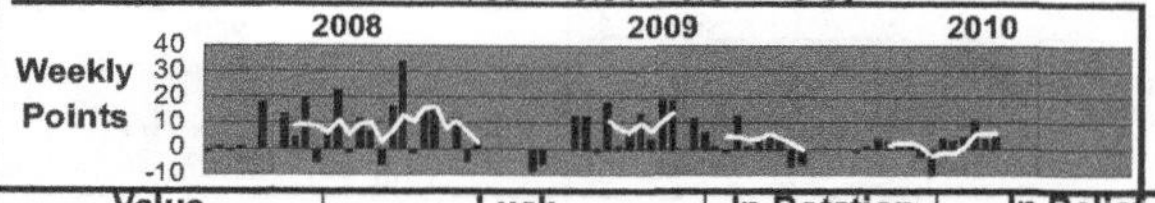
Weekly Points
2008
2009
2010
40
30
20
10
0
-10

| Level | Leag | W | L | Sv | IP | H | K | ERA | WHIP | K/9 | BB/9 | HR/9 | GB/F |
|---|---|---|---|---|---|---|---|---|---|---|---|---|---|
| | | Minors (2010) | | | | | | | | Skills | | | |
| A | — | — | — | — | — | — | — | — | — | — | — | — | — |
| AA | — | — | — | — | — | — | — | — | — | — | — | — | — |
| AAA | — | — | — | — | — | — | — | — | — | — | — | — | — |

| Yr | Team | W | L | Sv | IP | H | K | ERA | WHIP | K/9 | BB/9 | HR/9 | GB/F |
|---|---|---|---|---|---|---|---|---|---|---|---|---|---|
| | | Majors | | | | | | | | Skills | | | |
| 07 | HOU | 1 | 4 | 1 | 59 | 67 | 36 | 4.07 | 1.41 | 5.4 | 2.6 | 1.2 | 1.7 |
| 08 | HOU | 11 | 8 | 0 | 150 | 166 | 82 | 4.56 | 1.35 | 4.9 | 2.2 | 1.2 | 1.2 |
| 09 | HOU | 8 | 12 | 0 | 154 | 187 | 91 | 5.47 | 1.54 | 5.3 | 3.0 | 1.2 | 1.2 |
| 10 | HOU | 1 | 4 | 0 | 56 | 66 | 28 | 4.92 | 1.62 | 4.4 | 4.1 | 0.8 | 1.2 |

| Yr | $1L | $2L | Pts | RAA | H% | HR/fb | S% | FIP | GS | CG | QS/DS | GR | Hld | Bln | Lead | OPS | 1st Hf | 2nd Hf | vs RH | vs LH |
|---|---|---|---|---|---|---|---|---|---|---|---|---|---|---|---|---|---|---|---|---|
| | Value | | | | Luck | | | | In Rotation | | | In Relief | | | | OPS | | | | |
| 07 | -$1 | -$5 | 40 | –2 | 30% | 13% | 75% | 4.59 | — | — | — | 42 | 1 | 0 | –2.4 | .757 | .826 | .664 | .686 | .871 |
| 08 | $2 | -$6 | 160 | –12 | 29% | 11% | 69% | 4.56 | 26 | 0 | 9/4 | 5 | 0 | 0 | –0.4 | .772 | .777 | .768 | .679 | .877 |
| 09 | -$6 | -$11 | 110 | –31 | 32% | 11% | 66% | 4.78 | 29 | 1 | 11/8 | — | — | — | — | .843 | .859 | .827 | .857 | .828 |
| 10 | -$8 | -$18 | 20 | –7 | 33% | 7% | 70% | 4.74 | 8 | 0 | 2/1 | 12 | 0 | 0 | –2.4 | .799 | .799 | — | .807 | .789 |

## Carlos Monasterios

**40 IP | $-3 | 40 pts**

RP-19, SP-13 — Owned: 1% — RH

Given that Monasterios is a Rule 5 pick, simply the fact that he stuck with the Dodgers all season counts as a success. He made 13 starts, but he was far more effective from the 'pen (2.06 ERA). Now that he is Dodger property, he will get more minor-league seasoning, but he should pitch in for the parent, too. (MP)

| Player | Age | IP | W | Sv | K | ERA | WHIP | K/9 | BB/9 | $2L | Pts |
|---|---|---|---|---|---|---|---|---|---|---|---|
| | | Forecast | | | | | | | | | |
| Monasterios C | 25 | 40 | 2 | 0 | 32 | 4.98 | 1.56 | 7.2 | 3.2 | -$3 | 40 |
| **Mini-Browser** | **Age** | **IP** | **W** | **Sv** | **K** | **ERA** | **WHIP** | **K/9** | **BB/9** | **$2L** | **Pts** |
| Rodriguez F | 28 | 20 | 1 | 0 | 17 | 5.41 | 1.73 | 7.7 | 5.0 | -$3 | 20 |
| Bonine E | 29 | 60 | 3 | 0 | 30 | 5.38 | 1.50 | 4.6 | 2.5 | -$3 | 40 |
| Burres B | 29 | 40 | 2 | 0 | 26 | 5.03 | 1.51 | 5.8 | 3.5 | -$3 | 30 |
| Bell T | 24 | 80 | 4 | 0 | 62 | 5.12 | 1.61 | 7.0 | 3.3 | -$3 | 70 |
| Haeger C | 27 | 40 | 2 | 0 | 33 | 5.16 | 1.53 | 7.3 | 4.3 | -$3 | 40 |

**Competition at RP — Stats in 2010 as RP**

| Thr | Player | GR | ERA | IP/G | Sv-Hld |
|---|---|---|---|---|---|
| RH | Broxton J | 64 | 4.04 | 1.0 | 22-3 |
| RH | Belisario R | 59 | 5.04 | 0.9 | 2-16 |
| RH | Troncoso R | 52 | 4.33 | 1.0 | 0-8 |
| RH | Weaver J | 44 | 6.09 | 1.0 | 0-5 |

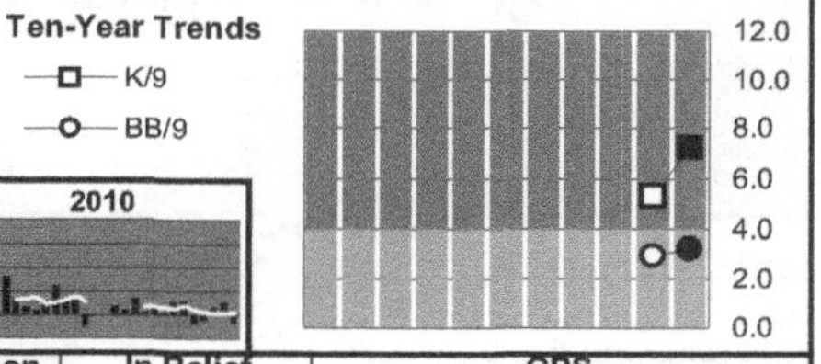
Ten-Year Trends
K/9
BB/9
12.0
10.0
8.0
6.0
4.0
2.0
0.0

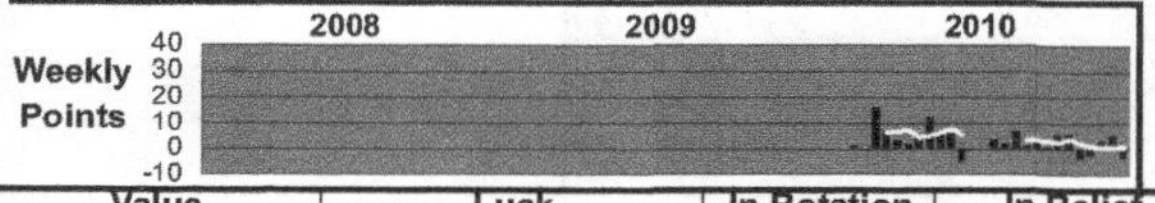
Weekly Points
2008
2009
2010
40
30
20
10
0
-10

| Level | Leag | W | L | Sv | IP | H | K | ERA | WHIP | K/9 | BB/9 | HR/9 | GB/F |
|---|---|---|---|---|---|---|---|---|---|---|---|---|---|
| | | Minors (2010) | | | | | | | | Skills | | | |
| A | — | — | — | — | — | — | — | — | — | — | — | — | — |
| AA | — | — | — | — | — | — | — | — | — | — | — | — | — |
| AAA | PCL | 0 | 0 | 0 | 6 | 7 | 5 | 5.40 | 1.50 | 6.8 | 4.1 | 1.4 | — |

| Yr | Team | W | L | Sv | IP | H | K | ERA | WHIP | K/9 | BB/9 | HR/9 | GB/F |
|---|---|---|---|---|---|---|---|---|---|---|---|---|---|
| | | Majors | | | | | | | | Skills | | | |
| 07 | — | — | — | — | — | — | — | — | — | — | — | — | — |
| 08 | — | — | — | — | — | — | — | — | — | — | — | — | — |
| 09 | — | — | — | — | — | — | — | — | — | — | — | — | — |
| 10 | LAD | 3 | 5 | 0 | 88 | 99 | 52 | 4.38 | 1.45 | 5.3 | 3.0 | 1.5 | 1.1 |

| Yr | $1L | $2L | Pts | RAA | H% | HR/fb | S% | FIP | GS | CG | QS/DS | GR | Hld | Bln | Lead | OPS | 1st Hf | 2nd Hf | vs RH | vs LH |
|---|---|---|---|---|---|---|---|---|---|---|---|---|---|---|---|---|---|---|---|---|
| | Value | | | | Luck | | | | In Rotation | | | In Relief | | | | OPS | | | | |
| 07 | — | — | — | — | — | — | — | — | — | — | — | — | — | — | — | — | — | — | — | — |
| 08 | — | — | — | — | — | — | — | — | — | — | — | — | — | — | — | — | — | — | — | — |
| 09 | — | — | — | — | — | — | — | — | — | — | — | — | — | — | — | — | — | — | — | — |
| 10 | -$5 | -$15 | 60 | –8 | 29% | 13% | 75% | 5.22 | 13 | 0 | 1/5 | 19 | 0 | 0 | –1.3 | .796 | .795 | .796 | .869 | .709 |

## Bryan Morris

**40 IP | $-4 | 30 pts**

No MLB games played in 2010 — Owned: 0% — RH

Morris opened 2010 by dominating High-A, and his rates stayed fairly steady on a subsequent promotion to Double-A. He will probably start the 2011 season in Triple-A, but if he continues to produce at this caliber, he could join Pittsburgh's rotation as early as June. (MB)

| Player | Age | IP | W | Sv | K | ERA | WHIP | K/9 | BB/9 | $2L | Pts |
|---|---|---|---|---|---|---|---|---|---|---|---|
| | | Forecast | | | | | | | | | |
| Morris B | 24 | 40 | 2 | 0 | 27 | 5.15 | 1.55 | 6.2 | 3.8 | -$4 | 30 |
| **Mini-Browser** | **Age** | **IP** | **W** | **Sv** | **K** | **ERA** | **WHIP** | **K/9** | **BB/9** | **$2L** | **Pts** |
| Herndon D | 25 | 40 | 1 | 0 | 28 | 4.95 | 1.53 | 6.2 | 2.5 | -$4 | 30 |
| Hardy B | 24 | 40 | 1 | 0 | 21 | 5.36 | 1.59 | 4.8 | 3.7 | -$4 | 20 |
| Stammen C | 27 | 60 | 2 | 0 | 39 | 5.14 | 1.47 | 5.8 | 2.8 | -$4 | 40 |
| Hernandez D | 25 | 60 | 4 | 0 | 56 | 5.64 | 1.64 | 8.5 | 4.6 | -$4 | 70 |
| Olson G | 27 | 50 | 2 | 0 | 35 | 5.51 | 1.58 | 6.3 | 4.4 | -$4 | 30 |

**Competition at SP — Stats in 2010 as SP**

| Thr | Player | GS | ERA | Supp | W-L |
|---|---|---|---|---|---|
| LH | Maholm P | 32 | 5.10 | 4.0 | 9-15 |
| LH | Duke Z | 29 | 5.72 | 3.8 | 8-15 |
| RH | Ohlendorf R | 21 | 4.07 | 2.9 | 1-11 |
| RH | Karstens J | 19 | 4.78 | 3.6 | 3-10 |

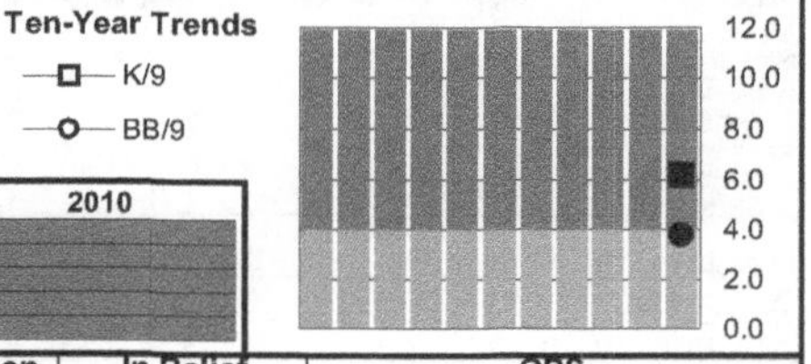
Ten-Year Trends
K/9
BB/9
12.0
10.0
8.0
6.0
4.0
2.0
0.0

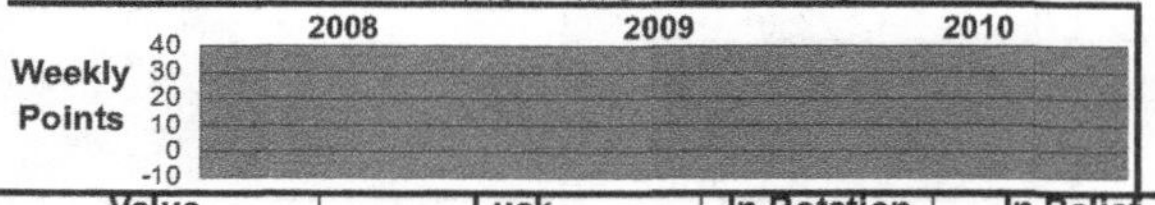
Weekly Points
2008
2009
2010
40
30
20
10
0
-10

| Level | Leag | W | L | Sv | IP | H | K | ERA | WHIP | K/9 | BB/9 | HR/9 | GB/F |
|---|---|---|---|---|---|---|---|---|---|---|---|---|---|
| | | Minors (2010) | | | | | | | | Skills | | | |
| A | FLO | 3 | 0 | 0 | 44 | 37 | 40 | 0.60 | 0.99 | 8.1 | 1.4 | 0.0 | — |
| AA | EL | 6 | 4 | 0 | 89 | 87 | 84 | 4.25 | 1.33 | 8.5 | 3.1 | 0.9 | — |
| AAA | — | — | — | — | — | — | — | — | — | — | — | — | — |

| Yr | Team | W | L | Sv | IP | H | K | ERA | WHIP | K/9 | BB/9 | HR/9 | GB/F |
|---|---|---|---|---|---|---|---|---|---|---|---|---|---|
| | | Majors | | | | | | | | Skills | | | |
| 07 | — | — | — | — | — | — | — | — | — | — | — | — | — |
| 08 | — | — | — | — | — | — | — | — | — | — | — | — | — |
| 09 | — | — | — | — | — | — | — | — | — | — | — | — | — |
| 10 | — | — | — | — | — | — | — | — | — | — | — | — | — |

| Yr | $1L | $2L | Pts | RAA | H% | HR/fb | S% | FIP | GS | CG | QS/DS | GR | Hld | Bln | Lead | OPS | 1st Hf | 2nd Hf | vs RH | vs LH |
|---|---|---|---|---|---|---|---|---|---|---|---|---|---|---|---|---|---|---|---|---|
| | Value | | | | Luck | | | | In Rotation | | | In Relief | | | | OPS | | | | |
| 07 | — | — | — | — | — | — | — | — | — | — | — | — | — | — | — | — | — | — | — | — |
| 08 | — | — | — | — | — | — | — | — | — | — | — | — | — | — | — | — | — | — | — | — |
| 09 | — | — | — | — | — | — | — | — | — | — | — | — | — | — | — | — | — | — | — | — |
| 10 | — | — | — | — | — | — | — | — | — | — | — | — | — | — | — | — | — | — | — | — |

## Brandon Morrow

**200 IP | $7 | 290 pts**

SP-26 — Owned: 66% — RH

In the face of a high H%, Morrow had a break-out 2010, posting the highest K/9 among MLB starters. He has the upside of a #2 starter, but his greenness is not behind him – his ERA was over 5.00 for three of the five months in which he pitched. Freed of an inning cap, he should be more prolific in 2011. (MH)

| Player | Age | IP | W | Sv | K | ERA | WHIP | K/9 | BB/9 | $2L | Pts |
|---|---|---|---|---|---|---|---|---|---|---|---|
| | | Forecast | | | | | | | | | |
| Morrow B | 26 | 200 | 13 | 0 | 215 | 4.60 | 1.45 | 9.7 | 4.8 | $7 | 290 |
| **Mini-Browser** | **Age** | **IP** | **W** | **Sv** | **K** | **ERA** | **WHIP** | **K/9** | **BB/9** | **$2L** | **Pts** |
| Meek E | 27 | 80 | 4 | 12 | 71 | 3.36 | 1.34 | 7.9 | 4.3 | $8 | 170 |
| Romero R | 26 | 200 | 12 | 0 | 157 | 4.32 | 1.42 | 7.1 | 4.0 | $8 | 240 |
| Slowey K | 26 | 140 | 10 | 0 | 104 | 4.51 | 1.25 | 6.7 | 1.6 | $8 | 190 |
| Downs S | 35 | 60 | 4 | 8 | 48 | 3.18 | 1.19 | 7.2 | 2.9 | $7 | 130 |
| Madson R | 30 | 60 | 4 | 9 | 53 | 3.49 | 1.17 | 8.0 | 2.5 | $7 | 150 |

**Competition at SP — Stats in 2010 as SP**

| Thr | Player | GS | ERA | Supp | W-L |
|---|---|---|---|---|---|
| LH | Romero R | 32 | 3.73 | 4.5 | 14-9 |
| RH | Marcum S | 31 | 3.64 | 4.5 | 13-8 |
| LH | Cecil B | 28 | 4.22 | 5.5 | 15-7 |
| ▶ RH | Morrow B | 26 | 4.49 | 4.6 | 10-7 |

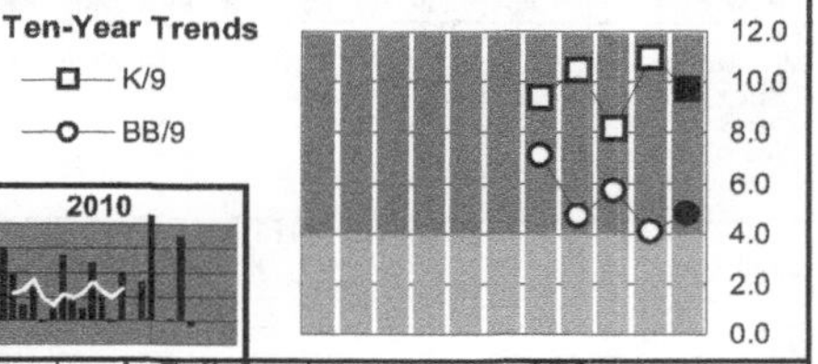
Ten-Year Trends
K/9
BB/9
12.0
10.0
8.0
6.0
4.0
2.0
0.0

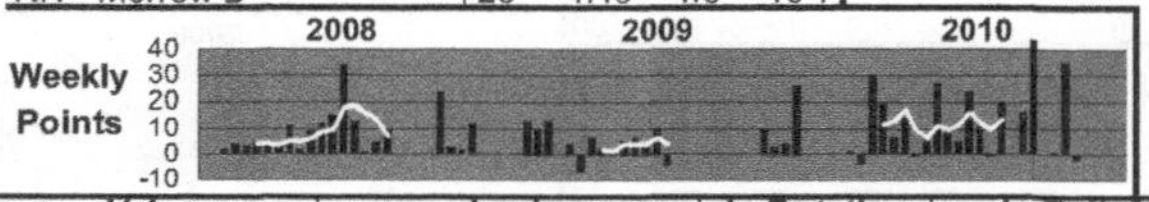
Weekly Points
2008
2009
2010
40
30
20
10
0
-10

| Level | Leag | W | L | Sv | IP | H | K | ERA | WHIP | K/9 | BB/9 | HR/9 | GB/F |
|---|---|---|---|---|---|---|---|---|---|---|---|---|---|
| | | Minors (2010) | | | | | | | | Skills | | | |
| A | — | — | — | — | — | — | — | — | — | — | — | — | — |
| AA | — | — | — | — | — | — | — | — | — | — | — | — | — |
| AAA | — | — | — | — | — | — | — | — | — | — | — | — | — |

| Yr | Team | W | L | Sv | IP | H | K | ERA | WHIP | K/9 | BB/9 | HR/9 | GB/F |
|---|---|---|---|---|---|---|---|---|---|---|---|---|---|
| | | Majors | | | | | | | | Skills | | | |
| 07 | SEA | 3 | 4 | 0 | 63 | 56 | 66 | 4.12 | 1.67 | 9.4 | 7.1 | 0.4 | 0.7 |
| 08 | SEA | 3 | 4 | 10 | 64 | 40 | 75 | 3.34 | 1.14 | 10.4 | 4.7 | 1.4 | 0.7 |
| 09 | SEA | 2 | 4 | 6 | 69 | 66 | 63 | 4.39 | 1.58 | 8.1 | 5.7 | 1.3 | 0.9 |
| 10 | TOR | 10 | 7 | 0 | 146 | 136 | 178 | 4.49 | 1.38 | 10.9 | 4.1 | 0.7 | 1.0 |

| Yr | $1L | $2L | Pts | RAA | H% | HR/fb | S% | FIP | GS | CG | QS/DS | GR | Hld | Bln | Lead | OPS | 1st Hf | 2nd Hf | vs RH | vs LH |
|---|---|---|---|---|---|---|---|---|---|---|---|---|---|---|---|---|---|---|---|---|
| | Value | | | | Luck | | | | In Rotation | | | In Relief | | | | OPS | | | | |
| 07 | -$1 | -$7 | 80 | +2 | 33% | 4% | 75% | 4.20 | — | — | — | 60 | 18 | 2 | +0.2 | .723 | .728 | .714 | .638 | .848 |
| 08 | $8 | $4 | 160 | +6 | 21% | 13% | 78% | 4.57 | 5 | 0 | 2/2 | 40 | 3 | 2 | 0.0 | .611 | .519 | .690 | .499 | .718 |
| 09 | $1 | -$3 | 90 | –4 | 29% | 11% | 76% | 5.25 | 10 | 0 | 2/0 | 16 | 1 | 2 | +0.4 | .755 | .846 | .554 | .628 | .854 |
| 10 | $6 | -$9 | 250 | –4 | 35% | 7% | 68% | 3.20 | 26 | 1 | 15/5 | — | — | — | — | .725 | .753 | .663 | .704 | .739 |

*For more stats, visit www.Rotolympus.com.*

## Clay Mortensen — 40 IP | $-3 | 30 pts
**SP-1** · Owned: 0% · RH

Mortensen in 2010 added a curveball to his repertoire and put together a strong season at Triple-A, though he faded in August. He also pitched well in one major-league outing. In most organizations, Mortensen would be a strong #5 SP candidate, but on the A's, he will have to overtake a handful of pitchers. (ML)

**Forecast**

| Player | Age | IP | W | Sv | K | ERA | WHIP | K/9 | BB/9 | $2L | Pts |
|---|---|---|---|---|---|---|---|---|---|---|---|
| Mortensen C | 25 | 40 | 2 | 0 | 30 | 5.58 | 1.54 | 6.7 | 3.9 | -$3 | 30 |

**Mini-Browser**

| Player | Age | IP | W | Sv | K | ERA | WHIP | K/9 | BB/9 | $2L | Pts |
|---|---|---|---|---|---|---|---|---|---|---|---|
| McCutchen D | 28 | 40 | 2 | 0 | 30 | 5.16 | 1.47 | 6.7 | 2.7 | -$3 | 40 |
| Ray R | 27 | 60 | 3 | 0 | 49 | 5.26 | 1.60 | 7.4 | 3.6 | -$3 | 50 |
| Igarashi R | 31 | 40 | 2 | 0 | 29 | 5.28 | 1.43 | 6.4 | 4.4 | -$3 | 50 |
| Berken J | 27 | 60 | 3 | 0 | 41 | 5.19 | 1.57 | 6.2 | 3.2 | -$3 | 50 |
| Parra M | 28 | 60 | 3 | 0 | 51 | 4.99 | 1.53 | 7.7 | 4.3 | -$3 | 60 |

**Competition at SP / Stats in 2010 as SP**

| Thr | Player | GS | ERA | Supp | W-L |
|---|---|---|---|---|---|
| LH | Gonzalez G | 33 | 3.23 | 4.3 | 15-9 |
| RH | Cahill T | 30 | 2.97 | 4.6 | 18-8 |
| LH | Braden D | 30 | 3.50 | 3.3 | 11-14 |
| RH | Sheets B | 20 | 4.53 | 4.6 | 4-9 |

**Minors (2010)**

| Level Leag | W | L | Sv | IP | H | K | ERA | WHIP | K/9 | BB/9 | HR/9 | GB/F |
|---|---|---|---|---|---|---|---|---|---|---|---|---|
| A — | | | | | | | | | | | | |
| AA — | | | | | | | | | | | | |
| AAA — | | | | | | | | | | | | |

**Majors**

| Yr Team | W | L | Sv | IP | H | K | ERA | WHIP | K/9 | BB/9 | HR/9 | GB/F |
|---|---|---|---|---|---|---|---|---|---|---|---|---|
| 07 — | | | | | | | | | | | | |
| 08 — | | | | | | | | | | | | |
| 09 2TM | 2 | 4 | 0 | 30 | 42 | 13 | 7.63 | 1.79 | 3.8 | 3.8 | 1.8 | 1.9 |
| 10 OAK | 0 | 0 | 0 | 6 | 6 | 7 | 4.50 | 1.33 | 10.5 | 3.0 | 1.5 | 0.7 |

**Value / Luck / In Rotation / In Relief / OPS**

| $1L | $2L | Pts | RAA | H% | HR/fb | S% | FIP | GS | CG | QS/DS | GR | Hld | Bln | Lead | OPS | 1st Hf | 2nd Hf | vs RH | vs LH |
|---|---|---|---|---|---|---|---|---|---|---|---|---|---|---|---|---|---|---|---|
| -$7 | -$7 | 10 | -19 | 32% | 19% | 59% | 6.22 | 6 | 0 | 1/3 | 1 | 0 | 0 | -0.6 | .962 | 1.300 | .927 | .887 | 1.047 |
| -$4 | -$11 | 10 | -1 | 31% | 14% | 71% | | | | 1/0 | | | | | .853 | .683 | .683 | .853 | .347 |

---

## Charlie Morton — 100 IP | $-5 | 80 pts
**SP-17** · Owned: 0% · RH

In a disastrous 2010 season, Morton steadied himself late (4.33 ERA in Sept.), and he finished the year with acceptable skills. The Pirates have little upside in their SP's, so Morton should get another chance. He will need to produce immediately, because the rotation could get crowded around mid-season. (MB)

**Forecast**

| Player | Age | IP | W | Sv | K | ERA | WHIP | K/9 | BB/9 | $2L | Pts |
|---|---|---|---|---|---|---|---|---|---|---|---|
| Morton C | 27 | 100 | 5 | 0 | 72 | 5.35 | 1.53 | 6.5 | 3.4 | -$5 | 80 |

**Mini-Browser**

| Player | Age | IP | W | Sv | K | ERA | WHIP | K/9 | BB/9 | $2L | Pts |
|---|---|---|---|---|---|---|---|---|---|---|---|
| Lynn L | 23 | 60 | 3 | 0 | 43 | 5.52 | 1.58 | 6.4 | 4.4 | -$5 | 50 |
| Medders B | 31 | 60 | 2 | 0 | 43 | 5.07 | 1.61 | 6.5 | 4.2 | -$5 | 40 |
| Moehler B | 39 | 60 | 2 | 0 | 30 | 5.43 | 1.50 | 4.5 | 3.0 | -$5 | 30 |
| Vasquez E | 27 | 60 | 3 | 0 | 54 | 5.26 | 1.65 | 8.1 | 5.4 | -$5 | 40 |
| Wellemeyer T | 32 | 60 | 3 | 0 | 37 | 5.70 | 1.52 | 5.5 | 4.1 | -$5 | 40 |

**Competition at SP / Stats in 2010 as SP**

| Thr | Player | GS | ERA | Supp | W-L |
|---|---|---|---|---|---|
| LH | Maholm P | 32 | 5.10 | 4.0 | 9-15 |
| LH | Duke Z | 29 | 5.72 | 3.8 | 8-15 |
| RH | Ohlendorf R | 21 | 4.07 | 2.9 | 1-11 |
| RH | Karstens J | 19 | 4.78 | 3.6 | 3-10 |

**Minors (2010)**

| Level Leag | W | L | Sv | IP | H | K | ERA | WHIP | K/9 | BB/9 | HR/9 | GB/F |
|---|---|---|---|---|---|---|---|---|---|---|---|---|
| A — | | | | | | | | | | | | |
| AA — | | | | | | | | | | | | |
| AAA — | | | | | | | | | | | | |

**Majors**

| Yr Team | W | L | Sv | IP | H | K | ERA | WHIP | K/9 | BB/9 | HR/9 | GB/F |
|---|---|---|---|---|---|---|---|---|---|---|---|---|
| 07 — | | | | | | | | | | | | |
| 08 ATL | 4 | 8 | 0 | 74 | 80 | 48 | 6.15 | 1.62 | 5.8 | 4.9 | 1.1 | 1.6 |
| 09 PIT | 5 | 9 | 0 | 97 | 102 | 62 | 4.55 | 1.46 | 5.8 | 3.7 | 0.6 | 1.5 |
| 10 PIT | 2 | 12 | 0 | 79 | 112 | 59 | 7.57 | 1.73 | 6.7 | 2.9 | 1.7 | 1.6 |

**Value / Luck / In Rotation / In Relief / OPS**

| $1L | $2L | Pts | RAA | H% | HR/fb | S% | FIP | GS | CG | QS/DS | GR | Hld | Bln | Lead | OPS | 1st Hf | 2nd Hf | vs RH | vs LH |
|---|---|---|---|---|---|---|---|---|---|---|---|---|---|---|---|---|---|---|---|
| -$8 | -$13 | 50 | -19 | 30% | 12% | 63% | 5.13 | 15 | 0 | 6/5 | 1 | 0 | 0 | 0.0 | .816 | .797 | .829 | .721 | .925 |
| -$1 | -$4 | 50 | -1 | 32% | 7% | 69% | 4.10 | 18 | 1 | 8/3 | | | | | .761 | .790 | .752 | .594 | .923 |
| -$16 | -$34 | 20 | -40 | 36% | 18% | 58% | 5.15 | 17 | 0 | 7/7 | | | | | .908 | .984 | .806 | .878 | .949 |

---

## Dustin Moseley — 60 IP | $-2 | 50 pts
**SP-9, RP-7** · Owned: 1% · RH

Moseley mostly filled in for Andy Pettitte and Javier Vazquez, and he fared OK in that role. He recorded no Disaster Starts, though he did allow 4+ ER in 6 of 9 starts, and hitters caught up to him on his second and (especially) third time through the line-up. Still, Moseley is arguably NY's best candidate for this job. (LS)

**Forecast**

| Player | Age | IP | W | Sv | K | ERA | WHIP | K/9 | BB/9 | $2L | Pts |
|---|---|---|---|---|---|---|---|---|---|---|---|
| Moseley D | 29 | 60 | 3 | 0 | 34 | 5.10 | 1.42 | 5.1 | 3.1 | -$2 | 50 |

**Mini-Browser**

| Player | Age | IP | W | Sv | K | ERA | WHIP | K/9 | BB/9 | $2L | Pts |
|---|---|---|---|---|---|---|---|---|---|---|---|
| Beimel J | 33 | 40 | 2 | 0 | 21 | 3.95 | 1.43 | 4.7 | 3.3 | -$1 | 30 |
| Durbin C | 33 | 60 | 3 | 0 | 45 | 4.59 | 1.41 | 6.8 | 3.9 | -$1 | 60 |
| Tomlin J | 26 | 60 | 4 | 0 | 52 | 5.23 | 1.47 | 7.8 | 2.6 | -$1 | 70 |
| Chavez J | 27 | 60 | 3 | 0 | 45 | 5.18 | 1.42 | 6.7 | 3.3 | -$2 | 60 |
| Cohoon M | 23 | 40 | 2 | 0 | 24 | 4.35 | 1.41 | 5.4 | 3.0 | -$2 | 40 |

**Competition at SP / Stats in 2010 as SP**

| Thr | Player | GS | ERA | Supp | W-L |
|---|---|---|---|---|---|
| LH | Sabathia C | 34 | 3.18 | 5.7 | 21-7 |
| RH | Burnett A | 33 | 5.26 | 4.3 | 10-15 |
| RH | Hughes P | 29 | 4.23 | 6.5 | 17-8 |
| RH | Vazquez J | 26 | 5.56 | 4.1 | 8-10 |

**Minors (2010)**

| Level Leag | W | L | Sv | IP | H | K | ERA | WHIP | K/9 | BB/9 | HR/9 | GB/F |
|---|---|---|---|---|---|---|---|---|---|---|---|---|
| A — | | | | | | | | | | | | |
| AA — | | | | | | | | | | | | |
| AAA IL | 4 | 4 | 0 | 72 | 83 | 55 | 4.21 | 1.39 | 6.8 | 2.2 | 0.7 | — |

**Majors**

| Yr Team | W | L | Sv | IP | H | K | ERA | WHIP | K/9 | BB/9 | HR/9 | GB/F |
|---|---|---|---|---|---|---|---|---|---|---|---|---|
| 07 LAA | 4 | 3 | 0 | 92 | 97 | 50 | 4.40 | 1.35 | 4.9 | 2.6 | 0.7 | 1.4 |
| 08 LAA | 2 | 4 | 0 | 50 | 70 | 37 | 6.79 | 1.79 | 6.6 | 3.6 | 1.1 | 1.5 |
| 09 LAA | 1 | 0 | 0 | 14 | 20 | 8 | 4.30 | 1.57 | 4.9 | 1.8 | 1.8 | 1.1 |
| 10 NYY | 4 | 4 | 0 | 65 | 66 | 33 | 4.96 | 1.42 | 4.5 | 3.7 | 1.8 | 1.4 |

**Value / Luck / In Rotation / In Relief / OPS**

| $1L | $2L | Pts | RAA | H% | HR/fb | S% | FIP | GS | CG | QS/DS | GR | Hld | Bln | Lead | OPS | 1st Hf | 2nd Hf | vs RH | vs LH |
|---|---|---|---|---|---|---|---|---|---|---|---|---|---|---|---|---|---|---|---|
| $1 | -$6 | 60 | +0 | 31% | 7% | 68% | 4.08 | 8 | 0 | 2/1 | 38 | 4 | 0 | +0.1 | .747 | .651 | .829 | .833 | .644 |
| -$9 | -$12 | 20 | -13 | 38% | 11% | 62% | 4.57 | 10 | 0 | 0/1 | 2 | 0 | 0 | -0.9 | .883 | .897 | .855 | .829 | .941 |
| -$2 | -$3 | 10 | -1 | 33% | 15% | 60% | 5.48 | 3 | 0 | 1/0 | | | | | .870 | .870 | | 1.020 | .730 |
| -$2 | -$15 | 60 | -4 | 26% | 18% | 71% | 6.12 | 9 | 0 | 3/0 | 7 | 0 | 0 | +0.3 | .807 | .500 | .819 | .747 | .862 |

---

## Jason Motte — 60 IP | $4 | 110 pts
**RP-56** · Owned: 1% · RH

This catcher-turned-reliever might be the favorite to fill the closer role in STL once Ryan Franklin vacates it. Showing LaRussa's bias, Motte's 2010 innings were higher-leverage than those of Mitchell Boggs and Kyle McClellan. Motte's velocity remains impressive, and his trends are heading in the right direction. (AB)

**Forecast**

| Player | Age | IP | W | Sv | K | ERA | WHIP | K/9 | BB/9 | $2L | Pts |
|---|---|---|---|---|---|---|---|---|---|---|---|
| Motte J | 28 | 60 | 3 | 4 | 62 | 3.63 | 1.27 | 9.2 | 3.2 | $4 | 110 |

**Mini-Browser**

| Player | Age | IP | W | Sv | K | ERA | WHIP | K/9 | BB/9 | $2L | Pts |
|---|---|---|---|---|---|---|---|---|---|---|---|
| Balfour G | 33 | 60 | 3 | 0 | 64 | 3.24 | 1.26 | 9.6 | 4.1 | $4 | 100 |
| Devine J | 27 | 45 | 3 | 2 | 51 | 2.87 | 1.25 | 10.2 | 3.8 | $4 | 90 |
| Wells R | 28 | 180 | 9 | 0 | 127 | 4.30 | 1.37 | 6.3 | 2.8 | $4 | 190 |
| Adams M | 32 | 40 | 2 | 2 | 42 | 2.57 | 1.10 | 9.4 | 2.9 | $4 | 80 |
| Guthrie J | 31 | 200 | 10 | 0 | 110 | 4.76 | 1.34 | 5.0 | 2.6 | $4 | 170 |

**Competition at RP / Stats in 2010 as RP**

| Thr | Player | GR | ERA | IP/G | Sv-Hld |
|---|---|---|---|---|---|
| RH | McClellan K | 68 | 2.27 | 1.1 | 2-19 |
| RH | Boggs M | 61 | 3.61 | 1.1 | 0-6 |
| RH | Franklin R | 59 | 3.46 | 1.1 | 27-0 |
| RH | Motte J | 56 | 2.24 | 0.9 | 2-12 |

**Minors (2010)**

| Level Leag | W | L | Sv | IP | H | K | ERA | WHIP | K/9 | BB/9 | HR/9 | GB/F |
|---|---|---|---|---|---|---|---|---|---|---|---|---|
| A — | | | | | | | | | | | | |
| AA — | | | | | | | | | | | | |
| AAA PCL | 0 | 0 | 0 | 2 | 2 | 2 | 3.38 | 1.13 | 6.8 | 3.4 | 0.0 | — |

**Majors**

| Yr Team | W | L | Sv | IP | H | K | ERA | WHIP | K/9 | BB/9 | HR/9 | GB/F |
|---|---|---|---|---|---|---|---|---|---|---|---|---|
| 07 — | | | | | | | | | | | | |
| 08 STL | 0 | 0 | 1 | 11 | 5 | 16 | 0.82 | 0.73 | 13.1 | 2.5 | 0.0 | 1.0 |
| 09 STL | 4 | 4 | 0 | 56 | 57 | 54 | 4.76 | 1.41 | 8.6 | 3.7 | 1.6 | 0.8 |
| 10 STL | 4 | 2 | 2 | 52 | 41 | 54 | 2.24 | 1.13 | 9.3 | 3.1 | 0.9 | 0.8 |

**Value / Luck / In Relief / OPS**

| $1L | $2L | Pts | RAA | H% | HR/fb | S% | FIP | GS | CG | QS/DS | GR | Hld | Bln | Lead | OPS | 1st Hf | 2nd Hf | vs RH | vs LH |
|---|---|---|---|---|---|---|---|---|---|---|---|---|---|---|---|---|---|---|---|
| $1 | $1 | 30 | +3 | 25% | 0% | 88% | 1.11 | — | — | — | 12 | 4 | 0 | +0.1 | .344 | — | .344 | .340 | .347 |
| -$1 | -$2 | 80 | -7 | 31% | 14% | 71% | 4.81 | — | — | — | 69 | 15 | 3 | +1.6 | .804 | .732 | .902 | .686 | .987 |
| $4 | $0 | 110 | +11 | 28% | 8% | 85% | 3.41 | — | — | — | 56 | 12 | 1 | +1.2 | .618 | .621 | .611 | .531 | .789 |

---

## Jamie Moyer — 100 IP | $1 | 100 pts
**SP-19** · Owned: 6% · LH

Moyer says that he wants to pitch again, despite an elbow injury that shelved him for the second half of 2010. If he does return, it won't be for the Phillies. Moyer is a free agent, and the market for 48-year-old, injury-prone soft-tossers will be rather slim. On the other hand, his control was a 24-season best! (BB)

**Forecast**

| Player | Age | IP | W | Sv | K | ERA | WHIP | K/9 | BB/9 | $2L | Pts |
|---|---|---|---|---|---|---|---|---|---|---|---|
| Moyer J | 48 | 100 | 6 | 0 | 53 | 4.89 | 1.25 | 4.8 | 2.3 | $1 | 100 |

**Mini-Browser**

| Player | Age | IP | W | Sv | K | ERA | WHIP | K/9 | BB/9 | $2L | Pts |
|---|---|---|---|---|---|---|---|---|---|---|---|
| Lopez J | 33 | 60 | 3 | 0 | 38 | 3.54 | 1.37 | 5.7 | 3.7 | $1 | 60 |
| Zito B | 32 | 200 | 10 | 0 | 138 | 4.59 | 1.42 | 6.2 | 3.9 | $1 | 190 |
| Blevins J | 27 | 50 | 2 | 0 | 48 | 3.98 | 1.37 | 8.7 | 3.1 | $1 | 60 |
| Ramirez R | 29 | 60 | 3 | 0 | 44 | 3.66 | 1.35 | 6.7 | 4.1 | $1 | 60 |
| Lopez W | 27 | 60 | 3 | 0 | 45 | 4.35 | 1.34 | 6.8 | 3.0 | $1 | 80 |

**Competition at SP / Stats in 2010 as SP**

| Thr | Player | GS | ERA | Supp | W-L |
|---|---|---|---|---|---|
| RH | Halladay R | 33 | 2.44 | 4.4 | 21-10 |
| LH | Hamels C | 33 | 3.06 | 3.8 | 12-11 |
| RH | Oswalt R | 32 | 2.73 | 3.0 | 13-13 |
| RH | Kendrick K | 31 | 4.81 | 5.5 | 11-10 |

**Minors (2010)**

| Level Leag | W | L | Sv | IP | H | K | ERA | WHIP | K/9 | BB/9 | HR/9 | GB/F |
|---|---|---|---|---|---|---|---|---|---|---|---|---|
| A — | | | | | | | | | | | | |
| AA — | | | | | | | | | | | | |
| AAA — | | | | | | | | | | | | |

**Majors**

| Yr Team | W | L | Sv | IP | H | K | ERA | WHIP | K/9 | BB/9 | HR/9 | GB/F |
|---|---|---|---|---|---|---|---|---|---|---|---|---|
| 07 PHI | 14 | 12 | 0 | 199 | 222 | 133 | 5.01 | 1.44 | 6.0 | 3.0 | 1.4 | 1.0 |
| 08 PHI | 16 | 7 | 0 | 196 | 199 | 123 | 3.71 | 1.33 | 5.6 | 2.8 | 0.9 | 1.3 |
| 09 PHI | 12 | 10 | 0 | 162 | 177 | 94 | 4.94 | 1.36 | 5.2 | 2.4 | 1.5 | 1.0 |
| 10 PHI | 9 | 9 | 0 | 111 | 103 | 63 | 4.84 | 1.10 | 5.1 | 1.6 | 1.6 | 1.1 |

**Value / Luck / In Rotation / In Relief / OPS**

| $1L | $2L | Pts | RAA | H% | HR/fb | S% | FIP | GS | CG | QS/DS | GR | Hld | Bln | Lead | OPS | 1st Hf | 2nd Hf | vs RH | vs LH |
|---|---|---|---|---|---|---|---|---|---|---|---|---|---|---|---|---|---|---|---|
| $0 | -$16 | 220 | -20 | 31% | 12% | 69% | 4.82 | 33 | 1 | 18/6 | — | — | — | — | .826 | .785 | .876 | .811 | .887 |
| $10 | $2 | 270 | +12 | 29% | 9% | 75% | 4.22 | 33 | 0 | 19/4 | — | — | — | — | .731 | .777 | .664 | .735 | .718 |
| $1 | -$4 | 180 | -11 | 29% | 13% | 68% | 5.00 | 25 | 0 | 11/4 | 5 | 1 | 0 | +0.4 | .795 | .895 | .646 | .831 | .681 |
| $2 | -$7 | 140 | -9 | 24% | 13% | 61% | 4.94 | 19 | 0 | 9/3 | — | — | — | — | .715 | .689 | 1.271 | .707 | .756 |

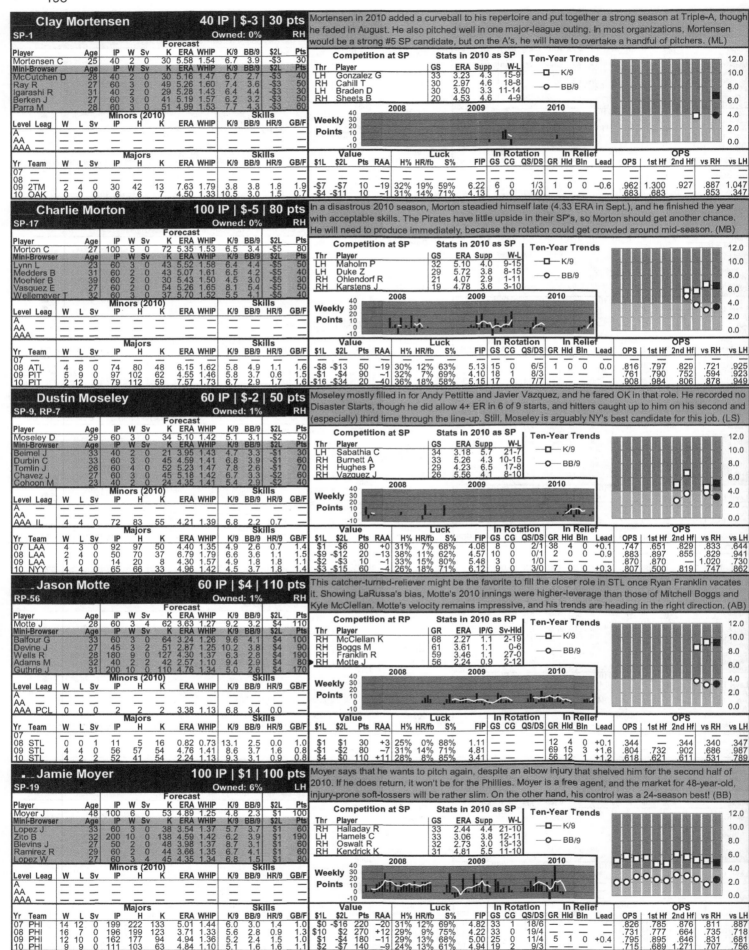

## Peter Moylan — 70 IP | $3 | 100 pts
RP-85    Owned: 18%    RH

Moylan in 2010 lost some velocity on his fastball, and with that went some of Bobby Cox's confidence in him. He did add a change-up, but his command of it was patchy. Those caveats aside, Moylan's high-K, high-GB combo remains potent. He'll find work in the 7th or 8th inning somewhere, if not in Atlanta. (MG)

### Forecast
| Player | Age | IP | W | Sv | K | ERA | WHIP | K/9 | BB/9 | $2L | Pts |
|---|---|---|---|---|---|---|---|---|---|---|---|
| Moylan P | 32 | 70 | 5 | 0 | 53 | 3.39 | 1.39 | 6.9 | 4.5 | $3 | 100 |

### Mini-Browser
| Player | Age | IP | W | Sv | K | ERA | WHIP | K/9 | BB/9 | $2L | Pts |
|---|---|---|---|---|---|---|---|---|---|---|---|
| Chapman A | 23 | 100 | 6 | 4 | 95 | 4.54 | 1.36 | 8.6 | 4.7 | $3 | 160 |
| McClellan K | 26 | 70 | 3 | 0 | 51 | 3.35 | 1.26 | 6.8 | 3.3 | $3 | 80 |
| Volquez E | 27 | 160 | 9 | 0 | 155 | 4.35 | 1.46 | 8.7 | 4.3 | $3 | 210 |
| Wuertz M | 32 | 50 | 3 | 2 | 51 | 3.67 | 1.27 | 9.2 | 3.9 | $3 | 90 |
| de la Rosa J | 29 | 160 | 10 | 0 | 140 | 4.59 | 1.39 | 7.9 | 4.0 | $3 | 200 |

### Competition at RP — Stats in 2010 as RP
| Thr | Player | GR | ERA | IP/G | Sv-Hld |
|---|---|---|---|---|---|
| RH | Moylan P | 85 | 2.97 | 0.7 | 1-21 |
| RH | Saito T | 56 | 2.83 | 1.0 | 1-17 |
| RH | Farnsworth K | 23 | 5.40 | 0.9 | 0-2 |
| RH | Kimbrel C | 21 | 0.44 | 1.0 | 1-2 |

Ten-Year Trends: K/9, BB/9

### Minors (2010)
| Level | Leag | W | L | Sv | IP | H | K | ERA | WHIP | K/9 | BB/9 | HR/9 | GB/F |
|---|---|---|---|---|---|---|---|---|---|---|---|---|---|
| A | — | — | — | — | — | — | — | — | — | — | — | — | — |
| AA | — | — | — | — | — | — | — | — | — | — | — | — | — |
| AAA | — | — | — | — | — | — | — | — | — | — | — | — | — |

### Majors / Skills / Value / Luck / In Rotation / In Relief / OPS
| Yr | Team | W | L | Sv | IP | H | K | ERA | WHIP | K/9 | BB/9 | HR/9 | GB/F | $1L | $2L | Pts | RAA | H% | HR/fb | S% | FIP | GS | CG | QS/DS | GR | Hld | Bln | Lead | OPS | 1st Hf | 2nd Hf | vs RH | vs LH |
|---|---|---|---|---|---|---|---|---|---|---|---|---|---|---|---|---|---|---|---|---|---|---|---|---|---|---|---|---|---|---|---|---|---|
| 07 | ATL | 5 | 3 | 1 | 90 | 65 | 63 | 1.80 | 1.07 | 6.3 | 3.1 | 0.6 | 2.5 | $12 | $12 | 140 | +14 | 24% | 10% | 87% | 3.70 | — | — | — | 80 | 8 | 1 | +0.2 | .597 | .619 | .572 | .537 | .679 |
| 08 | ATL | 0 | 1 | 1 | 5 | 5 | 5 | 1.59 | 1.06 | 7.9 | 1.6 | 1.6 | 3.0 | -$1 | -$1 | 10 | +2 | 24% | 25% | 100% | 4.26 | — | — | — | 7 | 4 | 1 | +1.1 | .628 | .628 | — | .647 | .606 |
| 09 | ATL | 6 | 2 | 0 | 73 | 65 | 61 | 2.84 | 1.37 | 7.5 | 4.3 | 0.0 | 3.2 | $5 | $2 | 120 | +4 | 32% | 0% | 77% | 2.97 | — | — | — | 87 | 25 | 5 | +1.1 | .651 | .716 | .581 | .534 | .851 |
| 10 | ATL | 6 | 2 | 1 | 63 | 53 | 52 | 2.97 | 1.41 | 7.4 | 5.2 | 0.7 | 3.2 | -$1 | -$5 | 110 | +5 | 28% | 14% | 81% | 4.33 | — | — | — | 85 | 21 | 3 | +0.8 | .693 | .708 | .674 | .593 | .981 |

---

## Edward Mujica — 60 IP | $3 | 70 pts
RP-59    Owned: 1%    RH

Mujica owned the strike zone (12.0 K/BB!), but the Padres rarely unleashed him in important spots. Their reluctance stemmed in part from his high HR/9, but he did raise his GB/F, and he is not likely to have an 18% HR/FB in 2011. Still, in San Diego, Mujica won't pass names like Adams, Bell, and Gregerson. (DG)

### Forecast
| Player | Age | IP | W | Sv | K | ERA | WHIP | K/9 | BB/9 | $2L | Pts |
|---|---|---|---|---|---|---|---|---|---|---|---|
| Mujica E | 26 | 60 | 2 | 0 | 51 | 4.04 | 1.08 | 7.7 | 1.5 | $3 | 70 |

### Mini-Browser
| Player | Age | IP | W | Sv | K | ERA | WHIP | K/9 | BB/9 | $2L | Pts |
|---|---|---|---|---|---|---|---|---|---|---|---|
| Sanchez A | 27 | 140 | 8 | 0 | 110 | 4.15 | 1.44 | 7.1 | 3.7 | $3 | 170 |
| Guerrier M | 32 | 80 | 4 | 0 | 49 | 4.08 | 1.27 | 5.5 | 3.0 | $3 | 80 |
| Oliver D | 40 | 60 | 3 | 0 | 50 | 3.57 | 1.28 | 7.5 | 2.8 | $3 | 80 |
| Thatcher J | 29 | 40 | 2 | 0 | 43 | 2.89 | 1.12 | 9.6 | 2.7 | $3 | 60 |
| Robertson D | 25 | 60 | 4 | 0 | 72 | 3.69 | 1.44 | 10.9 | 4.8 | $3 | 100 |

### Competition at RP — Stats in 2010 as RP
| Thr | Player | GR | ERA | IP/G | Sv-Hld |
|---|---|---|---|---|---|
| RH | Gregerson L | 80 | 3.22 | 1.0 | 2-40 |
| RH | Adams M | 70 | 1.76 | 1.0 | 0-38 |
| RH | Bell H | 67 | 1.93 | 1.0 | 47-0 |
| RH | Mujica E | 59 | 3.62 | 1.2 | 0-4 |

Ten-Year Trends: K/9, BB/9

### Minors (2010)
| Level | Leag | W | L | Sv | IP | H | K | ERA | WHIP | K/9 | BB/9 | HR/9 | GB/F |
|---|---|---|---|---|---|---|---|---|---|---|---|---|---|
| A | — | — | — | — | — | — | — | — | — | — | — | — | — |
| AA | — | — | — | — | — | — | — | — | — | — | — | — | — |
| AAA | — | — | — | — | — | — | — | — | — | — | — | — | — |

### Majors / Skills / Value / Luck / In Rotation / In Relief / OPS
| Yr | Team | W | L | Sv | IP | H | K | ERA | WHIP | K/9 | BB/9 | HR/9 | GB/F | $1L | $2L | Pts | RAA | H% | HR/fb | S% | FIP | GS | CG | QS/DS | GR | Hld | Bln | Lead | OPS | 1st Hf | 2nd Hf | vs RH | vs LH |
|---|---|---|---|---|---|---|---|---|---|---|---|---|---|---|---|---|---|---|---|---|---|---|---|---|---|---|---|---|---|---|---|---|---|
| 07 | CLE | 0 | 0 | 0 | 13 | 19 | 7 | 8.31 | 1.62 | 4.8 | 1.4 | 2.1 | 0.4 | -$4 | -$6 | 0 | -6 | 34% | 10% | 50% | 5.68 | — | — | — | 10 | 0 | 0 | -3.3 | .982 | .937 | 1.042 | 1.020 | .933 |
| 08 | CLE | 3 | 2 | 0 | 38 | 46 | 27 | 6.75 | 1.45 | 6.3 | 2.3 | 1.2 | 0.7 | -$4 | -$7 | 40 | -12 | 33% | 8% | 53% | 4.36 | — | — | — | 33 | 1 | 2 | -0.1 | .849 | .758 | .912 | .823 | .883 |
| 09 | SD | 3 | 5 | 2 | 93 | 101 | 76 | 3.94 | 1.28 | 7.3 | 1.8 | 1.3 | 1.0 | $3 | $0 | 110 | -5 | 32% | 11% | 75% | 4.13 | 4 | 0 | 0/1 | 63 | 11 | 4 | -0.6 | .747 | .689 | .790 | .682 | .815 |
| 10 | SD | 2 | 1 | 0 | 69 | 59 | 72 | 3.62 | 0.93 | 9.3 | 0.8 | 1.8 | 1.1 | $3 | -$1 | 100 | +2 | 26% | 18% | 73% | 4.00 | — | — | — | 59 | 4 | 1 | -0.5 | .684 | .710 | .646 | .727 | .625 |

---

## Brett Myers — 220 IP | $11 | 270 pts
SP-33    Owned: 80%    RH

Leaving Citizens Bank Park was the best thing to happen to Myers. Away from the barrage of HR, Myers used his savvy to pitch deep into games (he was one out shy of going 6 innings in every one of his starts!). He got an extension more fitting to a second-tier starter; if he's healthy, he should easily earn his pay. (BJ)

### Forecast
| Player | Age | IP | W | Sv | K | ERA | WHIP | K/9 | BB/9 | $2L | Pts |
|---|---|---|---|---|---|---|---|---|---|---|---|
| Myers B | 30 | 220 | 12 | 0 | 175 | 4.05 | 1.30 | 7.2 | 2.8 | $11 | 270 |

### Mini-Browser
| Player | Age | IP | W | Sv | K | ERA | WHIP | K/9 | BB/9 | $2L | Pts |
|---|---|---|---|---|---|---|---|---|---|---|---|
| Vazquez J | 34 | 200 | 14 | 0 | 172 | 4.52 | 1.27 | 7.8 | 2.8 | $12 | 280 |
| Braden D | 27 | 175 | 10 | 0 | 105 | 3.89 | 1.24 | 5.4 | 2.5 | $12 | 200 |
| Lidge B | 34 | 60 | 2 | 38 | 63 | 4.24 | 1.36 | 9.4 | 4.1 | $11 | 260 |
| Baker S | 29 | 200 | 13 | 0 | 155 | 4.41 | 1.28 | 7.0 | 2.2 | $11 | 260 |
| Jansen K | 23 | 60 | 2 | 9 | 85 | 1.56 | 1.18 | 12.7 | 5.4 | $11 | 170 |

### Competition at SP — Stats in 2010 as SP
| Thr | Player | GS | ERA | Supp | W-L |
|---|---|---|---|---|---|
| RH | Myers B | 33 | 3.14 | 4.3 | 14-8 |
| LH | Rodriguez W | 32 | 3.60 | 3.8 | 11-12 |
| RH | Norris B | 27 | 4.92 | 4.3 | 9-10 |
| LH | Happ J | 16 | 3.40 | 3.9 | 6-4 |

Ten-Year Trends: K/9, BB/9

### Minors (2010)
| Level | Leag | W | L | Sv | IP | H | K | ERA | WHIP | K/9 | BB/9 | HR/9 | GB/F |
|---|---|---|---|---|---|---|---|---|---|---|---|---|---|
| A | — | — | — | — | — | — | — | — | — | — | — | — | — |
| AA | — | — | — | — | — | — | — | — | — | — | — | — | — |
| AAA | — | — | — | — | — | — | — | — | — | — | — | — | — |

### Majors / Skills / Value / Luck / In Rotation / In Relief / OPS
| Yr | Team | W | L | Sv | IP | H | K | ERA | WHIP | K/9 | BB/9 | HR/9 | GB/F | $1L | $2L | Pts | RAA | H% | HR/fb | S% | FIP | GS | CG | QS/DS | GR | Hld | Bln | Lead | OPS | 1st Hf | 2nd Hf | vs RH | vs LH |
|---|---|---|---|---|---|---|---|---|---|---|---|---|---|---|---|---|---|---|---|---|---|---|---|---|---|---|---|---|---|---|---|---|---|
| 07 | PHI | 5 | 7 | 21 | 68 | 61 | 83 | 4.33 | 1.28 | 10.9 | 3.5 | 1.2 | 1.3 | $8 | $3 | 230 | +1 | 31% | 15% | 70% | 3.67 | 3 | 0 | 1/0 | 48 | 3 | 3 | +1.9 | .698 | .804 | .573 | .796 | .574 |
| 08 | PHI | 10 | 13 | 0 | 190 | 197 | 163 | 4.55 | 1.38 | 7.7 | 3.1 | 1.4 | 1.5 | $2 | -$7 | 230 | -9 | 31% | 16% | 71% | 4.49 | 30 | 2 | 15/5 | — | — | — | — | .791 | .907 | .649 | .835 | .739 |
| 09 | PHI | 4 | 3 | 0 | 70 | 74 | 50 | 4.84 | 1.37 | 6.4 | 2.9 | 2.3 | 1.4 | -$1 | -$7 | 30 | -3 | 27% | 23% | 75% | 6.07 | 10 | 0 | 6/4 | 8 | 3 | 0 | +0.3 | .872 | .872 | .879 | 1.118 | .674 |
| 10 | HOU | 14 | 8 | 0 | 223 | 212 | 180 | 3.14 | 1.24 | 7.2 | 2.7 | 0.8 | 1.4 | $17 | $11 | 330 | +22 | 29% | 9% | 78% | 3.64 | 33 | 2 | 24/2 | — | — | — | — | .683 | .709 | .651 | .678 | .688 |

---

## Chris Narveson — 180 IP | $2 | 230 pts
SP-28, RP-9    Owned: 0%    LH

The Brewers' decision to cut bait on Jeff Suppan thrust Narveson into the rotation full-time, and after some bumps, he settled down to a fine second half (3.89 ERA in 14 starts, only 1 Disaster). He misses bats with his breaking stuff and has good control. But he has to offer a prayer on his fly balls in Miller Park. (MS)

### Forecast
| Player | Age | IP | W | Sv | K | ERA | WHIP | K/9 | BB/9 | $2L | Pts |
|---|---|---|---|---|---|---|---|---|---|---|---|
| Narveson C | 29 | 180 | 12 | 0 | 152 | 4.87 | 1.39 | 7.6 | 3.3 | $2 | 230 |

### Mini-Browser
| Player | Age | IP | W | Sv | K | ERA | WHIP | K/9 | BB/9 | $2L | Pts |
|---|---|---|---|---|---|---|---|---|---|---|---|
| McDonald J | 26 | 160 | 7 | 0 | 160 | 4.35 | 1.44 | 9.0 | 3.8 | $3 | 200 |
| Stauffer T | 28 | 60 | 3 | 0 | 43 | 3.52 | 1.25 | 6.4 | 3.0 | $3 | 80 |
| Frasor J | 33 | 60 | 3 | 0 | 57 | 3.67 | 1.33 | 8.5 | 3.9 | $3 | 80 |
| Carmona F | 27 | 200 | 11 | 0 | 116 | 4.60 | 1.45 | 5.2 | 3.8 | $3 | 180 |
| Kintzler B | 26 | 40 | 3 | 0 | 29 | 3.07 | 1.14 | 6.5 | 1.6 | $3 | 60 |

### Competition at SP — Stats in 2010 as SP
| Thr | Player | GS | ERA | Supp | W-L |
|---|---|---|---|---|---|
| LH | Wolf R | 34 | 4.17 | 5.3 | 13-12 |
| RH | Gallardo Y | 31 | 3.84 | 5.3 | 14-7 |
| RH | Bush D | 31 | 4.55 | 4.0 | 8-13 |
| LH | Narveson C | 28 | 4.85 | 4.3 | 11-9 |

Ten-Year Trends: K/9, BB/9

### Minors (2010)
| Level | Leag | W | L | Sv | IP | H | K | ERA | WHIP | K/9 | BB/9 | HR/9 | GB/F |
|---|---|---|---|---|---|---|---|---|---|---|---|---|---|
| A | — | — | — | — | — | — | — | — | — | — | — | — | — |
| AA | — | — | — | — | — | — | — | — | — | — | — | — | — |
| AAA | — | — | — | — | — | — | — | — | — | — | — | — | — |

### Majors / Skills / Value / Luck / In Rotation / In Relief / OPS
| Yr | Team | W | L | Sv | IP | H | K | ERA | WHIP | K/9 | BB/9 | HR/9 | GB/F | $1L | $2L | Pts | RAA | H% | HR/fb | S% | FIP | GS | CG | QS/DS | GR | Hld | Bln | Lead | OPS | 1st Hf | 2nd Hf | vs RH | vs LH |
|---|---|---|---|---|---|---|---|---|---|---|---|---|---|---|---|---|---|---|---|---|---|---|---|---|---|---|---|---|---|---|---|---|---|
| 07 | | | | | | | | | | | | | | | | | | | | | | | | | | | | | | | | | |
| 08 | | | | | | | | | | | | | | | | | | | | | | | | | | | | | | | | | |
| 09 | MIL | 2 | 0 | 0 | 47 | 45 | 46 | 3.83 | 1.30 | 8.8 | 3.1 | 1.3 | 0.7 | -$1 | -$1 | 60 | +1 | 29% | 11% | 76% | 4.20 | 4 | 0 | 0/0 | 17 | 0 | 0 | -2.1 | .750 | .974 | .674 | .714 | .850 |
| 10 | MIL | 12 | 9 | 0 | 167 | 172 | 137 | 4.99 | 1.39 | 7.4 | 3.2 | 1.1 | 0.9 | -$1 | -$16 | 220 | -13 | 31% | 10% | 70% | 4.25 | 28 | 0 | 12/3 | 9 | 3 | 1 | +0.6 | .761 | .859 | .651 | .816 | .598 |

---

## Joe Nathan — 40 IP | $10 | 180 pts
No MLB games played in 2010    Owned: 9%    RH

Nathan tore an elbow ligament in Spring Training and missed all of 2010 following Tommy John surgery. Now that Joe is 36, a full recovery after one year is hardly a given (though we *have* seen aging closers such as Billy Wagner pull it off). In any case, all indications are that Nathan's rehab is going to plan. (NN)

### Forecast
| Player | Age | IP | W | Sv | K | ERA | WHIP | K/9 | BB/9 | $2L | Pts |
|---|---|---|---|---|---|---|---|---|---|---|---|
| Nathan J | 36 | 40 | 4 | 18 | 45 | 2.72 | 1.12 | 10.1 | 3.0 | $10 | 180 |

### Mini-Browser
| Player | Age | IP | W | Sv | K | ERA | WHIP | K/9 | BB/9 | $2L | Pts |
|---|---|---|---|---|---|---|---|---|---|---|---|
| Lilly T | 35 | 180 | 10 | 0 | 144 | 4.22 | 1.19 | 7.2 | 2.4 | $10 | 270 |
| Nolasco R | 28 | 180 | 13 | 0 | 158 | 4.43 | 1.25 | 7.9 | 2.4 | $10 | 270 |
| Garland J | 31 | 200 | 12 | 0 | 107 | 3.99 | 1.27 | 4.8 | 3.0 | $10 | 210 |
| Gregg K | 32 | 60 | 2 | 32 | 55 | 4.27 | 1.41 | 8.3 | 4.2 | $10 | 230 |
| Webb B | 31 | 160 | 11 | 0 | 113 | 3.86 | 1.28 | 6.3 | 2.5 | $10 | 210 |

### Competition at RP — Stats in 2010 as RP
| Thr | Player | GR | ERA | IP/G | Sv-Hld |
|---|---|---|---|---|---|
| RH | Guerrier M | 74 | 3.17 | 1.0 | 1-23 |
| RH | Crain J | 71 | 3.04 | 1.0 | 1-21 |
| RH | Rauch J | 59 | 3.12 | 1.0 | 21-2 |
| RH | Burnett A | 41 | 5.29 | 1.2 | 0-2 |

Ten-Year Trends: K/9, BB/9

### Minors (2010)
| Level | Leag | W | L | Sv | IP | H | K | ERA | WHIP | K/9 | BB/9 | HR/9 | GB/F |
|---|---|---|---|---|---|---|---|---|---|---|---|---|---|
| A | — | — | — | — | — | — | — | — | — | — | — | — | — |
| AA | — | — | — | — | — | — | — | — | — | — | — | — | — |
| AAA | — | — | — | — | — | — | — | — | — | — | — | — | — |

### Majors / Skills / Value / Luck / In Rotation / In Relief / OPS
| Yr | Team | W | L | Sv | IP | H | K | ERA | WHIP | K/9 | BB/9 | HR/9 | GB/F | $1L | $2L | Pts | RAA | H% | HR/fb | S% | FIP | GS | CG | QS/DS | GR | Hld | Bln | Lead | OPS | 1st Hf | 2nd Hf | vs RH | vs LH |
|---|---|---|---|---|---|---|---|---|---|---|---|---|---|---|---|---|---|---|---|---|---|---|---|---|---|---|---|---|---|---|---|---|---|
| 07 | MIN | 4 | 2 | 37 | 71 | 54 | 77 | 1.88 | 1.02 | 9.7 | 2.4 | 0.5 | 1.0 | $20 | $18 | 320 | +17 | 28% | 6% | 84% | 2.67 | — | — | — | 68 | 0 | 4 | +2.3 | .574 | .613 | .529 | .532 | .620 |
| 08 | MIN | 1 | 2 | 39 | 67 | 43 | 74 | 1.33 | 0.90 | 9.8 | 2.4 | 0.7 | 1.4 | $23 | $18 | 310 | +17 | 24% | 9% | 91% | 2.87 | — | — | — | 68 | 0 | 6 | +1.4 | .521 | .522 | .521 | .495 | .548 |
| 09 | MIN | 2 | 2 | 47 | 68 | 42 | 89 | 2.10 | 0.93 | 11.7 | 2.9 | 0.9 | 0.9 | $19 | $15 | 360 | +15 | 24% | 10% | 84% | 2.99 | — | — | — | 70 | 0 | 5 | +2.3 | .549 | .446 | .642 | .551 | .548 |

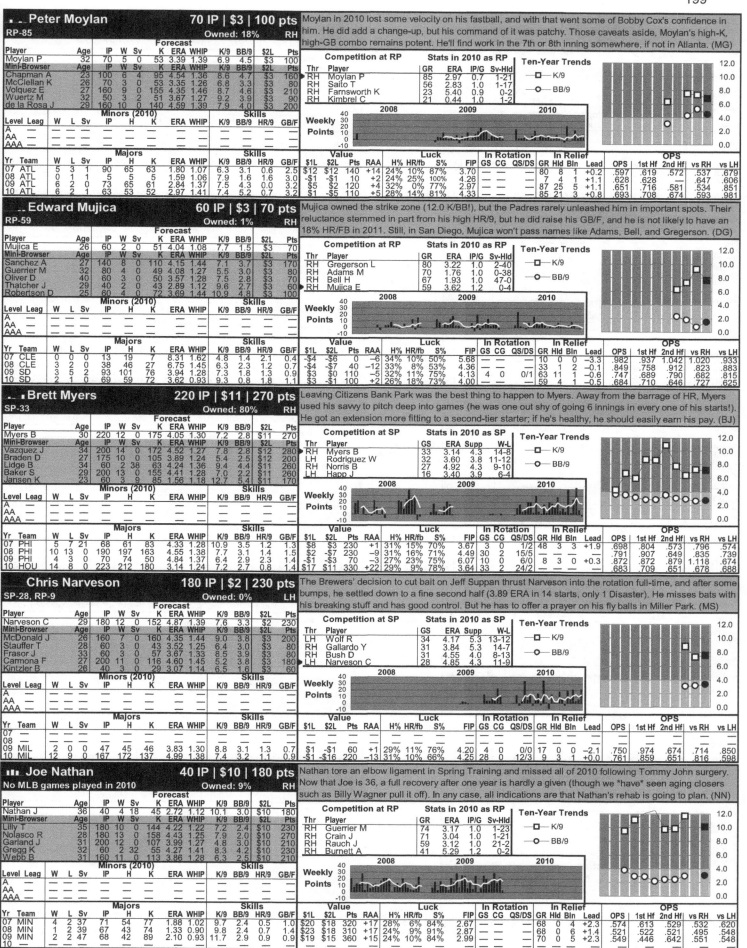

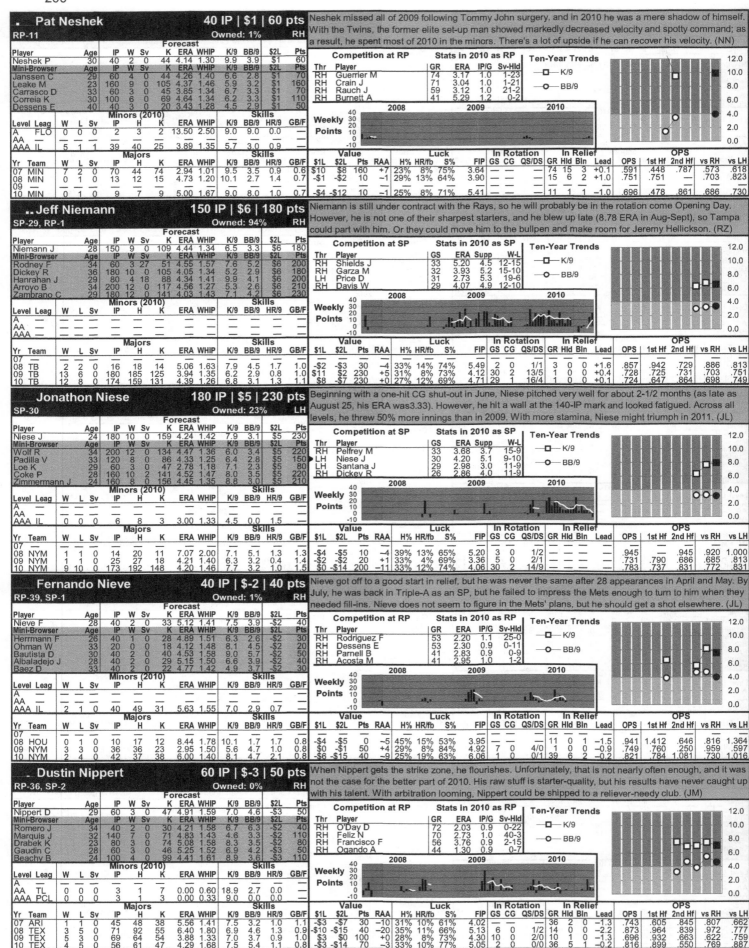

## . Pat Neshek — 40 IP | $1 | 60 pts

RP-11 — Owned: 1% — RH

Neshek missed all of 2009 following Tommy John surgery, and in 2010 he was a mere shadow of himself. With the Twins, the former elite set-up man showed markedly decreased velocity and spotty command; as a result, he spent most of 2010 in the minors. There's a lot of upside if he can recover his velocity. (NN)

| Player | Age | IP | W | Sv | K | ERA | WHIP | K/9 | BB/9 | $2L | Pts |
|---|---|---|---|---|---|---|---|---|---|---|---|
| Neshek P | 30 | 40 | 2 | 0 | 44 | 4.14 | 1.30 | 9.9 | 3.9 | $1 | 60 |
| **Mini-Browser** | **Age** | **IP** | **W** | **Sv** | **K** | **ERA** | **WHIP** | **K/9** | **BB/9** | **$2L** | **Pts** |
| Janssen C | 29 | 60 | 4 | 0 | 44 | 4.26 | 1.40 | 6.6 | 2.8 | $1 | 70 |
| Leake M | 23 | 160 | 9 | 0 | 105 | 4.37 | 1.46 | 5.9 | 3.2 | $1 | 160 |
| Carrasco D | 33 | 60 | 3 | 0 | 45 | 3.85 | 1.34 | 6.7 | 3.3 | $1 | 70 |
| Correia K | 30 | 100 | 6 | 0 | 69 | 4.64 | 1.34 | 6.2 | 3.3 | $1 | 110 |
| Dessens E | 40 | 40 | 3 | 0 | 20 | 3.43 | 1.28 | 4.5 | 2.9 | $1 | 50 |

Minors (2010) / Skills

| Level | Leag | W | L | Sv | IP | H | K | ERA | WHIP | K/9 | BB/9 | HR/9 | GB/F |
|---|---|---|---|---|---|---|---|---|---|---|---|---|---|
| A | FLO | 0 | 0 | 0 | 2 | 3 | 2 | 13.50 | 2.50 | 9.0 | 9.0 | 0.0 | — |
| AA | — | — | — | — | — | — | — | — | — | — | — | — | — |
| AAA | IL | 5 | 1 | 1 | 39 | 40 | 25 | 3.89 | 1.35 | 5.7 | 3.0 | 0.9 | — |

Competition at RP — Stats in 2010 as RP

| Thr | Player | GR | ERA | IP/G | Sv-Hld |
|---|---|---|---|---|---|
| RH | Guerrier M | 74 | 3.17 | 1.0 | 1-23 |
| RH | Crain J | 71 | 3.04 | 1.0 | 1-21 |
| RH | Rauch J | 59 | 3.12 | 1.0 | 21-2 |
| RH | Burnett A | 41 | 5.29 | 1.2 | 0-2 |

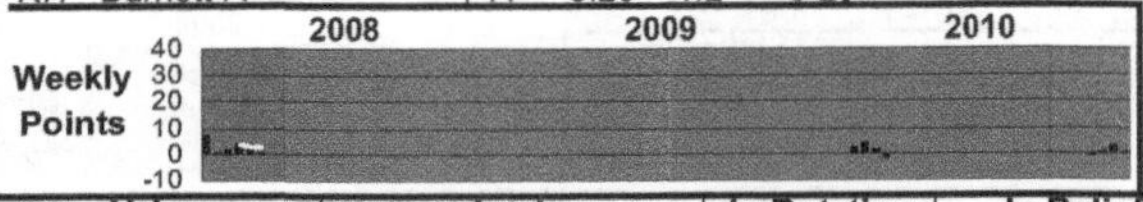


Ten-Year Trends

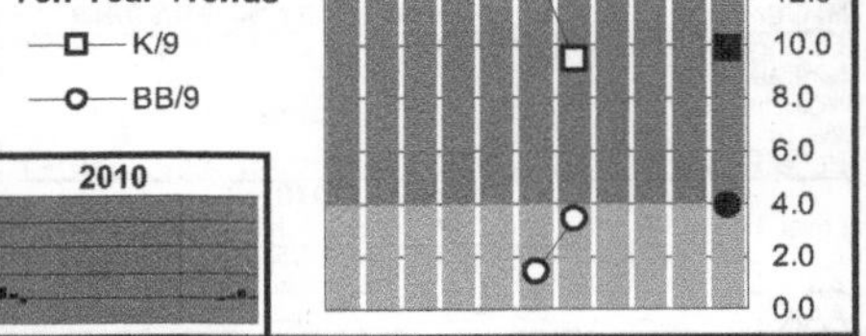


Majors / Skills / Value / Luck / In Rotation / In Relief / OPS

| Yr | Team | W | L | Sv | IP | H | K | ERA | WHIP | K/9 | BB/9 | HR/9 | GB/F | $1L | $2L | Pts | RAA | H% | HR/fb | S% | FIP | GS | CG | QS/DS | GR | Hld | Bln | Lead | OPS | 1st Hf | 2nd Hf | vs RH | vs LH |
|---|---|---|---|---|---|---|---|---|---|---|---|---|---|---|---|---|---|---|---|---|---|---|---|---|---|---|---|---|---|---|---|---|---|
| 07 | MIN | 7 | 2 | 0 | 70 | 44 | 74 | 2.94 | 1.01 | 9.5 | 3.5 | 0.9 | 0.6 | $10 | $8 | 160 | +7 | 23% | 8% | 75% | 3.64 | — | — | — | 74 | 15 | 3 | +0.1 | .591 | .448 | .787 | .573 | .618 |
| 08 | MIN | 0 | 1 | 0 | 13 | 12 | 15 | 4.73 | 1.20 | 10.1 | 2.7 | 1.4 | 0.7 | -$1 | -$2 | 10 | –1 | 29% | 13% | 64% | 3.90 | — | — | — | 15 | 6 | 2 | +1.0 | .751 | .751 | — | .703 | .823 |
| 09 | — | — | — | — | — | — | — | — | — | — | — | — | — | — | — | — | — | — | — | — | — | — | — | — | — | — | — | — | — | — | — | — | — |
| 10 | MIN | 0 | 1 | 0 | 9 | 7 | 9 | 5.00 | 1.67 | 9.0 | 8.0 | 1.0 | 0.7 | -$4 | -$12 | 10 | –1 | 25% | 8% | 71% | 5.41 | — | — | — | 11 | 1 | 1 | –1.0 | .696 | .478 | .861 | .686 | .730 |

## .. Jeff Niemann — 150 IP | $6 | 180 pts

SP-29, RP-1 — Owned: 94% — RH

Niemann is still under contract with the Rays, so he will probably be in the rotation come Opening Day. However, he is not one of their sharpest starters, and he blew up late (8.78 ERA in Aug-Sept), so Tampa could part with him. Or they could move him to the bullpen and make room for Jeremy Hellickson. (RZ)

| Player | Age | IP | W | Sv | K | ERA | WHIP | K/9 | BB/9 | $2L | Pts |
|---|---|---|---|---|---|---|---|---|---|---|---|
| Niemann J | 28 | 150 | 9 | 0 | 109 | 4.44 | 1.34 | 6.5 | 3.3 | $6 | 180 |
| **Mini-Browser** | **Age** | **IP** | **W** | **Sv** | **K** | **ERA** | **WHIP** | **K/9** | **BB/9** | **$2L** | **Pts** |
| Rodney F | 34 | 60 | 3 | 27 | 51 | 4.55 | 1.57 | 7.6 | 5.2 | $6 | 200 |
| Dickey R | 36 | 180 | 10 | 0 | 105 | 4.05 | 1.34 | 5.2 | 2.9 | $6 | 180 |
| Hanrahan J | 29 | 80 | 4 | 18 | 88 | 4.34 | 1.41 | 9.9 | 4.1 | $6 | 200 |
| Arroyo B | 34 | 200 | 12 | 0 | 117 | 4.56 | 1.27 | 5.3 | 2.6 | $6 | 210 |
| Zambrano C | 29 | 180 | 12 | 0 | 141 | 4.03 | 1.43 | 7.1 | 4.2 | $6 | 230 |

Minors (2010) / Skills

| Level | Leag | W | L | Sv | IP | H | K | ERA | WHIP | K/9 | BB/9 | HR/9 | GB/F |
|---|---|---|---|---|---|---|---|---|---|---|---|---|---|
| A | — | — | — | — | — | — | — | — | — | — | — | — | — |
| AA | — | — | — | — | — | — | — | — | — | — | — | — | — |
| AAA | — | — | — | — | — | — | — | — | — | — | — | — | — |

Competition at SP — Stats in 2010 as SP

| Thr | Player | GS | ERA | Supp | W-L |
|---|---|---|---|---|---|
| RH | Shields J | 33 | 5.20 | 4.5 | 12-15 |
| RH | Garza M | 32 | 3.93 | 5.2 | 15-10 |
| LH | Price D | 31 | 2.73 | 5.3 | 19-6 |
| RH | Davis W | 29 | 4.07 | 4.9 | 12-10 |

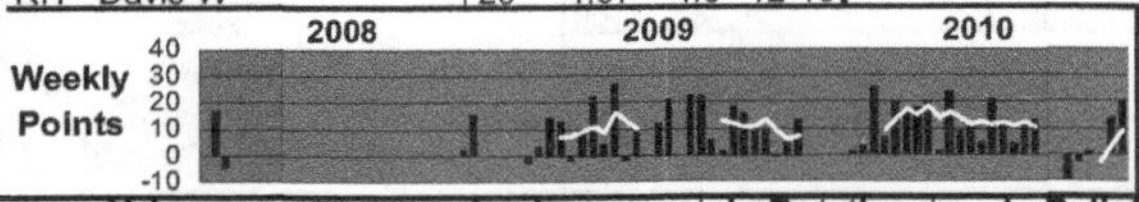


Ten-Year Trends

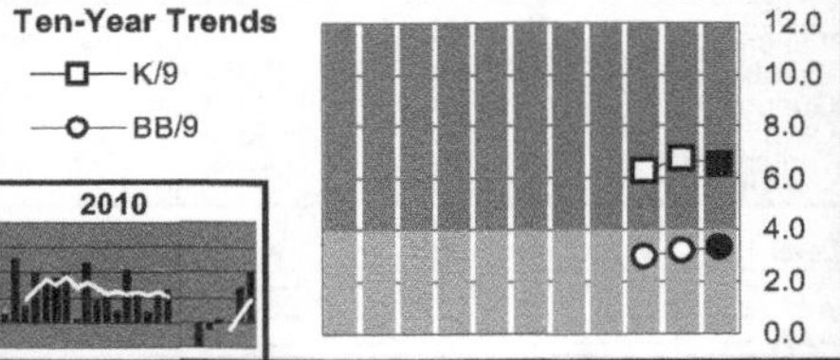


Majors / Skills / Value / Luck / In Rotation / In Relief / OPS

| Yr | Team | W | L | Sv | IP | H | K | ERA | WHIP | K/9 | BB/9 | HR/9 | GB/F | $1L | $2L | Pts | RAA | H% | HR/fb | S% | FIP | GS | CG | QS/DS | GR | Hld | Bln | Lead | OPS | 1st Hf | 2nd Hf | vs RH | vs LH |
|---|---|---|---|---|---|---|---|---|---|---|---|---|---|---|---|---|---|---|---|---|---|---|---|---|---|---|---|---|---|---|---|---|---|
| 07 | — | — | — | — | — | — | — | — | — | — | — | — | — | — | — | — | — | — | — | — | — | — | — | — | — | — | — | — | — | — | — | — | — |
| 08 | TB | 2 | 2 | 0 | 16 | 18 | 14 | 5.06 | 1.63 | 7.9 | 4.5 | 1.7 | 1.0 | -$2 | -$3 | 30 | –4 | 33% | 14% | 74% | 5.49 | 2 | 0 | 1/1 | 3 | 0 | 0 | +1.6 | .857 | .942 | .729 | .886 | .813 |
| 09 | TB | 13 | 6 | 0 | 180 | 185 | 125 | 3.94 | 1.35 | 6.2 | 2.9 | 0.8 | 1.0 | $11 | $2 | 230 | +5 | 31% | 8% | 73% | 4.12 | 30 | 2 | 13/5 | 1 | 0 | 0 | +0.4 | .728 | .725 | .731 | .703 | .751 |
| 10 | TB | 12 | 8 | 0 | 174 | 159 | 131 | 4.39 | 1.26 | 6.8 | 3.1 | 1.3 | 1.1 | $8 | -$7 | 230 | +0 | 27% | 12% | 69% | 4.71 | 29 | 1 | 16/4 | 1 | 0 | 0 | +0.1 | .724 | .647 | .864 | .698 | .749 |

## Jonathon Niese — 180 IP | $5 | 230 pts

SP-30 — Owned: 23% — LH

Beginning with a one-hit CG shut-out in June, Niese pitched very well for about 2-1/2 months (as late as August 25, his ERA was3.33). However, he hit a wall at the 140-IP mark and looked fatigued. Across all levels, he threw 50% more innings than in 2009. With more stamina, Niese might triumph in 2011. (JL)

| Player | Age | IP | W | Sv | K | ERA | WHIP | K/9 | BB/9 | $2L | Pts |
|---|---|---|---|---|---|---|---|---|---|---|---|
| Niese J | 24 | 180 | 10 | 0 | 159 | 4.24 | 1.42 | 7.9 | 3.1 | $5 | 230 |
| **Mini-Browser** | **Age** | **IP** | **W** | **Sv** | **K** | **ERA** | **WHIP** | **K/9** | **BB/9** | **$2L** | **Pts** |
| Wolf R | 34 | 200 | 12 | 0 | 134 | 4.47 | 1.36 | 6.0 | 3.4 | $5 | 220 |
| Padilla V | 33 | 120 | 8 | 0 | 86 | 4.33 | 1.25 | 6.4 | 2.8 | $5 | 150 |
| Loe K | 29 | 60 | 3 | 0 | 47 | 2.78 | 1.18 | 7.1 | 2.3 | $5 | 80 |
| Coke P | 28 | 160 | 10 | 2 | 141 | 4.52 | 1.47 | 8.0 | 3.5 | $5 | 220 |
| Zimmermann J | 24 | 160 | 8 | 0 | 156 | 4.45 | 1.35 | 8.8 | 3.0 | $5 | 210 |

Minors (2010) / Skills

| Level | Leag | W | L | Sv | IP | H | K | ERA | WHIP | K/9 | BB/9 | HR/9 | GB/F |
|---|---|---|---|---|---|---|---|---|---|---|---|---|---|
| A | — | — | — | — | — | — | — | — | — | — | — | — | — |
| AA | — | — | — | — | — | — | — | — | — | — | — | — | — |
| AAA | IL | 0 | 0 | 0 | 6 | 8 | 3 | 3.00 | 1.33 | 4.5 | 0.0 | 1.5 | — |

Competition at SP — Stats in 2010 as SP

| Thr | Player | GS | ERA | Supp | W-L |
|---|---|---|---|---|---|
| RH | Pelfrey M | 33 | 3.68 | 3.7 | 15-9 |
| LH | Niese J | 30 | 4.20 | 5.1 | 9-10 |
| LH | Santana J | 29 | 2.98 | 3.0 | 11-9 |
| RH | Dickey R | 26 | 2.86 | 4.0 | 11-9 |

Ten-Year Trends

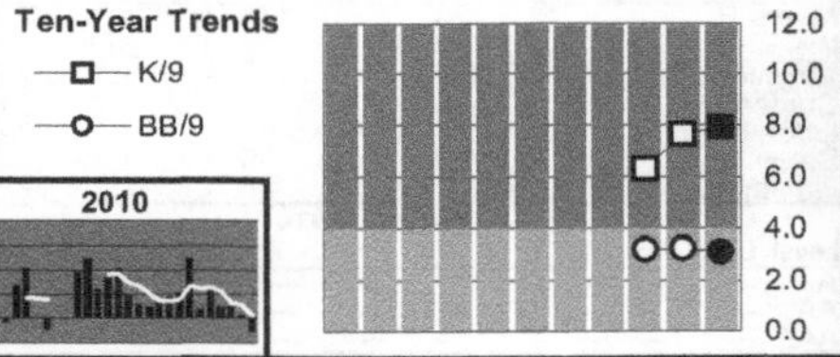


Majors / Skills / Value / Luck / In Rotation / In Relief / OPS

| Yr | Team | W | L | Sv | IP | H | K | ERA | WHIP | K/9 | BB/9 | HR/9 | GB/F | $1L | $2L | Pts | RAA | H% | HR/fb | S% | FIP | GS | CG | QS/DS | GR | Hld | Bln | Lead | OPS | 1st Hf | 2nd Hf | vs RH | vs LH |
|---|---|---|---|---|---|---|---|---|---|---|---|---|---|---|---|---|---|---|---|---|---|---|---|---|---|---|---|---|---|---|---|---|---|
| 07 | — | — | — | — | — | — | — | — | — | — | — | — | — | — | — | — | — | — | — | — | — | — | — | — | — | — | — | — | — | — | — | — | — |
| 08 | NYM | 1 | 1 | 0 | 14 | 20 | 11 | 7.07 | 2.00 | 7.1 | 5.1 | 1.3 | 1.3 | -$4 | -$5 | 10 | –4 | 39% | 13% | 65% | 5.20 | 3 | 0 | 1/2 | — | — | — | — | .945 | — | .945 | .920 | 1.000 |
| 09 | NYM | 1 | 1 | 0 | 25 | 27 | 18 | 4.21 | 1.40 | 6.3 | 3.2 | 0.4 | 1.4 | -$2 | -$2 | 20 | +1 | 33% | 4% | 69% | 3.36 | 5 | 0 | 2/1 | — | — | — | — | .731 | .790 | .686 | .685 | .813 |
| 10 | NYM | 9 | 10 | 0 | 173 | 192 | 148 | 4.20 | 1.46 | 7.7 | 3.2 | 1.0 | 1.5 | $0 | -$14 | 200 | –11 | 33% | 12% | 74% | 4.06 | 30 | 2 | 14/9 | — | — | — | — | .783 | .737 | .831 | .772 | .831 |

## Fernando Nieve — 40 IP | $-2 | 40 pts

RP-39, SP-1 — Owned: 1% — RH

Nieve got off to a good start in relief, but he was never the same after 28 appearances in April and May. By July, he was back in Triple-A as an SP, but he failed to impress the Mets enough to turn to him when they needed fill-ins. Nieve does not seem to figure in the Mets' plans, but he should get a shot elsewhere. (JL)

| Player | Age | IP | W | Sv | K | ERA | WHIP | K/9 | BB/9 | $2L | Pts |
|---|---|---|---|---|---|---|---|---|---|---|---|
| Nieve F | 28 | 40 | 2 | 0 | 33 | 5.12 | 1.41 | 7.5 | 3.9 | -$2 | 40 |
| **Mini-Browser** | **Age** | **IP** | **W** | **Sv** | **K** | **ERA** | **WHIP** | **K/9** | **BB/9** | **$2L** | **Pts** |
| Herrmann F | 26 | 40 | 1 | 0 | 28 | 4.89 | 1.51 | 6.3 | 2.6 | -$2 | 30 |
| Ohman W | 33 | 20 | 0 | 0 | 18 | 4.12 | 1.48 | 8.1 | 4.5 | -$2 | 20 |
| Bautista D | 30 | 40 | 2 | 0 | 40 | 4.53 | 1.58 | 9.0 | 5.7 | -$2 | 50 |
| Albaladejo J | 28 | 40 | 2 | 0 | 29 | 5.15 | 1.50 | 6.6 | 3.9 | -$2 | 40 |
| Baez D | 33 | 40 | 2 | 0 | 22 | 4.77 | 1.42 | 4.9 | 3.7 | -$2 | 30 |

Minors (2010) / Skills

| Level | Leag | W | L | Sv | IP | H | K | ERA | WHIP | K/9 | BB/9 | HR/9 | GB/F |
|---|---|---|---|---|---|---|---|---|---|---|---|---|---|
| A | — | — | — | — | — | — | — | — | — | — | — | — | — |
| AA | — | — | — | — | — | — | — | — | — | — | — | — | — |
| AAA | IL | 2 | 1 | 0 | 40 | 49 | 31 | 5.63 | 1.55 | 7.0 | 2.9 | 0.7 | — |

Competition at RP — Stats in 2010 as RP

| Thr | Player | GR | ERA | IP/G | Sv-Hld |
|---|---|---|---|---|---|
| RH | Rodriguez F | 53 | 2.20 | 1.1 | 25-0 |
| RH | Dessens E | 53 | 2.30 | 0.9 | 0-11 |
| RH | Parnell B | 41 | 2.83 | 0.9 | 0-9 |
| RH | Acosta M | 41 | 2.95 | 1.0 | 1-2 |

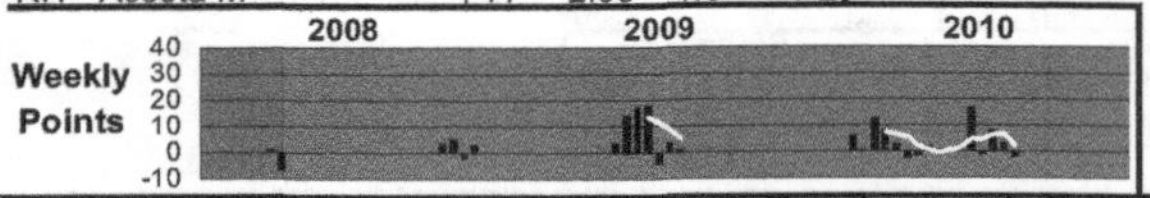


Ten-Year Trends

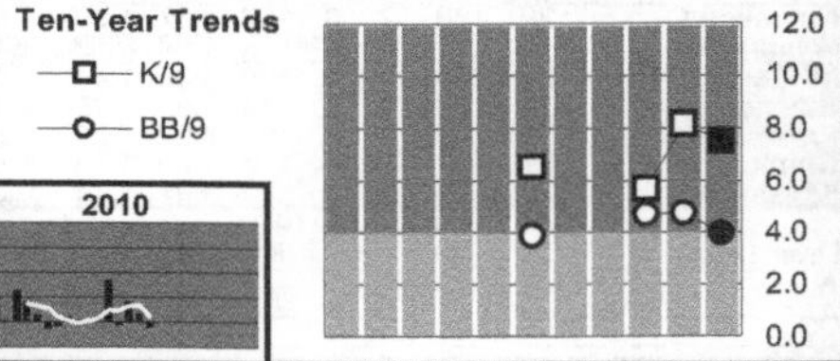


Majors / Skills / Value / Luck / In Rotation / In Relief / OPS

| Yr | Team | W | L | Sv | IP | H | K | ERA | WHIP | K/9 | BB/9 | HR/9 | GB/F | $1L | $2L | Pts | RAA | H% | HR/fb | S% | FIP | GS | CG | QS/DS | GR | Hld | Bln | Lead | OPS | 1st Hf | 2nd Hf | vs RH | vs LH |
|---|---|---|---|---|---|---|---|---|---|---|---|---|---|---|---|---|---|---|---|---|---|---|---|---|---|---|---|---|---|---|---|---|---|
| 07 | — | — | — | — | — | — | — | — | — | — | — | — | — | — | — | — | — | — | — | — | — | — | — | — | — | — | — | — | — | — | — | — | — |
| 08 | HOU | 0 | 1 | 0 | 10 | 17 | 12 | 8.44 | 1.78 | 10.1 | 1.7 | 1.7 | 0.8 | -$4 | -$5 | 0 | –5 | 45% | 15% | 53% | 3.95 | — | — | — | 11 | 0 | 1 | –1.5 | .941 | 1.412 | .646 | .816 | 1.364 |
| 09 | NYM | 3 | 3 | 0 | 36 | 36 | 23 | 2.95 | 1.50 | 5.6 | 4.7 | 1.0 | 0.8 | $0 | -$1 | 50 | +4 | 29% | 8% | 84% | 4.92 | 7 | 0 | 4/0 | 1 | 0 | 0 | –0.9 | .749 | .760 | .250 | .959 | .597 |
| 10 | NYM | 2 | 4 | 0 | 42 | 37 | 38 | 6.00 | 1.40 | 8.1 | 4.7 | 2.1 | 0.8 | -$6 | -$15 | 40 | –9 | 25% | 19% | 63% | 6.06 | 1 | 0 | 0/1 | 39 | 6 | 2 | –0.2 | .821 | .784 | 1.081 | .730 | 1.016 |

## . Dustin Nippert — 60 IP | $-3 | 50 pts

RP-36, SP-2 — Owned: 0% — RH

When Nippert gets the strike zone, he flourishes. Unfortunately, that is not nearly often enough, and it was not the case for the better part of 2010. His raw stuff is starter-quality, but his results have never caught up with his talent. With arbitration looming, Nippert could be shipped to a reliever-needy club. (JM)

| Player | Age | IP | W | Sv | K | ERA | WHIP | K/9 | BB/9 | $2L | Pts |
|---|---|---|---|---|---|---|---|---|---|---|---|
| Nippert D | 29 | 60 | 3 | 0 | 47 | 4.91 | 1.59 | 7.0 | 4.6 | -$3 | 50 |
| **Mini-Browser** | **Age** | **IP** | **W** | **Sv** | **K** | **ERA** | **WHIP** | **K/9** | **BB/9** | **$2L** | **Pts** |
| Romero J | 34 | 40 | 2 | 0 | 30 | 4.21 | 1.58 | 6.7 | 6.3 | -$2 | 40 |
| Marquis J | 32 | 140 | 7 | 0 | 71 | 4.83 | 1.43 | 4.6 | 3.3 | -$2 | 110 |
| Drabek K | 23 | 80 | 3 | 0 | 74 | 5.08 | 1.58 | 8.3 | 3.5 | -$2 | 80 |
| Gaudin C | 28 | 60 | 3 | 0 | 46 | 5.25 | 1.52 | 6.9 | 4.2 | -$3 | 50 |
| Beachy B | 24 | 100 | 4 | 0 | 99 | 4.41 | 1.61 | 8.9 | 3.6 | -$3 | 110 |

Minors (2010) / Skills

| Level | Leag | W | L | Sv | IP | H | K | ERA | WHIP | K/9 | BB/9 | HR/9 | GB/F |
|---|---|---|---|---|---|---|---|---|---|---|---|---|---|
| A | — | — | — | — | — | — | — | — | — | — | — | — | — |
| AA | TL | 0 | 0 | 0 | 3 | 1 | 7 | 0.00 | 0.60 | 18.9 | 2.7 | 0.0 | — |
| AAA | PCL | 0 | 0 | 0 | 3 | 1 | 3 | 0.00 | 0.33 | 9.0 | 0.0 | 0.0 | — |

Competition at RP — Stats in 2010 as RP

| Thr | Player | GR | ERA | IP/G | Sv-Hld |
|---|---|---|---|---|---|
| RH | O'Day D | 72 | 2.03 | 0.9 | 0-22 |
| RH | Feliz N | 70 | 2.73 | 1.0 | 40-3 |
| RH | Francisco F | 56 | 3.76 | 0.9 | 2-15 |
| RH | Ogando A | 44 | 1.30 | 0.9 | 0-7 |

Ten-Year Trends

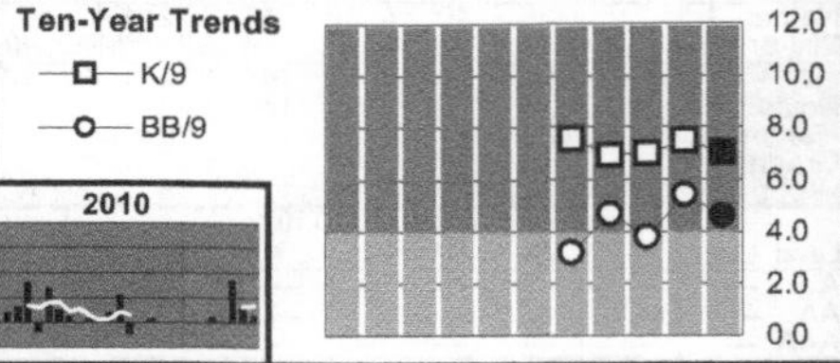


Majors / Skills / Value / Luck / In Rotation / In Relief / OPS

| Yr | Team | W | L | Sv | IP | H | K | ERA | WHIP | K/9 | BB/9 | HR/9 | GB/F | $1L | $2L | Pts | RAA | H% | HR/fb | S% | FIP | GS | CG | QS/DS | GR | Hld | Bln | Lead | OPS | 1st Hf | 2nd Hf | vs RH | vs LH |
|---|---|---|---|---|---|---|---|---|---|---|---|---|---|---|---|---|---|---|---|---|---|---|---|---|---|---|---|---|---|---|---|---|---|
| 07 | ARI | 1 | 1 | 0 | 45 | 48 | 38 | 5.56 | 1.41 | 7.5 | 3.2 | 1.0 | 1.1 | -$3 | -$7 | 30 | –10 | 31% | 10% | 61% | 4.02 | — | — | — | 36 | 2 | 0 | –1.3 | .743 | .605 | .845 | .807 | .662 |
| 08 | TEX | 3 | 5 | 0 | 71 | 92 | 55 | 6.40 | 1.80 | 6.9 | 4.6 | 1.3 | 0.9 | -$10 | -$15 | 40 | –20 | 35% | 11% | 66% | 5.13 | 6 | 0 | 1/2 | 14 | 0 | 0 | –2.2 | .873 | .964 | .839 | .972 | .777 |
| 09 | TEX | 5 | 3 | 0 | 69 | 64 | 54 | 3.88 | 1.33 | 7.0 | 3.7 | 0.9 | 1.0 | $3 | $0 | 100 | +0 | 28% | 8% | 73% | 4.30 | 10 | 0 | 2/0 | 10 | 1 | 0 | –1.3 | .696 | .932 | .663 | .622 | .759 |
| 10 | TEX | 4 | 5 | 0 | 56 | 61 | 47 | 4.29 | 1.68 | 7.5 | 5.4 | 1.1 | 0.8 | -$3 | -$14 | 70 | –3 | 33% | 10% | 77% | 5.05 | 2 | 0 | 0/0 | 36 | 5 | 1 | –0.2 | .816 | .899 | .550 | .769 | .887 |

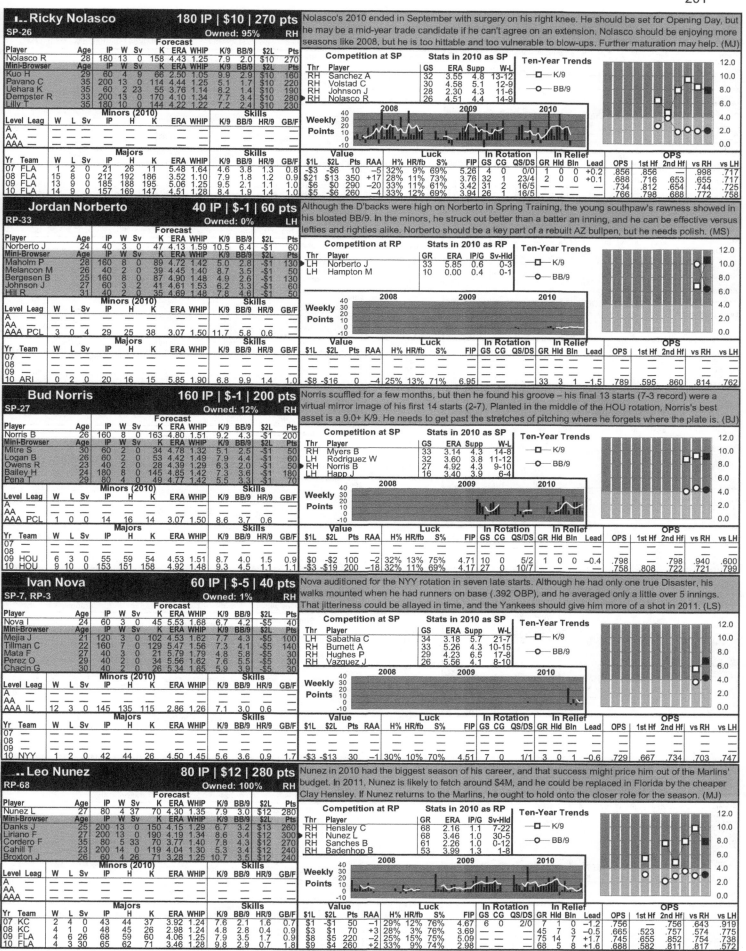

## Ricky Nolasco — 180 IP | $10 | 270 pts
SP-26    Owned: 95%    RH

Nolasco's 2010 ended in September with surgery on his right knee. He should be set for Opening Day, but he may be a mid-year trade candidate if he can't agree on an extension. Nolasco should be enjoying more seasons like 2008, but he is too hittable and too vulnerable to blow-ups. Further maturation may help. (MJ)

### Forecast
| Player | Age | IP | W | Sv | K | ERA | WHIP | K/9 | BB/9 | $2L | Pts |
|---|---|---|---|---|---|---|---|---|---|---|---|
| Nolasco R | 28 | 180 | 13 | 0 | 158 | 4.43 | 1.25 | 7.9 | 2.0 | $10 | 270 |

### Mini-Browser
| Player | Age | IP | W | Sv | K | ERA | WHIP | K/9 | BB/9 | $2L | Pts |
|---|---|---|---|---|---|---|---|---|---|---|---|
| Kuo H | 29 | 60 | 4 | 9 | 66 | 2.50 | 1.05 | 9.9 | 2.9 | $10 | 160 |
| Pavano C | 35 | 200 | 13 | 0 | 114 | 4.44 | 1.25 | 5.1 | 1.7 | $10 | 190 |
| Uehara K | 35 | 60 | 2 | 23 | 55 | 3.76 | 1.14 | 8.2 | 1.4 | $10 | 120 |
| Dempster R | 33 | 200 | 13 | 0 | 170 | 4.10 | 1.34 | 7.7 | 3.4 | $10 | 280 |
| Lilly T | 35 | 180 | 10 | 0 | 144 | 4.22 | 1.22 | 7.2 | 2.4 | $10 | 190 |

### Minors (2010)
| Level | Leag | W | L | Sv | IP | H | K | ERA | WHIP | K/9 | BB/9 | HR/9 | GB/F |
|---|---|---|---|---|---|---|---|---|---|---|---|---|---|
| A | — | — | — | — | — | — | — | — | — | — | — | — | — |
| AA | — | — | — | — | — | — | — | — | — | — | — | — | — |
| AAA | — | — | — | — | — | — | — | — | — | — | — | — | — |

### Majors
| Yr | Team | W | L | Sv | IP | H | K | ERA | WHIP | K/9 | BB/9 | HR/9 | GB/F |
|---|---|---|---|---|---|---|---|---|---|---|---|---|---|
| 07 | FLA | 1 | 2 | 0 | 21 | 26 | 11 | 5.48 | 1.64 | 4.6 | 3.8 | 1.3 | 0.8 |
| 08 | FLA | 15 | 8 | 0 | 212 | 192 | 186 | 3.52 | 1.10 | 7.9 | 1.8 | 1.2 | 1.0 |
| 09 | FLA | 13 | 9 | 0 | 185 | 188 | 195 | 5.06 | 1.25 | 9.5 | 2.1 | 1.1 | 1.0 |
| 10 | FLA | 14 | 9 | 0 | 157 | 169 | 147 | 4.51 | 1.28 | 8.4 | 1.9 | 1.4 | 1.0 |

### Competition at SP / Stats in 2010 as SP
| Thr | Player | GS | ERA | Supp | W-L |
|---|---|---|---|---|---|
| RH | Sanchez A | 32 | 3.55 | 4.8 | 13-12 |
| RH | Volstad C | 30 | 4.58 | 5.1 | 12-9 |
| RH | Johnson J | 28 | 2.30 | 4.3 | 11-6 |
| RH | Nolasco R | 26 | 4.51 | 4.4 | 14-9 |

### Value / Luck / In Rotation / In Relief / OPS
| $1L | $2L | Pts | RAA | H% | HR/fb | S% | FIP | GS | CG | QS/DS | GR | Hld | Bln | Lead | OPS | 1st Hf | 2nd Hf | vs RH | vs LH |
|---|---|---|---|---|---|---|---|---|---|---|---|---|---|---|---|---|---|---|---|
| -$3 | -$6 | 120 | -5 | 32% | 9% | 69% | 5.26 | 4 | 0 | 0/0 | 1 | 0 | 0 | +0.2 | .856 | .856 | | .998 | .717 |
| $21 | $13 | 350 | +17 | 28% | 11% | 73% | 3.76 | 32 | 1 | 23/4 | 2 | 0 | 0 | +0.1 | .688 | .716 | .653 | .655 | .717 |
| $6 | $0 | 290 | -20 | 33% | 11% | 60% | 3.42 | 31 | 2 | 16/5 | — | — | — | | .734 | .812 | .654 | .744 | .725 |
| $5 | -$6 | 290 | -4 | 33% | 12% | 69% | 3.94 | 26 | 1 | 16/5 | — | — | — | | .766 | .798 | .688 | .772 | .758 |

---

## Jordan Norberto — 40 IP | $-1 | 60 pts
RP-33    Owned: 0%    LH

Although the D'backs were high on Norberto in Spring Training, the young southpaw's rawness showed in his bloated BB/9. In the minors, he struck out better than a batter an inning, and he can be effective versus lefties and righties alike. Norberto should be a key part of a rebuilt AZ bullpen, but he needs polish. (MS)

### Forecast
| Player | Age | IP | W | Sv | K | ERA | WHIP | K/9 | BB/9 | $2L | Pts |
|---|---|---|---|---|---|---|---|---|---|---|---|
| Norberto J | 24 | 40 | 3 | 0 | 47 | 4.13 | 1.59 | 10.5 | 6.4 | -$1 | 60 |

### Mini-Browser
| Player | Age | IP | W | Sv | K | ERA | WHIP | K/9 | BB/9 | $2L | Pts |
|---|---|---|---|---|---|---|---|---|---|---|---|
| Maholm P | 28 | 160 | 8 | 0 | 89 | 4.72 | 1.42 | 5.0 | 2.8 | -$1 | 130 |
| Melancon M | 26 | 40 | 2 | 0 | 39 | 4.45 | 1.40 | 8.7 | 3.5 | -$1 | 50 |
| Bergesen B | 25 | 160 | 8 | 0 | 87 | 4.90 | 1.48 | 4.9 | 2.6 | -$1 | 130 |
| Johnson J | 27 | 60 | 3 | 2 | 41 | 4.61 | 1.53 | 6.2 | 3.3 | -$1 | 60 |
| Hill R | 31 | 40 | 2 | 0 | 35 | 4.69 | 1.48 | 7.8 | 4.6 | -$1 | 50 |

### Minors (2010)
| Level | Leag | W | L | Sv | IP | H | K | ERA | WHIP | K/9 | BB/9 | HR/9 | GB/F |
|---|---|---|---|---|---|---|---|---|---|---|---|---|---|
| A | — | — | — | — | — | — | — | — | — | — | — | — | — |
| AA | — | — | — | — | — | — | — | — | — | — | — | — | — |
| AAA | PCL | 3 | 0 | 4 | 29 | 25 | 38 | 3.07 | 1.50 | 11.7 | 5.8 | 0.6 | — |

### Majors
| Yr | Team | W | L | Sv | IP | H | K | ERA | WHIP | K/9 | BB/9 | HR/9 | GB/F |
|---|---|---|---|---|---|---|---|---|---|---|---|---|---|
| 07 | — | — | — | — | — | — | — | — | — | — | — | — | — |
| 08 | — | — | — | — | — | — | — | — | — | — | — | — | — |
| 09 | — | — | — | — | — | — | — | — | — | — | — | — | — |
| 10 | ARI | 0 | 2 | 0 | 20 | 16 | 15 | 5.85 | 1.90 | 6.8 | 9.9 | 1.4 | 1.0 |

### Competition at RP / Stats in 2010 as RP
| Thr | Player | GR | ERA | IP/G | Sv-Hld |
|---|---|---|---|---|---|
| LH | Norberto J | 33 | 5.85 | 0.6 | 0-3 |
| LH | Hampton M | 10 | 0.00 | 0.4 | 0-1 |

### Value / Luck / In Rotation / In Relief / OPS
| $1L | $2L | Pts | RAA | H% | HR/fb | S% | FIP | GS | CG | QS/DS | GR | Hld | Bln | Lead | OPS | 1st Hf | 2nd Hf | vs RH | vs LH |
|---|---|---|---|---|---|---|---|---|---|---|---|---|---|---|---|---|---|---|---|
| -$8 | -$16 | — | -4 | 25% | 13% | 71% | 6.95 | — | — | — | 33 | 3 | 1 | -1.5 | .789 | .595 | .860 | .814 | .762 |

---

## Bud Norris — 160 IP | $-1 | 200 pts
SP-27    Owned: 12%    RH

Norris scuffled for a few months, but then he found his groove – his final 13 starts (7-3 record) were a virtual mirror image of his first 14 starts (2-7). Planted in the middle of the HOU rotation, Norris's best asset is a 9.0+ K/9. He needs to get past the stretches of pitching where he forgets where the plate is. (BJ)

### Forecast
| Player | Age | IP | W | Sv | K | ERA | WHIP | K/9 | BB/9 | $2L | Pts |
|---|---|---|---|---|---|---|---|---|---|---|---|
| Norris B | 26 | 160 | 8 | 0 | 163 | 4.80 | 1.51 | 9.2 | 4.3 | -$1 | 200 |

### Mini-Browser
| Player | Age | IP | W | Sv | K | ERA | WHIP | K/9 | BB/9 | $2L | Pts |
|---|---|---|---|---|---|---|---|---|---|---|---|
| Mitre S | 30 | 60 | 2 | 0 | 34 | 4.78 | 1.32 | 5.1 | 2.5 | -$1 | 50 |
| Logan B | 26 | 60 | 2 | 0 | 53 | 4.42 | 1.49 | 7.9 | 4.4 | -$1 | 60 |
| Owens R | 23 | 40 | 2 | 0 | 28 | 4.39 | 1.29 | 6.3 | 2.0 | -$1 | 50 |
| Bailey H | 24 | 180 | 8 | 0 | 145 | 4.85 | 1.42 | 7.3 | 3.6 | -$1 | 180 |
| Pena T | 29 | 80 | 4 | 0 | 49 | 4.77 | 1.42 | 5.5 | 3.3 | -$1 | 70 |

### Minors (2010)
| Level | Leag | W | L | Sv | IP | H | K | ERA | WHIP | K/9 | BB/9 | HR/9 | GB/F |
|---|---|---|---|---|---|---|---|---|---|---|---|---|---|
| A | — | — | — | — | — | — | — | — | — | — | — | — | — |
| AA | — | — | — | — | — | — | — | — | — | — | — | — | — |
| AAA | PCL | 1 | 0 | 0 | 14 | 16 | 14 | 3.07 | 1.50 | 8.6 | 3.7 | 0.6 | — |

### Majors
| Yr | Team | W | L | Sv | IP | H | K | ERA | WHIP | K/9 | BB/9 | HR/9 | GB/F |
|---|---|---|---|---|---|---|---|---|---|---|---|---|---|
| 07 | — | — | — | — | — | — | — | — | — | — | — | — | — |
| 08 | — | — | — | — | — | — | — | — | — | — | — | — | — |
| 09 | HOU | 6 | 3 | 0 | 55 | 59 | 54 | 4.53 | 1.51 | 8.7 | 4.0 | 1.5 | 0.9 |
| 10 | HOU | 9 | 10 | 0 | 153 | 151 | 158 | 4.92 | 1.48 | 9.3 | 4.5 | 1.1 | 1.1 |

### Competition at SP / Stats in 2010 as SP
| Thr | Player | GS | ERA | Supp | W-L |
|---|---|---|---|---|---|
| RH | Myers B | 33 | 3.14 | 4.3 | 14-8 |
| LH | Rodriguez W | 32 | 3.60 | 3.8 | 11-12 |
| RH | Norris B | 27 | 4.92 | 4.3 | 9-10 |
| LH | Happ J | 16 | 3.40 | 3.9 | 6-4 |

### Value / Luck / In Rotation / In Relief / OPS
| $1L | $2L | Pts | RAA | H% | HR/fb | S% | FIP | GS | CG | QS/DS | GR | Hld | Bln | Lead | OPS | 1st Hf | 2nd Hf | vs RH | vs LH |
|---|---|---|---|---|---|---|---|---|---|---|---|---|---|---|---|---|---|---|---|
| $0 | -$2 | 100 | -2 | 32% | 13% | 75% | 4.71 | 10 | 0 | 5/2 | 1 | 0 | 0 | -0.4 | .798 | — | .798 | .940 | .600 |
| -$3 | -$19 | 200 | -18 | 32% | 11% | 69% | 4.17 | 27 | 0 | 10/7 | — | — | — | | .758 | .808 | .722 | .721 | .799 |

---

## Ivan Nova — 60 IP | $-5 | 40 pts
SP-7, RP-3    Owned: 1%    RH

Nova auditioned for the NYY rotation in seven late starts. Although he had only one true Disaster, his walks mounted when he had runners on base (.392 OBP), and he averaged only a little over 5 innings. That jitteriness could be allayed in time, and the Yankees should give him more of a shot in 2011. (LS)

### Forecast
| Player | Age | IP | W | Sv | K | ERA | WHIP | K/9 | BB/9 | $2L | Pts |
|---|---|---|---|---|---|---|---|---|---|---|---|
| Nova I | 24 | 60 | 3 | 0 | 45 | 5.53 | 1.68 | 6.7 | 4.2 | -$5 | 40 |

### Mini-Browser
| Player | Age | IP | W | Sv | K | ERA | WHIP | K/9 | BB/9 | $2L | Pts |
|---|---|---|---|---|---|---|---|---|---|---|---|
| Mejia J | 21 | 120 | 3 | 0 | 102 | 4.53 | 1.62 | 7.7 | 4.3 | -$5 | 100 |
| Tillman C | 22 | 160 | 7 | 0 | 129 | 5.47 | 1.56 | 7.3 | 4.1 | -$5 | 140 |
| Mata F | 27 | 40 | 2 | 0 | 21 | 5.79 | 1.79 | 4.8 | 5.8 | -$5 | 30 |
| Perez O | 29 | 40 | 2 | 0 | 34 | 5.56 | 1.62 | 7.6 | 5.5 | -$5 | 30 |
| Chacin G | 30 | 40 | 2 | 0 | 26 | 5.34 | 1.65 | 5.9 | 3.9 | -$5 | 30 |

### Minors (2010)
| Level | Leag | W | L | Sv | IP | H | K | ERA | WHIP | K/9 | BB/9 | HR/9 | GB/F |
|---|---|---|---|---|---|---|---|---|---|---|---|---|---|
| A | — | — | — | — | — | — | — | — | — | — | — | — | — |
| AA | — | — | — | — | — | — | — | — | — | — | — | — | — |
| AAA | IL | 12 | 3 | 0 | 145 | 135 | 115 | 2.86 | 1.26 | 7.1 | 3.0 | 0.6 | — |

### Majors
| Yr | Team | W | L | Sv | IP | H | K | ERA | WHIP | K/9 | BB/9 | HR/9 | GB/F |
|---|---|---|---|---|---|---|---|---|---|---|---|---|---|
| 07 | — | — | — | — | — | — | — | — | — | — | — | — | — |
| 08 | — | — | — | — | — | — | — | — | — | — | — | — | — |
| 09 | — | — | — | — | — | — | — | — | — | — | — | — | — |
| 10 | NYY | 1 | 2 | 0 | 42 | 49 | 26 | 4.50 | 1.45 | 5.6 | 3.6 | 0.9 | 1.7 |

### Competition at SP / Stats in 2010 as SP
| Thr | Player | GS | ERA | Supp | W-L |
|---|---|---|---|---|---|
| LH | Sabathia C | 34 | 3.18 | 5.7 | 21-7 |
| RH | Burnett A | 33 | 5.26 | 4.3 | 10-15 |
| RH | Hughes P | 29 | 4.23 | 6.5 | 17-8 |
| RH | Vazquez J | 26 | 5.56 | 4.1 | 8-10 |

### Value / Luck / In Rotation / In Relief / OPS
| $1L | $2L | Pts | RAA | H% | HR/fb | S% | FIP | GS | CG | QS/DS | GR | Hld | Bln | Lead | OPS | 1st Hf | 2nd Hf | vs RH | vs LH |
|---|---|---|---|---|---|---|---|---|---|---|---|---|---|---|---|---|---|---|---|
| -$3 | -$13 | 40 | -1 | 30% | 10% | 70% | 4.51 | 7 | 0 | 1/1 | 3 | 0 | 1 | -0.6 | .729 | .667 | .734 | .703 | .747 |

---

## Leo Nunez — 80 IP | $12 | 280 pts
RP-68    Owned: 100%    RH

Nunez in 2010 had the biggest season of his career, and that success might price him out of the Marlins' budget. In 2011, Nunez is likely to fetch around $4M, and he could be replaced in Florida by the cheaper Clay Hensley. If Nunez returns to the Marlins, he ought to hold onto the closer role for the season. (MJ)

### Forecast
| Player | Age | IP | W | Sv | K | ERA | WHIP | K/9 | BB/9 | $2L | Pts |
|---|---|---|---|---|---|---|---|---|---|---|---|
| Nunez L | 27 | 80 | 4 | 37 | 70 | 4.30 | 1.35 | 7.9 | 3.0 | $12 | 280 |

### Mini-Browser
| Player | Age | IP | W | Sv | K | ERA | WHIP | K/9 | BB/9 | $2L | Pts |
|---|---|---|---|---|---|---|---|---|---|---|---|
| Danks J | 25 | 200 | 13 | 0 | 150 | 4.15 | 1.29 | 6.7 | 3.2 | $13 | 260 |
| Liriano F | 27 | 200 | 13 | 0 | 190 | 4.19 | 1.34 | 8.6 | 3.4 | $12 | 300 |
| Cordero F | 35 | 80 | 5 | 33 | 70 | 3.77 | 1.40 | 7.8 | 4.3 | $12 | 270 |
| Cahill T | 23 | 200 | 14 | 0 | 119 | 4.04 | 1.30 | 5.3 | 3.4 | $12 | 240 |
| Broxton J | 26 | 60 | 4 | 26 | 71 | 3.28 | 1.24 | 10.7 | 3.5 | $12 | 240 |

### Minors (2010)
| Level | Leag | W | L | Sv | IP | H | K | ERA | WHIP | K/9 | BB/9 | HR/9 | GB/F |
|---|---|---|---|---|---|---|---|---|---|---|---|---|---|
| A | — | — | — | — | — | — | — | — | — | — | — | — | — |
| AA | — | — | — | — | — | — | — | — | — | — | — | — | — |
| AAA | — | — | — | — | — | — | — | — | — | — | — | — | — |

### Majors
| Yr | Team | W | L | Sv | IP | H | K | ERA | WHIP | K/9 | BB/9 | HR/9 | GB/F |
|---|---|---|---|---|---|---|---|---|---|---|---|---|---|
| 07 | KC | 2 | 4 | 0 | 43 | 44 | 37 | 3.92 | 1.24 | 7.6 | 2.1 | 1.6 | 0.7 |
| 08 | KC | 4 | 1 | 0 | 48 | 45 | 26 | 2.98 | 1.24 | 4.8 | 2.8 | 0.4 | 0.9 |
| 09 | FLA | 4 | 6 | 26 | 68 | 59 | 60 | 4.06 | 1.25 | 7.9 | 3.5 | 1.7 | 0.9 |
| 10 | FLA | 4 | 3 | 30 | 65 | 62 | 71 | 3.46 | 1.28 | 9.8 | 2.9 | 1.5 | 0.9 |

### Competition at RP / Stats in 2010 as RP
| Thr | Player | GR | ERA | IP/G | Sv-Hld |
|---|---|---|---|---|---|
| RH | Hensley C | 68 | 2.16 | 1.1 | 7-22 |
| RH | Nunez L | 68 | 3.46 | 1.0 | 30-5 |
| RH | Sanches B | 61 | 2.26 | 1.0 | 0-12 |
| RH | Badenhop B | 53 | 3.99 | 1.3 | 1-8 |

### Value / Luck / In Rotation / In Relief / OPS
| $1L | $2L | Pts | RAA | H% | HR/fb | S% | FIP | GS | CG | QS/DS | GR | Hld | Bln | Lead | OPS | 1st Hf | 2nd Hf | vs RH | vs LH |
|---|---|---|---|---|---|---|---|---|---|---|---|---|---|---|---|---|---|---|---|
| $1 | -$1 | 50 | -1 | 29% | 12% | 76% | 4.67 | 6 | — | 2/0 | 7 | 1 | 0 | -1.2 | .756 | — | .756 | .643 | .919 |
| $3 | -$1 | 70 | +3 | 28% | 3% | 76% | 3.69 | — | — | — | 45 | 7 | 3 | -0.5 | .665 | .523 | .757 | .574 | .775 |
| $8 | $5 | 220 | -2 | 25% | 15% | 75% | 5.09 | — | — | — | 75 | 14 | 7 | +1.7 | .745 | .655 | .852 | .754 | .738 |
| $9 | $4 | 260 | +2 | 33% | 9% | 74% | 2.98 | — | — | — | 68 | 5 | 8 | +1.6 | .688 | .582 | .811 | .817 | .572 |

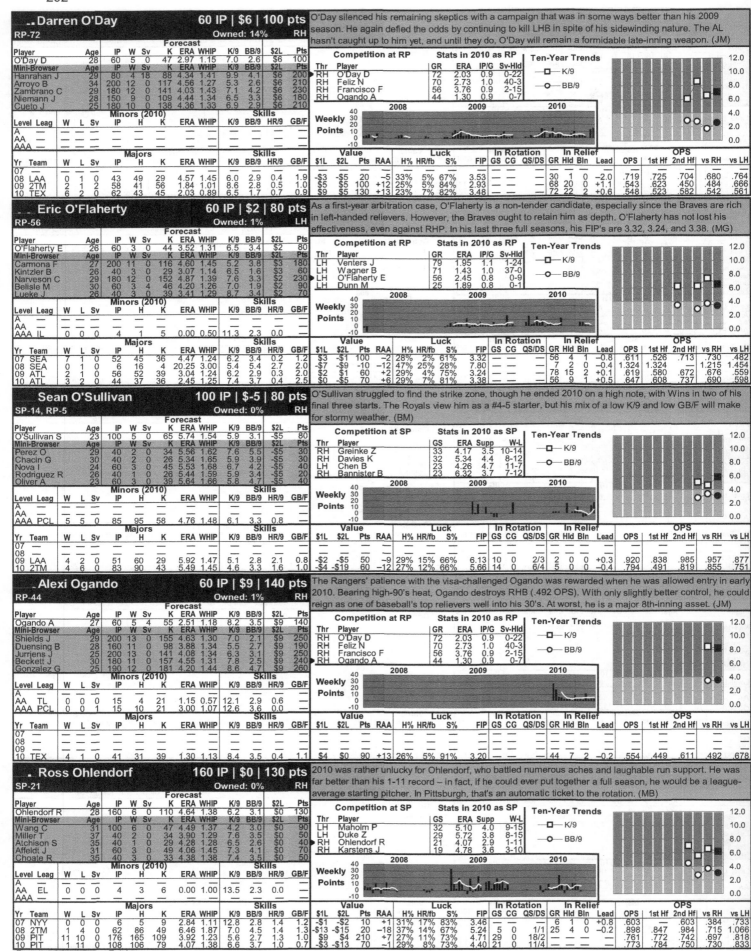

## Darren O'Day — 60 IP | $6 | 100 pts
RP-72 — Owned: 14% — RH

O'Day silenced his remaining skeptics with a campaign that was in some ways better than his 2009 season. He again defied the odds by continuing to kill LHB in spite of his sidewinding nature. The AL hasn't caught up to him yet, and until they do, O'Day will remain a formidable late-inning weapon. (JM)

### Forecast
| Player | Age | IP | W | Sv | K | ERA | WHIP | K/9 | BB/9 | $2L | Pts |
|---|---|---|---|---|---|---|---|---|---|---|---|
| O'Day D | 28 | 60 | 5 | 0 | 47 | 2.97 | 1.15 | 7.0 | 2.6 | $6 | 100 |
| **Mini-Browser** | **Age** | **IP** | **W** | **Sv** | **K** | **ERA** | **WHIP** | **K/9** | **BB/9** | **$2L** | **Pts** |
| Hanrahan J | 29 | 80 | 4 | 18 | 88 | 4.34 | 1.41 | 9.9 | 4.1 | $6 | 200 |
| Arroyo B | 34 | 200 | 12 | 0 | 117 | 4.56 | 1.27 | 5.3 | 2.6 | $6 | 210 |
| Zambrano C | 29 | 180 | 12 | 0 | 141 | 4.03 | 1.43 | 7.1 | 4.2 | $6 | 230 |
| Niemann J | 28 | 150 | 9 | 0 | 109 | 4.44 | 1.34 | 6.5 | 3.3 | $6 | 180 |
| Cueto J | 25 | 180 | 10 | 0 | 138 | 4.36 | 1.33 | 6.9 | 2.9 | $6 | 210 |

### Competition at RP / Stats in 2010 as RP
| Thr | Player | GR | ERA | IP/G | Sv-Hld |
|---|---|---|---|---|---|
| RH | O'Day D | 72 | 2.03 | 0.9 | 0-22 |
| RH | Feliz N | 70 | 2.73 | 1.0 | 40-3 |
| RH | Francisco F | 56 | 3.76 | 0.9 | 2-15 |
| RH | Ogando A | 44 | 1.30 | 0.9 | 0-7 |

Ten-Year Trends: K/9, BB/9

### Minors (2010) / Skills
| Level | Leag | W | L | Sv | IP | H | K | ERA | WHIP | K/9 | BB/9 | HR/9 | GB/F |
|---|---|---|---|---|---|---|---|---|---|---|---|---|---|
| A | — | — | — | — | — | — | — | — | — | — | — | — | — |
| AA | — | — | — | — | — | — | — | — | — | — | — | — | — |
| AAA | — | — | — | — | — | — | — | — | — | — | — | — | — |

### Majors / Skills / Value / Luck / In Rotation / In Relief / OPS
| Yr | Team | W | L | Sv | IP | H | K | ERA | WHIP | K/9 | BB/9 | HR/9 | GB/F | $1L | $2L | Pts | RAA | H% | HR/fb | S% | FIP | GS | CG | QS/DS | GR | Hld | Bln | Lead | OPS | 1st Hf | 2nd Hf | vs RH | vs LH |
|---|---|---|---|---|---|---|---|---|---|---|---|---|---|---|---|---|---|---|---|---|---|---|---|---|---|---|---|---|---|---|---|---|---|
| 07 | — | — | — | — | — | — | — | — | — | — | — | — | — | — | — | — | — | — | — | — | — | — | — | — | — | — | — | — | — | — | — | — | — |
| 08 | LAA | 0 | 1 | 0 | 43 | 49 | 29 | 4.57 | 1.45 | 6.0 | 2.9 | 0.4 | 1.9 | -$3 | -$5 | 20 | -5 | 33% | 5% | 67% | 3.53 | — | — | — | 30 | 1 | 0 | -2.0 | .719 | .725 | .704 | .680 | .764 |
| 09 | 2TM | 2 | 1 | 2 | 58 | 41 | 56 | 1.84 | 1.01 | 8.6 | 2.8 | 0.5 | 1.0 | $5 | -$5 | 100 | +12 | 25% | 5% | 84% | 2.93 | — | — | — | 68 | 20 | 0 | +1.1 | .543 | .623 | .450 | .484 | .666 |
| 10 | TEX | 6 | 2 | 0 | 62 | 43 | 45 | 2.03 | 0.89 | 6.5 | 1.7 | 0.7 | 0.9 | $5 | $5 | 130 | +13 | 23% | 7% | 81% | 2.93 | — | — | — | 72 | 22 | 2 | +0.6 | .548 | .582 | .523 | .542 | .561 |

## Eric O'Flaherty — 60 IP | $2 | 80 pts
RP-56 — Owned: 1% — LH

As a first-year arbitration case, O'Flaherty is a non-tender candidate, especially since the Braves are rich in left-handed relievers. However, the Braves ought to retain him as depth. O'Flaherty has not lost his effectiveness, even against RHP. In his last three full seasons, his FIP's are 3.32, 3.24, and 3.38. (MG)

### Forecast
| Player | Age | IP | W | Sv | K | ERA | WHIP | K/9 | BB/9 | $2L | Pts |
|---|---|---|---|---|---|---|---|---|---|---|---|
| O'Flaherty E | 26 | 60 | 3 | 0 | 44 | 3.52 | 1.31 | 6.5 | 3.4 | $2 | 80 |
| **Mini-Browser** | **Age** | **IP** | **W** | **Sv** | **K** | **ERA** | **WHIP** | **K/9** | **BB/9** | **$2L** | **Pts** |
| Carmona F | 27 | 200 | 11 | 0 | 116 | 4.60 | 1.45 | 5.2 | 3.8 | $3 | 180 |
| Kintzler B | 26 | 40 | 1 | 0 | 29 | 3.07 | 1.14 | 6.5 | 1.6 | $3 | 60 |
| Narveson C | 29 | 180 | 12 | 0 | 152 | 4.87 | 1.39 | 7.6 | 3.3 | $2 | 230 |
| Belisle M | 30 | 60 | 3 | 0 | 46 | 4.20 | 1.26 | 7.0 | 1.9 | $2 | 90 |
| Lueke J | 26 | 40 | 3 | 0 | 39 | 3.41 | 1.29 | 8.7 | 3.4 | $2 | 70 |

### Competition at RP / Stats in 2010 as RP
| Thr | Player | GR | ERA | IP/G | Sv-Hld |
|---|---|---|---|---|---|
| LH | Venters J | 79 | 1.95 | 1.1 | 1-24 |
| LH | Wagner B | 71 | 1.43 | 1.0 | 37-0 |
| LH | O'Flaherty E | 56 | 2.45 | 0.8 | 0-9 |
| LH | Dunn M | 25 | 1.89 | 0.8 | 0-1 |

Ten-Year Trends: K/9, BB/9

### Minors (2010) / Skills
| Level | Leag | W | L | Sv | IP | H | K | ERA | WHIP | K/9 | BB/9 | HR/9 | GB/F |
|---|---|---|---|---|---|---|---|---|---|---|---|---|---|
| A | — | — | — | — | — | — | — | — | — | — | — | — | — |
| AA | — | — | — | — | — | — | — | — | — | — | — | — | — |
| AAA | IL | 0 | 0 | 0 | 4 | 1 | 5 | 0.00 | 0.50 | 11.3 | 2.3 | 0.0 | — |

### Majors
| Yr | Team | W | L | Sv | IP | H | K | ERA | WHIP | K/9 | BB/9 | HR/9 | GB/F | $1L | $2L | Pts | RAA | H% | HR/fb | S% | FIP | GS | CG | QS/DS | GR | Hld | Bln | Lead | OPS | 1st Hf | 2nd Hf | vs RH | vs LH |
|---|---|---|---|---|---|---|---|---|---|---|---|---|---|---|---|---|---|---|---|---|---|---|---|---|---|---|---|---|---|---|---|---|---|
| 07 | SEA | 7 | 1 | 0 | 52 | 45 | 36 | 4.47 | 1.24 | 6.2 | 3.4 | 0.2 | 1.2 | $3 | -$1 | 100 | -2 | 28% | 2% | 61% | 3.32 | — | — | — | 56 | 4 | 1 | -0.8 | .611 | .526 | .713 | .730 | .482 |
| 08 | SEA | 0 | 1 | 0 | 6 | 16 | 4 | 20.25 | 3.00 | 5.4 | 5.4 | 2.7 | 2.0 | -$7 | -$9 | -10 | -12 | 47% | 25% | 28% | 7.80 | — | — | — | 7 | 2 | 0 | -0.4 | 1.324 | 1.324 | — | 1.215 | 1.454 |
| 09 | ATL | 1 | 3 | 0 | 56 | 50 | 39 | 3.04 | 1.24 | 6.2 | 2.9 | 0.3 | 2.0 | $2 | $1 | 60 | +2 | 29% | 4% | 75% | 3.24 | — | — | — | 78 | 15 | 2 | +0.1 | .619 | .580 | .672 | .676 | .559 |
| 10 | ATL | 3 | 2 | 0 | 44 | 37 | 36 | 2.45 | 1.25 | 7.4 | 3.7 | 0.4 | 2.5 | $0 | -$5 | 70 | +6 | 29% | 7% | 81% | 3.38 | — | — | — | 56 | 9 | 1 | +0.5 | .647 | .608 | .737 | .690 | .598 |

## Sean O'Sullivan — 100 IP | $-5 | 80 pts
SP-14, RP-5 — Owned: 0% — RH

O'Sullivan struggled to find the strike zone, though he ended 2010 on a high note, with Wins in two of his final three starts. The Royals view him as a #4-5 starter, but his mix of a low K/9 and low GB/F will make for stormy weather. (BM)

### Forecast
| Player | Age | IP | W | Sv | K | ERA | WHIP | K/9 | BB/9 | $2L | Pts |
|---|---|---|---|---|---|---|---|---|---|---|---|
| O'Sullivan S | 23 | 100 | 5 | 0 | 65 | 5.74 | 1.54 | 5.9 | 3.1 | -$5 | 80 |
| **Mini-Browser** | **Age** | **IP** | **W** | **Sv** | **K** | **ERA** | **WHIP** | **K/9** | **BB/9** | **$2L** | **Pts** |
| Perez O | 29 | 40 | 2 | 0 | 34 | 5.56 | 1.62 | 7.6 | 5.5 | -$5 | 30 |
| Chacin G | 30 | 40 | 2 | 0 | 26 | 5.34 | 1.65 | 5.9 | 3.9 | -$5 | 30 |
| Nova I | 24 | 60 | 3 | 0 | 45 | 5.53 | 1.68 | 6.7 | 4.2 | -$5 | 40 |
| Rodriguez R | 26 | 40 | 1 | 0 | 26 | 5.44 | 1.59 | 5.9 | 3.4 | -$5 | 20 |
| Oliver A | 23 | 60 | 3 | 0 | 39 | 5.64 | 1.66 | 5.8 | 4.7 | -$5 | 40 |

### Competition at SP / Stats in 2010 as SP
| Thr | Player | GS | ERA | Supp | W-L |
|---|---|---|---|---|---|
| RH | Greinke Z | 33 | 4.17 | 3.5 | 10-14 |
| RH | Davies K | 32 | 5.34 | 4.4 | 8-12 |
| LH | Chen B | 23 | 4.26 | 4.7 | 11-7 |
| RH | Bannister B | 23 | 6.32 | 3.7 | 7-12 |

Ten-Year Trends: K/9, BB/9

### Minors (2010) / Skills
| Level | Leag | W | L | Sv | IP | H | K | ERA | WHIP | K/9 | BB/9 | HR/9 | GB/F |
|---|---|---|---|---|---|---|---|---|---|---|---|---|---|
| A | — | — | — | — | — | — | — | — | — | — | — | — | — |
| AA | — | — | — | — | — | — | — | — | — | — | — | — | — |
| AAA | PCL | 5 | 5 | 0 | 85 | 95 | 58 | 4.76 | 1.48 | 6.1 | 3.3 | 0.8 | — |

### Majors
| Yr | Team | W | L | Sv | IP | H | K | ERA | WHIP | K/9 | BB/9 | HR/9 | GB/F | $1L | $2L | Pts | RAA | H% | HR/fb | S% | FIP | GS | CG | QS/DS | GR | Hld | Bln | Lead | OPS | 1st Hf | 2nd Hf | vs RH | vs LH |
|---|---|---|---|---|---|---|---|---|---|---|---|---|---|---|---|---|---|---|---|---|---|---|---|---|---|---|---|---|---|---|---|---|---|
| 07 | — | — | — | — | — | — | — | — | — | — | — | — | — | — | — | — | — | — | — | — | — | — | — | — | — | — | — | — | — | — | — | — | — |
| 08 | — | — | — | — | — | — | — | — | — | — | — | — | — | — | — | — | — | — | — | — | — | — | — | — | — | — | — | — | — | — | — | — | — |
| 09 | LAA | 4 | 4 | 0 | 51 | 60 | 29 | 5.92 | 1.47 | 5.1 | 2.8 | 2.1 | 0.8 | -$2 | -$5 | 60 | -2 | 29% | 15% | 66% | 6.13 | 10 | 0 | 2/3 | 2 | 0 | 0 | +0.3 | .920 | .838 | .985 | .957 | .877 |
| 10 | 2TM | 4 | 6 | 0 | 83 | 90 | 43 | 5.49 | 1.45 | 4.6 | 3.3 | 1.6 | 1.0 | -$4 | -$19 | 60 | -12 | 27% | 12% | 66% | 5.66 | 14 | 0 | 6/4 | 5 | 0 | 0 | -0.4 | .794 | .491 | .819 | .855 | .751 |

## Alexi Ogando — 60 IP | $9 | 140 pts
RP-44 — Owned: 1% — RH

The Rangers' patience with the visa-challenged Ogando was rewarded when he was allowed entry in early 2010. Bearing high-90's heat, Ogando destroys RHB (.492 OPS). With only slightly better control, he could reign as one of baseball's top relievers well into his 30's. At worst, he is a major 8th-inning asset. (JM)

### Forecast
| Player | Age | IP | W | Sv | K | ERA | WHIP | K/9 | BB/9 | $2L | Pts |
|---|---|---|---|---|---|---|---|---|---|---|---|
| Ogando A | 27 | 60 | 5 | 4 | 55 | 2.51 | 1.18 | 8.2 | 3.5 | $9 | 140 |
| **Mini-Browser** | **Age** | **IP** | **W** | **Sv** | **K** | **ERA** | **WHIP** | **K/9** | **BB/9** | **$2L** | **Pts** |
| Shields J | 29 | 200 | 13 | 0 | 155 | 4.63 | 1.30 | 7.0 | 2.1 | $9 | 250 |
| Duensing B | 28 | 160 | 11 | 0 | 98 | 3.88 | 1.34 | 5.5 | 2.7 | $9 | 190 |
| Jurrjens J | 25 | 200 | 13 | 0 | 141 | 4.08 | 1.34 | 6.3 | 3.1 | $9 | 250 |
| Beckett J | 30 | 180 | 11 | 0 | 157 | 4.55 | 1.31 | 7.8 | 2.5 | $9 | 240 |
| Gonzalez G | 25 | 190 | 12 | 0 | 181 | 4.20 | 1.44 | 8.6 | 4.7 | $9 | 260 |

### Competition at RP / Stats in 2010 as RP
| Thr | Player | GR | ERA | IP/G | Sv-Hld |
|---|---|---|---|---|---|
| RH | O'Day D | 72 | 2.03 | 0.9 | 0-22 |
| RH | Feliz N | 70 | 2.73 | 1.0 | 40-3 |
| RH | Francisco F | 56 | 3.76 | 0.9 | 2-15 |
| RH | Ogando A | 44 | 1.30 | 0.9 | 0-7 |

Ten-Year Trends: K/9, BB/9

### Minors (2010) / Skills
| Level | Leag | W | L | Sv | IP | H | K | ERA | WHIP | K/9 | BB/9 | HR/9 | GB/F |
|---|---|---|---|---|---|---|---|---|---|---|---|---|---|
| A | — | — | — | — | — | — | — | — | — | — | — | — | — |
| AA | TL | 0 | 0 | 0 | 15 | 10 | 21 | 1.15 | 0.57 | 12.1 | 2.9 | 0.6 | — |
| AAA | PCL | 0 | 0 | 1 | 15 | 10 | 21 | 3.00 | 1.07 | 12.6 | 3.6 | 0.0 | — |

### Majors
| Yr | Team | W | L | Sv | IP | H | K | ERA | WHIP | K/9 | BB/9 | HR/9 | GB/F | $1L | $2L | Pts | RAA | H% | HR/fb | S% | FIP | GS | CG | QS/DS | GR | Hld | Bln | Lead | OPS | 1st Hf | 2nd Hf | vs RH | vs LH |
|---|---|---|---|---|---|---|---|---|---|---|---|---|---|---|---|---|---|---|---|---|---|---|---|---|---|---|---|---|---|---|---|---|---|
| 07 | — | — | — | — | — | — | — | — | — | — | — | — | — | — | — | — | — | — | — | — | — | — | — | — | — | — | — | — | — | — | — | — | — |
| 08 | — | — | — | — | — | — | — | — | — | — | — | — | — | — | — | — | — | — | — | — | — | — | — | — | — | — | — | — | — | — | — | — | — |
| 09 | — | — | — | — | — | — | — | — | — | — | — | — | — | — | — | — | — | — | — | — | — | — | — | — | — | — | — | — | — | — | — | — | — |
| 10 | TEX | 4 | 1 | 0 | 41 | 31 | 39 | 1.30 | 1.13 | 8.4 | 3.5 | 0.4 | 1.1 | $4 | $0 | 90 | +13 | 26% | 5% | 91% | 3.20 | — | — | — | 44 | 7 | 2 | -0.2 | .554 | .449 | .611 | .492 | .678 |

## Ross Ohlendorf — 160 IP | $0 | 130 pts
SP-21 — Owned: 0% — RH

2010 was rather unlucky for Ohlendorf, who battled numerous aches and laughable run support. He was far better than his 1-11 record — in fact, if he could ever put together a full season, he would be a league-average starting pitcher. In Pittsburgh, that's an automatic ticket to the rotation. (MB)

### Forecast
| Player | Age | IP | W | Sv | K | ERA | WHIP | K/9 | BB/9 | $2L | Pts |
|---|---|---|---|---|---|---|---|---|---|---|---|
| Ohlendorf R | 28 | 160 | 6 | 0 | 110 | 4.64 | 1.38 | 6.2 | 3.1 | $0 | 130 |
| **Mini-Browser** | **Age** | **IP** | **W** | **Sv** | **K** | **ERA** | **WHIP** | **K/9** | **BB/9** | **$2L** | **Pts** |
| Wang C | 31 | 100 | 6 | 0 | 47 | 4.49 | 1.37 | 4.2 | 3.0 | $0 | 90 |
| Miller T | 37 | 40 | 2 | 0 | 34 | 3.90 | 1.29 | 7.6 | 3.5 | $0 | 50 |
| Atchison S | 35 | 40 | 1 | 0 | 29 | 4.28 | 1.28 | 6.5 | 2.6 | $0 | 40 |
| Affeldt J | 31 | 60 | 3 | 0 | 49 | 4.06 | 1.45 | 7.3 | 4.1 | $0 | 70 |
| Choate R | 35 | 40 | 3 | 0 | 33 | 4.38 | 1.38 | 7.4 | 3.5 | $0 | 50 |

### Competition at SP / Stats in 2010 as SP
| Thr | Player | GS | ERA | Supp | W-L |
|---|---|---|---|---|---|
| LH | Maholm P | 32 | 5.10 | 4.0 | 9-15 |
| LH | Duke Z | 29 | 5.72 | 3.8 | 8-15 |
| RH | Ohlendorf R | 21 | 4.07 | 2.9 | 1-11 |
| RH | Karstens J | 19 | 4.78 | 3.6 | 3-10 |

Ten-Year Trends: K/9, BB/9

### Minors (2010) / Skills
| Level | Leag | W | L | Sv | IP | H | K | ERA | WHIP | K/9 | BB/9 | HR/9 | GB/F |
|---|---|---|---|---|---|---|---|---|---|---|---|---|---|
| A | — | — | — | — | — | — | — | — | — | — | — | — | — |
| AA | EL | 0 | 0 | 0 | 4 | 3 | 6 | 0.00 | 1.00 | 13.5 | 2.3 | 0.0 | — |
| AAA | — | — | — | — | — | — | — | — | — | — | — | — | — |

### Majors
| Yr | Team | W | L | Sv | IP | H | K | ERA | WHIP | K/9 | BB/9 | HR/9 | GB/F | $1L | $2L | Pts | RAA | H% | HR/fb | S% | FIP | GS | CG | QS/DS | GR | Hld | Bln | Lead | OPS | 1st Hf | 2nd Hf | vs RH | vs LH |
|---|---|---|---|---|---|---|---|---|---|---|---|---|---|---|---|---|---|---|---|---|---|---|---|---|---|---|---|---|---|---|---|---|---|
| 07 | NYY | 1 | 0 | 0 | 6 | 5 | 9 | 2.84 | 1.17 | 12.8 | 2.8 | 1.4 | 1.2 | -$1 | -$2 | 10 | +1 | 31% | 17% | 83% | 3.46 | — | — | — | 6 | 1 | 0 | +0.8 | .603 | — | .603 | .384 | .733 |
| 08 | 2TM | 1 | 4 | 0 | 62 | 86 | 49 | 6.46 | 1.87 | 7.0 | 4.5 | 1.4 | 1.3 | -$13 | -$15 | 20 | -18 | 37% | 14% | 67% | 5.24 | 5 | 0 | 1/1 | 25 | 4 | 0 | -0.2 | .898 | .847 | .984 | .715 | 1.066 |
| 09 | PIT | 11 | 10 | 0 | 176 | 165 | 109 | 3.92 | 1.23 | 5.6 | 2.7 | 1.3 | 1.0 | $9 | $4 | 210 | +7 | 27% | 11% | 73% | 4.71 | 29 | 0 | 18/2 | — | — | — | — | .761 | .772 | .742 | .697 | .818 |
| 10 | PIT | 1 | 11 | 0 | 108 | 106 | 79 | 4.07 | 1.38 | 6.6 | 3.7 | 1.0 | 0.7 | -$3 | -$13 | 70 | -2 | 29% | 8% | 73% | 4.40 | 21 | 0 | 11/4 | — | — | — | — | .773 | .784 | .750 | .730 | .833 |

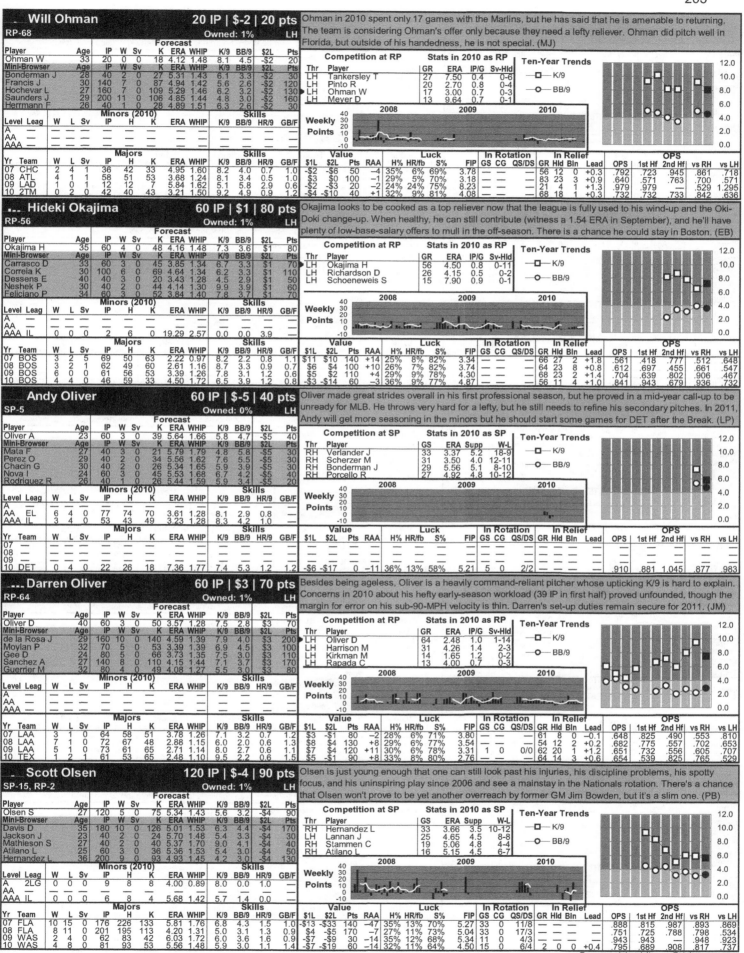

## Will Ohman — 20 IP | $-2 | 20 pts
RP-68  Owned: 1%  LH

Ohman in 2010 spent only 17 games with the Marlins, but he has said that he is amenable to returning. The team is considering Ohman's offer only because they need a lefty reliever. Ohman did pitch well in Florida, but outside of his handedness, he is not special. (MJ)

### Forecast
| Player | Age | IP | W | Sv | K | ERA | WHIP | K/9 | BB/9 | $2L | Pts |
|---|---|---|---|---|---|---|---|---|---|---|---|
| Ohman W | 33 | 20 | 0 | 0 | 18 | 4.12 | 1.48 | 8.1 | 4.5 | -$2 | 20 |

### Mini-Browser
| Player | Age | IP | W | Sv | K | ERA | WHIP | K/9 | BB/9 | $2L | Pts |
|---|---|---|---|---|---|---|---|---|---|---|---|
| Bonderman J | 28 | 40 | 4 | 0 | 27 | 5.31 | 1.43 | 6.1 | 3.3 | -$2 | 30 |
| Francis J | 30 | 140 | 7 | 0 | 87 | 4.94 | 1.42 | 5.6 | 2.6 | -$2 | 120 |
| Hochevar L | 27 | 160 | 7 | 0 | 109 | 5.29 | 1.46 | 6.2 | 3.2 | -$2 | 130 |
| Saunders J | 29 | 200 | 11 | 0 | 106 | 4.85 | 1.44 | 4.8 | 3.0 | -$2 | 160 |
| Herrmann F | 26 | — | — | 0 | 28 | 4.89 | 1.51 | 6.3 | 2.6 | -$2 | 30 |

### Competition at RP / Stats in 2010 as RP
| Thr | Player | GR | ERA | IP/G | Sv-Hld |
|---|---|---|---|---|---|
| LH | Tankersley T | 27 | 7.50 | 0.4 | 0-6 |
| LH | Pinto R | 20 | 2.70 | 0.8 | 0-4 |
| LH | Ohman W | 17 | 3.00 | 0.7 | 0-3 |
| LH | Meyer D | 13 | 9.64 | 0.7 | 0-1 |

### Minors (2010)
| Level | Leag | W | L | Sv | IP | H | K | ERA | WHIP | K/9 | BB/9 | HR/9 | GB/F |
|---|---|---|---|---|---|---|---|---|---|---|---|---|---|
| A | — | — | — | — | — | — | — | — | — | — | — | — | — |
| AA | — | — | — | — | — | — | — | — | — | — | — | — | — |
| AAA | — | — | — | — | — | — | — | — | — | — | — | — | — |

### Majors / Skills / Value / Luck / In Rotation / In Relief / OPS
| Yr | Team | W | L | Sv | IP | H | K | ERA | WHIP | K/9 | BB/9 | HR/9 | GB/F | $1L | $2L | Pts | RAA | H% | HR/fb | S% | FIP | GS | CG | QS/DS | GR | Hld | Bln | Lead | OPS | 1st Hf | 2nd Hf | vs RH | vs LH |
|---|---|---|---|---|---|---|---|---|---|---|---|---|---|---|---|---|---|---|---|---|---|---|---|---|---|---|---|---|---|---|---|---|---|
| 07 | CHC | 2 | 4 | 1 | 36 | 42 | 33 | 4.95 | 1.60 | 8.2 | 4.0 | 0.7 | 1.0 | -$2 | -$6 | 50 | -4 | 35% | 6% | 69% | 3.78 | — | — | — | 56 | 12 | 0 | +0.3 | .792 | .723 | .945 | .861 | .718 |
| 08 | ATL | 4 | 1 | 4 | 58 | 51 | 53 | 3.68 | 1.24 | 8.1 | 3.4 | 0.5 | 1.0 | $3 | $0 | 100 | -1 | 29% | 5% | 70% | 3.18 | — | — | — | 83 | 23 | 3 | +0.9 | .640 | .571 | .763 | .700 | .571 |
| 09 | LAD | 1 | 0 | 1 | 12 | 12 | 7 | 5.84 | 1.62 | 5.1 | 5.8 | 2.9 | 0.6 | -$2 | -$3 | 20 | -2 | 24% | 24% | 75% | 8.23 | — | — | — | 21 | 4 | 1 | +0.3 | .979 | .979 | — | .529 | 1.295 |
| 10 | 2TM | 0 | 2 | 0 | 42 | 40 | 43 | 3.21 | 1.50 | 9.2 | 4.9 | 0.9 | 1.2 | -$4 | -$10 | 40 | +1 | 32% | 9% | 81% | 4.08 | — | — | — | 68 | 18 | 1 | +0.3 | .732 | .732 | .733 | .842 | .606 |

## Hideki Okajima — 60 IP | $1 | 80 pts
RP-56  Owned: 1%  LH

Okajima looks to be cooked as a top reliever now that the league is fully used to his wind-up and the Oki-Doki change-up. When healthy, he can still contribute (witness a 1.54 ERA in September), and he'll have plenty of low-base-salary offers to mull in the off-season. There is a chance he could stay in Boston. (EB)

### Forecast
| Player | Age | IP | W | Sv | K | ERA | WHIP | K/9 | BB/9 | $2L | Pts |
|---|---|---|---|---|---|---|---|---|---|---|---|
| Okajima H | 35 | 60 | 4 | 0 | 48 | 4.16 | 1.48 | 7.3 | 3.6 | $1 | 80 |

### Mini-Browser
| Player | Age | IP | W | Sv | K | ERA | WHIP | K/9 | BB/9 | $2L | Pts |
|---|---|---|---|---|---|---|---|---|---|---|---|
| Carrasco D | 33 | 60 | 3 | 0 | 45 | 3.85 | 1.34 | 6.7 | 3.3 | $1 | 70 |
| Correia K | 30 | 100 | 6 | 0 | 69 | 4.64 | 1.34 | 6.2 | 3.3 | $1 | 110 |
| Dessens E | 40 | 40 | 3 | 0 | 20 | 3.43 | 1.28 | 4.5 | 2.9 | $1 | 50 |
| Neshek P | 30 | 40 | 2 | 0 | 44 | 4.14 | 1.30 | 9.9 | 3.9 | $1 | 60 |
| Feliciano P | 34 | 60 | 3 | 0 | 52 | 3.84 | 1.40 | 7.8 | 3.7 | $1 | 70 |

### Competition at RP / Stats in 2010 as RP
| Thr | Player | GR | ERA | IP/G | Sv-Hld |
|---|---|---|---|---|---|
| LH | Okajima H | 56 | 4.50 | 0.8 | 0-11 |
| LH | Richardson D | 26 | 4.15 | 0.5 | 0-2 |
| LH | Schoeneweis S | 15 | 7.90 | 0.9 | 0-1 |

### Minors (2010)
| Level | Leag | W | L | Sv | IP | H | K | ERA | WHIP | K/9 | BB/9 | HR/9 | GB/F |
|---|---|---|---|---|---|---|---|---|---|---|---|---|---|
| A | — | — | — | — | — | — | — | — | — | — | — | — | — |
| AA | — | — | — | — | — | — | — | — | — | — | — | — | — |
| AAA | IL | 0 | 0 | 0 | 2 | 6 | 0 | 19.29 | 2.57 | 0.0 | 0.0 | 3.9 | — |

### Majors
| Yr | Team | W | L | Sv | IP | H | K | ERA | WHIP | K/9 | BB/9 | HR/9 | GB/F | $1L | $2L | Pts | RAA | H% | HR/fb | S% | FIP | GS | CG | QS/DS | GR | Hld | Bln | Lead | OPS | 1st Hf | 2nd Hf | vs RH | vs LH |
|---|---|---|---|---|---|---|---|---|---|---|---|---|---|---|---|---|---|---|---|---|---|---|---|---|---|---|---|---|---|---|---|---|---|
| 07 | BOS | 3 | 2 | 5 | 69 | 50 | 63 | 2.22 | 0.97 | 8.2 | 2.2 | 0.8 | 1.1 | $11 | $10 | 140 | +14 | 25% | 8% | 82% | 3.34 | — | — | — | 66 | 27 | 2 | +1.8 | .561 | .418 | .777 | .512 | .648 |
| 08 | BOS | 3 | 2 | 1 | 62 | 49 | 60 | 2.61 | 1.16 | 8.7 | 3.3 | 0.9 | 0.7 | $6 | $4 | 100 | +10 | 26% | 7% | 82% | 3.74 | — | — | — | 64 | 23 | 8 | +0.8 | .612 | .697 | .455 | .661 | .547 |
| 09 | BOS | 6 | 0 | 0 | 61 | 56 | 53 | 3.39 | 1.26 | 7.8 | 3.1 | 1.2 | 0.6 | $5 | $2 | 110 | +4 | 29% | 9% | 78% | 4.30 | — | — | — | 68 | 23 | 4 | +1.4 | .704 | .639 | .802 | .906 | .467 |
| 10 | BOS | 4 | 0 | 0 | 46 | 59 | 33 | 4.50 | 1.72 | 6.5 | 3.9 | 1.2 | 0.8 | -$3 | -$14 | 60 | -3 | 36% | 9% | 77% | 4.87 | — | — | — | 56 | 11 | 4 | +1.0 | .841 | .943 | .679 | .936 | .732 |

## Andy Oliver — 60 IP | $-5 | 40 pts
SP-5  Owned: 0%  LH

Oliver made great strides overall in his first professional season, but he proved in a mid-year call-up to be unready for MLB. He throws very hard for a lefty, but he still needs to refine his secondary pitches. In 2011, Andy will get more seasoning in the minors but he should start some games for DET after the Break. (LP)

### Forecast
| Player | Age | IP | W | Sv | K | ERA | WHIP | K/9 | BB/9 | $2L | Pts |
|---|---|---|---|---|---|---|---|---|---|---|---|
| Oliver A | 23 | 60 | 3 | 0 | 39 | 5.64 | 1.66 | 5.8 | 4.7 | -$5 | 40 |

### Mini-Browser
| Player | Age | IP | W | Sv | K | ERA | WHIP | K/9 | BB/9 | $2L | Pts |
|---|---|---|---|---|---|---|---|---|---|---|---|
| Mata F | 27 | 40 | 3 | 0 | 21 | 5.79 | 1.79 | 4.8 | 5.8 | -$5 | 30 |
| Perez O | 29 | 40 | 2 | 0 | 34 | 5.56 | 1.62 | 7.6 | 5.5 | -$5 | 30 |
| Chacin G | 30 | 40 | 2 | 0 | 26 | 5.34 | 1.65 | 5.9 | 3.9 | -$5 | 30 |
| Nova I | 24 | 60 | 3 | 0 | 45 | 5.53 | 1.68 | 6.7 | 4.2 | -$5 | 40 |
| Rodriguez R | 26 | 40 | 1 | 0 | 26 | 5.44 | 1.59 | 5.9 | 3.4 | -$5 | 20 |

### Competition at SP / Stats in 2010 as SP
| Thr | Player | GS | ERA | Supp | W-L |
|---|---|---|---|---|---|
| RH | Verlander J | 33 | 3.37 | 5.2 | 18-9 |
| RH | Scherzer M | 31 | 3.50 | 4.0 | 12-11 |
| RH | Bonderman J | 29 | 5.56 | 5.1 | 8-10 |
| RH | Porcello R | 27 | 4.92 | 4.8 | 10-12 |

### Minors (2010)
| Level | Leag | W | L | Sv | IP | H | K | ERA | WHIP | K/9 | BB/9 | HR/9 | GB/F |
|---|---|---|---|---|---|---|---|---|---|---|---|---|---|
| A | — | — | — | — | — | — | — | — | — | — | — | — | — |
| AA | EL | 6 | 4 | 0 | 77 | 74 | 70 | 3.61 | 1.28 | 8.1 | 2.9 | 0.8 | — |
| AAA | IL | 3 | 4 | 0 | 53 | 43 | 49 | 3.23 | 1.28 | 8.3 | 4.2 | 1.0 | — |

### Majors
| Yr | Team | W | L | Sv | IP | H | K | ERA | WHIP | K/9 | BB/9 | HR/9 | GB/F | $1L | $2L | Pts | RAA | H% | HR/fb | S% | FIP | GS | CG | QS/DS | GR | Hld | Bln | Lead | OPS | 1st Hf | 2nd Hf | vs RH | vs LH |
|---|---|---|---|---|---|---|---|---|---|---|---|---|---|---|---|---|---|---|---|---|---|---|---|---|---|---|---|---|---|---|---|---|---|
| 07 | — | | | | | | | | | | | | | | | | | | | | | | | | | | | | | | | | |
| 08 | — | | | | | | | | | | | | | | | | | | | | | | | | | | | | | | | | |
| 09 | — | | | | | | | | | | | | | | | | | | | | | | | | | | | | | | | | |
| 10 | DET | 0 | 4 | 0 | 22 | 26 | 18 | 7.36 | 1.77 | 7.4 | 5.3 | 1.2 | 1.2 | -$6 | -$17 | 0 | -11 | 36% | 13% | 58% | 5.21 | 5 | 0 | 2/2 | — | — | — | — | .910 | .881 | 1.045 | .877 | .983 |

## Darren Oliver — 60 IP | $3 | 70 pts
RP-64  Owned: 1%  LH

Besides being ageless, Oliver is a heavily command-reliant pitcher whose upticking K/9 is hard to explain. Concerns in 2010 about his hefty early-season workload (39 IP in first half) proved unfounded, though the margin for error on his sub-90-MPH velocity is thin. Darren's set-up duties remain secure for 2011. (JM)

### Forecast
| Player | Age | IP | W | Sv | K | ERA | WHIP | K/9 | BB/9 | $2L | Pts |
|---|---|---|---|---|---|---|---|---|---|---|---|
| Oliver D | 40 | 60 | 3 | 0 | 50 | 3.57 | 1.28 | 7.5 | 2.8 | $3 | 70 |

### Mini-Browser
| Player | Age | IP | W | Sv | K | ERA | WHIP | K/9 | BB/9 | $2L | Pts |
|---|---|---|---|---|---|---|---|---|---|---|---|
| de la Rosa J | 29 | 160 | 10 | 0 | 140 | 4.59 | 1.39 | 7.9 | 4.0 | $3 | 200 |
| Moylan P | 32 | 70 | 5 | 0 | 53 | 3.39 | 1.39 | 6.9 | 4.5 | $3 | 100 |
| Gee D | 24 | 80 | 5 | 0 | 66 | 3.73 | 1.35 | 7.5 | 3.0 | $3 | 100 |
| Sanchez A | 27 | 140 | 8 | 0 | 110 | 4.15 | 1.44 | 7.1 | 3.7 | $3 | 170 |
| Guerrier M | 32 | 80 | 4 | 0 | 49 | 4.08 | 1.27 | 5.5 | 3.0 | $3 | 80 |

### Competition at RP / Stats in 2010 as RP
| Thr | Player | GR | ERA | IP/G | Sv-Hld |
|---|---|---|---|---|---|
| LH | Oliver D | 64 | 2.48 | 1.0 | 1-14 |
| LH | Harrison M | 31 | 4.26 | 1.4 | 2-3 |
| LH | Kirkman M | 14 | 1.65 | 1.2 | 0-2 |
| LH | Rapada C | 13 | 4.00 | 0.7 | 0-3 |

### Minors (2010)
| Level | Leag | W | L | Sv | IP | H | K | ERA | WHIP | K/9 | BB/9 | HR/9 | GB/F |
|---|---|---|---|---|---|---|---|---|---|---|---|---|---|
| A | — | — | — | — | — | — | — | — | — | — | — | — | — |
| AA | — | — | — | — | — | — | — | — | — | — | — | — | — |
| AAA | — | — | — | — | — | — | — | — | — | — | — | — | — |

### Majors
| Yr | Team | W | L | Sv | IP | H | K | ERA | WHIP | K/9 | BB/9 | HR/9 | GB/F | $1L | $2L | Pts | RAA | H% | HR/fb | S% | FIP | GS | CG | QS/DS | GR | Hld | Bln | Lead | OPS | 1st Hf | 2nd Hf | vs RH | vs LH |
|---|---|---|---|---|---|---|---|---|---|---|---|---|---|---|---|---|---|---|---|---|---|---|---|---|---|---|---|---|---|---|---|---|---|
| 07 | LAA | 3 | 1 | 0 | 64 | 58 | 51 | 3.78 | 1.26 | 7.1 | 3.2 | 0.7 | 1.2 | $3 | -$1 | 80 | -2 | 28% | 6% | 71% | 3.80 | — | — | — | 61 | 8 | 0 | -0.1 | .648 | .825 | .490 | .553 | .810 |
| 08 | LAA | 7 | 1 | 0 | 72 | 67 | 48 | 2.88 | 1.15 | 6.0 | 2.0 | 0.6 | 1.3 | $8 | $4 | 130 | +8 | 29% | 6% | 77% | 3.54 | — | — | — | 54 | 12 | 2 | +0.2 | .682 | .775 | .557 | .702 | .653 |
| 09 | LAA | 5 | 1 | 0 | 73 | 61 | 65 | 2.71 | 1.14 | 8.0 | 2.7 | 0.6 | 1.1 | $7 | $4 | 120 | +11 | 30% | 6% | 78% | 3.31 | 1 | 0 | 0/0 | 62 | 20 | 1 | +1.2 | .651 | .732 | .556 | .605 | .707 |
| 10 | TEX | 1 | 1 | 1 | 61 | 53 | 65 | 2.48 | 1.10 | 9.6 | 2.5 | 0.7 | 1.5 | $5 | $1 | 110 | +6 | 33% | 8% | 80% | 2.76 | — | — | — | 64 | 14 | 3 | +0.6 | .546 | .539 | .825 | .765 | .529 |

## Scott Olsen — 120 IP | $-4 | 90 pts
SP-15, RP-2  Owned: 1%  LH

Olsen is just young enough that one can still look past his injuries, his discipline problems, his spotty focus, and his uninspiring play since 2006 and see a mainstay in the Nationals rotation. There's a chance that Olsen won't prove to be yet another overreach by former GM Jim Bowden, but it's a slim one. (PB)

### Forecast
| Player | Age | IP | W | Sv | K | ERA | WHIP | K/9 | BB/9 | $2L | Pts |
|---|---|---|---|---|---|---|---|---|---|---|---|
| Olsen S | 27 | 120 | 5 | 0 | 75 | 5.34 | 1.43 | 5.6 | 3.2 | -$4 | 90 |

### Mini-Browser
| Player | Age | IP | W | Sv | K | ERA | WHIP | K/9 | BB/9 | $2L | Pts |
|---|---|---|---|---|---|---|---|---|---|---|---|
| Davis D | 35 | 180 | 10 | 0 | 126 | 5.01 | 1.53 | 6.3 | 4.4 | -$4 | 170 |
| Jackson J | 23 | 40 | 2 | 0 | 24 | 5.70 | 1.48 | 5.4 | 3.3 | -$4 | 20 |
| Mathieson S | 27 | 40 | 2 | 0 | 40 | 5.37 | 1.70 | 9.0 | 4.1 | -$4 | 40 |
| Atilano L | 25 | 60 | 3 | 0 | 36 | 5.36 | 1.53 | 5.4 | 4.0 | -$4 | 50 |
| Hernandez L | 36 | 200 | 9 | 0 | 93 | 4.93 | 1.45 | 4.2 | 3.0 | -$4 | 130 |

### Competition at SP / Stats in 2010 as SP
| Thr | Player | GS | ERA | Supp | W-L |
|---|---|---|---|---|---|
| RH | Hernandez L | 33 | 3.66 | 3.5 | 10-12 |
| LH | Lannan J | 25 | 4.65 | 4.5 | 8-8 |
| RH | Stammen C | 19 | 5.06 | 4.8 | 4-4 |
| RH | Atilano L | 16 | 5.15 | 4.5 | 6-7 |

### Minors (2010)
| Level | Leag | W | L | Sv | IP | H | K | ERA | WHIP | K/9 | BB/9 | HR/9 | GB/F |
|---|---|---|---|---|---|---|---|---|---|---|---|---|---|
| A | 2LG | 0 | 0 | 0 | 9 | 8 | 8 | 4.00 | 0.89 | 8.0 | 0.0 | 1.0 | — |
| AA | — | — | — | — | — | — | — | — | — | — | — | — | — |
| AAA | IL | 0 | 0 | 0 | 6 | 8 | 4 | 5.68 | 1.42 | 5.7 | 1.4 | 1.4 | — |

### Majors
| Yr | Team | W | L | Sv | IP | H | K | ERA | WHIP | K/9 | BB/9 | HR/9 | GB/F | $1L | $2L | Pts | RAA | H% | HR/fb | S% | FIP | GS | CG | QS/DS | GR | Hld | Bln | Lead | OPS | 1st Hf | 2nd Hf | vs RH | vs LH |
|---|---|---|---|---|---|---|---|---|---|---|---|---|---|---|---|---|---|---|---|---|---|---|---|---|---|---|---|---|---|---|---|---|---|
| 07 | FLA | 10 | 15 | 0 | 176 | 226 | 133 | 5.81 | 1.76 | 6.8 | 4.3 | 1.5 | 1.0 | -$13 | -$33 | 140 | -47 | 35% | 13% | 70% | 5.27 | 33 | 0 | 11/8 | — | — | — | — | .888 | .815 | .987 | .893 | .869 |
| 08 | FLA | 8 | 11 | 0 | 201 | 195 | 113 | 4.20 | 1.31 | 5.0 | 3.1 | 1.3 | 0.9 | $4 | -$5 | 170 | -7 | 27% | 11% | 73% | 5.04 | 33 | 0 | 17/3 | — | — | — | — | .751 | .725 | .788 | .798 | .534 |
| 09 | WAS | 2 | 7 | 0 | 62 | 83 | 42 | 6.03 | 1.72 | 6.0 | 3.6 | 1.6 | 0.9 | -$7 | -$9 | 20 | -14 | 35% | 12% | 68% | 5.34 | 11 | 0 | 4/3 | — | — | — | — | .943 | .943 | — | .948 | .923 |
| 10 | WAS | 4 | 8 | 0 | 81 | 93 | 53 | 5.56 | 1.48 | 5.9 | 3.6 | 1.6 | 1.4 | -$7 | -$19 | 60 | -14 | 32% | 11% | 64% | 4.50 | 15 | 0 | 6/4 | 2 | 0 | 0 | +0.4 | .795 | .689 | .908 | .817 | .737 |

## Garrett Olson — 50 IP | $-4 | 30 pts
**RP-35** — Owned: 0% — LH

Olson was better in his first full season in relief, notably (and predictably) in his strikeout rate, but he is still a mediocre pitcher, and he is likely to split time in 2011 between Triple-A and MLB. His left-handedness is perhaps his most redeeming quality, and he might be able to earn the lefty specialist role. (GC)

### Forecast
| Player | Age | IP | W | Sv | K | ERA | WHIP | K/9 | BB/9 | $2L | Pts |
|---|---|---|---|---|---|---|---|---|---|---|---|
| Olson G | 27 | 50 | 2 | 0 | 35 | 5.51 | 1.58 | 6.3 | 4.4 | -$4 | 30 |

### Mini-Browser
| Player | Age | IP | W | Sv | K | ERA | WHIP | K/9 | BB/9 | $2L | Pts |
|---|---|---|---|---|---|---|---|---|---|---|---|
| Duke Z | 27 | 160 | 8 | 0 | 79 | 5.01 | 1.43 | 4.5 | 2.4 | -$4 | 120 |
| Herndon D | 25 | 40 | 1 | 0 | 28 | 4.95 | 1.53 | 6.2 | 2.5 | -$4 | 30 |
| Hardy B | 24 | 40 | 1 | 0 | 21 | 5.36 | 1.59 | 4.8 | 3.7 | -$4 | 20 |
| Stammen C | 27 | 60 | 2 | 0 | 39 | 5.14 | 1.47 | 5.8 | 2.8 | -$4 | 40 |
| Hernandez D | 25 | 60 | 4 | 0 | 56 | 5.64 | 1.64 | 8.5 | 4.6 | -$4 | 70 |

### Competition at RP / Stats in 2010 as RP
| Thr | Player | GR | ERA | IP/G | Sv-Hld |
|---|---|---|---|---|---|
| LH | Olson G | 35 | 4.54 | 1.1 | 1-1 |
| LH | Seddon C | 14 | 5.64 | 1.6 | 0-0 |

### Minors (2010)
| Level | Leag | W | L | Sv | IP | H | K | ERA | WHIP | K/9 | BB/9 | HR/9 | GB/F |
|---|---|---|---|---|---|---|---|---|---|---|---|---|---|
| A | — | | | | | | | | | | | | |
| AA | — | | | | | | | | | | | | |
| AAA | PCL | 2 | 5 | 0 | 46 | 36 | 50 | 3.66 | 1.09 | 9.6 | 2.9 | 0.8 | — |

### Majors / Value / Luck / In Rotation / In Relief / OPS
| Yr | Team | W | L | Sv | IP | H | K | ERA | WHIP | K/9 | BB/9 | HR/9 | GB/F | $1L | $2L | Pts | RAA | H% | HR/fb | S% | FIP | GS | CG | QS/DS | GR | Hld | Bln | Lead | OPS | 1st Hf | 2nd Hf | vs RH | vs LH |
|---|---|---|---|---|---|---|---|---|---|---|---|---|---|---|---|---|---|---|---|---|---|---|---|---|---|---|---|---|---|---|---|---|---|
| 07 | BAL | 1 | 3 | 0 | 32 | 42 | 28 | 7.79 | 2.16 | 7.8 | 7.8 | 1.1 | 0.7 | -$8 | -$14 | 10 | -13 | 38% | 8% | 64% | 5.77 | 7 | 0 | 0/3 | — | — | — | — | .917 | .876 | .922 | .955 | .741 |
| 08 | BAL | 9 | 10 | 0 | 132 | 168 | 83 | 6.65 | 1.73 | 5.6 | 4.2 | 1.2 | 1.1 | -$17 | -$25 | 90 | -40 | 34% | 9% | 62% | 5.12 | 26 | 0 | 8/9 | — | — | — | — | .861 | .793 | .942 | .880 | .796 |
| 09 | SEA | 3 | 5 | 0 | 80 | 79 | 47 | 5.60 | 1.41 | 5.3 | 3.8 | 2.1 | 0.7 | -$1 | -$6 | 50 | -16 | 25% | 15% | 67% | 6.47 | 11 | 0 | 3/4 | 20 | 5 | 0 | -0.4 | .835 | .747 | 1.031 | .844 | .812 |
| 10 | SEA | 0 | 3 | 1 | 37 | 42 | 31 | 4.54 | 1.51 | 7.4 | 3.6 | 1.4 | 0.9 | -$3 | -$13 | 30 | -13 | 31% | 12% | 75% | 4.92 | — | — | — | 35 | 1 | 0 | -1.6 | .785 | .838 | .763 | .829 | .699 |

---

## Logan Ondrusek — 60 IP | $-2 | 70 pts
**RP-60** — Owned: 0% — RH

Ondrusek is a middle-relief type, with decent stuff but no chance of starting. His ceiling is as a set-up guy, but he is unlikely to achieve even that rank in the current Reds bullpen. Expect Ondrusek to fill in for a few years in Cincinnati and then move on when he hits arbitration eligibility. (SW)

### Forecast
| Player | Age | IP | W | Sv | K | ERA | WHIP | K/9 | BB/9 | $2L | Pts |
|---|---|---|---|---|---|---|---|---|---|---|---|
| Ondrusek L | 26 | 60 | 3 | 0 | 48 | 4.62 | 1.49 | 7.2 | 3.5 | -$2 | 70 |

### Mini-Browser
| Player | Age | IP | W | Sv | K | ERA | WHIP | K/9 | BB/9 | $2L | Pts |
|---|---|---|---|---|---|---|---|---|---|---|---|
| Purcey D | 28 | 60 | 3 | 0 | 53 | 4.96 | 1.53 | 7.9 | 4.9 | -$2 | 60 |
| Ring R | 30 | 20 | 1 | 0 | 17 | 4.49 | 1.44 | 7.7 | 4.0 | -$2 | 30 |
| Misch P | 29 | 40 | 2 | 0 | 25 | 4.72 | 1.33 | 5.7 | 2.3 | -$2 | 30 |
| Kendrick K | 26 | 80 | 5 | 0 | 38 | 4.85 | 1.39 | 4.3 | 2.6 | -$2 | 70 |
| Heilman A | 32 | 80 | 4 | 0 | 63 | 4.82 | 1.45 | 7.1 | 3.8 | -$2 | 80 |

### Competition at RP / Stats in 2010 as RP
| Thr | Player | GR | ERA | IP/G | Sv-Hld |
|---|---|---|---|---|---|
| RH | Masset N | 82 | 3.40 | 0.9 | 2-20 |
| RH | Cordero F | 75 | 3.84 | 1.0 | 40-1 |
| RH | Ondrusek L | 60 | 3.68 | 1.0 | 0-6 |
| RH | Smith J | 37 | 3.86 | 1.1 | 1-2 |

### Minors (2010)
| Level | Leag | W | L | Sv | IP | H | K | ERA | WHIP | K/9 | BB/9 | HR/9 | GB/F |
|---|---|---|---|---|---|---|---|---|---|---|---|---|---|
| A | — | | | | | | | | | | | | |
| AA | — | | | | | | | | | | | | |
| AAA | IL | 0 | 1 | 1 | 19 | 21 | 14 | 4.12 | 1.22 | 6.4 | 3.6 | 0.0 | — |

### Majors
| Yr | Team | W | L | Sv | IP | H | K | ERA | WHIP | K/9 | BB/9 | HR/9 | GB/F | $1L | $2L | Pts | RAA | H% | HR/fb | S% | FIP | GS | CG | QS/DS | GR | Hld | Bln | Lead | OPS | 1st Hf | 2nd Hf | vs RH | vs LH |
|---|---|---|---|---|---|---|---|---|---|---|---|---|---|---|---|---|---|---|---|---|---|---|---|---|---|---|---|---|---|---|---|---|---|
| 07 | — | | | | | | | | | | | | | | | | | | | | | | | | | | | | | | | | |
| 08 | — | | | | | | | | | | | | | | | | | | | | | | | | | | | | | | | | |
| 09 | — | | | | | | | | | | | | | | | | | | | | | | | | | | | | | | | | |
| 10 | CIN | 5 | 0 | 0 | 58 | 49 | 39 | 3.68 | 1.18 | 6.0 | 3.1 | 1.1 | 1.3 | $0 | -$6 | 90 | +1 | 24% | 10% | 73% | 4.44 | — | — | — | 60 | 6 | 2 | +0.6 | .669 | .731 | .626 | .725 | .561 |

---

## Roy Oswalt — 200 IP | $18 | 270 pts
**SP-32, RP-1** — Owned: 100% — RH

With a relatively affordable club option for 2012, the Phillies are likely to retain Oswalt's services for the entirety of 2011, slotting him behind Roy Halladay in the rotation. In 2010, Oswalt benefited from a 26% hit rate, but he also made legitimate gains, and he should be among the top starters again. (BB)

### Forecast
| Player | Age | IP | W | Sv | K | ERA | WHIP | K/9 | BB/9 | $2L | Pts |
|---|---|---|---|---|---|---|---|---|---|---|---|
| Oswalt R | 33 | 200 | 12 | 0 | 153 | 3.56 | 1.16 | 6.9 | 2.2 | $18 | 270 |

### Mini-Browser
| Player | Age | IP | W | Sv | K | ERA | WHIP | K/9 | BB/9 | $2L | Pts |
|---|---|---|---|---|---|---|---|---|---|---|---|
| Weaver J | 28 | 220 | 14 | 0 | 193 | 3.73 | 1.21 | 7.9 | 2.6 | $21 | 330 |
| Rivera M | 41 | 60 | 4 | 38 | 54 | 2.35 | 0.96 | 8.1 | 1.6 | $20 | 300 |
| Soriano R | 31 | 60 | 3 | 44 | 61 | 2.89 | 1.05 | 9.2 | 2.7 | $19 | 320 |
| Hamels C | 27 | 200 | 13 | 0 | 175 | 3.67 | 1.17 | 7.9 | 2.3 | $19 | 310 |
| Latos M | 23 | 160 | 11 | 0 | 160 | 3.31 | 1.15 | 9.0 | 2.7 | $18 | 280 |

### Competition at SP / Stats in 2010 as SP
| Thr | Player | GS | ERA | Supp | W-L |
|---|---|---|---|---|---|
| RH | Halladay R | 33 | 2.44 | 4.4 | 21-10 |
| LH | Hamels C | 33 | 3.06 | 3.8 | 12-11 |
| RH | Oswalt R | 32 | 2.73 | 3.0 | 13-13 |
| RH | Kendrick K | 31 | 4.81 | 5.5 | 11-10 |

### Minors (2010)
| Level | Leag | W | L | Sv | IP | H | K | ERA | WHIP | K/9 | BB/9 | HR/9 | GB/F |
|---|---|---|---|---|---|---|---|---|---|---|---|---|---|
| A | — | | | | | | | | | | | | |
| AA | — | | | | | | | | | | | | |
| AAA | — | | | | | | | | | | | | |

### Majors
| Yr | Team | W | L | Sv | IP | H | K | ERA | WHIP | K/9 | BB/9 | HR/9 | GB/F | $1L | $2L | Pts | RAA | H% | HR/fb | S% | FIP | GS | CG | QS/DS | GR | Hld | Bln | Lead | OPS | 1st Hf | 2nd Hf | vs RH | vs LH |
|---|---|---|---|---|---|---|---|---|---|---|---|---|---|---|---|---|---|---|---|---|---|---|---|---|---|---|---|---|---|---|---|---|---|
| 07 | HOU | 14 | 7 | 0 | 212 | 221 | 154 | 3.18 | 1.33 | 6.5 | 2.5 | 0.6 | 1.7 | $16 | $7 | 290 | +25 | 31% | 7% | 77% | 3.45 | 32 | 1 | 21/2 | 1 | 1 | 0 | +0.2 | .708 | .727 | .698 | .698 | .716 |
| 08 | HOU | 17 | 10 | 0 | 208 | 199 | 165 | 3.54 | 1.18 | 7.1 | 2.0 | 1.0 | 1.7 | $18 | $10 | 340 | +14 | 29% | 13% | 74% | 3.73 | 32 | 3 | 22/2 | — | — | — | — | .692 | .794 | .543 | .688 | .695 |
| 09 | HOU | 8 | 6 | 0 | 181 | 183 | 138 | 4.12 | 1.24 | 6.8 | 2.1 | 0.9 | 1.2 | $7 | $2 | 200 | +6 | 31% | 10% | 69% | 3.73 | 30 | 3 | 17/2 | — | — | — | — | .732 | .731 | .733 | .723 | .741 |
| 10 | 2TM | 13 | 13 | 0 | 211 | 162 | 193 | 2.76 | 1.03 | 8.2 | 2.3 | 0.8 | 1.2 | $26 | $26 | 360 | +34 | 26% | 9% | 77% | 3.37 | 32 | 2 | 24/3 | 1 | 0 | 0 | +0.2 | .614 | .613 | .615 | .580 | .653 |

---

## Josh Outman — 60 IP | $-1 | 70 pts
**No MLB games played in 2010** — Owned: 0% — LH

Outman missed all of 2010 after having Tommy John surgery in June 2009. He was outstanding in 2009 in 12 starts in Oakland's rotation, but in light of his injury history and the A's depth at SP, Outman may return to the bullpen. He should get a chance during Spring Training to at least compete for a starter's spot. (ML)

### Forecast
| Player | Age | IP | W | Sv | K | ERA | WHIP | K/9 | BB/9 | $2L | Pts |
|---|---|---|---|---|---|---|---|---|---|---|---|
| Outman J | 26 | 60 | 3 | 0 | 54 | 4.72 | 1.56 | 8.1 | 4.3 | -$1 | 70 |

### Mini-Browser
| Player | Age | IP | W | Sv | K | ERA | WHIP | K/9 | BB/9 | $2L | Pts |
|---|---|---|---|---|---|---|---|---|---|---|---|
| Salas F | 25 | 40 | 1 | 0 | 41 | 4.10 | 1.45 | 9.2 | 3.6 | -$1 | 50 |
| Gorzelanny T | 28 | 140 | 7 | 0 | 111 | 4.67 | 1.48 | 7.1 | 4.1 | -$1 | 150 |
| Judy J | 25 | 60 | 1 | 0 | 50 | 4.53 | 1.47 | 7.6 | 3.4 | -$1 | 50 |
| Sonnanstine A | 28 | 50 | 2 | 0 | 31 | 5.09 | 1.34 | 5.5 | 2.4 | -$1 | 40 |
| Thomas B | 33 | 40 | 3 | 0 | 21 | 4.29 | 1.55 | 4.7 | 3.6 | -$1 | 40 |

### Competition at RP / Stats in 2010 as RP
| Thr | Player | GR | ERA | IP/G | Sv-Hld |
|---|---|---|---|---|---|
| LH | Breslow C | 75 | 3.01 | 1.0 | 5-16 |
| LH | Blevins J | 63 | 3.70 | 0.8 | 1-11 |
| LH | Bowers C | 14 | 4.50 | 1.0 | 0-0 |

### Minors (2010)
| Level | Leag | W | L | Sv | IP | H | K | ERA | WHIP | K/9 | BB/9 | HR/9 | GB/F |
|---|---|---|---|---|---|---|---|---|---|---|---|---|---|
| A | — | | | | | | | | | | | | |
| AA | — | | | | | | | | | | | | |
| AAA | — | | | | | | | | | | | | |

### Majors
| Yr | Team | W | L | Sv | IP | H | K | ERA | WHIP | K/9 | BB/9 | HR/9 | GB/F | $1L | $2L | Pts | RAA | H% | HR/fb | S% | FIP | GS | CG | QS/DS | GR | Hld | Bln | Lead | OPS | 1st Hf | 2nd Hf | vs RH | vs LH |
|---|---|---|---|---|---|---|---|---|---|---|---|---|---|---|---|---|---|---|---|---|---|---|---|---|---|---|---|---|---|---|---|---|---|
| 07 | — | | | | | | | | | | | | | | | | | | | | | | | | | | | | | | | | |
| 08 | OAK | 1 | 2 | 0 | 25 | 34 | 19 | 4.56 | 1.64 | 6.7 | 2.8 | 0.4 | 1.0 | -$3 | -$4 | 20 | -2 | 39% | 14% | 71% | 3.26 | 4 | 0 | 2/0 | 2 | 0 | 0 | -1.0 | .860 | — | .860 | .937 | .584 |
| 09 | OAK | 4 | 1 | 0 | 67 | 53 | 53 | 3.48 | 1.16 | 7.1 | 3.3 | 1.2 | 0.9 | $5 | $2 | 100 | +0 | 24% | 11% | 75% | 4.58 | 12 | 0 | 7/1 | 2 | 0 | 0 | +0.1 | .640 | .640 | — | .717 | .373 |
| 10 | — | | | | | | | | | | | | | | | | | | | | | | | | | | | | | | | | |

---

## Rudy Owens — 40 IP | $-1 | 50 pts
**No MLB games played in 2010** — Owned: 0% — LH

After dominating Single-A in 2009, Owens posted nearly identical rates in Double-A in 2010. He does not have overwhelming stuff but rather gets success through strong command and an above-average change. Assuming the Pirates' starters keep flailing, Owens is likely to join the rotation around mid-season. (MB)

### Forecast
| Player | Age | IP | W | Sv | K | ERA | WHIP | K/9 | BB/9 | $2L | Pts |
|---|---|---|---|---|---|---|---|---|---|---|---|
| Owens R | 23 | 40 | 2 | 0 | 28 | 4.39 | 1.29 | 6.3 | 2.0 | -$1 | 50 |

### Mini-Browser
| Player | Age | IP | W | Sv | K | ERA | WHIP | K/9 | BB/9 | $2L | Pts |
|---|---|---|---|---|---|---|---|---|---|---|---|
| Reyes D | 33 | 40 | 2 | 0 | 29 | 3.72 | 1.43 | 6.4 | 4.5 | -$1 | 50 |
| Boggs M | 27 | 60 | 3 | 4 | 44 | 4.54 | 1.48 | 6.7 | 3.9 | -$1 | 80 |
| Cramer B | 31 | 40 | 3 | 0 | 35 | 4.33 | 1.48 | 8.0 | 3.2 | -$1 | 50 |
| Mitre S | 30 | 60 | 2 | 0 | 34 | 4.78 | 1.32 | 5.1 | 2.5 | -$1 | 50 |
| Logan B | 26 | 60 | 2 | 0 | 53 | 4.42 | 1.49 | 7.9 | 4.4 | -$1 | 60 |

### Competition at SP / Stats in 2010 as SP
| Thr | Player | GS | ERA | Supp | W-L |
|---|---|---|---|---|---|
| LH | Maholm P | 32 | 5.10 | 4.0 | 9-15 |
| LH | Duke Z | 29 | 5.72 | 3.8 | 8-15 |
| RH | Ohlendorf R | 21 | 4.07 | 2.9 | 1-11 |
| RH | Karstens J | 19 | 4.78 | 3.6 | 3-10 |

### Minors (2010)
| Level | Leag | W | L | Sv | IP | H | K | ERA | WHIP | K/9 | BB/9 | HR/9 | GB/F |
|---|---|---|---|---|---|---|---|---|---|---|---|---|---|
| A | — | | | | | | | | | | | | |
| AA | EL | 12 | 6 | 0 | 150 | 124 | 132 | 2.46 | 0.98 | 7.9 | 1.4 | 0.7 | — |
| AAA | — | | | | | | | | | | | | |

### Majors
| Yr | Team | W | L | Sv | IP | H | K | ERA | WHIP | K/9 | BB/9 | HR/9 | GB/F | $1L | $2L | Pts | RAA | H% | HR/fb | S% | FIP | GS | CG | QS/DS | GR | Hld | Bln | Lead | OPS | 1st Hf | 2nd Hf | vs RH | vs LH |
|---|---|---|---|---|---|---|---|---|---|---|---|---|---|---|---|---|---|---|---|---|---|---|---|---|---|---|---|---|---|---|---|---|---|
| 07 | — | | | | | | | | | | | | | | | | | | | | | | | | | | | | | | | | |
| 08 | — | | | | | | | | | | | | | | | | | | | | | | | | | | | | | | | | |
| 09 | — | | | | | | | | | | | | | | | | | | | | | | | | | | | | | | | | |
| 10 | — | | | | | | | | | | | | | | | | | | | | | | | | | | | | | | | | |

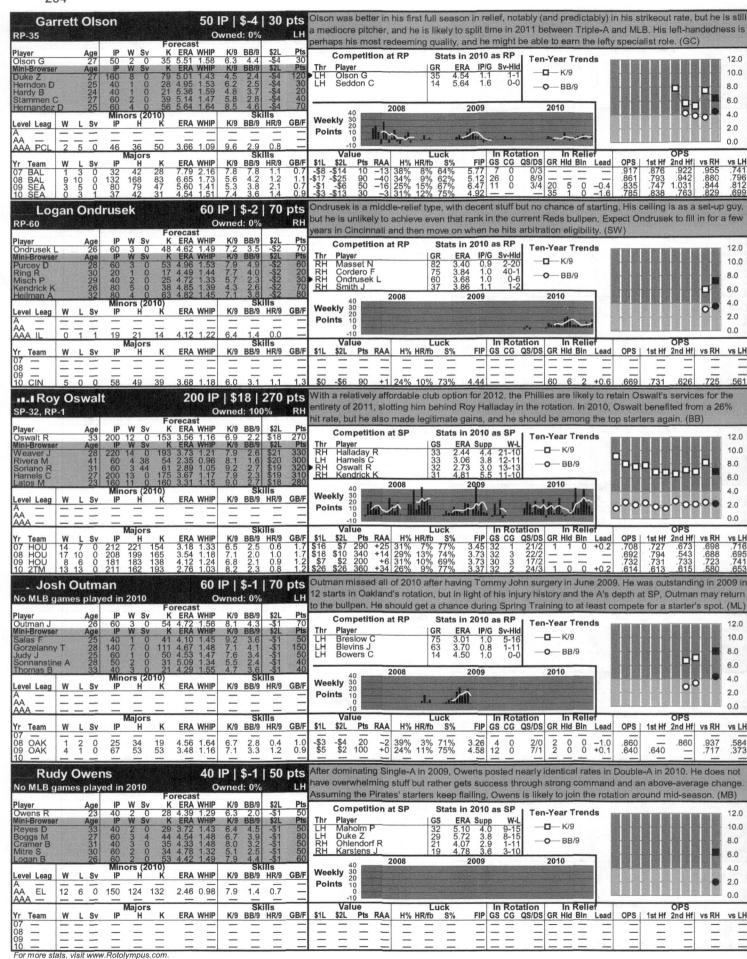

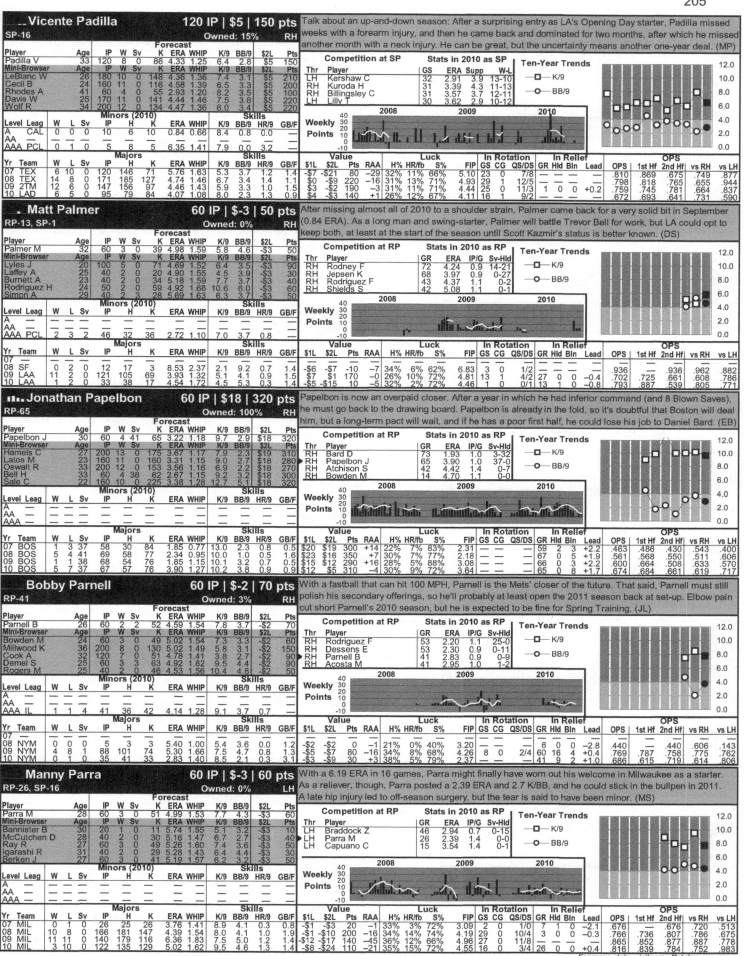

## Vicente Padilla — 120 IP | $5 | 150 pts
SP-16   Owned: 15%   RH

Talk about an up-and-down season: After a surprising entry as LA's Opening Day starter, Padilla missed weeks with a forearm injury, and then he came back and dominated for two months, after which he missed another month with a neck injury. He can be great, but the uncertainty means another one-year deal. (MP)

**Forecast**

| Player | Age | IP | W | Sv | K | ERA | WHIP | K/9 | BB/9 | $2L | Pts |
|---|---|---|---|---|---|---|---|---|---|---|---|
| Padilla V | 33 | 120 | 8 | 0 | 86 | 4.33 | 1.25 | 6.4 | 2.8 | $5 | 150 |

| Mini-Browser | Age | IP | W | Sv | K | ERA | WHIP | K/9 | BB/9 | $2L | Pts |
|---|---|---|---|---|---|---|---|---|---|---|---|
| LeBlanc W | 26 | 180 | 10 | 0 | 148 | 4.36 | 1.36 | 7.4 | 3.1 | $5 | 210 |
| Cecil B | 24 | 160 | 11 | 0 | 116 | 4.58 | 1.39 | 6.5 | 3.3 | $5 | 200 |
| Rhodes A | 41 | 60 | 4 | 0 | 55 | 2.93 | 1.20 | 8.2 | 3.5 | $5 | 200 |
| Davis W | 25 | 170 | 11 | 0 | 141 | 4.44 | 1.46 | 7.5 | 3.8 | $5 | 220 |
| Wolf R | 34 | 200 | 12 | 0 | 134 | 4.47 | 1.36 | 6.0 | 3.4 | $5 | 220 |

**Competition at SP**

| Thr | Player | GS | ERA | Supp | W-L |
|---|---|---|---|---|---|
| LH | Kershaw C | 32 | 2.91 | 3.9 | 13-10 |
| RH | Kuroda H | 31 | 3.39 | 4.3 | 11-13 |
| RH | Billingsley C | 31 | 3.57 | 3.7 | 12-11 |
| LH | Lilly T | 30 | 3.62 | 2.9 | 10-12 |

Ten-Year Trends: K/9, BB/9

**Minors (2010)**

| Level | Leag | W | L | Sv | IP | H | K | ERA | WHIP | K/9 | BB/9 | HR/9 | GB/F |
|---|---|---|---|---|---|---|---|---|---|---|---|---|---|
| A | CAL | 0 | 0 | 0 | 10 | 6 | 10 | 0.84 | 0.66 | 8.4 | 0.8 | 0.0 | — |
| AA | — | | | | | | | | | | | | |
| AAA | PCL | 0 | 1 | 0 | 5 | 8 | 5 | 6.35 | 1.41 | 7.9 | 0.0 | 3.2 | — |

**Majors**

| Yr | Team | W | L | Sv | IP | H | K | ERA | WHIP | K/9 | BB/9 | HR/9 | GB/F |
|---|---|---|---|---|---|---|---|---|---|---|---|---|---|
| 07 | TEX | 6 | 10 | 0 | 120 | 146 | 71 | 5.76 | 1.46 | 5.3 | 3.7 | 1.2 | 1.4 |
| 08 | TEX | 14 | 8 | 0 | 171 | 185 | 127 | 4.74 | 1.46 | 6.7 | 3.4 | 1.4 | 1.1 |
| 09 | 2TM | 12 | 6 | 0 | 147 | 156 | 97 | 4.46 | 1.43 | 5.9 | 3.3 | 1.0 | 1.5 |
| 10 | LAD | 6 | 5 | 0 | 95 | | 75 | 4.07 | 1.08 | 8.0 | 2.3 | 1.3 | 0.9 |

| Yr | $1L | $2L | Pts | RAA | H% | HR/fb | S% | FIP | GS | CG | QS/DS | GR | Hld | Bln | Lead | OPS | 1st Hf | 2nd Hf | vs RH | vs LH |
|---|---|---|---|---|---|---|---|---|---|---|---|---|---|---|---|---|---|---|---|---|
| 07 | -$7 | -$21 | 100 | -29 | 34% | 11% | 66% | 5.10 | 23 | 0 | 7/8 | — | — | — | — | .810 | .869 | .675 | .749 | .877 |
| 08 | -$0 | -$9 | 220 | -16 | 31% | 13% | 71% | 4.93 | 29 | 1 | 12/5 | — | — | — | — | .798 | .818 | .765 | .655 | .944 |
| 09 | $3 | -$2 | 190 | -3 | 31% | 11% | 71% | 4.44 | 25 | 0 | 11/3 | 1 | 0 | 0 | +0.2 | .759 | .745 | .781 | .664 | .837 |
| 10 | $4 | -$3 | 140 | +1 | 26% | 12% | 67% | 4.11 | 16 | 1 | | | | | | .672 | .693 | .641 | .731 | .590 |

## Matt Palmer — 60 IP | $-3 | 50 pts
RP-13, SP-1   Owned: 0%   RH

After missing almost all of 2010 to a shoulder strain, Palmer came back for a very solid bit in September (0.84 ERA). As a long man and swing-starter, Palmer will battle Trevor Bell for work, but LA could opt to keep both, at least at the start of the season until Scott Kazmir's status is better known. (DS)

**Forecast**

| Player | Age | IP | W | Sv | K | ERA | WHIP | K/9 | BB/9 | $2L | Pts |
|---|---|---|---|---|---|---|---|---|---|---|---|
| Palmer M | 32 | 60 | 3 | 0 | 39 | 4.98 | 1.59 | 5.8 | 4.6 | -$3 | 50 |

| Mini-Browser | Age | IP | W | Sv | K | ERA | WHIP | K/9 | BB/9 | $2L | Pts |
|---|---|---|---|---|---|---|---|---|---|---|---|
| Lyles J | 20 | 100 | 5 | 0 | 71 | 4.69 | 1.52 | 6.4 | 3.5 | -$3 | 90 |
| Laffey A | 25 | 40 | 2 | 0 | 20 | 4.90 | 1.55 | 4.5 | 3.9 | -$3 | 30 |
| Burnett A | 23 | 40 | 2 | 0 | 34 | 5.18 | 1.59 | 7.7 | 3.7 | -$3 | 40 |
| Rodriguez H | 24 | 50 | 2 | 0 | 59 | 4.92 | 1.68 | 10.6 | 6.0 | -$3 | 40 |
| Simon A | 29 | 40 | 2 | 3 | 28 | 5.69 | 1.63 | 6.3 | 3.7 | -$3 | 50 |

**Competition at RP**

| Thr | Player | GR | ERA | IP/G | Sv-Hld |
|---|---|---|---|---|---|
| RH | Rodney F | 72 | 4.24 | 0.9 | 14-21 |
| RH | Jepsen K | 68 | 3.97 | 0.9 | 0-27 |
| RH | Rodriguez F | 43 | 4.37 | 1.1 | 0-2 |
| RH | Shields S | 42 | 5.08 | 1.1 | 0-1 |

Ten-Year Trends: K/9, BB/9

**Minors (2010)**

| Level | Leag | W | L | Sv | IP | H | K | ERA | WHIP | K/9 | BB/9 | HR/9 | GB/F |
|---|---|---|---|---|---|---|---|---|---|---|---|---|---|
| A | — | | | | | | | | | | | | |
| AA | — | | | | | | | | | | | | |
| AAA | PCL | 2 | 3 | 2 | 46 | 32 | 36 | 2.72 | 1.10 | 7.0 | 3.7 | 0.8 | — |

**Majors**

| Yr | Team | W | L | Sv | IP | H | K | ERA | WHIP | K/9 | BB/9 | HR/9 | GB/F |
|---|---|---|---|---|---|---|---|---|---|---|---|---|---|
| 07 | — | | | | | | | | | | | | |
| 08 | SF | 0 | 2 | 0 | 12 | 17 | 3 | 8.53 | 2.37 | 2.1 | 9.2 | 0.7 | 1.4 |
| 09 | LAA | 11 | 2 | 0 | 121 | 105 | 69 | 3.93 | 1.32 | 5.1 | 4.1 | 0.9 | 1.5 |
| 10 | LAA | 1 | 0 | 0 | 33 | 38 | 17 | 4.54 | 1.72 | 4.5 | 5.3 | 1.3 | 1.4 |

| Yr | $1L | $2L | Pts | RAA | H% | HR/fb | S% | FIP | GS | CG | QS/DS | GR | Hld | Bln | Lead | OPS | 1st Hf | 2nd Hf | vs RH | vs LH |
|---|---|---|---|---|---|---|---|---|---|---|---|---|---|---|---|---|---|---|---|---|
| 08 | -$6 | -$7 | -10 | -7 | 34% | 6% | 62% | 6.83 | — | — | 0 1/2 | — | — | — | — | .936 | — | .936 | .962 | .882 |
| 09 | $7 | $1 | 170 | -0 | 26% | 10% | 72% | 4.81 | 13 | 1 | 0/2 | 27 | 0 | 0 | -0.4 | .702 | .725 | .661 | .608 | .786 |
| 10 | -$5 | -$15 | 10 | -5 | 32% | 2% | 72% | 4.46 | 1 | 0 | 0/1 | 13 | 1 | 0 | -0.8 | .793 | .887 | .539 | .805 | .771 |

## Jonathan Papelbon — 60 IP | $18 | 320 pts
RP-65   Owned: 100%   RH

Papelbon is now an overpaid closer. After a year in which he had inferior command (and 8 Blown Saves), he must go back to the drawing board. Papelbon is already in the fold, so it's doubtful that Boston will deal him, but a long-term pact will wait, and if he has a poor first half, he could lose his job to Daniel Bard. (EB)

**Forecast**

| Player | Age | IP | W | Sv | K | ERA | WHIP | K/9 | BB/9 | $2L | Pts |
|---|---|---|---|---|---|---|---|---|---|---|---|
| Papelbon J | 30 | 60 | 4 | 41 | 65 | 3.22 | 1.18 | 9.7 | 2.9 | $18 | 320 |

| Mini-Browser | Age | IP | W | Sv | K | ERA | WHIP | K/9 | BB/9 | $2L | Pts |
|---|---|---|---|---|---|---|---|---|---|---|---|
| Hamels C | 27 | 200 | 13 | 0 | 175 | 3.67 | 1.17 | 7.9 | 2.3 | $19 | 310 |
| Latos M | 23 | 160 | 11 | 0 | 160 | 3.31 | 1.15 | 9.0 | 2.7 | $18 | 280 |
| Oswalt R | 33 | 200 | 12 | 0 | 153 | 3.56 | 1.16 | 6.9 | 2.2 | $18 | 270 |
| Bell H | 33 | 60 | 4 | 38 | 62 | 2.67 | 1.15 | 9.2 | 3.2 | $18 | 300 |
| Sale C | 22 | 160 | 10 | 0 | 225 | 3.38 | 1.28 | 12.7 | 5.1 | $18 | 320 |

**Competition at RP**

| Thr | Player | GR | ERA | IP/G | Sv-Hld |
|---|---|---|---|---|---|
| RH | Bard D | 73 | 1.93 | 1.0 | 3-32 |
| RH | Papelbon J | 65 | 3.90 | 1.0 | 37-0 |
| RH | Atchison S | 42 | 4.42 | 1.4 | 0-7 |
| RH | Bowden M | 14 | 4.70 | 1.1 | 0-0 |

Ten-Year Trends: K/9, BB/9

**Minors (2010):** none

**Majors**

| Yr | Team | W | L | Sv | IP | H | K | ERA | WHIP | K/9 | BB/9 | HR/9 | GB/F |
|---|---|---|---|---|---|---|---|---|---|---|---|---|---|
| 07 | BOS | 1 | 3 | 37 | 58 | 30 | 84 | 1.85 | 0.77 | 13.0 | 2.3 | 0.8 | 0.5 |
| 08 | BOS | 5 | 4 | 41 | 69 | 58 | 77 | 2.34 | 0.95 | 10.0 | 1.0 | 0.5 | 0.6 |
| 09 | BOS | 1 | 1 | 38 | 68 | 54 | 76 | 1.85 | 1.15 | 10.1 | 3.2 | 0.7 | 0.5 |
| 10 | BOS | 5 | 7 | 37 | 67 | 57 | 76 | 3.90 | 1.27 | 10.1 | 3.8 | 0.9 | 0.9 |

| Yr | $1L | $2L | Pts | RAA | H% | HR/fb | S% | FIP | GS | CG | QS/DS | GR | Hld | Bln | Lead | OPS | 1st Hf | 2nd Hf | vs RH | vs LH |
|---|---|---|---|---|---|---|---|---|---|---|---|---|---|---|---|---|---|---|---|---|
| 07 | $20 | $19 | 300 | +14 | 22% | 7% | 83% | 2.31 | — | — | — | 59 | 2 | 3 | +2.2 | .463 | .486 | .430 | .543 | .400 |
| 08 | $23 | $19 | 350 | +7 | 30% | 7% | 77% | 2.18 | — | — | — | 67 | 0 | 5 | +1.9 | .561 | .568 | .550 | .511 | .606 |
| 09 | $15 | $12 | 290 | +16 | 28% | 5% | 88% | 3.08 | — | — | — | 66 | 0 | 3 | +2.2 | .600 | .664 | .508 | .633 | .570 |
| 10 | $12 | $5 | 310 | -4 | 30% | 9% | 72% | 3.64 | — | — | — | 65 | 0 | 8 | +1.7 | .674 | .684 | .661 | .619 | .717 |

## Bobby Parnell — 60 IP | $-2 | 70 pts
RP-41   Owned: 3%   RH

With a fastball that can hit 100 MPH, Parnell is the Mets' closer of the future. That said, Parnell must still polish his secondary offerings, so he'll probably at least open the 2011 season back at set-up. Elbow pain cut short Parnell's 2010 season, but he is expected to be fine for Spring Training. (JL)

**Forecast**

| Player | Age | IP | W | Sv | K | ERA | WHIP | K/9 | BB/9 | $2L | Pts |
|---|---|---|---|---|---|---|---|---|---|---|---|
| Parnell B | 26 | 60 | 2 | 2 | 52 | 4.59 | 1.54 | 7.8 | 3.7 | -$2 | 70 |

| Mini-Browser | Age | IP | W | Sv | K | ERA | WHIP | K/9 | BB/9 | $2L | Pts |
|---|---|---|---|---|---|---|---|---|---|---|---|
| Bowden M | 24 | 60 | 3 | 0 | 49 | 5.02 | 1.54 | 7.3 | 3.3 | -$2 | 60 |
| Millwood K | 36 | 200 | 8 | 0 | 130 | 5.02 | 1.49 | 5.8 | 3.1 | -$2 | 150 |
| Cook A | 32 | 120 | 7 | 0 | 51 | 4.78 | 1.41 | 3.8 | 2.7 | -$2 | 90 |
| Demel S | 25 | 60 | 3 | 3 | 63 | 4.92 | 1.62 | 9.5 | 4.4 | -$2 | 90 |
| Rogers M | 25 | 40 | 2 | 0 | 46 | 4.53 | 1.56 | 10.4 | 4.8 | -$2 | 50 |

**Competition at RP**

| Thr | Player | GR | ERA | IP/G | Sv-Hld |
|---|---|---|---|---|---|
| RH | Rodriguez F | 53 | 2.20 | 1.1 | 25-0 |
| RH | Dessens E | 53 | 2.30 | 0.9 | 0-11 |
| RH | Parnell B | 41 | 2.83 | 0.9 | 0-9 |
| RH | Acosta M | 41 | 2.95 | 1.0 | 1-2 |

Ten-Year Trends: K/9, BB/9

**Minors (2010)**

| Level | Leag | W | L | Sv | IP | H | K | ERA | WHIP | K/9 | BB/9 | HR/9 | GB/F |
|---|---|---|---|---|---|---|---|---|---|---|---|---|---|
| A | — | | | | | | | | | | | | |
| AA | — | | | | | | | | | | | | |
| AAA | IL | 1 | 1 | 4 | 41 | 36 | 42 | 4.14 | 1.28 | 9.1 | 3.7 | 0.7 | — |

**Majors**

| Yr | Team | W | L | Sv | IP | H | K | ERA | WHIP | K/9 | BB/9 | HR/9 | GB/F |
|---|---|---|---|---|---|---|---|---|---|---|---|---|---|
| 07 | — | | | | | | | | | | | | |
| 08 | NYM | 0 | 0 | 0 | 5 | 3 | 3 | 5.40 | 1.00 | 5.4 | 3.6 | 0.0 | 1.2 |
| 09 | NYM | 4 | 8 | 1 | 88 | 101 | 74 | 5.30 | 1.66 | 7.5 | 4.7 | 0.8 | 1.9 |
| 10 | NYM | 0 | 1 | 0 | 35 | 41 | 33 | 2.83 | 1.40 | 8.5 | 2.1 | 0.3 | 3.1 |

| Yr | $1L | $2L | Pts | RAA | H% | HR/fb | S% | FIP | GS | CG | QS/DS | GR | Hld | Bln | Lead | OPS | 1st Hf | 2nd Hf | vs RH | vs LH |
|---|---|---|---|---|---|---|---|---|---|---|---|---|---|---|---|---|---|---|---|---|
| 08 | -$2 | -$2 | 80 | -1 | 21% | 0% | 40% | 3.20 | — | — | — | 6 | 0 | 0 | -2.8 | .440 | — | .440 | .606 | .143 |
| 09 | -$5 | -$7 | 80 | -16 | 34% | 8% | 68% | 4.26 | 8 | 0 | 2/4 | 60 | 16 | 4 | +0.4 | .769 | .787 | .758 | .775 | .762 |
| 10 | $2 | $2 | 70 | +1 | 38% | 5% | 79% | 2.37 | — | — | — | 26 | 0 | 2 | +1.0 | .686 | .615 | .719 | .614 | .806 |

## Manny Parra — 60 IP | $-3 | 60 pts
RP-26, SP-16   Owned: 0%   LH

With a 6.19 ERA in 16 games, Parra might finally have worn out his welcome in Milwaukee as a starter. As a reliever, though, Parra posted a 2.39 ERA and 2.7 K/BB, and he could stick in the bullpen in 2011. A late hip injury led to off-season surgery, but the tear is said to have been minor. (MS)

**Forecast**

| Player | Age | IP | W | Sv | K | ERA | WHIP | K/9 | BB/9 | $2L | Pts |
|---|---|---|---|---|---|---|---|---|---|---|---|
| Parra M | 28 | 60 | 3 | 0 | 51 | 4.99 | 1.53 | 7.7 | 4.3 | -$3 | 60 |

| Mini-Browser | Age | IP | W | Sv | K | ERA | WHIP | K/9 | BB/9 | $2L | Pts |
|---|---|---|---|---|---|---|---|---|---|---|---|
| Bannister B | 30 | 20 | 1 | 0 | 11 | 5.74 | 1.55 | 5.1 | 3.2 | -$3 | 50 |
| McCutchen D | 28 | 40 | 2 | 0 | 30 | 5.16 | 1.47 | 6.7 | 2.7 | -$3 | 40 |
| Ray R | 27 | 60 | 3 | 0 | 49 | 5.26 | 1.60 | 7.4 | 3.6 | -$3 | 50 |
| Igarashi R | 31 | 40 | 2 | 0 | 29 | 5.28 | 1.43 | 6.4 | 4.4 | -$3 | 30 |
| Berken J | 27 | 60 | 3 | 0 | 41 | 5.19 | 1.57 | 6.2 | 3.2 | -$3 | 50 |

**Competition at RP**

| Thr | Player | GR | ERA | IP/G | Sv-Hld |
|---|---|---|---|---|---|
| LH | Braddock Z | 46 | 2.94 | 0.7 | 0-15 |
| LH | Parra M | 26 | 2.39 | 1.4 | 0-0 |
| LH | Capuano C | 15 | 3.54 | 1.4 | 0-1 |

Ten-Year Trends: K/9, BB/9

**Minors (2010):** A —, AA —, AAA —

**Majors**

| Yr | Team | W | L | Sv | IP | H | K | ERA | WHIP | K/9 | BB/9 | HR/9 | GB/F |
|---|---|---|---|---|---|---|---|---|---|---|---|---|---|
| 07 | MIL | 0 | 1 | 0 | 26 | 25 | 26 | 3.76 | 1.41 | 8.9 | 4.5 | 0.3 | 0.8 |
| 08 | MIL | 10 | 8 | 0 | 166 | 181 | 147 | 4.39 | 1.54 | 8.0 | 4.1 | 1.0 | 1.9 |
| 09 | MIL | 11 | 11 | 0 | 140 | 179 | 116 | 6.36 | 1.83 | 7.5 | 5.0 | 1.2 | 1.4 |
| 10 | MIL | 3 | 10 | 0 | 122 | 135 | 129 | 5.02 | 1.62 | 9.5 | 4.9 | 1.1 | 1.4 |

| Yr | $1L | $2L | Pts | RAA | H% | HR/fb | S% | FIP | GS | CG | QS/DS | GR | Hld | Bln | Lead | OPS | 1st Hf | 2nd Hf | vs RH | vs LH |
|---|---|---|---|---|---|---|---|---|---|---|---|---|---|---|---|---|---|---|---|---|
| 07 | -$1 | -$3 | 20 | -1 | 33% | 3% | 72% | 3.09 | 2 | 0 | 1/0 | — | — | — | -2.1 | .676 | — | .676 | .720 | .513 |
| 08 | -$1 | -$10 | 200 | -16 | 34% | 14% | 74% | 4.19 | 29 | 0 | 10/4 | 3 | 0 | 0 | -0.3 | .766 | .736 | .807 | .786 | .675 |
| 09 | -$12 | -$17 | 140 | -45 | 36% | 12% | 66% | 4.96 | 27 | 0 | 11/8 | — | — | — | | .865 | .852 | .877 | .887 | .778 |
| 10 | -$8 | -$24 | 140 | -21 | 35% | 15% | 72% | 4.55 | 16 | 0 | 3/4 | 26 | 0 | 0 | +0.4 | .816 | .839 | .784 | .752 | .983 |

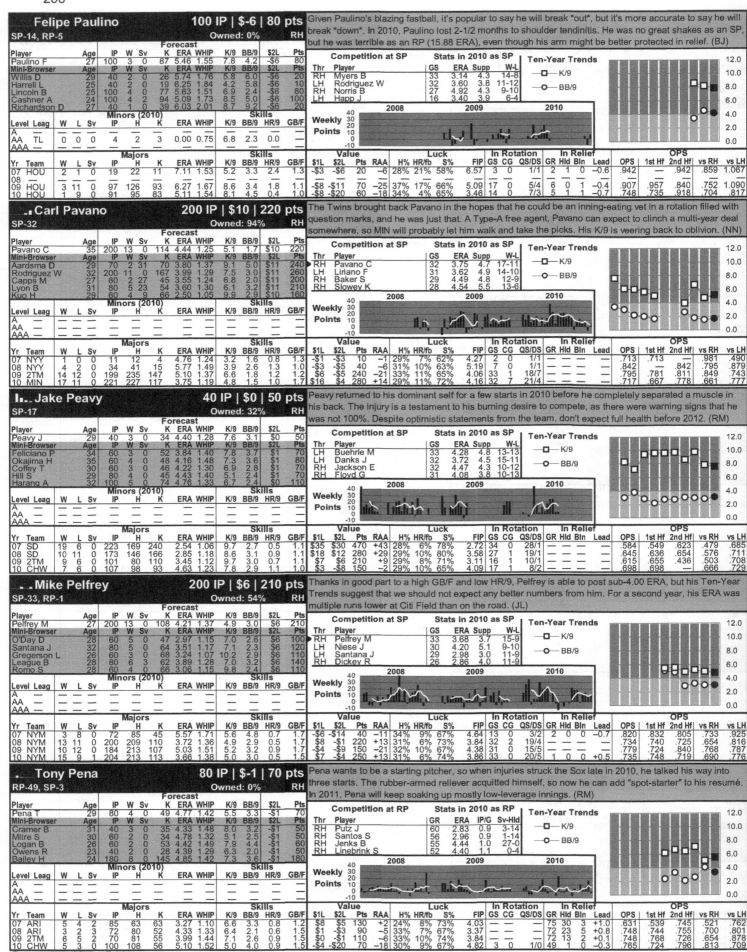

## Felipe Paulino — 100 IP | $-6 | 80 pts

SP-14, RP-5 — Owned: 0% — RH

Given Paulino's blazing fastball, it's popular to say he will break *out*, but it's more accurate to say he will break *down*. In 2010, Paulino lost 2-1/2 months to shoulder tendinitis. He was no great shakes as an SP, but he was terrible as an RP (15.88 ERA), even though his arm might be better protected in relief. (BJ)

| Player | Age | IP | W | Sv | K | ERA | WHIP | K/9 | BB/9 | $2L | Pts |
|---|---|---|---|---|---|---|---|---|---|---|---|
| Paulino F | 27 | 100 | 3 | 0 | 87 | 5.46 | 1.55 | 7.8 | 4.2 | -$6 | 80 |
| **Mini-Browser** | **Age** | **IP** | **W** | **Sv** | **K** | **ERA** | **WHIP** | **K/9** | **BB/9** | **$2L** | **Pts** |
| Willis D | 29 | 40 | 2 | 0 | 26 | 5.74 | 1.76 | 5.8 | 6.0 | -$6 | 20 |
| Harrell L | 25 | 40 | 2 | 0 | 19 | 6.25 | 1.84 | 4.2 | 5.8 | -$6 | 10 |
| Lincoln B | 25 | 100 | 4 | 0 | 77 | 5.63 | 1.51 | 6.9 | 2.4 | -$6 | 80 |
| Cashner A | 24 | 100 | 4 | 2 | 94 | 5.09 | 1.73 | 8.5 | 5.0 | -$6 | 100 |
| Richardson D | 27 | 40 | 1 | 0 | 39 | 6.03 | 2.01 | 8.7 | 9.2 | -$6 | 20 |

| Level | Leag | W | L | Sv | IP | H | K | ERA | WHIP | K/9 | BB/9 | HR/9 | GB/F |
|---|---|---|---|---|---|---|---|---|---|---|---|---|---|
| A | — | — | — | — | — | — | — | — | — | — | — | — | — |
| AA | TL | 0 | 0 | 0 | 4 | 2 | 3 | 0.00 | 0.75 | 6.8 | 2.3 | 0.0 | — |
| AAA | — | — | — | — | — | — | — | — | — | — | — | — | — |

Competition at SP — Stats in 2010 as SP

| Thr | Player | GS | ERA | Supp | W-L |
|---|---|---|---|---|---|
| RH | Myers B | 33 | 3.14 | 4.3 | 14-8 |
| LH | Rodriguez W | 32 | 3.60 | 3.8 | 11-12 |
| RH | Norris B | 27 | 4.92 | 4.3 | 9-10 |
| LH | Happ J | 16 | 3.40 | 3.9 | 6-4 |

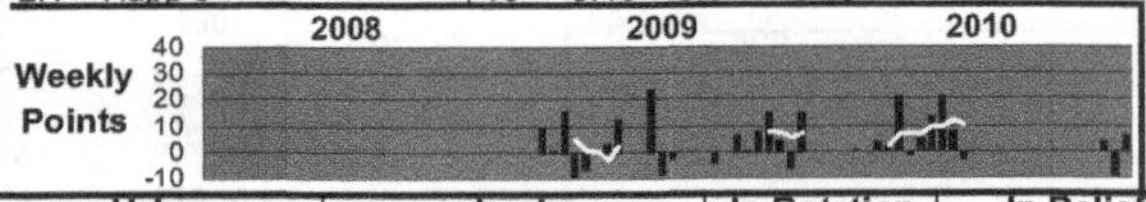

Weekly Points
2008
2009
2010
40
30
20
10
0
-10


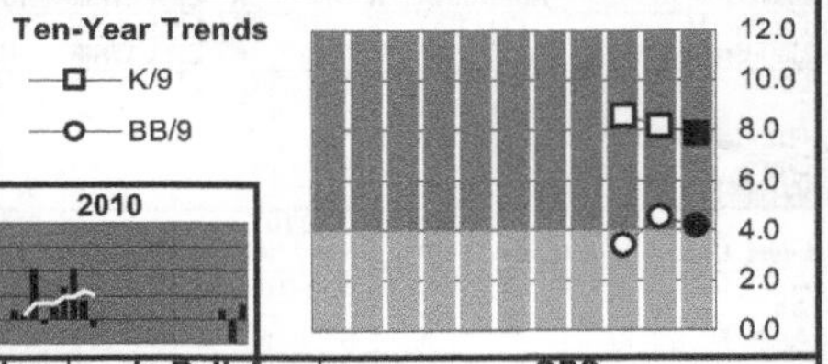

Ten-Year Trends
K/9
BB/9
12.0
10.0
8.0
6.0
4.0
2.0
0.0


| Yr | Team | W | L | Sv | IP | H | K | ERA | WHIP | K/9 | BB/9 | HR/9 | GB/F | $1L | $2L | Pts | RAA | H% | HR/fb | S% | FIP | GS | CG | QS/DS | GR | Hld | Bln | Lead | OPS | 1st Hf | 2nd Hf | vs RH | vs LH |
|---|---|---|---|---|---|---|---|---|---|---|---|---|---|---|---|---|---|---|---|---|---|---|---|---|---|---|---|---|---|---|---|---|---|
| 07 | HOU | 2 | 1 | 0 | 19 | 22 | 11 | 7.11 | 1.53 | 5.2 | 3.3 | 2.4 | 1.3 | -$3 | -$6 | 20 | −6 | 28% | 21% | 58% | 6.57 | 3 | 0 | 1/1 | 2 | 1 | 0 | −0.6 | .942 | — | .942 | .859 | 1.067 |
| 08 | — | — | — | — | — | — | — | — | — | — | — | — | — | — | — | — | — | — | — | — | — | — | — | — | — | — | — | — | — | — | — | — | — |
| 09 | HOU | 3 | 11 | 0 | 97 | 126 | 93 | 6.27 | 1.67 | 8.6 | 3.4 | 1.8 | 1.1 | -$8 | -$11 | 70 | −25 | 37% | 17% | 66% | 5.09 | 17 | 0 | 5/4 | 6 | 0 | 1 | −0.4 | .907 | .957 | .840 | .752 | 1.090 |
| 10 | HOU | 1 | 9 | 0 | 91 | 95 | 83 | 5.11 | 1.54 | 8.1 | 4.5 | 0.4 | 1.0 | -$8 | -$20 | 60 | −18 | 34% | 4% | 65% | 3.46 | 14 | 0 | 7/3 | 5 | 1 | 1 | −0.7 | .748 | .735 | .918 | .704 | .817 |

## Carl Pavano — 200 IP | $10 | 220 pts

SP-32 — Owned: 94% — RH

The Twins brought back Pavano in the hopes that he could be an inning-eating vet in a rotation filled with question marks, and he was just that. A Type-A free agent, Pavano can expect to clinch a multi-year deal somewhere, so MIN will probably let him walk and take the picks. His K/9 is veering back to oblivion. (NN)

| Player | Age | IP | W | Sv | K | ERA | WHIP | K/9 | BB/9 | $2L | Pts |
|---|---|---|---|---|---|---|---|---|---|---|---|
| Pavano C | 35 | 200 | 13 | 0 | 114 | 4.44 | 1.25 | 5.1 | 1.7 | $10 | 220 |
| **Mini-Browser** | **Age** | **IP** | **W** | **Sv** | **K** | **ERA** | **WHIP** | **K/9** | **BB/9** | **$2L** | **Pts** |
| Aardsma D | 29 | 70 | 2 | 31 | 70 | 3.80 | 1.37 | 9.1 | 5.0 | $11 | 240 |
| Rodriguez W | 32 | 200 | 11 | 0 | 167 | 3.99 | 1.29 | 7.5 | 3.0 | $11 | 260 |
| Capps M | 27 | 60 | 2 | 27 | 45 | 3.55 | 1.24 | 6.8 | 2.0 | $11 | 200 |
| Lyon B | 31 | 80 | 5 | 23 | 54 | 3.60 | 1.30 | 6.1 | 3.2 | $11 | 210 |
| Kuo H | 29 | 60 | 4 | 9 | 66 | 2.50 | 1.05 | 9.9 | 2.9 | $10 | 160 |

| Level | Leag | W | L | Sv | IP | H | K | ERA | WHIP | K/9 | BB/9 | HR/9 | GB/F |
|---|---|---|---|---|---|---|---|---|---|---|---|---|---|
| A | — | — | — | — | — | — | — | — | — | — | — | — | — |
| AA | — | — | — | — | — | — | — | — | — | — | — | — | — |
| AAA | — | — | — | — | — | — | — | — | — | — | — | — | — |

Competition at SP — Stats in 2010 as SP

| Thr | Player | GS | ERA | Supp | W-L |
|---|---|---|---|---|---|
| RH | Pavano C | 32 | 3.75 | 4.7 | 17-11 |
| LH | Liriano F | 31 | 3.62 | 4.9 | 14-10 |
| RH | Baker S | 29 | 4.49 | 4.8 | 12-9 |
| RH | Slowey K | 28 | 4.54 | 5.5 | 13-6 |

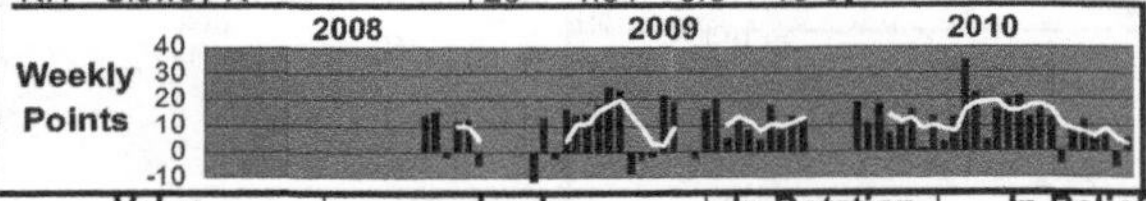

Weekly Points
2008
2009
2010
40
30
20
10
0
-10


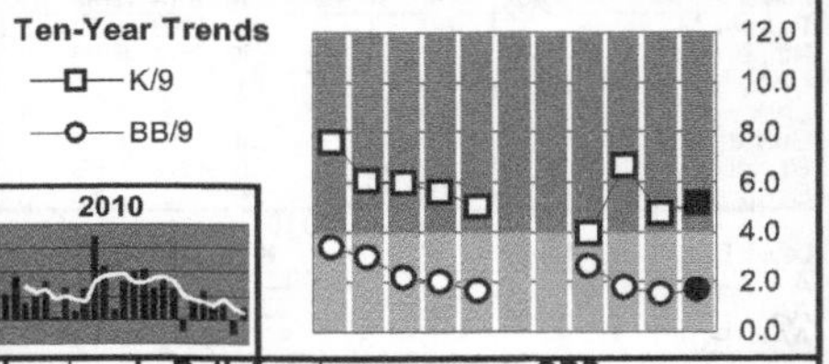

Ten-Year Trends
K/9
BB/9
12.0
10.0
8.0
6.0
4.0
2.0
0.0


| Yr | Team | W | L | Sv | IP | H | K | ERA | WHIP | K/9 | BB/9 | HR/9 | GB/F | $1L | $2L | Pts | RAA | H% | HR/fb | S% | FIP | GS | CG | QS/DS | GR | Hld | Bln | Lead | OPS | 1st Hf | 2nd Hf | vs RH | vs LH |
|---|---|---|---|---|---|---|---|---|---|---|---|---|---|---|---|---|---|---|---|---|---|---|---|---|---|---|---|---|---|---|---|---|---|
| 07 | NYY | 1 | 0 | 0 | 11 | 12 | 4 | 4.76 | 1.24 | 3.2 | 1.6 | 0.8 | 1.3 | -$1 | -$3 | 10 | −1 | 29% | 7% | 62% | 4.27 | 2 | 0 | 1/1 | — | — | — | — | .713 | .713 | — | .981 | .490 |
| 08 | NYY | 4 | 2 | 0 | 34 | 41 | 15 | 5.77 | 1.49 | 3.9 | 2.6 | 1.3 | 1.0 | -$3 | -$5 | 40 | −6 | 31% | 10% | 63% | 5.19 | 7 | 0 | 1/1 | — | — | — | — | .842 | — | .842 | .795 | .879 |
| 09 | 2TM | 14 | 12 | 0 | 199 | 235 | 147 | 5.10 | 1.37 | 6.6 | 1.8 | 1.2 | 1.2 | $6 | -$5 | 240 | −21 | 33% | 11% | 65% | 4.06 | 33 | 1 | 18/7 | — | — | — | — | .795 | .781 | .811 | .849 | .743 |
| 10 | MIN | 17 | 11 | 0 | 221 | 227 | 117 | 3.75 | 1.19 | 4.8 | 1.5 | 1.0 | 1.7 | $16 | $4 | 280 | +14 | 29% | 11% | 72% | 4.16 | 32 | 7 | 21/4 | — | — | — | — | .717 | .667 | .778 | .661 | .777 |

## Jake Peavy — 40 IP | $0 | 50 pts

SP-17 — Owned: 32% — RH

Peavy returned to his dominant self for a few starts in 2010 before he completely separated a muscle in his back. The injury is a testament to his burning desire to compete, as there were warning signs that he was not 100%. Despite optimistic statements from the team, don't expect full health before 2012. (RM)

| Player | Age | IP | W | Sv | K | ERA | WHIP | K/9 | BB/9 | $2L | Pts |
|---|---|---|---|---|---|---|---|---|---|---|---|
| Peavy J | 29 | 40 | 3 | 0 | 34 | 4.40 | 1.28 | 7.6 | 3.1 | $0 | 50 |
| **Mini-Browser** | **Age** | **IP** | **W** | **Sv** | **K** | **ERA** | **WHIP** | **K/9** | **BB/9** | **$2L** | **Pts** |
| Feliciano P | 34 | 60 | 3 | 0 | 52 | 3.84 | 1.40 | 7.8 | 3.7 | $1 | 70 |
| Okajima H | 35 | 60 | 4 | 0 | 48 | 4.16 | 1.48 | 7.3 | 3.6 | $1 | 80 |
| Coffey T | 30 | 60 | 3 | 0 | 46 | 4.22 | 1.30 | 6.9 | 2.8 | $1 | 70 |
| Hill S | 29 | 80 | 4 | 0 | 45 | 4.43 | 1.40 | 5.1 | 2.4 | $1 | 70 |
| Harang A | 32 | 100 | 5 | 0 | 74 | 4.76 | 1.33 | 6.7 | 2.4 | $0 | 110 |

| Level | Leag | W | L | Sv | IP | H | K | ERA | WHIP | K/9 | BB/9 | HR/9 | GB/F |
|---|---|---|---|---|---|---|---|---|---|---|---|---|---|
| A | — | — | — | — | — | — | — | — | — | — | — | — | — |
| AA | — | — | — | — | — | — | — | — | — | — | — | — | — |
| AAA | — | — | — | — | — | — | — | — | — | — | — | — | — |

Competition at SP — Stats in 2010 as SP

| Thr | Player | GS | ERA | Supp | W-L |
|---|---|---|---|---|---|
| LH | Buehrle M | 33 | 4.28 | 4.8 | 13-13 |
| LH | Danks J | 32 | 3.72 | 4.5 | 15-11 |
| RH | Jackson E | 32 | 4.47 | 4.3 | 10-12 |
| RH | Floyd G | 31 | 4.08 | 3.8 | 10-13 |

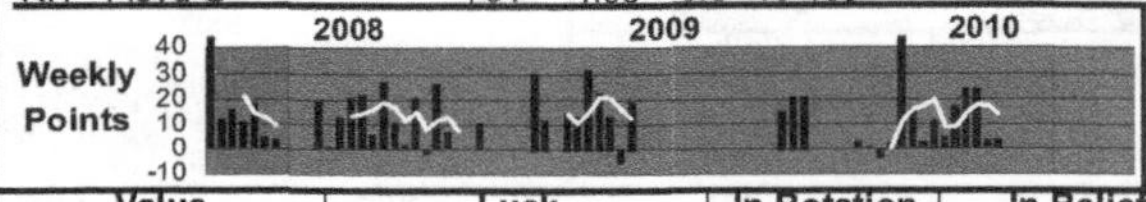

Weekly Points
2008
2009
2010
40
30
20
10
0
-10


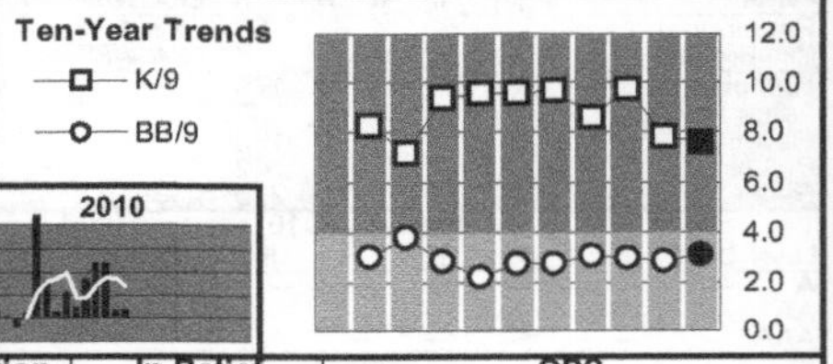

Ten-Year Trends
K/9
BB/9
12.0
10.0
8.0
6.0
4.0
2.0
0.0


| Yr | Team | W | L | Sv | IP | H | K | ERA | WHIP | K/9 | BB/9 | HR/9 | GB/F | $1L | $2L | Pts | RAA | H% | HR/fb | S% | FIP | GS | CG | QS/DS | GR | Hld | Bln | Lead | OPS | 1st Hf | 2nd Hf | vs RH | vs LH |
|---|---|---|---|---|---|---|---|---|---|---|---|---|---|---|---|---|---|---|---|---|---|---|---|---|---|---|---|---|---|---|---|---|---|
| 07 | SD | 19 | 6 | 0 | 223 | 169 | 240 | 2.54 | 1.06 | 9.7 | 2.7 | 0.5 | 1.1 | $35 | $30 | 470 | +43 | 28% | 6% | 78% | 2.72 | 34 | 0 | 28/1 | — | — | — | — | .584 | .549 | .623 | .479 | .685 |
| 08 | SD | 10 | 11 | 0 | 173 | 146 | 166 | 2.85 | 1.18 | 8.6 | 3.1 | 0.9 | 1.1 | $18 | $12 | 280 | +29 | 29% | 10% | 80% | 3.58 | 27 | 1 | 19/1 | — | — | — | — | .645 | .636 | .654 | .576 | .711 |
| 09 | 2TM | 9 | 6 | 0 | 101 | 80 | 110 | 3.45 | 1.12 | 9.7 | 3.0 | 0.7 | 1.1 | $7 | $6 | 210 | +9 | 29% | 8% | 71% | 3.11 | 16 | 1 | 10/1 | — | — | — | — | .615 | .655 | .436 | .503 | .708 |
| 10 | CHW | 7 | 6 | 0 | 107 | 98 | 93 | 4.63 | 1.23 | 7.8 | 2.9 | 1.1 | 1.0 | $3 | -$8 | 150 | −2 | 29% | 10% | 65% | 4.09 | 17 | 1 | 8/2 | — | — | — | — | .698 | .698 | — | .666 | .729 |

## Mike Pelfrey — 200 IP | $6 | 210 pts

SP-33, RP-1 — Owned: 54% — RH

Thanks in good part to a high GB/F and low HR/9, Pelfrey is able to post sub-4.00 ERA, but his Ten-Year Trends suggest that we should not expect any better numbers from him. For a second year, his ERA was multiple runs lower at Citi Field than on the road. (JL)

| Player | Age | IP | W | Sv | K | ERA | WHIP | K/9 | BB/9 | $2L | Pts |
|---|---|---|---|---|---|---|---|---|---|---|---|
| Pelfrey M | 27 | 200 | 13 | 0 | 108 | 4.21 | 1.37 | 4.9 | 3.0 | $6 | 210 |
| **Mini-Browser** | **Age** | **IP** | **W** | **Sv** | **K** | **ERA** | **WHIP** | **K/9** | **BB/9** | **$2L** | **Pts** |
| O'Day D | 28 | 60 | 5 | 0 | 47 | 2.97 | 1.15 | 7.0 | 2.6 | $6 | 100 |
| Santana J | 32 | 80 | 5 | 0 | 64 | 3.51 | 1.17 | 7.1 | 2.3 | $6 | 120 |
| Gregerson L | 26 | 60 | 3 | 0 | 68 | 3.24 | 1.07 | 10.2 | 2.9 | $6 | 110 |
| League B | 28 | 80 | 6 | 3 | 62 | 3.89 | 1.28 | 7.0 | 3.2 | $6 | 140 |
| Romo S | 28 | 60 | 4 | 0 | 66 | 3.06 | 1.15 | 9.8 | 2.4 | $6 | 110 |

| Level | Leag | W | L | Sv | IP | H | K | ERA | WHIP | K/9 | BB/9 | HR/9 | GB/F |
|---|---|---|---|---|---|---|---|---|---|---|---|---|---|
| A | — | — | — | — | — | — | — | — | — | — | — | — | — |
| AA | — | — | — | — | — | — | — | — | — | — | — | — | — |
| AAA | — | — | — | — | — | — | — | — | — | — | — | — | — |

Competition at SP — Stats in 2010 as SP

| Thr | Player | GS | ERA | Supp | W-L |
|---|---|---|---|---|---|
| RH | Pelfrey M | 33 | 3.68 | 3.7 | 15-9 |
| LH | Niese J | 30 | 4.20 | 5.1 | 9-10 |
| LH | Santana J | 29 | 2.98 | 3.0 | 11-9 |
| RH | Dickey R | 26 | 2.86 | 4.0 | 11-9 |

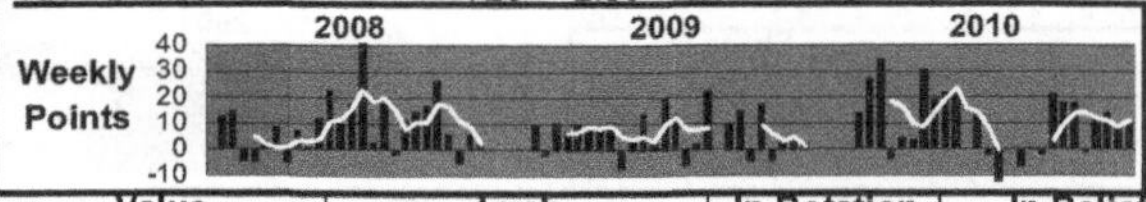

Weekly Points
2008
2009
2010
40
30
20
10
0
-10


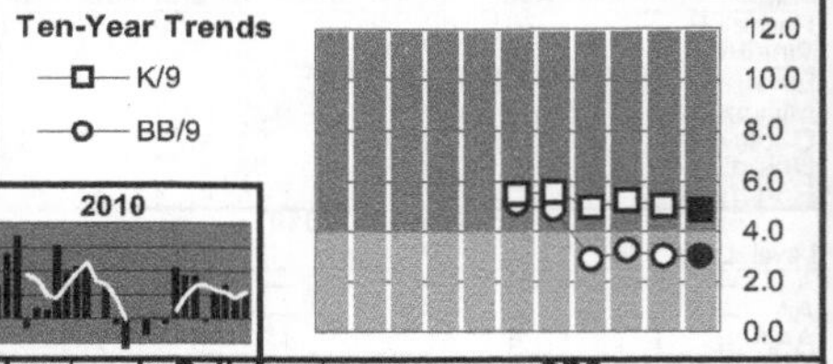

Ten-Year Trends
K/9
BB/9
12.0
10.0
8.0
6.0
4.0
2.0
0.0


| Yr | Team | W | L | Sv | IP | H | K | ERA | WHIP | K/9 | BB/9 | HR/9 | GB/F | $1L | $2L | Pts | RAA | H% | HR/fb | S% | FIP | GS | CG | QS/DS | GR | Hld | Bln | Lead | OPS | 1st Hf | 2nd Hf | vs RH | vs LH |
|---|---|---|---|---|---|---|---|---|---|---|---|---|---|---|---|---|---|---|---|---|---|---|---|---|---|---|---|---|---|---|---|---|---|
| 07 | NYM | 3 | 8 | 0 | 72 | 85 | 45 | 5.57 | 1.71 | 5.6 | 4.8 | 0.7 | 1.7 | -$6 | -$14 | 40 | −11 | 34% | 9% | 67% | 4.64 | 13 | 0 | 3/2 | 2 | 0 | 0 | −0.7 | .820 | .832 | .805 | .733 | .925 |
| 08 | NYM | 13 | 11 | 0 | 200 | 209 | 110 | 3.72 | 1.36 | 4.9 | 2.9 | 0.5 | 1.7 | $8 | -$1 | 220 | +13 | 31% | 6% | 73% | 3.84 | 32 | 2 | 19/4 | — | — | — | — | .734 | .740 | .725 | .654 | .816 |
| 09 | NYM | 10 | 12 | 0 | 184 | 213 | 107 | 5.03 | 1.51 | 5.2 | 3.2 | 0.9 | 1.7 | -$4 | -$9 | 150 | −21 | 32% | 10% | 67% | 4.38 | 31 | 0 | 15/5 | — | — | — | — | .779 | .724 | .840 | .768 | .787 |
| 10 | NYM | 15 | 9 | 1 | 204 | 213 | 113 | 3.66 | 1.38 | 5.0 | 3.0 | 0.5 | 1.5 | $7 | -$4 | 250 | +13 | 31% | 6% | 74% | 3.86 | 33 | 0 | 20/5 | 1 | 0 | 0 | +0.5 | .735 | .748 | .719 | .690 | .776 |

## Tony Pena — 80 IP | $-1 | 70 pts

RP-49, SP-3 — Owned: 0% — RH

Pena wants to be a starting pitcher, so when injuries struck the Sox late in 2010, he talked his way into three starts. The rubber-armed reliever acquitted himself, so now he can add "spot-starter" to his resumé. In 2011, Pena will keep soaking up mostly low-leverage innings. (RM)

| Player | Age | IP | W | Sv | K | ERA | WHIP | K/9 | BB/9 | $2L | Pts |
|---|---|---|---|---|---|---|---|---|---|---|---|
| Pena T | 29 | 80 | 4 | 0 | 49 | 4.77 | 1.42 | 5.5 | 3.3 | -$1 | 70 |
| **Mini-Browser** | **Age** | **IP** | **W** | **Sv** | **K** | **ERA** | **WHIP** | **K/9** | **BB/9** | **$2L** | **Pts** |
| Cramer B | 31 | 40 | 3 | 0 | 35 | 4.33 | 1.48 | 8.0 | 3.2 | -$1 | 50 |
| Mitre S | 30 | 60 | 2 | 0 | 34 | 4.78 | 1.32 | 5.1 | 2.5 | -$1 | 50 |
| Logan B | 26 | 60 | 2 | 0 | 53 | 4.42 | 1.49 | 7.9 | 4.4 | -$1 | 60 |
| Owens R | 23 | 40 | 2 | 0 | 28 | 4.39 | 1.29 | 6.3 | 2.0 | -$1 | 50 |
| Bailey H | 24 | 180 | 8 | 0 | 145 | 4.85 | 1.42 | 7.3 | 3.6 | -$1 | 180 |

| Level | Leag | W | L | Sv | IP | H | K | ERA | WHIP | K/9 | BB/9 | HR/9 | GB/F |
|---|---|---|---|---|---|---|---|---|---|---|---|---|---|
| A | — | — | — | — | — | — | — | — | — | — | — | — | — |
| AA | — | — | — | — | — | — | — | — | — | — | — | — | — |
| AAA | — | — | — | — | — | — | — | — | — | — | — | — | — |

Competition at RP — Stats in 2010 as RP

| Thr | Player | GR | ERA | IP/G | Sv-Hld |
|---|---|---|---|---|---|
| RH | Putz J | 60 | 2.83 | 0.9 | 3-14 |
| RH | Santos S | 56 | 2.96 | 0.9 | 1-14 |
| RH | Jenks B | 55 | 4.44 | 1.0 | 27-0 |
| RH | Linebrink S | 52 | 4.40 | 1.1 | 0-4 |

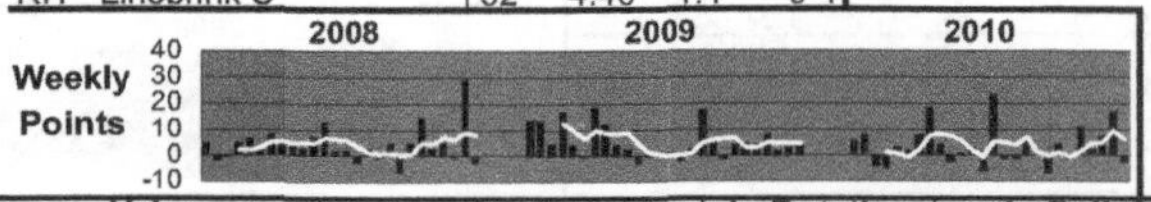

Weekly Points
2008
2009
2010
40
30
20
10
0
-10


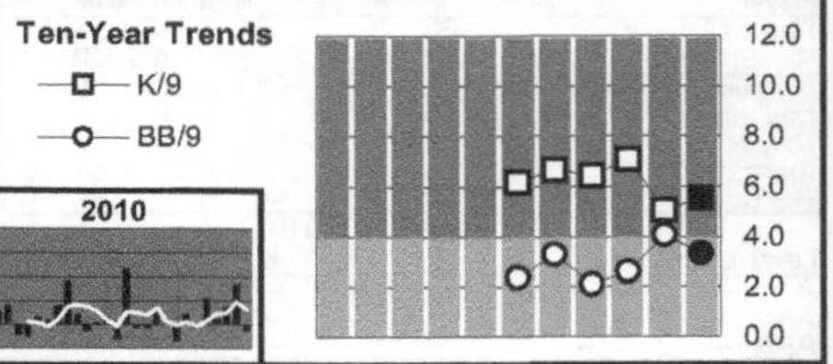

Ten-Year Trends
K/9
BB/9
12.0
10.0
8.0
6.0
4.0
2.0
0.0


| Yr | Team | W | L | Sv | IP | H | K | ERA | WHIP | K/9 | BB/9 | HR/9 | GB/F | $1L | $2L | Pts | RAA | H% | HR/fb | S% | FIP | GS | CG | QS/DS | GR | Hld | Bln | Lead | OPS | 1st Hf | 2nd Hf | vs RH | vs LH |
|---|---|---|---|---|---|---|---|---|---|---|---|---|---|---|---|---|---|---|---|---|---|---|---|---|---|---|---|---|---|---|---|---|---|
| 07 | ARI | 5 | 4 | 2 | 85 | 63 | 63 | 3.27 | 1.10 | 6.6 | 3.3 | 0.8 | 1.2 | $8 | $5 | 130 | +2 | 24% | 8% | 73% | 4.03 | — | — | — | 75 | 30 | 3 | +1.0 | .631 | .539 | .745 | .521 | .762 |
| 08 | ARI | 3 | 2 | 3 | 72 | 80 | 52 | 4.33 | 1.33 | 6.4 | 2.1 | 0.6 | 1.5 | $1 | -$3 | 90 | −5 | 33% | 7% | 67% | 3.37 | — | — | — | 72 | 23 | 5 | +0.8 | .748 | .744 | .755 | .700 | .801 |
| 09 | 2TM | 6 | 5 | 2 | 70 | 81 | 55 | 3.99 | 1.44 | 7.1 | 2.6 | 0.9 | 1.5 | $0 | -$1 | 110 | −6 | 33% | 10% | 74% | 3.84 | — | — | — | 72 | 13 | 2 | +0.1 | .748 | .768 | .726 | .654 | .878 |
| 10 | CHW | 5 | 3 | 0 | 100 | 108 | 56 | 5.10 | 1.52 | 5.0 | 4.0 | 0.9 | 1.5 | -$4 | -$20 | 70 | −18 | 30% | 9% | 67% | 4.82 | 3 | 0 | 1/0 | 49 | 1 | 0 | −0.3 | .765 | .724 | .796 | .813 | .709 |

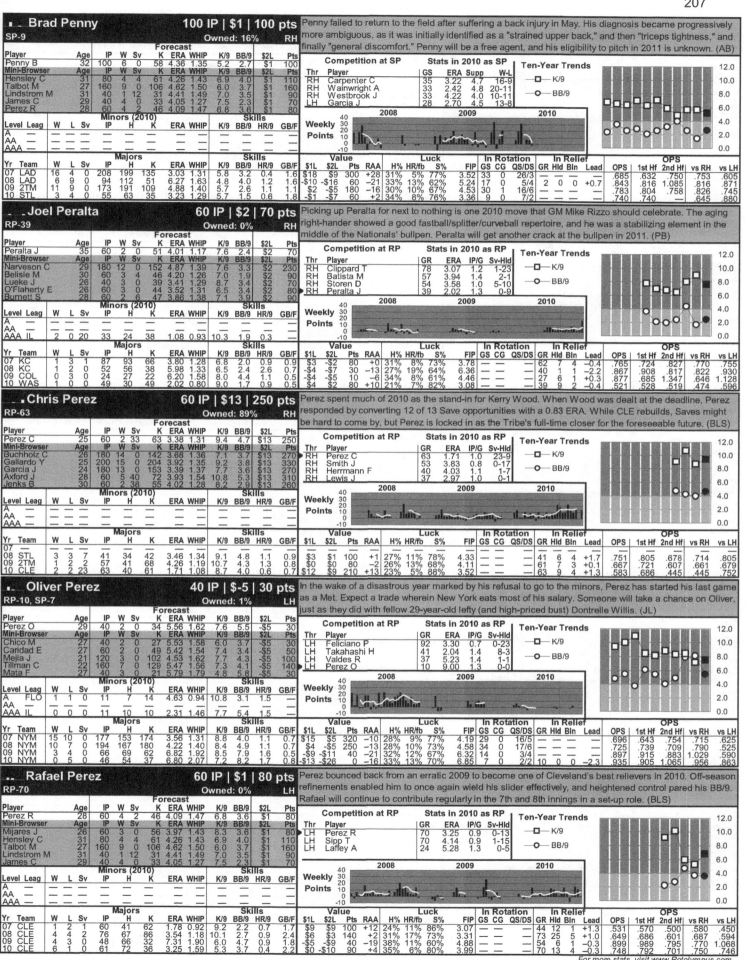

## Brad Penny

**100 IP | $1 | 100 pts**

SP-9 — Owned: 16% — RH

Penny failed to return to the field after suffering a back injury in May. His diagnosis became progressively more ambiguous, as it was initially identified as a "strained upper back," and then "triceps tightness," and finally "general discomfort." Penny will be a free agent, and his eligibility to pitch in 2011 is unknown. (AB)

| Player | Age | IP | W | Sv | K | ERA | WHIP | K/9 | BB/9 | $2L | Pts |
|---|---|---|---|---|---|---|---|---|---|---|---|
| | | Forecast | | | | | | | | | |
| Penny B | 32 | 100 | 6 | 0 | 58 | 4.36 | 1.35 | 5.2 | 2.7 | $1 | 100 |
| **Mini-Browser** | **Age** | **IP** | **W** | **Sv** | **K** | **ERA** | **WHIP** | **K/9** | **BB/9** | **$2L** | **Pts** |
| Hensley C | 31 | 80 | 4 | 4 | 61 | 4.26 | 1.43 | 6.9 | 4.0 | $1 | 110 |
| Talbot M | 27 | 160 | 9 | 0 | 106 | 4.62 | 1.50 | 6.0 | 3.7 | $1 | 160 |
| Lindstrom M | 31 | 40 | 1 | 12 | 31 | 4.41 | 1.49 | 7.0 | 3.5 | $1 | 90 |
| James C | 29 | 40 | 4 | 0 | 33 | 4.05 | 1.27 | 7.5 | 2.3 | $1 | 70 |
| Perez R | 28 | 60 | 4 | 2 | 46 | 4.09 | 1.47 | 6.8 | 3.6 | $1 | 80 |

| Level | Leag | W | L | Sv | IP | H | K | ERA | WHIP | K/9 | BB/9 | HR/9 | GB/F |
|---|---|---|---|---|---|---|---|---|---|---|---|---|---|
| | | Minors (2010) | | | | | | | | Skills | | | |
| A | — | — | — | — | — | — | — | — | — | — | — | — | — |
| AA | — | — | — | — | — | — | — | — | — | — | — | — | — |
| AAA | — | — | — | — | — | — | — | — | — | — | — | — | — |

| Yr | Team | W | L | Sv | IP | H | K | ERA | WHIP | K/9 | BB/9 | HR/9 | GB/F |
|---|---|---|---|---|---|---|---|---|---|---|---|---|---|
| | | Majors | | | | | | | | Skills | | | |
| 07 | LAD | 16 | 4 | 0 | 208 | 199 | 135 | 3.03 | 1.31 | 5.8 | 3.2 | 0.4 | 1.6 |
| 08 | LAD | 6 | 9 | 0 | 94 | 112 | 51 | 6.27 | 1.63 | 4.8 | 4.0 | 1.2 | 1.6 |
| 09 | 2TM | 11 | 9 | 0 | 173 | 191 | 109 | 4.88 | 1.40 | 5.7 | 2.6 | 1.1 | 1.1 |
| 10 | STL | 3 | 4 | 0 | 55 | 63 | 35 | 3.23 | 1.29 | 5.7 | 1.5 | 0.6 | 1.8 |

| Yr | $1L | $2L | Pts | RAA | H% | HR/fb | S% | FIP | GS | CG | QS/DS | GR | Hld | Bln | Lead | OPS | 1st Hf | 2nd Hf | vs RH | vs LH |
|---|---|---|---|---|---|---|---|---|---|---|---|---|---|---|---|---|---|---|---|---|
| | Value | | | | Luck | | | | In Rotation | | | In Relief | | | | OPS | | | | |
| 07 | $18 | $9 | 300 | +28 | 31% | 5% | 77% | 3.52 | 33 | 0 | 26/3 | — | — | — | — | .685 | .632 | .750 | .753 | .605 |
| 08 | -$10 | -$16 | 60 | −21 | 33% | 13% | 62% | 5.24 | 17 | 0 | 5/4 | 2 | 0 | 0 | +0.7 | .843 | .816 | 1.085 | .816 | .871 |
| 09 | $2 | -$5 | 180 | −16 | 30% | 10% | 67% | 4.53 | 30 | 1 | 16/6 | — | — | — | — | .783 | .804 | .758 | .826 | .745 |
| 10 | -$1 | -$7 | 60 | +2 | 34% | 8% | 76% | 3.36 | 9 | 0 | 7/2 | — | — | — | — | .740 | .740 | — | .645 | .880 |

**Competition at SP** — Stats in 2010 as SP

| Thr | Player | GS | ERA | Supp | W-L |
|---|---|---|---|---|---|
| RH | Carpenter C | 35 | 3.22 | 4.7 | 16-9 |
| RH | Wainwright A | 33 | 2.42 | 4.8 | 20-11 |
| RH | Westbrook J | 33 | 4.22 | 4.0 | 10-11 |
| LH | Garcia J | 28 | 2.70 | 4.5 | 13-8 |

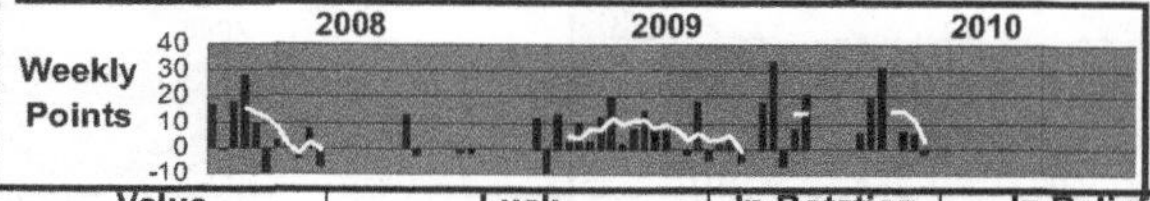


**Ten-Year Trends**

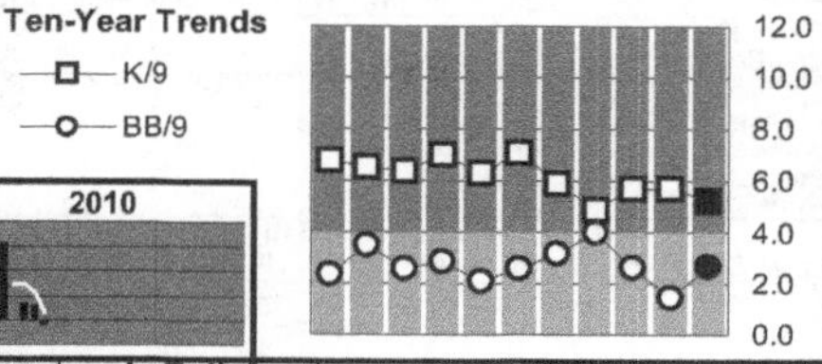


## Joel Peralta

**60 IP | $2 | 70 pts**

RP-39 — Owned: 0% — RH

Picking up Peralta for next to nothing is one 2010 move that GM Mike Rizzo should celebrate. The aging right-hander showed a good fastball/splitter/curveball repertoire, and he was a stabilizing element in the middle of the Nationals' bullpen. Peralta will get another crack at the bullpen in 2011. (PB)

| Player | Age | IP | W | Sv | K | ERA | WHIP | K/9 | BB/9 | $2L | Pts |
|---|---|---|---|---|---|---|---|---|---|---|---|
| | | Forecast | | | | | | | | | |
| Peralta J | 35 | 60 | 2 | 0 | 51 | 4.01 | 1.17 | 7.6 | 2.4 | $2 | 70 |
| **Mini-Browser** | **Age** | **IP** | **W** | **Sv** | **K** | **ERA** | **WHIP** | **K/9** | **BB/9** | **$2L** | **Pts** |
| Narveson C | 29 | 180 | 12 | 0 | 152 | 4.87 | 1.39 | 7.6 | 3.3 | $2 | 230 |
| Belisle M | 30 | 60 | 3 | 4 | 46 | 4.20 | 1.26 | 7.0 | 1.9 | $2 | 90 |
| Lueke J | 26 | 40 | 3 | 0 | 39 | 3.41 | 1.29 | 8.7 | 3.4 | $2 | 70 |
| O'Flaherty E | 26 | 60 | 3 | 0 | 44 | 3.52 | 1.31 | 6.5 | 3.4 | $2 | 80 |
| Burnett S | 28 | 60 | 2 | 6 | 47 | 3.86 | 1.38 | 7.1 | 3.9 | $2 | 90 |

| Level | Leag | W | L | Sv | IP | H | K | ERA | WHIP | K/9 | BB/9 | HR/9 | GB/F |
|---|---|---|---|---|---|---|---|---|---|---|---|---|---|
| | | Minors (2010) | | | | | | | | Skills | | | |
| A | — | — | — | — | — | — | — | — | — | — | — | — | — |
| AA | — | — | — | — | — | — | — | — | — | — | — | — | — |
| AAA | IL | 2 | 0 | 20 | 33 | 24 | 38 | 1.08 | 0.93 | 10.3 | 1.9 | 0.3 | — |

| Yr | Team | W | L | Sv | IP | H | K | ERA | WHIP | K/9 | BB/9 | HR/9 | GB/F |
|---|---|---|---|---|---|---|---|---|---|---|---|---|---|
| | | Majors | | | | | | | | Skills | | | |
| 07 | KC | 1 | 3 | 1 | 87 | 93 | 66 | 3.80 | 1.28 | 6.8 | 2.0 | 0.9 | 0.9 |
| 08 | KC | 1 | 2 | 0 | 52 | 56 | 38 | 5.98 | 1.33 | 6.5 | 2.4 | 2.6 | 0.7 |
| 09 | COL | 0 | 3 | 0 | 24 | 27 | 22 | 6.20 | 1.58 | 8.0 | 4.4 | 1.1 | 0.5 |
| 10 | WAS | 1 | 0 | 0 | 49 | 30 | 49 | 2.02 | 0.80 | 9.0 | 1.7 | 0.9 | 0.5 |

| Yr | $1L | $2L | Pts | RAA | H% | HR/fb | S% | FIP | GS | CG | QS/DS | GR | Hld | Bln | Lead | OPS | 1st Hf | 2nd Hf | vs RH | vs LH |
|---|---|---|---|---|---|---|---|---|---|---|---|---|---|---|---|---|---|---|---|---|
| | Value | | | | Luck | | | | In Rotation | | | In Relief | | | | OPS | | | | |
| 07 | $3 | -$2 | 80 | +0 | 31% | 8% | 73% | 3.78 | — | — | — | 62 | 7 | 4 | −0.4 | .765 | .724 | .827 | .770 | .755 |
| 08 | -$4 | -$7 | 30 | −13 | 27% | 19% | 64% | 6.36 | — | — | — | 40 | 1 | 1 | −2.2 | .867 | .908 | .817 | .822 | .930 |
| 09 | -$4 | -$5 | 10 | −6 | 34% | 8% | 61% | 4.46 | — | — | — | 27 | 6 | 1 | +0.3 | .877 | .685 | 1.347 | .646 | 1.128 |
| 10 | $4 | $2 | 80 | +10 | 21% | 7% | 82% | 3.08 | — | — | — | 39 | 9 | 2 | −0.4 | .521 | .528 | .519 | .474 | .596 |

**Competition at RP** — Stats in 2010 as RP

| Thr | Player | GR | ERA | IP/G | Sv-Hld |
|---|---|---|---|---|---|
| RH | Clippard T | 78 | 3.07 | 1.2 | 1-23 |
| RH | Batista M | 57 | 3.94 | 1.4 | 2-1 |
| RH | Storen D | 54 | 3.58 | 1.0 | 5-10 |
| RH | Peralta J | 39 | 2.02 | 1.3 | 0-9 |

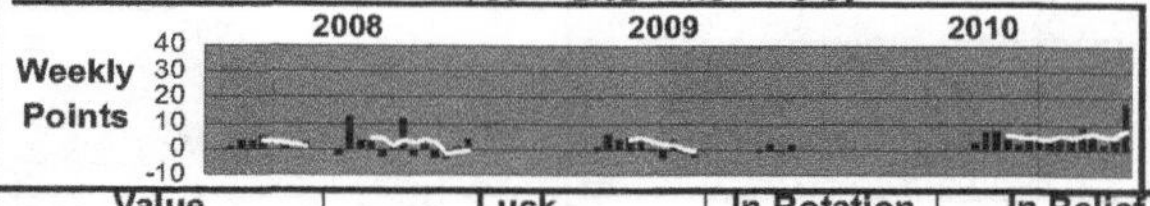


**Ten-Year Trends**

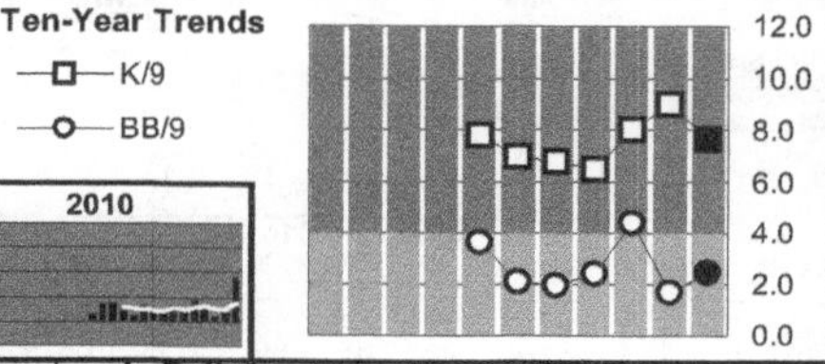


## Chris Perez

**60 IP | $13 | 250 pts**

RP-63 — Owned: 89% — RH

Perez spent much of 2010 as the stand-in for Kerry Wood. When Wood was dealt at the deadline, Perez responded by converting 12 of 13 Save opportunities with a 0.83 ERA. While CLE rebuilds, Saves might be hard to come by, but Perez is locked in as the Tribe's full-time closer for the foreseeable future. (BLS)

| Player | Age | IP | W | Sv | K | ERA | WHIP | K/9 | BB/9 | $2L | Pts |
|---|---|---|---|---|---|---|---|---|---|---|---|
| | | Forecast | | | | | | | | | |
| Perez C | 25 | 60 | 2 | 33 | 63 | 3.38 | 1.31 | 9.4 | 4.7 | $13 | 250 |
| **Mini-Browser** | **Age** | **IP** | **W** | **Sv** | **K** | **ERA** | **WHIP** | **K/9** | **BB/9** | **$2L** | **Pts** |
| Buchholz C | 26 | 180 | 14 | 0 | 142 | 3.68 | 1.36 | 7.1 | 3.7 | $13 | 270 |
| Gallardo Y | 25 | 200 | 15 | 0 | 204 | 3.92 | 1.35 | 9.2 | 3.8 | $13 | 330 |
| Garcia J | 24 | 180 | 13 | 0 | 153 | 3.39 | 1.37 | 7.7 | 3.6 | $13 | 270 |
| Axford J | 28 | 60 | 5 | 40 | 72 | 3.93 | 1.54 | 10.8 | 5.3 | $13 | 310 |
| Jenks B | 30 | 60 | 2 | 38 | 55 | 4.02 | 1.28 | 8.2 | 2.9 | $13 | 260 |

| Level | Leag | W | L | Sv | IP | H | K | ERA | WHIP | K/9 | BB/9 | HR/9 | GB/F |
|---|---|---|---|---|---|---|---|---|---|---|---|---|---|
| | | Minors (2010) | | | | | | | | Skills | | | |
| A | — | — | — | — | — | — | — | — | — | — | — | — | — |
| AA | — | — | — | — | — | — | — | — | — | — | — | — | — |
| AAA | — | — | — | — | — | — | — | — | — | — | — | — | — |

| Yr | Team | W | L | Sv | IP | H | K | ERA | WHIP | K/9 | BB/9 | HR/9 | GB/F |
|---|---|---|---|---|---|---|---|---|---|---|---|---|---|
| | | Majors | | | | | | | | Skills | | | |
| 07 | — | — | — | — | — | — | — | — | — | — | — | — | — |
| 08 | STL | 3 | 3 | 7 | 41 | 34 | 42 | 3.46 | 1.34 | 9.1 | 4.8 | 1.1 | 0.9 |
| 09 | 2TM | 1 | 2 | 2 | 57 | 41 | 68 | 4.26 | 1.19 | 10.7 | 4.3 | 1.3 | 0.8 |
| 10 | CLE | 2 | 2 | 23 | 63 | 40 | 61 | 1.71 | 1.08 | 8.7 | 4.0 | 0.6 | 0.7 |

| Yr | $1L | $2L | Pts | RAA | H% | HR/fb | S% | FIP | GS | CG | QS/DS | GR | Hld | Bln | Lead | OPS | 1st Hf | 2nd Hf | vs RH | vs LH |
|---|---|---|---|---|---|---|---|---|---|---|---|---|---|---|---|---|---|---|---|---|
| | Value | | | | Luck | | | | In Rotation | | | In Relief | | | | OPS | | | | |
| 07 | — | — | — | — | — | — | — | — | — | — | — | — | — | — | — | — | — | — | — | — |
| 08 | $3 | $1 | 100 | +1 | 27% | 11% | 78% | 4.33 | — | — | — | 41 | 6 | 4 | +1.7 | .751 | .805 | .678 | .714 | .805 |
| 09 | $0 | $0 | 80 | −2 | 26% | 13% | 68% | 4.11 | — | — | — | 61 | 7 | 3 | +0.1 | .667 | .721 | .607 | .661 | .679 |
| 10 | $12 | $9 | 210 | +13 | 23% | 5% | 88% | 3.52 | — | — | — | 63 | 9 | 4 | +1.3 | .583 | .686 | .445 | .445 | .752 |

**Competition at RP** — Stats in 2010 as RP

| Thr | Player | GR | ERA | IP/G | Sv-Hld |
|---|---|---|---|---|---|
| RH | Perez C | 63 | 1.71 | 1.0 | 23-9 |
| RH | Smith J | 53 | 3.83 | 0.8 | 0-17 |
| RH | Herrmann F | 40 | 4.03 | 1.1 | 1-7 |
| RH | Lewis J | 37 | 2.97 | 1.0 | 0-1 |

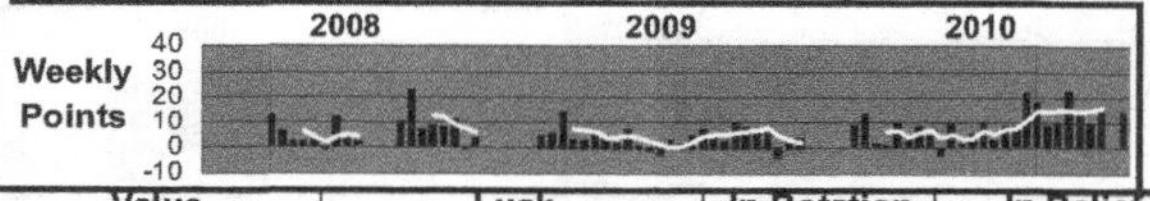


**Ten-Year Trends**

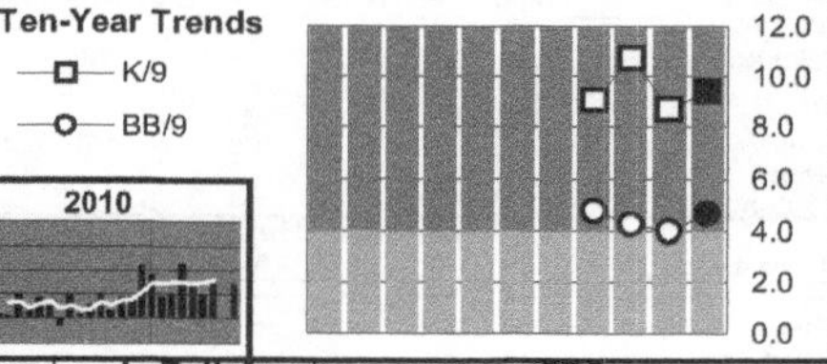


## Oliver Perez

**40 IP | $-5 | 30 pts**

RP-10, SP-7 — Owned: 1% — LH

In the wake of a disastrous year marked by his refusal to go to the minors, Perez has started his last game as a Met. Expect a trade wherein New York eats most of his salary. Someone will take a chance on Oliver, just as they did with fellow 29-year-old lefty (and high-priced bust) Dontrelle Willis. (JL)

| Player | Age | IP | W | Sv | K | ERA | WHIP | K/9 | BB/9 | $2L | Pts |
|---|---|---|---|---|---|---|---|---|---|---|---|
| | | Forecast | | | | | | | | | |
| Perez O | 29 | 40 | 2 | 0 | 34 | 5.56 | 1.62 | 7.6 | 5.5 | -$5 | 30 |
| **Mini-Browser** | **Age** | **IP** | **W** | **Sv** | **K** | **ERA** | **WHIP** | **K/9** | **BB/9** | **$2L** | **Pts** |
| Chico M | 27 | 40 | 2 | 0 | 27 | 5.53 | 1.58 | 6.0 | 3.7 | -$5 | 30 |
| Caridad E | 27 | 60 | 2 | 0 | 49 | 5.42 | 1.54 | 7.4 | 3.4 | -$5 | 50 |
| Mejia J | 21 | 120 | 3 | 0 | 102 | 4.53 | 1.62 | 7.7 | 4.3 | -$5 | 100 |
| Tillman C | 22 | 160 | 7 | 0 | 129 | 5.47 | 1.56 | 7.3 | 4.1 | -$5 | 140 |
| Mata F | 27 | 40 | 3 | 0 | 21 | 5.79 | 1.79 | 4.8 | 5.8 | -$5 | 30 |

| Level | Leag | W | L | Sv | IP | H | K | ERA | WHIP | K/9 | BB/9 | HR/9 | GB/F |
|---|---|---|---|---|---|---|---|---|---|---|---|---|---|
| | | Minors (2010) | | | | | | | | Skills | | | |
| A | FLO | 1 | 1 | 0 | 11 | 7 | 14 | 4.63 | 0.94 | 10.8 | 3.1 | 1.5 | — |
| AA | — | — | — | — | — | — | — | — | — | — | — | — | — |
| AAA | IL | 0 | 0 | 0 | 11 | 10 | 10 | 2.31 | 1.46 | 7.7 | 5.4 | 1.5 | — |

| Yr | Team | W | L | Sv | IP | H | K | ERA | WHIP | K/9 | BB/9 | HR/9 | GB/F |
|---|---|---|---|---|---|---|---|---|---|---|---|---|---|
| | | Majors | | | | | | | | Skills | | | |
| 07 | NYM | 15 | 10 | 0 | 177 | 153 | 174 | 3.56 | 1.31 | 8.8 | 4.0 | 1.1 | 0.7 |
| 08 | NYM | 10 | 7 | 0 | 194 | 167 | 180 | 4.22 | 1.40 | 8.4 | 4.9 | 1.1 | 0.7 |
| 09 | NYM | 3 | 4 | 0 | 66 | 69 | 62 | 6.82 | 1.92 | 8.5 | 7.9 | 1.6 | 0.5 |
| 10 | NYM | 0 | 5 | 0 | 46 | 54 | 37 | 6.80 | 2.07 | 7.2 | 8.2 | 1.7 | 0.8 |

| Yr | $1L | $2L | Pts | RAA | H% | HR/fb | S% | FIP | GS | CG | QS/DS | GR | Hld | Bln | Lead | OPS | 1st Hf | 2nd Hf | vs RH | vs LH |
|---|---|---|---|---|---|---|---|---|---|---|---|---|---|---|---|---|---|---|---|---|
| | Value | | | | Luck | | | | In Rotation | | | In Relief | | | | OPS | | | | |
| 07 | $15 | $5 | 320 | −10 | 28% | 9% | 77% | 4.19 | 29 | 0 | 16/5 | — | — | — | — | .696 | .643 | .754 | .715 | .625 |
| 08 | $4 | -$5 | 250 | −13 | 28% | 10% | 73% | 4.58 | 34 | 0 | 17/6 | — | — | — | — | .725 | .739 | .709 | .790 | .525 |
| 09 | -$9 | -$11 | 40 | −21 | 32% | 12% | 67% | 6.32 | 14 | 0 | 3/4 | — | — | — | — | .897 | .915 | .883 | 1.029 | .590 |
| 10 | -$13 | -$26 | 0 | −16 | 33% | 13% | 70% | 6.85 | 7 | 0 | 2/2 | 10 | 0 | 0 | −2.3 | .935 | .905 | 1.065 | .956 | .863 |

**Competition at RP** — Stats in 2010 as RP

| Thr | Player | GR | ERA | IP/G | Sv-Hld |
|---|---|---|---|---|---|
| LH | Feliciano P | 92 | 3.30 | 0.7 | 0-23 |
| LH | Takahashi H | 41 | 2.04 | 1.4 | 8-3 |
| LH | Valdes R | 37 | 5.23 | 1.4 | 1-1 |
| LH | Perez O | 10 | 9.00 | 1.3 | 0-0 |

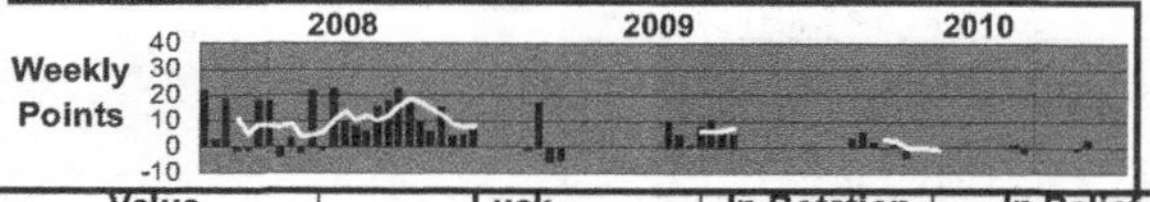


**Ten-Year Trends**

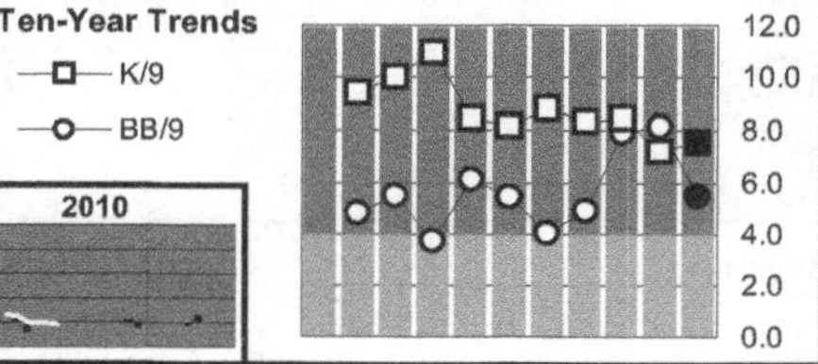


## Rafael Perez

**60 IP | $1 | 80 pts**

RP-70 — Owned: 0% — LH

Perez bounced back from an erratic 2009 to become one of Cleveland's best relievers in 2010. Off-season refinements enabled him to once again wield his slider effectively, and heightened control pared his BB/9. Rafael will continue to contribute regularly in the 7th and 8th innings in a set-up role. (BLS)

| Player | Age | IP | W | Sv | K | ERA | WHIP | K/9 | BB/9 | $2L | Pts |
|---|---|---|---|---|---|---|---|---|---|---|---|
| | | Forecast | | | | | | | | | |
| Perez R | 28 | 60 | 4 | 2 | 46 | 4.09 | 1.47 | 6.8 | 3.6 | $1 | 80 |
| **Mini-Browser** | **Age** | **IP** | **W** | **Sv** | **K** | **ERA** | **WHIP** | **K/9** | **BB/9** | **$2L** | **Pts** |
| Mijares J | 26 | 60 | 3 | 0 | 56 | 3.97 | 1.43 | 8.3 | 3.6 | $1 | 80 |
| Hensley C | 31 | 80 | 4 | 4 | 61 | 4.26 | 1.43 | 6.9 | 4.0 | $1 | 110 |
| Talbot M | 27 | 160 | 9 | 0 | 106 | 4.62 | 1.50 | 6.0 | 3.7 | $1 | 160 |
| Lindstrom M | 31 | 40 | 1 | 12 | 31 | 4.41 | 1.49 | 7.0 | 3.5 | $1 | 90 |
| James C | 29 | 40 | 4 | 0 | 33 | 4.05 | 1.27 | 7.5 | 2.3 | $1 | 70 |

| Level | Leag | W | L | Sv | IP | H | K | ERA | WHIP | K/9 | BB/9 | HR/9 | GB/F |
|---|---|---|---|---|---|---|---|---|---|---|---|---|---|
| | | Minors (2010) | | | | | | | | Skills | | | |
| A | — | — | — | — | — | — | — | — | — | — | — | — | — |
| AA | — | — | — | — | — | — | — | — | — | — | — | — | — |
| AAA | — | — | — | — | — | — | — | — | — | — | — | — | — |

| Yr | Team | W | L | Sv | IP | H | K | ERA | WHIP | K/9 | BB/9 | HR/9 | GB/F |
|---|---|---|---|---|---|---|---|---|---|---|---|---|---|
| | | Majors | | | | | | | | Skills | | | |
| 07 | CLE | 1 | 2 | 1 | 60 | 41 | 62 | 1.78 | 0.92 | 9.2 | 2.2 | 0.7 | 1.7 |
| 08 | CLE | 4 | 4 | 2 | 76 | 67 | 86 | 3.54 | 1.18 | 10.1 | 2.7 | 0.9 | 2.4 |
| 09 | CLE | 4 | 3 | 0 | 48 | 66 | 32 | 7.31 | 1.90 | 6.0 | 4.7 | 0.9 | 1.8 |
| 10 | CLE | 6 | 1 | 0 | 61 | 72 | 36 | 3.25 | 1.59 | 5.3 | 3.7 | 0.4 | 2.2 |

| Yr | $1L | $2L | Pts | RAA | H% | HR/fb | S% | FIP | GS | CG | QS/DS | GR | Hld | Bln | Lead | OPS | 1st Hf | 2nd Hf | vs RH | vs LH |
|---|---|---|---|---|---|---|---|---|---|---|---|---|---|---|---|---|---|---|---|---|
| | Value | | | | Luck | | | | In Rotation | | | In Relief | | | | OPS | | | | |
| 07 | $9 | $9 | 100 | +12 | 24% | 11% | 86% | 3.07 | — | — | — | 44 | 12 | 1 | +1.3 | .531 | .570 | .500 | .580 | .450 |
| 08 | $6 | $3 | 140 | +2 | 31% | 17% | 73% | 3.31 | — | — | — | 73 | 25 | 5 | +1.0 | .649 | .686 | .601 | .687 | .594 |
| 09 | -$5 | -$9 | 40 | −19 | 38% | 11% | 60% | 4.88 | — | — | — | 54 | 6 | 1 | −0.3 | .899 | .989 | .795 | .770 | 1.068 |
| 10 | $0 | -$10 | 90 | +4 | 35% | 6% | 80% | 3.99 | — | — | — | 70 | 13 | 4 | −0.3 | .748 | .792 | .701 | .750 | .746 |

**Competition at RP** — Stats in 2010 as RP

| Thr | Player | GR | ERA | IP/G | Sv-Hld |
|---|---|---|---|---|---|
| LH | Perez R | 70 | 3.25 | 0.9 | 0-13 |
| LH | Sipp T | 70 | 4.14 | 0.9 | 1-15 |
| LH | Laffey A | 24 | 5.28 | 1.3 | 0-5 |

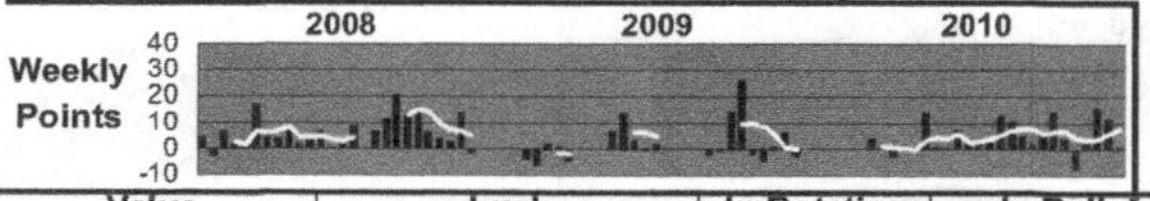


**Ten-Year Trends**

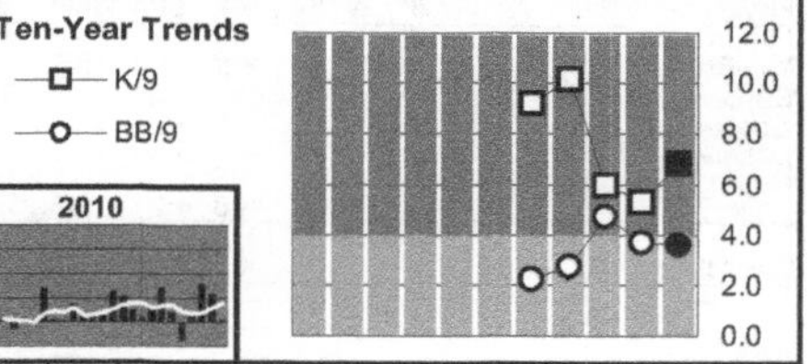

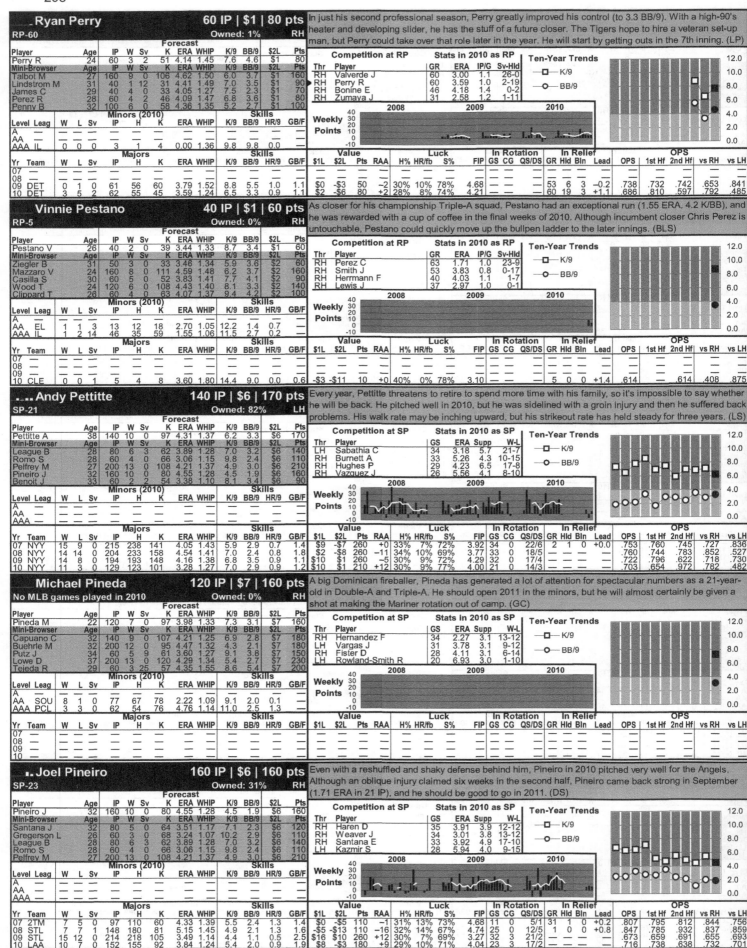

## Ryan Perry
**60 IP | $1 | 80 pts**
RP-60 | Owned: 1% | RH

In just his second professional season, Perry greatly improved his control (to 3.3 BB/9). With a high-90's heater and developing slider, he has the stuff of a future closer. The Tigers hope to hire a veteran set-up man, but Perry could take over that role later in the year. He will start by getting outs in the 7th inning. (LP)

| Player | Age | IP | W | Sv | K | ERA | WHIP | K/9 | BB/9 | $2L | Pts |
|---|---|---|---|---|---|---|---|---|---|---|---|
| Perry R | 24 | 60 | 3 | 2 | 51 | 4.14 | 1.45 | 7.6 | 4.6 | $1 | 80 |
| **Mini-Browser** | Age | IP | W | Sv | K | ERA | WHIP | K/9 | BB/9 | $2L | Pts |
| Talbot M | 27 | 160 | 9 | 0 | 106 | 4.62 | 1.50 | 6.0 | 3.7 | $1 | 160 |
| Lindstrom M | 31 | 40 | 1 | 12 | 31 | 4.41 | 1.49 | 7.0 | 3.5 | $1 | 90 |
| James C | 29 | 40 | 4 | 0 | 33 | 4.05 | 1.27 | 7.5 | 2.3 | $1 | 70 |
| Perez R | 28 | 60 | 4 | 2 | 46 | 4.09 | 1.47 | 6.8 | 3.6 | $1 | 80 |
| Penny B | 32 | 100 | 6 | 0 | 58 | 4.36 | 1.35 | 5.2 | 2.7 | $1 | 100 |

| Minors (2010) Level | Leag | W | L | Sv | IP | H | K | ERA | WHIP | K/9 | BB/9 | HR/9 | GB/F |
|---|---|---|---|---|---|---|---|---|---|---|---|---|---|
| A | — | — | — | — | — | — | — | — | — | — | — | — | — |
| AA | — | — | — | — | — | — | — | — | — | — | — | — | — |
| AAA | IL | 0 | 0 | 0 | 3 | 1 | 4 | 0.00 | 1.36 | 9.8 | 9.8 | 0.0 | — |

| Majors Yr | Team | W | L | Sv | IP | H | K | ERA | WHIP | K/9 | BB/9 | HR/9 | GB/F |
|---|---|---|---|---|---|---|---|---|---|---|---|---|---|
| 07 | — | — | — | — | — | — | — | — | — | — | — | — | — |
| 08 | — | — | — | — | — | — | — | — | — | — | — | — | — |
| 09 | DET | 0 | 1 | 0 | 61 | 56 | 60 | 3.79 | 1.52 | 8.8 | 5.5 | 1.0 | 1.1 |
| 10 | DET | 3 | 5 | 2 | 62 | 55 | 45 | 3.59 | 1.24 | 6.5 | 3.3 | 0.9 | 1.1 |

**Competition at RP** — Stats in 2010 as RP

| Thr | Player | GR | ERA | IP/G | Sv-Hld |
|---|---|---|---|---|---|
| RH | Valverde J | 60 | 3.00 | 1.1 | 26-0 |
| RH | Perry R | 60 | 3.59 | 1.0 | 2-19 |
| RH | Bonine E | 46 | 4.18 | 1.4 | 0-2 |
| RH | Zumaya J | 31 | 2.58 | 1.2 | 1-11 |

Weekly Points (2008, 2009, 2010)
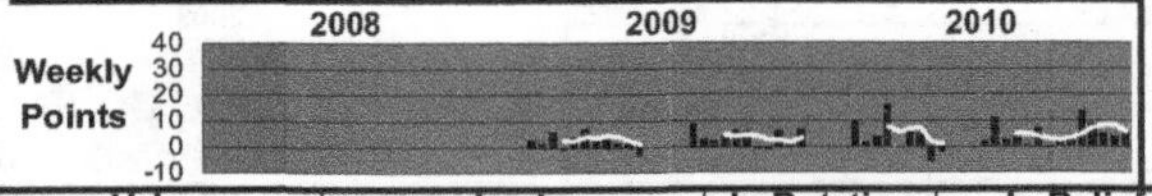

Ten-Year Trends: K/9, BB/9
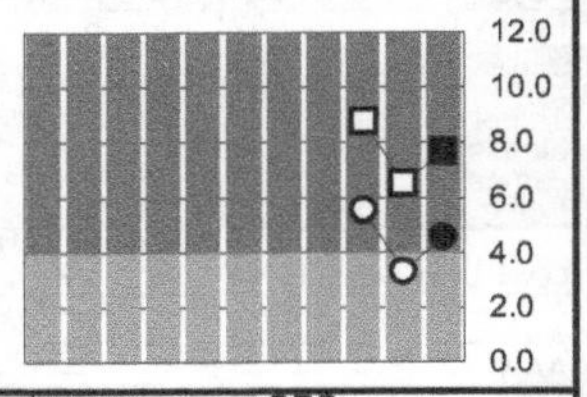

| Yr | $1L | $2L | Pts | RAA | H% | HR/fb | S% | FIP | GS | CG | QS/DS | GR | Hld | Bln | Lead | OPS | 1st Hf | 2nd Hf | vs RH | vs LH |
|---|---|---|---|---|---|---|---|---|---|---|---|---|---|---|---|---|---|---|---|---|
| 07 | — | — | — | — | — | — | — | — | — | — | — | — | — | — | — | — | — | — | — | — |
| 08 | — | — | — | — | — | — | — | — | — | — | — | — | — | — | — | — | — | — | — | — |
| 09 | $0 | -$3 | 50 | -2 | 30% | 10% | 78% | 4.68 | — | — | — | 53 | 6 | 3 | -0.2 | .738 | .732 | .742 | .653 | .841 |
| 10 | $2 | -$6 | 80 | +2 | 28% | 8% | 74% | 4.21 | — | — | — | 60 | 19 | 3 | +1.1 | .686 | .810 | .597 | .792 | .485 |

## Vinnie Pestano
**40 IP | $1 | 60 pts**
RP-5 | Owned: 0% | RH

As closer for his championship Triple-A squad, Pestano had an exceptional run (1.55 ERA, 4.2 K/BB), and he was rewarded with a cup of coffee in the final weeks of 2010. Although incumbent closer Chris Perez is untouchable, Pestano could quickly move up the bullpen ladder to the later innings. (BLS)

| Player | Age | IP | W | Sv | K | ERA | WHIP | K/9 | BB/9 | $2L | Pts |
|---|---|---|---|---|---|---|---|---|---|---|---|
| Pestano V | 26 | 40 | 2 | 0 | 39 | 3.44 | 1.33 | 8.7 | 3.4 | $1 | 60 |
| **Mini-Browser** | Age | IP | W | Sv | K | ERA | WHIP | K/9 | BB/9 | $2L | Pts |
| Ziegler B | 31 | 50 | 3 | 0 | 33 | 3.46 | 1.34 | 5.9 | 3.6 | $2 | 60 |
| Mazzaro V | 24 | 160 | 8 | 0 | 111 | 4.59 | 1.48 | 6.2 | 3.7 | $2 | 160 |
| Casilla S | 30 | 60 | 5 | 0 | 52 | 3.83 | 1.41 | 7.7 | 4.1 | $2 | 90 |
| Wood T | 24 | 120 | 6 | 0 | 108 | 4.43 | 1.40 | 8.1 | 3.3 | $2 | 140 |
| Clippard T | 26 | 60 | 4 | 0 | 63 | 4.07 | 1.37 | 9.4 | 4.2 | $2 | 100 |

| Minors (2010) Level | Leag | W | L | Sv | IP | H | K | ERA | WHIP | K/9 | BB/9 | HR/9 | GB/F |
|---|---|---|---|---|---|---|---|---|---|---|---|---|---|
| A | — | — | — | — | — | — | — | — | — | — | — | — | — |
| AA | EL | 1 | 1 | 3 | 13 | 12 | 18 | 2.70 | 1.05 | 12.2 | 1.4 | 0.7 | — |
| AAA | IL | 1 | 2 | 14 | 46 | 35 | 59 | 1.55 | 1.06 | 11.5 | 2.7 | 0.2 | — |

| Majors Yr | Team | W | L | Sv | IP | H | K | ERA | WHIP | K/9 | BB/9 | HR/9 | GB/F |
|---|---|---|---|---|---|---|---|---|---|---|---|---|---|
| 07 | — | — | — | — | — | — | — | — | — | — | — | — | — |
| 08 | — | — | — | — | — | — | — | — | — | — | — | — | — |
| 09 | — | — | — | — | — | — | — | — | — | — | — | — | — |
| 10 | CLE | 0 | 0 | 1 | 5 | 4 | 8 | 3.60 | 1.80 | 14.4 | 9.0 | 0.0 | 0.6 |

**Competition at RP** — Stats in 2010 as RP

| Thr | Player | GR | ERA | IP/G | Sv-Hld |
|---|---|---|---|---|---|
| RH | Perez C | 63 | 1.71 | 1.0 | 23-9 |
| RH | Smith J | 53 | 3.83 | 0.8 | 0-17 |
| RH | Herrmann F | 40 | 4.03 | 1.1 | 1-7 |
| RH | Lewis J | 37 | 2.97 | 1.0 | 0-1 |

Weekly Points (2008, 2009, 2010)
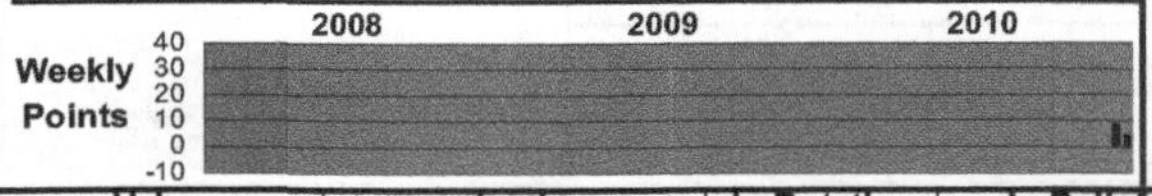

Ten-Year Trends: K/9, BB/9
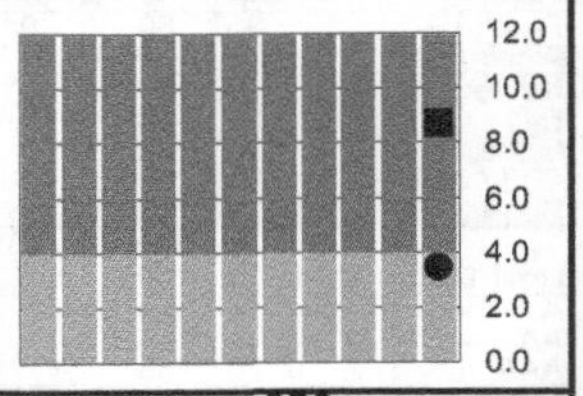

| Yr | $1L | $2L | Pts | RAA | H% | HR/fb | S% | FIP | GS | CG | QS/DS | GR | Hld | Bln | Lead | OPS | 1st Hf | 2nd Hf | vs RH | vs LH |
|---|---|---|---|---|---|---|---|---|---|---|---|---|---|---|---|---|---|---|---|---|
| 07 | — | — | — | — | — | — | — | — | — | — | — | — | — | — | — | — | — | — | — | — |
| 08 | — | — | — | — | — | — | — | — | — | — | — | — | — | — | — | — | — | — | — | — |
| 09 | — | — | — | — | — | — | — | — | — | — | — | — | — | — | — | — | — | — | — | — |
| 10 | -$3 | -$11 | 10 | +0 | 40% | 0% | 78% | 3.10 | — | — | — | 5 | 0 | 0 | +1.4 | .614 | — | .614 | .408 | .875 |

## Andy Pettitte
**140 IP | $6 | 170 pts**
SP-21 | Owned: 82% | LH

Every year, Pettitte threatens to retire to spend more time with his family, so it's impossible to say whether he will be back. He pitched well in 2010, but he was sidelined with a groin injury and then he suffered back problems. His walk rate may be inching upward, but his strikeout rate has held steady for three years. (LS)

| Player | Age | IP | W | Sv | K | ERA | WHIP | K/9 | BB/9 | $2L | Pts |
|---|---|---|---|---|---|---|---|---|---|---|---|
| Pettitte A | 38 | 140 | 10 | 0 | 97 | 4.31 | 1.37 | 6.2 | 3.3 | $6 | 170 |
| **Mini-Browser** | Age | IP | W | Sv | K | ERA | WHIP | K/9 | BB/9 | $2L | Pts |
| League B | 28 | 80 | 6 | 3 | 62 | 3.89 | 1.28 | 7.0 | 3.2 | $6 | 140 |
| Romo S | 28 | 60 | 4 | 0 | 66 | 3.06 | 1.15 | 9.8 | 2.4 | $6 | 110 |
| Pelfrey M | 27 | 200 | 13 | 0 | 108 | 4.21 | 1.37 | 4.9 | 3.0 | $6 | 210 |
| Pineiro J | 32 | 160 | 10 | 0 | 80 | 4.55 | 1.28 | 4.5 | 1.9 | $6 | 160 |
| Benoit J | 33 | 60 | 2 | 2 | 54 | 3.38 | 1.10 | 8.1 | 3.4 | $6 | 90 |

| Minors (2010) Level | Leag | W | L | Sv | IP | H | K | ERA | WHIP | K/9 | BB/9 | HR/9 | GB/F |
|---|---|---|---|---|---|---|---|---|---|---|---|---|---|
| A | — | — | — | — | — | — | — | — | — | — | — | — | — |
| AA | — | — | — | — | — | — | — | — | — | — | — | — | — |
| AAA | — | — | — | — | — | — | — | — | — | — | — | — | — |

| Majors Yr | Team | W | L | Sv | IP | H | K | ERA | WHIP | K/9 | BB/9 | HR/9 | GB/F |
|---|---|---|---|---|---|---|---|---|---|---|---|---|---|
| 07 | NYY | 15 | 9 | 0 | 215 | 238 | 141 | 4.05 | 1.43 | 5.9 | 2.9 | 0.7 | 1.4 |
| 08 | NYY | 14 | 14 | 0 | 204 | 233 | 158 | 4.54 | 1.41 | 7.0 | 2.4 | 0.8 | 1.8 |
| 09 | NYY | 14 | 8 | 0 | 194 | 193 | 148 | 4.16 | 1.38 | 6.8 | 3.5 | 0.9 | 1.1 |
| 10 | NYY | 11 | 3 | 0 | 129 | 123 | 101 | 3.28 | 1.27 | 7.0 | 2.9 | 0.9 | 1.2 |

**Competition at SP** — Stats in 2010 as SP

| Thr | Player | GS | ERA | Supp | W-L |
|---|---|---|---|---|---|
| LH | Sabathia C | 34 | 3.18 | 5.7 | 21-7 |
| RH | Burnett A | 33 | 5.26 | 4.3 | 10-15 |
| RH | Hughes P | 29 | 4.23 | 6.5 | 17-8 |
| RH | Vazquez J | 26 | 5.56 | 4.1 | 8-10 |

Weekly Points (2008, 2009, 2010)
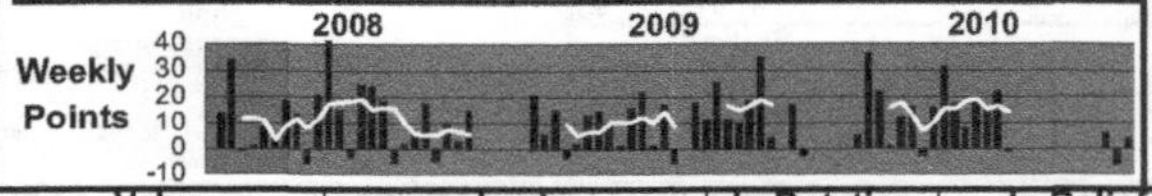

Ten-Year Trends: K/9, BB/9
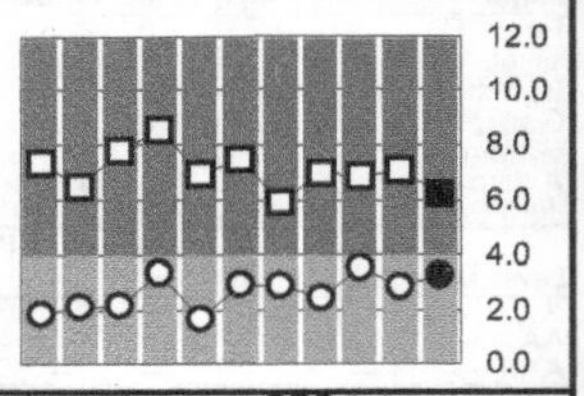

| Yr | $1L | $2L | Pts | RAA | H% | HR/fb | S% | FIP | GS | CG | QS/DS | GR | Hld | Bln | Lead | OPS | 1st Hf | 2nd Hf | vs RH | vs LH |
|---|---|---|---|---|---|---|---|---|---|---|---|---|---|---|---|---|---|---|---|---|
| 07 | $9 | -$7 | 260 | +0 | 33% | 7% | 72% | 3.92 | 34 | 0 | 22/6 | 2 | 1 | 0 | +0.0 | .753 | .760 | .745 | .727 | .836 |
| 08 | $2 | -$8 | 260 | -11 | 34% | 10% | 69% | 3.77 | 33 | 0 | 18/5 | — | — | — | — | .760 | .744 | .783 | .852 | .527 |
| 09 | $10 | $1 | 260 | -5 | 30% | 9% | 72% | 4.29 | 32 | 0 | 17/4 | — | — | — | — | .722 | .796 | .622 | .718 | .730 |
| 10 | $10 | $1 | 210 | +12 | 30% | 9% | 77% | 4.00 | 21 | 0 | 14/3 | — | — | — | — | .703 | .654 | .972 | .782 | .482 |

## Michael Pineda
**120 IP | $7 | 160 pts**
No MLB games played in 2010 | Owned: 0% | RH

A big Dominican fireballer, Pineda has generated a lot of attention for spectacular numbers as a 21-year-old in Double-A and Triple-A. He should open 2011 in the minors, but he will almost certainly be given a shot at making the Mariner rotation out of camp. (GC)

| Player | Age | IP | W | Sv | K | ERA | WHIP | K/9 | BB/9 | $2L | Pts |
|---|---|---|---|---|---|---|---|---|---|---|---|
| Pineda M | 22 | 120 | 7 | 0 | 97 | 3.98 | 1.33 | 7.3 | 3.1 | $7 | 160 |
| **Mini-Browser** | Age | IP | W | Sv | K | ERA | WHIP | K/9 | BB/9 | $2L | Pts |
| Capuano C | 32 | 140 | 9 | 0 | 107 | 4.21 | 1.25 | 6.9 | 2.8 | $7 | 180 |
| Buehrle M | 32 | 200 | 12 | 0 | 95 | 4.47 | 1.32 | 4.3 | 2.1 | $7 | 180 |
| Putz J | 34 | 60 | 5 | 9 | 61 | 3.60 | 1.27 | 9.1 | 3.8 | $7 | 150 |
| Lowe D | 37 | 200 | 13 | 0 | 120 | 4.29 | 1.34 | 5.4 | 2.7 | $7 | 230 |
| Tejeda R | 29 | 60 | 3 | 25 | 57 | 4.35 | 1.55 | 8.6 | 5.4 | $7 | 200 |

| Minors (2010) Level | Leag | W | L | Sv | IP | H | K | ERA | WHIP | K/9 | BB/9 | HR/9 | GB/F |
|---|---|---|---|---|---|---|---|---|---|---|---|---|---|
| A | — | — | — | — | — | — | — | — | — | — | — | — | — |
| AA | SOU | 8 | 1 | 0 | 77 | 67 | 78 | 2.22 | 1.09 | 9.1 | 2.0 | 0.1 | — |
| AAA | PCL | 3 | 3 | 0 | 62 | 54 | 76 | 4.76 | 1.14 | 11.0 | 2.5 | 1.3 | — |

| Majors Yr | Team | W | L | Sv | IP | H | K | ERA | WHIP | K/9 | BB/9 | HR/9 | GB/F |
|---|---|---|---|---|---|---|---|---|---|---|---|---|---|
| 07 | — | — | — | — | — | — | — | — | — | — | — | — | — |
| 08 | — | — | — | — | — | — | — | — | — | — | — | — | — |
| 09 | — | — | — | — | — | — | — | — | — | — | — | — | — |
| 10 | — | — | — | — | — | — | — | — | — | — | — | — | — |

**Competition at SP** — Stats in 2010 as SP

| Thr | Player | GS | ERA | Supp | W-L |
|---|---|---|---|---|---|
| RH | Hernandez F | 34 | 2.27 | 3.1 | 13-12 |
| LH | Vargas J | 31 | 3.78 | 3.1 | 9-12 |
| RH | Fister D | 28 | 4.11 | 3.1 | 6-14 |
| LH | Rowland-Smith R | 20 | 6.93 | 3.0 | 1-10 |

Weekly Points (2008, 2009, 2010)
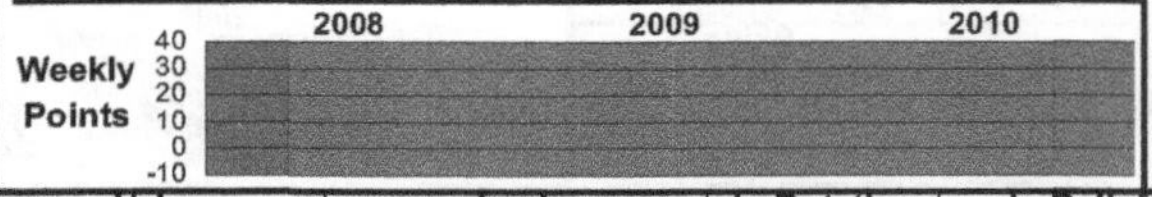

Ten-Year Trends: K/9, BB/9
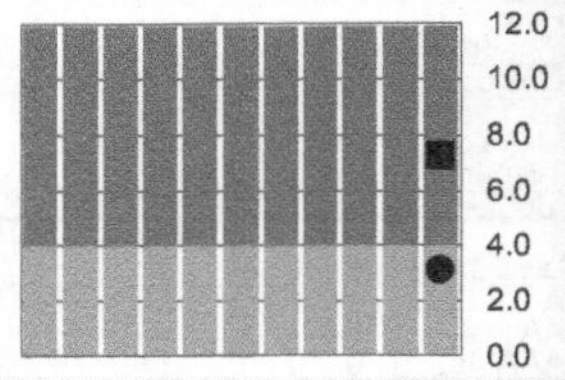

| Yr | $1L | $2L | Pts | RAA | H% | HR/fb | S% | FIP | GS | CG | QS/DS | GR | Hld | Bln | Lead | OPS | 1st Hf | 2nd Hf | vs RH | vs LH |
|---|---|---|---|---|---|---|---|---|---|---|---|---|---|---|---|---|---|---|---|---|
| 07 | — | — | — | — | — | — | — | — | — | — | — | — | — | — | — | — | — | — | — | — |
| 08 | — | — | — | — | — | — | — | — | — | — | — | — | — | — | — | — | — | — | — | — |
| 09 | — | — | — | — | — | — | — | — | — | — | — | — | — | — | — | — | — | — | — | — |
| 10 | — | — | — | — | — | — | — | — | — | — | — | — | — | — | — | — | — | — | — | — |

## Joel Pineiro
**160 IP | $6 | 160 pts**
SP-23 | Owned: 31% | RH

Even with a reshuffled and shaky defense behind him, Pineiro in 2010 pitched very well for the Angels. Although an oblique injury claimed six weeks in the second half, Pineiro came back strong in September (1.71 ERA in 21 IP), and he should be good to go in 2011. (DS)

| Player | Age | IP | W | Sv | K | ERA | WHIP | K/9 | BB/9 | $2L | Pts |
|---|---|---|---|---|---|---|---|---|---|---|---|
| Pineiro J | 32 | 160 | 10 | 0 | 80 | 4.55 | 1.28 | 4.5 | 1.9 | $6 | 160 |
| **Mini-Browser** | Age | IP | W | Sv | K | ERA | WHIP | K/9 | BB/9 | $2L | Pts |
| Santana J | 32 | 80 | 5 | 0 | 64 | 3.51 | 1.17 | 7.1 | 2.3 | $6 | 120 |
| Gregerson L | 26 | 60 | 3 | 0 | 68 | 3.24 | 1.07 | 10.2 | 2.9 | $6 | 110 |
| League B | 28 | 80 | 6 | 3 | 62 | 3.89 | 1.28 | 7.0 | 3.2 | $6 | 140 |
| Romo S | 28 | 60 | 4 | 0 | 66 | 3.06 | 1.15 | 9.8 | 2.4 | $6 | 110 |
| Pelfrey M | 27 | 200 | 13 | 0 | 108 | 4.21 | 1.37 | 4.9 | 3.0 | $6 | 210 |

| Minors (2010) Level | Leag | W | L | Sv | IP | H | K | ERA | WHIP | K/9 | BB/9 | HR/9 | GB/F |
|---|---|---|---|---|---|---|---|---|---|---|---|---|---|
| A | — | — | — | — | — | — | — | — | — | — | — | — | — |
| AA | — | — | — | — | — | — | — | — | — | — | — | — | — |
| AAA | — | — | — | — | — | — | — | — | — | — | — | — | — |

| Majors Yr | Team | W | L | Sv | IP | H | K | ERA | WHIP | K/9 | BB/9 | HR/9 | GB/F |
|---|---|---|---|---|---|---|---|---|---|---|---|---|---|
| 07 | 2TM | 7 | 5 | 0 | 97 | 110 | 60 | 4.33 | 1.39 | 5.5 | 2.4 | 1.3 | 1.4 |
| 08 | STL | 7 | 7 | 1 | 148 | 180 | 81 | 5.15 | 1.45 | 4.9 | 2.1 | 1.3 | 1.6 |
| 09 | STL | 15 | 12 | 0 | 214 | 218 | 105 | 3.49 | 1.14 | 4.4 | 1.1 | 0.5 | 2.5 |
| 10 | LAA | 10 | 7 | 0 | 152 | 155 | 92 | 3.84 | 1.24 | 5.4 | 2.0 | 0.9 | 1.9 |

**Competition at SP** — Stats in 2010 as SP

| Thr | Player | GS | ERA | Supp | W-L |
|---|---|---|---|---|---|
| RH | Haren D | 35 | 3.91 | 3.9 | 12-12 |
| RH | Weaver J | 34 | 3.01 | 3.8 | 13-13 |
| RH | Santana E | 33 | 3.92 | 4.9 | 17-10 |
| LH | Kazmir S | 28 | 5.94 | 4.0 | 9-15 |

Weekly Points (2008, 2009, 2010)
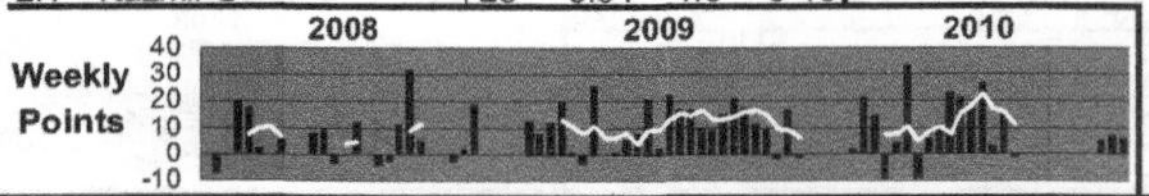

Ten-Year Trends: K/9, BB/9
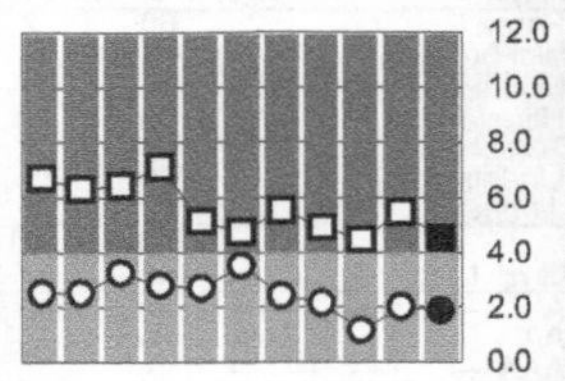

| Yr | $1L | $2L | Pts | RAA | H% | HR/fb | S% | FIP | GS | CG | QS/DS | GR | Hld | Bln | Lead | OPS | 1st Hf | 2nd Hf | vs RH | vs LH |
|---|---|---|---|---|---|---|---|---|---|---|---|---|---|---|---|---|---|---|---|---|
| 07 | $0 | -$5 | 110 | -1 | 31% | 13% | 73% | 4.68 | 11 | 0 | 5/1 | 31 | 1 | 0 | +0.2 | .807 | .795 | .812 | .844 | .756 |
| 08 | -$5 | -$13 | 110 | -16 | 32% | 14% | 67% | 4.74 | 25 | 0 | 12/5 | 1 | 0 | 0 | +0.8 | .847 | .785 | .932 | .837 | .859 |
| 09 | $16 | $10 | 260 | +12 | 30% | 7% | 69% | 3.27 | 32 | 3 | 21/2 | — | — | — | — | .673 | .659 | .691 | .655 | .693 |
| 10 | $8 | -$3 | 180 | +9 | 29% | 10% | 71% | 4.04 | 23 | 3 | 17/2 | — | — | — | — | .716 | .738 | .638 | .732 | .701 |

## Rick Porcello — 200 IP | $2 | 170 pts

SP-27 · Owned: 47% · RH

After a rough first half (6.14 ERA), Porcello got back on track after the Break with outstanding control (1.6 BB/9, 4.00 ERA). Porcello strikes out relatively few men; instead, he gets outs on ground balls, which can be problematic given the Tigers' middle infield. Still, with his control, he should be a capable #3 SP. (LP)

| Player | Age | IP | W | Sv | K | ERA | WHIP | K/9 | BB/9 | $2L | Pts |
|---|---|---|---|---|---|---|---|---|---|---|---|
| **Forecast** | | | | | | | | | | | |
| Porcello R | 22 | 200 | 11 | 0 | 100 | 4.92 | 1.39 | 4.5 | 2.5 | $2 | 170 |
| **Mini-Browser** | | | | | | | | | | | |
| Lueke J | 26 | 40 | 3 | 0 | 39 | 3.41 | 1.29 | 8.7 | 3.4 | $2 | 70 |
| O'Flaherty E | 26 | 60 | 3 | 0 | 44 | 3.52 | 1.31 | 6.5 | 3.4 | $2 | 80 |
| Burnett S | 28 | 60 | 2 | 6 | 47 | 3.86 | 1.38 | 7.1 | 3.9 | $2 | 90 |
| Peralta J | 35 | 60 | 2 | 0 | 51 | 4.01 | 1.17 | 7.6 | 2.4 | $2 | 70 |
| Wood K | 33 | 60 | 3 | 0 | 62 | 3.77 | 1.41 | 9.3 | 4.7 | $2 | 80 |

**Minors (2010)**

| Level | Leag | W | L | Sv | IP | H | K | ERA | WHIP | K/9 | BB/9 | HR/9 | GB/F |
|---|---|---|---|---|---|---|---|---|---|---|---|---|---|
| A | — | — | — | — | — | — | — | — | — | — | — | — | — |
| AA | — | — | — | — | — | — | — | — | — | — | — | — | — |
| AAA | IL | 1 | 2 | 0 | 28 | 24 | 19 | 3.21 | 1.21 | 6.1 | 3.2 | 0.0 | — |

**Competition at SP / Stats in 2010 as SP**

| Thr | Player | GS | ERA | Supp | W-L |
|---|---|---|---|---|---|
| RH | Verlander J | 33 | 3.37 | 5.2 | 18-9 |
| RH | Scherzer M | 31 | 3.50 | 4.0 | 12-11 |
| RH | Bonderman J | 29 | 5.56 | 5.1 | 8-10 |
| RH | Porcello R | 27 | 4.92 | 4.8 | 10-12 |

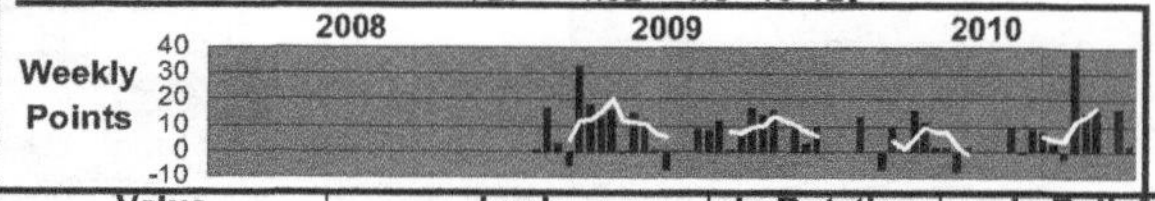
Weekly Points
2008
2009
2010
40
30
20
10
0
-10

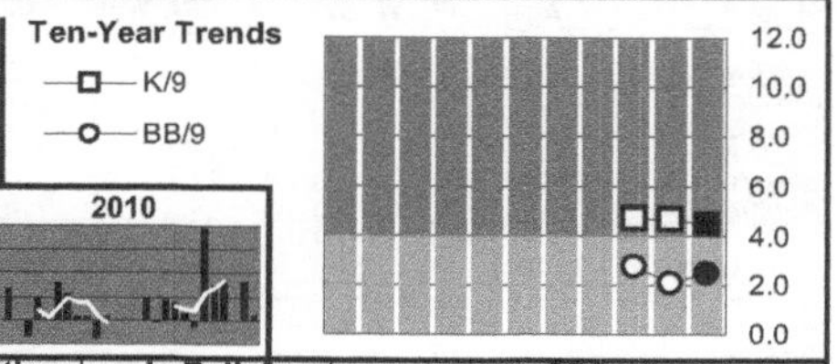
Ten-Year Trends
K/9
BB/9
12.0
10.0
8.0
6.0
4.0
2.0
0.0

**Majors / Skills**

| Yr | Team | W | L | Sv | IP | H | K | ERA | WHIP | K/9 | BB/9 | HR/9 | GB/F |
|---|---|---|---|---|---|---|---|---|---|---|---|---|---|
| 07 | — | — | — | — | — | — | — | — | — | — | — | — | — |
| 08 | — | — | — | — | — | — | — | — | — | — | — | — | — |
| 09 | DET | 14 | 9 | 0 | 170 | 176 | 89 | 3.96 | 1.34 | 4.7 | 2.7 | 1.2 | 1.9 |
| 10 | DET | 10 | 12 | 0 | 162 | 188 | 84 | 4.92 | 1.39 | 4.6 | 2.1 | 1.0 | 1.6 |

| Yr | $1L | $2L | Pts | RAA | H% | HR/fb | S% | FIP | GS | CG | QS/DS | GR | Hld | Bln | Lead | OPS | 1st Hf | 2nd Hf | vs RH | vs LH |
|---|---|---|---|---|---|---|---|---|---|---|---|---|---|---|---|---|---|---|---|---|
| 07 | — | — | — | — | — | — | — | — | — | — | — | — | — | — | — | — | — | — | — | — |
| 08 | — | — | — | — | — | — | — | — | — | — | — | — | — | — | — | — | — | — | — | — |
| 09 | $10 | $2 | 210 | +3 | 28% | 14% | 75% | 4.92 | 31 | 0 | 11/3 | — | — | — | — | .738 | .787 | .687 | .719 | .753 |
| 10 | $0 | -$19 | 140 | −16 | 31% | 10% | 66% | 4.41 | 27 | 0 | 13/6 | — | — | — | — | .752 | .867 | .654 | .717 | .784 |

(Value: $1L, $2L, Pts, RAA · Luck: H%, HR/fb, S%, FIP · In Rotation: GS, CG, QS/DS · In Relief: GR, Hld, Bln, Lead · OPS: OPS, 1st Hf, 2nd Hf, vs RH, vs LH)

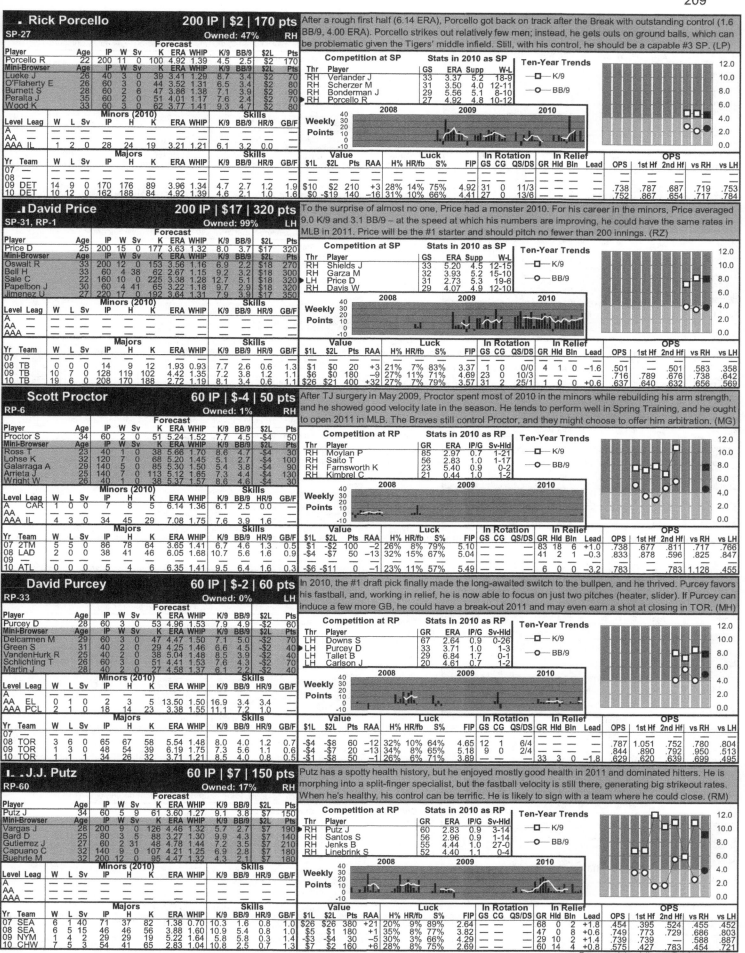

## David Price — 200 IP | $17 | 320 pts

SP-31, RP-1 · Owned: 99% · LH

To the surprise of almost no one, Price had a monster 2010. For his career in the minors, Price averaged 9.0 K/9 and 3.1 BB/9 – at the speed at which his numbers are improving, he could have the same rates in MLB in 2011. Price will be the #1 starter and should pitch no fewer than 200 innings. (RZ)

| Player | Age | IP | W | Sv | K | ERA | WHIP | K/9 | BB/9 | $2L | Pts |
|---|---|---|---|---|---|---|---|---|---|---|---|
| **Forecast** | | | | | | | | | | | |
| Price D | 25 | 200 | 15 | 0 | 177 | 3.63 | 1.32 | 8.0 | 3.7 | $17 | 320 |
| **Mini-Browser** | | | | | | | | | | | |
| Oswalt R | 33 | 200 | 12 | 0 | 153 | 3.56 | 1.16 | 6.9 | 2.2 | $18 | 270 |
| Bell H | 33 | 60 | 4 | 38 | 62 | 2.67 | 1.15 | 9.2 | 3.2 | $18 | 300 |
| Sale C | 22 | 160 | 10 | 0 | 225 | 3.38 | 1.28 | 12.7 | 5.1 | $18 | 320 |
| Papelbon J | 30 | 60 | 4 | 41 | 65 | 3.22 | 1.18 | 9.7 | 2.9 | $18 | 320 |
| Jimenez U | 27 | 220 | 17 | 0 | 192 | 3.64 | 1.31 | 7.9 | 3.9 | $17 | 350 |

**Minors (2010)**

| Level | Leag | W | L | Sv | IP | H | K | ERA | WHIP | K/9 | BB/9 | HR/9 | GB/F |
|---|---|---|---|---|---|---|---|---|---|---|---|---|---|
| A | — | — | — | — | — | — | — | — | — | — | — | — | — |
| AA | — | — | — | — | — | — | — | — | — | — | — | — | — |
| AAA | — | — | — | — | — | — | — | — | — | — | — | — | — |

**Competition at SP / Stats in 2010 as SP**

| Thr | Player | GS | ERA | Supp | W-L |
|---|---|---|---|---|---|
| RH | Shields J | 33 | 5.20 | 4.5 | 12-15 |
| RH | Garza M | 32 | 3.93 | 5.2 | 15-10 |
| LH | Price D | 31 | 2.73 | 5.3 | 19-6 |
| RH | Davis W | 29 | 4.07 | 4.9 | 12-10 |

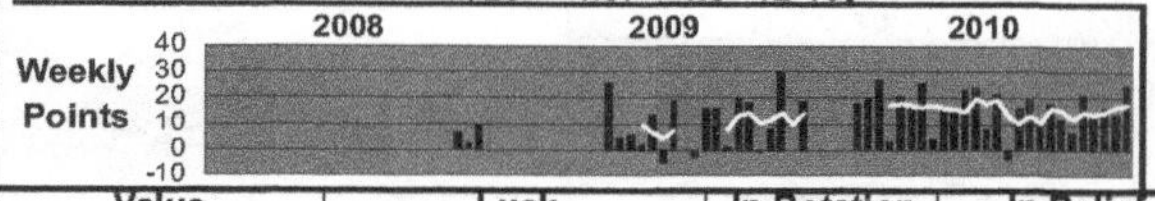
Weekly Points
2008
2009
2010
40
30
20
10
0
-10

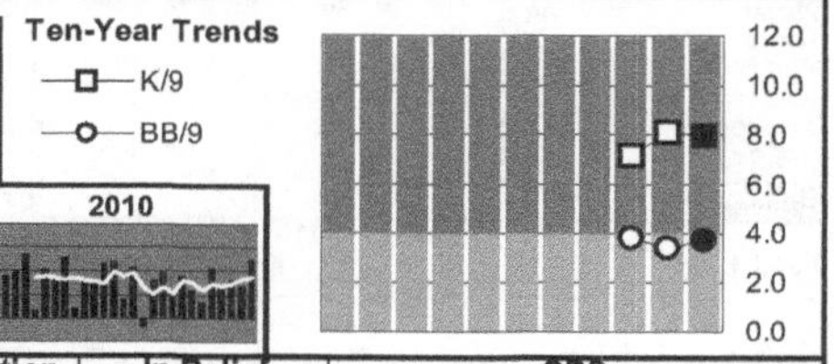
Ten-Year Trends
K/9
BB/9
12.0
10.0
8.0
6.0
4.0
2.0
0.0

**Majors / Skills**

| Yr | Team | W | L | Sv | IP | H | K | ERA | WHIP | K/9 | BB/9 | HR/9 | GB/F |
|---|---|---|---|---|---|---|---|---|---|---|---|---|---|
| 07 | — | — | — | — | — | — | — | — | — | — | — | — | — |
| 08 | TB | 0 | 0 | 0 | 14 | 9 | 12 | 1.93 | 0.93 | 7.7 | 2.6 | 0.6 | 1.3 |
| 09 | TB | 10 | 7 | 0 | 128 | 119 | 102 | 4.42 | 1.35 | 7.2 | 3.8 | 1.2 | 1.1 |
| 10 | TB | 19 | 6 | 0 | 208 | 170 | 188 | 2.72 | 1.19 | 8.1 | 3.4 | 0.6 | 1.1 |

| Yr | $1L | $2L | Pts | RAA | H% | HR/fb | S% | FIP | GS | CG | QS/DS | GR | Hld | Bln | Lead | OPS | 1st Hf | 2nd Hf | vs RH | vs LH |
|---|---|---|---|---|---|---|---|---|---|---|---|---|---|---|---|---|---|---|---|---|
| 07 | — | — | — | — | — | — | — | — | — | — | — | — | — | — | — | — | — | — | — | — |
| 08 | $1 | $0 | 20 | +3 | 21% | 7% | 83% | 3.37 | 1 | 0 | 0/0 | 4 | 1 | 0 | −1.6 | .501 | — | .501 | .583 | .358 |
| 09 | $6 | $0 | 180 | −9 | 27% | 11% | 71% | 4.69 | 23 | 0 | 10/3 | — | — | — | — | .716 | .789 | .676 | .738 | .642 |
| 10 | $26 | $21 | 400 | +32 | 27% | 7% | 79% | 3.57 | 31 | 2 | 25/1 | 1 | 0 | 0 | +0.6 | .637 | .640 | .632 | .656 | .569 |

## Scott Proctor — 60 IP | $-4 | 50 pts

RP-6 · Owned: 1% · RH

After TJ surgery in May 2009, Proctor spent most of 2010 in the minors while rebuilding his arm strength, and he showed good velocity late in the season. He tends to perform well in Spring Training, and he ought to open 2011 in MLB. The Braves still control Proctor, and they might choose to offer him arbitration. (MG)

| Player | Age | IP | W | Sv | K | ERA | WHIP | K/9 | BB/9 | $2L | Pts |
|---|---|---|---|---|---|---|---|---|---|---|---|
| **Forecast** | | | | | | | | | | | |
| Proctor S | 34 | 60 | 2 | 0 | 51 | 5.24 | 1.52 | 7.7 | 4.5 | -$4 | 50 |
| **Mini-Browser** | | | | | | | | | | | |
| Ross T | 23 | 40 | 1 | 0 | 38 | 5.66 | 1.70 | 8.6 | 4.7 | -$4 | 30 |
| Lohse K | 32 | 120 | 7 | 0 | 68 | 5.20 | 1.45 | 5.1 | 2.7 | -$4 | 100 |
| Galarraga A | 29 | 140 | 5 | 0 | 85 | 5.30 | 1.50 | 5.4 | 3.8 | -$4 | 90 |
| Arrieta J | 25 | 140 | 7 | 0 | 113 | 5.12 | 1.65 | 7.3 | 4.4 | -$4 | 130 |
| Wright W | 26 | 40 | 1 | 0 | 38 | 5.37 | 1.57 | 8.6 | 4.6 | -$4 | 30 |

**Minors (2010)**

| Level | Leag | W | L | Sv | IP | H | K | ERA | WHIP | K/9 | BB/9 | HR/9 | GB/F |
|---|---|---|---|---|---|---|---|---|---|---|---|---|---|
| A | CAR | 1 | 0 | 0 | 7 | 8 | 5 | 6.14 | 1.36 | 6.1 | 2.5 | 0.0 | — |
| AA | — | — | — | — | — | — | — | — | — | — | — | — | — |
| AAA | IL | 4 | 3 | 0 | 34 | 45 | 29 | 7.08 | 1.75 | 7.6 | 3.9 | 1.6 | — |

**Competition at RP / Stats in 2010 as RP**

| Thr | Player | GR | ERA | IP/G | Sv-Hld |
|---|---|---|---|---|---|
| RH | Moylan P | 85 | 2.97 | 0.7 | 1-21 |
| RH | Saito T | 56 | 2.83 | 1.0 | 1-17 |
| RH | Farnsworth K | 23 | 5.40 | 0.9 | 0-2 |
| RH | Kimbrel C | 21 | 0.44 | 1.0 | 1-2 |

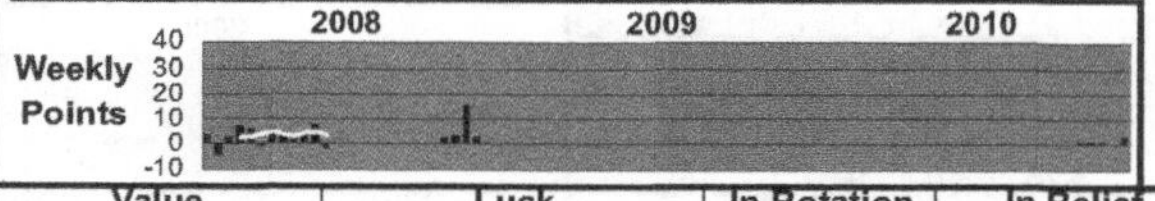
Weekly Points
2008
2009
2010
40
30
20
10
0
-10

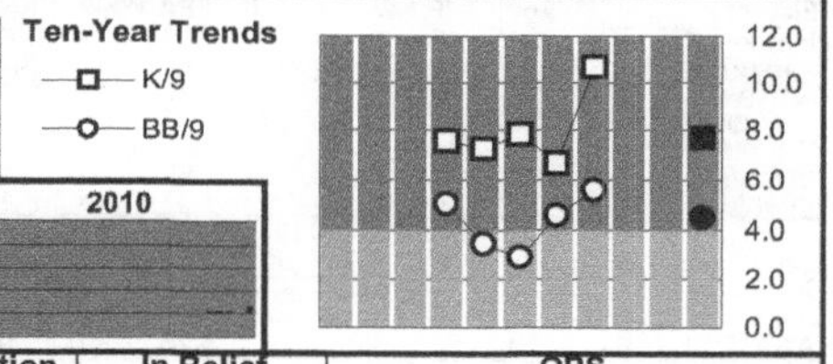
Ten-Year Trends
K/9
BB/9
12.0
10.0
8.0
6.0
4.0
2.0
0.0

**Majors / Skills**

| Yr | Team | W | L | Sv | IP | H | K | ERA | WHIP | K/9 | BB/9 | HR/9 | GB/F |
|---|---|---|---|---|---|---|---|---|---|---|---|---|---|
| 07 | 2TM | 5 | 5 | 0 | 86 | 78 | 64 | 3.65 | 1.41 | 6.7 | 4.6 | 1.3 | 0.5 |
| 08 | LAD | 2 | 0 | 0 | 38 | 41 | 46 | 6.05 | 1.68 | 10.7 | 5.6 | 1.6 | 0.9 |
| 09 | — | — | — | — | — | — | — | — | — | — | — | — | — |
| 10 | ATL | 0 | 0 | 0 | 5 | 4 | 6 | 6.35 | 1.41 | 9.5 | 6.4 | 1.6 | 0.3 |

| Yr | $1L | $2L | Pts | RAA | H% | HR/fb | S% | FIP | GS | CG | QS/DS | GR | Hld | Bln | Lead | OPS | 1st Hf | 2nd Hf | vs RH | vs LH |
|---|---|---|---|---|---|---|---|---|---|---|---|---|---|---|---|---|---|---|---|---|
| 07 | $1 | -$2 | 100 | −2 | 26% | 8% | 79% | 5.10 | — | — | — | 83 | 18 | 6 | +1.0 | .738 | .677 | .811 | .717 | .766 |
| 08 | -$4 | -$7 | 50 | −13 | 32% | 15% | 67% | 5.04 | — | — | — | 41 | 2 | 1 | −0.3 | .833 | .878 | .596 | .825 | .847 |
| 09 | | | | | | | | | | | | | | | | | | | | |
| 10 | -$6 | -$11 | 0 | −1 | 23% | 11% | 57% | 5.49 | — | — | — | 6 | 0 | 0 | −3.2 | .783 | — | .783 | 1.128 | .455 |

## David Purcey — 60 IP | $-2 | 60 pts

RP-33 · Owned: 0% · LH

In 2010, the #1 draft pick finally made the long-awaited switch to the bullpen, and he thrived. Purcey favors his fastball, and, working in relief, he is now able to focus on just two pitches (heater, slider). If Purcey can induce a few more GB, he could have a break-out 2011 and may even earn a shot at closing in TOR. (MH)

| Player | Age | IP | W | Sv | K | ERA | WHIP | K/9 | BB/9 | $2L | Pts |
|---|---|---|---|---|---|---|---|---|---|---|---|
| **Forecast** | | | | | | | | | | | |
| Purcey D | 28 | 60 | 3 | 0 | 53 | 4.96 | 1.53 | 7.9 | 4.9 | -$2 | 60 |
| **Mini-Browser** | | | | | | | | | | | |
| Delcarmen M | 29 | 60 | 3 | 0 | 47 | 4.47 | 1.50 | 7.1 | 5.0 | -$2 | 70 |
| Green S | 31 | 40 | 2 | 0 | 29 | 4.25 | 1.46 | 6.6 | 4.5 | -$2 | 40 |
| VandenHurk R | 25 | 40 | 2 | 0 | 38 | 5.04 | 1.48 | 8.5 | 3.9 | -$2 | 40 |
| Schlichting T | 26 | 60 | 3 | 0 | 51 | 4.41 | 1.53 | 7.6 | 4.3 | -$2 | 70 |
| Martin J | 28 | 40 | 2 | 0 | 27 | 4.58 | 1.37 | 6.1 | 2.2 | -$2 | 40 |

**Minors (2010)**

| Level | Leag | W | L | Sv | IP | H | K | ERA | WHIP | K/9 | BB/9 | HR/9 | GB/F |
|---|---|---|---|---|---|---|---|---|---|---|---|---|---|
| A | — | — | — | — | — | — | — | — | — | — | — | — | — |
| AA | EL | 0 | 1 | 0 | 2 | 3 | 5 | 13.50 | 1.50 | 16.9 | 3.4 | 3.4 | — |
| AAA | PCL | 2 | 1 | 0 | 18 | 14 | 23 | 3.38 | 1.55 | 11.1 | 7.2 | 1.0 | — |

**Competition at RP / Stats in 2010 as RP**

| Thr | Player | GR | ERA | IP/G | Sv-Hld |
|---|---|---|---|---|---|
| LH | Downs S | 67 | 2.64 | 0.9 | 0-26 |
| LH | Purcey D | 33 | 3.71 | 1.0 | 1-3 |
| LH | Tallet B | 29 | 6.84 | 1.7 | 0-1 |
| LH | Carlson J | 20 | 4.61 | 0.7 | 1-2 |

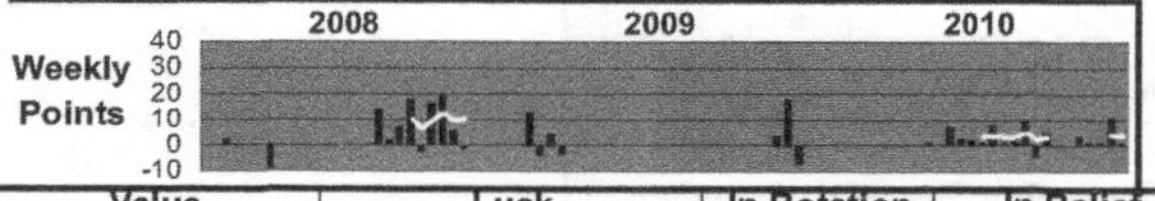
Weekly Points
2008
2009
2010
40
30
20
10
0
-10

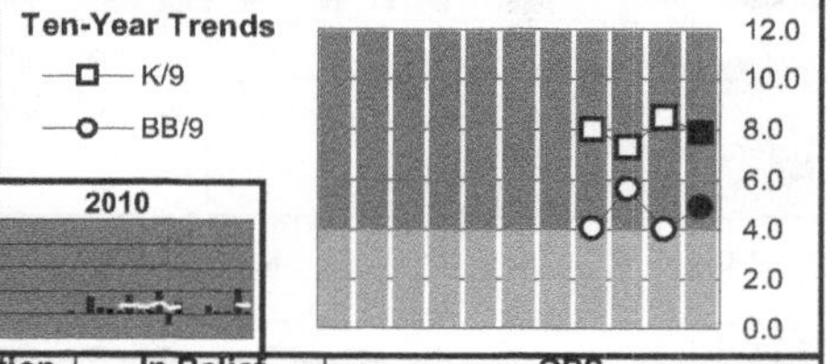
Ten-Year Trends
K/9
BB/9
12.0
10.0
8.0
6.0
4.0
2.0
0.0

**Majors / Skills**

| Yr | Team | W | L | Sv | IP | H | K | ERA | WHIP | K/9 | BB/9 | HR/9 | GB/F |
|---|---|---|---|---|---|---|---|---|---|---|---|---|---|
| 07 | — | — | — | — | — | — | — | — | — | — | — | — | — |
| 08 | TOR | 3 | 6 | 0 | 65 | 67 | 58 | 5.54 | 1.48 | 8.0 | 4.0 | 1.2 | 0.7 |
| 09 | TOR | 1 | 3 | 0 | 48 | 54 | 39 | 6.19 | 1.75 | 7.3 | 5.6 | 1.1 | 0.6 |
| 10 | TOR | 1 | 1 | 1 | 34 | 26 | 32 | 3.71 | 1.21 | 8.5 | 4.0 | 0.8 | 0.5 |

| Yr | $1L | $2L | Pts | RAA | H% | HR/fb | S% | FIP | GS | CG | QS/DS | GR | Hld | Bln | Lead | OPS | 1st Hf | 2nd Hf | vs RH | vs LH |
|---|---|---|---|---|---|---|---|---|---|---|---|---|---|---|---|---|---|---|---|---|
| 07 | — | — | — | — | — | — | — | — | — | — | — | — | — | — | — | — | — | — | — | — |
| 08 | -$4 | -$8 | 60 | −12 | 32% | 10% | 64% | 4.65 | 12 | 1 | 6/4 | — | — | — | — | .787 | 1.051 | .752 | .780 | .804 |
| 09 | -$4 | -$7 | 20 | −13 | 34% | 8% | 65% | 5.18 | 9 | 0 | 2/4 | — | — | — | — | .844 | .890 | .792 | .950 | .513 |
| 10 | -$1 | -$8 | 50 | −1 | 26% | 6% | 71% | 3.89 | — | — | — | 33 | 3 | 0 | −1.8 | .629 | .620 | .639 | .699 | .495 |

## J.J. Putz — 60 IP | $7 | 150 pts

RP-60 · Owned: 17% · RH

Putz has a spotty health history, but he enjoyed mostly good health in 2011 and dominated hitters. He is morphing into a split-finger specialist, but the fastball velocity is still there, generating big strikeout rates. When he's healthy, his control can be terrific. He is likely to sign with a team where he could close. (RM)

| Player | Age | IP | W | Sv | K | ERA | WHIP | K/9 | BB/9 | $2L | Pts |
|---|---|---|---|---|---|---|---|---|---|---|---|
| **Forecast** | | | | | | | | | | | |
| Putz J | 34 | 60 | 5 | 9 | 61 | 3.60 | 1.27 | 9.1 | 3.8 | $7 | 150 |
| **Mini-Browser** | | | | | | | | | | | |
| Vargas J | 28 | 200 | 9 | 0 | 126 | 4.46 | 1.32 | 5.7 | 2.7 | $7 | 190 |
| Bard D | 25 | 80 | 3 | 5 | 88 | 3.27 | 1.30 | 9.9 | 4.3 | $7 | 140 |
| Gutierrez J | 27 | 60 | 2 | 31 | 48 | 4.78 | 1.44 | 7.2 | 3.5 | $7 | 210 |
| Capuano C | 32 | 140 | 9 | 0 | 107 | 4.21 | 1.25 | 6.9 | 2.8 | $7 | 180 |
| Buehrle M | 32 | 200 | 12 | 0 | 95 | 4.47 | 1.32 | 4.3 | 2.1 | $7 | 180 |

**Minors (2010)**

| Level | Leag | W | L | Sv | IP | H | K | ERA | WHIP | K/9 | BB/9 | HR/9 | GB/F |
|---|---|---|---|---|---|---|---|---|---|---|---|---|---|
| A | — | — | — | — | — | — | — | — | — | — | — | — | — |
| AA | — | — | — | — | — | — | — | — | — | — | — | — | — |
| AAA | — | — | — | — | — | — | — | — | — | — | — | — | — |

**Competition at RP / Stats in 2010 as RP**

| Thr | Player | GR | ERA | IP/G | Sv-Hld |
|---|---|---|---|---|---|
| RH | Putz J | 60 | 2.83 | 0.9 | 3-14 |
| RH | Santos S | 56 | 2.96 | 0.9 | 1-14 |
| RH | Jenks B | 55 | 4.44 | 1.0 | 27-0 |
| RH | Linebrink S | 52 | 4.40 | 1.1 | 0-4 |

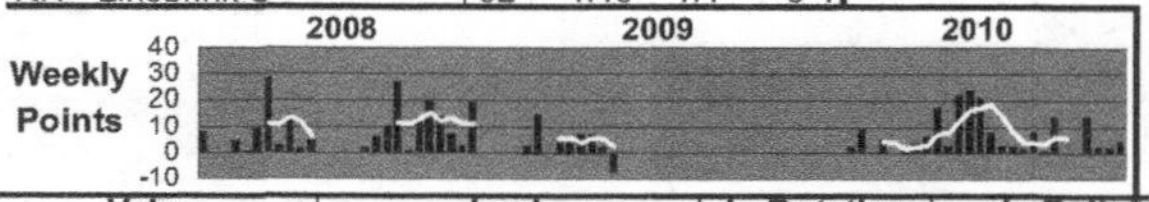
Weekly Points
2008
2009
2010
40
30
20
10
0
-10

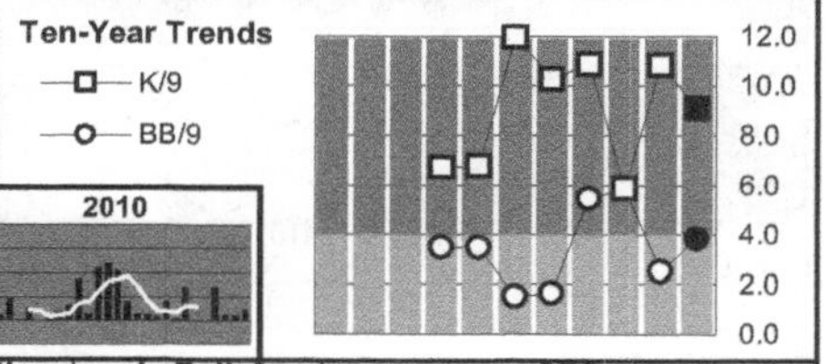
Ten-Year Trends
K/9
BB/9
12.0
10.0
8.0
6.0
4.0
2.0
0.0

**Majors / Skills**

| Yr | Team | W | L | Sv | IP | H | K | ERA | WHIP | K/9 | BB/9 | HR/9 | GB/F |
|---|---|---|---|---|---|---|---|---|---|---|---|---|---|
| 07 | SEA | 6 | 1 | 40 | 71 | 37 | 82 | 1.38 | 0.70 | 10.3 | 1.6 | 0.8 | 1.0 |
| 08 | SEA | 6 | 5 | 15 | 46 | 46 | 56 | 3.88 | 1.60 | 10.9 | 5.4 | 0.8 | 1.0 |
| 09 | NYM | 1 | 4 | 2 | 29 | 29 | 19 | 5.22 | 1.64 | 5.8 | 5.8 | 0.3 | 1.4 |
| 10 | CHW | 7 | 5 | 3 | 54 | 41 | 65 | 2.83 | 1.04 | 10.8 | 2.5 | 0.7 | 1.3 |

| Yr | $1L | $2L | Pts | RAA | H% | HR/fb | S% | FIP | GS | CG | QS/DS | GR | Hld | Bln | Lead | OPS | 1st Hf | 2nd Hf | vs RH | vs LH |
|---|---|---|---|---|---|---|---|---|---|---|---|---|---|---|---|---|---|---|---|---|
| 07 | $26 | $26 | 380 | +21 | 20% | 9% | 89% | 2.64 | — | — | — | 68 | 0 | 2 | +1.8 | .454 | .395 | .524 | .455 | .452 |
| 08 | $5 | $1 | 180 | +1 | 35% | 8% | 77% | 3.82 | — | — | — | 47 | 0 | 8 | +0.6 | .749 | .773 | .729 | .686 | .803 |
| 09 | -$3 | -$4 | 30 | −5 | 30% | 3% | 66% | 4.29 | — | — | — | 29 | 10 | 2 | +1.4 | .739 | .739 | — | .588 | .887 |
| 10 | $7 | $2 | 160 | +6 | 28% | 8% | 75% | 2.69 | — | — | — | 60 | 14 | 4 | +0.8 | .575 | .427 | .783 | .454 | .721 |

## ... Chad Qualls — 50 IP | $-2 | 40 pts

RP-70 — Owned: 59% — RH

A trade-deadline pick-up forTampa, Qualls was so-so in his time there (5.57 ERA but 2.5 K/BB and 2.0 GB/F). The cost of retaining him to pitch in middle relief might be too rich for TB, so Qualls will probably be an FA. In 2010, he might have still been suffering the effects of his 2009 knee injury and surgery. (RZ)

| Player | Age | IP | W | Sv | K | ERA | WHIP | K/9 | BB/9 | $2L | Pts |
|---|---|---|---|---|---|---|---|---|---|---|---|
| Qualls C | 32 | 50 | 2 | 0 | 39 | 5.14 | 1.44 | 7.1 | 2.5 | -$2 | 40 |
| **Mini-Browser** | Age | IP | W | Sv | K | ERA | WHIP | K/9 | BB/9 | $2L | Pts |
| Kendrick K | 26 | 80 | 5 | 0 | 38 | 4.85 | 1.39 | 4.3 | 2.6 | -$2 | 70 |
| Heilman A | 32 | 80 | 4 | 0 | 63 | 4.82 | 1.45 | 7.1 | 3.8 | -$2 | 80 |
| Ondrusek L | 26 | 60 | 3 | 0 | 48 | 4.62 | 1.49 | 7.2 | 3.5 | -$2 | 70 |
| Sanchez E | 22 | 40 | 1 | 0 | 35 | 4.07 | 1.48 | 8.0 | 4.8 | -$2 | 40 |
| Acosta M | 29 | 40 | 2 | 0 | 33 | 4.39 | 1.48 | 7.5 | 4.7 | -$2 | 40 |

| Level | Leag | W | L | Sv | IP | H | K | ERA | WHIP | K/9 | BB/9 | HR/9 | GB/F |
|---|---|---|---|---|---|---|---|---|---|---|---|---|---|
| A | — | — | — | — | — | — | — | — | — | — | — | — | — |
| AA | — | — | — | — | — | — | — | — | — | — | — | — | — |
| AAA | — | — | — | — | — | — | — | — | — | — | — | — | — |

| Yr | Team | W | L | Sv | IP | H | K | ERA | WHIP | K/9 | BB/9 | HR/9 | GB/F |
|---|---|---|---|---|---|---|---|---|---|---|---|---|---|
| 07 | HOU | 6 | 5 | 5 | 82 | 84 | 78 | 3.05 | 1.32 | 8.5 | 2.7 | 1.1 | 1.9 |
| 08 | ARI | 4 | 8 | 9 | 73 | 61 | 71 | 2.81 | 1.07 | 8.7 | 2.2 | 0.5 | 2.5 |
| 09 | ARI | 2 | 2 | 24 | 52 | 53 | 45 | 3.63 | 1.15 | 7.8 | 1.2 | 0.9 | 2.5 |
| 10 | 2TM | 3 | 4 | 12 | 59 | 85 | 49 | 7.32 | 1.80 | 7.5 | 3.2 | 1.1 | 1.9 |

| Yr | $1L | $2L | Pts | RAA | H% | HR/fb | S% | FIP | GS | CG | QS/DS | GR | Hld | Bln | Lead | OPS | 1st Hf | 2nd Hf | vs RH | vs LH |
|---|---|---|---|---|---|---|---|---|---|---|---|---|---|---|---|---|---|---|---|---|
| 07 | $7 | $4 | 160 | +8 | 33% | 15% | 82% | 3.79 | — | — | — | 79 | 21 | 5 | +0.8 | .732 | .804 | .643 | .833 | .590 |
| 08 | $10 | $7 | 170 | +4 | 29% | 9% | 75% | 2.71 | — | — | — | 77 | 22 | 8 | +1.2 | .601 | .687 | .455 | .640 | .559 |
| 09 | $8 | $5 | 190 | +0 | 31% | 14% | 71% | 3.12 | — | — | — | 51 | 0 | 5 | +2.0 | .683 | .684 | .681 | .638 | .728 |
| 10 | -$7 | -$23 | 100 | −29 | 40% | 12% | 59% | 4.20 | — | — | — | 70 | 11 | 7 | +0.3 | .894 | .983 | .782 | .766 | 1.031 |

Competition at RP — Stats in 2010 as RP

| Thr | Player | GR | ERA | IP/G | Sv-Hld |
|---|---|---|---|---|---|
| RH | Soriano R | 64 | 1.73 | 1.0 | 45-0 |
| RH | Wheeler D | 64 | 3.35 | 0.8 | 3-9 |
| RH | Benoit J | 63 | 1.34 | 1.0 | 1-25 |
| RH | Cormier L | 60 | 3.92 | 1.0 | 0-4 |

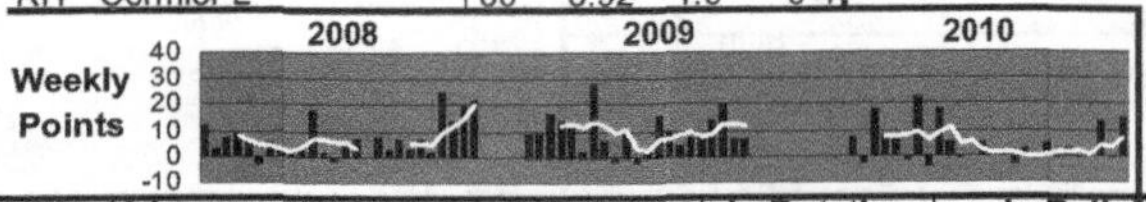


Ten-Year Trends

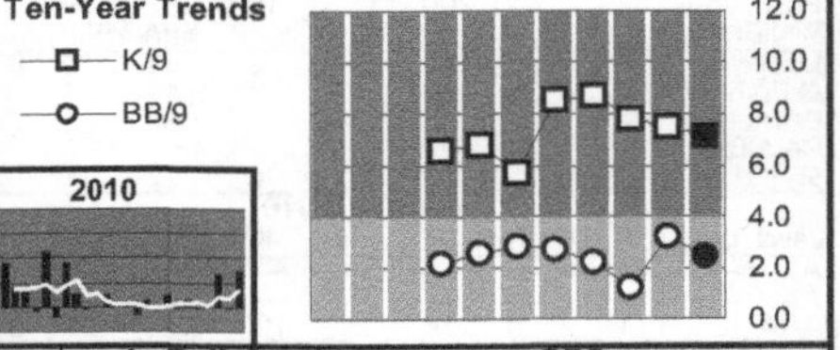


## ... Ramon Ramirez — 60 IP | $1 | 60 pts

RP-69 — Owned: 0% — RH

Ramirez is a time bomb. His very low ERA's from 2008-10 mask mediocre rates of strikeouts and walks; in fact, in the 2nd half of 2010, his rates worsened to 5.9 K/9 and 4.0 BB/9. And yet, he is lodged into a set-up role. If SF offers Ramirez $4-5M, we will know that they value "the touch" over underlying statistics. (PB)

| Player | Age | IP | W | Sv | K | ERA | WHIP | K/9 | BB/9 | $2L | Pts |
|---|---|---|---|---|---|---|---|---|---|---|---|
| Ramirez R | 29 | 60 | 2 | 0 | 44 | 3.66 | 1.35 | 6.7 | 4.1 | $1 | 60 |
| **Mini-Browser** | Age | IP | W | Sv | K | ERA | WHIP | K/9 | BB/9 | $2L | Pts |
| Kazmir S | 27 | 140 | 9 | 0 | 112 | 4.98 | 1.46 | 7.2 | 4.2 | $1 | 160 |
| Aceves A | 28 | 40 | 3 | 0 | 29 | 3.91 | 1.29 | 6.5 | 2.4 | $1 | 60 |
| Lopez J | 33 | 60 | 3 | 0 | 38 | 3.54 | 1.37 | 5.7 | 3.7 | $1 | 60 |
| Zito B | 32 | 200 | 10 | 0 | 138 | 4.59 | 1.42 | 6.2 | 3.9 | $1 | 190 |
| Blevins J | 27 | 50 | 2 | 0 | 48 | 3.98 | 1.37 | 8.7 | 3.1 | $1 | 60 |

| Level | Leag | W | L | Sv | IP | H | K | ERA | WHIP | K/9 | BB/9 | HR/9 | GB/F |
|---|---|---|---|---|---|---|---|---|---|---|---|---|---|
| A | — | — | — | — | — | — | — | — | — | — | — | — | — |
| AA | — | — | — | — | — | — | — | — | — | — | — | — | — |
| AAA | — | — | — | — | — | — | — | — | — | — | — | — | — |

| Yr | Team | W | L | Sv | IP | H | K | ERA | WHIP | K/9 | BB/9 | HR/9 | GB/F |
|---|---|---|---|---|---|---|---|---|---|---|---|---|---|
| 07 | COL | 2 | 2 | 0 | 17 | 21 | 15 | 8.31 | 1.56 | 7.8 | 3.1 | 1.0 | 0.6 |
| 08 | KC | 3 | 2 | 1 | 71 | 57 | 70 | 2.64 | 1.23 | 8.8 | 3.9 | 0.3 | 1.3 |
| 09 | BOS | 7 | 4 | 0 | 69 | 61 | 52 | 2.84 | 1.33 | 6.7 | 4.1 | 0.9 | 0.7 |
| 10 | 2TM | 1 | 3 | 3 | 69 | 52 | 46 | 2.99 | 1.14 | 6.0 | 3.5 | 0.9 | 0.8 |

| Yr | $1L | $2L | Pts | RAA | H% | HR/fb | S% | FIP | GS | CG | QS/DS | GR | Hld | Bln | Lead | OPS | 1st Hf | 2nd Hf | vs RH | vs LH |
|---|---|---|---|---|---|---|---|---|---|---|---|---|---|---|---|---|---|---|---|---|
| 07 | -$4 | -$6 | 20 | −8 | 37% | 7% | 44% | 4.01 | — | — | — | 22 | 3 | 0 | 0.0 | .891 | .975 | .679 | 1.053 | .624 |
| 08 | $7 | $4 | 110 | +9 | 30% | 3% | 78% | 3.01 | — | — | — | 71 | 21 | 4 | +0.5 | .590 | .548 | .663 | .455 | .745 |
| 09 | $6 | $3 | 120 | +5 | 27% | 7% | 83% | 4.49 | — | — | — | 70 | 12 | 4 | +0.5 | .711 | .614 | .814 | .623 | .794 |
| 10 | $2 | -$3 | 80 | +7 | 22% | 7% | 78% | 4.40 | — | — | — | 69 | 6 | 0 | −0.3 | .631 | .795 | .441 | .599 | .677 |

Competition at RP — Stats in 2010 as RP

| Thr | Player | GR | ERA | IP/G | Sv-Hld |
|---|---|---|---|---|---|
| RH | Wilson B | 70 | 1.81 | 1.1 | 48-0 |
| RH | Romo S | 68 | 2.18 | 0.9 | 0-21 |
| RH | Mota G | 56 | 4.33 | 1.0 | 1-8 |
| RH | Casilla S | 52 | 1.95 | 1.1 | 2-11 |

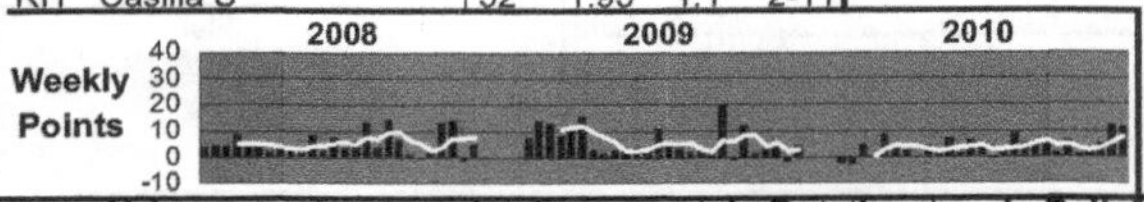


Ten-Year Trends

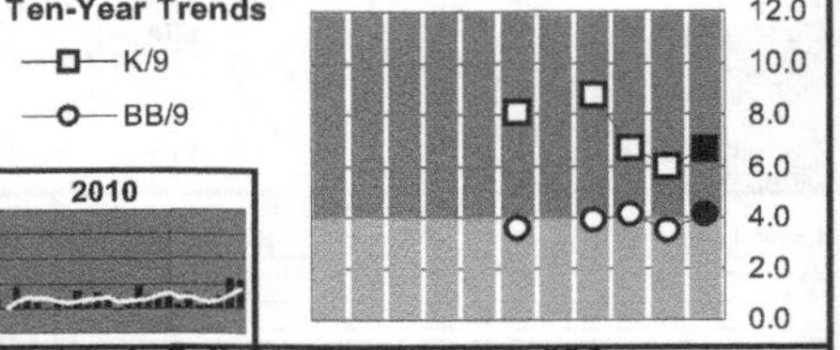


## Cesar Ramos — 40 IP | $-2 | 40 pts

RP-14 — Owned: 0% — LH

Ramos did tolerable work in a swing role at Triple-A, and he got thumped in limited big-league relief action with the Padres. His future probably lies in SD's bullpen, but there might not be room for him with the parent club at the start of 2011. Ramos's upside tops off at decent-middle-reliever/lefty-specialist. (DG)

| Player | Age | IP | W | Sv | K | ERA | WHIP | K/9 | BB/9 | $2L | Pts |
|---|---|---|---|---|---|---|---|---|---|---|---|
| Ramos C | 26 | 40 | 2 | 0 | 29 | 4.81 | 1.46 | 6.5 | 3.4 | -$2 | 40 |
| **Mini-Browser** | Age | IP | W | Sv | K | ERA | WHIP | K/9 | BB/9 | $2L | Pts |
| Nieve F | 28 | 40 | 2 | 0 | 33 | 5.12 | 1.41 | 7.5 | 3.9 | -$2 | 40 |
| Sanabia A | 22 | 100 | 6 | 0 | 74 | 4.83 | 1.50 | 6.7 | 3.0 | -$2 | 100 |
| Walters P | 26 | 40 | 2 | 0 | 38 | 5.02 | 1.49 | 8.5 | 3.6 | -$2 | 50 |
| Fulchino J | 31 | 40 | 2 | 0 | 33 | 4.80 | 1.45 | 7.4 | 3.6 | -$2 | 40 |
| Infante G | 23 | 60 | 3 | 0 | 47 | 4.31 | 1.75 | 7.1 | 7.0 | -$2 | 60 |

| Level | Leag | W | L | Sv | IP | H | K | ERA | WHIP | K/9 | BB/9 | HR/9 | GB/F |
|---|---|---|---|---|---|---|---|---|---|---|---|---|---|
| A | — | — | — | — | — | — | — | — | — | — | — | — | — |
| AA | — | — | — | — | — | — | — | — | — | — | — | — | — |
| AAA | PCL | 6 | 7 | 0 | 96 | 90 | 63 | 3.28 | 1.39 | 5.9 | 4.0 | 0.7 | — |

| Yr | Team | W | L | Sv | IP | H | K | ERA | WHIP | K/9 | BB/9 | HR/9 | GB/F |
|---|---|---|---|---|---|---|---|---|---|---|---|---|---|
| 07 | — | — | — | — | — | — | — | — | — | — | — | — | — |
| 08 | — | — | — | — | — | — | — | — | — | — | — | — | — |
| 09 | SD | 0 | 1 | 0 | 14 | 19 | 10 | 3.07 | 1.57 | 6.1 | 2.5 | 0.0 | 1.7 |
| 10 | SD | 0 | 1 | 0 | 8 | 18 | 9 | 11.88 | 2.64 | 9.7 | 4.3 | 1.1 | 1.3 |

| Yr | $1L | $2L | Pts | RAA | H% | HR/fb | S% | FIP | GS | CG | QS/DS | GR | Hld | Bln | Lead | OPS | 1st Hf | 2nd Hf | vs RH | vs LH |
|---|---|---|---|---|---|---|---|---|---|---|---|---|---|---|---|---|---|---|---|---|
| 07 | — | — | — | — | — | — | — | — | — | — | — | — | — | — | — | — | — | — | — | — |
| 08 | — | — | — | — | — | — | — | — | — | — | — | — | — | — | — | — | — | — | — | — |
| 09 | -$2 | -$2 | 10 | +2 | 41% | 0% | 78% | 2.65 | 2 | 0 | 0/0 | 3 | 0 | 0 | −0.8 | .750 | — | .750 | .954 | .235 |
| 10 | -$9 | -$17 | 0 | −7 | 52% | 8% | 52% | 4.04 | — | — | — | 14 | 2 | 0 | −2.3 | 1.049 | 1.258 | .701 | 1.330 | .697 |

Competition at RP — Stats in 2010 as RP

| Thr | Player | GR | ERA | IP/G | Sv-Hld |
|---|---|---|---|---|---|
| LH | Thatcher J | 65 | 1.29 | 0.5 | 0-11 |
| ▶ LH | Ramos C | 14 | 11.88 | 0.6 | 0-2 |

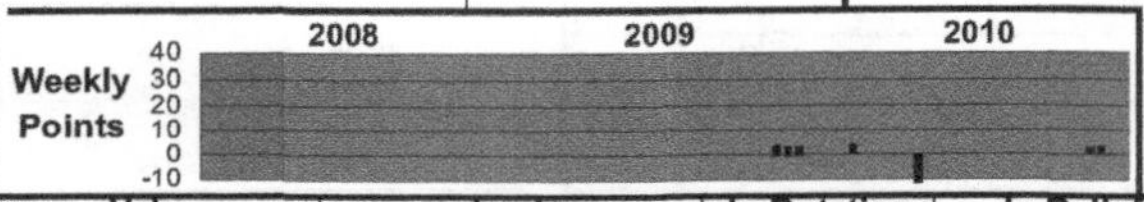


Ten-Year Trends

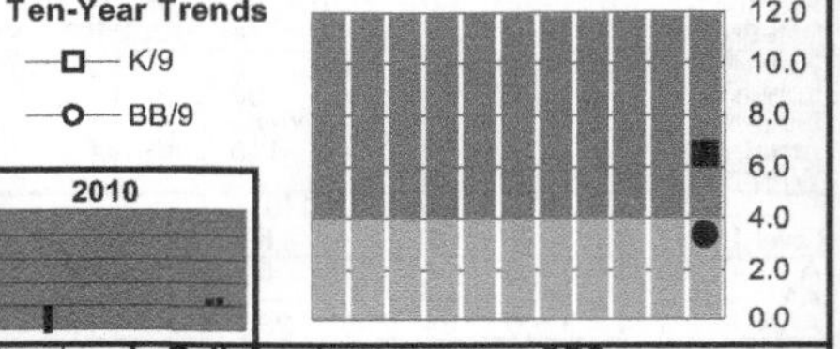


## ... Jon Rauch — 40 IP | $0 | 50 pts

RP-59 — Owned: 57% — RH

When their elite closer went down in Spring Training, the Twins turned to Rauch, and the sky-scraping reliever stepped up admirably for three months before being replaced by Matt Capps. A free agent, Rauch could entice some club to sign him as a closer, though the Twins would surely like to bring him back. (NN)

| Player | Age | IP | W | Sv | K | ERA | WHIP | K/9 | BB/9 | $2L | Pts |
|---|---|---|---|---|---|---|---|---|---|---|---|
| Rauch J | 32 | 40 | 2 | 0 | 30 | 4.01 | 1.31 | 6.7 | 2.6 | $0 | 50 |
| **Mini-Browser** | Age | IP | W | Sv | K | ERA | WHIP | K/9 | BB/9 | $2L | Pts |
| Coffey T | 30 | 60 | 3 | 0 | 46 | 4.22 | 1.30 | 6.9 | 2.8 | $1 | 70 |
| Hill S | 29 | 80 | 4 | 0 | 45 | 4.43 | 1.40 | 5.1 | 2.4 | $1 | 70 |
| Harang A | 32 | 100 | 5 | 0 | 74 | 4.76 | 1.33 | 6.7 | 2.4 | $0 | 110 |
| Peavy J | 29 | 40 | 3 | 0 | 34 | 4.40 | 1.28 | 7.6 | 3.1 | $0 | 50 |
| Harden R | 29 | 100 | 6 | 0 | 99 | 4.87 | 1.50 | 8.9 | 5.0 | $0 | 130 |

| Level | Leag | W | L | Sv | IP | H | K | ERA | WHIP | K/9 | BB/9 | HR/9 | GB/F |
|---|---|---|---|---|---|---|---|---|---|---|---|---|---|
| A | — | — | — | — | — | — | — | — | — | — | — | — | — |
| AA | — | — | — | — | — | — | — | — | — | — | — | — | — |
| AAA | — | — | — | — | — | — | — | — | — | — | — | — | — |

| Yr | Team | W | L | Sv | IP | H | K | ERA | WHIP | K/9 | BB/9 | HR/9 | GB/F |
|---|---|---|---|---|---|---|---|---|---|---|---|---|---|
| 07 | WAS | 8 | 4 | 4 | 87 | 75 | 71 | 3.61 | 1.10 | 7.3 | 2.2 | 0.7 | 0.6 |
| 08 | 2TM | 4 | 8 | 18 | 71 | 69 | 66 | 4.14 | 1.19 | 8.3 | 2.0 | 1.4 | 0.7 |
| 09 | 2TM | 7 | 3 | 2 | 70 | 70 | 49 | 3.60 | 1.33 | 6.3 | 3.0 | 0.8 | 0.8 |
| 10 | MIN | 3 | 1 | 21 | 57 | 61 | 46 | 3.12 | 1.30 | 7.2 | 2.2 | 0.5 | 0.9 |

| Yr | $1L | $2L | Pts | RAA | H% | HR/fb | S% | FIP | GS | CG | QS/DS | GR | Hld | Bln | Lead | OPS | 1st Hf | 2nd Hf | vs RH | vs LH |
|---|---|---|---|---|---|---|---|---|---|---|---|---|---|---|---|---|---|---|---|---|
| 07 | $9 | $6 | 180 | +2 | 28% | 5% | 69% | 3.34 | — | — | — | 88 | 33 | 6 | +0.6 | .619 | .599 | .642 | .618 | .622 |
| 08 | $7 | $3 | 190 | −4 | 30% | 12% | 70% | 4.07 | — | — | — | 74 | 6 | 6 | +0.6 | .742 | .627 | .958 | .734 | .750 |
| 09 | $2 | $1 | 120 | +2 | 30% | 6% | 75% | 3.95 | — | — | — | 75 | 17 | 3 | −0.5 | .722 | .734 | .704 | .718 | .724 |
| 10 | $7 | $0 | 180 | +6 | 32% | 4% | 76% | 3.11 | — | — | — | 59 | 2 | 4 | +1.3 | .671 | .671 | .669 | .607 | .739 |

Competition at RP — Stats in 2010 as RP

| Thr | Player | GR | ERA | IP/G | Sv-Hld |
|---|---|---|---|---|---|
| RH | Guerrier M | 74 | 3.17 | 1.0 | 1-23 |
| RH | Crain J | 71 | 3.04 | 1.0 | 1-21 |
| ▶ RH | Rauch J | 59 | 3.12 | 1.0 | 21-2 |
| RH | Burnett A | 41 | 5.29 | 1.2 | 0-2 |

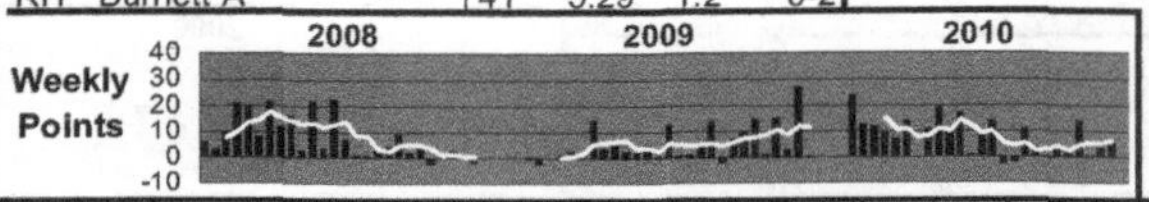


Ten-Year Trends

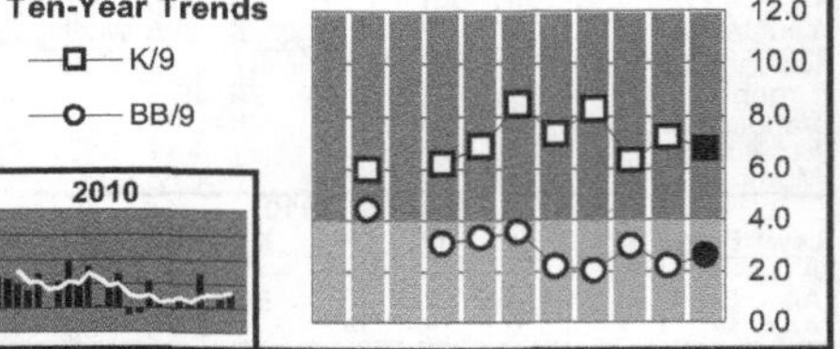


## . Chris Ray — 60 IP | $-2 | 60 pts

RP-63 — Owned: 0% — RH

Following Tommy John surgery in 2008, Ray recaptured his 93-94MLB fastball, but his control and the bite on his slider have yet to resurface. Until they do, Ray will be lucky to work the 6th and 7th innings for teams who are hoping that he regains his closer form. He is entering his third arbitration year. (PB)

| Player | Age | IP | W | Sv | K | ERA | WHIP | K/9 | BB/9 | $2L | Pts |
|---|---|---|---|---|---|---|---|---|---|---|---|
| Ray C | 29 | 60 | 4 | 0 | 43 | 4.84 | 1.48 | 6.5 | 4.6 | -$2 | 60 |
| **Mini-Browser** | Age | IP | W | Sv | K | ERA | WHIP | K/9 | BB/9 | $2L | Pts |
| Cook A | 32 | 120 | 7 | 0 | 51 | 4.78 | 1.41 | 3.8 | 2.7 | -$2 | 90 |
| Demel S | 25 | 60 | 3 | 3 | 63 | 4.92 | 1.62 | 9.5 | 4.4 | -$2 | 90 |
| Rogers M | 25 | 40 | 2 | 0 | 46 | 4.53 | 1.56 | 10.4 | 4.8 | -$2 | 50 |
| Parnell B | 26 | 60 | 2 | 2 | 52 | 4.59 | 1.54 | 7.8 | 3.7 | -$2 | 70 |
| Silva C | 31 | 160 | 10 | 0 | 76 | 5.24 | 1.35 | 4.3 | 1.8 | -$2 | 130 |

| Level | Leag | W | L | Sv | IP | H | K | ERA | WHIP | K/9 | BB/9 | HR/9 | GB/F |
|---|---|---|---|---|---|---|---|---|---|---|---|---|---|
| A | CAL | 0 | 1 | 0 | 1 | 7 | 1 | 10.80 | 4.20 | 5.4 | 0.0 | 0.0 | — |
| AA | — | — | — | — | — | — | — | — | — | — | — | — | — |
| AAA | — | — | — | — | — | — | — | — | — | — | — | — | — |

| Yr | Team | W | L | Sv | IP | H | K | ERA | WHIP | K/9 | BB/9 | HR/9 | GB/F |
|---|---|---|---|---|---|---|---|---|---|---|---|---|---|
| 07 | BAL | 5 | 6 | 16 | 42 | 35 | 44 | 4.43 | 1.24 | 9.3 | 3.8 | 1.1 | 1.2 |
| 08 | — | — | — | — | — | — | — | — | — | — | — | — | — |
| 09 | BAL | 0 | 4 | 0 | 43 | 64 | 39 | 7.27 | 2.01 | 8.1 | 4.8 | 1.7 | 1.1 |
| 10 | 2TM | 5 | 0 | 2 | 55 | 48 | 31 | 3.72 | 1.31 | 5.0 | 4.0 | 0.8 | 0.8 |

| Yr | $1L | $2L | Pts | RAA | H% | HR/fb | S% | FIP | GS | CG | QS/DS | GR | Hld | Bln | Lead | OPS | 1st Hf | 2nd Hf | vs RH | vs LH |
|---|---|---|---|---|---|---|---|---|---|---|---|---|---|---|---|---|---|---|---|---|
| 07 | $6 | $2 | 170 | −3 | 28% | 12% | 67% | 4.03 | — | — | — | 43 | 0 | 4 | +1.4 | .674 | .698 | .437 | .673 | .671 |
| 08 | — | — | — | — | — | — | — | — | — | — | — | — | — | — | — | — | — | — | — | — |
| 09 | -$6 | -$10 | 0 | −17 | 40% | 14% | 66% | 5.49 | — | — | — | 46 | 6 | 3 | −0.6 | .985 | 1.033 | .932 | .790 | 1.249 |
| 10 | -$1 | -$7 | 90 | +2 | 26% | 6% | 74% | 4.65 | — | — | — | 63 | 9 | 2 | +0.5 | .701 | .620 | .870 | .617 | .817 |

Competition at RP — Stats in 2010 as RP

| Thr | Player | GR | ERA | IP/G | Sv-Hld |
|---|---|---|---|---|---|
| RH | Wilson B | 70 | 1.81 | 1.1 | 48-0 |
| RH | Romo S | 68 | 2.18 | 0.9 | 0-21 |
| RH | Mota G | 56 | 4.33 | 1.0 | 1-8 |
| RH | Casilla S | 52 | 1.95 | 1.1 | 2-11 |

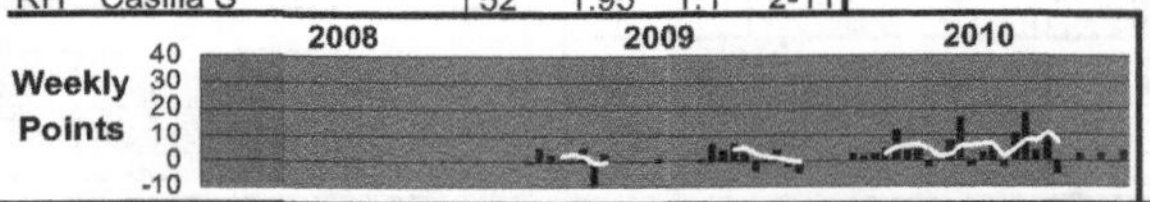


Ten-Year Trends

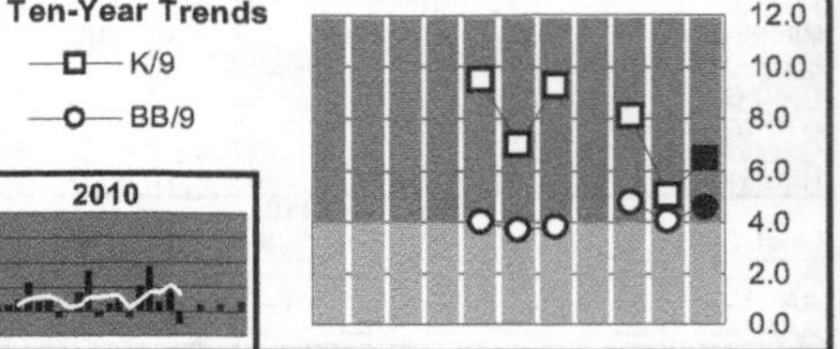


*For more stats, visit www.Rotolympus.com.*

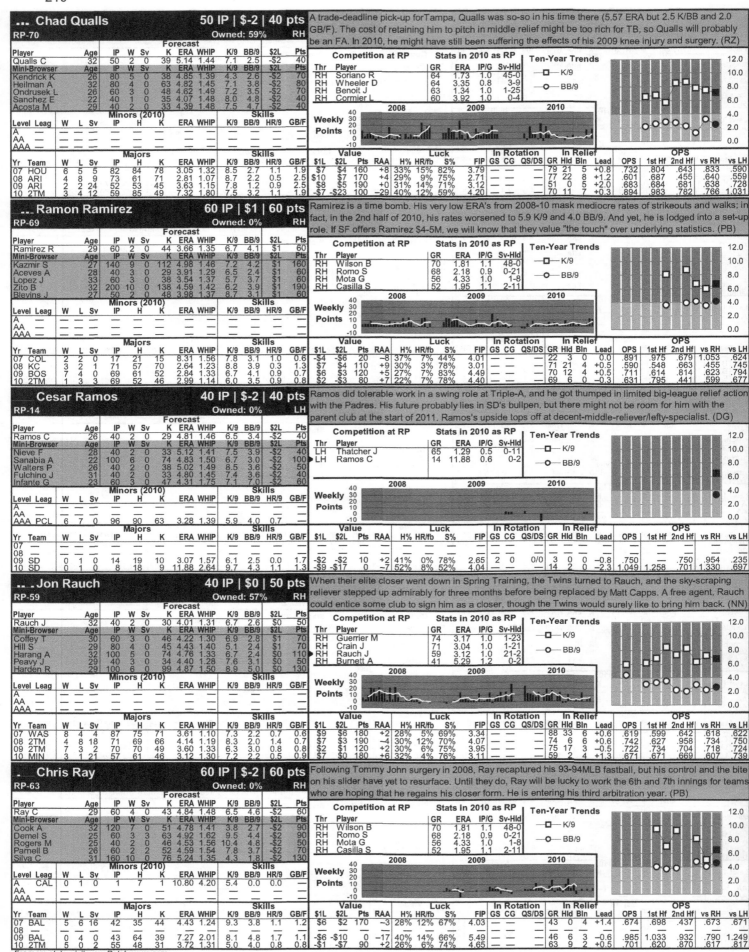

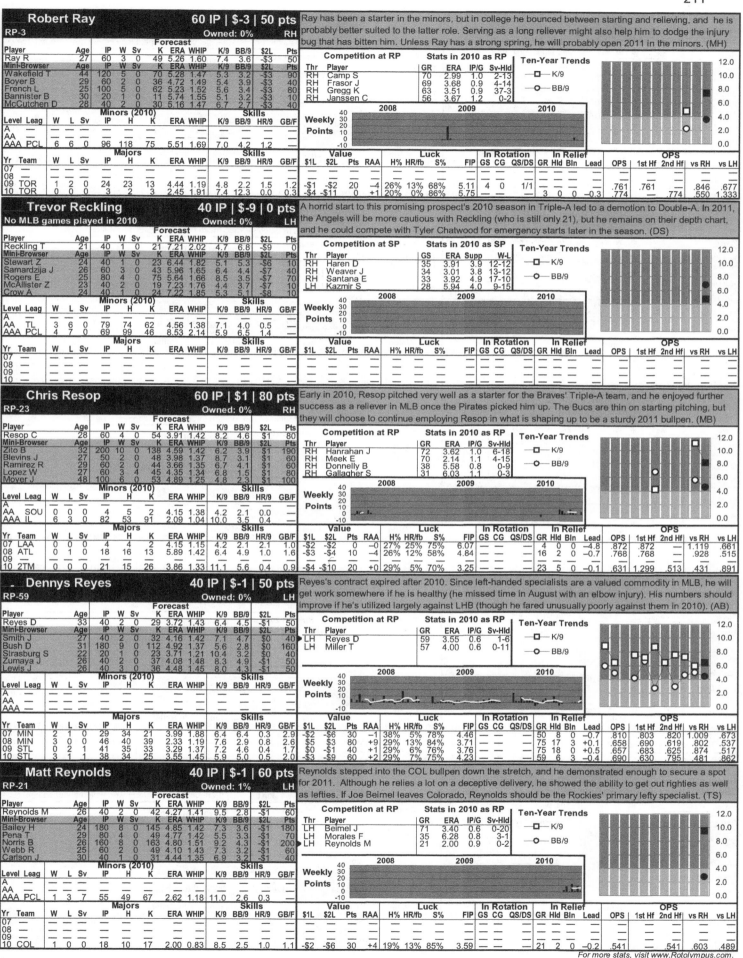

## Robert Ray — 60 IP | $-3 | 50 pts

RP-3 — Owned: 0% — RH

| Player | Age | IP | W | Sv | K | ERA | WHIP | K/9 | BB/9 | $2L | Pts |
|---|---|---|---|---|---|---|---|---|---|---|---|
| **Forecast** | | | | | | | | | | | |
| Ray R | 27 | 60 | 3 | 0 | 49 | 5.26 | 1.60 | 7.4 | 3.6 | -$3 | 50 |
| **Mini-Browser** | Age | IP | W | Sv | K | ERA | WHIP | K/9 | BB/9 | $2L | Pts |
| Wakefield T | 44 | 120 | 5 | 0 | 70 | 5.28 | 1.47 | 5.3 | 3.2 | -$3 | 90 |
| Boyer B | 29 | 60 | 2 | 0 | 36 | 4.72 | 1.49 | 5.4 | 3.9 | -$3 | 40 |
| French L | 25 | 100 | 5 | 0 | 62 | 5.23 | 1.52 | 5.6 | 3.4 | -$3 | 80 |
| Bannister B | 30 | 20 | 1 | 0 | 11 | 5.74 | 1.55 | 5.1 | 3.2 | -$3 | 10 |
| McCutchen D | 28 | 40 | 2 | 0 | 30 | 5.16 | 1.47 | 6.7 | 2.7 | -$3 | 40 |

Minors (2010) / Skills

| Level | Leag | W | L | Sv | IP | H | K | ERA | WHIP | K/9 | BB/9 | HR/9 | GB/F |
|---|---|---|---|---|---|---|---|---|---|---|---|---|---|
| A | — | — | — | — | — | — | — | — | — | — | — | — | — |
| AA | — | — | — | — | — | — | — | — | — | — | — | — | — |
| AAA | PCL | 6 | 6 | 0 | 96 | 118 | 75 | 5.51 | 1.69 | 7.0 | 4.2 | 1.2 | — |

Majors / Skills

| Yr | Team | W | L | Sv | IP | H | K | ERA | WHIP | K/9 | BB/9 | HR/9 | GB/F |
|---|---|---|---|---|---|---|---|---|---|---|---|---|---|
| 07 | — | — | — | — | — | — | — | — | — | — | — | — | — |
| 08 | — | — | — | — | — | — | — | — | — | — | — | — | — |
| 09 | TOR | 1 | 2 | 0 | 24 | 23 | 13 | 4.44 | 1.19 | 4.8 | 2.2 | 1.5 | 1.2 |
| 10 | TOR | 0 | 0 | 0 | 3 | 2 | 3 | 2.45 | 1.91 | 7.4 | 12.3 | 0.0 | 0.3 |

Ray has been a starter in the minors, but in college he bounced between starting and relieving, and he is probably better suited to the latter role. Serving as a long reliever might also help him to dodge the injury bug that has bitten him. Unless Ray has a strong spring, he will probably open 2011 in the minors. (MH)

Competition at RP — Stats in 2010 as RP

| Thr | Player | GR | ERA | IP/G | Sv-Hld |
|---|---|---|---|---|---|
| RH | Camp S | 70 | 2.99 | 1.0 | 2-13 |
| RH | Frasor J | 69 | 3.68 | 0.9 | 4-14 |
| RH | Gregg K | 63 | 3.51 | 0.9 | 37-3 |
| RH | Janssen C | 56 | 3.67 | 1.2 | 0-2 |

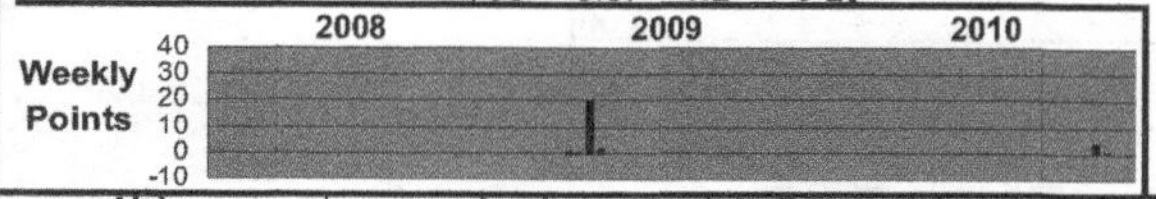
2008
2009
2010
Weekly Points
40
30
20
10
0
-10

Ten-Year Trends — K/9 — BB/9

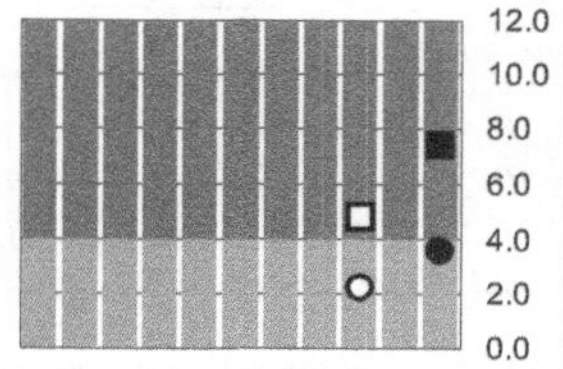
12.0
10.0
8.0
6.0
4.0
2.0
0.0

| Yr | $1L | $2L | Pts | RAA | H% | HR/fb | S% | FIP | GS | CG | QS/DS | GR | Hld | Bln | Lead | OPS | 1st Hf | 2nd Hf | vs RH | vs LH |
|---|---|---|---|---|---|---|---|---|---|---|---|---|---|---|---|---|---|---|---|---|
| | **Value** | | | | **Luck** | | | | **In Rotation** | | | **In Relief** | | | | **OPS** | | | | |
| 07 | — | — | — | — | — | — | — | — | — | — | — | — | — | — | — | — | — | — | — | — |
| 08 | — | — | — | — | — | — | — | — | — | — | — | — | — | — | — | — | — | — | — | — |
| 09 | -$1 | -$2 | 20 | −4 | 26% | 13% | 68% | 5.11 | 4 | 0 | 1/1 | — | — | — | — | .761 | .761 | — | .846 | .677 |
| 10 | -$4 | -$11 | 0 | +1 | 20% | 0% | 86% | 5.75 | — | — | — | 3 | 0 | 0 | −0.3 | .774 | — | .774 | .550 | 1.333 |

## Trevor Reckling — 40 IP | $-9 | 0 pts

No MLB games played in 2010 — Owned: 0% — LH

| Player | Age | IP | W | Sv | K | ERA | WHIP | K/9 | BB/9 | $2L | Pts |
|---|---|---|---|---|---|---|---|---|---|---|---|
| **Forecast** | | | | | | | | | | | |
| Reckling T | 21 | 40 | 1 | 0 | 21 | 7.21 | 2.02 | 4.7 | 6.8 | -$9 | 0 |
| **Mini-Browser** | Age | IP | W | Sv | K | ERA | WHIP | K/9 | BB/9 | $2L | Pts |
| Stewart Z | 24 | 40 | 1 | 0 | 23 | 6.44 | 1.82 | 5.1 | 5.3 | -$6 | 10 |
| Samardzija J | 26 | 60 | 3 | 0 | 43 | 5.96 | 1.65 | 6.4 | 4.4 | -$7 | 40 |
| Rogers E | 25 | 80 | 4 | 0 | 75 | 5.64 | 1.66 | 8.5 | 3.5 | -$7 | 70 |
| McAllister Z | 23 | 40 | 2 | 0 | 19 | 7.23 | 1.76 | 4.4 | 3.7 | -$7 | 10 |
| Crow A | 24 | 40 | 1 | 0 | 24 | 7.22 | 1.85 | 5.3 | 5.1 | -$8 | 10 |

Minors (2010) / Skills

| Level | Leag | W | L | Sv | IP | H | K | ERA | WHIP | K/9 | BB/9 | HR/9 | GB/F |
|---|---|---|---|---|---|---|---|---|---|---|---|---|---|
| A | — | — | — | — | — | — | — | — | — | — | — | — | — |
| AA | TL | 3 | 6 | 0 | 79 | 74 | 62 | 4.56 | 1.38 | 7.1 | 4.0 | 0.5 | — |
| AAA | PCL | 4 | 7 | 0 | 69 | 99 | 46 | 8.53 | 2.14 | 5.9 | 6.5 | 1.4 | — |

Majors / Skills

| Yr | Team | W | L | Sv | IP | H | K | ERA | WHIP | K/9 | BB/9 | HR/9 | GB/F |
|---|---|---|---|---|---|---|---|---|---|---|---|---|---|
| 07 | — | — | — | — | — | — | — | — | — | — | — | — | — |
| 08 | — | — | — | — | — | — | — | — | — | — | — | — | — |
| 09 | — | — | — | — | — | — | — | — | — | — | — | — | — |
| 10 | — | — | — | — | — | — | — | — | — | — | — | — | — |

A horrid start to this promising prospect's 2010 season in Triple-A led to a demotion to Double-A. In 2011, the Angels will be more cautious with Reckling (who is still only 21), but he remains on their depth chart, and he could compete with Tyler Chatwood for emergency starts later in the season. (DS)

Competition at SP — Stats in 2010 as SP

| Thr | Player | GS | ERA | Supp | W-L |
|---|---|---|---|---|---|
| RH | Haren D | 35 | 3.91 | 3.9 | 12-12 |
| RH | Weaver J | 34 | 3.01 | 3.8 | 13-12 |
| RH | Santana E | 33 | 3.92 | 4.9 | 17-10 |
| LH | Kazmir S | 28 | 5.94 | 4.0 | 9-15 |

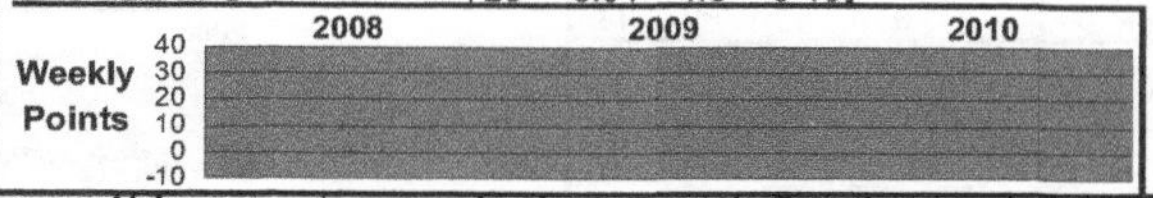
2008
2009
2010
Weekly Points
40
30
20
10
0
-10

Ten-Year Trends — K/9 — BB/9

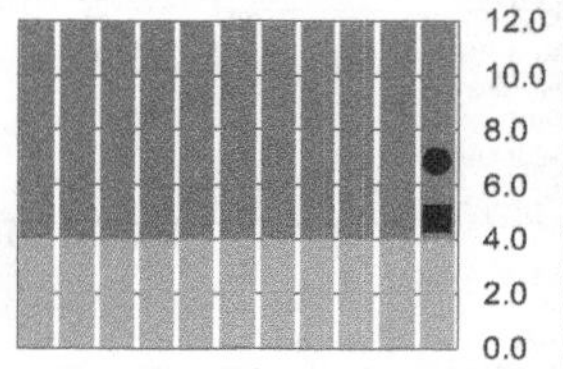
12.0
10.0
8.0
6.0
4.0
2.0
0.0

| Yr | $1L | $2L | Pts | RAA | H% | HR/fb | S% | FIP | GS | CG | QS/DS | GR | Hld | Bln | Lead | OPS | 1st Hf | 2nd Hf | vs RH | vs LH |
|---|---|---|---|---|---|---|---|---|---|---|---|---|---|---|---|---|---|---|---|---|
| | **Value** | | | | **Luck** | | | | **In Rotation** | | | **In Relief** | | | | **OPS** | | | | |
| 07 | — | — | — | — | — | — | — | — | — | — | — | — | — | — | — | — | — | — | — | — |
| 08 | — | — | — | — | — | — | — | — | — | — | — | — | — | — | — | — | — | — | — | — |
| 09 | — | — | — | — | — | — | — | — | — | — | — | — | — | — | — | — | — | — | — | — |
| 10 | — | — | — | — | — | — | — | — | — | — | — | — | — | — | — | — | — | — | — | — |

## Chris Resop — 60 IP | $1 | 80 pts

RP-23 — Owned: 0% — RH

| Player | Age | IP | W | Sv | K | ERA | WHIP | K/9 | BB/9 | $2L | Pts |
|---|---|---|---|---|---|---|---|---|---|---|---|
| **Forecast** | | | | | | | | | | | |
| Resop C | 28 | 60 | 4 | 0 | 54 | 3.91 | 1.42 | 8.2 | 4.6 | $1 | 80 |
| **Mini-Browser** | Age | IP | W | Sv | K | ERA | WHIP | K/9 | BB/9 | $2L | Pts |
| Zito B | 32 | 200 | 10 | 0 | 138 | 4.59 | 1.42 | 6.2 | 3.9 | $1 | 190 |
| Blevins J | 27 | 50 | 2 | 0 | 48 | 3.98 | 1.37 | 8.7 | 3.1 | $1 | 60 |
| Ramirez R | 29 | 60 | 2 | 0 | 44 | 3.66 | 1.35 | 6.7 | 4.1 | $1 | 60 |
| Lopez W | 27 | 60 | 3 | 4 | 45 | 4.35 | 1.34 | 6.8 | 1.5 | $1 | 80 |
| Moyer J | 48 | 100 | 6 | 0 | 53 | 4.89 | 1.25 | 4.8 | 2.3 | $1 | 100 |

Minors (2010) / Skills

| Level | Leag | W | L | Sv | IP | H | K | ERA | WHIP | K/9 | BB/9 | HR/9 | GB/F |
|---|---|---|---|---|---|---|---|---|---|---|---|---|---|
| A | — | — | — | — | — | — | — | — | — | — | — | — | — |
| AA | SOU | 0 | 0 | 0 | 4 | 5 | 2 | 4.15 | 1.38 | 4.2 | 2.1 | 0.0 | — |
| AAA | IL | 6 | 3 | 0 | 82 | 53 | 91 | 2.09 | 1.04 | 10.0 | 3.5 | 0.4 | — |

Majors / Skills

| Yr | Team | W | L | Sv | IP | H | K | ERA | WHIP | K/9 | BB/9 | HR/9 | GB/F |
|---|---|---|---|---|---|---|---|---|---|---|---|---|---|
| 07 | LAA | 0 | 0 | 0 | 4 | 4 | 2 | 4.15 | 1.15 | 4.2 | 2.1 | 2.1 | 1.0 |
| 08 | ATL | 0 | 1 | 0 | 18 | 16 | 13 | 5.89 | 1.42 | 6.4 | 4.9 | 1.0 | 1.6 |
| 09 | — | — | — | — | — | — | — | — | — | — | — | — | — |
| 10 | 2TM | 0 | 0 | 0 | 21 | 15 | 26 | 3.86 | 1.33 | 11.1 | 5.6 | 0.4 | 0.9 |

Early in 2010, Resop pitched very well as a starter for the Braves' Triple-A team, and he enjoyed further success as a reliever in MLB once the Pirates picked him up. The Bucs are thin on starting pitching, but they will choose to continue employing Resop in what is shaping up to be a sturdy 2011 bullpen. (MB)

Competition at RP — Stats in 2010 as RP

| Thr | Player | GR | ERA | IP/G | Sv-Hld |
|---|---|---|---|---|---|
| RH | Hanrahan J | 72 | 3.62 | 1.0 | 6-18 |
| RH | Meek E | 70 | 2.14 | 1.1 | 4-15 |
| RH | Donnelly B | 38 | 5.58 | 0.8 | 0-9 |
| RH | Gallagher S | 31 | 6.03 | 1.1 | 0-3 |

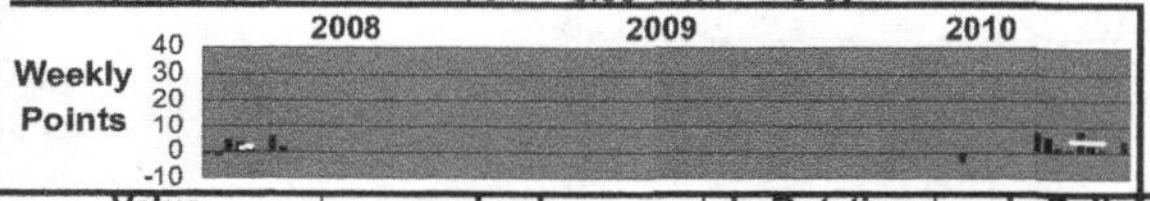
2008
2009
2010
Weekly Points
40
30
20
10
0
-10

Ten-Year Trends — K/9 — BB/9

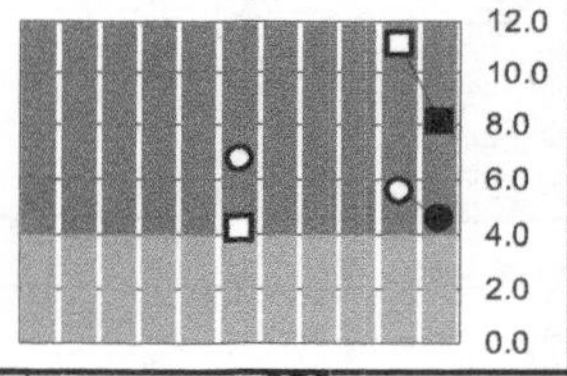
12.0
10.0
8.0
6.0
4.0
2.0
0.0

| Yr | $1L | $2L | Pts | RAA | H% | HR/fb | S% | FIP | GS | CG | QS/DS | GR | Hld | Bln | Lead | OPS | 1st Hf | 2nd Hf | vs RH | vs LH |
|---|---|---|---|---|---|---|---|---|---|---|---|---|---|---|---|---|---|---|---|---|
| | **Value** | | | | **Luck** | | | | **In Rotation** | | | **In Relief** | | | | **OPS** | | | | |
| 07 | -$2 | -$2 | 0 | −0 | 27% | 25% | 75% | 6.07 | — | — | — | 4 | 0 | 0 | −4.8 | .872 | .872 | — | 1.119 | .661 |
| 08 | -$3 | -$4 | 10 | −4 | 26% | 12% | 58% | 4.84 | — | — | — | 16 | 2 | 0 | −0.7 | .768 | .768 | — | .928 | .515 |
| 09 | — | — | — | — | — | — | — | — | — | — | — | — | — | — | — | — | — | — | — | — |
| 10 | -$4 | -$10 | 20 | +0 | 29% | 5% | 70% | 3.25 | — | — | — | 23 | 5 | 0 | −0.1 | .631 | 1.299 | .513 | .431 | .891 |

## Dennys Reyes — 40 IP | $-1 | 50 pts

RP-59 — Owned: 0% — LH

| Player | Age | IP | W | Sv | K | ERA | WHIP | K/9 | BB/9 | $2L | Pts |
|---|---|---|---|---|---|---|---|---|---|---|---|
| **Forecast** | | | | | | | | | | | |
| Reyes D | 33 | 40 | 2 | 0 | 29 | 3.72 | 1.43 | 6.4 | 4.5 | -$1 | 50 |
| **Mini-Browser** | Age | IP | W | Sv | K | ERA | WHIP | K/9 | BB/9 | $2L | Pts |
| Smith J | 27 | 40 | 2 | 0 | 32 | 4.16 | 1.42 | 7.1 | 4.7 | $0 | 40 |
| Bush D | 31 | 180 | 9 | 0 | 112 | 4.92 | 1.37 | 5.6 | 2.8 | $0 | 160 |
| Strasburg S | 22 | 20 | 1 | 0 | 23 | 3.71 | 1.21 | 10.4 | 3.2 | $0 | 40 |
| Zumaya J | 26 | 40 | 2 | 0 | 37 | 4.08 | 1.48 | 8.3 | 4.9 | -$1 | 50 |
| Lewis J | 26 | 40 | 3 | 0 | 36 | 4.48 | 1.45 | 8.0 | 4.3 | -$1 | 50 |

Minors (2010) / Skills

| Level | Leag | W | L | Sv | IP | H | K | ERA | WHIP | K/9 | BB/9 | HR/9 | GB/F |
|---|---|---|---|---|---|---|---|---|---|---|---|---|---|
| A | — | — | — | — | — | — | — | — | — | — | — | — | — |
| AA | — | — | — | — | — | — | — | — | — | — | — | — | — |
| AAA | — | — | — | — | — | — | — | — | — | — | — | — | — |

Majors / Skills

| Yr | Team | W | L | Sv | IP | H | K | ERA | WHIP | K/9 | BB/9 | HR/9 | GB/F |
|---|---|---|---|---|---|---|---|---|---|---|---|---|---|
| 07 | MIN | 2 | 1 | 0 | 29 | 34 | 21 | 3.99 | 1.88 | 6.4 | 6.4 | 0.3 | 2.9 |
| 08 | MIN | 3 | 0 | 0 | 46 | 40 | 39 | 2.33 | 1.19 | 7.6 | 2.9 | 0.8 | 2.6 |
| 09 | STL | 0 | 2 | 1 | 41 | 35 | 33 | 3.29 | 1.37 | 7.2 | 4.6 | 0.4 | 1.7 |
| 10 | STL | 3 | 1 | 1 | 38 | 34 | 25 | 3.55 | 1.45 | 5.9 | 5.0 | 0.5 | 2.0 |

Reyes's contract expired after 2010. Since left-handed specialists are a valued commodity in MLB, he will get work somewhere if he is healthy (he missed time in August with an elbow injury). His numbers should improve if he's utilized largely against LHB (though he fared unusually poorly against them in 2010). (AB)

Competition at RP — Stats in 2010 as RP

| Thr | Player | GR | ERA | IP/G | Sv-Hld |
|---|---|---|---|---|---|
| ▶ LH | Reyes D | 59 | 3.55 | 0.6 | 1-6 |
| LH | Miller T | 57 | 4.00 | 0.6 | 0-11 |

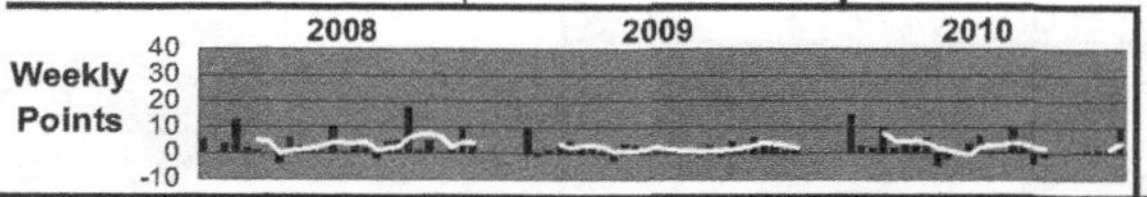
2008
2009
2010
Weekly Points
40
30
20
10
0
-10

Ten-Year Trends — K/9 — BB/9

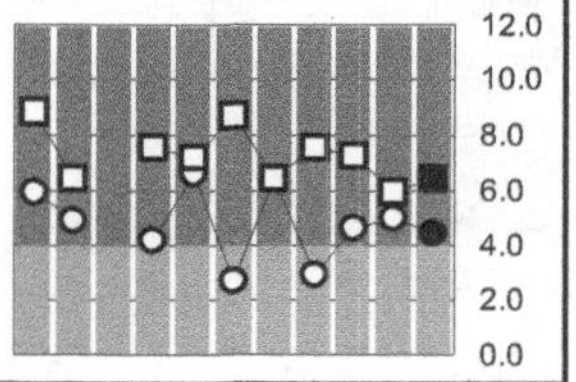
12.0
10.0
8.0
6.0
4.0
2.0
0.0

| Yr | $1L | $2L | Pts | RAA | H% | HR/fb | S% | FIP | GS | CG | QS/DS | GR | Hld | Bln | Lead | OPS | 1st Hf | 2nd Hf | vs RH | vs LH |
|---|---|---|---|---|---|---|---|---|---|---|---|---|---|---|---|---|---|---|---|---|
| | **Value** | | | | **Luck** | | | | **In Rotation** | | | **In Relief** | | | | **OPS** | | | | |
| 07 | -$2 | -$6 | 30 | −1 | 38% | 5% | 78% | 4.46 | — | — | — | 50 | 8 | 0 | −0.7 | .810 | .803 | .820 | 1.009 | .673 |
| 08 | $5 | $3 | 80 | +9 | 29% | 13% | 84% | 3.71 | — | — | — | 75 | 17 | 3 | +0.1 | .658 | .690 | .619 | .802 | .537 |
| 09 | $0 | -$1 | 40 | +1 | 29% | 6% | 76% | 3.76 | — | — | — | 75 | 18 | 0 | +0.5 | .657 | .683 | .625 | .874 | .517 |
| 10 | -$3 | -$9 | 60 | +2 | 29% | 7% | 75% | 4.23 | — | — | — | 59 | 6 | 3 | −0.4 | .690 | .630 | .795 | .481 | .862 |

## Matt Reynolds — 40 IP | $-1 | 60 pts

RP-21 — Owned: 1% — LH

| Player | Age | IP | W | Sv | K | ERA | WHIP | K/9 | BB/9 | $2L | Pts |
|---|---|---|---|---|---|---|---|---|---|---|---|
| **Forecast** | | | | | | | | | | | |
| Reynolds M | 26 | 40 | 2 | 0 | 42 | 4.27 | 1.41 | 9.5 | 2.8 | -$1 | 60 |
| **Mini-Browser** | Age | IP | W | Sv | K | ERA | WHIP | K/9 | BB/9 | $2L | Pts |
| Bailey H | 24 | 180 | 8 | 0 | 145 | 4.85 | 1.42 | 7.3 | 3.6 | -$1 | 180 |
| Pena T | 29 | 80 | 4 | 0 | 49 | 4.77 | 1.42 | 5.5 | 3.3 | -$1 | 70 |
| Norris B | 26 | 160 | 8 | 0 | 163 | 4.80 | 1.51 | 9.2 | 4.3 | -$1 | 200 |
| Webb R | 25 | 60 | 2 | 0 | 49 | 4.10 | 1.43 | 7.3 | 3.2 | -$1 | 60 |
| Carlson J | 30 | 40 | 1 | 0 | 31 | 4.44 | 1.35 | 6.9 | 3.2 | -$1 | 40 |

Minors (2010) / Skills

| Level | Leag | W | L | Sv | IP | H | K | ERA | WHIP | K/9 | BB/9 | HR/9 | GB/F |
|---|---|---|---|---|---|---|---|---|---|---|---|---|---|
| A | — | — | — | — | — | — | — | — | — | — | — | — | — |
| AA | — | — | — | — | — | — | — | — | — | — | — | — | — |
| AAA | PCL | 1 | 3 | 7 | 55 | 49 | 67 | 2.62 | 1.18 | 11.0 | 2.6 | 0.3 | — |

Majors / Skills

| Yr | Team | W | L | Sv | IP | H | K | ERA | WHIP | K/9 | BB/9 | HR/9 | GB/F |
|---|---|---|---|---|---|---|---|---|---|---|---|---|---|
| 07 | — | — | — | — | — | — | — | — | — | — | — | — | — |
| 08 | — | — | — | — | — | — | — | — | — | — | — | — | — |
| 09 | — | — | — | — | — | — | — | — | — | — | — | — | — |
| 10 | COL | 1 | 0 | 0 | 18 | 10 | 17 | 2.00 | 0.83 | 8.5 | 2.5 | 1.0 | 1.1 |

Reynolds stepped into the COL bullpen down the stretch, and he demonstrated enough to secure a spot for 2011. Although he relies a lot on a deceptive delivery, he showed the ability to get out righties as well as lefties. If Joe Beimel leaves Colorado, Reynolds should be the Rockies' primary lefty specialist. (TS)

Competition at RP — Stats in 2010 as RP

| Thr | Player | GR | ERA | IP/G | Sv-Hld |
|---|---|---|---|---|---|
| LH | Beimel J | 71 | 3.40 | 0.6 | 0-20 |
| LH | Morales F | 35 | 6.28 | 0.8 | 3-1 |
| ▶ LH | Reynolds M | 21 | 2.00 | 0.9 | 0-2 |

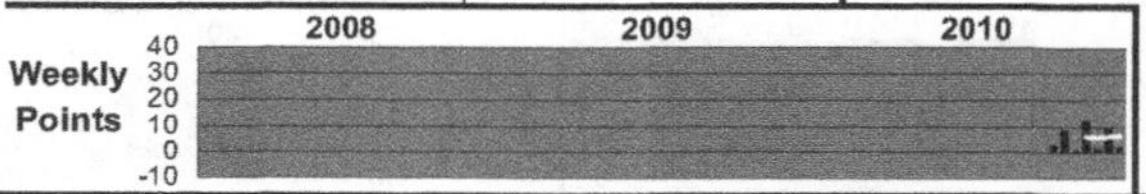
2008
2009
2010
Weekly Points
40
30
20
10
0
-10

Ten-Year Trends — K/9 — BB/9

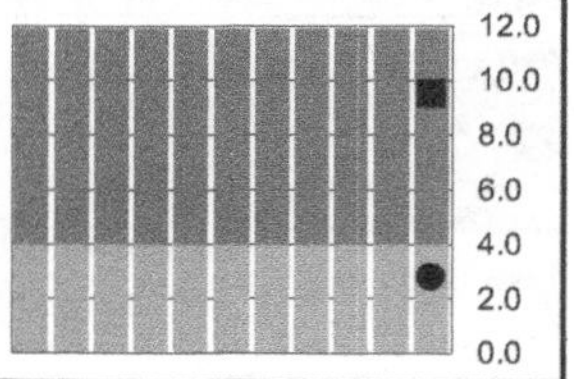
12.0
10.0
8.0
6.0
4.0
2.0
0.0

| Yr | $1L | $2L | Pts | RAA | H% | HR/fb | S% | FIP | GS | CG | QS/DS | GR | Hld | Bln | Lead | OPS | 1st Hf | 2nd Hf | vs RH | vs LH |
|---|---|---|---|---|---|---|---|---|---|---|---|---|---|---|---|---|---|---|---|---|
| | **Value** | | | | **Luck** | | | | **In Rotation** | | | **In Relief** | | | | **OPS** | | | | |
| 07 | — | — | — | — | — | — | — | — | — | — | — | — | — | — | — | — | — | — | — | — |
| 08 | — | — | — | — | — | — | — | — | — | — | — | — | — | — | — | — | — | — | — | — |
| 09 | — | — | — | — | — | — | — | — | — | — | — | — | — | — | — | — | — | — | — | — |
| 10 | -$2 | -$6 | 30 | +4 | 19% | 13% | 85% | 3.59 | — | — | — | 21 | 2 | 0 | −0.2 | .541 | — | .541 | .603 | .489 |

## Arthur Rhodes — 60 IP | $5 | 100 pts

RP-70 — Owned: 4% — LH

The old man was indispensable for the Reds for four months, until overuse wore out his 40-year-old body. Rhodes can still set down all types of hitters, but he needs more careful spotting (no more 35-inning first halves), and he cannot work on consecutive days. He's still one of the best lefty set-up guys around. (SW)

| Player | Age | IP | W | Sv | K | ERA | WHIP | K/9 | BB/9 | $2L | Pts |
|---|---|---|---|---|---|---|---|---|---|---|---|
| **Forecast** | | | | | | | | | | | |
| Rhodes A | 41 | 60 | 4 | 0 | 55 | 2.93 | 1.20 | 8.2 | 3.5 | $5 | 100 |
| **Mini-Browser** | **Age** | **IP** | **W** | **Sv** | **K** | **ERA** | **WHIP** | **K/9** | **BB/9** | **$2L** | **Pts** |
| Benoit J | 33 | 60 | 2 | 2 | 54 | 3.38 | 1.10 | 8.1 | 3.4 | $6 | 90 |
| Pettitte A | 38 | 140 | 10 | 0 | 97 | 4.31 | 1.37 | 6.2 | 3.3 | $6 | 170 |
| Breslow C | 30 | 75 | 4 | 2 | 65 | 3.61 | 1.24 | 7.7 | 3.9 | $6 | 110 |
| LeBlanc W | 26 | 180 | 10 | 0 | 148 | 4.36 | 1.36 | 7.4 | 3.1 | $5 | 210 |
| Cecil B | 24 | 160 | 11 | 0 | 116 | 4.58 | 1.39 | 6.5 | 3.3 | $5 | 200 |

Minors (2010)

| Level | Leag | W | L | Sv | IP | H | K | ERA | WHIP | K/9 | BB/9 | HR/9 | GB/F |
|---|---|---|---|---|---|---|---|---|---|---|---|---|---|
| A | — | — | — | — | — | — | — | — | — | — | — | — | — |
| AA | — | — | — | — | — | — | — | — | — | — | — | — | — |
| AAA | — | — | — | — | — | — | — | — | — | — | — | — | — |

Competition at RP / Stats in 2010 as RP

| Thr | Player | GR | ERA | IP/G | Sv-Hld |
|---|---|---|---|---|---|
| LH | Rhodes A | 70 | 2.29 | 0.8 | 0-26 |
| LH | Herrera D | 36 | 3.91 | 0.6 | 0-9 |
| LH | Bray B | 35 | 4.13 | 0.8 | 0-2 |
| LH | Chapman A | 15 | 2.03 | 0.9 | 0-4 |

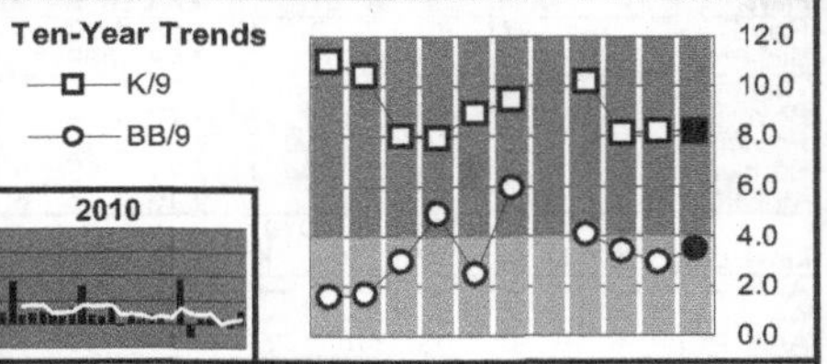


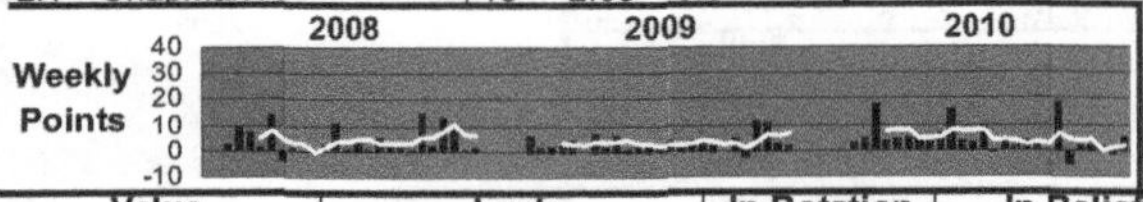


Majors

| Yr | Team | W | L | Sv | IP | H | K | ERA | WHIP | K/9 | BB/9 | HR/9 | GB/F | $1L | $2L | Pts | RAA | H% | HR/fb | S% | FIP | GS | CG | QS/DS | GR | Hld | Bln | Lead | OPS | 1st Hf | 2nd Hf | vs RH | vs LH |
|---|---|---|---|---|---|---|---|---|---|---|---|---|---|---|---|---|---|---|---|---|---|---|---|---|---|---|---|---|---|---|---|---|---|
| 07 | — | — | — | — | — | — | — | — | — | — | — | — | — | — | — | — | — | — | — | — | — | — | — | — | — | — | — | — | — | — | — | — | — |
| 08 | 2TM | 4 | 1 | 2 | 35 | 28 | 40 | 2.04 | 1.25 | 10.2 | 4.1 | 0.0 | 0.6 | $2 | $3 | 100 | +7 | 33% | 0% | 82% | 2.34 | — | — | — | 61 | 24 | 1 | +0.6 | .566 | .615 | .515 | .708 | .453 |
| 09 | CIN | 1 | 1 | 0 | 53 | 37 | 48 | 2.53 | 1.07 | 8.1 | 3.4 | 0.5 | 1.0 | $4 | $2 | 70 | +8 | 25% | 5% | 78% | 3.26 | — | — | — | 66 | 25 | 2 | +0.4 | .576 | .533 | .630 | .740 | .380 |
| 10 | CIN | 4 | 4 | 0 | 55 | 38 | 50 | 2.29 | 1.02 | 8.2 | 2.9 | 0.7 | 0.8 | $4 | $1 | 100 | +11 | 24% | 6% | 81% | 3.31 | — | — | — | 70 | 26 | 2 | +0.7 | .574 | .523 | .654 | .535 | .623 |

## Clayton Richard — 180 IP | $8 | 230 pts

SP-33 — Owned: 70% — LH

The big "get" in the Jake Peavy deal, Richard in 2010 topped the 200-inning mark and solidified himself as a solid mid-rotation starter. He is cheap and relatively effective, a combination that makes him valuable to the Padres. Richard joins Mat Latos in being locks to make San Diego's 2011 rotation. (DG)

| Player | Age | IP | W | Sv | K | ERA | WHIP | K/9 | BB/9 | $2L | Pts |
|---|---|---|---|---|---|---|---|---|---|---|---|
| **Forecast** | | | | | | | | | | | |
| Richard C | 27 | 180 | 11 | 0 | 134 | 3.95 | 1.36 | 6.7 | 3.4 | $8 | 230 |
| **Mini-Browser** | **Age** | **IP** | **W** | **Sv** | **K** | **ERA** | **WHIP** | **K/9** | **BB/9** | **$2L** | **Pts** |
| Beckett J | 30 | 180 | 11 | 0 | 157 | 4.55 | 1.31 | 7.8 | 2.5 | $9 | 240 |
| Gonzalez G | 25 | 190 | 12 | 0 | 181 | 4.20 | 1.44 | 8.6 | 4.7 | $9 | 260 |
| Ogando A | 27 | 60 | 5 | 4 | 55 | 2.51 | 1.18 | 8.2 | 3.5 | $9 | 140 |
| Happ J | 28 | 160 | 10 | 0 | 126 | 4.00 | 1.32 | 7.1 | 3.6 | $8 | 210 |
| Thornton M | 34 | 60 | 4 | 4 | 68 | 2.99 | 1.11 | 10.2 | 3.0 | $8 | 140 |

Minors (2010)

| Level | Leag | W | L | Sv | IP | H | K | ERA | WHIP | K/9 | BB/9 | HR/9 | GB/F |
|---|---|---|---|---|---|---|---|---|---|---|---|---|---|
| A | — | — | — | — | — | — | — | — | — | — | — | — | — |
| AA | — | — | — | — | — | — | — | — | — | — | — | — | — |
| AAA | — | — | — | — | — | — | — | — | — | — | — | — | — |

Competition at SP / Stats in 2010 as SP

| Thr | Player | GS | ERA | Supp | W-L |
|---|---|---|---|---|---|
| RH | Garland J | 33 | 3.47 | 3.8 | 14-12 |
| LH | Richard C | 33 | 3.75 | 4.1 | 14-9 |
| RH | Latos M | 31 | 2.92 | 3.5 | 14-10 |
| RH | Correia K | 26 | 5.52 | 5.6 | 10-10 |

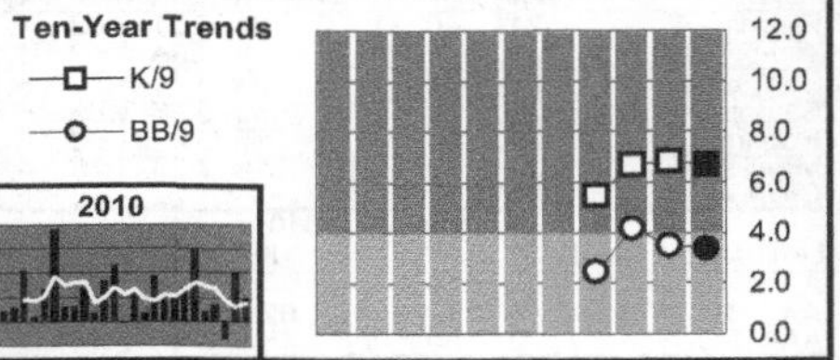


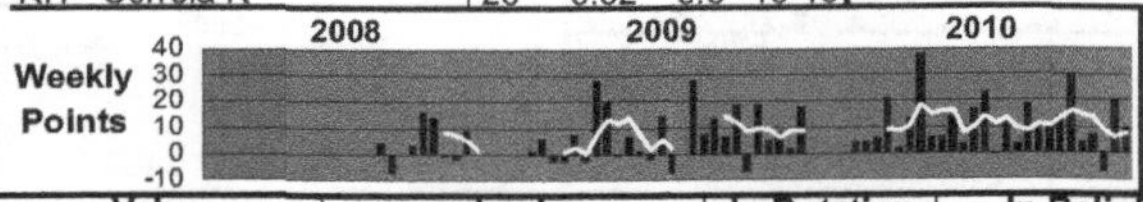


Majors

| Yr | Team | W | L | Sv | IP | H | K | ERA | WHIP | K/9 | BB/9 | HR/9 | GB/F | $1L | $2L | Pts | RAA | H% | HR/fb | S% | FIP | GS | CG | QS/DS | GR | Hld | Bln | Lead | OPS | 1st Hf | 2nd Hf | vs RH | vs LH |
|---|---|---|---|---|---|---|---|---|---|---|---|---|---|---|---|---|---|---|---|---|---|---|---|---|---|---|---|---|---|---|---|---|---|
| 07 | — | — | — | — | — | — | — | — | — | — | — | — | — | — | — | — | — | — | — | — | — | — | — | — | — | — | — | — | — | — | — | — | — |
| 08 | CHW | 2 | 5 | 0 | 47 | 61 | 29 | 6.04 | 1.55 | 5.5 | 2.5 | 0.9 | 1.8 | -$5 | -$8 | 30 | −13 | 34% | 11% | 61% | 4.27 | 8 | 0 | 3/4 | 5 | 0 | 0 | −0.2 | .802 | — | .802 | .888 | .650 |
| 09 | 2TM | 9 | 5 | 0 | 153 | 154 | 114 | 4.41 | 1.47 | 6.7 | 4.2 | 1.0 | 1.4 | $1 | -$4 | 170 | −6 | 31% | 11% | 72% | 4.60 | 26 | 1 | 10/6 | 12 | 0 | 0 | −0.3 | .756 | .835 | .678 | .788 | .645 |
| 10 | SD | 14 | 9 | 0 | 201 | 206 | 153 | 3.75 | 1.41 | 6.8 | 3.5 | 0.7 | 1.4 | $6 | -$6 | 270 | +10 | 32% | 8% | 75% | 3.87 | 33 | 1 | 20/4 | — | — | — | — | .718 | .682 | .763 | .770 | .574 |

## Dustin Richardson — 40 IP | $-6 | 20 pts

RP-26 — Owned: 0% — LH

Richardson's value took a hit in 2010 after he struggled big time with his control. He still has a future as a reliever, but he might have to spend another year in Pawtucket to achieve it. However, with the stuff at his disposal, he is certain to get some looks. A step forward in Spring Training could be all it takes. (EB)

| Player | Age | IP | W | Sv | K | ERA | WHIP | K/9 | BB/9 | $2L | Pts |
|---|---|---|---|---|---|---|---|---|---|---|---|
| **Forecast** | | | | | | | | | | | |
| Richardson D | 27 | 40 | 1 | 0 | 39 | 6.03 | 2.01 | 8.7 | 9.2 | -$6 | 20 |
| **Mini-Browser** | **Age** | **IP** | **W** | **Sv** | **K** | **ERA** | **WHIP** | **K/9** | **BB/9** | **$2L** | **Pts** |
| Chatwood T | 21 | 40 | 2 | 0 | 19 | 6.02 | 1.89 | 4.3 | 5.9 | -$6 | 20 |
| Willis D | 29 | 40 | 2 | 0 | 26 | 5.74 | 1.76 | 5.8 | 6.0 | -$6 | 20 |
| Harrell L | 25 | 40 | 2 | 0 | 19 | 6.25 | 1.84 | 4.2 | 5.8 | -$6 | 10 |
| Lincoln B | 25 | 100 | 4 | 0 | 77 | 5.63 | 1.51 | 6.9 | 2.4 | -$6 | 80 |
| Cashner A | 24 | 100 | 4 | 2 | 94 | 5.09 | 1.73 | 8.5 | 5.0 | -$6 | 100 |

Minors (2010)

| Level | Leag | W | L | Sv | IP | H | K | ERA | WHIP | K/9 | BB/9 | HR/9 | GB/F |
|---|---|---|---|---|---|---|---|---|---|---|---|---|---|
| A | — | — | — | — | — | — | — | — | — | — | — | — | — |
| AA | — | — | — | — | — | — | — | — | — | — | — | — | — |
| AAA | IL | 3 | 0 | 2 | 44 | 27 | 56 | 2.66 | 1.32 | 11.5 | 6.3 | 0.8 | — |

Competition at RP / Stats in 2010 as RP

| Thr | Player | GR | ERA | IP/G | Sv-Hld |
|---|---|---|---|---|---|
| LH | Okajima H | 56 | 4.50 | 0.8 | 0-11 |
| LH | Richardson D | 26 | 4.15 | 0.5 | 0-2 |
| LH | Schoeneweis S | 15 | 7.90 | 0.9 | 0-1 |

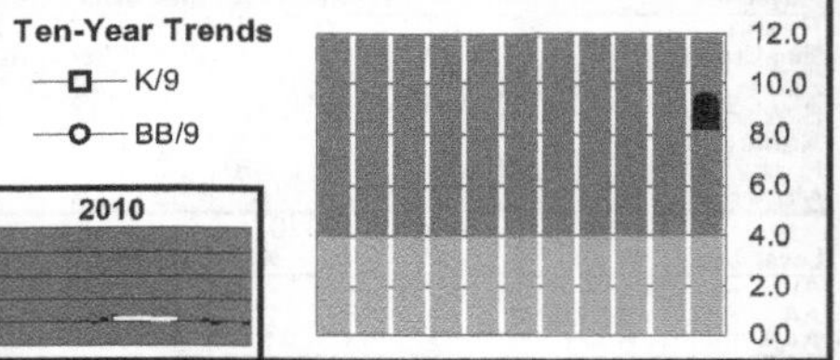


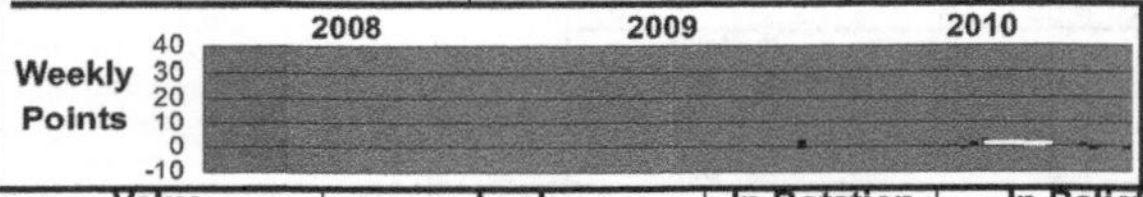


Majors

| Yr | Team | W | L | Sv | IP | H | K | ERA | WHIP | K/9 | BB/9 | HR/9 | GB/F | $1L | $2L | Pts | RAA | H% | HR/fb | S% | FIP | GS | CG | QS/DS | GR | Hld | Bln | Lead | OPS | 1st Hf | 2nd Hf | vs RH | vs LH |
|---|---|---|---|---|---|---|---|---|---|---|---|---|---|---|---|---|---|---|---|---|---|---|---|---|---|---|---|---|---|---|---|---|---|
| 07 | — | — | — | — | — | — | — | — | — | — | — | — | — | — | — | — | — | — | — | — | — | — | — | — | — | — | — | — | — | — | — | — | — |
| 08 | — | — | — | — | — | — | — | — | — | — | — | — | — | — | — | — | — | — | — | — | — | — | — | — | — | — | — | — | — | — | — | — | — |
| 09 | BOS | 0 | 0 | 0 | 3 | 3 | 0 | 0.00 | 1.20 | 0.0 | 2.7 | 0.0 | 0.5 | -$2 | -$2 | 0 | +2 | 23% | 0% | 100% | 4.20 | — | — | — | 3 | 0 | 0 | −3.0 | .536 | — | .536 | .619 | .400 |
| 10 | BOS | 0 | 0 | 0 | 13 | 15 | 12 | 4.15 | 2.23 | 8.3 | 9.7 | 1.4 | 1.2 | -$5 | -$14 | 0 | −0 | 36% | 14% | 85% | 6.68 | — | — | — | 26 | 2 | 0 | −0.4 | .915 | 1.011 | .821 | .695 | 1.129 |

## Royce Ring — 20 IP | $-2 | 20 pts

RP-5 — Owned: 0% — LH

Ring contributed 2.1 IP in relief for the Yankees as a September call-up; two bad outings against Boston were enough to inflate his ERA to over 15. Ring did not make NY's post-season roster, and it is unclear where (or whether) the 30-year-old fits into the Yankees' plans. (LS)

| Player | Age | IP | W | Sv | K | ERA | WHIP | K/9 | BB/9 | $2L | Pts |
|---|---|---|---|---|---|---|---|---|---|---|---|
| **Forecast** | | | | | | | | | | | |
| Ring R | 30 | 20 | 1 | 0 | 17 | 4.49 | 1.44 | 7.7 | 4.0 | -$2 | 20 |
| **Mini-Browser** | **Age** | **IP** | **W** | **Sv** | **K** | **ERA** | **WHIP** | **K/9** | **BB/9** | **$2L** | **Pts** |
| Green S | 31 | 40 | 2 | 0 | 29 | 4.25 | 1.46 | 6.6 | 4.5 | -$2 | 40 |
| VandenHurk R | 25 | 40 | 2 | 0 | 38 | 5.04 | 1.48 | 8.5 | 3.9 | -$2 | 40 |
| Schlichting T | 26 | 60 | 3 | 0 | 51 | 4.41 | 1.53 | 7.6 | 4.3 | -$2 | 70 |
| Martin J | 28 | 40 | 2 | 0 | 27 | 4.58 | 1.37 | 6.1 | 2.2 | -$2 | 40 |
| Purcey D | 28 | 60 | 3 | 0 | 53 | 4.96 | 1.53 | 7.9 | 4.9 | -$2 | 60 |

Minors (2010)

| Level | Leag | W | L | Sv | IP | H | K | ERA | WHIP | K/9 | BB/9 | HR/9 | GB/F |
|---|---|---|---|---|---|---|---|---|---|---|---|---|---|
| A | — | — | — | — | — | — | — | — | — | — | — | — | — |
| AA | — | — | — | — | — | — | — | — | — | — | — | — | — |
| AAA | IL | 2 | 1 | 2 | 42 | 35 | 39 | 1.93 | 1.10 | 8.4 | 2.4 | 0.4 | — |

Competition at RP / Stats in 2010 as RP

| Thr | Player | GR | ERA | IP/G | Sv-Hld |
|---|---|---|---|---|---|
| LH | Logan B | 51 | 2.93 | 0.8 | 0-13 |
| LH | Marte D | 30 | 4.08 | 0.6 | 0-9 |

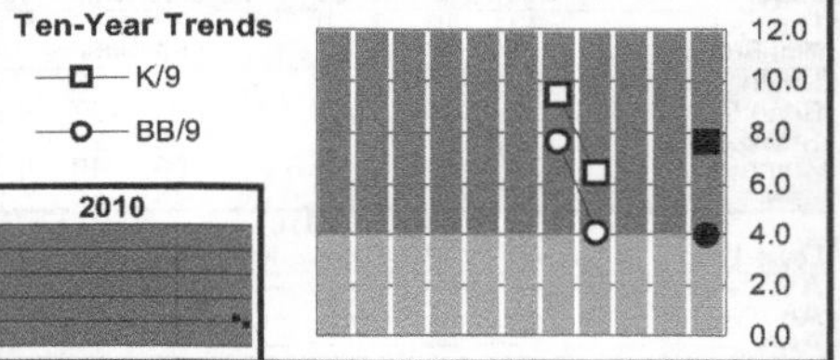


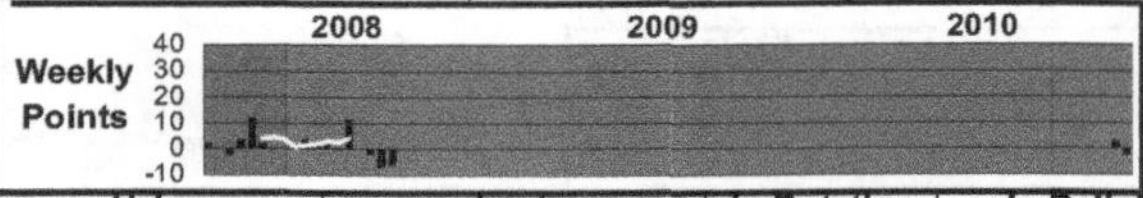


Majors

| Yr | Team | W | L | Sv | IP | H | K | ERA | WHIP | K/9 | BB/9 | HR/9 | GB/F | $1L | $2L | Pts | RAA | H% | HR/fb | S% | FIP | GS | CG | QS/DS | GR | Hld | Bln | Lead | OPS | 1st Hf | 2nd Hf | vs RH | vs LH |
|---|---|---|---|---|---|---|---|---|---|---|---|---|---|---|---|---|---|---|---|---|---|---|---|---|---|---|---|---|---|---|---|---|---|
| 07 | 2TM | 1 | 0 | 0 | 20 | 13 | 21 | 2.70 | 1.50 | 9.5 | 7.7 | 0.5 | 2.0 | -$1 | -$2 | 30 | +1 | 24% | 7% | 83% | 4.35 | — | — | — | 26 | 0 | 0 | −1.4 | .584 | .458 | .720 | .469 | .701 |
| 08 | ATL | 2 | 1 | 0 | 22 | 32 | 16 | 8.46 | 1.88 | 6.4 | 4.0 | 0.8 | 2.3 | -$6 | -$8 | 20 | −15 | 38% | 10% | 53% | 4.27 | — | — | — | 42 | 4 | 0 | −1.1 | .921 | .753 | 1.290 | 1.145 | .735 |
| 09 | — | — | — | — | — | — | — | — | — | — | — | — | — | — | — | — | — | — | — | — | — | — | — | — | — | — | — | — | — | — | — | — | — |
| 10 | NYY | 0 | 0 | 0 | 2 | 3 | 2 | 15.43 | 2.14 | 7.7 | 7.7 | 0.0 | 5.0 | -$5 | -$13 | 0 | −3 | 43% | 0% | 20% | 4.16 | — | — | — | 5 | 1 | 0 | −2.2 | .717 | — | .717 | .333 | .819 |

## Mariano Rivera — 60 IP | $20 | 300 pts

RP-61 — Owned: 100% — RH

The all-time great fended off aging for most of 2010, but he struggled in September (4.76 ERA), and his strikeout rate was down (only 4.2 K/9 in 2nd half). On the plus side, his control was unharmed. Rivera will be the Yankees' closer in 2011, but we don't know if it will be his last year or who would succeed him. (LS)

| Player | Age | IP | W | Sv | K | ERA | WHIP | K/9 | BB/9 | $2L | Pts |
|---|---|---|---|---|---|---|---|---|---|---|---|
| **Forecast** | | | | | | | | | | | |
| Rivera M | 41 | 60 | 4 | 38 | 54 | 2.35 | 0.96 | 8.1 | 1.6 | $20 | 300 |
| **Mini-Browser** | **Age** | **IP** | **W** | **Sv** | **K** | **ERA** | **WHIP** | **K/9** | **BB/9** | **$2L** | **Pts** |
| Lester J | 27 | 220 | 18 | 0 | 208 | 3.55 | 1.27 | 8.5 | 3.4 | $22 | 380 |
| Kershaw C | 23 | 220 | 15 | 0 | 214 | 3.30 | 1.26 | 8.8 | 3.9 | $22 | 370 |
| Carpenter C | 35 | 200 | 15 | 0 | 146 | 3.22 | 1.17 | 6.5 | 2.2 | $22 | 300 |
| Greinke Z | 27 | 220 | 13 | 0 | 192 | 3.60 | 1.21 | 7.9 | 2.3 | $21 | 320 |
| Weaver J | 28 | 220 | 14 | 0 | 193 | 3.73 | 1.21 | 7.9 | 2.6 | $21 | 330 |

Minors (2010)

| Level | Leag | W | L | Sv | IP | H | K | ERA | WHIP | K/9 | BB/9 | HR/9 | GB/F |
|---|---|---|---|---|---|---|---|---|---|---|---|---|---|
| A | — | — | — | — | — | — | — | — | — | — | — | — | — |
| AA | — | — | — | — | — | — | — | — | — | — | — | — | — |
| AAA | — | — | — | — | — | — | — | — | — | — | — | — | — |

Competition at RP / Stats in 2010 as RP

| Thr | Player | GR | ERA | IP/G | Sv-Hld |
|---|---|---|---|---|---|
| RH | Chamberlain J | 73 | 4.40 | 1.0 | 3-26 |
| RH | Robertson D | 64 | 3.82 | 1.0 | 1-14 |
| RH | Rivera M | 61 | 1.80 | 1.0 | 33-0 |
| RH | Gaudin C | 30 | 4.50 | 1.6 | 0-0 |

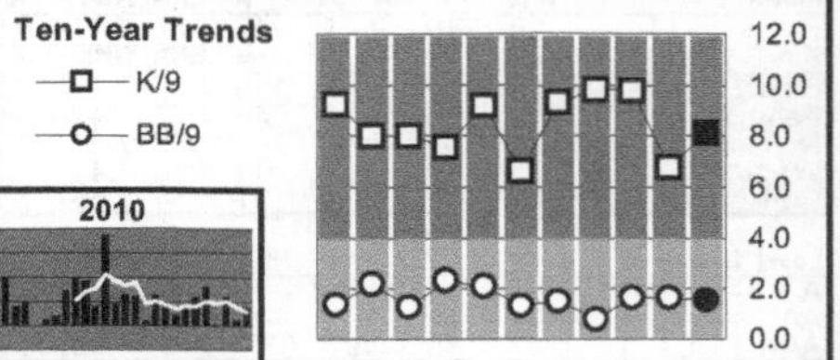


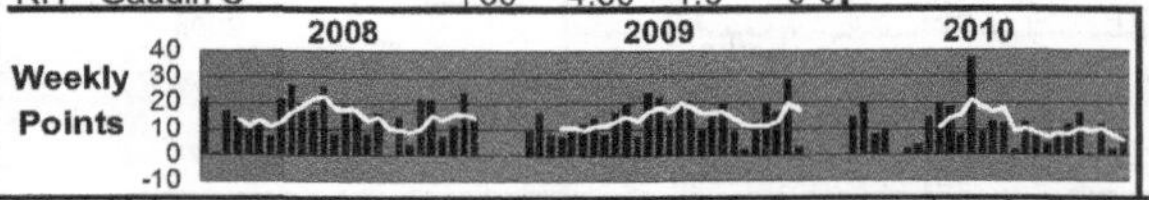


Majors

| Yr | Team | W | L | Sv | IP | H | K | ERA | WHIP | K/9 | BB/9 | HR/9 | GB/F | $1L | $2L | Pts | RAA | H% | HR/fb | S% | FIP | GS | CG | QS/DS | GR | Hld | Bln | Lead | OPS | 1st Hf | 2nd Hf | vs RH | vs LH |
|---|---|---|---|---|---|---|---|---|---|---|---|---|---|---|---|---|---|---|---|---|---|---|---|---|---|---|---|---|---|---|---|---|---|
| 07 | NYY | 3 | 4 | 30 | 71 | 68 | 74 | 3.15 | 1.12 | 9.3 | 1.5 | 0.5 | 1.9 | $14 | $10 | 260 | +7 | 33% | 7% | 72% | 2.46 | — | — | — | 67 | 0 | 4 | +2.5 | .644 | .654 | .634 | .680 | .608 |
| 08 | NYY | 6 | 5 | 39 | 70 | 41 | 77 | 1.40 | 0.67 | 9.8 | 0.8 | 0.5 | 1.8 | $28 | $23 | 370 | +21 | 22% | 8% | 84% | 2.11 | — | — | — | 64 | 0 | 1 | +1.6 | .423 | .416 | .433 | .474 | .376 |
| 09 | NYY | 3 | 3 | 44 | 66 | 48 | 72 | 1.76 | 0.90 | 9.8 | 1.6 | 0.9 | 1.9 | $19 | $15 | 350 | +16 | 25% | 15% | 89% | 3.04 | — | — | — | 66 | 0 | 2 | +2.0 | .549 | .581 | .505 | .586 | .511 |
| 10 | NYY | 3 | 3 | 33 | 60 | 39 | 45 | 1.80 | 0.83 | 6.8 | 1.7 | 0.3 | 1.5 | $16 | $14 | 260 | +13 | 22% | 4% | 79% | 2.78 | — | — | — | 61 | 0 | 5 | +2.2 | .493 | .397 | .608 | .433 | .554 |

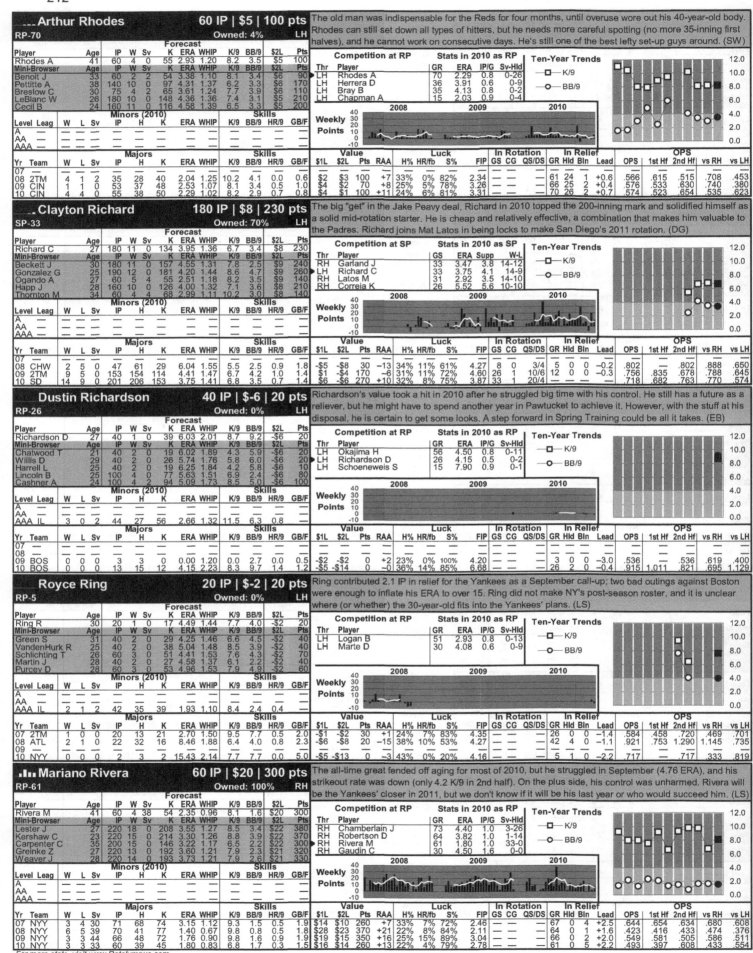

## David Robertson

**60 IP | $3 | 100 pts**

RP-64 Owned: 1% RH

2010 was a breakout season for Robertson, who became one of the arms to which Joe Girardi turned most. Robertson had the best K/9 of any Yankee, and he seemed to rank higher on the depth chart than Joba Chamberlain. Unfortunately, with 4.5+ BB/9, Robertson will probably never have an elite ERA. (LS)

| Player | Age | IP | W | Sv | K | ERA | WHIP | K/9 | BB/9 | $2L | Pts |
|---|---|---|---|---|---|---|---|---|---|---|---|
| Robertson D | 25 | 60 | 4 | 0 | 72 | 3.69 | 1.44 | 10.9 | 4.8 | $3 | 100 |
| **Mini-Browser** | **Age** | **IP** | **W** | **Sv** | **K** | **ERA** | **WHIP** | **K/9** | **BB/9** | **$2L** | **Pts** |
| Gee D | 24 | 80 | 5 | 0 | 66 | 3.73 | 1.35 | 7.5 | 3.0 | $3 | 110 |
| Sanchez A | 27 | 140 | 8 | 0 | 110 | 4.15 | 1.44 | 7.1 | 3.7 | $3 | 170 |
| Guerrier M | 32 | 80 | 4 | 0 | 49 | 4.08 | 1.27 | 5.5 | 3.0 | $3 | 80 |
| Oliver D | 40 | 60 | 3 | 0 | 50 | 3.57 | 1.28 | 7.5 | 2.8 | $3 | 70 |
| Thatcher J | 29 | 40 | 2 | 0 | 43 | 2.89 | 1.12 | 9.6 | 2.7 | $3 | 60 |

| Competition at RP | | Stats in 2010 as RP | | | |
|---|---|---|---|---|---|
| Thr | Player | GR | ERA | IP/G | Sv-Hld |
| RH | Chamberlain J | 73 | 4.40 | 1.0 | 3-26 |
| RH | Robertson D | 64 | 3.82 | 1.0 | 1-14 |
| RH | Rivera M | 61 | 1.80 | 1.0 | 33-0 |
| RH | Gaudin C | 30 | 4.50 | 1.6 | 0-0 |

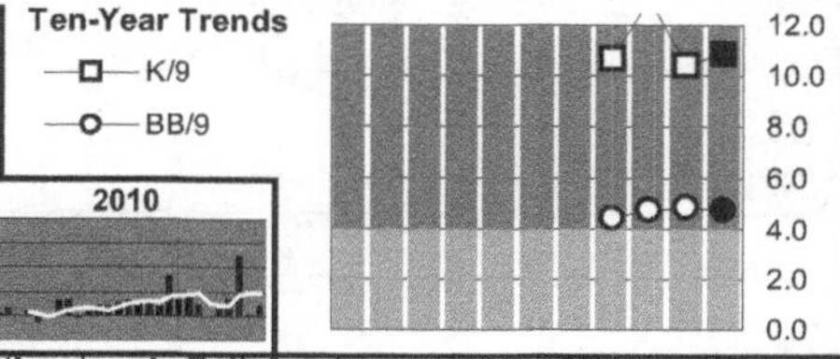


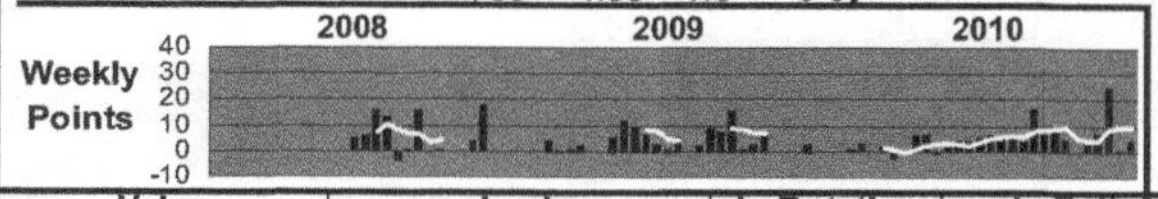


| Minors (2010) Level | Leag | W | L | Sv | IP | H | K | ERA | WHIP | Skills K/9 | BB/9 | HR/9 | GB/F |
|---|---|---|---|---|---|---|---|---|---|---|---|---|---|
| A | — | — | — | — | — | — | — | — | — | — | — | — | — |
| AA | — | — | — | — | — | — | — | — | — | — | — | — | — |
| AAA | — | — | — | — | — | — | — | — | — | — | — | — | — |

| Majors Yr | Team | W | L | Sv | IP | H | K | ERA | WHIP | Skills K/9 | BB/9 | HR/9 | GB/F |
|---|---|---|---|---|---|---|---|---|---|---|---|---|---|
| 07 | — | — | — | — | — | — | — | — | — | — | — | — | — |
| 08 | NYY | 4 | 0 | 0 | 30 | 29 | 36 | 5.34 | 1.45 | 10.7 | 4.5 | 0.9 | 1.0 |
| 09 | NYY | 2 | 1 | 1 | 43 | 36 | 63 | 3.30 | 1.35 | 13.0 | 4.7 | 0.8 | 0.9 |
| 10 | NYY | 4 | 5 | 1 | 61 | 59 | 71 | 3.82 | 1.50 | 10.4 | 4.8 | 0.7 | 1.1 |

| Yr | Value $1L | $2L | Pts | RAA | Luck H% | HR/fb | S% | FIP | In Rotation GS | CG | QS/DS | In Relief GR | Hld | Bln | Lead | OPS | 1st Hf | 2nd Hf | vs RH | vs LH |
|---|---|---|---|---|---|---|---|---|---|---|---|---|---|---|---|---|---|---|---|---|
| 07 | — | — | — | — | — | — | — | — | — | — | — | — | — | — | — | — | — | — | — | — |
| 08 | -$1 | -$3 | 70 | –4 | 34% | 9% | 63% | 3.70 | — | — | — | 25 | 0 | 0 | –0.6 | .690 | .531 | .742 | .747 | .627 |
| 09 | $3 | $0 | 90 | +1 | 32% | 9% | 78% | 3.19 | — | — | — | 45 | 5 | 0 | –0.0 | .685 | .673 | .697 | .751 | .601 |
| 10 | $0 | -$9 | 110 | +2 | 35% | 9% | 76% | 3.66 | — | — | — | 64 | 14 | 2 | +1.8 | .721 | .825 | .612 | .693 | .759 |

## Fernando Rodney

**60 IP | $6 | 200 pts**

RP-72 Owned: 63% RH

Attitude and work ethic are the issues with Rodney, and he was on the wrong side of both of them. If the Angels could move him, they would, but that seems unlikely. Rodney will get a chance to close in 2011, but if he continues to defy the team or underwhelm on play, he will be replaced by Jordan Walden. (DS)

| Player | Age | IP | W | Sv | K | ERA | WHIP | K/9 | BB/9 | $2L | Pts |
|---|---|---|---|---|---|---|---|---|---|---|---|
| Rodney F | 34 | 60 | 3 | 27 | 51 | 4.55 | 1.57 | 7.6 | 5.2 | $6 | 200 |
| **Mini-Browser** | **Age** | **IP** | **W** | **Sv** | **K** | **ERA** | **WHIP** | **K/9** | **BB/9** | **$2L** | **Pts** |
| Putz J | 34 | 60 | 5 | 9 | 61 | 3.60 | 1.27 | 9.1 | 3.8 | $7 | 150 |
| Lowe D | 37 | 200 | 13 | 0 | 120 | 4.29 | 1.34 | 5.4 | 2.7 | $7 | 230 |
| Tejeda R | 29 | 60 | 3 | 25 | 57 | 4.35 | 1.55 | 8.6 | 5.4 | $7 | 200 |
| Pineda M | 22 | 120 | 7 | 0 | 97 | 3.98 | 1.33 | 7.3 | 3.1 | $7 | 160 |
| Hellickson J | 23 | 120 | 9 | 0 | 129 | 4.39 | 1.35 | 9.7 | 2.6 | $6 | 200 |

| Competition at RP | | Stats in 2010 as RP | | | |
|---|---|---|---|---|---|
| Thr | Player | GR | ERA | IP/G | Sv-Hld |
| RH | Rodney F | 72 | 4.24 | 0.9 | 14-21 |
| RH | Jepsen K | 68 | 3.97 | 0.9 | 0-27 |
| RH | Rodriguez F | 43 | 4.37 | 1.1 | 0-2 |
| RH | Shields S | 42 | 5.08 | 1.1 | 0-1 |

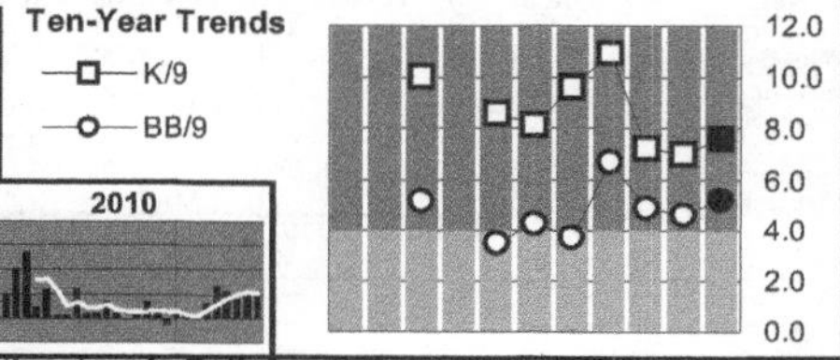


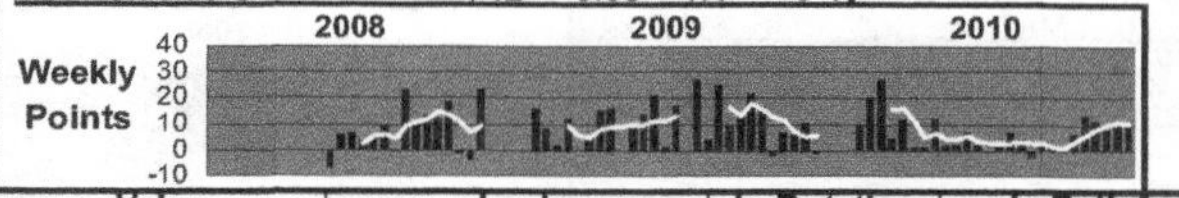


| Minors (2010) Level | Leag | W | L | Sv | IP | H | K | ERA | WHIP | Skills K/9 | BB/9 | HR/9 | GB/F |
|---|---|---|---|---|---|---|---|---|---|---|---|---|---|
| A | — | — | — | — | — | — | — | — | — | — | — | — | — |
| AA | — | — | — | — | — | — | — | — | — | — | — | — | — |
| AAA | — | — | — | — | — | — | — | — | — | — | — | — | — |

| Majors Yr | Team | W | L | Sv | IP | H | K | ERA | WHIP | Skills K/9 | BB/9 | HR/9 | GB/F |
|---|---|---|---|---|---|---|---|---|---|---|---|---|---|
| 07 | DET | 2 | 6 | 1 | 50 | 46 | 54 | 4.26 | 1.32 | 9.6 | 3.7 | 0.9 | 1.3 |
| 08 | DET | 0 | 6 | 13 | 40 | 34 | 49 | 4.91 | 1.59 | 10.9 | 6.7 | 0.7 | 1.2 |
| 09 | DET | 2 | 5 | 37 | 75 | 70 | 61 | 4.40 | 1.47 | 7.3 | 4.9 | 1.0 | 1.9 |
| 10 | LAA | 4 | 3 | 14 | 68 | 70 | 53 | 4.24 | 1.54 | 7.0 | 4.6 | 0.5 | 1.7 |

| Yr | Value $1L | $2L | Pts | RAA | Luck H% | HR/fb | S% | FIP | In Rotation GS | CG | QS/DS | In Relief GR | Hld | Bln | Lead | OPS | 1st Hf | 2nd Hf | vs RH | vs LH |
|---|---|---|---|---|---|---|---|---|---|---|---|---|---|---|---|---|---|---|---|---|
| 07 | $1 | -$3 | 70 | –4 | 31% | 10% | 69% | 3.69 | — | — | — | 48 | 12 | 2 | +1.4 | .698 | .807 | .533 | .686 | .712 |
| 08 | $0 | -$3 | 100 | –4 | 31% | 9% | 69% | 4.07 | — | — | — | 38 | 5 | 6 | +1.3 | .733 | .841 | .697 | .748 | .720 |
| 09 | $8 | $3 | 250 | –4 | 29% | 12% | 72% | 4.69 | — | — | — | 73 | 0 | 1 | +2.1 | .731 | .673 | .790 | .737 | .727 |
| 10 | $2 | -$9 | 150 | –2 | 32% | 6% | 72% | 4.05 | — | — | — | 72 | 21 | 7 | +1.8 | .739 | .718 | .761 | .750 | .728 |

## Francisco Rodriguez

**20 IP | $-3 | 20 pts**

RP-43 Owned: 0% RH

Amid all the injuries to the Angels' bullpen in 2010, Rodriguez briefly emerged as a favorite of Scioscia. Unfortunately, the shine was erased by horrid control after the Break and by the emergence of Kohn and Walden. With the return of Bulger and Jepsen, Rodriguez will probably be relegated to the minors. (DS)

| Player | Age | IP | W | Sv | K | ERA | WHIP | K/9 | BB/9 | $2L | Pts |
|---|---|---|---|---|---|---|---|---|---|---|---|
| Rodriguez F | 28 | 20 | 1 | 0 | 17 | 5.41 | 1.73 | 7.7 | 5.0 | -$3 | 20 |
| **Mini-Browser** | **Age** | **IP** | **W** | **Sv** | **K** | **ERA** | **WHIP** | **K/9** | **BB/9** | **$2L** | **Pts** |
| Igarashi R | 31 | 40 | 2 | 0 | 29 | 5.28 | 1.43 | 6.4 | 4.4 | -$3 | 30 |
| Berken J | 27 | 60 | 3 | 0 | 41 | 5.19 | 1.57 | 6.2 | 3.2 | -$3 | 50 |
| Parra M | 28 | 60 | 3 | 0 | 51 | 4.99 | 1.53 | 7.7 | 4.3 | -$3 | 60 |
| Mortensen C | 25 | 40 | 2 | 0 | 30 | 5.58 | 1.54 | 6.7 | 3.9 | -$3 | 30 |
| Manship J | 26 | 60 | 2 | 0 | 48 | 5.18 | 1.59 | 7.2 | 3.3 | -$3 | 50 |

| Competition at RP | | Stats in 2010 as RP | | | |
|---|---|---|---|---|---|
| Thr | Player | GR | ERA | IP/G | Sv-Hld |
| RH | Rodney F | 72 | 4.24 | 0.9 | 14-21 |
| RH | Jepsen K | 68 | 3.97 | 0.9 | 0-27 |
| RH | Rodriguez F | 43 | 4.37 | 1.1 | 0-2 |
| RH | Shields S | 42 | 5.08 | 1.1 | 0-1 |

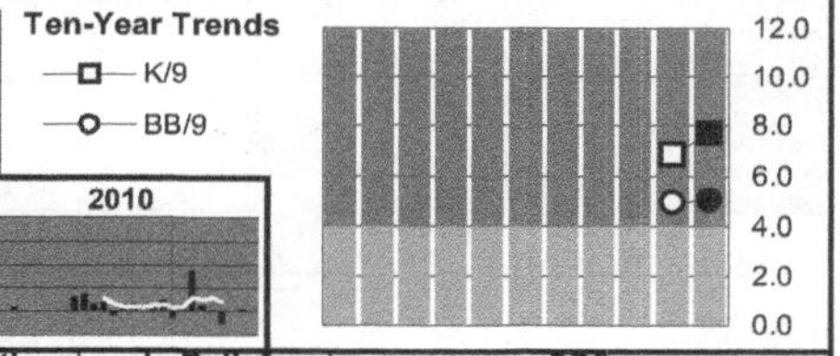


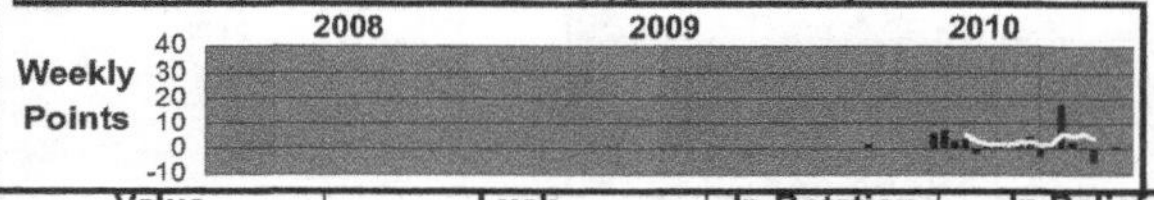


| Minors (2010) Level | Leag | W | L | Sv | IP | H | K | ERA | WHIP | Skills K/9 | BB/9 | HR/9 | GB/F |
|---|---|---|---|---|---|---|---|---|---|---|---|---|---|
| A | — | — | — | — | — | — | — | — | — | — | — | — | — |
| AA | — | — | — | — | — | — | — | — | — | — | — | — | — |
| AAA | — | — | — | — | — | — | — | — | — | — | — | — | — |

| Majors Yr | Team | W | L | Sv | IP | H | K | ERA | WHIP | Skills K/9 | BB/9 | HR/9 | GB/F |
|---|---|---|---|---|---|---|---|---|---|---|---|---|---|
| 07 | — | — | — | — | — | — | — | — | — | — | — | — | — |
| 08 | — | — | — | — | — | — | — | — | — | — | — | — | — |
| 09 | — | — | — | — | — | — | — | — | — | — | — | — | — |
| 10 | LAA | 1 | 3 | 0 | 47 | 46 | 36 | 4.37 | 1.52 | 6.8 | 4.9 | 1.0 | 1.4 |

| Yr | Value $1L | $2L | Pts | RAA | Luck H% | HR/fb | S% | FIP | In Rotation GS | CG | QS/DS | In Relief GR | Hld | Bln | Lead | OPS | 1st Hf | 2nd Hf | vs RH | vs LH |
|---|---|---|---|---|---|---|---|---|---|---|---|---|---|---|---|---|---|---|---|---|
| 07 | — | — | — | — | — | — | — | — | — | — | — | — | — | — | — | — | — | — | — | — |
| 08 | — | — | — | — | — | — | — | — | — | — | — | — | — | — | — | — | — | — | — | — |
| 09 | — | — | — | — | — | — | — | — | — | — | — | — | — | — | — | — | — | — | — | — |
| 10 | -$3 | -$14 | 30 | –2 | 30% | 10% | 73% | 4.80 | — | — | — | 43 | 2 | 1 | +0.2 | .732 | .666 | .784 | .539 | .984 |

## Francisco Rodriguez

**60 IP | $10 | 200 pts**

RP-53 Owned: 47% RH

The Mets still hope to trade Rodriguez, who was arrested over an alleged altercation that left him with a season-ending thumb injury. If the Mets can't find a taker until Rodriguez proves that he is stable and fit, expect them to act before he finishes 55 games (which would kick in a $17.5M option for 2012). (JL)

| Player | Age | IP | W | Sv | K | ERA | WHIP | K/9 | BB/9 | $2L | Pts |
|---|---|---|---|---|---|---|---|---|---|---|---|
| Rodriguez F | 29 | 60 | 3 | 21 | 66 | 3.14 | 1.27 | 9.9 | 4.2 | $10 | 200 |
| **Mini-Browser** | **Age** | **IP** | **W** | **Sv** | **K** | **ERA** | **WHIP** | **K/9** | **BB/9** | **$2L** | **Pts** |
| Nolasco R | 28 | 180 | 13 | 0 | 158 | 4.43 | 1.25 | 7.9 | 2.0 | $10 | 270 |
| Garland J | 31 | 200 | 12 | 0 | 107 | 3.99 | 1.27 | 4.8 | 3.0 | $10 | 210 |
| Gregg K | 32 | 60 | 2 | 32 | 55 | 4.27 | 1.41 | 8.3 | 4.2 | $10 | 230 |
| Webb B | 31 | 160 | 11 | 0 | 113 | 3.86 | 1.28 | 6.3 | 2.5 | $10 | 210 |
| Nathan J | 36 | 40 | 4 | 18 | 45 | 2.72 | 1.12 | 10.1 | 3.0 | $10 | 180 |

| Competition at RP | | Stats in 2010 as RP | | | |
|---|---|---|---|---|---|
| Thr | Player | GR | ERA | IP/G | Sv-Hld |
| RH | Rodriguez F | 53 | 2.20 | 1.1 | 25-0 |
| RH | Dessens E | 53 | 2.30 | 0.9 | 0-11 |
| RH | Parnell B | 41 | 2.83 | 0.9 | 0-9 |
| RH | Acosta M | 41 | 2.95 | 1.0 | 1-2 |

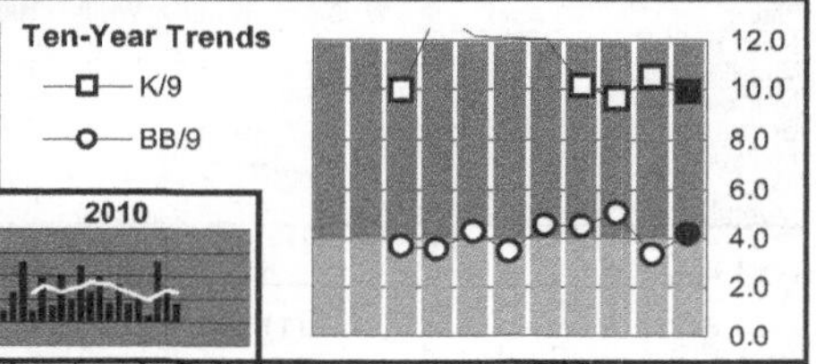


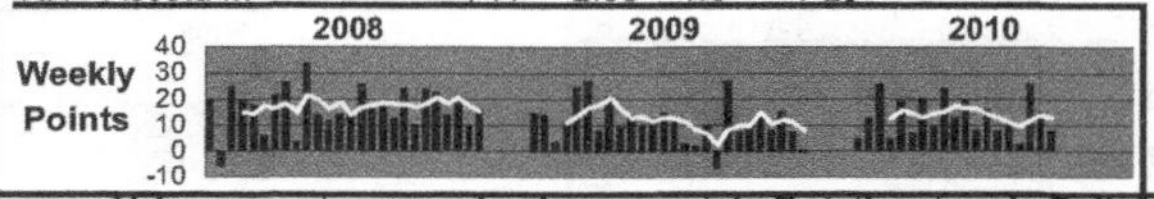


| Minors (2010) Level | Leag | W | L | Sv | IP | H | K | ERA | WHIP | Skills K/9 | BB/9 | HR/9 | GB/F |
|---|---|---|---|---|---|---|---|---|---|---|---|---|---|
| A | — | — | — | — | — | — | — | — | — | — | — | — | — |
| AA | — | — | — | — | — | — | — | — | — | — | — | — | — |
| AAA | — | — | — | — | — | — | — | — | — | — | — | — | — |

| Majors Yr | Team | W | L | Sv | IP | H | K | ERA | WHIP | Skills K/9 | BB/9 | HR/9 | GB/F |
|---|---|---|---|---|---|---|---|---|---|---|---|---|---|
| 07 | LAA | 5 | 2 | 40 | 67 | 50 | 90 | 2.81 | 1.25 | 12.0 | 4.5 | 0.4 | 1.1 |
| 08 | LAA | 2 | 3 | 62 | 68 | 54 | 77 | 2.24 | 1.29 | 10.1 | 4.5 | 0.5 | 1.1 |
| 09 | NYM | 3 | 6 | 35 | 68 | 51 | 73 | 3.71 | 1.31 | 9.7 | 5.0 | 0.9 | 0.8 |
| 10 | NYM | 4 | 2 | 25 | 57 | 45 | 67 | 2.20 | 1.15 | 10.5 | 3.3 | 0.5 | 1.1 |

| Yr | Value $1L | $2L | Pts | RAA | Luck H% | HR/fb | S% | FIP | In Rotation GS | CG | QS/DS | In Relief GR | Hld | Bln | Lead | OPS | 1st Hf | 2nd Hf | vs RH | vs LH |
|---|---|---|---|---|---|---|---|---|---|---|---|---|---|---|---|---|---|---|---|---|
| 07 | $17 | $13 | 340 | +8 | 31% | 5% | 78% | 2.72 | — | — | — | 64 | 0 | 6 | +1.8 | .605 | .591 | .624 | .649 | .549 |
| 08 | $24 | $15 | 410 | +10 | 30% | 6% | 85% | 3.30 | — | — | — | 76 | 0 | 7 | +1.8 | .630 | .582 | .700 | .571 | .682 |
| 09 | $11 | $6 | 270 | –3 | 26% | 9% | 74% | 4.07 | — | — | — | 70 | 0 | 7 | +1.8 | .644 | .559 | .781 | .750 | .541 |
| 10 | $10 | $8 | 240 | +12 | 30% | 5% | 83% | 2.64 | — | — | — | 53 | 0 | 5 | +1.7 | .597 | .649 | .404 | .531 | .680 |

## Henry Rodriguez

**50 IP | $-3 | 60 pts**

RP-29 Owned: 0% RH

Rodriguez is out of options, so he should be in the majors to stay, at least in the near term. His command is still shaky, though it did improve some in 2010. Rodriguez is a singular talent, with stuff on par with the Neftali Felizes of the world. However, his command will probably limit him to set-up or middle relief. (ML)

| Player | Age | IP | W | Sv | K | ERA | WHIP | K/9 | BB/9 | $2L | Pts |
|---|---|---|---|---|---|---|---|---|---|---|---|
| Rodriguez H | 24 | 50 | 2 | 0 | 59 | 4.92 | 1.68 | 10.6 | 6.0 | -$3 | 60 |
| **Mini-Browser** | **Age** | **IP** | **W** | **Sv** | **K** | **ERA** | **WHIP** | **K/9** | **BB/9** | **$2L** | **Pts** |
| Nippert D | 29 | 60 | 3 | 0 | 47 | 4.91 | 1.59 | 7.0 | 4.6 | -$3 | 50 |
| Carrasco C | 24 | 180 | 8 | 0 | 160 | 5.14 | 1.57 | 8.0 | 3.8 | -$3 | 180 |
| Lyles J | 20 | 100 | 5 | 0 | 71 | 4.69 | 1.52 | 6.4 | 3.5 | -$3 | 90 |
| Laffey A | 25 | 40 | 2 | 0 | 20 | 4.90 | 1.55 | 4.5 | 3.9 | -$3 | 30 |
| Burnett A | 23 | 40 | 2 | 0 | 34 | 5.18 | 1.59 | 7.7 | 3.7 | -$3 | 40 |

| Competition at RP | | Stats in 2010 as RP | | | |
|---|---|---|---|---|---|
| Thr | Player | GR | ERA | IP/G | Sv-Hld |
| RH | Ziegler B | 64 | 3.26 | 0.9 | 0-18 |
| RH | Wuertz M | 48 | 4.31 | 0.8 | 6-11 |
| RH | Bailey A | 47 | 1.47 | 1.0 | 25-0 |
| RH | Rodriguez H | 29 | 4.55 | 1.0 | 0-3 |

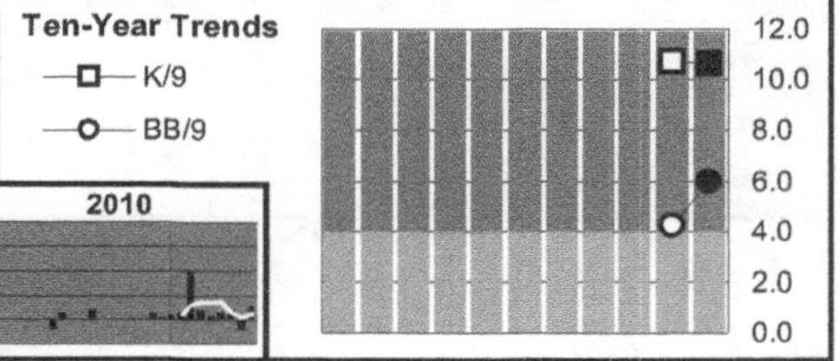


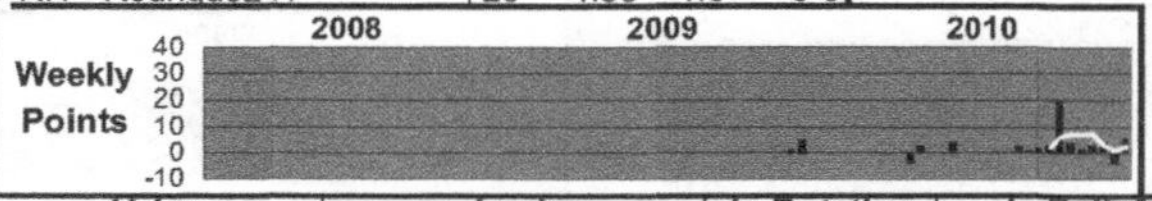


| Minors (2010) Level | Leag | W | L | Sv | IP | H | K | ERA | WHIP | Skills K/9 | BB/9 | HR/9 | GB/F |
|---|---|---|---|---|---|---|---|---|---|---|---|---|---|
| A | — | — | — | — | — | — | — | — | — | — | — | — | — |
| AA | — | — | — | — | — | — | — | — | — | — | — | — | — |
| AAA | PCL | 0 | 2 | 11 | 21 | 10 | 31 | 1.69 | 0.89 | 13.1 | 3.8 | 0.4 | — |

| Majors Yr | Team | W | L | Sv | IP | H | K | ERA | WHIP | Skills K/9 | BB/9 | HR/9 | GB/F |
|---|---|---|---|---|---|---|---|---|---|---|---|---|---|
| 07 | — | — | — | — | — | — | — | — | — | — | — | — | — |
| 08 | — | — | — | — | — | — | — | — | — | — | — | — | — |
| 09 | OAK | 0 | 0 | 0 | 4 | 4 | 4 | 2.25 | 1.50 | 9.0 | 4.5 | 0.0 | 1.8 |
| 10 | OAK | 1 | 0 | 0 | 27 | 25 | 33 | 4.55 | 1.37 | 10.7 | 4.2 | 0.7 | 0.9 |

| Yr | Value $1L | $2L | Pts | RAA | Luck H% | HR/fb | S% | FIP | In Rotation GS | CG | QS/DS | In Relief GR | Hld | Bln | Lead | OPS | 1st Hf | 2nd Hf | vs RH | vs LH |
|---|---|---|---|---|---|---|---|---|---|---|---|---|---|---|---|---|---|---|---|---|
| 07 | — | — | — | — | — | — | — | — | — | — | — | — | — | — | — | — | — | — | — | — |
| 08 | — | — | — | — | — | — | — | — | — | — | — | — | — | — | — | — | — | — | — | — |
| 09 | -$2 | -$2 | 0 | –0 | 31% | 0% | 83% | 2.80 | — | — | — | 3 | 0 | 0 | –6.0 | .585 | — | .585 | .282 | .984 |
| 10 | -$2 | -$11 | 40 | –4 | 33% | 6% | 67% | 3.26 | — | — | — | 29 | 3 | 1 | –0.7 | .664 | .825 | .625 | .587 | .758 |

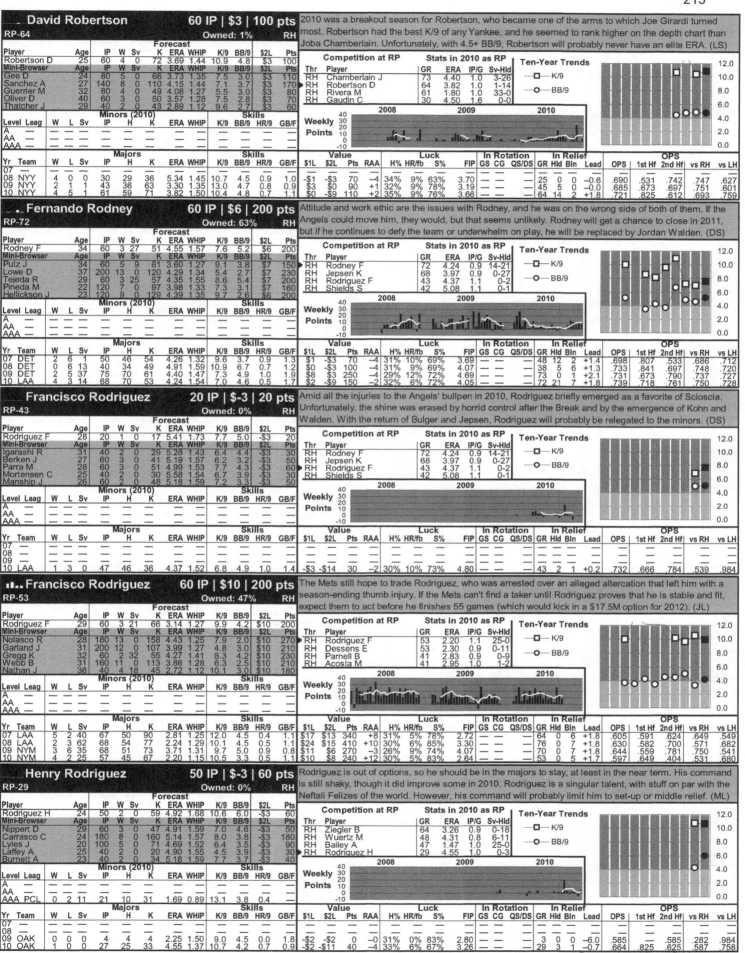

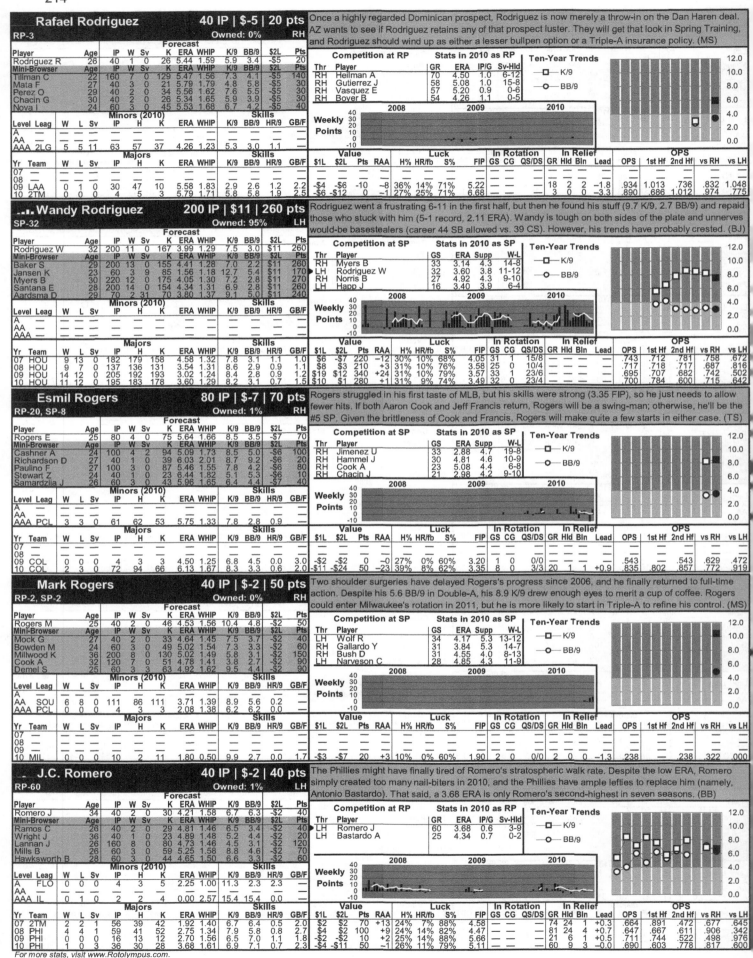

## Rafael Rodriguez — 40 IP | $-5 | 20 pts
RP-3 · Owned: 0% · RH

Once a highly regarded Dominican prospect, Rodriguez is now merely a throw-in on the Dan Haren deal. AZ wants to see if Rodriguez retains any of that prospect luster. They will get that look in Spring Training, and Rodriguez should wind up as either a lesser bullpen option or a Triple-A insurance policy. (MS)

### Forecast
| Player | Age | IP | W | Sv | K | ERA | WHIP | K/9 | BB/9 | $2L | Pts |
|---|---|---|---|---|---|---|---|---|---|---|---|
| Rodriguez R | 26 | 40 | 1 | 0 | 26 | 5.44 | 1.59 | 5.9 | 3.4 | -$5 | 20 |
| Mini-Browser | Age | IP | W | Sv | K | ERA | WHIP | K/9 | BB/9 | $2L | Pts |
| Tillman C | 22 | 160 | 7 | 0 | 129 | 5.47 | 1.56 | 7.3 | 4.1 | -$5 | 140 |
| Mata F | 27 | 40 | 3 | 0 | 21 | 5.79 | 1.79 | 4.8 | 5.8 | -$5 | 30 |
| Perez O | 29 | 40 | 2 | 0 | 34 | 5.56 | 1.62 | 7.6 | 5.5 | -$5 | 30 |
| Chacin G | 30 | 40 | 2 | 0 | 26 | 5.34 | 1.65 | 5.9 | 3.9 | -$5 | 30 |
| Nova I | 24 | 60 | 3 | 0 | 45 | 5.53 | 1.68 | 6.7 | 4.2 | -$5 | 40 |

### Minors (2010) / Skills
| Level | Leag | W | L | Sv | IP | H | K | ERA | WHIP | K/9 | BB/9 | HR/9 | GB/F |
|---|---|---|---|---|---|---|---|---|---|---|---|---|---|
| A | — | — | — | — | — | — | — | — | — | — | — | — | — |
| AA | — | — | — | — | — | — | — | — | — | — | — | — | — |
| AAA | 2LG | 5 | 5 | 11 | 63 | 57 | 37 | 4.26 | 1.23 | 5.3 | 3.0 | 1.1 | — |

### Majors / Skills / Value / Luck / In Rotation / In Relief / OPS
| Yr | Team | W | L | Sv | IP | H | K | ERA | WHIP | K/9 | BB/9 | HR/9 | GB/F | $1L | $2L | Pts | RAA | H% | HR/fb | S% | FIP | GS | CG | QS/DS | GR | Hld | Bln | Lead | OPS | 1st Hf | 2nd Hf | vs RH | vs LH |
|---|---|---|---|---|---|---|---|---|---|---|---|---|---|---|---|---|---|---|---|---|---|---|---|---|---|---|---|---|---|---|---|---|---|
| 07 | — | — | | | | | | | | | | | | | | | | | | | | | | | | | | | | | | | |
| 08 | — | — | | | | | | | | | | | | | | | | | | | | | | | | | | | | | | | |
| 09 | LAA | 0 | 1 | 0 | 30 | 47 | 10 | 5.58 | 1.83 | 2.9 | 2.6 | 1.2 | 2.2 | -$4 | -$6 | -10 | -8 | 36% | 14% | 71% | 5.22 | — | — | — | 18 | 2 | 2 | -1.8 | .934 | 1.013 | .736 | .832 | 1.048 |
| 10 | 2TM | 0 | 0 | 0 | 4 | 5 | 3 | 5.79 | 1.71 | 5.8 | 5.8 | 1.9 | 2.5 | -$6 | -$12 | 0 | -1 | 27% | 25% | 71% | 6.68 | — | — | — | 3 | 0 | 0 | -3.3 | .890 | .686 | 1.012 | .974 | .775 |

**Competition at RP — Stats in 2010 as RP**
| Thr | Player | GR | ERA | IP/G | Sv-Hld |
|---|---|---|---|---|---|
| RH | Heilman A | 70 | 4.50 | 1.0 | 6-12 |
| RH | Gutierrez J | 58 | 5.08 | 1.0 | 15-8 |
| RH | Vasquez E | 57 | 5.20 | 0.9 | 0-6 |
| RH | Boyer B | 54 | 4.26 | 1.1 | 0-5 |

---

## Wandy Rodriguez — 200 IP | $11 | 260 pts
SP-32 · Owned: 95% · LH

Rodriguez went a frustrating 6-11 in the first half, but then he found his stuff (9.7 K/9, 2.7 BB/9) and repaid those who stuck with him (5-1 record, 2.11 ERA). Wandy is tough on both sides of the plate and unnerves would-be basestealers (career 44 SB allowed vs. 39 CS). However, his trends have probably crested. (BJ)

### Forecast
| Player | Age | IP | W | Sv | K | ERA | WHIP | K/9 | BB/9 | $2L | Pts |
|---|---|---|---|---|---|---|---|---|---|---|---|
| Rodriguez W | 32 | 200 | 11 | 0 | 167 | 3.99 | 1.29 | 7.5 | 3.0 | $11 | 260 |
| Mini-Browser | Age | IP | W | Sv | K | ERA | WHIP | K/9 | BB/9 | $2L | Pts |
| Baker S | 29 | 200 | 13 | 0 | 155 | 4.41 | 1.28 | 7.0 | 2.2 | $11 | 260 |
| Jansen K | 23 | 60 | 3 | 9 | 85 | 1.56 | 1.18 | 12.7 | 5.4 | $11 | 170 |
| Myers B | 30 | 220 | 12 | 0 | 175 | 4.05 | 1.30 | 7.2 | 2.8 | $11 | 270 |
| Santana E | 28 | 200 | 14 | 0 | 154 | 4.34 | 1.31 | 6.9 | 2.8 | $11 | 260 |
| Aardsma D | 29 | 70 | 2 | 31 | 70 | 3.80 | 1.37 | 9.1 | 5.0 | $11 | 240 |

### Minors (2010) / Skills
| Level | Leag | W | L | Sv | IP | H | K | ERA | WHIP | K/9 | BB/9 | HR/9 | GB/F |
|---|---|---|---|---|---|---|---|---|---|---|---|---|---|
| A | — | — | — | — | — | — | — | — | — | — | — | — | — |
| AA | — | — | — | — | — | — | — | — | — | — | — | — | — |
| AAA | — | — | — | — | — | — | — | — | — | — | — | — | — |

### Majors
| Yr | Team | W | L | Sv | IP | H | K | ERA | WHIP | K/9 | BB/9 | HR/9 | GB/F | $1L | $2L | Pts | RAA | H% | HR/fb | S% | FIP | GS | CG | QS/DS | GR | Hld | Bln | Lead | OPS | 1st Hf | 2nd Hf | vs RH | vs LH |
|---|---|---|---|---|---|---|---|---|---|---|---|---|---|---|---|---|---|---|---|---|---|---|---|---|---|---|---|---|---|---|---|---|---|
| 07 | HOU | 9 | 13 | 0 | 182 | 179 | 158 | 4.58 | 1.32 | 7.8 | 3.1 | 1.1 | 1.0 | $6 | -$7 | 220 | -12 | 30% | 10% | 68% | 4.05 | 31 | 1 | 15/8 | — | — | — | — | .743 | .712 | .781 | .758 | .672 |
| 08 | HOU | 9 | 7 | 0 | 137 | 136 | 131 | 3.54 | 1.31 | 8.6 | 2.9 | 0.9 | 1.1 | $8 | $3 | 210 | +3 | 31% | 10% | 76% | 3.58 | 25 | 0 | 10/4 | — | — | — | — | .717 | .718 | .707 | .687 | .816 |
| 09 | HOU | 14 | 12 | 0 | 205 | 192 | 193 | 3.02 | 1.24 | 8.4 | 2.8 | 0.9 | 1.2 | $19 | $12 | 340 | +24 | 31% | 10% | 79% | 3.57 | 33 | 1 | 23/6 | — | — | — | — | .695 | .707 | .682 | .742 | .502 |
| 10 | HOU | 11 | 12 | 0 | 195 | 183 | 178 | 3.60 | 1.29 | 8.2 | 3.1 | 0.7 | 1.5 | $10 | $1 | 280 | +1 | 31% | 9% | 74% | 3.49 | 32 | 0 | 23/4 | — | — | — | — | .700 | .784 | .600 | .715 | .642 |

**Competition at SP — Stats in 2010 as SP**
| Thr | Player | GS | ERA | Supp | W-L |
|---|---|---|---|---|---|
| RH | Myers B | 33 | 3.14 | 4.3 | 14-8 |
| LH | Rodriguez W | 32 | 3.60 | 3.8 | 11-12 |
| RH | Norris B | 27 | 4.92 | 4.3 | 9-10 |
| LH | Happ J | 16 | 3.40 | 3.9 | 6-4 |

---

## Esmil Rogers — 80 IP | $-7 | 70 pts
RP-20, SP-8 · Owned: 1% · RH

Rogers struggled in his first taste of MLB, but his skills were strong (3.35 FIP), so he just needs to allow fewer hits. If both Aaron Cook and Jeff Francis return, Rogers will be a swing-man; otherwise, he'll be the #5 SP. Given the brittleness of Cook and Francis, Rogers will make quite a few starts in either case. (TS)

### Forecast
| Player | Age | IP | W | Sv | K | ERA | WHIP | K/9 | BB/9 | $2L | Pts |
|---|---|---|---|---|---|---|---|---|---|---|---|
| Rogers E | 25 | 80 | 4 | 0 | 75 | 5.64 | 1.66 | 8.5 | 3.5 | -$7 | 70 |
| Mini-Browser | Age | IP | W | Sv | K | ERA | WHIP | K/9 | BB/9 | $2L | Pts |
| Cashner A | 24 | 100 | 4 | 2 | 94 | 5.09 | 1.73 | 8.5 | 5.0 | -$6 | 100 |
| Richardson D | 27 | 40 | 1 | 0 | 39 | 6.03 | 2.01 | 8.7 | 9.2 | -$6 | 20 |
| Paulino F | 27 | 100 | 3 | 0 | 87 | 5.46 | 1.55 | 7.8 | 4.2 | -$6 | 80 |
| Stewart Z | 24 | 40 | 1 | 0 | 23 | 6.44 | 1.82 | 5.1 | 5.3 | -$7 | 10 |
| Samardzija J | 26 | 60 | 3 | 0 | 43 | 5.96 | 1.65 | 6.4 | 4.4 | -$6 | 40 |

### Minors (2010) / Skills
| Level | Leag | W | L | Sv | IP | H | K | ERA | WHIP | K/9 | BB/9 | HR/9 | GB/F |
|---|---|---|---|---|---|---|---|---|---|---|---|---|---|
| A | — | — | — | — | — | — | — | — | — | — | — | — | — |
| AA | — | — | — | — | — | — | — | — | — | — | — | — | — |
| AAA | PCL | 3 | 3 | 0 | 61 | 62 | 53 | 5.75 | 1.33 | 7.8 | 2.8 | 0.9 | — |

### Majors
| Yr | Team | W | L | Sv | IP | H | K | ERA | WHIP | K/9 | BB/9 | HR/9 | GB/F | $1L | $2L | Pts | RAA | H% | HR/fb | S% | FIP | GS | CG | QS/DS | GR | Hld | Bln | Lead | OPS | 1st Hf | 2nd Hf | vs RH | vs LH |
|---|---|---|---|---|---|---|---|---|---|---|---|---|---|---|---|---|---|---|---|---|---|---|---|---|---|---|---|---|---|---|---|---|---|
| 07 | — | — | | | | | | | | | | | | | | | | | | | | | | | | | | | | | | | |
| 08 | — | — | | | | | | | | | | | | | | | | | | | | | | | | | | | | | | | |
| 09 | COL | 0 | 0 | 0 | 4 | 3 | 4 | 4.50 | 1.25 | 6.8 | 4.5 | 0.0 | 3.0 | -$2 | -$2 | 0 | -0 | 27% | 0% | 60% | 3.20 | 1 | 0 | 0/0 | — | — | — | — | .543 | — | .543 | .629 | .472 |
| 10 | COL | 2 | 3 | 0 | 72 | 94 | 66 | 6.13 | 1.67 | 8.3 | 3.3 | 0.6 | 2.0 | -$11 | -$24 | 50 | -23 | 39% | 8% | 62% | 3.35 | 8 | 0 | 3/3 | 20 | 1 | 1 | +0.9 | .835 | .802 | .857 | .772 | .919 |

**Competition at SP — Stats in 2010 as SP**
| Thr | Player | GS | ERA | Supp | W-L |
|---|---|---|---|---|---|
| RH | Jimenez U | 33 | 2.88 | 4.7 | 19-8 |
| RH | Hammel J | 30 | 4.81 | 4.6 | 10-9 |
| RH | Cook A | 23 | 5.08 | 4.4 | 6-8 |
| RH | Chacin J | 21 | 2.98 | 4.2 | 9-10 |

---

## Mark Rogers — 40 IP | $-2 | 50 pts
RP-2, SP-2 · Owned: 0% · RH

Two shoulder surgeries have delayed Rogers's progress since 2006, and he finally returned to full-time action. Despite his 5.6 BB/9 in Double-A, his 8.9 K/9 drew enough eyes to merit a cup of coffee. Rogers could enter Milwaukee's rotation in 2011, but he is more likely to start in Triple-A to refine his control. (MS)

### Forecast
| Player | Age | IP | W | Sv | K | ERA | WHIP | K/9 | BB/9 | $2L | Pts |
|---|---|---|---|---|---|---|---|---|---|---|---|
| Rogers M | 25 | 40 | 2 | 0 | 46 | 4.53 | 1.56 | 10.4 | 4.8 | -$2 | 50 |
| Mini-Browser | Age | IP | W | Sv | K | ERA | WHIP | K/9 | BB/9 | $2L | Pts |
| Mock G | 27 | 40 | 2 | 0 | 33 | 4.64 | 1.45 | 7.5 | 3.7 | -$2 | 40 |
| Bowden M | 24 | 60 | 3 | 0 | 49 | 5.02 | 1.54 | 7.3 | 3.3 | -$2 | 60 |
| Millwood K | 36 | 200 | 8 | 0 | 130 | 5.02 | 1.49 | 5.8 | 3.1 | -$2 | 150 |
| Cook A | 32 | 120 | 7 | 0 | 51 | 4.78 | 1.41 | 3.8 | 2.7 | -$2 | 90 |
| Demel S | 25 | 60 | 3 | 3 | 63 | 4.92 | 1.62 | 9.5 | 4.4 | -$2 | 90 |

### Minors (2010) / Skills
| Level | Leag | W | L | Sv | IP | H | K | ERA | WHIP | K/9 | BB/9 | HR/9 | GB/F |
|---|---|---|---|---|---|---|---|---|---|---|---|---|---|
| A | — | — | — | — | — | — | — | — | — | — | — | — | — |
| AA | SOU | 6 | 8 | 0 | 111 | 86 | 111 | 3.71 | 1.39 | 8.9 | 5.6 | 0.2 | — |
| AAA | PCL | 0 | 0 | 0 | 4 | 3 | 3 | 2.08 | 1.38 | 6.2 | 6.2 | 0.0 | — |

### Majors
| Yr | Team | W | L | Sv | IP | H | K | ERA | WHIP | K/9 | BB/9 | HR/9 | GB/F | $1L | $2L | Pts | RAA | H% | HR/fb | S% | FIP | GS | CG | QS/DS | GR | Hld | Bln | Lead | OPS | 1st Hf | 2nd Hf | vs RH | vs LH |
|---|---|---|---|---|---|---|---|---|---|---|---|---|---|---|---|---|---|---|---|---|---|---|---|---|---|---|---|---|---|---|---|---|---|
| 07 | — | — | | | | | | | | | | | | | | | | | | | | | | | | | | | | | | | |
| 08 | — | — | | | | | | | | | | | | | | | | | | | | | | | | | | | | | | | |
| 09 | — | — | | | | | | | | | | | | | | | | | | | | | | | | | | | | | | | |
| 10 | MIL | 0 | 0 | 0 | 10 | 2 | 11 | 1.80 | 0.50 | 9.9 | 2.7 | 0.0 | 1.7 | -$3 | -$7 | 20 | +3 | 10% | 0% | 60% | 1.90 | 2 | 0 | 0/0 | 2 | 0 | 0 | -1.3 | .238 | — | .238 | .322 | .160 |

**Competition at SP — Stats in 2010 as SP**
| Thr | Player | GS | ERA | Supp | W-L |
|---|---|---|---|---|---|
| LH | Wolf R | 34 | 4.17 | 5.3 | 13-12 |
| RH | Gallardo Y | 31 | 3.84 | 5.3 | 14-7 |
| RH | Bush D | 31 | 4.55 | 4.0 | 8-13 |
| LH | Narveson C | 28 | 4.85 | 4.3 | 11-9 |

---

## J.C. Romero — 40 IP | $-2 | 40 pts
RP-60 · Owned: 1% · LH

The Phillies might have finally tired of Romero's stratospheric walk rate. Despite the low ERA, Romero simply created too many nail-biters in 2010, and the Phillies have ample lefties to replace him (namely, Antonio Bastardo). That said, a 3.68 ERA is only Romero's second-highest in seven seasons. (BB)

### Forecast
| Player | Age | IP | W | Sv | K | ERA | WHIP | K/9 | BB/9 | $2L | Pts |
|---|---|---|---|---|---|---|---|---|---|---|---|
| Romero J | 34 | 40 | 2 | 0 | 30 | 4.21 | 1.58 | 6.7 | 6.3 | -$2 | 40 |
| Mini-Browser | Age | IP | W | Sv | K | ERA | WHIP | K/9 | BB/9 | $2L | Pts |
| Ramos C | 26 | 40 | 2 | 0 | 29 | 4.81 | 1.46 | 6.5 | 3.4 | -$2 | 40 |
| Wright J | 36 | 40 | 1 | 0 | 23 | 4.89 | 1.48 | 5.2 | 4.4 | -$2 | 40 |
| Lannan J | 26 | 160 | 8 | 0 | 80 | 4.73 | 1.46 | 4.5 | 3.1 | -$2 | 120 |
| Mills B | 26 | 60 | 3 | 0 | 59 | 5.25 | 1.58 | 8.8 | 4.6 | -$2 | 70 |
| Hawksworth B | 28 | 60 | 3 | 0 | 44 | 4.65 | 1.50 | 6.6 | 3.3 | -$2 | 60 |

### Minors (2010) / Skills
| Level | Leag | W | L | Sv | IP | H | K | ERA | WHIP | K/9 | BB/9 | HR/9 | GB/F |
|---|---|---|---|---|---|---|---|---|---|---|---|---|---|
| A | FLO | 0 | 0 | 0 | 4 | 3 | 5 | 2.25 | 1.00 | 11.3 | 2.3 | 2.3 | — |
| AA | — | — | — | — | — | — | — | — | — | — | — | — | — |
| AAA | IL | 0 | 1 | 0 | 2 | 4 | 2 | 0.00 | 2.57 | 15.4 | 15.4 | 0.0 | — |

### Majors
| Yr | Team | W | L | Sv | IP | H | K | ERA | WHIP | K/9 | BB/9 | HR/9 | GB/F | $1L | $2L | Pts | RAA | H% | HR/fb | S% | FIP | GS | CG | QS/DS | GR | Hld | Bln | Lead | OPS | 1st Hf | 2nd Hf | vs RH | vs LH |
|---|---|---|---|---|---|---|---|---|---|---|---|---|---|---|---|---|---|---|---|---|---|---|---|---|---|---|---|---|---|---|---|---|---|
| 07 | 2TM | 2 | 2 | 1 | 56 | 54 | 42 | 1.92 | 1.40 | 6.7 | 6.4 | 0.5 | 2.0 | $2 | $2 | 70 | +13 | 24% | 7% | 88% | 4.58 | — | — | — | 74 | 24 | 1 | +0.3 | .664 | .891 | .472 | .677 | .645 |
| 08 | PHI | 4 | 4 | 1 | 59 | 41 | 52 | 2.75 | 1.34 | 7.9 | 5.8 | 0.8 | 2.7 | $4 | $2 | 100 | +9 | 24% | 14% | 82% | 4.47 | — | — | — | 81 | 24 | 4 | +0.7 | .647 | .667 | .611 | .906 | .342 |
| 09 | PHI | 1 | 1 | 0 | 16 | 13 | 12 | 2.70 | 1.56 | 6.5 | 7.0 | 1.1 | 1.8 | -$2 | -$2 | 10 | +2 | 25% | 14% | 88% | 5.66 | — | — | — | 21 | 6 | 1 | +0.5 | .711 | .744 | .522 | .498 | .976 |
| 10 | PHI | 1 | 0 | 3 | 36 | 30 | 28 | 3.68 | 1.61 | 6.9 | 7.1 | 0.7 | 2.3 | -$4 | -$11 | 50 | -1 | 25% | 11% | 79% | 5.11 | — | — | — | 60 | 9 | 3 | -0.0 | .690 | .603 | .778 | .817 | .600 |

**Competition at RP — Stats in 2010 as RP**
| Thr | Player | GR | ERA | IP/G | Sv-Hld |
|---|---|---|---|---|---|
| LH | Romero J | 60 | 3.68 | 0.6 | 3-9 |
| LH | Bastardo A | 25 | 4.34 | 0.7 | 0-2 |

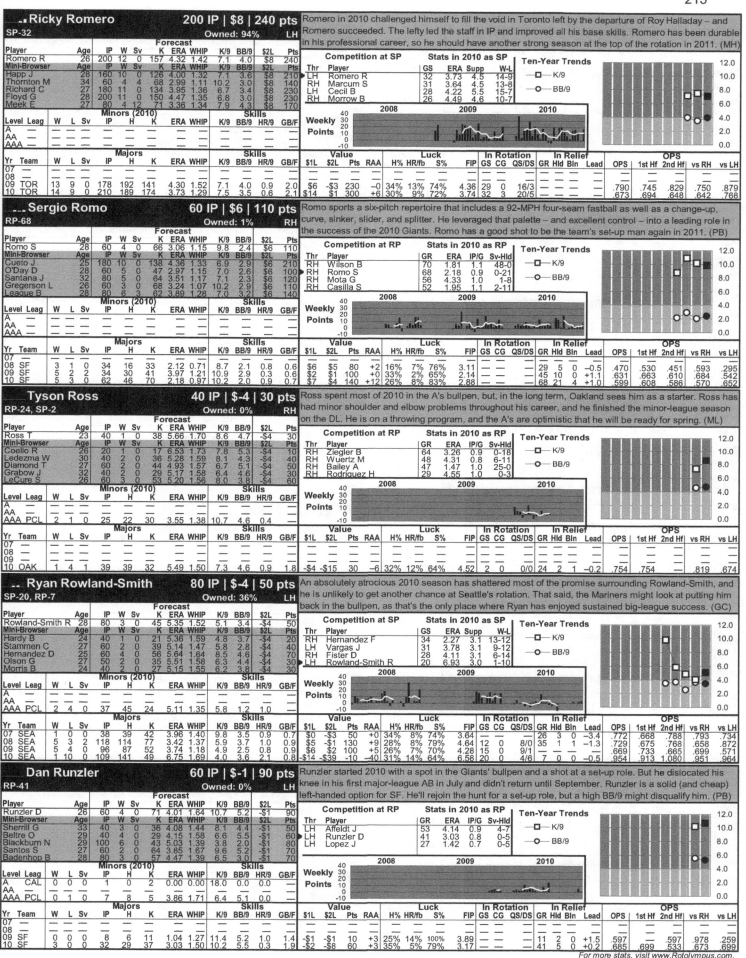

## Ricky Romero — 200 IP | $8 | 240 pts

SP-32 — Owned: 94% — LH

Romero in 2010 challenged himself to fill the void in Toronto left by the departure of Roy Halladay – and Romero succeeded. The lefty led the staff in IP and improved all his base skills. Romero has been durable in his professional career, so he should have another strong season at the top of the rotation in 2011. (MH)

| Player | Age | IP | W | Sv | K | ERA | WHIP | K/9 | BB/9 | $2L | Pts |
|---|---|---|---|---|---|---|---|---|---|---|---|
| **Forecast** | | | | | | | | | | | |
| Romero R | 26 | 200 | 12 | 0 | 157 | 4.32 | 1.42 | 7.1 | 4.0 | $8 | 240 |
| **Mini-Browser** | Age | IP | W | Sv | K | ERA | WHIP | K/9 | BB/9 | $2L | Pts |
| Happ J | 28 | 160 | 10 | 0 | 126 | 4.00 | 1.32 | 7.1 | 3.6 | $8 | 210 |
| Thornton M | 34 | 60 | 4 | 4 | 68 | 2.99 | 1.11 | 10.2 | 3.0 | $8 | 140 |
| Richard C | 27 | 180 | 11 | 0 | 134 | 3.95 | 1.36 | 6.7 | 3.4 | $8 | 230 |
| Floyd G | 28 | 200 | 11 | 0 | 150 | 4.47 | 1.35 | 6.8 | 3.0 | $8 | 230 |
| Meek E | 27 | 80 | 4 | 12 | 71 | 3.36 | 1.34 | 7.9 | 4.3 | $8 | 170 |

Minors (2010)

| Level | Leag | W | L | Sv | IP | H | K | ERA | WHIP | K/9 | BB/9 | HR/9 | GB/F |
|---|---|---|---|---|---|---|---|---|---|---|---|---|---|
| A | — | — | — | — | — | — | — | — | — | — | — | — | — |
| AA | — | — | — | — | — | — | — | — | — | — | — | — | — |
| AAA | — | — | — | — | — | — | — | — | — | — | — | — | — |

Competition at SP — Stats in 2010 as SP

| Thr | Player | GS | ERA | Supp | W-L |
|---|---|---|---|---|---|
| LH | Romero R | 32 | 3.73 | 4.5 | 14-9 |
| RH | Marcum S | 31 | 3.64 | 4.5 | 13-8 |
| LH | Cecil B | 28 | 4.22 | 5.5 | 15-7 |
| RH | Morrow B | 26 | 4.49 | 4.6 | 10-7 |

Weekly Points

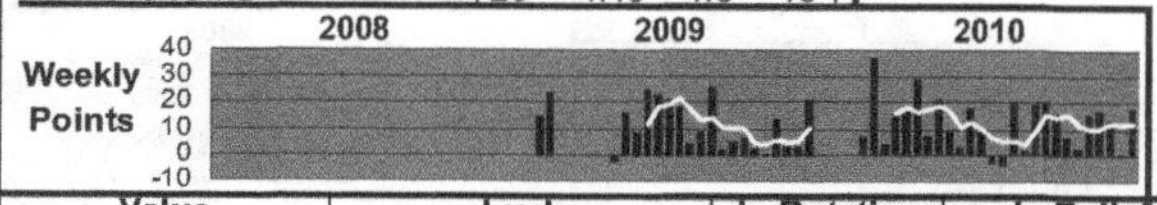

2008
2009
2010
40
30
20
10
0
-10


Ten-Year Trends

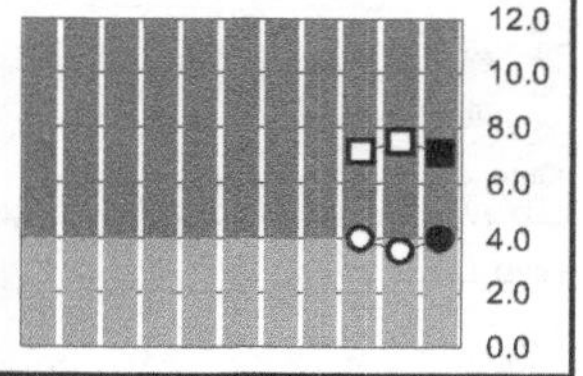

K/9
BB/9
12.0
10.0
8.0
6.0
4.0
2.0
0.0


| Yr | Team | W | L | Sv | IP | H | K | ERA | WHIP | K/9 | BB/9 | HR/9 | GB/F | $1L | $2L | Pts | RAA | H% | HR/fb | S% | FIP | GS | CG | QS/DS | GR | Hld | Bln | Lead | OPS | 1st Hf | 2nd Hf | vs RH | vs LH |
|---|---|---|---|---|---|---|---|---|---|---|---|---|---|---|---|---|---|---|---|---|---|---|---|---|---|---|---|---|---|---|---|---|---|
| | | Majors | | | | | | | | Skills | | | | Value | | | | Luck | | | | In Rotation | | | In Relief | | | | OPS | | | | |
| 07 | — | — | — | — | — | — | — | — | — | — | — | — | — | — | — | — | — | — | — | — | — | — | — | — | — | — | — | — | — | — | — | — | — |
| 08 | — | — | — | — | — | — | — | — | — | — | — | — | — | — | — | — | — | — | — | — | — | — | — | — | — | — | — | — | — | — | — | — | — |
| 09 | TOR | 13 | 9 | 0 | 178 | 192 | 141 | 4.30 | 1.52 | 7.1 | 4.0 | 0.9 | 2.0 | $6 | -$3 | 230 | –0 | 34% | 13% | 74% | 4.36 | 29 | 0 | 16/3 | — | — | — | — | .790 | .745 | .829 | .750 | .879 |
| 10 | TOR | 14 | 9 | 0 | 210 | 189 | 174 | 3.73 | 1.29 | 7.5 | 3.5 | 0.6 | 2.1 | $14 | $1 | 300 | +6 | 30% | 9% | 72% | 3.74 | 32 | 3 | 20/5 | — | — | — | — | .673 | .694 | .648 | .642 | .768 |

## Sergio Romo — 60 IP | $6 | 110 pts

RP-68 — Owned: 1% — RH

Romo sports a six-pitch repertoire that includes a 92-MPH four-seam fastball as well as a change-up, curve, sinker, slider, and splitter. He leveraged that palette – and excellent control – into a leading role in the success of the 2010 Giants. Romo has a good shot to be the team's set-up man again in 2011. (PB)

| Player | Age | IP | W | Sv | K | ERA | WHIP | K/9 | BB/9 | $2L | Pts |
|---|---|---|---|---|---|---|---|---|---|---|---|
| **Forecast** | | | | | | | | | | | |
| Romo S | 28 | 60 | 4 | 0 | 66 | 3.06 | 1.15 | 9.8 | 2.4 | $6 | 110 |
| **Mini-Browser** | Age | IP | W | Sv | K | ERA | WHIP | K/9 | BB/9 | $2L | Pts |
| Cueto J | 25 | 180 | 10 | 0 | 138 | 4.36 | 1.33 | 6.9 | 2.9 | $6 | 210 |
| O'Day D | 28 | 60 | 5 | 0 | 47 | 2.97 | 1.15 | 7.0 | 2.6 | $6 | 100 |
| Santana J | 32 | 80 | 5 | 0 | 64 | 3.51 | 1.17 | 7.1 | 2.3 | $6 | 120 |
| Gregerson L | 26 | 60 | 3 | 0 | 68 | 3.24 | 1.07 | 10.2 | 2.9 | $6 | 110 |
| League B | 28 | 80 | 6 | 3 | 62 | 3.89 | 1.28 | 7.0 | 3.2 | $6 | 140 |

Minors (2010)

| Level | Leag | W | L | Sv | IP | H | K | ERA | WHIP | K/9 | BB/9 | HR/9 | GB/F |
|---|---|---|---|---|---|---|---|---|---|---|---|---|---|
| A | — | — | — | — | — | — | — | — | — | — | — | — | — |
| AA | — | — | — | — | — | — | — | — | — | — | — | — | — |
| AAA | — | — | — | — | — | — | — | — | — | — | — | — | — |

Competition at RP — Stats in 2010 as RP

| Thr | Player | GR | ERA | IP/G | Sv-Hld |
|---|---|---|---|---|---|
| RH | Wilson B | 70 | 1.81 | 1.1 | 48-0 |
| RH | Romo S | 68 | 2.18 | 0.9 | 0-21 |
| RH | Mota G | 56 | 4.33 | 1.0 | 1-8 |
| RH | Casilla S | 52 | 1.95 | 1.1 | 2-11 |

Weekly Points

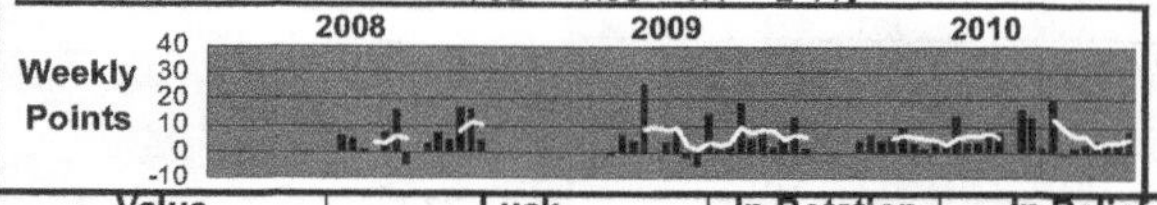

2008
2009
2010
40
30
20
10
0
-10


Ten-Year Trends

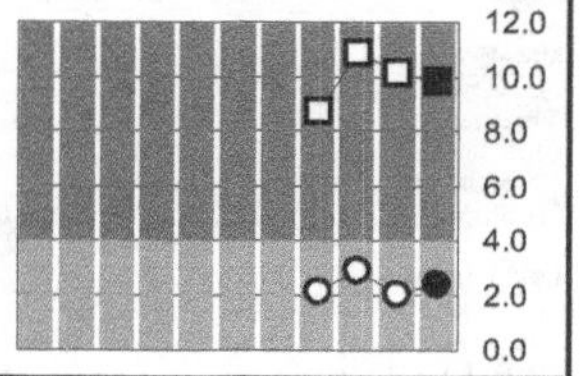

K/9
BB/9
12.0
10.0
8.0
6.0
4.0
2.0
0.0


| Yr | Team | W | L | Sv | IP | H | K | ERA | WHIP | K/9 | BB/9 | HR/9 | GB/F | $1L | $2L | Pts | RAA | H% | HR/fb | S% | FIP | GS | CG | QS/DS | GR | Hld | Bln | Lead | OPS | 1st Hf | 2nd Hf | vs RH | vs LH |
|---|---|---|---|---|---|---|---|---|---|---|---|---|---|---|---|---|---|---|---|---|---|---|---|---|---|---|---|---|---|---|---|---|---|
| | | Majors | | | | | | | | Skills | | | | Value | | | | Luck | | | | In Rotation | | | In Relief | | | | OPS | | | | |
| 07 | — | — | — | — | — | — | — | — | — | — | — | — | — | — | — | — | — | — | — | — | — | — | — | — | — | — | — | — | — | — | — | — | — |
| 08 | SF | 3 | 1 | 0 | 34 | 16 | 33 | 2.12 | 0.71 | 8.7 | 2.1 | 0.8 | 0.6 | $6 | $5 | 80 | +2 | 16% | 7% | 76% | 3.11 | — | — | — | 29 | 5 | 0 | –0.5 | .470 | .530 | .451 | .593 | .295 |
| 09 | SF | 5 | 2 | 2 | 34 | 30 | 41 | 3.97 | 1.21 | 10.9 | 2.9 | 0.3 | 0.6 | $2 | $1 | 100 | +0 | 33% | 2% | 65% | 2.14 | — | — | — | 45 | 10 | 0 | +1.1 | .631 | .663 | .610 | .684 | .542 |
| 10 | SF | 5 | 3 | 0 | 62 | 46 | 70 | 2.18 | 0.97 | 10.2 | 2.0 | 0.9 | 0.7 | $7 | $4 | 140 | +12 | 26% | 8% | 83% | 2.88 | — | — | — | 68 | 21 | 4 | +1.0 | .599 | .608 | .586 | .570 | .652 |

## Tyson Ross — 40 IP | $-4 | 30 pts

RP-24, SP-2 — Owned: 0% — RH

Ross spent most of 2010 in the A's bullpen, but, in the long term, Oakland sees him as a starter. Ross has had minor shoulder and elbow problems throughout his career, and he finished the minor-league season on the DL. He is on a throwing program, and the A's are optimistic that he will be ready for spring. (ML)

| Player | Age | IP | W | Sv | K | ERA | WHIP | K/9 | BB/9 | $2L | Pts |
|---|---|---|---|---|---|---|---|---|---|---|---|
| **Forecast** | | | | | | | | | | | |
| Ross T | 23 | 40 | 1 | 0 | 38 | 5.66 | 1.70 | 8.6 | 4.7 | -$4 | 30 |
| **Mini-Browser** | Age | IP | W | Sv | K | ERA | WHIP | K/9 | BB/9 | $2L | Pts |
| Coello R | 26 | 20 | 1 | 0 | 17 | 6.53 | 1.73 | 7.8 | 5.3 | -$4 | 10 |
| Ledezma W | 30 | 40 | 2 | 0 | 36 | 5.28 | 1.59 | 8.1 | 4.3 | -$4 | 40 |
| Diamond T | 27 | 60 | 2 | 0 | 44 | 4.93 | 1.57 | 6.7 | 5.1 | -$4 | 50 |
| Grabow J | 32 | 40 | 2 | 0 | 29 | 5.17 | 1.58 | 6.4 | 4.6 | -$4 | 30 |
| LeCure S | 26 | 60 | 3 | 0 | 53 | 5.20 | 1.56 | 8.0 | 3.8 | -$4 | 60 |

Minors (2010)

| Level | Leag | W | L | Sv | IP | H | K | ERA | WHIP | K/9 | BB/9 | HR/9 | GB/F |
|---|---|---|---|---|---|---|---|---|---|---|---|---|---|
| A | — | — | — | — | — | — | — | — | — | — | — | — | — |
| AA | — | — | — | — | — | — | — | — | — | — | — | — | — |
| AAA | PCL | 2 | 1 | 0 | 25 | 22 | 30 | 3.55 | 1.38 | 10.7 | 4.6 | 0.4 | — |

Competition at RP — Stats in 2010 as RP

| Thr | Player | GR | ERA | IP/G | Sv-Hld |
|---|---|---|---|---|---|
| RH | Ziegler B | 64 | 3.26 | 0.9 | 0-18 |
| RH | Wuertz M | 48 | 4.31 | 0.8 | 6-11 |
| RH | Bailey A | 47 | 1.47 | 1.0 | 25-0 |
| RH | Rodriguez H | 29 | 4.55 | 1.0 | 0-3 |

Weekly Points

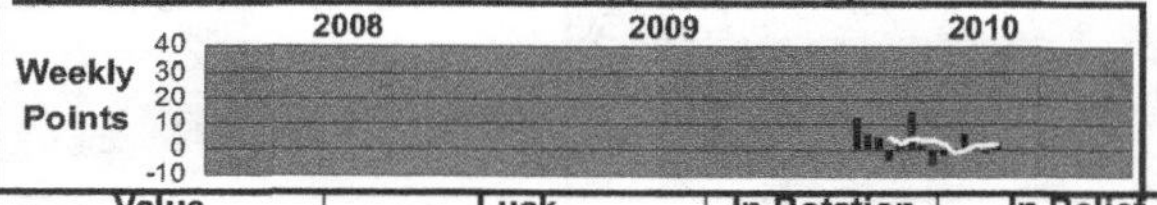

2008
2009
2010
40
30
20
10
0
-10


Ten-Year Trends

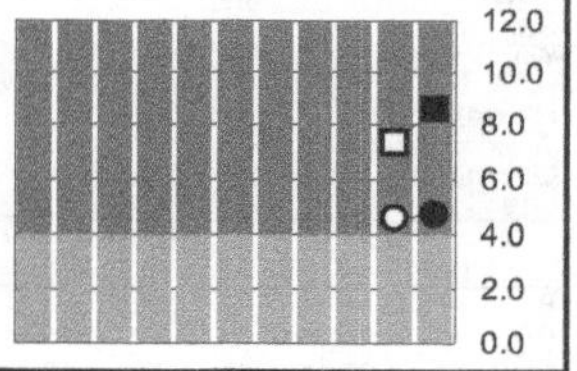

K/9
BB/9
12.0
10.0
8.0
6.0
4.0
2.0
0.0


| Yr | Team | W | L | Sv | IP | H | K | ERA | WHIP | K/9 | BB/9 | HR/9 | GB/F | $1L | $2L | Pts | RAA | H% | HR/fb | S% | FIP | GS | CG | QS/DS | GR | Hld | Bln | Lead | OPS | 1st Hf | 2nd Hf | vs RH | vs LH |
|---|---|---|---|---|---|---|---|---|---|---|---|---|---|---|---|---|---|---|---|---|---|---|---|---|---|---|---|---|---|---|---|---|---|
| | | Majors | | | | | | | | Skills | | | | Value | | | | Luck | | | | In Rotation | | | In Relief | | | | OPS | | | | |
| 07 | — | — | — | — | — | — | — | — | — | — | — | — | — | — | — | — | — | — | — | — | — | — | — | — | — | — | — | — | — | — | — | — | — |
| 08 | — | — | — | — | — | — | — | — | — | — | — | — | — | — | — | — | — | — | — | — | — | — | — | — | — | — | — | — | — | — | — | — | — |
| 09 | — | — | — | — | — | — | — | — | — | — | — | — | — | — | — | — | — | — | — | — | — | — | — | — | — | — | — | — | — | — | — | — | — |
| 10 | OAK | 1 | 4 | 1 | 39 | 39 | 32 | 5.49 | 1.50 | 7.3 | 4.6 | 0.9 | 1.8 | -$4 | -$15 | 30 | –6 | 32% | 12% | 64% | 4.52 | 2 | 0 | 0/0 | 24 | 2 | 1 | –0.2 | .754 | .754 | — | .819 | .674 |

## Ryan Rowland-Smith — 80 IP | $-4 | 50 pts

SP-20, RP-7 — Owned: 36% — LH

An absolutely atrocious 2010 season has shattered most of the promise surrounding Rowland-Smith, and he is unlikely to get another chance at Seattle's rotation. That said, the Mariners might look at putting him back in the bullpen, as that's the only place where Ryan has enjoyed sustained big-league success. (GC)

| Player | Age | IP | W | Sv | K | ERA | WHIP | K/9 | BB/9 | $2L | Pts |
|---|---|---|---|---|---|---|---|---|---|---|---|
| **Forecast** | | | | | | | | | | | |
| Rowland-Smith R | 28 | 80 | 3 | 0 | 45 | 5.35 | 1.52 | 5.1 | 3.4 | -$4 | 50 |
| **Mini-Browser** | Age | IP | W | Sv | K | ERA | WHIP | K/9 | BB/9 | $2L | Pts |
| Hardy B | 24 | 40 | 1 | 0 | 21 | 5.36 | 1.59 | 4.8 | 3.7 | -$4 | 20 |
| Stammen C | 27 | 60 | 2 | 0 | 39 | 5.14 | 1.47 | 5.8 | 2.8 | -$4 | 40 |
| Hernandez D | 25 | 60 | 4 | 0 | 56 | 5.64 | 1.64 | 8.5 | 4.6 | -$4 | 70 |
| Olson G | 27 | 50 | 2 | 0 | 35 | 5.51 | 1.58 | 6.3 | 4.4 | -$4 | 30 |
| Morris B | 24 | 40 | 2 | 0 | 27 | 5.15 | 1.55 | 6.2 | 3.8 | -$4 | 30 |

Minors (2010)

| Level | Leag | W | L | Sv | IP | H | K | ERA | WHIP | K/9 | BB/9 | HR/9 | GB/F |
|---|---|---|---|---|---|---|---|---|---|---|---|---|---|
| A | — | — | — | — | — | — | — | — | — | — | — | — | — |
| AA | — | — | — | — | — | — | — | — | — | — | — | — | — |
| AAA | PCL | 2 | 4 | 0 | 37 | 45 | 24 | 5.11 | 1.35 | 5.8 | 1.2 | 1.0 | — |

Competition at SP — Stats in 2010 as SP

| Thr | Player | GS | ERA | Supp | W-L |
|---|---|---|---|---|---|
| RH | Hernandez F | 34 | 2.27 | 3.1 | 13-12 |
| LH | Vargas J | 31 | 3.78 | 3.1 | 9-12 |
| RH | Fister D | 28 | 4.11 | 3.1 | 6-14 |
| LH | Rowland-Smith R | 20 | 6.93 | 3.0 | 1-10 |

Weekly Points

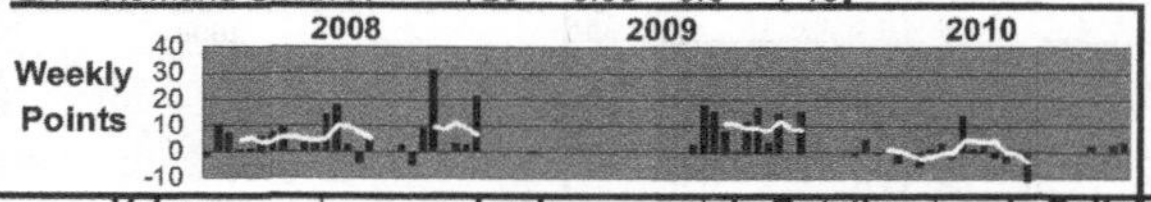

2008
2009
2010
40
30
20
10
0
-10


Ten-Year Trends

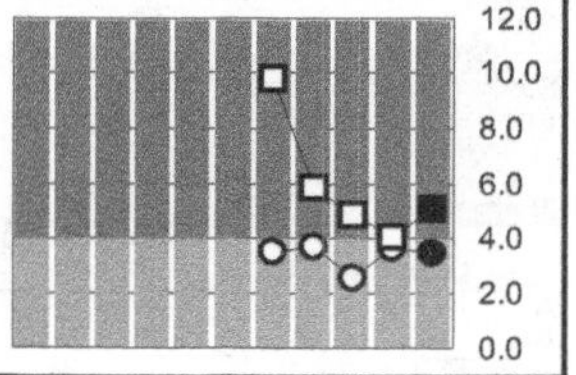

K/9
BB/9
12.0
10.0
8.0
6.0
4.0
2.0
0.0


| Yr | Team | W | L | Sv | IP | H | K | ERA | WHIP | K/9 | BB/9 | HR/9 | GB/F | $1L | $2L | Pts | RAA | H% | HR/fb | S% | FIP | GS | CG | QS/DS | GR | Hld | Bln | Lead | OPS | 1st Hf | 2nd Hf | vs RH | vs LH |
|---|---|---|---|---|---|---|---|---|---|---|---|---|---|---|---|---|---|---|---|---|---|---|---|---|---|---|---|---|---|---|---|---|---|
| | | Majors | | | | | | | | Skills | | | | Value | | | | Luck | | | | In Rotation | | | In Relief | | | | OPS | | | | |
| 07 | SEA | 1 | 0 | 0 | 38 | 39 | 42 | 3.96 | 1.40 | 9.8 | 3.5 | 0.9 | 0.7 | $0 | -$3 | 50 | +0 | 34% | 8% | 74% | 3.64 | — | — | — | 26 | 3 | 0 | –3.4 | .772 | .668 | .788 | .793 | .734 |
| 08 | SEA | 5 | 3 | 2 | 118 | 114 | 77 | 3.42 | 1.37 | 5.9 | 3.7 | 1.0 | 0.9 | $5 | -$1 | 130 | +9 | 28% | 8% | 79% | 4.64 | 12 | 0 | 8/0 | 35 | 1 | 1 | –1.3 | .729 | .675 | .768 | .658 | .872 |
| 09 | SEA | 5 | 4 | 0 | 96 | 87 | 52 | 3.74 | 1.18 | 4.9 | 2.5 | 0.8 | 0.9 | $6 | $2 | 100 | +5 | 26% | 7% | 70% | 4.28 | 15 | 0 | 9/1 | — | — | — | — | .669 | .733 | .665 | .699 | .571 |
| 10 | SEA | 1 | 10 | 0 | 109 | 141 | 49 | 6.75 | 1.69 | 4.0 | 3.6 | 2.1 | 0.8 | -$14 | -$39 | -10 | –40 | 31% | 14% | 64% | 6.58 | 20 | 0 | 4/6 | 7 | 0 | 0 | –0.5 | .954 | .913 | 1.080 | .951 | .964 |

## Dan Runzler — 60 IP | $-1 | 90 pts

RP-41 — Owned: 0% — LH

Runzler started 2010 with a spot in the Giants' bullpen and a shot at a set-up role. But he dislocated his knee in his first major-league AB in July and didn't return until September. Runzler is a solid (and cheap) left-handed option for SF. He'll rejoin the hunt for a set-up role, but a high BB/9 might disqualify him. (PB)

| Player | Age | IP | W | Sv | K | ERA | WHIP | K/9 | BB/9 | $2L | Pts |
|---|---|---|---|---|---|---|---|---|---|---|---|
| **Forecast** | | | | | | | | | | | |
| Runzler D | 26 | 60 | 4 | 0 | 71 | 4.01 | 1.64 | 10.7 | 5.2 | -$1 | 90 |
| **Mini-Browser** | Age | IP | W | Sv | K | ERA | WHIP | K/9 | BB/9 | $2L | Pts |
| Sherrill G | 33 | 40 | 3 | 0 | 36 | 4.08 | 1.44 | 8.1 | 4.4 | -$1 | 50 |
| Beltre O | 29 | 40 | 4 | 0 | 29 | 4.15 | 1.58 | 6.6 | 5.5 | -$1 | 60 |
| Blackburn N | 29 | 100 | 6 | 0 | 43 | 5.03 | 1.39 | 3.8 | 2.0 | -$1 | 80 |
| Santos S | 27 | 60 | 2 | 0 | 64 | 3.85 | 1.67 | 9.6 | 5.2 | -$1 | 70 |
| Badenhop B | 28 | 80 | 3 | 0 | 57 | 4.47 | 1.39 | 6.5 | 3.0 | -$1 | 70 |

Minors (2010)

| Level | Leag | W | L | Sv | IP | H | K | ERA | WHIP | K/9 | BB/9 | HR/9 | GB/F |
|---|---|---|---|---|---|---|---|---|---|---|---|---|---|
| A | CAL | 0 | 0 | 0 | 1 | 0 | 2 | 0.00 | 0.00 | 18.0 | 0.0 | 0.0 | — |
| AA | — | — | — | — | — | — | — | — | — | — | — | — | — |
| AAA | PCL | 0 | 1 | 0 | 7 | 8 | 5 | 3.86 | 1.71 | 6.4 | 5.1 | 0.0 | — |

Competition at RP — Stats in 2010 as RP

| Thr | Player | GR | ERA | IP/G | Sv-Hld |
|---|---|---|---|---|---|
| LH | Affeldt J | 53 | 4.14 | 0.9 | 4-7 |
| LH | Runzler D | 41 | 3.03 | 0.8 | 0-5 |
| LH | Lopez J | 27 | 1.42 | 0.7 | 0-5 |

Weekly Points

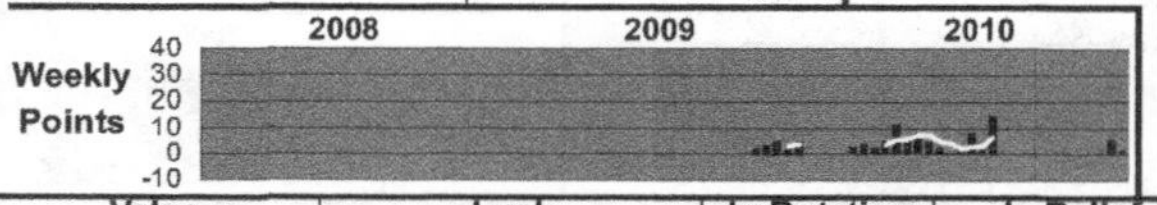

2008
2009
2010
40
30
20
10
0
-10


Ten-Year Trends

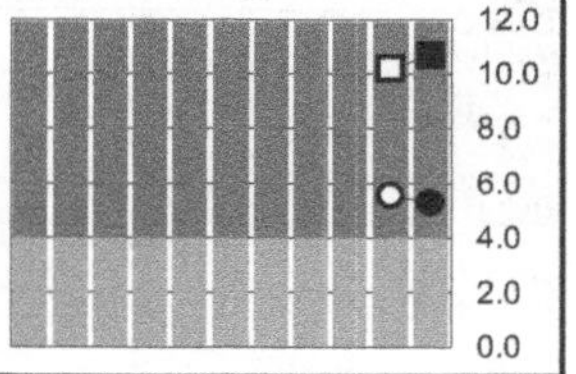

K/9
BB/9
12.0
10.0
8.0
6.0
4.0
2.0
0.0


| Yr | Team | W | L | Sv | IP | H | K | ERA | WHIP | K/9 | BB/9 | HR/9 | GB/F | $1L | $2L | Pts | RAA | H% | HR/fb | S% | FIP | GS | CG | QS/DS | GR | Hld | Bln | Lead | OPS | 1st Hf | 2nd Hf | vs RH | vs LH |
|---|---|---|---|---|---|---|---|---|---|---|---|---|---|---|---|---|---|---|---|---|---|---|---|---|---|---|---|---|---|---|---|---|---|
| | | Majors | | | | | | | | Skills | | | | Value | | | | Luck | | | | In Rotation | | | In Relief | | | | OPS | | | | |
| 07 | — | — | — | — | — | — | — | — | — | — | — | — | — | — | — | — | — | — | — | — | — | — | — | — | — | — | — | — | — | — | — | — | — |
| 08 | — | — | — | — | — | — | — | — | — | — | — | — | — | — | — | — | — | — | — | — | — | — | — | — | — | — | — | — | — | — | — | — | — |
| 09 | SF | 0 | 0 | 0 | 8 | 6 | 11 | 1.04 | 1.27 | 11.4 | 5.2 | 1.0 | 1.4 | -$1 | -$1 | 10 | +3 | 25% | 14% | 100% | 3.89 | — | — | — | 11 | 2 | 0 | +1.5 | .597 | — | .597 | .978 | .259 |
| 10 | SF | 3 | 0 | 0 | 32 | 29 | 37 | 3.03 | 1.50 | 10.2 | 5.5 | 0.3 | 1.9 | -$2 | -$8 | 60 | +3 | 35% | 5% | 79% | 3.17 | — | — | — | 41 | 5 | 0 | +0.2 | .685 | .699 | .533 | .673 | .699 |

## Adam Russell

**40 IP | $-1 | 40 pts**

RP-12 | Owned: 1% | RH

The hulking former White Sox prospect performed well in 15 IP with San Diego, but he had a mediocre year in Triple-A, missing bats but walking the yard. Russell needs dependable control to secure a relief spot with the Pads. A promising sign is the rise in his GB/F (he has a career 0.7 HR/9 in the minors). (DG)

| Player | Age | IP | W | Sv | K | ERA | WHIP | K/9 | BB/9 | $2L | Pts |
|---|---|---|---|---|---|---|---|---|---|---|---|
| Russell A | 27 | 40 | 2 | 0 | 36 | 4.27 | 1.43 | 8.1 | 4.0 | -$1 | 40 |
| **Mini-Browser** | Age | IP | W | Sv | K | ERA | WHIP | K/9 | BB/9 | $2L | Pts |
| Judy J | 25 | 60 | 1 | 0 | 50 | 4.53 | 1.47 | 7.6 | 3.4 | -$1 | 50 |
| Sonnanstine A | 28 | 50 | 2 | 0 | 31 | 5.09 | 1.34 | 5.5 | 2.4 | -$1 | 40 |
| Thomas B | 33 | 40 | 3 | 0 | 21 | 4.29 | 1.55 | 4.7 | 3.6 | -$1 | 40 |
| Outman J | 26 | 60 | 3 | 0 | 54 | 4.72 | 1.56 | 8.1 | 4.3 | -$1 | 70 |
| Hawkins L | 38 | 40 | 2 | 0 | 27 | 4.60 | 1.33 | 6.1 | 2.8 | -$1 | 40 |

Competition at RP / Stats in 2010 as RP

| Thr | Player | GR | ERA | IP/G | Sv-Hld |
|---|---|---|---|---|---|
| RH | Gregerson L | 80 | 3.22 | 1.0 | 2-40 |
| RH | Adams M | 70 | 1.76 | 1.0 | 0-38 |
| RH | Bell H | 67 | 1.93 | 1.0 | 47-0 |
| RH | Mujica E | 59 | 3.62 | 1.2 | 0-4 |

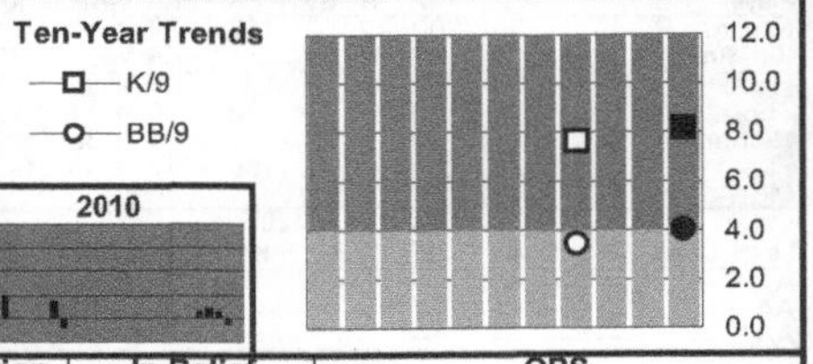


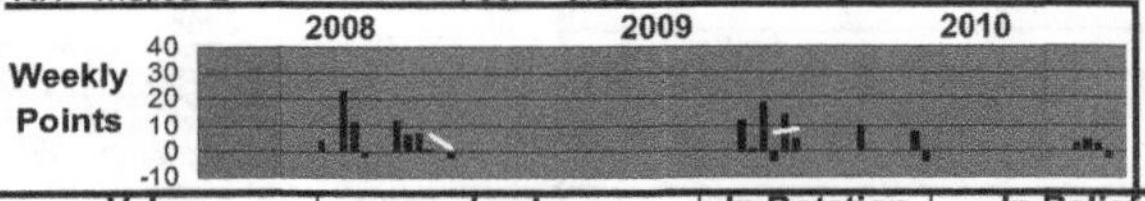


Minors (2010)

| Level | Leag | W | L | Sv | IP | H | K | ERA | WHIP | K/9 | BB/9 | HR/9 | GB/F |
|---|---|---|---|---|---|---|---|---|---|---|---|---|---|
| A | — | — | — | — | — | — | — | — | — | — | — | — | — |
| AA | — | — | — | — | — | — | — | — | — | — | — | — | — |
| AAA | PCL | 4 | 9 | 14 | 51 | 58 | 51 | 4.88 | 1.74 | 8.9 | 5.6 | 0.7 | — |

Majors

| Yr | Team | W | L | Sv | IP | H | K | ERA | WHIP | K/9 | BB/9 | HR/9 | GB/F |
|---|---|---|---|---|---|---|---|---|---|---|---|---|---|
| 07 | — | — | — | — | — | — | — | — | — | — | — | — | — |
| 08 | CHW | 4 | 0 | 0 | 26 | 30 | 22 | 5.19 | 1.54 | 7.6 | 3.5 | 0.3 | 1.1 |
| 09 | SD | 3 | 1 | 0 | 12 | 13 | 14 | 3.65 | 1.95 | 10.2 | 8.0 | 0.0 | 1.2 |
| 10 | SD | 0 | 0 | 0 | 15 | 14 | 18 | 4.02 | 1.21 | 10.3 | 2.9 | 0.0 | 2.3 |

| Yr | Value $1L | $2L | Pts | RAA | Luck H% | HR/fb | S% | FIP | In Rotation GS | CG | QS/DS | In Relief GR | Hld | Bln | Lead | OPS | 1st Hf | 2nd Hf | vs RH | vs LH |
|---|---|---|---|---|---|---|---|---|---|---|---|---|---|---|---|---|---|---|---|---|
| 07 | — | — | — | — | — | — | — | — | — | — | — | — | — | — | — | — | — | — | — | — |
| 08 | -$1 | -$3 | 50 | −3 | 36% | 3% | 64% | 3.26 | — | — | — | 22 | 0 | 0 | 0.0 | .741 | .869 | .684 | .677 | .813 |
| 09 | -$1 | -$2 | 40 | −0 | 36% | 0% | 79% | 3.61 | — | — | — | 15 | 4 | 0 | +0.5 | .673 | — | .673 | .630 | .733 |
| 10 | -$4 | -$10 | 20 | −1 | 38% | 0% | 63% | 1.86 | — | — | — | 12 | 0 | 0 | −2.6 | .602 | .639 | .547 | .734 | .393 |

## Marc Rzepczynski

**80 IP | $-1 | 100 pts**

SP-12, RP-2 | Owned: 0% | LH

Rzepczynski looked to follow up on a strong rookie campaign, but a fractured finger delayed the start of his 2010 season. When he finally took the field, he was tentative and didn't trust his stuff as much as in 2009. With TOR's depth at SP, Zep could end up in the bullpen, but it is early to write him off completely. (MH)

| Player | Age | IP | W | Sv | K | ERA | WHIP | K/9 | BB/9 | $2L | Pts |
|---|---|---|---|---|---|---|---|---|---|---|---|
| Rzepczynski M | 25 | 80 | 5 | 0 | 82 | 4.79 | 1.63 | 9.3 | 4.7 | -$1 | 100 |
| **Mini-Browser** | Age | IP | W | Sv | K | ERA | WHIP | K/9 | BB/9 | $2L | Pts |
| Sonnanstine A | 28 | 50 | 2 | 0 | 31 | 5.09 | 1.34 | 5.5 | 2.4 | -$1 | 40 |
| Thomas B | 33 | 40 | 3 | 0 | 21 | 4.29 | 1.55 | 4.7 | 3.6 | -$1 | 40 |
| Outman J | 26 | 60 | 3 | 0 | 54 | 4.72 | 1.56 | 8.1 | 4.3 | -$1 | 70 |
| Hawkins L | 38 | 40 | 2 | 0 | 27 | 4.60 | 1.33 | 6.1 | 2.8 | -$1 | 40 |
| Russell A | 27 | 40 | 2 | 0 | 36 | 4.27 | 1.43 | 8.1 | 4.0 | -$1 | 40 |

Competition at RP / Stats in 2010 as RP

| Thr | Player | GR | ERA | IP/G | Sv-Hld |
|---|---|---|---|---|---|
| LH | Downs S | 67 | 2.64 | 0.9 | 0-26 |
| LH | Purcey D | 33 | 3.71 | 1.0 | 1-3 |
| LH | Tallet B | 29 | 6.84 | 1.7 | 0-1 |
| LH | Carlson J | 20 | 4.61 | 0.7 | 1-2 |

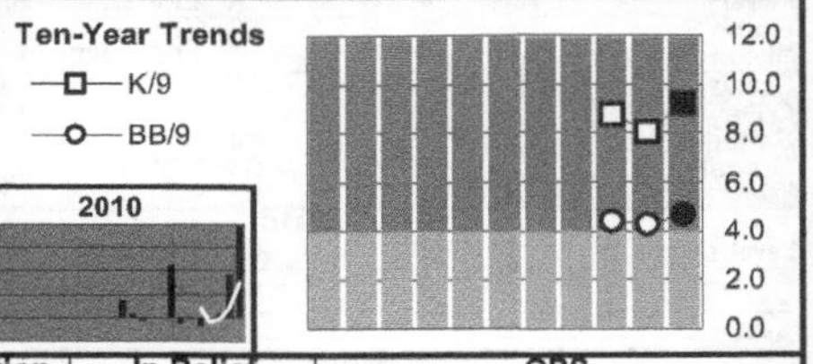


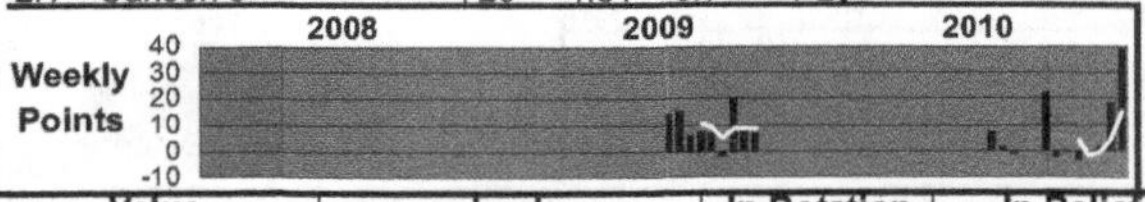


Minors (2010)

| Level | Leag | W | L | Sv | IP | H | K | ERA | WHIP | K/9 | BB/9 | HR/9 | GB/F |
|---|---|---|---|---|---|---|---|---|---|---|---|---|---|
| A | — | — | — | — | — | — | — | — | — | — | — | — | — |
| AA | — | — | — | — | — | — | — | — | — | — | — | — | — |
| AAA | PCL | 5 | 5 | 0 | 67 | 81 | 61 | 6.04 | 1.61 | 8.2 | 3.6 | 1.3 | — |

Majors

| Yr | Team | W | L | Sv | IP | H | K | ERA | WHIP | K/9 | BB/9 | HR/9 | GB/F |
|---|---|---|---|---|---|---|---|---|---|---|---|---|---|
| 07 | — | — | — | — | — | — | — | — | — | — | — | — | — |
| 08 | — | — | — | — | — | — | — | — | — | — | — | — | — |
| 09 | TOR | 2 | 4 | 0 | 61 | 51 | 60 | 3.67 | 1.32 | 8.8 | 4.4 | 1.0 | 1.8 |
| 10 | TOR | 4 | 4 | 0 | 63 | 72 | 57 | 4.95 | 1.60 | 8.1 | 4.2 | 1.1 | 1.6 |

| Yr | Value $1L | $2L | Pts | RAA | Luck H% | HR/fb | S% | FIP | In Rotation GS | CG | QS/DS | In Relief GR | Hld | Bln | Lead | OPS | 1st Hf | 2nd Hf | vs RH | vs LH |
|---|---|---|---|---|---|---|---|---|---|---|---|---|---|---|---|---|---|---|---|---|
| 07 | — | — | — | — | — | — | — | — | — | — | — | — | — | — | — | — | — | — | — | — |
| 08 | — | — | — | — | — | — | — | — | — | — | — | — | — | — | — | — | — | — | — | — |
| 09 | $3 | $0 | 80 | +1 | 28% | 15% | 76% | 4.29 | 11 | 0 | 7/1 | — | — | — | — | .682 | .571 | .708 | .691 | .651 |
| 10 | -$3 | -$16 | 70 | −8 | 34% | 13% | 71% | 4.56 | 12 | 0 | 3/3 | 2 | 2 | 0 | +0.3 | .840 | .954 | .828 | .895 | .671 |

## CC Sabathia

**240 IP | $27 | 400 pts**

SP-34 | Owned: 100% | LH

2010 was a landmark year for Sabathia, who won 20 games for the first time. That said, although his ERA dipped from 2009, his FIP rose and was quite higher (3.18 ERA vs. 3.67 FIP). Sabathia's Ten-Year Trends support the idea that 2010 was not a replay of 2008 but was another small step down from that peak. (LS)

| Player | Age | IP | W | Sv | K | ERA | WHIP | K/9 | BB/9 | $2L | Pts |
|---|---|---|---|---|---|---|---|---|---|---|---|
| Sabathia C | 30 | 240 | 20 | 0 | 198 | 3.45 | 1.18 | 7.4 | 2.5 | $27 | 400 |
| **Mini-Browser** | Age | IP | W | Sv | K | ERA | WHIP | K/9 | BB/9 | $2L | Pts |
| Halladay R | 33 | 240 | 20 | 0 | 189 | 2.96 | 1.06 | 7.1 | 1.2 | $35 | 420 |
| Hernandez F | 24 | 250 | 16 | 0 | 221 | 3.00 | 1.17 | 7.9 | 2.8 | $31 | 400 |
| Wainwright A | 29 | 240 | 19 | 0 | 196 | 3.15 | 1.17 | 7.4 | 2.4 | $28 | 400 |
| Lincecum T | 26 | 220 | 17 | 0 | 232 | 3.19 | 1.22 | 9.5 | 3.1 | $26 | 410 |
| Lee C | 32 | 220 | 14 | 0 | 164 | 3.52 | 1.13 | 6.7 | 1.5 | $23 | 310 |

Competition at SP / Stats in 2010 as SP

| Thr | Player | GS | ERA | Supp | W-L |
|---|---|---|---|---|---|
| LH | Sabathia C | 34 | 3.18 | 5.7 | 21-7 |
| RH | Burnett A | 33 | 5.26 | 4.3 | 10-15 |
| RH | Hughes P | 29 | 4.23 | 6.5 | 17-8 |
| RH | Vazquez J | 26 | 5.56 | 4.1 | 8-10 |

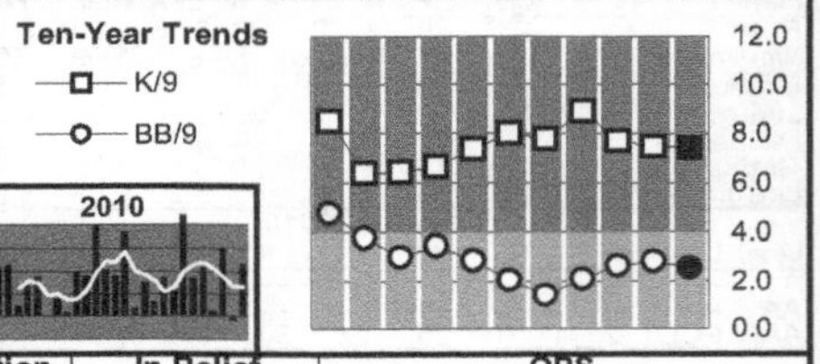


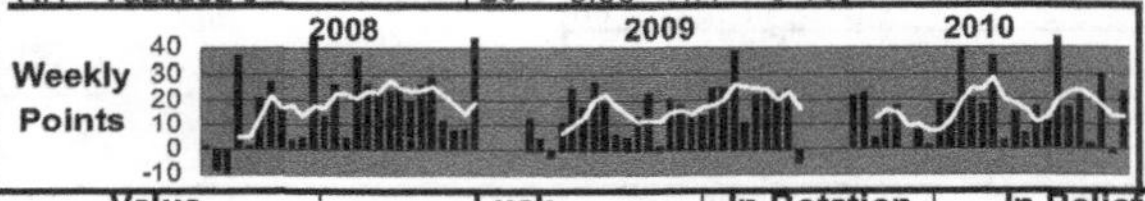


Minors (2010)

| Level | Leag | W | L | Sv | IP | H | K | ERA | WHIP | K/9 | BB/9 | HR/9 | GB/F |
|---|---|---|---|---|---|---|---|---|---|---|---|---|---|
| A | — | — | — | — | — | — | — | — | — | — | — | — | — |
| AA | — | — | — | — | — | — | — | — | — | — | — | — | — |
| AAA | — | — | — | — | — | — | — | — | — | — | — | — | — |

Majors

| Yr | Team | W | L | Sv | IP | H | K | ERA | WHIP | K/9 | BB/9 | HR/9 | GB/F |
|---|---|---|---|---|---|---|---|---|---|---|---|---|---|
| 07 | CLE | 19 | 7 | 0 | 241 | 238 | 209 | 3.21 | 1.14 | 7.8 | 1.4 | 0.7 | 1.2 |
| 08 | 2TM | 17 | 10 | 0 | 253 | 223 | 251 | 2.70 | 1.11 | 8.9 | 2.1 | 0.7 | 1.5 |
| 09 | NYY | 19 | 8 | 0 | 230 | 197 | 197 | 3.37 | 1.15 | 7.7 | 2.6 | 0.7 | 1.2 |
| 10 | NYY | 21 | 7 | 0 | 237 | 209 | 197 | 3.18 | 1.19 | 7.5 | 2.8 | 0.8 | 1.5 |

| Yr | Value $1L | $2L | Pts | RAA | Luck H% | HR/fb | S% | FIP | In Rotation GS | CG | QS/DS | In Relief GR | Hld | Bln | Lead | OPS | 1st Hf | 2nd Hf | vs RH | vs LH |
|---|---|---|---|---|---|---|---|---|---|---|---|---|---|---|---|---|---|---|---|---|
| 07 | $28 | $19 | 420 | +25 | 32% | 8% | 74% | 3.10 | 34 | 4 | 25/1 | — | — | — | — | .684 | .717 | .643 | .723 | .545 |
| 08 | $31 | $25 | 460 | +40 | 31% | 9% | 78% | 2.94 | 35 | 10 | 25/2 | — | — | — | — | .625 | .695 | .539 | .643 | .569 |
| 09 | $24 | $15 | 400 | +17 | 28% | 7% | 72% | 3.48 | 34 | 2 | 21/5 | — | — | — | — | .653 | .650 | .656 | .681 | .560 |
| 10 | $26 | $18 | 420 | +25 | 29% | 9% | 76% | 3.67 | 34 | 2 | 26/2 | — | — | — | — | .656 | .645 | .668 | .649 | .678 |

## Fernando Salas

**40 IP | $-1 | 50 pts**

RP-27 | Owned: 0% | RH

Salas in 2010 made frequent trips between Memphis and STL. His sophomore season in Triple-A featured heightened dominance and control, and his innings with the parent club were far from an embarrassment. All indications point to Salas sticking in the Cardinals' bullpen in 2011, initially in low-leverage duties. (AB)

| Player | Age | IP | W | Sv | K | ERA | WHIP | K/9 | BB/9 | $2L | Pts |
|---|---|---|---|---|---|---|---|---|---|---|---|
| Salas F | 25 | 40 | 1 | 0 | 41 | 4.10 | 1.45 | 9.2 | 3.6 | -$1 | 50 |
| **Mini-Browser** | Age | IP | W | Sv | K | ERA | WHIP | K/9 | BB/9 | $2L | Pts |
| Melancon M | 26 | 40 | 2 | 0 | 39 | 4.45 | 1.40 | 8.7 | 3.5 | -$1 | 50 |
| Bergesen B | 25 | 160 | 8 | 0 | 87 | 4.90 | 1.48 | 4.9 | 2.6 | -$1 | 130 |
| Johnson J | 27 | 60 | 3 | 2 | 41 | 4.61 | 1.53 | 6.2 | 3.3 | -$1 | 60 |
| Hill R | 31 | 40 | 2 | 0 | 35 | 4.69 | 1.48 | 7.8 | 4.6 | -$1 | 50 |
| Norberto J | 24 | 40 | 3 | 0 | 47 | 4.13 | 1.59 | 10.5 | 6.4 | -$1 | 60 |

Competition at RP / Stats in 2010 as RP

| Thr | Player | GR | ERA | IP/G | Sv-Hld |
|---|---|---|---|---|---|
| RH | McClellan K | 68 | 2.27 | 1.1 | 2-19 |
| RH | Boggs M | 61 | 3.61 | 1.1 | 0-6 |
| RH | Franklin R | 59 | 3.46 | 1.1 | 27-0 |
| RH | Motte J | 56 | 2.24 | 0.9 | 2-12 |

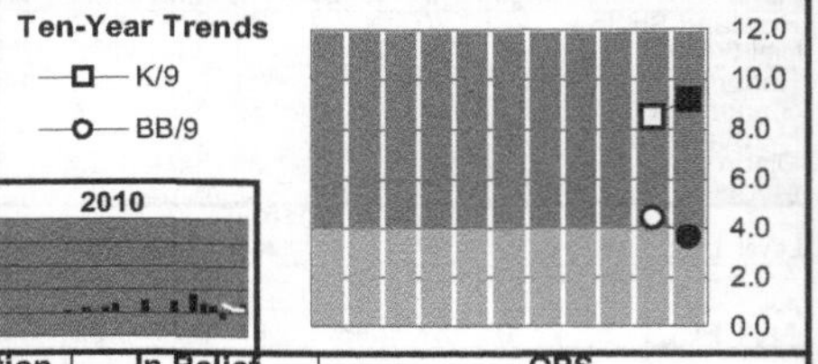


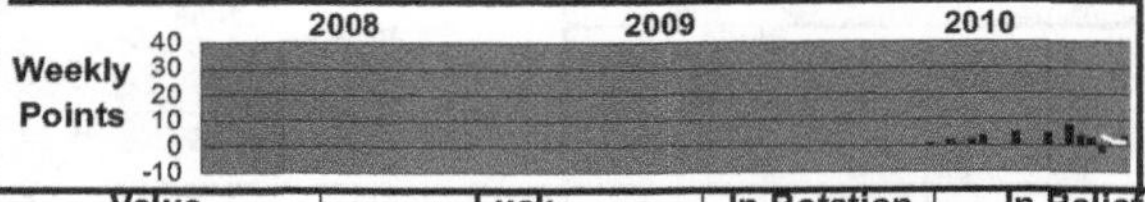


Minors (2010)

| Level | Leag | W | L | Sv | IP | H | K | ERA | WHIP | K/9 | BB/9 | HR/9 | GB/F |
|---|---|---|---|---|---|---|---|---|---|---|---|---|---|
| A | — | — | — | — | — | — | — | — | — | — | — | — | — |
| AA | — | — | — | — | — | — | — | — | — | — | — | — | — |
| AAA | PCL | 1 | 0 | 19 | 35 | 26 | 44 | 3.79 | 0.98 | 11.1 | 2.3 | 0.5 | — |

Majors

| Yr | Team | W | L | Sv | IP | H | K | ERA | WHIP | K/9 | BB/9 | HR/9 | GB/F |
|---|---|---|---|---|---|---|---|---|---|---|---|---|---|
| 07 | — | — | — | — | — | — | — | — | — | — | — | — | — |
| 08 | — | — | — | — | — | — | — | — | — | — | — | — | — |
| 09 | — | — | — | — | — | — | — | — | — | — | — | — | — |
| 10 | STL | 0 | 0 | 0 | 30 | 28 | 29 | 3.52 | 1.40 | 8.5 | 4.4 | 1.2 | 0.7 |

| Yr | Value $1L | $2L | Pts | RAA | Luck H% | HR/fb | S% | FIP | In Rotation GS | CG | QS/DS | In Relief GR | Hld | Bln | Lead | OPS | 1st Hf | 2nd Hf | vs RH | vs LH |
|---|---|---|---|---|---|---|---|---|---|---|---|---|---|---|---|---|---|---|---|---|
| 07 | — | — | — | — | — | — | — | — | — | — | — | — | — | — | — | — | — | — | — | — |
| 08 | — | — | — | — | — | — | — | — | — | — | — | — | — | — | — | — | — | — | — | — |
| 09 | — | — | — | — | — | — | — | — | — | — | — | — | — | — | — | — | — | — | — | — |
| 10 | -$4 | -$10 | 30 | +1 | 29% | 10% | 79% | 4.47 | — | — | — | 27 | 1 | 1 | +0.4 | .748 | .548 | .805 | .665 | .866 |

## Chris Sale

**160 IP | $18 | 320 pts**

RP-21 | Owned: 1% | LH

Scouted in the 2010 draft as rarely hitting 94 MPH, Sale topped 100 on hot guns, and his funky delivery had him closing games in Chicago by year's end. "Plan A" is for Sale to move back to the rotation, but if Jake Peavy and Freddy Garcia squeeze him out, he could morph into one of the great lefty closers. (RM)

| Player | Age | IP | W | Sv | K | ERA | WHIP | K/9 | BB/9 | $2L | Pts |
|---|---|---|---|---|---|---|---|---|---|---|---|
| Sale C | 22 | 160 | 10 | 0 | 225 | 3.38 | 1.28 | 12.7 | 5.1 | $18 | 320 |
| **Mini-Browser** | Age | IP | W | Sv | K | ERA | WHIP | K/9 | BB/9 | $2L | Pts |
| Soriano R | 31 | 60 | 3 | 44 | 61 | 2.89 | 1.05 | 9.2 | 2.7 | $19 | 320 |
| Hamels C | 27 | 200 | 13 | 0 | 175 | 3.67 | 1.17 | 7.9 | 2.3 | $19 | 310 |
| Latos M | 23 | 160 | 11 | 0 | 160 | 3.31 | 1.15 | 9.0 | 2.7 | $18 | 280 |
| Oswalt R | 33 | 200 | 12 | 0 | 153 | 3.56 | 1.16 | 6.9 | 2.2 | $18 | 270 |
| Bell H | 33 | 60 | 4 | 38 | 62 | 2.67 | 1.15 | 9.2 | 3.2 | $18 | 300 |

Competition at SP / Stats in 2010 as SP

| Thr | Player | GS | ERA | Supp | W-L |
|---|---|---|---|---|---|
| LH | Buehrle M | 33 | 4.28 | 4.8 | 13-13 |
| LH | Danks J | 32 | 3.72 | 4.5 | 15-11 |
| RH | Jackson E | 32 | 4.47 | 4.3 | 10-12 |
| RH | Floyd G | 31 | 4.08 | 3.8 | 10-13 |

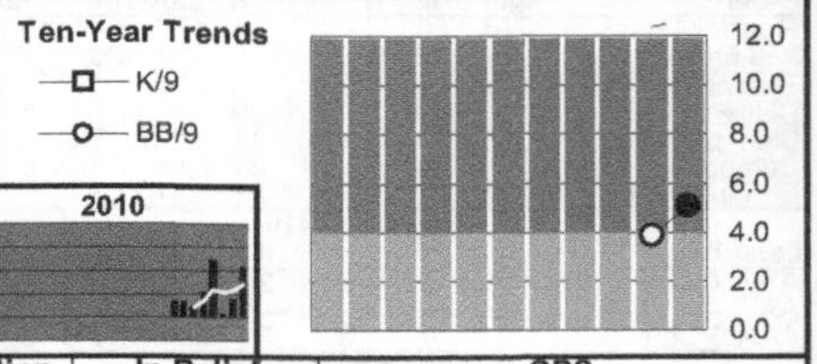


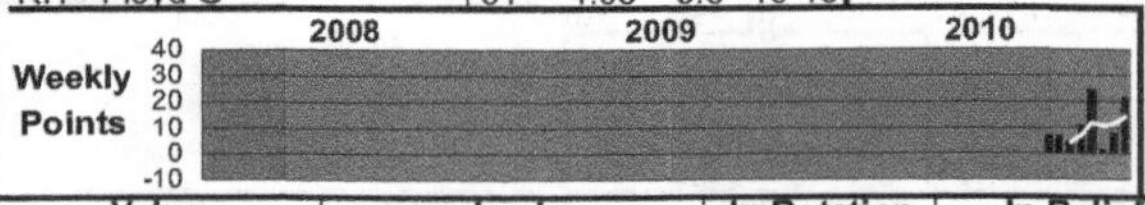


Minors (2010)

| Level | Leag | W | L | Sv | IP | H | K | ERA | WHIP | K/9 | BB/9 | HR/9 | GB/F |
|---|---|---|---|---|---|---|---|---|---|---|---|---|---|
| A | CAR | 0 | 0 | 0 | 4 | 3 | 4 | 2.25 | 1.25 | 9.0 | 4.5 | 0.0 | — |
| AA | — | — | — | — | — | — | — | — | — | — | — | — | — |
| AAA | IL | 0 | 0 | 0 | 6 | 3 | 15 | 2.84 | 1.11 | 21.3 | 5.7 | 2.8 | — |

Majors

| Yr | Team | W | L | Sv | IP | H | K | ERA | WHIP | K/9 | BB/9 | HR/9 | GB/F |
|---|---|---|---|---|---|---|---|---|---|---|---|---|---|
| 07 | — | — | — | — | — | — | — | — | — | — | — | — | — |
| 08 | — | — | — | — | — | — | — | — | — | — | — | — | — |
| 09 | — | — | — | — | — | — | — | — | — | — | — | — | — |
| 10 | CHW | 2 | 1 | 4 | 23 | 15 | 32 | 1.93 | 1.07 | 12.3 | 3.9 | 0.8 | 1.4 |

| Yr | Value $1L | $2L | Pts | RAA | Luck H% | HR/fb | S% | FIP | In Rotation GS | CG | QS/DS | In Relief GR | Hld | Bln | Lead | OPS | 1st Hf | 2nd Hf | vs RH | vs LH |
|---|---|---|---|---|---|---|---|---|---|---|---|---|---|---|---|---|---|---|---|---|
| 07 | — | — | — | — | — | — | — | — | — | — | — | — | — | — | — | — | — | — | — | — |
| 08 | — | — | — | — | — | — | — | — | — | — | — | — | — | — | — | — | — | — | — | — |
| 09 | — | — | — | — | — | — | — | — | — | — | — | — | — | — | — | — | — | — | — | — |
| 10 | $2 | -$4 | 80 | +7 | 28% | 11% | 87% | 2.96 | — | — | — | 21 | 2 | 0 | +0.2 | .546 | — | .546 | .454 | .694 |

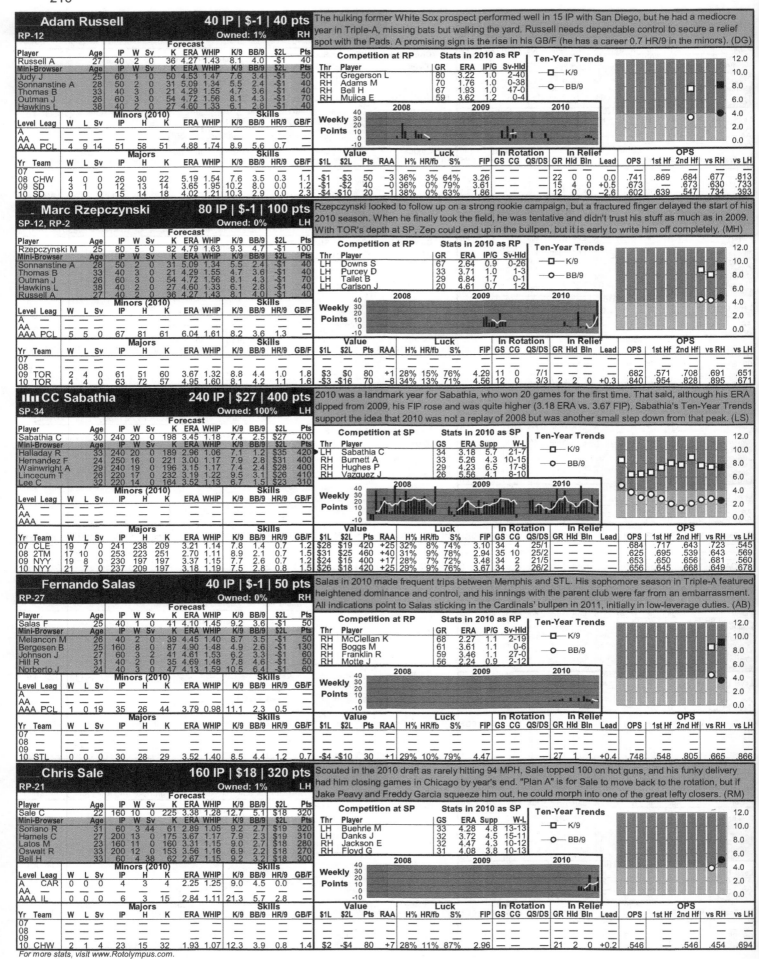

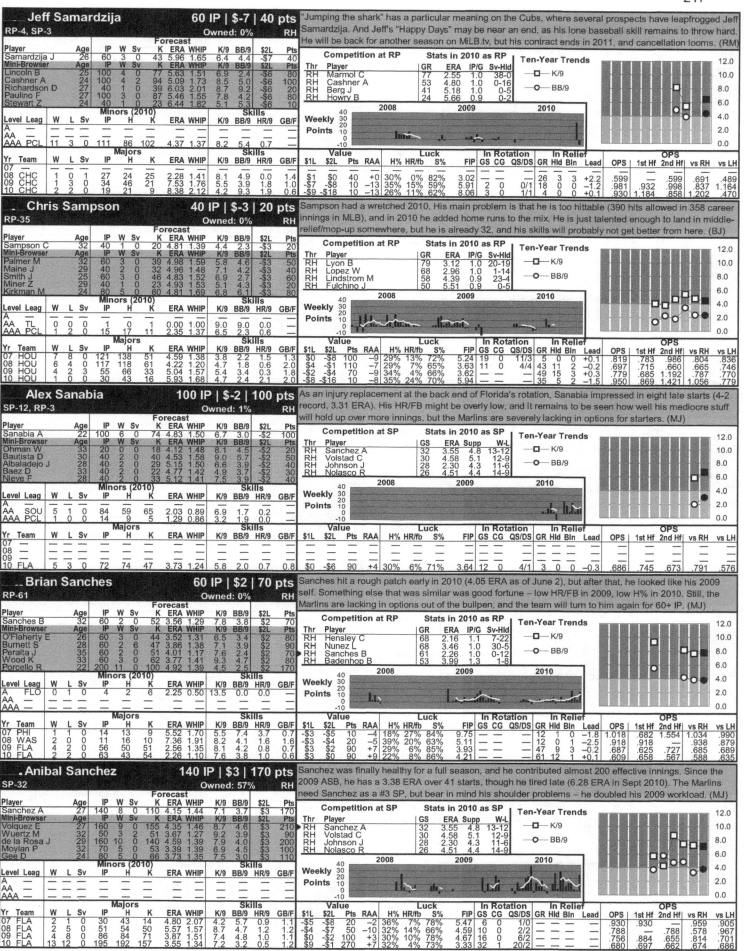

## Jeff Samardzija — 60 IP | $-7 | 40 pts

RP-4, SP-3 — Owned: 0% — RH

"Jumping the shark" has a particular meaning on the Cubs, where several prospects have leapfrogged Jeff Samardzija. And Jeff's "Happy Days" may be near an end, as his lone baseball skill remains to throw hard. He will be back for another season on MiLB.tv, but his contract ends in 2011, and cancellation looms. (RM)

| Player | Age | IP | W | Sv | K | ERA | WHIP | K/9 | BB/9 | $2L | Pts |
|---|---|---|---|---|---|---|---|---|---|---|---|
| Samardzija J | 26 | 60 | 3 | 0 | 43 | 5.96 | 1.65 | 6.4 | 4.4 | -$7 | 40 |
| **Mini-Browser** | **Age** | **IP** | **W** | **Sv** | **K** | **ERA** | **WHIP** | **K/9** | **BB/9** | **$2L** | **Pts** |
| Lincoln B | 25 | 100 | 4 | 0 | 77 | 5.63 | 1.51 | 6.9 | 2.4 | -$6 | 80 |
| Cashner A | 24 | 100 | 4 | 2 | 94 | 5.09 | 1.73 | 8.5 | 5.0 | -$6 | 100 |
| Richardson D | 27 | 40 | 1 | 0 | 39 | 6.03 | 2.01 | 8.7 | 9.2 | -$6 | 20 |
| Paulino F | 27 | 100 | 3 | 0 | 87 | 5.46 | 1.55 | 7.8 | 4.2 | -$6 | 80 |
| Stewart Z | 24 | 40 | 1 | 0 | 23 | 6.44 | 1.82 | 5.1 | 5.3 | -$6 | 10 |

Minors (2010) / Skills

| Level | Leag | W | L | Sv | IP | H | K | ERA | WHIP | K/9 | BB/9 | HR/9 | GB/F |
|---|---|---|---|---|---|---|---|---|---|---|---|---|---|
| A | — | — | — | — | — | — | — | — | — | — | — | — | — |
| AA | — | — | — | — | — | — | — | — | — | — | — | — | — |
| AAA | PCL | 11 | 3 | 0 | 111 | 86 | 102 | 4.37 | 1.37 | 8.2 | 5.4 | 0.7 | — |

Majors / Skills

| Yr | Team | W | L | Sv | IP | H | K | ERA | WHIP | K/9 | BB/9 | HR/9 | GB/F |
|---|---|---|---|---|---|---|---|---|---|---|---|---|---|
| 07 | — | — | — | — | — | — | — | — | — | — | — | — | — |
| 08 | CHC | 1 | 0 | 1 | 27 | 24 | 25 | 2.28 | 1.41 | 8.1 | 4.9 | 0.0 | 1.4 |
| 09 | CHC | 1 | 3 | 0 | 34 | 46 | 21 | 7.53 | 1.76 | 5.5 | 3.9 | 1.8 | 1.0 |
| 10 | CHC | 2 | 2 | 0 | 19 | 21 | 9 | 8.38 | 2.12 | 4.2 | 9.3 | 1.9 | 0.6 |

Competition at RP / Stats in 2010 as RP

| Thr | Player | GR | ERA | IP/G | Sv-Hld |
|---|---|---|---|---|---|
| RH | Marmol C | 77 | 2.55 | 1.0 | 38-0 |
| RH | Cashner A | 53 | 4.80 | 1.0 | 0-16 |
| RH | Berg J | 41 | 5.18 | 1.0 | 0-5 |
| RH | Howry B | 24 | 5.66 | 0.9 | 0-2 |

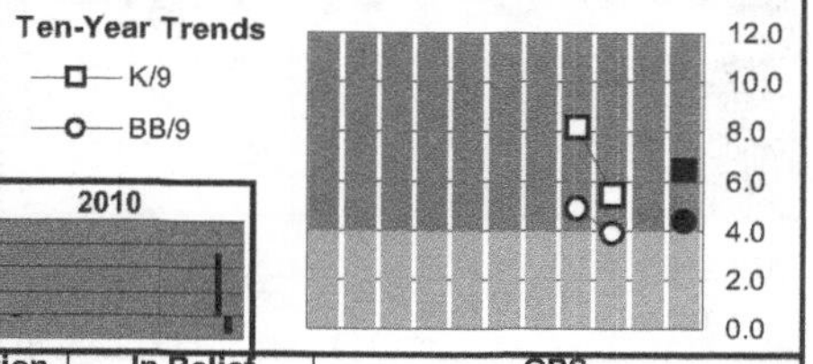


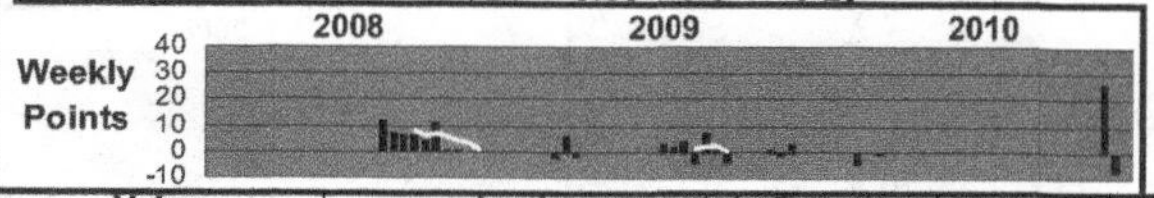


| Yr | $1L | $2L | Pts | RAA | H% | HR/fb | S% | FIP | GS | CG | QS/DS | GR | Hld | Bln | Lead | OPS | 1st Hf | 2nd Hf | vs RH | vs LH |
|---|---|---|---|---|---|---|---|---|---|---|---|---|---|---|---|---|---|---|---|---|
| 07 | — | — | — | — | — | — | — | — | — | — | — | — | — | — | — | — | — | — | — | — |
| 08 | $1 | $0 | 40 | +0 | 30% | 0% | 82% | 3.02 | — | — | — | 26 | 3 | 3 | +2.2 | .599 | — | .599 | .691 | .489 |
| 09 | -$7 | -$8 | 10 | –13 | 35% | 15% | 59% | 5.91 | 2 | 0 | 0/1 | 18 | 0 | 0 | –1.2 | .981 | .932 | .998 | .837 | 1.164 |
| 10 | -$9 | -$18 | 10 | –13 | 26% | 11% | 62% | 8.06 | 3 | 0 | 1/1 | 4 | 0 | 0 | +0.1 | .930 | 1.184 | .858 | 1.202 | .470 |

## Chris Sampson — 40 IP | $-3 | 20 pts

RP-35 — Owned: 0% — RH

Sampson had a wretched 2010. His main problem is that he is too hittable (390 hits allowed in 358 career innings in MLB), and in 2010 he added home runs to the mix. He is just talented enough to land in middle-relief/mop-up somewhere, but he is already 32, and his skills will probably not get better from here. (BJ)

| Player | Age | IP | W | Sv | K | ERA | WHIP | K/9 | BB/9 | $2L | Pts |
|---|---|---|---|---|---|---|---|---|---|---|---|
| Sampson C | 32 | 40 | 1 | 0 | 20 | 4.81 | 1.39 | 4.4 | 2.3 | -$3 | 20 |
| **Mini-Browser** | **Age** | **IP** | **W** | **Sv** | **K** | **ERA** | **WHIP** | **K/9** | **BB/9** | **$2L** | **Pts** |
| Palmer M | 32 | 60 | 3 | 0 | 39 | 4.98 | 1.59 | 5.8 | 4.6 | -$3 | 50 |
| Maine J | 29 | 40 | 2 | 0 | 32 | 4.96 | 1.48 | 7.1 | 4.2 | -$3 | 40 |
| Smith J | 25 | 60 | 3 | 0 | 46 | 4.83 | 1.52 | 6.9 | 2.7 | -$3 | 60 |
| Miner Z | 29 | 40 | 1 | 0 | 23 | 4.93 | 1.53 | 5.1 | 4.3 | -$3 | 20 |
| Kirkman M | 24 | 80 | 5 | 0 | 60 | 4.81 | 1.69 | 6.8 | 6.1 | -$3 | 80 |

Minors (2010) / Skills

| Level | Leag | W | L | Sv | IP | H | K | ERA | WHIP | K/9 | BB/9 | HR/9 | GB/F |
|---|---|---|---|---|---|---|---|---|---|---|---|---|---|
| A | — | — | — | — | — | — | — | — | — | — | — | — | — |
| AA | TL | 0 | 0 | 0 | 1 | 0 | 1 | 0.00 | 1.00 | 9.0 | 9.0 | 0.0 | — |
| AAA | PCL | 1 | 2 | 0 | 15 | 17 | 11 | 2.35 | 1.37 | 6.5 | 2.3 | 0.6 | — |

Majors / Skills

| Yr | Team | W | L | Sv | IP | H | K | ERA | WHIP | K/9 | BB/9 | HR/9 | GB/F |
|---|---|---|---|---|---|---|---|---|---|---|---|---|---|
| 07 | HOU | 7 | 8 | 0 | 121 | 138 | 51 | 4.59 | 1.38 | 3.8 | 2.2 | 1.5 | 1.3 |
| 08 | HOU | 6 | 4 | 0 | 117 | 118 | 61 | 4.22 | 1.20 | 4.7 | 1.8 | 0.6 | 2.0 |
| 09 | HOU | 4 | 2 | 3 | 55 | 66 | 33 | 5.04 | 1.57 | 5.4 | 3.4 | 0.3 | 1.8 |
| 10 | HOU | 1 | 0 | 0 | 30 | 43 | 16 | 5.93 | 1.68 | 4.7 | 2.4 | 2.1 | 2.0 |

Competition at RP / Stats in 2010 as RP

| Thr | Player | GR | ERA | IP/G | Sv-Hld |
|---|---|---|---|---|---|
| RH | Lyon B | 79 | 3.12 | 1.0 | 20-19 |
| RH | Lopez W | 68 | 2.96 | 1.0 | 1-14 |
| RH | Lindstrom M | 58 | 4.39 | 0.9 | 23-4 |
| RH | Fulchino J | 50 | 5.51 | 0.9 | 0-5 |

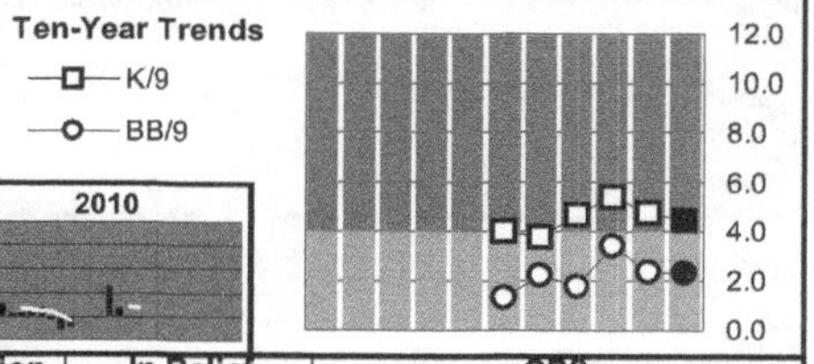


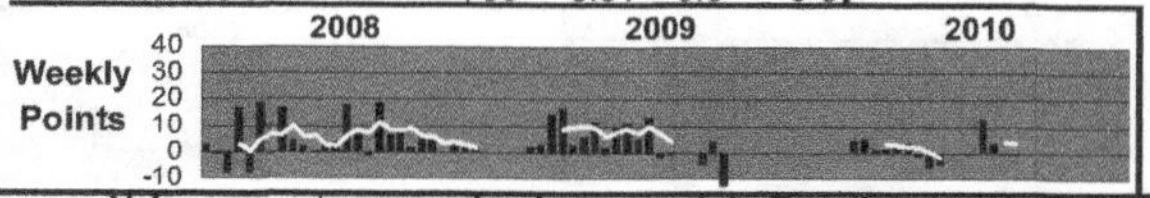


| Yr | $1L | $2L | Pts | RAA | H% | HR/fb | S% | FIP | GS | CG | QS/DS | GR | Hld | Bln | Lead | OPS | 1st Hf | 2nd Hf | vs RH | vs LH |
|---|---|---|---|---|---|---|---|---|---|---|---|---|---|---|---|---|---|---|---|---|
| 07 | $0 | -$8 | 100 | –9 | 29% | 13% | 72% | 5.24 | 19 | 0 | 11/3 | 5 | 0 | 0 | +0.1 | .819 | .783 | .986 | .804 | .836 |
| 08 | $4 | -$1 | 110 | –7 | 29% | 7% | 65% | 3.63 | 11 | 0 | 4/4 | 43 | 11 | 2 | –0.2 | .697 | .715 | .660 | .665 | .746 |
| 09 | -$2 | -$4 | 70 | –9 | 34% | 4% | 66% | 3.62 | — | — | — | 49 | 15 | 3 | +0.3 | .779 | .685 | 1.192 | .787 | .770 |
| 10 | -$8 | -$16 | 10 | –8 | 35% | 24% | 70% | 5.94 | — | — | — | 35 | 5 | 2 | –1.5 | .950 | .869 | 1.421 | 1.056 | .779 |

## Alex Sanabia — 100 IP | $-2 | 100 pts

SP-12, RP-3 — Owned: 1% — RH

As an injury replacement at the back end of Florida's rotation, Sanabia impressed in eight late starts (4-2 record, 3.31 ERA). His HR/FB might be overly low, and it remains to be seen how well his mediocre stuff will hold up over more innings, but the Marlins are severely lacking in options for starters. (MJ)

| Player | Age | IP | W | Sv | K | ERA | WHIP | K/9 | BB/9 | $2L | Pts |
|---|---|---|---|---|---|---|---|---|---|---|---|
| Sanabia A | 22 | 100 | 6 | 0 | 74 | 4.83 | 1.50 | 6.7 | 3.0 | -$2 | 100 |
| **Mini-Browser** | **Age** | **IP** | **W** | **Sv** | **K** | **ERA** | **WHIP** | **K/9** | **BB/9** | **$2L** | **Pts** |
| Ohman W | 33 | 20 | 0 | 0 | 18 | 4.12 | 1.48 | 8.1 | 4.5 | -$2 | 20 |
| Bautista D | 30 | 40 | 2 | 0 | 40 | 4.53 | 1.58 | 9.0 | 5.7 | -$2 | 50 |
| Albaladejo J | 28 | 40 | 2 | 0 | 29 | 5.15 | 1.50 | 6.6 | 3.9 | -$2 | 40 |
| Baez D | 33 | 40 | 2 | 0 | 22 | 4.77 | 1.42 | 4.9 | 3.7 | -$2 | 30 |
| Nieve F | 28 | 40 | 2 | 0 | 33 | 5.12 | 1.41 | 7.5 | 3.9 | -$2 | 40 |

Minors (2010) / Skills

| Level | Leag | W | L | Sv | IP | H | K | ERA | WHIP | K/9 | BB/9 | HR/9 | GB/F |
|---|---|---|---|---|---|---|---|---|---|---|---|---|---|
| A | — | — | — | — | — | — | — | — | — | — | — | — | — |
| AA | SOU | 5 | 1 | 0 | 84 | 59 | 65 | 2.03 | 0.89 | 6.9 | 1.7 | 0.2 | — |
| AAA | PCL | 1 | 0 | 0 | 14 | 9 | 5 | 1.29 | 0.86 | 3.2 | 1.9 | 0.0 | — |

Majors / Skills

| Yr | Team | W | L | Sv | IP | H | K | ERA | WHIP | K/9 | BB/9 | HR/9 | GB/F |
|---|---|---|---|---|---|---|---|---|---|---|---|---|---|
| 07 | — | — | — | — | — | — | — | — | — | — | — | — | — |
| 08 | — | — | — | — | — | — | — | — | — | — | — | — | — |
| 09 | — | — | — | — | — | — | — | — | — | — | — | — | — |
| 10 | FLA | 5 | 3 | 0 | 72 | 74 | 47 | 3.73 | 1.24 | 5.8 | 2.0 | 0.7 | 0.8 |

Competition at SP / Stats in 2010 as SP

| Thr | Player | GS | ERA | Supp | W-L |
|---|---|---|---|---|---|
| RH | Sanchez A | 32 | 3.55 | 4.8 | 13-12 |
| RH | Volstad C | 30 | 4.58 | 5.1 | 12-9 |
| RH | Johnson J | 28 | 2.30 | 4.3 | 11-6 |
| RH | Nolasco R | 26 | 4.51 | 4.4 | 14-9 |

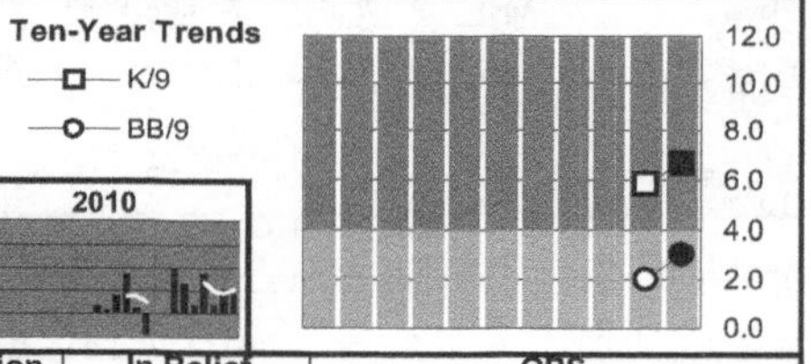


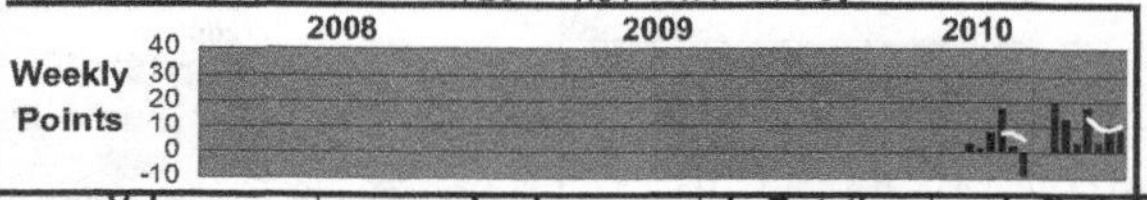


| Yr | $1L | $2L | Pts | RAA | H% | HR/fb | S% | FIP | GS | CG | QS/DS | GR | Hld | Bln | Lead | OPS | 1st Hf | 2nd Hf | vs RH | vs LH |
|---|---|---|---|---|---|---|---|---|---|---|---|---|---|---|---|---|---|---|---|---|
| 07 | — | — | — | — | — | — | — | — | — | — | — | — | — | — | — | — | — | — | — | — |
| 08 | — | — | — | — | — | — | — | — | — | — | — | — | — | — | — | — | — | — | — | — |
| 09 | — | — | — | — | — | — | — | — | — | — | — | — | — | — | — | — | — | — | — | — |
| 10 | $0 | -$6 | 90 | +4 | 30% | 6% | 71% | 3.64 | 12 | 0 | 4/1 | 3 | 0 | 0 | –0.3 | .686 | .745 | .673 | .791 | .576 |

## Brian Sanches — 60 IP | $2 | 70 pts

RP-61 — Owned: 0% — RH

Sanches hit a rough patch early in 2010 (4.05 ERA as of June 2), but after that, he looked like his 2009 self. Something else that was similar was good fortune – low HR/FB in 2009, low H% in 2010. Still, the Marlins are lacking in options out of the bullpen, and the team will turn to him again for 60+ IP. (MJ)

| Player | Age | IP | W | Sv | K | ERA | WHIP | K/9 | BB/9 | $2L | Pts |
|---|---|---|---|---|---|---|---|---|---|---|---|
| Sanches B | 32 | 60 | 2 | 0 | 52 | 3.56 | 1.29 | 7.8 | 3.8 | $2 | 70 |
| **Mini-Browser** | **Age** | **IP** | **W** | **Sv** | **K** | **ERA** | **WHIP** | **K/9** | **BB/9** | **$2L** | **Pts** |
| O'Flaherty E | 26 | 60 | 3 | 0 | 44 | 3.52 | 1.31 | 6.5 | 3.4 | $2 | 80 |
| Burnett S | 28 | 60 | 2 | 6 | 47 | 3.86 | 1.38 | 7.1 | 3.9 | $2 | 90 |
| Peralta J | 35 | 60 | 2 | 0 | 51 | 4.01 | 1.17 | 7.6 | 2.4 | $2 | 70 |
| Wood K | 33 | 60 | 3 | 0 | 62 | 3.77 | 1.41 | 9.3 | 4.7 | $2 | 80 |
| Porcello R | 22 | 200 | 11 | 0 | 100 | 4.92 | 1.39 | 4.5 | 2.5 | $2 | 170 |

Minors (2010) / Skills

| Level | Leag | W | L | Sv | IP | H | K | ERA | WHIP | K/9 | BB/9 | HR/9 | GB/F |
|---|---|---|---|---|---|---|---|---|---|---|---|---|---|
| A | FLO | 0 | 1 | 0 | 4 | 2 | 6 | 2.25 | 0.50 | 13.5 | 0.0 | 0.0 | — |
| AA | — | — | — | — | — | — | — | — | — | — | — | — | — |
| AAA | — | — | — | — | — | — | — | — | — | — | — | — | — |

Majors / Skills

| Yr | Team | W | L | Sv | IP | H | K | ERA | WHIP | K/9 | BB/9 | HR/9 | GB/F |
|---|---|---|---|---|---|---|---|---|---|---|---|---|---|
| 07 | PHI | 1 | 1 | 0 | 14 | 13 | 9 | 5.52 | 1.70 | 5.5 | 7.4 | 3.7 | 0.7 |
| 08 | WAS | 2 | 0 | 0 | 11 | 16 | 10 | 7.36 | 1.91 | 8.2 | 4.1 | 1.6 | 1.6 |
| 09 | FLA | 4 | 2 | 0 | 56 | 50 | 51 | 2.56 | 1.35 | 8.1 | 4.2 | 0.8 | 0.7 |
| 10 | FLA | 2 | 2 | 0 | 63 | 43 | 54 | 2.26 | 1.10 | 7.6 | 3.8 | 1.0 | 0.6 |

Competition at RP / Stats in 2010 as RP

| Thr | Player | GR | ERA | IP/G | Sv-Hld |
|---|---|---|---|---|---|
| RH | Hensley C | 68 | 2.16 | 1.1 | 7-22 |
| RH | Nunez L | 68 | 3.46 | 1.0 | 30-5 |
| RH | Sanches B | 61 | 2.26 | 1.0 | 0-12 |
| RH | Badenhop B | 53 | 3.99 | 1.3 | 1-8 |

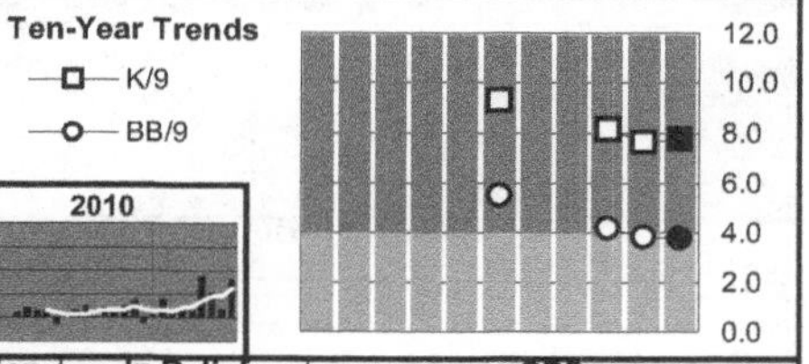


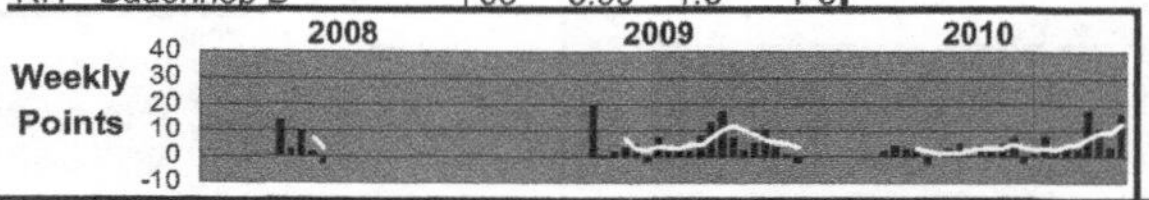


| Yr | $1L | $2L | Pts | RAA | H% | HR/fb | S% | FIP | GS | CG | QS/DS | GR | Hld | Bln | Lead | OPS | 1st Hf | 2nd Hf | vs RH | vs LH |
|---|---|---|---|---|---|---|---|---|---|---|---|---|---|---|---|---|---|---|---|---|
| 07 | -$3 | -$5 | 10 | –4 | 18% | 27% | 84% | 9.75 | — | — | — | 12 | 1 | 0 | –1.8 | 1.018 | .682 | 1.554 | 1.034 | .990 |
| 08 | -$3 | -$4 | 20 | –5 | 39% | 20% | 63% | 5.11 | — | — | — | 12 | 0 | 1 | –2.5 | .918 | .918 | — | .938 | .879 |
| 09 | $3 | $2 | 90 | +7 | 29% | 6% | 85% | 3.93 | — | — | — | 47 | 9 | 3 | –0.2 | .687 | .625 | .727 | .685 | .689 |
| 10 | $3 | $0 | 90 | +9 | 22% | 8% | 86% | 4.21 | — | — | — | 61 | 12 | 1 | +0.1 | .609 | .658 | .567 | .588 | .635 |

## Anibal Sanchez — 140 IP | $3 | 170 pts

SP-32 — Owned: 57% — RH

Sanchez was finally healthy for a full season, and he contributed almost 200 effective innings. Since the 2009 ASB, he has a 3.38 ERA over 41 starts, though he tired late (6.28 ERA in Sept 2010). The Marlins need Sanchez as a #3 SP, but bear in mind his shoulder problems – he doubled his 2009 workload. (MJ)

| Player | Age | IP | W | Sv | K | ERA | WHIP | K/9 | BB/9 | $2L | Pts |
|---|---|---|---|---|---|---|---|---|---|---|---|
| Sanchez A | 27 | 140 | 8 | 0 | 110 | 4.15 | 1.44 | 7.1 | 3.7 | $3 | 170 |
| **Mini-Browser** | **Age** | **IP** | **W** | **Sv** | **K** | **ERA** | **WHIP** | **K/9** | **BB/9** | **$2L** | **Pts** |
| Volquez E | 27 | 160 | 9 | 0 | 155 | 4.35 | 1.46 | 8.7 | 4.6 | $3 | 210 |
| Wuertz M | 32 | 50 | 3 | 2 | 51 | 3.67 | 1.27 | 9.2 | 3.9 | $3 | 90 |
| de la Rosa J | 29 | 160 | 10 | 0 | 140 | 4.59 | 1.39 | 7.9 | 4.0 | $3 | 200 |
| Moylan P | 32 | 70 | 5 | 0 | 53 | 3.39 | 1.39 | 6.9 | 4.5 | $3 | 100 |
| Gee D | 24 | 80 | 5 | 0 | 66 | 3.73 | 1.35 | 7.5 | 3.0 | $3 | 110 |

Minors (2010) / Skills

| Level | Leag | W | L | Sv | IP | H | K | ERA | WHIP | K/9 | BB/9 | HR/9 | GB/F |
|---|---|---|---|---|---|---|---|---|---|---|---|---|---|
| A | — | — | — | — | — | — | — | — | — | — | — | — | — |
| AA | — | — | — | — | — | — | — | — | — | — | — | — | — |
| AAA | — | — | — | — | — | — | — | — | — | — | — | — | — |

Majors / Skills

| Yr | Team | W | L | Sv | IP | H | K | ERA | WHIP | K/9 | BB/9 | HR/9 | GB/F |
|---|---|---|---|---|---|---|---|---|---|---|---|---|---|
| 07 | FLA | 2 | 1 | 0 | 30 | 43 | 14 | 4.80 | 2.07 | 4.2 | 5.7 | 0.9 | 1.1 |
| 08 | FLA | 2 | 5 | 0 | 51 | 54 | 50 | 5.57 | 1.57 | 8.7 | 4.7 | 1.2 | 1.2 |
| 09 | FLA | 4 | 8 | 0 | 86 | 84 | 71 | 3.87 | 1.51 | 7.4 | 4.8 | 1.0 | 1.1 |
| 10 | FLA | 13 | 12 | 0 | 195 | 192 | 157 | 3.55 | 1.34 | 7.2 | 3.2 | 0.5 | 1.2 |

Competition at SP / Stats in 2010 as SP

| Thr | Player | GS | ERA | Supp | W-L |
|---|---|---|---|---|---|
| RH | Sanchez A | 32 | 3.55 | 4.8 | 13-12 |
| RH | Volstad C | 30 | 4.58 | 5.1 | 12-9 |
| RH | Johnson J | 28 | 2.30 | 4.3 | 11-6 |
| RH | Nolasco R | 26 | 4.51 | 4.4 | 14-9 |

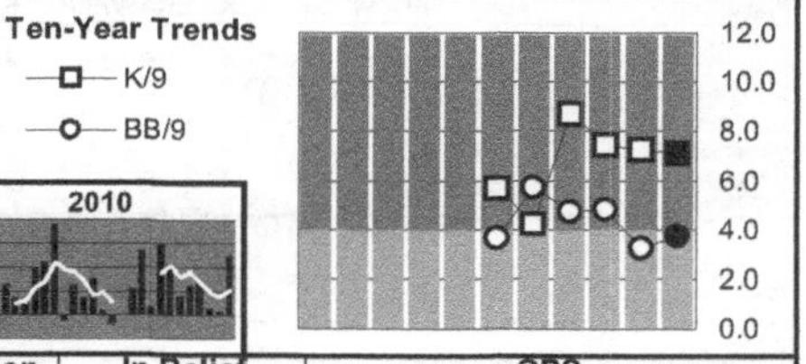


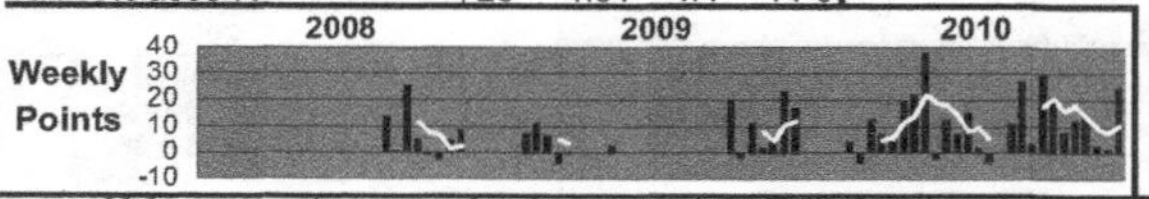


| Yr | $1L | $2L | Pts | RAA | H% | HR/fb | S% | FIP | GS | CG | QS/DS | GR | Hld | Bln | Lead | OPS | 1st Hf | 2nd Hf | vs RH | vs LH |
|---|---|---|---|---|---|---|---|---|---|---|---|---|---|---|---|---|---|---|---|---|
| 07 | -$5 | -$8 | 20 | –2 | 36% | 7% | 78% | 5.47 | 6 | 0 | 1/0 | — | — | — | — | .930 | .930 | — | .959 | .905 |
| 08 | -$4 | -$7 | 50 | –10 | 32% | 14% | 66% | 4.59 | 10 | 0 | 2/2 | — | — | — | — | .788 | — | .788 | .578 | .967 |
| 09 | $0 | -$2 | 100 | +3 | 30% | 10% | 78% | 4.67 | 16 | 0 | 6/2 | — | — | — | — | .756 | .884 | .655 | .814 | .701 |
| 10 | $9 | -$1 | 270 | +7 | 32% | 4% | 73% | 3.33 | 32 | 1 | 20/2 | — | — | — | — | .680 | .697 | .662 | .674 | .686 |

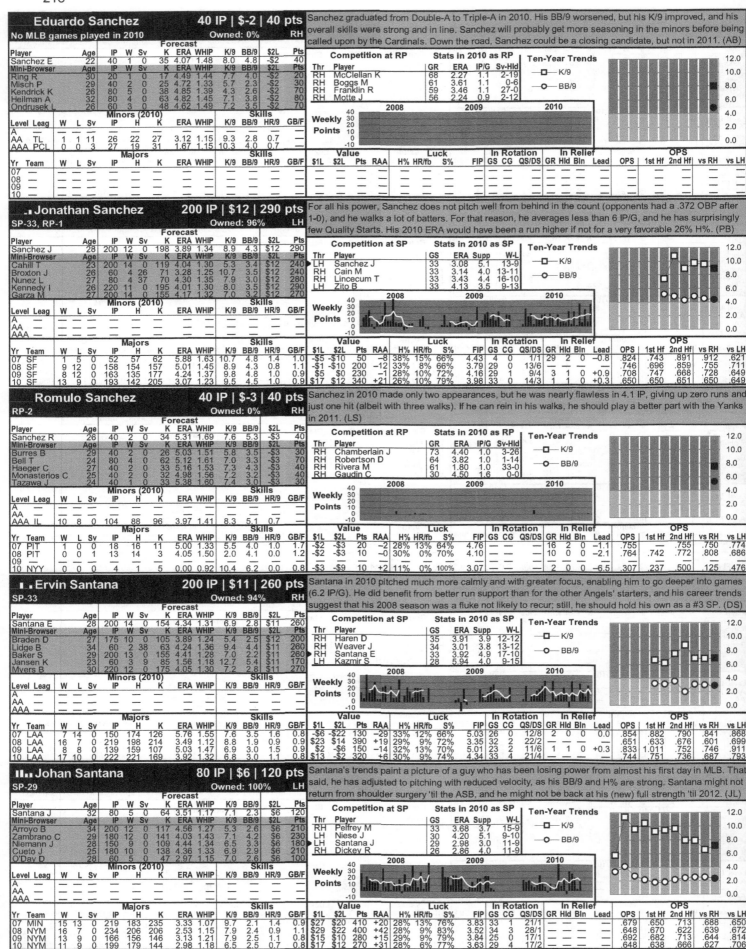

## Eduardo Sanchez — 40 IP | $-2 | 40 pts

No MLB games played in 2010 — Owned: 0% — RH

Sanchez graduated from Double-A to Triple-A in 2010. His BB/9 worsened, but his K/9 improved, and his overall skills were strong and in line. Sanchez will probably get more seasoning in the minors before being called upon by the Cardinals. Down the road, Sanchez could be a closing candidate, but not in 2011. (AB)

### Forecast
| Player | Age | IP | W | Sv | K | ERA | WHIP | K/9 | BB/9 | $2L | Pts |
|---|---|---|---|---|---|---|---|---|---|---|---|
| Sanchez E | 22 | 40 | 1 | 0 | 35 | 4.07 | 1.48 | 8.0 | 4.8 | -$2 | 40 |
| Mini-Browser | Age | IP | W | Sv | K | ERA | WHIP | K/9 | BB/9 | $2L | Pts |
| Ring R | 30 | 20 | 1 | 0 | 17 | 4.49 | 1.44 | 7.7 | 4.0 | -$2 | 20 |
| Misch P | 29 | 40 | 2 | 0 | 25 | 4.72 | 1.33 | 5.7 | 2.3 | -$2 | 30 |
| Kendrick K | 26 | 80 | 5 | 0 | 38 | 4.85 | 1.39 | 4.3 | 2.6 | -$2 | 50 |
| Heilman A | 32 | 80 | 4 | 0 | 63 | 4.82 | 1.45 | 7.1 | 3.8 | -$2 | 80 |
| Ondrusek L | 26 | 60 | 3 | 0 | 48 | 4.62 | 1.49 | 7.2 | 3.5 | -$2 | 70 |

### Minors (2010) / Skills
| Level | Leag | W | L | Sv | IP | H | K | ERA | WHIP | K/9 | BB/9 | HR/9 | GB/F |
|---|---|---|---|---|---|---|---|---|---|---|---|---|---|
| A | — | | | | | | | | | | | | |
| AA | TL | 1 | 1 | 11 | 26 | 22 | 27 | 3.12 | 1.15 | 9.3 | 2.8 | 0.7 | — |
| AAA | PCL | 0 | 0 | 3 | 27 | 19 | 31 | 1.67 | 1.15 | 10.3 | 4.0 | 0.7 | — |

### Majors / Skills
| Yr | Team | W | L | Sv | IP | H | K | ERA | WHIP | K/9 | BB/9 | HR/9 | GB/F |
|---|---|---|---|---|---|---|---|---|---|---|---|---|---|
| 07 | — | — | — | — | — | — | — | — | — | — | — | — | — |
| 08 | — | — | — | — | — | — | — | — | — | — | — | — | — |
| 09 | — | — | — | — | — | — | — | — | — | — | — | — | — |
| 10 | — | — | — | — | — | — | — | — | — | — | — | — | — |

### Competition at RP / Stats in 2010 as RP
| Thr | Player | GR | ERA | IP/G | Sv-Hld |
|---|---|---|---|---|---|
| RH | McClellan K | 68 | 2.27 | 1.1 | 2-19 |
| RH | Boggs M | 61 | 3.61 | 1.1 | 0-6 |
| RH | Franklin R | 59 | 3.46 | 1.1 | 27-0 |
| RH | Motte J | 56 | 2.24 | 0.9 | 2-12 |

Ten-Year Trends: ☐ K/9 ⬤ BB/9

---

## ◢ Jonathan Sanchez — 200 IP | $12 | 290 pts

SP-33, RP-1 — Owned: 96% — LH

For all his power, Sanchez does not pitch well from behind in the count (opponents had a .372 OBP after 1-0), and he walks a lot of batters. For that reason, he averages less than 6 IP/G, and he has surprisingly few Quality Starts. His 2010 ERA would have been a run higher if not for a very favorable 26% H%. (PB)

### Forecast
| Player | Age | IP | W | Sv | K | ERA | WHIP | K/9 | BB/9 | $2L | Pts |
|---|---|---|---|---|---|---|---|---|---|---|---|
| Sanchez J | 28 | 200 | 12 | 0 | 198 | 3.89 | 1.34 | 8.9 | 4.3 | $12 | 290 |
| Mini-Browser | Age | IP | W | Sv | K | ERA | WHIP | K/9 | BB/9 | $2L | Pts |
| Cahill T | 23 | 200 | 14 | 0 | 119 | 4.04 | 1.30 | 5.3 | 3.4 | $12 | 240 |
| Broxton J | 26 | 60 | 4 | 26 | 71 | 3.28 | 1.25 | 10.7 | 3.5 | $12 | 240 |
| Nunez L | 27 | 80 | 4 | 37 | 70 | 4.30 | 1.35 | 7.9 | 3.0 | $12 | 280 |
| Kennedy I | 26 | 220 | 11 | 0 | 195 | 4.01 | 1.30 | 8.0 | 3.5 | $12 | 290 |
| Garza M | 27 | 200 | 14 | 0 | 155 | 4.17 | 1.32 | 7.0 | 3.5 | $12 | 270 |

### Minors (2010) / Skills
| Level | Leag | W | L | Sv | IP | H | K | ERA | WHIP | K/9 | BB/9 | HR/9 | GB/F |
|---|---|---|---|---|---|---|---|---|---|---|---|---|---|
| A | — | — | — | — | — | — | — | — | — | — | — | — | — |
| AA | — | — | — | — | — | — | — | — | — | — | — | — | — |
| AAA | — | — | — | — | — | — | — | — | — | — | — | — | — |

### Majors / Skills
| Yr | Team | W | L | Sv | IP | H | K | ERA | WHIP | K/9 | BB/9 | HR/9 | GB/F |
|---|---|---|---|---|---|---|---|---|---|---|---|---|---|
| 07 | SF | 1 | 5 | 0 | 52 | 57 | 62 | 5.88 | 1.63 | 10.7 | 4.8 | 1.4 | 1.0 |
| 08 | SF | 9 | 12 | 0 | 158 | 154 | 157 | 5.01 | 1.45 | 8.9 | 4.3 | 0.8 | 1.1 |
| 09 | SF | 8 | 12 | 0 | 163 | 135 | 177 | 4.24 | 1.37 | 9.8 | 4.8 | 1.0 | 0.9 |
| 10 | SF | 13 | 9 | 0 | 193 | 142 | 205 | 3.07 | 1.23 | 9.5 | 4.5 | 1.0 | 0.9 |

### Competition at SP / Stats in 2010 as SP
| Thr | Player | GS | ERA | Supp | W-L |
|---|---|---|---|---|---|
| LH | Sanchez J | 33 | 3.08 | 5.1 | 13-9 |
| RH | Cain M | 33 | 3.14 | 4.4 | 13-11 |
| RH | Lincecum T | 33 | 3.43 | 4.4 | 16-10 |
| LH | Zito B | 33 | 4.13 | 3.5 | 9-13 |

Ten-Year Trends: ☐ K/9 ⬤ BB/9

### Value / Luck / In Rotation / In Relief / OPS
| Yr | Team | $1L | $2L | Pts | RAA | H% | HR/fb | S% | FIP | GS | CG | QS/DS | GR | Hld | Bln | Lead | OPS | 1st Hf | 2nd Hf | vs RH | vs LH |
|---|---|---|---|---|---|---|---|---|---|---|---|---|---|---|---|---|---|---|---|---|---|
| 07 | SF | -$5 | -$10 | 50 | -8 | 38% | 15% | 66% | 4.43 | 4 | 0 | 1/1 | 29 | 2 | 0 | -0.8 | .824 | .743 | .891 | .912 | .621 |
| 08 | SF | -$1 | -$10 | 200 | -12 | 33% | 8% | 66% | 3.79 | 29 | 0 | 13/6 | — | — | — | — | .746 | .696 | .859 | .755 | .711 |
| 09 | SF | $5 | $0 | 230 | -1 | 28% | 10% | 72% | 4.16 | 29 | 1 | 9/4 | 3 | 1 | 0 | +0.9 | .708 | .747 | .668 | .728 | .649 |
| 10 | SF | $17 | $12 | 340 | +21 | 26% | 10% | 79% | 3.98 | 33 | 0 | 14/3 | 1 | 1 | 0 | +0.3 | .650 | .650 | .651 | .650 | .649 |

---

## Romulo Sanchez — 40 IP | $-3 | 40 pts

RP-2 — Owned: 0% — RH

Sanchez in 2010 made only two appearances, but he was nearly flawless in 4.1 IP, giving up zero runs and just one hit (albeit with three walks). If he can rein in his walks, he should play a better part with the Yanks in 2011. (LS)

### Forecast
| Player | Age | IP | W | Sv | K | ERA | WHIP | K/9 | BB/9 | $2L | Pts |
|---|---|---|---|---|---|---|---|---|---|---|---|
| Sanchez R | 26 | 40 | 2 | 0 | 34 | 5.31 | 1.69 | 7.6 | 5.3 | -$3 | 40 |
| Mini-Browser | Age | IP | W | Sv | K | ERA | WHIP | K/9 | BB/9 | $2L | Pts |
| Burres B | 29 | 40 | 2 | 0 | 26 | 5.03 | 1.51 | 5.8 | 3.5 | -$3 | 30 |
| Bell T | 24 | 80 | 4 | 0 | 62 | 5.12 | 1.61 | 7.0 | 3.3 | -$3 | 70 |
| Haeger C | 27 | 40 | 2 | 0 | 33 | 5.16 | 1.53 | 7.3 | 4.3 | -$3 | 40 |
| Monasterios C | 25 | 40 | 2 | 0 | 32 | 4.98 | 1.56 | 7.2 | 3.2 | -$3 | 40 |
| Tazawa J | 24 | 40 | 1 | 0 | 33 | 5.38 | 1.60 | 7.4 | 3.3 | -$3 | 30 |

### Minors (2010) / Skills
| Level | Leag | W | L | Sv | IP | H | K | ERA | WHIP | K/9 | BB/9 | HR/9 | GB/F |
|---|---|---|---|---|---|---|---|---|---|---|---|---|---|
| A | — | — | — | — | — | — | — | — | — | — | — | — | — |
| AA | — | — | — | — | — | — | — | — | — | — | — | — | — |
| AAA | IL | 10 | 8 | 0 | 104 | 88 | 96 | 3.97 | 1.41 | 8.3 | 5.1 | 0.7 | — |

### Majors / Skills
| Yr | Team | W | L | Sv | IP | H | K | ERA | WHIP | K/9 | BB/9 | HR/9 | GB/F |
|---|---|---|---|---|---|---|---|---|---|---|---|---|---|
| 07 | PIT | 1 | 0 | 0 | 18 | 16 | 11 | 5.00 | 1.33 | 5.5 | 4.0 | 1.0 | 1.7 |
| 08 | PIT | 0 | 0 | 1 | 13 | 14 | 3 | 4.05 | 1.50 | 2.0 | 4.1 | 1.0 | 1.2 |
| 09 | — | — | — | — | — | — | — | — | — | — | — | — | — |
| 10 | NYY | 0 | 0 | 0 | 4 | 1 | 5 | 0.00 | 0.92 | 10.4 | 6.2 | 0.0 | 0.8 |

### Competition at RP / Stats in 2010 as RP
| Thr | Player | GR | ERA | IP/G | Sv-Hld |
|---|---|---|---|---|---|
| RH | Chamberlain J | 73 | 4.40 | 1.0 | 3-26 |
| RH | Robertson D | 64 | 3.82 | 1.0 | 1-14 |
| RH | Rivera M | 61 | 1.80 | 1.0 | 33-0 |
| RH | Gaudin C | 30 | 4.50 | 1.6 | 0-0 |

Ten-Year Trends: ☐ K/9 ⬤ BB/9

### Value / Luck / In Rotation / In Relief / OPS
| Yr | Team | $1L | $2L | Pts | RAA | H% | HR/fb | S% | FIP | GS | CG | QS/DS | GR | Hld | Bln | Lead | OPS | 1st Hf | 2nd Hf | vs RH | vs LH |
|---|---|---|---|---|---|---|---|---|---|---|---|---|---|---|---|---|---|---|---|---|---|
| 07 | PIT | -$2 | -$3 | 20 | -2 | 28% | 13% | 64% | 4.76 | — | — | — | 16 | 2 | 0 | -1.1 | .755 | — | .755 | .750 | .774 |
| 08 | PIT | -$2 | -$3 | 10 | -0 | 30% | 0% | 70% | 4.10 | — | — | — | 10 | 0 | 0 | -2.1 | .764 | .742 | .772 | .808 | .686 |
| 09 | — | — | — | — | — | — | — | — | — | — | — | — | — | — | — | — | — | — | — | — | — |
| 10 | NYY | -$3 | -$9 | 10 | +2 | 11% | 0% | 100% | 3.07 | — | — | — | 2 | 0 | 0 | -6.5 | .307 | .237 | .500 | .125 | .476 |

---

## ◢ Ervin Santana — 200 IP | $11 | 260 pts

SP-33 — Owned: 94% — RH

Santana in 2010 pitched much more calmly and with greater focus, enabling him to go deeper into games (6.2 IP/G). He did benefit from better run support than for the other Angels' starters, and his career trends suggest that his 2008 season was a fluke not likely to recur; still, he should hold his own as a #3 SP. (DS)

### Forecast
| Player | Age | IP | W | Sv | K | ERA | WHIP | K/9 | BB/9 | $2L | Pts |
|---|---|---|---|---|---|---|---|---|---|---|---|
| Santana E | 28 | 200 | 14 | 0 | 154 | 4.34 | 1.31 | 6.9 | 2.8 | $11 | 260 |
| Mini-Browser | Age | IP | W | Sv | K | ERA | WHIP | K/9 | BB/9 | $2L | Pts |
| Braden D | 27 | 175 | 10 | 0 | 105 | 3.89 | 1.24 | 5.4 | 2.5 | $12 | 200 |
| Lidge B | 34 | 60 | 2 | 38 | 63 | 4.24 | 1.36 | 9.4 | 4.4 | $11 | 260 |
| Baker S | 29 | 200 | 13 | 0 | 155 | 4.41 | 1.28 | 7.0 | 2.2 | $11 | 260 |
| Jansen K | 23 | 60 | 3 | 9 | 85 | 1.56 | 1.18 | 12.7 | 5.4 | $11 | 170 |
| Myers B | 30 | 220 | 12 | 0 | 175 | 4.05 | 1.30 | 7.2 | 2.8 | $11 | 270 |

### Minors (2010) / Skills
| Level | Leag | W | L | Sv | IP | H | K | ERA | WHIP | K/9 | BB/9 | HR/9 | GB/F |
|---|---|---|---|---|---|---|---|---|---|---|---|---|---|
| A | — | — | — | — | — | — | — | — | — | — | — | — | — |
| AA | — | — | — | — | — | — | — | — | — | — | — | — | — |
| AAA | — | — | — | — | — | — | — | — | — | — | — | — | — |

### Majors / Skills
| Yr | Team | W | L | Sv | IP | H | K | ERA | WHIP | K/9 | BB/9 | HR/9 | GB/F |
|---|---|---|---|---|---|---|---|---|---|---|---|---|---|
| 07 | LAA | 7 | 14 | 0 | 150 | 174 | 126 | 5.76 | 1.55 | 7.6 | 3.5 | 1.6 | 0.8 |
| 08 | LAA | 16 | 7 | 0 | 219 | 198 | 214 | 3.49 | 1.12 | 8.8 | 1.9 | 0.9 | 0.9 |
| 09 | LAA | 8 | 8 | 0 | 139 | 159 | 107 | 5.03 | 1.47 | 6.9 | 3.0 | 1.5 | 0.9 |
| 10 | LAA | 17 | 10 | 0 | 222 | 221 | 169 | 3.92 | 1.32 | 6.8 | 3.0 | 1.1 | 0.8 |

### Competition at SP / Stats in 2010 as SP
| Thr | Player | GS | ERA | Supp | W-L |
|---|---|---|---|---|---|
| RH | Haren D | 35 | 3.91 | 3.9 | 12-12 |
| RH | Weaver J | 34 | 3.01 | 3.8 | 13-12 |
| RH | Santana E | 33 | 3.92 | 4.9 | 17-10 |
| LH | Kazmir S | 28 | 5.94 | 4.0 | 9-15 |

Ten-Year Trends: ☐ K/9 ⬤ BB/9

### Value / Luck / In Rotation / In Relief / OPS
| Yr | Team | $1L | $2L | Pts | RAA | H% | HR/fb | S% | FIP | GS | CG | QS/DS | GR | Hld | Bln | Lead | OPS | 1st Hf | 2nd Hf | vs RH | vs LH |
|---|---|---|---|---|---|---|---|---|---|---|---|---|---|---|---|---|---|---|---|---|---|
| 07 | LAA | -$6 | -$22 | 130 | -29 | 33% | 12% | 66% | 5.03 | 26 | 0 | 12/8 | 2 | 0 | 0 | 0.0 | .854 | .882 | .790 | .841 | .868 |
| 08 | LAA | $23 | $14 | 390 | +19 | 29% | 9% | 72% | 3.35 | 32 | 2 | 22/2 | — | — | — | — | .651 | .633 | .676 | .601 | .699 |
| 09 | LAA | -$2 | -$6 | 150 | -14 | 32% | 13% | 70% | 5.01 | 23 | 1 | 11/6 | 1 | 1 | 0 | +0.3 | .833 | 1.011 | .752 | .746 | .911 |
| 10 | LAA | $13 | $2 | 320 | +6 | 30% | 9% | 74% | 4.34 | 33 | 0 | 21/4 | — | — | — | — | .744 | .751 | .736 | .687 | .793 |

---

## ◢◢ Johan Santana — 80 IP | $6 | 120 pts

SP-29 — Owned: 100% — LH

Santana's trends paint a picture of a guy who has been losing power from almost his first day in MLB. That said, he has adjusted to pitching with reduced velocity, as his BB/9 and H% are strong. Santana might not return from shoulder surgery 'til the ASB, and he might not be back at his (new) full strength 'til 2012. (JL)

### Forecast
| Player | Age | IP | W | Sv | K | ERA | WHIP | K/9 | BB/9 | $2L | Pts |
|---|---|---|---|---|---|---|---|---|---|---|---|
| Santana J | 32 | 80 | 5 | 0 | 64 | 3.51 | 1.17 | 7.1 | 2.3 | $6 | 120 |
| Mini-Browser | Age | IP | W | Sv | K | ERA | WHIP | K/9 | BB/9 | $2L | Pts |
| Arroyo B | 34 | 200 | 12 | 0 | 117 | 4.56 | 1.27 | 5.3 | 2.6 | $6 | 210 |
| Zambrano C | 29 | 180 | 12 | 0 | 141 | 4.49 | 1.34 | 7.1 | 4.2 | $6 | 230 |
| Niemann J | 28 | 150 | 9 | 0 | 109 | 4.44 | 1.34 | 6.5 | 3.3 | $6 | 180 |
| Cueto J | 25 | 180 | 10 | 0 | 138 | 4.36 | 1.33 | 6.9 | 2.9 | $6 | 210 |
| O'Day D | 28 | 80 | 6 | 0 | 47 | 2.97 | 1.15 | 7.0 | 2.5 | $6 | 100 |

### Minors (2010) / Skills
| Level | Leag | W | L | Sv | IP | H | K | ERA | WHIP | K/9 | BB/9 | HR/9 | GB/F |
|---|---|---|---|---|---|---|---|---|---|---|---|---|---|
| A | — | — | — | — | — | — | — | — | — | — | — | — | — |
| AA | — | — | — | — | — | — | — | — | — | — | — | — | — |
| AAA | — | — | — | — | — | — | — | — | — | — | — | — | — |

### Majors / Skills
| Yr | Team | W | L | Sv | IP | H | K | ERA | WHIP | K/9 | BB/9 | HR/9 | GB/F |
|---|---|---|---|---|---|---|---|---|---|---|---|---|---|
| 07 | MIN | 15 | 13 | 0 | 219 | 183 | 235 | 3.33 | 1.07 | 9.7 | 2.1 | 1.4 | 0.9 |
| 08 | NYM | 16 | 7 | 0 | 234 | 206 | 206 | 2.53 | 1.15 | 7.9 | 2.4 | 0.9 | 1.1 |
| 09 | NYM | 13 | 9 | 0 | 166 | 156 | 146 | 3.13 | 1.21 | 7.9 | 2.5 | 1.1 | 0.8 |
| 10 | NYM | 11 | 9 | 0 | 199 | 179 | 144 | 2.98 | 1.18 | 6.5 | 2.5 | 0.7 | 0.8 |

### Competition at SP / Stats in 2010 as SP
| Thr | Player | GS | ERA | Supp | W-L |
|---|---|---|---|---|---|
| RH | Pelfrey M | 33 | 3.68 | 3.7 | 15-9 |
| LH | Niese J | 30 | 4.20 | 5.1 | 9-10 |
| LH | Santana J | 29 | 2.98 | 3.0 | 11-9 |
| RH | Dickey R | 26 | 2.86 | 4.0 | 11-9 |

Ten-Year Trends: ☐ K/9 ⬤ BB/9

### Value / Luck / In Rotation / In Relief / OPS
| Yr | Team | $1L | $2L | Pts | RAA | H% | HR/fb | S% | FIP | GS | CG | QS/DS | GR | Hld | Bln | Lead | OPS | 1st Hf | 2nd Hf | vs RH | vs LH |
|---|---|---|---|---|---|---|---|---|---|---|---|---|---|---|---|---|---|---|---|---|---|
| 07 | MIN | $37 | $20 | 410 | +20 | 28% | 13% | 76% | 3.83 | 33 | 2 | 21/1 | — | — | — | — | .679 | .713 | .649 | .688 | .650 |
| 08 | NYM | $29 | $22 | 400 | +42 | 28% | 9% | 83% | 3.52 | 34 | 3 | 28/1 | — | — | — | — | .648 | .670 | .622 | .639 | .672 |
| 09 | NYM | $15 | $10 | 280 | +15 | 29% | 9% | 81% | 3.84 | 25 | 0 | 17/1 | — | — | — | — | .692 | .682 | .713 | .644 | .814 |
| 10 | NYM | $17 | $12 | 270 | +31 | 28% | 6% | 77% | 3.63 | 29 | 4 | 17/2 | — | — | — | — | .648 | .638 | .666 | .627 | .706 |

## Sergio Santos — 60 IP | $-1 | 70 pts

RP-56 — Owned: 1% — RH

| Player | Age | IP | W | Sv | K | ERA | WHIP | K/9 | BB/9 | $2L | Pts |
|---|---|---|---|---|---|---|---|---|---|---|---|
| **Forecast** | | | | | | | | | | | |
| Santos S | 27 | 60 | 2 | 0 | 64 | 3.85 | 1.67 | 9.6 | 5.2 | -$1 | 70 |
| **Mini-Browser** | Age | IP | W | Sv | K | ERA | WHIP | K/9 | BB/9 | $2L | Pts |
| Holland D | 24 | 140 | 7 | 0 | 120 | 5.19 | 1.47 | 7.7 | 3.5 | -$1 | 150 |
| Villanueva C | 27 | 60 | 2 | 0 | 53 | 4.70 | 1.32 | 8.0 | 3.2 | -$1 | 70 |
| Sherrill G | 33 | 40 | 3 | 0 | 36 | 4.08 | 1.44 | 8.1 | 4.4 | -$1 | 50 |
| Beltre O | 29 | 40 | 4 | 0 | 29 | 4.15 | 1.58 | 6.6 | 5.5 | -$1 | 60 |
| Blackburn N | 29 | 100 | 6 | 0 | 43 | 5.03 | 1.39 | 3.8 | 2.0 | -$1 | 80 |

Minors (2010)

| Level | Leag | W | L | Sv | IP | H | K | ERA | WHIP | K/9 | BB/9 | HR/9 | GB/F |
|---|---|---|---|---|---|---|---|---|---|---|---|---|---|
| A | — | — | — | — | — | — | — | — | — | — | — | — | — |
| AA | — | — | — | — | — | — | — | — | — | — | — | — | — |
| AAA | — | — | — | — | — | — | — | — | — | — | — | — | — |

Into August, Santos was living a movie script, as his ERA dipped under 1.50 in his first full season since converting to pitching in 2009. In the final six weeks, though, the plot turned to "disaster flick" (7.24 ERA). The Sox hope it was merely growing pains and not an undisclosed injury to their unripe set-up man. (RM)

Competition at RP — Stats in 2010 as RP

| Thr | Player | GR | ERA | IP/G | Sv-Hld |
|---|---|---|---|---|---|
| RH | Putz J | 60 | 2.83 | 0.9 | 3-14 |
| RH | Santos S | 56 | 2.96 | 0.9 | 1-14 |
| RH | Jenks B | 55 | 4.44 | 1.0 | 27-0 |
| RH | Linebrink S | 52 | 4.40 | 1.1 | 0-4 |

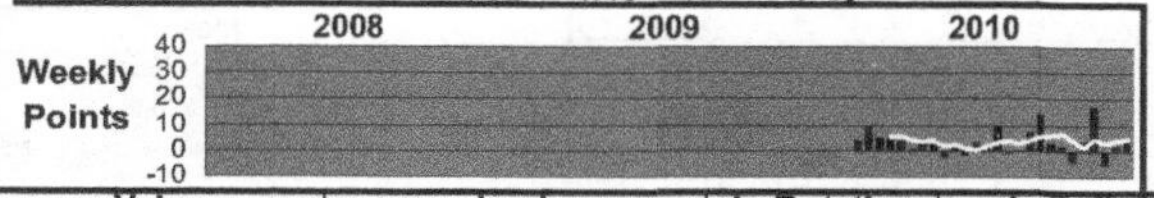


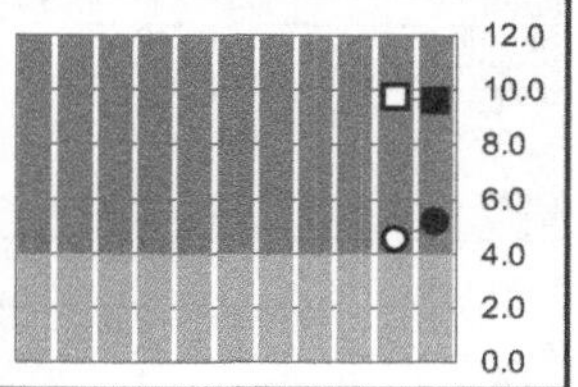


Majors

| Yr | Team | W | L | Sv | IP | H | K | ERA | WHIP | K/9 | BB/9 | HR/9 | GB/F | $1L | $2L | Pts | RAA | H% | HR/fb | S% | FIP | GS | CG | QS/DS | GR | Hld | Bln | Lead | OPS | 1st Hf | 2nd Hf | vs RH | vs LH |
|---|---|---|---|---|---|---|---|---|---|---|---|---|---|---|---|---|---|---|---|---|---|---|---|---|---|---|---|---|---|---|---|---|---|
| 07 | — | — | — | — | — | — | — | — | — | — | — | — | — | — | — | — | — | — | — | — | — | — | — | — | — | — | — | — | — | — | — | — | — |
| 08 | — | — | — | — | — | — | — | — | — | — | — | — | — | — | — | — | — | — | — | — | — | — | — | — | — | — | — | — | — | — | — | — | — |
| 09 | — | — | — | — | — | — | — | — | — | — | — | — | — | — | — | — | — | — | — | — | — | — | — | — | — | — | — | — | — | — | — | — | — |
| 10 | CHW | 2 | 2 | 1 | 51 | 53 | 56 | 2.96 | 1.53 | 9.8 | 4.5 | 0.3 | 1.2 | $0 | -$8 | 80 | +5 | 36% | 4% | 81% | 3.15 | — | — | — | 56 | 14 | 2 | +0.5 | .692 | .605 | .781 | .812 | .513 |

## Joe Saunders — 200 IP | $-2 | 160 pts

SP-33 — Owned: 12% — LH

| Player | Age | IP | W | Sv | K | ERA | WHIP | K/9 | BB/9 | $2L | Pts |
|---|---|---|---|---|---|---|---|---|---|---|---|
| **Forecast** | | | | | | | | | | | |
| Saunders J | 29 | 200 | 11 | 0 | 106 | 4.85 | 1.44 | 4.8 | 3.0 | -$2 | 160 |
| **Mini-Browser** | Age | IP | W | Sv | K | ERA | WHIP | K/9 | BB/9 | $2L | Pts |
| Silva C | 31 | 160 | 10 | 0 | 76 | 5.24 | 1.35 | 4.3 | 1.8 | -$2 | 130 |
| Ray C | 29 | 60 | 4 | 0 | 43 | 4.84 | 1.48 | 6.5 | 4.6 | -$2 | 60 |
| Bonderman J | 28 | 40 | 2 | 0 | 27 | 5.31 | 1.43 | 6.1 | 3.3 | -$2 | 30 |
| Francis J | 30 | 140 | 7 | 0 | 87 | 4.94 | 1.42 | 5.6 | 2.6 | -$2 | 120 |
| Hochevar L | 27 | 160 | 7 | 0 | 109 | 5.29 | 1.46 | 6.2 | 3.2 | -$2 | 130 |

Minors (2010)

| Level | Leag | W | L | Sv | IP | H | K | ERA | WHIP | K/9 | BB/9 | HR/9 | GB/F |
|---|---|---|---|---|---|---|---|---|---|---|---|---|---|
| A | — | — | — | — | — | — | — | — | — | — | — | — | — |
| AA | — | — | — | — | — | — | — | — | — | — | — | — | — |
| AAA | — | — | — | — | — | — | — | — | — | — | — | — | — |

He's not Dan Haren, but Saunders – acquired in the Haren trade – does give AZ a durable, reliable, middle-of-the-pack starter (4.25 ERA, 2.6 K/BB in 13 NL starts) who is three years from FA. He doesn't belong any higher than #3, but he has post-season experience and should mentor Arizona's younger starters. (MS)

Competition at SP — Stats in 2010 as SP

| Thr | Player | GS | ERA | Supp | W-L |
|---|---|---|---|---|---|
| LH | Saunders J | 33 | 4.47 | 3.9 | 9-17 |
| RH | Lopez R | 33 | 5.00 | 4.4 | 7-16 |
| RH | Kennedy I | 32 | 3.80 | 5.1 | 9-10 |
| RH | Enright B | 17 | 3.91 | 3.4 | 6-7 |

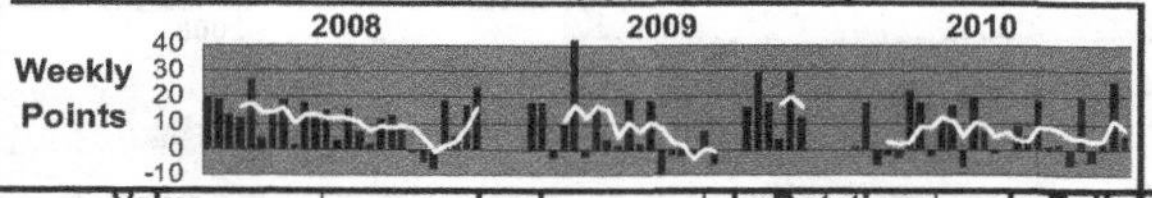


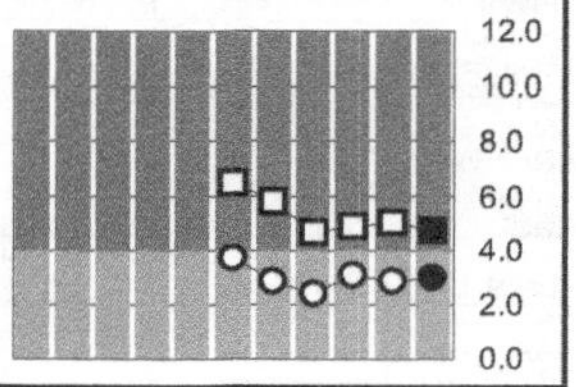


Majors

| Yr | Team | W | L | Sv | IP | H | K | ERA | WHIP | K/9 | BB/9 | HR/9 | GB/F | $1L | $2L | Pts | RAA | H% | HR/fb | S% | FIP | GS | CG | QS/DS | GR | Hld | Bln | Lead | OPS | 1st Hf | 2nd Hf | vs RH | vs LH |
|---|---|---|---|---|---|---|---|---|---|---|---|---|---|---|---|---|---|---|---|---|---|---|---|---|---|---|---|---|---|---|---|---|---|
| 07 | LAA | 8 | 5 | 0 | 107 | 129 | 69 | 4.44 | 1.52 | 5.8 | 2.9 | 0.9 | 1.3 | $1 | -$9 | 120 | −3 | 33% | 9% | 72% | 4.30 | 18 | 0 | 8/1 | — | — | — | — | .792 | .738 | .812 | .833 | .620 |
| 08 | LAA | 17 | 7 | 0 | 198 | 187 | 103 | 3.41 | 1.21 | 4.7 | 2.4 | 1.0 | 1.2 | $16 | $8 | 280 | +16 | 27% | 9% | 75% | 4.44 | 31 | 1 | 22/3 | — | — | — | — | .691 | .657 | .740 | .708 | .633 |
| 09 | LAA | 16 | 7 | 0 | 186 | 202 | 101 | 4.60 | 1.43 | 4.9 | 3.1 | 1.4 | 1.3 | $6 | -$3 | 220 | −10 | 29% | 13% | 72% | 5.27 | 31 | 1 | 13/6 | — | — | — | — | .794 | .786 | .807 | .829 | .696 |
| 10 | 2TM | 9 | 17 | 0 | 203 | 232 | 114 | 4.47 | 1.46 | 5.0 | 2.8 | 1.1 | 1.2 | -$4 | -$21 | 160 | −20 | 32% | 10% | 72% | 4.67 | 33 | 3 | 15/7 | — | — | — | — | .801 | .797 | .805 | .829 | .715 |

## Max Scherzer — 200 IP | $14 | 290 pts

SP-31 — Owned: 85% — RH

| Player | Age | IP | W | Sv | K | ERA | WHIP | K/9 | BB/9 | $2L | Pts |
|---|---|---|---|---|---|---|---|---|---|---|---|
| **Forecast** | | | | | | | | | | | |
| Scherzer M | 26 | 200 | 12 | 0 | 193 | 3.97 | 1.31 | 8.7 | 3.4 | $14 | 290 |
| **Mini-Browser** | Age | IP | W | Sv | K | ERA | WHIP | K/9 | BB/9 | $2L | Pts |
| Marmol C | 28 | 80 | 3 | 36 | 108 | 3.45 | 1.38 | 12.1 | 5.8 | $15 | 310 |
| Bailey A | 26 | 75 | 3 | 33 | 77 | 3.16 | 1.29 | 9.2 | 3.5 | $15 | 270 |
| Wilson C | 30 | 180 | 13 | 0 | 157 | 3.60 | 1.32 | 7.9 | 4.3 | $15 | 270 |
| Kimbrel C | 22 | 60 | 6 | 30 | 91 | 2.83 | 1.45 | 13.6 | 6.0 | $15 | 300 |
| Billingsley C | 26 | 220 | 14 | 0 | 189 | 3.84 | 1.31 | 7.7 | 3.5 | $15 | 320 |

Minors (2010)

| Level | Leag | W | L | Sv | IP | H | K | ERA | WHIP | K/9 | BB/9 | HR/9 | GB/F |
|---|---|---|---|---|---|---|---|---|---|---|---|---|---|
| A | — | — | — | — | — | — | — | — | — | — | — | — | — |
| AA | — | — | — | — | — | — | — | — | — | — | — | — | — |
| AAA | IL | 2 | 0 | 0 | 15 | 4 | 17 | 0.60 | 0.40 | 10.2 | 1.2 | 0.0 | — |

After a brief stint in the minors to improve his mechanics, Scherzer was one of the AL's top starters in the second half (2.47 ERA). Scherzer has the arm to be a perennial top-of-the-rotation starter, and he proved in 2010 that he is correctible. He is the Tigers' #2 SP and is under team control through 2014. (LP)

Competition at SP — Stats in 2010 as SP

| Thr | Player | GS | ERA | Supp | W-L |
|---|---|---|---|---|---|
| RH | Verlander J | 33 | 3.37 | 5.2 | 18-9 |
| RH | Scherzer M | 31 | 3.50 | 4.0 | 12-11 |
| RH | Bonderman J | 29 | 5.56 | 5.1 | 8-10 |
| RH | Porcello R | 27 | 4.92 | 4.8 | 10-12 |

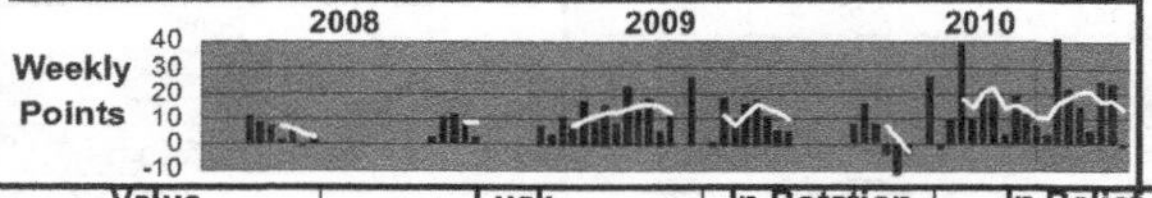


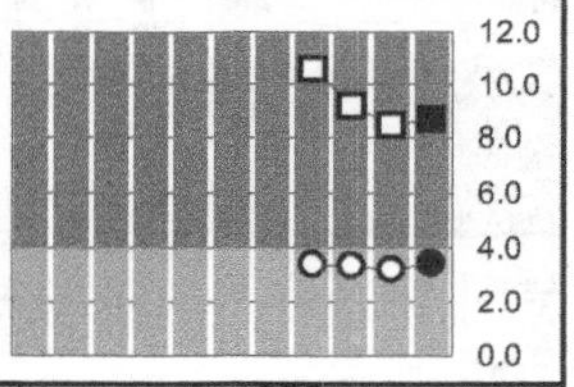


Majors

| Yr | Team | W | L | Sv | IP | H | K | ERA | WHIP | K/9 | BB/9 | HR/9 | GB/F | $1L | $2L | Pts | RAA | H% | HR/fb | S% | FIP | GS | CG | QS/DS | GR | Hld | Bln | Lead | OPS | 1st Hf | 2nd Hf | vs RH | vs LH |
|---|---|---|---|---|---|---|---|---|---|---|---|---|---|---|---|---|---|---|---|---|---|---|---|---|---|---|---|---|---|---|---|---|---|
| 07 | — | — | — | — | — | — | — | — | — | — | — | — | — | — | — | — | — | — | — | — | — | — | — | — | — | — | — | — | — | — | — | — | — |
| 08 | ARI | 0 | 4 | 0 | 56 | 48 | 66 | 3.05 | 1.23 | 10.6 | 3.4 | 0.8 | 1.4 | $3 | $1 | 70 | +4 | 32% | 12% | 78% | 3.13 | 7 | 0 | 3/1 | 9 | 0 | 0 | −0.9 | .649 | .651 | .645 | .515 | .814 |
| 09 | ARI | 9 | 11 | 0 | 170 | 166 | 174 | 4.12 | 1.34 | 9.2 | 3.3 | 1.1 | 1.0 | $7 | $1 | 240 | −10 | 32% | 10% | 72% | 3.79 | 30 | 0 | 14/3 | — | — | — | — | .751 | .722 | .789 | .702 | .793 |
| 10 | DET | 12 | 11 | 0 | 195 | 174 | 184 | 3.50 | 1.25 | 8.5 | 3.2 | 0.9 | 1.0 | $16 | $5 | 300 | +13 | 31% | 10% | 75% | 3.82 | 31 | 0 | 18/3 | — | — | — | — | .700 | .782 | .621 | .737 | .666 |

## Daniel Schlereth — 40 IP | $-2 | 50 pts

RP-18 — Owned: 0% — LH

| Player | Age | IP | W | Sv | K | ERA | WHIP | K/9 | BB/9 | $2L | Pts |
|---|---|---|---|---|---|---|---|---|---|---|---|
| **Forecast** | | | | | | | | | | | |
| Schlereth D | 24 | 40 | 2 | 0 | 46 | 4.33 | 1.72 | 10.3 | 6.1 | -$2 | 50 |
| **Mini-Browser** | Age | IP | W | Sv | K | ERA | WHIP | K/9 | BB/9 | $2L | Pts |
| Sanchez E | 22 | 40 | 1 | 0 | 35 | 4.07 | 1.48 | 8.0 | 4.8 | -$2 | 40 |
| Acosta M | 29 | 40 | 2 | 0 | 33 | 4.39 | 1.48 | 7.5 | 4.7 | -$2 | 40 |
| Qualls C | 32 | 50 | 2 | 0 | 39 | 5.14 | 1.44 | 7.1 | 2.5 | -$2 | 40 |
| Corpas M | 28 | 20 | 1 | 0 | 13 | 4.34 | 1.33 | 6.0 | 2.6 | -$2 | 20 |
| Elbert S | 25 | 40 | 2 | 0 | 48 | 4.59 | 1.51 | 10.8 | 4.2 | -$2 | 50 |

Minors (2010)

| Level | Leag | W | L | Sv | IP | H | K | ERA | WHIP | K/9 | BB/9 | HR/9 | GB/F |
|---|---|---|---|---|---|---|---|---|---|---|---|---|---|
| A | — | — | — | — | — | — | — | — | — | — | — | — | — |
| AA | — | — | — | — | — | — | — | — | — | — | — | — | — |
| AAA | IL | 1 | 3 | 0 | 49 | 40 | 60 | 2.37 | 1.50 | 10.9 | 6.2 | 0.0 | — |

Schlereth showed a lot of promise in his late season call-up, and the Tigers think that he could some day be a closer. In Triple-A, he was practically unhittable at times, but he relinquishes his edge with walks. He may start 2011 in the minors, but he should be one of the lefties in the DET bullpen by season's end. (LP)

Competition at RP — Stats in 2010 as RP

| Thr | Player | GR | ERA | IP/G | Sv-Hld |
|---|---|---|---|---|---|
| LH | Coke P | 73 | 3.57 | 0.9 | 2-17 |
| LH | Thomas B | 47 | 3.41 | 1.3 | 0-3 |
| LH | Ni F | 22 | 6.65 | 1.0 | 0-1 |
| LH | Schlereth D | 18 | 2.89 | 1.0 | 1-1 |

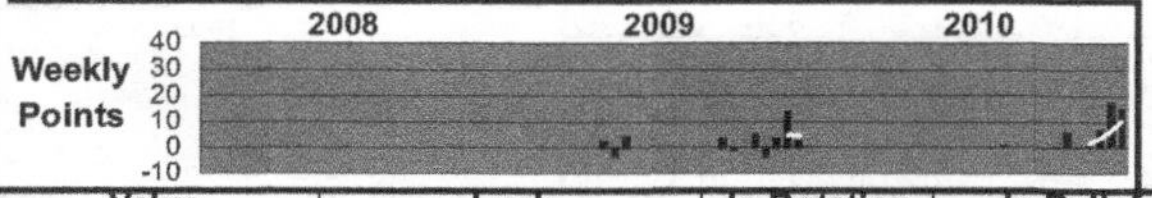


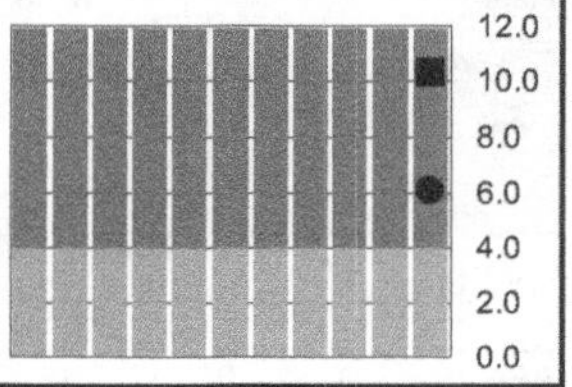


Majors

| Yr | Team | W | L | Sv | IP | H | K | ERA | WHIP | K/9 | BB/9 | HR/9 | GB/F | $1L | $2L | Pts | RAA | H% | HR/fb | S% | FIP | GS | CG | QS/DS | GR | Hld | Bln | Lead | OPS | 1st Hf | 2nd Hf | vs RH | vs LH |
|---|---|---|---|---|---|---|---|---|---|---|---|---|---|---|---|---|---|---|---|---|---|---|---|---|---|---|---|---|---|---|---|---|---|
| 07 | — | — | — | — | — | — | — | — | — | — | — | — | — | — | — | — | — | — | — | — | — | — | — | — | — | — | — | — | — | — | — | — | — |
| 08 | — | — | — | — | — | — | — | — | — | — | — | — | — | — | — | — | — | — | — | — | — | — | — | — | — | — | — | — | — | — | — | — | — |
| 09 | ARI | 1 | 4 | 0 | 18 | 15 | 22 | 5.89 | 1.64 | 10.8 | 7.4 | 0.5 | 1.8 | -$3 | -$3 | 20 | −5 | 31% | 7% | 62% | 3.96 | — | — | — | 21 | 0 | 3 | −1.7 | .648 | .641 | .651 | .566 | .770 |
| 10 | DET | 2 | 0 | 1 | 18 | 20 | 19 | 2.89 | 1.61 | 9.2 | 4.8 | 1.0 | 1.3 | -$2 | -$9 | 40 | +1 | 33% | 10% | 86% | 4.26 | — | — | — | 18 | 1 | 1 | −0.2 | .752 | .937 | .706 | .594 | .998 |

## Travis Schlichting — 60 IP | $-2 | 70 pts

RP-14 — Owned: 0% — RH

| Player | Age | IP | W | Sv | K | ERA | WHIP | K/9 | BB/9 | $2L | Pts |
|---|---|---|---|---|---|---|---|---|---|---|---|
| **Forecast** | | | | | | | | | | | |
| Schlichting T | 26 | 60 | 3 | 0 | 51 | 4.41 | 1.53 | 7.6 | 4.3 | -$2 | 70 |
| **Mini-Browser** | Age | IP | W | Sv | K | ERA | WHIP | K/9 | BB/9 | $2L | Pts |
| Braddock Z | 23 | 40 | 1 | 0 | 48 | 4.20 | 1.54 | 10.8 | 4.7 | -$2 | 50 |
| Volstad C | 24 | 160 | 10 | 0 | 101 | 4.89 | 1.45 | 5.7 | 3.2 | -$2 | 150 |
| Delcarmen M | 29 | 60 | 3 | 0 | 47 | 4.47 | 1.50 | 7.1 | 5.0 | -$2 | 70 |
| Green S | 31 | 40 | 2 | 0 | 29 | 4.25 | 1.46 | 6.6 | 4.5 | -$2 | 40 |
| VandenHurk R | 25 | 40 | 2 | 0 | 38 | 5.04 | 1.48 | 8.5 | 3.9 | -$2 | 40 |

Minors (2010)

| Level | Leag | W | L | Sv | IP | H | K | ERA | WHIP | K/9 | BB/9 | HR/9 | GB/F |
|---|---|---|---|---|---|---|---|---|---|---|---|---|---|
| A | — | — | — | — | — | — | — | — | — | — | — | — | — |
| AA | — | — | — | — | — | — | — | — | — | — | — | — | — |
| AAA | PCL | 3 | 0 | 1 | 47 | 55 | 29 | 4.75 | 1.44 | 5.5 | 2.5 | 1.0 | — |

In his time with the Dodgers in 2010, converted 3B Schlichting flashed a live arm, but he needs both more strikeouts and fewer walks in order to thrive. He'll also need to prove that he can rebound from late-season shoulder pain that cost him the final six weeks. Schlichting will be in the mix for a 2011 bullpen spot. (MP)

Competition at RP — Stats in 2010 as RP

| Thr | Player | GR | ERA | IP/G | Sv-Hld |
|---|---|---|---|---|---|
| RH | Broxton J | 64 | 4.04 | 1.0 | 22-3 |
| RH | Belisario R | 59 | 5.04 | 0.9 | 2-16 |
| RH | Troncoso R | 52 | 4.33 | 1.0 | 0-8 |
| RH | Weaver J | 44 | 6.09 | 1.0 | 0-5 |

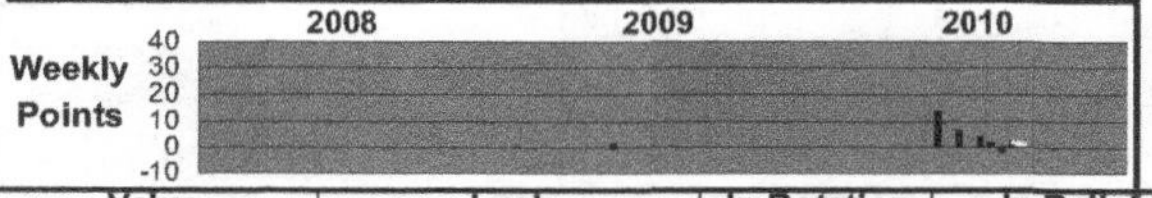


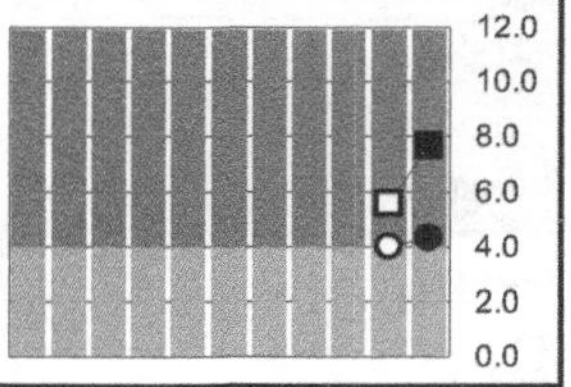


Majors

| Yr | Team | W | L | Sv | IP | H | K | ERA | WHIP | K/9 | BB/9 | HR/9 | GB/F | $1L | $2L | Pts | RAA | H% | HR/fb | S% | FIP | GS | CG | QS/DS | GR | Hld | Bln | Lead | OPS | 1st Hf | 2nd Hf | vs RH | vs LH |
|---|---|---|---|---|---|---|---|---|---|---|---|---|---|---|---|---|---|---|---|---|---|---|---|---|---|---|---|---|---|---|---|---|---|
| 07 | — | — | — | — | — | — | — | — | — | — | — | — | — | — | — | — | — | — | — | — | — | — | — | — | — | — | — | — | — | — | — | — | — |
| 08 | — | — | — | — | — | — | — | — | — | — | — | — | — | — | — | — | — | — | — | — | — | — | — | — | — | — | — | — | — | — | — | — | — |
| 09 | LAD | 0 | 0 | 0 | 2 | 1 | 2 | 3.38 | 2.25 | 6.8 | 16.9 | 3.4 | 0.8 | -$3 | -$3 | 0 | −1 | 0% | 25% | 100% | 12.20 | — | — | — | 2 | 0 | 0 | −4.5 | .844 | .844 | — | .500 | .905 |
| 10 | LAD | 1 | 0 | 0 | 22 | 20 | 14 | 3.57 | 1.32 | 5.6 | 4.0 | 0.0 | 1.4 | -$4 | -$10 | 20 | +1 | 27% | 0% | 70% | 3.29 | — | — | — | 14 | 0 | 0 | −0.2 | .588 | .490 | .724 | .670 | .465 |

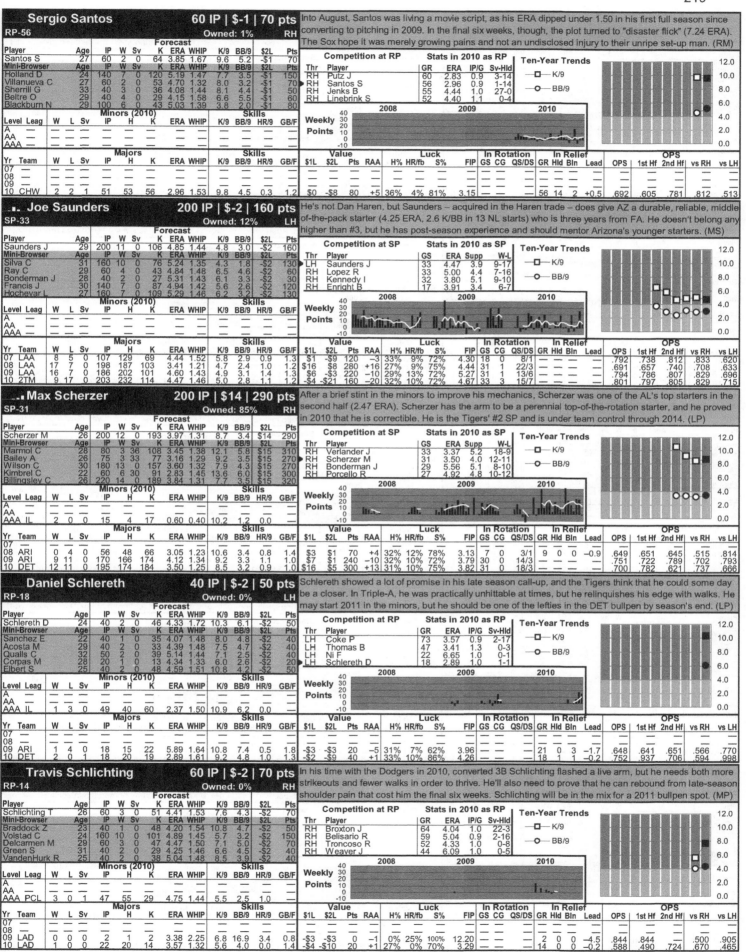

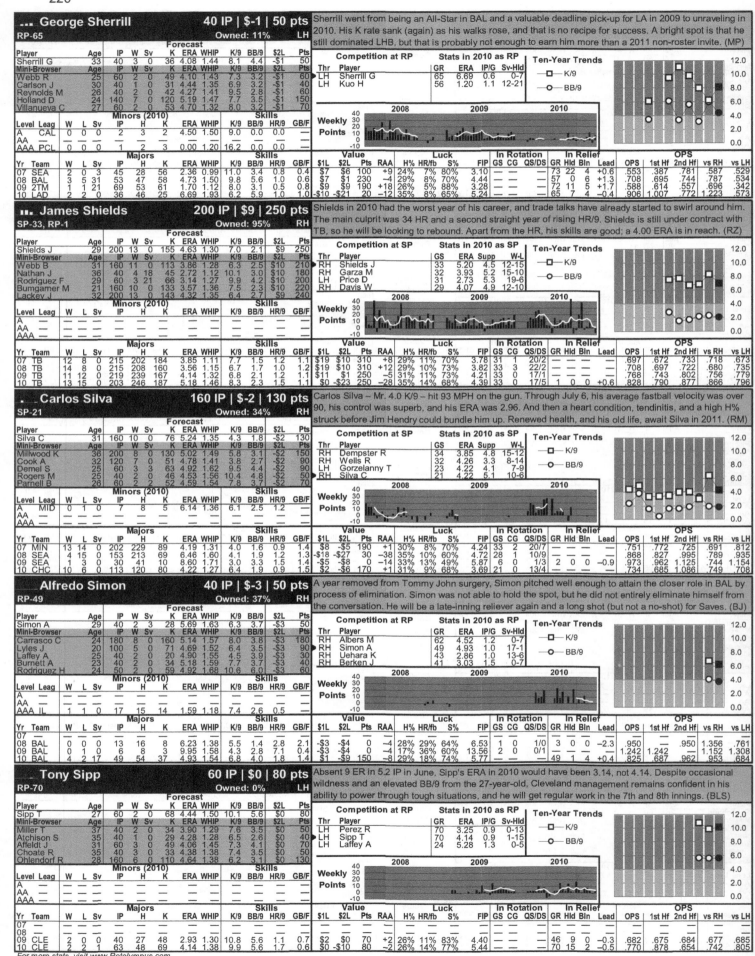

## ... George Sherrill — 40 IP | $-1 | 50 pts

RP-65 — Owned: 11% — LH

Sherrill went from being an All-Star in BAL and a valuable deadline pick-up for LA in 2009 to unraveling in 2010. His K rate sank (again) as his walks rose, and that is no recipe for success. A bright spot is that he still dominated LHB, but that is probably not enough to earn him more than a 2011 non-roster invite. (MP)

| Player | Age | IP | W | Sv | K | ERA | WHIP | K/9 | BB/9 | $2L | Pts |
|---|---|---|---|---|---|---|---|---|---|---|---|
| Sherrill G | 33 | 40 | 3 | 0 | 36 | 4.08 | 1.44 | 8.1 | 4.4 | -$1 | 50 |
| **Mini-Browser** | **Age** | **IP** | **W** | **Sv** | **K** | **ERA** | **WHIP** | **K/9** | **BB/9** | **$2L** | **Pts** |
| Webb R | 25 | 60 | 2 | 0 | 49 | 4.10 | 1.43 | 7.3 | 3.2 | -$1 | 60 |
| Carlson J | 30 | 40 | 1 | 0 | 31 | 4.44 | 1.35 | 6.9 | 3.2 | -$1 | 40 |
| Reynolds M | 26 | 40 | 2 | 0 | 42 | 4.27 | 1.41 | 9.5 | 2.8 | -$1 | 60 |
| Holland D | 24 | 140 | 7 | 0 | 120 | 5.19 | 1.47 | 7.7 | 3.5 | -$1 | 150 |
| Villanueva C | 27 | 60 | 2 | 0 | 53 | 4.70 | 1.32 | 8.0 | 3.2 | -$1 | 70 |

| Level | Leag | W | L | Sv | IP | H | K | ERA | WHIP | K/9 | BB/9 | HR/9 | GB/F |
|---|---|---|---|---|---|---|---|---|---|---|---|---|---|
| A | CAL | 0 | 0 | 0 | 2 | 3 | 2 | 4.50 | 1.50 | 9.0 | 0.0 | 0.0 | — |
| AA | — | — | — | — | — | — | — | — | — | — | — | — | — |
| AAA | PCL | 0 | 0 | 0 | 1 | 2 | 3 | 0.00 | 1.20 | 16.2 | 0.0 | 0.0 | — |

**Competition at RP** / **Stats in 2010 as RP**

| Thr | Player | GR | ERA | IP/G | Sv-Hld |
|---|---|---|---|---|---|
| LH | Sherrill G | 65 | 6.69 | 0.6 | 0-7 |
| LH | Kuo H | 56 | 1.20 | 1.1 | 12-21 |

**Ten-Year Trends** — K/9, BB/9

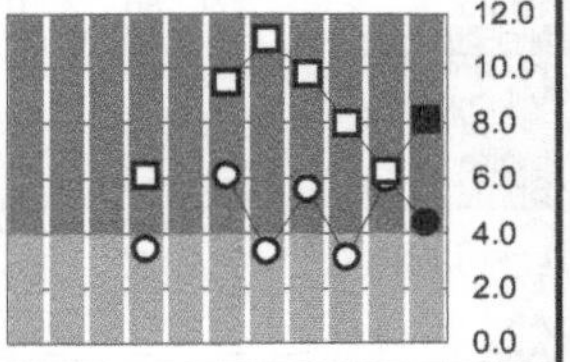


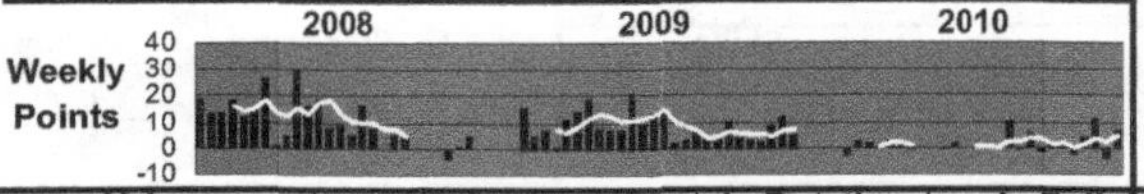


| Yr | Team | W | L | Sv | IP | H | K | ERA | WHIP | K/9 | BB/9 | HR/9 | GB/F | $1L | $2L | Pts | RAA | H% | HR/fb | S% | FIP | GS | CG | QS/DS | GR | Hld | Bln | Lead | OPS | 1st Hf | 2nd Hf | vs RH | vs LH |
|---|---|---|---|---|---|---|---|---|---|---|---|---|---|---|---|---|---|---|---|---|---|---|---|---|---|---|---|---|---|---|---|---|---|
| 07 | SEA | 2 | 0 | 3 | 45 | 28 | 56 | 2.36 | 0.99 | 11.0 | 3.4 | 0.8 | 0.4 | $7 | $6 | 100 | +9 | 24% | 7% | 80% | 3.10 | — | — | — | 73 | 22 | 4 | +0.6 | .553 | .387 | .781 | .587 | .529 |
| 08 | BAL | 3 | 5 | 31 | 53 | 47 | 58 | 4.73 | 1.50 | 9.8 | 5.6 | 1.0 | 0.6 | $7 | $1 | 230 | –4 | 29% | 8% | 70% | 4.44 | — | — | — | 57 | 0 | 6 | +1.3 | .708 | .695 | .744 | .787 | .534 |
| 09 | 2TM | 1 | 1 | 21 | 69 | 53 | 61 | 1.70 | 1.12 | 8.0 | 3.1 | 0.5 | 0.8 | $9 | $9 | 190 | +18 | 26% | 5% | 88% | 3.28 | — | — | — | 72 | 11 | 5 | +1.7 | .588 | .614 | .557 | .696 | .342 |
| 10 | LAD | 2 | 2 | 0 | 36 | 46 | 25 | 6.69 | 1.93 | 6.2 | 5.9 | 1.0 | 1.0 | -$10 | -$21 | 20 | –12 | 35% | 8% | 65% | 5.24 | — | — | — | 65 | 7 | 4 | –0.4 | .906 | 1.007 | .772 | 1.223 | .573 |

## ıı. James Shields — 200 IP | $9 | 250 pts

SP-33, RP-1 — Owned: 95% — RH

Shields in 2010 had the worst year of his career, and trade talks have already started to swirl around him. The main culprit was 34 HR and a second straight year of rising HR/9. Shields is still under contract with TB, so he will be looking to rebound. Apart from the HR, his skills are good; a 4.00 ERA is in reach. (RZ)

| Player | Age | IP | W | Sv | K | ERA | WHIP | K/9 | BB/9 | $2L | Pts |
|---|---|---|---|---|---|---|---|---|---|---|---|
| Shields J | 29 | 200 | 13 | 0 | 155 | 4.63 | 1.30 | 7.0 | 2.1 | $9 | 250 |
| **Mini-Browser** | **Age** | **IP** | **W** | **Sv** | **K** | **ERA** | **WHIP** | **K/9** | **BB/9** | **$2L** | **Pts** |
| Webb B | 31 | 160 | 11 | 0 | 113 | 3.86 | 1.28 | 6.3 | 2.5 | $10 | 210 |
| Nathan J | 36 | 40 | 4 | 18 | 45 | 2.72 | 1.12 | 10.1 | 3.0 | $10 | 180 |
| Rodriguez F | 29 | 60 | 3 | 21 | 66 | 3.14 | 1.27 | 9.9 | 4.2 | $10 | 200 |
| Bumgarner M | 21 | 160 | 10 | 0 | 133 | 3.57 | 1.36 | 7.5 | 2.3 | $10 | 220 |
| Lackey J | 32 | 200 | 13 | 0 | 143 | 4.32 | 1.35 | 6.4 | 2.7 | $9 | 240 |

| Level | Leag | W | L | Sv | IP | H | K | ERA | WHIP | K/9 | BB/9 | HR/9 | GB/F |
|---|---|---|---|---|---|---|---|---|---|---|---|---|---|
| A | — | — | — | — | — | — | — | — | — | — | — | — | — |
| AA | — | — | — | — | — | — | — | — | — | — | — | — | — |
| AAA | — | — | — | — | — | — | — | — | — | — | — | — | — |

**Competition at SP** / **Stats in 2010 as SP**

| Thr | Player | GS | ERA | Supp | W-L |
|---|---|---|---|---|---|
| RH | Shields J | 33 | 5.20 | 4.5 | 12-15 |
| RH | Garza M | 32 | 3.93 | 5.2 | 15-10 |
| LH | Price D | 31 | 2.73 | 5.3 | 19-6 |
| RH | Davis W | 29 | 4.07 | 4.9 | 12-10 |

**Ten-Year Trends** — K/9, BB/9

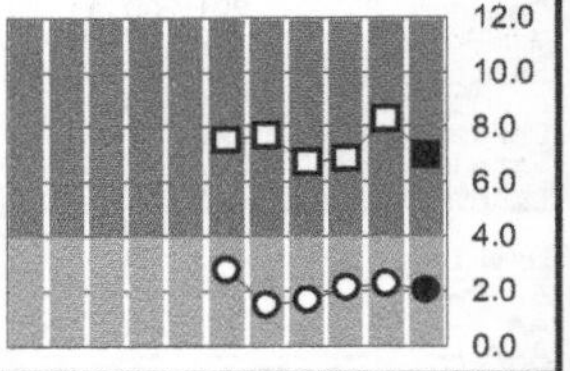


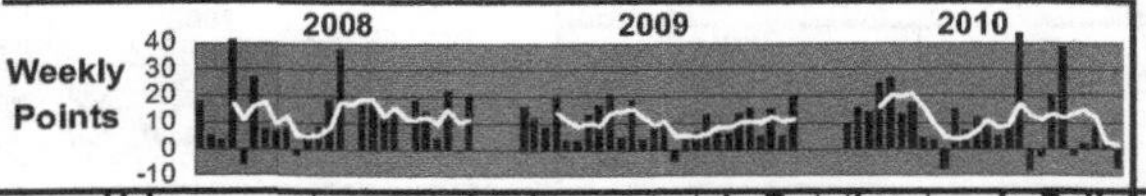


| Yr | Team | W | L | Sv | IP | H | K | ERA | WHIP | K/9 | BB/9 | HR/9 | GB/F | $1L | $2L | Pts | RAA | H% | HR/fb | S% | FIP | GS | CG | QS/DS | GR | Hld | Bln | Lead | OPS | 1st Hf | 2nd Hf | vs RH | vs LH |
|---|---|---|---|---|---|---|---|---|---|---|---|---|---|---|---|---|---|---|---|---|---|---|---|---|---|---|---|---|---|---|---|---|---|
| 07 | TB | 12 | 8 | 0 | 215 | 202 | 184 | 3.85 | 1.11 | 7.7 | 1.5 | 1.2 | 1.1 | $19 | $10 | 310 | +8 | 29% | 11% | 70% | 3.78 | 31 | 1 | 20/2 | — | — | — | — | .697 | .672 | .733 | .718 | .673 |
| 08 | TB | 14 | 8 | 0 | 215 | 208 | 160 | 3.56 | 1.15 | 6.7 | 1.7 | 1.0 | 1.2 | $19 | $10 | 310 | +12 | 29% | 10% | 73% | 3.82 | 33 | 3 | 22/2 | — | — | — | — | .708 | .697 | .722 | .680 | .735 |
| 09 | TB | 11 | 12 | 0 | 219 | 239 | 167 | 4.14 | 1.32 | 6.8 | 2.1 | 1.2 | 1.1 | $11 | $1 | 250 | –5 | 31% | 11% | 73% | 4.21 | 33 | 0 | 17/1 | — | — | — | — | .768 | .743 | .802 | .756 | .779 |
| 10 | TB | 13 | 15 | 0 | 203 | 246 | 187 | 5.18 | 1.46 | 8.3 | 2.3 | 1.5 | 1.1 | $0 | -$23 | 250 | –28 | 35% | 14% | 68% | 4.39 | 33 | 0 | 17/5 | 1 | 0 | 0 | +0.6 | .828 | .790 | .877 | .866 | .796 |

## . Carlos Silva — 160 IP | $-2 | 130 pts

SP-21 — Owned: 34% — RH

Carlos Silva – Mr. 4.0 K/9 – hit 93 MPH on the gun. Through July 6, his average fastball velocity was over 90, his control was superb, and his ERA was 2.96. And then a heart condition, tendinitis, and a high H% struck before Jim Hendry could bundle him up. Renewed health, and his old life, await Silva in 2011. (RM)

| Player | Age | IP | W | Sv | K | ERA | WHIP | K/9 | BB/9 | $2L | Pts |
|---|---|---|---|---|---|---|---|---|---|---|---|
| Silva C | 31 | 160 | 10 | 0 | 76 | 5.24 | 1.35 | 4.3 | 1.8 | -$2 | 130 |
| **Mini-Browser** | **Age** | **IP** | **W** | **Sv** | **K** | **ERA** | **WHIP** | **K/9** | **BB/9** | **$2L** | **Pts** |
| Millwood K | 36 | 200 | 8 | 0 | 130 | 5.02 | 1.49 | 5.8 | 3.1 | -$2 | 150 |
| Cook A | 32 | 120 | 7 | 0 | 51 | 4.78 | 1.41 | 3.8 | 2.7 | -$2 | 90 |
| Demel S | 25 | 60 | 3 | 3 | 63 | 4.92 | 1.62 | 9.5 | 4.4 | -$2 | 90 |
| Rogers M | 25 | 40 | 2 | 0 | 46 | 4.53 | 1.56 | 10.4 | 4.8 | -$2 | 50 |
| Parnell B | 26 | 60 | 2 | 2 | 52 | 4.59 | 1.54 | 7.8 | 3.7 | -$2 | 70 |

| Level | Leag | W | L | Sv | IP | H | K | ERA | WHIP | K/9 | BB/9 | HR/9 | GB/F |
|---|---|---|---|---|---|---|---|---|---|---|---|---|---|
| A | MID | 0 | 1 | 0 | 7 | 8 | 5 | 6.14 | 1.36 | 6.1 | 2.5 | 1.2 | — |
| AA | — | — | — | — | — | — | — | — | — | — | — | — | — |
| AAA | — | — | — | — | — | — | — | — | — | — | — | — | — |

**Competition at SP** / **Stats in 2010 as SP**

| Thr | Player | GS | ERA | Supp | W-L |
|---|---|---|---|---|---|
| RH | Dempster R | 34 | 3.85 | 4.8 | 15-12 |
| RH | Wells R | 32 | 4.26 | 3.3 | 8-14 |
| LH | Gorzelanny T | 23 | 4.22 | 4.1 | 7-9 |
| RH | Silva C | 21 | 4.22 | 5.1 | 10-6 |

**Ten-Year Trends** — K/9, BB/9

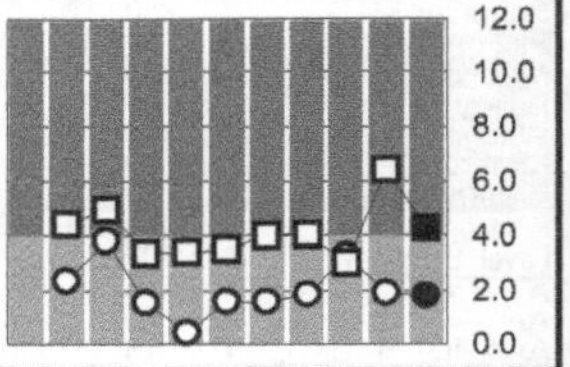


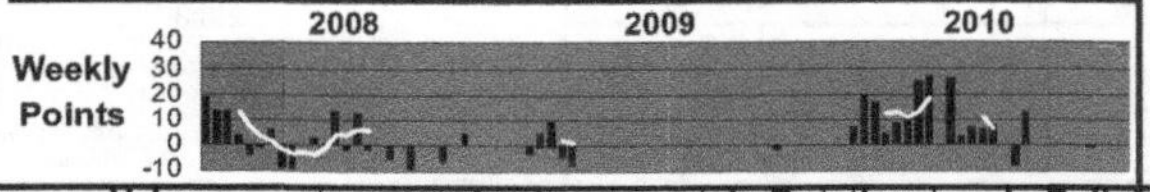


| Yr | Team | W | L | Sv | IP | H | K | ERA | WHIP | K/9 | BB/9 | HR/9 | GB/F | $1L | $2L | Pts | RAA | H% | HR/fb | S% | FIP | GS | CG | QS/DS | GR | Hld | Bln | Lead | OPS | 1st Hf | 2nd Hf | vs RH | vs LH |
|---|---|---|---|---|---|---|---|---|---|---|---|---|---|---|---|---|---|---|---|---|---|---|---|---|---|---|---|---|---|---|---|---|---|
| 07 | MIN | 13 | 14 | 0 | 202 | 229 | 89 | 4.19 | 1.31 | 4.0 | 1.6 | 0.9 | 1.4 | $8 | -$5 | 190 | +1 | 30% | 8% | 70% | 4.24 | 33 | 2 | 20/7 | — | — | — | — | .751 | .772 | .725 | .691 | .812 |
| 08 | SEA | 4 | 15 | 0 | 153 | 213 | 69 | 6.46 | 1.60 | 4.1 | 1.9 | 1.2 | 1.3 | -$18 | -$27 | 30 | –38 | 35% | 10% | 60% | 4.72 | 28 | 1 | 10/9 | — | — | — | — | .868 | .827 | .995 | .789 | .935 |
| 09 | SEA | 1 | 3 | 0 | 30 | 41 | 10 | 8.60 | 1.71 | 3.0 | 3.3 | 1.5 | 1.4 | -$5 | -$8 | 0 | –14 | 33% | 13% | 49% | 5.87 | 6 | 0 | 1/3 | 2 | 0 | 0 | –0.9 | .973 | .962 | 1.125 | .744 | 1.154 |
| 10 | CHC | 10 | 6 | 0 | 113 | 120 | 80 | 4.22 | 1.27 | 6.4 | 1.9 | 0.9 | 1.5 | $2 | -$6 | 170 | +1 | 31% | 9% | 68% | 3.69 | 21 | 0 | 13/4 | — | — | — | — | .734 | .685 | 1.086 | .749 | .708 |

## Alfredo Simon — 40 IP | $-3 | 50 pts

RP-49 — Owned: 37% — RH

A year removed from Tommy John surgery, Simon pitched well enough to attain the closer role in BAL by process of elimination. Simon was not able to hold the spot, but he did not entirely eliminate himself from the conversation. He will be a late-inning reliever again and a long shot (but not a no-shot) for Saves. (BJ)

| Player | Age | IP | W | Sv | K | ERA | WHIP | K/9 | BB/9 | $2L | Pts |
|---|---|---|---|---|---|---|---|---|---|---|---|
| Simon A | 29 | 40 | 2 | 3 | 28 | 5.69 | 1.63 | 6.3 | 3.7 | -$3 | 50 |
| **Mini-Browser** | **Age** | **IP** | **W** | **Sv** | **K** | **ERA** | **WHIP** | **K/9** | **BB/9** | **$2L** | **Pts** |
| Carrasco C | 24 | 180 | 8 | 0 | 160 | 5.14 | 1.57 | 8.0 | 3.8 | -$3 | 180 |
| Lyles J | 20 | 100 | 5 | 0 | 71 | 4.69 | 1.52 | 6.4 | 3.5 | -$3 | 90 |
| Laffey A | 25 | 40 | 2 | 0 | 20 | 4.90 | 1.55 | 4.5 | 3.9 | -$3 | 30 |
| Burnett A | 23 | 40 | 2 | 0 | 34 | 5.18 | 1.59 | 7.7 | 3.7 | -$3 | 40 |
| Rodriguez H | 24 | 50 | 2 | 0 | 59 | 4.92 | 1.68 | 10.6 | 6.0 | -$3 | 60 |

| Level | Leag | W | L | Sv | IP | H | K | ERA | WHIP | K/9 | BB/9 | HR/9 | GB/F |
|---|---|---|---|---|---|---|---|---|---|---|---|---|---|
| A | — | — | — | — | — | — | — | — | — | — | — | — | — |
| AA | — | — | — | — | — | — | — | — | — | — | — | — | — |
| AAA | IL | 1 | 1 | 0 | 17 | 15 | 14 | 1.59 | 1.18 | 7.4 | 2.6 | 0.5 | — |

**Competition at RP** / **Stats in 2010 as RP**

| Thr | Player | GR | ERA | IP/G | Sv-Hld |
|---|---|---|---|---|---|
| RH | Albers M | 62 | 4.52 | 1.2 | 0-7 |
| RH | Simon A | 49 | 4.93 | 1.0 | 17-1 |
| RH | Uehara K | 43 | 2.86 | 1.0 | 13-6 |
| RH | Berken J | 41 | 3.03 | 1.5 | 0-7 |

**Ten-Year Trends** — K/9, BB/9

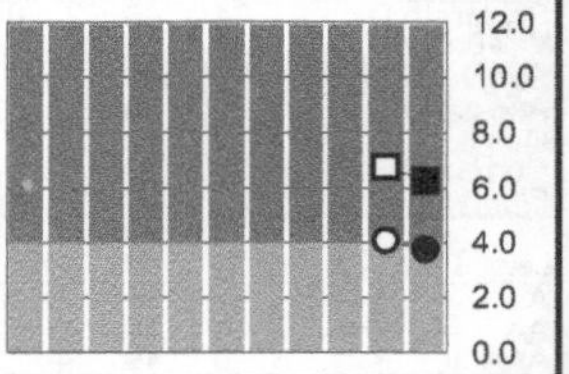


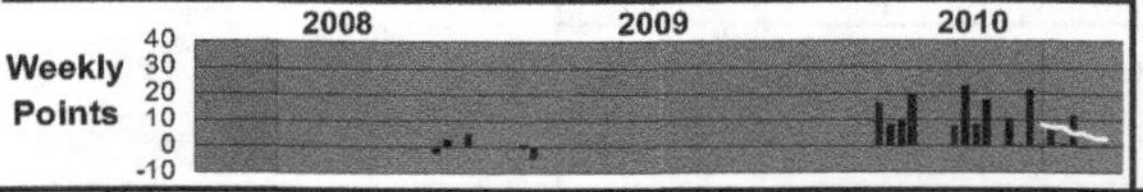


| Yr | Team | W | L | Sv | IP | H | K | ERA | WHIP | K/9 | BB/9 | HR/9 | GB/F | $1L | $2L | Pts | RAA | H% | HR/fb | S% | FIP | GS | CG | QS/DS | GR | Hld | Bln | Lead | OPS | 1st Hf | 2nd Hf | vs RH | vs LH |
|---|---|---|---|---|---|---|---|---|---|---|---|---|---|---|---|---|---|---|---|---|---|---|---|---|---|---|---|---|---|---|---|---|---|
| 07 | — | — | — | — | — | — | — | — | — | — | — | — | — | — | — | — | — | — | — | — | — | — | — | — | — | — | — | — | — | — | — | — | — |
| 08 | BAL | 0 | 0 | 0 | 13 | 16 | 8 | 6.23 | 1.38 | 5.5 | 1.4 | 2.8 | 2.1 | -$3 | -$4 | 0 | –4 | 28% | 29% | 64% | 6.53 | 1 | 0 | 1/0 | 3 | 0 | 0 | –2.3 | .950 | — | .950 | 1.356 | .761 |
| 09 | BAL | 0 | 1 | 0 | 6 | 8 | 3 | 9.95 | 1.58 | 4.3 | 2.8 | 7.1 | 0.4 | -$3 | -$4 | 0 | –4 | 17% | 36% | 60% | 13.56 | 2 | 0 | 0/1 | — | — | — | — | 1.242 | 1.242 | — | 1.152 | 1.308 |
| 10 | BAL | 4 | 2 | 17 | 49 | 54 | 37 | 4.93 | 1.54 | 6.8 | 4.0 | 1.8 | 1.4 | $1 | -$9 | 150 | –8 | 29% | 18% | 74% | 5.77 | — | — | — | 49 | 1 | 4 | +0.4 | .825 | .687 | .962 | .953 | .684 |

## Tony Sipp — 60 IP | $0 | 80 pts

RP-70 — Owned: 0% — LH

Absent 9 ER in 5.2 IP in June, Sipp's ERA in 2010 would have been 3.14, not 4.14. Despite occasional wildness and an elevated BB/9 from the 27-year-old, Cleveland management remains confident in his ability to power through tough situations, and he will get regular work in the 7th and 8th innings. (BLS)

| Player | Age | IP | W | Sv | K | ERA | WHIP | K/9 | BB/9 | $2L | Pts |
|---|---|---|---|---|---|---|---|---|---|---|---|
| Sipp T | 27 | 60 | 2 | 0 | 68 | 4.44 | 1.50 | 10.1 | 5.6 | $0 | 80 |
| **Mini-Browser** | **Age** | **IP** | **W** | **Sv** | **K** | **ERA** | **WHIP** | **K/9** | **BB/9** | **$2L** | **Pts** |
| Miller T | 37 | 40 | 2 | 0 | 34 | 3.90 | 1.29 | 7.6 | 3.5 | $0 | 50 |
| Atchison S | 35 | 40 | 1 | 0 | 29 | 4.28 | 1.28 | 6.5 | 2.6 | $0 | 40 |
| Affeldt J | 31 | 60 | 3 | 0 | 49 | 4.06 | 1.45 | 7.3 | 4.1 | $0 | 70 |
| Choate R | 35 | 40 | 3 | 0 | 33 | 4.38 | 1.38 | 7.4 | 3.5 | $0 | 50 |
| Ohlendorf R | 28 | 160 | 6 | 0 | 110 | 4.64 | 1.38 | 6.2 | 3.1 | $0 | 130 |

| Level | Leag | W | L | Sv | IP | H | K | ERA | WHIP | K/9 | BB/9 | HR/9 | GB/F |
|---|---|---|---|---|---|---|---|---|---|---|---|---|---|
| A | — | — | — | — | — | — | — | — | — | — | — | — | — |
| AA | — | — | — | — | — | — | — | — | — | — | — | — | — |
| AAA | — | — | — | — | — | — | — | — | — | — | — | — | — |

**Competition at RP** / **Stats in 2010 as RP**

| Thr | Player | GR | ERA | IP/G | Sv-Hld |
|---|---|---|---|---|---|
| LH | Perez R | 70 | 3.25 | 0.9 | 0-13 |
| LH | Sipp T | 70 | 4.14 | 0.9 | 1-15 |
| LH | Laffey A | 24 | 5.28 | 1.3 | 0-5 |

**Ten-Year Trends** — K/9, BB/9

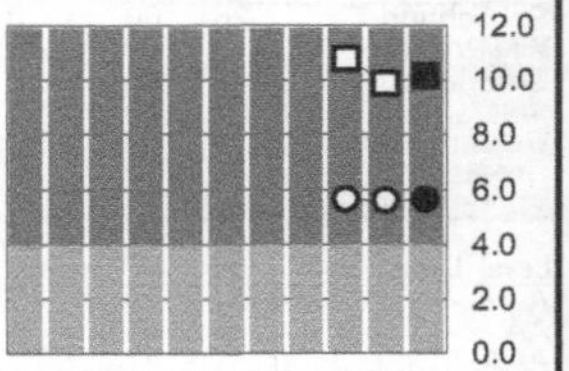


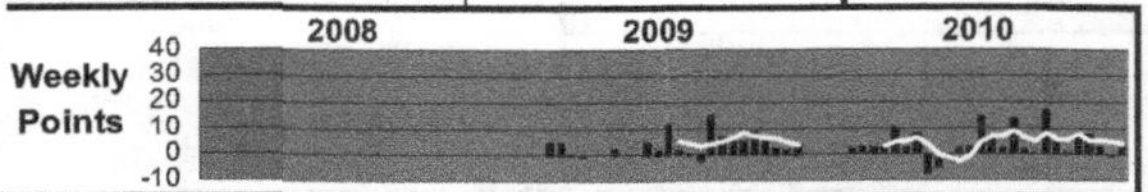


| Yr | Team | W | L | Sv | IP | H | K | ERA | WHIP | K/9 | BB/9 | HR/9 | GB/F | $1L | $2L | Pts | RAA | H% | HR/fb | S% | FIP | GS | CG | QS/DS | GR | Hld | Bln | Lead | OPS | 1st Hf | 2nd Hf | vs RH | vs LH |
|---|---|---|---|---|---|---|---|---|---|---|---|---|---|---|---|---|---|---|---|---|---|---|---|---|---|---|---|---|---|---|---|---|---|
| 07 | — | — | — | — | — | — | — | — | — | — | — | — | — | — | — | — | — | — | — | — | — | — | — | — | — | — | — | — | — | — | — | — | — |
| 08 | — | — | — | — | — | — | — | — | — | — | — | — | — | — | — | — | — | — | — | — | — | — | — | — | — | — | — | — | — | — | — | — | — |
| 09 | CLE | 2 | 0 | 0 | 40 | 27 | 48 | 2.93 | 1.30 | 10.8 | 5.6 | 1.1 | 0.7 | $2 | $0 | 70 | +2 | 26% | 11% | 83% | 4.40 | — | — | — | 46 | 9 | 0 | –0.3 | .682 | .675 | .684 | .677 | .685 |
| 10 | CLE | 2 | 2 | 1 | 63 | 48 | 69 | 4.14 | 1.38 | 9.9 | 5.6 | 1.7 | 0.6 | $0 | -$10 | 80 | –2 | 26% | 14% | 77% | 5.44 | — | — | — | 70 | 15 | 2 | –0.5 | .770 | .878 | .654 | .742 | .805 |

*For more stats, visit www.Rotolympus.com.*

## Doug Slaten — 40 IP | $0 | 50 pts

RP-49 — Owned: 0% — LH

Slaten in 2011 did what a lefty specialist should and nothing more. If the Nationals were in more close or meaningful games, Slaten's work would mean more than it does. Slaten should be able to perform this role for a couple more years, but he is arb-eligible and is more valuable to almost any other team. (PB)

| Player | Age | IP | W | Sv | K | ERA | WHIP | K/9 | BB/9 | $2L | Pts |
|---|---|---|---|---|---|---|---|---|---|---|---|
| **Forecast** | | | | | | | | | | | |
| Slaten D | 31 | 40 | 2 | 0 | 33 | 3.92 | 1.37 | 7.5 | 3.7 | $0 | 50 |
| **Mini-Browser** | **Age** | **IP** | **W** | **Sv** | **K** | **ERA** | **WHIP** | **K/9** | **BB/9** | **$2L** | **Pts** |
| Ohlendorf R | 28 | 160 | 6 | 0 | 110 | 4.64 | 1.38 | 6.2 | 3.1 | $0 | 130 |
| Sipp T | 27 | 60 | 2 | 0 | 68 | 4.44 | 1.50 | 10.1 | 5.6 | $0 | 80 |
| Jepsen K | 26 | 40 | 1 | 4 | 38 | 4.50 | 1.52 | 8.6 | 4.6 | $0 | 60 |
| Litsch J | 26 | 80 | 4 | 0 | 42 | 4.93 | 1.33 | 4.8 | 2.3 | $0 | 60 |
| Duchscherer J | 33 | 20 | 1 | 0 | 13 | 3.40 | 1.21 | 5.9 | 2.7 | $0 | 30 |

| Level | Leag | W | L | Sv | IP | H | K | ERA | WHIP | K/9 | BB/9 | HR/9 | GB/F |
|---|---|---|---|---|---|---|---|---|---|---|---|---|---|
| **Minors (2010)** | | | | | | | | | | **Skills** | | | |
| A | — | — | — | — | — | — | — | — | — | — | — | — | — |
| AA | — | — | — | — | — | — | — | — | — | — | — | — | — |
| AAA | IL | 1 | 0 | 0 | 17 | 12 | 17 | 0.00 | 0.76 | 9.0 | 0.5 | 0.0 | — |

| Yr | Team | W | L | Sv | IP | H | K | ERA | WHIP | K/9 | BB/9 | HR/9 | GB/F |
|---|---|---|---|---|---|---|---|---|---|---|---|---|---|
| **Majors** | | | | | | | | | | **Skills** | | | |
| 07 | ARI | 3 | 2 | 0 | 36 | 41 | 28 | 2.72 | 1.51 | 6.9 | 3.5 | 1.0 | 1.1 |
| 08 | ARI | 0 | 3 | 0 | 32 | 33 | 20 | 4.73 | 1.45 | 5.6 | 3.9 | 1.1 | 0.9 |
| 09 | ARI | 0 | 0 | 0 | 6 | 10 | 4 | 7.11 | 1.74 | 5.7 | 1.4 | 1.4 | 1.4 |
| 10 | WAS | 4 | 1 | 0 | 40 | 34 | 36 | 3.10 | 1.30 | 8.0 | 4.2 | 0.4 | 1.2 |

| Thr | Player | GR | ERA | IP/G | Sv-Hld |
|---|---|---|---|---|---|
| **Competition at RP** | | **Stats in 2010 as RP** | | | |
| LH | Burnett S | 73 | 2.14 | 0.9 | 3-20 |
| LH | Slaten D | 49 | 3.10 | 0.8 | 0-4 |

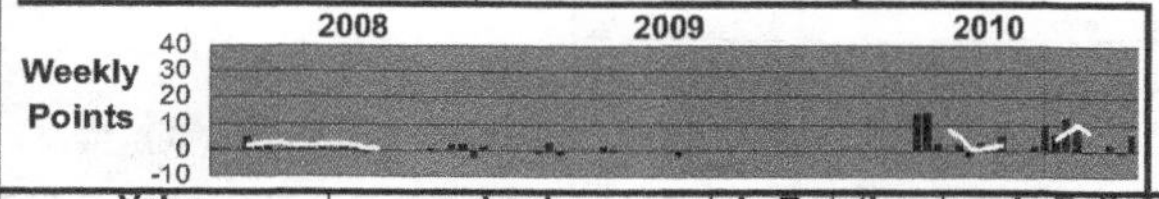


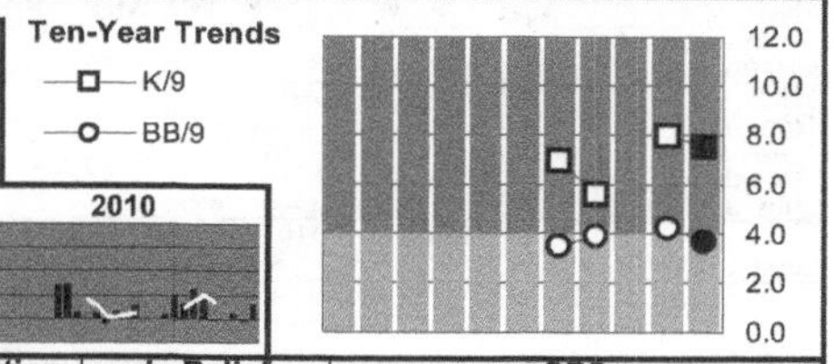


| Yr | $1L | $2L | Pts | RAA | H% | HR/fb | S% | FIP | GS | CG | QS/DS | GR | Hld | Bln | Lead | OPS | 1st Hf | 2nd Hf | vs RH | vs LH |
|---|---|---|---|---|---|---|---|---|---|---|---|---|---|---|---|---|---|---|---|---|
| | **Value** | | | | **Luck** | | | | **In Rotation** | | | **In Relief** | | | | **OPS** | | | | |
| 07 | $1 | -$1 | 60 | +1 | 32% | 9% | 86% | 4.25 | — | — | — | 61 | 7 | 1 | −0.4 | .760 | .762 | .758 | .820 | .711 |
| 08 | -$3 | -$5 | 10 | −5 | 28% | 9% | 70% | 4.87 | — | — | — | 45 | 4 | 0 | −1.7 | .790 | .728 | 1.026 | .866 | .692 |
| 09 | -$3 | -$3 | 0 | −2 | 38% | 13% | 60% | 4.46 | — | — | — | 11 | 0 | 0 | −0.8 | .953 | .953 | — | .788 | 1.056 |
| 10 | -$1 | -$6 | 80 | +0 | 29% | 4% | 76% | 3.47 | — | — | — | 49 | 4 | 0 | −1.3 | .626 | .658 | .595 | .844 | .385 |

## Kevin Slowey — 140 IP | $8 | 190 pts

SP-28, RP-2 — Owned: 73% — RH

2010 was a frustrating season for Slowey, who could never seem to stay healthy or reliable for any stretch, and who was left off the post-season roster despite a 13-6 record. There are a number of reasons that the Twins might seek to move Slowey. Having 4.00-ERA stuff hardly matters when you can't top 160 IP. (NN)

| Player | Age | IP | W | Sv | K | ERA | WHIP | K/9 | BB/9 | $2L | Pts |
|---|---|---|---|---|---|---|---|---|---|---|---|
| **Forecast** | | | | | | | | | | | |
| Slowey K | 26 | 140 | 10 | 0 | 104 | 4.51 | 1.25 | 6.7 | 1.6 | $8 | 190 |
| **Mini-Browser** | **Age** | **IP** | **W** | **Sv** | **K** | **ERA** | **WHIP** | **K/9** | **BB/9** | **$2L** | **Pts** |
| Thornton M | 34 | 60 | 4 | 4 | 68 | 2.99 | 1.11 | 10.2 | 3.0 | $8 | 140 |
| Richard C | 27 | 180 | 11 | 0 | 134 | 3.95 | 1.36 | 6.7 | 3.4 | $8 | 230 |
| Floyd G | 28 | 200 | 11 | 0 | 150 | 4.47 | 1.35 | 6.8 | 3.0 | $8 | 230 |
| Meek E | 27 | 80 | 4 | 12 | 71 | 3.36 | 1.34 | 7.9 | 4.3 | $8 | 170 |
| Romero R | 26 | 200 | 12 | 0 | 157 | 4.32 | 1.42 | 7.1 | 4.0 | $8 | 240 |

| Level | Leag | W | L | Sv | IP | H | K | ERA | WHIP | K/9 | BB/9 | HR/9 | GB/F |
|---|---|---|---|---|---|---|---|---|---|---|---|---|---|
| **Minors (2010)** | | | | | | | | | | **Skills** | | | |
| A | — | — | — | — | — | — | — | — | — | — | — | — | — |
| AA | — | — | — | — | — | — | — | — | — | — | — | — | — |
| AAA | — | — | — | — | — | — | — | — | — | — | — | — | — |

| Yr | Team | W | L | Sv | IP | H | K | ERA | WHIP | K/9 | BB/9 | HR/9 | GB/F |
|---|---|---|---|---|---|---|---|---|---|---|---|---|---|
| **Majors** | | | | | | | | | | **Skills** | | | |
| 07 | MIN | 4 | 1 | 0 | 66 | 82 | 47 | 4.73 | 1.40 | 6.3 | 1.5 | 2.2 | 0.6 |
| 08 | MIN | 12 | 11 | 0 | 160 | 161 | 123 | 3.99 | 1.15 | 6.9 | 1.3 | 1.2 | 0.8 |
| 09 | MIN | 10 | 3 | 0 | 90 | 113 | 75 | 4.86 | 1.41 | 7.4 | 1.5 | 1.5 | 0.7 |
| 10 | MIN | 13 | 6 | 0 | 155 | 172 | 116 | 4.45 | 1.29 | 6.7 | 1.7 | 1.2 | 0.6 |

| Thr | Player | GS | ERA | Supp | W-L |
|---|---|---|---|---|---|
| **Competition at SP** | | **Stats in 2010 as SP** | | | |
| RH | Pavano C | 32 | 3.75 | 4.7 | 17-11 |
| LH | Liriano F | 31 | 3.62 | 4.9 | 14-10 |
| RH | Baker S | 29 | 4.49 | 4.8 | 12-9 |
| RH | Slowey K | 28 | 4.54 | 5.5 | 13-6 |

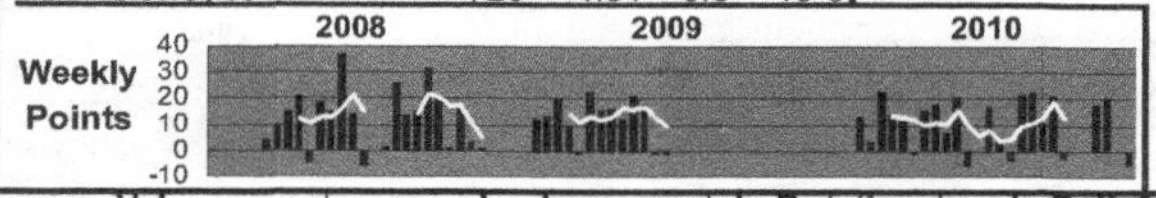


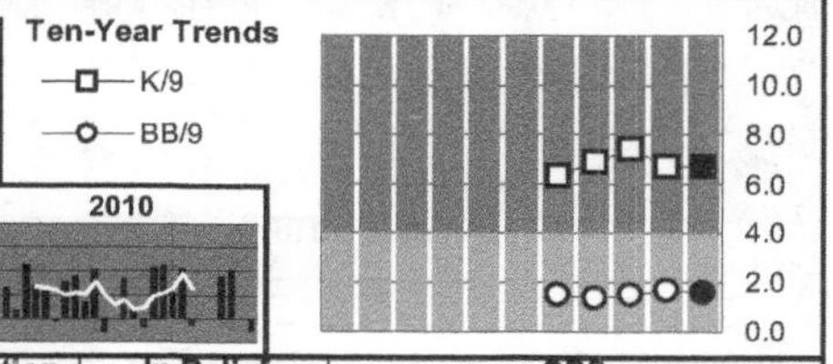


| Yr | $1L | $2L | Pts | RAA | H% | HR/fb | S% | FIP | GS | CG | QS/DS | GR | Hld | Bln | Lead | OPS | 1st Hf | 2nd Hf | vs RH | vs LH |
|---|---|---|---|---|---|---|---|---|---|---|---|---|---|---|---|---|---|---|---|---|
| | **Value** | | | | **Luck** | | | | **In Rotation** | | | **In Relief** | | | | **OPS** | | | | |
| 07 | $0 | -$6 | 70 | −6 | 30% | 13% | 75% | 5.51 | 11 | 0 | 4/1 | 2 | 0 | 0 | 0.0 | .850 | .984 | .665 | .878 | .823 |
| 08 | $12 | $5 | 240 | +5 | 29% | 10% | 70% | 4.00 | 27 | 3 | 13/4 | — | — | — | — | .728 | .748 | .707 | .637 | .832 |
| 09 | $3 | -$2 | 150 | −5 | 35% | 11% | 70% | 4.29 | 16 | 0 | 9/2 | — | — | — | — | .843 | .843 | — | .746 | .946 |
| 10 | $7 | -$7 | 220 | −3 | 31% | 8% | 69% | 4.12 | 28 | 0 | 9/6 | 2 | 0 | 0 | +0.4 | .770 | .819 | .687 | .807 | .734 |

## Chris Smith — 40 IP | $-3 | 30 pts

RP-3 — Owned: 0% — RH

As the closer for the Nashville Sounds, Smith has notched 43 Saves over the past two years, with 11.0 K/9 and 2.7 BB/9. He has not wowed in the majors, but it will be hard for MIL to keep him down much longer. If Smith is not in the bullpen after Spring Training, he will be called up any time the Brewers need help. (MS)

| Player | Age | IP | W | Sv | K | ERA | WHIP | K/9 | BB/9 | $2L | Pts |
|---|---|---|---|---|---|---|---|---|---|---|---|
| **Forecast** | | | | | | | | | | | |
| Smith C | 29 | 40 | 1 | 0 | 32 | 5.15 | 1.41 | 7.3 | 3.0 | -$3 | 30 |
| **Mini-Browser** | **Age** | **IP** | **W** | **Sv** | **K** | **ERA** | **WHIP** | **K/9** | **BB/9** | **$2L** | **Pts** |
| Smith J | 25 | 60 | 3 | 0 | 46 | 4.83 | 1.52 | 6.9 | 2.7 | -$3 | 60 |
| Miner Z | 29 | 40 | 1 | 0 | 23 | 4.93 | 1.53 | 5.1 | 4.3 | -$3 | 20 |
| Kirkman M | 24 | 80 | 5 | 0 | 60 | 4.81 | 1.69 | 6.8 | 6.1 | -$3 | 80 |
| Sampson C | 32 | 40 | 1 | 0 | 20 | 4.81 | 1.39 | 4.4 | 2.3 | -$3 | 20 |
| Feldman S | 28 | 160 | 9 | 0 | 84 | 5.13 | 1.51 | 4.7 | 3.3 | -$3 | 120 |

| Level | Leag | W | L | Sv | IP | H | K | ERA | WHIP | K/9 | BB/9 | HR/9 | GB/F |
|---|---|---|---|---|---|---|---|---|---|---|---|---|---|
| **Minors (2010)** | | | | | | | | | | **Skills** | | | |
| A | — | — | — | — | — | — | — | — | — | — | — | — | — |
| AA | — | — | — | — | — | — | — | — | — | — | — | — | — |
| AAA | PCL | 4 | 3 | 26 | 48 | 47 | 62 | 3.56 | 1.42 | 11.6 | 3.9 | 1.3 | — |

| Yr | Team | W | L | Sv | IP | H | K | ERA | WHIP | K/9 | BB/9 | HR/9 | GB/F |
|---|---|---|---|---|---|---|---|---|---|---|---|---|---|
| **Majors** | | | | | | | | | | **Skills** | | | |
| 07 | — | — | — | — | — | — | — | — | — | — | — | — | — |
| 08 | BOS | 1 | 0 | 0 | 18 | 18 | 13 | 7.85 | 1.36 | 6.4 | 3.4 | 2.9 | 0.5 |
| 09 | MIL | 0 | 0 | 0 | 46 | 41 | 35 | 4.11 | 1.30 | 6.8 | 3.7 | 2.2 | 0.6 |
| 10 | MIL | 0 | 0 | 0 | 3 | 4 | 4 | 5.40 | 1.50 | 10.8 | 2.7 | 0.0 | 5.0 |

| Thr | Player | GR | ERA | IP/G | Sv-Hld |
|---|---|---|---|---|---|
| **Competition at RP** | | **Stats in 2010 as RP** | | | |
| RH | Coffey T | 69 | 4.76 | 0.9 | 0-13 |
| RH | Loe K | 53 | 2.78 | 1.1 | 0-22 |
| RH | Axford J | 50 | 2.48 | 1.2 | 24-3 |
| RH | Villanueva C | 50 | 4.61 | 1.1 | 1-14 |

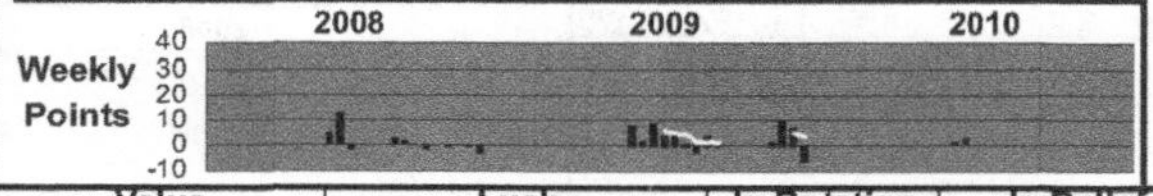


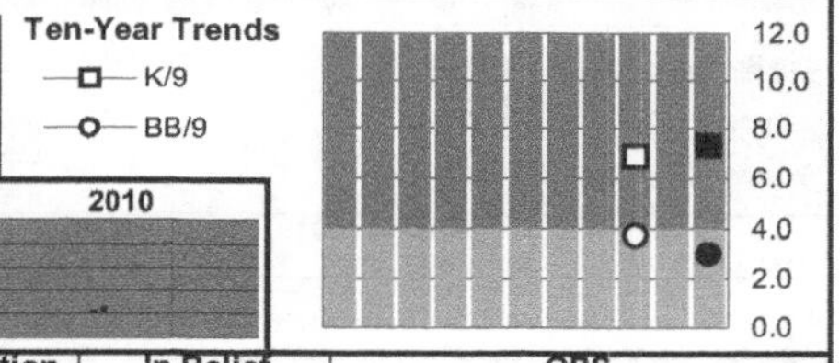


| Yr | $1L | $2L | Pts | RAA | H% | HR/fb | S% | FIP | GS | CG | QS/DS | GR | Hld | Bln | Lead | OPS | 1st Hf | 2nd Hf | vs RH | vs LH |
|---|---|---|---|---|---|---|---|---|---|---|---|---|---|---|---|---|---|---|---|---|
| | **Value** | | | | **Luck** | | | | **In Rotation** | | | **In Relief** | | | | **OPS** | | | | |
| 07 | — | — | — | — | — | — | — | — | — | — | — | — | — | — | — | — | — | — | — | — |
| 08 | -$4 | -$5 | 10 | −8 | 24% | 20% | 47% | 7.28 | — | — | — | 12 | 0 | 0 | +0.7 | .904 | .592 | 1.034 | 1.308 | .606 |
| 09 | -$1 | -$2 | 30 | −0 | 23% | 15% | 80% | 6.03 | — | — | — | 35 | 0 | 1 | −3.5 | .780 | .720 | .833 | .744 | .819 |
| 10 | -$5 | -$11 | 0 | −1 | 44% | 0% | 60% | 1.70 | — | — | — | 3 | 0 | 0 | +0.7 | .819 | .819 | — | .573 | 1.667 |

## Joe Smith — 40 IP | $0 | 40 pts

RP-53 — Owned: 0% — RH

Smith was shipped to Triple-A in April primarily to clear a spot in Cleveland for Rule-5 pick Hector Ambriz. In the meantime, the side-armer broke out of an early slump by re-acquainting himself with his customary worm-killing ways. Control issues and an extreme split paint Smith as a specialized middle reliever. (BLS)

| Player | Age | IP | W | Sv | K | ERA | WHIP | K/9 | BB/9 | $2L | Pts |
|---|---|---|---|---|---|---|---|---|---|---|---|
| **Forecast** | | | | | | | | | | | |
| Smith J | 27 | 40 | 2 | 0 | 32 | 4.16 | 1.42 | 7.1 | 4.7 | $0 | 40 |
| **Mini-Browser** | **Age** | **IP** | **W** | **Sv** | **K** | **ERA** | **WHIP** | **K/9** | **BB/9** | **$2L** | **Pts** |
| Slaten D | 31 | 40 | 2 | 0 | 33 | 3.92 | 1.37 | 7.5 | 3.7 | $0 | 50 |
| Bulger J | 32 | 40 | 2 | 0 | 44 | 4.22 | 1.46 | 9.8 | 5.0 | $0 | 50 |
| Bedard E | 32 | 20 | 1 | 0 | 19 | 3.68 | 1.27 | 8.6 | 3.6 | $0 | 30 |
| Belisario R | 28 | 80 | 4 | 0 | 62 | 4.55 | 1.40 | 7.0 | 3.6 | $0 | 90 |
| Linebrink S | 34 | 60 | 2 | 0 | 50 | 4.83 | 1.36 | 7.5 | 3.0 | $0 | 60 |

| Level | Leag | W | L | Sv | IP | H | K | ERA | WHIP | K/9 | BB/9 | HR/9 | GB/F |
|---|---|---|---|---|---|---|---|---|---|---|---|---|---|
| **Minors (2010)** | | | | | | | | | | **Skills** | | | |
| A | — | — | — | — | — | — | — | — | — | — | — | — | — |
| AA | — | — | — | — | — | — | — | — | — | — | — | — | — |
| AAA | IL | 2 | 1 | 2 | 23 | 17 | 19 | 1.96 | 1.17 | 7.4 | 3.9 | 0.0 | — |

| Yr | Team | W | L | Sv | IP | H | K | ERA | WHIP | K/9 | BB/9 | HR/9 | GB/F |
|---|---|---|---|---|---|---|---|---|---|---|---|---|---|
| **Majors** | | | | | | | | | | **Skills** | | | |
| 07 | NYM | 3 | 2 | 0 | 44 | 48 | 45 | 3.45 | 1.56 | 9.1 | 4.3 | 0.6 | 3.0 |
| 08 | NYM | 6 | 3 | 0 | 63 | 51 | 52 | 3.55 | 1.29 | 7.4 | 4.4 | 0.6 | 3.5 |
| 09 | CLE | 0 | 0 | 0 | 34 | 30 | 30 | 3.44 | 1.26 | 7.9 | 3.4 | 1.1 | 2.0 |
| 10 | CLE | 2 | 2 | 0 | 40 | 30 | 32 | 3.83 | 1.35 | 7.2 | 5.4 | 0.9 | 2.0 |

| Thr | Player | GR | ERA | IP/G | Sv-Hld |
|---|---|---|---|---|---|
| **Competition at RP** | | **Stats in 2010 as RP** | | | |
| RH | Perez C | 63 | 1.71 | 1.0 | 23-9 |
| RH | Smith J | 53 | 3.83 | 0.8 | 0-17 |
| RH | Herrmann F | 40 | 4.03 | 1.1 | 1-7 |
| RH | Lewis J | 37 | 2.97 | 1.0 | 0-1 |

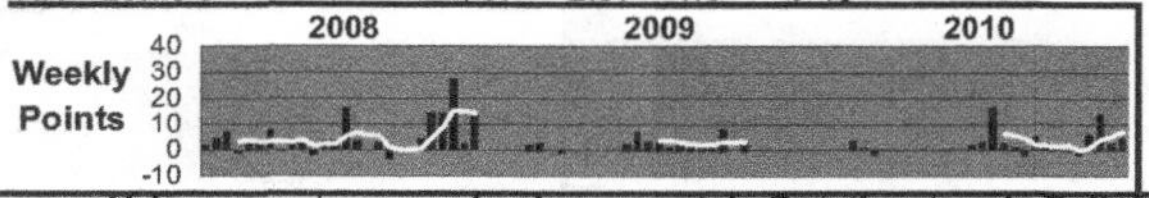


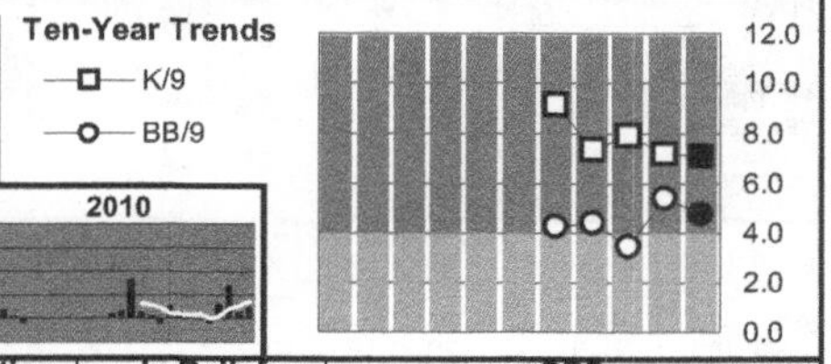


| Yr | $1L | $2L | Pts | RAA | H% | HR/fb | S% | FIP | GS | CG | QS/DS | GR | Hld | Bln | Lead | OPS | 1st Hf | 2nd Hf | vs RH | vs LH |
|---|---|---|---|---|---|---|---|---|---|---|---|---|---|---|---|---|---|---|---|---|
| | **Value** | | | | **Luck** | | | | **In Rotation** | | | **In Relief** | | | | **OPS** | | | | |
| 07 | $0 | -$3 | 70 | +2 | 35% | 11% | 79% | 3.47 | — | — | — | 54 | 10 | 0 | −0.3 | .757 | .686 | .982 | .720 | .858 |
| 08 | $3 | $1 | 110 | +1 | 27% | 13% | 73% | 3.85 | — | — | — | 82 | 18 | 3 | +1.0 | .658 | .614 | .722 | .589 | .903 |
| 09 | $0 | -$1 | 30 | −1 | 28% | 15% | 77% | 4.21 | — | — | — | 37 | 10 | 1 | +0.1 | .707 | .763 | .608 | .615 | .992 |
| 10 | -$1 | -$10 | 50 | 0 | 24% | 13% | 74% | 4.80 | — | — | — | 53 | 17 | 1 | +0.1 | .659 | .839 | .534 | .538 | .979 |

## Jordan Smith — 60 IP | $-3 | 60 pts

RP-37 — Owned: 0% — RH

Smith will probably get crowded out of the Reds' staff. At best, he will be an 11th or 12th pitcher in Cincy, and he could get dealt at the end of Spring Training to open a spot for someone else. In the right situation, Smith could hold down a set-up role. (SW)

| Player | Age | IP | W | Sv | K | ERA | WHIP | K/9 | BB/9 | $2L | Pts |
|---|---|---|---|---|---|---|---|---|---|---|---|
| **Forecast** | | | | | | | | | | | |
| Smith J | 25 | 60 | 3 | 0 | 46 | 4.83 | 1.52 | 6.9 | 2.7 | -$3 | 60 |
| **Mini-Browser** | **Age** | **IP** | **W** | **Sv** | **K** | **ERA** | **WHIP** | **K/9** | **BB/9** | **$2L** | **Pts** |
| Burnett A | 23 | 40 | 2 | 0 | 34 | 5.18 | 1.59 | 7.7 | 3.7 | -$3 | 40 |
| Rodriguez H | 24 | 50 | 2 | 0 | 59 | 4.92 | 1.68 | 10.6 | 6.0 | -$3 | 60 |
| Simon A | 29 | 40 | 2 | 3 | 28 | 5.69 | 1.63 | 6.3 | 3.7 | -$3 | 50 |
| Palmer M | 32 | 60 | 3 | 0 | 39 | 4.98 | 1.59 | 5.8 | 4.6 | -$3 | 50 |
| Maine J | 29 | 40 | 2 | 0 | 32 | 4.96 | 1.48 | 7.1 | 4.2 | -$3 | 40 |

| Level | Leag | W | L | Sv | IP | H | K | ERA | WHIP | K/9 | BB/9 | HR/9 | GB/F |
|---|---|---|---|---|---|---|---|---|---|---|---|---|---|
| **Minors (2010)** | | | | | | | | | | **Skills** | | | |
| A | — | — | — | — | — | — | — | — | — | — | — | — | — |
| AA | SOU | 1 | 3 | 9 | 28 | 38 | 14 | 5.08 | 1.62 | 4.4 | 2.5 | 1.0 | — |
| AAA | IL | 0 | 0 | 0 | 3 | 5 | 0 | 8.10 | 1.80 | 0.0 | 2.7 | 2.7 | — |

| Yr | Team | W | L | Sv | IP | H | K | ERA | WHIP | K/9 | BB/9 | HR/9 | GB/F |
|---|---|---|---|---|---|---|---|---|---|---|---|---|---|
| **Majors** | | | | | | | | | | **Skills** | | | |
| 07 | — | — | — | — | — | — | — | — | — | — | — | — | — |
| 08 | — | — | — | — | — | — | — | — | — | — | — | — | — |
| 09 | — | — | — | — | — | — | — | — | — | — | — | — | — |
| 10 | CIN | 3 | 2 | 1 | 42 | 45 | 26 | 3.86 | 1.33 | 5.6 | 2.4 | 1.5 | 1.6 |

| Thr | Player | GR | ERA | IP/G | Sv-Hld |
|---|---|---|---|---|---|
| **Competition at RP** | | **Stats in 2010 as RP** | | | |
| RH | Masset N | 82 | 3.40 | 0.9 | 2-20 |
| RH | Cordero F | 75 | 3.84 | 1.0 | 40-1 |
| RH | Ondrusek L | 60 | 3.68 | 1.0 | 0-6 |
| RH | Smith J | 37 | 3.86 | 1.1 | 1-2 |

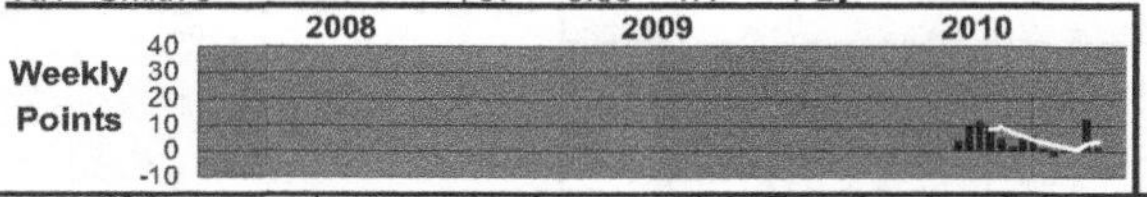


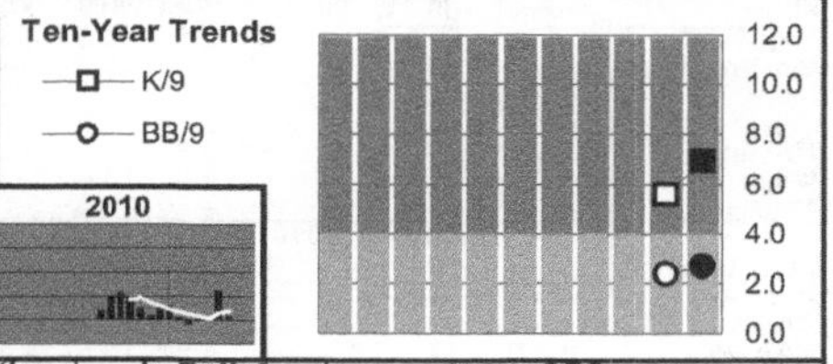


| Yr | $1L | $2L | Pts | RAA | H% | HR/fb | S% | FIP | GS | CG | QS/DS | GR | Hld | Bln | Lead | OPS | 1st Hf | 2nd Hf | vs RH | vs LH |
|---|---|---|---|---|---|---|---|---|---|---|---|---|---|---|---|---|---|---|---|---|
| | **Value** | | | | **Luck** | | | | **In Rotation** | | | **In Relief** | | | | **OPS** | | | | |
| 07 | — | — | — | — | — | — | — | — | — | — | — | — | — | — | — | — | — | — | — | — |
| 08 | — | — | — | — | — | — | — | — | — | — | — | — | — | — | — | — | — | — | — | — |
| 09 | — | — | — | — | — | — | — | — | — | — | — | — | — | — | — | — | — | — | — | — |
| 10 | -$3 | -$9 | 60 | +1 | 29% | 16% | 78% | 4.91 | — | — | — | 37 | 2 | 1 | −0.3 | .768 | .778 | .764 | .691 | .913 |

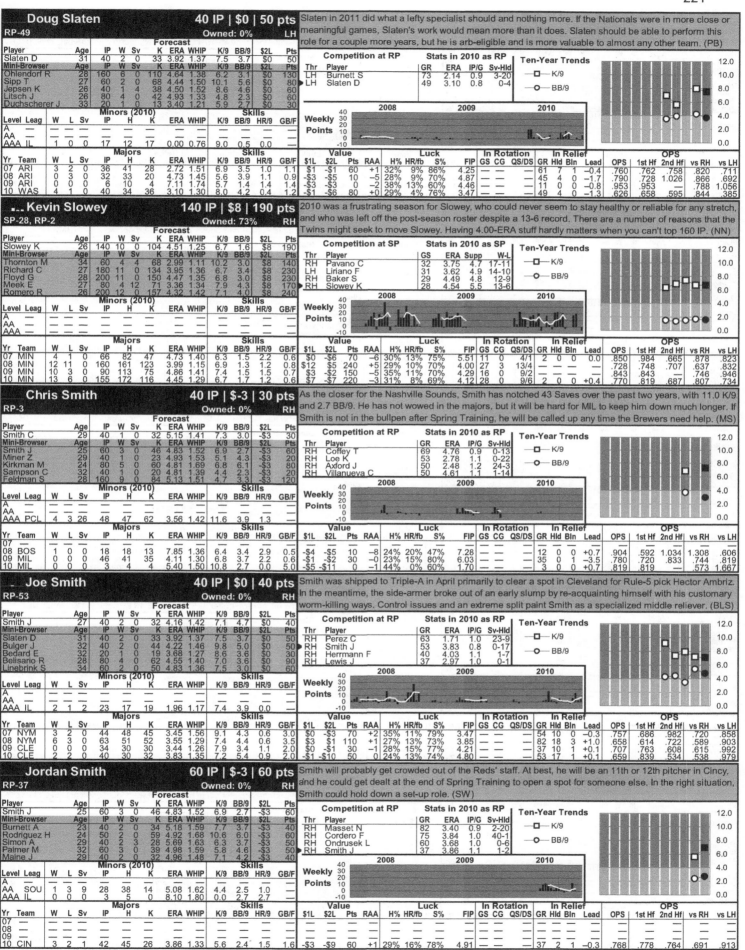

*For more stats, visit www.Rotolympus.com.*

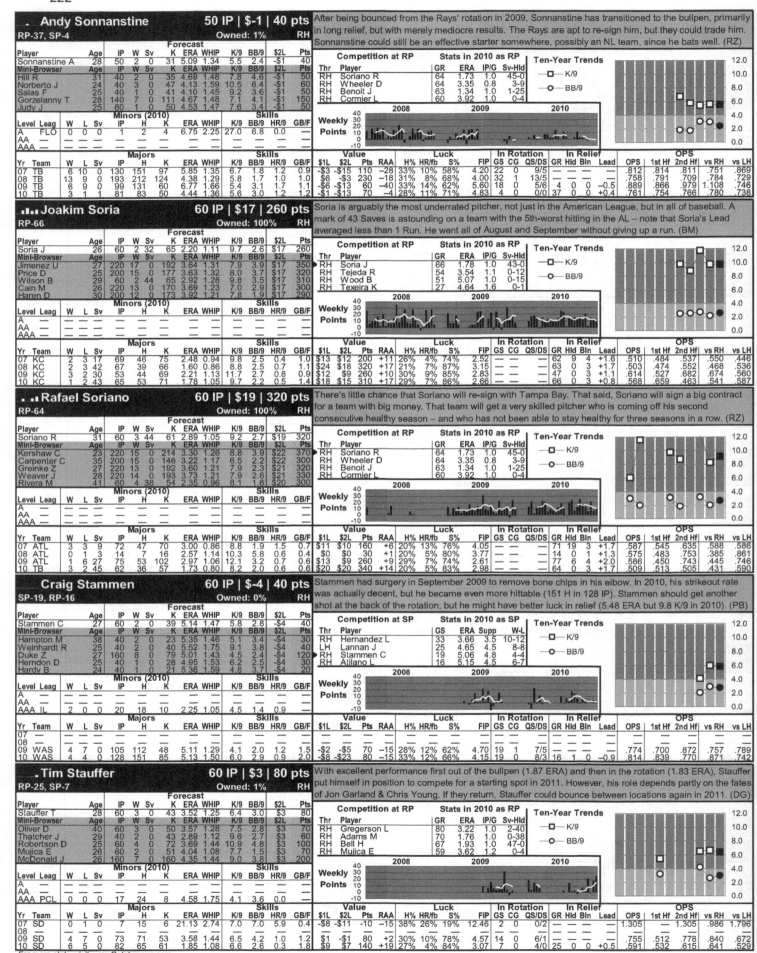

## Andy Sonnanstine — 50 IP | $-1 | 40 pts
RP-37, SP-4  Owned: 1%  RH

After being bounced from the Rays' rotation in 2009, Sonnanstine has transitioned to the bullpen, primarily in long relief, but with merely mediocre results. The Rays are apt to re-sign him, but they could trade him. Sonnanstine could still be an effective starter somewhere, possibly an NL team, since he bats well. (RZ)

### Forecast
| Player | Age | IP | W | Sv | K | ERA | WHIP | K/9 | BB/9 | $2L | Pts |
|---|---|---|---|---|---|---|---|---|---|---|---|
| Sonnanstine A | 28 | 50 | 2 | 0 | 31 | 5.09 | 1.34 | 5.5 | 2.4 | -$1 | 40 |
| Mini-Browser | Age | IP | W | Sv | K | ERA | WHIP | K/9 | BB/9 | $2L | Pts |
| Hill R | 31 | 40 | 2 | 0 | 35 | 4.69 | 1.48 | 7.8 | 4.6 | -$1 | 50 |
| Norberto J | 24 | 40 | 3 | 0 | 47 | 4.13 | 1.59 | 10.5 | 6.4 | -$1 | 60 |
| Salas F | 25 | 40 | 1 | 0 | 41 | 4.10 | 1.45 | 9.2 | 3.6 | -$1 | 50 |
| Gorzelanny T | 28 | 140 | 7 | 0 | 111 | 4.67 | 1.48 | 7.1 | 4.1 | -$1 | 150 |
| Judy J | 25 | 40 | 3 | 0 | 50 | 4.53 | 1.47 | 7.6 | 3.4 | -$1 | 50 |

### Minors (2010) / Skills
| Level | Leag | W | L | Sv | IP | H | K | ERA | WHIP | K/9 | BB/9 | HR/9 | GB/F |
|---|---|---|---|---|---|---|---|---|---|---|---|---|---|
| A | FLO | 0 | 0 | 0 | 1 | 2 | 4 | 6.75 | 2.25 | 27.0 | 6.8 | 0.0 | |
| AA | — | | | | | | | | | | | | |
| AAA | — | | | | | | | | | | | | |

### Majors / Skills / Value / Luck / In Rotation / In Relief / OPS
| Yr | Team | W | L | Sv | IP | H | K | ERA | WHIP | K/9 | BB/9 | HR/9 | GB/F | $1L | $2L | Pts | RAA | H% | HR/fb | S% | FIP | GS | CG | QS/DS | GR | Hld | Bln | Lead | OPS | 1st Hf | 2nd Hf | vs RH | vs LH |
|---|---|---|---|---|---|---|---|---|---|---|---|---|---|---|---|---|---|---|---|---|---|---|---|---|---|---|---|---|---|---|---|---|---|
| 07 | TB | 6 | 10 | 0 | 130 | 151 | 97 | 5.85 | 1.35 | 6.7 | 1.8 | 1.2 | 0.9 | -$3 | -$15 | 110 | -28 | 33% | 10% | 58% | 4.20 | 22 | 0 | 9/5 | — | — | — | — | .812 | .814 | .811 | .751 | .869 |
| 08 | TB | 13 | 9 | 0 | 193 | 212 | 124 | 4.38 | 1.29 | 5.8 | 1.7 | 1.0 | 1.0 | -$6 | -$33 | 230 | -18 | 31% | 8% | 68% | 4.00 | 32 | 1 | 13/5 | — | — | — | — | .758 | .791 | .709 | .784 | .729 |
| 09 | TB | 6 | 9 | 0 | 99 | 131 | 60 | 6.77 | 1.66 | 5.4 | 3.1 | 1.7 | 1.1 | -$6 | -$13 | 60 | -40 | 33% | 14% | 62% | 5.60 | 18 | 0 | 5/6 | 4 | 0 | 0 | -0.5 | .889 | .866 | .979 | 1.108 | .746 |
| 10 | TB | 3 | 1 | 1 | 81 | 83 | 50 | 4.44 | 1.36 | 5.6 | 3.0 | 1.2 | 1.2 | -$1 | -$13 | 70 | -4 | 28% | 11% | 71% | 4.83 | 4 | 0 | 0/0 | 37 | 0 | 0 | +0.4 | .761 | .754 | .766 | .780 | .738 |

### Competition at RP / Stats in 2010 as RP
| Thr | Player | GR | ERA | IP/G | Sv-Hld |
|---|---|---|---|---|---|
| RH | Soriano R | 64 | 1.73 | 1.0 | 45-0 |
| RH | Wheeler D | 64 | 3.35 | 0.8 | 3-9 |
| RH | Benoit J | 63 | 1.34 | 1.0 | 1-25 |
| RH | Cormier L | 60 | 3.92 | 1.0 | 0-4 |

## Joakim Soria — 60 IP | $17 | 260 pts
RP-66  Owned: 100%  RH

Soria is arguably the most underrated pitcher, not just in the American League, but in all of baseball. A mark of 43 Saves is astounding on a team with the 5th-worst hitting in the AL – note that Soria's Lead averaged less than 1 Run. He went all of August and September without giving up a run. (BM)

### Forecast
| Player | Age | IP | W | Sv | K | ERA | WHIP | K/9 | BB/9 | $2L | Pts |
|---|---|---|---|---|---|---|---|---|---|---|---|
| Soria J | 26 | 60 | 2 | 32 | 65 | 2.20 | 1.11 | 9.7 | 2.6 | $17 | 260 |
| Mini-Browser | Age | IP | W | Sv | K | ERA | WHIP | K/9 | BB/9 | $2L | Pts |
| Jimenez U | 27 | 220 | 17 | 0 | 192 | 3.64 | 1.31 | 7.9 | 3.9 | $17 | 350 |
| Price D | 25 | 200 | 15 | 0 | 177 | 3.63 | 1.32 | 8.0 | 3.7 | $17 | 320 |
| Wilson B | 29 | 60 | 2 | 44 | 65 | 2.92 | 1.28 | 9.8 | 3.5 | $17 | 310 |
| Cain M | 26 | 220 | 13 | 0 | 170 | 3.69 | 1.23 | 7.0 | 2.9 | $17 | 300 |
| Haren D | 30 | 200 | 12 | 0 | 173 | 3.92 | 1.21 | 7.8 | 1.9 | $17 | 290 |

### Minors (2010) / Skills
| Level | Leag | W | L | Sv | IP | H | K | ERA | WHIP | K/9 | BB/9 | HR/9 | GB/F |
|---|---|---|---|---|---|---|---|---|---|---|---|---|---|
| A | — | | | | | | | | | | | | |
| AA | — | | | | | | | | | | | | |
| AAA | — | | | | | | | | | | | | |

### Majors
| Yr | Team | W | L | Sv | IP | H | K | ERA | WHIP | K/9 | BB/9 | HR/9 | GB/F | $1L | $2L | Pts | RAA | H% | HR/fb | S% | FIP | GS | CG | QS/DS | GR | Hld | Bln | Lead | OPS | 1st Hf | 2nd Hf | vs RH | vs LH |
|---|---|---|---|---|---|---|---|---|---|---|---|---|---|---|---|---|---|---|---|---|---|---|---|---|---|---|---|---|---|---|---|---|---|
| 07 | KC | 2 | 3 | 17 | 69 | 46 | 75 | 2.48 | 0.94 | 9.8 | 2.5 | 0.4 | 1.0 | $13 | $12 | 200 | +11 | 26% | 4% | 74% | 2.52 | — | — | — | 62 | 9 | 4 | +1.6 | .510 | .484 | .537 | .550 | .446 |
| 08 | KC | 2 | 3 | 42 | 67 | 39 | 66 | 1.60 | 0.86 | 8.8 | 2.5 | 0.7 | 1.1 | $24 | $18 | 320 | +17 | 21% | 7% | 87% | 3.15 | — | — | — | 63 | 0 | 3 | +1.7 | .503 | .474 | .552 | .468 | .536 |
| 09 | KC | 3 | 2 | 30 | 53 | 44 | 69 | 2.21 | 1.13 | 11.7 | 2.7 | 0.8 | 0.9 | $12 | $9 | 260 | +10 | 30% | 9% | 85% | 2.83 | — | — | — | 47 | 0 | 3 | +1.1 | .614 | .527 | .682 | .674 | .560 |
| 10 | KC | 1 | 2 | 43 | 65 | 53 | 71 | 1.78 | 1.05 | 9.7 | 2.2 | 0.5 | 1.4 | $18 | $15 | 310 | +17 | 29% | 7% | 86% | 2.66 | — | — | — | 66 | 0 | 3 | +0.8 | .568 | .659 | .463 | .541 | .587 |

### Competition at RP / Stats in 2010 as RP
| Thr | Player | GR | ERA | IP/G | Sv-Hld |
|---|---|---|---|---|---|
| RH | Soria J | 66 | 1.78 | 1.0 | 43-0 |
| RH | Tejeda R | 54 | 3.54 | 1.1 | 0-12 |
| RH | Wood B | 51 | 5.07 | 1.0 | 0-15 |
| RH | Texeira K | 27 | 4.64 | 1.6 | 0-1 |

## Rafael Soriano — 60 IP | $19 | 320 pts
RP-64  Owned: 100%  RH

There's little chance that Soriano will re-sign with Tampa Bay. That said, Soriano will sign a big contract for a team with big money. That team will get a very skilled pitcher who is coming off his second consecutive healthy season – and who has not been able to stay healthy for three seasons in a row. (RZ)

### Forecast
| Player | Age | IP | W | Sv | K | ERA | WHIP | K/9 | BB/9 | $2L | Pts |
|---|---|---|---|---|---|---|---|---|---|---|---|
| Soriano R | 31 | 60 | 3 | 44 | 61 | 2.89 | 1.05 | 9.2 | 2.7 | $19 | 320 |
| Mini-Browser | Age | IP | W | Sv | K | ERA | WHIP | K/9 | BB/9 | $2L | Pts |
| Kershaw C | 23 | 220 | 15 | 0 | 214 | 3.30 | 1.26 | 8.8 | 3.9 | $22 | 370 |
| Carpenter C | 35 | 200 | 15 | 0 | 146 | 3.22 | 1.17 | 6.5 | 2.2 | $22 | 300 |
| Greinke Z | 27 | 220 | 13 | 0 | 192 | 3.60 | 1.21 | 7.9 | 2.3 | $21 | 320 |
| Weaver J | 28 | 220 | 14 | 0 | 193 | 3.73 | 1.21 | 7.9 | 2.6 | $21 | 330 |
| Rivera M | 41 | 60 | 4 | 38 | 54 | 2.35 | 0.96 | 8.1 | 1.6 | $20 | 300 |

### Minors (2010) / Skills
| Level | Leag | W | L | Sv | IP | H | K | ERA | WHIP | K/9 | BB/9 | HR/9 | GB/F |
|---|---|---|---|---|---|---|---|---|---|---|---|---|---|
| A | — | | | | | | | | | | | | |
| AA | — | | | | | | | | | | | | |
| AAA | — | | | | | | | | | | | | |

### Majors
| Yr | Team | W | L | Sv | IP | H | K | ERA | WHIP | K/9 | BB/9 | HR/9 | GB/F | $1L | $2L | Pts | RAA | H% | HR/fb | S% | FIP | GS | CG | QS/DS | GR | Hld | Bln | Lead | OPS | 1st Hf | 2nd Hf | vs RH | vs LH |
|---|---|---|---|---|---|---|---|---|---|---|---|---|---|---|---|---|---|---|---|---|---|---|---|---|---|---|---|---|---|---|---|---|---|
| 07 | ATL | 3 | 3 | 9 | 72 | 47 | 70 | 3.00 | 0.86 | 8.8 | 1.9 | 1.5 | 0.7 | $11 | $10 | 160 | +6 | 20% | 13% | 76% | 4.05 | — | — | — | 71 | 19 | 3 | +1.7 | .587 | .545 | .635 | .588 | .586 |
| 08 | ATL | 0 | 1 | 3 | 14 | 7 | 16 | 2.57 | 1.14 | 10.3 | 5.8 | 0.6 | 0.4 | $0 | $0 | 30 | +1 | 20% | 5% | 80% | 3.77 | — | — | — | 14 | 0 | 1 | +1.3 | .575 | .483 | .753 | .385 | .861 |
| 09 | ATL | 1 | 6 | 27 | 75 | 53 | 102 | 2.97 | 1.06 | 12.1 | 3.2 | 0.7 | 0.6 | $13 | $9 | 260 | +9 | 29% | 7% | 74% | 2.61 | — | — | — | 77 | 6 | 4 | +2.0 | .586 | .450 | .743 | .445 | .746 |
| 10 | TB | 3 | 2 | 45 | 62 | 36 | 57 | 1.73 | 0.80 | 8.2 | 2.0 | 0.6 | 0.6 | $20 | $20 | 340 | +14 | 29% | 7% | 84% | 2.98 | — | — | — | 64 | 0 | 3 | +1.7 | .509 | .513 | .505 | .431 | .590 |

### Competition at RP / Stats in 2010 as RP
| Thr | Player | GR | ERA | IP/G | Sv-Hld |
|---|---|---|---|---|---|
| RH | Soriano R | 64 | 1.73 | 1.0 | 45-0 |
| RH | Wheeler D | 64 | 3.35 | 0.8 | 3-9 |
| RH | Benoit J | 63 | 1.34 | 1.0 | 1-25 |
| RH | Cormier L | 60 | 3.92 | 1.0 | 0-4 |

## Craig Stammen — 60 IP | $-4 | 40 pts
SP-19, RP-16  Owned: 0%  RH

Stammen had surgery in September 2009 to remove bone chips in his elbow. In 2010, his strikeout rate was actually decent, but he became even more hittable (151 H in 128 IP). Stammen should get another shot at the back of the rotation, but he might have better luck in relief (5.48 ERA but 9.8 K/9 in 2010). (PB)

### Forecast
| Player | Age | IP | W | Sv | K | ERA | WHIP | K/9 | BB/9 | $2L | Pts |
|---|---|---|---|---|---|---|---|---|---|---|---|
| Stammen C | 27 | 60 | 2 | 0 | 39 | 5.14 | 1.47 | 5.8 | 2.8 | -$4 | 40 |
| Mini-Browser | Age | IP | W | Sv | K | ERA | WHIP | K/9 | BB/9 | $2L | Pts |
| Hampton M | 38 | 40 | 2 | 0 | 23 | 5.35 | 1.46 | 5.1 | 3.4 | -$4 | 30 |
| Weinhardt R | 25 | 40 | 2 | 0 | 40 | 5.52 | 1.75 | 9.1 | 4.9 | -$4 | 60 |
| Duke Z | 27 | 160 | 8 | 0 | 79 | 5.01 | 1.43 | 4.5 | 2.4 | -$4 | 120 |
| Herndon D | 25 | 40 | 1 | 0 | 28 | 4.95 | 1.53 | 6.2 | 2.5 | -$4 | 30 |
| Hardy B | 24 | 40 | 1 | 0 | 21 | 5.36 | 1.59 | 4.8 | 3.1 | -$4 | 20 |

### Minors (2010) / Skills
| Level | Leag | W | L | Sv | IP | H | K | ERA | WHIP | K/9 | BB/9 | HR/9 | GB/F |
|---|---|---|---|---|---|---|---|---|---|---|---|---|---|
| A | — | | | | | | | | | | | | |
| AA | — | | | | | | | | | | | | |
| AAA | IL | 2 | 0 | 0 | 20 | 18 | 10 | 2.25 | 1.05 | 4.5 | 1.4 | 0.9 | |

### Majors
| Yr | Team | W | L | Sv | IP | H | K | ERA | WHIP | K/9 | BB/9 | HR/9 | GB/F | $1L | $2L | Pts | RAA | H% | HR/fb | S% | FIP | GS | CG | QS/DS | GR | Hld | Bln | Lead | OPS | 1st Hf | 2nd Hf | vs RH | vs LH |
|---|---|---|---|---|---|---|---|---|---|---|---|---|---|---|---|---|---|---|---|---|---|---|---|---|---|---|---|---|---|---|---|---|---|
| 07 | — | | | | | | | | | | | | | | | | | | | | | | | | | | | | | | | | |
| 08 | — | | | | | | | | | | | | | | | | | | | | | | | | | | | | | | | | |
| 09 | WAS | 4 | 7 | 0 | 105 | 112 | 48 | 5.11 | 1.29 | 4.1 | 2.0 | 1.2 | 1.5 | -$2 | -$5 | 70 | -15 | 28% | 12% | 62% | 4.70 | 19 | 1 | 7/5 | — | — | — | — | .774 | .700 | .872 | .757 | .789 |
| 10 | WAS | 4 | 4 | 0 | 128 | 151 | 85 | 5.13 | 1.50 | 6.0 | 2.9 | 0.9 | 2.0 | -$8 | -$23 | 80 | -15 | 33% | 12% | 66% | 4.15 | 19 | 0 | 8/3 | 16 | 1 | 0 | -0.9 | .814 | .839 | .770 | .871 | .742 |

### Competition at SP / Stats in 2010 as SP
| Thr | Player | GS | ERA | Supp | W-L |
|---|---|---|---|---|---|
| RH | Hernandez L | 33 | 3.66 | 3.5 | 10-12 |
| LH | Lannan J | 25 | 4.65 | 4.5 | 8-8 |
| RH | Stammen C | 19 | 5.06 | 4.8 | 4-4 |
| RH | Atilano L | 16 | 5.15 | 4.5 | 6-7 |

## Tim Stauffer — 60 IP | $3 | 80 pts
RP-25, SP-7  Owned: 1%  RH

With excellent performance first out of the bullpen (1.87 ERA) and then in the rotation (1.83 ERA), Stauffer put himself in position to compete for a starting spot in 2011. However, his role depends partly on the fates of Jon Garland & Chris Young. If they return, Stauffer could bounce between locations again in 2011. (DG)

### Forecast
| Player | Age | IP | W | Sv | K | ERA | WHIP | K/9 | BB/9 | $2L | Pts |
|---|---|---|---|---|---|---|---|---|---|---|---|
| Stauffer T | 28 | 60 | 3 | 0 | 43 | 3.52 | 1.25 | 6.4 | 3.0 | $3 | 80 |
| Mini-Browser | Age | IP | W | Sv | K | ERA | WHIP | K/9 | BB/9 | $2L | Pts |
| Oliver D | 40 | 60 | 3 | 0 | 50 | 3.57 | 1.28 | 7.5 | 2.8 | $3 | 70 |
| Thatcher J | 29 | 40 | 2 | 0 | 43 | 2.89 | 1.12 | 9.6 | 2.7 | $3 | 60 |
| Robertson D | 25 | 60 | 4 | 0 | 72 | 3.69 | 1.44 | 10.9 | 4.5 | $3 | 100 |
| Mujica E | 26 | 60 | 2 | 0 | 51 | 4.04 | 1.08 | 7.7 | 1.5 | $3 | 70 |
| McDonald J | 26 | 160 | 7 | 0 | 160 | 4.35 | 1.44 | 9.0 | 3.5 | $3 | 200 |

### Minors (2010) / Skills
| Level | Leag | W | L | Sv | IP | H | K | ERA | WHIP | K/9 | BB/9 | HR/9 | GB/F |
|---|---|---|---|---|---|---|---|---|---|---|---|---|---|
| A | — | | | | | | | | | | | | |
| AA | — | | | | | | | | | | | | |
| AAA | PCL | 0 | 0 | 0 | 17 | 24 | 8 | 4.58 | 1.75 | 4.1 | 3.6 | 0.0 | |

### Majors
| Yr | Team | W | L | Sv | IP | H | K | ERA | WHIP | K/9 | BB/9 | HR/9 | GB/F | $1L | $2L | Pts | RAA | H% | HR/fb | S% | FIP | GS | CG | QS/DS | GR | Hld | Bln | Lead | OPS | 1st Hf | 2nd Hf | vs RH | vs LH |
|---|---|---|---|---|---|---|---|---|---|---|---|---|---|---|---|---|---|---|---|---|---|---|---|---|---|---|---|---|---|---|---|---|---|
| 07 | SD | 0 | 1 | 0 | 7 | 15 | 6 | 21.13 | 2.74 | 7.0 | 7.0 | 5.9 | 0.4 | -$8 | -$11 | -10 | -15 | 38% | 26% | 19% | 12.46 | 2 | 0 | 0/2 | — | — | — | — | 1.305 | — | 1.305 | .986 | 1.796 |
| 08 | — | | | | | | | | | | | | | | | | | | | | | | | | | | | | | | | | |
| 09 | SD | 0 | 0 | 0 | 73 | 71 | 53 | 3.58 | 1.44 | 6.5 | 4.2 | 1.0 | 1.2 | $1 | -$1 | 80 | +2 | 30% | 10% | 78% | 4.57 | 14 | 0 | 6/1 | — | — | — | — | .755 | .512 | .778 | .840 | .672 |
| 10 | SD | 6 | 5 | 0 | 82 | 65 | 61 | 1.85 | 1.08 | 6.7 | 2.6 | 0.3 | 1.8 | $9 | $7 | 140 | +19 | 27% | 9% | 84% | 3.07 | 7 | 0 | 4/0 | 25 | 0 | 0 | +0.5 | .591 | .532 | .615 | .641 | .590 |

### Competition at RP / Stats in 2010 as RP
| Thr | Player | GR | ERA | IP/G | Sv-Hld |
|---|---|---|---|---|---|
| RH | Gregerson L | 80 | 3.22 | 1.0 | 2-40 |
| RH | Adams M | 70 | 1.76 | 1.0 | 0-38 |
| RH | Bell H | 67 | 1.93 | 1.0 | 47-0 |
| RH | Mujica E | 59 | 3.62 | 1.2 | 0-4 |

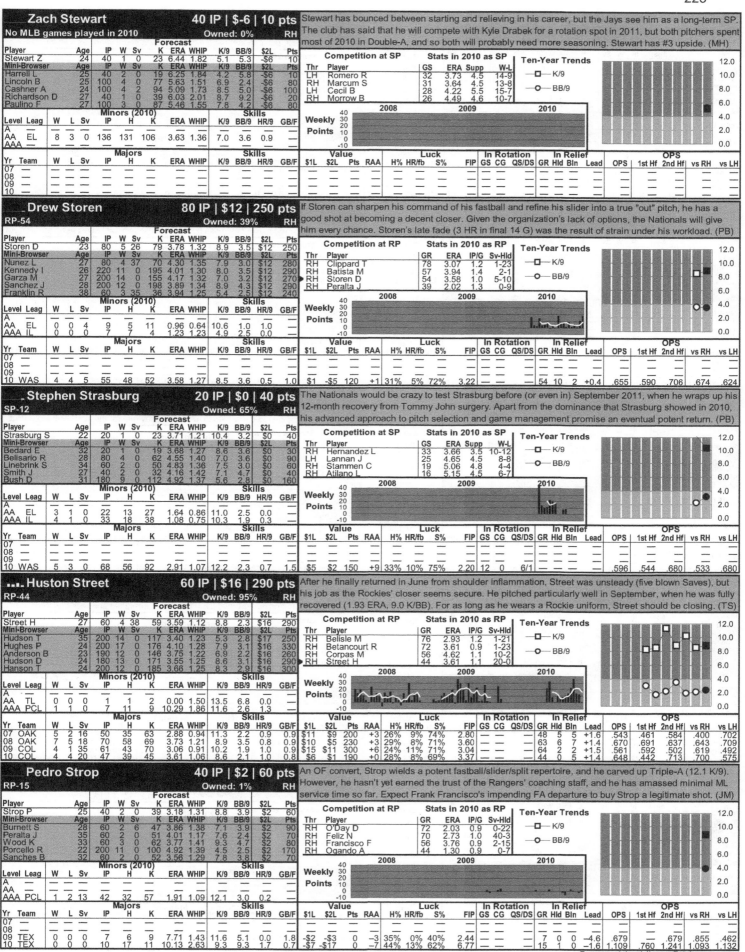

## Zach Stewart — 40 IP | $-6 | 10 pts

No MLB games played in 2010    Owned: 0%    RH

Stewart has bounced between starting and relieving in his career, but the Jays see him as a long-term SP. The club has said that he will compete with Kyle Drabek for a rotation spot in 2011, but both pitchers spent most of 2010 in Double-A, and so both will probably need more seasoning. Stewart has #3 upside. (MH)

**Forecast**

| Player | Age | IP | W | Sv | K | ERA | WHIP | K/9 | BB/9 | $2L | Pts |
|---|---|---|---|---|---|---|---|---|---|---|---|
| Stewart Z | 24 | 40 | 1 | 0 | 23 | 6.44 | 1.82 | 5.1 | 5.3 | -$6 | 10 |

| Mini-Browser | Age | IP | W | Sv | K | ERA | WHIP | K/9 | BB/9 | $2L | Pts |
|---|---|---|---|---|---|---|---|---|---|---|---|
| Harrell L | 25 | 40 | 2 | 0 | 19 | 6.25 | 1.84 | 4.2 | 5.8 | -$6 | 10 |
| Lincoln B | 25 | 100 | 4 | 0 | 77 | 5.63 | 1.51 | 6.9 | 2.4 | -$6 | 40 |
| Cashner A | 24 | 100 | 4 | 2 | 94 | 5.09 | 1.73 | 8.5 | 5.0 | -$6 | 100 |
| Richardson D | 27 | 40 | 1 | 0 | 39 | 6.03 | 2.01 | 8.7 | 9.2 | -$6 | 20 |
| Paulino F | 27 | 100 | 3 | 0 | 87 | 5.46 | 1.55 | 7.8 | 4.2 | -$6 | 80 |

**Minors (2010)** / **Skills**

| Level | Leag | W | L | Sv | IP | H | K | ERA | WHIP | K/9 | BB/9 | HR/9 | GB/F |
|---|---|---|---|---|---|---|---|---|---|---|---|---|---|
| A | — | — | — | — | — | — | — | — | — | — | — | — | — |
| AA | EL | 8 | 3 | 0 | 136 | 131 | 106 | 3.63 | 1.36 | 7.0 | 3.6 | 0.9 | — |
| AAA | — | — | — | — | — | — | — | — | — | — | — | — | — |

**Majors** / **Skills**

| Yr | Team | W | L | Sv | IP | H | K | ERA | WHIP | K/9 | BB/9 | HR/9 | GB/F |
|---|---|---|---|---|---|---|---|---|---|---|---|---|---|
| 07 | — | — | — | — | — | — | — | — | — | — | — | — | — |
| 08 | — | — | — | — | — | — | — | — | — | — | — | — | — |
| 09 | — | — | — | — | — | — | — | — | — | — | — | — | — |
| 10 | — | — | — | — | — | — | — | — | — | — | — | — | — |

**Competition at SP — Stats in 2010 as SP**

| Thr | Player | GS | ERA | Supp | W-L |
|---|---|---|---|---|---|
| LH | Romero R | 32 | 3.73 | 4.5 | 14-9 |
| RH | Marcum S | 31 | 3.64 | 4.5 | 13-8 |
| LH | Cecil B | 28 | 4.22 | 5.5 | 15-7 |
| RH | Morrow B | 26 | 4.49 | 4.6 | 10-7 |

**Value / Luck / In Rotation / In Relief / OPS**

| $1L | $2L | Pts | RAA | H% | HR/fb | S% | FIP | GS | CG | QS/DS | GR | Hld | Bln | Lead | OPS | 1st Hf | 2nd Hf | vs RH | vs LH |
|---|---|---|---|---|---|---|---|---|---|---|---|---|---|---|---|---|---|---|---|
| — | — | — | — | — | — | — | — | — | — | — | — | — | — | — | — | — | — | — | — |

---

## Drew Storen — 80 IP | $12 | 250 pts

RP-54    Owned: 39%    RH

If Storen can sharpen his command of his fastball and refine his slider into a true "out" pitch, he has a good shot at becoming a decent closer. Given the organization's lack of options, the Nationals will give him every chance. Storen's late fade (3 HR in final 14 G) was the result of strain under his workload. (PB)

**Forecast**

| Player | Age | IP | W | Sv | K | ERA | WHIP | K/9 | BB/9 | $2L | Pts |
|---|---|---|---|---|---|---|---|---|---|---|---|
| Storen D | 23 | 80 | 5 | 26 | 79 | 3.78 | 1.32 | 8.9 | 3.5 | $12 | 250 |

| Mini-Browser | Age | IP | W | Sv | K | ERA | WHIP | K/9 | BB/9 | $2L | Pts |
|---|---|---|---|---|---|---|---|---|---|---|---|
| Nunez L | 27 | 80 | 4 | 37 | 70 | 4.30 | 1.35 | 7.9 | 3.0 | $12 | 280 |
| Kennedy I | 26 | 220 | 11 | 0 | 195 | 4.01 | 1.30 | 8.0 | 3.5 | $12 | 290 |
| Garza M | 27 | 200 | 14 | 0 | 155 | 4.17 | 1.32 | 7.0 | 3.2 | $12 | 270 |
| Sanchez J | 28 | 200 | 12 | 0 | 198 | 3.89 | 1.34 | 8.9 | 4.3 | $12 | 290 |
| Franklin R | 38 | 60 | 3 | 35 | 36 | 3.94 | 1.25 | 5.4 | 2.5 | $12 | 240 |

**Minors (2010)** / **Skills**

| Level | Leag | W | L | Sv | IP | H | K | ERA | WHIP | K/9 | BB/9 | HR/9 | GB/F |
|---|---|---|---|---|---|---|---|---|---|---|---|---|---|
| A | — | — | — | — | — | — | — | — | — | — | — | — | — |
| AA | EL | 0 | 0 | 4 | 9 | 5 | 11 | 0.96 | 0.64 | 10.6 | 1.0 | 1.0 | — |
| AAA | IL | 0 | 0 | 0 | 7 | 7 | 4 | 1.23 | 1.23 | 4.9 | 2.5 | 0.0 | — |

**Majors** / **Skills**

| Yr | Team | W | L | Sv | IP | H | K | ERA | WHIP | K/9 | BB/9 | HR/9 | GB/F |
|---|---|---|---|---|---|---|---|---|---|---|---|---|---|
| 07 | — | — | — | — | — | — | — | — | — | — | — | — | — |
| 08 | — | — | — | — | — | — | — | — | — | — | — | — | — |
| 09 | — | — | — | — | — | — | — | — | — | — | — | — | — |
| 10 | WAS | 4 | 4 | 5 | 55 | 48 | 52 | 3.58 | 1.27 | 8.5 | 3.6 | 0.5 | 1.0 |

**Competition at RP — Stats in 2010 as RP**

| Thr | Player | GR | ERA | IP/G | Sv-Hld |
|---|---|---|---|---|---|
| RH | Clippard T | 78 | 3.07 | 1.2 | 1-23 |
| RH | Batista M | 57 | 3.94 | 1.4 | 2-1 |
| RH | Storen D | 54 | 3.58 | 1.0 | 5-10 |
| RH | Peralta J | 39 | 2.02 | 1.3 | 0-9 |

**Value / Luck / In Rotation / In Relief / OPS**

| $1L | $2L | Pts | RAA | H% | HR/fb | S% | FIP | GS | CG | QS/DS | GR | Hld | Bln | Lead | OPS | 1st Hf | 2nd Hf | vs RH | vs LH |
|---|---|---|---|---|---|---|---|---|---|---|---|---|---|---|---|---|---|---|---|
| $1 | -$5 | 120 | +1 | 31% | 5% | 72% | 3.22 | — | — | — | 54 | 10 | 2 | +0.4 | .655 | .590 | .706 | .674 | .624 |

---

## Stephen Strasburg — 20 IP | $0 | 40 pts

SP-12    Owned: 65%    RH

The Nationals would be crazy to test Strasburg before (or even in) September 2011, when he wraps up his 12-month recovery from Tommy John surgery. Apart from the dominance that Strasburg showed in 2010, his advanced approach to pitch selection and game management promise an eventual potent return. (PB)

**Forecast**

| Player | Age | IP | W | Sv | K | ERA | WHIP | K/9 | BB/9 | $2L | Pts |
|---|---|---|---|---|---|---|---|---|---|---|---|
| Strasburg S | 22 | 20 | 1 | 0 | 23 | 3.71 | 1.21 | 10.4 | 3.2 | $0 | 40 |

| Mini-Browser | Age | IP | W | Sv | K | ERA | WHIP | K/9 | BB/9 | $2L | Pts |
|---|---|---|---|---|---|---|---|---|---|---|---|
| Bedard E | 32 | 20 | 1 | 0 | 19 | 3.68 | 1.27 | 8.6 | 3.6 | $0 | 30 |
| Belisario R | 28 | 80 | 4 | 0 | 62 | 4.55 | 1.40 | 7.0 | 3.6 | $0 | 90 |
| Linebrink S | 34 | 60 | 2 | 0 | 50 | 4.83 | 1.36 | 7.5 | 3.0 | $0 | 60 |
| Smith J | 27 | 40 | 2 | 0 | 32 | 4.16 | 1.42 | 7.1 | 4.7 | $0 | 40 |
| Bush D | 31 | 180 | 9 | 0 | 112 | 4.92 | 1.37 | 5.6 | 2.8 | $0 | 160 |

**Minors (2010)** / **Skills**

| Level | Leag | W | L | Sv | IP | H | K | ERA | WHIP | K/9 | BB/9 | HR/9 | GB/F |
|---|---|---|---|---|---|---|---|---|---|---|---|---|---|
| A | — | — | — | — | — | — | — | — | — | — | — | — | — |
| AA | EL | 3 | 1 | 0 | 22 | 13 | 27 | 1.64 | 0.86 | 11.0 | 2.5 | 0.0 | — |
| AAA | IL | 4 | 1 | 0 | 33 | 18 | 38 | 1.08 | 0.75 | 10.3 | 1.9 | 0.3 | — |

**Majors** / **Skills**

| Yr | Team | W | L | Sv | IP | H | K | ERA | WHIP | K/9 | BB/9 | HR/9 | GB/F |
|---|---|---|---|---|---|---|---|---|---|---|---|---|---|
| 07 | — | — | — | — | — | — | — | — | — | — | — | — | — |
| 08 | — | — | — | — | — | — | — | — | — | — | — | — | — |
| 09 | — | — | — | — | — | — | — | — | — | — | — | — | — |
| 10 | WAS | 5 | 3 | 0 | 68 | 56 | 92 | 2.91 | 1.07 | 12.2 | 2.3 | 0.7 | 1.5 |

**Competition at SP — Stats in 2010 as SP**

| Thr | Player | GS | ERA | Supp | W-L |
|---|---|---|---|---|---|
| RH | Hernandez L | 33 | 3.66 | 3.5 | 10-12 |
| LH | Lannan J | 25 | 4.65 | 4.5 | 8-8 |
| RH | Stammen C | 19 | 5.06 | 4.8 | 4-4 |
| RH | Atilano L | 16 | 5.15 | 4.5 | 6-7 |

**Value / Luck / In Rotation / In Relief / OPS**

| $1L | $2L | Pts | RAA | H% | HR/fb | S% | FIP | GS | CG | QS/DS | GR | Hld | Bln | Lead | OPS | 1st Hf | 2nd Hf | vs RH | vs LH |
|---|---|---|---|---|---|---|---|---|---|---|---|---|---|---|---|---|---|---|---|
| $5 | $2 | 150 | +9 | 33% | 10% | 75% | 2.20 | 12 | 0 | 6/1 | — | — | — | — | .596 | .544 | .680 | .533 | .680 |

---

## Huston Street — 60 IP | $16 | 290 pts

RP-44    Owned: 95%    RH

After he finally returned in June from shoulder inflammation, Street was unsteady (five blown Saves), but his job as the Rockies' closer seems secure. He pitched particularly well in September, when he was fully recovered (1.93 ERA, 9.0 K/BB). For as long as he wears a Rockie uniform, Street should be closing. (TS)

**Forecast**

| Player | Age | IP | W | Sv | K | ERA | WHIP | K/9 | BB/9 | $2L | Pts |
|---|---|---|---|---|---|---|---|---|---|---|---|
| Street H | 27 | 60 | 4 | 38 | 59 | 3.59 | 1.12 | 8.8 | 2.3 | $16 | 290 |

| Mini-Browser | Age | IP | W | Sv | K | ERA | WHIP | K/9 | BB/9 | $2L | Pts |
|---|---|---|---|---|---|---|---|---|---|---|---|
| Hudson T | 35 | 200 | 14 | 0 | 117 | 3.40 | 1.23 | 5.3 | 2.8 | $17 | 250 |
| Hughes P | 24 | 200 | 17 | 0 | 176 | 4.10 | 1.28 | 7.9 | 3.1 | $16 | 330 |
| Anderson B | 23 | 190 | 12 | 0 | 146 | 3.75 | 1.22 | 6.9 | 2.2 | $16 | 260 |
| Hudson D | 24 | 180 | 13 | 0 | 171 | 3.55 | 1.25 | 8.6 | 3.1 | $16 | 290 |
| Hanson T | 24 | 200 | 12 | 0 | 185 | 3.66 | 1.25 | 8.3 | 2.9 | $16 | 300 |

**Minors (2010)** / **Skills**

| Level | Leag | W | L | Sv | IP | H | K | ERA | WHIP | K/9 | BB/9 | HR/9 | GB/F |
|---|---|---|---|---|---|---|---|---|---|---|---|---|---|
| A | — | — | — | — | — | — | — | — | — | — | — | — | — |
| AA | TL | 0 | 0 | 0 | 1 | 1 | 2 | 0.00 | 1.50 | 13.5 | 6.8 | 0.0 | — |
| AAA | PCL | 1 | 1 | 0 | 7 | 11 | 9 | 10.29 | 1.86 | 11.6 | 2.6 | 1.3 | — |

**Majors** / **Skills**

| Yr | Team | W | L | Sv | IP | H | K | ERA | WHIP | K/9 | BB/9 | HR/9 | GB/F |
|---|---|---|---|---|---|---|---|---|---|---|---|---|---|
| 07 | OAK | 5 | 2 | 16 | 50 | 35 | 63 | 2.88 | 0.94 | 11.3 | 2.2 | 0.9 | 0.9 |
| 08 | OAK | 7 | 5 | 18 | 70 | 58 | 69 | 3.73 | 1.21 | 8.9 | 3.5 | 0.8 | 0.9 |
| 09 | COL | 4 | 1 | 35 | 61 | 43 | 70 | 3.06 | 0.91 | 10.2 | 1.9 | 1.0 | 0.9 |
| 10 | COL | 4 | 4 | 20 | 47 | 39 | 45 | 3.61 | 1.06 | 8.6 | 2.1 | 1.0 | 0.8 |

**Competition at RP — Stats in 2010 as RP**

| Thr | Player | GR | ERA | IP/G | Sv-Hld |
|---|---|---|---|---|---|
| RH | Belisle M | 76 | 2.93 | 1.2 | 1-21 |
| RH | Betancourt R | 72 | 3.61 | 0.9 | 1-23 |
| RH | Corpas M | 56 | 4.62 | 1.1 | 10-2 |
| RH | Street H | 44 | 3.61 | 1.1 | 20-0 |

**Value / Luck / In Rotation / In Relief / OPS**

| $1L | $2L | Pts | RAA | H% | HR/fb | S% | FIP | GS | CG | QS/DS | GR | Hld | Bln | Lead | OPS | 1st Hf | 2nd Hf | vs RH | vs LH |
|---|---|---|---|---|---|---|---|---|---|---|---|---|---|---|---|---|---|---|---|
| $11 | $9 | 200 | +3 | 26% | 9% | 74% | 2.80 | — | — | — | 48 | 5 | 5 | +1.6 | .543 | .461 | .584 | .400 | .702 |
| $10 | $5 | 230 | +3 | 29% | 8% | 71% | 3.60 | — | — | — | 63 | 6 | 7 | +1.4 | .670 | .691 | .637 | .643 | .709 |
| $15 | $7 | 300 | +6 | 24% | 11% | 71% | 3.04 | — | — | — | 64 | 2 | 2 | +1.5 | .561 | .592 | .502 | .619 | .492 |
| $6 | $0 | 190 | +2 | 28% | 8% | 69% | 3.72 | — | — | — | 40 | 4 | 4 | +1.4 | .548 | .442 | .710 | .700 | .575 |

---

## Pedro Strop — 40 IP | $2 | 60 pts

RP-15    Owned: 1%    RH

An OF convert, Strop wields a potent fastball/slider/split repertoire, and he carved up Triple-A (12.1 K/9). However, he hasn't yet earned the trust of the Rangers' coaching staff, and he has amassed minimal ML service time so far. Expect Frank Francisco's impending FA departure to buy Strop a legitimate shot. (JM)

**Forecast**

| Player | Age | IP | W | Sv | K | ERA | WHIP | K/9 | BB/9 | $2L | Pts |
|---|---|---|---|---|---|---|---|---|---|---|---|
| Strop P | 25 | 40 | 2 | 0 | 39 | 3.18 | 1.31 | 8.8 | 3.9 | $2 | 60 |

| Mini-Browser | Age | IP | W | Sv | K | ERA | WHIP | K/9 | BB/9 | $2L | Pts |
|---|---|---|---|---|---|---|---|---|---|---|---|
| Burnett S | 28 | 60 | 2 | 6 | 47 | 3.86 | 1.38 | 7.1 | 3.9 | $2 | 90 |
| Peralta J | 35 | 60 | 2 | 0 | 51 | 4.01 | 1.17 | 7.6 | 2.4 | $2 | 80 |
| Wood K | 33 | 60 | 3 | 0 | 62 | 3.77 | 1.43 | 9.3 | 4.7 | $2 | 80 |
| Porcello R | 22 | 200 | 11 | 0 | 100 | 4.92 | 1.39 | 4.5 | 2.5 | $2 | 170 |
| Sanches B | 32 | 60 | 2 | 0 | 52 | 3.56 | 1.29 | 7.8 | 3.8 | $2 | 70 |

**Minors (2010)** / **Skills**

| Level | Leag | W | L | Sv | IP | H | K | ERA | WHIP | K/9 | BB/9 | HR/9 | GB/F |
|---|---|---|---|---|---|---|---|---|---|---|---|---|---|
| A | — | — | — | — | — | — | — | — | — | — | — | — | — |
| AA | — | — | — | — | — | — | — | — | — | — | — | — | — |
| AAA | PCL | 1 | 2 | 13 | 42 | 32 | 57 | 1.91 | 1.09 | 12.1 | 3.0 | 0.2 | — |

**Majors** / **Skills**

| Yr | Team | W | L | Sv | IP | H | K | ERA | WHIP | K/9 | BB/9 | HR/9 | GB/F |
|---|---|---|---|---|---|---|---|---|---|---|---|---|---|
| 07 | — | — | — | — | — | — | — | — | — | — | — | — | — |
| 08 | — | — | — | — | — | — | — | — | — | — | — | — | — |
| 09 | TEX | 0 | 0 | 0 | 7 | 6 | 9 | 7.71 | 1.43 | 11.6 | 5.1 | 0.0 | 1.8 |
| 10 | TEX | 0 | 0 | 0 | 10 | 17 | 11 | 10.13 | 2.63 | 9.3 | 9.3 | 1.7 | 0.7 |

**Competition at RP — Stats in 2010 as RP**

| Thr | Player | GR | ERA | IP/G | Sv-Hld |
|---|---|---|---|---|---|
| RH | O'Day D | 72 | 2.03 | 0.9 | 0-22 |
| RH | Feliz N | 70 | 2.73 | 1.0 | 40-3 |
| RH | Francisco F | 56 | 3.76 | 0.9 | 2-15 |
| RH | Ogando A | 44 | 1.30 | 0.9 | 0-7 |

**Value / Luck / In Rotation / In Relief / OPS**

| $1L | $2L | Pts | RAA | H% | HR/fb | S% | FIP | GS | CG | QS/DS | GR | Hld | Bln | Lead | OPS | 1st Hf | 2nd Hf | vs RH | vs LH |
|---|---|---|---|---|---|---|---|---|---|---|---|---|---|---|---|---|---|---|---|
| -$2 | -$3 | 0 | -3 | 35% | 0% | 40% | 2.44 | — | — | — | 7 | 0 | 0 | -4.6 | .679 | — | .679 | .855 | .462 |
| -$7 | -$17 | 0 | -7 | 44% | 13% | 62% | 6.77 | — | — | — | 15 | 1 | 0 | -1.6 | 1.109 | .760 | 1.241 | 1.093 | 1.132 |

## Jeff Suppan — 60 IP | $-6 | 30 pts
RP-15, SP-15 — Owned: 0% — RH

There is a popular perception that Suppan "held his own" in 2010 after being acquired by the Cards. The truth is that his 7.84 ERA in Milwaukee was unfairly high, but his 3.84 ERA in St. Louis was unfairly low. He barely averaged 5 IP per start. Still, don't be surprised if he latches on somewhere as a #5 SP. (AB)

### Forecast
| Player | Age | IP | W | Sv | K | ERA | WHIP | K/9 | BB/9 | $2L | Pts |
|---|---|---|---|---|---|---|---|---|---|---|---|
| Suppan J | 36 | 60 | 3 | 0 | 28 | 5.58 | 1.55 | 4.1 | 3.5 | -$6 | 30 |

### Mini-Browser
| Player | Age | IP | W | Sv | K | ERA | WHIP | K/9 | BB/9 | $2L | Pts |
|---|---|---|---|---|---|---|---|---|---|---|---|
| Wellemeyer T | 32 | 60 | 3 | 0 | 37 | 5.70 | 1.52 | 5.5 | 4.1 | -$5 | 40 |
| Morton C | 27 | 100 | 5 | 0 | 72 | 5.35 | 1.53 | 6.5 | 3.4 | -$5 | 80 |
| Davies K | 27 | 140 | 6 | 0 | 95 | 5.36 | 1.59 | 6.1 | 4.3 | -$5 | 100 |
| Wood B | 25 | 60 | 2 | 0 | 50 | 5.71 | 1.73 | 7.5 | 4.1 | -$6 | 40 |
| Lopez R | 35 | 180 | 7 | 0 | 104 | 5.25 | 1.43 | 5.2 | 3.2 | -$6 | 120 |

### Minors (2010)
| Level | Leag | W | L | Sv | IP | H | K | ERA | WHIP | K/9 | BB/9 | HR/9 | GB/F |
|---|---|---|---|---|---|---|---|---|---|---|---|---|---|
| A | MID | 0 | 0 | 0 | 4 | 7 | 4 | 2.08 | 2.31 | 8.3 | 6.2 | 0.0 | — |
| AA | — | | | | — | — | — | — | — | — | — | — | — |
| AAA | — | | | | — | — | — | — | — | — | — | — | — |

### Majors
| Yr | Team | W | L | Sv | IP | H | K | ERA | WHIP | K/9 | BB/9 | HR/9 | GB/F |
|---|---|---|---|---|---|---|---|---|---|---|---|---|---|
| 07 | MIL | 12 | 12 | 0 | 206 | 243 | 114 | 4.62 | 1.50 | 5.0 | 3.0 | 0.8 | 1.3 |
| 08 | MIL | 10 | 10 | 0 | 177 | 207 | 90 | 4.96 | 1.54 | 4.6 | 3.4 | 1.5 | 1.4 |
| 09 | MIL | 7 | 12 | 0 | 161 | 200 | 80 | 5.29 | 1.69 | 4.5 | 4.1 | 1.4 | 1.5 |
| 10 | 2TM | 3 | 8 | 0 | 101 | 130 | 51 | 5.06 | 1.65 | 4.5 | 3.3 | 1.2 | 1.0 |

**Competition at SP — Stats in 2010 as SP**
| Thr | Player | GS | ERA | Supp | W-L |
|---|---|---|---|---|---|
| RH | Carpenter C | 35 | 3.22 | 4.7 | 16-9 |
| RH | Wainwright A | 33 | 2.42 | 4.8 | 20-11 |
| RH | Westbrook J | 33 | 4.22 | 4.0 | 10-11 |
| LH | Garcia J | 28 | 2.70 | 4.5 | 13-8 |

**Value / Luck / In Rotation / In Relief / OPS**
| $1L | $2L | Pts | RAA | H% | HR/fb | S% | FIP | GS | CG | QS/DS | GR | Hld | Bln | Lead | OPS | 1st Hf | 2nd Hf | vs RH | vs LH |
|---|---|---|---|---|---|---|---|---|---|---|---|---|---|---|---|---|---|---|---|
| -$1 | -$17 | 180 | -11 | 33% | 7% | 70% | 4.22 | 34 | 1 | 15/1 | — | — | — | | .801 | .810 | .790 | .736 | .890 |
| -$1 | -$17 | 130 | -22 | 31% | 16% | 72% | 5.51 | 31 | 0 | 14/7 | — | — | — | | .844 | .817 | .881 | .877 | .814 |
| -$10 | -$14 | 80 | -26 | 32% | 13% | 72% | 5.59 | 30 | 0 | 12/8 | — | — | — | | .899 | .860 | .958 | .896 | .902 |
| -$10 | -$25 | 40 | -11 | 35% | 10% | 71% | 5.01 | 15 | 0 | 2/1 | 15 | 0 | 0 | -0.8 | .878 | .847 | .731 | .906 | .836 |

---

## .Hisanori Takahashi — 60 IP | $4 | 150 pts
RP-41, SP-12 — Owned: 27% — LH

When Francisco Rodriguez got hurt, Takahashi became the Mets' closer, and he converted all eight Save chances. The Japanese export had a 2.04 ERA and 9.4 K/9 in relief, vs. 5.01 ERA and 7.5 K/9 as a starter. If NY can deal Rodriguez, Takahashi will close, otherwise he'll set-up — unless he leaves to be an SP. (JL)

### Forecast
| Player | Age | IP | W | Sv | K | ERA | WHIP | K/9 | BB/9 | $2L | Pts |
|---|---|---|---|---|---|---|---|---|---|---|---|
| Takahashi H | 35 | 60 | 4 | 15 | 46 | 4.43 | 1.38 | 7.0 | 3.5 | $4 | 150 |

### Mini-Browser
| Player | Age | IP | W | Sv | K | ERA | WHIP | K/9 | BB/9 | $2L | Pts |
|---|---|---|---|---|---|---|---|---|---|---|---|
| Zimmermann J | 24 | 160 | 8 | 0 | 156 | 4.45 | 1.35 | 8.8 | 3.0 | -$5 | 210 |
| Niese J | 24 | 180 | 10 | 0 | 159 | 4.24 | 1.42 | 7.9 | 3.1 | -$5 | 230 |
| Germano J | 28 | 40 | 0 | 0 | 32 | 2.16 | 0.84 | 7.3 | 2.2 | -$5 | 50 |
| Figueroa N | 36 | 100 | 7 | 0 | 79 | 3.86 | 1.32 | 7.1 | 3.0 | -$5 | 140 |
| Matusz B | 24 | 180 | 10 | 0 | 156 | 4.54 | 1.44 | 7.8 | 3.5 | -$5 | 210 |

### Minors (2010)
| Level | Leag | W | L | Sv | IP | H | K | ERA | WHIP | K/9 | BB/9 | HR/9 | GB/F |
|---|---|---|---|---|---|---|---|---|---|---|---|---|---|
| A | — | | | | — | — | — | — | — | — | — | — | — |
| AA | — | | | | — | — | — | — | — | — | — | — | — |
| AAA | — | | | | — | — | — | — | — | — | — | — | — |

### Majors
| Yr | Team | W | L | Sv | IP | H | K | ERA | WHIP | K/9 | BB/9 | HR/9 | GB/F |
|---|---|---|---|---|---|---|---|---|---|---|---|---|---|
| 07 | — | | | | — | — | — | — | — | — | — | — | — |
| 08 | — | | | | — | — | — | — | — | — | — | — | — |
| 09 | — | | | | — | — | — | — | — | — | — | — | — |
| 10 | NYM | 10 | 6 | 8 | 122 | 116 | 114 | 3.61 | 1.30 | 8.4 | 3.2 | 1.0 | 0.9 |

**Competition at RP — Stats in 2010 as RP**
| Thr | Player | GR | ERA | IP/G | Sv-Hld |
|---|---|---|---|---|---|
| LH | Feliciano P | 92 | 3.30 | 0.7 | 0-23 |
| LH | Takahashi H | 41 | 2.04 | 1.4 | 8-3 |
| LH | Valdes R | 37 | 5.23 | 1.4 | 1-1 |
| LH | Perez O | 10 | 9.00 | 1.3 | 0-0 |

**Value / Luck / In Rotation / In Relief / OPS**
| $1L | $2L | Pts | RAA | H% | HR/fb | S% | FIP | GS | CG | QS/DS | GR | Hld | Bln | Lead | OPS | 1st Hf | 2nd Hf | vs RH | vs LH |
|---|---|---|---|---|---|---|---|---|---|---|---|---|---|---|---|---|---|---|---|
| $8 | $0 | 250 | +4 | 31% | 8% | 75% | 3.77 | 12 | 0 | 6/4 | 41 | 3 | 0 | -0.4 | .712 | .757 | .630 | .768 | .544 |

---

## Mitch Talbot — 160 IP | $1 | 160 pts
SP-28 — Owned: 5% — RH

Talbot started strong, but he faded after the Break as the wear-and-tear of his first full season took its toll. He averaged 6-1/2 IP in his first 15 starts (3.88 ERA) but less than 5 IP over his final 13 (5.23 ERA). The Indians are confident that Mitch will adjust to the workload, and he's a favorite for their 2011 rotation. (BLS)

### Forecast
| Player | Age | IP | W | Sv | K | ERA | WHIP | K/9 | BB/9 | $2L | Pts |
|---|---|---|---|---|---|---|---|---|---|---|---|
| Talbot M | 27 | 160 | 9 | 0 | 106 | 4.62 | 1.50 | 6.0 | 3.7 | $1 | 160 |

### Mini-Browser
| Player | Age | IP | W | Sv | K | ERA | WHIP | K/9 | BB/9 | $2L | Pts |
|---|---|---|---|---|---|---|---|---|---|---|---|
| Hammel J | 28 | 180 | 10 | 0 | 130 | 4.80 | 1.38 | 6.5 | 2.5 | $1 | 190 |
| Young C | 31 | 80 | 4 | 0 | 60 | 4.26 | 1.34 | 6.8 | 4.1 | $1 | 90 |
| Walden J | 23 | 40 | 2 | 13 | 44 | 5.06 | 1.67 | 9.9 | 4.2 | $1 | 70 |
| Mijares J | 26 | 60 | 3 | 0 | 56 | 3.97 | 1.43 | 8.3 | 3.6 | $1 | 80 |
| Hensley C | 31 | 80 | 4 | 0 | 61 | 4.26 | 1.43 | 6.9 | 4.0 | $1 | 110 |

### Minors (2010)
| Level | Leag | W | L | Sv | IP | H | K | ERA | WHIP | K/9 | BB/9 | HR/9 | GB/F |
|---|---|---|---|---|---|---|---|---|---|---|---|---|---|
| A | NYP | 0 | 0 | 0 | 3 | 2 | 0 | 3.00 | 1.00 | 0.0 | 3.0 | 0.0 | — |
| AA | — | | | | — | — | — | — | — | — | — | — | — |
| AAA | — | | | | — | — | — | — | — | — | — | — | — |

### Majors
| Yr | Team | W | L | Sv | IP | H | K | ERA | WHIP | K/9 | BB/9 | HR/9 | GB/F |
|---|---|---|---|---|---|---|---|---|---|---|---|---|---|
| 07 | — | | | | — | — | — | — | — | — | — | — | — |
| 08 | TB | 0 | 0 | 0 | 9 | 16 | 5 | 11.17 | 2.79 | 4.7 | 10.2 | 2.8 | 1.1 |
| 09 | — | | | | — | — | — | — | — | — | — | — | — |
| 10 | CLE | 10 | 13 | 0 | 159 | 169 | 88 | 4.41 | 1.49 | 5.0 | 3.9 | 0.7 | 1.4 |

**Competition at SP — Stats in 2010 as SP**
| Thr | Player | GS | ERA | Supp | W-L |
|---|---|---|---|---|---|
| RH | Carmona F | 33 | 3.77 | 3.5 | 13-14 |
| RH | Masterson J | 29 | 4.78 | 4.3 | 6-12 |
| RH | Talbot M | 28 | 4.41 | 4.1 | 10-13 |
| LH | Huff D | 15 | 6.21 | 3.6 | 2-11 |

**Value / Luck / In Rotation / In Relief / OPS**
| $1L | $2L | Pts | RAA | H% | HR/fb | S% | FIP | GS | CG | QS/DS | GR | Hld | Bln | Lead | OPS | 1st Hf | 2nd Hf | vs RH | vs LH |
|---|---|---|---|---|---|---|---|---|---|---|---|---|---|---|---|---|---|---|---|
| -$6 | -$8 | -10 | -7 | 38% | 23% | 63% | 9.71 | 1 | 0 | 0/0 | 2 | 0 | 0 | -1.7 | 1.233 | — | 1.233 | 1.085 | 1.611 |
| $0 | -$18 | 150 | -9 | 30% | 7% | 71% | 4.56 | 28 | 1 | 11/4 | — | — | — | | .761 | .733 | .814 | .794 | .725 |

---

## Brian Tallet — 60 IP | $-3 | 50 pts
RP-29, SP-5 — Owned: 0% — LH

2010 was an ugly year for Tallet, who entered the season as Toronto's #5 SP but then strained his forearm and pitched poorly out of the bullpen. A lack of fastball command was at the heart of the problem. Tallet is not expected back in TOR, and the fading hurler could labor to find a guaranteed contract anywhere. (MH)

### Forecast
| Player | Age | IP | W | Sv | K | ERA | WHIP | K/9 | BB/9 | $2L | Pts |
|---|---|---|---|---|---|---|---|---|---|---|---|
| Tallet B | 33 | 60 | 3 | 0 | 41 | 5.35 | 1.51 | 6.2 | 4.4 | -$3 | 50 |

### Mini-Browser
| Player | Age | IP | W | Sv | K | ERA | WHIP | K/9 | BB/9 | $2L | Pts |
|---|---|---|---|---|---|---|---|---|---|---|---|
| Detwiler R | 25 | 100 | 5 | 0 | 76 | 4.55 | 1.57 | 6.9 | 3.9 | -$3 | 100 |
| Valdes R | 33 | 40 | 2 | 0 | 29 | 5.02 | 1.49 | 6.6 | 4.1 | -$3 | 40 |
| White S | 29 | 40 | 1 | 0 | 18 | 4.89 | 1.53 | 4.1 | 3.3 | -$3 | 20 |
| Castro S | 22 | 40 | 2 | 0 | 27 | 4.77 | 1.49 | 6.1 | 3.9 | -$3 | 40 |
| Britton Z | 23 | 100 | 5 | 0 | 59 | 4.83 | 1.59 | 5.3 | 4.0 | -$3 | 80 |

### Minors (2010)
| Level | Leag | W | L | Sv | IP | H | K | ERA | WHIP | K/9 | BB/9 | HR/9 | GB/F |
|---|---|---|---|---|---|---|---|---|---|---|---|---|---|
| A | FLO | 0 | 0 | 0 | 4 | 2 | 3 | 0.00 | 0.75 | 6.8 | 2.3 | 0.0 | — |
| AA | — | | | | — | — | — | — | — | — | — | — | — |
| AAA | PCL | 0 | 1 | 0 | 1 | 9 | 1 | 54.00 | 7.50 | 6.8 | 6.8 | 13.5 | — |

### Majors
| Yr | Team | W | L | Sv | IP | H | K | ERA | WHIP | K/9 | BB/9 | HR/9 | GB/F |
|---|---|---|---|---|---|---|---|---|---|---|---|---|---|
| 07 | TOR | 2 | 4 | 0 | 62 | 49 | 54 | 3.47 | 1.24 | 7.8 | 4.0 | 0.1 | 1.0 |
| 08 | TOR | 1 | 2 | 0 | 56 | 52 | 47 | 2.88 | 1.31 | 7.5 | 3.5 | 0.6 | 1.2 |
| 09 | TOR | 7 | 9 | 0 | 160 | 169 | 120 | 5.32 | 1.50 | 6.7 | 4.0 | 1.1 | 0.8 |
| 10 | TOR | 2 | 6 | 0 | 77 | 84 | 53 | 6.40 | 1.58 | 6.2 | 4.4 | 2.3 | 0.7 |

**Competition at RP — Stats in 2010 as RP**
| Thr | Player | GR | ERA | IP/G | Sv-Hld |
|---|---|---|---|---|---|
| LH | Downs S | 67 | 2.64 | 0.9 | 0-26 |
| LH | Purcey D | 33 | 3.71 | 1.0 | 1-3 |
| LH | Tallet B | 29 | 6.84 | 1.7 | 0-1 |
| LH | Carlson J | 20 | 4.61 | 0.7 | 1-2 |

**Value / Luck / In Rotation / In Relief / OPS**
| $1L | $2L | Pts | RAA | H% | HR/fb | S% | FIP | GS | CG | QS/DS | GR | Hld | Bln | Lead | OPS | 1st Hf | 2nd Hf | vs RH | vs LH |
|---|---|---|---|---|---|---|---|---|---|---|---|---|---|---|---|---|---|---|---|
| $3 | $0 | 70 | +2 | 27% | 1% | 70% | 3.12 | — | — | — | 48 | 1 | 3 | -1.1 | .611 | .514 | .766 | .555 | .697 |
| $3 | $0 | 60 | +6 | 29% | 7% | 80% | 3.73 | — | — | — | 51 | 4 | 0 | -0.9 | .664 | .694 | .600 | .673 | .654 |
| $0 | -$9 | 140 | -27 | 30% | 9% | 66% | 4.77 | 25 | 0 | 11/3 | 12 | 0 | 0 | -0.2 | .789 | .739 | .875 | .748 | .893 |
| -$8 | -$25 | 30 | -25 | 27% | 16% | 66% | 6.77 | 10 | 0 | 1/1 | 29 | 1 | 2 | -0.7 | .881 | .926 | .827 | 1.031 | .807 |

---

## Junichi Tazawa — 40 IP | $-3 | 30 pts
No MLB games played in 2010 — Owned: 0% — RH

Tazawa is recovering from Tommy John surgery in April 2010, and he could spend all of 2011 in Triple-A building up his arm as a starter. There is a chance that Tazawa gets a look in Boston later in 2011 as an injury replacement, but significant major-league action won't come until 2012. (EB)

### Forecast
| Player | Age | IP | W | Sv | K | ERA | WHIP | K/9 | BB/9 | $2L | Pts |
|---|---|---|---|---|---|---|---|---|---|---|---|
| Tazawa J | 24 | 40 | 1 | 0 | 33 | 5.38 | 1.60 | 7.4 | 3.0 | -$3 | 30 |

### Mini-Browser
| Player | Age | IP | W | Sv | K | ERA | WHIP | K/9 | BB/9 | $2L | Pts |
|---|---|---|---|---|---|---|---|---|---|---|---|
| Bonine E | 29 | 60 | 3 | 0 | 30 | 5.38 | 1.50 | 4.6 | 2.5 | -$3 | 40 |
| Burres B | 29 | 40 | 2 | 0 | 26 | 5.03 | 1.51 | 5.8 | 3.5 | -$3 | 30 |
| Bell T | 24 | 80 | 4 | 0 | 62 | 5.12 | 1.61 | 7.0 | 3.3 | -$3 | 70 |
| Haeger C | 27 | 40 | 2 | 0 | 33 | 5.16 | 1.53 | 7.3 | 4.3 | -$3 | 40 |
| Monasterios C | 25 | 40 | 2 | 0 | 32 | 4.98 | 1.56 | 7.2 | 3.3 | -$3 | 40 |

### Minors (2010)
| Level | Leag | W | L | Sv | IP | H | K | ERA | WHIP | K/9 | BB/9 | HR/9 | GB/F |
|---|---|---|---|---|---|---|---|---|---|---|---|---|---|
| A | — | | | | — | — | — | — | — | — | — | — | — |
| AA | — | | | | — | — | — | — | — | — | — | — | — |
| AAA | — | | | | — | — | — | — | — | — | — | — | — |

### Majors
| Yr | Team | W | L | Sv | IP | H | K | ERA | WHIP | K/9 | BB/9 | HR/9 | GB/F |
|---|---|---|---|---|---|---|---|---|---|---|---|---|---|
| 07 | — | | | | — | — | — | — | — | — | — | — | — |
| 08 | — | | | | — | — | — | — | — | — | — | — | — |
| 09 | BOS | 2 | 3 | 0 | 25 | 43 | 13 | 7.46 | 2.05 | 4.6 | 3.2 | 1.4 | 0.5 |
| 10 | — | | | | — | — | — | — | — | — | — | — | — |

**Competition at SP — Stats in 2010 as SP**
| Thr | Player | GS | ERA | Supp | W-L |
|---|---|---|---|---|---|
| RH | Lackey J | 33 | 4.40 | 5.1 | 14-11 |
| LH | Lester J | 32 | 3.25 | 5.0 | 19-9 |
| RH | Buchholz C | 28 | 2.33 | 4.7 | 17-7 |
| RH | Matsuzaka D | 25 | 4.69 | 5.6 | 9-6 |

**Value / Luck / In Rotation / In Relief / OPS**
| $1L | $2L | Pts | RAA | H% | HR/fb | S% | FIP | GS | CG | QS/DS | GR | Hld | Bln | Lead | OPS | 1st Hf | 2nd Hf | vs RH | vs LH |
|---|---|---|---|---|---|---|---|---|---|---|---|---|---|---|---|---|---|---|---|
| -$4 | -$7 | 10 | -11 | 40% | 7% | 65% | 5.39 | 4 | 0 | 1/1 | 0 | 0 | 0 | -1.2 | .997 | — | .997 | 1.291 | .770 |

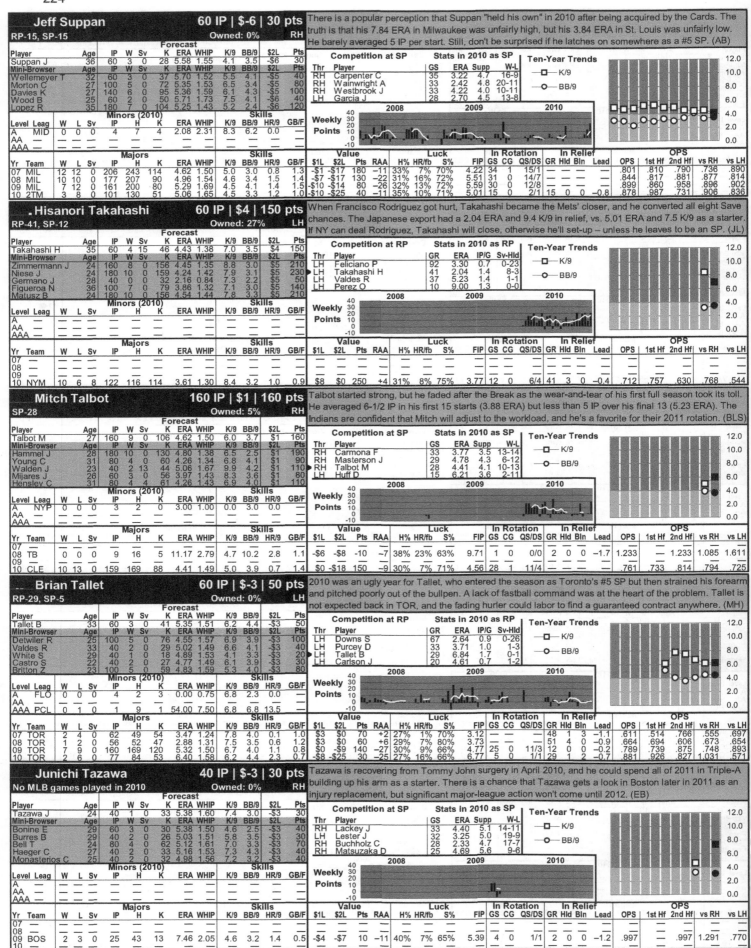

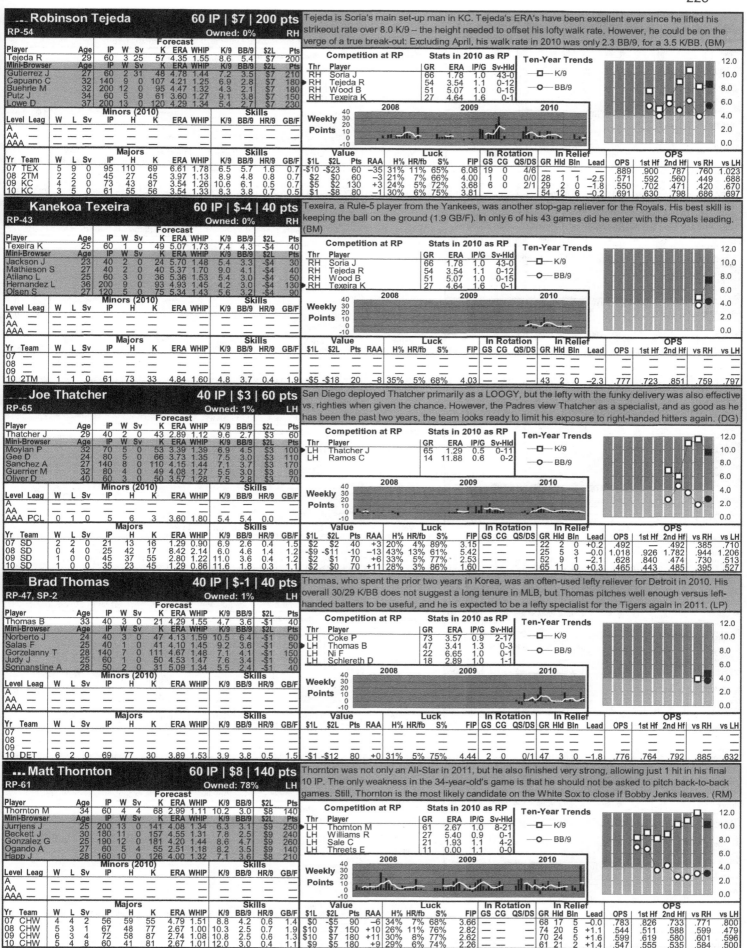

## Robinson Tejeda — 60 IP | $7 | 200 pts

RP-54 — Owned: 0% — RH

Tejeda is Soria's main set-up man in KC. Tejeda's ERA's have been excellent ever since he lifted his strikeout rate over 8.0 K/9 – the height needed to offset his lofty walk rate. However, he could be on the verge of a true break-out: Excluding April, his walk rate in 2010 was only 2.3 BB/9, for a 3.5 K/BB. (BM)

| Player | Age | IP | W | Sv | K | ERA | WHIP | K/9 | BB/9 | $2L | Pts |
|---|---|---|---|---|---|---|---|---|---|---|---|
| Tejeda R | 29 | 60 | 3 | 25 | 57 | 4.35 | 1.55 | 8.6 | 5.4 | $7 | 200 |
| **Mini-Browser** | **Age** | **IP** | **W** | **Sv** | **K** | **ERA** | **WHIP** | **K/9** | **BB/9** | **$2L** | **Pts** |
| Gutierrez J | 27 | 60 | 2 | 31 | 48 | 4.78 | 1.44 | 7.2 | 3.5 | $7 | 210 |
| Capuano C | 32 | 140 | 9 | 0 | 107 | 4.21 | 1.25 | 6.9 | 2.8 | $7 | 180 |
| Buehrle M | 32 | 200 | 12 | 0 | 95 | 4.47 | 1.32 | 4.3 | 2.1 | $7 | 180 |
| Putz J | 34 | 60 | 5 | 9 | 61 | 3.60 | 1.27 | 9.1 | 3.8 | $7 | 150 |
| Lowe D | 37 | 200 | 13 | 0 | 120 | 4.29 | 1.34 | 5.4 | 2.7 | $7 | 230 |

Minors (2010)

| Level | Leag | W | L | Sv | IP | H | K | ERA | WHIP | K/9 | BB/9 | HR/9 | GB/F |
|---|---|---|---|---|---|---|---|---|---|---|---|---|---|
| A | — | — | — | — | — | — | — | — | — | — | — | — | — |
| AA | — | — | — | — | — | — | — | — | — | — | — | — | — |
| AAA | — | — | — | — | — | — | — | — | — | — | — | — | — |

Majors

| Yr | Team | W | L | Sv | IP | H | K | ERA | WHIP | K/9 | BB/9 | HR/9 | GB/F |
|---|---|---|---|---|---|---|---|---|---|---|---|---|---|
| 07 | TEX | 5 | 9 | 0 | 95 | 110 | 69 | 6.61 | 1.78 | 6.5 | 5.7 | 1.6 | 0.7 |
| 08 | 2TM | 2 | 2 | 0 | 45 | 27 | 45 | 3.97 | 1.13 | 8.9 | 4.8 | 0.8 | 0.7 |
| 09 | KC | 4 | 2 | 0 | 73 | 43 | 87 | 3.54 | 1.26 | 10.6 | 6.1 | 0.5 | 0.7 |
| 10 | KC | 3 | 5 | 0 | 61 | 55 | 56 | 3.54 | 1.33 | 8.3 | 3.8 | 0.7 | 0.5 |

Competition at RP — Stats in 2010 as RP

| Thr | Player | GR | ERA | IP/G | Sv-Hld |
|---|---|---|---|---|---|
| RH | Soria J | 66 | 1.78 | 1.0 | 43-0 |
| RH | Tejeda R | 54 | 3.54 | 1.1 | 0-12 |
| RH | Wood B | 51 | 5.07 | 1.0 | 0-15 |
| RH | Texeira K | 27 | 4.64 | 1.6 | 0-1 |

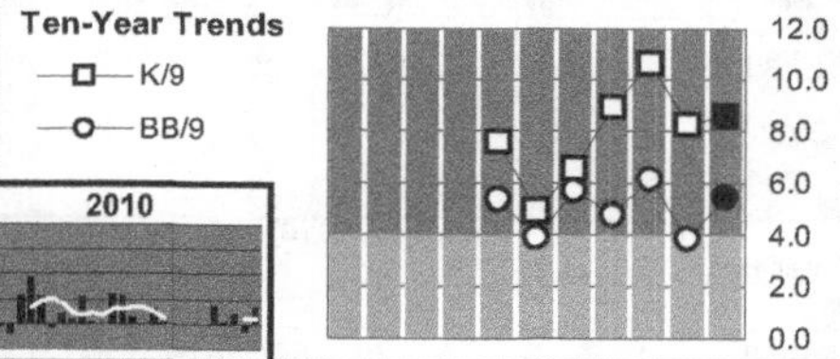
Ten-Year Trends
K/9
BB/9
12.0
10.0
8.0
6.0
4.0
2.0
0.0

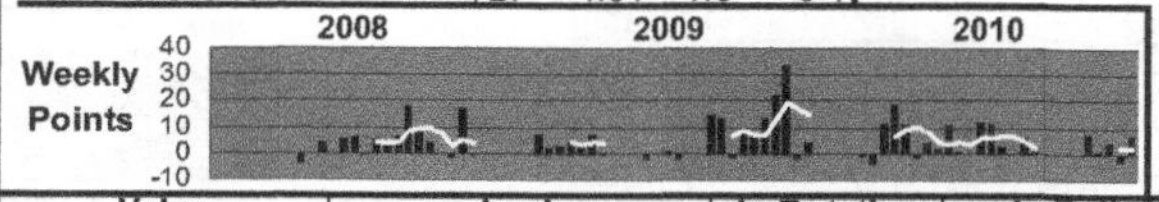
2008
2009
2010
Weekly
Points
40
30
20
10
0
-10

| Yr | $1L | $2L | Pts | RAA | H% | HR/fb | S% | FIP | GS | CG | QS/DS | GR | Hld | Bln | Lead | OPS | 1st Hf | 2nd Hf | vs RH | vs LH |
|---|---|---|---|---|---|---|---|---|---|---|---|---|---|---|---|---|---|---|---|---|
| 07 | -$10 | -$23 | 60 | −35 | 31% | 11% | 65% | 6.06 | 19 | 0 | 4/6 | — | — | — | — | .889 | .900 | .787 | .760 | 1.023 |
| 08 | $2 | $0 | 60 | −3 | 21% | 7% | 66% | 4.00 | 1 | 0 | 0/0 | 28 | 1 | 1 | −2.5 | .571 | .592 | .560 | .449 | .688 |
| 09 | $5 | $2 | 130 | +3 | 24% | 5% | 72% | 3.68 | 6 | 0 | 2/1 | 29 | 2 | 0 | −1.8 | .550 | .702 | .471 | .420 | .670 |
| 10 | $1 | -$8 | 80 | −1 | 30% | 6% | 75% | 3.81 | — | — | — | 54 | 12 | 6 | −0.2 | .691 | .630 | .798 | .686 | .697 |

## Kanekoa Texeira — 60 IP | $-4 | 40 pts

RP-43 — Owned: 0% — RH

Texeira, a Rule-5 player from the Yankees, was another stop-gap reliever for the Royals. His best skill is keeping the ball on the ground (1.9 GB/F). In only 6 of his 43 games did he enter with the Royals leading. (BM)

| Player | Age | IP | W | Sv | K | ERA | WHIP | K/9 | BB/9 | $2L | Pts |
|---|---|---|---|---|---|---|---|---|---|---|---|
| Texeira K | 25 | 60 | 1 | 0 | 49 | 5.07 | 1.73 | 7.4 | 4.3 | -$4 | 40 |
| **Mini-Browser** | **Age** | **IP** | **W** | **Sv** | **K** | **ERA** | **WHIP** | **K/9** | **BB/9** | **$2L** | **Pts** |
| Jackson J | 23 | 40 | 2 | 0 | 24 | 5.70 | 1.48 | 5.4 | 3.3 | -$4 | 30 |
| Mathieson S | 27 | 40 | 2 | 0 | 40 | 5.37 | 1.70 | 9.0 | 4.1 | -$4 | 40 |
| Atilano L | 25 | 60 | 3 | 0 | 36 | 5.36 | 1.53 | 5.4 | 3.0 | -$4 | 50 |
| Hernandez L | 36 | 200 | 9 | 0 | 93 | 4.93 | 1.45 | 4.2 | 3.0 | -$4 | 130 |
| Olsen S | 27 | 120 | 5 | 0 | 75 | 5.34 | 1.43 | 5.6 | 3.2 | -$4 | 90 |

Minors (2010)

| Level | Leag | W | L | Sv | IP | H | K | ERA | WHIP | K/9 | BB/9 | HR/9 | GB/F |
|---|---|---|---|---|---|---|---|---|---|---|---|---|---|
| A | — | — | — | — | — | — | — | — | — | — | — | — | — |
| AA | — | — | — | — | — | — | — | — | — | — | — | — | — |
| AAA | — | — | — | — | — | — | — | — | — | — | — | — | — |

Majors

| Yr | Team | W | L | Sv | IP | H | K | ERA | WHIP | K/9 | BB/9 | HR/9 | GB/F |
|---|---|---|---|---|---|---|---|---|---|---|---|---|---|
| 07 | — | — | — | — | — | — | — | — | — | — | — | — | — |
| 08 | — | — | — | — | — | — | — | — | — | — | — | — | — |
| 09 | — | — | — | — | — | — | — | — | — | — | — | — | — |
| 10 | 2TM | 1 | 1 | 0 | 61 | 73 | 33 | 4.84 | 1.60 | 4.8 | 3.7 | 0.4 | 1.9 |

Competition at RP — Stats in 2010 as RP

| Thr | Player | GR | ERA | IP/G | Sv-Hld |
|---|---|---|---|---|---|
| RH | Soria J | 66 | 1.78 | 1.0 | 43-0 |
| RH | Tejeda R | 54 | 3.54 | 1.1 | 0-12 |
| RH | Wood B | 51 | 5.07 | 1.0 | 0-15 |
| RH | Texeira K | 27 | 4.64 | 1.6 | 0-1 |

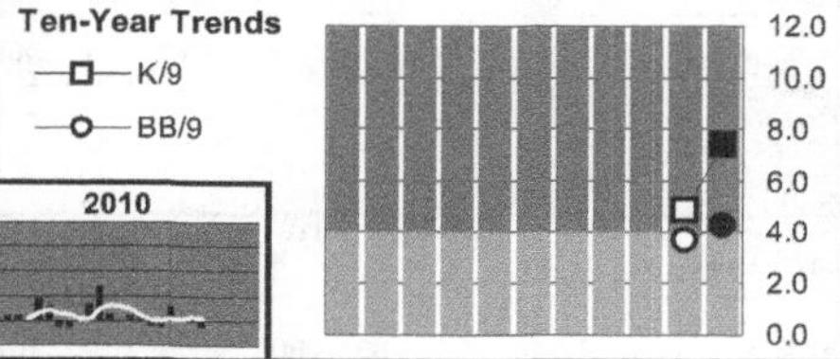
Ten-Year Trends
K/9
BB/9
12.0
10.0
8.0
6.0
4.0
2.0
0.0

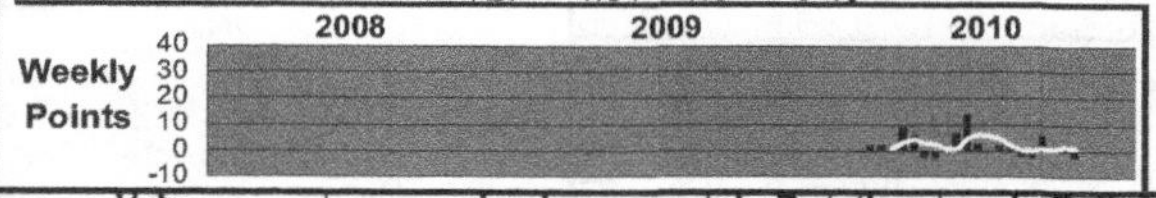
2008
2009
2010
Weekly
Points
40
30
20
10
0
-10

| Yr | $1L | $2L | Pts | RAA | H% | HR/fb | S% | FIP | GS | CG | QS/DS | GR | Hld | Bln | Lead | OPS | 1st Hf | 2nd Hf | vs RH | vs LH |
|---|---|---|---|---|---|---|---|---|---|---|---|---|---|---|---|---|---|---|---|---|
| 07 | — | — | — | — | — | — | — | — | — | — | — | — | — | — | — | — | — | — | — | — |
| 08 | — | — | — | — | — | — | — | — | — | — | — | — | — | — | — | — | — | — | — | — |
| 09 | — | — | — | — | — | — | — | — | — | — | — | — | — | — | — | — | — | — | — | — |
| 10 | -$5 | -$18 | 20 | −8 | 35% | 5% | 68% | 4.03 | — | — | — | 43 | 2 | 0 | −2.3 | .777 | .723 | .851 | .759 | .797 |

## Joe Thatcher — 40 IP | $3 | 60 pts

RP-65 — Owned: 1% — LH

San Diego deployed Thatcher primarily as a LOOGY, but the lefty with the funky delivery was also effective vs. righties when given the chance. However, the Padres view Thatcher as a specialist, and as good as he has been the past two years, the team looks ready to limit his exposure to right-handed hitters again. (DG)

| Player | Age | IP | W | Sv | K | ERA | WHIP | K/9 | BB/9 | $2L | Pts |
|---|---|---|---|---|---|---|---|---|---|---|---|
| Thatcher J | 29 | 40 | 2 | 0 | 43 | 2.89 | 1.12 | 9.6 | 2.7 | $3 | 60 |
| **Mini-Browser** | **Age** | **IP** | **W** | **Sv** | **K** | **ERA** | **WHIP** | **K/9** | **BB/9** | **$2L** | **Pts** |
| Moylan P | 32 | 70 | 5 | 0 | 53 | 3.39 | 1.39 | 6.9 | 4.5 | $3 | 100 |
| Gee D | 24 | 80 | 5 | 0 | 66 | 3.73 | 1.35 | 7.5 | 3.0 | $3 | 110 |
| Sanchez A | 27 | 140 | 8 | 0 | 110 | 4.15 | 1.44 | 7.1 | 3.7 | $3 | 170 |
| Guerrier M | 32 | 80 | 4 | 0 | 49 | 4.08 | 1.27 | 5.5 | 3.0 | $3 | 80 |
| Oliver D | 40 | 60 | 3 | 0 | 50 | 3.57 | 1.28 | 7.5 | 2.8 | $3 | 70 |

Minors (2010)

| Level | Leag | W | L | Sv | IP | H | K | ERA | WHIP | K/9 | BB/9 | HR/9 | GB/F |
|---|---|---|---|---|---|---|---|---|---|---|---|---|---|
| A | — | — | — | — | — | — | — | — | — | — | — | — | — |
| AA | — | — | — | — | — | — | — | — | — | — | — | — | — |
| AAA | PCL | 0 | 1 | 0 | 5 | 6 | 3 | 3.60 | 1.80 | 5.4 | 5.4 | 0.0 | — |

Majors

| Yr | Team | W | L | Sv | IP | H | K | ERA | WHIP | K/9 | BB/9 | HR/9 | GB/F |
|---|---|---|---|---|---|---|---|---|---|---|---|---|---|
| 07 | SD | 2 | 2 | 0 | 21 | 13 | 16 | 1.29 | 0.90 | 6.9 | 2.6 | 0.4 | 1.5 |
| 08 | SD | 0 | 4 | 0 | 25 | 42 | 17 | 8.42 | 2.14 | 6.0 | 4.6 | 1.4 | 1.2 |
| 09 | SD | 1 | 0 | 0 | 45 | 37 | 55 | 2.80 | 1.22 | 11.0 | 3.6 | 0.4 | 1.2 |
| 10 | SD | 1 | 0 | 0 | 35 | 23 | 45 | 1.29 | 0.86 | 11.6 | 1.8 | 0.3 | 1.1 |

Competition at RP — Stats in 2010 as RP

| Thr | Player | GR | ERA | IP/G | Sv-Hld |
|---|---|---|---|---|---|
| LH | Thatcher J | 65 | 1.29 | 0.5 | 0-11 |
| LH | Ramos C | 14 | 11.88 | 0.6 | 0-2 |

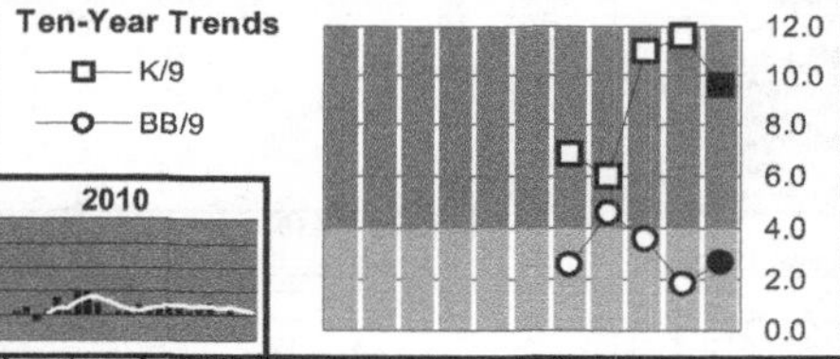
Ten-Year Trends
K/9
BB/9
12.0
10.0
8.0
6.0
4.0
2.0
0.0

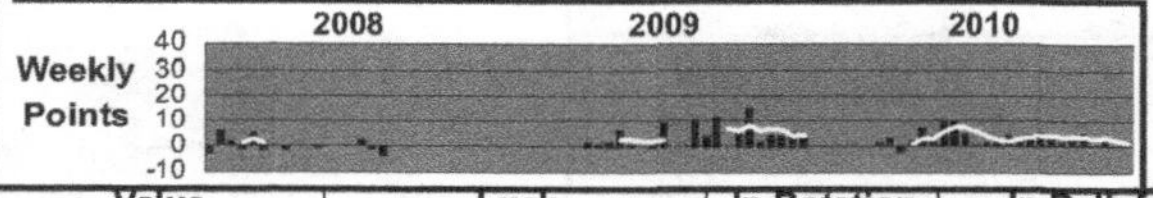
2008
2009
2010
Weekly
Points
40
30
20
10
0
-10

| Yr | $1L | $2L | Pts | RAA | H% | HR/fb | S% | FIP | GS | CG | QS/DS | GR | Hld | Bln | Lead | OPS | 1st Hf | 2nd Hf | vs RH | vs LH |
|---|---|---|---|---|---|---|---|---|---|---|---|---|---|---|---|---|---|---|---|---|
| 07 | $2 | $2 | 40 | +3 | 20% | 4% | 89% | 3.15 | — | — | — | 22 | 2 | 0 | +0.2 | .492 | — | .492 | .385 | .710 |
| 08 | -$9 | -$11 | -10 | −13 | 43% | 13% | 61% | 5.42 | — | — | — | 25 | 5 | 3 | −0.0 | 1.018 | .926 | 1.782 | .944 | 1.206 |
| 09 | $2 | $1 | 70 | +6 | 33% | 5% | 77% | 2.53 | — | — | — | 52 | 9 | 1 | −2.1 | .628 | .840 | .474 | .730 | .513 |
| 10 | $2 | $0 | 70 | +11 | 28% | 3% | 86% | 1.60 | — | — | — | 65 | 11 | 0 | +0.3 | .465 | .443 | .485 | .395 | .527 |

## Brad Thomas — 40 IP | $-1 | 40 pts

RP-47, SP-2 — Owned: 1% — LH

Thomas, who spent the prior two years in Korea, was an often-used lefty reliever for Detroit in 2010. His overall 30/29 K/BB does not suggest a long tenure in MLB, but Thomas pitches well enough versus left-handed batters to be useful, and he is expected to be a lefty specialist for the Tigers again in 2011. (LP)

| Player | Age | IP | W | Sv | K | ERA | WHIP | K/9 | BB/9 | $2L | Pts |
|---|---|---|---|---|---|---|---|---|---|---|---|
| Thomas B | 33 | 40 | 3 | 0 | 21 | 4.29 | 1.55 | 4.7 | 3.6 | -$1 | 40 |
| **Mini-Browser** | **Age** | **IP** | **W** | **Sv** | **K** | **ERA** | **WHIP** | **K/9** | **BB/9** | **$2L** | **Pts** |
| Norberto J | 24 | 40 | 3 | 0 | 47 | 4.13 | 1.59 | 10.5 | 6.4 | -$1 | 60 |
| Salas F | 25 | 40 | 1 | 0 | 41 | 4.10 | 1.45 | 9.2 | 3.6 | -$1 | 50 |
| Gorzelanny T | 28 | 140 | 7 | 0 | 111 | 4.67 | 1.48 | 7.1 | 4.1 | -$1 | 150 |
| Judy J | 25 | 60 | 1 | 0 | 50 | 4.53 | 1.47 | 7.6 | 3.4 | -$1 | 50 |
| Sonnanstine A | 28 | 50 | 2 | 0 | 31 | 5.09 | 1.34 | 5.5 | 2.4 | -$1 | 40 |

Minors (2010)

| Level | Leag | W | L | Sv | IP | H | K | ERA | WHIP | K/9 | BB/9 | HR/9 | GB/F |
|---|---|---|---|---|---|---|---|---|---|---|---|---|---|
| A | — | — | — | — | — | — | — | — | — | — | — | — | — |
| AA | — | — | — | — | — | — | — | — | — | — | — | — | — |
| AAA | — | — | — | — | — | — | — | — | — | — | — | — | — |

Majors

| Yr | Team | W | L | Sv | IP | H | K | ERA | WHIP | K/9 | BB/9 | HR/9 | GB/F |
|---|---|---|---|---|---|---|---|---|---|---|---|---|---|
| 07 | — | — | — | — | — | — | — | — | — | — | — | — | — |
| 08 | — | — | — | — | — | — | — | — | — | — | — | — | — |
| 09 | — | — | — | — | — | — | — | — | — | — | — | — | — |
| 10 | DET | 6 | 2 | 0 | 69 | 77 | 30 | 3.89 | 1.53 | 3.9 | 3.8 | 0.5 | 1.5 |

Competition at RP — Stats in 2010 as RP

| Thr | Player | GR | ERA | IP/G | Sv-Hld |
|---|---|---|---|---|---|
| LH | Coke P | 73 | 3.57 | 0.9 | 2-17 |
| LH | Thomas B | 47 | 3.41 | 1.3 | 0-3 |
| LH | Ni F | 22 | 6.65 | 1.0 | 0-1 |
| LH | Schlereth D | 18 | 2.89 | 1.0 | 1-1 |

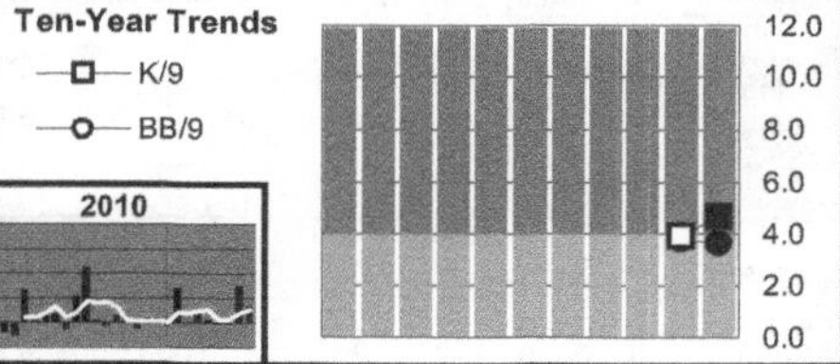
Ten-Year Trends
K/9
BB/9
12.0
10.0
8.0
6.0
4.0
2.0
0.0

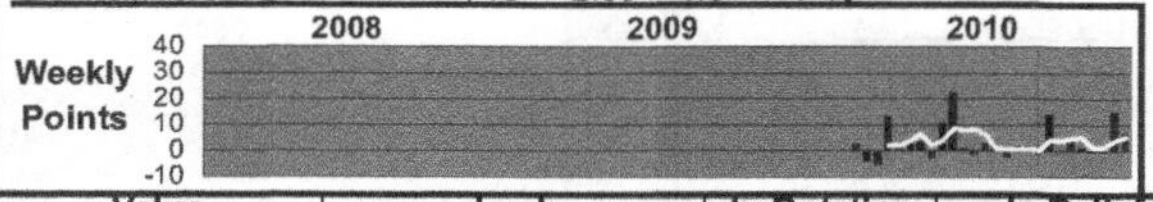
2008
2009
2010
Weekly
Points
40
30
20
10
0
-10

| Yr | $1L | $2L | Pts | RAA | H% | HR/fb | S% | FIP | GS | CG | QS/DS | GR | Hld | Bln | Lead | OPS | 1st Hf | 2nd Hf | vs RH | vs LH |
|---|---|---|---|---|---|---|---|---|---|---|---|---|---|---|---|---|---|---|---|---|
| 07 | — | — | — | — | — | — | — | — | — | — | — | — | — | — | — | — | — | — | — | — |
| 08 | — | — | — | — | — | — | — | — | — | — | — | — | — | — | — | — | — | — | — | — |
| 09 | — | — | — | — | — | — | — | — | — | — | — | — | — | — | — | — | — | — | — | — |
| 10 | -$1 | -$12 | 80 | +0 | 31% | 5% | 75% | 4.44 | 2 | 0 | 0/1 | 47 | 3 | 0 | −1.8 | .776 | .764 | .792 | .885 | .632 |

## Matt Thornton — 60 IP | $8 | 140 pts

RP-61 — Owned: 78% — LH

Thornton was not only an All-Star in 2011, but he also finished very strong, allowing just 1 hit in his final 10 IP. The only weakness in the 34-year-old's game is that he should not be asked to pitch back-to-back games. Still, Thornton is the most likely candidate on the White Sox to close if Bobby Jenks leaves. (RM)

| Player | Age | IP | W | Sv | K | ERA | WHIP | K/9 | BB/9 | $2L | Pts |
|---|---|---|---|---|---|---|---|---|---|---|---|
| Thornton M | 34 | 60 | 4 | 4 | 68 | 2.99 | 1.11 | 10.2 | 3.0 | $8 | 140 |
| **Mini-Browser** | **Age** | **IP** | **W** | **Sv** | **K** | **ERA** | **WHIP** | **K/9** | **BB/9** | **$2L** | **Pts** |
| Jurrjens J | 25 | 200 | 13 | 0 | 141 | 4.08 | 1.34 | 6.3 | 3.1 | $9 | 250 |
| Beckett J | 30 | 180 | 11 | 0 | 157 | 4.55 | 1.31 | 7.8 | 2.5 | $9 | 240 |
| Gonzalez G | 25 | 190 | 12 | 0 | 181 | 4.20 | 1.44 | 8.6 | 4.7 | $9 | 260 |
| Ogando A | 27 | 60 | 5 | 4 | 55 | 2.51 | 1.18 | 8.2 | 3.5 | $9 | 140 |
| Happ J | 28 | 160 | 10 | 0 | 126 | 4.00 | 1.32 | 7.1 | 3.6 | $8 | 210 |

Minors (2010)

| Level | Leag | W | L | Sv | IP | H | K | ERA | WHIP | K/9 | BB/9 | HR/9 | GB/F |
|---|---|---|---|---|---|---|---|---|---|---|---|---|---|
| A | — | — | — | — | — | — | — | — | — | — | — | — | — |
| AA | — | — | — | — | — | — | — | — | — | — | — | — | — |
| AAA | — | — | — | — | — | — | — | — | — | — | — | — | — |

Majors

| Yr | Team | W | L | Sv | IP | H | K | ERA | WHIP | K/9 | BB/9 | HR/9 | GB/F |
|---|---|---|---|---|---|---|---|---|---|---|---|---|---|
| 07 | CHW | 4 | 4 | 2 | 56 | 59 | 55 | 4.79 | 1.51 | 8.8 | 4.2 | 0.6 | 1.4 |
| 08 | CHW | 5 | 3 | 1 | 67 | 48 | 77 | 2.67 | 1.00 | 10.3 | 2.5 | 0.7 | 1.9 |
| 09 | CHW | 6 | 3 | 4 | 72 | 58 | 87 | 2.74 | 1.08 | 10.8 | 2.5 | 0.6 | 1.3 |
| 10 | CHW | 5 | 4 | 8 | 60 | 41 | 81 | 2.67 | 1.01 | 12.0 | 3.0 | 0.4 | 1.1 |

Competition at RP — Stats in 2010 as RP

| Thr | Player | GR | ERA | IP/G | Sv-Hld |
|---|---|---|---|---|---|
| LH | Thornton M | 61 | 2.67 | 1.0 | 8-21 |
| LH | Williams R | 27 | 5.40 | 0.9 | 0-1 |
| LH | Sale C | 21 | 1.93 | 1.1 | 4-2 |
| LH | Threets E | 11 | 0.00 | 1.1 | 0-0 |

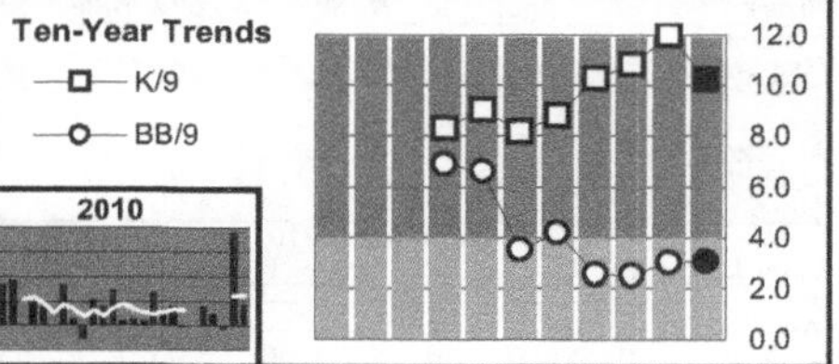
Ten-Year Trends
K/9
BB/9
12.0
10.0
8.0
6.0
4.0
2.0
0.0

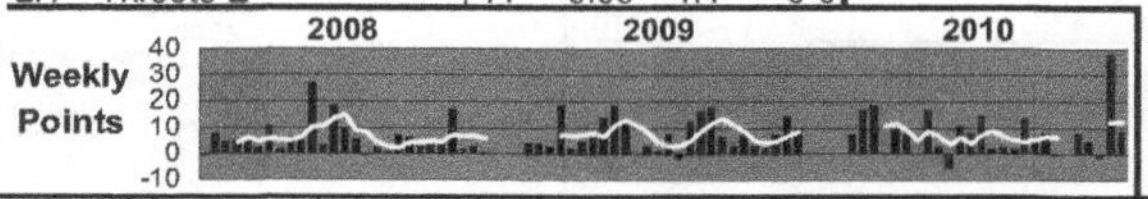
2008
2009
2010
Weekly
Points
40
30
20
10
0
-10

| Yr | $1L | $2L | Pts | RAA | H% | HR/fb | S% | FIP | GS | CG | QS/DS | GR | Hld | Bln | Lead | OPS | 1st Hf | 2nd Hf | vs RH | vs LH |
|---|---|---|---|---|---|---|---|---|---|---|---|---|---|---|---|---|---|---|---|---|
| 07 | $0 | -$5 | 90 | −6 | 34% | 7% | 68% | 3.66 | — | — | — | 68 | 17 | 5 | −0.0 | .783 | .826 | .733 | .771 | .800 |
| 08 | $10 | $7 | 150 | +10 | 26% | 11% | 76% | 2.82 | — | — | — | 74 | 20 | 5 | +1.1 | .544 | .511 | .588 | .599 | .479 |
| 09 | $10 | $7 | 180 | +11 | 30% | 8% | 77% | 2.62 | — | — | — | 70 | 24 | 5 | +1.6 | .599 | .619 | .580 | .601 | .596 |
| 10 | $9 | $5 | 180 | +9 | 29% | 6% | 74% | 2.26 | — | — | — | 61 | 21 | 2 | +1.4 | .547 | .555 | .535 | .584 | .500 |

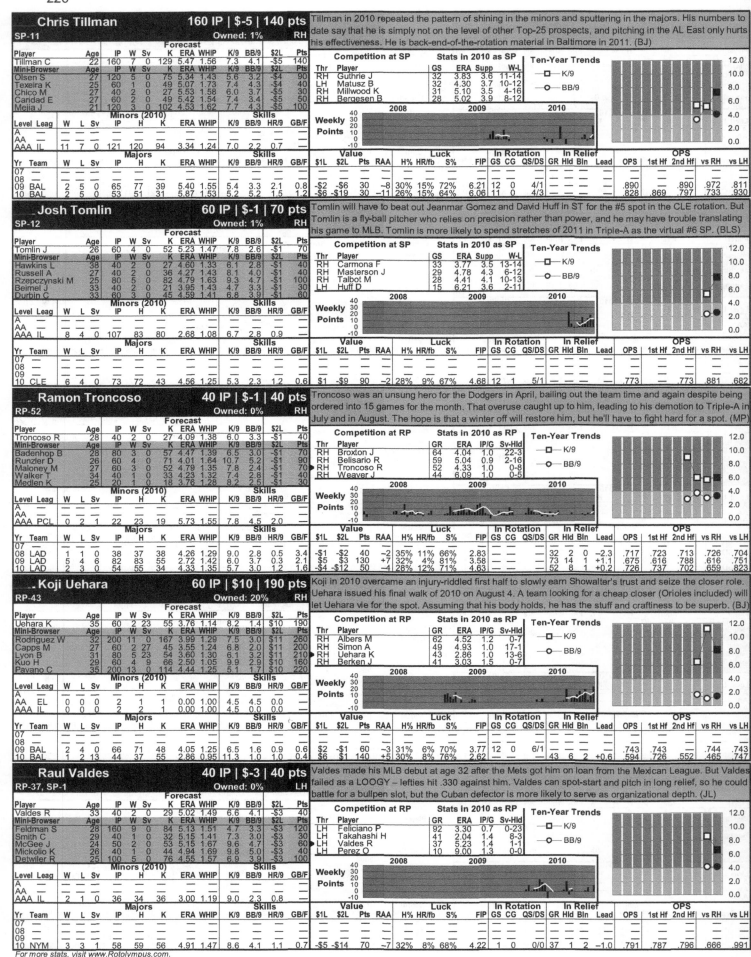

## Chris Tillman 160 IP | $-5 | 140 pts

SP-11 Owned: 1% RH

Tillman in 2010 repeated the pattern of shining in the minors and sputtering in the majors. His numbers to date say that he is simply not on the level of other Top-25 prospects, and pitching in the AL East only hurts his effectiveness. He is back-end-of-the-rotation material in Baltimore in 2011. (BJ)

**Forecast**

| Player | Age | IP | W | Sv | K | ERA | WHIP | K/9 | BB/9 | $2L | Pts |
|---|---|---|---|---|---|---|---|---|---|---|---|
| Tillman C | 22 | 160 | 7 | 0 | 129 | 5.47 | 1.56 | 7.3 | 4.1 | -$5 | 140 |
| **Mini-Browser** | **Age** | **IP** | **W** | **Sv** | **K** | **ERA** | **WHIP** | **K/9** | **BB/9** | **$2L** | **Pts** |
| Olsen S | 27 | 120 | 5 | 0 | 75 | 5.34 | 1.43 | 5.6 | 3.2 | -$4 | 90 |
| Texeira K | 25 | 60 | 1 | 0 | 49 | 5.07 | 1.73 | 7.4 | 4.3 | -$4 | 40 |
| Chico M | 27 | 40 | 2 | 0 | 27 | 5.53 | 1.58 | 6.0 | 3.7 | -$5 | 30 |
| Caridad E | 27 | 60 | 2 | 0 | 49 | 5.42 | 1.54 | 7.4 | 3.4 | -$5 | 50 |
| Mejia J | 21 | 120 | 3 | 0 | 102 | 4.53 | 1.62 | 7.7 | 4.3 | -$5 | 100 |

**Competition at SP** — Stats in 2010 as SP

| Thr | Player | GS | ERA | Supp | W-L |
|---|---|---|---|---|---|
| RH | Guthrie J | 32 | 3.83 | 3.6 | 11-14 |
| LH | Matusz B | 32 | 4.30 | 3.7 | 10-12 |
| RH | Millwood K | 31 | 5.10 | 3.5 | 4-16 |
| RH | Bergesen B | 28 | 5.02 | 3.9 | 8-12 |

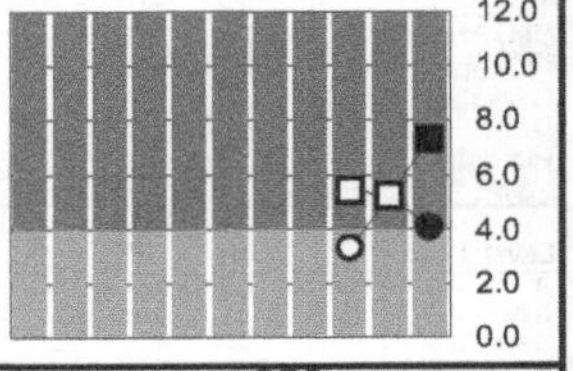


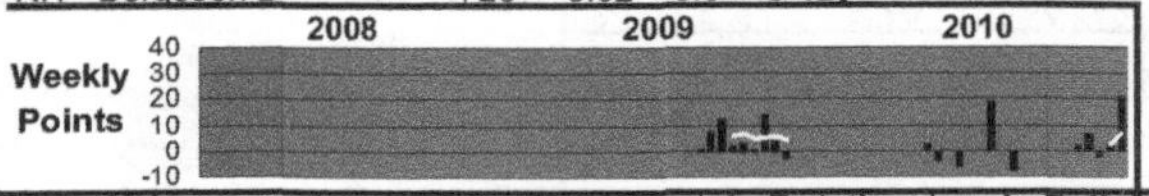


**Minors (2010)**

| Level | Leag | W | L | Sv | IP | H | K | ERA | WHIP | K/9 | BB/9 | HR/9 | GB/F |
|---|---|---|---|---|---|---|---|---|---|---|---|---|---|
| A | — | — | — | — | — | — | — | — | — | — | — | — | — |
| AA | — | — | — | — | — | — | — | — | — | — | — | — | — |
| AAA | IL | 11 | 7 | 0 | 121 | 120 | 94 | 3.34 | 1.24 | 7.0 | 2.2 | 0.7 | — |

**Majors**

| Yr | Team | W | L | Sv | IP | H | K | ERA | WHIP | K/9 | BB/9 | HR/9 | GB/F | $1L | $2L | Pts | RAA | H% | HR/fb | S% | FIP | GS | CG | QS/DS | GR | Hld | Bln | Lead | OPS | 1st Hf | 2nd Hf | vs RH | vs LH |
|---|---|---|---|---|---|---|---|---|---|---|---|---|---|---|---|---|---|---|---|---|---|---|---|---|---|---|---|---|---|---|---|---|---|
| 07 | — | — | — | — | — | — | — | — | — | — | — | — | — | — | — | — | — | — | — | — | — | — | — | — | — | — | — | — | — | — | — | — | — |
| 08 | — | — | — | — | — | — | — | — | — | — | — | — | — | — | — | — | — | — | — | — | — | — | — | — | — | — | — | — | — | — | — | — | — |
| 09 | BAL | 2 | 5 | 0 | 65 | 77 | 39 | 5.40 | 1.55 | 5.4 | 3.3 | 2.1 | 0.8 | -$2 | -$6 | 30 | −8 | 30% | 15% | 72% | 6.21 | 12 | 0 | 4/1 | — | — | — | — | .890 | — | .890 | .972 | .811 |
| 10 | BAL | 2 | 5 | 0 | 53 | 51 | 31 | 5.87 | 1.53 | 5.2 | 5.2 | 1.5 | 1.2 | -$6 | -$19 | 30 | −11 | 26% | 15% | 64% | 6.06 | 11 | 0 | 4/3 | — | — | — | — | .828 | .869 | .797 | .733 | .930 |

## Josh Tomlin 60 IP | $-1 | 70 pts

SP-12 Owned: 1% RH

Tomlin will have to beat out Jeanmar Gomez and David Huff in ST for the #5 spot in the CLE rotation. But Tomlin is a fly-ball pitcher who relies on precision rather than power, and he may have trouble translating his game to MLB. Tomlin is more likely to spend stretches of 2011 in Triple-A as the virtual #6 SP. (BLS)

**Forecast**

| Player | Age | IP | W | Sv | K | ERA | WHIP | K/9 | BB/9 | $2L | Pts |
|---|---|---|---|---|---|---|---|---|---|---|---|
| Tomlin J | 26 | 60 | 4 | 0 | 52 | 5.23 | 1.47 | 7.8 | 2.6 | -$1 | 70 |
| **Mini-Browser** | **Age** | **IP** | **W** | **Sv** | **K** | **ERA** | **WHIP** | **K/9** | **BB/9** | **$2L** | **Pts** |
| Hawkins L | 38 | 40 | 2 | 0 | 27 | 4.60 | 1.33 | 6.1 | 2.8 | -$1 | 40 |
| Russell A | 27 | 40 | 2 | 0 | 36 | 4.27 | 1.43 | 8.1 | 4.0 | -$1 | 40 |
| Rzepczynski M | 25 | 80 | 5 | 0 | 82 | 4.79 | 1.63 | 9.3 | 4.7 | -$1 | 100 |
| Beimel J | 33 | 40 | 2 | 0 | 21 | 3.95 | 1.43 | 4.7 | 3.3 | -$1 | 30 |
| Durbin C | 33 | 60 | 3 | 0 | 45 | 4.59 | 1.41 | 6.8 | 3.9 | -$1 | 60 |

**Competition at SP** — Stats in 2010 as SP

| Thr | Player | GS | ERA | Supp | W-L |
|---|---|---|---|---|---|
| RH | Carmona F | 33 | 3.77 | 3.5 | 13-14 |
| RH | Masterson J | 29 | 4.78 | 4.3 | 6-12 |
| RH | Talbot M | 28 | 4.41 | 4.1 | 10-13 |
| LH | Huff D | 15 | 6.21 | 3.6 | 2-11 |

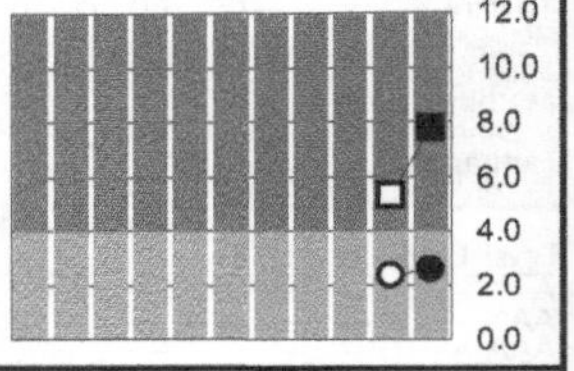

**Minors (2010)**

| Level | Leag | W | L | Sv | IP | H | K | ERA | WHIP | K/9 | BB/9 | HR/9 | GB/F |
|---|---|---|---|---|---|---|---|---|---|---|---|---|---|
| A | — | — | — | — | — | — | — | — | — | — | — | — | — |
| AA | — | — | — | — | — | — | — | — | — | — | — | — | — |
| AAA | IL | 8 | 4 | 0 | 107 | 83 | 80 | 2.68 | 1.08 | 6.7 | 2.8 | 0.9 | — |

**Majors**

| Yr | Team | W | L | Sv | IP | H | K | ERA | WHIP | K/9 | BB/9 | HR/9 | GB/F | $1L | $2L | Pts | RAA | H% | HR/fb | S% | FIP | GS | CG | QS/DS | GR | Hld | Bln | Lead | OPS | 1st Hf | 2nd Hf | vs RH | vs LH |
|---|---|---|---|---|---|---|---|---|---|---|---|---|---|---|---|---|---|---|---|---|---|---|---|---|---|---|---|---|---|---|---|---|---|
| 07 | — | — | — | — | — | — | — | — | — | — | — | — | — | — | — | — | — | — | — | — | — | — | — | — | — | — | — | — | — | — | — | — | — |
| 08 | — | — | — | — | — | — | — | — | — | — | — | — | — | — | — | — | — | — | — | — | — | — | — | — | — | — | — | — | — | — | — | — | — |
| 09 | — | — | — | — | — | — | — | — | — | — | — | — | — | — | — | — | — | — | — | — | — | — | — | — | — | — | — | — | — | — | — | — | — |
| 10 | CLE | 6 | 4 | 0 | 73 | 72 | 43 | 4.56 | 1.25 | 5.3 | 2.3 | 1.2 | 0.6 | $1 | -$9 | 90 | −2 | 28% | 9% | 67% | 4.68 | 12 | 1 | 5/1 | — | — | — | — | .773 | — | .773 | .881 | .682 |

## Ramon Troncoso 40 IP | $-1 | 40 pts

RP-52 Owned: 0% RH

Troncoso was an unsung hero for the Dodgers in April, bailing out the team time and again despite being ordered into 15 games for the month. That overuse caught up to him, leading to his demotion to Triple-A in July and in August. The hope is that a winter off will restore him, but he'll have to fight hard for a spot. (MP)

**Forecast**

| Player | Age | IP | W | Sv | K | ERA | WHIP | K/9 | BB/9 | $2L | Pts |
|---|---|---|---|---|---|---|---|---|---|---|---|
| Troncoso R | 28 | 40 | 2 | 0 | 27 | 4.09 | 1.38 | 6.0 | 3.3 | -$1 | 40 |
| **Mini-Browser** | **Age** | **IP** | **W** | **Sv** | **K** | **ERA** | **WHIP** | **K/9** | **BB/9** | **$2L** | **Pts** |
| Badenhop B | 28 | 80 | 3 | 0 | 57 | 4.47 | 1.39 | 6.5 | 3.0 | -$1 | 70 |
| Runzler D | 26 | 60 | 4 | 0 | 71 | 4.01 | 1.64 | 10.7 | 5.2 | -$1 | 90 |
| Maloney M | 27 | 60 | 3 | 0 | 52 | 4.79 | 1.35 | 7.8 | 2.4 | -$1 | 70 |
| Walker T | 34 | 40 | 1 | 0 | 33 | 4.23 | 1.32 | 7.4 | 2.8 | -$1 | 40 |
| Medlen K | 25 | 20 | 1 | 0 | 18 | 3.76 | 1.28 | 8.2 | 2.5 | -$1 | 30 |

**Competition at RP** — Stats in 2010 as RP

| Thr | Player | GR | ERA | IP/G | Sv-Hld |
|---|---|---|---|---|---|
| RH | Broxton J | 64 | 4.04 | 1.0 | 22-3 |
| RH | Belisario R | 59 | 5.04 | 0.9 | 2-16 |
| RH | Troncoso R | 52 | 4.33 | 1.0 | 0-8 |
| RH | Weaver J | 44 | 6.09 | 1.0 | 0-5 |

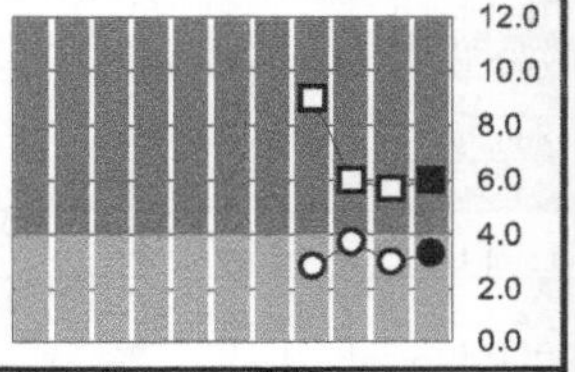


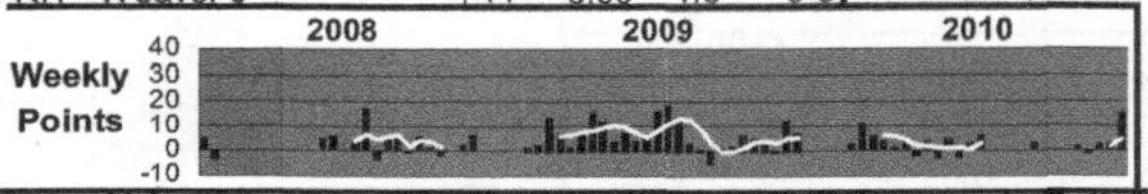


**Minors (2010)**

| Level | Leag | W | L | Sv | IP | H | K | ERA | WHIP | K/9 | BB/9 | HR/9 | GB/F |
|---|---|---|---|---|---|---|---|---|---|---|---|---|---|
| A | — | — | — | — | — | — | — | — | — | — | — | — | — |
| AA | — | — | — | — | — | — | — | — | — | — | — | — | — |
| AAA | PCL | 0 | 2 | 1 | 22 | 23 | 19 | 5.73 | 1.55 | 7.8 | 4.5 | 2.0 | — |

**Majors**

| Yr | Team | W | L | Sv | IP | H | K | ERA | WHIP | K/9 | BB/9 | HR/9 | GB/F | $1L | $2L | Pts | RAA | H% | HR/fb | S% | FIP | GS | CG | QS/DS | GR | Hld | Bln | Lead | OPS | 1st Hf | 2nd Hf | vs RH | vs LH |
|---|---|---|---|---|---|---|---|---|---|---|---|---|---|---|---|---|---|---|---|---|---|---|---|---|---|---|---|---|---|---|---|---|---|
| 07 | — | — | — | — | — | — | — | — | — | — | — | — | — | — | — | — | — | — | — | — | — | — | — | — | — | — | — | — | — | — | — | — | — |
| 08 | LAD | 1 | 1 | 0 | 38 | 37 | 38 | 4.26 | 1.29 | 9.0 | 2.8 | 0.5 | 3.4 | -$1 | -$2 | 40 | −2 | 35% | 11% | 66% | 2.83 | — | — | — | 32 | 2 | 0 | −2.3 | .717 | .723 | .713 | .726 | .704 |
| 09 | LAD | 5 | 4 | 6 | 82 | 83 | 55 | 2.72 | 1.42 | 6.0 | 3.7 | 0.3 | 2.1 | $5 | $3 | 130 | +7 | 32% | 4% | 81% | 3.58 | — | — | — | 73 | 14 | 1 | +1.1 | .675 | .616 | .788 | .616 | .751 |
| 10 | LAD | 2 | 3 | 0 | 54 | 55 | 34 | 4.33 | 1.35 | 5.7 | 3.0 | 1.2 | 1.6 | -$4 | -$12 | 50 | −4 | 28% | 12% | 71% | 4.63 | — | — | — | 52 | 8 | 1 | +0.2 | .726 | .737 | .702 | .659 | .823 |

## Koji Uehara 60 IP | $10 | 190 pts

RP-43 Owned: 20% RH

Koji in 2010 overcame an injury-riddled first half to slowly earn Showalter's trust and seize the closer role. Uehara issued his final walk of 2010 on August 4. A team looking for a cheap closer (Orioles included) will let Uehara vie for the spot. Assuming that his body holds, he has the stuff and craftiness to be superb. (BJ)

**Forecast**

| Player | Age | IP | W | Sv | K | ERA | WHIP | K/9 | BB/9 | $2L | Pts |
|---|---|---|---|---|---|---|---|---|---|---|---|
| Uehara K | 35 | 60 | 2 | 23 | 55 | 3.76 | 1.14 | 8.2 | 1.4 | $10 | 190 |
| **Mini-Browser** | **Age** | **IP** | **W** | **Sv** | **K** | **ERA** | **WHIP** | **K/9** | **BB/9** | **$2L** | **Pts** |
| Rodriguez W | 32 | 200 | 11 | 0 | 167 | 3.99 | 1.29 | 7.5 | 3.0 | $11 | 260 |
| Capps M | 27 | 60 | 2 | 27 | 45 | 3.55 | 1.24 | 6.8 | 2.0 | $11 | 200 |
| Lyon B | 31 | 80 | 5 | 23 | 54 | 3.60 | 1.30 | 6.1 | 3.2 | $11 | 210 |
| Kuo H | 29 | 60 | 4 | 9 | 66 | 2.50 | 1.05 | 9.9 | 2.9 | $10 | 160 |
| Pavano C | 35 | 200 | 13 | 0 | 114 | 4.44 | 1.25 | 5.1 | 1.7 | $10 | 220 |

**Competition at RP** — Stats in 2010 as RP

| Thr | Player | GR | ERA | IP/G | Sv-Hld |
|---|---|---|---|---|---|
| RH | Albers M | 62 | 4.52 | 1.2 | 0-7 |
| RH | Simon A | 49 | 4.93 | 1.0 | 17-1 |
| RH | Uehara K | 43 | 2.86 | 1.0 | 13-6 |
| RH | Berken J | 41 | 3.03 | 1.5 | 0-7 |

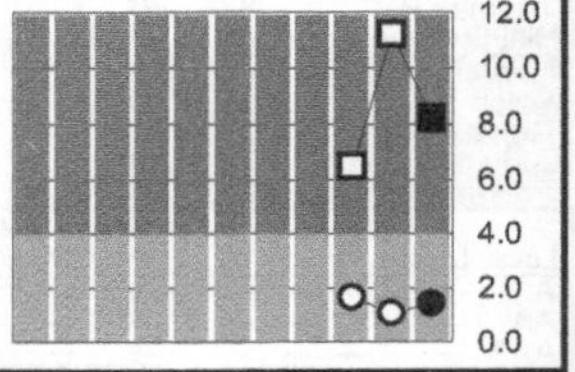

**Minors (2010)**

| Level | Leag | W | L | Sv | IP | H | K | ERA | WHIP | K/9 | BB/9 | HR/9 | GB/F |
|---|---|---|---|---|---|---|---|---|---|---|---|---|---|
| A | — | — | — | — | — | — | — | — | — | — | — | — | — |
| AA | EL | 0 | 0 | 0 | 2 | 1 | 1 | 0.00 | 1.00 | 4.5 | 4.5 | 0.0 | — |
| AAA | IL | 0 | 0 | 0 | 2 | 2 | 1 | 0.00 | 1.00 | 4.5 | 0.0 | 0.0 | — |

**Majors**

| Yr | Team | W | L | Sv | IP | H | K | ERA | WHIP | K/9 | BB/9 | HR/9 | GB/F | $1L | $2L | Pts | RAA | H% | HR/fb | S% | FIP | GS | CG | QS/DS | GR | Hld | Bln | Lead | OPS | 1st Hf | 2nd Hf | vs RH | vs LH |
|---|---|---|---|---|---|---|---|---|---|---|---|---|---|---|---|---|---|---|---|---|---|---|---|---|---|---|---|---|---|---|---|---|---|
| 07 | — | — | — | — | — | — | — | — | — | — | — | — | — | — | — | — | — | — | — | — | — | — | — | — | — | — | — | — | — | — | — | — | — |
| 08 | — | — | — | — | — | — | — | — | — | — | — | — | — | — | — | — | — | — | — | — | — | — | — | — | — | — | — | — | — | — | — | — | — |
| 09 | BAL | 2 | 4 | 0 | 66 | 71 | 48 | 4.05 | 1.25 | 6.5 | 1.6 | 0.9 | 0.6 | $2 | -$1 | 60 | −3 | 31% | 6% | 70% | 3.77 | 12 | 0 | 6/1 | — | — | — | — | .743 | .743 | — | .744 | .743 |
| 10 | BAL | 1 | 2 | 13 | 44 | 37 | 55 | 2.86 | 0.95 | 11.3 | 1.0 | 1.0 | 0.4 | $6 | $1 | 140 | +5 | 30% | 8% | 76% | 2.62 | — | — | — | 43 | 6 | 2 | +0.6 | .594 | .726 | .552 | .465 | .747 |

## Raul Valdes 40 IP | $-3 | 40 pts

RP-37, SP-1 Owned: 0% LH

Valdes made his MLB debut at age 32 after the Mets got him on loan from the Mexican League. But Valdes failed as a LOOGY – lefties hit .330 against him. Valdes can spot-start and pitch in long relief, so he could battle for a bullpen slot, but the Cuban defector is more likely to serve as organizational depth. (JL)

**Forecast**

| Player | Age | IP | W | Sv | K | ERA | WHIP | K/9 | BB/9 | $2L | Pts |
|---|---|---|---|---|---|---|---|---|---|---|---|
| Valdes R | 33 | 40 | 2 | 0 | 29 | 5.02 | 1.49 | 6.6 | 4.1 | -$3 | 40 |
| **Mini-Browser** | **Age** | **IP** | **W** | **Sv** | **K** | **ERA** | **WHIP** | **K/9** | **BB/9** | **$2L** | **Pts** |
| Feldman S | 28 | 160 | 9 | 0 | 84 | 5.13 | 1.51 | 4.7 | 3.3 | -$3 | 120 |
| Smith C | 29 | 40 | 1 | 0 | 32 | 5.15 | 1.41 | 7.3 | 3.0 | -$3 | 30 |
| McGee J | 24 | 50 | 2 | 0 | 53 | 5.15 | 1.67 | 9.6 | 4.7 | -$3 | 60 |
| Mickolio K | 26 | 40 | 1 | 0 | 44 | 4.94 | 1.69 | 9.8 | 5.0 | -$3 | 40 |
| Detwiler R | 25 | 100 | 5 | 0 | 76 | 4.55 | 1.57 | 6.9 | 3.9 | -$3 | 100 |

**Competition at RP** — Stats in 2010 as RP

| Thr | Player | GR | ERA | IP/G | Sv-Hld |
|---|---|---|---|---|---|
| LH | Feliciano P | 92 | 3.30 | 0.7 | 0-23 |
| LH | Takahashi H | 41 | 2.04 | 1.4 | 8-3 |
| LH | Valdes R | 37 | 5.23 | 1.4 | 1-1 |
| LH | Perez O | 10 | 9.00 | 1.3 | 0-0 |

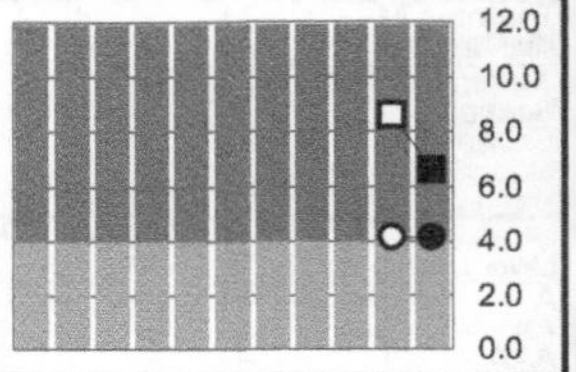


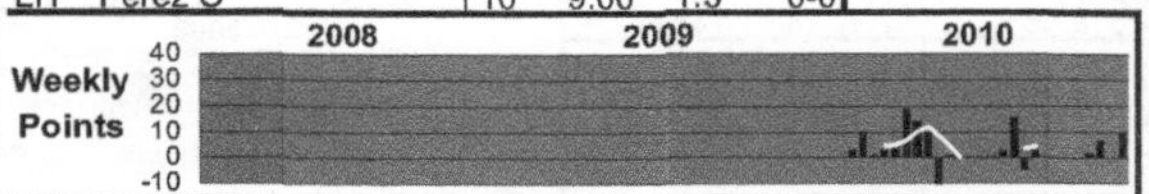


**Minors (2010)**

| Level | Leag | W | L | Sv | IP | H | K | ERA | WHIP | K/9 | BB/9 | HR/9 | GB/F |
|---|---|---|---|---|---|---|---|---|---|---|---|---|---|
| A | — | — | — | — | — | — | — | — | — | — | — | — | — |
| AA | — | — | — | — | — | — | — | — | — | — | — | — | — |
| AAA | IL | 2 | 1 | 0 | 36 | 34 | 36 | 3.00 | 1.19 | 9.0 | 2.3 | 0.8 | — |

**Majors**

| Yr | Team | W | L | Sv | IP | H | K | ERA | WHIP | K/9 | BB/9 | HR/9 | GB/F | $1L | $2L | Pts | RAA | H% | HR/fb | S% | FIP | GS | CG | QS/DS | GR | Hld | Bln | Lead | OPS | 1st Hf | 2nd Hf | vs RH | vs LH |
|---|---|---|---|---|---|---|---|---|---|---|---|---|---|---|---|---|---|---|---|---|---|---|---|---|---|---|---|---|---|---|---|---|---|
| 07 | — | — | — | — | — | — | — | — | — | — | — | — | — | — | — | — | — | — | — | — | — | — | — | — | — | — | — | — | — | — | — | — | — |
| 08 | — | — | — | — | — | — | — | — | — | — | — | — | — | — | — | — | — | — | — | — | — | — | — | — | — | — | — | — | — | — | — | — | — |
| 09 | — | — | — | — | — | — | — | — | — | — | — | — | — | — | — | — | — | — | — | — | — | — | — | — | — | — | — | — | — | — | — | — | — |
| 10 | NYM | 3 | 3 | 1 | 58 | 59 | 56 | 4.91 | 1.47 | 8.6 | 4.1 | 1.1 | 0.7 | -$5 | -$14 | 70 | −7 | 32% | 8% | 68% | 4.22 | 1 | 0 | 0/0 | 37 | 1 | 2 | −1.0 | .791 | .787 | .796 | .666 | .991 |

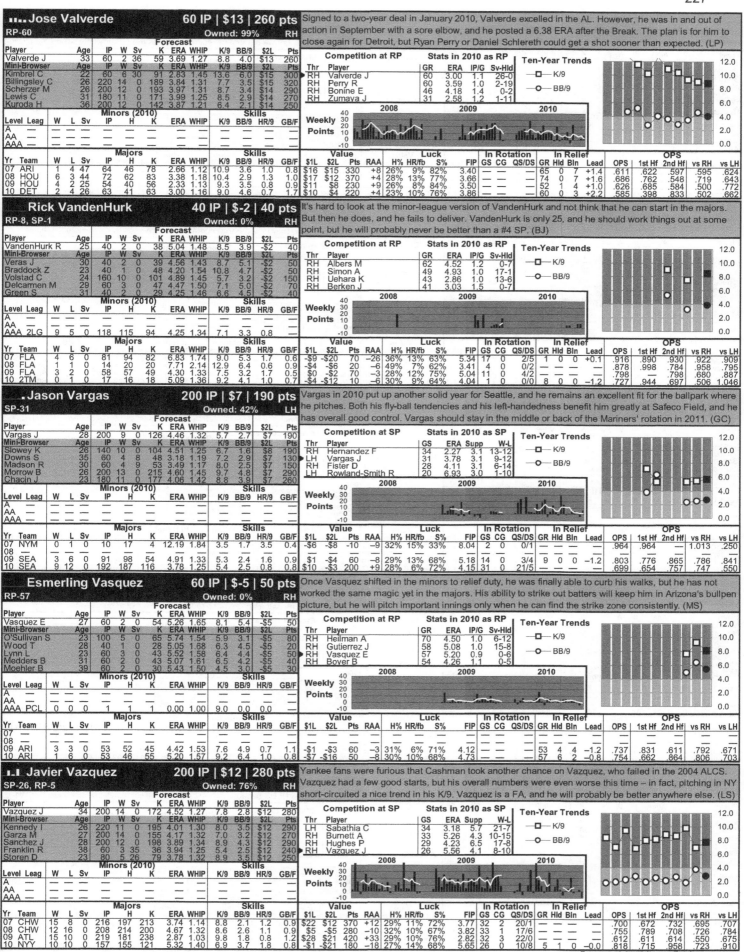

## Jose Valverde — 60 IP | $13 | 260 pts
RP-60 · Owned: 99% · RH

Signed to a two-year deal in January 2010, Valverde excelled in the AL. However, he was in and out of action in September with a sore elbow, and he posted a 6.38 ERA after the Break. The plan is for him to close again for Detroit, but Ryan Perry or Daniel Schlereth could get a shot sooner than expected. (LP)

### Forecast
| Player | Age | IP | W | Sv | K | ERA | WHIP | K/9 | BB/9 | $2L | Pts |
|---|---|---|---|---|---|---|---|---|---|---|---|
| Valverde J | 33 | 60 | 2 | 36 | 59 | 3.69 | 1.27 | 8.8 | 4.0 | $13 | 260 |

### Mini-Browser
| Player | Age | IP | W | Sv | K | ERA | WHIP | K/9 | BB/9 | $2L | Pts |
|---|---|---|---|---|---|---|---|---|---|---|---|
| Kimbrel C | 22 | 60 | 6 | 30 | 91 | 2.83 | 1.45 | 13.6 | 6.0 | $15 | 300 |
| Billingsley C | 26 | 220 | 14 | 0 | 189 | 3.84 | 1.27 | 7.7 | 3.5 | $15 | 320 |
| Scherzer M | 26 | 200 | 12 | 0 | 193 | 3.97 | 1.31 | 8.7 | 3.4 | $14 | 290 |
| Lewis C | 31 | 180 | 11 | 0 | 171 | 3.99 | 1.25 | 8.5 | 2.9 | $14 | 270 |
| Kuroda H | 36 | 200 | 12 | 0 | 142 | 3.87 | 1.21 | 6.4 | 2.1 | $14 | 250 |

### Competition at RP
| Thr | Player | GR | ERA | IP/G | Sv-Hld |
|---|---|---|---|---|---|
| RH | Valverde J | 60 | 3.00 | 1.1 | 26-0 |
| RH | Perry R | 60 | 3.59 | 1.0 | 2-19 |
| RH | Bonine E | 46 | 4.18 | 1.4 | 0-2 |
| RH | Zumaya J | 31 | 2.58 | 1.2 | 1-11 |

Ten-Year Trends: K/9, BB/9

### Majors
| Yr | Team | W | L | Sv | IP | H | K | ERA | WHIP | K/9 | BB/9 | HR/9 | GB/F |
|---|---|---|---|---|---|---|---|---|---|---|---|---|---|
| 07 | ARI | 1 | 4 | 47 | 64 | 46 | 78 | 2.66 | 1.12 | 10.9 | 3.6 | 1.0 | 0.8 |
| 08 | HOU | 6 | 3 | 44 | 72 | 62 | 83 | 3.38 | 1.18 | 10.4 | 2.9 | 1.3 | 1.0 |
| 09 | HOU | 4 | 2 | 25 | 54 | 40 | 56 | 2.33 | 1.13 | 9.3 | 3.5 | 0.8 | 0.9 |
| 10 | DET | 2 | 4 | 26 | 63 | 41 | 63 | 3.00 | 1.16 | 9.0 | 4.6 | 0.7 | 1.7 |

| $1L | $2L | Pts | RAA | H% | HR/fb | S% | FIP | GS | CG | QS/DS | GR | Hld | Bln | Lead | OPS | 1st Hf | 2nd Hf | vs RH | vs LH |
|---|---|---|---|---|---|---|---|---|---|---|---|---|---|---|---|---|---|---|---|
| $16 | $15 | 330 | +8 | 26% | 9% | 82% | 3.40 | — | — | — | 65 | 0 | 7 | +1.4 | .611 | .622 | .597 | .595 | .624 |
| $17 | $12 | 370 | +4 | 28% | 13% | 77% | 3.66 | — | — | — | 74 | 6 | 7 | +1.6 | .686 | .762 | .548 | .719 | .643 |
| $12 | $8 | 230 | +9 | 26% | 8% | 84% | 3.50 | — | — | — | 52 | 1 | 4 | +1.0 | .626 | .685 | .584 | .500 | .772 |
| $10 | $4 | 220 | +4 | 23% | 10% | 76% | 3.86 | — | — | — | 60 | 0 | 3 | +2.2 | .585 | .398 | .833 | .502 | .662 |

## Rick VandenHurk — 40 IP | $-2 | 40 pts
RP-8, SP-1 · Owned: 0% · RH

It's hard to look at the minor-league version of VandenHurk and not think that he can start in the majors. But then he does, and he fails to deliver. VandenHurk is only 25, and he should work things out at some point, but he will probably never be better than a #4 SP. (BJ)

### Forecast
| Player | Age | IP | W | Sv | K | ERA | WHIP | K/9 | BB/9 | $2L | Pts |
|---|---|---|---|---|---|---|---|---|---|---|---|
| VandenHurk R | 25 | 40 | 2 | 0 | 38 | 5.04 | 1.48 | 8.5 | 3.9 | -$2 | 40 |

### Mini-Browser
| Player | Age | IP | W | Sv | K | ERA | WHIP | K/9 | BB/9 | $2L | Pts |
|---|---|---|---|---|---|---|---|---|---|---|---|
| Veras J | 30 | 40 | 2 | 0 | 39 | 4.56 | 1.43 | 8.7 | 5.1 | -$2 | 50 |
| Braddock Z | 23 | 40 | 1 | 0 | 48 | 4.20 | 1.54 | 10.8 | 4.7 | -$2 | 50 |
| Volstad C | 24 | 160 | 10 | 0 | 101 | 4.89 | 1.45 | 5.7 | 3.2 | -$2 | 150 |
| Delcarmen M | 29 | 60 | 3 | 0 | 47 | 4.47 | 1.50 | 7.1 | 5.0 | -$2 | 40 |
| Green S | 31 | 40 | 2 | 0 | 29 | 4.25 | 1.46 | 6.6 | 4.5 | -$2 | 40 |

### Competition at RP
| Thr | Player | GR | ERA | IP/G | Sv-Hld |
|---|---|---|---|---|---|
| RH | Albers M | 62 | 4.52 | 1.2 | 0-7 |
| RH | Simon A | 49 | 4.93 | 1.0 | 17-1 |
| RH | Uehara K | 43 | 2.86 | 1.0 | 13-6 |
| RH | Berken J | 41 | 3.03 | 1.5 | 0-7 |

Ten-Year Trends: K/9, BB/9

### Majors
| Yr | Team | W | L | Sv | IP | H | K | ERA | WHIP | K/9 | BB/9 | HR/9 | GB/F |
|---|---|---|---|---|---|---|---|---|---|---|---|---|---|
| 07 | FLA | 4 | 6 | 0 | 81 | 94 | 82 | 6.83 | 1.74 | 9.0 | 5.3 | 1.7 | 0.6 |
| 08 | FLA | 1 | 1 | 0 | 14 | 20 | 20 | 7.71 | 2.14 | 12.9 | 6.4 | 0.6 | 0.9 |
| 09 | FLA | 3 | 2 | 0 | 58 | 57 | 49 | 4.30 | 1.33 | 7.5 | 3.2 | 1.7 | 0.8 |
| 10 | 2TM | 0 | 0 | 0 | 17 | 16 | 18 | 5.09 | 1.36 | 9.2 | 4.1 | 1.0 | 0.7 |

| $1L | $2L | Pts | RAA | H% | HR/fb | S% | FIP | GS | CG | QS/DS | GR | Hld | Bln | Lead | OPS | 1st Hf | 2nd Hf | vs RH | vs LH |
|---|---|---|---|---|---|---|---|---|---|---|---|---|---|---|---|---|---|---|---|
| -$9 | -$20 | 70 | -26 | 36% | 13% | 63% | 5.34 | 17 | 0 | 2/5 | 1 | 0 | 0 | +0.1 | .916 | .890 | .930 | .922 | .909 |
| -$4 | -$6 | 20 | -6 | 49% | 7% | 62% | 3.41 | 4 | 0 | 0/2 | — | — | — | — | .878 | .998 | .784 | .958 | .795 |
| -$0 | -$2 | 70 | -3 | 28% | 12% | 75% | 5.04 | 11 | 0 | 4/2 | — | — | — | — | .798 | — | .798 | .680 | .887 |
| -$4 | -$12 | 10 | -6 | 30% | 9% | 64% | 4.04 | 3 | 0 | 0/0 | 0 | 0 | 0 | -1.2 | .727 | .944 | .697 | .506 | 1.046 |

## Jason Vargas — 200 IP | $7 | 190 pts
SP-31 · Owned: 42% · LH

Vargas in 2010 put up another solid year for Seattle, and he remains an excellent fit for the ballpark where he pitches. Both his fly-ball tendencies and his left-handedness benefit him greatly at Safeco Field, and he has overall good control. Vargas should stay in the middle or back of the Mariners' rotation in 2011. (GC)

### Forecast
| Player | Age | IP | W | Sv | K | ERA | WHIP | K/9 | BB/9 | $2L | Pts |
|---|---|---|---|---|---|---|---|---|---|---|---|
| Vargas J | 28 | 200 | 9 | 0 | 126 | 4.46 | 1.32 | 5.7 | 2.7 | $7 | 190 |

### Mini-Browser
| Player | Age | IP | W | Sv | K | ERA | WHIP | K/9 | BB/9 | $2L | Pts |
|---|---|---|---|---|---|---|---|---|---|---|---|
| Slowey K | 26 | 140 | 10 | 0 | 104 | 4.51 | 1.25 | 6.7 | 1.6 | $8 | 190 |
| Downs S | 35 | 60 | 4 | 8 | 48 | 3.18 | 1.19 | 7.2 | 2.9 | $7 | 130 |
| Madson R | 30 | 60 | 4 | 9 | 53 | 3.49 | 1.17 | 8.0 | 2.5 | $7 | 150 |
| Morrow B | 26 | 200 | 13 | 0 | 215 | 4.60 | 1.45 | 9.7 | 4.8 | $7 | 290 |
| Chacin J | 23 | 180 | 11 | 0 | 177 | 4.06 | 1.42 | 8.8 | 3.9 | $7 | 260 |

### Competition at SP
| Thr | Player | GS | ERA | Supp | W-L |
|---|---|---|---|---|---|
| RH | Hernandez F | 34 | 2.27 | 3.1 | 13-12 |
| LH | Vargas J | 31 | 3.78 | 3.1 | 9-12 |
| RH | Fister D | 28 | 4.11 | 3.1 | 6-14 |
| LH | Rowland-Smith R | 20 | 6.93 | 3.0 | 1-10 |

Ten-Year Trends: K/9, BB/9

### Majors
| Yr | Team | W | L | Sv | IP | H | K | ERA | WHIP | K/9 | BB/9 | HR/9 | GB/F |
|---|---|---|---|---|---|---|---|---|---|---|---|---|---|
| 07 | NYM | 0 | 1 | 0 | 10 | 17 | 4 | 12.19 | 1.84 | 3.5 | 1.7 | 3.5 | 0.4 |
| 08 | — | | | | | | | | | | | | |
| 09 | SEA | 3 | 6 | 0 | 91 | 98 | 54 | 4.91 | 1.35 | 5.3 | 2.4 | 1.6 | 0.9 |
| 10 | SEA | 9 | 12 | 0 | 192 | 187 | 116 | 3.78 | 1.25 | 5.4 | 2.5 | 0.8 | 0.8 |

| $1L | $2L | Pts | RAA | H% | HR/fb | S% | FIP | GS | CG | QS/DS | GR | Hld | Bln | Lead | OPS | 1st Hf | 2nd Hf | vs RH | vs LH |
|---|---|---|---|---|---|---|---|---|---|---|---|---|---|---|---|---|---|---|---|
| -$6 | -$8 | -10 | -9 | 32% | 15% | 33% | 8.04 | 2 | 0 | 0/1 | — | — | — | — | .964 | .964 | — | 1.013 | .250 |
| -$4 | -$4 | 60 | -8 | 29% | 13% | 68% | 5.18 | 14 | 0 | 3/4 | 9 | 0 | 0 | -1.2 | .803 | .776 | .865 | .786 | .841 |
| $10 | -$3 | 200 | +9 | 28% | 6% | 72% | 4.15 | 31 | 0 | 21/5 | — | — | — | — | .699 | .654 | .757 | .747 | .550 |

## Esmerling Vasquez — 60 IP | $-5 | 50 pts
RP-57 · Owned: 0% · RH

Once Vasquez shifted in the minors to relief duty, he was finally able to curb his walks, but he has not worked the same magic yet in the majors. His ability to strike out batters will keep him in Arizona's bullpen picture, but he will pitch important innings only when he can find the strike zone consistently. (MS)

### Forecast
| Player | Age | IP | W | Sv | K | ERA | WHIP | K/9 | BB/9 | $2L | Pts |
|---|---|---|---|---|---|---|---|---|---|---|---|
| Vasquez E | 27 | 60 | 2 | 0 | 54 | 5.26 | 1.65 | 8.1 | 5.4 | -$5 | 50 |

### Mini-Browser
| Player | Age | IP | W | Sv | K | ERA | WHIP | K/9 | BB/9 | $2L | Pts |
|---|---|---|---|---|---|---|---|---|---|---|---|
| O'Sullivan S | 23 | 100 | 5 | 0 | 65 | 5.74 | 1.54 | 5.9 | 3.1 | -$5 | 80 |
| Wood T | 28 | 40 | 1 | 0 | 28 | 5.05 | 1.68 | 6.3 | 4.5 | -$5 | 20 |
| Lynn L | 23 | 60 | 3 | 0 | 43 | 5.52 | 1.58 | 6.4 | 4.4 | -$5 | 50 |
| Medders B | 31 | 60 | 2 | 0 | 43 | 5.07 | 1.61 | 6.5 | 4.2 | -$5 | 40 |
| Moehler B | 39 | 60 | 2 | 0 | 30 | 5.43 | 1.50 | 4.5 | 3.0 | -$5 | 30 |

### Competition at RP
| Thr | Player | GR | ERA | IP/G | Sv-Hld |
|---|---|---|---|---|---|
| RH | Heilman A | 70 | 4.50 | 1.0 | 6-12 |
| RH | Gutierrez J | 58 | 5.08 | 1.0 | 15-8 |
| RH | Vasquez E | 57 | 5.20 | 0.9 | 0-6 |
| RH | Boyer B | 54 | 4.26 | 1.1 | 0-5 |

Ten-Year Trends: K/9, BB/9

### Majors
| Yr | Team | W | L | Sv | IP | H | K | ERA | WHIP | K/9 | BB/9 | HR/9 | GB/F |
|---|---|---|---|---|---|---|---|---|---|---|---|---|---|
| 07 | — | | | | | | | | | | | | |
| 08 | — | | | | | | | | | | | | |
| 09 | ARI | 3 | 3 | 0 | 53 | 52 | 45 | 4.42 | 1.53 | 7.6 | 4.9 | 0.7 | 1.1 |
| 10 | ARI | 0 | 0 | 0 | 53 | 46 | 55 | 5.20 | 1.57 | 9.2 | 4.6 | 1.0 | 0.8 |

| $1L | $2L | Pts | RAA | H% | HR/fb | S% | FIP | GS | CG | QS/DS | GR | Hld | Bln | Lead | OPS | 1st Hf | 2nd Hf | vs RH | vs LH |
|---|---|---|---|---|---|---|---|---|---|---|---|---|---|---|---|---|---|---|---|
| -$1 | -$3 | 60 | -3 | 31% | 6% | 71% | 4.12 | — | — | — | 53 | 4 | 4 | -1.2 | .737 | .831 | .611 | .792 | .671 |
| -$4 | -$12 | 50 | -6 | 30% | 10% | 66% | 4.73 | — | — | — | 57 | 6 | 2 | -0.0 | .754 | .662 | .864 | .806 | .703 |

## Javier Vazquez — 200 IP | $12 | 280 pts
SP-26, RP-5 · Owned: 76% · RH

Yankee fans were furious that Cashman took another chance on Vazquez, who failed in the 2004 ALCS. Vazquez had a few good starts, but his overall numbers were even worse this time — in fact, pitching in NY short-circuited a nice trend in his K/9. Vazquez is a FA, and he will probably be better anywhere else. (LS)

### Forecast
| Player | Age | IP | W | Sv | K | ERA | WHIP | K/9 | BB/9 | $2L | Pts |
|---|---|---|---|---|---|---|---|---|---|---|---|
| Vazquez J | 34 | 200 | 14 | 0 | 172 | 4.52 | 1.27 | 7.8 | 2.8 | $12 | 280 |

### Mini-Browser
| Player | Age | IP | W | Sv | K | ERA | WHIP | K/9 | BB/9 | $2L | Pts |
|---|---|---|---|---|---|---|---|---|---|---|---|
| Kennedy I | 26 | 220 | 11 | 0 | 195 | 4.01 | 1.30 | 8.0 | 3.5 | $12 | 290 |
| Garza M | 27 | 200 | 14 | 0 | 155 | 4.17 | 1.32 | 7.0 | 3.2 | $12 | 270 |
| Sanchez J | 28 | 200 | 12 | 0 | 198 | 3.89 | 1.34 | 8.9 | 4.3 | $12 | 290 |
| Franklin R | 38 | 60 | 3 | 35 | 36 | 3.94 | 1.25 | 5.4 | 2.5 | $12 | 240 |
| Storen D | 23 | 80 | 5 | 26 | 79 | 3.78 | 1.34 | 8.9 | 3.3 | $12 | 250 |

### Competition at SP
| Thr | Player | GS | ERA | Supp | W-L |
|---|---|---|---|---|---|
| LH | Sabathia C | 34 | 3.18 | 5.7 | 21-7 |
| RH | Burnett A | 33 | 5.26 | 4.3 | 10-15 |
| RH | Hughes P | 29 | 4.23 | 6.5 | 17-8 |
| RH | Vazquez J | 26 | 5.56 | 4.1 | 8-10 |

Ten-Year Trends: K/9, BB/9

### Majors
| Yr | Team | W | L | Sv | IP | H | K | ERA | WHIP | K/9 | BB/9 | HR/9 | GB/F |
|---|---|---|---|---|---|---|---|---|---|---|---|---|---|
| 07 | CHW | 15 | 8 | 0 | 216 | 197 | 213 | 3.74 | 1.14 | 8.8 | 2.1 | 1.2 | 0.9 |
| 08 | CHW | 12 | 16 | 0 | 208 | 214 | 200 | 4.67 | 1.32 | 8.6 | 2.6 | 1.1 | 0.9 |
| 09 | ATL | 15 | 10 | 0 | 219 | 181 | 238 | 2.87 | 1.03 | 9.8 | 1.8 | 0.8 | 1.2 |
| 10 | NYY | 10 | 10 | 0 | 157 | 155 | 121 | 5.32 | 1.40 | 6.9 | 3.7 | 1.8 | 0.8 |

| $1L | $2L | Pts | RAA | H% | HR/fb | S% | FIP | GS | CG | QS/DS | GR | Hld | Bln | Lead | OPS | 1st Hf | 2nd Hf | vs RH | vs LH |
|---|---|---|---|---|---|---|---|---|---|---|---|---|---|---|---|---|---|---|---|
| $22 | $12 | 370 | +12 | 29% | 11% | 72% | 3.77 | 32 | 2 | 20/1 | — | — | — | — | .700 | .672 | .732 | .695 | .707 |
| $5 | -$5 | 280 | -10 | 32% | 10% | 67% | 3.82 | 33 | 1 | 17/6 | — | — | — | — | .755 | .789 | .708 | .726 | .784 |
| $28 | $21 | 420 | +33 | 29% | 10% | 76% | 2.82 | 32 | 3 | 22/0 | — | — | — | — | .612 | .611 | .614 | .550 | .675 |
| -$4 | -$21 | 180 | -18 | 27% | 14% | 68% | 5.65 | 26 | 0 | 10/8 | 5 | 1 | 0 | -0.0 | .818 | .715 | .958 | .723 | .910 |

*For more stats, visit www.Rotolympus.com.*

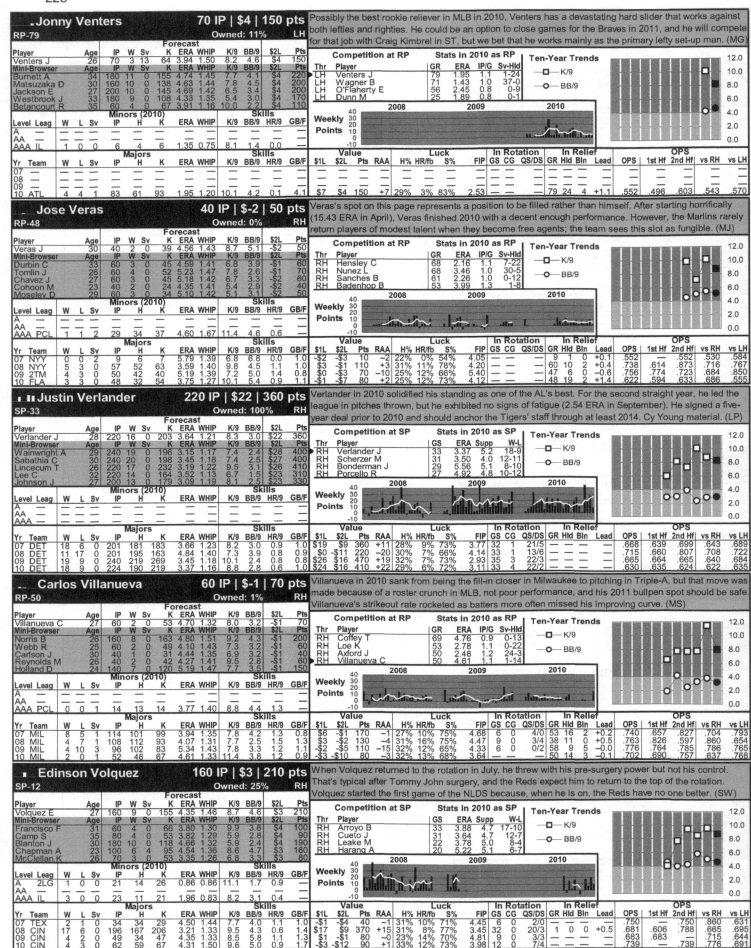

## Jonny Venters — 70 IP | $4 | 150 pts

RP-79    Owned: 11%    LH

Possibly the best rookie reliever in MLB in 2010, Venters has a devastating hard slider that works against both lefties and righties. He could be an option to close games for the Braves in 2011, and he will compete for that job with Craig Kimbrel in ST, but we bet that he works mainly as the primary lefty set-up man. (MG)

### Forecast

| Player | Age | IP | W | Sv | K | ERA | WHIP | K/9 | BB/9 | $2L | Pts |
|---|---|---|---|---|---|---|---|---|---|---|---|
| Venters J | 26 | 70 | 3 | 13 | 64 | 3.94 | 1.50 | 8.2 | 4.6 | $4 | 150 |
| Mini-Browser | Age | IP | W | Sv | K | ERA | WHIP | K/9 | BB/9 | $2L | Pts |
| Burnett A | 34 | 180 | 11 | 0 | 155 | 4.74 | 1.45 | 7.7 | 4.1 | $4 | 220 |
| Matsuzaka D | 30 | 160 | 10 | 0 | 138 | 4.63 | 1.44 | 7.8 | 4.5 | $4 | 200 |
| Jackson E | 27 | 200 | 10 | 0 | 145 | 4.69 | 1.42 | 6.5 | 3.4 | $4 | 200 |
| Westbrook J | 33 | 180 | 9 | 0 | 108 | 4.33 | 1.35 | 5.4 | 3.0 | $4 | 170 |
| Betancourt R | 35 | 60 | 4 | 0 | 67 | 3.91 | 1.16 | 10.0 | 2.2 | $4 | 110 |

### Competition at RP / Stats in 2010 as RP

| Thr | Player | GR | ERA | IP/G | Sv-Hld |
|---|---|---|---|---|---|
| LH | Venters J | 79 | 1.95 | 1.1 | 1-24 |
| LH | Wagner B | 71 | 1.43 | 1.0 | 37-0 |
| LH | O'Flaherty E | 56 | 2.45 | 0.8 | 0-9 |
| LH | Dunn M | 25 | 1.89 | 0.8 | 0-1 |

Ten-Year Trends: K/9, BB/9

### Minors (2010) / Skills

| Level Leag | W | L | Sv | IP | H | K | ERA | WHIP | K/9 | BB/9 | HR/9 | GB/F |
|---|---|---|---|---|---|---|---|---|---|---|---|---|
| A | — | | | | | | | | | | | — |
| AA | — | | | | | | | | | | | — |
| AAA IL | 1 | 0 | 0 | 6 | 4 | 6 | 1.35 | 0.75 | 8.1 | 1.4 | 0.0 | — |

### Majors / Skills / Value / Luck / In Rotation / In Relief / OPS

| Yr Team | W | L | Sv | IP | H | K | ERA | WHIP | K/9 | BB/9 | HR/9 | GB/F | $1L | $2L | Pts | RAA | H% | HR/fb | S% | FIP | GS | CG | QS/DS | GR | Hld | Bln | Lead | OPS | 1st Hf | 2nd Hf | vs RH | vs LH |
|---|---|---|---|---|---|---|---|---|---|---|---|---|---|---|---|---|---|---|---|---|---|---|---|---|---|---|---|---|---|---|---|---|
| 07 | — | | | | | | | | | | | | | | | | | | | | | | | | | | | | | | | |
| 08 | — | | | | | | | | | | | | | | | | | | | | | | | | | | | | | | | |
| 09 | — | | | | | | | | | | | | | | | | | | | | | | | | | | | | | | | |
| 10 ATL | 4 | 4 | 1 | 83 | 61 | 93 | 1.95 | 1.20 | 10.1 | 4.2 | 0.1 | 4.1 | $7 | $4 | 150 | +7 | 29% | 3% | 83% | 2.53 | — | — | — | 79 | 24 | 4 | +1.1 | .552 | .496 | .603 | .543 | .570 |

## Jose Veras — 40 IP | $-2 | 50 pts

RP-48    Owned: 0%    RH

Veras's spot on this page represents a position to be filled rather than himself. After starting horrifically (15.43 ERA in April), Veras finished 2010 with a decent enough performance. However, the Marlins rarely return players of modest talent when they become free agents; the team sees this slot as fungible. (MJ)

### Forecast

| Player | Age | IP | W | Sv | K | ERA | WHIP | K/9 | BB/9 | $2L | Pts |
|---|---|---|---|---|---|---|---|---|---|---|---|
| Veras J | 30 | 40 | 2 | 0 | 39 | 4.56 | 1.43 | 8.7 | 5.1 | -$2 | 50 |
| Mini-Browser | Age | IP | W | Sv | K | ERA | WHIP | K/9 | BB/9 | $2L | Pts |
| Durbin C | 33 | 60 | 3 | 0 | 45 | 4.59 | 1.41 | 6.8 | 3.9 | -$1 | 60 |
| Tomlin J | 26 | 60 | 4 | 0 | 52 | 5.23 | 1.47 | 7.8 | 2.6 | -$1 | 70 |
| Chavez J | 27 | 60 | 3 | 0 | 45 | 5.18 | 1.42 | 6.7 | 3.3 | -$2 | 60 |
| Cohoon M | 23 | 40 | 2 | 0 | 24 | 4.35 | 1.41 | 5.4 | 2.9 | -$2 | 40 |
| Moseley D | 29 | 60 | 3 | 0 | 34 | 5.10 | 1.42 | 5.1 | 3.1 | -$2 | 50 |

### Competition at RP / Stats in 2010 as RP

| Thr | Player | GR | ERA | IP/G | Sv-Hld |
|---|---|---|---|---|---|
| RH | Hensley C | 68 | 2.16 | 1.1 | 7-22 |
| RH | Nunez L | 68 | 3.46 | 1.0 | 30-5 |
| RH | Sanches B | 61 | 2.26 | 1.0 | 0-12 |
| RH | Badenhop B | 53 | 3.99 | 1.3 | 1-8 |

Ten-Year Trends: K/9, BB/9

### Minors (2010) / Skills

| Level Leag | W | L | Sv | IP | H | K | ERA | WHIP | K/9 | BB/9 | HR/9 | GB/F |
|---|---|---|---|---|---|---|---|---|---|---|---|---|
| A | — | | | | | | | | | | | — |
| AA | — | | | | | | | | | | | — |
| AAA PCL | 1 | 1 | 2 | 29 | 34 | 37 | 4.60 | 1.67 | 11.4 | 4.6 | 0.6 | — |

### Majors / Skills / Value / Luck / In Rotation / In Relief / OPS

| Yr Team | W | L | Sv | IP | H | K | ERA | WHIP | K/9 | BB/9 | HR/9 | GB/F | $1L | $2L | Pts | RAA | H% | HR/fb | S% | FIP | GS | CG | QS/DS | GR | Hld | Bln | Lead | OPS | 1st Hf | 2nd Hf | vs RH | vs LH |
|---|---|---|---|---|---|---|---|---|---|---|---|---|---|---|---|---|---|---|---|---|---|---|---|---|---|---|---|---|---|---|---|---|
| 07 NYY | 0 | 0 | 2 | 9 | 6 | 7 | 5.79 | 1.39 | 6.8 | 6.8 | 0.0 | 1.0 | -$2 | -$3 | 10 | -2 | 22% | 0% | 54% | 4.05 | — | — | — | 9 | 1 | 0 | +0.1 | .552 | — | .552 | .530 | .584 |
| 08 NYY | 5 | 3 | 0 | 57 | 52 | 63 | 3.59 | 1.40 | 9.8 | 4.5 | 1.1 | 1.0 | -$3 | -$1 | 110 | +3 | 31% | 11% | 78% | 4.20 | — | — | — | 60 | 10 | 2 | +0.4 | .738 | .614 | .873 | .716 | .767 |
| 09 2TM | 3 | 3 | 0 | 50 | 42 | 40 | 5.19 | 1.39 | 7.2 | 5.0 | 1.4 | 0.8 | $0 | -$3 | 70 | -10 | 25% | 12% | 66% | 5.40 | — | — | — | 47 | 6 | 0 | -0.6 | .756 | .774 | .723 | .684 | .850 |
| 10 FLA | 3 | 3 | 0 | 48 | 32 | 54 | 3.75 | 1.27 | 10.1 | 5.4 | 0.9 | 1.1 | -$1 | -$7 | 80 | +2 | 25% | 12% | 73% | 4.12 | — | — | — | 48 | 19 | 2 | +1.4 | .622 | .594 | .633 | .686 | .555 |

## Justin Verlander — 220 IP | $22 | 360 pts

SP-33    Owned: 100%    RH

Verlander in 2010 solidified his standing as one of the AL's best. For the second straight year, he led the league in pitches thrown, but he exhibited no signs of fatigue (2.54 ERA in September). He signed a five-year deal prior to 2010 and should anchor the Tigers' staff through at least 2014. Cy Young material. (LP)

### Forecast

| Player | Age | IP | W | Sv | K | ERA | WHIP | K/9 | BB/9 | $2L | Pts |
|---|---|---|---|---|---|---|---|---|---|---|---|
| Verlander J | 28 | 220 | 16 | 0 | 203 | 3.64 | 1.21 | 8.3 | 3.0 | $22 | 360 |
| Mini-Browser | Age | IP | W | Sv | K | ERA | WHIP | K/9 | BB/9 | $2L | Pts |
| Wainwright A | 29 | 240 | 19 | 0 | 196 | 3.15 | 1.17 | 7.4 | 2.4 | $28 | 400 |
| Sabathia C | 30 | 240 | 20 | 0 | 198 | 3.45 | 1.18 | 7.4 | 2.5 | $27 | 400 |
| Lincecum T | 26 | 220 | 17 | 0 | 232 | 3.19 | 1.22 | 9.5 | 3.0 | $26 | 410 |
| Lee C | 32 | 220 | 14 | 0 | 164 | 3.52 | 1.13 | 6.7 | 1.5 | $23 | 310 |
| Johnson J | 27 | 200 | 12 | 0 | 179 | 3.09 | 1.19 | 8.1 | 2.5 | $23 | 330 |

### Competition at SP / Stats in 2010 as SP

| Thr | Player | GS | ERA | Supp | W-L |
|---|---|---|---|---|---|
| RH | Verlander J | 33 | 3.37 | 5.2 | 18-9 |
| RH | Scherzer M | 31 | 3.50 | 4.0 | 12-11 |
| RH | Bonderman J | 29 | 5.56 | 5.1 | 8-10 |
| RH | Porcello R | 27 | 4.92 | 4.8 | 10-12 |

Ten-Year Trends: K/9, BB/9

### Minors (2010) / Skills

| Level Leag | W | L | Sv | IP | H | K | ERA | WHIP | K/9 | BB/9 | HR/9 | GB/F |
|---|---|---|---|---|---|---|---|---|---|---|---|---|
| A | — | | | | | | | | | | | — |
| AA | — | | | | | | | | | | | — |
| AAA | — | | | | | | | | | | | — |

### Majors / Skills / Value / Luck / In Rotation / In Relief / OPS

| Yr Team | W | L | Sv | IP | H | K | ERA | WHIP | K/9 | BB/9 | HR/9 | GB/F | $1L | $2L | Pts | RAA | H% | HR/fb | S% | FIP | GS | CG | QS/DS | GR | Hld | Bln | Lead | OPS | 1st Hf | 2nd Hf | vs RH | vs LH |
|---|---|---|---|---|---|---|---|---|---|---|---|---|---|---|---|---|---|---|---|---|---|---|---|---|---|---|---|---|---|---|---|---|
| 07 DET | 18 | 6 | 0 | 201 | 181 | 183 | 3.66 | 1.23 | 8.2 | 3.0 | 0.9 | 1.0 | $19 | -$9 | 360 | +11 | 28% | 9% | 73% | 3.77 | 32 | 1 | 21/5 | — | — | — | — | .668 | .639 | .699 | .643 | .689 |
| 08 DET | 11 | 17 | 0 | 201 | 195 | 163 | 4.84 | 1.40 | 7.3 | 3.9 | 0.8 | 1.0 | $0 | -$11 | 220 | -20 | 30% | 7% | 66% | 4.14 | 33 | 1 | 13/6 | — | — | — | — | .715 | .660 | .807 | .708 | .722 |
| 09 DET | 19 | 9 | 0 | 240 | 219 | 269 | 3.45 | 1.18 | 10.1 | 2.4 | 0.8 | 0.8 | $26 | $16 | 470 | +19 | 32% | 7% | 73% | 2.93 | 35 | 3 | 22/3 | — | — | — | — | .665 | .664 | .665 | .640 | .684 |
| 10 DET | 18 | 9 | 0 | 224 | 190 | 219 | 3.37 | 1.16 | 8.8 | 2.8 | 0.6 | 1.0 | $24 | $16 | 410 | +22 | 29% | 6% | 72% | 3.11 | 33 | 4 | 22/3 | — | — | — | — | .630 | .635 | .624 | .622 | .635 |

## Carlos Villanueva — 60 IP | $-1 | 70 pts

RP-50    Owned: 1%    RH

Villanueva in 2010 sank from being the fill-in closer in Milwaukee to pitching in Triple-A, but that move was made because of a roster crunch in MLB, not poor performance, and his 2011 bullpen spot should be safe. Villanueva's strikeout rate rocketed as batters more often missed his improving curve. (MS)

### Forecast

| Player | Age | IP | W | Sv | K | ERA | WHIP | K/9 | BB/9 | $2L | Pts |
|---|---|---|---|---|---|---|---|---|---|---|---|
| Villanueva C | 27 | 60 | 2 | 0 | 53 | 4.70 | 1.32 | 8.0 | 3.2 | -$1 | 70 |
| Mini-Browser | Age | IP | W | Sv | K | ERA | WHIP | K/9 | BB/9 | $2L | Pts |
| Norris B | 26 | 160 | 8 | 0 | 163 | 4.80 | 1.51 | 9.2 | 4.3 | -$1 | 200 |
| Webb R | 25 | 60 | 2 | 0 | 49 | 4.10 | 1.43 | 7.3 | 3.2 | -$1 | 60 |
| Carlson J | 30 | 40 | 1 | 0 | 31 | 4.44 | 1.35 | 6.9 | 3.2 | -$1 | 40 |
| Reynolds M | 26 | 40 | 2 | 0 | 42 | 4.27 | 1.41 | 9.5 | 2.8 | -$1 | 60 |
| Holland D | 24 | 140 | 7 | 0 | 120 | 5.19 | 1.47 | 7.7 | 3.5 | -$1 | 150 |

### Competition at RP / Stats in 2010 as RP

| Thr | Player | GR | ERA | IP/G | Sv-Hld |
|---|---|---|---|---|---|
| RH | Coffey T | 69 | 4.76 | 0.9 | 0-13 |
| RH | Loe K | 53 | 2.78 | 1.1 | 0-22 |
| RH | Axford J | 50 | 2.48 | 1.2 | 24-3 |
| RH | Villanueva C | 50 | 4.61 | 1.1 | 1-14 |

Ten-Year Trends: K/9, BB/9

### Minors (2010) / Skills

| Level Leag | W | L | Sv | IP | H | K | ERA | WHIP | K/9 | BB/9 | HR/9 | GB/F |
|---|---|---|---|---|---|---|---|---|---|---|---|---|
| A | — | | | | | | | | | | | — |
| AA | — | | | | | | | | | | | — |
| AAA PCL | 0 | 0 | 1 | 14 | 13 | 14 | 3.77 | 1.40 | 8.8 | 4.4 | 1.3 | — |

### Majors / Skills / Value / Luck / In Rotation / In Relief / OPS

| Yr Team | W | L | Sv | IP | H | K | ERA | WHIP | K/9 | BB/9 | HR/9 | GB/F | $1L | $2L | Pts | RAA | H% | HR/fb | S% | FIP | GS | CG | QS/DS | GR | Hld | Bln | Lead | OPS | 1st Hf | 2nd Hf | vs RH | vs LH |
|---|---|---|---|---|---|---|---|---|---|---|---|---|---|---|---|---|---|---|---|---|---|---|---|---|---|---|---|---|---|---|---|---|
| 07 MIL | 8 | 5 | 1 | 114 | 101 | 99 | 3.94 | 1.35 | 7.8 | 4.2 | 1.3 | 0.8 | $6 | -$1 | 170 | -1 | 27% | 10% | 75% | 4.68 | 6 | 0 | 4/0 | 53 | 16 | 2 | +0.2 | .740 | .657 | .827 | .704 | .793 |
| 08 MIL | 4 | 7 | 1 | 108 | 112 | 93 | 4.07 | 1.31 | 7.7 | 2.5 | 1.5 | 1.3 | $3 | -$2 | 130 | -4 | 31% | 16% | 75% | 4.47 | 9 | 0 | 3/4 | 38 | 11 | 0 | +0.5 | .763 | .826 | .597 | .860 | .654 |
| 09 MIL | 4 | 10 | 3 | 96 | 102 | 83 | 5.34 | 1.43 | 7.8 | 3.3 | 1.2 | 1.1 | -$2 | -$5 | 110 | -15 | 32% | 12% | 65% | 4.33 | 6 | 0 | 0/2 | 58 | 9 | 5 | -0.0 | .776 | .764 | .785 | .786 | .765 |
| 10 MIL | 2 | 3 | 0 | 52 | 48 | 67 | 4.61 | 1.33 | 11.4 | 3.8 | 1.2 | 0.9 | -$3 | -$10 | 80 | -3 | 32% | 13% | 68% | 3.64 | — | — | — | 50 | 14 | 3 | -0.1 | .702 | .590 | .757 | .693 | .718 |

## Edinson Volquez — 160 IP | $3 | 210 pts

SP-12    Owned: 25%    RH

When Volquez returned to the rotation in July, he threw with his pre-surgery power but not his control. That's typical after Tommy John surgery, and the Reds expect him to return to the top of the rotation. Volquez started the first game of the NLDS because, when he is on, the Reds have no one better. (SW)

### Forecast

| Player | Age | IP | W | Sv | K | ERA | WHIP | K/9 | BB/9 | $2L | Pts |
|---|---|---|---|---|---|---|---|---|---|---|---|
| Volquez E | 27 | 160 | 9 | 0 | 155 | 4.35 | 1.46 | 8.7 | 4.6 | $3 | 210 |
| Mini-Browser | Age | IP | W | Sv | K | ERA | WHIP | K/9 | BB/9 | $2L | Pts |
| Francisco F | 31 | 60 | 4 | 0 | 66 | 3.80 | 1.30 | 9.9 | 3.6 | $4 | 100 |
| Camp S | 35 | 80 | 4 | 0 | 53 | 3.82 | 1.29 | 5.9 | 2.8 | $4 | 90 |
| Blanton J | 30 | 180 | 10 | 0 | 118 | 4.66 | 1.32 | 5.9 | 2.4 | $4 | 190 |
| Chapman A | 23 | 100 | 6 | 4 | 95 | 4.54 | 1.36 | 8.6 | 4.7 | $3 | 160 |
| McClellan K | 26 | 70 | 3 | 0 | 53 | 3.35 | 1.26 | 6.8 | 3.3 | $3 | 80 |

### Competition at SP / Stats in 2010 as SP

| Thr | Player | GS | ERA | Supp | W-L |
|---|---|---|---|---|---|
| RH | Arroyo B | 33 | 3.88 | 4.7 | 17-10 |
| RH | Cueto J | 31 | 3.64 | 4.7 | 12-7 |
| RH | Leake M | 22 | 3.78 | 5.0 | 8-4 |
| RH | Harang A | 20 | 5.22 | 5.1 | 6-7 |

Ten-Year Trends: K/9, BB/9

### Minors (2010) / Skills

| Level Leag | W | L | Sv | IP | H | K | ERA | WHIP | K/9 | BB/9 | HR/9 | GB/F |
|---|---|---|---|---|---|---|---|---|---|---|---|---|
| A 2LG | 1 | 0 | 0 | 21 | 14 | 26 | 0.86 | 0.86 | 11.1 | 1.7 | 0.9 | — |
| AA | — | | | | | | | | | | | — |
| AAA IL | 3 | 0 | 0 | 23 | 11 | 21 | 1.96 | 0.83 | 8.2 | 3.1 | 0.4 | — |

### Majors / Skills / Value / Luck / In Rotation / In Relief / OPS

| Yr Team | W | L | Sv | IP | H | K | ERA | WHIP | K/9 | BB/9 | HR/9 | GB/F | $1L | $2L | Pts | RAA | H% | HR/fb | S% | FIP | GS | CG | QS/DS | GR | Hld | Bln | Lead | OPS | 1st Hf | 2nd Hf | vs RH | vs LH |
|---|---|---|---|---|---|---|---|---|---|---|---|---|---|---|---|---|---|---|---|---|---|---|---|---|---|---|---|---|---|---|---|---|
| 07 TEX | 2 | 1 | 0 | 34 | 34 | 29 | 4.50 | 1.44 | 7.7 | 4.0 | 1.0 | 1.0 | -$3 | -$4 | 40 | -1 | 31% | 10% | 70% | 4.45 | 6 | 0 | 2/0 | — | — | — | — | — | — | .750 | .860 | .631 |
| 08 CIN | 17 | 6 | 0 | 196 | 167 | 206 | 3.21 | 1.33 | 9.5 | 4.3 | 0.6 | 1.4 | $17 | $9 | 370 | +15 | 31% | 8% | 77% | 3.45 | 32 | 0 | 20/3 | 1 | 0 | 0 | +0.5 | .681 | .606 | .788 | .665 | .695 |
| 09 CIN | 4 | 2 | 0 | 49 | 34 | 47 | 4.35 | 1.33 | 8.5 | 5.8 | 1.1 | 1.3 | -$3 | -$1 | 80 | -0 | 23% | 14% | 70% | 4.81 | 9 | 0 | 3/3 | — | — | — | — | .683 | .683 | — | .715 | .644 |
| 10 CIN | 4 | 3 | 0 | 62 | 59 | 67 | 4.31 | 1.50 | 9.6 | 5.0 | 1.0 | 1.7 | -$3 | -$12 | 90 | +1 | 27% | 13% | 73% | 3.98 | 12 | 0 | 7/4 | — | — | — | — | .739 | — | .739 | .776 | .691 |

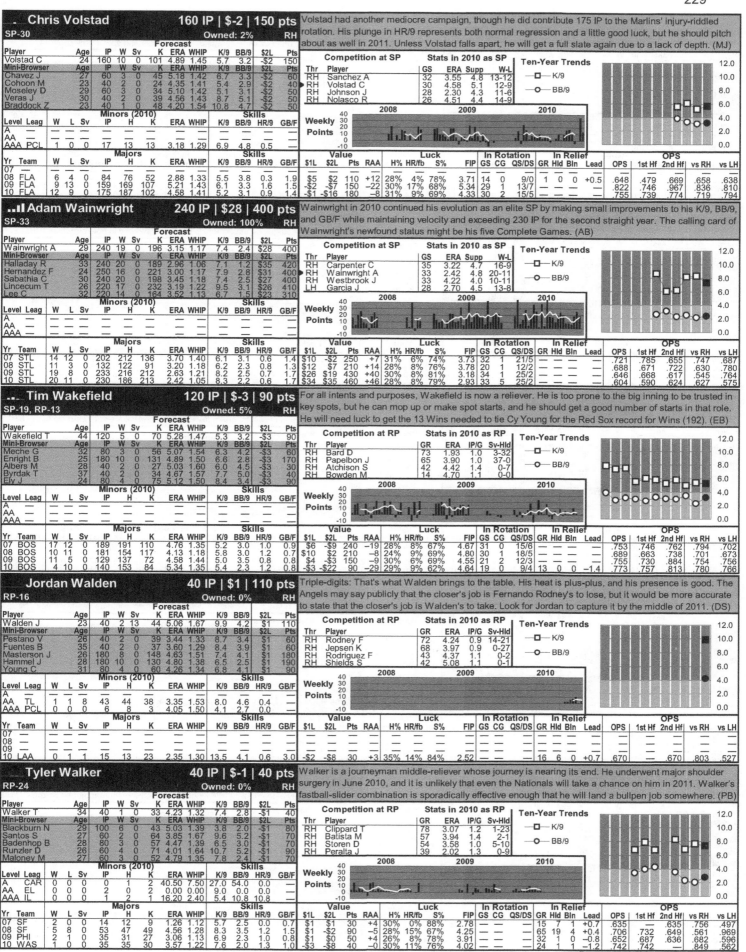

## Chris Volstad — SP-30
**160 IP | $-2 | 150 pts** — Owned: 2% — RH

Volstad had another mediocre campaign, though he did contribute 175 IP to the Marlins' injury-riddled rotation. His plunge in HR/9 represents both normal regression and a little good luck, but he should pitch about as well in 2011. Unless Volstad falls apart, he will get a full slate again due to a lack of depth. (MJ)

### Forecast
| Player | Age | IP | W | Sv | K | ERA | WHIP | K/9 | BB/9 | $2L | Pts |
|---|---|---|---|---|---|---|---|---|---|---|---|
| Volstad C | 24 | 160 | 10 | 0 | 101 | 4.89 | 1.45 | 5.7 | 3.2 | -2 | 150 |

### Mini-Browser
| Player | Age | IP | W | Sv | K | ERA | WHIP | K/9 | BB/9 | $2L | Pts |
|---|---|---|---|---|---|---|---|---|---|---|---|
| Chavez J | 27 | 60 | 3 | 0 | 45 | 5.18 | 1.42 | 6.7 | 3.3 | -2 | 60 |
| Cohoon M | 23 | 40 | 2 | 0 | 24 | 4.35 | 1.41 | 5.4 | 2.9 | -2 | 40 |
| Moseley D | 29 | 60 | 3 | 0 | 34 | 5.10 | 1.42 | 5.1 | 3.1 | -2 | 50 |
| Veras J | 30 | 40 | 2 | 0 | 39 | 4.56 | 1.43 | 8.7 | 5.1 | -2 | 50 |
| Braddock Z | 23 | 40 | 2 | 0 | 48 | 4.20 | 1.54 | 10.8 | 4.7 | -2 | 50 |

### Minors (2010)
| Level Leag | W | L | Sv | IP | H | K | ERA | WHIP | K/9 | BB/9 | HR/9 | GB/F |
|---|---|---|---|---|---|---|---|---|---|---|---|---|
| A | — | | | | | | | | | | | |
| AA | — | | | | | | | | | | | |
| AAA PCL | 1 | 0 | 0 | 17 | 13 | 13 | 3.18 | 1.29 | 6.9 | 4.8 | 0.5 | — |

### Majors
| Yr Team | W | L | Sv | IP | H | K | ERA | WHIP | K/9 | BB/9 | HR/9 | GB/F |
|---|---|---|---|---|---|---|---|---|---|---|---|---|
| 07 | — | | | | | | | | | | | |
| 08 FLA | 6 | 4 | 0 | 84 | 76 | 52 | 2.88 | 1.33 | 5.5 | 3.8 | 0.3 | 1.9 |
| 09 FLA | 9 | 13 | 0 | 159 | 169 | 107 | 5.21 | 1.43 | 6.1 | 3.3 | 1.6 | 1.5 |
| 10 FLA | 12 | 9 | 0 | 175 | 187 | 102 | 4.58 | 1.41 | 5.2 | 3.1 | 0.9 | 1.5 |

### Competition at SP / Stats in 2010 as SP
| Thr | Player | GS | ERA | Supp | W-L |
|---|---|---|---|---|---|
| RH | Sanchez A | 32 | 3.55 | 4.8 | 13-12 |
| RH | Volstad C | 30 | 4.58 | 5.1 | 12-9 |
| RH | Johnson J | 28 | 2.30 | 4.3 | 11-6 |
| RH | Nolasco R | 26 | 4.51 | 4.4 | 14-9 |

### Value / Luck / In Rotation / In Relief / OPS
| Yr | $1L | $2L | Pts | RAA | H% | HR/fb | S% | FIP | GS | CG | QS/DS | GR | Hld | Bln | Lead | OPS | 1st Hf | 2nd Hf | vs RH | vs LH |
|---|---|---|---|---|---|---|---|---|---|---|---|---|---|---|---|---|---|---|---|---|
| 07 | | | | | | | | | | | | | | | | | | | | |
| 08 | $5 | $2 | 110 | +12 | 28% | 4% | 78% | 3.71 | 14 | 0 | 9/0 | 1 | 0 | 0 | +0.5 | .648 | .479 | .669 | .658 | .638 |
| 09 | -$2 | -$7 | 150 | -22 | 30% | 17% | 68% | 5.34 | 29 | 1 | 13/7 | — | — | — | — | .822 | .746 | .967 | .836 | .810 |
| 10 | -$1 | -$16 | 180 | -8 | 31% | 9% | 69% | 4.33 | 30 | 2 | 15/5 | — | — | — | — | .755 | .739 | .774 | .719 | .794 |

Ten-Year Trends: K/9, BB/9

---

## Adam Wainwright — SP-33
**240 IP | $28 | 400 pts** — Owned: 100% — RH

Wainwright in 2010 continued his evolution as an elite SP by making small improvements to his K/9, BB/9, and GB/F while maintaining velocity and exceeding 230 IP for the second straight year. The calling card of Wainwright's newfound status might be his five Complete Games. (AB)

### Forecast
| Player | Age | IP | W | Sv | K | ERA | WHIP | K/9 | BB/9 | $2L | Pts |
|---|---|---|---|---|---|---|---|---|---|---|---|
| Wainwright A | 29 | 240 | 19 | 0 | 196 | 3.15 | 1.17 | 7.4 | 2.4 | 28 | 400 |

### Mini-Browser
| Player | Age | IP | W | Sv | K | ERA | WHIP | K/9 | BB/9 | $2L | Pts |
|---|---|---|---|---|---|---|---|---|---|---|---|
| Halladay R | 33 | 240 | 20 | 0 | 189 | 2.96 | 1.06 | 7.1 | 1.2 | 35 | 420 |
| Hernandez F | 24 | 250 | 16 | 0 | 221 | 3.00 | 1.17 | 7.9 | 2.8 | 31 | 400 |
| Sabathia C | 30 | 240 | 20 | 0 | 198 | 3.45 | 1.18 | 7.4 | 2.5 | 27 | 400 |
| Lincecum T | 26 | 220 | 17 | 0 | 232 | 3.19 | 1.22 | 9.5 | 3.1 | 26 | 410 |
| Lee C | 32 | 220 | 14 | 0 | 164 | 3.52 | 1.13 | 6.7 | 1.5 | 23 | 310 |

### Minors (2010)
| Level Leag | W | L | Sv | IP | H | K | ERA | WHIP | K/9 | BB/9 | HR/9 | GB/F |
|---|---|---|---|---|---|---|---|---|---|---|---|---|
| A | — | | | | | | | | | | | |
| AA | — | | | | | | | | | | | |
| AAA | — | | | | | | | | | | | |

### Majors
| Yr Team | W | L | Sv | IP | H | K | ERA | WHIP | K/9 | BB/9 | HR/9 | GB/F |
|---|---|---|---|---|---|---|---|---|---|---|---|---|
| 07 STL | 14 | 12 | 0 | 202 | 212 | 136 | 3.70 | 1.40 | 6.1 | 3.1 | 0.6 | 1.4 |
| 08 STL | 11 | 3 | 0 | 132 | 122 | 91 | 3.20 | 1.18 | 6.2 | 2.3 | 0.8 | 1.3 |
| 09 STL | 19 | 8 | 0 | 233 | 216 | 212 | 2.63 | 1.21 | 8.2 | 2.5 | 0.7 | 1.1 |
| 10 STL | 20 | 11 | 0 | 230 | 186 | 213 | 2.42 | 1.05 | 8.3 | 2.2 | 0.6 | 1.7 |

### Competition at SP / Stats in 2010 as SP
| Thr | Player | GS | ERA | Supp | W-L |
|---|---|---|---|---|---|
| RH | Carpenter C | 35 | 3.22 | 4.7 | 16-9 |
| RH | Wainwright A | 33 | 2.42 | 4.8 | 20-11 |
| RH | Westbrook J | 33 | 4.22 | 4.0 | 10-11 |
| LH | Garcia J | 28 | 2.70 | 4.5 | 13-8 |

### Value / Luck / In Rotation / In Relief / OPS
| Yr | $1L | $2L | Pts | RAA | H% | HR/fb | S% | FIP | GS | CG | QS/DS | GR | Hld | Bln | Lead | OPS | 1st Hf | 2nd Hf | vs RH | vs LH |
|---|---|---|---|---|---|---|---|---|---|---|---|---|---|---|---|---|---|---|---|---|
| 07 STL | $10 | -$2 | 250 | +7 | 31% | 6% | 74% | 3.73 | 32 | 1 | 21/5 | — | — | — | — | .721 | .785 | .655 | .747 | .687 |
| 08 STL | $12 | $7 | 210 | +14 | 26% | 8% | 76% | 3.78 | 20 | 1 | 12/2 | — | — | — | — | .688 | .671 | .722 | .630 | .780 |
| 09 STL | $26 | $19 | 430 | +40 | 30% | 8% | 81% | 3.18 | 34 | 1 | 25/2 | — | — | — | — | .646 | .668 | .617 | .545 | .764 |
| 10 STL | $34 | $35 | 460 | +46 | 28% | 9% | 79% | 2.93 | 33 | 5 | 25/2 | — | — | — | — | .604 | .590 | .624 | .627 | .575 |

Ten-Year Trends: K/9, BB/9

---

## Tim Wakefield — SP-19, RP-13
**120 IP | $-3 | 90 pts** — Owned: 5% — RH

For all intents and purposes, Wakefield is now a reliever. He is too prone to the big inning to be trusted in key spots, but he can mop up or make spot starts, and he should get a good number of starts in that role. He will need luck to get the 13 Wins needed to tie Cy Young for the Red Sox record for Wins (192). (EB)

### Forecast
| Player | Age | IP | W | Sv | K | ERA | WHIP | K/9 | BB/9 | $2L | Pts |
|---|---|---|---|---|---|---|---|---|---|---|---|
| Wakefield T | 44 | 120 | 5 | 0 | 70 | 5.28 | 1.47 | 5.3 | 3.2 | -3 | 90 |

### Mini-Browser
| Player | Age | IP | W | Sv | K | ERA | WHIP | K/9 | BB/9 | $2L | Pts |
|---|---|---|---|---|---|---|---|---|---|---|---|
| Meche G | 32 | 80 | 4 | 0 | 56 | 5.07 | 1.54 | 6.3 | 4.2 | -3 | 40 |
| Enright B | 25 | 180 | 10 | 0 | 131 | 4.89 | 1.50 | 6.6 | 2.8 | -3 | 170 |
| Albers M | 28 | 40 | 2 | 0 | 27 | 5.03 | 1.60 | 6.0 | 4.5 | -3 | 30 |
| Byrdak T | 37 | 40 | 2 | 0 | 34 | 4.67 | 1.57 | 7.7 | 5.0 | -3 | 40 |
| Ely J | 24 | 80 | 4 | 0 | 75 | 5.12 | 1.50 | 8.4 | 3.4 | -3 | 90 |

### Minors (2010)
| Level Leag | W | L | Sv | IP | H | K | ERA | WHIP | K/9 | BB/9 | HR/9 | GB/F |
|---|---|---|---|---|---|---|---|---|---|---|---|---|
| A | — | | | | | | | | | | | |
| AA | — | | | | | | | | | | | |
| AAA | — | | | | | | | | | | | |

### Majors
| Yr Team | W | L | Sv | IP | H | K | ERA | WHIP | K/9 | BB/9 | HR/9 | GB/F |
|---|---|---|---|---|---|---|---|---|---|---|---|---|
| 07 BOS | 17 | 12 | 0 | 189 | 191 | 110 | 4.76 | 1.35 | 5.2 | 3.0 | 1.0 | 0.9 |
| 08 BOS | 10 | 11 | 0 | 181 | 154 | 117 | 4.13 | 1.18 | 5.8 | 3.0 | 1.2 | 0.8 |
| 09 BOS | 11 | 5 | 0 | 129 | 137 | 72 | 4.58 | 1.44 | 5.0 | 3.5 | 0.8 | 0.8 |
| 10 BOS | 4 | 10 | 0 | 140 | 153 | 84 | 5.34 | 1.35 | 5.4 | 2.3 | 1.2 | 0.8 |

### Competition at RP / Stats in 2010 as RP
| Thr | Player | GR | ERA | IP/G | Sv-Hld |
|---|---|---|---|---|---|
| RH | Bard D | 73 | 1.93 | 1.0 | 3-32 |
| RH | Papelbon J | 65 | 3.90 | 1.0 | 37-0 |
| RH | Atchison S | 42 | 4.42 | 1.4 | 0-7 |
| RH | Bowden M | 14 | 4.70 | 1.1 | 0-0 |

### Value / Luck / In Rotation / In Relief / OPS
| Yr | $1L | $2L | Pts | RAA | H% | HR/fb | S% | FIP | GS | CG | QS/DS | GR | Hld | Bln | Lead | OPS | 1st Hf | 2nd Hf | vs RH | vs LH |
|---|---|---|---|---|---|---|---|---|---|---|---|---|---|---|---|---|---|---|---|---|
| 07 BOS | $6 | -$9 | 240 | -19 | 28% | 8% | 67% | 4.67 | 31 | 0 | 15/6 | — | — | — | — | .753 | .746 | .762 | .794 | .702 |
| 08 BOS | $10 | $2 | 210 | -8 | 24% | 9% | 69% | 4.80 | 30 | 1 | 18/5 | — | — | — | — | .689 | .663 | .738 | .701 | .673 |
| 09 BOS | $4 | -$3 | 150 | -9 | 30% | 6% | 69% | 4.55 | 21 | 2 | 12/3 | — | — | — | — | .755 | .730 | .884 | .754 | .756 |
| 10 BOS | -$3 | -$22 | 90 | -7 | 29% | 9% | 62% | 4.64 | 19 | 0 | 9/4 | 13 | 0 | 0 | -1.4 | .773 | .757 | .813 | .780 | .766 |

Ten-Year Trends: K/9, BB/9

---

## Jordan Walden — RP-16
**40 IP | $1 | 110 pts** — Owned: 0% — RH

Triple-digits: That's what Walden brings to the table. His heat is plus-plus, and his presence is good. The Angels may say publicly that the closer's job is Fernando Rodney's to lose, but it would be more accurate to state that the closer's job is Walden's to take. Look for Jordan to capture it by the middle of 2011. (DS)

### Forecast
| Player | Age | IP | W | Sv | K | ERA | WHIP | K/9 | BB/9 | $2L | Pts |
|---|---|---|---|---|---|---|---|---|---|---|---|
| Walden J | 23 | 40 | 2 | 13 | 44 | 5.06 | 1.67 | 9.9 | 4.2 | 1 | 110 |

### Mini-Browser
| Player | Age | IP | W | Sv | K | ERA | WHIP | K/9 | BB/9 | $2L | Pts |
|---|---|---|---|---|---|---|---|---|---|---|---|
| Pestano V | 26 | 40 | 2 | 0 | 39 | 3.44 | 1.33 | 8.7 | 3.4 | 1 | 60 |
| Fuentes B | 35 | 40 | 2 | 0 | 37 | 3.60 | 1.29 | 8.4 | 3.9 | 1 | 60 |
| Masterson J | 26 | 180 | 8 | 0 | 148 | 4.63 | 1.51 | 7.4 | 4.1 | 1 | 180 |
| Hammel J | 28 | 180 | 10 | 0 | 130 | 4.80 | 1.38 | 6.5 | 2.5 | 1 | 190 |
| Young C | 31 | 80 | 4 | 0 | 60 | 4.26 | 1.34 | 6.8 | 4.1 | 1 | 90 |

### Minors (2010)
| Level Leag | W | L | Sv | IP | H | K | ERA | WHIP | K/9 | BB/9 | HR/9 | GB/F |
|---|---|---|---|---|---|---|---|---|---|---|---|---|
| A | — | | | | | | | | | | | |
| AA TL | 1 | 1 | 8 | 43 | 44 | 38 | 3.35 | 1.53 | 8.0 | 4.6 | 0.4 | — |
| AAA PCL | 0 | 0 | 0 | 6 | 8 | 3 | 4.05 | 1.50 | 4.1 | 2.7 | 0.0 | — |

### Majors
| Yr Team | W | L | Sv | IP | H | K | ERA | WHIP | K/9 | BB/9 | HR/9 | GB/F |
|---|---|---|---|---|---|---|---|---|---|---|---|---|
| 07 | — | | | | | | | | | | | |
| 08 | — | | | | | | | | | | | |
| 09 | — | | | | | | | | | | | |
| 10 LAA | 0 | 1 | 0 | 15 | 13 | 23 | 2.35 | 1.30 | 13.5 | 4.1 | 0.6 | 3.0 |

### Competition at RP / Stats in 2010 as RP
| Thr | Player | GR | ERA | IP/G | Sv-Hld |
|---|---|---|---|---|---|
| RH | Rodney F | 72 | 4.24 | 0.9 | 14-21 |
| RH | Jepsen K | 68 | 3.97 | 0.9 | 0-27 |
| RH | Rodriguez F | 43 | 4.37 | 1.1 | 0-2 |
| RH | Shields S | 42 | 5.08 | 1.1 | 0-1 |

### Value / Luck / In Rotation / In Relief / OPS
| Yr | $1L | $2L | Pts | RAA | H% | HR/fb | S% | FIP | GS | CG | QS/DS | GR | Hld | Bln | Lead | OPS | 1st Hf | 2nd Hf | vs RH | vs LH |
|---|---|---|---|---|---|---|---|---|---|---|---|---|---|---|---|---|---|---|---|---|
| 10 LAA | -$2 | -$2 | 30 | +3 | 35% | 14% | 84% | 2.52 | — | — | — | 15 | 1 | 0 | +0.7 | .670 | — | .670 | .803 | .527 |

Ten-Year Trends: K/9, BB/9

---

## Tyler Walker — RP-24
**40 IP | $-1 | 40 pts** — Owned: 0% — RH

Walker is a journeyman middle-reliever whose journey is nearing its end. He underwent major shoulder surgery in June 2010, and it is unlikely that even the Nationals will take a chance on him in 2011. Walker's fastball-slider combination is sporadically effective enough that he will land a bullpen job somewhere. (PB)

### Forecast
| Player | Age | IP | W | Sv | K | ERA | WHIP | K/9 | BB/9 | $2L | Pts |
|---|---|---|---|---|---|---|---|---|---|---|---|
| Walker T | 34 | 40 | 1 | 0 | 33 | 4.23 | 1.32 | 7.4 | 2.8 | -1 | 40 |

### Mini-Browser
| Player | Age | IP | W | Sv | K | ERA | WHIP | K/9 | BB/9 | $2L | Pts |
|---|---|---|---|---|---|---|---|---|---|---|---|
| Blackburn N | 29 | 100 | 6 | 0 | 43 | 5.03 | 1.39 | 3.8 | 2.0 | -1 | 80 |
| Santos S | 27 | 60 | 2 | 0 | 64 | 3.85 | 1.67 | 9.6 | 5.2 | -1 | 70 |
| Badenhop B | 28 | 80 | 3 | 0 | 57 | 4.47 | 1.39 | 6.5 | 3.0 | -1 | 70 |
| Runzler D | 26 | 60 | 4 | 0 | 71 | 4.01 | 1.64 | 10.7 | 5.2 | -1 | 90 |
| Maloney M | 27 | 60 | 2 | 0 | 52 | 4.79 | 1.35 | 7.8 | 2.4 | -1 | 70 |

### Minors (2010)
| Level Leag | W | L | Sv | IP | H | K | ERA | WHIP | K/9 | BB/9 | HR/9 | GB/F |
|---|---|---|---|---|---|---|---|---|---|---|---|---|
| A CAR | 0 | 0 | 0 | 0 | 1 | 2 | 40.50 | 7.50 | 27.0 | 54.0 | 0.0 | — |
| AA EL | 0 | 0 | 0 | 2 | 0 | 2 | 0.00 | 0.00 | 9.0 | 0.0 | 0.0 | — |
| AAA IL | 0 | 0 | 1 | 3 | 2 | 1 | 16.20 | 2.40 | 5.4 | 10.8 | 10.8 | — |

### Majors
| Yr Team | W | L | Sv | IP | H | K | ERA | WHIP | K/9 | BB/9 | HR/9 | GB/F |
|---|---|---|---|---|---|---|---|---|---|---|---|---|
| 07 SF | 2 | 0 | 0 | 14 | 12 | 9 | 1.26 | 1.12 | 5.7 | 2.5 | 0.7 | 0.7 |
| 08 SF | 5 | 8 | 0 | 53 | 47 | 49 | 4.56 | 1.28 | 8.3 | 3.5 | 1.2 | 1.5 |
| 09 PHI | 3 | 3 | 0 | 35 | 31 | 27 | 3.06 | 1.13 | 6.9 | 2.3 | 1.0 | 0.8 |
| 10 WAS | 1 | 0 | 0 | 35 | 35 | 30 | 3.57 | 1.22 | 7.7 | 2.0 | 1.3 | 1.0 |

### Competition at RP / Stats in 2010 as RP
| Thr | Player | GR | ERA | IP/G | Sv-Hld |
|---|---|---|---|---|---|
| RH | Clippard T | 78 | 3.07 | 1.2 | 1-23 |
| RH | Batista M | 57 | 3.94 | 1.4 | 2-1 |
| RH | Storen D | 54 | 3.58 | 1.0 | 5-10 |
| RH | Peralta J | 39 | 2.02 | 1.3 | 0-9 |

### Value / Luck / In Rotation / In Relief / OPS
| Yr | $1L | $2L | Pts | RAA | H% | HR/fb | S% | FIP | GS | CG | QS/DS | GR | Hld | Bln | Lead | OPS | 1st Hf | 2nd Hf | vs RH | vs LH |
|---|---|---|---|---|---|---|---|---|---|---|---|---|---|---|---|---|---|---|---|---|
| 07 SF | $1 | $1 | 30 | +4 | 30% | 0% | 88% | 2.78 | — | — | — | — | — | — | — | .635 | — | .635 | .756 | .497 |
| 08 SF | $1 | -$2 | 90 | -5 | 28% | 15% | 67% | 4.25 | — | — | — | 65 | 19 | 4 | +0.4 | .706 | .732 | .649 | .561 | .969 |
| 09 PHI | $1 | $0 | 50 | +4 | 26% | 8% | 78% | 3.91 | — | — | — | 32 | 1 | 0 | -0.8 | .652 | .687 | .636 | .682 | .596 |
| 10 WAS | -$3 | -$8 | 40 | 0 | 30% | 11% | 76% | 4.02 | — | — | — | 24 | 1 | 1 | -1.2 | .742 | .742 | — | .849 | .562 |

Ten-Year Trends: K/9, BB/9

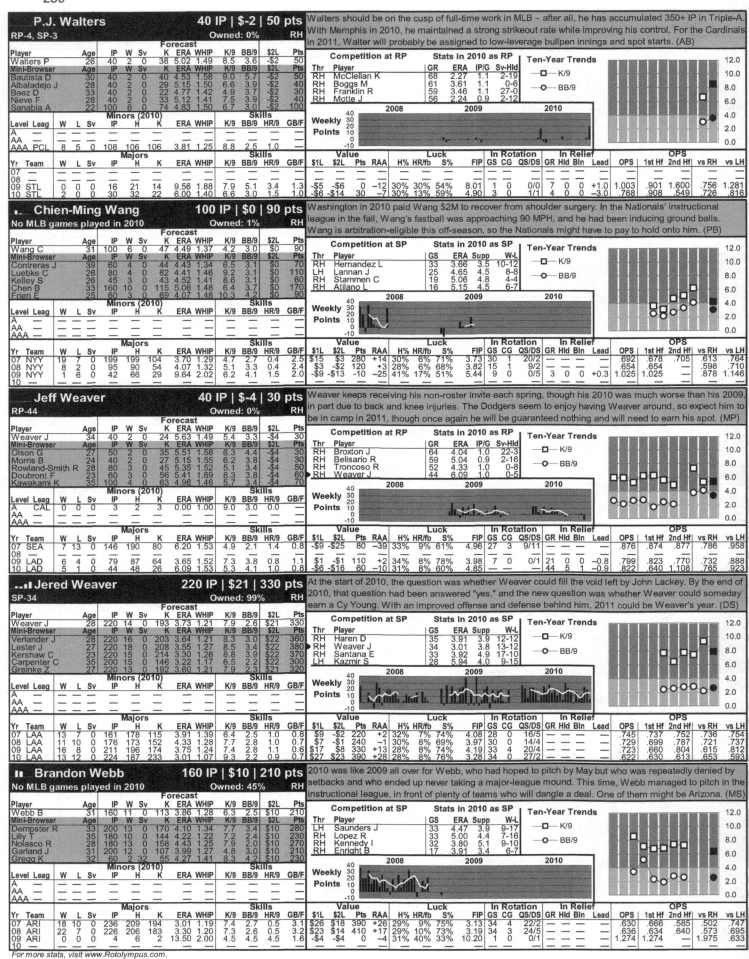

## P.J. Walters — 40 IP | $-2 | 50 pts
RP-4, SP-3 | Owned: 0% | RH

Walters should be on the cusp of full-time work in MLB – after all, he has accumulated 350+ IP in Triple-A. With Memphis in 2010, he maintained a strong strikeout rate while improving his control. For the Cardinals in 2011, Walter will probably be assigned to low-leverage bullpen innings and spot starts. (AB)

### Forecast
| Player | Age | IP | W | Sv | K | ERA | WHIP | K/9 | BB/9 | $2L | Pts |
|---|---|---|---|---|---|---|---|---|---|---|---|
| Walters P | 26 | 40 | 2 | 0 | 38 | 5.02 | 1.49 | 8.5 | 3.6 | -$2 | 50 |
| Mini-Browser | Age | IP | W | Sv | K | ERA | WHIP | K/9 | BB/9 | $2L | Pts |
| Bautista D | 30 | 40 | 2 | 0 | 40 | 4.53 | 1.58 | 9.0 | 5.7 | -$2 | 50 |
| Albaladejo J | 28 | 40 | 2 | 0 | 29 | 5.15 | 1.50 | 6.6 | 3.9 | -$2 | 40 |
| Baez D | 33 | 40 | 2 | 0 | 22 | 4.77 | 1.42 | 4.9 | 3.7 | -$2 | 40 |
| Nieve F | 28 | 40 | 2 | 0 | 33 | 5.12 | 1.41 | 7.5 | 3.9 | -$2 | 40 |
| Sanabia A | 22 | 100 | 6 | 0 | 74 | 4.83 | 1.50 | 6.7 | 3.0 | -$2 | 100 |

### Competition at RP | Stats in 2010 as RP
| Thr | Player | GR | ERA | IP/G | Sv-Hld |
|---|---|---|---|---|---|
| RH | McClellan K | 68 | 2.27 | 1.1 | 2-19 |
| RH | Boggs M | 61 | 3.61 | 1.1 | 0-6 |
| RH | Franklin R | 59 | 3.46 | 1.1 | 27-0 |
| RH | Motte J | 56 | 2.24 | 0.9 | 2-12 |

### Minors (2010)
| Level | Leag | W | L | Sv | IP | H | K | ERA | WHIP | K/9 | BB/9 | HR/9 | GB/F |
|---|---|---|---|---|---|---|---|---|---|---|---|---|---|
| A | — | | | | | | | | | | | | |
| AA | — | | | | | | | | | | | | |
| AAA | PCL | 8 | 5 | 0 | 108 | 106 | 106 | 3.81 | 1.25 | 8.8 | 2.5 | 1.0 | — |

### Majors / Value
| Yr | Team | W | L | Sv | IP | H | K | ERA | WHIP | K/9 | BB/9 | HR/9 | GB/F | $1L | $2L | Pts | RAA | H% | HR/fb | S% | FIP | GS | CG | QS/DS | GR | Hld | Bln | Lead | OPS | 1st Hf | 2nd Hf | vs RH | vs LH |
|---|---|---|---|---|---|---|---|---|---|---|---|---|---|---|---|---|---|---|---|---|---|---|---|---|---|---|---|---|---|---|---|---|---|
| 07 | — | | | | | | | | | | | | | | | | | | | | | | | | | | | | | | | | |
| 08 | — | | | | | | | | | | | | | | | | | | | | | | | | | | | | | | | | |
| 09 | STL | 0 | 0 | 0 | 16 | 21 | 14 | 9.56 | 1.88 | 7.9 | 5.1 | 3.4 | 1.3 | -$5 | -$6 | 0 | -12 | 30% | 30% | 54% | 8.01 | 1 | 0 | 0/0 | 7 | 0 | 0 | +1.0 | 1.003 | .901 | 1.600 | .756 | 1.281 |
| 10 | STL | 2 | 0 | 0 | 30 | 32 | 22 | 6.00 | 1.40 | 6.6 | 3.0 | 1.5 | 1.0 | -$6 | -$14 | 30 | -7 | 30% | 13% | 59% | 4.90 | 0 | 0 | 1/1 | 0 | 0 | 0 | -3.0 | .768 | .908 | .549 | .726 | .816 |

---

## Chien-Ming Wang — 100 IP | $0 | 90 pts
No MLB games played in 2010 | Owned: 1% | RH

Washington in 2010 paid Wang $2M to recover from shoulder surgery. In the Nationals' instructional league in the fall, Wang's fastball was approaching 90 MPH, and he had been inducing ground balls. Wang is arbitration-eligible this off-season, so the Nationals might have to pay to hold onto him. (PB)

### Forecast
| Player | Age | IP | W | Sv | K | ERA | WHIP | K/9 | BB/9 | $2L | Pts |
|---|---|---|---|---|---|---|---|---|---|---|---|
| Wang C | 31 | 100 | 6 | 0 | 47 | 4.49 | 1.37 | 4.2 | 3.0 | $0 | 90 |
| Mini-Browser | Age | IP | W | Sv | K | ERA | WHIP | K/9 | BB/9 | $2L | Pts |
| Contreras J | 39 | 60 | 4 | 0 | 44 | 4.43 | 1.34 | 6.5 | 3.1 | $0 | 90 |
| Luebke C | 26 | 80 | 4 | 0 | 82 | 4.41 | 1.46 | 9.2 | 3.1 | $0 | 110 |
| Kelley S | 26 | 45 | 3 | 0 | 43 | 4.52 | 1.41 | 8.6 | 3.1 | $0 | 60 |
| Chen B | 33 | 160 | 10 | 0 | 115 | 5.06 | 1.48 | 6.4 | 3.7 | $0 | 170 |
| Frieri E | 25 | 60 | 3 | 0 | 69 | 4.07 | 1.48 | 10.3 | 4.9 | $0 | 90 |

### Competition at SP | Stats in 2010 as SP
| Thr | Player | GS | ERA | Supp | W-L |
|---|---|---|---|---|---|
| RH | Hernandez L | 33 | 3.66 | 3.5 | 10-12 |
| LH | Lannan J | 25 | 4.65 | 4.5 | 8-8 |
| RH | Stammen C | 19 | 5.06 | 4.8 | 4-4 |
| RH | Atilano L | 16 | 5.15 | 4.5 | 6-7 |

### Minors (2010)
| Level | Leag | W | L | Sv | IP | H | K | ERA | WHIP | K/9 | BB/9 | HR/9 | GB/F |
|---|---|---|---|---|---|---|---|---|---|---|---|---|---|
| A | — | | | | | | | | | | | | |
| AA | — | | | | | | | | | | | | |
| AAA | — | | | | | | | | | | | | |

### Majors / Value
| Yr | Team | W | L | Sv | IP | H | K | ERA | WHIP | K/9 | BB/9 | HR/9 | GB/F | $1L | $2L | Pts | RAA | H% | HR/fb | S% | FIP | GS | CG | QS/DS | GR | Hld | Bln | Lead | OPS | 1st Hf | 2nd Hf | vs RH | vs LH |
|---|---|---|---|---|---|---|---|---|---|---|---|---|---|---|---|---|---|---|---|---|---|---|---|---|---|---|---|---|---|---|---|---|---|
| 07 | NYY | 19 | 7 | 0 | 199 | 199 | 104 | 3.70 | 1.29 | 4.7 | 2.7 | 0.4 | 2.5 | $15 | $3 | 280 | +14 | 30% | 6% | 71% | 3.73 | 30 | 1 | 20/2 | — | — | — | — | .692 | .678 | .705 | .613 | .764 |
| 08 | NYY | 8 | 2 | 0 | 95 | 90 | 54 | 4.07 | 1.32 | 5.1 | 3.3 | 0.4 | 2.4 | $3 | -$2 | 120 | +3 | 28% | 6% | 68% | 3.82 | 15 | 1 | 9/2 | — | — | — | — | .654 | .654 | — | .598 | .710 |
| 09 | NYY | 1 | 6 | 0 | 42 | 66 | 29 | 9.64 | 2.02 | 6.2 | 4.1 | 1.5 | 2.0 | -$9 | -$13 | -10 | -25 | 41% | 17% | 51% | 5.44 | 9 | 0 | 0/5 | 3 | 0 | 0 | +0.3 | 1.025 | 1.025 | — | .878 | 1.146 |
| 10 | — | | | | | | | | | | | | | | | | | | | | | | | | | | | | | | | | |

---

## Jeff Weaver — 40 IP | $-4 | 30 pts
RP-44 | Owned: 0% | RH

Weaver keeps receiving his non-roster invite each spring, though his 2010 was much worse than his 2009, in part due to back and knee injuries. The Dodgers seem to enjoy having Weaver around, so expect him to be in camp in 2011, though once again he will be guaranteed nothing and will need to earn his spot. (MP)

### Forecast
| Player | Age | IP | W | Sv | K | ERA | WHIP | K/9 | BB/9 | $2L | Pts |
|---|---|---|---|---|---|---|---|---|---|---|---|
| Weaver J | 34 | 40 | 2 | 0 | 24 | 5.63 | 1.49 | 5.4 | 3.3 | -$4 | 30 |
| Mini-Browser | Age | IP | W | Sv | K | ERA | WHIP | K/9 | BB/9 | $2L | Pts |
| Olson G | 27 | 50 | 2 | 0 | 35 | 5.51 | 1.58 | 6.3 | 4.4 | -$4 | 30 |
| Morris B | 24 | 40 | 2 | 0 | 27 | 5.15 | 1.55 | 6.2 | 3.8 | -$4 | 30 |
| Rowland-Smith R | 28 | 80 | 3 | 0 | 45 | 5.35 | 1.52 | 5.1 | 3.4 | -$4 | 50 |
| Doubront F | 23 | 60 | 3 | 0 | 56 | 5.41 | 1.69 | 8.3 | 3.8 | -$4 | 60 |
| Kawakami K | 35 | 100 | 4 | 0 | 63 | 4.96 | 1.46 | 5.7 | 3.4 | -$4 | 70 |

### Competition at RP | Stats in 2010 as RP
| Thr | Player | GR | ERA | IP/G | Sv-Hld |
|---|---|---|---|---|---|
| RH | Broxton J | 64 | 4.04 | 1.0 | 22-3 |
| RH | Belisario R | 59 | 5.04 | 0.9 | 2-16 |
| RH | Troncoso R | 52 | 4.33 | 1.0 | 0-8 |
| RH | Weaver J | 44 | 6.09 | 1.0 | 0-5 |

### Minors (2010)
| Level | Leag | W | L | Sv | IP | H | K | ERA | WHIP | K/9 | BB/9 | HR/9 | GB/F |
|---|---|---|---|---|---|---|---|---|---|---|---|---|---|
| A | CAL | 0 | 0 | 0 | 3 | 2 | 3 | 0.00 | 1.00 | 9.0 | 3.0 | 0.0 | — |
| AA | — | | | | | | | | | | | | |
| AAA | — | | | | | | | | | | | | |

### Majors / Value
| Yr | Team | W | L | Sv | IP | H | K | ERA | WHIP | K/9 | BB/9 | HR/9 | GB/F | $1L | $2L | Pts | RAA | H% | HR/fb | S% | FIP | GS | CG | QS/DS | GR | Hld | Bln | Lead | OPS | 1st Hf | 2nd Hf | vs RH | vs LH |
|---|---|---|---|---|---|---|---|---|---|---|---|---|---|---|---|---|---|---|---|---|---|---|---|---|---|---|---|---|---|---|---|---|---|
| 07 | SEA | 7 | 13 | 0 | 146 | 190 | 80 | 6.20 | 1.53 | 4.9 | 2.1 | 1.4 | 0.8 | -$9 | -$25 | 80 | -39 | 33% | 9% | 61% | 4.96 | 27 | 3 | 9/11 | — | — | — | — | .876 | .874 | .877 | .786 | .958 |
| 08 | — | | | | | | | | | | | | | | | | | | | | | | | | | | | | | | | | |
| 09 | LAD | 6 | 4 | 0 | 79 | 87 | 64 | 3.65 | 1.52 | 7.3 | 3.8 | 0.8 | 1.1 | -$1 | -$1 | 110 | +2 | 34% | 8% | 78% | 3.98 | 7 | 0 | 0/1 | 21 | 0 | 0 | -0.8 | .799 | .823 | .770 | .732 | .888 |
| 10 | LAD | 5 | 1 | 0 | 44 | 48 | 26 | 6.09 | 1.53 | 5.3 | 4.1 | 1.0 | 0.8 | -$6 | -$16 | 60 | -10 | 31% | 8% | 60% | 4.85 | — | — | — | 44 | 5 | 1 | -0.9 | .822 | .640 | 1.108 | .765 | .923 |

---

## Jered Weaver — 220 IP | $21 | 330 pts
SP-34 | Owned: 99% | RH

At the start of 2010, the question was whether Weaver could fill the void left by John Lackey. By the end of 2010, that question had been answered "yes," and the new question was whether Weaver could someday earn a Cy Young. With an improved offense and defense behind him, 2011 could be Weaver's year. (DS)

### Forecast
| Player | Age | IP | W | Sv | K | ERA | WHIP | K/9 | BB/9 | $2L | Pts |
|---|---|---|---|---|---|---|---|---|---|---|---|
| Weaver J | 28 | 220 | 14 | 0 | 193 | 3.73 | 1.21 | 7.9 | 2.6 | $21 | 330 |
| Mini-Browser | Age | IP | W | Sv | K | ERA | WHIP | K/9 | BB/9 | $2L | Pts |
| Verlander J | 28 | 220 | 16 | 0 | 203 | 3.64 | 1.21 | 8.3 | 3.0 | $22 | 360 |
| Lester J | 27 | 220 | 18 | 0 | 208 | 3.55 | 1.27 | 8.5 | 3.4 | $22 | 380 |
| Kershaw C | 23 | 220 | 15 | 0 | 214 | 3.30 | 1.26 | 8.8 | 3.9 | $22 | 370 |
| Carpenter C | 35 | 200 | 15 | 0 | 146 | 3.22 | 1.17 | 6.5 | 2.2 | $22 | 300 |
| Greinke Z | 27 | 220 | 13 | 0 | 192 | 3.60 | 1.21 | 7.9 | 2.3 | $21 | 320 |

### Competition at SP | Stats in 2010 as SP
| Thr | Player | GS | ERA | Supp | W-L |
|---|---|---|---|---|---|
| RH | Haren D | 35 | 3.91 | 3.9 | 12-12 |
| RH | Weaver J | 34 | 3.01 | 3.8 | 13-12 |
| RH | Santana E | 33 | 3.92 | 4.9 | 17-10 |
| LH | Kazmir S | 28 | 5.94 | 4.0 | 9-15 |

### Minors (2010)
| Level | Leag | W | L | Sv | IP | H | K | ERA | WHIP | K/9 | BB/9 | HR/9 | GB/F |
|---|---|---|---|---|---|---|---|---|---|---|---|---|---|
| A | — | | | | | | | | | | | | |
| AA | — | | | | | | | | | | | | |
| AAA | — | | | | | | | | | | | | |

### Majors / Value
| Yr | Team | W | L | Sv | IP | H | K | ERA | WHIP | K/9 | BB/9 | HR/9 | GB/F | $1L | $2L | Pts | RAA | H% | HR/fb | S% | FIP | GS | CG | QS/DS | GR | Hld | Bln | Lead | OPS | 1st Hf | 2nd Hf | vs RH | vs LH |
|---|---|---|---|---|---|---|---|---|---|---|---|---|---|---|---|---|---|---|---|---|---|---|---|---|---|---|---|---|---|---|---|---|---|
| 07 | LAA | 13 | 7 | 0 | 161 | 178 | 115 | 3.91 | 1.39 | 6.4 | 2.5 | 1.0 | 0.8 | $9 | -$2 | 220 | +2 | 32% | 7% | 74% | 4.08 | 28 | 0 | 16/5 | — | — | — | — | .745 | .737 | .752 | .736 | .754 |
| 08 | LAA | 11 | 10 | 0 | 176 | 173 | 152 | 4.33 | 1.28 | 7.7 | 2.8 | 1.0 | 0.7 | -$1 | -$1 | 240 | -1 | 30% | 8% | 69% | 3.97 | 30 | 0 | 14/4 | — | — | — | — | .729 | .699 | .787 | .721 | .737 |
| 09 | LAA | 16 | 8 | 0 | 211 | 196 | 174 | 3.75 | 1.24 | 7.4 | 2.8 | 1.1 | 0.6 | $17 | $8 | 330 | +13 | 28% | 8% | 74% | 4.19 | 33 | 0 | 20/4 | — | — | — | — | .723 | .660 | .804 | .615 | .812 |
| 10 | LAA | 13 | 12 | 0 | 224 | 187 | 233 | 3.01 | 1.07 | 9.3 | 2.2 | 0.9 | 0.7 | $27 | $23 | 390 | +28 | 28% | 8% | 76% | 3.28 | 34 | 0 | 27/2 | — | — | — | — | .622 | .630 | .613 | .653 | .583 |

---

## Brandon Webb — 160 IP | $10 | 210 pts
No MLB games played in 2010 | Owned: 45% | RH

2010 was like 2009 all over for Webb, who had hoped to pitch by May but who was repeatedly denied by setbacks and who ended up never taking a major-league mound. This time, Webb managed to pitch in the instructional league, in front of plenty of teams who will dangle a deal. One of them might be Arizona. (MS)

### Forecast
| Player | Age | IP | W | Sv | K | ERA | WHIP | K/9 | BB/9 | $2L | Pts |
|---|---|---|---|---|---|---|---|---|---|---|---|
| Webb B | 31 | 160 | 11 | 0 | 113 | 3.86 | 1.28 | 6.3 | 2.5 | $10 | 210 |
| Mini-Browser | Age | IP | W | Sv | K | ERA | WHIP | K/9 | BB/9 | $2L | Pts |
| Dempster R | 33 | 200 | 13 | 0 | 170 | 4.10 | 1.34 | 7.7 | 3.4 | $10 | 280 |
| Lilly T | 35 | 180 | 10 | 0 | 144 | 4.22 | 1.22 | 7.2 | 2.4 | $10 | 230 |
| Nolasco R | 28 | 180 | 13 | 0 | 158 | 4.43 | 1.25 | 7.9 | 2.0 | $10 | 270 |
| Garland J | 31 | 200 | 12 | 0 | 107 | 3.99 | 1.27 | 4.8 | 3.0 | $10 | 210 |
| Gregg K | 32 | 60 | 2 | 32 | 55 | 4.27 | 1.41 | 8.3 | 4.2 | $10 | 230 |

### Competition at SP | Stats in 2010 as SP
| Thr | Player | GS | ERA | Supp | W-L |
|---|---|---|---|---|---|
| LH | Saunders J | 33 | 4.47 | 3.9 | 9-17 |
| RH | Lopez R | 33 | 5.00 | 4.4 | 7-16 |
| RH | Kennedy I | 32 | 3.80 | 5.1 | 9-10 |
| RH | Enright B | 17 | 3.91 | 3.4 | 6-7 |

### Minors (2010)
| Level | Leag | W | L | Sv | IP | H | K | ERA | WHIP | K/9 | BB/9 | HR/9 | GB/F |
|---|---|---|---|---|---|---|---|---|---|---|---|---|---|
| A | — | | | | | | | | | | | | |
| AA | — | | | | | | | | | | | | |
| AAA | — | | | | | | | | | | | | |

### Majors / Value
| Yr | Team | W | L | Sv | IP | H | K | ERA | WHIP | K/9 | BB/9 | HR/9 | GB/F | $1L | $2L | Pts | RAA | H% | HR/fb | S% | FIP | GS | CG | QS/DS | GR | Hld | Bln | Lead | OPS | 1st Hf | 2nd Hf | vs RH | vs LH |
|---|---|---|---|---|---|---|---|---|---|---|---|---|---|---|---|---|---|---|---|---|---|---|---|---|---|---|---|---|---|---|---|---|---|
| 07 | ARI | 18 | 10 | 0 | 236 | 209 | 194 | 3.01 | 1.19 | 7.4 | 2.7 | 0.5 | 3.1 | $26 | $18 | 390 | +26 | 29% | 9% | 75% | 3.13 | 34 | 4 | 22/2 | — | — | — | — | .630 | .666 | .585 | .502 | .747 |
| 08 | ARI | 22 | 7 | 0 | 226 | 206 | 183 | 3.30 | 1.20 | 7.3 | 2.6 | 0.5 | 3.2 | $23 | $14 | 410 | +17 | 29% | 10% | 73% | 3.19 | 34 | 3 | 24/2 | — | — | — | — | .636 | .634 | .640 | .573 | .695 |
| 09 | ARI | 0 | 0 | 0 | 4 | 6 | 3 | 13.50 | 2.00 | 4.5 | 4.5 | 4.5 | 1.6 | -$4 | -$4 | 0 | -4 | 31% | 40% | 33% | 10.20 | 1 | 0 | 0/1 | — | — | — | — | 1.274 | 1.274 | — | 1.975 | .633 |
| 10 | — | | | | | | | | | | | | | | | | | | | | | | | | | | | | | | | | |

## Ryan Webb — 60 IP | $-1 | 60 pts
**RP-54** | Owned: 0% | RH

Webb in 2010 used his power sinker and slider to burn worms like few others (3.7 GB/F), and he proved that he can step into critical situations. In the Padres' stacked bullpen, however, getting meaningful work is easier said than done, so Webb in 2011 will probably toil in middle relief and be effective there. (DG)

### Forecast
| Player | Age | IP | W | Sv | K | ERA | WHIP | K/9 | BB/9 | $2L | Pts |
|---|---|---|---|---|---|---|---|---|---|---|---|
| Webb R | 25 | 60 | 2 | 0 | 49 | 4.10 | 1.43 | 7.3 | 3.2 | -$1 | 60 |
| Mini-Browser | Age | IP | W | Sv | K | ERA | WHIP | K/9 | BB/9 | $2L | Pts |
| Logan B | 26 | 60 | 2 | 0 | 53 | 4.42 | 1.49 | 7.9 | 4.4 | -$1 | 60 |
| Owens R | 23 | 40 | 2 | 0 | 28 | 4.39 | 1.29 | 6.3 | 2.0 | -$1 | 50 |
| Bailey H | 24 | 180 | 8 | 0 | 145 | 4.85 | 1.42 | 7.3 | 3.6 | -$1 | 180 |
| Pena T | 29 | 80 | 4 | 0 | 49 | 4.77 | 1.42 | 5.5 | 3.3 | -$1 | 70 |
| Norris B | 26 | 160 | 8 | 0 | 163 | 4.80 | 1.51 | 9.2 | 4.3 | -$1 | 200 |

### Minors (2010)
| Level | Leag | W | L | Sv | IP | H | K | ERA | WHIP | K/9 | BB/9 | HR/9 | GB/F |
|---|---|---|---|---|---|---|---|---|---|---|---|---|---|
| A | — | | | | | | | | | | | | |
| AA | — | | | | | | | | | | | | |
| AAA | PCL | 1 | 0 | 1 | 20 | 12 | 23 | 0.87 | 0.82 | 10.0 | 2.2 | 0.4 | — |

### Majors
| Yr | Team | W | L | Sv | IP | H | K | ERA | WHIP | K/9 | BB/9 | HR/9 | GB/F |
|---|---|---|---|---|---|---|---|---|---|---|---|---|---|
| 07 | — | | | | | | | | | | | | |
| 08 | — | | | | | | | | | | | | |
| 09 | SD | 2 | 3 | 0 | 25 | 27 | 19 | 3.86 | 1.48 | 6.7 | 3.9 | 1.1 | 2.3 |
| 10 | SD | 3 | 1 | 0 | 59 | 64 | 44 | 2.90 | 1.41 | 6.7 | 3.1 | 0.2 | 3.7 |

| | Competition at RP | | Stats in 2010 as RP | | | |
|---|---|---|---|---|---|---|
| Thr | Player | GR | ERA | IP/G | Sv-Hld | |
| RH | Gregerson L | 80 | 3.22 | 1.0 | 2-40 | |
| RH | Adams M | 70 | 1.76 | 1.0 | 0-38 | |
| RH | Bell H | 67 | 1.93 | 1.0 | 47-0 | |
| RH | Mujica E | 59 | 3.62 | 1.2 | 0-4 | |

### Value / Luck / In Rotation / In Relief / OPS
| $1L | $2L | Pts | RAA | H% | HR/fb | S% | FIP | GS | CG | QS/DS | GR | Hld | Bln | Lead | OPS | 1st Hf | 2nd Hf | vs RH | vs LH |
|---|---|---|---|---|---|---|---|---|---|---|---|---|---|---|---|---|---|---|---|
| -$1 | -$2 | 30 | -2 | 30% | 14% | 77% | 4.52 | — | — | — | 28 | 6 | 0 | -1.3 | .771 | 1.000 | .753 | .662 | .889 |
| -$1 | -$7 | 70 | +6 | 35% | 3% | 2% | 2.89 | — | — | — | 54 | 9 | 2 | +0.1 | .680 | .581 | .806 | .566 | .846 |

---

## Robbie Weinhardt — 40 IP | $-4 | 40 pts
**RP-28** | Owned: 0% | RH

One of the Tigers' best relief prospects, Weinhardt showed flashes of his potential in MLB in 2010. He has good control, and he generates a lot of grounders, but he was hit hard at times with Detroit. He'll compete for a middle-relief job in Spring Training, and he should spend much of 2011 up with the parent club. (LP)

### Forecast
| Player | Age | IP | W | Sv | K | ERA | WHIP | K/9 | BB/9 | $2L | Pts |
|---|---|---|---|---|---|---|---|---|---|---|---|
| Weinhardt R | 25 | 40 | 2 | 0 | 40 | 5.52 | 1.75 | 9.1 | 3.8 | -$4 | 40 |
| Mini-Browser | Age | IP | W | Sv | K | ERA | WHIP | K/9 | BB/9 | $2L | Pts |
| Jeffress J | 23 | 20 | 1 | 0 | 22 | 5.20 | 1.77 | 9.8 | 5.9 | -$3 | 20 |
| Dunn M | 25 | 40 | 2 | 0 | 48 | 4.71 | 1.79 | 10.9 | 5.9 | -$3 | 20 |
| Coleman C | 23 | 40 | 2 | 0 | 26 | 4.94 | 1.59 | 5.8 | 3.7 | -$3 | 30 |
| Gomez J | 23 | 60 | 3 | 0 | 49 | 5.24 | 1.66 | 7.4 | 3.5 | -$3 | 50 |
| Hampton M | 38 | 40 | 2 | 0 | 23 | 5.35 | 1.46 | 5.1 | 3.4 | -$4 | 30 |

### Minors (2010)
| Level | Leag | W | L | Sv | IP | H | K | ERA | WHIP | K/9 | BB/9 | HR/9 | GB/F |
|---|---|---|---|---|---|---|---|---|---|---|---|---|---|
| A | NYP | 1 | 0 | 0 | 4 | 2 | 5 | 2.25 | 1.00 | 11.3 | 4.5 | 0.0 | — |
| AA | — | | | | | | | | | | | | |
| AAA | IL | 1 | 1 | 1 | 34 | 26 | 25 | 1.57 | 0.96 | 6.6 | 1.8 | 0.0 | — |

### Majors
| Yr | Team | W | L | Sv | IP | H | K | ERA | WHIP | K/9 | BB/9 | HR/9 | GB/F |
|---|---|---|---|---|---|---|---|---|---|---|---|---|---|
| 07 | — | | | | | | | | | | | | |
| 08 | — | | | | | | | | | | | | |
| 09 | — | | | | | | | | | | | | |
| 10 | DET | 2 | 2 | 0 | 29 | 40 | 21 | 6.14 | 1.64 | 6.4 | 2.5 | 0.6 | 2.3 |

| | Competition at RP | | Stats in 2010 as RP | | | |
|---|---|---|---|---|---|---|
| Thr | Player | GR | ERA | IP/G | Sv-Hld | |
| RH | Valverde J | 60 | 3.00 | 1.0 | 26-0 | |
| RH | Perry R | 60 | 3.59 | 1.0 | 2-19 | |
| RH | Bonine E | 46 | 4.18 | 1.4 | 0-2 | |
| RH | Zumaya J | 31 | 2.58 | 1.2 | 1-11 | |

### Value / Luck / In Rotation / In Relief / OPS
| $1L | $2L | Pts | RAA | H% | HR/fb | S% | FIP | GS | CG | QS/DS | GR | Hld | Bln | Lead | OPS | 1st Hf | 2nd Hf | vs RH | vs LH |
|---|---|---|---|---|---|---|---|---|---|---|---|---|---|---|---|---|---|---|---|
| -$5 | -$15 | 30 | -10 | 39% | 8% | 61% | 3.57 | — | — | — | 28 | 5 | 2 | +0.4 | .831 | .439 | .870 | .949 | .616 |

---

## Todd Wellemeyer — 60 IP | $-5 | 40 pts
**SP-11, RP-2** | Owned: 0% | RH

It's hard to remember now that the Giants' #5 SP when they broke camp in 2010 was Todd Wellemeyer. Wellemeyer was released by SF in August, and his days of being an option in anyone's rotation are over. Wellemeyer's fastball might regain its lost oomph if he was moved to a bullpen. (PB)

### Forecast
| Player | Age | IP | W | Sv | K | ERA | WHIP | K/9 | BB/9 | $2L | Pts |
|---|---|---|---|---|---|---|---|---|---|---|---|
| Wellemeyer T | 32 | 60 | 3 | 0 | 37 | 5.70 | 1.52 | 5.5 | 4.1 | -$5 | 40 |
| Mini-Browser | Age | IP | W | Sv | K | ERA | WHIP | K/9 | BB/9 | $2L | Pts |
| Wood T | 28 | 40 | 1 | 0 | 28 | 5.05 | 1.68 | 6.3 | 4.5 | -$5 | 20 |
| Lynn L | 23 | 60 | 3 | 0 | 43 | 5.52 | 1.58 | 6.4 | 4.4 | -$5 | 50 |
| Medders B | 31 | 60 | 3 | 0 | 43 | 5.07 | 1.61 | 6.5 | 4.2 | -$5 | 50 |
| Moehler B | 39 | 60 | 2 | 0 | 30 | 5.43 | 1.50 | 4.5 | 3.0 | -$5 | 30 |
| Vasquez E | 27 | 60 | 2 | 0 | 54 | 5.26 | 1.65 | 8.1 | 5.4 | -$5 | 50 |

### Minors (2010)
| Level | Leag | W | L | Sv | IP | H | K | ERA | WHIP | K/9 | BB/9 | HR/9 | GB/F |
|---|---|---|---|---|---|---|---|---|---|---|---|---|---|
| A | — | | | | | | | | | | | | |
| AA | — | | | | | | | | | | | | |
| AAA | PCL | 1 | 0 | 0 | 16 | 9 | 12 | 2.25 | 1.31 | 6.8 | 6.8 | 0.6 | — |

### Majors
| Yr | Team | W | L | Sv | IP | H | K | ERA | WHIP | K/9 | BB/9 | HR/9 | GB/F |
|---|---|---|---|---|---|---|---|---|---|---|---|---|---|
| 07 | 2TM | 3 | 3 | 0 | 79 | 77 | 60 | 4.54 | 1.47 | 6.8 | 4.5 | 1.2 | 1.0 |
| 08 | STL | 13 | 9 | 0 | 191 | 178 | 134 | 3.71 | 1.25 | 6.3 | 2.9 | 1.2 | 1.0 |
| 09 | STL | 7 | 10 | 0 | 122 | 160 | 78 | 5.89 | 1.77 | 5.7 | 4.2 | 1.4 | 0.9 |
| 10 | SF | 3 | 5 | 0 | 58 | 57 | 41 | 5.68 | 1.57 | 6.3 | 5.4 | 1.8 | 0.7 |

| | Competition at RP | | Stats in 2010 as RP | | | |
|---|---|---|---|---|---|---|
| Thr | Player | GR | ERA | IP/G | Sv-Hld | |
| RH | Wilson B | 70 | 1.81 | 1.1 | 48-0 | |
| RH | Romo S | 68 | 2.18 | 0.9 | 0-21 | |
| RH | Mota G | 56 | 4.33 | 1.0 | 1-8 | |
| RH | Casilla S | 52 | 1.95 | 1.1 | 2-11 | |

### Value / Luck / In Rotation / In Relief / OPS
| $1L | $2L | Pts | RAA | H% | HR/fb | S% | FIP | GS | CG | QS/DS | GR | Hld | Bln | Lead | OPS | 1st Hf | 2nd Hf | vs RH | vs LH |
|---|---|---|---|---|---|---|---|---|---|---|---|---|---|---|---|---|---|---|---|
| -$3 | -$7 | 250 | -28 | 27% | 11% | 73% | 5.05 | 11 | 0 | 2/1 | 21 | 2 | 0 | -1.1 | .752 | .867 | .317 | .628 | .882 |
| $12 | $4 | 260 | +2 | 27% | 11% | 75% | 4.47 | 32 | 0 | 17/2 | — | — | — | | .724 | .728 | .720 | .699 | .759 |
| -$10 | -$14 | 80 | -33 | 36% | 11% | 69% | 5.34 | 21 | 0 | 5/6 | 7 | 0 | 0 | +0.4 | .907 | .874 | 1.047 | .742 | 1.068 |
| -$8 | -$18 | 50 | -11 | 27% | 14% | 69% | 6.25 | 11 | 0 | 4/2 | 2 | 0 | 0 | -0.4 | .837 | .817 | 2.000 | .689 | 1.027 |

---

## Randy Wells — 180 IP | $4 | 190 pts
**SP-32** | Owned: 65% | RH

On May 28, Randy Wells allowed hits to the first six Cardinal hitters, and he was pulled from his start. He returned to play three days later, unfazed and en route to a near-200 IP season. Under Mike Quade, Wells posted a 3.12 ERA in 4 of 6 starts vs. play-off teams, and he is a solid mid-rotation starter for 2011. (RM)

### Forecast
| Player | Age | IP | W | Sv | K | ERA | WHIP | K/9 | BB/9 | $2L | Pts |
|---|---|---|---|---|---|---|---|---|---|---|---|
| Wells R | 28 | 180 | 9 | 0 | 127 | 4.30 | 1.37 | 6.3 | 2.8 | $4 | 190 |
| Mini-Browser | Age | IP | W | Sv | K | ERA | WHIP | K/9 | BB/9 | $2L | Pts |
| Figueroa N | 36 | 100 | 7 | 0 | 79 | 3.86 | 1.32 | 7.1 | 3.0 | $5 | 140 |
| Matusz B | 24 | 180 | 10 | 0 | 156 | 4.54 | 1.44 | 7.8 | 3.3 | $5 | 210 |
| Takahashi H | 35 | 60 | 4 | 15 | 46 | 4.43 | 1.38 | 7.0 | 3.5 | $4 | 100 |
| Balfour G | 33 | 60 | 3 | 2 | 64 | 3.24 | 1.26 | 9.6 | 4.1 | $4 | 100 |
| Devine J | 27 | 45 | 3 | 2 | 51 | 2.87 | 1.25 | 10.2 | 3.8 | $4 | 90 |

### Minors (2010)
| Level | Leag | W | L | Sv | IP | H | K | ERA | WHIP | K/9 | BB/9 | HR/9 | GB/F |
|---|---|---|---|---|---|---|---|---|---|---|---|---|---|
| A | — | | | | | | | | | | | | |
| AA | — | | | | | | | | | | | | |
| AAA | — | | | | | | | | | | | | |

### Majors
| Yr | Team | W | L | Sv | IP | H | K | ERA | WHIP | K/9 | BB/9 | HR/9 | GB/F |
|---|---|---|---|---|---|---|---|---|---|---|---|---|---|
| 07 | — | | | | | | | | | | | | |
| 08 | 2TM | 0 | 0 | 0 | 5 | 4 | 1 | 0.00 | 0.56 | 1.7 | 5.1 | 0.0 | 1.8 |
| 09 | CHC | 12 | 10 | 0 | 165 | 165 | 104 | 3.05 | 1.28 | 5.7 | 2.5 | 0.8 | 1.4 |
| 10 | CHC | 8 | 14 | 0 | 194 | 209 | 144 | 4.26 | 1.40 | 6.7 | 2.9 | 0.9 | 1.4 |

| | Competition at SP | | Stats in 2010 as SP | | |
|---|---|---|---|---|---|
| Thr | Player | GS | ERA | Supp | W-L |
| RH | Dempster R | 34 | 3.85 | 4.8 | 15-12 |
| RH | Wells R | 32 | 4.26 | 3.3 | 8-14 |
| LH | Gorzelanny T | 23 | 4.22 | 4.1 | 7-9 |
| RH | Silva C | 21 | 4.22 | 5.1 | 10-6 |

### Value / Luck / In Rotation / In Relief / OPS
| $1L | $2L | Pts | RAA | H% | HR/fb | S% | FIP | GS | CG | QS/DS | GR | Hld | Bln | Lead | OPS | 1st Hf | 2nd Hf | vs RH | vs LH |
|---|---|---|---|---|---|---|---|---|---|---|---|---|---|---|---|---|---|---|---|
| -$3 | -$1 | 0 | +3 | 0% | 0% | 100% | 4.56 | — | — | — | 4 | 0 | 0 | +1.3 | .167 | .250 | .143 | .273 | .000 |
| $12 | $7 | 230 | +15 | 29% | 8% | 79% | 3.88 | 27 | 0 | 18/4 | — | — | — | | .680 | .641 | .711 | .575 | .806 |
| $0 | -$14 | 190 | -1 | 32% | 9% | 71% | 3.96 | 32 | 0 | 18/6 | — | — | — | | .745 | .738 | .754 | .775 | .700 |

---

## Sean West — 120 IP | $-9 | 100 pts
**SP-2** | Owned: 0% | LH

West pitched well in Triple-A for most of 2010 before starting two games for the Marlins and then yielding to knee inflammation. He should get ample opportunity to start again in 2011, as he is the only left-hander in the organization who is near to being MLB-ready. If West has decent command, he should stick. (MJ)

### Forecast
| Player | Age | IP | W | Sv | K | ERA | WHIP | K/9 | BB/9 | $2L | Pts |
|---|---|---|---|---|---|---|---|---|---|---|---|
| West S | 24 | 120 | 6 | 0 | 100 | 5.57 | 1.69 | 7.5 | 4.3 | -$9 | 100 |
| Mini-Browser | Age | IP | W | Sv | K | ERA | WHIP | K/9 | BB/9 | $2L | Pts |
| Samardzija J | 26 | 60 | 3 | 0 | 43 | 5.96 | 1.65 | 6.4 | 4.4 | -$7 | 40 |
| Rogers E | 25 | 80 | 4 | 0 | 75 | 5.64 | 1.66 | 8.5 | 3.5 | -$7 | 70 |
| McAllister Z | 23 | 40 | 2 | 0 | 19 | 7.23 | 1.76 | 4.4 | 3.7 | -$7 | 10 |
| Crow A | 24 | 40 | 1 | 0 | 24 | 7.22 | 1.85 | 5.3 | 5.1 | -$8 | 10 |
| Reckling T | 21 | 40 | 1 | 0 | 21 | 7.21 | 2.02 | 4.7 | 6.8 | -$9 | — |

### Minors (2010)
| Level | Leag | W | L | Sv | IP | H | K | ERA | WHIP | K/9 | BB/9 | HR/9 | GB/F |
|---|---|---|---|---|---|---|---|---|---|---|---|---|---|
| A | — | | | | | | | | | | | | |
| AA | — | | | | | | | | | | | | |
| AAA | PCL | 4 | 3 | 0 | 57 | 60 | 46 | 3.12 | 1.37 | 7.2 | 3.0 | 0.6 | — |

### Majors
| Yr | Team | W | L | Sv | IP | H | K | ERA | WHIP | K/9 | BB/9 | HR/9 | GB/F |
|---|---|---|---|---|---|---|---|---|---|---|---|---|---|
| 07 | — | | | | | | | | | | | | |
| 08 | — | | | | | | | | | | | | |
| 09 | FLA | 8 | 6 | 0 | 103 | 115 | 70 | 4.79 | 1.54 | 6.1 | 3.8 | 1.0 | 1.0 |
| 10 | FLA | 0 | 2 | 0 | 9 | 15 | 8 | 7.71 | 2.04 | 7.7 | 3.9 | 1.9 | 1.0 |

| | Competition at SP | | Stats in 2010 as SP | | |
|---|---|---|---|---|---|
| Thr | Player | GS | ERA | Supp | W-L |
| RH | Sanchez A | 32 | 3.55 | 4.8 | 13-12 |
| RH | Volstad C | 30 | 4.58 | 5.1 | 12-9 |
| RH | Johnson J | 28 | 2.30 | 4.3 | 11-6 |
| RH | Nolasco R | 26 | 4.51 | 4.4 | 14-9 |

### Value / Luck / In Rotation / In Relief / OPS
| $1L | $2L | Pts | RAA | H% | HR/fb | S% | FIP | GS | CG | QS/DS | GR | Hld | Bln | Lead | OPS | 1st Hf | 2nd Hf | vs RH | vs LH |
|---|---|---|---|---|---|---|---|---|---|---|---|---|---|---|---|---|---|---|---|
| -$1 | -$5 | 120 | -11 | 32% | 8% | 70% | 4.51 | 20 | 0 | 7/6 | — | — | — | | .801 | .773 | .831 | .782 | .889 |
| -$7 | -$14 | 0 | -4 | 43% | 15% | 65% | 5.56 | 2 | 0 | — | — | — | — | | 1.032 | — | 1.032 | 1.039 | 1.000 |

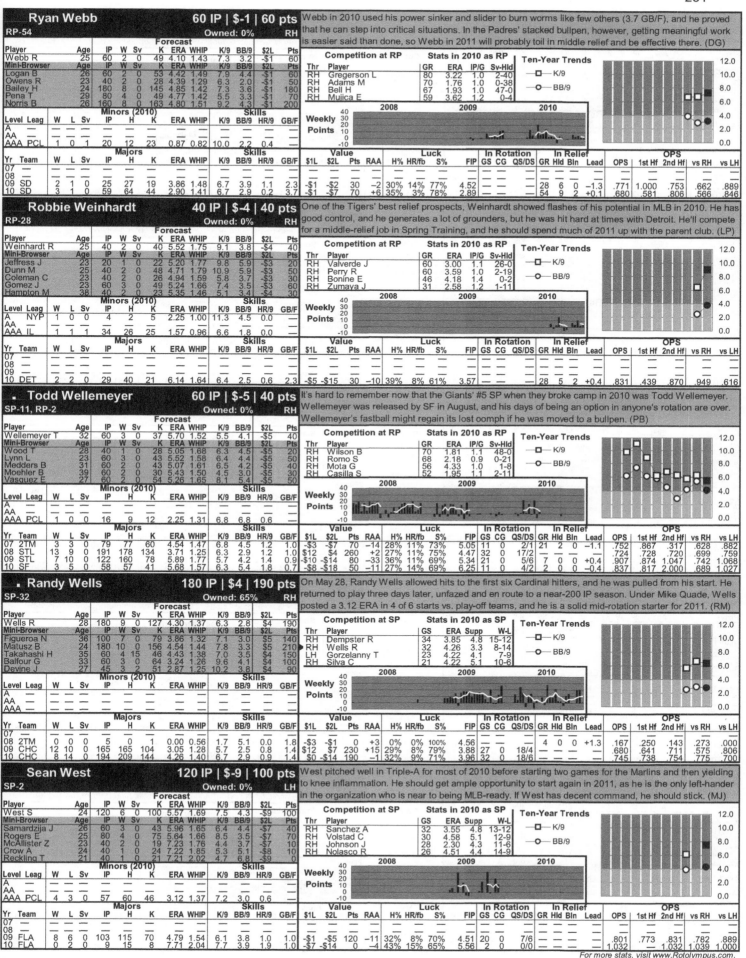

*For more stats, visit www.Rotolympus.com.*

## Jake Westbrook — 180 IP | $4 | 170 pts
SP-33 · Owned: 9% · RH

Finally returned from TJ surgery, Westbrook performed well after switching to the NL at the deadline – his ability to coax a lot of GB meshes well with St. Louis's pitch-to-contact philosophy. The Cards would like to keep him, but their payroll flexibility might be limited depending on their upcoming decision on Pujols. (AB)

### Forecast
| Player | Age | IP | W | Sv | K | ERA | WHIP | K/9 | BB/9 | $2L | Pts |
|---|---|---|---|---|---|---|---|---|---|---|---|
| Westbrook J | 33 | 180 | 9 | 0 | 108 | 4.33 | 1.35 | 5.4 | 3.0 | $4 | 170 |

### Mini-Browser
| Player | Age | IP | W | Sv | K | ERA | WHIP | K/9 | BB/9 | $2L | Pts |
|---|---|---|---|---|---|---|---|---|---|---|---|
| Chamberlain J | 25 | 60 | 4 | 10 | 57 | 4.29 | 1.38 | 8.5 | 3.9 | $4 | 130 |
| Hunter T | 24 | 140 | 10 | 0 | 83 | 4.55 | 1.38 | 5.4 | 2.6 | $4 | 160 |
| Burnett A | 34 | 180 | 11 | 0 | 155 | 4.74 | 1.45 | 7.7 | 4.1 | $4 | 220 |
| Matsuzaka D | 30 | 160 | 10 | 0 | 138 | 4.63 | 1.44 | 7.8 | 4.5 | $4 | 200 |
| Jackson E | 27 | 200 | 10 | 0 | 145 | 4.69 | 1.42 | 6.5 | 3.4 | $4 | 200 |

### Competition at SP / Stats in 2010 as SP
| Thr | Player | GS | ERA | Supp | W-L |
|---|---|---|---|---|---|
| RH | Carpenter C | 35 | 3.22 | 4.7 | 16-9 |
| RH | Wainwright A | 33 | 2.42 | 4.8 | 20-11 |
| RH | Westbrook J | 33 | 4.22 | 4.0 | 10-11 |
| LH | Garcia J | 28 | 2.70 | 4.5 | 13-8 |

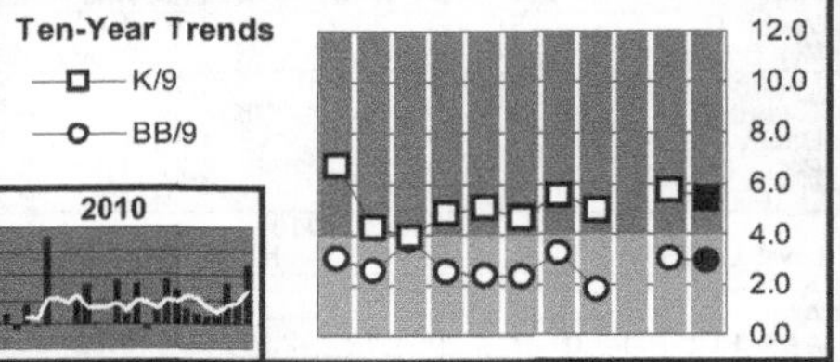

### Minors (2010)
| Level | Leag | W | L | Sv | IP | H | K | ERA | WHIP | K/9 | BB/9 | HR/9 | GB/F |
|---|---|---|---|---|---|---|---|---|---|---|---|---|---|
| A | — | — | — | — | — | — | — | — | — | — | — | — | — |
| AA | — | — | — | — | — | — | — | — | — | — | — | — | — |
| AAA | — | — | — | — | — | — | — | — | — | — | — | — | — |

### Majors / Value / Luck / In Rotation / In Relief / OPS
| Yr | Team | W | L | Sv | IP | H | K | ERA | WHIP | K/9 | BB/9 | HR/9 | GB/F | $1L | $2L | Pts | RAA | H% | HR/fb | S% | FIP | GS | CG | QS/DS | GR | Hld | Bln | Lead | OPS | 1st Hf | 2nd Hf | vs RH | vs LH |
|---|---|---|---|---|---|---|---|---|---|---|---|---|---|---|---|---|---|---|---|---|---|---|---|---|---|---|---|---|---|---|---|---|---|
| 07 | CLE | 6 | 9 | 0 | 152 | 159 | 93 | 4.32 | 1.41 | 5.5 | 3.3 | 0.8 | 2.0 | $2 | -$9 | 120 | -3 | 31% | 10% | 70% | 4.27 | 25 | 0 | 15/2 | — | — | — | — | .729 | .788 | .701 | .669 | .783 |
| 08 | CLE | 1 | 2 | 0 | 34 | 33 | 19 | 3.12 | 1.15 | 4.9 | 1.8 | 1.3 | 2.0 | $1 | $0 | 30 | +4 | 27% | 17% | 80% | 4.68 | 5 | 1 | 4/0 | — | — | — | — | .698 | .698 | — | .785 | .607 |
| 09 | — | — | — | — | — | — | — | — | — | — | — | — | — | — | — | — | — | — | — | — | — | — | — | — | — | — | — | — | — | — | — | — | — |
| 10 | 2TM | 10 | 11 | 0 | 202 | 203 | 128 | 4.22 | 1.34 | 5.7 | 3.0 | 0.9 | 2.1 | $3 | -$11 | 200 | +1 | 29% | 12% | 72% | 4.21 | 33 | 0 | 18/4 | — | — | — | — | .727 | .786 | .658 | .694 | .767 |

## Dan Wheeler — 50 IP | $2 | 60 pts
RP-64 · Owned: 2% · RH

It would be hard for the Rays to pick up the $4M option for a pitcher who was used almost entirely against right-handers and who pitched only sporadically at the end of the season. If the Rays really want Wheeler, they might buy out his contract and then re-sign him at a lower rate. It's not a question of his talent. (RZ)

### Forecast
| Player | Age | IP | W | Sv | K | ERA | WHIP | K/9 | BB/9 | $2L | Pts |
|---|---|---|---|---|---|---|---|---|---|---|---|
| Wheeler D | 33 | 50 | 2 | 0 | 42 | 4.23 | 1.18 | 7.6 | 2.6 | $2 | 60 |

### Mini-Browser
| Player | Age | IP | W | Sv | K | ERA | WHIP | K/9 | BB/9 | $2L | Pts |
|---|---|---|---|---|---|---|---|---|---|---|---|
| Peralta J | 35 | 60 | 2 | 0 | 51 | 4.01 | 1.17 | 7.6 | 2.4 | $2 | 70 |
| Wood K | 33 | 60 | 3 | 0 | 62 | 3.77 | 1.41 | 9.3 | 4.7 | $2 | 80 |
| Porcello R | 22 | 200 | 11 | 0 | 100 | 4.92 | 1.39 | 4.5 | 2.5 | $2 | 170 |
| Sanches B | 32 | 60 | 2 | 0 | 52 | 3.56 | 1.29 | 7.8 | 3.8 | $2 | 70 |
| Strop P | 25 | 40 | 2 | 0 | 39 | 3.18 | 1.31 | 8.8 | 3.9 | $2 | 60 |

### Competition at RP / Stats in 2010 as RP
| Thr | Player | GR | ERA | IP/G | Sv-Hld |
|---|---|---|---|---|---|
| RH | Soriano R | 64 | 1.73 | 1.0 | 45-0 |
| RH | Wheeler D | 64 | 3.35 | 0.8 | 3-9 |
| RH | Benoit R | 63 | 1.34 | 1.0 | 1-25 |
| RH | Cormier L | 60 | 3.92 | 1.0 | 0-4 |

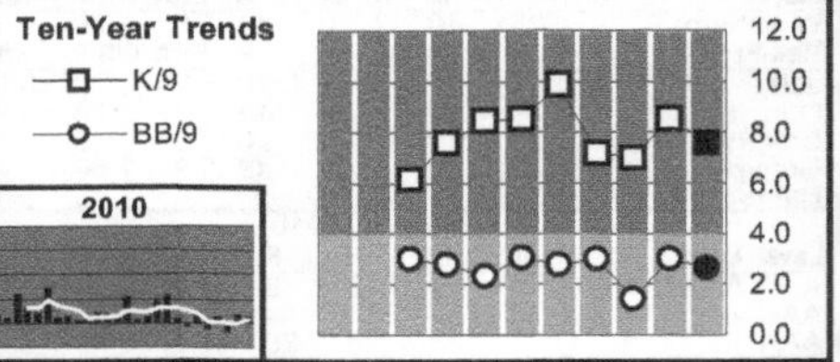

### Minors (2010)
| Level | Leag | W | L | Sv | IP | H | K | ERA | WHIP | K/9 | BB/9 | HR/9 | GB/F |
|---|---|---|---|---|---|---|---|---|---|---|---|---|---|
| A | — | — | — | — | — | — | — | — | — | — | — | — | — |
| AA | — | — | — | — | — | — | — | — | — | — | — | — | — |
| AAA | — | — | — | — | — | — | — | — | — | — | — | — | — |

### Majors / Value / Luck / In Rotation / In Relief / OPS
| Yr | Team | W | L | Sv | IP | H | K | ERA | WHIP | K/9 | BB/9 | HR/9 | GB/F | $1L | $2L | Pts | RAA | H% | HR/fb | S% | FIP | GS | CG | QS/DS | GR | Hld | Bln | Lead | OPS | 1st Hf | 2nd Hf | vs RH | vs LH |
|---|---|---|---|---|---|---|---|---|---|---|---|---|---|---|---|---|---|---|---|---|---|---|---|---|---|---|---|---|---|---|---|---|---|
| 07 | 2TM | 1 | 9 | 11 | 74 | 74 | 82 | 5.30 | 1.30 | 9.9 | 2.8 | 1.3 | 0.8 | -$1 | -$5 | 130 | -14 | 32% | 12% | 62% | 3.89 | — | — | — | 70 | 18 | 7 | +0.9 | .757 | .762 | .750 | .745 | .773 |
| 08 | TB | 5 | 6 | 13 | 66 | 44 | 53 | 3.12 | 0.99 | 7.2 | 3.0 | 1.4 | 0.5 | $11 | $7 | 180 | +5 | 20% | 10% | 77% | 4.66 | — | — | — | 70 | 26 | 5 | +0.9 | .608 | .555 | .694 | .570 | .669 |
| 09 | TB | 4 | 5 | 2 | 57 | 41 | 45 | 3.28 | 0.87 | 7.0 | 1.4 | 1.7 | 0.6 | $7 | $4 | 110 | +4 | 20% | 12% | 74% | 4.69 | — | — | — | 69 | 16 | 4 | +0.7 | .659 | .655 | .662 | .511 | 1.020 |
| 10 | TB | 2 | 4 | 3 | 48 | 36 | 46 | 3.35 | 1.08 | 8.6 | 3.0 | 1.3 | 0.8 | $3 | -$4 | 90 | +2 | 24% | 12% | 76% | 4.27 | — | — | — | 64 | 9 | 3 | +0.1 | .681 | .651 | .726 | .687 | .663 |

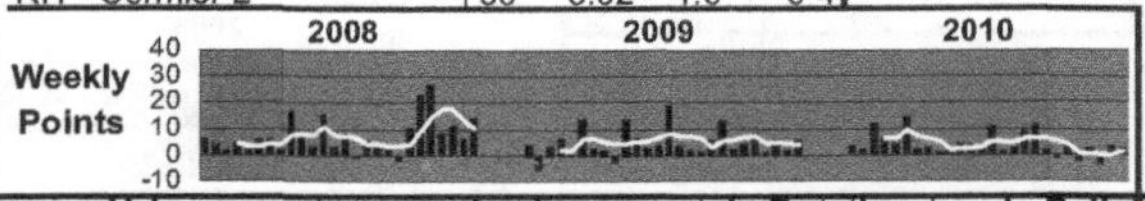

## Sean White — 40 IP | $-3 | 20 pts
RP-38 · Owned: 0% · RH

White was mediocre at best in MLB in 2010, and he should be back in Triple-A, where he has only 153 IP. There is a chance that White will be back in the bullpen in 2011, but he might have finally done enough to earn himself a one-way ticket to Tacoma. (GC)

### Forecast
| Player | Age | IP | W | Sv | K | ERA | WHIP | K/9 | BB/9 | $2L | Pts |
|---|---|---|---|---|---|---|---|---|---|---|---|
| White S | 29 | 40 | 1 | 0 | 18 | 4.89 | 1.53 | 4.1 | 3.3 | -$3 | 20 |

### Mini-Browser
| Player | Age | IP | W | Sv | K | ERA | WHIP | K/9 | BB/9 | $2L | Pts |
|---|---|---|---|---|---|---|---|---|---|---|---|
| Smith C | 29 | 40 | 1 | 0 | 32 | 5.15 | 1.41 | 7.3 | 3.0 | -$3 | 30 |
| McGee J | 24 | 50 | 2 | 0 | 53 | 5.15 | 1.67 | 9.6 | 4.7 | -$3 | 60 |
| Mickolio K | 26 | 40 | 1 | 0 | 44 | 4.94 | 1.69 | 9.8 | 5.0 | -$3 | 40 |
| Detwiler R | 25 | 100 | 5 | 0 | 76 | 4.55 | 1.57 | 6.9 | 3.9 | -$3 | 100 |
| Valdes R | 33 | 40 | 2 | 0 | 29 | 5.02 | 1.49 | 6.6 | 4.1 | -$3 | 40 |

### Competition at RP / Stats in 2010 as RP
| Thr | Player | GR | ERA | IP/G | Sv-Hld |
|---|---|---|---|---|---|
| RH | League B | 70 | 3.42 | 1.1 | 6-13 |
| RH | Aardsma D | 53 | 3.44 | 0.9 | 31-0 |
| RH | White S | 38 | 5.24 | 0.9 | 0-5 |
| RH | Wright J | 28 | 3.41 | 1.3 | 0-8 |

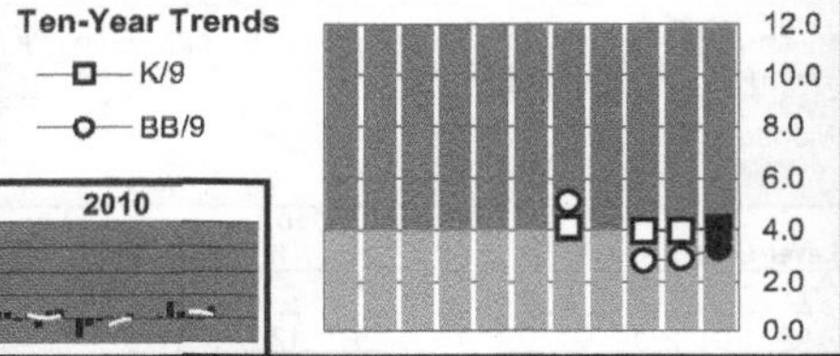

### Minors (2010)
| Level | Leag | W | L | Sv | IP | H | K | ERA | WHIP | K/9 | BB/9 | HR/9 | GB/F |
|---|---|---|---|---|---|---|---|---|---|---|---|---|---|
| A | — | — | — | — | — | — | — | — | — | — | — | — | — |
| AA | — | — | — | — | — | — | — | — | — | — | — | — | — |
| AAA | PCL | 1 | 0 | 0 | 13 | 7 | 10 | 0.00 | 1.15 | 6.9 | 5.5 | 0.0 | — |

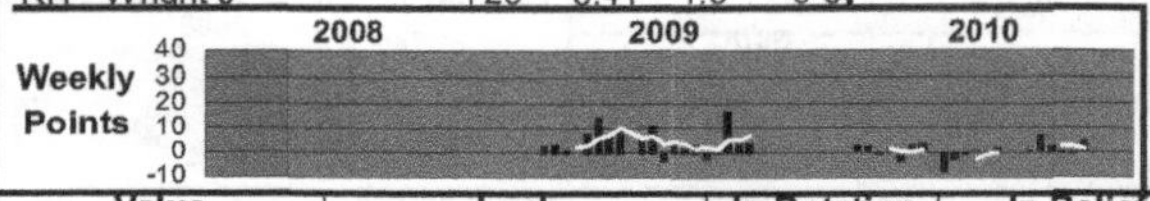

### Majors / Value / Luck / In Rotation / In Relief / OPS
| Yr | Team | W | L | Sv | IP | H | K | ERA | WHIP | K/9 | BB/9 | HR/9 | GB/F | $1L | $2L | Pts | RAA | H% | HR/fb | S% | FIP | GS | CG | QS/DS | GR | Hld | Bln | Lead | OPS | 1st Hf | 2nd Hf | vs RH | vs LH |
|---|---|---|---|---|---|---|---|---|---|---|---|---|---|---|---|---|---|---|---|---|---|---|---|---|---|---|---|---|---|---|---|---|---|
| 07 | SEA | 1 | 1 | 0 | 35 | 35 | 16 | 5.60 | 1.56 | 4.1 | 5.1 | 0.5 | 1.5 | -$4 | -$8 | 10 | -8 | 28% | 5% | 62% | 4.83 | — | — | — | 15 | 0 | 0 | -3.5 | .777 | .761 | .810 | .777 | .778 |
| 08 | — | — | — | — | — | — | — | — | — | — | — | — | — | — | — | — | — | — | — | — | — | — | — | — | — | — | — | — | — | — | — | — | — |
| 09 | SEA | 3 | 2 | 1 | 64 | 50 | 28 | 2.80 | 1.09 | 3.9 | 2.8 | 0.4 | 1.4 | $5 | $3 | 70 | +6 | 23% | 4% | 75% | 3.97 | — | — | — | 52 | 15 | 2 | -0.6 | .581 | .588 | .565 | .626 | .531 |
| 10 | SEA | 0 | 1 | 0 | 34 | 45 | 15 | 5.24 | 1.63 | 3.9 | 2.9 | 1.1 | 1.4 | -$5 | -$16 | 20 | -10 | 31% | 10% | 69% | 4.90 | — | — | — | 38 | 5 | 3 | -2.0 | .891 | 1.025 | .643 | .810 | 1.001 |

## Dontrelle Willis — 40 IP | $-6 | 20 pts
SP-13, RP-2 · Owned: 1% · LH

Neither Detroit nor Arizona could restore the D-Train's magic, and he looked awful in almost every way each time he took the mound. His past successes and infectious enthusiasm might earn him a minor-league deal with a team desperate for a southpaw, but he is unlikely to be a factor in MLB again. (MS)

### Forecast
| Player | Age | IP | W | Sv | K | ERA | WHIP | K/9 | BB/9 | $2L | Pts |
|---|---|---|---|---|---|---|---|---|---|---|---|
| Willis D | 29 | 40 | 2 | 0 | 26 | 5.74 | 1.76 | 5.8 | 6.0 | -$6 | 20 |

### Mini-Browser
| Player | Age | IP | W | Sv | K | ERA | WHIP | K/9 | BB/9 | $2L | Pts |
|---|---|---|---|---|---|---|---|---|---|---|---|
| Wood B | 25 | 60 | 2 | 0 | 50 | 5.71 | 1.73 | 7.5 | 4.1 | -$6 | 40 |
| Lopez R | 35 | 180 | 7 | 0 | 104 | 5.25 | 1.43 | 5.2 | 2.4 | -$6 | 120 |
| Suppan J | 36 | 60 | 3 | 0 | 28 | 5.58 | 1.55 | 4.1 | 3.5 | -$6 | 30 |
| Leroux C | 26 | 40 | 2 | 0 | 39 | 5.67 | 1.80 | 8.7 | 4.5 | -$6 | 30 |
| Chatwood T | 21 | 40 | 2 | 0 | 19 | 6.02 | 1.89 | 4.3 | 5.4 | -$6 | 20 |

### Competition at SP / Stats in 2010 as SP
| Thr | Player | GS | ERA | Supp | W-L |
|---|---|---|---|---|---|
| LH | Saunders J | 33 | 4.47 | 3.9 | 9-17 |
| RH | Lopez R | 33 | 5.00 | 4.4 | 7-16 |
| RH | Kennedy I | 32 | 3.80 | 5.1 | 9-10 |
| RH | Enright B | 17 | 3.91 | 3.4 | 6-7 |

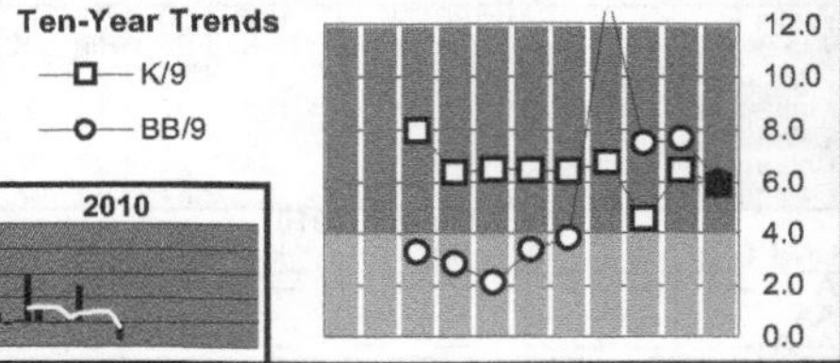

### Minors (2010)
| Level | Leag | W | L | Sv | IP | H | K | ERA | WHIP | K/9 | BB/9 | HR/9 | GB/F |
|---|---|---|---|---|---|---|---|---|---|---|---|---|---|
| A | — | — | — | — | — | — | — | — | — | — | — | — | — |
| AA | — | — | — | — | — | — | — | — | — | — | — | — | — |
| AAA | PCL | 0 | 0 | 0 | 5 | 2 | 6 | 5.06 | 1.13 | 10.1 | 6.8 | 1.7 | — |

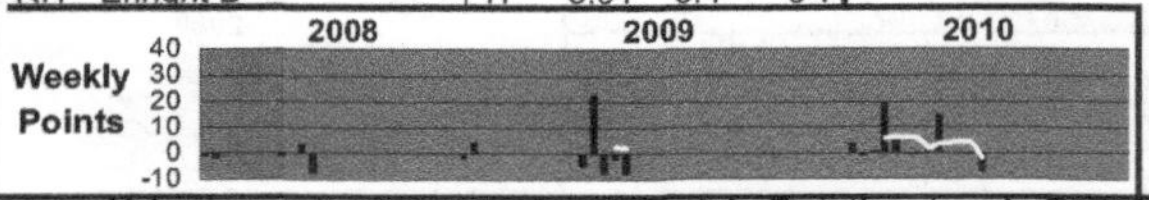

### Majors / Value / Luck / In Rotation / In Relief / OPS
| Yr | Team | W | L | Sv | IP | H | K | ERA | WHIP | K/9 | BB/9 | HR/9 | GB/F | $1L | $2L | Pts | RAA | H% | HR/fb | S% | FIP | GS | CG | QS/DS | GR | Hld | Bln | Lead | OPS | 1st Hf | 2nd Hf | vs RH | vs LH |
|---|---|---|---|---|---|---|---|---|---|---|---|---|---|---|---|---|---|---|---|---|---|---|---|---|---|---|---|---|---|---|---|---|---|
| 07 | FLA | 10 | 15 | 0 | 205 | 241 | 146 | 5.17 | 1.60 | 6.4 | 3.8 | 1.3 | 1.4 | -$7 | -$26 | 170 | -30 | 33% | 13% | 70% | 4.89 | 35 | 0 | 16/6 | — | — | — | — | .846 | .798 | .907 | .919 | .356 |
| 08 | DET | 0 | 2 | 0 | 24 | 18 | 18 | 9.38 | 2.21 | 6.8 | 13.1 | 1.5 | 0.9 | -$9 | -$12 | -10 | -13 | 22% | 13% | 57% | 8.34 | 7 | 0 | 0/3 | 1 | 0 | 0 | -0.6 | .884 | .915 | .855 | 1.005 | .550 |
| 09 | DET | 1 | 4 | 0 | 33 | 37 | 17 | 7.49 | 1.93 | 4.5 | 7.5 | 1.1 | 1.7 | -$5 | -$8 | 0 | -11 | 31% | 12% | 61% | 6.33 | 7 | 0 | 2/3 | — | — | — | — | .854 | .854 | — | .785 | 1.028 |
| 10 | 2TM | 2 | 3 | 0 | 65 | 72 | 47 | 5.62 | 1.95 | 6.4 | 7.7 | 0.8 | 1.6 | -$12 | -$26 | 30 | -9 | 34% | 11% | 71% | 5.56 | 13 | 0 | 4/2 | 2 | 0 | 0 | -0.8 | .836 | .836 | — | .937 | .581 |

## Brian Wilson — 60 IP | $17 | 310 pts
RP-70 · Owned: 100% · RH

Wilson's command of his fastball is still occasionally an issue, but when that fastball is coupled with a pitch that has morphed over the past couple years from a 90-MPH slider into a cutter, Wilson dominates. 2010 almost certainly represents Wilson's peak performance, but his rates held up over the season. (PB)

### Forecast
| Player | Age | IP | W | Sv | K | ERA | WHIP | K/9 | BB/9 | $2L | Pts |
|---|---|---|---|---|---|---|---|---|---|---|---|
| Wilson B | 29 | 60 | 2 | 44 | 65 | 2.92 | 1.28 | 9.8 | 3.5 | $17 | 310 |

### Mini-Browser
| Player | Age | IP | W | Sv | K | ERA | WHIP | K/9 | BB/9 | $2L | Pts |
|---|---|---|---|---|---|---|---|---|---|---|---|
| Bell H | 33 | 60 | 4 | 38 | 62 | 2.67 | 1.15 | 9.2 | 3.2 | $18 | 300 |
| Sale C | 22 | 160 | 10 | 0 | 225 | 3.38 | 1.28 | 12.7 | 5.1 | $18 | 320 |
| Papelbon J | 30 | 60 | 4 | 41 | 65 | 3.22 | 1.18 | 9.7 | 2.9 | $18 | 320 |
| Jimenez U | 27 | 220 | 17 | 0 | 192 | 3.64 | 1.31 | 7.9 | 3.9 | $17 | 350 |
| Price D | 25 | 200 | 15 | 0 | 177 | 3.63 | 1.32 | 8.0 | 3.7 | $17 | 320 |

### Competition at RP / Stats in 2010 as RP
| Thr | Player | GR | ERA | IP/G | Sv-Hld |
|---|---|---|---|---|---|
| RH | Wilson B | 70 | 1.81 | 1.1 | 48-0 |
| RH | Romo S | 68 | 2.18 | 0.9 | 0-21 |
| RH | Mota G | 56 | 4.33 | 1.0 | 1-8 |
| RH | Casilla S | 52 | 1.95 | 1.1 | 2-11 |

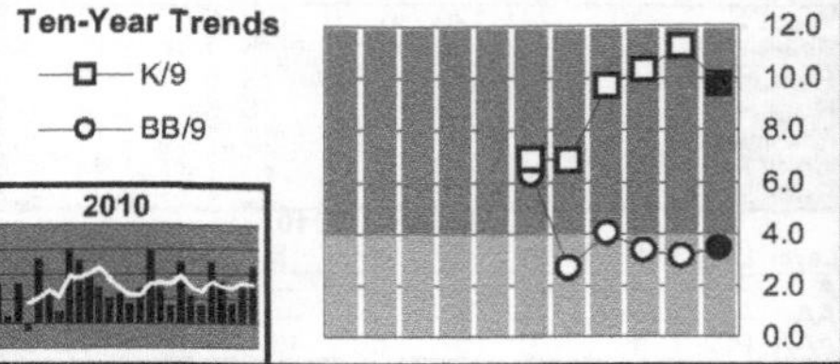

### Minors (2010)
| Level | Leag | W | L | Sv | IP | H | K | ERA | WHIP | K/9 | BB/9 | HR/9 | GB/F |
|---|---|---|---|---|---|---|---|---|---|---|---|---|---|
| A | — | — | — | — | — | — | — | — | — | — | — | — | — |
| AA | — | — | — | — | — | — | — | — | — | — | — | — | — |
| AAA | — | — | — | — | — | — | — | — | — | — | — | — | — |

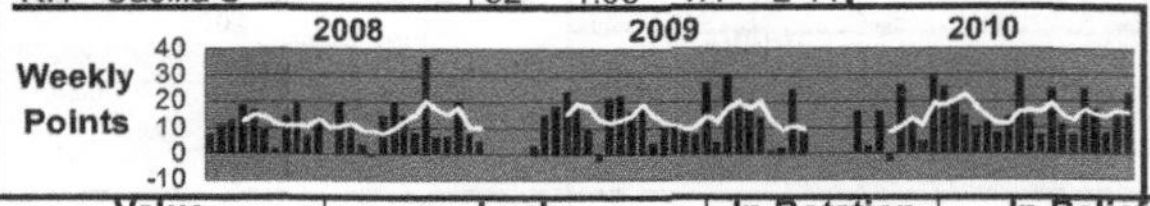

### Majors / Value / Luck / In Rotation / In Relief / OPS
| Yr | Team | W | L | Sv | IP | H | K | ERA | WHIP | K/9 | BB/9 | HR/9 | GB/F | $1L | $2L | Pts | RAA | H% | HR/fb | S% | FIP | GS | CG | QS/DS | GR | Hld | Bln | Lead | OPS | 1st Hf | 2nd Hf | vs RH | vs LH |
|---|---|---|---|---|---|---|---|---|---|---|---|---|---|---|---|---|---|---|---|---|---|---|---|---|---|---|---|---|---|---|---|---|---|
| 07 | SF | 1 | 2 | 6 | 23 | 16 | 18 | 2.28 | 0.97 | 6.8 | 2.7 | 0.4 | 1.9 | $3 | $2 | 60 | +5 | 23% | 5% | 77% | 3.12 | — | — | — | 24 | 9 | 1 | +1.8 | .529 | — | .529 | .336 | .988 |
| 08 | SF | 3 | 2 | 41 | 62 | 62 | 67 | 4.62 | 1.44 | 9.7 | 4.0 | 1.0 | 1.7 | $9 | $4 | 290 | -4 | 33% | 14% | 70% | 3.86 | — | — | — | 63 | 0 | 6 | +1.5 | .732 | .713 | .758 | .889 | .564 |
| 09 | SF | 5 | 6 | 38 | 72 | 60 | 83 | 2.74 | 1.20 | 10.3 | 3.4 | 0.4 | 1.3 | $16 | $11 | 330 | +6 | 31% | 4% | 77% | 2.56 | — | — | — | 68 | 1 | 7 | +1.6 | .595 | .634 | .548 | .657 | .532 |
| 10 | SF | 3 | 3 | 48 | 75 | 50 | 93 | 1.81 | 1.18 | 11.2 | 3.1 | 0.4 | 1.3 | $19 | $18 | 380 | +18 | 32% | 4% | 86% | 2.28 | — | — | — | 70 | 0 | 5 | +1.5 | .597 | .611 | .580 | .587 | .607 |

## C.J. Wilson — 180 IP | $15 | 270 pts
SP-33    Owned: 95%    LH

Wilson had clamored for an opportunity to start, and he justified the Rangers' acquiescence in 2010 with a stellar 200-IP campaign. Wilson's 0.4 HR/9 seems unsustainable, but he has a history in TEX of low rates. Wilson could attain true "ace" status if he lowered his BB/9, but his trend does not support that hope. (JM)

### Forecast
| Player | Age | IP | W | Sv | K | ERA | WHIP | K/9 | BB/9 | $2L | Pts |
|---|---|---|---|---|---|---|---|---|---|---|---|
| Wilson C | 30 | 180 | 13 | 0 | 157 | 3.60 | 1.32 | 7.9 | 4.3 | $15 | 270 |

| Mini-Browser | Age | IP | W | Sv | K | ERA | WHIP | K/9 | BB/9 | $2L | Pts |
|---|---|---|---|---|---|---|---|---|---|---|---|
| Street H | 27 | 60 | 4 | 38 | 59 | 3.59 | 1.12 | 8.8 | 2.3 | $16 | 290 |
| Marcum S | 29 | 200 | 13 | 0 | 164 | 4.02 | 1.22 | 7.4 | 2.5 | $16 | 280 |
| Feliz N | 22 | 60 | 4 | 39 | 62 | 3.50 | 1.21 | 9.3 | 3.3 | $16 | 290 |
| Marmol C | 28 | 80 | 3 | 36 | 108 | 3.45 | 1.38 | 12.1 | 5.8 | $15 | 310 |
| Bailey A | 26 | 75 | 3 | 33 | 77 | 3.16 | 1.29 | 9.2 | 3.5 | $15 | 270 |

### Minors (2010)
| Level | Leag | W | L | Sv | IP | H | K | ERA | WHIP | K/9 | BB/9 | HR/9 | GB/F |
|---|---|---|---|---|---|---|---|---|---|---|---|---|---|
| A | — | — | — | — | — | — | — | — | — | — | — | — | — |
| AA | — | — | — | — | — | — | — | — | — | — | — | — | — |
| AAA | — | — | — | — | — | — | — | — | — | — | — | — | — |

### Majors / Skills
| Yr | Team | W | L | Sv | IP | H | K | ERA | WHIP | K/9 | BB/9 | HR/9 | GB/F |
|---|---|---|---|---|---|---|---|---|---|---|---|---|---|
| 07 | TEX | 2 | 1 | 12 | 68 | 50 | 63 | 3.03 | 1.21 | 8.3 | 4.3 | 0.5 | 1.8 |
| 08 | TEX | 2 | 2 | 24 | 46 | 49 | 41 | 6.02 | 1.64 | 8.0 | 5.2 | 1.6 | 1.4 |
| 09 | TEX | 5 | 6 | 14 | 73 | 66 | 84 | 2.81 | 1.13 | 10.3 | 3.9 | 0.4 | 2.3 |
| 10 | TEX | 15 | 8 | 0 | 204 | 161 | 170 | 3.35 | 1.25 | 7.5 | 4.1 | 0.4 | 1.5 |

### Competition at SP | Stats in 2010 as SP
| Thr | Player | GS | ERA | Supp | W-L |
|---|---|---|---|---|---|
| LH | Wilson C | 33 | 3.35 | 4.6 | 15-8 |
| LH | Lewis C | 32 | 3.72 | 4.1 | 12-13 |
| LH | Lee C | 28 | 3.18 | 4.3 | 12-9 |
| RH | Hunter T | 22 | 3.75 | 6.0 | 13-4 |

Ten-Year Trends — K/9, BB/9

Weekly Points 2008 2009 2010

### Value / Luck / In Rotation / In Relief / OPS
| $1L | $2L | Pts | RAA | H% | HR/fb | S% | FIP | GS | CG | QS/DS | GR | Hld | Bln | Lead | OPS | 1st Hf | 2nd Hf | vs RH | vs LH |
|---|---|---|---|---|---|---|---|---|---|---|---|---|---|---|---|---|---|---|---|
| $5 | $5 | 150 | +9 | 26% | 8% | 76% | 3.67 | — | — | — | 66 | 15 | 2 | -0.2 | .622 | .615 | .584 | .754 | .381 |
| $1 | -$4 | 160 | -12 | 31% | 16% | 66% | 5.52 | — | — | — | 50 | 1 | 4 | +1.4 | .842 | .789 | 1.250 | .836 | .853 |
| $9 | $5 | 210 | +7 | 33% | 6% | 79% | 2.85 | — | — | — | 74 | 19 | 4 | +1.4 | .651 | .714 | .584 | .701 | .556 |
| $18 | $8 | 320 | +18 | 27% | 5% | 73% | 3.64 | 33 | 3 | 20/5 | — | — | — | — | .622 | .625 | .618 | .679 | .400 |

---

## Randy Wolf — 200 IP | $5 | 220 pts
SP-34    Owned: 60%    LH

Wolf's 2010 season hinged on a mid-year adjustment following a 12-run outburst on July 21. Beyond that, he had a 2.67 ERA in 13 starts, 10 of which were Quality Starts. The Brewers hope that Wolf will continue performing at that level for the remaining two years on his deal as a solid #2 behind Yovani Gallardo. (MS)

### Forecast
| Player | Age | IP | W | Sv | K | ERA | WHIP | K/9 | BB/9 | $2L | Pts |
|---|---|---|---|---|---|---|---|---|---|---|---|
| Wolf R | 34 | 200 | 12 | 0 | 134 | 4.47 | 1.36 | 6.0 | 3.4 | $5 | 220 |

| Mini-Browser | Age | IP | W | Sv | K | ERA | WHIP | K/9 | BB/9 | $2L | Pts |
|---|---|---|---|---|---|---|---|---|---|---|---|
| Breslow C | 30 | 75 | 4 | 2 | 65 | 3.61 | 1.24 | 7.7 | 3.9 | $6 | 110 |
| LeBlanc W | 26 | 180 | 10 | 0 | 148 | 4.36 | 1.36 | 7.4 | 3.1 | $5 | 210 |
| Cecil B | 24 | 160 | 11 | 0 | 116 | 4.58 | 1.39 | 6.5 | 3.3 | $5 | 200 |
| Rhodes A | 41 | 60 | 4 | 0 | 55 | 2.93 | 1.20 | 8.2 | 3.5 | $5 | 100 |
| Davis W | 25 | 170 | 11 | 0 | 141 | 4.44 | 1.46 | 7.5 | 3.8 | $5 | 220 |

### Minors (2010)
| Level | Leag | W | L | Sv | IP | H | K | ERA | WHIP | K/9 | BB/9 | HR/9 | GB/F |
|---|---|---|---|---|---|---|---|---|---|---|---|---|---|
| A | — | — | — | — | — | — | — | — | — | — | — | — | — |
| AA | — | — | — | — | — | — | — | — | — | — | — | — | — |
| AAA | — | — | — | — | — | — | — | — | — | — | — | — | — |

### Majors / Skills
| Yr | Team | W | L | Sv | IP | H | K | ERA | WHIP | K/9 | BB/9 | HR/9 | GB/F |
|---|---|---|---|---|---|---|---|---|---|---|---|---|---|
| 07 | LAD | 9 | 6 | 0 | 102 | 110 | 94 | 4.73 | 1.45 | 8.2 | 3.4 | 0.9 | 1.0 |
| 08 | 2TM | 12 | 12 | 0 | 190 | 191 | 162 | 4.30 | 1.38 | 7.7 | 3.4 | 1.0 | 1.0 |
| 09 | LAD | 11 | 7 | 0 | 214 | 178 | 160 | 3.23 | 1.10 | 6.7 | 2.4 | 1.0 | 0.9 |
| 10 | MIL | 13 | 12 | 0 | 215 | 213 | 142 | 4.17 | 1.39 | 5.9 | 3.3 | 1.2 | 0.9 |

### Competition at SP | Stats in 2010 as SP
| Thr | Player | GS | ERA | Supp | W-L |
|---|---|---|---|---|---|
| LH | Wolf R | 34 | 4.17 | 5.3 | 13-12 |
| RH | Gallardo Y | 31 | 3.84 | 5.3 | 14-7 |
| RH | Bush D | 31 | 4.55 | 4.0 | 8-13 |
| LH | Narveson C | 28 | 4.85 | 4.3 | 11-9 |

Ten-Year Trends — K/9, BB/9

Weekly Points 2008 2009 2010

### Value / Luck / In Rotation / In Relief / OPS
| $1L | $2L | Pts | RAA | H% | HR/fb | S% | FIP | GS | CG | QS/DS | GR | Hld | Bln | Lead | OPS | 1st Hf | 2nd Hf | vs RH | vs LH |
|---|---|---|---|---|---|---|---|---|---|---|---|---|---|---|---|---|---|---|---|
| $2 | -$7 | 160 | -4 | 33% | 8% | 68% | 3.77 | 18 | 0 | 8/2 | — | — | — | — | .762 | .762 | — | .760 | .762 |
| $5 | -$4 | 250 | -6 | 32% | 10% | 71% | 4.10 | 33 | 1 | 18/8 | — | — | — | — | .746 | .755 | .732 | .728 | .815 |
| $19 | $13 | 290 | +25 | 26% | 9% | 75% | 3.97 | 34 | 0 | 24/1 | — | — | — | — | .660 | .700 | .612 | .727 | .417 |
| $3 | -$12 | 240 | -1 | 28% | 10% | 74% | 4.84 | 34 | 1 | 20/3 | — | — | — | — | .764 | .820 | .696 | .728 | .889 |

---

## Blake Wood — 60 IP | $-6 | 40 pts
RP-51    Owned: 0%    RH

Wood posted solid rates in Triple-A, but he struggled to strike out guys in his debut with KC. Wood won't be anything special in MLB, but he could eventually have a 3.50-4.00 ERA. His strikeout numbers should rise (his career rate in the minors is 7.8 K/9). (BM)

### Forecast
| Player | Age | IP | W | Sv | K | ERA | WHIP | K/9 | BB/9 | $2L | Pts |
|---|---|---|---|---|---|---|---|---|---|---|---|
| Wood B | 25 | 60 | 2 | 0 | 50 | 5.71 | 1.73 | 7.5 | 4.1 | -$6 | 40 |

| Mini-Browser | Age | IP | W | Sv | K | ERA | WHIP | K/9 | BB/9 | $2L | Pts |
|---|---|---|---|---|---|---|---|---|---|---|---|
| Moehler B | 39 | 60 | 2 | 0 | 30 | 5.43 | 1.50 | 4.5 | 3.0 | -$5 | 30 |
| Vasquez E | 27 | 60 | 2 | 0 | 54 | 5.26 | 1.65 | 8.1 | 5.4 | -$5 | 50 |
| Wellemeyer T | 32 | 60 | 3 | 0 | 37 | 5.70 | 1.52 | 5.5 | 4.1 | -$5 | 40 |
| Morton C | 27 | 100 | 5 | 0 | 72 | 5.35 | 1.53 | 6.5 | 3.4 | -$5 | 80 |
| Davies K | 27 | 140 | 6 | 0 | 95 | 5.36 | 1.59 | 6.1 | 4.3 | -$5 | 100 |

### Minors (2010)
| Level | Leag | W | L | Sv | IP | H | K | ERA | WHIP | K/9 | BB/9 | HR/9 | GB/F |
|---|---|---|---|---|---|---|---|---|---|---|---|---|---|
| A | — | — | — | — | — | — | — | — | — | — | — | — | — |
| AA | — | — | — | — | — | — | — | — | — | — | — | — | — |
| AAA | PCL | 2 | 1 | 5 | 16 | 12 | 12 | 2.16 | 1.14 | 6.5 | 3.8 | 0.0 | — |

### Majors / Skills
| Yr | Team | W | L | Sv | IP | H | K | ERA | WHIP | K/9 | BB/9 | HR/9 | GB/F |
|---|---|---|---|---|---|---|---|---|---|---|---|---|---|
| 07 | — | — | — | — | — | — | — | — | — | — | — | — | — |
| 08 | — | — | — | — | — | — | — | — | — | — | — | — | — |
| 09 | — | — | — | — | — | — | — | — | — | — | — | — | — |
| 10 | KC | 1 | 3 | 0 | 49 | 54 | 31 | 5.07 | 1.53 | 5.6 | 4.0 | 1.1 | 1.5 |

### Competition at RP | Stats in 2010 as RP
| Thr | Player | GR | ERA | IP/G | Sv-Hld |
|---|---|---|---|---|---|
| RH | Soria J | 66 | 1.78 | 1.0 | 43-0 |
| RH | Tejeda R | 54 | 3.54 | 1.1 | 0-12 |
| RH | Wood B | 51 | 5.07 | 1.0 | 0-15 |
| RH | Texeira K | 27 | 4.64 | 1.6 | 0-1 |

Ten-Year Trends — K/9, BB/9

Weekly Points 2008 2009 2010

### Value / Luck / In Rotation / In Relief / OPS
| $1L | $2L | Pts | RAA | H% | HR/fb | S% | FIP | GS | CG | QS/DS | GR | Hld | Bln | Lead | OPS | 1st Hf | 2nd Hf | vs RH | vs LH |
|---|---|---|---|---|---|---|---|---|---|---|---|---|---|---|---|---|---|---|---|
| — | — | — | — | — | — | — | — | — | — | — | — | — | — | — | — | — | — | — | — |
| — | — | — | — | — | — | — | — | — | — | — | — | — | — | — | — | — | — | — | — |
| — | — | — | — | — | — | — | — | — | — | — | — | — | — | — | — | — | — | — | — |
| -$4 | -$16 | 20 | -7 | 30% | 11% | 69% | 4.95 | — | — | — | 51 | 15 | 4 | +0.1 | .798 | .759 | .830 | .767 | .827 |

---

## Kerry Wood — 60 IP | $2 | 80 pts
RP-47    Owned: 20%    RH

Wood was arguably Brian Cashman's best deadline pick-up. The pitcher was solid in Joba Chamberlain's previous role as the Yankees' 8th-inning reliever. It is unclear whether Wood will return to New York, but he played well enough to justify a good deal. For all his woes, Wood's skills have not rotted away. (LS)

### Forecast
| Player | Age | IP | W | Sv | K | ERA | WHIP | K/9 | BB/9 | $2L | Pts |
|---|---|---|---|---|---|---|---|---|---|---|---|
| Wood K | 33 | 60 | 3 | 0 | 62 | 3.77 | 1.41 | 9.3 | 4.7 | $2 | 80 |

| Mini-Browser | Age | IP | W | Sv | K | ERA | WHIP | K/9 | BB/9 | $2L | Pts |
|---|---|---|---|---|---|---|---|---|---|---|---|
| Belisle M | 30 | 60 | 3 | 4 | 46 | 4.20 | 1.26 | 7.0 | 1.9 | $2 | 90 |
| Lueke J | 26 | 60 | 3 | 0 | 39 | 3.41 | 1.29 | 8.7 | 3.4 | $2 | 70 |
| O'Flaherty E | 26 | 60 | 3 | 0 | 44 | 3.52 | 1.31 | 6.5 | 3.4 | $2 | 70 |
| Burnett S | 28 | 60 | 2 | 6 | 47 | 3.86 | 1.38 | 7.1 | 3.9 | $2 | 90 |
| Peralta J | 35 | 60 | 2 | 0 | 51 | 4.01 | 1.17 | 7.6 | 2.4 | $2 | 70 |

### Minors (2010)
| Level | Leag | W | L | Sv | IP | H | K | ERA | WHIP | K/9 | BB/9 | HR/9 | GB/F |
|---|---|---|---|---|---|---|---|---|---|---|---|---|---|
| A | — | — | — | — | — | — | — | — | — | — | — | — | — |
| AA | EL | 0 | 1 | 0 | 2 | 4 | 2 | 20.25 | 2.63 | 6.8 | 10.1 | 0.0 | — |
| AAA | — | — | — | — | — | — | — | — | — | — | — | — | — |

### Majors / Skills
| Yr | Team | W | L | Sv | IP | H | K | ERA | WHIP | K/9 | BB/9 | HR/9 | GB/F |
|---|---|---|---|---|---|---|---|---|---|---|---|---|---|
| 07 | CHC | 1 | 1 | 0 | 24 | 18 | 24 | 3.33 | 1.27 | 8.9 | 4.8 | 0.0 | 0.7 |
| 08 | CHC | 5 | 4 | 34 | 66 | 54 | 84 | 3.26 | 1.09 | 11.4 | 2.4 | 0.4 | 1.0 |
| 09 | CLE | 3 | 3 | 20 | 55 | 48 | 63 | 4.25 | 1.38 | 10.3 | 4.6 | 1.1 | 0.9 |
| 10 | 2TM | 3 | 4 | 8 | 46 | 35 | 49 | 3.13 | 1.39 | 9.6 | 5.7 | 0.8 | 0.9 |

### Competition at RP | Stats in 2010 as RP
| Thr | Player | GR | ERA | IP/G | Sv-Hld |
|---|---|---|---|---|---|
| RH | Chamberlain J | 73 | 4.40 | 1.0 | 3-26 |
| RH | Robertson D | 64 | 3.82 | 1.0 | 1-14 |
| RH | Rivera M | 61 | 1.80 | 1.0 | 33-0 |
| RH | Gaudin C | 30 | 4.50 | 1.6 | 0-0 |

Ten-Year Trends — K/9, BB/9

Weekly Points 2008 2009 2010

### Value / Luck / In Rotation / In Relief / OPS
| $1L | $2L | Pts | RAA | H% | HR/fb | S% | FIP | GS | CG | QS/DS | GR | Hld | Bln | Lead | OPS | 1st Hf | 2nd Hf | vs RH | vs LH |
|---|---|---|---|---|---|---|---|---|---|---|---|---|---|---|---|---|---|---|---|
| $0 | -$1 | 30 | +2 | 29% | 0% | 71% | 2.83 | — | — | — | 22 | 0 | 0 | -0.9 | .609 | — | .609 | .683 | .443 |
| $15 | $11 | 310 | +6 | 32% | 5% | 70% | 2.07 | — | — | — | 65 | 0 | 6 | +2.5 | .632 | .598 | .696 | .657 | .604 |
| $6 | $2 | 180 | -1 | 30% | 11% | 72% | 4.19 | — | — | — | 58 | 0 | 6 | +0.4 | .703 | .796 | .590 | .676 | .727 |
| $4 | -$1 | 80 | +4 | 27% | 8% | 80% | 4.14 | — | — | — | 47 | 11 | 4 | +0.3 | .654 | .816 | .507 | .639 | .654 |

---

## Tim Wood — 40 IP | $-5 | 20 pts
RP-26    Owned: 0%    RH

Like Jose Veras, Wood is here in name only; he more represents an opening to be filled in Florida. Wood was outrighted off Florida's 40-man roster, meaning that the team has no interest in him beyond as organizational filler. They could still turn to him if necessary, but the club is looking to upgrade. (MJ)

### Forecast
| Player | Age | IP | W | Sv | K | ERA | WHIP | K/9 | BB/9 | $2L | Pts |
|---|---|---|---|---|---|---|---|---|---|---|---|
| Wood T | 28 | 40 | 1 | 0 | 28 | 5.05 | 1.68 | 6.3 | 4.5 | -$5 | 20 |

| Mini-Browser | Age | IP | W | Sv | K | ERA | WHIP | K/9 | BB/9 | $2L | Pts |
|---|---|---|---|---|---|---|---|---|---|---|---|
| Chacin G | 30 | 40 | 2 | 0 | 26 | 5.34 | 1.65 | 5.9 | 3.9 | -$5 | 30 |
| Nova I | 24 | 60 | 3 | 0 | 45 | 5.53 | 1.68 | 6.7 | 4.2 | -$5 | 40 |
| Rodriguez R | 26 | 40 | 1 | 0 | 26 | 5.44 | 1.59 | 5.9 | 3.4 | -$5 | 30 |
| Oliver A | 23 | 60 | 2 | 0 | 39 | 5.64 | 1.66 | 5.8 | 4.7 | -$5 | 40 |
| O'Sullivan S | 23 | 100 | 5 | 0 | 65 | 5.74 | 1.54 | 5.9 | 3.1 | -$5 | 80 |

### Minors (2010)
| Level | Leag | W | L | Sv | IP | H | K | ERA | WHIP | K/9 | BB/9 | HR/9 | GB/F |
|---|---|---|---|---|---|---|---|---|---|---|---|---|---|
| A | — | — | — | — | — | — | — | — | — | — | — | — | — |
| AA | — | — | — | — | — | — | — | — | — | — | — | — | — |
| AAA | PCL | 0 | 1 | 0 | 14 | 19 | 12 | 6.43 | 1.64 | 7.7 | 2.6 | 2.6 | — |

### Majors / Skills
| Yr | Team | W | L | Sv | IP | H | K | ERA | WHIP | K/9 | BB/9 | HR/9 | GB/F |
|---|---|---|---|---|---|---|---|---|---|---|---|---|---|
| 07 | — | — | — | — | — | — | — | — | — | — | — | — | — |
| 08 | — | — | — | — | — | — | — | — | — | — | — | — | — |
| 09 | FLA | 1 | 0 | 0 | 22 | 22 | 16 | 2.82 | 1.43 | 6.4 | 4.0 | 0.8 | 1.4 |
| 10 | FLA | 0 | 1 | 1 | 27 | 33 | 10 | 5.53 | 1.73 | 3.3 | 4.9 | 0.7 | 0.9 |

### Competition at RP | Stats in 2010 as RP
| Thr | Player | GR | ERA | IP/G | Sv-Hld |
|---|---|---|---|---|---|
| RH | Hensley C | 68 | 2.16 | 1.1 | 7-22 |
| RH | Nunez L | 68 | 3.46 | 1.0 | 30-5 |
| RH | Sanches B | 61 | 2.26 | 1.0 | 0-12 |
| RH | Badenhop B | 53 | 3.99 | 1.3 | 1-8 |

Ten-Year Trends — K/9, BB/9

Weekly Points 2008 2009 2010

### Value / Luck / In Rotation / In Relief / OPS
| $1L | $2L | Pts | RAA | H% | HR/fb | S% | FIP | GS | CG | QS/DS | GR | Hld | Bln | Lead | OPS | 1st Hf | 2nd Hf | vs RH | vs LH |
|---|---|---|---|---|---|---|---|---|---|---|---|---|---|---|---|---|---|---|---|
| — | — | — | — | — | — | — | — | — | — | — | — | — | — | — | — | — | — | — | — |
| — | — | — | — | — | — | — | — | — | — | — | — | — | — | — | — | — | — | — | — |
| -$1 | -$1 | 30 | +2 | 31% | 9% | 83% | 4.27 | — | — | — | 18 | 1 | 0 | -0.1 | .742 | .412 | .909 | .768 | .703 |
| -$8 | -$16 | 0 | -7 | 32% | 5% | 67% | 5.04 | — | — | — | 26 | 3 | 2 | -1.0 | .819 | .819 | — | .894 | .718 |

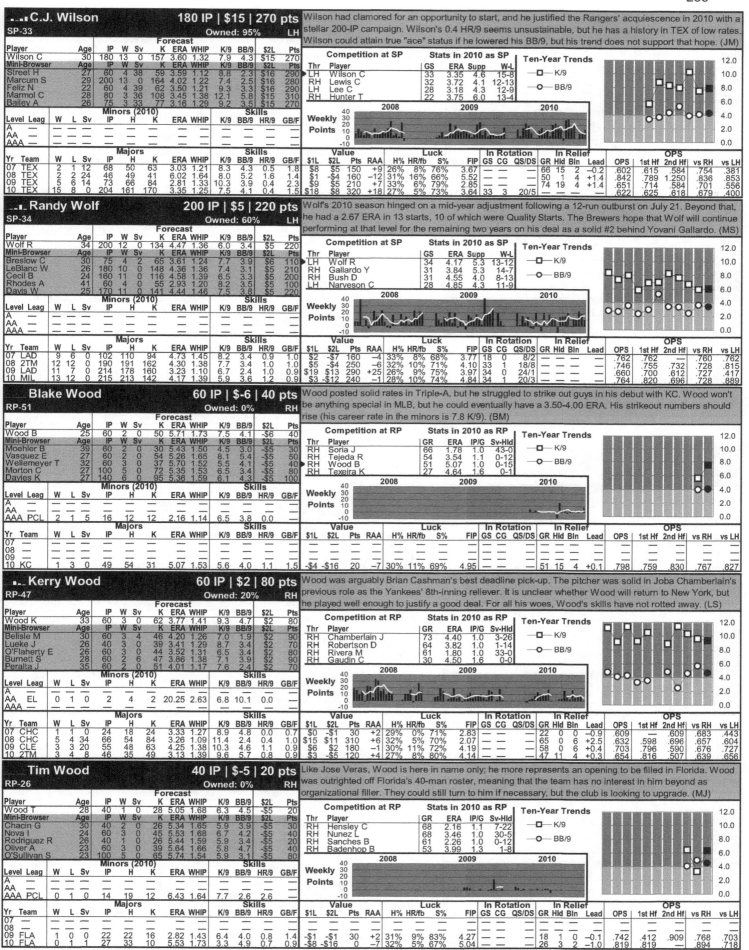

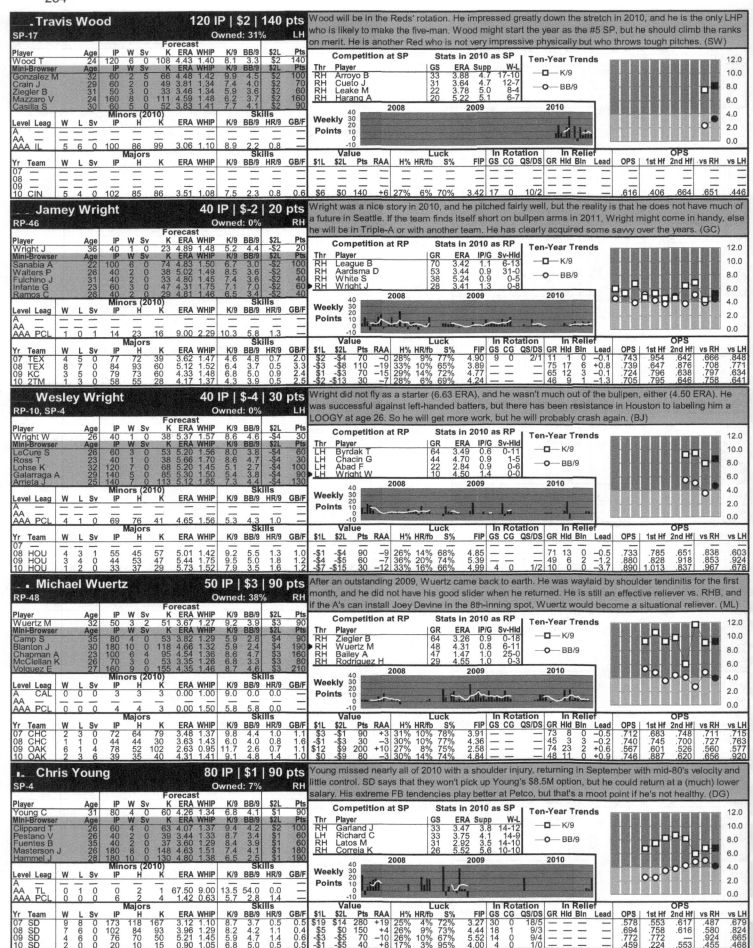

## Travis Wood — 120 IP | $2 | 140 pts
SP-17 — Owned: 31% — LH

Wood will be in the Reds' rotation. He impressed greatly down the stretch in 2010, and he is the only LHP who is likely to make the five-man. Wood might start the year as the #5 SP, but he should climb the ranks on merit. He is another Red who is not very impressive physically but who throws tough pitches. (SW)

### Forecast
| Player | Age | IP | W | Sv | K | ERA | WHIP | K/9 | BB/9 | $2L | Pts |
|---|---|---|---|---|---|---|---|---|---|---|---|
| Wood T | 24 | 120 | 6 | 0 | 108 | 4.43 | 1.40 | 8.1 | 3.3 | $2 | 140 |

| Mini-Browser | Age | IP | W | Sv | K | ERA | WHIP | K/9 | BB/9 | $2L | Pts |
|---|---|---|---|---|---|---|---|---|---|---|---|
| Gonzalez M | 32 | 60 | 2 | 5 | 66 | 4.48 | 1.42 | 9.9 | 4.5 | $2 | 100 |
| Crain J | 29 | 60 | 2 | 0 | 49 | 3.81 | 1.34 | 7.4 | 4.0 | $2 | 70 |
| Ziegler B | 31 | 50 | 3 | 0 | 33 | 3.46 | 1.34 | 5.9 | 3.6 | $2 | 60 |
| Mazzaro V | 24 | 160 | 8 | 0 | 111 | 4.59 | 1.48 | 6.2 | 3.7 | $2 | 160 |
| Casilla S | 30 | 60 | 5 | 0 | 52 | 3.83 | 1.41 | 7.7 | 4.1 | $2 | 90 |

### Minors (2010) / Skills
| Level | Leag | W | L | Sv | IP | H | K | ERA | WHIP | K/9 | BB/9 | HR/9 | GB/F |
|---|---|---|---|---|---|---|---|---|---|---|---|---|---|
| A | — | — | — | — | — | — | — | — | — | — | — | — | — |
| AA | — | — | — | — | — | — | — | — | — | — | — | — | — |
| AAA | IL | 5 | 6 | 0 | 100 | 86 | 99 | 3.06 | 1.10 | 8.9 | 2.2 | 0.8 | — |

### Majors / Skills
| Yr | Team | W | L | Sv | IP | H | K | ERA | WHIP | K/9 | BB/9 | HR/9 | GB/F |
|---|---|---|---|---|---|---|---|---|---|---|---|---|---|
| 07 | — | — | — | — | — | — | — | — | — | — | — | — | — |
| 08 | — | — | — | — | — | — | — | — | — | — | — | — | — |
| 09 | — | — | — | — | — | — | — | — | — | — | — | — | — |
| 10 | CIN | 5 | 4 | 0 | 102 | 85 | 86 | 3.51 | 1.08 | 7.5 | 2.3 | 0.8 | 0.6 |

### Competition at SP / Stats in 2010 as SP
| Thr | Player | GS | ERA | Supp | W-L |
|---|---|---|---|---|---|
| RH | Arroyo B | 33 | 3.88 | 4.7 | 17-10 |
| RH | Cueto J | 31 | 3.64 | 4.7 | 12-7 |
| RH | Leake M | 22 | 3.78 | 5.0 | 8-4 |
| RH | Harang A | 20 | 5.22 | 5.1 | 6-7 |

### Value / Luck / In Rotation / In Relief / OPS
| $1L | $2L | Pts | RAA | H% | HR/fb | S% | FIP | GS | CG | QS/DS | GR | Hld | Bln | Lead | OPS | 1st Hf | 2nd Hf | vs RH | vs LH |
|---|---|---|---|---|---|---|---|---|---|---|---|---|---|---|---|---|---|---|---|
| $6 | $0 | 140 | +6 | 27% | 6% | 70% | 3.42 | 17 | 0 | 10/2 | — | — | — | — | .616 | .406 | .664 | .651 | .446 |

---

## Jamey Wright — 40 IP | $-2 | 20 pts
RP-46 — Owned: 0% — RH

Wright was a nice story in 2010, and he pitched fairly well, but the reality is that he does not have much of a future in Seattle. If the team finds itself short on bullpen arms in 2011, Wright might come in handy, else he will be in Triple-A or with another team. He has clearly acquired some savvy over the years. (GC)

### Forecast
| Player | Age | IP | W | Sv | K | ERA | WHIP | K/9 | BB/9 | $2L | Pts |
|---|---|---|---|---|---|---|---|---|---|---|---|
| Wright J | 36 | 40 | 1 | 0 | 23 | 4.89 | 1.48 | 5.2 | 4.4 | -$2 | 20 |

| Mini-Browser | Age | IP | W | Sv | K | ERA | WHIP | K/9 | BB/9 | $2L | Pts |
|---|---|---|---|---|---|---|---|---|---|---|---|
| Sanabia A | 22 | 100 | 6 | 0 | 74 | 4.83 | 1.50 | 6.7 | 3.0 | -$2 | 100 |
| Walters P | 26 | 40 | 2 | 0 | 38 | 5.02 | 1.49 | 8.5 | 3.6 | -$2 | 50 |
| Fulchino J | 31 | 40 | 2 | 0 | 33 | 4.80 | 1.45 | 7.4 | 3.6 | -$2 | 40 |
| Infante G | 23 | 60 | 3 | 0 | 47 | 4.31 | 1.75 | 7.1 | 7.0 | -$2 | 60 |
| Ramos C | 26 | 40 | 2 | 0 | 29 | 4.81 | 1.46 | 6.5 | 4.3 | -$2 | 40 |

### Minors (2010) / Skills
| Level | Leag | W | L | Sv | IP | H | K | ERA | WHIP | K/9 | BB/9 | HR/9 | GB/F |
|---|---|---|---|---|---|---|---|---|---|---|---|---|---|
| A | — | — | — | — | — | — | — | — | — | — | — | — | — |
| AA | — | — | — | — | — | — | — | — | — | — | — | — | — |
| AAA | PCL | 1 | 0 | 1 | 14 | 23 | 16 | 9.00 | 2.29 | 10.3 | 5.8 | 1.3 | — |

### Majors / Skills
| Yr | Team | W | L | Sv | IP | H | K | ERA | WHIP | K/9 | BB/9 | HR/9 | GB/F |
|---|---|---|---|---|---|---|---|---|---|---|---|---|---|
| 07 | TEX | 4 | 5 | 0 | 77 | 72 | 39 | 3.62 | 1.47 | 4.6 | 4.8 | 0.7 | 2.0 |
| 08 | TEX | 8 | 7 | 0 | 84 | 93 | 60 | 5.12 | 1.52 | 6.4 | 3.7 | 0.5 | 3.3 |
| 09 | KC | 3 | 5 | 0 | 79 | 73 | 60 | 4.33 | 1.48 | 6.8 | 5.0 | 0.9 | 2.4 |
| 10 | 2TM | 1 | 3 | 0 | 58 | 55 | 28 | 4.17 | 1.37 | 4.3 | 3.9 | 0.5 | 2.5 |

### Competition at RP / Stats in 2010 as RP
| Thr | Player | GR | ERA | IP/G | Sv-Hld |
|---|---|---|---|---|---|
| RH | League B | 70 | 3.42 | 1.1 | 6-13 |
| RH | Aardsma D | 53 | 3.44 | 0.9 | 31-0 |
| RH | White S | 38 | 5.24 | 0.9 | 0-5 |
| RH | Wright J | 28 | 3.41 | 1.3 | 0-8 |

### Value / Luck / In Rotation / In Relief / OPS
| $1L | $2L | Pts | RAA | H% | HR/fb | S% | FIP | GS | CG | QS/DS | GR | Hld | Bln | Lead | OPS | 1st Hf | 2nd Hf | vs RH | vs LH |
|---|---|---|---|---|---|---|---|---|---|---|---|---|---|---|---|---|---|---|---|
| $2 | -$4 | 70 | -0 | 28% | 9% | 77% | 4.90 | 9 | 0 | 2/1 | 11 | 1 | 0 | -0.1 | .743 | .954 | .642 | .666 | .848 |
| -$3 | -$8 | 110 | -19 | 33% | 10% | 60% | 3.89 | — | — | — | 75 | 17 | 6 | +0.8 | .739 | .647 | .876 | .708 | .771 |
| -$1 | -$3 | 70 | -15 | 29% | 14% | 72% | 4.77 | — | — | — | 65 | 12 | 3 | -0.1 | .724 | .796 | .638 | .797 | .634 |
| -$2 | -$13 | 30 | -7 | 28% | 6% | 69% | 4.24 | — | — | — | 46 | 9 | 1 | -1.3 | .705 | .795 | .646 | .758 | .641 |

---

## Wesley Wright — 40 IP | $-4 | 30 pts
RP-10, SP-4 — Owned: 0% — LH

Wright did not fly as a starter (6.63 ERA), and he wasn't much out of the bullpen, either (4.50 ERA). He was successful against left-handed batters, but there has been resistance in Houston to labeling him a LOOGY at age 26. So he will get more work, and he will probably crash again. (BJ)

### Forecast
| Player | Age | IP | W | Sv | K | ERA | WHIP | K/9 | BB/9 | $2L | Pts |
|---|---|---|---|---|---|---|---|---|---|---|---|
| Wright W | 26 | 40 | 1 | 0 | 38 | 5.37 | 1.57 | 8.6 | 4.6 | -$4 | 30 |

| Mini-Browser | Age | IP | W | Sv | K | ERA | WHIP | K/9 | BB/9 | $2L | Pts |
|---|---|---|---|---|---|---|---|---|---|---|---|
| LeCure S | 26 | 60 | 3 | 0 | 53 | 5.20 | 1.56 | 8.0 | 3.8 | -$4 | 60 |
| Ross T | 23 | 40 | 1 | 0 | 38 | 5.66 | 1.70 | 8.6 | 4.7 | -$4 | 40 |
| Lohse K | 32 | 120 | 7 | 0 | 68 | 5.20 | 1.45 | 5.1 | 2.7 | -$4 | 100 |
| Galarraga A | 29 | 140 | 5 | 0 | 85 | 5.30 | 1.50 | 5.4 | 3.8 | -$4 | 90 |
| Arrieta J | 25 | 140 | 7 | 0 | 113 | 5.12 | 1.65 | 7.3 | 4.4 | -$4 | 130 |

### Minors (2010) / Skills
| Level | Leag | W | L | Sv | IP | H | K | ERA | WHIP | K/9 | BB/9 | HR/9 | GB/F |
|---|---|---|---|---|---|---|---|---|---|---|---|---|---|
| A | — | — | — | — | — | — | — | — | — | — | — | — | — |
| AA | — | — | — | — | — | — | — | — | — | — | — | — | — |
| AAA | PCL | 4 | 1 | 0 | 69 | 76 | 41 | 4.65 | 1.56 | 5.3 | 4.3 | 1.0 | — |

### Majors / Skills
| Yr | Team | W | L | Sv | IP | H | K | ERA | WHIP | K/9 | BB/9 | HR/9 | GB/F |
|---|---|---|---|---|---|---|---|---|---|---|---|---|---|
| 07 | — | — | — | — | — | — | — | — | — | — | — | — | — |
| 08 | HOU | 4 | 3 | 1 | 55 | 45 | 57 | 5.01 | 1.42 | 9.2 | 5.5 | 1.3 | 1.0 |
| 09 | HOU | 3 | 4 | 0 | 44 | 53 | 47 | 5.44 | 1.75 | 9.5 | 5.0 | 1.8 | 1.2 |
| 10 | HOU | 1 | 2 | 0 | 33 | 37 | 29 | 5.73 | 1.52 | 7.9 | 3.5 | 1.6 | 1.2 |

### Competition at RP / Stats in 2010 as RP
| Thr | Player | GR | ERA | IP/G | Sv-Hld |
|---|---|---|---|---|---|
| LH | Byrdak T | 64 | 3.49 | 0.6 | 0-11 |
| LH | Chacin G | 44 | 4.70 | 0.9 | 1-5 |
| LH | Abad F | 22 | 2.84 | 0.9 | 0-6 |
| LH | Wright W | 10 | 4.50 | 1.4 | 0-0 |

### Value / Luck / In Rotation / In Relief / OPS
| $1L | $2L | Pts | RAA | H% | HR/fb | S% | FIP | GS | CG | QS/DS | GR | Hld | Bln | Lead | OPS | 1st Hf | 2nd Hf | vs RH | vs LH |
|---|---|---|---|---|---|---|---|---|---|---|---|---|---|---|---|---|---|---|---|
| -$1 | -$4 | 90 | -9 | 26% | 14% | 68% | 4.85 | — | — | — | 71 | 13 | 0 | -0.5 | .733 | .785 | .651 | .838 | .603 |
| -$4 | -$5 | 60 | -7 | 36% | 20% | 74% | 5.39 | — | — | — | 49 | 6 | 2 | -1.2 | .880 | .828 | .918 | .853 | .924 |
| -$7 | -$15 | 30 | -12 | 33% | 16% | 66% | 4.99 | 4 | 0 | 1/2 | 10 | 0 | 0 | -3.7 | .890 | 1.013 | .837 | .967 | .678 |

---

## Michael Wuertz — 50 IP | $3 | 90 pts
RP-48 — Owned: 38% — RH

After an outstanding 2009, Wuertz came back to earth. He was waylaid by shoulder tendinitis for the first month, and he did not have his good slider when he returned. He is still an effective reliever vs. RHB, and if the A's can install Joey Devine in the 8th-inning spot, Wuertz would become a situational reliever. (ML)

### Forecast
| Player | Age | IP | W | Sv | K | ERA | WHIP | K/9 | BB/9 | $2L | Pts |
|---|---|---|---|---|---|---|---|---|---|---|---|
| Wuertz M | 32 | 50 | 3 | 2 | 51 | 3.67 | 1.27 | 9.2 | 3.9 | $3 | 90 |

| Mini-Browser | Age | IP | W | Sv | K | ERA | WHIP | K/9 | BB/9 | $2L | Pts |
|---|---|---|---|---|---|---|---|---|---|---|---|
| Camp S | 35 | 80 | 4 | 0 | 53 | 3.82 | 1.29 | 5.9 | 2.8 | $4 | 90 |
| Blanton J | 30 | 180 | 10 | 0 | 118 | 4.66 | 1.32 | 5.9 | 2.4 | $4 | 190 |
| Chapman A | 23 | 100 | 6 | 0 | 95 | 4.54 | 1.36 | 8.6 | 4.7 | $3 | 160 |
| McClellan K | 26 | 70 | 3 | 0 | 53 | 3.35 | 1.26 | 6.8 | 3.3 | $3 | 80 |
| Volquez E | 27 | 160 | 9 | 0 | 155 | 4.35 | 1.46 | 8.7 | 4.8 | $3 | 210 |

### Minors (2010) / Skills
| Level | Leag | W | L | Sv | IP | H | K | ERA | WHIP | K/9 | BB/9 | HR/9 | GB/F |
|---|---|---|---|---|---|---|---|---|---|---|---|---|---|
| A | CAL | 0 | 0 | 0 | 3 | 3 | 3 | 0.00 | 1.00 | 9.0 | 0.0 | 0.0 | — |
| AA | — | — | — | — | — | — | — | — | — | — | — | — | — |
| AAA | PCL | 0 | 0 | 0 | 4 | 4 | 3 | 0.00 | 1.50 | 5.8 | 5.8 | 0.0 | — |

### Majors / Skills
| Yr | Team | W | L | Sv | IP | H | K | ERA | WHIP | K/9 | BB/9 | HR/9 | GB/F |
|---|---|---|---|---|---|---|---|---|---|---|---|---|---|
| 07 | CHC | 2 | 3 | 0 | 72 | 64 | 79 | 3.48 | 1.37 | 9.8 | 4.4 | 1.0 | 1.1 |
| 08 | CHC | 1 | 1 | 0 | 44 | 44 | 30 | 3.63 | 1.43 | 6.0 | 4.0 | 0.8 | 1.6 |
| 09 | OAK | 6 | 1 | 4 | 78 | 52 | 102 | 2.63 | 0.95 | 11.7 | 2.6 | 0.7 | 1.1 |
| 10 | OAK | 2 | 3 | 6 | 39 | 35 | 40 | 4.31 | 1.41 | 9.1 | 4.8 | 1.4 | 1.0 |

### Competition at RP / Stats in 2010 as RP
| Thr | Player | GR | ERA | IP/G | Sv-Hld |
|---|---|---|---|---|---|
| RH | Ziegler B | 64 | 3.26 | 0.9 | 0-18 |
| RH | Wuertz M | 48 | 4.31 | 0.8 | 6-11 |
| RH | Bailey A | 47 | 1.47 | 1.0 | 25-0 |
| RH | Rodriguez H | 29 | 4.55 | 1.0 | 0-3 |

### Value / Luck / In Rotation / In Relief / OPS
| $1L | $2L | Pts | RAA | H% | HR/fb | S% | FIP | GS | CG | QS/DS | GR | Hld | Bln | Lead | OPS | 1st Hf | 2nd Hf | vs RH | vs LH |
|---|---|---|---|---|---|---|---|---|---|---|---|---|---|---|---|---|---|---|---|
| $3 | -$1 | 90 | +3 | 31% | 10% | 78% | 3.91 | — | — | — | 73 | 8 | 0 | -0.5 | .712 | .683 | .748 | .711 | .715 |
| -$1 | -$3 | 30 | -3 | 30% | 10% | 77% | 4.36 | — | — | — | 45 | 3 | 3 | -1.2 | .740 | .745 | .700 | .727 | .763 |
| $12 | $9 | 200 | +10 | 27% | 8% | 75% | 2.58 | — | — | — | 74 | 23 | 2 | +0.6 | .567 | .601 | .526 | .560 | .577 |
| $0 | -$3 | 90 | -3 | 30% | 14% | 74% | 4.84 | — | — | — | 48 | 11 | 0 | +0.8 | .746 | .887 | .620 | .656 | .920 |

---

## Chris Young — 80 IP | $1 | 90 pts
SP-4 — Owned: 7% — RH

Young missed nearly all of 2010 with a shoulder injury, returning in September with mid-80's velocity and little control. SD says that they won't pick up Young's $8.5M option, but he could return at a (much) lower salary. His extreme FB tendencies play better at Petco, but that's a moot point if he's not healthy. (DG)

### Forecast
| Player | Age | IP | W | Sv | K | ERA | WHIP | K/9 | BB/9 | $2L | Pts |
|---|---|---|---|---|---|---|---|---|---|---|---|
| Young C | 31 | 80 | 4 | 0 | 60 | 4.26 | 1.34 | 6.8 | 4.1 | $1 | 90 |

| Mini-Browser | Age | IP | W | Sv | K | ERA | WHIP | K/9 | BB/9 | $2L | Pts |
|---|---|---|---|---|---|---|---|---|---|---|---|
| Clippard T | 26 | 60 | 4 | 0 | 63 | 4.07 | 1.37 | 9.4 | 4.2 | $1 | 100 |
| Pestano V | 26 | 40 | 2 | 0 | 39 | 3.44 | 1.33 | 8.7 | 3.4 | $1 | 60 |
| Fuentes B | 35 | 40 | 2 | 0 | 37 | 3.60 | 1.29 | 8.4 | 3.9 | $1 | 60 |
| Masterson J | 26 | 180 | 8 | 0 | 148 | 4.63 | 1.51 | 7.4 | 4.1 | $1 | 180 |
| Hammel J | 28 | 180 | 10 | 0 | 130 | 4.80 | 1.38 | 6.5 | 2.5 | $1 | 190 |

### Minors (2010) / Skills
| Level | Leag | W | L | Sv | IP | H | K | ERA | WHIP | K/9 | BB/9 | HR/9 | GB/F |
|---|---|---|---|---|---|---|---|---|---|---|---|---|---|
| A | — | — | — | — | — | — | — | — | — | — | — | — | — |
| AA | TL | 0 | 1 | 0 | 0 | 2 | 1 | 67.50 | 9.00 | 13.5 | 54.0 | 0.0 | — |
| AAA | PCL | 0 | 0 | 0 | 6 | 2 | 4 | 1.42 | 0.63 | 5.7 | 2.8 | 1.4 | — |

### Majors / Skills
| Yr | Team | W | L | Sv | IP | H | K | ERA | WHIP | K/9 | BB/9 | HR/9 | GB/F |
|---|---|---|---|---|---|---|---|---|---|---|---|---|---|
| 07 | SD | 9 | 8 | 0 | 173 | 118 | 167 | 3.12 | 1.10 | 8.7 | 3.7 | 0.5 | 0.5 |
| 08 | SD | 7 | 6 | 0 | 102 | 84 | 93 | 3.96 | 1.29 | 8.2 | 4.2 | 1.1 | 0.4 |
| 09 | SD | 4 | 6 | 0 | 76 | 70 | 50 | 5.21 | 1.45 | 5.9 | 4.7 | 1.4 | 0.6 |
| 10 | SD | 2 | 0 | 0 | 20 | 10 | 15 | 0.90 | 1.05 | 6.8 | 5.0 | 0.5 | 0.5 |

### Competition at SP / Stats in 2010 as SP
| Thr | Player | GS | ERA | Supp | W-L |
|---|---|---|---|---|---|
| RH | Garland J | 33 | 3.47 | 3.8 | 14-12 |
| LH | Richard C | 33 | 3.75 | 4.1 | 14-9 |
| RH | Latos M | 31 | 2.92 | 3.5 | 14-10 |
| RH | Correia K | 26 | 5.52 | 5.6 | 10-10 |

### Value / Luck / In Rotation / In Relief / OPS
| $1L | $2L | Pts | RAA | H% | HR/fb | S% | FIP | GS | CG | QS/DS | GR | Hld | Bln | Lead | OPS | 1st Hf | 2nd Hf | vs RH | vs LH |
|---|---|---|---|---|---|---|---|---|---|---|---|---|---|---|---|---|---|---|---|
| $19 | $14 | 280 | +19 | 25% | 4% | 72% | 3.27 | 30 | 0 | 18/5 | — | — | — | — | .578 | .553 | .617 | .487 | .679 |
| $5 | $0 | 150 | +4 | 26% | 9% | 73% | 4.44 | 18 | 1 | 9/3 | — | — | — | — | .694 | .758 | .616 | .580 | .824 |
| -$3 | -$5 | 70 | -10 | 26% | 10% | 67% | 5.52 | 14 | 0 | 9/4 | — | — | — | — | .772 | .772 | — | .924 | .665 |
| $0 | -$1 | 40 | +8 | 17% | 3% | 95% | 4.00 | 4 | 0 | 1/0 | — | — | — | — | .459 | .224 | .553 | .455 | .462 |

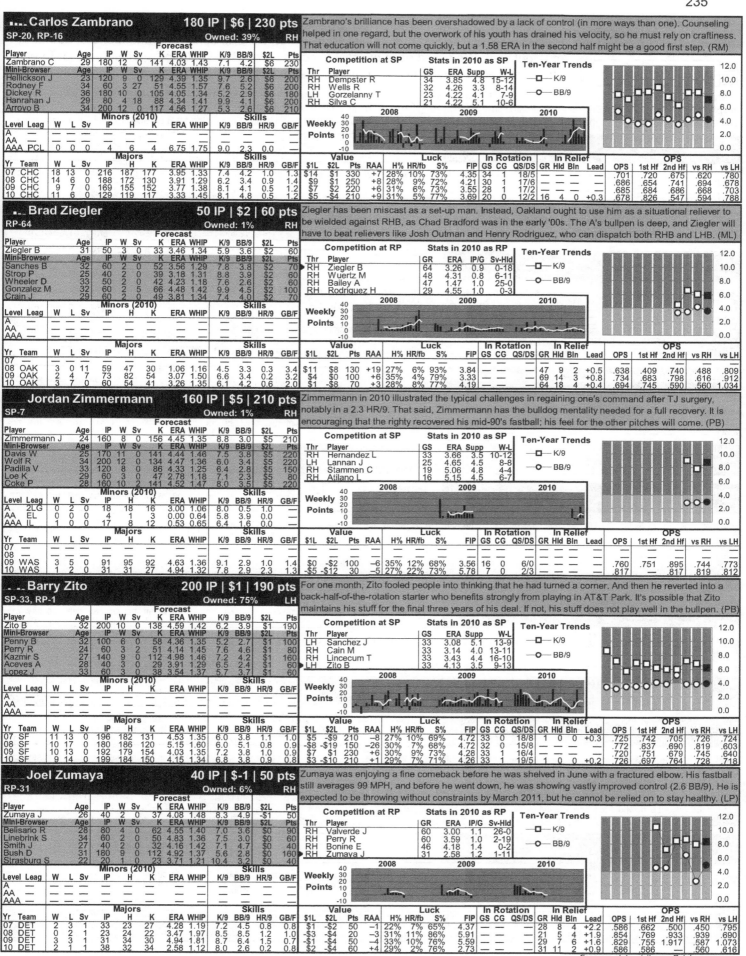

For more stats, visit www.Rotolympus.com.

# Prospects

| | 1B | 2B | 3B | SS | OF | CA | Tot |
|---|---|---|---|---|---|---|---|
| AL | 4 | 3 | 5 | 8 | 9 | 9 | 38 |
| NL | 6 | 1 | 5 | 3 | 8 | 6 | 29 |

We have the good fortune to welcome back all three of our prospect mavens from last year: **Matt Hagen**, of The Hardball Times; **Marc Hulet**, of Fangraphs.com; and **Melissa Lockard**, of Scout.com. We asked each panelist to submit his or her top 60 prospects for 2011. Every player who appeared on at least one list — a total of 118 distinct names — is covered here.

Every expert commented on and ranked every prospect. Hitters and pitchers are ranked separately (hitters from #1-#67, pitchers from #1-#51). The rank reflects the player's eventual caliber. "ETA" is the estimated time of arrival for good in the majors. Level "A" comprises both low-A and high-A (rookie ball is not included). The listed age is as of April 1, 2011. If the prospect entered more than one draft, the listed result is the latest. Forecasted MLB playing time is by the team writer.

## 2B Dustin Ackley — Seattle | AL

LH | 23 yrs, 1 mo — Drafted 2009, #2 overall

Last year's rankings: #28 | #10 | #15 — Latest league: Pacific Coast

**MLB Forecast 2011**

| AB | R | H | 2B | 3B | HR | RBI | SB | BA | OBP | SLG | BB% | CT% |
|---|---|---|---|---|---|---|---|---|---|---|---|---|
| 354 | 54 | 89 | 17 | 4 | 11 | 35 | 8 | .251 | .338 | .409 | 11% | 83% |

**2008**

| Level | AB | R | H | 2B | 3B | HR | RBI | SB | BA | OBP | SLG | BB% | CT% |
|---|---|---|---|---|---|---|---|---|---|---|---|---|---|
| A | — | — | — | — | — | — | — | — | — | — | — | — | — |
| AA | — | — | — | — | — | — | — | — | — | — | — | — | — |
| AAA | — | — | — | — | — | — | — | — | — | — | — | — | — |
| MLB | — | — | — | — | — | — | — | — | — | — | — | — | — |

**2009**

| Level | AB | R | H | 2B | 3B | HR | RBI | SB | BA | OBP | SLG | BB% | CT% |
|---|---|---|---|---|---|---|---|---|---|---|---|---|---|
| A | — | — | — | — | — | — | — | — | — | — | — | — | — |
| AA | — | — | — | — | — | — | — | — | — | — | — | — | — |
| AAA | — | — | — | — | — | — | — | — | — | — | — | — | — |
| MLB | — | — | — | — | — | — | — | — | — | — | — | — | — |

**2010**

| Level | AB | R | H | 2B | 3B | HR | RBI | SB | BA | OBP | SLG | BB% | CT% |
|---|---|---|---|---|---|---|---|---|---|---|---|---|---|
| A | — | — | — | — | — | — | — | — | — | — | — | — | — |
| AA | 289 | 42 | 76 | 21 | 4 | 2 | 28 | 8 | .263 | .389 | .384 | 16% | 86% |
| AAA | 212 | 37 | 58 | 12 | 4 | 5 | 23 | 2 | .274 | .338 | .439 | 8% | 82% |
| MLB | — | — | — | — | — | — | — | — | — | — | — | — | — |

| Rank | Comment | ETA |
|---|---|---|
| #25 | His move from 1B/OF to 2B helps, but owing to paltry power and speed numbers, Ackley has yet to resemble the star that he was drafted to be. (Hagen) | ETA: Late 2011 |
| #30 | Ackley overcame a slow start to earn a promotion to Triple-A; once there, though, he sacrificed patience for power. His glove might not play at 2B. (Hulet) | ETA: Late 2011 |
| #9 | Coming from college, Ackley transitioned to a new position and then held his own in the advanced leagues. He is a future lead-off or #2 hitter. (Lockard) | ETA: Mid-2011 |

## 1B Yonder Alonso — Cincinnati | NL

LH | 23 yrs, 11 mo — Drafted 2008, #7 overall

Last year's rankings: #35 | #17 | #34 — Latest league: International

**MLB Forecast 2011**

| AB | R | H | 2B | 3B | HR | RBI | SB | BA | OBP | SLG | BB% | CT% |
|---|---|---|---|---|---|---|---|---|---|---|---|---|
| 94 | 8 | 21 | 6 | 0 | 4 | 13 | 0 | .224 | .298 | .408 | 10% | 79% |

**2008**

| Level | AB | R | H | 2B | 3B | HR | RBI | SB | BA | OBP | SLG | BB% | CT% |
|---|---|---|---|---|---|---|---|---|---|---|---|---|---|
| A | 19 | 1 | 6 | 1 | 0 | 0 | 2 | 0 | .316 | .440 | .368 | 20% | 74% |
| AA | — | — | — | — | — | — | — | — | — | — | — | — | — |
| AAA | — | — | — | — | — | — | — | — | — | — | — | — | — |
| MLB | — | — | — | — | — | — | — | — | — | — | — | — | — |

**2009**

| Level | AB | R | H | 2B | 3B | HR | RBI | SB | BA | OBP | SLG | BB% | CT% |
|---|---|---|---|---|---|---|---|---|---|---|---|---|---|
| A | 175 | 21 | 53 | 13 | 0 | 7 | 38 | 0 | .303 | .383 | .497 | 12% | 83% |
| AA | 105 | 12 | 31 | 11 | 0 | 2 | 14 | 1 | .295 | .372 | .457 | 12% | 86% |
| AAA | — | — | — | — | — | — | — | — | — | — | — | — | — |
| MLB | — | — | — | — | — | — | — | — | — | — | — | — | — |

**2010**

| Level | AB | R | H | 2B | 3B | HR | RBI | SB | BA | OBP | SLG | BB% | CT% |
|---|---|---|---|---|---|---|---|---|---|---|---|---|---|
| A | — | — | — | — | — | — | — | — | — | — | — | — | — |
| AA | 101 | 19 | 27 | 5 | 0 | 3 | 13 | 4 | .267 | .388 | .406 | 16% | 84% |
| AAA | 406 | 50 | 120 | 31 | 2 | 12 | 56 | 9 | .296 | .355 | .470 | 8% | 81% |
| MLB | 29 | 2 | 6 | 2 | 0 | 0 | 3 | 0 | .207 | .207 | .276 | 0% | 66% |

| Rank | Comment | ETA |
|---|---|---|
| #46 | Alonso's weak HR numbers continue to hamper his value. His future would be much brighter if he could merely hold down a spot in the outfield. (Hagen) | ETA: Mid-2011 |
| #33 | Despite a solid season in Triple-A, Alonso is blocked by incumbent 1B Joey Votto. But Alonso's OF defense comes up short. He's a trading chip. (Hulet) | ETA: Mid-2011 |
| #39 | Don't let his overall numbers fool you: Alonso was slowed early while recovering from a broken hamate. Still, he is blocked at 1B in Cincinnati. (Lockard) | ETA: Mid-2011 |

## 1B Lars Anderson — Boston | AL

LH | 23 yrs, 6 mo — Drafted 2006, 18th round

Last year's rankings: #19 | #42 | #40 — Latest league: International

**MLB Forecast 2011**

| AB | R | H | 2B | 3B | HR | RBI | SB | BA | OBP | SLG | BB% | CT% |
|---|---|---|---|---|---|---|---|---|---|---|---|---|
| 44 | 5 | 10 | 3 | 0 | 2 | 5 | 0 | .228 | .320 | .384 | 12% | 73% |

**2008**

| Level | AB | R | H | 2B | 3B | HR | RBI | SB | BA | OBP | SLG | BB% | CT% |
|---|---|---|---|---|---|---|---|---|---|---|---|---|---|
| A | 306 | 58 | 97 | 19 | 1 | 13 | 50 | 0 | .317 | .408 | .513 | 13% | 79% |
| AA | 133 | 27 | 42 | 13 | 0 | 5 | 30 | 1 | .316 | .436 | .526 | 18% | 68% |
| AAA | — | — | — | — | — | — | — | — | — | — | — | — | — |
| MLB | — | — | — | — | — | — | — | — | — | — | — | — | — |

**2009**

| Level | AB | R | H | 2B | 3B | HR | RBI | SB | BA | OBP | SLG | BB% | CT% |
|---|---|---|---|---|---|---|---|---|---|---|---|---|---|
| A | — | — | — | — | — | — | — | — | — | — | — | — | — |
| AA | 447 | 50 | 104 | 23 | 0 | 9 | 51 | 2 | .233 | .328 | .345 | 12% | 74% |
| AAA | — | — | — | — | — | — | — | — | — | — | — | — | — |
| MLB | — | — | — | — | — | — | — | — | — | — | — | — | — |

**2010**

| Level | AB | R | H | 2B | 3B | HR | RBI | SB | BA | OBP | SLG | BB% | CT% |
|---|---|---|---|---|---|---|---|---|---|---|---|---|---|
| A | — | — | — | — | — | — | — | — | — | — | — | — | — |
| AA | 62 | 13 | 22 | 5 | 0 | 5 | 16 | 1 | .355 | .408 | .677 | 10% | 74% |
| AAA | 409 | 49 | 107 | 32 | 3 | 10 | 53 | 2 | .262 | .340 | .428 | 10% | 73% |
| MLB | 35 | 4 | 7 | 1 | 0 | 0 | 4 | 0 | .200 | .326 | .229 | 16% | 77% |

| Rank | Comment | ETA |
|---|---|---|
| #36 | I'm souring on Anderson: His home run power and patience at the plate have not taken off as expected, leaving him somewhat lost in the shuffle. (Hagen) | ETA: Late 2011 |
| #66 | After two straight poor offensive seasons, Anderson has been passed on the depth chart by Anthony Rizzo. But Lars is young enough to rebound. (Hulet) | ETA: Mid-2012 |
| #61 | Anderson bombed in Double-A in '09 and was only average in Triple-A this year. He still has his believers, but he must re-capture his '08 form. (Lockard) | ETA: Early 2011 |

## 3B Nolan Arenado — Colorado | NL

RH | 19 yrs, 11 mo — Drafted 2009, 2nd round

Last year's rankings: — | — | — — Latest league: South Atlantic

**MLB Forecast 2011**

| AB | R | H | 2B | 3B | HR | RBI | SB | BA | OBP | SLG | BB% | CT% |
|---|---|---|---|---|---|---|---|---|---|---|---|---|
| — | — | — | — | — | — | — | — | — | — | — | — | — |

**2008**

| Level | AB | R | H | 2B | 3B | HR | RBI | SB | BA | OBP | SLG | BB% | CT% |
|---|---|---|---|---|---|---|---|---|---|---|---|---|---|
| A | — | — | — | — | — | — | — | — | — | — | — | — | — |
| AA | — | — | — | — | — | — | — | — | — | — | — | — | — |
| AAA | — | — | — | — | — | — | — | — | — | — | — | — | — |
| MLB | — | — | — | — | — | — | — | — | — | — | — | — | — |

**2009**

| Level | AB | R | H | 2B | 3B | HR | RBI | SB | BA | OBP | SLG | BB% | CT% |
|---|---|---|---|---|---|---|---|---|---|---|---|---|---|
| A | — | — | — | — | — | — | — | — | — | — | — | — | — |
| AA | — | — | — | — | — | — | — | — | — | — | — | — | — |
| AAA | — | — | — | — | — | — | — | — | — | — | — | — | — |
| MLB | — | — | — | — | — | — | — | — | — | — | — | — | — |

**2010**

| Level | AB | R | H | 2B | 3B | HR | RBI | SB | BA | OBP | SLG | BB% | CT% |
|---|---|---|---|---|---|---|---|---|---|---|---|---|---|
| A | 373 | 45 | 115 | 41 | 1 | 12 | 65 | 1 | .308 | .338 | .520 | 5% | 86% |
| AA | — | — | — | — | — | — | — | — | — | — | — | — | — |
| AAA | — | — | — | — | — | — | — | — | — | — | — | — | — |
| MLB | — | — | — | — | — | — | — | — | — | — | — | — | — |

| Rank | Comment | ETA |
|---|---|---|
| #53 | Arenado posted a stellar full-season debut, showing off his contact skills and gap power. Greater long-ball power and plate discipline are needed. (Hagen) | ETA: Late 2013 |
| #29 | Many of Arenado's doubles could turn into homers in 2011, making him a player to monitor. At present, the biggest weakness is a lack of patience. (Hulet) | ETA: Late 2013 |
| #35 | Arenado is a rare hitter who generates big power without a lot of whiffs. He has the arm to stick at third base but his footwork needs refinement. (Lockard) | ETA: Early 2013 |

## CA J.P. Arencibia — Toronto | AL

RH | 25 yrs, 2 mo — Drafted 2007, #21 overall

Last year's rankings: — | — | — — Latest league: Pacific Coast

**MLB Forecast 2011**

| AB | R | H | 2B | 3B | HR | RBI | SB | BA | OBP | SLG | BB% | CT% |
|---|---|---|---|---|---|---|---|---|---|---|---|---|
| 369 | 36 | 80 | 24 | 0 | 16 | 52 | 0 | .217 | .254 | .420 | 4% | 73% |

**2008**

| Level | AB | R | H | 2B | 3B | HR | RBI | SB | BA | OBP | SLG | BB% | CT% |
|---|---|---|---|---|---|---|---|---|---|---|---|---|---|
| A | 248 | 38 | 78 | 22 | 0 | 13 | 62 | 0 | .315 | .344 | .560 | 4% | 81% |
| AA | 262 | 32 | 74 | 14 | 0 | 14 | 43 | 0 | .282 | .302 | .496 | 3% | 79% |
| AAA | — | — | — | — | — | — | — | — | — | — | — | — | — |
| MLB | — | — | — | — | — | — | — | — | — | — | — | — | — |

**2009**

| Level | AB | R | H | 2B | 3B | HR | RBI | SB | BA | OBP | SLG | BB% | CT% |
|---|---|---|---|---|---|---|---|---|---|---|---|---|---|
| A | — | — | — | — | — | — | — | — | — | — | — | — | — |
| AA | — | — | — | — | — | — | — | — | — | — | — | — | — |
| AAA | 466 | 67 | 110 | 32 | 1 | 21 | 75 | 0 | .236 | .284 | .444 | 5% | 76% |
| MLB | — | — | — | — | — | — | — | — | — | — | — | — | — |

**2010**

| Level | AB | R | H | 2B | 3B | HR | RBI | SB | BA | OBP | SLG | BB% | CT% |
|---|---|---|---|---|---|---|---|---|---|---|---|---|---|
| A | — | — | — | — | — | — | — | — | — | — | — | — | — |
| AA | — | — | — | — | — | — | — | — | — | — | — | — | — |
| AAA | 412 | 76 | 124 | 36 | 1 | 32 | 85 | 0 | .301 | .359 | .626 | 8% | 79% |
| MLB | 35 | 3 | 5 | 1 | 0 | 2 | 4 | 0 | .143 | .189 | .343 | 5% | 69% |

| Rank | Comment | ETA |
|---|---|---|
| #26 | After a lousy 2009, Arencibia put himself on the short list for 2010 Minor League MVP. He could become a respectable power hitter in the majors. (Hagen) | ETA: Mid-2011 |
| #24 | Arencibia posted a whopping .325 ISO in Triple-A, but a stint in MLB spotlighted his over-aggressive approach. That rashness will hurt him in '11. (Hulet) | ETA: Mid-2011 |
| #36 | Arencibia recovered from a poor 2009 to put up spectacular numbers in '10. His approach is just OK, but he has plus power and a good glove. (Lockard) | ETA: Early 2011 |

## 1B Brandon Belt — San Francisco | NL

LH | 22 yrs, 11 mo — Drafted 2009, 5th round

Last year's rankings: — | — | — — Latest league: Pacific Coast

**MLB Forecast 2011**

| AB | R | H | 2B | 3B | HR | RBI | SB | BA | OBP | SLG | BB% | CT% |
|---|---|---|---|---|---|---|---|---|---|---|---|---|
| 129 | 19 | 35 | 8 | 2 | 4 | 20 | 4 | .270 | .364 | .457 | 12% | 77% |

**2008**

| Level | AB | R | H | 2B | 3B | HR | RBI | SB | BA | OBP | SLG | BB% | CT% |
|---|---|---|---|---|---|---|---|---|---|---|---|---|---|
| A | — | — | — | — | — | — | — | — | — | — | — | — | — |
| AA | — | — | — | — | — | — | — | — | — | — | — | — | — |
| AAA | — | — | — | — | — | — | — | — | — | — | — | — | — |
| MLB | — | — | — | — | — | — | — | — | — | — | — | — | — |

**2009**

| Level | AB | R | H | 2B | 3B | HR | RBI | SB | BA | OBP | SLG | BB% | CT% |
|---|---|---|---|---|---|---|---|---|---|---|---|---|---|
| A | — | — | — | — | — | — | — | — | — | — | — | — | — |
| AA | — | — | — | — | — | — | — | — | — | — | — | — | — |
| AAA | — | — | — | — | — | — | — | — | — | — | — | — | — |
| MLB | — | — | — | — | — | — | — | — | — | — | — | — | — |

**2010**

| Level | AB | R | H | 2B | 3B | HR | RBI | SB | BA | OBP | SLG | BB% | CT% |
|---|---|---|---|---|---|---|---|---|---|---|---|---|---|
| A | 269 | 62 | 103 | 28 | 4 | 10 | 62 | 18 | .383 | .492 | .628 | 17% | 81% |
| AA | 175 | 26 | 59 | 11 | 6 | 9 | 40 | 2 | .337 | .413 | .623 | 11% | 81% |
| AAA | 48 | 11 | 11 | 4 | 0 | 4 | 10 | 2 | .229 | .393 | .563 | 21% | 69% |
| MLB | — | — | — | — | — | — | — | — | — | — | — | — | — |

| Rank | Comment | ETA |
|---|---|---|
| #65 | Unheralded leaving the University of Texas, Belt opened everyone's eyes in 2010. However, most of his numbers are bloated beyond his skill set. (Hagen) | ETA: Late 2012 |
| #43 | Belt came out of nowhere to reach Triple-A in his first season. He displayed power, patience, and even some baserunning acumen for a 6'5" guy. (Hulet) | ETA: Late 2011 |
| #24 | Belt began the year off the prospect radar but he finished on the verge of the big leagues. He has good gap power and ability to hit for average. (Lockard) | ETA: Early 2011 |

## CF Engel Beltre — Texas | AL

LH | 21 yrs, 5 mo — Signed as non-drafted free agent, 2006

Last year's rankings: — | — | — — Latest league: Texas

**MLB Forecast 2011**

| AB | R | H | 2B | 3B | HR | RBI | SB | BA | OBP | SLG | BB% | CT% |
|---|---|---|---|---|---|---|---|---|---|---|---|---|
| — | — | — | — | — | — | — | — | — | — | — | — | — |

**2008**

| Level | AB | R | H | 2B | 3B | HR | RBI | SB | BA | OBP | SLG | BB% | CT% |
|---|---|---|---|---|---|---|---|---|---|---|---|---|---|
| A | 566 | 87 | 160 | 26 | 9 | 8 | 47 | 31 | .283 | .308 | .403 | 3% | 81% |
| AA | — | — | — | — | — | — | — | — | — | — | — | — | — |
| AAA | — | — | — | — | — | — | — | — | — | — | — | — | — |
| MLB | — | — | — | — | — | — | — | — | — | — | — | — | — |

**2009**

| Level | AB | R | H | 2B | 3B | HR | RBI | SB | BA | OBP | SLG | BB% | CT% |
|---|---|---|---|---|---|---|---|---|---|---|---|---|---|
| A | 357 | 44 | 81 | 13 | 5 | 3 | 23 | 17 | .227 | .281 | .317 | 4% | 78% |
| AA | 14 | 1 | 1 | 1 | 0 | 0 | 1 | 1 | .071 | .133 | .143 | 0% | 86% |
| AAA | — | — | — | — | — | — | — | — | — | — | — | — | — |
| MLB | — | — | — | — | — | — | — | — | — | — | — | — | — |

**2010**

| Level | AB | R | H | 2B | 3B | HR | RBI | SB | BA | OBP | SLG | BB% | CT% |
|---|---|---|---|---|---|---|---|---|---|---|---|---|---|
| A | 263 | 38 | 87 | 11 | 4 | 5 | 35 | 10 | .331 | .376 | .460 | 4% | 87% |
| AA | 181 | 14 | 46 | 4 | 4 | 1 | 14 | 8 | .254 | .301 | .337 | 5% | 87% |
| AAA | — | — | — | — | — | — | — | — | — | — | — | — | — |
| MLB | — | — | — | — | — | — | — | — | — | — | — | — | — |

| Rank | Comment | ETA |
|---|---|---|
| #66 | Beltre owns plus speed and bat control beyond his 21 years, but the hyped power potential has quieted. Poor plate discipline will be his downfall. (Hagen) | ETA: Late 2013 |
| #65 | Always known for possessing impressive tools, Beltre finally started to develop actual baseball skills. But his patience needs a lot of improvement. (Hulet) | ETA: Late 2012 |
| #38 | Beltre recaptured his prospect status by improving his contact rate and hitting for more pop. He has huge tools but he's still a work-in-progress. (Lockard) | ETA: Late 2012 |

## RF Domonic Brown — Philadelphia | NL

LH | 23 yrs, 6 mo — Drafted 2006, 20th round

Last year's rankings: #47 | #4 | #3 — Latest league: International

| MLB Forecast 2011 | AB | R | H | 2B | 3B | HR | RBI | SB | BA | OBP | SLG | BB% | CT% |
|---|---|---|---|---|---|---|---|---|---|---|---|---|---|
| | 531 | 66 | 120 | 24 | 6 | 18 | 66 | 24 | .226 | .307 | .401 | 10% | 76% |

| 2008 Level | AB | R | H | 2B | 3B | HR | RBI | SB | BA | OBP | SLG | BB% | CT% |
|---|---|---|---|---|---|---|---|---|---|---|---|---|---|
| A | 444 | 77 | 129 | 23 | 3 | 9 | 54 | 22 | .291 | .382 | .417 | 12% | 84% |
| AA | — | — | — | — | — | — | — | — | — | — | — | — | — |
| AAA | — | — | — | — | — | — | — | — | — | — | — | — | — |
| MLB | — | — | — | — | — | — | — | — | — | — | — | — | — |

| 2009 Level | AB | R | H | 2B | 3B | HR | RBI | SB | BA | OBP | SLG | BB% | CT% |
|---|---|---|---|---|---|---|---|---|---|---|---|---|---|
| A | 238 | 41 | 72 | 12 | 3 | 11 | 44 | 15 | .303 | .386 | .517 | 12% | 80% |
| AA | 147 | 20 | 41 | 9 | 4 | 3 | 20 | 8 | .279 | .346 | .456 | 9% | 75% |
| AAA | — | — | — | — | — | — | — | — | — | — | — | — | — |
| MLB | — | — | — | — | — | — | — | — | — | — | — | — | — |

| 2010 Level | AB | R | H | 2B | 3B | HR | RBI | SB | BA | OBP | SLG | BB% | CT% |
|---|---|---|---|---|---|---|---|---|---|---|---|---|---|
| A | — | — | — | — | — | — | — | — | — | — | — | — | — |
| AA | 236 | 50 | 75 | 16 | 3 | 15 | 47 | 12 | .318 | .391 | .602 | 11% | 78% |
| AAA | 107 | 15 | 37 | 6 | 1 | 5 | 21 | 5 | .346 | .390 | .561 | 7% | 79% |
| MLB | 62 | 8 | 13 | 3 | 0 | 2 | 13 | 2 | .210 | .257 | .355 | 7% | 61% |

| Rank | Comment | ETA |
|---|---|---|
| #7 | I've come around on Brown, but my skepticism is not fully gone. He destroyed the minors, but his big-league debut highlighted his weaknesses. (Hagen) | ETA: Mid-2011 |
| #8 | Brown did not impress in his stint in MLB, which could hurt his chances of opening '11 in Philly. He has undeniably impressive power and speed. (Hulet) | ETA: Mid-2011 |
| #1 | Brown is a legitimate five-tool talent who profiles as a future superstar. Already a power threat, Brown's HR totals will rise as his body fills out. (Lockard) | ETA: Early 2011 |

## 1B Chris Carter — Oakland | AL

RH | 24 yrs, 3 mo — Drafted 2005, 15th round

Last year's rankings: #25 | #14 | #18 — Latest league: Pacific Coast

| MLB Forecast 2011 | AB | R | H | 2B | 3B | HR | RBI | SB | BA | OBP | SLG | BB% | CT% |
|---|---|---|---|---|---|---|---|---|---|---|---|---|---|
| | 442 | 55 | 95 | 25 | 0 | 25 | 65 | 5 | .215 | .306 | .437 | 11% | 69% |

| 2008 Level | AB | R | H | 2B | 3B | HR | RBI | SB | BA | OBP | SLG | BB% | CT% |
|---|---|---|---|---|---|---|---|---|---|---|---|---|---|
| A | 506 | 101 | 131 | 32 | 4 | 39 | 104 | 4 | .259 | .361 | .569 | 13% | 69% |
| AA | — | — | — | — | — | — | — | — | — | — | — | — | — |
| AAA | — | — | — | — | — | — | — | — | — | — | — | — | — |
| MLB | — | — | — | — | — | — | — | — | — | — | — | — | — |

| 2009 Level | AB | R | H | 2B | 3B | HR | RBI | SB | BA | OBP | SLG | BB% | CT% |
|---|---|---|---|---|---|---|---|---|---|---|---|---|---|
| A | — | — | — | — | — | — | — | — | — | — | — | — | — |
| AA | 490 | 108 | 165 | 41 | 2 | 24 | 101 | 13 | .337 | .435 | .576 | 14% | 76% |
| AAA | 54 | 7 | 14 | 2 | 0 | 4 | 14 | 0 | .259 | .293 | .519 | 5% | 74% |
| MLB | — | — | — | — | — | — | — | — | — | — | — | — | — |

| 2010 Level | AB | R | H | 2B | 3B | HR | RBI | SB | BA | OBP | SLG | BB% | CT% |
|---|---|---|---|---|---|---|---|---|---|---|---|---|---|
| A | — | — | — | — | — | — | — | — | — | — | — | — | — |
| AA | — | — | — | — | — | — | — | — | — | — | — | — | — |
| AAA | 465 | 92 | 120 | 29 | 2 | 31 | 94 | 1 | .258 | .365 | .529 | 13% | 70% |
| MLB | 70 | 8 | 13 | 1 | 0 | 3 | 7 | 1 | .186 | .256 | .329 | 9% | 70% |

| Rank | Comment | ETA |
|---|---|---|
| #30 | Carter has elite power and little else. Surprisingly, he might be able to man the outfield, but his terrible MLB debut leads me to turn the other way. (Hagen) | ETA: Late 2011 |
| #54 | After a so-so season in Triple-A, Carter kicked off his MLB career by going 0-for-33. He'll keep swinging for good power, but his BA will be modest. (Hulet) | ETA: Mid-2011 |
| #18 | Carter is streaky but he has legit 30-HR power. He might never hit higher than .270 in the majors, but his power and walk rate will make up for it. (Lockard) | ETA: Early 2011 |

## RF Johermyn Chavez — Seattle | AL

RH | 22 yrs, 2 mo — Signed as non-drafted free agent, 2005

Last year's rankings: — | — | — — Latest league: California

| MLB Forecast 2011 | AB | R | H | 2B | 3B | HR | RBI | SB | BA | OBP | SLG | BB% | CT% |
|---|---|---|---|---|---|---|---|---|---|---|---|---|---|
| | — | — | — | — | — | — | — | — | — | — | — | — | — |

| 2008 Level | AB | R | H | 2B | 3B | HR | RBI | SB | BA | OBP | SLG | BB% | CT% |
|---|---|---|---|---|---|---|---|---|---|---|---|---|---|
| A | 402 | 40 | 85 | 20 | 2 | 7 | 39 | 9 | .211 | .272 | .323 | 6% | 68% |
| AA | — | — | — | — | — | — | — | — | — | — | — | — | — |
| AAA | — | — | — | — | — | — | — | — | — | — | — | — | — |
| MLB | — | — | — | — | — | — | — | — | — | — | — | — | — |

| 2009 Level | AB | R | H | 2B | 3B | HR | RBI | SB | BA | OBP | SLG | BB% | CT% |
|---|---|---|---|---|---|---|---|---|---|---|---|---|---|
| A | 508 | 87 | 144 | 22 | 6 | 21 | 89 | 10 | .283 | .346 | .474 | 7% | 73% |
| AA | — | — | — | — | — | — | — | — | — | — | — | — | — |
| AAA | — | — | — | — | — | — | — | — | — | — | — | — | — |
| MLB | — | — | — | — | — | — | — | — | — | — | — | — | — |

| 2010 Level | AB | R | H | 2B | 3B | HR | RBI | SB | BA | OBP | SLG | BB% | CT% |
|---|---|---|---|---|---|---|---|---|---|---|---|---|---|
| A | 534 | 109 | 168 | 30 | 7 | 32 | 96 | 6 | .315 | .387 | .577 | 9% | 75% |
| AA | — | — | — | — | — | — | — | — | — | — | — | — | — |
| AAA | — | — | — | — | — | — | — | — | — | — | — | — | — |
| MLB | — | — | — | — | — | — | — | — | — | — | — | — | — |

| Rank | Comment | ETA |
|---|---|---|
| #40 | Chavez posted a second straight stellar campaign, beating up the California League. He's under the radar, but his bat has holes that need fixing. (Hagen) | ETA: Late 2012 |
| #55 | A sleeper prospect, Chavez's HR total was aided by his environment, but he does own pop and a strong arm. His batting eye needs improvement. (Hulet) | ETA: Late 2012 |
| #41 | Chavez used a smooth swing and power to all fields to put up a huge season. He benefited from a good hitters' park, so Double-A will be a test. (Lockard) | ETA: Late 2012 |

## 3B Lonnie Chisenhall — Cleveland | AL

LH | 22 yrs, 5 mo — Drafted 2008, #29 overall

Last year's rankings: #21 | #21 | #46 — Latest league: Eastern

| MLB Forecast 2011 | AB | R | H | 2B | 3B | HR | RBI | SB | BA | OBP | SLG | BB% | CT% |
|---|---|---|---|---|---|---|---|---|---|---|---|---|---|
| | — | — | — | — | — | — | — | — | — | — | — | — | — |

| 2008 Level | AB | R | H | 2B | 3B | HR | RBI | SB | BA | OBP | SLG | BB% | CT% |
|---|---|---|---|---|---|---|---|---|---|---|---|---|---|
| A | 276 | 38 | 80 | 20 | 3 | 5 | 45 | 7 | .290 | .355 | .438 | 8% | 88% |
| AA | — | — | — | — | — | — | — | — | — | — | — | — | — |
| AAA | — | — | — | — | — | — | — | — | — | — | — | — | — |
| MLB | — | — | — | — | — | — | — | — | — | — | — | — | — |

| 2009 Level | AB | R | H | 2B | 3B | HR | RBI | SB | BA | OBP | SLG | BB% | CT% |
|---|---|---|---|---|---|---|---|---|---|---|---|---|---|
| A | 388 | 59 | 107 | 26 | 2 | 18 | 79 | 2 | .276 | .346 | .492 | 9% | 79% |
| AA | 93 | 13 | 17 | 5 | 1 | 4 | 13 | 1 | .183 | .238 | .387 | 7% | 83% |
| AAA | — | — | — | — | — | — | — | — | — | — | — | — | — |
| MLB | — | — | — | — | — | — | — | — | — | — | — | — | — |

| 2010 Level | AB | R | H | 2B | 3B | HR | RBI | SB | BA | OBP | SLG | BB% | CT% |
|---|---|---|---|---|---|---|---|---|---|---|---|---|---|
| A | — | — | — | — | — | — | — | — | — | — | — | — | — |
| AA | 460 | 81 | 128 | 22 | 3 | 17 | 84 | 3 | .278 | .351 | .450 | 9% | 83% |
| AAA | — | — | — | — | — | — | — | — | — | — | — | — | — |
| MLB | — | — | — | — | — | — | — | — | — | — | — | — | — |

| Rank | Comment | ETA |
|---|---|---|
| #35 | Chisenhall adjusted to Double-A pitching in his second attempt. Still, his upside as a third baseman appears more limited with each passing year. (Hagen) | ETA: Late 2011 |
| #52 | Chisenhall continues to post good – but not great – numbers in the minors. He needs to step up if he will be a first-division starter at the hot corner. (Hulet) | ETA: Late 2011 |
| #37 | A shoulder injury curbed Chisenhall's overall stats. Once he was healthy, Lonnie showed off the easy, powerful stroke that has excited scouts. (Lockard) | ETA: Mid-2011 |

## CF Michael Choice — Oakland | AL

RH | 21 yrs, 4 mo — Drafted 2010, #10 overall

Last year's rankings: — | — | — — Latest league: Northwest

| MLB Forecast 2011 | AB | R | H | 2B | 3B | HR | RBI | SB | BA | OBP | SLG | BB% | CT% |
|---|---|---|---|---|---|---|---|---|---|---|---|---|---|
| | — | — | — | — | — | — | — | — | — | — | — | — | — |

| 2008 Level | AB | R | H | 2B | 3B | HR | RBI | SB | BA | OBP | SLG | BB% | CT% |
|---|---|---|---|---|---|---|---|---|---|---|---|---|---|
| A | — | — | — | — | — | — | — | — | — | — | — | — | — |
| AA | — | — | — | — | — | — | — | — | — | — | — | — | — |
| AAA | — | — | — | — | — | — | — | — | — | — | — | — | — |
| MLB | — | — | — | — | — | — | — | — | — | — | — | — | — |

| 2009 Level | AB | R | H | 2B | 3B | HR | RBI | SB | BA | OBP | SLG | BB% | CT% |
|---|---|---|---|---|---|---|---|---|---|---|---|---|---|
| A | — | — | — | — | — | — | — | — | — | — | — | — | — |
| AA | — | — | — | — | — | — | — | — | — | — | — | — | — |
| AAA | — | — | — | — | — | — | — | — | — | — | — | — | — |
| MLB | — | — | — | — | — | — | — | — | — | — | — | — | — |

| 2010 Level | AB | R | H | 2B | 3B | HR | RBI | SB | BA | OBP | SLG | BB% | CT% |
|---|---|---|---|---|---|---|---|---|---|---|---|---|---|
| A | 102 | 20 | 29 | 10 | 2 | 7 | 26 | 6 | .284 | .388 | .627 | 12% | 58% |
| AA | — | — | — | — | — | — | — | — | — | — | — | — | — |
| AAA | — | — | — | — | — | — | — | — | — | — | — | — | — |
| MLB | — | — | — | — | — | — | — | — | — | — | — | — | — |

| Rank | Comment | ETA |
|---|---|---|
| #15 | Apart from Bryce Harper, Choice is the best power hitter from the 2010 draft. Choice has speed to work with, too, but also quite a bit to clean up. (Hagen) | ETA: Early 2013 |
| #53 | Choice exhibited great power – and similarly large strikeout numbers. He owns clear talent, but he also has a lot of work to do on making contact. (Hulet) | ETA: Late 2013 |
| #30 | Choice showed prodigious power and above-average speed in his pro debut. He possesses a good eye, but his strikeouts need to come down. (Lockard) | ETA: Mid-2012 |

## SS Christian Colon — Kansas City | AL

RH | 21 yrs, 10 mo — Drafted 2010, #4 overall

Last year's rankings: — | — | — — Latest league: Carolina

| MLB Forecast 2011 | AB | R | H | 2B | 3B | HR | RBI | SB | BA | OBP | SLG | BB% | CT% |
|---|---|---|---|---|---|---|---|---|---|---|---|---|---|
| | — | — | — | — | — | — | — | — | — | — | — | — | — |

| 2008 Level | AB | R | H | 2B | 3B | HR | RBI | SB | BA | OBP | SLG | BB% | CT% |
|---|---|---|---|---|---|---|---|---|---|---|---|---|---|
| A | — | — | — | — | — | — | — | — | — | — | — | — | — |
| AA | — | — | — | — | — | — | — | — | — | — | — | — | — |
| AAA | — | — | — | — | — | — | — | — | — | — | — | — | — |
| MLB | — | — | — | — | — | — | — | — | — | — | — | — | — |

| 2009 Level | AB | R | H | 2B | 3B | HR | RBI | SB | BA | OBP | SLG | BB% | CT% |
|---|---|---|---|---|---|---|---|---|---|---|---|---|---|
| A | — | — | — | — | — | — | — | — | — | — | — | — | — |
| AA | — | — | — | — | — | — | — | — | — | — | — | — | — |
| AAA | — | — | — | — | — | — | — | — | — | — | — | — | — |
| MLB | — | — | — | — | — | — | — | — | — | — | — | — | — |

| 2010 Level | AB | R | H | 2B | 3B | HR | RBI | SB | BA | OBP | SLG | BB% | CT% |
|---|---|---|---|---|---|---|---|---|---|---|---|---|---|
| A | 245 | 38 | 68 | 12 | 2 | 3 | 30 | 2 | .278 | .326 | .380 | 5% | 87% |
| AA | — | — | — | — | — | — | — | — | — | — | — | — | — |
| AAA | — | — | — | — | — | — | — | — | — | — | — | — | — |
| MLB | — | — | — | — | — | — | — | — | — | — | — | — | — |

| Rank | Comment | ETA |
|---|---|---|
| #33 | Colon was an overdraft at #4, but we could see the appeal. He doesn't offer much in terms of tools, but he has polish and could advance quickly. (Hagen) | ETA: Mid-2012 |
| #56 | You have to love the fact that Colon got signed and moved into pro ball so quickly. Unfortunately, he was a singles hitter with little power or speed. (Hulet) | ETA: Mid-2012 |
| #26 | A shortstop in college, Colon is seen by most scouts as eventually sticking at 2B. He does everything moderately well but has no stand-out tool. (Lockard) | ETA: Mid-2012 |

## CA Hank Conger — Los Angeles | AL

BH | 23 yrs, 2 mo — Drafted 2006, #25 overall

Last year's rankings: #46 | #59 | #54 — Latest league: Pacific Coast

| MLB Forecast 2011 | AB | R | H | 2B | 3B | HR | RBI | SB | BA | OBP | SLG | BB% | CT% |
|---|---|---|---|---|---|---|---|---|---|---|---|---|---|
| | 276 | 27 | 66 | 15 | 3 | 9 | 42 | 3 | .239 | .299 | .415 | 8% | 79% |

| 2008 Level | AB | R | H | 2B | 3B | HR | RBI | SB | BA | OBP | SLG | BB% | CT% |
|---|---|---|---|---|---|---|---|---|---|---|---|---|---|
| A | 294 | 47 | 89 | 20 | 2 | 13 | 75 | 2 | .303 | .333 | .517 | 4% | 81% |
| AA | — | — | — | — | — | — | — | — | — | — | — | — | — |
| AAA | — | — | — | — | — | — | — | — | — | — | — | — | — |
| MLB | — | — | — | — | — | — | — | — | — | — | — | — | — |

| 2009 Level | AB | R | H | 2B | 3B | HR | RBI | SB | BA | OBP | SLG | BB% | CT% |
|---|---|---|---|---|---|---|---|---|---|---|---|---|---|
| A | — | — | — | — | — | — | — | — | — | — | — | — | — |
| AA | 458 | 61 | 135 | 20 | 3 | 11 | 68 | 4 | .295 | .369 | .424 | 10% | 85% |
| AAA | — | — | — | — | — | — | — | — | — | — | — | — | — |
| MLB | — | — | — | — | — | — | — | — | — | — | — | — | — |

| 2010 Level | AB | R | H | 2B | 3B | HR | RBI | SB | BA | OBP | SLG | BB% | CT% |
|---|---|---|---|---|---|---|---|---|---|---|---|---|---|
| A | — | — | — | — | — | — | — | — | — | — | — | — | — |
| AA | — | — | — | — | — | — | — | — | — | — | — | — | — |
| AAA | 387 | 56 | 116 | 26 | 2 | 11 | 49 | 0 | .300 | .385 | .463 | 12% | 85% |
| MLB | 29 | 2 | 5 | 1 | 1 | 0 | 5 | 0 | .172 | .294 | .276 | 15% | 69% |

| Rank | Comment | ETA |
|---|---|---|
| #27 | From nearly every standpoint, Conger impressed in 2010. However, the details of where, how, and when he fits onto the Angels is still to be seen. (Hagen) | ETA: Late 2011 |
| #34 | With his modest defensive skills, Conger may have a difficult time cracking Anaheim's roster. However, he has a sweet swing and power potential. (Hulet) | ETA: Mid-2011 |
| #25 | Despite fighting injuries for much of his career, Conger is arguably the most well-rounded catcher on either side of the ball on the Angels' roster. (Lockard) | ETA: Early 2011 |

## 3B Zach Cox — St. Louis | NL

LH | 21 yrs, 10 mo — Drafted 2010, #25 overall

Last year's rankings: — | — | — — Latest league: Gulf Coast

| MLB Forecast 2011 | AB | R | H | 2B | 3B | HR | RBI | SB | BA | OBP | SLG | BB% | CT% |
|---|---|---|---|---|---|---|---|---|---|---|---|---|---|
| | — | — | — | — | — | — | — | — | — | — | — | — | — |

| 2008 Level | AB | R | H | 2B | 3B | HR | RBI | SB | BA | OBP | SLG | BB% | CT% |
|---|---|---|---|---|---|---|---|---|---|---|---|---|---|
| A | — | — | — | — | — | — | — | — | — | — | — | — | — |
| AA | — | — | — | — | — | — | — | — | — | — | — | — | — |
| AAA | — | — | — | — | — | — | — | — | — | — | — | — | — |
| MLB | — | — | — | — | — | — | — | — | — | — | — | — | — |

| 2009 Level | AB | R | H | 2B | 3B | HR | RBI | SB | BA | OBP | SLG | BB% | CT% |
|---|---|---|---|---|---|---|---|---|---|---|---|---|---|
| A | — | — | — | — | — | — | — | — | — | — | — | — | — |
| AA | — | — | — | — | — | — | — | — | — | — | — | — | — |
| AAA | — | — | — | — | — | — | — | — | — | — | — | — | — |
| MLB | — | — | — | — | — | — | — | — | — | — | — | — | — |

| 2010 Level | AB | R | H | 2B | 3B | HR | RBI | SB | BA | OBP | SLG | BB% | CT% |
|---|---|---|---|---|---|---|---|---|---|---|---|---|---|
| A | — | — | — | — | — | — | — | — | — | — | — | — | — |
| AA | — | — | — | — | — | — | — | — | — | — | — | — | — |
| AAA | — | — | — | — | — | — | — | — | — | — | — | — | — |
| MLB | — | — | — | — | — | — | — | — | — | — | — | — | — |

| Rank | Comment | ETA |
|---|---|---|
| #24 | Cox was drafted for his professionalism, polish, bat speed, and plate approach. Nonetheless, his questionable power potential may yet limit him. (Hagen) | ETA: Late 2012 |
| #15 | One of the top hitters in the draft, Cox brings a lot of talent to St. Louis, and he could develop into an impact bat at the MLB level for the Cardinals. (Hulet) | ETA: Late 2013 |
| #42 | Some scouts viewed Cox as the best college hitter in the draft, but others questioned his power potential and overall threat as a corner infielder. (Lockard) | ETA: Late 2012 |

## CA Travis d'Arnaud — Toronto | AL
RH | 22 yrs, 1 mo — Drafted 2007, #37 overall
Last year's rankings: — — — | Latest league: Florida State
MLB Forecast 2011: — — — — — — — — — — — — —

| Year | Level | AB | R | H | 2B | 3B | HR | RBI | SB | BA | OBP | SLG | BB% | CT% |
|---|---|---|---|---|---|---|---|---|---|---|---|---|---|---|
| 2008 | A | 239 | 33 | 73 | 18 | 1 | 6 | 30 | 1 | .305 | .367 | .464 | 9% | 84% |
| 2009 | A | 482 | 71 | 123 | 38 | 1 | 13 | 71 | 8 | .255 | .319 | .419 | 8% | 84% |
| 2010 | A | 263 | 36 | 68 | 20 | 1 | 6 | 38 | 3 | .259 | .315 | .411 | 7% | 76% |

#52 D'Arnaud has the skills to excel defensively, but for the most part his bat grades out as average, with some decent power potential still looming. (Hagen) — ETA: Mid-2013
#42 D'Arnaud's 2010 was hampered by back problems, and his season ended prematurely to surgery. That's not good resumé material for a catcher. (Hulet) — ETA: Late 2012
#45 Injuries hurt d'Arnaud at the plate. He remains above-average as a receiver, so even with a mediocre offensive profile, he would be valuable. (Lockard) — ETA: Early 2013

## 3B Matt Davidson — Arizona | NL
RH | 20 yrs, 0 mo — Drafted 2009, #35 overall
Last year's rankings: — — — | Latest league: California
MLB Forecast 2011: — — — — — — — — — — — — —

| Year | Level | AB | R | H | 2B | 3B | HR | RBI | SB | BA | OBP | SLG | BB% | CT% |
|---|---|---|---|---|---|---|---|---|---|---|---|---|---|---|
| 2009 | A | 270 | 29 | 65 | 15 | 0 | 2 | 28 | 0 | .241 | .312 | .319 | 7% | 72% |
| 2010 | A | 486 | 64 | 132 | 36 | 3 | 18 | 90 | 0 | .272 | .360 | .469 | 10% | 72% |

#57 Davidson has plenty to work on, and it's safe to question his glove, but no one can doubt the 20-year-old's raw power at this point. (Hagen) — ETA: Early 2013
#31 Davidson in 2010 surpassed fellow 3B prospect (and teenager) Bobby Borchering in Arizona. Matt has power, but his BA was unrealistically high. (Hulet) — ETA: Mid-2014
#62 Davidson is a 3B in the "Troy Glaus" mold, with big power and a big arm but also big strikeouts. He might never have the young Glaus's range. (Lockard) — ETA: Late 2012

## LF Jaff Decker — San Diego | NL
LH | 21 yrs, 1 mo — Drafted 2008, #42 overall
Last year's rankings: #32 #28 #14 | Latest league: California
MLB Forecast 2011: — — — — — — — — — — — — —

| Year | Level | AB | R | H | 2B | 3B | HR | RBI | SB | BA | OBP | SLG | BB% | CT% |
|---|---|---|---|---|---|---|---|---|---|---|---|---|---|---|
| 2008 | A | 10 | 2 | 2 | 0 | 0 | 0 | 0 | 0 | .200 | .333 | .200 | 17% | 50% |
| 2009 | A | 358 | 78 | 107 | 25 | 2 | 16 | 64 | 10 | .299 | .442 | .514 | 19% | 74% |
| 2010 | A | 290 | 53 | 76 | 14 | 2 | 17 | 58 | 5 | .262 | .374 | .500 | 14% | 72% |

#23 In the eyes of many, Decker had a lousy 2011, but he's a natural hitter with tremendous pitch recognition. His bat will adjust anywhere he plays. (Hagen) — ETA: Early 2012
#64 A hamstring injury delayed the start of Decker's season, and he struggled with his batting average. On the plus side, his power rose even further. (Hulet) — ETA: Late 2013
#34 Decker resembles Matt Stairs but is a much better athlete. He has surprising pop, and he moves better than you would think by looking at him. (Lockard) — ETA: Late 2011

## 3B Matt Dominguez — Florida | NL
RH | 21 yrs, 7 mo — Drafted 2007, #12 overall
Last year's rankings: #57 #26 #48 | Latest league: Southern
MLB Forecast 2011: — — — — — — — — — — — — —

| Year | Level | AB | R | H | 2B | 3B | HR | RBI | SB | BA | OBP | SLG | BB% | CT% |
|---|---|---|---|---|---|---|---|---|---|---|---|---|---|---|
| 2008 | A | 345 | 59 | 102 | 16 | 0 | 18 | 70 | 0 | .296 | .354 | .499 | 7% | 80% |
| 2009 | A | 381 | 49 | 100 | 25 | 1 | 11 | 53 | 1 | .262 | .333 | .420 | 9% | 82% |
| 2009 | AA | 97 | 10 | 18 | 7 | 0 | 2 | 9 | 0 | .186 | .292 | .320 | 12% | 75% |
| 2010 | AA | 504 | 61 | 127 | 34 | 2 | 14 | 81 | 0 | .252 | .333 | .411 | 10% | 81% |

#64 Dominguez for his career has shown little growth, and he sported another rotten batting average. He doesn't own a single above-average bat skill. (Hagen) — ETA: Late 2013
#37 Dominguez continues to offer more on defense than on offense. With each promotion, his power has retreated, and he might never hit for average. (Hulet) — ETA: Late 2012
#64 Dominguez has a plus glove but his bat has not developed as some expected. He'll need to improve at the plate to be an above-average regular. (Lockard) — ETA: Late 2011

## SS Danny Espinosa — Washington | NL
BH | 23 yrs, 11 mo — Drafted 2008, 3rd round
Last year's rankings: — — — | Latest league: International
MLB Forecast 2011: 417 60 90 20 5 20 60 15 .216 .315 .429 11% 70%

| Year | Level | AB | R | H | 2B | 3B | HR | RBI | SB | BA | OBP | SLG | BB% | CT% |
|---|---|---|---|---|---|---|---|---|---|---|---|---|---|---|
| 2008 | A | 64 | 8 | 21 | 2 | 0 | 0 | 4 | 2 | .328 | .476 | .359 | 20% | 73% |
| 2009 | A | 474 | 90 | 125 | 31 | 4 | 18 | 72 | 29 | .264 | .375 | .460 | 13% | 73% |
| 2010 | AA | 386 | 66 | 101 | 16 | 4 | 18 | 54 | 20 | .262 | .334 | .464 | 8% | 76% |
| 2010 | AAA | 95 | 14 | 28 | 2 | 1 | 4 | 15 | 5 | .295 | .349 | .463 | 7% | 77% |
| 2010 | MLB | 103 | 16 | 22 | 4 | 1 | 6 | 15 | 0 | .214 | .277 | .447 | 8% | 71% |

#18 Espinosa took his game to the next level and even enjoyed some big-league success. His versatility on defense stabilizes his long-term chances. (Hagen) — ETA: Early 2011
#60 Espinosa failed to build on his breakout '09 campaign and now looks like a utility or platoon player. His power numbers will probably drop in MLB. (Hulet) — ETA: Late 2011
#31 Espinosa is a strong defensive middle-infielder with power and decent speed. His swing can get a little long, but thus far he has made it work. (Lockard) — ETA: Early 2011

## SS Wilmer Flores — New York | NL
RH | 19 yrs, 7 mo — Signed as non-drafted free agent, 2007
Last year's rankings: #53 #39 #23 | Latest league: Florida State
MLB Forecast 2011: — — — — — — — — — — — — —

| Year | Level | AB | R | H | 2B | 3B | HR | RBI | SB | BA | OBP | SLG | BB% | CT% |
|---|---|---|---|---|---|---|---|---|---|---|---|---|---|---|
| 2009 | A | 488 | 44 | 129 | 20 | 2 | 3 | 36 | 3 | .264 | .305 | .332 | 4% | 85% |
| 2010 | A | 554 | 62 | 160 | 36 | 3 | 11 | 84 | 4 | .289 | .333 | .424 | 5% | 86% |

#13 I demanded improvement, and Flores delivered, maturing across the board. Make no mistake, though, he'll eventually be moved (probably to 3B). (Hagen) — ETA: Mid-2013
#22 Flores is still only a teenager, and he has shown good improvement each season. However, he still has to develop a better game plan at the plate. (Hulet) — ETA: Late 2012
#13 Flores was just 18 for much of 2010 and yet he held his own against players two years his senior. He's a smart hitter with the tools to be special. (Lockard) — ETA: Early 2013

## SS Nick Franklin — Seattle | AL
BH | 20 yrs, 0 mo — Drafted 2009, #27 overall
Last year's rankings: — — — | Latest league: Southern
MLB Forecast 2011: — — — — — — — — — — — — —

| Year | Level | AB | R | H | 2B | 3B | HR | RBI | SB | BA | OBP | SLG | BB% | CT% |
|---|---|---|---|---|---|---|---|---|---|---|---|---|---|---|
| 2009 | A | 20 | 4 | 8 | 2 | 1 | 0 | 2 | 1 | .400 | .429 | .600 | 5% | 90% |
| 2010 | A | 513 | 89 | 144 | 22 | 7 | 23 | 65 | 25 | .281 | .351 | .485 | 9% | 76% |
| 2010 | AA | 3 | 3 | 2 | 0 | 0 | 0 | 0 | 0 | .667 | .750 | .667 | 25% | 67% |

#20 No one saw Franklin's power coming, at least not this fast. He has plenty of work to do and challenges to overcome, but his potential is immense. (Hagen) — ETA: Late 2012
#27 One of the biggest surprises of 2010, Franklin had a 20-20 season in Low-A. A switch-hitter, he batted only .174 against southpaws with no power. (Hulet) — ETA: Late 2013
#19 Franklin surprised all observers with a big power year in a pitchers' league. If he can maintain that power, he could be a Miguel Tejada-type SS. (Lockard) — ETA: Early 2013

## 1B Freddie Freeman — Atlanta | NL
LH | 21 yrs, 6 mo — Drafted 2007, 2nd round
Last year's rankings: #22 #22 #22 | Latest league: International
MLB Forecast 2011: 537 60 132 30 6 18 72 0 .246 .313 .425 8% 81%

| Year | Level | AB | R | H | 2B | 3B | HR | RBI | SB | BA | OBP | SLG | BB% | CT% |
|---|---|---|---|---|---|---|---|---|---|---|---|---|---|---|
| 2008 | A | 491 | 70 | 155 | 33 | 7 | 18 | 95 | 5 | .316 | .378 | .521 | 9% | 83% |
| 2009 | A | 255 | 43 | 77 | 19 | 0 | 6 | 34 | 1 | .302 | .394 | .447 | 9% | 84% |
| 2009 | AA | 149 | 15 | 37 | 8 | 0 | 2 | 24 | 0 | .248 | .308 | .342 | 7% | 87% |
| 2010 | AAA | 461 | 73 | 147 | 35 | 2 | 18 | 87 | 6 | .319 | .378 | .521 | 8% | 82% |
| 2010 | MLB | 24 | 3 | 4 | 1 | 0 | 1 | 1 | 0 | .167 | .167 | .333 | 0% | 67% |

#12 Freeman's power has not developed much since '08, and his plate approach needs refinement. That said, he may become an asset at first base. (Hagen) — ETA: Mid-2011
#14 At age 20, Freeman had an impressive Triple-A season, and he made a case that he is MLB-ready. He should hit for average with modest power. (Hulet) — ETA: Mid-2011
#10 If 2010 was the year of Jason Heyward in Atlanta, 2011 should be the year of Freeman, who's poised to take over 1B for Atlanta for a long time. (Lockard) — ETA: Early 2011

## SS Dee Gordon — Los Angeles | NL

LH | 22 yrs, 11 mo — Drafted 2008, 4th round

Last year's rankings: #58 #53 #41 — Latest league: Southern

MLB Forecast 2011

| AB | R | H | 2B | 3B | HR | RBI | SB | BA | OBP | SLG | BB% | CT% |
|---|---|---|---|---|---|---|---|---|---|---|---|---|
| — | — | — | — | — | — | — | — | — | — | — | — | — |

| | 2008 | | | | | | | | | | | | | 2009 | | | | | | | | | | | | | 2010 | | | | | | | | | | | | |
|---|---|---|---|---|---|---|---|---|---|---|---|---|---|---|---|---|---|---|---|---|---|---|---|---|---|---|---|---|---|---|---|---|---|---|---|---|---|---|---|
| Level | AB | R | H | 2B | 3B | HR | RBI | SB | BA | OBP | SLG | BB% | CT% | AB | R | H | 2B | 3B | HR | RBI | SB | BA | OBP | SLG | BB% | CT% | AB | R | H | 2B | 3B | HR | RBI | SB | BA | OBP | SLG | BB% | CT% |
| A | — | — | — | — | — | — | — | — | — | — | — | — | — | 538 | 96 | 162 | 17 | 12 | 3 | 35 | 73 | .301 | .362 | .394 | 7% | 83% | — | — | — | — | — | — | — | — | — | — | — | — | — |
| AA | — | — | — | — | — | — | — | — | — | — | — | — | — | — | — | — | — | — | — | — | — | — | — | — | — | — | 555 | 86 | 154 | 17 | 10 | 2 | 39 | 53 | .277 | .332 | .355 | 7% | 84% |
| AAA | — | — | — | — | — | — | — | — | — | — | — | — | — | — | — | — | — | — | — | — | — | — | — | — | — | — | — | — | — | — | — | — | — | — | — | — | — | — | — |
| MLB | — | — | — | — | — | — | — | — | — | — | — | — | — | — | — | — | — | — | — | — | — | — | — | — | — | — | — | — | — | — | — | — | — | — | — | — | — | — | — |

| | | |
|---|---|---|
| #28 | Gordon impressed me in 2010 with his seamless transition to the Southern League. Yet the only outstanding tool that he possesses is his speed. (Hagen) | ETA: Late 2012 |
| #17 | The Dodgers gave Gordon an ill-advised jump from non-advanced Single-A to Double-A; his OPS dropped 70 points. He still showed good speed. (Hulet) | ETA: Mid-2012 |
| #20 | One of the fastest players in the minors, Gordon projects as an above-average defensive shortstop with pop. He has a lot of refining to do first. (Lockard) | ETA: Mid-2012 |

## CA Yasmani Grandal — Cincinnati | NL

BH | 22 yrs, 4 mo — Drafted 2010, #12 overall

Last year's rankings: — — — — Latest league: Arizona

MLB Forecast 2011

| AB | R | H | 2B | 3B | HR | RBI | SB | BA | OBP | SLG | BB% | CT% |
|---|---|---|---|---|---|---|---|---|---|---|---|---|
| — | — | — | — | — | — | — | — | — | — | — | — | — |

| | 2008 | | | | | | | | | | | | | 2009 | | | | | | | | | | | | | 2010 | | | | | | | | | | | | |
|---|---|---|---|---|---|---|---|---|---|---|---|---|---|---|---|---|---|---|---|---|---|---|---|---|---|---|---|---|---|---|---|---|---|---|---|---|---|---|---|
| Level | AB | R | H | 2B | 3B | HR | RBI | SB | BA | OBP | SLG | BB% | CT% | AB | R | H | 2B | 3B | HR | RBI | SB | BA | OBP | SLG | BB% | CT% | AB | R | H | 2B | 3B | HR | RBI | SB | BA | OBP | SLG | BB% | CT% |
| A | — | — | — | — | — | — | — | — | — | — | — | — | — | — | — | — | — | — | — | — | — | — | — | — | — | — | — | — | — | — | — | — | — | — | — | — | — | — | — |
| AA | — | — | — | — | — | — | — | — | — | — | — | — | — | — | — | — | — | — | — | — | — | — | — | — | — | — | — | — | — | — | — | — | — | — | — | — | — | — | — |
| AAA | — | — | — | — | — | — | — | — | — | — | — | — | — | — | — | — | — | — | — | — | — | — | — | — | — | — | — | — | — | — | — | — | — | — | — | — | — | — | — |
| MLB | — | — | — | — | — | — | — | — | — | — | — | — | — | — | — | — | — | — | — | — | — | — | — | — | — | — | — | — | — | — | — | — | — | — | — | — | — | — | — |

| | | |
|---|---|---|
| #37 | By my estimation, Grandal does only one thing well with the bat: hit for power. He is mildly intriguing, but he is far too raw coming out of college. (Hagen) | ETA: Mid-2013 |
| #16 | Grandal is one of the top CA prospects in baseball, with a balanced attack at the plate and behind the dish. He has just 28 pro AB (in rookie ball). (Hulet) | ETA: Mid-2012 |
| #60 | Grandal is an excellent defensive catcher and a switch-hitter with power potential, though his calling card is his glove. He could advance quickly. (Lockard) | ETA: Mid-2012 |

## SS Grant Green — Oakland | AL

RH | 23 yrs, 6 mo — Drafted 2009, #13 overall

Last year's rankings: — — — — Latest league: California

MLB Forecast 2011

| AB | R | H | 2B | 3B | HR | RBI | SB | BA | OBP | SLG | BB% | CT% |
|---|---|---|---|---|---|---|---|---|---|---|---|---|
| — | — | — | — | — | — | — | — | — | — | — | — | — |

| | 2008 | | | | | | | | | | | | | 2009 | | | | | | | | | | | | | 2010 | | | | | | | | | | | | |
|---|---|---|---|---|---|---|---|---|---|---|---|---|---|---|---|---|---|---|---|---|---|---|---|---|---|---|---|---|---|---|---|---|---|---|---|---|---|---|---|
| Level | AB | R | H | 2B | 3B | HR | RBI | SB | BA | OBP | SLG | BB% | CT% | AB | R | H | 2B | 3B | HR | RBI | SB | BA | OBP | SLG | BB% | CT% | AB | R | H | 2B | 3B | HR | RBI | SB | BA | OBP | SLG | BB% | CT% |
| A | — | — | — | — | — | — | — | — | — | — | — | — | — | 19 | 2 | 6 | 1 | 0 | 0 | 3 | 1 | .316 | .350 | .368 | 5% | 74% | 548 | 107 | 174 | 39 | 6 | 20 | 87 | 9 | .318 | .363 | .520 | 6% | 79% |
| AA | — | — | — | — | — | — | — | — | — | — | — | — | — | — | — | — | — | — | — | — | — | — | — | — | — | — | — | — | — | — | — | — | — | — | — | — | — | — | — |
| AAA | — | — | — | — | — | — | — | — | — | — | — | — | — | — | — | — | — | — | — | — | — | — | — | — | — | — | — | — | — | — | — | — | — | — | — | — | — | — | — |
| MLB | — | — | — | — | — | — | — | — | — | — | — | — | — | — | — | — | — | — | — | — | — | — | — | — | — | — | — | — | — | — | — | — | — | — | — | — | — | — | — |

| | | |
|---|---|---|
| #19 | Green played well in 2010, and he showed better than expected power, albeit in the California League. He has greater upside than I credited him. (Hagen) | ETA: Late 2011 |
| #18 | Green took advantage of his league and exhibited good power potential. A high .366 BABIP inflated his batting average. Double-A will be a big test. (Hulet) | ETA: Mid-2012 |
| #11 | Green profiles as a Troy Tulowitzki-type offensive SS, but he may lack the glove for there. Even with a shift to 2B, Green should still be valuable. (Lockard) | ETA: Early 2012 |

## RF Bryce Harper — Washington | NL

LH | 18 yrs, 5 mo — Drafted 2010, #1 overall

Last year's rankings: — — — — Latest league: N/A

MLB Forecast 2011

| AB | R | H | 2B | 3B | HR | RBI | SB | BA | OBP | SLG | BB% | CT% |
|---|---|---|---|---|---|---|---|---|---|---|---|---|
| — | — | — | — | — | — | — | — | — | — | — | — | — |

| | 2008 | | | | | | | | | | | | | 2009 | | | | | | | | | | | | | 2010 | | | | | | | | | | | | |
|---|---|---|---|---|---|---|---|---|---|---|---|---|---|---|---|---|---|---|---|---|---|---|---|---|---|---|---|---|---|---|---|---|---|---|---|---|---|---|---|
| Level | AB | R | H | 2B | 3B | HR | RBI | SB | BA | OBP | SLG | BB% | CT% | AB | R | H | 2B | 3B | HR | RBI | SB | BA | OBP | SLG | BB% | CT% | AB | R | H | 2B | 3B | HR | RBI | SB | BA | OBP | SLG | BB% | CT% |
| A | — | — | — | — | — | — | — | — | — | — | — | — | — | — | — | — | — | — | — | — | — | — | — | — | — | — | — | — | — | — | — | — | — | — | — | — | — | — | — |
| AA | — | — | — | — | — | — | — | — | — | — | — | — | — | — | — | — | — | — | — | — | — | — | — | — | — | — | — | — | — | — | — | — | — | — | — | — | — | — | — |
| AAA | — | — | — | — | — | — | — | — | — | — | — | — | — | — | — | — | — | — | — | — | — | — | — | — | — | — | — | — | — | — | — | — | — | — | — | — | — | — | — |
| MLB | — | — | — | — | — | — | — | — | — | — | — | — | — | — | — | — | — | — | — | — | — | — | — | — | — | — | — | — | — | — | — | — | — | — | — | — | — | — | — |

| | | |
|---|---|---|
| #5 | I'm disappointed that Harper will not get a chance to demonstrate his superstar bat at catcher. That's the only thing that I can find to criticize. (Hagen) | ETA: Late 2012 |
| #3 | Harper won't reach MLB as quickly as Stephen Strasburg did, but Bryce has a ton of potential with a powerful bat. Just don't expect him to catch. (Hulet) | ETA: Late 2013 |
| #6 | Harper is arguably the most hyped hitter to be drafted since A-Rod. His scouting reports are off the charts, but he has a long journey ahead. (Lockard) | ETA: Mid-2013 |

## SS Adeiny Hechavarria — Toronto | AL

RH | 21 yrs, 11 mo — Signed as international free agent, 2010

Last year's rankings: — — — — Latest league: Eastern

MLB Forecast 2011

| AB | R | H | 2B | 3B | HR | RBI | SB | BA | OBP | SLG | BB% | CT% |
|---|---|---|---|---|---|---|---|---|---|---|---|---|
| — | — | — | — | — | — | — | — | — | — | — | — | — |

| | 2008 | | | | | | | | | | | | | 2009 | | | | | | | | | | | | | 2010 | | | | | | | | | | | | |
|---|---|---|---|---|---|---|---|---|---|---|---|---|---|---|---|---|---|---|---|---|---|---|---|---|---|---|---|---|---|---|---|---|---|---|---|---|---|---|---|
| Level | AB | R | H | 2B | 3B | HR | RBI | SB | BA | OBP | SLG | BB% | CT% | AB | R | H | 2B | 3B | HR | RBI | SB | BA | OBP | SLG | BB% | CT% | AB | R | H | 2B | 3B | HR | RBI | SB | BA | OBP | SLG | BB% | CT% |
| A | — | — | — | — | — | — | — | — | — | — | — | — | — | — | — | — | — | — | — | — | — | — | — | — | — | — | 161 | 21 | 31 | 7 | 3 | 1 | 7 | 7 | .193 | .217 | .292 | 3% | 84% |
| AA | — | — | — | — | — | — | — | — | — | — | — | — | — | — | — | — | — | — | — | — | — | — | — | — | — | — | 253 | 36 | 69 | 11 | 1 | 3 | 34 | 6 | .273 | .305 | .360 | 4% | 84% |
| AAA | — | — | — | — | — | — | — | — | — | — | — | — | — | — | — | — | — | — | — | — | — | — | — | — | — | — | — | — | — | — | — | — | — | — | — | — | — | — | — |
| MLB | — | — | — | — | — | — | — | — | — | — | — | — | — | — | — | — | — | — | — | — | — | — | — | — | — | — | — | — | — | — | — | — | — | — | — | — | — | — | — |

| | | |
|---|---|---|
| #58 | Hechavarria is in desperate need of polish across the board – I'm concerned mainly with his long swing. However, the tools are there to succeed. (Hagen) | ETA: Late 2012 |
| #32 | Hechavarria improved when he reached Double-A, where he had a Latin mentor. He is a slick fielder who must do a better job of selecting pitches. (Hulet) | ETA: Mid-2012 |
| #29 | Adeiny's glove is ahead of his bat, but he still projects offensively as a speedster with line-drive pop. He could be a regular Gold Glove winner. (Lockard) | ETA: Early 2012 |

## CF Aaron Hicks — Minnesota | AL

BH | 21 yrs, 5 mo — Drafted 2008, #14 overall

Last year's rankings: #38 #41 #28 — Latest league: Midwest

MLB Forecast 2011

| AB | R | H | 2B | 3B | HR | RBI | SB | BA | OBP | SLG | BB% | CT% |
|---|---|---|---|---|---|---|---|---|---|---|---|---|
| — | — | — | — | — | — | — | — | — | — | — | — | — |

| | 2008 | | | | | | | | | | | | | 2009 | | | | | | | | | | | | | 2010 | | | | | | | | | | | | |
|---|---|---|---|---|---|---|---|---|---|---|---|---|---|---|---|---|---|---|---|---|---|---|---|---|---|---|---|---|---|---|---|---|---|---|---|---|---|---|---|
| Level | AB | R | H | 2B | 3B | HR | RBI | SB | BA | OBP | SLG | BB% | CT% | AB | R | H | 2B | 3B | HR | RBI | SB | BA | OBP | SLG | BB% | CT% | AB | R | H | 2B | 3B | HR | RBI | SB | BA | OBP | SLG | BB% | CT% |
| A | — | — | — | — | — | — | — | — | — | — | — | — | — | 251 | 43 | 63 | 15 | 3 | 4 | 29 | 10 | .251 | .353 | .382 | 13% | 78% | 423 | 86 | 118 | 27 | 6 | 8 | 49 | 21 | .279 | .401 | .428 | 17% | 74% |
| AA | — | — | — | — | — | — | — | — | — | — | — | — | — | — | — | — | — | — | — | — | — | — | — | — | — | — | — | — | — | — | — | — | — | — | — | — | — | — | — |
| AAA | — | — | — | — | — | — | — | — | — | — | — | — | — | — | — | — | — | — | — | — | — | — | — | — | — | — | — | — | — | — | — | — | — | — | — | — | — | — | — |
| MLB | — | — | — | — | — | — | — | — | — | — | — | — | — | — | — | — | — | — | — | — | — | — | — | — | — | — | — | — | — | — | — | — | — | — | — | — | — | — | — |

| | | |
|---|---|---|
| #31 | Hicks continues to disappoint. He is surely mature with a bat, and his tools are too much for A-ball, so his earthbound stats are head-scratching. (Hagen) | ETA: Late 2012 |
| #19 | Asked to repeat Low-A ball, Hicks showed improvement, but he did not break out in a big way as expected. Look for that to occur in '11 at High-A. (Hulet) | ETA: Late 2013 |
| #23 | Hicks has eye-popping talent and is starting to add polish, displaying a better approach in his second year in Low-A. His ceiling is still sky-high. (Lockard) | ETA: Late 2012 |

## 1B Eric Hosmer — Kansas City | AL

LH | 21 yrs, 5 mo — Drafted 2008, #3 overall

Last year's rankings: #26 #27 #26 — Latest league: Texas

MLB Forecast 2011

| AB | R | H | 2B | 3B | HR | RBI | SB | BA | OBP | SLG | BB% | CT% |
|---|---|---|---|---|---|---|---|---|---|---|---|---|
| 129 | 11 | 29 | 6 | 2 | 3 | 17 | 0 | .221 | .303 | .359 | 10% | 72% |

| | 2008 | | | | | | | | | | | | | 2009 | | | | | | | | | | | | | 2010 | | | | | | | | | | | | |
|---|---|---|---|---|---|---|---|---|---|---|---|---|---|---|---|---|---|---|---|---|---|---|---|---|---|---|---|---|---|---|---|---|---|---|---|---|---|---|---|
| Level | AB | R | H | 2B | 3B | HR | RBI | SB | BA | OBP | SLG | BB% | CT% | AB | R | H | 2B | 3B | HR | RBI | SB | BA | OBP | SLG | BB% | CT% | AB | R | H | 2B | 3B | HR | RBI | SB | BA | OBP | SLG | BB% | CT% |
| A | — | — | — | — | — | — | — | — | — | — | — | — | — | 377 | 40 | 91 | 19 | 4 | 6 | 59 | 3 | .241 | .334 | .361 | 12% | 76% | 325 | 48 | 115 | 29 | 6 | 7 | 51 | 11 | .354 | .429 | .545 | 12% | 88% |
| AA | — | — | — | — | — | — | — | — | — | — | — | — | — | — | — | — | — | — | — | — | — | — | — | — | — | — | 195 | 39 | 61 | 14 | 3 | 13 | 35 | 3 | .313 | .365 | .615 | 7% | 86% |
| AAA | — | — | — | — | — | — | — | — | — | — | — | — | — | — | — | — | — | — | — | — | — | — | — | — | — | — | — | — | — | — | — | — | — | — | — | — | — | — | — |
| MLB | — | — | — | — | — | — | — | — | — | — | — | — | — | — | — | — | — | — | — | — | — | — | — | — | — | — | — | — | — | — | — | — | — | — | — | — | — | — | — |

| | | |
|---|---|---|
| #6 | Just as I was questioning Hosmer's power, he took the Texas League by storm. If he is asked to, his arm *could* handle a move to the outfield. (Hagen) | ETA: Late 2011 |
| #5 | At age 20, Hosmer turned into one of the top prospects in baseball. He showed massive power and run production after a promotion to Double-A. (Hulet) | ETA: Mid-2012 |
| #15 | Off-season eye surgery worked wonders for Hosmer. His approach at the plate is very mature and he is continuing to add power as he fills out. (Lockard) | ETA: Late 2011 |

## SS Jose Iglesias — Boston | AL

RH | 21 yrs, 2 mo — Signed as international free agent, 2009

Last year's rankings: — — — — Latest league: Eastern

MLB Forecast 2011

| AB | R | H | 2B | 3B | HR | RBI | SB | BA | OBP | SLG | BB% | CT% |
|---|---|---|---|---|---|---|---|---|---|---|---|---|
| 47 | 6 | 11 | 2 | 1 | 0 | 2 | 1 | .236 | .272 | .296 | 4% | 75% |

| | 2008 | | | | | | | | | | | | | 2009 | | | | | | | | | | | | | 2010 | | | | | | | | | | | | |
|---|---|---|---|---|---|---|---|---|---|---|---|---|---|---|---|---|---|---|---|---|---|---|---|---|---|---|---|---|---|---|---|---|---|---|---|---|---|---|---|
| Level | AB | R | H | 2B | 3B | HR | RBI | SB | BA | OBP | SLG | BB% | CT% | AB | R | H | 2B | 3B | HR | RBI | SB | BA | OBP | SLG | BB% | CT% | AB | R | H | 2B | 3B | HR | RBI | SB | BA | OBP | SLG | BB% | CT% |
| A | — | — | — | — | — | — | — | — | — | — | — | — | — | — | — | — | — | — | — | — | — | — | — | — | — | — | 40 | 8 | 14 | 2 | 2 | 0 | 7 | 2 | .350 | .458 | .500 | 15% | 80% |
| AA | — | — | — | — | — | — | — | — | — | — | — | — | — | — | — | — | — | — | — | — | — | — | — | — | — | — | 221 | 29 | 63 | 10 | 3 | 0 | 13 | 5 | .285 | .315 | .357 | 3% | 78% |
| AAA | — | — | — | — | — | — | — | — | — | — | — | — | — | — | — | — | — | — | — | — | — | — | — | — | — | — | — | — | — | — | — | — | — | — | — | — | — | — | — |
| MLB | — | — | — | — | — | — | — | — | — | — | — | — | — | — | — | — | — | — | — | — | — | — | — | — | — | — | — | — | — | — | — | — | — | — | — | — | — | — | — |

| | | |
|---|---|---|
| #42 | Iglesias has room to grow, but he has a big-league future. He might turn into one of those players who is better in real life than in fantasy terms. (Hagen) | ETA: Mid-2012 |
| #26 | Iglesias neither hit for power nor stole bases, and his batting average was aided by unsustainably high BABIP's. Next year could be disappointing. (Hulet) | ETA: Late 2012 |
| #48 | A premier defender at SS, Iglesias is a work-in-progress at the plate. He has a quick bat but swings at everything. His power is still developing. (Lockard) | ETA: Early 2012 |

## CF Brett Jackson — Chicago | NL
LH | 22 yrs, 7 mo — Drafted 2009, #31 overall
Last year's rankings: — — —
Latest league: Southern

**MLB Forecast 2011:** AB 133, R 23, H 32, 2B 5, 3B 2, HR 6, RBI 17, SB 5, BA .237, OBP .331, SLG .433, BB% 10%, CT% 72%

| Year/Level | AB | R | H | 2B | 3B | HR | RBI | SB | BA | OBP | SLG | BB% | CT% |
|---|---|---|---|---|---|---|---|---|---|---|---|---|---|
| 2009 A | 211 | 50 | 67 | 6 | 3 | 8 | 36 | 13 | .318 | .418 | .488 | 12% | 73% |
| 2010 A | 263 | 56 | 83 | 19 | 6 | 8 | 38 | 12 | .316 | .420 | .517 | 14% | 76% |
| 2010 AA | 228 | 47 | 63 | 13 | 6 | 6 | 28 | 18 | .276 | .366 | .465 | 11% | 72% |

#43 Jackson's plate discipline and defensive prowess are true assets, but I'm skeptical that his power and speed will translate to the higher levels. (Hagen) — ETA: Late 2012
#20 Jackson's batting average in his young career has been boosted by high BABIP's. His speed is nifty, but he needs to put more balls into play. (Hulet) — ETA: Mid-2012
#28 Since turning pro, Jackson has done nothing but impress. His offensive game is well-rounded, he has speed, and he's a plus defender in CF. (Lockard) — ETA: Mid-2011

## CF Desmond Jennings — Tampa Bay | AL
RH | 24 yrs, 5 mo — Drafted 2006, 10th round
Last year's rankings: #10 #5 #2
Latest league: International

**MLB Forecast 2011:** AB 293, R 39, H 72, 2B 13, 3B 7, HR 7, RBI 26, SB 20, BA .244, OBP .322, SLG .403, BB% 9%, CT% 82%

| Year/Level | AB | R | H | 2B | 3B | HR | RBI | SB | BA | OBP | SLG | BB% | CT% |
|---|---|---|---|---|---|---|---|---|---|---|---|---|---|
| 2008 A | 85 | 17 | 22 | 5 | 1 | 2 | 6 | 5 | .259 | .360 | .412 | 14% | 81% |
| 2009 AA | 383 | 69 | 121 | 25 | 8 | 8 | 45 | 37 | .316 | .395 | .486 | 11% | 86% |
| 2009 AAA | 114 | 23 | 37 | 6 | 2 | 3 | 17 | 15 | .325 | .419 | .491 | 14% | 87% |
| 2010 AAA | 399 | 82 | 111 | 25 | 6 | 3 | 36 | 37 | .278 | .362 | .393 | 10% | 83% |
| 2010 MLB | 21 | 5 | 4 | 1 | 1 | 0 | 2 | 2 | .190 | .292 | .333 | 8% | 81% |

#3 It wasn't always pretty, but Jennings didn't lose a thing from his potential star status of 2009. Tampa Bay simply couldn't find a spot for him. (Hagen) — ETA: Early 2011
#10 Injuries (wrist, shoulder) continue to plague Jennings, and his power took a big step back with an ISO of only .115. He does have that speed. (Hulet) — ETA: Early 2011
#8 The Rays might lose Carl Crawford, but their team speed won't diminish with Jennings filling his shoes. He could top 50 SB with regularity. (Lockard) — ETA: Early 2011

## CF Ryan Kalish — Boston | AL
LH | 23 yrs, 0 mo — Drafted 2006, 9th round
Last year's rankings: — — —
Latest league: International

**MLB Forecast 2011:** AB 182, R 22, H 42, 2B 10, 3B 2, HR 6, RBI 22, SB 8, BA .231, OBP .306, SLG .394, BB% 9%, CT% 76%

| Year/Level | AB | R | H | 2B | 3B | HR | RBI | SB | BA | OBP | SLG | BB% | CT% |
|---|---|---|---|---|---|---|---|---|---|---|---|---|---|
| 2008 A | 433 | 57 | 118 | 22 | 1 | 5 | 46 | 19 | .273 | .365 | .363 | 12% | 77% |
| 2009 A | 115 | 21 | 35 | 5 | 2 | 5 | 21 | 7 | .304 | .434 | .513 | 18% | 83% |
| 2009 AA | 391 | 63 | 106 | 19 | 4 | 13 | 56 | 14 | .271 | .341 | .440 | 10% | 78% |
| 2010 AA | 150 | 35 | 44 | 9 | 1 | 8 | 29 | 13 | .293 | .404 | .527 | 15% | 86% |
| 2010 AAA | 143 | 22 | 42 | 9 | 1 | 5 | 18 | 12 | .294 | .356 | .476 | 9% | 78% |
| 2010 MLB | 163 | 26 | 41 | 11 | 1 | 4 | 24 | 10 | .252 | .305 | .405 | 7% | 77% |

#45 Kalish is a hard-working, under-the-radar outfielder. Still, it's fair to question whether his power, speed, or plate approach will work in the majors. (Hagen) — ETA: Mid-2011
#38 Kalish offers a nice combination of power and speed, as well as solid defensive skills. He could make it as a 4th outfielder on a first-division team. (Hulet) — ETA: Early 2011
#33 Kalish doesn't have any one standout tool, but he does everything pretty well. He profiles to be a steady top-of-the-order hitter with a solid glove. (Lockard) — ETA: Early 2011

## 2B Jason Kipnis — Cleveland | AL
LH | 23 yrs, 11 mo — Drafted 2009, 2nd round
Last year's rankings: — — —
Latest league: Eastern

**MLB Forecast 2011:** — (no forecast)

| Year/Level | AB | R | H | 2B | 3B | HR | RBI | SB | BA | OBP | SLG | BB% | CT% |
|---|---|---|---|---|---|---|---|---|---|---|---|---|---|
| 2009 A | 111 | 19 | 34 | 8 | 3 | 1 | 19 | 3 | .306 | .388 | .459 | 12% | 84% |
| 2010 A | 203 | 33 | 61 | 12 | 3 | 6 | 31 | 2 | .300 | .387 | .478 | 10% | 77% |
| 2010 AA | 315 | 63 | 98 | 20 | 5 | 10 | 43 | 7 | .311 | .385 | .502 | 9% | 81% |

#59 Kipnis lacks a plus tool, but he posted strong overall numbers in '10. It would be rude to ask for better offense than this from a second baseman. (Hagen) — ETA: Late 2012
#50 Converted from center field, Kipnis should provide at least average offense at the keystone, and he could eventually settle into a utility role. (Hulet) — ETA: Late 2011
#17 Cleveland has been looking for an answer at 2B, and they might have found it in Kipnis, who can handle second base but hits like an outfielder. (Lockard) — ETA: Mid-2011

## LF Marc Krauss — Arizona | NL
LH | 23 yrs, 5 mo — Drafted 2009, 2nd round
Last year's rankings: — — —
Latest league: California

**MLB Forecast 2011:** — (no forecast)

| Year/Level | AB | R | H | 2B | 3B | HR | RBI | SB | BA | OBP | SLG | BB% | CT% |
|---|---|---|---|---|---|---|---|---|---|---|---|---|---|
| 2009 A | 115 | 14 | 35 | 12 | 1 | 2 | 17 | 0 | .304 | .377 | .478 | 11% | 82% |
| 2010 A | 530 | 107 | 160 | 27 | 4 | 25 | 87 | 1 | .302 | .371 | .509 | 10% | 73% |

#56 Krauss did everything expected of him in the California League, but Double-A will be a true test of his plate approach, power, and mechanics. (Hagen) — ETA: Late 2012
#57 Krauss played in a good hitters' environment in 2010, so temper your enthusiasm. As far as projecting him, 2011 will be a telling season. (Hulet) — ETA: Mid-2012
#66 Krauss is a polished hitter with good power. He should move steadily up the ladder, though his lack of athleticism limits his ceiling. (Lockard) — ETA: Mid-2012

## 2B Brett Lawrie — Milwaukee | NL
RH | 21 yrs, 2 mo — Drafted 2008, #16 overall
Last year's rankings: #17 #45 #24
Latest league: Southern

**MLB Forecast 2011:** — (no forecast)

| Year/Level | AB | R | H | 2B | 3B | HR | RBI | SB | BA | OBP | SLG | BB% | CT% |
|---|---|---|---|---|---|---|---|---|---|---|---|---|---|
| 2009 A | 372 | 48 | 102 | 18 | 5 | 13 | 65 | 19 | .274 | .348 | .454 | 10% | 81% |
| 2009 AA | 52 | 6 | 14 | 0 | 1 | 0 | 0 | 0 | .269 | .283 | .308 | 0% | 73% |
| 2010 AA | 554 | 90 | 158 | 36 | 16 | 8 | 63 | 30 | .285 | .346 | .451 | 8% | 79% |

#9 Even though Lawrie did not "wow" in 2010, he was still one of the more dangerous hitters in the Southern League. Bigger things could lie ahead. (Hagen) — ETA: Mid-2011
#12 Lawrie has an advanced bat for his age, and he's an astute baserunner. He has defensive shortcomings at second base and could wind up in LF. (Hulet) — ETA: Mid-2011
#12 Lawrie is a bit over-aggressive at the plate, and he's just starting to grow into his power, but he has the potential to be a perennial 20/20 player. (Lockard) — ETA: Early 2012

## 3B Alex Liddi — Seattle | AL
RH | 22 yrs, 7 mo — Signed as non-drafted free agent, 2005
Last year's rankings: — — —
Latest league: Southern

**MLB Forecast 2011:** — (no forecast)

| Year/Level | AB | R | H | 2B | 3B | HR | RBI | SB | BA | OBP | SLG | BB% | CT% |
|---|---|---|---|---|---|---|---|---|---|---|---|---|---|
| 2008 A | 447 | 65 | 109 | 26 | 4 | 6 | 53 | 17 | .244 | .313 | .360 | 8% | 74% |
| 2009 A | 493 | 97 | 170 | 44 | 5 | 23 | 104 | 10 | .345 | .411 | .594 | 9% | 75% |
| 2010 AA | 502 | 78 | 141 | 37 | 8 | 15 | 92 | 5 | .281 | .353 | .476 | 9% | 71% |

#55 After a slow start, Liddi completed a strong Southern League season. He needs to build on that success and dramatically cut down on his K's. (Hagen) — ETA: Late 2012
#59 Liddi posted good offensive numbers, but (not unexpectedly) his power dropped, and his strikeouts went through the roof. He needs more time. (Hulet) — ETA: Late 2011
#50 With a second solid season, Liddi proved that he wasn't a fluke. He strikes out too much, and his defense needs help, but he has gap power. (Lockard) — ETA: Late 2012

## SS Manny Machado — Baltimore | AL
RH | 18 yrs, 8 mo — Drafted 2010, #3 overall
Last year's rankings: — — —
Latest league: New York-Penn

**MLB Forecast 2011:** — (no forecast)

| Year/Level | AB | R | H | 2B | 3B | HR | RBI | SB | BA | OBP | SLG | BB% | CT% |
|---|---|---|---|---|---|---|---|---|---|---|---|---|---|
| 2010 A | 29 | 2 | 10 | 1 | 1 | 0 | 3 | 0 | .345 | .406 | .448 | 9% | 93% |

#14 Regardless of the position he ends up at, Machado has the tools to be a star with the bat. But the power might be more of a hope than a reality. (Hagen) — ETA: Early 2013
#9 Perhaps the top SS prospect in the minors, Machado should advance quickly through the system. He could help fill the void left by Cal Ripken Jr. (Hulet) — ETA: Mid-2014
#22 In a year without Bryce Harper, Machado would have gone first in the draft. He has a plus offensive profile and the requisite athleticism for SS. (Lockard) — ETA: Mid-2013

## RF Fernando Martinez — New York | NL
LH | 22 yrs, 5 mo — Signed as non-drafted free agent, 2005

Last year's rankings: #30 #23 #17
Latest league: International

**MLB Forecast 2011**

| AB | R | H | 2B | 3B | HR | RBI | SB | BA | OBP | SLG | BB% | CT% |
|---|---|---|---|---|---|---|---|---|---|---|---|---|
| 188 | 22 | 46 | 10 | 2 | 6 | 20 | 2 | .245 | .299 | .410 | 6% | 78% |

| Level | AB | R | H | 2B | 3B | HR | RBI | SB | BA | OBP | SLG | BB% | CT% |
|---|---|---|---|---|---|---|---|---|---|---|---|---|---|
| **2008** | | | | | | | | | | | | | |
| A | — | — | — | — | — | — | — | — | — | — | — | — | — |
| AA | 352 | 48 | 101 | 19 | 4 | 8 | 43 | 6 | .287 | .340 | .432 | 7% | 79% |
| AAA | — | — | — | — | — | — | — | — | — | — | — | — | — |
| MLB | — | — | — | — | — | — | — | — | — | — | — | — | — |
| **2009** | | | | | | | | | | | | | |
| A | — | — | — | — | — | — | — | — | — | — | — | — | — |
| AA | 176 | 24 | 51 | 16 | 2 | 8 | 28 | 2 | .290 | .337 | .540 | 6% | 81% |
| AAA | — | — | — | — | — | — | — | — | — | — | — | — | — |
| MLB | 91 | 11 | 16 | 6 | 0 | 1 | 8 | 2 | .176 | .242 | .275 | 5% | 85% |
| **2010** | | | | | | | | | | | | | |
| A | 15 | 1 | 4 | 1 | 0 | 0 | 0 | 0 | .267 | .313 | .333 | 6% | 87% |
| AA | — | — | — | — | — | — | — | — | — | — | — | — | — |
| AAA | 257 | 39 | 65 | 16 | 0 | 12 | 33 | 1 | .253 | .317 | .455 | 6% | 75% |
| MLB | 18 | 1 | 3 | 0 | 0 | 0 | 2 | 0 | .167 | .273 | .167 | 5% | 72% |

#38 We witnessed more power from Martinez in 2010 than in past years, but it seems as if he has been around forever with little growth to show for it. (Hagen) — ETA: Mid-2011
#51 Still just 22, Martinez continues to show flashes of brilliance, but he simply can't put it all together. He might be helped by a change of scenery. (Hulet) — ETA: Late 2011
#51 Injuries have really stalled Martinez the past two seasons. His approach needs work, but he has to stay on the field if he is going to improve. (Lockard) — ETA: Early 2011

## CA Devin Mesoraco — Cincinnati | NL
RH | 22 yrs, 9 mo — Drafted 2007, #15 overall

Last year's rankings: — — —
Latest league: International

**MLB Forecast 2011**

| AB | R | H | 2B | 3B | HR | RBI | SB | BA | OBP | SLG | BB% | CT% |
|---|---|---|---|---|---|---|---|---|---|---|---|---|---|
| — | — | — | — | — | — | — | — | — | — | — | — | — |

| Level | AB | R | H | 2B | 3B | HR | RBI | SB | BA | OBP | SLG | BB% | CT% |
|---|---|---|---|---|---|---|---|---|---|---|---|---|---|
| **2008** | | | | | | | | | | | | | |
| A | 306 | 29 | 80 | 13 | 1 | 9 | 42 | 2 | .261 | .311 | .399 | 6% | 79% |
| AA | — | — | — | — | — | — | — | — | — | — | — | — | — |
| AAA | — | — | — | — | — | — | — | — | — | — | — | — | — |
| MLB | — | — | — | — | — | — | — | — | — | — | — | — | — |
| **2009** | | | | | | | | | | | | | |
| A | 312 | 32 | 71 | 22 | 1 | 8 | 37 | 0 | .228 | .311 | .381 | 10% | 76% |
| **2010** | | | | | | | | | | | | | |
| A | 158 | 24 | 53 | 11 | 2 | 10 | 31 | 2 | .335 | .414 | .620 | 10% | 82% |
| AA | 187 | 42 | 55 | 11 | 3 | 13 | 31 | 1 | .294 | .363 | .594 | 8% | 80% |
| MLB | 52 | 5 | 12 | 3 | 0 | 3 | 13 | 0 | .231 | .310 | .462 | 10% | 73% |

#29 Mesoraco busted out of his shell in grand fashion – he improved his conditioning and brought a new, shorter swing to the ballpark. (Hagen) — ETA: Late 2011
#11 Mesoraco will be pushed by Yasmani Grandal, but Mesoraco has a head start of 1,100 AB, as well as a nice offensive attack and good power. (Hulet) — ETA: Mid-2011
#40 Previously a disappointment, Mesoraco hit for power and average. He has a strong arm and could be above-average on both sides of the ball. (Lockard) — ETA: Late 2011

## CF Jared Mitchell — Chicago | AL
LH | 22 yrs, 5 mo — Drafted 2009, #23 overall

Last year's rankings: — — —
Latest league: South Atlantic

**MLB Forecast 2011**

| AB | R | H | 2B | 3B | HR | RBI | SB | BA | OBP | SLG | BB% | CT% |
|---|---|---|---|---|---|---|---|---|---|---|---|---|---|
| — | — | — | — | — | — | — | — | — | — | — | — | — |

| Level | AB | R | H | 2B | 3B | HR | RBI | SB | BA | OBP | SLG | BB% | CT% |
|---|---|---|---|---|---|---|---|---|---|---|---|---|---|
| **2009** | | | | | | | | | | | | | |
| A | 115 | 13 | 34 | 12 | 2 | 0 | 10 | 5 | .296 | .417 | .435 | 17% | 65% |

#67 Mitchell was an over-draft in 2009, and I have never believed in his power or speed. Ankle surgery kept him from proving me wrong in 2010. (Hagen) — ETA: Late 2013
#67 Mitchell's 2010 season was derailed by an injury, but the college product was already raw for his experience. Don't expect wonders in 2011. (Hulet) — ETA: Late 2013
#58 Mitchell lost a year of a development to an ankle injury. He is a raw prospect, but he has the potential to put up Carl Crawford-like numbers. (Lockard) — ETA: Early 2013

## CA Jesus Montero — New York | AL
RH | 21 yrs, 4 mo — Signed as non-drafted free agent, 2006

Last year's rankings: #3 #7 #8
Latest league: International

**MLB Forecast 2011**

| AB | R | H | 2B | 3B | HR | RBI | SB | BA | OBP | SLG | BB% | CT% |
|---|---|---|---|---|---|---|---|---|---|---|---|---|---|
| 183 | 22 | 48 | 10 | 0 | 10 | 28 | 0 | .263 | .316 | .484 | 6% | 82% |

| Level | AB | R | H | 2B | 3B | HR | RBI | SB | BA | OBP | SLG | BB% | CT% |
|---|---|---|---|---|---|---|---|---|---|---|---|---|---|
| **2008** | | | | | | | | | | | | | |
| A | 525 | 86 | 171 | 34 | 1 | 17 | 87 | 2 | .326 | .376 | .491 | 7% | 84% |
| **2009** | | | | | | | | | | | | | |
| A | 180 | 26 | 64 | 15 | 1 | 8 | 37 | 0 | .356 | .406 | .583 | 7% | 86% |
| AA | 167 | 19 | 53 | 10 | 0 | 9 | 33 | 0 | .317 | .370 | .539 | 8% | 87% |
| **2010** | | | | | | | | | | | | | |
| AAA | 453 | 66 | 131 | 34 | 3 | 21 | 75 | 0 | .289 | .353 | .517 | 9% | 80% |

#2 The Yankees have *two* defense-oriented catchers nearly ready to take over, so Montero might move his beastly bat to a new position (COF?). (Hagen) — ETA: Mid-2011
#7 Montero got off to a slow start in 2010 but then exploded as a 20-year-old at Triple-A. In the final two months of the season, he hit 15 home runs. (Hulet) — ETA: Late 2011
#5 Montero's power impressed even the veterans at Spring Training. He's a below-average receiver, but the Yanks could leave him there for now. (Lockard) — ETA: Mid-2011

## LF Logan Morrison — Florida | NL
LH | 23 yrs, 7 mo — Drafted 2005, 22nd round

Last year's rankings: #13 #15 #38
Latest league: Pacific Coast

**MLB Forecast 2011**

| AB | R | H | 2B | 3B | HR | RBI | SB | BA | OBP | SLG | BB% | CT% |
|---|---|---|---|---|---|---|---|---|---|---|---|---|---|
| 535 | 72 | 138 | 36 | 6 | 18 | 66 | 6 | .258 | .354 | .438 | 13% | 80% |

| Level | AB | R | H | 2B | 3B | HR | RBI | SB | BA | OBP | SLG | BB% | CT% |
|---|---|---|---|---|---|---|---|---|---|---|---|---|---|
| **2008** | | | | | | | | | | | | | |
| A | 488 | 71 | 162 | 38 | 1 | 13 | 74 | 9 | .332 | .402 | .494 | 10% | 84% |
| **2009** | | | | | | | | | | | | | |
| A | 11 | 0 | 3 | 1 | 0 | 0 | 2 | 0 | .273 | .333 | .364 | 8% | 82% |
| AA | 278 | 48 | 77 | 18 | 2 | 8 | 47 | 9 | .277 | .411 | .442 | 18% | 83% |
| **2010** | | | | | | | | | | | | | |
| A | 21 | 3 | 8 | 2 | 2 | 0 | 2 | 0 | .381 | .381 | .667 | 0% | 86% |
| AAA | 238 | 36 | 73 | 17 | 4 | 6 | 45 | 1 | .307 | .427 | .487 | 16% | 85% |
| MLB | 244 | 34 | 69 | 20 | 7 | 2 | 18 | 0 | .283 | .390 | .447 | 14% | 79% |

#8 Morrison's move to left field jump-started his stock for me. Morrison is perhaps the most polished hitter on this list, with plus power to back it up. (Hagen) — ETA: Arrived
#6 Morrison had an outstanding offensive rookie season while playing an unfamiliar position. He's blocked at 1B, but LF might not be the right home. (Hulet) — ETA: Early 2011
#27 Morrison is an on-base machine. There are questions about how much power he'll produce, but he has the physique to add power as he ages. (Lockard) — ETA: Early 2011

## 3B Mike Moustakas — Kansas City | AL
LH | 22 yrs, 6 mo — Drafted 2007, #2 overall

Last year's rankings: #18 #16 #13
Latest league: Pacific Coast

**MLB Forecast 2011**

| AB | R | H | 2B | 3B | HR | RBI | SB | BA | OBP | SLG | BB% | CT% |
|---|---|---|---|---|---|---|---|---|---|---|---|---|---|
| 368 | 47 | 97 | 24 | 2 | 17 | 60 | 3 | .262 | .304 | .465 | 5% | 81% |

| Level | AB | R | H | 2B | 3B | HR | RBI | SB | BA | OBP | SLG | BB% | CT% |
|---|---|---|---|---|---|---|---|---|---|---|---|---|---|
| **2008** | | | | | | | | | | | | | |
| A | 496 | 77 | 135 | 25 | 3 | 22 | 71 | 8 | .272 | .337 | .468 | 8% | 83% |
| **2009** | | | | | | | | | | | | | |
| A | 492 | 66 | 123 | 32 | 2 | 16 | 86 | 10 | .250 | .297 | .421 | 6% | 82% |
| **2010** | | | | | | | | | | | | | |
| AA | 259 | 58 | 90 | 25 | 0 | 21 | 76 | 0 | .347 | .413 | .687 | 9% | 84% |
| AAA | 225 | 36 | 66 | 16 | 0 | 15 | 48 | 2 | .293 | .314 | .564 | 3% | 89% |

#4 It would be nice if Moustakas could draw a few more walks, but it's hard to argue with the talent and production of my 2010 Minor League MVP. (Hagen) — ETA: Mid-2011
#4 Like Eric Hosmer, Moustakas had a breakout 2010, and he should be set by mid-2011. Poor defense, though, means he probably won't stick at 3B. (Hulet) — ETA: Mid-2011
#7 Moose recovered from a poor 2009 to post a spectacular '10 season. His power is plus-plus; his glove will need to catch up with his bat in '11. (Lockard) — ETA: Mid-2011

## CA Wil Myers — Kansas City | AL
RH | 20 yrs, 3 mo — Drafted 2009, 3rd round

Last year's rankings: — — —
Latest league: Carolina

**MLB Forecast 2011**

| AB | R | H | 2B | 3B | HR | RBI | SB | BA | OBP | SLG | BB% | CT% |
|---|---|---|---|---|---|---|---|---|---|---|---|---|---|
| — | — | — | — | — | — | — | — | — | — | — | — | — |

| Level | AB | R | H | 2B | 3B | HR | RBI | SB | BA | OBP | SLG | BB% | CT% |
|---|---|---|---|---|---|---|---|---|---|---|---|---|---|
| **2010** | | | | | | | | | | | | | |
| A | 447 | 70 | 141 | 37 | 3 | 14 | 83 | 12 | .315 | .429 | .506 | 16% | 79% |

#10 Nineteen-year-old hitters are supposed to have weaknesses; Myers does not. His upside is unknown, as is his playing position. (Hagen) — ETA: Mid-2012
#13 Myers had awesome productivity in High-A as a teenager, though his BA was aided by a .400+ BABIP. Believe in the power but expect fewer hits. (Hulet) — ETA: Mid-2013
#4 There is nothing to dislike about Myers's approach at the plate. He might not stick at catcher, but his bat could play anywhere. (Lockard) — ETA: Early 2012

## CF Kirk Nieuwenhuis — New York | NL
LH | 23 yrs, 7 mo — Drafted 2008, 3rd round

Last year's rankings: — — —
Latest league: International

**MLB Forecast 2011**

| AB | R | H | 2B | 3B | HR | RBI | SB | BA | OBP | SLG | BB% | CT% |
|---|---|---|---|---|---|---|---|---|---|---|---|---|---|
| 45 | 6 | 10 | 3 | 1 | 2 | 6 | 2 | .222 | .306 | .426 | 10% | 72% |

| Level | AB | R | H | 2B | 3B | HR | RBI | SB | BA | OBP | SLG | BB% | CT% |
|---|---|---|---|---|---|---|---|---|---|---|---|---|---|
| **2008** | | | | | | | | | | | | | |
| A | 285 | 34 | 79 | 15 | 5 | 3 | 29 | 11 | .277 | .348 | .396 | 9% | 75% |
| **2009** | | | | | | | | | | | | | |
| A | 482 | 91 | 132 | 35 | 5 | 16 | 71 | 16 | .274 | .357 | .467 | 10% | 76% |
| AA | 32 | 8 | 13 | 3 | 1 | 1 | 2 | 1 | .406 | .472 | .656 | 11% | 72% |
| **2010** | | | | | | | | | | | | | |
| AA | 394 | 81 | 114 | 35 | 2 | 16 | 60 | 13 | .289 | .337 | .510 | 7% | 76% |
| AAA | 120 | 10 | 27 | 8 | 1 | 2 | 17 | 0 | .225 | .295 | .358 | 8% | 68% |

#63 Nieuwenhuis has solid power as well as some speed to work with, but he needs to clean up his approach at the plate and create more contact. (Hagen) — ETA: Late 2012
#49 I prefer Nieuwenhuis to Fernando Martinez (another sleeper prospect), but Kirk needs to make more contact to be an everyday player in the bigs. (Hulet) — ETA: Mid-2012
#63 Long term, Nieuwenhuis probably is not a centerfielder, but he can play there in a pinch. He has the potential to be a 20 HR/.280 hitter in MLB. (Lockard) — ETA: Mid-2011

## CA Derek Norris — Washington | NL

RH | 22 yrs, 1 mo — Drafted 2007, 4th round

Last year's rankings: #33 | #20 | #35 — Latest league: Carolina

MLB Forecast 2011

| AB | R | H | 2B | 3B | HR | RBI | SB | BA | OBP | SLG | BB% | CT% |
|---|---|---|---|---|---|---|---|---|---|---|---|---|
| — | — | — | — | — | — | — | — | — | — | — | — | — |

| | 2008 | | | | | | | | | | | | | 2009 | | | | | | | | | | | | | 2010 | | | | | | | | | | | | |
|---|---|---|---|---|---|---|---|---|---|---|---|---|---|---|---|---|---|---|---|---|---|---|---|---|---|---|---|---|---|---|---|---|---|---|---|---|---|---|---|
| Level | AB | R | H | 2B | 3B | HR | RBI | SB | BA | OBP | SLG | BB% | CT% | AB | R | H | 2B | 3B | HR | RBI | SB | BA | OBP | SLG | BB% | CT% | AB | R | H | 2B | 3B | HR | RBI | SB | BA | OBP | SLG | BB% | CT% |
| A | 227 | 42 | 63 | 12 | 0 | 10 | 38 | 11 | .278 | .444 | .463 | 21% | 75% | 437 | 78 | 125 | 30 | 0 | 23 | 84 | 6 | .286 | .413 | .513 | 17% | 73% | 298 | 67 | 70 | 19 | 0 | 12 | 49 | 6 | .235 | .419 | .419 | 22% | 68% |
| AA | — | — | — | — | — | — | — | — | — | — | — | — | — | — | — | — | — | — | — | — | — | — | — | — | — | — | — | — | — | — | — | — | — | — | — | — | — | — | — |
| AAA | — | — | — | — | — | — | — | — | — | — | — | — | — | — | — | — | — | — | — | — | — | — | — | — | — | — | — | — | — | — | — | — | — | — | — | — | — | — | — |
| MLB | — | — | — | — | — | — | — | — | — | — | — | — | — | — | — | — | — | — | — | — | — | — | — | — | — | — | — | — | — | — | — | — | — | — | — | — | — | — | — |

| | | |
|---|---|---|
| #39 | Norris's career took a step backward in 2010, but with his power he still could be a game-changer. He has his work cut out for him, though. (Hagen) | ETA: Late 2012 |
| #41 | Norris was snake-bitten in 2010 as he recovered from wrist surgery. He might not hit for a great BA, but he hits for power and collects walks. (Hulet) | ETA: Late 2013 |
| #32 | Hampered by a sore wrist and concussion, Norris took a step back, but there's still a lot to like about his approach. His defense improved. (Lockard) | ETA: Mid-2012 |

## CA Carlos Perez — Toronto | AL

RH | 20 yrs, 5 mo — Signed as international free agent, 2007

Last year's rankings: — | — | — — Latest league: New York-Penn

MLB Forecast 2011

| AB | R | H | 2B | 3B | HR | RBI | SB | BA | OBP | SLG | BB% | CT% |
|---|---|---|---|---|---|---|---|---|---|---|---|---|
| — | — | — | — | — | — | — | — | — | — | — | — | — |

| | 2008 | | | | | | | | | | | | | 2009 | | | | | | | | | | | | | 2010 | | | | | | | | | | | | |
|---|---|---|---|---|---|---|---|---|---|---|---|---|---|---|---|---|---|---|---|---|---|---|---|---|---|---|---|---|---|---|---|---|---|---|---|---|---|---|---|
| Level | AB | R | H | 2B | 3B | HR | RBI | SB | BA | OBP | SLG | BB% | CT% | AB | R | H | 2B | 3B | HR | RBI | SB | BA | OBP | SLG | BB% | CT% | AB | R | H | 2B | 3B | HR | RBI | SB | BA | OBP | SLG | BB% | CT% |
| A | — | — | — | — | — | — | — | — | — | — | — | — | — | — | — | — | — | — | — | — | — | — | — | — | — | — | 235 | 44 | 70 | 11 | 8 | 2 | 41 | 7 | .298 | .396 | .438 | 12% | 83% |
| AA | — | — | — | — | — | — | — | — | — | — | — | — | — | — | — | — | — | — | — | — | — | — | — | — | — | — | — | — | — | — | — | — | — | — | — | — | — | — | — |
| AAA | — | — | — | — | — | — | — | — | — | — | — | — | — | — | — | — | — | — | — | — | — | — | — | — | — | — | — | — | — | — | — | — | — | — | — | — | — | — | — |
| MLB | — | — | — | — | — | — | — | — | — | — | — | — | — | — | — | — | — | — | — | — | — | — | — | — | — | — | — | — | — | — | — | — | — | — | — | — | — | — | — |

| | | |
|---|---|---|
| #54 | Perez is an athletic catcher with solid tools across the board. He has a bright future, though he does not have the huge upside that some foresee. (Hagen) | ETA: Mid-2014 |
| #25 | A lesser-known prospect, Perez is poised to take a big step forward for Toronto in 2011. He is a good defender and an advanced hitter for his age. (Hulet) | ETA: Late 2014 |
| #43 | Despite his age, Perez is a very mature hitter, and he has the tools to be an above-average fielding catcher. He will be pushed slowly, however. (Lockard) | ETA: Mid-2013 |

## CA Wilson Ramos — Washington | NL

RH | 23 yrs, 7 mo — Signed as non-drafted free agent, 2004

Last year's rankings: #54 | #55 | #62 — Latest league: International

MLB Forecast 2011

| AB | R | H | 2B | 3B | HR | RBI | SB | BA | OBP | SLG | BB% | CT% |
|---|---|---|---|---|---|---|---|---|---|---|---|---|
| 277 | 27 | 66 | 15 | 0 | 9 | 36 | 0 | .238 | .279 | .389 | 5% | 77% |

| | 2008 | | | | | | | | | | | | | 2009 | | | | | | | | | | | | | 2010 | | | | | | | | | | | | |
|---|---|---|---|---|---|---|---|---|---|---|---|---|---|---|---|---|---|---|---|---|---|---|---|---|---|---|---|---|---|---|---|---|---|---|---|---|---|---|---|
| Level | AB | R | H | 2B | 3B | HR | RBI | SB | BA | OBP | SLG | BB% | CT% | AB | R | H | 2B | 3B | HR | RBI | SB | BA | OBP | SLG | BB% | CT% | AB | R | H | 2B | 3B | HR | RBI | SB | BA | OBP | SLG | BB% | CT% |
| A | 452 | 50 | 130 | 23 | 2 | 13 | 78 | 0 | .288 | .346 | .434 | 7% | 77% | — | — | — | — | — | — | — | — | — | — | — | — | — | — | — | — | — | — | — | — | — | — | — | — | — | — |
| AA | — | — | — | — | — | — | — | — | — | — | — | — | — | 205 | 31 | 65 | 16 | 0 | 4 | 29 | 0 | .317 | .341 | .454 | 3% | 89% | — | — | — | — | — | — | — | — | — | — | — | — | — |
| AAA | — | — | — | — | — | — | — | — | — | — | — | — | — | — | — | — | — | — | — | — | — | — | — | — | — | — | 357 | 39 | 92 | 17 | 1 | 8 | 38 | 1 | .258 | .293 | .378 | 4% | 83% |
| MLB | — | — | — | — | — | — | — | — | — | — | — | — | — | — | — | — | — | — | — | — | — | — | — | — | — | — | 79 | 5 | 22 | 7 | 0 | 1 | 5 | 0 | .278 | .305 | .405 | 2% | 85% |

| | | |
|---|---|---|
| #47 | Ramos is the definition of a solid, all-around catching prospect. The potential in his bat is not infinite, but it's good enough to start every day. (Hagen) | ETA: Late 2011 |
| #39 | A bit over-hyped, Ramos is a solid catching prospect, but his power is modest, and his walk rates have been brutal throughout his pro career. (Hulet) | ETA: Mid-2011 |
| #67 | A strong fielding catcher, Ramos played well in limited big-league time in '10. His glove is ahead of his bat, but he has offensive projection. (Lockard) | ETA: Mid-2011 |

## 1B Anthony Rizzo — Boston | AL

LH | 21 yrs, 7 mo — Drafted 2007, 6th round

Last year's rankings: — | — | — — Latest league: Eastern

MLB Forecast 2011

| AB | R | H | 2B | 3B | HR | RBI | SB | BA | OBP | SLG | BB% | CT% |
|---|---|---|---|---|---|---|---|---|---|---|---|---|
| 44 | 5 | 11 | 4 | 0 | 2 | 6 | 0 | .251 | .313 | .424 | 8% | 74% |

| | 2008 | | | | | | | | | | | | | 2009 | | | | | | | | | | | | | 2010 | | | | | | | | | | | | |
|---|---|---|---|---|---|---|---|---|---|---|---|---|---|---|---|---|---|---|---|---|---|---|---|---|---|---|---|---|---|---|---|---|---|---|---|---|---|---|---|
| Level | AB | R | H | 2B | 3B | HR | RBI | SB | BA | OBP | SLG | BB% | CT% | AB | R | H | 2B | 3B | HR | RBI | SB | BA | OBP | SLG | BB% | CT% | AB | R | H | 2B | 3B | HR | RBI | SB | BA | OBP | SLG | BB% | CT% |
| A | 83 | 9 | 31 | 6 | 0 | 0 | 11 | 0 | .373 | .402 | .446 | 3% | 82% | 445 | 63 | 132 | 37 | 0 | 12 | 66 | 4 | .297 | .368 | .461 | 10% | 78% | 117 | 26 | 29 | 12 | 0 | 5 | 20 | 3 | .248 | .333 | .479 | 12% | 73% |
| AA | — | — | — | — | — | — | — | — | — | — | — | — | — | — | — | — | — | — | — | — | — | — | — | — | — | — | 414 | 66 | 109 | 30 | 0 | 20 | 80 | 7 | .263 | .334 | .481 | 10% | 76% |
| AAA | — | — | — | — | — | — | — | — | — | — | — | — | — | — | — | — | — | — | — | — | — | — | — | — | — | — | — | — | — | — | — | — | — | — | — | — | — | — | — |
| MLB | — | — | — | — | — | — | — | — | — | — | — | — | — | — | — | — | — | — | — | — | — | — | — | — | — | — | — | — | — | — | — | — | — | — | — | — | — | — | — |

| | | |
|---|---|---|
| #49 | Rizzo looks awful against good breaking stuff, and his home run total in 2010 was inflated, but he has skill, and there is room to grow as a hitter. (Hagen) | ETA: Early 2013 |
| #40 | Rizzo had a nice season, but it remains to be seen if he owns enough of the overall package to be a starter in the majors. 2011 will be a big year. (Hulet) | ETA: Late 2011 |
| #44 | Two years removed from a cancer fight, Rizzo displayed solid power and an excellent glove at first base; however, his on-base skills took a hit. (Lockard) | ETA: Late 2011 |

## CA Austin Romine — New York | AL

RH | 22 yrs, 4 mo — Drafted 2007, 2nd round

Last year's rankings: #61 | #31 | #59 — Latest league: Eastern

MLB Forecast 2011

| AB | R | H | 2B | 3B | HR | RBI | SB | BA | OBP | SLG | BB% | CT% |
|---|---|---|---|---|---|---|---|---|---|---|---|---|
| — | — | — | — | — | — | — | — | — | — | — | — | — |

| | 2008 | | | | | | | | | | | | | 2009 | | | | | | | | | | | | | 2010 | | | | | | | | | | | | |
|---|---|---|---|---|---|---|---|---|---|---|---|---|---|---|---|---|---|---|---|---|---|---|---|---|---|---|---|---|---|---|---|---|---|---|---|---|---|---|---|
| Level | AB | R | H | 2B | 3B | HR | RBI | SB | BA | OBP | SLG | BB% | CT% | AB | R | H | 2B | 3B | HR | RBI | SB | BA | OBP | SLG | BB% | CT% | AB | R | H | 2B | 3B | HR | RBI | SB | BA | OBP | SLG | BB% | CT% |
| A | 407 | 66 | 122 | 24 | 1 | 10 | 49 | 3 | .300 | .344 | .437 | 6% | 86% | 442 | 61 | 122 | 28 | 3 | 13 | 72 | 11 | .276 | .322 | .441 | 6% | 82% | — | — | — | — | — | — | — | — | — | — | — | — | — |
| AA | — | — | — | — | — | — | — | — | — | — | — | — | — | — | — | — | — | — | — | — | — | — | — | — | — | — | 455 | 61 | 122 | 31 | 0 | 10 | 69 | 2 | .268 | .324 | .402 | 7% | 79% |
| AAA | — | — | — | — | — | — | — | — | — | — | — | — | — | — | — | — | — | — | — | — | — | — | — | — | — | — | — | — | — | — | — | — | — | — | — | — | — | — | — |
| MLB | — | — | — | — | — | — | — | — | — | — | — | — | — | — | — | — | — | — | — | — | — | — | — | — | — | — | — | — | — | — | — | — | — | — | — | — | — | — | — |

| | | |
|---|---|---|
| #51 | Romine continues to post solid production wherever he goes, matching his skill level. He has the make-up of a typical big-league catcher. (Hagen) | ETA: Early 2012 |
| #23 | Over-shadowed, Romine is a solid defensive player, and he is NYY's true "catcher of the future." He does need to drive the ball more consistently. (Hulet) | ETA: Mid-2012 |
| #54 | Romine struggles badly at the plate against righties, and his throwing game needs work behind the plate. That said, he was young for his level. (Lockard) | ETA: Late 2012 |

## CA Wilin Rosario — Colorado | NL

RH | 22 yrs, 1 mo — Signed as non-drafted free agent, 2006

Last year's rankings: — | — | — — Latest league: Texas

MLB Forecast 2011

| AB | R | H | 2B | 3B | HR | RBI | SB | BA | OBP | SLG | BB% | CT% |
|---|---|---|---|---|---|---|---|---|---|---|---|---|
| — | — | — | — | — | — | — | — | — | — | — | — | — |

| | 2008 | | | | | | | | | | | | | 2009 | | | | | | | | | | | | | 2010 | | | | | | | | | | | | |
|---|---|---|---|---|---|---|---|---|---|---|---|---|---|---|---|---|---|---|---|---|---|---|---|---|---|---|---|---|---|---|---|---|---|---|---|---|---|---|---|
| Level | AB | R | H | 2B | 3B | HR | RBI | SB | BA | OBP | SLG | BB% | CT% | AB | R | H | 2B | 3B | HR | RBI | SB | BA | OBP | SLG | BB% | CT% | AB | R | H | 2B | 3B | HR | RBI | SB | BA | OBP | SLG | BB% | CT% |
| A | — | — | — | — | — | — | — | — | — | — | — | — | — | 203 | 17 | 54 | 12 | 2 | 4 | 33 | 2 | .266 | .297 | .404 | 5% | 73% | — | — | — | — | — | — | — | — | — | — | — | — | — |
| AA | — | — | — | — | — | — | — | — | — | — | — | — | — | — | — | — | — | — | — | — | — | — | — | — | — | — | 270 | 42 | 77 | 13 | 1 | 19 | 52 | 1 | .285 | .342 | .552 | 7% | 79% |
| AAA | — | — | — | — | — | — | — | — | — | — | — | — | — | — | — | — | — | — | — | — | — | — | — | — | — | — | — | — | — | — | — | — | — | — | — | — | — | — | — |
| MLB | — | — | — | — | — | — | — | — | — | — | — | — | — | — | — | — | — | — | — | — | — | — | — | — | — | — | — | — | — | — | — | — | — | — | — | — | — | — | — |

| | | |
|---|---|---|
| #50 | Rosario needs a lot of refinement behind the plate, but his raw power took hold this year before a season-ending knee injury. He is one to watch. (Hagen) | ETA: Early 2013 |
| #48 | Despite playing only 73 games, Rosario's power made a big jump, with an ISO of .267. He needs to prove his durability and improve his receiving. (Hulet) | ETA: Late 2012 |
| #16 | Rosario has lost consecutive seasons to an inflamed wrist and a torn ACL. He shows promise on both sides of the ball but he must stay healthy. (Lockard) | ETA: Early 2013 |

## CA Gary Sanchez — New York | AL

RH | 18 yrs, 3 mo — Signed as international free agent, 2009

Last year's rankings: — | — | — — Latest league: New York-Penn

MLB Forecast 2011

| AB | R | H | 2B | 3B | HR | RBI | SB | BA | OBP | SLG | BB% | CT% |
|---|---|---|---|---|---|---|---|---|---|---|---|---|
| — | — | — | — | — | — | — | — | — | — | — | — | — |

| | 2008 | | | | | | | | | | | | | 2009 | | | | | | | | | | | | | 2010 | | | | | | | | | | | | |
|---|---|---|---|---|---|---|---|---|---|---|---|---|---|---|---|---|---|---|---|---|---|---|---|---|---|---|---|---|---|---|---|---|---|---|---|---|---|---|---|
| Level | AB | R | H | 2B | 3B | HR | RBI | SB | BA | OBP | SLG | BB% | CT% | AB | R | H | 2B | 3B | HR | RBI | SB | BA | OBP | SLG | BB% | CT% | AB | R | H | 2B | 3B | HR | RBI | SB | BA | OBP | SLG | BB% | CT% |
| A | — | — | — | — | — | — | — | — | — | — | — | — | — | — | — | — | — | — | — | — | — | — | — | — | — | — | 54 | 8 | 15 | 2 | 0 | 2 | 7 | 1 | .278 | .333 | .426 | 5% | 70% |
| AA | — | — | — | — | — | — | — | — | — | — | — | — | — | — | — | — | — | — | — | — | — | — | — | — | — | — | — | — | — | — | — | — | — | — | — | — | — | — | — |
| AAA | — | — | — | — | — | — | — | — | — | — | — | — | — | — | — | — | — | — | — | — | — | — | — | — | — | — | — | — | — | — | — | — | — | — | — | — | — | — | — |
| MLB | — | — | — | — | — | — | — | — | — | — | — | — | — | — | — | — | — | — | — | — | — | — | — | — | — | — | — | — | — | — | — | — | — | — | — | — | — | — | — |

| | | |
|---|---|---|
| #48 | Sanchez in his debut did everything that one could ask of him. He has the basis for an exceptional bat with average glove, but let's take it slow. (Hagen) | ETA: Mid-2014 |
| #21 | The next coming of Jesus Montero, Sanchez dominated rookie ball at age 17 with good power. His defensive game still has a lot of rough edges. (Hulet) | ETA: Mid-2014 |
| #49 | Sanchez wowed offensively in rookie ball, but the real tests with the bat will come at higher levels. His glove needs work, but he is very young. (Lockard) | ETA: Late 2013 |

## CA Tony Sanchez — Pittsburgh | NL

RH | 22 yrs, 10 mo — Drafted 2009, #4 overall

Last year's rankings: #44 | #32 | #58 — Latest league: Florida State

MLB Forecast 2011

| AB | R | H | 2B | 3B | HR | RBI | SB | BA | OBP | SLG | BB% | CT% |
|---|---|---|---|---|---|---|---|---|---|---|---|---|
| — | — | — | — | — | — | — | — | — | — | — | — | — |

| | 2008 | | | | | | | | | | | | | 2009 | | | | | | | | | | | | | 2010 | | | | | | | | | | | | |
|---|---|---|---|---|---|---|---|---|---|---|---|---|---|---|---|---|---|---|---|---|---|---|---|---|---|---|---|---|---|---|---|---|---|---|---|---|---|---|---|
| Level | AB | R | H | 2B | 3B | HR | RBI | SB | BA | OBP | SLG | BB% | CT% | AB | R | H | 2B | 3B | HR | RBI | SB | BA | OBP | SLG | BB% | CT% | AB | R | H | 2B | 3B | HR | RBI | SB | BA | OBP | SLG | BB% | CT% |
| A | — | — | — | — | — | — | — | — | — | — | — | — | — | 178 | 33 | 55 | 18 | 1 | 7 | 48 | 1 | .309 | .409 | .539 | 11% | 78% | 207 | 31 | 65 | 17 | 0 | 4 | 35 | 2 | .314 | .416 | .454 | 11% | 80% |
| AA | — | — | — | — | — | — | — | — | — | — | — | — | — | — | — | — | — | — | — | — | — | — | — | — | — | — | — | — | — | — | — | — | — | — | — | — | — | — | — |
| AAA | — | — | — | — | — | — | — | — | — | — | — | — | — | — | — | — | — | — | — | — | — | — | — | — | — | — | — | — | — | — | — | — | — | — | — | — | — | — | — |
| MLB | — | — | — | — | — | — | — | — | — | — | — | — | — | — | — | — | — | — | — | — | — | — | — | — | — | — | — | — | — | — | — | — | — | — | — | — | — | — | — |

| | | |
|---|---|---|
| #41 | Sanchez's power potential is limited, but he's a team leader and a strong defender, and he has a reputation for finding ways to get on base. (Hagen) | ETA: Mid-2012 |
| #35 | A beaning injury ended Sanchez's season early, but he had excellent production in 59 games. Look for him to get a taste of the majors in 2011. (Hulet) | ETA: Late 2012 |
| #21 | Sanchez broke his jaw on an errant pitch, cutting short his season. He is already MLB-ready behind the plate, and his bat should play fine. (Lockard) | ETA: Late 2011 |

## SS Miguel Sano — Minnesota | AL
RH | 17 yrs, 10 mo — Signed as international free agent, 2009

Last year's rankings: — — —
Latest league: Gulf Coast

**MLB Forecast 2011**

| AB | R | H | 2B | 3B | HR | RBI | SB | BA | OBP | SLG | BB% | CT% |
|----|---|---|----|----|----|-----|----|----|-----|-----|-----|-----|
| — | — | — | — | — | — | — | — | — | — | — | — | — |

| Level | AB | R | H | 2B | 3B | HR | RBI | SB | BA | OBP | SLG | BB% | CT% | AB | R | H | 2B | 3B | HR | RBI | SB | BA | OBP | SLG | BB% | CT% | AB | R | H | 2B | 3B | HR | RBI | SB | BA | OBP | SLG | BB% | CT% |
|---|---|---|---|---|---|---|---|---|---|---|---|---|---|---|---|---|---|---|---|---|---|---|---|---|---|---|---|---|---|---|---|---|---|---|---|---|---|---|---|
| | | | | 2008 | | | | | | | | | | | | | | 2009 | | | | | | | | | | | | | 2010 | | | | | | | | |
| A | — | — | — | — | — | — | — | — | — | — | — | — | — | — | — | — | — | — | — | — | — | — | — | — | — | — | — | — | — | — | — | — | — | — | — | — | — | — |
| AA | — | — | — | — | — | — | — | — | — | — | — | — | — | — | — | — | — | — | — | — | — | — | — | — | — | — | — | — | — | — | — | — | — | — | — | — | — | — |
| AAA | — | — | — | — | — | — | — | — | — | — | — | — | — | — | — | — | — | — | — | — | — | — | — | — | — | — | — | — | — | — | — | — | — | — | — | — | — | — |
| MLB | — | — | — | — | — | — | — | — | — | — | — | — | — | — | — | — | — | — | — | — | — | — | — | — | — | — | — | — | — | — | — | — | — | — | — | — | — | — |

#21 Sano's rookie-ball debut (.307/.379/.491) is promising. His bat has plus potential across the board, and he is fleet enough to attack the basepaths. (Hagen) — ETA: Early 2014
#46 Sano, 17, is still a long way from the majors, but he exhibits impressive tools, so just be patient. His power has been above-average for his age. (Hulet) — ETA: Mid-2015
#14 Sano is years away from the majors, but he already has scouts dreaming about his potential, which some have compared to Miguel Cabrera. (Lockard) — ETA: Late 2013

## CA Carlos Santana — Cleveland | AL
BH | 24 yrs, 11 mo — Signed as non-drafted free agent, 2004

Last year's rankings: #4 #11 #10
Latest league: International

**MLB Forecast 2011**

| AB | R | H | 2B | 3B | HR | RBI | SB | BA | OBP | SLG | BB% | CT% |
|----|---|---|----|----|----|-----|----|----|-----|-----|-----|-----|
| 519 | 66 | 120 | 36 | 0 | 24 | 78 | 6 | .231 | .342 | .435 | 14% | 78% |

| Level | AB | R | H | 2B | 3B | HR | RBI | SB | BA | OBP | SLG | BB% | CT% | AB | R | H | 2B | 3B | HR | RBI | SB | BA | OBP | SLG | BB% | CT% | AB | R | H | 2B | 3B | HR | RBI | SB | BA | OBP | SLG | BB% | CT% |
|---|---|---|---|---|---|---|---|---|---|---|---|---|---|---|---|---|---|---|---|---|---|---|---|---|---|---|---|---|---|---|---|---|---|---|---|---|---|---|---|
| | | | | 2008 | | | | | | | | | | | | | | 2009 | | | | | | | | | | | | | 2010 | | | | | | | | |
| A | 463 | 125 | 151 | 39 | 5 | 21 | 117 | 10 | .326 | .431 | .568 | 16% | 82% | — | — | — | — | — | — | — | — | — | — | — | — | — | — | — | — | — | — | — | — | — | — | — | — | — | — |
| AA | — | — | — | — | — | — | — | — | — | — | — | — | — | 428 | 91 | 124 | 30 | 2 | 23 | 97 | 2 | .290 | .413 | .530 | 17% | 81% | — | — | — | — | — | — | — | — | — | — | — | — | — |
| AAA | — | — | — | — | — | — | — | — | — | — | — | — | — | — | — | — | — | — | — | — | — | — | — | — | — | — | 196 | 39 | 62 | 14 | 1 | 13 | 51 | 6 | .316 | .447 | .597 | 18% | 80% |
| MLB | — | — | — | — | — | — | — | — | — | — | — | — | — | — | — | — | — | — | — | — | — | — | — | — | — | — | 150 | 23 | 39 | 13 | 0 | 6 | 22 | 3 | .260 | .401 | .467 | 19% | 81% |

#1 The August knee surgery doesn't scare me off – Santana possesses absolutely everything necessary to be a perennial All Star at catcher. (Hagen) — ETA: Arrived
#1 Santana was well on his way to being Rookie of the Year before a nasty knee injury. Look for him to be a top offensive player at his position in '11. (Hulet) — ETA: Early 2011
#3 A collision at home plate ended Santana's season, but he had been playing like a star. He will make Cleveland forget Victor Martinez in a hurry. (Lockard) — ETA: Early 2011

## 1B Jonathan Singleton — Philadelphia | NL
LH | 19 yrs, 6 mo — Drafted 2009, 8th round

Last year's rankings: — — —
Latest league: South Atlantic

**MLB Forecast 2011**

| AB | R | H | 2B | 3B | HR | RBI | SB | BA | OBP | SLG | BB% | CT% |
|----|---|---|----|----|----|-----|----|----|-----|-----|-----|-----|
| — | — | — | — | — | — | — | — | — | — | — | — | — |

| Level | AB | R | H | 2B | 3B | HR | RBI | SB | BA | OBP | SLG | BB% | CT% | AB | R | H | 2B | 3B | HR | RBI | SB | BA | OBP | SLG | BB% | CT% | AB | R | H | 2B | 3B | HR | RBI | SB | BA | OBP | SLG | BB% | CT% |
|---|---|---|---|---|---|---|---|---|---|---|---|---|---|---|---|---|---|---|---|---|---|---|---|---|---|---|---|---|---|---|---|---|---|---|---|---|---|---|---|
| | | | | 2008 | | | | | | | | | | | | | | 2009 | | | | | | | | | | | | | 2010 | | | | | | | | |
| A | — | — | — | — | — | — | — | — | — | — | — | — | — | — | — | — | — | — | — | — | — | — | — | — | — | — | 376 | 64 | 109 | 25 | 2 | 14 | 77 | 9 | .290 | .393 | .479 | 14% | 80% |
| AA | — | — | — | — | — | — | — | — | — | — | — | — | — | — | — | — | — | — | — | — | — | — | — | — | — | — | — | — | — | — | — | — | — | — | — | — | — | — | — |
| AAA | — | — | — | — | — | — | — | — | — | — | — | — | — | — | — | — | — | — | — | — | — | — | — | — | — | — | — | — | — | — | — | — | — | — | — | — | — | — | — |
| MLB | — | — | — | — | — | — | — | — | — | — | — | — | — | — | — | — | — | — | — | — | — | — | — | — | — | — | — | — | — | — | — | — | — | — | — | — | — | — | — |

#44 Singleton was one of the minors' breakout hitters of 2010. He has a big bat and plate patience, but I'm not sure how he'll adjust to off-speed stuff. (Hagen) — ETA: Mid-2013
#63 Singleton came out of nowhere in '10. Unfortunately, his numbers dropped off dramatically in the second half. He'll have something to prove in '11. (Hulet) — ETA: Mid-2013
#46 Scouts are split on Singleton, who was stellar in the 1st half but ordinary in the 2nd half. He has power and patience but also holes in his swing. (Lockard) — ETA: Late 2012

## CF Donavan Tate — San Diego | NL
RH | 20 yrs, 6 mo — Drafted 2009, #3 overall

Last year's rankings: #7 #47 #21
Latest league: Arizona

**MLB Forecast 2011**

| AB | R | H | 2B | 3B | HR | RBI | SB | BA | OBP | SLG | BB% | CT% |
|----|---|---|----|----|----|-----|----|----|-----|-----|-----|-----|
| — | — | — | — | — | — | — | — | — | — | — | — | — |

| Level | AB | R | H | 2B | 3B | HR | RBI | SB | BA | OBP | SLG | BB% | CT% | AB | R | H | 2B | 3B | HR | RBI | SB | BA | OBP | SLG | BB% | CT% | AB | R | H | 2B | 3B | HR | RBI | SB | BA | OBP | SLG | BB% | CT% |
|---|---|---|---|---|---|---|---|---|---|---|---|---|---|---|---|---|---|---|---|---|---|---|---|---|---|---|---|---|---|---|---|---|---|---|---|---|---|---|---|
| | | | | 2008 | | | | | | | | | | | | | | 2009 | | | | | | | | | | | | | 2010 | | | | | | | | |
| A | — | — | — | — | — | — | — | — | — | — | — | — | — | — | — | — | — | — | — | — | — | — | — | — | — | — | — | — | — | — | — | — | — | — | — | — | — | — |
| AA | — | — | — | — | — | — | — | — | — | — | — | — | — | — | — | — | — | — | — | — | — | — | — | — | — | — | — | — | — | — | — | — | — | — | — | — | — | — |
| AAA | — | — | — | — | — | — | — | — | — | — | — | — | — | — | — | — | — | — | — | — | — | — | — | — | — | — | — | — | — | — | — | — | — | — | — | — | — | — |
| MLB | — | — | — | — | — | — | — | — | — | — | — | — | — | — | — | — | — | — | — | — | — | — | — | — | — | — | — | — | — | — | — | — | — | — | — | — | — | — |

#16 Tate was my favorite hitter of the 2009 draft, but our first sightings of him (.222/.336/.344 in rookie ball) aren't good. The five-tool talent remains. (Hagen) — ETA: Late 2013
#36 Random injuries again haunted Tate. Despite a high .375 BABIP, he hit for a terrible BA due to a strikeout rate near 40%. A lot of work is needed. (Hulet) — ETA: Mid-2015
#47 Tate has not been able to stay on the field since being drafted. The talent is there, and time is on his side, but he needs to get his act together. (Lockard) — ETA: Late 2012

## SS Carlos Triunfel — Seattle | AL
RH | 21 yrs, 1 mo — Signed as non-drafted free agent, 2006

Last year's rankings: #23 #40 #39
Latest league: Southern

**MLB Forecast 2011**

| AB | R | H | 2B | 3B | HR | RBI | SB | BA | OBP | SLG | BB% | CT% |
|----|---|---|----|----|----|-----|----|----|-----|-----|-----|-----|
| — | — | — | — | — | — | — | — | — | — | — | — | — |

| Level | AB | R | H | 2B | 3B | HR | RBI | SB | BA | OBP | SLG | BB% | CT% | AB | R | H | 2B | 3B | HR | RBI | SB | BA | OBP | SLG | BB% | CT% | AB | R | H | 2B | 3B | HR | RBI | SB | BA | OBP | SLG | BB% | CT% |
|---|---|---|---|---|---|---|---|---|---|---|---|---|---|---|---|---|---|---|---|---|---|---|---|---|---|---|---|---|---|---|---|---|---|---|---|---|---|---|---|
| | | | | 2008 | | | | | | | | | | | | | | 2009 | | | | | | | | | | | | | 2010 | | | | | | | | |
| A | 436 | 75 | 125 | 20 | 4 | 8 | 49 | 30 | .287 | .336 | .406 | 6% | 88% | — | — | — | — | — | — | — | — | — | — | — | — | — | — | — | — | — | — | — | — | — | — | — | — | — | — |
| AA | — | — | — | — | — | — | — | — | — | — | — | — | — | 26 | 2 | 6 | 1 | 0 | 0 | 4 | 0 | .231 | .286 | .269 | 4% | 92% | 470 | 51 | 121 | 12 | 1 | 7 | 42 | 2 | .257 | .286 | .332 | 3% | 89% |
| AAA | — | — | — | — | — | — | — | — | — | — | — | — | — | — | — | — | — | — | — | — | — | — | — | — | — | — | — | — | — | — | — | — | — | — | — | — | — | — | — |
| MLB | — | — | — | — | — | — | — | — | — | — | — | — | — | — | — | — | — | — | — | — | — | — | — | — | — | — | — | — | — | — | — | — | — | — | — | — | — | — | — |

#32 Triunfel still possesses the tools necessary to become a star, but his speed and power evaporated in 2010. He has taken two steps back. (Hagen) — ETA: Early 2012
#61 Age 20 in Double-A, Triunfel had a brutal season with an over-aggressive approach. He lacks the power for third base but the range for shortstop. (Hulet) — ETA: Mid-2012
#59 Scouts have been waiting for two years for Triunfel to live up to his potential. At some point, age will stop being an excuse for his performance. (Lockard) — ETA: Mid-2012

## CF Mike Trout — Los Angeles | AL
RH | 19 yrs, 7 mo — Drafted 2009, #25 overall

Last year's rankings: — — —
Latest league: California

**MLB Forecast 2011**

| AB | R | H | 2B | 3B | HR | RBI | SB | BA | OBP | SLG | BB% | CT% |
|----|---|---|----|----|----|-----|----|----|-----|-----|-----|-----|
| — | — | — | — | — | — | — | — | — | — | — | — | — |

| Level | AB | R | H | 2B | 3B | HR | RBI | SB | BA | OBP | SLG | BB% | CT% | AB | R | H | 2B | 3B | HR | RBI | SB | BA | OBP | SLG | BB% | CT% | AB | R | H | 2B | 3B | HR | RBI | SB | BA | OBP | SLG | BB% | CT% |
|---|---|---|---|---|---|---|---|---|---|---|---|---|---|---|---|---|---|---|---|---|---|---|---|---|---|---|---|---|---|---|---|---|---|---|---|---|---|---|---|
| | | | | 2008 | | | | | | | | | | | | | | 2009 | | | | | | | | | | | | | 2010 | | | | | | | | |
| A | — | — | — | — | — | — | — | — | — | — | — | — | — | 15 | 1 | 4 | 0 | 0 | 0 | 0 | 0 | .267 | .421 | .267 | 20% | 60% | 508 | 106 | 173 | 28 | 9 | 10 | 58 | 56 | .341 | .428 | .490 | 12% | 83% |
| AA | — | — | — | — | — | — | — | — | — | — | — | — | — | — | — | — | — | — | — | — | — | — | — | — | — | — | — | — | — | — | — | — | — | — | — | — | — | — | — |
| AAA | — | — | — | — | — | — | — | — | — | — | — | — | — | — | — | — | — | — | — | — | — | — | — | — | — | — | — | — | — | — | — | — | — | — | — | — | — | — | — |
| MLB | — | — | — | — | — | — | — | — | — | — | — | — | — | — | — | — | — | — | — | — | — | — | — | — | — | — | — | — | — | — | — | — | — | — | — | — | — | — | — |

#11 Trout's power seems to be merely OK, but his speed and plate discipline set A-ball on fire. The Angels could have a star in the making. (Hagen) — ETA: Mid-2012
#2 Perhaps the top hitting prospect in the minors, Trout has a solid all-around game and a gamer mentality. The organization has a real find. (Hulet) — ETA: Late 2012
#2 Trout is one of the fastest players in the minors, and he has the batting eye to put that skill to good use. He also has developing power. (Lockard) — ETA: Late 2011

## 3B Dayan Viciedo — Chicago | AL
RH | 22 yrs, 0 mo — Signed as international free agent, 2008

Last year's rankings: #56 #51 #51
Latest league: International

**MLB Forecast 2011**

| AB | R | H | 2B | 3B | HR | RBI | SB | BA | OBP | SLG | BB% | CT% |
|----|---|---|----|----|----|-----|----|----|-----|-----|-----|-----|
| 293 | 36 | 75 | 12 | 0 | 12 | 36 | 3 | .256 | .288 | .419 | 4% | 80% |

| Level | AB | R | H | 2B | 3B | HR | RBI | SB | BA | OBP | SLG | BB% | CT% | AB | R | H | 2B | 3B | HR | RBI | SB | BA | OBP | SLG | BB% | CT% | AB | R | H | 2B | 3B | HR | RBI | SB | BA | OBP | SLG | BB% | CT% |
|---|---|---|---|---|---|---|---|---|---|---|---|---|---|---|---|---|---|---|---|---|---|---|---|---|---|---|---|---|---|---|---|---|---|---|---|---|---|---|---|
| | | | | 2008 | | | | | | | | | | | | | | 2009 | | | | | | | | | | | | | 2010 | | | | | | | | |
| A | — | — | — | — | — | — | — | — | — | — | — | — | — | — | — | — | — | — | — | — | — | — | — | — | — | — | — | — | — | — | — | — | — | — | — | — | — | — |
| AA | — | — | — | — | — | — | — | — | — | — | — | — | — | 504 | 72 | 141 | 20 | 0 | 12 | 78 | 5 | .280 | .317 | .391 | 4% | 82% | — | — | — | — | — | — | — | — | — | — | — | — | — |
| AAA | — | — | — | — | — | — | — | — | — | — | — | — | — | — | — | — | — | — | — | — | — | — | — | — | — | — | 343 | 42 | 94 | 15 | 0 | 20 | 47 | 1 | .274 | .308 | .493 | 3% | 77% |
| MLB | — | — | — | — | — | — | — | — | — | — | — | — | — | — | — | — | — | — | — | — | — | — | — | — | — | — | 104 | 17 | 32 | 7 | 0 | 5 | 13 | 1 | .308 | .321 | .519 | 2% | 76% |

#61 Viciedo has some tools, but I am not sure that his power is anything better than ordinary. His overly aggressive nature at the plate is killing him. (Hagen) — ETA: Early 2011
#44 Like a lot of young hitters, Viciedo lacks sufficient selectivity, and major-league pitchers picked him apart. He might not have enough pop for 1B. (Hulet) — ETA: Mid 2011
#55 Viciedo recovered from a poor first season in the U.S., but his free-swinging approach is not likely to produce consistent numbers in the bigs. (Lockard) — ETA: Early 2011

## 3B Kolbrin Vitek — Boston | AL
RH | 22 yrs, 0 mo — Drafted 2010, #20 overall

Last year's rankings: — — —
Latest league: South Atlantic

**MLB Forecast 2011**

| AB | R | H | 2B | 3B | HR | RBI | SB | BA | OBP | SLG | BB% | CT% |
|----|---|---|----|----|----|-----|----|----|-----|-----|-----|-----|
| — | — | — | — | — | — | — | — | — | — | — | — | — |

| Level | AB | R | H | 2B | 3B | HR | RBI | SB | BA | OBP | SLG | BB% | CT% | AB | R | H | 2B | 3B | HR | RBI | SB | BA | OBP | SLG | BB% | CT% | AB | R | H | 2B | 3B | HR | RBI | SB | BA | OBP | SLG | BB% | CT% |
|---|---|---|---|---|---|---|---|---|---|---|---|---|---|---|---|---|---|---|---|---|---|---|---|---|---|---|---|---|---|---|---|---|---|---|---|---|---|---|---|
| | | | | 2008 | | | | | | | | | | | | | | 2009 | | | | | | | | | | | | | 2010 | | | | | | | | |
| A | — | — | — | — | — | — | — | — | — | — | — | — | — | — | — | — | — | — | — | — | — | — | — | — | — | — | 244 | 37 | 66 | 16 | 4 | 4 | 33 | 17 | .270 | .364 | .418 | 12% | 70% |
| AA | — | — | — | — | — | — | — | — | — | — | — | — | — | — | — | — | — | — | — | — | — | — | — | — | — | — | — | — | — | — | — | — | — | — | — | — | — | — | — |
| AAA | — | — | — | — | — | — | — | — | — | — | — | — | — | — | — | — | — | — | — | — | — | — | — | — | — | — | — | — | — | — | — | — | — | — | — | — | — | — | — |
| MLB | — | — | — | — | — | — | — | — | — | — | — | — | — | — | — | — | — | — | — | — | — | — | — | — | — | — | — | — | — | — | — | — | — | — | — | — | — | — | — |

#22 Vitek has bat speed to burn, workable speed, and a decent plate approach. The big question marks are his power and position. (Hagen) — ETA: Late 2012
#28 Vitek has a high ceiling with good hitting skills, power, and speed. His defensive home is in question, and he could wind up in the outfield. (Hulet) — ETA: Late 2012
#53 Vitek was one of the most polished hitters in the draft, with good speed and power potential. He could move to second base or even center field. (Lockard) — ETA: Late 2012

## 3B Josh Vitters — Chicago | NL

RH | 21 yrs, 7 mo — Drafted 2007, #3 overall

Last year's rankings: #50 | #37 | #16 — Latest league: Southern

| MLB Forecast 2011 | AB | R | H | 2B | 3B | HR | RBI | SB | BA | OBP | SLG | BB% | CT% |
|---|---|---|---|---|---|---|---|---|---|---|---|---|---|
| | — | — | — | — | — | — | — | — | — | — | — | — | — |

| 2008 Level | AB | R | H | 2B | 3B | HR | RBI | SB | BA | OBP | SLG | BB% | CT% |
|---|---|---|---|---|---|---|---|---|---|---|---|---|---|
| A | 273 | 39 | 88 | 28 | 2 | 5 | 38 | 1 | .322 | .357 | .495 | 4% | 82% |
| AA | — | — | — | — | — | — | — | — | — | — | — | — | — |
| AAA | — | — | — | — | — | — | — | — | — | — | — | — | — |
| MLB | — | — | — | — | — | — | — | — | — | — | — | — | — |

| 2009 Level | AB | R | H | 2B | 3B | HR | RBI | SB | BA | OBP | SLG | BB% | CT% |
|---|---|---|---|---|---|---|---|---|---|---|---|---|---|
| A | 458 | 63 | 130 | 19 | 3 | 18 | 68 | 6 | .284 | .314 | .456 | 2% | 86% |
| AA | — | — | — | — | — | — | — | — | — | — | — | — | — |
| AAA | — | — | — | — | — | — | — | — | — | — | — | — | — |
| MLB | — | — | — | — | — | — | — | — | — | — | — | — | — |

| 2010 Level | AB | R | H | 2B | 3B | HR | RBI | SB | BA | OBP | SLG | BB% | CT% |
|---|---|---|---|---|---|---|---|---|---|---|---|---|---|
| A | 110 | 16 | 32 | 8 | 0 | 3 | 13 | 4 | .291 | .350 | .445 | 7% | 80% |
| AA | 206 | 28 | 46 | 12 | 0 | 7 | 26 | 2 | .223 | .292 | .383 | 6% | 80% |
| AAA | — | — | — | — | — | — | — | — | — | — | — | — | — |
| MLB | — | — | — | — | — | — | — | — | — | — | — | — | — |

| Rank | Comment | ETA |
|---|---|---|
| #62 | Despite another lackluster year, Vitters could eventually post plus power in the majors. But the rest of his bat is undeveloped and unimpressive. (Hagen) | ETA: Late 2012 |
| #45 | Vitters continues to struggle as a hitter owing to an extreme lack of selectivity. He needs to adjust his approach if he is going to reach his ceiling. (Hulet) | ETA: Mid-2013 |
| #56 | Vitters has not progressed the way that the Cubs hoped he would, but he is still young for his level. Plate discipline remains an issue for him. (Lockard) | ETA: Mid-2012 |

## 1B Brett Wallace — Houston | NL

LH | 24 yrs, 7 mo — Drafted 2008, #13 overall

Last year's rankings: #14 | #9 | #11 — Latest league: Pacific Coast

| MLB Forecast 2011 | AB | R | H | 2B | 3B | HR | RBI | SB | BA | OBP | SLG | BB% | CT% |
|---|---|---|---|---|---|---|---|---|---|---|---|---|---|
| | 421 | 48 | 100 | 19 | 0 | 14 | 43 | 0 | .237 | .309 | .397 | 7% | 74% |

| 2008 Level | AB | R | H | 2B | 3B | HR | RBI | SB | BA | OBP | SLG | BB% | CT% |
|---|---|---|---|---|---|---|---|---|---|---|---|---|---|
| A | 153 | 28 | 50 | 8 | 1 | 5 | 25 | 0 | .327 | .418 | .490 | 10% | 79% |
| AA | 49 | 13 | 18 | 5 | 0 | 3 | 11 | 0 | .367 | .456 | .653 | 4% | 86% |
| AAA | — | — | — | — | — | — | — | — | — | — | — | — | — |
| MLB | — | — | — | — | — | — | — | — | — | — | — | — | — |

| 2009 Level | AB | R | H | 2B | 3B | HR | RBI | SB | BA | OBP | SLG | BB% | CT% |
|---|---|---|---|---|---|---|---|---|---|---|---|---|---|
| A | — | — | — | — | — | — | — | — | — | — | — | — | — |
| AA | 128 | 22 | 36 | 5 | 0 | 5 | 16 | 0 | .281 | .403 | .438 | 12% | 73% |
| AAA | 404 | 54 | 120 | 21 | 0 | 15 | 47 | 1 | .297 | .355 | .460 | 7% | 80% |
| MLB | — | — | — | — | — | — | — | — | — | — | — | — | — |

| 2010 Level | AB | R | H | 2B | 3B | HR | RBI | SB | BA | OBP | SLG | BB% | CT% |
|---|---|---|---|---|---|---|---|---|---|---|---|---|---|
| A | — | — | — | — | — | — | — | — | — | — | — | — | — |
| AA | — | — | — | — | — | — | — | — | — | — | — | — | — |
| AAA | 385 | 64 | 116 | 24 | 1 | 18 | 61 | 1 | .301 | .359 | .509 | 6% | 78% |
| MLB | 144 | 14 | 32 | 6 | 1 | 2 | 13 | 0 | .222 | .296 | .319 | 5% | 65% |

| Rank | Comment | ETA |
|---|---|---|
| #17 | Wallace's MLB debut left much to be desired. With his power flattening out, he looks like a middling first baseman, albeit one with potential. (Hagen) | ETA: Mid-2011 |
| #58 | For good or bad, Wallace has switched multiple teams in the last 12 months. He had a rough intro to the majors but has a solid ceiling at 1B. (Hulet) | ETA: Early 2011 |
| #57 | Wallace is on his third organization in less than two years. He was steady but not spectacular at Triple-A, but he should get his shot in '11. (Lockard) | ETA: Early 2011 |

## 2B Jemile Weeks — Oakland | AL

BH | 24 yrs, 2 mo — Drafted 2008, #12 overall

Last year's rankings: #40 | #36 | #53 — Latest league: Texas

| MLB Forecast 2011 | AB | R | H | 2B | 3B | HR | RBI | SB | BA | OBP | SLG | BB% | CT% |
|---|---|---|---|---|---|---|---|---|---|---|---|---|---|
| | — | — | — | — | — | — | — | — | — | — | — | — | — |

| 2008 Level | AB | R | H | 2B | 3B | HR | RBI | SB | BA | OBP | SLG | BB% | CT% |
|---|---|---|---|---|---|---|---|---|---|---|---|---|---|
| A | 74 | 11 | 22 | 3 | 1 | 1 | 8 | 6 | .297 | .422 | .405 | 14% | 84% |
| AA | — | — | — | — | — | — | — | — | — | — | — | — | — |
| AAA | — | — | — | — | — | — | — | — | — | — | — | — | — |
| MLB | — | — | — | — | — | — | — | — | — | — | — | — | — |

| 2009 Level | AB | R | H | 2B | 3B | HR | RBI | SB | BA | OBP | SLG | BB% | CT% |
|---|---|---|---|---|---|---|---|---|---|---|---|---|---|
| A | 201 | 29 | 60 | 9 | 2 | 7 | 31 | 5 | .299 | .385 | .468 | 11% | 80% |
| AA | 105 | 10 | 25 | 5 | 0 | 2 | 13 | 4 | .238 | .303 | .343 | 8% | 85% |
| AAA | — | — | — | — | — | — | — | — | — | — | — | — | — |
| MLB | — | — | — | — | — | — | — | — | — | — | — | — | — |

| 2010 Level | AB | R | H | 2B | 3B | HR | RBI | SB | BA | OBP | SLG | BB% | CT% |
|---|---|---|---|---|---|---|---|---|---|---|---|---|---|
| A | — | — | — | — | — | — | — | — | — | — | — | — | — |
| AA | 273 | 43 | 73 | 14 | 7 | 3 | 33 | 11 | .267 | .335 | .403 | 9% | 86% |
| AAA | — | — | — | — | — | — | — | — | — | — | — | — | — |
| MLB | — | — | — | — | — | — | — | — | — | — | — | — | — |

| Rank | Comment | ETA |
|---|---|---|
| #34 | The No. 1 problem with Weeks is that he can't stay healthy. In a full season unhindered by injury, his athleticism and bat speed might flourish. (Hagen) | ETA: Late 2011 |
| #62 | Weeks has struggled with injuries throughout his career, a fact that has tempered enthusiasm. When healthy, he is an above-average hitter. (Hulet) | ETA: Mid-2012 |
| #52 | Weeks has been battling hip issues since 2008, and there is concern that the problem is chronic. He could still be a top-of-the-order threat. (Lockard) | ETA: Late 2011 |

## LF Nick Weglarz — Cleveland | AL

LH | 23 yrs, 3 mo — Drafted 2005, 3rd round

Last year's rankings: — | — | — — Latest league: International

| MLB Forecast 2011 | AB | R | H | 2B | 3B | HR | RBI | SB | BA | OBP | SLG | BB% | CT% |
|---|---|---|---|---|---|---|---|---|---|---|---|---|---|
| | — | — | — | — | — | — | — | — | — | — | — | — | — |

| 2008 Level | AB | R | H | 2B | 3B | HR | RBI | SB | BA | OBP | SLG | BB% | CT% |
|---|---|---|---|---|---|---|---|---|---|---|---|---|---|
| A | 375 | 68 | 102 | 20 | 5 | 10 | 41 | 9 | .272 | .396 | .432 | 16% | 79% |
| AA | — | — | — | — | — | — | — | — | — | — | — | — | — |
| AAA | — | — | — | — | — | — | — | — | — | — | — | — | — |
| MLB | — | — | — | — | — | — | — | — | — | — | — | — | — |

| 2009 Level | AB | R | H | 2B | 3B | HR | RBI | SB | BA | OBP | SLG | BB% | CT% |
|---|---|---|---|---|---|---|---|---|---|---|---|---|---|
| A | — | — | — | — | — | — | — | — | — | — | — | — | — |
| AA | 339 | 69 | 77 | 17 | 2 | 16 | 65 | 2 | .227 | .377 | .431 | 18% | 77% |
| AAA | — | — | — | — | — | — | — | — | — | — | — | — | — |
| MLB | — | — | — | — | — | — | — | — | — | — | — | — | — |

| 2010 Level | AB | R | H | 2B | 3B | HR | RBI | SB | BA | OBP | SLG | BB% | CT% |
|---|---|---|---|---|---|---|---|---|---|---|---|---|---|
| A | — | — | — | — | — | — | — | — | — | — | — | — | — |
| AA | 137 | 21 | 39 | 10 | 0 | 7 | 27 | 1 | .285 | .387 | .511 | 13% | 81% |
| AAA | 175 | 30 | 50 | 17 | 1 | 6 | 20 | 2 | .286 | .392 | .497 | 13% | 75% |
| MLB | — | — | — | — | — | — | — | — | — | — | — | — | — |

| Rank | Comment | ETA |
|---|---|---|
| #60 | Patience at the plate and raw power have always been Weglarz's calling cards. The rest of his game (notably free-swingingness) hurts his stock. (Hagen) | ETA: Mid-2012 |
| #47 | Weglarz had a nice bounce-back season. His skills are decidedly "old player" – i.e., power and a good eye at the plate. He reached Triple-A at 22. (Hulet) | ETA: Late 2011 |
| #65 | Weglarz hits for power and exhibits OK contact skills and a good eye. He is limited to the corner outfield positions, but his bat should play there. (Lockard) | ETA: mid-2011 |

# Pitchers

| | SP | RP | Tot |
|---|---|---|---|
| AL | 22 | 5 | 27 |
| NL | 24 | 0 | 24 |

## SP Stetson Allie — Pittsburgh | NL

RH | 20 yrs, 0 mo — Drafted 2010, 2nd round

Last year's rankings: — | — | — — Latest league: N/A

| MLB Forecast 2011 | W | L | Sv | IP | H | K | ERA | WHIP | K/9 | BB/9 | HR/9 |
|---|---|---|---|---|---|---|---|---|---|---|---|
| | — | — | — | — | — | — | — | — | — | — | — |

| 2008 Level | W | L | Sv | IP | H | K | ERA | WHIP | K/9 | BB/9 | HR/9 |
|---|---|---|---|---|---|---|---|---|---|---|---|
| A | — | — | — | — | — | — | — | — | — | — | — |
| AA | — | — | — | — | — | — | — | — | — | — | — |
| AAA | — | — | — | — | — | — | — | — | — | — | — |
| MLB | — | — | — | — | — | — | — | — | — | — | — |

| 2009 Level | W | L | Sv | IP | H | K | ERA | WHIP | K/9 | BB/9 | HR/9 |
|---|---|---|---|---|---|---|---|---|---|---|---|
| A | — | — | — | — | — | — | — | — | — | — | — |
| AA | — | — | — | — | — | — | — | — | — | — | — |
| AAA | — | — | — | — | — | — | — | — | — | — | — |
| MLB | — | — | — | — | — | — | — | — | — | — | — |

| 2010 Level | W | L | Sv | IP | H | K | ERA | WHIP | K/9 | BB/9 | HR/9 |
|---|---|---|---|---|---|---|---|---|---|---|---|
| A | — | — | — | — | — | — | — | — | — | — | — |
| AA | — | — | — | — | — | — | — | — | — | — | — |
| AAA | — | — | — | — | — | — | — | — | — | — | — |
| MLB | — | — | — | — | — | — | — | — | — | — | — |

| Rank | Comment | ETA |
|---|---|---|
| #45 | Allie brings tremendous velocity to the mound, but little else. The upside is unquestioned, but he has an awful lot to learn about pitching. (Hagen) | ETA: Early 2014 |
| #31 | One of the top prep arms in the 2010 draft, Allie was bought away from college. By 2015, Allie could form a dangerous duo with Jameson Taillon. (Hulet) | ETA: Late 2014 |
| #32 | Allie was one of the hardest throwers in the draft. He has the build of a starter, but his secondary pitches need work – he could end up in relief. (Lockard) | ETA: Early 2013 |

## SP Chris Archer — Chicago | NL

RH | 22 yrs, 6 mo — Drafted 2006, 5th round

Last year's rankings: — | — | — — Latest league: Southern

| MLB Forecast 2011 | W | L | Sv | IP | H | K | ERA | WHIP | K/9 | BB/9 | HR/9 |
|---|---|---|---|---|---|---|---|---|---|---|---|
| | — | — | — | — | — | — | — | — | — | — | — |

| 2008 Level | W | L | Sv | IP | H | K | ERA | WHIP | K/9 | BB/9 | HR/9 |
|---|---|---|---|---|---|---|---|---|---|---|---|
| A | 4 | 8 | 0 | 115.1 | 92 | 106 | 4.29 | 1.53 | 8.3 | 6.6 | 0.6 |
| AA | — | — | — | — | — | — | — | — | — | — | — |
| AAA | — | — | — | — | — | — | — | — | — | — | — |
| MLB | — | — | — | — | — | — | — | — | — | — | — |

| 2009 Level | W | L | Sv | IP | H | K | ERA | WHIP | K/9 | BB/9 | HR/9 |
|---|---|---|---|---|---|---|---|---|---|---|---|
| A | 6 | 4 | 0 | 109.0 | 78 | 119 | 2.81 | 1.32 | 9.8 | 5.4 | 0.0 |
| AA | — | — | — | — | — | — | — | — | — | — | — |
| AAA | — | — | — | — | — | — | — | — | — | — | — |
| MLB | — | — | — | — | — | — | — | — | — | — | — |

| 2010 Level | W | L | Sv | IP | H | K | ERA | WHIP | K/9 | BB/9 | HR/9 |
|---|---|---|---|---|---|---|---|---|---|---|---|
| A | 7 | 1 | 0 | 72.1 | 54 | 82 | 2.86 | 1.11 | 10.2 | 3.2 | 0.5 |
| AA | 8 | 2 | 0 | 70.0 | 48 | 67 | 1.80 | 1.24 | 8.6 | 5.0 | 0.3 |
| AAA | — | — | — | — | — | — | — | — | — | — | — |
| MLB | — | — | — | — | — | — | — | — | — | — | — |

| Rank | Comment | ETA |
|---|---|---|
| #40 | Archer's velocity and command continue to improve, but he is currently lacking the "out" pitch necessary to take his game to the next level. (Hagen) | ETA: Mid-2012 |
| #43 | Archer took a big step forward, though his control struggles resumed after a promotion to Double-A. He has good strikeout and ground-ball rates. (Hulet) | ETA: Mid-2012 |
| #41 | Archer can be wild, but he has above-average stuff and a fearless approach. If he doesn't take to starting, he would be a good fit in the bullpen. (Lockard) | ETA: Late 2011 |

## SP Manuel Banuelos — New York | AL

LH | 20 yrs, 0 mo — Signed as non-drafted free agent, 2008

Last year's rankings: #31 | #43 | #29 — Latest league: Eastern

| MLB Forecast 2011 | W | L | Sv | IP | H | K | ERA | WHIP | K/9 | BB/9 | HR/9 |
|---|---|---|---|---|---|---|---|---|---|---|---|
| | — | — | — | — | — | — | — | — | — | — | — |

| 2008 Level | W | L | Sv | IP | H | K | ERA | WHIP | K/9 | BB/9 | HR/9 |
|---|---|---|---|---|---|---|---|---|---|---|---|
| A | — | — | — | — | — | — | — | — | — | — | — |
| AA | — | — | — | — | — | — | — | — | — | — | — |
| AAA | — | — | — | — | — | — | — | — | — | — | — |
| MLB | — | — | — | — | — | — | — | — | — | — | — |

| 2009 Level | W | L | Sv | IP | H | K | ERA | WHIP | K/9 | BB/9 | HR/9 |
|---|---|---|---|---|---|---|---|---|---|---|---|
| A | 9 | 5 | 0 | 109.0 | 88 | 106 | 2.64 | 1.06 | 8.8 | 2.3 | 0.3 |
| AA | — | — | — | — | — | — | — | — | — | — | — |
| AAA | — | — | — | — | — | — | — | — | — | — | — |
| MLB | — | — | — | — | — | — | — | — | — | — | — |

| 2010 Level | W | L | Sv | IP | H | K | ERA | WHIP | K/9 | BB/9 | HR/9 |
|---|---|---|---|---|---|---|---|---|---|---|---|
| A | 0 | 3 | 0 | 44.1 | 38 | 62 | 2.23 | 1.17 | 12.6 | 2.8 | 0.2 |
| AA | 0 | 1 | 0 | 15.1 | 15 | 17 | 3.52 | 1.50 | 10.0 | 4.7 | 1.2 |
| AAA | — | — | — | — | — | — | — | — | — | — | — |
| MLB | — | — | — | — | — | — | — | — | — | — | — |

| Rank | Comment | ETA |
|---|---|---|
| #28 | Banuelos placed his poise and command on display in the second half of 2010. He already has excellent mastery of a plus three-pitch arsenal. (Hagen) | ETA: Early 2013 |
| #46 | Banuelos reached Double-A as a teen while exhibiting solid strikeout and ground-ball rates. But durability is a concern after he made only 15 starts. (Hulet) | ETA: Mid-2012 |
| #3 | Only 19, Banuelos already has three plus pitches, the best a change-up. He added 2 MPH to his fastball and now regularly sits in the mid-90's. (Lockard) | ETA: Mid-2012 |

## SP Nick Barnese — Tampa Bay | AL
RH | 22 yrs, 3 mo — Drafted 2007, 3rd round

Last year's rankings: — — —
Latest league: Florida State

**MLB Forecast 2011**

| W | L | Sv | IP | H | K | ERA | WHIP | K/9 | BB/9 | HR/9 |
|---|---|----|----|---|---|-----|------|-----|------|------|
| — | — | — | — | — | — | — | — | — | — | — |

| Level | 2008 W | L | Sv | IP | H | K | ERA | WHIP | K/9 | BB/9 | HR/9 | 2009 W | L | Sv | IP | H | K | ERA | WHIP | K/9 | BB/9 | HR/9 | 2010 W | L | Sv | IP | H | K | ERA | WHIP | K/9 | BB/9 | HR/9 |
|---|---|---|---|---|---|---|---|---|---|---|---|---|---|---|---|---|---|---|---|---|---|---|---|---|---|---|---|---|---|---|---|---|---|
| A | 5 | 3 | 0 | 66.0 | 52 | 84 | 2.45 | 1.15 | 11.5 | 3.3 | 0.1 | 6 | 5 | 0 | 74.2 | 56 | 62 | 2.53 | 1.09 | 7.5 | 3.0 | 0.4 | 8 | 4 | 0 | 122.1 | 114 | 100 | 3.02 | 1.14 | 7.4 | 1.9 | 0.4 |
| AA | — | — | — | — | — | — | — | — | — | — | — | — | — | — | — | — | — | — | — | — | — | — | — | — | — | — | — | — | — | — | — | — | — |
| AAA | — | — | — | — | — | — | — | — | — | — | — | — | — | — | — | — | — | — | — | — | — | — | — | — | — | — | — | — | — | — | — | — | — |
| MLB | — | — | — | — | — | — | — | — | — | — | — | — | — | — | — | — | — | — | — | — | — | — | — | — | — | — | — | — | — | — | — | — | — |

#34 Barnese is getting by with impressive command of his lively fastball. To survive, he'll need to develop his secondary stuff, as Double-A is up next. (Hagen) — **ETA: Late 2012**
#36 Although not as talked about as other arms in Tampa's system, Barnese shows solid control for his age as well as an impressive ground-ball rate. (Hulet) — **ETA: Late 2012**
#49 Injuries have hurt Barnese throughout his career, and he ended 2010 on the DL. His upside is Trevor Cahill, though Barnese misses fewer bats. (Lockard) — **ETA: Early 2013**

## SP Brandon Beachy — Atlanta | NL
RH | 24 yrs, 6 mo — Signed as non-drafted free agent, 2008

Last year's rankings: — — —
Latest league: International

**MLB Forecast 2011**

| W | L | Sv | IP | H | K | ERA | WHIP | K/9 | BB/9 | HR/9 |
|---|---|----|----|---|---|-----|------|-----|------|------|
| 4 | 9 | 0 | 100.0 | 120 | 98 | 4.41 | 1.61 | 8.9 | 3.6 | 0.6 |

| Level | 2008 W | L | Sv | IP | H | K | ERA | WHIP | K/9 | BB/9 | HR/9 | 2009 W | L | Sv | IP | H | K | ERA | WHIP | K/9 | BB/9 | HR/9 | 2010 W | L | Sv | IP | H | K | ERA | WHIP | K/9 | BB/9 | HR/9 |
|---|---|---|---|---|---|---|---|---|---|---|---|---|---|---|---|---|---|---|---|---|---|---|---|---|---|---|---|---|---|---|---|---|---|
| A | — | — | — | — | — | — | — | — | — | — | — | 4 | 3 | 1 | 76.2 | 80 | 64 | 3.87 | 1.29 | 7.5 | 2.2 | 0.2 | — | — | — | — | — | — | — | — | — | — | — |
| AA | — | — | — | — | — | — | — | — | — | — | — | — | — | — | — | — | — | — | — | — | — | — | 3 | 1 | 1 | 73.2 | 53 | 100 | 1.47 | 1.02 | 12.2 | 2.7 | 0.4 |
| AAA | — | — | — | — | — | — | — | — | — | — | — | — | — | — | — | — | — | — | — | — | — | — | 2 | 0 | 0 | 45.2 | 40 | 48 | 2.17 | 1.01 | 9.5 | 1.2 | 0.4 |
| MLB | — | — | — | — | — | — | — | — | — | — | — | — | — | — | — | — | — | — | — | — | — | — | 0 | 2 | 0 | 15.0 | 16 | 15 | 3.00 | 1.53 | 9.0 | 4.2 | 0.0 |

#50 Beachy is a hard worker who sports solid command of merely average stuff. His mechanics and stamina are not what you look for in a starter. (Hagen) — **ETA: Mid-2011**
#40 Don't get carried away after Beachy's excellent 2010 season. He succeeds thanks to solid control, but his overall repertoire is fairly pedestrian. (Hulet) — **ETA: Mid-2011**
#40 Rising from "undrafted" to the majors, Beachy has excellent command of three pitches and decent velocity. He projects as a #3 or #4 starter. (Lockard) — **ETA: Early 2011**

## SP Dellin Betances — New York | AL
RH | 23 yrs, 0 mo — Drafted 2006, 8th round

Last year's rankings: — — —
Latest league: Eastern

**MLB Forecast 2011**

| W | L | Sv | IP | H | K | ERA | WHIP | K/9 | BB/9 | HR/9 |
|---|---|----|----|---|---|-----|------|-----|------|------|
| — | — | — | — | — | — | — | — | — | — | — |

| Level | 2008 W | L | Sv | IP | H | K | ERA | WHIP | K/9 | BB/9 | HR/9 | 2009 W | L | Sv | IP | H | K | ERA | WHIP | K/9 | BB/9 | HR/9 | 2010 W | L | Sv | IP | H | K | ERA | WHIP | K/9 | BB/9 | HR/9 |
|---|---|---|---|---|---|---|---|---|---|---|---|---|---|---|---|---|---|---|---|---|---|---|---|---|---|---|---|---|---|---|---|---|---|
| A | 9 | 4 | 0 | 115.1 | 87 | 135 | 3.67 | 1.27 | 10.5 | 4.6 | 0.7 | 2 | 5 | 0 | 44.1 | 48 | 44 | 5.48 | 1.69 | 8.9 | 5.5 | 0.4 | 8 | 1 | 0 | 71.0 | 43 | 88 | 1.77 | 0.87 | 11.2 | 2.4 | 0.1 |
| AA | — | — | — | — | — | — | — | — | — | — | — | — | — | — | — | — | — | — | — | — | — | — | 0 | 0 | 0 | 14.1 | 10 | 20 | 3.77 | 0.91 | 12.6 | 1.9 | 1.9 |
| AAA | — | — | — | — | — | — | — | — | — | — | — | — | — | — | — | — | — | — | — | — | — | — | — | — | — | — | — | — | — | — | — | — | — |
| MLB | — | — | — | — | — | — | — | — | — | — | — | — | — | — | — | — | — | — | — | — | — | — | — | — | — | — | — | — | — | — | — | — | — |

#36 If elbow surgery is truly behind him, Betances could become an elite prospect. I want to see the restrictions lifted and his stamina tested. (Hagen) — **ETA: Late 2012**
#23 Betances had a monster season, but durability is a concern – he has reached 100 IP in a season just once. He might pan out as a reliever. (Hulet) — **ETA: Late 2011**
#12 Recovered from elbow surgery, Betances is armed with a mid-90's fastball and a good curve. His ceiling is "ace," but he needs one more pitch. (Lockard) — **ETA: Mid-2012**

## SP Zach Britton — Baltimore | AL
LH | 23 yrs, 3 mo — Drafted 2006, 3rd round

Last year's rankings: — — —
Latest league: International

**MLB Forecast 2011**

| W | L | Sv | IP | H | K | ERA | WHIP | K/9 | BB/9 | HR/9 |
|---|---|----|----|---|---|-----|------|-----|------|------|
| 5 | 7 | 0 | 100.0 | 113 | 59 | 4.83 | 1.59 | 5.3 | 4.0 | 1.0 |

| Level | 2008 W | L | Sv | IP | H | K | ERA | WHIP | K/9 | BB/9 | HR/9 | 2009 W | L | Sv | IP | H | K | ERA | WHIP | K/9 | BB/9 | HR/9 | 2010 W | L | Sv | IP | H | K | ERA | WHIP | K/9 | BB/9 | HR/9 |
|---|---|---|---|---|---|---|---|---|---|---|---|---|---|---|---|---|---|---|---|---|---|---|---|---|---|---|---|---|---|---|---|---|---|
| A | 12 | 7 | 0 | 147.1 | 118 | 114 | 3.12 | 1.13 | 7.0 | 3.0 | 0.5 | 9 | 6 | 0 | 140.0 | 123 | 131 | 2.70 | 1.27 | 8.4 | 3.5 | 0.4 | — | — | — | — | — | — | — | — | — | — | — |
| AA | — | — | — | — | — | — | — | — | — | — | — | — | — | — | — | — | — | — | — | — | — | — | 7 | 3 | 0 | 87.0 | 76 | 68 | 2.48 | 1.20 | 7.0 | 2.9 | 0.4 |
| AAA | — | — | — | — | — | — | — | — | — | — | — | — | — | — | — | — | — | — | — | — | — | — | 3 | 4 | 0 | 66.1 | 63 | 56 | 2.98 | 1.30 | 7.6 | 3.1 | 0.4 |
| MLB | — | — | — | — | — | — | — | — | — | — | — | — | — | — | — | — | — | — | — | — | — | — | — | — | — | — | — | — | — | — | — | — | — |

#39 Britton lacks a high ceiling, but he gets results wherever he goes. He's a ground-ball machine staring at a future in the middle of a rotation. (Hagen) — **ETA: Late 2011**
#10 One of the most underrated young arms, Britton is a LH with great sink on his fastball. Look for him to be as good as (or better than) Brian Matusz. (Hulet) — **ETA: Mid-2011**
#29 Worms hunker down when Britton is on the hill – there are few more extreme ground-ball pitchers. He should be well-suited for Camden. (Lockard) — **ETA: Mid-2011**

## SP Simon Castro — San Diego | NL
RH | 22 yrs, 11 mo — Signed as international free agent, 2006

Last year's rankings: #37 #24 #20
Latest league: Pacific Coast

**MLB Forecast 2011**

| W | L | Sv | IP | H | K | ERA | WHIP | K/9 | BB/9 | HR/9 |
|---|---|----|----|---|---|-----|------|-----|------|------|
| 2 | 3 | 0 | 40.0 | 38 | 24 | 4.77 | 1.49 | 6.1 | 3.9 | 1.1 |

| Level | 2008 W | L | Sv | IP | H | K | ERA | WHIP | K/9 | BB/9 | HR/9 | 2009 W | L | Sv | IP | H | K | ERA | WHIP | K/9 | BB/9 | HR/9 | 2010 W | L | Sv | IP | H | K | ERA | WHIP | K/9 | BB/9 | HR/9 |
|---|---|---|---|---|---|---|---|---|---|---|---|---|---|---|---|---|---|---|---|---|---|---|---|---|---|---|---|---|---|---|---|---|---|
| A | 2 | 3 | 0 | 65.1 | 54 | 64 | 3.99 | 1.27 | 8.8 | 4.0 | 0.4 | 10 | 6 | 0 | 140.1 | 118 | 157 | 3.33 | 1.11 | 10.1 | 2.4 | 0.6 | — | — | — | — | — | — | — | — | — | — | — |
| AA | — | — | — | — | — | — | — | — | — | — | — | — | — | — | — | — | — | — | — | — | — | — | 7 | 6 | 0 | 129.2 | 107 | 107 | 2.92 | 1.10 | 7.4 | 2.5 | 0.6 |
| AAA | — | — | — | — | — | — | — | — | — | — | — | — | — | — | — | — | — | — | — | — | — | — | 0 | 1 | 0 | 10.1 | 16 | 6 | 7.84 | 2.13 | 5.2 | 5.2 | 0.9 |
| MLB | — | — | — | — | — | — | — | — | — | — | — | — | — | — | — | — | — | — | — | — | — | — | — | — | — | — | — | — | — | — | — | — | — |

#20 Castro has more work to do, but he continues to improve every year. His excellent fastball/slider combo should carry him to success. (Hagen) — **ETA: Late 2011**
#32 Perhaps the biggest arm in the Padres system, Castro could have a lot of success at Petco. His secondary pitches need work to stick as a starter. (Hulet) — **ETA: Mid-2011**
#16 Castro's strikeouts were down, but the reports on his stuff remained positive. He has three solid pitches and could soon be following Mat Latos. (Lockard) — **ETA: Mid-2011**

## SP Aroldis Chapman — Cincinnati | NL
LH | 23 yrs, 1 mo — Signed as international free agent, 2010

Last year's rankings: — — —
Latest league: International

**MLB Forecast 2011**

| W | L | Sv | IP | H | K | ERA | WHIP | K/9 | BB/9 | HR/9 |
|---|---|----|----|---|---|-----|------|-----|------|------|
| 6 | 8 | 4 | 100.0 | 83 | 94 | 4.54 | 1.36 | 8.6 | 4.7 | 1.1 |

| Level | 2008 W | L | Sv | IP | H | K | ERA | WHIP | K/9 | BB/9 | HR/9 | 2009 W | L | Sv | IP | H | K | ERA | WHIP | K/9 | BB/9 | HR/9 | 2010 W | L | Sv | IP | H | K | ERA | WHIP | K/9 | BB/9 | HR/9 |
|---|---|---|---|---|---|---|---|---|---|---|---|---|---|---|---|---|---|---|---|---|---|---|---|---|---|---|---|---|---|---|---|---|---|
| A | — | — | — | — | — | — | — | — | — | — | — | — | — | — | — | — | — | — | — | — | — | — | — | — | — | — | — | — | — | — | — | — | — |
| AA | — | — | — | — | — | — | — | — | — | — | — | — | — | — | — | — | — | — | — | — | — | — | — | — | — | — | — | — | — | — | — | — | — |
| AAA | — | — | — | — | — | — | — | — | — | — | — | — | — | — | — | — | — | — | — | — | — | — | 9 | 6 | 8 | 95.2 | 77 | 125 | 3.57 | 1.35 | 11.8 | 4.9 | 0.7 |
| MLB | — | — | — | — | — | — | — | — | — | — | — | — | — | — | — | — | — | — | — | — | — | — | 2 | 2 | 0 | 13.1 | 9 | 19 | 2.03 | 1.05 | 12.8 | 3.4 | 0.0 |

#14 It'll be tempting for the Reds to leave Chapman in the bullpen where his velocity could make him a star. His upside as a starter is still a mystery. (Hagen) — **ETA: Early 2011**
#9 Chapman needs a bit more seasoning to become an impact MLB'er. It would be wise for Cincy to settle on a role for him, preferably as a starter. (Hulet) — **ETA: Mid-2011**
#1 No doubt, Chapman can be a dominant force next season out of the bullpen, but it would be a waste of his talents to limit him to 60 innings. (Lockard) — **ETA: Early 2011**

## SP Brody Colvin — Philadelphia | NL
RH | 22 yrs, 7 mo — Drafted 2009, 7th round

Last year's rankings: — — —
Latest league: South Atlantic

**MLB Forecast 2011**

| W | L | Sv | IP | H | K | ERA | WHIP | K/9 | BB/9 | HR/9 |
|---|---|----|----|---|---|-----|------|-----|------|------|
| — | — | — | — | — | — | — | — | — | — | — |

| Level | 2008 W | L | Sv | IP | H | K | ERA | WHIP | K/9 | BB/9 | HR/9 | 2009 W | L | Sv | IP | H | K | ERA | WHIP | K/9 | BB/9 | HR/9 | 2010 W | L | Sv | IP | H | K | ERA | WHIP | K/9 | BB/9 | HR/9 |
|---|---|---|---|---|---|---|---|---|---|---|---|---|---|---|---|---|---|---|---|---|---|---|---|---|---|---|---|---|---|---|---|---|---|
| A | — | — | — | — | — | — | — | — | — | — | — | — | — | — | — | — | — | — | — | — | — | — | 6 | 8 | 0 | 138.0 | 138 | 120 | 3.39 | 1.30 | 7.8 | 2.7 | 0.5 |
| AA | — | — | — | — | — | — | — | — | — | — | — | — | — | — | — | — | — | — | — | — | — | — | — | — | — | — | — | — | — | — | — | — | — |
| AAA | — | — | — | — | — | — | — | — | — | — | — | — | — | — | — | — | — | — | — | — | — | — | — | — | — | — | — | — | — | — | — | — | — |
| MLB | — | — | — | — | — | — | — | — | — | — | — | — | — | — | — | — | — | — | — | — | — | — | — | — | — | — | — | — | — | — | — | — | — |

#42 Colvin has above-average velocity along with a developing change-up and slider. He needs polish across the board, but the talent is apparent. (Hagen) — **ETA: Mid-2013**
#18 Philly worked Colvin hard in 2010 as he threw a lot of innings. Despite that, he posted a better ERA after the Break and had heightened control. (Hulet) — **ETA: Mid-2014**
#48 A few mechanical adjustments allowed Colvin to overcome a rough April. He exhibited excellent command and ground-ball tendencies. (Lockard) — **ETA: Mid-2013**

## SP Jarred Cosart — Philadelphia | NL
RH | 20 yrs, 10 mo — Drafted 2008, 38th round

Last year's rankings: — — —
Latest league: South Atlantic

**MLB Forecast 2011**

| W | L | Sv | IP | H | K | ERA | WHIP | K/9 | BB/9 | HR/9 |
|---|---|----|----|---|---|-----|------|-----|------|------|
| — | — | — | — | — | — | — | — | — | — | — |

| Level | 2008 W | L | Sv | IP | H | K | ERA | WHIP | K/9 | BB/9 | HR/9 | 2009 W | L | Sv | IP | H | K | ERA | WHIP | K/9 | BB/9 | HR/9 | 2010 W | L | Sv | IP | H | K | ERA | WHIP | K/9 | BB/9 | HR/9 |
|---|---|---|---|---|---|---|---|---|---|---|---|---|---|---|---|---|---|---|---|---|---|---|---|---|---|---|---|---|---|---|---|---|---|
| A | — | — | — | — | — | — | — | — | — | — | — | — | — | — | — | — | — | — | — | — | — | — | 7 | 3 | 0 | 71.1 | 60 | 77 | 3.79 | 1.07 | 9.7 | 2.0 | 0.4 |
| AA | — | — | — | — | — | — | — | — | — | — | — | — | — | — | — | — | — | — | — | — | — | — | — | — | — | — | — | — | — | — | — | — | — |
| AAA | — | — | — | — | — | — | — | — | — | — | — | — | — | — | — | — | — | — | — | — | — | — | — | — | — | — | — | — | — | — | — | — | — |
| MLB | — | — | — | — | — | — | — | — | — | — | — | — | — | — | — | — | — | — | — | — | — | — | — | — | — | — | — | — | — | — | — | — | — |

#37 For his age, the athletic Cosart has a plus fastball and sharp command. However, his mechanics need help, and his secondary offerings are raw. (Hagen) — **ETA: Late 2013**
#15 Cosart hurt his elbow in June and missed the remainder of the year, but he's expected to be back in 2011. Keep an eye on him – he could surprise. (Hulet) — **ETA: Mid-2014**
#50 Cosart's season ended with a sore elbow. He has battled injuries throughout his career, and he simply might not be durable enough to start. (Lockard) — **ETA: Mid-2013**

## SP Randall Delgado — Atlanta | NL

RH | 21 yrs, 1 mo — Signed as non-drafted free agent, 2006

Last year's rankings: — | — | — Latest league: Southern

| MLB Forecast 2011 | W | L | Sv | IP | H | K | ERA | WHIP | K/9 | BB/9 | HR/9 |
|---|---|---|---|---|---|---|---|---|---|---|---|
| | — | — | — | — | — | — | — | — | — | — | — |

| | 2008 | | | | | | | | | | | 2009 | | | | | | | | | | | 2010 | | | | | | | | | | |
|---|---|---|---|---|---|---|---|---|---|---|---|---|---|---|---|---|---|---|---|---|---|---|---|---|---|---|---|---|---|---|---|---|---|
| Level | W | L | Sv | IP | H | K | ERA | WHIP | K/9 | BB/9 | HR/9 | W | L | Sv | IP | H | K | ERA | WHIP | K/9 | BB/9 | HR/9 | W | L | Sv | IP | H | K | ERA | WHIP | K/9 | BB/9 | HR/9 |
| A | — | — | — | — | — | — | — | — | — | — | — | 5 | 10 | 0 | 124.0 | 123 | 141 | 4.35 | 1.39 | 10.2 | 3.6 | 0.7 | 4 | 7 | 0 | 117.1 | 89 | 120 | 2.76 | 1.03 | 9.2 | 2.5 | 0.5 |
| AA | — | — | — | — | — | — | — | — | — | — | — | — | — | — | — | — | — | — | — | — | — | — | 3 | 5 | 0 | 43.2 | 36 | 42 | 4.74 | 1.28 | 8.7 | 4.1 | 0.4 |
| AAA | — | — | — | — | — | — | — | — | — | — | — | — | — | — | — | — | — | — | — | — | — | — | — | — | — | — | — | — | — | — | — | — | — |
| MLB | — | — | — | — | — | — | — | — | — | — | — | — | — | — | — | — | — | — | — | — | — | — | — | — | — | — | — | — | — | — | — | — | — |

| | | |
|---|---|---|
| #25 | Improved command and movement of Delgado's fastball carried him in 2010. Now, improved secondary stuff is needed to reach the next level. (Hagen) | ETA: Late 2012 |
| #13 | For a flame-thrower, Delgado does a better job of keeping the ball down than do most of his kind. He has room to add bulk/muscle to his frame. (Hulet) | ETA: Mid-2012 |
| #13 | Delgado has a plus sinking fastball, and he has sharpened his secondary pitches. He is comparable to Derek Lowe, but with greater velocity. (Lockard) | ETA: Early 2013 |

## SP Kyle Drabek — Toronto | AL

RH | 23 yrs, 3 mo — Drafted 2006, #18 overall

Last year's rankings: #27 | #6 | #9 Latest league: Eastern

| MLB Forecast 2011 | W | L | Sv | IP | H | K | ERA | WHIP | K/9 | BB/9 | HR/9 |
|---|---|---|---|---|---|---|---|---|---|---|---|
| | 3 | 6 | 0 | 80.0 | 86 | 66 | 5.08 | 1.58 | 8.3 | 3.5 | 1.3 |

| | 2008 | | | | | | | | | | | 2009 | | | | | | | | | | | 2010 | | | | | | | | | | |
|---|---|---|---|---|---|---|---|---|---|---|---|---|---|---|---|---|---|---|---|---|---|---|---|---|---|---|---|---|---|---|---|---|---|
| Level | W | L | Sv | IP | H | K | ERA | WHIP | K/9 | BB/9 | HR/9 | W | L | Sv | IP | H | K | ERA | WHIP | K/9 | BB/9 | HR/9 | W | L | Sv | IP | H | K | ERA | WHIP | K/9 | BB/9 | HR/9 |
| A | 1 | 2 | 0 | 20.1 | 11 | 10 | 2.21 | 0.84 | 4.4 | 2.7 | 0.4 | 4 | 1 | 0 | 61.2 | 49 | 74 | 2.48 | 1.10 | 10.8 | 2.8 | 0.0 | — | — | — | — | — | — | — | — | — | — | — |
| AA | — | — | — | — | — | — | — | — | — | — | — | 8 | 2 | 0 | 96.1 | 92 | 76 | 3.64 | 1.28 | 7.1 | 2.9 | 0.8 | 14 | 9 | 0 | 162.0 | 126 | 132 | 2.94 | 1.20 | 7.3 | 3.8 | 0.7 |
| AAA | — | — | — | — | — | — | — | — | — | — | — | — | — | — | — | — | — | — | — | — | — | — | — | — | — | — | — | — | — | — | — | — | — |
| MLB | — | — | — | — | — | — | — | — | — | — | — | — | — | — | — | — | — | — | — | — | — | — | 0 | 3 | 0 | 17.0 | 18 | 12 | 4.76 | 1.35 | 6.4 | 2.6 | 1.1 |

| | | |
|---|---|---|
| #24 | Drabek flaunts a fastball/curveball combo that will certainly generate strikeouts in the majors. But his command will never be better than average. (Hagen) | ETA: Mid-2011 |
| #14 | Drabek had a solid season in Double-A, but his brief stint in MLB showed that he has work to do on his command and secondary pitches. (Hulet) | ETA: Late 2011 |
| #36 | Drabek has a classic power-starter's arsenal: hard fastball, spike curveball, and change-up. He has been durable since elbow surgery in 2008. (Lockard) | ETA: Early 2011 |

## SP Danny Duffy — Kansas City | AL

LH | 22 yrs, 3 mo — Drafted 2007, 3rd round

Last year's rankings: #29 | #25 | #31 Latest league: Texas

| MLB Forecast 2011 | W | L | Sv | IP | H | K | ERA | WHIP | K/9 | BB/9 | HR/9 |
|---|---|---|---|---|---|---|---|---|---|---|---|
| | — | — | — | — | — | — | — | — | — | — | — |

| | 2008 | | | | | | | | | | | 2009 | | | | | | | | | | | 2010 | | | | | | | | | | |
|---|---|---|---|---|---|---|---|---|---|---|---|---|---|---|---|---|---|---|---|---|---|---|---|---|---|---|---|---|---|---|---|---|---|
| Level | W | L | Sv | IP | H | K | ERA | WHIP | K/9 | BB/9 | HR/9 | W | L | Sv | IP | H | K | ERA | WHIP | K/9 | BB/9 | HR/9 | W | L | Sv | IP | H | K | ERA | WHIP | K/9 | BB/9 | HR/9 |
| A | 8 | 4 | 0 | 81.2 | 56 | 102 | 2.20 | 0.99 | 11.2 | 2.8 | 0.4 | 9 | 3 | 0 | 126.2 | 108 | 125 | 2.98 | 1.18 | 8.9 | 2.9 | 0.4 | 0 | 0 | 0 | 14.0 | 8 | 18 | 2.57 | 1.07 | 11.6 | 4.5 | 1.3 |
| AA | — | — | — | — | — | — | — | — | — | — | — | — | — | — | — | — | — | — | — | — | — | — | 5 | 2 | 0 | 39.2 | 38 | 41 | 2.95 | 1.19 | 9.3 | 2.0 | 0.7 |
| AAA | — | — | — | — | — | — | — | — | — | — | — | — | — | — | — | — | — | — | — | — | — | — | — | — | — | — | — | — | — | — | — | — | — |
| MLB | — | — | — | — | — | — | — | — | — | — | — | — | — | — | — | — | — | — | — | — | — | — | — | — | — | — | — | — | — | — | — | — | — |

| | | |
|---|---|---|
| #19 | After some uncertainty about his future, Duffy returned at mid-season and excelled with the always-sharp command of his natural movement. (Hagen) | ETA: Late 2011 |
| #42 | After a hiatus from baseball, Duffy came back better than ever and reached Double-A. Expect the lefty to top out as a solid #3 starter for the Royals. (Hulet) | ETA: Late 2011 |
| #17 | Duffy took a leave of absence early in the year, but his game didn't miss a beat on his return. He can change speeds and has good velocity. (Lockard) | ETA: Late 2011 |

## SP Chris Dwyer — Kansas City | AL

LH | 22 yrs, 11 mo — Drafted 2009, 4th round

Last year's rankings: — | — | — Latest league: Texas

| MLB Forecast 2011 | W | L | Sv | IP | H | K | ERA | WHIP | K/9 | BB/9 | HR/9 |
|---|---|---|---|---|---|---|---|---|---|---|---|
| | — | — | — | — | — | — | — | — | — | — | — |

| | 2008 | | | | | | | | | | | 2009 | | | | | | | | | | | 2010 | | | | | | | | | | |
|---|---|---|---|---|---|---|---|---|---|---|---|---|---|---|---|---|---|---|---|---|---|---|---|---|---|---|---|---|---|---|---|---|---|
| Level | W | L | Sv | IP | H | K | ERA | WHIP | K/9 | BB/9 | HR/9 | W | L | Sv | IP | H | K | ERA | WHIP | K/9 | BB/9 | HR/9 | W | L | Sv | IP | H | K | ERA | WHIP | K/9 | BB/9 | HR/9 |
| A | — | — | — | — | — | — | — | — | — | — | — | — | — | — | — | — | — | — | — | — | — | — | 6 | 3 | 0 | 84.1 | 79 | 93 | 2.99 | 1.33 | 9.9 | 3.5 | 0.3 |
| AA | — | — | — | — | — | — | — | — | — | — | — | — | — | — | — | — | — | — | — | — | — | — | 2 | 1 | 0 | 17.2 | 11 | 20 | 3.06 | 1.19 | 10.2 | 5.1 | 1.0 |
| AAA | — | — | — | — | — | — | — | — | — | — | — | — | — | — | — | — | — | — | — | — | — | — | — | — | — | — | — | — | — | — | — | — | — |
| MLB | — | — | — | — | — | — | — | — | — | — | — | — | — | — | — | — | — | — | — | — | — | — | — | — | — | — | — | — | — | — | — | — | — |

| | | |
|---|---|---|
| #43 | Despite demonstrating only ordinary velocity on his fastball, Dwyer has a nice three-pitch repertoire, good command, and easy mechanics. (Hagen) | ETA: Early 2012 |
| #37 | Dwyer impressed in 2010 before he was sidelined by a bad back. He might make a good closer, but he also the upside of a #2 or #3 starter. (Hulet) | ETA: Mid-2012 |
| #30 | Dwyer looked to be on the fast track until a back injury cut short his season. He has three solid pitches, with the curveball as his out-pitch. (Lockard) | ETA: Early 2012 |

## SP Christian Friedrich — Colorado | NL

LH | 23 yrs, 8 mo — Drafted 2008, #25 overall

Last year's rankings: #10 | #11 | #10 Latest league: Texas

| MLB Forecast 2011 | W | L | Sv | IP | H | K | ERA | WHIP | K/9 | BB/9 | HR/9 |
|---|---|---|---|---|---|---|---|---|---|---|---|
| | — | — | — | — | — | — | — | — | — | — | — |

| | 2008 | | | | | | | | | | | 2009 | | | | | | | | | | | 2010 | | | | | | | | | | |
|---|---|---|---|---|---|---|---|---|---|---|---|---|---|---|---|---|---|---|---|---|---|---|---|---|---|---|---|---|---|---|---|---|---|
| Level | W | L | Sv | IP | H | K | ERA | WHIP | K/9 | BB/9 | HR/9 | W | L | Sv | IP | H | K | ERA | WHIP | K/9 | BB/9 | HR/9 | W | L | Sv | IP | H | K | ERA | WHIP | K/9 | BB/9 | HR/9 |
| A | 2 | 2 | 0 | 48.0 | 45 | 65 | 4.31 | 1.25 | 12.2 | 2.8 | 0.8 | 6 | 5 | 0 | 119.2 | 94 | 159 | 2.41 | 1.15 | 12.0 | 3.2 | 0.4 | — | — | — | — | — | — | — | — | — | — | — |
| AA | — | — | — | — | — | — | — | — | — | — | — | — | — | — | — | — | — | — | — | — | — | — | 3 | 6 | 0 | 87.1 | 100 | 78 | 5.05 | 1.55 | 8.0 | 3.6 | 1.0 |
| AAA | — | — | — | — | — | — | — | — | — | — | — | — | — | — | — | — | — | — | — | — | — | — | — | — | — | — | — | — | — | — | — | — | — |
| MLB | — | — | — | — | — | — | — | — | — | — | — | — | — | — | — | — | — | — | — | — | — | — | — | — | — | — | — | — | — | — | — | — | — |

| | | |
|---|---|---|
| #6 | Friedrich did not adjust well to Double-A, owing mostly to a dip in his command. His outstanding repertoire is still present and accounted for. (Hagen) | ETA: Late 2011 |
| #38 | Injuries and inconsistencies marred Friedrich's 2010 season. Despite those hiccups, he has one of the highest upsides in the Rockies system. (Hulet) | ETA: Late 2011 |
| #22 | Friedrich is much too good to put up the kind of numbers he did in '10. He battled some injuries & mechanical issues and should rebound in '11. (Lockard) | ETA: Late 2011 |

## SP Joseph Gardner — Cleveland | AL

RH | 23 yrs, 0 mo — Drafted 2009, 3rd round

Last year's rankings: — | — | — Latest league: Carolina

| MLB Forecast 2011 | W | L | Sv | IP | H | K | ERA | WHIP | K/9 | BB/9 | HR/9 |
|---|---|---|---|---|---|---|---|---|---|---|---|
| | — | — | — | — | — | — | — | — | — | — | — |

| | 2008 | | | | | | | | | | | 2009 | | | | | | | | | | | 2010 | | | | | | | | | | |
|---|---|---|---|---|---|---|---|---|---|---|---|---|---|---|---|---|---|---|---|---|---|---|---|---|---|---|---|---|---|---|---|---|---|
| Level | W | L | Sv | IP | H | K | ERA | WHIP | K/9 | BB/9 | HR/9 | W | L | Sv | IP | H | K | ERA | WHIP | K/9 | BB/9 | HR/9 | W | L | Sv | IP | H | K | ERA | WHIP | K/9 | BB/9 | HR/9 |
| A | — | — | — | — | — | — | — | — | — | — | — | — | — | — | — | — | — | — | — | — | — | — | 13 | 6 | 0 | 147.1 | 102 | 142 | 2.75 | 1.11 | 8.7 | 3.8 | 0.4 |
| AA | — | — | — | — | — | — | — | — | — | — | — | — | — | — | — | — | — | — | — | — | — | — | — | — | — | — | — | — | — | — | — | — | — |
| AAA | — | — | — | — | — | — | — | — | — | — | — | — | — | — | — | — | — | — | — | — | — | — | — | — | — | — | — | — | — | — | — | — | — |
| MLB | — | — | — | — | — | — | — | — | — | — | — | — | — | — | — | — | — | — | — | — | — | — | — | — | — | — | — | — | — | — | — | — | — |

| | | |
|---|---|---|
| #51 | Gardner's control will never be perfect, and his mediocre three-pitch mix might land in the bullpen, but he sure knows how to keep the ball down. (Hagen) | ETA: Early 2013 |
| #24 | An extreme ground-ball pitcher, Gardner profiles similarly to Justin Masterson. Joseph needs to sharpen his control as he moves up the ladder. (Hulet) | ETA: Mid-2013 |
| #47 | Despite being a ground-ball pitcher, Gardner can be wild. He has an unusual three-quarters delivery and a disconcerting mound presence. (Lockard) | ETA: Mid-2012 |

## SP Kyle Gibson — Minnesota | AL

RH | 23 yrs, 5 mo — Drafted 2009, #22 overall

Last year's rankings: — | — | — Latest league: International

| MLB Forecast 2011 | W | L | Sv | IP | H | K | ERA | WHIP | K/9 | BB/9 | HR/9 |
|---|---|---|---|---|---|---|---|---|---|---|---|
| | — | — | — | — | — | — | — | — | — | — | — |

| | 2008 | | | | | | | | | | | 2009 | | | | | | | | | | | 2010 | | | | | | | | | | |
|---|---|---|---|---|---|---|---|---|---|---|---|---|---|---|---|---|---|---|---|---|---|---|---|---|---|---|---|---|---|---|---|---|---|
| Level | W | L | Sv | IP | H | K | ERA | WHIP | K/9 | BB/9 | HR/9 | W | L | Sv | IP | H | K | ERA | WHIP | K/9 | BB/9 | HR/9 | W | L | Sv | IP | H | K | ERA | WHIP | K/9 | BB/9 | HR/9 |
| A | — | — | — | — | — | — | — | — | — | — | — | — | — | — | — | — | — | — | — | — | — | — | 4 | 1 | 0 | 43.1 | 33 | 40 | 1.87 | 1.04 | 8.3 | 2.5 | 0.4 |
| AA | — | — | — | — | — | — | — | — | — | — | — | — | — | — | — | — | — | — | — | — | — | — | 7 | 5 | 0 | 93.0 | 91 | 77 | 3.68 | 1.22 | 7.5 | 2.1 | 0.5 |
| AAA | — | — | — | — | — | — | — | — | — | — | — | — | — | — | — | — | — | — | — | — | — | — | 0 | 0 | 0 | 15.2 | 12 | 9 | 1.72 | 1.09 | 5.2 | 2.9 | 0.0 |
| MLB | — | — | — | — | — | — | — | — | — | — | — | — | — | — | — | — | — | — | — | — | — | — | — | — | — | — | — | — | — | — | — | — | — |

| | | |
|---|---|---|
| #8 | Gibson's health was in question heading into 2010, but he proved to be fit, and he took the opportunity to put his advanced repertoire on display. (Hagen) | ETA: Mid-2011 |
| #3 | Gibson zoomed through the minors in 2010. His K rate dropped at each step, but his control stayed solid throughout. He could be a #2 starter. (Hulet) | ETA: Mid-2011 |
| #31 | Gibson cuts an intimidating figure on the mound. He is fully recovered from a stress fracture in his elbow and looks to be nearly MLB-ready. (Lockard) | ETA: Mid-2011 |

## SP Jeremy Hellickson — Tampa Bay | AL

RH | 23 yrs, 11 mo — Drafted 2005, 4th round

Last year's rankings: #14 | #9 | #14 Latest league: International

| MLB Forecast 2011 | W | L | Sv | IP | H | K | ERA | WHIP | K/9 | BB/9 | HR/9 |
|---|---|---|---|---|---|---|---|---|---|---|---|
| | 9 | 5 | 0 | 120.0 | 125 | 129 | 4.39 | 1.35 | 9.7 | 2.6 | 1.4 |

| | 2008 | | | | | | | | | | | 2009 | | | | | | | | | | | 2010 | | | | | | | | | | |
|---|---|---|---|---|---|---|---|---|---|---|---|---|---|---|---|---|---|---|---|---|---|---|---|---|---|---|---|---|---|---|---|---|---|
| Level | W | L | Sv | IP | H | K | ERA | WHIP | K/9 | BB/9 | HR/9 | W | L | Sv | IP | H | K | ERA | WHIP | K/9 | BB/9 | HR/9 | W | L | Sv | IP | H | K | ERA | WHIP | K/9 | BB/9 | HR/9 |
| A | 7 | 1 | 0 | 76.2 | 64 | 83 | 2.00 | 0.90 | 9.7 | 0.6 | 0.8 | — | — | — | — | — | — | — | — | — | — | — | — | — | — | — | — | — | — | — | — | — | — |
| AA | 4 | 4 | 0 | 75.1 | 84 | 79 | 3.94 | 1.31 | 9.4 | 1.8 | 1.8 | 3 | 1 | 0 | 56.2 | 41 | 62 | 2.38 | 0.97 | 9.8 | 2.2 | 0.6 | — | — | — | — | — | — | — | — | — | — | — |
| AAA | — | — | — | — | — | — | — | — | — | — | — | 6 | 1 | 0 | 57.1 | 31 | 70 | 2.51 | 0.80 | 11.0 | 2.4 | 0.6 | 12 | 3 | 0 | 117.2 | 103 | 123 | 2.45 | 1.17 | 9.4 | 2.7 | 0.4 |
| MLB | — | — | — | — | — | — | — | — | — | — | — | — | — | — | — | — | — | — | — | — | — | — | 4 | 0 | 0 | 36.1 | 32 | 33 | 3.47 | 1.10 | 8.2 | 2.0 | 1.2 |

| | | |
|---|---|---|
| #1 | Hellickson is rare: an elite prospect who doesn't beat you with speed; rather, he comes at hitters with poise and pinpoint control of a plus arsenal. (Hagen) | ETA: Arrived |
| #1 | Hellickson could be a #2 starter with good control. His remaining tasks are to perfect his breaking ball and find a way to get more ground-ball outs. (Hulet) | ETA: Early 2011 |
| #2 | Jeremy spent '10 tuning his already-outstanding palette. He has great movement, good location, and a knack for missing bats. What's to dislike? (Lockard) | ETA: Early 2011 |

## SP Casey Kelly — Boston | AL
RH | 21 yrs, 5 mo — Drafted 2008, #30 overall

Last year's rankings: #18 #7 #15 | Latest league: Eastern | MLB Forecast 2011: — — — — — — — — — — — —

| Year | Level | W | L | Sv | IP | H | K | ERA | WHIP | K/9 | BB/9 | HR/9 |
|---|---|---|---|---|---|---|---|---|---|---|---|---|
| 2009 | AA | 7 | 5 | 0 | 95.0 | 65 | 74 | 2.08 | 0.85 | 7.0 | 1.5 | 0.4 |
| 2010 | AA | 3 | 5 | 0 | 95.0 | 118 | 81 | 5.31 | 1.61 | 7.7 | 3.3 | 0.9 |

#16 Kelly had trouble adjusting to Double-A: His command, mechanics, and poise stayed strong, but he is too reliant on his ordinary fastball. (Hagen) — ETA: Late 2012
#39 Kelly was pushed, and he stumbled, but he is still young. True, his control slipped, but he also suffered from an unfortunately high BABIP. (Hulet) — ETA: Mid-2012
#19 Kelly had a disappointing season that was cut short by a shoulder strain, but many still believe that he can be John Lackey-type starter. (Lockard) — ETA: Late 2012

## SP Jason Knapp — Cleveland | AL
RH | 20 yrs, 7 mo — Drafted 2008, 2nd round

Last year's rankings: #20 #42 #22 | Latest league: Midwest | MLB Forecast 2011: — — — — — — — — — — — —

| Year | Level | W | L | Sv | IP | H | K | ERA | WHIP | K/9 | BB/9 | HR/9 |
|---|---|---|---|---|---|---|---|---|---|---|---|---|
| 2009 | A | 2 | 7 | 0 | 97.0 | 73 | 123 | 4.18 | 1.24 | 11.4 | 4.4 | 0.3 |
| 2010 | A | 1 | 0 | 0 | 16.0 | 12 | 29 | 3.94 | 1.25 | 16.3 | 4.5 | 0.0 |

#32 Cleveland's patience with Knapp's shoulder surgery paid off. Knapp hasn't lost a thing, and he was too much for lower leagues late in the year. (Hagen) — ETA: Late 2012
#47 Whenever he takes to the mound, Knapp dominates. Unfortunately, injuries have been a major issue, and he threw just 28 total innings in 2010. (Hulet) — ETA: Mid-2014
#21 Knapp finally made it back on the mound in July after arm trouble, but he ended the year on the DL after a drop in velocity. A stud when healthy. (Lockard) — ETA: Early 2013

## SP John Lamb — Kansas City | AL
LH | 20 yrs, 8 mo — Drafted 2008, 5th round

Last year's rankings: — — — | Latest league: Texas | MLB Forecast 2011: — — — — — — — — — — — —

| Year | Level | W | L | Sv | IP | H | K | ERA | WHIP | K/9 | BB/9 | HR/9 |
|---|---|---|---|---|---|---|---|---|---|---|---|---|
| 2010 | A | 8 | 6 | 0 | 114.2 | 85 | 133 | 1.49 | 1.02 | 10.4 | 2.5 | 0.2 |
| 2010 | AA | 2 | 1 | 0 | 33.0 | 37 | 26 | 5.45 | 1.52 | 7.1 | 3.5 | 0.5 |

#29 Lamb found the Texas League hard to handle, but overall 2010 was a success. He brings a varied, developing arsenal and sharp command. (Hagen) — ETA: Late 2012
#4 Lamb needs more work in the upper minors, but he remains one of the top pitching prospects. KC has a profusion of interesting young southpaws. (Hulet) — ETA: Mid-2012
#11 Lamb has three major-league-caliber pitches, and he garners high praise for his maturity on the mound. He should be a reliable arm for years. (Lockard) — ETA: Early 2012

## SP Jordan Lyles — Houston | NL
RH | 20 yrs, 5 mo — Drafted 2008, #38 overall

Last year's rankings: #15 #23 #39 | Latest league: Pacific Coast | MLB Forecast 2011: 5 7 0 100.0 113 71 4.69 1.52 6.4 3.5 1.2

| Year | Level | W | L | Sv | IP | H | K | ERA | WHIP | K/9 | BB/9 | HR/9 |
|---|---|---|---|---|---|---|---|---|---|---|---|---|
| 2008 | A | 0 | 0 | 0 | 5.2 | 7 | 4 | 6.35 | 2.47 | 6.4 | 11.1 | 3.2 |
| 2009 | A | 7 | 11 | 0 | 144.2 | 134 | 167 | 3.24 | 1.19 | 10.4 | 2.4 | 0.3 |
| 2010 | AA | 7 | 9 | 0 | 127.0 | 133 | 115 | 3.12 | 1.32 | 8.1 | 2.5 | 0.7 |
| 2010 | AAA | 0 | 3 | 0 | 31.2 | 48 | 22 | 5.40 | 1.86 | 6.3 | 3.1 | 0.6 |

#7 Lyles is a big, athletic kid who has solid command of his often-dominating fastball/change-up combo. His curveball is still a work in progress. (Hagen) — ETA: Mid-2011
#33 Lyles might reach the majors as a 20-year-old, but he ought to receive a little more fine-tuning. He is Houston's brightest hope for the future. (Hulet) — ETA: Mid-2012
#25 Lyles doesn't throw hard, he simply knows how to pitch. It remains to be seen if he can dominate at the highest levels with his repertoire. (Lockard) — ETA: Mid-2011

## SP Ethan Martin — Los Angeles | NL
RH | 21 yrs, 9 mo — Drafted 2008, #15 overall

Last year's rankings: — — — | Latest league: California | MLB Forecast 2011: — — — — — — — — — — — —

| Year | Level | W | L | Sv | IP | H | K | ERA | WHIP | K/9 | BB/9 | HR/9 |
|---|---|---|---|---|---|---|---|---|---|---|---|---|
| 2009 | A | 6 | 8 | 1 | 100.0 | 85 | 120 | 3.87 | 1.46 | 10.8 | 5.5 | 0.4 |
| 2010 | A | 9 | 14 | 0 | 113.1 | 120 | 105 | 6.35 | 1.77 | 8.3 | 6.4 | 0.8 |

#48 Big-league velocity will get you only so far. Martin's command is regressing, and a future in the bullpen looks likely if he does not improve. (Hagen) — ETA: Mid-2013
#50 A 6.35 ERA with a walk rate of 6.4 BB/9 is a bad year no matter how you slice it. However, that ERA was a little unfair, and he's still just 21. (Hulet) — ETA: Mid-2013
#45 Martin can still hit the high 90's, but he was often all over the place. There's still time, but if the wildness continues, he will move to relief. (Lockard) — ETA: Late 2012

## SP Carlos Matias — St. Louis | NL
RH | 19 yrs, 6 mo — Signed as non-drafted free agent, 2010

Last year's rankings: — — — | Latest league: Dominican Sum. | MLB Forecast 2011: — — — — — — — — — — — —

(No statistics listed)

#38 Matias looks to be the best international signing of the year. He sports a ridiculous, well-rounded fastball for his size and outstanding command. (Hagen) — ETA: Mid-2014
#49 Matias is about as distant from the major leagues as you can get, but he dominated the Dominican Summer League, and he has a fine repertoire. (Hulet) — ETA: Mid-2015
#44 Matias will probably make his highly anticipated U.S. debut in 2011. There are murmurs about his real age, but his fastball is reportedly electric. (Lockard) — ETA: Late 2013

## SP Tyler Matzek — Colorado | NL
LH | 20 yrs, 5 mo — Drafted 2009, #11 overall

Last year's rankings: #17 #29 #28 | Latest league: South Atlantic | MLB Forecast 2011: — — — — — — — — — — — —

| Year | Level | W | L | Sv | IP | H | K | ERA | WHIP | K/9 | BB/9 | HR/9 |
|---|---|---|---|---|---|---|---|---|---|---|---|---|
| 2010 | A | 5 | 1 | 0 | 89.1 | 62 | 88 | 2.92 | 1.39 | 8.9 | 6.2 | 0.6 |

#12 Matzek is fearless on the mound, throwing any pitch on any count to any location. The course and placement of his fastball is his best asset. (Hagen) — ETA: Late 2012
#11 Matzek is the most talented arm in the Rockies system, but he struggled with his control in 2010. He still has the ceiling of a #1 or #2 starter. (Hulet) — ETA: Mid-2014
#23 Matzek's rising BB/9 and declining velocity are both concerns, but he did post a strong K rate. His ceiling remains that of a top-line starter. (Lockard) — ETA: Late 2012

## SP Trevor May — Philadelphia | NL
RH | 21 yrs, 6 mo — Drafted 2008, 4th round

Last year's rankings: — — — | Latest league: Florida State | MLB Forecast 2011: — — — — — — — — — — — —

| Year | Level | W | L | Sv | IP | H | K | ERA | WHIP | K/9 | BB/9 | HR/9 |
|---|---|---|---|---|---|---|---|---|---|---|---|---|
| 2009 | A | 4 | 1 | 0 | 77.1 | 58 | 95 | 2.56 | 1.31 | 11.1 | 5.0 | 0.3 |
| 2010 | A | 12 | 8 | 0 | 135.0 | 104 | 182 | 4.00 | 1.37 | 12.1 | 5.4 | 0.7 |

#41 May combines good movement with a plus repertoire, but poor control and a high fly-ball rate will destroy his career if he doesn't wise up. (Hagen) — ETA: Late 2012
#22 May's control deserted him on a promotion to High-A. Despite that, he kept blowing the ball past hitters, and he racked up outstanding K numbers. (Hulet) — ETA: Late 2013
#43 May struggled with his mechanics early in the year, but he finished strong. He has a projectable frame and figures to add velocity as he fills out. (Lockard) — ETA: Early 2013

## RP Jacob McGee — Tampa Bay | AL

LH | 24 yrs, 7 mo — Drafted 2004, 5th round

Last year's rankings: — | — | — — Latest league: International

| MLB Forecast 2011 | W | L | Sv | IP | H | K | ERA | WHIP | K/9 | BB/9 | HR/9 |
|---|---|---|---|---|---|---|---|---|---|---|---|
| | 2 | 3 | 0 | 50.0 | 51 | 53 | 5.15 | 1.67 | 9.6 | 4.7 | 1.2 |

| | 2008 | | | | | | | | | | | 2009 | | | | | | | | | | | 2010 | | | | | | | | | | |
|---|---|---|---|---|---|---|---|---|---|---|---|---|---|---|---|---|---|---|---|---|---|---|---|---|---|---|---|---|---|---|---|---|---|
| Level | W | L | Sv | IP | H | K | ERA | WHIP | K/9 | BB/9 | HR/9 | W | L | Sv | IP | H | K | ERA | WHIP | K/9 | BB/9 | HR/9 | W | L | Sv | IP | H | K | ERA | WHIP | K/9 | BB/9 | HR/9 |
| A | — | — | — | — | — | — | — | — | — | — | — | 0 | 2 | 0 | 22.1 | 26 | 26 | 6.45 | 1.57 | 10.5 | 3.6 | 0.8 | — | — | — | — | — | — | — | — | — | — | — |
| AA | 6 | 4 | 0 | 77.2 | 65 | 65 | 3.94 | 1.31 | 7.5 | 4.3 | 0.7 | — | — | — | — | — | — | — | — | — | — | — | 3 | 7 | 0 | 88.1 | 81 | 100 | 3.57 | 1.29 | 10.2 | 3.4 | 0.3 |
| AAA | — | — | — | — | — | — | — | — | — | — | — | — | — | — | — | — | — | — | — | — | — | — | 1 | 1 | 1 | 17.1 | 9 | 27 | 0.52 | 0.69 | 14.0 | 1.6 | 0.0 |
| MLB | — | — | — | — | — | — | — | — | — | — | — | — | — | — | — | — | — | — | — | — | — | — | 0 | 0 | 0 | 5.0 | 2 | 6 | 1.80 | 1.00 | 10.8 | 5.4 | 0.0 |

| Rank | Comment | ETA |
|---|---|---|
| #21 | McGee showed no ill effects from elbow surgery. His move to the 'pen may be permanent, but he hasn't lost a thing and could regain his status. (Hagen) | ETA: Early 2011 |
| #45 | McGee's long-suspected conversion to reliever began this season, and he looks like a solid closer prospect. His command needs some work. (Hulet) | ETA: Mid-2011 |
| #15 | Fully recovered from Tommy John surgery, McGee finished 2010 as a reliever. A crowded Tampa rotation could keep him there in 2011. (Lockard) | ETA: Early 2011 |

## SP Deck McGuire — Toronto | AL

RH | 21 yrs, 9 mo — Drafted 2010, #11 overall

Last year's rankings: — | — | — — Latest league: N/A

| MLB Forecast 2011 | W | L | Sv | IP | H | K | ERA | WHIP | K/9 | BB/9 | HR/9 |
|---|---|---|---|---|---|---|---|---|---|---|---|
| | — | — | — | — | — | — | — | — | — | — | — |

| | 2008 | | | | | | | | | | | 2009 | | | | | | | | | | | 2010 | | | | | | | | | | |
|---|---|---|---|---|---|---|---|---|---|---|---|---|---|---|---|---|---|---|---|---|---|---|---|---|---|---|---|---|---|---|---|---|---|
| Level | W | L | Sv | IP | H | K | ERA | WHIP | K/9 | BB/9 | HR/9 | W | L | Sv | IP | H | K | ERA | WHIP | K/9 | BB/9 | HR/9 | W | L | Sv | IP | H | K | ERA | WHIP | K/9 | BB/9 | HR/9 |
| A | — | — | — | — | — | — | — | — | — | — | — | — | — | — | — | — | — | — | — | — | — | — | — | — | — | — | — | — | — | — | — | — | — |
| AA | — | — | — | — | — | — | — | — | — | — | — | — | — | — | — | — | — | — | — | — | — | — | — | — | — | — | — | — | — | — | — | — | — |
| AAA | — | — | — | — | — | — | — | — | — | — | — | — | — | — | — | — | — | — | — | — | — | — | — | — | — | — | — | — | — | — | — | — | — |
| MLB | — | — | — | — | — | — | — | — | — | — | — | — | — | — | — | — | — | — | — | — | — | — | — | — | — | — | — | — | — | — | — | — | — |

| Rank | Comment | ETA |
|---|---|---|
| #26 | McGuire is a poised, big-bodied starter who's known for pumping the strike zone with a solid three-pitch mix. That said, his upside is limited. (Hagen) | ETA: Late 2012 |
| #34 | McGuire has yet to throw a pitch in pro ball, but he projects to be durable workhorse with a typical repertoire. He should be a #2 or #3 starter. (Hulet) | ETA: Mid-2013 |
| #39 | McGuire does not have the highest ceiling, but he should reach the big leagues quickly and settle into the third or fourth slot of the rotation. (Lockard) | ETA: Early 2012 |

## SP Jenrry Mejia — New York | NL

RH | 21 yrs, 5 mo — Signed as non-drafted free agent, 2007

Last year's rankings: #13 | #17 | #26 — Latest league: International

| MLB Forecast 2011 | W | L | Sv | IP | H | K | ERA | WHIP | K/9 | BB/9 | HR/9 |
|---|---|---|---|---|---|---|---|---|---|---|---|
| | 3 | 9 | 0 | 120.0 | 133 | 102 | 4.53 | 1.62 | 7.7 | 4.3 | 0.9 |

| | 2008 | | | | | | | | | | | 2009 | | | | | | | | | | | 2010 | | | | | | | | | | |
|---|---|---|---|---|---|---|---|---|---|---|---|---|---|---|---|---|---|---|---|---|---|---|---|---|---|---|---|---|---|---|---|---|---|
| Level | W | L | Sv | IP | H | K | ERA | WHIP | K/9 | BB/9 | HR/9 | W | L | Sv | IP | H | K | ERA | WHIP | K/9 | BB/9 | HR/9 | W | L | Sv | IP | H | K | ERA | WHIP | K/9 | BB/9 | HR/9 |
| A | 3 | 2 | 0 | 56.2 | 42 | 52 | 3.49 | 1.15 | 8.3 | 3.7 | 0.6 | 4 | 1 | 0 | 50.1 | 41 | 44 | 1.97 | 1.13 | 7.9 | 2.9 | 0.0 | 0 | 0 | 0 | 4.0 | 1 | 7 | 0.00 | 0.25 | 15.8 | 0.0 | 0.0 |
| AA | — | — | — | — | — | — | — | — | — | — | — | 0 | 5 | 0 | 44.1 | 44 | 47 | 4.47 | 1.51 | 9.5 | 4.7 | 0.4 | 2 | 0 | 0 | 27.1 | 19 | 26 | 1.32 | 1.21 | 8.6 | 4.6 | 0.0 |
| AAA | — | — | — | — | — | — | — | — | — | — | — | — | — | — | — | — | — | — | — | — | — | — | 0 | 0 | 0 | 8.0 | 5 | 9 | 1.12 | 0.75 | 10.1 | 1.1 | 1.1 |
| MLB | — | — | — | — | — | — | — | — | — | — | — | — | — | — | — | — | — | — | — | — | — | — | 0 | 4 | 0 | 39.0 | 46 | 22 | 4.62 | 1.69 | 5.1 | 4.6 | 0.7 |

| Rank | Comment | ETA |
|---|---|---|
| #13 | The Mets want to see Mejia and his electric fastball in the rotation. However, his mechanics and shaky control may force him back to the bullpen. (Hagen) | ETA: Early 2011 |
| #35 | Mejia was one of the top arms entering 2010, but his development was stunted when the club stuck him in relief. He's back where he belongs now. (Hulet) | ETA: Mid-2011 |
| #27 | Mejia began 2010 in the bullpen, but his future is in the rotation. His control was wobbly in the bigs but he has had good command generally. (Lockard) | ETA: Mid-2011 |

## SP Aaron Miller — Los Angeles | NL

LH | 23 yrs, 6 mo — Drafted 2009, #36 overall

Last year's rankings: — | — | — — Latest league: Southern

| MLB Forecast 2011 | W | L | Sv | IP | H | K | ERA | WHIP | K/9 | BB/9 | HR/9 |
|---|---|---|---|---|---|---|---|---|---|---|---|
| | — | — | — | — | — | — | — | — | — | — | — |

| | 2008 | | | | | | | | | | | 2009 | | | | | | | | | | | 2010 | | | | | | | | | | |
|---|---|---|---|---|---|---|---|---|---|---|---|---|---|---|---|---|---|---|---|---|---|---|---|---|---|---|---|---|---|---|---|---|---|
| Level | W | L | Sv | IP | H | K | ERA | WHIP | K/9 | BB/9 | HR/9 | W | L | Sv | IP | H | K | ERA | WHIP | K/9 | BB/9 | HR/9 | W | L | Sv | IP | H | K | ERA | WHIP | K/9 | BB/9 | HR/9 |
| A | — | — | — | — | — | — | — | — | — | — | — | 3 | 1 | 0 | 30.1 | 22 | 38 | 2.08 | 1.06 | 11.3 | 3.0 | 0.9 | 6 | 4 | 0 | 101.2 | 76 | 99 | 2.92 | 1.22 | 8.8 | 4.2 | 0.5 |
| AA | — | — | — | — | — | — | — | — | — | — | — | — | — | — | — | — | — | — | — | — | — | — | 1 | 4 | 0 | 23.0 | 28 | 22 | 7.04 | 2.00 | 8.6 | 7.0 | 1.2 |
| AAA | — | — | — | — | — | — | — | — | — | — | — | — | — | — | — | — | — | — | — | — | — | — | — | — | — | — | — | — | — | — | — | — | — |
| MLB | — | — | — | — | — | — | — | — | — | — | — | — | — | — | — | — | — | — | — | — | — | — | — | — | — | — | — | — | — | — | — | — | — |

| Rank | Comment | ETA |
|---|---|---|
| #35 | Miller's fastball/slider combo might be one of the best in baseball, but his lack of command is a killer and might consign him to the bullpen. (Hagen) | ETA: Mid-2012 |
| #29 | Miller is one of the few arms in the Dodgers system who didn't take a step back in 2010. The lefty held his own against right-handed hitters. (Hulet) | ETA: Late 2012 |
| #38 | A two-way player in college, Miller is athletic and has good movement on his fastball. He had a hiccup at Double-A, but he'll get another crack. (Lockard) | ETA: Late 2012 |

## SP Shelby Miller — St. Louis | NL

RH | 20 yrs, 5 mo — Drafted 2009, #19 overall

Last year's rankings: #19 | #31 | #30 — Latest league: Midwest

| MLB Forecast 2011 | W | L | Sv | IP | H | K | ERA | WHIP | K/9 | BB/9 | HR/9 |
|---|---|---|---|---|---|---|---|---|---|---|---|
| | — | — | — | — | — | — | — | — | — | — | — |

| | 2008 | | | | | | | | | | | 2009 | | | | | | | | | | | 2010 | | | | | | | | | | |
|---|---|---|---|---|---|---|---|---|---|---|---|---|---|---|---|---|---|---|---|---|---|---|---|---|---|---|---|---|---|---|---|---|---|
| Level | W | L | Sv | IP | H | K | ERA | WHIP | K/9 | BB/9 | HR/9 | W | L | Sv | IP | H | K | ERA | WHIP | K/9 | BB/9 | HR/9 | W | L | Sv | IP | H | K | ERA | WHIP | K/9 | BB/9 | HR/9 |
| A | — | — | — | — | — | — | — | — | — | — | — | 0 | 0 | 0 | 3.0 | 5 | 2 | 6.00 | 2.33 | 6.0 | 6.0 | 0.0 | 7 | 5 | 0 | 104.1 | 97 | 140 | 3.62 | 1.25 | 12.1 | 2.8 | 0.6 |
| AA | — | — | — | — | — | — | — | — | — | — | — | — | — | — | — | — | — | — | — | — | — | — | — | — | — | — | — | — | — | — | — | — | — |
| AAA | — | — | — | — | — | — | — | — | — | — | — | — | — | — | — | — | — | — | — | — | — | — | — | — | — | — | — | — | — | — | — | — | — |
| MLB | — | — | — | — | — | — | — | — | — | — | — | — | — | — | — | — | — | — | — | — | — | — | — | — | — | — | — | — | — | — | — | — | — |

| Rank | Comment | ETA |
|---|---|---|
| #11 | It's hard to find a fault with Miller – his command got better as the year went on, and he has a slick repertoire, complete with a nasty curveball. (Hagen) | ETA: Early 2013 |
| #16 | The teen whiffed a lot of batters in his debut, and he dominated left-handed hitters. Miller showed off superb control for his age and experience. (Hulet) | ETA: Mid-2013 |
| #7 | Miller showed good growth through a dominant '10 season, improving his location and delivery as the season progressed. He's a potential ace. (Lockard) | ETA: Mid-2013 |

## SP Mike Minor — Atlanta | NL

LH | 23 yrs, 3 mo — Drafted 2009, #7 overall

Last year's rankings: — | — | — — Latest league: International

| MLB Forecast 2011 | W | L | Sv | IP | H | K | ERA | WHIP | K/9 | BB/9 | HR/9 |
|---|---|---|---|---|---|---|---|---|---|---|---|
| | 7 | 11 | 0 | 150.0 | 183 | 158 | 5.62 | 1.52 | 9.5 | 2.2 | 1.2 |

| | 2008 | | | | | | | | | | | 2009 | | | | | | | | | | | 2010 | | | | | | | | | | |
|---|---|---|---|---|---|---|---|---|---|---|---|---|---|---|---|---|---|---|---|---|---|---|---|---|---|---|---|---|---|---|---|---|---|
| Level | W | L | Sv | IP | H | K | ERA | WHIP | K/9 | BB/9 | HR/9 | W | L | Sv | IP | H | K | ERA | WHIP | K/9 | BB/9 | HR/9 | W | L | Sv | IP | H | K | ERA | WHIP | K/9 | BB/9 | HR/9 |
| A | — | — | — | — | — | — | — | — | — | — | — | 0 | 1 | 0 | 14.0 | 10 | 17 | 0.64 | 0.71 | 10.9 | 0.0 | 0.0 | — | — | — | — | — | — | — | — | — | — | — |
| AA | — | — | — | — | — | — | — | — | — | — | — | — | — | — | — | — | — | — | — | — | — | — | 2 | 6 | 0 | 87.0 | 74 | 109 | 4.03 | 1.24 | 11.3 | 3.5 | 0.8 |
| AAA | — | — | — | — | — | — | — | — | — | — | — | — | — | — | — | — | — | — | — | — | — | — | 4 | 1 | 0 | 33.1 | 19 | 37 | 1.89 | 0.93 | 10.0 | 3.2 | 0.3 |
| MLB | — | — | — | — | — | — | — | — | — | — | — | — | — | — | — | — | — | — | — | — | — | — | 3 | 2 | 0 | 40.2 | 53 | 43 | 5.98 | 1.57 | 9.5 | 2.4 | 1.3 |

| Rank | Comment | ETA |
|---|---|---|
| #9 | Minor has a good repertoire, and he trusts any pitch in any situation. The strikeouts should taper off, but his success should not. (Hagen) | ETA: Early 2011 |
| #2 | Minor's fastball velocity took a big jump in 2010, and his value rose with it. If he can maintain the radar gun readings, he could be a solid #2. (Hulet) | ETA: Early 2011 |
| #20 | When drafted, Minor was considered a safe pick – a #3 or #4 starter. Since then, he has added velocity, and now he looks like a rotation anchor. (Lockard) | ETA: Early 2011 |

## SP Mike Montgomery — Kansas City | AL

LH | 21 yrs, 9 mo — Drafted 2008, #36 overall

Last year's rankings: #36 | #20 | #25 — Latest league: Texas

| MLB Forecast 2011 | W | L | Sv | IP | H | K | ERA | WHIP | K/9 | BB/9 | HR/9 |
|---|---|---|---|---|---|---|---|---|---|---|---|
| | — | — | — | — | — | — | — | — | — | — | — |

| | 2008 | | | | | | | | | | | 2009 | | | | | | | | | | | 2010 | | | | | | | | | | |
|---|---|---|---|---|---|---|---|---|---|---|---|---|---|---|---|---|---|---|---|---|---|---|---|---|---|---|---|---|---|---|---|---|---|
| Level | W | L | Sv | IP | H | K | ERA | WHIP | K/9 | BB/9 | HR/9 | W | L | Sv | IP | H | K | ERA | WHIP | K/9 | BB/9 | HR/9 | W | L | Sv | IP | H | K | ERA | WHIP | K/9 | BB/9 | HR/9 |
| A | — | — | — | — | — | — | — | — | — | — | — | 6 | 4 | 0 | 110.0 | 80 | 98 | 2.21 | 1.06 | 8.0 | 2.9 | 0.1 | 2 | 0 | 0 | 24.2 | 14 | 33 | 1.09 | 0.73 | 12.0 | 1.5 | 0.0 |
| AA | — | — | — | — | — | — | — | — | — | — | — | — | — | — | — | — | — | — | — | — | — | — | 5 | 4 | 0 | 59.2 | 56 | 48 | 3.47 | 1.37 | 7.2 | 3.9 | 0.6 |
| AAA | — | — | — | — | — | — | — | — | — | — | — | — | — | — | — | — | — | — | — | — | — | — | — | — | — | — | — | — | — | — | — | — | — |
| MLB | — | — | — | — | — | — | — | — | — | — | — | — | — | — | — | — | — | — | — | — | — | — | — | — | — | — | — | — | — | — | — | — | — |

| Rank | Comment | ETA |
|---|---|---|
| #10 | Montgomery has a sick fastball/curveball combination. His command dimmed when he entered the Texas League, but his future remains bright. (Hagen) | ETA: Late 2011 |
| #21 | In KC, John Lamb has passed Montgomery, partly due to concerns about the latter's durability. If Mike can stay healthy, he has plenty of promise. (Hulet) | ETA: Mid 2011 |
| #4 | Montgomery has a lively fastball and an aggressive mindset. His secondary pitches and command need refinement, but he could be special. (Lockard) | ETA: Mid-2012 |

## SP Matthew Moore — Tampa Bay | AL

LH | 21 yrs, 9 mo — Drafted 2007, 8th round

Last year's rankings: #34 | #21 | #27 — Latest league: Florida State

| MLB Forecast 2011 | W | L | Sv | IP | H | K | ERA | WHIP | K/9 | BB/9 | HR/9 |
|---|---|---|---|---|---|---|---|---|---|---|---|
| | — | — | — | — | — | — | — | — | — | — | — |

| | 2008 | | | | | | | | | | | 2009 | | | | | | | | | | | 2010 | | | | | | | | | | |
|---|---|---|---|---|---|---|---|---|---|---|---|---|---|---|---|---|---|---|---|---|---|---|---|---|---|---|---|---|---|---|---|---|---|
| Level | W | L | Sv | IP | H | K | ERA | WHIP | K/9 | BB/9 | HR/9 | W | L | Sv | IP | H | K | ERA | WHIP | K/9 | BB/9 | HR/9 | W | L | Sv | IP | H | K | ERA | WHIP | K/9 | BB/9 | HR/9 |
| A | — | — | — | — | — | — | — | — | — | — | — | 8 | 5 | 0 | 123.0 | 86 | 176 | 3.15 | 1.27 | 12.9 | 5.1 | 0.4 | 6 | 11 | 0 | 144.2 | 109 | 208 | 3.36 | 1.18 | 12.9 | 3.8 | 0.4 |
| AA | — | — | — | — | — | — | — | — | — | — | — | — | — | — | — | — | — | — | — | — | — | — | — | — | — | — | — | — | — | — | — | — | — |
| AAA | — | — | — | — | — | — | — | — | — | — | — | — | — | — | — | — | — | — | — | — | — | — | — | — | — | — | — | — | — | — | — | — | — |
| MLB | — | — | — | — | — | — | — | — | — | — | — | — | — | — | — | — | — | — | — | — | — | — | — | — | — | — | — | — | — | — | — | — | — |

| Rank | Comment | ETA |
|---|---|---|
| #23 | Moore's curveball continues to generate video-game strikeout numbers. Yet, I am more impressed with his command upon entering High-A ball. (Hagen) | ETA: Late 2012 |
| #5 | Moore led the minors in K in '10. That's all the more impressive when you consider he had a slow start – his ERA in his first 12 games was 6.08. (Hulet) | ETA: Mid-2012 |
| #24 | Moore was the far-and-away the minor-league K leader. He is very hard to hit, but his control needs to be tightened before he reaches the bigs. (Lockard) | ETA: Mid-2012 |

## SP Jacob Odorizzi — Milwaukee | NL

RH | 21 yrs, 0 mo — Drafted 2008, #32 overall

Last year's rankings: — | — | — — Latest league: Midwest

| MLB Forecast 2011 | | | | | | | | | | |
|---|---|---|---|---|---|---|---|---|---|---|
| W | L | Sv | IP | H | K | ERA | WHIP | K/9 | BB/9 | HR/9 |
| — | — | — | — | — | — | — | — | — | — | — |

| Level | 2008 | | | | | | | | | | | 2009 | | | | | | | | | | | 2010 | | | | | | | | | | |
|---|---|---|---|---|---|---|---|---|---|---|---|---|---|---|---|---|---|---|---|---|---|---|---|---|---|---|---|---|---|---|---|---|---|
| | W | L | Sv | IP | H | K | ERA | WHIP | K/9 | BB/9 | HR/9 | W | L | Sv | IP | H | K | ERA | WHIP | K/9 | BB/9 | HR/9 | W | L | Sv | IP | H | K | ERA | WHIP | K/9 | BB/9 | HR/9 |
| A | — | — | — | — | — | — | — | — | — | — | — | — | — | — | — | — | — | — | — | — | — | — | 7 | 3 | 1 | 120.2 | 99 | 135 | 3.43 | 1.15 | 10.1 | 3.0 | 0.5 |
| AA | — | — | — | — | — | — | — | — | — | — | — | — | — | — | — | — | — | — | — | — | — | — | — | — | — | — | — | — | — | — | — | — | — |
| AAA | — | — | — | — | — | — | — | — | — | — | — | — | — | — | — | — | — | — | — | — | — | — | — | — | — | — | — | — | — | — | — | — | — |
| MLB | — | — | — | — | — | — | — | — | — | — | — | — | — | — | — | — | — | — | — | — | — | — | — | — | — | — | — | — | — | — | — | — | — |

| | | |
|---|---|---|
| #30 | Odorizzi delivers four reliable pitches, highlighted by a potentially plus curveball. If his ball location doesn't improve, he will meet resistance soon. (Hagen) | ETA: Early 2013 |
| #27 | Odorizzi took a big step forward in '10 and justified his draft status. The Brewers have not enjoyed a ton of luck developing pitchers in recent years. (Hulet) | ETA: Mid-2013 |
| #33 | Odorizzi handled the rigors of full-season ball well and fields potentially four big-league-caliber offerings. At present, his best pitch is his slider. (Lockard) | ETA: Mid-2012 |

## SP Jarrod Parker — Arizona | NL

RH | 22 yrs, 4 mo — Drafted 2007, #9 overall

Last year's rankings: #9 | #10 | #13 — Latest league: Southern

| MLB Forecast 2011 | | | | | | | | | | |
|---|---|---|---|---|---|---|---|---|---|---|
| W | L | Sv | IP | H | K | ERA | WHIP | K/9 | BB/9 | HR/9 |
| — | — | — | — | — | — | — | — | — | — | — |

| Level | 2008 | | | | | | | | | | | 2009 | | | | | | | | | | | 2010 | | | | | | | | | | |
|---|---|---|---|---|---|---|---|---|---|---|---|---|---|---|---|---|---|---|---|---|---|---|---|---|---|---|---|---|---|---|---|---|---|
| | W | L | Sv | IP | H | K | ERA | WHIP | K/9 | BB/9 | HR/9 | W | L | Sv | IP | H | K | ERA | WHIP | K/9 | BB/9 | HR/9 | W | L | Sv | IP | H | K | ERA | WHIP | K/9 | BB/9 | HR/9 |
| A | 12 | 5 | 0 | 117.2 | 113 | 117 | 3.44 | 1.24 | 8.9 | 2.5 | 0.6 | 1 | 0 | 0 | 19.0 | 12 | 21 | 0.95 | 0.84 | 9.9 | 1.9 | 0.0 | — | — | — | — | — | — | — | — | — | — | — |
| AA | — | — | — | — | — | — | — | — | — | — | — | 4 | 6 | 0 | 78.1 | 82 | 74 | 3.68 | 1.48 | 8.5 | 3.9 | 0.2 | — | — | — | — | — | — | — | — | — | — | — |
| AAA | — | — | — | — | — | — | — | — | — | — | — | — | — | — | — | — | — | — | — | — | — | — | — | — | — | — | — | — | — | — | — | — | — |
| MLB | — | — | — | — | — | — | — | — | — | — | — | — | — | — | — | — | — | — | — | — | — | — | — | — | — | — | — | — | — | — | — | — | — |

| | | |
|---|---|---|
| #27 | Reports say that Parker looks good coming back from Tommy John surgery. Jarrod will start fresh in 2011 in pursuit of his previous elite status. (Hagen) | ETA: Early 2012 |
| #28 | Parker missed all of 2010 owing to Tommy John surger,y but he still owns one of the most electric arms in the minors and definitely in the system. (Hulet) | ETA: Late 2012 |
| #14 | Parker is coming off a missed year after elbow surgery, but assuming that he regains his pre-surgery stuff, he is one of the top arms in baseball. (Lockard) | ETA: Mid-2012 |

## SP Martin Perez — Texas | AL

LH | 19 yrs, 11 mo — Signed as non-drafted free agent, 2007

Last year's rankings: #7 | #15 | #7 — Latest league: Texas

| MLB Forecast 2011 | | | | | | | | | | |
|---|---|---|---|---|---|---|---|---|---|---|
| W | L | Sv | IP | H | K | ERA | WHIP | K/9 | BB/9 | HR/9 |
| — | — | — | — | — | — | — | — | — | — | — |

| Level | 2008 | | | | | | | | | | | 2009 | | | | | | | | | | | 2010 | | | | | | | | | | |
|---|---|---|---|---|---|---|---|---|---|---|---|---|---|---|---|---|---|---|---|---|---|---|---|---|---|---|---|---|---|---|---|---|---|
| | W | L | Sv | IP | H | K | ERA | WHIP | K/9 | BB/9 | HR/9 | W | L | Sv | IP | H | K | ERA | WHIP | K/9 | BB/9 | HR/9 | W | L | Sv | IP | H | K | ERA | WHIP | K/9 | BB/9 | HR/9 |
| A | 1 | 2 | 0 | 61.2 | 66 | 53 | 3.65 | 1.52 | 7.7 | 4.1 | 0.4 | 5 | 5 | 1 | 93.2 | 82 | 105 | 2.31 | 1.23 | 10.1 | 3.2 | 0.3 | — | — | — | — | — | — | — | — | — | — | — |
| AA | — | — | — | — | — | — | — | — | — | — | — | 1 | 3 | 0 | 21.0 | 29 | 14 | 5.57 | 1.62 | 6.0 | 2.1 | 0.9 | 5 | 8 | 0 | 99.2 | 117 | 101 | 5.96 | 1.68 | 9.1 | 4.5 | 1.1 |
| AAA | — | — | — | — | — | — | — | — | — | — | — | — | — | — | — | — | — | — | — | — | — | — | — | — | — | — | — | — | — | — | — | — | — |
| MLB | — | — | — | — | — | — | — | — | — | — | — | — | — | — | — | — | — | — | — | — | — | — | — | — | — | — | — | — | — | — | — | — | — |

| | | |
|---|---|---|
| #5 | Perez needs to work on his control, as he found it difficult to fool Texas League hitters, but his curveball and change-up have immense promise. (Hagen) | ETA: Late 2011 |
| #26 | In terms of skills, Perez's season was not as bad as his 5.96 ERA suggests. Perez is young, and he must learn to be more efficient and consistent. (Hulet) | ETA: Mid-2012 |
| #8 | Perez was hit around at Double-A, but he was 19 in a sea of 24-year-olds. He might need another year but he'll one day anchor Texas's rotation. (Lockard) | ETA: Early 2012 |

## SP Michael Pineda — Seattle | AL

RH | 22 yrs, 2 mo — Signed as non-drafted free agent, 2005

Last year's rankings: — | — | — — Latest league: Pacific Coast

| MLB Forecast 2011 | | | | | | | | | | |
|---|---|---|---|---|---|---|---|---|---|---|
| W | L | Sv | IP | H | K | ERA | WHIP | K/9 | BB/9 | HR/9 |
| 7 | 6 | 0 | 120.0 | 115 | 97 | 3.98 | 1.33 | 7.3 | 3.1 | 1.0 |

| Level | 2008 | | | | | | | | | | | 2009 | | | | | | | | | | | 2010 | | | | | | | | | | |
|---|---|---|---|---|---|---|---|---|---|---|---|---|---|---|---|---|---|---|---|---|---|---|---|---|---|---|---|---|---|---|---|---|---|
| | W | L | Sv | IP | H | K | ERA | WHIP | K/9 | BB/9 | HR/9 | W | L | Sv | IP | H | K | ERA | WHIP | K/9 | BB/9 | HR/9 | W | L | Sv | IP | H | K | ERA | WHIP | K/9 | BB/9 | HR/9 |
| A | 8 | 6 | 0 | 138.1 | 109 | 128 | 1.95 | 1.04 | 8.3 | 2.3 | 0.5 | 4 | 2 | 0 | 44.1 | 29 | 48 | 2.84 | 0.79 | 9.7 | 1.2 | 0.6 | — | — | — | — | — | — | — | — | — | — | — |
| AA | — | — | — | — | — | — | — | — | — | — | — | — | — | — | — | — | — | — | — | — | — | — | 8 | 1 | 0 | 77.0 | 67 | 78 | 2.22 | 1.09 | 9.1 | 2.0 | 0.1 |
| AAA | — | — | — | — | — | — | — | — | — | — | — | — | — | — | — | — | — | — | — | — | — | — | 3 | 3 | 0 | 62.1 | 54 | 76 | 4.76 | 1.14 | 11.0 | 2.5 | 1.3 |
| MLB | — | — | — | — | — | — | — | — | — | — | — | — | — | — | — | — | — | — | — | — | — | — | — | — | — | — | — | — | — | — | — | — | — |

| | | |
|---|---|---|
| #17 | Pineda has always possessed ace potential, and in 2010 he was able to put an injury-plagued '09 behind him and effortlessly raise his velocity. (Hagen) | ETA: Mid-2011 |
| #17 | Pineda's stats in Triple-A were tarnished by one bad month. He combines solid control with a good fastball and should enjoy success in Seattle. (Hulet) | ETA: Mid-2011 |
| #6 | Pineda tired at the end of the season, but he retained impeccable command against much older competition. He is a future #1 or #2 starter. (Lockard) | ETA: Mid-2011 |

## SP Drew Pomeranz — Cleveland | AL

LH | 22 yrs, 4 mo — Drafted 2010, #5 overall

Last year's rankings: — | — | — — Latest league: N/A

| MLB Forecast 2011 | | | | | | | | | | |
|---|---|---|---|---|---|---|---|---|---|---|
| W | L | Sv | IP | H | K | ERA | WHIP | K/9 | BB/9 | HR/9 |
| — | — | — | — | — | — | — | — | — | — | — |

| Level | 2008 | | | | | | | | | | | 2009 | | | | | | | | | | | 2010 | | | | | | | | | | |
|---|---|---|---|---|---|---|---|---|---|---|---|---|---|---|---|---|---|---|---|---|---|---|---|---|---|---|---|---|---|---|---|---|---|
| | W | L | Sv | IP | H | K | ERA | WHIP | K/9 | BB/9 | HR/9 | W | L | Sv | IP | H | K | ERA | WHIP | K/9 | BB/9 | HR/9 | W | L | Sv | IP | H | K | ERA | WHIP | K/9 | BB/9 | HR/9 |
| A | — | — | — | — | — | — | — | — | — | — | — | — | — | — | — | — | — | — | — | — | — | — | — | — | — | — | — | — | — | — | — | — | — |
| AA | — | — | — | — | — | — | — | — | — | — | — | — | — | — | — | — | — | — | — | — | — | — | — | — | — | — | — | — | — | — | — | — | — |
| AAA | — | — | — | — | — | — | — | — | — | — | — | — | — | — | — | — | — | — | — | — | — | — | — | — | — | — | — | — | — | — | — | — | — |
| MLB | — | — | — | — | — | — | — | — | — | — | — | — | — | — | — | — | — | — | — | — | — | — | — | — | — | — | — | — | — | — | — | — | — |

| | | |
|---|---|---|
| #33 | Pomeranz has the potential for as many as three plus pitches, but his command is shaky, and he currently lacks movement on those pitches. (Hagen) | ETA: Mid-2012 |
| #30 | The left-handed Pomeranz will not make his pro debut until 2011, but once there, he could rise quickly. He has the ceiling of a #2 or #3 starter. (Hulet) | ETA: Mid-2012 |
| #34 | Pomeranz is a polished starter with three solid pitches, good command, and above-average velocity for a southpaw. He has a workhorse build. (Lockard) | ETA: Mid-2012 |

## RP Chris Sale — Chicago | AL

LH | 22 yrs, 0 mo — Drafted 2010, #13 overall

Last year's rankings: — | — | — — Latest league: International

| MLB Forecast 2011 | | | | | | | | | | |
|---|---|---|---|---|---|---|---|---|---|---|
| W | L | Sv | IP | H | K | ERA | WHIP | K/9 | BB/9 | HR/9 |
| 10 | 5 | 0 | 160.0 | 110 | 225 | 3.38 | 1.28 | 12.7 | 5.1 | 1.4 |

| Level | 2008 | | | | | | | | | | | 2009 | | | | | | | | | | | 2010 | | | | | | | | | | |
|---|---|---|---|---|---|---|---|---|---|---|---|---|---|---|---|---|---|---|---|---|---|---|---|---|---|---|---|---|---|---|---|---|---|
| | W | L | Sv | IP | H | K | ERA | WHIP | K/9 | BB/9 | HR/9 | W | L | Sv | IP | H | K | ERA | WHIP | K/9 | BB/9 | HR/9 | W | L | Sv | IP | H | K | ERA | WHIP | K/9 | BB/9 | HR/9 |
| A | — | — | — | — | — | — | — | — | — | — | — | — | — | — | — | — | — | — | — | — | — | — | 0 | 0 | 0 | 4.0 | 3 | 4 | 2.25 | 1.25 | 9.0 | 4.5 | 0.0 |
| AA | — | — | — | — | — | — | — | — | — | — | — | — | — | — | — | — | — | — | — | — | — | — | — | — | — | — | — | — | — | — | — | — | — |
| AAA | — | — | — | — | — | — | — | — | — | — | — | — | — | — | — | — | — | — | — | — | — | — | 0 | 0 | 0 | 6.1 | 3 | 15 | 2.84 | 1.11 | 21.3 | 5.7 | 2.8 |
| MLB | — | — | — | — | — | — | — | — | — | — | — | — | — | — | — | — | — | — | — | — | — | — | 2 | 1 | 4 | 23.1 | 15 | 32 | 1.93 | 1.07 | 12.3 | 3.9 | 0.8 |

| | | |
|---|---|---|
| #15 | The big question with Sale is whether he will stay in the bullpen or return to starting. I think that his plus three-pitch mix belongs in the rotation. (Hagen) | ETA: Early 2011 |
| #20 | Sale in 2010 got his feet wet as a reliever, but he has more value as a starter. Perhaps the White Sox will actually hold onto this pitching prospect! (Hulet) | ETA: Mid-2011 |
| #18 | Sale excelled as a reliever in the bigs mere months after being drafted, but he has starter stuff and should receive a chance in that role in 2011. (Lockard) | ETA: Early 2011 |

## RP Tanner Scheppers — Texas | AL

RH | 24 yrs, 2 mo — Drafted 2009, #44 overall

Last year's rankings: — | — | — — Latest league: Pacific Coast

| MLB Forecast 2011 | | | | | | | | | | |
|---|---|---|---|---|---|---|---|---|---|---|
| W | L | Sv | IP | H | K | ERA | WHIP | K/9 | BB/9 | HR/9 |
| — | — | — | — | — | — | — | — | — | — | — |

| Level | 2008 | | | | | | | | | | | 2009 | | | | | | | | | | | 2010 | | | | | | | | | | |
|---|---|---|---|---|---|---|---|---|---|---|---|---|---|---|---|---|---|---|---|---|---|---|---|---|---|---|---|---|---|---|---|---|---|
| | W | L | Sv | IP | H | K | ERA | WHIP | K/9 | BB/9 | HR/9 | W | L | Sv | IP | H | K | ERA | WHIP | K/9 | BB/9 | HR/9 | W | L | Sv | IP | H | K | ERA | WHIP | K/9 | BB/9 | HR/9 |
| A | — | — | — | — | — | — | — | — | — | — | — | — | — | — | — | — | — | — | — | — | — | — | — | — | — | — | — | — | — | — | — | — | — |
| AA | — | — | — | — | — | — | — | — | — | — | — | 1 | 1 | 0 | 19.0 | 17 | 20 | 3.32 | 1.47 | 9.5 | 5.2 | 0.5 | 0 | 0 | 2 | 11.0 | 3 | 19 | 0.82 | 0.27 | 15.5 | 0.0 | 0.8 |
| AAA | — | — | — | — | — | — | — | — | — | — | — | — | — | — | — | — | — | — | — | — | — | — | 1 | 3 | 4 | 69.0 | 82 | 71 | 5.48 | 1.62 | 9.3 | 3.9 | 0.7 |
| MLB | — | — | — | — | — | — | — | — | — | — | — | — | — | — | — | — | — | — | — | — | — | — | — | — | — | — | — | — | — | — | — | — | — |

| | | |
|---|---|---|
| #31 | My guess is Scheppers settles in as a reliever. Working from the bullpen could mask his control issues and let his fastball/curveball combo shine. (Hagen) | ETA: Mid-2011 |
| #48 | A seven-game stint as a starter in Triple-A didn't agree with Scheppers. Also, there are big question marks surrounding the health of his shoulder. (Hulet) | ETA: Mid-2011 |
| #35 | Texas flirted with the idea of turning Scheppers into a starter, but his future lies in relief, where his at-times-wild power arsenal will play better. (Lockard) | ETA: Mid-2011 |

## RP Daniel Schlereth — Detroit | AL

LH | 24 yrs, 10 mo — Drafted 2008, #26 overall

Last year's rankings: #44 | #38 | #44 — Latest league: International

| MLB Forecast 2011 | | | | | | | | | | |
|---|---|---|---|---|---|---|---|---|---|---|
| W | L | Sv | IP | H | K | ERA | WHIP | K/9 | BB/9 | HR/9 |
| 2 | 1 | 0 | 40.0 | 38 | 46 | 4.33 | 1.72 | 10.3 | 6.1 | 1.0 |

| Level | 2008 | | | | | | | | | | | 2009 | | | | | | | | | | | 2010 | | | | | | | | | | |
|---|---|---|---|---|---|---|---|---|---|---|---|---|---|---|---|---|---|---|---|---|---|---|---|---|---|---|---|---|---|---|---|---|---|
| | W | L | Sv | IP | H | K | ERA | WHIP | K/9 | BB/9 | HR/9 | W | L | Sv | IP | H | K | ERA | WHIP | K/9 | BB/9 | HR/9 | W | L | Sv | IP | H | K | ERA | WHIP | K/9 | BB/9 | HR/9 |
| A | 1 | 0 | 0 | 9.0 | 3 | 14 | 2.00 | 0.78 | 14.0 | 4.0 | 0.0 | — | — | — | — | — | — | — | — | — | — | — | — | — | — | — | — | — | — | — | — | — | — |
| AA | — | — | — | — | — | — | — | — | — | — | — | 0 | 0 | 4 | 26.2 | 14 | 39 | 1.01 | 1.13 | 13.2 | 5.4 | 0.3 | — | — | — | — | — | — | — | — | — | — | — |
| AAA | — | — | — | — | — | — | — | — | — | — | — | 0 | 0 | 0 | 1.0 | 1 | 1 | 0.00 | 2.00 | 9.0 | 9.0 | 0.0 | 1 | 3 | 0 | 49.1 | 40 | 60 | 2.37 | 1.50 | 10.9 | 6.2 | 0.0 |
| MLB | — | — | — | — | — | — | — | — | — | — | — | 1 | 4 | 0 | 18.1 | 15 | 22 | 5.89 | 1.64 | 10.8 | 7.4 | 0.5 | 2 | 0 | 1 | 18.2 | 20 | 19 | 2.89 | 1.61 | 9.2 | 4.8 | 1.0 |

| | | |
|---|---|---|
| #47 | Schlereth is a power reliever who wields a devastating curveball, but his command isn't improving. That's keeping him from a prominent MLB job. (Hagen) | ETA: Arrived |
| #51 | Schlereth was rushed through the minors by Arizona, and his control has yet to catch up. Detroit is being more cautious with the future closer. (Hulet) | ETA: Mid-2011 |
| #51 | Schlereth regularly misses bats, but he just as regularly misses the strike zone. His poor command will probably keep him from being a closer. (Lockard) | ETA: Early 2011 |

## SP Jameson Taillon — Pittsburgh | NL

RH | 19 yrs, 4 mo — Drafted 2010, #2 overall

Last year's rankings: — | — | — — Latest league: N/A

| MLB Forecast 2011 | W | L | Sv | IP | H | K | ERA | WHIP | K/9 | BB/9 | HR/9 |
|---|---|---|---|---|---|---|---|---|---|---|---|
| | — | — | — | — | — | — | — | — | — | — | — |

| Level | 2008 W | L | Sv | IP | H | K | ERA | WHIP | K/9 | BB/9 | HR/9 | 2009 W | L | Sv | IP | H | K | ERA | WHIP | K/9 | BB/9 | HR/9 | 2010 W | L | Sv | IP | H | K | ERA | WHIP | K/9 | BB/9 | HR/9 |
|---|---|---|---|---|---|---|---|---|---|---|---|---|---|---|---|---|---|---|---|---|---|---|---|---|---|---|---|---|---|---|---|---|---|
| A | — | — | — | — | — | — | — | — | — | — | — | — | — | — | — | — | — | — | — | — | — | — | — | — | — | — | — | — | — | — | — | — | — |
| AA | — | — | — | — | — | — | — | — | — | — | — | — | — | — | — | — | — | — | — | — | — | — | — | — | — | — | — | — | — | — | — | — | — |
| AAA | — | — | — | — | — | — | — | — | — | — | — | — | — | — | — | — | — | — | — | — | — | — | — | — | — | — | — | — | — | — | — | — | — |
| MLB | — | — | — | — | — | — | — | — | — | — | — | — | — | — | — | — | — | — | — | — | — | — | — | — | — | — | — | — | — | — | — | — | — |

| Rank | Comment | ETA |
|---|---|---|
| #4 | What more do you want in a high school arm? Taillon has velocity, movement, size, poise, and the basis of a four-pitch arsenal at his disposal. (Hagen) | ETA: Late 2013 |
| #12 | Taillon in five years could combine with Stetson Allie and Luis Heredia in a killer 1-2-3 punch. If he can avoid injuries, Taillon has #1 potential. (Hulet) | ETA: Mid-2014 |
| #10 | Regarded as the top HS arm in the draft, Taillon is a classic Texas flame-thrower. In many ways, he's a taller version of Josh Beckett. (Lockard) | ETA: Late 2013 |

## SP Julio Teheran — Atlanta | NL

RH | 20 yrs, 2 mo — Signed as non-drafted free agent, 2007

Last year's rankings: #35 | #22 | #12 — Latest league: Southern

| MLB Forecast 2011 | W | L | Sv | IP | H | K | ERA | WHIP | K/9 | BB/9 | HR/9 |
|---|---|---|---|---|---|---|---|---|---|---|---|
| | — | — | — | — | — | — | — | — | — | — | — |

| Level | 2008 W | L | Sv | IP | H | K | ERA | WHIP | K/9 | BB/9 | HR/9 | 2009 W | L | Sv | IP | H | K | ERA | WHIP | K/9 | BB/9 | HR/9 | 2010 W | L | Sv | IP | H | K | ERA | WHIP | K/9 | BB/9 | HR/9 |
|---|---|---|---|---|---|---|---|---|---|---|---|---|---|---|---|---|---|---|---|---|---|---|---|---|---|---|---|---|---|---|---|---|---|
| A | — | — | — | — | — | — | — | — | — | — | — | 1 | 3 | 0 | 37.2 | 42 | 28 | 4.78 | 1.41 | 6.7 | 2.6 | 0.5 | 6 | 6 | 0 | 102.2 | 79 | 121 | 2.28 | 0.99 | 10.6 | 2.0 | 0.6 |
| AA | — | — | — | — | — | — | — | — | — | — | — | — | — | — | — | — | — | — | — | — | — | — | 3 | 2 | 0 | 40.0 | 29 | 38 | 3.38 | 1.15 | 8.6 | 3.8 | 0.4 |
| AAA | — | — | — | — | — | — | — | — | — | — | — | — | — | — | — | — | — | — | — | — | — | — | — | — | — | — | — | — | — | — | — | — | — |
| MLB | — | — | — | — | — | — | — | — | — | — | — | — | — | — | — | — | — | — | — | — | — | — | — | — | — | — | — | — | — | — | — | — | — |

| Rank | Comment | ETA |
|---|---|---|
| #2 | Teheran's curveball hit a new level, giving him a third plus offering. Pitching is about velocity, movement, and location, and Teheran has them all. (Hagen) | ETA: Early 2012 |
| #6 | A former top international free agent signee, Teheran made good on his potential in 2010. He could be a staff ace for ATL so long as he's healthy. (Hulet) | ETA: Mid-2012 |
| #5 | Teheran has mound maturity well beyond his 20 years. He has excellent command and the stuff to be a top-of-the-rotation starter for years. (Lockard) | ETA: Late 2011 |

## SP Jacob Turner — Detroit | AL

RH | 19 yrs, 10 mo — Drafted 2009, #9 overall

Last year's rankings: #22 | #32 | #23 — Latest league: Florida State

| MLB Forecast 2011 | W | L | Sv | IP | H | K | ERA | WHIP | K/9 | BB/9 | HR/9 |
|---|---|---|---|---|---|---|---|---|---|---|---|
| | — | — | — | — | — | — | — | — | — | — | — |

| Level | 2008 W | L | Sv | IP | H | K | ERA | WHIP | K/9 | BB/9 | HR/9 | 2009 W | L | Sv | IP | H | K | ERA | WHIP | K/9 | BB/9 | HR/9 | 2010 W | L | Sv | IP | H | K | ERA | WHIP | K/9 | BB/9 | HR/9 |
|---|---|---|---|---|---|---|---|---|---|---|---|---|---|---|---|---|---|---|---|---|---|---|---|---|---|---|---|---|---|---|---|---|---|
| A | — | — | — | — | — | — | — | — | — | — | — | — | — | — | — | — | — | — | — | — | — | — | 6 | 5 | 0 | 115.1 | 106 | 102 | 3.28 | 1.12 | 8.0 | 1.8 | 0.5 |
| AA | — | — | — | — | — | — | — | — | — | — | — | — | — | — | — | — | — | — | — | — | — | — | — | — | — | — | — | — | — | — | — | — | — |
| AAA | — | — | — | — | — | — | — | — | — | — | — | — | — | — | — | — | — | — | — | — | — | — | — | — | — | — | — | — | — | — | — | — | — |
| MLB | — | — | — | — | — | — | — | — | — | — | — | — | — | — | — | — | — | — | — | — | — | — | — | — | — | — | — | — | — | — | — | — | — |

| Rank | Comment | ETA |
|---|---|---|
| #3 | I may be idealistic about Turner, but he brings poise and ace velocity, and his curveball has improved since he was drafted. Next: the change-up. (Hagen) | ETA: Late 2012 |
| #19 | Turner bears an advanced approach for his age along with good control. He has a fine fastball, but it would be good to see more sink on it. (Hulet) | ETA: Late 2012 |
| #9 | Turner is a rare young power-pitcher who has plus command. He breezed through A-ball and could be in the majors before he turns 21. (Lockard) | ETA: Late 2011 |

## RP Jordan Walden — Los Angeles | AL

RH | 23 yrs, 4 mo — Drafted 2006, 12th round

Last year's rankings: — | — | — — Latest league: Pacific Coast

| MLB Forecast 2011 | W | L | Sv | IP | H | K | ERA | WHIP | K/9 | BB/9 | HR/9 |
|---|---|---|---|---|---|---|---|---|---|---|---|
| | 2 | 2 | 13 | 40.0 | 43 | 44 | 5.06 | 1.67 | 9.9 | 4.2 | 1.1 |

| Level | 2008 W | L | Sv | IP | H | K | ERA | WHIP | K/9 | BB/9 | HR/9 | 2009 W | L | Sv | IP | H | K | ERA | WHIP | K/9 | BB/9 | HR/9 | 2010 W | L | Sv | IP | H | K | ERA | WHIP | K/9 | BB/9 | HR/9 |
|---|---|---|---|---|---|---|---|---|---|---|---|---|---|---|---|---|---|---|---|---|---|---|---|---|---|---|---|---|---|---|---|---|---|
| A | 9 | 8 | 0 | 156.1 | 122 | 141 | 2.76 | 1.14 | 8.1 | 3.2 | 0.4 | — | — | — | — | — | — | — | — | — | — | — | — | — | — | — | — | — | — | — | — | — | — |
| AA | — | — | — | — | — | — | — | — | — | — | — | 1 | 5 | 0 | 60.0 | 72 | 57 | 5.25 | 1.68 | 8.6 | 4.4 | 0.6 | 1 | 1 | 8 | 43.0 | 44 | 38 | 3.35 | 1.54 | 8.0 | 4.6 | 0.4 |
| AAA | — | — | — | — | — | — | — | — | — | — | — | — | — | — | — | — | — | — | — | — | — | — | 0 | 0 | 0 | 6.2 | 8 | 3 | 4.05 | 1.50 | 4.0 | 2.7 | 0.0 |
| MLB | — | — | — | — | — | — | — | — | — | — | — | — | — | — | — | — | — | — | — | — | — | — | 0 | 1 | 1 | 15.1 | 13 | 23 | 2.35 | 1.30 | 13.5 | 4.1 | 0.6 |

| Rank | Comment | ETA |
|---|---|---|
| #46 | Walden has transitioned into relief, where his wicked fastball will serve him best. His control needs work, but in time he will play a key role for LA. (Hagen) | ETA: Arrived |
| #44 | Walden moved to the bullpen in 2010 and blossomed; he could be the Angels' closer of the future in short order. He summons a high-90's fastball. (Hulet) | ETA: Mid-2011 |
| #46 | Despite a move to the bullpen, Walden's command hasn't improved. He retains the stuff to be a late-inning force if he can just reduce his walks. (Lockard) | ETA: Mid-2011 |

## SP Allen Webster — Los Angeles | NL

RH | 21 yrs, 1 mo — Drafted 2008, 18th round

Last year's rankings: — | — | — — Latest league: Midwest

| MLB Forecast 2011 | W | L | Sv | IP | H | K | ERA | WHIP | K/9 | BB/9 | HR/9 |
|---|---|---|---|---|---|---|---|---|---|---|---|
| | — | — | — | — | — | — | — | — | — | — | — |

| Level | 2008 W | L | Sv | IP | H | K | ERA | WHIP | K/9 | BB/9 | HR/9 | 2009 W | L | Sv | IP | H | K | ERA | WHIP | K/9 | BB/9 | HR/9 | 2010 W | L | Sv | IP | H | K | ERA | WHIP | K/9 | BB/9 | HR/9 |
|---|---|---|---|---|---|---|---|---|---|---|---|---|---|---|---|---|---|---|---|---|---|---|---|---|---|---|---|---|---|---|---|---|---|
| A | — | — | — | — | — | — | — | — | — | — | — | — | — | — | — | — | — | — | — | — | — | — | 12 | 9 | 0 | 131.1 | 119 | 114 | 2.88 | 1.31 | 7.8 | 3.6 | 0.4 |
| AA | — | — | — | — | — | — | — | — | — | — | — | — | — | — | — | — | — | — | — | — | — | — | — | — | — | — | — | — | — | — | — | — | — |
| AAA | — | — | — | — | — | — | — | — | — | — | — | — | — | — | — | — | — | — | — | — | — | — | — | — | — | — | — | — | — | — | — | — | — |
| MLB | — | — | — | — | — | — | — | — | — | — | — | — | — | — | — | — | — | — | — | — | — | — | — | — | — | — | — | — | — | — | — | — | — |

| Rank | Comment | ETA |
|---|---|---|
| #49 | Webster is a young man with a good frame and developing arsenal. His full-season debut displayed promise, yet much more work is called for. (Hagen) | ETA: Late 2013 |
| #41 | Webster is not as electric as some of the other arms in the system, but he has had success. He needs to develop his secondary pitches. (Hulet) | ETA: Late 2013 |
| #42 | Webster dominated the Midwest League at a young age. He features a hard-sinking fastball and the beginnings of two solid off-speed pitches. (Lockard) | ETA: Late 2012 |

## SP Zack Wheeler — San Francisco | NL

RH | 20 yrs, 10 mo — Drafted 2009, #6 overall

Last year's rankings: #12 | #30 | #36 — Latest league: South Atlantic

| MLB Forecast 2011 | W | L | Sv | IP | H | K | ERA | WHIP | K/9 | BB/9 | HR/9 |
|---|---|---|---|---|---|---|---|---|---|---|---|
| | — | — | — | — | — | — | — | — | — | — | — |

| Level | 2008 W | L | Sv | IP | H | K | ERA | WHIP | K/9 | BB/9 | HR/9 | 2009 W | L | Sv | IP | H | K | ERA | WHIP | K/9 | BB/9 | HR/9 | 2010 W | L | Sv | IP | H | K | ERA | WHIP | K/9 | BB/9 | HR/9 |
|---|---|---|---|---|---|---|---|---|---|---|---|---|---|---|---|---|---|---|---|---|---|---|---|---|---|---|---|---|---|---|---|---|---|
| A | — | — | — | — | — | — | — | — | — | — | — | — | — | — | — | — | — | — | — | — | — | — | 3 | 3 | 0 | 58.2 | 47 | 70 | 3.99 | 1.45 | 10.7 | 5.8 | 0.0 |
| AA | — | — | — | — | — | — | — | — | — | — | — | — | — | — | — | — | — | — | — | — | — | — | — | — | — | — | — | — | — | — | — | — | — |
| AAA | — | — | — | — | — | — | — | — | — | — | — | — | — | — | — | — | — | — | — | — | — | — | — | — | — | — | — | — | — | — | — | — | — |
| MLB | — | — | — | — | — | — | — | — | — | — | — | — | — | — | — | — | — | — | — | — | — | — | — | — | — | — | — | — | — | — | — | — | — |

| Rank | Comment | ETA |
|---|---|---|
| #22 | Wheeler's fastball touches the mid-90's, and he has plenty of movement on his pitches. The trick will be to harness that movement consistently. (Hagen) | ETA: Mid-2013 |
| #7 | Wheeler carries an exciting combination of fastball velocity and ground-ball tendencies. His workload was closely monitored, but he's a future #1. (Hulet) | ETA: Mid-2013 |
| #37 | Wheeler struggled in his first pro season and missed time with a fingernail issue. His mechanics need work, but he has time to develop. (Lockard) | ETA: Late 2013 |

## SP Alex White — Cleveland | AL

RH | 22 yrs, 7 mo — Drafted 2009, #15 overall

Last year's rankings: #25 | #27 | #43 — Latest league: Eastern

| MLB Forecast 2011 | W | L | Sv | IP | H | K | ERA | WHIP | K/9 | BB/9 | HR/9 |
|---|---|---|---|---|---|---|---|---|---|---|---|
| | — | — | — | — | — | — | — | — | — | — | — |

| Level | 2008 W | L | Sv | IP | H | K | ERA | WHIP | K/9 | BB/9 | HR/9 | 2009 W | L | Sv | IP | H | K | ERA | WHIP | K/9 | BB/9 | HR/9 | 2010 W | L | Sv | IP | H | K | ERA | WHIP | K/9 | BB/9 | HR/9 |
|---|---|---|---|---|---|---|---|---|---|---|---|---|---|---|---|---|---|---|---|---|---|---|---|---|---|---|---|---|---|---|---|---|---|
| A | — | — | — | — | — | — | — | — | — | — | — | — | — | — | — | — | — | — | — | — | — | — | 2 | 3 | 0 | 44.0 | 32 | 41 | 2.86 | 1.16 | 8.4 | 3.9 | 0.8 |
| AA | — | — | — | — | — | — | — | — | — | — | — | — | — | — | — | — | — | — | — | — | — | — | 8 | 7 | 0 | 106.2 | 91 | 76 | 2.28 | 1.11 | 6.4 | 2.3 | 0.7 |
| AAA | — | — | — | — | — | — | — | — | — | — | — | — | — | — | — | — | — | — | — | — | — | — | — | — | — | — | — | — | — | — | — | — | — |
| MLB | — | — | — | — | — | — | — | — | — | — | — | — | — | — | — | — | — | — | — | — | — | — | — | — | — | — | — | — | — | — | — | — | — |

| Rank | Comment | ETA |
|---|---|---|
| #18 | White has the necessary control of his lively fastball, but at least another of his pitches will have to mature into a quality offering for him to thrive. (Hagen) | ETA: Late 2011 |
| #8 | White breezed through the lower minors, but he often pitched to contact. That tendency could place his success on the shoulders of his defenders. (Hulet) | ETA: Late 2011 |
| #26 | Some see White as a closer, but he excelled as the starter in Double-A. He has three good pitches and the build to take the ball every fifth day. (Lockard) | ETA: Late 2011 |

## SP Alex Wimmers — Minnesota | AL

RH | 22 yrs, 5 mo — Drafted 2010, #21 overall

Last year's rankings: — | — | — — Latest league: Florida State

| MLB Forecast 2011 | W | L | Sv | IP | H | K | ERA | WHIP | K/9 | BB/9 | HR/9 |
|---|---|---|---|---|---|---|---|---|---|---|---|
| | — | — | — | — | — | — | — | — | — | — | — |

| Level | 2008 W | L | Sv | IP | H | K | ERA | WHIP | K/9 | BB/9 | HR/9 | 2009 W | L | Sv | IP | H | K | ERA | WHIP | K/9 | BB/9 | HR/9 | 2010 W | L | Sv | IP | H | K | ERA | WHIP | K/9 | BB/9 | HR/9 |
|---|---|---|---|---|---|---|---|---|---|---|---|---|---|---|---|---|---|---|---|---|---|---|---|---|---|---|---|---|---|---|---|---|---|
| A | — | — | — | — | — | — | — | — | — | — | — | — | — | — | — | — | — | — | — | — | — | — | 2 | 0 | 0 | 15.2 | 6 | 23 | 0.57 | 0.70 | 13.2 | 2.9 | 0.0 |
| AA | — | — | — | — | — | — | — | — | — | — | — | — | — | — | — | — | — | — | — | — | — | — | — | — | — | — | — | — | — | — | — | — | — |
| AAA | — | — | — | — | — | — | — | — | — | — | — | — | — | — | — | — | — | — | — | — | — | — | — | — | — | — | — | — | — | — | — | — | — |
| MLB | — | — | — | — | — | — | — | — | — | — | — | — | — | — | — | — | — | — | — | — | — | — | — | — | — | — | — | — | — | — | — | — | — |

| Rank | Comment | ETA |
|---|---|---|
| #44 | Wimmers doesn't blow 'em away, which caps his ceiling, but his curveball will get strikeouts. His control is an asset; he could progress quickly. (Hagen) | ETA: Mid-2012 |
| #25 | Wimmers lacks a killer fastball, but he lays claim to good command and a solid repertoire, and he should rise fast. His best pitch is his change-up. (Hulet) | ETA: Late 2012 |
| #28 | Wimmers brandished his polish when he breezed through his first taste of pro ball. He should enter the Twins' rotation at some point in 2011. (Lockard) | ETA: Late 2011 |

# ORGANIZATIONS

Each MLB team spans one half (the top or the bottom) of two pages, The page on the left shows where the 2010 version of the team fits among the other teams in the league and among recent incarnations of the same team.

Under "Playing Time Leaders by Period," we give the positional leaders by month and then again for all of 2010. Players are ranked by Plate Appearances or Innings Pitched, not by Games Played. We are tabulating the appearances of players, not the frequency of certain line-ups. It is not impossible for a player to be the leader at two positions in the same period.

The facing page features full team stats for everyone who played in the majors in 2010. The listed stats are the player's stats on that team; comprehensive stats for players who played on multiple teams can be found in the player profiles.

Writer: Michael Street
www.aasportsexaminer.com

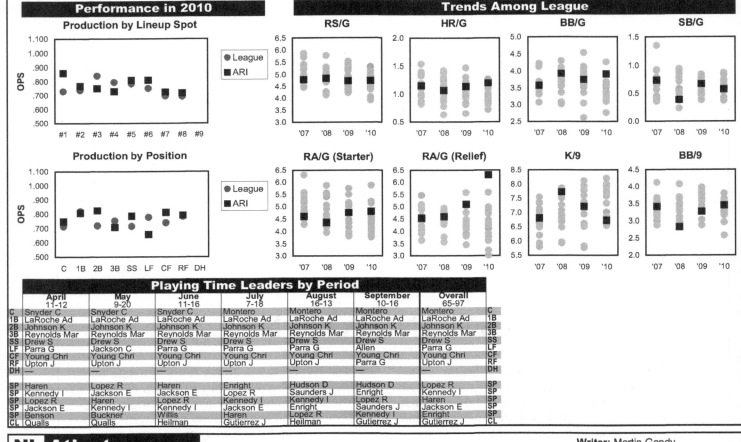

## Performance in 2010
### Production by Lineup Spot
### Production by Position

## Trends Among League
RS/G  HR/G  BB/G  SB/G
RA/G (Starter)  RA/G (Relief)  K/9  BB/9

### Playing Time Leaders by Period

| | April 11-12 | May 9-20 | June 11-16 | July 7-18 | August 16-13 | September 10-16 | Overall 65-97 | |
|---|---|---|---|---|---|---|---|---|
| C | Snyder C | Snyder C | Snyder C | Montero | Montero | Montero | Montero | C |
| 1B | LaRoche Ad | LaRoche Ad | LaRoche Ad | LaRoche Ad | LaRoche Ad | LaRoche Ad | LaRoche Ad | 1B |
| 2B | Johnson K | Johnson K | Johnson K | Johnson K | Johnson K | Johnson K | Johnson K | 2B |
| 3B | Reynolds Mar | Reynolds Mar | Reynolds Mar | Reynolds Mar | Reynolds Mar | Reynolds Mar | Reynolds Mar | 3B |
| SS | Drew S | Drew S | Drew S | Drew S | Drew S | Drew S | Drew S | SS |
| LF | Parra G | Jackson C | Parra G | Parra G | Parra G | Allen | Parra G | LF |
| CF | Young Chri | Young Chri | Young Chri | Young Chri | Young Chri | Young Chri | Young Chri | CF |
| RF | Upton J | Upton J | Upton J | Upton J | Upton J | Parra G | Upton J | RF |
| DH | — | — | — | — | — | — | — | DH |
| SP | Haren | Lopez R | Haren | Enright | Hudson D | Hudson D | Lopez R | SP |
| SP | Kennedy I | Jackson E | Jackson E | Lopez R | Saunders J | Enright | Kennedy I | SP |
| SP | Lopez R | Haren | Lopez R | Kennedy I | Kennedy I | Lopez R | Haren | SP |
| SP | Jackson E | Kennedy I | Kennedy I | Jackson E | Enright | Saunders J | Jackson E | SP |
| SP | Benson | Buckner | Willis | Haren | Lopez R | Kennedy I | Enright | SP |
| CL | Qualls | Qualls | Heilman | Gutierrez J | Heilman | Gutierrez J | Gutierrez J | CL |

Writer: Martin Gandy
www.talkingchop.com

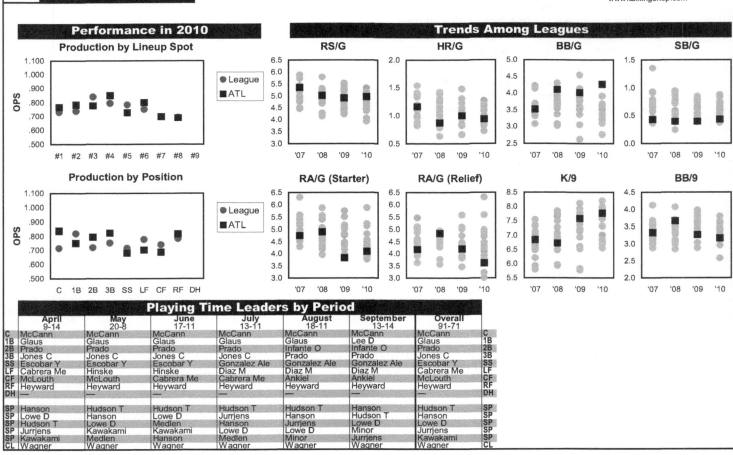

## Performance in 2010
### Production by Lineup Spot
### Production by Position

## Trends Among Leagues
RS/G  HR/G  BB/G  SB/G
RA/G (Starter)  RA/G (Relief)  K/9  BB/9

### Playing Time Leaders by Period

| | April 9-14 | May 20-8 | June 17-11 | July 13-11 | August 18-11 | September 13-14 | Overall 91-71 | |
|---|---|---|---|---|---|---|---|---|
| C | McCann | McCann | McCann | McCann | McCann | McCann | McCann | C |
| 1B | Glaus | Glaus | Glaus | Glaus | Glaus | Lee D | Glaus | 1B |
| 2B | Prado | Prado | Prado | Prado | Infante O | Infante O | Prado | 2B |
| 3B | Jones C | Jones C | Jones C | Jones C | Prado | Prado | Jones C | 3B |
| SS | Escobar Y | Escobar Y | Escobar Y | Gonzalez Ale | Gonzalez Ale | Gonzalez Ale | Escobar Y | SS |
| LF | Cabrera Me | Hinske | Hinske | Diaz M | Diaz M | Diaz M | Cabrera Me | LF |
| CF | McLouth | McLouth | Cabrera Me | Cabrera Me | Ankiel | Ankiel | McLouth | CF |
| RF | Heyward | Heyward | Heyward | Heyward | Heyward | Heyward | Heyward | RF |
| DH | | | | | | | | DH |
| SP | Hanson | Hudson T | Hudson T | Hudson T | Hudson T | Hanson | Hudson T | SP |
| SP | Lowe D | Hanson | Lowe D | Jurrjens | Hanson | Hudson T | Hanson | SP |
| SP | Hudson T | Lowe D | Medlen | Hanson | Jurrjens | Lowe D | Lowe D | SP |
| SP | Jurrjens | Kawakami | Kawakami | Lowe D | Lowe D | Minor | Jurrjens | SP |
| SP | Kawakami | Medlen | Hanson | Medlen | Minor | Jurrjens | Kawakami | SP |
| CL | Wagner | Wagner | Wagner | Wagner | Wagner | Wagner | Wagner | CL |

## Hitters — Arizona Diamondbacks 2010

| Hitters | Arizona Diamondbacks 2010 | | | | | | | | | | | | | 1st Half | | | | | | 2nd Half | | | | | | Rates | | | | | Productiveness | | |
|---|---|---|---|---|---|---|---|---|---|---|---|---|---|---|---|---|---|---|---|---|---|---|---|---|---|---|---|---|---|---|---|---|---|
| | G | AB | R | H | 2B | 3B | HR | RBI | BA | OBP | SLG | SB | CS | AB | R | HR | BI | BA | SB | AB | R | HR | BI | BA | SB | CT% | H% | BB% | Bash | GB% | OPS | vs RH | vs LH |
| Abreu T | 81 | 193 | 16 | 45 | 11 | 1 | 1 | 13 | .233 | .244 | .316 | 2 | 1 | 120 | 11 | 0 | 6 | .242 | 1 | 73 | 5 | 1 | 7 | .219 | 1 | 76% | 31% | 2% | 1.4 | 47% | .560 | .517 | .635 |
| Allen B | 22 | 45 | 5 | 12 | 3 | 0 | 1 | 6 | .267 | .393 | .400 | 0 | 0 | -- | -- | -- | -- | -- | -- | 45 | 5 | 1 | 6 | .267 | 0 | 56% | 48% | 18% | 1.5 | 28% | .793 | .839 | .543 |
| Church R | 37 | 49 | 9 | 13 | 5 | 0 | 2 | 7 | .265 | .345 | .490 | 0 | 0 | -- | -- | -- | -- | -- | -- | 49 | 9 | 2 | 7 | .265 | 0 | 61% | 43% | 7% | 1.8 | 23% | .835 | .967 | .000 |
| Crosby B | 9 | 12 | 0 | 2 | 2 | 0 | 0 | 2 | .167 | .214 | .333 | 0 | 1 | -- | -- | -- | -- | -- | -- | 12 | 0 | 0 | 2 | .167 | 0 | 58% | 29% | 7% | 2.0 | 43% | .548 | .000 | .800 |
| Drew S | 151 | 565 | 83 | 157 | 33 | 12 | 15 | 61 | .278 | .352 | .458 | 10 | 5 | 298 | 43 | 4 | 29 | .275 | 6 | 267 | 40 | 11 | 32 | .281 | 4 | 81% | 34% | 10% | 1.6 | 40% | .810 | .817 | .794 |
| Gillespie C | 45 | 104 | 11 | 24 | 8 | 0 | 2 | 12 | .231 | .283 | .365 | 1 | 1 | 67 | 8 | 1 | 6 | .239 | 0 | 37 | 3 | 1 | 6 | .216 | 1 | 72% | 32% | 6% | 1.6 | 56% | .649 | .766 | .515 |
| Hester J | 38 | 95 | 9 | 20 | 7 | 0 | 2 | 7 | .211 | .292 | .347 | 1 | 0 | 48 | 6 | 0 | 3 | .188 | 1 | 47 | 3 | 2 | 4 | .234 | 0 | 66% | 32% | 10% | 1.7 | 35% | .640 | .623 | .661 |
| Jackson C | 42 | 151 | 19 | 36 | 11 | 0 | 1 | 11 | .238 | .326 | .331 | 4 | 1 | 151 | 19 | 1 | 11 | .238 | 4 | -- | -- | -- | -- | -- | -- | 88% | 27% | 11% | 1.4 | 38% | .657 | .612 | .833 |
| Johnson K | 154 | 585 | 93 | 166 | 36 | 5 | 26 | 71 | .284 | .370 | .496 | 13 | 7 | 312 | 52 | 14 | 43 | .276 | 8 | 273 | 41 | 12 | 28 | .293 | 5 | 75% | 38% | 12% | 1.7 | 42% | .865 | .825 | .953 |
| LaRoche A | 151 | 560 | 75 | 146 | 37 | 2 | 25 | 100 | .261 | .320 | .468 | 0 | 1 | 296 | 44 | 13 | 55 | .253 | 0 | 264 | 31 | 12 | 45 | .269 | 0 | 69% | 38% | 8% | 1.8 | 38% | .788 | .802 | .758 |
| Montero M | 85 | 297 | 36 | 79 | 20 | 2 | 9 | 43 | .266 | .332 | .438 | 0 | 1 | 89 | 10 | 2 | 13 | .348 | 0 | 208 | 26 | 7 | 30 | .231 | 0 | 76% | 35% | 9% | 1.6 | 38% | .770 | .811 | .661 |
| Ojeda A | 59 | 79 | 6 | 15 | 3 | 0 | 0 | 5 | .190 | .258 | .228 | 0 | 1 | 40 | 2 | 0 | 2 | .125 | 0 | 39 | 4 | 0 | 3 | .256 | 0 | 90% | 21% | 9% | 1.2 | 52% | .486 | .406 | .614 |
| Parra G | 133 | 364 | 31 | 95 | 19 | 6 | 3 | 30 | .261 | .308 | .371 | 1 | 0 | 174 | 16 | 2 | 15 | .270 | 0 | 190 | 15 | 1 | 15 | .253 | 1 | 79% | 33% | 6% | 1.4 | 51% | .679 | .674 | .701 |
| Reynolds M | 145 | 499 | 79 | 99 | 17 | 2 | 32 | 85 | .198 | .320 | .433 | 7 | 4 | 294 | 49 | 20 | 56 | .214 | 5 | 205 | 30 | 12 | 29 | .176 | 2 | 58% | 34% | 14% | 2.2 | 32% | .753 | .694 | .913 |
| Roberts R | 36 | 66 | 8 | 13 | 4 | 0 | 2 | 9 | .197 | .229 | .348 | 0 | 0 | 17 | 1 | 0 | 3 | .176 | 0 | 49 | 7 | 2 | 6 | .204 | 0 | 74% | 27% | 4% | 1.8 | 39% | .577 | .849 | .420 |
| Ryal R | 104 | 207 | 19 | 54 | 7 | 1 | 3 | 11 | .261 | .308 | .348 | 0 | 3 | 103 | 9 | 2 | 6 | .282 | 0 | 104 | 10 | 1 | 5 | .240 | 0 | 68% | 39% | 4% | 1.3 | 45% | .656 | .596 | .712 |
| Schmidt K | 4 | 8 | 0 | 1 | 0 | 0 | 0 | 0 | .125 | .222 | .125 | 0 | 0 | -- | -- | -- | -- | -- | -- | 8 | 0 | 0 | 0 | .125 | 0 | 100% | 13% | 11% | 1.0 | 63% | .347 | .650 | .000 |
| Snyder C | 65 | 195 | 22 | 45 | 8 | 0 | 10 | 32 | .231 | .352 | .426 | 0 | 0 | 183 | 21 | 10 | 31 | .240 | 0 | 12 | 1 | 0 | 1 | .083 | 0 | 69% | 34% | 15% | 1.8 | 43% | .778 | .790 | .738 |
| Upton J | 133 | 495 | 73 | 135 | 27 | 3 | 17 | 69 | .273 | .356 | .442 | 18 | 8 | 328 | 48 | 14 | 42 | .259 | 11 | 167 | 25 | 3 | 27 | .299 | 7 | 69% | 39% | 11% | 1.6 | 42% | .799 | .808 | .768 |
| Young C | 156 | 584 | 94 | 150 | 33 | 0 | 27 | 91 | .257 | .341 | .452 | 28 | 7 | 320 | 48 | 15 | 61 | .266 | 17 | 264 | 46 | 12 | 30 | .246 | 11 | 75% | 34% | 11% | 1.8 | 34% | .793 | .781 | .826 |

## Pitchers — Arizona Diamondbacks 2010

| Pitchers | Arizona Diamondbacks 2010 | | | | | | | | | | | | | 1st Half | | | | | | 2nd Half | | | | | | Rates | | | Productiveness | | |
|---|---|---|---|---|---|---|---|---|---|---|---|---|---|---|---|---|---|---|---|---|---|---|---|---|---|---|---|---|---|---|---|
| | G | GS | W | L | Hld | Sv | IP | H | HR | ERA | WHIP | K | BB | W | L | Sv | IP | ERA | WHIP | W | L | Sv | IP | ERA | WHIP | K/9 | BB/9 | HR/9 | opOPS | vs RH | vs LH |
| Benson K | 3 | 3 | 1 | 1 | 0 | 0 | 14.0 | 18 | 2 | 5.14 | 1.71 | 8 | 6 | 1 | 1 | 0 | 14.0 | 5.14 | 1.71 | -- | -- | -- | -- | -- | -- | 5.1 | 3.9 | 1.3 | .853 | .797 | .911 |
| Boyer B | 54 | 0 | 3 | 2 | 5 | 0 | 57.0 | 59 | 3 | 4.26 | 1.54 | 29 | 29 | 1 | 2 | 0 | 28.0 | 4.82 | 1.82 | 2 | 0 | 0 | 29.0 | 3.72 | 1.28 | 4.6 | 4.6 | 0.5 | .734 | .585 | .895 |
| Buckner B | 3 | 3 | 0 | 3 | 0 | 0 | 13.0 | 26 | 4 | 11.08 | 2.38 | 11 | 5 | 0 | 3 | 0 | 13.0 | 11.08 | 2.38 | -- | -- | -- | -- | -- | -- | 7.6 | 3.5 | 2.8 | 1.115 | 1.389 | .593 |
| Carrasco D | 18 | 0 | 1 | 0 | 2 | 0 | 22.2 | 18 | 1 | 3.18 | 1.32 | 20 | 12 | -- | -- | -- | -- | -- | -- | 1 | 0 | 0 | 22.2 | 3.18 | 1.32 | 7.9 | 4.8 | 0.4 | .642 | .639 | .646 |
| Demel S | 37 | 0 | 2 | 1 | 4 | 2 | 37.0 | 42 | 5 | 5.35 | 1.46 | 33 | 12 | 0 | 0 | 0 | 12.0 | 3.00 | 1.00 | 2 | 1 | 2 | 25.0 | 6.48 | 1.68 | 8.0 | 2.9 | 1.2 | .817 | .838 | .784 |
| Enright B | 17 | 17 | 6 | 7 | 0 | 0 | 99.0 | 97 | 20 | 3.91 | 1.27 | 49 | 29 | 1 | 2 | 0 | 15.2 | 3.45 | 1.34 | 5 | 5 | 0 | 83.1 | 4.00 | 1.26 | 4.5 | 2.6 | 1.8 | .806 | .841 | .766 |
| Gutierrez J | 58 | 0 | 0 | 6 | 8 | 15 | 56.2 | 55 | 13 | 5.08 | 1.38 | 47 | 23 | 0 | 5 | 2 | 32.1 | 6.96 | 1.52 | 0 | 1 | 13 | 24.1 | 2.59 | 1.19 | 7.5 | 3.7 | 2.1 | .806 | .715 | .927 |
| Hampton M | 10 | 0 | 0 | 0 | 1 | 0 | 4.1 | 3 | 0 | 0.00 | 0.92 | 3 | 1 | -- | -- | -- | -- | -- | -- | 0 | 0 | 0 | 4.1 | 0.00 | 0.92 | 6.2 | 2.1 | 0.0 | .464 | .143 | .667 |
| Haren D | 21 | 21 | 7 | 8 | 0 | 0 | 141.0 | 161 | 23 | 4.60 | 1.35 | 141 | 29 | 7 | 7 | 0 | 130.0 | 4.36 | 1.33 | 0 | 1 | 0 | 11.0 | 7.36 | 1.55 | 9.0 | 1.9 | 1.5 | .792 | .758 | .837 |
| Heilman A | 70 | 0 | 5 | 8 | 12 | 6 | 72.0 | 73 | 9 | 4.50 | 1.38 | 55 | 26 | 2 | 3 | 3 | 40.0 | 3.83 | 1.48 | 3 | 5 | 3 | 32.0 | 5.34 | 1.25 | 6.9 | 3.3 | 1.1 | .755 | .860 | .647 |
| Howry B | 14 | 0 | 1 | 0 | 1 | 0 | 14.1 | 18 | 6 | 10.67 | 1.67 | 6 | 6 | 1 | 0 | 0 | 14.1 | 10.67 | 1.67 | -- | -- | -- | -- | -- | -- | 3.8 | 3.8 | 3.8 | 1.008 | 1.056 | .950 |
| Hudson D | 11 | 11 | 7 | 1 | 0 | 0 | 79.2 | 51 | 7 | 1.69 | 0.84 | 70 | 16 | -- | -- | -- | -- | -- | -- | 7 | 1 | 0 | 79.2 | 1.69 | 0.84 | 7.9 | 1.8 | 0.8 | .531 | .546 | .510 |
| Jackson E | 21 | 21 | 6 | 10 | 0 | 0 | 134.1 | 141 | 13 | 5.16 | 1.50 | 104 | 60 | 6 | 7 | 0 | 117.0 | 4.92 | 1.44 | 0 | 3 | 0 | 17.1 | 6.75 | 1.90 | 7.0 | 4.0 | 0.9 | .775 | .727 | .827 |
| Kennedy I | 32 | 32 | 9 | 10 | 0 | 0 | 194.0 | 163 | 26 | 3.80 | 1.20 | 168 | 70 | 4 | 7 | 0 | 111.1 | 4.12 | 1.25 | 5 | 3 | 0 | 82.2 | 3.38 | 1.14 | 7.8 | 3.2 | 1.2 | .696 | .716 | .674 |
| Kroenke Z | 3 | 1 | 1 | 0 | 0 | 0 | 6.2 | 9 | 2 | 6.75 | 1.95 | 2 | 4 | -- | -- | -- | -- | -- | -- | 1 | 0 | 0 | 6.2 | 6.75 | 1.95 | 2.7 | 5.4 | 2.7 | 1.012 | 1.200 | .429 |
| Lopez R | 33 | 33 | 7 | 16 | 0 | 0 | 200.0 | 227 | 37 | 5.00 | 1.42 | 116 | 56 | 5 | 7 | 0 | 116.2 | 4.40 | 1.35 | 2 | 9 | 0 | 83.1 | 5.83 | 1.51 | 5.2 | 2.5 | 1.7 | .833 | .812 | .856 |
| Mulvey K | 2 | 0 | 0 | 0 | 0 | 0 | 3.0 | 5 | 2 | 6.00 | 2.33 | 1 | 2 | 0 | 0 | 0 | 3.0 | 6.00 | 2.33 | -- | -- | -- | -- | -- | -- | 3.0 | 6.0 | 6.0 | 1.256 | 1.657 | .533 |
| Norberto J | 33 | 0 | 0 | 2 | 3 | 0 | 20.0 | 16 | 3 | 5.85 | 1.90 | 15 | 22 | 0 | 0 | 0 | 5.2 | 4.76 | 1.76 | 0 | 2 | 0 | 14.1 | 6.28 | 1.95 | 6.8 | 9.9 | 1.4 | .789 | .814 | .762 |
| Qualls C | 43 | 0 | 1 | 4 | 3 | 12 | 38.0 | 61 | 5 | 8.29 | 2.00 | 34 | 15 | 1 | 4 | 12 | 30.1 | 8.60 | 2.11 | 0 | 0 | 0 | 7.2 | 7.04 | 1.57 | 8.1 | 3.6 | 1.2 | .956 | .896 | 1.020 |
| Rivera S | 4 | 0 | 0 | 0 | 0 | 0 | 3.2 | 11 | 2 | 22.09 | 3.82 | 1 | 3 | 0 | 0 | 0 | 3.2 | 22.09 | 3.82 | -- | -- | -- | -- | -- | -- | 2.5 | 7.4 | 4.9 | 1.433 | 1.647 | .929 |
| Rodriguez R | 2 | 0 | 0 | 0 | 0 | 0 | 2.2 | 4 | 1 | 6.75 | 1.88 | 2 | 1 | -- | -- | -- | -- | -- | -- | 0 | 0 | 0 | 2.2 | 6.75 | 1.88 | 6.8 | 3.4 | 3.4 | 1.012 | 1.194 | .650 |
| Rosa C | 22 | 0 | 2 | 1 | 0 | 0 | 20.0 | 20 | 1 | 4.50 | 1.60 | 9 | 12 | 0 | 2 | 0 | 13.1 | 6.75 | 1.88 | 0 | 0 | 0 | 6.2 | 0.00 | 1.05 | 4.1 | 5.4 | 0.5 | .721 | .497 | 1.043 |
| Rosales L | 16 | 0 | 2 | 0 | 2 | 0 | 16.1 | 25 | 2 | 7.16 | 2.08 | 12 | 9 | 2 | 0 | 0 | 10.0 | 8.10 | 2.10 | 0 | 0 | 0 | 6.1 | 5.68 | 2.05 | 6.6 | 5.0 | 1.1 | .976 | .950 | 1.013 |
| Saunders J | 13 | 13 | 3 | 7 | 0 | 0 | 82.2 | 97 | 11 | 4.25 | 1.40 | 50 | 19 | -- | -- | -- | -- | -- | -- | 3 | 7 | 0 | 82.2 | 4.25 | 1.40 | 5.4 | 2.1 | 1.2 | .792 | .834 | .639 |
| Stange D | 4 | 0 | 0 | 0 | 0 | 0 | 4.0 | 4 | 1 | 13.50 | 2.50 | 2 | 6 | 0 | 0 | 0 | 4.0 | 13.50 | 2.50 | -- | -- | -- | -- | -- | -- | 4.5 | 13.5 | 2.3 | .955 | 1.667 | .311 |
| Valdez C | 9 | 2 | 1 | 2 | 0 | 0 | 20.0 | 29 | 2 | 7.65 | 1.95 | 13 | 10 | 1 | 2 | 0 | 20.0 | 7.65 | 1.95 | -- | -- | -- | -- | -- | -- | 5.9 | 4.5 | 0.9 | .889 | .829 | .969 |
| Vasquez E | 57 | 0 | 1 | 6 | 6 | 0 | 53.2 | 46 | 6 | 5.20 | 1.57 | 55 | 38 | 1 | 2 | 0 | 30.1 | 4.75 | 1.29 | 0 | 4 | 0 | 23.1 | 5.79 | 1.93 | 9.2 | 6.4 | 1.0 | .754 | .806 | .703 |
| Willis D | 6 | 5 | 1 | 1 | 0 | 0 | 22.1 | 24 | 3 | 6.85 | 2.28 | 14 | 27 | 1 | 1 | 0 | 22.1 | 6.85 | 2.28 | -- | -- | -- | -- | -- | -- | 5.6 | 10.9 | 1.2 | .946 | 1.140 | .476 |

## Hitters — Atlanta Braves 2010

| Hitters | Atlanta Braves 2010 | | | | | | | | | | | | | 1st Half | | | | | | 2nd Half | | | | | | Rates | | | | | Productiveness | | |
|---|---|---|---|---|---|---|---|---|---|---|---|---|---|---|---|---|---|---|---|---|---|---|---|---|---|---|---|---|---|---|---|---|---|
| | G | AB | R | H | 2B | 3B | HR | RBI | BA | OBP | SLG | SB | CS | AB | R | HR | BI | BA | SB | AB | R | HR | BI | BA | SB | CT% | H% | BB% | Bash | GB% | OPS | vs RH | vs LH |
| Ankiel R | 47 | 119 | 17 | 25 | 6 | 1 | 2 | 9 | .210 | .324 | .328 | 2 | 1 | -- | -- | -- | -- | -- | -- | 119 | 17 | 2 | 9 | .210 | 2 | 65% | 32% | 13% | 1.6 | 57% | .651 | .693 | .505 |
| Blanco G | 36 | 58 | 9 | 18 | 1 | 1 | 0 | 3 | .310 | .394 | .362 | 1 | 2 | 55 | 9 | 0 | 3 | .327 | 1 | 3 | 0 | 0 | 0 | .000 | 0 | 74% | 42% | 12% | 1.2 | 42% | .756 | .749 | .788 |
| Cabrera M | 147 | 458 | 50 | 117 | 27 | 3 | 4 | 42 | .255 | .317 | .354 | 7 | 1 | 270 | 29 | 3 | 24 | .259 | 4 | 188 | 21 | 1 | 18 | .250 | 3 | 86% | 30% | 8% | 1.4 | 49% | .671 | .685 | .642 |
| Clevlen B | 4 | 4 | 2 | 1 | 1 | 0 | 0 | 0 | .250 | .250 | .500 | 0 | 0 | 4 | 2 | 0 | 0 | .250 | 0 | -- | -- | -- | -- | -- | -- | 75% | 33% | 0% | 2.0 | 67% | .750 | 3.000 | .000 |
| Conrad B | 103 | 156 | 31 | 39 | 11 | 1 | 8 | 33 | .250 | .324 | .487 | 5 | 1 | 72 | 16 | 4 | 16 | .250 | 4 | 84 | 15 | 4 | 17 | .250 | 1 | 71% | 35% | 9% | 1.9 | 32% | .811 | .811 | .810 |
| Diaz M | 84 | 224 | 27 | 56 | 17 | 2 | 7 | 31 | .250 | .302 | .438 | 3 | 1 | 97 | 8 | 1 | 8 | .227 | 2 | 127 | 19 | 6 | 23 | .268 | 1 | 80% | 31% | 5% | 1.8 | 44% | .739 | .633 | .830 |
| Escobar Y | 75 | 261 | 28 | 62 | 12 | 0 | 0 | 19 | .238 | .334 | .284 | 5 | 1 | 261 | 28 | 0 | 19 | .238 | 5 | -- | -- | -- | -- | -- | -- | 88% | 27% | 12% | 1.2 | 50% | .618 | .600 | .671 |
| Freeman F | 20 | 24 | 3 | 4 | 1 | 0 | 1 | 1 | .167 | .167 | .333 | 0 | 0 | -- | -- | -- | -- | -- | -- | 24 | 3 | 1 | 1 | .167 | 0 | 67% | 25% | 0% | 2.0 | 44% | .500 | .333 | 1.667 |
| Glaus T | 128 | 412 | 52 | 99 | 18 | 0 | 16 | 71 | .240 | .344 | .400 | 0 | 0 | 295 | 43 | 14 | 58 | .254 | 0 | 117 | 9 | 2 | 13 | .205 | 0 | 76% | 32% | 13% | 1.7 | 40% | .744 | .735 | .762 |
| Gonzalez A | 72 | 267 | 27 | 64 | 17 | 2 | 6 | 38 | .240 | .291 | .386 | 0 | 2 | -- | -- | -- | -- | -- | -- | 267 | 27 | 6 | 38 | .240 | 0 | 80% | 30% | 5% | 1.6 | 36% | .676 | .680 | .666 |
| Hernandez D | 20 | 9 | 5 | 1 | 0 | 0 | 1 | 1 | .111 | .111 | .444 | 0 | 0 | -- | -- | -- | -- | -- | -- | 9 | 5 | 1 | 1 | .111 | 0 | 56% | 20% | 0% | 4.0 | 40% | .556 | .000 | 1.000 |
| Heyward J | 142 | 520 | 83 | 144 | 29 | 5 | 18 | 72 | .277 | .393 | .456 | 11 | 6 | 255 | 41 | 11 | 45 | .251 | 5 | 265 | 42 | 7 | 27 | .302 | 6 | 75% | 37% | 15% | 1.6 | 55% | .849 | .895 | .755 |
| Hicks B | 16 | 5 | 7 | 0 | 0 | 0 | 0 | 0 | .000 | .167 | .000 | 0 | 0 | 5 | 5 | 0 | 0 | .000 | 0 | -- | -- | -- | -- | -- | -- | 60% | 0% | 17% | --- | 67% | .167 | .000 | .500 |
| Hinske E | 131 | 281 | 38 | 72 | 21 | 1 | 11 | 51 | .256 | .338 | .456 | 0 | 0 | 175 | 26 | 6 | 34 | .274 | 0 | 106 | 12 | 5 | 17 | .226 | 0 | 73% | 35% | 10% | 1.8 | 33% | .793 | .759 | 1.219 |
| Infante O | 134 | 471 | 65 | 151 | 15 | 3 | 8 | 47 | .321 | .359 | .416 | 7 | 6 | 193 | 26 | 2 | 24 | .332 | 3 | 278 | 39 | 6 | 23 | .313 | 4 | 87% | 37% | 6% | 1.3 | 46% | .775 | .827 | .665 |
| Jones C | 95 | 317 | 47 | 84 | 21 | 0 | 10 | 46 | .265 | .381 | .426 | 5 | 0 | 242 | 33 | 6 | 33 | .252 | 5 | 75 | 14 | 4 | 13 | .307 | 0 | 85% | 31% | 16% | 1.6 | 39% | .806 | .828 | .766 |
| Lee D | 39 | 129 | 17 | 37 | 14 | 0 | 3 | 24 | .287 | .384 | .465 | 0 | 0 | -- | -- | -- | -- | -- | -- | 129 | 17 | 3 | 24 | .287 | 0 | 74% | 39% | 14% | 1.6 | 44% | .849 | .809 | .958 |
| McCann B | 143 | 479 | 63 | 129 | 25 | 0 | 21 | 77 | .269 | .375 | .453 | 5 | 2 | 255 | 40 | 10 | 37 | .267 | 3 | 224 | 23 | 11 | 40 | .272 | 2 | 80% | 34% | 13% | 1.7 | 37% | .828 | .845 | .783 |
| McLouth N | 85 | 242 | 30 | 46 | 12 | 1 | 6 | 24 | .190 | .298 | .322 | 7 | 2 | 170 | 20 | 3 | 14 | .176 | 4 | 72 | 10 | 3 | 10 | .222 | 3 | 76% | 25% | 11% | 1.7 | 40% | .620 | .685 | .378 |
| Prado M | 140 | 599 | 100 | 184 | 40 | 3 | 15 | 66 | .307 | .350 | .459 | 5 | 3 | 372 | 61 | 10 | 39 | .325 | 4 | 227 | 39 | 5 | 27 | .278 | 1 | 86% | 36% | 6% | 1.5 | 49% | .809 | .834 | .747 |
| Ross D | 59 | 121 | 15 | 35 | 13 | 2 | 2 | 28 | .289 | .392 | .479 | 0 | 1 | 68 | 8 | 0 | 17 | .279 | 0 | 53 | 7 | 2 | 11 | .302 | 0 | 77% | 38% | 14% | 1.7 | 38% | .871 | .834 | .886 |

## Pitchers — Atlanta Braves 2010

| Pitchers | Atlanta Braves 2010 | | | | | | | | | | | | | 1st Half | | | | | | 2nd Half | | | | | | Rates | | | Productiveness | | |
|---|---|---|---|---|---|---|---|---|---|---|---|---|---|---|---|---|---|---|---|---|---|---|---|---|---|---|---|---|---|---|---|
| | G | GS | W | L | Hld | Sv | IP | H | HR | ERA | WHIP | K | BB | W | L | Sv | IP | ERA | WHIP | W | L | Sv | IP | ERA | WHIP | K/9 | BB/9 | HR/9 | opOPS | vs RH | vs LH |
| Beachy B | 3 | 3 | 0 | 2 | 0 | 0 | 15.0 | 16 | 0 | 3.00 | 1.53 | 15 | 7 | -- | -- | -- | -- | -- | -- | 0 | 2 | 0 | 15.0 | 3.00 | 1.53 | 9.0 | 4.2 | 0.0 | .677 | .704 | .654 |
| Chavez J | 28 | 0 | 3 | 2 | 0 | 0 | 36.2 | 40 | 6 | 5.89 | 1.42 | 29 | 12 | 1 | 1 | 0 | 32.0 | 5.63 | 1.28 | 2 | 1 | 0 | 4.2 | 7.71 | 2.36 | 7.1 | 2.9 | 1.5 | .813 | .785 | .863 |
| Dunn M | 25 | 0 | 2 | 0 | 1 | 0 | 19.0 | 15 | 1 | 1.89 | 1.68 | 27 | 17 | -- | -- | -- | -- | -- | -- | 2 | 0 | 0 | 19.0 | 1.89 | 1.68 | 12.8 | 8.1 | 0.5 | .659 | .742 | .581 |
| Farnsworth K | 23 | 0 | 0 | 2 | 2 | 0 | 20.0 | 15 | 2 | 5.40 | 1.10 | 25 | 7 | -- | -- | -- | -- | -- | -- | 0 | 2 | 0 | 20.0 | 5.40 | 1.10 | 11.3 | 3.2 | 0.9 | .636 | .409 | .914 |
| Hanson T | 34 | 34 | 10 | 11 | 0 | 0 | 202.2 | 182 | 14 | 3.33 | 1.17 | 173 | 56 | 8 | 5 | 0 | 102.1 | 4.13 | 1.37 | 2 | 6 | 0 | 100.1 | 2.51 | 0.98 | 7.7 | 2.5 | 0.6 | .648 | .685 | .606 |
| Hudson T | 34 | 34 | 17 | 9 | 0 | 0 | 228.2 | 189 | 20 | 2.83 | 1.15 | 139 | 74 | 9 | 4 | 0 | 121.1 | 2.30 | 1.13 | 8 | 5 | 0 | 107.1 | 3.44 | 1.17 | 5.5 | 2.9 | 0.8 | .641 | .616 | .667 |
| Jurrjens J | 20 | 20 | 7 | 6 | 0 | 0 | 116.1 | 120 | 13 | 4.64 | 1.39 | 86 | 42 | 1 | 3 | 0 | 35.0 | 5.40 | 1.31 | 6 | 3 | 0 | 81.1 | 4.32 | 1.43 | 6.7 | 3.2 | 1.0 | .791 | .725 | .873 |
| Kawakami K | 18 | 16 | 1 | 10 | 0 | 0 | 87.1 | 98 | 10 | 5.15 | 1.49 | 59 | 32 | 1 | 9 | 0 | 82.1 | 4.48 | 1.40 | 0 | 1 | 0 | 5.0 | 16.20 | 3.00 | 6.1 | 3.3 | 1.0 | .830 | .788 | .880 |
| Kimbrel C | 21 | 0 | 4 | 0 | 2 | 1 | 20.2 | 9 | 0 | 0.44 | 1.21 | 40 | 16 | 2 | 0 | 0 | 8.1 | 1.08 | 1.68 | 2 | 0 | 1 | 12.1 | 0.00 | 0.89 | 17.4 | 7.0 | 0.0 | .437 | .361 | .523 |
| Lowe D | 33 | 33 | 16 | 12 | 0 | 0 | 193.2 | 204 | 18 | 4.00 | 1.37 | 136 | 61 | 9 | 8 | 0 | 113.2 | 4.35 | 1.41 | 7 | 4 | 0 | 80.0 | 3.49 | 1.31 | 6.3 | 2.8 | 0.8 | .728 | .715 | .741 |
| Martinez C | 18 | 0 | 0 | 0 | 0 | 0 | 26.0 | 28 | 3 | 4.85 | 1.31 | 22 | 6 | 0 | 0 | 0 | 10.2 | 5.06 | 1.22 | 0 | 0 | 0 | 15.1 | 4.70 | 1.37 | 7.6 | 2.1 | 1.0 | .746 | .630 | .890 |
| Medlen K | 31 | 14 | 6 | 2 | 1 | 0 | 107.2 | 108 | 13 | 3.68 | 1.20 | 83 | 21 | 6 | 1 | 0 | 88.1 | 3.16 | 1.15 | 0 | 1 | 0 | 19.1 | 6.05 | 1.40 | 6.9 | 1.8 | 1.1 | .725 | .693 | .765 |
| Minor M | 9 | 8 | 3 | 2 | 0 | 0 | 40.2 | 53 | 6 | 5.98 | 1.57 | 43 | 11 | -- | -- | -- | -- | -- | -- | 3 | 2 | 0 | 40.2 | 5.98 | 1.57 | 9.5 | 2.4 | 1.3 | .880 | .907 | .795 |
| Moylan P | 85 | 0 | 6 | 2 | 21 | 1 | 63.2 | 53 | 5 | 2.97 | 1.41 | 52 | 37 | 3 | 1 | 1 | 34.0 | 2.91 | 1.50 | 3 | 1 | 0 | 29.2 | 3.03 | 1.31 | 7.4 | 5.2 | 0.7 | .693 | .593 | .981 |
| O'Flaherty E | 56 | 0 | 3 | 2 | 9 | 0 | 44.0 | 37 | 2 | 2.45 | 1.25 | 36 | 18 | 3 | 1 | 0 | 31.1 | 2.30 | 1.21 | 0 | 1 | 0 | 12.2 | 2.84 | 1.34 | 7.4 | 3.7 | 0.4 | .647 | .690 | .598 |
| Proctor S | 6 | 0 | 0 | 0 | 0 | 0 | 5.2 | 4 | 1 | 6.35 | 1.41 | 6 | 4 | -- | -- | -- | -- | -- | -- | 0 | 0 | 0 | 5.2 | 6.35 | 1.41 | 9.5 | 6.4 | 1.6 | .783 | 1.128 | .455 |
| Resop C | 1 | 0 | 0 | 0 | 0 | 0 | 2.0 | 5 | 0 | 22.50 | 4.00 | 2 | 3 | 0 | 0 | 0 | 2.0 | 22.50 | 4.00 | -- | -- | -- | -- | -- | -- | 9.0 | 13.5 | 0.0 | 1.299 | .750 | 1.557 |
| Reyes J | 1 | 0 | 0 | 0 | 0 | 0 | 3.1 | 10 | 2 | 24.30 | 3.90 | 2 | 3 | 0 | 0 | 0 | 3.1 | 24.30 | 3.90 | -- | -- | -- | -- | -- | -- | 5.4 | 8.1 | 5.4 | 1.465 | 1.482 | 1.429 |
| Saito T | 56 | 0 | 2 | 3 | 17 | 1 | 54.0 | 41 | 4 | 2.83 | 1.07 | 69 | 17 | 1 | 3 | 0 | 34.0 | 3.71 | 1.21 | 1 | 0 | 1 | 20.0 | 1.35 | 0.85 | 11.5 | 2.8 | 0.7 | .577 | .513 | .660 |
| Venters J | 79 | 0 | 4 | 4 | 24 | 1 | 83.0 | 61 | 1 | 1.95 | 1.20 | 93 | 39 | 3 | 0 | 1 | 41.2 | 1.30 | 1.10 | 1 | 4 | 0 | 41.1 | 2.61 | 1.31 | 10.1 | 4.2 | 0.1 | .552 | .543 | .570 |
| Wagner B | 71 | 0 | 7 | 2 | 0 | 37 | 69.1 | 38 | 5 | 1.43 | 0.87 | 104 | 22 | 5 | 0 | 20 | 37.1 | 1.21 | 0.86 | 2 | 2 | 17 | 32.0 | 1.69 | 0.88 | 13.5 | 2.9 | 0.6 | .493 | .569 | .246 |

## Performance in 2010

### Production by Lineup Spot

### Production by Position

## Trends Among League

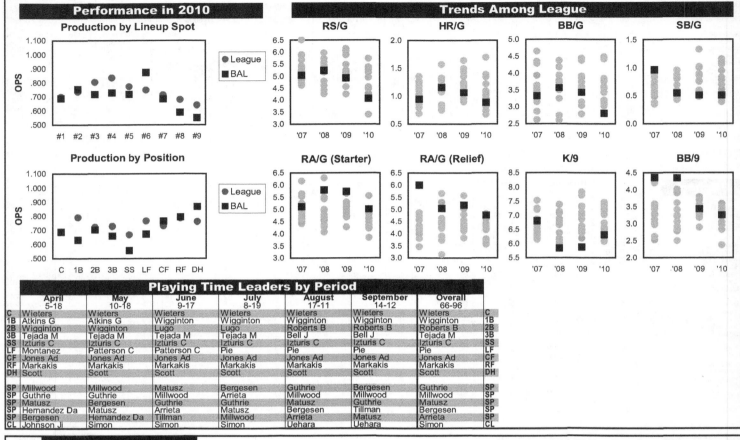

### Playing Time Leaders by Period

| | April 5-18 | May 10-18 | June 9-17 | July 8-19 | August 17-11 | September 14-12 | Overall 66-96 | |
|---|---|---|---|---|---|---|---|---|
| C | Wieters | Wieters | Wieters | Wieters | Wieters | Wieters | Wieters | C |
| 1B | Atkins G | Atkins G | Wigginton | Wigginton | Wigginton | Wigginton | Wigginton | 1B |
| 2B | Wigginton | Wigginton | Lugo | Lugo | Roberts B | Roberts B | Roberts B | 2B |
| 3B | Tejada M | Tejada M | Tejada M | Tejada M | Bell J | Bell J | Tejada M | 3B |
| SS | Izturis C | Izturis C | Izturis C | Izturis C | Izturis C | Izturis C | Izturis C | SS |
| LF | Montanez | Patterson C | Patterson C | Pie | Pie | Pie | Pie | LF |
| CF | Jones Ad | Jones Ad | Jones Ad | Jones Ad | Jones Ad | Jones Ad | Jones Ad | CF |
| RF | Markakis | Markakis | Markakis | Markakis | Markakis | Markakis | Markakis | RF |
| DH | Scott | Scott | Scott | Scott | Scott | Scott | Scott | DH |
| | | | | | | | | |
| SP | Millwood | Millwood | Matusz | Bergesen | Guthrie | Bergesen | Guthrie | SP |
| SP | Guthrie | Guthrie | Millwood | Arrieta | Millwood | Millwood | Millwood | SP |
| SP | Matusz | Bergesen | Guthrie | Guthrie | Matusz | Guthrie | Matusz | SP |
| SP | Hernandez Da | Matusz | Arrieta | Matusz | Bergesen | Tillman | Bergesen | SP |
| SP | Bergesen | Hernandez Da | Tillman | Millwood | Arrieta | Matusz | Arrieta | SP |
| CL | Johnson Ji | Simon | Simon | Simon | Uehara | Uehara | Simon | CL |

## Performance in 2010

### Production by Lineup Spot

### Production by Position

## Trends Among Leagues

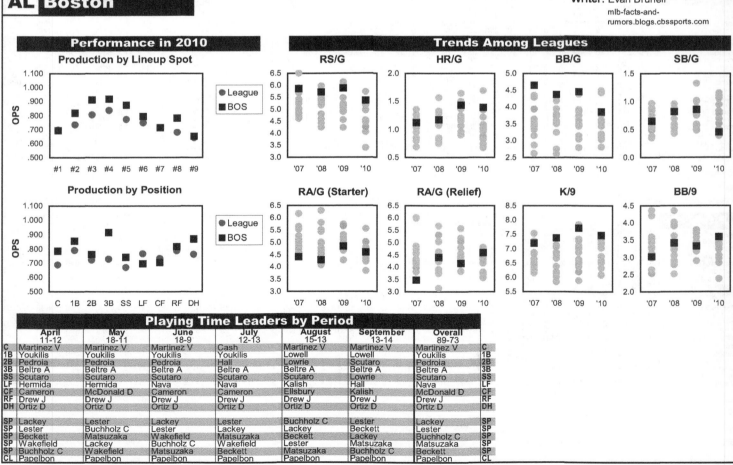

### Playing Time Leaders by Period

| | April 11-12 | May 18-11 | June 18-9 | July 12-13 | August 15-13 | September 13-14 | Overall 89-73 | |
|---|---|---|---|---|---|---|---|---|
| C | Martinez V | Martinez V | Martinez V | Cash | Martinez V | Martinez V | Martinez V | C |
| 1B | Youkilis | Youkilis | Youkilis | Youkilis | Lowell | Lowell | Youkilis | 1B |
| 2B | Pedroia | Pedroia | Pedroia | Hall | Lowrie | Scutaro | Pedroia | 2B |
| 3B | Beltre A | Beltre A | Beltre A | Beltre A | Beltre A | Beltre A | Beltre A | 3B |
| SS | Scutaro | Scutaro | Scutaro | Scutaro | Scutaro | Lowrie | Scutaro | SS |
| LF | Hermida | Hermida | Nava | Nava | Kalish | Hall | Nava | LF |
| CF | Cameron | McDonald D | Cameron | Cameron | Ellsbury | Kalish | McDonald D | CF |
| RF | Drew J | Drew J | Drew J | Drew J | Drew J | Drew J | Drew J | RF |
| DH | Ortiz D | Ortiz D | Ortiz D | Ortiz D | Ortiz D | Ortiz D | Ortiz D | DH |
| | | | | | | | | |
| SP | Lackey | Lester | Lackey | Lester | Buchholz C | Lester | Lackey | SP |
| SP | Lester | Buchholz C | Lester | Lackey | Lackey | Beckett | Lester | SP |
| SP | Beckett | Matsuza | Wakefield | Matsuzaka | Beckett | Lackey | Buchholz C | SP |
| SP | Wakefield | Lackey | Buchholz C | Wakefield | Lester | Matsuzaka | Matsuzaka | SP |
| SP | Buchholz C | Wakefield | Matsuzaka | Beckett | Matsuzaka | Buchholz C | Beckett | SP |
| CL | Papelbon | Papelbon | Papelbon | Papelbon | Papelbon | Papelbon | Papelbon | CL |

| Hitters | Baltimore Orioles 2010 | | | | | | | | | | | | | 1st Half | | | | | | 2nd Half | | | | | | Rates | | | | | Productiveness | | |
|---|---|---|---|---|---|---|---|---|---|---|---|---|---|---|---|---|---|---|---|---|---|---|---|---|---|---|---|---|---|---|---|---|---|
| | G | AB | R | H | 2B | 3B | HR | RBI | BA | OBP | SLG | SB | CS | AB | R | HR | BI | BA | SB | AB | R | HR | BI | BA | SB | CT% | H% | BB% | Bash | GB% | OPS | vs RH | vs LH |
| Andino R | 16 | 61 | 6 | 18 | 4 | 0 | 2 | 6 | .295 | .333 | .459 | 1 | 1 | --- | -- | -- | -- | --- | -- | 61 | 6 | 2 | 6 | .295 | 1 | 79% | 38% | 5% | 1.6 | 44% | .792 | .738 | .900 |
| Atkins G | 44 | 140 | 5 | 30 | 7 | 0 | 1 | 9 | .214 | .276 | .286 | 0 | 0 | 140 | 5 | 1 | 9 | .214 | 0 | --- | -- | -- | -- | --- | -- | 79% | 27% | 8% | 1.3 | 42% | .562 | .590 | .508 |
| Bell J | 53 | 159 | 15 | 34 | 5 | 0 | 3 | 12 | .214 | .224 | .302 | 0 | 1 | 15 | 1 | 0 | 0 | .200 | 0 | 144 | 14 | 3 | 12 | .215 | 0 | 67% | 32% | 1% | 1.4 | 57% | .525 | .474 | .652 |
| Fox J | 38 | 100 | 10 | 22 | 5 | 1 | 5 | 10 | .220 | .257 | .440 | 0 | 0 | 28 | 6 | 3 | 4 | .250 | 0 | 72 | 4 | 2 | 6 | .208 | 0 | 77% | 29% | 3% | 2.0 | 31% | .697 | .969 | .403 |
| Hughes R | 14 | 47 | 3 | 10 | 2 | 0 | 0 | 4 | .213 | .275 | .255 | 0 | 0 | 47 | 3 | 0 | 4 | .213 | 0 | --- | -- | -- | -- | --- | -- | 60% | 36% | 8% | 1.2 | 50% | .530 | .517 | .650 |
| Izturis C | 150 | 473 | 42 | 109 | 13 | 1 | 1 | 28 | .230 | .277 | .268 | 11 | 5 | 251 | 25 | 1 | 14 | .239 | 7 | 222 | 17 | 0 | 14 | .221 | 4 | 89% | 26% | 5% | 1.2 | 45% | .545 | .561 | .504 |
| Jones A | 149 | 581 | 76 | 165 | 25 | 5 | 19 | 69 | .284 | .325 | .442 | 7 | 7 | 351 | 44 | 14 | 39 | .276 | 3 | 230 | 32 | 5 | 30 | .296 | 4 | 80% | 36% | 4% | 1.6 | 45% | .767 | .804 | .666 |
| Lugo J | 93 | 241 | 26 | 60 | 4 | 2 | 0 | 20 | .249 | .298 | .282 | 5 | 7 | 169 | 19 | 0 | 13 | .260 | 5 | 72 | 7 | 0 | 7 | .222 | 0 | 79% | 31% | 6% | 1.1 | 48% | .581 | .487 | .716 |
| Markakis N | 160 | 629 | 79 | 187 | 45 | 3 | 12 | 60 | .297 | .370 | .436 | 7 | 2 | 334 | 40 | 6 | 31 | .308 | 3 | 295 | 39 | 6 | 29 | .285 | 4 | 85% | 35% | 10% | 1.5 | 46% | .805 | .762 | .906 |
| Montanez L | 26 | 57 | 2 | 8 | 0 | 0 | 0 | 3 | .140 | .155 | .140 | 1 | 0 | 57 | 2 | 0 | 3 | .140 | 1 | --- | -- | -- | -- | --- | -- | 84% | 17% | 2% | 1.0 | 48% | .296 | .368 | .153 |
| Moore S | 41 | 86 | 8 | 18 | 2 | 0 | 3 | 10 | .209 | .274 | .337 | 3 | 0 | 71 | 7 | 3 | 9 | .254 | 3 | 15 | 1 | 0 | 1 | .000 | 0 | 78% | 27% | 8% | 1.6 | 46% | .611 | .631 | .286 |
| Patterson C | 90 | 308 | 43 | 83 | 16 | 1 | 8 | 32 | .269 | .315 | .406 | 21 | 4 | 201 | 28 | 5 | 21 | .289 | 16 | 107 | 15 | 3 | 11 | .234 | 5 | 76% | 36% | 6% | 1.5 | 42% | .721 | .794 | .516 |
| Pie F | 82 | 288 | 39 | 79 | 15 | 5 | 5 | 31 | .274 | .305 | .413 | 5 | 2 | 36 | 5 | 2 | 4 | .333 | 0 | 252 | 34 | 3 | 27 | .266 | 5 | 82% | 33% | 4% | 1.5 | 51% | .718 | .730 | .676 |
| Reimold N | 39 | 116 | 9 | 24 | 5 | 0 | 3 | 14 | .207 | .282 | .328 | 0 | 0 | 83 | 7 | 2 | 10 | .205 | 0 | 33 | 2 | 1 | 4 | .212 | 0 | 78% | 27% | 9% | 1.6 | 50% | .610 | .519 | .735 |
| Roberts B | 59 | 230 | 28 | 64 | 14 | 0 | 4 | 15 | .278 | .354 | .391 | 12 | 2 | 14 | 1 | 0 | 0 | .143 | 2 | 216 | 27 | 4 | 15 | .287 | 10 | 83% | 34% | 10% | 1.4 | 34% | .745 | .726 | .801 |
| Scott L | 131 | 447 | 70 | 127 | 29 | 1 | 27 | 72 | .284 | .368 | .535 | 2 | 0 | 223 | 35 | 12 | 30 | .274 | 1 | 224 | 35 | 15 | 42 | .295 | 1 | 78% | 36% | 11% | 1.9 | 41% | .902 | .935 | .787 |
| Snyder B | 10 | 20 | 1 | 6 | 2 | 0 | 0 | 3 | .300 | .300 | .400 | 0 | 1 | --- | -- | -- | -- | --- | -- | 20 | 1 | 0 | 3 | .300 | 0 | 85% | 35% | 0% | 1.3 | 47% | .700 | .400 | 1.000 |
| Tatum C | 43 | 114 | 11 | 32 | 4 | 0 | 0 | 9 | .281 | .349 | .316 | 1 | 0 | 61 | 8 | 0 | 5 | .246 | 1 | 53 | 3 | 0 | 4 | .321 | 0 | 82% | 34% | 10% | 1.1 | 52% | .665 | .749 | .521 |
| Tejada M | 97 | 401 | 40 | 108 | 16 | 0 | 7 | 39 | .269 | .308 | .362 | 0 | 0 | 348 | 34 | 7 | 35 | .276 | 0 | 53 | 6 | 0 | 4 | .226 | 0 | 90% | 30% | 3% | 1.3 | 49% | .670 | .677 | .651 |
| Turner J | 5 | 9 | 0 | 0 | 0 | 0 | 0 | 0 | .000 | .000 | .000 | 0 | 0 | 9 | 0 | 0 | 0 | .000 | 0 | --- | -- | -- | -- | --- | -- | 67% | 0% | 0% | --- | 83% | .000 | .000 | .000 |
| Wieters M | 130 | 446 | 37 | 111 | 22 | 1 | 11 | 55 | .249 | .319 | .377 | 0 | 1 | 269 | 22 | 6 | 29 | .245 | 0 | 177 | 15 | 5 | 26 | .254 | 0 | 79% | 32% | 9% | 1.5 | 47% | .695 | .741 | .564 |
| Wigginton T | 154 | 581 | 63 | 144 | 29 | 1 | 22 | 76 | .248 | .312 | .415 | 0 | 1 | 302 | 32 | 14 | 45 | .252 | 0 | 279 | 31 | 8 | 31 | .244 | 0 | 80% | 31% | 8% | 1.7 | 48% | .727 | .743 | .679 |

| Pitchers | Baltimore Orioles 2010 | | | | | | | | | | | | | | 1st Half | | | | | | 2nd Half | | | | | | Rates | | | Productiveness | | |
|---|---|---|---|---|---|---|---|---|---|---|---|---|---|---|---|---|---|---|---|---|---|---|---|---|---|---|---|---|---|---|---|---|
| | G | GS | W | L | Hld | Sv | IP | H | HR | ERA | WHIP | K | BB | W | L | Sv | IP | ERA | WHIP | W | L | Sv | IP | ERA | WHIP | K/9 | BB/9 | HR/9 | opOPS | vs RH | vs LH |
| Albers M | 62 | 0 | 5 | 3 | 7 | 0 | 75.2 | 78 | 6 | 4.52 | 1.48 | 49 | 34 | 3 | 3 | 0 | 43.2 | 4.74 | 1.51 | 2 | 0 | 0 | 32.0 | 4.22 | 1.44 | 5.8 | 4.0 | 0.7 | .726 | .662 | .819 |
| Arrieta J | 18 | 18 | 6 | 6 | 0 | 0 | 100.1 | 106 | 9 | 4.66 | 1.53 | 52 | 48 | 3 | 2 | 0 | 39.0 | 4.38 | 1.54 | 3 | 4 | 0 | 61.1 | 4.84 | 1.53 | 4.7 | 4.3 | 0.8 | .767 | .594 | .898 |
| Bergesen B | 30 | 28 | 8 | 12 | 0 | 0 | 170.0 | 193 | 26 | 4.98 | 1.44 | 81 | 51 | 3 | 6 | 0 | 71.2 | 6.40 | 1.67 | 5 | 6 | 0 | 98.1 | 3.94 | 1.26 | 4.3 | 2.7 | 1.4 | .828 | .752 | .902 |
| Berken J | 41 | 0 | 3 | 3 | 7 | 0 | 62.1 | 64 | 5 | 3.03 | 1.33 | 45 | 19 | 2 | 1 | 0 | 50.2 | 1.95 | 1.13 | 1 | 2 | 0 | 11.2 | 7.71 | 2.23 | 6.5 | 2.7 | 0.7 | .728 | .780 | .632 |
| Castillo A | 14 | 0 | 1 | 0 | 1 | 0 | 10.2 | 16 | 5 | 10.13 | 2.06 | 11 | 6 | 1 | 0 | 0 | 10.2 | 10.13 | 2.06 | -- | -- | -- | ---- | ---- | --- | 9.3 | 5.1 | 4.2 | 1.187 | .990 | 1.373 |
| Gabino A | 5 | 0 | 0 | 0 | 0 | 0 | 4.2 | 9 | 3 | 13.50 | 2.57 | 2 | 3 | -- | -- | -- | ---- | ---- | --- | 0 | 0 | 0 | 4.2 | 13.50 | 2.57 | 3.9 | 5.8 | 5.8 | 1.288 | 1.000 | 1.843 |
| Gonzalez M | 29 | 0 | 1 | 3 | 10 | 1 | 24.2 | 18 | 1 | 4.01 | 1.30 | 31 | 14 | 0 | 2 | 1 | 2.0 | 18.00 | 4.50 | 1 | 1 | 0 | 22.2 | 2.78 | 1.01 | 11.3 | 5.1 | 0.4 | .629 | .495 | .849 |
| Guthrie J | 32 | 32 | 11 | 14 | 0 | 0 | 209.1 | 193 | 25 | 3.83 | 1.16 | 119 | 50 | 3 | 10 | 0 | 111.1 | 4.77 | 1.31 | 8 | 4 | 0 | 98.0 | 2.76 | 0.99 | 5.1 | 2.1 | 1.1 | .714 | .643 | .783 |
| Hendrickson M | 52 | 1 | 1 | 6 | 8 | 0 | 75.1 | 97 | 9 | 5.26 | 1.55 | 55 | 20 | 1 | 4 | 0 | 45.0 | 5.40 | 1.58 | 0 | 2 | 0 | 30.1 | 5.04 | 1.52 | 6.6 | 2.4 | 1.1 | .812 | .815 | .807 |
| Hernandez D | 41 | 8 | 8 | 8 | 2 | 2 | 79.1 | 72 | 9 | 4.31 | 1.44 | 72 | 42 | 4 | 7 | 2 | 60.2 | 4.45 | 1.48 | 4 | 1 | 0 | 18.2 | 3.86 | 1.29 | 8.2 | 4.8 | 1.0 | .733 | .726 | .743 |
| Johnson J | 26 | 0 | 1 | 1 | 11 | 1 | 26.1 | 32 | 2 | 3.42 | 1.41 | 22 | 5 | 1 | 1 | 1 | 9.2 | 6.52 | 1.97 | 0 | 0 | 0 | 16.2 | 1.62 | 1.08 | 7.5 | 1.7 | 0.7 | .722 | .773 | .668 |
| Mata F | 15 | 0 | 0 | 0 | 1 | 0 | 17.1 | 24 | 2 | 7.79 | 1.85 | 9 | 8 | 0 | 0 | 0 | 14.1 | 8.79 | 1.95 | 0 | 0 | 0 | 3.0 | 3.00 | 1.33 | 4.7 | 4.2 | 1.0 | .900 | .891 | .913 |
| Matusz B | 32 | 32 | 10 | 12 | 0 | 0 | 175.2 | 173 | 19 | 4.30 | 1.34 | 143 | 63 | 3 | 9 | 0 | 103.2 | 4.77 | 1.45 | 7 | 3 | 0 | 72.0 | 3.63 | 1.19 | 7.3 | 3.2 | 1.0 | .718 | .755 | .581 |
| Meredith C | 21 | 0 | 0 | 2 | 3 | 1 | 15.0 | 18 | 4 | 5.40 | 1.47 | 7 | 4 | 0 | 2 | 1 | 15.0 | 5.40 | 1.47 | -- | -- | -- | ---- | ---- | --- | 4.2 | 2.4 | 2.4 | .932 | .952 | .881 |
| Mickolio K | 3 | 0 | 0 | 0 | 0 | 0 | 3.2 | 5 | 1 | 7.36 | 2.18 | 4 | 3 | 0 | 0 | 0 | 3.2 | 7.36 | 2.18 | -- | -- | -- | ---- | ---- | --- | 9.8 | 7.4 | 2.5 | 1.046 | 1.250 | .833 |
| Millwood K | 31 | 31 | 4 | 16 | 0 | 0 | 190.2 | 223 | 30 | 5.10 | 1.51 | 132 | 65 | 2 | 8 | 0 | 107.2 | 5.77 | 1.58 | 2 | 8 | 0 | 83.0 | 4.23 | 1.42 | 6.2 | 3.1 | 1.4 | .813 | .788 | .836 |
| Ohman W | 51 | 0 | 0 | 0 | 15 | 0 | 30.0 | 30 | 3 | 3.30 | 1.60 | 29 | 18 | 0 | 0 | 0 | 26.1 | 2.73 | 1.52 | 0 | 0 | 0 | 3.2 | 7.36 | 2.18 | 8.7 | 5.4 | 0.9 | .765 | .934 | .631 |
| Patton T | 1 | 0 | 0 | 0 | 0 | 0 | 0.2 | 1 | 0 | 0.00 | 3.00 | 1 | 1 | -- | -- | -- | ---- | ---- | --- | 0 | 0 | 0 | 0.2 | 0.00 | 3.00 | 13.5 | 13.5 | 0.0 | 1.167 | ---- | 1.000 |
| Simon A | 49 | 0 | 4 | 2 | 1 | 17 | 49.1 | 54 | 10 | 4.93 | 1.54 | 37 | 22 | 2 | 1 | 13 | 25.0 | 3.24 | 1.48 | 2 | 1 | 4 | 24.1 | 6.66 | 1.60 | 6.8 | 4.0 | 1.8 | .825 | .953 | .684 |
| Tillman C | 11 | 11 | 2 | 5 | 0 | 0 | 53.2 | 51 | 9 | 5.87 | 1.53 | 31 | 31 | 1 | 3 | 0 | 22.1 | 5.64 | 1.61 | 1 | 2 | 0 | 31.1 | 6.03 | 1.47 | 5.2 | 5.2 | 1.5 | .828 | .733 | .930 |
| Uehara K | 43 | 0 | 1 | 2 | 6 | 13 | 44.0 | 37 | 5 | 2.86 | 0.95 | 55 | 5 | 0 | 0 | 0 | 9.0 | 4.00 | 1.67 | 1 | 2 | 13 | 35.0 | 2.57 | 0.77 | 11.3 | 1.0 | 1.0 | .594 | .465 | .747 |
| VandenHurk R | 7 | 1 | 0 | 1 | 0 | 0 | 16.1 | 13 | 2 | 4.96 | 1.22 | 17 | 7 | -- | -- | -- | ---- | ---- | --- | 0 | 1 | 0 | 16.1 | 4.96 | 1.22 | 9.4 | 3.9 | 1.1 | .697 | .475 | 1.053 |
| Viola P | 2 | 0 | 0 | 0 | 0 | 0 | 1.1 | 1 | 1 | 13.50 | 1.50 | 3 | 1 | -- | -- | -- | ---- | ---- | --- | 0 | 0 | 0 | 1.1 | 13.50 | 1.50 | 20.3 | 6.8 | 6.8 | 1.133 | 5.000 | .200 |

| Hitters | Boston Red Sox 2010 | | | | | | | | | | | | | 1st Half | | | | | | 2nd Half | | | | | | Rates | | | | | Productiveness | | |
|---|---|---|---|---|---|---|---|---|---|---|---|---|---|---|---|---|---|---|---|---|---|---|---|---|---|---|---|---|---|---|---|---|---|
| | G | AB | R | H | 2B | 3B | HR | RBI | BA | OBP | SLG | SB | CS | AB | R | HR | BI | BA | SB | AB | R | HR | BI | BA | SB | CT% | H% | BB% | Bash | GB% | OPS | vs RH | vs LH |
| Anderson L | 18 | 35 | 4 | 7 | 1 | 0 | 0 | 4 | .200 | .326 | .229 | 0 | 0 | --- | -- | -- | -- | --- | -- | 35 | 4 | 0 | 4 | .200 | 0 | 77% | 26% | 16% | 1.1 | 48% | .554 | .574 | .333 |
| Beltre A | 154 | 589 | 84 | 189 | 49 | 2 | 28 | 102 | .321 | .365 | .553 | 2 | 1 | 324 | 44 | 13 | 55 | .330 | 1 | 265 | 40 | 15 | 47 | .309 | 1 | 86% | 37% | 6% | 1.7 | 41% | .919 | .908 | .943 |
| Brown D | 7 | 12 | 0 | 3 | 1 | 0 | 0 | 2 | .250 | .250 | .333 | 0 | 0 | --- | -- | -- | -- | --- | -- | 12 | 0 | 0 | 2 | .250 | 0 | 83% | 30% | 0% | 1.3 | 40% | .583 | .800 | .429 |
| Cameron M | 48 | 162 | 24 | 42 | 11 | 0 | 4 | 15 | .259 | .328 | .401 | 0 | 1 | 120 | 19 | 3 | 14 | .283 | 0 | 42 | 5 | 1 | 1 | .190 | 0 | 73% | 36% | 8% | 1.5 | 29% | .729 | .588 | 1.128 |
| Cash K | 29 | 60 | 1 | 8 | 1 | 0 | 0 | 1 | .133 | .224 | .150 | 0 | 0 | 22 | 1 | 0 | 0 | .136 | 0 | 38 | 0 | 0 | 1 | .132 | 0 | 73% | 18% | 9% | 1.1 | 52% | .374 | .291 | .620 |
| Drew J | 139 | 478 | 69 | 122 | 24 | 2 | 22 | 68 | .255 | .341 | .452 | 3 | 1 | 262 | 46 | 10 | 42 | .275 | 2 | 216 | 23 | 12 | 26 | .231 | 1 | 78% | 33% | 11% | 1.8 | 45% | .793 | .875 | .611 |
| Ellsbury J | 18 | 78 | 10 | 15 | 4 | 0 | 0 | 5 | .192 | .241 | .244 | 7 | 1 | 44 | 7 | 0 | 3 | .250 | 2 | 34 | 3 | 0 | 2 | .118 | 5 | 88% | 22% | 5% | 1.3 | 49% | .485 | .488 | .471 |
| Hall B | 120 | 344 | 44 | 85 | 16 | 1 | 18 | 46 | .247 | .316 | .456 | 9 | 1 | 163 | 23 | 7 | 24 | .239 | 3 | 181 | 21 | 11 | 22 | .254 | 6 | 70% | 35% | 9% | 1.8 | 38% | .772 | .841 | .680 |
| Hermida J | 52 | 158 | 14 | 32 | 8 | 0 | 5 | 27 | .203 | .257 | .348 | 1 | 0 | 138 | 13 | 5 | 27 | .217 | 1 | 20 | 1 | 0 | 0 | .100 | 0 | 72% | 28% | 7% | 1.7 | 38% | .605 | .633 | .436 |
| Kalish R | 53 | 163 | 26 | 41 | 11 | 1 | 4 | 24 | .252 | .305 | .405 | 10 | 1 | --- | -- | -- | -- | --- | -- | 163 | 26 | 4 | 24 | .252 | 10 | 77% | 33% | 7% | 1.6 | 46% | .710 | .748 | .599 |
| Lopez F | 4 | 15 | 2 | 4 | 0 | 0 | 1 | 1 | .267 | .313 | .467 | 0 | 0 | --- | -- | -- | -- | --- | -- | 15 | 2 | 1 | 1 | .267 | 0 | 73% | 36% | 6% | 1.8 | 45% | .779 | .808 | .667 |
| Lowell M | 73 | 218 | 23 | 52 | 13 | 0 | 5 | 26 | .239 | .307 | .367 | 0 | 0 | 80 | 5 | 2 | 12 | .213 | 0 | 138 | 18 | 3 | 14 | .254 | 0 | 84% | 28% | 9% | 1.5 | 32% | .674 | .700 | .641 |
| Lowrie J | 55 | 171 | 31 | 49 | 14 | 0 | 9 | 24 | .287 | .381 | .526 | 1 | 1 | --- | -- | -- | -- | --- | -- | 171 | 31 | 9 | 24 | .287 | 1 | 85% | 34% | 13% | 1.8 | 29% | .907 | .823 | 1.025 |
| Martinez V | 127 | 493 | 64 | 149 | 32 | 1 | 20 | 79 | .302 | .351 | .493 | 1 | 0 | 246 | 36 | 9 | 38 | .289 | 1 | 247 | 28 | 11 | 41 | .316 | 0 | 89% | 34% | 7% | 1.6 | 41% | .844 | .694 | 1.173 |
| McDonald D | 117 | 319 | 40 | 86 | 18 | 3 | 9 | 34 | .270 | .336 | .429 | 9 | 1 | 192 | 22 | 6 | 24 | .271 | 6 | 127 | 18 | 3 | 10 | .268 | 3 | 73% | 37% | 8% | 1.6 | 42% | .766 | .715 | .821 |
| Nava D | 60 | 161 | 23 | 39 | 14 | 1 | 1 | 26 | .242 | .351 | .360 | 1 | 1 | 80 | 13 | 1 | 16 | .300 | 0 | 81 | 10 | 0 | 10 | .185 | 1 | 71% | 34% | 10% | 1.5 | 39% | .711 | .727 | .637 |
| Navarro Y | 20 | 42 | 4 | 6 | 0 | 0 | 0 | 5 | .143 | .174 | .143 | 0 | 0 | --- | -- | -- | -- | --- | -- | 42 | 4 | 0 | 5 | .143 | 0 | 60% | 24% | 4% | 1.0 | 48% | .317 | .215 | .494 |
| Ortiz D | 145 | 518 | 86 | 140 | 36 | 1 | 32 | 102 | .270 | .370 | .529 | 0 | 1 | 251 | 46 | 18 | 57 | .263 | 0 | 267 | 40 | 14 | 45 | .277 | 0 | 72% | 38% | 13% | 2.0 | 38% | .899 | 1.059 | .599 |
| Patterson E | 45 | 84 | 13 | 19 | 3 | 3 | 2 | 7 | .226 | .293 | .405 | 5 | 1 | 26 | 6 | 2 | 3 | .269 | 0 | 58 | 7 | 0 | 4 | .207 | 5 | 63% | 36% | 8% | 1.8 | 28% | .698 | .628 | 1.183 |
| Pedroia D | 75 | 302 | 53 | 87 | 24 | 1 | 12 | 41 | .288 | .367 | .493 | 9 | 1 | 295 | 52 | 12 | 41 | .292 | 8 | 7 | 1 | 0 | 0 | .143 | 1 | 87% | 33% | 11% | 1.7 | 40% | .860 | .910 | .700 |
| Reddick J | 29 | 62 | 5 | 12 | 3 | 1 | 1 | 5 | .194 | .206 | .323 | 1 | 0 | 25 | 2 | 0 | 2 | .160 | 1 | 37 | 3 | 1 | 3 | .216 | 0 | 76% | 26% | 2% | 1.7 | 45% | .529 | .488 | 1.000 |
| Saltalamacchia J | 10 | 19 | 2 | 3 | 3 | 0 | 0 | 1 | .158 | .360 | .316 | 0 | 0 | --- | -- | -- | -- | --- | -- | 19 | 2 | 0 | 1 | .158 | 0 | 79% | 20% | 24% | 2.0 | 47% | .676 | .733 | .654 |
| Scutaro M | 150 | 632 | 92 | 174 | 38 | 0 | 11 | 56 | .275 | .333 | .388 | 5 | 4 | 357 | 52 | 4 | 28 | .283 | 2 | 275 | 40 | 7 | 28 | .265 | 3 | 89% | 31% | 8% | 1.4 | 41% | .721 | .711 | .743 |
| Shealy R | 5 | 7 | 0 | 0 | 0 | 0 | 0 | 0 | .000 | .000 | .000 | 0 | 0 | 3 | 0 | 0 | 0 | .000 | 0 | 4 | 0 | 0 | 0 | .000 | 0 | 71% | 0% | 0% | --- | 40% | .000 | .000 | .000 |
| Van Every J | 22 | 19 | 6 | 4 | 1 | 0 | 1 | 1 | .211 | .286 | .421 | 0 | 0 | 19 | 6 | 1 | 1 | .211 | 0 | --- | -- | -- | -- | --- | -- | 53% | 40% | 10% | 2.0 | 50% | .707 | .886 | .000 |
| Varitek J | 39 | 112 | 18 | 26 | 6 | 0 | 7 | 16 | .232 | .293 | .473 | 0 | 0 | 95 | 18 | 7 | 16 | .263 | 0 | 17 | 0 | 0 | 0 | .059 | 0 | 69% | 34% | 8% | 2.0 | 27% | .766 | .733 | .868 |
| Youkilis K | 102 | 362 | 77 | 111 | 26 | 5 | 19 | 62 | .307 | .411 | .564 | 4 | 1 | 294 | 67 | 18 | 57 | .293 | 3 | 68 | 10 | 1 | 5 | .368 | 1 | 81% | 38% | 13% | 1.8 | 38% | .975 | .863 | 1.311 |

| Pitchers | Boston Red Sox 2010 | | | | | | | | | | | | | | 1st Half | | | | | | 2nd Half | | | | | | Rates | | | Productiveness | | |
|---|---|---|---|---|---|---|---|---|---|---|---|---|---|---|---|---|---|---|---|---|---|---|---|---|---|---|---|---|---|---|---|---|
| | G | GS | W | L | Hld | Sv | IP | H | HR | ERA | WHIP | K | BB | W | L | Sv | IP | ERA | WHIP | W | L | Sv | IP | ERA | WHIP | K/9 | BB/9 | HR/9 | opOPS | vs RH | vs LH |
| Atchison S | 43 | 1 | 2 | 3 | 7 | 0 | 60.0 | 58 | 9 | 4.50 | 1.28 | 41 | 19 | 1 | 1 | 0 | 28.2 | 4.71 | 1.19 | 1 | 2 | 0 | 31.1 | 4.31 | 1.37 | 6.2 | 2.9 | 1.4 | .736 | .645 | .839 |
| Bard D | 73 | 0 | 1 | 2 | 32 | 3 | 74.2 | 45 | 6 | 1.93 | 1.00 | 76 | 30 | 1 | 2 | 3 | 42.2 | 1.90 | 0.82 | 0 | 0 | 0 | 32.0 | 1.97 | 1.25 | 9.2 | 3.6 | 0.7 | .540 | .627 | .462 |
| Beckett J | 21 | 21 | 6 | 6 | 0 | 0 | 127.2 | 151 | 20 | 5.78 | 1.54 | 116 | 45 | 1 | 1 | 0 | 45.2 | 7.29 | 1.66 | 5 | 5 | 0 | 82.0 | 4.94 | 1.46 | 8.2 | 3.2 | 1.4 | .848 | .726 | .940 |
| Bonser B | 2 | 0 | 0 | 0 | 0 | 0 | 2.0 | 6 | 0 | 18.00 | 4.00 | 0 | 2 | 0 | 0 | 0 | 2.0 | 18.00 | 4.00 | -- | -- | -- | ---- | ---- | --- | 0.0 | 9.0 | 0.0 | 1.161 | 1.071 | 1.267 |
| Bowden M | 14 | 0 | 0 | 1 | 0 | 0 | 15.1 | 20 | 2 | 4.70 | 1.57 | 13 | 4 | -- | -- | -- | ---- | ---- | --- | 0 | 1 | 0 | 15.1 | 4.70 | 1.57 | 7.6 | 2.3 | 1.2 | .912 | .809 | 1.024 |
| Buchholz C | 28 | 28 | 17 | 7 | 0 | 0 | 173.2 | 142 | 9 | 2.33 | 1.20 | 120 | 67 | 10 | 4 | 0 | 92.0 | 2.45 | 1.25 | 7 | 3 | 0 | 81.2 | 2.20 | 1.15 | 6.2 | 3.5 | 0.5 | .615 | .571 | .651 |
| Cabrera F | 1 | 0 | 0 | 0 | 0 | 0 | 1.1 | 2 | 1 | 20.25 | 3.00 | 0 | 2 | -- | -- | -- | ---- | ---- | --- | 0 | 0 | 0 | 1.1 | 20.25 | 3.00 | 0.0 | 13.5 | 6.8 | 1.571 | 1.850 | .500 |
| Coello R | 6 | 0 | 0 | 0 | 0 | 0 | 5.2 | 4 | 0 | 4.76 | 1.59 | 5 | 5 | -- | -- | -- | ---- | ---- | --- | 0 | 0 | 0 | 5.2 | 4.76 | 1.59 | 7.9 | 7.9 | 0.0 | .537 | .200 | .990 |
| Delcarmen M | 48 | 0 | 3 | 2 | 8 | 0 | 44.0 | 33 | 7 | 4.70 | 1.39 | 32 | 28 | 2 | 2 | 0 | 33.1 | 4.59 | 1.41 | 1 | 0 | 0 | 10.2 | 5.06 | 1.31 | 6.5 | 5.7 | 1.4 | .687 | .817 | .551 |
| Doubront F | 12 | 3 | 2 | 2 | 1 | 2 | 25.0 | 27 | 3 | 4.32 | 1.48 | 23 | 10 | 1 | 1 | 0 | 10.2 | 4.22 | 1.59 | 1 | 1 | 2 | 14.1 | 4.40 | 1.40 | 8.3 | 3.6 | 1.1 | .789 | .911 | .576 |
| Fox M | 3 | 0 | 0 | 0 | 0 | 0 | 1.2 | 4 | 0 | 10.80 | 3.00 | 0 | 1 | -- | -- | -- | ---- | ---- | --- | 0 | 0 | 0 | 1.2 | 10.80 | 3.00 | 0.0 | 5.4 | 0.0 | 1.125 | 1.667 | .250 |
| Hill R | 6 | 0 | 1 | 0 | 1 | 0 | 4.0 | 5 | 0 | 0.00 | 1.50 | 3 | 1 | -- | -- | -- | ---- | ---- | --- | 1 | 0 | 0 | 4.0 | 0.00 | 1.50 | 6.8 | 2.3 | 0.0 | .627 | .944 | .250 |
| Lackey J | 33 | 33 | 14 | 11 | 0 | 0 | 215.0 | 233 | 18 | 4.40 | 1.42 | 156 | 72 | 9 | 5 | 0 | 113.0 | 4.78 | 1.60 | 5 | 6 | 0 | 102.0 | 3.97 | 1.22 | 6.5 | 3.0 | 0.8 | .765 | .719 | .802 |
| Lester J | 32 | 32 | 19 | 9 | 0 | 0 | 208.0 | 167 | 14 | 3.25 | 1.20 | 225 | 83 | 11 | 3 | 0 | 120.0 | 2.78 | 1.09 | 8 | 6 | 0 | 88.0 | 3.89 | 1.35 | 9.7 | 3.6 | 0.6 | .628 | .620 | .651 |
| Manuel R | 10 | 0 | 1 | 0 | 0 | 0 | 12.2 | 10 | 5 | 4.26 | 1.34 | 5 | 7 | 0 | 0 | 0 | 4.1 | 6.23 | 1.15 | 1 | 0 | 0 | 8.1 | 3.24 | 1.44 | 3.6 | 5.0 | 3.6 | .911 | 1.088 | .670 |
| Matsuzaka D | 25 | 25 | 9 | 6 | 0 | 0 | 153.2 | 137 | 13 | 4.69 | 1.37 | 133 | 74 | 6 | 3 | 0 | 71.0 | 4.56 | 1.39 | 3 | 3 | 0 | 82.2 | 4.79 | 1.35 | 7.8 | 4.3 | 0.8 | .706 | .626 | .770 |
| Nelson J | 8 | 0 | 0 | 0 | 0 | 0 | 8.1 | 14 | 2 | 9.72 | 2.40 | 9 | 6 | 0 | 0 | 0 | 8.1 | 9.72 | 2.40 | -- | -- | -- | ---- | ---- | --- | 9.7 | 6.5 | 2.2 | 1.060 | .707 | 1.262 |
| Okajima H | 56 | 0 | 4 | 4 | 11 | 0 | 46.0 | 59 | 6 | 4.50 | 1.72 | 33 | 20 | 2 | 2 | 0 | 27.0 | 6.00 | 1.89 | 2 | 2 | 0 | 19.0 | 2.37 | 1.47 | 6.5 | 3.9 | 1.2 | .841 | .936 | .732 |
| Papelbon J | 65 | 0 | 5 | 7 | 0 | 37 | 67.0 | 57 | 7 | 3.90 | 1.27 | 76 | 28 | 3 | 4 | 20 | 36.0 | 3.50 | 1.11 | 2 | 3 | 17 | 31.0 | 4.35 | 1.45 | 10.2 | 3.8 | 0.9 | .674 | .619 | .717 |
| Ramirez R | 44 | 0 | 0 | 3 | 2 | 2 | 42.1 | 39 | 6 | 4.46 | 1.30 | 31 | 16 | 0 | 2 | 1 | 35.2 | 4.79 | 1.32 | 0 | 1 | 1 | 6.2 | 2.70 | 1.20 | 6.6 | 3.4 | 1.3 | .768 | .758 | .780 |
| Richardson D | 26 | 0 | 0 | 0 | 2 | 0 | 13.0 | 15 | 2 | 4.15 | 2.23 | 12 | 14 | 0 | 0 | 0 | 5.1 | 3.38 | 1.69 | 0 | 0 | 0 | 7.2 | 4.70 | 2.61 | 8.3 | 9.7 | 1.4 | .915 | .695 | 1.129 |
| Schoeneweis S | 15 | 0 | 1 | 0 | 1 | 0 | 13.2 | 19 | 2 | 7.90 | 2.12 | 13 | 10 | 1 | 0 | 0 | 13.2 | 7.90 | 2.12 | -- | -- | -- | ---- | ---- | --- | 8.6 | 6.6 | 1.3 | .935 | .952 | .914 |
| Wakefield T | 32 | 19 | 4 | 10 | 0 | 0 | 140.0 | 153 | 19 | 5.34 | 1.35 | 84 | 36 | 3 | 7 | 0 | 100.0 | 5.22 | 1.32 | 1 | 3 | 0 | 40.0 | 5.63 | 1.43 | 5.4 | 2.3 | 1.2 | .773 | .780 | .766 |

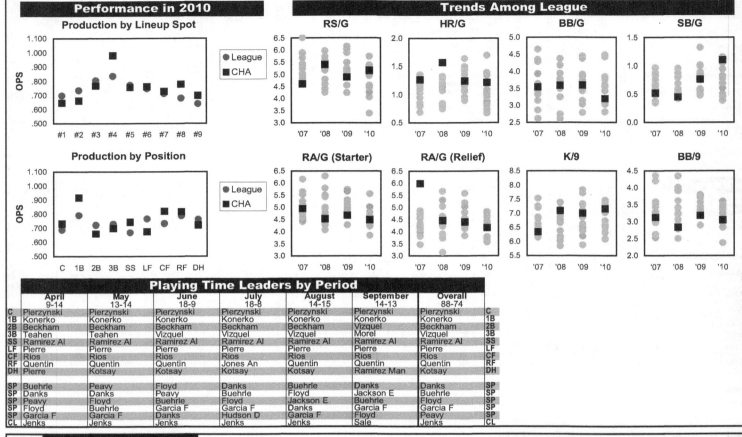

## Performance in 2010 / Trends Among League

### Playing Time Leaders by Period

| | April 9-14 | May 13-14 | June 18-9 | July 18-8 | August 14-15 | September 14-13 | Overall 88-74 | |
|---|---|---|---|---|---|---|---|---|
| C | Pierzynski | Pierzynski | Pierzynski | Pierzynski | Pierzynski | Pierzynski | Pierzynski | C |
| 1B | Konerko | Konerko | Konerko | Konerko | Konerko | Konerko | Konerko | 1B |
| 2B | Beckham | Beckham | Beckham | Beckham | Beckham | Vizquel | Beckham | 2B |
| 3B | Teahen | Teahen | Vizquel | Vizquel | Vizquel | Morel | Vizquel | 3B |
| SS | Ramirez Al | Ramirez Al | Ramirez Al | Ramirez Al | Ramirez Al | Ramirez Al | Ramirez Al | SS |
| LF | Pierre | Pierre | Pierre | Pierre | Pierre | Pierre | Pierre | LF |
| CF | Rios | Rios | Rios | Rios | Rios | Rios | Rios | CF |
| RF | Quentin | Quentin | Quentin | Jones An | Quentin | Quentin | Quentin | RF |
| DH | Pierre | Kotsay | Kotsay | Kotsay | Kotsay | Ramirez Man | Kotsay | DH |
| | | | | | | | | |
| SP | Buehrle | Peavy | Floyd | Danks | Buehrle | Danks | Danks | SP |
| SP | Danks | Danks | Peavy | Buehrle | Floyd | Jackson E | Buehrle | SP |
| SP | Peavy | Floyd | Buehrle | Floyd | Jackson E | Buehrle | Floyd | SP |
| SP | Floyd | Buehrle | Garcia F | Garcia F | Danks | Garcia F | Garcia F | SP |
| SP | Garcia F | Garcia F | Danks | Hudson D | Garcia F | Floyd | Peavy | SP |
| CL | Jenks | Jenks | Jenks | Jenks | Jenks | Sale | Jenks | CL |

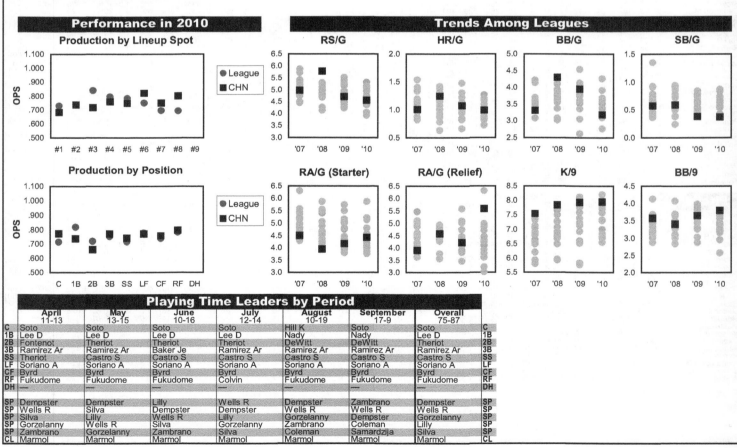

## Performance in 2010 / Trends Among Leagues

### Playing Time Leaders by Period

| | April 11-13 | May 13-15 | June 10-16 | July 12-14 | August 10-19 | September 17-9 | Overall 75-87 | |
|---|---|---|---|---|---|---|---|---|
| C | Soto | Soto | Soto | Soto | Hill K | Soto | Soto | C |
| 1B | Lee D | Lee D | Lee D | Lee D | Nady | Nady | Lee D | 1B |
| 2B | Fontenot | Theriot | Theriot | Theriot | DeWitt | DeWitt | Theriot | 2B |
| 3B | Ramirez Ar | Ramirez Ar | Baker Je | Ramirez Ar | Ramirez Ar | Ramirez Ar | Ramirez Ar | 3B |
| SS | Theriot | Castro S | Castro S | Castro S | Castro S | Castro S | Castro S | SS |
| LF | Soriano A | Soriano A | Soriano A | Soriano A | Soriano A | Soriano A | Soriano A | LF |
| CF | Byrd | Byrd | Byrd | Byrd | Byrd | Byrd | Byrd | CF |
| RF | Fukudome | Fukudome | Fukudome | Colvin | Fukudome | Fukudome | Fukudome | RF |
| DH | — | — | — | — | — | — | — | DH |
| | | | | | | | | |
| SP | Dempster | Dempster | Lilly | Wells R | Dempster | Zambrano | Dempster | SP |
| SP | Wells R | Silva | Dempster | Dempster | Wells R | Wells R | Wells R | SP |
| SP | Silva | Lilly | Wells R | Lilly | Gorzelanny | Dempster | Gorzelanny | SP |
| SP | Gorzelanny | Wells R | Silva | Gorzelanny | Zambrano | Coleman | Lilly | SP |
| SP | Zambrano | Gorzelanny | Zambrano | Silva | Coleman | Samardzija | Silva | SP |
| CL | Marmol | Marmol | Marmol | Marmol | Marmol | Marmol | Marmol | CL |

| Hitters | Chicago White Sox 2010 | | | | | | | | | | | | | 1st Half | | | | | | 2nd Half | | | | | | Rates | | | | | Productiveness | | |
|---|---|---|---|---|---|---|---|---|---|---|---|---|---|---|---|---|---|---|---|---|---|---|---|---|---|---|---|---|---|---|---|---|---|
| | G | AB | R | H | 2B | 3B | HR | RBI | BA | OBP | SLG | SB | CS | AB | R | HR | BI | BA | SB | AB | R | HR | BI | BA | SB | CT% | H% | BB% | Bash | GB% | OPS | vs RH | vs LH |
| Beckham G | 131 | 444 | 58 | 112 | 25 | 2 | 9 | 49 | .252 | .317 | .378 | 4 | 6 | 273 | 35 | 3 | 22 | .216 | 4 | 171 | 23 | 6 | 27 | .310 | 0 | 79% | 32% | 7% | 1.5 | 45% | .695 | .705 | .667 |
| Castro R | 37 | 115 | 18 | 32 | 2 | 0 | 8 | 21 | .278 | .328 | .504 | 1 | 0 | 43 | 6 | 2 | 8 | .302 | 1 | 72 | 12 | 6 | 13 | .264 | 0 | 77% | 36% | 7% | 1.8 | 43% | .832 | .780 | .953 |
| De Aza A | 19 | 30 | 7 | 9 | 3 | 0 | 0 | 2 | .300 | .323 | .400 | 2 | 1 | --- | -- | -- | -- | --- | -- | 30 | 7 | 0 | 2 | .300 | 2 | 87% | 35% | 3% | 1.3 | 54% | .723 | .692 | .900 |
| Flowers T | 8 | 11 | 2 | 1 | 0 | 0 | 0 | 0 | .091 | .333 | .091 | 0 | 0 | --- | -- | -- | -- | --- | -- | 11 | 2 | 0 | 0 | .091 | 0 | 55% | 17% | 27% | 1.0 | 33% | .424 | .542 | .000 |
| Jones A | 107 | 278 | 41 | 64 | 12 | 1 | 19 | 48 | .230 | .341 | .486 | 9 | 2 | 186 | 24 | 12 | 29 | .210 | 8 | 92 | 17 | 7 | 19 | .272 | 1 | 74% | 31% | 14% | 2.1 | 45% | .827 | .781 | .931 |
| Konerko P | 149 | 548 | 89 | 171 | 30 | 1 | 39 | 111 | .312 | .393 | .584 | 0 | 1 | 291 | 50 | 20 | 63 | .299 | 0 | 257 | 39 | 19 | 48 | .327 | 0 | 80% | 39% | 11% | 1.9 | 36% | .977 | .941 | 1.102 |
| Kotsay M | 107 | 327 | 30 | 78 | 17 | 2 | 8 | 31 | .239 | .306 | .376 | 1 | 3 | 187 | 20 | 6 | 19 | .230 | 1 | 140 | 10 | 2 | 12 | .250 | 0 | 89% | 27% | 9% | 1.6 | 44% | .683 | .733 | .074 |
| Lillibridge B | 64 | 98 | 19 | 22 | 5 | 2 | 2 | 16 | .224 | .248 | .378 | 5 | 3 | 22 | 5 | 1 | 10 | .455 | 1 | 76 | 14 | 1 | 6 | .158 | 4 | 63% | 35% | 3% | 1.7 | 34% | .625 | .459 | .949 |
| Lucy D | 7 | 15 | 2 | 5 | 3 | 0 | 1 | 2 | .333 | .444 | .733 | 1 | 0 | 15 | 2 | 1 | 2 | .333 | 1 | --- | -- | -- | -- | --- | -- | 80% | 42% | 11% | 2.2 | 42% | 1.178 | .733 | 1.400 |
| Morel B | 21 | 65 | 9 | 15 | 3 | 0 | 3 | 7 | .231 | .271 | .415 | 2 | 0 | --- | -- | -- | -- | --- | -- | 65 | 9 | 3 | 7 | .231 | 2 | 74% | 31% | 6% | 1.8 | 50% | .687 | .594 | .974 |
| Nix J | 24 | 49 | 3 | 8 | 1 | 0 | 1 | 5 | .163 | .268 | .245 | 0 | 0 | 49 | 3 | 1 | 5 | .163 | 0 | --- | -- | -- | -- | --- | -- | 76% | 22% | 12% | 1.5 | 32% | .513 | .851 | .259 |
| Pierre J | 160 | 651 | 96 | 179 | 18 | 3 | 1 | 47 | .275 | .341 | .316 | 68 | 18 | 339 | 46 | 0 | 14 | .257 | 32 | 312 | 50 | 1 | 33 | .295 | 36 | 93% | 30% | 6% | 1.2 | 55% | .657 | .642 | .700 |
| Pierzynski A | 128 | 474 | 43 | 128 | 29 | 0 | 9 | 56 | .270 | .300 | .388 | 3 | 4 | 263 | 23 | 6 | 25 | .247 | 0 | 211 | 20 | 3 | 31 | .299 | 3 | 92% | 29% | 3% | 1.4 | 49% | .688 | .702 | .642 |
| Quentin C | 131 | 453 | 73 | 110 | 25 | 2 | 26 | 87 | .243 | .342 | .479 | 2 | 2 | 262 | 48 | 19 | 61 | .244 | 0 | 191 | 25 | 7 | 26 | .241 | 2 | 82% | 30% | 9% | 2.0 | 37% | .821 | .838 | .764 |
| Ramirez A | 156 | 585 | 83 | 165 | 29 | 2 | 18 | 70 | .282 | .313 | .431 | 13 | 8 | 299 | 33 | 8 | 33 | .274 | 3 | 286 | 50 | 10 | 37 | .290 | 10 | 86% | 33% | 4% | 1.5 | 48% | .744 | .751 | .725 |
| Ramirez M | 24 | 69 | 6 | 18 | 1 | 0 | 1 | 2 | .261 | .420 | .319 | 0 | 0 | --- | -- | -- | -- | --- | -- | 69 | 6 | 1 | 2 | .261 | 0 | 67% | 39% | 16% | 1.2 | 41% | .739 | .736 | .752 |
| Rios A | 147 | 567 | 89 | 161 | 29 | 3 | 21 | 88 | .284 | .334 | .457 | 34 | 14 | 311 | 55 | 15 | 49 | .305 | 23 | 256 | 34 | 6 | 39 | .258 | 11 | 84% | 34% | 6% | 1.6 | 46% | .791 | .814 | .717 |
| Teahen M | 77 | 233 | 31 | 60 | 13 | 2 | 4 | 25 | .258 | .327 | .382 | 3 | 5 | 137 | 16 | 3 | 14 | .255 | 3 | 96 | 15 | 1 | 11 | .260 | 0 | 74% | 35% | 10% | 1.5 | 48% | .709 | .761 | .433 |
| Viciedo D | 38 | 104 | 17 | 32 | 7 | 0 | 5 | 13 | .308 | .321 | .519 | 1 | 0 | 40 | 8 | 2 | 5 | .300 | 1 | 64 | 9 | 3 | 8 | .313 | 0 | 76% | 41% | 2% | 1.7 | 42% | .840 | .729 | .960 |
| Vizquel O | 108 | 344 | 36 | 95 | 11 | 1 | 2 | 30 | .276 | .341 | .331 | 11 | 7 | 138 | 19 | 1 | 15 | .254 | 2 | 206 | 17 | 1 | 15 | .291 | 9 | 87% | 32% | 9% | 1.2 | 46% | .673 | .695 | .559 |

| Pitchers | Chicago White Sox 2010 | | | | | | | | | | | | | 1st Half | | | | | | 2nd Half | | | | | | Rates | | | Productiveness | | |
|---|---|---|---|---|---|---|---|---|---|---|---|---|---|---|---|---|---|---|---|---|---|---|---|---|---|---|---|---|---|---|---|
| | G | GS | W | L | Hld | Sv | IP | H | HR | ERA | WHIP | K | BB | W | L | Sv | IP | ERA | WHIP | W | L | Sv | IP | ERA | WHIP | K/9 | BB/9 | HR/9 | opOPS | vs RH | vs LH |
| Buehrle M | 33 | 33 | 13 | 13 | 0 | 0 | 210.1 | 246 | 17 | 4.28 | 1.40 | 99 | 49 | 8 | 7 | 0 | 110.1 | 4.24 | 1.43 | 5 | 6 | 0 | 100.0 | 4.32 | 1.37 | 4.2 | 2.1 | 0.7 | .751 | .751 | .749 |
| Danks J | 32 | 32 | 15 | 11 | 0 | 0 | 213.0 | 189 | 18 | 3.72 | 1.22 | 162 | 70 | 8 | 7 | 0 | 112.0 | 3.29 | 1.13 | 7 | 4 | 0 | 101.0 | 4.19 | 1.31 | 6.8 | 3.0 | 0.8 | .657 | .640 | .694 |
| Floyd G | 31 | 31 | 10 | 13 | 0 | 0 | 187.1 | 199 | 14 | 4.08 | 1.37 | 151 | 58 | 5 | 7 | 0 | 111.1 | 4.20 | 1.29 | 5 | 6 | 0 | 76.0 | 3.91 | 1.49 | 7.3 | 2.8 | 0.7 | .719 | .775 | .673 |
| Garcia F | 28 | 28 | 12 | 6 | 0 | 0 | 157.0 | 171 | 23 | 4.64 | 1.38 | 89 | 45 | 9 | 3 | 0 | 97.0 | 4.36 | 1.33 | 3 | 3 | 0 | 60.0 | 5.10 | 1.45 | 5.1 | 2.6 | 1.3 | .804 | .826 | .784 |
| Harrell L | 8 | 3 | 1 | 0 | 0 | 0 | 24.0 | 34 | 2 | 4.88 | 2.13 | 15 | 17 | -- | -- | -- | ---- | ---- | --- | 1 | 0 | 0 | 24.0 | 4.88 | 2.13 | 5.6 | 6.4 | 0.8 | .898 | .727 | 1.047 |
| Hudson D | 3 | 3 | 1 | 1 | 0 | 0 | 15.2 | 17 | 1 | 6.32 | 1.79 | 14 | 11 | 0 | 0 | 0 | 4.0 | 11.25 | 2.25 | 1 | 1 | 0 | 11.2 | 4.63 | 1.63 | 8.0 | 6.3 | 0.6 | .797 | .816 | .780 |
| Infante G | 5 | 0 | 0 | 0 | 0 | 0 | 4.2 | 2 | 0 | 0.00 | 1.29 | 5 | 4 | -- | -- | -- | ---- | ---- | --- | 0 | 0 | 0 | 4.2 | 0.00 | 1.29 | 9.6 | 7.7 | 0.0 | .449 | .111 | .786 |
| Jackson E | 11 | 11 | 4 | 2 | 0 | 0 | 75.0 | 73 | 8 | 3.24 | 1.21 | 77 | 18 | -- | -- | -- | ---- | ---- | --- | 4 | 2 | 0 | 75.0 | 3.24 | 1.21 | 9.2 | 2.2 | 1.0 | .663 | .718 | .636 |
| Jenks B | 55 | 0 | 1 | 3 | 0 | 27 | 52.2 | 54 | 3 | 4.44 | 1.37 | 61 | 18 | 1 | 1 | 19 | 32.2 | 3.86 | 1.44 | 0 | 2 | 8 | 20.0 | 5.40 | 1.25 | 10.4 | 3.1 | 0.5 | .668 | .689 | .648 |
| Linebrink S | 52 | 0 | 3 | 2 | 4 | 0 | 57.1 | 59 | 11 | 4.40 | 1.33 | 52 | 17 | 1 | 0 | 0 | 29.1 | 4.91 | 1.43 | 2 | 2 | 0 | 28.0 | 3.86 | 1.21 | 8.2 | 2.7 | 1.7 | .780 | .647 | .901 |
| Marquez J | 1 | 0 | 0 | 0 | 0 | 0 | 1.0 | 2 | 1 | 18.00 | 2.00 | 0 | 0 | 0 | 0 | 0 | 1.0 | 18.00 | 2.00 | -- | -- | -- | ---- | ---- | --- | 0.0 | 0.0 | 9.0 | 1.400 | 1.667 | 1.000 |
| Peavy J | 17 | 17 | 7 | 6 | 0 | 0 | 107.0 | 98 | 13 | 4.63 | 1.23 | 93 | 34 | 7 | 6 | 0 | 107.0 | 4.63 | 1.23 | -- | -- | -- | ---- | ---- | --- | 7.8 | 2.9 | 1.1 | .698 | .666 | .729 |
| Pena T | 52 | 3 | 5 | 3 | 1 | 0 | 100.2 | 108 | 10 | 5.10 | 1.52 | 56 | 45 | 3 | 1 | 0 | 44.2 | 4.63 | 1.39 | 2 | 2 | 0 | 56.0 | 5.46 | 1.63 | 5.0 | 4.0 | 0.9 | .765 | .813 | .709 |
| Putz J | 60 | 0 | 7 | 5 | 14 | 3 | 54.0 | 41 | 4 | 2.83 | 1.04 | 65 | 15 | 5 | 2 | 2 | 34.0 | 1.59 | 0.74 | 2 | 3 | 1 | 20.0 | 4.95 | 1.55 | 10.8 | 2.5 | 0.7 | .575 | .454 | .721 |
| Sale C | 21 | 0 | 2 | 1 | 2 | 4 | 23.1 | 15 | 2 | 1.93 | 1.07 | 32 | 10 | -- | -- | -- | ---- | ---- | --- | 2 | 1 | 4 | 23.1 | 1.93 | 1.07 | 12.3 | 3.9 | 0.8 | .546 | .454 | .694 |
| Santos S | 56 | 0 | 2 | 2 | 14 | 1 | 51.2 | 53 | 2 | 2.96 | 1.53 | 56 | 26 | 0 | 0 | 1 | 28.0 | 1.93 | 1.32 | 2 | 2 | 0 | 23.2 | 4.18 | 1.77 | 9.8 | 4.5 | 0.3 | .692 | .812 | .513 |
| Thornton M | 61 | 0 | 5 | 4 | 21 | 8 | 60.2 | 41 | 3 | 2.67 | 1.01 | 81 | 20 | 2 | 3 | 5 | 36.2 | 2.70 | 1.04 | 3 | 1 | 3 | 24.0 | 2.63 | 0.96 | 12.0 | 3.0 | 0.4 | .547 | .584 | .500 |
| Threets E | 11 | 0 | 0 | 0 | 0 | 0 | 12.1 | 9 | 0 | 0.00 | 0.97 | 6 | 3 | 0 | 0 | 0 | 2.0 | 0.00 | 1.00 | 0 | 0 | 0 | 10.1 | 0.00 | 0.97 | 4.4 | 2.2 | 0.0 | .486 | .364 | .697 |
| Torres C | 5 | 1 | 0 | 1 | 0 | 0 | 13.2 | 23 | 2 | 8.56 | 2.34 | 13 | 9 | -- | -- | -- | ---- | ---- | --- | 0 | 1 | 0 | 13.2 | 8.56 | 2.34 | 8.6 | 5.9 | 1.3 | 1.041 | 1.041 | 1.039 |
| Williams R | 27 | 0 | 0 | 1 | 1 | 0 | 25.0 | 37 | 2 | 5.40 | 2.32 | 22 | 21 | 0 | 1 | 0 | 25.0 | 5.40 | 2.32 | -- | -- | -- | ---- | ---- | --- | 7.9 | 7.6 | 0.7 | .995 | 1.083 | .890 |

| Hitters | Chicago Cubs 2010 | | | | | | | | | | | | | 1st Half | | | | | | 2nd Half | | | | | | Rates | | | | | Productiveness | | |
|---|---|---|---|---|---|---|---|---|---|---|---|---|---|---|---|---|---|---|---|---|---|---|---|---|---|---|---|---|---|---|---|---|---|
| | G | AB | R | H | 2B | 3B | HR | RBI | BA | OBP | SLG | SB | CS | AB | R | HR | BI | BA | SB | AB | R | HR | BI | BA | SB | CT% | H% | BB% | Bash | GB% | OPS | vs RH | vs LH |
| Baker J | 79 | 206 | 29 | 56 | 13 | 2 | 4 | 21 | .272 | .326 | .413 | 1 | 0 | 120 | 14 | 3 | 12 | .233 | 0 | 86 | 15 | 1 | 9 | .326 | 1 | 76% | 36% | 7% | 1.5 | 42% | .739 | .302 | .945 |
| Barney D | 30 | 79 | 12 | 19 | 4 | 0 | 0 | 2 | .241 | .294 | .291 | 0 | 0 | --- | -- | -- | -- | --- | -- | 79 | 12 | 0 | 2 | .241 | 0 | 85% | 28% | 7% | 1.2 | 54% | .585 | .528 | .699 |
| Byrd M | 152 | 580 | 84 | 170 | 39 | 2 | 12 | 66 | .293 | .346 | .429 | 5 | 1 | 331 | 47 | 9 | 40 | .317 | 4 | 249 | 37 | 3 | 26 | .261 | 1 | 83% | 35% | 5% | 1.5 | 52% | .775 | .717 | .916 |
| Castillo W | 7 | 20 | 3 | 6 | 4 | 0 | 1 | 5 | .300 | .333 | .650 | 0 | 0 | --- | -- | -- | -- | --- | -- | 20 | 3 | 1 | 5 | .300 | 0 | 65% | 46% | 5% | 2.2 | 23% | .983 | 1.167 | .708 |
| Castro S | 125 | 463 | 53 | 139 | 31 | 5 | 3 | 41 | .300 | .347 | .408 | 10 | 8 | 196 | 19 | 2 | 24 | .270 | 1 | 267 | 34 | 1 | 17 | .322 | 9 | 85% | 35% | 6% | 1.4 | 52% | .755 | .701 | .897 |
| Colvin T | 135 | 358 | 60 | 91 | 18 | 5 | 20 | 56 | .254 | .316 | .500 | 6 | 1 | 179 | 29 | 12 | 32 | .263 | 2 | 179 | 31 | 8 | 24 | .246 | 4 | 72% | 35% | 8% | 2.0 | 43% | .816 | .813 | .820 |
| DeWitt B | 53 | 184 | 18 | 46 | 9 | 1 | 4 | 22 | .250 | .314 | .375 | 1 | 0 | --- | -- | -- | -- | --- | -- | 184 | 18 | 4 | 22 | .250 | 1 | 80% | 31% | 8% | 1.5 | 45% | .689 | .672 | .763 |
| Fontenot M | 75 | 169 | 14 | 48 | 11 | 3 | 1 | 20 | .284 | .332 | .402 | 1 | 2 | 154 | 11 | 1 | 18 | .292 | 1 | 15 | 3 | 0 | 2 | .200 | 0 | 83% | 34% | 5% | 1.4 | 44% | .734 | .735 | .714 |
| Fukudome K | 130 | 358 | 45 | 94 | 20 | 2 | 13 | 44 | .263 | .371 | .439 | 7 | 8 | 222 | 28 | 8 | 26 | .252 | 4 | 136 | 17 | 5 | 18 | .279 | 3 | 81% | 32% | 15% | 1.7 | 50% | .809 | .804 | .850 |
| Fuld S | 19 | 28 | 3 | 4 | 1 | 0 | 0 | 3 | .143 | .226 | .179 | 0 | 0 | --- | -- | -- | -- | --- | -- | 28 | 3 | 0 | 3 | .143 | 0 | 82% | 17% | 10% | 1.3 | 43% | .404 | .374 | .667 |
| Hill K | 77 | 215 | 18 | 46 | 13 | 1 | 1 | 17 | .214 | .254 | .298 | 1 | 0 | 89 | 6 | 0 | 8 | .213 | 0 | 126 | 12 | 1 | 9 | .214 | 1 | 72% | 30% | 5% | 1.4 | 49% | .552 | .523 | .694 |
| Hoffpauir M | 24 | 52 | 5 | 9 | 3 | 0 | 0 | 5 | .173 | .246 | .231 | 0 | 0 | --- | -- | -- | -- | --- | -- | 52 | 5 | 0 | 5 | .173 | 0 | 71% | 24% | 9% | 1.3 | 51% | .476 | .408 | .873 |
| Lee D | 109 | 418 | 63 | 105 | 21 | 0 | 16 | 56 | .251 | .335 | .416 | 1 | 3 | 322 | 42 | 10 | 36 | .233 | 1 | 96 | 21 | 6 | 20 | .313 | 0 | 76% | 33% | 11% | 1.7 | 39% | .751 | .762 | .723 |
| Nady X | 119 | 317 | 33 | 81 | 13 | 0 | 6 | 33 | .256 | .306 | .353 | 0 | 0 | 138 | 12 | 4 | 19 | .225 | 0 | 179 | 21 | 2 | 14 | .279 | 0 | 73% | 35% | 5% | 1.4 | 47% | .660 | .667 | .649 |
| Ramirez A | 124 | 465 | 61 | 112 | 21 | 1 | 25 | 83 | .241 | .294 | .452 | 0 | 0 | 237 | 29 | 10 | 32 | .207 | 0 | 228 | 32 | 15 | 51 | .276 | 0 | 81% | 30% | 7% | 1.9 | 28% | .745 | .722 | .816 |
| Scales B | 10 | 13 | 4 | 4 | 0 | 0 | 0 | 2 | .308 | .550 | .308 | 1 | 0 | --- | -- | -- | -- | --- | -- | 13 | 4 | 0 | 2 | .308 | 1 | 62% | 50% | 35% | 1.0 | 63% | .858 | .776 | 2.000 |
| Snyder B | 12 | 27 | 1 | 5 | 1 | 0 | 0 | 5 | .185 | .214 | .222 | 0 | 0 | --- | -- | -- | -- | --- | -- | 27 | 1 | 0 | 5 | .185 | 0 | 56% | 33% | 4% | 1.2 | 40% | .437 | .511 | .000 |
| Soriano A | 147 | 496 | 67 | 128 | 40 | 3 | 24 | 79 | .258 | .322 | .496 | 5 | 1 | 268 | 44 | 15 | 44 | .269 | 4 | 228 | 23 | 9 | 35 | .246 | 1 | 75% | 34% | 8% | 1.9 | 29% | .818 | .764 | .944 |
| Soto G | 105 | 322 | 47 | 90 | 19 | 0 | 17 | 53 | .280 | .393 | .497 | 0 | 1 | 204 | 29 | 9 | 27 | .284 | 0 | 118 | 18 | 8 | 26 | .271 | 0 | 74% | 38% | 16% | 1.8 | 36% | .890 | .796 | 1.072 |
| Theriot R | 96 | 388 | 45 | 110 | 10 | 2 | 1 | 21 | .284 | .320 | .327 | 16 | 6 | 335 | 39 | 0 | 18 | .278 | 16 | 53 | 6 | 1 | 3 | .321 | 0 | 88% | 32% | 5% | 1.2 | 54% | .647 | .644 | .654 |
| Tracy C | 28 | 44 | 6 | 11 | 2 | 0 | 0 | 5 | .250 | .327 | .295 | 0 | 0 | 44 | 6 | 0 | 5 | .250 | 0 | --- | -- | -- | -- | --- | -- | 66% | 38% | 10% | 1.2 | 41% | .622 | .650 | .000 |

| Pitchers | Chicago Cubs 2010 | | | | | | | | | | | | | 1st Half | | | | | | 2nd Half | | | | | | Rates | | | Productiveness | | |
|---|---|---|---|---|---|---|---|---|---|---|---|---|---|---|---|---|---|---|---|---|---|---|---|---|---|---|---|---|---|---|---|
| | G | GS | W | L | Hld | Sv | IP | H | HR | ERA | WHIP | K | BB | W | L | Sv | IP | ERA | WHIP | W | L | Sv | IP | ERA | WHIP | K/9 | BB/9 | HR/9 | opOPS | vs RH | vs LH |
| Atkins M | 5 | 0 | 0 | 0 | 0 | 0 | 10.0 | 12 | 2 | 6.30 | 1.80 | 10 | 6 | 0 | 0 | 0 | 3.0 | 6.00 | 2.33 | 0 | 0 | 0 | 7.0 | 6.43 | 1.57 | 9.0 | 5.4 | 1.8 | .864 | .580 | 1.313 |
| Berg J | 41 | 0 | 0 | 1 | 5 | 0 | 40.0 | 45 | 3 | 5.18 | 1.63 | 14 | 20 | 0 | 0 | 0 | 16.2 | 5.40 | 1.44 | 0 | 1 | 0 | 23.1 | 5.01 | 1.76 | 3.2 | 4.5 | 0.7 | .738 | .756 | .694 |
| Caridad E | 8 | 0 | 0 | 1 | 1 | 0 | 4.0 | 4 | 1 | 11.25 | 2.25 | 4 | 5 | 0 | 1 | 0 | 4.0 | 11.25 | 2.25 | -- | -- | -- | ---- | ---- | --- | 9.0 | 11.3 | 2.3 | .862 | .806 | 1.000 |
| Cashner A | 53 | 0 | 2 | 6 | 16 | 0 | 54.1 | 55 | 8 | 4.80 | 1.56 | 50 | 30 | 0 | 3 | 0 | 18.2 | 2.41 | 1.39 | 2 | 3 | 0 | 35.2 | 6.06 | 1.65 | 8.3 | 5.0 | 1.3 | .795 | .726 | .904 |
| Coleman C | 12 | 8 | 4 | 2 | 0 | 0 | 57.0 | 56 | 3 | 4.11 | 1.42 | 27 | 25 | -- | -- | -- | ---- | ---- | --- | 4 | 2 | 0 | 57.0 | 4.11 | 1.42 | 4.3 | 3.9 | 0.5 | .705 | .643 | .807 |
| Dempster R | 34 | 34 | 15 | 12 | 0 | 0 | 215.1 | 198 | 25 | 3.85 | 1.32 | 208 | 86 | 7 | 7 | 0 | 122.0 | 3.61 | 1.20 | 8 | 5 | 0 | 93.1 | 4.15 | 1.48 | 8.7 | 3.6 | 1.0 | .712 | .717 | .704 |
| Diamond T | 16 | 3 | 1 | 3 | 0 | 0 | 29.0 | 33 | 5 | 6.83 | 1.76 | 36 | 18 | -- | -- | -- | ---- | ---- | --- | 1 | 3 | 0 | 29.0 | 6.83 | 1.76 | 11.2 | 5.6 | 1.6 | .875 | .945 | .754 |
| Gorzelanny T | 29 | 23 | 7 | 9 | 1 | 1 | 136.1 | 136 | 11 | 4.09 | 1.50 | 119 | 68 | 4 | 5 | 1 | 74.0 | 3.16 | 1.41 | 3 | 4 | 0 | 62.1 | 5.20 | 1.60 | 7.9 | 4.5 | 0.7 | .742 | .716 | .823 |
| Grabow J | 28 | 0 | 1 | 3 | 7 | 0 | 25.2 | 35 | 5 | 7.36 | 1.87 | 20 | 13 | 1 | 3 | 0 | 25.2 | 7.36 | 1.87 | -- | -- | -- | ---- | ---- | --- | 7.0 | 4.6 | 1.8 | .930 | .983 | .811 |
| Gray J | 7 | 0 | 1 | 0 | 0 | 0 | 9.1 | 12 | 1 | 6.75 | 1.82 | 4 | 5 | 1 | 0 | 0 | 9.1 | 6.75 | 1.82 | -- | -- | -- | ---- | ---- | --- | 3.9 | 4.8 | 1.0 | .935 | .866 | 1.055 |
| Howry B | 24 | 0 | 0 | 3 | 2 | 0 | 20.2 | 29 | 2 | 5.66 | 1.74 | 8 | 7 | 0 | 2 | 0 | 16.0 | 1.69 | 1.25 | 0 | 1 | 0 | 4.2 | 19.29 | 3.43 | 3.5 | 3.0 | 0.9 | .917 | .985 | .755 |
| Lilly T | 18 | 18 | 3 | 8 | 0 | 0 | 117.0 | 104 | 19 | 3.69 | 1.14 | 89 | 29 | 3 | 8 | 0 | 97.0 | 4.08 | 1.15 | 0 | 0 | 0 | 20.0 | 1.80 | 1.05 | 6.8 | 2.2 | 1.5 | .697 | .677 | .781 |
| Maine S | 13 | 0 | 0 | 0 | 2 | 0 | 13.0 | 9 | 1 | 2.08 | 1.08 | 11 | 5 | -- | -- | -- | ---- | ---- | --- | 0 | 0 | 0 | 13.0 | 2.08 | 1.08 | 7.6 | 3.5 | 0.7 | .572 | .404 | 1.185 |
| Marmol C | 77 | 0 | 2 | 3 | 0 | 38 | 77.2 | 40 | 1 | 2.55 | 1.18 | 138 | 52 | 2 | 1 | 16 | 41.2 | 2.16 | 1.22 | 0 | 2 | 22 | 36.0 | 3.00 | 1.14 | 16.0 | 6.0 | 0.1 | .500 | .508 | .490 |
| Marshall S | 80 | 0 | 7 | 5 | 22 | 1 | 74.2 | 58 | 3 | 2.65 | 1.11 | 90 | 25 | 5 | 2 | 1 | 44.1 | 2.03 | 1.06 | 2 | 3 | 0 | 30.1 | 3.56 | 1.19 | 10.8 | 3.0 | 0.4 | .569 | .585 | .539 |
| Mateo M | 21 | 0 | 0 | 1 | 1 | 0 | 21.2 | 20 | 6 | 5.82 | 1.34 | 26 | 9 | -- | -- | -- | ---- | ---- | --- | 0 | 1 | 0 | 21.2 | 5.82 | 1.34 | 10.8 | 3.7 | 2.5 | .829 | .780 | .900 |
| Russell J | 57 | 0 | 1 | 1 | 6 | 0 | 49.0 | 55 | 11 | 4.96 | 1.35 | 42 | 11 | 0 | 1 | 0 | 27.1 | 3.62 | 1.21 | 1 | 0 | 0 | 21.2 | 6.65 | 1.52 | 7.7 | 2.0 | 2.0 | .822 | .887 | .726 |
| Samardzija J | 7 | 3 | 2 | 2 | 0 | 0 | 19.1 | 21 | 4 | 8.38 | 2.12 | 9 | 20 | 0 | 1 | 0 | 3.1 | 18.90 | 3.30 | 2 | 1 | 0 | 16.0 | 6.19 | 1.88 | 4.2 | 9.3 | 1.9 | .930 | 1.202 | .470 |
| Schlitter B | 7 | 0 | 0 | 1 | 0 | 0 | 8.0 | 18 | 2 | 12.38 | 2.88 | 7 | 5 | 0 | 0 | 0 | 3.0 | 15.00 | 2.00 | 0 | 1 | 0 | 5.0 | 10.80 | 3.40 | 7.9 | 5.6 | 2.3 | 1.167 | .906 | 1.478 |
| Silva C | 21 | 21 | 10 | 6 | 0 | 0 | 113.0 | 120 | 11 | 4.22 | 1.27 | 80 | 24 | 9 | 3 | 0 | 101.2 | 3.45 | 1.14 | 1 | 3 | 0 | 11.1 | 11.12 | 2.47 | 6.4 | 1.9 | 0.9 | .734 | .749 | .708 |
| Stevens J | 18 | 0 | 0 | 0 | 1 | 0 | 17.2 | 21 | 4 | 6.11 | 1.75 | 15 | 10 | 0 | 0 | 0 | 17.1 | 5.71 | 1.67 | 0 | 0 | 0 | 0.1 | 27.00 | 6.00 | 7.6 | 5.1 | 2.0 | .931 | .788 | 1.577 |
| Wells R | 32 | 32 | 8 | 14 | 0 | 0 | 194.1 | 209 | 19 | 4.26 | 1.40 | 144 | 63 | 4 | 7 | 0 | 105.1 | 4.61 | 1.40 | 4 | 7 | 0 | 89.0 | 3.84 | 1.40 | 6.7 | 2.9 | 0.9 | .745 | .775 | .700 |
| Zambrano C | 36 | 20 | 11 | 6 | 4 | 0 | 129.2 | 119 | 7 | 3.33 | 1.45 | 117 | 69 | 3 | 6 | 0 | 55.2 | 5.66 | 1.69 | 8 | 0 | 0 | 74.0 | 1.58 | 1.27 | 8.1 | 4.8 | 0.5 | .678 | .594 | .788 |

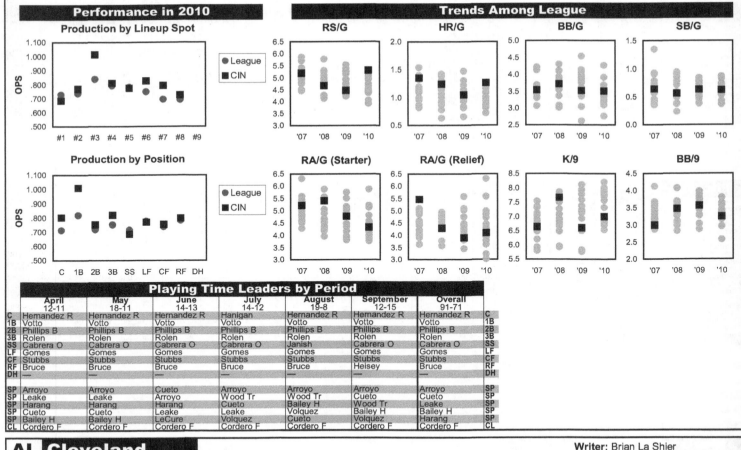

## Performance in 2010

### Production by Lineup Spot

### Production by Position

## Trends Among League

RS/G | HR/G | BB/G | SB/G

RA/G (Starter) | RA/G (Relief) | K/9 | BB/9

### Playing Time Leaders by Period

| | April 12-11 | May 18-11 | June 14-13 | July 14-12 | August 19-8 | September 12-15 | Overall 91-71 | |
|---|---|---|---|---|---|---|---|---|
| C | Hernandez R | Hernandez R | Hernandez R | Hanigan | Hernandez R | Hernandez R | Hernandez R | C |
| 1B | Votto | Votto | Votto | Votto | Votto | Votto | Votto | 1B |
| 2B | Phillips B | Phillips B | Phillips B | Phillips B | Phillips B | Phillips B | Phillips B | 2B |
| 3B | Rolen | Rolen | Rolen | Rolen | Rolen | Rolen | Rolen | 3B |
| SS | Cabrera O | Cabrera O | Cabrera O | Cabrera O | Janish | Cabrera O | Cabrera O | SS |
| LF | Gomes | Gomes | Gomes | Gomes | Gomes | Gomes | Gomes | LF |
| CF | Stubbs | Stubbs | Stubbs | Stubbs | Stubbs | Stubbs | Stubbs | CF |
| RF | Bruce | Bruce | Bruce | Bruce | Bruce | Heisey | Bruce | RF |
| DH | — | — | — | — | — | — | — | DH |
| SP | Arroyo | Arroyo | Cueto | Arroyo | Arroyo | Arroyo | Arroyo | SP |
| SP | Leake | Leake | Arroyo | Wood Tr | Wood Tr | Cueto | Cueto | SP |
| SP | Harang | Harang | Harang | Cueto | Bailey H | Wood Tr | Leake | SP |
| SP | Cueto | Cueto | Leake | Leake | Volquez | Bailey H | Bailey H | SP |
| SP | Bailey H | Bailey H | LeCure | Volquez | Cueto | Volquez | Harang | SP |
| CL | Cordero F | Cordero F | Cordero F | Cordero F | Cordero F | Cordero F | Cordero F | CL |

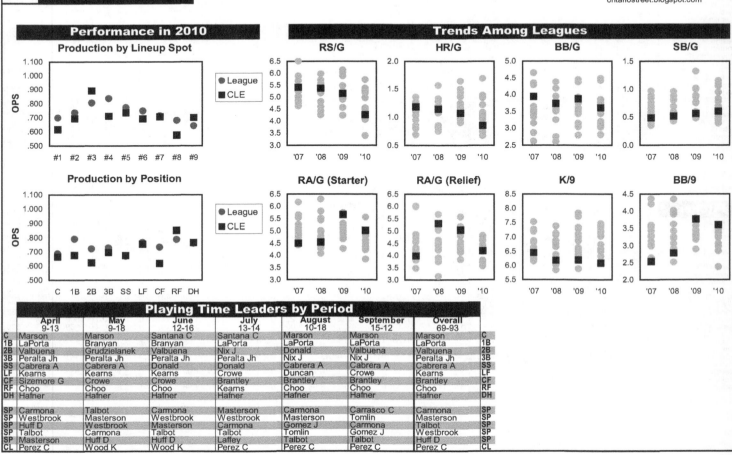

## Performance in 2010

### Production by Lineup Spot

### Production by Position

## Trends Among Leagues

RS/G | HR/G | BB/G | SB/G

RA/G (Starter) | RA/G (Relief) | K/9 | BB/9

### Playing Time Leaders by Period

| | April 9-13 | May 9-18 | June 12-16 | July 13-14 | August 10-18 | September 15-12 | Overall 69-93 | |
|---|---|---|---|---|---|---|---|---|
| C | Marson | Marson | Santana C | Santana C | Marson | Marson | Marson | C |
| 1B | LaPorta | Branyan | Branyan | LaPorta | LaPorta | LaPorta | LaPorta | 1B |
| 2B | Valbuena | Grudzielanek | Valbuena | Nix J | Donald | Valbuena | Valbuena | 2B |
| 3B | Peralta Jh | Peralta Jh | Peralta Jh | Peralta Jh | Nix J | Nix J | Peralta Jh | 3B |
| SS | Cabrera A | Cabrera A | Donald | Donald | Cabrera A | Cabrera A | Cabrera A | SS |
| LF | Kearns | Kearns | Kearns | Crowe | Duncan | Crowe | Kearns | LF |
| CF | Sizemore G | Crowe | Crowe | Brantley | Brantley | Brantley | Brantley | CF |
| RF | Choo | Choo | Choo | Kearns | Choo | Choo | Choo | RF |
| DH | Hafner | Hafner | Hafner | Hafner | Hafner | Hafner | Hafner | DH |
| SP | Carmona | Talbot | Carmona | Masterson | Carmona | Carrasco C | Carmona | SP |
| SP | Westbrook | Masterson | Westbrook | Westbrook | Masterson | Tomlin | Masterson | SP |
| SP | Huff D | Westbrook | Masterson | Carmona | Gomez J | Carmona | Talbot | SP |
| SP | Talbot | Carmona | Talbot | Talbot | Tomlin | Gomez J | Westbrook | SP |
| SP | Masterson | Huff D | Huff D | Laffey | Talbot | Talbot | Huff D | SP |
| CL | Perez C | Wood K | Wood K | Perez C | Perez C | Perez C | Perez C | CL |

| Hitters | Cincinnati Reds 2010 | | | | | | | | | | | | | 1st Half | | | | | | 2nd Half | | | | | | Rates | | | | | Productiveness | | |
|---|---|---|---|---|---|---|---|---|---|---|---|---|---|---|---|---|---|---|---|---|---|---|---|---|---|---|---|---|---|---|---|---|---|
| | G | AB | R | H | 2B | 3B | HR | RBI | BA | OBP | SLG | SB | CS | AB | R | HR | BI | BA | SB | AB | R | HR | BI | BA | SB | CT% | H% | BB% | Bash | GB% | OPS | vs RH | vs LH |
| Alonso Y | 22 | 29 | 2 | 6 | 2 | 0 | 0 | 3 | .207 | .207 | .276 | 0 | 0 | --- | -- | -- | -- | --- | -- | 29 | 2 | 0 | 3 | .207 | 0 | 66% | 32% | 0% | 1.3 | 47% | .483 | .600 | .222 |
| Bloomquist W | 11 | 17 | 0 | 5 | 0 | 0 | 0 | 0 | .294 | .333 | .294 | 0 | 0 | --- | -- | -- | -- | --- | -- | 17 | 0 | 0 | 0 | .294 | 0 | 82% | 36% | 6% | 1.0 | 50% | .627 | 1.196 | .200 |
| Bruce J | 148 | 509 | 80 | 143 | 23 | 5 | 25 | 70 | .281 | .353 | .493 | 5 | 4 | 323 | 50 | 10 | 36 | .266 | 5 | 186 | 30 | 15 | 34 | .306 | 0 | 73% | 38% | 10% | 1.8 | 36% | .846 | .821 | .899 |
| Cabrera O | 123 | 494 | 64 | 130 | 33 | 0 | 4 | 42 | .263 | .303 | .354 | 11 | 4 | 347 | 41 | 3 | 31 | .245 | 10 | 147 | 23 | 1 | 11 | .306 | 1 | 89% | 29% | 5% | 1.3 | 45% | .657 | .601 | .804 |
| Cairo M | 91 | 200 | 30 | 58 | 12 | 0 | 4 | 28 | .290 | .353 | .410 | 4 | 0 | 108 | 14 | 2 | 13 | .306 | 1 | 92 | 16 | 2 | 15 | .272 | 3 | 85% | 34% | 8% | 1.4 | 44% | .763 | .813 | .659 |
| Dickerson C | 20 | 44 | 9 | 9 | 1 | 1 | 0 | 0 | .205 | .222 | .273 | 3 | 0 | 44 | 9 | 0 | 0 | .205 | 3 | --- | -- | -- | -- | --- | -- | 57% | 36% | 2% | 1.3 | 52% | .495 | .558 | .000 |
| Edmonds J | 13 | 29 | 6 | 6 | 2 | 0 | 3 | 3 | .207 | .281 | .586 | 0 | 0 | --- | -- | -- | -- | --- | -- | 29 | 6 | 3 | 3 | .207 | 0 | 76% | 27% | 9% | 2.8 | 18% | .867 | .964 | .000 |
| Francisco J | 36 | 55 | 3 | 15 | 3 | 0 | 1 | 7 | .273 | .322 | .382 | 0 | 1 | 6 | 0 | 0 | 1 | .167 | 0 | 49 | 3 | 1 | 6 | .286 | 0 | 64% | 43% | 7% | 1.4 | 60% | .704 | .753 | .444 |
| Gomes J | 148 | 511 | 77 | 136 | 24 | 3 | 18 | 86 | .266 | .327 | .431 | 5 | 3 | 278 | 36 | 11 | 60 | .277 | 2 | 233 | 41 | 7 | 26 | .253 | 3 | 76% | 35% | 7% | 1.6 | 30% | .758 | .709 | .856 |
| Hanigan R | 70 | 203 | 25 | 61 | 11 | 0 | 5 | 40 | .300 | .405 | .429 | 0 | 0 | 81 | 9 | 2 | 17 | .333 | 0 | 122 | 16 | 3 | 23 | .279 | 0 | 90% | 34% | 13% | 1.4 | 48% | .834 | .771 | .993 |
| Heisey C | 97 | 201 | 33 | 51 | 10 | 1 | 8 | 21 | .254 | .324 | .433 | 1 | 2 | 70 | 14 | 5 | 7 | .286 | 0 | 131 | 19 | 3 | 14 | .237 | 1 | 72% | 35% | 7% | 1.7 | 34% | .757 | .925 | .546 |
| Hernandez R | 97 | 313 | 30 | 93 | 18 | 1 | 7 | 48 | .297 | .364 | .428 | 0 | 0 | 181 | 16 | 3 | 23 | .287 | 0 | 132 | 14 | 4 | 25 | .311 | 0 | 84% | 35% | 8% | 1.4 | 52% | .792 | .786 | .811 |
| Janish P | 82 | 200 | 23 | 52 | 10 | 0 | 5 | 25 | .260 | .338 | .385 | 1 | 3 | 54 | 7 | 2 | 9 | .296 | 0 | 146 | 16 | 3 | 16 | .247 | 1 | 85% | 31% | 10% | 1.5 | 29% | .723 | .667 | .838 |
| Miller C | 32 | 74 | 5 | 18 | 5 | 0 | 2 | 9 | .243 | .282 | .392 | 0 | 0 | 58 | 4 | 1 | 6 | .224 | 0 | 16 | 1 | 1 | 3 | .313 | 0 | 78% | 31% | 3% | 1.6 | 34% | .674 | .798 | .472 |
| Nix L | 97 | 165 | 16 | 48 | 11 | 2 | 4 | 18 | .291 | .350 | .455 | 0 | 1 | 107 | 8 | 4 | 12 | .234 | 0 | 58 | 8 | 0 | 6 | .397 | 0 | 76% | 38% | 8% | 1.6 | 40% | .805 | .795 | .889 |
| Phillips B | 155 | 626 | 100 | 172 | 33 | 5 | 18 | 59 | .275 | .332 | .430 | 16 | 12 | 367 | 66 | 12 | 30 | .294 | 10 | 259 | 34 | 6 | 29 | .247 | 6 | 87% | 32% | 7% | 1.6 | 51% | .762 | .741 | .810 |
| Rolen S | 133 | 471 | 66 | 134 | 34 | 3 | 20 | 83 | .285 | .358 | .497 | 1 | 2 | 283 | 43 | 17 | 57 | .290 | 0 | 188 | 23 | 3 | 26 | .277 | 1 | 83% | 34% | 9% | 1.7 | 38% | .854 | .860 | .840 |
| Stubbs D | 150 | 514 | 91 | 131 | 19 | 6 | 22 | 77 | .255 | .329 | .444 | 30 | 6 | 293 | 47 | 11 | 43 | .235 | 17 | 221 | 44 | 11 | 34 | .281 | 13 | 67% | 38% | 9% | 1.7 | 43% | .773 | .765 | .789 |
| Sutton D | 2 | 3 | 1 | 2 | 0 | 0 | 1 | 4 | .667 | .667 | 1.667 | 0 | 0 | 3 | 1 | 1 | 4 | .667 | 0 | --- | -- | -- | -- | --- | -- | 67% | 100% | 0% | 2.5 | 50% | 2.333 | 1.000 | 5.000 |
| Valaika C | 19 | 38 | 3 | 10 | 1 | 0 | 1 | 2 | .263 | .282 | .368 | 0 | 0 | --- | -- | -- | -- | --- | -- | 38 | 3 | 1 | 2 | .263 | 0 | 76% | 34% | 3% | 1.4 | 41% | .650 | .348 | 1.104 |
| Votto J | 150 | 547 | 106 | 177 | 36 | 2 | 37 | 113 | .324 | .424 | .600 | 16 | 5 | 309 | 59 | 22 | 60 | .314 | 7 | 238 | 47 | 15 | 53 | .336 | 9 | 77% | 42% | 14% | 1.9 | 45% | 1.024 | 1.115 | .863 |

| Pitchers | Cincinnati Reds 2010 | | | | | | | | | | | | | 1st Half | | | | | | 2nd Half | | | | | | Rates | | | Productiveness | | |
|---|---|---|---|---|---|---|---|---|---|---|---|---|---|---|---|---|---|---|---|---|---|---|---|---|---|---|---|---|---|---|---|
| | G | GS | W | L | Hld | Sv | IP | H | HR | ERA | WHIP | K | BB | W | L | Sv | IP | ERA | WHIP | W | L | Sv | IP | ERA | WHIP | K/9 | BB/9 | HR/9 | opOPS | vs RH | vs LH |
| Arroyo B | 33 | 33 | 17 | 10 | 0 | 0 | 215.2 | 188 | 29 | 3.88 | 1.15 | 121 | 59 | 9 | 4 | 0 | 120.1 | 4.04 | 1.23 | 8 | 6 | 0 | 95.1 | 3.68 | 1.04 | 5.0 | 2.5 | 1.2 | .679 | .576 | .786 |
| Bailey H | 19 | 19 | 4 | 3 | 0 | 0 | 109.0 | 109 | 11 | 4.46 | 1.37 | 100 | 40 | 1 | 2 | 0 | 50.2 | 5.51 | 1.48 | 3 | 1 | 0 | 58.1 | 3.55 | 1.27 | 8.3 | 3.3 | 0.9 | .744 | .781 | .677 |
| Bray B | 35 | 0 | 0 | 2 | 2 | 0 | 28.1 | 21 | 4 | 4.13 | 1.09 | 30 | 10 | 0 | 1 | 0 | 6.0 | 4.50 | 0.83 | 0 | 1 | 0 | 22.1 | 4.03 | 1.16 | 9.5 | 3.2 | 1.3 | .626 | .724 | .505 |
| Burton J | 4 | 0 | 0 | 0 | 1 | 0 | 3.1 | 0 | 0 | 0.00 | 0.00 | 1 | 0 | -- | -- | -- | ---- | ---- | --- | 0 | 0 | 0 | 3.1 | 0.00 | 0.00 | 2.7 | 0.0 | 0.0 | .000 | .000 | .000 |
| Chapman A | 15 | 0 | 2 | 2 | 4 | 0 | 13.1 | 9 | 0 | 2.03 | 1.05 | 19 | 5 | -- | -- | -- | ---- | ---- | --- | 2 | 2 | 0 | 13.1 | 2.03 | 1.05 | 12.8 | 3.4 | 0.0 | .492 | .540 | .368 |
| Cordero F | 75 | 0 | 6 | 5 | 1 | 40 | 72.2 | 68 | 5 | 3.84 | 1.43 | 59 | 36 | 3 | 3 | 24 | 40.2 | 4.20 | 1.55 | 3 | 2 | 16 | 32.0 | 3.38 | 1.28 | 7.3 | 4.5 | 0.6 | .681 | .631 | .743 |
| Cueto J | 31 | 31 | 12 | 7 | 0 | 0 | 185.2 | 181 | 19 | 3.64 | 1.28 | 138 | 56 | 8 | 2 | 0 | 110.2 | 3.42 | 1.28 | 4 | 5 | 0 | 75.0 | 3.96 | 1.27 | 6.7 | 2.7 | 0.9 | .727 | .741 | .710 |
| Del Rosario E | 9 | 0 | 1 | 1 | 0 | 0 | 8.2 | 13 | 0 | 2.08 | 1.96 | 3 | 4 | 1 | 1 | 0 | 8.2 | 2.08 | 1.96 | -- | -- | -- | ---- | ---- | --- | 3.1 | 4.2 | 0.0 | .936 | .933 | .932 |
| Fisher C | 18 | 0 | 1 | 1 | 0 | 0 | 22.1 | 22 | 1 | 5.64 | 1.57 | 21 | 13 | 1 | 1 | 0 | 11.0 | 9.82 | 2.09 | 0 | 0 | 0 | 11.1 | 1.59 | 1.06 | 8.5 | 5.2 | 0.4 | .720 | .672 | .790 |
| Harang A | 22 | 20 | 6 | 7 | 0 | 0 | 111.2 | 139 | 16 | 5.32 | 1.59 | 82 | 38 | 6 | 7 | 0 | 100.1 | 5.02 | 1.46 | 0 | 0 | 0 | 11.1 | 7.94 | 2.74 | 6.6 | 3.1 | 1.3 | .841 | .873 | .800 |
| Herrera D | 36 | 0 | 1 | 3 | 9 | 0 | 23.0 | 31 | 2 | 3.91 | 1.61 | 14 | 6 | 1 | 3 | 0 | 23.0 | 3.91 | 1.61 | -- | -- | -- | ---- | ---- | --- | 5.5 | 2.3 | 0.8 | .793 | .836 | .728 |
| Leake M | 24 | 22 | 8 | 4 | 0 | 0 | 138.1 | 158 | 19 | 4.23 | 1.50 | 91 | 49 | 6 | 1 | 0 | 109.2 | 3.53 | 1.40 | 2 | 3 | 0 | 28.2 | 6.91 | 1.88 | 5.9 | 3.2 | 1.2 | .804 | .779 | .832 |
| LeCure S | 15 | 6 | 2 | 5 | 0 | 0 | 48.0 | 50 | 6 | 4.50 | 1.56 | 37 | 25 | 1 | 4 | 0 | 33.1 | 4.86 | 1.71 | 1 | 1 | 0 | 14.2 | 3.68 | 1.23 | 6.9 | 4.7 | 1.1 | .800 | .720 | .928 |
| Lincoln M | 19 | 0 | 1 | 0 | 3 | 0 | 19.2 | 25 | 1 | 7.32 | 1.78 | 12 | 10 | 1 | 0 | 0 | 19.2 | 7.32 | 1.78 | -- | -- | -- | ---- | ---- | --- | 5.5 | 4.6 | 0.5 | .813 | .910 | .619 |
| Maloney M | 7 | 2 | 2 | 2 | 0 | 0 | 20.2 | 20 | 2 | 3.05 | 1.21 | 13 | 5 | 0 | 2 | 0 | 11.2 | 3.09 | 1.11 | 2 | 0 | 0 | 9.0 | 3.00 | 1.33 | 5.7 | 2.2 | 0.9 | .681 | .705 | .641 |
| Masset N | 82 | 0 | 4 | 4 | 20 | 2 | 76.2 | 64 | 7 | 3.40 | 1.27 | 85 | 33 | 3 | 3 | 1 | 39.1 | 5.26 | 1.65 | 1 | 1 | 1 | 37.1 | 1.45 | 0.86 | 10.0 | 3.9 | 0.8 | .643 | .660 | .608 |
| Ondrusek L | 60 | 0 | 5 | 0 | 6 | 0 | 58.2 | 49 | 7 | 3.68 | 1.18 | 39 | 20 | 0 | 0 | 0 | 24.0 | 4.50 | 1.29 | 5 | 0 | 0 | 34.2 | 3.12 | 1.10 | 6.0 | 3.1 | 1.1 | .669 | .725 | .561 |
| Owings M | 22 | 0 | 3 | 2 | 0 | 0 | 33.1 | 28 | 3 | 5.40 | 1.59 | 35 | 25 | 3 | 2 | 0 | 32.2 | 4.41 | 1.53 | 0 | 0 | 0 | 0.2 | 54.00 | 4.50 | 9.5 | 6.8 | 0.8 | .748 | .582 | 1.048 |
| Rhodes A | 70 | 0 | 4 | 4 | 26 | 0 | 55.0 | 38 | 4 | 2.29 | 1.02 | 50 | 18 | 3 | 3 | 0 | 35.0 | 1.54 | 0.94 | 1 | 1 | 0 | 20.0 | 3.60 | 1.15 | 8.2 | 2.9 | 0.7 | .574 | .535 | .623 |
| Smith J | 37 | 0 | 3 | 2 | 2 | 1 | 42.0 | 45 | 7 | 3.86 | 1.33 | 26 | 11 | 2 | 2 | 1 | 13.0 | 4.15 | 1.31 | 1 | 0 | 0 | 29.0 | 3.72 | 1.34 | 5.6 | 2.4 | 1.5 | .768 | .691 | .913 |
| Springer R | 2 | 0 | 0 | 0 | 0 | 0 | 1.2 | 2 | 0 | 5.40 | 1.20 | 1 | 0 | -- | -- | -- | ---- | ---- | --- | 0 | 0 | 0 | 1.2 | 5.40 | 1.20 | 5.4 | 0.0 | 0.0 | .571 | .333 | 2.000 |
| Volquez E | 12 | 12 | 4 | 3 | 0 | 0 | 62.2 | 59 | 6 | 4.31 | 1.50 | 67 | 35 | -- | -- | -- | ---- | ---- | --- | 4 | 3 | 0 | 62.2 | 4.31 | 1.50 | 9.6 | 5.0 | 0.9 | .739 | .776 | .691 |
| Wood T | 17 | 17 | 5 | 4 | 0 | 0 | 102.2 | 85 | 9 | 3.51 | 1.08 | 86 | 26 | 0 | 0 | 0 | 20.2 | 2.18 | 0.68 | 5 | 4 | 0 | 82.0 | 3.84 | 1.18 | 7.5 | 2.3 | 0.8 | .616 | .651 | .446 |

| Hitters | Cleveland Indians 2010 | | | | | | | | | | | | | 1st Half | | | | | | 2nd Half | | | | | | Rates | | | | | Productiveness | | |
|---|---|---|---|---|---|---|---|---|---|---|---|---|---|---|---|---|---|---|---|---|---|---|---|---|---|---|---|---|---|---|---|---|---|
| | G | AB | R | H | 2B | 3B | HR | RBI | BA | OBP | SLG | SB | CS | AB | R | HR | BI | BA | SB | AB | R | HR | BI | BA | SB | CT% | H% | BB% | Bash | GB% | OPS | vs RH | vs LH |
| Brantley M | 72 | 297 | 38 | 73 | 9 | 3 | 3 | 22 | .246 | .296 | .327 | 10 | 2 | 68 | 6 | 1 | 5 | .118 | 0 | 229 | 32 | 2 | 17 | .284 | 10 | 87% | 28% | 7% | 1.3 | 48% | .623 | .665 | .467 |
| Branyan R | 52 | 171 | 24 | 45 | 9 | 0 | 10 | 24 | .263 | .328 | .491 | 0 | 0 | 171 | 24 | 10 | 24 | .263 | 0 | --- | -- | -- | -- | --- | -- | 71% | 37% | 8% | 1.9 | 39% | .819 | .867 | .654 |
| Brown J | 26 | 87 | 9 | 20 | 7 | 0 | 0 | 2 | .230 | .272 | .310 | 0 | 0 | --- | -- | -- | -- | --- | -- | 87 | 9 | 0 | 2 | .230 | 0 | 89% | 26% | 4% | 1.4 | 51% | .582 | .554 | .800 |
| Cabrera A | 97 | 381 | 39 | 105 | 16 | 1 | 3 | 29 | .276 | .326 | .346 | 6 | 4 | 136 | 16 | 1 | 7 | .287 | 1 | 245 | 23 | 2 | 22 | .269 | 5 | 84% | 33% | 6% | 1.3 | 51% | .673 | .685 | .647 |
| Carlin L | 6 | 14 | 4 | 5 | 0 | 0 | 2 | 3 | .357 | .438 | .786 | 0 | 0 | --- | -- | -- | -- | --- | -- | 14 | 4 | 2 | 3 | .357 | 0 | 64% | 56% | 13% | 2.2 | 78% | 1.223 | 1.264 | 1.100 |
| Choo S | 144 | 550 | 81 | 165 | 31 | 2 | 22 | 90 | .300 | .401 | .484 | 22 | 7 | 301 | 48 | 13 | 43 | .286 | 12 | 249 | 33 | 9 | 47 | .317 | 10 | 79% | 38% | 13% | 1.6 | 45% | .885 | .998 | .670 |
| Crowe T | 122 | 442 | 48 | 111 | 24 | 3 | 2 | 36 | .251 | .302 | .333 | 20 | 7 | 209 | 25 | 1 | 20 | .249 | 10 | 233 | 23 | 1 | 16 | .253 | 10 | 83% | 30% | 6% | 1.3 | 52% | .634 | .679 | .490 |
| Donald J | 88 | 296 | 39 | 75 | 19 | 3 | 4 | 24 | .253 | .312 | .378 | 5 | 1 | 146 | 15 | 2 | 12 | .274 | 2 | 150 | 24 | 2 | 12 | .233 | 3 | 76% | 33% | 7% | 1.5 | 47% | .690 | .643 | .833 |
| Duncan S | 85 | 229 | 29 | 53 | 10 | 0 | 11 | 36 | .231 | .317 | .419 | 1 | 0 | 73 | 7 | 5 | 13 | .260 | 0 | 156 | 22 | 6 | 23 | .218 | 1 | 67% | 35% | 10% | 1.8 | 29% | .736 | .662 | .857 |
| Gimenez C | 28 | 58 | 6 | 11 | 5 | 0 | 1 | 8 | .190 | .288 | .328 | 0 | 0 | 3 | 0 | 0 | 0 | .000 | 0 | 55 | 6 | 1 | 8 | .200 | 0 | 62% | 31% | 12% | 1.7 | 39% | .615 | .572 | .698 |
| Grudzielanek M | 30 | 110 | 10 | 30 | 0 | 0 | 0 | 11 | .273 | .328 | .273 | 2 | 0 | 110 | 10 | 0 | 11 | .273 | 2 | --- | -- | -- | -- | --- | -- | 91% | 30% | 7% | 1.0 | 54% | .600 | .607 | .588 |
| Hafner T | 118 | 396 | 46 | 110 | 29 | 0 | 13 | 50 | .278 | .374 | .449 | 2 | 1 | 241 | 28 | 8 | 29 | .245 | 1 | 155 | 18 | 5 | 21 | .329 | 1 | 76% | 36% | 11% | 1.6 | 43% | .824 | .863 | .706 |
| Hernandez A | 22 | 61 | 6 | 15 | 3 | 0 | 0 | 2 | .246 | .270 | .295 | 1 | 0 | 57 | 6 | 0 | 2 | .228 | 1 | 4 | 0 | 0 | 0 | .500 | 0 | 85% | 29% | 3% | 1.2 | 44% | .565 | .646 | .321 |
| Kearns A | 84 | 301 | 42 | 82 | 18 | 1 | 8 | 42 | .272 | .354 | .419 | 4 | 1 | 270 | 39 | 7 | 38 | .270 | 4 | 31 | 3 | 1 | 4 | .290 | 0 | 74% | 37% | 10% | 1.5 | 44% | .772 | .798 | .720 |
| LaPorta M | 110 | 376 | 41 | 83 | 15 | 1 | 12 | 41 | .221 | .306 | .362 | 0 | 0 | 161 | 20 | 5 | 18 | .255 | 0 | 215 | 21 | 7 | 23 | .195 | 0 | 78% | 28% | 11% | 1.6 | 43% | .668 | .679 | .635 |
| Marson L | 87 | 262 | 29 | 51 | 15 | 0 | 3 | 22 | .195 | .274 | .286 | 8 | 1 | 141 | 15 | 1 | 12 | .191 | 4 | 121 | 14 | 2 | 10 | .198 | 4 | 79% | 25% | 9% | 1.5 | 56% | .560 | .488 | .759 |
| Marte A | 81 | 170 | 18 | 39 | 7 | 2 | 5 | 19 | .229 | .298 | .382 | 0 | 3 | 65 | 9 | 2 | 9 | .185 | 0 | 105 | 9 | 3 | 10 | .257 | 0 | 79% | 29% | 9% | 1.7 | 35% | .680 | .656 | .724 |
| Nix J | 78 | 282 | 29 | 66 | 14 | 0 | 13 | 29 | .234 | .283 | .422 | 1 | 2 | 59 | 8 | 6 | 9 | .237 | 0 | 223 | 21 | 7 | 20 | .233 | 1 | 73% | 32% | 4% | 1.8 | 37% | .705 | .657 | .877 |
| Peralta J | 91 | 334 | 37 | 82 | 23 | 2 | 7 | 43 | .246 | .308 | .389 | 1 | 0 | 306 | 32 | 6 | 39 | .252 | 1 | 28 | 5 | 1 | 4 | .179 | 0 | 79% | 31% | 9% | 1.6 | 35% | .698 | .688 | .720 |
| Redmond M | 22 | 63 | 7 | 13 | 4 | 0 | 0 | 5 | .206 | .242 | .270 | 0 | 0 | 63 | 7 | 0 | 5 | .206 | 0 | --- | -- | -- | -- | --- | -- | 84% | 25% | 3% | 1.3 | 43% | .512 | .496 | .583 |
| Santana C | 46 | 150 | 23 | 39 | 13 | 0 | 6 | 22 | .260 | .401 | .467 | 3 | 0 | 95 | 17 | 5 | 16 | .284 | 1 | 55 | 6 | 1 | 6 | .218 | 2 | 81% | 32% | 19% | 1.8 | 36% | .868 | 1.002 | .582 |
| Sizemore G | 33 | 128 | 15 | 27 | 6 | 2 | 0 | 13 | .211 | .271 | .289 | 4 | 2 | 128 | 15 | 0 | 13 | .211 | 4 | --- | -- | -- | -- | --- | -- | 73% | 29% | 6% | 1.4 | 39% | .560 | .706 | .326 |
| Sutton D | 11 | 36 | 4 | 8 | 1 | 0 | 1 | 4 | .222 | .282 | .333 | 0 | 0 | --- | -- | -- | -- | --- | -- | 36 | 4 | 1 | 4 | .222 | 0 | 67% | 33% | 8% | 1.5 | 58% | .615 | .506 | 1.167 |
| Valbuena L | 91 | 275 | 22 | 53 | 12 | 0 | 2 | 24 | .193 | .273 | .258 | 1 | 2 | 151 | 13 | 2 | 14 | .166 | 1 | 124 | 9 | 0 | 10 | .226 | 0 | 78% | 25% | 9% | 1.3 | 46% | .531 | .467 | .855 |

| Pitchers | Cleveland Indians 2010 | | | | | | | | | | | | | 1st Half | | | | | | 2nd Half | | | | | | Rates | | | Productiveness | | |
|---|---|---|---|---|---|---|---|---|---|---|---|---|---|---|---|---|---|---|---|---|---|---|---|---|---|---|---|---|---|---|---|
| | G | GS | W | L | Hld | Sv | IP | H | HR | ERA | WHIP | K | BB | W | L | Sv | IP | ERA | WHIP | W | L | Sv | IP | ERA | WHIP | K/9 | BB/9 | HR/9 | opOPS | vs RH | vs LH |
| Ambriz H | 34 | 0 | 0 | 2 | 0 | 0 | 48.1 | 68 | 10 | 5.59 | 1.76 | 37 | 17 | 0 | 1 | 0 | 27.2 | 5.86 | 1.92 | 0 | 1 | 0 | 20.2 | 5.23 | 1.55 | 6.9 | 3.2 | 1.9 | .960 | 1.084 | .845 |
| Carmona F | 33 | 33 | 13 | 14 | 0 | 0 | 210.1 | 203 | 17 | 3.77 | 1.31 | 124 | 72 | 8 | 7 | 0 | 116.1 | 3.64 | 1.29 | 5 | 7 | 0 | 94.0 | 3.93 | 1.33 | 5.3 | 3.1 | 0.7 | .703 | .681 | .722 |
| Carrasco C | 7 | 7 | 2 | 2 | 0 | 0 | 44.2 | 47 | 6 | 3.83 | 1.37 | 38 | 14 | -- | -- | -- | ---- | ---- | --- | 2 | 2 | 0 | 44.2 | 3.83 | 1.37 | 7.7 | 2.8 | 1.2 | .816 | 1.042 | .581 |
| Germano J | 23 | 1 | 0 | 3 | 2 | 0 | 35.1 | 27 | 6 | 3.31 | 0.99 | 29 | 8 | -- | -- | -- | ---- | ---- | --- | 0 | 3 | 0 | 35.1 | 3.31 | 0.99 | 7.4 | 2.0 | 1.5 | .664 | .716 | .606 |
| Gomez J | 11 | 11 | 4 | 5 | 0 | 0 | 57.2 | 73 | 7 | 4.68 | 1.65 | 34 | 22 | -- | -- | -- | ---- | ---- | --- | 4 | 5 | 0 | 57.2 | 4.68 | 1.65 | 5.3 | 3.4 | 1.1 | .841 | .961 | .752 |
| Herrmann F | 40 | 0 | 0 | 1 | 7 | 1 | 44.2 | 48 | 6 | 4.03 | 1.28 | 24 | 9 | 0 | 0 | 1 | 16.0 | 2.81 | 1.06 | 0 | 1 | 0 | 28.2 | 4.71 | 1.40 | 4.8 | 1.8 | 1.2 | .775 | .629 | .920 |
| Huff D | 15 | 15 | 2 | 11 | 0 | 0 | 79.2 | 101 | 14 | 6.21 | 1.69 | 37 | 34 | 2 | 9 | 0 | 70.0 | 6.04 | 1.69 | 0 | 2 | 0 | 9.2 | 7.45 | 1.76 | 4.2 | 3.8 | 1.6 | .917 | .880 | 1.040 |
| Laffey A | 29 | 5 | 2 | 3 | 5 | 0 | 55.2 | 62 | 1 | 4.53 | 1.62 | 28 | 28 | 1 | 3 | 0 | 45.2 | 5.12 | 1.66 | 1 | 0 | 0 | 10.0 | 1.80 | 1.40 | 4.5 | 4.5 | 0.2 | .744 | .724 | .779 |
| Lewis J | 37 | 0 | 4 | 2 | 1 | 0 | 36.1 | 28 | 1 | 2.97 | 1.29 | 29 | 19 | 2 | 2 | 0 | 21.0 | 3.86 | 1.62 | 2 | 0 | 0 | 15.1 | 1.76 | 0.85 | 7.2 | 4.7 | 0.2 | .611 | .532 | .727 |
| Masterson J | 34 | 29 | 6 | 13 | 2 | 0 | 180.0 | 197 | 14 | 4.70 | 1.50 | 140 | 73 | 3 | 8 | 0 | 105.0 | 5.31 | 1.63 | 3 | 5 | 0 | 75.0 | 3.84 | 1.32 | 7.0 | 3.7 | 0.7 | .738 | .681 | .784 |
| Perez C | 63 | 0 | 2 | 2 | 9 | 23 | 63.0 | 40 | 4 | 1.71 | 1.08 | 61 | 28 | 0 | 2 | 7 | 34.1 | 2.62 | 1.25 | 2 | 0 | 16 | 28.2 | 0.63 | 0.87 | 8.7 | 4.0 | 0.6 | .583 | .445 | .752 |
| Perez R | 70 | 0 | 6 | 1 | 13 | 0 | 61.0 | 72 | 3 | 3.25 | 1.59 | 36 | 25 | 1 | 0 | 0 | 31.0 | 4.06 | 1.77 | 5 | 1 | 0 | 30.0 | 2.40 | 1.40 | 5.3 | 3.7 | 0.4 | .748 | .750 | .746 |
| Pestano V | 5 | 0 | 0 | 0 | 0 | 1 | 5.0 | 4 | 0 | 3.60 | 1.80 | 8 | 5 | -- | -- | -- | ---- | ---- | --- | 0 | 0 | 1 | 5.0 | 3.60 | 1.80 | 14.4 | 9.0 | 0.0 | .614 | .408 | .875 |
| Sipp T | 70 | 0 | 2 | 2 | 15 | 1 | 63.0 | 48 | 12 | 4.14 | 1.38 | 69 | 39 | 1 | 2 | 0 | 31.0 | 5.52 | 1.71 | 1 | 0 | 1 | 32.0 | 2.81 | 1.06 | 9.9 | 5.6 | 1.7 | .770 | .742 | .805 |
| Smith J | 53 | 0 | 2 | 2 | 17 | 0 | 40.0 | 30 | 4 | 3.83 | 1.35 | 32 | 24 | 1 | 1 | 0 | 15.2 | 5.17 | 1.53 | 1 | 1 | 0 | 24.1 | 2.96 | 1.23 | 7.2 | 5.4 | 0.9 | .659 | .538 | .979 |
| Talbot M | 28 | 28 | 10 | 13 | 0 | 0 | 159.1 | 169 | 13 | 4.41 | 1.49 | 88 | 69 | 8 | 8 | 0 | 108.1 | 3.99 | 1.38 | 2 | 5 | 0 | 51.0 | 5.29 | 1.73 | 5.0 | 3.9 | 0.7 | .761 | .794 | .725 |
| Todd J | 5 | 0 | 0 | 0 | 0 | 0 | 6.0 | 9 | 0 | 7.50 | 2.00 | 9 | 3 | -- | -- | -- | ---- | ---- | --- | 0 | 0 | 0 | 6.0 | 7.50 | 2.00 | 13.5 | 4.5 | 0.0 | .844 | .800 | .883 |
| Tomlin J | 12 | 12 | 6 | 4 | 0 | 0 | 73.0 | 72 | 10 | 4.56 | 1.25 | 43 | 19 | -- | -- | -- | ---- | ---- | --- | 6 | 4 | 0 | 73.0 | 4.56 | 1.25 | 5.3 | 2.3 | 1.2 | .773 | .881 | .682 |
| Westbrook J | 21 | 21 | 6 | 7 | 0 | 0 | 127.2 | 133 | 15 | 4.65 | 1.39 | 73 | 44 | 5 | 5 | 0 | 108.0 | 4.75 | 1.43 | 1 | 2 | 0 | 19.2 | 4.12 | 1.17 | 5.1 | 3.1 | 1.1 | .772 | .767 | .776 |
| Wood K | 23 | 0 | 1 | 4 | 1 | 8 | 20.0 | 21 | 3 | 6.30 | 1.60 | 18 | 11 | 1 | 4 | 8 | 20.0 | 6.30 | 1.60 | -- | -- | -- | ---- | ---- | --- | 8.1 | 5.0 | 1.4 | .816 | .955 | .669 |
| Wright J | 18 | 0 | 1 | 2 | 1 | 0 | 21.1 | 25 | 1 | 5.48 | 1.59 | 9 | 9 | 1 | 2 | 0 | 21.1 | 5.48 | 1.59 | -- | -- | -- | ---- | ---- | --- | 3.8 | 3.8 | 0.4 | .795 | .746 | .853 |

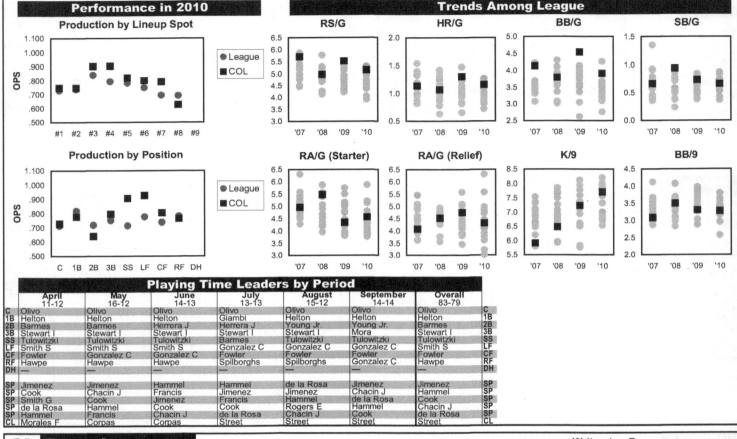

### Performance in 2010
**Production by Lineup Spot**

**Production by Position**

### Trends Among League
RS/G • HR/G • BB/G • SB/G
RA/G (Starter) • RA/G (Relief) • K/9 • BB/9

● League ■ COL

| | Playing Time Leaders by Period | | | | | | | |
|---|---|---|---|---|---|---|---|---|
| | April 11-12 | May 16-12 | June 14-13 | July 13-13 | August 15-12 | September 14-14 | Overall 83-79 | |
| C | Olivo | Olivo | Olivo | Olivo | Helton | Olivo | Olivo | C |
| 1B | Helton | Helton | Helton | Giambi | Helton | Helton | Helton | 1B |
| 2B | Barmes | Barmes | Herrera J | Herrera J | Young Jr. | Young Jr. | Barmes | 2B |
| 3B | Stewart I | Stewart I | Stewart I | Stewart I | Stewart I | Mora | Stewart I | 3B |
| SS | Tulowitzki | Tulowitzki | Tulowitzki | Barmes | Tulowitzki | Tulowitzki | Tulowitzki | SS |
| LF | Smith S | Smith S | Smith S | Gonzalez C | Gonzalez C | Gonzalez C | Smith S | LF |
| CF | Fowler | Gonzalez C | Gonzalez C | Fowler | Fowler | Fowler | Fowler | CF |
| RF | Hawpe | Hawpe | Hawpe | Spilborghs | Spilborghs | Gonzalez C | Hawpe | RF |
| DH | — | — | — | — | — | — | — | DH |
| | | | | | | | | |
| SP | Jimenez | Jimenez | Hammel | Hammel | de la Rosa | Jimenez | Jimenez | SP |
| SP | Cook | Chacin J | Francis | Jimenez | Jimenez | Chacin J | Hammel | SP |
| SP | Smith G | Cook | Jimenez | Francis | Hammel | de la Rosa | Cook | SP |
| SP | de la Rosa | Hammel | Cook | Cook | Rogers E | Hammel | Chacin J | SP |
| SP | Hammel | Francis | Chacin J | de la Rosa | Chacin J | Cook | de la Rosa | SP |
| CL | Morales F | Corpas | Corpas | Street | Street | Street | Street | CL |

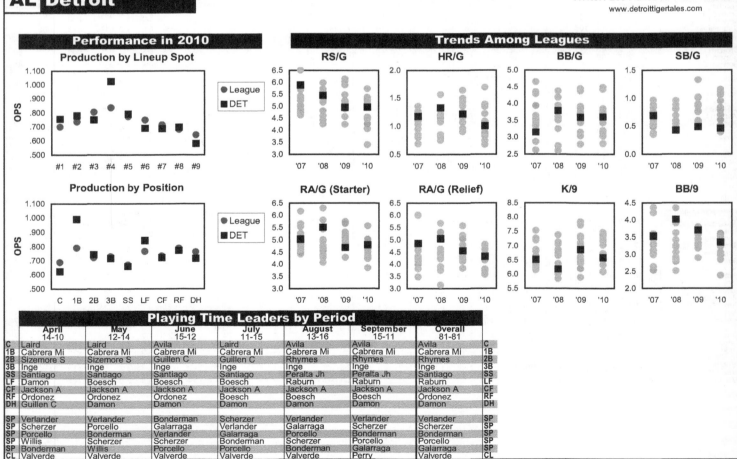

### Performance in 2010
**Production by Lineup Spot**

**Production by Position**

### Trends Among Leagues
RS/G • HR/G • BB/G • SB/G
RA/G (Starter) • RA/G (Relief) • K/9 • BB/9

● League ■ DET

| | Playing Time Leaders by Period | | | | | | | |
|---|---|---|---|---|---|---|---|---|
| | April 14-10 | May 12-14 | June 15-12 | July 11-15 | August 13-16 | September 15-11 | Overall 81-81 | |
| C | Laird | Laird | Avila | Laird | Avila | Avila | Avila | C |
| 1B | Cabrera Mi | Cabrera Mi | Cabrera Mi | Cabrera Mi | Cabrera Mi | Cabrera Mi | Cabrera Mi | 1B |
| 2B | Sizemore S | Sizemore S | Guillen C | Guillen C | Rhymes | Rhymes | Rhymes | 2B |
| 3B | Inge | Inge | Inge | Inge | Inge | Inge | Inge | 3B |
| SS | Santiago | Santiago | Santiago | Santiago | Peralta Jh | Peralta Jh | Santiago | SS |
| LF | Damon | Boesch | Boesch | Boesch | Raburn | Raburn | Raburn | LF |
| CF | Jackson A | Jackson A | Jackson A | Jackson A | Jackson A | Jackson A | Jackson A | CF |
| RF | Ordonez | Ordonez | Ordonez | Boesch | Boesch | Boesch | Ordonez | RF |
| DH | Guillen C | Damon | Damon | Damon | Damon | Damon | Damon | DH |
| | | | | | | | | |
| SP | Verlander | Verlander | Bonderman | Scherzer | Verlander | Verlander | Verlander | SP |
| SP | Scherzer | Porcello | Galarraga | Verlander | Galarraga | Scherzer | Scherzer | SP |
| SP | Porcello | Bonderman | Verlander | Galarraga | Porcello | Bonderman | Bonderman | SP |
| SP | Willis | Scherzer | Scherzer | Bonderman | Scherzer | Porcello | Porcello | SP |
| SP | Bonderman | Willis | Porcello | Porcello | Bonderman | Galarraga | Galarraga | SP |
| CL | Valverde | Valverde | Valverde | Valverde | Valverde | Perry | Valverde | CL |

## Hitters — Colorado Rockies 2010

| Hitters | G | AB | R | H | 2B | 3B | HR | RBI | BA | OBP | SLG | SB | CS | 1st Half AB | R | HR | BI | BA | SB | 2nd Half AB | R | HR | BI | BA | SB | Rates CT% | H% | BB% | Bash | GB% | Productiveness OPS | vs RH | vs LH |
|---|---|---|---|---|---|---|---|---|---|---|---|---|---|---|---|---|---|---|---|---|---|---|---|---|---|---|---|---|---|---|---|---|---|
| Barmes C | 133 | 387 | 43 | 91 | 21 | 0 | 8 | 50 | .235 | .305 | .351 | 3 | 2 | 268 | 31 | 7 | 42 | .257 | 2 | 119 | 12 | 1 | 8 | .185 | 1 | 83% | 28% | 8% | 1.5 | 30% | .656 | .612 | .748 |
| Eldred B | 11 | 24 | 4 | 6 | 1 | 0 | 1 | 3 | .250 | .333 | .417 | 0 | 0 | 13 | 4 | 1 | 2 | .385 | 0 | 11 | 0 | 0 | 1 | .091 | 0 | 58% | 43% | 7% | 1.7 | 43% | .750 | .417 | 1.050 |
| Fowler D | 132 | 439 | 73 | 114 | 20 | 14 | 6 | 36 | .260 | .347 | .410 | 13 | 7 | 189 | 32 | 2 | 10 | .233 | 8 | 250 | 41 | 4 | 26 | .280 | 5 | 76% | 34% | 11% | 1.6 | 44% | .757 | .764 | .744 |
| Giambi J | 87 | 176 | 17 | 43 | 9 | 0 | 6 | 35 | .244 | .378 | .398 | 2 | 0 | 102 | 13 | 3 | 19 | .275 | 1 | 74 | 4 | 3 | 16 | .203 | 1 | 73% | 33% | 15% | 1.6 | 33% | .776 | .739 | .879 |
| Gonzalez C | 145 | 587 | 111 | 197 | 34 | 9 | 34 | 117 | .336 | .376 | .598 | 26 | 8 | 325 | 56 | 17 | 60 | .314 | 12 | 262 | 55 | 17 | 57 | .363 | 14 | 77% | 44% | 6% | 1.8 | 43% | .974 | 1.003 | .925 |
| Hawpe B | 88 | 259 | 24 | 66 | 21 | 2 | 7 | 37 | .255 | .343 | .432 | 2 | 1 | 201 | 17 | 5 | 33 | .274 | 1 | 58 | 7 | 2 | 4 | .190 | 1 | 74% | 35% | 12% | 1.7 | 41% | .776 | .756 | .821 |
| Helton T | 118 | 398 | 48 | 102 | 18 | 1 | 8 | 37 | .256 | .362 | .367 | 0 | 0 | 248 | 29 | 2 | 16 | .246 | 0 | 150 | 19 | 6 | 21 | .273 | 0 | 77% | 33% | 14% | 1.4 | 35% | .728 | .735 | .714 |
| Herrera J | 76 | 222 | 34 | 63 | 6 | 2 | 1 | 21 | .284 | .352 | .342 | 2 | 2 | 113 | 14 | 0 | 10 | .319 | 1 | 109 | 20 | 1 | 11 | .248 | 1 | 84% | 34% | 10% | 1.2 | 49% | .694 | .680 | .722 |
| Iannetta C | 61 | 188 | 20 | 37 | 6 | 1 | 9 | 27 | .197 | .318 | .383 | 1 | 0 | 87 | 9 | 6 | 13 | .207 | 1 | 101 | 11 | 3 | 14 | .188 | 0 | 74% | 26% | 13% | 1.9 | 41% | .701 | .683 | .737 |
| McKenry M | 6 | 8 | 0 | 0 | 0 | 0 | 0 | 0 | .000 | .111 | .000 | 0 | 0 | -- | -- | -- | -- | -- | -- | 8 | 0 | 0 | 0 | .000 | 0 | 38% | 0% | 11% | -- | 67% | .111 | .000 | -- |
| Mora M | 113 | 316 | 39 | 90 | 12 | 5 | 7 | 45 | .285 | .358 | .421 | 2 | 1 | 140 | 14 | 1 | 14 | .257 | 1 | 176 | 25 | 6 | 31 | .307 | 1 | 83% | 34% | 9% | 1.5 | 44% | .779 | .760 | .804 |
| Nelson C | 17 | 25 | 7 | 7 | 1 | 0 | 0 | 0 | .280 | .308 | .320 | 1 | 0 | 5 | 2 | 0 | 0 | .400 | 0 | 20 | 5 | 0 | 0 | .250 | 1 | 84% | 33% | 4% | 1.1 | 52% | .628 | .485 | .889 |
| Olivo M | 112 | 394 | 55 | 106 | 17 | 6 | 14 | 58 | .269 | .315 | .449 | 7 | 4 | 228 | 42 | 11 | 42 | .325 | 4 | 166 | 13 | 3 | 16 | .193 | 3 | 70% | 38% | 6% | 1.7 | 42% | .765 | .749 | .801 |
| Payton J | 20 | 35 | 3 | 12 | 4 | 1 | 0 | 1 | .343 | .361 | .514 | 1 | 0 | -- | -- | -- | -- | -- | -- | 35 | 3 | 0 | 1 | .343 | 1 | 89% | 39% | 3% | 1.5 | 45% | .875 | 1.026 | .667 |
| Phillips P | 12 | 23 | 4 | 5 | 0 | 0 | 0 | 1 | .217 | .280 | .217 | 0 | 0 | 17 | 4 | 0 | 1 | .294 | 0 | 6 | 0 | 0 | 0 | .000 | 0 | 70% | 31% | 8% | 1.0 | 38% | .497 | .513 | .452 |
| Smith S | 133 | 358 | 55 | 88 | 19 | 5 | 17 | 52 | .246 | .314 | .469 | 2 | 1 | 202 | 36 | 12 | 38 | .287 | 2 | 156 | 19 | 5 | 14 | .192 | 0 | 81% | 30% | 9% | 1.9 | 36% | .783 | .848 | .393 |
| Spilborghs R | 134 | 341 | 41 | 95 | 20 | 2 | 10 | 39 | .279 | .360 | .437 | 4 | 5 | 173 | 22 | 8 | 17 | .260 | 1 | 168 | 19 | 2 | 22 | .298 | 3 | 76% | 37% | 10% | 1.6 | 42% | .797 | .814 | .774 |
| Stewart I | 121 | 386 | 54 | 99 | 14 | 2 | 18 | 61 | .256 | .338 | .443 | 5 | 2 | 256 | 40 | 11 | 44 | .258 | 5 | 130 | 14 | 7 | 17 | .254 | 0 | 72% | 36% | 10% | 1.7 | 37% | .781 | .811 | .683 |
| Tulowitzki T | 122 | 470 | 89 | 148 | 32 | 3 | 27 | 95 | .315 | .381 | .568 | 11 | 2 | 235 | 47 | 9 | 34 | .306 | 7 | 235 | 42 | 18 | 61 | .323 | 4 | 83% | 38% | 9% | 1.8 | 45% | .949 | .930 | .990 |
| Young Jr. E | 51 | 172 | 26 | 42 | 5 | 1 | 0 | 8 | .244 | .312 | .285 | 17 | 6 | 32 | 7 | 0 | 3 | .250 | 4 | 140 | 19 | 0 | 5 | .243 | 13 | 81% | 30% | 9% | 1.2 | 51% | .597 | .623 | .552 |

## Pitchers — Colorado Rockies 2010

| Pitchers | G | GS | W | L | Hld | Sv | IP | H | HR | ERA | WHIP | K | BB | 1st Half W | L | Sv | IP | ERA | WHIP | 2nd Half W | L | Sv | IP | ERA | WHIP | Rates K/9 | BB/9 | HR/9 | Productiveness opOPS | vs RH | vs LH |
|---|---|---|---|---|---|---|---|---|---|---|---|---|---|---|---|---|---|---|---|---|---|---|---|---|---|---|---|---|---|---|---|
| Beimel J | 71 | 0 | 1 | 2 | 20 | 0 | 45.0 | 46 | 5 | 3.40 | 1.36 | 21 | 15 | 1 | 0 | 0 | 27.2 | 2.28 | 0.94 | 0 | 2 | 0 | 17.1 | 5.19 | 2.02 | 4.2 | 3.0 | 1.0 | .747 | .862 | .653 |
| Belisle M | 76 | 0 | 7 | 5 | 21 | 1 | 92.0 | 84 | 7 | 2.93 | 1.09 | 91 | 16 | 4 | 4 | 1 | 54.2 | 2.63 | 1.08 | 3 | 1 | 0 | 37.1 | 3.38 | 1.10 | 8.9 | 1.6 | 0.7 | .646 | .659 | .620 |
| Betancourt R | 72 | 0 | 5 | 1 | 23 | 1 | 62.1 | 52 | 9 | 3.61 | 0.96 | 89 | 8 | 1 | 1 | 1 | 32.0 | 5.06 | 1.38 | 4 | 0 | 0 | 30.1 | 2.08 | 0.53 | 12.9 | 1.2 | 1.3 | .626 | .515 | .819 |
| Buchholz T | 7 | 0 | 1 | 0 | 0 | 0 | 10.0 | 10 | 2 | 4.50 | 1.60 | 9 | 6 | -- | -- | -- | -- | -- | -- | 1 | 0 | 0 | 10.0 | 4.50 | 1.60 | 8.1 | 5.4 | 1.8 | .937 | 1.014 | .833 |
| Chacin J | 28 | 21 | 9 | 11 | 0 | 0 | 137.1 | 114 | 10 | 3.28 | 1.27 | 138 | 61 | 5 | 7 | 0 | 77.0 | 4.09 | 1.32 | 4 | 4 | 0 | 60.1 | 2.24 | 1.21 | 9.0 | 4.0 | 0.7 | .650 | .612 | .705 |
| Cook A | 23 | 23 | 6 | 8 | 0 | 0 | 127.2 | 147 | 11 | 5.08 | 1.56 | 62 | 52 | 3 | 5 | 0 | 99.2 | 4.88 | 1.48 | 3 | 3 | 0 | 28.0 | 5.79 | 1.82 | 4.4 | 3.7 | 0.8 | .759 | .670 | .882 |
| Corpas M | 56 | 0 | 3 | 5 | 2 | 10 | 62.1 | 66 | 7 | 4.62 | 1.41 | 47 | 22 | 3 | 5 | 10 | 47.0 | 4.60 | 1.23 | 0 | 0 | 0 | 15.1 | 4.70 | 1.96 | 6.8 | 3.2 | 1.0 | .772 | .652 | .990 |
| Daley M | 28 | 0 | 0 | 1 | 6 | 0 | 23.1 | 27 | 2 | 4.24 | 1.59 | 18 | 10 | 0 | 1 | 0 | 21.2 | 3.74 | 1.52 | 0 | 0 | 0 | 1.2 | 10.80 | 2.40 | 6.9 | 3.9 | 0.8 | .845 | .825 | .889 |
| de la Rosa J | 20 | 20 | 8 | 7 | 0 | 0 | 121.2 | 105 | 15 | 4.22 | 1.32 | 113 | 55 | 3 | 1 | 0 | 27.1 | 4.94 | 1.46 | 5 | 6 | 0 | 94.1 | 4.01 | 1.27 | 8.4 | 4.1 | 1.1 | .737 | .755 | .671 |
| Deduno S | 4 | 0 | 0 | 0 | 1 | 0 | 2.2 | 3 | 1 | 3.38 | 1.50 | 3 | 1 | -- | -- | -- | -- | -- | -- | 0 | 0 | 0 | 2.2 | 3.38 | 1.50 | 10.1 | 3.4 | 3.4 | .879 | 1.262 | .400 |
| Delcarmen M | 9 | 0 | 0 | 2 | 0 | 0 | 8.1 | 12 | 1 | 6.48 | 1.92 | 6 | 4 | -- | -- | -- | -- | -- | -- | 0 | 2 | 0 | 8.1 | 6.48 | 1.92 | 6.5 | 4.3 | 1.1 | .850 | .863 | .829 |
| Dotel O | 8 | 0 | 0 | 1 | 1 | 0 | 5.1 | 6 | 1 | 5.06 | 1.88 | 6 | 4 | -- | -- | -- | -- | -- | -- | 0 | 1 | 0 | 5.1 | 5.06 | 1.88 | 10.1 | 6.8 | 1.7 | .857 | .821 | .946 |
| Escalona E | 5 | 0 | 0 | 0 | 0 | 0 | 6.0 | 4 | 0 | 1.50 | 1.33 | 2 | 4 | -- | -- | -- | -- | -- | -- | 0 | 0 | 0 | 6.0 | 1.50 | 1.33 | 3.0 | 6.0 | 0.0 | .546 | .354 | 1.025 |
| Flores R | 47 | 0 | 2 | 0 | 4 | 0 | 27.1 | 22 | 4 | 2.96 | 1.28 | 18 | 13 | 2 | 0 | 0 | 20.1 | 3.10 | 1.08 | 0 | 0 | 0 | 7.0 | 2.57 | 1.86 | 5.9 | 4.3 | 1.3 | .754 | .716 | .791 |
| Francis J | 20 | 19 | 4 | 6 | 0 | 0 | 104.1 | 119 | 11 | 5.00 | 1.36 | 67 | 23 | 2 | 3 | 0 | 63.0 | 5.14 | 1.43 | 2 | 3 | 0 | 41.1 | 4.79 | 1.26 | 5.8 | 2.0 | 0.9 | .777 | .768 | .823 |
| Hammel J | 30 | 30 | 10 | 9 | 0 | 0 | 177.2 | 201 | 18 | 4.81 | 1.40 | 141 | 47 | 7 | 3 | 0 | 90.1 | 4.08 | 1.34 | 3 | 6 | 0 | 87.1 | 5.56 | 1.45 | 7.1 | 2.4 | 0.9 | .755 | .750 | .761 |
| Jimenez U | 33 | 33 | 19 | 8 | 0 | 0 | 221.2 | 164 | 10 | 2.88 | 1.15 | 214 | 92 | 15 | 1 | 0 | 127.0 | 2.20 | 1.05 | 4 | 7 | 0 | 94.2 | 3.80 | 1.30 | 8.7 | 3.7 | 0.4 | .610 | .638 | .582 |
| Morales F | 35 | 0 | 0 | 4 | 1 | 3 | 28.2 | 28 | 5 | 6.28 | 1.81 | 27 | 24 | 0 | 3 | 3 | 21.1 | 6.75 | 1.88 | 0 | 1 | 0 | 7.1 | 4.91 | 1.64 | 8.5 | 7.5 | 1.6 | .810 | .889 | .636 |
| Reynolds M | 21 | 0 | 1 | 0 | 2 | 0 | 18.0 | 10 | 2 | 2.00 | 0.83 | 17 | 5 | -- | -- | -- | -- | -- | -- | 1 | 0 | 0 | 18.0 | 2.00 | 0.83 | 8.5 | 2.5 | 1.0 | .541 | .603 | .489 |
| Rincon J | 2 | 0 | 0 | 0 | 0 | 0 | 2.0 | 3 | 0 | 4.50 | 2.50 | 3 | 2 | 0 | 0 | 0 | 2.0 | 4.50 | 2.50 | -- | -- | -- | -- | -- | -- | 13.5 | 9.0 | 0.0 | .899 | .800 | 1.000 |
| Rogers E | 28 | 8 | 2 | 3 | 1 | 0 | 72.0 | 94 | 5 | 6.13 | 1.67 | 66 | 26 | 1 | 2 | 0 | 29.2 | 4.85 | 1.55 | 1 | 1 | 0 | 42.1 | 7.02 | 1.75 | 8.3 | 3.3 | 0.6 | .835 | .772 | .919 |
| Smith G | 8 | 8 | 1 | 2 | 0 | 0 | 39.0 | 49 | 8 | 6.23 | 1.87 | 31 | 24 | 1 | 2 | 0 | 39.0 | 6.23 | 1.87 | -- | -- | -- | -- | -- | -- | 7.2 | 5.5 | 1.8 | 1.003 | 1.101 | .574 |
| Street H | 44 | 0 | 4 | 4 | 0 | 20 | 47.1 | 39 | 5 | 3.61 | 1.06 | 45 | 11 | 1 | 1 | 5 | 12.1 | 2.19 | 0.57 | 3 | 3 | 15 | 35.0 | 4.11 | 1.23 | 8.6 | 2.1 | 1.0 | .648 | .700 | .575 |

## Hitters — Detroit Tigers 2010

| Hitters | G | AB | R | H | 2B | 3B | HR | RBI | BA | OBP | SLG | SB | CS | 1st Half AB | R | HR | BI | BA | SB | 2nd Half AB | R | HR | BI | BA | SB | Rates CT% | H% | BB% | Bash | GB% | Productiveness OPS | vs RH | vs LH |
|---|---|---|---|---|---|---|---|---|---|---|---|---|---|---|---|---|---|---|---|---|---|---|---|---|---|---|---|---|---|---|---|---|---|
| Avila A | 104 | 294 | 28 | 67 | 12 | 0 | 7 | 31 | .228 | .316 | .340 | 2 | 2 | 144 | 12 | 4 | 14 | .222 | 2 | 150 | 16 | 3 | 17 | .233 | 0 | 76% | 30% | 11% | 1.5 | 43% | .656 | .676 | .502 |
| Boesch B | 133 | 464 | 49 | 119 | 26 | 3 | 14 | 67 | .256 | .320 | .416 | 7 | 1 | 243 | 34 | 12 | 49 | .342 | 2 | 221 | 15 | 2 | 18 | .163 | 5 | 79% | 33% | 8% | 1.6 | 45% | .736 | .673 | .951 |
| Cabrera M | 150 | 548 | 111 | 180 | 45 | 1 | 38 | 126 | .328 | .420 | .622 | 3 | 3 | 312 | 64 | 22 | 77 | .346 | 2 | 236 | 47 | 16 | 49 | .305 | 1 | 83% | 40% | 13% | 1.9 | 40% | 1.042 | 1.054 | 1.000 |
| Damon J | 145 | 539 | 81 | 146 | 36 | 5 | 8 | 51 | .271 | .355 | .401 | 11 | 1 | 292 | 54 | 6 | 28 | .274 | 7 | 247 | 27 | 2 | 23 | .267 | 4 | 83% | 33% | 11% | 1.5 | 44% | .756 | .760 | .740 |
| Everett A | 31 | 81 | 6 | 15 | 5 | 0 | 0 | 4 | .185 | .221 | .247 | 2 | 1 | 81 | 6 | 0 | 4 | .185 | 2 | -- | -- | -- | -- | -- | -- | 78% | 24% | 4% | 1.3 | 33% | .468 | .382 | .630 |
| Frazier J | 9 | 23 | 3 | 5 | 1 | 0 | 0 | 1 | .217 | .250 | .261 | 0 | 0 | -- | -- | -- | -- | -- | -- | 23 | 3 | 0 | 1 | .217 | 0 | 74% | 29% | 4% | 1.2 | 47% | .511 | .697 | .333 |
| Guillen C | 68 | 253 | 26 | 69 | 17 | 1 | 6 | 34 | .273 | .327 | .419 | 1 | 2 | 201 | 22 | 5 | 28 | .289 | 1 | 52 | 4 | 1 | 6 | .212 | 0 | 84% | 33% | 8% | 1.5 | 50% | .746 | .786 | .629 |
| Inge B | 144 | 514 | 47 | 127 | 28 | 5 | 13 | 70 | .247 | .321 | .397 | 4 | 3 | 299 | 21 | 6 | 39 | .264 | 1 | 215 | 26 | 7 | 31 | .223 | 3 | 74% | 33% | 9% | 1.6 | 39% | .718 | .681 | .817 |
| Jackson A | 151 | 618 | 103 | 181 | 34 | 10 | 4 | 41 | .293 | .345 | .400 | 27 | 6 | 313 | 52 | 1 | 20 | .300 | 14 | 305 | 51 | 3 | 21 | .285 | 13 | 72% | 40% | 7% | 1.4 | 48% | .745 | .798 | .600 |
| Kelly D | 119 | 238 | 30 | 58 | 4 | 0 | 9 | 27 | .244 | .272 | .374 | 3 | 0 | 100 | 11 | 1 | 8 | .220 | 1 | 138 | 19 | 8 | 19 | .261 | 2 | 82% | 30% | 3% | 1.5 | 32% | .646 | .663 | .487 |
| Laird G | 89 | 270 | 22 | 56 | 11 | 0 | 5 | 25 | .207 | .263 | .304 | 3 | 1 | 167 | 14 | 2 | 13 | .192 | 2 | 103 | 8 | 3 | 12 | .233 | 1 | 79% | 26% | 6% | 1.5 | 42% | .567 | .611 | .501 |
| Larish J | 3 | 10 | 0 | 2 | 0 | 0 | 0 | 1 | .200 | .200 | .200 | 0 | 0 | -- | -- | -- | -- | -- | -- | 10 | 0 | 0 | 1 | .200 | 0 | 60% | 33% | 0% | 1.0 | 100% | .400 | .333 | .500 |
| Ordonez M | 84 | 323 | 56 | 98 | 17 | 1 | 12 | 59 | .303 | .378 | .474 | 1 | 0 | 291 | 53 | 11 | 56 | .313 | 1 | 32 | 3 | 1 | 3 | .219 | 0 | 88% | 34% | 11% | 1.6 | 47% | .852 | .763 | 1.171 |
| Peralta J | 57 | 217 | 23 | 55 | 7 | 0 | 8 | 38 | .253 | .314 | .396 | 0 | 0 | -- | -- | -- | -- | -- | -- | 217 | 23 | 8 | 38 | .253 | 0 | 84% | 30% | 9% | 1.6 | 36% | .710 | .659 | .858 |
| Raburn R | 113 | 371 | 54 | 104 | 25 | 1 | 15 | 62 | .280 | .340 | .474 | 2 | 2 | 120 | 15 | 2 | 16 | .208 | 1 | 251 | 39 | 13 | 46 | .315 | 1 | 75% | 37% | 7% | 1.7 | 39% | .814 | .753 | .929 |
| Rhymes W | 54 | 191 | 30 | 58 | 12 | 3 | 1 | 19 | .304 | .350 | .414 | 0 | 3 | -- | -- | -- | -- | -- | -- | 191 | 30 | 1 | 19 | .304 | 0 | 92% | 33% | 7% | 1.4 | 42% | .763 | .741 | .855 |
| Santiago R | 112 | 320 | 38 | 84 | 9 | 1 | 3 | 22 | .263 | .337 | .325 | 2 | 2 | 190 | 25 | 2 | 12 | .268 | 1 | 130 | 13 | 1 | 10 | .254 | 1 | 83% | 32% | 8% | 1.2 | 47% | .662 | .635 | .763 |
| Sizemore S | 48 | 143 | 19 | 32 | 7 | 0 | 3 | 14 | .224 | .296 | .336 | 0 | 0 | 97 | 12 | 1 | 8 | .206 | 0 | 46 | 7 | 2 | 6 | .261 | 0 | 72% | 31% | 9% | 1.5 | 38% | .631 | .610 | .671 |
| St. Pierre M | 6 | 9 | 1 | 2 | 1 | 0 | 0 | 0 | .222 | .222 | .333 | 0 | 0 | -- | -- | -- | -- | -- | -- | 9 | 1 | 0 | 0 | .222 | 0 | 78% | 29% | 0% | 1.5 | 43% | .556 | .000 | .833 |
| Wells C | 36 | 93 | 14 | 30 | 6 | 1 | 4 | 17 | .323 | .364 | .538 | 0 | 1 | 9 | 0 | 0 | 2 | .222 | 0 | 84 | 14 | 4 | 15 | .333 | 0 | 80% | 41% | 6% | 1.7 | 46% | .901 | 1.130 | .695 |
| Worth D | 39 | 106 | 10 | 27 | 5 | 0 | 2 | 8 | .255 | .295 | .358 | 1 | 2 | 73 | 6 | 1 | 7 | .274 | 1 | 33 | 4 | 1 | 1 | .212 | 0 | 88% | 29% | 5% | 1.4 | 46% | .653 | .563 | .766 |

## Pitchers — Detroit Tigers 2010

| Pitchers | G | GS | W | L | Hld | Sv | IP | H | HR | ERA | WHIP | K | BB | 1st Half W | L | Sv | IP | ERA | WHIP | 2nd Half W | L | Sv | IP | ERA | WHIP | Rates K/9 | BB/9 | HR/9 | Productiveness opOPS | vs RH | vs LH |
|---|---|---|---|---|---|---|---|---|---|---|---|---|---|---|---|---|---|---|---|---|---|---|---|---|---|---|---|---|---|---|---|
| Bonderman J | 30 | 29 | 8 | 10 | 1 | 0 | 171.0 | 187 | 25 | 5.53 | 1.44 | 112 | 60 | 5 | 6 | 0 | 97.2 | 4.79 | 1.32 | 3 | 4 | 0 | 73.1 | 6.50 | 1.61 | 5.9 | 3.2 | 1.3 | .790 | .673 | .905 |
| Bonine E | 47 | 1 | 4 | 1 | 2 | 0 | 68.0 | 84 | 7 | 4.63 | 1.56 | 26 | 22 | 4 | 0 | 0 | 41.2 | 2.81 | 1.25 | 0 | 1 | 0 | 26.1 | 7.52 | 2.05 | 3.4 | 2.9 | 0.9 | .818 | .889 | .726 |
| Coke P | 74 | 1 | 7 | 5 | 17 | 2 | 64.2 | 67 | 2 | 3.76 | 1.44 | 53 | 26 | 5 | 0 | 1 | 36.1 | 2.48 | 1.32 | 2 | 5 | 1 | 28.1 | 5.40 | 1.59 | 7.4 | 3.6 | 0.3 | .699 | .713 | .681 |
| Fien C | 2 | 0 | 0 | 0 | 0 | 0 | 2.2 | 4 | 2 | 10.13 | 1.50 | 0 | 0 | 0 | 0 | 0 | 2.0 | 0.00 | 0.50 | 0 | 0 | 0 | 0.2 | 40.50 | 4.50 | 0.0 | 0.0 | 6.8 | 1.364 | 1.333 | 1.400 |
| Figaro A | 8 | 1 | 0 | 2 | 0 | 0 | 14.2 | 18 | 1 | 6.75 | 1.77 | 5 | 8 | 0 | 0 | 0 | 0.2 | 27.00 | 7.50 | 0 | 2 | 0 | 14.0 | 5.79 | 1.50 | 3.1 | 4.9 | 0.6 | .871 | .902 | .820 |
| Galarraga A | 25 | 24 | 4 | 9 | 0 | 0 | 144.1 | 143 | 21 | 4.49 | 1.34 | 74 | 51 | 3 | 2 | 0 | 54.2 | 4.45 | 1.32 | 1 | 7 | 0 | 89.2 | 4.52 | 1.36 | 4.6 | 3.2 | 1.3 | .765 | .745 | .785 |
| Gonzalez E | 18 | 0 | 0 | 1 | 0 | 0 | 26.0 | 21 | 4 | 3.81 | 1.46 | 13 | 17 | 0 | 0 | 0 | 12.0 | 2.25 | 1.25 | 0 | 1 | 0 | 14.0 | 5.14 | 1.64 | 4.5 | 5.9 | 1.4 | .771 | .669 | .876 |
| Ni F | 22 | 0 | 0 | 1 | 1 | 0 | 23.0 | 27 | 2 | 6.65 | 2.00 | 22 | 19 | 0 | 1 | 0 | 23.0 | 6.65 | 2.00 | -- | -- | -- | -- | -- | -- | 8.6 | 7.4 | 0.8 | .869 | .865 | .876 |
| Oliver A | 5 | 5 | 0 | 4 | 0 | 0 | 22.0 | 26 | 3 | 7.36 | 1.77 | 18 | 13 | 0 | 3 | 0 | 18.1 | 6.38 | 1.64 | 0 | 1 | 0 | 3.2 | 12.27 | 2.45 | 7.4 | 5.3 | 1.2 | .910 | .877 | .983 |
| Perry R | 60 | 0 | 3 | 5 | 19 | 2 | 62.2 | 55 | 6 | 3.59 | 1.24 | 45 | 23 | 2 | 4 | 1 | 24.2 | 5.47 | 1.62 | 1 | 1 | 1 | 38.0 | 2.37 | 1.00 | 6.5 | 3.3 | 0.9 | .686 | .792 | .485 |
| Porcello R | 27 | 27 | 10 | 12 | 0 | 0 | 162.2 | 188 | 18 | 4.92 | 1.39 | 84 | 38 | 4 | 7 | 0 | 70.1 | 6.14 | 1.69 | 6 | 5 | 0 | 92.1 | 4.00 | 1.16 | 4.6 | 2.1 | 1.0 | .752 | .717 | .784 |
| Sborz J | 1 | 0 | 0 | 0 | 0 | 0 | 0.2 | 3 | 0 | 67.50 | 4.50 | 1 | 0 | 0 | 0 | 0 | 0.2 | 67.50 | 4.50 | -- | -- | -- | -- | -- | -- | 13.5 | 0.0 | 0.0 | 1.314 | 1.250 | 1.333 |
| Scherzer M | 31 | 31 | 12 | 11 | 0 | 0 | 195.2 | 174 | 20 | 3.50 | 1.25 | 184 | 70 | 6 | 6 | 0 | 93.2 | 4.61 | 1.37 | 6 | 5 | 0 | 102.0 | 2.47 | 1.14 | 8.5 | 3.2 | 0.9 | .700 | .737 | .666 |
| Schlereth D | 18 | 0 | 2 | 0 | 1 | 1 | 18.2 | 20 | 2 | 2.89 | 1.61 | 19 | 10 | 0 | 0 | 0 | 2.2 | 3.38 | 3.00 | 2 | 0 | 1 | 16.0 | 2.81 | 1.38 | 9.2 | 4.8 | 1.0 | .752 | .594 | .998 |
| Thomas B | 49 | 2 | 6 | 2 | 3 | 0 | 69.1 | 77 | 4 | 3.89 | 1.53 | 30 | 29 | 4 | 0 | 0 | 39.1 | 4.12 | 1.65 | 2 | 2 | 0 | 30.0 | 3.60 | 1.37 | 3.9 | 3.8 | 0.5 | .776 | .885 | .632 |
| Valverde J | 60 | 0 | 2 | 4 | 0 | 26 | 63.0 | 41 | 5 | 3.00 | 1.16 | 63 | 32 | 1 | 1 | 19 | 39.0 | 0.92 | 0.82 | 1 | 3 | 7 | 24.0 | 6.38 | 1.71 | 9.0 | 4.6 | 0.7 | .585 | .502 | .662 |
| Verlander J | 33 | 33 | 18 | 9 | 0 | 0 | 224.1 | 190 | 14 | 3.37 | 1.16 | 219 | 71 | 11 | 5 | 0 | 115.1 | 3.82 | 1.19 | 7 | 4 | 0 | 109.0 | 2.89 | 1.14 | 8.8 | 2.8 | 0.6 | .630 | .622 | .635 |
| Weinhardt R | 28 | 0 | 2 | 2 | 5 | 0 | 29.1 | 40 | 2 | 6.14 | 1.64 | 21 | 8 | 0 | 0 | 0 | 4.0 | 2.25 | 0.25 | 2 | 2 | 0 | 25.1 | 6.75 | 1.86 | 6.4 | 2.5 | 0.6 | .831 | .949 | .616 |
| Willis D | 9 | 8 | 1 | 2 | 0 | 0 | 43.1 | 48 | 3 | 4.98 | 1.78 | 33 | 29 | 1 | 2 | 0 | 43.1 | 4.98 | 1.78 | -- | -- | -- | -- | -- | -- | 6.9 | 6.0 | 0.6 | .780 | .836 | .636 |
| Zumaya J | 31 | 0 | 2 | 1 | 11 | 1 | 38.1 | 32 | 1 | 2.58 | 1.12 | 34 | 11 | 2 | 1 | 1 | 38.1 | 2.58 | 1.12 | -- | -- | -- | -- | -- | -- | 8.0 | 2.6 | 0.2 | .586 | .560 | .616 |

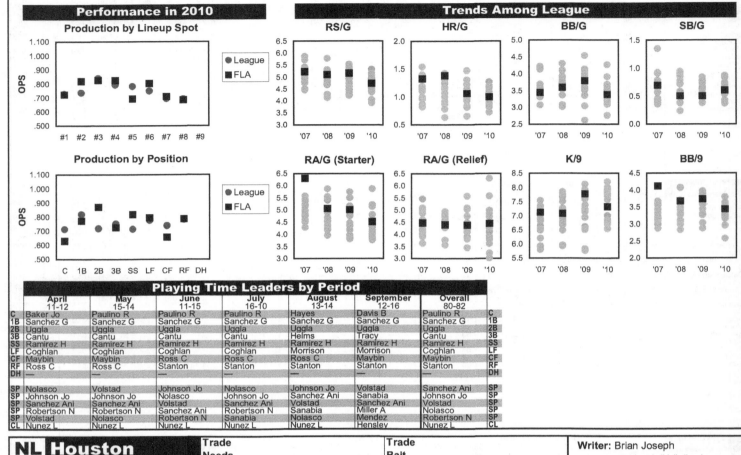

### Performance in 2010
**Production by Lineup Spot**
**Production by Position**

### Trends Among League
RS/G | HR/G | BB/G | SB/G
RA/G (Starter) | RA/G (Relief) | K/9 | BB/9

| Playing Time Leaders by Period | | | | | | | |
|---|---|---|---|---|---|---|---|
| | April 11-12 | May 15-14 | June 11-15 | July 16-10 | August 13-14 | September 12-16 | Overall 80-82 |
| C | Baker Jo | Paulino R | Paulino R | Paulino R | Hayes | Davis B | Paulino R |
| 1B | Sanchez G | Sanchez G | Sanchez G | Sanchez G | Sanchez G | Sanchez G | Sanchez G |
| 2B | Uggla | Uggla | Uggla | Uggla | Uggla | Uggla | Uggla |
| 3B | Cantu | Cantu | Cantu | Cantu | Helms | Tracy | Cantu |
| SS | Ramirez H | Ramirez H | Coghlan | Ramirez H | Ramirez H | Ramirez H | Ramirez H |
| LF | Coghlan | Coghlan | Coghlan | Coghlan | Morrison | Morrison | Coghlan |
| CF | Maybin | Maybin | Ross C | Ross C | Ross C | Maybin | Maybin |
| RF | Ross C | Ross C | Stanton | Stanton | Stanton | Stanton | Stanton |
| DH | — | — | — | — | — | — | — |
| SP | Nolasco | Volstad | Johnson Jo | Nolasco | Johnson Jo | Volstad | Sanchez Ani |
| SP | Johnson Jo | Johnson Jo | Nolasco | Johnson Jo | Sanchez Ani | Sanabia | Johnson Jo |
| SP | Sanchez Ani | Sanchez Ani | Volstad | Sanchez Ani | Volstad | Sanchez Ani | Volstad |
| SP | Robertson N | Robertson N | Sanchez Ani | Robertson N | Sanabia | Miller A | Nolasco |
| SP | Volstad | Nolasco | Robertson N | Sanabia | Nolasco | Mendez | Robertson N |
| CL | Nunez L | Nunez L | Nunez L | Nunez L | Nunez L | Hensley | Nunez L |

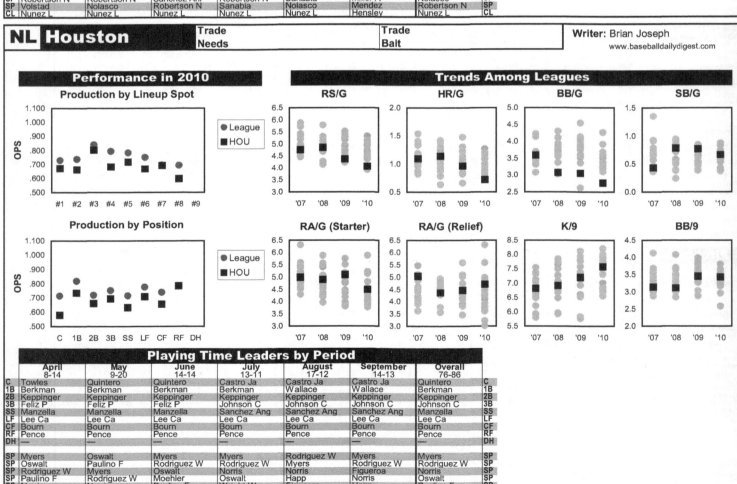

### Performance in 2010
**Production by Lineup Spot**
**Production by Position**

### Trends Among Leagues
RS/G | HR/G | BB/G | SB/G
RA/G (Starter) | RA/G (Relief) | K/9 | BB/9

| Playing Time Leaders by Period | | | | | | | |
|---|---|---|---|---|---|---|---|
| | April 8-14 | May 9-20 | June 14-14 | July 13-11 | August 17-12 | September 14-13 | Overall 76-86 |
| C | Towles | Quintero | Quintero | Castro Ja | Castro Ja | Castro Ja | Quintero |
| 1B | Berkman | Berkman | Berkman | Berkman | Wallace | Wallace | Berkman |
| 2B | Keppinger | Keppinger | Keppinger | Keppinger | Keppinger | Keppinger | Keppinger |
| 3B | Feliz P | Feliz P | Feliz P | Johnson C | Johnson C | Johnson C | Johnson C |
| SS | Manzella | Manzella | Manzella | Sanchez Ang | Sanchez Ang | Sanchez Ang | Manzella |
| LF | Lee Ca | Lee Ca | Lee Ca | Lee Ca | Lee Ca | Lee Ca | Lee Ca |
| CF | Bourn | Bourn | Bourn | Bourn | Bourn | Bourn | Bourn |
| RF | Pence | Pence | Pence | Pence | Pence | Pence | Pence |
| DH | — | — | — | — | — | — | — |
| SP | Myers | Oswalt | Myers | Myers | Rodriguez W | Myers | Myers |
| SP | Oswalt | Paulino F | Rodriguez W | Rodriguez W | Myers | Rodriguez W | Rodriguez W |
| SP | Rodriguez W | Myers | Oswalt | Norris | Norris | Figueroa | Norris |
| SP | Paulino F | Rodriguez W | Moehler | Oswalt | Happ | Norris | Oswalt |
| SP | Norris | Norris | Paulino F | Wright W | Figueroa | Happ | Paulino F |
| CL | Lindstrom | Lindstrom | Lindstrom | Lindstrom | Lyon | Lyon | Lindstrom |

## Hitters — Florida Marlins 2010

| Hitters | G | AB | R | H | 2B | 3B | HR | RBI | BA | OBP | SLG | SB | CS | 1st Half AB | R | HR | BI | BA | SB | 2nd Half AB | R | HR | BI | BA | SB | Rates CT% | H% | BB% | Bash | GB% | Productiveness OPS | vs RH | vs LH |
|---|---|---|---|---|---|---|---|---|---|---|---|---|---|---|---|---|---|---|---|---|---|---|---|---|---|---|---|---|---|---|---|---|---|
| Baker J | 23 | 78 | 7 | 17 | 3 | 1 | 0 | 6 | .218 | .307 | .282 | 0 | 0 | 78 | 7 | 0 | 6 | .218 | 0 | — | — | — | — | — | — | 77% | 28% | 10% | 1.3 | 52% | .589 | .625 | .250 |
| Barden B | 35 | 28 | 2 | 5 | 0 | 0 | 0 | 3 | .179 | .281 | .179 | 0 | 2 | 28 | 2 | 0 | 3 | .179 | 0 | — | — | — | — | — | — | 57% | 31% | 9% | 1.0 | 50% | .460 | .485 | .400 |
| Bonifacio E | 73 | 180 | 30 | 47 | 6 | 3 | 0 | 10 | .261 | .320 | .328 | 12 | 0 | 21 | 1 | 0 | 1 | .238 | 3 | 159 | 29 | 0 | 9 | .264 | 9 | 77% | 34% | 8% | 1.3 | 48% | .648 | .586 | .827 |
| Cantu J | 97 | 374 | 41 | 98 | 25 | 0 | 10 | 54 | .262 | .310 | .409 | 0 | 0 | 330 | 37 | 10 | 52 | .261 | 0 | 44 | 4 | 0 | 2 | .273 | 0 | 80% | 33% | 6% | 1.6 | 40% | .719 | .719 | .718 |
| Carroll B | 32 | 76 | 13 | 15 | 4 | 0 | 2 | 7 | .197 | .311 | .329 | 2 | 1 | 76 | 13 | 2 | 7 | .197 | 2 | — | — | — | — | — | — | 62% | 32% | 6% | 1.7 | 51% | .640 | .626 | .661 |
| Coghlan C | 91 | 358 | 60 | 96 | 20 | 3 | 5 | 28 | .268 | .335 | .383 | 10 | 3 | 332 | 55 | 5 | 28 | .268 | 9 | 26 | 5 | 0 | 0 | .269 | 1 | 77% | 35% | 8% | 1.4 | 51% | .718 | .720 | .709 |
| Cousins S | 27 | 37 | 2 | 11 | 2 | 2 | 0 | 2 | .297 | .316 | .459 | 0 | 0 | — | — | — | — | — | — | 37 | 2 | 0 | 2 | .297 | 0 | 65% | 46% | 3% | 1.5 | 46% | .775 | .727 | 1.100 |
| Davis B | 33 | 109 | 8 | 23 | 7 | 1 | 3 | 16 | .211 | .270 | .376 | 2 | 0 | — | — | — | — | — | — | 109 | 8 | 3 | 16 | .211 | 2 | 66% | 32% | 7% | 1.8 | 47% | .647 | .653 | .627 |
| Hatcher C | 5 | 6 | 0 | 0 | 0 | 0 | 0 | 0 | .000 | .250 | .000 | 0 | 0 | — | — | — | — | — | — | 6 | 0 | 0 | 0 | .000 | 0 | 17% | 0% | 22% | — | 100% | .250 | .400 | .000 |
| Hayes B | 26 | 77 | 6 | 16 | 6 | 1 | 2 | 6 | .208 | .265 | .390 | 0 | 0 | 31 | 1 | 1 | 2 | .226 | 0 | 46 | 5 | 1 | 4 | .196 | 0 | 66% | 31% | 7% | 1.9 | 31% | .655 | .692 | .486 |
| Helms W | 127 | 254 | 25 | 56 | 12 | 4 | 4 | 39 | .220 | .300 | .346 | 0 | 2 | 115 | 11 | 3 | 15 | .243 | 0 | 139 | 14 | 1 | 24 | .201 | 0 | 70% | 31% | 9% | 1.6 | 45% | .646 | .525 | .942 |
| Lamb M | 39 | 38 | 2 | 7 | 1 | 1 | 0 | 4 | .184 | .225 | .263 | 0 | 0 | 36 | 2 | 0 | 4 | .194 | 0 | 2 | 0 | 0 | 0 | .000 | 0 | 84% | 22% | 5% | 1.4 | 50% | .488 | .488 | — |
| Luna H | 27 | 29 | 2 | 4 | 1 | 0 | 2 | 4 | .138 | .133 | .379 | 0 | 1 | — | — | — | — | — | — | 29 | 2 | 2 | 4 | .138 | 0 | 55% | 25% | 0% | 2.8 | 25% | .513 | .464 | .583 |
| Martinez O | 14 | 43 | 8 | 14 | 4 | 1 | 0 | 2 | .326 | .383 | .465 | 1 | 0 | — | — | — | — | — | — | 43 | 8 | 0 | 2 | .326 | 1 | 86% | 38% | 8% | 1.4 | 51% | .848 | .895 | .771 |
| Maybin C | 82 | 291 | 46 | 68 | 7 | 3 | 8 | 28 | .234 | .302 | .361 | 9 | 2 | 182 | 31 | 5 | 19 | .225 | 6 | 109 | 15 | 3 | 9 | .248 | 3 | 68% | 34% | 7% | 1.5 | 51% | .663 | .694 | .584 |
| Morrison L | 62 | 244 | 43 | 69 | 20 | 7 | 2 | 18 | .283 | .390 | .447 | 0 | 1 | — | — | — | — | — | — | 244 | 43 | 2 | 18 | .283 | 0 | 79% | 36% | 14% | 1.6 | 48% | .837 | .797 | .926 |
| Murphy D | 29 | 44 | 9 | 14 | 6 | 1 | 3 | 16 | .318 | .348 | .705 | 0 | 0 | 2 | 1 | 0 | 0 | .500 | 0 | 42 | 8 | 3 | 16 | .310 | 0 | 57% | 56% | 4% | 2.2 | 32% | 1.052 | .844 | 1.571 |
| Paulino R | 91 | 316 | 31 | 82 | 18 | 0 | 4 | 37 | .259 | .311 | .354 | 1 | 0 | 234 | 25 | 3 | 30 | .282 | 1 | 82 | 6 | 1 | 7 | .195 | 0 | 84% | 31% | 7% | 1.4 | 43% | .665 | .568 | .896 |
| Petersen B | 23 | 24 | 1 | 2 | 0 | 0 | 0 | 2 | .083 | .120 | .083 | 0 | 0 | 16 | 1 | 0 | 0 | .063 | 0 | 8 | 0 | 0 | 2 | .125 | 0 | 75% | 11% | 4% | 1.0 | 50% | .203 | .212 | .000 |
| Ramirez H | 142 | 543 | 92 | 163 | 28 | 2 | 21 | 76 | .300 | .378 | .475 | 32 | 10 | 326 | 50 | 13 | 53 | .301 | 18 | 217 | 42 | 8 | 23 | .300 | 14 | 83% | 36% | 10% | 1.6 | 51% | .853 | .858 | .838 |
| Rivera M | 7 | 14 | 0 | 0 | 0 | 0 | 0 | 0 | .000 | .176 | .000 | 0 | 0 | — | — | — | — | — | — | 14 | 0 | 0 | 0 | .000 | 0 | 79% | 0% | 12% | — | 55% | .176 | .214 | .000 |
| Ross C | 120 | 452 | 60 | 120 | 24 | 3 | 11 | 58 | .265 | .316 | .405 | 9 | 1 | 330 | 45 | 7 | 46 | .282 | 8 | 122 | 15 | 4 | 12 | .221 | 1 | 78% | 34% | 6% | 1.5 | 45% | .721 | .677 | .864 |
| Sanchez G | 151 | 572 | 72 | 156 | 37 | 3 | 19 | 85 | .273 | .341 | .448 | 5 | 1 | 315 | 43 | 9 | 38 | .302 | 3 | 257 | 29 | 10 | 47 | .237 | 2 | 82% | 33% | 9% | 1.6 | 37% | .788 | .742 | .925 |
| Stanton M | 100 | 359 | 45 | 93 | 21 | 1 | 22 | 59 | .259 | .326 | .507 | 5 | 2 | 108 | 16 | 5 | 20 | .231 | 3 | 251 | 29 | 17 | 39 | .271 | 2 | 66% | 39% | 8% | 2.0 | 43% | .833 | .892 | .644 |
| Tracy C | 41 | 102 | 5 | 25 | 6 | 0 | 1 | 10 | .245 | .297 | .333 | 0 | 0 | — | — | — | — | — | — | 102 | 5 | 1 | 10 | .245 | 0 | 79% | 31% | 5% | 1.4 | 38% | .631 | .623 | .833 |
| Uggla D | 159 | 589 | 100 | 169 | 31 | 0 | 33 | 105 | .287 | .369 | .508 | 4 | 1 | 323 | 56 | 16 | 52 | .285 | 2 | 266 | 44 | 17 | 53 | .289 | 2 | 75% | 38% | 12% | 1.8 | 40% | .877 | .845 | .983 |

## Pitchers — Florida Marlins 2010

| Pitchers | G | GS | W | L | Hld | Sv | IP | H | HR | ERA | WHIP | K | BB | 1st Half W | L | Sv | IP | ERA | WHIP | 2nd Half W | L | Sv | IP | ERA | WHIP | Rates K/9 | BB/9 | HR/9 | Productiveness opOPS | vs RH | vs LH |
|---|---|---|---|---|---|---|---|---|---|---|---|---|---|---|---|---|---|---|---|---|---|---|---|---|---|---|---|---|---|---|---|
| Badenhop B | 53 | 0 | 2 | 5 | 8 | 1 | 67.2 | 62 | 5 | 3.99 | 1.23 | 47 | 21 | 1 | 5 | 1 | 23.2 | 5.70 | 1.35 | 1 | 0 | 0 | 44.0 | 3.07 | 1.16 | 6.3 | 2.8 | 0.7 | .681 | .667 | .700 |
| Buente J | 8 | 0 | 0 | 0 | 0 | 0 | 11.0 | 16 | 0 | 6.55 | 2.45 | 9 | 11 | 0 | 0 | 0 | 5.1 | 6.75 | 2.81 | 0 | 0 | 0 | 5.2 | 6.35 | 2.12 | 7.4 | 9.0 | 0.0 | .848 | .973 | .711 |
| Ceda J | 8 | 0 | 0 | 0 | 0 | 0 | 8.2 | 8 | 1 | 5.19 | 2.19 | 9 | 11 | — | — | — | — | — | — | 0 | 0 | 0 | 8.2 | 5.19 | 2.19 | 9.3 | 11.4 | 1.0 | .808 | .568 | 1.010 |
| Cishek S | 3 | 0 | 0 | 0 | 0 | 0 | 4.1 | 1 | 0 | 0.00 | 0.46 | 3 | 1 | — | — | — | — | — | — | 0 | 0 | 0 | 4.1 | 0.00 | 0.46 | 6.2 | 2.1 | 0.0 | .276 | .333 | .167 |
| Hensley C | 68 | 0 | 3 | 4 | 22 | 7 | 75.0 | 54 | 3 | 2.16 | 1.11 | 77 | 29 | 1 | 3 | 0 | 37.2 | 2.39 | 1.12 | 2 | 1 | 7 | 37.1 | 1.93 | 1.10 | 9.2 | 3.5 | 0.4 | .568 | .523 | .612 |
| Houser J | 1 | 0 | 0 | 0 | 0 | 0 | 1.1 | 3 | 1 | 20.25 | 3.00 | 1 | 1 | 0 | 0 | 0 | 1.1 | 20.25 | 3.00 | — | — | — | — | — | — | 6.8 | 6.8 | 6.8 | 1.792 | 1.500 | 3.000 |
| Johnson J | 28 | 28 | 11 | 6 | 0 | 0 | 183.2 | 155 | 7 | 2.30 | 1.11 | 186 | 48 | 9 | 3 | 0 | 122.0 | 1.70 | 0.96 | 2 | 3 | 0 | 61.2 | 3.50 | 1.39 | 9.1 | 2.4 | 0.3 | .607 | .602 | .612 |
| Jones H | 3 | 0 | 0 | 0 | 0 | 0 | 1.2 | 0 | 0 | 0.00 | 0.60 | 3 | 1 | 0 | 0 | 0 | 1.2 | 0.00 | 0.60 | — | — | — | — | — | — | 16.2 | 5.4 | 0.0 | .286 | .200 | .500 |
| Leroux C | 17 | 0 | 0 | 0 | 3 | 0 | 18.0 | 24 | 1 | 7.00 | 1.94 | 18 | 11 | 0 | 0 | 0 | 15.0 | 6.60 | 1.87 | 0 | 0 | 0 | 3.0 | 9.00 | 2.33 | 9.0 | 5.5 | 0.5 | .931 | .941 | .902 |
| Marinez J | 4 | 0 | 1 | 1 | 0 | 0 | 2.2 | 3 | 1 | 6.75 | 2.25 | 3 | 3 | — | — | — | — | — | — | 1 | 1 | 0 | 2.2 | 6.75 | 2.25 | 10.1 | 10.1 | 3.4 | .974 | .600 | 1.000 |
| Mendez A | 5 | 5 | 1 | 3 | 0 | 0 | 24.2 | 28 | 7 | 5.11 | 1.62 | 11 | 12 | — | — | — | — | — | — | 1 | 3 | 0 | 24.2 | 5.11 | 1.62 | 4.0 | 4.4 | 2.6 | .964 | .971 | .959 |
| Meyer D | 13 | 0 | 0 | 1 | 1 | 0 | 9.1 | 15 | 1 | 9.64 | 2.89 | 4 | 12 | 0 | 1 | 0 | 9.1 | 9.64 | 2.89 | — | — | — | — | — | — | 3.9 | 11.6 | 1.0 | 1.031 | .962 | 1.150 |
| Miller A | 9 | 7 | 1 | 5 | 0 | 0 | 32.2 | 51 | 6 | 8.54 | 2.36 | 28 | 26 | — | — | — | — | — | — | 1 | 5 | 0 | 32.2 | 8.54 | 2.36 | 7.7 | 7.2 | 1.7 | 1.054 | .975 | 1.262 |
| Nolasco R | 26 | 26 | 14 | 9 | 0 | 0 | 157.2 | 169 | 24 | 4.51 | 1.28 | 147 | 33 | 9 | 6 | 0 | 110.2 | 4.55 | 1.29 | 5 | 3 | 0 | 47.0 | 4.40 | 1.26 | 8.4 | 1.9 | 1.4 | .766 | .772 | .758 |
| Nunez L | 68 | 0 | 4 | 3 | 5 | 30 | 65.0 | 62 | 5 | 3.46 | 1.28 | 71 | 21 | 3 | 2 | 20 | 36.2 | 2.95 | 1.04 | 1 | 1 | 10 | 28.1 | 4.13 | 1.59 | 9.8 | 2.9 | 0.7 | .688 | .817 | .572 |
| Ohman W | 17 | 0 | 0 | 2 | 3 | 0 | 12.0 | 10 | 1 | 3.00 | 1.25 | 14 | 5 | — | — | — | — | — | — | 0 | 2 | 0 | 12.0 | 3.00 | 1.25 | 10.5 | 3.8 | 0.8 | .650 | .644 | .653 |
| Pinto R | 20 | 0 | 0 | 0 | 4 | 0 | 16.2 | 16 | 1 | 2.70 | 1.50 | 16 | 9 | 0 | 0 | 0 | 16.2 | 2.70 | 1.50 | — | — | — | — | — | — | 8.6 | 4.9 | 0.5 | .736 | .558 | 1.072 |
| Robertson N | 19 | 18 | 6 | 8 | 0 | 0 | 100.1 | 110 | 11 | 5.47 | 1.50 | 61 | 40 | 6 | 7 | 0 | 95.1 | 5.10 | 1.49 | 0 | 1 | 0 | 5.0 | 12.60 | 1.60 | 5.5 | 3.6 | 1.0 | .806 | .834 | .696 |
| Rosario S | 2 | 0 | 0 | 0 | 0 | 0 | 1.0 | 9 | 2 | 54.00 | 10.00 | 0 | 1 | — | — | — | — | — | — | 0 | 0 | 0 | 1.0 | 54.00 | 10.00 | 0.0 | 9.0 | 18.0 | 2.288 | 2.333 | 2.233 |
| Sanabia A | 15 | 12 | 5 | 3 | 0 | 0 | 72.1 | 74 | 6 | 3.73 | 1.24 | 47 | 16 | 0 | 1 | 0 | 11.2 | 3.09 | 1.46 | 5 | 2 | 0 | 60.2 | 3.86 | 1.20 | 5.8 | 2.0 | 0.7 | .686 | .791 | .576 |
| Sanches B | 61 | 0 | 2 | 2 | 12 | 0 | 63.2 | 43 | 7 | 2.26 | 1.10 | 54 | 27 | 0 | 1 | 0 | 29.0 | 3.10 | 1.34 | 2 | 1 | 0 | 34.2 | 1.56 | 0.89 | 7.6 | 3.8 | 1.0 | .609 | .588 | .635 |
| Sanchez A | 32 | 32 | 13 | 12 | 0 | 0 | 195.0 | 192 | 10 | 3.55 | 1.34 | 157 | 70 | 7 | 6 | 0 | 103.1 | 3.66 | 1.43 | 6 | 6 | 0 | 91.2 | 3.44 | 1.24 | 7.2 | 3.2 | 0.5 | .680 | .674 | .686 |
| Sinkbeil B | 3 | 0 | 0 | 0 | 0 | 0 | 2.0 | 2 | 0 | 13.50 | 3.50 | 1 | 5 | — | — | — | — | — | — | 0 | 0 | 0 | 2.0 | 13.50 | 3.50 | 4.5 | 22.5 | 0.0 | .913 | .829 | 1.000 |
| Sosa J | 22 | 2 | 2 | 3 | 0 | 0 | 36.2 | 39 | 4 | 4.66 | 1.55 | 19 | 18 | 1 | 2 | 0 | 9.1 | 7.71 | 1.39 | 1 | 1 | 0 | 27.1 | 3.62 | 1.61 | 4.7 | 4.4 | 1.0 | .764 | .642 | .944 |
| Strickland S | 3 | 0 | 0 | 0 | 0 | 0 | 2.0 | 5 | 0 | 9.00 | 3.00 | 0 | 1 | 0 | 0 | 0 | 2.0 | 9.00 | 3.00 | — | — | — | — | — | — | 0.0 | 4.5 | 0.0 | 1.245 | 1.833 | .600 |
| Tankersley T | 27 | 0 | 0 | 0 | 6 | 0 | 12.0 | 12 | 4 | 7.50 | 1.58 | 7 | 7 | 0 | 0 | 0 | 7.2 | 3.52 | 1.43 | 0 | 0 | 0 | 4.1 | 14.54 | 1.85 | 5.3 | 5.3 | 3.0 | .913 | 1.232 | .719 |
| VandenHurk R | 2 | 0 | 0 | 0 | 0 | 0 | 1.1 | 3 | 0 | 6.75 | 3.00 | 1 | 1 | 0 | 0 | 0 | 1.1 | 6.75 | 3.00 | — | — | — | — | — | — | 6.8 | 6.8 | 0.0 | .944 | .833 | 1.000 |
| Veras J | 48 | 0 | 3 | 3 | 19 | 0 | 48.0 | 32 | 5 | 3.75 | 1.27 | 54 | 29 | 1 | 0 | 0 | 14.2 | 4.91 | 1.09 | 2 | 3 | 0 | 33.1 | 3.24 | 1.35 | 10.1 | 5.4 | 0.9 | .622 | .686 | .555 |
| Volstad C | 30 | 30 | 12 | 9 | 0 | 0 | 175.0 | 187 | 17 | 4.58 | 1.41 | 102 | 60 | 4 | 8 | 0 | 98.0 | 4.78 | 1.39 | 8 | 1 | 0 | 77.0 | 4.32 | 1.44 | 5.2 | 3.1 | 0.9 | .755 | .719 | .794 |
| West S | 2 | 2 | 0 | 2 | 0 | 0 | 9.1 | 15 | 2 | 7.71 | 2.04 | 8 | 4 | — | — | — | — | — | — | 0 | 2 | 0 | 9.1 | 7.71 | 2.04 | 7.7 | 3.9 | 1.9 | 1.032 | 1.039 | 1.000 |
| Wood T | 26 | 0 | 0 | 1 | 3 | 1 | 27.2 | 33 | 2 | 5.53 | 1.73 | 10 | 15 | 0 | 1 | 1 | 27.2 | 5.53 | 1.73 | — | — | — | — | — | — | 3.3 | 4.9 | 0.7 | .819 | .894 | .718 |

## Hitters — Houston Astros 2010

| Hitters | G | AB | R | H | 2B | 3B | HR | RBI | BA | OBP | SLG | SB | CS | 1st Half AB | R | HR | BI | BA | SB | 2nd Half AB | R | HR | BI | BA | SB | Rates CT% | H% | BB% | Bash | GB% | Productiveness OPS | vs RH | vs LH |
|---|---|---|---|---|---|---|---|---|---|---|---|---|---|---|---|---|---|---|---|---|---|---|---|---|---|---|---|---|---|---|---|---|---|
| Berkman L | 85 | 298 | 39 | 73 | 16 | 1 | 13 | 49 | .245 | .372 | .436 | 3 | 2 | 259 | 32 | 12 | 43 | .255 | 3 | 39 | 7 | 1 | 6 | .179 | 0 | 77% | 32% | 17% | 1.8 | 47% | .808 | .874 | .559 |
| Blum G | 93 | 202 | 22 | 54 | 10 | 1 | 2 | 22 | .267 | .321 | .356 | 0 | 0 | 137 | 15 | 0 | 14 | .241 | 0 | 65 | 7 | 2 | 8 | .323 | 0 | 84% | 32% | 7% | 1.3 | 44% | .678 | .722 | .415 |
| Bogusevic B | 19 | 28 | 5 | 5 | 3 | 0 | 0 | 3 | .179 | .258 | .286 | 1 | 1 | — | — | — | — | — | — | 28 | 5 | 0 | 3 | .179 | 1 | 57% | 31% | 9% | 1.6 | 69% | .544 | .584 | .000 |
| Bourgeois J | 69 | 123 | 16 | 27 | 4 | 1 | 0 | 3 | .220 | .294 | .268 | 12 | 4 | 19 | 1 | 0 | 1 | .316 | 3 | 104 | 15 | 0 | 2 | .202 | 9 | 87% | 25% | 10% | 1.2 | 44% | .562 | .546 | .580 |
| Bourn M | 141 | 535 | 84 | 142 | 25 | 6 | 2 | 38 | .265 | .341 | .346 | 52 | 12 | 321 | 52 | 1 | 20 | .255 | 28 | 214 | 32 | 1 | 18 | .280 | 24 | 80% | 33% | 10% | 1.3 | 57% | .686 | .723 | .555 |
| Cash K | 20 | 54 | 3 | 11 | 1 | 0 | 2 | 4 | .204 | .271 | .333 | 0 | 0 | 54 | 3 | 2 | 4 | .204 | 0 | — | — | — | — | — | — | 76% | 27% | 8% | 1.6 | 39% | .605 | .624 | .538 |
| Castro J | 67 | 195 | 26 | 40 | 8 | 1 | 2 | 8 | .205 | .286 | .287 | 0 | 0 | 47 | 7 | 1 | 1 | .170 | 0 | 148 | 19 | 1 | 7 | .216 | 0 | 79% | 26% | 10% | 1.4 | 41% | .573 | .670 | .223 |
| Downs M | 11 | 19 | 2 | 2 | 0 | 0 | 0 | 0 | .105 | .190 | .105 | 0 | 0 | — | — | — | — | — | — | 19 | 2 | 0 | 0 | .105 | 0 | 89% | 12% | 5% | 1.0 | 47% | .296 | .220 | .452 |
| Esposito B | 2 | 3 | 0 | 0 | 0 | 0 | 0 | 0 | .000 | .000 | .000 | 0 | 0 | — | — | — | — | — | — | 3 | 0 | 0 | 0 | .000 | 0 | 67% | 0% | 0% | — | 50% | .000 | .000 | .000 |
| Feliz P | 97 | 289 | 22 | 64 | 12 | 1 | 4 | 31 | .221 | .243 | .311 | 1 | 1 | 255 | 18 | 3 | 26 | .220 | 1 | 34 | 4 | 1 | 5 | .235 | 0 | 89% | 25% | 3% | 1.4 | 43% | .555 | .497 | .723 |
| Hernandez A | 32 | 48 | 7 | 9 | 2 | 0 | 0 | 1 | .188 | .304 | .229 | 2 | 0 | — | — | — | — | — | — | 48 | 7 | 0 | 1 | .188 | 2 | 79% | 24% | 14% | 1.2 | 58% | .533 | .530 | .542 |
| Johnson C | 94 | 341 | 40 | 105 | 22 | 2 | 11 | 52 | .308 | .337 | .481 | 3 | 0 | 78 | 7 | 0 | 8 | .282 | 1 | 263 | 33 | 11 | 44 | .316 | 2 | 73% | 42% | 4% | 1.6 | 42% | .818 | .848 | .735 |
| Keppinger J | 137 | 514 | 62 | 148 | 34 | 1 | 6 | 59 | .288 | .351 | .393 | 4 | 1 | 317 | 36 | 3 | 31 | .284 | 2 | 197 | 26 | 3 | 28 | .294 | 2 | 93% | 31% | 9% | 1.4 | 51% | .744 | .719 | .810 |
| Lee C | 157 | 605 | 67 | 149 | 29 | 1 | 24 | 89 | .246 | .291 | .417 | 3 | 3 | 329 | 35 | 12 | 45 | .240 | 1 | 276 | 32 | 12 | 44 | .254 | 2 | 90% | 27% | 6% | 1.7 | 39% | .708 | .689 | .771 |
| Manzella T | 83 | 258 | 17 | 58 | 7 | 0 | 1 | 21 | .225 | .267 | .264 | 0 | 1 | 189 | 13 | 1 | 16 | .212 | 0 | 69 | 4 | 0 | 5 | .261 | 0 | 72% | 31% | 5% | 1.2 | 52% | .531 | .474 | .686 |
| Matsui K | 27 | 71 | 4 | 10 | 1 | 0 | 0 | 1 | .141 | .197 | .155 | 1 | 1 | 71 | 4 | 0 | 1 | .141 | 1 | — | — | — | — | — | — | 86% | 16% | 5% | 1.1 | 67% | .352 | .367 | .000 |
| Michaels J | 106 | 186 | 23 | 47 | 14 | 1 | 8 | 26 | .253 | .310 | .468 | 0 | 0 | 95 | 10 | 5 | 14 | .242 | 0 | 91 | 13 | 3 | 12 | .264 | 0 | 84% | 30% | 6% | 1.9 | 34% | .778 | .685 | .876 |
| Navarro O | 14 | 20 | 2 | 1 | 0 | 0 | 0 | 0 | .050 | .240 | .050 | 0 | 0 | 19 | 2 | 0 | 0 | .053 | 0 | 1 | 0 | 0 | 0 | .000 | 0 | 80% | 6% | 20% | 1.0 | 31% | .290 | .327 | .222 |
| Pence H | 156 | 614 | 93 | 173 | 29 | 3 | 25 | 91 | .282 | .325 | .461 | 18 | 9 | 323 | 47 | 12 | 40 | .263 | 11 | 291 | 46 | 13 | 51 | .302 | 7 | 83% | 34% | 6% | 1.6 | 53% | .786 | .776 | .820 |
| Quintero H | 88 | 265 | 13 | 62 | 10 | 0 | 4 | 20 | .234 | .262 | .317 | 0 | 0 | 159 | 9 | 3 | 10 | .233 | 0 | 106 | 4 | 1 | 10 | .236 | 0 | 78% | 30% | 3% | 1.4 | 45% | .579 | .665 | .375 |
| Sanchez A | 65 | 250 | 30 | 70 | 9 | 4 | 0 | 25 | .280 | .316 | .348 | 0 | 1 | 22 | 0 | 0 | 0 | .227 | 0 | 228 | 30 | 0 | 25 | .285 | 0 | 82% | 34% | 4% | 1.2 | 43% | .664 | .670 | .648 |
| Sullivan C | 57 | 64 | 6 | 12 | 1 | 1 | 0 | 4 | .188 | .257 | .234 | 0 | 0 | 64 | 6 | 0 | 4 | .188 | 0 | — | — | — | — | — | — | 72% | 26% | 8% | 1.3 | 48% | .492 | .515 | .000 |
| Towles J | 17 | 47 | 3 | 9 | 3 | 0 | 1 | 8 | .191 | .235 | .319 | 0 | 0 | 47 | 3 | 1 | 8 | .191 | 0 | — | — | — | — | — | — | 74% | 26% | 4% | 1.7 | 34% | .554 | .612 | .311 |
| Wallace B | 51 | 144 | 14 | 32 | 6 | 1 | 2 | 13 | .222 | .296 | .319 | 0 | 0 | — | — | — | — | — | — | 144 | 14 | 2 | 13 | .222 | 0 | 65% | 34% | 5% | 1.4 | 39% | .615 | .623 | .576 |

## Pitchers — Houston Astros 2010

| Pitchers | G | GS | W | L | Hld | Sv | IP | H | HR | ERA | WHIP | K | BB | 1st Half W | L | Sv | IP | ERA | WHIP | 2nd Half W | L | Sv | IP | ERA | WHIP | Rates K/9 | BB/9 | HR/9 | Productiveness opOPS | vs RH | vs LH |
|---|---|---|---|---|---|---|---|---|---|---|---|---|---|---|---|---|---|---|---|---|---|---|---|---|---|---|---|---|---|---|---|
| Abad F | 22 | 0 | 0 | 1 | 6 | 0 | 19.0 | 14 | 3 | 2.84 | 1.00 | 12 | 5 | — | — | — | — | — | — | 0 | 1 | 0 | 19.0 | 2.84 | 1.00 | 5.7 | 2.4 | 1.4 | .636 | .648 | .619 |
| Banks J | 1 | 1 | 0 | 1 | 0 | 0 | 4.0 | 8 | 1 | 13.50 | 3.00 | 1 | 4 | 0 | 1 | 0 | 4.0 | 13.50 | 3.00 | — | — | — | — | — | — | 2.3 | 9.0 | 2.3 | 1.200 | 1.329 | .829 |
| Byrdak T | 64 | 0 | 2 | 2 | 11 | 0 | 38.2 | 40 | 4 | 3.49 | 1.55 | 29 | 20 | 1 | 0 | 0 | 22.0 | 4.50 | 1.55 | 1 | 2 | 0 | 16.2 | 2.16 | 1.56 | 6.8 | 4.7 | 0.9 | .795 | .949 | .644 |
| Chacin G | 44 | 0 | 2 | 2 | 5 | 1 | 38.1 | 51 | 3 | 4.70 | 1.85 | 31 | 20 | 1 | 1 | 0 | 21.2 | 4.57 | 1.62 | 1 | 1 | 1 | 16.2 | 4.86 | 2.16 | 7.3 | 4.7 | 0.7 | .814 | .828 | .790 |
| Daigle C | 13 | 0 | 1 | 1 | 3 | 0 | 10.1 | 25 | 3 | 11.32 | 3.00 | 6 | 6 | 1 | 1 | 0 | 9.0 | 7.00 | 2.33 | 0 | 0 | 0 | 1.1 | 40.50 | 7.50 | 5.2 | 5.2 | 2.6 | 1.246 | .980 | 1.748 |
| Del Rosario E | 2 | 0 | 0 | 0 | 0 | 0 | 1.1 | 4 | 0 | 20.25 | 3.00 | 1 | 0 | — | — | — | — | — | — | 0 | 0 | 0 | 1.1 | 20.25 | 3.00 | 6.8 | 0.0 | 0.0 | 1.181 | .733 | 2.000 |
| Figueroa N | 18 | 10 | 5 | 3 | 0 | 0 | 67.0 | 64 | 9 | 3.22 | 1.33 | 58 | 25 | — | — | — | — | — | — | 5 | 3 | 0 | 67.0 | 3.22 | 1.33 | 7.8 | 3.4 | 1.2 | .735 | .585 | .953 |
| Fulchino J | 50 | 0 | 2 | 1 | 5 | 0 | 47.1 | 53 | 7 | 5.51 | 1.58 | 46 | 22 | 0 | 0 | 0 | 29.0 | 6.83 | 1.79 | 2 | 1 | 0 | 18.1 | 3.44 | 1.25 | 8.7 | 4.2 | 1.3 | .793 | .775 | .817 |
| Gervacio S | 6 | 0 | 0 | 1 | 0 | 0 | 3.2 | 4 | 1 | 12.27 | 2.45 | 3 | 5 | 0 | 1 | 0 | 3.2 | 12.27 | 2.45 | — | — | — | — | — | — | 7.4 | 12.3 | 2.5 | .983 | 1.083 | .821 |
| Happ J | 13 | 13 | 5 | 4 | 0 | 0 | 72.0 | 60 | 7 | 3.75 | 1.32 | 61 | 35 | — | — | — | — | — | — | 5 | 4 | 0 | 72.0 | 3.75 | 1.32 | 7.6 | 4.4 | 0.9 | .684 | .728 | .506 |
| Lindstrom M | 58 | 0 | 2 | 5 | 4 | 23 | 53.1 | 68 | 5 | 4.39 | 1.65 | 43 | 20 | 2 | 1 | 21 | 35.1 | 2.80 | 1.53 | 0 | 4 | 2 | 18.0 | 7.50 | 1.89 | 7.3 | 3.4 | 0.8 | .792 | .809 | .769 |
| Lopez W | 68 | 0 | 5 | 2 | 14 | 1 | 67.0 | 66 | 4 | 2.96 | 1.06 | 50 | 5 | 3 | 0 | 0 | 33.1 | 4.05 | 1.23 | 2 | 2 | 1 | 33.2 | 1.87 | 0.89 | 6.7 | 0.7 | 0.5 | .653 | .624 | .694 |
| Lyon B | 79 | 0 | 6 | 6 | 19 | 20 | 78.0 | 68 | 2 | 3.12 | 1.27 | 54 | 31 | 5 | 3 | 1 | 39.1 | 3.66 | 1.42 | 1 | 3 | 19 | 38.2 | 2.56 | 1.11 | 6.2 | 3.6 | 0.2 | .622 | .657 | .576 |
| Majewski G | 2 | 0 | 0 | 0 | 0 | 0 | 2.0 | 5 | 1 | 22.50 | 3.00 | 1 | 1 | — | — | — | — | — | — | 0 | 0 | 0 | 2.0 | 22.50 | 3.00 | 4.5 | 4.5 | 4.5 | 1.212 | 1.091 | 2.000 |
| Melancon M | 20 | 0 | 2 | 0 | 8 | 0 | 17.1 | 12 | 1 | 3.12 | 1.15 | 19 | 8 | — | — | — | — | — | — | 2 | 0 | 0 | 17.1 | 3.12 | 1.15 | 9.9 | 4.2 | 0.5 | .586 | .677 | .433 |
| Moehler B | 20 | 8 | 1 | 4 | 0 | 0 | 56.2 | 66 | 5 | 4.92 | 1.62 | 28 | 26 | 1 | 4 | 0 | 56.2 | 4.92 | 1.62 | — | — | — | — | — | — | 4.4 | 4.1 | 0.8 | .799 | .807 | .789 |
| Myers B | 33 | 33 | 14 | 8 | 0 | 0 | 223.2 | 212 | 20 | 3.14 | 1.24 | 180 | 66 | 6 | 6 | 0 | 121.1 | 3.41 | 1.31 | 8 | 2 | 0 | 102.1 | 2.81 | 1.16 | 7.2 | 2.7 | 0.8 | .683 | .678 | .688 |
| Norris B | 27 | 27 | 9 | 10 | 0 | 0 | 153.2 | 151 | 18 | 4.92 | 1.48 | 158 | 77 | 2 | 6 | 0 | 63.1 | 5.97 | 1.59 | 7 | 4 | 0 | 90.1 | 4.18 | 1.41 | 9.3 | 4.5 | 1.1 | .758 | .721 | .799 |
| Oswalt R | 20 | 20 | 6 | 12 | 0 | 0 | 129.0 | 109 | 13 | 3.42 | 1.11 | 120 | 34 | 6 | 10 | 0 | 120.0 | 3.08 | 1.05 | 0 | 2 | 0 | 9.0 | 8.00 | 1.89 | 8.4 | 2.4 | 0.9 | .652 | .601 | .709 |
| Paulino F | 19 | 14 | 1 | 9 | 1 | 0 | 91.2 | 95 | 4 | 5.11 | 1.54 | 83 | 46 | 1 | 8 | 0 | 86.0 | 4.40 | 1.51 | 0 | 1 | 0 | 5.2 | 15.88 | 1.94 | 8.1 | 4.5 | 0.4 | .748 | .704 | .817 |
| Rodriguez W | 32 | 32 | 11 | 12 | 0 | 0 | 195.0 | 183 | 16 | 3.60 | 1.29 | 178 | 68 | 6 | 11 | 0 | 101.1 | 4.97 | 1.52 | 5 | 1 | 0 | 93.2 | 2.11 | 1.04 | 8.2 | 3.1 | 0.7 | .700 | .715 | .642 |
| Sampson C | 35 | 0 | 1 | 0 | 5 | 0 | 30.1 | 43 | 7 | 5.93 | 1.68 | 16 | 8 | 1 | 0 | 0 | 26.1 | 5.47 | 1.59 | 0 | 0 | 0 | 4.0 | 9.00 | 2.25 | 4.7 | 2.4 | 2.1 | .950 | 1.056 | .779 |
| Villar H | 8 | 0 | 0 | 0 | 1 | 0 | 6.0 | 5 | 0 | 4.50 | 1.33 | 3 | 3 | — | — | — | — | — | — | 0 | 0 | 0 | 6.0 | 4.50 | 1.33 | 4.5 | 4.5 | 0.0 | .561 | .675 | .167 |
| Wright W | 14 | 4 | 1 | 2 | 0 | 0 | 33.0 | 37 | 6 | 5.73 | 1.52 | 29 | 13 | 0 | 0 | 0 | 9.2 | 5.59 | 1.55 | 1 | 2 | 0 | 23.1 | 5.79 | 1.50 | 7.9 | 3.5 | 1.6 | .890 | .967 | .678 |

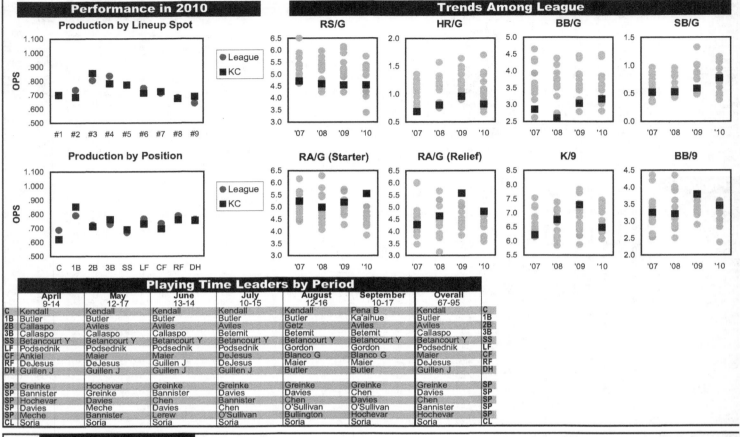

## Performance in 2010 / Trends Among League

### Playing Time Leaders by Period

| | April 9-14 | May 12-17 | June 13-14 | July 10-15 | August 12-16 | September 10-17 | Overall 67-95 | |
|---|---|---|---|---|---|---|---|---|
| C | Kendall | Kendall | Kendall | Kendall | Kendall | Pena B | Kendall | C |
| 1B | Butler | Butler | Butler | Butler | Butler | Ka'aihue | Butler | 1B |
| 2B | Callaspo | Aviles | Aviles | Aviles | Getz | Aviles | Aviles | 2B |
| 3B | Callaspo | Callaspo | Callaspo | Betemit | Betemit | Betemit | Callaspo | 3B |
| SS | Betancourt Y | Betancourt Y | Betancourt Y | Betancourt Y | Betancourt Y | Betancourt Y | Betancourt Y | SS |
| LF | Podsednik | Podsednik | Podsednik | Podsednik | Gordon | Gordon | Podsednik | LF |
| CF | Ankiel | Maier | Maier | DeJesus | Blanco G | Blanco G | Maier | CF |
| RF | DeJesus | DeJesus | Guillen J | DeJesus | Maier | Maier | DeJesus | RF |
| DH | Guillen J | Guillen J | Guillen J | Guillen J | Butler | Butler | Guillen J | DH |
| | | | | | | | | |
| SP | Greinke | Hochevar | Greinke | Greinke | Greinke | Greinke | Greinke | SP |
| SP | Bannister | Greinke | Bannister | Davies | Davies | Chen | Davies | SP |
| SP | Hochevar | Davies | Chen | Bannister | Chen | Davies | Chen | SP |
| SP | Davies | Meche | Davies | Chen | O'Sullivan | O'Sullivan | Bannister | SP |
| SP | Meche | Bannister | Lerew | O'Sullivan | Bullington | Hochevar | Hochevar | SP |
| CL | Soria | Soria | Soria | Soria | Soria | Soria | Soria | CL |

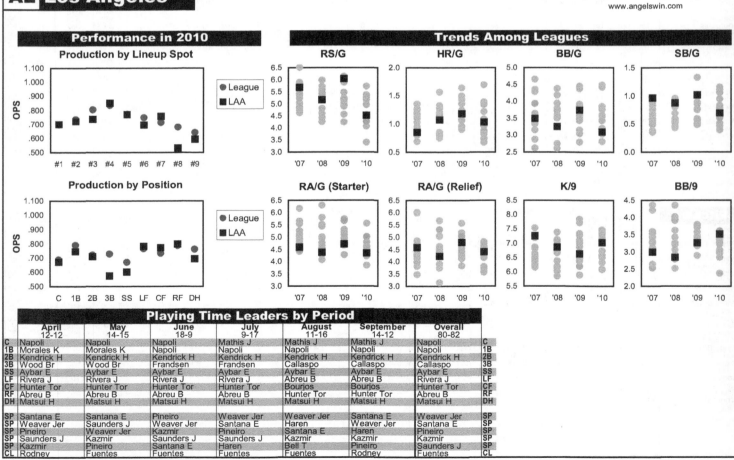

## Performance in 2010 / Trends Among Leagues

### Playing Time Leaders by Period

| | April 12-12 | May 14-15 | June 18-9 | July 9-17 | August 11-16 | September 14-12 | Overall 80-82 | |
|---|---|---|---|---|---|---|---|---|
| C | Napoli | Napoli | Napoli | Mathis J | Mathis J | Mathis J | Napoli | C |
| 1B | Morales K | Morales K | Napoli | Napoli | Napoli | Napoli | Napoli | 1B |
| 2B | Kendrick H | Kendrick H | Kendrick H | Kendrick H | Kendrick H | Kendrick H | Kendrick H | 2B |
| 3B | Wood Br | Wood Br | Frandsen | Frandsen | Callaspo | Callaspo | Callaspo | 3B |
| SS | Aybar E | Aybar E | Aybar E | Aybar E | Aybar E | Aybar E | Aybar E | SS |
| LF | Rivera J | Rivera J | Rivera J | Rivera J | Abreu B | Abreu B | Rivera J | LF |
| CF | Hunter Tor | Hunter Tor | Hunter Tor | Hunter Tor | Bourjos | Bourjos | Hunter Tor | CF |
| RF | Abreu B | Abreu B | Abreu B | Abreu B | Hunter Tor | Hunter Tor | Abreu B | RF |
| DH | Matsui H | Matsui H | Matsui H | Matsui H | Matsui H | Matsui H | Matsui H | DH |
| | | | | | | | | |
| SP | Santana E | Santana E | Pineiro | Weaver Jer | Weaver Jer | Santana E | Weaver Jer | SP |
| SP | Weaver Jer | Saunders J | Weaver Jer | Santana E | Haren | Weaver Jer | Santana E | SP |
| SP | Pineiro | Weaver Jer | Kazmir | Pineiro | Santana E | Haren | Pineiro | SP |
| SP | Saunders J | Kazmir | Saunders J | Saunders J | Kazmir | Kazmir | Kazmir | SP |
| SP | Kazmir | Pineiro | Santana E | Haren | Bell T | Pineiro | Saunders J | SP |
| CL | Rodney | Fuentes | Fuentes | Fuentes | Fuentes | Rodney | Fuentes | CL |

| Hitters | Kansas City Royals 2010 | | | | | | | | | | | | | 1st Half | | | | | | 2nd Half | | | | | | Rates | | | | | Productiveness | | |
|---|---|---|---|---|---|---|---|---|---|---|---|---|---|---|---|---|---|---|---|---|---|---|---|---|---|---|---|---|---|---|---|---|---|
| | G | AB | R | H | 2B | 3B | HR | RBI | BA | OBP | SLG | SB | CS | AB | R | HR | BI | BA | SB | AB | R | HR | BI | BA | SB | CT% | H% | BB% | Bash | GB% | OPS | vs RH | vs LH |
| Ankiel R | 27 | 92 | 14 | 24 | 7 | 0 | 4 | 15 | .261 | .317 | .467 | 1 | 0 | 62 | 7 | 3 | 9 | .210 | 1 | 30 | 7 | 1 | 6 | .367 | 0 | 68% | 38% | 7% | 1.8 | 49% | .784 | .960 | .398 |
| Aviles M | 110 | 424 | 63 | 129 | 16 | 3 | 8 | 32 | .304 | .335 | .413 | 14 | 5 | 210 | 29 | 2 | 14 | .305 | 2 | 214 | 34 | 6 | 18 | .304 | 12 | 88% | 34% | 4% | 1.4 | 43% | .748 | .787 | .642 |
| Betancourt Y | 151 | 556 | 60 | 144 | 29 | 2 | 16 | 78 | .259 | .288 | .405 | 2 | 3 | 302 | 40 | 6 | 36 | .258 | 0 | 254 | 20 | 10 | 42 | .260 | 2 | 88% | 29% | 4% | 1.6 | 40% | .692 | .666 | .778 |
| Betemit W | 84 | 276 | 36 | 82 | 20 | 0 | 13 | 43 | .297 | .378 | .511 | 0 | 0 | 54 | 10 | 4 | 10 | .389 | 0 | 222 | 26 | 9 | 33 | .275 | 0 | 73% | 41% | 11% | 1.7 | 41% | .889 | .873 | .930 |
| Blanco G | 49 | 179 | 22 | 49 | 8 | 3 | 1 | 11 | .274 | .348 | .369 | 10 | 2 | -- | -- | -- | -- | -- | -- | 179 | 22 | 1 | 11 | .274 | 10 | 80% | 34% | 10% | 1.3 | 51% | .717 | .836 | .380 |
| Bloomquist W | 72 | 170 | 31 | 45 | 10 | 1 | 3 | 17 | .265 | .296 | .388 | 8 | 5 | 83 | 18 | 2 | 10 | .229 | 5 | 87 | 13 | 1 | 7 | .299 | 3 | 85% | 31% | 4% | 1.5 | 44% | .684 | .567 | .838 |
| Butler B | 158 | 595 | 77 | 189 | 45 | 0 | 15 | 78 | .318 | .388 | .469 | 0 | 0 | 329 | 44 | 9 | 46 | .322 | 0 | 266 | 33 | 6 | 32 | .312 | 0 | 87% | 37% | 10% | 1.5 | 49% | .857 | .888 | .727 |
| Callaspo A | 88 | 349 | 40 | 96 | 19 | 2 | 8 | 43 | .275 | .308 | .410 | 3 | 1 | 325 | 38 | 8 | 41 | .274 | 3 | 24 | 2 | 0 | 2 | .292 | 0 | 92% | 30% | 5% | 1.5 | 43% | .718 | .738 | .648 |
| DeJesus D | 91 | 352 | 46 | 112 | 23 | 3 | 5 | 37 | .318 | .384 | .443 | 3 | 3 | 328 | 45 | 5 | 36 | .326 | 3 | 24 | 1 | 0 | 1 | .208 | 0 | 87% | 37% | 9% | 1.4 | 46% | .827 | .864 | .725 |
| Dyson J | 18 | 57 | 11 | 12 | 4 | 2 | 1 | 5 | .211 | .286 | .404 | 9 | 1 | -- | -- | -- | -- | -- | -- | 57 | 11 | 1 | 5 | .211 | 9 | 72% | 29% | 9% | 1.9 | 63% | .689 | .783 | .273 |
| Fields J | 13 | 49 | 5 | 15 | 0 | 0 | 3 | 6 | .306 | .320 | .490 | 0 | 0 | -- | -- | -- | -- | -- | -- | 49 | 5 | 3 | 6 | .306 | 0 | 82% | 38% | 2% | 1.6 | 58% | .810 | .545 | 1.136 |
| Getz C | 72 | 224 | 23 | 53 | 9 | 0 | 0 | 18 | .237 | .302 | .277 | 15 | 2 | 112 | 12 | 0 | 10 | .232 | 8 | 112 | 11 | 0 | 8 | .241 | 7 | 88% | 27% | 8% | 1.2 | 49% | .579 | .548 | .699 |
| Gordon A | 74 | 242 | 34 | 52 | 10 | 0 | 8 | 20 | .215 | .315 | .355 | 1 | 5 | 31 | 5 | 1 | 1 | .194 | 0 | 211 | 29 | 7 | 19 | .218 | 1 | 74% | 29% | 12% | 1.7 | 38% | .671 | .660 | .704 |
| Guillen J | 106 | 396 | 46 | 101 | 17 | 2 | 16 | 62 | .255 | .314 | .429 | 1 | 0 | 323 | 43 | 15 | 54 | .279 | 1 | 73 | 3 | 1 | 8 | .151 | 0 | 79% | 32% | 6% | 1.7 | 42% | .743 | .775 | .621 |
| Ka'aihue K | 52 | 180 | 22 | 39 | 6 | 1 | 8 | 25 | .217 | .307 | .394 | 0 | 1 | 4 | 0 | 0 | 1 | .250 | 0 | 176 | 22 | 8 | 24 | .216 | 0 | 78% | 28% | 12% | 1.8 | 35% | .702 | .684 | .754 |
| Kendall J | 118 | 434 | 39 | 111 | 18 | 0 | 0 | 37 | .256 | .318 | .297 | 12 | 7 | 303 | 27 | 0 | 30 | .271 | 5 | 131 | 12 | 0 | 7 | .221 | 7 | 90% | 29% | 8% | 1.2 | 47% | .615 | .576 | .756 |
| Maier M | 117 | 373 | 41 | 98 | 15 | 6 | 5 | 39 | .263 | .333 | .375 | 3 | 2 | 207 | 26 | 3 | 27 | .251 | 0 | 166 | 15 | 2 | 12 | .277 | 3 | 82% | 32% | 10% | 1.4 | 39% | .709 | .720 | .659 |
| May L | 12 | 37 | 3 | 7 | 1 | 0 | 0 | 6 | .189 | .205 | .216 | 0 | 1 | -- | -- | -- | -- | -- | -- | 37 | 3 | 0 | 6 | .189 | 0 | 73% | 26% | 0% | 1.1 | 41% | .421 | .501 | .200 |
| Miller J | 20 | 55 | 5 | 13 | 3 | 0 | 1 | 4 | .236 | .300 | .345 | 1 | 0 | -- | -- | -- | -- | -- | -- | 55 | 5 | 1 | 4 | .236 | 1 | 58% | 41% | 7% | 1.5 | 28% | .645 | .565 | .745 |
| Pena B | 60 | 158 | 11 | 40 | 10 | 0 | 1 | 19 | .253 | .306 | .335 | 2 | 0 | 29 | 1 | 0 | 3 | .172 | 1 | 129 | 10 | 1 | 16 | .271 | 1 | 83% | 31% | 7% | 1.3 | 44% | .642 | .701 | .509 |
| Podsednik S | 95 | 390 | 46 | 121 | 8 | 6 | 5 | 44 | .310 | .353 | .400 | 30 | 12 | 336 | 39 | 3 | 35 | .301 | 25 | 54 | 7 | 2 | 9 | .370 | 5 | 85% | 36% | 7% | 1.3 | 50% | .753 | .774 | .697 |

| Pitchers | Kansas City Royals 2010 | | | | | | | | | | | | | 1st Half | | | | | | 2nd Half | | | | | | Rates | | | Productiveness | | |
|---|---|---|---|---|---|---|---|---|---|---|---|---|---|---|---|---|---|---|---|---|---|---|---|---|---|---|---|---|---|---|---|
| | G | GS | W | L | Hld | Sv | IP | H | HR | ERA | WHIP | K | BB | W | L | Sv | IP | ERA | WHIP | W | L | Sv | IP | ERA | WHIP | K/9 | BB/9 | HR/9 | opOPS | vs RH | vs LH |
| Bannister B | 24 | 23 | 7 | 12 | 0 | 0 | 127.2 | 158 | 23 | 6.34 | 1.63 | 77 | 50 | 7 | 7 | 0 | 102.0 | 5.56 | 1.50 | 0 | 5 | 0 | 25.2 | 9.47 | 2.14 | 5.4 | 3.5 | 1.6 | .868 | .980 | .752 |
| Bullington B | 13 | 5 | 1 | 4 | 0 | 0 | 42.2 | 51 | 6 | 6.12 | 1.59 | 29 | 17 | 0 | 1 | 0 | 3.0 | 12.00 | 4.00 | 1 | 3 | 0 | 39.2 | 5.67 | 1.41 | 6.1 | 3.6 | 1.3 | .846 | .778 | .902 |
| Chavez J | 23 | 0 | 2 | 3 | 6 | 0 | 26.0 | 29 | 5 | 5.88 | 1.54 | 16 | 11 | -- | -- | -- | -- | -- | -- | 2 | 3 | 0 | 26.0 | 5.88 | 1.54 | 5.5 | 3.8 | 1.7 | .864 | .821 | .905 |
| Chen B | 33 | 23 | 12 | 7 | 0 | 1 | 140.1 | 136 | 17 | 4.17 | 1.38 | 98 | 57 | 5 | 3 | 1 | 52.0 | 3.81 | 1.31 | 7 | 4 | 0 | 88.1 | 4.38 | 1.42 | 6.3 | 3.7 | 1.1 | .735 | .727 | .756 |
| Colon R | 5 | 0 | 0 | 0 | 0 | 0 | 2.0 | 5 | 0 | 18.00 | 3.50 | 1 | 2 | 0 | 0 | 0 | 2.0 | 18.00 | 3.50 | -- | -- | -- | -- | -- | -- | 4.5 | 9.0 | 0.0 | 1.208 | 1.524 | .650 |
| Cruz J | 5 | 0 | 0 | 0 | 0 | 0 | 5.1 | 9 | 0 | 3.38 | 2.44 | 7 | 4 | 0 | 0 | 0 | 5.1 | 3.38 | 2.44 | -- | -- | -- | -- | -- | -- | 11.8 | 6.8 | 0.0 | .960 | 1.000 | .899 |
| Davies K | 32 | 32 | 8 | 12 | 0 | 0 | 183.2 | 206 | 20 | 5.34 | 1.56 | 126 | 80 | 4 | 6 | 0 | 95.1 | 5.57 | 1.52 | 4 | 6 | 0 | 88.1 | 5.09 | 1.60 | 6.2 | 3.9 | 1.0 | .793 | .745 | .836 |
| Farnsworth K | 37 | 0 | 3 | 0 | 7 | 0 | 44.2 | 40 | 2 | 2.42 | 1.16 | 36 | 12 | 2 | 0 | 0 | 37.1 | 2.41 | 1.13 | 1 | 0 | 0 | 7.1 | 2.45 | 1.36 | 7.3 | 2.4 | 0.4 | .634 | .596 | .676 |
| Greinke Z | 33 | 33 | 10 | 14 | 0 | 0 | 220.0 | 219 | 18 | 4.17 | 1.25 | 181 | 55 | 5 | 8 | 0 | 119.0 | 3.71 | 1.16 | 5 | 6 | 0 | 101.0 | 4.72 | 1.35 | 7.4 | 2.3 | 0.7 | .696 | .601 | .774 |
| Hochevar L | 18 | 17 | 6 | 6 | 0 | 0 | 103.0 | 110 | 9 | 4.81 | 1.43 | 76 | 37 | 5 | 4 | 0 | 78.0 | 4.96 | 1.38 | 1 | 2 | 0 | 25.0 | 4.32 | 1.56 | 6.6 | 3.2 | 0.8 | .754 | .712 | .796 |
| Holland G | 15 | 0 | 0 | 1 | 0 | 0 | 18.2 | 23 | 3 | 6.75 | 1.66 | 23 | 8 | -- | -- | -- | -- | -- | -- | 0 | 1 | 0 | 18.2 | 6.75 | 1.66 | 11.1 | 3.9 | 1.4 | .835 | .832 | .838 |
| Hughes D | 57 | 0 | 1 | 3 | 7 | 0 | 56.1 | 59 | 3 | 3.83 | 1.47 | 34 | 24 | 1 | 1 | 0 | 29.1 | 3.99 | 1.50 | 0 | 2 | 0 | 27.0 | 3.67 | 1.44 | 5.4 | 3.8 | 0.5 | .730 | .775 | .674 |
| Humber P | 8 | 1 | 2 | 1 | 1 | 0 | 21.2 | 22 | 1 | 4.15 | 1.34 | 16 | 7 | -- | -- | -- | -- | -- | -- | 2 | 1 | 0 | 21.2 | 4.15 | 1.34 | 6.6 | 2.9 | 0.4 | .637 | .587 | .693 |
| Lerew A | 6 | 6 | 1 | 4 | 0 | 0 | 26.1 | 34 | 9 | 8.54 | 1.63 | 18 | 9 | 1 | 3 | 0 | 25.0 | 7.56 | 1.52 | 0 | 1 | 0 | 1.1 | 27.00 | 3.75 | 6.2 | 3.1 | 3.1 | .998 | 1.247 | .686 |
| Marte V | 22 | 0 | 3 | 0 | 1 | 0 | 27.2 | 38 | 8 | 9.76 | 1.92 | 19 | 15 | 3 | 0 | 0 | 22.2 | 5.56 | 1.32 | 0 | 0 | 0 | 5.0 | 28.80 | 4.60 | 6.2 | 4.9 | 2.6 | 1.001 | 1.039 | .945 |
| Meche G | 20 | 9 | 0 | 5 | 6 | 0 | 61.2 | 65 | 9 | 5.69 | 1.67 | 41 | 38 | 0 | 4 | 0 | 48.2 | 6.66 | 1.85 | 0 | 1 | 0 | 13.0 | 2.08 | 1.00 | 6.0 | 5.5 | 1.3 | .822 | .877 | .768 |
| Mendoza L | 4 | 0 | 0 | 1 | 0 | 0 | 4.0 | 10 | 4 | 22.50 | 3.25 | 1 | 3 | 0 | 1 | 0 | 4.0 | 22.50 | 3.25 | -- | -- | -- | -- | -- | -- | 2.3 | 6.8 | 9.0 | 1.656 | 1.796 | 1.357 |
| O'Sullivan S | 14 | 13 | 3 | 6 | 0 | 0 | 70.2 | 83 | 14 | 6.11 | 1.56 | 37 | 27 | -- | -- | -- | -- | -- | -- | 3 | 6 | 0 | 70.2 | 6.11 | 1.56 | 4.7 | 3.4 | 1.8 | .838 | .943 | .771 |
| Parrish J | 9 | 0 | 1 | 1 | 2 | 0 | 6.0 | 4 | 2 | 3.00 | 1.50 | 4 | 5 | 1 | 1 | 0 | 6.0 | 3.00 | 1.50 | -- | -- | -- | -- | -- | -- | 6.0 | 7.5 | 3.0 | .822 | .649 | 1.017 |
| Rupe J | 11 | 0 | 1 | 1 | 5 | 0 | 9.2 | 14 | 1 | 5.59 | 2.17 | 8 | 7 | 1 | 1 | 0 | 9.2 | 5.59 | 2.17 | -- | -- | -- | -- | -- | -- | 7.4 | 6.5 | 0.9 | .925 | 1.109 | .683 |
| Soria J | 66 | 0 | 1 | 2 | 0 | 43 | 65.2 | 53 | 4 | 1.78 | 1.05 | 71 | 16 | 0 | 1 | 25 | 35.0 | 2.31 | 1.14 | 1 | 1 | 18 | 30.2 | 1.17 | 0.95 | 9.7 | 2.2 | 0.5 | .568 | .541 | .587 |
| Tejeda R | 54 | 0 | 3 | 5 | 12 | 0 | 61.0 | 55 | 5 | 3.54 | 1.33 | 56 | 26 | 3 | 3 | 0 | 40.1 | 3.35 | 1.34 | 0 | 2 | 0 | 20.2 | 3.92 | 1.31 | 8.3 | 3.8 | 0.7 | .691 | .686 | .697 |
| Texeira K | 27 | 0 | 1 | 0 | 1 | 0 | 42.2 | 51 | 3 | 4.64 | 1.55 | 19 | 15 | 1 | 0 | 0 | 18.0 | 2.00 | 1.22 | 0 | 0 | 0 | 24.2 | 6.57 | 1.78 | 4.0 | 3.2 | 0.6 | .788 | .757 | .825 |
| Thompson B | 16 | 0 | 0 | 4 | 1 | 0 | 19.2 | 25 | 4 | 6.41 | 1.47 | 10 | 4 | 0 | 4 | 0 | 19.2 | 6.41 | 1.47 | -- | -- | -- | -- | -- | -- | 4.6 | 1.8 | 1.8 | .877 | .656 | 1.183 |
| Wood B | 51 | 0 | 1 | 3 | 15 | 0 | 49.2 | 54 | 6 | 5.07 | 1.53 | 31 | 22 | 0 | 1 | 0 | 25.0 | 3.96 | 1.36 | 1 | 2 | 0 | 24.2 | 6.20 | 1.70 | 5.6 | 4.0 | 1.1 | .798 | .767 | .827 |

| Hitters | Los Angeles Angels 2010 | | | | | | | | | | | | | 1st Half | | | | | | 2nd Half | | | | | | Rates | | | | | Productiveness | | |
|---|---|---|---|---|---|---|---|---|---|---|---|---|---|---|---|---|---|---|---|---|---|---|---|---|---|---|---|---|---|---|---|---|---|
| | G | AB | R | H | 2B | 3B | HR | RBI | BA | OBP | SLG | SB | CS | AB | R | HR | BI | BA | SB | AB | R | HR | BI | BA | SB | CT% | H% | BB% | Bash | GB% | OPS | vs RH | vs LH |
| Abreu B | 154 | 573 | 88 | 146 | 41 | 1 | 20 | 78 | .255 | .352 | .435 | 24 | 10 | 331 | 50 | 10 | 47 | .257 | 15 | 242 | 38 | 10 | 31 | .252 | 9 | 77% | 33% | 13% | 1.7 | 48% | .787 | .856 | .639 |
| Aldridge C | 5 | 13 | 0 | 1 | 0 | 1 | 0 | 1 | .077 | .077 | .231 | 0 | 0 | 13 | 0 | 0 | 1 | .077 | 0 | -- | -- | -- | -- | -- | -- | 62% | 13% | 0% | 3.0 | 75% | .308 | .444 | .000 |
| Aybar E | 138 | 534 | 69 | 135 | 18 | 4 | 5 | 29 | .253 | .306 | .330 | 22 | 8 | 325 | 52 | 3 | 16 | .283 | 14 | 209 | 17 | 2 | 13 | .206 | 8 | 85% | 30% | 6% | 1.3 | 44% | .636 | .646 | .609 |
| Bourjos P | 51 | 181 | 19 | 37 | 6 | 4 | 6 | 15 | .204 | .237 | .381 | 10 | 3 | -- | -- | -- | -- | -- | -- | 181 | 19 | 6 | 15 | .204 | 10 | 78% | 26% | 3% | 1.9 | 48% | .618 | .679 | .480 |
| Budde R | 6 | 10 | 2 | 4 | 1 | 0 | 1 | 3 | .400 | .455 | .800 | 0 | 0 | 10 | 2 | 1 | 3 | .400 | 0 | -- | -- | -- | -- | -- | -- | 50% | 80% | 9% | 2.0 | 0% | 1.255 | .714 | 2.333 |
| Callaspo A | 58 | 213 | 21 | 53 | 8 | 0 | 2 | 13 | .249 | .291 | .315 | 2 | 2 | -- | -- | -- | -- | -- | -- | 213 | 21 | 2 | 13 | .249 | 2 | 94% | 27% | 5% | 1.3 | 49% | .605 | .643 | .439 |
| Conger H | 13 | 29 | 2 | 5 | 1 | 1 | 0 | 5 | .172 | .294 | .276 | 0 | 0 | -- | -- | -- | -- | -- | -- | 29 | 2 | 0 | 5 | .172 | 0 | 69% | 25% | 15% | 1.6 | 55% | .570 | .587 | .333 |
| Evans T | 1 | 1 | 0 | 0 | 0 | 0 | 0 | 0 | .000 | .000 | .000 | 0 | 0 | 1 | 0 | 0 | 0 | .000 | 0 | -- | -- | -- | -- | -- | -- | 0% | -- | 0% | -- | -- | .000 | .000 | -- |
| Frandsen K | 54 | 160 | 24 | 40 | 11 | 0 | 0 | 14 | .250 | .294 | .319 | 2 | 2 | 119 | 21 | 0 | 9 | .286 | 2 | 41 | 3 | 0 | 5 | .146 | 0 | 94% | 27% | 5% | 1.3 | 53% | .613 | .625 | .589 |
| Hunter T | 152 | 573 | 76 | 161 | 36 | 0 | 23 | 90 | .281 | .354 | .464 | 9 | 12 | 309 | 51 | 15 | 62 | .298 | 7 | 264 | 25 | 8 | 28 | .261 | 2 | 82% | 34% | 9% | 1.7 | 48% | .819 | .838 | .775 |
| Izturis M | 61 | 212 | 27 | 53 | 13 | 1 | 3 | 27 | .250 | .321 | .363 | 7 | 3 | 103 | 15 | 2 | 15 | .233 | 4 | 109 | 12 | 1 | 12 | .266 | 3 | 87% | 29% | 9% | 1.5 | 42% | .684 | .680 | .697 |
| Kendrick H | 158 | 616 | 67 | 172 | 41 | 4 | 10 | 75 | .279 | .313 | .407 | 14 | 4 | 355 | 39 | 7 | 52 | .273 | 9 | 261 | 28 | 3 | 23 | .287 | 5 | 85% | 33% | 4% | 1.5 | 53% | .721 | .741 | .673 |
| Mathis J | 68 | 205 | 19 | 40 | 6 | 1 | 3 | 18 | .195 | .219 | .278 | 3 | 0 | 89 | 10 | 2 | 8 | .236 | 2 | 116 | 9 | 1 | 10 | .164 | 1 | 71% | 27% | 3% | 1.4 | 38% | .497 | .467 | .580 |
| Matsui H | 145 | 482 | 55 | 132 | 24 | 1 | 21 | 84 | .274 | .361 | .459 | 0 | 1 | 294 | 24 | 10 | 47 | .252 | 0 | 188 | 31 | 11 | 37 | .309 | 0 | 80% | 34% | 12% | 1.7 | 40% | .820 | .868 | .692 |
| McAnulty P | 9 | 22 | 2 | 3 | 0 | 0 | 1 | 2 | .136 | .208 | .273 | 0 | 0 | 18 | 1 | 1 | 2 | .056 | 0 | 4 | 1 | 0 | 0 | .500 | 0 | 50% | 27% | 8% | 2.0 | 36% | .481 | .481 | -- |
| Morales K | 51 | 193 | 29 | 56 | 5 | 0 | 11 | 39 | .290 | .346 | .487 | 0 | 1 | 193 | 29 | 11 | 39 | .290 | 0 | -- | -- | -- | -- | -- | -- | 84% | 35% | 6% | 1.7 | 48% | .833 | 1.002 | .548 |
| Napoli M | 140 | 453 | 60 | 108 | 24 | 1 | 26 | 68 | .238 | .316 | .468 | 4 | 2 | 260 | 33 | 14 | 37 | .246 | 3 | 193 | 27 | 12 | 31 | .228 | 1 | 70% | 34% | 8% | 2.0 | 38% | .784 | .700 | .966 |
| Quinlan R | 23 | 33 | 4 | 4 | 2 | 0 | 0 | 2 | .121 | .171 | .182 | 2 | 0 | 33 | 4 | 0 | 2 | .121 | 2 | -- | -- | -- | -- | -- | -- | 82% | 15% | 6% | 1.5 | 52% | .353 | .186 | .641 |
| Rivera J | 124 | 416 | 53 | 105 | 20 | 0 | 15 | 52 | .252 | .312 | .409 | 2 | 2 | 254 | 38 | 10 | 34 | .240 | 1 | 162 | 15 | 5 | 18 | .272 | 1 | 86% | 29% | 7% | 1.6 | 46% | .721 | .707 | .746 |
| Romine A | 5 | 11 | 0 | 1 | 0 | 0 | 0 | 0 | .091 | .091 | .091 | 0 | 0 | -- | -- | -- | -- | -- | -- | 11 | 0 | 0 | 0 | .091 | 0 | 64% | 14% | 0% | 1.0 | 57% | .182 | .200 | .000 |
| Ryan M | 22 | 39 | 3 | 8 | 4 | 0 | 0 | 2 | .205 | .220 | .308 | 0 | 0 | 39 | 3 | 0 | 2 | .205 | 0 | -- | -- | -- | -- | -- | -- | 87% | 24% | 2% | 1.5 | 41% | .527 | .541 | .000 |
| Trumbo M | 8 | 15 | 2 | 1 | 0 | 0 | 0 | 2 | .067 | .125 | .067 | 0 | 0 | -- | -- | -- | -- | -- | -- | 15 | 2 | 0 | 2 | .067 | 0 | 47% | 14% | 6% | 1.0 | 43% | .192 | .200 | .167 |
| Willits R | 97 | 159 | 23 | 41 | 7 | 0 | 0 | 8 | .258 | .341 | .302 | 2 | 4 | 76 | 11 | 0 | 5 | .237 | 1 | 83 | 12 | 0 | 3 | .277 | 1 | 84% | 31% | 10% | 1.2 | 32% | .643 | .648 | .630 |
| Wilson B | 40 | 96 | 12 | 22 | 6 | 0 | 4 | 15 | .229 | .288 | .417 | 0 | 0 | 47 | 8 | 1 | 4 | .191 | 0 | 49 | 4 | 3 | 11 | .265 | 0 | 76% | 30% | 8% | 1.8 | 40% | .705 | .624 | .947 |
| Wood B | 81 | 226 | 20 | 33 | 2 | 0 | 4 | 14 | .146 | .174 | .208 | 1 | 0 | 170 | 17 | 3 | 12 | .171 | 1 | 56 | 3 | 1 | 2 | .071 | 0 | 69% | 21% | 2% | 1.4 | 35% | .382 | .377 | .392 |

| Pitchers | Los Angeles Angels 2010 | | | | | | | | | | | | | 1st Half | | | | | | 2nd Half | | | | | | Rates | | | Productiveness | | |
|---|---|---|---|---|---|---|---|---|---|---|---|---|---|---|---|---|---|---|---|---|---|---|---|---|---|---|---|---|---|---|---|
| | G | GS | W | L | Hld | Sv | IP | H | HR | ERA | WHIP | K | BB | W | L | Sv | IP | ERA | WHIP | W | L | Sv | IP | ERA | WHIP | K/9 | BB/9 | HR/9 | opOPS | vs RH | vs LH |
| Bell T | 25 | 7 | 2 | 5 | 1 | 0 | 61.0 | 77 | 2 | 4.72 | 1.61 | 45 | 21 | 1 | 1 | 0 | 18.1 | 6.38 | 1.75 | 1 | 4 | 0 | 42.2 | 4.01 | 1.55 | 6.6 | 3.1 | 0.3 | .792 | .769 | .811 |
| Bulger J | 25 | 0 | 0 | 0 | 2 | 0 | 24.0 | 25 | 3 | 4.88 | 1.67 | 25 | 15 | 0 | 0 | 0 | 21.2 | 3.74 | 1.57 | 0 | 0 | 0 | 2.1 | 15.43 | 2.57 | 9.4 | 5.6 | 1.1 | .823 | .752 | .912 |
| Cassevah B | 16 | 0 | 1 | 2 | 0 | 0 | 20.0 | 23 | 0 | 3.15 | 1.55 | 8 | 8 | 0 | 0 | 0 | 11.1 | 5.56 | 1.50 | 1 | 2 | 0 | 8.2 | 0.00 | 1.62 | 3.6 | 3.6 | 0.0 | .730 | .463 | .963 |
| Fuentes B | 39 | 0 | 4 | 1 | 0 | 23 | 38.1 | 28 | 5 | 3.52 | 1.20 | 39 | 18 | 3 | 1 | 16 | 25.1 | 4.26 | 1.22 | 1 | 0 | 7 | 13.0 | 2.08 | 1.15 | 9.2 | 4.2 | 1.2 | .677 | .793 | .367 |
| Haren D | 14 | 14 | 5 | 4 | 0 | 0 | 94.0 | 84 | 8 | 2.87 | 1.16 | 75 | 25 | -- | -- | -- | -- | -- | -- | 5 | 4 | 0 | 94.0 | 2.87 | 1.16 | 7.2 | 2.4 | 0.8 | .648 | .632 | .663 |
| Jepsen K | 68 | 0 | 2 | 4 | 27 | 0 | 59.0 | 54 | 2 | 3.97 | 1.41 | 61 | 29 | 1 | 1 | 0 | 30.0 | 4.50 | 1.47 | 1 | 3 | 0 | 29.0 | 3.41 | 1.34 | 9.3 | 4.4 | 0.3 | .665 | .661 | .669 |
| Kazmir S | 28 | 28 | 9 | 15 | 0 | 0 | 150.0 | 158 | 25 | 5.94 | 1.58 | 93 | 79 | 7 | 9 | 0 | 92.1 | 6.92 | 1.64 | 2 | 6 | 0 | 57.2 | 4.37 | 1.49 | 5.6 | 4.7 | 1.5 | .841 | .855 | .790 |
| Kohn M | 24 | 0 | 2 | 0 | 1 | 1 | 21.1 | 17 | 0 | 2.11 | 1.55 | 20 | 16 | -- | -- | -- | -- | -- | -- | 2 | 0 | 1 | 21.1 | 2.11 | 1.55 | 8.4 | 6.8 | 0.0 | .616 | .454 | .763 |
| O'Sullivan S | 5 | 1 | 1 | 0 | 0 | 0 | 13.0 | 7 | 1 | 2.08 | 0.85 | 6 | 4 | 0 | 0 | 0 | 7.0 | 1.29 | 0.86 | 1 | 0 | 0 | 6.0 | 3.00 | 0.83 | 4.2 | 2.8 | 0.7 | .513 | .481 | .551 |
| Palmer M | 14 | 1 | 1 | 2 | 1 | 0 | 33.2 | 38 | 1 | 4.54 | 1.72 | 17 | 20 | 0 | 1 | 0 | 23.0 | 6.26 | 2.04 | 1 | 1 | 0 | 10.2 | 0.84 | 1.03 | 4.5 | 5.3 | 0.3 | .793 | .805 | .771 |
| Pineiro J | 23 | 23 | 10 | 7 | 0 | 0 | 152.1 | 155 | 15 | 3.84 | 1.24 | 92 | 34 | 9 | 6 | 0 | 118.1 | 3.95 | 1.28 | 1 | 1 | 0 | 34.0 | 3.44 | 1.09 | 5.4 | 2.0 | 0.9 | .716 | .732 | .701 |
| Rodney F | 72 | 0 | 4 | 3 | 21 | 14 | 68.0 | 70 | 4 | 4.24 | 1.54 | 53 | 35 | 4 | 0 | 6 | 35.1 | 3.57 | 1.53 | 0 | 3 | 8 | 32.2 | 4.96 | 1.56 | 7.0 | 4.6 | 0.5 | .739 | .750 | .728 |
| Rodriguez F | 43 | 0 | 1 | 3 | 2 | 0 | 47.1 | 46 | 5 | 4.37 | 1.52 | 36 | 26 | 0 | 1 | 0 | 21.0 | 4.29 | 1.24 | 1 | 2 | 0 | 26.1 | 4.44 | 1.75 | 6.8 | 4.9 | 1.0 | .732 | .539 | .984 |
| Rodriguez R | 1 | 0 | 0 | 0 | 0 | 0 | 2.0 | 1 | 0 | 4.50 | 1.50 | 1 | 2 | 0 | 0 | 0 | 2.0 | 4.50 | 1.50 | -- | -- | -- | -- | -- | -- | 4.5 | 9.0 | 0.0 | .686 | .400 | .900 |
| Santana E | 33 | 33 | 17 | 10 | 0 | 0 | 222.2 | 221 | 27 | 3.92 | 1.32 | 169 | 73 | 8 | 7 | 0 | 122.0 | 3.76 | 1.30 | 9 | 3 | 0 | 100.2 | 4.11 | 1.34 | 6.8 | 3.0 | 1.1 | .744 | .687 | .793 |
| Saunders J | 20 | 20 | 6 | 10 | 0 | 0 | 120.2 | 135 | 14 | 4.62 | 1.49 | 64 | 45 | 6 | 9 | 0 | 107.2 | 4.76 | 1.50 | 0 | 1 | 0 | 13.0 | 3.46 | 1.38 | 4.8 | 3.4 | 1.0 | .807 | .825 | .758 |
| Shields S | 43 | 1 | 0 | 3 | 1 | 0 | 46.0 | 45 | 6 | 5.28 | 1.72 | 39 | 34 | 0 | 3 | 0 | 29.2 | 4.85 | 1.69 | 0 | 0 | 0 | 16.1 | 6.06 | 1.78 | 7.6 | 6.7 | 1.2 | .765 | .907 | .619 |
| Stokes B | 16 | 0 | 0 | 0 | 0 | 0 | 16.2 | 26 | 4 | 8.10 | 2.52 | 16 | 16 | 0 | 0 | 0 | 16.0 | 7.31 | 2.50 | 0 | 0 | 0 | 0.2 | 27.00 | 3.00 | 8.6 | 8.6 | 2.2 | 1.131 | 1.062 | 1.206 |
| Thompson R | 13 | 0 | 2 | 0 | 1 | 0 | 19.2 | 12 | 2 | 1.37 | 0.81 | 15 | 4 | 0 | 0 | 0 | 2.2 | 3.38 | 1.88 | 2 | 0 | 0 | 17.0 | 1.06 | 0.65 | 6.9 | 1.8 | 0.9 | .516 | .679 | .296 |
| Walden J | 16 | 0 | 0 | 1 | 6 | 1 | 15.1 | 13 | 1 | 2.35 | 1.30 | 23 | 7 | -- | -- | -- | -- | -- | -- | 0 | 1 | 1 | 15.1 | 2.35 | 1.30 | 13.5 | 4.1 | 0.6 | .670 | .803 | .527 |
| Weaver J | 34 | 34 | 13 | 12 | 0 | 0 | 224.1 | 187 | 23 | 3.01 | 1.07 | 233 | 54 | 8 | 5 | 0 | 121.0 | 3.20 | 1.08 | 5 | 7 | 0 | 103.1 | 2.79 | 1.06 | 9.3 | 2.2 | 0.9 | .622 | .653 | .593 |

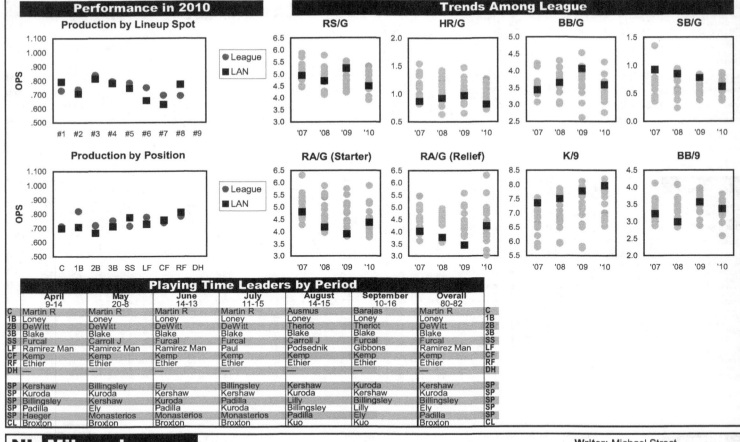

### Performance in 2010

**Production by Lineup Spot**

**Production by Position**

### Trends Among League

RS/G | HR/G | BB/G | SB/G

RA/G (Starter) | RA/G (Relief) | K/9 | BB/9

Legend: ● League ■ LAN

### Playing Time Leaders by Period

| | April 9-14 | May 20-8 | June 14-13 | July 11-15 | August 14-15 | September 10-16 | Overall 80-82 | |
|---|---|---|---|---|---|---|---|---|
| C | Martin R | Martin R | Martin R | Martin R | Ausmus | Barajas | Martin R | C |
| 1B | Loney | Loney | Loney | Loney | Loney | Loney | Loney | 1B |
| 2B | DeWitt | DeWitt | DeWitt | DeWitt | Theriot | Theriot | DeWitt | 2B |
| 3B | Blake | Blake | Blake | Blake | Blake | Blake | Blake | 3B |
| SS | Furcal | Carroll J | Furcal | Furcal | Carroll J | Furcal | Furcal | SS |
| LF | Ramirez Man | Ramirez Man | Ramirez Man | Paul | Podsednik | Gibbons | Ramirez Man | LF |
| CF | Kemp | Kemp | Kemp | Kemp | Kemp | Kemp | Kemp | CF |
| RF | Ethier | Ethier | Ethier | Ethier | Ethier | Ethier | Ethier | RF |
| DH | — | | — | | | | — | DH |
| | | | | | | | | |
| SP | Kershaw | Billingsley | Ely | Billingsley | Kershaw | Kuroda | Kershaw | SP |
| SP | Kuroda | Kuroda | Kershaw | Kershaw | Kuroda | Kershaw | Kuroda | SP |
| SP | Billingsley | Kershaw | Kuroda | Padilla | Lilly | Billingsley | Billingsley | SP |
| SP | Padilla | Ely | Padilla | Kuroda | Billingsley | Lilly | Ely | SP |
| SP | Haeger | Monasterios | Monasterios | Monasterios | Padilla | Ely | Padilla | SP |
| CL | Broxton | Broxton | Broxton | Broxton | Kuo | Kuo | Broxton | CL |

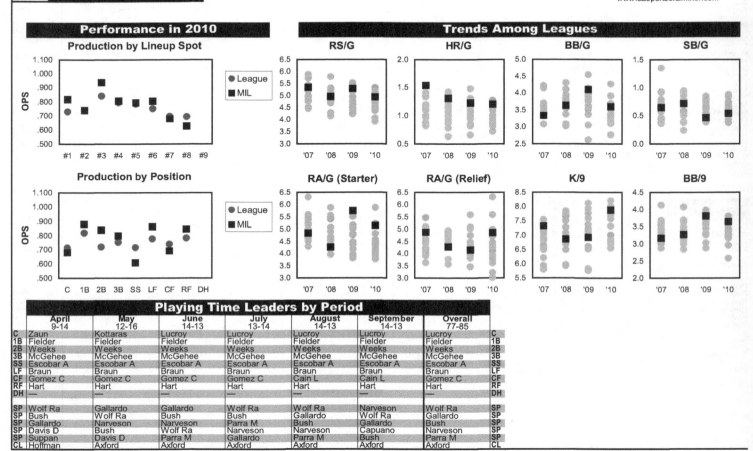

### Performance in 2010

**Production by Lineup Spot**

**Production by Position**

### Trends Among Leagues

RS/G | HR/G | BB/G | SB/G

RA/G (Starter) | RA/G (Relief) | K/9 | BB/9

Legend: ● League ■ MIL

### Playing Time Leaders by Period

| | April 9-14 | May 12-16 | June 14-13 | July 13-14 | August 14-13 | September 14-13 | Overall 77-85 | |
|---|---|---|---|---|---|---|---|---|
| C | Zaun | Kottaras | Lucroy | Lucroy | Lucroy | Lucroy | Lucroy | C |
| 1B | Fielder | Fielder | Fielder | Fielder | Fielder | Fielder | Fielder | 1B |
| 2B | Weeks | Weeks | Weeks | Weeks | Weeks | Weeks | Weeks | 2B |
| 3B | McGehee | McGehee | McGehee | McGehee | McGehee | McGehee | McGehee | 3B |
| SS | Escobar A | Escobar A | Escobar A | Escobar A | Escobar A | Escobar A | Escobar A | SS |
| LF | Braun | Braun | Braun | Braun | Braun | Braun | Braun | LF |
| CF | Gomez C | Gomez C | Gomez C | Gomez C | Cain L | Cain L | Gomez C | CF |
| RF | Hart | Hart | Hart | Hart | Hart | Hart | Hart | RF |
| DH | — | | | | | | — | DH |
| | | | | | | | | |
| SP | Wolf Ra | Gallardo | Gallardo | Wolf Ra | Wolf Ra | Narveson | Wolf Ra | SP |
| SP | Bush | Wolf Ra | Bush | Bush | Gallardo | Wolf Ra | Gallardo | SP |
| SP | Gallardo | Narveson | Narveson | Parra M | Bush | Gallardo | Bush | SP |
| SP | Davis D | Bush | Wolf Ra | Narveson | Narveson | Capuano | Narveson | SP |
| SP | Suppan | Davis D | Parra M | Gallardo | Parra M | Bush | Parra M | SP |
| CL | Hoffman | Axford | Axford | Axford | Axford | Axford | Axford | CL |

## Hitters — Los Angeles Dodgers 2010

| Hitters | G | AB | R | H | 2B | 3B | HR | RBI | BA | OBP | SLG | SB | CS | 1st Half AB | R | HR | BI | BA | SB | 2nd Half AB | R | HR | BI | BA | SB | Rates CT% | H% | BB% | Bash | GB% | Productiveness OPS | vs RH | vs LH |
|---|---|---|---|---|---|---|---|---|---|---|---|---|---|---|---|---|---|---|---|---|---|---|---|---|---|---|---|---|---|---|---|---|---|
| Anderson G | 80 | 155 | 8 | 28 | 6 | 1 | 2 | 12 | .181 | .204 | .271 | 1 | 0 | 134 | 6 | 2 | 11 | .179 | 1 | 21 | 2 | 0 | 1 | .190 | 0 | 78% | 23% | 3% | 1.5 | 43% | .475 | .481 | .448 |
| Ausmus B | 21 | 63 | 4 | 14 | 2 | 0 | 0 | 2 | .222 | .310 | .254 | 0 | 0 | 4 | 0 | 0 | 0 | .250 | 0 | 59 | 4 | 0 | 2 | .220 | 0 | 76% | 29% | 10% | 1.1 | 50% | .564 | .581 | .497 |
| Barajas R | 25 | 64 | 9 | 19 | 3 | 0 | 5 | 13 | .297 | .361 | .578 | 0 | 0 | — | — | — | — | — | — | 64 | 9 | 5 | 13 | .297 | 0 | 77% | 39% | 7% | 1.9 | 14% | .939 | 1.026 | .748 |
| Belliard R | 82 | 162 | 24 | 35 | 10 | 1 | 2 | 19 | .216 | .295 | .327 | 2 | 2 | 108 | 16 | 2 | 14 | .222 | 1 | 54 | 8 | 0 | 5 | .204 | 1 | 78% | 28% | 10% | 1.5 | 41% | .622 | .667 | .554 |
| Blake C | 146 | 509 | 56 | 126 | 28 | 1 | 17 | 64 | .248 | .320 | .407 | 0 | 4 | 274 | 30 | 9 | 36 | .259 | 0 | 235 | 26 | 8 | 28 | .234 | 0 | 73% | 34% | 8% | 1.6 | 43% | .727 | .663 | .895 |
| Carroll J | 133 | 351 | 48 | 102 | 15 | 1 | 0 | 23 | .291 | .379 | .339 | 12 | 4 | 179 | 30 | 0 | 11 | .291 | 6 | 172 | 18 | 0 | 12 | .291 | 6 | 82% | 36% | 12% | 1.2 | 54% | .718 | .713 | .733 |
| Castro J | 1 | 3 | 0 | 0 | 0 | 0 | 0 | 0 | .000 | .250 | .000 | 0 | 0 | — | — | — | — | — | — | 3 | 0 | 0 | 0 | .000 | 0 | 33% | 0% | 25% | — | 0% | .250 | .250 | — |
| DeWitt B | 82 | 256 | 29 | 69 | 15 | 4 | 1 | 30 | .270 | .352 | .371 | 2 | 2 | 219 | 26 | 1 | 29 | .269 | 2 | 37 | 3 | 0 | 1 | .270 | 0 | 81% | 33% | 10% | 1.4 | 47% | .723 | .752 | .582 |
| Ellis A | 44 | 108 | 6 | 30 | 5 | 0 | 0 | 16 | .278 | .363 | .324 | 0 | 0 | 42 | 2 | 0 | 8 | .214 | 0 | 66 | 4 | 0 | 8 | .318 | 0 | 83% | 33% | 11% | 1.2 | 52% | .687 | .688 | .673 |
| Ethier A | 139 | 517 | 71 | 151 | 33 | 1 | 23 | 82 | .292 | .364 | .493 | 2 | 1 | 275 | 43 | 14 | 54 | .324 | 1 | 242 | 28 | 9 | 28 | .256 | 1 | 80% | 36% | 10% | 1.7 | 39% | .857 | .960 | .625 |
| Furcal R | 97 | 383 | 66 | 115 | 23 | 7 | 8 | 43 | .300 | .366 | .460 | 22 | 4 | 243 | 51 | 6 | 35 | .333 | 14 | 140 | 15 | 2 | 8 | .243 | 8 | 84% | 36% | 9% | 1.5 | 46% | .826 | .847 | .774 |
| Gibbons J | 37 | 75 | 11 | 21 | 2 | 0 | 5 | 17 | .280 | .313 | .507 | 0 | 1 | — | — | — | — | — | — | 75 | 11 | 5 | 17 | .280 | 0 | 81% | 34% | 5% | 1.8 | 49% | .819 | .808 | .867 |
| Green N | 5 | 8 | 0 | 1 | 0 | 0 | 0 | 1 | .125 | .222 | .125 | 0 | 0 | 8 | 0 | 0 | 1 | .125 | 0 | — | — | — | — | — | — | 75% | 17% | 0% | 1.0 | 0% | .347 | .000 | .393 |
| Hu C | 14 | 23 | 2 | 3 | 1 | 0 | 0 | 1 | .130 | .160 | .174 | 1 | 0 | — | — | — | — | — | — | 23 | 2 | 0 | 1 | .130 | 1 | 78% | 17% | 0% | 1.3 | 33% | .334 | .236 | .571 |
| Johnson R | 102 | 202 | 24 | 53 | 11 | 2 | 2 | 15 | .262 | .291 | .366 | 2 | 2 | 127 | 16 | 0 | 7 | .291 | 1 | 75 | 8 | 2 | 8 | .213 | 1 | 75% | 35% | 2% | 1.4 | 43% | .657 | .520 | .790 |
| Kemp M | 162 | 602 | 82 | 150 | 25 | 6 | 28 | 89 | .249 | .310 | .450 | 19 | 15 | 349 | 58 | 16 | 51 | .261 | 15 | 253 | 24 | 12 | 38 | .233 | 4 | 72% | 35% | 8% | 1.8 | 41% | .760 | .743 | .809 |
| Lindsey J | 11 | 12 | 0 | 1 | 0 | 0 | 0 | 0 | .083 | .154 | .083 | 0 | 0 | — | — | — | — | — | — | 12 | 0 | 0 | 0 | .083 | 0 | 75% | 11% | 0% | 1.0 | 44% | .237 | .393 | .000 |
| Loney J | 161 | 588 | 67 | 157 | 41 | 2 | 10 | 88 | .267 | .329 | .395 | 10 | 5 | 337 | 47 | 6 | 63 | .309 | 9 | 251 | 20 | 4 | 25 | .211 | 1 | 84% | 32% | 8% | 1.5 | 44% | .723 | .785 | .575 |
| Martin R | 97 | 331 | 45 | 82 | 13 | 0 | 5 | 26 | .248 | .347 | .332 | 6 | 2 | 283 | 43 | 5 | 22 | .244 | 6 | 48 | 2 | 0 | 4 | .271 | 0 | 82% | 30% | 12% | 1.3 | 51% | .679 | .678 | .682 |
| Mitchell R | 15 | 42 | 3 | 6 | 0 | 0 | 2 | 4 | .143 | .140 | .286 | 0 | 0 | — | — | — | — | — | — | 42 | 3 | 2 | 4 | .143 | 0 | 81% | 18% | 0% | 2.0 | 35% | .425 | .226 | .750 |
| Oeltjen T | 15 | 23 | 5 | 5 | 1 | 1 | 0 | 1 | .217 | .357 | .348 | 0 | 0 | — | — | — | — | — | — | 23 | 5 | 0 | 1 | .217 | 0 | 65% | 33% | 13% | 1.6 | 20% | .705 | .734 | .000 |
| Paul X | 44 | 121 | 16 | 28 | 8 | 1 | 0 | 11 | .231 | .277 | .314 | 3 | 1 | 85 | 13 | 0 | 9 | .259 | 3 | 36 | 3 | 0 | 2 | .167 | 0 | 80% | 29% | 6% | 1.4 | 40% | .591 | .591 | .590 |
| Podsednik S | 39 | 149 | 17 | 39 | 6 | 1 | 1 | 7 | .262 | .313 | .336 | 5 | 3 | — | — | — | — | — | — | 149 | 17 | 1 | 7 | .262 | 5 | 83% | 32% | 7% | 1.3 | 46% | .648 | .705 | .463 |
| Ramirez M | 66 | 196 | 32 | 61 | 15 | 0 | 8 | 40 | .311 | .405 | .510 | 1 | 1 | 183 | 31 | 8 | 39 | .322 | 1 | 13 | 1 | 0 | 1 | .154 | 0 | 81% | 39% | 14% | 1.6 | 44% | .915 | .928 | .858 |
| Theriot R | 54 | 198 | 27 | 48 | 5 | 0 | 1 | 8 | .242 | .323 | .283 | 4 | 3 | — | — | — | — | — | — | 198 | 27 | 1 | 8 | .242 | 4 | 86% | 28% | 10% | 1.2 | 49% | .606 | .567 | .713 |

## Pitchers — Los Angeles Dodgers 2010

| Pitchers | G | GS | W | L | Hld | Sv | IP | H | HR | ERA | WHIP | K | BB | 1st Half W | L | Sv | IP | ERA | WHIP | 2nd Half W | L | Sv | IP | ERA | WHIP | Rates K/9 | BB/9 | HR/9 | Productiveness opOPS | vs RH | vs LH |
|---|---|---|---|---|---|---|---|---|---|---|---|---|---|---|---|---|---|---|---|---|---|---|---|---|---|---|---|---|---|---|---|
| Belisario R | 59 | 0 | 3 | 1 | 16 | 2 | 55.1 | 52 | 6 | 5.04 | 1.28 | 38 | 19 | 1 | 1 | 1 | 35.2 | 3.79 | 1.21 | 2 | 0 | 1 | 19.2 | 7.32 | 1.42 | 6.2 | 3.1 | 1.0 | .702 | .649 | .793 |
| Billingsley C | 31 | 31 | 12 | 11 | 0 | 0 | 191.2 | 176 | 8 | 3.57 | 1.28 | 171 | 69 | 7 | 4 | 0 | 95.2 | 4.14 | 1.39 | 5 | 7 | 0 | 96.0 | 3.00 | 1.17 | 8.0 | 3.2 | 0.4 | .668 | .629 | .703 |
| Broxton J | 64 | 0 | 5 | 6 | 3 | 22 | 62.1 | 64 | 4 | 4.04 | 1.48 | 73 | 28 | 3 | 0 | 19 | 38.1 | 2.11 | 1.07 | 2 | 6 | 3 | 24.0 | 7.13 | 2.13 | 10.5 | 4.0 | 0.6 | .718 | .794 | .626 |
| Dotel O | 19 | 0 | 1 | 1 | 3 | 1 | 18.2 | 11 | 3 | 3.38 | 1.18 | 21 | 11 | — | — | — | — | — | — | 1 | 1 | 1 | 18.2 | 3.38 | 1.18 | 10.1 | 5.3 | 1.4 | .661 | .566 | .835 |
| Elbert S | 1 | 0 | 0 | 0 | 0 | 0 | 0.2 | 1 | 0 | 13.50 | 6.00 | 0 | 3 | 0 | 0 | 0 | 0.2 | 13.50 | 6.00 | — | — | — | — | — | — | 0.0 | 40.5 | 0.0 | 1.000 | .000 | 2.000 |
| Ely J | 18 | 18 | 4 | 10 | 0 | 0 | 100.0 | 105 | 12 | 5.49 | 1.45 | 76 | 40 | 4 | 7 | 0 | 79.2 | 4.63 | 1.32 | 0 | 3 | 0 | 20.1 | 8.85 | 1.97 | 6.8 | 3.6 | 1.1 | .803 | .837 | .749 |
| Haeger C | 9 | 6 | 0 | 4 | 0 | 0 | 30.0 | 36 | 4 | 8.40 | 2.07 | 30 | 26 | 0 | 4 | 0 | 30.0 | 8.40 | 2.07 | — | — | — | — | — | — | 9.0 | 7.8 | 1.2 | .905 | .835 | 1.004 |
| Jansen K | 25 | 0 | 1 | 0 | 4 | 4 | 27.0 | 12 | 0 | 0.67 | 1.00 | 41 | 15 | — | — | — | — | — | — | 1 | 0 | 4 | 27.0 | 0.67 | 1.00 | 13.7 | 5.0 | 0.0 | .422 | .273 | .586 |
| Kershaw C | 32 | 32 | 13 | 10 | 0 | 0 | 204.1 | 160 | 13 | 2.91 | 1.18 | 212 | 81 | 9 | 4 | 0 | 112.1 | 2.96 | 1.20 | 4 | 6 | 0 | 92.0 | 2.84 | 1.15 | 9.3 | 3.6 | 0.6 | .615 | .599 | .673 |
| Kuo H | 56 | 0 | 3 | 2 | 21 | 12 | 60.0 | 29 | 1 | 1.20 | 0.78 | 73 | 18 | 3 | 1 | 2 | 27.1 | 0.99 | 0.77 | 0 | 1 | 10 | 32.2 | 1.38 | 0.80 | 11.0 | 2.7 | 0.2 | .403 | .460 | .271 |
| Kuroda H | 31 | 31 | 11 | 13 | 0 | 0 | 196.1 | 180 | 15 | 3.39 | 1.16 | 159 | 48 | 7 | 7 | 0 | 102.1 | 3.87 | 1.37 | 4 | 6 | 0 | 94.0 | 2.87 | 0.94 | 7.3 | 2.2 | 0.7 | .642 | .623 | .664 |
| Lilly T | 12 | 12 | 7 | 4 | 0 | 0 | 76.2 | 61 | 13 | 3.52 | 0.99 | 77 | 15 | — | — | — | — | — | — | 7 | 4 | 0 | 76.2 | 3.52 | 0.99 | 9.0 | 1.8 | 1.5 | .700 | .624 | 1.089 |
| Link J | 9 | 0 | 0 | 0 | 0 | 0 | 8.2 | 12 | 0 | 4.15 | 1.85 | 4 | 4 | 0 | 0 | 0 | 4.1 | 4.15 | 1.85 | 0 | 0 | 0 | 4.1 | 4.15 | 1.85 | 4.2 | 4.2 | 0.0 | .789 | .681 | .962 |
| McDonald J | 4 | 1 | 0 | 1 | 1 | 0 | 7.2 | 11 | 1 | 8.22 | 2.09 | 7 | 5 | — | — | — | — | — | — | 0 | 1 | 0 | 7.2 | 8.22 | 2.09 | 8.2 | 5.9 | 1.2 | .952 | .600 | 1.265 |
| Miller J | 19 | 0 | 1 | 0 | 1 | 0 | 24.1 | 22 | 4 | 4.44 | 1.23 | 30 | 8 | 0 | 0 | 0 | 23.2 | 4.18 | 1.18 | 0 | 0 | 0 | 0.2 | 13.50 | 3.00 | 11.1 | 3.0 | 1.5 | .754 | .741 | .754 |
| Monasterios C | 32 | 13 | 3 | 5 | 0 | 0 | 88.1 | 99 | 15 | 4.38 | 1.45 | 52 | 29 | 3 | 2 | 0 | 48.1 | 3.91 | 1.34 | 0 | 3 | 0 | 40.0 | 4.95 | 1.58 | 5.3 | 3.0 | 1.5 | .796 | .869 | .709 |
| Ortiz R | 16 | 2 | 1 | 2 | 1 | 0 | 30.0 | 33 | 5 | 6.30 | 1.63 | 21 | 16 | 1 | 2 | 0 | 30.0 | 6.30 | 1.63 | — | — | — | — | — | — | 6.3 | 4.8 | 1.5 | .874 | .582 | 1.179 |
| Ortiz R | 6 | 0 | 0 | 1 | 0 | 0 | 7.0 | 10 | 0 | 10.29 | 2.14 | 6 | 5 | 0 | 1 | 0 | 7.0 | 10.29 | 2.14 | — | — | — | — | — | — | 7.7 | 6.4 | 0.0 | .808 | .911 | .683 |
| Padilla V | 16 | 16 | 6 | 5 | 0 | 0 | 95.0 | 79 | 14 | 4.07 | 1.08 | 84 | 24 | 4 | 2 | 0 | 55.2 | 4.04 | 1.02 | 2 | 3 | 0 | 39.1 | 4.12 | 1.17 | 8.0 | 2.3 | 1.3 | .672 | .731 | .590 |
| Schlichting T | 14 | 0 | 1 | 0 | 0 | 0 | 22.2 | 20 | 0 | 3.57 | 1.32 | 14 | 10 | 1 | 0 | 0 | 14.0 | 0.64 | 1.00 | 0 | 0 | 0 | 8.2 | 8.31 | 1.85 | 5.6 | 4.0 | 0.0 | .588 | .670 | .465 |
| Sherrill G | 65 | 0 | 2 | 2 | 7 | 0 | 36.1 | 46 | 4 | 6.69 | 1.93 | 25 | 24 | 0 | 1 | 0 | 19.2 | 7.32 | 2.24 | 2 | 1 | 0 | 16.2 | 5.94 | 1.56 | 6.2 | 5.9 | 1.0 | .906 | 1.223 | .573 |
| Taschner J | 3 | 0 | 0 | 0 | 0 | 0 | 0.1 | 1 | 0 | 27.00 | 12.00 | 0 | 3 | — | — | — | — | — | — | 0 | 0 | 0 | 0.1 | 27.00 | 12.00 | 0.0 | 81.0 | 0.0 | 1.000 | .833 | — |
| Troncoso R | 52 | 0 | 2 | 3 | 8 | 0 | 54.0 | 55 | 7 | 4.33 | 1.35 | 34 | 18 | 1 | 2 | 0 | 36.2 | 5.15 | 1.31 | 1 | 1 | 0 | 17.1 | 2.60 | 1.44 | 5.7 | 3.0 | 1.2 | .726 | .659 | .823 |
| Weaver J | 44 | 0 | 5 | 1 | 5 | 0 | 44.1 | 48 | 5 | 6.09 | 1.53 | 26 | 20 | 5 | 1 | 0 | 28.0 | 3.54 | 1.25 | 0 | 0 | 0 | 16.1 | 10.47 | 2.02 | 5.3 | 4.1 | 1.0 | .822 | .765 | .923 |

## Hitters — Milwaukee Brewers 2010

| Hitters | G | AB | R | H | 2B | 3B | HR | RBI | BA | OBP | SLG | SB | CS | 1st Half AB | R | HR | BI | BA | SB | 2nd Half AB | R | HR | BI | BA | SB | Rates CT% | H% | BB% | Bash | GB% | Productiveness OPS | vs RH | vs LH |
|---|---|---|---|---|---|---|---|---|---|---|---|---|---|---|---|---|---|---|---|---|---|---|---|---|---|---|---|---|---|---|---|---|---|
| Braun R | 157 | 619 | 101 | 188 | 45 | 1 | 25 | 103 | .304 | .365 | .501 | 14 | 3 | 349 | 55 | 13 | 54 | .292 | 12 | 270 | 46 | 12 | 49 | .319 | 2 | 83% | 37% | 8% | 1.6 | 48% | .866 | .893 | .786 |
| Cain L | 43 | 147 | 17 | 45 | 11 | 1 | 1 | 13 | .306 | .348 | .415 | 7 | 1 | — | — | — | — | — | — | 147 | 17 | 1 | 13 | .306 | 7 | 81% | 38% | 6% | 1.4 | 42% | .763 | .805 | .668 |
| Counsell C | 102 | 204 | 16 | 51 | 8 | 0 | 2 | 21 | .250 | .322 | .319 | 1 | 1 | 130 | 10 | 1 | 13 | .238 | 1 | 74 | 6 | 1 | 8 | .270 | 0 | 86% | 29% | 9% | 1.3 | 42% | .640 | .660 | .543 |
| Cruz L | 7 | 17 | 2 | 4 | 0 | 1 | 0 | 1 | .235 | .235 | .353 | 0 | 0 | — | — | — | — | — | — | 17 | 2 | 0 | 1 | .235 | 0 | 88% | 27% | 0% | 1.5 | 53% | .588 | 1.333 | .182 |
| Dickerson C | 25 | 53 | 2 | 11 | 1 | 1 | 0 | 5 | .208 | .271 | .264 | 1 | 0 | — | — | — | — | — | — | 53 | 2 | 0 | 5 | .208 | 1 | 72% | 29% | 8% | 1.3 | 50% | .535 | .571 | .000 |
| Edmonds J | 73 | 217 | 38 | 62 | 21 | 0 | 8 | 20 | .286 | .350 | .493 | 2 | 2 | 172 | 28 | 4 | 12 | .273 | 2 | 45 | 10 | 4 | 8 | .333 | 0 | 76% | 38% | 9% | 1.7 | 30% | .843 | .858 | .784 |
| Escobar A | 145 | 506 | 57 | 119 | 14 | 10 | 4 | 41 | .235 | .288 | .326 | 10 | 4 | 283 | 35 | 2 | 24 | .244 | 7 | 223 | 22 | 2 | 17 | .224 | 3 | 86% | 27% | 6% | 1.4 | 44% | .614 | .614 | .614 |
| Fielder P | 161 | 578 | 94 | 151 | 25 | 0 | 32 | 83 | .261 | .401 | .471 | 1 | 0 | 324 | 53 | 20 | 39 | .265 | 1 | 254 | 41 | 12 | 44 | .256 | 0 | 76% | 34% | 16% | 1.8 | 43% | .871 | .975 | .668 |
| Gamel M | 12 | 15 | 1 | 3 | 1 | 0 | 0 | 1 | .200 | .294 | .267 | 0 | 0 | — | — | — | — | — | — | 15 | 1 | 0 | 1 | .200 | 0 | 47% | 43% | 6% | 1.3 | 45% | .561 | .497 | 1.000 |
| Gerut J | 32 | 71 | 7 | 14 | 4 | 1 | 2 | 8 | .197 | .230 | .366 | 0 | 1 | 71 | 7 | 2 | 8 | .197 | 0 | — | — | — | — | — | — | 76% | 26% | 4% | 1.9 | 57% | .596 | .444 | .981 |
| Gomez C | 97 | 291 | 38 | 72 | 11 | 3 | 5 | 24 | .247 | .298 | .357 | 18 | 3 | 205 | 28 | 5 | 20 | .229 | 10 | 86 | 10 | 0 | 4 | .291 | 8 | 75% | 33% | 5% | 1.4 | 43% | .655 | .694 | .580 |
| Hart C | 145 | 558 | 91 | 158 | 34 | 4 | 31 | 102 | .283 | .340 | .525 | 7 | 6 | 306 | 44 | 21 | 65 | .288 | 4 | 252 | 47 | 10 | 37 | .278 | 3 | 75% | 38% | 7% | 1.9 | 39% | .865 | .827 | .973 |
| Inglett J | 102 | 142 | 15 | 36 | 8 | 5 | 1 | 8 | .254 | .331 | .401 | 1 | 0 | 67 | 9 | 0 | 2 | .328 | 1 | 75 | 6 | 1 | 6 | .187 | 0 | 76% | 33% | 9% | 1.6 | 34% | .733 | .782 | .419 |
| Kottaras G | 67 | 212 | 24 | 43 | 12 | 1 | 9 | 26 | .203 | .305 | .396 | 2 | 0 | 135 | 16 | 7 | 21 | .207 | 2 | 77 | 8 | 2 | 5 | .195 | 0 | 79% | 26% | 13% | 2.0 | 44% | .701 | .691 | .726 |
| Lucroy J | 75 | 277 | 24 | 70 | 9 | 0 | 4 | 26 | .253 | .300 | .329 | 4 | 2 | 86 | 11 | 2 | 5 | .267 | 2 | 191 | 13 | 2 | 21 | .246 | 2 | 84% | 30% | 6% | 1.3 | 44% | .628 | .589 | .735 |
| McGehee C | 157 | 610 | 70 | 174 | 38 | 1 | 23 | 104 | .285 | .337 | .464 | 1 | 1 | 325 | 38 | 13 | 53 | .274 | 1 | 285 | 32 | 10 | 51 | .298 | 0 | 83% | 34% | 7% | 1.6 | 48% | .801 | .750 | .947 |
| Stern A | 6 | 8 | 0 | 0 | 0 | 0 | 0 | 1 | .000 | .000 | .000 | 0 | 0 | 8 | 0 | 0 | 1 | .000 | 0 | — | — | — | — | — | — | 75% | 0% | 0% | — | 83% | .000 | .000 | .000 |
| Weeks R | 160 | 651 | 112 | 175 | 32 | 4 | 29 | 83 | .269 | .366 | .464 | 11 | 4 | 361 | 56 | 15 | 53 | .269 | 6 | 290 | 56 | 14 | 30 | .269 | 5 | 72% | 37% | 10% | 1.7 | 49% | .830 | .769 | 1.025 |
| Zaun G | 28 | 102 | 11 | 27 | 7 | 0 | 2 | 14 | .265 | .350 | .392 | 0 | 0 | 102 | 11 | 2 | 14 | .265 | 0 | — | — | — | — | — | — | 88% | 30% | 9% | 1.5 | 49% | .743 | .840 | .523 |

## Pitchers — Milwaukee Brewers 2010

| Pitchers | G | GS | W | L | Hld | Sv | IP | H | HR | ERA | WHIP | K | BB | 1st Half W | L | Sv | IP | ERA | WHIP | 2nd Half W | L | Sv | IP | ERA | WHIP | Rates K/9 | BB/9 | HR/9 | Productiveness opOPS | vs RH | vs LH |
|---|---|---|---|---|---|---|---|---|---|---|---|---|---|---|---|---|---|---|---|---|---|---|---|---|---|---|---|---|---|---|---|
| Axford J | 50 | 0 | 8 | 2 | 3 | 24 | 58.0 | 42 | 1 | 2.48 | 1.19 | 76 | 27 | 5 | 1 | 10 | 26.0 | 3.12 | 1.27 | 3 | 1 | 14 | 32.0 | 1.97 | 1.13 | 11.8 | 4.2 | 0.2 | .588 | .483 | .692 |
| Braddock Z | 46 | 0 | 1 | 2 | 15 | 0 | 33.2 | 29 | 1 | 2.94 | 1.43 | 41 | 19 | 1 | 1 | 0 | 17.2 | 4.08 | 1.47 | 0 | 1 | 0 | 16.0 | 1.69 | 1.38 | 11.0 | 5.1 | 0.3 | .656 | .812 | .440 |
| Bush D | 32 | 31 | 8 | 13 | 1 | 0 | 174.1 | 198 | 28 | 4.54 | 1.51 | 107 | 65 | 4 | 6 | 0 | 95.2 | 4.14 | 1.49 | 4 | 7 | 0 | 78.2 | 5.03 | 1.53 | 5.5 | 3.4 | 1.4 | .826 | .799 | .857 |
| Capuano C | 24 | 9 | 4 | 4 | 1 | 0 | 66.0 | 65 | 9 | 3.95 | 1.30 | 54 | 21 | 0 | 1 | 0 | 10.1 | 4.35 | 1.84 | 4 | 3 | 0 | 55.2 | 3.88 | 1.20 | 7.4 | 2.9 | 1.2 | .755 | .780 | .685 |
| Coffey T | 69 | 0 | 2 | 4 | 13 | 0 | 62.1 | 65 | 8 | 4.76 | 1.41 | 56 | 23 | 2 | 2 | 0 | 34.2 | 4.41 | 1.38 | 0 | 2 | 0 | 27.2 | 5.20 | 1.45 | 8.1 | 3.3 | 1.2 | .783 | .737 | .893 |
| Davis D | 8 | 8 | 1 | 4 | 0 | 0 | 38.1 | 55 | 6 | 7.51 | 1.98 | 34 | 21 | 1 | 4 | 0 | 38.1 | 7.51 | 1.98 | — | — | — | — | — | — | 8.0 | 4.9 | 1.4 | .915 | .972 | .699 |
| Estrada M | 7 | 1 | 0 | 0 | 0 | 0 | 11.1 | 14 | 3 | 9.53 | 1.76 | 13 | 6 | 0 | 0 | 0 | 11.1 | 9.53 | 1.76 | — | — | — | — | — | — | 10.3 | 4.8 | 2.4 | .908 | .571 | 1.348 |
| Gallardo Y | 31 | 31 | 14 | 7 | 0 | 0 | 185.0 | 178 | 12 | 3.84 | 1.37 | 200 | 75 | 8 | 4 | 0 | 111.2 | 2.58 | 1.26 | 6 | 3 | 0 | 73.1 | 5.77 | 1.53 | 9.7 | 3.6 | 0.6 | .693 | .620 | .781 |
| Hawkins L | 18 | 0 | 0 | 3 | 6 | 0 | 16.0 | 21 | 2 | 8.44 | 1.69 | 18 | 6 | 0 | 3 | 0 | 11.2 | 9.26 | 1.71 | 0 | 0 | 0 | 4.1 | 6.23 | 1.62 | 10.1 | 3.4 | 1.1 | .890 | .957 | .783 |
| Hoffman T | 50 | 0 | 2 | 7 | 2 | 10 | 47.1 | 49 | 8 | 5.89 | 1.44 | 30 | 19 | 2 | 4 | 5 | 27.0 | 8.33 | 1.74 | 0 | 3 | 5 | 20.1 | 2.66 | 1.03 | 5.7 | 3.6 | 1.5 | .832 | .780 | .892 |
| Jeffress J | 10 | 0 | 1 | 0 | 0 | 0 | 10.0 | 8 | 0 | 2.70 | 1.40 | 8 | 6 | — | — | — | — | — | — | 1 | 0 | 0 | 10.0 | 2.70 | 1.40 | 7.2 | 5.4 | 0.0 | .676 | .644 | .748 |
| Kintzler B | 7 | 0 | 0 | 1 | 0 | 0 | 7.1 | 10 | 2 | 7.36 | 1.91 | 9 | 4 | — | — | — | — | — | — | 0 | 1 | 0 | 7.1 | 7.36 | 1.91 | 11.0 | 4.9 | 2.5 | 1.045 | 1.087 | .964 |
| Loe K | 53 | 0 | 3 | 5 | 22 | 0 | 58.1 | 54 | 6 | 2.78 | 1.18 | 46 | 15 | 0 | 1 | 0 | 22.2 | 1.59 | 0.88 | 3 | 4 | 0 | 35.2 | 3.53 | 1.37 | 7.1 | 2.3 | 0.9 | .661 | .612 | .740 |
| McClendon M | 17 | 0 | 2 | 0 | 3 | 0 | 21.0 | 15 | 2 | 3.00 | 1.05 | 21 | 7 | — | — | — | — | — | — | 2 | 0 | 0 | 21.0 | 3.00 | 1.05 | 9.0 | 3.0 | 0.9 | .587 | .549 | .638 |
| Narveson C | 37 | 28 | 12 | 9 | 3 | 0 | 167.2 | 172 | 21 | 4.99 | 1.38 | 137 | 59 | 7 | 6 | 0 | 86.2 | 6.02 | 1.57 | 5 | 3 | 0 | 81.0 | 3.89 | 1.17 | 7.4 | 3.2 | 1.1 | .761 | .816 | .598 |
| Parra M | 42 | 16 | 3 | 10 | 0 | 0 | 122.0 | 135 | 18 | 5.02 | 1.62 | 129 | 63 | 3 | 6 | 0 | 69.2 | 4.65 | 1.71 | 0 | 4 | 0 | 52.1 | 5.50 | 1.51 | 9.5 | 4.6 | 1.3 | .816 | .752 | .983 |
| Riske D | 23 | 0 | 0 | 0 | 0 | 0 | 23.1 | 25 | 2 | 5.01 | 1.41 | 16 | 8 | 0 | 0 | 0 | 11.2 | 2.31 | 0.86 | 0 | 0 | 0 | 11.2 | 7.71 | 1.97 | 6.2 | 3.1 | 0.8 | .745 | .913 | .366 |
| Rogers M | 4 | 2 | 0 | 0 | 0 | 0 | 10.0 | 2 | 0 | 1.80 | 0.50 | 11 | 3 | — | — | — | — | — | — | 0 | 0 | 0 | 10.0 | 1.80 | 0.50 | 9.9 | 2.7 | 0.0 | .238 | .322 | .000 |
| Smith C | 3 | 0 | 0 | 0 | 0 | 0 | 3.1 | 4 | 0 | 5.40 | 1.50 | 4 | 1 | 0 | 0 | 0 | 3.1 | 5.40 | 1.50 | — | — | — | — | — | — | 10.8 | 2.7 | 0.0 | .819 | .573 | 1.667 |
| Stetter M | 9 | 0 | 0 | 0 | 3 | 0 | 3.2 | 7 | 1 | 14.73 | 2.73 | 3 | 3 | 0 | 0 | 0 | 3.2 | 14.73 | 2.73 | — | — | — | — | — | — | 7.4 | 7.4 | 2.5 | 1.056 | 1.167 | 1.009 |
| Suppan J | 15 | 2 | 0 | 2 | 0 | 0 | 31.0 | 50 | 4 | 7.84 | 2.00 | 18 | 12 | 0 | 2 | 0 | 31.0 | 7.84 | 2.00 | — | — | — | — | — | — | 5.2 | 3.5 | 1.2 | 1.019 | .980 | 1.069 |
| Vargas C | 17 | 0 | 1 | 0 | 0 | 0 | 19.2 | 28 | 3 | 7.32 | 1.93 | 18 | 10 | 1 | 0 | 0 | 19.2 | 7.32 | 1.93 | — | — | — | — | — | — | 8.2 | 4.6 | 1.4 | .903 | 1.067 | .686 |
| Villanueva C | 50 | 0 | 2 | 0 | 14 | 1 | 52.2 | 48 | 7 | 4.61 | 1.33 | 67 | 22 | 0 | 0 | 1 | 44.1 | 4.26 | 1.31 | 2 | 0 | 0 | 8.1 | 6.48 | 1.44 | 11.4 | 3.8 | 1.2 | .702 | .637 | .768 |
| Wolf R | 34 | 34 | 13 | 12 | 0 | 0 | 215.2 | 213 | 29 | 4.17 | 1.39 | 142 | 87 | 6 | 8 | 0 | 116.1 | 4.56 | 1.50 | 7 | 4 | 0 | 99.1 | 3.71 | 1.26 | 5.9 | 3.6 | 1.2 | .764 | .728 | .889 |

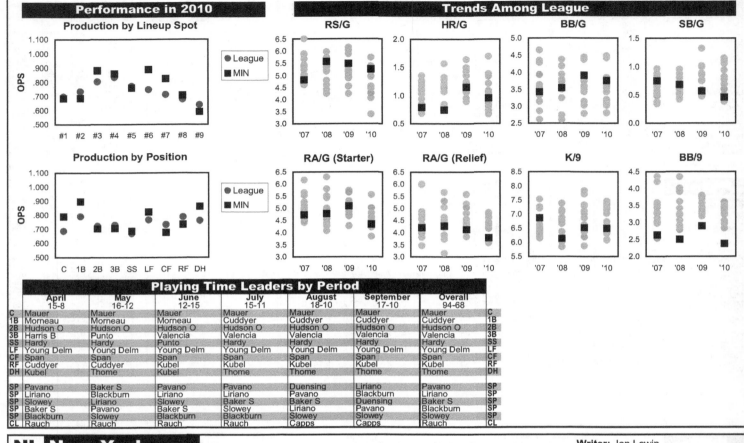

### Performance in 2010

**Production by Lineup Spot**

**Production by Position**

### Trends Among League

RS/G · HR/G · BB/G · SB/G

RA/G (Starter) · RA/G (Relief) · K/9 · BB/9

### Playing Time Leaders by Period

| | April 15-8 | May 16-12 | June 12-15 | July 15-11 | August 18-10 | September 17-10 | Overall 94-68 | |
|---|---|---|---|---|---|---|---|---|
| C | Mauer | Mauer | Mauer | Mauer | Mauer | Mauer | Mauer | C |
| 1B | Morneau | Morneau | Morneau | Cuddyer | Cuddyer | Cuddyer | Cuddyer | 1B |
| 2B | Hudson O | Hudson O | Hudson O | Hudson O | Hudson O | Hudson O | Hudson O | 2B |
| 3B | Harris B | Punto | Valencia | Valencia | Valencia | Valencia | Valencia | 3B |
| SS | Hardy | Hardy | Punto | Hardy | Hardy | Hardy | Hardy | SS |
| LF | Young Delm | Young Delm | Young Delm | Young Delm | Young Delm | Young Delm | Young Delm | LF |
| CF | Span | Span | Span | Span | Span | Span | Span | CF |
| RF | Cuddyer | Cuddyer | Kubel | Kubel | Kubel | Kubel | Kubel | RF |
| DH | Kubel | Thome | Kubel | Thome | Thome | Thome | Thome | DH |
| | | | | | | | | |
| SP | Pavano | Baker S | Pavano | Pavano | Duensing | Liriano | Pavano | SP |
| SP | Liriano | Blackburn | Liriano | Liriano | Pavano | Blackburn | Liriano | SP |
| SP | Slowey | Liriano | Slowey | Baker S | Baker S | Duensing | Baker S | SP |
| SP | Baker S | Pavano | Baker S | Slowey | Liriano | Pavano | Blackburn | SP |
| SP | Blackburn | Slowey | Blackburn | Blackburn | Slowey | Slowey | Slowey | SP |
| CL | Rauch | Rauch | Rauch | Rauch | Capps | Capps | Rauch | CL |

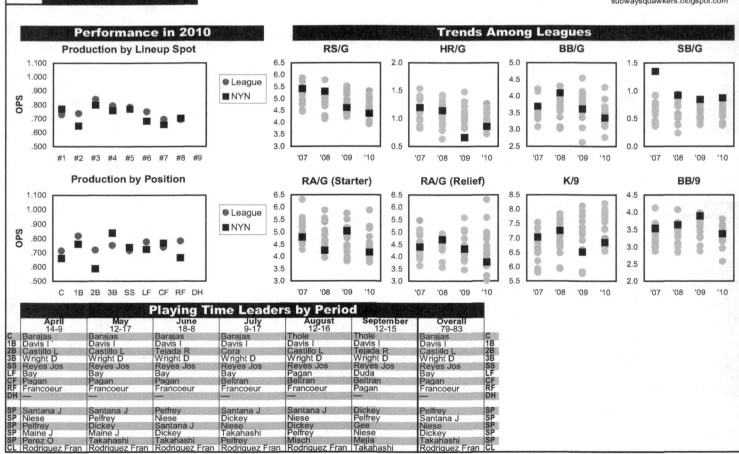

### Performance in 2010

**Production by Lineup Spot**

**Production by Position**

### Trends Among Leagues

RS/G · HR/G · BB/G · SB/G

RA/G (Starter) · RA/G (Relief) · K/9 · BB/9

### Playing Time Leaders by Period

| | April 14-9 | May 12-17 | June 18-8 | July 9-17 | August 12-16 | September 12-15 | Overall 79-83 | |
|---|---|---|---|---|---|---|---|---|
| C | Barajas | Barajas | Barajas | Barajas | Thole | Thole | Barajas | C |
| 1B | Davis I ' | Davis I | Davis I | Davis I | Davis I | Davis I | Davis I | 1B |
| 2B | Castillo L | Castillo L | Tejada R | Cora | Castillo L | Tejada R | Castillo L | 2B |
| 3B | Wright D | Wright D | Wright D | Wright D | Wright D | Wright D | Wright D | 3B |
| SS | Reyes Jos | Reyes Jos | Reyes Jos | Reyes Jos | Reyes Jos | Reyes Jos | Reyes Jos | SS |
| LF | Bay | Bay | Bay | Bay | Pagan | Duda | Bay | LF |
| CF | Pagan | Pagan | Pagan | Beltran | Beltran | Beltran | Pagan | CF |
| RF | Francoeur | Francoeur | Francoeur | Francoeur | Francoeur | Pagan | Francoeur | RF |
| DH | — | | | | | | | DH |
| | | | | | | | | |
| SP | Santana J | Santana J | Pelfrey | Santana J | Santana J | Dickey | Pelfrey | SP |
| SP | Niese | Pelfrey | Niese | Dickey | Niese | Pelfrey | Santana J | SP |
| SP | Pelfrey | Dickey | Santana J | Niese | Dickey | Gee | Niese | SP |
| SP | Maine J | Maine J | Dickey | Takahashi | Pelfrey | Niese | Dickey | SP |
| SP | Perez O | Takahashi | Pelfrey | Pelfrey | Misch | Mejia | Takahashi | SP |
| CL | Rodriguez Fran | Rodriguez Fran | Rodriguez Fran | Rodriguez Fran | Rodriguez Fran | Takahashi | Rodriguez Fran | CL |

| Hitters | Minnesota Twins 2010 | | | | | | | | | | | | | 1st Half | | | | | | 2nd Half | | | | | | Rates | | | | | Productiveness | | |
|---|---|---|---|---|---|---|---|---|---|---|---|---|---|---|---|---|---|---|---|---|---|---|---|---|---|---|---|---|---|---|---|---|---|
| | G | AB | R | H | 2B | 3B | HR | RBI | BA | OBP | SLG | SB | CS | AB | R | HR | BI | BA | SB | AB | R | HR | BI | BA | SB | CT% | H% | BB% | Bash | GB% | OPS | vs RH | vs LH |
| Butera D | 49 | 142 | 12 | 28 | 6 | 1 | 2 | 13 | .197 | .237 | .296 | 0 | 0 | 51 | 3 | 1 | 5 | .157 | 0 | 91 | 9 | 1 | 8 | .220 | 0 | 82% | 24% | 3% | 1.5 | 40% | .533 | .591 | .453 |
| Casilla A | 69 | 152 | 26 | 42 | 7 | 4 | 1 | 20 | .276 | .331 | .395 | 6 | 1 | 39 | 7 | 0 | 2 | .256 | 0 | 113 | 19 | 1 | 18 | .283 | 6 | 89% | 31% | 8% | 1.4 | 47% | .726 | .702 | .813 |
| Cuddyer M | 157 | 609 | 93 | 165 | 37 | 5 | 14 | 81 | .271 | .336 | .417 | 7 | 3 | 322 | 50 | 9 | 40 | .267 | 2 | 287 | 43 | 5 | 41 | .275 | 5 | 85% | 32% | 9% | 1.5 | 50% | .753 | .700 | .875 |
| Hardy J | 101 | 340 | 44 | 91 | 19 | 3 | 6 | 38 | .268 | .320 | .394 | 1 | 1 | 159 | 14 | 3 | 14 | .226 | 0 | 181 | 30 | 3 | 24 | .304 | 1 | 84% | 32% | 7% | 1.5 | 50% | .714 | .759 | .614 |
| Harris B | 43 | 108 | 11 | 17 | 3 | 0 | 1 | 4 | .157 | .233 | .213 | 0 | 0 | 108 | 11 | 1 | 4 | .157 | 0 | --- | -- | -- | -- | --- | -- | 79% | 20% | 8% | 1.4 | 59% | .446 | .469 | .413 |
| Hudson O | 126 | 497 | 80 | 133 | 24 | 5 | 6 | 37 | .268 | .338 | .372 | 10 | 3 | 288 | 49 | 4 | 24 | .281 | 6 | 209 | 31 | 2 | 13 | .249 | 4 | 82% | 32% | 9% | 1.4 | 48% | .710 | .711 | .707 |
| Hughes L | 2 | 7 | 1 | 2 | 0 | 0 | 1 | 1 | .286 | .286 | .714 | 0 | 1 | 7 | 1 | 1 | 1 | .286 | 0 | --- | -- | -- | -- | --- | -- | 57% | 50% | 0% | 2.5 | 25% | 1.000 | 1.667 | .500 |
| Kubel J | 143 | 518 | 68 | 129 | 23 | 3 | 21 | 92 | .249 | .323 | .427 | 0 | 1 | 276 | 31 | 11 | 49 | .264 | 0 | 242 | 37 | 10 | 43 | .231 | 0 | 78% | 32% | 10% | 1.7 | 38% | .750 | .792 | .655 |
| Mauer J | 137 | 510 | 88 | 167 | 43 | 1 | 9 | 75 | .327 | .402 | .469 | 1 | 4 | 290 | 47 | 4 | 35 | .293 | 1 | 220 | 41 | 5 | 40 | .373 | 0 | 90% | 37% | 11% | 1.4 | 47% | .871 | .978 | .711 |
| Morales J | 19 | 36 | 4 | 7 | 2 | 0 | 0 | 7 | .194 | .295 | .250 | 0 | 0 | --- | -- | -- | -- | --- | -- | 36 | 4 | 0 | 7 | .194 | 0 | 61% | 32% | 14% | 1.3 | 50% | .545 | .558 | .450 |
| Morneau J | 81 | 296 | 53 | 102 | 25 | 1 | 18 | 56 | .345 | .437 | .618 | 0 | 0 | 296 | 53 | 18 | 56 | .345 | 0 | --- | -- | -- | -- | --- | -- | 79% | 44% | 14% | 1.8 | 33% | 1.055 | 1.113 | .966 |
| Plouffe T | 22 | 41 | 7 | 6 | 1 | 0 | 2 | 6 | .146 | .143 | .317 | 0 | 0 | 23 | 1 | 0 | 3 | .130 | 0 | 18 | 6 | 2 | 3 | .167 | 0 | 66% | 22% | 0% | 2.2 | 52% | .460 | .468 | .400 |
| Punto N | 88 | 252 | 24 | 60 | 11 | 1 | 1 | 20 | .238 | .313 | .302 | 6 | 2 | 199 | 19 | 1 | 18 | .241 | 5 | 53 | 5 | 0 | 2 | .226 | 1 | 80% | 30% | 10% | 1.3 | 51% | .615 | .618 | .608 |
| Ramos W | 7 | 27 | 2 | 8 | 3 | 0 | 0 | 1 | .296 | .321 | .407 | 0 | 0 | 27 | 2 | 0 | 1 | .296 | 0 | --- | -- | -- | -- | --- | -- | 89% | 33% | 0% | 1.4 | 46% | .729 | .433 | 1.333 |
| Repko J | 58 | 127 | 19 | 29 | 6 | 0 | 3 | 9 | .228 | .324 | .346 | 3 | 2 | 9 | 0 | 0 | 0 | .333 | 0 | 118 | 19 | 3 | 9 | .220 | 3 | 70% | 33% | 9% | 1.5 | 37% | .671 | .767 | .523 |
| Revere B | 13 | 28 | 1 | 5 | 0 | 0 | 0 | 2 | .179 | .233 | .179 | 0 | 1 | --- | -- | -- | -- | --- | -- | 28 | 1 | 0 | 2 | .179 | 0 | 82% | 22% | 7% | 1.0 | 65% | .412 | .450 | .368 |
| Span D | 153 | 629 | 85 | 166 | 24 | 10 | 3 | 58 | .264 | .331 | .348 | 26 | 4 | 355 | 54 | 3 | 37 | .273 | 16 | 274 | 31 | 0 | 21 | .252 | 10 | 88% | 30% | 9% | 1.3 | 53% | .679 | .670 | .696 |
| Thome J | 108 | 276 | 48 | 78 | 16 | 2 | 25 | 59 | .283 | .412 | .627 | 0 | 0 | 145 | 20 | 10 | 29 | .255 | 0 | 131 | 28 | 15 | 30 | .313 | 0 | 70% | 40% | 17% | 2.2 | 41% | 1.039 | 1.154 | .769 |
| Tolbert M | 48 | 87 | 8 | 20 | 4 | 3 | 1 | 18 | .230 | .293 | .379 | 1 | 1 | 46 | 4 | 1 | 8 | .217 | 0 | 41 | 4 | 0 | 10 | .244 | 1 | 79% | 29% | 9% | 1.7 | 43% | .672 | .797 | .198 |
| Valencia D | 85 | 299 | 30 | 93 | 18 | 1 | 7 | 40 | .311 | .351 | .448 | 2 | 0 | 58 | 4 | 0 | 3 | .310 | 1 | 241 | 26 | 7 | 37 | .311 | 1 | 85% | 37% | 6% | 1.4 | 43% | .799 | .713 | .967 |
| Young D | 153 | 570 | 77 | 170 | 46 | 1 | 21 | 112 | .298 | .333 | .493 | 5 | 4 | 279 | 38 | 10 | 58 | .305 | 4 | 291 | 39 | 11 | 54 | .292 | 1 | 86% | 35% | 5% | 1.7 | 46% | .826 | .781 | .927 |

| Pitchers | Minnesota Twins 2010 | | | | | | | | | | | | | 1st Half | | | | | | 2nd Half | | | | | | Rates | | | Productiveness | | |
|---|---|---|---|---|---|---|---|---|---|---|---|---|---|---|---|---|---|---|---|---|---|---|---|---|---|---|---|---|---|---|---|
| | G | GS | W | L | Hld | Sv | IP | H | HR | ERA | WHIP | K | BB | W | L | Sv | IP | ERA | WHIP | W | L | Sv | IP | ERA | WHIP | K/9 | BB/9 | HR/9 | opOPS | vs RH | vs LH |
| Baker S | 29 | 29 | 12 | 9 | 0 | 0 | 170.1 | 186 | 23 | 4.49 | 1.34 | 148 | 43 | 7 | 8 | 0 | 109.0 | 4.87 | 1.31 | 5 | 1 | 0 | 61.1 | 3.82 | 1.40 | 7.8 | 2.3 | 1.2 | .793 | .756 | .830 |
| Blackburn N | 28 | 26 | 10 | 12 | 0 | 0 | 161.0 | 194 | 25 | 5.42 | 1.45 | 68 | 40 | 7 | 7 | 0 | 97.0 | 6.40 | 1.66 | 3 | 5 | 0 | 64.0 | 3.94 | 1.14 | 3.8 | 2.2 | 1.4 | .839 | .836 | .843 |
| Burnett A | 41 | 0 | 2 | 2 | 2 | 0 | 47.2 | 52 | 6 | 5.29 | 1.57 | 37 | 23 | 1 | 1 | 0 | 40.0 | 3.60 | 1.40 | 1 | 1 | 0 | 7.2 | 14.09 | 2.48 | 7.0 | 4.3 | 1.1 | .847 | .794 | .946 |
| Capps M | 27 | 0 | 2 | 0 | 0 | 16 | 27.0 | 24 | 1 | 2.00 | 1.19 | 21 | 8 | -- | -- | -- | ---- | ---- | --- | 2 | 0 | 16 | 27.0 | 2.00 | 1.19 | 7.0 | 2.7 | 0.3 | .624 | .629 | .616 |
| Crain J | 71 | 0 | 1 | 1 | 21 | 1 | 68.0 | 53 | 5 | 3.04 | 1.18 | 62 | 27 | 1 | 0 | 0 | 34.1 | 3.93 | 1.34 | 0 | 1 | 1 | 33.2 | 2.14 | 1.01 | 8.2 | 3.6 | 0.7 | .627 | .635 | .614 |
| Delaney R | 1 | 0 | 0 | 0 | 0 | 0 | 1.0 | 2 | 1 | 9.00 | 3.00 | 0 | 1 | -- | -- | -- | ---- | ---- | --- | 0 | 0 | 0 | 1.0 | 9.00 | 3.00 | 0.0 | 9.0 | 9.0 | 1.850 | 2.333 | .500 |
| Duensing B | 53 | 13 | 10 | 3 | 9 | 0 | 130.2 | 122 | 11 | 2.62 | 1.20 | 78 | 35 | 2 | 1 | 0 | 39.0 | 1.62 | 0.95 | 8 | 2 | 0 | 91.2 | 3.04 | 1.31 | 5.4 | 2.4 | 0.8 | .666 | .751 | .457 |
| Flores R | 11 | 0 | 0 | 0 | 3 | 0 | 3.2 | 10 | 2 | 4.91 | 3.27 | 2 | 2 | -- | -- | -- | ---- | ---- | --- | 0 | 0 | 0 | 3.2 | 4.91 | 3.27 | 4.9 | 4.9 | 4.9 | 1.372 | 1.333 | 1.370 |
| Fox M | 1 | 1 | 0 | 0 | 0 | 0 | 5.2 | 4 | 0 | 3.18 | 0.88 | 0 | 1 | -- | -- | -- | ---- | ---- | --- | 0 | 0 | 0 | 5.2 | 3.18 | 0.88 | 0.0 | 1.6 | 0.0 | .449 | .333 | .619 |
| Fuentes B | 9 | 0 | 0 | 0 | 3 | 1 | 9.2 | 3 | 0 | 0.00 | 0.52 | 8 | 2 | -- | -- | -- | ---- | ---- | --- | 0 | 0 | 1 | 9.2 | 0.00 | 0.52 | 7.4 | 1.9 | 0.0 | .296 | .255 | .384 |
| Guerrier M | 74 | 0 | 5 | 7 | 23 | 1 | 71.0 | 56 | 7 | 3.17 | 1.10 | 42 | 22 | 1 | 5 | 1 | 39.1 | 2.97 | 1.14 | 4 | 2 | 0 | 31.2 | 3.41 | 1.04 | 5.3 | 2.8 | 0.9 | .625 | .611 | .649 |
| Liriano F | 31 | 31 | 14 | 10 | 0 | 0 | 191.2 | 184 | 9 | 3.62 | 1.26 | 201 | 58 | 6 | 7 | 0 | 107.1 | 3.86 | 1.28 | 8 | 3 | 0 | 84.1 | 3.31 | 1.25 | 9.4 | 2.7 | 0.4 | .670 | .713 | .517 |
| Mahay R | 41 | 0 | 1 | 1 | 2 | 0 | 34.0 | 33 | 5 | 3.44 | 1.21 | 25 | 8 | 0 | 1 | 0 | 26.0 | 3.81 | 1.19 | 1 | 0 | 0 | 8.0 | 2.25 | 1.25 | 6.6 | 2.1 | 1.3 | .675 | .820 | .520 |
| Manship J | 13 | 1 | 2 | 1 | 0 | 0 | 29.0 | 34 | 3 | 5.28 | 1.38 | 21 | 6 | 0 | 0 | 0 | 12.2 | 2.84 | 1.03 | 2 | 1 | 0 | 16.1 | 7.16 | 1.65 | 6.5 | 1.9 | 0.9 | .773 | .861 | .676 |
| Mijares J | 47 | 0 | 1 | 1 | 9 | 0 | 32.2 | 34 | 4 | 3.31 | 1.32 | 28 | 9 | 1 | 0 | 0 | 18.2 | 2.41 | 1.18 | 0 | 1 | 0 | 14.0 | 4.50 | 1.50 | 7.7 | 2.5 | 1.1 | .768 | .761 | .776 |
| Neshek P | 11 | 0 | 0 | 1 | 1 | 0 | 9.0 | 7 | 1 | 5.00 | 1.67 | 9 | 8 | 0 | 0 | 0 | 4.1 | 4.15 | 0.92 | 0 | 1 | 0 | 4.2 | 5.79 | 2.36 | 9.0 | 8.0 | 1.0 | .696 | .686 | .730 |
| Pavano C | 32 | 32 | 17 | 11 | 0 | 0 | 221.0 | 227 | 24 | 3.75 | 1.19 | 117 | 37 | 10 | 6 | 0 | 125.2 | 3.58 | 1.05 | 7 | 5 | 0 | 95.1 | 3.97 | 1.38 | 4.8 | 1.5 | 1.0 | .717 | .661 | .777 |
| Perkins G | 13 | 1 | 1 | 1 | 0 | 0 | 21.2 | 29 | 3 | 5.82 | 1.57 | 14 | 5 | -- | -- | -- | ---- | ---- | --- | 1 | 1 | 0 | 21.2 | 5.82 | 1.57 | 5.8 | 2.1 | 1.2 | .938 | 1.080 | .657 |
| Rauch J | 59 | 0 | 3 | 1 | 2 | 21 | 57.2 | 61 | 3 | 3.12 | 1.30 | 46 | 14 | 2 | 1 | 20 | 34.0 | 2.38 | 1.15 | 1 | 0 | 1 | 23.2 | 4.18 | 1.52 | 7.2 | 2.2 | 0.5 | .671 | .607 | .739 |
| Slama A | 5 | 0 | 0 | 1 | 0 | 0 | 4.2 | 6 | 1 | 7.71 | 2.36 | 5 | 5 | -- | -- | -- | ---- | ---- | --- | 0 | 1 | 0 | 4.2 | 7.71 | 2.36 | 9.6 | 9.6 | 1.9 | .990 | .657 | 1.389 |
| Slowey K | 30 | 28 | 13 | 6 | 0 | 0 | 155.2 | 172 | 21 | 4.45 | 1.29 | 116 | 29 | 8 | 5 | 0 | 97.0 | 4.64 | 1.36 | 5 | 1 | 0 | 58.2 | 4.14 | 1.18 | 6.7 | 1.7 | 1.2 | .770 | .807 | .734 |

| Hitters | New York Mets 2010 | | | | | | | | | | | | | 1st Half | | | | | | 2nd Half | | | | | | Rates | | | | | Productiveness | | |
|---|---|---|---|---|---|---|---|---|---|---|---|---|---|---|---|---|---|---|---|---|---|---|---|---|---|---|---|---|---|---|---|---|---|
| | G | AB | R | H | 2B | 3B | HR | RBI | BA | OBP | SLG | SB | CS | AB | R | HR | BI | BA | SB | AB | R | HR | BI | BA | SB | CT% | H% | BB% | Bash | GB% | OPS | vs RH | vs LH |
| Arias J | 22 | 30 | 5 | 6 | 1 | 0 | 0 | 4 | .200 | .250 | .233 | 0 | 0 | --- | -- | -- | -- | --- | -- | 30 | 5 | 0 | 4 | .200 | 0 | 80% | 25% | 6% | 1.2 | 46% | .483 | .310 | .944 |
| Barajas R | 74 | 249 | 30 | 56 | 11 | 0 | 12 | 34 | .225 | .263 | .414 | 0 | 0 | 227 | 29 | 11 | 32 | .238 | 0 | 22 | 1 | 1 | 2 | .091 | 0 | 84% | 27% | 3% | 1.8 | 21% | .677 | .737 | .482 |
| Bay J | 95 | 348 | 48 | 90 | 20 | 6 | 6 | 47 | .259 | .347 | .402 | 10 | 0 | 309 | 46 | 6 | 44 | .265 | 10 | 39 | 2 | 0 | 3 | .205 | 0 | 74% | 35% | 11% | 1.6 | 36% | .749 | .748 | .750 |
| Beltran C | 64 | 220 | 21 | 56 | 11 | 3 | 7 | 27 | .255 | .341 | .427 | 3 | 1 | --- | -- | -- | -- | --- | -- | 220 | 21 | 7 | 27 | .255 | 3 | 82% | 31% | 12% | 1.7 | 43% | .768 | .701 | 1.009 |
| Blanco H | 50 | 130 | 10 | 28 | 5 | 0 | 2 | 8 | .215 | .271 | .300 | 1 | 0 | 74 | 9 | 2 | 7 | .284 | 1 | 56 | 1 | 0 | 1 | .125 | 0 | 80% | 27% | 8% | 1.4 | 35% | .571 | .629 | .451 |
| Carter C | 100 | 167 | 15 | 44 | 9 | 0 | 4 | 24 | .263 | .317 | .389 | 1 | 2 | 70 | 7 | 2 | 12 | .257 | 0 | 97 | 8 | 2 | 12 | .268 | 1 | 90% | 29% | 7% | 1.5 | 39% | .706 | .724 | .286 |
| Castillo L | 86 | 247 | 28 | 58 | 4 | 2 | 0 | 17 | .235 | .337 | .267 | 8 | 3 | 141 | 13 | 0 | 14 | .241 | 7 | 106 | 15 | 0 | 3 | .226 | 1 | 90% | 26% | 13% | 1.1 | 68% | .604 | .602 | .608 |
| Catalanotto F | 25 | 25 | 2 | 4 | 1 | 0 | 0 | 1 | .160 | .192 | .200 | 0 | 0 | 25 | 2 | 0 | 1 | .160 | 0 | --- | -- | -- | -- | --- | -- | 80% | 20% | 4% | 1.3 | 60% | .392 | .408 | .000 |
| Cora A | 62 | 169 | 14 | 35 | 6 | 3 | 0 | 20 | .207 | .265 | .278 | 4 | 1 | 144 | 14 | 0 | 20 | .222 | 2 | 25 | 0 | 0 | 0 | .120 | 2 | 91% | 23% | 5% | 1.3 | 48% | .543 | .568 | .401 |
| Davis I | 147 | 523 | 73 | 138 | 33 | 1 | 19 | 71 | .264 | .351 | .440 | 3 | 2 | 275 | 43 | 11 | 40 | .258 | 1 | 248 | 30 | 8 | 31 | .270 | 2 | 74% | 36% | 12% | 1.7 | 44% | .791 | .787 | .805 |
| Duda L | 29 | 84 | 11 | 17 | 6 | 0 | 4 | 13 | .202 | .261 | .417 | 0 | 0 | --- | -- | -- | -- | --- | -- | 84 | 11 | 4 | 13 | .202 | 0 | 74% | 27% | 7% | 2.1 | 35% | .678 | .749 | .421 |
| Evans N | 20 | 36 | 5 | 11 | 3 | 0 | 1 | 5 | .306 | .324 | .472 | 0 | 0 | 2 | 0 | 0 | 0 | .000 | 0 | 34 | 5 | 1 | 5 | .324 | 0 | 72% | 42% | 3% | 1.5 | 50% | .797 | .533 | .983 |
| Feliciano J | 54 | 108 | 12 | 25 | 4 | 1 | 0 | 3 | .231 | .276 | .287 | 1 | 0 | 55 | 7 | 0 | 2 | .291 | 1 | 53 | 5 | 0 | 1 | .170 | 0 | 89% | 26% | 5% | 1.2 | 63% | .563 | .588 | .400 |
| Francoeur J | 124 | 401 | 43 | 95 | 16 | 2 | 11 | 54 | .237 | .293 | .369 | 8 | 2 | 293 | 34 | 8 | 42 | .253 | 7 | 108 | 9 | 3 | 12 | .194 | 1 | 81% | 29% | 6% | 1.6 | 42% | .662 | .629 | .761 |
| Hernandez L | 17 | 44 | 4 | 11 | 1 | 0 | 2 | 6 | .250 | .298 | .409 | 1 | 0 | --- | -- | -- | -- | --- | -- | 44 | 4 | 2 | 6 | .250 | 1 | 84% | 30% | 4% | 1.6 | 49% | .707 | .584 | 1.500 |
| Hessman M | 32 | 55 | 6 | 7 | 2 | 1 | 1 | 6 | .127 | .262 | .255 | 0 | 0 | --- | -- | -- | -- | --- | -- | 55 | 6 | 1 | 6 | .127 | 0 | 58% | 22% | 12% | 2.0 | 41% | .516 | .284 | .757 |
| Jacobs M | 7 | 24 | 1 | 5 | 1 | 0 | 1 | 2 | .208 | .296 | .375 | 0 | 0 | 24 | 1 | 1 | 2 | .208 | 0 | --- | -- | -- | -- | --- | -- | 71% | 29% | 11% | 1.8 | 29% | .671 | .699 | .000 |
| Martinez F | 7 | 18 | 1 | 3 | 0 | 0 | 0 | 2 | .167 | .273 | .167 | 0 | 1 | --- | -- | -- | -- | --- | -- | 18 | 1 | 0 | 2 | .167 | 0 | 72% | 23% | 5% | 1.0 | 54% | .439 | .439 | ---- |
| Matthews Jr. G | 36 | 58 | 9 | 11 | 3 | 0 | 0 | 1 | .190 | .266 | .241 | 1 | 0 | 58 | 9 | 0 | 1 | .190 | 1 | --- | -- | -- | -- | --- | -- | 59% | 32% | 9% | 1.3 | 50% | .507 | .544 | .393 |
| Nickeas M | 5 | 10 | 0 | 2 | 0 | 0 | 0 | 0 | .200 | .200 | .200 | 0 | 0 | --- | -- | -- | -- | --- | -- | 10 | 0 | 0 | 0 | .200 | 0 | 50% | 40% | 0% | 1.0 | 40% | .400 | .571 | .000 |
| Pagan A | 151 | 579 | 80 | 168 | 31 | 7 | 11 | 69 | .290 | .340 | .425 | 37 | 9 | 298 | 46 | 6 | 40 | .315 | 19 | 281 | 34 | 5 | 29 | .263 | 18 | 83% | 35% | 7% | 1.5 | 35% | .765 | .788 | .692 |
| Reyes J | 133 | 563 | 83 | 159 | 29 | 10 | 11 | 54 | .282 | .321 | .428 | 30 | 10 | 324 | 52 | 6 | 33 | .275 | 19 | 239 | 31 | 5 | 21 | .293 | 11 | 89% | 32% | 5% | 1.5 | 42% | .749 | .750 | .744 |
| Tatis F | 41 | 65 | 6 | 12 | 4 | 0 | 2 | 6 | .185 | .254 | .338 | 0 | 0 | 65 | 6 | 2 | 6 | .185 | 0 | --- | -- | -- | -- | --- | -- | 71% | 26% | 8% | 1.8 | 39% | .592 | .321 | .722 |
| Tejada R | 78 | 216 | 28 | 46 | 12 | 0 | 1 | 15 | .213 | .305 | .282 | 2 | 2 | 92 | 16 | 0 | 5 | .217 | 1 | 124 | 12 | 1 | 10 | .210 | 1 | 82% | 26% | 9% | 1.3 | 40% | .588 | .541 | .729 |
| Thole J | 73 | 202 | 17 | 56 | 7 | 1 | 3 | 17 | .277 | .357 | .366 | 1 | 0 | 17 | 0 | 0 | 5 | .529 | 0 | 185 | 17 | 3 | 12 | .254 | 1 | 88% | 32% | 11% | 1.3 | 44% | .723 | .783 | .343 |
| Turner J | 4 | 8 | 1 | 1 | 1 | 0 | 0 | 0 | .125 | .222 | .250 | 0 | 0 | --- | -- | -- | -- | --- | -- | 8 | 1 | 0 | 0 | .125 | 0 | 100% | 13% | 11% | 2.0 | 38% | .472 | .750 | .200 |
| Wright D | 157 | 587 | 87 | 166 | 36 | 3 | 29 | 103 | .283 | .354 | .503 | 19 | 11 | 325 | 52 | 14 | 65 | .314 | 15 | 262 | 35 | 15 | 38 | .244 | 4 | 73% | 39% | 10% | 1.8 | 39% | .856 | .798 | 1.066 |

| Pitchers | New York Mets 2010 | | | | | | | | | | | | | 1st Half | | | | | | 2nd Half | | | | | | Rates | | | Productiveness | | |
|---|---|---|---|---|---|---|---|---|---|---|---|---|---|---|---|---|---|---|---|---|---|---|---|---|---|---|---|---|---|---|---|
| | G | GS | W | L | Hld | Sv | IP | H | HR | ERA | WHIP | K | BB | W | L | Sv | IP | ERA | WHIP | W | L | Sv | IP | ERA | WHIP | K/9 | BB/9 | HR/9 | opOPS | vs RH | vs LH |
| Acosta M | 41 | 0 | 3 | 2 | 2 | 1 | 39.2 | 30 | 4 | 2.95 | 1.21 | 42 | 18 | 1 | 1 | 0 | 12.0 | 3.00 | 1.33 | 2 | 1 | 1 | 27.2 | 2.93 | 1.16 | 9.5 | 4.1 | 0.9 | .636 | .707 | .473 |
| Dessens E | 53 | 0 | 4 | 2 | 11 | 0 | 47.0 | 41 | 4 | 2.30 | 1.21 | 16 | 16 | 2 | 1 | 0 | 18.1 | 1.47 | 0.98 | 2 | 1 | 0 | 28.2 | 2.83 | 1.36 | 3.1 | 3.1 | 0.8 | .694 | .709 | .664 |
| Dickey R | 27 | 26 | 11 | 9 | 1 | 0 | 174.1 | 165 | 13 | 2.84 | 1.19 | 104 | 42 | 6 | 2 | 0 | 65.0 | 2.77 | 1.31 | 5 | 7 | 0 | 109.1 | 2.88 | 1.12 | 5.4 | 2.2 | 0.7 | .660 | .700 | .605 |
| Feliciano P | 92 | 0 | 3 | 6 | 23 | 0 | 62.2 | 66 | 1 | 3.30 | 1.53 | 56 | 30 | 2 | 4 | 0 | 34.2 | 2.34 | 1.62 | 1 | 2 | 0 | 28.0 | 4.50 | 1.43 | 8.0 | 4.3 | 0.1 | .702 | .831 | .574 |
| Gee D | 5 | 5 | 2 | 2 | 0 | 0 | 33.0 | 25 | 2 | 2.18 | 1.21 | 17 | 15 | -- | -- | -- | ---- | ---- | --- | 2 | 2 | 0 | 33.0 | 2.18 | 1.21 | 4.6 | 4.1 | 0.5 | .631 | .618 | .653 |
| Green S | 11 | 0 | 0 | 0 | 2 | 0 | 9.1 | 7 | 1 | 3.86 | 1.61 | 12 | 8 | 0 | 0 | 0 | 1.0 | 9.00 | 2.00 | 0 | 0 | 0 | 8.1 | 3.24 | 1.56 | 11.6 | 7.7 | 1.0 | .719 | .644 | .970 |
| Igarashi R | 34 | 0 | 1 | 1 | 2 | 0 | 30.1 | 29 | 4 | 7.12 | 1.55 | 25 | 18 | 0 | 1 | 0 | 19.1 | 7.91 | 1.71 | 1 | 0 | 0 | 11.0 | 5.73 | 1.27 | 7.4 | 5.3 | 1.2 | .796 | .724 | .915 |
| Maine J | 9 | 9 | 1 | 3 | 0 | 0 | 39.2 | 47 | 8 | 6.13 | 1.82 | 39 | 25 | 1 | 3 | 0 | 39.2 | 6.13 | 1.82 | -- | -- | -- | ---- | ---- | --- | 8.8 | 5.7 | 1.8 | .904 | 1.035 | .688 |
| Mejia J | 33 | 3 | 0 | 4 | 2 | 0 | 39.0 | 46 | 3 | 4.62 | 1.69 | 22 | 20 | 0 | 2 | 0 | 27.2 | 3.25 | 1.59 | 0 | 2 | 0 | 11.1 | 7.94 | 1.94 | 5.1 | 4.6 | 0.7 | .773 | .882 | .590 |
| Misch P | 12 | 6 | 0 | 4 | 0 | 0 | 37.2 | 43 | 4 | 3.82 | 1.25 | 23 | 4 | -- | -- | -- | ---- | ---- | --- | 0 | 4 | 0 | 37.2 | 3.82 | 1.25 | 5.5 | 1.0 | 1.0 | .703 | .671 | .814 |
| Niese J | 30 | 30 | 9 | 10 | 0 | 0 | 173.2 | 192 | 20 | 4.20 | 1.46 | 148 | 62 | 6 | 3 | 0 | 89.2 | 3.61 | 1.36 | 3 | 7 | 0 | 84.0 | 4.82 | 1.57 | 7.7 | 3.2 | 1.0 | .783 | .772 | .831 |
| Nieve F | 40 | 1 | 2 | 4 | 6 | 0 | 42.0 | 37 | 10 | 6.00 | 1.40 | 38 | 22 | 2 | 3 | 0 | 37.2 | 5.26 | 1.35 | 0 | 1 | 0 | 4.1 | 12.46 | 1.85 | 8.1 | 4.7 | 2.1 | .821 | .730 | 1.016 |
| Parnell B | 41 | 0 | 0 | 1 | 9 | 0 | 35.0 | 41 | 1 | 2.83 | 1.40 | 33 | 8 | 0 | 0 | 0 | 11.0 | 1.64 | 1.36 | 0 | 1 | 0 | 24.0 | 3.38 | 1.42 | 8.5 | 2.1 | 0.3 | .686 | .614 | .806 |
| Pelfrey M | 34 | 33 | 15 | 9 | 0 | 1 | 204.0 | 213 | 12 | 3.66 | 1.38 | 113 | 68 | 10 | 4 | 1 | 113.0 | 3.58 | 1.44 | 5 | 5 | 0 | 91.0 | 3.76 | 1.30 | 5.0 | 3.0 | 0.5 | .735 | .690 | .776 |
| Perez O | 17 | 7 | 0 | 5 | 0 | 0 | 46.1 | 54 | 9 | 6.80 | 2.07 | 37 | 42 | 0 | 3 | 0 | 38.2 | 6.28 | 1.97 | 0 | 2 | 0 | 7.2 | 9.39 | 2.61 | 7.2 | 8.2 | 1.7 | .935 | .956 | .863 |
| Rodriguez F | 53 | 0 | 4 | 2 | 0 | 25 | 57.1 | 45 | 3 | 2.20 | 1.15 | 67 | 21 | 2 | 2 | 21 | 44.0 | 2.45 | 1.27 | 2 | 0 | 4 | 13.1 | 1.35 | 0.75 | 10.5 | 3.3 | 0.5 | .597 | .531 | .680 |
| Santana J | 29 | 29 | 11 | 9 | 0 | 0 | 199.0 | 179 | 16 | 2.98 | 1.18 | 144 | 55 | 7 | 5 | 0 | 127.0 | 2.98 | 1.20 | 4 | 4 | 0 | 72.0 | 3.00 | 1.14 | 6.5 | 2.5 | 0.7 | .648 | .627 | .706 |
| Stoner T | 1 | 0 | 0 | 1 | 0 | 0 | 2.1 | 3 | 0 | 3.86 | 1.71 | 0 | 1 | 0 | 1 | 0 | 2.1 | 3.86 | 1.71 | -- | -- | -- | ---- | ---- | --- | 0.0 | 3.9 | 0.0 | .864 | 1.069 | .000 |
| Takahashi H | 53 | 12 | 10 | 6 | 3 | 8 | 122.0 | 116 | 13 | 3.61 | 1.30 | 114 | 43 | 7 | 3 | 0 | 78.0 | 4.15 | 1.41 | 3 | 3 | 8 | 44.0 | 2.66 | 1.11 | 8.4 | 3.2 | 1.0 | .712 | .768 | .544 |
| Valdes R | 38 | 1 | 3 | 3 | 1 | 1 | 58.2 | 59 | 7 | 4.91 | 1.47 | 56 | 27 | 2 | 2 | 1 | 30.1 | 5.04 | 1.55 | 1 | 1 | 0 | 28.1 | 4.76 | 1.38 | 8.6 | 4.1 | 1.1 | .791 | .666 | .991 |

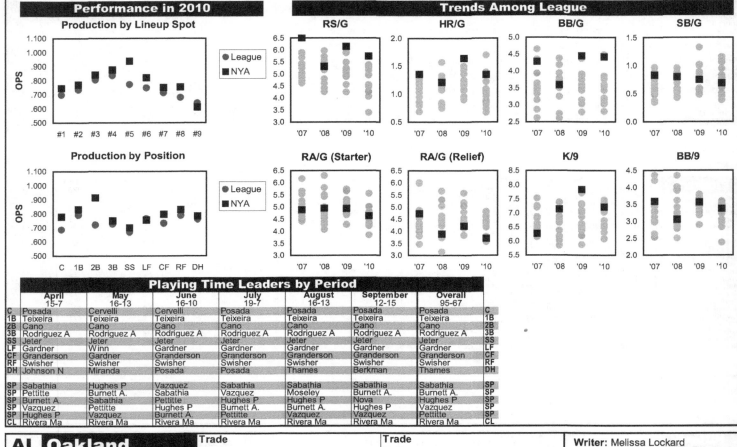

## Performance in 2010
### Production by Lineup Spot
### Production by Position

## Trends Among League
### RS/G
### HR/G
### BB/G
### SB/G
### RA/G (Starter)
### RA/G (Relief)
### K/9
### BB/9

### Playing Time Leaders by Period

| | April 15-7 | May 16-13 | June 16-10 | July 19-7 | August 16-13 | September 12-15 | Overall 95-67 | |
|---|---|---|---|---|---|---|---|---|
| C | Posada | Cervelli | Cervelli | Posada | Posada | Posada | Posada | C |
| 1B | Teixeira | Teixeira | Teixeira | Teixeira | Teixeira | Teixeira | Teixeira | 1B |
| 2B | Cano | Cano | Cano | Cano | Cano | Cano | Cano | 2B |
| 3B | Rodriguez A | Rodriguez A | Rodriguez A | Rodriguez A | Rodriguez A | Rodriguez A | Rodriguez A | 3B |
| SS | Jeter | Jeter | Jeter | Jeter | Jeter | Jeter | Jeter | SS |
| LF | Gardner | Winn | Gardner | Gardner | Gardner | Gardner | Gardner | LF |
| CF | Granderson | Gardner | Granderson | Granderson | Granderson | Granderson | Granderson | CF |
| RF | Swisher | Swisher | Swisher | Swisher | Swisher | Swisher | Swisher | RF |
| DH | Johnson N | Miranda | Posada | Posada | Thames | Berkman | Thames | DH |
| | | | | | | | | |
| SP | Sabathia | Hughes P | Vazquez | Sabathia | Sabathia | Sabathia | Sabathia | SP |
| SP | Pettitte | Burnett A. | Sabathia | Vazquez | Moseley | Burnett A. | Burnett A. | SP |
| SP | Burnett A. | Sabathia | Pettitte | Hughes P | Hughes P | Nova | Hughes P | SP |
| SP | Vazquez | Pettitte | Hughes P | Burnett A. | Burnett A. | Hughes P | Vazquez | SP |
| SP | Hughes P | Vazquez | Burnett A. | Pettitte | Vazquez | Vazquez | Pettitte | SP |
| CL | Rivera Ma | Rivera Ma | Rivera Ma | Rivera Ma | Rivera Ma | Rivera Ma | Rivera Ma | CL |

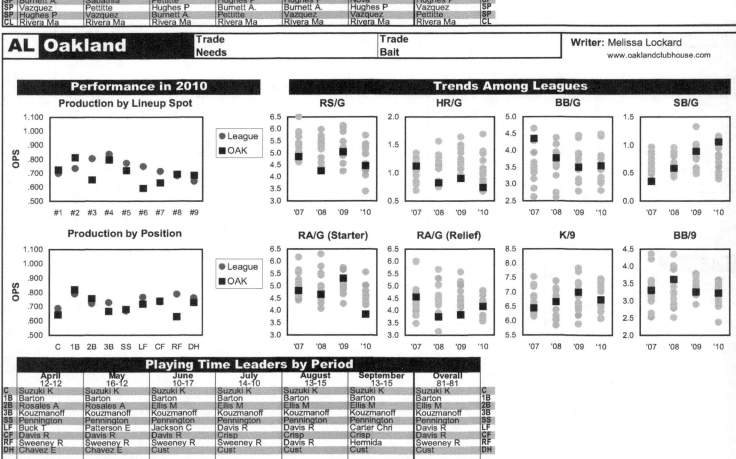

## Performance in 2010
### Production by Lineup Spot
### Production by Position

## Trends Among Leagues
### RS/G
### HR/G
### BB/G
### SB/G
### RA/G (Starter)
### RA/G (Relief)
### K/9
### BB/9

### Playing Time Leaders by Period

| | April 12-12 | May 16-12 | June 16-12 | July 10-17 | August 13-15 | September 13-15 | Overall 81-81 | |
|---|---|---|---|---|---|---|---|---|
| C | Suzuki K | Suzuki K | Suzuki K | Suzuki K | Suzuki K | Suzuki K | Suzuki K | C |
| 1B | Barton | Barton | Barton | Barton | Barton | Barton | Barton | 1B |
| 2B | Rosales A | Rosales A | Ellis M | Ellis M | Ellis M | Ellis M | Ellis M | 2B |
| 3B | Kouzmanoff | Kouzmanoff | Kouzmanoff | Kouzmanoff | Kouzmanoff | Kouzmanoff | Kouzmanoff | 3B |
| SS | Pennington | Pennington | Pennington | Pennington | Pennington | Pennington | Pennington | SS |
| LF | Buck T | Patterson E | Jackson C | Davis R | Davis R | Carter Chri | Davis R | LF |
| CF | Davis R | Davis R | Davis R | Crisp | Crisp | Crisp | Davis R | CF |
| RF | Sweeney R | Sweeney R | Sweeney R | Sweeney R | Davis R | Hermida | Sweeney R | RF |
| DH | Chavez E | Chavez E | Cust | Cust | Cust | Cust | Cust | DH |
| | | | | | | | | |
| SP | Braden | Braden | Sheets | Cahill | Cahill | Anderson Bre | Gonzalez G | SP |
| SP | Duchscherer | Gonzalez G | Gonzalez G | Mazzaro | Gonzalez G | Braden | Cahill | SP |
| SP | Sheets | Cahill | Cahill | Gonzalez G | Braden | Gonzalez G | Braden | SP |
| SP | Anderson Bre | Sheets | Mazzaro | Braden | Mazzaro | Cahill | Sheets | SP |
| SP | Gonzalez G | Ross T | Braden | Sheets | Anderson Bre | Cramer | Anderson Bre | SP |
| CL | Bailey A | Bailey A | Bailey A | Bailey A | Wuertz | Bailey A | Bailey A | CL |

| Hitters | New York Yankees 2010 | | | | | | | | | | | | | 1st Half | | | | | | 2nd Half | | | | | | Rates | | | | | Productiveness | | |
|---|---|---|---|---|---|---|---|---|---|---|---|---|---|---|---|---|---|---|---|---|---|---|---|---|---|---|---|---|---|---|---|---|---|
| | G | AB | R | H | 2B | 3B | HR | RBI | BA | OBP | SLG | SB | CS | AB | R | HR | BI | BA | SB | AB | R | HR | BI | BA | SB | CT% | H% | BB% | Bash | GB% | OPS | vs RH | vs LH |
| Berkman L | 37 | 106 | 9 | 27 | 7 | 0 | 1 | 9 | .255 | .358 | .349 | 0 | 0 | --- | -- | -- | -- | --- | -- | 106 | 9 | 1 | 9 | .255 | 0 | 86% | 30% | 13% | 1.4 | 48% | .707 | .775 | .367 |
| Cano R | 160 | 626 | 103 | 200 | 41 | 3 | 29 | 109 | .319 | .381 | .534 | 3 | 2 | 342 | 61 | 16 | 58 | .336 | 2 | 284 | 42 | 13 | 51 | .299 | 1 | 88% | 36% | 8% | 1.7 | 45% | .914 | .944 | .857 |
| Cervelli F | 93 | 266 | 27 | 72 | 11 | 3 | 0 | 38 | .271 | .359 | .335 | 1 | 1 | 177 | 15 | 0 | 30 | .266 | 0 | 89 | 12 | 0 | 8 | .281 | 1 | 84% | 32% | 10% | 1.2 | 47% | .694 | .617 | .846 |
| Curtis C | 31 | 59 | 7 | 11 | 3 | 0 | 1 | 8 | .186 | .250 | .288 | 0 | 0 | 25 | 1 | 0 | 4 | .200 | 0 | 34 | 6 | 1 | 4 | .176 | 0 | 75% | 25% | 6% | 1.5 | 48% | .538 | .521 | .633 |
| Gardner B | 150 | 477 | 97 | 132 | 20 | 7 | 5 | 47 | .277 | .383 | .379 | 47 | 9 | 275 | 56 | 5 | 29 | .309 | 25 | 202 | 41 | 0 | 18 | .233 | 22 | 79% | 35% | 14% | 1.4 | 52% | .762 | .778 | .725 |
| Golson G | 24 | 23 | 3 | 6 | 2 | 0 | 0 | 2 | .261 | .261 | .348 | 0 | 2 | 5 | 0 | 0 | 0 | .400 | 0 | 18 | 3 | 0 | 2 | .222 | 0 | 87% | 30% | 0% | 1.3 | 30% | .609 | .000 | .824 |
| Granderson C | 136 | 466 | 76 | 115 | 17 | 7 | 24 | 67 | .247 | .324 | .468 | 12 | 2 | 225 | 32 | 7 | 24 | .240 | 7 | 241 | 44 | 17 | 43 | .253 | 5 | 75% | 33% | 10% | 1.9 | 33% | .792 | .866 | .647 |
| Huffman C | 9 | 18 | 1 | 3 | 0 | 0 | 0 | 2 | .167 | .286 | .167 | 0 | 0 | 18 | 1 | 0 | 2 | .167 | 0 | --- | -- | -- | -- | --- | -- | 72% | 23% | 10% | 1.0 | 46% | .452 | .730 | .258 |
| Jeter D | 157 | 663 | 111 | 179 | 30 | 3 | 10 | 67 | .270 | .340 | .370 | 18 | 5 | 365 | 60 | 8 | 43 | .274 | 9 | 298 | 51 | 2 | 24 | .265 | 9 | 84% | 32% | 8% | 1.4 | 65% | .710 | .632 | .874 |
| Johnson N | 24 | 72 | 12 | 12 | 4 | 0 | 2 | 8 | .167 | .388 | .306 | 0 | 1 | 72 | 12 | 2 | 8 | .167 | 0 | --- | -- | -- | -- | --- | -- | 68% | 24% | 24% | 1.8 | 37% | .693 | .697 | .679 |
| Kearns A | 36 | 102 | 13 | 24 | 3 | 0 | 2 | 7 | .235 | .345 | .324 | 0 | 0 | --- | -- | -- | -- | --- | -- | 102 | 13 | 2 | 7 | .235 | 0 | 63% | 38% | 10% | 1.4 | 47% | .668 | .572 | .779 |
| Miranda J | 33 | 64 | 7 | 14 | 2 | 1 | 3 | 10 | .219 | .296 | .422 | 0 | 0 | 46 | 6 | 2 | 7 | .217 | 0 | 18 | 1 | 1 | 3 | .222 | 0 | 81% | 27% | 10% | 1.9 | 33% | .718 | .717 | .708 |
| Moeller C | 9 | 14 | 2 | 3 | 3 | 0 | 0 | 0 | .214 | .267 | .429 | 0 | 0 | 11 | 2 | 0 | 0 | .182 | 0 | 3 | 0 | 0 | 0 | .333 | 0 | 71% | 30% | 7% | 2.0 | 30% | .695 | .422 | 1.200 |
| Nunez E | 30 | 50 | 12 | 14 | 1 | 0 | 1 | 7 | .280 | .321 | .360 | 5 | 0 | --- | -- | -- | -- | --- | -- | 50 | 12 | 1 | 7 | .280 | 5 | 96% | 29% | 6% | 1.3 | 65% | .681 | .662 | .692 |
| Pena R | 85 | 154 | 18 | 35 | 1 | 1 | 0 | 18 | .227 | .258 | .247 | 7 | 1 | 82 | 12 | 0 | 10 | .195 | 3 | 72 | 6 | 0 | 8 | .264 | 4 | 82% | 28% | 4% | 1.1 | 41% | .504 | .545 | .343 |
| Posada J | 120 | 383 | 49 | 95 | 23 | 1 | 18 | 57 | .248 | .357 | .454 | 3 | 1 | 196 | 26 | 9 | 29 | .265 | 0 | 187 | 23 | 9 | 28 | .230 | 3 | 74% | 33% | 13% | 1.8 | 43% | .811 | .799 | .833 |
| Rodriguez A | 137 | 522 | 74 | 141 | 29 | 2 | 30 | 125 | .270 | .341 | .506 | 4 | 3 | 312 | 46 | 14 | 70 | .269 | 2 | 210 | 28 | 16 | 55 | .271 | 2 | 81% | 33% | 10% | 1.9 | 47% | .847 | .883 | .755 |
| Russo K | 31 | 49 | 5 | 9 | 2 | 0 | 0 | 4 | .184 | .245 | .224 | 1 | 0 | 48 | 5 | 0 | 4 | .188 | 1 | 1 | 0 | 0 | 0 | .000 | 0 | 82% | 23% | 6% | 1.2 | 43% | .470 | .451 | .481 |
| Swisher N | 150 | 566 | 91 | 163 | 33 | 3 | 29 | 89 | .288 | .359 | .511 | 1 | 2 | 315 | 55 | 15 | 49 | .298 | 1 | 251 | 36 | 14 | 40 | .275 | 0 | 75% | 38% | 9% | 1.8 | 36% | .870 | .877 | .848 |
| Teixeira M | 158 | 601 | 113 | 154 | 36 | 0 | 33 | 108 | .256 | .365 | .481 | 0 | 1 | 342 | 63 | 17 | 60 | .254 | 0 | 259 | 50 | 16 | 48 | .259 | 0 | 80% | 32% | 13% | 1.9 | 36% | .846 | .804 | .940 |
| Thames M | 82 | 212 | 22 | 61 | 7 | 0 | 12 | 33 | .288 | .350 | .491 | 0 | 0 | 85 | 9 | 3 | 13 | .294 | 0 | 127 | 13 | 9 | 20 | .283 | 0 | 71% | 40% | 8% | 1.7 | 33% | .841 | .896 | .806 |
| Winn R | 29 | 61 | 7 | 13 | 0 | 1 | 1 | 8 | .213 | .300 | .295 | 1 | 0 | 61 | 7 | 1 | 8 | .213 | 1 | --- | -- | -- | -- | --- | -- | 75% | 28% | 11% | 1.4 | 50% | .595 | .716 | .000 |

| Pitchers | New York Yankees 2010 | | | | | | | | | | | | | 1st Half | | | | | | 2nd Half | | | | | | Rates | | | Productiveness | | |
|---|---|---|---|---|---|---|---|---|---|---|---|---|---|---|---|---|---|---|---|---|---|---|---|---|---|---|---|---|---|---|---|
| | G | GS | W | L | Hld | Sv | IP | H | HR | ERA | WHIP | K | BB | W | L | Sv | IP | ERA | WHIP | W | L | Sv | IP | ERA | WHIP | K/9 | BB/9 | HR/9 | opOPS | vs RH | vs LH |
| Aceves A | 10 | 0 | 3 | 0 | 1 | 1 | 12.0 | 10 | 1 | 3.00 | 1.17 | 2 | 4 | 3 | 0 | 1 | 12.0 | 3.00 | 1.17 | -- | -- | -- | ---- | ---- | --- | 1.5 | 3.0 | 0.8 | .575 | .565 | .585 |
| Albaladejo J | 10 | 0 | 0 | 0 | 0 | 0 | 11.1 | 9 | 1 | 3.97 | 1.50 | 8 | 8 | -- | -- | -- | ---- | ---- | --- | 0 | 0 | 0 | 11.1 | 3.97 | 1.50 | 6.4 | 6.4 | 0.8 | .713 | .821 | .586 |
| Burnett A | 33 | 33 | 10 | 15 | 0 | 0 | 186.2 | 204 | 25 | 5.26 | 1.51 | 145 | 78 | 7 | 7 | 0 | 108.0 | 4.75 | 1.47 | 3 | 8 | 0 | 78.2 | 5.95 | 1.56 | 7.0 | 3.8 | 1.2 | .824 | .827 | .820 |
| Chamberlain J | 73 | 0 | 3 | 4 | 26 | 3 | 71.2 | 71 | 6 | 4.40 | 1.30 | 77 | 22 | 1 | 4 | 2 | 37.1 | 5.79 | 1.50 | 2 | 0 | 1 | 34.1 | 2.88 | 1.08 | 9.7 | 2.8 | 0.8 | .693 | .675 | .713 |
| Gaudin C | 30 | 0 | 1 | 2 | 0 | 0 | 48.0 | 46 | 11 | 4.50 | 1.38 | 33 | 20 | 0 | 1 | 0 | 17.1 | 4.67 | 1.38 | 1 | 1 | 0 | 30.2 | 4.40 | 1.37 | 6.2 | 3.8 | 2.1 | .824 | .724 | .908 |
| Hughes P | 31 | 29 | 18 | 8 | 0 | 0 | 176.1 | 162 | 25 | 4.19 | 1.25 | 146 | 58 | 11 | 2 | 0 | 101.0 | 3.65 | 1.18 | 7 | 6 | 0 | 75.1 | 4.90 | 1.34 | 7.5 | 3.0 | 1.3 | .702 | .674 | .728 |
| Logan B | 51 | 0 | 2 | 0 | 13 | 0 | 40.0 | 34 | 3 | 2.93 | 1.35 | 38 | 20 | 0 | 0 | 0 | 18.1 | 3.93 | 1.75 | 2 | 0 | 0 | 21.2 | 2.08 | 1.02 | 8.6 | 4.5 | 0.7 | .659 | .842 | .501 |
| Marte D | 30 | 0 | 0 | 0 | 9 | 0 | 17.2 | 10 | 2 | 4.08 | 1.19 | 12 | 11 | 0 | 0 | 0 | 17.2 | 4.08 | 1.19 | -- | -- | -- | ---- | ---- | --- | 6.1 | 5.6 | 1.0 | .580 | .753 | .468 |
| Melancon M | 2 | 0 | 0 | 0 | 0 | 0 | 4.0 | 7 | 1 | 9.00 | 1.75 | 3 | 0 | 0 | 0 | 0 | 4.0 | 9.00 | 1.75 | -- | -- | -- | ---- | ---- | --- | 6.8 | 0.0 | 2.3 | .980 | 1.273 | .536 |
| Mitre S | 27 | 3 | 0 | 3 | 1 | 1 | 54.0 | 43 | 7 | 3.33 | 1.09 | 29 | 16 | 0 | 1 | 0 | 25.0 | 2.88 | 1.00 | 0 | 2 | 1 | 29.0 | 3.72 | 1.17 | 4.8 | 2.7 | 1.2 | .666 | .708 | .629 |
| Moseley D | 16 | 9 | 4 | 4 | 0 | 0 | 65.1 | 66 | 13 | 4.96 | 1.42 | 33 | 27 | 0 | 0 | 0 | 3.0 | 3.00 | 0.33 | 4 | 4 | 0 | 62.1 | 5.05 | 1.48 | 4.5 | 3.7 | 1.8 | .807 | .747 | .862 |
| Nova I | 10 | 7 | 1 | 2 | 0 | 0 | 42.0 | 44 | 4 | 4.50 | 1.45 | 26 | 17 | 0 | 0 | 0 | 3.0 | 0.00 | 1.33 | 1 | 2 | 0 | 39.0 | 4.85 | 1.46 | 5.6 | 3.6 | 0.9 | .729 | .703 | .747 |
| Park C | 27 | 0 | 2 | 1 | 0 | 0 | 35.1 | 40 | 7 | 5.60 | 1.47 | 29 | 12 | 1 | 1 | 0 | 27.2 | 6.18 | 1.48 | 1 | 0 | 0 | 7.2 | 3.52 | 1.43 | 7.4 | 3.1 | 1.8 | .822 | .699 | .963 |
| Pettitte A | 21 | 21 | 11 | 3 | 0 | 0 | 129.0 | 123 | 13 | 3.28 | 1.27 | 101 | 41 | 11 | 2 | 0 | 113.1 | 2.70 | 1.15 | 0 | 1 | 0 | 15.2 | 7.47 | 2.17 | 7.0 | 2.9 | 0.9 | .703 | .782 | .482 |
| Ring R | 5 | 0 | 0 | 0 | 1 | 0 | 2.1 | 3 | 0 | 15.43 | 2.14 | 2 | 2 | -- | -- | -- | ---- | ---- | --- | 0 | 0 | 0 | 2.1 | 15.43 | 2.14 | 7.7 | 7.7 | 0.0 | .717 | .333 | .819 |
| Rivera M | 61 | 0 | 3 | 3 | 0 | 33 | 60.0 | 39 | 2 | 1.80 | 0.83 | 45 | 11 | 2 | 1 | 20 | 34.1 | 1.05 | 0.64 | 1 | 2 | 13 | 25.2 | 2.81 | 1.09 | 6.8 | 1.7 | 0.3 | .493 | .433 | .554 |
| Robertson D | 64 | 0 | 4 | 5 | 14 | 1 | 61.1 | 59 | 5 | 3.82 | 1.50 | 71 | 33 | 1 | 3 | 0 | 29.2 | 5.46 | 1.79 | 3 | 2 | 1 | 31.2 | 2.27 | 1.23 | 10.4 | 4.8 | 0.7 | .721 | .693 | .759 |
| Sabathia C | 34 | 34 | 21 | 7 | 0 | 0 | 237.2 | 209 | 20 | 3.18 | 1.19 | 197 | 74 | 12 | 3 | 0 | 131.0 | 3.09 | 1.14 | 9 | 4 | 0 | 106.2 | 3.29 | 1.26 | 7.5 | 2.8 | 0.8 | .656 | .649 | .678 |
| Sanchez R | 2 | 0 | 0 | 0 | 0 | 0 | 4.1 | 1 | 0 | 0.00 | 0.92 | 5 | 3 | 0 | 0 | 0 | 3.2 | 0.00 | 0.55 | 0 | 0 | 0 | 0.2 | 0.00 | 3.00 | 10.4 | 6.2 | 0.0 | .307 | .125 | .476 |
| Vazquez J | 31 | 26 | 10 | 10 | 1 | 0 | 157.1 | 155 | 32 | 5.32 | 1.40 | 121 | 65 | 7 | 7 | 0 | 95.0 | 4.45 | 1.22 | 3 | 3 | 0 | 62.1 | 6.64 | 1.67 | 6.9 | 3.7 | 1.8 | .818 | .723 | .910 |
| Wood K | 24 | 0 | 2 | 0 | 10 | 0 | 26.0 | 14 | 1 | 0.69 | 1.23 | 31 | 18 | -- | -- | -- | ---- | ---- | --- | 2 | 0 | 0 | 26.0 | 0.69 | 1.23 | 10.7 | 6.2 | 0.3 | .507 | .373 | .634 |

| Hitters | Oakland Athletics 2010 | | | | | | | | | | | | | 1st Half | | | | | | 2nd Half | | | | | | Rates | | | | | Productiveness | | |
|---|---|---|---|---|---|---|---|---|---|---|---|---|---|---|---|---|---|---|---|---|---|---|---|---|---|---|---|---|---|---|---|---|---|
| | G | AB | R | H | 2B | 3B | HR | RBI | BA | OBP | SLG | SB | CS | AB | R | HR | BI | BA | SB | AB | R | HR | BI | BA | SB | CT% | H% | BB% | Bash | GB% | OPS | vs RH | vs LH |
| Barton D | 159 | 556 | 79 | 152 | 33 | 5 | 10 | 57 | .273 | .393 | .405 | 7 | 3 | 320 | 38 | 5 | 32 | .272 | 0 | 236 | 41 | 5 | 25 | .275 | 7 | 82% | 33% | 16% | 1.5 | 39% | .798 | .761 | .895 |
| Buck T | 14 | 42 | 6 | 7 | 2 | 0 | 1 | 2 | .167 | .255 | .286 | 1 | 0 | 32 | 6 | 1 | 2 | .219 | 1 | 10 | 0 | 0 | 0 | .000 | 0 | 67% | 25% | 8% | 1.7 | 25% | .541 | .552 | .500 |
| Carson M | 36 | 79 | 7 | 14 | 2 | 0 | 4 | 9 | .177 | .193 | .354 | 4 | 0 | 13 | 1 | 1 | 1 | .154 | 0 | 66 | 6 | 3 | 8 | .182 | 4 | 71% | 25% | 2% | 2.0 | 38% | .547 | .474 | .571 |
| Carter C | 24 | 70 | 8 | 13 | 1 | 0 | 3 | 7 | .186 | .256 | .329 | 1 | 0 | --- | -- | -- | -- | --- | -- | 70 | 8 | 3 | 7 | .186 | 1 | 70% | 27% | 9% | 1.8 | 35% | .585 | .606 | .520 |
| Chavez E | 33 | 111 | 10 | 26 | 8 | 0 | 1 | 10 | .234 | .276 | .333 | 0 | 0 | 111 | 10 | 1 | 10 | .234 | 0 | --- | -- | -- | -- | --- | -- | 72% | 33% | 7% | 1.4 | 51% | .610 | .635 | .322 |
| Crisp C | 75 | 290 | 51 | 81 | 14 | 4 | 8 | 38 | .279 | .342 | .438 | 32 | 3 | 65 | 14 | 3 | 17 | .277 | 5 | 225 | 37 | 5 | 21 | .280 | 27 | 83% | 34% | 9% | 1.6 | 47% | .779 | .716 | .949 |
| Cust J | 112 | 349 | 50 | 95 | 19 | 0 | 13 | 52 | .272 | .395 | .438 | 2 | 2 | 136 | 22 | 4 | 18 | .294 | 1 | 213 | 28 | 9 | 34 | .258 | 1 | 64% | 43% | 16% | 1.6 | 40% | .834 | .880 | .638 |
| Davis R | 143 | 525 | 66 | 149 | 28 | 3 | 5 | 52 | .284 | .320 | .377 | 50 | 11 | 269 | 36 | 3 | 26 | .268 | 27 | 256 | 30 | 2 | 26 | .301 | 23 | 85% | 33% | 5% | 1.3 | 47% | .697 | .666 | .784 |
| Donaldson J | 14 | 32 | 1 | 5 | 1 | 0 | 1 | 4 | .156 | .206 | .281 | 0 | 0 | 26 | 1 | 1 | 3 | .154 | 0 | 6 | 0 | 0 | 1 | .167 | 0 | 63% | 25% | 6% | 1.8 | 50% | .487 | .000 | .768 |
| Ellis M | 124 | 436 | 45 | 127 | 24 | 0 | 5 | 49 | .291 | .358 | .381 | 7 | 6 | 180 | 22 | 2 | 22 | .278 | 3 | 256 | 23 | 3 | 27 | .301 | 4 | 87% | 33% | 8% | 1.3 | 42% | .739 | .706 | .839 |
| Fox J | 39 | 98 | 11 | 21 | 5 | 0 | 2 | 12 | .214 | .264 | .327 | 0 | 0 | 98 | 11 | 2 | 12 | .214 | 0 | --- | -- | -- | -- | --- | -- | 73% | 29% | 5% | 1.5 | 49% | .591 | .447 | .675 |
| Gross G | 105 | 222 | 27 | 53 | 11 | 1 | 1 | 25 | .239 | .290 | .311 | 5 | 1 | 155 | 14 | 1 | 18 | .265 | 2 | 67 | 13 | 0 | 7 | .179 | 3 | 82% | 29% | 7% | 1.3 | 47% | .601 | .610 | .552 |
| Hermida J | 21 | 64 | 5 | 16 | 4 | 0 | 1 | 2 | .250 | .294 | .359 | 0 | 0 | --- | -- | -- | -- | --- | -- | 64 | 5 | 1 | 2 | .250 | 0 | 80% | 31% | 6% | 1.4 | 41% | .653 | .676 | .558 |
| Iwamura A | 10 | 31 | 3 | 4 | 1 | 0 | 0 | 4 | .129 | .250 | .161 | 0 | 0 | --- | -- | -- | -- | --- | -- | 31 | 3 | 0 | 4 | .129 | 0 | 68% | 19% | 14% | 1.3 | 57% | .411 | .417 | .393 |
| Jackson C | 18 | 57 | 6 | 13 | 2 | 0 | 1 | 5 | .228 | .362 | .316 | 2 | 0 | 45 | 5 | 0 | 4 | .267 | 1 | 12 | 1 | 1 | 1 | .083 | 1 | 84% | 27% | 16% | 1.4 | 35% | .678 | .722 | .364 |
| Kouzmanoff K | 143 | 551 | 59 | 136 | 32 | 1 | 16 | 71 | .247 | .283 | .396 | 2 | 1 | 338 | 36 | 8 | 40 | .266 | 1 | 213 | 23 | 8 | 31 | .216 | 1 | 83% | 30% | 4% | 1.6 | 43% | .679 | .663 | .724 |
| Larish J | 24 | 57 | 5 | 10 | 3 | 0 | 2 | 8 | .175 | .277 | .333 | 1 | 0 | --- | -- | -- | -- | --- | -- | 57 | 5 | 2 | 8 | .175 | 1 | 65% | 27% | 11% | 1.9 | 54% | .610 | .678 | .125 |
| Patterson E | 45 | 103 | 13 | 21 | 5 | 2 | 4 | 9 | .204 | .255 | .408 | 6 | 0 | 103 | 13 | 4 | 9 | .204 | 6 | --- | -- | -- | -- | --- | -- | 70% | 29% | 6% | 2.0 | 35% | .662 | .781 | .221 |
| Pennington C | 156 | 508 | 64 | 127 | 26 | 8 | 6 | 46 | .250 | .319 | .368 | 29 | 5 | 288 | 38 | 3 | 27 | .264 | 13 | 220 | 26 | 3 | 19 | .232 | 16 | 81% | 31% | 9% | 1.5 | 35% | .687 | .697 | .655 |
| Powell L | 41 | 112 | 13 | 24 | 4 | 0 | 2 | 11 | .214 | .305 | .304 | 1 | 0 | 64 | 7 | 1 | 6 | .250 | 1 | 48 | 6 | 1 | 5 | .167 | 0 | 74% | 29% | 12% | 1.4 | 37% | .608 | .602 | .624 |
| Rosales A | 80 | 255 | 31 | 69 | 8 | 2 | 7 | 31 | .271 | .321 | .400 | 2 | 2 | 217 | 26 | 6 | 27 | .276 | 2 | 38 | 5 | 1 | 4 | .237 | 0 | 75% | 36% | 7% | 1.5 | 38% | .721 | .681 | .794 |
| Sogard E | 4 | 7 | 0 | 3 | 0 | 0 | 0 | 0 | .429 | .556 | .429 | 0 | 1 | --- | -- | -- | -- | --- | -- | 7 | 0 | 0 | 0 | .429 | 0 | 86% | 50% | 22% | 1.0 | 50% | .984 | .533 | 2.000 |
| Suzuki K | 131 | 495 | 55 | 120 | 18 | 2 | 13 | 71 | .242 | .303 | .366 | 3 | 2 | 246 | 28 | 10 | 37 | .252 | 1 | 249 | 27 | 3 | 34 | .233 | 2 | 90% | 27% | 6% | 1.5 | 42% | .669 | .701 | .575 |
| Sweeney R | 82 | 303 | 41 | 89 | 20 | 2 | 1 | 36 | .294 | .342 | .383 | 1 | 1 | 303 | 41 | 1 | 36 | .294 | 1 | --- | -- | -- | -- | --- | -- | 86% | 34% | 7% | 1.3 | 52% | .725 | .754 | .623 |
| Tolleson S | 25 | 49 | 5 | 14 | 3 | 0 | 1 | 4 | .286 | .340 | .408 | 0 | 0 | 4 | 0 | 0 | 0 | .250 | 0 | 45 | 5 | 1 | 4 | .289 | 0 | 82% | 35% | 8% | 1.4 | 33% | .748 | .459 | 1.048 |
| Watson M | 12 | 30 | 2 | 6 | 2 | 0 | 1 | 4 | .200 | .273 | .367 | 0 | 0 | 4 | 0 | 0 | 0 | .000 | 0 | 26 | 2 | 1 | 4 | .231 | 0 | 83% | 24% | 9% | 1.8 | 28% | .639 | .639 | --- |

| Pitchers | Oakland Athletics 2010 | | | | | | | | | | | | | 1st Half | | | | | | 2nd Half | | | | | | Rates | | | Productiveness | | |
|---|---|---|---|---|---|---|---|---|---|---|---|---|---|---|---|---|---|---|---|---|---|---|---|---|---|---|---|---|---|---|---|
| | G | GS | W | L | Hld | Sv | IP | H | HR | ERA | WHIP | K | BB | W | L | Sv | IP | ERA | WHIP | W | L | Sv | IP | ERA | WHIP | K/9 | BB/9 | HR/9 | opOPS | vs RH | vs LH |
| Anderson B | 19 | 19 | 7 | 6 | 0 | 0 | 112.1 | 112 | 6 | 2.80 | 1.19 | 75 | 22 | 2 | 1 | 0 | 30.2 | 2.35 | 1.04 | 5 | 5 | 0 | 81.2 | 2.98 | 1.25 | 6.0 | 1.8 | 0.5 | .655 | .646 | .685 |
| Bailey A | 47 | 0 | 1 | 3 | 0 | 25 | 49.0 | 34 | 3 | 1.47 | 0.96 | 42 | 13 | 0 | 3 | 18 | 37.0 | 1.70 | 1.00 | 1 | 0 | 7 | 12.0 | 0.75 | 0.83 | 7.7 | 2.4 | 0.6 | .544 | .523 | .569 |
| Blevins J | 63 | 0 | 2 | 1 | 11 | 1 | 48.2 | 54 | 7 | 3.70 | 1.48 | 46 | 18 | 2 | 1 | 0 | 31.0 | 3.77 | 1.52 | 0 | 0 | 1 | 17.2 | 3.57 | 1.42 | 8.5 | 3.3 | 1.3 | .758 | .892 | .598 |
| Bonser B | 13 | 0 | 1 | 0 | 3 | 0 | 23.0 | 27 | 2 | 5.09 | 1.43 | 17 | 6 | -- | -- | -- | ---- | ---- | --- | 1 | 0 | 0 | 23.0 | 5.09 | 1.43 | 6.7 | 2.3 | 0.8 | .744 | .730 | .756 |
| Bowers C | 14 | 0 | 0 | 1 | 0 | 0 | 14.0 | 12 | 4 | 4.50 | 1.29 | 18 | 6 | 0 | 1 | 0 | 12.2 | 4.26 | 1.18 | 0 | 0 | 0 | 1.1 | 6.75 | 2.25 | 11.6 | 3.9 | 2.6 | .779 | .568 | 1.206 |
| Braden D | 30 | 30 | 11 | 14 | 0 | 0 | 192.2 | 180 | 17 | 3.50 | 1.16 | 113 | 43 | 4 | 7 | 0 | 94.0 | 3.83 | 1.19 | 7 | 7 | 0 | 98.2 | 3.19 | 1.13 | 5.3 | 2.0 | 0.8 | .668 | .655 | .706 |
| Breslow C | 75 | 0 | 4 | 4 | 16 | 5 | 74.2 | 53 | 9 | 3.01 | 1.10 | 71 | 29 | 3 | 2 | 0 | 40.2 | 3.32 | 1.08 | 1 | 2 | 5 | 34.0 | 2.65 | 1.12 | 8.6 | 3.5 | 1.1 | .620 | .637 | .586 |
| Cahill T | 30 | 30 | 18 | 8 | 0 | 0 | 196.2 | 155 | 19 | 2.97 | 1.11 | 118 | 63 | 9 | 3 | 0 | 95.0 | 2.94 | 1.03 | 9 | 5 | 0 | 101.2 | 3.01 | 1.18 | 5.4 | 2.9 | 0.9 | .619 | .605 | .630 |
| Cramer B | 4 | 4 | 2 | 1 | 0 | 0 | 23.2 | 20 | 5 | 3.04 | 1.10 | 13 | 6 | -- | -- | -- | ---- | ---- | --- | 2 | 1 | 0 | 23.2 | 3.04 | 1.10 | 4.9 | 2.3 | 1.9 | .736 | .705 | .875 |
| Duchscherer J | 5 | 5 | 2 | 1 | 0 | 0 | 28.0 | 26 | 3 | 2.89 | 1.36 | 18 | 12 | 2 | 1 | 0 | 28.0 | 2.89 | 1.36 | -- | -- | -- | ---- | ---- | --- | 5.8 | 3.9 | 1.0 | .699 | .770 | .633 |
| Gaudin C | 12 | 0 | 0 | 2 | 1 | 0 | 17.1 | 27 | 5 | 8.83 | 1.85 | 20 | 5 | 0 | 2 | 0 | 17.1 | 8.83 | 1.85 | -- | -- | -- | ---- | ---- | --- | 10.4 | 2.6 | 2.6 | 1.057 | 1.107 | .976 |
| Gonzalez G | 33 | 33 | 15 | 9 | 0 | 0 | 200.2 | 171 | 15 | 3.23 | 1.31 | 171 | 92 | 7 | 6 | 0 | 107.0 | 3.79 | 1.38 | 8 | 3 | 0 | 93.2 | 2.59 | 1.23 | 7.7 | 4.1 | 0.7 | .644 | .653 | .615 |
| James J | 5 | 0 | 0 | 0 | 0 | 0 | 4.0 | 7 | 0 | 4.50 | 2.75 | 5 | 4 | -- | -- | -- | ---- | ---- | --- | 0 | 0 | 0 | 4.0 | 4.50 | 2.75 | 11.3 | 9.0 | 0.0 | .911 | .944 | .872 |
| Kilby B | 5 | 0 | 0 | 0 | 0 | 0 | 8.1 | 7 | 2 | 2.16 | 0.84 | 8 | 0 | 0 | 0 | 0 | 8.1 | 2.16 | 0.84 | -- | -- | -- | ---- | ---- | --- | 8.6 | 0.0 | 2.2 | .688 | .789 | .538 |
| Mazzaro V | 24 | 18 | 6 | 8 | 0 | 0 | 122.1 | 127 | 19 | 4.27 | 1.45 | 79 | 50 | 4 | 2 | 0 | 56.2 | 3.81 | 1.43 | 2 | 6 | 0 | 65.2 | 4.66 | 1.46 | 5.8 | 3.7 | 1.4 | .765 | .733 | .797 |
| Mortensen C | 1 | 1 | 0 | 0 | 0 | 0 | 6.0 | 6 | 1 | 4.50 | 1.33 | 7 | 2 | 0 | 0 | 0 | 6.0 | 4.50 | 1.33 | -- | -- | -- | ---- | ---- | --- | 10.5 | 3.0 | 1.5 | .683 | .853 | .347 |
| Ramirez E | 7 | 0 | 1 | 0 | 0 | 0 | 11.0 | 9 | 1 | 4.91 | 1.73 | 10 | 10 | 1 | 0 | 0 | 11.0 | 4.91 | 1.73 | -- | -- | -- | ---- | ---- | --- | 8.2 | 8.2 | 0.8 | .658 | .598 | .743 |
| Rodriguez H | 29 | 0 | 1 | 0 | 3 | 0 | 27.2 | 25 | 2 | 4.55 | 1.37 | 33 | 13 | 0 | 0 | 0 | 5.1 | 5.06 | 1.69 | 1 | 0 | 0 | 22.1 | 4.43 | 1.30 | 10.7 | 4.2 | 0.7 | .664 | .587 | .758 |
| Ross T | 26 | 2 | 1 | 4 | 2 | 1 | 39.1 | 39 | 4 | 5.49 | 1.50 | 32 | 20 | 1 | 4 | 1 | 39.1 | 5.49 | 1.50 | -- | -- | -- | ---- | ---- | --- | 7.3 | 4.6 | 0.9 | .754 | .819 | .674 |
| Sheets B | 20 | 20 | 4 | 9 | 0 | 0 | 119.1 | 123 | 18 | 4.53 | 1.39 | 84 | 43 | 4 | 8 | 0 | 112.2 | 4.63 | 1.39 | 0 | 1 | 0 | 6.2 | 2.70 | 1.35 | 6.3 | 3.2 | 1.4 | .813 | .825 | .801 |
| Wolf R | 11 | 0 | 0 | 0 | 0 | 0 | 12.2 | 12 | 1 | 4.26 | 1.42 | 9 | 6 | 0 | 0 | 0 | 1.0 | 9.00 | 2.00 | 0 | 0 | 0 | 11.2 | 3.86 | 1.37 | 6.4 | 4.3 | 0.7 | .741 | .569 | .945 |
| Wuertz M | 48 | 0 | 2 | 3 | 11 | 6 | 39.2 | 35 | 6 | 4.31 | 1.41 | 40 | 21 | 2 | 1 | 1 | 17.2 | 5.60 | 1.70 | 0 | 2 | 5 | 22.0 | 3.27 | 1.18 | 9.1 | 4.8 | 1.4 | .746 | .656 | .920 |
| Ziegler B | 64 | 0 | 3 | 7 | 18 | 0 | 60.2 | 54 | 4 | 3.26 | 1.35 | 41 | 28 | 2 | 4 | 0 | 39.1 | 3.43 | 1.40 | 1 | 3 | 0 | 21.1 | 2.95 | 1.27 | 6.1 | 4.2 | 0.6 | .694 | .560 | 1.034 |

## Performance in 2010

### Production by Lineup Spot

### Trends Among League

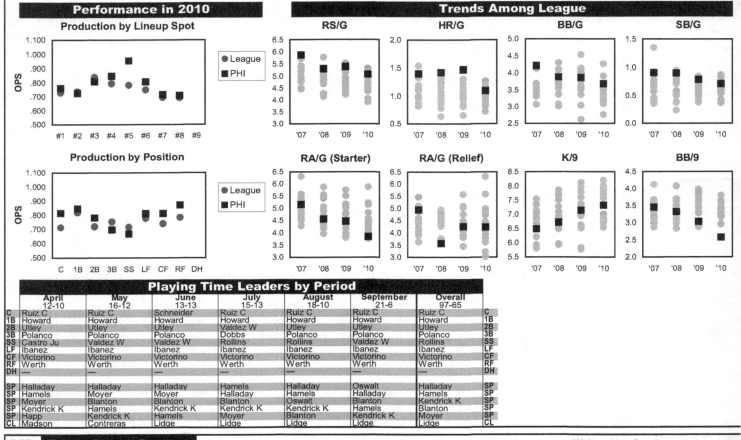

### Production by Position

### Playing Time Leaders by Period

| | April 12-10 | May 16-12 | June 13-13 | July 15-13 | August 18-10 | September 21-6 | Overall 97-65 | |
|---|---|---|---|---|---|---|---|---|
| C | Ruiz C | Ruiz C | Schneider | Ruiz C | Ruiz C | Ruiz C | Ruiz C | C |
| 1B | Howard | Howard | Howard | Howard | Howard | Howard | Howard | 1B |
| 2B | Utley | Utley | Utley | Valdez W | Utley | Utley | Utley | 2B |
| 3B | Polanco | Polanco | Polanco | Dobbs | Polanco | Polanco | Polanco | 3B |
| SS | Castro Ju | Valdez W | Valdez W | Rollins | Rollins | Valdez W | Rollins | SS |
| LF | Ibanez | Ibanez | Ibanez | Ibanez | Ibanez | Ibanez | Ibanez | LF |
| CF | Victorino | Victorino | Victorino | Victorino | Victorino | Victorino | Victorino | CF |
| RF | Werth | Werth | Werth | Werth | Werth | Werth | Werth | RF |
| DH | — | — | — | — | — | — | — | DH |
| SP | Halladay | Halladay | Halladay | Hamels | Halladay | Oswalt | Halladay | SP |
| SP | Hamels | Moyer | Moyer | Halladay | Hamels | Halladay | Hamels | SP |
| SP | Moyer | Blanton | Blanton | Blanton | Oswalt | Blanton | Kendrick K | SP |
| SP | Kendrick K | Hamels | Kendrick K | Kendrick K | Kendrick K | Hamels | Blanton | SP |
| SP | Happ | Kendrick K | Hamels | Moyer | Blanton | Kendrick K | Moyer | SP |
| CL | Madson | Contreras | Lidge | Lidge | Lidge | Lidge | Lidge | CL |

## Performance in 2010

### Production by Lineup Spot

### Trends Among Leagues

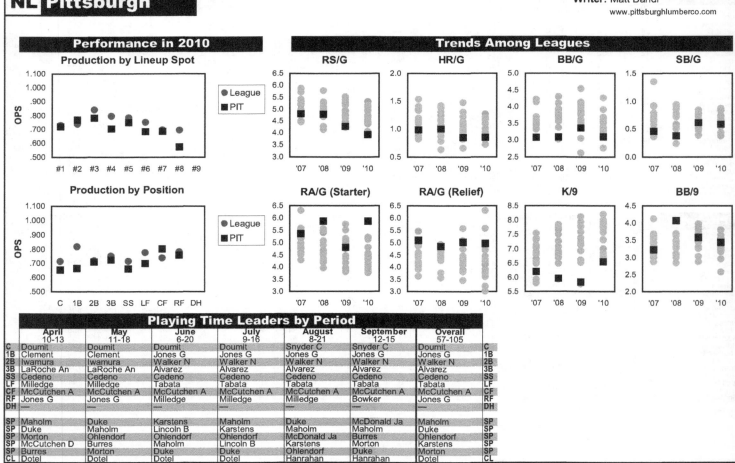

### Production by Position

### Playing Time Leaders by Period

| | April 10-13 | May 11-18 | June 6-20 | July 9-16 | August 8-21 | September 12-15 | Overall 57-105 | |
|---|---|---|---|---|---|---|---|---|
| C | Doumit | Doumit | Doumit | Doumit | Snyder C | Snyder C | Doumit | C |
| 1B | Clement | Clement | Jones G | Jones G | Jones G | Jones G | Jones G | 1B |
| 2B | Iwamura | Iwamura | Walker N | Walker N | Walker N | Walker N | Walker N | 2B |
| 3B | LaRoche An | LaRoche An | Alvarez | Alvarez | Alvarez | Alvarez | Alvarez | 3B |
| SS | Cedeno | Cedeno | Cedeno | Cedeno | Cedeno | Cedeno | Cedeno | SS |
| LF | Milledge | Milledge | Tabata | Tabata | Tabata | Tabata | Tabata | LF |
| CF | McCutchen A | McCutchen A | McCutchen A | McCutchen A | McCutchen A | McCutchen A | McCutchen A | CF |
| RF | Jones G | Jones G | Milledge | Milledge | Milledge | Bowker | Jones G | RF |
| DH | — | — | — | — | — | — | — | DH |
| SP | Maholm | Duke | Karstens | Maholm | Duke | McDonald Ja | Maholm | SP |
| SP | Duke | Maholm | Lincoln B | Karstens | Maholm | Maholm | Duke | SP |
| SP | Morton | Ohlendorf | Ohlendorf | Ohlendorf | McDonald Ja | Burres | Ohlendorf | SP |
| SP | McCutchen D | Burres | Maholm | Lincoln B | Karstens | Morton | Karstens | SP |
| SP | Burres | Morton | Duke | Duke | Ohlendorf | Duke | Morton | SP |
| CL | Dotel | Dotel | Dotel | Dotel | Hanrahan | Hanrahan | Dotel | CL |

| Hitters | Philadelphia Phillies 2010 | | | | | | | | | | | | | 1st Half | | | | | | 2nd Half | | | | | | Rates | | | | | Productiveness | | |
|---|---|---|---|---|---|---|---|---|---|---|---|---|---|---|---|---|---|---|---|---|---|---|---|---|---|---|---|---|---|---|---|---|---|
| | G | AB | R | H | 2B | 3B | HR | RBI | BA | OBP | SLG | SB | CS | AB | R | HR | BI | BA | SB | AB | R | HR | BI | BA | SB | CT% | H% | BB% | Bash | GB% | OPS | vs RH | vs LH |
| Bocock B | 6 | 5 | 2 | 0 | 0 | 0 | 0 | 0 | .000 | .000 | .000 | 0 | 0 | --- | -- | -- | -- | --- | -- | 5 | 2 | 0 | 0 | .000 | 0 | 40% | 0% | 0% | --- | 50% | .000 | .000 | --- |
| Brown D | 35 | 62 | 8 | 13 | 3 | 0 | 2 | 13 | .210 | .257 | .355 | 2 | 1 | --- | -- | -- | -- | --- | -- | 62 | 8 | 2 | 13 | .210 | 2 | 61% | 34% | 7% | 1.7 | 45% | .612 | .732 | .148 |
| Castro J | 54 | 126 | 7 | 25 | 5 | 0 | 0 | 13 | .198 | .237 | .238 | 0 | 1 | 124 | 7 | 0 | 13 | .202 | 0 | 2 | 0 | 0 | 0 | .000 | 0 | 82% | 24% | 5% | 1.2 | 51% | .475 | .465 | .506 |
| Dobbs G | 88 | 163 | 13 | 32 | 7 | 0 | 5 | 15 | .196 | .251 | .331 | 1 | 1 | 99 | 7 | 3 | 12 | .192 | 1 | 64 | 6 | 2 | 3 | .203 | 0 | 76% | 26% | 7% | 1.7 | 33% | .583 | .598 | .438 |
| Francisco B | 88 | 179 | 24 | 48 | 13 | 0 | 6 | 28 | .268 | .327 | .441 | 8 | 0 | 94 | 10 | 1 | 12 | .245 | 3 | 85 | 14 | 5 | 16 | .294 | 5 | 80% | 33% | 7% | 1.6 | 38% | .768 | .640 | .901 |
| Gload R | 94 | 128 | 16 | 36 | 8 | 0 | 6 | 22 | .281 | .328 | .484 | 1 | 0 | 70 | 5 | 3 | 12 | .243 | 1 | 58 | 11 | 3 | 10 | .328 | 0 | 88% | 32% | 6% | 1.7 | 42% | .813 | .818 | .748 |
| Hoover P | 9 | 22 | 6 | 5 | 2 | 0 | 0 | 2 | .227 | .320 | .318 | 0 | 0 | 18 | 6 | 0 | 2 | .278 | 0 | 4 | 0 | 0 | 0 | .000 | 0 | 77% | 29% | 11% | 1.4 | 53% | .638 | .619 | .664 |
| Howard R | 143 | 550 | 87 | 152 | 23 | 5 | 31 | 108 | .276 | .353 | .505 | 1 | 1 | 344 | 55 | 17 | 65 | .294 | 0 | 206 | 32 | 14 | 43 | .248 | 1 | 71% | 39% | 9% | 1.8 | 40% | .859 | .876 | .826 |
| Ibanez R | 155 | 561 | 75 | 154 | 37 | 5 | 16 | 83 | .275 | .349 | .444 | 4 | 3 | 292 | 36 | 7 | 39 | .243 | 2 | 269 | 39 | 9 | 44 | .309 | 2 | 81% | 34% | 11% | 1.6 | 45% | .793 | .822 | .728 |
| Mayberry J | 11 | 12 | 4 | 4 | 0 | 0 | 2 | 6 | .333 | .385 | .833 | 0 | 1 | --- | -- | -- | -- | --- | -- | 12 | 4 | 2 | 6 | .333 | 0 | 67% | 50% | 8% | 2.5 | 50% | 1.218 | .952 | 1.500 |
| Polanco P | 132 | 554 | 76 | 165 | 27 | 2 | 6 | 52 | .298 | .339 | .386 | 5 | 0 | 261 | 39 | 5 | 27 | .318 | 3 | 293 | 37 | 1 | 25 | .280 | 2 | 92% | 33% | 5% | 1.3 | 46% | .726 | .749 | .668 |
| Ransom C | 22 | 42 | 6 | 8 | 0 | 0 | 2 | 5 | .190 | .244 | .333 | 1 | 0 | 14 | 2 | 1 | 3 | .214 | 0 | 28 | 4 | 1 | 2 | .179 | 1 | 74% | 26% | 7% | 1.8 | 42% | .578 | 1.035 | .412 |
| Rollins J | 88 | 350 | 48 | 85 | 16 | 3 | 8 | 41 | .243 | .320 | .374 | 17 | 1 | 118 | 18 | 4 | 18 | .254 | 3 | 232 | 30 | 4 | 23 | .237 | 14 | 91% | 27% | 10% | 1.5 | 46% | .694 | .657 | .773 |
| Ruiz C | 121 | 371 | 43 | 112 | 28 | 1 | 8 | 53 | .302 | .400 | .447 | 0 | 1 | 159 | 18 | 2 | 13 | .283 | 0 | 212 | 25 | 6 | 40 | .316 | 0 | 85% | 35% | 12% | 1.5 | 45% | .847 | .808 | .940 |
| Sardinha D | 13 | 39 | 5 | 8 | 2 | 0 | 3 | 8 | .205 | .225 | .487 | 0 | 0 | 39 | 5 | 3 | 8 | .205 | 0 | --- | -- | -- | -- | --- | -- | 67% | 31% | 3% | 2.4 | 27% | .712 | .726 | .667 |
| Schneider B | 47 | 125 | 17 | 30 | 4 | 1 | 4 | 15 | .240 | .345 | .384 | 0 | 0 | 72 | 10 | 3 | 7 | .236 | 0 | 53 | 7 | 1 | 8 | .245 | 0 | 80% | 30% | 13% | 1.6 | 45% | .729 | .820 | .161 |
| Sweeney M | 26 | 52 | 10 | 12 | 2 | 0 | 2 | 8 | .231 | .310 | .385 | 1 | 0 | --- | -- | -- | -- | --- | -- | 52 | 10 | 2 | 8 | .231 | 1 | 87% | 27% | 9% | 1.7 | 49% | .695 | .675 | .702 |
| Utley C | 115 | 425 | 75 | 117 | 20 | 2 | 16 | 65 | .275 | .387 | .445 | 13 | 2 | 264 | 49 | 11 | 37 | .277 | 5 | 161 | 26 | 5 | 28 | .273 | 8 | 85% | 32% | 12% | 1.6 | 42% | .832 | .752 | 1.003 |
| Valdez W | 111 | 333 | 37 | 86 | 16 | 3 | 4 | 35 | .258 | .306 | .360 | 7 | 0 | 168 | 23 | 4 | 21 | .250 | 3 | 165 | 14 | 0 | 14 | .267 | 4 | 87% | 30% | 6% | 1.4 | 58% | .667 | .689 | .610 |
| Victorino S | 147 | 587 | 84 | 152 | 26 | 10 | 18 | 69 | .259 | .327 | .429 | 34 | 6 | 352 | 54 | 14 | 48 | .250 | 17 | 235 | 30 | 4 | 21 | .272 | 17 | 87% | 30% | 8% | 1.7 | 45% | .756 | .692 | .921 |
| Werth J | 156 | 554 | 106 | 164 | 46 | 2 | 27 | 85 | .296 | .388 | .532 | 13 | 3 | 294 | 52 | 13 | 49 | .282 | 5 | 260 | 54 | 14 | 36 | .312 | 8 | 73% | 40% | 12% | 1.8 | 38% | .921 | .937 | .881 |

| Pitchers | Philadelphia Phillies 2010 | | | | | | | | | | | | | 1st Half | | | | | | 2nd Half | | | | | | Rates | | | Productiveness | | |
|---|---|---|---|---|---|---|---|---|---|---|---|---|---|---|---|---|---|---|---|---|---|---|---|---|---|---|---|---|---|---|---|
| | G | GS | W | L | Hld | Sv | IP | H | HR | ERA | WHIP | K | BB | W | L | Sv | IP | ERA | WHIP | W | L | Sv | IP | ERA | WHIP | K/9 | BB/9 | HR/9 | opOPS | vs RH | vs LH |
| Baez D | 51 | 0 | 3 | 4 | 6 | 0 | 47.2 | 55 | 6 | 5.48 | 1.64 | 28 | 23 | 2 | 3 | 0 | 32.1 | 4.45 | 1.52 | 1 | 1 | 0 | 15.1 | 7.63 | 1.89 | 5.3 | 4.3 | 1.1 | .863 | .807 | .949 |
| Bastardo A | 25 | 0 | 2 | 0 | 2 | 0 | 18.2 | 19 | 1 | 4.34 | 1.50 | 26 | 9 | 0 | 0 | 0 | 12.1 | 5.11 | 1.22 | 2 | 0 | 0 | 6.1 | 2.84 | 2.05 | 12.5 | 4.3 | 0.5 | .669 | .678 | .660 |
| Blanton J | 29 | 28 | 9 | 6 | 0 | 0 | 175.2 | 206 | 27 | 4.82 | 1.42 | 134 | 43 | 3 | 5 | 0 | 80.0 | 6.41 | 1.51 | 6 | 1 | 0 | 95.2 | 3.48 | 1.34 | 6.9 | 2.2 | 1.4 | .796 | .815 | .774 |
| Carpenter D | 1 | 0 | 0 | 1 | 0 | 0 | 3.0 | 5 | 1 | 9.00 | 1.67 | 2 | 0 | -- | -- | -- | ---- | ---- | --- | 0 | 1 | 0 | 3.0 | 9.00 | 1.67 | 6.0 | 0.0 | 3.0 | 1.077 | .625 | 1.800 |
| Contreras J | 67 | 0 | 6 | 4 | 13 | 4 | 56.2 | 53 | 5 | 3.34 | 1.22 | 57 | 16 | 4 | 3 | 3 | 29.0 | 2.79 | 1.10 | 2 | 1 | 1 | 27.2 | 3.90 | 1.34 | 9.1 | 2.5 | 0.8 | .699 | .658 | .754 |
| Durbin C | 64 | 0 | 4 | 1 | 15 | 0 | 68.2 | 63 | 7 | 3.80 | 1.31 | 63 | 27 | 0 | 1 | 0 | 35.1 | 3.31 | 1.19 | 4 | 0 | 0 | 33.1 | 4.32 | 1.44 | 8.3 | 3.5 | 0.9 | .738 | .604 | .936 |
| Figueroa N | 13 | 1 | 2 | 1 | 0 | 1 | 26.0 | 20 | 1 | 3.46 | 1.12 | 15 | 9 | 2 | 1 | 1 | 26.0 | 3.46 | 1.12 | -- | -- | -- | ---- | ---- | --- | 5.2 | 3.1 | 0.3 | .609 | .514 | .726 |
| Halladay R | 33 | 33 | 21 | 10 | 0 | 0 | 250.2 | 231 | 24 | 2.44 | 1.04 | 219 | 30 | 10 | 7 | 0 | 148.0 | 2.19 | 1.05 | 11 | 3 | 0 | 102.2 | 2.81 | 1.02 | 7.9 | 1.1 | 0.9 | .645 | .610 | .682 |
| Hamels C | 33 | 33 | 12 | 11 | 0 | 0 | 208.2 | 185 | 26 | 3.06 | 1.18 | 211 | 61 | 7 | 7 | 0 | 112.0 | 3.78 | 1.33 | 5 | 4 | 0 | 96.2 | 2.23 | 1.00 | 9.1 | 2.6 | 1.1 | .693 | .704 | .645 |
| Happ J | 3 | 3 | 1 | 0 | 0 | 0 | 15.1 | 13 | 1 | 1.76 | 1.63 | 9 | 12 | 1 | 0 | 0 | 10.1 | 0.00 | 1.65 | 0 | 0 | 0 | 5.0 | 5.40 | 1.60 | 5.3 | 7.0 | 0.6 | .702 | .703 | .701 |
| Herndon D | 47 | 0 | 1 | 3 | 1 | 0 | 52.1 | 67 | 2 | 4.30 | 1.61 | 29 | 17 | 0 | 2 | 0 | 30.1 | 3.86 | 1.65 | 1 | 1 | 0 | 22.0 | 4.91 | 1.55 | 5.0 | 2.9 | 0.3 | .814 | .771 | .905 |
| Kendrick K | 33 | 31 | 11 | 10 | 0 | 0 | 180.2 | 199 | 26 | 4.73 | 1.37 | 84 | 49 | 5 | 3 | 0 | 102.1 | 4.49 | 1.29 | 6 | 7 | 0 | 78.1 | 5.06 | 1.48 | 4.2 | 2.4 | 1.3 | .807 | .713 | .902 |
| Lidge B | 50 | 0 | 1 | 1 | 0 | 27 | 45.2 | 32 | 5 | 2.96 | 1.23 | 52 | 24 | 1 | 0 | 6 | 15.2 | 4.60 | 1.40 | 0 | 1 | 21 | 30.0 | 2.10 | 1.13 | 10.2 | 4.7 | 1.0 | .627 | .564 | .685 |
| Madson R | 55 | 0 | 6 | 2 | 15 | 5 | 53.0 | 42 | 4 | 2.55 | 1.04 | 64 | 13 | 2 | 0 | 4 | 11.0 | 6.55 | 1.64 | 4 | 2 | 1 | 42.0 | 1.50 | 0.88 | 10.9 | 2.2 | 0.7 | .582 | .556 | .613 |
| Mathieson S | 2 | 0 | 0 | 0 | 0 | 0 | 1.2 | 5 | 0 | 10.80 | 4.20 | 1 | 2 | 0 | 0 | 0 | 0.2 | 27.00 | 4.50 | 0 | 0 | 0 | 1.0 | 0.00 | 4.00 | 5.4 | 10.8 | 0.0 | 1.192 | 1.314 | 1.000 |
| Moyer J | 19 | 19 | 9 | 9 | 0 | 0 | 111.2 | 103 | 20 | 4.84 | 1.10 | 63 | 20 | 9 | 8 | 0 | 107.2 | 4.51 | 1.08 | 0 | 1 | 0 | 4.0 | 13.50 | 1.75 | 5.1 | 1.6 | 1.6 | .715 | .707 | .756 |
| Oswalt R | 13 | 12 | 7 | 1 | 0 | 0 | 82.2 | 53 | 6 | 1.74 | 0.90 | 73 | 21 | -- | -- | -- | ---- | ---- | --- | 7 | 1 | 0 | 82.2 | 1.74 | 0.90 | 7.9 | 2.3 | 0.7 | .550 | .545 | .556 |
| Robertson N | 2 | 0 | 0 | 0 | 0 | 0 | 1.0 | 5 | 1 | 54.00 | 7.00 | 2 | 2 | -- | -- | -- | ---- | ---- | --- | 0 | 0 | 0 | 1.0 | 54.00 | 7.00 | 18.0 | 18.0 | 9.0 | 1.825 | 1.792 | --- |
| Romero J | 60 | 0 | 1 | 0 | 9 | 3 | 36.2 | 30 | 3 | 3.68 | 1.61 | 28 | 29 | 1 | 0 | 3 | 18.2 | 2.41 | 1.50 | 0 | 0 | 0 | 18.0 | 5.00 | 1.72 | 6.9 | 7.1 | 0.7 | .690 | .817 | .600 |
| Worley V | 5 | 2 | 1 | 1 | 0 | 0 | 13.0 | 8 | 1 | 1.38 | 0.92 | 12 | 4 | -- | -- | -- | ---- | ---- | --- | 1 | 1 | 0 | 13.0 | 1.38 | 0.92 | 8.3 | 2.8 | 0.7 | .512 | .520 | .500 |
| Zagurski M | 8 | 0 | 0 | 0 | 0 | 0 | 7.0 | 8 | 1 | 10.29 | 1.86 | 11 | 5 | 0 | 0 | 0 | 5.1 | 3.38 | 1.13 | 0 | 0 | 0 | 1.2 | 32.40 | 4.20 | 14.1 | 6.4 | 1.3 | 1.015 | 1.026 | .973 |

| Hitters | Pittsburgh Pirates 2010 | | | | | | | | | | | | | 1st Half | | | | | | 2nd Half | | | | | | Rates | | | | | Productiveness | | |
|---|---|---|---|---|---|---|---|---|---|---|---|---|---|---|---|---|---|---|---|---|---|---|---|---|---|---|---|---|---|---|---|---|---|
| | G | AB | R | H | 2B | 3B | HR | RBI | BA | OBP | SLG | SB | CS | AB | R | HR | BI | BA | SB | AB | R | HR | BI | BA | SB | CT% | H% | BB% | Bash | GB% | OPS | vs RH | vs LH |
| Alvarez P | 95 | 347 | 42 | 89 | 21 | 1 | 16 | 64 | .256 | .326 | .461 | 0 | 0 | 84 | 8 | 3 | 11 | .214 | 0 | 263 | 34 | 13 | 53 | .270 | 0 | 66% | 39% | 10% | 1.8 | 46% | .788 | .858 | .644 |
| Bowker J | 26 | 69 | 7 | 16 | 5 | 0 | 2 | 13 | .232 | .312 | .391 | 0 | 1 | --- | -- | -- | -- | --- | -- | 69 | 7 | 2 | 13 | .232 | 0 | 86% | 27% | 10% | 1.7 | 46% | .703 | .691 | .804 |
| Cedeno R | 139 | 468 | 42 | 120 | 29 | 3 | 8 | 38 | .256 | .293 | .382 | 12 | 3 | 240 | 15 | 4 | 16 | .229 | 8 | 228 | 27 | 4 | 22 | .285 | 4 | 77% | 33% | 5% | 1.5 | 48% | .675 | .647 | .767 |
| Church R | 69 | 170 | 16 | 31 | 11 | 1 | 3 | 18 | .182 | .240 | .312 | 1 | 0 | 156 | 15 | 3 | 16 | .186 | 1 | 14 | 1 | 0 | 2 | .143 | 0 | 73% | 25% | 7% | 1.7 | 40% | .552 | .575 | .459 |
| Ciriaco P | 8 | 6 | 3 | 3 | 1 | 1 | 0 | 1 | .500 | .500 | 1.000 | 0 | 0 | --- | -- | -- | -- | --- | -- | 6 | 3 | 0 | 1 | .500 | 0 | 50% | 100% | 0% | 2.0 | 33% | 1.500 | 1.500 | --- |
| Clement J | 54 | 144 | 11 | 29 | 3 | 0 | 7 | 12 | .201 | .237 | .368 | 0 | 0 | 127 | 9 | 5 | 9 | .189 | 0 | 17 | 2 | 2 | 3 | .294 | 0 | 74% | 27% | 4% | 1.8 | 47% | .605 | .561 | .743 |
| Crosby B | 61 | 156 | 9 | 35 | 8 | 0 | 1 | 11 | .224 | .301 | .295 | 0 | 2 | 148 | 9 | 1 | 11 | .236 | 0 | 8 | 0 | 0 | 0 | .000 | 0 | 79% | 28% | 9% | 1.3 | 51% | .595 | .599 | .589 |
| Diaz A | 22 | 33 | 0 | 8 | 1 | 0 | 0 | 2 | .242 | .306 | .273 | 0 | 1 | 2 | 0 | 0 | 0 | .000 | 0 | 31 | 0 | 0 | 2 | .258 | 0 | 70% | 35% | 8% | 1.1 | 52% | .578 | .633 | .200 |
| Doumit R | 124 | 406 | 42 | 102 | 22 | 1 | 13 | 45 | .251 | .331 | .406 | 1 | 0 | 265 | 25 | 8 | 31 | .260 | 1 | 141 | 17 | 5 | 14 | .234 | 0 | 79% | 32% | 9% | 1.6 | 41% | .738 | .832 | .532 |
| Iwamura A | 54 | 165 | 18 | 30 | 6 | 1 | 2 | 9 | .182 | .292 | .267 | 3 | 1 | 165 | 18 | 2 | 9 | .182 | 3 | --- | -- | -- | -- | --- | -- | 81% | 22% | 13% | 1.5 | 56% | .558 | .617 | .326 |
| Jaramillo J | 33 | 87 | 2 | 13 | 2 | 0 | 1 | 6 | .149 | .227 | .207 | 0 | 0 | 67 | 2 | 1 | 6 | .164 | 0 | 20 | 0 | 0 | 0 | .100 | 0 | 84% | 18% | 8% | 1.4 | 51% | .434 | .332 | .741 |
| Jones G | 158 | 592 | 64 | 146 | 34 | 1 | 21 | 86 | .247 | .306 | .414 | 7 | 3 | 327 | 35 | 11 | 52 | .272 | 6 | 265 | 29 | 10 | 34 | .215 | 1 | 79% | 31% | 8% | 1.7 | 45% | .720 | .775 | .621 |
| Kratz E | 9 | 34 | 2 | 4 | 0 | 0 | 0 | 1 | .118 | .167 | .118 | 0 | 0 | --- | -- | -- | -- | --- | -- | 34 | 2 | 0 | 1 | .118 | 0 | 74% | 16% | 6% | 1.0 | 28% | .284 | .284 | .286 |
| LaRoche A | 102 | 247 | 26 | 51 | 8 | 0 | 4 | 16 | .206 | .268 | .287 | 1 | 1 | 201 | 24 | 3 | 13 | .229 | 1 | 46 | 2 | 1 | 3 | .109 | 0 | 83% | 25% | 7% | 1.4 | 50% | .555 | .485 | .683 |
| McCutchen A | 154 | 570 | 94 | 163 | 35 | 5 | 16 | 56 | .286 | .365 | .449 | 33 | 10 | 324 | 52 | 8 | 29 | .287 | 20 | 246 | 42 | 8 | 27 | .285 | 13 | 84% | 34% | 11% | 1.6 | 44% | .814 | .784 | .903 |
| Milledge L | 113 | 379 | 38 | 105 | 21 | 3 | 4 | 34 | .277 | .332 | .380 | 5 | 3 | 250 | 23 | 3 | 26 | .276 | 5 | 129 | 15 | 1 | 8 | .279 | 0 | 84% | 33% | 7% | 1.4 | 48% | .712 | .602 | .926 |
| Moss B | 17 | 26 | 2 | 4 | 1 | 0 | 0 | 2 | .154 | .185 | .192 | 0 | 0 | --- | -- | -- | -- | --- | -- | 26 | 2 | 0 | 2 | .154 | 0 | 77% | 20% | 4% | 1.3 | 55% | .377 | .392 | .000 |
| Pearce S | 15 | 29 | 4 | 8 | 2 | 1 | 0 | 5 | .276 | .395 | .414 | 0 | 0 | 29 | 4 | 0 | 5 | .276 | 0 | --- | -- | -- | -- | --- | -- | 79% | 35% | 18% | 1.5 | 48% | .809 | .583 | .964 |
| Presley A | 19 | 23 | 2 | 6 | 1 | 0 | 0 | 0 | .261 | .292 | .304 | 1 | 1 | --- | -- | -- | -- | --- | -- | 23 | 2 | 0 | 0 | .261 | 1 | 65% | 40% | 4% | 1.2 | 60% | .596 | .511 | 1.500 |
| Raynor J | 11 | 10 | 1 | 2 | 0 | 0 | 0 | 0 | .200 | .273 | .200 | 0 | 0 | 10 | 1 | 0 | 0 | .200 | 0 | --- | -- | -- | -- | --- | -- | 70% | 29% | 9% | 1.0 | 71% | .473 | .833 | .286 |
| Snyder C | 40 | 124 | 12 | 21 | 1 | 0 | 5 | 16 | .169 | .268 | .298 | 0 | 0 | --- | -- | -- | -- | --- | -- | 124 | 12 | 5 | 16 | .169 | 0 | 73% | 23% | 11% | 1.8 | 42% | .566 | .506 | .773 |
| Tabata J | 102 | 405 | 61 | 121 | 21 | 4 | 4 | 35 | .299 | .346 | .400 | 19 | 7 | 116 | 12 | 1 | 6 | .241 | 8 | 289 | 49 | 3 | 29 | .322 | 11 | 86% | 35% | 6% | 1.3 | 58% | .746 | .767 | .682 |
| Walker N | 110 | 426 | 57 | 126 | 29 | 3 | 12 | 66 | .296 | .349 | .462 | 2 | 3 | 142 | 19 | 3 | 12 | .275 | 2 | 284 | 38 | 9 | 54 | .306 | 0 | 81% | 37% | 7% | 1.6 | 36% | .811 | .813 | .809 |
| Young D | 110 | 191 | 22 | 45 | 11 | 1 | 7 | 28 | .236 | .286 | .414 | 1 | 0 | 116 | 9 | 3 | 18 | .233 | 1 | 75 | 13 | 4 | 10 | .240 | 0 | 73% | 32% | 6% | 1.8 | 47% | .700 | .663 | 1.000 |

| Pitchers | Pittsburgh Pirates 2010 | | | | | | | | | | | | | 1st Half | | | | | | 2nd Half | | | | | | Rates | | | Productiveness | | |
|---|---|---|---|---|---|---|---|---|---|---|---|---|---|---|---|---|---|---|---|---|---|---|---|---|---|---|---|---|---|---|---|
| | G | GS | W | L | Hld | Sv | IP | H | HR | ERA | WHIP | K | BB | W | L | Sv | IP | ERA | WHIP | W | L | Sv | IP | ERA | WHIP | K/9 | BB/9 | HR/9 | opOPS | vs RH | vs LH |
| Bass B | 4 | 0 | 0 | 0 | 0 | 0 | 7.1 | 9 | 0 | 12.27 | 2.59 | 5 | 10 | 0 | 0 | 0 | 6.1 | 12.79 | 2.68 | 0 | 0 | 0 | 1.0 | 9.00 | 2.00 | 6.1 | 12.3 | 0.0 | .902 | .832 | 1.127 |
| Burres B | 20 | 13 | 4 | 5 | 0 | 0 | 79.1 | 87 | 9 | 4.99 | 1.53 | 45 | 34 | 2 | 3 | 0 | 41.2 | 5.62 | 1.70 | 2 | 2 | 0 | 37.2 | 4.30 | 1.33 | 5.1 | 3.9 | 1.0 | .835 | .810 | .912 |
| Carrasco D | 45 | 0 | 2 | 2 | 5 | 0 | 55.2 | 50 | 4 | 3.88 | 1.29 | 45 | 22 | 1 | 2 | 0 | 45.2 | 3.74 | 1.36 | 1 | 0 | 0 | 10.0 | 4.50 | 1.00 | 7.3 | 3.6 | 0.6 | .693 | .669 | .742 |
| Donnelly B | 38 | 0 | 3 | 1 | 9 | 0 | 30.2 | 26 | 6 | 5.58 | 1.66 | 26 | 25 | 3 | 1 | 0 | 27.0 | 5.33 | 1.70 | 0 | 0 | 0 | 3.2 | 7.36 | 1.36 | 7.6 | 7.3 | 1.8 | .804 | .680 | 1.049 |
| Dotel O | 41 | 0 | 2 | 2 | 0 | 21 | 40.0 | 35 | 5 | 4.28 | 1.30 | 48 | 17 | 2 | 2 | 19 | 35.0 | 4.89 | 1.37 | 0 | 0 | 2 | 5.0 | 0.00 | 0.80 | 10.8 | 3.8 | 1.1 | .761 | .532 | 1.055 |
| Duke Z | 29 | 29 | 8 | 15 | 0 | 0 | 159.0 | 212 | 25 | 5.72 | 1.65 | 96 | 51 | 3 | 8 | 0 | 80.1 | 5.49 | 1.72 | 5 | 7 | 0 | 78.2 | 5.95 | 1.59 | 5.4 | 2.9 | 1.4 | .881 | .864 | .947 |
| Eveland D | 3 | 1 | 0 | 1 | 0 | 0 | 9.2 | 15 | 0 | 8.38 | 2.07 | 3 | 5 | 0 | 1 | 0 | 9.2 | 8.38 | 2.07 | -- | -- | -- | ---- | ---- | --- | 2.8 | 4.7 | 0.0 | .949 | .968 | .833 |
| Gallagher S | 31 | 0 | 2 | 1 | 3 | 0 | 34.1 | 38 | 2 | 6.03 | 1.75 | 22 | 22 | 0 | 0 | 0 | 0.2 | 0.00 | 3.00 | 2 | 1 | 0 | 33.2 | 6.15 | 1.72 | 5.8 | 5.8 | 0.5 | .768 | .843 | .675 |
| Hanrahan J | 72 | 0 | 4 | 1 | 18 | 6 | 69.2 | 58 | 6 | 3.62 | 1.21 | 100 | 26 | 2 | 1 | 0 | 37.2 | 4.06 | 1.12 | 2 | 0 | 6 | 32.0 | 3.09 | 1.31 | 12.9 | 3.4 | 0.8 | .649 | .589 | .750 |
| Jackson S | 11 | 0 | 0 | 1 | 0 | 0 | 11.1 | 17 | 4 | 8.74 | 2.03 | 7 | 6 | 0 | 1 | 0 | 2.1 | 3.86 | 1.71 | 0 | 0 | 0 | 9.0 | 10.00 | 2.11 | 5.6 | 4.8 | 3.2 | 1.043 | 1.180 | .879 |
| Jakubauskas C | 1 | 1 | 0 | 1 | 0 | 0 | 0.2 | 2 | 0 | 27.00 | 3.00 | 0 | 0 | 0 | 1 | 0 | 0.2 | 27.00 | 3.00 | -- | -- | -- | ---- | ---- | --- | 0.0 | 0.0 | 0.0 | 1.000 | .000 | 2.000 |
| Karstens J | 26 | 19 | 3 | 10 | 0 | 0 | 122.2 | 146 | 21 | 4.92 | 1.41 | 72 | 27 | 2 | 4 | 0 | 77.2 | 4.87 | 1.48 | 1 | 6 | 0 | 45.0 | 5.00 | 1.29 | 5.3 | 2.0 | 1.5 | .837 | .683 | 1.027 |
| Ledezma W | 27 | 0 | 0 | 3 | 3 | 0 | 19.2 | 25 | 2 | 6.86 | 1.58 | 22 | 6 | -- | -- | -- | ---- | ---- | --- | 0 | 3 | 0 | 19.2 | 6.86 | 1.58 | 10.1 | 2.7 | 0.9 | .807 | .723 | .958 |
| Leroux C | 6 | 0 | 0 | 1 | 0 | 0 | 4.2 | 4 | 0 | 5.79 | 1.50 | 4 | 3 | -- | -- | -- | ---- | ---- | --- | 0 | 1 | 0 | 4.2 | 5.79 | 1.50 | 7.7 | 5.8 | 0.0 | .611 | 1.045 | .200 |
| Lincoln B | 11 | 9 | 1 | 4 | 0 | 0 | 52.2 | 66 | 9 | 6.66 | 1.54 | 25 | 15 | 1 | 3 | 0 | 42.0 | 5.14 | 1.40 | 0 | 1 | 0 | 10.2 | 12.66 | 2.06 | 4.3 | 2.6 | 1.5 | .893 | .870 | .922 |
| Lopez J | 50 | 0 | 2 | 2 | 6 | 0 | 38.2 | 39 | 2 | 2.79 | 1.47 | 22 | 18 | 1 | 1 | 0 | 32.1 | 2.78 | 1.36 | 1 | 1 | 0 | 6.1 | 2.84 | 2.05 | 5.1 | 4.2 | 0.5 | .756 | .807 | .675 |
| Maholm P | 32 | 32 | 9 | 15 | 0 | 0 | 185.1 | 228 | 15 | 5.10 | 1.56 | 102 | 62 | 5 | 7 | 0 | 105.0 | 4.37 | 1.53 | 4 | 8 | 0 | 80.1 | 6.05 | 1.61 | 5.0 | 3.0 | 0.7 | .812 | .842 | .645 |
| Martinez J | 5 | 0 | 0 | 0 | 0 | 0 | 8.2 | 11 | 0 | 3.12 | 1.62 | 6 | 3 | -- | -- | -- | ---- | ---- | --- | 0 | 0 | 0 | 8.2 | 3.12 | 1.62 | 6.2 | 3.1 | 0.0 | .744 | .705 | .778 |
| McCutchen D | 28 | 9 | 2 | 5 | 0 | 0 | 67.2 | 83 | 13 | 6.12 | 1.64 | 38 | 28 | 1 | 4 | 0 | 28.1 | 8.58 | 1.69 | 1 | 1 | 0 | 39.1 | 4.35 | 1.60 | 5.1 | 3.7 | 1.7 | .887 | .855 | .927 |
| McDonald J | 11 | 11 | 4 | 5 | 0 | 0 | 64.0 | 59 | 3 | 3.52 | 1.30 | 61 | 24 | -- | -- | -- | ---- | ---- | --- | 4 | 5 | 0 | 64.0 | 3.52 | 1.30 | 8.6 | 3.4 | 0.4 | .678 | .700 | .658 |
| Meek E | 70 | 0 | 5 | 4 | 15 | 4 | 80.0 | 53 | 5 | 2.14 | 1.05 | 70 | 31 | 4 | 3 | 1 | 48.2 | 1.11 | 0.95 | 1 | 1 | 3 | 31.1 | 3.73 | 1.21 | 7.9 | 3.5 | 0.6 | .546 | .611 | .462 |
| Morton C | 17 | 17 | 2 | 12 | 0 | 0 | 79.2 | 112 | 15 | 7.57 | 1.73 | 59 | 26 | 1 | 9 | 0 | 43.1 | 9.35 | 1.89 | 1 | 3 | 0 | 36.1 | 5.45 | 1.54 | 6.7 | 2.9 | 1.7 | .908 | .878 | .949 |
| Ohlendorf R | 21 | 21 | 1 | 11 | 0 | 0 | 108.1 | 106 | 12 | 4.07 | 1.38 | 79 | 44 | 1 | 7 | 0 | 74.2 | 4.22 | 1.42 | 0 | 4 | 0 | 33.2 | 3.74 | 1.31 | 6.6 | 3.7 | 1.0 | .773 | .730 | .833 |
| Park C | 26 | 0 | 2 | 2 | 1 | 0 | 28.1 | 25 | 2 | 3.49 | 1.13 | 23 | 7 | -- | -- | -- | ---- | ---- | --- | 2 | 2 | 0 | 28.1 | 3.49 | 1.13 | 7.3 | 2.2 | 0.6 | .620 | .690 | .515 |
| Penn H | 3 | 0 | 0 | 0 | 0 | 0 | 2.1 | 8 | 0 | 30.86 | 4.71 | 0 | 3 | 0 | 0 | 0 | 2.1 | 30.86 | 4.71 | -- | -- | -- | ---- | ---- | --- | 0.0 | 11.6 | 0.0 | 1.534 | 1.413 | 1.690 |
| Resop C | 22 | 0 | 0 | 0 | 5 | 0 | 19.0 | 10 | 1 | 1.89 | 1.05 | 24 | 10 | -- | -- | -- | ---- | ---- | --- | 0 | 0 | 0 | 19.0 | 1.89 | 1.05 | 11.4 | 4.7 | 0.5 | .513 | .400 | .688 |
| Taschner J | 17 | 0 | 1 | 0 | 2 | 0 | 19.1 | 22 | 3 | 6.05 | 1.55 | 17 | 8 | 1 | 0 | 0 | 19.1 | 6.05 | 1.55 | -- | -- | -- | ---- | ---- | --- | 7.9 | 3.7 | 1.4 | .828 | .837 | .810 |
| Thomas J | 12 | 0 | 0 | 1 | 0 | 0 | 13.0 | 21 | 3 | 6.23 | 2.00 | 5 | 5 | 0 | 0 | 0 | 5.0 | 10.80 | 1.60 | 0 | 1 | 0 | 8.0 | 3.38 | 2.25 | 3.5 | 3.5 | 2.1 | 1.026 | .920 | 1.333 |

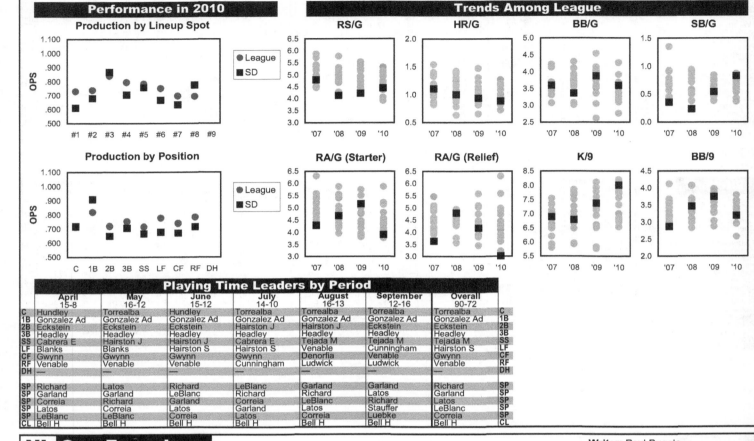

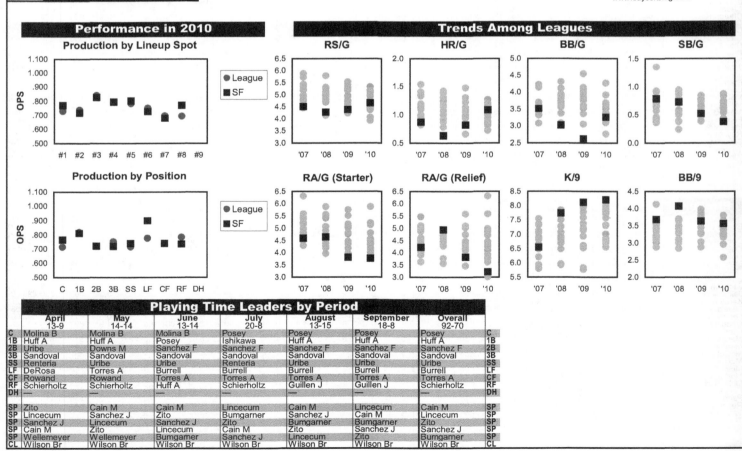

# NL San Diego

Writer: David Golebiewski
www.fangraphs.com

## Performance in 2010

### Production by Lineup Spot

### Production by Position

## Trends Among League

RS/G  HR/G  BB/G  SB/G

RA/G (Starter)  RA/G (Relief)  K/9  BB/9

### Playing Time Leaders by Period

| | April 15-8 | May 16-12 | June 15-12 | July 14-10 | August 16-13 | September 12-16 | Overall 90-72 | |
|---|---|---|---|---|---|---|---|---|
| C | Hundley | Torrealba | Hundley | Torrealba | Torrealba | Torrealba | Torrealba | C |
| 1B | Gonzalez Ad | Gonzalez Ad | Gonzalez Ad | Gonzalez Ad | Gonzalez Ad | Gonzalez Ad | Gonzalez Ad | 1B |
| 2B | Eckstein | Eckstein | Eckstein | Hairston J | Hairston J | Eckstein | Eckstein | 2B |
| 3B | Headley | Headley | Headley | Headley | Headley | Headley | Headley | 3B |
| SS | Cabrera E | Hairston J | Hairston J | Cabrera E | Tejada M | Tejada M | Tejada M | SS |
| LF | Blanks | Blanks | Hairston S | Hairston S | Venable | Cunningham | Hairston S | LF |
| CF | Gwynn | Gwynn | Gwynn | Gwynn | Denorfia | Venable | Gwynn | CF |
| RF | Venable | Venable | Venable | Cunningham | Ludwick | Ludwick | Venable | RF |
| DH | — | — | — | — | — | — | — | DH |
| SP | Richard | Latos | Richard | LeBlanc | Garland | Garland | Richard | SP |
| SP | Garland | Garland | LeBlanc | Richard | Richard | Latos | Garland | SP |
| SP | Correia | Richard | Garland | Correia | LeBlanc | Richard | Latos | SP |
| SP | Latos | Correia | Latos | Garland | Latos | Stauffer | LeBlanc | SP |
| SP | LeBlanc | LeBlanc | Correia | Latos | Correia | Luebke | Correia | SP |
| CL | Bell H | Bell H | Bell H | Bell H | Bell H | Bell H | Bell H | CL |

# NL San Francisco

www.baysoxblog.com

## Performance in 2010

### Production by Lineup Spot

### Production by Position

## Trends Among Leagues

RS/G  HR/G  BB/G  SB/G

RA/G (Starter)  RA/G (Relief)  K/9  BB/9

### Playing Time Leaders by Period

| | April 13-9 | May 14-14 | June 13-14 | July 20-8 | August 13-15 | September 18-8 | Overall 92-70 | |
|---|---|---|---|---|---|---|---|---|
| C | Molina B | Molina B | Molina B | Posey | Posey | Posey | Posey | C |
| 1B | Huff A | Huff A | Posey | Ishikawa | Huff A | Huff A | Huff A | 1B |
| 2B | Uribe | Downs M | Sanchez F | Sanchez F | Sanchez F | Sanchez F | Sanchez F | 2B |
| 3B | Sandoval | Sandoval | Sandoval | Sandoval | Sandoval | Sandoval | Sandoval | 3B |
| SS | Renteria | Uribe | Uribe | Renteria | Uribe | Uribe | Uribe | SS |
| LF | DeRosa | Torres A | Burrell | Burrell | Burrell | Burrell | Burrell | LF |
| CF | Rowand | Rowand | Torres A | Torres A | Torres A | Torres A | Torres A | CF |
| RF | Schierholtz | Schierholtz | Huff A | Schierholtz | Guillen J | Guillen J | Schierholtz | RF |
| DH | | | | | | | | DH |
| SP | Zito | Cain M | Cain M | Lincecum | Cain M | Lincecum | Cain M | SP |
| SP | Lincecum | Sanchez J | Zito | Bumgarner | Sanchez J | Cain M | Lincecum | SP |
| SP | Sanchez J | Lincecum | Sanchez J | Zito | Bumgarner | Bumgarner | Zito | SP |
| SP | Cain M | Zito | Lincecum | Cain M | Zito | Sanchez J | Sanchez J | SP |
| SP | Wellemeyer | Wellemeyer | Bumgarner | Sanchez J | Lincecum | Zito | Bumgarner | SP |
| CL | Wilson Br | Wilson Br | Wilson Br | Wilson Br | Wilson Br | Wilson Br | Wilson Br | CL |

| Hitters | San Diego Padres 2010 | | | | | | | | | | | | | 1st Half | | | | | | 2nd Half | | | | | | Rates | | | | | Productiveness | | |
|---|---|---|---|---|---|---|---|---|---|---|---|---|---|---|---|---|---|---|---|---|---|---|---|---|---|---|---|---|---|---|---|---|---|
| | G | AB | R | H | 2B | 3B | HR | RBI | BA | OBP | SLG | SB | CS | AB | R | HR | BI | BA | SB | AB | R | HR | BI | BA | SB | CT% | H% | BB% | Bash | GB% | OPS | vs RH | vs LH |
| Baxter M | 9 | 8 | 0 | 1 | 0 | 0 | 0 | 1 | .125 | .111 | .125 | 0 | 0 | --- | -- | -- | -- | --- | -- | 8 | 0 | 0 | 1 | .125 | 0 | 75% | 17% | 0% | 1.0 | 50% | .236 | .236 | --- |
| Blanks K | 33 | 102 | 14 | 16 | 6 | 1 | 3 | 15 | .157 | .283 | .324 | 1 | 0 | 102 | 14 | 3 | 15 | .157 | 1 | --- | -- | -- | -- | --- | -- | 55% | 29% | 13% | 2.1 | 41% | .607 | .526 | .865 |
| Cabrera E | 76 | 212 | 22 | 44 | 6 | 3 | 1 | 22 | .208 | .279 | .278 | 10 | 6 | 141 | 13 | 1 | 16 | .199 | 7 | 71 | 9 | 0 | 6 | .225 | 3 | 75% | 28% | 8% | 1.3 | 51% | .557 | .545 | .607 |
| Cunningham A | 53 | 132 | 17 | 38 | 12 | 1 | 1 | 15 | .288 | .331 | .417 | 1 | 3 | 59 | 10 | 1 | 12 | .339 | 0 | 73 | 7 | 0 | 3 | .247 | 1 | 79% | 37% | 5% | 1.4 | 46% | .748 | .606 | 1.022 |
| Denorfia C | 99 | 284 | 41 | 77 | 15 | 2 | 9 | 36 | .271 | .335 | .433 | 8 | 4 | 110 | 14 | 2 | 15 | .255 | 2 | 174 | 27 | 7 | 21 | .282 | 6 | 82% | 33% | 8% | 1.6 | 59% | .769 | .769 | .763 |
| Durango L | 28 | 48 | 8 | 12 | 0 | 0 | 0 | 4 | .250 | .308 | .250 | 5 | 0 | 13 | 3 | 0 | 2 | .385 | 0 | 35 | 5 | 0 | 2 | .200 | 5 | 85% | 29% | 8% | 1.0 | 80% | .558 | .560 | .539 |
| Eckstein D | 116 | 442 | 49 | 118 | 23 | 0 | 1 | 29 | .267 | .321 | .326 | 8 | 1 | 297 | 29 | 1 | 22 | .279 | 5 | 145 | 20 | 0 | 7 | .241 | 3 | 92% | 29% | 5% | 1.2 | 48% | .647 | .642 | .658 |
| Gonzalez A | 160 | 591 | 87 | 176 | 33 | 0 | 31 | 101 | .298 | .393 | .511 | 0 | 0 | 319 | 49 | 18 | 56 | .301 | 0 | 272 | 38 | 13 | 45 | .294 | 0 | 81% | 37% | 13% | 1.7 | 40% | .904 | .887 | .937 |
| Gwynn T | 117 | 289 | 30 | 59 | 9 | 3 | 3 | 20 | .204 | .304 | .287 | 17 | 4 | 222 | 22 | 2 | 16 | .221 | 13 | 67 | 8 | 1 | 4 | .149 | 4 | 83% | 25% | 12% | 1.4 | 44% | .591 | .547 | .872 |
| Hairston J | 119 | 430 | 53 | 105 | 13 | 2 | 10 | 50 | .244 | .299 | .353 | 9 | 6 | 286 | 31 | 6 | 32 | .248 | 6 | 144 | 22 | 4 | 18 | .236 | 3 | 87% | 28% | 6% | 1.4 | 40% | .652 | .642 | .678 |
| Hairston S | 104 | 295 | 34 | 62 | 10 | 0 | 10 | 36 | .210 | .295 | .346 | 6 | 1 | 212 | 29 | 8 | 28 | .241 | 6 | 83 | 5 | 2 | 8 | .133 | 0 | 77% | 27% | 9% | 1.6 | 35% | .640 | .633 | .655 |
| Headley C | 161 | 610 | 77 | 161 | 29 | 3 | 11 | 58 | .264 | .327 | .375 | 17 | 5 | 349 | 48 | 6 | 31 | .269 | 11 | 261 | 29 | 5 | 27 | .257 | 6 | 77% | 34% | 8% | 1.4 | 46% | .702 | .753 | .589 |
| Hundley N | 85 | 273 | 33 | 68 | 18 | 2 | 8 | 43 | .249 | .308 | .418 | 0 | 5 | 179 | 26 | 5 | 26 | .257 | 0 | 94 | 7 | 3 | 17 | .234 | 0 | 76% | 33% | 8% | 1.7 | 42% | .726 | .692 | .830 |
| Ludwick R | 59 | 209 | 19 | 44 | 7 | 0 | 6 | 26 | .211 | .301 | .330 | 0 | 1 | --- | -- | -- | -- | --- | -- | 209 | 19 | 6 | 26 | .211 | 0 | 73% | 29% | 10% | 1.6 | 36% | .631 | .695 | .498 |
| Salazar O | 85 | 131 | 19 | 31 | 4 | 0 | 3 | 19 | .237 | .318 | .336 | 1 | 2 | 106 | 13 | 2 | 15 | .226 | 1 | 25 | 6 | 1 | 4 | .280 | 0 | 82% | 29% | 11% | 1.4 | 44% | .653 | .685 | .625 |
| Stairs M | 78 | 99 | 14 | 23 | 6 | 0 | 6 | 16 | .232 | .306 | .475 | 2 | 0 | 50 | 7 | 2 | 8 | .200 | 2 | 49 | 7 | 4 | 8 | .265 | 0 | 68% | 34% | 10% | 2.0 | 39% | .781 | .798 | .250 |
| Tejada M | 59 | 235 | 31 | 63 | 10 | 0 | 8 | 32 | .268 | .317 | .413 | 2 | 0 | --- | -- | -- | -- | --- | -- | 235 | 31 | 8 | 32 | .268 | 2 | 88% | 30% | 6% | 1.5 | 49% | .730 | .570 | 1.147 |
| Torrealba Y | 95 | 325 | 31 | 88 | 14 | 0 | 7 | 37 | .271 | .343 | .378 | 7 | 5 | 152 | 16 | 1 | 17 | .289 | 4 | 173 | 15 | 6 | 20 | .254 | 3 | 79% | 34% | 9% | 1.4 | 54% | .721 | .729 | .698 |
| Venable W | 131 | 392 | 60 | 96 | 11 | 7 | 13 | 51 | .245 | .324 | .408 | 29 | 7 | 214 | 35 | 8 | 32 | .238 | 14 | 178 | 25 | 5 | 19 | .253 | 15 | 67% | 36% | 10% | 1.7 | 39% | .732 | .764 | .523 |
| Zawadzki L | 20 | 35 | 4 | 7 | 2 | 0 | 0 | 1 | .200 | .300 | .257 | 1 | 0 | 35 | 4 | 0 | 1 | .200 | 1 | --- | -- | -- | -- | --- | -- | 80% | 25% | 11% | 1.3 | 50% | .557 | .387 | .714 |

| Pitchers | San Diego Padres 2010 | | | | | | | | | | | | | 1st Half | | | | | | 2nd Half | | | | | | Rates | | | Productiveness | | |
|---|---|---|---|---|---|---|---|---|---|---|---|---|---|---|---|---|---|---|---|---|---|---|---|---|---|---|---|---|---|---|---|
| | G | GS | W | L | Hld | Sv | IP | H | HR | ERA | WHIP | K | BB | W | L | Sv | IP | ERA | WHIP | W | L | Sv | IP | ERA | WHIP | K/9 | BB/9 | HR/9 | opOPS | vs RH | vs LH |
| Adams M | 70 | 0 | 4 | 1 | 38 | 0 | 66.2 | 48 | 2 | 1.76 | 1.07 | 73 | 23 | 2 | 1 | 0 | 41.1 | 2.18 | 0.94 | 2 | 0 | 0 | 25.1 | 1.07 | 1.26 | 9.9 | 3.1 | 0.3 | .526 | .513 | .540 |
| Bell H | 67 | 0 | 6 | 1 | 0 | 47 | 70.0 | 56 | 1 | 1.93 | 1.20 | 86 | 28 | 4 | 0 | 24 | 38.1 | 1.88 | 1.33 | 2 | 1 | 23 | 31.2 | 1.99 | 1.04 | 11.1 | 3.6 | 0.1 | .585 | .612 | .554 |
| Correia K | 28 | 26 | 10 | 10 | 0 | 0 | 145.0 | 152 | 20 | 5.40 | 1.49 | 115 | 64 | 5 | 6 | 0 | 92.1 | 5.26 | 1.48 | 5 | 4 | 0 | 52.2 | 5.64 | 1.50 | 7.1 | 4.0 | 1.2 | .783 | .795 | .769 |
| Frieri E | 33 | 0 | 1 | 1 | 7 | 0 | 31.2 | 18 | 2 | 1.71 | 1.11 | 41 | 17 | -- | -- | -- | ---- | ---- | --- | 1 | 1 | 0 | 31.2 | 1.71 | 1.11 | 11.7 | 4.8 | 0.6 | .553 | .469 | .731 |
| Gallagher S | 15 | 0 | 0 | 0 | 0 | 0 | 23.1 | 24 | 5 | 5.40 | 1.84 | 21 | 19 | 0 | 0 | 0 | 23.1 | 5.40 | 1.84 | -- | -- | -- | ---- | ---- | --- | 8.1 | 7.3 | 1.9 | .922 | 1.209 | .590 |
| Garland J | 33 | 33 | 14 | 12 | 0 | 0 | 200.0 | 176 | 20 | 3.47 | 1.32 | 136 | 87 | 8 | 6 | 0 | 108.2 | 3.56 | 1.38 | 6 | 6 | 0 | 91.1 | 3.35 | 1.24 | 6.1 | 3.9 | 0.9 | .694 | .674 | .717 |
| Gregerson L | 80 | 0 | 4 | 7 | 40 | 2 | 78.1 | 47 | 8 | 3.22 | 0.83 | 89 | 18 | 3 | 5 | 1 | 43.1 | 2.91 | 0.74 | 1 | 2 | 1 | 35.0 | 3.60 | 0.94 | 10.2 | 2.1 | 0.9 | .524 | .511 | .540 |
| Latos M | 31 | 31 | 14 | 10 | 0 | 0 | 184.2 | 150 | 16 | 2.92 | 1.08 | 189 | 50 | 10 | 4 | 0 | 106.2 | 2.45 | 0.97 | 4 | 6 | 0 | 78.0 | 3.58 | 1.24 | 9.2 | 2.4 | 0.8 | .601 | .623 | .580 |
| LeBlanc W | 26 | 25 | 8 | 12 | 0 | 0 | 146.0 | 157 | 24 | 4.25 | 1.42 | 110 | 51 | 4 | 7 | 0 | 92.2 | 3.30 | 1.44 | 4 | 5 | 0 | 53.1 | 5.91 | 1.41 | 6.8 | 3.1 | 1.5 | .818 | .803 | .860 |
| Luebke C | 4 | 3 | 1 | 1 | 0 | 0 | 17.2 | 17 | 3 | 4.08 | 1.30 | 18 | 6 | -- | -- | -- | ---- | ---- | --- | 1 | 1 | 0 | 17.2 | 4.08 | 1.30 | 9.2 | 3.1 | 1.5 | .751 | .719 | .867 |
| Mujica E | 59 | 0 | 2 | 1 | 4 | 0 | 69.2 | 59 | 14 | 3.62 | 0.93 | 72 | 6 | 2 | 1 | 0 | 42.0 | 3.00 | 0.90 | 0 | 0 | 0 | 27.2 | 4.55 | 0.98 | 9.3 | 0.8 | 1.8 | .684 | .727 | .625 |
| Perdomo L | 1 | 0 | 0 | 0 | 0 | 0 | 1.0 | 1 | 1 | 9.00 | 1.00 | 0 | 0 | -- | -- | -- | ---- | ---- | --- | 0 | 0 | 0 | 1.0 | 9.00 | 1.00 | 0.0 | 0.0 | 9.0 | 1.250 | 2.500 | .000 |
| Ramos C | 14 | 0 | 0 | 1 | 2 | 0 | 8.1 | 18 | 1 | 11.88 | 2.64 | 9 | 4 | 0 | 1 | 0 | 4.2 | 21.21 | 3.21 | 0 | 0 | 0 | 3.2 | 0.00 | 1.91 | 9.7 | 4.3 | 1.1 | 1.049 | 1.330 | .697 |
| Richard C | 33 | 33 | 14 | 9 | 0 | 0 | 201.2 | 206 | 16 | 3.75 | 1.41 | 153 | 78 | 6 | 4 | 0 | 113.2 | 3.33 | 1.34 | 8 | 5 | 0 | 88.0 | 4.30 | 1.50 | 6.8 | 3.5 | 0.7 | .718 | .770 | .574 |
| Russell A | 12 | 0 | 0 | 0 | 0 | 0 | 15.2 | 14 | 0 | 4.02 | 1.21 | 18 | 5 | 0 | 0 | 0 | 9.2 | 3.72 | 1.14 | 0 | 0 | 0 | 6.0 | 4.50 | 1.33 | 10.3 | 2.9 | 0.0 | .602 | .734 | .393 |
| Stauffer T | 32 | 7 | 6 | 5 | 0 | 0 | 82.2 | 65 | 3 | 1.85 | 1.08 | 61 | 24 | 2 | 1 | 0 | 24.1 | 0.37 | 0.90 | 4 | 4 | 0 | 58.1 | 2.47 | 1.15 | 6.6 | 2.6 | 0.3 | .591 | .641 | .529 |
| Thatcher J | 65 | 0 | 1 | 0 | 11 | 0 | 35.0 | 23 | 1 | 1.29 | 0.86 | 45 | 7 | 1 | 0 | 0 | 17.2 | 2.04 | 0.74 | 0 | 0 | 0 | 17.1 | 0.52 | 0.98 | 11.6 | 1.8 | 0.3 | .465 | .395 | .527 |
| Webb R | 54 | 0 | 3 | 1 | 9 | 0 | 59.0 | 64 | 1 | 2.90 | 1.41 | 44 | 19 | 3 | 1 | 0 | 35.2 | 2.27 | 1.12 | 0 | 0 | 0 | 23.1 | 3.86 | 1.84 | 6.7 | 2.9 | 0.2 | .680 | .566 | .846 |
| Young C | 4 | 4 | 2 | 0 | 0 | 0 | 20.0 | 10 | 1 | 0.90 | 1.05 | 15 | 11 | 1 | 0 | 0 | 6.0 | 0.00 | 0.67 | 1 | 0 | 0 | 14.0 | 1.29 | 1.21 | 6.8 | 5.0 | 0.5 | .459 | .455 | .468 |

| Hitters | San Francisco Giants 2010 | | | | | | | | | | | | | 1st Half | | | | | | 2nd Half | | | | | | Rates | | | | | Productiveness | | |
|---|---|---|---|---|---|---|---|---|---|---|---|---|---|---|---|---|---|---|---|---|---|---|---|---|---|---|---|---|---|---|---|---|---|
| | G | AB | R | H | 2B | 3B | HR | RBI | BA | OBP | SLG | SB | CS | AB | R | HR | BI | BA | SB | AB | R | HR | BI | BA | SB | CT% | H% | BB% | Bash | GB% | OPS | vs RH | vs LH |
| Bowker J | 41 | 82 | 9 | 17 | 3 | 0 | 3 | 8 | .207 | .256 | .354 | 0 | 0 | 82 | 9 | 3 | 8 | .207 | 0 | --- | -- | -- | -- | --- | -- | 72% | 29% | 7% | 1.7 | 53% | .609 | .672 | .000 |
| Burrell P | 96 | 289 | 41 | 77 | 16 | 0 | 18 | 51 | .266 | .364 | .509 | 0 | 2 | 91 | 13 | 5 | 11 | .286 | 0 | 198 | 28 | 13 | 40 | .258 | 0 | 73% | 36% | 14% | 1.9 | 34% | .872 | .888 | .822 |
| Burriss E | 7 | 5 | 3 | 2 | 0 | 0 | 0 | 0 | .400 | .400 | .400 | 0 | 0 | --- | -- | -- | -- | --- | -- | 5 | 3 | 0 | 0 | .400 | 0 | 80% | 50% | 0% | 1.0 | 75% | .800 | 1.000 | .000 |
| DeRosa M | 26 | 93 | 9 | 18 | 3 | 0 | 1 | 10 | .194 | .279 | .258 | 0 | 2 | 93 | 9 | 1 | 10 | .194 | 0 | --- | -- | -- | -- | --- | -- | 83% | 23% | 9% | 1.3 | 44% | .537 | .421 | .840 |
| Downs M | 29 | 78 | 6 | 19 | 7 | 0 | 1 | 7 | .244 | .318 | .372 | 0 | 0 | 78 | 6 | 1 | 7 | .244 | 0 | --- | -- | -- | -- | --- | -- | 77% | 32% | 9% | 1.5 | 35% | .690 | .644 | .740 |
| Fontenot M | 28 | 71 | 10 | 20 | 2 | 0 | 0 | 5 | .282 | .329 | .310 | 0 | 2 | --- | -- | -- | -- | --- | -- | 71 | 10 | 0 | 5 | .282 | 0 | 82% | 34% | 7% | 1.1 | 52% | .639 | .666 | .393 |
| Guillen J | 42 | 128 | 9 | 34 | 5 | 0 | 3 | 15 | .266 | .317 | .375 | 0 | 0 | --- | -- | -- | -- | --- | -- | 128 | 9 | 3 | 15 | .266 | 0 | 77% | 34% | 4% | 1.4 | 57% | .692 | .696 | .671 |
| Huff A | 157 | 569 | 100 | 165 | 35 | 5 | 26 | 86 | .290 | .385 | .506 | 7 | 0 | 305 | 55 | 17 | 54 | .295 | 3 | 264 | 45 | 9 | 32 | .284 | 4 | 84% | 35% | 12% | 1.7 | 45% | .891 | .894 | .884 |
| Ishikawa T | 116 | 158 | 18 | 42 | 11 | 0 | 3 | 22 | .266 | .320 | .392 | 0 | 0 | 65 | 11 | 2 | 15 | .354 | 0 | 93 | 7 | 1 | 7 | .204 | 0 | 82% | 33% | 7% | 1.5 | 43% | .712 | .768 | .269 |
| Molina B | 61 | 202 | 17 | 52 | 6 | 0 | 3 | 17 | .257 | .312 | .332 | 0 | 0 | 202 | 17 | 3 | 17 | .257 | 0 | --- | -- | -- | -- | --- | -- | 91% | 28% | 6% | 1.3 | 39% | .644 | .534 | .926 |
| Posey B | 108 | 406 | 58 | 124 | 23 | 2 | 18 | 67 | .305 | .357 | .505 | 0 | 2 | 137 | 22 | 7 | 25 | .350 | 0 | 269 | 36 | 11 | 42 | .283 | 0 | 86% | 35% | 7% | 1.7 | 49% | .862 | .832 | .955 |
| Renteria E | 72 | 243 | 26 | 67 | 11 | 2 | 3 | 22 | .276 | .332 | .374 | 3 | 0 | 147 | 13 | 1 | 13 | .299 | 3 | 96 | 13 | 2 | 9 | .240 | 0 | 82% | 34% | 8% | 1.4 | 47% | .707 | .671 | .794 |
| Rohlinger R | 12 | 15 | 1 | 3 | 0 | 0 | 0 | 1 | .200 | .294 | .200 | 0 | 0 | 14 | 1 | 0 | 1 | .214 | 0 | 1 | 0 | 0 | 0 | .000 | 0 | 67% | 30% | 11% | 1.0 | 40% | .494 | .222 | .833 |
| Ross C | 33 | 73 | 11 | 21 | 4 | 0 | 3 | 7 | .288 | .354 | .466 | 0 | 1 | --- | -- | -- | -- | --- | -- | 73 | 11 | 3 | 7 | .288 | 0 | 71% | 40% | 9% | 1.6 | 54% | .819 | .753 | .969 |
| Rowand A | 105 | 331 | 42 | 76 | 12 | 2 | 11 | 34 | .230 | .281 | .378 | 5 | 3 | 240 | 30 | 8 | 27 | .238 | 2 | 91 | 12 | 3 | 7 | .209 | 3 | 78% | 30% | 4% | 1.6 | 49% | .659 | .649 | .682 |
| Sanchez F | 111 | 431 | 55 | 126 | 22 | 1 | 7 | 47 | .292 | .342 | .397 | 3 | 1 | 186 | 27 | 1 | 26 | .285 | 1 | 245 | 28 | 6 | 21 | .298 | 2 | 84% | 35% | 7% | 1.4 | 44% | .739 | .689 | .888 |
| Sandoval P | 152 | 563 | 61 | 151 | 34 | 3 | 13 | 63 | .268 | .323 | .409 | 3 | 2 | 335 | 42 | 6 | 34 | .263 | 2 | 228 | 19 | 7 | 29 | .276 | 1 | 86% | 31% | 7% | 1.5 | 45% | .732 | .779 | .589 |
| Schierholtz N | 137 | 227 | 34 | 55 | 13 | 3 | 3 | 17 | .242 | .311 | .366 | 4 | 5 | 160 | 24 | 2 | 12 | .250 | 4 | 67 | 10 | 1 | 5 | .224 | 0 | 83% | 29% | 8% | 1.5 | 44% | .676 | .678 | .671 |
| Torres A | 139 | 507 | 84 | 136 | 43 | 8 | 16 | 63 | .268 | .343 | .479 | 26 | 7 | 263 | 46 | 7 | 29 | .281 | 17 | 244 | 38 | 9 | 34 | .254 | 9 | 75% | 36% | 10% | 1.8 | 38% | .823 | .881 | .659 |
| Uribe J | 148 | 521 | 64 | 129 | 24 | 2 | 24 | 85 | .248 | .310 | .440 | 1 | 2 | 283 | 39 | 12 | 50 | .251 | 1 | 238 | 25 | 12 | 35 | .244 | 0 | 82% | 30% | 8% | 1.8 | 41% | .749 | .766 | .682 |
| Velez E | 29 | 55 | 7 | 9 | 2 | 0 | 2 | 8 | .164 | .246 | .309 | 0 | 0 | 46 | 6 | 2 | 8 | .196 | 0 | 9 | 1 | 0 | 0 | .000 | 0 | 84% | 20% | 9% | 1.9 | 59% | .555 | .576 | .481 |
| Whiteside E | 56 | 126 | 19 | 30 | 6 | 1 | 4 | 10 | .238 | .299 | .397 | 1 | 2 | 95 | 14 | 4 | 10 | .263 | 1 | 31 | 5 | 0 | 0 | .161 | 0 | 72% | 33% | 6% | 1.7 | 46% | .696 | .754 | .502 |

| Pitchers | San Francisco Giants 2010 | | | | | | | | | | | | | 1st Half | | | | | | 2nd Half | | | | | | Rates | | | Productiveness | | |
|---|---|---|---|---|---|---|---|---|---|---|---|---|---|---|---|---|---|---|---|---|---|---|---|---|---|---|---|---|---|---|---|
| | G | GS | W | L | Hld | Sv | IP | H | HR | ERA | WHIP | K | BB | W | L | Sv | IP | ERA | WHIP | W | L | Sv | IP | ERA | WHIP | K/9 | BB/9 | HR/9 | opOPS | vs RH | vs LH |
| Affeldt J | 53 | 0 | 4 | 3 | 7 | 4 | 50.0 | 56 | 4 | 4.14 | 1.60 | 44 | 24 | 2 | 3 | 2 | 31.2 | 4.55 | 1.77 | 2 | 0 | 2 | 18.1 | 3.44 | 1.31 | 7.9 | 4.3 | 0.7 | .795 | .784 | .815 |
| Bautista D | 31 | 0 | 2 | 0 | 0 | 0 | 33.2 | 25 | 4 | 3.74 | 1.54 | 44 | 27 | 2 | 0 | 0 | 28.0 | 2.89 | 1.57 | 0 | 0 | 0 | 5.2 | 7.94 | 1.41 | 11.8 | 7.2 | 1.1 | .685 | .694 | .671 |
| Bumgarner M | 18 | 18 | 7 | 6 | 0 | 0 | 111.0 | 119 | 11 | 3.00 | 1.31 | 86 | 26 | 2 | 2 | 0 | 28.0 | 2.57 | 1.04 | 5 | 4 | 0 | 83.0 | 3.14 | 1.40 | 7.0 | 2.1 | 0.9 | .732 | .751 | .678 |
| Cain M | 33 | 33 | 13 | 11 | 0 | 0 | 223.1 | 181 | 22 | 3.14 | 1.08 | 177 | 61 | 6 | 8 | 0 | 121.1 | 3.34 | 1.21 | 7 | 3 | 0 | 102.0 | 2.91 | 0.93 | 7.1 | 2.5 | 0.9 | .646 | .629 | .663 |
| Casilla S | 52 | 0 | 7 | 2 | 11 | 2 | 55.1 | 40 | 2 | 1.95 | 1.19 | 56 | 26 | 2 | 2 | 2 | 17.1 | 2.08 | 1.62 | 5 | 0 | 0 | 38.0 | 1.89 | 1.00 | 9.1 | 4.2 | 0.3 | .600 | .564 | .678 |
| Joaquin W | 4 | 0 | 0 | 0 | 1 | 0 | 4.2 | 6 | 0 | 9.64 | 2.79 | 2 | 7 | 0 | 0 | 0 | 4.2 | 9.64 | 2.79 | -- | -- | -- | ---- | ---- | --- | 3.9 | 13.5 | 0.0 | .927 | .778 | 1.267 |
| Lincecum T | 33 | 33 | 16 | 10 | 0 | 0 | 212.1 | 194 | 18 | 3.43 | 1.27 | 231 | 76 | 9 | 4 | 0 | 116.2 | 3.16 | 1.28 | 7 | 6 | 0 | 95.2 | 3.76 | 1.26 | 9.8 | 3.2 | 0.8 | .674 | .609 | .730 |
| Lopez J | 27 | 0 | 2 | 0 | 5 | 0 | 19.0 | 11 | 0 | 1.42 | 0.68 | 16 | 2 | -- | -- | -- | ---- | ---- | --- | 2 | 0 | 0 | 19.0 | 1.42 | 0.68 | 7.6 | 0.9 | 0.0 | .368 | .591 | .260 |
| Martinez J | 4 | 1 | 0 | 1 | 0 | 0 | 11.0 | 15 | 1 | 4.91 | 1.91 | 3 | 6 | 0 | 1 | 0 | 9.0 | 4.00 | 1.89 | 0 | 0 | 0 | 2.0 | 9.00 | 2.00 | 2.5 | 4.9 | 0.8 | .904 | 1.128 | .535 |
| Medders B | 14 | 0 | 0 | 0 | 0 | 0 | 15.0 | 26 | 3 | 7.20 | 2.13 | 8 | 6 | 0 | 0 | 0 | 15.0 | 7.20 | 2.13 | -- | -- | -- | ---- | ---- | --- | 4.8 | 3.6 | 1.8 | 1.080 | 1.018 | 1.166 |
| Mota G | 56 | 0 | 1 | 3 | 8 | 1 | 54.0 | 49 | 4 | 4.33 | 1.31 | 38 | 22 | 0 | 3 | 1 | 33.2 | 3.21 | 1.37 | 1 | 0 | 0 | 20.1 | 6.20 | 1.23 | 6.3 | 3.7 | 0.7 | .727 | .682 | .794 |
| Ramirez R | 25 | 0 | 1 | 0 | 4 | 1 | 27.0 | 13 | 1 | 0.67 | 0.89 | 15 | 11 | -- | -- | -- | ---- | ---- | --- | 1 | 0 | 1 | 27.0 | 0.67 | 0.89 | 5.0 | 3.7 | 0.3 | .405 | .359 | .481 |
| Ray C | 28 | 0 | 3 | 0 | 2 | 1 | 24.0 | 24 | 1 | 4.13 | 1.38 | 15 | 9 | 0 | 0 | 0 | 6.2 | 1.35 | 0.60 | 3 | 0 | 1 | 17.1 | 5.19 | 1.67 | 5.6 | 3.4 | 0.4 | .735 | .706 | .783 |
| Romo S | 68 | 0 | 5 | 3 | 21 | 0 | 62.0 | 46 | 6 | 2.18 | 0.97 | 70 | 14 | 2 | 3 | 0 | 36.2 | 2.21 | 0.93 | 3 | 0 | 0 | 25.1 | 2.13 | 1.03 | 10.2 | 2.0 | 0.9 | .599 | .570 | .652 |
| Runzler D | 41 | 0 | 3 | 0 | 5 | 0 | 32.2 | 29 | 1 | 3.03 | 1.50 | 37 | 20 | 3 | 0 | 0 | 30.0 | 3.30 | 1.53 | 0 | 0 | 0 | 2.2 | 0.00 | 1.13 | 10.2 | 5.5 | 0.3 | .685 | .673 | .699 |
| Sanchez J | 34 | 33 | 13 | 9 | 1 | 0 | 193.1 | 142 | 21 | 3.07 | 1.23 | 205 | 96 | 7 | 6 | 0 | 103.2 | 3.47 | 1.29 | 6 | 3 | 0 | 89.2 | 2.61 | 1.16 | 9.5 | 4.5 | 1.0 | .650 | .650 | .649 |
| Wellemeyer T | 13 | 11 | 3 | 5 | 0 | 0 | 58.2 | 57 | 12 | 5.68 | 1.57 | 41 | 35 | 3 | 5 | 0 | 58.2 | 5.52 | 1.50 | -- | -- | -- | ---- | ---- | --- | 6.3 | 5.4 | 1.8 | .837 | .689 | 1.027 |
| Wilson B | 70 | 0 | 3 | 3 | 0 | 48 | 74.2 | 62 | 3 | 1.81 | 1.18 | 93 | 26 | 2 | 0 | 23 | 37.2 | 1.91 | 1.33 | 1 | 3 | 25 | 37.0 | 1.70 | 1.03 | 11.2 | 3.1 | 0.4 | .597 | .587 | .607 |
| Zito B | 34 | 33 | 9 | 14 | 0 | 0 | 199.1 | 184 | 20 | 4.15 | 1.34 | 150 | 84 | 7 | 4 | 0 | 115.0 | 3.76 | 1.31 | 2 | 10 | 0 | 84.1 | 4.70 | 1.39 | 6.8 | 3.8 | 0.9 | .726 | .728 | .718 |

**Writer:** Griffin Cooper
www.sodomojo.com

## AL Seattle

### Performance in 2010

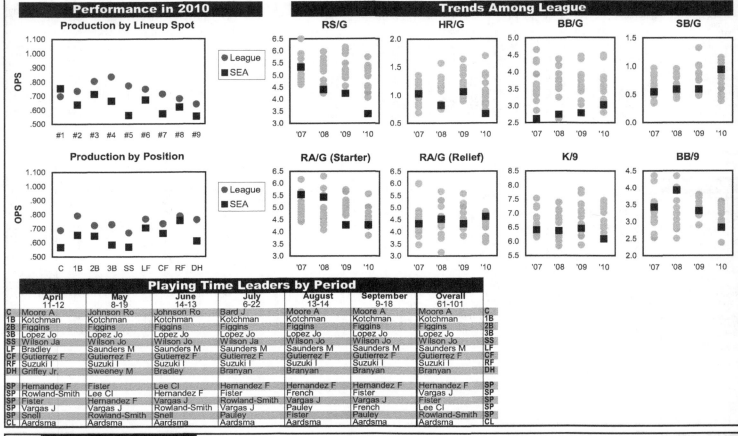

### Trends Among League

RS/G | HR/G | BB/G | SB/G | RA/G (Starter) | RA/G (Relief) | K/9 | BB/9

Production by Lineup Spot · Production by Position · League · SEA

### Playing Time Leaders by Period

|     | April 11-12 | May 8-19 | June 14-13 | July 6-22 | August 13-14 | September 9-18 | Overall 61-101 |     |
| --- | --- | --- | --- | --- | --- | --- | --- | --- |
| C | Moore A | Johnson Ro | Johnson Ro | Bard J | Moore A | Moore A | Moore A | C |
| 1B | Kotchman | Kotchman | Kotchman | Kotchman | Kotchman | Kotchman | Kotchman | 1B |
| 2B | Figgins | Figgins | Figgins | Figgins | Figgins | Figgins | Figgins | 2B |
| 3B | Lopez Jo | Lopez Jo | Lopez Jo | Lopez Jo | Lopez Jo | Lopez Jo | Lopez Jo | 3B |
| SS | Wilson Ja | Wilson Jo | Wilson Jo | Wilson Ja | Wilson Jo | Wilson Jo | Wilson Jo | SS |
| LF | Bradley | Saunders M | Saunders M | Saunders M | Saunders M | Saunders M | Saunders M | LF |
| CF | Gutierrez F | Gutierrez F | Gutierrez F | Gutierrez F | Gutierrez F | Gutierrez F | Gutierrez F | CF |
| RF | Suzuki I | Suzuki I | Suzuki I | Suzuki I | Suzuki I | Suzuki I | Suzuki I | RF |
| DH | Griffey Jr. | Sweeney M | Bradley | Branyan | Branyan | Branyan | Branyan | DH |
| | | | | | | | | |
| SP | Hernandez F | Fister | Lee Cl | Hernandez F | Hernandez F | Hernandez F | Hernandez F | SP |
| SP | Rowland-Smith | Lee Cl | Hernandez F | Fister | French | Fister | Vargas J | SP |
| SP | Fister | Hernandez F | Vargas J | Rowland-Smith | Vargas J | Vargas J | Fister | SP |
| SP | Vargas J | Vargas J | Rowland-Smith | Vargas J | Pauley | French | Lee Cl | SP |
| SP | Snell | Rowland-Smith | Snell | Pauley | Fister | Pauley | Rowland-Smith | SP |
| CL | Aardsma | Aardsma | Aardsma | Aardsma | Aardsma | Aardsma | Aardsma | CL |

## NL St. Louis

**Writer:** Andy Beard
playahardnine.wordpress.com

### Performance in 2010

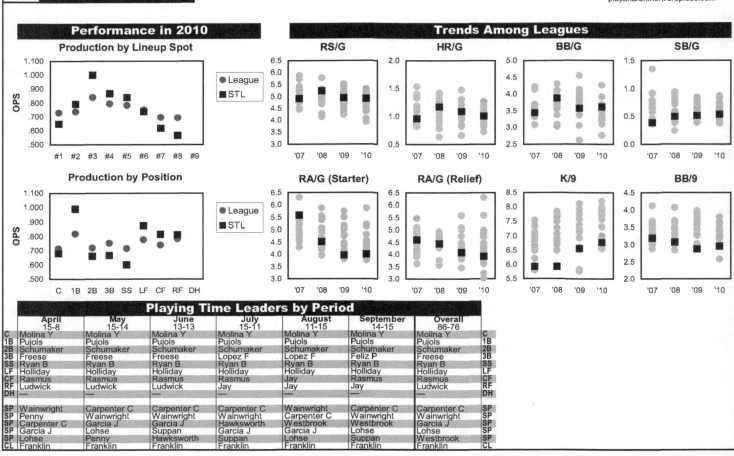

### Trends Among Leagues

RS/G | HR/G | BB/G | SB/G | RA/G (Starter) | RA/G (Relief) | K/9 | BB/9

Production by Lineup Spot · Production by Position · League · STL

### Playing Time Leaders by Period

|     | April 15-8 | May 15-14 | June 13-13 | July 15-11 | August 11-15 | September 14-15 | Overall 86-76 |     |
| --- | --- | --- | --- | --- | --- | --- | --- | --- |
| C | Molina Y | Molina Y | Molina Y | Molina Y | Molina Y | Molina Y | Molina Y | C |
| 1B | Pujols | Pujols | Pujols | Pujols | Pujols | Pujols | Pujols | 1B |
| 2B | Schumaker | Schumaker | Schumaker | Schumaker | Schumaker | Schumaker | Schumaker | 2B |
| 3B | Freese | Freese | Freese | Lopez F | Lopez F | Feliz P | Freese | 3B |
| SS | Ryan B | Ryan B | Ryan B | Ryan B | Ryan B | Ryan B | Ryan B | SS |
| LF | Holliday | Holliday | Holliday | Holliday | Holliday | Holliday | Holliday | LF |
| CF | Rasmus | Rasmus | Rasmus | Rasmus | Jay | Rasmus | Rasmus | CF |
| RF | Ludwick | Ludwick | Ludwick | Jay | Jay | Jay | Ludwick | RF |
| DH | — | | | | | | — | DH |
| | | | | | | | | |
| SP | Wainwright | Carpenter C | Carpenter C | Carpenter C | Wainwright | Carpenter C | Carpenter C | SP |
| SP | Penny | Wainwright | Wainwright | Wainwright | Carpenter C | Wainwright | Wainwright | SP |
| SP | Carpenter C | Garcia J | Garcia J | Hawksworth | Westbrook | Westbrook | Garcia J | SP |
| SP | Garcia J | Lohse | Suppan | Garcia J | Garcia J | Lohse | Lohse | SP |
| SP | Lohse | Penny | Hawksworth | Suppan | Lohse | Suppan | Westbrook | SP |
| CL | Franklin | Franklin | Franklin | Franklin | Franklin | Franklin | Franklin | CL |

## Hitters — Seattle Mariners 2010

| Hitters | G | AB | R | H | 2B | 3B | HR | RBI | BA | OBP | SLG | SB | CS | 1st Half AB | R | HR | BI | BA | SB | 2nd Half AB | R | HR | BI | BA | SB | Rates CT% | H% | BB% | Bash | GB% | Productiveness OPS | vs RH | vs LH |
|---|---|---|---|---|---|---|---|---|---|---|---|---|---|---|---|---|---|---|---|---|---|---|---|---|---|---|---|---|---|---|---|---|---|
| Alfonzo E | 13 | 41 | 4 | 9 | 1 | 0 | 1 | 4 | .220 | .220 | .317 | 0 | 0 | 41 | 4 | 1 | 4 | .220 | 0 | --- | -- | -- | -- | --- | -- | 76% | 29% | 0% | 1.4 | 39% | .537 | .520 | .563 |
| Bard J | 39 | 112 | 9 | 24 | 7 | 0 | 3 | 10 | .214 | .276 | .357 | 0 | 0 | 38 | 6 | 1 | 4 | .184 | 0 | 74 | 3 | 2 | 6 | .230 | 0 | 76% | 28% | 8% | 1.7 | 38% | .634 | .521 | .797 |
| Bradley M | 73 | 244 | 28 | 50 | 9 | 1 | 8 | 29 | .205 | .292 | .348 | 8 | 2 | 210 | 24 | 8 | 28 | .210 | 6 | 34 | 4 | 0 | 1 | .176 | 2 | 69% | 30% | 10% | 1.7 | 37% | .641 | .608 | .705 |
| Branyan R | 57 | 205 | 23 | 44 | 10 | 0 | 15 | 33 | .215 | .319 | .483 | 1 | 0 | 42 | 6 | 3 | 9 | .238 | 0 | 163 | 17 | 12 | 24 | .209 | 1 | 60% | 36% | 13% | 2.3 | 31% | .802 | .880 | .608 |
| Byrnes E | 15 | 32 | 1 | 3 | 2 | 0 | 0 | 0 | .094 | .237 | .156 | 1 | 0 | 32 | 1 | 0 | 0 | .094 | 1 | --- | -- | -- | -- | --- | -- | 72% | 13% | 16% | 1.7 | 35% | .393 | .596 | .071 |
| Carp M | 14 | 37 | 1 | 7 | 2 | 0 | 0 | 0 | .189 | .268 | .243 | 0 | 0 | 30 | 1 | 0 | 0 | .167 | 0 | 7 | 0 | 0 | 0 | .286 | 0 | 78% | 24% | 10% | 1.3 | 31% | .512 | .496 | .556 |
| Figgins C | 161 | 602 | 62 | 156 | 21 | 2 | 1 | 35 | .259 | .340 | .306 | 42 | 15 | 319 | 38 | 0 | 22 | .235 | 24 | 283 | 24 | 1 | 13 | .286 | 18 | 81% | 32% | 11% | 1.2 | 46% | .646 | .617 | .708 |
| Griffey Jr. K | 33 | 98 | 6 | 18 | 2 | 0 | 0 | 7 | .184 | .250 | .204 | 0 | 0 | 98 | 6 | 0 | 7 | .184 | 0 | --- | -- | -- | -- | --- | -- | 83% | 22% | 8% | 1.1 | 35% | .454 | .436 | .583 |
| Gutierrez F | 152 | 568 | 61 | 139 | 25 | 3 | 12 | 64 | .245 | .303 | .363 | 25 | 3 | 312 | 35 | 8 | 36 | .256 | 10 | 256 | 26 | 4 | 28 | .230 | 15 | 76% | 32% | 8% | 1.5 | 43% | .666 | .653 | .704 |
| Halman G | 9 | 29 | 1 | 4 | 1 | 0 | 0 | 3 | .138 | .167 | .172 | 1 | 0 | --- | -- | -- | -- | --- | -- | 29 | 1 | 0 | 3 | .138 | 1 | 62% | 22% | 3% | 1.3 | 22% | .339 | .000 | .690 |
| Johnson R | 61 | 178 | 24 | 34 | 10 | 0 | 2 | 13 | .191 | .293 | .281 | 1 | 1 | 151 | 23 | 2 | 13 | .205 | 1 | 27 | 1 | 0 | 0 | .111 | 0 | 74% | 26% | 12% | 1.5 | 52% | .574 | .562 | .610 |
| Kotchman C | 125 | 414 | 37 | 90 | 20 | 1 | 9 | 51 | .217 | .280 | .336 | 0 | 0 | 216 | 20 | 7 | 29 | .218 | 0 | 198 | 17 | 2 | 22 | .217 | 0 | 86% | 25% | 8% | 1.5 | 56% | .616 | .670 | .460 |
| Langerhans R | 60 | 107 | 16 | 21 | 2 | 1 | 3 | 4 | .196 | .344 | .318 | 4 | 1 | 41 | 8 | 2 | 3 | .195 | 3 | 66 | 8 | 1 | 1 | .197 | 1 | 52% | 38% | 18% | 1.6 | 38% | .661 | .810 | .322 |
| Lopez J | 150 | 593 | 49 | 142 | 29 | 0 | 10 | 58 | .239 | .270 | .339 | 3 | 2 | 350 | 28 | 6 | 37 | .240 | 3 | 243 | 21 | 4 | 21 | .239 | 0 | 89% | 27% | 4% | 1.4 | 43% | .609 | .584 | .681 |
| Mangini M | 11 | 38 | 2 | 8 | 0 | 0 | 0 | 1 | .211 | .250 | .211 | 0 | 0 | --- | -- | -- | -- | --- | -- | 38 | 2 | 0 | 1 | .211 | 0 | 66% | 32% | 5% | 1.0 | 60% | .461 | .581 | .267 |
| Moore A | 60 | 205 | 12 | 40 | 6 | 0 | 4 | 15 | .195 | .230 | .283 | 0 | 1 | 57 | 4 | 1 | 4 | .193 | 0 | 148 | 8 | 3 | 11 | .196 | 0 | 69% | 28% | 4% | 1.5 | 57% | .513 | .474 | .629 |
| Quiroz G | 2 | 7 | 1 | 2 | 1 | 0 | 0 | 0 | .286 | .286 | .429 | 0 | 0 | --- | -- | -- | -- | --- | -- | 7 | 1 | 0 | 0 | .286 | 0 | 86% | 33% | 0% | 1.5 | 17% | .714 | .500 | 1.000 |
| Saunders M | 100 | 289 | 29 | 61 | 11 | 2 | 10 | 33 | .211 | .295 | .367 | 6 | 3 | 139 | 20 | 7 | 21 | .216 | 2 | 150 | 9 | 3 | 12 | .207 | 4 | 71% | 30% | 11% | 1.7 | 34% | .662 | .686 | .601 |
| Smoak J | 30 | 113 | 11 | 27 | 4 | 0 | 5 | 14 | .239 | .287 | .407 | 0 | 0 | 8 | 0 | 0 | 0 | .125 | 0 | 105 | 11 | 5 | 14 | .248 | 0 | 70% | 34% | 7% | 1.7 | 35% | .694 | .519 | .987 |
| Suzuki I | 162 | 680 | 74 | 214 | 30 | 3 | 6 | 43 | .315 | .359 | .394 | 42 | 9 | 362 | 35 | 3 | 24 | .326 | 22 | 318 | 39 | 3 | 19 | .302 | 20 | 87% | 36% | 6% | 1.3 | 56% | .754 | .789 | .684 |
| Sweeney M | 30 | 99 | 11 | 26 | 3 | 0 | 6 | 18 | .263 | .327 | .475 | 2 | 0 | 99 | 11 | 6 | 18 | .263 | 2 | --- | -- | -- | -- | --- | -- | 86% | 31% | 8% | 1.8 | 40% | .802 | .882 | .701 |
| Tuiasosopo M | 50 | 127 | 12 | 22 | 5 | 0 | 4 | 11 | .173 | .234 | .307 | 0 | 0 | 54 | 4 | 1 | 2 | .167 | 0 | 73 | 8 | 3 | 9 | .178 | 0 | 61% | 28% | 7% | 1.8 | 44% | .541 | .571 | .487 |
| Wilson J | 61 | 193 | 17 | 48 | 11 | 1 | 0 | 14 | .249 | .282 | .316 | 1 | 2 | 124 | 10 | 0 | 10 | .250 | 1 | 69 | 7 | 0 | 4 | .246 | 0 | 82% | 30% | 3% | 1.3 | 39% | .598 | .597 | .600 |
| Wilson J | 108 | 361 | 22 | 82 | 14 | 2 | 2 | 25 | .227 | .278 | .294 | 5 | 0 | 189 | 14 | 1 | 14 | .265 | 3 | 172 | 8 | 1 | 11 | .186 | 2 | 80% | 29% | 4% | 1.3 | 35% | .572 | .596 | .508 |
| Woodward C | 8 | 19 | 0 | 3 | 1 | 0 | 0 | 0 | .158 | .273 | .211 | 0 | 0 | --- | -- | -- | -- | --- | -- | 19 | 0 | 0 | 0 | .158 | 0 | 53% | 30% | 14% | 1.3 | 50% | .483 | .404 | .667 |

## Pitchers — Seattle Mariners 2010

| Pitchers | G | GS | W | L | Hld | Sv | IP | H | HR | ERA | WHIP | K | BB | 1st Half W | L | Sv | IP | ERA | WHIP | 2nd Half W | L | Sv | IP | ERA | WHIP | Rates K/9 | BB/9 | HR/9 | Productiveness opOPS | vs RH | vs LH |
|---|---|---|---|---|---|---|---|---|---|---|---|---|---|---|---|---|---|---|---|---|---|---|---|---|---|---|---|---|---|---|---|
| Aardsma D | 53 | 0 | 0 | 6 | 0 | 31 | 49.2 | 33 | 5 | 3.44 | 1.17 | 49 | 25 | 0 | 6 | 16 | 28.1 | 5.40 | 1.34 | 0 | 0 | 15 | 21.1 | 0.84 | 0.94 | 8.9 | 4.5 | 0.9 | .631 | .568 | .688 |
| Colome J | 12 | 0 | 0 | 1 | 0 | 0 | 17.0 | 15 | 1 | 5.29 | 1.53 | 16 | 11 | 0 | 1 | 0 | 17.0 | 5.29 | 1.53 | -- | -- | -- | ---- | ---- | --- | 8.5 | 5.8 | 0.5 | .722 | .520 | .890 |
| Cordero C | 9 | 0 | 0 | 1 | 0 | 0 | 9.2 | 10 | 1 | 6.52 | 1.55 | 6 | 5 | 0 | 1 | 0 | 9.2 | 6.52 | 1.55 | -- | -- | -- | ---- | ---- | --- | 5.6 | 4.7 | 0.9 | .994 | .968 | 1.017 |
| Cortes D | 4 | 0 | 0 | 1 | 0 | 0 | 5.1 | 3 | 0 | 3.38 | 1.13 | 6 | 3 | -- | -- | -- | ---- | ---- | --- | 0 | 1 | 0 | 5.1 | 3.38 | 1.13 | 10.1 | 5.1 | 0.0 | .471 | .267 | .697 |
| Fister D | 28 | 28 | 6 | 14 | 0 | 0 | 171.0 | 187 | 13 | 4.11 | 1.28 | 93 | 32 | 3 | 4 | 0 | 84.1 | 3.09 | 1.07 | 3 | 10 | 0 | 86.2 | 5.09 | 1.49 | 4.9 | 1.7 | 0.7 | .698 | .685 | .710 |
| French L | 16 | 13 | 5 | 7 | 0 | 0 | 87.2 | 88 | 13 | 4.83 | 1.33 | 37 | 29 | 0 | 1 | 0 | 12.2 | 6.39 | 1.66 | 5 | 6 | 0 | 75.0 | 4.56 | 1.28 | 3.8 | 3.0 | 1.3 | .779 | .761 | .830 |
| Hernandez F | 34 | 34 | 13 | 12 | 0 | 0 | 249.2 | 194 | 17 | 2.27 | 1.06 | 232 | 70 | 7 | 5 | 0 | 137.2 | 2.88 | 1.15 | 6 | 7 | 0 | 112.0 | 1.53 | 0.94 | 8.4 | 2.5 | 0.6 | .585 | .576 | .593 |
| Kelley S | 22 | 0 | 3 | 1 | 3 | 0 | 25.0 | 26 | 5 | 3.96 | 1.52 | 26 | 12 | 3 | 1 | 0 | 25.0 | 3.96 | 1.52 | -- | -- | -- | ---- | ---- | --- | 9.4 | 4.3 | 1.8 | .841 | .968 | .696 |
| League B | 70 | 0 | 9 | 7 | 13 | 6 | 79.0 | 67 | 7 | 3.42 | 1.19 | 56 | 27 | 5 | 6 | 2 | 44.1 | 3.86 | 1.26 | 4 | 1 | 4 | 34.2 | 2.86 | 1.10 | 6.4 | 3.1 | 0.8 | .630 | .556 | .714 |
| Lee C | 13 | 13 | 8 | 3 | 0 | 0 | 103.2 | 92 | 5 | 2.34 | 0.95 | 89 | 6 | 8 | 3 | 0 | 103.2 | 2.34 | 0.95 | -- | -- | -- | ---- | ---- | --- | 7.7 | 0.5 | 0.4 | .572 | .529 | .713 |
| Lowe M | 11 | 0 | 1 | 3 | 4 | 0 | 10.1 | 11 | 1 | 3.48 | 1.55 | 7 | 5 | 1 | 3 | 0 | 10.1 | 3.48 | 1.55 | -- | -- | -- | ---- | ---- | --- | 6.1 | 4.4 | 0.9 | .766 | .671 | .911 |
| Olson G | 35 | 0 | 0 | 3 | 1 | 1 | 37.2 | 42 | 6 | 4.54 | 1.51 | 31 | 15 | 0 | 2 | 0 | 10.2 | 5.91 | 1.78 | 0 | 1 | 1 | 27.0 | 4.00 | 1.41 | 7.4 | 3.6 | 1.4 | .785 | .829 | .699 |
| Pauley D | 19 | 15 | 4 | 9 | 0 | 0 | 90.2 | 89 | 13 | 4.07 | 1.31 | 51 | 30 | 0 | 1 | 0 | 9.0 | 1.00 | 1.00 | 4 | 8 | 0 | 81.2 | 4.41 | 1.35 | 5.1 | 3.0 | 1.3 | .713 | .762 | .669 |
| Rowland-Smith R | 27 | 20 | 1 | 10 | 0 | 0 | 109.1 | 141 | 25 | 6.75 | 1.69 | 49 | 44 | 1 | 9 | 0 | 84.0 | 5.89 | 1.64 | 0 | 1 | 0 | 25.1 | 9.59 | 1.86 | 4.0 | 3.6 | 2.1 | .954 | .951 | .964 |
| Seddon C | 14 | 0 | 1 | 0 | 0 | 0 | 22.1 | 21 | 4 | 5.64 | 1.39 | 16 | 10 | -- | -- | -- | ---- | ---- | --- | 1 | 0 | 0 | 22.1 | 5.64 | 1.39 | 6.4 | 4.0 | 1.6 | .826 | .816 | .846 |
| Snell I | 12 | 8 | 0 | 5 | 0 | 0 | 46.1 | 60 | 10 | 6.41 | 1.83 | 26 | 25 | 0 | 5 | 0 | 46.1 | 6.41 | 1.83 | -- | -- | -- | ---- | ---- | --- | 5.1 | 4.9 | 1.9 | .948 | .890 | 1.007 |
| Sweeney B | 24 | 0 | 1 | 2 | 1 | 0 | 37.0 | 33 | 5 | 3.16 | 1.05 | 14 | 6 | 1 | 0 | 0 | 12.0 | 2.25 | 0.67 | 0 | 2 | 0 | 25.0 | 3.60 | 1.24 | 3.4 | 1.5 | 1.2 | .644 | .559 | .782 |
| Texeira K | 16 | 0 | 0 | 1 | 1 | 0 | 18.2 | 22 | 0 | 5.30 | 1.71 | 14 | 10 | 0 | 1 | 0 | 18.2 | 5.30 | 1.71 | -- | -- | -- | ---- | ---- | --- | 6.8 | 4.8 | 0.0 | .753 | .764 | .742 |
| Vargas J | 31 | 31 | 9 | 12 | 0 | 0 | 192.2 | 187 | 18 | 3.78 | 1.25 | 116 | 54 | 6 | 4 | 0 | 107.2 | 3.09 | 1.19 | 3 | 8 | 0 | 85.0 | 4.66 | 1.33 | 5.4 | 2.5 | 0.8 | .699 | .747 | .550 |
| Varvaro A | 4 | 0 | 0 | 1 | 0 | 0 | 4.0 | 6 | 2 | 11.25 | 3.00 | 5 | 6 | -- | -- | -- | ---- | ---- | --- | 0 | 1 | 0 | 4.0 | 11.25 | 3.00 | 11.3 | 13.5 | 4.5 | 1.167 | 1.115 | 1.300 |
| White S | 38 | 0 | 0 | 1 | 5 | 0 | 34.1 | 45 | 4 | 5.24 | 1.63 | 15 | 11 | 0 | 0 | 0 | 21.0 | 6.86 | 2.10 | 0 | 1 | 0 | 13.1 | 2.70 | 0.90 | 3.9 | 2.9 | 1.0 | .891 | .810 | 1.001 |
| Wright J | 28 | 0 | 0 | 1 | 8 | 0 | 37.0 | 30 | 2 | 3.41 | 1.24 | 19 | 16 | -- | -- | -- | ---- | ---- | --- | 0 | 1 | 0 | 37.0 | 3.41 | 1.24 | 4.6 | 3.9 | 0.5 | .646 | .765 | .504 |

## Hitters — St. Louis Cardinals 2010

| Hitters | G | AB | R | H | 2B | 3B | HR | RBI | BA | OBP | SLG | SB | CS | 1st Half AB | R | HR | BI | BA | SB | 2nd Half AB | R | HR | BI | BA | SB | Rates CT% | H% | BB% | Bash | GB% | Productiveness OPS | vs RH | vs LH |
|---|---|---|---|---|---|---|---|---|---|---|---|---|---|---|---|---|---|---|---|---|---|---|---|---|---|---|---|---|---|---|---|---|---|
| Anderson B | 15 | 32 | 1 | 9 | 2 | 0 | 0 | 4 | .281 | .314 | .344 | 0 | 0 | 7 | 1 | 0 | 1 | .286 | 0 | 25 | 0 | 0 | 3 | .280 | 0 | 78% | 36% | 3% | 1.2 | 28% | .658 | .588 | 1.100 |
| Craig A | 44 | 114 | 12 | 28 | 7 | 0 | 4 | 18 | .246 | .298 | .412 | 0 | 1 | 19 | 0 | 0 | 0 | .053 | 0 | 95 | 12 | 4 | 18 | .284 | 0 | 77% | 32% | 7% | 1.7 | 39% | .711 | .739 | .674 |
| Descalso D | 11 | 34 | 6 | 9 | 2 | 0 | 0 | 4 | .265 | .324 | .324 | 1 | 0 | --- | -- | -- | -- | --- | -- | 34 | 6 | 0 | 4 | .265 | 1 | 82% | 32% | 5% | 1.2 | 61% | .648 | .559 | 1.000 |
| Feliz P | 40 | 120 | 14 | 25 | 0 | 1 | 1 | 9 | .208 | .232 | .250 | 0 | 0 | --- | -- | -- | -- | --- | -- | 120 | 14 | 1 | 9 | .208 | 0 | 92% | 23% | 3% | 1.2 | 49% | .482 | .514 | .431 |
| Freese D | 70 | 240 | 28 | 71 | 12 | 1 | 4 | 36 | .296 | .361 | .404 | 1 | 1 | 240 | 28 | 4 | 36 | .296 | 1 | --- | -- | -- | -- | --- | -- | 75% | 39% | 8% | 1.4 | 49% | .765 | .721 | .873 |
| Greene T | 44 | 104 | 14 | 23 | 3 | 1 | 2 | 10 | .221 | .328 | .327 | 2 | 0 | 52 | 7 | 2 | 6 | .269 | 1 | 52 | 7 | 0 | 4 | .173 | 1 | 77% | 29% | 10% | 1.5 | 40% | .655 | .634 | .678 |
| Hamilton M | 9 | 14 | 0 | 2 | 0 | 0 | 0 | 0 | .143 | .200 | .143 | 0 | 0 | --- | -- | -- | -- | --- | -- | 14 | 0 | 0 | 0 | .143 | 0 | 64% | 22% | 7% | 1.0 | 33% | .343 | .343 | ---- |
| Hill S | 1 | 3 | 1 | 1 | 0 | 0 | 1 | 1 | .333 | .333 | 1.333 | 0 | 0 | --- | -- | -- | -- | --- | -- | 3 | 1 | 1 | 1 | .333 | 0 | 67% | 50% | 0% | 4.0 | 50% | 1.667 | 1.667 | ---- |
| Holliday M | 158 | 596 | 95 | 186 | 45 | 1 | 28 | 103 | .312 | .390 | .532 | 9 | 5 | 327 | 52 | 16 | 51 | .300 | 6 | 269 | 43 | 12 | 52 | .327 | 3 | 84% | 37% | 10% | 1.7 | 42% | .922 | .900 | .982 |
| Jay J | 105 | 287 | 47 | 86 | 19 | 2 | 4 | 27 | .300 | .359 | .422 | 2 | 4 | 69 | 12 | 3 | 9 | .377 | 0 | 218 | 35 | 1 | 18 | .275 | 2 | 83% | 36% | 7% | 1.4 | 48% | .780 | .791 | .741 |
| LaRue J | 29 | 56 | 3 | 11 | 1 | 0 | 2 | 5 | .196 | .274 | .321 | 0 | 0 | 46 | 3 | 2 | 5 | .196 | 0 | 10 | 0 | 0 | 0 | .200 | 0 | 88% | 22% | 8% | 1.6 | 47% | .596 | .523 | .857 |
| Lopez F | 109 | 376 | 50 | 87 | 18 | 1 | 7 | 36 | .231 | .310 | .340 | 8 | 2 | 212 | 30 | 5 | 22 | .269 | 5 | 164 | 20 | 2 | 14 | .183 | 3 | 80% | 29% | 10% | 1.5 | 48% | .651 | .617 | .719 |
| Ludwick R | 77 | 281 | 44 | 79 | 20 | 2 | 11 | 43 | .281 | .343 | .484 | 0 | 3 | 264 | 40 | 11 | 42 | .273 | 0 | 17 | 4 | 0 | 1 | .412 | 0 | 77% | 36% | 8% | 1.7 | 30% | .827 | .872 | .707 |
| Mather J | 36 | 60 | 7 | 13 | 4 | 0 | 0 | 3 | .217 | .242 | .283 | 1 | 1 | 47 | 4 | 0 | 2 | .191 | 1 | 13 | 3 | 0 | 1 | .308 | 0 | 82% | 27% | 3% | 1.3 | 39% | .525 | .563 | .492 |
| Miles A | 79 | 139 | 14 | 39 | 5 | 0 | 0 | 9 | .281 | .311 | .317 | 0 | 1 | 35 | 5 | 0 | 2 | .314 | 0 | 104 | 9 | 0 | 7 | .269 | 0 | 90% | 31% | 4% | 1.1 | 54% | .627 | .635 | .616 |
| Molina Y | 136 | 465 | 34 | 122 | 19 | 0 | 6 | 62 | .262 | .329 | .342 | 8 | 4 | 265 | 17 | 3 | 33 | .223 | 6 | 200 | 17 | 3 | 29 | .315 | 2 | 89% | 29% | 8% | 1.3 | 52% | .671 | .714 | .570 |
| Pagnozzi M | 15 | 39 | 4 | 14 | 2 | 0 | 1 | 10 | .359 | .405 | .487 | 0 | 0 | --- | -- | -- | -- | --- | -- | 39 | 4 | 1 | 10 | .359 | 0 | 79% | 45% | 5% | 1.4 | 52% | .892 | .904 | .857 |
| Pujols A | 159 | 587 | 115 | 183 | 39 | 1 | 42 | 118 | .312 | .414 | .596 | 14 | 4 | 321 | 55 | 21 | 64 | .308 | 9 | 266 | 60 | 21 | 54 | .316 | 5 | 87% | 36% | 14% | 1.9 | 39% | 1.011 | .983 | 1.076 |
| Rasmus C | 144 | 464 | 85 | 128 | 28 | 3 | 23 | 66 | .276 | .361 | .498 | 12 | 8 | 264 | 51 | 16 | 42 | .284 | 9 | 200 | 34 | 7 | 24 | .265 | 3 | 68% | 41% | 12% | 1.8 | 32% | .859 | .875 | .810 |
| Ryan B | 139 | 439 | 50 | 98 | 19 | 3 | 2 | 36 | .223 | .279 | .294 | 11 | 4 | 217 | 20 | 2 | 16 | .194 | 7 | 222 | 30 | 0 | 20 | .252 | 4 | 86% | 26% | 7% | 1.3 | 47% | .573 | .575 | .568 |
| Schumaker S | 137 | 476 | 66 | 126 | 18 | 1 | 5 | 42 | .265 | .328 | .338 | 5 | 3 | 278 | 42 | 2 | 20 | .255 | 4 | 198 | 24 | 3 | 22 | .278 | 1 | 87% | 31% | 8% | 1.3 | 59% | .667 | .691 | .541 |
| Stavinoha N | 79 | 121 | 11 | 31 | 4 | 0 | 2 | 9 | .256 | .286 | .339 | 0 | 0 | 90 | 8 | 2 | 7 | .256 | 0 | 31 | 3 | 0 | 2 | .258 | 0 | 77% | 33% | 3% | 1.3 | 47% | .625 | .641 | .608 |
| Winn R | 87 | 144 | 16 | 36 | 8 | 1 | 3 | 17 | .250 | .311 | .382 | 5 | 0 | 56 | 5 | 0 | 2 | .232 | 2 | 88 | 11 | 3 | 15 | .261 | 3 | 85% | 30% | 8% | 1.5 | 49% | .693 | .737 | .564 |

## Pitchers — St. Louis Cardinals 2010

| Pitchers | G | GS | W | L | Hld | Sv | IP | H | HR | ERA | WHIP | K | BB | 1st Half W | L | Sv | IP | ERA | WHIP | 2nd Half W | L | Sv | IP | ERA | WHIP | Rates K/9 | BB/9 | HR/9 | Productiveness opOPS | vs RH | vs LH |
|---|---|---|---|---|---|---|---|---|---|---|---|---|---|---|---|---|---|---|---|---|---|---|---|---|---|---|---|---|---|---|---|
| Boggs M | 61 | 0 | 2 | 3 | 6 | 0 | 67.1 | 60 | 5 | 3.61 | 1.29 | 52 | 27 | 1 | 2 | 0 | 39.0 | 2.54 | 1.10 | 1 | 1 | 0 | 28.1 | 5.08 | 1.55 | 7.0 | 3.6 | 0.7 | .696 | .664 | .763 |
| Carpenter C | 35 | 35 | 16 | 9 | 0 | 0 | 235.0 | 214 | 21 | 3.22 | 1.18 | 179 | 63 | 9 | 3 | 0 | 125.2 | 3.29 | 1.24 | 7 | 6 | 0 | 109.1 | 3.13 | 1.11 | 6.9 | 2.4 | 0.8 | .680 | .696 | .659 |
| Franklin R | 59 | 0 | 6 | 2 | 0 | 27 | 65.0 | 57 | 7 | 3.46 | 1.03 | 42 | 10 | 3 | 1 | 16 | 34.2 | 3.63 | 1.15 | 3 | 1 | 11 | 30.1 | 3.26 | 0.89 | 5.8 | 1.4 | 1.0 | .661 | .597 | .750 |
| Garcia J | 28 | 28 | 13 | 8 | 0 | 0 | 163.1 | 151 | 9 | 2.70 | 1.32 | 132 | 64 | 8 | 4 | 0 | 99.2 | 2.17 | 1.25 | 5 | 4 | 0 | 63.2 | 3.53 | 1.41 | 7.3 | 3.5 | 0.5 | .638 | .660 | .550 |
| Hawksworth B | 45 | 8 | 4 | 8 | 4 | 0 | 90.1 | 113 | 15 | 4.98 | 1.64 | 61 | 35 | 3 | 5 | 0 | 53.1 | 4.73 | 1.73 | 1 | 3 | 0 | 37.0 | 5.35 | 1.51 | 6.1 | 3.5 | 1.5 | .848 | .818 | .886 |
| Lohse K | 18 | 18 | 4 | 8 | 0 | 0 | 92.0 | 129 | 9 | 6.55 | 1.78 | 54 | 35 | 1 | 4 | 0 | 47.1 | 5.89 | 1.71 | 3 | 4 | 0 | 44.2 | 7.25 | 1.86 | 5.3 | 3.4 | 0.9 | .905 | .849 | .979 |
| MacDougal M | 17 | 0 | 1 | 1 | 0 | 0 | 18.2 | 23 | 1 | 7.23 | 1.88 | 14 | 12 | -- | -- | -- | ---- | ---- | --- | 1 | 1 | 0 | 18.2 | 7.23 | 1.88 | 6.8 | 5.8 | 0.5 | .844 | .512 | 1.353 |
| MacLane E | 2 | 0 | 0 | 1 | 0 | 0 | 1.0 | 1 | 1 | 9.00 | 2.00 | 0 | 1 | -- | -- | -- | ---- | ---- | --- | 0 | 0 | 0 | 1.0 | 0.00 | 1.00 | 0.0 | 9.0 | 9.0 | 1.833 | 1.667 | ---- |
| McClellan K | 68 | 0 | 1 | 4 | 19 | 2 | 75.1 | 58 | 9 | 2.27 | 1.08 | 60 | 23 | 0 | 2 | 1 | 42.1 | 2.13 | 1.02 | 1 | 2 | 1 | 33.0 | 2.45 | 1.15 | 7.2 | 2.7 | 1.1 | .621 | .640 | .592 |
| Miller T | 57 | 0 | 1 | 1 | 11 | 0 | 36.0 | 30 | 2 | 4.00 | 1.28 | 22 | 16 | 0 | 1 | 0 | 20.0 | 4.05 | 1.20 | 0 | 0 | 0 | 16.0 | 3.94 | 1.38 | 5.5 | 4.0 | 0.5 | .640 | .759 | .551 |
| Motte J | 56 | 0 | 4 | 2 | 12 | 2 | 52.1 | 41 | 5 | 2.24 | 1.13 | 54 | 18 | 3 | 2 | 2 | 35.2 | 2.27 | 1.07 | 1 | 0 | 0 | 16.2 | 2.16 | 1.26 | 9.3 | 3.1 | 0.9 | .618 | .531 | .789 |
| Ottavino A | 5 | 3 | 0 | 2 | 0 | 0 | 22.1 | 37 | 5 | 8.46 | 2.06 | 12 | 9 | 0 | 2 | 0 | 22.1 | 8.46 | 2.06 | -- | -- | -- | ---- | ---- | --- | 4.8 | 3.6 | 2.0 | 1.072 | .973 | 1.213 |
| Penny B | 9 | 9 | 3 | 4 | 0 | 0 | 55.2 | 63 | 4 | 3.23 | 1.29 | 35 | 9 | 3 | 4 | 0 | 55.2 | 3.23 | 1.29 | -- | -- | -- | ---- | ---- | --- | 5.7 | 1.5 | 0.6 | .740 | .645 | .880 |
| Reyes D | 59 | 0 | 3 | 1 | 6 | 1 | 38.0 | 34 | 2 | 3.55 | 1.45 | 25 | 21 | 2 | 1 | 0 | 25.1 | 3.55 | 1.34 | 1 | 0 | 1 | 12.2 | 3.55 | 1.66 | 5.9 | 5.0 | 0.5 | .690 | .481 | .862 |
| Salas F | 27 | 0 | 0 | 0 | 1 | 0 | 30.2 | 28 | 4 | 3.52 | 1.40 | 29 | 15 | 0 | 0 | 0 | 7.1 | 1.23 | 0.82 | 0 | 0 | 0 | 23.1 | 4.24 | 1.59 | 8.5 | 4.4 | 1.2 | .748 | .665 | .866 |
| Suppan J | 15 | 13 | 3 | 6 | 0 | 0 | 70.1 | 80 | 9 | 3.84 | 1.49 | 33 | 25 | 0 | 3 | 0 | 24.0 | 4.88 | 1.88 | 3 | 3 | 0 | 46.1 | 3.30 | 1.29 | 4.2 | 3.2 | 1.2 | .810 | .873 | .710 |
| Wainwright A | 33 | 33 | 20 | 11 | 0 | 0 | 230.1 | 186 | 15 | 2.42 | 1.05 | 213 | 56 | 13 | 5 | 0 | 136.1 | 2.11 | 1.00 | 7 | 6 | 0 | 94.0 | 2.87 | 1.12 | 8.3 | 2.2 | 0.6 | .604 | .627 | .575 |
| Walters P | 7 | 3 | 2 | 0 | 0 | 0 | 30.0 | 32 | 5 | 6.00 | 1.40 | 22 | 10 | 1 | 0 | 0 | 17.0 | 7.94 | 1.76 | 1 | 0 | 0 | 13.0 | 3.46 | 0.92 | 6.6 | 3.0 | 1.5 | .768 | .726 | .816 |
| Westbrook J | 12 | 12 | 4 | 4 | 0 | 0 | 75.0 | 70 | 5 | 3.48 | 1.25 | 55 | 24 | -- | -- | -- | ---- | ---- | --- | 4 | 4 | 0 | 75.0 | 3.48 | 1.25 | 6.6 | 2.9 | 0.6 | .651 | .583 | .749 |

## AL Tampa Bay

**Writer:** Ricky Zanker
www.draysbay.com

### Performance in 2010

### Trends Among League

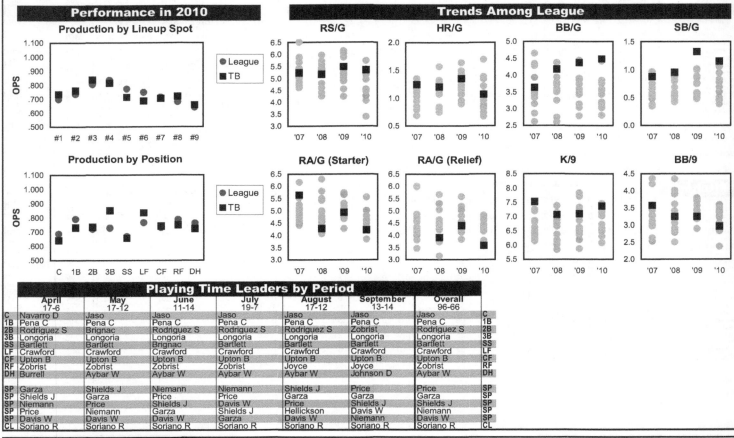

### Playing Time Leaders by Period

| | April 17-6 | May 17-12 | June 11-14 | July 19-7 | August 17-12 | September 13-14 | Overall 96-66 | |
|---|---|---|---|---|---|---|---|---|
| C | Navarro D | Jaso | Jaso | Jaso | Jaso | Jaso | Jaso | C |
| 1B | Pena C | Pena C | Pena C | Pena C | Pena C | Pena C | Pena C | 1B |
| 2B | Rodriguez S | Brignac | Rodriguez S | Rodriguez S | Rodriguez S | Zobrist | Rodriguez S | 2B |
| 3B | Longoria | Longoria | Longoria | Longoria | Longoria | Longoria | Longoria | 3B |
| SS | Bartlett | Bartlett | Brignac | Bartlett | Bartlett | Bartlett | Bartlett | SS |
| LF | Crawford | Crawford | Crawford | Crawford | Crawford | Crawford | Crawford | LF |
| CF | Upton B | Upton B | Upton B | Upton B | Upton B | Upton B | Upton B | CF |
| RF | Zobrist | Zobrist | Zobrist | Zobrist | Joyce | Joyce | Zobrist | RF |
| DH | Burrell | Aybar W | Aybar W | Aybar W | Aybar W | Johnson D | Aybar W | DH |
| | | | | | | | | |
| SP | Garza | Shields J | Niemann | Niemann | Shields J | Price | Price | SP |
| SP | Shields J | Garza | Price | Price | Garza | Garza | Garza | SP |
| SP | Niemann | Price | Shields J | Davis W | Price | Shields J | Shields J | SP |
| SP | Price | Niemann | Garza | Shields J | Hellickson | Davis W | Niemann | SP |
| SP | Davis W | Davis W | Davis W | Garza | Davis W | Niemann | Davis W | SP |
| CL | Soriano R | Soriano R | Soriano R | Soriano R | Soriano R | Soriano R | Soriano R | CL |

## AL Texas

**Writer:** Joey Matschulat
www.bbtia.com

### Performance in 2010

### Trends Among Leagues

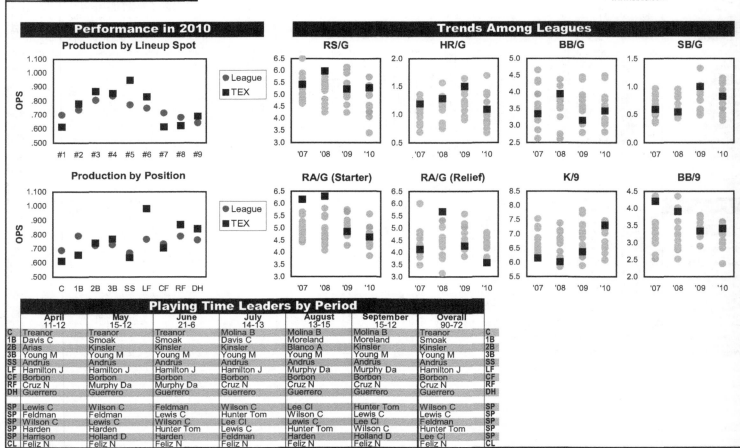

### Playing Time Leaders by Period

| | April 11-12 | May 15-12 | June 21-6 | July 14-13 | August 13-15 | September 15-12 | Overall 90-72 | |
|---|---|---|---|---|---|---|---|---|
| C | Treanor | Treanor | Treanor | Molina B | Molina B | Molina B | Treanor | C |
| 1B | Davis C | Smoak | Smoak | Davis C | Moreland | Moreland | Smoak | 1B |
| 2B | Arias | Kinsler | Kinsler | Kinsler | Blanco A | Kinsler | Kinsler | 2B |
| 3B | Young M | Young M | Young M | Young M | Young M | Young M | Young M | 3B |
| SS | Andrus | Andrus | Andrus | Andrus | Andrus | Andrus | Andrus | SS |
| LF | Hamilton J | Hamilton J | Hamilton J | Hamilton J | Murphy Da | Murphy Da | Hamilton J | LF |
| CF | Borbon | Borbon | Borbon | Borbon | Borbon | Borbon | Borbon | CF |
| RF | Cruz N | Murphy Da | Murphy Da | Cruz N | Cruz N | Cruz N | Cruz N | RF |
| DH | Guerrero | Guerrero | Guerrero | Guerrero | Guerrero | Guerrero | Guerrero | DH |
| | | | | | | | | |
| SP | Lewis C | Wilson C | Feldman | Wilson C | Lee Cl | Hunter Tom | Wilson C | SP |
| SP | Feldman | Feldman | Lewis C | Hunter Tom | Wilson C | Lewis C | Lewis C | SP |
| SP | Wilson C | Lewis C | Wilson C | Lee Cl | Lewis C | Lee Cl | Feldman | SP |
| SP | Harden | Harden | Hunter Tom | Lewis C | Hunter Tom | Wilson C | Hunter Tom | SP |
| SP | Harrison | Holland D | Harden | Feldman | Harden | Holland D | Lee Cl | SP |
| CL | Feliz N | Feliz N | Feliz N | Feliz N | Feliz N | Feliz N | Feliz N | CL |

## Hitters — Tampa Bay Rays 2010

| Hitters | Tampa Bay Rays 2010 | | | | | | | | | | | | | 1st Half | | | | | | 2nd Half | | | | | | Rates | | | | | Productiveness | | |
|---|---|---|---|---|---|---|---|---|---|---|---|---|---|---|---|---|---|---|---|---|---|---|---|---|---|---|---|---|---|---|---|---|---|
| | G | AB | R | H | 2B | 3B | HR | RBI | BA | OBP | SLG | SB | CS | AB | R | HR | BI | BA | SB | AB | R | HR | BI | BA | SB | CT% | H% | BB% | Bash | GB% | OPS | vs RH | vs LH |
| Aybar W | 100 | 270 | 22 | 62 | 13 | 0 | 6 | 43 | .230 | .309 | .344 | 0 | 0 | 144 | 12 | 5 | 23 | .250 | 0 | 126 | 10 | 1 | 20 | .206 | 0 | 77% | 30% | 10% | 1.5 | 43% | .654 | .609 | .696 |
| Baldelli R | 10 | 24 | 3 | 5 | 1 | 0 | 1 | 5 | .208 | .240 | .375 | 1 | 0 | --- | -- | -- | -- | --- | -- | 24 | 3 | 1 | 5 | .208 | 1 | 79% | 26% | 4% | 1.8 | 42% | .615 | .000 | .816 |
| Bartlett J | 135 | 468 | 71 | 119 | 27 | 3 | 4 | 47 | .254 | .324 | .350 | 11 | 6 | 242 | 31 | 2 | 33 | .231 | 4 | 226 | 40 | 2 | 14 | .279 | 7 | 82% | 31% | 8% | 1.4 | 45% | .675 | .647 | .725 |
| Blalock H | 26 | 63 | 8 | 16 | 3 | 0 | 1 | 7 | .254 | .319 | .349 | 1 | 1 | 63 | 8 | 1 | 7 | .254 | 1 | --- | -- | -- | -- | --- | -- | 76% | 33% | 9% | 1.4 | 52% | .668 | .714 | .286 |
| Brignac R | 113 | 301 | 39 | 77 | 13 | 1 | 8 | 45 | .256 | .307 | .385 | 3 | 3 | 189 | 23 | 2 | 25 | .265 | 2 | 112 | 16 | 6 | 20 | .241 | 1 | 74% | 34% | 6% | 1.5 | 38% | .692 | .706 | .609 |
| Burrell P | 24 | 84 | 9 | 17 | 5 | 0 | 2 | 13 | .202 | .292 | .333 | 0 | 0 | 84 | 9 | 2 | 13 | .202 | 0 | --- | -- | -- | -- | --- | -- | 67% | 30% | 10% | 1.6 | 38% | .625 | .744 | .227 |
| Crawford C | 154 | 600 | 110 | 184 | 30 | 13 | 19 | 90 | .307 | .356 | .495 | 47 | 10 | 330 | 70 | 11 | 50 | .321 | 31 | 270 | 40 | 8 | 40 | .289 | 16 | 83% | 37% | 7% | 1.6 | 48% | .851 | .930 | .696 |
| Hawpe B | 15 | 39 | 7 | 7 | 0 | 0 | 2 | 7 | .179 | .304 | .333 | 0 | 0 | --- | -- | -- | -- | --- | -- | 39 | 7 | 2 | 7 | .179 | 0 | 56% | 32% | 13% | 1.9 | 45% | .638 | .564 | .818 |
| Jaso J | 109 | 339 | 57 | 89 | 18 | 3 | 5 | 44 | .263 | .372 | .378 | 4 | 0 | 175 | 25 | 3 | 29 | .274 | 3 | 164 | 32 | 2 | 15 | .250 | 1 | 88% | 30% | 15% | 1.4 | 46% | .750 | .772 | .610 |
| Jennings D | 17 | 21 | 5 | 4 | 1 | 1 | 0 | 2 | .190 | .292 | .333 | 2 | 2 | --- | -- | -- | -- | --- | -- | 21 | 5 | 0 | 2 | .190 | 2 | 81% | 24% | 8% | 1.8 | 47% | .625 | .350 | .879 |
| Johnson D | 40 | 111 | 15 | 22 | 3 | 0 | 7 | 23 | .198 | .343 | .414 | 1 | 0 | --- | -- | -- | -- | --- | -- | 111 | 15 | 7 | 23 | .198 | 1 | 76% | 26% | 18% | 2.1 | 39% | .757 | .738 | .862 |
| Joyce M | 77 | 216 | 30 | 52 | 15 | 3 | 10 | 40 | .241 | .360 | .477 | 2 | 2 | 40 | 4 | 1 | 5 | .175 | 1 | 176 | 26 | 9 | 35 | .256 | 1 | 75% | 32% | 15% | 2.0 | 34% | .837 | .910 | .263 |
| Kapler G | 59 | 124 | 19 | 26 | 4 | 0 | 2 | 14 | .210 | .288 | .290 | 1 | 1 | 95 | 18 | 1 | 12 | .221 | 1 | 29 | 1 | 1 | 2 | .172 | 0 | 81% | 26% | 8% | 1.4 | 42% | .578 | .640 | .560 |
| Longoria E | 151 | 574 | 96 | 169 | 46 | 5 | 22 | 104 | .294 | .372 | .507 | 15 | 5 | 337 | 54 | 13 | 61 | .300 | 13 | 237 | 42 | 9 | 43 | .287 | 2 | 78% | 38% | 11% | 1.7 | 37% | .879 | .845 | .956 |
| Navarro D | 48 | 124 | 11 | 24 | 5 | 0 | 1 | 7 | .194 | .270 | .258 | 0 | 1 | 105 | 11 | 1 | 7 | .210 | 0 | 19 | 0 | 0 | 0 | .105 | 0 | 84% | 23% | 8% | 1.3 | 46% | .528 | .535 | .518 |
| Pena C | 144 | 484 | 64 | 95 | 18 | 0 | 28 | 84 | .196 | .325 | .407 | 5 | 1 | 301 | 43 | 18 | 54 | .203 | 3 | 183 | 21 | 10 | 30 | .186 | 2 | 67% | 29% | 15% | 2.1 | 45% | .732 | .759 | .675 |
| Rodriguez S | 118 | 343 | 53 | 86 | 19 | 2 | 9 | 40 | .251 | .308 | .397 | 13 | 3 | 219 | 34 | 6 | 30 | .265 | 7 | 124 | 19 | 3 | 10 | .226 | 6 | 72% | 35% | 6% | 1.6 | 40% | .705 | .642 | .817 |
| Shoppach K | 63 | 158 | 17 | 31 | 8 | 0 | 5 | 17 | .196 | .308 | .342 | 0 | 0 | 55 | 5 | 1 | 5 | .200 | 0 | 103 | 12 | 4 | 12 | .194 | 0 | 55% | 36% | 11% | 1.7 | 45% | .650 | .432 | .823 |
| Upton B | 154 | 536 | 89 | 127 | 38 | 4 | 18 | 62 | .237 | .322 | .424 | 42 | 9 | 291 | 50 | 7 | 31 | .230 | 25 | 245 | 39 | 11 | 31 | .245 | 17 | 69% | 34% | 11% | 1.8 | 40% | .745 | .664 | .919 |
| Zobrist B | 151 | 541 | 77 | 129 | 28 | 2 | 10 | 75 | .238 | .346 | .353 | 24 | 3 | 309 | 47 | 5 | 41 | .285 | 19 | 232 | 30 | 5 | 34 | .177 | 5 | 80% | 30% | 14% | 1.5 | 44% | .699 | .700 | .695 |

## Pitchers — Tampa Bay Rays 2010

| Pitchers | Tampa Bay Rays 2010 | | | | | | | | | | | | | 1st Half | | | | | | 2nd Half | | | | | | Rates | | | Productiveness | | |
|---|---|---|---|---|---|---|---|---|---|---|---|---|---|---|---|---|---|---|---|---|---|---|---|---|---|---|---|---|---|---|---|
| | G | GS | W | L | Hld | Sv | IP | H | HR | ERA | WHIP | K | BB | W | L | Sv | IP | ERA | WHIP | W | L | Sv | IP | ERA | WHIP | K/9 | BB/9 | HR/9 | opOPS | vs RH | vs LH |
| Balfour G | 57 | 0 | 2 | 1 | 16 | 0 | 55.1 | 43 | 3 | 2.28 | 1.08 | 56 | 17 | 1 | 1 | 0 | 37.2 | 2.15 | 1.09 | 1 | 0 | 0 | 17.2 | 2.55 | 1.08 | 9.1 | 2.8 | 0.5 | .619 | .496 | .771 |
| Benoit J | 63 | 0 | 1 | 2 | 25 | 1 | 60.1 | 30 | 6 | 1.34 | 0.68 | 75 | 11 | 0 | 0 | 1 | 27.2 | 0.65 | 0.51 | 1 | 2 | 0 | 32.2 | 1.93 | 0.83 | 11.2 | 1.6 | 0.9 | .454 | .419 | .491 |
| Choate R | 85 | 0 | 4 | 3 | 18 | 0 | 44.2 | 41 | 3 | 4.23 | 1.30 | 40 | 17 | 2 | 2 | 0 | 22.2 | 5.96 | 1.10 | 2 | 1 | 0 | 22.0 | 2.45 | 1.50 | 8.1 | 3.4 | 0.6 | .686 | 1.162 | .529 |
| Cormier L | 60 | 0 | 4 | 3 | 4 | 0 | 62.0 | 68 | 7 | 3.92 | 1.65 | 30 | 34 | 3 | 1 | 0 | 35.0 | 4.37 | 1.86 | 1 | 2 | 0 | 27.0 | 3.33 | 1.37 | 4.4 | 4.9 | 1.0 | .810 | .936 | .718 |
| Davis W | 29 | 29 | 12 | 10 | 0 | 0 | 168.0 | 165 | 24 | 4.07 | 1.35 | 113 | 62 | 6 | 9 | 0 | 94.0 | 4.69 | 1.46 | 6 | 1 | 0 | 74.0 | 3.28 | 1.22 | 6.1 | 3.3 | 1.3 | .756 | .732 | .776 |
| Ekstrom M | 15 | 0 | 0 | 1 | 0 | 0 | 16.1 | 12 | 0 | 3.31 | 1.29 | 10 | 9 | 0 | 1 | 0 | 6.1 | 8.53 | 2.05 | 0 | 0 | 0 | 10.0 | 0.00 | 0.80 | 5.5 | 5.0 | 0.0 | .570 | .599 | .538 |
| Garza M | 33 | 32 | 15 | 10 | 0 | 1 | 204.2 | 193 | 28 | 3.91 | 1.25 | 150 | 63 | 10 | 5 | 1 | 113.1 | 4.05 | 1.31 | 5 | 5 | 0 | 91.1 | 3.74 | 1.18 | 6.6 | 2.8 | 1.2 | .728 | .726 | .730 |
| Hellickson J | 10 | 4 | 4 | 0 | 0 | 0 | 36.1 | 32 | 5 | 3.47 | 1.10 | 33 | 8 | -- | -- | -- | ---- | ---- | --- | 4 | 0 | 0 | 36.1 | 3.47 | 1.10 | 8.2 | 2.0 | 1.2 | .666 | .391 | .906 |
| McGee J | 8 | 0 | 0 | 0 | 0 | 0 | 5.0 | 2 | 0 | 1.80 | 1.00 | 6 | 3 | -- | -- | -- | ---- | ---- | --- | 0 | 0 | 0 | 5.0 | 1.80 | 1.00 | 10.8 | 5.4 | 0.0 | .426 | .111 | .697 |
| Niemann J | 30 | 29 | 12 | 8 | 0 | 0 | 174.1 | 159 | 25 | 4.39 | 1.26 | 131 | 61 | 7 | 2 | 0 | 117.0 | 2.77 | 1.09 | 5 | 6 | 0 | 57.1 | 7.69 | 1.62 | 6.8 | 3.1 | 1.3 | .724 | .698 | .749 |
| Price D | 32 | 31 | 19 | 6 | 0 | 0 | 208.2 | 170 | 15 | 2.72 | 1.19 | 188 | 79 | 12 | 4 | 0 | 115.1 | 2.42 | 1.20 | 7 | 2 | 0 | 93.1 | 3.09 | 1.19 | 8.1 | 3.4 | 0.6 | .637 | .656 | .569 |
| Qualls C | 27 | 0 | 2 | 0 | 8 | 0 | 21.0 | 24 | 2 | 5.57 | 1.43 | 15 | 6 | -- | -- | -- | ---- | ---- | --- | 2 | 0 | 0 | 21.0 | 5.57 | 1.43 | 6.4 | 2.6 | 0.9 | .767 | .494 | 1.052 |
| Shields J | 34 | 33 | 13 | 15 | 0 | 0 | 203.1 | 246 | 34 | 5.18 | 1.46 | 187 | 51 | 7 | 9 | 0 | 116.1 | 4.87 | 1.37 | 6 | 6 | 0 | 87.0 | 5.59 | 1.59 | 8.3 | 2.3 | 1.5 | .828 | .866 | .796 |
| Sonnanstine A | 41 | 4 | 3 | 1 | 0 | 1 | 81.0 | 83 | 11 | 4.44 | 1.36 | 50 | 27 | 2 | 0 | 1 | 45.1 | 4.17 | 1.15 | 1 | 1 | 0 | 35.2 | 4.79 | 1.63 | 5.6 | 3.0 | 1.2 | .761 | .780 | .738 |
| Soriano R | 64 | 0 | 3 | 2 | 0 | 45 | 62.1 | 36 | 4 | 1.73 | 0.80 | 57 | 14 | 2 | 0 | 23 | 33.2 | 1.60 | 0.80 | 1 | 2 | 22 | 28.2 | 1.88 | 0.80 | 8.2 | 2.0 | 0.6 | .509 | .431 | .590 |
| Thayer D | 1 | 0 | 0 | 0 | 0 | 0 | 2.0 | 7 | 1 | 27.00 | 3.50 | 2 | 0 | -- | -- | -- | ---- | ---- | --- | 0 | 0 | 0 | 2.0 | 27.00 | 3.50 | 9.0 | 0.0 | 4.5 | 1.385 | 1.556 | 1.000 |
| Wheeler D | 64 | 0 | 2 | 4 | 9 | 3 | 48.1 | 36 | 7 | 3.35 | 1.08 | 46 | 16 | 2 | 0 | 1 | 28.1 | 3.18 | 1.09 | 0 | 4 | 2 | 20.0 | 3.60 | 1.05 | 8.6 | 3.0 | 1.3 | .681 | .687 | .663 |

## Hitters — Texas Rangers 2010

| Hitters | Texas Rangers 2010 | | | | | | | | | | | | | 1st Half | | | | | | 2nd Half | | | | | | Rates | | | | | Productiveness | | |
|---|---|---|---|---|---|---|---|---|---|---|---|---|---|---|---|---|---|---|---|---|---|---|---|---|---|---|---|---|---|---|---|---|---|
| | G | AB | R | H | 2B | 3B | HR | RBI | BA | OBP | SLG | SB | CS | AB | R | HR | BI | BA | SB | AB | R | HR | BI | BA | SB | CT% | H% | BB% | Bash | GB% | OPS | vs RH | vs LH |
| Andrus E | 148 | 588 | 88 | 156 | 15 | 3 | 0 | 35 | .265 | .342 | .301 | 32 | 15 | 329 | 57 | 0 | 25 | .280 | 23 | 259 | 31 | 0 | 10 | .247 | 9 | 84% | 32% | 9% | 1.1 | 59% | .643 | .644 | .642 |
| Arias J | 50 | 98 | 18 | 27 | 5 | 1 | 0 | 9 | .276 | .290 | .347 | 1 | 0 | 83 | 14 | 0 | 9 | .277 | 1 | 15 | 4 | 0 | 0 | .267 | 0 | 83% | 33% | 2% | 1.3 | 42% | .637 | .613 | .706 |
| Blanco A | 68 | 166 | 17 | 46 | 10 | 1 | 0 | 13 | .277 | .330 | .349 | 0 | 2 | 67 | 6 | 0 | 3 | .239 | 0 | 99 | 11 | 0 | 10 | .303 | 0 | 86% | 32% | 6% | 1.3 | 44% | .679 | .739 | .539 |
| Boggs B | 4 | 7 | 0 | 0 | 0 | 0 | 0 | 0 | .000 | .125 | .000 | 0 | 0 | --- | -- | -- | -- | --- | -- | 7 | 0 | 0 | 0 | .000 | 0 | 43% | 0% | 13% | --- | 33% | .125 | .500 | .000 |
| Borbon J | 137 | 438 | 60 | 121 | 11 | 4 | 3 | 42 | .276 | .309 | .340 | 15 | 7 | 254 | 37 | 3 | 25 | .280 | 8 | 184 | 23 | 0 | 17 | .272 | 7 | 87% | 32% | 4% | 1.2 | 51% | .649 | .660 | .609 |
| Cantu J | 30 | 98 | 9 | 23 | 4 | 1 | 1 | 2 | .235 | .279 | .327 | 0 | 0 | --- | -- | -- | -- | --- | -- | 98 | 9 | 1 | 2 | .235 | 0 | 81% | 29% | 6% | 1.4 | 43% | .605 | .696 | .523 |
| Cora A | 4 | 7 | 0 | 2 | 0 | 0 | 0 | 0 | .286 | .286 | .286 | 0 | 0 | --- | -- | -- | -- | --- | -- | 7 | 0 | 0 | 0 | .286 | 0 | 100% | 29% | 0% | 1.0 | 29% | .571 | 2.000 | .333 |
| Cruz N | 108 | 399 | 60 | 127 | 31 | 3 | 22 | 78 | .318 | .374 | .576 | 17 | 4 | 174 | 25 | 11 | 41 | .299 | 9 | 225 | 35 | 11 | 37 | .333 | 8 | 80% | 40% | 8% | 1.8 | 38% | .950 | .941 | .976 |
| Davis C | 45 | 120 | 7 | 23 | 9 | 0 | 1 | 4 | .192 | .279 | .292 | 3 | 0 | 56 | 2 | 0 | 2 | .214 | 1 | 64 | 5 | 1 | 2 | .172 | 2 | 67% | 29% | 11% | 1.5 | 43% | .571 | .618 | .411 |
| Francoeur J | 15 | 53 | 9 | 18 | 2 | 0 | 2 | 11 | .340 | .357 | .491 | 0 | 1 | --- | -- | -- | -- | --- | -- | 53 | 9 | 2 | 11 | .340 | 0 | 91% | 38% | 2% | 1.4 | 42% | .848 | .739 | 1.029 |
| Garko R | 15 | 33 | 0 | 3 | 0 | 0 | 0 | 3 | .091 | .167 | .091 | 0 | 0 | 33 | 0 | 0 | 3 | .091 | 0 | --- | -- | -- | -- | --- | -- | 88% | 10% | 8% | 1.0 | 48% | .258 | .237 | .269 |
| Gentry C | 20 | 33 | 4 | 7 | 0 | 0 | 0 | 3 | .212 | .229 | .212 | 1 | 0 | 33 | 4 | 0 | 3 | .212 | 1 | --- | -- | -- | -- | --- | -- | 67% | 32% | 3% | 1.0 | 45% | .441 | .633 | .348 |
| German E | 13 | 13 | 5 | 3 | 0 | 0 | 0 | 1 | .231 | .375 | .231 | 4 | 1 | --- | -- | -- | -- | --- | -- | 13 | 5 | 0 | 1 | .231 | 4 | 85% | 27% | 19% | 1.0 | 36% | .606 | .539 | 1.000 |
| Guerrero V | 152 | 593 | 83 | 178 | 27 | 1 | 29 | 115 | .300 | .345 | .496 | 4 | 5 | 323 | 55 | 20 | 75 | .319 | 4 | 270 | 28 | 9 | 40 | .278 | 0 | 90% | 33% | 5% | 1.7 | 45% | .841 | .810 | .932 |
| Guzman C | 15 | 46 | 4 | 7 | 1 | 0 | 0 | 1 | .152 | .204 | .174 | 0 | 0 | --- | -- | -- | -- | --- | -- | 46 | 4 | 0 | 1 | .152 | 0 | 78% | 19% | 6% | 1.1 | 53% | .378 | .361 | .432 |
| Hamilton J | 133 | 518 | 95 | 186 | 40 | 3 | 32 | 100 | .359 | .411 | .633 | 8 | 1 | 341 | 59 | 22 | 64 | .346 | 7 | 177 | 36 | 10 | 36 | .384 | 1 | 82% | 44% | 7% | 1.8 | 42% | 1.044 | 1.163 | .789 |
| Kinsler I | 103 | 391 | 73 | 112 | 20 | 1 | 9 | 45 | .286 | .382 | .412 | 15 | 5 | 239 | 46 | 4 | 30 | .310 | 8 | 152 | 27 | 5 | 15 | .250 | 7 | 85% | 34% | 12% | 1.4 | 40% | .794 | .743 | .957 |
| Molina B | 57 | 175 | 10 | 42 | 6 | 1 | 2 | 19 | .240 | .279 | .320 | 0 | 0 | 23 | 2 | 0 | 0 | .174 | 0 | 152 | 8 | 2 | 19 | .250 | 0 | 91% | 26% | 5% | 1.3 | 33% | .599 | .558 | .716 |
| Moreland M | 47 | 145 | 20 | 37 | 4 | 0 | 9 | 25 | .255 | .364 | .469 | 3 | 1 | --- | -- | -- | -- | --- | -- | 145 | 20 | 9 | 25 | .255 | 3 | 75% | 34% | 14% | 1.8 | 40% | .833 | .869 | .604 |
| Murphy D | 138 | 419 | 54 | 122 | 26 | 2 | 12 | 65 | .291 | .358 | .449 | 14 | 2 | 207 | 27 | 3 | 24 | .271 | 4 | 212 | 27 | 9 | 41 | .311 | 10 | 83% | 35% | 10% | 1.5 | 45% | .806 | .847 | .696 |
| Ramirez M | 28 | 69 | 8 | 15 | 3 | 0 | 2 | 8 | .217 | .341 | .348 | 0 | 0 | 69 | 8 | 2 | 8 | .217 | 0 | --- | -- | -- | -- | --- | -- | 68% | 32% | 14% | 1.6 | 53% | .689 | .745 | .516 |
| Saltalamacchia J | 2 | 5 | 0 | 1 | 0 | 0 | 0 | 1 | .200 | .200 | .200 | 0 | 0 | 5 | 0 | 0 | 1 | .200 | 0 | --- | -- | -- | -- | --- | -- | 80% | 25% | 0% | 1.0 | 25% | .400 | .400 | ---- |
| Smoak J | 70 | 235 | 29 | 49 | 10 | 0 | 8 | 34 | .209 | .316 | .353 | 1 | 0 | 235 | 29 | 8 | 34 | .209 | 1 | --- | -- | -- | -- | --- | -- | 76% | 28% | 14% | 1.7 | 39% | .670 | .764 | .473 |
| Teagarden T | 28 | 71 | 10 | 11 | 1 | 0 | 4 | 6 | .155 | .259 | .338 | 0 | 0 | 27 | 3 | 0 | 0 | .037 | 0 | 44 | 7 | 4 | 6 | .227 | 0 | 52% | 30% | 9% | 2.2 | 41% | .597 | .542 | .686 |
| Treanor M | 82 | 237 | 22 | 50 | 6 | 1 | 5 | 27 | .211 | .287 | .308 | 1 | 2 | 171 | 19 | 5 | 23 | .228 | 1 | 66 | 3 | 0 | 4 | .167 | 0 | 82% | 26% | 8% | 1.5 | 43% | .595 | .677 | .408 |
| Young M | 157 | 656 | 99 | 186 | 36 | 3 | 21 | 91 | .284 | .330 | .444 | 4 | 2 | 362 | 57 | 12 | 54 | .301 | 3 | 294 | 42 | 9 | 37 | .262 | 1 | 82% | 34% | 7% | 1.6 | 48% | .774 | .739 | .871 |

## Pitchers — Texas Rangers 2010

| Pitchers | Texas Rangers 2010 | | | | | | | | | | | | | 1st Half | | | | | | 2nd Half | | | | | | Rates | | | Productiveness | | |
|---|---|---|---|---|---|---|---|---|---|---|---|---|---|---|---|---|---|---|---|---|---|---|---|---|---|---|---|---|---|---|---|
| | G | GS | W | L | Hld | Sv | IP | H | HR | ERA | WHIP | K | BB | W | L | Sv | IP | ERA | WHIP | W | L | Sv | IP | ERA | WHIP | K/9 | BB/9 | HR/9 | opOPS | vs RH | vs LH |
| Beltre O | 2 | 2 | 0 | 1 | 0 | 0 | 7.0 | 9 | 3 | 9.00 | 2.29 | 9 | 7 | 0 | 1 | 0 | 7.0 | 9.00 | 2.29 | -- | -- | -- | ---- | ---- | --- | 11.6 | 9.0 | 3.9 | 1.129 | 1.065 | 1.178 |
| Feldman S | 29 | 22 | 7 | 11 | 0 | 0 | 141.1 | 181 | 18 | 5.48 | 1.60 | 75 | 45 | 5 | 8 | 0 | 108.1 | 5.32 | 1.60 | 2 | 3 | 0 | 33.0 | 6.00 | 1.61 | 4.8 | 2.9 | 1.1 | .849 | .904 | .790 |
| Feliz N | 70 | 0 | 4 | 3 | 3 | 40 | 69.1 | 43 | 5 | 2.73 | 0.88 | 71 | 18 | 1 | 2 | 23 | 37.2 | 3.82 | 1.06 | 3 | 1 | 17 | 31.2 | 1.42 | 0.66 | 9.2 | 2.3 | 0.6 | .516 | .616 | .409 |
| Francisco F | 56 | 0 | 6 | 4 | 15 | 2 | 52.2 | 49 | 5 | 3.76 | 1.27 | 60 | 18 | 6 | 4 | 2 | 40.0 | 4.28 | 1.33 | 0 | 0 | 0 | 12.2 | 2.13 | 1.11 | 10.3 | 3.1 | 0.9 | .681 | .765 | .549 |
| Harden R | 20 | 18 | 5 | 5 | 0 | 0 | 92.0 | 91 | 18 | 5.58 | 1.66 | 75 | 62 | 3 | 3 | 0 | 65.0 | 5.68 | 1.68 | 2 | 2 | 0 | 27.0 | 5.33 | 1.63 | 7.3 | 6.1 | 1.8 | .842 | .759 | .915 |
| Harrison M | 37 | 6 | 3 | 2 | 3 | 2 | 78.1 | 80 | 10 | 4.71 | 1.52 | 46 | 39 | 1 | 1 | 1 | 50.1 | 4.47 | 1.37 | 2 | 1 | 1 | 28.0 | 5.14 | 1.79 | 5.3 | 4.5 | 1.1 | .755 | .770 | .716 |
| Holland D | 14 | 10 | 3 | 4 | 1 | 0 | 57.1 | 55 | 6 | 4.08 | 1.38 | 54 | 24 | 2 | 1 | 0 | 19.1 | 4.19 | 1.29 | 1 | 3 | 0 | 38.0 | 4.03 | 1.42 | 8.5 | 3.8 | 0.9 | .727 | .818 | .362 |
| Hunter T | 23 | 22 | 13 | 4 | 0 | 0 | 128.0 | 126 | 21 | 3.73 | 1.24 | 68 | 33 | 5 | 0 | 0 | 42.1 | 2.34 | 1.18 | 8 | 4 | 0 | 85.2 | 4.41 | 1.27 | 4.8 | 2.3 | 1.5 | .740 | .708 | .765 |
| Kirkman M | 14 | 0 | 0 | 0 | 2 | 0 | 16.1 | 9 | 0 | 1.65 | 1.16 | 16 | 10 | -- | -- | -- | ---- | ---- | --- | 0 | 0 | 0 | 16.1 | 1.65 | 1.16 | 8.8 | 5.5 | 0.0 | .458 | .357 | .563 |
| Lee C | 15 | 15 | 4 | 6 | 0 | 0 | 108.2 | 103 | 11 | 3.98 | 1.06 | 96 | 12 | 0 | 1 | 0 | 9.0 | 6.00 | 1.00 | 4 | 5 | 0 | 99.2 | 3.79 | 1.06 | 8.0 | 1.0 | 0.9 | .662 | .650 | .699 |
| Lewis C | 32 | 32 | 12 | 13 | 0 | 0 | 201.0 | 174 | 21 | 3.72 | 1.19 | 196 | 65 | 8 | 5 | 0 | 110.2 | 3.33 | 1.12 | 4 | 8 | 0 | 90.1 | 4.18 | 1.27 | 8.8 | 2.9 | 0.9 | .660 | .627 | .693 |
| Lowe M | 3 | 0 | 0 | 0 | 0 | 0 | 3.0 | 7 | 1 | 12.00 | 2.67 | 5 | 1 | -- | -- | -- | ---- | ---- | --- | 0 | 0 | 0 | 3.0 | 12.00 | 2.67 | 15.0 | 3.0 | 3.0 | 1.233 | 1.400 | 1.145 |
| Mathis D | 13 | 0 | 1 | 1 | 0 | 0 | 22.1 | 30 | 7 | 6.04 | 1.84 | 10 | 11 | 1 | 1 | 0 | 19.1 | 6.98 | 1.97 | 0 | 0 | 0 | 3.0 | 0.00 | 1.00 | 4.0 | 4.4 | 2.8 | 1.017 | 1.163 | .843 |
| Moscoso G | 1 | 0 | 0 | 0 | 0 | 0 | 0.2 | 2 | 0 | 27.00 | 6.00 | 2 | 2 | 0 | 0 | 0 | 0.2 | 27.00 | 6.00 | -- | -- | -- | ---- | ---- | --- | 27.0 | 27.0 | 0.0 | 1.464 | 1.250 | ---- |
| Nippert D | 38 | 2 | 4 | 5 | 5 | 0 | 56.2 | 61 | 7 | 4.29 | 1.68 | 47 | 34 | 3 | 4 | 0 | 41.2 | 5.40 | 1.97 | 1 | 1 | 0 | 15.0 | 1.20 | 0.87 | 7.5 | 5.4 | 1.1 | .816 | .769 | .887 |
| O'Day D | 72 | 0 | 6 | 2 | 22 | 0 | 62.0 | 43 | 5 | 2.03 | 0.89 | 45 | 12 | 3 | 2 | 0 | 36.1 | 1.49 | 0.88 | 3 | 0 | 0 | 25.2 | 2.81 | 0.90 | 6.5 | 1.7 | 0.7 | .548 | .542 | .561 |
| Ogando A | 44 | 0 | 4 | 1 | 7 | 0 | 41.2 | 31 | 2 | 1.30 | 1.13 | 39 | 16 | 3 | 0 | 0 | 15.2 | 0.57 | 0.83 | 1 | 1 | 0 | 26.0 | 1.73 | 1.31 | 8.4 | 3.5 | 0.4 | .554 | .492 | .678 |
| Oliver D | 64 | 0 | 1 | 2 | 14 | 1 | 61.2 | 53 | 4 | 2.48 | 1.10 | 65 | 15 | 0 | 0 | 1 | 39.2 | 1.36 | 0.88 | 1 | 2 | 0 | 22.0 | 4.50 | 1.50 | 9.5 | 2.2 | 0.6 | .654 | .765 | .529 |
| Rapada C | 13 | 0 | 0 | 0 | 3 | 0 | 9.0 | 6 | 2 | 4.00 | 1.44 | 5 | 7 | -- | -- | -- | ---- | ---- | --- | 0 | 0 | 0 | 9.0 | 4.00 | 1.44 | 5.0 | 7.0 | 2.0 | .708 | 1.402 | .195 |
| Ray C | 35 | 0 | 2 | 0 | 7 | 1 | 31.2 | 24 | 4 | 3.41 | 1.26 | 16 | 16 | 2 | 0 | 1 | 31.2 | 3.41 | 1.26 | -- | -- | -- | ---- | ---- | --- | 4.5 | 4.5 | 1.1 | .677 | .543 | .839 |
| Strop P | 15 | 0 | 0 | 0 | 1 | 0 | 10.2 | 17 | 2 | 10.13 | 2.63 | 11 | 11 | 0 | 0 | 0 | 3.2 | 2.45 | 1.64 | 0 | 0 | 0 | 7.0 | 14.14 | 3.14 | 9.3 | 9.3 | 1.7 | 1.109 | 1.093 | 1.132 |
| Wilson C | 33 | 33 | 15 | 8 | 0 | 0 | 204.0 | 161 | 10 | 3.35 | 1.25 | 170 | 93 | 7 | 5 | 0 | 113.0 | 3.35 | 1.25 | 8 | 3 | 0 | 91.0 | 3.36 | 1.24 | 7.5 | 4.1 | 0.4 | .622 | .679 | .400 |

# AL Toronto

**Writer:** Marc Hulet
www.battersbox.ca

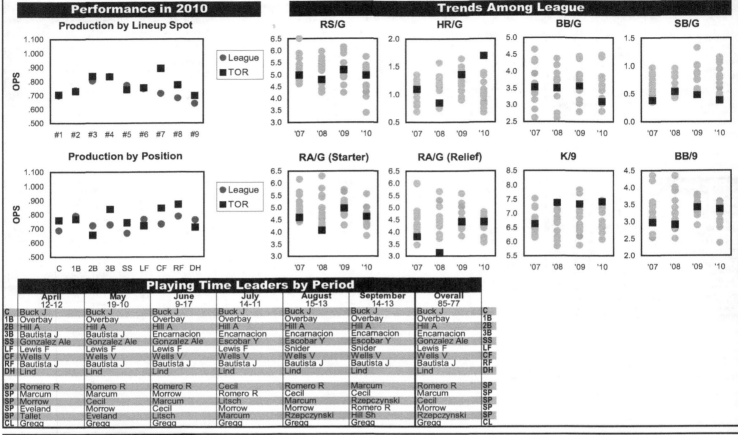

## Performance in 2010
### Production by Lineup Spot
### Production by Position

## Trends Among League
RS/G    HR/G    BB/G    SB/G
RA/G (Starter)    RA/G (Relief)    K/9    BB/9

### Playing Time Leaders by Period

|     | April 12–12 | May 19–10 | June 9–17 | July 14–11 | August 15–13 | September 14–13 | Overall 85–77 |     |
|-----|-------------|-----------|-----------|------------|--------------|-----------------|---------------|-----|
| C   | Buck J | Buck J | Buck J | Buck J | Buck J | Buck J | Buck J | C |
| 1B  | Overbay | Overbay | Overbay | Overbay | Overbay | Overbay | Overbay | 1B |
| 2B  | Hill A | Hill A | Hill A | Hill A | Hill A | Hill A | Hill A | 2B |
| 3B  | Bautista J | Bautista J | Encarnacion | Encarnacion | Encarnacion | Encarnacion | Encarnacion | 3B |
| SS  | Gonzalez Ale | Gonzalez Ale | Gonzalez Ale | Escobar Y | Escobar Y | Escobar Y | Gonzalez Ale | SS |
| LF  | Lewis F | Lewis F | Lewis F | Lewis F | Snider | Snider | Lewis F | LF |
| CF  | Wells V | Wells V | Wells V | Wells V | Wells V | Wells V | Wells V | CF |
| RF  | Bautista J | Bautista J | Bautista J | Bautista J | Bautista J | Bautista J | Bautista J | RF |
| DH  | Lind | Lind | Lind | Lind | Lind | Lind | Lind | DH |
|     |        |        |        |        |        |        |        |    |
| SP  | Romero R | Romero R | Romero R | Cecil | Romero R | Marcum | Romero R | SP |
| SP  | Marcum | Marcum | Morrow | Romero R | Cecil | Cecil | Marcum | SP |
| SP  | Morrow | Cecil | Marcum | Litsch | Marcum | Rzepczynski | Cecil | SP |
| SP  | Eveland | Morrow | Cecil | Morrow | Morrow | Romero R | Morrow | SP |
| SP  | Tallet | Eveland | Litsch | Marcum | Rzepczynski | Hill Sh | Rzepczynski | SP |
| CL  | Gregg | Gregg | Gregg | Gregg | Gregg | Gregg | Gregg | CL |

# NL Washington

**Writer:** Paul Bugala
www.baysoxblog.com

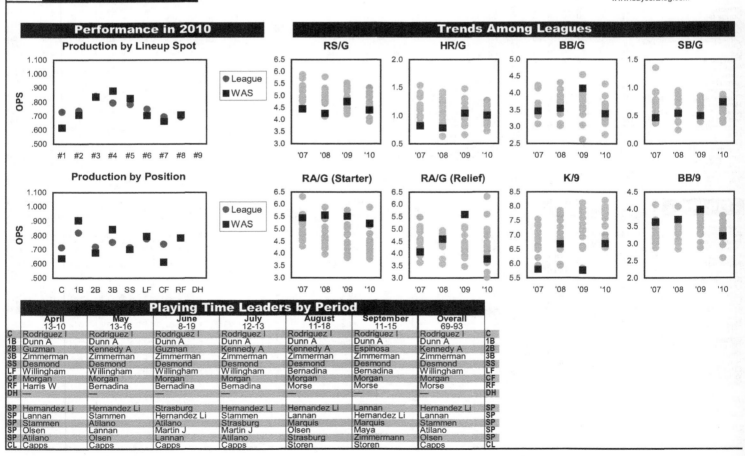

## Performance in 2010
### Production by Lineup Spot
### Production by Position

## Trends Among Leagues
RS/G    HR/G    BB/G    SB/G
RA/G (Starter)    RA/G (Relief)    K/9    BB/9

### Playing Time Leaders by Period

|     | April 13–10 | May 13–16 | June 8–19 | July 12–13 | August 11–18 | September 11–15 | Overall 69–93 |     |
|-----|-------------|-----------|-----------|------------|--------------|-----------------|---------------|-----|
| C   | Rodriguez I | Rodriguez I | Rodriguez I | Rodriguez I | Rodriguez I | Rodriguez I | Rodriguez I | C |
| 1B  | Dunn A | Dunn A | Dunn A | Dunn A | Dunn A | Dunn A | Dunn A | 1B |
| 2B  | Guzman | Kennedy A | Guzman | Kennedy A | Kennedy A | Espinosa | Kennedy A | 2B |
| 3B  | Zimmerman | Zimmerman | Zimmerman | Zimmerman | Zimmerman | Zimmerman | Zimmerman | 3B |
| SS  | Desmond | Desmond | Desmond | Desmond | Desmond | Desmond | Desmond | SS |
| LF  | Willingham | Willingham | Willingham | Willingham | Bernadina | Bernadina | Willingham | LF |
| CF  | Morgan | Morgan | Morgan | Morgan | Morgan | Morgan | Morgan | CF |
| RF  | Harris W | Bernadina | Bernadina | Bernadina | Morse | Morse | Morse | RF |
| DH  | — | — | — | — | — | — | — | DH |
|     |        |        |        |        |        |        |        |    |
| SP  | Hernandez Li | Hernandez Li | Strasburg | Hernandez Li | Hernandez Li | Lannan | Hernandez Li | SP |
| SP  | Lannan | Stammen | Hernandez Li | Stammen | Lannan | Hernandez Li | Lannan | SP |
| SP  | Stammen | Atilano | Atilano | Strasburg | Marquis | Marquis | Stammen | SP |
| SP  | Olsen | Lannan | Martin J | Martin J | Olsen | Maya | Atilano | SP |
| SP  | Atilano | Olsen | Lannan | Atilano | Strasburg | Zimmermann | Olsen | SP |
| CL  | Capps | Capps | Capps | Capps | Storen | Storen | Capps | CL |

| Hitters | Toronto Blue Jays 2010 | | | | | | | | | | | | | 1st Half | | | | | | 2nd Half | | | | | | Rates | | | | | Productiveness | | |
|---|---|---|---|---|---|---|---|---|---|---|---|---|---|---|---|---|---|---|---|---|---|---|---|---|---|---|---|---|---|---|---|---|---|
| | G | AB | R | H | 2B | 3B | HR | RBI | BA | OBP | SLG | SB | CS | AB | R | HR | BI | BA | SB | AB | R | HR | BI | BA | SB | CT% | H% | BB% | Bash | GB% | OPS | vs RH | vs LH |
| Arencibia J | 11 | 35 | 3 | 5 | 1 | 0 | 2 | 4 | .143 | .189 | .343 | 0 | 0 | --- | -- | -- | -- | --- | -- | 35 | 3 | 2 | 4 | .143 | 0 | 69% | 21% | 5% | 2.4 | 29% | .532 | .772 | .077 |
| Bautista J | 161 | 569 | 109 | 148 | 35 | 3 | 54 | 124 | .260 | .378 | .617 | 9 | 2 | 304 | 55 | 24 | 56 | .237 | 3 | 265 | 54 | 30 | 68 | .287 | 6 | 80% | 33% | 15% | 2.4 | 31% | .995 | 1.030 | .843 |
| Buck J | 118 | 409 | 53 | 115 | 25 | 0 | 20 | 66 | .281 | .314 | .489 | 0 | 0 | 235 | 27 | 13 | 41 | .272 | 0 | 174 | 26 | 7 | 25 | .293 | 0 | 73% | 39% | 4% | 1.7 | 40% | .802 | .718 | 1.116 |
| Encarnacion E | 96 | 332 | 47 | 81 | 16 | 0 | 21 | 51 | .244 | .305 | .482 | 1 | 0 | 149 | 20 | 10 | 24 | .221 | 1 | 183 | 27 | 11 | 27 | .262 | 0 | 82% | 30% | 8% | 2.0 | 32% | .787 | .755 | .914 |
| Escobar Y | 60 | 236 | 32 | 65 | 7 | 0 | 4 | 16 | .275 | .340 | .356 | 1 | 1 | --- | -- | -- | -- | --- | -- | 236 | 32 | 4 | 16 | .275 | 1 | 89% | 31% | 7% | 1.3 | 55% | .696 | .669 | .821 |
| Gonzalez A | 85 | 328 | 47 | 85 | 25 | 1 | 17 | 50 | .259 | .296 | .497 | 1 | 0 | 328 | 47 | 17 | 50 | .259 | 1 | --- | -- | -- | -- | --- | -- | 80% | 32% | 5% | 1.9 | 30% | .793 | .816 | .714 |
| Green N | 9 | 13 | 2 | 2 | 0 | 0 | 0 | 1 | .154 | .214 | .154 | 0 | 0 | 13 | 2 | 0 | 1 | .154 | 0 | --- | -- | -- | -- | --- | -- | 77% | 20% | 7% | 1.0 | 50% | .368 | .250 | .533 |
| Hill A | 138 | 528 | 70 | 108 | 22 | 0 | 26 | 68 | .205 | .271 | .394 | 2 | 2 | 281 | 33 | 12 | 33 | .189 | 1 | 247 | 37 | 14 | 35 | .223 | 1 | 84% | 24% | 7% | 1.9 | 35% | .665 | .729 | .451 |
| Hoffpauir J | 13 | 34 | 1 | 7 | 1 | 0 | 0 | 0 | .206 | .250 | .235 | 0 | 0 | 28 | 1 | 0 | 0 | .214 | 0 | 6 | 0 | 0 | 0 | .167 | 0 | 85% | 24% | 5% | 1.1 | 45% | .485 | .372 | .665 |
| Lewis F | 110 | 428 | 70 | 112 | 31 | 5 | 8 | 36 | .262 | .332 | .414 | 17 | 6 | 279 | 44 | 5 | 25 | .276 | 10 | 149 | 26 | 3 | 11 | .235 | 7 | 76% | 35% | 8% | 1.6 | 48% | .745 | .776 | .636 |
| Lind A | 150 | 569 | 57 | 135 | 32 | 3 | 23 | 72 | .237 | .287 | .425 | 0 | 0 | 322 | 33 | 12 | 40 | .214 | 0 | 247 | 24 | 11 | 32 | .267 | 0 | 75% | 32% | 6% | 1.8 | 41% | .712 | .829 | .341 |
| McCoy M | 46 | 82 | 9 | 16 | 4 | 0 | 0 | 3 | .195 | .267 | .244 | 5 | 1 | 50 | 6 | 0 | 2 | .200 | 4 | 32 | 3 | 0 | 1 | .188 | 1 | 76% | 26% | 9% | 1.3 | 40% | .511 | .370 | .745 |
| McDonald J | 63 | 152 | 27 | 38 | 9 | 2 | 6 | 23 | .250 | .273 | .454 | 2 | 1 | 65 | 11 | 2 | 6 | .231 | 0 | 87 | 16 | 4 | 17 | .264 | 2 | 83% | 30% | 4% | 1.8 | 35% | .727 | .721 | .743 |
| Molina J | 57 | 167 | 13 | 41 | 4 | 0 | 6 | 12 | .246 | .304 | .377 | 1 | 0 | 85 | 9 | 2 | 6 | .282 | 0 | 82 | 4 | 4 | 6 | .207 | 1 | 78% | 31% | 5% | 1.5 | 43% | .681 | .763 | .464 |
| Overbay L | 154 | 534 | 75 | 130 | 37 | 2 | 20 | 67 | .243 | .329 | .433 | 1 | 0 | 312 | 43 | 10 | 31 | .250 | 1 | 222 | 32 | 10 | 36 | .234 | 0 | 75% | 32% | 11% | 1.8 | 45% | .762 | .781 | .700 |
| Reed J | 14 | 21 | 1 | 3 | 0 | 0 | 1 | 3 | .143 | .217 | .286 | 1 | 0 | 21 | 1 | 1 | 3 | .143 | 1 | --- | -- | -- | -- | --- | -- | 62% | 23% | 9% | 2.0 | 38% | .503 | .490 | .500 |
| Ruiz R | 13 | 40 | 3 | 6 | 2 | 0 | 1 | 1 | .150 | .150 | .275 | 1 | 0 | 40 | 3 | 1 | 1 | .150 | 1 | --- | -- | -- | -- | --- | -- | 73% | 21% | 0% | 1.8 | 45% | .425 | .435 | .412 |
| Snider T | 82 | 298 | 36 | 76 | 20 | 0 | 14 | 32 | .255 | .304 | .463 | 6 | 3 | 116 | 16 | 6 | 15 | .241 | 3 | 182 | 20 | 8 | 17 | .264 | 3 | 73% | 35% | 7% | 1.8 | 41% | .767 | .783 | .702 |
| Wells V | 157 | 590 | 79 | 161 | 44 | 3 | 31 | 88 | .273 | .331 | .515 | 6 | 4 | 328 | 46 | 19 | 49 | .265 | 4 | 262 | 33 | 12 | 39 | .282 | 2 | 86% | 32% | 8% | 1.9 | 42% | .847 | .895 | .643 |
| Wise D | 52 | 112 | 20 | 28 | 3 | 2 | 3 | 14 | .250 | .282 | .393 | 4 | 0 | 30 | 6 | 2 | 9 | .233 | 2 | 82 | 14 | 1 | 5 | .256 | 2 | 74% | 34% | 3% | 1.6 | 41% | .675 | .679 | .641 |

| Pitchers | Toronto Blue Jays 2010 | | | | | | | | | | | | | 1st Half | | | | | | 2nd Half | | | | | | Rates | | | Productiveness | | |
|---|---|---|---|---|---|---|---|---|---|---|---|---|---|---|---|---|---|---|---|---|---|---|---|---|---|---|---|---|---|---|---|
| | G | GS | W | L | Hld | Sv | IP | H | HR | ERA | WHIP | K | BB | W | L | Sv | IP | ERA | WHIP | W | L | Sv | IP | ERA | WHIP | K/9 | BB/9 | HR/9 | opOPS | vs RH | vs LH |
| Accardo J | 5 | 0 | 0 | 1 | 0 | 0 | 6.2 | 12 | 0 | 8.10 | 2.25 | 3 | 3 | 0 | 1 | 0 | 6.2 | 8.10 | 2.25 | -- | -- | -- | ---- | ---- | --- | 4.1 | 4.1 | 0.0 | 1.004 | .801 | 1.255 |
| Buchholz T | 2 | 0 | 0 | 0 | 0 | 0 | 2.0 | 0 | 0 | 0.00 | 0.00 | 0 | 0 | -- | -- | -- | ---- | ---- | --- | 0 | 0 | 0 | 2.0 | 0.00 | 0.00 | 0.0 | 0.0 | 0.0 | .000 | .000 | .000 |
| Camp S | 70 | 0 | 4 | 3 | 13 | 2 | 72.1 | 71 | 8 | 2.99 | 1.23 | 46 | 18 | 3 | 1 | 0 | 46.1 | 2.53 | 1.04 | 1 | 2 | 2 | 26.0 | 3.81 | 1.58 | 5.7 | 2.2 | 1.0 | .728 | .661 | .832 |
| Carlson J | 20 | 0 | 0 | 0 | 2 | 1 | 13.2 | 13 | 3 | 4.61 | 1.32 | 8 | 5 | -- | -- | -- | ---- | ---- | --- | 0 | 0 | 1 | 13.2 | 4.61 | 1.32 | 5.3 | 3.3 | 2.0 | .808 | 1.015 | .449 |
| Cecil B | 28 | 28 | 15 | 7 | 0 | 0 | 172.2 | 175 | 18 | 4.22 | 1.33 | 117 | 54 | 8 | 5 | 0 | 93.0 | 3.97 | 1.16 | 7 | 2 | 0 | 79.2 | 4.52 | 1.52 | 6.1 | 2.8 | 0.9 | .733 | .773 | .597 |
| Downs S | 67 | 0 | 5 | 5 | 26 | 0 | 61.1 | 47 | 3 | 2.64 | 0.99 | 48 | 14 | 3 | 5 | 0 | 37.1 | 2.65 | 1.02 | 2 | 0 | 0 | 24.0 | 2.63 | 0.96 | 7.0 | 2.1 | 0.4 | .584 | .637 | .488 |
| Drabek K | 3 | 3 | 0 | 3 | 0 | 0 | 17.0 | 18 | 2 | 4.76 | 1.35 | 12 | 5 | -- | -- | -- | ---- | ---- | --- | 0 | 3 | 0 | 17.0 | 4.76 | 1.35 | 6.4 | 2.6 | 1.1 | .781 | .913 | .744 |
| Eveland D | 9 | 9 | 3 | 4 | 0 | 0 | 44.2 | 57 | 4 | 6.45 | 1.88 | 21 | 27 | 3 | 4 | 0 | 44.2 | 6.45 | 1.88 | -- | -- | -- | ---- | ---- | --- | 4.2 | 5.4 | 0.8 | .854 | .870 | .797 |
| Frasor J | 69 | 0 | 3 | 4 | 14 | 4 | 63.2 | 61 | 4 | 3.68 | 1.38 | 65 | 27 | 3 | 2 | 3 | 34.2 | 4.67 | 1.62 | 0 | 2 | 1 | 29.0 | 2.48 | 1.10 | 9.2 | 3.8 | 0.6 | .691 | .671 | .718 |
| Gregg K | 63 | 0 | 2 | 6 | 3 | 37 | 59.0 | 52 | 4 | 3.51 | 1.39 | 58 | 30 | 0 | 3 | 20 | 34.1 | 3.67 | 1.37 | 2 | 3 | 17 | 24.2 | 3.28 | 1.42 | 8.8 | 4.6 | 0.6 | .712 | .692 | .732 |
| Hill S | 4 | 4 | 1 | 2 | 0 | 0 | 20.2 | 24 | 1 | 2.61 | 1.35 | 14 | 4 | -- | -- | -- | ---- | ---- | --- | 1 | 2 | 0 | 20.2 | 2.61 | 1.35 | 6.1 | 1.7 | 0.4 | .683 | .589 | .773 |
| Janssen C | 56 | 0 | 5 | 2 | 2 | 0 | 68.2 | 74 | 8 | 3.67 | 1.38 | 63 | 21 | 4 | 0 | 0 | 41.2 | 4.10 | 1.20 | 1 | 2 | 0 | 27.0 | 3.00 | 1.67 | 8.3 | 2.8 | 1.0 | .748 | .709 | .798 |
| Lewis R | 14 | 0 | 0 | 0 | 0 | 0 | 18.2 | 20 | 4 | 6.75 | 1.50 | 15 | 8 | 0 | 0 | 0 | 18.1 | 4.91 | 1.25 | 0 | 0 | 0 | 0.1 | 108.00 | 15.00 | 7.2 | 3.9 | 1.9 | .841 | .799 | .903 |
| Litsch J | 9 | 9 | 1 | 5 | 0 | 0 | 46.2 | 53 | 7 | 5.79 | 1.46 | 16 | 15 | 0 | 4 | 0 | 31.2 | 6.54 | 1.39 | 1 | 1 | 0 | 15.0 | 4.20 | 1.60 | 3.1 | 2.9 | 1.4 | .822 | .805 | .833 |
| Marcum S | 31 | 31 | 13 | 8 | 0 | 0 | 195.1 | 181 | 24 | 3.64 | 1.15 | 165 | 43 | 7 | 4 | 0 | 107.1 | 3.44 | 1.16 | 6 | 4 | 0 | 88.0 | 3.89 | 1.13 | 7.6 | 2.0 | 1.1 | .691 | .859 | .532 |
| Mills B | 7 | 3 | 1 | 0 | 1 | 0 | 22.1 | 20 | 2 | 5.64 | 1.48 | 18 | 13 | -- | -- | -- | ---- | ---- | --- | 1 | 0 | 0 | 22.1 | 5.64 | 1.48 | 7.3 | 5.2 | 0.8 | .745 | .684 | .836 |
| Morrow B | 26 | 26 | 10 | 7 | 0 | 0 | 146.1 | 136 | 11 | 4.49 | 1.38 | 178 | 66 | 5 | 6 | 0 | 100.0 | 4.86 | 1.46 | 5 | 1 | 0 | 46.1 | 3.69 | 1.21 | 10.9 | 4.1 | 0.7 | .725 | .704 | .739 |
| Purcey D | 33 | 0 | 1 | 1 | 3 | 1 | 34.0 | 26 | 3 | 3.71 | 1.21 | 32 | 15 | 0 | 1 | 0 | 17.0 | 2.12 | 1.12 | 1 | 0 | 1 | 17.0 | 5.29 | 1.29 | 8.5 | 4.0 | 0.8 | .629 | .699 | .495 |
| Ray R | 3 | 0 | 0 | 0 | 0 | 0 | 3.2 | 2 | 0 | 2.45 | 1.91 | 3 | 5 | -- | -- | -- | ---- | ---- | --- | 0 | 0 | 0 | 3.2 | 2.45 | 1.91 | 7.4 | 12.3 | 0.0 | .774 | .550 | 1.333 |
| Roenicke J | 16 | 0 | 1 | 0 | 2 | 0 | 19.0 | 18 | 1 | 5.68 | 1.63 | 18 | 13 | 1 | 0 | 0 | 12.2 | 4.97 | 1.74 | 0 | 0 | 0 | 6.1 | 7.11 | 1.42 | 8.5 | 6.2 | 0.5 | .718 | .809 | .592 |
| Romero R | 32 | 32 | 14 | 9 | 0 | 0 | 210.0 | 189 | 15 | 3.73 | 1.29 | 174 | 82 | 6 | 6 | 0 | 116.1 | 3.71 | 1.32 | 8 | 3 | 0 | 93.2 | 3.75 | 1.25 | 7.5 | 3.5 | 0.6 | .673 | .642 | .768 |
| Rzepczynski M | 14 | 12 | 4 | 4 | 2 | 0 | 63.2 | 72 | 8 | 4.95 | 1.60 | 57 | 30 | 0 | 0 | 0 | 6.1 | 5.68 | 1.42 | 4 | 4 | 0 | 57.1 | 4.87 | 1.62 | 8.1 | 4.2 | 1.1 | .840 | .895 | .671 |
| Tallet B | 34 | 5 | 2 | 6 | 1 | 0 | 77.1 | 84 | 20 | 6.40 | 1.58 | 53 | 38 | 1 | 3 | 0 | 42.1 | 6.59 | 1.63 | 1 | 3 | 0 | 35.0 | 6.17 | 1.51 | 6.2 | 4.4 | 2.3 | .881 | 1.031 | .571 |
| Valdez M | 2 | 0 | 0 | 0 | 0 | 0 | 1.1 | 2 | 0 | 20.25 | 3.75 | 0 | 3 | 0 | 0 | 0 | 1.1 | 20.25 | 3.75 | -- | -- | -- | ---- | ---- | --- | 0.0 | 20.3 | 0.0 | .889 | .667 | 1.000 |

| Hitters | Washington Nationals 2010 | | | | | | | | | | | | | 1st Half | | | | | | 2nd Half | | | | | | Rates | | | | | Productiveness | | |
|---|---|---|---|---|---|---|---|---|---|---|---|---|---|---|---|---|---|---|---|---|---|---|---|---|---|---|---|---|---|---|---|---|---|
| | G | AB | R | H | 2B | 3B | HR | RBI | BA | OBP | SLG | SB | CS | AB | R | HR | BI | BA | SB | AB | R | HR | BI | BA | SB | CT% | H% | BB% | Bash | GB% | OPS | vs RH | vs LH |
| Bernadina R | 134 | 414 | 52 | 102 | 18 | 3 | 11 | 47 | .246 | .307 | .384 | 16 | 2 | 181 | 19 | 5 | 24 | .282 | 7 | 233 | 33 | 6 | 23 | .219 | 9 | 78% | 32% | 8% | 1.6 | 46% | .691 | .681 | .757 |
| Desmond I | 154 | 525 | 59 | 141 | 27 | 4 | 10 | 65 | .269 | .308 | .392 | 17 | 5 | 271 | 31 | 6 | 36 | .255 | 8 | 254 | 28 | 4 | 29 | .283 | 9 | 79% | 34% | 5% | 1.5 | 52% | .700 | .664 | .799 |
| Dunn A | 158 | 558 | 85 | 145 | 36 | 2 | 38 | 103 | .260 | .356 | .536 | 0 | 1 | 320 | 51 | 22 | 59 | .288 | 0 | 238 | 34 | 16 | 44 | .223 | 0 | 64% | 40% | 12% | 2.1 | 33% | .892 | .965 | .719 |
| Espinosa D | 28 | 103 | 16 | 22 | 4 | 1 | 6 | 15 | .214 | .277 | .447 | 0 | 2 | --- | -- | -- | -- | --- | -- | 103 | 16 | 6 | 15 | .214 | 0 | 71% | 30% | 8% | 2.1 | 45% | .723 | .684 | .846 |
| Gonzalez A | 115 | 186 | 19 | 46 | 8 | 1 | 0 | 5 | .247 | .277 | .301 | 0 | 0 | 76 | 9 | 0 | 3 | .289 | 0 | 110 | 10 | 0 | 2 | .218 | 0 | 84% | 29% | 4% | 1.2 | 56% | .578 | .568 | .595 |
| Guzman C | 89 | 319 | 44 | 90 | 11 | 4 | 2 | 25 | .282 | .327 | .361 | 4 | 2 | 282 | 41 | 1 | 22 | .294 | 3 | 37 | 3 | 1 | 3 | .189 | 1 | 83% | 34% | 5% | 1.3 | 51% | .687 | .637 | .784 |
| Harris W | 132 | 224 | 25 | 41 | 6 | 2 | 10 | 32 | .183 | .291 | .362 | 5 | 2 | 122 | 11 | 4 | 19 | .180 | 2 | 102 | 14 | 6 | 13 | .186 | 3 | 73% | 25% | 13% | 2.0 | 41% | .653 | .642 | .778 |
| Kennedy A | 135 | 342 | 43 | 85 | 16 | 1 | 3 | 31 | .249 | .327 | .327 | 14 | 2 | 178 | 22 | 2 | 16 | .242 | 9 | 164 | 21 | 1 | 15 | .256 | 5 | 87% | 29% | 9% | 1.3 | 44% | .655 | .635 | .803 |
| Maldonado C | 4 | 11 | 1 | 3 | 0 | 0 | 1 | 3 | .273 | .333 | .545 | 0 | 0 | 11 | 1 | 1 | 3 | .273 | 0 | --- | -- | -- | -- | --- | -- | 82% | 33% | 8% | 2.0 | 67% | .879 | 1.286 | .200 |
| Maxwell J | 67 | 104 | 16 | 15 | 6 | 0 | 3 | 12 | .144 | .305 | .288 | 5 | 1 | 38 | 6 | 1 | 3 | .105 | 3 | 66 | 10 | 2 | 9 | .167 | 2 | 59% | 25% | 19% | 2.0 | 36% | .594 | .407 | .729 |
| Mench K | 27 | 27 | 2 | 3 | 0 | 0 | 0 | 1 | .111 | .172 | .111 | 0 | 0 | --- | -- | -- | -- | --- | -- | 27 | 2 | 0 | 1 | .111 | 0 | 78% | 14% | 7% | 1.0 | 52% | .284 | .269 | .311 |
| Morgan N | 136 | 509 | 60 | 129 | 17 | 7 | 0 | 24 | .253 | .319 | .314 | 34 | 17 | 329 | 40 | 0 | 14 | .252 | 20 | 180 | 20 | 0 | 10 | .256 | 14 | 83% | 31% | 7% | 1.2 | 49% | .633 | .669 | .532 |
| Morse M | 98 | 266 | 36 | 77 | 12 | 2 | 15 | 41 | .289 | .352 | .519 | 0 | 1 | 71 | 6 | 4 | 9 | .310 | 0 | 195 | 30 | 11 | 32 | .282 | 0 | 76% | 38% | 7% | 1.8 | 47% | .870 | .806 | .999 |
| Nieves W | 59 | 158 | 10 | 32 | 8 | 0 | 3 | 16 | .203 | .244 | .310 | 0 | 0 | 113 | 5 | 1 | 11 | .186 | 0 | 45 | 5 | 2 | 5 | .244 | 0 | 82% | 25% | 5% | 1.5 | 54% | .554 | .537 | .621 |
| Ramos W | 15 | 52 | 3 | 14 | 4 | 0 | 1 | 4 | .269 | .296 | .404 | 0 | 0 | --- | -- | -- | -- | --- | -- | 52 | 3 | 1 | 4 | .269 | 0 | 83% | 33% | 4% | 1.5 | 42% | .700 | .589 | 1.429 |
| Rodriguez I | 111 | 398 | 32 | 106 | 18 | 1 | 4 | 49 | .266 | .294 | .347 | 2 | 3 | 216 | 19 | 1 | 27 | .296 | 2 | 182 | 13 | 3 | 22 | .231 | 0 | 83% | 32% | 4% | 1.3 | 62% | .640 | .616 | .716 |
| Taveras W | 27 | 35 | 7 | 7 | 0 | 1 | 0 | 4 | .200 | .243 | .257 | 1 | 2 | 35 | 7 | 0 | 4 | .200 | 1 | --- | -- | -- | -- | --- | -- | 83% | 24% | 5% | 1.3 | 55% | .500 | .056 | .921 |
| Willingham J | 114 | 370 | 54 | 99 | 19 | 2 | 16 | 56 | .268 | .389 | .459 | 8 | 0 | 281 | 45 | 15 | 46 | .281 | 7 | 89 | 9 | 1 | 10 | .225 | 1 | 77% | 35% | 15% | 1.7 | 31% | .848 | .828 | .909 |
| Zimmerman R | 142 | 525 | 85 | 161 | 32 | 0 | 25 | 85 | .307 | .388 | .510 | 4 | 1 | 289 | 52 | 16 | 48 | .294 | 1 | 236 | 33 | 9 | 37 | .322 | 3 | 81% | 38% | 11% | 1.7 | 42% | .899 | .879 | .957 |

| Pitchers | Washington Nationals 2010 | | | | | | | | | | | | | 1st Half | | | | | | 2nd Half | | | | | | Rates | | | Productiveness | | |
|---|---|---|---|---|---|---|---|---|---|---|---|---|---|---|---|---|---|---|---|---|---|---|---|---|---|---|---|---|---|---|---|
| | G | GS | W | L | Hld | Sv | IP | H | HR | ERA | WHIP | K | BB | W | L | Sv | IP | ERA | WHIP | W | L | Sv | IP | ERA | WHIP | K/9 | BB/9 | HR/9 | opOPS | vs RH | vs LH |
| Atilano L | 16 | 16 | 6 | 7 | 0 | 0 | 85.2 | 96 | 11 | 5.15 | 1.49 | 40 | 32 | 6 | 6 | 0 | 81.2 | 4.85 | 1.47 | 0 | 1 | 0 | 4.0 | 11.25 | 2.00 | 4.2 | 3.4 | 1.2 | .813 | .770 | .867 |
| Balester C | 17 | 0 | 0 | 1 | 0 | 0 | 21.0 | 15 | 2 | 2.57 | 1.24 | 28 | 11 | -- | -- | -- | ---- | ---- | --- | 0 | 1 | 0 | 21.0 | 2.57 | 1.24 | 12.0 | 4.7 | 0.9 | .633 | .492 | .790 |
| Batista M | 58 | 1 | 1 | 2 | 1 | 2 | 82.2 | 71 | 9 | 3.70 | 1.33 | 55 | 39 | 0 | 2 | 1 | 47.0 | 4.60 | 1.38 | 1 | 0 | 1 | 35.2 | 2.52 | 1.26 | 6.0 | 4.2 | 1.0 | .693 | .651 | .758 |
| Bergmann J | 4 | 0 | 0 | 1 | 1 | 0 | 2.1 | 3 | 2 | 15.43 | 1.71 | 2 | 1 | 0 | 1 | 0 | 2.1 | 15.43 | 1.71 | -- | -- | -- | ---- | ---- | --- | 7.7 | 3.9 | 7.7 | 1.364 | 1.700 | 1.000 |
| Bisenius J | 5 | 0 | 0 | 0 | 0 | 0 | 4.2 | 6 | 1 | 9.64 | 2.57 | 5 | 6 | -- | -- | -- | ---- | ---- | --- | 0 | 0 | 0 | 4.2 | 9.64 | 2.57 | 9.6 | 11.6 | 1.9 | 1.012 | 1.080 | .833 |
| Bruney B | 19 | 0 | 1 | 2 | 3 | 0 | 17.2 | 21 | 1 | 7.64 | 2.32 | 16 | 20 | 1 | 2 | 0 | 17.2 | 7.64 | 2.32 | -- | -- | -- | ---- | ---- | --- | 8.2 | 10.2 | 0.5 | .867 | .974 | .722 |
| Burnett S | 73 | 0 | 1 | 7 | 20 | 3 | 63.0 | 52 | 3 | 2.14 | 1.14 | 62 | 20 | 0 | 4 | 0 | 30.2 | 2.64 | 1.34 | 1 | 3 | 3 | 32.1 | 1.67 | 0.96 | 8.9 | 2.9 | 0.4 | .581 | .487 | .711 |
| Capps M | 47 | 0 | 3 | 3 | 0 | 26 | 46.0 | 51 | 5 | 2.74 | 1.30 | 38 | 9 | 3 | 3 | 23 | 39.2 | 3.18 | 1.41 | 0 | 0 | 3 | 6.1 | 0.00 | 0.63 | 7.4 | 1.8 | 1.0 | .722 | .763 | .673 |
| Chico M | 1 | 1 | 0 | 0 | 0 | 0 | 5.0 | 6 | 0 | 3.60 | 1.20 | 3 | 0 | 0 | 0 | 0 | 5.0 | 3.60 | 1.20 | -- | -- | -- | ---- | ---- | --- | 5.4 | 0.0 | 0.0 | .699 | .668 | 1.000 |
| Clippard T | 78 | 0 | 11 | 8 | 23 | 1 | 91.0 | 69 | 8 | 3.07 | 1.21 | 112 | 41 | 8 | 6 | 1 | 51.2 | 3.31 | 1.30 | 3 | 2 | 0 | 39.1 | 2.75 | 1.09 | 11.1 | 4.1 | 0.8 | .646 | .594 | .708 |
| Detwiler R | 8 | 5 | 1 | 3 | 0 | 0 | 29.2 | 34 | 5 | 4.25 | 1.62 | 17 | 14 | -- | -- | -- | ---- | ---- | --- | 1 | 3 | 0 | 29.2 | 4.25 | 1.62 | 5.2 | 4.2 | 1.5 | .826 | .780 | 1.024 |
| English J | 7 | 0 | 0 | 0 | 0 | 0 | 7.0 | 10 | 0 | 3.86 | 1.71 | 4 | 2 | 0 | 0 | 0 | 7.0 | 3.86 | 1.71 | -- | -- | -- | ---- | ---- | --- | 5.1 | 2.6 | 0.0 | .783 | 1.100 | .485 |
| Hernandez L | 33 | 33 | 10 | 12 | 0 | 0 | 211.2 | 216 | 16 | 3.66 | 1.32 | 114 | 64 | 6 | 5 | 0 | 117.2 | 3.37 | 1.28 | 4 | 7 | 0 | 94.0 | 4.02 | 1.37 | 4.8 | 2.7 | 0.7 | .716 | .640 | .803 |
| Lannan J | 25 | 25 | 8 | 8 | 0 | 0 | 143.1 | 175 | 14 | 4.65 | 1.56 | 71 | 49 | 2 | 5 | 0 | 75.0 | 5.76 | 1.85 | 6 | 3 | 0 | 68.1 | 3.42 | 1.24 | 4.5 | 3.1 | 0.9 | .799 | .817 | .747 |
| Marquis J | 13 | 13 | 2 | 9 | 0 | 0 | 58.2 | 76 | 9 | 6.60 | 1.70 | 31 | 24 | 0 | 3 | 0 | 8.1 | 20.52 | 2.88 | 2 | 6 | 0 | 50.1 | 4.29 | 1.51 | 4.8 | 3.7 | 1.4 | .877 | .783 | .977 |
| Martin J | 9 | 9 | 1 | 5 | 0 | 0 | 48.0 | 56 | 9 | 4.13 | 1.40 | 31 | 11 | 1 | 4 | 0 | 40.1 | 3.35 | 1.29 | 0 | 1 | 0 | 7.2 | 8.22 | 1.96 | 5.8 | 2.1 | 1.7 | .820 | .721 | .934 |
| Maya Y | 5 | 5 | 0 | 3 | 0 | 0 | 26.0 | 30 | 3 | 5.88 | 1.58 | 12 | 11 | -- | -- | -- | ---- | ---- | --- | 0 | 3 | 0 | 26.0 | 5.88 | 1.58 | 4.2 | 3.8 | 1.0 | .831 | .774 | .883 |
| Mock G | 1 | 1 | 0 | 0 | 0 | 0 | 3.1 | 4 | 2 | 5.40 | 2.70 | 3 | 5 | 0 | 0 | 0 | 3.1 | 5.40 | 2.70 | -- | -- | -- | ---- | ---- | --- | 8.1 | 13.5 | 5.4 | 1.188 | 1.500 | .429 |
| Olsen S | 17 | 15 | 4 | 8 | 0 | 0 | 81.0 | 93 | 10 | 5.56 | 1.48 | 53 | 27 | 2 | 2 | 0 | 43.0 | 3.77 | 1.37 | 2 | 6 | 0 | 38.0 | 7.58 | 1.61 | 5.9 | 3.0 | 1.1 | .795 | .817 | .737 |
| Peralta J | 39 | 0 | 1 | 0 | 9 | 0 | 49.0 | 30 | 5 | 2.02 | 0.80 | 49 | 9 | 0 | 0 | 0 | 10.1 | 0.87 | 0.77 | 1 | 0 | 0 | 38.2 | 2.33 | 0.80 | 9.0 | 1.7 | 0.9 | .521 | .474 | .596 |
| Slaten D | 49 | 0 | 4 | 1 | 4 | 0 | 40.2 | 34 | 2 | 3.10 | 1.30 | 36 | 19 | 2 | 1 | 0 | 19.1 | 2.79 | 1.29 | 2 | 0 | 0 | 21.1 | 3.38 | 1.31 | 8.0 | 4.2 | 0.4 | .626 | .844 | .385 |
| Stammen C | 35 | 19 | 4 | 4 | 1 | 0 | 128.0 | 151 | 13 | 5.13 | 1.50 | 85 | 41 | 2 | 3 | 0 | 82.1 | 5.79 | 1.48 | 2 | 1 | 0 | 45.2 | 3.94 | 1.53 | 6.0 | 2.9 | 0.9 | .814 | .871 | .742 |
| Storen D | 54 | 0 | 4 | 4 | 10 | 5 | 55.1 | 48 | 3 | 3.58 | 1.27 | 52 | 22 | 2 | 1 | 0 | 25.2 | 2.45 | 1.21 | 2 | 3 | 5 | 29.2 | 4.55 | 1.31 | 8.5 | 3.6 | 0.5 | .655 | .674 | .624 |
| Strasburg S | 12 | 12 | 5 | 3 | 0 | 0 | 68.0 | 56 | 5 | 2.91 | 1.07 | 92 | 17 | 3 | 2 | 0 | 42.2 | 2.32 | 1.01 | 2 | 1 | 0 | 25.1 | 3.91 | 1.18 | 12.2 | 2.3 | 0.7 | .596 | .533 | .680 |
| Walker T | 24 | 0 | 1 | 0 | 1 | 0 | 35.1 | 35 | 5 | 3.57 | 1.22 | 30 | 8 | 1 | 0 | 0 | 35.1 | 3.57 | 1.22 | -- | -- | -- | ---- | ---- | --- | 7.6 | 2.0 | 1.3 | .742 | .849 | .562 |
| Zimmermann J | 7 | 7 | 1 | 2 | 0 | 0 | 31.0 | 31 | 8 | 4.94 | 1.32 | 27 | 10 | -- | -- | -- | ---- | ---- | --- | 1 | 2 | 0 | 31.0 | 4.94 | 1.32 | 7.8 | 2.9 | 2.3 | .817 | .819 | .812 |

## Free Bill James Daily Match-Ups
## E-mailed to You
## Every Day of the Season

A CTA Sports is offering our customers a free subscription to *The Bill James Daily Match-Ups*. Each day you'll receive a PDF file in your e-mail inbox showing lifetime batter vs. pitcher statistics for your favorite team against your team's next opponent. These match-ups are updated daily throughout the season.

If you would like to receive a free subscription to *The Bill James Daily Match-Ups* for the 2011 season, please send an email to **matchups@actasports.com** with your name and favorite team and where you usually buy your sports books. Limit one team per customer.

Thanks for your patronage.

Play ball!

Greg Pierce
Co-Publisher

# CONTRIBUTORS

**Bill Baer (PHI)** – Bill runs the sabermetrically inclined Phillies blog Crashburn Alley (crashburnalley.com), which is part of Rob Neyer's ESPN SweetSpot network. A contributor to HEATER, he also writes pitcher-centric fantasy baseball articles for Baseball Prospectus.

**Andy Beard (STL)** – Andy moved to St Louis in the summer of 2007 after finishing graduate school with a master's degree in clinical psychology. Although he has a full-time job working in the mental health field, he spends his free time contributing at Play A Hard Nine (playahardnine.wordpress.com). He enjoys road tripping with friends to various baseball stadiums throughout the summers.

**Matt Bandi (PIT)** – Matt has spent all of his 26 years in Pittsburgh, graduating from the University of Pittsburgh in 2006. He is a lifelong Pirates fan, and he has covered the Bucs at Pittsburgh Lumber Co. (pittsburghlumberco.com) since 2007.

**Evan Brunell (BOS)** – Evan covers baseball for CBS Sports at *MLB Facts and Rumors*, and he is writer emeritus/director of Fire Brand of the American League, a Red Sox blog he started in 2003 that is affiliated with the ESPN SweetSpot Network.

**Paul Bugala (SF, WAS)** – Paul covers the Eastern League (Double-A) at baysoxblog.com. He has also written for Baseball Daily Digest.

**Griffin Cooper (SEA)** – Griffin covers the Mariners at SoDo Mojo (www.sodomojo.com).

**Martin Gandy (ATL)** – Martin covers the Braves for SBNation at TalkingChop.com. He has appeared in Sports Weekly and has written for BaseballDailyDigest.com. Rare for a blogger, he has been able to get credentialed as media to several major-league clubhouses and has had the opportunity to interview just about every Atlanta Braves player as well as many other current and former big leaguers.

**David Golebiewski (SD)** – A journalism student at Duquesne University, David is a writer for Heater Magazine, Fangraphs, and The Hardball Times. His work for Inside Edge Scouting Services has appeared on ESPN.com and Yahoo.com, and he worked as a fantasy baseball writer for Rotoworld in 2009 and 2010. He recently contributed an article to *The Hardball Times Annual 2011*.

**Matt Hagen (minors)** – A writer for The Hardball Times, Matt is an expert in minor-league baseball, which he calls "the unrivaled system that keeps major-league baseball competitive and the fans coming back for more."

**Marc Hulet (TOR, minors)** – Marc is a freelance writer in Ontario, Canada. He writes for Fangraphs.com (mostly about prospects) while also managing the site's fantasy coverage. He helps cover the Blue Jays organization at Battersbox.ca.

**Michael Jong (FLA)** – Michael is a long-time Marlins fan, having jumped on the team's bandwagon in 1997 and ridden it through the highs and lows of the last 13 years. He covers the Marlins daily at Marlin Maniac (www.marlinmaniac.com) and has also written for Beyond the Box Score and Baseball Prospectus Fantasy.

**Brian Joseph (BAL, HOU)** – Brian is a freelance sports writer who lives in the Philadelphia area. Currently, he is the managing editor of Baseball Daily Digest as well as the Philadelphia 76ers blogger at FanHuddle.com. His work has appeared at Seamheads.com and the Most Valuable Network and on Scout.com and Rivals.com.

**Brian La Shier (CLE)** – Brian is a lifelong Cleveland fan who has covered the Indians at Ontario Street (www.ontariostreet.blogspot.com) since 2007.

**Jon Lewin (NYM)** – Jon co-writes the Subway Squawkers Mets-Yankees fan blog with Lisa Swan (www.subwaysquawkers.com). He is also the fantasy baseball columnist for TheFasterTimes.com and a contributor to The Huffington Post's sports section. Jon wrote on the origins of free agency for "The Cambridge Companion to Baseball."

**Melissa Lockard (OAK, minors)** – Melissa has been covering the Athletics, with a specific focus on the team's minor-league system, for Scout.com since 2004. Ms. Lockard, a graduate of Northwestern University, has more than 10 years of journalism and business writing experience.

**Erik Manning (STL)** – Erik is a lifelong Cardinals fan and the founder of the prospect-centric blog FutureRedbirds.net. His writing can also be found at FanGraphs.com and BeyondtheBoxscore.com. He is married with two children and lives in Eastern Iowa.

**Joey Matschulat (TEX)** – A college student by day and diehard analyst of the Texas Rangers by night, Joey writes for Baseball Time in Arlington at http://bbtia.com.

**Rob McQuown (CHC, CHW, projections)** – SABR member Rob is a lifelong Cubs fan who was inspired by a Bill James Abstract to join STATS, Inc. as one of its first full-time employees. A simulation and fantasy baseball expert, Rob programs for Rotolympus, writes for Heater, and does both for Baseball Prospectus.

**Brian McGannon (KC)** – Born and raised in Kansas City, Missouri, Brian, a 24-year-old student, is the writer and proprietor of Royals Kingdom, a Kansas City Royals blog (royalskingdom.blogspot.com). He was the host of Royals Kingdom Radio for the 2010 season.

**Nick Nelson (MIN)** – Nick resides in Minneapolis and has blogged about the Twins regularly for over five years at Nick's Twins Blog (www.nickstwinsblog.com), which is featured on ESPN.com. He also contributes to the baseball and football coverage for the fantasy Web site Rotoworld.com.

**Lee Panas (DET)** – Lee works as a research analyst at Brandeis University in Massachusetts. He is the author of the book *Beyond Batting Average*, a comprehensive sabermetrics primer. He has been following the Tigers since 1968 and covers his favorite team at www.DetroitTigerTales.com.

**Mike Petriello (LAD)** – Mike blogs daily about the Dodgers at www.MikeSciosciasTragicIllness.com.

**David Saltzer (ANA)** – David is a lifelong Angels fan and the Senior Writer at AngelsWin.com, which covers the Angels' major- and minor-league squads and is the internet home for Angels fans. When David isn't spending time with his three sons, he is a high school teacher and can be found at the ballpark or with his family and friends

**Tom Stephenson (COL)** – Tom covers the Rockies at "Up in the Rockies," part of the Real Clear Sports network (www.realclearsports.com). He is a licensed attorney in the state of Texas.

**Michael Street (ARI, MIL)** – Michael has been playing fantasy baseball and writing baseball fiction and non-fiction for over 15 years. He covers Asian-American sports at Examiner.com (aasportsexaminer.com) and concentrates on Asian baseball players in his "Pacific Perspectives" column on BaseballDailyDigest.com. He has written fantasy analysis for The Hardball Times and Baseball Prospectus, as well as reviewed baseball books for Lovemyteam.com.

**Lisa Swan (NYY)** – Lisa co-writes the Subway Squawkers Yankees-Mets fan blog with Jon Lewin (www.subwaysquawkers.com). She is also the MLB columnist for TheFasterTimes.

**Shawn Weaver (CIN)** – A Reds fan since the days of the Big Red Machine, Shawn is a science teacher by day and blogger by night. He operates the original blog on the Cincinnati Reds, Cincinnati Reds Blog (www.shawns.blogspot.com). He also writes on MLB history, covering the MVP and Cy Young awards (www.baseballawards.blogspot.com) as well as baseball's legends (www.baseballsgreatest.blogspot.com).

**Ricky Zanker (TB)** – When not out cycling, Ricky writes for DRaysBay.com and TheHardballTimes.com.

# SABR

## Society for American Baseball Research

### *WHERE BASEBALL FANS COME TOGETHER*
### WWW.SABR.ORG

The Society for American Baseball Research (SABR) is a member-driven nonprofit dedicated to fostering the study of baseball past and present and providing an outlet for educational, historical, and research information about the game.

**www.sabr.org**

# KEY TERMS

**BB%**: Walk rate = BB/PA. *(featured on hitter pages)*

**Bash**: Bases/Hit. The average Bash in 2010 for batters with at least 300 AB was 1.6. Rates run from 1.1 (Elvis Andrus) to 2.4 (Jose Bautista). *(featured on hitter pages)*

**Bln**: Blown Save. *(featured on pitcher pages)*

**CG**: Complete Game. *(featured on pitcher pages)*

**CT%**: Contact rate = (AB-K)/AB. Few hitters hold down jobs with CT% < 72%. *(featured on hitter pages)*

**DS**: Disaster Start = an outing in which the starting pitcher allows more runs than innings. [Rob Neyer]

**FB-LD-GB**: Rates of fly balls, line drives, and ground balls per fair ball. The three numbers total 100%. For power hitters, look for a rising FB%. *(featured on hitter pages)*

**FIP** (Fielding-Independent ERA): A measure that isolates a pitcher's skill from events beyond his control. Our formula is (13*HR+3*(BB+HBP-IBB)-2*K)/IP, plus a factor of 3.30 for the AL and 3.20 for the NL. [Tom Tango] *(featured on pitcher pages)*

**GB/F**: Ground balls per fly ball. *(featured on pitcher pages)*

**GR**: Games in Relief. *(featured on pitcher pages)*

**GS**: Games Started. *(featured on pitcher pages)*

**GSvR, GSvL**: Games started by hitters against right-handed SP's or left-handed SP's. *(featured on hitter pages)*

**H%** (Hit Rate):

**For batters**, H% = H/(AB-K). So BA = CT% * H%. Hitters' hit rate tends toward their level of the past few years.

**For pitchers**, H% = (H-HR)/(Balls in Play). Pitchers' H% tends toward 30%, but defense, GB rate, health, and in-experience all matter.

**Hld**: Hold. *(featured on pitcher pages)*

**HR/fb** : Home runs per fly ball. The rate tends toward 10% for pitchers, though opponents and parks play a role. The rate does not tend toward 10% for hitters – hitters have varied strengths. *(featured on hitter and pitcher pages)*

**Lead**: The average run differential (Own Score - Opponent Score) when a reliever entered the game. Note that leads and deficits can cancel out when calculating the average. *(featured on pitcher pages)*

**MOB** (Men on Base): The average number of men on base when a hitter steps to the plate. MOB represents RBI opportunities and also hints at where the hitter bats in the lineup and how well his place-setting hitters reach base. *(featured on hitter pages)*

**Owned**: In a sampling of 200 online fantasy leagues, the percentage in which a given player was owned in the final weekend of August (before September call-ups, and before fantasy play-offs). All of the leagues were 12-team, mixed leagues, with the usual 5x5 categories (HR, R, RBI, SB, and BA for hitters; W, Sv, K, ERA, and WHIP for pitchers).

**$1L**: A player's Roto value in an AL- or NL-only 5x5 league.

**$2L**: A player's Roto value in a combined AL/NL 5x5 league.

**Pts** (Points): A player's value in a typical points league. For readability, point totals are rounded to the nearest 10.
**Hitter**: 1 pt for each base, Run, and RBI, SB=2, K=-1, CS=-1.
**Pitcher**: 10 pts for Win, 5 pts for Save, IP+K=1, H+BB=-0.5.

**QS** (Quality Start): A start when the pitcher lasts at least 6 IP and allows no more than 3 ER. *(featured on pitcher pages)*

**RA** (Run Average): A measure of run allowance by pitchers = Runs per Nine Innings. *(featured on pitcher pages)*

**RAA**: Runs Above Average = the theoretical number of runs created by a hitter (or saved by a pitcher) vs. the average player at same position, whose rate is pwOBA (or pRA). Positive RAA means better than average, negative RAA means worse than average.

**For batters**, RAA = (wOBA-pwOBA)/1.15 * PA. See **wOBA**.

**For pitchers**, RAA = (pRA-RA)*IP/9. See **RA**.

**RBI%**: Rate of RBI generation for runners other than oneself = (RBI-HR)/(RBI+LOB-HR). *(on hitter pages)*

**RS%**: Rate of Run Scoring, per instance on base, other than on one's HR = (R-HR)/(H+BB+HBP-HR). *(on hitter pages)*

**S%** (Strand Rate): fraction of a pitcher's baserunners who do not turned into earned runs = (H+BB-ER)/(H+BB-HR). [Ron Shandler] *(featured on pitcher pages)*

**Supp**: Average run support of a starting pitcher's backing offense in games he started. *(featured on pitcher pages)*

**Sub** (Substitutions): The number of times in which a hitter entered a game for another hitter. Players with high Sub tend to be either very good from one side of the plate, or plus defenders, or versatile. *(featured on hitter pages)*

**Scoresheet**: A specialized fantasy game in which your team plays 162 complete games (plate appearance by plate appearance), and in which the production of your players is based largely on their stats in MLB for the previous week. (You can read more on the game at www.Scoresheet.com.) Certain information about players is fixed before a season:

**Rnge** (Range) = Fielding range of a hitter in Scoresheet. For non-catchers, higher numbers are better. For catchers, this number represents their tendency to allow SB, so lower numbers are better.

**vRH, vLH** = Adjustment to OPS of a hitter vs. right-handed or left-handed pitchers. Positive adjustments indicate better hitting vs. that handedness of opposing pitcher.

*(featured on hitter pages)*

**wOBA** (Weighted On-Base Average): A measure of expected run creation. We use a static, simplified form = (0.7*BB + 0.9*1B + 1.3*(2B+3B)+2.0*HR + SB/4 - CS/2)/PA. The coefficients represent the run impact of each event (relative to an out), inflated by 15% so that wOBA is on the scale of OBP. A typical wOBA is .330-.340, a bad one is .300, and a fine one is .400. [Tom Tango] *(featured on hitter pages)*

# THE RUNDOWN

In honor of the "Year of the Pitcher," here are the box scores for the nine most dominant regular-season pitching performances for 2010. The games are presented in the order in which they were played. In each box score, the "Season" stats are as of the date of the game.

## April 17, 2010
Ubaldo Jimenez throws the first no-hitter in Rockies history.
**COLORADO 4, ATLANTA 0**

| | 1 | 2 | 3 | 4 | 5 | 6 | 7 | 8 | 9 | | R | H | E |
|---|---|---|---|---|---|---|---|---|---|---|---|---|---|
| COL | 1 | 0 | 0 | 3 | 0 | 0 | 0 | 0 | 0 | | 4 | 9 | 0 |
| ATL | 0 | 0 | 0 | 0 | 0 | 0 | 0 | 0 | 0 | | 0 | 0 | 0 |

| Colorado Rockies | AB | R | H | HR | BI | SB | BB-K | HR | RBI | SB | BA |
|---|---|---|---|---|---|---|---|---|---|---|---|
| Gonzalez lf | 5 | 1 | 2 | 0 | 2 | 0 | 0-1 | 0 | 5 | 0 | .382 |
| Fowler cf | 5 | 0 | 0 | 0 | 0 | 0 | 0-0 | 0 | 2 | 0 | .167 |
| Helton 1b | 2 | 0 | 1 | 0 | 0 | 0 | 2-0 | 0 | 2 | 0 | .324 |
| Tulowitzki ss | 3 | 0 | 0 | 0 | 1 | 0 | 0-0 | 0 | 6 | 1 | .250 |
| Hawpe rf | 4 | 1 | 3 | 0 | 0 | 0 | 0-0 | 2 | 5 | 0 | .393 |
| Olivo c | 4 | 0 | 0 | 0 | 0 | 0 | 0-1 | 2 | 3 | 1 | .348 |
| Stewart 3b | 3 | 1 | 1 | 0 | 0 | 0 | 1-1 | 2 | 6 | 1 | .293 |
| Barmes 2b | 4 | 0 | 1 | 0 | 0 | 0 | 0-0 | 1 | 6 | 0 | .226 |
| Jimenez p | 4 | 1 | 1 | 0 | 1 | 0 | 0-2 | 0 | 1 | 0 | .125 |

| Atlanta Braves | AB | R | H | HR | BI | SB | BB-K | HR | RBI | SB | BA |
|---|---|---|---|---|---|---|---|---|---|---|---|
| McLouth cf | 4 | 0 | 0 | 0 | 0 | 0 | 0-2 | 1 | 6 | 0 | .148 |
| Prado 2b | 2 | 0 | 0 | 0 | 0 | 0 | 2-1 | 1 | 2 | 0 | .442 |
| Jones 3b | 3 | 0 | 0 | 0 | 0 | 0 | 1-0 | 2 | 4 | 2 | .192 |
| McCann c | 4 | 0 | 0 | 0 | 0 | 0 | 0-1 | 2 | 6 | 1 | .300 |
| Glaus 1b | 2 | 0 | 0 | 0 | 0 | 0 | 1-1 | 1 | 6 | 0 | .216 |
| Escobar ss | 3 | 0 | 0 | 0 | 0 | 0 | 1-0 | 0 | 8 | 2 | .227 |
| Heyward rf | 2 | 0 | 0 | 0 | 0 | 0 | 1-2 | 3 | 12 | 0 | .300 |
| Cabrera lf | 2 | 0 | 0 | 0 | 0 | 0 | 1-0 | 0 | 4 | 0 | .125 |
| Kawakami p | 1 | 0 | 0 | 0 | 0 | 0 | 0-0 | 0 | 0 | 0 | .000 |
|  Conrad ph | 1 | 0 | 0 | 0 | 0 | 0 | 0-0 | 0 | 0 | 0 | .000 |
|  Hinske ph | 1 | 0 | 0 | 0 | 0 | 0 | 0-1 | 0 | 6 | 0 | .333 |

| Colorado Rockies | IP | H | R | ER | BB | K | HR | W | Sv | K | ERA |
|---|---|---|---|---|---|---|---|---|---|---|---|
| Jimenez, W 3-0 | 9.0 | 0 | 0 | 0 | 6 | 7 | 0 | 3 | 0 | 20 | 1.29 |

| Atlanta Braves | IP | H | R | ER | BB | K | HR | W | Sv | K | ERA |
|---|---|---|---|---|---|---|---|---|---|---|---|
| Kawakami, L 0-2 | 5.0 | 8 | 4 | 4 | 2 | 2 | 0 | 0 | 0 | 4 | 3.91 |
| Venters | 3.0 | 1 | 0 | 0 | 1 | 2 | 0 | 0 | 0 | 2 | 0.00 |
| Chavez | 1.0 | 0 | 0 | 0 | 0 | 1 | 0 | 0 | 0 | 7 | 1.69 |

## May 7, 2010
Jamie Moyer becomes the oldest pitcher to hurl a shut-out.
**PHILADELPHIA 7, ATLANTA 0**

| | 1 | 2 | 3 | 4 | 5 | 6 | 7 | 8 | 9 | | R | H | E |
|---|---|---|---|---|---|---|---|---|---|---|---|---|---|
| ATL | 0 | 0 | 0 | 0 | 0 | 0 | 0 | 0 | 0 | | 0 | 2 | 0 |
| PHI | 0 | 0 | 3 | 0 | 4 | 0 | 0 | 0 | - | | 7 | 12 | 0 |

| Atlanta Braves | AB | R | H | HR | BI | SB | BB-K | HR | RBI | SB | BA |
|---|---|---|---|---|---|---|---|---|---|---|---|
| Infante ss | 4 | 0 | 0 | 0 | 0 | 0 | 0-1 | 1 | 7 | 2 | .276 |
| Prado 2b | 3 | 0 | 0 | 0 | 0 | 0 | 0-0 | 1 | 7 | 0 | .319 |
| Jones 3b | 3 | 0 | 2 | 0 | 0 | 0 | 0-0 | 2 | 7 | 2 | .222 |
| Glaus 1b | 3 | 0 | 0 | 0 | 0 | 0 | 0-0 | 2 | 15 | 0 | .242 |
| Diaz lf | 3 | 0 | 0 | 0 | 0 | 0 | 0-0 | 0 | 4 | 2 | .180 |
| Ross c | 3 | 0 | 0 | 0 | 0 | 0 | 0-0 | 0 | 4 | 0 | .231 |
| Cabrera rf | 3 | 0 | 0 | 0 | 0 | 0 | 0-0 | 0 | 6 | 0 | .185 |
| McLouth cf | 3 | 0 | 0 | 0 | 0 | 0 | 0-2 | 1 | 5 | 1 | .179 |
| Lowe p | 1 | 0 | 0 | 0 | 0 | 0 | 0-1 | 0 | 0 | 0 | .091 |
|  Hicks ph | 1 | 0 | 0 | 0 | 0 | 0 | 0-1 | 0 | 0 | 0 | .000 |
|  Hinske ph | 1 | 0 | 0 | 0 | 0 | 0 | 0-0 | 0 | 8 | 0 | .276 |

| Philadelph. Phillies | AB | R | H | HR | BI | SB | BB-K | HR | RBI | SB | BA |
|---|---|---|---|---|---|---|---|---|---|---|---|
| Victorino cf | 5 | 0 | 0 | 0 | 0 | 0 | 0-0 | 6 | 23 | 3 | .240 |
| Polanco 3b | 5 | 1 | 2 | 0 | 0 | 0 | 0-0 | 4 | 16 | 1 | .280 |
| Utley 2b | 2 | 2 | 2 | 0 | 0 | 0 | 2-0 | 8 | 18 | 1 | .302 |
| Howard 1b | 4 | 2 | 2 | 0 | 0 | 0 | 0-1 | 5 | 20 | 0 | .287 |
| Werth rf | 4 | 1 | 2 | 1 | 3 | 0 | 0-1 | 6 | 24 | 1 | .359 |
| Ibanez lf | 4 | 1 | 2 | 2 | 0 | 0 | 0-1 | 2 | 15 | 0 | .250 |
| Ruiz c | 3 | 0 | 1 | 0 | 0 | 0 | 1-1 | 1 | 9 | 0 | .315 |
| Valdez ss | 4 | 0 | 1 | 0 | 2 | 0 | 0-0 | 0 | 3 | 0 | .227 |
| Moyer p | 3 | 0 | 0 | 0 | 0 | 0 | 0-1 | 0 | 1 | 0 | .182 |

| Atlanta Braves | IP | H | R | ER | BB | K | HR | W | Sv | K | ERA |
|---|---|---|---|---|---|---|---|---|---|---|---|
| Lowe, L 4-3 | 5.0 | 11 | 7 | 7 | 2 | 2 | 1 | 4 | 0 | 23 | 6.16 |
| Venters | 1.0 | 0 | 0 | 0 | 1 | 0 | 0 | 0 | 0 | 7 | 1.69 |
| Kimbrel | 1.0 | 1 | 0 | 0 | 2 | 0 | 0 | 0 | 0 | 2 | 0.00 |
| Chavez | 1.0 | 0 | 0 | 0 | 0 | 0 | 0 | 0 | 0 | 13 | 4.73 |

| Philadelph. Phillies | IP | H | R | ER | BB | K | HR | W | Sv | K | ERA |
|---|---|---|---|---|---|---|---|---|---|---|---|
| Moyer, W 4-2 | 9.0 | 2 | 0 | 0 | 0 | 5 | 0 | 4 | 0 | 20 | 4.38 |

## May 9, 2010
Dallas Braden throws the second perfect game in A's history.
**OAKLAND 4, TAMPA BAY 0**

| | 1 | 2 | 3 | 4 | 5 | 6 | 7 | 8 | 9 | | R | H | E |
|---|---|---|---|---|---|---|---|---|---|---|---|---|---|
| TB | 0 | 0 | 0 | 0 | 0 | 0 | 0 | 0 | 0 | | 0 | 0 | 0 |
| OAK | 0 | 1 | 1 | 2 | 0 | 0 | 0 | 0 | - | | 4 | 12 | 0 |

| Tampa Bay Rays | AB | R | H | HR | BI | SB | BB-K | HR | RBI | SB | BA |
|---|---|---|---|---|---|---|---|---|---|---|---|
| Bartlett ss | 3 | 0 | 0 | 0 | 0 | 0 | 0-0 | 1 | 18 | 2 | .248 |
| Crawford lf | 3 | 0 | 0 | 0 | 0 | 0 | 0-1 | 3 | 15 | 7 | .308 |
| Zobrist 2b | 3 | 0 | 0 | 0 | 0 | 0 | 0-0 | 1 | 13 | 6 | .259 |
| Longoria 3b | 3 | 0 | 0 | 0 | 0 | 0 | 0-1 | 7 | 23 | 5 | .325 |
| Pena 1b | 3 | 0 | 0 | 0 | 0 | 0 | 0-0 | 5 | 22 | 1 | .183 |
| Upton cf | 3 | 0 | 0 | 0 | 0 | 0 | 0-2 | 4 | 17 | 7 | .223 |
| Aybar dh | 3 | 0 | 0 | 0 | 0 | 0 | 0-2 | 2 | 7 | 0 | .273 |
| Navarro c | 3 | 0 | 0 | 0 | 0 | 0 | 0-0 | 0 | 2 | 0 | .150 |
| Kapler rf | 3 | 0 | 0 | 0 | 0 | 0 | 0-1 | 1 | 6 | 1 | .220 |

| Oakland A's | AB | R | H | HR | BI | SB | BB-K | HR | RBI | SB | BA |
|---|---|---|---|---|---|---|---|---|---|---|---|
| Pennington ss | 5 | 1 | 1 | 0 | 0 | 0 | 0-0 | 3 | 16 | 4 | .269 |
| Barton 1b | 5 | 2 | 3 | 0 | 0 | 0 | 0-0 | 1 | 12 | 0 | .296 |
| Sweeney rf | 4 | 0 | 2 | 0 | 1 | 0 | 0-1 | 1 | 19 | 0 | .304 |
| Kouzmanoff 3b | 4 | 1 | 2 | 0 | 1 | 0 | 0-2 | 2 | 18 | 0 | .275 |
| Chavez dh | 3 | 0 | 1 | 0 | 0 | 0 | 0-1 | 0 | 7 | 0 | .239 |
| Rosales 2b | 3 | 0 | 1 | 0 | 0 | 0 | 0-1 | 2 | 12 | 0 | .273 |
| Patterson lf | 4 | 0 | 0 | 0 | 0 | 0 | 0-2 | 2 | 5 | 2 | .143 |
| Powell c | 4 | 0 | 2 | 0 | 1 | 0 | 0-1 | 0 | 7 | 0 | .143 |
| Davis cf | 4 | 0 | 0 | 0 | 0 | 0 | 0-1 | 1 | 10 | 12 | .227 |

| Tampa Bay Rays | IP | H | R | ER | BB | K | HR | W | Sv | K | ERA |
|---|---|---|---|---|---|---|---|---|---|---|---|
| Shields, L 4-1 | 6.0 | 11 | 4 | 3 | 1 | 6 | 0 | 4 | 0 | 49 | 3.33 |
| Wheeler | 1.0 | 0 | 0 | 0 | 0 | 1 | 0 | 0 | 0 | 10 | 1.86 |
| Sonnanstine | 1.0 | 1 | 0 | 0 | 0 | 0 | 0 | 0 | 0 | 6 | 2.51 |

| Oakland A's | IP | H | R | ER | BB | K | HR | W | Sv | K | ERA |
|---|---|---|---|---|---|---|---|---|---|---|---|
| Braden, W 4-2 | 9.0 | 0 | 0 | 0 | 0 | 6 | 0 | 4 | 0 | 28 | 3.33 |

## May 29, 2010
Roy Halladay throws the 2nd perfect game in Phillies history.
**PHILADELPHIA 1, FLORIDA 0**

| | 1 | 2 | 3 | 4 | 5 | 6 | 7 | 8 | 9 | | R | H | E |
|---|---|---|---|---|---|---|---|---|---|---|---|---|---|
| PHI | 0 | 0 | 1 | 0 | 0 | 0 | 0 | 0 | 0 | | 1 | 7 | 0 |
| FLA | 0 | 0 | 0 | 0 | 0 | 0 | 0 | 0 | 0 | | 0 | 0 | 1 |

| Philadelph. Phillies | AB | R | H | HR | BI | SB | BB-K | HR | RBI | SB | BA |
|---|---|---|---|---|---|---|---|---|---|---|---|
| Victorino cf | 4 | 0 | 1 | 0 | 0 | 0 | 0-0 | 8 | 33 | 10 | .257 |
| Valdez ss | 4 | 1 | 2 | 0 | 0 | 0 | 0-1 | 0 | 5 | 1 | .262 |
| Utley 2b | 4 | 0 | 0 | 0 | 0 | 0 | 0-0 | 10 | 24 | 2 | .276 |
| Howard 1b | 3 | 0 | 0 | 0 | 0 | 0 | 1-1 | 8 | 33 | 0 | .287 |
| Werth rf | 4 | 0 | 0 | 0 | 0 | 0 | 0-2 | 9 | 33 | 2 | .302 |
| Ibanez lf | 4 | 0 | 0 | 0 | 0 | 0 | 0-1 | 3 | 21 | 0 | .247 |
| Castro 3b | 4 | 0 | 2 | 0 | 0 | 0 | 0-0 | 1 | 10 | 0 | .265 |
| Ruiz c | 4 | 0 | 2 | 0 | 0 | 0 | 0-0 | 2 | 11 | 0 | .298 |
| Halladay p | 3 | 0 | 0 | 0 | 0 | 0 | 0-1 | 0 | 1 | 0 | .111 |

| Florida Marlins | AB | R | H | HR | BI | SB | BB-K | HR | RBI | SB | BA |
|---|---|---|---|---|---|---|---|---|---|---|---|
| Coghlan lf | 3 | 0 | 0 | 0 | 0 | 0 | 0-2 | 2 | 12 | 5 | .216 |
| Sanchez 1b | 3 | 0 | 0 | 0 | 0 | 0 | 0-1 | 4 | 21 | 1 | .268 |
| Ramirez ss | 3 | 0 | 0 | 0 | 0 | 0 | 0-1 | 8 | 26 | 5 | .297 |
| Cantu 3b | 3 | 0 | 0 | 0 | 0 | 0 | 0-1 | 8 | 36 | 0 | .287 |
| Uggla 2b | 3 | 0 | 0 | 0 | 0 | 0 | 0-2 | 12 | 31 | 1 | .267 |
| Ross rf | 3 | 0 | 0 | 0 | 0 | 0 | 0-0 | 4 | 26 | 2 | .301 |
| Hayes c | 2 | 0 | 0 | 0 | 0 | 0 | 0-0 | 0 | 0 | 0 | .250 |
|  Lamb ph | 1 | 0 | 0 | 0 | 0 | 0 | 0-0 | 0 | 3 | 0 | .200 |
| Maybin cf | 2 | 0 | 0 | 0 | 0 | 0 | 0-1 | 4 | 16 | 4 | .227 |
|  Helms ph | 1 | 0 | 0 | 0 | 0 | 0 | 0-1 | 0 | 4 | 0 | .293 |
| Johnson p | 2 | 0 | 0 | 0 | 0 | 0 | 0-1 | 0 | 0 | 0 | .190 |
|  Paulino ph | 1 | 0 | 0 | 0 | 0 | 0 | 0-0 | 3 | 15 | 0 | .308 |

| Philadelph. Phillies | IP | H | R | ER | BB | K | HR | W | Sv | K | ERA |
|---|---|---|---|---|---|---|---|---|---|---|---|
| Halladay, W 7-3 | 9.0 | 0 | 0 | 0 | 0 | 11 | 0 | 7 | 0 | 70 | 1.99 |

| Florida Marlins | IP | H | R | ER | BB | K | HR | W | Sv | K | ERA |
|---|---|---|---|---|---|---|---|---|---|---|---|
| Johnson, L 5-2 | 7.0 | 7 | 1 | 0 | 1 | 6 | 0 | 5 | 0 | 69 | 2.19 |
| Hensley | 1.0 | 0 | 0 | 0 | 0 | 1 | 0 | 1 | 0 | 34 | 1.35 |
| Nunez | 1.0 | 0 | 0 | 0 | 0 | 0 | 0 | 0 | 2 | 9 | 2.18 |

## June 2, 2010
Armando Galarraga throws the "28-out perfect game."
**DETROIT 3, CLEVELAND 0**

| | 1 | 2 | 3 | 4 | 5 | 6 | 7 | 8 | 9 | | R | H | E |
|---|---|---|---|---|---|---|---|---|---|---|---|---|---|
| CLE | 0 | 0 | 0 | 0 | 0 | 0 | 0 | 0 | 0 | | 0 | 1 | 1 |
| DET | 0 | 1 | 0 | 0 | 0 | 0 | 0 | 2 | - | | 3 | 9 | 0 |

| Cleveland Indians | AB | R | H | HR | BI | SB | BB-K | HR | RBI | SB | BA |
|---|---|---|---|---|---|---|---|---|---|---|---|
| Crowe cf | 4 | 0 | 0 | 0 | 0 | 0 | 0-0 | 1 | 9 | 4 | .240 |
| Choo rf | 3 | 0 | 0 | 0 | 0 | 0 | 0-0 | 8 | 26 | 9 | .275 |
| Kearns lf | 3 | 0 | 0 | 0 | 0 | 0 | 0-1 | 3 | 22 | 2 | .282 |
| Hafner dh | 3 | 0 | 0 | 0 | 0 | 0 | 0-1 | 4 | 17 | 0 | .258 |
| Peralta 3b | 3 | 0 | 0 | 0 | 0 | 0 | 0-1 | 4 | 22 | 1 | .243 |
| Branyan 1b | 3 | 0 | 0 | 0 | 0 | 0 | 0-1 | 7 | 14 | 0 | .235 |
| Grudzielanek 2b | 3 | 0 | 0 | 0 | 0 | 0 | 0-0 | 0 | 11 | 2 | .283 |
| Redmond c | 3 | 0 | 0 | 0 | 0 | 0 | 0-0 | 0 | 5 | 0 | .220 |
| Donald ss | 3 | 0 | 1 | 0 | 0 | 0 | 0-0 | 0 | 5 | 0 | .182 |

| Detroit Tigers | AB | R | H | HR | BI | SB | BB-K | HR | RBI | SB | BA |
|---|---|---|---|---|---|---|---|---|---|---|---|
| Jackson cf | 4 | 1 | 3 | 0 | 1 | 0 | 0-0 | 1 | 14 | 8 | .332 |
| Damon lf | 4 | 1 | 1 | 0 | 0 | 0 | 0-0 | 3 | 18 | 3 | .277 |
|  Kelly lf | 0 | 0 | 0 | 0 | 0 | 0 | 0-0 | 1 | 3 | 1 | .277 |
| Ordonez rf | 4 | 0 | 1 | 0 | 1 | 0 | 0-0 | 1 | 35 | 1 | .307 |
| Cabrera 1b | 4 | 1 | 2 | 1 | 1 | 0 | 0-1 | 15 | 49 | 2 | .351 |
| Boesch dh | 3 | 0 | 1 | 0 | 0 | 0 | 0-0 | 4 | 22 | 1 | .319 |
| Guillen 2b | 3 | 0 | 0 | 0 | 0 | 0 | 0-2 | 2 | 10 | 1 | .265 |
| Inge 3b | 3 | 0 | 0 | 0 | 0 | 0 | 0-0 | 6 | 23 | 0 | .232 |
| Avila c | 3 | 0 | 1 | 0 | 0 | 0 | 0-0 | 2 | 3 | 1 | .192 |
| Santiago ss | 3 | 0 | 0 | 0 | 0 | 0 | 0-1 | 1 | 7 | 1 | .239 |

| Cleveland Indians | IP | H | R | ER | BB | K | HR | W | Sv | K | ERA |
|---|---|---|---|---|---|---|---|---|---|---|---|
| Camona, L 4-4 | 8.0 | 9 | 3 | 2 | 0 | 3 | 1 | 4 | 0 | 36 | 3.53 |

| Detroit Tigers | IP | H | R | ER | BB | K | HR | W | Sv | K | ERA |
|---|---|---|---|---|---|---|---|---|---|---|---|
| Galarraga, W 2-1 | 9.0 | 1 | 0 | 0 | 0 | 3 | 0 | 2 | 0 | 11 | 2.57 |

## June 8, 2010
Stephen Strasburg has 14 K, one shy of the record for a debut.
**WASHINGTON 5, PITTSBURGH 2**

| | 1 | 2 | 3 | 4 | 5 | 6 | 7 | 8 | 9 | | R | H | E |
|---|---|---|---|---|---|---|---|---|---|---|---|---|---|
| PIT | 0 | 0 | 0 | 0 | 0 | 0 | 0 | 2 | 0 | | 2 | 5 | 0 |
| WAS | 1 | 0 | 0 | 0 | 0 | 3 | 0 | 1 | - | | 5 | 11 | 0 |

| Pittsburgh Pirates | AB | R | H | HR | BI | SB | BB-K | HR | RBI | SB | BA |
|---|---|---|---|---|---|---|---|---|---|---|---|
| McCutchen cf | 4 | 0 | 0 | 0 | 0 | 0 | 0-1 | 7 | 17 | 13 | .306 |
| Walker 2b | 4 | 1 | 1 | 0 | 0 | 0 | 0-2 | 1 | 6 | 1 | .320 |
| Milledge lf | 4 | 0 | 1 | 0 | 0 | 0 | 0-2 | 8 | 35 | 3 | .246 |
| Jones 1b | 4 | 0 | 1 | 0 | 0 | 0 | 0-1 | 8 | 35 | 3 | .256 |
| Young rf | 3 | 1 | 1 | 1 | 2 | 0 | 0-1 | 3 | 13 | 1 | .241 |
| LaRoche 3b | 3 | 0 | 1 | 0 | 0 | 0 | 0-1 | 3 | 11 | 0 | .244 |
| Cedeno ss | 3 | 0 | 0 | 0 | 0 | 0 | 0-2 | 1 | 14 | 6 | .242 |
| Jaramillo c | 3 | 0 | 0 | 0 | 0 | 0 | 0-0 | 0 | 5 | 0 | .220 |
| Karstens p | 2 | 0 | 0 | 0 | 0 | 0 | 0-2 | 0 | 0 | 0 | .182 |
|  Church ph | 1 | 0 | 0 | 0 | 0 | 0 | 0-1 | 2 | 9 | 0 | .192 |

| Washington Nat'ls | AB | R | H | HR | BI | SB | BB-K | HR | RBI | SB | BA |
|---|---|---|---|---|---|---|---|---|---|---|---|
| Guzman 2b | 4 | 0 | 1 | 0 | 0 | 0 | 0-0 | 0 | 18 | 2 | .332 |
| Morgan cf | 4 | 0 | 1 | 0 | 0 | 0 | 0-0 | 0 | 9 | 12 | .258 |
| Zimmerman 3b | 4 | 3 | 3 | 1 | 1 | 0 | 0-0 | 12 | 33 | 1 | .316 |
| Dunn 1b | 4 | 1 | 3 | 1 | 2 | 0 | 0-0 | 11 | 30 | 0 | .280 |
|  Kennedy pr-1b | 0 | 0 | 0 | 0 | 0 | 0 | 0-0 | 2 | 15 | 7 | .243 |
| Willingham lf | 3 | 1 | 1 | 1 | 1 | 0 | 1-0 | 11 | 38 | 5 | .278 |
| Rodriguez c | 4 | 0 | 2 | 0 | 0 | 0 | 0-0 | 1 | 16 | 2 | .311 |
| Bernadina rf | 4 | 0 | 0 | 0 | 0 | 0 | 0-0 | 2 | 15 | 3 | .250 |
| Desmond ss | 3 | 0 | 0 | 0 | 0 | 0 | 0-1 | 4 | 30 | 4 | .271 |
| Strasburg p | 2 | 0 | 0 | 0 | 0 | 0 | 0-0 | 0 | 0 | 0 | .000 |
|  Harris ph | 1 | 0 | 0 | 0 | 0 | 0 | 0-1 | 4 | 18 | 2 | .180 |

| Pittsburgh Pirates | IP | H | R | ER | BB | K | HR | W | Sv | K | ERA |
|---|---|---|---|---|---|---|---|---|---|---|---|
| Karstens, L 1-2 | 5.0 | 9 | 4 | 4 | 0 | 3 | 1 | 1 | 0 | 22 | 4.81 |
| Meek | 2.0 | 0 | 0 | 0 | 0 | 1 | 0 | 3 | 1 | 33 | 0.78 |
| Lopez | 1.0 | 2 | 1 | 1 | 1 | 0 | 0 | 1 | 0 | 12 | 1.94 |

| Washington Nat'ls | IP | H | R | ER | BB | K | HR | W | Sv | K | ERA |
|---|---|---|---|---|---|---|---|---|---|---|---|
| Strasburg, W 1-0 | 7.0 | 4 | 2 | 2 | 0 | 14 | 1 | 1 | 0 | 14 | 2.57 |
| Clippard, H 13 | 1.0 | 1 | 0 | 0 | 0 | 2 | 0 | 8 | 0 | 46 | 1.80 |

## June 25, 2010
Edwin Jackson throws a no-hitter in 149 pitches, the most ever.
**ARIZONA 1, TAMPA BAY 0**

| | 1 | 2 | 3 | 4 | 5 | 6 | 7 | 8 | 9 | | R | H | E |
|---|---|---|---|---|---|---|---|---|---|---|---|---|---|
| ARI | 0 | 1 | 0 | 0 | 0 | 0 | 0 | 0 | 0 | | 1 | 7 | 1 |
| TB | 0 | 0 | 0 | 0 | 0 | 0 | 0 | 0 | 0 | | 0 | 0 | 0 |

| Arizona D'backs | AB | R | H | HR | BI | SB | BB-K | HR | RBI | SB | BA |
|---|---|---|---|---|---|---|---|---|---|---|---|
| Johnson dh | 3 | 0 | 2 | 0 | 0 | 0 | 1-1 | 13 | 35 | 5 | .268 |
| Drew ss | 4 | 0 | 1 | 0 | 0 | 0 | 0-0 | 4 | 28 | 5 | .270 |
| Upton rf | 3 | 0 | 2 | 0 | 0 | 0 | 1-1 | 13 | 38 | 11 | .266 |
| Montero c | 4 | 0 | 0 | 0 | 0 | 0 | 0-2 | 2 | 10 | 0 | .396 |
| Young cf | 4 | 0 | 0 | 0 | 0 | 0 | 0-2 | 12 | 49 | 13 | .269 |
| LaRoche 1b | 3 | 1 | 1 | 1 | 1 | 0 | 0-1 | 11 | 51 | 0 | .266 |
| Reynolds 3b | 3 | 0 | 0 | 0 | 0 | 0 | 0-0 | 17 | 48 | 4 | .212 |
| Parra lf | 3 | 0 | 0 | 0 | 0 | 0 | 0-2 | 1 | 12 | 0 | .255 |
| Abreu 2b | 3 | 0 | 1 | 0 | 0 | 0 | 0-0 | 0 | 5 | 1 | .273 |

| Tampa Bay Rays | AB | R | H | HR | BI | SB | BB-K | HR | RBI | SB | BA |
|---|---|---|---|---|---|---|---|---|---|---|---|
| Jaso c | 4 | 0 | 0 | 0 | 0 | 0 | 0-0 | 3 | 25 | 3 | .275 |
| Zobrist rf-1b | 2 | 0 | 0 | 0 | 0 | 1 | 2-0 | 5 | 38 | 10 | .297 |
| Longoria 3b | 3 | 0 | 0 | 0 | 0 | 0 | 0-1 | 12 | 52 | 11 | .301 |
| Pena 1b | 2 | 0 | 0 | 0 | 0 | 0 | 2-0 | 16 | 47 | 2 | .199 |
|  Crawford pr | 0 | 0 | 0 | 0 | 0 | 0 | 0-0 | 7 | 38 | 26 | .306 |
|  Brignac 2b | 0 | 0 | 0 | 0 | 0 | 0 | 0-0 | 4 | 24 | 2 | .277 |
| Joyce lf | 4 | 0 | 0 | 0 | 0 | 0 | 0-0 | 0 | 0 | 0 | .000 |
| Upton cf | 2 | 0 | 0 | 0 | 0 | 0 | 1-1 | 7 | 29 | 24 | .229 |
| Blalock dh | 4 | 0 | 0 | 0 | 0 | 0 | 0-0 | 1 | 7 | 0 | .246 |
| Rodriguez 2b-rf | 3 | 0 | 0 | 0 | 0 | 0 | 0-3 | 5 | 24 | 3 | .255 |
|  Aybar ph | 0 | 0 | 0 | 0 | 0 | 0 | 1-0 | 4 | 18 | 0 | .239 |
| Bartlett ss | 3 | 0 | 0 | 0 | 0 | 0 | 0-0 | 1 | 24 | 3 | .225 |

| Arizona D'backs | IP | H | R | ER | BB | K | HR | W | Sv | K | ERA |
|---|---|---|---|---|---|---|---|---|---|---|---|
| Jackson, W 5-6 | 9.0 | 0 | 0 | 0 | 8 | 6 | 0 | 5 | 0 | 85 | 4.93 |

| Tampa Bay Rays | IP | H | R | ER | BB | K | HR | W | Sv | K | ERA |
|---|---|---|---|---|---|---|---|---|---|---|---|
| Niemann, L 6-2 | 7.1 | 6 | 1 | 1 | 2 | 8 | 1 | 6 | 0 | 70 | 2.72 |
| Choate | 0.2 | 0 | 0 | 0 | 0 | 0 | 0 | 0 | 0 | 20 | 5.50 |
| Balfour | 1.0 | 1 | 0 | 0 | 0 | 2 | 0 | 0 | 0 | 31 | 1.69 |

## July 26, 2010
Matt Garza throws the first no-hitter in Rays history.
**TAMPA BAY 5, DETROIT 0**

| | 1 | 2 | 3 | 4 | 5 | 6 | 7 | 8 | 9 | | R | H | E |
|---|---|---|---|---|---|---|---|---|---|---|---|---|---|
| DET | 0 | 0 | 0 | 0 | 0 | 0 | 0 | 0 | 0 | | 0 | 0 | 1 |
| TB | 0 | 0 | 0 | 0 | 0 | 4 | 0 | 1 | - | | 5 | 3 | 0 |

| Detroit Tigers | AB | R | H | HR | BI | SB | BB-K | HR | RBI | SB | BA |
|---|---|---|---|---|---|---|---|---|---|---|---|
| Jackson cf | 3 | 0 | 0 | 0 | 0 | 0 | 0-1 | 1 | 21 | 16 | .316 |
| Rhymes 2b | 3 | 0 | 0 | 0 | 0 | 0 | 0-0 | 0 | 0 | 0 | .000 |
| Damon dh | 3 | 0 | 0 | 0 | 0 | 0 | 0-0 | 6 | 30 | 7 | .279 |
| Cabrera 1b | 3 | 0 | 0 | 0 | 0 | 0 | 0-1 | 24 | 88 | 2 | .347 |
| Boesch rf | 2 | 0 | 0 | 0 | 0 | 0 | 0-1 | 12 | 51 | 3 | .310 |
| Raburn lf | 3 | 0 | 0 | 0 | 0 | 0 | 0-1 | 8 | 22 | 1 | .204 |
| Kelly 3b | 3 | 0 | 0 | 0 | 0 | 0 | 0-2 | 1 | 8 | 1 | .206 |
| Laird c | 3 | 0 | 0 | 0 | 0 | 0 | 0-2 | 3 | 16 | 2 | .182 |
| Worth ss | 2 | 0 | 0 | 0 | 0 | 0 | 0-0 | 2 | 8 | 1 | .250 |
|  Santiago ph | 1 | 0 | 0 | 0 | 0 | 0 | 0-0 | 2 | 12 | 1 | .272 |

| Tampa Bay Rays | AB | R | H | HR | BI | SB | BB-K | HR | RBI | SB | BA |
|---|---|---|---|---|---|---|---|---|---|---|---|
| Jaso c | 3 | 1 | 1 | 0 | 0 | 0 | 1-0 | 6 | 47 | 19 | .271 |
| Zobrist rf | 3 | 2 | 1 | 1 | 1 | 0 | 0-0 | 12 | 54 | 34 | .311 |
| Crawford lf | 3 | 1 | 0 | 0 | 0 | 0 | 0-0 | 14 | 65 | 14 | .293 |
| Longoria 3b | 4 | 0 | 0 | 0 | 0 | 0 | 0-2 | 15 | 70 | 15 | .285 |
| Pena 1b | 4 | 0 | 0 | 0 | 0 | 0 | 0-2 | 21 | 61 | 5 | .204 |
| Joyce dh | 4 | 1 | 1 | 1 | 4 | 0 | 0-2 | 5 | 20 | 1 | .204 |
| Bartlett ss | 2 | 0 | 1 | 0 | 0 | 0 | 2-1 | 1 | 33 | 3 | .247 |
| Brignac 2b | 3 | 0 | 0 | 0 | 0 | 0 | 0-0 | 6 | 35 | 2 | .278 |
| Upton cf | 2 | 0 | 0 | 0 | 0 | 0 | 1-2 | 8 | 35 | 27 | .227 |
|  Shoppach c | 3 | 0 | 0 | 0 | 0 | 0 | 0-0 | 5 | 12 | 0 | .194 |

| Detroit Tigers | IP | H | R | ER | BB | K | HR | W | Sv | K | ERA |
|---|---|---|---|---|---|---|---|---|---|---|---|
| Scherzer, L 7-8 | 5.2 | 2 | 4 | 3 | 4 | 8 | 1 | 7 | 0 | 108 | 4.45 |
| Thomas | 0.1 | 0 | 0 | 0 | 0 | 0 | 0 | 4 | 0 | 17 | 4.46 |
| Gonzalez | 2.0 | 1 | 1 | 1 | 0 | 3 | 1 | 0 | 0 | 9 | 3.12 |

| Tampa Bay Rays | IP | H | R | ER | BB | K | HR | W | Sv | K | ERA |
|---|---|---|---|---|---|---|---|---|---|---|---|
| Garza, W 11-5 | 9.0 | 0 | 0 | 0 | 1 | 6 | 0 | 11 | 1 | 97 | 4.06 |

## August 8, 2010
Brandon Morrow logs 17 K and gets within an out of a no-hitter.
**TORONTO 1, TAMPA BAY 0**

| | 1 | 2 | 3 | 4 | 5 | 6 | 7 | 8 | 9 | | R | H | E |
|---|---|---|---|---|---|---|---|---|---|---|---|---|---|
| TB | 0 | 0 | 0 | 0 | 0 | 0 | 0 | 1 | 0 | | 1 | 1 | 0 |
| TOR | 1 | 0 | 0 | 0 | 0 | 0 | 0 | 0 | - | | 1 | 5 | 1 |

| Tampa Bay Rays | AB | R | H | HR | BI | SB | BB-K | HR | RBI | SB | BA |
|---|---|---|---|---|---|---|---|---|---|---|---|
| Zobrist rf | 3 | 0 | 0 | 0 | 0 | 0 | 1-2 | 6 | 47 | 22 | .264 |
| Crawford lf | 4 | 0 | 0 | 0 | 0 | 0 | 0-3 | 12 | 58 | 38 | .299 |
| Longoria 3b | 4 | 0 | 1 | 0 | 0 | 0 | 0-2 | 15 | 70 | 15 | .285 |
| Johnson 1b | 3 | 0 | 0 | 0 | 0 | 0 | 1-2 | 1 | 0 | 0 | .214 |
| Joyce dh | 3 | 0 | 0 | 0 | 0 | 0 | 0-2 | 5 | 20 | 1 | .204 |
| Jaso c | 3 | 0 | 0 | 0 | 0 | 0 | 0-1 | 5 | 33 | 3 | .247 |
| Upton cf | 4 | 0 | 0 | 0 | 0 | 0 | 0-2 | 10 | 41 | 32 | .233 |
| Brignac 2b | 2 | 0 | 0 | 0 | 0 | 0 | 0-1 | 6 | 36 | 3 | .262 |
|  Aybar ph-2b | 1 | 0 | 0 | 0 | 0 | 0 | 0-0 | 4 | 20 | 0 | .247 |
| Bartlett ss | 3 | 0 | 0 | 0 | 0 | 0 | 0-1 | 1 | 41 | 9 | .249 |

| Toronto Blue Jays | AB | R | H | HR | BI | SB | BB-K | HR | RBI | SB | BA |
|---|---|---|---|---|---|---|---|---|---|---|---|
| Wise lf-cf | 4 | 0 | 1 | 0 | 0 | 0 | 0-2 | 3 | 11 | 2 | .271 |
| Escobar ss | 3 | 1 | 1 | 0 | 0 | 0 | 1-0 | 3 | 29 | 5 | .252 |
| Bautista rf | 3 | 1 | 1 | 1 | 1 | 0 | 1-0 | 34 | 85 | 6 | .254 |
| Wells cf | 2 | 0 | 1 | 0 | 0 | 0 | 1-1 | 22 | 60 | 5 | .274 |
|  Snider ph-lf | 2 | 0 | 0 | 0 | 0 | 0 | 0-1 | 8 | 22 | 4 | .252 |
| Lind dh | 4 | 0 | 0 | 0 | 0 | 0 | 0-2 | 15 | 50 | 0 | .224 |
| Hill 2b | 3 | 0 | 0 | 0 | 0 | 0 | 0-1 | 18 | 45 | 1 | .213 |
| Overbay 1b | 3 | 0 | 0 | 0 | 0 | 0 | 0-1 | 13 | 45 | 1 | .252 |
| Encarnacion 3b | 3 | 0 | 0 | 0 | 0 | 0 | 0-1 | 12 | 32 | 1 | .249 |
| Molina c | 2 | 0 | 0 | 0 | 0 | 0 | 0-1 | 4 | 9 | 1 | .270 |

| Tampa Bay Rays | IP | H | R | ER | BB | K | HR | W | Sv | K | ERA |
|---|---|---|---|---|---|---|---|---|---|---|---|
| Sonnanstine, L 2-1 | 5.1 | 3 | 1 | 1 | 3 | 1 | 0 | 2 | 1 | 36 | 3.98 |
| Choate | 0.2 | 0 | 0 | 0 | 0 | 1 | 0 | 0 | 0 | 29 | 5.10 |
| Wheeler | 1.0 | 0 | 0 | 0 | 1 | 2 | 0 | 3 | 3 | 40 | 2.70 |
| Cormier | 0.1 | 1 | 0 | 0 | 0 | 2 | 0 | 3 | 0 | 16 | 4.24 |

| Toronto Blue Jays | IP | H | R | ER | BB | K | HR | W | Sv | K | ERA |
|---|---|---|---|---|---|---|---|---|---|---|---|
| Morrow, W 9-6 | 9.0 | 1 | 0 | 0 | 2 | 17 | 0 | 9 | 0 | 151 | 4.45 |

One final outing for the ages: On August 23, 2010, Rays closer Rafael Soriano retired the Angels with three strikeouts — on nine pitches. It was the 44th such "perfect inning" in MLB history. Soriano struck out Erick Aybar, Mike Napoli, and Peter Bourjos on nine fastballs.